FOOTBALL YEARBOOK 2019–2020

SPECIAL 50TH ANNIVERSARY EDITION 1970–2020

IN ASSOCIATION WITH THE SUN

COMPILED BY JOHN ANDERSON

HEADLINE

First published in 2019
by HEADLINE PUBLISHING GROUP

1

Spine photograph:
Liverpool manager Jurgen Klopp with the Champions League trophy, June 2019 –
Marc Atkins/Getty Images

Cataloguing in Publication Data is available from the British Library

ISBN 9781472261106 (Hardback)
ISBN 9781472261113 (Trade Paperback)

Typeset by Wearset Ltd, Boldon, Tyne & Wear

Printed and bound by Clays Ltd, Elcograf S.p.A.

FSC www.fsc.org MIX Paper from responsible sources FSC® C104740

Headline's policy is to use papers that are natural, renewable and recyclable products and made from wood grown in sustainable forests. The logging and manufacturing processes are expected to conform to the environmental regulations of the country of origin.

HEADLINE PUBLISHING GROUP
An Hachette UK Company
Carmelite House
50 Victoria Embankment
London EC4Y 0DZ

www.headline.co.uk
www.hachette.co.uk

CONTENTS

EUROPEAN FOOTBALL

INTERNATIONAL FOOTBALL

NON-LEAGUE FOOTBALL

INFORMATION AND RECORDS

WELCOME

Happy 50th birthday to football's 'bible'.

For five decades the iconic reference book has faithfully recorded every detail of the game that entrances millions. So much has changed but so much is the same. Beautiful, intoxicating, football is a constant, bookending those 50 years.

In 1970, the world huddled around new colour television sets, thrilled by the flashing golden shirts of Pelé's Brazil, arguably the finest World Cup team of all time. Fast forward to 2019, and we've been privileged to witness perhaps the most remarkable denouement of any English football season.

One giddy and breathless week in May, starting with the purest of Vincent Kompany strikes and rolling into the craziest of fight-backs from Liverpool and Spurs, encapsulated a thrilling year. City held their nerve to retain the title and Liverpool ended the season with glory in Madrid. Pep Guardiola, Mauricio Pochettino and Jurgen Klopp have elevated football in this country to a new level of technical and tactical excellence. The way the game is played has changed. But its ability to capture our hearts and minds is undiminished.

Those magnificent games are just the headlines. The joy of the *Football Yearbook* is that it tells the whole story: it records every detail of every team, however painful that may be for some of us.

In these pages, the 'Voice of Football', John Motson, reflects on what 50 years of the *Yearbook* mean to him, and you can also read the thoughts of *The Sun*'s Head of Sport and Chief Football Reporter, Shaun Custis and Neil Ashton respectively, about the events of last season.

Then relax into more than a thousand pages inside the *Football Yearbook*'s distinctive cover and luxuriate in the minutiae that made up a magnificent year of football. Yes, the summer is for dreaming about who our team will sign and what they can do next season: but before that, take time to soak up season 2018–19.

The Sun was proud to rescue the *Football Yearbook* last season – indeed our football-mad readers would never have forgiven us if we had not – and we are delighted to be its sponsor in this special golden anniversary year.

In an age when facts and stats spill in their thousands from our TVs and our phones, and when pundits bicker over the inexorable march of VAR technology, there's something comforting about sliding the latest edition onto the bookshelf alongside those 49 others.

Motty calls this tome his 'bible'. If it's good enough for him...

Tony Gallagher, Editor-in-Chief, *The Sun*

Rothmans
Football Yearbook
1970-71
All the essential facts and figures of the World's most popular game 992 pages 32 pages of illustrations
18s

Cover of the first edition of the *Football Yearbook*, 1970–71.

INTRODUCTION

The 50th edition of the *Football Yearbook* is our second in association with *The Sun* and includes every game of the inaugural UEFA Nations League, plus full coverage of the European Qualifying campaign for Euro 2020 including match line-ups and league tables. Other international football at various levels is also well catered for in this edition.

The concise feature entitled Cups and Ups and Downs Diary is included with dates of those events affecting cup finals, promotion and relegation issues. The Managers In and Out section is once again included, with a diary of managerial changes throughout the year.

At European level, the Champions League has its usual comprehensive details included, with results, goalscorers, attendances, full line-ups and formations from the qualifying rounds onwards and also including all the league tables from the respective group stages. The Europa League includes full line-ups and formations from the group stages onwards.

The 2018–19 season ended as another record-breaking one for Pep Guardiola's Manchester City, winning all three domestic trophies and reaching the semi-final of the Champions League. Raheem Sterling of Manchester City and England won the Football Writers' Footballer of the Year award and Liverpool's Virgil van Dijk won the PFA Player of the Year award. The Championship season ended with Norwich City and Sheffield United promoted automatically, and they were joined by Aston Villa who won the Championship Play-Off 2-1 against Derby County at Wembley.

All of these statistics are reproduced in the pages devoted not only to the Premier League, but the three Football League competitions too, as well as all major allied cup competitions.

In women's football, the Women's FIFA World Cup European qualification campaign and the FIFA World Cup Finals from France are covered. The Women's Super League, Championship and National Leagues are included, together with the domestic cup competitions: Women's FA Cup and League Cup. The Women's UEFA Champions League is also covered. England Women's Internationals since 1974 and all of the 2018–19 season's games are included.

While transfer fees are invariably those reported at the time and rarely given as official figures, the edition reflects those listed at the time.

In the club-by-club pages that contain the line-ups of all league matches, appearances are split into starting and substitute appearances. In the Players Directory the totals show figures combined.

The Players Directory and its accompanying A to Z index enables the reader to quickly find the club of any specific player.

Throughout the book players sent off are designated with ■; substitutes in the club pages are 12, 13 and 14. Included again in main cup competitions are the formations for each team.

In addition to competitions already mentioned there is full coverage of Scottish Premiership, Scottish Football League and Scottish domestic cup competitions. There are also sections devoted to Welsh and Irish football, Under-21s and various other UEFA youth levels, schools, reserve team, academies, referees and the leading non-league competitions as well as the work of club chaplains. The chief tournaments outside the UK at club and national level are not forgotten. The International Directory itself features Europe in some depth as well as every FIFA-affiliated country's international results for the year since July 2018; every reigning league and cup champion worldwide is listed.

Naturally there are international appearances and goals scored by players for England, Scotland, Northern Ireland, Wales and the Republic of Ireland. For easy reference, those players making appearances and scoring goals in the season covered are picked out in bold type.

The *Football Yearbook* would like to extend its appreciation to the publishers Headline for excellent support in the preparation of this edition, particularly Jonathan Taylor for photographic selection throughout the book and to Graham Green for his continued support.

ACKNOWLEDGEMENTS

In addition the *Football Yearbook* is also keen to thank the following individuals and organisations for their co-operation.

Special thanks to Tony Gallagher and Shaun Custis from *The Sun* for their contributions, Neil Ashton for his Team of the Season and to John Motson for his Foreword.

Thanks are also due to Ian Nannestad for the Obituaries, Did You Know? and Fact File features in the club section. Many thanks also to John English for his conscientious proof reading and compilation of the International Directory.

The *Football Yearbook* is grateful to the Football Association, the Scottish Professional Football League, the Football League, Rev. Nigel Sands for his contribution to the Chaplain's page and Bob Bannister, Paul Anderson, Riley Davison and Martin Cooper for their help.

Sincere thanks to George Schley and Simon Dunnington for their excellent work on the database, and to Andy Cordiner, Geoff Turner, Brian Tait, Robin Middlemiss and the staff at Wearset for their much appreciated efforts in the production of the book throughout the year.

In this, its 50th year, the *Football Yearbook* would like to pay special thanks to Jack and Glenda Rollin, who were editors for many years. Their unwavering dedication, diligence and attention to detail are the cornerstone of its continued success. All of the contributors over the past 50 years are also thanked.

DREAM TEAM

The 2018–19 Dream Team season really belonged to a genius who blitzed the rest of the field.

Eden Hazard's parting gifts to Chelsea before his long-awaited move to Real Madrid this summer were securing a top-four spot and the Europa League trophy. And his spellbinding performances across the season saw him rack up a stunning 360 points on Dream Team – a full 48 ahead of his nearest challenger.

Hazard notched 21 goals, 17 assists and an incredible 18 Star Man awards in all competitions, registering the eighth highest individual points total in Dream Team history. In fact, the brilliant Belgian effectively scooped the Man of the Match award more than once every three appearances across the season.

FWA Footballer of the Year Raheem Sterling was Hazard's closest rival after the Manchester City and England man's stunning individual term. Sterling made waves on and off the field in 2018–19 and was the only other player to break the 300-point barrier as City became the first English club to win the domestic treble.

Behind Sterling came last season's leading points-scorer Mo Salah, Arsenal hitman Pierre-Emerick Aubameyang and City's all-time top goal getter Sergio Aguero.

PFA Player of the Year Virgil van Dijk recorded the second highest total ever for a defender with 282 points, but was still some way short of John Terry's record of 368 in the 2004–05 season.

Van Dijk's Liverpool team-mates Trent Alexander-Arnold and Andy Robertson were Dream Team must-haves too, amassing an incredible 446 points between them.

Salah was by far the most picked player on the game with 60.8% ownership, with van Dijk, Aguero, Sadio Mané and Hazard making up the rest of the top five.

Away from the household names there was joy for some less familiar faces. Wolves full-back Matt Doherty rose to prominence with some hugely impressive performances, whilst Ryan Fraser matched Hazard for assists and outscored Riyad Mahrez for points.

Liverpool goalkeeper Alisson was the highest-scoring new signing with 209 points, closely followed by Wolves striker Raul Jimenez and Everton full-back Lucas Digne.

But it wasn't a success story for everyone this season. Alexis Sanchez smashed 348 points back in the 2016–17 campaign, but his fall from grace in the last couple of years has been drastic. The Manchester United flop managed just 36 points in the entirety of 2018–19 – just six points more than Gerard Deulofeu recorded in one game for Watford against Cardiff.

It wasn't much better for Sanchez's disgruntled United team-mate David de Gea.

The Spaniard's clean sheets dried up massively and he was outscored by the likes of Neil Etheridge, Martin Dubravka and Vicente Guaita. Mesut Özil's anonymity was evident with just 72 points, while the less said about Christian Benteke the better. But spare a thought for Huddersfield's Chris Löwe, who finished rock bottom of the player rankings with an eye-watering 28 points. Blimey.

So what can we expect on Dream Team next season? Well the usual suspects will be popular again, with the likes of Salah, Sterling and Harry Kane all vying to fill the Hazard-shaped hole at the top of the player rankings. Salah and Kane were the joint most expensive players before the season started last summer, but the latter's injury record will be a worry for both Spurs fans and Dream Team managers.

We are anticipating even bigger things from some of the younger contingent, with the likes of Alexander-Arnold, Bernardo Silva and James Maddison all ready to take the next step.

Big things are expected of Chelsea new boy Christian Pulisic: will the American feel burdened by replacing Hazard amidst the Blues' debilitating transfer ban?

And after an injury-ravaged campaign, everyone will be hoping City maestro Kevin De Bruyne can sprinkle his magic again by returning to full fitness.

Dream Team has some bold and exciting new plans for the 2019–20 season, with not one, not two, but THREE different game formats available to play.

As well as the classic Season game and the hugely popular short-form version Weekender, Dream Team is launching a Draft game too to bring a completely different dimension to fantasy football. Unlike traditional formats, Draft really tests your managerial nous with an NFL-style player selection process taking place before the season starts. Only one manager in each mini-league can own a player. So if you snap up Salah in the draft, nobody else can have him. Simple as that.

It all makes for a mouth-watering new season on Dream Team, which gets underway when European champions Liverpool host newly promoted Norwich City on 9 August. To get involved and for any further details, head to dreamteamfc.com.

Adam Jones

TEAM OF THE SEASON 2018–19

NEIL ASHTON, CHIEF FOOTBALL REPORTER, *THE SUN*

Alisson Becker
(Liverpool)

Trent Alexander-Arnold *(Liverpool)* | **Virgil van Dijk** *(Liverpool)* | **Joel Matip** *(Liverpool)* | **Andy Robertson** *(Liverpool)*

Raheem Sterling *(Manchester City)* | **Jordan Henderson** *(Liverpool)* | **Bernardo Silva** *(Manchester City)*

Mo Salah *(Liverpool)* | **Sergio Aguero** *(Manchester City)* | **Sadio Mané** *(Liverpool)*

Manager: Pep Guardiola
(Manchester City)

Alisson Becker: it is a close call with Manchester City's keeper Ederson, but Alisson's commanding debut season at Liverpool ended with a Champions League medal swinging around his neck. Liverpool conceded just 22 goals in the Premier League, but Alisson's composure and presence in Europe was telling.

Trent Alexander-Arnold: humble, down-to-earth kid who claims he is just a normal boy from Liverpool. The reality is that Alexander-Arnold is redefining the role of right-back by adding a steady supply of crosses and match-winning moments. His cheeky, improvised corner against Barcelona in the Champions League semi-final was further proof of his game intelligence.

Virgil van Dijk: the PFA Player of the Year will be remembered for his immaculate interception of Son Heung-Min during the Champions League final against Tottenham. He laughed when he was compared to the great centre-halves – Nesta, Maldini, Baresi – but he is well on the way to becoming one of the best defenders of all time.

Joel Matip: turned into the enforcer after winning a place alongside van Dijk in the centre of Liverpool's defence. While van Dijk drops deep to sweep up, Matip is sent in to make the first challenge when Liverpool try to win the ball back. A true warrior, this Sami Hyypia-style defender gets the nod over Manchester City's much-improved Aymeric Laporte.

Andy Robertson: involved in his own friendly battle with team-mate Trent Alexander-Arnold to provide the most assists from his position at full-back. He got 11 last season in the Premier League, adding another dynamic element to this intoxicating, compelling Liverpool side. Finished the season in style by captaining his country, Scotland.

Raheem Sterling: finished the season with the richly deserved FWA Footballer of the Year award to commemorate another successful season with Manchester City. As well as scoring 17 times in their title defence, Sterling also made people think with a challenging Instagram post about discrimination. He is a classy footballer and a measured campaigner.

Jordan Henderson: his endless, ceaseless, selfless running during Liverpool's incredible journey to a sixth European Cup merits inclusion. He has risen to Jurgen Klopp's challenge, influencing Liverpool's attacks in their spellbinding run to the final and adding a layer of protection to their back four. An outstanding individual.

Bernardo Silva: scored just seven goals for City in their title-winning season, but the feeling is that Bernardo is only just getting going. As the influence of David Silva starts to fade after his glorious career at the Etihad, Bernardo's performances last season suggest he will go on to win the hearts of City supporters in the years to come.

Mo Salah: followed up on his double of FWA and PFA awards in 2018 by scoring 22 times in the Premier League. Although many felt that his form dipped, Salah was instrumental in keeping Liverpool's title challenge alive and played a crucial role in their run to the Champions League final. A true great.

Sergio Aguero: he has scored 20-plus goals for Manchester City in each of his last five seasons. His appetite is undiminished, continuing to score goals as Pep Guardiola's side hunted down a domestic quadruple of Community Shield, FA Cup, Carabao Cup and the defence of the Premier League. When his career finally turns full circle and Aguero returns to finish his career in Argentina, the Premier League will miss him.

Sadio Mané: his Liverpool career really took off last season after scoring 22 times in 37 Premier League appearances. With his fast, direct, ruthless running, Mané has emerged as an alternative attacking threat for this great Liverpool side. Finished the season winning the penalty for Liverpool after just 23 seconds of the Champions League final.

Manager, Pep Guardiola: sees off Jurgen Klopp – his obvious and only rival – because he held his nerve in the final weeks of the season to successfully defend Manchester City's Premier League title. To win four trophies in domestic football is exceptional, but Liverpool's Champions League success means the pressure is on City to finally land the European Cup this season.

FOREWORD

talkSPORT's JOHN MOTSON

In the summer of 1970 I received an invitation to a small book launch at the old Rothmans building in Pall Mall. Rothmans was a tobacco manufacturer at the time but had decided to put money behind a new football yearbook. I travelled down to London with Gerald Sinstadt. Gerald was already an extremely established commentator at ITV, while I was still making my way as a young reporter on the BBC. Back then, there weren't so many people covering football. Gerald and I were joined by a handful of journalists and a couple of television presenters who shuffled into the Rothmans showroom for the launch.

Rothmans had made a bit of a show of it by bringing along one or two football personalities. Who they were, I couldn't tell you now. What I do remember, and so vividly, is getting my hands on the first edition and flicking through all the facts and stats in amazement. Gerald was a big statistician. He looked at me and said: 'Wow! We've been waiting for something like this for years.'

Half a century on and I own all 49 editions. The collection has pride of place on the bookcase in my study. Every year, as the new season dawned, the first thing I thought of was getting the latest *Football Yearbook*. As the years have gone by the book has grown with new sections because there's much more information to be absorbed now. Nothing on the internet can quite match the delight in pulling one of the past editions off the shelf and referring to the printed word, which I do every day.

For those of us covering sport, the *Football Yearbook* changed the game. There were other annuals that came out before it, but the Rothmans broke new ground because it was far more comprehensive and far more detailed than any others. It covered everything, from the European game to youth football. But it was the section on clubs which was revolutionary compared to what we had seen before. Every player was listed and every match recorded from the previous season. There were the most obscure facts in there, records that we had never seen before in print. For those of us who collected these books, it was an eye-opener; for reporters covering the game, it was an absolute godsend because you had it all in front of you. It became a bible for us.

I had not really graduated into full-time commentary at that stage, though. I was a sports news reporter on the old BBC Radio 2, reading everything from the racing results to news from leagues across the country. But, funnily enough, my move to *Match of the Day* came in September 1971 after the *Football Yearbook*'s first full season, so I really was a football commentator from the start of the Rothmans series.

In the beginning, I used to take it to all the games. Be it Hillsborough or The Hawthorns, the *Football Yearbook* was in my bag. It was fairly heavy to carry about but it was my insurance, a trusty back-up. As a commentator it was invaluable: it gave us much more information and saved us a lot of time. In the later years, I wouldn't take it out of the house too often through fear of losing it and not being able to get another copy. Instead, the *Yearbook* would come into its own on a Thursday and Friday as I flicked through it in preparation for the weekend. It had everything I needed on the two teams I was covering. By the time Saturday came, all of that homework was done and I could rest assured my facts were correct.

The world has changed nowadays but it is special to have everything in a beautifully bound book, to turn the page and get the reference you need. It became the *Wisden* of football. *Wisden* was a recognised source of reference for a cricket enthusiast that fans wanted to see; 'the Rothmans' became exactly that for football due to the extent of detail and reliability.

If something is in print, even these days, you tend to think you can trust it because it has been published in ink. We would talk about the Rothmans as a reference point. 'That's what the Rothmans tells me,' we'd say, because of its accuracy. Nothing has ever matched it. In those 50 years, no other football book – and certainly no other football reference book – has come near it.

Credit for such exceptional success belongs to two individuals in particular. Jack Rollin, the former *Sunday Telegraph* columnist, who I worked with at the BBC, edited the book for decades; his daughter, Glenda, became involved in later years. If anyone deserves the most plaudits for the way the *Football Yearbook* has been written and developed over the years it is Jack and Glenda. Without their devotion and dedication, it would not have continued to be produced to such a high standard.

There was a threat of the book dying out in 2018, however. I remember it all very clearly. It was *The Sun* that broke the story: they rung me up for my thoughts and I said how horrified I was, that it was a bad day in the history of football journalism. It was, then, *The Sun* who stepped in to keep the annual going and I'm absolutely thrilled that it's still where it is today, celebrating half a century.

All I can say is, I hope there's another 50 years to come.

John Motson

FOOTBALL AWARDS 2018–19

THE FOOTBALL WRITERS' FOOTBALLER OF THE YEAR 2019

The Football Writers' Association Sir Stanley Matthews Trophy for the Footballer of the Year was awarded to Raheem Sterling of Manchester C and England. Virgil van Dijk (Liverpool and Netherlands) was runner-up and Sergio Aguero (Manchester C and Argentina) came third.

Past Winners
1947–48 Stanley Matthews (Blackpool), 1948–49 Johnny Carey (Manchester U), 1949–50 Joe Mercer (Arsenal), 1950–51 Harry Johnston (Blackpool), 1951–52 Billy Wright (Wolverhampton W), 1952–53 Nat Lofthouse (Bolton W), 1953–54 Tom Finney (Preston NE), 1954–55 Don Revie (Manchester C), 1955–56 Bert Trautmann (Manchester C), 1956–57 Tom Finney (Preston NE), 1957–58 Danny Blanchflower (Tottenham H), 1958–59 Syd Owen (Luton T), 1959–60 Bill Slater (Wolverhampton W), 1960–61 Danny Blanchflower (Tottenham H), 1961–62 Jimmy Adamson (Burnley), 1962–63 Stanley Matthews (Stoke C), 1963–64 Bobby Moore (West Ham U), 1964–65 Bobby Collins (Leeds U), 1965–66 Bobby Charlton (Manchester U), 1966–67 Jackie Charlton (Leeds U), 1967–68 George Best (Manchester U), 1968–69 Dave Mackay (Derby Co) shared with Tony Book (Manchester C), 1969–70 Billy Bremner (Leeds U), 1970–71 Frank McLintock (Arsenal), 1971–72 Gordon Banks (Stoke C), 1972–73 Pat Jennings (Tottenham H), 1973–74 Ian Callaghan (Liverpool), 1974–75 Alan Mullery (Fulham), 1975–76 Kevin Keegan (Liverpool), 1976–77 Emlyn Hughes (Liverpool), 1977–78 Kenny Burns (Nottingham F), 1978–79 Kenny Dalglish (Liverpool), 1979–80 Terry McDermott (Liverpool), 1980–81 Frans Thijssen (Ipswich T), 1981–82 Steve Perryman (Tottenham H), 1982–83 Kenny Dalglish (Liverpool), 1983–84 Ian Rush (Liverpool), 1984–85 Neville Southall (Everton), 1985–86 Gary Lineker (Everton), 1986–87 Clive Allen (Tottenham H), 1987–88 John Barnes (Liverpool), 1988–89 Steve Nicol (Liverpool), 1989–90 John Barnes (Liverpool), 1990–91 Gordon Strachan (Leeds U), 1991–92 Gary Lineker (Tottenham H), 1992–93 Chris Waddle (Sheffield W), 1993–94 Alan Shearer (Blackburn R), 1994–95 Jurgen Klinsmann (Tottenham H), 1995–96 Eric Cantona (Manchester U), 1996–97 Gianfranco Zola (Chelsea), 1997–98 Dennis Bergkamp (Arsenal), 1998–99 David Ginola (Tottenham H), 1999–2000 Roy Keane (Manchester U), 2000–01 Teddy Sheringham (Manchester U), 2001–02 Robert Pires (Arsenal), 2002–03 Thierry Henry (Arsenal), 2003–04 Thierry Henry (Arsenal), 2004–05 Frank Lampard (Chelsea), 2005–06 Thierry Henry (Arsenal), 2006–07 Cristiano Ronaldo (Manchester U), 2007–08 Cristiano Ronaldo (Manchester U), 2008–09 Ryan Giggs (Manchester U), 2009–10 Wayne Rooney (Manchester U), 2010–11 Scott Parker (West Ham U), 2011–12 Robin van Persie (Arsenal), 2012–13 Gareth Bale (Tottenham H), 2013–14 Luis Suárez (Liverpool), 2014–15 Eden Hazard (Chelsea), 2015–16 Jamie Vardy (Leicester C), 2016–17 N'Golo Kanté (Chelsea and France), 2017–18 Mohamed Salah (Liverpool and Egypt), 2018–19 Raheem Sterling (Manchester C and England).

THE FOOTBALL WRITERS' WOMEN'S FOOTBALLER OF THE YEAR 2019

Nikita Parris (Manchester C and England)

THE PFA AWARDS 2019

Player of the Year: Virgil van Dijk, Liverpool and Netherlands.
Young Player of the Year: Raheem Stirling, Manchester C and England.
Women's Player of the Year: Vivianne Miedema, Arsenal and Netherlands.
Women's Young Player of the Year: Georgia Stanway, Manchester C and England.
PFA Merit Award: Steph Houghton, Manchester C and England.

PFA Premier League Team of the Year 2019 in association with Panini
Ederson Moraes (Manchester C); Trent Alexander-Arnold (Liverpool), Virgil van Dijk (Liverpool), Aymeric Laporte (Manchester C), Andrew Robertson (Liverpool), Paul Pogba (Manchester U), Fernandinho (Manchester C), Bernardo Silva (Manchester C), Raheem Sterling (Manchester C), Sergio Aguero (Manchester C), Sadio Mane (Liverpool).

PFA Championship Team of the Year 2019 in association with Panini
Darren Randolph (Middlesbrough); Max Aarons (Norwich C), Liam Cooper (Leeds U), Pontus Jansson (Leeds U), Jamal Lewis (Norwich C), Pablo Hernandez (Leeds U), Oliver Norwood (Sheffield U), Jack Grealish (Aston Villa), Billy Sharp (Sheffield U), Tammy Abraham (Aston Villa), Teemu Pukki (Norwich C).

PFA League One Team of the Year 2019 in association with Panini
Adam Davies (Barnsley); Dimitri Cavare (Barnsley), Ethan Pinnock (Barnsley), Matthew Clarke (Portsmouth), James Justin (Luton T), Jamal Lowe (Portsmouth), Alex Mowatt (Barnsley), Aiden McGeady (Sunderland), James Collins (Luton T), John Marquis (Doncaster R), Kieffer Moore (Barnsley).

PFA League Two Team of the Year 2019 in association with Panini
Joe Murphy (Bury), Neal Eardley (Lincoln C), Jason Shackell (Lincoln C), Krystian Pearce (Mansfield T), Harry Toffolo (Lincoln C), Reece Brown (Forest Green R), Jay O'Shea (Bury), Danny Mayor (Bury), James Norwood (Tranmere R), John Akinde (Lincoln C), Tyler Walker (Mansfield T).

SCOTTISH AWARDS 2018–19

SCOTTISH PFA PLAYER OF THE YEAR AWARDS 2019

Player of the Year: James Forrest, Celtic and Scotland.
Young Player of the Year: Ryan Kent, Rangers.
Manager of the Year: Steve Clarke, Kilmarnock.
Championship Player of the Year: Stephen Dobbie, Queen of the South.
League One Player of the Year: Bobby Lin, Arbroath.
League Two Player of the Year: Blair Henderson, Edinburgh C.
Goal of the Season: Alfred Morelos, Aberdeen v Rangers, Scottish Premiership, 6 February 2019.
Special Merit Award: Dr John MacLean, Hampden Sports Clinic, Clyde and Scotland.

SCOTTISH FOOTBALL WRITERS' ASSOCIATION AWARDS 2019

Player of the Year: James Forrest, Celtic and Scotland.
Young Player of the Year: David Turnbull, Motherwell and Scotland U21.
International Player of the Year: James Forrest, Celtic and Scotland.
Manager of the Year: Steve Clarke, Kilmarnock.

PREMIER LEAGUE AWARDS 2018–19

PLAYER OF THE MONTH AWARDS 2018–19

August	Lucas Moura (Tottenham H)
September	Eden Hazard (Chelsea)
October	Pierre-Emerick Aubameyang (Arsenal)
November	Raheem Sterling (Manchester C)
December	Virgil van Dijk (Liverpool)
January	Marcus Rashford (Manchester U)
February	Sergio Aguero (Manchester C)
March	Sadio Mane (Liverpool)
April	Jamie Vardy (Leicester C)

MANAGER OF THE MONTH AWARDS 2018–19

Javi Gracia (Watford)
Nuno Espirito Santo (Wolverhampton W)
Eddie Howe (Bournemouth)
Rafael Benitez (Newcastle U)
Jurgen Klopp (Liverpool)
Ole Gunnar Solskjaer (Manchester U)
Pep Guardiola (Manchester C)
Jurgen Klopp (Liverpool)
Pep Guardiola (Manchester C)

SKY BET LEAGUE AWARDS 2018–19

LEAGUE PLAYER OF THE MONTH AWARDS 2018–19

	Championship	*League One*	*League Two*
August	Kemar Roofe (Leeds U)	Jason Cummings (Peterborough U)	James Norwood (Tranmere R)
September	Dwight Gayle (WBA)	John Marquis (Doncaster R)	Sam Surridge (Oldham Ath)
October	Lukas Jutkiewicz (Birmingham C)	Freddie Ladapo (Plymouth Arg)	James McKeown (Grimsby T)
November	Tammy Abraham (Aston Villa)	Elliott Lee (Luton T)	Jay O'Shea (Bury)
December	Jarrod Bowen (Hull C)	Ivan Toney (Peterborough U)	Danny Grainger (Carlisle U)
January	Adam Armstrong (Blackburn R)	James Collins (Luton T)	Jay O'Shea (Bury)
February	Che Adams (Birmingham C)	Aiden McGeady (Sunderland)	Bruno Andrade (Lincoln C)
March	Semi Ajayi (Rotherham U)	Jonson Clarke-Harris (Bristol R)	Reece Brown (Forest Green R)
April	Dwight Gayle (WBA)	Joe Piggott (AFC Wimbledon)	Joe Day (Newport Co)
Player of the Season	Teemu Pukki (Norwich C)	James Collins (Luton T)	James Norwood (Tranmere R)

SKY BET FOOTBALL LEAGUE MANAGER OF THE MONTH AWARDS 2018–19

	Championship	*League One*	*League Two*
August	Marcelo Bielsa (Leeds U)	Steve Evans (Peterborough U)	Danny Cowley (Lincoln C)
September	Darren Moore (WBA)	Grant McCann (Doncaster R)	Michael Flynn (Newport Co)
October	Steve McClaren (QPR)	Mark Robins (Coventry C)	Paul Tidsdale (Milton Keynes D)
November	Daniel Farke (Norwich C)	Lee Bowyer (Charlton Ath)	Ryan Lowe (Bury)
December	Nigel Adkins (Hull C)	Nathan Jones (Luton T)	Michael Jolley (Grimsby T)
January	Tony Mowbray (Blackburn R)	Stuart McCall (Scunthorpe U)	Ryan Lowe (Bury)
February	Chris Wilder (Sheffield U)	Jack Ross (Sunderland)	Ryan Lowe (Bury)
March	Dean Smith (Aston Villa)	Mick Harford (Luton T)	Micky Mellon (Tranmere R)
April	Chris Wilder (Sheffield U)	Lee Bowyer (Charlton Ath)	Michael Flynn (Newport Co)
Manager of the Season	Chris Wilder (Sheffield U)		

LEAGUE MANAGERS ASSOCIATION AWARDS 2018–19

SIR ALEX FERGUSON TROPHY FOR LMA MANAGER OF THE YEAR SPONSORED BY EVEREST
Chris Wilder (Sheffield U)

PREMIER LEAGUE MANAGER OF THE YEAR SPONSORED BY BARCLAYS
Pep Guardiola (Manchester C)

SKY BET FOOTBALL LEAGUE CHAMPIONSHIP MANAGER OF THE YEAR
Chris Wilder (Sheffield U)

SKY BET FOOTBALL LEAGUE ONE MANAGER OF THE YEAR
Mick Harford (Luton T)

SKY BET FOOTBALL LEAGUE TWO MANAGER OF THE YEAR
Danny Cowley (Lincoln C)

FA WOMEN'S SUPER LEAGUE MANAGER OF THE YEAR
Joe Montemurro (Arsenal)

FA WOMEN'S CHAMPIONSHIP MANAGER OF THE YEAR
Karen Hills (Tottenham H)

LMA SPECIAL ACHIEVEMENT AWARD SPONSORED BY PROSTATE CANCER UK
John Still

LMA SERVICE TO FOOTBALL AWARD
Pat Godbold (Ipswich T)

LMA SPECIAL RECOGNITION AWARD
Richard Scudamore CBE

OTHER AWARDS

EUROPEAN FOOTBALLER OF THE YEAR 2018
Luca Modric, Real Madrid and Croatia

EUROPEAN WOMEN'S PLAYER OF THE YEAR 2018
Pernille Harder, Wolfsburg and Denmark

FIFA BALLON D'OR PLAYER OF THE YEAR 2018
Luca Modric, Real Madrid and Croatia

FIFA BALLON D'OR WOMEN'S PLAYER OF THE YEAR 2018
Ada Hegerberg, Lyon and Norway

FIFA PUSKAS AWARD GOAL OF THE YEAR 2018
Mohamed Salah, Liverpool v Everton, Premier League, 10 December 2017

PREMIER LEAGUE 2018–19

(P) *Promoted into division at end of 2017–18 season.*

			Home					*Away*					*Total*						
		P	*W*	*D*	*L*	*F*	*A*	*W*	*D*	*L*	*F*	*A*	*W*	*D*	*L*	*F*	*A*	*GD*	*Pts*
1	Manchester C	38	18	0	1	57	12	14	2	3	38	11	32	2	4	95	23	72	98
2	Liverpool	38	17	2	0	55	10	13	5	1	34	12	30	7	1	89	22	67	97
3	Chelsea	38	12	6	1	39	12	9	3	7	24	27	21	9	8	63	39	24	72
4	Tottenham H	38	12	2	5	34	16	11	0	8	33	23	23	2	13	67	39	28	71
5	Arsenal	38	14	3	2	42	16	7	4	8	31	35	21	7	10	73	51	22	70
6	Manchester U	38	10	6	3	33	25	9	3	7	32	29	19	9	10	65	54	11	66
7	Wolverhampton W (P)	38	10	4	5	28	21	6	5	8	19	25	16	9	13	47	46	1	57
8	Everton	38	10	4	5	30	21	5	5	9	24	25	15	9	14	54	46	8	54
9	Leicester C	38	8	3	8	24	20	7	4	8	27	28	15	7	16	51	48	3	52
10	West Ham U	38	9	4	6	32	27	6	3	10	20	28	15	7	16	52	55	–3	52
11	Watford	38	8	3	8	26	28	6	5	8	26	31	14	8	16	52	59	–7	50
12	Crystal Palace	38	5	5	9	19	23	9	2	8	32	30	14	7	17	51	53	–2	49
13	Newcastle U	38	8	1	10	24	25	4	8	7	18	23	12	9	17	42	48	–6	45
14	Bournemouth	38	8	5	6	30	25	5	1	13	26	45	13	6	19	56	70	–14	45
15	Burnley	38	7	2	10	24	32	4	5	10	21	36	11	7	20	45	68	–23	40
16	Southampton	38	5	8	6	27	30	4	4	11	18	35	9	12	17	45	65	–20	39
17	Brighton & HA	38	6	5	8	19	28	3	4	12	16	32	9	9	20	35	60	–25	36
18	Cardiff C (P)	38	6	2	11	21	38	4	2	13	13	31	10	4	24	34	69	–35	34
19	Fulham (P)	38	6	3	10	22	36	1	2	16	12	45	7	5	26	34	81	–47	26
20	Huddersfield T	38	2	3	14	10	31	1	4	14	12	45	3	7	28	22	76	–54	16

PREMIER LEAGUE LEADING GOALSCORERS 2018–19

Qualification 10 league goals	*League*	*FA Cup*	*EFL Cup*	*Other*	*Total*
Sergio Aguero *(Manchester C)*	21	2	1	8	32
Pierre-Emerick Aubameyang *(Arsenal)*	22	1	0	8	31
Mohamed Salah *(Liverpool)*	22	0	0	5	27
Sadio Mane *(Liverpool)*	22	0	0	4	26
Raheem Sterling *(Manchester C)*	17	3	0	5	25
Harry Kane *(Tottenham H)*	17	1	1	5	24
Eden Hazard *(Chelsea)*	16	0	3	2	21
Son Heung-Min *(Tottenham H)*	12	1	3	4	20
Alexandre Lacazette *(Arsenal)*	13	0	1	5	19
Jamie Vardy *(Leicester C)*	18	0	0	0	18
Raul Jimenez *(Wolverhampton W)*	13	4	0	0	17
Roberto Firmino *(Liverpool)*	12	0	0	4	16
Leroy Sane *(Manchester C)*	10	2	0	4	16
Paul Pogba *(Manchester U)*	13	1	0	2	16
Callum Wilson *(Bournemouth)*	14	0	1	0	15
Glenn Murray *(Brighton & HA)*	13	2	0	0	15
Romelu Lukaku *(Manchester U)*	12	1	0	2	15
Lucas Moura *(Tottenham H)*	10	0	0	5	15
Richarlison *(Everton)*	13	1	0	0	14
Gylfi Sigurdsson *(Everton)*	13	0	1	0	14
Ashley Barnes *(Burnley)*	12	0	0	1	13
Chris Wood *(Burnley)*	10	1	0	2	13
Marcus Rashford *(Manchester U)*	10	1	0	2	13
Ayoze Perez *(Newcastle U)*	12	1	0	0	13
Josh King *(Bournemouth)*	12	0	0	0	12
Luka Milivojevic *(Crystal Palace)*	12	0	0	0	12
Anthony Martial *(Manchester U)*	10	1	0	1	12
Salomon Rondon *(Newcastle U)*	11	0	1	0	12
Gerard Deulofeu *(Watford)*	10	2	0	0	12
Aleksandar Mitrovic *(Fulham)*	11	0	0	0	11
Marko Arnautovic *(West Ham U)*	10	1	0	0	11
Wilfried Zaha *(Crystal Palace)*	10	0	0	0	10

Other matches consist of European games, Community Shield.

SKY BET CHAMPIONSHIP 2018–19

(P) *Promoted into division at end of 2017–18 season.* (R) *Relegated into division at end of 2017–18 season.*

		Home						Away					Total						
		P	W	D	L	F	A	W	D	L	F	A	W	D	L	F	A	GD	Pts
1	Norwich C	46	15	4	4	51	34	12	9	2	42	23	27	13	6	93	57	36	94
2	Sheffield U	46	15	4	4	42	17	11	7	5	36	24	26	11	9	78	41	37	89
3	Leeds U	46	14	4	5	38	21	11	4	8	35	29	25	8	13	73	50	23	83
4	WBA (R)	46	12	7	4	53	31	11	4	8	34	31	23	11	12	87	62	25	80
5	Aston Villa¶	46	11	8	4	50	36	9	8	6	32	25	20	16	10	82	61	21	76
6	Derby Co	46	13	7	3	40	20	7	7	9	29	34	20	14	12	69	54	15	74
7	Middlesbrough	46	10	6	7	23	17	10	7	6	26	24	20	13	13	49	41	8	73
8	Bristol C	46	8	8	7	28	26	11	5	7	31	27	19	13	14	59	53	6	70
9	Nottingham F	46	13	4	6	34	21	4	11	8	27	33	17	15	14	61	54	7	66
10	Swansea C (R)	46	12	6	5	42	28	6	5	12	23	34	18	11	17	65	62	3	65
11	Brentford†	46	14	4	5	50	23	3	9	11	23	36	17	13	16	73	59	14	64
12	Sheffield W	46	10	8	5	34	27	6	8	9	26	35	16	16	14	60	62	−2	64
13	Hull C	46	11	6	6	37	24	6	5	12	29	44	17	11	18	66	68	−2	62
14	Preston NE	46	8	10	5	41	30	8	3	12	26	37	16	13	17	67	67	0	61
15	Blackburn R (P)	46	10	7	6	32	21	6	5	12	32	48	16	12	18	64	69	−5	60
16	Stoke C (R)	46	8	9	6	26	24	3	13	7	19	28	11	22	13	45	52	−7	55
17	Birmingham C*	46	7	11	5	31	24	7	8	8	33	34	14	19	13	64	58	6	52
18	Wigan Ath (P)	46	11	8	4	29	20	2	5	16	22	44	13	13	20	51	64	−13	52
19	QPR	46	9	3	11	33	31	5	6	12	20	40	14	9	23	53	71	−18	51
20	Reading	46	8	6	9	29	31	2	11	10	20	35	10	17	19	49	66	−17	47
21	Millwall	46	7	9	7	26	27	3	5	15	22	37	10	14	22	48	64	−16	44
22	Rotherham U (P)	46	7	8	8	32	38	1	8	14	20	45	8	16	22	52	83	−31	40
23	Bolton W†	46	4	4	15	13	35	4	4	15	16	43	8	8	30	29	78	−49	32
24	Ipswich T	46	3	11	9	22	31	2	5	16	14	46	5	16	25	36	77	−41	31

¶Aston Villa promoted via play-offs.
**Birmingham C deducted 9 points for breach of rules.*
†Brentford awarded a 1-0 win in match to be played at Bolton W on Saturday 27 April. Bolton W unable to fulfil fixture.

SKY BET CHAMPIONSHIP LEADING GOALSCORERS 2018–19

Qualification 10 league goals	*League*	*FA Cup*	*EFL Cup*	*Play-offs*	*Total*
Temmu Pukki *(Norwich C)*	29	0	1	0	30
Neal Maupay *(Brentford)*	25	3	0	0	28
Tammy Abraham *(Aston Villa)*	25	0	0	1	26
Billy Sharp *(Sheffield U)*	23	0	1	0	24
Oliver McBurnie *(Swansea C)*	22	2	0	0	24
Dwight Gayle *(WBA)*	23	0	0	1	24
Che Adams *(Birmingham C)*	22	0	0	0	22
Jarrod Bowen *(Hull C)*	22	0	0	0	22
Jay Rodriguez *(WBA)*	22	0	0	0	22
Bradley Dack *(Blackburn R)*	15	1	2	0	18
Harry Wilson *(Derby C)*	15	1	1	1	18
Lewis Grabban *(Nottingham F)*	16	0	1	0	17
Danny Graham *(Blackburn R)*	15	0	1	0	16
Britt Assombalonga *(Middlesbrough)*	14	2	0	0	16
Kemar Roofe *(Leeds U)*	14	0	0	1	15
David McGoldrick *(Sheffield U)*	15	0	0	0	15
Lukas Jutkiewicz *(Birmingham C)*	14	0	0	0	14
Famara Diedhiou *(Bristol C)*	13	0	0	0	13
Lee Gregory *(Millwall)*	10	1	2	0	13
Callum Robinson *(Preston NE)*	12	0	1	0	13
Yakou Meite *(Reading)*	12	0	1	0	13
Ollie Watkins *(Brentford)*	10	2	0	0	12
Fraizer Campbell *(Hull C)*	12	0	0	0	12
Pablo Hernandez *(Leeds U)*	12	0	0	0	12
Joe Lolley *(Nottingham F)*	11	0	1	0	12
Alan Browne *(Preston NE)*	12	0	0	0	12
Said Benrahma *(Brentford)*	10	0	1	0	11
Steven Fletcher *(Sheffield W)*	11	0	0	0	11
Charlie Mulgrew *(Blackburn R)*	10	0	0	0	10
Andreas Weimann *(Bristol C)*	10	0	0	0	10
Mateusz Klich *(Leeds U)*	10	0	0	0	10
Mario Vrancic *(Norwich C)*	10	0	0	0	10

SKY BET LEAGUE ONE 2018–19

(P) *Promoted into division at end of 2017–18 season.* (R) *Relegated into division at end of 2017–18 season.*

			Home					Away					Total						
		P	W	D	L	F	A	W	D	L	F	A	W	D	L	F	A	GD	Pts
1	Luton T (P)	46	16	7	0	57	19	11	6	6	33	23	27	13	6	90	42	48	94
2	Barnsley (R)	46	15	8	0	40	16	11	5	7	40	23	26	13	7	80	39	41	91
3	Charlton Ath¶	46	16	5	2	41	15	10	5	8	32	25	26	10	10	73	40	33	88
4	Portsmouth	46	12	7	4	42	22	13	6	4	41	29	25	13	8	83	51	32	88
5	Sunderland (R)	46	12	10	1	46	25	10	9	4	34	22	22	19	5	80	47	33	85
6	Doncaster R	46	13	7	3	45	21	7	6	10	31	37	20	13	13	76	58	18	73
7	Peterborough U	46	9	7	7	31	28	11	5	7	40	34	20	12	14	71	62	9	72
8	Coventry C (P)	46	9	7	7	24	20	9	4	10	30	34	18	11	17	54	54	0	65
9	Burton Alb (R)	46	11	5	7	35	23	6	7	10	31	34	17	12	17	66	57	9	63
10	Blackpool	46	8	8	7	28	26	7	9	7	22	26	15	17	14	50	52	–2	62
11	Fleetwood T	46	9	9	5	33	27	7	4	12	25	25	16	13	17	58	52	6	61
12	Oxford U	46	11	4	8	34	27	4	11	8	24	37	15	15	16	58	64	–6	60
13	Gillingham	46	7	4	12	27	36	8	6	9	34	36	15	10	21	61	72	–11	55
14	Accrington S (P)	46	7	6	10	26	33	7	7	9	25	34	14	13	19	51	67	–16	55
15	Bristol R	46	6	6	11	24	28	7	9	7	23	22	13	15	18	47	50	–3	54
16	Rochdale	46	8	4	11	25	37	7	5	11	29	50	15	9	22	54	87	–33	54
17	Wycombe W (P)	46	10	5	8	28	26	4	6	13	27	41	14	11	21	55	67	–12	53
18	Shrewsbury T	46	8	9	6	25	25	4	7	12	26	34	12	16	18	51	59	–8	52
19	Southend U	46	8	2	13	32	34	6	6	11	23	34	14	8	24	55	68	–13	50
20	AFC Wimbledon	46	6	5	12	24	37	7	6	10	18	26	13	11	22	42	63	–21	50
21	Plymouth Arg	46	9	6	8	36	38	4	5	14	20	42	13	11	22	56	80	–24	50
22	Walsall	46	7	5	11	30	37	5	6	12	19	34	12	11	23	49	71	–22	47
23	Scunthorpe U	46	6	7	10	31	42	6	3	14	22	41	12	10	24	53	83	–30	46
24	Bradford C	46	7	4	12	25	31	4	4	15	24	46	11	8	27	49	77	–28	41

¶*Charlton Ath promoted via play-offs.*

SKY BET LEAGUE ONE LEADING GOALSCORERS 2018–19

Qualification 10 league goals	*League*	*FA Cup*	*EFL Cup*	*EFL Trophy*	*Play-Offs*	*Total*
John Marquis *(Doncaster R)*	21	3	0	1	1	26
Lyle Taylor *(Charlton Ath)*	21	3	0	0	1	25
James Collins *(Luton T)*	25	0	0	0	0	25
Ivan Toney *(Peterborough U)*	16	4	0	3	0	23
Tom Eaves *(Gillingham)*	21	1	0	0	0	22
Ian Henderson *(Rochdale)*	20	1	0	0	0	21
Kieffer Moore *(Barnsley)*	17	2	0	0	0	19
Cauley Woodrow *(Barnsley)*	16	3	0	0	0	19
Paddy Madden *(Fleetwood T)*	15	4	0	0	0	19
Freddie Ladapo *(Plymouth Arg)*	18	0	1	0	0	19
Joe Pigott *(AFC Wimbledon)*	15	1	2	0	0	18
Ched Evans *(Fleetwood T)*	17	1	0	0	0	18
Matt Godden *(Peterborough U)*	14	2	0	2	0	18
Andy Cook *(Walsall)*	13	3	1	1	0	18
Jamal Lowe *(Portsmouth)*	15	1	0	1	0	17
Simon Cox *(Southend U)*	15	2	0	0	0	17
Billy Kee *(Accrington S)*	13	2	0	1	0	16
Mallik Wilks *(Doncaster R)*	14	1	1	0	0	16
Fejiri Okenabirhie *(Shrewsbury T)*	10	3	0	3	0	16
Sean McConville *(Accrington S)*	15	0	0	0	0	15
James Henry *(Oxford U)*	11	2	0	2	0	15
Josh Maja *(Sunderland)*	15	0	0	0	0	15
Armand Gnanduillet *(Blackpool)*	10	1	2	1	0	14
Lucas Akins *(Burton Alb)*	13	0	1	0	0	14
Liam Boyce *(Burton Alb)*	11	1	2	0	0	14
Karlan Ahearne-Grant *(Charlton Ath)*	14	0	0	0	0	14
Aiden McGeady *(Sunderland)*	11	1	0	2	0	14
Jordy Hiwula-Mayifuila *(Coventry C)*	12	0	0	1	0	13
Brett Pitman *(Portsmouth)*	11	0	0	2	0	13
Gareth Evans *(Portsmouth)*	10	0	0	3	0	13
Lee Novak *(Scunthorpe U)*	12	1	0	0	0	13
Elliot Lee *(Luton T)*	12	0	0	0	0	12
Ruben Lameiras *(Plymouth Arg)*	11	1	0	0	0	12
Ronan Curtis *(Portsmouth)*	11	0	0	1	0	12
Eoin Doyle *(Bradford C)*	11	0	0	0	0	11
Jonson Clarke-Harris *(Bristol R)*	11	0	0	0	0	11

SKY BET LEAGUE TWO 2018–19

(P) *Promoted into division at end of 2017–18 season.* (R) *Relegated into division at end of 2017–18 season.*

			Home					*Away*					*Total*						
		P	*W*	*D*	*L*	*F*	*A*	*W*	*D*	*L*	*F*	*A*	*W*	*D*	*L*	*F*	*A*	*GD*	*Pts*
1	Lincoln C	46	11	10	2	35	23	12	6	5	38	20	23	16	7	73	43	30	85
2	Bury (R)	46	14	6	3	52	26	8	7	8	30	30	22	13	11	82	56	26	79
3	Milton Keynes D (R)	46	14	5	4	35	14	9	5	9	36	35	23	10	13	71	49	22	79
4	Mansfield T	46	14	5	4	38	15	6	11	6	31	26	20	16	10	69	41	28	76
5	Forest Green R	46	8	9	6	28	20	12	5	6	40	27	20	14	12	68	47	21	74
6	Tranmere R¶ (P)	46	14	5	4	33	13	6	8	9	30	37	20	13	13	63	50	13	73
7	Newport Co	46	14	6	3	32	22	6	5	12	27	37	20	11	15	59	59	0	71
8	Colchester U	46	12	4	7	39	23	8	6	9	26	30	20	10	16	65	53	12	70
9	Exeter C	46	12	3	8	34	25	7	10	6	26	24	19	13	14	60	49	11	70
10	Stevenage	46	12	3	8	28	23	8	7	8	31	32	20	10	16	59	55	4	70
11	Carlisle U	46	12	3	8	42	31	8	5	10	25	31	20	8	18	67	62	5	68
12	Crewe Alex	46	15	2	6	45	25	4	6	13	15	34	19	8	19	60	59	1	65
13	Swindon T	46	8	9	6	31	27	8	7	8	28	29	16	16	14	59	56	3	64
14	Oldham Ath (R)	46	10	6	7	42	33	6	8	9	25	27	16	14	16	67	60	7	62
15	Northampton T (R)	46	7	12	4	30	27	7	7	9	34	36	14	19	13	64	63	1	61
16	Cheltenham T	46	10	7	6	34	29	5	5	13	23	39	15	12	19	57	68	−11	57
17	Grimsby T	46	11	4	8	26	21	5	4	14	19	35	16	8	22	45	56	−11	56
18	Morecambe	46	8	5	10	33	31	6	7	10	21	39	14	12	20	54	70	−16	54
19	Crawley T	46	10	5	8	34	31	5	3	15	17	37	15	8	23	51	68	−17	53
20	Port Vale	46	7	3	13	24	36	5	10	8	15	19	12	13	21	39	55	−16	49
21	Cambridge U	46	7	7	9	21	26	5	4	14	19	40	12	11	23	40	66	−26	47
22	Macclesfield T (P)	46	5	11	7	26	35	5	3	15	22	39	10	14	22	48	74	−26	44
23	Notts Co	46	5	9	9	23	34	4	5	14	25	50	9	14	23	48	84	−36	41
24	Yeovil T	46	4	9	10	20	34	5	4	14	21	32	9	13	24	41	66	−25	40

¶*Tranmere R promoted via play-offs.*

SKY BET LEAGUE TWO LEADING GOALSCORERS 2018–19

Qualification 10 league goals	*League*	*FA Cup*	*EFL Cup*	*EFL Trophy*	*Play-Offs*	*Total*
James Norwood *(Tranmere R)*	29	2	0	0	0	31
Tyler Walker *(Mansfield T)*	22	0	3	1	0	26
Nicky Maynard *(Bury)*	21	0	0	1	0	22
Kieran Agard *(Milton Keynes D)*	20	1	0	1	0	22
Padraig Amond *(Newport Co)*	14	5	2	1	0	22
Jamille Matt *(Newport Co)*	14	3	1	2	0	20
Chuks Aneke *(Milton Keynes D)*	17	0	0	2	0	19
John Akinde *(Lincoln C)*	15	1	1	0	0	17
Jay O'Shea *(Bury)*	15	1	0	0	0	16
Ollie Palmer *(Crawley T)*	14	2	0	0	0	16
Jayden Stockley *(Exeter C)*	16	0	0	0	0	16
Callum Lang *(Oldham Ath)*	13	2	0	1	0	16
Hallum Hope *(Carlisle U)*	14	0	1	0	0	15
Sammie Szmodics *(Colchester U)*	14	0	1	0	0	15
Chris Porter *(Crewe Alex)*	13	0	0	2	0	15
Luke Varney *(Cheltenham T)*	14	0	0	0	0	14
Christian Doidge *(Forest Green R)*	14	0	0	0	0	14
Kane Hemmings *(Notts Co)*	14	0	0	0	0	14
Tom Pope *(Port Vale)*	11	1	0	2	0	14
Kurtis Guthrie *(Stevenage)*	11	0	0	3	0	14
Michael Doughty *(Swindon T)*	13	0	0	1	0	14
CJ Hamilton *(Mansfield T)*	11	1	1	0	1	14
Jamie Devitt *(Carlisle U)*	11	1	0	0	0	12
Wes Thomas *(Grimsby T)*	11	1	0	0	0	12
Andy Williams *(Northampton T)*	12	0	0	0	0	12
Charlie Kirk *(Crewe Alex)*	11	0	0	0	0	11
Reece Brown *(Forest Green R)*	11	0	0	0	0	11
Bruno Andrade *(Lincoln C)*	10	1	0	0	0	11
Scott Wilson *(Macclesfield T)*	10	0	0	1	0	11
Nicky Law *(Exeter C)*	10	0	0	0	0	10

FOOTBALL LEAGUE PLAY-OFFS 2018–19

▪ *Denotes player sent off.*

SKY BET CHAMPIONSHIP SEMI-FINALS FIRST LEG

Saturday, 11 May 2019

Aston Villa (0) 2 *(Hourihane 75, Abraham 79 (pen))*
WBA (1) 1 *(Gayle 16)* 40,754
Aston Villa: (4141) Steer; Elmohamady, Tuanzebe, Mings, Taylor; Whelan (Hourihane 67); Adomah (Green 67), McGinn, Grealish, El Ghazi (Kodjia 90); Abraham.
WBA: (343) Johnstone; Dawson (Mears 46), Bartley, Hegazi; Holgate, Brunt, Johansen (Morrison 85), Gibbs; Phillips (Murphy 66), Rodriguez, Gayle▪.
Referee: Graham Scott.

Derby Co (0) 0
Leeds U (0) 1 *(Roofe 55)* 31,723
Derby Co: (4231) Roos; Bogle, Tomori, Keogh, Malone; Mount, Johnson; Wilson H, Holmes (Bennett 70), Lawrence (Huddlestone 86); Nugent (Marriott 64).
Leeds U: (4141) Casilla; Ayling, Berardi, Cooper, Dallas; Phillips; Hernandez, Forshaw (Shackleton 24), Klich, Harrison; Roofe (Clarke 81).
Referee: Craig Pawson.

SKY BET CHAMPIONSHIP SEMI-FINALS SECOND LEG

Tuesday, 14 May 2019

WBA (1) 1 *(Dawson 29)*
Aston Villa (0) 0 25,702
WBA: (541) Johnstone; Holgate, Dawson, Bartley, Hegazi, Gibbs; Phillips (Harper 75), Johansen (Morrison 71), Brunt▪, Murphy (Adarabioyo 82); Rodriguez (Leko 93).
Aston Villa: (433) Steer; Elmohamady (Davis 114), Tuanzebe (Jedinak 120), Mings, Taylor; McGinn, Hourihane, Grealish; Green (Adomah 75), Abraham, El Ghazi (Kodjia 101).
aet; Aston Villa won 4-3 on penalties.
Referee: Chris Kavanagh.

Wednesday, 15 May 2019

Leeds U (1) 2 *(Dallas 24, 62)*
Derby Co (1) 4 *(Marriott 45, 85, Mount 46, Wilson H 58 (pen))* 36,326
Leeds U: (4141) Casilla; Ayling, Berardi▪, Cooper, Dallas; Phillips; Hernandez, Shackleton, Klich (Clarke 86), Harrison; Bamford (Brown 88).
Derby Co: (4231) Roos; Bogle, Keogh, Tomori, Malone▪; Holmes (Marriott 44), Johnson; Wilson H (Cole 90), Mount, Lawrence; Bennett (Huddlestone 59).
Derby Co won 4-3 on aggregate. Referee: Anthony Taylor.

SKY BET CHAMPIONSHIP FINAL

Wembley, Monday, 27 May 2019

Aston Villa (1) 2 *(El Ghazi 44, McGinn 59)*
Derby Co (0) 1 *(Marriott 81)* 85,826
Aston Villa: (433) Steer; Elmohamady, Tuanzebe, Mings (Hause 86), Taylor; McGinn, Hourihane, Grealish; Adomah (Green 73), Abraham, El Ghazi.
Derby Co: (4312) Roos; Bogle, Keogh, Tomori, Cole; Mount, Huddlestone (Marriott 63), Johnson; Wilson H; Lawrence (Jozefzoon 73), Bennett (Waghorn 69).
Referee: Paul Tierney.

SKY BET LEAGUE ONE SEMI-FINALS FIRST LEG

Saturday, 11 May 2019

Sunderland (0) 1 *(Maguire 62)*
Portsmouth (0) 0 26,610
Sunderland: (4231) McLaughlin; O'Nien, Ozturk▪, Flanagan, Oviedo; Power, Cattermole; Gooch (Dunne 70), Honeyman, Morgan (Maguire 58); Wyke.
Portsmouth: (4231) MacGillivray; Thompson N, Burgess, Clarke, Walkes; Naylor, Close; Lowe, Evans, Curtis (Bogle 69); Hawkins (Solomon-Otabor 69).
Referee: Andy Woolmer.

Sunday, 12 May 2019

Doncaster R (0) 1 *(Blair 87)*
Charlton Ath (2) 2 *(Taylor 32, Aribo 34)* 11,140
Doncaster R: (4231) Marosi; Blair, Downing, Butler, Andrew; Whiteman, Kane; Wilks, Coppinger (Rowe 46), Sadlier (May 84); Marquis.
Charlton Ath: (532) Phillips; Dijksteel, Bielik, Bauer, Sarr, Purrington; Morgan (Pratley 61), Cullen, Aribo; Taylor, Parker (Pearce 67).
Referee: Oliver Langford.

SKY BET LEAGUE ONE SEMI-FINALS SECOND LEG

Thursday, 16 May 2019

Portsmouth (0) 0
Sunderland (0) 0 18,077
Portsmouth: (4231) MacGillivray; Thompson N, Burgess, Clarke, Brown; Naylor, Close; Solomon-Otabor (Lowe 53), Pitman B, Evans; Hawkins (Vaughan 68).
Sunderland: (433) McLaughlin; O'Nien, Ozturk, Flanagan, Oviedo; Power (Morgan 80), Cattermole, Leadbitter; Honeyman, Wyke (Grigg 83), Maguire (Gooch 69).
Sunderland won 1-0 on aggregate.
Referee: Peter Bankes.

Aston Villa's John McGinn scores at Wembley as Villa secure promotion to the Premier League by beating Derby County 2-1 in the Championship Play-Off final on 27 May. (Action Images via Reuters/Ed Sykes)

The Charlton Athletic players celebrate their dramatic, last-gasp victory over Sunderland in the League One Play-Off final on 26 May. (Steven Paston/EMPICS Sport)

Friday, 17 May 2019

Charlton Ath (1) 2 *(Bielik 2, Pratley 101)*

Doncaster R (1) 3 *(Rowe 11, Butler 88, Marquis 100)* 25,428

Charlton Ath: (4312) Phillips; Dijksteel, Bauer, Sarr, Purrington; Cullen, Bielik (Solly 110), Morgan (Pratley 46); Aribo; Parker (Williams 95), Taylor.
Doncaster R: (433) Marosi; Blair (May 86), Downing, Butler, Andrew; Kane (Crawford 80), Rowe, Whiteman; Coppinger (Sadlier 96), Marquis, Wilks (Wright 106).
aet; Charlton Ath won 4-3 on penalties.
Referee: Gavin Ward.

SKY BET LEAGUE ONE FINAL

Wembley, Sunday, 26 May 2019

Charlton Ath (1) 2 *(Purrington 35, Bauer 90)*

Sunderland (1) 1 *(Sarr 5 (og))* 76,155

Charlton Ath: (352) Phillips; Bielik, Bauer, Sarr (Pearce 46); Dijksteel, Pratley (Williams 71), Cullen, Aribo, Purrington; Taylor, Parker.
Sunderland: (433) McLaughlin; O'Nien, Ozturk, Flanagan, Oviedo; Cattermole, Power (Morgan 9), Leadbitter; Honeyman, Wyke (McGeady 72), Maguire (Grigg 57).
Referee: Andrew Madley.

SKY BET LEAGUE TWO SEMI-FINALS FIRST LEG

Thursday, 9 May 2019

Newport Co (0) 1 *(Amond 83)*

Mansfield T (1) 1 *(Hamilton 12)* 6035

Newport Co: (3142) Day; Poole, O'Brien, Demetriou; Sheehan; Willmott, Bennett (Labadie 72), Dolan (Azeez 58), Butler; Matt, Amond (Crofts 84).
Mansfield T: (352) Logan; Pearce, Turner, Sweeney; Jones, MacDonald, Bishop, Mellis, Hamilton; Rose (Benning 77), Walker.
Referee: Matthew Donohue.

Friday, 10 May 2019

Tranmere R (1) 1 *(Banks 26)*

Forest Green R (0) 0 9579

Tranmere R: (4141) Davies; Caprice, Nelson, Monthe, Ridehalgh; Banks (Gilmour 76); Morris (Smith 62), Harris, Perkins, Jennings; Norwood.
Forest Green R: (4231) Ward; Shephard, Rawson, McGinley, Mills; Winchester, Gunning■; Mondal (Collins 32), Brown (Digby 88), Grubb (Williams 66); Doidge.
Referee: John Busby.

SKY BET LEAGUE TWO SEMI-FINALS SECOND LEG

Sunday, 12 May 2019

Mansfield T (0) 0

Newport Co (0) 0 7361

Mansfield T: (352) Logan; Pearce, Turner, Sweeney; Jones (Grant 120), Tomlinson (Benning 46), MacDonald, Mellis (Atkinson 91), Hamilton; Walker, Rose (Ajose 105).
Newport Co: (433) Day; Poole, O'Brien, Demetriou, Butler; Bennett, Sheehan (Dolan 110), Labadie (Azeez 76 (McKirdy 111)); Amond, Matt, Willmott.
aet; Newport Co won 5-3 on penalties.
Referee: Michael Salisbury.

Monday, 13 May 2019

Forest Green R (1) 1 *(Mills 12)*

Tranmere R (1) 1 *(Norwood 27)* 4492

Forest Green R: (4231) Ward; Shephard, Rawson, McGinley, Mills; Winchester■, Collins (McCoulsky 81); Mondal (Williams 46), Brown, Grubb (James 70); Doidge.
Tranmere R: (4141) Davies; Caprice, Nelson, Monthe, Ridehalgh; Banks; Morris (Gilmour 66), Harris, Perkins, Jennings; Norwood.
Tranmere R won 2-1 on aggregate.
Referee: Eddie Ilderton.

SKY BET LEAGUE TWO FINAL

Wembley, Saturday, 25 May 2019

Newport Co (0) 0

Tranmere R (0) 1 *(Jennings 119)* 25,217

Newport Co: (4312) Day; Poole, O'Brien■, Demetriou, Butler; Willmott (Marsh-Brown 106), Sheehan (Bakinson 91), Bennett; Labadie (Dolan 72); Matt (Azeez 103), Amond.
Tranmere R: (4141) Davies; Caprice, Nelson (Buxton 115), Monthe, Ridehalgh; Banks; Morris (McNulty 82), Harris (Pringle 53), Perkins, Jennings; Norwood.
aet.
Referee: Ross Joyce.

REVIEW OF THE SEASON 2018–19

It was a season unlike any other that had gone before as Manchester City landed an unprecedented domestic treble of Premier League title, Carabao Cup and FA Cup.

According to their charismatic boss Pep Guardiola, it ought to have been recognised as a quadruple: the Community Shield victory against Chelsea should be counted in the trophy haul too, he argued. Hence City were labelled 'The Fourmidables'.

It was an astonishing achievement. This was a team which, a year earlier, had set a Premier League records for points (100) and goals scored (106). In winning the title again, they were only two points and 11 goals adrift of those marks. But while 2017–18 had been something of a canter as they romped in 19 points clear of second-placed Manchester United, this was a battle right to the very end.

Jurgen Klopp's Liverpool were still chasing City hard on the last day, only to finish an agonising one point behind in their quest for a first Premier League crown. City had to win their final 14 games in a row to see them off. The Reds, marshalled by PFA Player of the Year Virgil van Dijk, only lost once in the entire campaign, a January defeat at the home of the champions which turned out to be pivotal. Mind you, the long-range late rocket by City captain Vincent Kompany against Leicester in their penultimate match will be the goal which defines their title win in the same way Sergio Aguero's did in 2012.

It was a special way for Kompany to end his City career as he departed for Anderlecht after 11 years at the club. 'I knew then I was done,' he said. 'I couldn't do anything better.'

City claimed the Carabao Cup on penalties against Chelsea in a final which will be remembered for Blues' keeper Kepa Arrizabalaga refusing to come off when manager Maurizio Sarri wanted to substitute him ahead of the shoot-out, believing him to be injured.

The FA Cup final may not be fondly recalled by Watford keeper Heurelho Gomes either. He conceded six as City equalled Bury's 1903 record victory. Raheem Sterling was

Sadio Mané's 22 Premier League goals played a major part in Liverpool pushing Manchester City so close for the Premier League title. Here he is scoring against Cardiff City at Anfield on 27 October.
(Action Images via Reuters/Lee Smith)

The PFA's Player of the Season, Liverpool's Virgil van Dijk, scores against Newcastle United at St James' Park on 4 May. (Action Images via Reuters/Lee Smith)

denied a first final hat-trick since Stan Mortensen in 1953 when it was ruled that a Gabriel Jesus shot was already over the line before he smashed it into the net. Had he been awarded the third goal it would have been some conclusion to a season in which Sterling was at the forefront of the campaign to clamp down hard on racism in football. His work on and off the field earned him the FWA's Footballer of the Year award.

Strangely for City, it was still a case of what could have been. They were knocked out of the Champions League, the trophy their Abu Dhabi paymasters wanted most of all, after a dramatic night in the quarter-final against Tottenham. Sterling thought he had scored the goal in added time to put them through but the celebrations were cut short by VAR technology which ruled Sergio Aguero was a fraction offside in the build-up.

That meant Tottenham progressed on away goals and, after another heart-stopping semi-final against Ajax, which was settled when Lucas Moura completed his hat-trick in injury time, they reached their first ever Champions League final. But that was the high point for Spurs: Liverpool finished their season in style with a 2-0 win in the all-English finale in Madrid. It was a game which could not possibly have lived up to the drama of their semi-final against Barcelona when they recovered from a 3-0 deficit in the first leg to win an incredible second leg by 4-0. This was a sixth European Cup for Liverpool and 750,000 people lined the streets of the city to welcome their heroes home.

There was a feeling that Liverpool and Manchester City would happily have swapped places and taken each other's trophy but it was fitting that they should each win a big prize.

Chelsea and Arsenal finished a long way back in the title chase but they did have the consolation of a Europa League final which was controversially staged in the Azerbaijan capital, Baku. For the first time a Champions League place was up for grabs for the winners but with Chelsea having already qualified, it was more important to Arsenal to win. In the end it was hardly a contest as an Eden Hazard-inspired Chelsea ran out easy winners by 4-1.

As for Manchester United, it was another miserable season as they continued to flounder in the post-Sir Alex Ferguson era. Fans and players turned against manager Jose Mourinho, who had been highly critical of the club's transfer policy, and the board felt the 'toxic' atmosphere had to change. Mourinho was sacked in December and in came the hero of their 1999 Champions League win, Ole Gunnar Solskjaer.

The Norwegian initially arrived as a loan boss from his club Molde but he made a good start to his reign at Old Trafford, winning his first six League games and pulling off a 3-1 Champions League win over PSG in Paris (after losing the first leg 2-0) to advance to the quarter-finals. There was a clamour from former players and pundits to give Solskjaer the job on a permanent basis and he eventually signed a three-year deal in March. But, by the end of the season, Solskjaer was coming under pressure, having won only two of his last 12 matches.

Though they finished one place below United, the season was a success for newly promoted Wolves. Boss Nuno Espirito Santo had them playing with a style which earned plaudits around the country and they thoroughly deserved the last Europa League qualifying spot. It could have been an even better season but they imploded in the FA Cup semi-final against Watford. Having been 2-0 up, they eventually lost 3-2 after extra time.

Down at the bottom, Brighton sacked boss Chris Hughton and replaced him with Swansea's Graham Potter. Owner Tony Bloom was not satisfied by seventeenth place, one spot above the drop zone. Huddersfield never looked likely to complete a second successive season in the Premier League and manager David Wagner left by mutual agreement five months into the campaign.

Fulham spent £100m in a bid to establish themselves in the top flight but sacked boss Slavisa Jokanovic then brought in Leicester title winner Claudio Ranieiri who couldn't work another miracle and left after three months. Scott Parker oversaw the last rites but they were already doomed.

Cardiff completed the trio of relegated clubs after a fraught season in which the tragic death in a plane crash of newly-signed £15m Argentinian striker Emiliano Sala from Nantes overshadowed events on the pitch.

Another air tragedy occurred at Leicester where owner Vichai Srivaddhanaprabha was one of five people killed in a helicopter crash within seconds of taking off from the centre circle following a game against West Ham in October. The city came out in force to

Vincent Kompany's wonder strike gives Manchester City a crucial late victory over Leicester City at the Etihad Stadium on 6 May. (Action Images via Reuters/Jason Cairnduff)

The FWA's Footballer of the Year, Raheem Sterling of Manchester City, scores against Schalke in the Champions League in Gelsenkirchen on 20 February. (Action Images via Reuters/Matthew Childs)

mourn the popular owner who had given the locals such joy in helping to mastermind their 2016 title win.

In the Championship, Norwich went up as title winners while Sheffield United became the new kings of Yorkshire having taken advantage of a fading Leeds. Up from the play-offs came Aston Villa who beat Derby at Wembley.

Rotherham, Bolton and Ipswich plunged into League One. Bolton's season was characterised by behind-the-scenes arguments over the ownership and they eventually went into administration: they will start the new season on minus 12 points.

Up from League One came Luton and Barnsley, joined by Charlton from the play-off final. Wimbledon produced an incredible escape at the bottom under former player Wally Downes: at one point they were ten points adrift of safety. Plymouth, Walsall, Scunthorpe and Bradford were relegated.

Lincoln continued their rise under Danny Cowley as they took the League Two title and were joined on the promotion podium by Bury, MK Dons and Tranmere – the last promoted for a second season running. However, it was a sad demise for the oldest League club of them all, Notts County: they dropped into the National League with Yeovil as Sol Campbell orchestrated a great escape for Macclesfield.

National League champions Leyton Orient returned to the Football League after a two-year absence, along with Salford City who triumphed over Fylde in the Wembley play-off. David Beckham, Gary and Phil Neville, Nicky Butt and Ryan Giggs from the Class of 92 had backed Salford and were all there to see it. They had enjoyed many a Wembley triumph between them but this was a day to rival any from their playing days.

Shaun Custis, Head of Sport, *The Sun*

CUPS AND UPS AND DOWNS DIARY

AUGUST 2018

5 FA Community Shield: Manchester C 2 Chelsea 0.
15 European Super Cup 2018: Atletico Madrid 4 v Real Madrid 2 *(aet)*.

NOVEMBER 2018

2 Betfred Scottish League Cup Final: Celtic 1 Aberdeen 0.

DECEMBER 2018

22 FIFA Club World Cup Final: Real Madrid 4 Al-Ain 1.

JANUARY 2019

19 Nathaniel MG Welsh League Cup Final: Cardiff Metropolitan 2 Cambrian & Clydach Vale 0.

FEBRUARY 2019

16 BetMcLean League Cup Final: Linfield 1 Ballymena U 0.
23 Women's Continental Tyres Cup Final: Manchester C 0 Arsenal 0 *(aet; Manchester C won 4-2 on penalties)*.
24 Carabao Cup Final: Manchester C 0 Chelsea 0 *(aet; Manchester C won 4-3 on penalties)*.

MARCH 2019

10 University Football 2018: Cambridge 1 Oxford 1 *(Cambridge won 4-3 on penalties)*.
24 Irn-Bru Scottish League Challenge Cup Final: Ross Co 3 Connah's Quay Nomads 1.
30 Huddersfield T relegated from Premier League to EFL Championship. Braintree T relegated from National League.
31 EFL Checkatrade Trophy Final: Portsmouth 2 Sunderland 2 *(aet; Portsmouth won 5-4 on penalties)*.

APRIL 2019

2 Fulham relegated from Premier League to EFL Championship.
6 Maidstone U relegated from National League.
13 Ipswich T relegated from EFL Championship to EFL League One. Lincoln C promoted from EFL League Two to EFL League One. Aldershot T and Havant & Waterlooville relegated from National League. Arbroath promoted from Scottish League One to Scottish Championship.
13 The FA County Youth Cup Final: Manchester 3 Norfolk 0. The FAW Trophy Final: Cefn Alb 4 Pontardawe T 0.
19 Bolton W relegated from EFL Championship to EFL League One. Bradford C relegated from EFL League One to EFL League Two.
22 Lincoln C champions of EFL League Two.
25 The FA Youth Cup Final: Manchester C 1 Liverpool 1 *(aet; Liverpool won 5-3 on penalties)*.
26 Ross Co promoted from Scottish Championship to Scottish Premiership.
27 Norwich C promoted from EFL Championship to Premier League. Rotherham U relegated from EFL Championship to EFL League One. Yeovil T relegated from EFL League Two to National League. Leyton Orient champions of National League and promoted to EFL League Two. Berwick Rangers bottom of Scottish League Two and into play-off.
28 Sheffield U promoted from EFL Championship to Premier League. The FA Sunday Cup Final: Aylesbury Flooring 3 Birstall Stamford 1.
30 Luton T and Barnsley promoted from EFL League One to EFL Championship. Bury promoted from EFL League Two to EFL League One.

MAY 2019

2 Premier League International Cup Final: Bayern Munich 2 Dinamo Zagreb 0.
4 Celtic champions of Scottish Premiership. Cardiff C relegated from Premier League to EFL Championship. Luton champions of EFL One. Milton Keynes D promoted from EFL League Two to EFL League One. Walsall relegated from EFL League One to EFL League Two. Plymouth Arg relegated from EFL League One to EFL League Two. Scunthorpe U relegated from EFL League One to EFL League Two. Notts Co relegated from EFL League Two to National League. Dundee relegated from Scottish Premiership to Scottish Championship. Falkirk relegated from Scottish Championship to Scottish League One. Brechin C relegated from Scottish League One to Scottish League Two. Peterhead promoted from Scottish League Two to Scottish League One. The SSE Women's FA Cup Final: Manchester C 3 West Ham U 0. JD Welsh FA Cup Final: The New Saints 3 Connah's Quay Nomads 0. Tennent's Irish FA Cup Final: Crusaders 3 Ballinamallard U 0.
5 Norwich C champions of EFL Championship.
11 Stenhousemuir relegated from Scottish League One to Scottish League Two. Scottish League Two Play-Off Final First Leg: Cove Rangers 4 Berwick Rangers 0.
12 Manchester C champions of Premier League. National League Play-Off Final: Salford C 3 AFC Fylde 0 (*Salford C promoted to EFL League Two*). National League North Play-Off Final: Chorley 1 Spennymoor T 1 (*aet; Chorley won 4-3 on penalties and promoted to National League*). National League South Play-Off Final: Woking 1 Welling U 0 (*Woking promoted to National League*).
14 Scottish League One Play-Off Final First Leg: Annan Ath 1 Clyde 0.
15 Scottish Championship Play-Off Final First Leg: Raith R 1 Queen of the South 3.
18 The Emirates FA Cup Final: Manchester C 6 Watford 0. Scottish Championship Play-Off Final Second Leg: Queen of the South 0 Raith R 0. (*Queen of the South won 3-1 on aggregate and remain in Scottish Championship*). Scottish League One Play-Off Final Second Leg: Clyde 2 Annan Ath 0 (*Clyde won 2-1 on aggregate and promoted to Scottish League One*). Scottish League Two Play-Off Final Second Leg: Berwick Rangers 0 Cove Rangers 3 (*Cove Rangers won 7-0 on aggregate and promoted to Scottish League Two. Berwick Rangers relegated to the Lowland League*). UEFA Women's Champions League Final: Lyon 4 Barcelona 1.
19 The Buildbase FA Trophy Final: AFC Fylde 2 Leyton Orient 0. The Buildbase FA Vase Final: Chertsey T 3 Cray Valley (PM) 1 (*aet*).
23 Scottish Premiership Play-Off Final First Leg: Dundee U 0 St Mirren 0.
25 William Hill Scottish FA Cup Final: Celtic 2 Hearts 1. EFL League Two Play-Off Final: Tranmere R 1 v Newport Co 0 (*aet; Tranmere R promoted to EFL League One*).
26 EFL League One Play-Off Final: Charlton Ath 2 Sunderland 1 (*Charlton Ath promoted to EFL Championship*). Scottish Premiership Play-Off Final Second Leg: St Mirren 1 Dundee U 1 (*aet; St Mirren won 2-0 on penalties and remain in Scottish Premiership*).
27 EFL Championship Play-Off Final: Aston Villa 2 Derby Co 1 (*Aston Villa promoted to Premier League*).
29 UEFA Europa League Final: Chelsea 4 Arsenal 1.

JUNE 2019

1 UEFA Champions League Final: Liverpool 2 Tottenham H 0.
26 UEFA Regions Cup Final: Dolny Slask 3 Bavaria 2.

JULY 2019

7 Women's World Cup Final: USA 2 Netherlands 0.

THE FA COMMUNITY SHIELD WINNERS 1908–2018

CHARITY SHIELD 1908–2001

1908	Manchester U v QPR	1-1
Replay	Manchester U v QPR	4-0
1909	Newcastle U v Northampton T	2-0
1910	Brighton v Aston Villa	1-0
1911	Manchester U v Swindon T	8-4
1912	Blackburn R v QPR	2-1
1913	Professionals v Amateurs	7-2
1920	WBA v Tottenham H	2-0
1921	Tottenham H v Burnley	2-0
1922	Huddersfield T v Liverpool	1-0
1923	Professionals v Amateurs	2-0
1924	Professionals v Amateurs	3-1
1925	Amateurs v Professionals	6-1
1926	Amateurs v Professionals	6-3
1927	Cardiff C v Corinthians	2-1
1928	Everton v Blackburn R	2-1
1929	Professionals v Amateurs	3-0
1930	Arsenal v Sheffield W	2-1
1931	Arsenal v WBA	1-0
1932	Everton v Newcastle U	5-3
1933	Arsenal v Everton	3-0
1934	Arsenal v Manchester C	4-0
1935	Sheffield W v Arsenal	1-0
1936	Sunderland v Arsenal	2-1
1937	Manchester C v Sunderland	2-0
1938	Arsenal v Preston NE	2-1
1948	Arsenal v Manchester U	4-3
1949	Portsmouth v Wolverhampton W	1-1*
1950	English World Cup XI v FA Canadian Touring Team	4-2
1951	Tottenham H v Newcastle U	2-1
1952	Manchester U v Newcastle U	4-2
1953	Arsenal v Blackpool	3-1
1954	Wolverhampton W v WBA	4-4*
1955	Chelsea v Newcastle U	3-0
1956	Manchester U v Manchester C	1-0
1957	Manchester U v Aston Villa	4-0
1958	Bolton W v Wolverhampton W	4-1
1959	Wolverhampton W v Nottingham F	3-1
1960	Burnley v Wolverhampton W	2-2*
1961	Tottenham H v FA XI	3-2
1962	Tottenham H v Ipswich T	5-1
1963	Everton v Manchester U	4-0
1964	Liverpool v West Ham U	2-2*
1965	Manchester U v Liverpool	2-2*
1966	Liverpool v Everton	1-0
1967	Manchester U v Tottenham H	3-3*
1968	Manchester C v WBA	6-1
1969	Leeds U v Manchester C	2-1
1970	Everton v Chelsea	2-1
1971	Leicester C v Liverpool	1-0
1972	Manchester C v Aston Villa	1-0
1973	Burnley v Manchester C	1-0
1974	Liverpool v Leeds U	1-1
	Liverpool won 6-5 on penalties.	
1975	Derby Co v West Ham U	2-0
1976	Liverpool v Southampton	1-0
1977	Liverpool v Manchester U	0-0*
1978	Nottingham F v Ipswich T	5-0
1979	Liverpool v Arsenal	3-1
1980	Liverpool v West Ham U	1-0
1981	Aston Villa v Tottenham H	2-2*
1982	Liverpool v Tottenham H	1-0
1983	Manchester U v Liverpool	2-0
1984	Everton v Liverpool	1-0
1985	Everton v Manchester U	2-0
1986	Everton v Liverpool	1-1*
1987	Everton v Coventry C	1-0
1988	Liverpool v Wimbledon	2-1
1989	Liverpool v Arsenal	1-0
1990	Liverpool v Manchester U	1-1*
1991	Arsenal v Tottenham H	0-0*
1992	Leeds U v Liverpool	4-3
1993	Manchester U v Arsenal	1-1
	Manchester U won 5-4 on penalties.	
1994	Manchester U v Blackburn R	2-0
1995	Everton v Blackburn R	1-0
1996	Manchester U v Newcastle U	4-0
1997	Manchester U v Chelsea	1-1
	Manchester U won 4-2 on penalties.	
1998	Arsenal v Manchester U	3-0
1999	Arsenal v Manchester U	2-1
2000	Chelsea v Manchester U	2-0
2001	Liverpool v Manchester U	2-1

COMMUNITY SHIELD 2002–18

2002	Arsenal v Liverpool	1-0
2003	Manchester U v Arsenal	1-1
	Manchester U won 4-3 on penalties.	
2004	Arsenal v Manchester U	3-1
2005	Chelsea v Arsenal	2-1
2006	Liverpool v Chelsea	2-1
2007	Manchester U v Chelsea	1-1
	Manchester U won 3-0 on penalties.	
2008	Manchester U v Portsmouth	0-0
	Manchester U won 3-1 on penalties.	
2009	Chelsea v Manchester U	2-2
	Chelsea won 4-1 on penalties.	
2010	Manchester U v Chelsea	3-1
2011	Manchester U v Manchester C	3-2
2012	Manchester C v Chelsea	3-2
2013	Manchester U v Wigan Ath	2-0
2014	Arsenal v Manchester C	3-0
2015	Arsenal v Chelsea	1-0
2016	Manchester U v Leicester C	2-1
2017	Arsenal v Chelsea	1-1
	Arsenal won 4-1 on penalties.	
2018	Manchester C v Chelsea	2-0

** Each club retained shield for six months.* ▪ *Denotes player sent off.*

THE FA COMMUNITY SHIELD 2018

Manchester C (1) 2, Chelsea (0) 0

at Wembley, Sunday 5 August 2018, attendance 72,724

Manchester C: Bravo; Walker, Stones (Gomez 90), Laporte (Otamendi 87), Mendy, Foden (Diaz 76), Fernandinho, Bernardo Silva, Sane (Gundogan 46), Aguero (Kompany 80), Mahrez (Jesus 68).
Scorers: Aguero 13, 58.

Chelsea: Caballero; Azpilicueta, Luiz, Rudiger, Alonso, Jorginho, Barkley, Fabregas (Drinkwater 59), Hudson-Odoi (Willian 59), Pedro, Morata (Abraham 69).

Referee: Jonathan Moss.

ACCRINGTON STANLEY

FOUNDATION

Accrington Football Club, founder members of the Football League in 1888, were not connected with Accrington Stanley. In fact both clubs ran concurrently between 1891 when Stanley were formed and 1895 when Accrington FC folded. Actually Stanley Villa was the original name, those responsible for forming the club living in Stanley Street and using the Stanley Arms as their meeting place. They became Accrington Stanley in 1893. In 1894–95 they joined the Accrington & District League, playing at Moorhead Park. Subsequently they played in the North-East Lancashire Combination and the Lancashire Combination before becoming founder members of the Third Division (North) in 1921, two years after moving to Peel Park. In 1962 they resigned from the Football League, were wound up, re-formed in 1963, disbanded in 1966 only to restart as Accrington Stanley (1968), returning to the Lancashire Combination in 1970.

Wham Stadium, Livingstone Road, Accrington, Lancashire BB5 5BX.

Telephone: (01254) 356 950. ***Fax:*** (01254) 356 951.

Website: www.accringtonstanley.co.uk

Email: info@accringtonstanley.co.uk

Ground Capacity: 5,450.

Record Attendance: 13,181 v Hull C, Division 3 (N), 28 September 1948 (at Peel Park); 5,397 v Derby Co, FA Cup 4th rd, 26 January 2019.

Pitch Measurements: 102m × 66m (111.5yd × 72yd).

Chairman: Andy Holt.

Managing Director: David Burgess.

Manager: John Coleman.

Assistant Manager: Jimmy Bell.

Colours: Red shirts with white trim, white shorts with red trim, red socks with white trim.

Year Formed: 1891, reformed 1968.

Turned Professional: 1919.

Club Nickname: 'The Reds', 'Stanley'.

Previous Names: 1891, Stanley Villa; 1893, Accrington Stanley.

Grounds: 1891, Moorhead Park; 1897, Bell's Ground; 1919, Peel Park; 1970, Crown Ground (renamed Interlink Express Stadium, Fraser Eagle Stadium, Store First Stadium 2013, Wham Stadium 2015).

First Football League Game: 27 August 1921, Division 3 (N), v Rochdale (a) L 3-6 – Tattersall; Newton, Baines, Crawshaw, Popplewell, Burkinshaw, Oxley, Makin, Green (1), Hosker (2), Hartles.

Record League Victory: 8–0 v New Brighton, Division 3 (N), 17 March 1934 – Maidment; Armstrong (pen), Price, Dodds, Crawshaw, McCulloch, Wyper, Lennox (2), Cheetham (4), Leedham (1), Watson.

Record Cup Victory: 7–0 v Spennymoor U, FA Cup 2nd rd, 8 December 1938 – Tootill; Armstrong, Whittaker, Latham, Curran, Lee, Parry (2), Chadwick, Jepson (3), McLoughlin (2), Barclay.

Record Defeat: 1–9 v Lincoln C, Division 3 (N), 3 March 1951.

HONOURS

League Champions: FL 2 – 2017–18; Conference – 2005–06.
Runners-up: Division 3N – 1954–55, 1957–58.

FA Cup: 4th rd – 1927, 1937, 1959, 2010, 2017, 2019.

League Cup: 3rd rd – 2016–17.

THE Sun FACT FILE

The current Accrington Stanley club reached the first round proper of the FA Cup for the first time in the 1992–93 season, eliminating former Football League clubs Bradford Park Avenue and Stalybridge Celtic in the qualifying rounds. In Round One they defeated another former Football League club, Gateshead, before going down 6-1 at home to Crewe Alexandra in a match played at Ewood Park.

Most League Points (2 for a win): 61, Division 3 (N), 1954–55.

Most League Points (3 for a win): 93, FL 2, 2017–18.

Most League Goals: 96, Division 3 (N), 1954–55.

Highest League Scorer in Season: George Stewart, 35, Division 3 (N), 1955–56; George Hudson, 35, Division 4, 1960–61.

Most League Goals in Total Aggregate: George Stewart, 136, 1954–58.

Most League Goals in One Match: 5, Billy Harker v Gateshead, Division 3 (N), 16 November 1935; George Stewart v Gateshead, Division 3 (N), 27 November 1954.

Most Capped Player: Romuald Boco, 19 (48), Benin.

Most League Appearances: Andy Procter, 275, 2006–12, 2014–16.

Youngest League Player: Ian Gibson, 15 years 358 days, v Norwich C, 23 March 1959.

Record Transfer Fee Received: £1,000,000 from Ipswich T for Kayden Jackson, August 2018.

Record Transfer Fee Paid: £85,000 (rising to £150,000) to Swansea C for Ian Craney, January 2008.

Football League Record: 1921 Original Member of Division 3 (N); 1958–60 Division 3; 1960–62 Division 4; 2006–18 FL 2; 2018– FL 1.

LATEST SEQUENCES

Longest Sequence of League Wins: 7, 24.2.2018 – 7.4.2018.

Longest Sequence of League Defeats: 9, 8.3.1930 – 21.4.1930.

Longest Sequence of League Draws: 4, 25.8.2018 – 15.9.2018.

Longest Sequence of Unbeaten League Matches: 15, 3.2.2018 – 21.4.2018.

Longest Sequence Without a League Win: 18, 17.9.1938 – 31.12.1938.

Successive Scoring Runs: 24 from 23.12.2017.

Successive Non-scoring Runs: 6 from 29.12.2018.

MANAGERS

William Cronshaw *c.*1894
John Haworth 1897–1910
Johnson Haworth *c.*1916
Sam Pilkingson 1919–24
(*Tommy Booth p-m 1923–24*)
Ernie Blackburn 1924–32
Amos Wade 1932–35
John Hacking 1935–49
Jimmy Porter 1949–51
Walter Crook 1951–53
Walter Galbraith 1953–58
George Eastham Snr 1958–59
Harold Bodle 1959–60
James Harrower 1960–61
Harold Mather 1962–63
Jimmy Hinksman 1963–64
Terry Neville 1964–65
Ian Bryson 1965
Danny Parker 1965–66
Gerry Keenan
Gary Pierce
Dave Thornley
Phil Staley
Eric Whalley
Stan Allen 1995–96
Tony Greenwood 1996–98
Billy Rodaway 1998
Wayne Harrison 1998–99
John Coleman 1999–2012
Paul Cook 2012
Leam Richardson 2012–13
James Beattie 2013–14
John Coleman September 2014–

TEN YEAR LEAGUE RECORD

		P	W	D	L	F	A	Pts	Pos
2009-10	FL 2	46	18	7	21	62	74	61	15
2010-11	FL 2	46	18	19	9	73	55	73	5
2011-12	FL 2	46	14	15	17	54	66	57	14
2012-13	FL 2	46	14	12	20	51	68	54	18
2013-14	FL 2	46	14	15	17	54	56	57	15
2014-15	FL 2	46	15	11	20	58	77	56	17
2015-16	FL 2	46	24	13	9	74	48	85	4
2016-17	FL 2	46	17	14	15	59	56	65	13
2017-18	FL 2	46	29	6	11	76	46	93	1
2018-19	FL 1	46	14	13	19	51	67	55	14

DID YOU KNOW ?

Winger Mike Ferguson, who appeared in the original Accrington Stanley's final game against Crewe Alexandra in March 1962, continued playing at senior level until the 1976–77 season. He was the last of the Accrington players from that season to retire from playing.

ACCRINGTON STANLEY – SKY BET LEAGUE ONE 2018–19 LEAGUE RECORD

Match No.	*Date*	*Venue*	*Opponents*	*Result*		*H/T Score*	*Lg Pos.*	*Goalscorers*	*Atten-dance*
1	Aug 4	H	Gillingham	L	0-2	0-2	23		2201
2	11	A	Bristol R	W	2-1	1-0	12	McConville 2 [6, 89]	8683
3	18	H	Charlton Ath	D	1-1	0-1	14	Clark [78]	2265
4	21	A	Oxford U	W	3-2	1-1	7	Sykes [43], Kee 2 (1 pen) [62, 79 (p)]	5748
5	25	A	Blackpool	D	1-1	0-0	8	Hughes [90]	3354
6	Sept 1	H	Scunthorpe U	D	1-1	0-0	8	Conneely [82]	2059
7	8	H	Burton Alb	D	1-1	0-1	10	Kee (pen) [84]	1943
8	15	A	Fleetwood T	D	1-1	0-1	11	McConville [69]	3355
9	22	H	AFC Wimbledon	W	2-1	1-0	9	Kee [6], McConville [60]	1732
10	29	A	Walsall	W	1-0	1-0	8	Kee (pen) [7]	4257
11	Oct 2	H	Doncaster R	W	1-0	0-0	5	Zanzala [87]	2327
12	6	A	Shrewsbury T	L	0-1	0-0	7		4353
13	13	H	Bradford C	W	3-1	1-0	6	Kee (pen) [39], Zanzala [54], McConville [66]	3346
14	20	A	Peterborough U	W	1-0	1-0	4	McConville [11]	6141
15	23	A	Luton T	L	1-4	1-1	4	Zanzala [27]	8454
16	27	H	Portsmouth	D	1-1	0-0	6	Ihiekwe [64]	3558
17	Nov 3	A	Coventry C	D	1-1	0-0	6	Zanzala [58]	10,653
18	17	H	Barnsley	L	0-2	0-1	10		4801
19	24	A	Rochdale	L	0-1	0-0	10		3497
20	27	H	Wycombe W	L	1-2	1-0	11	McConville [15]	1740
21	Dec 15	A	Southend U	L	0-3	0-2	14		6286
22	22	A	Plymouth Arg	W	3-0	0-0	10	Finley [61], McConville [65], Clark [77]	10,193
23	26	H	Shrewsbury T	W	2-1	2-0	9	Clark [1], Kee [21]	3061
24	29	H	Peterborough U	L	0-4	0-2	10		2672
25	Jan 1	A	Bradford C	L	0-3	0-2	12		16,318
26	12	H	Bristol R	D	0-0	0-0	14		2246
27	19	A	Charlton Ath	L	0-1	0-0	14		11,877
28	29	A	Gillingham	D	0-0	0-0	15		3423
29	Feb 9	A	Scunthorpe U	L	0-2	0-2	16		4824
30	15	A	Sunderland	D	2-2	1-0	15	Kee (pen) [30], Smyth [52]	28,937
31	19	H	Oxford U	W	4-2	1-0	14	Kee [36], McConville [57], Clark [73], Armstrong [90]	2095
32	23	H	Southend U	D	1-1	0-1	15	Barlaser [60]	2472
33	Mar 2	H	Coventry C	L	0-1	0-0	14		3083
34	5	H	Blackpool	L	1-2	1-1	15	Armstrong [23]	3792
35	9	A	Barnsley	L	0-2	0-2	17		11,533
36	12	A	Wycombe W	W	3-1	1-1	14	Kee 2 (2 pens) [45, 66], Smyth [71]	3819
37	23	A	Burton Alb	L	2-5	2-1	17	McConville [37], Kee (pen) [40]	2916
38	30	H	Fleetwood T	L	0-1	0-0	18		2485
39	Apr 3	H	Sunderland	L	0-3	0-2	18		3802
40	6	A	AFC Wimbledon	D	1-1	1-1	17	Clark [34]	4565
41	9	H	Rochdale	L	0-1	0-0	17		2824
42	13	H	Walsall	W	2-1	1-1	16	Sykes 2 [11, 69]	2662
43	20	H	Luton T	L	0-3	0-1	16		3271
44	23	A	Doncaster R	W	2-1	2-0	14	McConville [17], Smyth [44]	7222
45	27	H	Plymouth Arg	W	5-1	3-0	13	Kee (pen) [20], McConville 3 [36, 43, 51], Armstrong [66]	3134
46	May 4	A	Portsmouth	D	1-1	0-0	14	McConville [46]	18,439

Final League Position: 14

GOALSCORERS

League (51): McConville 15, Kee 13 (9 pens), Clark 5, Zanzala 4, Armstrong 3, Smyth 3, Sykes 3, Barlaser 1, Conneely 1, Finley 1, Hughes 1, Ihiekwe 1.
FA Cup (5): Kee 2 (1 pen), Barlaser 1, Clark 1, Zanzala 1.
Carabao Cup (1): Finley 1.
Checkatrade Trophy (12): Clark 3, Hall 2 (1 pen), Barlaser 1, Brown 1, Finley 1, Kee 1, Sykes 1, Zanzala 1, own goal 1.

Maxted J 16 + 3	Johnson C 40 + 1	Richards-Everton B 13 + 4	Hughes M 46	Sykes R 19 + 1	Clark J 43	Conneely S 25 + 2	Brown S 18 + 11	McConville S 45	Jackson K 1	Kee B 42 + 2	Finley S 32 + 5	Zanzala O 12 + 15	Ripley C 21	Anderton N 20 + 2	Ihiekwe M 20	Nolan L — + 2	Mangan A — + 3	Mingoia P 2 + 2	Barlaser D 33 + 6	Hall C 1 + 12	Sousa E — + 4	Gibson L 4 + 1	Armstrong L 8 + 8	Wood W 1 + 3	Evtimov D 9 + 2	Donacien J 19	Smyth P 11 + 4	Rodgers H 5 + 1	Williams D — + 1	Match No.
1	2^{2}	3	4	5	6	7	8	9	10^{1}	11	12	13																		1
	2	5	3	4	6	8	7	9		11	12	10^{1}	1																	2
	2	5^{1}	3	4	6	7	8	9		11^{2}	10	12	1	13																3
	2	5^{1}	3	4	6	7	8^{2}	9		11	10	12	1	13																4
	2^{1}		4	3	9	8^{2}	7^{3}	6		11	10	12	1		5	13	14													5
	2^{3}	14	3^{1}		9	8	7	6			10^{2}	11	1	5	4		13	12												6
	2^{3}		3	4	6	7^{2}	8^{1}	9		11	10	13	1	5					12	14										7
	2		4		6	7^{2}	8^{1}	9		11	10	13	1	5	3				12											8
	2		4		6	13	14	9		11	7^{2}	10^{1}	1	5	3				8^{3}	12										9
	7		3		6	2^{1}	10	9		11	8^{2}	13	1	5	4				12											10
	2		3		6		8^{1}	9		11	10	12	1	5	4				7											11
12	2^{2}		3		6		7	9		11	10^{1}	13	1■	5	4				8											12
1	2		4		6		13	9		11	7	10^{1}		5	3				8^{2}	12										13
1	2		3		6		12	9		10	8	11^{4}		5	4				7^{1}	13										14
1	2^{1}		3		6		12	9		10	8^{3}	11^{2}		5	4		14		7	13										15
	2		3					9		10	8	11^{1}	1	5	4			6	7	12										16
	2		3		9	13				11^{1}	8	10^{2}	1	5	4			6	7	12										17
	2^{2}		4		6		13	7		11	9	10	1	5	3				8^{1}	12										18
	2^{2}		4		6	8^{3}		9		11	12	10^{1}	1	5	3			13	7	14										19
	2		4		6	8^{1}		9		11	10	12	1	5	3				7											20
	2		3^{1}	13	6		14	9		10	8^{2}	11^{3}	1	5	4				7	12										21
	2		3		6	8	12	10		11	9		1	5	4				7^{1}											22
	2		4		6			9		11	7	12	1	5	3				8	10^{1}										23
	2		4		6	7^{3}		10^{2}		11^{1}	8	12	1	5	3				9	13	14									24
	2^{1}	12	4		6			9		11	7	10■	1	5^{2}	3				8	13										25
1	2		3	4	6			9		10	7								8			5^{1}	11	12						26
1■	2		3	4	6			9		10	7								8			5^{1}	11^{2}	13	12					27
1	2	5	3	4^{1}	7	9	8	10		11																6	12			28
1	2^{1}	4	3		6	8^{2}	12	9		11		14							7				13			5	10^{3}			29
1	2	14	3	4^{3}	6	8^{2}	12	9		10									7				13			5	11^{1}			30
1	2	4	3		6		7	9^{2}		11									8			12	13			5	10^{1}			31
1^{1}	2	4	3		6		7	9		11									8				13		12	5	10^{2}			32
	2		3		6		13	9		10	7^{3}	14							8			5^{1}	12		1	4	11^{2}			33
13	2		3		6^{3}			10		14	8								7			9^{2}	11	12	1■	4		5^{1}		34
1	2		3		6^{3}			10		13	8	14							9				11^{1}	7^{2}		4	12	5		35
1	2		3		9			6		11	7								8							4	10	5		36
1	2^{1}		4		9		10	6		11	7								8				12			5		3		37
	14		3	4		8^{2}		9		11	7								13		12		6^{3}		1	5	10	2^{1}		38
	7	3^{1}	2	4		8^{2}	14	9		10	6^{3}								13		12				1	5	11			39
		3	2	4	5	8	6^{2}	9		10	12								13						1	7	11^{1}			40
			4	2	5	8	6^{2}	9		11^{1}	13								10				3		1	7	12			41
	2	12	4	3	6	8		9		11	10								7						1	5^{1}				42
12	2		4	3	6	8	7^{3}	10		11^{2}						14			9^{1}				13		1■	5				43
1		2	4	3	6	8		9		10									7				12			5	11^{1}			44
1		2	4	3^{1}	6	8		9		10^{3}									7				11			5^{2}	13	12	14	45
		2	4	3	6^{1}	8		9											7		12		11		1	5	10			46

FA Cup

First Round	Colchester U	(h)	1-0
Second Round	Cheltenham T	(h)	3-1
Third Round	Ipswich T	(h)	1-0
Fourth Round	Derby Co	(h)	0-1

Carabao Cup

First Round	Mansfield T	(a)	1-6

Checkatrade Trophy

Group C (N)	Macclesfield T	(h)	4-1
Group C (N)	WBA U21	(h)	2-1
Group C (N)	Blackpool	(a)	2-3
Second Round (N)	Lincoln C	(h)	2-2
(Accrington S won 4-2 on penalties)			
Third Round	Bury	(h)	2-4

AFC WIMBLEDON

FOUNDATION

While the history of AFC Wimbledon is straightforward since it was a new club formed in 2002, there were in effect two clubs operating for two years with Wimbledon connections. The other club was MK Dons, of course. In August 2001, the Football League had rejected the existing Wimbledon's application to move to Milton Keynes. In May 2002, they rejected local sites and were given permission to move by an independent commission set up by the Football League. AFC Wimbledon was founded in the summer of 2002 and held its first trials on Wimbledon Common. In subsequent years, there was considerable debate over the rightful home of the trophies obtained by the former Wimbledon football club. In October 2006, an agreement was reached between Milton Keynes Dons FC, its Supporters Association, the Wimbledon Independent Supporters Association and the Football Supporters Federation to transfer such trophies and honours to the London Borough of Merton.

The Cherry Red Records Stadium, Kingsmeadow, Jack Goodchild Way, 422a Kingston Road, Kingston-upon-Thames, Surrey KT1 3PB.

Telephone: (0208) 547 3528.

Fax: (0808) 2800 816.

Website: www.afcwimbledon.co.uk

Email: info@afcwimbledon.co.uk

Ground Capacity: 4,850.

Record Attendance: 4,870 v Accrington S, FL 2 Play-Offs, 14 May 2016.

Pitch Measurements: 104m × 66m (114yd × 72yd).

President: Dickie Guy.

Chief Executive: Joe Palmer.

Manager: Wally Downes.

Assistant Manager: Glyn Hodges.

First-Team Coach: Vaughan Ryan.

Club Nickname: 'The Dons'.

Colours: Blue shirts with yellow trim, blue shorts with yellow trim, blue socks with yellow trim.

Year Formed: 2002.

Turned Professional: 2002.

HONOURS

League: *Runners-up:* FL 2 – (7th) 2015–16 *(promoted via play-offs)*; Conference – (2nd) 2010–11 *(promoted via play-offs)*.

FA Cup: 5th rd – 2019.

League Cup: never past 1st rd.

THE SUN FACT FILE

AFC Wimbledon are probably unique in English football in that their story has been presented at the 2005 Edinburgh Festival. The play, titled *A Fan's Club*, tells the tale of how the club was born.

Grounds: 2002, Kingsmeadow (renamed The Cherry Red Records Stadium).

First Football League Game: 6 August 2011, FL 2 v Bristol R (h) L 2–3 – Brown; Hatton, Gwillim (Bush), Porter (Minshull), Stuart (1), Johnson B, Moore L, Wellard, Jolley (Ademeno (1)), Midson, Yussuff.

Record League Victory: 5–1 v Bury, FL 2, 19 November 2016 – Shea; Fuller, Robertson, Robinson (Taylor), Owens, Francomb (2 (1 pen)), Reeves, Parrett, Whelpdale (1), Elliott (1) (Nightingale), Poleon (1), (Barrett).

MANAGERS

Terry Eames 2002–04
Nicky English *(Caretaker)* 2004
Dave Anderson 2004–07
Terry Brown 2007–12
Neal Ardley 2012–18
Wally Downes December 2018–

Record Cup Victory: 5–0 v Bury, FA Cup 1st rd replay, 5 November 2016 – Shea; Fuller (Owens), Robertson, Robinson (1), Francomb. Parrett (1), Reeves, Bulman (Beere), Whelpdale, Barcham (Poleon (2)), Taylor (1).

Record Defeat: 2–6 v Burton Alb, FL 2, 25 August 2012.

Most League Points (3 for a win): 75, FL 2, 2015–16.

Most League Goals: 64, FL 2, 2015–16.

Highest League Scorer in Season: Lyle Taylor, 20, 2015–16.

Most League Goals in Total Aggregate: Kevin Cooper, 107, 2002–04.

Most League Goals in One Match: 3, Lyle Taylor v Rotherham U, FL 1, 17 October 2017; 3, Joe Pigott v Rochdale, FL 1, 19 February 2019.

Most Capped Player: Shane Smeltz, 5 (58), New Zealand.

Most League Appearances: Barry Fuller, 205, 2013–18.

Youngest League Player: Ben Harrison, 17 years 195 days v Accrington S, 13 September 2014.

Record Transfer Fee Received: £150,000 from Bradford C for Jake Reeves, July 2017.

Record Transfer Fee Paid: £25,000 (in excess of) to Stevenage for Byron Harrison, January 2012.

Football League Record: 2011 Promoted from Conference Premier; 2011–16 FL 2; 2016– FL 1.

LATEST SEQUENCES

Longest Sequence of League Wins: 5, 2.4.2016 – 23.4.2016.

Longest Sequence of League Defeats: 8, 2.10.2018 – 17.11.2018.

Longest Sequence of League Draws: 4, 6.4.2019 – 23.4.2019.

Longest Sequence of Unbeaten League Matches: 10, 7.4.2018 – 18.8.2018.

Longest Sequence Without a League Win: 12, 15.10.2011 – 2.1.2012.

Successive Scoring Runs: 10 from 28.12.2016.

Successive Non-scoring Runs: 6 from 1.4.2017.

TEN YEAR LEAGUE RECORD

		P	W	D	L	F	A	Pts	Pos
2009-10	Conf P	44	18	10	16	61	47	64	8
2010-11	Conf P	46	27	9	10	83	47	90	2
2011-12	FL 2	46	15	9	22	62	78	54	16
2012-13	FL 2	46	14	11	21	54	76	53	20
2013-14	FL 2	46	14	14	18	49	57	53*	20
2014-15	FL 2	46	14	16	16	54	60	58	15
2015-16	FL 2	46	21	12	13	64	50	75	7
2016-17	FL 1	46	13	18	15	52	55	57	15
2017-18	FL 1	46	13	14	19	47	58	53	18
2018-19	FL 1	46	13	11	22	42	63	50	20

** 3 pts deducted.*

DID YOU KNOW ?

AFC Wimbledon's home fixture with Plymouth Argyle on Boxing Day 2018 was the club's 400th competitive game as a Football League club. Of these, 129 were won and 107 drawn with 164 defeats.

AFC WIMBLEDON – SKY BET LEAGUE ONE 2018–19 LEAGUE RECORD

Match No.	Date	Venue	Opponents	Result		H/T Score	Lg Pos.	Goalscorers	Attendance
1	Aug 4	A	Fleetwood T	W	1-0	0-0	9	Pigott [60]	3236
2	11	H	Coventry C	D	0-0	0-0	9		4768
3	18	A	Barnsley	D	0-0	0-0	7		11,607
4	21	H	Walsall	L	1-3	0-1	11	Appiah [87]	3887
5	25	H	Sunderland	L	1-2	1-0	15	Pigott [9]	4848
6	Sept 1	A	Burton Alb	L	0-3	0-1	20		2814
7	8	A	Gillingham	W	1-0	0-0	12	Pigott [53]	5246
8	15	H	Scunthorpe U	L	2-3	0-2	16	Trotter [49], Appiah [55]	3885
9	22	A	Accrington S	L	1-2	0-1	19	Wagstaff [64]	1732
10	29	H	Oxford U	W	2-1	2-1	16	Wagstaff [20], Pigott [32]	4068
11	Oct 2	H	Bradford C	L	0-1	0-1	17		3630
12	6	A	Plymouth Arg	L	0-1	0-0	20		8542
13	13	H	Portsmouth	L	1-2	0-2	20	Hanson [63]	4569
14	20	A	Blackpool	L	0-2	0-1	21		3246
15	23	A	Bristol R	L	0-2	0-1	22		7184
16	27	H	Luton T	L	0-2	0-0	23		4202
17	Nov 3	H	Shrewsbury T	L	1-2	1-0	23	Hanson [35]	4066
18	17	A	Doncaster R	L	1-2	1-1	23	Pinnock [26]	7843
19	24	H	Southend U	W	2-1	1-1	23	Oshilaja [45], Pinnock [70]	4195
20	27	A	Peterborough U	L	0-1	0-0	23		5064
21	Dec 8	H	Rochdale	D	1-1	0-1	23	Barcham [70]	3988
22	15	A	Charlton Ath	L	0-2	0-0	24		10,691
23	22	A	Wycombe W	W	2-1	1-0	24	Appiah [29], Jervis [90]	5814
24	26	H	Plymouth Arg	W	2-1	1-1	22	Wordsworth [32], Pinnock [75]	4434
25	29	H	Blackpool	D	0-0	0-0	23		4416
26	Jan 1	A	Portsmouth	L	1-2	0-1	24	Appiah [75]	18,732
27	12	A	Coventry C	D	1-1	1-0	24	Jervis [2]	10,420
28	19	H	Barnsley	L	1-4	1-1	24	Pigott [36]	4795
29	22	H	Fleetwood T	L	0-3	0-2	24		3499
30	Feb 2	A	Sunderland	L	0-1	0-0	24		30,424
31	9	H	Burton Alb	L	0-2	0-1	24		4003
32	12	A	Walsall	W	1-0	0-0	24	Seddon [48]	3287
33	19	A	Rochdale	W	4-3	1-2	24	Pigott 3 (1 pen) [36, 46, 90 (p)], Wordsworth [76]	2410
34	23	H	Charlton Ath	L	1-2	1-0	24	Folivi [24]	4532
35	Mar 2	A	Shrewsbury T	D	0-0	0-0	24		6166
36	9	H	Doncaster R	W	2-0	0-0	24	Seddon [67], McLoughlin [90]	4203
37	12	H	Peterborough U	W	1-0	0-0	24	Pigott (pen) [87]	3737
38	16	A	Southend U	W	1-0	0-0	22	Pigott [67]	7570
39	23	H	Gillingham	L	2-4	1-2	23	Folivi [22], Hanson [90]	4847
40	30	A	Scunthorpe U	W	2-1	2-0	22	Hanson 2 [23, 29]	3955
41	Apr 6	H	Accrington S	D	1-1	1-1	21	Pigott [21]	4565
42	13	A	Oxford U	D	0-0	0-0	21		7678
43	19	H	Bristol R	D	1-1	1-0	21	Pigott [22]	4850
44	23	A	Luton T	D	2-2	1-2	21	Pigott [28], Seddon [90]	10,070
45	27	H	Wycombe W	W	2-1	1-0	19	Pigott 2 [38, 53]	4850
46	May 4	A	Bradford C	D	0-0	0-0	20		17,817

Final League Position: 20

GOALSCORERS

League (42): Pigott 15 (2 pens), Hanson 5, Appiah 4, Pinnock 3, Seddon 3, Folivi 2, Jervis 2, Wagstaff 2, Wordsworth 2, Barcham 1, McLoughlin 1, Oshilaja 1, Trotter 1.
FA Cup (11): Appiah 2, Wagstaff 2, Barcham 1, Hartigan 1, Pigott 1, Pinnock 1, Purrington 1, Sibbick 1, Wordsworth 1.
Carabao Cup (3): Pigott 2, own goal 1.
Checkatrade Trophy (7): Wordsworth 2, Appiah 1, Egan 1, Garratt 1, Hartigan 1, Soares 1.

King T 12	Watson T 22 + 2	Oshilaja A 25	Nightingale W 37 + 2	Purrington B 26	Pinnock M 19 + 15	Soares T 19 + 4	Trotter L 17 + 2	Barcham A 21 + 6	Pigott J 31 + 9	Appiah K 18 + 8	Hanson J 18 + 11	Wagstaff S 28 + 7	Garrett T 1 + 5	Wordsworth A 29 + 8	Sibbick T 18 + 5	McDonald R 22 + 1	Hartigan A 27 + 4	Jervis J 12 + 11	McDonnell J 14	Thomas T 20 + 3	Burey T — + 3	Kalambayi P 17	Egan A — + 1	Ramsdale A 20	Seddon S 18	Connolly D 2 + 10	Wood T — + 1	Folivi M B + 2	McLoughlin S 5 + 5	*Match No.*
1	2	3	4	5	6^3	7	8	9^2	10	11^1	12	13	14																	1
1	2	3	4	5	6^1	7^3	8	9	11^2	10	12	13		14																2
1	2^2	3	4	5		7	8	9	12	10^1	11	6			13															3
1			3	5	6		7	9	11^2	10^3	12	14		8^1	2	4	13													4
1		4	3	5	6^1		8	9^2	11		10	12	13	7	2															5
1	2^3	3	4	5	14		7	9	11	10^2	13	6^1		8				12												6
1	2	3		5	14	8^2	7	9	11	12	10^1	6^3		13		4														7
1	2^3	4		5	12	8	7	9^2	11	10		6^1			14	3		13												8
	2	4		5	6^2	7	8	9^1	11		10	12				3		13	1											9
	2^3	3	14	5		8	7	10^2	9^1	12		6		13		4		11	1											10
	2^2	3		5	9^1	8	7^3	13	11	12		6		14		4		10	1											11
	2^1	3		5		8	7	9^2	11	12		6		13		4		10	1											12
	2^1	3	13	5		8	7	9^2	11^3	10	14					4	12	6	1											13
		3^1	2	5^3	12	8	14		13	11^2	10	9				4	7	6	1											14
		2	3	5^2	13	7			12	11	10	6				4	8	9^1	1											15
		2	3	5^2	12	9	7		13	10^1	11	6				4	8		1											16
		4		5	9	8			11	13	10^2	6			2		7^1	12	1	3										17
		2	3	5	9^2	7	8	12	13	11^3		10		6^1		4		14	1											18
		2	3	5	9^2	7	8	14	12	11^1		10		6^3		4	13		1											19
		2	3	5	9	8	7^3	10^1	11	14				6^2		4	12	13	1											20
	2		3	5	9	8^2		13			10	6		12		4	7	11^1	1											21
	2		3	5	10■	8		11^1			14	9^2		6			7^3	12	1	4	13									22
1	2		3	5		13		9^3		10	11^1	6^2	14	7			8	12		4										23
1	2		3	5	12			9^3		10	11^1		14	7			8	6^2		4	13									24
1	2^2		3	5	6	13		9		10				8	14		7^1	11^3		4	12									25
1	2		6	5^3	7			10^2		11			13	9			8^1	14		4		3	12							26
	2	3	6		7		12	10	13				5^2	9			8	11^1				4		1						27
	2	4	3		6			9^1	10^2					13				11		5		7		1	8	12				28
	2	5	6		9			10^2	11^3					13			7	8^1		4		3		1		12	14			29
	2^2	4	6		10^1				14	11		9		7	13			12		3				1	5	8^3				30
	2	3	6		7				12	11^3		9		8^1	14					4^2				1	5	10		13		31
		2	3		12				11^7					8	5^1	4	7			13				1	9			10	6	32
			3		14				10			12		8^3	5	4	7	13		2				1	9			11^2	6^1	33
			3					14	10		13	6		8^1	5		7^2			2		4		1	9			11^3	12	34
			3		13				11		12	6^1		8	5		7			4		2		1	9			10^2		35
			3					12	10^2		14	6^1		8	5^3		7			4		2		1	9			11	13	36
			3						10		13	6^3		8	5		7^2			4		2		1	9	12		11^1	14	37
	12		2^1		14				11^2			6		8	5		7			3		4		1	9	13		10^3		38
									10		13	6^3		8	5	3	7^2			4		2		1	9	14		11^1	12	39
			4		14				10^1	12	11^3	13		9	2	5	8					3		1	6				7^2	40
			3						11^1	13	10	6		8	5	4	7			14		2^3		1	9^2	12				41
			3		14				10^1		11	7^3		9	2		8^2			5		4		1	6	13			12	42
			3			14			11^3		10	6^1		8	5	4	7^2					2		1	9	13		12		43
			3		14				11		10	6^2		8	5	4^3	7^1			12		2		1	9	13				44
	12		3			14			11^2		10			8	5		7^1			4		2^3		1	9	13			6	45
			3		12				10^2		11			8	5	13	7			4		2		1	9				6^1	46

FA Cup

First Round	Haringey Boro	(a)	1-0
Second Round	FC Halifax T	(a)	3-1
Third Round	Fleetwood T	(a)	3-2
Fourth Round	West Ham U	(h)	4-2
Fifth Round	Millwall	(h)	0-1

Carabao Cup

First Round	Portsmouth	(a)	2-1
Second Round	West Ham U	(h)	1-3

Checkatrade Trophy

Group G (S)	Charlton Ath	(a)	2-2
(AFC Wimbledon won 4-2 on penalties)			
Group G (S)	Swansea C U21	(h)	0-1
Group G (S)	Stevenage	(h)	4-0
Second Round (S)	Chelsea U21	(a)	1-2

ARSENAL

FOUNDATION

Formed by workers at the Royal Arsenal, Woolwich in 1886, they began as Dial Square (name of one of the workshops), and included two former Nottingham Forest players, Fred Beardsley and Morris Bates. Beardsley wrote to his old club seeking help and they provided the new club with a full set of red jerseys and a ball. The club became known as the 'Woolwich Reds' although their official title soon after formation was Woolwich Arsenal.

Emirates Stadium, Highbury House, 75 Drayton Park, Islington, London N5 1BU.

Telephone: (020) 7619 5003.

Fax: (020) 7704 4001.

Ticket Office: (020) 7619 5000.

Website: www.arsenal.com

Email: info@arsenal.co.uk

Ground Capacity: 60,260.

Record Attendance: 73,295 v Sunderland, Div 1, 9 March 1935 (at Highbury); 73,707 v RC Lens, UEFA Champions League, 25 November 1998 (at Wembley); 60,162 v Manchester U, Premier League, 3 November 2007 (at Emirates).

Pitch Measurements: 105m × 68m (115yd × 74.5yd).

Chairman: Sir John 'Chips' Keswick.

Head Coach: Unai Emery.

Assistant Head Coach: Juan Carlos Carcedo.

Colours: Red shirts with white sleeves, white shorts with red trim, white socks with red trim.

Year Formed: 1886.

Turned Professional: 1891.

Previous Names: 1886, Dial Square; 1886, Royal Arsenal; 1891, Woolwich Arsenal; 1914, Arsenal.

Club Nickname: 'The Gunners'.

Grounds: 1886, Plumstead Common; 1887, Sportsman Ground; 1888, Manor Ground; 1890, Invicta Ground; 1893, Manor Ground; 1913, Highbury; 2006, Emirates Stadium.

HONOURS

League Champions: Premier League – 1997–98, 2001–02, 2003–04; Division 1 – 1930–31, 1932–33, 1933–34, 1934–35, 1937–38, 1947–48, 1952–53, 1970–71, 1988–89, 1990–91.
Runners-up: Premier League – 1998–99, 1999–2000, 2000–01, 2002–03, 2004–05, 2015–16; Division 1 – 1925–26, 1931–32, 1972–73; Division 2 – 1903–04.

FA Cup Winners: 1930, 1936, 1950, 1971, 1979, 1993, 1998, 2002, 2003, 2005, 2014, 2015, 2017.
Runners-up: 1927, 1932, 1952, 1972, 1978, 1980, 2001.

League Cup Winners: 1987, 1993.
Runners-up: 1968, 1969, 1988, 2007, 2011, 2018.

Double performed: 1970–71, 1997–98, 2001–02.

European Competitions
European Cup: 1971–72 *(qf)*, 1991–92.
UEFA Champions League: 1998–99, 1999–2000, 2000–01, 2001–02, 2002–03, 2003–04, 2004–05, 2005–06 *(runners-up)*, 2006–07, 2007–08 *(qf)*, 2008–09 *(sf)*, 2009–10*(qf)*, 2010–11, 2011–12, 2012–13, 2013–14, 2014–15, 2015–16, 2016–17.
Fairs Cup: 1963–64, 1969–70 *(winners)*, 1970–71.
UEFA Cup: 1978–79, 1981–82, 1982–83, 1996–97, 1997–98, 1999–2000 *(runners-up)*.
Europa League: 2017–18 *(sf)*, 2018–19 *(runners-up)*.
European Cup-Winners' Cup: 1979–80 *(runners-up)*, 1993–94 *(winners)*, 1994–95 *(runners-up)*.
Super Cup: 1994 *(runners-up)*.

THE SUN FACT FILE

Arsenal have had many talented cricketers on their books over the years. They were three times winners of the London *Evening News* Cricket Cup for Footballers, being successful in 1930, 1931 and 1933. On the latter occasion Joe Hulme, who also featured for Middlesex at cricket, almost defeated Crystal Palace in the final on his own, taking 6 wickets for 34 runs and then contributing to an unbeaten third-wicket partnership of 225.

First Football League Game: 2 September 1893, Division 2, v Newcastle U (h) D 2–2 – Williams; Powell, Jeffrey; Devine, Buist, Howat; Gemmell, Henderson, Shaw (1), Elliott (1), Booth.

Record League Victory: 12–0 v Loughborough T, Division 2, 12 March 1900 – Orr; McNichol, Jackson; Moir, Dick (2), Anderson (1); Hunt, Cottrell (2), Main (2), Gaudie (3), Tennant (2).

Record Cup Victory: 11–1 v Darwen, FA Cup 3rd rd, 9 January 1932 – Moss; Parker, Hapgood; Jones, Roberts, John; Hulme (2), Jack (3), Lambert (2), James, Bastin (4).

Record Defeat: 0–8 v Loughborough T, Division 2, 12 December 1896.

Most League Points (2 for a win): 66, Division 1, 1930–31.

Most League Points (3 for a win): 90, Premier League, 2003–04.

Most League Goals: 127, Division 1, 1930–31.

Highest League Scorer in Season: Ted Drake, 42, 1934–35.

Most League Goals in Total Aggregate: Thierry Henry, 175, 1999–2007; 2011–12.

Most League Goals in One Match: 7, Ted Drake v Aston Villa, Division 1, 14 December 1935.

Most Capped Player: Thierry Henry, 81 (123), France.

Most League Appearances: David O'Leary, 558, 1975–93.

Youngest League Player: Jack Wilshere, 16 years 256 days v Blackburn R, 13 September 2008.

Record Transfer Fee Received: £40,000,000 from Liverpool for Alex Oxlade-Chamberlain, August 2017.

Record Transfer Fee Paid: £55,000,000 (rising to £60,000,000) to Borussia Dortmund for Pierre-Emerick Aubameyang, January 2018.

Football League Record: 1893 Elected to Division 2; 1904–13 Division 1; 1913–19 Division 2; 1919–92 Division 1; 1992– Premier League.

MANAGERS

Sam Hollis 1894–97
Tom Mitchell 1897–98
George Elcoat 1898–99
Harry Bradshaw 1899–1904
Phil Kelso 1904–08
George Morrell 1908–15
Leslie Knighton 1919–25
Herbert Chapman 1925–34
George Allison 1934–47
Tom Whittaker 1947–56
Jack Crayston 1956–58
George Swindin 1958–62
Billy Wright 1962–66
Bertie Mee 1966–76
Terry Neill 1976–83
Don Howe 1984–86
George Graham 1986–95
Bruce Rioch 1995–96
Arsène Wenger 1996–2018
Unai Emery May 2018–

LATEST SEQUENCES

Longest Sequence of League Wins: 14, 10.2.2002 – 18.8.2002.

Longest Sequence of League Defeats: 7, 12.2.1977 – 12.3.1977.

Longest Sequence of League Draws: 6, 4.3.1961 – 1.4.1961.

Longest Sequence of Unbeaten League Matches: 49, 7.5.2003 – 24.10.2004.

Longest Sequence Without a League Win: 23, 28.9.1912 – 1.3.1913.

Successive Scoring Runs: 55 from 19.5.2001.

Successive Non-scoring Runs: 6 from 25.2.1987.

TEN YEAR LEAGUE RECORD

		P	*W*	*D*	*L*	*F*	*A*	*Pts*	*Pos*
2009-10	PR Lge	38	23	6	9	83	41	75	3
2010-11	PR Lge	38	19	11	8	72	43	68	4
2011-12	PR Lge	38	21	7	10	74	49	70	3
2012-13	PR Lge	38	21	10	7	72	37	73	4
2013-14	PR Lge	38	24	7	7	68	41	79	4
2014-15	PR Lge	38	22	9	7	71	36	75	3
2015-16	PR Lge	38	20	11	7	65	36	71	2
2016-17	PR Lge	38	23	6	9	77	44	75	5
2017-18	PR Lge	38	19	6	13	74	51	63	6
2018-19	PR Lge	38	21	7	10	73	51	70	5

DID YOU KNOW ?

Arsenal were the best supported Football League club for every season from 1929–30 to 1937–38, a run of nine consecutive seasons. The Gunners' highest average attendance achieved during this period was 46,252 in 1934–35 when they won the First Division title for the third season in a row.

ARSENAL – PREMIER LEAGUE 2018–19 LEAGUE RECORD

Match No.	Date	Venue	Opponents	Result	H/T Score	Lg Pos.	Goalscorers	Attendance
1	Aug 12	H	Manchester C	L 0-2	0-1	15		59,934
2	18	A	Chelsea	L 2-3	2-2	17	Mkhitaryan ^{37}, Iwobi ^{41}	40,491
3	25	H	West Ham U	W 3-1	1-1	11	Monreal ^{30}, Diop (og) ^{70}, Welbeck ^{90}	59,830
4	Sept 2	A	Cardiff C	W 3-2	1-1	9	Mustafi ^{11}, Aubameyang ^{62}, Lacazette ^{81}	32,316
5	15	A	Newcastle U	W 2-1	0-0	7	Xhaka ^{49}, Ozil ^{58}	52,165
6	23	H	Everton	W 2-0	0-0	6	Lacazette ^{56}, Aubameyang ^{59}	59,964
7	29	H	Watford	W 2-0	0-0	5	Cathcart (og) ^{81}, Ozil ^{83}	60,019
8	Oct 7	A	Fulham	W 5-1	1-1	4	Lacazette 2 $^{29, 49}$, Ramsey ^{67}, Aubameyang 2 $^{79, 90}$	25,401
9	22	H	Leicester C	W 3-1	1-1	4	Ozil ^{45}, Aubameyang 2 $^{63, 66}$	59,886
10	28	A	Crystal Palace	D 2-2	0-1	4	Xhaka ^{51}, Aubameyang ^{56}	25,718
11	Nov 3	H	Liverpool	D 1-1	0-0	5	Lacazette ^{82}	59,993
12	11	H	Wolverhampton W	D 1-1	0-1	5	Mkhitaryan ^{86}	60,030
13	25	A	Bournemouth	W 2-1	1-1	5	Lerma (og) ^{30}, Aubameyang ^{67}	10,792
14	Dec 2	H	Tottenham H	W 4-2	1-2	4	Aubameyang 2 (1 pen) $^{10 (p), 56}$, Lacazette ^{74}, Torreira ^{77}	59,973
15	5	A	Manchester U	D 2-2	1-1	5	Mustafi ^{26}, Rojo (og) ^{68}	74,507
16	8	H	Huddersfield T	W 1-0	0-0	5	Torreira ^{83}	59,893
17	16	A	Southampton	L 2-3	1-2	5	Mkhitaryan 2 $^{28, 53}$	29,497
18	22	H	Burnley	W 3-1	1-0	5	Aubameyang 2 $^{14, 48}$, Iwobi ^{90}	59,493
19	26	A	Brighton & HA	D 1-1	1-1	5	Aubameyang ^{7}	30,608
20	29	A	Liverpool	L 1-5	1-4	5	Maitland-Niles ^{11}	53,326
21	Jan 1	H	Fulham	W 4-1	1-0	5	Xhaka ^{25}, Lacazette ^{55}, Ramsey ^{79}, Aubameyang ^{83}	59,887
22	12	A	West Ham U	L 0-1	0-0	5		59,946
23	19	H	Chelsea	W 2-0	2-0	5	Lacazette ^{14}, Koscielny ^{39}	59,979
24	29	H	Cardiff C	W 2-1	0-0	5	Aubameyang (pen) ^{66}, Lacazette ^{83}	59,933
25	Feb 3	A	Manchester C	L 1-3	1-2	6	Koscielny ^{11}	54,483
26	9	A	Huddersfield T	W 2-1	2-0	6	Iwobi ^{16}, Lacazette ^{44}	24,182
27	24	H	Southampton	W 2-0	2-0	4	Lacazette ^{6}, Mkhitaryan ^{17}	59,877
28	27	H	Bournemouth	W 5-1	2-1	4	Ozil ^{4}, Mkhitaryan ^{27}, Koscielny ^{47}, Aubameyang ^{59}, Lacazette ^{78}	59,618
29	Mar 2	A	Tottenham H	D 1-1	1-0	5	Ramsey ^{16}	81,332
30	10	H	Manchester U	W 2-0	1-0	4	Xhaka ^{12}, Aubameyang (pen) ^{69}	60,000
31	Apr 1	H	Newcastle U	W 2-0	1-0	3	Ramsey ^{30}, Lacazette ^{83}	59,869
32	7	A	Everton	L 0-1	0-1	4		39,400
33	15	A	Watford	W 1-0	1-0	4	Aubameyang ^{10}	20,480
34	21	H	Crystal Palace	L 2-3	0-1	4	Ozil ^{47}, Aubameyang ^{77}	59,929
35	24	A	Wolverhampton W	L 1-3	0-3	5	Papastathopoulos ^{80}	31,436
36	28	A	Leicester C	L 0-3	0-0	5		32,037
37	May 5	H	Brighton & HA	D 1-1	1-0	5	Aubameyang (pen) ^{9}	59,965
38	12	A	Burnley	W 3-1	0-0	5	Aubameyang 2 $^{52, 63}$, Nketiah ^{90}	21,461

Final League Position: 5

GOALSCORERS

League (73): Aubameyang 22 (4 pens), Lacazette 13, Mkhitaryan 6, Ozil 5, Ramsey 4, Xhaka 4, Iwobi 3, Koscielny 3, Mustafi 2, Torreira 2, Maitland-Niles 1, Monreal 1, Nketiah 1, Papastathopoulos 1, Welbeck 1, own goals 4.
FA Cup (4): Willock 2, Aubameyang 1, Iwobi 1.
Carabao Cup (5): Welbeck 2, Lacazette 1, Lichtsteiner 1, Smith-Rowe 1.
Europa League (30): Aubameyang 8, Lacazette 5, Iwobi 2, Papastathopoulos 2, Ramsey 2 (1 pen), Smith-Rowe 2, Welbeck 2, Guendouzi 1, Maitland-Niles 1, Mustafi 1, Ozil 1, Willock 1, own goals 2.
Checkatrade Trophy (9): Willock 3 (1 pen), John-Jules 2, Gilmour 1 (1 pen), Nketiah 1, Saka 1, Smith-Rowe 1.

Cech P 7	Bellerin H 18 + 1	Mustafi S 31	Papastathopoulos S 25	Maitland-Niles A 11 + 5	Guendouzi M 23 + 10	Xhaka G 29	Ozil M 20 + 4	Ramsey A 14 + 14	Mkhitaryan H 19 + 6	Aubameyang P 30 + 6	Lichtsteiner S 10 + 4	Lacazette A 27 + 8	Torreira L 24 + 10	Monreal N 21 + 1	Iwobi A 22 + 13	Welbeck D 1 + 7	Holding R 9 + 1	Leno B 31 + 1	Kolasinac S 22 + 2	Nketiah E — + 5	Koscielny L 13 + 4	Elneny M 5 + 3	Saka B — + 1	Jenkinson C 2 + 1	Suarez D — + 4	Mavropanos K 3 + 1	Willock J 1 + 1	*Match No.*
1	2	3	4	5^{1}	6	7^{3}	8	9^{2}	10	11	12	13	14															1
1	2	3	4		7	6^{3}	9^{1}	13	8	11		14	12	5	10^{2}													2
1	2	3	4		6^{2}	7		9	8	11^{3}		12	13	5	10^{1}	14												3
1	2	3	4		6^{3}	7	8^{1}	9	14	10^{2}		11	12	5		13												4
1	2	3	4		6^{3}	7	8	9^{2}	13	10^{1}		11	12	5		14												5
1	2	3	4^{2}			7	8	9^{1}		10^{3}		11	6	5	13	14	12											6
1^{1}	2	3				7	8	9^{2}		10^{3}		11	6	5	13	14	4	12										7
	2	3			14	8		13	6	12		11^{3}	7	5	9^{1}	10^{2}	4	1										8
	2	3			12	7	9^{1}	14	8^{2}	13	5^{3}	11	6		10		4	1										9
	2^{3}	3			7	5	9^{2}	14		10^{1}	12	11	6		8	13	4	1										10
	2	3				7	9	13	8^{3}	10^{1}		11	6		12	14	4	1	5^{2}									11
	2	3			12	7	9^{2}	13	14	10		11	6		8^{3}		4	1	5^{1}									12
	5	2	3		12	7		13	9	11^{1}			6^{3}		10^{2}		4	1	8	14								13
	5	2^{3}	3		14	7		13	9^{2}	10		12	6		11^{1}		4	1	8									14
	5	2	3		7			9^{1}	13	11	12	14	6		10^{2}		4^{3}	1	8									15
	6	3^{1}	4		8	5			12	10	2^{2}	11^{3}	7	14	13			1	9									16
	5^{3}			14	7	4	13		9	10	2^{2}	12	6	8	11^{1}			1			3							17
			3	2	8	7	9			10	12	11^{1}	13	4^{2}	14			1	5			6^{3}						18
			3	14	8	6	9^{2}	13		10	2	11^{3}	7		12			1	5		4^{1}							19
		3^{2}	4	8	14	7		9		11^{1}	2	13	6		10			1	5^{3}		12							20
		2^{2}	3	5	6	7		13		10		11^{3}	12		9^{1}			1	8		4		14					21
	14	2^{3}	3	5^{2}	6	7^{1}		13		9		11	12		10			1	8		4							22
	2^{2}		3	12	8	6		9^{1}		11		10^{3}	7		13			1	5		4	14						23
		3			8		9^{3}	14		11	2^{2}	10	6	4	12			1	5			7^{1}		13				24
		3^{1}			8			13		11	2	10	7	5	6^{3}			1	9^{2}		4				12	14		25
		2		5	7				9^{1}			10	6^{2}	4	11^{3}			1	8		3	12			13		14	26
		3	4			7	13	9^{1}	8	14	2^{2}	11	6		10^{3}			1	5		12							27
			2		7		9		10^{1}	11^{2}		13	6	4	12			1	8^{3}		3			5	14			28
		2	3		6^{3}	7	14	9^{1}	8	13		11^{2}	12■	5	10			1			4							29
			2	5		7	9^{1}	6		11^{2}		10^{3}		4	12			1	8	14	3				13			30
		2	3	5	7		9^{1}	6^{3}	14	12		11		4	10^{2}			1	8			13						31
		2	3	5	7		9^{2}	13	10	12		11		4	14			1	8^{1}			6^{3}						32
		2		14	13	7	12	9^{3}	8	11			6^{1}	5	10			1			4					3^{2}		33
		2		13	6		9			11		10	14		12			1	8		3	7^{2}		5^{1}		4^{3}		34
			3	2	13	7	9		8^{2}			11	6^{1}	5	10^{3}			1	12	14	4							35
		3	4	2■	13	8			6^{1}	10		11^{2}	7		9^{3}			1	5	14	12							36
		3	4		12	7^{2}	9		8^{3}	11	2^{1}	10	6	5	13			1	14									37
		3			7				8	11	2			5	10			1		13	12	6				4^{2}	9^{1}	38

FA Cup

Third Round	Blackpool	(a)	3-0
Fourth Round	Manchester U	(h)	1-3

Carabao Cup

Third Round	Brentford	(h)	3-1
Fourth Round	Blackpool	(h)	2-1
Quarter-Final	Tottenham H	(h)	0-2

Checkatrade Trophy (Arsenal U21)

Group E (S)	Coventry C	(a)	3-0
Group E (S)	Cheltenham T	(a)	2-6
Group E (S)	Forest Green R	(a)	3-1
Second Round (S)	Portsmouth	(a)	1-2

Europa League

Group E	Vorskla	(h)	4-2
Group E	Qarabag	(a)	3-0
Group E	Sporting Lisbon	(a)	1-0
Group E	Sporting Lisbon	(h)	0-0
Group E	Vorskla	(a)	3-0
Group E	Qarabag	(h)	1-0
Round of 32 1st leg	BATE Borisov	(a)	0-1
Round of 32 2nd leg	BATE Borisov	(h)	3-0
Round of 16 1st leg	Rennes	(a)	1-3
Round of 16 2nd leg	Rennes	(h)	3-0
Quarter-Final 1st leg	Napoli	(h)	2-0
Quarter-Final 2nd leg	Napoli	(a)	1-0
Semi-Final 1st leg	Valencia	(h)	3-1
Semi-Final 2nd leg	Valencia	(a)	4-2
Final	Chelsea	(Baku)	1-4

ASTON VILLA

FOUNDATION

Cricketing enthusiasts of Villa Cross Wesleyan Chapel, Aston, Birmingham decided to form a football club during the winter of 1874–75. Football clubs were few and far between in the Birmingham area and in their first game against Aston Brook St Mary's rugby team they played one half rugby and the other soccer. In 1876 they were joined by Scottish soccer enthusiast George Ramsay who was immediately appointed captain and went on to lead Aston Villa from obscurity to one of the country's top clubs in a period of less than ten years.

Villa Park, Trinity Road, Birmingham B6 6HE.

Telephone: (0121) 327 2299.

Fax: (0121) 322 2107.

Ticket Office: (0333) 323 1874.

Website: www.avfc.co.uk

Email: postmaster@avfc.co.uk

Ground Capacity: 42,777.

Record Attendance: 76,588 v Derby Co, FA Cup 6th rd, 2 March 1946.

Pitch Measurements: 105m × 68m (115yd × 74.5yd).

Executive Chairman: Nassef Sawiris.

Co-Chairman: Wes Edens.

Chief Executive: Christian Purslow.

Head Coach: Dean Smith.

Assistant Head Coaches: Richard O'Kelly, John Terry.

Colours: Claret shirts with sky blue trim, white shorts with claret trim, sky blue socks with claret trim.

Year Formed: 1874.

Turned Professional: 1885.

Club Nickname: 'The Villans'.

Grounds: 1874, Wilson Road and Aston Park (also used Aston Lower Grounds for some matches); 1876, Wellington Road, Perry Barr; 1897, Villa Park.

First Football League Game: 8 September 1888, Football League, v Wolverhampton W (a) D 1–1 – Warner; Cox, Coulton; Yates, Harry Devey, Dawson; Albert Brown, Green (1), Allen, Garvey, Hodgetts.

Record League Victory: 12–2 v Accrington S, Division 1, 12 March 1892 – Warner; Evans, Cox; Harry Devey, Jimmy Cowan, Baird; Athersmith (1), Dickson (2), John Devey (4), Lewis Campbell (4), Hodgetts (1).

HONOURS

League Champions: Division 1 – 1893–94, 1895–96, 1896–97, 1898–99, 1899–1900, 1909–10, 1980–81; Division 2 – 1937–38, 1959–60; Division 3 – 1971–72.
Runners-up: Premier League – 1992–93; Division 1 – 1902–03, 1907–08, 1910–11, 1912–13, 1913–14, 1930–31, 1932–33, 1989–90; Football League 1888–89; Division 2 – 1974–75, 1987–88.

FA Cup Winners: 1887, 1895, 1897, 1905, 1913, 1920, 1957.
Runners-up: 1892, 1924, 2000, 2015.

League Cup Winners: 1961, 1975, 1977, 1994, 1996.
Runners-up: 1963, 1971, 2010.

Double Performed: 1896–97.

European Competitions
European Cup: 1981–82 *(winners)*, 1982–83 *(qf)*.
UEFA Cup: 1975–76, 1977–78 *(qf)*, 1983–84, 1990–91, 1993–94, 1994–95, 1996–97, 1997–98 *(qf)*, 1998–99, 2001–02, 2008–09.
Europa League: 2009–10, 2010–11.
Intertoto Cup: 2000, 2001 *(winners)*, 2002 *(sf)*, 2008 *(qualified for UEFA Cup)*.
Super Cup: 1982 *(winners)*.
World Club Championship: 1982.

THE Sun FACT FILE

Aston Villa shocked reigning Football League champions Liverpool with a stunning display of attacking football when the teams met at Villa Park in December 1976. Goals from Andy Gray (2), Brian Little and John Deehan (2) helped the Villa to a 5-1 half-time lead and with no further scoring it marked Liverpool's heaviest League defeat in over a decade.

Record Cup Victory: 13–0 v Wednesbury Old Ath, FA Cup 1st rd, 30 October 1886 – Warner; Coulton, Simmonds; Yates, Robertson, Burton (2); Richard Davis (1), Albert Brown (3), Hunter (3), Loach (2), Hodgetts (2).

Record Defeat: 0–8 v Chelsea, Premier League, 23 December 2012.

Most League Points (2 for a win): 70, Division 3, 1971–72.

Most League Points (3 for a win): 83, FL C, 2017–18.

Most League Goals: 128, Division 1, 1930–31.

Highest League Scorer in Season: 'Pongo' Waring, 49, Division 1, 1930–31.

Most League Goals in Total Aggregate: Harry Hampton, 215, 1904–15.

Most League Goals in One Match: 5, Harry Hampton v Sheffield W, Division 1, 5 October 1912; 5, Harold Halse v Derby Co, Division 1, 19 October 1912; 5, Len Capewell v Burnley, Division 1, 29 August 1925; 5, George Brown v Leicester C, Division 1, 2 January 1932; 5, Gerry Hitchens v Charlton Ath, Division 2, 18 November 1959.

Most Capped Player: Steve Staunton, 64 (102), Republic of Ireland.

Most League Appearances: Charlie Aitken, 561, 1961–76.

Youngest League Player: Jimmy Brown, 15 years 349 days v Bolton W, 17 September 1969.

Record Transfer Fee Received: £32,500,000 from Liverpool for Christian Benteke, July 2015.

Record Transfer Fee Paid: £22,000,000 to Club Brugge for Wesley Moraes, June 2019.

Football League Record: 1888 Founder Member of the League; 1936–38 Division 2; 1938–59 Division 1; 1959–60 Division 2; 1960–67 Division 1; 1967–70 Division 2; 1970–72 Division 3; 1972–75 Division 2; 1975–87 Division 1; 1987–88 Division 2; 1988–92 Division 1; 1992–2016 Premier League; 2016–19 FL C; 2019– Premier League.

MANAGERS

George Ramsay 1884–1926 (*Secretary-Manager*)
W. J. Smith 1926–34 (*Secretary-Manager*)
Jimmy McMullan 1934–35
Jimmy Hogan 1936–44
Alex Massie 1945–50
George Martin 1950–53
Eric Houghton 1953–58
Joe Mercer 1958–64
Dick Taylor 1964–67
Tommy Cummings 1967–68
Tommy Docherty 1968–70
Vic Crowe 1970–74
Ron Saunders 1974–82
Tony Barton 1982–84
Graham Turner 1984–86
Billy McNeill 1986–87
Graham Taylor 1987–90
Dr Jozef Venglos 1990–91
Ron Atkinson 1991–94
Brian Little 1994–98
John Gregory 1998–2002
Graham Taylor OBE 2002–03
David O'Leary 2003–06
Martin O'Neill 2006–10
Gerard Houllier 2010–11
Alex McLeish 2011–12
Paul Lambert 2012–15
Tim Sherwood 2015
Remi Garde 2015–16
Roberto Di Matteo 2016
Steve Bruce 2016–18
Dean Smith October 2018–

LATEST SEQUENCES

Longest Sequence of League Wins: 10, 2.3.2019 – 22.4.2019.

Longest Sequence of League Defeats: 11, 14.2.2016 – 30.4.2016.

Longest Sequence of League Draws: 6, 12.9.1981 – 10.10.1981.

Longest Sequence of Unbeaten League Matches: 15, 12.3.1949 – 27.8.1949.

Longest Sequence Without a League Win: 19, 14.8.2015 – 2.1.2016.

Successive Scoring Runs: 35 from 10.11.1895.

Successive Non-scoring Runs: 6 from 26.12.2014.

TEN YEAR LEAGUE RECORD

		P	*W*	*D*	*L*	*F*	*A*	*Pts*	*Pos*
2009-10	PR Lge	38	17	13	8	52	39	64	6
2010-11	PR Lge	38	12	12	14	48	59	48	9
2011-12	PR Lge	38	7	17	14	37	53	38	16
2012-13	PR Lge	38	10	11	17	47	69	41	15
2013-14	PR Lge	38	10	8	20	39	61	38	15
2014-15	PR Lge	38	10	8	20	31	57	38	17
2015-16	PR Lge	38	3	8	27	27	76	17	20
2016-17	FL C	46	16	14	16	47	48	62	13
2017-18	FL C	46	24	11	11	72	42	83	4
2018-19	FL C	46	20	16	10	82	61	76	5

DID YOU KNOW ?

Although history records that Aston Villa were the first winners of the Football League Cup in the 1960–61 season, both legs of the final tie against Rotherham United were actually played at the start of the following campaign. Peter McParland's extra-time goal finally clinched the trophy for Villa in a game that was played on 5 September 1961.

ASTON VILLA – SKY BET CHAMPIONSHIP 2018–19 LEAGUE RECORD

Match No.	Date	Venue	Opponents	Result	H/T Score	Lg Pos.	Goalscorers	Attendance
1	Aug 6	A	Hull C	W 3-1	1-1	2	Elphick [14], Elmohamady [70], Hutton [75]	14,071
2	11	H	Wigan Ath	W 3-2	1-1	3	Chester [13], Dunkley (og) [63], Bjarnason [90]	34,331
3	18	A	Ipswich T	D 1-1	1-1	4	Kodjia [21]	17,824
4	22	H	Brentford	D 2-2	1-1	5	Kodjia 2 [39, 90]	30,011
5	25	H	Reading	D 1-1	0-0	4	Elmohamady [51]	33,405
6	Sept 1	A	Sheffield U	L 1-4	0-3	12	El Ghazi [61]	26,030
7	15	A	Blackburn R	D 1-1	0-0	12	Hourihane [90]	15,982
8	18	H	Rotherham U	W 2-0	1-0	6	Abraham [27], Bolasie [82]	27,991
9	22	H	Sheffield W	L 1-2	0-0	13	McGinn [53]	35,572
10	28	A	Bristol C	D 1-1	1-1	11	Bjarnason [45]	24,224
11	Oct 2	H	Preston NE	D 3-3	2-0	12	Kodjia [26], Abraham [37], Bolasie [90]	27,331
12	6	A	Millwall	L 1-2	1-1	15	Abraham [7]	14,491
13	20	H	Swansea C	W 1-0	1-0	13	Abraham [8]	41,326
14	23	A	Norwich C	L 1-2	1-0	16	Chester [19]	24,977
15	26	A	QPR	L 0-1	0-1	16		16,036
16	Nov 2	H	Bolton W	W 2-0	1-0	13	Grealish [4], Chester [57]	30,802
17	10	A	Derby Co	W 3-0	0-0	11	McGinn [74], Abraham [78], Hourihane [84]	30,400
18	25	H	Birmingham C	W 4-2	2-1	8	Kodjia [37], Grealish [39], Abraham (pen) [51], Hutton [76]	41,200
19	28	H	Nottingham F	D 5-5	3-3	8	Abraham 4 (1 pen) [11, 14, 36 (p), 71], El Ghazi [75]	32,868
20	Dec 1	A	Middlesbrough	W 3-0	1-0	8	Chester [20], Abraham [64], Whelan [83]	23,424
21	7	A	WBA	D 2-2	1-1	8	El Ghazi 2 [12, 59]	26,513
22	15	H	Stoke C	D 2-2	0-0	8	Abraham (pen) [73], Kodjia [84]	36,999
23	23	H	Leeds U	L 2-3	2-0	11	Abraham [5], Hourihane [17]	41,411
24	26	A	Swansea C	W 1-0	0-0	9	Hourihane [65]	20,775
25	29	A	Preston NE	D 1-1	1-0	9	Abraham [45]	19,126
26	Jan 1	H	QPR	D 2-2	1-1	10	Abraham 2 [21, 75]	37,760
27	12	A	Wigan Ath	L 0-3	0-1	12		13,882
28	19	H	Hull C	D 2-2	1-2	13	Chester [45], Abraham [64]	33,619
29	26	H	Ipswich T	W 2-1	1-0	10	Abraham 2 (1 pen) [6, 61 (p)]	33,653
30	Feb 2	A	Reading	D 0-0	0-0	9		17,458
31	8	H	Sheffield U	D 3-3	0-1	8	Mings [82], Abraham [86], Green [90]	34,892
32	13	A	Brentford	L 0-1	0-0	10		9636
33	16	H	WBA	L 0-2	0-2	10		39,263
34	23	A	Stoke C	D 1-1	0-1	11	Adomah [62]	27,975
35	Mar 2	H	Derby Co	W 4-0	4-0	11	Hourihane 2 [9, 44], Abraham [37], Grealish [45]	37,273
36	10	A	Birmingham C	W 1-0	0-0	9	Grealish [67]	26,631
37	13	A	Nottingham F	W 3-1	2-1	8	McGinn 2 [7, 15], Hause [61]	29,224
38	16	H	Middlesbrough	W 3-0	2-0	6	El Ghazi [28], McGinn [44], Adomah [88]	36,263
39	30	H	Blackburn R	W 2-1	1-0	5	Abraham [8], Mings [61]	39,687
40	Apr 6	A	Sheffield W	W 3-1	1-1	5	McGinn [22], Abraham [90], Adomah [90]	29,458
41	10	A	Rotherham U	W 2-1	0-1	5	Kodjia (pen) [48], Grealish [51]	10,558
42	13	H	Bristol C	W 2-1	0-0	5	Abraham (pen) [55], Hourihane [66]	41,418
43	19	A	Bolton W	W 2-0	0-0	5	Grealish [47], Abraham [57]	17,344
44	22	H	Millwall	W 1-0	1-0	5	Kodjia [30]	39,839
45	28	A	Leeds U	D 1-1	0-0	5	Adomah [77]	36,786
46	May 5	H	Norwich C	L 1-2	1-1	5	Kodjia [14]	41,696

Final League Position: 5

GOALSCORERS

League (82): Abraham 25 (5 pens), Kodjia 9 (1 pen), Hourihane 7, Grealish 6, McGinn 6, Chester 5, El Ghazi 5, Adomah 4, Bjarnason 2, Bolasie 2, Elmohamady 2, Hutton 2, Mings 2, Elphick 1, Green 1, Hause 1, Whelan 1, own goal 1.
FA Cup (0).
Carabao Cup (1): Hourihane 1.
Championship Play-offs (4): Abraham 1 (1 pen), El Ghazi 1, Hourihane 1, McGinn 1.

Steer J 15 + 1	Hutton A 33	Elphick T 11	Chester J 28	Taylor N 28 + 3	Elmohamady A 32 + 6	Whelan G 23 + 12	Hourihane C 33 + 10	Adomah A 22 + 14	Grealish J 31	Kodjia J 22 + 17	Green A 8 + 10	Hepburn-Murphy R — + 5	Bjarnason B 11 + 6	Nyland O 23	Tuanzebe A 24 + 1	Jedinak M 12 + 5	McGinn J 39 + 1	El Ghazi A 25 + 6	Abraham T 37	Bolasie Y 9 + 12	Bree J 6 + 2	Bunn M 1	Hogan S — + 6	Lansbury H 1 + 2	Kalinic L 7	Hause K 10 + 1	Mings T 15	Carroll T — + 2	Ramsey J — + 1	Davis K — + 5	Match No.
1	2	3	4	5	6	7	8	9^{2}	10^{1}	11^{3}	12	13	14																		1
	5		3		6		14	12	10	11^{3}	9^{1}	13	8	1	2^{2}	4	7														2
	5		3		6		13	9^{1}	10	11	12	14	8^{3}	1	2^{2}	4	7														3
	5		3		6	7^{1}	13	9^{2}	10	11	12	14		1	2^{3}	4	8														4
	5		3	14	6		12	13	10^{1}	11^{2}			7	1	2	4	8	9^{3}													5
	5^{1}		3	14	6	7	12		10	11		13		1	2^{2}	4	8^{3}	9													6
	2		4	5	6^{3}		14	9^{2}	10	12				1	3	7^{1}	8		11	13											7
	5		3		2		8	13	9	10^{1}				1		4	7	6^{3}	11^{2}	12	14										8
	5		3		2		7	6^{1}	9	10^{2}				1		4	8	13	11	12											9
	5		3				9	13	8	10^{2}			7	1	2	4	6		11^{1}	12											10
	5		4■		2	14	9^{3}		10	8^{2}			6		3		7		11^{1}	13	12	1									11
	4			5	6^{3}		9^{1}	14	10	12			7	1	3		8^{2}		11	13	2										12
	2		4	5	6^{1}		14	9^{3}	10^{2}	13			7	1	3		8		11	12											13
	2		4	5	6	8	7^{3}	9^{1}	10	14				1	3			12	11^{2}				13								14
	2		4	5	6^{2}	12			10	9			7^{1}	1	3		8		11	13											15
	2		4	5		14	8	6^{1}	10^{2}	9				1	3		7		11^{3}	12			13								16
	2		4	5^{3}	12		8	6	10	9^{2}				1	3		7		11^{1}	13			14								17
	2		4	5	14	0^{7}	7	6^{1}	10	8				1	3				11	12				13^{3}							18
	2		4	5	14	13	7		8	11^{3}				1	3		6^{2}	12	10	9^{1}											19
			4	5	2	14	8		10	12				1	3		7^{3}	6	11^{2}	9^{1}			13								20
	2		4	5^{2}	12	14	7		8^{3}	13				1	3		6	9	10	11^{1}											21
	5		4		2	6^{1}	8			12				1	3		9	7^{2}	11	10			13								22
	5		4		2	6^{3}	9			7^{1}			13	1			8	12	11	10^{2}	3		14								23
	5		4		2	6	8^{1}	12		13			14	1			9	7	11^{3}	10^{2}	3										24
	5		4		2	6^{2}	8	12					13	1			9	7	11	10^{1}	3										25
1	5	3	4			14	6^{1}	9^{2}		11^{3}			8				7	13	10	12	2										26
		3^{1}	4	5		14	9	12					6^{2}				8	7^{3}	11	10	2				1	13					27
	2	3	4	5			7	9^{1}		14	13		8^{2}				6	12	10	11^{3}					1						28
	2	3	4	5	12	6^{2}	8	7^{1}		13						14	9	10^{3}	11						1						29
	2	3		5		6^{3}	8	7^{2}		12						14	9^{1}	10	11						1		4	13			30
	2	3^{1}		5		13	8			10^{2}	12					6^{1}	9	7	11						1		4				31
	2	3			12	8	8^{1}	10^{2}		14	13						9	7^{3}	11						1	5	4				32
12	2	3			7	6	8^{2}			14	10^{3}						9		11						1^{1}	5	4		13		33
1	2^{1}	3			6	7	8	12^{2}		10	13							9	11							5	4				34
1		3^{3}		12	2	7	6	9	8^{1}		14							11^{2}	10							5	4	13			35
1				5	2	7^{2}	6	9^{3}	8^{1}		12		14				13	11	10							3	4				36
1				5	2	14	7	12	8^{2}	13	9						6	11^{3}	10^{1}							3	4				37
1				5	2	6		12	9	13	7^{3}						8	10^{2}	11^{1}							3	4			14	38
1				5	2	6	13	12	9^{2}		7^{1}						8	10	11							3	4				39
1				5	2	6		13	9	14	7^{2}				12		8	10^{1}	11							3^{3}	4				40
1				5	2	14	6	7^{3}	9^{2}	13					3	12	8	10^{1}	11								4■				41
1				5	2	7	6^{2}	9							3	4	8	11	10^{1}					13						12	42
1				5	2	6	13	7	9						3^{3}	14	8^{2}	10	11^{1}								4			12	43
1				5	2	6^{1}	13	7^{3}	9	11^{2}	12					3	8	10									4			14	44
1				5	2	14	7	12	8^{3}	10^{1}	9^{2}				3	13	6	11■									4				45
1	2			5		6	9	7		11^{2}	10		13		3									8^{1}		4				12	46

FA Cup

Third Round	Swansea C	(h)	0-3

Carabao Cup

First Round	Yeovil T	(a)	1-0
Second Round	Burton Alb	(a)	0-1

Championship Play-offs

Semi-Final 1st leg	WBA	(h)	2-1
Semi-Final 2nd leg	WBA	(a)	0-1

(aet; Aston Villa won 4-3 on penalties)

Final	Derby Co	(Wembley)	2-1

BARNSLEY

FOUNDATION

Many clubs owe their inception to the Church and Barnsley are among them, for they were formed in 1887 by the Rev. T. T. Preedy, curate of Barnsley St Peter's, and went under that name until it was dropped in 1897 a year before being admitted to the Second Division of the Football League.

Oakwell Stadium, Grove Street, Barnsley, South Yorkshire S71 1ET.

Telephone: (01226) 211 211.

Fax: (01226) 211 444.

Ticket Office: (01226) 211 183.

Website: www.barnsleyfc.co.uk

Email: thereds@barnsleyfc.co.uk

Ground Capacity: 22,815.

Record Attendance: 40,255 v Stoke C, FA Cup 5th rd, 15 February 1936.

Pitch Measurements: 100.5m × 67m (110yd × 73.5yd).

Co-Chairmen: Chien Lee, Paul Conway.

Head Coach: Daniel Stendel.

Assistant First-Team Coaches: Christopher Stern, Dale Tonge.

Colours: Red shirts with white trim, white shorts with red trim, red socks with white trim.

Year Formed: 1887.

Turned Professional: 1888.

Previous Name: 1887, Barnsley St Peter's; 1897, Barnsley.

Club Nickname: 'The Tykes', 'The Reds', 'The Colliers'.

Ground: 1887, Oakwell.

First Football League Game: 1 September 1898, Division 2, v Lincoln C (a) L 0–1 – Fawcett; McArtney, Nixon; King, Burleigh, Porteous; Davis, Lees, Murray, McCullough, McGee.

Record League Victory: 9–0 v Loughborough T, Division 2, 28 January 1899 – Greaves; McArtney, Nixon; Porteous, Burleigh, Howard; Davis (4), Hepworth (1), Lees (1), McCullough (1), Jones (2). 9–0 v Accrington S, Division 3 (N), 3 February 1934 – Ellis; Cookson, Shotton; Harper, Henderson, Whitworth; Spence (2), Smith (1), Blight (4), Andrews (1), Ashton (1).

Record Cup Victory: 6–0 v Blackpool, FA Cup 1st rd replay, 20 January 1910 – Mearns; Downs, Ness; Glendinning, Boyle (1), Utley; Bartrop, Gadsby (1), Lillycrop (2), Tufnell (2), Forman. 6–0 v Peterborough U, League Cup 1st rd 2nd leg, 15 September 1981 – Horn; Joyce, Chambers, Glavin (2), Banks, McCarthy, Evans, Parker (2), Aylott (1), McHale, Barrowclough (1).

Record Defeat: 0–9 v Notts Co, Division 2, 19 November 1927.

Most League Points (2 for a win): 67, Division 3 (N), 1938–39.

Most League Points (3 for a win): 91, FL 1, 2018–19.

HONOURS

League Champions: Division 3N – 1933–34, 1938–39, 1954–55.
Runners-up: First Division – 1996–97; FL 1 – 2018–19; Division 3 – 1980–81; Division 3N – 1953–54; Division 4 – 1967–68.

FA Cup Winners: 1912.
Runners-up: 1910.

League Cup: quarter-final – 1982.

League Trophy Winners: 2016.

THE Sun FACT FILE

Barnsley won promotion to top-flight football for the first time in their 110-year history when they defeated Bradford City at Oakwell on 26 April 1996. The game attracted a season's best attendance of 18,605 with goals from Paul Wilkinson and Clint Marcelle. The Reds went on to lose their remaining game, going down to a 5-1 defeat at Oxford United on the last day of the season, but finished second in the table to go up automatically.

Most League Goals: 118, Division 3 (N), 1933–34.

Highest League Scorer in Season: Cecil McCormack, 33, Division 2, 1950–51.

Most League Goals in Total Aggregate: Ernest Hine, 123, 1921–26 and 1934–38.

Most League Goals in One Match: 5, Frank Eaton v South Shields, Division 3 (N), 9 April 1927; 5, Peter Cunningham v Darlington, Division 3 (N), 4 February 1933; 5, Beau Asquith v Darlington, Division 3 (N), 12 November 1938; 5, Cecil McCormack v Luton T, Division 2, 9 September 1950.

Most Capped Player: Gerry Taggart, 35 (51), Northern Ireland.

Most League Appearances: Barry Murphy, 514, 1962–78.

Youngest League Player: Reuben Noble-Lazarus, 15 years 45 days v Ipswich T, 30 September 2008.

Record Transfer Fee Received: £3,000,000 (rising to £10,125,000) from Everton for John Stones, January 2013.

Record Transfer Fee Paid: £1,500,000 to Partizan Belgrade for Georgi Hristov, July 1997; £1,500,000 to QPR for Mike Sheron, January 1999.

Football League Record: 1898 Elected to Division 2; 1932–34 Division 3 (N); 1934–38 Division 2; 1938–39 Division 3 (N); 1946–53 Division 2; 1953–55 Division 3 (N); 1955–59 Division 2; 1959–65 Division 3; 1965–68 Division 4; 1968–72 Division 3; 1972–79 Division 4; 1979–81 Division 3; 1981–92 Division 2; 1992–97 Division 1; 1997–98 Premier League; 1998–2002 Division 1; 2002–04 Division 2; 2004–06 FL 1; 2006–14 FL C; 2014–16 FL 1; 2016–18 FL C; 2018–19 FL 1; 2019– FL C.

LATEST SEQUENCES

Longest Sequence of League Wins: 10, 5.3.1955 – 23.4.1955.

Longest Sequence of League Defeats: 9, 14.3.1953 – 25.4.1953.

Longest Sequence of League Draws: 7, 28.3.1911 – 22.4.1911.

Longest Sequence of Unbeaten League Matches: 21, 1.1.1934 – 5.5.1934.

Longest Sequence Without a League Win: 26, 13.12.1952 – 26.8.1953.

Successive Scoring Runs: 44 from 2.10.1926.

Successive Non-scoring Runs: 6 from 27.11.1971.

MANAGERS

Arthur Fairclough 1898–1901 (*Secretary-Manager*)
John McCartney 1901–04 (*Secretary-Manager*)
Arthur Fairclough 1904–12
John Hastie 1912–14
Percy Lewis 1914–19
Peter Sant 1919–26
John Commins 1926–29
Arthur Fairclough 1929–30
Brough Fletcher 1930–37
Angus Seed 1937–53
Tim Ward 1953–60
Johnny Steele 1960–71 (*continued as General Manager*)
John McSeveney 1971–72
Johnny Steele (*General Manager*) 1972–73
Jim Iley 1973–78
Allan Clarke 1978–80
Norman Hunter 1980–84
Bobby Collins 1984–85
Allan Clarke 1985–89
Mel Machin 1989–93
Viv Anderson 1993–94
Danny Wilson 1994–98
John Hendrie 1998–99
Dave Bassett 1999–2000
Nigel Spackman 2001
Steve Parkin 2001–02
Glyn Hodges 2002–03
Gudjon Thordarson 2003–04
Paul Hart 2004–05
Andy Ritchie 2005–06
Simon Davey 2007–09 (*Caretaker from November 2006*)
Mark Robins 2009–11
Keith Hill 2011–12
David Flitcroft 2012–13
Danny Wilson 2013–15
Lee Johnson 2015–16
Paul Heckingbottom 2016–18
Jose Morais 2018
Daniel Stendel June 2018–

TEN YEAR LEAGUE RECORD

		P	W	D	L	F	A	Pts	Pos
2009-10	FL C	46	14	12	20	53	69	54	18
2010-11	FL C	46	14	14	18	55	66	56	17
2011-12	FL C	46	13	9	24	49	74	48	21
2012-13	FL C	46	14	13	19	56	70	55	21
2013-14	FL C	46	9	12	25	44	77	39	23
2014-15	FL 1	46	17	11	18	62	61	62	11
2015-16	FL 1	46	22	8	16	70	54	74	6
2016-17	FL C	46	15	13	18	64	67	58	14
2017-18	FL C	46	9	14	23	48	72	41	22
2018-19	FL 1	46	26	13	7	80	39	91	2

DID YOU KNOW ?

Barnsley were one of the last Football League teams to install floodlights. The lights at Oakwell were switched on for the first time on 23 January 1962 when Barnsley met Bolton Wanderers in a friendly match to mark the occasion. The Reds, bolstered by the inclusion of the recently retired former England winger Tom Finney, won the game 2-0 with Finney scoring the first goal.

BARNSLEY – SKY BET LEAGUE ONE 2018–19 LEAGUE RECORD

Match No.	Date	Venue	Opponents	Result		H/T Score	Lg Pos.	Goalscorers	Attendance
1	Aug 4	H	Oxford U	W	4-0	2-0	1	Thiam 2 [20, 29], Potts [77], Adeboyejo [89]	12,820
2	11	A	Bradford C	W	2-0	1-0	1	Bradshaw [7], Adeboyejo [70]	18,986
3	18	H	AFC Wimbledon	D	0-0	0-0	3		11,607
4	21	A	Rochdale	W	4-0	2-0	3	Potts [35], Moore 3 [42, 48, 68]	4359
5	25	A	Scunthorpe U	D	2-2	0-1	5	Moore [59], Cavare [69]	5579
6	Sept 1	H	Gillingham	W	2-1	2-0	3	Moore 2 (1 pen) [13, 34 (p)]	11,434
7	8	H	Walsall	D	1-1	0-0	3	Fitzwater (og) [55]	11,468
8	15	A	Coventry C	L	0-1	0-0	3		11,465
9	29	A	Fleetwood T	W	3-1	2-1	5	Brown [32], Moore [41], Thiam [90]	3756
10	Oct 2	H	Plymouth Arg	D	1-1	1-1	6	Mowatt [8]	10,717
11	6	A	Peterborough U	W	4-0	2-0	4	Moncur [14], Potts 2 [45, 59], Brown [90]	7683
12	13	H	Luton T	W	3-2	2-1	3	Potts [5], McGeehan [26], Thiam [79]	12,688
13	20	A	Charlton Ath	L	0-2	0-1	5		12,416
14	23	A	Shrewsbury T	L	1-3	0-2	5	Pinnock [49]	5587
15	27	H	Bristol R	W	1-0	1-0	4	Mowatt [11]	10,966
16	Nov 3	H	Southend U	W	1-0	0-0	4	Moore [87]	10,709
17	17	A	Accrington S	W	2-0	1-0	3	Woodrow [36], Moore [90]	4801
18	24	H	Doncaster R	D	1-1	0-0	3	Woodrow [62]	13,573
19	27	A	Sunderland	L	2-4	1-3	5	Moore 2 [41, 61]	28,514
20	Dec 8	A	Wycombe W	L	0-1	0-0	5		5225
21	15	H	Portsmouth	D	1-1	0-1	7	Woodrow [61]	12,441
22	22	A	Blackpool	W	1-0	0-0	6	McGeehan [59]	4054
23	26	H	Peterborough U	W	2-0	1-0	5	Mowatt [24], Woodrow [49]	12,843
24	29	H	Charlton Ath	W	2-1	2-0	4	Potts [5], Thiam [14]	11,978
25	Jan 1	A	Luton T	D	0-0	0-0	4		9926
26	12	H	Bradford C	W	3-0	2-0	5	Brown [28], Moore [38], Mowatt [90]	14,962
27	19	A	AFC Wimbledon	W	4-1	1-1	5	Woodrow [19], Moore [51], Thiam [65], McGeehan [90]	4795
28	26	H	Rochdale	W	2-1	0-0	3	Moore [54], Woodrow [75]	11,379
29	29	A	Oxford U	D	2-2	0-1	3	Thiam [70], Moore [79]	5794
30	Feb 2	H	Scunthorpe U	W	2-0	2-0	2	Mowatt [16], McGeehan [41]	12,150
31	9	A	Gillingham	W	4-1	2-0	2	Moore [1], Woodrow 2 [45, 71], Brown [90]	4791
32	16	H	Wycombe W	W	2-1	1-0	2	Woodrow 2 (1 pen) [13 (p), 64]	11,821
33	19	H	Burton Alb	D	0-0	0-0	2		11,778
34	23	A	Portsmouth	D	0-0	0-0	2		18,624
35	Mar 2	A	Southend U	W	3-0	0-0	2	McGeehan [50], Woodrow [73], Green [90]	6217
36	9	H	Accrington S	W	2-0	2-0	2	Cavare [41], Wood (og) [45]	11,533
37	12	H	Sunderland	D	0-0	0-0	2		18,282
38	15	A	Doncaster R	D	0-0	0-0	2		11,710
39	23	A	Walsall	W	1-0	0-0	2	Brown [90]	4969
40	30	H	Coventry C	D	2-2	1-1	2	Mowatt [9], Woodrow [48]	13,593
41	Apr 6	A	Burton Alb	L	1-3	0-1	2	Woodrow (pen) [85]	4310
42	13	H	Fleetwood T	W	4-2	2-0	2	Bahre [21], Woodrow [34], McGeehan [70], Brown [79]	11,243
43	19	H	Shrewsbury T	W	2-1	1-1	2	Mowatt [23], Brown [55]	13,426
44	22	A	Plymouth Arg	W	3-0	3-0	2	Woodrow [15], Brown [21], Mowatt [28]	10,898
45	27	H	Blackpool	W	2-1	1-1	2	Woodrow [40], Lindsay [59]	14,703
46	May 4	A	Bristol R	L	1-2	1-0	2	Moore [12]	9859

Final League Position: 2

GOALSCORERS

League (80): Moore 17 (1 pen), Woodrow 16 (2 pens), Brown 8, Mowatt 8, Thiam 7, McGeehan 6, Potts 6, Adeboyejo 2, Cavare 2, Bahre 1, Bradshaw 1, Green 1, Lindsay 1, Moncur 1, Pinnock 1, own goals 2.
FA Cup (8): Woodrow 3, Moore 2, Bahre 1, Fryers 1, Potts 1.
Carabao Cup (1): Moncur 1.
Checkatrade Trophy (8): Moncur 3, Adeboyejo 2, Hedges 1, Lindsay 1, Williams J 1.

Davies A 42	Cavare D 40 + 1	Pinnock E 46	Lindsay L 41	Pinillos D 32 + 3	Potts B 20 + 2	Dougall K 19 + 8	Mowatt A 46	Thiam M 36 + 10	Moore K 26 + 5	Bradshaw T 4	Moncur G 10 + 11	McGeehan C 32 + 7	Adeboyejo V 2 + 23	Isgrove L — + 2	Williams J 6 + 5	Brown J 22 + 10	Walton J 3	Bahre M 23 + 12	Jackson A 5 + 1	Hedges R 5 + 16	Williams B 11	Woodrow C 29 + 2	Smith J 1	Fryers Z 3 + 2	Green J 2 + 8	Styles C — + 7	Match No.
1	2	3	4	5	6	7	8^{2}	9^{3}	10^{1}	11	12	13	14														1
1	2	3	4	5	9^{1}	8	7	6^{3}	10^{2}	11	13		12	14													2
1	2	3	4	5	6^{3}	7	8	11^{1}	10	9^{2}	12		14		13												3
1	2^{3}	3	4	5	6	7^{1}	8	9^{2}	11	10	12	13			14												4
1	2	3	4	5^{3}	6	7	8	9^{1}	11		10^{2}	14	12			13											5
1	2	3	4	5	7^{1}	6	8	10^{3}	11		9^{2}	13	12			14											6
	2	3	4	5			8	11	10		7	6^{1}	12				1	9									7
1	2	3	4^{2}	5		7	8	9	11		12	14	13			10^{3}		6^{1}									8
1	2	3		5		7	8	12	11		9^{2}	14	13			10^{1}		6^{3}	4								9
1	2	4		5^{1}	12	7	8	9^{3}	11		14		10^{2}					13	3	6							10
1	2	3	4		8^{2}	7	6	14	11^{3}		10					12		9^{1}		13	5						11
	2	3	4	13	6		7	12			10^{2}	8				11	1	9^{1}		14	5^{3}						12
1	2	3	4	5^{2}	8	6	7	14	12		10^{3}	9^{1}				11				13							13
1	2	4	3		8^{1}	6^{3}	7	10^{2}	11		13	12						9		14	5						14
1	2	3	4	5	6		8	12	10^{1}		9^{2}	7				13		11^{3}		14							15
1	2	3	4	5^{3}	11		8	9^{2}	10		14	7						6^{1}		12		13					16
	2	4	3	12	6		7^{1}	9^{2}	10			8				13		14				11^{3}	1	5■			17
1	2	3	4	5^{1}	11^{3}		8	14	10		13	7^{2}						6		9		12					18
1	2	3	4		6^{1}		8	9	11		13	7	14			12						10^{3}		5^{2}			19
1		3	4		13		7	14	11		9	8			12	2		6^{1}				10^{2}		5^{3}			20
1	2^{3}	4		5	6^{1}		8	14	10		9^{2}	7		13		12			3			11					21
1	2	4	3	5	6	13	8^{1}	9^{3}	10			7	14					12				11^{2}					22
1	2	3	4	5	9^{1}	7^{3}	8	13				6	14			12		10^{2}				11					23
1	2	3	4	5	7^{3}	13	8	10^{2}				6				12		9^{1}		14		11					24
1	2	3	4		10^{3}	8^{1}	9	7^{2}				6	14			13		12			5	11					25
1	2	3	4				8	9^{3}	10^{2}		14	7	13			6		12			5	11^{1}					26
1	2	3	4	13		12	8	7	9^{3}			6	14			10					5^{1}	11^{2}					27
1	2	3	4			12	8	9^{2}	10^{1}			7	14			6					5	11^{3}			13		28
1	2	3	4			8^{3}	9	10^{1}	12			7				6		14			5	11^{2}			13		29
1	6	2	3	8			9	10^{2}	7^{1}			4	14			11		13		12		5^{3}					30
1	2	3	4	5		13	8^{2}	9	11^{3}			7				6		12				10^{1}			14		31
1	5	4	3	2		14	6^{2}	9^{1}				7	13			11		8^{3}		12		10					32
1	5	4	3	2		14	6	12				7^{3}	13			11		8^{2}		9^{1}		10					33
1	2	4	3	5		14	6	11^{1}				7^{2}	12			9		8^{3}		13		10					34
1	2	3	4	5		7^{2}	8	11^{3}				6				9■		12	14			10^{1}			13		35
1	2	4	3	5		7	6	11^{3}							12			9^{2}		14		10			8^{1}	13	36
1	2	4	3	5		7	6	11					13		12			9^{1}				10			8^{2}		37
1	2	4	3			7^{2}	8	10^{3}					6		5^{1}			13		14	9	11		12			38
	2	3	4				8	9^{1}				7^{3}	13			10	1	6^{2}			5	11			14	12	39
1	2	3	4				6	9^{3}				7	14			8^{1}		12		10^{2}	5	11			13		40
1	5	4	3	2^{1}			7	9^{3}				6	14			8^{2}		12		10		11				13	41
1		4		5			8	9^{3}				7			2	6^{1}		10^{2}	3	13		11			14	12	42
1		4		5			8	9^{1}	12			7			2	6		10^{3}	3	13		11^{2}				14	43
1		3	4	5			7	10^{2}	12			6			2	8		9^{1}		13		11^{3}				14	44
1		3	4	5			7	10^{1}	12			6			2	8^{3}		9^{2}		13		11				14	45
1	12	3	4■	5			7	10^{2}	8^{3}			6			2			9^{1}				11		13	14		46

FA Cup

First Round	Notts Co	(h)	4-0
Second Round	Southend U	(a)	4-2
Third Round	Burnley	(a)	0-1

Carabao Cup

First Round	Blackpool	(a)	1-3

Checkatrade Trophy

Group F (N)	Oldham Ath	(a)	2-1
Group F (N)	Everton U21	(h)	1-1
(Barnsley won 4-2 on penalties)			
Group F (N)	Bradford C	(h)	2-1
Second Round (N)	Manchester C U21	(h)	3-3
(Manchester C U21 won 5-3 on penalties)			

BIRMINGHAM CITY

FOUNDATION

In 1875, cricketing enthusiasts who were largely members of Trinity Church, Bordesley, determined to continue their sporting relationships throughout the year by forming a football club which they called Small Heath Alliance. For their earliest games played on waste land in Arthur Street, the team included three Edden brothers and two James brothers.

St Andrew's Trillion Trophy Stadium, Cattell Road, Birmingham B9 4RL.

Telephone: (0121) 772 0101.

Fax: (0121) 766 7866.

Ticket Office: (0121) 772 0101 (option 2).

Website: www.bcfc.com

Email: reception@bcfc.com

Ground Capacity: 29,409.

Record Attendance: 66,844 v Everton, FA Cup 5th rd, 11 February 1939.

Pitch Measurements: 100m × 65m (109.5yd × 71yd).

Directors: Wenqing Zhao, Chun Kong Yiu, Gannan Zheng, Yao Wang, Xuandong Ren.

Manager: Pep Clotet (caretaker).

Colours: Blue shirts with white trim, white shorts with blue trim, blue socks with white trim.

Year Formed: 1875.

Turned Professional: 1885.

Previous Names: 1875, Small Heath Alliance; 1888, dropped 'Alliance'; 1905, Birmingham; 1945, Birmingham City.

Club Nickname: 'Blues'.

Grounds: 1875, waste ground near Arthur St; 1877, Muntz St, Small Heath; 1906, St Andrew's (renamed St Andrew's Trillion Trophy Stadium 2018).

First Football League Game: 3 September 1892, Division 2, v Burslem Port Vale (h) W 5–1 – Charsley; Bayley, Speller; Ollis, Jenkyns, Devey; Hallam (1), Edwards (1), Short (1), Wheldon (2), Hands.

Record League Victory: 12–0 v Walsall T Swifts, Division 2, 17 December 1892 – Charsley; Bayley, Jones; Ollis, Jenkyns, Devey; Hallam (2), Walton (3), Mobley (3), Wheldon (2), Hands (2). 12–0 v Doncaster R, Division 2, 11 April 1903 – Dorrington; Goldie, Wassell; Beer, Dougherty (1), Howard; Athersmith, Leonard (4), McRoberts (1), Wilcox (4), Field (1), (1 og).

Record Cup Victory: 9–2 v Burton W, FA Cup 1st rd, 31 October 1885 – Hedges; Jones, Evetts (1); Fred James, Felton, Arthur James (1); Davenport (2), Stanley (4), Simms, Figures, Morris (1).

Record Defeat: 1–9 v Blackburn R, Division 1, 5 January 1895; 1–9 v Sheffield W, Division 1, 13 December 1930; 0–8 v Bournemouth, FLC, 25 October 2014.

HONOURS

League Champions: Division 2 – 1892–93, 1920–21, 1947–48, 1954–55; Second Division – 1994–95.
Runners-up: FL C – 2006–07, 2008–09; Division 2 – 1893–94, 1900–01, 1902–03; 1971–72, 1984–85; Division 3 – 1991–92.

FA Cup: *Runners-up:* 1931, 1956.

League Cup Winners: 1963, 2011.
Runners-up: 2001.

League Trophy Winners: 1991, 1995.

European Competitions
Fairs Cup: 1955–58, 1958–60 *(runners-up)*, 1960–61 *(runners-up)*, 1961–62.
Europa League: 2011–12.

THE Sun FACT FILE

Birmingham player Frank Osborne created something of a record in the 1918–19 season when he featured in four consecutive games at St Andrew's, each time turning out as a 'guest' for the opposition team. Later that season he scored the winner for Lincoln City against Blues, a result that effectively cost his team the Midland Section title.

Most League Points (2 for a win): 59, Division 2, 1947–48.

Most League Points (3 for a win): 89, Division 2, 1994–95.

Most League Goals: 103, Division 2, 1893–94 (only 28 games).

Highest League Scorer in Season: Walter Abbott, 34, Division 2, 1898–99 (Small Heath); Joe Bradford, 29, Division 1, 1927–28 (Birmingham City).

Most League Goals in Total Aggregate: Joe Bradford, 249, 1920–35.

Most League Goals in One Match: 5, Walter Abbott v Darwen, Division 2, 26 November, 1898; 5, John McMillan v Blackpool, Division 2, 2 March 1901; 5, James Windridge v Glossop, Division 2, 23 January 1915.

Most Capped Player: Maik Taylor, 58 (including 8 on loan at Fulham) (88), Northern Ireland.

Most League Appearances: Frank Womack, 491, 1908–28.

Youngest League Player: Trevor Francis, 16 years 139 days v Cardiff C, 5 September 1970.

Record Transfer Fee Received: £15,000,000 from Southampton for Che Adams, July 2019.

Record Transfer Fee Paid: £6,250,000 to Brentford for Jota, August 2017.

Football League Record: 1892 Elected to Division 2; 1894–96 Division 1; 1896–1901 Division 2; 1901–02 Division 1; 1902–03 Division 2; 1903–08 Division 1; 1908–21 Division 2; 1921–39 Division 1; 1946–48 Division 2; 1948–50 Division 1; 1950–55 Division 2; 1955–65 Division 1; 1965–72 Division 2; 1972–79 Division 1; 1979–80 Division 2; 1980–84 Division 1; 1984–85 Division 2; 1985–86 Division 1; 1986–89 Division 2; 1989–92 Division 3; 1992–94 Division 1; 1994–95 Division 2; 1995–2002 Division 1; 2002–06 Premier League; 2006–07 FL C; 2007–08 Premier League; 2008–09 FL C; 2009–11 Premier League; 2011– FL C.

LATEST SEQUENCES

Longest Sequence of League Wins: 13, 17.12.1892 – 16.9.1893.

Longest Sequence of League Defeats: 8, 28.9.1985 – 23.11.1985.

Longest Sequence of League Draws: 8, 18.9.1990 – 23.10.1990.

Longest Sequence of Unbeaten League Matches: 20, 3.9.1994 – 2.1.1995.

Longest Sequence Without a League Win: 17, 28.9.1985 – 18.1.1986.

Successive Scoring Runs: 24 from 24.9.1892.

Successive Non-scoring Runs: 6 from 11.2.1989.

MANAGERS

Alfred Jones 1892–1908
(*Secretary-Manager*)
Alec Watson 1908–10
Bob McRoberts 1910–15
Frank Richards 1915–23
Billy Beer 1923–27
William Harvey 1927–28
Leslie Knighton 1928–33
George Liddell 1933–39
William Camkin and Ted Goodier 1939–45
Harry Storer 1945–48
Bob Brocklebank 1949–54
Arthur Turner 1954–58
Pat Beasley 1959–60
Gil Merrick 1960–64
Joe Mallett 1964–65
Stan Cullis 1965–70
Fred Goodwin 1970–75
Willie Bell 1975–77
Sir Alf Ramsay 1977–78
Jim Smith 1978–82
Ron Saunders 1982–86
John Bond 1986–87
Garry Pendrey 1987–89
Dave Mackay 1989–91
Lou Macari 1991
Terry Cooper 1991–93
Barry Fry 1993–96
Trevor Francis 1996–2001
Steve Bruce 2001–07
Alex McLeish 2007–11
Chris Hughton 2011–12
Lee Clark 2012–14
Gary Rowett 2014–16
Gianfranco Zola 2016–17
Harry Redknapp 2017
Steve Cotterill 2017–18
Garry Monk 2018–19
Pep Clotet June 2019–

TEN YEAR LEAGUE RECORD

		P	*W*	*D*	*L*	*F*	*A*	*Pts*	*Pos*
2009-10	PR Lge	38	13	11	14	38	47	50	9
2010-11	PR Lge	38	8	15	15	37	58	39	18
2011-12	FL C	46	20	16	10	78	51	76	4
2012-13	FL C	46	15	16	15	63	69	61	12
2013-14	FL C	46	11	11	24	58	74	44	21
2014-15	FL C	46	16	15	15	54	64	63	10
2015-16	FL C	46	16	15	15	53	49	63	10
2016-17	FL C	46	13	14	19	45	64	53	19
2017-18	FL C	46	13	7	26	38	68	46	19
2018-19	FL C	46	14	19	13	64	58	52*	17

** 9 pts deducted.*

DID YOU KNOW ?

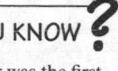

Cammie Fraser was the first player to wear the number 12 shirt in a Football League match for Birmingham City when he lined up against Crystal Palace on the opening day of the 1965–66 season, although he was not called into action. Local newspaper the *Sports Argus* listed him as 'twelfth man' in their line-ups.

BIRMINGHAM CITY – SKY BET CHAMPIONSHIP 2018–19 LEAGUE RECORD

Match No.	*Date*	*Venue*	*Opponents*	*Result*		*H/T Score*	*Lg Pos.*	*Goalscorers*	*Attendance*
1	Aug 4	H	Norwich C	D	2-2	0-0	7	Maghoma [56], Solomon-Otabor [89]	22,677
2	11	A	Middlesbrough	L	0-1	0-1	19		23,748
3	17	H	Swansea C	D	0-0	0-0	17		20,083
4	22	A	Bolton W	L	0-1	0-0	20		13,821
5	25	A	Nottingham F	D	2-2	1-0	20	Jutkiewicz [21], Adams [72]	26,799
6	Sept 1	H	QPR	D	0-0	0-0	19		21,155
7	14	H	WBA	D	1-1	1-1	17	Jota [26]	22,715
8	19	A	Sheffield U	D	0-0	0-0	20		23,525
9	22	A	Leeds U	W	2-1	2-0	17	Adams 2 [8, 29]	34,800
10	29	H	Ipswich T	D	2-2	0-2	16	Jutkiewicz 2 [48, 68]	21,612
11	Oct 2	A	Brentford	D	1-1	1-1	18	Morrison [26]	9715
12	6	H	Rotherham U	W	3-1	2-0	17	Jutkiewicz 3 [20, 23, 68]	19,795
13	20	A	Stoke C	W	1-0	0-0	14	Adams [81]	28,160
14	23	H	Reading	W	2-1	0-0	9	Gardner, G [49], Jutkiewicz [70]	22,126
15	27	H	Sheffield W	W	3-1	1-1	9	Mahoney [43], Jutkiewicz [80], Adams [84]	23,659
16	Nov 3	A	Derby Co	L	1-3	1-0	10	Jutkiewicz [10]	28,114
17	10	H	Hull C	D	3-3	2-0	12	Adams 3 [21, 45, 84]	21,468
18	25	A	Aston Villa	L	2-4	1-2	12	Jutkiewicz [28], Pedersen [57]	41,200
19	28	A	Millwall	W	2-0	1-0	10	Meredith (og) [11], Morrison [76]	11,644
20	Dec 1	H	Preston NE	W	3-0	0-0	9	Kieftenbeld [46], Maghoma [61], Adams [77]	20,523
21	8	H	Bristol C	L	0-1	0-0	9		20,961
22	15	A	Blackburn R	D	2-2	0-1	10	Gardner, C (pen) [78], Adams [80]	13,622
23	22	A	Wigan Ath	W	3-0	2-0	8	Adams [26], Morrison [45], Maghoma [61]	13,774
24	26	H	Stoke C	W	2-0	1-0	7	Maghoma [43], Bogle [87]	26,344
25	29	H	Brentford	D	0-0	0-0	7		23,909
26	Jan 1	A	Sheffield W	D	1-1	0-1	8	Adams [48]	29,462
27	12	H	Middlesbrough	L	1-2	0-1	8	Adams [79]	21,420
28	18	A	Norwich C	L	1-3	1-3	9	Adams [14]	25,932
29	29	A	Swansea C	D	3-3	1-1	12	Maghoma [35], Morrison [67], Adams [71]	18,194
30	Feb 2	H	Nottingham F	W	2-0	1-0	8	Jota [13], Adams (pen) [90]	24,235
31	9	A	QPR	W	4-3	4-1	8	Adams 3 [21, 26, 42], Dean [36]	14,234
32	12	H	Bolton W	L	0-1	0-0	8		21,682
33	23	H	Blackburn R	D	2-2	1-0	8	Adams 2 [16, 85]	21,869
34	26	A	Bristol C	W	2-1	1-0	8	Mahoney [42], Morrison [47]	19,777
35	Mar 2	A	Hull C	L	0-2	0-1	8		12,551
36	10	H	Aston Villa	L	0-1	0-0	11		26,631
37	13	H	Millwall	L	0-2	0-2	12		20,151
38	16	A	Preston NE	L	0-1	0-0	13		17,509
39	29	A	WBA	L	2-3	1-0	18	Gardner, G [7], Jutkiewicz [59]	24,789
40	Apr 6	H	Leeds U	W	1-0	1-0	17	Adams [29]	24,197
41	10	H	Sheffield U	D	1-1	1-1	17	Morrison [42]	22,351
42	13	A	Ipswich T	D	1-1	1-0	18	Jutkiewicz [7]	17,248
43	19	H	Derby Co	D	2-2	2-2	18	Jutkiewicz [2], Morrison [18]	23,902
44	22	A	Rotherham U	W	3-1	0-1	17	Maghoma [56], Jota [63], Mrbati [90]	10,703
45	27	H	Wigan Ath	D	1-1	1-1	17	Jutkiewicz [2]	23,645
46	May 5	A	Reading	D	0-0	0-0	17		17,247

Final League Position: 17

GOALSCORERS

League (64): Adams 22 (1 pen), Jutkiewicz 14, Morrison 7, Maghoma 6, Jota 3, Gardner G 2, Mahoney 2, Bogle 1, Dean 1, Gardner C 1 (1 pen), Kieftenbeld 1, Mrbati 1, Pedersen 1, Solomon-Otabor 1, own goal 1.
FA Cup (0).
Carabao Cup (0).

Trueman C 2	Colin M 43	Morrison M 43	Dean H 44	Pedersen K 39	Jota R 33 + 7	Kieftenbeld M 34 + 2	Gardner C 5 + 16	Maghoma J 35 + 7	Adams C 43 + 3	Jutkiewicz L 44 + 2	N'Doye C 1 + 1	Solomon-Otabor V — + 8	Lubula B — + 3	Bogle O 3 + 12	Mahoney C 17 + 13	Camp L 44	Gardner G 39 + 1	Lakin C 5 + 5	Harding W 13 + 14	Roberts M 3 + 5	Dacres-Cogley J — + 1	Vassell I 2 + 12	Mrbati K 6 + 6	Davis D 8 + 3	Match No.
1	2	3	4	5	6^{3}	7	8^{2}	9	10^{1}	11	12	13	14												1
1	2	3	4	5	6^{2}		8■	9^{3}	10^{1}	11	7	13		12	14										2
	2	3	4	5	6	8		9	12	10				11^{1}		1	7^{2}	13							3
	2	3	4	5	6	8		9^{1}	12	10^{2}		13		11		1	7								4
	2	3	4	5	6^{1}	8		9^{2}	12	10		13		11^{3}	14	1	7								5
	2^{3}	3	4	5	9	8		6	10^{1}	11^{2}		13		14		1	7		12						6
	2	3	4	5	6	7		9	10^{2}	11^{1}		13		12		1	8								7
	2	3	4	5	6			9^{1}	11^{3}	10				12	13	1	8	7^{2}	14						8
	2	3	4	5	6^{3}	12		9	11	10^{2}				13		1	7^{1}	8	14						9
	2	3	4	5	6	12		9	11	10					13	1	8^{2}	7^{1}							10
	2	3	4	5	6^{1}	7■		9	11^{3}	10^{2}				13	14	1	8	12							11
	2	3^{2}	4	5	6	7		9^{1}	11^{3}	10			14		12	1	8			13					12
	2	3	4	5^{2}	6	7		12	10^{1}	11					9^{3}	1	8		13	14					13
	2	3	4	5	6^{1}	8		9^{2}	10	11^{3}		13	14		12	1	7								14
	2	3	4^{3}	5	6	7			11	10					9^{2}	1	8^{1}	14	13	12					15
	2	3	4	5	6	8			10	11					9	1	7^{1}		12						16
	2	3	4	5	6^{2}	8	13		10	11		12^{3}			9	1		7^{1}	14						17
	2	3	4	9		7	8^{2}	12	11	10^{1}				14	6^{3}	1		13	5						18
	2	3	4	5		8^{2}	13	9^{1}	11	10				14	6^{3}	1	7		12						19
	2	3	4	5		7		9^{2}	10	11^{3}				13	6^{1}	1	8		12		14				20
	2	3^{2}	4	5		8^{1}		9	10	11					6	1	7		13	12					21
	2		4	5	14	7^{3}	13	9	10	11					6^{2}	1	8		12	3^{1}					22
	5	3	4		12	8	14	9	10	11^{2}				13	6^{3}	1	7^{1}		2						23
	5	3	4		6	8	13	9	10^{1}	11				12		1	7^{2}		2						24
	5	3	4		6^{1}	8		9	10^{2}	11				12	13	1	7		2						25
	5	3	4		6	8	13	9^{2}	11	10					12	1	7^{1}		2						26
	2	3	4	5	6	8^{1}	12	9	11	10						1	7^{2}					13			27
	2	3	4	5	6^{3}	8^{1}	12	9	10	11^{2}					14	1	7					13			28
	2	3	4	5■	6	8	7^{2}	9^{3}	10	11^{1}						1	14		12			13			29
	5	3	4		9^{1}	8	14	6^{3}	10	11^{2}						1	7		2			12	13		30
	5	3	4		6	8	13	9^{3}	10^{2}	11^{1}						1	7		2			14	12		31
	5	3	4		6^{2}	7^{1}		9	10	11						1	8^{3}		2			13	12	14	32
	2	3	4	5	6^{2}	7		9^{1}	10	11^{3}					13	1	8					14	12		33
	2	4	3	5	13	7		12	10^{3}	11					9^{2}	1	8					14	6^{1}		34
	2^{2}	3	4	5			13	14	10	11					9^{1}	1	7		12				6	8^{3}	35
		3	4	5	6^{2}	7	14	9^{1}	10	11					13	1			2				12	8^{3}	36
		3	4	5		8^{2}	12	14	11	13					6	1	7		2			10^{3}	9^{1}		37
		4	3	5	12	8		9	10	11					6^{1}	1	7		2						38
	2	3	4	5	14		12	9^{2}	10^{1}	11					6	1	7					13		8^{3}	39
	2	4	3	5	14	8^{1}		9	10	11					6^{3}	1	7^{2}		13					12	40
	2	3	4	5	12		13	9	10	11					6^{7}	1	8							7^{1}	41
	2	4	3	5	6^{2}			13	10	11					12	1	7						9^{1}	8	42
	2	4	3	5	6			9	10	11^{1}						1	7					12		8	43
	2	4	3	5	6^{3}			9	11^{1}	10^{2}						1	7			14		13	12	8	44
	2			5	6		12		10^{2}	11						1	7^{1}	14	4	3		13	9	8^{3}	45
	2			5	6		7	14	10	12						1		8^{3}	4	3		11^{2}	9^{1}	13	46

FA Cup
Third Round West Ham U (a) 0-2

Carabao Cup
First Round Reading (a) 0-2

BLACKBURN ROVERS

FOUNDATION

It was in 1875 that some public school old boys called a meeting at which the Blackburn Rovers club was formed and the colours blue and white adopted. The leading light was John Lewis, later to become a founder of the Lancashire FA, a famous referee who was in charge of two FA Cup finals, and a vice-president of both the FA and the Football League.

Ewood Park, Blackburn, Lancashire BB2 4JF.

Telephone: (01254) 372 001.

Fax: (01254) 671 042.

Ticket Office: (01254) 372 000.

Website: www.rovers.co.uk

Email: enquiries@rovers.co.uk

Ground Capacity: 31,363.

Record Attendance: 62,522 v Bolton W, FA Cup 6th rd, 2 March 1929.

Pitch Measurements: 105m × 66m (115yd × 72yd).

Chief Executive: Steve Waggott.

Manager: Tony Mowbray.

Assistant Manager: Mark Venus.

Colours: Light blue and white halved shirts, white shorts, blue socks with white trim.

Year Formed: 1875.

Turned Professional: 1880.

Club Nickname: 'Rovers'.

Grounds: 1875, all matches played away; 1876, Oozehead Ground; 1877, Pleasington Cricket Ground; 1878, Alexandra Meadows; 1881, Leamington Road; 1890, Ewood Park.

First Football League Game: 15 September 1888, Football League, v Accrington (h) D 5–5 – Arthur; Beverley, James Southworth; Douglas, Almond, Forrest; Beresford (1), Walton, John Southworth (1), Fecitt (1), Townley (2).

Record League Victory: 9–0 v Middlesbrough, Division 2, 6 November 1954 – Elvy; Suart, Eckersley; Clayton, Kelly, Bell; Mooney (3), Crossan (2), Briggs, Quigley (3), Langton (1).

Record Cup Victory: 11–0 v Rossendale, FA Cup 1st rd, 13 October 1884 – Arthur; Hopwood, McIntyre; Forrest, Blenkhorn, Lofthouse; Sowerbutts (2), Jimmy Brown (1), Fecitt (4), Barton (3), Birtwistle (1).

Record Defeat: 0–8 v Arsenal, Division 1, 25 February 1933; 0-8 v Lincoln C, Division 2, 29 August 1953.

HONOURS

League Champions: Premier League – 1994–95; Division 1 – 1911–12, 1913–14; Division 2 – 1938–39; Division 3 – 1974–75.
Runners-up: Premier League – 1993–94; FL 1 – 2017–18; First Division – 2000–01; Division 2 – 1957–58; Division 3 – 1979–80.

FA Cup Winners: 1884, 1885, 1886, 1890, 1891, 1928.
Runners-up: 1882, 1960.

League Cup Winners: 2002.

Full Members' Cup Winners: 1987.

European Competitions
European Cup: 1995–96.
UEFA Cup: 1994–95, 1998–99, 2002–03, 2003–04, 2006–07, 2007–08.
Intertoto Cup: 2007.

THE SUN FACT FILE

Blackburn Rovers fans witnessed a total of 30 goals during three consecutive games at Ewood Park during the 1954–55 season. Successive matches saw Rovers beat Doncaster Rovers 7-2, lose 6-4 to Notts County and then beat Bristol Rovers 8-3. Tommy Briggs scored 10 of Rovers' 19 goals during this spell.

Most League Points (2 for a win): 60, Division 3, 1974–75.

Most League Points (3 for a win): 96, FL 1, 2017–18.

Most League Goals: 114, Division 2, 1954–55.

Highest League Scorer in Season: Ted Harper, 43, Division 1, 1925–26.

Most League Goals in Total Aggregate: Simon Garner, 168, 1978–92.

Most League Goals in One Match: 7, Tommy Briggs v Bristol R, Division 2, 5 February 1955.

Most Capped Player: Morten Gamst Pedersen, 70 (83), Norway.

Most League Appearances: Derek Fazackerley, 596, 1970–86.

Youngest League Player: Harry Dennison, 16 years 155 days v Bristol C, 8 April 1911.

Record Transfer Fee Received: £18,000,000 from Manchester C for Roque Santa Cruz, June 2009.

Record Transfer Fee Paid: £3,000,000 (rising to £10,000,000) to Arsenal for David Bentley, January 2006.

Football League Record: 1888 Founder Member of the League; 1936–39 Division 2; 1946–48 Division 1; 1948–58 Division 2; 1958–66 Division 1; 1966–71 Division 2; 1971–75 Division 3; 1975–79 Division 2; 1979–80 Division 3; 1980–92 Division 2; 1992–99 Premier League; 1999–2001 Division 1; 2001–12 Premier League; 2012–17 FL C; 2017–18 FL 1; 2018– FL C.

LATEST SEQUENCES

Longest Sequence of League Wins: 8, 1.3.1980 – 7.4.1980.

Longest Sequence of League Defeats: 7, 12.3.1966 – 16.4.1966.

Longest Sequence of League Draws: 5, 11.10.1975 – 1.11.1975.

Longest Sequence of Unbeaten League Matches: 23, 30.9.1987 – 27.2.1988.

Longest Sequence Without a League Win: 16, 11.11.1978 – 24.3.1979.

Successive Scoring Runs: 32 from 24.4.1954.

Successive Non-scoring Runs: 4 from 14.12.2015.

MANAGERS

Thomas Mitchell 1884–96
(*Secretary-Manager*)
J. Walmsley 1896–1903
(*Secretary-Manager*)
R. B. Middleton 1903–25
Jack Carr 1922–26
(*Team Manager under Middleton to 1925*)
Bob Crompton 1926–31
(*Hon. Team Manager*)
Arthur Barritt 1931–36
(*had been Secretary from 1927*)
Reg Taylor 1936–38
Bob Crompton 1938–41
Eddie Hapgood 1944–47
Will Scott 1947
Jack Bruton 1947–49
Jackie Bestall 1949–53
Johnny Carey 1953–58
Dally Duncan 1958–60
Jack Marshall 1960–67
Eddie Quigley 1967–70
Johnny Carey 1970–71
Ken Furphy 1971–73
Gordon Lee 1974–75
Jim Smith 1975–78
Jim Iley 1978
John Pickering 1978–79
Howard Kendall 1979–81
Bobby Saxton 1981–86
Don Mackay 1987–91
Kenny Dalglish 1991–95
Ray Harford 1995–96
Roy Hodgson 1997–98
Brian Kidd 1998–99
Graeme Souness 2000–04
Mark Hughes 2004–08
Paul Ince 2008
Sam Allardyce 2008–10
Steve Kean 2010–12
Henning Berg 2012
Michael Appleton 2013
Gary Bowyer 2013–15
Paul Lambert 2015–16
Owen Coyle 2016–17
Tony Mowbray February 2017–

TEN YEAR LEAGUE RECORD

		P	*W*	*D*	*L*	*F*	*A*	*Pts*	*Pos*
2009-10	PR Lge	38	13	11	14	41	55	50	10
2010-11	PR Lge	38	11	10	17	46	59	43	15
2011-12	PR Lge	38	8	7	23	48	78	31	19
2012-13	FL C	46	14	16	16	55	62	58	17
2013-14	FL C	46	18	16	12	70	62	70	8
2014-15	FL C	46	17	16	13	66	59	67	9
2015-16	FL C	46	13	16	17	46	46	55	15
2016-17	FL C	46	12	15	19	53	65	51	22
2017-18	FL 1	46	28	12	6	82	40	96	2
2018-19	FL C	46	16	12	18	64	69	60	15

DID YOU KNOW ?

Blackburn Rovers acted quickly when Accrington Stanley folded in 1962, signing up Mike Ferguson whose registration had transferred to the Football League. Ferguson went on to make more than 250 appearances for Rovers before moving on to Aston Villa in May 1968.

BLACKBURN ROVERS – SKY BET CHAMPIONSHIP 2018–19 LEAGUE RECORD

Match No.	Date	Venue	Opponents	Result	H/T Score	Lg Pos.	Goalscorers	Attendance
1	Aug 4	A	Ipswich T	D 2-2	2-1	7	Graham 20, Dack 29	18,940
2	11	H	Millwall	D 0-0	0-0	15		13,239
3	18	A	Hull C	W 1-0	1-0	10	Dack 43	12,233
4	22	H	Reading	D 2-2	0-2	9	Mulgrew 2 (2 pens) 51, 76	11,818
5	25	H	Brentford	W 1-0	0-0	5	Palmer 54	12,094
6	Sept 2	A	Bristol C	L 1-4	1-1	13	Mulgrew 13	19,769
7	15	H	Aston Villa	D 1-1	0-0	13	Dack 76	15,982
8	18	A	Derby Co	D 0-0	0-0	13		23,580
9	22	A	Stoke C	W 3-2	2-0	12	Dack 26, Graham 44, Reed 46	25,673
10	29	H	Nottingham F	D 2-2	0-0	13	Armstrong 65, Dack 74	14,440
11	Oct 3	H	Sheffield U	L 0-2	0-0	14		14,440
12	6	A	Bolton W	W 1-0	1-0	9	Dack 22	15,461
13	20	H	Leeds U	W 2-1	1-1	7	Graham 2, Lenihan 70	20,929
14	23	A	Swansea C	L 1-3	1-0	7	Mulgrew (pen) 26	18,035
15	27	A	WBA	D 1-1	0-1	12	Reed 71	23,820
16	Nov 3	H	QPR	W 1-0	0-0	8	Dack (pen) 87	13,294
17	10	H	Rotherham U	D 1-1	0-0	9	Dack 81	12,847
18	24	A	Preston NE	L 1-4	0-2	10	Graham 48	19,912
19	28	A	Wigan Ath	L 1-3	0-1	13	Burn (og) 83	10,777
20	Dec 1	H	Sheffield W	W 4-2	1-0	10	Graham 3 11, 66, 90, Dack 53	15,154
21	8	A	Middlesbrough	D 1-1	1-0	11	Mulgrew 22	21,985
22	15	H	Birmingham C	D 2-2	1-0	12	Graham 19, Armstrong 46	13,622
23	22	H	Norwich C	L 0-1	0-0	14		14,202
24	26	A	Leeds U	L 2-3	0-1	14	Mulgrew 2 (1 pen) 47 (p), 90	34,863
25	29	A	Sheffield U	L 0-3	0-0	15		27,384
26	Jan 1	H	WBA	W 2-1	0-0	15	Mulgrew 53, Dack 58	14,258
27	12	A	Millwall	W 2-0	0-0	14	Nuttall 86, Armstrong 87	13,862
28	19	H	Ipswich T	W 2-0	0-0	10	Graham (pen) 65, Nuttall 74	12,762
29	26	H	Hull C	W 3-0	2-0	8	Armstrong 10, Rodwell 18, Reed 73	13,589
30	Feb 2	A	Brentford	L 2-5	2-1	11	Dack 2, Graham 7	9972
31	9	H	Bristol C	L 0-1	0-0	13		13,593
32	13	A	Reading	L 1-2	0-1	14	Bell 82	11,271
33	17	H	Middlesbrough	L 0-1	0-1	14		13,249
34	23	A	Birmingham C	D 2-2	0-1	14	Mulgrew 52, Graham 83	21,869
35	Mar 2	A	Rotherham U	L 2-3	0-1	17	Bell 51, Mulgrew (pen) 90	9663
36	9	H	Preston NE	L 0-1	0-1	17		21,577
37	12	H	Wigan Ath	W 3-0	1-0	16	Graham 2 (1 pen) 39 (p), 54, Dack 86	12,763
38	16	A	Sheffield W	L 2-4	0-1	17	Conway 72, Bennett 88	24,608
39	30	A	Aston Villa	L 1-2	0-1	16	Bell 74	39,687
40	Apr 6	H	Stoke C	L 0-1	0-1	16		17,478
41	9	H	Derby Co	W 2-0	0-0	16	Rothwell 76, Dack 90	12,590
42	13	A	Nottingham F	W 2-1	1-0	15	Rothwell 29, Graham 49	27,786
43	19	A	QPR	W 2-1	1-0	14	Graham (pen) 22, Dack 46	13,632
44	22	H	Bolton W	W 2-0	1-0	14	Brereton 30, Armstrong 50	14,495
45	27	A	Norwich C	L 1-2	1-2	14	Travis 23	26,848
46	May 5	H	Swansea C	D 2-2	1-2	15	Lenihan 21, Dack 47	16,227

Final League Position: 15

GOALSCORERS

League (64): Dack 15 (1 pen), Graham 15 (3 pens), Mulgrew 10 (5 pens), Armstrong 5, Bell 3, Reed 3, Lenihan 2, Nuttall 2, Rothwell 2, Bennett 1, Brereton 1, Conway 1, Palmer 1, Rodwell 1, Travis 1, own goal 1.
FA Cup (3): Armstrong 1, Dack 1, Lenihan 1.
Carabao Cup (11): Armstrong 3 (1 pen), Dack 2, Palmer 2, Conway 1, Downing 1, Graham 1, Nuttall 1.

Raya D 41	Nyambe R 25 + 4	Lenihan D 34	Mulgrew C 28 + 1	Williams D 23 + 4	Smallwood R 29 + 3	Evans C 33 + 2	Samuel D 1 + 1	Dack B 40 + 2	Bennett E 38 + 2	Graham D 37 + 6	Palmer K 10 + 4	Nuttall J 2 + 13	Conway C 9 + 12	Bell A 35 + 3	Rothwell J 13 + 20	Armstrong A 31 + 13	Travis L 19 + 7	Brereton B 4 + 21	Reed H 28 + 5	Downing P 3	Rodwell J 16 + 5	Leutwiler J 5	Magliore T 2	Buckley J — + 2	Butterworth D — + 1	Chapman H — + 2	Davenport J — + 1	Match No.
1	2	3	4	5	6	7	8^2	9^3	10	11^1	12	13	14															1
1	2	3	4		7^2	6		9	8^3	11	10^1			5	12	13	14											2
1	2	3	4		6	7		9^3	10	12	8^2			5	14	11^1	13											3
1	2	3	4		6^2	7	13^3		8	11		14	12	5	10	9^1												4
1	2	3	4		6	7^1			10	12	8^2	11^3	13	5	9		14											5
1	2^3	3	4		6	7			8	11^2	10^1	14		5	13	9		12										6
1	2	3	4	14	6^3	7^1		10	8	11				5		9^2		12	13									7
1	2	3		4	6	7		9	13	12	10^3		8^1	5		11^1			14									8
1	2	3		4	6	7		9^2	8	11^3				5	12	14		13	10^1									9
1	2^2	4			6	7^1		9	10	11				5	14	12			8	3^3	13							10
1		3	12	4	7^3	6		9	2	11^1				5^2	14	10		13	8									11
1		3	4	5	12	13		9	2	11	8^1				10^3	14			7		6^2							12
1		3	4		6^3	7		9	2	11^2			14	5		10		13	8^1		12							13
1		3^1	4		7	6^2		9	2	11^3				5	14	10		13	8		12							14
1			4^3	5	6			11	2		8^2		9	12	10	14	13		7		3^1							15
		3		4	6^1	7		9	2	11^2	12			5	13	10^3		14	8			1						16
1	12	3			7^1			9	2	11^3	8			5	14	10		13	6^2		4							17
1	2	3	4	5	7^1			9	8	12	10^2				13	11^3		14	6									18
1	2^3		4	12	6^1	7		9		11^2			14	5		10		13	8		3							19
1	2		4	5	7	6^3		9^1		11^2			10			14	12	13	8	3								20
1	2		4	5	7^1	6		9		11			10^3		13	12		14	8^2	3								21
1	2	3	4		7	6		9		11^2			10^1	5		12		13	8									22
1	2	3	4^2	12	7	6^3		9		11	13			5		10^1		14	8									23
1	2^2	3	4	5	13	7		9		11				10	14	8^3			12		6^1							24
1		3	4	5	7■			12	2		8^2				10	13	9	11^1	6									25
1		3	4			7		9^2	2	11^1	14		12	5		10^3	6	13	8									26
1	12	3				6^1		9^3	2	13		11	10^2	5		14	7		8		4							27
1		3			14	6^1		9	2	11^3		13		5	12	10	7		8^2		4							28
1		3				6		9	2	11^2		12	13	5	14	8^1	7		10^3		4							29
1		3				7^2		9^1	2	11^3		13	12	5		8	6	14	10		4							30
1	12		3	5	6^2			9^3	2	11		14			13	10	7^1		8		4							31
1			4		7^2	8		12	2	14			11^3	5	13	10	6	9^1			3							32
1	14		4	5■		6^1		9	2	11				12		10	13	8^3	7		3^2							33
1	2		3		6			9	10	11				5		12	7		8^1		4							34
1	2		4		6^1			9	8^3	11		13		5	12	10^2	7		14		3							35
1	2		3^3	4	6^2	7		9	8	10		12		13	14	11			5^1									36
1	2			4				9	5	10^3		13	12	8^2	14	11^1	7		6				3					37
1	2			4		7^2		9	8	10^3			12		11	13	6		5^1				3	14				38
1	2	3	4					9^1	7^3	11^2			8	5	14	10	6	13	12									39
1	2^1	3	4^3	12	8^2	7			10	11				5	9	6	13	14										40
1		3		4		13		9	2	11^1		14	8	5	10^2	12	7		6^3									41
1		3		4		6^1		9^3	2	11^2		12		5	8	10	7	14			13							42
		3		4		6^3		9	2	11^2		13		5	8	10^1	7	14			12	1						43
	2	3		4				9^2	12					5	10	8	6^1	11			7^3	1		13	14			44
		3		4				9^1	2	11^3			13	5	10	8	6	12			7^2	1				14		45
		3		4		7^3		9	2^2	11^1			13	5	10	8	6					1				14	12	46

FA Cup

Third Round	Newcastle U	(a)	1-1
Replay	Newcastle U	(h)	2-4
(*aet*)			

Carabao Cup

First Round	Carlisle U	(a)	5-1
Second Round	Lincoln C	(h)	4-1
Third Round	Bournemouth	(a)	2-3

BLACKPOOL

FOUNDATION

Old boys of St John's School, who had formed themselves into a football club, decided to establish a club bearing the name of their town and Blackpool FC came into being at a meeting at the Stanley Arms Hotel in the summer of 1887. In their first season playing at Raikes Hall Gardens, the club won both the Lancashire Junior Cup and the Fylde Cup.

Bloomfield Road, Seasiders Way, Blackpool, Lancashire FY1 6JJ.

Telephone: (01253) 401 953 (option 1).

Fax: (01253) 405 011.

Ticket Office: (01253) 599 745.

Website: www.blackpoolfc.co.uk

Email: via website.

Ground Capacity: 17,338.

Record Attendance: 38,098 v Wolverhampton W, Division 1, 17 September 1955.

Pitch Measurements: 100m × 64m (109.5yd × 70yd).

Owner: Simon Sadler.

Managing Director: Ben Hatton.

Manager: Simon Grayson.

First-Team Coach: Ian Dawes.

Colours: Tangerine shirts with white trim, white shorts with tangerine trim, tangerine socks with white hoops.

Year Formed: 1887.

Turned Professional: 1887.

Previous Name: 'South Shore' combined with Blackpool in 1899, twelve years after the latter had been formed on the breaking up of the old 'Blackpool St John's' club.

Club Nickname: 'The Seasiders'.

Grounds: 1887, Raikes Hall Gardens; 1897, Athletic Grounds; 1899, Raikes Hall Gardens; 1899, Bloomfield Road.

First Football League Game: 5 September 1896, Division 2, v Lincoln C (a) L 1–3 – Douglas; Parr, Bowman; Stuart, Stirzaker, Norris; Clarkin, Donnelly, Robert Parkinson, Mount (1), Jack Parkinson.

Record League Victory: 7–0 v Reading, Division 2, 10 November 1928 – Mercer; Gibson, Hamilton, Watson, Wilson, Grant, Ritchie, Oxberry (2), Hampson (5), Tufnell, Neal. 7–0 v Preston NE (away), Division 1, 1 May 1948 – Robinson; Shimwell, Crosland; Buchan, Hayward, Kelly; Hobson, Munro (1), McIntosh (5), McCall, Rickett (1). 7–0 v Sunderland, Division 1, 5 October 1957 – Farm; Armfield, Garrett, Kelly J, Gratrix, Kelly H, Matthews, Taylor (2), Charnley (2), Durie (2), Perry (1).

Record Cup Victory: 7–1 v Charlton Ath, League Cup 2nd rd, 25 September 1963 – Harvey; Armfield, Martin; Crawford, Gratrix, Cranston; Lea, Ball (1), Charnley (4), Durie (1), Oates (1).

HONOURS

League Champions: Division 2 – 1929–30.
Runners-up: Division 1 – 1955–56; Division 2 – 1936–37, 1969–70; Division 4 – 1984–85.

FA Cup Winners: 1953.
Runners-up: 1948, 1951.

League Cup: semi-final – 1962.

League Trophy Winners: 2002, 2004.

Anglo-Italian Cup Winners: 1971.
Runners-up: 1972.

THE SUN FACT FILE

Cheung Chi Doy, who spent two years on Blackpool's books in the early 1960s, was only the second player of Chinese origin to appear in the Football League. Recruited from Hong Kong football he did well with the Seasiders' Central League team, scoring 23 goals from 44 appearances, and played two first-team games, finding the net in the 3-1 defeat to Sheffield Wednesday in November 1961.

Record Defeat: 1–10 v Small Heath, Division 2, 2 March 1901 and v Huddersfield T, Division 1, 13 December 1930.

Most League Points (2 for a win): 58, Division 2, 1929–30 and Division 2, 1967–68.

Most League Points (3 for a win): 86, Division 4, 1984–85.

Most League Goals: 98, Division 2, 1929–30.

Highest League Scorer in Season: Jimmy Hampson, 45, Division 2, 1929–30.

Most League Goals in Total Aggregate: Jimmy Hampson, 248, 1927–38.

Most League Goals in One Match: 5, Jimmy Hampson v Reading, Division 2, 10 November 1928; 5, Jimmy McIntosh v Preston NE, Division 1, 1 May 1948.

Most Capped Player: Jimmy Armfield, 43, England.

Most League Appearances: Jimmy Armfield, 568, 1952–71.

Youngest League Player: Matty Kay, 16 years 32 days v Scunthorpe U, 13 November 2005.

Record Transfer Fee Received: £6,750,000 from Liverpool for Charlie Adam, July 2011.

Record Transfer Fee Paid: £1,250,000 to Leicester C for D.J. Campbell, August 2010.

Football League Record: 1896 Elected to Division 2; 1899 Failed re-election; 1900 Re-elected; 1900–30 Division 2; 1930–33 Division 1; 1933–37 Division 2; 1937–67 Division 1; 1967–70 Division 2; 1970–71 Division 1; 1971–78 Division 2; 1978–81 Division 3; 1981–85 Division 4; 1985–90 Division 3; 1990–92 Division 4; 1992–2000 Division 2; 2000–01 Division 3; 2001–04 Division 2; 2004–07 FL 1; 2007–10 FL C; 2010–11 Premier League; 2011–15 FL C; 2015–16 FL 1; 2016–17 FL 2; 2017– FL 1.

MANAGERS

Tom Barcroft 1903–33 (*Secretary-Manager*)
John Cox 1909–11
Bill Norman 1919–23
Maj. Frank Buckley 1923–27
Sid Beaumont 1927–28
Harry Evans 1928–33 (*Hon. Team Manager*)
Alex 'Sandy' Macfarlane 1933–35
Joe Smith 1935–58
Ronnie Suart 1958–67
Stan Mortensen 1967–69
Les Shannon 1969–70
Bob Stokoe 1970–72
Harry Potts 1972–76
Allan Brown 1976–78
Bob Stokoe 1978–79
Stan Ternent 1979–80
Alan Ball 1980–81
Allan Brown 1981–82
Sam Ellis 1982–89
Jimmy Mullen 1989–90
Graham Carr 1990
Bill Ayre 1990–94
Sam Allardyce 1994–96
Gary Megson 1996–97
Nigel Worthington 1997–99
Steve McMahon 2000–04
Colin Hendry 2004–05
Simon Grayson 2005–08
Ian Holloway 2009–12
Michael Appleton 2012–13
Paul Ince 2013–14
José Riga 2014
Lee Clark 2014–15
Neil McDonald 2015–16
Gary Bowyer 2016–18
Terry McPhillips 2018–19
Simon Grayson July 2019–

LATEST SEQUENCES

Longest Sequence of League Wins: 9, 21.11.1936 – 1.1.1937.

Longest Sequence of League Defeats: 8, 26.11.1898 – 7.1.1899.

Longest Sequence of League Draws: 5, 4.12.1976 – 1.1.1977.

Longest Sequence of Unbeaten League Matches: 17, 6.4.1968 – 21.9.1968.

Longest Sequence Without a League Win: 23, 7.2.2015 – 29.8.2015.

Successive Scoring Runs: 33 from 23.2.1929.

Successive Non-scoring Runs: 5 from 25.11.1989.

TEN YEAR LEAGUE RECORD

		P	W	D	L	F	A	Pts	Pos
2009-10	FL C	46	19	13	14	74	58	70	6
2010-11	PR Lge	38	10	9	19	55	78	39	19
2011-12	FL C	46	20	15	11	79	59	75	5
2012-13	FL C	46	14	17	15	62	63	59	15
2013-14	FL C	46	11	13	22	38	66	46	20
2014-15	FL C	46	4	14	28	36	91	26	24
2015-16	FL 1	46	12	10	24	40	63	46	22
2016-17	FL 2	46	18	16	12	69	46	70	7
2017-18	FL 1	46	15	15	16	60	55	60	12
2018-19	FL 1	46	15	17	14	50	52	62	10

DID YOU KNOW ?

Blackpool attracted an average attendance of more than 20,000 for each of the first 14 post-war seasons. The club's highest ever average attendance of 26,336 was recorded during this period in the 1949–50 season.

BLACKPOOL – SKY BET LEAGUE ONE 2018–19 LEAGUE RECORD

Match No.	Date	Venue	Opponents	Result		H/T Score	Lg Pos.	Goalscorers	Attendance
1	Aug 4	A	Wycombe W	D	0-0	0-0	12		5115
2	11	H	Portsmouth	L	1-2	0-1	17	Cullen 81	4154
3	18	A	Shrewsbury T	D	0-0	0-0	19		5216
4	21	H	Coventry C	W	2-0	0-0	10	Cullen 48, Dodoo 80	3656
5	25	H	Accrington S	D	1-1	0-0	12	Delfouneso 66	3354
6	Sept 1	A	Walsall	D	0-0	0-0	11		4762
7	8	H	Bradford C	W	3-2	0-0	9	Spearing 2 (1 pen) 84 (p), 88, Tilt 90	4393
8	15	A	Plymouth Arg	W	1-0	1-0	9	Cullen 14	8658
9	22	H	Luton T	D	0-0	0-0	8		4124
10	29	A	Peterborough U	D	2-2	0-1	9	Gnanduillet 58, Delfouneso 66	6269
11	Oct 6	H	Rochdale	D	2-2	2-1	13	Thompson 5, Tilt 29	3520
12	20	H	AFC Wimbledon	W	2-0	1-0	13	Tilt 7, Bola 84	3246
13	23	H	Scunthorpe U	W	1-0	1-0	10	Gnanduillet 19	2769
14	27	A	Fleetwood T	L	2-3	1-2	12	Thompson 34, Delfouneso 59	5035
15	Nov 3	H	Bristol R	L	0-3	0-0	13		3227
16	6	A	Gillingham	W	1-0	0-0	9	Delfouneso 49	4055
17	17	A	Southend U	W	2-1	1-0	7	Turton 14, Gnanduillet 83	6882
18	24	H	Burton Alb	W	3-0	0-0	7	Gnanduillet 46, Thompson 49, Dodoo 57	3163
19	27	A	Doncaster R	L	0-2	0-1	8		6473
20	Dec 8	H	Charlton Ath	W	2-1	1-0	8	Gnanduillet 16, Delfouneso 87	3024
21	15	A	Oxford U	L	0-2	0-2	8		6003
22	22	H	Barnsley	L	0-1	0-0	8		4054
23	26	A	Rochdale	L	1-2	1-1	8	Nottingham 35	4006
24	29	A	AFC Wimbledon	D	0-0	0-0	8		4416
25	Jan 1	H	Sunderland	L	0-1	0-1	10		10,994
26	12	A	Portsmouth	W	1-0	0-0	9	Long 74	18,403
27	19	H	Shrewsbury T	D	0-0	0-0	8		3186
28	26	A	Coventry C	W	2-0	0-0	8	Delfouneso 47, Gnanduillet 52	9786
29	29	H	Wycombe W	D	2-2	0-1	8	Heneghan 50, Pritchard (pen) 83	2388
30	Feb 9	H	Walsall	W	2-0	1-0	8	Long 14, Pritchard 88	3252
31	12	A	Sunderland	D	1-1	1-0	8	Gnanduillet 31	27,580
32	16	A	Charlton Ath	D	0-0	0-0	8		17,267
33	23	H	Oxford U	L	0-1	0-1	9		4003
34	Mar 2	A	Bristol R	L	0-4	0-2	10		8496
35	5	A	Accrington S	W	2-1	1-1	8	Virtue 5, Spearing (pen) 81	3792
36	9	H	Southend U	D	2-2	1-1	8	Gnanduillet 27, Moore (og) 90	15,871
37	12	H	Doncaster R	D	1-1	0-0	8	Nottingham 49	7404
38	16	A	Burton Alb	L	0-3	0-2	9		2715
39	23	A	Bradford C	W	4-1	1-0	8	Gnanduillet 2 24, 68, Virtue 50, Taylor 80	16,307
40	30	H	Plymouth Arg	D	2-2	0-1	8	Bola 84, Tilt 90	8343
41	Apr 6	A	Luton T	D	2-2	1-1	8	Kirby 30, Virtue 62	10,028
42	13	H	Peterborough U	L	0-1	0-1	10		7477
43	19	A	Scunthorpe U	D	0-0	0-0	10		3795
44	22	H	Fleetwood T	W	2-1	1-1	9	Spearing (pen) 31, Delfouneso 90	11,713
45	27	A	Barnsley	L	1-2	1-1	10	Pritchard 15	14,703
46	May 4	H	Gillingham	L	0-3	0-3	10		9571

Final League Position: 10

GOALSCORERS

League (50): Gnanduillet 10, Delfouneso 7, Spearing 4 (3 pens), Tilt 4, Cullen 3, Pritchard 3 (1 pen), Thompson 3, Virtue 3, Bola 2, Dodoo 2, Long 2, Nottingham 2, Heneghan 1, Kirby 1, Taylor 1, Turton 1, own goal 1.
FA Cup (6): Dodoo 2, Cullen 1, Gnanduillet 1, Pritchard 1, Spearing 1 (1 pen).
Carabao Cup (8): Gnanduillet 2, Nottingham 2, Pritchard 2, O'Connor 1, Spearing 1.
Checkatrade Trophy (7): Dodoo 2, Davies 1, Gnanduillet 1, Guy 1, O'Connor 1, O'Sullivan 1.

Howard M 32	Turton O 32	O'Connor P 7 + 3	Heneghan B 41 + 1	Bunney J 4 – 1	Pritchard H 17 + 20	Spearing J 42	Taylor C 7 + 5	Nottingham M 15 + 14	Dodoo J 10 + 8	Delfouneso N 32 + 7	O'Sullivan J 4 + 9	Thompson J 31 + 7	Gnanduillet A 35 + 8	Bola M 35	Cullen M 8 + 4	Tilt C 37	Daniels D 21 + 3	Feeney L 24 + 10	McLaughlin R 1 + 5	Guy C 13 + 2	Mafoumbi C 14	Davies S — + 2	Anderton N 10	Long C 8 + 9	Sorensen E — + 1	Kirby N 6 + 5	Virtue M 11 + 2	Evans A 9 + 3	Boney M — + 1	Ryan J — + 1	Match No.
1	2	3	4	5	6	7	8^3	9^1	10^2	11	12	13	14																		1
1	2	4	3	5	6^2	7	8		10^1	11	12		14	9^3	13																2
1	5	4^1	2	9		7	8^2			10	6	13	11			3	12														3
1	8	13			11^1	6		2	9	12	14	7		5	10^3	4	3^2														4
1	8	3	4			6		2	9^1	11	13	7	14	5^2	10^3			12													5
1	8		4		13	6		2	11^1	9		7^3	14	5	10^2	3		12													6
1	2				9^1	6		14		8		7	12	5	11^3	4	3	10^2	13												7
1	2				9^2	6				8	12	7	14	5■	11^3	4	3■	10^1	13												8
1	2		3			6		13		8^1	9^3	7	14	5	11^2	4		10		12											9
1	2		3			7		12		9		6	10	5		4		11^1	13	8^2											10
1	2		3			6		12		8^1		9	11	5	14	4		10^2	13	7^3											11
1	2		14		11^1	6		13		9^2		8^3	10	5		4	3	12		7											12
1	5				14	6		2		9	13	8^1	10^2		12	4	3	11^3		7											13
1	2		3		12	8		14		11^1		6	10■	5	13	4		9^2		7^3											14
	2		3		6	7		12	14	8		9^3		5	11^2	4		10^1	13		1										15
	6		3		13	8	9^1	2		10		12		5	11^2	4				7	1										16
1	5		4		12	7		13	11^2	9			10	8		3	2			6^1											17
1	9^1		3		12	6^2	13	5	10^3			7	11	8		4	2	14													18
1			3	8^3	7^2	6	14	12	13	11		9	10			4	2		5^1												19
1	2	12	5				6^1		11^3	14		9	10	8		4^2	3	7		13											20
1	2^1		4		14	6			11^3	8	13	9	12	5			3	7		10^2											21
1		12	3		7	6		13			10^2	9	11	8		4^3	2	5^1				14									22
1		4	3	13	12	7		2		11^1	14	6■	10	5				9^3		8^2											23
1		4	3		12	7^1	9^3	2		11	6^2		10	5				13		8		14									24
1		3	4		13	6	5^1		12	9^2			10	8			2	11		7											25
			4		13	7		14		10^3		6	11	5			2	9^2		8^1	1		3	12							26
			4		12	7		13			14	6	10	5		3	2	9^3		8^1	1			11^2							27
	8^1		2		13	7				10		6	11	9		3	5	12			1		4^2								28
	6		2		12	7^3		4		10		8^1	11	9		3		5^2			1				13	14					29
1	8		3		6				14	9^3		7	10^1	5		4	2							11^2			12	13			30
1	8		3		6					9		7	10	5^1		4		12						13		14	11^2	2^3			31
1	8		3		9		13		12	14			10			4	2						5	11^1		7^2		6^3			32
1	8		3		9	7		14	13			12	10			4	2						5^2	11^1				6^3			33
1	8		3		9^1	7	14		13	11		6^3	10			4	2						5^2				12				34
1	2		4		14	6			10^3			13	11			3		9					5	12			7^1	8^2			35
1	2		3		9^1	7				11^3		14	10			4	12	6					5^2	13			8				36
1			3		13	6		12				7	11			4^2	2^3	10					5	8			9^1	14			37
1^3			4			6		2	13			7^2	11				3	10					5	8^1		14	9		12		38
			3		12	7^3	13	2		10			11^2	5		4		6			1					14	8	9^1			39
			3		14	7		2		10^1			11	5		4		6			1			12		13	8^3	9^2			40
	2		3		13	7				10^1		12	11	5		4		6^3			1			14		9^2	8				41
	2		3			7				10^1			11	5		4	13	6^2			1			12		9	8				42
	2^1		3			6				13		8	11	5		4		12			1			14		10^2	7	9^3			43
			3		13	7		2		12		6^1	10	5		4					1			11		9^3	8^2	14			44
			3		7^2	8		2		12		6	11	5		4		13			1			14		9^3		10^1			45
			3		11	7				13		6^3	9	8		2		14			1		4	10^1				5^2		12	46

FA Cup

First Round	Exeter C	(a)	3-2
Second Round	Solihull Moors	(a)	0-0
Replay	Solihull Moors	(h)	3-2
(*aet*)			
Third Round	Arsenal	(h)	0-3

Carabao Cup

First Round	Barnsley	(h)	3-1
Second Round	Doncaster R	(a)	2-1
Third Round	QPR	(h)	2-0
Fourth Round	Arsenal	(a)	1-2

Checkatrade Trophy

Group C (N)	Macclesfield T	(a)	3-3
(Macclesfield T won 5-3 on penalties)			
Group C (N)	WBA U21	(h)	1-2
Group C (N)	Accrington S	(h)	3-2

BOLTON WANDERERS

FOUNDATION

In 1874 boys of Christ Church Sunday School, Blackburn Street, led by their master Thomas Ogden, established a football club which went under the name of the school and whose president was vicar of Christ Church. Membership was 6d (two and a half pence). When their president began to lay down too many rules about the use of church premises, the club broke away and formed Bolton Wanderers in 1877, holding their earliest meetings at the Gladstone Hotel.

University of Bolton Stadium, Burnden Way, Lostock, Bolton BL6 6JW.

Telephone: (01204) 673 673. ***Fax:*** (01204) 673 773.

Ticket Office: (0844) 871 2932.

Website: www.bwfc.co.uk

Email: reception@bwfc.co.uk (or via website).

Ground Capacity: 28,723.

Record Attendance: 69,912 v Manchester C, FA Cup 5th rd, 18 February 1933 (at Burnden Park); 28,353 v Leicester C, Premier League, 23 December 2003 (at The Reebok Stadium).

Pitch Measurements: 102m × 65m (111.5yd × 71yd).

Manager: Phil Parkinson.

Assistant Manager: Steve Parkin.

Colours: White shirts with faint grey stripes and blue and red trim, blue shorts with white and red trim, white socks with red and blue trim.

Year Formed: 1874.

Turned Professional: 1880.

Previous Name: 1874, Christ Church FC; 1877, Bolton Wanderers.

Club Nickname: 'The Trotters'.

Grounds: Park Recreation Ground and Cockle's Field before moving to Pike's Lane ground 1881; 1895, Burnden Park; 1997, Reebok Stadium (renamed Macron Stadium 2014; University of Bolton Stadium 2018).

First Football League Game: 8 September 1888, Football League, v Derby Co (h) L 3–6 – Harrison; Robinson, Mitchell; Roberts, Weir, Bullough, Davenport (2), Milne, Coupar, Barbour, Brogan (1).

Record League Victory: 8–0 v Barnsley, Division 2, 6 October 1934 – Jones; Smith, Finney; Goslin, Atkinson, George Taylor; George T. Taylor (2), Eastham, Milsom (1), Westwood (4), Cook, (1 og).

Record Cup Victory: 13–0 v Sheffield U, FA Cup 2nd rd, 1 February 1890 – Parkinson; Robinson (1), Jones; Bullough, Davenport, Roberts; Rushton, Brogan (3), Cassidy (5), McNee, Weir (4).

HONOURS

League Champions: First Division – 1996–97; Division 2 – 1908–09, 1977–78; Division 3 – 1972–73.
Runners-up: Division 2 – 1899–1900, 1904–05, 1910–11, 1934–35; Second Division – 1992–93; FL 1 – 2016–17.

FA Cup Winners: 1923, 1926, 1929, 1958.
Runners-up: 1894, 1904, 1953.

League Cup: *Runners-up:* 1995, 2004.

League Trophy Winners: 1989.
Runners-up: 1986.

European Competitions
UEFA Cup: 2005–06, 2007–08.

THE SUN FACT FILE

Bolton Wanderers were required to play two games in the emergency wartime competitions on Good Friday of 1917. Kicking off at 11.30am, Wanderers lost 2-0 at Stockport County then quickly made their way over to Oldham for an afternoon fixture where they ran out 2-1 winners.

Record Defeat: 1–9 v Preston NE, FA Cup 2nd rd, 5 November 1887.

Most League Points (2 for a win): 61, Division 3, 1972–73.

Most League Points (3 for a win): 98, Division 1, 1996–97.

Most League Goals: 100, Division 1, 1996–97.

Highest League Scorer in Season: Joe Smith, 38, Division 1, 1920–21.

Most League Goals in Total Aggregate: Nat Lofthouse, 255, 1946–61.

Most League Goals in One Match: 5, Tony Caldwell v Walsall, Division 3, 10 September 1983.

Most Capped Player: Ricardo Gardner, 72 (112), Jamaica.

Most League Appearances: Eddie Hopkinson, 519, 1956–70.

Youngest League Player: Ray Parry, 15 years 267 days v Wolverhampton W, 13 October 1951.

Record Transfer Fee Received: £15,000,000 from Chelsea for Nicolas Anelka, January 2008.

Record Transfer Fee Paid: £8,250,000 to Toulouse for Johan Elmander, June 2008.

Football League Record: 1888 Founder Member of the League; 1899–1900 Division 2; 1900–03 Division 1; 1903–05 Division 2; 1905–08 Division 1; 1908–09 Division 2; 1909–10 Division 1; 1910–11 Division 2; 1911–33 Division 1; 1933–35 Division 2; 1935–64 Division 1; 1964–71 Division 2; 1971–73 Division 3; 1973–78 Division 2; 1978–80 Division 1; 1980–83 Division 2; 1983–87 Division 3; 1987–88 Division 4; 1988–92 Division 3; 1992–93 Division 2; 1993–95 Division 1; 1995–96 Premier League; 1996–97 Division 1; 1997–98 Premier League; 1998–2001 Division 1; 2001–12 Premier League; 2012–16 FL C; 2016–17 FL 1; 2017–19 FL C; 2019– FL 1.

LATEST SEQUENCES

Longest Sequence of League Wins: 11, 5.11.1904 – 2.1.1905.

Longest Sequence of League Defeats: 11, 7.4.1902 – 18.10.1902.

Longest Sequence of League Draws: 6, 25.1.1913 – 8.3.1913.

Longest Sequence of Unbeaten League Matches: 23, 13.10.1990 – 9.3.1991.

Longest Sequence Without a League Win: 26, 7.4.1902 – 10.1.1903.

Successive Scoring Runs: 24 from 22.11.1996.

Successive Non-scoring Runs: 7 from 25.8.2017.

MANAGERS

Tom Rawthorne 1874–85 (*Secretary*)
J. J. Bentley 1885–86 (*Secretary*)
W. G. Struthers 1886–87 (*Secretary*)
Fitzroy Norris 1887 (*Secretary*)
J. J. Bentley 1887–95 (*Secretary*)
Harry Downs 1895–96 (*Secretary*)
Frank Brettell 1896–98 (*Secretary*)
John Somerville 1898–1910
Will Settle 1910–15
Tom Mather 1915–19
Charles Foweraker 1919–44
Walter Rowley 1944–50
Bill Ridding 1951–68
Nat Lofthouse 1968–70
Jimmy McIlroy 1970
Jimmy Meadows 1971
Nat Lofthouse 1971 (*then Admin. Manager to 1972*)
Jimmy Armfield 1971–74
Ian Greaves 1974–80
Stan Anderson 1980–81
George Mulhall 1981–82
John McGovern 1982–85
Charlie Wright 1985
Phil Neal 1985–92
Bruce Rioch 1992–95
Roy McFarland 1995–96
Colin Todd 1996–99
Roy McFarland and Colin Todd 1995–96
Sam Allardyce 1999–2007
Sammy Lee 2007
Gary Megson 2007–09
Owen Coyle 2010–12
Dougie Freedman 2012–14
Neil Lennon 2014–16
Phil Parkinson June 2016–

TEN YEAR LEAGUE RECORD

		P	W	D	L	F	A	Pts	Pos
2009-10	PR Lge	38	10	9	19	42	67	39	14
2010-11	PR Lge	38	12	10	16	52	56	46	14
2011-12	PR Lge	38	10	6	22	46	77	36	18
2012-13	FL C	46	18	14	14	69	61	68	7
2013-14	FL C	46	14	17	15	59	60	59	14
2014-15	FL C	46	13	12	21	54	67	51	18
2015-16	FL C	46	5	15	26	41	81	30	24
2016-17	FL 1	46	25	11	10	68	36	86	2
2017-18	FL C	46	10	13	23	39	74	43	21
2018-19	FL C	46	8	8	30	29	78	32	23

DID YOU KNOW ?

On the first two occasions that Bolton were relegated to the third tier of English football their fate was sealed by Charlton Athletic. The games took place on 17 April 1971 and 14 May 1983 and on both occasions the Trotters went down to a 4-1 defeat at The Valley.

BOLTON WANDERERS – SKY BET CHAMPIONSHIP 2018–19 LEAGUE RECORD

Match No.	Date	Venue	Opponents	Result		H/T Score	Lg Pos.	Goalscorers	Attendance
1	Aug 4	A	WBA	W	2-1	1-1	3	Magennis [18], Wildschut [89]	25,901
2	11	H	Bristol C	D	2-2	0-0	7	Buckley [57], Magennis [60]	14,112
3	18	A	Reading	W	1-0	0-0	5	Wildschut [48]	13,318
4	22	H	Birmingham C	W	1-0	0-0	3	Magennis [73]	13,821
5	25	H	Sheffield U	L	0-3	0-2	3		14,848
6	Sept 1	A	Preston NE	D	2-2	2-2	7	Ameobi [38], Olkowski [40]	16,331
7	15	H	QPR	L	1-2	0-1	10	Magennis [69]	13,581
8	19	A	Middlesbrough	L	0-2	0-1	15		21,345
9	22	A	Ipswich T	D	0-0	0-0	15		14,755
10	29	H	Derby Co	W	1-0	1-0	14	Noone [10]	14,096
11	Oct 2	A	Stoke C	L	0-2	0-1	15		22,116
12	6	H	Blackburn R	L	0-1	0-1	16		15,461
13	20	A	Rotherham U	D	1-1	0-0	18	Doidge [84]	10,011
14	24	H	Nottingham F	L	0-3	0-1	18		13,195
15	27	H	Hull C	L	0-1	0-1	19		13,108
16	Nov 2	A	Aston Villa	L	0-2	0-1	19		30,802
17	10	H	Swansea C	L	0-1	0-1	23		14,090
18	24	A	Millwall	D	1-1	1-0	22	Beevers [12]	12,554
19	27	A	Sheffield W	L	0-1	0-0	23		20,861
20	Dec 1	H	Wigan Ath	D	1-1	1-1	22	Buckley [7]	15,237
21	8	A	Norwich C	L	2-3	0-1	23	Ameobi [63], Beevers [88]	25,811
22	15	H	Leeds U	L	0-1	0-0	23		17,484
23	22	A	Brentford	L	0-1	0-0	23		10,512
24	26	H	Rotherham U	W	2-1	1-1	22	Ameobi [33], O'Neil [65]	15,255
25	29	H	Stoke C	D	0-0	0-0	21		15,309
26	Jan 1	A	Hull C	L	0-6	0-1	22		12,418
27	12	A	Bristol C	L	1-2	0-0	23	Buckley [58]	19,730
28	21	H	WBA	L	0-2	0-1	23		14,750
29	29	H	Reading	D	1-1	0-0	23	Hobbs [90]	12,195
30	Feb 2	A	Sheffield U	L	0-2	0-0	23		26,131
31	9	H	Preston NE	L	1-2	0-1	23	Donaldson [90]	17,381
32	12	A	Birmingham C	W	1-0	0-0	23	Connolly [71]	21,682
33	16	H	Norwich C	L	0-4	0-3	23		14,006
34	23	A	Leeds U	L	1-2	1-1	23	Beevers [22]	34,144
35	Mar 2	A	Swansea C	L	0-2	0-0	23		17,880
36	9	H	Millwall	W	2-1	0-0	23	Olkowski [48], O'Neil [60]	13,035
37	12	H	Sheffield W	L	0-2	0-1	23		13,624
38	16	A	Wigan Ath	L	2-5	0-1	23	O'Neil [62], Ameobi [80]	13,664
39	30	A	QPR	W	2-1	1-0	23	Buckley [35], Connolly [71]	13,603
40	Apr 6	H	Ipswich T	L	1-2	0-2	23	Emmanuel (og) [90]	17,811
41	9	H	Middlesbrough	L	0-2	0-2	23		12,259
42	13	A	Derby Co	L	0-4	0-2	23		26,602
43	19	H	Aston Villa	L	0-2	0-0	23		17,344
44	22	A	Blackburn R	L	0-2	0-1	23		14,495
45	May 5	A	Nottingham F	L	0-1	0-1	23		27,578
46	7	H	Brentford	Match cancelled and Brentford awarded 0-1 win.					

Final League Position: 23

GOALSCORERS

League (29): Ameobi 4, Buckley 4, Magennis 4, Beevers 3, O'Neil 3, Connolly 2, Olkowski 2, Wildschut 2, Doidge 1, Donaldson 1, Hobbs 1, Noone 1, own goal 1.
FA Cup (6): Magennis 3, Beevers 1, Donaldson 1, own goal 1.
Carabao Cup (1): Oztumer 1.

Alnwick B 27	Olkowski P 34 + 3	Wheater D 32 + 1	Beevers M 31 + 1	Taylor A 26	Lowe J 35	Murphy L 7 + 4	Ameobi S 26 + 4	Vela J 12 + 5	Buckley W 23 + 10	Magennis J 29 + 13	Noone C 25 + 11	O'Neil G 24 + 5	Wildschut Y 4 + 12	Le Fondre A — + 1	Donaldson C 18 + 13	Oztumer E 8 + 9	Grounds J 12 + 1	Williams J 29 + 1	Doidge C 8 + 9	Hobbs J 24 + 1	Wilson M 13 + 3	Matthews R 18	Dyer L 2 + 5	Little M 1 + 1	Pritchard J 1 + 3	Connell L 8 + 2	Connolly C 15 + 1	Brockbank H 3	Muscatt J — + 1	Darcy R — + 1	Earing J — + 1	Match No.
1	2	3	4	5	6	7^1	8^3	9	10^2	11	12	13	14																			1
1	2	3	4	5	7	8^2		6	11^3	10	9^1	12	13	14																		2
1	2	3	4	5	7	8^2		6	11^3	10	9^1	13	12		14																	3
1	2	3	4	5	6		13		12	11	8^1	7	10^3		14	9^2																4
1	2	3	4		6	7^2	8	9	10^1	11^3			13		14	12	5															5
1	2	3	4	5^1	6		8			11	12	7	10^2				13	9														6
1	2	3	4		7^1		8^3			13	10	6	12			14	5^2	9	11													7
1	2	4	5		8			11^1		10		9	14			13	6^2	7		3^3	12											8
1	2	12			6				10^2	11	7^1		13		14	9^3	5	8		3	4■											9
	2	3			7			14	10	11^1	8^2	12				9^3	5	6	13	4		1										10
	2				7				10^3	11^1	8^2		12		13	9	5	6	14	3	4	1										11
	2	3			7				10^1	11	8^2		12			9	5^3	6	14	4		1	13									12
1	5	3			6			12		11		7^1	13		10			8^2	14	2	4		9^3									13
1		3		5^1	7^3			9		11	8		10^2		12	13		6	14	4				2								14
1	5^1		4					7	12	13					10	9		6	11	3	2		8^2									15
1	2	3		5	7				10^3	13	8				11^1	9^2		6	14	4			12									16
1	2		4	5^1	7		8		10^2	13	12				11^2	9		6	14	3												17
1	2	3	4	5	9		7		10^1	11^2	13				12			8			6											18
1	2^1		4	5	9		7		14	11^3			10		12			8	13	3	6^2											19
1	2		4	5	7		8^2		10^1	12	9		13					6	11	3												20
1	2^3		4	5	7		9■		10^2	13	8^1	14						6	11	3			12									21
1	2	3		5	7			9	10^1	11^3	8		12			14		6^2	13	4												22
1	2^1	3		5	8		10		9^3	13	12	6			14				11^2	4	7											23
1	12	3	4	5^1	2		9^2		14	13		6			11^3			8	10		7											24
1		3	4		2		10	9^1		12	13				8^2		5	7	11		6											25
1	14	3	4		2		10^1	9			13	8			7^2	12	5		11		6^3											26
1	2	3	4		7	6^2	10	13	8^3	11	9				12		5^1						14									27
1	2		4	5	7	8^3	6		12	13	9^2	10			11^1					3					14							28
	2^3	3		5	6		8		12	14	10^1	9			11					4		1			13	7^2						29
		3		5	2		10	9^1		12		8			11					4		1				7	6					30
		4			2		10	12		11	6^1	7			13		5^2				3	1			14	9^3	8					31
	2	4	5		8	12		13		10	6	7^1			11						3^2	1					9					32
	2	4	5		3	8	13	7^3	14	11	6^1				10^2			12				1					9					33
	2	3	4		7	14	12		13	11	9^1	6			10^2			8^3				1					5					34
	2	3■	4			13	6		12	10^1	9■	7			11^2					14		1				8^3	5					35
	2		4	5			10		9^1	11		6						7^2		3	13	1	12				8					36
	2		4		7		10		12	11	9^2	6^3			13			8^1		3		1				14	5					37
	12		4	5	2^2		13		9^1	11	14	6			10^3			7		3		1					8					38
	2	3	4	5			6^1		8^2	11	12	10			13			7				1					8					39
	2	3	4	5^3			6		9^2	11	14	10^1				13		7				1				12	8					40
	5	3	4				10			11	9	8				12		6^1			2	1				7^2	13					41
		3	4	5			6^1		9^2		13	10			11			7				1		12		8	2					42
1		3^1	12	5					9	13		6^3			11^2	14		7		4						8	10	2				43
1			4^2	5		13	7				10				11			8^1		3	12					6	9	2^3	14			44
				5					6	11	10^2	7					4			3		1			8^1		9	2		12	13	45
																																46

FA Cup
Third Round Walsall (h) 5-2
Fourth Round Bristol C (a) 1-2

Carabao Cup
First Round Leeds U (a) 1-2

AFC BOURNEMOUTH

FOUNDATION

There was a Bournemouth FC as early as 1875, but the present club arose out of the remnants of the Boscombe St John's club (formed 1890). The meeting at which Boscombe FC came into being was held at a house in Gladstone Road in 1899. They began by playing in the Boscombe and District Junior League.

Vitality Stadium, Dean Court, Kings Park, Bournemouth, Dorset BH7 7AF.

Telephone: (0344) 576 1910.

Fax: (01202) 726 373.

Ticket Office: (0344) 576 1910.

Website: www.afcb.co.uk

Email: enquiries@afcb.co.uk

Ground Capacity: 11,329.

Record Attendance: 28,799 v Manchester U, FA Cup 6th rd, 2 March 1957.

Pitch Measurements: 105m × 68m (115yd × 74.5yd).

Chairman: Jeff Mostyn.

Chief Executive: Neill Blake.

Manager: Eddie Howe.

Assistant Manager: Jason Tindall.

Colours: Red and black striped shirts, black shorts with red trim, black socks with red trim.

Year Formed: 1899.

Turned Professional: 1910.

Previous Names: 1890, Boscombe St John's; 1899, Boscombe FC; 1923, Bournemouth & Boscombe Ath FC; 1972, AFC Bournemouth.

Club Nickname: 'Cherries'.

Grounds: 1899, Castlemain Road, Pokesdown; 1910, Dean Court (renamed Fitness First Stadium 2001, Seward Stadium 2011, Goldsands Stadium 2012, Vitality Stadium 2015).

First Football League Game: 25 August 1923, Division 3 (S), v Swindon T (a) L 1–3 – Heron; Wingham, Lamb; Butt, Charles Smith, Voisey; Miller, Lister (1), Davey, Simpson, Robinson.

Record League Victory: 8–0 v Birmingham C, FL C, 25 October 2014 – Boruc; Francis, Elphick, Cook, Daniels; Ritchie (1), Arter (Gosling), Surman, Pugh (3); Pitman (1) (Rantie 2 (1 pen)), Wilson (1) (Fraser). 10–0 win v Northampton T at start of 1939–40 expunged from the records on outbreak of war.

Record Cup Victory: 11–0 v Margate, FA Cup 1st rd, 20 November 1971 – Davies; Machin (1), Kitchener, Benson, Jones, Powell, Cave (1), Boyer, MacDougall (9 incl. 1p), Miller, Scott (De Garis).

Record Defeat: 0–9 v Lincoln C, Division 3, 18 December 1982.

HONOURS

League Champions: FL C – 2014–15; Division 3 – 1986–87.
Runners-up: FL 1 – 2012–13; Division 3S – 1947–48; FL 2 – 2009–10; Division 4 – 1970–71.

FA Cup: 6th rd – 1957.

League Cup: quarter-final – 2015, 2018, 2019.

League Trophy Winners: 1984.
Runners-up: 1998.

THE Sun FACT FILE

Following relegation to the fourth tier of English football Bournemouth & Boscombe Athletic underwent a major rebranding in the summer of 1970. The club name was changed to the snappier AFC Bournemouth, the team adopted red and black striped shirts based on those of AC Milan and a Public Relations officer was appointed. The changes were successful and the Cherries were promoted back to the Third Division at the first attempt.

Most League Points (2 for a win): 62, Division 3, 1971–72.

Most League Points (3 for a win): 97, Division 3, 1986–87.

Most League Goals: 98, FL C, 2014–15.

Highest League Scorer in Season: Ted MacDougall, 42, 1970–71.

Most League Goals in Total Aggregate: Ron Eyre, 202, 1924–33.

Most League Goals in One Match: 4, Jack Russell v Clapton Orient, Division 3 (S), 7 January 1933; 4, Jack Russell v Bristol C, Division 3 (S), 28 January 1933; 4, Harry Mardon v Southend U, Division 3 (S), 1 January 1938; 4, Jack McDonald v Torquay U, Division 3 (S), 8 November 1947; 4, Ted MacDougall v Colchester U, 18 September 1970; 4, Brian Clark v Rotherham U, 10 October 1972; 4, Luther Blissett v Hull C, 29 November 1988; 4, James Hayter v Bury, Division 2, 21 October 2000.

Most Capped Player: Tokelo Rantie, 24 (41), South Africa.

Most League Appearances: Steve Fletcher, 628, 1992–2007; 2008–13.

Youngest League Player: Jimmy White, 15 years 321 days v Brentford, 30 April 1958.

Record Transfer Fee Received: £20,000,000 (rising to £25,000,000) from Aston Villa for Tyrone Mings, July 2019.

Record Transfer Fee Paid: £25,000,000 to Levante for Jefferson Lerma, August 2018.

Football League Record: 1923 Elected to Division 3 (S) and remained a Third Division club for record number of years until 1970; 1970–71 Division 4; 1971–75 Division 3; 1975–82 Division 4; 1982–87 Division 3; 1987–90 Division 2; 1990–92 Division 3; 1992–2002 Division 2; 2002–03 Division 3; 2003–04 Division 2; 2004–08 FL 1; 2008–10 FL 2; 2010–13 FL 1; 2013–15 FL C; 2015– Premier League.

MANAGERS

Vincent Kitcher 1914–23 (*Secretary-Manager*)
Harry Kinghorn 1923–25
Leslie Knighton 1925–28
Frank Richards 1928–30
Billy Birrell 1930–35
Bob Crompton 1935–36
Charlie Bell 1936–39
Harry Kinghorn 1939–47
Harry Lowe 1947–50
Jack Bruton 1950–56
Fred Cox 1956–58
Don Welsh 1958–61
Bill McGarry 1961–63
Reg Flewin 1963–65
Fred Cox 1965–70
John Bond 1970–73
Trevor Hartley 1974–75
John Benson 1975–78
Alec Stock 1979–80
David Webb 1980–82
Don Megson 1983
Harry Redknapp 1983–92
Tony Pulis 1992–94
Mel Machin 1994–2000
Sean O'Driscoll 2000–06
Kevin Bond 2006–08
Jimmy Quinn 2008
Eddie Howe 2008–11
Lee Bradbury 2011–12
Paul Groves 2012
Eddie Howe October 2012–

LATEST SEQUENCES

Longest Sequence of League Wins: 8, 12.3.2013 – 20.4.2013.

Longest Sequence of League Defeats: 7, 13.8.1994 – 13.9.1994.

Longest Sequence of League Draws: 5, 25.4.2000 – 19.8.2000.

Longest Sequence of Unbeaten League Matches: 18, 6.3.1982 – 28.8.1982.

Longest Sequence Without a League Win: 14, 6.3.1974 – 27.4.1974.

Successive Scoring Runs: 31 from 28.10.2000.

Successive Non-scoring Runs: 6 from 1.2.1975.

TEN YEAR LEAGUE RECORD

		P	*W*	*D*	*L*	*F*	*A*	*Pts*	*Pos*
2009-10	FL 2	46	25	8	13	61	44	83	2
2010-11	FL 1	46	19	14	13	75	54	71	6
2011-12	FL 1	46	15	13	18	48	52	58	11
2012-13	FL 1	46	24	11	11	76	53	83	2
2013-14	FL C	46	18	12	16	67	66	66	10
2014-15	FL C	46	26	12	8	98	45	90	1
2015-16	PR Lge	38	11	9	18	45	67	42	16
2016-17	PR Lge	38	12	10	16	55	67	46	9
2017-18	PR Lge	38	11	11	16	45	61	44	12
2018-19	PR Lge	38	13	6	19	56	70	45	14

DID YOU KNOW ?

AFC Bournemouth reached their first final of a significant competition in the 1945–46 season, defeating Queens Park Rangers in the semi-final. The final was played at Stamford Bridge in front of an attendance of 19,715 with an early goal from Jack MacDonald giving the Cherries a 1-0 victory over Walsall.

AFC BOURNEMOUTH – PREMIER LEAGUE 2018–19 LEAGUE RECORD

Match No.	*Date*	*Venue*	*Opponents*	*Result*	*H/T Score*	*Lg Pos.*	*Goalscorers*	*Attendance*
1	Aug 11	H	Cardiff C	W 2-0	1-0	2	Fraser [24], Wilson [90]	10,353
2	18	A	West Ham U	W 2-1	0-1	3	Wilson [60], Cook, S [66]	56,888
3	25	H	Everton	D 2-2	0-0	3	King (pen) [75], Ake [79]	10,654
4	Sept 1	A	Chelsea	L 0-2	0-0	6		40,178
5	15	H	Leicester C	W 4-2	3-0	5	Fraser 2 [19, 37], King (pen) [41], Smith [81]	10,543
6	22	A	Burnley	L 0-4	0-2	7		18,636
7	Oct 1	H	Crystal Palace	W 2-1	1-0	7	Brooks [5], Stanislas (pen) [87]	10,199
8	6	A	Watford	W 4-0	3-0	5	Brooks [14], King 2 (1 pen) [33 (p), 45], Wilson [47]	20,139
9	20	H	Southampton	D 0-0	0-0	6		10,986
10	27	A	Fulham	W 3-0	1-0	6	Wilson 2 (1 pen) [14 (p), 85], Brooks [72]	25,071
11	Nov 3	H	Manchester U	L 1-2	1-1	6	Wilson [11]	10,792
12	10	A	Newcastle U	L 1-2	1-2	6	Lerma [45]	49,266
13	25	H	Arsenal	L 1-2	1-1	8	King [45]	10,792
14	Dec 1	A	Manchester C	L 1-3	1-1	9	Wilson [44]	54,409
15	4	H	Huddersfield T	W 2-1	2-1	6	Wilson [5], Fraser [22]	9980
16	8	H	Liverpool	L 0-4	0-1	8		10,752
17	15	A	Wolverhampton W	L 0-2	0-1	11		30,997
18	22	H	Brighton & HA	W 2-0	1-0	8	Brooks 2 [21, 77]	10,491
19	26	A	Tottenham H	L 0-5	0-3	11		45,154
20	30	A	Manchester U	L 1-4	1-3	12	Ake [45]	74,556
21	Jan 2	H	Watford	D 3-3	3-3	12	Ake [34], Wilson [37], Fraser [40]	10,261
22	13	A	Everton	L 0-2	0-0	12		38,113
23	19	H	West Ham U	W 2-0	0-0	12	Wilson [53], King [90]	10,495
24	30	H	Chelsea	W 4-0	0-0	10	King 2 [47, 74], Brooks [63], Daniels [90]	10,227
25	Feb 2	A	Cardiff C	L 0-2	0-1	10		31,939
26	9	A	Liverpool	L 0-3	0-2	11		53,178
27	23	H	Wolverhampton W	D 1-1	1-0	10	King (pen) [14]	10,671
28	27	A	Arsenal	L 1-5	1-2	12	Mousset [30]	59,618
29	Mar 2	H	Manchester C	L 0-1	0-0	12		10,699
30	9	A	Huddersfield T	W 2-0	1-0	12	Wilson [20], Fraser [66]	22,304
31	16	H	Newcastle U	D 2-2	0-1	11	King 2 (1 pen) [48 (p), 81]	10,625
32	30	A	Leicester C	L 0-2	0-1	12		31,530
33	Apr 6	H	Burnley	L 1-3	1-2	13	Barnes (og) [4]	10,446
34	13	A	Brighton & HA	W 5-0	1-0	12	Gosling [33], Fraser [55], Brooks [74], Wilson [82], Stanislas [90]	30,460
35	20	H	Fulham	L 0-1	0-0	13		10,511
36	27	A	Southampton	D 3-3	2-1	14	Gosling [20], Wilson 2 [32, 86]	31,310
37	May 4	H	Tottenham H	W 1-0	0-0	13	Ake [90]	10,630
38	12	A	Crystal Palace	L 3-5	1-3	14	Lerma [45], Ibe [56], King [73]	25,433

Final League Position: 14

GOALSCORERS

League (56): Wilson 14 (1 pen), King 12 (5 pens), Brooks 7, Fraser 7, Ake 4, Gosling 2, Lerma 2, Stanislas 2 (1 pen), Cook S 1, Daniels 1, Ibe 1, Mousset 1, Smith 1, own goal 1.
FA Cup (1): Pugh 1.
Carabao Cup (8): Ibe 2 (1 pen), Stanislas 2, Cook S 1, Fraser 1, Mousset 1, Wilson 1.

Begovic A 24	Smith A 25	Cook S 31	Ake N 38	Daniels C 17 + 4	Brooks D 29 + 1	Surman A 16 + 2	Gosling D 19 + 6	Fraser R 35 + 3	Wilson C 29 + 1	King J 34 + 1	Francis S 13 + 4	Mousset L 1 + 23	Defoe J — + 4	Cook L 8 + 5	Ibe J 9 + 10	Lerma J 29 + 1	Rico D 5 + 7	Stanislas J 11 + 12	Mings T 2 + 3	Clyne N 13 + 1	Boruc A 12	Mepham C 10 + 3	Solanke D 2 + 8	Surridge S — + 2	Simpson J 4 + 2	Hyndman E — + 1	Travers M 2	*Match No.*
1	2^{7}	3	4	5	6^{3}	7	8	9	10^{1}	11	12	13	14															1
1	2	3	4	5	6^{2}	7	8	9	10	11^{1}	12			13														2
1	2	3	4	5	6^{3}	7^{2}	8	9	10	11^{1}		14		13	12													3
1	5^{1}	3	4				7	9	10	11^{2}	2	12		14	13	6^{3}	8											4
1	2	3	4		6^{2}		8	9	11	10^{3}	12	14		13		7^{1}	5											5
1	2^{3}	3	4		6	8		9	10^{2}	11	12		14			7	5^{1}	13										6
1	5	3	4		6^{1}		12	9	11	10^{2}	2			8		7		13										7
1	5	3	4		8^{1}	14	13	9^{3}	11	10	2			8^{2}		7		12										8
1	5	3	4		6^{1}		14	9^{3}	11	10^{2}	2			8	13	7		12										9
1	5	3	4	8	9^{2}		12	11^{3}	10		2		14	6^{1}		7		13										10
1	5	3	4		10	14	12	9^{1}	11		2			7^{2}	13	8		6^{3}										11
1	5^{1}	3	4	12	10		13	9	11		2		14	7	6^{2}	8^{3}												12
1		3	4	5	6^{3}		7^{2}	9	10	11^{1}	2	14		13		8		12										13
1		3	4	6	12	9		10^{3}	11^{1}	7^{2}	2	13		8				14	5									14
1		3	4	5	6^{3}			9^{1}	11	10^{2}	2	13		7		8		12	14									15
1		3	4	5^{3}	6^{2}	8		10		11	2	12				7	13	9^{1}	14									16
1		2	3	8		6		10	13	11		14			5^{1}	7	12	9^{2}	4^{3}									17
1		3	4	5	6^{1}	8		12	10	11^{3}	2	13			14	7		9^{2}										18
1		3	4	5	6^{1}	7		9	11^{2}	14	2^{3}	13				8	12	10										19
1		2	3^{3}	4	6^{2}	7		13	11^{1}	10		12			5		9	8	14									20
1		3	4	5	6		7	9^{2}	10^{1}	11		13			12	8		2										21
1	5	3	4		10^{2}		7	9		11		12			13	8		6^{1}		2								22
	5	3	4	13	6^{3}		7	9^{2}	11^{1}	10		14				8		12		2	1							23
	5	3	4	13	10^{3}	8	7	9^{2}		11					12			6^{1}		2	1	14						24
	5	3	4			8	7^{3}	9		10		12			13	14		6^{2}		2	1		11^{1}					25
	2	3	4			9	7	10		11		13			6^{2}	8^{3}	5^{1}				1	14	12					26
	5		4				8	9		10		12			6	7				2	1	3	11^{1}					27
	5^{3}		4	12		8	7	9^{2}		10		11			6^{1}		13			2	1	3		14				28
	7		5	6	8^{3}	9		10		11		12			13		14			2^{2}	1	3			4^{1}			29
	2^{3}		4	5	6^{2}	8		9	10	11^{1}		14				7				12	1	3	13					30
			4	5	7			9	10	11					6^{1}	8				2	1	3	12					31
1			4	5^{3}	6		7	9	11	10^{1}						8^{2}	12	14		2		3	13					32
1	5		4		6		7^{3}	9	11	10						8^{2}	12	14		2^{1}		3	13					33
	5	3^{2}	4		9		6	8	11^{1}	10^{3}						7		13			1	2	12		14			34
		4	5		6		7	9	11	10^{3}		14				8		2^{1}			1	3^{2}	13		12			35
		4	5		7		9^{2}	12	11	10						8				2^{3}	1	3^{1}	14		6	13		36
	2	3	8					6	11	9		12			10^{1}	7				5					4		1	37
	2	3	8					9	11	10		13			6^{2}	7				5^{3}		12		14	4^{1}		1	38

FA Cup

Third Round	Brighton & HA	(h)	1-3

Carabao Cup

Second Round	Milton Keynes D	(h)	3-0
Third Round	Blackburn R	(h)	3-2
Fourth Round	Norwich C	(h)	2-1
Quarter-Final	Chelsea	(a)	0-1

BRADFORD CITY

FOUNDATION

Bradford was a rugby stronghold around the turn of the 20th century but after Manningham RFC held an archery contest to help them out of financial difficulties in 1903, they were persuaded to give up the handling code and turn to soccer. So they formed Bradford City and continued at Valley Parade. Recognising this as an opportunity to spread the dribbling code in this part of Yorkshire, the Football League immediately accepted the new club's first application for membership of the Second Division.

Northern Commercials Stadium, Valley Parade, Bradford, West Yorkshire BD8 7DY.

Telephone: (01274) 773 355.

Fax: (01274) 773 356.

Ticket Office: (01274) 770 012.

Website: www.bradfordcityfc.co.uk

Email: support@bradfordcityfc.co.uk

Ground Capacity: 25,136.

Record Attendance: 39,146 v Burnley, FA Cup 4th rd, 11 March 1911.

Pitch Measurements: 103.5m × 64m (113yd × 70yd).

Chief Executive Officer: Julian Rhodes.

Manager: Gary Bowyer.

Assistant Manager: Martin Drury.

Colours: Claret shirts with black and amber trim, claret shorts with amber trim, claret socks with amber trim.

Year Formed: 1903.

Turned Professional: 1903.

Club Nickname: 'The Bantams'.

Ground: 1903, Valley Parade (renamed Bradford & Bingley Stadium 1999, Intersonic Stadium 2007, Coral Windows Stadium 2007, Northern Commercials Stadium 2016).

First Football League Game: 1 September 1903, Division 2, v Grimsby T (a) L 0–2 – Seymour; Wilson, Halliday; Robinson, Millar, Farnall; Guy, Beckram, Forrest, McMillan, Graham.

Record League Victory: 11–1 v Rotherham U, Division 3 (N), 25 August 1928 – Sherlaw; Russell, Watson; Burkinshaw (1), Summers, Bauld; Harvey (2), Edmunds (3), White (3), Cairns, Scriven (2).

Record Cup Victory: 11–3 v Walker Celtic, FA Cup 1st rd (replay), 1 December 1937 – Parker; Rookes, McDermott; Murphy, Mackie, Moore; Bagley (1), Whittingham (1), Deakin (4 incl. 1p), Cooke (1), Bartholomew (4).

Record Defeat: 1–9 v Colchester U, Division 4, 30 December 1961.

Most League Points (2 for a win): 63, Division 3 (N), 1928–29.

HONOURS

League Champions: Division 2 – 1907–08; Division 3 – 1984–85; Division 3N – 1928–29.
Runners-up: First Division – 1998–99; Division 4 – 1981–82.

FA Cup Winners: 1911.

League Cup: *Runners-up:* 2013.

European Competitions
Intertoto Cup: 2000.

THE SUN FACT FILE

Bradford City went on a tour of Continental Europe in May 1914 after winning promotion to Division One. They won nine out of the ten games they played in Belgium, Germany and Switzerland with the only defeat coming against a representative team from the Frankfurt Union League. The biggest victory was 9-1 against a Munich team when Jimmy McIlvenney netted four goals and Oscar Fox a hat-trick. It was the third time the Bantams had toured Europe.

Most League Points (3 for a win): 94, Division 3, 1984–85.

Most League Goals: 128, Division 3 (N), 1928–29.

Highest League Scorer in Season: David Layne, 34, Division 4, 1961–62.

Most League Goals in Total Aggregate: Bobby Campbell, 121, 1981–84, 1984–86.

Most League Goals in One Match: 7, Albert Whitehurst v Tranmere R, Division 3 (N), 6 March 1929.

Most Capped Player: Jamie Lawrence, 19 (24), Jamaica.

Most League Appearances: Cec Podd, 502, 1970–84.

Youngest League Player: Robert Cullingford, 16 years 141 days v Mansfield T, 22 April 1970.

Record Transfer Fee Received: £2,000,000 from Newcastle U for Des Hamilton, March 1997; £2,000,000 from Newcastle U for Andrew O'Brien, March 2001.

Record Transfer Fee Paid: £2,500,000 to Leeds U for David Hopkin, July 2000.

Football League Record: 1903 Elected to Division 2; 1908–22 Division 1; 1922–27 Division 2; 1927–29 Division 3 (N); 1929–37 Division 2; 1937–61 Division 3; 1961–69 Division 4; 1969–72 Division 3; 1972–77 Division 4; 1977–78 Division 3; 1978–82 Division 4; 1982–85 Division 3; 1985–90 Division 2; 1990–92 Division 3; 1992–96 Division 2; 1996–99 Division 1; 1999–2001 Premier League; 2001–04 Division 1; 2004–07 FL 1; 2007–13 FL 2; 2013–19 FL 1; 2019– FL 2.

LATEST SEQUENCES

Longest Sequence of League Wins: 10, 26.11.1983 – 3.2.1984.

Longest Sequence of League Defeats: 8, 21.1.1933 – 11.3.1933.

Longest Sequence of League Draws: 6, 30.1.1976 – 13.3.1976.

Longest Sequence of Unbeaten League Matches: 21, 11.1.1969 – 2.5.1969.

Longest Sequence Without a League Win: 16, 28.8.1948 – 20.11.1948.

Successive Scoring Runs: 30 from 26.12.1961.

Successive Non-scoring Runs: 7 from 18.4.1925.

MANAGERS

Robert Campbell 1903–05
Peter O'Rourke 1905–21
David Menzies 1921–26
Colin Veitch 1926–28
Peter O'Rourke 1928–30
Jack Peart 1930–35
Dick Ray 1935–37
Fred Westgarth 1938–43
Bob Sharp 1943–46
Jack Barker 1946–47
John Milburn 1947–48
David Steele 1948–52
Albert Harris 1952
Ivor Powell 1952–55
Peter Jackson 1955–61
Bob Brocklebank 1961–64
Bill Harris 1965–66
Willie Watson 1966–69
Grenville Hair 1967–68
Jimmy Wheeler 1968–71
Bryan Edwards 1971–75
Bobby Kennedy 1975–78
John Napier 1978
George Mulhall 1978–81
Roy McFarland 1981–82
Trevor Cherry 1982–87
Terry Dolan 1987–89
Terry Yorath 1989–90
John Docherty 1990–91
Frank Stapleton 1991–94
Lennie Lawrence 1994–95
Chris Kamara 1995–98
Paul Jewell 1998–2000
Chris Hutchings 2000
Jim Jefferies 2000–01
Nicky Law 2001–03
Bryan Robson 2003–04
Colin Todd 2004–07
Stuart McCall 2007–10
Peter Taylor 2010–11
Peter Jackson 2011
Phil Parkinson 2011–16
Stuart McCall 2016–18
Simon Grayson 2018
Michael Collins 2018–19
David Hopkin 2019
Gary Bowyer March 2019–

TEN YEAR LEAGUE RECORD

		P	W	D	L	F	A	Pts	Pos
2009-10	FL 2	46	16	14	16	59	62	62	14
2010-11	FL 2	46	15	7	24	43	68	52	18
2011-12	FL 2	46	12	14	20	54	59	50	18
2012-13	FL 2	46	18	15	13	63	52	69	7
2013-14	FL 1	46	14	17	15	57	54	59	11
2014-15	FL 1	46	17	14	15	55	55	65	7
2015-16	FL 1	46	23	11	12	55	40	80	5
2016-17	FL 1	46	20	19	7	62	43	79	5
2017-18	FL 1	46	18	9	19	57	67	63	11
2018-19	FL 1	46	11	8	27	49	77	41	24

DID YOU KNOW ?

Bradford City had an indifferent start to the 1981–82 season but turned things round with a 6-2 victory over York City on 12 September. That was the first of a run of nine consecutive League wins, which equalled the then club record and took them to the top of Division Four. The Bantams remained among the leaders throughout the season and won promotion after finishing second to Sheffield United.

BRADFORD CITY – SKY BET LEAGUE ONE 2018–19 LEAGUE RECORD

Match No.	*Date*	*Venue*	*Opponents*	*Result*		*H/T Score*	*Lg Pos.*	*Goalscorers*	*Attendance*
1	Aug 4	A	Shrewsbury T	W	1-0	1-0	9	Payne ^{19}	7625
2	11	H	Barnsley	L	0-2	0-1	13		18,986
3	18	A	Southend U	L	0-2	0-0	18		6295
4	21	H	Burton Alb	W	1-0	1-0	9	Payne ^{32}	15,302
5	25	H	Wycombe W	L	1-2	0-1	13	Colville ^{90}	15,563
6	Sept 1	A	Fleetwood T	L	1-2	1-1	17	Doyle (pen) ^{23}	3347
7	8	A	Blackpool	L	2-3	0-0	19	Doyle (pen) ^{59}, Payne ^{64}	4393
8	15	H	Charlton Ath	L	0-2	0-1	21		15,709
9	22	A	Doncaster R	L	1-2	0-1	22	Miller ^{81}	8481
10	29	H	Bristol R	D	0-0	0-0	22		15,916
11	Oct 2	A	AFC Wimbledon	W	1-0	1-0	19	Payne (pen) ^{45}	3630
12	6	H	Sunderland	L	1-2	0-1	22	O'Connor, A ^{52}	19,487
13	13	A	Accrington S	L	1-3	0-1	22	Doyle ^{62}	3346
14	20	H	Rochdale	L	0-2	0-0	23		15,875
15	23	H	Coventry C	L	2-4	0-2	24	O'Connor, A 2 $^{62, 78}$	11,075
16	27	A	Gillingham	L	0-4	0-0	24		4399
17	Nov 3	H	Portsmouth	L	0-1	0-1	24		16,393
18	17	A	Peterborough U	D	1-1	1-0	24	O'Connor, A ^{10}	8046
19	24	H	Oxford U	W	2-0	2-0	24	Ball ^{25}, Payne ^{28}	19,084
20	27	A	Luton T	L	0-4	0-3	24		8568
21	Dec 8	A	Plymouth Arg	D	3-3	2-1	24	Payne 2 $^{4, 18}$, Miller ^{53}	9092
22	15	H	Walsall	W	4-0	1-0	22	Caddis ^{34}, Ball 2 $^{52, 61}$, Doyle ^{83}	15,314
23	22	H	Scunthorpe U	W	2-0	2-0	20	Payne ^{10}, Doyle (pen) ^{27}	16,130
24	26	A	Sunderland	L	0-1	0-1	21		46,039
25	29	A	Rochdale	W	4-0	1-0	21	Knight-Percival ^{23}, O'Connor, A ^{48}, Doyle (pen) ^{60}, Miller ^{89}	5673
26	Jan 1	H	Accrington S	W	3-0	2-0	20	O'Brien, L ^{21}, Doyle ^{30}, Wood ^{49}	16,318
27	12	A	Barnsley	L	0-3	0-2	22		14,962
28	19	H	Southend U	L	0-4	0-2	23		15,517
29	26	A	Burton Alb	D	1-1	0-1	23	Akpan ^{68}	3162
30	29	H	Shrewsbury T	W	4-3	2-1	21	Payne ^{19}, O'Brien, L ^{38}, Doyle ^{60}, Ball ^{90}	14,906
31	Feb 2	A	Wycombe W	D	0-0	0-0	22		4586
32	9	H	Fleetwood T	L	0-1	0-1	23		15,365
33	16	H	Plymouth Arg	D	0-0	0-0	23		15,855
34	23	A	Walsall	L	2-3	1-1	23	Doyle ^{12}, O'Connor, A ^{53}	5503
35	Mar 2	A	Portsmouth	L	1-5	0-2	23	Akpan ^{65}	17,657
36	9	H	Peterborough U	W	3-1	0-0	23	Butterfield ^{70}, Doyle ^{83}, O'Brien, L ^{86}	15,890
37	12	H	Luton T	L	0-1	0-1	23		15,992
38	16	A	Oxford U	L	0-1	0-0	24		6681
39	23	H	Blackpool	L	1-4	0-1	24	Ball ^{90}	16,307
40	30	A	Charlton Ath	L	0-1	0-1	24		11,630
41	Apr 6	H	Doncaster R	L	0-1	0-0	24		16,496
42	13	A	Bristol R	L	2-3	1-1	24	O'Brien, L ^{16}, Knight-Percival ^{90}	8418
43	19	A	Coventry C	L	0-2	0-1	24		11,711
44	22	H	Gillingham	D	1-1	1-0	24	Mellor ^{10}	15,686
45	27	A	Scunthorpe U	W	3-2	3-0	24	Clarke ^{2}, Anderson ^{12}, Doyle ^{15}	4528
46	May 4	H	AFC Wimbledon	D	0-0	0-0	24		17,817

Final League Position: 24

GOALSCORERS

League (49): Doyle 11 (4 pens), Payne 9 (1 pen), O'Connor A 6, Ball 5, O'Brien L 4, Miller 3, Akpan 2, Knight-Percival 2, Anderson 1, Butterfield 1, Caddis 1, Clarke 1, Colville 1, Mellor 1, Wood 1.
FA Cup (8): Miller 2, Ball 1, Caddis 1, Colville 1, Knight-Percival 1, Mellor 1, own goal 1.
Carabao Cup (1): Colville 1.
Checkatrade Trophy (3): Ball 1, Brunker 1, Miller 1.

O'Donnell R 42	Mellor K 17 + 3	O'Connor A 41 + 1	Knight-Percival N 34 + 1	Chicksen A 26 + 2	Wright J 15 + 3	Akpan H 24 + 4	Riley J 5 + 1	Payne J 33 + 6	Scannell S 15 + 1	Miller G 18 + 21	Doyle E 40 + 4	Robinson T — + 2	Seedorf S 1 + 5	McGowan R 22 + 1	Colville L 3 + 8	Gibson J 1 + 10	Wood C 18 + 4	Brunker K 4 + 13	Ball D 30 + 5	O'Brien L 38 + 2	O'Brien J 5 + 6	Poppler-Isherwood T 1 + 2	Jones A — + 2	Caddis P 25 + 2	Henry K 3 + 1	Goldthorp E — + 2	O'Connor P 8 + 1	Anderson J 9 + 4	Woods C 5 + 1	Butterfield J 11 + 4	Clarke B 6 + 8	Patrick O — + 1	Wilson B 4	Devine D 2 + 1	Match No.
1	2	3	4	5	6	7^{3}	8^{1}	9	10^{2}	11	12	13	14																						1
1	4	3	2^{1}	8	6	7	5^{2}	11	9^{3}	14	10	13	12																						2
1	12	4		2	7	6^{1}	5^{2}	9^{3}	10	14	11			3	8	13																			3
1	2^{2}	3		5	8	7	13	9^{1}	6	10^{3}	11			4	14	12																			4
1		4		5	8	7^{3}	2	9	6^{1}	12	10		11^{2}	3	13	14																			5
1	2	4		5	8^{2}	7		9^{3}		11	10			3^{1}	6	13	12	14																	6
1	2	4	5		8^{1}			9		11^{2}	10			3	6^{3}	14	7		12	13															7
1		3	4					9	5^{3}		10			2		13	8	12	11^{2}	6	7^{1}	14													8
1		4	6					9^{2}	2	12	10			3		13	7	14	11^{1}	8^{3}	5														9
1	2	3						12	6	10^{3}	11^{2}			4		9^{1}	5	14	13	8	7														10
1	2	4	5					12	6	10^{2}				3			9	11^{3}	13	8	7^{1}	14													11
1	2	4	9					11	6▪	10^{3}			14	3		13	8	12	7^{2}	5^{1}															12
1	3	7	5		14		2^{2}	8		12	11^{1}			4			6	10^{3}	13	9															13
1	2^{1}	3	12		7			9		10	11^{3}			4			5	14	8^{2}	6			13												14
1		3	4		6	7^{1}		11		9▪	10^{2}			2		12	5		14	8			13^{3}												15
1		3	4		6	7		11			10^{3}		13			14	2	12	9^{1}	8		5^{2}													16
1		3	4	5▪	6^{3}	8		12		11^{2}	10^{1}		14	2				13	9	7															17
1		4	3	5		8^{2}		11		13	10^{1}			2					6	7	12			9											18
1		4	3▪	5				7^{1}		12	10^{2}			14				11^{3}	2	8	13			9	6										19
1	7			5				13		14	10^{3}			3			4^{2}	11^{1}	2	8	12			9	6										20
1	4	3		5		13		9^{3}		11	10^{1}				14				7	8	12			2	6^{2}										21
1	6	3	4	5		7^{2}		10^{3}		11^{1}	13							14	9	8				2	12										22
1			3	5		7		6^{2}		11^{1}	10^{3}			4				12	9	8	13			2		14									23
1		14	3	5^{3}		7^{4}		6		11	10^{1}			4				13	9	8	12			2											24
1		3	4	5				6^{2}		12	10^{1}			8				13	11	9	7			2											25
1		6	3	5				7^{2}		11^{1}	10			4			12	13	9	8^{3}				2		14									26
1		3	4	8▪		13		9^{2}		12	11			5			14		10	7				6^{3}			2^{1}								27
1		4^{2}	5			7		9		11^{1}	10^{3}			3	13		12		6	8				2				14							28
1		3	4			6		9^{1}		13	11^{2}				12		10		8	7				2					5						29
1		4	3	12		7		9^{1}		13	11^{3}						10		8	6				2			14		5^{2}						30
1		3	4	5		6		9^{2}		12	11^{1}						10		8^{3}	7				2						13	14				31
1		4	3	5		7^{3}		11^{1}		10^{2}	12				14				9	6				2						8	13				32
1		4	3	5		12		10^{1}		14	11^{2}								8	7				2				13		6^{3}	9				33
1	13	3	4	5				9		14	11								8	7^{2}				2^{1}				12		6	10^{3}				34
1	12	3	4			7		9^{3}		13	11						5^{1}		10	8				2^{2}						6	14				35
1	2^{3}	4	3	13		7					11								10^{2}	8				12				9	5^{1}	6	14				36
1		4	3	5		7					11^{1}								8^{2}	6				2				10		9	12	13			37
1		4	3	5		7		14		12	11								8^{1}	13				2				10		9^{2}	6^{3}				38
1		4	3	5	13	7		9^{3}			11^{2}								8	6				2				10^{1}		12	14				39
1		4			12	7^{1}				14	11						5		8	6				2			3	10^{2}		9^{3}	13				40
1			4	5		14		12	13		10								9^{2}	8				2			3	6^{1}		7	11^{3}				41
1			4	5	6			11	9^{1}	12	10^{2}									8				2			3			7	13				42
		5	4▪		9				7	12	11^{2}						6			10				2^{3}			3	13		8^{1}			1	14	43
	2	3			7				10	11^{3}	13						5^{2}			8							4	6	12	14	9^{1}		1		44
	2	4							11		10				12					8				13			3	7	5^{2}		9^{1}		1	6	45
	2	4			7				11	12	10^{3}				14					9^{2}							3	6	5	13			1	8^{1}	46

FA Cup

First Round	Aldershot T	(a)	1-1
Replay	Aldershot T	(h)	1-1
(aet; Bradford C won 4-1 on penalties)			
Second Round	Peterborough U	(a)	2-2
Replay	Peterborough U	(h)	4-4
(aet; Peterborough U won 3-2 on penalties)			

Carabao Cup

First Round	Macclesfield T	(a)	1-1
(Macclesfield T won 4-2 on penalties)			

Checkatrade Trophy

Group F (N)	Everton U21	(h)	1-1
(Bradford C won 6-5 on penalties)			
Group F (N)	Oldham Ath	(h)	1-4
Group F (N)	Barnsley	(a)	1-2

BRENTFORD

FOUNDATION

Formed as a small amateur concern in 1889 they were very successful in local circles. They won the championship of the West London Alliance in 1893 and a year later the West Middlesex Junior Cup before carrying off the Senior Cup in 1895. After winning both the London Senior Amateur Cup and the Middlesex Senior Cup in 1898 they were admitted to the Second Division of the Southern League.

Griffin Park, Braemar Road, Brentford, Middlesex TW8 0NT.

Telephone: (0208) 847 2511.

Ticket Office: (0333) 005 8521.

Website: www.brentfordfc.com

Email: enquiries@brentfordfc.com

Ground Capacity: 12,300.

Record Attendance: 38,678 v Leicester C, FA Cup 6th rd, 26 February 1949.

Pitch Measurements: 100m × 67m (109.5yd × 73.5yd).

Chairman: Cliff Crown.

Chief Executive: Jon Varney.

Head Coach: Thomas Frank.

Assistant Head Coach: Brian Riemer.

HONOURS

League Champions: Division 2 – 1934–35; Division 3 – 1991–92; Division 3S – 1932–33; FL 2 – 2008–09; Third Division – 1998–99; Division 4 – 1962–63.
Runners-up: FL 1 – 2013–14; Second Division – 1994–95; Division 3S – 1929–30, 1957–58.

FA Cup: 6th rd – 1938, 1946, 1949, 1989.

League Cup: 4th rd – 1983, 2011.

League Trophy: *Runners-up:* 1985, 2001, 2011.

Colours: Red and white striped shirts with black trim, black shorts with white trim, black socks with white trim.

Year Formed: 1889.

Turned Professional: 1899.

Club Nickname: 'The Bees'.

Grounds: 1889, Clifden Road; 1891, Benns Fields, Little Ealing; 1895, Shotters Field; 1898, Cross Road, S. Ealing; 1900, Boston Park; 1904, Griffin Park.

First Football League Game: 28 August 1920, Division 3, v Exeter C (a) L 0–3 – Young; Hodson, Rosier, Jimmy Elliott, Levitt, Amos, Smith, Thompson, Spreadbury, Morley, Henery.

Record League Victory: 9–0 v Wrexham, Division 3, 15 October 1963 – Cakebread; Coote, Jones; Slater, Scott, Higginson; Summers (1), Brooks (2), McAdams (2), Ward (2), Hales (1), (1 og).

Record Cup Victory: 7–0 v Windsor & Eton (away), FA Cup 1st rd, 20 November 1982 – Roche; Rowe, Harris (Booker), McNichol (1), Whitehead, Hurlock (2), Kamara, Joseph (1), Mahoney (3), Bowles, Roberts. *N.B.* 8–0 v Uxbridge: Frail, Jock Watson, Caie, Bellingham, Parsonage (1), Jay, Atherton, Leigh (1), Bell (2), Buchanan (2), Underwood (2), FA Cup, 3rd Qual rd, 31 October 1903.

Record Defeat: 0–7 v Swansea T, Division 3 (S), 8 November 1924; v Walsall, Division 3 (S), 19 January 1957; v Peterborough U, 24 November 2007.

Most League Points (2 for a win): 62, Division 3 (S), 1932–33 and Division 4, 1962–63.

THE SUN FACT FILE

Former Brentford forward Ian Lawther is probably the only player to claim to have signed for his club in the House of Commons. Lawther moved from Scunthorpe to Griffin Park in November 1964, signing up at Westminster as the Bees' chairman Jack Dunnett was MP for Nottingham Central at the time.

Most League Points (3 for a win): 94, FL 1, 2013–14.

Most League Goals: 98, Division 4, 1962–63.

Highest League Scorer in Season: Jack Holliday, 38, Division 3 (S), 1932–33.

Most League Goals in Total Aggregate: Jim Towers, 153, 1954–61.

Most League Goals in One Match: 5, Jack Holliday v Luton T, Division 3 (S), 28 January 1933; 5, Billy Scott v Barnsley, Division 2, 15 December 1934; 5, Peter McKennan v Bury, Division 2, 18 February 1949.

Most Capped Player: John Buttigieg, 22 (98), Malta.

Most League Appearances: Ken Coote, 514, 1949–64.

Youngest League Player: Danis Salman, 15 years 248 days v Watford, 15 November 1975.

Record Transfer Fee Received: £12,000,000 from AFC Bournemouth for Chris Mepham, January 2019; £12,000,000 from Aston Villa for Ezri Konsa, July 2019.

Record Transfer Fee Paid: £3,000,000 to Barnsley for Ethan Pinnock, July 2019.

Football League Record: 1920 Original Member of Division 3; 1921–33 Division 3 (S); 1933–35 Division 2; 1935–47 Division 1; 1947–54 Division 2; 1954–62 Division 3 (S); 1962–63 Division 4; 1963–66 Division 3; 1966–72 Division 4; 1972–73 Division 3; 1973–78 Division 4; 1978–92 Division 3; 1992–93 Division 1; 1993–98 Division 2; 1998–99 Division 3; 1999–2004 Division 2; 2004–07 FL 1; 2007–09 FL 2; 2009–14 FL 1; 2014– FL C.

LATEST SEQUENCES

Longest Sequence of League Wins: 9, 30.4.1932 – 24.9.1932.

Longest Sequence of League Defeats: 9, 20.10.1928 – 25.12.1928.

Longest Sequence of League Draws: 5, 16.3.1957 – 6.4.1957.

Longest Sequence of Unbeaten League Matches: 26, 20.2.1999 – 16.10.1999.

Longest Sequence Without a League Win: 18, 9.9.2006 – 26.12.2006.

Successive Scoring Runs: 26 from 4.3.1963.

Successive Non-scoring Runs: 7 from 7.3.2000.

MANAGERS

Will Lewis 1900–03
(*Secretary-Manager*)
Dick Molyneux 1902–06
W. G. Brown 1906–08
Fred Halliday 1908–12, 1915–21, 1924–26
(*only Secretary to 1922*)
Ephraim Rhodes 1912–15
Archie Mitchell 1921–24
Harry Curtis 1926–49
Jackie Gibbons 1949–52
Jimmy Bain 1952–53
Tommy Lawton 1953
Bill Dodgin Snr 1953–57
Malcolm Macdonald 1957–65
Tommy Cavanagh 1965–66
Billy Gray 1966–67
Jimmy Sirrel 1967–69
Frank Blunstone 1969–73
Mike Everitt 1973–75
John Docherty 1975–76
Bill Dodgin Jnr 1976–80
Fred Callaghan 1980–84
Frank McLintock 1984–87
Steve Perryman 1987–90
Phil Holder 1990–93
David Webb 1993–97
Eddie May 1997
Micky Adams 1997–98
Ron Noades 1998–2000
Ray Lewington 2000–01
Steve Coppell 2001–02
Wally Downes 2002–04
Martin Allen 2004–06
Leroy Rosenior 2006
Scott Fitzgerald 2006–07
Terry Butcher 2007
Andy Scott 2007–11
Nicky Forster 2011
Uwe Rosler 2011–13
Mark Warburton 2013–15
Marinus Dijkhuizen 2015
Dean Smith 2015–18
Thomas Frank October 2018–

TEN YEAR LEAGUE RECORD

		P	W	D	L	F	A	Pts	Pos
2009-10	FL 1	46	14	20	12	55	52	62	9
2010-11	FL 1	46	17	10	19	55	62	61	11
2011-12	FL 1	46	18	13	15	63	52	67	9
2012-13	FL 1	46	21	16	9	62	47	79	3
2013-14	FL 1	46	28	10	8	72	43	94	2
2014-15	FL C	46	23	9	14	78	59	78	5
2015-16	FL C	46	19	8	19	72	67	65	9
2016-17	FL C	46	18	10	18	75	65	64	10
2017-18	FL C	46	18	15	13	62	52	69	9
2018-19	FL C	46	17	13	16	73	59	64	11

DID YOU KNOW ?

Brentford played in the first ever Football League game held at the original Wembley Stadium when they faced temporary tenants Clapton Orient on 22 November 1930. The Bees went down to a 3-0 defeat in front of a crowd of 8,319.

BRENTFORD – SKY BET CHAMPIONSHIP 2018–19 LEAGUE RECORD

Match No.	Date	Venue	Opponents	Result	H/T Score	Lg Pos.	Goalscorers	Attendance
1	Aug 4	H	Rotherham U	W 5-1	2-0	1	Maupay 2 [4, 60], Canos [44], Watkins [48], Macleod [89]	10,297
2	11	A	Stoke C	D 1-1	0-1	6	Watkins [66]	24,806
3	19	H	Sheffield W	W 2-0	1-0	4	Maupay (pen) [20], Watkins [61]	10,134
4	22	A	Aston Villa	D 2-2	1-1	4	Maupay 2 [23, 82]	30,011
5	25	A	Blackburn R	L 0-1	0-0	8		12,094
6	Sept 1	H	Nottingham F	W 2-1	1-0	5	Macleod [45], Watkins [84]	10,186
7	15	H	Wigan Ath	W 2-0	1-0	2	Maupay 2 [24, 63]	9951
8	18	A	Ipswich T	D 1-1	1-0	2	Maupay [31]	14,897
9	22	A	Derby Co	L 1-3	1-3	7	Dalsgaard [1]	25,110
10	29	H	Reading	D 2-2	1-1	6	Maupay [11], Barbet [90]	10,045
11	Oct 2	H	Birmingham C	D 1-1	1-1	5	McEachran [42]	9715
12	6	A	Leeds U	D 1-1	0-0	6	Maupay (pen) [62]	31,880
13	20	H	Bristol C	L 0-1	0-0	12		11,182
14	24	A	Preston NE	L 3-4	1-3	15	Canos [29], Watkins [56], Maupay [85]	10,882
15	27	A	Norwich C	L 0-1	0-1	16		25,443
16	Nov 3	H	Millwall	W 2-0	0-0	13	Canos [48], Watkins [85]	9476
17	10	A	QPR	L 2-3	1-0	15	Maupay [22], Dalsgaard [81]	17,609
18	24	H	Middlesbrough	L 1-2	0-0	15	Judge [75]	9430
19	27	H	Sheffield U	L 2-3	1-2	17	Maupay [6], Fleck (og) [65]	8903
20	Dec 3	A	WBA	D 1-1	0-0	17	Macleod [90]	20,949
21	8	H	Swansea C	L 2-3	1-3	18	Watkins [45], Benrahma [69]	9442
22	15	A	Hull C	L 0-2	0-2	19		10,530
23	22	H	Bolton W	W 1-0	0-0	18	Maupay [62]	10,512
24	26	A	Bristol C	D 1-1	0-1	18	Maupay [53]	21,207
25	29	A	Birmingham C	D 0-0	0-0	18		23,909
26	Jan 1	H	Norwich C	D 1-1	1-0	18	Jeanvier [22]	9524
27	12	H	Stoke C	W 3-1	2-1	17	Shawcross (og) [7], Benrahma [17], Henry [54]	9439
28	19	A	Rotherham U	W 4-2	1-1	17	Mokotjo 2 [2, 75], Benrahma [53], Maupay [85]	8319
29	Feb 2	H	Blackburn R	W 5-2	1-2	17	Benrahma [13], Watkins 2 [58, 73], Maupay [79], Canos [90]	9972
30	9	A	Nottingham F	L 1-2	0-1	18	Canos [89]	27,829
31	13	H	Aston Villa	W 1-0	0-0	15	Maupay [90]	9636
32	23	H	Hull C	W 5-1	3-1	16	Mokotjo [28], Benrahma 3 [33, 43, 81], Maupay [52]	9675
33	26	A	Sheffield W	L 0-2	0-1	16		23,094
34	Mar 2	H	QPR	W 3-0	0-0	15	Maupay (pen) [50], Benrahma [71], Canos [90]	11,771
35	9	A	Middlesbrough	W 2-1	0-1	12	Shotton (og) [70], Benrahma [73]	22,069
36	12	A	Sheffield U	L 0-2	0-1	14		24,463
37	16	H	WBA	L 0-1	0-0	14		11,488
38	30	A	Wigan Ath	D 0-0	0-0	13		9953
39	Apr 2	A	Swansea C	L 0-3	0-2	13		17,197
40	6	H	Derby Co	D 3-3	2-2	14	Jeanvier [23], Maupay [31], Benrahma [83]	12,225
41	10	H	Ipswich T	W 2-0	2-0	14	Maupay [20], Watkins [28]	10,039
42	13	A	Reading	L 1-2	1-2	14	Maupay [45]	16,892
43	19	A	Millwall	D 1-1	1-1	15	Da Silva [20]	14,530
44	22	H	Leeds U	W 2-0	1-0	15	Maupay [45], Canos [62]	11,580
45	May 5	H	Preston NE	W 3-0	1-0	13	Konsa [45], Maupay [54], Forss [83]	11,289
46	7	A	Bolton W	Match cancelled and Brentford awarded 1-0 win.				

Final League Position: 11

GOALSCORERS

League (73): Maupay 25 (3 pens), Benrahma 10, Watkins 10, Canos 7, Macleod 3, Mokotjo 3, Dalsgaard 2, Jeanvier 2, Barbet 1, Da Silva 1, Forss 1, Henry 1, Judge 1, Konsa 1, McEachran 1, own goals 3, awarded 1 (match 46).
FA Cup (8): Maupay 3 (2 pens), Canos 2, Watkins 2, Jeanvier 1.
Carabao Cup (6): Jeanvier 2, Benrahma 1, Forss 1, Judge 1, Mokotjo 1.

Bentley D 33	Dalsgaard H 40	Konsa E 42	Mepham C 22	Barbet Y 30 + 2	Macleod L 12 + 5	McEachran J 19 + 5	Canos S 25 + 19	Sawyers R 41 + 1	Watkins O 35 + 6	Maupay N 43	Benrahma S 29 + 9	Judge A 4 + 16	Mokotjo K 24 + 10	Yennaris N 9 + 8	Forss M 1 + 5	Jeanvier J 23 + 1	Daniels L 12	Odubajo M 22 + 8	Da Silva J 5 + 12	Clarke J — + 1	Marcondes E 3 + 10	Henry R 13 + 1	Ogbene C — + 4	Field T — + 1	Zamburek J — + 1	Sorensen M 7 + 1	Gunnarsson P — + 1	Racic L 1 + 1	Oksanen J — + 1	*Match No.*
1	2	3	4	5	6	7	8^{2}	9	10^{1}	11^{3}	12	13	14																	1
1	2	3	4	5	6^{2}	7^{1}	8^{3}	9	10	11	14		12	13																2
1	2	3	4	5	6^{3}	7	9^{2}	8	11^{1}	10	13	14	12																	3
1	2	3	4	5	6^{1}	7^{3}	8^{2}	9	10	11	14		12	13																4
1	2	3	4	5	14		13	8^{1}	11		9^{2}	12	7	6	10^{3}															5
1	2	3	4	5	6^{3}	7^{1}	11^{2}	8	10		9	12	13	14																6
1	2	3	4^{1}	5	9	6	12	7	10	11^{3}	8^{2}	13				14														7
1	2	3	4	5		7^{1}	12	9	10	11^{1}	8^{2}	14	6	13																8
1	2		4	5	6^{2}	7^{3}	12	9	10	11	8^{1}		13	14		3														9
1	2	3	4	5	9	6^{3}	12	7^{1}	10^{2}	11	8■	14	13																	10
	2	3	4	5	9^{2}	6	8	7^{1}		11		10^{3}	13	14			1	12												11
	2	3	4	12			8^{1}	6	10^{3}	11	13	14	7	9			1	5^{2}												12
1	2	3	4■	5	9^{2}	6^{1}	8^{3}	7	10	11			12	14				13												13
1	2	3		4	13		8^{3}	7^{2}	10^{1}	11	12	14	9	6				5												14
1	2	3	4	5	14	12	8^{1}	9	10	11	13		6^{3}	7^{2}																15
1	2	3	4			6^{2}	8^{1}	9	12	11	10^{3}	13		7				5	14											16
1	2	3	4			6^{3}	8	9		11^{1}	10^{2}	12		7				5	13	14										17
1	2	3	4		9^{1}	6^{2}	8			11		10		7				5^{3}	13		12	14								18
1	2	3	4	5	9^{3}	6^{2}	10^{1}	7		11		8						14	13		12									19
1	2	3	4		14	6^{1}		9	7^{3}	11	13	10						12			8	5^{2}								20
1	2	3	4			6^{2}	14	9	8	11	10^{1}	12	13	7^{3}								5								21
1	2^{2}		3				12	9	8	11	10		6^{3}	7^{1}		4		13	14			5								22
1		3	5^{3}	12			14	9	7^{1}	11	10^{2}	13	8			4		2				6								23
1	5	2		4			12	7	11^{1}	10	9^{2}	13	6			3		8												24
1		2		4		7^{2}	11^{1}	6	9	10^{3}	12	14		13		3		5				8								25
1	5	2		4		14	9^{2}	7^{3}	12	10	11^{1}	13	6			3						8								26
1	5	2		4			12	6	11^{1}	10	9^{2}		7			3						8	13							27
1	5	2		4			12	6	9^{2}	10	11^{3}		7^{1}			3			13			8	14							28
1	5	2		4		14	13	7	9	10	11^{3}		6^{2}			3		12				8^{1}								29
1	5	2^{1}		4		13	12	7	9	10	11^{3}		6^{2}		14	3		8												30
1		2		4			5^{2}	7	9	10	11^{1}		6			3		8					13	12						31
1	2			4		13	5	7	9	10^{3}	11^{1}		6^{2}			3		8	12						14					32
1	5	2		4		6^{2}	9^{1}	7	13	10	11					3		8	12											33
1	5	2		4			13	7	9^{1}	10	11^{2}		6			3		8			12									34
1^{3}	5	2		4			9^{1}	7	13	10	11^{2}		6					8			14					3	12			35
	5^{1}	2^{3}		4			13	6	9	10	11		7		14	3	1	8^{2}			12									36
	5	2		4			9^{1}	6	12	10	11		7^{3}			3	1	8^{2}	13		14									37
	5	2		4^{3}	14		13		9^{2}	10	11		6			3	1	8	7^{1}							12				38
	5	2					9^{3}	7	12	11	10^{2}		6^{1}			3	1	8	14		13					4				39
	5	2					14	6	9^{2}	10	11		7^{1}			3	1	13	12			8^{3}				4				40
		2					12	7	9^{2}	11^{3}	10^{1}				14	3	1	5	6		13	8				4				41
	5	2					12	7	9	10	11^{1}				14	3	1	8^{2}	6^{3}		13					4				42
	2■	3					5^{1}	13	11^{2}	10			7				1	8	6		9^{3}		14			4		12		43
		2					11^{2}	7	9^{1}	10			6			3	1	5	13		12	8				4				44
	5	2					9^{3}		11^{1}	10					14	3^{2}	1	12	7		6	8						4	13	45
																														46

FA Cup

Third Round	Oxford U	(h)	1-0
Fourth Round	Barnet	(a)	3-3
Replay	Barnet	(h)	3-1
Fifth Round	Swansea C	(a)	1-4

Carabao Cup

First Round	Southend U	(a)	4-2
Second Round	Cheltenham T	(h)	1-0
Third Round	Arsenal	(a)	1-3

BRIGHTON & HOVE ALBION

FOUNDATION

A professional club Brighton United was formed in November 1897 at the Imperial Hotel, Queen's Road, but folded in March 1900 after less than two seasons in the Southern League at the County Ground. An amateur team Brighton & Hove Rangers was then formed by some prominent United supporters and after one season at Withdean, decided to turn semi-professional and play at the County Ground. Rangers were accepted into the Southern League but folded in June 1901. John Jackson, the former United manager, organised a meeting at the Seven Stars public house, Ship Street on 24 June 1901 at which a new third club Brighton & Hove United was formed. They took over Rangers' place in the Southern League and pitch at County Ground. The name was changed to Brighton & Hove Albion before a match was played because of objections by Hove FC.

American Express Community Stadium, Village Way, Falmer, Brighton BN1 9BL.

Telephone: (0344) 324 6282.

Fax: (01273) 878 238.

Ticket Office: (0844) 327 1901.

Website: www.brightonandhovealbion.com

Email: supporter.services@bhafc.co.uk

Ground Capacity: 30,750.

Record Attendance: 36,747 v Fulham, Division 2, 27 December 1958 (at Goldstone Ground); 8,691 v Leeds U, FL 1, 20 October 2007 (at Withdean); 30,682 v Liverpool, Premier League, 12 January 2019 (at Amex).

Pitch Measurements: 105m × 68m (115yd × 74.5yd).

Chairman: Tony Bloom.

Chief Executive: Paul Barber.

Head Coach: Graham Potter.

Assistant Head Coach: Billy Reid.

Colours: Blue and white striped shirts with white sleeves, white shorts with blue trim, blue socks.

Year Formed: 1901.

Turned Professional: 1901.

Club Nickname: 'The Seagulls'.

Grounds: 1901, County Ground; 1902, Goldstone Ground; 1997, groundshare at Gillingham FC; 1999, Withdean Stadium; 2011, American Express Community Stadium.

First Football League Game: 28 August 1920, Division 3, v Southend U (a) L 0–2 – Hayes; Woodhouse, Little; Hall, Comber, Bentley; Longstaff, Ritchie, Doran, Rodgerson, March.

Record League Victory: 9–1 v Newport Co, Division 3 (S), 18 April 1951 – Ball; Tennant (1p), Mansell (1p); Willard, McCoy, Wilson; Reed, McNichol (4), Garbutt, Bennett (2), Keene (1). 9–1 v Southend U, Division 3, 27 November 1965 – Powney; Magill, Baxter; Leck, Gall, Turner; Gould (1), Collins (1), Livesey (2), Smith (3), Goodchild (2).

HONOURS

League Champions: FL 1 – 2010–11; Second Division – 2001–02; Division 3S – 1957–58; Third Division – 2000–01; Division 4 – 1964–65.
Runners-up: FL C – 2016–17; Division 2 – 1978–79; Division 3 – 1971–72, 1976–77, 1987–88; Division 3S – 1953–54, 1955–56.

FA Cup: *Runners-up:* 1983.

League Cup: 5th rd – 1979.

THE Sun FACT FILE

In 1929–30 both Hugh Vallance and Dan Kirkwood broke Brighton's then club record of Football League goals scored in a season. Vallance netted 30 goals including four hat-tricks before Christmas while Kirkwood's total of 28 goals included two occasions when he scored four in a match. Despite their efforts Albion missed out on promotion to Division Two.

Record Cup Victory: 10–1 v Wisbech, FA Cup 1st rd, 13 November 1965 – Powney; Magill, Baxter; Collins (1), Gall, Turner; Gould, Smith (2), Livesey (3), Cassidy (2), Goodchild (1), (1 og).

Record Defeat: 0–9 v Middlesbrough, Division 2, 23 August 1958.

Most League Points (2 for a win): 65, Division 3 (S), 1955–56 and Division 3, 1971–72.

Most League Points (3 for a win): 95, FL 1, 2010–11.

Most League Goals: 112, Division 3 (S), 1955–56.

Highest League Scorer in Season: Peter Ward, 32, Division 3, 1976–77.

Most League Goals in Total Aggregate: Tommy Cook, 114, 1922–29.

Most League Goals in One Match: 5, Jack Doran v Northampton T, Division 3 (S), 5 November 1921; 5, Adrian Thorne v Watford, Division 3 (S), 30 April 1958.

Most Capped Player: Shane Duffy, 24 (29), Republic of Ireland.

Most League Appearances: Ernie 'Tug' Wilson, 509, 1922–36.

Youngest League Player: Ian Chapman, 16 years 259 days v Birmingham C, 14 February 1987.

Record Transfer Fee Received: £8,000,000 from Leicester C for Leonardo Ulloa, July 2014.

Record Transfer Fee Paid: £17,000,000 to AZ Alkmaar for Alireza Jahanbakhsh, July 2018.

Football League Record: 1920 Original Member of Division 3; 1921–58 Division 3 (S); 1958–62 Division 2; 1962–63 Division 3; 1963–65 Division 4; 1965–72 Division 3; 1972–73 Division 2; 1973–77 Division 3; 1977–79 Division 2; 1979–83 Division 1; 1983–87 Division 2; 1987–88 Division 3; 1988–96 Division 2; 1996–2001 Division 3; 2001–02 Division 2; 2002–03 Division 1; 2003–04 Division 2; 2004–06 FL C; 2006–11 FL 1; 2011–17 FL C; 2017– Premier League.

MANAGERS

John Jackson 1901–05
Frank Scott-Walford 1905–08
John Robson 1908–14
Charles Webb 1919–47
Tommy Cook 1947
Don Welsh 1947–51
Billy Lane 1951–61
George Curtis 1961–63
Archie Macaulay 1963–68
Fred Goodwin 1968–70
Pat Saward 1970–73
Brian Clough 1973–74
Peter Taylor 1974–76
Alan Mullery 1976–81
Mike Bailey 1981–82
Jimmy Melia 1982–83
Chris Cattlin 1983–86
Alan Mullery 1986–87
Barry Lloyd 1987–93
Liam Brady 1993–95
Jimmy Case 1995–96
Steve Gritt 1996–98
Brian Horton 1998–99
Jeff Wood 1999
Micky Adams 1999–2001
Peter Taylor 2001–02
Martin Hinshelwood 2002
Steve Coppell 2002–03
Mark McGhee 2003–06
Dean Wilkins 2006–08
Micky Adams 2008–09
Russell Slade 2009
Gus Poyet 2009–13
Óscar Garcia 2013–14
Sammi Hyypia 2014
Chris Hughton 2014–19
Graham Potter May 2019–

LATEST SEQUENCES

Longest Sequence of League Wins: 9, 2.10.1926 – 20.11.1926.

Longest Sequence of League Defeats: 12, 17.8.2002 – 26.10.2002.

Longest Sequence of League Draws: 6, 16.2.1980 – 15.3.1980.

Longest Sequence of Unbeaten League Matches: 22, 2.5.2015 – 15.12.2015.

Longest Sequence Without a League Win: 15, 21.10.1972 – 27.1.1973.

Successive Scoring Runs: 31 from 4.2.1956.

Successive Non-scoring Runs: 6 from 30.3.2019.

TEN YEAR LEAGUE RECORD

		P	*W*	*D*	*L*	*F*	*A*	*Pts*	*Pos*
2009-10	FL 1	46	15	14	17	56	60	59	13
2010-11	FL 1	46	28	11	7	85	40	95	1
2011-12	FL C	46	17	15	14	52	52	66	10
2012-13	FL C	46	19	18	9	69	43	75	4
2013-14	FL C	46	19	15	12	55	40	72	6
2014-15	FL C	46	10	17	19	44	54	47	20
2015-16	FL C	46	24	17	5	72	42	89	3
2016-17	FL C	46	28	9	9	74	40	93	2
2017-18	PR Lge	38	9	13	16	34	54	40	15
2018-19	PR Lge	38	9	9	20	35	60	36	17

DID YOU KNOW ?

The most Brighton & Hove Albion players to have been included in the PFA divisional team of the season is four, which was achieved in the 2016–17 season, when the Seagulls won promotion from the Championship. The Brighton players selected by their peers were David Stockdale, Bruno, Lewis Dunk and Anthony Knockaert.

BRIGHTON & HOVE ALBION – PREMIER LEAGUE 2018–19 LEAGUE RECORD

Match No.	Date	Venue	Opponents	Result		H/T Score	Lg Pos.	Goalscorers	Attendance
1	Aug 11	A	Watford	L	0-2	0-1	17		20,051
2	19	H	Manchester U	W	3-2	3-1	11	Murray [25], Duffy [27], Gross (pen) [44]	30,592
3	25	A	Liverpool	L	0-1	0-1	12		53,294
4	Sept 1	H	Fulham	D	2-2	0-1	12	Murray 2 (1 pen) [67, 84 (p)]	30,526
5	17	A	Southampton	D	2-2	0-1	14	Duffy [67], Murray (pen) [90]	28,811
6	22	H	Tottenham H	L	1-2	0-1	13	Knockaert [90]	30,531
7	29	A	Manchester C	L	0-2	0-1	14		54,152
8	Oct 5	H	West Ham U	W	1-0	1-0	12	Murray [25]	30,544
9	20	A	Newcastle U	W	1-0	1-0	12	Kayal [29]	50,329
10	27	H	Wolverhampton W	W	1-0	0-0	11	Murray [48]	30,654
11	Nov 3	A	Everton	L	1-3	1-1	12	Dunk [33]	38,966
12	10	A	Cardiff C	L	1-2	1-1	12	Dunk [6]	29,402
13	24	H	Leicester C	D	1-1	1-0	12	Murray [15]	30,553
14	Dec 1	A	Huddersfield T	W	2-1	1-1	11	Duffy [45], Andone [69]	22,973
15	4	H	Crystal Palace	W	3-1	3-0	10	Murray (pen) [24], Balogun [31], Andone [45]	29,663
16	8	A	Burnley	L	0-1	0-1	11		18,497
17	16	H	Chelsea	L	1-2	0-2	13	March [66]	30,645
18	22	A	Bournemouth	L	0-2	0-1	13		10,491
19	26	H	Arsenal	D	1-1	1-1	13	Locadia [35]	30,608
20	29	H	Everton	W	1-0	0-0	13	Locadia [59]	30,597
21	Jan 2	A	West Ham U	D	2-2	0-0	13	Stephens [56], Duffy [58]	59,870
22	12	H	Liverpool	L	0-1	0-0	13		30,682
23	19	A	Manchester U	L	1-2	0-2	13	Gross [72]	74,532
24	29	A	Fulham	L	2-4	2-0	13	Murray 2 [3, 17]	22,008
25	Feb 2	H	Watford	D	0-0	0-0	13		30,414
26	9	H	Burnley	L	1-3	0-1	14	Duffy [76]	29,323
27	26	A	Leicester C	L	1-2	0-1	16	Propper [66]	30,558
28	Mar 2	H	Huddersfield T	W	1-0	0-0	15	Andone [79]	30,182
29	9	A	Crystal Palace	W	2-1	1-0	15	Murray [19], Knockaert [74]	24,972
30	30	H	Southampton	L	0-1	0-0	15		30,636
31	Apr 3	A	Chelsea	L	0-3	0-1	15		38,593
32	13	H	Bournemouth	L	0-5	0-1	17		30,460
33	16	H	Cardiff C	L	0-2	0-1	17		30,226
34	20	A	Wolverhampton W	D	0-0	0-0	17		31,096
35	23	A	Tottenham H	L	0-1	0-0	17		56,251
36	27	H	Newcastle U	D	1-1	0-1	17	Gross [75]	30,587
37	May 5	A	Arsenal	D	1-1	0-1	17	Murray (pen) [61]	59,965
38	12	H	Manchester C	L	1-4	1-2	17	Murray [27]	30,662

Final League Position: 17

GOALSCORERS

League (35): Murray 13 (4 pens), Duffy 5, Andone 3, Gross 3 (1 pen), Dunk 2, Knockaert 2, Locadia 2, Balogun 1, Kayal 1, March 1, Propper 1, Stephens 1.
FA Cup (10): Andone 2, Knockaert 2, Locadia 2, Murray 2, Bissouma 1, March 1.
Carabao Cup (0).
Checkatrade Trophy (6): Connolly 5, Davies J 1.

Ryan M 34	Saltor B 14	Duffy S 35	Dunk L 36	Bernardo J 19 + 3	Knockaert A 18 + 12	Stephens D 29 + 1	Propper D 30	March S 30 + 5	Gross P 24 + 1	Murray G 30 + 8	Bong G 19 + 3	Bissouma Y 17 + 11	Jahanbakhsh A 12 + 7	Montoya M 24 + 1	Balogun L 5 + 3	Locadia J 12 + 14	Kayal B 9 + 9	Izquierdo J 9 + 6	Andone F 8 + 15	Button D 4	Match No.
1	2^{1}	3	4	5	6	7	8	9^{2}	10^{3}	11	12	13	14								1
1		3	4^{2}		6	7	8	9	10^{1}	11^{3}	5			2	12	13	14				2
1		3			6^{3}	8	7	10^{2}	14	11	5	9^{1}	13	2	4	12					3
1		3	4		6^{1}	7	8^{3}	9	10^{2}	11	5	12	14	2		13					4
1		3	4		7	6	8	10^{1}		11	5	9^{2}	12	2		13					5
1		3	4		7	6^{3}	8	10^{4}		11	5	9^{1}	13	2		14	12				6
1		3	4		7^{3}		6	10^{2}		12	5	9	13	2		11^{1}	8	14			7
1	2	3	4		6		7^{3}	10^{1}		11	5	13	9^{2}			14	8	12			8
1	2^{3}	3	4	13		7		10		11^{2}	5	14	6			12	8	9^{1}			9
1	2	3	4		13	7		10^{1}		11	5	12	6				8	9^{2}			10
1	2	3	4		12	7		10^{1}		11	5	13	6				8^{3}	9^{2}	14		11
1		3	4		6	7■		10^{1}		11^{2}	5	12		2			8	9	13		12
1	2	3	4	5	6^{7}		7	12	10^{1}	11^{3}						14	8	9	13		13
1	2^{3}	3	4	5			6	8	9	13		7^{1}			12		14	10	11^{2}		14
1		3■	4	5	14		7	6	10^{3}	11^{1}		8		2	12			9^{2}	13		15
1	2		4	5	6^{2}	14	7	9	10^{3}	12		8			3	13			11^{1}		16
1			4	5	6^{3}	7	8	9	10^{1}	11^{2}		13		2	3	14			12		17
1			4■	5	12		6	7	8^{3}	14	13	9		2	3	10^{2}			11^{1}		18
1		3		5	13	8	9	6	7	11^{1}				2	4	10^{2}			12		19
		3	4	5		8	9	6	7	12				2		10			11^{1}	1	20
		3	4	5^{1}		8	9	6	7	11^{2}	12			2		10			13	1	21
		3	4		13	8	9	6^{3}	7^{2}	11^{1}	5			2		10	14		12	1	22
		3	4		13	8	9	6^{3}	7^{1}	11^{2}	5			2		10	14		12	1	23
1		3	4		12	7	8	9	6^{1}	10	5			2		11^{2}			13		24
1		3	4				7	9	6	10^{1}	5	8		2		11			12		25
1		3	4		12	7	8	9^{1}	6^{2}	10	5	14	13	2		11^{3}					26
1		3	4		9	7^{1}	8	11^{3}	6^{2}	10	5	12		2		13		14			27
1		3	4	5	9	7	8			10^{2}		6^{1}	11^{3}	2			14	13	12		28
1		3	4	5	6^{1}	8	9	12		11		7	10^{2}	2		13					29
1		3	4	5	9	7	8^{1}	12		10		6	11^{2}	2		13					30
1	2	3	4	14	12	7	6	11^{2}		13	5	8	9^{1}						10^{3}		31
1		3	4	5	9■	7	8^{1}			12		6		2		11		13	10^{2}		32
1	2	3	4	5		7	8	11	6^{2}	10			9^{1}					13	12		33
1	2^{1}	3	4	13		7	8^{2}	9	6	10	5						12	11			34
1		3	4	5		7		13	6	12		8^{2}	9^{1}	2		11	14		10^{3}		35
1	2	3	4	5	14	7		12	6	11		13					8^{1}	9^{3}	10^{2}		36
1	2	3	4	5	12	8		10	7^{2}	11^{1}		9	6^{3}				14		13		37
1	2^{1}	3	4	5	6				7	11^{2}		9	10^{3}	14		13	8		12		38

FA Cup

Third Round	Bournemouth	(a)	3-1
Fourth Round	WBA	(h)	0-0
Replay	WBA	(a)	3-1
(aet)			
Fifth Round	Derby Co	(h)	2-1
Sixth Round	Millwall	(a)	2-2
(aet; Brighton & HA won 5-4 on penalties)			
Semi-Final	Manchester C	(Wembley)	0-1

Carabao Cup

Second Round	Southampton	(h)	0-1

Checkatrade Trophy (Brighton & HA U21)

Group H (S)	Luton T	(a)	1-2
Group H (S)	Peterborough U	(a)	2-2
(Brighton & HA U21 won 5-4 on penalties)			
Group H (S)	Milton Keynes D	(a)	3-2

BRISTOL CITY

FOUNDATION

The name Bristol City came into being in 1897 when the Bristol South End club, formed three years earlier, decided to adopt professionalism and apply for admission to the Southern League after competing in the Western League. The historic meeting was held at the Albert Hall, Bedminster. Bristol City employed Sam Hollis from Woolwich Arsenal as manager and gave him £40 to buy players. In 1900 they merged with Bedminster, another leading Bristol club.

Ashton Gate Stadium, Ashton Road, Bristol BS3 2EJ.

Telephone: (0117) 963 0600.

Fax: (0117) 963 0700.

Ticket Office: (0117) 963 0600 (option 1).

Website: www.bcfc.co.uk

Email: supporterservices@bristol-sport.co.uk

Ground Capacity: 27,000.

Record Attendance: 43,335 v Preston NE, FA Cup 5th rd, 16 February 1935.

Pitch Measurements: 105m × 67m (115yd × 73.5yd).

Chairman: Keith Dawe.

Chief Executive Officer: Mark Ashton.

Head Coach: Lee Johnson.

Assistant Head Coaches: Dean Holden, Jamie McAllister.

Colours: Red shirts with white trim, white shorts with red trim, red socks with white trim.

Year Formed: 1894.

Turned Professional: 1897.

Previous Name: 1894, Bristol South End; 1897, Bristol City.

Club Nickname: 'Robins'.

Grounds: 1894, St John's Lane; 1904, Ashton Gate.

First Football League Game: 7 September 1901, Division 2, v Blackpool (a) W 2–0 – Moles; Tuft, Davies; Jones, McLean, Chambers; Bradbury, Connor, Boucher, O'Brien (2), Flynn.

Record League Victory: 9–0 v Aldershot, Division 3 (S), 28 December 1946 – Eddols; Morgan, Fox; Peacock, Roberts, Jones (1); Chilcott, Thomas, Clark (4 incl. 1p), Cyril Williams (1), Hargreaves (3).

Record Cup Victory: 11–0 v Chichester C, FA Cup 1st rd, 5 November 1960 – Cook; Collinson, Thresher; Connor, Alan Williams, Etheridge; Tait (1), Bobby Williams (1), Atyeo (5), Adrian Williams (3), Derrick, (1 og).

Record Defeat: 0–9 v Coventry C, Division 3 (S), 28 April 1934.

HONOURS

League Champions: Division 2 – 1905–06; FL 1 – 2014–15; Division 3S – 1922–23, 1926–27, 1954–55.
Runners-up: Division 1 – 1906–07; Division 2 – 1975–76; FL 1 – 2006–07; Second Division – 1997–98; Division 3 – 1964–65, 1989–90; Division 3S – 1937–38.

FA Cup: *Runners-up:* 1909.

League Cup: semi-final – 1971, 1989, 2018.

League Trophy Winners: 1986, 2003, 2015.
Runners-up: 1987, 2000.

Welsh Cup Winners: 1934.

Anglo-Scottish Cup Winners: 1978.

THE Sun FACT FILE

The first two Bristol City players to be rewarded with a place in the PFA team of the season were Geoff Merrick and Paul Cheesley, both of whom appeared in the Second Division team for 1975–76 when City won promotion to the top flight. Although only in his early 20s, this more or less marked the end of Cheesley's career as he suffered a career-ending injury shortly after the start of the following season.

Most League Points (2 for a win): 70, Division 3 (S), 1954–55.

Most League Points (3 for a win): 99, FL 1, 2014–15.

Most League Goals: 104, Division 3 (S), 1926–27.

Highest League Scorer in Season: Don Clark, 36, Division 3 (S), 1946–47.

Most League Goals in Total Aggregate: John Atyeo, 314, 1951–66.

Most League Goals in One Match: 6, Tommy 'Tot' Walsh v Gillingham, Division 3 (S), 15 January 1927.

Most Capped Player: Billy Wedlock, 26, England.

Most League Appearances: John Atyeo, 596, 1951–66.

Youngest League Player: Marvin Brown, 16 years 105 days v Bristol R, 17 October 1999.

Record Transfer Fee Received: £11,000,000 (rising to £15,000,000) from Aston Villa for Jonathan Kodjia, August 2016.

Record Transfer Fee Paid: £5,300,000 to Angers for Famara Diedhiou, June 2017.

Football League Record: 1901 Elected to Division 2; 1906–11 Division 1; 1911–22 Division 2; 1922–23 Division 3 (S); 1923–24 Division 2; 1924–27 Division 3 (S); 1927–32 Division 2; 1932–55 Division 3 (S); 1955–60 Division 2; 1960–65 Division 3; 1965–76 Division 2; 1976–80 Division 1; 1980–81 Division 2; 1981–82 Division 3; 1982–84 Division 4; 1984–90 Division 3; 1990–92 Division 2; 1992–95 Division 1; 1995–98 Division 2; 1998–99 Division 1; 1999–2004 Division 2; 2004–07 FL 1; 2007–13 FL C; 2013–15 FL 1; 2015– FL C.

MANAGERS

Sam Hollis 1897–99
Bob Campbell 1899–1901
Sam Hollis 1901–05
Harry Thickett 1905–10
Frank Bacon 1910–11
Sam Hollis 1911–13
George Hedley 1913–17
Jack Hamilton 1917–19
Joe Palmer 1919–21
Alex Raisbeck 1921–29
Joe Bradshaw 1929–32
Bob Hewison 1932–49 (*under suspension 1938–39*)
Bob Wright 1949–50
Pat Beasley 1950–58
Peter Doherty 1958–60
Fred Ford 1960–67
Alan Dicks 1967–80
Bobby Houghton 1980–82
Roy Hodgson 1982
Terry Cooper 1982–88 (*Director from 1983*)
Joe Jordan 1988–90
Jimmy Lumsden 1990–92
Denis Smith 1992–93
Russell Osman 1993–94
Joe Jordan 1994–97
John Ward 1997–98
Benny Lennartsson 1998–99
Tony Pulis 1999–2000
Tony Fawthrop 2000
Danny Wilson 2000–04
Brian Tinnion 2004–05
Gary Johnson 2005–10
Steve Coppell 2010
Keith Millen 2010–11
Derek McInnes 2011–13
Sean O'Driscoll 2013
Steve Cotterill 2013–16
Lee Johnson February 2016–

LATEST SEQUENCES

Longest Sequence of League Wins: 14, 9.9.1905 – 2.12.1905.

Longest Sequence of League Defeats: 8, 10.12.2016 – 21.1.2017.

Longest Sequence of League Draws: 4, 6.11.1999 – 27.11.1999.

Longest Sequence of Unbeaten League Matches: 24, 9.9.1905 – 10.2.1906.

Longest Sequence Without a League Win: 21, 16.3.2013 – 22.10.2013.

Successive Scoring Runs: 25 from 26.12.1905.

Successive Non-scoring Runs: 6 from 20.12.1980.

TEN YEAR LEAGUE RECORD

		P	*W*	*D*	*L*	*F*	*A*	*Pts*	*Pos*
2009-10	FL C	46	15	18	13	56	65	63	10
2010-11	FL C	46	17	9	20	62	65	60	15
2011-12	FL C	46	12	13	21	44	68	49	20
2012-13	FL C	46	11	8	27	59	84	41	24
2013-14	FL 1	46	13	19	14	70	67	58	12
2014-15	FL 1	46	29	12	5	96	38	99	1
2015-16	FL C	46	13	13	20	54	71	52	18
2016-17	FL C	46	15	9	22	60	66	54	17
2017-18	FL C	46	17	16	13	67	58	67	11
2018-19	FL C	46	19	13	14	59	53	70	8

DID YOU KNOW ?

Bristol City's Ashton Gate stadium hosted both rugby union and soccer internationals between England and Wales in the period before the First World War. Around 25,000 saw Wales beat England at rugby by 25 points to 18 in January 1908. In contrast only around 7–8,000 turned out to see England defeat Wales 4-3 in the Home International Championship in March 1913.

BRISTOL CITY – SKY BET CHAMPIONSHIP 2018–19 LEAGUE RECORD

Match No.	Date	Venue	Opponents	Result	H/T Score	Lg Pos.	Goalscorers	Attendance
1	Aug 4	H	Nottingham F	D 1-1	1-0	13	Weimann [5]	22,395
2	11	A	Bolton W	D 2-2	0-0	14	Weimann [64], Paterson [81]	14,112
3	18	H	Middlesbrough	L 0-2	0-2	19		19,455
4	21	A	QPR	W 3-0	1-0	11	Taylor [41], Weimann 2 [50, 90]	11,739
5	25	A	Swansea C	W 1-0	1-0	9	Weimann [1]	20,522
6	Sept 2	H	Blackburn R	W 4-1	1-1	6	Brownhill [38], Watkins [55], Diedhiou [73], Pack [82]	19,769
7	15	H	Sheffield U	W 1-0	0-0	3	Watkins [81]	20,540
8	18	A	WBA	L 2-4	0-3	5	Kelly [60], Diedhiou [68]	22,051
9	21	A	Wigan Ath	L 0-1	0-0	6		10,192
10	28	H	Aston Villa	D 1-1	1-1	8	Brownhill [16]	24,224
11	Oct 3	A	Rotherham U	D 0-0	0-0	10		8187
12	7	H	Sheffield W	L 1-2	0-0	13	Taylor (pen) [80]	20,102
13	20	A	Brentford	W 1-0	0-0	10	Eliasson [89]	11,182
14	24	H	Hull C	W 1-0	0-0	8	Diedhiou [90]	19,149
15	27	H	Stoke C	L 0-1	0-1	11		22,456
16	Nov 3	A	Reading	L 2-3	2-2	12	Pack [23], Brownhill [45]	14,455
17	10	H	Preston NE	L 0-1	0-1	13		19,797
18	24	A	Leeds U	L 0-2	0-0	14		34,333
19	28	A	Ipswich T	W 3-2	0-1	14	Bialkowski (og) [55], Paterson [59], Diedhiou [64]	13,726
20	Dec 2	H	Millwall	D 1-1	0-0	14	Cooper (og) [52]	18,814
21	8	A	Birmingham C	W 1-0	0-0	13	Diedhiou [63]	20,961
22	15	H	Norwich C	D 2-2	1-1	14	Diedhiou [45], O'Dowda [53]	19,851
23	22	A	Derby Co	D 1-1	1-1	13	Paterson [24]	26,719
24	26	H	Brentford	D 1-1	1-0	12	Pisano [20]	21,207
25	29	H	Rotherham U	W 1-0	0-0	11	Webster [86]	21,207
26	Jan 1	A	Stoke C	W 2-0	1-0	11	Diedhiou [39], O'Dowda [81]	23,912
27	12	H	Bolton W	W 2-1	0-0	7	Taylor [64], Palmer [66]	19,730
28	19	A	Nottingham F	W 1-0	0-0	7	Diedhiou [70]	28,922
29	Feb 2	H	Swansea C	W 2-0	0-0	6	Weimann [46], O'Dowda [74]	23,560
30	9	A	Blackburn R	W 1-0	0-0	6	Pisano [80]	13,593
31	12	H	QPR	W 2-1	0-1	5	Eliasson [73], Diedhiou (pen) [90]	19,183
32	23	A	Norwich C	L 2-3	2-1	6	Paterson [12], O'Dowda [37]	26,338
33	26	H	Birmingham C	L 1-2	0-1	6	Diedhiou [66]	19,777
34	Mar 2	A	Preston NE	D 1-1	0-1	6	Diedhiou [69]	12,863
35	9	H	Leeds U	L 0-1	0-1	7		24,832
36	12	H	Ipswich T	D 1-1	1-0	6	Webster [32]	18,411
37	30	A	Sheffield U	W 3-2	1-1	7	Weimann 3 [30, 77, 83]	30,030
38	Apr 2	A	Middlesbrough	W 1-0	1-0	5	Webster [31]	21,016
39	6	H	Wigan Ath	D 2-2	0-1	6	Taylor [65], Palmer [68]	20,931
40	9	H	WBA	W 3-2	3-0	5	Brownhill [2], Weimann [16], Hunt [19]	20,581
41	13	A	Aston Villa	L 1-2	0-0	6	Diedhiou [74]	41,418
42	19	H	Reading	D 1-1	0-0	7	Brownhill [72]	23,309
43	22	A	Sheffield W	L 0-2	0-2	8		23,998
44	27	H	Derby Co	L 0-2	0-1	8		25,556
45	30	A	Millwall	W 2-1	0-1	8	Paterson [76], Diedhiou [81]	12,261
46	May 5	A	Hull C	D 1-1	0-0	8	Henriksen (og) [90]	12,165

Final League Position: 8

GOALSCORERS

League (59): Diedhiou 13 (1 pen), Weimann 10, Brownhill 5, Paterson 5, O'Dowda 4, Taylor 4 (1 pen), Webster 3, Eliasson 2, Pack 2, Palmer 2, Pisano 2, Watkins 2, Hunt 1, Kelly 1, own goals 3.
FA Cup (3): Brownhill 1, Eliasson 1, O'Dowda 1.
Carabao Cup (0).

Maenpaa N 26	Hunt J 32 + 1	Webster A 43 + 1	Baker N 12 + 4	Bryan J 1	Eliasson N 21 + 12	Pack M 46	Brownhill J 45	O'Dowda C 20 + 11	Weimann A 40 + 4	Paterson J 31 + 9	Taylor M 10 + 23	Smith K 3 + 2	Eisa M — + 5	Kelly L 26 + 6	Watkins M 5 + 11	Pisano E 11 + 4	Dasilva J 21 + 7	Kalas T 38	Diedhiou F 35 + 6	O'Leary M 14 + 1	Walsh L 4 + 5	Adelakun H 3 + 2	Morrell J — + 1	Wright B 10 + 2	Palmer K 2 + 13	Fielding F 5	Semenyo A 1 + 3	Marinovic S 1	*Match No.*
1	2	3	4	5	6^3	7	0	9^1	10	11^2	12	13	14																1
1	2	3	4		6^1	8	7	9^3	11^2	10	13		14	5	12														2
1	2^2	3				7	6	13	11	10^1	12	8^3		4	9	5	14												3
1	2	4			9	8	7	12	11		10^1		13	5	6^2	3													4
1	2^2	4			9	7	8	12	11		10			5	6^1	13		3											5
1	2	4			9	7	8	12	11^1	14	10^2			5	6^3			3	13										6
1	2	3			7^2	8	9	12	11		14			5	13		6^1	4	10^3										7
1	2^3	4			13	8	7	9	11	14	10^1			5	6^2			3	12										8
1	2	4	14		6^3	7	8	12	11	9^1				5	13			3^2	10										9
1	2	3	4		9^1	8	7	6^2	11	13	10^3			5	14				12										10
1	2	3	4		9^1	0	7	6^3	11^2	14	12			5	13				10										11
1	2	3	4			8	7	12	14	9^3	10			5^2	13		6		11^1										12
	2	3	4^2		6	8	7^3		11	9	10^1			5			12		13	1	14								13
	2	4			6^3	8	7	12	11^2	9^1	14				13		5	3	10	1									14
	2	4			6	8	7^1	9^2		11	14			5^3			13	3	10	1	12								15
	2^1	4			9^2	8	6		12	14	10^3			13			5	3	11	1	7								16
1	2	5	4^1		13	8	7		11	12	14						6	3	10^3		9^2								17
1	2	4			6^3	7	8■		11	10^1			14	5				3	12		13	9^2							18
1	14	4			6	8			11	10				5		2^1		3	12		7^2	9^3	13						19
1		4			10	7	6	12	8^3	9^2			14	5	13	2		3	11^1										20
1		4			10^2	7	6	12	8^1	9				5	13	2		3	11										21
1			4			6	8	10	7^1	9				5	12	2		3	11										22
1		12	4^2		13	6	8	10	7^3	9^1				5		2		3	11			14							23
1		4			14	6	8	10^3	7^1	9	12			5^2		2	13	3	11										24
1	2	4			13	6	8	7^1	14	9	12						5^2	3	11			10^3							25
1	2	4^2				6	8	10	7^3	9^1	13			5				3	11			14		12					26
1	2	4				6	8	10	7^3	9^1	13			5^2			14	3	11						12				27
			4			6	8	10	7	9^3				13		2	5^1	3	11^2					14	12	1			28
		4			12	6	9	10^2	7	8^3	13						5	3	11^1					2	14	1			29
		4				7	6	9	8^1	10^2	13					12	5	3	11					2^3	14	1			30
		4			12	6^1	8	10	7^3	9	14			5^2		2	13	3	11							1			31
		4				6	8	10	7	9^2	12				14		5^3	3	11^1					2	13	1			32
1		4			13	6	8	10^3	7^2	14	12					2	5	3	11						9^1				33
1^2	2	4				6	8	10^3	7	9				5^1			13	3	11	14							12		34
		4				7^3	6	8^1	13	10	12						5	3	11	1				2	14		9^2		35
	2	4			7^2	6	8	12	10^1	9^3	14			5				3	11						13			1	36
	5	4	14			7	9		10^3	13		6^2					8	2	11	1				3^1	12				37
	5	4	14			7	6		10^2	8^1		12^3		13			9	2	11	1				3					38
	5	4^3			14	7	6			8^2	10			13			9^1	2	11	1				3	12				39
	2^3	6	4		10	9	8		7^1		13			14		12	5^2	3	11	1									40
	2^2	4	13		9^3	8	7		6	14	10^1						5	3	11	1					12				41
	5	4			13	7	8		10^1		14	6^3					9	2	11	1	12			3^2					42
	5	4			10^3	7^1	6		9								8	2	11	1	14			3^2	12		13		43
1	2	7	4^3		14	6	8		9^1	10^2							5	3	11						13		12■		44
	2^1	4				7	9		8	10	14			5		12^3		3	11	1	6^2				13				45
		4^3			14	7	6		8	10	13			12			5	3	11^1	1				2	9^2				46

FA Cup

Third Round	Huddersfield T	(h)	1-0
Fourth Round	Bolton W	(h)	2-1
Fifth Round	Wolverhampton W	(h)	0-1

Carabao Cup

First Round	Plymouth Arg	(h)	0-1

BRISTOL ROVERS

FOUNDATION

Bristol Rovers were formed at a meeting in Stapleton Road, Eastville, in 1883. However, they first went under the name of the Black Arabs (wearing black shirts). Changing their name to Eastville Rovers in their second season in 1888–89, they won the Gloucestershire Senior Cup. Original members of the Bristol & District League in 1892, this eventually became the Western League and Eastville Rovers adopted professionalism in 1897.

The Memorial Stadium, Filton Avenue, Horfield, Bristol BS7 0BF.
Telephone: (0117) 909 6648.
Fax: (0117) 907 4312.
Ticket Office: (0117) 952 4001.
Website: www.bristolrovers.co.uk
Email: via website.
Ground Capacity: 11,906.
Record Attendance: 38,472 v Preston NE, FA Cup 4th rd, 30 January 1960 (at Eastville); 9,464 v Liverpool, FA Cup 4th rd, 8 February 1992 (at Twerton Park); 12,011 v WBA, FA Cup 6th rd, 9 March 2008 (at Memorial Stadium).
Pitch Measurements: 100m × 68m (109.5yd × 74.5yd).
Chairman: Steve Hamer.
Manager: Graham Coughlan.
Assistant Manager: Joe Dunne.
Colours: Blue and white quartered shirts, white shorts with blue trim, blue socks.
Year Formed: 1883.
Turned Professional: 1897.
Previous Names: 1883, Black Arabs; 1884, Eastville Rovers; 1897, Bristol Eastville Rovers; 1898, Bristol Rovers. ***Club Nicknames:*** 'The Pirates', 'The Gas'.
Grounds: 1883, Purdown; Three Acres, Ashley Hill; Rudgeway, Fishponds; 1897, Eastville; 1986, Twerton Park; 1996, The Memorial Stadium.
First Football League Game: 28 August 1920, Division 3, v Millwall (a) L 0–2 – Stansfield; Bethune, Panes; Boxley, Kenny, Steele; Chance, Bird, Sims, Bell, Palmer.
Record League Victory: 7–0 v Brighton & HA, Division 3 (S), 29 November 1952 – Hoyle; Bamford, Fox; Pitt, Warren, Sampson; McIlvenny, Roost (2), Lambden (1), Bradford (1), Petherbridge (2), (1 og). 7–0 v Swansea T, Division 2, 2 October 1954 – Radford; Bamford, Watkins; Pitt, Muir, Anderson; Petherbridge, Bradford (2), Meyer, Roost (1), Hooper (2), (2 og). 7–0 v Shrewsbury T, Division 3, 21 March 1964 – Hall; Hillard, Gwyn Jones; Oldfield, Stone (1), Mabbutt; Jarman (2), Brown (1), Biggs (1p), Hamilton, Bobby Jones (2).
Record Cup Victory: 7–1 v Dorchester, FA Cup 4th qualifying rd, 25 October 2014 – Midenhall; Locyer, Trotman (McChrystal), Parkes, Monkhouse (2), Clarke, Mansell (1) (Thomas), Brown, Gosling, Harrison (3), Taylor (1) (White).
Record Defeat: 0–12 v Luton T, Division 3 (S), 13 April 1936.
Most League Points (2 for a win): 64, Division 3 (S), 1952–53.

HONOURS

League Champions: Division 3 – 1989–90; Division 3S – 1952–53.
Runners-up: Division 3 – 1973–74; Conference – (2nd) 2014–15 *(promoted via play-offs)*.
FA Cup: 6th rd – 1951, 1958, 2008.
League Cup: 5th rd – 1971, 1972.
League Trophy: *Runners-up:* 1990, 2007.

THE SUN FACT FILE

In May 1956 Bristol Rovers travelled to Jersey to play Cardiff City in a match to mark Liberation Day, an event to commemorate the end of German occupation of the Channel Islands in the Second World War. Rovers finished 1-0 winners thanks to a second-half own goal by a Cardiff defender.

Most League Points (3 for a win): 93, Division 3, 1989–90.

Most League Goals: 92, Division 3 (S), 1952–53.

Highest League Scorer in Season: Geoff Bradford, 33, Division 3 (S), 1952–53.

Most League Goals in Total Aggregate: Geoff Bradford, 242, 1949–64.

Most League Goals in One Match: 4, Sidney Leigh v Exeter C, Division 3 (S), 2 May 1921; 4, Jonah Wilcox v Bournemouth, Division 3 (S), 12 December 1925; 4, Bill Culley v QPR, Division 3 (S), 5 March 1927; 4, Frank Curran v Swindon T, Division 3 (S), 25 March 1939; 4, Vic Lambden v Aldershot, Division 3 (S), 29 March 1947; 4, George Petherbridge v Torquay U, Division 3 (S), 1 December 1951; 4, Vic Lambden v Colchester U, Division 3 (S), 14 May 1952; 4, Geoff Bradford v Rotherham U, Division 2, 14 March 1959; 4, Robin Stubbs v Gillingham, Division 2, 10 October 1970; 4, Alan Warboys v Brighton & HA, Division 3, 1 December 1973; 4, Jamie Cureton v Reading, Division 2, 16 January 1999; 4, Ellis Harrison v Northampton T, FL 1, 7 January 2017.

Most Capped Player: Vitalijs Astafjevs, 31 (167), Latvia.

Most League Appearances: Stuart Taylor, 546, 1966–80.

Youngest League Player: Ronnie Dix, 15 years 173 days v Charlton Ath, 25 February 1928.

Record Transfer Fee Received: £2,000,000 from Fulham for Barry Hayles, November 1998; £2,000,000 from WBA for Jason Roberts, July 2000.

Record Transfer Fee Paid: £370,000 to QPR for Andy Tillson, November 1992.

Football League Record: 1920 Original Member of Division 3; 1921–53 Division 3 (S); 1953–62 Division 2; 1962–74 Division 3; 1974–81 Division 2; 1981–90 Division 3; 1990–92 Division 2. 1992–93 Division 1; 1993–2001 Division 2; 2001–04 Division 3; 2004–07 FL 2; 2007–11 FL 1; 2011–14 FL 2; 2014–15 Conference Premier; 2015–16 FL 2; 2016– FL 1.

MANAGERS

Alfred Homer 1899–1920 (*continued as Secretary to 1928*)
Ben Hall 1920–21
Andy Wilson 1921–26
Joe Palmer 1926–29
Dave McLean 1929–30
Albert Prince-Cox 1930–36
Percy Smith 1936–37
Brough Fletcher 1938–49
Bert Tann 1950–68 (*continued as General Manager to 1972*)
Fred Ford 1968–69
Bill Dodgin Snr 1969–72
Don Megson 1972–77
Bobby Campbell 1978–79
Harold Jarman 1979–80
Terry Cooper 1980–81
Bobby Gould 1981–83
David Williams 1983–85
Bobby Gould 1985–87
Gerry Francis 1987–91
Martin Dobson 1991
Dennis Rofe 1992
Malcolm Allison 1992–93
John Ward 1993–96
Ian Holloway 1996–2001
Garry Thompson 2001
Gerry Francis 2001
Garry Thompson 2001–02
Ray Graydon 2002–04
Ian Atkins 2004–05
Paul Trollope 2005–10
Dave Penney 2011
Paul Buckle 2011–12
Mark McGhee 2012
John Ward 2012–14
Darrell Clarke 2014–18
Graham Coughlan December 2018–

LATEST SEQUENCES

Longest Sequence of League Wins: 12, 18.10.1952 – 17.1.1953.

Longest Sequence of League Defeats: 8, 26.10.2002 – 21.12.2002.

Longest Sequence of League Draws: 6, 4.2.2017 – 28.2.2017.

Longest Sequence of Unbeaten League Matches: 32, 7.4.1973 – 27.1.1974.

Longest Sequence Without a League Win: 20, 5.4.1980 – 1.11.1980.

Successive Scoring Runs: 26 from 26.3.1927.

Successive Non-scoring Runs: 6 from 14.10.1922.

TEN YEAR LEAGUE RECORD

		P	W	D	L	F	A	Pts	Pos
2009-10	FL 1	46	19	5	22	59	70	62	11
2010-11	FL 1	46	11	12	23	48	82	45	22
2011-12	FL 2	46	15	12	19	60	70	57	13
2012-13	FL 2	46	16	12	18	60	69	60	14
2013-14	FL 2	46	12	14	20	43	54	50	23
2014-15	Conf P	46	25	16	5	73	34	91	2
2015-16	FL 2	46	26	7	13	77	46	85	3
2016-17	FL 1	46	18	12	16	68	70	66	10
2017-18	FL 1	46	16	11	19	60	66	59	13
2018-19	FL 1	46	13	15	18	47	50	54	15

DID YOU KNOW ?

Inside-forward Barrie Meyer made over 100 first-team appearances for Bristol Rovers in the 1950s but was better known for his cricketing exploits. He made over 400 First Class appearances as a wicket keeper for Gloucestershire and went on to become an umpire, standing in 26 Test Matches.

BRISTOL ROVERS – SKY BET LEAGUE ONE 2018–19 LEAGUE RECORD

Match No.	Date	Venue	Opponents	Result		H/T Score	Lg Pos.	Goalscorers	Attendance
1	Aug 4	A	Peterborough U	L	1-2	0-2	15	Lockyer [90]	6439
2	11	H	Accrington S	L	1-2	0-1	21	Payne [83]	8683
3	18	A	Wycombe W	W	2-1	2-0	16	Clarke, J [4], Craig [20]	4858
4	21	H	Portsmouth	L	1-2	0-1	19	Lines (pen) [76]	9073
5	25	H	Southend U	L	0-1	0-1	20		8172
6	Sept 1	A	Shrewsbury T	D	1-1	0-0	21	Payne (pen) [53]	5759
7	8	H	Plymouth Arg	D	0-0	0-0	20		9006
8	15	A	Luton T	L	0-1	0-0	22		8912
9	22	H	Coventry C	W	3-1	3-1	17	Reilly [7], Lockyer [19], Clarke, O [23]	8385
10	29	A	Bradford C	D	0-0	0-0	18		15,916
11	Oct 2	A	Rochdale	D	0-0	0-0	18		2301
12	6	H	Walsall	L	0-1	0-0	21		7768
13	13	A	Burton Alb	L	0-1	0-0	21		3171
14	20	H	Oxford U	D	0-0	0-0	20		8506
15	23	H	AFC Wimbledon	W	2-0	1-0	19	Upson [35], Nightingale (og) [53]	7184
16	27	A	Barnsley	L	0-1	0-1	20		10,966
17	Nov 3	A	Blackpool	W	3-0	0-0	20	Clarke, O 2 [48, 85], Craig [77]	3227
18	17	H	Scunthorpe U	L	1-2	1-1	21	Sercombe [45]	8003
19	24	A	Charlton Ath	L	1-3	1-2	21	Martin [30]	10,328
20	27	H	Gillingham	L	1-2	0-1	21	Sercombe [87]	6983
21	Dec 8	H	Doncaster R	L	0-4	0-2	21		7356
22	15	A	Sunderland	L	1-2	1-1	23	Rodman [11]	28,971
23	22	H	Fleetwood T	W	2-1	1-1	22	Reilly [36], Clarke, J [90]	7159
24	26	A	Walsall	W	3-1	2-1	20	Lockyer [7], Rodman [10], Holmes-Dennis [52]	5069
25	29	A	Oxford U	W	2-0	1-0	19	Jakubiak 2 [15, 63]	8135
26	Jan 1	H	Burton Alb	D	0-0	0-0	19		9060
27	12	A	Accrington S	D	0-0	0-0	20		2246
28	19	H	Wycombe W	L	0-1	0-0	22		8163
29	29	H	Peterborough U	D	2-2	2-1	23	Nichols (pen) [8], Clarke, O [43]	6851
30	Feb 2	A	Southend U	W	2-1	2-1	20	Sercombe [20], Reilly [32]	5982
31	9	H	Shrewsbury T	D	1-1	0-1	19	Rodman [53]	8322
32	19	A	Portsmouth	D	1-1	1-0	19	Clarke-Harris (pen) [37]	17,880
33	23	H	Sunderland	L	0-2	0-1	21		10,009
34	Mar 2	H	Blackpool	W	4-0	2-0	21	Clarke-Harris 3 [6, 37, 68], Sercombe [90]	8496
35	9	A	Scunthorpe U	W	1-0	1-0	19	Clarke-Harris [35]	3877
36	12	A	Gillingham	W	1-0	0-0	16	Clarke-Harris [57]	3938
37	16	H	Charlton Ath	D	0-0	0-0	13		8343
38	23	A	Plymouth Arg	D	2-2	0-0	15	Clarke-Harris [72], Reilly [90]	12,003
39	26	A	Doncaster R	L	1-4	0-3	15	Clarke-Harris (pen) [66]	6907
40	30	H	Luton T	L	1-2	1-2	16	Clarke-Harris [45]	9037
41	Apr 7	A	Coventry C	D	0-0	0-0	16		12,664
42	13	H	Bradford C	W	3-2	1-1	14	Clarke-Harris 2 [38, 90], Clarke, O [72]	8418
43	19	A	AFC Wimbledon	D	1-1	0-1	14	Clarke, O [78]	4850
44	22	H	Rochdale	L	0-1	0-0	15		8516
45	27	A	Fleetwood T	D	0-0	0-0	16		3488
46	May 4	H	Barnsley	W	2-1	0-1	15	Rodman 2 [71, 90]	9859

Final League Position: 15

GOALSCORERS

League (47): Clarke-Harris 11 (2 pens), Clarke O 6, Rodman 5, Reilly 4, Sercombe 4, Lockyer 3, Clarke J 2, Craig 2, Jakubiak 2, Payne 2 (1 pen), Holmes-Dennis 1, Lines 1 (1 pen), Martin 1, Nichols 1 (1 pen), Upson 1, own goal 1.
FA Cup (2): Lines 1 (1 pen), Nichols 1.
Carabao Cup (3): Bennett 1, Clarke O 1, Upson 1.
Checkatrade Trophy (11): Jakubiak 3, Rodman 2, Broadbent 1, Clarke O 1, Craig 1, Lockyer 1, Nichols 1 (1 pen), Payne 1.

Slocombe S 2	Leadbitter D 11	Lockyer T 40	Craig T 46	Clarke J 38+4	Upson E 34+1	Lines C 12+7	Sercombe L 33+6	Bennett K 12+7	Nichols T 26+10	Rodman A 18+9	Reilly G 16+14	Matthews S 5+11	Mensah B —+1	Broadbent T 4+3	Clarke O 40	Payne S 14+6	Smith A 4+1	Jakubiak A 12+26	Bonham J 40	Martin J 8+2	Kelly M 20+1	Sinclair S 9+9	Partington J 13+1	Holmes-Dennis T 18	Ogogo A 16	Clarke-Harris J 14+2	Kilgour A 1+3	Moore D —+1	Match No.
1	2^{2}	3	4	5	6	7	8	9^{3}	10^{1}	11	12	13	14																1
1		4	5^{2}	2	7^{1}	12	8	11	13	9^{3}		14		3	6	10													2
		3	5	2	4		9^{2}	12	10^{1}	14	13	6^{3}		8	7	11	1												3
	2	3	4	5	8^{1}	12■	6	9	10^{2}	14					7	11^{3}	1	13											4
	2		4	5	8		9^{2}	6	10^{3}	12	14			3	7	11^{1}	1	13											5
	2	4	3		7			12	10^{2}	9		6^{1}		13	8	11			1	5■									6
	2^{3}		4	3		8		9	12		11^{1}	6^{2}		14	7	10			1		5	13							7
		4	3	2	7	9		10^{1}	12		13	6^{2}			8	11^{3}		14	1	5									8
		3	4	2		7		6	10^{2}		11^{1}	14			8	12		13	1		5	9^{3}							9
		3^{3}	4	2	8		13		10^{1}		11			12	9			14	1		5	6	7^{2}						10
			5^{2}	3		7	6	9			12			4	8	11^{3}		13	1	14		10^{1}	2						11
	3		4	2		7	12	6^{2}	11^{3}		10	14			8			13	1	5		9^{1}							12
		4	3	2	8		7^{1}			10^{2}	14	12			9			11	1		13	6	5^{3}						13
		3	4		8		9	13	10^{2}			12			7^{3}	14		11^{1}	1		5	6	2						14
	2	3	4	12	7		6	11^{1}	10^{2}			9^{3}			8	14		13	1		5								15
	5^{1}	2	3	4		6	8	13		12	11^{3}	14			7^{2}	10			1		9								16
	6	3	4	5	8^{1}		2		9						10	11^{3}		14	1	13	7^{2}	12							17
	2		3^{1}	4		7	9	6^{2}	10	13		12			8^{3}	11		14	1	5									18
	2	7	3	4	6^{1}	14	11	13	9	12					8^{2}	10^{3}			1	5									19
		3	4			7	6	9	10	11^{2}		14				12	13		1^{3}	5		8^{1}	2						20
		4	5	3^{2}		8	9	12	10	13					7^{1}	11^{3}		14	1	6			2						21
		4	5	3	8		9^{3}	12	13	10^{2}					7	14		11	1		6			2^{1}					22
		4	5	3	8	14		12		9	11^{2}	13			7^{1}			10	1		6			2^{3}					23
		3	4	2	8		12		13	6	11^{3}				7	14		10^{2}	1		5			9^{1}					24
		5	4	3	9		12		13	8	11^{2}				7			10	1		6			2^{1}					25
		3	4	2	8^{1}	13	12		14	6	10^{2}							11	1	9	5^{3}	7							26
		3	4	2	6		8			9	12				7			10	1		5			11^{1}					27
		3	4	2	7^{2}	13				6	12	14			8	11^{1}		10	1		5			9^{3}					28
		3	4	13		7	9		10^{1}	6	11^{2}				8			12	1				2	5					29
		4	3	14			9^{2}		11^{3}	6	10^{1}				8			13	1				2	5	7	12			30
		3	4	14		7	9		10^{3}	6	11^{1}							12	1				2^{2}	5	8	13			31
		3	4	5	7		6				12							11^{2}	1			13	2	9^{1}	8	10			32
		3	4	2	13		9^{3}		14	6	11^{2}				8^{1}			12	1					5	7	10			33
		3	4		8		6		11^{1}		13				9^{3}			12	1			14	2	5	7	10^{2}			34
		3	4	2	7		9^{2}		10^{1}						6			12	1		5	13			8	11			35
		3	4	2	7		9^{1}		10^{3}						6			13	1		5	12			8^{2}	11	14		36
		3	4	2	6		9^{1}		10^{2}						8			12	1		5	13			7	11			37
			4	2	6		9		10^{1}		13				8			12	1					5	7^{2}	11	3		38
		3	4	2	6^{1}						11				8			9^{4}	1			13	12	5^{3}	7	10		14	39
		3	4	2	6		9		11^{2}		13				7			12	1		5				8^{1}	10			40
		3	4	2	8		6^{2}		13		11^{1}							12	1		5	9^{3}			7	10	14		41
		3	4	2	6		9^{3}		11^{1}	12					7^{2}			14	1			13		5	8	10			42
		6	3	5	7		14			12	8^{1}				9			13	1				2^{3}	4^{2}	11	10			43
		3	4	2	7		6		10^{1}	9^{2}	13				8			12	1					5		11			44
		3	4	5	7		6								8			12	1				2	10^{1}	9	11			45
		3^{2}	4	5	7^{1}	13	6			10	12				8		1	11			2				9^{3}		14		46

FA Cup
First Round | Barnet | (a) | 1-1
Replay | Barnet | (h) | 1-2

Carabao Cup
First Round | Crawley T | (h) | 2-1
Second Round | QPR | (a) | 1-3

Checkatrade Trophy
Group D (S) | West Ham U U21 | (h) | 2-0
Group D (S) | Yeovil T | (h) | 2-0
Group D (S) | Exeter C | (a) | 0-2
Second Round (S) | Swansea C U21 | (a) | 2-1
Third Round | Northampton T | (a) | 2-1
Quarter-Final | Port Vale | (h) | 3-0
Semi-Final | Sunderland | (h) | 0-2

BURNLEY

FOUNDATION

On 18 May 1882 Burnley (Association) Football Club was still known as Burnley Rovers as members of that rugby club had decided on that date to play Association Football in the future. It was only a matter of days later that the members met again and decided to drop Rovers from the club's name.

Turf Moor, Harry Potts Way, Burnley, Lancashire BB10 4BX.

Telephone: (01282) 446 800.

Fax: (01282) 700 014.

Ticket Office: (0844) 807 1882.

Website: www.burnleyfc.com

Email: info@burnleyfc.com

Ground Capacity: 21,944.

Record Attendance: 54,775 v Huddersfield T, FA Cup 3rd rd, 23 February 1924.

Pitch Measurements: 105m × 68m (115yd × 74.5yd).

Chairman: Mike Garlick.

Chief Executive: Dave Baldwin.

Manager: Sean Dyche.

Assistant Manager: Ian Woan.

Colours: Claret shirts with sky blue trim, white shorts with sky blue trim, white socks with claret trim.

Year Formed: 1882.

Turned Professional: 1883.

Previous Name: 1882, Burnley Rovers; 1882, Burnley.

Club Nickname: 'The Clarets'.

Grounds: 1882, Calder Vale; 1883, Turf Moor.

First Football League Game: 8 September 1888, Football League, v Preston NE (a) L 2–5 – Smith; Lang, Bury, Abrahams, Friel, Keenan, Brady, Tait, Poland (1), Gallocher (1), Yates.

Record League Victory: 9–0 v Darwen, Division 1, 9 January 1892 – Hillman; Walker, McFettridge, Lang, Matthews, Keenan, Nicol (3), Bowes, Espie (1), McLardie (3), Hill (2).

Record Cup Victory: 9–0 v Crystal Palace, FA Cup 2nd rd (replay), 10 February 1909 – Dawson; Barron, McLean; Cretney (2), Leake, Moffat; Morley, Ogden, Smith (3), Abbott (2), Smethams (1). 9–0 v New Brighton, FA Cup 4th rd, 26 January 1957 – Blacklaw; Angus, Winton; Seith, Adamson, Miller; Newlands (1), McIlroy (3), Lawson (3), Cheesebrough (1), Pilkington (1). 9–0 v Penrith, FA Cup 1st rd, 17 November 1984 – Hansbury; Miller, Hampton, Phelan, Overson (Kennedy), Hird (3 incl. 1p), Grewcock (1), Powell (2), Taylor (3), Biggins, Hutchison.

Record Defeat: 0–11 v Darwen, FA Cup 1st rd, 17 October 1885.

Most League Points (2 for a win): 62, Division 2, 1972–73.

HONOURS

League Champions: Division 1 – 1920–21, 1959–60; FL C – 2015–16; Division 2 – 1897–98, 1972–73; Division 3 – 1981–82; Division 4 – 1991–92.
Runners-up: Division 1 – 1919–20, 1961–62; FL C – 2013–14; Division 2 – 1912–13, 1946–47; Second Division – 1999–2000.

FA Cup Winners: 1914.
Runners-up: 1947, 1962.

League Cup: semi-final – 1961, 1969, 1983, 2009.

League Trophy: *Runners-up:* 1988.

Anglo-Scottish Cup Winners: 1979.

European Competitions
European Cup: 1960–61 *(qf)*.
Fairs Cup: 1966–67.
Europa League: 2018–19.

THE Sun FACT FILE

With relegation to the Football Conference introduced for the 1986–87 season, Burnley found themselves bottom of the Fourth Division table with just one match remaining, seemingly doomed to face oblivion. However, the Clarets beat Orient 2-1 with goals from Neil Grewcock and Ian Britton and with 21st place Lincoln City losing at Swansea City, Burnley were saved as the Imps went out the League.

Most League Points (3 for a win): 93, FL C, 2013–14; FL C, 2015–16.

Most League Goals: 102, Division 1, 1960–61.

Highest League Scorer in Season: George Beel, 35, Division 1, 1927–28.

Most League Goals in Total Aggregate: George Beel, 179, 1923–32.

Most League Goals in One Match: 6, Louis Page v Birmingham C, Division 1, 10 April 1926.

Most Capped Player: Jimmy McIlroy, 51 (55), Northern Ireland.

Most League Appearances: Jerry Dawson, 522, 1907–28.

Youngest League Player: Tommy Lawton, 16 years 174 days v Doncaster R, 28 March 1936.

Record Transfer Fee Received: £25,000,000 (rising to £30,000,000) from Everton for Michael Keane, July 2017.

Record Transfer Fee Paid: £15,000,000 to Leeds U for Chris Wood, August 2017; £15,000,000 to Middlesbrough for Ben Gibson, August 2018.

Football League Record: 1888 Original Member of the Football League; 1897–98 Division 2; 1898–1900 Division 1; 1900–13 Division 2; 1913–30 Division 1; 1930–47 Division 2; 1947–71 Division 1; 1971–73 Division 2; 1973–76 Division 1; 1976–80 Division 2; 1980–82 Division 3; 1982–83 Division 2; 1983–85 Division 3; 1985–92 Division 4; 1992–94 Division 2; 1994–95 Division 1; 1995–2000 Division 2; 2000–04 Division 1; 2004–09 FL C; 2009–10 Premier League; 2010–14 FL C; 2014–15 Premier League; 2015–16 FL C; 2016– Premier League.

MANAGERS

Harry Bradshaw 1894–99
(*Secretary-Manager from 1897*)
Club Directors 1899–1900
J. Ernest Mangnall 1900–03
(*Secretary-Manager*)
Spen Whittaker 1903–10
(*Secretary-Manager*)
John Haworth 1910–24
(*Secretary-Manager*)
Albert Pickles 1925–31
(*Secretary-Manager*)
Tom Bromilow 1932–35
Selection Committee 1935–45
Cliff Britton 1945–48
Frank Hill 1948–54
Alan Brown 1954–57
Billy Dougall 1957–58
Harry Potts 1958–70
(*General Manager to 1972*)
Jimmy Adamson 1970–76
Joe Brown 1976–77
Harry Potts 1977–79
Brian Miller 1979–83
John Bond 1983–84
John Benson 1984–85
Martin Buchan 1985
Tommy Cavanagh 1985–86
Brian Miller 1986–89
Frank Casper 1989–91
Jimmy Mullen 1991–96
Adrian Heath 1996–97
Chris Waddle 1997–98
Stan Ternent 1998–2004
Steve Cotterill 2004–07
Owen Coyle 2007–10
Brian Laws 2010
Eddie Howe 2011–12
Sean Dyche October 2012–

LATEST SEQUENCES

Longest Sequence of League Wins: 10, 16.11.1912 – 18.1.1913.

Longest Sequence of League Defeats: 8, 2.1.1995 – 25.2.1995.

Longest Sequence of League Draws: 6, 21.2.1931 – 28.3.1931.

Longest Sequence of Unbeaten League Matches: 30, 6.9.1920 – 25.3.1921.

Longest Sequence Without a League Win: 24, 16.4.1979 – 17.11.1979.

Successive Scoring Runs: 27 from 13.2.1926.

Successive Non-scoring Runs: 6 from 21.3.2015.

TEN YEAR LEAGUE RECORD

		P	*W*	*D*	*L*	*F*	*A*	*Pts*	*Pos*
2009-10	PR Lge	38	8	6	24	42	82	30	18
2010-11	FL C	46	18	14	14	65	61	68	8
2011-12	FL C	46	17	11	18	61	58	62	13
2012-13	FL C	46	16	13	17	62	60	61	11
2013-14	FL C	46	26	15	5	72	37	93	2
2014-15	PR Lge	38	7	12	19	28	53	33	19
2015-16	FL C	46	26	15	5	72	35	93	1
2016-17	PR Lge	38	11	7	20	39	55	40	16
2017-18	PR Lge	38	14	12	12	36	39	54	7
2018-19	PR Lge	38	11	7	20	45	68	40	15

DID YOU KNOW ?

Although he was an early supporter of televised football, Burnley chairman Bob Lord quickly became a fierce opponent of the cameras. When the BBC announced they would show highlights of the Clarets' FA Cup replay against Bournemouth in January 1966, Lord banned the cameras from the ground and threatened to sue both the BBC and the Football Association.

BURNLEY – PREMIER LEAGUE 2018–19 LEAGUE RECORD

Match No.	Date	Venue	Opponents	Result		H/T Score	Lg Pos.	Goalscorers	Attendance
1	Aug 12	A	Southampton	D	0-0	0-0	11		30,784
2	19	H	Watford	L	1-3	1-1	15	Tarkowski ^{6}	18,822
3	26	A	Fulham	L	2-4	2-3	18	Hendrick ^{10}, Tarkowski ^{41}	23,438
4	Sept 2	H	Manchester U	L	0-2	0-2	19		21,525
5	16	A	Wolverhampton W	L	0-1	0-0	20		30,406
6	22	H	Bournemouth	W	4-0	2-0	16	Vydra ^{39}, Lennon ^{41}, Barnes 2 $^{83, 88}$	18,636
7	30	A	Cardiff C	W	2-1	0-0	12	Gudmundsson ^{51}, Vokes ^{70}	30,411
8	Oct 6	H	Huddersfield T	D	1-1	1-0	12	Vokes ^{20}	20,533
9	20	A	Manchester C	L	0-5	0-1	13		54,094
10	28	H	Chelsea	L	0-4	0-1	15		21,430
11	Nov 3	A	West Ham U	L	2-4	1-1	15	Gudmundsson ^{45}, Wood ^{77}	56,862
12	10	A	Leicester C	D	0-0	0-0	15		32,184
13	26	H	Newcastle U	L	1-2	1-2	17	Vokes ^{40}	20,628
14	Dec 1	A	Crystal Palace	L	0-2	0-1	19		25,098
15	5	H	Liverpool	L	1-3	0-0	19	Cork ^{54}	21,741
16	8	H	Brighton & HA	W	1-0	1-0	17	Tarkowski ^{40}	18,497
17	15	A	Tottenham H	L	0-1	0-0	17		41,645
18	22	A	Arsenal	L	1-3	0-1	18	Barnes ^{63}	59,493
19	26	H	Everton	L	1-5	1-3	18	Gibson ^{36}	21,484
20	30	H	West Ham U	W	2-0	2-0	18	Wood ^{15}, McNeil ^{34}	20,933
21	Jan 2	A	Huddersfield T	W	2-1	1-1	16	Wood ^{40}, Barnes ^{74}	23,715
22	12	H	Fulham	W	2-1	2-1	15	Hendrick ^{20}, Odoi (og) ^{23}	19,316
23	19	A	Watford	D	0-0	0-0	16		19,510
24	29	A	Manchester U	D	2-2	0-0	15	Barnes ^{51}, Wood ^{81}	74,529
25	Feb 2	H	Southampton	D	1-1	0-0	17	Barnes (pen) ^{90}	19,787
26	9	A	Brighton & HA	W	3-1	1-0	15	Wood 2 $^{26, 61}$, Barnes (pen) ^{74}	29,323
27	23	H	Tottenham H	W	2-1	0-0	14	Wood ^{57}, Barnes ^{83}	21,338
28	26	A	Newcastle U	L	0-2	0-2	15		48,323
29	Mar 2	H	Crystal Palace	L	1-3	0-1	16	Barnes ^{90}	19,223
30	10	A	Liverpool	L	2-4	1-2	17	Westwood ^{6}, Gudmundsson ^{90}	53,310
31	16	H	Leicester C	L	1-2	1-1	17	McNeil ^{38}	20,719
32	30	H	Wolverhampton W	W	2-0	1-0	17	Coady (og) ^{2}, McNeil ^{77}	20,990
33	Apr 6	A	Bournemouth	W	3-1	2-1	14	Barnes ^{56}, Wood ^{18}, Westwood ^{20}	10,446
34	13	H	Cardiff C	W	2-0	1-0	14	Wood 2 $^{31, 90}$	21,480
35	22	A	Chelsea	D	2-2	2-2	15	Hendrick ^{8}, Barnes ^{24}	40,642
36	28	H	Manchester C	L	0-1	0-0	15		21,605
37	May 3	A	Everton	L	0-2	0-2	15		39,303
38	12	H	Arsenal	L	1-3	0-0	15	Barnes ^{65}	21,461

Final League Position: 15

GOALSCORERS

League (45): Barnes 12 (2 pens), Wood 10, Gudmundsson 3, Hendrick 3, McNeil 3, Tarkowski 3, Vokes 3, Westwood 2, Cork 1, Gibson 1, Lennon 1, Vydra 1, own goals 2.
FA Cup (1): Wood 1 (1 pen).
Carabao Cup (1): Long 1.
Europa League (7): Cork 2, Wood 2 (1 pen), Barnes 1 (1 pen), Vokes 1, Vydra 1.

Hart J 19	Lowton M 19 + 2	Tarkowski J 35	Mee B 38	Ward S 3	Lennon A 14 + 2	Westwood A 31 + 3	Cork J 37	Gudmundsson J 19 + 10	Hendrick J 25 + 7	Wood C 29 + 9	Vokes S 10 + 10	Barnes A 26 + 11	Taylor C 35 + 3	Bardsley P 19	McNeil D 19 + 2	Vydra M 3 + 10	Long K 5 + 1	Defour S 6	Brady R 6 + 10	Gibson B 1	Heaton T 19	Crouch P — + 6	*Match No.*
1	2	3	4	5	6	7	8	9^{2}	10^{3}	11^{1}	12	13	14										1
1	2	3	4	5^{2}	6	8	7	9	10^{1}	11^{3}	13	12	14										2
1	2	3	4	5^{1}	6	8	7	9^{2}	10	11^{3}	14	13	12										3
1		3	4		6	7	8		10^{1}	11^{2}	12	13	5	2	9^{3}	14							4
1		3	4		6	14	7	9	8^{1}	13	11^{3}	10^{2}	5	2		12							5
1	2	3	4		9	7	8	6		12	11^{2}	13	5			10^{1}							6
1	2	3^{2}	4		9	8	7	6		13	11		5			10^{1}	12						7
1	2	3	4		9	7^{3}	8	6	13	12	11^{2}	10^{1}	5			14							8
1	2	3	4		9^{2}	12	8	6	10	13	11^{1}	14	5					7^{3}					9
1	2	3	4			14	7^{2}	6	10^{3}	12	11^{1}	13	5					8	9				10
1	2	3	4		9^{1}	7		6		13	11^{3}	12	5			10^{2}		8	14				11
1	2		4		6		8	9^{1}	12	11	10^{2}	14	5				3	7^{3}	13				12
1	2		4		6		8		12	11	10	13	5				3	7^{1}	9^{2}				13
1	2		4		6^{3}		8	9	10	11^{2}	13	14	5				3	7^{1}	12				14
1		3	4		12	7	8	6		11^{2}	13	10^{3}	5	2		14			9^{1}				15
1		3	4		12	7	8	6^{1}	13	10		11^{2}	5	2					9				16
1		4	5		7^{3}	8	9		13	12	14	11^{2}	6	2			3		10^{1}				17
1	14	4	5			7	8		9	11^{1}	13	10^{3}	6	2^{2}		12	3						18
1	2	3	4			7	8	13	9^{1}	14	10^{2}	11	6		12					5^{3}			19
		3	4			7	8	6		11^{1}	12	10	5	2	9						1		20
	12	3	4			7	8	6	14	10		11^{2}	5	2^{1}	9^{3}				13■		1		21
		3	4			7	8		6	10^{1}	12	11	5	2	9						1		22
		3	4			7	8		6	11		10	5	2	9						1		23
		3	4			7	8	12	6	11		10	5	2	9^{1}						1		24
		3	4			7	8	12	6^{3}	11^{2}		10	5	2	9^{1}				14		1	13	25
		3	4			7	8		6	11		10	5	2	9						1		26
		3	4			7	8	12	6^{2}	11		10	5	2	9^{1}				13		1		27
		3	4				8	6	7	10^{2}		11^{3}	5	2	9^{1}	14			12		1	13	28
		3	4			7	8	12	6^{3}	11^{1}		10	5	2	9^{2}				13		1	14	29
		3	4			7	8	13	6^{2}	11^{1}		10^{3}	5	2	9	14					1	12	30
		3	4			7	8	6^{3}		10^{2}		11	5	2	9^{1}	14			13		1	12	31
		3	4			7	8	12	6	11		10	5	2	9^{1}						1		32
	2	3	4			7	8	12	6^{1}	10		11	5		9						1		33
	2	3	4			7	8		6	11		10	5		9						1		34
	2	3	4			7	8		6	11		10	5		9						1		35
	2	3	4			7	8	13	6^{1}	11^{2}		10	5		9	12					1		36
	2	3	4			7	8	6^{1}	14	11		10^{3}	5		12	13			9^{2}		1		37
	2	3	4			7	8	12	6^{3}	11^{2}		10	5		9^{1}				14		1	13	38

FA Cup

Third Round	Barnsley	(h)	1-0
Fourth Round	Manchester C	(a)	0-5

Carabao Cup

Third Round	Burton Alb	(a)	1-2

Europa League

Second Qual 1st leg	Aberdeen	(a)	1-1
Second Qual 2nd leg (*aet*)	Aberdeen	(h)	3-1
Third Qual 1st leg	Istanbul Basaksehir	(a)	0-0
Third Qual 2nd leg (*aet*)	Istanbul Basaksehir	(h)	1-0
Play-off Round 1st leg	Olympiacos	(a)	1-3
Play-off Round 2nd leg	Olympiacos	(h)	1-1

BURTON ALBION

FOUNDATION

Once upon a time there were three Football League clubs bearing the name Burton. Then there were none. In reality it had been two. Originally Burton Swifts and Burton Wanderers competed in it until 1901 when they amalgamated to form Burton United. This club disbanded in 1910. There was no senior club representing the town until 1924 when Burton Town, formerly known as Burton All Saints, played in the Birmingham & District League, subsequently joining the Midland League in 1935–36. When the Second World War broke out the club fielded a team in a truncated version of the Birmingham & District League taking over from the club's reserves. But it was not revived in peacetime. So it was not until a further decade that a club bearing the name of Burton reappeared. Founded in 1950 Burton Albion made progress from the Birmingham & District League, too, then into the Southern League and because of its geographical situation later had spells in the Northern Premier League. In April 2009 Burton Albion restored the name of the town to the Football League competition as champions of the Blue Square Premier League.

Pirelli Stadium, Princess Way, Burton-on-Trent, Staffordshire DE13 0AR.

Telephone: (01283) 565 938.

Fax: (01283) 523 199.

Ticket Office: (01283) 565 938.

Website: www.burtonalbionfc.co.uk

Email: bafc@burtonalbionfc.co.uk

Ground Capactiy: 6,912.

Record Attendance: 5,806 v Weymouth, Southern League Cup final 2nd leg, 1964 (at Eton Park); 6,746 v Derby Co, FL C, 26 August 2016 (at Pirelli Stadium).

Pitch Measurements: 100m × 67m (109.5yd × 73.5yd).

Chairman: Ben Robinson.

Manager: Nigel Clough.

Assistant Manager: Gary Crosby.

Colours: Yellow shirts with black trim, black shorts with yellow trim, yellow socks with black trim.

Year Formed: 1950.

Turned Professional: 1950.

Club Nickname: 'The Brewers'.

Grounds: 1950, Eton Park; 2005, Pirelli Stadium.

HONOURS

League Champions: FL 2 – 2014–15; Conference – 2008–09.
Runners-up: FL 1 – 2015–16.

FA Cup: 4th rd – 2011.

League Cup: semi-final 2019.

THE Sun FACT FILE

Burton Albion's Pirelli Stadium was officially opened in November 2005 when the Brewers, then in the Football Conference, defeated a Manchester United XI 2-1 in front of a then record crowd of 6,065. The teams met again at the stadium two months later after being drawn together in the third round of the FA Cup. This time Albion held their Premier League opponents to a goalless draw with the attendance record once more being broken with 6,191 spectators watching the game.

First Football League Game: 8 August 2009, FL 2, v Shrewsbury T (a) L 1–3 – Redmond; Edworthy, Boertien, Austin, Branston, McGrath, Maghoma, Penn, Phillips (Stride), Walker, Shroot (Pearson) (1).

Record League Victory: 6-1 v Aldershot T, FL 2, 12 December 2009 – Krysiak; James, Boertien, Stride, Webster, McGrath, Jackson, Penn, Kabba (2), Pearson (3) (Harrad) (1), Gilroy (Maghoma).

Record Cup Victory: 12–1 v Coalville T, Birmingham Senior Cup, 6 September 1954.

Record Defeat: 0–10 v Barnet, Southern League, 7 February 1970.

Most League Points (3 for a win): 94, FL 2, 2014–15.

Most League Goals: 71, FL 2, 2009–10; 2012–13.

Highest League Scorer in Season: Shaun Harrad, 21, 2009–10.

Most League Goals in Total Aggregate: Lucas Akins, 44, 2014–19.

Most League Goals in One Match: 3, Greg Pearson v Aldershot T, FL 2, 12 December 2009; 3, Shaun Harrad v Rotherham U, FL 2, 11 September 2010; 3, Lucas Akins v Colchester U, FL 1, 23 April 2016; 3, Marcus Harness v Rochdale, FL 1, 5 January 2019.

Most Capped Player: Jackson Irvine 9 (30), Australia.

Most League Appearances: Lucas Akins, 205, 2014–19.

Youngest League Player: Sam Austin, 17 years 310 days v Stevenage, 25 October 2014.

Record Transfer Fee Received: £2,000,000 from Hull C for Jackson Irvine, August 2017.

Record Transfer Fee Paid: £500,000 to Ross Co for Liam Boyce, June 2017.

Football League Record: 2009 Promoted from Blue Square Premier; 2009–15 FL 2; 2015–16 FL 1; 2016–18 FL C; 2018– FL 1.

MANAGERS

Reg Weston 1953–57
Sammy Crooks 1957
Eddie Shimwell 1958
Bill Townsend 1959–62
Peter Taylor 1962–65
Alex Tait 1965–70
Richie Norman 1970–73
Ken Gutteridge 1973–74
Harold Bodle 1974–76
Ian Storey-Moore 1978–81
Neil Warnock 1981–86
Brian Fidler 1986–88
Vic Halom 1988
Bobby Hope 1988
Chris Wright 1988–89
Ken Blair 1989–90
Steve Powell 1990–91
Brian Fidler 1991–92
Brian Kenning 1992–94
John Barton 1994–98
Nigel Clough 1998–2009
Roy McFarland 2009
Paul Peschisolido 2009–12
Gary Rowett 2012–14
Jimmy Floyd Hasselbaink 2014–15
Nigel Clough December 2015–

LATEST SEQUENCES

Longest Sequence of League Wins: 4, 24.11.2015 – 12.12.2015.

Longest Sequence of League Defeats: 8, 25.2.2012 – 24.3.2012.

Longest Sequence of League Draws: 6, 25.4.2011 – 16.8.2011.

Longest Sequence of Unbeaten League Matches: 13, 7.3.2015 – 8.8.2015.

Longest Sequence Without a League Win: 16, 31.12.2011 – 24.3.2012.

Successive Scoring Runs: 18 from 16.4.2011 – 8.10.2011.

Successive Non-scoring Runs: 5 from 23.9.2017.

TEN YEAR LEAGUE RECORD

		P	W	D	L	F	A	Pts	Pos
2009-10	FL 2	46	17	11	18	71	71	62	13
2010-11	FL 2	46	12	15	19	56	70	51	19
2011-12	FL 2	46	14	12	20	54	81	54	17
2012-13	FL 2	46	22	10	14	71	65	76	4
2013-14	FL 2	46	19	15	12	47	42	72	6
2014-15	FL 2	46	28	10	8	69	39	94	1
2015-16	FL 1	46	25	10	11	57	37	85	2
2016-17	FL C	46	13	13	20	49	63	52	20
2017-18	FL C	46	10	11	25	38	81	41	23
2018-19	FL 1	46	17	12	17	66	57	63	9

DID YOU KNOW ?

After losing to Trowbridge on 15 March 1971, Burton Albion were undefeated in their next 31 games in Division One North of the Southern League. The run ended on 26 February 1972 when the Brewers went down 1-0 at home to Ilkeston Town. The club lost only two more games during the season and finished second in the table to earn promotion to the Premier Division.

BURTON ALBION – SKY BET LEAGUE ONE 2018–19 LEAGUE RECORD

Match No.	*Date*	*Venue*	*Opponents*	*Result*	*H/T Score*	*Lg Pos.*	*Goalscorers*	*Attendance*
1	Aug 4	H	Rochdale	L 1-2	0-2	15	Boyce[71]	2987
2	11	A	Gillingham	L 1-3	1-1	23	Boyce[26]	5016
3	18	H	Doncaster R	W 1-0	0-0	17	Boyce[47]	3129
4	21	A	Bradford C	L 0-1	0-1	20		15,302
5	25	A	Oxford U	L 1-3	1-1	21	Sordell[39]	6026
6	Sept 1	H	AFC Wimbledon	W 3-0	1-0	15	Quinn[34], Templeton[54], Boyce[60]	2814
7	8	A	Accrington S	D 1-1	1-0	16	Fraser[11]	1943
8	15	H	Sunderland	W 2-1	2-0	14	Allen[19], McFadzean[36]	4566
9	29	H	Scunthorpe U	D 0-0	0-0	15		2797
10	Oct 2	H	Southend U	L 1-2	1-0	16	Boyce[21]	2149
11	6	A	Wycombe W	L 1-2	0-2	18	Sordell[47]	4022
12	13	H	Bristol R	W 1-0	0-0	15	Fox[90]	3171
13	20	A	Plymouth Arg	W 3-2	2-2	14	McFadzean 2[19, 84], Akins[39]	8190
14	23	A	Portsmouth	D 2-2	0-1	15	Cole[48], Hesketh[52]	18,200
15	27	H	Peterborough U	L 1-2	0-1	16	Allen[60]	3600
16	Nov 3	A	Walsall	W 3-1	2-0	14	Allen[13], Cole[25], Fraser[47]	5297
17	17	H	Coventry C	W 1-0	0-0	13	Bayliss (og)[66]	4681
18	24	A	Blackpool	L 0-3	0-0	14		3163
19	27	H	Charlton Ath	L 1-2	1-1	16	Akins (pen)[25]	2438
20	Dec 8	H	Shrewsbury T	W 2-1	1-0	14	Boyce[3], Fraser[81]	3062
21	15	A	Fleetwood T	L 0-1	0-0	15		2563
22	22	A	Luton T	L 0-2	0-1	16		9538
23	26	H	Wycombe W	W 3-1	3-1	15	Akins 2[33, 45], Templeton[34]	3679
24	29	H	Plymouth Arg	D 1-1	1-0	15	Miller[4]	3577
25	Jan 1	A	Bristol R	D 0-0	0-0	13		9060
26	5	A	Rochdale	W 4-0	2-0	9	Harness 3[19, 30, 86], Boyce[78]	2666
27	12	H	Gillingham	L 2-3	0-2	11	Fraser 2[52, 60]	2634
28	19	A	Doncaster R	D 2-2	1-0	13	Brayford 2[8, 90]	7202
29	26	H	Bradford C	D 1-1	1-0	13	Akins[45]	3162
30	Feb 2	H	Oxford U	D 0-0	0-0	13		3197
31	9	A	AFC Wimbledon	W 2-0	1-0	12	Allen[14], Templeton[57]	4003
32	16	A	Shrewsbury T	D 1-1	1-1	12	Templeton[11]	6254
33	19	A	Barnsley	D 0-0	0-0	11		11,778
34	23	H	Fleetwood T	L 0-1	0-0	11		2634
35	Mar 2	H	Walsall	D 0-0	0-0	11		3924
36	8	A	Coventry C	W 2-1	1-0	11	Akins[19], Allen[60]	11,468
37	12	A	Charlton Ath	L 1-2	1-2	11	Akins (pen)[19]	9505
38	16	H	Blackpool	W 3-0	2-0	11	Boyce[6], Allen[34], Akins[68]	2715
39	23	H	Accrington S	W 5-2	1-2	10	Fraser[44], McFadzean[68], Akins 2 (2 pens)[78, 90], Templeton[82]	2916
40	Apr 6	H	Barnsley	W 3-1	1-0	10	Allen[5], Boyce[81], Harness[89]	4310
41	9	A	Sunderland	D 1-1	1-1	10	Flanagan (og)[19]	29,513
42	13	A	Scunthorpe U	W 3-0	1-0	9	Wallace[39], Akins[68], Boyce[74]	3698
43	19	H	Portsmouth	L 1-2	0-1	9	Boyce[47]	4034
44	22	A	Southend U	L 2-3	0-1	10	Brayford[60], Harness[86]	6169
45	27	H	Luton T	W 2-1	0-1	9	Akins 2[62, 73]	4903
46	May 4	A	Peterborough U	L 1-3	0-2	9	Bradley[85]	9019

Final League Position: 9

GOALSCORERS

League (66): Akins 13 (4 pens), Boyce 11, Allen 7, Fraser 6, Harness 5, Templeton 5, McFadzean 4, Brayford 3, Cole 2, Sordell 2, Bradley 1, Fox 1, Hesketh 1, Miller 1, Quinn 1, Wallace 1, own goals 2.
FA Cup (1): Boyce 1.
Carabao Cup (9): Boyce 2, Hesketh 2, Akins 1 (1 pen), Allen 1, Fraser 1, Templeton 1, own goal 1.
Checkatrade Trophy (1): Harness 1.

Bywater S 8	Brayford J 38 + 3	Turner B 18 + 1	McFadzean K 35	Buxton J 21 + 9	McCrory D 10 + 5	Allen J 41 + 1	Fraser S 39 + 3	Akins L 46	Sordell M 10 + 2	Boyce L 33 + 4	Fox B 14 + 13	Templeton D 17 + 11	Sbarra J 2 + 7	Hutchinson R 16 + 9	Harness M 21 + 11	Hodge E — + 2	Quinn S 41 + 1	Collins B 31	Hesketh J 14 + 2	Cole D 6 + 7	Campbell H — + 1	Evtimov D 7	Miller W 10 + 12	Beardsley C — + 1	Wallace K 8 + 14	Clarke J 3 + 3	Daniel C 17	Bradley A — + 7	*Match No.*
1	2	3	4	5^2	6	7^1	8	9	10	11	12	13																	1
1	2	4	3^2	14	5^3		8^1	9	11	10	7	13	6	12															2
1	2	5	4	3			6	9	10	11^1	8	12	7^2		13														3
1	2	5	4	3			6	9	10^2	11	8	7^1			12	13													4
1	2	5	4	3		13■	6	9	10^2	11	8^3	7^1				14	12												5
		4				7	8	3	9^1	10	2	11^3		5	14		6^2	1	12	13									6
		4	3			8	7	10	9		2	11^3		5			6^2	1^1	13	14	12								7
		4	3		2^1	6	5	7	11^2	10	12	8^3	13	14			9					1							8
	12	4	3		5	7	8	2	9^1	10		11					6					1							9
	4		3		5^3	7	8^1	2	13	10		11	14				6^2		9	12		1							10
	5	4	3		12	7^1	6^3	2	9	10			14				8		11^2	13		1							11
	2	4	3		5	6	8^2	10			12		13				7		9^1	14		1	11^3						12
	2	4^1	3	14		6		9		10	12			5			7		8^3	13		1	11^2						13
	3		4	13		8^1		2		10	6^2			5			7		9	12		1	11^3	14					14
	3		4			8	13	2		10	14	12		5^3			7	1	6^1	9			11^2						15
	3		4	13	5^2	8^1	6	2	12	11	14						7	1	9^3	10									16
	3		4	13	5	6	8	2				11^3			14		7	1	9^1	10^2			12						17
	3		4		5^3	6	8	2		10			14	12	13		7^2	1	9^1	11									18
	3		4		5^1	6	8	2		10			14		13		7	1	9^2	11^3			12						19
	3	13	4^2	12		6	8	2		10				5	14		7	1	9^1				11^3						20
	3	4		12		6	8^2	2		10^1		14		5	13		7	1	9^3				11						21
	3	4				6	8	2			12			5	9		7^1	1	11^3	10^2			14		13				22
	2	4		3		6	8	11			14	12^3		5	10^2		7	1	9^1						13				23
	3			4	13	6^1	8	10			2	14		5^3	9		7	1					11^2		12				24
	2	3		4			12	8			7^2	9^1		5	11		6	1					13		10				25
		4		3		8	6	10		13	2	11^3		5^2	9		7^1	1					14		12				26
	3	4				6	8	9		10	2^2	12		5			7	1					11^1			13			27
	3			4		6^3	8^1	11		10		13		5	9		7	1					14		12	2^2			28
	3			4		6^2	8	9		10		14		5^3	12		7	1							13	2^1	11		29
	3■		4	12		6^1	8^2	9		10		11^3			13		7	1							14	2	5		30
			4	3		6^1	8	2		10		11^3			9^2		7	1					13		12		5	14	31
	12		4	3		9	7^2	2		11		10^1			8^3		6	1					14		13		5		32
	2		3	5		9	4	11		12				14	8^2		7	1					10^1		13		6^3		33
	2^2		4	3		7^1	12	11		10		9^3	13		6		8	1									5	14	34
	12		4	3		6^1	8	2		10^3		11^2			9		7	1							13		5	14	35
	2		4	3		6	8^2	10		12		11^1			9		7	1							13		5		36
	2		3	4^2		8	6	10		12		11^3			9^1		7	1					13			14	5		37
	3		5	4		7		11		10				13	12		8^2	1					9^1		2^3		6	14	38
	2		3	4		7	9^1	10			13	12			11^2		8	1					14		6^3		5		39
	2		3	4		6^1	7^2	11		10^3	12				9		8	1					13		14		5		40
	2		3	4^1	14	6	7^3	11		10	12				9^2		8	1							13		5		41
	2		4			8	9^1	7		11^2	14			13	10^3		6	1							3		5	12	42
1	2		4			8	9^3	7		11	12			14	10^1		6^2						13		3		5		43
1	2^3		4		13	9		6		11^1	7			5	10		8^2								3	14		12	44
1	2		4		13	8	9^2	10			6^1			12	11		7								3		5		45
	2			12		7	5^1	10		11^2	6			14	9		8^3	1							3		4	13	46

FA Cup

First Round	Scunthorpe U	(a)	1-2

Carabao Cup

First Round	Shrewsbury T	(a)	2-1
Second Round	Aston Villa	(h)	1-0
Third Round	Burnley	(h)	2-1
Fourth Round	Nottingham F	(h)	3-2
Quarter-Final	Middlesbrough	(a)	1-0
Semi-Final 1st leg	Manchester C	(a)	0-9
Semi-Final 2nd leg	Manchester C	(h)	0-1

Checkatrade Trophy

Group E (N)	Walsall	(h)	1-2
Group E (N)	Port Vale	(a)	0-1
Group E (N)	Middlesbrough U21	(h)	0-1

BURY

FOUNDATION

A meeting at the Waggon & Horses Hotel, attended largely by members of Bury Wesleyans and Bury Unitarians football clubs, decided to form a new Bury club. This was officially formed at a subsequent gathering at the Old White Horse Hotel, Fleet Street, Bury on 24 April 1885.

The Energy Check Stadium@Gigg Lane, Bury, Lancashire BL9 9HR.

Telephone: (0161) 764 4881.

Fax: (0161) 764 5521.

Ticket Office: (0161) 764 4881 (option 1).

Website: www.buryfc.co.uk

Email: info@buryfc.co.uk

Ground Capacity: 11,376.

Record Attendance: 35,000 v Bolton W, FA Cup 3rd rd, 9 January 1960.

Pitch Measurements: 103m × 67m (112.5yd × 73.5yd).

Chairman: Steve Dale.

Chief Executive: Karl Evans.

Manager: Paul Wilkinson.

First-Team Coach: TBC.

Colours: White shirts with blue trim, blue shorts with white trim, blue socks with white hoops.

Year Formed: 1885.

Turned Professional: 1885.

Club Nickname: 'The Shakers'.

Ground: 1885, Gigg Lane (renamed JD Stadium 2013); 2015 Gigg Lane (renamed The Energy Check Stadium@Gigg Lane 2017).

First Football League Game: 1 September 1894, Division 2, v Manchester C (h) W 4–2 – Lowe; Gillespie, Davies; White, Clegg, Ross; Wylie, Barbour (2), Millar (1), Ostler (1), Plant.

Record League Victory: 8–0 v Tranmere R, Division 3, 10 January 1970 – Forrest; Tinney, Saile; Anderson, Turner, McDermott; Hince (1), Arrowsmith (1), Jones (4), Kerr (1), Grundy, (1 og).

Record Cup Victory: 12–1 v Stockton, FA Cup 1st rd (replay), 2 February 1897 – Montgomery; Darroch, Barbour; Hendry (1), Clegg, Ross (1); Wylie (3), Pangbourn, Millar (4), Henderson (2), Plant, (1 og).

Record Defeat: 0–10 v Blackburn R, FA Cup pr rd, 1 October 1887. 0–10 v West Ham U, Milk Cup 2nd rd 2nd leg, 25 October 1983.

Most League Points (2 for a win): 68, Division 3, 1960–61.

Most League Points (3 for a win): 85, FL 2, 2014–15.

HONOURS

League Champions: Division 2 – 1894–95; Second Division – 1996–97; Division 3 – 1960–61.
Runners-up: Division 2 – 1923–24; Division 3 – 1967–68; FL 2 – 2010–11, 2018–19.

FA Cup Winners: 1900, 1903.

League Cup: semi-final – 1963.

THE Sun FACT FILE

George Jones is the only player to score four goals in a game for Bury on three occasions. He netted all four in the home victory over Bournemouth in 1967–68 and repeated the feat against Tranmere Rovers in 1969–70 and Reading the following season. He also scored two hat-tricks during his time at Gigg Lane.

Most League Goals: 108, Division 3, 1960–61.

Highest League Scorer in Season: Craig Madden, 35, Division 4, 1981–82.

Most League Goals in Total Aggregate: Craig Madden, 129, 1978–86.

Most League Goals in One Match: 5, Eddie Quigley v Millwall, Division 2, 15 February 1947; 5, Ray Pointer v Rotherham U, Division 2, 2 October 1965.

Most Capped Player: Bill Gorman, 11 (13), Republic of Ireland and (4), Northern Ireland.

Most League Appearances: Norman Bullock, 505, 1920–35.

Youngest League Player: Brian Williams, 16 years 133 days v Stockport Co, 18 March 1972; Callum Styles, 16 years 41 days v Southend U, 8 May 2016 (later found to be an ineligible player).

Record Transfer Fee Received: £1,100,000 from Ipswich T for David Johnson, November 1997.

Record Transfer Fee Paid: £200,000 to Ipswich T for Chris Swailes, November 1997; £200,000 to Swindon T for Darren Bullock, February 1999.

Football League Record: 1894 Elected to Division 2; 1895–1912 Division 1; 1912–24 Division 2; 1924–29 Division 1; 1929–57 Division 2; 1957–61 Division 3; 1961–67 Division 2; 1967–68 Division 3; 1968–69 Division 2; 1969–71 Division 3; 1971–74 Division 4; 1974–80 Division 3; 1980–85 Division 4; 1985–96 Division 3; 1996–97 Division 2; 1997–99 Division 1; 1999–2002 Division 2; 2002–04 Division 3; 2004–11 FL 2; 2011–13 FL 1; 2013–15 FL 2; 2015–18 FL 1; 2018–19 FL 2; 2019– FL 1.

LATEST SEQUENCES

Longest Sequence of League Wins: 9, 26.9.1960 – 19.11.1960.

Longest Sequence of League Defeats: 12, 1.10.2016 – 17.12.2016.

Longest Sequence of League Draws: 6, 6.3.1999 – 3.4.1999.

Longest Sequence of Unbeaten League Matches: 18, 4.2.1961 – 29.4.1961.

Longest Sequence Without a League Win: 19, 1.4.1911 – 2.12.1911.

Successive Scoring Runs: 24 from 1.9.1894.

Successive Non-scoring Runs: 8 from 25.11.2017.

MANAGERS

T. Hargreaves 1887 (*Secretary Manager*)
H. S. Hamer 1887–1907 (*Secretary-Manager*)
Archie Montgomery 1907–15
William Cameron 1919–23
James Hunter Thompson 1923–27
Percy Smith 1927–30
Arthur Paine 1930–34
Norman Bullock 1934–38
Charlie Dean 1938–44
Jim Porter 1944–45
Norman Bullock 1945–49
John McNeil 1950–53
Dave Russell 1953–61
Bob Stokoe 1961–65
Bert Head 1965–66
Les Shannon 1966–69
Jack Marshall 1969
Colin McDonald 1970
Les Hart 1970
Tommy McAnearney 1970–72
Alan Brown 1972–73
Bobby Smith 1973–77
Bob Stokoe 1977–78
David Hatton 1978–79
Dave Connor 1979–80
Jim Iley 1980–84
Martin Dobson 1984–89
Sam Ellis 1989–90
Mike Walsh 1990–95
Stan Ternent 1995–98
Neil Warnock 1998–99
Andy Preece 1999–2003
Graham Barrow 2003–05
Chris Casper 2005–08
Alan Knill 2008–11
Richie Barker 2011–12
Kevin Blackwell 2012–13
David Flitcroft 2013–16
Chris Brass 2016–17
Lee Clark 2017
Chris Lucketti 2017–18
Ryan Lowe 2018–19
Paul Wilkinson July 2019–

TEN YEAR LEAGUE RECORD

		P	*W*	*D*	*L*	*F*	*A*	*Pts*	*Pos*
2009-10	FL 2	46	19	12	15	54	59	69	9
2010-11	FL 2	46	23	12	11	82	50	81	2
2011-12	FL 1	46	15	11	20	60	79	56	14
2012-13	FL 1	46	9	14	23	45	73	41	22
2013-14	FL 2	46	13	20	13	59	51	59	12
2014-15	FL 2	46	26	7	13	60	40	85	3
2015-16	FL 1	46	16	12	18	56	73	57*	16
2016-17	FL 1	46	13	11	22	61	73	50	19
2017-18	FL 1	46	8	12	26	41	71	36	24
2018-19	FL 2	46	22	13	11	82	56	79	2

**3 pts deducted.*

DID YOU KNOW ?

When Bury won promotion from the Fourth Division in 1984–85 they used just 16 players. Four of the team were ever-present including leading scorer Craig Madden, while Chris Grimshaw's only appearance was from the substitute's bench on the final day of the season.

BURY – SKY BET LEAGUE TWO 2018–19 LEAGUE RECORD

Match No.	*Date*	*Venue*	*Opponents*	*Result*		*H/T Score*	*Lg Pos.*	*Goalscorers*	*Attendance*
1	Aug 4	H	Yeovil T	W	1-0	0-0	8	Omotayo [89]	3151
2	11	A	Milton Keynes D	L	0-1	0-0	11		6867
3	18	H	Forest Green R	D	1-1	0-1	14	Aimson [90]	2853
4	21	A	Lincoln C	L	1-2	1-0	17	O'Connell [31]	8016
5	25	A	Crawley T	L	2-3	0-1	19	Dagnall [56], Mayor [78]	2036
6	Sept 1	H	Morecambe	W	3-2	2-1	15	Thompson [29], Telford 2 [44, 86]	3242
7	8	H	Grimsby T	W	4-0	2-0	13	Mayor 2 [14, 70], Aimson [34], Collins (og) [63]	3677
8	15	A	Swindon T	W	2-1	1-0	7	Moore 2 [19, 56]	6087
9	22	H	Carlisle U	L	0-1	0-0	11		3657
10	29	A	Colchester U	W	2-1	1-0	8	Moore [35], Dagnall [52]	3161
11	Oct 2	A	Northampton T	D	0-0	0-0	9		4073
12	6	H	Mansfield T	D	2-2	0-1	11	Maynard 2 [56, 90]	3880
13	13	A	Crewe Alex	D	1-1	0-1	9	Maynard [54]	3777
14	20	H	Notts Co	W	4-0	2-0	7	Maynard [11], Telford [18], O'Shea (pen) [65], Adams, N [88]	4103
15	23	H	Newport Co	D	1-1	1-0	8	Maynard [24]	3072
16	27	A	Port Vale	L	0-1	0-0	9		4375
17	Nov 3	A	Macclesfield T	W	4-1	3-1	9	Danns 2 [14, 18], O'Shea [44], Maynard [60]	2485
18	17	H	Stevenage	W	4-0	0-0	8	O'Shea 2 [63, 78], Mayor [68], O'Connell [83]	3385
19	24	A	Cambridge U	D	2-2	2-1	9	O'Shea [23], Aimson [26]	3846
20	27	H	Cheltenham T	W	4-1	2-1	5	Stokes [14], Maynard 2 [39, 79], Moore [72]	2779
21	Dec 8	H	Exeter C	W	2-0	1-0	4	O'Shea [39], Moore [76]	3328
22	15	A	Oldham Ath	L	2-4	0-3	4	Lavery 2 [46, 56]	5018
23	22	H	Tranmere R	W	2-1	0-0	4	Maynard [52], Lavery [90]	4748
24	26	A	Mansfield T	L	1-2	0-0	6	O'Shea (pen) [90]	4959
25	29	A	Notts Co	D	0-0	0-0	5		7014
26	Jan 1	H	Crewe Alex	W	3-1	0-1	4	Lavery [50], O'Shea 2 (1 pen) [58 (p), 76]	3812
27	5	A	Yeovil T	W	1-0	1-0	3	Maynard [24]	2426
28	12	H	Milton Keynes D	W	4-3	1-2	2	O'Shea (pen) [33], Telford [72], Mayor [77], Maynard [90]	4072
29	19	A	Forest Green R	W	2-1	0-1	2	O'Shea [69], Maynard [83]	2940
30	26	H	Lincoln C	D	3-3	2-2	3	O'Shea [15], Adams, N [42], Aimson [86]	5169
31	Feb 2	H	Crawley T	D	1-1	0-0	3	Maynard [83]	3625
32	9	A	Morecambe	W	3-2	2-0	3	Mayor [17], O'Shea 2 [45, 59]	2665
33	16	A	Exeter C	W	1-0	0-0	2	Maynard [66]	4607
34	23	H	Oldham Ath	W	3-1	0-1	2	Maynard 2 [72, 90], Lavery [76]	7784
35	Mar 2	H	Macclesfield T	W	3-0	1-0	2	Maynard [24], O'Shea (pen) [75], Wharton [90]	4277
36	5	A	Cheltenham T	D	1-1	1-1	2	Wharton [13]	2409
37	9	A	Stevenage	W	1-0	0-0	2	Maynard [90]	3530
38	23	A	Grimsby T	D	0-0	0-0	2		4375
39	30	H	Swindon T	L	1-3	1-1	3	Maynard [28]	3997
40	Apr 2	H	Cambridge U	L	0-3	0-2	3		3386
41	6	A	Carlisle U	L	2-3	2-1	4	Stokes 2 [8, 43]	4656
42	13	H	Colchester U	W	2-0	0-0	2	Telford 2 [49, 66]	3898
43	19	A	Newport Co	L	1-3	1-2	4	Maynard [7]	4433
44	22	H	Northampton T	W	3-1	1-1	2	Stokes [39], Mayor [65], Maynard [90]	4407
45	30	A	Tranmere R	D	1-1	0-1	2	Mayor [56]	9145
46	May 4	H	Port Vale	D	1-1	1-1	2	Rossiter [45]	6719

Final League Position: 2

GOALSCORERS

League (82): Maynard 21, O'Shea 15 (5 pens), Mayor 8, Telford 6, Lavery 5, Moore 5, Aimson 4, Stokes 4, Adams N 2, Dagnall 2, Danns 2, O'Connell 2, Wharton 2, Omotayo 1, Rossiter 1, Thompson 1, own goal 1.
FA Cup (5): Moore 2, Mayor 1, O'Shea 1, Telford 1.
Carabao Cup (1): O'Connell 1.
Checkatrade Trophy (16): Telford 7 (1 pen), Mayor 3, Adams N 1, Dagnall 1, Lavery 1 (1 pen), Maynard 1, Moore 1, Thompson 1.

Murphy J 46	Miller T 3 + 4	Aimson W 36 + 1	Thompson A 44	O'Connell E 18 + 13	Stokes C 36 + 1	Danns N 28 + 6	Styles C 8 + 8	Mayor D 38 + 1	Dagnall C 12 + 5	Adams N 44 + 2	Moore B 18 + 18	Telford D 16 + 22	Omotayo G 2 + 11	O'Shea J 42 + 2	McFadzean C 36 + 4	Bunn H — + 1	Dawson S 4 + 1	Lavery C 9 + 14	Hulme C — + 1	Barjonas J — + 4	Beckford J — + 1	Maynard N 34 + 3	Adams J — + 1	Cooney R 2 + 7	Wharton S 15	Rossiter J 15 + 1	Match No.
1	2^{3}	3	4	5	6^{2}	7	8	9	10^{1}	11	12	13	14														1
1	2^{1}	3	4	5	6	7	8	9^{3}	10^{2}	11		13	12	14													2
1		2	3	4	9^{3}	7		8		5	14	10^{2}	11	6^{1}	12	13											3
1		2■	3	4	9	7		8^{1}	10^{2}	5	14		11^{3}	12	13		6										4
1			2	3^{2}	4	7	13	12	10^{3}	5		11	14	8^{1}	9		6										5
1	14	2	3		4	8	12	7^{2}	10^{1}	5		11			9		6^{3}	13									6
1		2	3		4	13	6^{3}	7^{1}	10	5	12			8	9			11^{2}	14								7
1		2	3		4	6^{2}		9^{1}	10	5	11			7	8		13			12							8
1		2	3		4	6	12	9	10^{2}	5	11^{1}		13	7^{3}	8						14						9
1		2	3	4^{1}	8	7		9	11^{2}	5	10^{3}	14		6	12							13					10
1		3	4		2	7		9		5	10	12		6	8							11^{1}					11
1		2	3		4^{1}	7^{2}	13	9	10^{3}	5		12		6	8					14		11					12
1		3	4		2	7^{2}	13	9	11^{1}	5		12		6	8							10					13
1		2	3		4	7^{1}		8	12	5		10^{2}		6	9					13		11^{3}	14				14
1		2	3		4	7^{2}		8	12	5		10^{1}		6	9					13		11					15
1		3	2		4	6^{2}	14	9	11^{1}	5^{3}	13	12		7	8							10					16
1		2	3		4	7^{1}	14	9	13	5	12	11^{3}		6	8							10^{2}					17
1		2	3	13	4		6^{2}	7		5^{1}	10^{3}	12		8	9							11		14			18
1		2	3	12	4		6^{2}	7		5	10	13		8	9							11^{1}					19
1	13	2^{2}	3	12	4	7		9	14	5^{1}	11^{3}			6	8							10					20
1	14	12	2	3^{2}	4	11		9		5^{1}	10	13		6	8							7^{3}					21
1	14		3	4	2^{2}	8		6		5^{1}	10	12		9	7			13				11^{3}					22
1		2	3	13	4	7	8			5	10^{3}	14		6	9^{1}			12				11^{2}					23
1	5^{3}	2	4	3	9	13	8^{2}			12		10		6			7^{1}	11				14					24
1		2	3		4^{1}	8^{3}	12	7		5	11	14		6	9			13				10^{2}					25
1		2^{2}	3		4		7	8	14	5		12		6	9			10^{1}				11^{3}		13			26
1		3	4	13	2	8^{2}		6		5	12	14		7	9			11^{1}				10^{3}					27
1		2	3	12	4^{3}	8^{1}		7		5	13	10^{2}	14	6	9							11					28
1		2	3	13	4	8^{1}		7		5	12	11^{2}		6	9^{3}			14				10					29
1		2	3	7^{3}	4^{1}	14		8		5	12	10^{2}		6	9			13				11					30
1		2	3	6^{3}		7^{2}				5	13	10^{1}		8	9			14				11			4	12	31
1		2	3	13				7^{3}		5^{1}	10^{2}	14		6	9							11		12	4	8	32
1		2	3	14	12			7		5	10	13		8	9							11^{3}			4^{2}	6^{1}	33
1		2	3	13	4^{3}			7^{1}		5	10		14	8	9			12				11^{2}				6	34
1			2	3		14		6^{1}		5	13	12		8	9			10^{2}				11^{3}			4	7	35
1			3	2				7		5^{2}	10^{3}	11^{1}		8	9			13				12		14	4	6	36
1			3	2		7^{2}				5^{3}	12	13	14	8	9			10^{1}				11			4	6	37
1			3	2				8		5^{3}	12		13	6	9^{1}			10^{2}				11		14	4	7	38
1			3^{2}	2				8■		6^{1}	12		14	8	9			10^{3}				11		13	4	7	39
1		2^{2}	3	12		6				5^{1}	10	14		8	9							11		13	4^{3}	7	40
1			4	7^{2}	6					2^{3}	10	12		9	14			13				11		3	5^{1}	8	41
1		2			4	6				5	12	10^{1}	14	8	9^{2}			13				11^{3}			3	7	42
1		2			4	14		8		5	9^{3}	10^{2}	12	6^{1}				13				11			3	7	43
1		2	3	14	9^{2}			8		5	12	10^{3}		6^{1}				13				11			4	7	44
1		2^{2}	3	12	9	14		8		5		10^{3}		6				13				11			4	7^{1}	45
1			3	2				8		14	12	13		6	9			10^{1}				11		5^{3}	4^{2}	7	46

FA Cup

First Round	Dover Ath	(h)	5-0
Second Round	Luton T	(h)	0-1

Carabao Cup

First Round	Nottingham F	(a)	1-1

(Nottingham F won 10-9 on penalties)

Checkatrade Trophy

Group B (N)	Rochdale	(a)	1-2
Group B (N)	Leicester C U21	(h)	2-1
Group B (N)	Fleetwood T	(h)	3-1
Second Round (N)	Mansfield T	(a)	1-0
Third Round	Accrington S	(a)	4-2
Quarter-Final	Oxford U	(h)	5-2
Semi-Final	Portsmouth	(h)	0-3

CAMBRIDGE UNITED

FOUNDATION

The football revival in Cambridge began soon after World War II when the Abbey United club (formed 1912) decided to turn professional in 1949. In 1951 they changed their name to Cambridge United. They were competing in the United Counties League before graduating to the Eastern Counties League in 1951 and the Southern League in 1958.

The Abbey Stadium, Newmarket Road, Cambridge CB5 8LN.

Telephone: (01223) 566 500.

Ticket Office: (01223) 566 500 (option 1).

Website: www.cambridge-united.co.uk

Email: info@cambridge-united.co.uk

Ground Capacity: 8,127.

Record Attendance: 14,000 v Chelsea, Friendly, 1 May 1970.

Pitch Measurements: 100.5m × 67.5m (110yd × 74yd).

Vice-Chairman: Eddie Clark.

Chief Operating Officer: Henry Comfort.

Head Coach: Colin Calderwood.

Assistant Head Coach: Mark Bonner.

HONOURS

League Champions: Division 3 – 1990–91; Division 4 – 1976–77.
Runners-up: Division 3 – 1977–78; Fourth Division – (6th) 1989–90 *(promoted via play-offs)*; Third Division – 1998–99; Conference – (2nd) 2013–14 *(promoted via play-offs)*.

FA Cup: 6th rd – 1990, 1991.

League Cup: quarter-final – 1993.

League Trophy: *Runners-up:* 2002.

Colours: Amber and black striped shirts, black shorts with amber trim, black socks with amber trim.

Year Formed: 1912.

Turned Professional: 1949.

Ltd Co.: 1948.

Previous Name: 1919, Abbey United; 1951, Cambridge United.

Club Nickname: The 'U's'.

Grounds: 1932, Abbey Stadium (renamed R Costings Abbey Stadium 2009, Cambs Glass Stadium 2016, The Abbey Stadium 2017).

First Football League Game: 15 August 1970, Division 4, v Lincoln C (h) D 1–1 – Roberts; Thompson, Meldrum (1), Slack, Eades, Hardy, Leggett, Cassidy, Lindsey, McKinven, Harris.

Record League Victory: 7–0 v Morecambe, FL 2, 19 April 2016 – Norris; Roberts (1), Coulson, Clark, Dunne (Williams), Ismail (1), Berry (2 pens), Ledson (Spencer), Dunk (2), Williamson (1) (Simpson).

Record Cup Victory: 5–1 v Bristol C, FA Cup 5th rd second replay, 27 February 1990 – Vaughan; Fensome, Kimble, Bailie (O'Shea), Chapple, Daish, Cheetham (Robinson), Leadbitter (1), Dublin (2), Taylor (1), Philpott (1).

Record Defeat: 0–7 v Sunderland, League Cup 2nd rd, 1 October 2002; 0–7 v Luton T, FL 2, 18 November 2017.

THE SUN FACT FILE

Abbey United, as the U's were then known, won their first game in Division Three of the Cambridgeshire Senior League after being accepted into the competition in 1920–21, only for the 2-1 victory to be wiped from the records when their opponents Abbey Crusaders withdrew from the league. United went on to win the title and then gained a second consecutive promotion the following season.

Most League Points (2 for a win): 65, Division 4, 1976–77.

Most League Points (3 for a win): 86, Division 3, 1990–91.

Most League Goals: 87, Division 4, 1976–77.

Highest League Scorer in Season: David Crown, 24, Division 4, 1985–86.

Most League Goals in Total Aggregate: John Taylor, 86, 1988–92; 1996–2001.

Most League Goals in One Match: 5, Steve Butler v Exeter C, Division 2, 4 April 1994.

Most Capped Player: Tom Finney, 7 (15), Northern Ireland.

Most League Appearances: Steve Spriggs, 416, 1975–87.

Youngest League Player: Andy Sinton, 16 years 228 days v Wolverhampton W, 2 November 1982.

Record Transfer Fee Received: £1,300,000 from Leicester C for Trevor Benjamin, July 2000.

Record Transfer Fee Paid: £190,000 to Luton T for Steve Claridge, November 1992.

Football League Record: 1970 Elected to Division 4; 1973–74 Division 3; 1974–77 Division 4; 1977–78 Division 3; 1978–84 Division 2; 1984–85 Division 3; 1985–90 Division 4; 1990–91 Division 3; 1991–92 Division 2; 1992–93 Division 1; 1993–95 Division 2; 1995–99 Division 3; 1999–2002 Division 2; 2002–04 Division 3; 2004–05 FL2; 2005–14 Conference Premier; 2014– FL 2.

MANAGERS

Bill Whittaker 1949–55
Gerald Williams 1955
Bert Johnson 1955–59
Bill Craig 1959–60
Alan Moore 1960–63
Roy Kirk 1964–66
Bill Leivers 1967–74
Ron Atkinson 1974–78
John Docherty 1978–83
John Ryan 1984–85
Ken Shellito 1985
Chris Turner 1985–90
John Beck 1990–92
Ian Atkins 1992–93
Gary Johnson 1993–95
Tommy Taylor 1995–96
Roy McFarland 1996–2001
John Beck 2001
John Taylor 2001–04
Claude Le Roy 2004
Herve Renard 2004
Steve Thompson 2004–05
Rob Newman 2005–06
Jimmy Quinn 2006–08
Gary Brabin 2008–09
Martin Ling 2009–11
Jez George 2011–12
Richard Money 2012–15
Shaun Derry 2015–18
Joe Dunne 2018
Colin Calderwood December 2018–

LATEST SEQUENCES

Longest Sequence of League Wins: 7, 19.2.1977 – 1.4.1977.

Longest Sequence of League Defeats: 7, 8.4.1985 – 30.4.1985.

Longest Sequence of League Draws: 6, 6.9.1986 – 30.9.1986.

Longest Sequence of Unbeaten League Matches: 14, 9.9.1972 – 10.11.1972.

Longest Sequence Without a League Win: 31, 8.10.1983 – 23.4.1984.

Successive Scoring Runs: 26 from 9.4.2002.

Successive Non-scoring Runs: 5 from 29.9.1973.

TEN YEAR LEAGUE RECORD

		P	*W*	*D*	*L*	*F*	*A*	*Pts*	*Pos*
2009-10	Conf P	44	15	14	15	65	53	59	10
2010-11	Conf P	46	11	17	18	53	61	50	17
2011-12	Conf P	46	19	14	13	57	41	71	9
2012-13	Conf P	46	15	14	17	68	69	59	14
2013-14	Conf P	46	23	13	10	72	35	82	2
2014-15	FL 2	46	13	12	21	61	66	51	19
2015-16	FL 2	46	18	14	14	66	55	68	9
2016-17	FL 2	46	19	9	18	58	50	66	11
2017-18	FL 2	46	17	13	16	56	60	64	12
2018-19	FL 2	46	12	11	23	40	66	47	21

DID YOU KNOW ?

Cambridge United's first win in the Football League Cup came when they defeated 3-0 in a first-round replay against Aldershot in September 1973 at the Abbey Stadium. The result earned United a second-round tie at Bury. The U's had lost in the opening round in each of their first three seasons in Division Four following their election to the Football League in May 1970.

CAMBRIDGE UNITED – SKY BET LEAGUE TWO 2018–19 LEAGUE RECORD

Match No.	Date	Venue	Opponents	Result		H/T Score	Lg Pos.	Goalscorers	Attendance
1	Aug 4	A	Port Vale	L	0-3	0-1	22		5559
2	11	H	Notts Co	W	3-2	0-1	15	Azeez 2 [46, 61], Corr [90]	4372
3	18	A	Northampton T	D	2-2	0-0	17	Maris [70], Deegan [86]	5047
4	21	H	Exeter C	L	0-2	0-2	19		3662
5	25	H	Cheltenham T	L	0-1	0-0	21		3660
6	Sept 1	A	Stevenage	W	1-0	1-0	17	Amoo [17]	2998
7	8	H	Carlisle U	L	1-2	1-1	19	Brown [23]	4234
8	15	A	Colchester U	L	0-3	0-2	19		4108
9	22	H	Mansfield T	D	1-1	0-1	19	Maris [88]	3909
10	29	A	Newport Co	L	2-4	2-1	20	Lambe 2 [4, 21]	3104
11	Oct 2	H	Forest Green R	L	1-3	1-1	23	Brown [21]	3059
12	6	A	Crawley T	L	0-2	0-0	23		2151
13	13	H	Milton Keynes D	L	0-1	0-1	23		5106
14	20	A	Lincoln C	D	1-1	1-1	23	Brown [11]	9108
15	23	A	Swindon T	W	2-0	2-0	21	Lambe [11], Brown [12]	5824
16	27	H	Macclesfield T	W	1-0	0-0	20	Ibehre [80]	3946
17	Nov 3	H	Grimsby T	W	1-0	0-0	19	Lewis [83]	4096
18	17	A	Oldham Ath	L	1-3	1-0	21	Maris [7]	3818
19	24	H	Bury	D	2-2	1-2	21	Lewis [39], Taylor [86]	3846
20	27	A	Crewe Alex	L	0-2	0-1	21		2569
21	Dec 8	A	Tranmere R	L	0-1	0-0	22		5016
22	15	H	Yeovil T	D	0-0	0-0	22		3807
23	22	A	Morecambe	L	0-3	0-0	22		1439
24	26.	H	Crawley T	W	2-1	1-1	22	Maris [27], Ibehre [88]	4601
25	29	H	Lincoln C	L	1-2	1-0	22	Ibehre [28]	6858
26	Jan 1	A	Milton Keynes D	L	0-6	0-3	22		8128
27	5	H	Stevenage	W	2-0	2-0	21	Amoo [35], Brown [45]	4235
28	12	A	Notts Co	W	1-0	1-0	20	Taylor [41]	15,026
29	19	H	Northampton T	W	3-2	1-1	19	Brown [45], Taft [64], Amoo [90]	4849
30	26	A	Exeter C	L	0-1	0-0	20		3996
31	Feb 9	H	Port Vale	W	1-0	1-0	19	Amoo [19]	4193
32	16	H	Tranmere R	D	0-0	0-0	18		4872
33	19	A	Cheltenham T	L	0-2	0-1	19		2339
34	23	A	Yeovil T	L	0-1	0-1	19		2596
35	Mar 2	A	Grimsby T	W	2-0	1-0	19	Taft [42], Hepburn-Murphy [82]	4772
36	9	H	Oldham Ath	D	1-1	0-1	19	Brown [46]	4758
37	12	H	Crewe Alex	D	0-0	0-0	20		3448
38	23	A	Carlisle U	D	2-2	1-2	20	Hepburn-Murphy [3], Ibehre [68]	4673
39	30	H	Colchester U	L	0-1	0-0	21		5515
40	Apr 2	A	Bury	W	3-0	2-0	19	Jones [16], Amoo [34], Maris [72]	3386
41	6	A	Mansfield T	L	0-1	0-0	20		4789
42	13	H	Newport Co	L	0-3	0-2	21		4294
43	19	H	Swindon T	D	0-0	0-0	21		4380
44	22	A	Forest Green R	L	1-2	0-1	21	Lewis [66]	2699
45	27	H	Morecambe	L	1-2	0-1	21	Knowles [90]	4083
46	May 4	A	Macclesfield T	D	1-1	1-0	21	Lewis [44]	3986

Final League Position: 21

GOALSCORERS

League (40): Brown 7, Amoo 5, Maris 5, Ibehre 4, Lewis 4, Lambe 3, Azeez 2, Hepburn-Murphy 2, Taft 2, Taylor 2, Corr 1, Deegan 1, Jones 1, Knowles 1.
FA Cup (3): Ibehre 2, Maris 1.
Carabao Cup (1): Azeez 1 (1 pen).
Checkatrade Trophy (9): Azeez 5 (1 pen), Brown 1, Lambe 1, Maris 1, Osadebe 1.

Forde D 25	Davies L 5 + 1	Taylor G 39	Taft G 35 + 2	Carroll J 31 + 1	Amoo D 25 + 18	Deegan G 40 + 1	Maris G 39	Dunk H 15 + 11	Lambe R 27 + 5	Azeez A 12 + 14	Corr B 1 + 8	Osaoabe E 1 + 11	O'Neil L 15 + 4	Mitov D 21	Halliday B 37 + 1	Darling H 12	Ibehre J 32 + 4	John L 17 + 5	Brown J 40 + 3	Lewis P 12 + 11	Knowles T — + 3	Hepburn-Murphy R 10 + 6	Jones A 5 + 7	Doyle-Hayes J 4 + 2	Coulson H 6 + 8	Worman B — + 1	Match No.
1	2	3	4	5	6¹	7	8	9²	10³	11	12	13	14														1
	12		3	5	6¹	7	8		9	10	13			1	2²	4³	11	14									2
			4	5	12	6	8		9³	10²	14		7¹	1	2	3	11		13								3
			4	5	12	7	8	14		10¹	13		6²	1	2		11	3	9³								4
1			3	5³	12	6	8	13	14	10¹			7²		2		11	4	9								5
1			4	5	6¹	7	8²		9³	12		13	14		2		11	3	10								6
1			3	5	7	6¹	8			10²	12				2		11	4	9	13							7
1		3	4	5	8	6	7		10¹	13	12				2		11²		9								8
1		3		5	8²	6	7		10	12	11¹		14		2			4	9³	13							9
1		7	4³	5			8		11	13	14		6²		2		10	3	9¹	12							10
1		3		5■	12	6	8		10	13	14		7³		2		11²	4	9¹								11
1		4	3		12	5	9		8	6			7¹		2			10	11								12
1		5	3		8	6¹	9			11			7		2			4	10		12						13
1		5	3		12	6	8²		9	10¹		13	7³		2			4	11	14							14
1		2	4	5	10²	7	8³		11	12		13	6¹					3	9	14							15
1		2	4	5	10¹	7	6²		11	14			8		12		13	3³	9								16
1		3	4	5	12	6	10¹	14	8³				7²		2		11		9	13							17
1		3	4	5	13	6	8	14		11³					2²		10	12	9	7¹							18
1	2¹	4	3	5	12	6	8³	14	11²			13					10		9	7■							19
1		3	4		12	7³	6	5	11	13		8¹	14		2		9²		10								20
1		3		5	13	7	8	9¹	12						2	4	11		10	6²							21
1		3			13	7	6	5	11¹	12					2	4	10		9²	8							22
1		3		5	12	8	10	9³	14	11²		13	7		2	4				6¹							23
1		4	14	5	12	6	10³		8²			13	7¹		2	3	11		9								24
1		3		5	8²			13	10	14		12	6³		2	4	11		9¹	7							25
1		4		5			8	14	10²	13		12	6		2	3	11³		9¹	7							26
1		4	3	5	8²	6	10³	13		12		14			2		11		9¹	7							27
1		4	3	5	7³	6	8	13		12		14			2		11		9¹			10²					28
		3	4	5¹	7	6	8²	12		13				1	2		11	14	9			10³					29
		3	4	5²	6¹	7	8	12		11³				1	2				9	13		10	14				30
		4	3	5	7³	6	8		12					1	2		11²		9			10¹	13	14			31
		4	3		7²	6	8	5	14					1	2		11		9³			10¹	13		12		32
		3	4	5■	12	8¹								1			11³	2	10	6		13	14	7	9²		33
		5	3		6	7	8		9					1		4	10	2¹	13			12	11²				34
		4	3		6¹	7	8	5	9³					1	2		10²		11	13		12			14		35
		4	3		8²	6	7	5	9					1	2		11		10¹			13			12		36
	2	4	3		7¹	6	8	5	11³					1			10²		9			13	14		12		37
		4	3	5	12	8	7							1	2		11¹		6	14		10²	13		9³		38
		4	3	5¹	14	7²	8	9						1	2		11		10	12³				13	6		39
		4	3³		8²		7	5	9					1	2		14	12	10				11¹	8	13		40
		4	3	5	6	12	7²		9					1	2				10			13	11¹	8³	14		41
		4	3		12	6		5	8²					1	2				9			10	11¹	7	13		42
		4	3		7²	6		5	8³					1	2		11	14	9	13		10¹			12		43
	2¹	5³		6	7²	8								1		4	12	3	13	9	14	11			10		44
	2				8	7		5³						1		3	13	4	9	6¹	14	11²	12		10		45
		8	13	12				5²						1	2³	4	11¹	3	9	7			10		6	14	46

FA Cup

First Round	Guiseley	(a)	3-4

Carabao Cup

First Round	Newport Co	(h)	1-4

Checkatrade Trophy

Group B (S)	Southend U	(a)	1-3
Group B (S)	Southampton U21	(h)	4-0
Group B (S)	Colchester U	(h)	3-1
Second Round (S)	Northampton T	(h)	1-1

(Northampton T won 4-2 on penalties)

CARDIFF CITY

FOUNDATION

Credit for the establishment of a first class professional football club in such a rugby stronghold as Cardiff is due to members of the Riverside club formed in 1899 out of a cricket club of that name. Cardiff became a city in 1905 and in 1908 the South Wales and Monmouthshire FA granted Riverside permission to call themselves Cardiff City. The club turned professional under that name in 1910.

Cardiff City Stadium, Leckwith Road, Cardiff CF11 8AZ.

Telephone: (0845) 365 1115. ***Fax:*** (0845) 365 1116.

Ticket Office: (0845) 345 1400.

Website: www.cardiffcityfc.co.uk

Email: club@cardiffcityfc.co.uk

Ground Capacity: 33,316.

Record Attendance: 57,893 v Arsenal, Division 1, 22 April 1953 (at Ninian Park); 32,478 v Reading, FL C, 6 May 2018 (at Cardiff City Stadium).

Ground Record Attendance: 62,634, Wales v England, 17 October 1959 (at Ninian Park); 33,280, Wales v Belgium, 12 June 2015 (at Cardiff City Stadium).

Pitch Measurements: 105m × 68m (115yd × 74.5yd).

Chairman: Mehmet Dalman.

Chief Executive: Ken Choo.

Manager: Neil Warnock.

Assistant Manager: Kevin Blackwell

Colours: Blue shirts with white trim, blue shorts with white trim, blue socks with white trim.

Year Formed: 1899.

Turned Professional: 1910.

Previous Names: 1899, Riverside; 1902, Riverside Albion; 1908, Cardiff City.

Club Nickname: 'The Bluebirds'.

Grounds: Riverside, Sophia Gardens, Old Park and Fir Gardens; 1910, Ninian Park; 2009, Cardiff City Stadium.

First Football League Game: 28 August 1920, Division 2, v Stockport Co (a) W 5–2 – Kneeshaw; Brittan, Leyton; Keenor (1), Smith, Hardy; Grimshaw (1), Gill (2), Cashmore, West, Evans (1).

Record League Victory: 9–2 v Thames, Division 3 (S), 6 February 1932 – Farquharson; Eric Morris, Roberts; Galbraith, Harris, Ronan; Emmerson (1), Keating (1), Jones (1), McCambridge (1), Robbins (5).

Record Cup Victory: 8–0 v Enfield, FA Cup 1st rd, 28 November 1931 – Farquharson; Smith, Roberts; Harris (1), Galbraith, Ronan; Emmerson (2), Keating (3); O'Neill (2), Robbins, McCambridge.

HONOURS

League Champions: FL C – 2012–13; Division 3S – 1946–47; Third Division – 1992–93.
Runners-up: FL C – 2017–18; Division 1 – 1923–24; Division 2 – 1920–21, 1951–52, 1959–60; Division 3 – 1975–76, 1982–83; Third Division – 2000–01; Division 4 – 1987–88.

FA Cup Winners: 1927.
Runners-up: 1925, 2008.

League Cup: *Runners-up:* 2012.

Welsh Cup Winners: 22 times.

European Competitions
European Cup-Winners' Cup: 1964–65 *(qf)*, 1965–66, 1967–68 *(sf)*, 1968–69, 1969–70, 1970–71 *(qf)*, 1971–72, 1973–74, 1974–75, 1976–77, 1977–78, 1988–89, 1992–93, 1993–94.

THE SUN FACT FILE

Goalkeeper Graham Vearncombe, who made over 200 appearances for Cardiff City between 1952 and 1964, was a double international for Wales. Capped for England against Wales at baseball in July 1957, he went on to represent his country twice at soccer, making his debut against East Germany in September 1957.

Record Defeat: 2–11 v Sheffield U, Division 1, 1 January 1926.

Most League Points (2 for a win): 66, Division 3 (S), 1946–47.

Most League Points (3 for a win): 90, FL C, 2017–18.

Most League Goals: 95, Division 3, 2000–01.

Highest League Scorer in Season: Robert Earnshaw, 31, Division 2, 2002–03.

Most League Goals in Total Aggregate: Len Davies, 128, 1920–31.

Most League Goals in One Match: 5, Hugh Ferguson v Burnley, Division 1, 1 September 1928; 5, Walter Robbins v Thames, Division 3 (S), 6 February 1932; 5, William Henderson v Northampton T, Division 3 (S), 22 April 1933.

Most Capped Player: Aron Gunnarsson, 59 (85), Iceland.

Most League Appearances: Phil Dwyer, 471, 1972–85.

Youngest League Player: Bob Adams, 15 years 355 days v Southend U, 18 February 1933.

Record Transfer Fee Received: £10,000,000 from Internazionale for Gary Medel, August 2014.

Record Transfer Fee Paid: £15,000,000 to Nantes for Emiliano Sala, January 2019.

Football League Record: 1920 Elected to Division 2; 1921–29 Division 1; 1929–31 Division 2; 1931–47 Division 3 (S); 1947–52 Division 2; 1952–57 Division 1; 1957–60 Division 2; 1960–62 Division 1; 1962–75 Division 2; 1975–76 Division 3; 1976–82 Division 2; 1982–83 Division 3; 1983–85 Division 2; 1985–86 Division 3; 1986–88 Division 4; 1988–90 Division 3; 1990–92 Division 4; 1992–93 Division 3; 1993–95 Division 2; 1995–99 Division 3; 1999–2000 Division 2; 2000–01 Division 3; 2001–03 Division 2; 2003–04 Division 1; 2004–13 FL C; 2013–14 Premier League; 2014–18 FL C; 2018–19 Premier League; 2019– FL C.

LATEST SEQUENCES

Longest Sequence of League Wins: 9, 26.10.1946 – 28.12.1946.

Longest Sequence of League Defeats: 7, 4.11.1933 – 25.12.1933.

Longest Sequence of League Draws: 6, 29.11.1980 – 17.1.1981.

Longest Sequence of Unbeaten League Matches: 21, 21.9.1946 – 1.3.1947.

Longest Sequence Without a League Win: 15, 21.11.1936 – 6.3.1937.

Successive Scoring Runs: 24 from 25.8.2012.

Successive Non-scoring Runs: 8 from 20.12.1952.

MANAGERS

Davy McDougall 1910–11
Fred Stewart 1911–33
Bartley Wilson 1933–34
B. Watts-Jones 1934–37
Bill Jennings 1937–39
Cyril Spiers 1939–46
Billy McCandless 1946–48
Cyril Spiers 1948–54
Trevor Morris 1954–58
Bill Jones 1958–62
George Swindin 1962–64
Jimmy Scoular 1964–73
Frank O'Farrell 1973–74
Jimmy Andrews 1974–78
Richie Morgan 1978–81
Graham Williams 1981–82
Len Ashurst 1982–84
Jimmy Goodfellow 1984
Alan Durban 1984–86
Frank Burrows 1986–89
Len Ashurst 1989–91
Eddie May 1991–94
Terry Yorath 1994–95
Eddie May 1995
Kenny Hibbitt (*Chief Coach*) 1995–96
Phil Neal 1996
Russell Osman 1996–97
Kenny Hibbitt 1997–98
Frank Burrows 1998–2000
Billy Ayre 2000
Bobby Gould 2000
Alan Cork 2000–02
Lennie Lawrence 2002–05
Dave Jones 2005–11
Malky Mackay 2011–13
Ole Gunnar Solskjaer 2014
Russell Slade 2014–16
Paul Trollope 2016
Neil Warnock October 2016–

TEN YEAR LEAGUE RECORD

		P	W	D	L	F	A	Pts	Pos
2009-10	FL C	46	22	10	14	73	54	76	4
2010-11	FL C	46	23	11	12	76	54	80	4
2011-12	FL C	46	19	18	9	66	53	75	6
2012-13	FL C	46	25	12	9	72	45	87	1
2013-14	PR Lge	38	7	9	22	32	74	30	20
2014-15	FL C	46	16	14	16	57	61	62	11
2015-16	FL C	46	17	17	12	56	51	68	8
2016-17	FL C	46	17	11	18	60	61	62	12
2017-18	FL C	46	27	9	10	69	39	90	2
2018-19	PR Lge	38	10	4	24	34	69	34	18

DID YOU KNOW ?

Cardiff City played their first games in European competition in the short-lived Friendship Cup in the 1961–62 season. The Bluebirds won 4-2 away to French club RC Lens and followed up with a 2-0 win at Ninian Park, leaving them 6-2 winners on aggregate.

CARDIFF CITY – PREMIER LEAGUE 2018–19 LEAGUE RECORD

Match No.	*Date*	*Venue*	*Opponents*	*Result*		*H/T Score*	*Lg Pos.*	*Goalscorers*	*Attendance*
1	Aug 11	A	Bournemouth	L	0-2	0-1	17		10,353
2	18	H	Newcastle U	D	0-0	0-0	15		30,720
3	25	A	Huddersfield T	D	0-0	0-0	14		23,787
4	Sept 2	H	Arsenal	L	2-3	1-1	16	Victor Camarasa [45], Ward [70]	32,316
5	15	A	Chelsea	L	1-4	1-2	16	Bamba [16]	40,499
6	22	H	Manchester C	L	0-5	0-3	19		32,321
7	30	H	Burnley	L	1-2	0-0	19	Murphy, J [60]	30,411
8	Oct 6	A	Tottenham H	L	0-1	0-1	20		43,268
9	20	H	Fulham	W	4-2	2-2	17	Murphy, J [15], Reid [20], Paterson [65], Harris, K [87]	29,681
10	27	A	Liverpool	L	1-4	0-1	17	Paterson [77]	53,373
11	Nov 3	H	Leicester C	L	0-1	0-0	18		30,877
12	10	H	Brighton & HA	W	2-1	1-1	18	Paterson [28], Bamba [90]	29,402
13	24	A	Everton	L	0-1	0-0	18		39,139
14	30	H	Wolverhampton W	W	2-1	0-1	15	Gunnarsson [65], Hoilett [77]	30,213
15	Dec 4	A	West Ham U	L	1-3	0-0	16	Murphy, J [90]	56,811
16	8	H	Southampton	W	1-0	0-0	14	Paterson [74]	30,067
17	15	A	Watford	L	2-3	0-1	16	Hoilett [80], Reid [82]	20,032
18	22	H	Manchester U	L	1-5	1-3	17	Victor Camarasa (pen) [38]	33,028
19	26	A	Crystal Palace	D	0-0	0-0	17		25,206
20	29	A	Leicester C	W	1-0	0-0	16	Victor Camarasa [90]	32,047
21	Jan 1	H	Tottenham H	L	0-3	0-3	16		32,485
22	12	H	Huddersfield T	D	0-0	0-0	17		30,725
23	19	A	Newcastle U	L	0-3	0-1	18		49,864
24	29	A	Arsenal	L	1-2	0-0	18	Mendez-Laing [90]	59,933
25	Feb 2	H	Bournemouth	W	2-0	1-0	18	Reid 2 (1 pen) [5 (p), 46]	31,939
26	9	A	Southampton	W	2-1	0-0	16	Bamba [69], Zohore [90]	31,438
27	22	H	Watford	L	1-5	0-1	17	Bamba [82]	30,387
28	26	H	Everton	L	0-3	0-1	17		31,849
29	Mar 2	A	Wolverhampton W	L	0-2	0-2	18		31,309
30	9	H	West Ham U	W	2-0	1-0	18	Hoilett [4], Victor Camarasa [52]	32,458
31	31	H	Chelsea	L	1-2	0-0	18	Victor Camarasa [46]	32,657
32	Apr 3	A	Manchester C	L	0-2	0-2	18		53,559
33	13	A	Burnley	L	0-2	0-1	18		21,480
34	16	A	Brighton & HA	W	2-0	1-0	18	Mendez-Laing [22], Morrison [50]	30,226
35	21	H	Liverpool	L	0-2	0-0	18		33,082
36	27	A	Fulham	L	0-1	0-0	18		23,822
37	May 4	H	Crystal Palace	L	2-3	1-2	18	Kelly (og) [31], Reid [90]	32,133
38	12	A	Manchester U	W	2-0	1-0	18	Mendez-Laing 2 (1 pen) [23 (p), 54]	74,457

Final League Position: 18

GOALSCORERS

League (34): Reid 5 (1 pen), Victor Camarasa 5 (1 pen), Bamba 4, Mendez-Laing 4 (1 pen), Paterson 4, Hoilett 3, Murphy J 3, Gunnarsson 1, Harris K 1, Morrison 1, Ward 1, Zohore 1, own goal 1.
FA Cup (0).
Carabao Cup (1): Ecuele Manga 1.

Etheridge N 38	Peltier L 17 + 3	Morrison S 34	Ecuele Manga B 37 + 1	Bennett J 30	Bamba S 28	Mendez-Laing N 11 + 9	Paterson C 21 + 6	Ralls J 22 + 6	Hoilett J 23 + 9	Reid B 16 + 11	Ward D 4 + 10	Murphy J 22 + 7	Madine G — + 5	Victor Camarasa F 31 + 1	Arter H 24 + 1	Zohore K 7 + 12	Richards A — + 4	Cunningham G 7	Harris K 3 + 10	Gunnarsson A 27 + 1	Damour L — + 2	Healey R — + 3	Niasse O 12 + 1	Bacuna L 4 + 7	*Match No.*
1	2	3	4	5	6	7¹	8³	9	10	11²	12	13	14												1
1		3	2	5	4	13	14	7	9³	12		11²		6¹	8	10									2
1		3	2	5	4	7²	12	6		14	13	10		8¹	9	11³									3
1		3	2	5	4			8	9	10	11²		13	6¹	7	12									4
1		3	2	5	4		13	7	9	10²	11¹		14	6	0³		12								5
1	2⁴	3	4					8	6³	10	11¹	14		7	9	13	12	5							6
1		3	2		4		10	8¹			12	9	13	6	7	11²		5							7
1		3	2	5	4		11¹	6	7²	14	13³	10		8	9				12						8
1		3	2	5	4		11			10		9²		6	8¹		12		13	7³	14				9
1		3	2	5	4		11		6	10¹		9²		7		14			13	8³	12				10
1		3	2	5	4		11		12	10³	13	9²	14	6	8¹					7					11
1	12	3³	2		4		11	9¹	13	14		10²		8				5	7	6					12
1		3	2		4		11	9	13		14	12		8¹	10²			5	7³	6					13
1		3	2		4		10	7	9	12		11¹		6	8²				13	5					14
1		3	2	5	4	12	11³	8²	10¹			13		7	9				14	6					15
1		3	2	5	4	7¹	11	14	12			10²		8	9³				13	6					16
1	13	3	2	5¹	4	12	11		7	14		10³		8	9					6²					17
1		3	2		4		11	14	7¹			10		8	9²	12		5	13	6³					18
1	2	4	3	6	5			9	10¹	11				8²	12				7	13					19
1	14	3	2		4		11		7¹	13		10²		8	9³			5	12	6					20
1		3	2		4	14	7	13	12	11¹		10³		8²	9			5		6					21
1		3	2	5	4	7¹	11	12	10					8²	9					6		13			22
1	2		3	5	4	6¹	10³	8	9	12	14	13		7									11²		23
1	2		3	5	4	12	6	9		10³					7²	13			14	8			11¹		24
1	2		3	5	4		6	8	12	10³		9²				13				7			11¹	14	25
1	2		3	8	4		5	7		10²				14	9	13				6¹			11³	12	26
1		3	2	8	4	13	9	7²	12			11¹			6	14							10³	5	27
1		3	2	5	4	6²	13		9³	10	14	12				11¹				8				7	28
1	2	3	12	5	4³		13	8		9²				7		11				6		14	10¹		29
1	2	3	4	5³			14	13	10			8		9¹	7²					6			11	12	30
1	2	3	4	5		14		12	10			8¹		9	7³	13				6			11²		31
1	2	3	4	5		12		8	9	14		6²		10³						7¹			11	13	32
1	2	3	4	5		12			10³	14		8		9	7²	11¹				6			13		33
1	2	3	4	5		8³		7	10					9		14			13	6¹			11²	12	34
1	2	3	4	5		10		9¹	7²			14		8		12				6			11³	13	35
1	2	3	4	5		10			8	14	12			9¹						6³		13	11²	7	36
1	2	3	4	5		6			14	10	11²	9¹		8³		13				7				12	37
1	2	3	4	5		6³			14	10	13	9				11¹	12			8²				7	38

FA Cup
Third Round Gillingham (a) 0-1

Carabao Cup
Second Round Norwich C (h) 1-3

CARLISLE UNITED

FOUNDATION

Carlisle United came into being when members of Shaddongate United voted to change its name on 17 May 1904. The new club was admitted to the Second Division of the Lancashire Combination in 1905–06, winning promotion the following season. Devonshire Park was officially opened on 2 September 1905, when St Helens Town were the visitors. Despite defeat in a disappointing 3–2 start, a respectable mid-table position was achieved.

Brunton Park, Warwick Road, Carlisle, Cumbria CA1 1LL.

Telephone: (01228) 526 237.

Ticket Office: (0844) 371 1921.

Website: www.carlisleunited.co.uk

Email: enquiries@carlisleunited.co.uk

Ground Capacity: 17,949.

Record Attendance: 27,500 v Birmingham C, FA Cup 3rd rd, 5 January 1957 and v Middlesbrough, FA Cup 5th rd, 7 February 1970.

Pitch Measurements: 102m × 68m (111.5yd × 74.5yd).

Chairman: Andrew Jenkins.

Chief Executive: Nigel Clibbens.

Manager: Steven Pressley.

Assistant Manager: Gavin Skelton.

Colours: Blue shirts with white and red trim, white shorts with blue trim, blue socks with white trim.

Year Formed: 1904. ***Turned Professional:*** 1921.

Previous Name: 1904, Shaddongate United; 1904, Carlisle United.

Club Nicknames: 'The Cumbrians', 'The Blues'.

Grounds: 1904, Milholme Bank; 1905, Devonshire Park; 1909, Brunton Park.

First Football League Game: 25 August 1928, Division 3 (N), v Accrington S (a) W 3–2 – Prout; Coulthard, Cook; Harrison, Ross, Pigg; Agar (1), Hutchison, McConnell (1), Ward (1), Watson.

Record League Victory: 8–0 v Hartlepool U, Division 3 (N), 1 September 1928 – Prout; Smiles, Cook; Robinson (1) Ross, Pigg; Agar (1), Hutchison (1), McConnell (4), Ward (1), Watson. 8–0 v Scunthorpe U, Division 3 (N), 25 December 1952 – MacLaren; Hill, Scott; Stokoe, Twentyman, Waters; Harrison (1), Whitehouse (5), Ashman (2), Duffett, Bond.

Record Cup Victory: 6–0 v Shepshed Dynamo, FA Cup 1st rd, 16 November 1996 – Caig; Hopper, Archdeacon (pen), Walling, Robinson, Pounewatchy, Peacock (1), Conway (1) (Jansen), Smart (McAlindon (1)), Hayward, Aspinall (Thorpe), (2 og). 6–0 v Tipton T, FA Cup 1st rd, 6 November 2010 – Collin; Simek, Murphy, Chester, Cruise, Robson (McKenna), Berrett, Taiwo (Hurst), Marshall, Zoko (Curran) (2), Madine (4).

Record Defeat: 1–11 v Hull C, Division 3 (N), 14 January 1939.

HONOURS

League Champions: Division 3 – 1964–65; FL 2 – 2005–06; Third Division – 1994–95.
Runners-up: Division 3 – 1981–82; Division 4 – 1963–64; Conference – (3rd) 2004–05 *(promoted via play-offs)*.

FA Cup: 6th rd – 1975.

League Cup: semi-final – 1970.

League Trophy Winners: 1997, 2011.
Runners-up: 1995, 2003, 2006, 2010.

THE Sun FACT FILE

When Bill Shankly took over as manager of Carlisle United in the summer of 1949 he was able to rebuild the team using cash from the sale of his predecessor Ivor Broadis to Sunderland as a player. Record signing Billy Hogan, a £4,000 buy from Manchester City, was one of six new men brought in at the start of the season but United's bid to earn promotion fell short as they finished the season ninth in Division Three North.

Most League Points (2 for a win): 62, Division 3 (N), 1950–51.

Most League Points (3 for a win): 91, Division 3, 1994–95.

Most League Goals: 113, Division 4, 1963–64.

Highest League Scorer in Season: Jimmy McConnell, 42, Division 3 (N), 1928–29.

Most League Goals in Total Aggregate: Jimmy McConnell, 124, 1928–32.

Most League Goals in One Match: 5, Hugh Mills v Halifax T, Division 3 (N), 11 September 1937; 5, Jim Whitehouse v Scunthorpe U, Division 3 (N), 25 December 1952.

Most Capped Player: Reggie Lambe, 6 (34), Bermuda.

Most League Appearances: Allan Ross, 466, 1963–79.

Youngest League Player: John Slaven, 16 years 162 days v Scunthorpe U, 16 March 2002.

Record Transfer Fee Received: £1,000,000 from Crystal Palace for Matt Jansen, February 1998.

Record Transfer Fee Paid: £140,000 to Blackburn R for Joe Garner, August 2007.

Football League Record: 1928 Elected to Division 3 (N); 1958–62 Division 4; 1962–63 Division 3; 1963–64 Division 4; 1964–65 Division 3; 1965–74 Division 2; 1974–75 Division 1; 1975–77 Division 2; 1977–82 Division 3; 1982–86 Division 2; 1986–87 Division 3; 1987–92 Division 4; 1992–95 Division 3; 1995–96 Division 2; 1996–97 Division 3; 1997–98 Division 2; 1998–2004 Division 3; 2004–05 Conference; 2005–06 FL 2; 2006–14 FL 1; 2014– FL 2.

LATEST SEQUENCES

Longest Sequence of League Wins: 7, 18.2.2006 – 8.4.2006.

Longest Sequence of League Defeats: 12, 27.9.2003 – 13.12.2003.

Longest Sequence of League Draws: 6, 11.2.1978 – 11.3.1978.

Longest Sequence of Unbeaten League Matches: 19, 1.10.1994 – 11.2.1995.

Longest Sequence Without a League Win: 15, 12.4.2014 – 20.9.2014.

Successive Scoring Runs: 26 from 23.8.1947.

Successive Non-scoring Runs: 7 from 25.2.2017.

MANAGERS

Harry Kirkbride 1904–05 (*Secretary-Manager*)
McCumiskey 1905–06 (*Secretary-Manager*)
Jack Houston 1906–08 (*Secretary-Manager*)
Bert Stansfield 1908–10
Jack Houston 1910–12
Davie Graham 1912–13
George Bristow 1913–30
Billy Hampson 1930–33
Bill Clarke 1933–35
Robert Kelly 1935–36
Fred Westgarth 1936–38
David Taylor 1938–40
Howard Harkness 1940–45
Bill Clark 1945–46 (*Secretary-Manager*)
Ivor Broadis 1946–49
Bill Shankly 1949–51
Fred Emery 1951–58
Andy Beattie 1958–60
Ivor Powell 1960–63
Alan Ashman 1963–67
Tim Ward 1967–68
Bob Stokoe 1968–70
Ian MacFarlane 1970–72
Alan Ashman 1972–75
Dick Young 1975–76
Bobby Moncur 1976–80
Martin Harvey 1980
Bob Stokoe 1980–85
Bryan 'Pop' Robson 1985
Bob Stokoe 1985–86
Harry Gregg 1986–87
Cliff Middlemass 1987–91
Aidan McCaffery 1991–92
David McCreery 1992–93
Mick Wadsworth (*Director of Coaching*) 1993–96
Mervyn Day 1996–97
David Wilkes and John Halpin (*Directors of Coaching*), and **Michael Knighton** 1997–99
Nigel Pearson 1998–99
Keith Mincher 1999
Martin Wilkinson 1999–2000
Ian Atkins 2000–01
Roddy Collins 2001–02; 2002–03
Paul Simpson 2003–06
Neil McDonald 2006–07
John Ward 2007–08
Greg Abbott 2008–13
Graham Kavanagh 2013–14
Keith Curle 2014–18
John Sheridan 2018–19
Steven Pressley January 2019–

TEN YEAR LEAGUE RECORD

		P	W	D	L	F	A	Pts	Pos
2009-10	FL 1	46	15	13	18	63	66	58	14
2010-11	FL 1	46	16	11	19	60	62	59	12
2011-12	FL 1	46	18	15	13	65	66	69	8
2012-13	FL 1	46	14	13	19	56	77	55	17
2013-14	FL 1	46	11	12	23	43	76	45	22
2014-15	FL 2	46	14	8	24	56	74	50	20
2015-16	FL 2	46	17	16	13	67	62	67	10
2016-17	FL 2	46	18	17	11	69	68	71	6
2017-18	FL 2	46	17	16	13	62	54	67	10
2018-19	FL 2	46	20	8	18	67	62	68	11

DID YOU KNOW ?

Carlisle United won the Cumberland League championship in 1904–05, their first season of existence, finishing six points clear of their nearest rivals Carlisle Red Rose. They completed a double by defeating Red Rose 2-0 in the final of the Cumberland Cup and were elected to the Lancashire Combination for the following season.

CARLISLE UNITED – SKY BET LEAGUE TWO 2018–19 LEAGUE RECORD

Match No.	Date	Venue	Opponents	Result		H/T Score	Lg Pos.	Goalscorers	Attendance
1	Aug 4	A	Exeter C	L	1-3	1-2	20	Bennett [37]	4266
2	11	H	Northampton T	D	2-2	1-1	21	Devitt [30], Hope [63]	4521
3	18	A	Cheltenham T	W	1-0	1-0	15	Bennett [39]	2455
4	21	H	Port Vale	W	2-1	1-0	6	Grainger (pen) [30], Parkes [84]	3688
5	25	H	Crewe Alex	W	1-0	0-0	4	Nadesan [69]	4238
6	Sept 1	A	Mansfield T	L	0-1	0-0	10		4470
7	8	A	Cambridge U	W	2-1	1-1	4	Bennett [43], Nadesan [69]	4234
8	15	H	Tranmere R	L	0-2	0-0	11		5187
9	22	A	Bury	W	1-0	0-0	5	Bennett [52]	3657
10	29	H	Stevenage	L	0-1	0-0	11		4200
11	Oct 2	H	Grimsby T	L	0-1	0-1	13		3316
12	6	A	Oldham Ath	W	3-1	1-0	10	Hope [21], Nadesan [56], Sowerby [57]	4730
13	13	H	Morecambe	L	0-2	0-2	11		4569
14	20	A	Macclesfield T	L	1-2	0-0	11	Nadesan [50]	2153
15	23	A	Lincoln C	D	2-2	2-2	13	Nadesan 2 [6, 27]	9119
16	27	H	Yeovil T	L	0-1	0-0	16		3928
17	Nov 3	H	Newport Co	W	3-2	2-1	11	Devitt 2 [9, 12], Grainger [90]	3541
18	17	A	Swindon T	W	4-0	1-0	11	Nadesan [41], Slater 2 [46, 65], Devitt [54]	6722
19	24	H	Forest Green R	L	1-2	0-1	11	Devitt (pen) [77]	4166
20	27	A	Notts Co	D	1-1	0-0	11	Yates [84]	4119
21	Dec 8	A	Milton Keynes D	L	0-2	0-0	13		6849
22	15	H	Colchester U	W	4-0	1-0	12	Hope [33], Yates [51], Devitt [57], Grainger [90]	3547
23	22	A	Crawley T	W	3-2	2-2	10	Yates [14], Grainger (pen) [37], Sowerby [56]	2176
24	26	H	Oldham Ath	W	6-0	2-0	9	Hope [18], Yates 2 [30, 71], Nadesan [60], Grainger [64], Liddle [90]	5465
25	29	H	Macclesfield T	W	2-1	1-1	8	Hope [44], Yates [88]	4884
26	Jan 1	A	Morecambe	W	2-0	1-0	7	Devitt [15], Sowerby [76]	3749
27	5	H	Mansfield T	W	3-2	2-0	5	Sowerby [4], Hope 2 [26, 79]	4563
28	12	A	Northampton T	L	0-3	0-0	6		4875
29	19	H	Cheltenham T	W	2-0	0-0	4	Devitt [49], Hope [56]	4458
30	26	A	Port Vale	W	1-0	0-0	4	Simpson [79]	3881
31	Feb 9	H	Exeter C	D	1-1	0-1	5	Devitt [78]	4851
32	12	A	Crewe Alex	L	1-2	1-1	6	Miller [29]	3476
33	16	H	Milton Keynes D	L	2-3	1-1	7	Scougall (pen) [14], Hope [90]	10,459
34	23	A	Colchester U	D	1-1	0-0	8	Hope [57]	3626
35	Mar 2	A	Newport Co	L	0-2	0-1	9		3432
36	9	H	Swindon T	W	2-1	1-1	7	Hope [13], O'Hare [79]	4629
37	12	H	Notts Co	L	1-3	0-1	8	Hope [76]	3514
38	16	A	Forest Green R	D	1-1	0-1	9	Thomas [49]	2381
39	23	H	Cambridge U	D	2-2	2-1	8	Devitt [37], Thomas [45]	4673
40	30	A	Tranmere R	L	0-3	0-1	9		8095
41	Apr 6	H	Bury	W	3-2	1-2	8	Devitt [1], O'Hare [50], Hope [89]	4656
42	13	A	Stevenage	L	0-3	0-1	8		2770
43	19	H	Lincoln C	W	1-0	0-0	8	Jones [76]	6819
44	22	A	Grimsby T	L	0-1	0-0	9		3647
45	27	H	Crawley T	W	4-2	4-1	9	Thomas 2 [7, 9], O'Hare [20], Hope [31]	4514
46	May 4	A	Yeovil T	D	0-0	0-0	11		3418

Final League Position: 11

GOALSCORERS

League (67): Hope 14, Devitt 11 (1 pen), Nadesan 8, Yates 6, Grainger 5 (2 pens), Bennett 4, Sowerby 4, Thomas 4, O'Hare 3, Slater 2, Jones 1, Liddle 1, Miller 1, Parkes 1, Scougall 1 (1 pen), Simpson 1.
FA Cup (1): Devitt 1.
Carabao Cup (1): Hope 1.
Checkatrade Trophy (5): Gillesphey 1, Glendon 1, Nadesan 1, Sowerby 1, Yates 1.

Fryer J 5	Miller G 17 + 1	Liddle G 38 + 1	Parkes T 37 + 2	Grainger D 23	Slater R 24 + 11	Glendon G 5 + 11	Etuhu K 34 + 5	Yates J 23	Bennett R 13 + 8	Hope H 39 + 1	Devitt J 32 + 3	Jones M 19 + 5	Campbell A 2 + 11	Gerrard A 41	Nadesan A 23 + 2	Gillespey M 20 + 4	Collin A 41 + 1	Sowerby J 22 + 3	McCarron L 3 + 13	Adewusi S — + 1	Kennedy J — + 6	Simpson C 1 + 7	Gnahoua A — + 1	O'Hare C 16	Thomas N 11 + 5	Scougall S 10 + 5	Cullen M 3 + 6	Grant P 4	*Match No.*
1	2	3	4	5	6^{3}	7^{1}	8	9^{2}	10	11	12	13	14																1
1		3	4	5	12	7^{1}	2	9	10	11	6	8^{2}	13																2
1		2	3	5	13	12	8^{2}	6	10	9	7			4	11^{1}														3
1		2	4	5		12	7	6	10	9	8			3	11^{1}														4
1^{1}		2	4	5^{2}		14	7	6	11	9	8			3	10^{3}	12	13												5
		2	4			7^{1}	9	6	11^{3}	10	8^{2}		14	3	12	5	1	13											6
		2	4			7^{1}	8	6	10		9		12	3	11^{2}	5	1	13											7
		2	4				7	6^{2}	11^{1}	9	8		13	3	10^{3}	5	1	12	14										8
		2	4			12	9	6■	11^{2}	10	8			3	13	5	1	7^{1}											9
		2	4			12	7		11^{1}	9	8		13	3	10	5^{2}	1	6^{3}	14										10
		2	4		6^{2}		8			11	7^{3}	14	12	3	10	5	1	9^{1}	13										11
		2	4		14	13	8	9		11		7^{1}	12	3	10^{2}	5	1	6^{3}											12
	2	3	4		14	13	8	9	11^{2}			7^{1}			10	5^{3}	1	6	12										13
	2^{2}		4^{3}			12	9	10	11			7		3	8^{1}	5	1	6	14	13									14
					4		2	9	11			8	7	3	10	5	1	6											15
		3			8^{3}		2	9^{1}	13		12	7	10^{7}	4	11	5	1	6	14										16
		2		5	13	7^{1}		10	12		8	9^{2}		3	11	4	1	6											17
	14	2			7			6		10	9^{2}	8	13	3^{3}	11^{1}	4	1	5	12										18
		2			6		12	9	13	11^{1}	8	7^{2}		3	10	4	1	5											19
		2			7		14	6	13	11	9^{1}	8^{3}		3	10^{2}	4	1	5	12										20
		2	12		7^{2}		9	6^{3}	14	10	13	8		3	11^{1}	4	1	5											21
		2	12	9	14		6^{2}	8		10	7		13	3	11^{1}	4^{3}	1	5											22
		5	3	6	12		7	9		11	8^{1}			4	10		1	2											23
		3	5	6^{2}	12		7^{1}	9		11	8			4	10^{3}	14	1	2	13										24
		2	4	5	14		8	10^{1}	13	11	7^{3}		12	3	9^{2}		1	6											25
		2	5	6	12		9		13	11	8^{2}			3	10	4^{3}	1	7^{1}			14								26
		2	4	6			8			11^{1}	9			3	10	5	1	7	12										27
		2	4	10	14		9		13	11^{3}	7			3		5^{1}	1	8	6^{2}			12							28
	2^{2}		4	5	10	13	9			11	7^{1}	12		3			1	8	6^{3}			14							29
	2		4	5	10		9			11	7	13		3			1	8^{2}	6^{1}			14	12^{3}						30
	2		4	5	6^{2}		8			11	7			3			1							9	10^{1}	12	13		31
	2^{1}	12	4	5	8		7			11	10■			3			1							6^{3}	9^{2}	13	14		32
	5	2			7^{3}		8			11				3			1		13		14			9	6^{1}	10^{2}	12	4	33
		2	4	5	7		8			10		13		3			1		14					9^{1}	12	6^{3}	11^{2}		34
		5	4	2	6		8^{2}			10^{1}				3			1		13					7	12	9	11		35
		2	4	5	7		13			10	8^{3}			3			1					14		9	12	6^{2}	11^{1}		36
		2	4	5^{1}	7		8			11	6			3			1					13		9	12	10^{2}			37
	2		4	5	7					11^{2}	6^{1}	8		3			1					13		9	10	12			38
	2		4	5	8					10^{1}	11^{2}	7		3			1				13			9	6	12			39
	5^{1}	4	9		8		13			12	11^{2}	6		2			1							7	10			3	40
	2	3	5		7^{2}		12			10	11^{3}	8■					1					14		9	6^{1}	13		4	41
	2	3	5		7^{1}	12				10							1				13	11^{2}		9	6	8		4	42
	2^{2}	3	5				8			10	11^{1}	7		4		13	1							9	12	6			43
	5	2	4			12	8^{1}			10^{2}		6		3			1				14			7	9	11^{3}	13		44
	5	2	4		8					10		6		3		14	1				12^{3}			7^{2}	9	11^{1}	13		45
	5	2	4		7^{1}					10		6		3			1							8	9	11	12		46

FA Cup

First Round	Crewe Alex	(a)	1-0
Second Round	Lincoln C	(a)	0-2

Carabao Cup

First Round	Blackburn R	(h)	1-5

Checkatrade Trophy

Group A (N)	Morecambe	(h)	3-2
Group A (N)	Sunderland	(a)	1-3
Group A (N)	Stoke C U21	(h)	1-1

(Stoke C U21 won 5-4 on penalties)

CHARLTON ATHLETIC

FOUNDATION

The club was formed on 9 June 1905, by a group of 14- and 15-year-old youths living in streets by the Thames in the area which now borders the Thames Barrier. The club's progress through local leagues was so rapid that after the First World War they joined the Kent League where they spent a season before turning professional and joining the Southern League in 1920. A year later they were elected to the Football League's Division 3 (South).

The Valley, Floyd Road, Charlton, London SE7 8BL.

Telephone: (020) 8333 4000.

Ticket Office: (020) 8333 4094.

Website: www.cafc.co.uk

Email: info@cafc.co.uk

Ground Capacity: 27,111.

Record Attendance: 75,031 v Aston Villa, FA Cup 5th rd, 12 February 1938 (at The Valley).

Pitch Measurements: 102.5m × 67.5m (112yd × 74yd).

Owner: Roland Duchâtelet.

Chairman: Richard Murray.

Chief Operating Officer: Terry Keohane.

Manager: Lee Bowyer.

Assistant Manager: Johnnie Jackson.

Colours: Red shirts with white trim, white shorts with red trim, red socks with white trim.

Year Formed: 1905.

Turned Professional: 1920.

Club Nickname: 'The Addicks'.

Grounds: 1906, Siemen's Meadow; 1907, Woolwich Common; 1909, Pound Park; 1913, Horn Lane; 1920, The Valley; 1923, Catford (The Mount); 1924, The Valley; 1985, Selhurst Park; 1991, Upton Park; 1992, The Valley.

First Football League Game: 27 August 1921, Division 3 (S), v Exeter C (h) W 1–0 – Hughes; Johnny Mitchell, Goodman; Dowling (1), Hampson, Dunn; Castle, Bailey, Halse, Green, Wilson.

Record League Victory: 8–1 v Middlesbrough, Division 1, 12 September 1953 – Bartram; Campbell, Ellis; Fenton, Ufton, Hammond; Hurst (2), O'Linn (2), Leary (1), Firmani (3), Kiernan.

Record Cup Victory: 8–0 v Stevenage, FL Trophy, 9 October 2018 – Phillips; Marshall, Dijksteel, Sarr, Stevenson (3) (Reeves), Lapslie (1), Maloney, Ward (Morgan), Pratley (1), Vetokele (2), Ajose (1).

Record Defeat: 1–11 v Aston Villa, Division 2, 14 November 1959.

Most League Points (2 for a win): 61, Division 3 (S), 1934–35.

HONOURS

League Champions: First Division – 1999–2000; FL 1 – 2011–12; Division 3S – 1928–29, 1934–35.
Runners-up: Division 1 – 1936–37; Division 2 – 1935–36, 1985–86.

FA Cup Winners: 1947.
Runners-up: 1946.

League Cup: quarter-final – 2007.

Full Members' Cup:
Runners-up 1987.

THE Sun FACT FILE

Although Charlton Athletic have traditionally worn a predominantly red outfit, for the 1923–24 season they switched to light and dark blue stripes with dark blue shorts. The reason was that the Addicks were considering a merger with Catford South End at the time, but this proved to be unsuccessful and they returned to their traditional red shirts with white shorts the following season.

Most League Points (3 for a win): 101, FL 1, 2011–12.

Most League Goals: 107, Division 2, 1957–58.

Highest League Scorer in Season: Ralph Allen, 32, Division 3 (S), 1934–35.

Most League Goals in Total Aggregate: Stuart Leary, 153, 1953–62.

Most League Goals in One Match: 5, Wilson Lennox v Exeter C, Division 3 (S), 2 February 1929; 5, Eddie Firmani v Aston Villa, Division 1, 5 February 1955; 5, John Summers v Huddersfield T, Division 2, 21 December 1957; 5, John Summers v Portsmouth, Division 2, 1 October 1960.

Most Capped Player: Jonatan Johansson, 42 (106), Finland.

Most League Appearances: Sam Bartram, 579, 1934–56.

Youngest League Player: Jonjo Shelvey, 16 years 59 days v Burnley, 26 April 2008.

Record Transfer Fee Received: £16,500,000 from Tottenham H for Darren Bent, June 2007.

Record Transfer Fee Paid: £4,750,000 to Wimbledon for Jason Euell, January 2001.

Football League Record: 1921 Elected to Division 3 (S); 1929–33 Division 2; 1933–35 Division 3 (S); 1935–36 Division 2; 1936–57 Division 1; 1957–72 Division 2; 1972–75 Division 3; 1975–80 Division 2; 1980–81 Division 3; 1981–86 Division 2; 1986–90 Division 1; 1990–92 Division 2; 1992–98 Division 1; 1998–99 Premier League; 1999–2000 Division 1; 2000–07 Premier League; 2007–09 FL C; 2009–12 FL 1; 2012–16 FL C; 2016–19 FL 1; 2019– FL C.

MANAGERS

Walter Rayner 1920–25
Alex Macfarlane 1925–27
Albert Lindon 1928
Alex Macfarlane 1928–32
Albert Lindon 1932–33
Jimmy Seed 1933–56
Jimmy Trotter 1956–61
Frank Hill 1961–65
Bob Stokoe 1965–67
Eddie Firmani 1967–70
Theo Foley 1970–74
Andy Nelson 1974–79
Mike Bailey 1979–81
Alan Mullery 1981–82
Ken Craggs 1982
Lennie Lawrence 1982–91
Steve Gritt and Alan Curbishley 1991–95
Alan Curbishley 1995–2006
Iain Dowie 2006
Les Reed 2006
Alan Pardew 2006–08
Phil Parkinson 2008–11
Chris Powell 2011–14
José Riga 2014
Bob Peeters 2014–15
Guy Luzon 2015
Karel Fraeye 2015–16
José Riga 2016
Russell Slade 2016
Karl Robinson 2016–18
Lee Bowyer September 2018–

LATEST SEQUENCES

Longest Sequence of League Wins: 12, 26.12.1999 – 7.3.2000.

Longest Sequence of League Defeats: 10, 11.4.1990 – 15.9.1990.

Longest Sequence of League Draws: 6, 13.12.1992 – 16.1.1993.

Longest Sequence of Unbeaten League Matches: 15, 4.10.1980 – 20.12.1980.

Longest Sequence Without a League Win: 18, 18.10.2008 – 17.1.2009.

Successive Scoring Runs: 25 from 26.12.1935.

Successive Non-scoring Runs: 5 from 17.10.2015.

TEN YEAR LEAGUE RECORD

		P	W	D	L	F	A	Pts	Pos
2009-10	FL 1	46	23	15	8	71	48	84	4
2010-11	FL 1	46	15	14	17	62	66	59	13
2011-12	FL 1	46	30	11	5	82	36	101	1
2012-13	FL C	46	17	14	15	65	59	65	9
2013-14	FL C	46	13	12	21	41	61	51	18
2014-15	FL C	46	14	18	14	54	60	60	12
2015-16	FL C	46	9	13	24	40	80	40	22
2016-17	FL 1	46	14	18	14	60	53	60	13
2017-18	FL 1	46	20	11	15	58	51	71	6
2018-19	FL 1	46	26	10	10	73	40	88	3

DID YOU KNOW?

Although they were a First Division team at the time, Charlton Athletic were required to take part in the end-of-season play-offs in 1986–87 to retain their top-flight position. The Addicks drew 1-1 on aggregate in the two-legged final against Leeds United. In the replay Peter Shirtliff's two extra-time goals ensured they avoided the drop.

CHARLTON ATHLETIC – SKY BET LEAGUE ONE 2018–19 LEAGUE RECORD

Match No.	Date	Venue	Opponents	Result		H/T Score	Lg Pos.	Goalscorers	Attendance
1	Aug 4	A	Sunderland	L	1-2	1-0	15	Taylor (pen) [10]	31,075
2	11	H	Shrewsbury T	W	2-1	0-0	11	Taylor [62], Ahearne-Grant [90]	9429
3	18	A	Accrington S	D	1-1	1-0	12	Ahearne-Grant [15]	2265
4	21	H	Peterborough U	L	0-1	0-0	15		9762
5	25	H	Fleetwood T	D	0-0	0-0	14		8810
6	Sept 1	A	Southend U	W	2-1	0-0	10	Taylor [57], Bielik [87]	7923
7	8	H	Wycombe W	W	3-2	1-1	8	Jombati (og) [32], Taylor [71], Sarr [80]	10,358
8	15	A	Bradford C	W	2-0	1-0	7	Ahearne-Grant [3], Taylor [81]	15,709
9	22	H	Plymouth Arg	W	2-1	1-1	6	Ahearne-Grant 2 [12, 88]	10,818
10	29	A	Luton T	D	2-2	1-0	6	Fosu (pen) [23], Solly [90]	9502
11	Oct 2	A	Scunthorpe U	L	3-5	2-3	8	Taylor [18], Aribo 2 [22, 69]	3341
12	6	H	Coventry C	L	1-2	1-0	9	Taylor (pen) [45]	11,743
13	20	H	Barnsley	W	2-0	1-0	9	Ahearne-Grant 2 [8, 52]	12,416
14	23	H	Oxford U	D	1-1	1-0	11	Taylor (pen) [25]	9984
15	27	A	Rochdale	L	0-1	0-1	13		3109
16	Nov 3	H	Doncaster R	W	2-0	2-0	8	Aribo [18], Ahearne-Grant [33]	9873
17	6	A	Walsall	W	2-0	1-0	6	Taylor (pen) [6], Bielik [51]	3719
18	24	H	Bristol R	W	3-1	2-1	6	Ward [10], Aribo [45], Ahearne-Grant [90]	10,328
19	27	A	Burton Alb	W	2-1	1-1	6	Ahearne-Grant (pen) [32], Pearce [88]	2438
20	Dec 8	A	Blackpool	L	1-2	0-1	7	Aribo [55]	3024
21	11	A	Portsmouth	W	2-1	2-0	5	Ahearne-Grant [23], Ajose [43]	17,891
22	15	H	AFC Wimbledon	W	2-0	0-0	5	Taylor [60], Marshall [86]	10,691
23	22	H	Gillingham	W	2-0	2-0	4	Reeves [6], Fosu [39]	12,836
24	26	A	Coventry C	L	1-2	0-1	4	Pratley [58]	13,013
25	29	A	Barnsley	L	1-2	0-2	6	Reeves [73]	11,978
26	Jan 1	H	Walsall	W	2-1	2-0	5	Ahearne-Grant [6], Taylor (pen) [9]	10,421
27	5	H	Sunderland	D	1-1	0-1	4	James, Reece (og) [50]	16,317
28	12	A	Shrewsbury T	W	3-0	1-0	4	Taylor [26], Pratley [54], Ahearne-Grant (pen) [79]	5995
29	19	H	Accrington S	W	1-0	0-0	4	Ahearne-Grant (pen) [90]	11,877
30	26	A	Peterborough U	D	0-0	0-0	4		9002
31	Feb 2	A	Fleetwood T	L	0-1	0-0	5		2742
32	9	H	Southend U	D	1-1	0-1	5	Reeves [59]	12,389
33	16	H	Blackpool	D	0-0	0-0	5		17,267
34	23	A	AFC Wimbledon	W	2-1	0-1	5	Sarr [51], Vetokele [90]	4532
35	Mar 2	A	Doncaster R	D	1-1	0-0	5	Marquis (og) [72]	8385
36	9	H	Portsmouth	W	2-1	1-1	5	Aribo [41], Taylor [51]	14,451
37	12	H	Burton Alb	W	2-1	2-1	5	Taylor (pen) [6], Reeves [33]	9505
38	16	A	Bristol R	D	0-0	0-0	5		8343
39	30	H	Bradford C	W	1-0	1-0	5	Taylor [19]	11,630
40	Apr 6	A	Plymouth Arg	W	2-0	1-0	5	Taylor [41], Canavan (og) [49]	10,696
41	9	A	Wycombe W	W	1-0	1-0	5	Pearce [35]	5487
42	13	H	Luton T	W	3-1	0-1	5	Taylor 2 (1 pen) [54 (p), 72], Vetokele [70]	16,449
43	19	A	Oxford U	L	1-2	1-2	5	Taylor (pen) [5]	8680
44	22	H	Scunthorpe U	W	4-0	1-0	5	Dijksteel [24], Aribo [57], Vetokele [63], Taylor [66]	11,973
45	27	A	Gillingham	W	2-0	2-0	5	Aribo [24], Cullen [42]	8047
46	May 4	H	Rochdale	W	4-0	3-0	3	Aribo [19], Andrew (og) [32], Taylor [40], Bielik [75]	12,705

Final League Position: 3

GOALSCORERS

League (73): Taylor 21 (8 pens), Ahearne-Grant 14 (3 pens), Aribo 9, Reeves 4, Bielik 3, Vetokele 3, Fosu 2 (1 pen), Pearce 2, Pratley 2, Sarr 2, Ajose 1, Cullen 1, Dijksteel 1, Marshall 1, Solly 1, Ward 1, own goals 5.
FA Cup (6): Taylor 3, Ajose 1, Marshall 1, Stevenson 1.
Carabao Cup (0).
Checkatrade Trophy (10): Stevenson 3 (1 pen), Vetokele 2, Ajose 1, Lapslie 1, Mascoll 1, Pratley 1, Sarr 1.
League One Play-offs (6): Aribo 1, Bauer 1, Bielik 1, Pratley 1, Purrington 1, Taylor 1.

Phillips D 27	Marshall M 6 + 16	Bauer P 35	Page L 11	Solly C 36 + 1	Pratley D 20 + 8	Pearce J 25 + 1	Lapslie G 11 + 16	Aribo J 35 + 1	Taylor L 41	Ahearne-Grant K 25 + 3	Sarr N 31 + 5	Morgan A 6 + 2	Dijksteel A 21 + 9	Hackett-Fairchild R 1 + 6	Bielik K 30 + 1	Maloney T — + 1	Ajose N 6 + 3	Vetokele I 12 + 11	Cullen J 29	Fosu T 14 + 13	Steer J 19	Reeves B 22 + 7	Ward J 6 + 3	Stevenson T 2 + 1	Williams J 14 + 2	Purrington B 18	Parker J 3 + 7	Forster-Caskey J — + 1	Match No.
1	2	3	4	5	6	7¹	8	9	10	11	12																		1
1	2¹	3	4	5	6		8²	9	10³	11	7	12	13	14															2
1	12	3	5	2	6		7¹	9	10	11	8				4²	13													3
1		3	5	2	6			9	10	11	8	7¹			4		12												4
1	7¹	3	5	2	8		13	9²	10	11	4				6			12											5
1		3³	5	2	6¹	4	13		10	8					7		11²	14	9	12■									6
		2	8	5	6²	3	13	7	10³	9	4		14				11¹				1	12							7
		2	8	5		3	12	6	10	9²	14							13	7		1	11³	4¹						8
			5	2		3		7	11	10	4							12	6		1	9	8¹						9
			5	2		3	13	7	10	12	4						14	11³	8	9¹	1	6²							10
			5¹	2	6³	3		8	10	11	4		12					14	7	9²	1	13							11
				2		3	12	9	10	11	4		5						8	7²	1	6¹	13						12
				5		4	13	8	10	11	14		2		3¹				6	12	1	7²	9³						13
				5	3	4		8	10	11			2		13				6	9¹	1	7²	12						14
				5	3	4		8	11	10¹			2		7²			14	6	13	1	12	9³						15
	13			5		4		8	10²	11	14		2¹		3			12	6		1	7³	9						16
	14			2	6	4	13	7	10	12	5				3			11²	8¹	9³	1								17
	13	3		5		4	7³	8		11			2	14	6		10²			12	1		9¹						18
	13	3		2		4	7³	9	11	10	5		14		6¹					8²	1		12						19
	12	3		2		4	6²	8	10	11					7					9¹	1	13		5					20
	13	3		14		4	6	8	10	11¹	5		2		7²		12				1	9³							21
	12	3		2		4		8	10		5■		13		6		11²			7	1	9¹							22
	14	3		5	12	4		8²	11¹				2	13	7		10			6³	1	9							23
	13	3		5	8	4	14		10	12			2		6¹		11²			7	1	9³							24
	9³	3		5■	7¹	4²			11	10			2	14	6					12	1	8		13					25
1	13	3			12				11	10	4	7	2		6					9²		8¹		5					26
1		3		5	8				10	11	4	7¹	2		6					9					12				27
1	13	3		5	8		12		10	11	4	7²	14		6¹										9³	2			28
1		3		2	7²				10■	11	4				6				8	13		12			9¹	5			29
1		3		2	6¹					11	4			12	7				8	13		9			10²	5			30
1		3■		2			6²				4			11³	7			13	8	14		9¹			10	5	12		31
1	7¹			2			14				4			13	3			10	6	11		8³			9	5²	12		32
1	12	3					13	8	10		4		2					14	6			7³			9²	5	11¹		33
1	11²	3		2³			8¹	6	10		4		14					13	7	12					9	5			34
1	13	4		2				8	11		3		14		6¹			10³	7	12					9²	5			35
1		3			14			8	10		4		2		6¹			11²	7	13		12			9³	5			36
1	14	3		2			12	8³	10		4							13	6	9²		7¹				5	11		37
1		3			8¹	2		13	10				5		4			11²	8	14		7³				9	12		38
1		3			13	14		8	10		4		2					11³	6	12		7¹			9²	5			39
1		3		2	12		13	8	10		4				6²			11¹	7						9³	5	14		40
1		3			7	4	8²	9	10		12		2					11¹	6							5	13		41
1		3		2	13		12	9	10		4		14		7³			11²	6						8¹	5			42
1		4		2■		3	13	9	11				5¹		8				6			7²			10		12		43
1		3			13			7²	10		4	8	2					11³	6			9¹			12	5		14	44
1					7	3	8²	10			4	13	2					11	6						9¹	5	12		45
1	12	4			13			11¹	10³		5	7	2		3²				8			14				9	6		46

FA Cup

First Round	Mansfield T	(a)	1-1
Replay	Mansfield T	(h)	5-0
Second Round	Doncaster R	(h)	0-2

Carabao Cup

First Round	Milton Keynes D	(a)	0-3

Checkatrade Trophy

Group G (S)	AFC Wimbledon	(h)	2-2
(AFC Wimbledon won 4-2 on penalties)			
Group G (S)	Stevenage	(a)	8-0
Group G (S)	Swansea C U21	(h)	0-1

League One Play-offs

Semi-Final 1st leg	Doncaster R	(a)	2-1
Semi-Final 2nd leg	Doncaster R	(h)	2-3
(aet; Charlton Ath won 4-3 on penalties)			
Final	Sunderland	(Wembley)	2-1

CHELSEA

FOUNDATION

Chelsea may never have existed but for the fact that Fulham rejected an offer to rent the Stamford Bridge ground from Mr H. A. Mears who had owned it since 1904. Fortunately he was determined to develop it as a football stadium rather than sell it to the Great Western Railway and got together with Frederick Parker, who persuaded Mears of the financial advantages of developing a major sporting venue. Chelsea FC was formed in 1905 and applications made to join both the Southern League and Football League. The latter competition was decided upon because of its comparatively meagre representation in the south of England.

Stamford Bridge, Fulham Road, London SW6 1HS.

Telephone: (0371) 811 1955. ***Fax:*** (020) 7381 4831.

Ticket Office: (0371) 811 1905.

Website: www.chelseafc.com

Email: enquiries@chelseafc.com

Ground Capacity: 40,853.

Record Attendance: 82,905 v Arsenal, Division 1, 12 October 1935.

Pitch Measurements: 103m × 67.5m (112.5yd × 74yd).

Chairman: Bruce Buck.

Chief Executive: Guy Laurence.

Manager: Frank Lampard.

Assistant Managers: Jody Morris, Eddie Newton.

Colours: Rush blue shirt with pimento red and white trim, rush blue shorts with white trim, white socks with rush blue and pimento red trim.

Year Formed: 1905. ***Turned Professional:*** 1905.

Club Nickname: 'The Blues'.

Ground: 1905, Stamford Bridge.

First Football League Game: 2 September 1905, Division 2, v Stockport Co (a) L 0–1 – Foulke; Mackie, McEwan; Key, Harris, Miller; Moran, Jack Robertson, Copeland, Windridge, Kirwan.

Record League Victory: 8–0 v Wigan Ath, Premier League, 9 May 2010 – Cech; Ivanovic (Belletti), Ashley Cole (1), Ballack (Matic), Terry, Alex, Kalou (1) (Joe Cole), Lampard (pen), Anelka (2), Drogba (3, 1 pen), Malouda; 8–0 v Aston Villa, Premier League, 23 December 2012 – Cech; Azpilicueta, Ivanovic (1), Cahill, Cole, Luiz (1), Lampard (1) (Ramirez (2)), Moses, Mata (Piazon), Hazard (1), Torres (1) (Oscar (1)).

HONOURS

League Champions: Premier League – 2004–05, 2005–06, 2009–10, 2014–15, 2016–17; Division 1 – 1954–55; Division 2 – 1983–84, 1988–89.
Runners-up: Premier League – 2003–04, 2006–07, 2007–08, 2010–11; Division 2 – 1906–07, 1911–12, 1929–30, 1962–63, 1976–77.

FA Cup Winners: 1970, 1997, 2000, 2007, 2009, 2010, 2012, 2018.
Runners-up: 1915, 1967, 1994, 2002, 2017.

League Cup Winners: 1965, 1998, 2005, 2007, 2015.
Runners-up: 1972, 2008, 2019.
Full Members' Cup Winners: 1986, 1990.

European Competitions
Champions League: 1999–2000, 2003–04 *(sf)*, 2004–05 *(sf)*, 2005–06, 2006–07 *(sf)*, 2007–08 *(runners-up)*, 2008–09 *(sf)*, 2009–10, 2010–11 *(qf)*, 2011–12 *(winners)*, 2012–13, 2013–14 *(sf)*, 2014–15, 2015–16, 2017–18.
Fairs Cup: 1958–60, 1965–66, 1968–69.
UEFA Cup: 2000–01, 2001–02, 2002–03.
Europa League: 2012–13 *(winners)*, 2018–19 *(winners)*.
European Cup-Winners' Cup: 1970–71 *(winners)*, 1971–72, 1994–95 *(sf)*, 1997–98 *(winners)*, 1998–99 *(sf)*.
Super Cup: 1998 *(winners)*, 2012, 2013.
Club World Cup: 2012 *(runners-up)*.

THE Sun FACT FILE

The first Chelsea game to be broadcast live on radio was the FA Cup fifth-round tie against Burnley played at Stamford Bridge on 19 February 1927. Running commentary was provided by Rex Palmer, an early broadcasting pioneer who was better known at the time as presenter of children's programmes under the name 'Uncle Rex'.

Record Cup Victory: 13–0 v Jeunesse Hautcharage, ECWC, 1st rd 2nd leg, 29 September 1971 – Bonetti; Boyle, Harris (1), Hollins (1p), Webb (1), Hinton, Cooke, Baldwin (3), Osgood (5), Hudson (1), Houseman (1).

Record Defeat: 1–8 v Wolverhampton W, Division 1, 26 September 1953; 0–7 v Nottingham F, Division 1, 20 April 1991.

Most League Points (2 for a win): 57, Division 2, 1906–07.

Most League Points (3 for a win): 99, Division 2, 1988–89.

Most League Goals: 103, Premier League, 2009–10.

Highest League Scorer in Season: Jimmy Greaves, 41, 1960–61.

Most League Goals in Total Aggregate: Bobby Tambling, 164, 1958–70.

Most League Goals in One Match: 5, George Hilsdon v Glossop, Division 2, 1 September 1906; 5, Jimmy Greaves v Wolverhampton W, Division 1, 30 August 1958; 5, Jimmy Greaves v Preston NE, Division 1, 19 December 1959; 5, Jimmy Greaves v WBA, Division 1, 3 December 1960; 5, Bobby Tambling v Aston Villa, Division 1, 17 September 1966; 5, Gordon Durie v Walsall, Division 2, 4 February 1989.

Most Capped Player: Frank Lampard, 104 (106), England.

Most League Appearances: Ron Harris, 655, 1962–80.

Youngest League Player: Ian Hamilton, 16 years 138 days v Tottenham H, 18 March 1967.

Record Transfer Fee Received: £88,500,000 from Real Madrid for Eden Hazard, June 2019.

Record Transfer Fee Paid: £71,600,000 to Athletic Bilbao for Kepa Arrizabalaga, August 2018.

Football League Record: 1905 Elected to Division 2; 1907–10 Division 1; 1910–12 Division 2; 1912–24 Division 1; 1924–30 Division 2; 1930–62 Division 1; 1962–63 Division 2; 1963–75 Division 1; 1975–77 Division 2; 1977–79 Division 1; 1979–84 Division 2; 1984–88 Division 1; 1988–89 Division 2; 1989–92 Division 1; 1992– Premier League.

MANAGERS

John Tait Robertson 1905–07
David Calderhead 1907–33
Leslie Knighton 1933–39
Billy Birrell 1939–52
Ted Drake 1952–61
Tommy Docherty 1961–67
Dave Sexton 1967–74
Ron Suart 1974–75
Eddie McCreadie 1975–77
Ken Shellito 1977–78
Danny Blanchflower 1978–79
Geoff Hurst 1979–81
John Neal 1981–85 (*Director to 1986*)
John Hollins 1985–88
Bobby Campbell 1988–91
Ian Porterfield 1991–93
David Webb 1993
Glenn Hoddle 1993–96
Ruud Gullit 1996–98
Gianluca Vialli 1998–2000
Claudio Ranieri 2000–04
Jose Mourinho 2004–07
Avram Grant 2007–08
Luiz Felipe Scolari 2008–09
Guus Hiddink 2009
Carlo Ancelotti 2009–11
Andre Villas-Boas 2011–12
Roberto Di Matteo 2012
Rafael Benitez 2012–13
Jose Mourinho 2013–15
Guus Hiddink 2015–16
Antonio Conte 2016–18
Maurizio Sarri 2018–19
Frank Lampard July 2019–

LATEST SEQUENCES

Longest Sequence of League Wins: 13, 1.10.2016 – 31.12.2016.

Longest Sequence of League Defeats: 7, 1.11.1952 – 20.12.1952.

Longest Sequence of League Draws: 6, 20.8.1969 – 13.9.1969.

Longest Sequence of Unbeaten League Matches: 40, 23.10.2004 – 29.10.2005.

Longest Sequence Without a League Win: 21, 3.11.1987 – 2.4.1988.

Successive Scoring Runs: 27 from 29.10.1988.

Successive Non-scoring Runs: 9 from 14.3.1981.

TEN YEAR LEAGUE RECORD

		P	*W*	*D*	*L*	*F*	*A*	*Pts*	*Pos*
2009-10	PR Lge	38	27	5	6	103	32	86	1
2010-11	PR Lge	38	21	8	9	69	33	71	2
2011-12	PR Lge	38	18	10	10	65	46	64	6
2012-13	PR Lge	38	22	9	7	75	39	75	3
2013-14	PR Lge	38	25	7	6	71	27	82	3
2014-15	PR Lge	38	26	9	3	73	32	87	1
2015-16	PR Lge	38	12	14	12	59	53	50	10
2016-17	PR Lge	38	30	3	5	85	33	93	1
2017-18	PR Lge	38	21	7	10	62	38	70	5
2018-19	PR Lge	38	21	9	8	63	39	72	3

DID YOU KNOW ?

Goalkeeper Peter Bonetti was selected as Chelsea's first ever Player of the Year, receiving the Joe Mears Memorial Trophy in May 1967. The supporters' club organised a series of six ballots over the season and Bonetti received the most votes followed by Bobby Tambling in second place.

CHELSEA – PREMIER LEAGUE 2018–19 LEAGUE RECORD

Match No.	*Date*	*Venue*	*Opponents*	*Result*		*H/T Score*	*Lg Pos.*	*Goalscorers*	*Attendance*
1	Aug 11	A	Huddersfield T	W	3-0	2-0	1	Kante ^{34}, Jorginho (pen) ^{45}, Pedro ^{80}	24,121
2	18	H	Arsenal	W	3-2	2-2	1	Pedro ^{9}, Morata ^{20}, Alonso ^{81}	40,491
3	26	A	Newcastle U	W	2-1	0-0	2	Hazard (pen) ^{76}, Yedlin (og) ^{87}	51,791
4	Sept 1	H	Bournemouth	W	2-0	0-0	2	Pedro ^{72}, Hazard ^{85}	40,178
5	15	H	Cardiff C	W	4-1	2-1	1	Hazard 3 (1 pen) $^{37, 43, 80 (p)}$, Willian ^{83}	40,499
6	23	A	West Ham U	D	0-0	0-0	3		56,875
7	29	H	Liverpool	D	1-1	1-0	3	Hazard ^{25}	40,625
8	Oct 7	A	Southampton	W	3-0	1-0	2	Hazard ^{30}, Barkley ^{57}, Morata ^{90}	30,663
9	20	H	Manchester U	D	2-2	1-0	3	Rudiger ^{21}, Barkley ^{90}	40,721
10	28	A	Burnley	W	4-0	1-0	2	Morata ^{22}, Barkley ^{57}, Willian ^{62}, Loftus-Cheek ^{90}	21,430
11	Nov 4	H	Crystal Palace	W	3-1	1-0	2	Morata 2 $^{32, 65}$, Pedro ^{70}	40,407
12	11	H	Everton	D	0-0	0-0	3		40,345
13	24	A	Tottenham H	L	1-3	0-2	4	Giroud ^{85}	55,465
14	Dec 2	H	Fulham	W	2-0	1-0	3	Pedro ^{4}, Loftus-Cheek ^{82}	40,551
15	5	A	Wolverhampton W	L	1-2	1-0	4	Loftus-Cheek ^{18}	31,300
16	8	H	Manchester C	W	2-0	1-0	4	Kante ^{45}, Luiz ^{78}	40,571
17	16	A	Brighton & HA	W	2-1	2-0	4	Pedro ^{17}, Hazard ^{33}	30,645
18	22	H	Leicester C	L	0-1	0-0	4		40,558
19	26	A	Watford	W	2-1	1-1	4	Hazard 2 (1 pen) $^{45, 58 (p)}$	20,415
20	30	A	Crystal Palace	W	1-0	0-0	4	Kante ^{51}	25,781
21	Jan 2	H	Southampton	D	0-0	0-0	4		40,668
22	12	H	Newcastle U	W	2-1	1-1	4	Pedro ^{9}, Willian ^{57}	40,491
23	19	A	Arsenal	L	0-2	0-2	4		59,979
24	30	A	Bournemouth	L	0-4	0-0	5		10,227
25	Feb 2	H	Huddersfield T	W	5-0	2-0	4	Higuain 2 $^{16, 69}$, Hazard 2 (1 pen) $^{45 (p), 66}$, Luiz ^{86}	40,626
26	10	A	Manchester C	L	0-6	0-4	6		54,452
27	27	H	Tottenham H	W	2-0	0-0	6	Pedro ^{57}, Trippier (og) ^{84}	40,542
28	Mar 3	A	Fulham	W	2-1	2-1	6	Higuain ^{20}, Jorginho ^{31}	24,900
29	10	H	Wolverhampton W	D	1-1	0-0	6	Hazard ^{90}	40,692
30	17	A	Everton	L	0-2	0-0	6		39,356
31	31	A	Cardiff C	W	2-1	0-0	6	Azpilicueta ^{84}, Loftus-Cheek ^{90}	32,657
32	Apr 3	H	Brighton & HA	W	3-0	1-0	5	Giroud ^{38}, Hazard ^{60}, Loftus-Cheek ^{63}	38,593
33	8	H	West Ham U	W	2-0	1-0	3	Hazard 2 $^{24, 90}$	40,537
34	14	A	Liverpool	L	0-2	0-0	4		53,279
35	22	H	Burnley	D	2-2	2-2	4	Kante ^{12}, Higuain ^{14}	40,642
36	28	A	Manchester U	D	1-1	1-1	4	Alonso ^{43}	74,526
37	May 5	H	Watford	W	3-0	0-0	3	Loftus-Cheek ^{48}, Luiz ^{51}, Higuain ^{75}	40,650
38	12	A	Leicester C	D	0-0	0-0	3		32,140

Final League Position: 3

GOALSCORERS

League (63): Hazard 16 (4 pens), Pedro 8, Loftus-Cheek 6, Higuain 5, Morata 5, Kante 4, Barkley 3, Luiz 3, Willian 3, Alonso 2, Giroud 2, Jorginho 2 (1 pen), Azpilicueta 1, Rudiger 1, own goals 2.
FA Cup (5): Morata 2, Willian 2 (1 pen), Hudson-Odoi 1.
Carabao Cup (8): Hazard 3, Emerson Palmieri 1, Fabregas 1, Kante 1, own goals 2.
Europa League (36): Giroud 11, Pedro 5, Hudson-Odoi 4, Loftus-Cheek 4, Willian 3, Alonso 2, Barkley 2, Hazard 2 (1 pen), Morata 2, own goal 1.
Checkatrade Trophy (12): Brown 4 (1 pen), Redan 2, Anjorin 1, Musonda 1 (1 pen), Nartey 1, Taylor-Crossdale 1, Ugbo 1, own goal 1.

Arrizabalaga K 36	Azpilicueta C 38	Rudiger A 33	Luiz D 36	Alonso M 31	Kante N 36	Jorginho F 37	Barkley R 13 + 14	Pedro R 21 + 10	Morata A 11 + 5	Willian 26 + 6	Loftus-Cheek R 6 + 18	Hazard E 32 + 5	Moses V — + 2	Kovacic M 21 + 11	Giroud O 7 + 20	Zappacosta D 1 + 3	Cahill G — + 2	Fabregas F 1 + 5	Christensen A 6 + 2	Hudson-Odoi C 4 + 6	Emerson 7 + 3	Higuain G 13 + 1	Caballero W 2	*Match No.*
1	2	3	4	5	6	7	8^2	9^3	10	11^1	12	13	14											1
1	2	3	4	5	6	7	8^3	9	10^1	11^2		13		12	14									2
1	2	3	4	5	6	7	14	9^3	10^1	13		11		8^2	12									3
1	2	3	4	5	6	7		13	10^2	9^3	14	11		8^1	12									4
1	2	3	4	5	6	7	12	9^1		13		11^2		8^3	10	14								5
1	2	3^3	4	5	6	7	14		12	9		11		8^1	10^2		13							6
1	2	3	4	5	6	7	14		12	9^3		11	13	8^1	10^2									7
1	2	3	4	5	6	7	8^3	13	12	9^1		11		14	10^2									8
1	2	3	4	5	6	7	12	13	10^2	9^1		11		8^3	14									9
1	2	3	4	5	6	7^2	8	9^3	10^1	11	12				13			14						10
1	2	3	4	5	6	7^1	8^3	9	10	11^2		12		13				14						11
1	2	3	4	5	6	7^1	14	13	10	9^3		11		8^2				12						12
1	2	3	4	5	6	7	13	12	10^1	9^3		11		8^2	14									13
1	2	3	4	5^3	6	7		9	13		12	11		8^1	10^2	14								14
1	2	3		5	6^2			13	10^1	9^3	8	11		14	12			7	4					15
1	2	3	4	5	6	7	12	9		11^3	13	10^2		8^1	14									16
1	2	3	4	5	6	7	13	9^3		11	12	10^1		8^2	14									17
1	2	3	4	5	6	7^3		9		11^1	13	10		8^2	12			14						18
1	2	3	4	5	6	7	13	9^2		11		10		8^1						12^3	14			19
1	2	3	4	5	6	7	8^2		12	9^3		11		14	10^1						13			20
1	2	3	4	5	6	7	8^1		10	9^2	12	11						13						21
1	2	3	4	5	6	7	12	9^1		11		10^3		8^2	14					13				22
1	2	3	4	5	6	7	12	9^3		11^1		10		8^2	13					14				23
1	2	3	4		6	7		9^2		12	14	11		8^1	13						5	10^3		24
1	2		4	5	6^2	7^1	8			9	14	11^3		12					3	13		10		25
1	2	3	4	5^1	6	7	8^2	9^3			13	11		12							14	10		26
	2	3	4	5	6	7		9		12	13	11^2		8^3	14							10^1	1	27
1	2	3			6	7^3	8^2	13		9	14	11^1		12					4		5	10		28
1	2	3	4		6	7^2		9^3		14	12	11		8^1						13	5	10		29
1	2	3	4	5	6	7^1	8^3	9			12	11			13					14		10^2		30
1	2	3	4	5		7^2	8	9^3		11	13	12		6	14							10^1		31
1	2^2		4		6	7				14	8^1	11^3		13	10	12			3	9	5			32
1	2	3	4		6	7	12	14			8^3	11			13					9^2	5	10^1		33
1	2	3^1	4		6	7	14			11	8^3	10							12	9^2	5	13		34
1	2		4		6^2	7		12			8	11		13	14				3	9^1	5	10^3		35
1	2	3^3	4	5	6	7		14		9^2	13	11		8^1					12			10		36
1	2		4^2	5	6^1	7		9			12	11		8	13		14		3			10^3		37
	3		4	5		7	6^3	9		11^2	8	12		13	14	2						10^1	1	38

FA Cup

Third Round	Nottingham F	(h)	2-0
Fourth Round	Sheffield W	(h)	3-0
Fifth Round	Manchester U	(h)	0-2

Carabao Cup

Third Round	Liverpool	(a)	2-1
Fourth Round	Derby Co	(h)	3-2
Quarter-Final	Bournemouth	(h)	1-0
Semi-Final 1st leg	Tottenham H	(a)	0-1
Semi-Final 2nd leg	Tottenham H	(h)	2-1
(Chelsea won 4-2 on penalties)			
Final	Manchester C	(Wembley)	0-0
(aet; Manchester C won 4-3 on penalties)			

Checkatrade Trophy (Chelsea U21)

Group C (S)	Swindon T	(a)	4-0
Group C (S)	Newport Co	(a)	0-3
Group C (S)	Plymouth Arg	(a)	5-0
Second Round (S)	AFC Wimbledon	(h)	2-1
Third Round	Peterborough U	(h)	1-3

Europa League

Group L	PAOK Salonika	(a)	1-0
Group L	Vidi	(h)	1-0
Group L	BATE Borisov	(h)	3-1
Group L	BATE Borisov	(a)	1-0
Group L	PAOK Salonika	(h)	4-0
Group L	Vidi	(a)	2-2
Round of 32 1st leg	Malmo	(a)	2-1
Round of 32 2nd leg	Malmo	(h)	3-0
Round of 16 1st leg	Dynamo Kyiv	(h)	3-0
Round of 16 2nd leg	Dynamo Kyiv	(a)	5-0
Quarter-Final 1st leg	Slavia Prague	(a)	1-0
Quarter-Final 2nd leg	Slavia Prague	(h)	4-3
Semi-Final 1st leg	Eintracht Frankfurt	(a)	1-1
Semi-Final 2nd leg	Eintracht Frankfurt	(h)	1-1
(aet; Chelsea won 4-3 on penalties)			
Final	Arsenal	(Baku)	4-1

CHELTENHAM TOWN

FOUNDATION

Although a scratch team representing Cheltenham played a match against Gloucester in 1884, the earliest recorded match for Cheltenham Town FC was a friendly against Dean Close School on 12 March 1892. The School won 4–3 and the match was played at Prestbury (half a mile from Whaddon Road). Cheltenham Town played Wednesday afternoon friendlies at a local cricket ground until entering the Mid Gloucester League. In those days the club played in deep red coloured shirts and were nicknamed 'the Rubies'. The club moved to Whaddon Lane for season 1901–02 and changed to red and white colours two years later.

The Jonny-Rocks Stadium, Whaddon Road, Cheltenham, Gloucestershire GL52 5NA.

Telephone: (01242) 573 558.

Fax: (01242) 224 675.

Ticket Office: (01242) 573 558 (option 1).

Website: www.ctfc.com

Email: info@ctfc.com

Ground Capacity: 7,200.

Record Attendance: 10,389 v Blackpool, FA Cup 3rd rd, 13 January 1934 (at Cheltenham Athletic Ground); 8,326 v Reading, FA Cup 1st rd, 17 November 1956 (at Whaddon Road).

Pitch Measurements: 102m × 65m (111.5yd × 71yd).

Chairman: Andy Wilcox.

Vice-Chairman: David Bloxham.

Manager: Michael Duff.

Assistant Manager: Russell Milton.

Colours: Red and white striped shirts, white shorts with red trim, red socks with white trim.

Year Formed: 1892.

Turned Professional: 1932.

Club Nickname: 'The Robins'.

Grounds: Pre-1932, Agg-Gardner's Recreation Ground; Whaddon Lane; Carter's Lane; 1932, Whaddon Road (renamed The Abbey Business Stadium 2009, World of Smile Stadium 2015, LCI Rail Stadium 2016, Jonny-Rocks Stadium 2019).

First Football League Game: 7 August 1999, Division 3, v Rochdale (h) L 0–2 – Book; Griffin, Victory, Banks, Freeman, Brough (Howarth), Howells, Bloomer (Devaney), Grayson, Watkins (McAuley), Yates.

Record League Victory: 5–0 v Mansfield T, FL 2, 6 May 2006 – Higgs; Gallinagh, Bell, McCann (1) (Connolly), Caines, Duff, Wilson, Bird (1p), Gillespie (1) (Spencer), Guinan (Odejayi (1)), Vincent (1).

Record Cup Victory: 12–0 v Chippenham R, FA Cup 3rd qual. rd, 2 November 1935 – Bowles; Whitehouse, Williams; Lang, Devonport (1), Partridge (2); Perkins, Hackett, Jones (4), Black (4), Griffiths (1).

HONOURS

League Champions: Conference – 1998–99, 2015–16.
Runners-up: Conference – 1997–98.

FA Cup: 5th rd – 2002.

League Cup: never past 2nd rd.

THE Sun FACT FILE

George Blackburn, the first professional to sign for Cheltenham Town, was recruited as player-coach in the summer of 1932 when the club moved up from the Gloucestershire Northern Senior League to play in the Birmingham Combination. Blackburn was a former England international who played for Aston Villa, Cardiff City and Mansfield Town before joining the Robins. He stayed with the club for two seasons before retiring from football.

Record Defeat: 1–8 v Crewe Alex, FL 2, 2 April 2011; 0–7 v Crystal Palace, League Cup 2nd rd, 2 October 2002. *N.B.* 1–10 v Merthyr T, Southern League, 8 March 1952.

Most League Points (2 for a win): 60, Southern League Division 1, 1963–64.

Most League Points (3 for a win): 78, Division 3, 2001–02.

Most League Goals: 67, FL 2, 2017–18.

Highest League Scorer in Season: Mo Eisa, 23, FL 2, 2017–18.

Most League Goals in Total Aggregate: Julian Alsop, 39, 2000–03; 2009–10.

Most League Goals in One Match: 3, Martin Devaney v Plymouth Arg, Division 3, 23 September 2000; 3, Neil Grayson v Cardiff C, Division 3, 1 April 2001; 3, Damien Spencer v Hull C, Division 3, 23 August 2003; 3, Damien Spencer v Milton Keynes D, FL 1, 31 January 2009; 3, Michael Pook v Burton Alb, FL 2, 13 March 2010; 3, Mohamed Eisa v Port Vale, FL 2, 10 February 2018.

Most Capped Player: Grant McCann, 7 (40), Northern Ireland.

Most League Appearances: David Bird, 288, 2001–11.

Youngest League Player: Kyle Haynes, 17 years 85 days v Oldham Ath, 24 March 2009.

Record Transfer Fee Received: £1,400,000 from Bristol C for Mo Eisa, July 2018.

Record Transfer Fee Paid: £60,000 to Aldershot T for Jermaine McGlashan, January 2012.

Football League Record: 1999 Promoted to Division 3; 2002 Division 2; 2003–04 Division 3; 2004–06 FL 2; 2006–09 FL 1; 2009–15 FL 2; 2015–16 National League; 2016– FL 2.

MANAGERS

George Blackburn 1932–34
George Carr 1934–37
Jimmy Brain 1937–48
Cyril Dean 1948–50
George Summerbee 1950–52
William Raeside 1952–53
Arch Anderson 1953–58
Ron Lewin 1958–60
Peter Donnelly 1960–61
Tommy Cavanagh 1961
Arch Anderson 1961–65
Harold Fletcher 1965–66
Bob Etheridge 1966–73
Willie Penman 1973–74
Dennis Allen 1974–79
Terry Paine 1979
Alan Grundy 1979–82
Alan Wood 1982–83
John Murphy 1983–88
Jim Barron 1988–90
John Murphy 1990
Dave Lewis 1990–91
Ally Robertson 1991–92
Lindsay Parsons 1992–95
Chris Robinson 1995–97
Steve Cotterill 1997–2002
Graham Allner 2002–03
Bobby Gould 2003
John Ward 2003–07
Keith Downing 2007–08
Martin Allen 2008–09
Mark Yates 2009–14
Paul Buckle 2014–15
Gary Johnson 2015–18
Michael Duff September 2018–

LATEST SEQUENCES

Longest Sequence of League Wins: 5, 29.10.2011 – 10.12.2011.

Longest Sequence of League Defeats: 7, 14.4.2018 – 18.8.2018.

Longest Sequence of League Draws: 5, 5.4.2003 – 21.4.2003.

Longest Sequence of Unbeaten League Matches: 16, 1.12.2001 – 12.3.2002.

Longest Sequence Without a League Win: 14, 20.12.2008 – 7.3.2009.

Successive Scoring Runs: 17 from 16.2.2008.

Successive Non-scoring Runs: 5 from 10.3.2012 – 30.3.2012.

TEN YEAR LEAGUE RECORD

		P	*W*	*D*	*L*	*F*	*A*	*Pts*	*Pos*
2009-10	FL 2	46	10	18	18	54	71	48	22
2010-11	FL 2	46	13	13	20	56	77	52	17
2011-12	FL 2	46	23	8	15	66	50	77	6
2012-13	FL 2	46	20	15	11	58	51	75	5
2013-14	FL 2	46	13	16	17	53	63	55	17
2014-15	FL 2	46	9	14	23	40	67	41	23
2015-16	NL	46	30	11	5	87	30	101	1
2016-17	FL 2	46	12	14	20	49	69	50	21
2017-18	FL 2	46	13	12	21	67	73	51	17
2018-19	FL 2	46	15	12	19	57	68	57	16

DID YOU KNOW ?

Cheltenham Town's first promotion as a Football League club came via the play-offs at the end of the 2001–02 season. The Robins finished fourth in what was then Division Three and went on to defeat Hartlepool United in a penalty shoot-out before achieving a 3-1 victory over Rushden & Diamonds in the play-off final at the Millennium Stadium.

CHELTENHAM TOWN – SKY BET LEAGUE TWO 2018–19 LEAGUE RECORD

Match No.	Date	Venue	Opponents	Result	H/T Score	Lg Pos.	Goalscorers	Attendance
1	Aug 4	H	Crawley T	L 0-1	0-0	17		2719
2	11	A	Tranmere R	L 0-1	0-1	22		6736
3	18	H	Carlisle U	L 0-1	0-1	22		2455
4	21	A	Macclesfield T	D 1-1	0-1	22	Duku [85]	1496
5	25	A	Cambridge U	W 1-0	0-0	20	Jones [66]	3660
6	Sept 1	H	Colchester U	L 1-3	0-2	21	Dawson [56]	2789
7	8	A	Northampton T	W 3-1	1-0	18	Boyle [36], Thomas (pen) [77], Mooney [83]	4608
8	15	H	Crewe Alex	D 0-0	0-0	18		2921
9	22	A	Exeter C	L 1-3	1-0	18	Broom [42]	3723
10	29	H	Lincoln C	L 0-2	0-0	19		3202
11	Oct 2	H	Morecambe	D 2-2	1-1	19	Varney 2 [44, 90]	2095
12	6	A	Milton Keynes D	L 0-3	0-1	21		6503
13	20	A	Forest Green R	D 1-1	1-0	22	Barnett [26]	3582
14	23	A	Oldham Ath	L 0-2	0-0	23		2865
15	27	H	Stevenage	L 0-2	0-2	23		2382
16	Nov 3	H	Mansfield T	D 2-2	2-1	23	Tozer [10], Boyle [45]	2828
17	17	A	Notts Co	W 3-0	1-0	22	Varney 2 [35, 66], Barnett [87]	6109
18	24	H	Newport Co	W 2-1	2-0	22	Boyle [18], Barnett [44]	3672
19	27	A	Bury	L 1-4	1-2	22	Clements [25]	2779
20	Dec 8	H	Grimsby T	W 2-1	1-0	21	Broom [29], Thomas (pen) [90]	2775
21	15	A	Port Vale	D 2-2	1-1	21	Jones [26], Atangana [89]	3109
22	22	A	Swindon T	D 0-0	0-0	21		7026
23	26	H	Milton Keynes D	W 3-1	2-1	19	Atangana [14], Barnett [44], Clements [86]	3266
24	29	H	Forest Green R	D 2-2	0-0	19	Varney [78], Thomas [80]	5125
25	Jan 1	A	Yeovil T	W 4-1	2-0	18	Varney [24], Thomas (pen) [34], Forster [77], Dawson [87]	2883
26	5	A	Crawley T	L 0-1	0-1	18		2623
27	12	H	Tranmere R	L 1-3	1-0	18	Varney [42]	3104
28	19	A	Carlisle U	L 0-2	0-0	21		4458
29	26	H	Macclesfield T	W 3-2	0-2	18	Varney [54], Maddox [61], Raglan [79]	3041
30	Feb 5	H	Yeovil T	W 1-0	0-0	18	Varney [59]	2457
31	9	A	Colchester U	L 0-3	0-2	18		3026
32	16	A	Grimsby T	L 0-1	0-1	19		4940
33	19	H	Cambridge U	W 2-0	1-0	18	Taft (og) [23], Thomas (pen) [58]	2339
34	23	H	Port Vale	W 1-0	1-0	17	Varney [34]	3079
35	Mar 2	A	Mansfield T	L 2-4	0-2	17	Hussey [59], Raglan [68]	5276
36	5	H	Bury	D 1-1	1-1	17	Waters [33]	2409
37	9	H	Notts Co	W 4-1	2-0	17	Boyle [29], Varney (pen) [36], Waters [55], Barnett [88]	3514
38	15	A	Newport Co	L 0-1	0-0	17		3192
39	23	H	Northampton T	W 3-1	2-0	17	Varney 2 (1 pen) [18, 41 (p)], Barnett [73]	3513
40	30	A	Crewe Alex	W 3-1	1-1	16	Dawson [45], Waters [74], Varney [83]	3495
41	Apr 6	H	Exeter C	D 1-1	0-1	16	Thomas (pen) [60]	4079
42	13	A	Lincoln C	D 1-1	0-1	16	Lloyd [73]	9820
43	19	H	Oldham Ath	D 0-0	0-0	16		4022
44	22	A	Morecambe	L 0-4	0-0	16		3066
45	27	H	Swindon T	W 3-2	3-0	16	Woolfenden (og) [26], Waters [30], Dawson [37]	4306
46	May 4	A	Stevenage	L 0-2	0-0	16		3071

Final League Position: 16

GOALSCORERS

League (57): Varney 14 (2 pens), Barnett 6, Thomas 6 (5 pens), Boyle 4, Dawson 4, Waters 4, Atangana 2, Broom 2, Clements 2, Jones 2, Raglan 2, Duku 1, Forster 1, Hussey 1, Lloyd 1, Maddox 1, Mooney 1, Tozer 1, own goals 2.
FA Cup (3): Addai 2, Barnett 1.
Carabao Cup (2): Broom 1, Thomas 1 (1 pen).
Checkatrade Trophy (10): Maddox 3, Boyle 2, Addai 1, Broom 1, Clements 1, Dawson 1, Mooney 1.

Flinders S 46	Baldwin A 3 + 1	Mullins J 18 + 1	Boyle W 36 + 2	Debayo J 4 + 1	Addai A 10 + 11	Tozer B 34 + 3	Atangana N 25 + 1	Maddox J 29 + 9	Duku I 6 + 5	McAlinden L 4 + 2	Broom R 33 + 6	Dawson K 22 + 10	Lumbombo Kalala K 1 + 6	Forster J 23 + 3	Thomas C 26 + 6	Hussey C 31 + 3	Jones S 6 + 6	Field T 5 + 2	Mooney K 3 + 5	Barnett T 19 + 11	Lloyd G 3 + 4	Alcock C 6 + 2	Varney L 30 + 5	Clements C 26 + 4	Pring C 7 + 1	Waters B 10 + 8	Bower M 1 + 1	Raglan C 19	Tillson J 12 + 2	Bingham R 4 + 6	Long S 4 + 1	*Match No.*
1	2^{2}	3	4	5	6^{3}	7	8	9	10	11^{1}	12	13	14																			1
1	2	3	4	5	14	7	8	9	10^{2}	11^{3}	13	6^{1}	12																			2
1		3	4	5^{1}	10	12	7	9		14	6	13	11^{2}	2	8^{3}																	3
1		3	4	5^{2}	10		7^{1}	9	13	11	6		14	2^{3}	8	12																4
1		3	4	14			8	9	10	11^{2}	6	12		2	7^{3}	5^{1}	13															5
1		3	4^{1}				7	10	11^{3}		6	8	14	2^{2}			9	5	12	13												6
1		3	4			14	6	9^{3}	13		7			2	12			5	8	11^{1}	10^{2}											7
1	12	4	3				6	8	14		9	7		2			13		10^{1}	11^{3}		5^{2}										8
1		3	4				7	9	10^{1}		8	6^{2}	14	2			12	13		11		5^{3}										9
1		3	4				7	9	11^{2}		8^{1}	6	14	2				5^{3}		10		12	13									10
1		3	4				8	9				6^{1}		2		12		5^{3}	14	11^{2}	13		10	7								11
1	2^{2}	3	4			7	11	6			9					12		5^{1}		13			10	8								12
1		3	4			14	8	9^{1}		12	7	6^{3}				5			13	11^{2}		2	10									13
1		3	4		13		7	9^{2}			6					5	11■			12		2	10	8^{1}								14
1		3	4				7^{2}	9			6			13		5			12	10		2^{1}	11	8								15
1			4		13	3	12	7			5			2	8	9			10^{2}	14			11^{3}	6^{1}								16
1			4			3	6	7^{2}			5			2	8	9	13			10			11^{1}	12								17
1			4		12	3	7				6			2	8	5				10			11	9^{1}								18
1			4^{3}		12	3	6				5			2	7	9	14	13		10^{1}			11^{2}	8								19
1		3	4		13	2	7^{2}	6^{1}			5				12	9	14			10			11^{3}	8								20
1		13	4		12	3	7				2			5	8	6	10						11^{2}	9^{1}								21
1			4		9^{2}	3	6							2	5	8	11		13	12			10^{1}	7								22
1			4		11^{2}	3	7					13		2	5	8	9^{1}			10			12	6								23
1		4			10	3	7	12				14		2	5^{1}	8	9^{3}			11^{2}			13	6								24
1		3^{1}			10	2	7	8^{3}				14		4	5	9				13		12	11^{2}	6								25
1					11^{2}	2	8^{3}	6^{1}			13	14		3	5	9				10			12	7	4							26
1					13	3		7^{2}			5			2	8	4				10^{3}			11	6	9^{1}	12	14					27
1					12	3		13			9	14			5	4				10		6^{2}	11^{3}	7		2^{1}		8				28
1					10	3		8^{2}			9	12		2^{1}	5^{3}	4							11	6	14	13		7				29
1					10^{1}	3		8			5	13		2^{2}	14	9							11	6^{3}				4	7	12		30
1						3		14			5^{1}	7		4		9				12			10	6^{3}		13		2	8	11^{2}		31
1			14			4		9	13			7			2	5							11^{1}		6^{2}	12		3	8	10^{3}		32
1			4			3		8	12		5	7			6	9					13					10^{1}		2		11^{2}		33
1			3			4		6^{2}			5	7			8	9				13			11^{3}	12		10^{1}		2	14			34
1			5			4^{2}		10^{1}			2	7^{3}			8	6				12	14		11			13		3	9			35
1			4			3		14			5	8^{1}			13					10^{3}			12	7^{2}	6	11		2	9			36
1			4			3		13			5	6^{3}				9				12			11^{2}	7		10^{1}		2	8	14		37
1			4■			3		14			5	6^{3}				9				13			10^{2}	8		11^{1}		2	7	12		38
1			4			3					5^{1}	6		14	12	9				11			10^{3}	8^{2}				2	7	13		39
1			4			3		14			5	7^{3}			12	9				11^{1}			10	8^{2}		13		2	6			40
1			3			2		12			5^{1}	7			6	8							11^{2}	9^{3}		10		4		13	14	41
1			4			3					13	7		14	6	9					12					10		2	8^{2}	11^{1}	5^{3}	42
1			4			3		13			14	7			6	9					10^{1}		11			12		2	8^{3}		5^{2}	43
1			13			3					5				6						9^{3}		11	12	8	10^{1}	4^{2}	2	7	14		44
1			4		13	3		9^{3}				6^{2}			7								10	12	8	11^{1}		2	14		5	45
1			6		12	3^{2}		7			14	5^{3}			4								11	9	10	13		8			2^{1}	46

FA Cup

First Round	Ebbsfleet U	(a)	0-0
Replay	Ebbsfleet U	(h)	2-0
Second Round	Accrington S	(a)	1-3

Carabao Cup

First Round	Colchester U	(h)	2-2
(Cheltenham T won 6-5 on penalties)			
Second Round	Brentford	(a)	0-1

Checkatrade Trophy

Group E (S)	Forest Green R	(a)	0-4
Group E (S)	Arsenal U21	(h)	6-2
Group E (S)	Coventry C	(h)	2-0
Second Round (S)	Newport Co	(h)	1-1
(Cheltenham T won 7-6 on penalties)			
Third Round	Oxford U	(h)	1-1

COLCHESTER UNITED

FOUNDATION

Colchester United was formed in 1937 when a number of enthusiasts of the much older Colchester Town club decided to establish a professional concern as a limited liability company. The new club continued at Layer Road which had been the amateur club's home since 1909.

JobServe Community Stadium, United Way, Colchester, Essex CO4 5UP.

Telephone: (01206) 755 100.

Ticket Office: (01206) 755 161.

Website: www.cu-fc.com

Email: media@colchesterunited.net

Ground Capacity: 10,105.

Record Attendance: 19,072 v Reading, FA Cup 1st rd, 27 November 1948 (at Layer Road); 10,064 v Norwich C, FL 1, 16 January 2010 (at Community Stadium).

Pitch Measurements: 100m × 65m (109.5yd × 71yd).

Executive Chairman: Robbie Cowling.

Head Coach: John McGreal.

Assistant Coach: Steve Ball.

Colours: Royal blue and white striped shirts, white shorts with royal blue trim, white socks with royal blue hoops.

Year Formed: 1937.

Turned Professional: 1937.

Club Nickname: 'The U's'.

Grounds: 1937, Layer Road; 2008, Weston Homes Community Stadium (renamed JobServe Community Stadium 2018).

First Football League Game: 19 August 1950, Division 3 (S), v Gillingham (a) D 0–0 – Wright; Kettle, Allen; Bearryman, Stewart, Elder; Jones, Curry, Turner, McKim, Church.

Record League Victory: 9–1 v Bradford C, Division 4, 30 December 1961 – Ames; Millar, Fowler; Harris, Abrey, Ron Hunt; Foster, Bobby Hunt (4), King (4), Hill (1), Wright.

Record Cup Victory: 9-1 v Leamington, FA Cup 1st rd, 5 November 2005 – Davison; Stockley (Garcia), Duguid, Brown (1), Chilvers, Watson (1), Halford (1), Izzet (Danns) (2), Iwelumo (1) (Williams), Cureton (2), Yeates (1).

Record Defeat: 0–8 v Leyton Orient, Division 4, 15 October 1988.

Most League Points (2 for a win): 60, Division 4, 1973–74.

HONOURS

League Champions: Conference – 1991–92.
Runners-up: FL 1 – 2005–06; Division 4 – 1961–62; Conference – 1990–91.

FA Cup: 6th rd – 1971.

League Cup: 5th rd – 1975.

League Trophy: *Runners-up:* 1997.

THE Sun FACT FILE

Colchester United lost their final game at their Layer Road ground in April 2008, going down 1-0 to Stoke City in a Championship fixture in front of a crowd of 6,300. Richard Cresswell scored the last Football League goal on the ground that had been United's home since their formation. Stoke went on to win promotion to the Premier League while Colchester finished bottom of the table and were relegated.

Most League Points (3 for a win): 81, Division 4, 1982–83.

Most League Goals: 104, Division 4, 1961–62.

Highest League Scorer in Season: Bobby Hunt, 38, Division 4, 1961–62.

Most League Goals in Total Aggregate: Martyn King, 130, 1956–64.

Most League Goals in One Match: 4, Bobby Hunt v Bradford C, Division 4, 30 December 1961; 4, Martyn King v Bradford C, Division 4, 30 December 1961; 4, Bobby Hunt v Doncaster R, Division 4, 30 April 1962.

Most Capped Player: Brandon Comley, 3, Montserrat.

Most League Appearances: Micky Cook, 613, 1969–84.

Youngest League Player: Todd Miller, 16 years 166 days v Exeter C, 16 March 2019.

Record Transfer Fee Received: £2,500,000 from Reading for Greg Halford, January 2007.

Record Transfer Fee Paid: £400,000 to Cheltenham T for Steve Gillespie, July 2008.

Football League Record: 1950 Elected to Division 3 (S); 1958–61 Division 3; 1961–62 Division 4; 1962–65 Division 3; 1965–66 Division 4; 1966–68 Division 3; 1968–74 Division 4; 1974–76 Division 3, 1976–77 Division 4; 1977–81 Division 3; 1981–90 Division 4; 1990–92 Conference; 1992–98 Division 3; 1998–2004 Division 2; 2004–06 FL 1; 2006–08 FL C; 2008–16 FL 1; 2016– FL 2.

MANAGERS

Ted Fenton 1946–48
Jimmy Allen 1948–53
Jack Butler 1953–55
Benny Fenton 1955–63
Neil Franklin 1963–68
Dick Graham 1968–72
Jim Smith 1972–75
Bobby Roberts 1975–82
Allan Hunter 1982–83
Cyril Lea 1983–86
Mike Walker 1986–87
Roger Brown 1987–88
Jock Wallace 1989
Mick Mills 1990
Ian Atkins 1990–91
Roy McDonough 1991–94
George Burley 1994
Steve Wignall 1995–99
Mick Wadsworth 1999
Steve Whitton 1999–2003
Phil Parkinson 2003–06
Geraint Williams 2006–08
Paul Lambert 2008–09
Aidy Boothroyd 2009–10
John Ward 2010–12
Joe Dunne 2012–14
Tony Humes 2014–15
Kevin Keen 2015–16
John McGreal May 2016–

LATEST SEQUENCES

Longest Sequence of League Wins: 7, 31.12.2005 – 7.2.2006.

Longest Sequence of League Defeats: 9, 31.10.2015 – 28.12.2015.

Longest Sequence of League Draws: 6, 21.3.1977 – 11.4.1977.

Longest Sequence of Unbeaten League Matches: 20, 22.12.1956 – 19.4.1957.

Longest Sequence Without a League Win: 20, 2.3.1968 – 31.8.1968.

Successive Scoring Runs: 24 from 15.9.1962.

Successive Non-scoring Runs: 5 from 11.2.2006.

TEN YEAR LEAGUE RECORD

		P	W	D	L	F	A	Pts	Pos
2009-10	FL 1	46	20	12	14	64	52	72	8
2010-11	FL 1	46	16	14	16	57	63	62	10
2011-12	FL 1	46	13	20	13	61	66	59	10
2012-13	FL 1	46	14	9	23	47	68	51	20
2013-14	FL 1	46	13	14	19	53	61	53	16
2014-15	FL 1	46	14	10	22	58	77	52	19
2015-16	FL 1	46	9	13	24	57	99	40	23
2016-17	FL 2	46	19	12	15	67	57	69	8
2017-18	FL 2	46	16	14	16	53	52	62	13
2018-19	FL 2	46	20	10	16	65	53	70	8

DID YOU KNOW ?

Colchester United's home FA Cup tie against Leyton Orient in December 1990 was the first Sunday night professional fixture scheduled in the UK. The game was due to be shown live on BSB television with the kick-off at 8pm but was postponed due to a snowstorm. The fixture was played on the following Wednesday, ending in a goalless draw with Orient progressing with a win in the replay.

COLCHESTER UNITED – SKY BET LEAGUE TWO 2018–19 LEAGUE RECORD

Match No.	*Date*	*Venue*	*Opponents*	*Result*		*H/T Score*	*Lg Pos.*	*Goalscorers*	*Attendance*
1	Aug 4	A	Notts Co	D	0-0	0-0	13		7136
2	11	H	Port Vale	W	2-0	2-0	7	Senior [8], Jackson [23]	3183
3	18	A	Mansfield T	D	1-1	0-0	9	Szmidics [90]	3909
4	21	H	Crewe Alex	W	6-0	3-0	3	Kent [4], Dickenson 2 [8, 26], Jackson [59], Norris [74], Lapslie [77]	2842
5	25	H	Northampton T	L	1-2	0-0	6	Pierre (og) [90]	3791
6	Sept 1	A	Cheltenham T	W	3-1	2-0	4	Norris 2 (1 pen) [12 (p), 26], Pell (pen) [88]	2789
7	8	A	Tranmere R	D	1-1	0-1	5	Pell [61]	5885
8	15	H	Cambridge U	W	3-0	2-0	4	Szmidics [23], Nouble [35], Senior [80]	4108
9	22	A	Oldham Ath	D	3-3	1-0	4	Norris 2 [15, 68], Pell [50]	4017
10	29	H	Bury	L	1-2	0-1	5	Norris (pen) [81]	3161
11	Oct 2	H	Yeovil T	W	3-1	1-0	4	Eastman [25], Nouble 2 [59, 84]	2435
12	6	A	Stevenage	L	1-3	1-1	8	Szmidics [2]	2763
13	13	H	Crawley T	W	3-1	1-1	6	Szmidics [27], Nouble [57], Norris [90]	3208
14	20	A	Morecambe	W	1-0	1-0	5	Senior [45]	1839
15	23	A	Grimsby T	L	0-1	0-0	5		3662
16	27	H	Lincoln C	W	1-0	1-0	5	Kent [28]	4962
17	Nov 3	H	Swindon T	W	1-0	1-0	3	Szmidics [45]	3227
18	17	A	Newport Co	L	0-2	0-0	4		3512
19	24	H	Exeter C	D	1-1	0-0	3	Szmidics [67]	3384
20	27	A	Forest Green R	W	1-0	1-0	3	Szmidics [25]	1600
21	Dec 8	H	Macclesfield T	W	1-0	1-0	3	Mandron [29]	3099
22	15	A	Carlisle U	L	0-4	0-1	3		3547
23	22	A	Milton Keynes D	W	1-0	1-0	3	Prosser [11]	7765
24	26	H	Stevenage	L	1-2	0-2	4	Prosser [83]	5032
25	29	H	Morecambe	D	0-0	0-0	4		3653
26	Jan 1	A	Crawley T	L	0-2	0-0	8		2765
27	5	H	Notts Co	D	3-3	2-3	8	Szmidics [8], Mandron [45], Pell (pen) [67]	3181
28	12	A	Port Vale	W	3-0	2-0	4	Senior [5], Pell 2 [18, 69]	3636
29	19	H	Mansfield T	L	2-3	2-0	6	Eastman [14], Senior [30]	3546
30	26	A	Crewe Alex	L	1-2	1-0	8	Szmidics [11]	3306
31	Feb 2	A	Northampton T	W	4-0	1-0	8	Nouble [25], Eisa [50], Vincent-Young [53], Szmidics [67]	4796
32	9	H	Cheltenham T	W	3-0	2-0	4	Vincent-Young [30], Nouble [43], Eisa [56]	3026
33	16	A	Macclesfield T	D	1-1	0-1	6	Nouble (pen) [47]	2092
34	23	H	Carlisle U	D	1-1	0-0	5	Kent [84]	3626
35	Mar 2	A	Swindon T	L	0-3	0-2	8		6082
36	9	H	Newport Co	W	3-0	2-0	6	Szmidics [20], Senior [45], Nouble [63]	3213
37	12	H	Forest Green R	L	0-3	0-2	7		2871
38	16	A	Exeter C	L	0-3	0-1	8		3951
39	23	H	Tranmere R	L	0-2	0-1	9		2800
40	30	A	Cambridge U	W	1-0	0-0	8	Vincent-Young [90]	5515
41	Apr 6	H	Oldham Ath	L	0-2	0-2	9		3975
42	13	A	Bury	L	0-2	0-0	9		3898
43	19	H	Grimsby T	W	1-0	1-0	9	Nouble [25]	3677
44	22	A	Yeovil T	D	1-1	0-0	8	Eastman [75]	3370
45	27	H	Milton Keynes D	W	2-0	1-0	8	Szmidics [2], Kent [47]	5000
46	May 4	A	Lincoln C	W	3-0	3-0	8	Dickenson [22], Szmidics 2 [27, 44]	9832

Final League Position: 8

GOALSCORERS

League (65): Szmidics 14, Nouble 9 (1 pen), Norris 7 (2 pens), Pell 6 (2 pens), Senior 6, Kent 4, Dickenson 3, Eastman 3, Vincent-Young 3, Eisa 2, Jackson 2, Mandron 2, Prosser 2, Lapslie 1, own goal 1.
FA Cup (0).
Carabao Cup (2): Norris 1, Szmodics 1.
Checkatrade Trophy (3): Collins 1, Kent 1, Pell 1.

Barnes D 22	Kent F 39 + 1	Prosser L 38	Eastman T 22 + 9	Jackson R 46	Pell H 30 + 1	Lapslie T 34 + 1	Dickenson B 19 + 23	Collins A 1 + 6	Szmidics S 43	Nouble F 42 + 1	Mandron M 16 + 25	Vincent-Young K 38 + 2	Senior C 37 + 5	Comley B 5 + 8	Norris L 21 + 13	Wright D 4 + 5	Gilmartin R 22	Gondoh R — + 4	Kensadale O 1 + 1	Ogedi-Uzokwe J — + 1	Stevenson B 11 + 3	Eisa A 8 + 6	Roberts C — + 3	Chilvers N — + 2	Miller T — + 1	Saunders S 5 + 1	Ross E 2 + 1	Match No.
1	2	3	4	5	6	7	8	9^{1}	10	11	12																	1
1	3	4		2	8	7	9	13	10	11^{3}	12	5^{1}	6^{2}	14														2
1	3	4	13	2	7	6	10		9	11^{2}	14	5^{3}	8^{1}		12													3
1	3	4^{1}	14	2	8	7	9	13	10	11^{3}		5	6^{2}		12													4
1	3	4	13	2	8	7	9		10	11^{1}	12	5^{3}	6^{2}		14													5
1	3	4	6	2	8				11	10	12	5		7^{1}	9^{2}	13												6
1	4		3	2	6		10^{1}		8	11	13	5	12		9^{2}	7												7
1	3	4		2	7		10^{1}	13	8^{3}	11	14	5	12	6	9^{2}													8
1	3	4	13	2	6		10^{2}		9	8	12	5		7	11^{1}													9
1	3^{1}	4	12^{3}	2	8		13		10	6	14	5	9	7^{2}	11													10
1		4	3	2	7	6^{1}	12		9	10	14	5	8^{3}		11^{2}	13												11
1		4	3	2	7	6	12	13	9^{2}	10		5	8^{1}		11													12
	12	4	3	2	8^{3}	7	13		10	9		5^{2}	6^{1}		11	14	1											13
	4	3	2	5	6	7^{2}	13	12		9		8^{3}	10^{1}	14	11		1											14
	4	3	2	5^{2}	6	7^{3}	12			9	13	8	11		10^{1}	14	1											15
	3	4	12	2	8	7			10^{1}	9	13	5	6^{2}		11		1											16
	3	4		2	7	6	12		9^{3}	10	14	5	8^{2}	13	11^{1}		1											17
1	3	4		2		7^{2}	10^{1}	14	9	11	12	5	8^{3}			6		13										18
1	3			2	7	6	13		9	11	10^{1}	5	8^{2}					12	4									19
1	3	4		2^{1}	7	6	12		9	10	11	5	8^{2}	13														20
1	3	4		2	8	7	12		10^{1}	9	11^{2}	5	6^{3}	14	13													21
1	4^{1}	3		2	7	6	12		9	10	11^{3}	5^{2}	8		13				14									22
	3	4	5	2	6	7	10		9^{2}	8	12			13	11^{1}		1											23
	4^{2}	3	2	5	7	6^{1}	8		9	10	14	12	13		11^{3}		1											24
	3	4		2	13	6	10^{2}		9	8	14	5	12	7^{3}	11^{1}		1											25
	2■	3^{1}	4	5	6	7^{3}	13		9	10	14	8^{2}	12		11		1											26
		4	3	2	6	7	14		9^{1}	10	11^{3}	5	8^{2}		13		1	12										27
		3	4	2	7	6	5		9^{1}	10^{2}	11		8^{3}	12	13		1	14										28
		4	3	2	7	6^{1}	5^{3}		9	10	11	12	8^{2}	13			1			14								29
		4	3	2	6	7^{1}	12		9	10	11	5	8				1											30
	4	3		2	7		13		8^{1}	9	11^{3}	5	10^{2}				1				6	12	14					31
	3	4		2	6^{1}	12^{3}	13		10	9	14	5	8				1				7	11^{2}						32
	4	3	12	2		6^{1}			9	11		5	8^{2}			13	1				7	10^{3}	14					33
	4	3		2^{1}			12		9	11	13	5	8		14	7^{2}	1				6	10^{3}						34
	4	3	12	2			10^{2}			11^{1}	9	5	8		13	7^{3}	1				6		14					35
	3		4	2			12		8^{2}	9^{3}	10	5	6^{1}		11		1				7	13		14				36
	3		4	2			12		7	9■	10^{1}	5	8		11		1				6^{2}	13						37
	4	3^{1}	2	5					9		6	8	10^{2}		11		1				7	12			13			38
1	4	3		2		6^{2}	13		9		11^{1}	5	8		12						7	10						39
1	4	3		2		6^{3}	14		9		12	5	8		11^{1}						7	10^{2}				13		40
1	3	4		2		6^{3}	14		9	12	13	5	8		11^{1}						7	10^{2}						41
	4	3^{2}	12	2		6^{3}	13		9	10	11^{1}	5	8		14		1									7		42
1	4		3	2		6	10^{1}		9^{3}	11	12	5	8^{2}								14	13				7		43
1■	3		4	2		7	5		8	11	13		6^{2}		14							9^{3}				10^{1}	12	44
	4		3	2		7	5		9	11^{1}	12		8^{2}		14						13	10^{3}				6	1	45
	4		3	2		6^{3}	5		9	11	10		8^{2}								12	13		14		7^{1}	1	46

FA Cup
First Round Accrington S (a) 0-1

Carabao Cup
First Round Cheltenham T (a) 2-2
(Cheltenham T won 6-5 on penalties)

Checkatrade Trophy
Group B (S) Southampton U21 (h) 0-2
Group B (S) Southend U (h) 2-0
Group B (S) Cambridge U (a) 1-3

COVENTRY CITY

FOUNDATION

Workers at Singers' cycle factory formed a club in 1883. The first success of Singers' FC was to win the Birmingham Junior Cup in 1891 and this led in 1894 to their election to the Birmingham & District League. Four years later they changed their name to Coventry City and joined the Southern League in 1908 at which time they were playing in blue and white quarters.

Ricoh Arena, Judds Lane, Longford, Coventry CV6 6AQ.

Groundsharing with Birmingham C for 2019–20 season.

Sky Blue Lodge, Leamington Road, Coventry CV8 3FL

Telephone: (02476) 991 987.

Fax: (02476) 303 872.

Ticket Office: (02476) 991 987.

Website: www.ccfc.co.uk

Email: info@ccfc.co.uk

Ground Capacity: 32,609.

Record Attendance: 51,455 v Wolverhampton W, Division 2, 29 April 1967 (at Highfield Road); 31,407 v Chelsea, FA Cup 6th rd, 7 March 2009 (at Ricoh Arena).

Pitch Measurements: 100m × 68m (109.5yd × 74.5yd).

Chairman: Tim Fisher.

Chief Executive: David Boddy.

Manager: Mark Robins.

Assistant Manager: Adi Viveash.

Colours: Sky blue shirts with white trim, sky blue shorts, sky blue socks.

Year Formed: 1883.

Turned Professional: 1893.

Previous Name: 1883, Singers' FC; 1898, Coventry City.

Club Nickname: 'Sky Blues'.

Grounds: 1883, Binley Road; 1887, Stoke Road; 1899, Highfield Road; 2005, Ricoh Arena; 2013, Sixfields Stadium (groundshare with Northampton T); 2014, Ricoh Arena; 2019, St Andrew's Trillion Trophy Stadium (groundshare with Birmingham C).

First Football League Game: 30 August 1919, Division 2, v Tottenham H (h) L 0–5 – Lindon; Roberts, Chaplin, Allan, Hawley, Clarke, Sheldon, Mercer, Sambrooke, Lowes, Gibson.

Record League Victory: 9–0 v Bristol C, Division 3 (S), 28 April 1934 – Pearson; Brown, Bisby; Perry, Davidson, Frith; White (2), Lauderdale, Bourton (5), Jones (2), Lake.

Record Cup Victory: 8–0 v Rushden & D, League Cup 2nd rd, 2 October 2002 – Debec; Caldwell, Quinn, Betts (1p), Konjic (Shaw), Davenport, Pipe, Safri (Stanford), Mills (2) (Bothroyd (2)), McSheffery (3), Partridge.

HONOURS

League Champions: Division 2 – 1966–67; Division 3 – 1963–64; Division 3S – 1935–36.
Runners-up: Division 3S – 1933–34; Division 4 – 1958–59.

FA Cup Winners: 1987.

League Cup: semi-final – 1981, 1990.

League Trophy Winners: 2017.

European Competitions
Fairs Cup: 1970–71.

THE SUN FACT FILE

The first time Coventry City reached a 'Wembley final' was in November 1977 when they lost out to Ipswich Town in the *Daily Express* Five-a-Side National Championships at Wembley Pool. The Sky Blues had previously beaten Everton, Manchester United and Arsenal, but were unable to keep their run going to take the trophy.

Record Defeat: 2–10 v Norwich C, Division 3 (S), 15 March 1930.

Most League Points (2 for a win): 60, Division 4, 1958–59 and Division 3, 1963–64.

Most League Points (3 for a win): 75, FL 2, 2017–18.

Most League Goals: 108, Division 3 (S), 1931–32.

Highest League Scorer in Season: Clarrie Bourton, 49, Division 3 (S), 1931–32.

Most League Goals in Total Aggregate: Clarrie Bourton, 173, 1931–37.

Most League Goals in One Match: 5, Clarrie Bourton v Bournemouth, Division 3 (S), 17 October 1931; 5, Arthur Bacon v Gillingham, Division 3 (S), 30 December 1933.

Most Capped Player: Magnus Hedman, 44 (58), Sweden.

Most League Appearances: Steve Ogrizovic, 507, 1984–2000.

Youngest League Player: Ben Mackey, 16 years 167 days v Ipswich T, 12 April 2003.

Record Transfer Fee Received: £13,000,000 from Internazionale for Robbie Keane, July 2000.

Record Transfer Fee Paid: £6,500,000 to Norwich C for Craig Bellamy, August 2000.

Football League Record: 1919 Elected to Division 2; 1925–26 Division 3 (N); 1926–36 Division 3 (S); 1936–52 Division 2; 1952–58 Division 3 (S); 1958–59 Division 4; 1959–64 Division 3; 1964–67 Division 2; 1967–92 Division 1; 1992–2001 Premier League; 2001–04 Division 1; 2004–12 FL C; 2012–17 FL 1; 2017–18 FL 2; 2018– FL 1.

LATEST SEQUENCES

Longest Sequence of League Wins: 6, 25.4.1964 – 5.9.1964.

Longest Sequence of League Defeats: 9, 30.8.1919 – 11.10.1919.

Longest Sequence of League Draws: 6, 1.11.2003 – 29.11.2003.

Longest Sequence of Unbeaten League Matches: 25, 26.11.1966 – 13.5.1967.

Longest Sequence Without a League Win: 19, 30.8.1919 – 20.12.1919.

Successive Scoring Runs: 25 from 10.9.1966.

Successive Non-scoring Runs: 11 from 11.10.1919.

MANAGERS

H. R. Buckle 1909–10
Robert Wallace 1910–13
(*Secretary-Manager*)
Frank Scott-Walford 1913–15
William Clayton 1917–19
H. Pollitt 1919–20
Albert Evans 1920–24
Jimmy Kerr 1924–28
James McIntyre 1928–31
Harry Storer 1931–45
Dick Bayliss 1945–47
Billy Frith 1947–48
Harry Storer 1948–53
Jack Fairbrother 1953–54
Charlie Elliott 1954–55
Jesse Carver 1955–56
George Raynor 1956
Harry Warren 1956–57
Billy Frith 1957–61
Jimmy Hill 1961–67
Noel Cantwell 1967–72
Bob Dennison 1972
Joe Mercer 1972–75
Gordon Milne 1972–81
Dave Sexton 1981–83
Bobby Gould 1983–84
Don Mackay 1985–86
George Curtis 1986–87
(*became Managing Director*)
John Sillett 1987–90
Terry Butcher 1990–92
Don Howe 1992
Bobby Gould 1992–93
(*with Don Howe, June 1992*)
Phil Neal 1993–95
Ron Atkinson 1995–96
(*became Director of Football*)
Gordon Strachan 1996–2001
Roland Nilsson 2001–02
Gary McAllister 2002–04
Eric Black 2004
Peter Reid 2004–05
Micky Adams 2005–07
Iain Dowie 2007–08
Chris Coleman 2008–10
Aidy Boothroyd 2010–11
Andy Thorn 2011–12
Mark Robins 2012–13
Steven Pressley 2013–15
Tony Mowbray 2015–16
Russell Slade 2016–17
Mark Robins March 2017–

TEN YEAR LEAGUE RECORD

		P	W	D	L	F	A	Pts	Pos
2009-10	FL C	46	13	15	18	47	64	54	19
2010-11	FL C	46	14	13	19	54	58	55	18
2011-12	FL C	46	9	13	24	41	65	40	23
2012-13	FL 1	46	18	11	17	66	59	55*	15
2013-14	FL 1	46	16	13	17	74	77	51*	18
2014-15	FL 1	46	13	16	17	49	60	55	17
2015-16	FL 1	46	19	12	15	67	49	69	8
2016-17	FL 1	46	9	12	25	37	68	39	23
2017-18	FL 2	46	22	9	15	64	47	75	6
2018-19	FL 1	46	18	11	17	54	54	65	8

** 10 pts deducted.*

DID YOU KNOW ?

Following Coventry City's adjourned annual meeting in February 1922 they were presented with a new strip in the local authority's colours of red, green and gold. This was worn for a couple of seasons but then discarded as it was believed to be the cause of bad luck.

COVENTRY CITY – SKY BET LEAGUE ONE 2018–19 LEAGUE RECORD

Match No.	Date	Venue	Opponents	Result		H/T Score	Lg Pos.	Goalscorers	Attendance
1	Aug 4	H	Scunthorpe U	L	1-2	0-0	15	Andreu [52]	12,964
2	11	A	AFC Wimbledon	D	0-0	0-0	17		4768
3	18	H	Plymouth Arg	W	1-0	1-0	13	Bakayoko (pen) [43]	11,453
4	21	A	Blackpool	L	0-2	0-0	17		3656
5	25	A	Gillingham	D	1-1	0-0	16	Clarke-Harris [46]	4880
6	Sept 1	H	Rochdale	L	0-1	0-0	19		9879
7	9	A	Oxford U	W	2-1	0-0	12	Mousinho (og) [64], Chaplin (pen) [81]	7519
8	15	H	Barnsley	W	1-0	0-0	12	Willis [80]	11,465
9	22	A	Bristol R	L	1-3	1-3	13	Hyam [44]	8385
10	29	H	Sunderland	D	1-1	0-0	14	Clarke-Harris [68]	16,407
11	Oct 2	H	Portsmouth	L	0-1	0-1	14		11,102
12	6	A	Charlton Ath	W	2-1	0-1	14	Bakayoko 2 [81, 90]	11,743
13	13	H	Wycombe W	W	1-0	0-0	12	Chaplin [82]	10,480
14	20	A	Southend U	W	2-1	1-0	10	Hiwula [20], Jones [90]	7775
15	23	A	Bradford C	W	4-2	2-0	8	Clarke-Harris [2], Chaplin [11], Hiwula [65], Bayliss [70]	11,075
16	27	H	Doncaster R	W	2-1	2-0	7	Hiwula [21], Thomas [41]	11,006
17	Nov 3	H	Accrington S	D	1-1	0-0	7	Doyle [87]	10,653
18	17	A	Burton Alb	L	0-1	0-0	9		4681
19	23	H	Peterborough U	D	1-1	0-0	6	Chaplin [90]	11,719
20	27	A	Fleetwood T	L	0-3	0-0	9		2570
21	Dec 8	A	Walsall	L	1-2	1-0	11	Thomas [18]	5926
22	15	H	Luton T	L	1-2	0-1	13	Clarke-Harris (pen) [90]	12,559
23	22	A	Shrewsbury T	L	0-1	0-0	14		8083
24	26	H	Charlton Ath	W	2-1	1-0	13	Hiwula [41], Bayliss [89]	13,013
25	29	H	Southend U	W	1-0	0-0	9	Hiwula [54]	11,395
26	Jan 1	A	Wycombe W	W	2-0	1-0	8	Chaplin (pen) [34], Clarke-Harris [62]	6183
27	5	A	Scunthorpe U	L	1-2	0-0	8	Chaplin [78]	4692
28	12	H	AFC Wimbledon	D	1-1	0-1	8	Thomas [61]	10,420
29	19	A	Plymouth Arg	L	1-2	0-0	9	Chaplin [55]	10,686
30	26	H	Blackpool	L	0-2	0-0	11		9786
31	Feb 2	H	Gillingham	D	1-1	0-0	11	Enobakhare [68]	26,741
32	9	A	Rochdale	W	1-0	0-0	11	Hiwula [68]	3661
33	16	H	Walsall	W	3-0	2-0	9	Bakayoko [29], Hiwula [36], Enobakhare (pen) [73]	10,646
34	24	A	Luton T	D	1-1	1-1	10	Shipley [34]	9810
35	Mar 2	A	Accrington S	W	1-0	0-0	8	Enobakhare [60]	3083
36	8	H	Burton Alb	L	1-2	0-1	9	Bayliss [51]	11,468
37	12	H	Fleetwood T	W	2-1	2-1	9	Bakayoko [6], Hiwula [42]	9220
38	16	A	Peterborough U	W	2-1	1-0	7	Bakayoko [42], Enobakhare [49]	7084
39	23	H	Oxford U	L	0-1	0-0	9		14,044
40	30	A	Barnsley	D	2-2	1-1	9	Hiwula [35], Thomas [62]	13,593
41	Apr 7	H	Bristol R	D	0-0	0-0	9		12,664
42	13	A	Sunderland	W	5-4	3-3	8	Enobakhare [12], Bakayoko [18], Hiwula [25], Shipley [55], Chaplin [78]	36,134
43	19	H	Bradford C	W	2-0	1-0	8	Hiwula [9], Enobakhare [88]	11,711
44	22	A	Portsmouth	L	1-2	1-0	8	Hiwula [9]	18,884
45	28	H	Shrewsbury T	D	1-1	1-0	8	Shipley [16]	13,549
46	May 4	A	Doncaster R	L	0-2	0-1	8		12,794

Final League Position: 8

GOALSCORERS

League (54): Hiwula 12, Chaplin 8 (2 pens), Bakayoko 7 (1 pen), Enobakhare 6 (1 pen), Clarke-Harris 5 (1 pen), Thomas 4, Bayliss 3, Shipley 3, Andreu 1, Doyle 1, Hyam 1, Jones 1, Willis 1, own goal 1.
FA Cup (2): Clarke-Harris 1, Thomas 1.
Carabao Cup (0).
Checkatrade Trophy (1): Hiwula 1.

O'Brien L 4	Sterling D 37 + 1	Willis J 36 + 2	Hyam D 37 + 1	Mason B 25	Doyle M 21 + 2	Ogogo A 6 + 4	Hiwula J 35 + 4	Andreu T 6 + 4	Bayliss T 37 + 1	Biamou M 2 + 2	Thompson J 1 + 3	Clarke-Harris J 18 + 9	Shipley J 22 + 11	Davies T 19 + 4	Bakayoko A 18 + 13	Brown J 17 + 5	Thomas L 41 + 2	Burge L 40	Grimmer J 8 + 3	Allassani R — + 5	Ponticelli J — + 5	Chaplin C 22 + 9	Kelly L 25 + 5	Jones J — + 8	Westbrooke Z 3 + 4	McCallum S 3 + 4	Enobakhare B 18	Meyler D 2 + 3	Wakefield C — + 8	Stockdale D 2	Williams M 1	Match No.
1	2	3^{2}	4	5	6	7	8	9	10^{1}	11^{3}	12	13	14																			1
1	2		4	5^{1}	6	7	9	10	8	12				3	11^{2}	13																2
1	2	3	4	5	7	6	8^{1}	9^{3}	10	13			14		11^{2}		12															3
1	5	2	3		7	4	13	14	8	10^{1}			6^{2}		12^{3}	9	11															4
		3	4	5	7			9	6			11^{1}	10^{2}		14		8^{3}	1	2	12	13											5
		3	4	5	8			10^{1}	7			11^{3}	9^{2}		14		6	1	2	13		12										6
	12	3	4		8	13		14	7			11	9^{3}			5	6	1	2^{1}			10^{2}										7
	2	3	4		8				7			11	9^{1}		13	5	6^{2}	1				10	12									8
	2^{3}	6	4		7			13			12	11^{2}	10		14	5	8	1				9	3^{1}									9
	2	4	3		8				7			10	9	12		5^{2}	6^{1}	1				11		13								10
	5	2	4^{2}		8		14	11^{1}	7		12	10	9^{3}	3			6	1						13								11
	5	2			8		13		7			10^{3}	14	3	12	9	6^{2}	1				11	4^{1}									12
	2	3			8		9^{1}		7^{2}			11		4	13	5	6	1				10	12									13
	2	3			7		9^{3}		8			10^{2}	12	4	14	5	6	1				11^{1}		13								14
	2		4		7		9^{2}		8^{2}			10	14	3		5	6^{1}	1				11	13	12								15
	2	3			8	14	9^{3}		7^{2}			11		4		5	6	1				10^{1}	12	13								16
		3			8	7^{2}	9				2	11		4		5	6	1				10^{1}	13	12								17
		3	4		8^{3}	13	9		7			10^{2}			12	5	6	1	2			11^{1}		14								18
		3	4		8		9^{1}		7			11			13	5	6	1	2			10		12^{2}								19
		3^{1}	4		8		9^{2}	13	7			11		12	14	5	6	1	2			10^{3}										20
	2	3				13			7^{2}			12	8	4	10	5	9	1				11^{1}	6									21
		3^{3}	12				11^{2}		6^{1}			10	8	4		5	9	1	2	14		13	7									22
	2	3	11			9^{2}	12		8			4	14			5^{3}	6^{1}	1		13		10	7									23
	2	3	4	5^{3}			11		6			12	8^{1}	14		13	9^{2}	1				10	7									24
	2	3	4	5^{3}	14		11		6			12	8^{1}					1				10	7		9^{2}	13						25
	2	3	4	5	13		11^{1}		7			12	9				6	1				10^{2}	8^{3}			14						26
	2	3	4	5^{3}	7^{1}		11^{2}		6			12	10				8	1		13		9				14						27
	2	4	3				8		6			12					10	1	13			9	7			5^{1}	11^{2}					28
			4	5^{2}			11^{3}		6^{1}			12		3			8	1	2			9	7		13	14	10					29
	2		3	5			10^{2}					13		4	12		8	1				11	6		7		9^{1}					30
	2	3	4				11		13				9		12		6	1							7^{3}	5	10^{1}	8^{2}	14			31
	2	3	4	5			10		7^{1}				12	13	11		8						6				9^{2}			1		32
	2	3	4	5			10		6^{1}						11		8^{3}					12	7				9^{2}	13	14	1		33
	2	3	4	5			10		6				12		11^{1}		8^{3}	1					7				9^{2}	13	14			34
	2	4	3	5			10		7				8^{1}		11		12	1					6				9					35
	2	3		5^{2}			10		7				12	4	11^{1}		8	1	13				6				9^{1}					36
	2			5^{1}			9		7				10	4	11	12	8^{2}	1	14									6	13		3^{3}	37
	2	3	4	5^{2}			10		7				13		11	12	8^{1}	1					6				9					38
	2	3	4	5			10		6^{2}				12		11		8^{1}	1			13		7				9					39
	2	4	3	5^{2}			9		7						11	12	6^{1}	1					8				10		13			40
	2		4	5			10		6^{1}					3	11^{2}		8	1			14	13	7				9	12^{3}				41
	2		4	5			10^{1}						7	3	11		8^{3}	1				13	6		14		9^{2}		12			42
	2		4				10^{2}						7^{1}	3	11^{3}		8	1			14	12	6		13	5	9					43
	2	13	4	5			10						7^{1}	3^{2}	11		8^{3}	1				12	6				9		14			44
	2^{1}	13	4	5^{3}			10						7	3	11^{2}		8	1				12	6				9		14			45
	2	4	3	5			10						7^{2}		11^{1}		8	1			14	12	6		13		9^{3}					46

FA Cup

First Round	Walsall	(a)	2-3

Carabao Cup

First Round	Oxford U	(a)	0-2

Checkatrade Trophy

Group E (S)	Arsenal U21	(h)	0-3
Group E (S)	Forest Green R	(h)	1-1
(Coventry C won 4-2 on penalties)			
Group E (S)	Cheltenham T	(a)	0-2

CRAWLEY TOWN

FOUNDATION

Formed in 1896, Crawley Town initially entered the West Sussex League before switching to the mid-Sussex League in 1901, winning the Second Division in its second season. The club remained at such level until 1951 when it became members of the Sussex County League and five years later moved to the Metropolitan League while remaining as an amateur club. It was not until 1962 that the club turned semi-professional and a year later, joined the Southern League. Many honours came the club's way, but the most successful run was achieved in 2010–11 when they reached the fifith round of the FA Cup and played before a crowd of 74,778 spectators at Old Trafford against Manchester United. Crawley Town spent 48 years at the Town Mead ground before a new site was occupied at Broadfield in 1997, ideally suited to access from the neighbouring motorway. History was also made on 9 April when the team won promotion to the Football League after beating Tamworth 3-0 to stretch their unbeaten League record to 26 games. They finished the season with a Conference record points total of 105 and at the same time, established another milestone for the longest unbeaten run, having extended it to 30 matches by the end of the season.

The People's Pension Stadium, Winfield Way, Crawley, West Sussex RH11 9RX.

Telephone: (01293) 410 000.

Ticket Office: (01293) 410 005.

Website: www.crawleytownfc.com

Email: feedback@crawleytownfc.com

Ground Capacity: 6,134.

Record Attendance: 5,880 v Reading, FA Cup 3rd rd, 5 January 2013.

Pitch Measurements: 103.5m × 66m (113yd × 72yd).

Chairman: Ziya Eren.

Operations Director: Kelly Derham.

Head Coach: Gabriele Cioffi.

Assistant Head Coach: Nathan Rooney.

Colours: Red shirts with white trim, red shorts with white trim, red socks with white trim.

Year Formed: 1896. ***Turned Professional:*** 1962.

Club Nickname: 'The Red Devils'.

Grounds: Up to 1997, Town Mead; 1997 Broadfield Stadium (renamed Checkatrade.com Stadium 2013, The People's Pension Stadium 2018).

HONOURS

League Champions: Conference – 2010–11.
FL 2 – (3rd) 2011–12 *(promoted).*

FA Cup: 5th rd – 2011, 2012.

League Cup: 3rd rd – 2013.

THE Sun FACT FILE

Former Chelsea defender Steve Wicks broke the club's transfer record twice in his first seven days as manager of Crawley Town after being appointed in May 1992. Both Daren O'Neill and Dave Thompson were signed from Wokingham as Wicks started rebuilding the team. But after quick exits from both the FA Cup and FA Trophy he was asked to reduce the wage bill and resigned after just seven months in charge.

First Football League Game: 6 August 2011, FL 2 v Port Vale (a) D 2-2 – Shearer; Hunt, Howell, Bulman, McFadzean (1), Dempster (Thomas), Simpson, Torres, Tubbs (Neilson), Barnett (1) (Wassmer), Smith.

Record League Victory: 5–1 v Barnsley, FL 1, 14 February 2015 – Price; Dickson, Bradley (1), Ward, Fowler (Smith); Young, Elliott (1), Edwards, Wordsworth (Morgan), Pogba (Tomlin); McLeod (3).

Record League Defeat: 6-0 v Morecambe, FL 2, 10 September 2011.

Most League Points (3 for a win): 84, FL 2, 2011–12.

Most League Goals: 76, FL 2, 2011–12.

Highest League Scorer in Season: James Collins, 20, FL 2, 2016–17.

Most League Goals in Total Aggregate: Billy Clarke, 20, 2011–14; Matt Tubbs, 20, 2011–12, 2013–14; James Collins, 20, 2016–17.

Most League Goals in One Match: 3, Izale McLeod v Barnsley, FL 1, 14 February 2015; 3, Jimmy Smith v Colchester U, FL 2, 14 February 2017.

Most Capped Player: Dean Morgan, 1 (3), Montserrat.

Most League Appearances: Lewis Young, 198, 2014–19.

Youngest League Player: Brian Galach, 17 years 353 days v Tranmere R, 4 May 2019.

Record Transfer Fee Received: £1,100,000 from Peterborough U for Tyrone Barnett, July 2012.

Record Transfer Fee Paid: £220,000 to York C for Richard Brodie, August 2010.

Football League Record: 2011 Promoted from Conference Premier; 2011–12 FL 2; 2012–15 FL 1; 2015– FL 2.

MANAGERS

John Maggs 1978–90
Brian Sparrow 1990–92
Steve Wicks 1992–93
Ted Shepherd 1993–95
Colin Pates 1995–96
Billy Smith 1997–99
Cliff Cant 1999–2000
Billy Smith 2000–03
Francis Vines 2003–05
John Hollins 2005–06
David Woozley, Ben Judge and John Yems 2006–07
Steve Evans 2007–12
Sean O'Driscoll 2012
Richie Barker 2012–13
John Gregory 2013–14
Dean Saunders 2014–15
Mark Yates 2015–16
Dermot Drummy 2016–17
Harry Kewell 2017–18
Gabriele Cioffi September 2018–

LATEST SEQUENCES

Longest Sequence of League Wins: 7, 17.9.2011 – 25.10.2011.

Longest Sequence of League Defeats: 8, 28.3.2016 – 7.5.2016.

Longest Sequence of League Draws: 5, 25.10.2014 – 29.11.2014.

Longest Sequence of Unbeaten League Matches: 13, 17.9.2011 – 17.12.2011.

Longest Sequence Without a League Win: 13, 25.10.2014 – 27.1.2015.

Successive Scoring Runs: 16 from 17.9.2011.

Successive Non-scoring Runs: 4 from 14.10.2017.

TEN YEAR LEAGUE RECORD

		P	W	D	L	F	A	Pts	Pos
2009-10	Conf P	44	19	9	16	50	57	66	7
2010-11	Conf P	46	31	12	3	93	50	105	1
2011-12	FL 2	46	23	15	8	76	54	84	3
2012-13	FL 1	46	18	14	14	59	58	68	10
2013-14	FL 1	46	14	15	17	48	54	57	14
2014-15	FL 1	46	13	11	22	53	79	50	22
2015-16	FL 2	46	13	8	25	45	78	47	20
2016-17	FL 2	46	13	12	21	53	71	51	19
2017-18	FL 2	46	16	11	19	58	66	59	14
2018-19	FL 2	46	15	8	23	51	68	53	19

DID YOU KNOW ?

When Crawley Town reached Round One of the FA Cup for the first time in their history, goalkeeper John Maggs played despite having suffered a broken bone in his hand. Maggs, the only experienced keeper on Crawley's books at the time, helped the club gain a 1-1 draw in the tie against Chelmsford City in November 1970 but they lost the replay and so missed out on a home game against Torquay United.

CRAWLEY TOWN – SKY BET LEAGUE TWO 2018–19 LEAGUE RECORD

Match No.	Date	Venue	Opponents	Result		H/T Score	Lg Pos.	Goalscorers	Attendance
1	Aug 4	A	Cheltenham T	W	1-0	0-0	8	Palmer [63]	2719
2	11	H	Stevenage	L	1-3	0-0	13	Palmer [53]	2102
3	18	A	Port Vale	L	0-1	0-1	19		4159
4	21	H	Swindon T	D	2-2	0-2	18	Palmer 2 (1 pen) [51, 90 (p)]	2050
5	25	H	Bury	W	3-2	1-0	14	Smith [4], Camara [81], Palmer [88]	2036
6	Sept 1	A	Oldham Ath	L	1-2	1-1	16	Bulman [22]	4160
7	8	A	Lincoln C	W	1-0	1-0	15	Bostwick (og) [45]	8321
8	15	H	Morecambe	W	2-0	0-0	10	Nathaniel-George [52], Camara [55]	1895
9	22	A	Forest Green R	L	0-1	0-0	15		2089
10	29	H	Yeovil T	W	3-1	1-1	10	Palmer [25], Nathaniel-George [68], Morais [90]	2142
11	Oct 2	A	Notts Co	L	1-3	0-2	12	Poleon [90]	5098
12	6	H	Cambridge U	W	2-0	0-0	9	Gambin [71], Palmer [77]	2151
13	13	A	Colchester U	L	1-3	1-1	10	Morais (pen) [40]	3208
14	20	H	Newport Co	W	4-1	1-0	8	Maguire [1], Morais (pen) [64], Palmer [72], Nathaniel-George [79]	2157
15	23	H	Exeter C	D	1-1	0-0	9	Morais [61]	2095
16	27	A	Tranmere R	L	1-5	0-2	10	Palmer [65]	5445
17	Nov 3	H	Milton Keynes D	L	0-4	0-3	12		2667
18	17	A	Grimsby T	L	0-1	0-0	13		4459
19	24	H	Crewe Alex	W	3-0	1-0	12	Payne (pen) [15], McNerney [81], Bulman [90]	1734
20	Dec 8	H	Northampton T	L	0-1	0-0	16		2389
21	15	A	Macclesfield T	L	0-2	0-1	16		1362
22	22	H	Carlisle U	L	2-3	2-2	17	Poleon 2 [8, 40]	2176
23	26	A	Cambridge U	L	1-2	1-1	18	Poleon [16]	4601
24	29	A	Newport Co	D	0-0	0-0	18		3166
25	Jan 1	H	Colchester U	W	2-0	0-0	17	Gambin 2 [60, 90]	2765
26	5	H	Cheltenham T	W	1-0	1-0	15	Palmer (pen) [39]	2623
27	12	A	Stevenage	L	1-2	1-2	17	Poleon [36]	2347
28	15	A	Mansfield T	L	0-1	0-0	17		3739
29	19	H	Port Vale	L	0-1	0-1	17		2089
30	26	A	Swindon T	W	1-0	1-0	16	Morais [45]	6026
31	Feb 2	A	Bury	D	1-1	0-0	16	Palmer [87]	3625
32	9	H	Oldham Ath	L	0-3	0-0	17		2058
33	16	A	Northampton T	D	0-0	0-0	17		4581
34	23	H	Macclesfield T	D	1-1	0-1	18	Young [84]	2190
35	Mar 2	A	Milton Keynes D	L	0-1	0-1	18		6889
36	9	H	Grimsby T	W	2-1	2-1	18	Palmer 2 [26, 40]	2043
37	12	H	Mansfield T	D	0-0	0-0	18		1909
38	16	A	Crewe Alex	L	1-6	1-4	18	Palmer (pen) [13]	3220
39	23	H	Lincoln C	L	0-3	0-1	18		3335
40	30	A	Morecambe	L	0-1	0-0	20		2445
41	Apr 6	H	Forest Green R	L	1-2	1-1	21	Bulman [24]	2088
42	13	A	Yeovil T	W	1-0	0-0	20	Morais [72]	3232
43	19	A	Exeter C	W	3-1	2-0	18	Morais [26], Grego-Cox 2 [34, 60]	5054
44	22	H	Notts Co	D	1-1	1-1	19	Nathaniel-George [19]	2800
45	27	A	Carlisle U	L	2-4	1-4	19	Nathaniel-George [44], Gerrard (og) [77]	4514
46	May 4	H	Tranmere R	W	3-1	2-0	19	Nathaniel-George [36], Morais [42], Camara [90]	3183

Final League Position: 19

GOALSCORERS

League (51): Palmer 14 (3 pens), Morais 8 (2 pens), Nathaniel-George 6, Poleon 5, Bulman 3, Camara 3, Gambin 3, Grego-Cox 2, Maguire 1, McNerney 1, Payne 1 (1 pen), Smith 1, Young 1, own goals 2.
FA Cup (3): Palmer 2, own goal 1.
Carabao Cup (1): Connolly 1.
Checkatrade Trophy (2): N'Gala 1, Poleon 1.

Morris G 46	Francomb G 39 + 2	Connolly M 23	Vincelot R 12	Doherty J 12 + 6	Young L 34 + 4	Payne J 24 + 3	Bulman D 29 + 7	Morais F 31 + 3	Palmer O 39 + 1	Poleon D 21 + 9	Grego-Cox R 15 + 13	Randall M 2 + 4	Camara P 34 + 11	Milsom R 2 + 1	Nathaniel-George A 15 + 15	Smith J 3 + 1	N'Gala B 12 + 1	Maguire J 24 + 3	McNerney J 26 + 3	Gambin L 21 + 5	Allarakhia T — + 5	Sesay D 16 + 2	Dallison T 19	German R — + 4	Willock M 7 + 4	Meite I — + 2	Galach B — + 1	*Match No.*
1	2	3	4	5	6	7	8^3	9	10^2	11^1	12	13	14															1
1	2	4	3	5	9^1	8^2	7	6	10	11	13	12																2
1	2	3	4	5	9^2		7^1	6	11		10^3	13	14	8	12													3
1	2	4	3^2	5		12■		6	10	11	14		13	8^3	9	7^1												4
1	2	4	3	5	12		8	6^3	10	11^1			13	14	9	7^2												5
1	2	3	4^1	5			6	9	11	7^2			13		10	8	12											6
1	2^2	4		12	6		8	7	11				10		9^1		3	5	13									7
1	6^1	4		14	2	13	8^2	7	11	12			10		9^3		3	5										8
1	6	4^1			2		7^2	9	10	14			11		8^3		3	5	12■	13								9
1			4		2	7		6	10	13		8^2	11		12		3	5		9^1								10
1			4	5^3	2	7^1		6	10	9		14	11^4					12	3	8	13							11
1	14	4			2	3		8	10	11^1		7^2	12				6	5		9^3	13							12
1	6	3			2	7^1		8	10	11^2			12				4■	5	14	9^3	13							13
1	6	3	4	12	2	7^1	14	8	10				9		13			5^2		11^3								14
1	6	3	4	12	2	7^1	14	8	11				9		13			5^2		10^3								15
1	6^1	3	4	13	2		7^3	8	11				9^2		12			5		10	14							16
1	6	3	4		2^1	8		7	10	13			12		9			5		11^2								17
1	4	2			5	8	6^1		11		12		10		7			9	3									18
1	5				13	8	7			10^2	12		11		6^1		4	2	3	9^3	14							19
1	5					8^1	7		11■	10^2	12		6		13		3	2	4	9								20
1	2			13		8	7			11	10^2		9		12		4	5^1	3	6								21
1	2					8	7			10	12		11^1		6		4	5	3	9								22
1	2	7		5^2		8	12			11	13		10		6^1		4	14	3	9^3								23
1	2	4		5		7	8			10	9^1		11						3	12		6						24
1	2	3		5		7^1	12			11	9		10						4■	8		6						25
1	2	3		4	12	8^1	14		11	10^3	13		7					5		9		6^2						26
1	2	3		9	13	7^2		12	11	10^3	14		8					4		6		5^1						27
1	3	4			2^1	7		8	11	10^2	14		12					5		9^3		13	6					28
1	2	3			5		7	6^3	10	11^1			8^2		13			9		12			4	14				29
1	3				5		7	6	11				8						2	10		9	4					30
1	2				5	7^1	12	8^2	11	14			6		13				3	10^3		9	4					31
1	2				5	6^2		10	11	14			8		12				3	9^1		7^3	4		13			32
1	2				5	12	6	7^1	11	8			10						3			9	4					33
1	2				5	8^3	7		11	10^2	14		13		12				3			9	4		6^1			34
1	2				5		6		11	13	7^1		8		12				3			9	4		10^2			35
1	2				5		7	12	10		8^1		11						3			9	4		6^2	13		36
1	2				5	7^2	12	13	10		11		6^1						3			9	4		8			37
1	2				5		7	6^1	10		11^3		13						3			9	4	12	8^2	14■		38
1					5		6		11^1	12	7		9				2		3			8	4	13	10^2			39
1	13				2		8	6^2	10		11		7^3		9^1			5	3			12	4	14				40
1	2				5		7	8^1	10	12	11^2		6		13			9	3				4					41
1	2				5		7	8^1	10		11^3		6^2		12			9	3	14			4		13			42
1	2^1				5		6	7	10^2		11		8		12			13	3			9^3	4		14			43
1					2		7	6	10		12		8		9			5	3	11^1			4					44
1					2		7	6^2	11^1		10		8		9			5	3	12			4		13			45
1	7				2			6^1	12		10		9		11^2	14			3			5	4		8^3		13	46

FA Cup

First Round	Southend U	(a)	1-1
Replay	Southend U	(h)	2-6
(*aet*)			

Carabao Cup

First Round	Bristol R	(a)	1-2

Checkatrade Trophy

Group A (S)	Tottenham H U21	(h)	1-1
(Crawley T won 5-3 on penalties)			
Group A (S)	Portsmouth	(h)	0-1
Group A (S)	Gillingham	(a)	1-2

CREWE ALEXANDRA

FOUNDATION

The first match played at Crewe was on 1 December 1877 against Basford, the leading North Staffordshire team of that time. During the club's history they have also played in a number of other leagues including the Football Alliance, Football Combination, Lancashire League, Manchester League, Central League and Lancashire Combination. Two former players, Aaron Scragg in 1899 and Jackie Pearson in 1911, had the distinction of refereeing FA Cup finals. Pearson was also capped for England against Ireland in 1892.

The Alexandra Stadium, Gresty Road, Crewe, Cheshire CW2 6EB.

Telephone: (01270) 213 014.

Fax: (01270) 216 320.

Ticket Office: (01270) 252 610.

Website: www.crewealex.net

Email: info@crewealex.net

Ground Capacity: 10,109.

Record Attendance: 20,000 v Tottenham H, FA Cup 4th rd, 30 January 1960.

Pitch Measurements: 100.5m × 67m (110yd × 73.5yd).

Chairman: John Bowler MBE.

Vice-Chairman: David Rowlinson.

Manager: David Artell.

Assistant Manager: Kenny Lunt.

Colours: Red shirts with black and white trim, white shorts with black and red trim, red socks with white trim.

Year Formed: 1877. ***Turned Professional:*** 1893. ***Club Nickname:*** 'The Railwaymen'.

Ground: 1898, Gresty Road.

First Football League Game: 3 September 1892, Division 2, v Burton Swifts (a) L 1–7 – Hickton; Moore, Cope; Linnell, Johnson, Osborne; Bennett, Pearson (1), Bailey, Barnett, Roberts.

Record League Victory: 8–0 v Rotherham U, Division 3 (N), 1 October 1932 – Foster; Pringle, Dawson; Ward, Keenor (1), Turner (1); Gillespie, Swindells (1), McConnell (2), Deacon (2), Weale (1).

Record Cup Victory: 8–0 v Hartlepool U, Auto Windscreens Shield 1st rd, 17 October 1995 – Gayle; Collins (1), Booty, Westwood (Unsworth), Macauley (1), Whalley (1), Garvey (1), Murphy (1), Savage (1) (Rivers (1p)), Lennon, Edwards, (1 og). 8–0 v Doncaster R, LDV Vans Trophy 3rd rd, 10 November 2002 – Bankole; Wright, Walker, Foster, Tierney; Lunt (1), Brammer, Sorvel, Vaughan (1) (Bell); Ashton (3) (Miles), Jack (2) (Jones (1)).

Record Defeat: 2–13 v Tottenham H, FA Cup 4th rd replay, 3 February 1960.

HONOURS

League: *Runners-up:* Second Division – 2002–03.

FA Cup: semi-final – 1888.

League Cup: never past 3rd rd.

League Trophy Winners: 2013.

Welsh Cup Winners: 1936, 1937.

THE Sun FACT FILE

It was during his spell at Crewe Alexandra in 1979–80 that goalkeeper Bruce Grobbelaar scored his only Football League goal when he netted from the penalty spot in a 2-0 win over York City on the final day of the season. The win extended Crewe's unbeaten run to six games in Division Four but they still ended up 23rd in the table and had to seek re-election.

Most League Points (2 for a win): 59, Division 4, 1962–63.

Most League Points (3 for a win): 86, Division 2, 2002–03.

Most League Goals: 95, Division 3 (N), 1931–32.

Highest League Scorer in Season: Terry Harkin, 35, Division 4, 1964–65.

Most League Goals in Total Aggregate: Bert Swindells, 126, 1928–37.

Most League Goals in One Match: 5, Tony Naylor v Colchester U, Division 3, 24 April 1993.

Most Capped Player: Clayton Ince, 38 (79), Trinidad & Tobago.

Most League Appearances: Tommy Lowry, 436, 1966–78.

Youngest League Player: Steve Walters, 16 years 119 days v Peterborough U, 6 May 1988.

Record Transfer Fee Received: £3,000,000 (rising to £6,000,000) from Manchester U for Nick Powell, June 2012.

Record Transfer Fee Paid: £650,000 to Torquay U for Rodney Jack, July 1998.

Football League Record: 1892 Original Member of Division 2; 1896 Failed re-election; 1921 Re-entered Division (N); 1958–63 Division 4; 1963–64 Division 3; 1964–68 Division 4; 1968–69 Division 3; 1969–89 Division 4; 1989–91 Division 3; 1991–92 Division 4; 1992–94 Division 3; 1994–97 Division 2; 1997–2002 Division 1; 2002–03 Division 2; 2003–04 Division 1; 2004–06 FL C; 2006–09 FL 1; 2009–12 FL 2; 2012–16 FL 1; 2016– FL 2.

LATEST SEQUENCES

Longest Sequence of League Wins: 7, 30.4.1994 – 3.9.1994.

Longest Sequence of League Defeats: 10, 16.4.1979 – 22.8.1979.

Longest Sequence of League Draws: 5, 18.9.2010 – 9.10.2010.

Longest Sequence of Unbeaten League Matches: 17, 25.3.1995 – 16.9.1995.

Longest Sequence Without a League Win: 30, 22.9.1956 – 6.4.1957.

Successive Scoring Runs: 26 from 7.4.1934.

Successive Non-scoring Runs: 9 from 6.11.1974.

MANAGERS

W. C. McNeill 1892–94 (*Secretary-Manager*)
J. G. Hall 1895–96 (*Secretary-Manager*)
R. Roberts (*1st team Secretary-Manager*) 1897
J. B. Blomerley 1898–1911 (*Secretary-Manager, continued as Hon. Secretary to 1925*)
Tom Bailey (*Secretary only*) 1925–38
George Lillycrop (*Trainer*) 1938–44
Frank Hill 1944–48
Arthur Turner 1948–51
Harry Catterick 1951–53
Ralph Ward 1953–55
Maurice Lindley 1956–57
Willie Cook 1957–58
Harry Ware 1958–60
Jimmy McGuigan 1960–64
Ernie Tagg 1964–71 (*continued as Secretary to 1972*)
Dennis Viollet 1971
Jimmy Melia 1972–74
Ernie Tagg 1974
Harry Gregg 1975–78
Warwick Rimmer 1978–79
Tony Waddington 1979–81
Arfon Griffiths 1981–82
Peter Morris 1982–83
Dario Gradi 1983–2007
Steve Holland 2007–08
Gudjon Thordarson 2008–09
Dario Gradi 2009–11
Steve Davis 2011–17
David Artell January 2017–

TEN YEAR LEAGUE RECORD

		P	*W*	*D*	*L*	*F*	*A*	*Pts*	*Pos*
2009-10	FL 2	46	15	10	21	68	73	55	18
2010-11	FL 2	46	18	11	17	87	65	65	10
2011-12	FL 2	46	20	12	14	67	59	72	7
2012-13	FL 1	46	18	10	18	54	62	64	13
2013-14	FL 1	46	13	12	21	54	80	51	19
2014-15	FL 1	46	14	10	22	43	75	52	20
2015-16	FL 1	46	7	13	26	46	83	34	24
2016-17	FL 2	46	14	13	19	58	67	55	17
2017-18	FL 2	46	17	5	24	62	75	56	15
2018-19	FL 2	46	19	8	19	60	59	65	12

DID YOU KNOW ?

Crewe Alexandra's 1-0 win at Southport in Division Three North on 24 April 1957 was their first away victory in the League for 58 games. The crucial goal came after just four minutes when Harry Mosby scored direct from a corner. Crewe had not won away from home since a 2-1 victory at Tranmere Rovers on Christmas Day 1954.

CREWE ALEXANDRA – SKY BET LEAGUE TWO 2018–19 LEAGUE RECORD

Match No.	*Date*	*Venue*	*Opponents*	*Result*		*H/T Score*	*Lg Pos.*	*Goalscorers*	*Attendance*
1	Aug 4	H	Morecambe	W	6-0	2-0	1	Kirk [6], Nicholls 2 [10, 63], Jones 2 [72, 90], Porter [87]	3559
2	11	A	Newport Co	L	0-1	0-1	9		3243
3	18	H	Milton Keynes D	D	0-0	0-0	10		3505
4	21	A	Colchester U	L	0-6	0-3	16		2842
5	25	A	Carlisle U	L	0-1	0-0	18		4238
6	Sept 1	H	Macclesfield T	W	3-0	2-0	14	Kirk [17], Bowery 2 [40, 68]	3915
7	15	A	Cheltenham T	D	0-0	0-0	17		2921
8	22	H	Port Vale	L	0-1	0-0	17		6180
9	29	A	Notts Co	L	1-2	1-1	18	Bowery [14]	6117
10	Oct 2	H	Swindon T	W	1-0	1-0	17	Kirk [30]	2761
11	6	A	Lincoln C	L	0-1	0-0	18		8718
12	13	H	Bury	D	1-1	1-0	18	Kirk [37]	3777
13	20	A	Stevenage	W	1-0	0-0	17	Bowery [61]	2164
14	23	A	Yeovil T	D	1-1	1-1	17	Bowery [14]	2397
15	27	H	Grimsby T	W	2-0	0-0	17	Whelan [70], Miller [77]	3725
16	30	H	Mansfield T	L	0-3	0-2	17		2973
17	Nov 3	A	Northampton T	L	0-2	0-1	18		5401
18	17	H	Tranmere R	W	3-2	1-1	15	Ainley 2 [20, 51], Kirk [67]	5154
19	24	A	Crawley T	L	0-3	0-1	16		1734
20	27	H	Cambridge U	W	2-0	1-0	15	Ainley [34], Miller [86]	2569
21	Dec 8	H	Oldham Ath	L	0-2	0-2	17		4168
22	15	A	Exeter C	L	0-1	0-1	17		3505
23	22	A	Forest Green R	L	0-1	0-1	18		2388
24	26	H	Lincoln C	W	2-1	0-0	17	Porter [47], Jones [72]	4440
25	29	H	Stevenage	W	1-0	1-0	15	Porter (pen) [21]	3625
26	Jan 1	A	Bury	L	1-3	1-0	15	Porter [3]	3812
27	5	A	Morecambe	D	2-2	1-0	16	Jones [27], Porter (pen) [90]	1662
28	12	H	Newport Co	W	3-2	1-0	14	Bowery [34], Porter (pen) [88], Ainley [90]	3104
29	19	A	Milton Keynes D	W	1-0	1-0	14	Kirk [32]	8347
30	26	H	Colchester U	W	2-1	0-1	11	Kirk [48], Nolan [87]	3306
31	Feb 9	A	Macclesfield T	D	3-3	2-1	15	Bowery [3], Porter (pen) [32], Ray [90]	3772
32	12	H	Carlisle U	W	2-1	1-1	13	Porter [3], Miller [73]	3476
33	16	A	Oldham Ath	D	1-1	0-1	13	Ray [90]	5288
34	23	H	Exeter C	L	1-2	0-1	14	Porter [48]	3841
35	Mar 2	H	Northampton T	L	0-2	0-2	15		4096
36	8	A	Tranmere R	L	0-1	0-0	15		7898
37	12	A	Cambridge U	D	0-0	0-0	15		3448
38	16	H	Crawley T	W	6-1	4-1	14	Bowery [36], Dallison (og) [38], Porter [42], Green [43], Kirk [47], Dale [83]	3220
39	23	A	Mansfield T	W	2-1	0-0	12	Ainley 2 [71, 84]	4675
40	30	H	Cheltenham T	L	1-3	1-1	13	Taylor-Sinclair [34]	3495
41	Apr 6	A	Port Vale	L	0-1	0-0	15		6823
42	13	H	Notts Co	W	3-0	1-0	14	Taylor-Sinclair [31], Wintle [77], Jones [83]	4316
43	19	H	Yeovil T	W	2-0	1-0	14	Kirk [4], Lowery [65]	3410
44	22	A	Swindon T	W	2-1	2-0	13	Porter 2 [3, 45]	6107
45	27	H	Forest Green R	W	4-3	1-1	12	Porter [19], Mills (og) [63], Kirk 2 [87, 89]	3906
46	May 4	A	Grimsby T	L	0-2	0-2	12		4248

Final League Position: 12

GOALSCORERS

League (60): Porter 13 (4 pens), Kirk 11, Bowery 8, Ainley 6, Jones 5, Miller 3, Nicholls 2, Ray 2, Taylor-Sinclair 2, Dale 1, Green 1, Lowery 1, Nolan 1, Whelan 1, Wintle 1, own goals 2.
FA Cup (0).
Carabao Cup (1): Wintle 1.
Checkatrade Trophy (6): Nicholls 2, Porter 2, Bowery 1, Jones 1.

Richards D 4	Ng P 44	Ray G 31 + 1	Nolan E 32 + 1	Pickering H 31 + 1	Jones J 33 + 5	Green P 25 + 1	Wintle R 46	Kirk C 40 + 2	Nicholls A 7 + 14	Bowery J 38 + 6	Hunt N 18 + 4	Ainley C 35 + 8	Porter C 27 + 13	Raynes M 1 + 4	Miller S 13 + 16	Walker B — + 1	Garratt B 38	O'Connor K 5 + 1	Whelan C 16	Lowery T 6 + 9	Finney O 4 + 13	Dale O — + 16	Reilly L 1 + 2	Taylor-Sinclair A 4 + 4	Sterry J 1	Jaaskelainen W 4	Sass-Davies B 2	*Match No.*
1	2	3^{2}	4	5	6	7	8	9^{3}	10^{1}	11	12	13	14															1
1	3		4	5	6	7	8	9^{1}	11	10	2^{2}	12		13														2
1	4		5	3	6	8	9	12	11^{2}	10^{1}	2	7^{3}	13		14													3
1	5	3^{3}	4	9^{1}	6	8	7		11	13	2^{2}		10	12		14												4
	2		4		12	7^{1}	8	9^{2}	13	10^{3}	5	6	14	3	11		1											5
	2	3	4^{3}		7		8	9	14	11	12	6^{2}		13	10		1	5^{1}										6
	3	4			8		7	9	10^{2}	11	5	6^{1}	12		13		1		2									7
	4	3			7		8	9	14	10^{2}	5^{1}	6^{3}	11		13		1	12	2									8
	4	3			7^{1}		8	9	11^{2}	10		12	13				1	5	2	6^{3}	14							9
		4			7		6	11	12	9	3	8^{1}	10				1	5	2									10
	3	4		12	7^{3}		6	11	14	9		8	10^{2}				1	5^{1}	2		13							11
	4	3		5	7		6	11		9	2	8	10^{1}		12		1											12
	4	3		7	12		8^{3}	9		11^{2}	14	6	13		10		1	5^{1}	2									13
	4	3		5	8		7	9	13	11^{1}		6	12		10^{2}		1		2									14
		3		5	7		8	9		10^{1}	4	6^{2}	12		11		1		2		13							15
	4	3		5	7^{2}		8	9	13	10		6^{1}			11		1		2		12							16
	3	4	13	5			8	6^{3}	14	11^{1}		9	12		10		1		2^{2}		7							17
	3		4	5	7		8	9	12	11		6^{1}	13		10^{2}		1		2									18
	3		4	5	7		8	6^{3}	13	11^{2}		9^{1}	12		10		1		2		14							19
	3		4	5	7		8	9	13	11^{3}		6^{1}	12		10^{2}		1		2		14							20
	3	14	4^{3}	5	7		8	9^{2}		11^{1}		6	13		10		1		2			12						21
	2	3	4	5	7		9	10^{3}	6^{2}	11		8^{1}			13		1				14	12						22
	6	3	4	5	7	13	8	14		10		9^{1}			11^{3}		1		2^{2}				12					23
	2	3	4	5	8	6^{1}	7	11^{3}	14	10		12	9^{2}		13		1											24
	2	3	4	5	8	6	7	9^{1}		11		12	10				1											25
	4	3		5	6	7^{2}	8	9^{3}		11^{1}			10		13		1		2	12		14						26
	2	3		5	6	7	8^{3}	9^{2}		11^{1}	4	12	10		13		1					14						27
	2	3		5	7		8	11^{2}		9	4^{1}	6^{3}	10	14			1				13	12						28
	2	3	4	5	7		8	11^{1}	13	10		8^{2}	9				1			12								29
	2	3	4	5		7	8	11^{2}	13	9		6^{1}	10				1			12								30
	2	3	4	5		7	8	11^{1}		9		6^{2}	10				1			13		12						31
	2	3	4	5		7	8	11^{1}		9^{3}		6^{2}	10		12		1			13		14						32
	2	3	4	5^{2}		7	8	11		9^{3}		6^{1}	10		14		1			12				13				33
	2	3	4	5		7	8	11^{2}		9^{1}		6	10		13		1					12						34
	2	3	4			7^{3}	8	11^{2}		9^{1}		6	10		12		1				14	13			5			35
	2	3	4	5	9	7^{3}	8	11^{1}		12		6^{2}	10		13		1					14						36
	2	3	4	5	6^{1}	8^{2}	7			13		9	11		10^{3}		1			12	14							37
	2		4	5^{3}	14	7^{1}	6	9^{2}		10	3		11				1				8	12		13				38
	2		4		8^{1}	7	6			10^{3}	3	12	11		13		1			14	9^{2}			5				39
	2	3^{1}	4		12	7^{1}	8	9^{2}		10	13	6^{3}	11		14		1							5				40
	2		3		6^{3}	7^{1}	8			11	4	13	10		14		1			12	9^{2}			5				41
	2		4		14	8	6	11			3	9^{3}	10^{2}				1			7		12	13	5^{1}				42
	2		4		8^{2}		6	11		14	3	9^{1}	10^{3}							7	13	12				1	5	43
	2		4		8	6^{1}	3	11^{2}		13	5	9^{3}	10							7	14	12				1		44
	2		4		7^{2}	6^{1}	3	11			5	9^{3}	10							8	13	12		14		1		45
	2		4	5^{2}		8	7	11		12		9^{3}								6		14	10^{1}	13		1	3	46

FA Cup
First Round | Carlisle U | (h) | 0-1

Carabao Cup
First Round | Fleetwood T | (h) | 1-1
(Fleetwood T won 4-3 on penalties)

Checkatrade Trophy
Group D (N) | Tranmere R | (a) | 4-3
Group D (N) | Manchester C U21 | (h) | 1-4
Group D (N) | Shrewsbury T | (h) | 1-2

CRYSTAL PALACE

FOUNDATION

There was a Crystal Palace club as early as 1861 but the present organisation was born in 1905 after the formation of a club by the company that controlled the Crystal Palace (building) had been rejected by the FA, who did not like the idea of the Cup Final hosts running their own club. A separate company had to be formed and they had their home on the old Cup Final ground until 1915.

Selhurst Park Stadium, Whitehorse Lane, London SE25 6PU.

Telephone: (020) 8768 6000.

Fax: (020) 8771 5311.

Ticket Office: (0871) 200 0071.

Website: www.cpfc.co.uk

Email: info@cpfc.co.uk

Ground Capacity: 26,074.

Record Attendance: 51,482 v Burnley, Division 2, 11 May 1979 (at Selhurst Park).

Pitch Measurements: 101m × 68m (110.5yd × 74.5yd).

Chairman: Steve Parish.

Chief Executive: Phil Alexander.

Manager: Roy Hodgson.

Assistant Manager: Ray Lewington.

Colours: Red and blue striped shirts, blue shorts with red trim, blue socks with red trim.

Year Formed: 1905.

Turned Professional: 1905.

Club Nickname: 'The Eagles'.

Grounds: 1905, Crystal Palace; 1915, Herne Hill; 1918, The Nest; 1924, Selhurst Park.

First Football League Game: 28 August 1920, Division 3, v Merthyr T (a) L 1–2 – Alderson; Little, Rhodes; McCracken, Jones, Feebury; Bateman, Conner, Smith, Milligan (1), Whibley.

Record League Victory: 9–0 v Barrow, Division 4, 10 October 1959 – Rouse; Long, Noakes; Truett, Evans, McNichol; Gavin (1), Summersby (4 incl. 1p), Sexton, Byrne (2), Colfar (2).

Record Cup Victory: 8–0 v Southend U, Rumbelows League Cup 2nd rd (1st leg), 25 September 1990 – Martyn; Humphrey (Thompson (1)), Shaw, Pardew, Young, Thorn, McGoldrick, Thomas, Bright (3), Wright (3), Barber (Hodges (1)).

Record Defeat: 0–9 v Burnley, FA Cup 2nd rd replay, 10 February 1909; 0–9 v Liverpool, Division 1, 12 September 1990.

Most League Points (2 for a win): 64, Division 4, 1960–61.

HONOURS

League Champions: First Division – 1993–94; Division 2 – 1978–79; Division 3S – 1920–21.
Runners-up: Division 2 – 1968–69; Division 3 – 1963–64; Division 3S – 1928–29, 1930–31, 1938–39; Division 4 – 1960–61.

FA Cup: *Runners-up:* 1990, 2016.

League Cup: semi-final – 1993, 1995, 2001, 2012.

Full Members' Cup Winners: 1991.

European Competition
Intertoto Cup: 1998.

THE SUN FACT FILE

Crystal Palace were bottom of the First Division table with just three wins from 20 games when they hosted Manchester United on 16 December 1972. Palace recorded a remarkable 5-0 victory with two goals apiece from Don Rogers and Paddy Mulligan and one from Alan Whittle, but nevertheless they were relegated at the end of the season.

Most League Points (3 for a win): 90, Division 1, 1993–94.

Most League Goals: 110, Division 4, 1960–61.

Highest League Scorer in Season: Peter Simpson, 46, Division 3 (S), 1930–31.

Most League Goals in Total Aggregate: Peter Simpson, 153, 1930–36.

Most League Goals in One Match: 6, Peter Simpson v Exeter C, Division 3 (S), 4 October 1930.

Most Capped Player: Wayne Hennessey, 42 (84), Wales.

Most League Appearances: Jim Cannon, 571, 1973–88.

Youngest League Player: John Bostock, 15 years 287 days v Watford, 29 October 2007.

Record Transfer Fee Received: £45,000,000 from Manchester U for Aaron Wan-Bissaka, July 2019.

Record Transfer Fee Paid: £27,000,000 to Liverpool for Christian Benteke, August 2016.

Football League Record: 1920 Original Members of Division 3; 1921–25 Division 2; 1925–58 Division 3 (S); 1958–61 Division 4; 1961–64 Division 3; 1964–69 Division 2; 1969–73 Division 1; 1973–74 Division 2; 1974–77 Division 3; 1977–79 Division 2; 1979–81 Division 1; 1981–89 Division 2; 1989–92 Division 1; 1992–93 Premier League; 1993–94 Division 1; 1994–95 Premier League; 1995–97 Division 1; 1997–98 Premier League; 1998–2004 Division 1; 2004–05 Premier League; 2005–13 FL C; 2013– Premier League.

LATEST SEQUENCES

Longest Sequence of League Wins: 8, 21.5.2017 – 30.9.2017.

Longest Sequence of League Defeats: 8, 10.1.1998 – 14.3.1998.

Longest Sequence of League Draws: 5, 21.9.2002 – 19.10.2002.

Longest Sequence of Unbeaten League Matches: 18, 22.2.1969 – 13.8.1969.

Longest Sequence Without a League Win: 20, 3.3.1962 – 8.9.1962.

Successive Scoring Runs: 24 from 27.4.1929.

Successive Non-scoring Runs: 9 from 19.11.1994.

MANAGERS

John T. Robson 1905–07
Edmund Goodman 1907–25 (*Secretary 1905–33*)
Alex Maley 1925–27
Fred Mavin 1927–30
Jack Tresadern 1930–35
Tom Bromilow 1935–36
R. S. Moyes 1936
Tom Bromilow 1936–39
George Irwin 1939–47
Jack Butler 1947–49
Ronnie Rooke 1949–50
Charlie Slade and Fred Dawes (*Joint Managers*) 1950–51
Laurie Scott 1951–54
Cyril Spiers 1954–58
George Smith 1958–60
Arthur Rowe 1960–62
Dick Graham 1962–66
Bert Head 1966–72 (*continued as General Manager to 1973*)
Malcolm Allison 1973–76
Terry Venables 1976–80
Ernie Walley 1980
Malcolm Allison 1980–81
Dario Gradi 1981
Steve Kember 1981–82
Alan Mullery 1982–84
Steve Coppell 1984–93
Alan Smith 1993–95
Steve Coppell (*Technical Director*) 1995–96
Dave Bassett 1996–97
Steve Coppell 1997–98
Attilio Lombardo 1998
Terry Venables (*Head Coach*) 1998–99
Steve Coppell 1999–2000
Alan Smith 2000–01
Steve Bruce 2001
Trevor Francis 2001–03
Steve Kember 2003
Iain Dowie 2003–06
Peter Taylor 2006–07
Neil Warnock 2007–10
Paul Hart 2010
George Burley 2010–11
Dougie Freedman 2011–12
Ian Holloway 2012–13
Tony Pulis 2013–14
Neil Warnock 2014
Alan Pardew 2015–16
Sam Allardyce 2016–17
Frank de Boer 2017
Roy Hodgson September 2017–

TEN YEAR LEAGUE RECORD

		P	W	D	L	F	A	Pts	Pos
2009-10	FL C	46	14	17	15	50	53	49*	21
2010-11	FL C	46	12	12	22	44	69	48	20
2011-12	FL C	46	13	17	16	46	51	56	17
2012-13	FL C	46	19	15	12	73	62	72	5
2013-14	PR Lge	38	13	6	19	33	48	45	11
2014-15	PR Lge	38	13	9	16	47	51	48	10
2015-16	PR Lge	38	11	9	18	39	51	42	15
2016-17	PR Lge	38	12	5	21	50	63	41	14
2017-18	PR Lge	38	11	11	16	45	55	44	11
2018-19	PR Lge	38	14	7	17	51	53	49	12

** 10 pts deducted.*

DID YOU KNOW ?

Crystal Palace had a successful supporters' club in the 1930s and provided both the secretary (Leslie Davis) and the vice-president (D.W. Oliver) of the National Federation of Football Supporters' Clubs. In 1939 they had 1,550 members including 208 women.

CRYSTAL PALACE – PREMIER LEAGUE 2018–19 LEAGUE RECORD

Match No.	*Date*	*Venue*	*Opponents*	*Result*		*H/T Score*	*Lg Pos.*	*Goalscorers*	*Atten-dance*
1	Aug 11	A	Fulham	W	2-0	1-0	2	Schlupp [41], Zaha [79]	24,821
2	20	H	Liverpool	L	0-2	0-1	10		25,750
3	26	A	Watford	L	1-2	0-0	11	Zaha [78]	20,014
4	Sept 1	H	Southampton	L	0-2	0-0	15		25,495
5	15	A	Huddersfield T	W	1-0	1-0	11	Zaha [38]	23,696
6	22	H	Newcastle U	D	0-0	0-0	11		25,679
7	Oct 1	A	Bournemouth	L	1-2	0-1	13	Van Aanholt [55]	10,199
8	6	H	Wolverhampton W	L	0-1	0-0	14		25,715
9	21	A	Everton	L	0-2	0-0	15		38,668
10	28	H	Arsenal	D	2-2	1-0	14	Milivojevic 2 (2 pens) [45, 83]	25,718
11	Nov 4	A	Chelsea	L	1-3	0-1	14	Townsend [53]	40,407
12	10	H	Tottenham H	L	0-1	0-0	16		25,685
13	24	A	Manchester U	D	0-0	0-0	15		74,516
14	Dec 1	H	Burnley	W	2-0	1-0	14	McArthur [16], Townsend [77]	25,098
15	4	A	Brighton & HA	L	1-3	0-3	15	Milivojevic (pen) [81]	29,663
16	8	A	West Ham U	L	2-3	1-0	16	McArthur [6], Schlupp [76]	56,995
17	15	H	Leicester C	W	1-0	1-0	15	Milivojevic [39]	24,738
18	22	A	Manchester C	W	3-2	2-1	14	Schlupp [33], Townsend [35], Milivojevic (pen) [51]	54,340
19	26	H	Cardiff C	D	0-0	0-0	14		25,206
20	30	H	Chelsea	L	0-1	0-0	14		25,781
21	Jan 2	A	Wolverhampton W	W	2-0	0-0	14	Ayew [83], Milivojevic (pen) [90]	30,666
22	12	H	Watford	L	1-2	1-0	14	Cathcart (og) [38]	25,010
23	19	A	Liverpool	L	3-4	1-0	14	Townsend [34], Tomkins [65], Meyer [90]	53,171
24	30	A	Southampton	D	1-1	1-0	15	Zaha [41]	28,339
25	Feb 2	H	Fulham	W	2-0	1-0	14	Milivojevic (pen) [25], Schlupp [87]	25,355
26	9	H	West Ham U	D	1-1	0-1	13	Zaha [76]	25,552
27	23	A	Leicester C	W	4-1	1-0	13	Batshuayi [40], Zaha 2 [70, 90], Milivojevic (pen) [81]	31,778
28	27	H	Manchester U	L	1-3	0-1	14	Ward [66]	25,754
29	Mar 2	A	Burnley	W	3-1	1-0	13	Bardsley (og) [15], Batshuayi [48], Zaha [76]	19,223
30	9	H	Brighton & HA	L	1-2	0-1	14	Milivojevic (pen) [50]	24,972
31	30	H	Huddersfield T	W	2-0	0-0	13	Milivojevic (pen) [76], Van Aanholt [88]	25,193
32	Apr 3	A	Tottenham H	L	0-2	0-0	13		59,215
33	6	A	Newcastle U	W	1-0	0-0	12	Milivojevic (pen) [81]	51,926
34	14	H	Manchester C	L	1-3	0-1	13	Milivojevic [81]	25,721
35	21	A	Arsenal	W	3-2	1-0	12	Benteke [17], Zaha [61], McArthur [69]	59,929
36	27	H	Everton	D	0-0	0-0	12		25,789
37	May 4	A	Cardiff C	W	3-2	2-1	12	Zaha [28], Batshuayi [39], Townsend [70]	32,133
38	12	H	Bournemouth	W	5-3	3-1	12	Batshuayi 2 [24, 32], Simpson (og) [37], Van Aanholt [65], Townsend [80]	25,433

Final League Position: 12

GOALSCORERS

League (51): Milivojevic 12 (10 pens), Zaha 10, Townsend 6, Batshuayi 5, Schlupp 4, McArthur 3, Van Aanholt 3, Ayew 1, Benteke 1, Meyer 1, Tomkins 1, Ward 1, own goals 3.
FA Cup (6): Ayew 1, Batshuayi 1, Meyer 1, Schlupp 1, Townsend 1 (1 pen), Wickham 1.
Carabao Cup (4): Townsend 2, Sorloth 1, Van Aanholt 1.

Hennessey W 17 + 1	Wan Bissaka A 35	Tomkins J 29	Sakho M 27	Van Aanholt P 36	Townsend A 34 + 4	Milivojevic L 38	McArthur J 36 + 2	Schlupp J 18 + 12	Benteke C 9 + 7	Zaha W 34	Sorloth A — + 12	Kouyate C 21 + 10	Souare P — + 1	Ward J 6 + 1	Meyer M 15 + 14	Kelly M 12 + 1	Ayew J 14 + 6	Wickham C — + 6	Puncheon J — + 5	Guaita V 20	Speroni J 1	Dann S 7 + 3	Batshuayi M 9 + 2	Sako B — + 4	Dreher L — + 1	Match No.
1	2	3	4	5^{1}	6^{3}	7	8	9	10^{2}	11	12	13	14													1
1	2■	3	4	5	6^{1}	7	8	9^{2}	10^{3}	11	12			13	14											2
1			4	5	6	7	8	9^{1}	10^{2}	11	13			2	12	3										3
1	2		4	5	6^{3}	8	7	9^{2}	10		14	12			13	3	11^{1}									4
1	2	3	4	5	9^{1}	7	8	12		11		6					10									5
1	2	3	4	5	9	7	8			11	13	6^{1}			12		10^{2}									6
1	2	3	4	5	9	7	8^{2}	12		11	13	14			6^{3}		10^{1}									7
1	2	3	4	5	6	7	8^{2}	9^{3}		11	14	13			12		10^{1}									8
1	2	3	4	5	10	7	6^{1}	9		11		8						12								9
1	2	3	4	5	9	7	8^{2}			11	13	6^{1}			12		10^{3}		14							10
1	2	3	4	5	10	8	6^{1}	13		11		7			9^{2}		12									11
1	2	3^{1}	4	5	10	8	6^{2}	13			14	7			9^{3}	12	11									12
1	2	3	4	5	10^{1}	8	6	12		11^{2}		7			9		13									13
1	2	3	4	5	10^{3}	7	6^{2}	12		11	13	8			9^{1}				14							14
1	2	3	4	5	10	8	6^{2}	13		11	12	7^{1}			9											15
1	2	3	4	5^{1}	10	7	6^{3}	12		11		8			9^{2}		13		14							16
	2		4	5	10	8	6	12			13	7^{2}			9^{3}	3	11^{1}		14	1						17
	2	3	4	5	6	8	7	9		11^{1}					10^{2}		12		13	1						18
	2	3	4	5	11	8	6			10		7			9^{1}			12		1						19
	2	3	4	5	6	8	7	10^{2}		11		9^{1}			13			12		1						20
	2	3	4	5	9	7	8			11		6					10^{1}	12		1						21
12	2	3	4	5	9	7	8^{3}	14	13	11		6					10^{2}			1^{1}						22
	2	3	4	5	6	8	7^{2}	12		10		9^{1}			13		11^{3}	14			1					23
	2	3^{1}	4	5	9	7	8	12		11■		6^{2}					10			1		13				24
	2	3	4	5	6	8	7	9^{2}	11^{3}						12		10^{1}			1			13	14		25
	2		4	5	9	7	6^{2}	8	10^{1}	11					13	3				1			12			26
		3	4^{3}	5	9^{2}	7	6	8		11		13		2			14			1		12	10^{1}			27
		4		5^{2}	9	7	6^{3}	8	13	11		14		2	12	3				1			10^{1}			28
1	2	3		5	13	8	12	10	14	6^{3}		7			9^{1}							4	11^{2}			29
	2	3		5	9^{1}	7	6^{2}	8	13	11					12					1		4	10			30
	2	3		5	9^{2}	7	12	8	13	11		14			6^{3}					1		4	10^{1}			31
	2	4		5	12	7	6	11	13	9		8^{2}				3				1			10^{1}			32
	2	4^{2}		5	6^{3}	8	7	9	12	11		14				3				1		13	10^{1}			33
	2			5	6^{1}	8	7^{3}	9^{2}	11	10		12			13	3				1		4		14		34
	2				13	7	6		10^{1}	11		8		5	9^{2}	3	12			1		4				35
	2			5	12	7	6		10	11		8			9^{1}	3				1		4				36
	2				6^{2}	8	7			9		14		5	13	3	11^{1}			1		4	10^{3}	12		37
	2			5	6^{1}	8	7			11^{3}				4	9	3		13		1			10^{2}	12	14	38

FA Cup

Third Round	Grimsby T	(h)	1-0
Fourth Round	Tottenham H	(h)	2-0
Fifth Round	Doncaster R	(a)	2-0
Sixth Round	Watford	(a)	1-2

Carabao Cup

Second Round	Swansea C	(a)	1-0
Third Round	WBA	(a)	3-0
Fourth Round	Middlesbrough	(a)	0-1

DERBY COUNTY

FOUNDATION

Derby County was formed by members of the Derbyshire County Cricket Club in 1884, when football was booming in the area and the cricketers thought that a football club would help boost finances for the summer game. To begin with, they sported the cricket club's colours of amber, chocolate and pale blue, and went into the game at the top immediately entering the FA Cup.

Pride Park Stadium, Pride Park, Derby DE24 8XL.

Telephone: (0871) 472 1884.

Fax: (0871) 472 1884

Ticket Office: (0871) 472 1884 (option 1).

Website: www.dcfc.co.uk

Email: derby.county@dcfc.co.uk

Ground Capacity: 33,597.

Record Attendance: 41,826 v Tottenham H, Division 1, 20 September 1969 (at Baseball Ground); 33,378 v Liverpool, Premier League, 18 March 2000 (at Pride Park).

Stadium Record Attendance: 33,597, England v Mexico, 25 May 2001 (at Pride Park).

Pitch Measurements: 105m × 68m (115yd × 74.5yd).

Executive Chairman: Mel Morris CBE.

Chief Executive Officer: Stephen Pearce.

Manager: Phillip Cocu.

Assistant Manager: Chris van der Weerden.

Colours: White shirts with black trim, black shorts with white trim, white socks with black trim.

Year Formed: 1884.

Turned Professional: 1884.

Club Nickname: 'The Rams'.

Grounds: 1884, Racecourse Ground; 1895, Baseball Ground; 1997, Pride Park (renamed The iPro Stadium 2013; Pride Park Stadium 2016).

First Football League Game: 8 September 1888, Football League, v Bolton W (a) W 6–3 – Marshall; Latham, Ferguson, Williamson; Monks, Walter Roulstone; Bakewell (2), Cooper (2), Higgins, Harry Plackett, Lol Plackett (2).

Record League Victory: 9–0 v Wolverhampton W, Division 1, 10 January 1891 – Bunyan; Archie Goodall, Roberts; Walker, Chalmers, Walter Roulstone (1); Bakewell, McLachlan, Johnny Goodall (1), Holmes (2), McMillan (5). 9–0 v Sheffield W, Division 1, 21 January 1899 – Fryer; Methven, Staley; Cox, Archie Goodall, May; Oakden (1), Bloomer (6), Boag, McDonald (1), Allen, (1 og).

HONOURS

League Champions: Division 1 – 1971–72, 1974–75; Division 2 – 1911–12, 1914–15, 1968–69, 1986–87; Division 3N – 1956–57.
Runners-up: Division 1 – 1895–96, 1929–30, 1935–36; First Division – 1995–96; Division 2 – 1925–26; Division 3N – 1955–56.

FA Cup Winners: 1946.
Runners-up: 1898, 1899, 1903.

League Cup: semi-final – 1968, 2009.

Texaco Cup Winners: 1972.

Anglo-Italian Cup: *Runners-up:* 1993–94, 1994–95.

European Competitions
European Cup: 1972–73 *(sf)*, 1975–76.
UEFA Cup: 1974–75, 1976–77.

THE SUN FACT FILE

Derby County finished in fourth place in the old First Division in 1969–70 which would normally have qualified them for the following season's Inter-Cities Fairs Cup. However, a joint commission of the FA and Football League found the club to be in breach of rules on a number of administrative issues and they were fined £10,000 and banned from playing European opposition for a season.

Record Cup Victory: 12–0 v Finn Harps, UEFA Cup 1st rd 1st leg, 15 September 1976 – Moseley; Thomas, Nish, Rioch (1), McFarland, Todd (King), Macken, Gemmill, Hector (5), George (3), James (3).

Record Defeat: 2–11 v Everton, FA Cup 1st rd, 1889–90.

Most League Points (2 for a win): 63, Division 2, 1968–69 and Division 3 (N), 1955–56 and 1956–57.

Most League Points (3 for a win): 85, FL C, 2013–14.

Most League Goals: 111, Division 3 (N), 1956–57.

Highest League Scorer in Season: Jack Bowers, 37, Division 1, 1930–31; Ray Straw, 37 Division 3 (N), 1956–57.

Most League Goals in Total Aggregate: Steve Bloomer, 292, 1892–1906 and 1910–14.

Most League Goals in One Match: 6, Steve Bloomer v Sheffield W, Division 1, 2 January 1899.

Most Capped Player: Deon Burton, 42 (59), Jamaica.

Most League Appearances: Kevin Hector, 486, 1966–78 and 1980–82.

Youngest League Player: Mason Bennett, 15 years 99 days v Middlesbrough 22 October 2011.

Record Transfer Fee Received: £8,500,000 (rising to £11,000,000) from Huddersfield T for Tom Ince, July 2017.

Record Transfer Fee Paid: £8,000,000 to Watford for Matej Vydra, August 2016.

Football League Record: 1888 Founder Member of the Football League; 1907–12 Division 2; 1912–14 Division 1; 1914–15 Division 2; 1915–21 Division 1; 1921–26 Division 2; 1926–53 Division 1; 1953–55 Division 2; 1955–57 Division 3 (N); 1957–69 Division 2; 1969–80 Division 1; 1980–84 Division 2; 1984–86 Division 3; 1986–87 Division 2; 1987–91 Division 1; 1991–92 Division 2; 1992–96 Division 1; 1996–2002 Premier League; 2002–04 Division 1; 2004–07 FL C; 2007–08 Premier League; 2008– FL C.

MANAGERS

W. D. Clark 1896–1900
Harry Newbould 1900–06
Jimmy Methven 1906–22
Cecil Potter 1922–25
George Jobey 1925–41
Ted Magner 1944–46
Stuart McMillan 1946–53
Jack Barker 1953–55
Harry Storer 1955–62
Tim Ward 1962–67
Brian Clough 1967–73
Dave Mackay 1973–76
Colin Murphy 1977
Tommy Docherty 1977–79
Colin Addison 1979–82
Johnny Newman 1982
Peter Taylor 1982–84
Roy McFarland 1984
Arthur Cox 1984–93
Roy McFarland 1993–95
Jim Smith 1995–2001
Colin Todd 2001–02
John Gregory 2002–03
George Burley 2003–05
Phil Brown 2005–06
Billy Davies 2006–07
Paul Jewell 2007–08
Nigel Clough 2009–13
Steve McClaren 2013–15
Paul Clement 2015–16
Darren Wassall 2016
Nigel Pearson 2016
Steve McClaren 2016–17
Gary Rowett 2017–18
Frank Lampard 2018–19
Phillip Cocu July 2019–

LATEST SEQUENCES

Longest Sequence of League Wins: 9, 15.3.1969 – 19.4.1969.

Longest Sequence of League Defeats: 8, 12.12.1987 – 10.2.1988.

Longest Sequence of League Draws: 6, 26.3.1927 – 18.4.1927.

Longest Sequence of Unbeaten League Matches: 22, 8.3.1969 – 20.9.1969.

Longest Sequence Without a League Win: 36, 22.9.2007 – 30.8.2008.

Successive Scoring Runs: 29 from 3.12.1960.

Successive Non-scoring Runs: 8 from 30.10.1920.

TEN YEAR LEAGUE RECORD

		P	W	D	L	F	A	Pts	Pos
2009-10	FL C	46	15	11	20	53	63	56	14
2010-11	FL C	46	13	10	23	58	71	49	19
2011-12	FL C	46	18	10	18	50	58	64	12
2012-13	FL C	46	16	13	17	65	62	61	10
2013-14	FL C	46	25	10	11	84	52	85	3
2014-15	FL C	46	21	14	11	85	56	77	8
2015-16	FL C	46	21	15	10	66	43	78	5
2016-17	FL C	46	18	13	15	54	50	67	9
2017-18	FL C	46	20	15	11	70	48	75	6
2018-19	FL C	46	20	14	12	69	54	74	6

DID YOU KNOW ?

Albert Mays who made over 250 appearances as a half-back for Derby County was a talented all-round sportsman who also excelled at cricket, billiards and snooker. He represented Derbyshire seconds at cricket while in 1966 he reached the quarter-finals of the English Amateur Snooker Championship.

DERBY COUNTY – SKY BET CHAMPIONSHIP 2018–19 LEAGUE RECORD

Match No.	*Date*		*Venue*	*Opponents*	*Result*		*H/T Score*	*Lg Pos.*	*Goalscorers*	*Attendance*
1	Aug	3	A	Reading	W	2-1	0-0	1	Mount[60], Lawrence[90]	16,923
2		11	H	Leeds U	L	1-4	1-2	11	Lawrence[12]	27,311
3		18	A	Millwall	L	1-2	0-2	14	Nugent[73]	13,557
4		21	H	Ipswich T	W	2-0	0-0	9	Ledley[59], Lawrence[68]	24,362
5		25	H	Preston NE	W	2-0	1-0	7	Mount[38], Keogh[78]	25,257
6	Sept	1	A	Hull C	W	2-1	1-0	4	Waghorn (pen)[23], Jozefzoon[88]	12,285
7		15	A	Rotherham U	L	0-1	0-0	7		10,707
8		18	H	Blackburn R	D	0-0	0-0	8		23,580
9		22	H	Brentford	W	3-1	3-1	6	Wilson, H[14], Nugent[21], Mount[28]	25,110
10		29	A	Bolton W	L	0-1	0-1	9		14,096
11	Oct	3	H	Norwich C	D	1-1	0-0	9	Bryson[86]	24,236
12		6	A	QPR	D	1-1	1-0	7	Marriott[24]	14,727
13		20	H	Sheffield U	W	2-1	1-1	5	Bryson[1], Marriott[77]	27,927
14		24	A	WBA	W	4-1	2-0	5	Marriott[10], Lawrence[15], Wilson, H[51], Malone[71]	22,848
15		27	A	Middlesbrough	D	1-1	1-0	6	Friend (og)[19]	22,907
16	Nov	3	H	Birmingham C	W	3-1	0-1	4	Bennett[53], Wilson, H[55], Marriott[73]	28,114
17		10	H	Aston Villa	L	0-3	0-0	6		30,400
18		24	A	Sheffield W	W	2-1	2-1	6	Wilson, H[29], Marriott[35]	25,204
19		28	A	Stoke C	L	1-2	0-1	7	Wilson, H[50]	25,147
20	Dec	1	H	Swansea C	W	2-1	2-0	7	Wilson, H 2[30, 40]	26,167
21		8	A	Wigan Ath	W	1-0	1-0	4	Marriott[21]	10,768
22		17	H	Nottingham F	D	0-0	0-0	4		31,160
23		22	H	Bristol C	D	1-1	1-1	5	Waghorn[37]	26,719
24		26	A	Sheffield U	L	1-3	0-1	6	Wilson, H[53]	28,974
25		29	A	Norwich C	W	4-3	2-2	6	Tomori[36], Mount[45], Jozefzoon[87], Marriott[90]	26,866
26	Jan	1	H	Middlesbrough	D	1-1	1-0	6	Wilson, H[2]	28,123
27		11	A	Leeds U	L	0-2	0-1	6		34,668
28		19	H	Reading	W	2-1	2-0	6	Holmes[3], Wilson, H[40]	26,404
29	Feb	1	A	Preston NE	D	0-0	0-0	6		12,124
30		9	H	Hull C	W	2-0	1-0	7	Waghorn 2[41, 71]	28,211
31		13	A	Ipswich T	D	1-1	1-0	7	Lawrence[2]	18,604
32		20	H	Millwall	L	0-1	0-0	7		24,907
33		25	A	Nottingham F	L	0-1	0-1	7		29,421
34	Mar	2	A	Aston Villa	L	0-4	0-4	7		37,273
35		5	H	Wigan Ath	W	2-1	0-1	7	Bennett[62], Malone[78]	23,655
36		9	H	Sheffield W	D	1-1	1-0	6	Johnson[10]	28,574
37		13	H	Stoke C	D	0-0	0-0	6		25,685
38		30	H	Rotherham U	W	6-1	3-0	6	Waghorn 3 (2 pens)[13 (p), 42, 71 (p)], Johnson[39], Mount[48], Holmes[62]	27,003
39	Apr	6	A	Brentford	D	3-3	2-2	7	Wilson, H 2[13, 78], Bogle[26]	12,225
40		9	A	Blackburn R	L	0-2	0-0	8		12,590
41		13	H	Bolton W	W	4-0	2-0	8	Bryson[37], Mount 3[45, 55, 82]	26,602
42		19	A	Birmingham C	D	2-2	2-2	8	Waghorn[7], Keogh[28]	23,902
43		22	H	QPR	W	2-0	0-0	6	Wilson, H 2 (1 pen)[90 (p), 90]	25,986
44		27	A	Bristol C	W	2-0	1-0	6	Lawrence[18], Bogle[77]	25,556
45	May	1	A	Swansea C	D	1-1	1-0	6	Keogh[21]	18,434
46		5	H	WBA	W	3-1	1-0	6	Waghorn[19], Bennett[70], Wilson, H (pen)[73]	32,055

Final League Position: 6

GOALSCORERS

League (69): Wilson H 15 (2 pens), Waghorn 9 (3 pens), Mount 8, Marriott 7, Lawrence 6, Bennett 3, Bryson 3, Keogh 3, Bogle 2, Holmes 2, Johnson 2, Jozefzoon 2, Malone 2, Nugent 2, Ledley 1, Tomori 1, own goal 1.
FA Cup (6): Waghorn 2, Cole 1, Lawrence 1, Marriott 1, Wilson H 1.
Carabao Cup (10): Marriott 2, Mount 2, Waghorn 2, Jozefzoon 1, Tomori 1, Wilson H 1, own goal 1.
Championship Play-offs (5): Marriott 3, Mount 1, Wilson H 1 (1 pen).

Carson S 30	Wisdom A 9 + 2	Keogh R 46	Davies C 3 + 2	Lowe M 3	Bryson C 25 + 3	Ledley J 3 + 1	Mount M 35	Wilson H 37 + 3	Nugent D 11 + 20	Lawrence T 28 + 5	Johnson B 22 + 6	Bennett M 9 + 21	Pearce A — + 1	Tomori F 43 + 1	Waghorn M 29 + 7	Jozefzoon F 13 + 14	Bogle J 39 + 1	Malone S 24 + 3	Forsyth C 10 + 3	Evans G 6 + 5	Marriott J 19 + 14	Huddlestone T 21 + 3	Holmes D 16 + 9	Bird M 1 + 3	Roos K 16	King A 2 + 2	Cole A 6 + 3	Mitchell-Lawson J — + 1	*Match No.*
1	2	3	4	5	6	7^{1}	8	9	10^{3}	11^{2}	12	13	14																1
1	2	3		5	6	7^{2}	8^{1}	9^{3}		11	12	14		4	10	13													2
1		3			6		9		14	10	7	13		4	11^{2}	8^{3}	2	5^{1}	12										3
1		3			6	12	8		10^{1}	11		9^{3}		4		13	2		5	7^{2}	14								4
1	12	3			6	7^{1}	8		10	11	13	9^{2}		4		14	2^{3}		5										5
1	2	3			6		8		10^{1}	12	7	14		4	9^{3}	11		5^{2}	13										6
1		3					9			10	7	13		4	11^{2}	8^{3}	2		5		12	6^{1}	14						7
1		3			6		9	12	11^{3}		7	8^{2}		4	13	10^{1}	2		5		14								8
1		3			6		9	10^{2}	11^{3}		7	8^{1}		4		12	2	14	5		13								9
1		3			6		9	10^{1}	11^{3}	12	7	8^{2}		4	14		2		5		13								10
1		3			6		9	10^{1}	11^{3}	12	7	8^{2}		4	14		2	5			13								11
1		3			6		9	12		10^{3}	7^{1}			4	14	8^{2}	2		5		11	13							12
1		3	14		6^{1}		9	10		12				4	8^{2}	13	2		5		11^{3}	7							13
1		3					8	6	13	11		12		4	9^{2}		2	5^{3}	14		10^{1}	7							14
1		3					8^{1}	6	13	11	12			4	9		2	5			10^{2}	7							15
1		3	4					6		11	14	12			9^{2}	13	2		5		10^{3}	7	8^{1}						16
1		3						6	14	11		9^{2}		4		12	2	13	5^{1}		10	7	8^{3}						17
1	2	3	12		13		9^{1}	10		14				4^{3}		8^{2}		5			11	6	7						18
1		3	4^{1}		6^{3}		8	9		11	7^{2}			12	14		2	5			10	13							19
1		3			8		6^{3}	9^{2}	10^{1}	11				4		12	2	5				7	14	13					20
1		3			6^{3}		8	9^{1}	14	11				4		12	2	5			10^{2}	7	13						21
1		3			6		8^{2}	9	12	11^{1}				4			2	5			10	7	13						22
1		3					8	6	10^{1}					4	11^{2}	9	2	5			12	7	13						23
1	5^{1}	3			6		8	11	12					4	14	9^{3}	2			13	10	7^{2}							24
1	5^{3}	3					7	6	13					4	9^{1}	11	2			8	10^{2}		12	14					25
1	5	3					8	6^{1}	14					4	9^{3}	11	2			7^{2}	10	12	13						26
1	2^{2}	3		5	6		8		12	11				4	14	13				7^{3}	10^{1}		9						27
		3					8	6^{2}	13			12		4	9		2	5		14	10^{3}	7	11^{1}		1				28
	13	3			6			9	11^{1}	10		12		4	8^{2}			5		7			2		1				29
		3			6			9				12		4	10^{3}	11^{2}	2	5				7	8^{1}		1	13	14		30
		3			14			9^{1}	12	10	7	13		4	11		2	5					8^{2}		1	6^{3}			31
		3			6			8^{3}	14					4	10	12	2				11	7^{2}	5		1	13	9^{1}		32
		3						11^{3}			13	14		4	9	12	2				10	7^{2}	6		1	8^{1}	5		33
1	2	3						12				10^{2}		4		8	14	13		7^{1}	11		9	6			5^{3}		34
1		3						9^{2}	14		6	12		4	8	10^{3}	2	5			11^{1}	7	13						35
1		3						8^{3}	14		7	10^{2}		4	11^{1}	12	2	5			13	6	9						36
		3						8		10^{2}	7			4	11^{1}		2	5			12	6	9		1			13	37
		3					8^{2}	9		11	7	12		4	10^{1}		2	5^{3}			14		6		1		13		38
		3			14		8	9		11	7	13		4	10^{1}		2	5^{3}					6^{2}		1		12		39
		3			7^{1}		9^{3}	8	14	10	6	12		4	11^{2}		2						13		1		5		40
		3			6^{2}		8	9^{3}		11	7			4	10^{1}	14	2				13			12	1		5		41
		3			6		8	9^{3}	14	11^{1}	7	13		4	10^{2}		2				12				1		5		42
		3			6^{3}		8	9	14	11^{1}	7	12		4	10^{2}		2	5			13				1				43
		3					9	8^{1}	14	10	7	13		4^{2}	11^{3}		2	5		12		6			1				44
		3^{1}					9	8		10	7	12		4	11^{3}		2	5		13	14	6^{2}			1				45
		3					8	9^{3}	12	11	7	13		4	10^{1}		2	5		14			6^{2}		1				46

FA Cup

Third Round	Southampton	(h)	2-2
Replay	Southampton	(a)	2-2
(aet; Derby Co won 5-3 on penalties)			
Fourth Round	Accrington S	(a)	1-0
Fifth Round	Brighton & HA	(a)	1-2

Carabao Cup

First Round	Oldham Ath	(a)	2-0
Second Round	Hull C	(a)	4-0
Third Round	Manchester U	(a)	2-2
(Derby Co won 8-7 on penalties)			
Fourth Round	Chelsea	(a)	2-3

Championship Play-offs

Semi-Final 1st leg	Leeds U	(h)	0-1
Semi-Final 2nd leg	Leeds U	(a)	4-2
Final	Aston Villa	(Wembley)	1-2

DONCASTER ROVERS

FOUNDATION

In 1879, Mr Albert Jenkins assembled a team to play a match against the Yorkshire Institution for the Deaf. The players remained together as Doncaster Rovers, joining the Midland Alliance in 1889 and the Midland Counties League in 1891.

Keepmoat Stadium, Stadium Way, Lakeside, Doncaster, South Yorkshire DN4 5JW.

Telephone: (01302) 764 664.

Ticket Office: (01302) 762 576.

Website: www.doncasterroversfc.co.uk

Email: info@clubdoncaster.co.uk

Ground Capacity: 15,231.

Record Attendance: 37,149 v Hull C, Division 3 (N), 2 October 1948 (at Belle Vue); 15,001 v Leeds U, FL 1, 1 April 2008 (at Keepmoat Stadium).

Pitch Measurements: 100m × 66m (109.5yd × 72yd).

Chairman: David Blunt.

Chief Executive: Gavin Baldwin.

Manager: Darren Moore.

Assistant Manager: TBC.

Colours: Red and white hooped shirts, white shorts with red and black trim, white socks with red trim.

Year Formed: 1879.

Turned Professional: 1885.

Club Nickname: 'Rovers', 'Donny'.

Grounds: 1880–1916, Intake Ground; 1920, Benetthorpe Ground; 1922, Low Pasture, Belle Vue; 2007, Keepmoat Stadium.

First Football League Game: 7 September 1901, Division 2, v Burslem Port Vale (h) D 3–3 – Eggett; Simpson, Layton; Longden, Jones, Wright, Langham, Murphy, Price, Goodson (2), Bailey (1).

Record League Victory: 10–0 v Darlington, Division 4, 25 January 1964 – Potter; Raine, Meadows, Windross (1), White, Ripley (2), Robinson, Booth (2), Hale (4), Jeffrey, Broadbent (1).

Record Cup Victory: 7–0 v Blyth Spartans, FA Cup 1st rd, 27 November 1937 – Imrie; Shaw, Rodgers, McFarlane, Bycroft, Cyril Smith, Burton (1), Killourhy (4), Morgan (2), Malam, Dutton; 7–0 v Chorley, FA Cup 1st rd replay, 20 November 2018 – Lawlor; Mason, Butler, Anderson T■, Andrew, Whiteman (Rowe), Coppinger (Taylor), Kane (1) (Crawford), May (4), Marquis (1), Blair (1).

Record Defeat: 0–12 v Small Heath, Division 2, 11 April 1903.

HONOURS

League Champions: FL 1 – 2012–13; Division 3N – 1934–35, 1946–47, 1949–50; Third Division – 2003–04; Division 4 – 1965–66, 1968–69.
Runners-up: Division 3N – 1937–38, 1938–39; Division 4 – 1983–84; Conference – (3rd) 2002–03 *(promoted via play-offs (and golden goal)).*

FA Cup: 5th rd – 1952, 1954, 1955, 1956, 2019.

League Cup: 5th rd – 1976, 2006.

League Trophy Winners: 2007.

THE SUN FACT FILE

The first substitute selected for Doncaster Rovers was Keith Ripley, who sat on the bench for the home game with Lincoln City on 21 August 1965. Although he did not feature that day he replaced Laurie Sheffield the following week against Southport and went on to make a total of five substitute appearances that season.

Most League Points (2 for a win): 72, Division 3 (N), 1946–47.

Most League Points (3 for a win): 92, Division 3, 2003–04.

Most League Goals: 123, Division 3 (N), 1946–47.

Highest League Scorer in Season: Clarrie Jordan, 42, Division 3 (N), 1946–47.

Most League Goals in Total Aggregate: Tom Keetley, 180, 1923–29.

Most League Goals in One Match: 6, Tom Keetley v Ashington, Division 3 (N), 16 February 1929.

Most Capped Player: Len Graham, 14, Northern Ireland.

Most League Appearances: James Coppinger, 553, 2004–19.

Youngest League Player: Alick Jeffrey, 15 years 229 days v Fulham, 15 September 1954.

Record Transfer Fee Received: £2,000,000 from Reading for Matthew Mills, July 2009.

Record Transfer Fee Paid: £1,150,000 to Sheffield U for Billy Sharp, August 2010.

Football League Record: 1901 Elected to Division 2; 1903 Failed re-election; 1904 Re-elected; 1905 Failed re-election; 1923 Re-elected to Division 3 (N); 1935–37 Division 2; 1937–47 Division 3 (N); 1947–48 Division 2; 1948–50 Division 3 (N); 1950–58 Division 2; 1958–59 Division 3; 1959–66 Division 4; 1966–67 Division 3; 1967–69 Division 4; 1969–71 Division 3; 1971–81 Division 4; 1981–83 Division 3; 1983–84 Division 4; 1984–88 Division 3; 1988–92 Division 4; 1992–98 Division 3; 1998–2003 Conference; 2003–04 Division 3; 2004–08 FL 1; 2008–12 FL C; 2012–13 FL 1; 2013–14 FL C; 2014–16 FL 1; 2016–17 FL 2; 2017– FL 1.

LATEST SEQUENCES

Longest Sequence of League Wins: 10, 22.1.1947 – 4.4.1947.

Longest Sequence of League Defeats: 9, 14.1.1905 – 1.4.1905.

Longest Sequence of League Draws: 4, 1.1.2018 – 23.1.2018.

Longest Sequence of Unbeaten League Matches: 20, 26.12.1968 – 12.4.1969.

Longest Sequence Without a League Win: 20, 9.8.1997 – 29.11.1997.

Successive Scoring Runs: 27 from 10.11.1934.

Successive Non-scoring Runs: 7 from 27.9.1947.

MANAGERS

Arthur Porter 1920–21
Harry Tufnell 1921–22
Arthur Porter 1922–23
Dick Ray 1923–27
David Menzies 1928–36
Fred Emery 1936–40
Bill Marsden 1944–46
Jackie Bestall 1946–49
Peter Doherty 1949–58
Jack Hodgson and Sid Bycroft (*Joint Managers*) 1958
Jack Crayston 1958–59 (*continued as Secretary-Manager to 1961*)
Jackie Bestall 1959–60
Norman Curtis 1960–61
Danny Malloy 1961–62
Oscar Hold 1962–64
Bill Leivers 1964–66
Keith Kettleborough 1966–67
George Raynor 1967–68
Lawrie McMenemy 1968–71
Maurice Setters 1971–74
Stan Anderson 1975–78
Billy Bremner 1978–85
Dave Cusack 1985–87
Dave Mackay 1987–89
Billy Bremner 1989–91
Steve Beaglehole 1991–93
Ian Atkins 1994
Sammy Chung 1994–96
Kerry Dixon (*Player-Manager*) 1996–97
Dave Cowling 1997
Mark Weaver 1997–98
Ian Snodin 1998–99
Steve Wignall 1999–2001
Dave Penney 2002–06
Sean O'Driscoll 2006–11
Dean Saunders 2011–13
Brian Flynn 2013
Paul Dickov 2013–15
Darren Ferguson 2015–18
Grant McCann 2018–19
Darren Moore July 2019–

TEN YEAR LEAGUE RECORD

		P	W	D	L	F	A	Pts	Pos
2009-10	FL C	46	15	15	16	59	58	60	12
2010-11	FL C	46	11	15	20	55	81	48	21
2011-12	FL C	46	8	12	26	43	80	36	24
2012-13	FL 1	46	25	9	12	62	44	84	1
2013-14	FL C	46	11	11	24	39	70	44	22
2014-15	FL 1	46	16	13	17	58	62	61	13
2015-16	FL 1	46	11	13	22	48	64	46	21
2016-17	FL 2	46	25	10	11	85	55	85	3
2017-18	FL 1	46	13	17	16	52	52	56	15
2018-19	FL 1	46	20	13	13	76	58	73	6

DID YOU KNOW ?

The highest average attendance recorded by Doncaster Rovers was 22,838 at the old Belle Vue ground in 1950–51. The only other occasions the club has achieved a 20,000 plus average attendance are 1947–48 (22,317) and 1951–52 (21,078).

DONCASTER ROVERS – SKY BET LEAGUE ONE 2018–19 LEAGUE RECORD

Match No.	Date	Venue	Opponents	Result	H/T Score	Lg Pos.	Goalscorers	Attendance
1	Aug 4	A	Southend U	W 3-2	0-0	3	Marquis [51], Wilks [58], Rowe [70]	7147
2	11	H	Wycombe W	W 3-0	0-0	2	Wilks [55], Wright [78], Marquis [80]	7122
3	18	A	Burton Alb	L 0-1	0-0	5		3129
4	21	H	Shrewsbury T	D 0-0	0-0	6		6943
5	25	H	Portsmouth	D 0-0	0-0	7		7618
6	Sept 1	A	Peterborough U	D 1-1	1-0	7	Marquis [40]	7060
7	8	H	Luton T	W 2-1	1-1	7	Blair [6], Whiteman [46]	7526
8	15	A	Walsall	W 4-1	1-1	5	Marquis (pen) [33], Wilks [58], Coppinger [66], Blair [90]	4546
9	22	H	Bradford C	W 2-1	1-0	4	Marquis 2 [23, 52]	8481
10	29	A	Plymouth Arg	W 3-2	1-1	3	Marquis 2 [18, 90], Blair [57]	8532
11	Oct 2	A	Accrington S	L 0-1	0-0	3		2327
12	6	H	Fleetwood T	L 0-4	0-3	6		6846
13	13	A	Rochdale	W 3-2	1-0	4	Crawford [20], Butler [50], Anderson, J [68]	3600
14	20	H	Gillingham	D 3-3	0-2	6	Marquis [51], Wilks [67], Taylor [90]	6891
15	23	H	Sunderland	L 0-1	0-0	7		11,881
16	27	A	Coventry C	L 1-2	0-2	8	Wright [69]	11,006
17	Nov 3	A	Charlton Ath	L 0-2	0-2	9		9873
18	17	H	AFC Wimbledon	W 2-1	1-1	8	Crawford [35], Rowe [86]	7843
19	24	A	Barnsley	D 1-1	0-0	8	Kane [52]	13,573
20	27	H	Blackpool	W 2-0	1-0	7	Kane [45], Marquis [78]	6473
21	Dec 8	A	Bristol R	W 4-0	2-0	6	Marquis [10], Wilks 2 [43, 59], Anderson, T [54]	7356
22	15	H	Scunthorpe U	W 3-0	2-0	6	Whiteman [6], Kane [10], Marquis [85]	7969
23	22	H	Oxford U	D 2-2	1-0	7	Whiteman (pen) [20], May [90]	7425
24	26	A	Fleetwood T	L 0-3	0-1	7		2908
25	29	A	Gillingham	W 3-1	1-0	7	Marquis [28], Wilks [54], Andrew [61]	4791
26	Jan 1	H	Rochdale	W 5-0	3-0	6	May [1], Crawford [23], Marquis 2 [34, 75], Coppinger [82]	7408
27	12	A	Wycombe W	L 2-3	0-0	7	Marquis [60], Rowe [70]	4747
28	19	H	Burton Alb	D 2-2	0-1	7	Smith 2 [53, 75]	7202
29	Feb 2	A	Portsmouth	D 1-1	1-0	7	Wilks [30]	17,800
30	9	H	Peterborough U	W 3-1	0-1	6	White (og) [62], Marquis [65], Sadlier [74]	9627
31	12	H	Southend U	W 3-0	1-0	6	Marquis [14], Wilks [55], Kane [73]	6557
32	23	A	Scunthorpe U	D 1-1	1-0	6	Wilks [25]	6255
33	26	A	Shrewsbury T	L 0-2	0-2	6		5394
34	Mar 2	H	Charlton Ath	D 1-1	0-0	6	Wilks [76]	8385
35	9	A	AFC Wimbledon	L 0-2	0-0	6		4203
36	12	A	Blackpool	D 1-1	0-0	6	Rowe [73]	7404
37	15	H	Barnsley	D 0-0	0-0	6		11,710
38	23	A	Luton T	L 0-4	0-1	7		10,071
39	26	H	Bristol R	W 4-1	3-0	6	Coppinger 2 [3, 12], Wilks [31], Sadlier [46]	6907
40	30	H	Walsall	W 3-1	3-1	6	Marquis (pen) [3], Wilks [4], Andrew [39]	7630
41	Apr 6	A	Bradford C	W 1-0	0-0	6	Wilks [73]	16,496
42	13	H	Plymouth Arg	W 2-0	2-0	6	Rowe [7], Andrew [44]	7795
43	19	A	Sunderland	L 0-2	0-2	6		34,287
44	23	H	Accrington S	L 1-2	0-2	6	Andrew [90]	7222
45	27	A	Oxford U	D 2-2	1-1	6	Marquis [7], Jones (og) [61]	9000
46	May 4	H	Coventry C	W 2-0	1-0	6	Sadlier [31], Marquis [85]	12,794

Final League Position: 6

GOALSCORERS

League (76): Marquis 21 (2 pens), Wilks 14, Rowe 5, Andrew 4, Coppinger 4, Kane 4, Blair 3, Crawford 3, Sadlier 3, Whiteman 3 (1 pen), May 2, Smith 2, Wright 2, Anderson J 1, Anderson T 1, Butler 1, Taylor 1, own goals 2.
FA Cup (16): May 4, Kane 3, Marquis 3, Whiteman 2 (1 pen), Anderson 1, Blair 1, Butler 1, Wilks 1.
Carabao Cup (3): Andrew 1, May 1, Wilks 1.
Checkatrade Trophy (5): May 4 (1 pen), Marquis 1.
League One Play-offs (4): Blair 1, Butler 1, Marquis 1, Rowe 1.

Marosi M 36	Mason N 19 + 1	Wright J 14	Butler A 39 + 1	Andrew D 46	Whiteman B 39 + 1	Crawford A 25 + 10	Rowe T 18 + 14	Coppinger J 38 + 5	Marquis J 44	Wilks M 42 + 4	Kiwomya A 1 + 2	Amos D — + 1	Blair M 31 + 11	Kane H 37 + 1	Taylor P 1 + 13	May A 8 + 26	Anderson T 21 + 2	Anderson J 1 + 8	Beestin A — + 5	Lawlor I 10	Cummings S 4	Boocock R — + 1	Smith T 2 + 12	Lewis A 7	Downing P 17 + 1	Sadlier K 6 + 8	Hasani L — + 2	*Match No*
1	2	3	4	5^{2}	6	7^{1}	8	9^{3}	10	11	12	13	14															1
1	2^{2}	3	4	5	6		8	12	10	9^{3}	11^{1}		13	7	14													2
1	2	3	4	5	7		8	9^{1}	10	11^{3}			12	6^{2}	13	14												3
1	2	3^{1}	4	5	7		8^{3}	9^{2}	10	11			13	6	12		14											4
1■	2	3	4	5	7		13	12	10	11^{3}	14		6^{2}	8		9^{1}												5
1	2		3	5	6		9	8	10	11^{1}				7		12	4											6
1	2	3	4	5	7			11^{1}	10	9^{3}			6	8^{2}	14	12		13										7
1	2	3	4	5	7			11^{1}	10	9^{3}			6	8^{2}	14	12		13										8
1	2	4	3	5	7			11^{1}	10	9^{4}			8	6	13	12												9
1	2	3	4	5		13		11^{1}	10	9^{2}			6	7		12		8^{3}	14									10
1	2	3	4	5	7	13		11^{1}	10	9^{2}			8^{3}	6	14	12												11
1	2^{2}	3	4	5	7	12		9^{1}	10	11^{3}			6	8		13			14									12
1	2	3	4	5	7	8^{1}		11^{2}	10	13			6		14	9^{3}		12										13
1	2		4	5	7	12		9^{2}	10	11			6^{3}	8^{1}	14		3	13										14
1	2	3	4	5	7			9^{2}	10	11^{1}			6^{3}	8	14	13		12										15
1		3		5	7	6^{2}		9	10	11^{1}			2	8	13		4	12										16
1	2		3	5	7			9^{3}	10	13			6^{1}	8	11^{2}	12	4	14										17
	2		4	5	7	6^{3}	14	9^{1}	10	11^{2}			13	8		12	3			1								18
	3		4	5	7	6^{1}	12	9	10	13			2	8		11^{2}				1								19
	2		4	5	7	8^{1}	12	9^{2}	10	14			13	6		11^{3}	3			1								20
			4	5	7	6^{2}	12	9^{1}	10	11^{3}				8	14	13	3			1	2							21
			4	5	7	6^{3}	13	9^{1}	10	11^{2}			14	8		12	3			1	2							22
			4	5	7	6^{1}	12	9^{3}	10	11			13	8		14	3			1	2^{2}							23
			4	5	7	6^{2}	12	9	10	11				8		13	3			1	2^{1}							24
			4	5	7	12	6^{1}		10	9^{2}			2	8		11^{3}	3	13		1		14						25
			4	5	7	6^{1}	12	13	10	9			2	8^{3}	14	11^{2}	3			1								26
	12		3	5	7	6^{2}	13	11^{1}	10	9			2^{3}	8		14	4			1								27
1			4	5	7	6	8^{2}	9	10	11^{1}			2			12	3						13					28
1				5	7^{3}	13	14		10	11			6^{1}	8		12	4						9^{2}	2	3			29
1				5	7	6		9^{1}	10	11^{2}			12	8			3						14	2^{3}	4	13		30
1				5	7	6		9^{2}	10	11			12	8^{1}			4						14	2^{3}	3	13		31
1				5	7	6^{2}	14	9^{3}	10	11^{1}			2	8			4						12		3	13		32
1			12	5	7	6^{1}	8	13	10	9							4^{2}						11^{3}	2	3	14		33
1			4	5	7	6^{1}	13	11^{3}	10	9			12	8^{2}		14								2	3			34
1			4	5	7	12		11	10■	9^{2}			6	8^{1}		13							14	2^{3}	3			35
1			4	5	7^{3}	11	10	13		9			6	14		8^{2}							12		3	2^{1}		36
1			4	5	7	12	8^{2}	11^{3}	10	9^{1}			2	8		14									3	13		37
1			4	5		7	8^{4}	9	11	10^{3}			2										12	6^{1}	3	13	14	38
1			4	5		7	8	6^{3}	10	9^{2}			2			12			13				14		3	11^{1}		39
1			4	5		7	8	6^{2}	10	9^{3}			2			14							12		3	11^{1}	13	40
1			3	5		7	6	8^{3}	10	11^{2}			2			12	4		13						14	9^{1}		41
1			4	5		7^{3}	8	9^{1}		10			2	6		12			13				14		3	11^{2}		42
1			4	5	7^{2}	13	8	11^{1}	10	9^{3}			2	6		12							14		3			43
1				5	12	7^{1}	8		10	9			2	6		11^{2}	3								4	13		44
1			4	5	6		7^{1}	11	10	9			2	8			12								3^{2}	13		45
1			4	5	7	12	14	6^{2}	10	9^{1}			2	8									13		3	11^{3}		46

FA Cup

First Round	Chorley	(a)	2 2
Replay	Chorley	(h)	7-0
Second Round	Charlton Ath	(a)	2-0
Third Round	Preston NE	(a)	3-1
Fourth Round	Oldham Ath	(h)	2-1
Fifth Round	Crystal Palace	(h)	0-2

Carabao Cup

First Round	Scunthorpe U	(a)	2-1
Second Round	Blackpool	(h)	1-2

Checkatrade Trophy

Group G (N)	Newcastle U U21	(h)	1-3
Group G (N)	Grimsby T	(h)	2-0
Group G (N)	Notts Co	(a)	2-4

League One Play-offs

Semi-Final 1st leg	Charlton Ath	(h)	1-2
Semi-Final 2nd leg	Charlton Ath	(a)	3-2

(aet; Charlton Ath won 4-3 on penalties)

EVERTON

FOUNDATION

St Domingo Church Sunday School formed a football club in 1878 which played at Stanley Park. Enthusiasm was so great that in November 1879 they decided to expand membership and changed the name to Everton, playing in black shirts with a scarlet sash and nicknamed the 'Black Watch'. After wearing several other colours, royal blue was adopted in 1901.

Goodison Park, Goodison Road, Liverpool L4 4EL.

Telephone: (0151) 556 1878.

Fax: (0151) 286 9112.

Ticket Office: (0151) 556 1878.

Website: www.evertonfc.com

Email: everton@evertonfc.com

Ground Capacity: 39,221.

Record Attendance: 78,299 v Liverpool, Division 1, 18 September 1948.

Pitch Measurements: 100.48m × 68m (110yd × 74.5yd).

Chairman: Bill Kenwright CBE.

Chief Executive: Dr Denise Barrett-Baxendale MBE.

Manager: Marco Silva.

Assistant Manager: Luis Boa Morte.

Colours: Blue shirts with white trim, white shorts with blue trim, white socks with blue trim.

Year Formed: 1878.

Turned Professional: 1885.

Previous Name: 1878, St Domingo FC; 1879, Everton.

Club Nickname: 'The Toffees'.

Grounds: 1878, Stanley Park; 1882, Priory Road; 1884, Anfield Road; 1892, Goodison Park.

First Football League Game: 8 September 1888, Football League, v Accrington (h) W 2–1 – Smalley; Dick, Ross; Holt, Jones, Dobson; Fleming (2), Waugh, Lewis, Edgar Chadwick, Farmer.

Record League Victory: 9–1 v Manchester C, Division 1, 3 September 1906 – Scott; Balmer, Crelley; Booth, Taylor (1), Abbott (1); Sharp, Bolton (1), Young (4), Settle (2), George Wilson; 9–1 v Plymouth Arg, Division 2, 27 December 1930 – Coggins; Williams, Cresswell; McPherson, Griffiths, Thomson; Critchley, Dunn, Dean (4), Johnson (1), Stein (4).

HONOURS

League Champions: Division 1 – 1914–15, 1927–28, 1931–32, 1938–39, 1962–63, 1969–70, 1984–85, 1986–87; Football League 1890–91; Division 2 – 1930–31.
Runners-up: Division 1 – 1894–95, 1901–02, 1904–05, 1908–09, 1911–12, 1985–86; Football League 1889–90; Division 2 – 1953–54.

FA Cup Winners: 1906, 1933, 1966, 1984, 1995.
Runners-up: 1893, 1897, 1907, 1968, 1985, 1986, 1989, 2009.

League Cup: *Runners-up:* 1977, 1984.

League Super Cup: *Runners-up:* 1986.

Full Members' Cup: *Runners-up:* 1989, 1991.

European Competitions
European Cup: 1963–64, 1970–71 *(qf)*.
Champions League: 2005–06.
Fairs Cup: 1962–63, 1964–65, 1965–66.
UEFA Cup: 1975–76, 1978–79, 1979–80, 2005–06, 2007–08, 2008–09.
Europa League: 2009–10, 2014–15, 2017–18.
European Cup-Winners' Cup: 1966–67, 1984–85 *(winners)*, 1995–96.

THE Sun FACT FILE

The Everton Toffee Lady was introduced as a club mascot by the Everton Supporters' Club in the early 1950s as a feature of the pre-match routine at Goodison. Initially one person held the title role until eventually 'retiring' and passing it on, but in more recent years different members of the Supporters' Club have been selected on a match-by-match basis.

Record Cup Victory: 11–2 v Derby Co, FA Cup 1st rd, 18 January 1890 – Smalley; Hannah, Doyle (1); Kirkwood, Holt (1), Parry; Latta, Brady (3), Geary (3), Edgar Chadwick, Millward (3).

Record Defeat: 4–10 v Tottenham H, Division 1, 11 October 1958.

Most League Points (2 for a win): 66, Division 1, 1969–70.

Most League Points (3 for a win): 90, Division 1, 1984–85.

Most League Goals: 121, Division 2, 1930–31.

Highest League Scorer in Season: William Ralph 'Dixie' Dean, 60, Division 1, 1927–28 (All-time League record).

Most League Goals in Total Aggregate: William Ralph 'Dixie' Dean, 349, 1925–37.

Most League Goals in One Match: 6, Jack Southworth v WBA, Division 1, 30 December 1893.

Most Capped Player: Tim Howard, 93 (121), USA.

Most League Appearances: Neville Southall, 578, 1981–98.

Youngest League Player: Jose Baxter, 16 years 191 days v Blackburn R, 16 August 2008.

Record Transfer Fee Received: £75,000,000 from Manchester U for Romelu Lukaku, July 2017.

Record Transfer Fee Paid: £40,000,000 (rising to £45,000,000) to Swansea C for Gylfi Sigurdsson, August 2017.

Football League Record: 1888 Founder Member of the Football League; 1930–31 Division 2; 1931–51 Division 1; 1951–54 Division 2; 1954–92 Division 1; 1992– Premier League.

MANAGERS

W. E. Barclay 1888–89
(Secretary-Manager)
Dick Molyneux 1889–1901
(Secretary-Manager)
William C. Cuff 1901–18
(Secretary-Manager)
W. J. Sawyer 1918–19
(Secretary-Manager)
Thomas H. McIntosh 1919–35
(Secretary-Manager)
Theo Kelly 1936–48
Cliff Britton 1948–56
Ian Buchan 1956–58
Johnny Carey 1958–61
Harry Catterick 1961–73
Billy Bingham 1973–77
Gordon Lee 1977–81
Howard Kendall 1981–87
Colin Harvey 1987–90
Howard Kendall 1990–93
Mike Walker 1994
Joe Royle 1994–97
Howard Kendall 1997–98
Walter Smith 1998–2002
David Moyes 2002–13
Roberto Martinez 2013–16
Ronald Koeman 2016–17
Sam Allardyce 2017–18
Marco Silva May 2018–

LATEST SEQUENCES

Longest Sequence of League Wins: 12, 24.3.1894 – 13.10.1894.

Longest Sequence of League Defeats: 6, 27.8.2005– 15.10.2005.

Longest Sequence of League Draws: 5, 4.5.1977 – 16.5.1977.

Longest Sequence of Unbeaten League Matches: 20, 29.4.1978 – 16.12.1978.

Longest Sequence Without a League Win: 14, 6.3.1937 – 4.9.1937.

Successive Scoring Runs: 40 from 15.3.1930.

Successive Non-scoring Runs: 6 from 27.8.2005.

TEN YEAR LEAGUE RECORD

		P	W	D	L	F	A	Pts	Pos
2009-10	PR Lge	38	16	13	9	60	49	61	8
2010-11	PR Lge	38	13	15	10	51	45	54	7
2011-12	PR Lge	38	15	11	12	50	40	56	7
2012-13	PR Lge	38	16	15	7	55	40	63	6
2013-14	PR Lge	38	21	9	8	61	39	72	5
2014-15	PR Lge	38	12	11	15	48	50	47	11
2015-16	PR Lge	38	11	14	13	59	55	47	11
2016-17	PR Lge	38	17	10	11	62	44	61	7
2017-18	PR Lge	38	13	10	15	44	58	49	8
2018-19	PR Lge	38	15	9	14	54	46	54	8

DID YOU KNOW ?

Everton's Goodison Park hosted a baseball match between two of America's top professional sides in October 1924. The Chicago White Sox beat the New York Giants by 16 runs to 11 in the first match of a European tour made by the two clubs.

EVERTON – PREMIER LEAGUE 2018–19 LEAGUE RECORD

Match No.	*Date*	*Venue*	*Opponents*	*Result*	*H/T Score*	*Lg Pos.*	*Goalscorers*	*Attendance*
1	Aug 11	A	Wolverhampton W	D 2-2	1-1	7	Richarlison 2 [17, 67]	31,231
2	18	H	Southampton	W 2-1	2-0	4	Walcott [15], Richarlison [31]	38,601
3	25	A	Bournemouth	D 2-2	0-0	8	Walcott [56], Keane [66]	10,654
4	Sept 1	H	Huddersfield T	D 1-1	1-1	7	Calvert-Lewin [36]	38,767
5	16	H	West Ham U	L 1-3	1-2	10	Sigurdsson [45]	39,161
6	23	A	Arsenal	L 0-2	0-0	12		59,964
7	29	H	Fulham	W 3-0	0-0	11	Sigurdsson 2 [56, 89], Tosun [66]	38,788
8	Oct 6	A	Leicester C	W 2-1	1-1	11	Richarlison [7], Sigurdsson [77]	32,007
9	21	H	Crystal Palace	W 2-0	0-0	8	Calvert-Lewin [87], Tosun [89]	38,668
10	28	A	Manchester U	L 1-2	0-1	9	Sigurdsson (pen) [77]	74,525
11	Nov 3	H	Brighton & HA	W 3-1	1-1	9	Richarlison 2 [26, 77], Coleman [50]	38,966
12	11	A	Chelsea	D 0-0	0-0	9		40,345
13	24	H	Cardiff C	W 1-0	0-0	6	Sigurdsson [59]	39,139
14	Dec 2	A	Liverpool	L 0-1	0-0	6		51,756
15	5	H	Newcastle U	D 1-1	1-1	6	Richarlison [38]	39,350
16	10	H	Watford	D 2-2	1-0	7	Richarlison [15], Digne [90]	38,400
17	15	A	Manchester C	L 1-3	0-1	8	Calvert-Lewin [65]	54,173
18	23	H	Tottenham H	L 2-6	1-3	11	Walcott [21], Sigurdsson [51]	39,319
19	26	A	Burnley	W 5-1	3-1	8	Mina [2], Digne 2 [13, 71], Sigurdsson (pen) [22], Richarlison [90]	21,484
20	29	A	Brighton & HA	L 0-1	0-0	10		30,597
21	Jan 1	H	Leicester C	L 0-1	0-0	10		39,052
22	13	H	Bournemouth	W 2-0	0-0	10	Zouma [61], Calvert-Lewin [90]	38,113
23	19	A	Southampton	L 1-2	0-0	11	Sigurdsson [90]	29,989
24	29	A	Huddersfield T	W 1-0	1-0	8	Richarlison [3]	23,699
25	Feb 2	H	Wolverhampton W	L 1-3	1-2	9	Andre Gomes [27]	39,380
26	6	H	Manchester C	L 0-2	0-1	9		39,322
27	9	A	Watford	L 0-1	0-0	9		20,333
28	26	A	Cardiff C	W 3-0	1-0	9	Sigurdsson 2 [41, 66], Calvert-Lewin [90]	31,849
29	Mar 3	H	Liverpool	D 0-0	0-0	10		39,335
30	9	A	Newcastle U	L 2-3	2-0	11	Calvert-Lewin [18], Richarlison [32]	52,242
31	17	H	Chelsea	W 2-0	0-0	11	Richarlison [49], Sigurdsson [72]	39,356
32	30	A	West Ham U	W 2-0	2-0	9	Zouma [5], Bernard [33]	59,988
33	Apr 7	H	Arsenal	W 1-0	1-0	9	Jagielka [10]	39,400
34	13	A	Fulham	L 0-2	0-0	9		24,971
35	21	H	Manchester U	W 4-0	2-0	7	Richarlison [13], Sigurdsson [28], Digne [56], Walcott [64]	39,395
36	27	A	Crystal Palace	D 0-0	0-0	8		25,789
37	May 3	H	Burnley	W 2-0	2-0	8	Mee (og) [17], Coleman [20]	39,303
38	12	A	Tottenham H	D 2-2	0-1	8	Walcott [69], Tosun [72]	60,124

Final League Position: 8

GOALSCORERS

League (54): Richarlison 13, Sigurdsson 13 (2 pens), Calvert-Lewin 6, Walcott 5, Digne 4, Tosun 3, Coleman 2, Zouma 2, Andre Gomes 1, Bernard 1, Jagielka 1, Keane 1, Mina 1, own goal 1.
FA Cup (4): Bernard 1, Lookman 1, Richarlison 1, Tosun 1.
Carabao Cup (4): Calvert-Lewin 2, Sigurdsson 1, Walcott 1.
Checkatrade Trophy (4): Sambou 2, Lavery 1, Markelo 1.

Pickford J 38	Coleman S 29	Jagielka P 4 + 3	Keane M 33	Baines L 5 + 1	Schneiderlin M 10 + 4	Gana I 32 + 1	Walcott T 24 + 13	Sigurdsson G 36 + 2	Richarlison 32 + 3	Tosun C 10 + 15	Holgate M 4 + 1	Niasse O — + 5	Digne L 33 + 2	Davies T 10 + 6	Calvert-Lewin D 19 + 16	Bernard C 25 + 9	Zouma K 29 + 3	Lookman A 3 + 18	Kenny J 8 + 2	Andre Gomes F 24 + 3	Mina Y 10 + 3	McCarthy J — + 1	Match No.
1	2	3■	4	5	6	7	8	9^{1}	10^{3}	11^{2}	12	13	14										1
1	2		4	5	7^{1}	6	8	9	10^{2}	11^{3}	3	14		12	13								2
1	2		4^{1}	5		8	6^{2}	10	9■	11^{3}	3			7	12	13	14						3
1	2			13	7		8^{3}	9^{2}		11	3	14	5^{1}	6	10		4	12					4
1					7^{1}	6	8^{2}	9		11^{3}	3	13	5		10	12	4	14	2				5
1			3			6	8^{1}	9	10	12			5	7	11^{2}	13	4		2				6
1			3		14	7	8	9^{2}	10^{3}	12			5	6	11^{1}	13	4		2				7
1			3		13	7	8^{3}	9	11	12			5	6^{1}	14	10^{2}	4		2				8
1	2		3			7	8^{1}	9	11	12			5		14	10^{2}	4	13		6^{3}			9
1	2		3			7^{3}	8^{1}	9	11	13			5		14	10^{2}	4	12		6			10
1	2		3			7	8^{1}	9^{3}	11				5		13	10^{2}	4	12		6	14		11
1	2	13	3			7	8	9^{1}	11^{2}				5		14	10^{3}		12		6	4		12
1	2		3			7	8^{2}	9^{1}	11	13			5			10^{3}	14	12		6	4		13
1	2		3			8	6^{2}	10^{3}	11				5		13	9^{1}	14	12		7	4		14
1	2					6	13	9^{1}	10	11^{4}			5		14	12	3	8^{3}		7	4		15
1	2		3			7^{1}	8^{2}	9	11	14			5		13	10^{3}		12		6	4		16
1	2^{1}		4				13	9^{3}	7				6	14	11	10^{2}	3	12		8	5		17
1	2		3		12		8	9^{2}	10^{3}	14			5	6	11	13	4			7^{1}			18
1	5		3			13	9	6	12				8	14	11^{2}	10^{3}	4			7^{1}	2		19
1	5		3			7	9	12	11			14	8		13	10^{2}	4			6^{3}	2^{1}		20
1			3			7	8^{1}	9	10	13			5		11	12	4		2	6^{2}			21
1	2		3			6	12	9^{3}	11^{1}				5		13	10^{2}	4	8		7	14		22
1	2		3			7	14	9	11^{1}	13			5		12	10^{2}	4	8		6^{3}			23
1	2		3	5^{3}				9	10^{2}	11^{1}			12■	8	14	7	4		13	6			24
1	2^{1}		3	5^{2}			7^{3}	9	10	11				8	14		4	13	12	6			25
1			3			6	8^{3}	12	13	14			5	9	11	10^{2}	4		2	7^{1}			26
1			3			6	12	10^{2}	8^{3}	11			5	9	14	13	4■		2	7^{1}			27
1	2	4	3		6	7	8^{3}	9^{2}	10^{1}				5		11	12		13		14			28
1	2		3		8^{1}	7	6^{2}	10	12	13			5		11^{3}	9	4			14			29
1			3			7	14	9	8^{2}				5		11	10^{3}	4	13	2^{1}	6	12		30
1	2		3		12	6	13	9^{1}	8				5	14	11	10^{2}				7^{3}	4		31
1	2		3			6	14	9^{1}	8^{2}	13			5	12	11^{3}	10	4			7			32
1	2	3				7	12	9^{3}	8^{1}				5	14	11	10^{2}	4	13		6			33
1	2	3				7	13	9^{3}	8^{2}	14			5		11	10^{1}	4	12		6			34
1	2	14	3		6	7^{3}	12	9	8^{2}				5^{1}		11	10	4					13	35
1	2		3		6	7	14	9^{1}	8	12			5		11^{3}	10^{2}	4	13					36
1	2	14	3		6	7	12	9^{1}	8^{3}				5		11	10^{3}	4	13					37
1			3		7	8^{1}	6	10		11			5			9^{2}	2	12		13	4		38

FA Cup

Third Round	Lincoln C	(h)	2-1
Fourth Round	Millwall	(a)	2-3

Carabao Cup

Second Round	Rotherham U	(h)	3-1
Third Round	Southampton	(h)	1-1

(Southampton won 4-3 on penalties)

Checkatrade Trophy (Everton U21)

Group F (N)	Bradford C	(a)	1-1

(Bradford C won 6-5 on penalties)

Group F (N)	Oldham Ath	(a)	2-3
Group F (N)	Barnsley	(a)	1-1

(Barnsley won 4-2 on penalties)

EXETER CITY

FOUNDATION

Exeter City was formed in 1904 by the amalgamation of St Sidwell's United and Exeter United. The club first played in the East Devon League and then the Plymouth & District League. After an exhibition match between West Bromwich Albion and Woolwich Arsenal, which was held to test interest as Exeter was then a rugby stronghold, it was decided to form Exeter City. At a meeting at the Red Lion Hotel in 1908, the club turned professional.

St James Park, Stadium Way, Exeter, Devon EX4 6PX.

Telephone: (01392) 411 243.

Fax: (01392) 413 959.

Ticket Office: (01392) 411 243.

Website: www.exetercityfc.co.uk

Email: reception@ecfc.co.uk

Ground Capacity: 8,714.

Record Attendance: 20,984 v Sunderland, FA Cup 6th rd (replay), 4 March 1931.

Pitch Measurements: 103m × 64m (112.5yd × 70yd).

Chairman: Julian Tagg.

Chief Operating Officer (interim): Justin Quick.

Manager: Matt Taylor.

Assistant Manager: Wayne Carlisle.

Colours: Red and white striped shirts with white sleeves, black shorts with white trim, white socks with black hoops.

Year Formed: 1904.

Turned Professional: 1908.

Club Nickname: 'The Grecians'.

Ground: 1904, St James Park.

First Football League Game: 28 August 1920, Division 3, v Brentford (h) W 3–0 – Pym; Coleburne, Feebury (1p); Crawshaw, Carrick, Mitton; Appleton, Makin, Wright (1), Vowles (1), Dockray.

Record League Victory: 8–1 v Coventry C, Division 3 (S), 4 December 1926 – Bailey; Pollard, Charlton; Pullen, Pool, Garrett; Purcell (2), McDevitt, Blackmore (2), Dent (2), Compton (2). 8–1 v Aldershot, Division 3 (S), 4 May 1935 – Chesters; Gray, Miller; Risdon, Webb, Angus; Jack Scott (1), Wrightson (1), Poulter (3), McArthur (1), Dryden (1), (1 og).

Record Cup Victory: 14–0 v Weymouth, FA Cup 1st qual rd, 3 October 1908 – Fletcher; Craig, Bulcock; Ambler, Chadwick, Wake; Parnell (1), Watson (1), McGuigan (4), Bell (6), Copestake (2).

Record Defeat: 0–9 v Notts Co, Division 3 (S), 16 October 1948. 0–9 v Northampton T, Division 3 (S), 12 April 1958.

HONOURS

League Champions: Division 4 – 1989–90.
Runners-up: Division 3S – 1932–33; FL 2 – 2008–09; Division 4 – 1976–77; Conference – (4th) 2007–08 *(promoted via play-offs)*.

FA Cup: 6th rd replay – 1931; 6th rd – 1981.

League Cup: never past 4th rd.

THE SUN FACT FILE

Exeter City hit double-figure scores in each of the opening two rounds of their first FA Cup campaign back in 1908–09. They won 14-0 in their first qualifying round game against amateur club Weymouth in what still stands as their record score in the competition. In the next qualifying round they were held to a draw by Longfleet St Mary but won the replay 10-1. The Grecians went on to reach the second round proper before going out to Plymouth Argyle in front of a 20,000 crowd.

Most League Points (2 for a win): 62, Division 4, 1976–77.

Most League Points (3 for a win): 89, Division 4, 1989–90.

Most League Goals: 88, Division 3 (S), 1932–33.

Highest League Scorer in Season: Fred Whitlow, 33, Division 3 (S), 1932–33.

Most League Goals in Total Aggregate: Tony Kellow, 129, 1976–78, 1980–83, 1985–88.

Most League Goals in One Match: 4, Harold 'Jazzo' Kirk v Portsmouth, Division 3 (S), 3 March 1923; 4, Fred Dent v Bristol R, Division 3 (S), 5 November 1927; 4, Fred Whitlow v Watford, Division 3 (S), 29 October 1932.

Most Capped Player: Joel Grant, 2 (14), Jamaica.

Most League Appearances: Arnold Mitchell, 495, 1952–66.

Youngest League Player: Ethan Ampadu, 15 years 337 days v Crawley T, 16 August 2016.

Record Transfer Fee Received: £1,800,000 from Brentford for Ollie Watkins, July 2017.

Record Transfer Fee Paid: £100,000 to Aberdeen for Jayden Stockley, August 2017.

Football League Record: 1920 Elected to Division 3; 1921–58 Division 3 (S); 1958–64 Division 4; 1964–66 Division 3; 1966–77 Division 4; 1977–84 Division 3; 1984–90 Division 4; 1990–92 Division 3; 1992–94 Division 2; 1994–2003 Division 3; 2003–08 Conference; 2008–09 FL 2; 2009–12 FL 1; 2012– FL 2.

LATEST SEQUENCES

Longest Sequence of League Wins: 7, 31.12.2016 – 4.2.2017.

Longest Sequence of League Defeats: 7, 14.1.1984 – 25.2.1984.

Longest Sequence of League Draws: 6, 13.9.1986 – 4.10.1986.

Longest Sequence of Unbeaten League Matches: 13, 23.8.1986 – 25.10.1986.

Longest Sequence Without a League Win: 18, 21.2.1995 – 19.8.1995.

Successive Scoring Runs: 22 from 15.9.1958.

Successive Non-scoring Runs: 6 from 17.1.1986.

MANAGERS

Arthur Chadwick 1910–22
Fred Mavin 1923–27
Dave Wilson 1928–29
Billy McDevitt 1929–35
Jack English 1935–39
George Roughton 1945–52
Norman Kirkman 1952–53
Norman Dodgin 1953–57
Bill Thompson 1957–58
Frank Broome 1958–60
Glen Wilson 1960–62
Cyril Spiers 1962–63
Jack Edwards 1963–65
Ellis Stuttard 1965–66
Jock Basford 1966–67
Frank Broome 1967–69
Johnny Newman 1969–76
Bobby Saxton 1977–79
Brian Godfrey 1979–83
Gerry Francis 1983–84
Jim Iley 1984–85
Colin Appleton 1985–87
Terry Cooper 1988–91
Alan Ball 1991–94
Terry Cooper 1994–95
Peter Fox 1995–2000
Noel Blake 2000–01
John Cornforth 2001–02
Neil McNab 2002–03
Gary Peters 2003
Eamonn Dolan 2003–04
Alex Inglethorpe 2004–06
Paul Tisdale 2006–18
Matt Taylor June 2018–

TEN YEAR LEAGUE RECORD

		P	W	D	L	F	A	Pts	Pos
2009-10	FL 1	46	11	18	17	48	60	51	18
2010-11	FL 1	46	20	10	16	66	73	70	8
2011-12	FL 1	46	10	12	24	46	75	42	23
2012-13	FL 2	46	18	10	18	63	62	64	10
2013-14	FL 2	46	14	13	19	54	57	55	16
2014-15	FL 2	46	17	13	16	61	65	64	10
2015-16	FL 2	46	17	13	16	63	65	64	14
2016-17	FL 2	46	21	8	17	75	56	71	5
2017-18	FL 2	46	24	8	14	64	54	80	4
2018-19	FL 2	46	19	13	14	60	49	70	9

DID YOU KNOW ?

Exeter City finished bottom of the Football League in 1994–95 but were spared automatic relegation as Conference champions Macclesfield Town's ground was ruled unfit to stage League football. The decision was a relief for the Grecians who failed to win any of their last 16 games in the run-in to the end of the season.

EXETER CITY – SKY BET LEAGUE TWO 2018–19 LEAGUE RECORD

Match No.	*Date*	*Venue*	*Opponents*	*Result*	*H/T Score*	*Lg Pos.*	*Goalscorers*	*Atten-dance*
1	Aug 4	H	Carlisle U	W 3-1	2-1	5	Law [16], Forte [26], Abrahams [90]	4266
2	11	A	Morecambe	W 2-0	1-0	2	Sweeney (pen) [43], Stockley [66]	1654
3	18	H	Newport Co	D 1-1	1-0	2	Stockley [21]	4239
4	21	A	Cambridge U	W 2-0	2-0	1	Forte [8], Stockley [14]	3662
5	25	A	Milton Keynes D	L 0-1	0-0	3		7672
6	Sept 1	H	Lincoln C	L 0-3	0-2	9		4067
7	8	H	Notts Co	W 5-1	2-1	3	Sweeney 2 (1 pen) [16, 58 (p)], Stockley 2 [18, 74], Martin, A [90]	3916
8	15	A	Mansfield T	W 2-1	1-0	2	Moxey [31], Law [57]	4443
9	22	H	Cheltenham T	W 3-1	0-1	2	Sweeney [46], Stockley [80], Forte [88]	3723
10	29	A	Port Vale	D 1-1	0-0	3	Law [48]	4615
11	Oct 2	H	Stevenage	W 1-0	1-0	2	Moxey [45]	3671
12	6	A	Yeovil T	D 2-2	1-0	2	Stockley 2 [9, 75]	4223
13	13	H	Swindon T	W 2-0	1-0	2	Forte [14], Stockley [63]	4506
14	20	A	Grimsby T	D 0-0	0-0	2		4038
15	23	A	Crawley T	D 1-1	0-0	3	Holmes [79]	2095
16	27	H	Forest Green R	L 1-2	0-0	3	Martin, A [90]	4983
17	Nov 3	A	Tranmere R	L 0-2	0-1	5		6209
18	17	H	Northampton T	D 2-2	2-1	6	Taylor [14], Stockley [43]	4332
19	24	A	Colchester U	D 1-1	0-0	6	Stockley [70]	3384
20	27	H	Macclesfield T	L 0-1	0-0	7		3070
21	Dec 8	A	Bury	L 0-2	0-1	9		3328
22	15	H	Crewe Alex	W 1-0	1-0	7	Martin, L [42]	3505
23	22	A	Oldham Ath	W 3-2	1-1	6	Stockley 3 [38, 64, 70]	4079
24	26	H	Yeovil T	W 2-1	1-0	5	Holmes [34], Stockley [88]	5974
25	29	H	Grimsby T	L 1-2	0-1	7	Stockley [78]	4956
26	Jan 1	A	Swindon T	W 2-0	1-0	6	Forte (pen) [37], Collins [69]	6755
27	12	H	Morecambe	D 0-0	0-0	8		4113
28	19	A	Newport Co	L 0-1	0-0	8		3791
29	26	H	Cambridge U	W 1-0	0-0	7	Law [82]	3996
30	Feb 2	H	Milton Keynes D	W 3-1	2-0	7	Law 2 [7, 72], Taylor [17]	5766
31	9	A	Carlisle U	D 1-1	1-0	7	Law [19]	4851
32	16	H	Bury	L 0-1	0-0	8		4607
33	23	A	Crewe Alex	W 2-1	1-0	7	Taylor [7], Jay [66]	3841
34	26	A	Lincoln C	D 1-1	1-0	5	Jay [22]	8589
35	Mar 2	H	Tranmere R	L 0-1	0-1	5		4855
36	9	A	Northampton T	L 1-2	0-1	8	Martin, A [61]	4954
37	16	H	Colchester U	W 3-0	1-0	7	Jay [45], Holmes [66], Law [76]	3951
38	23	A	Notts Co	W 1-0	0-0	7	Law [90]	9505
39	30	H	Mansfield T	L 1-4	1-2	7	Jay [21]	5017
40	Apr 6	A	Cheltenham T	D 1-1	1-0	7	Moxey [36]	4079
41	9	A	Macclesfield T	L 2-3	2-2	7	Bowman 2 [27, 34]	1588
42	13	H	Port Vale	W 2-0	1-0	7	Law (pen) [2], Boateng [55]	4013
43	19	H	Crawley T	L 1-3	0-2	7	Bowman [50]	5054
44	22	A	Stevenage	D 1-1	1-1	7	Bowman [40]	3195
45	27	H	Oldham Ath	W 1-0	0-0	7	Bowman [79]	5040
46	May 4	A	Forest Green R	D 0-0	0-0	9		4537

Final League Position: 9

GOALSCORERS

League (60): Stockley 16, Law 10 (1 pen), Bowman 5, Forte 5 (1 pen), Jay 4, Sweeney 4 (2 pens), Holmes 3, Martin A 3, Moxey 3, Taylor 3, Abrahams 1, Boateng 1, Collins 1, Martin L 1.
FA Cup (2): Abrahams 1, Tillson 1.
Carabao Cup (1): Brown 1.
Checkatrade Trophy (4): Forte 3, Randall 1.

Pym C 43	Sweeney P 42 + 1	Martin A 22 + 1	Brown T 9 + 2	Moxey D 37 + 1	Taylor J 46	Boateng H 21 + 6	Law N 39 + 4	Holmes L 29 + 5	Stockley J 24 + 1	Forte J 18 + 9	Abrahams T 4 + 12	Martin L 19 + 16	Tillson J 13 + 8	Woodman C 28 + 4	Croll L 11 + 2	Ogbene C 3 + 11	Jay M 10 + 8	Collins A 23 + 3	O'Shea D 26 + 1	Hamon J 3 + 1	Hartridge A 2 + 1	Bowman R 13 + 5	Wilson K 12 + 5	Williams R 6 + 4	Wilson D 3 + 7	Match No.
1	2	3	4	5	6	7³	8	9²	10	11¹	12	13	14													1
1	2	3	4	5	6	7	8³	9¹	10	11²	14	13	12													2
1	2	4	3	5	8	9¹	13	6³	11	10²	12	14	7													3
1	2	3		4	9	8	7¹	13	10	11²		6	12	5												4
1	2	3		4▪	7	8	9	6³	10	11¹	14	12		5²	13											5
1	2	4	3	5	6	8	7³	9²	10		11¹	13				12	14									6
1	2	3		4	6	7²	9	10¹	11			13	8	5³	12		14									7
1	2	3		5	8	6²	9	10¹	11			12	7		4	13										8
1	2	3		5	7	10²	6		11	12		9¹	8		4			13								9
1	2	3		5	8	6¹	9		11			10²	7³		4	12		13	14							10
1	2	3		5	6	8	7	9¹	10	11²		12			4	13										11
1	2	4		5	9	8	6³	13	10	12		11²	7¹		3		14									12
1	2	5		3	7	8	6	9²	11	10¹		14	12		4	13³										13
1	2	4		5	7	8³	6	9¹	10	11²	14	12	13		3											14
1	2	3		5	6		8	13	12	10¹	14	9	7³		4		11²									15
	2	3		5	6		8¹		11	10³	13	9	7²	14	4		12			1						16
	2	3		5▪	9		6		10		12	11		13	4		7²	8¹		1						17
1	2	4			9		8	6¹	11	12	10²		7	5		13			3							18
1	2	4			9		7	8¹	10		11²	13	6	5		12			3							19
1	2			5	8		9	6	10	11³	12		7¹	14	4²	13			3							20
1	2	4		12	8		6	9	11	14		13	7³	5²		10¹			3							21
1	2			4	7		9	6¹	10			11		5		12		8	3							22
1	2			4	7		6	9²	11			10¹		5		12	13	8	3							23
1	2			4	7		6¹	9²	11		13	10³	14	5		12		8	3							24
1	2			4	6		12		11	13	10²	14	8¹			9		7	3		5³					25
1	2			4	7		9²			11¹	13	10³	14	5		6	12	8	3							26
1	2			4	7		9	6¹		11²		10		5			13	8	3			12				27
1	2			4	8		9	13		11¹	14			5²				7	3			10	6³	12		28
1	2			4	7		9	6		10³		11¹	14					8²	3			13	5	12		29
1	2			4	7		9	6¹		10²		11		5				8	3			13	12			30
1	2	13			7		9			10²		11		5				8	3			12	4	6¹		31
1	2			4	6		9	8²						5¹				7	3			11	12	10	13	32
1	2			4	7			9¹						12			11	8	3			10	5	6²	13	33
1	2	4			6	13				12				7			11¹	8	3		14	10²	5		9³	34
1	3				6	13	14	8		12				5			9	7¹	4				2	10³	11²	35
1		2			7	12	6³	13		11				4			10	8¹	3		9²	14	5			36
1			13	4	8	7¹	9	6³						5			10	12	3			11²	2		14	37
1	12		3	4	8	7¹	9	6²						5			10					11▪	2		13	38
1			14	4	7	8³	9	6¹				13		5			11		3				2	12	10²	39
1▪	2		3	4	6	13	8							9¹			11³	7²		14		10	5		12	40
	2		3	4	7	9¹	13			14		11³		5²			12	8		1		10	6			41
1	2		4		8	9¹	10	6²				13		5				7	3			11		12		42
1	2		3		9	7²	10	6				12		5³				8¹	4			11	13		14	43
1	2			4	7	12	6					11¹		5				8	3			10		9		44
1	2			4	6	12	10²					9		5				7	3			11	13	8¹		45
1	2			4	8	9		6		14		10²		5³				7¹	3			11	12		13	46

FA Cup

First Round	Blackpool	(h)	2-3

Carabao Cup

First Round	Ipswich T	(h)	1-1
(Exeter C won 4-2 on penalties)			
Second Round	Fulham	(a)	0-2

Checkatrade Trophy

Group D (S)	Yeovil T	(a)	0-0
(Exeter C won 5-2 on penalties)			
Group D (S)	West Ham U U21	(h)	2-0
Group D (S)	Bristol R	(h)	2-0
Second Round (S)	Peterborough U	(h)	0-2

FLEETWOOD TOWN

FOUNDATION

Originally formed in 1908 as Fleetwood FC, it was liquidated in 1976. Re-formed as Fleetwood Town in 1977, it folded again in 1996. Once again, it was re-formed a year later as Fleetwood Wanderers, but a sponsorship deal saw the club's name immediately changed to Fleetwood Freeport through the local retail outlet centre. This sponsorship ended in 2002, but since then local energy businessman Andy Pilley took charge and the club has risen through the non-league pyramid until finally achieving Football League status in 2012 as Fleetwood Town.

Highbury Stadium, Park Avenue, Fleetwood, Lancashire FY7 6TX.

Telephone: (01253) 775 080.

Ticket Office: (01253) 775 080.

Website: www.fleetwoodtownfc.com

Email: info@fleetwoodtownfc.com

Ground Capacity: 5,327.

Record Attendance: (Before 1997) 6,150 v Rochdale, FA Cup 1st rd, 13 November 1965; (Since 1997) 5,194 v York C, FL 2 Play-Off semi-final 2nd leg, 16 May 2014.

Pitch Measurements: 100m × 65m (109.5yd × 71yd).

Chairman: Andy Pilley.

Chief Executive: Steve Curwood.

Head Coach: Joey Barton.

Assistant Head Coach: Clint Hill.

Colours: Red shirts with white sleeves and red trim, white shorts with red trim, red socks.

Year Formed: 1908 (re-formed 1997).

Previous Names: 1908, Fleetwood FC; 1977, Fleetwood Town; 1997, Fleetwood Wanderers; 2002 Fleetwood Town.

Club Nicknames: 'The Trawlermen', 'The Cod Army'.

Grounds: 1908, North Euston Hotel; 1934, Memorial Park (now Highbury Stadium).

First Football League Game: 18 August 2012, FL 2, v Torquay U (h) D 0–0 – Davies; Beeley, Mawene, McNulty, Howell, Nicolson, Johnson, McGuire, Ball, Parkin, Mangan.

HONOURS

League Champions: Conference – 2011–12.

FA Cup: 3rd rd – 2012, 2017, 2018, 2019.

League Cup: never past 2nd rd.

THE Sun FACT FILE

Fleetwood Town have appeared at both the 'old' and 'new' Wembley Stadiums. In April 1985 they lost out to Halesowen Town at the original stadium in the FA Vase final, a game that attracted an attendance of 16,715, while in May 2014 they defeated Burton Albion to win the League Two play-off final at the new stadium in front of 14,007.

Record League Victory: 13–0 v Oldham T, North West Counties Div 2, 5 December 1998.

Record Defeat: 0–7 v Billingham T, FA Cup 1st qual rd, 15 September 2001.

Most League Points (3 for a win): 82, FL 1, 2016–17.

Most League Goals: 66, FL 2, 2013–14.

Highest League Scorer in Season: Ched Evans, 17, FL 1, 2018–19.

Most League Goals in Total Aggregate: David Ball, 41, 2012–17.

Most League Goals in One Match: 3, Steven Schumacher v Newport Co, FL 2, 2 November 2013.

Most Capped Player: Conor McLaughlin, 25 (35), Northern Ireland.

Most League Appearances: David Ball, 179, 2012–17.

Youngest League Player: Barry Baggley, 17 years 26 days v Walsall, 9 March 2019.

Record Transfer Fee Received: £1,000,000 (rising to £1,700,000) from Leicester C for Jamie Vardy, May 2012.

Record Transfer Fee Paid: £300,000 to Kidderminster H for Jamille Matt, January 2013; £300,000 to Huddersfield T for Kyle Dempsey, May 2017.

Football League Record: 2012 Promoted from Conference Premier; 2012–14 FL 2; 2014– FL 1.

MANAGER

Alan Tinsley 1997
Mark Hughes 1998
Brian Wilson 1998–99
Mick Hoyle 1999–2001
Les Attwood 2001
Mark Hughes 2001
Alan Tinsley 2001–02
Mick Hoyle 2002–03
Tony Greenwood 2003–08
Micky Mellon 2008–12
Graham Alexander 2012–15
Steven Pressley 2015–16
Uwe Rosler 2016–18
John Sheridan 2018
Joey Barton June 2018–

LATEST SEQUENCES

Longest Sequence of League Wins: 5, 31.12.2016 – 24.1.2017.

Longest Sequence of League Defeats: 6, 20.1.2018 – 20.2.2018.

Longest Sequence of League Draws: 3, 1.1.2019 – 19.1.2019.

Longest Sequence of Unbeaten League Matches: 18, 19.11.2016 – 4.3.2017.

Longest Sequence Without a League Win: 9, 20.1.2018 – 17.3.2018.

Successive Scoring Runs: 24 from 2.5.2016.

Successive Non-scoring Runs: 4 from 22.2.2014.

TEN YEAR LEAGUE RECORD

		P	*W*	*D*	*L*	*F*	*A*	*Pts*	*Pos*
2009-10	Conf N	42	26	7	7	86	44	85	2
2010-11	Conf P	46	22	12	12	68	42	78	5
2011-12	Conf P	46	31	10	5	102	48	103	1
2012-13	FL 2	46	15	15	16	55	57	60	13
2013-14	FL 2	46	22	10	14	66	52	76	4
2014-15	FL 1	46	17	12	17	49	52	63	10
2015-16	FL 1	46	12	15	19	52	56	51	19
2016-17	FL 1	46	23	13	10	64	43	82	4
2017-18	FL 1	46	16	9	21	59	68	57	14
2018-19	FL 1	46	16	13	17	58	52	61	11

DID YOU KNOW?

The highest average attendance recorded by Fleetwood Town since their promotion to the EFL is 3,522 in 2014–15, the club's first season playing in League One. Average attendances have not dropped below 3,000 since then.

FLEETWOOD TOWN – SKY BET LEAGUE ONE 2018–19 LEAGUE RECORD

Match No.	*Date*	*Venue*	*Opponents*	*Result*		*H/T Score*	*Lg Pos.*	*Goalscorers*	*Atten-dance*
1	Aug 4	H	AFC Wimbledon	L	0-1	0-0	20		3236
2	11	A	Oxford U	W	2-0	1-0	10	Evans [34], Madden (pen) [89]	6689
3	18	H	Rochdale	D	2-2	1-0	9	Madden [29], Evans [56]	3565
4	22	A	Scunthorpe U	W	5-0	4-0	6	Evans 2 [16, 18], Burns 2 [21, 29], Hunter [56]	3465
5	25	A	Charlton Ath	D	0-0	0-0	6		8810
6	Sept 1	H	Bradford C	W	2-1	1-1	6	Evans [12], Hunter [48]	3347
7	8	A	Sunderland	D	1-1	1-1	6	Madden [9]	29,367
8	15	H	Accrington S	D	1-1	1-0	8	Bolger [37]	3355
9	22	A	Southend U	L	0-1	0-0	10		5712
10	29	H	Barnsley	L	1-3	1-2	11	Biggins [19]	3756
11	Oct 2	H	Wycombe W	D	1-1	1-0	13	Madden [37]	2304
12	6	A	Doncaster R	W	4-0	3-0	10	Evans (pen) [4], Wallace, J [34], Eastham [45], Hunter [49]	6846
13	13	H	Shrewsbury T	W	2-1	2-0	8	Madden [19], Burns [28]	2983
14	20	A	Portsmouth	L	0-1	0-0	11		18,046
15	23	A	Peterborough U	L	0-1	0-0	13		5347
16	27	H	Blackpool	W	3-2	2-1	10	Burns [4], Wallace, R [11], Madden [57]	5035
17	Nov 3	A	Gillingham	L	0-3	0-2	11		3916
18	17	H	Walsall	D	0-0	0-0	12		3090
19	24	A	Plymouth Arg	L	1-2	0-0	13	Madden [84]	8301
20	27	H	Coventry C	W	3-0	0-0	12	Marney [53], Burns [71], Evans [73]	2570
21	Dec 8	A	Luton T	L	0-2	0-1	13		8528
22	15	H	Burton Alb	W	1-0	0-0	10	Evans (pen) [51]	2563
23	22	A	Bristol R	L	1-2	1-1	12	Hunter [28]	7159
24	26	H	Doncaster R	W	3-0	1-0	10	Madden 2 [11, 90], Hunter [48]	2908
25	29	H	Portsmouth	L	2-5	2-1	11	Madden [39], Evans (pen) [43]	3494
26	Jan 1	A	Shrewsbury T	D	0-0	0-0	11		5919
27	12	H	Oxford U	D	2-2	2-0	10	Burns [8], Madden [26]	2789
28	19	A	Rochdale	D	1-1	1-0	12	Madden [36]	2713
29	22	A	AFC Wimbledon	W	3-0	2-0	8	Evans 2 [19, 30], Hunter [83]	3499
30	26	H	Scunthorpe U	L	0-1	0-0	10		2637
31	Feb 2	H	Charlton Ath	W	1-0	0-0	10	Evans [68]	2742
32	9	A	Bradford C	W	1-0	1-0	9	Madden [9]	15,365
33	16	H	Luton T	L	1-2	0-1	10	Madden [90]	3651
34	23	A	Burton Alb	W	1-0	0-0	8	Nadesan [57]	2634
35	Mar 2	H	Gillingham	D	1-1	0-0	9	Husband [90]	3019
36	9	A	Walsall	L	0-2	0-0	10		4986
37	12	A	Coventry C	L	1-2	1-2	10	Evans [33]	9220
38	16	H	Plymouth Arg	W	2-0	0-0	10	Holt [77], Hunter [80]	2711
39	30	A	Accrington S	W	1-0	0-0	10	Soutar [50]	2485
40	Apr 6	H	Southend U	D	2-2	0-1	11	Evans 2 (1 pen) [59, 84 (p)]	2761
41	13	A	Barnsley	L	2-4	0-2	11	Evans [64], Burns [77]	11,243
42	19	H	Peterborough U	D	1-1	0-0	11	Hunter [90]	2774
43	22	A	Blackpool	L	1-2	1-1	12	Evans [37]	11,713
44	27	H	Bristol R	D	0-0	0-0	12		3488
45	30	H	Sunderland	W	2-1	0-1	11	Madden [73], Eastham [90]	4011
46	May 4	A	Wycombe W	L	0-1	0-0	11		5575

Final League Position: 11

GOALSCORERS

League (58): Evans 17 (4 pens), Madden 15 (1 pen), Hunter 8, Burns 7, Eastham 2, Biggins 1, Bolger 1, Holt 1, Husband 1, Marney 1, Nadesan 1, Soutar 1, Wallace J 1, Wallace R 1.
FA Cup (8): Madden 4 (1 pen), Burns 1, Evans 1 (1 pen), Garner 1, Hunter 1.
Carabao Cup (1): Holt 1.
Checkatrade Trophy (3): Dempsey 1, Long 1, McAleny 1.

Cairns A 46	Coyle L 41	Bolger C 5+6	Morgan C 21+2	Spurr T 2+2	Sowerby J 10+5	Dempsey K 5+9	Burns W 34+5	McAleny C 6+8	Grant R 2+2	Evans C 37+2	Marney D 15+1	Madden P 38+6	Hunter A 29+14	Holt J 29+4	Eastham A 43+2	Jones G 3	Sheron N 17+9	Husband J 32+1	Long C 1+7	Wallace J 11+7	Biggins H 8+15	Wallace R 34+2	Taylor R 8+2	Nadesan A 12+8	Soutar H 11	Garner G —+1	Rydel R 3+2	Baggley B —+3	Hill J 1+1	Clarke E 2	Southam M —+1	Mooney D —+1	*Match No.*
1	2^{3}	3	4	5	6^{2}	7	8	9^{1}	10	11	12	13	14																				1
1	5		4			8	12		9^{1}	10^{3}	6^{2}	14	11	2	3	7	13																2
1	5	13	4			8	12	14		10^{2}	11	7	9^{3}	2^{1}	3	6																	3
1	2		4				6	13	12	10^{1}	8	11^{3}	9^{2}	7	3			5	14														4
1	2		4				6	13		10^{1}	8	11^{2}	9	7	3			5	12														5
1	2		4	14			6■			10^{3}	8	11^{1}	9^{2}	7	3			5	13	12													6
1	2		4^{2}	12		13		6^{1}		11	8	10	9^{3}	7	3			5		14													7
1	2	4				12		10^{2}			8^{1}	6	9	7	3			5	11^{3}	13	14												8
1	2	4				8^{3}			14	11	6^{2}	10	9	7	3	5^{1}				12■		13											9
1	2	12		4^{1}		14	9			10				8^{2}	3			5	13		7^{3}	11	6										10
1	2						9					10	11		3		4	5		7^{1}	12	8	6										11
1	2		13				14			10^{1}		11	9	12	3		4	5^{3}		8^{2}		6	7										12
1	6		4			14	11					10	9	13	3		2		12^{3}	7^{1}		8^{2}	5										13
1	5^{3}	14	4			13	9			12		10	11	6^{2}	3		2■					8^{1}	7										14
1	2		4			6^{2}	9			10	7^{3}		11	13	3				14		12	8	5^{1}										15
1	2	13	4				11			10		12	9^{1}	7	3		6	5				8^{2}											16
1	2		4			14	10^{2}			11		12	9	7^{3}	3		6	5^{1}	13			8											17
1	6	4					10^{2}	13		12		9	11^{1}	7	3		2	5			14	8^{3}											18
1	5	4					12	13		11		10	9^{1}	8^{3}	3		7^{2}			14		6	2										19
1	2	12	4				6	8^{3}		11	7	10		14	3^{2}			5		9^{1}		13											20
1			4			12^{3}		14		11	7	10	13	8	3		2	5^{2}				9	6^{1}										21
1	2					13		9^{2}		10	6	11	5^{3}	7^{1}	3		4				12	8	14										22
1	2		13					9^{2}		10■	8	11	6^{3}	7^{1}	4		3				12	5	14										23
1	5		3				14			11	7	10	6^{1}	8^{2}	4		2^{3}			13	12	9											24
1	2	14	3			13	9^{2}			10	7■	11	6^{1}		4					12	8^{3}	5											25
1	2		3				6	14		11^{3}		10	12		4		13	5		7^{1}	8	9^{2}											26
1	2		4				9					10	12	7^{2}	3		14	5		8	13	6^{1}		11^{3}									27
1	2■		4				11					10^{1}	14	7	3		12	5		8	13	6^{3}		9^{2}									28
1			4				2^{3}			10		11	13	7^{2}	3		14	5		8	12	6		9^{1}									29
1			3				2	13		10		11	12	6^{2}	4			5		8		7		9^{1}									30
1					12		2^{1}			10		11	13	7^{2}	3			5		8	14	6		9^{3}	4								31
1	2				7					10		9	11^{1}		3		12	5		6^{2}	14	8^{3}		13	4								32
1	2				7^{3}		11			10		9	13	6^{1}	3		14	5				8^{2}		12	4								33
1	6				8^{2}		2			10		11	12	7^{1}	3		13	5			14			9^{3}	4								34
1	6				7		2			10		9	11^{2}		3		8^{1}	5						12	4	13							35
1					8		2			9		10^{3}	11^{1}	7	3			5				6^{2}		12	4		13	14					36
1	2				12		6			10		11	13	7	3		8^{1}					5^{3}		9^{2}	4		14						37
1	6				8		2			10		11^{1}	14	7	3			12				5^{2}		13	4		9^{3}						38
1	2				8		6			10		9		7^{1}	13		12	4				5^{3}		14	3		11^{2}						39
1	2				8^{1}		6			10		9	13		14			4			7^{3}	5		12	3		11^{2}						40
1	6						5			10		12	9^{1}		3		7	4			13	8^{2}		11^{3}	2■			14					41
1	6						2			10		9	13		3		7^{2}	4			8	5		11^{1}					12				42
1	2				14		6			11		10^{2}	9^{3}		4		8■	5			12	7^{1}		13					3				43
1	2				13		6			11		12	9		3			4			7	8		10^{2}						5^{1}			44
1	2				12		6					11	9		4			3			7	8		10						5^{1}			45
1	2				5		6^{1}					11	9		4			3			7^{2}	8		10^{3}				12			13	14	46

FA Cup
First Round Alfreton T (a) 4-1
Second Round Guiseley (a) 2-1
Third Round AFC Wimbledon (h) 2-3

Carabao Cup
First Round Crewe Alex (a) 1-1
(Fleetwood T won 4-3 on penalties)
Second Round Leicester C (a) 0-4

Checkatrade Trophy
Group B (N) Leicester C U21 (h) 2-2
(Leicester C U21 won 7-6 on penalties)
Group B (N) Rochdale (h) 0-2
Group B (N) Bury (a) 1-3

FOREST GREEN ROVERS

FOUNDATION

A football club was recorded at Forest Green as early as October 1889, established by Rev Edward Peach, a local Congregationalist minister. This club joined the Mid-Gloucestershire League for 1894–95 but disappeared around 1896 and was reformed as Forest Green Rovers in 1898. Rovers affiliated to the Gloucestershire county FA from 1899–1900 and competed in local leagues, mostly the Stroud & District and Dursley & District Leagues before joining the Gloucestershire Senior League North in 1937, where they remained until 1968. They became founder members of the Gloucestershire County League in 1968 and progressed to the Hellenic League in 1975. Success over Rainworth MW in the 1982 FA Vase final at Wembley was the start of the club's rise up the pyramid, firstly to the Southern League for the 1982–83 season and then the Football Conference from 1998–99. Rovers reached the play-offs in 2014–15 and 2015–16, losing to Bristol Rovers and Grimsby Town respectively, before finally achieving their goal of a place in the Football League with their 3-1 Play-Off victory over Tranmere Rovers on 14 May 2017.

The New Lawn Stadium, Another Way, Nailsworth, GL6 0FG.

Telephone: (0333) 123 1889.

Fax: (01453) 835 291.

Ticket Office: (0333) 123 1889.

Website: fgr.co.uk

Email: via website.

Ground Capacity: 5,012.

Record Attendance: 4,836 v Derby Co, FA Cup 3rd rd, 3 January 2009.

Pitch Measurements: 100m × 66m (109.5yd × 72yd).

Chairman: Dale Vince.

Chief Executive: Henry Staelens.

Manager: Mark Cooper.

Assistant Manager: Scott Lindsey.

Colours: Green and black hooped shirts, green shorts with black trim, green and black hooped socks.

Year Formed: 1889.

Previous Names: 1889, Forest Green; 1898, Forest Green Rovers; 1911, Nailsworth & Forest Green United; 1919 Forest Green Rovers; 1989, Stroud; 1992, Forest Green Rovers.

HONOURS

League Champions: Southern League – 1997–98.

FA Cup: 3rd rd – 2009, 2010.

League Cup: never past 2nd rd.

FA Trophy: *Runners-up:* 1998–99, 2000–01.

FA Vase: *Winners:* 1981–82.

THE SUN FACT FILE

Forest Green Rovers swept all before them in the 1920–21 season with their first team finishing as champions of both North Gloucestershire League and the Stroud & District League. In addition the club won the Gloucestershire Northern Junior Cup, defeating Cheltenham Town 3-0 in the final. The reserves were also successful, winning Division Three of the Stroud League.

Club Nicknames: Rovers, The Green, FGR, The Little Club on the Hill, Green Army, The Green Devils.

Grounds: 1890, The Lawn Ground; 2006, The New Lawn.

Record Victory: 8–0 v Fareham T, Southern League Southern Division, 1996–97; 8–0 v Hyde U, Football Conference, 10 August 2013.

Record Defeat: 0–10 v Gloucester, Mid-Gloucestershire League, 13 January 1900.

Most League Points (3 for a win): 74, FL 2, 2018–19.

Most League Goals: 68, FL 2, 2018–19.

Highest League Scorer in Season: Christian Doidge, 20, FL 2, 2017–18.

Most League Goals in Total Aggregate: Christian Doidge, 34, 2017–19.

Most League Goals in One Match: 3, George Williams v Newport Co, FL 2, 26 December 2018.

Most Capped Player: Omar Chaaban, 1 (5), Lebanon.

Most League Appearances: Reece Brown, 78, 2017–19.

Youngest League Player: Jordan Stevens, 17 years 171 days v Lincoln C, 12 September 2017.

Record Transfer Fee Received: £500,000 from Barnsley for Ethan Pinnock, June 2017.

Record Transfer Fee Paid: £25,000 to Bury for Adrian Randall, August 1999.

Football League Record: 2017 Promoted from National League; 2017– FL 2.

MANAGERS

Bill Thomas 1955–56
Eddie Cowley 1957–58
Don Cowley 1958–60
Jimmy Sewell 1966–67
Alan Morris 1967–68
Peter Goring 1968–79
Tony Morris 1979–80
Bob Mursell 1980–82
Roy Hillman 1982
Steve Millard 1983–87
John Evans 1987–90
Jeff Evans 1990
Bobby Jones 1990–91
Tim Harris 1991–92
Pat Casey 1992–94
Frank Gregan 1994–2000
Nigel Spink and David Norton 2000–01
Nigel Spink 2001–02
Colin Addison 2002–03
Tim Harris 2003–04
Alan Lewer 2004–05
Gary Owers 2005–06
Jim Harvey 2006–09
Dave Hockaday 2009–13
Adrian Pennock 2013–16
Mark Cooper May 2016–

LATEST SEQUENCES

Longest Sequence of League Wins: 4, 6.4.2019 – 22.4.2019.

Longest Sequence of League Defeats: 5, 9.12.2017 – 1.1.2018.

Longest Sequence of League Draws: 4, 11.8.2018 – 25.8.2018.

Longest Sequence of Unbeaten League Matches: 12, 4.8.2018 – 6.10.2018.

Longest Sequence Without a League Win: 10, 26.8.2017 – 14.10.2017.

Successive Scoring Runs: 13 from 25.8.2018.

Successive Non-scoring Runs: 3 from 9.12.2017.

TEN YEAR LEAGUE RECORD

		P	W	D	L	F	A	Pts	Pos
2009-10	Conf	46	12	9	23	50	76	45	21
2010-11	Conf	46	10	16	20	53	72	46	20
2011-12	Conf	46	19	13	14	66	45	70	10
2012-13	Conf	46	18	11	17	63	49	65	10
2013-14	Conf	46	19	10	17	80	66	67	10
2014-15	Conf	46	22	16	8	80	54	79*	5
2015-16	NL	46	26	11	9	69	42	89	2
2016-17	NL	46	25	11	10	88	56	86	3
2017-18	FL 2	46	13	8	25	54	77	47	21
2018-19	FL 2	46	20	14	12	68	47	74	5

**3 pts deducted.*

DID YOU KNOW ?

The first game at Forest Green Rovers' New Lawn Stadium saw Swindon Town visit for a pre-season friendly match in July 2006. Swindon won the game 3-2. The official opening came two months later when the occasion was marked by the England C international team playing against Forest Green.

FOREST GREEN ROVERS – SKY BET LEAGUE TWO 2018–19 LEAGUE RECORD

Match No.	*Date*	*Venue*	*Opponents*	*Result*		*H/T Score*	*Lg Pos.*	*Goalscorers*	*Attendance*
1	Aug 4	A	Grimsby T	W	4-1	0-1	2	Winchester [51], Collins (og) [67], Doidge 2 [70, 83]	5879
2	11	H	Oldham Ath	D	1-1	1-0	4	Reid [22]	2759
3	18	A	Bury	D	1-1	1-0	7	Doidge [29]	2853
4	21	H	Stevenage	D	0-0	0-0	9		1834
5	25	H	Swindon T	D	1-1	1-1	12	Doidge [5]	3458
6	Sept 1	A	Notts Co	W	3-1	1-0	7	Shephard [29], Reid [59], Grubb [84]	6049
7	8	H	Port Vale	D	1-1	1-0	9	Winchester [15]	2263
8	15	A	Milton Keynes D	D	1-1	0-1	12	Reid (pen) [80]	6638
9	22	H	Crawley T	W	1-0	0-0	7	Reid [70]	2089
10	29	A	Macclesfield T	D	1-1	0-0	7	Grubb [48]	1503
11	Oct 2	A	Cambridge U	W	3-1	1-1	5	Digby [34], Grubb [55], Worthington [88]	3059
12	6	H	Newport Co	D	1-1	1-1	6	Bennett (og) [18]	3081
13	13	A	Northampton T	L	1-2	1-0	8	Reid [43]	5073
14	20	H	Cheltenham T	D	1-1	0-1	9	Mills [75]	3582
15	23	H	Tranmere R	W	3-1	2-0	6	Brown [11], Shephard [39], Campbell [90]	2181
16	27	A	Exeter C	W	2-1	0-0	6	Brown [50], Shephard [72]	4983
17	Nov 3	A	Lincoln C	L	1-2	1-1	8	Brown [12]	8542
18	17	H	Morecambe	L	0-1	0-0	10		3085
19	24	A	Carlisle U	W	2-1	1-0	10	Morris [12], Winchester [71]	4166
20	27	H	Colchester U	L	0-1	0-1	10		1600
21	Dec 8	A	Yeovil T	W	2-1	0-0	8	Reid [90], Williams [90]	2529
22	22	H	Crewe Alex	W	1-0	1-0	7	Mills [45]	2388
23	26	A	Newport Co	W	4-1	2-1	7	Williams 3 [3, 52, 57], Campbell [43]	4203
24	29	A	Cheltenham T	D	2-2	0-0	6	Campbell [61], Williams [67]	5125
25	Jan 1	H	Northampton T	W	2-1	1-0	5	Williams [1], Archibald [90]	2909
26	12	A	Oldham Ath	D	0-0	0-0	7		4194
27	19	H	Bury	L	1-2	1-0	7	Brown [28]	2940
28	22	H	Grimsby T	W	3-0	2-0	6	Doidge 2 [29, 45], Brown [50]	1810
29	26	A	Stevenage	W	2-0	1-0	5	Shephard [13], Doidge [55]	2494
30	29	H	Mansfield T	D	1-1	0-1	4	Reid [70]	2428
31	Feb 9	H	Notts Co	L	1-2	0-0	6	Mills [63]	2871
32	12	A	Swindon T	L	0-2	0-2	7		6261
33	16	H	Yeovil T	W	3-0	2-0	5	Mondal [22], Doidge [31], Collins [58]	2449
34	23	A	Mansfield T	L	0-1	0-0	6		5256
35	Mar 2	H	Lincoln C	L	1-2	1-1	7	Brown [7]	3165
36	9	A	Morecambe	L	0-3	0-2	9		1528
37	12	A	Colchester U	W	3-0	2-0	6	Shephard [21], Brown [33], Doidge [81]	2871
38	16	H	Carlisle U	D	1-1	1-0	6	Brown [31]	2381
39	23	A	Port Vale	W	2-0	0-0	6	Brown 2 [69, 90]	4429
40	30	H	Milton Keynes D	L	1-2	0-1	6	Williams [63]	3220
41	Apr 6	A	Crawley T	W	2-1	1-1	6	Doidge 2 [34, 88]	2088
42	13	H	Macclesfield T	W	2-0	0-0	6	Doidge [56], Mills [88]	2386
43	19	A	Tranmere R	W	1-0	0-0	6	Mondal [47]	9468
44	22	H	Cambridge U	W	2-1	1-0	5	Gunning [24], Doidge [76]	2699
45	27	A	Crewe Alex	L	3-4	1-1	5	Brown [36], Mondal [47], Doidge [52]	3906
46	May 4	H	Exeter C	D	0-0	0-0	5		4537

Final League Position: 5

GOALSCORERS

League (68): Doidge 14, Brown 11, Reid 7 (1 pen), Williams 7, Shephard 5, Mills 4, Campbell 3, Grubb 3, Mondal 3, Winchester 3, Archibald 1, Collins 1, Digby 1, Gunning 1, Morris 1, Worthington 1, own goals 2.
FA Cup (0).
Carabao Cup (3): Campbell 1, Grubb 1, Winchester 1.
Checkatrade Trophy (6): Grubb 2, Pearce 2, Campbell 1, Williams 1.
League Two Play-offs (1): Mills 1.

Sanchez R 17	Shephard L 37 + 2	Rawson F 38	Gunning G 37 + 5	Mills J 44	Brown R 43 + 2	James L 31 + 4	Winchester C 44 + 1	Reid R 20 + 9	Doidge C 24 + 1	Williams G 25 + 13	Archibald T 4 + 10	Digby P 30 + 7	Grubb D 13 + 15	Campbell T 10 + 8	McGinley N 34 + 4	Worthington M 3 + 6	Morris B 2 + 2	Pearce I 1 + 3	Montgomery J 18	Collins L 6 + 5	McCoulsky S 3 + 10	Mondal J 8 + 10	Ward L 11 + 1	Liddle B — + 2	Godwin-Malife U 3 + 2	*Match No.*
1	2	3	4	5	6^{2}	7	8	9	10	11^{1}	12^{3}	13	14													1
1	2	3	4	5	6^{1}	7^{3}	8	9	10	11^{2}	13	12	14													2
1	2	3	4■	5	6^{2}	7	8	9^{1}	10	11^{3}		12	13	14												3
1	2	4		5	8	7	6	11	10	12	9^{1}	3														4
1	2	3		5	7	8	6	11^{2}	10	9^{1}		4	12	13												5
1	5	2	7	9	6^{3}	8^{2}	10^{1}	11		12		3	13		4	14										6
1	2	5■	8	6	11^{1}	9	7^{2}	10		12		4	13		3											7
1	5		4	8	6	7^{2}	11	10		14	13	2	9^{3}	12	3^{1}											8
1	5		3	9	7^{2}	8	6	11		12		2		10^{1}	4	13										9
1	5		2	9^{3}	7	8^{1}	6^{2}	11		10	12	3	13		4	14										10
1	5	3^{3}	13	8	7^{1}	6^{2}	12	11				2	9	10	4	14										11
1	2	3	4	5	6^{1}		8	10				7	11	9^{2}		13	12									12
1	5	3	12	9	7^{3}	6^{1}	8	11^{2}		13		2	10		4			14								13
1	2	3	13	5	14		6			11^{2}	9	7	10	12	4^{1}	8^{3}										14
	2	3	4	5	7^{2}	8	9^{3}					6	11^{1}	10	14	12		13	1							15
1	2		3	5	9	7	8^{1}				12	6	11^{2}	10	4					13						16
1			3	5	9	7	2	12		13	8^{3}	6	10^{1}	11^{2}	4			14								17
		3		5	9	7^{1}	2	11		8	10	6		12	4				1							18
		3	4	10	8^{1}	6	2	13		14	12	7			5	9^{2}	11^{3}		1							19
		2	4	9	10	7	6^{2}	13		14	12	3			5	8^{3}	11^{1}		1							20
1	2	3		5^{2}	10^{1}	6	7	11		13	14	8■	9^{3}		4		12									21
	5	2	3	9	6^{1}	7	8	11^{2}		10^{3}	13		12	14	4				1							22
	5	2	4	9	6	8	7	13		10^{3}			12	11^{2}	3^{1}				1	14						23
	5	2	3	9	7	6	8	13		10^{2}			12	11^{3}	4^{1}				1	14						24
	5	2	3	9	8	6^{2}	7			10	14	12	13	11^{3}	4^{1}				1							25
	5	4	3	9	7	8	6		13	10^{2}				11^{1}	2				1		12					26
	5	4	3	9	7	8^{2}	6		11^{3}	10^{1}				13	2				1		12	14				27
	5	2	3	9	7^{1}	14	6^{2}		11	10^{3}		8		13	4				1		12					28
	5	2	3	9	7	6	8^{2}		11	10^{1}		12			4				1			13				29
	5	2	3	9	7	12	8	13	11	10^{3}		6			4^{2}				1^{1}				14			30
	7	4	3	5	8	7^{2}	9^{3}	10^{1}	11	12		6									13	14	1			31
	5		3	9	7	6^{1}	8		10	11^{2}		4^{3}			2						13	14	1	12		32
		3	4	5^{2}	9		2		11	8		7			12					6^{1}	13	10^{3}	1	14		33
		3	4^{1}	5	9		2		11	8		6^{2}			13					7^{3}	12	10	1		14	34
		2	4	5	7^{2}		8		11	9		6	14		3^{3}				1	12	10^{1}	13				35
	14		4	2	13	5^{2}	6		10	9		8	7^{3}								11^{1}	12	1		3	36
	2^{2}	5	4	3	6	12	7	10^{3}	11						9					8^{1}		13	1		14	37
	5	2	6	9	7		8	10^{2}	11	12					4							13	1		3^{1}	38
	5	2	3		7	0^{1}	8	11^{2}	10	13		4			9							12	1			39
	2	3	8	5	7		6		10	11^{1}		4^{3}	13		12						14	9^{2}	1			40
	5	2	3^{1}	9	8		6		10	11^{2}		7^{3}	14		4					13		12	1			41
	2	3	12	5	9	14	6		11	10^{2}					4					7^{1}	13	8^{3}	1			42
	2	3	13	5	9		6		11	10^{2}		14	12		4				1	7^{1}		8^{3}				43
	2	3	4	5	9^{1}		6	12	11			13	10		7				1			8^{2}				44
	2	3	4	5	9		6	13	11				10^{2}		7				1		12	8^{1}				45
	13		7			6		12				4	10		5			9	1	3	11	8^{1}			2^{2}	46

FA Cup

First Round	Oxford U	(a)	0-0
Replay	Oxford U	(h)	0-3

Carabao Cup

First Round	Swindon T	(a)	1-0
Second Round	Wycombe W	(a)	2-2

(Wycombe W won 4-3 on penalties)

Checkatrade Trophy

Group E (S)	Cheltenham T	(h)	4-0
Group E (S)	Coventry C	(a)	1-1

(Coventry C won 4-2 on penalties)

Group E (S)	Arsenal U21	(h)	1-3

League Two Play-offs

Semi-Final 1st leg	Tranmere R	(a)	0-1
Semi-Final 2nd leg	Tranmere R	(h)	1-1

FULHAM

FOUNDATION

Churchgoers were responsible for the foundation of Fulham, which first saw the light of day as Fulham St Andrew's Church Sunday School FC in 1879. They won the West London Amateur Cup in 1887 and the championship of the West London League in its initial season of 1892–93. The name Fulham had been adopted in 1888.

Craven Cottage, Stevenage Road, London SW6 6HH.

Telephone: (0843) 208 1222.

Fax: (0870) 442 0236.

Ticket Office: (0843) 208 1234.

Website: www.fulhamfc.com

Email: enquiries@fulhamfc.com

Ground Capacity: 25,700.

Record Attendance: 49,335 v Millwall, Division 2, 8 October 1938.

Pitch Measurements: 100m × 65m (109.5yd × 71yd).

Chairman: Shahid Khan.

Chief Executive: Alistair Mackintosh.

Head Coach: Scott Parker.

Assistant Head Coach: Stuart Gray.

Colours: White shirts with black trim, black shorts with white trim, white socks with black trim.

Year Formed: 1879.

Turned Professional: 1898.

Reformed: 1987.

Previous Name: 1879, Fulham St Andrew's; 1888, Fulham.

Club Nickname: 'The Cottagers'.

Grounds: 1879, Star Road, Fulham; c.1883, Eel Brook Common, 1884, Lillie Road; 1885, Putney Lower Common; 1886, Ranelagh House, Fulham; 1888, Barn Elms, Castelnau; 1889, Purser's Cross (Roskell's Field), Parsons Green Lane; 1891, Eel Brook Common; 1891, Half Moon, Putney; 1895, Captain James Field, West Brompton; 1896, Craven Cottage.

First Football League Game: 3 September 1907, Division 2, v Hull C (h) L 0–1 – Skene; Ross, Lindsay; Collins, Morrison, Goldie; Dalrymple, Freeman, Bevan, Hubbard, Threlfall.

Record League Victory: 10–1 v Ipswich T, Division 1, 26 December 1963 – Macedo; Cohen, Langley; Mullery (1), Keetch, Robson (1); Key, Cook (1), Leggat (4), Haynes, Howfield (3).

Record Cup Victory: 7–0 v Swansea C, FA Cup 1st rd, 11 November 1995 – Lange; Jupp (1), Herrera, Barkus (Brooker (1)), Moore, Angus, Thomas (1), Morgan, Brazil (Hamill), Conroy (3) (Bolt), Cusack (1).

Record Defeat: 0–10 v Liverpool, League Cup 2nd rd 1st leg, 23 September 1986.

Most League Points (2 for a win): 60, Division 2, 1958–59 and Division 3, 1970–71.

HONOURS

League Champions: First Division – 2000–01; Division 2 – 1948–49; Second Division – 1998–99; Division 3S – 1931–32.
Runners-up: Division 2 – 1958–59; Division 3 – 1970–71; Third Division – 1996–97.

FA Cup: *Runners-up:* 1975.

League Cup: quarter-final – 1968, 1971, 2000, 2005.

European Competitions
UEFA Cup: 2002–03.
Europa League: 2009–10 *(runners-up)*, 2011–12.
Intertoto Cup: 2002 *(winners)*.

THE SUN FACT FILE

Bob Dennison was a versatile player with Fulham in the 1930s, but in the close season he would return to the North East of England to take part in professional sprint handicaps. Competing under the name R. Roberts (Amble) his greatest success was to win the 110-yard handicap at the Morpeth Olympic Games in 1938, worth £100 to the winner (equivalent to over £6,000 today).

Most League Points (3 for a win): 101, Division 2, 1998–99. 101, Division 1, 2000–01.

Most League Goals: 111, Division 3 (S), 1931–32.

Highest League Scorer in Season: Frank Newton, 43, Division 3 (S), 1931–32.

Most League Goals in Total Aggregate: Gordon Davies, 159, 1978–84, 1986–91.

Most League Goals in One Match: 5, Fred Harrison v Stockport Co, Division 2, 5 September 1908; 5, Bedford Jezzard v Hull C, Division 2, 8 October 1955; 5, Jimmy Hill v Doncaster R, Division 2, 15 March 1958; 5, Steve Earle v Halifax T, Division 3, 16 September 1969.

Most Capped Player: Johnny Haynes, 56, England.

Most League Appearances: Johnny Haynes, 594, 1952–70.

Youngest League Player: Harvey Elliott, 16 years 30 days v Wolverhampton W, 4 May 2019.

Record Transfer Fee Received: £15,000,000 from Tottenham H for Mousa Dembélé, August 2012.

Record Transfer Fee Paid: £22,800,000 to Marseille for André-Frank Zambo Anguissa, August 2018.

Football League Record: 1907 Elected to Division 2; 1928–32 Division 3 (S); 1932–49 Division 2; 1949–52 Division 1; 1952–59 Division 2; 1959–68 Division 1; 1968–69 Division 2; 1969–71 Division 3; 1971–80 Division 2; 1980–82 Division 3; 1982–86 Division 2; 1986–92 Division 3; 1992–94 Division 2; 1994–97 Division 3; 1997–99 Division 2; 1999–2001 Division 1; 2001–14 Premier League; 2014–18 FL C; 2018–19 Premier League; 2019– FL C.

LATEST SEQUENCES

Longest Sequence of League Wins: 12, 7.5.2000 – 18.10.2000.

Longest Sequence of League Defeats: 11, 2.12.1961 – 24.2.1962.

Longest Sequence of League Draws: 6, 23.12.2006 – 20.1.2007.

Longest Sequence of Unbeaten League Matches: 23, 23.12.2017 – 27.4.2018.

Longest Sequence Without a League Win: 15, 25.2.1950 – 23.8.1950.

Successive Scoring Runs: 26 from 28.3.1931.

Successive Non-scoring Runs: 6 from 21.8.1971.

MANAGERS

Harry Bradshaw 1904–09
Phil Kelso 1909–24
Andy Ducat 1924–26
Joe Bradshaw 1926–29
Ned Liddell 1929–31
Jim McIntyre 1931–34
Jimmy Hogan 1934–35
Jack Peart 1935–48
Frank Osborne 1948–64
(was Secretary-Manager or General Manager for most of this period and Team Manager 1953–56)
Bill Dodgin Snr 1949–53
Duggie Livingstone 1956–58
Bedford Jezzard 1958–64
(General Manager for last two months)
Vic Buckingham 1965–68
Bobby Robson 1968
Bill Dodgin Jnr 1968–72
Alec Stock 1972–76
Bobby Campbell 1976–80
Malcolm Macdonald 1980–84
Ray Harford 1984–96
Ray Lewington 1986–90
Alan Dicks 1990–91
Don Mackay 1991–94
Ian Branfoot 1994–96
(continued as General Manager)
Micky Adams 1996–97
Ray Wilkins 1997–98
Kevin Keegan 1998–99
(Chief Operating Officer)
Paul Bracewell 1999–2000
Jean Tigana 2000–03
Chris Coleman 2003–07
Lawrie Sanchez 2007
Roy Hodgson 2007–10
Mark Hughes 2010–11
Martin Jol 2011–13
Rene Muelenstein 2013–14
Felix Magath 2014
Kit Symons 2014–15
Slavisa Jokanovic 2015–18
Claudio Ranieri 2018–19
Scott Parker February 2019–

TEN YEAR LEAGUE RECORD

		P	W	D	L	F	A	Pts	Pos
2009-10	PR Lge	38	12	10	16	39	46	46	12
2010-11	PR Lge	38	11	16	11	49	43	49	8
2011-12	PR Lge	38	14	10	14	48	51	52	9
2012-13	PR Lge	38	11	10	17	50	60	43	12
2013-14	PR Lge	38	9	5	24	40	85	32	19
2014-15	FL C	46	14	10	22	62	83	52	17
2015-16	FL C	46	12	15	19	66	79	51	20
2016-17	FL C	46	22	14	10	85	57	80	6
2017-18	FL C	46	25	13	8	79	46	88	3
2018-19	PR Lge	38	7	5	26	34	81	26	19

DID YOU KNOW ?

Fulham had one of the strongest teams of footballing cricketers in London in the years between the wars. The Cottagers reached the final of the London *Evening News* Cricket Cup for Footballers in four of the first five seasons it was contested, winning the trophy in both 1927 and 1928.

FULHAM – PREMIER LEAGUE 2018–19 LEAGUE RECORD

Match No.	*Date*	*Venue*	*Opponents*	*Result*		*H/T Score*	*Lg Pos.*	*Goalscorers*	*Attendance*
1	Aug 11	H	Crystal Palace	L	0-2	0-1	17		24,821
2	18	A	Tottenham H	L	1-3	0-1	19	Mitrovic [52]	58,297
3	26	H	Burnley	W	4-2	3-2	12	Seri [4], Mitrovic 2 [36, 38], Schurrle [83]	23,438
4	Sept 1	A	Brighton & HA	D	2-2	1-0	11	Schurrle [43], Mitrovic [62]	30,526
5	15	A	Manchester C	L	0-3	0-2	15		53,307
6	22	H	Watford	D	1-1	0-1	15	Mitrovic [78]	23,418
7	29	A	Everton	L	0-3	0-0	16		38,788
8	Oct 7	H	Arsenal	L	1-5	1-1	17	Schurrle [44]	25,401
9	20	A	Cardiff C	L	2-4	2-2	18	Schurrle [11], Sessegnon, R [34]	29,681
10	27	H	Bournemouth	L	0-3	0-1	18		25,071
11	Nov 5	A	Huddersfield T	L	0-1	0-1	20		17,082
12	11	A	Liverpool	L	0-2	0-1	20		53,128
13	24	H	Southampton	W	3-2	2-1	19	Mitrovic 2 [33, 63], Schurrle [43]	24,603
14	Dec 2	A	Chelsea	L	0-2	0-1	20		40,551
15	5	H	Leicester C	D	1-1	1-0	20	Kamara [42]	22,881
16	8	A	Manchester U	L	1-4	0-3	20	Kamara (pen) [67]	74,523
17	15	H	West Ham U	L	0-2	0-2	20		24,081
18	22	A	Newcastle U	D	0-0	0-0	20		51,237
19	26	H	Wolverhampton W	D	1-1	0-0	19	Sessegnon, R [74]	24,382
20	29	H	Huddersfield T	W	1-0	0-0	18	Mitrovic [90]	24,423
21	Jan 1	A	Arsenal	L	1-4	0-1	19	Kamara [69]	59,887
22	12	A	Burnley	L	1-2	1-2	19	Schurrle [2]	19,316
23	20	H	Tottenham H	L	1-2	1-0	19	Llorente (og) [17]	24,807
24	29	H	Brighton & HA	W	4-2	0-2	19	Chambers [47], Mitrovic 2 [58, 74], Vietto [79]	22,008
25	Feb 2	A	Crystal Palace	L	0-2	0-1	19		25,355
26	9	H	Manchester U	L	0-3	0-2	19		25,001
27	22	A	West Ham U	L	1-3	1-2	19	Babel [3]	59,950
28	27	A	Southampton	L	0-2	0-2	19		27,597
29	Mar 3	H	Chelsea	L	1-2	1-2	19	Chambers [27]	24,900
30	9	A	Leicester C	L	1-3	0-1	19	Ayite [51]	32,017
31	17	H	Liverpool	L	1-2	0-1	19	Babel [74]	25,043
32	30	H	Manchester C	L	0-2	0-2	19		25,001
33	Apr 2	A	Watford	L	1-4	1-1	19	Babel [33]	17,301
34	13	H	Everton	W	2-0	0-0	19	Cairney [46], Babel [69]	24,971
35	20	A	Bournemouth	W	1-0	0-0	19	Mitrovic (pen) [53]	10,511
36	27	H	Cardiff C	W	1-0	0-0	19	Babel [79]	23,822
37	May 4	A	Wolverhampton W	L	0-1	0-0	19		30,456
38	12	H	Newcastle U	L	0-4	0-2	19		24,979

Final League Position: 19

GOALSCORERS

League (34): Mitrovic 11 (1 pen), Schurrle 6, Babel 5, Kamara 3 (1 pen), Chambers 2, Sessegnon R 2, Ayite 1, Cairney 1, Seri 1, Vietto 1, own goal 1.
FA Cup (1): Odoi 1.
Carabao Cup (5): Kamara 2, Bryan 1, Christie 1, De La Torre 1.
Checkatrade Trophy (1): Thompson 1.

Ramirez F 2	Christie C 19 + 9	Chambers C 29 + 2	Le Marchand M 25 + 1	Bryan J 27 + 1	Cairney T 24 + 7	McDonald K 10 + 5	Seri J 27 + 5	Schurrle A 21 + 3	Mitrovic A 37	Sessegnon R 26 + 9	Kamara A 5 + 8	Vietto L 10 + 10	Johansen S 4 + 8	Fosu-Mensah T 10 + 2	Zambo A 16 + 6	Bettinelli M 7	Odoi D 29 + 2	Mawson A 13 + 2	Ayite F 3 + 13	Ream T 25 + 1	Sergio Rico G 29	Kebano N — + 7	Cisse I 1 + 2	Babel R 15 + 1	Nordtveit H 4 + 1	Markovic L — + 1	Elliott H — + 2	*Match No.*
1	2	3	4	5^{1}	6	7	8^{2}	9^{3}	10	11	12	13	14															1
1	13	3	4	5^{3}	6^{1}		8	14	10	9	11^{2}		12	2	7													2
		12	4	5^{2}	8^{1}	7	6	9^{3}	10	14		11		2	13	1	3											3
		14	5			7	8	11^{3}	10	13		9^{1}	12	2	6^{2}	1	3	4										4
	2					7	6^{1}	11	10	5		9^{2}	8		12	1	3	4	13									5
		4				7^{3}	8	11	10	5		9	6^{2}	2	14	1	12	3^{1}	13									6
	12			5	13		8^{1}	10	11	9		6^{2}		2^{3}	7	1	3		14	4								7
	5		4			13	7	11	10	8	12	9^{2}	14		6^{3}	1	2			3^{1}								8
		2^{2}	5			7	8^{3}	9	10	11		14	6^{1}			1	3	12	13	4								9
			5^{2}		12	6▪	7^{1}	9	11	10	8			2	13		3			4	1							10
	13		4		7	12^{3}	8	11	10	5		9^{1}	14	2^{2}	6		3				1							11
	2	7	5		9^{1}		12	8^{2}	11	10		13	14		6^{3}		3	4			1							12
	2	6	5		9		7^{3}	8^{2}	11^{1}	10	13		12				3	4	14		1							13
	2	7	5		9^{1}		6		11	10^{3}	12		8^{2}				3	4	13		1	14						14
	2^{1}	6	5^{2}	13	12		7		11	10	8	9^{3}					3	4		14	1							15
				5	9^{1}		6	8^{3}	11^{2}	10	12	13			7▪		2	3		4	1		14					16
	12	6		5	8		7^{1}	10^{2}	11		9		13				2	3		4^{3}	1	14						17
	5	6		8	9^{1}		7	11^{2}	10		12						2	3	13	4	1							18
	5	6		8	13	14	7^{1}	11^{2}	10	12	9^{3}						2	3		4	1							19
	5	6	13	8	9		7^{1}		11	14	12	10^{2}					2	3^{3}		4	1							20
	5^{1}		3	8	6		14	11^{2}	10	9	13			12			2			4	1		7^{3}					21
	5	6	3	8^{3}	13		7	9^{2}	10	11^{1}		12					2			4	1	14						22
	5	6	3	8			7^{2}	9^{3}	10	12							2			4	1	13	14	11^{1}				23
	5	6	3	8^{2}	12		7	9^{3}	10	14		13					2			4^{1}	1			11				24
	5^{2}	6	3	8	9		7		10			12		13			2		14	4^{3}	1			11^{1}				25
	12	6	3	5^{1}	13		7	8^{3}	11	14		9					2			4	1			10^{2}				26
		7		5	6		8^{2}		11	9^{1}					13		2			4	1			10	3	12		27
		6		5	9^{1}	7^{2}			11	13		12			8		2			4	1			10	3			28
		6		5	9^{2}	7^{1}			11	10		14			12		2		13	4	1			8^{3}	3			29
		6		5	8	7^{2}	13		10	11^{1}		14					2		12	4	1			9^{3}	3			30
	13	3		5	6^{3}		8^{1}		10	12				2^{2}	7				9	4	1	14		11				31
	2	5	4	6	9^{3}	14		13		10				3	8				7^{2}		1	12		11^{1}				32
	5	2	3	8	7^{1}	14	12	13	10	9					6					4^{3}	1			11^{2}				33
	12	6	3	5	9		13		11	8				2^{1}	7^{3}		14			4	1			10^{2}				34
	12	6	3	5			9^{3}		11	8					7^{1}		2		13	4	1			10^{2}	14			35
	12	6	3	5	9				11	8^{2}					7		2^{3}	13	14	4	1			10^{1}				36
	3	8	4	6	7				10	2^{2}					9^{1}				12	5	1			11			13	37
	2^{1}	8	4	5	9				11	10^{2}					7			3	8^{3}		1	14		12			13	38

FA Cup

Third Round	Oldham Ath	(h)	1-2

Carabao Cup

Second Round	Exeter C	(h)	2-0
Third Round	Millwall	(a)	3-1
Fourth Round	Manchester C	(a)	0-2

Checkatrade Trophy (Fulham U21)

Group F (S)	Oxford U	(a)	0-3
Group F (S)	Wycombe W	(a)	1-2
Group F (S)	Northampton T	(a)	0-2

GILLINGHAM

FOUNDATION

The success of the pioneering Royal Engineers of Chatham excited the interest of the residents of the Medway Towns and led to the formation of many clubs including Excelsior. After winning the Kent Junior Cup and the Chatham District League in 1893, Excelsior decided to go for bigger things and it was at a meeting in the Napier Arms, Brompton, in 1893 that New Brompton FC came into being, buying and developing the ground which is now Priestfield Stadium. They changed their name to Gillingham in 1913, when they also changed their strip from black and white stripes to predominantly blue.

MEMS Priestfield Stadium, Redfern Avenue, Gillingham, Kent ME7 4DD.

Telephone: (01634) 300 000.

Fax: (01634) 850 986.

Ticket Office: (01634) 300 000 (option 1).

Website: www.gillinghamfootballclub.com

Email: info@gillinghamfootballclub.com

Ground Capacity: 10,500.

Record Attendance: 23,002 v QPR, FA Cup 3rd rd, 10 January 1948.

Pitch Measurements: 100.5m × 64m (110yd × 70yd).

Chairman: Paul Scally.

Manager: Steve Evans.

First-Team Coach: Mark Patterson.

Colours: Blue shirts with black stripes, blue shorts with black trim, blue socks with white trim.

Year Formed: 1893.

Turned Professional: 1894.

Previous Name: 1893, New Brompton; 1913, Gillingham.

Club Nickname: 'The Gills'.

Ground: 1893, Priestfield Stadium (renamed KRBS Priestfield Stadium 2009, MEMS Priestfield Stadium 2011).

First Football League Game: 28 August 1920, Division 3, v Southampton (h) D 1–1 – Branfield; Robertson, Sissons; Battiste, Baxter, Wigmore; Holt, Hall, Gilbey (1), Roe, Gore.

Record League Victory: 10–0 v Chesterfield, Division 3, 5 September 1987 – Kite; Haylock, Pearce, Shipley (2) (Lillis), West, Greenall (1), Pritchard (2), Shearer (2), Lovell, Elsey (2), David Smith (1).

Record Cup Victory: 10–1 v Gorleston, FA Cup 1st rd, 16 November 1957 – Brodie; Parry, Hannaway; Riggs, Boswell, Laing; Payne, Fletcher (2), Saunders (5), Morgan (1), Clark (2).

Record Defeat: 2–9 v Nottingham F, Division 3 (S), 18 November 1950.

Most League Points (2 for a win): 62, Division 4, 1973–74.

HONOURS

League Champions: FL 2 – 2012–13; Division 4 – 1963–64.
Runners-up: Third Division – 1995–96; Division 4 – 1973–74.

FA Cup: 6th rd – 2000.

League Cup: 4th rd – 1964, 1997.

THE Sun FACT FILE

After losing their Football League place in 1938, Gillingham dropped into the Southern League for the following season. Over the next five peacetime seasons they finished in the top five each time and when the Football League expanded to 92 clubs for the 1950–51 campaign the Gills were elected to one of the vacancies.

Most League Points (3 for a win): 85, Division 2, 1999–2000.

Most League Goals: 90, Division 4, 1973–74.

Highest League Scorer in Season: Ernie Morgan, 31, Division 3 (S), 1954–55; Brian Yeo, 31, Division 4, 1973–74.

Most League Goals in Total Aggregate: Brian Yeo, 135, 1963–75.

Most League Goals in One Match: 6, Fred Cheesmur v Merthyr T, Division 3 (S), 26 April 1930.

Most Capped Player: Andrew Crofts, 13 (includes 1 on loan from Brighton & HA) (29), Wales.

Most League Appearances: John Simpson, 571, 1957–72.

Youngest League Player: Luke Freeman, 15 years 247 days v Hartlepool U, 24 November 2007.

Record Transfer Fee Received: £1,500,000 from Manchester C for Robert Taylor, November 1999.

Record Transfer Fee Paid: £600,000 to Reading for Carl Asaba, August 1998.

Football League Record: 1920 Original Member of Division 3; 1921 Division 3 (S); 1938 Failed re-election; Southern League 1938–44; Kent League 1944–46; Southern League 1946–50; 1950 Re-elected to Division 3 (S); 1958–64 Division 4; 1964–71 Division 3; 1971–74 Division 4; 1974–89 Division 3; 1989–92 Division 4; 1992–96; Division 3; 1996–2000 Division 2; 2000–04 Division 1; 2004–05 FL C; 2005–08 FL 1; 2008–09 FL 2; 2009–10 FL 1; 2010–13 FL 2; 2013– FL 1.

LATEST SEQUENCES

Longest Sequence of League Wins: 7, 18.12.1954 – 29.1.1955.

Longest Sequence of League Defeats: 10, 20.9.1988 – 5.11.1988.

Longest Sequence of League Draws: 5, 21.1.2017 – 14.2.2017.

Longest Sequence of Unbeaten League Matches: 20, 13.10.1973 – 10.2.1974.

Longest Sequence Without a League Win: 15, 1.4.1972 – 2.9.1972.

Successive Scoring Runs: 20 from 31.10.1959.

Successive Non-scoring Runs: 6 from 11.2.1961.

MANAGERS

W. Ironside Groombridge 1896–1906 *(Secretary-Manager)* *(previously Financial Secretary)*
Steve Smith 1906–08
W. I. Groombridge 1908–19 *(Secretary-Manager)*
George Collins 1919–20
John McMillan 1920–23
Harry Curtis 1923–26
Albert Hoskins 1926–29
Dick Hendrie 1929–31
Fred Mavin 1932–37
Alan Ure 1937–38
Bill Harvey 1938–39
Archie Clark 1939–58
Harry Barratt 1958–62
Freddie Cox 1962–65
Basil Hayward 1966–71
Andy Nelson 1971–74
Len Ashurst 1974–75
Gerry Summers 1975–81
Keith Peacock 1981–87
Paul Taylor 1988
Keith Burkinshaw 1988–89
Damien Richardson 1989–92
Glenn Roeder 1992–93
Mike Flanagan 1993–95
Neil Smillie 1995
Tony Pulis 1995–99
Peter Taylor 1999–2000
Andy Hessenthaler 2000–04
Stan Ternent 2004–05
Neale Cooper 2005
Ronnie Jepson 2005–07
Mark Stimson 2007–10
Andy Hessenthaler 2010–12
Martin Allen 2012–13
Peter Taylor 2013–14
Justin Edinburgh 2015–17
Adrian Pennock 2017
Steve Lovell 2017–19
Steve Evans May 2019–

TEN YEAR LEAGUE RECORD

		P	W	D	L	F	A	Pts	Pos
2009-10	FL 1	46	12	14	20	48	64	50	21
2010-11	FL 2	46	17	17	12	67	57	68	8
2011-12	FL 2	46	20	10	16	79	62	70	8
2012-13	FL 2	46	23	14	9	66	39	83	1
2013-14	FL 1	46	15	8	23	60	79	53	17
2014-15	FL 1	46	16	14	16	65	66	62	12
2015-16	FL 1	46	19	12	15	71	56	69	9
2016-17	FL 1	46	12	14	20	59	79	50	20
2017-18	FL 1	46	13	17	16	50	55	56	17
2018-19	FL 1	46	15	10	21	61	72	55	13

DID YOU KNOW ?

Gillingham attracted their best ever attendances in 1951–52, their second season back in the Football League. An average of 12,576 was attracted to Priestfield Stadium, a significant improvement on the club's pre-war attendance figures which were generally around half this figure.

GILLINGHAM – SKY BET LEAGUE ONE 2018–19 LEAGUE RECORD

Match No.	*Date*	*Venue*	*Opponents*	*Result*		*H/T Score*	*Lg Pos.*	*Goalscorers*	*Atten-dance*
1	Aug 4	A	Accrington S	W	2-0	2-0	2	Hanlan [23], Parker [43]	2201
2	11	H	Burton Alb	W	3-1	1-1	4	Eaves 2 [35, 77], O'Neill [51]	5016
3	18	A	Walsall	L	1-2	0-2	5	Eaves [90]	4361
4	22	H	Sunderland	L	1-4	1-3	9	Eaves [3]	8438
5	25	H	Coventry C	D	1-1	0-0	9	List [70]	4880
6	Sept 1	A	Barnsley	L	1-2	0-2	12	Parker [61]	11,434
7	8	H	AFC Wimbledon	L	0-1	0-0	14		5246
8	15	A	Rochdale	L	0-3	0-2	20		2925
9	22	H	Peterborough U	L	2-4	0-1	21	Reilly [50], Byrne [53]	4407
10	29	A	Shrewsbury T	D	2-2	1-0	21	Hanlan [18], Eaves [90]	5695
11	Oct 6	A	Portsmouth	W	2-0	2-0	19	Eaves [26], Lacey [45]	18,158
12	13	H	Southend U	L	0-2	0-0	19		5584
13	20	A	Doncaster R	D	3-3	2-0	19	Fuller [7], Eaves [25], Ehmer [88]	6891
14	23	A	Plymouth Arg	L	1-3	0-2	20	O'Neill [76]	8754
15	27	H	Bradford C	W	4-0	0-0	18	Charles [48], Eaves 2 [65, 90], List [69]	4399
16	Nov 3	H	Fleetwood T	W	3-0	2-0	17	Hanlan [11], Eaves 2 [18, 55]	3916
17	6	H	Blackpool	L	0-1	0-0	17		4055
18	17	A	Oxford U	L	0-1	0-0	19		6628
19	24	H	Luton T	L	1-3	0-1	19	Eaves [72]	5671
20	27	A	Bristol R	W	2-1	1-0	18	List [8], Reilly [59]	6983
21	Dec 8	A	Scunthorpe U	W	2-0	0-0	16	Eaves [54], Parrett [56]	3054
22	15	H	Wycombe W	D	2-2	0-2	16	Eaves [56], Parker [76]	4687
23	22	A	Charlton Ath	L	0-2	0-2	19		12,836
24	26	H	Portsmouth	W	2-0	1-0	17	Parker [45], Reilly (pen) [90]	6940
25	29	H	Doncaster R	L	1-3	0-1	18	Reilly [88]	4791
26	Jan 1	A	Southend U	L	0-2	0-1	18		7903
27	12	A	Burton Alb	W	3-2	2-0	17	List [24], Reilly (pen) [45], Rees [90]	2634
28	19	H	Walsall	L	0-3	0-2	18		3975
29	29	H	Accrington S	D	0-0	0-0	18		3423
30	Feb 2	A	Coventry C	D	1-1	0-0	19	Eaves (pen) [90]	26,741
31	9	H	Barnsley	L	1-4	0-2	21	List [81]	4791
32	16	H	Scunthorpe U	W	1-0	1-0	17	Byrne [30]	4170
33	19	A	Sunderland	L	2-4	2-2	17	Eaves [6], Hanlan [40]	28,364
34	23	A	Wycombe W	W	1-0	0-0	17	Charles [83]	4879
35	Mar 2	A	Fleetwood T	D	1-1	0-0	18	Eaves [83]	3019
36	9	H	Oxford U	W	1-0	0-0	13	Hanlan [89]	4991
37	12	H	Bristol R	L	0-1	0-0	17		3938
38	16	A	Luton T	D	2-2	0-1	16	Eaves [53], O'Neill [79]	9963
39	23	A	AFC Wimbledon	W	4-2	2-1	12	Hanlan [40], Burke [42], Da Silva Lopes [50], Eaves [83]	4847
40	30	H	Rochdale	D	1-1	1-1	13	Byrne [45]	4686
41	Apr 6	A	Peterborough U	L	0-2	0-0	13		8331
42	13	H	Shrewsbury T	L	0-2	0-0	15		4109
43	19	H	Plymouth Arg	W	3-1	0-1	13	Charles [56], Byrne [58], Hanlan [90]	5987
44	22	A	Bradford C	D	1-1	0-1	13	Hanlan [53]	15,686
45	27	H	Charlton Ath	L	0-2	0-2	15		8047
46	May 4	A	Blackpool	W	3-0	3-0	13	Hanlan [7], Eaves 2 [30, 39]	9571

Final League Position: 13

GOALSCORERS

League (61): Eaves 21 (1 pen), Hanlan 9, List 5, Reilly 5 (2 pens), Byrne 4, Parker 4, Charles 3, O'Neill 3, Burke 1, Da Silva Lopes 1, Ehmer 1, Fuller 1, Lacey 1, Parrett 1, Rees 1.
FA Cup (7): List 2, Eaves 1 (1 pen), Ehmer 1, O'Neill 1, Oldaker 1, Rees 1.
Carabao Cup (0).
Checkatrade Trophy (2): List 1, Stevenson 1.

Holy T 46	O'Neill L 33 + 5	Ehmer M 39 + 1	Zakuani G 29	Garmston B 13 + 6	Charles R 16 + 10	Bingham B 15 + 6	Parrett D 19 + 8	Byrne M 45	Hanlan B 35 + 4	Parker J 19 + 2	Eaves T 35 + 8	Wilkinson C 2 + 5	Reilly C 18 + 7	Fuller B 37 + 2	List E 17 + 20	Stevenson B 1 + 2	Lacey A 13 + 3	Rees J 7 + 11	Nasseri D — + 4	Ogilvie C 29 + 2	Oldaker D 11 + 2	M'Bo N — + 1	Burke G 12	Da Silva Lopes L 12 + 2	King B 1 + 2	Campbell T 2 + 3	Match No.
1	2	3	4	5	6	7	8	9	10¹	11	12																1
1	2	3	4	5	6	7	9¹	8	10	11	12																2
1	2³	3	4	5	7	6¹		8	10²	9	11	12	13	14													3
1	2³	3	4	5	6	8²		7	10¹	9	11		13		12	14											4
1	2	3	4	5	7³	6		8¹	10²	9	11	14	12		13												5
1		4	3²	5		8			6³	9	10	14	7	2	11¹		12	13									6
1	12	3		5				7	11²		10	9	8	2	13		4	6¹									7
1	9³	3		5			6¹	7	14	11²	10		8	2	12		4		13								8
1		3	4		9³		6	7	10¹	11	12	14	8²	2				13		5							9
1	5	3	4	9¹			7²	6	11	10³	14		8	12			2	13									10
1	5	3	4				7	6	11¹		10		8	9	12		2										11
1	2	3	4³	13			9	7			10	14	8¹	5	11	12	6²										12
1	2²	3	4			13		7		11	10		8	5		9³	6¹		14	12							13
1	2	3	4	12		14		6			9	11¹	8²	5	10			7³	13								14
1	2	3	4		9¹	6³	14	8	10²		11			5	12				13		7						15
1	2	3	4		9²	6¹	14	8	10³		11			5	13					12	7						16
1	5²	2	3		9³		13	6	10	14	11			4	12					8¹	7						17
1	2	3	4		8	6		9	10		11			5	7												18
1	2	3	4	14		8³	6¹	7		13	10			5	11			9²			12						19
1	13	4	3²	12		14		6		11	10		7■	2	9¹					5	8³						20
1		4¹	3			13	6²	7		11	10			2	9		12			5	8						21
1			4	12			7	8	13	9	10			2	11²		3			5	6¹						22
1	13		4		14		8	7	10³	11			12	2²	9		3			5	6¹						23
1	13		4			12	6²	7	10¹	9³			8	2	11		3			5		14					24
1	14		4			12	6¹	8	10³	9	13		7	2²	11		3			5							25
1	5		3	9		7¹		6		11	10		8²		13		2	12		4							26
1	5	14	3²	8	9³			6	12	11			7		10		2	13		4¹							27
1	5		3	9	13			7	14	10²	12		8¹		11		2³	6		4							28
1		3	4		12			8	11		10			2	9¹			6		5	7						29
1		3	4					8	11		10			2	9²			6		5¹			7	12	13		30
1		3	4		14		13	7	8		11			2	12			6²		5¹			9		10³		31
1	2	3				8²		6	10		11		13	5	14					4	12		9¹	7³			32
1	2	3			12		14	6	11		10			5	13					4	8³		9¹	7²			33
1	2	3			14	6²	12	7	11		10¹			5						4			9³	8		13	34
1	2	3					6	7	11¹		10			5	12					4			9	8			35
1	2	3			12		6¹	7	10		11		13	5	14					4			9²	8³			36
1	2	3			9¹			7	10		11		8	5	12					4	6⁷			13			37
1	2	3						8	11		10		8	5				12		4			9	7¹			38
1	2	3			12		14	7	11²		10		8	5	13					4			9³	6¹			39
1	2	3			12		6¹	7	10		11			5				13		4			9²	8			40
1	2	3			12³		6	7²	10		11			5	13					4			9¹	8	14		41
1	2	3				8²	6³	7	11		10			5	12			13		4			9¹			14	42
1	2	3			9³	8¹	7	6	11		10²			5	13			14		4						12	43
1	2	3		12	9			7	10		14			5³	11			13		4				6²		8¹	44
1	2	3			7¹		13	6	10		12			5	9²			14		4				8		11³	45
1		3		5	6			7	10		11¹		13	2	14		12			4	8³			9²			46

FA Cup

First Round	Hartlepool U	(h)	0-0
Replay (*aet*)	Hartlepool U	(a)	4-3
Second Round	Slough	(a)	1-0
Third Round	Cardiff C	(h)	1-0
Fourth Round	Swansea C	(a)	1-4

Carabao Cup

First Round	Millwall	(a)	0-0

(Millwall won 3-1 on penalties)

Checkatrade Trophy

Group A (S)	Portsmouth	(a)	0-4
Group A (S)	Tottenham H U21	(h)	0-4
Group A (S)	Crawley T	(h)	2-1

GRIMSBY TOWN

FOUNDATION

Grimsby Pelham FC, as they were first known, came into being at a meeting held at the Wellington Arms in September 1878. Pelham is the family name of big landowners in the area, the Earls of Yarborough. The receipts for their first game amounted to 6s. 9d. (equivalent to approx. £25 today). After a year, the club name was changed to Grimsby Town.

Blundell Park, Cleethorpes, North East Lincolnshire DN35 7PY.

Telephone: (01472) 605 050.

Ticket Office: (01472) 605 050 (option 4).

Website: www.grimsby-townfc.co.uk

Email: enquiries@gtfc.co.uk

Ground Capacity: 8,933.

Record Attendance: 31,651 v Wolverhampton W, FA Cup 5th rd, 20 February 1937.

Pitch Measurements: 101.5m × 68.5m (111yd × 75yd).

Head Director: John Fenty.

Chief Executive: Ian Fleming.

Manager: Michael Jolley.

Assistant Manager: Anthony Limbrick.

Colours: Black and white striped shirts with red trim, black shorts with red and white trim, red socks with black and white trim.

Year Formed. 1878. ***Turned Professional:*** 1890. ***Ltd Co.:*** 1890.

Previous Name: 1878, Grimsby Pelham; 1879, Grimsby Town.

Club Nickname: 'The Mariners'.

Grounds: 1880, Clee Park; 1889, Abbey Park; 1899, Blundell Park.

First Football League Game: 3 September 1892, Division 2, v Northwich Victoria (h) W 2–1 – Whitehouse; Lundie, T. Frith; C. Frith, Walker, Murrell; Higgins, Henderson, Brayshaw, Riddoch (2), Ackroyd.

Record League Victory: 9–2 v Darwen, Division 2, 15 April 1899 – Bagshaw; Lockie, Nidd; Griffiths, Bell (1), Nelmes; Jenkinson (3), Richards (1), Cockshutt (3), Robinson, Chadburn (1).

Record Cup Victory: 8–0 v Darlington, FA Cup 2nd rd, 21 November 1885 – G. Atkinson; J. H. Taylor, H. Taylor; Hall, Kimpson, Hopewell; H. Atkinson (1), Garnham, Seal (3), Sharman, Monument (4).

Record Defeat: 1–9 v Arsenal, Division 1, 28 January 1931.

Most League Points (2 for a win): 68, Division 3 (N), 1955–56.

Most League Points (3 for a win): 83, Division 3, 1990–91.

HONOURS

League Champions: Division 2 – 1900–01, 1933–34; Division 3 – 1979–80; Division 3N – 1925–26, 1955–56; Division 4 – 1971–72.
Runners-up: Division 2 – 1928–29; Division 3 – 1961–62; Division 3N – 1951–52; Division 4 – 1978–79, 1989–90. Conference – (4th) 2015–16 *(promoted via play-offs).*

FA Cup: semi-final – 1936, 1939.

League Cup: 5th rd – 1980, 1985.

League Trophy Winners: 1998.
Runners-up: 2008.

THE SUN FACT FILE

Grimsby Town adopted their traditional black and white shirts for the start of their 1910–11 campaign in the Midland League after the club's directors looked for a change of luck following their failure to be re-elected to the Football League. The Mariners, who previously sported chocolate and blue quartered shirts, were elected back to the Football League 12 months later and the black and white stripes were retained.

Most League Goals: 103, Division 2, 1933–34.

Highest League Scorer in Season: Pat Glover, 42, Division 2, 1933–34.

Most League Goals in Total Aggregate: Pat Glover, 180, 1930–39.

Most League Goals in One Match: 6, Tommy McCairns v Leicester Fosse, Division 2, 11 April 1896.

Most Capped Player: Pat Glover, 7, Wales.

Most League Appearances: John McDermott, 647, 1987–2007.

Youngest League Player: Tony Ford, 16 years 143 days v Walsall, 4 October 1975.

Record Transfer Fee Received: £1,500,000 from Everton for John Oster, July 1997.

Record Transfer Fee Paid: £500,000 to Preston NE for Lee Ashcroft, August 1998.

Football League Record: 1892 Original Member of Division 2; 1901–03 Division 1; 1903 Division 2; 1910 Failed re-election; 1911 re-elected Division 2; 1920–21 Division 3; 1921–26 Division 3 (N); 1926–29 Division 2; 1929–32 Division 1; 1932–34 Division 2; 1934–48 Division 1; 1948–51 Division 2; 1951–56 Division 3 (N); 1956–59 Division 2; 1959–62 Division 3; 1962–64 Division 2; 1964–68 Division 3; 1968–72 Division 4; 1972–77 Division 3; 1977–79 Division 4; 1979–80 Division 3; 1980–87 Division 2; 1987–88 Division 3; 1988–90 Division 4; 1990–91 Division 3; 1991–92 Division 2; 1992–97 Division 1; 1997–98 Division 2; 1998–2003 Division 1; 2003–04 Division 2; 2004–10 FL 2; 2010–16 Conference/National League; 2016– FL 2.

LATEST SEQUENCES

Longest Sequence of League Wins: 11, 19.1.1952 – 29.3.1952.

Longest Sequence of League Defeats: 9, 30.11.1907 – 18.1.1908.

Longest Sequence of League Draws: 5, 6.2.1965 – 6.3.1965.

Longest Sequence of Unbeaten League Matches: 19, 16.2.1980 – 30.8.1980.

Longest Sequence Without a League Win: 22, 24.3.2008 – 1.11.2008.

Successive Scoring Runs: 33 from 6.10.1928.

Successive Non-scoring Runs: 6 from 11.3.2000.

MANAGERS

H. N. Hickson 1902–20 *(Secretary-Manager)*
Haydn Price 1920
George Fraser 1921–24
Wilf Gillow 1924–32
Frank Womack 1932–36
Charles Spencer 1937–51
Bill Shankly 1951–53
Billy Walsh 1954–55
Allenby Chilton 1955–59
Tim Ward 1960–62
Tom Johnston 1962–64
Jimmy McGuigan 1964–67
Don McEvoy 1967–68
Bill Harvey 1968–69
Bobby Kennedy 1969–71
Lawrie McMenemy 1971–73
Ron Ashman 1973–75
Tom Casey 1975–76
Johnny Newman 1976–79
George Kerr 1979–82
David Booth 1982–85
Mike Lyons 1985–87
Bobby Roberts 1987–88
Alan Buckley 1988–94
Brian Laws 1994–96
Kenny Swain 1997
Alan Buckley 1997–2000
Lennie Lawrence 2000–01
Paul Groves 2001–04
Nicky Law 2004
Russell Slade 2004–06
Graham Rodger 2006
Alan Buckley 2006–08
Mike Newell 2008–09
Neil Woods 2009–11
Rob Scott and Paul Hurst 2011–13
Paul Hurst 2013–16
Marcus Bignot 2016–17
Russell Slade 2017–18
Michael Jolley March 2018–

TEN YEAR LEAGUE RECORD

		P	*W*	*D*	*L*	*F*	*A*	*Pts*	*Pos*
2009-10	FL 2	46	9	17	20	45	71	44	23
2010-11	Conf	46	15	17	14	72	62	62	11
2011-12	Conf	46	19	13	14	79	60	70	11
2012-13	Conf	46	23	14	9	70	38	83	4
2013-14	Conf	46	22	12	12	65	46	78	4
2014-15	Conf	46	25	11	10	74	40	86	3
2015-16	NL	46	22	14	10	82	45	80	4
2016-17	FL 2	46	17	11	18	59	63	62	14
2017-18	FL 2	46	13	12	21	42	66	51	18
2018-19	FL 2	46	16	8	22	45	56	56	17

DID YOU KNOW ?

Grimsby Town's first visit to Wembley was in April 1998 for the final of the Auto Windscreens Shield when they defeated Bournemouth 2-1 with a golden goal from Wayne Burnett which won the trophy under the sudden-death rule that operated at the time. The Mariners were back at Wembley four weeks later when they defeated Northampton Town in the Division Two play-off final.

GRIMSBY TOWN – SKY BET LEAGUE TWO 2018–19 LEAGUE RECORD

Match No.	*Date*	*Venue*	*Opponents*	*Result*	*H/T Score*	*Lg Pos.*	*Goalscorers*	*Attendance*
1	Aug 4	H	Forest Green R	L 1-4	1-0	21	Rose, M (pen) [31]	5879
2	11	A	Macclesfield T	W 2-0	1-0	12	Cook [29], Vernam [90]	2589
3	18	H	Lincoln C	D 1-1	1-0	16	Woolford [33]	7201
4	21	A	Milton Keynes D	D 1-1	1-0	15	Cook [35]	6800
5	25	A	Newport Co	L 0-1	0-1	17		3288
6	Sept 1	H	Yeovil T	L 0-1	0-0	20		4284
7	8	A	Bury	L 0-4	0-2	21		3677
8	15	H	Oldham Ath	L 0-3	0-0	21		4746
9	22	A	Stevenage	L 0-1	0-0	22		2332
10	29	H	Morecambe	L 1-2	1-0	23	Embleton [9]	3972
11	Oct 2	A	Carlisle U	W 1-0	1-0	22	Hendrie [38]	3316
12	6	H	Port Vale	W 2-0	1-0	19	Thomas [1], Hooper [53]	3842
13	20	H	Exeter C	D 0-0	0-0	20		4038
14	23	H	Colchester U	W 1-0	0-0	19	Thomas [65]	3662
15	27	A	Crewe Alex	L 0-2	0-0	19		3725
16	Nov 3	A	Cambridge U	L 0-1	0-0	21		4096
17	6	A	Mansfield T	L 1-2	1-0	21	Benning (og) [36]	4118
18	17	H	Crawley T	W 1-0	0-0	20	Rose, A [86]	4459
19	24	A	Northampton T	D 2-2	1-1	20	Vernam [36], Cardwell [80]	5594
20	27	H	Tranmere R	W 5-2	2-1	18	Clifton [33], Thomas [40], Davis [48], Rose, M (pen) [82], Embleton [90]	3293
21	Dec 8	A	Cheltenham T	L 1-2	0-1	18	Embleton [63]	2775
22	15	H	Swindon T	W 2-1	1-1	18	Thomas 2 (1 pen) [26 (p), 61]	3809
23	22	H	Notts Co	W 4-0	2-0	16	Clifton [4], Davis 2 [37, 66], Thomas [88]	4946
24	26	A	Port Vale	W 1-0	0-0	14	Thomas [62]	5129
25	29	A	Exeter C	W 2-1	1-0	13	Woolford [14], Rose, M (pen) [80]	4956
26	Jan 1	H	Mansfield T	L 0-1	0-1	13		5931
27	12	H	Macclesfield T	L 0-2	0-2	15		4694
28	19	A	Lincoln C	L 0-1	0-1	15		9650
29	22	A	Forest Green R	L 0-3	0-2	15		1810
30	26	H	Milton Keynes D	W 1-0	1-0	15	Thomas [27]	3862
31	Feb 2	H	Newport Co	W 3-0	1-0	12	Cook 2 [17, 56], Demetriou (og) [84]	3712
32	9	A	Yeovil T	W 3-1	2-0	11	Thomas [9], Gafaiti (og) [35], Dennis [87]	2692
33	16	H	Cheltenham T	W 1-0	1-0	12	Thomas (pen) [41]	4940
34	23	A	Swindon T	D 1-1	0-0	11	Hendrie [76]	6434
35	Mar 2	H	Cambridge U	L 0-2	0-1	14		4772
36	9	A	Crawley T	L 1-2	1-2	15	Thomas [6]	2043
37	12	A	Tranmere R	L 1-4	1-4	16	Woolford [33]	5269
38	16	H	Northampton T	D 0-0	0-0	16		3890
39	23	H	Bury	D 0-0	0-0	15		4375
40	30	A	Oldham Ath	L 0-2	0-1	17		3998
41	Apr 6	H	Stevenage	L 0-2	0-1	17		3689
42	13	A	Morecambe	D 1-1	0-0	17	Vernam [88]	1897
43	19	A	Colchester U	L 0-1	0-1	17		3677
44	22	H	Carlisle U	W 1-0	0-0	17	Grayson [90]	3647
45	27	A	Notts Co	L 1-2	0-0	17	Whitmore [90]	8519
46	May 4	H	Crewe Alex	W 2-0	2-0	17	Davis [26], Grayson [34]	4248

Final League Position: 17

GOALSCORERS

League (45): Thomas 11 (2 pens), Cook 4, Davis 4, Embleton 3, Rose M 3 (3 pens), Vernam 3, Woolford 3, Clifton 2, Grayson 2, Hendrie 2, Cardwell 1, Dennis 1, Hooper 1, Rose A 1, Whitmore 1, own goals 3.
FA Cup (5): Vernam 2, Clifton 1, Embleton 1, Thomas 1.
Carabao Cup (0).
Checkatrade Trophy (4): Cook 1, Hessenthaler 1, Hooper 1, Rose M 1 (1 pen).

McKeown J 43	Collins D 28 + 2	Whitmore A 25 + 6	Davis H 33 + 2	Dixon P 3	Welsh J 9 + 4	Rose M 15 + 10	Woolford M 25 + 10	Clifton H 30 + 9	Hooper J 12 + 3	Cook J 18 + 6	Hessenthaler J 39 + 5	Hall-Johnson R 23 + 5	Vernam C 19 + 16	Robles L — + 1	Fanewo A 7 + 3	Thomas W 33 + 3	Hendrie L 40 + 1	Fox A 11 + 1	Embleton E 26 + 1	Pringle B 11 + 4	Cardwell H 11 + 8	Rose A 2 + 14	Pollock M — + 2	Ring S 14 + 1	Ohman L 12 + 1	Russell S 3 + 2	Grayson J 6 + 2	Dennis K 7 + 6	Burrell R — + 4	Wright M 1 + 1	*Match No.*
1	2	3	4^{2}	5^{3}	6	7	8^{1}	9	10	11	12	13	14																		1
1	4	8	2	3	6	7■	9		11^{1}	10^{2}	5		12	13																	2
1	4	3	2		8		9	6^{2}	10	11^{1}	7		12		5	13															3
1		3	2	4■	7		9	8^{2}	10^{1}	11^{3}	5		12		6	14	13														4
1		3	2		7	12	9^{3}	6^{2}	11^{1}	10	8		14		4	13■	5														5
1		3	2^{2}		7	14	9^{1}	13	11^{3}	10	8		6		4		5	12													6
1	3	4	2		7^{1}	9	11	6^{2}	14	10	8		13		12			5^{3}													7
1	3		4			7	11		13	10^{1}	8		12		5^{3}	9	2		6^{2}	14											8
1	4	3	5		8	7^{1}	10^{3}	6^{2}	14		9		13			11	2			12											9
1	4	3	2^{2}		8^{1}	13	7^{3}			11	9	12				10	5		6	14											10
1	4	3				7	12	8	11			2	9^{1}			10	5		6^{2}		13										11
1	4	3				7	12	8	11^{1}			2	9^{2}			10	5		6			13									12
1	4	3				7		8	11	12	13	2	9^{1}			10^{3}	5		6^{2}			14									13
1	4	3			13	7		8	11^{3}		12	2^{2}	9^{1}		14	10	5		6												14
1	3	4				8		7^{2}	6^{3}	12	14	5	10			11	2		9^{1}	13											15
1	3	4^{3}				7		8^{2}	9	14	13	2			12	10	5		6	11^{1}											16
1	4					7	6^{2}			10^{3}	8	2	13		3	11	5		12	9^{1}		14									17
1	4		3		14		12	8			7		9^{3}			10	2	5		6^{2}	11^{1}	13									18
1	4■	14	3					8			7		10^{3}			11^{2}	2	5	6	9^{1}	12	13									19
1		3	4		14	13		8			7		10^{3}			11^{2}	2	5	6	9^{1}	12										20
1	3		4			14		9^{1}		12	6		7^{3}			11	2	5	8	10^{2}	13										21
1	4^{3}	12	3			13		8			7		11^{1}			10^{2}	2	5	9	6	14										22
1		4	3			13	14	8			7	12				10	2^{2}	5	9	6^{1}	11^{3}										23
1		4	3^{2}			14	12	7			8	2				11^{3}		5	10	9^{1}	6	13									24
1		4■				14	9^{3}	7			8^{1}	3				10^{2}	2	5	6		11	13	12								25
1						2	12	8			7	3	14			10	4	5^{1}	6	9^{2}	11^{3}	13									26
1						12		7^{2}			8	3	6		4^{1}	11	2		10	9^{3}		13		5	14						27
1■		7^{1}	8			6					9		12			11	2		5		10^{3}	14		4	3^{2}	13					28
			3			8^{3}	14	12			6		7^{1}			11	5				10^{2}	13		9	2	1	4				29
		12	2■		14		8			10^{2}.	6	13				11	5	9	7^{3}						3	1	4^{1}				30
	4	13					8	12		10	6	2^{2}				11^{1}	5		7^{3}					9	3	1		14			31
1	4		14				7	12		10^{3}	8	2				11^{2}	5		6					9^{1}	3			13			32
1	3		14				7^{2}	12		11	6	2				10^{3}	5		9^{1}					8	4			13			33
1	4^{3}	13	2				8^{2}	12		10^{1}	7					11	5		6					9	3■			14			34
1	4		3					6^{2}		12	8	2^{1}	13			10	5		7^{3}		14			9				11			35
1	4^{1}		3				6^{3}	13		12	8		14			10	5		7					9	2			11^{2}			36
1		9	2				8^{3}	6		10^{1}	7	4^{2}				11	5							12	3	13		14			37
1	4		2				7			10	6		12			11^{1}	5		9^{2}					8	3			13			38
1	14		4				8	6		10^{3}	7	2^{1}	12			11^{2}	5					13		9	3						39
1			4				8	6^{2}			7	2	12			11	5				14	13		9	3^{3}			10^{1}			40
1	4	3	7^{2}				13	8			6	5^{3}	9				2				11^{1}						12	10	14		41
1	4	14	3				8^{3}	12			7	13	6				2				11^{2}			5^{1}			9	10			42
1	4■		3				8^{1}	13			7	5^{3}	6				2				10	12					9^{2}	11	14		43
1		4	3				12	9			7	2	8				6					10^{2}	14	5^{1}			13	11^{3}			44
1		4	3				11	9			7	2^{1}	8^{2}				6				13	10^{3}					5		14	12	45
1	14	4	3				12	8^{3}			7	5	10^{1}				2				11						9		13	6^{2}	46

FA Cup

First Round	Milton Keynes D	(h)	3-1
Second Round	Chesterfield	(a)	2-0
Third Round	Crystal Palace	(a)	0-1

Carabao Cup

First Round	Rochdale	(h)	0-2

Checkatrade Trophy

Group G (N)	Notts Co	(h)	2-1
Group G (N)	Doncaster R	(a)	0-2
Group G (N)	Newcastle U U21	(h)	2-3

HUDDERSFIELD TOWN

FOUNDATION

A meeting, attended largely by members of the Huddersfield & District FA, was held at the Imperial Hotel in 1906 to discuss the feasibility of establishing a football club in this rugby stronghold. However, it was not until a man with both the enthusiasm and the money to back the scheme came on the scene that real progress was made. This benefactor was Mr Hilton Crowther and it was at a meeting at the Albert Hotel in 1908 that the club formally came into existence with an investment of £2,000 and joined the North-Eastern League.

The John Smith's Stadium, Stadium Way, Leeds Road, Huddersfield, West Yorkshire HD1 6PX.

Telephone: (01484) 960 607.

Fax: (01484) 484 101.

Ticket Office: (01484) 960 601.

Website: www.htafc.com

Email: info@htafc.com

Ground Capacity: 24,169.

Record Attendance: 67,037 v Arsenal, FA Cup 6th rd, 27 February 1932 (at Leeds Road); 24,169 v Tottenham H, Premier League, 30 September 2017; 24,169 v Manchester U, Premier League, 21 October 2017; 24,169 v WBA, Premier League, 4 November 2017; 24,169 v Chelsea, Premier League, 12 December 2017 (at John Smith's Stadium).

Pitch Measurements: 106m × 68m (116yd × 74.5yd).

Chairman: Paul Hodgkinson.

Chief Executive: Julian Winter.

Head Coach: Jan Siewert.

Assistant Head Coach: Colin Bell.

Colours: Blue and white striped shirts, white shorts with blue trim, white socks with blue trim.

Year Formed: 1908.

Turned Professional: 1908.

Club Nickname: 'The Terriers'.

Grounds: 1908, Leeds Road; 1994, The Alfred McAlpine Stadium (renamed the Galpharm Stadium 2004, John Smith's Stadium 2012).

First Football League Game: 3 September 1910, Division 2, v Bradford PA (a) W 1–0 – Mutch; Taylor, Morris; Beaton, Hall, Bartlett; Blackburn, Wood, Hamilton (1), McCubbin, Jee.

Record League Victory: 10–1 v Blackpool, Division 1, 13 December 1930 – Turner; Goodall, Spencer; Redfern, Wilson, Campbell; Bob Kelly (1), McLean (4), Robson (3), Davies (1), Smailes (1).

Record Cup Victory: 7–0 v Lincoln U, FA Cup 1st rd, 16 November 1991 – Clarke; Trevitt, Charlton, Donovan (2), Mitchell, Doherty, O'Regan (1), Stapleton (1) (Wright), Roberts (2), Onuora (1), Barnett (Ireland). *N.B.* 11–0 v Heckmondwike (a), FA Cup pr rd, 18 September 1909 – Doggart; Roberts, Ewing; Hooton, Stevenson, Randall; Kenworthy (2), McCreadie (1), Foster (4), Stacey (4), Jee.

HONOURS

League Champions: Division 1 – 1923–24, 1924–25, 1925–26; Division 2 – 1969–70; Division 4 – 1979–80.
Runners-up: Division 1 – 1926–27, 1927–28, 1933–34; Division 2 – 1919–20, 1952–53.

FA Cup Winners: 1922.
Runners-up: 1920, 1928, 1930, 1938.

League Cup: semi-final – 1968.

League Trophy: *Runners-up:* 1994.

THE SUN FACT FILE

Huddersfield Town's Leeds Road ground was home to what is believed to have been the first electric scoreboard in English football. The board was a gift from Dutch club PSV Eindhoven who played against the Terriers in a Festival of Britain match in May 1951. The scoreboard stood at the open end behind the goal until it was damaged around 1970 and then replaced with a manual version.

Record Defeat: 1–10 v Manchester C, Division 2, 7 November 1987.

Most League Points (2 for a win): 66, Division 4, 1979–80.

Most League Points (3 for a win): 87, FL 1, 2010–11.

Most League Goals: 101, Division 4, 1979–80.

Highest League Scorer in Season: Sam Taylor, 35, Division 2, 1919–20; George Brown, 35, Division 1, 1925–26; Jordan Rhodes, 35, 2011–12.

Most League Goals in Total Aggregate: George Brown, 142, 1921–29; Jimmy Glazzard, 142, 1946–56.

Most League Goals in One Match: 5, Dave Mangnall v Derby Co, Division 1, 21 November 1931; 5, Alf Lythgoe v Blackburn R, Division 1, 13 April 1935; 5, Jordan Rhodes v Wycombe W, FL 1, 6 January 2012.

Most Capped Player: Jimmy Nicholson, 31 (41), Northern Ireland.

Most League Appearances: Billy Smith, 521, 1914–34.

Youngest League Player: Denis Law, 16 years 303 days v Notts Co, 24 December 1956.

Record Transfer Fee Received: £10,000,000 (rising to £12,000,000) from Stoke C for Tom Ince, July 2018.

Record Transfer Fee Paid: £17,500,000 to Monaco for Terence Kongolo, June 2018.

Football League Record: 1910 Elected to Division 2; 1920–52 Division 1; 1952–53 Division 2; 1953–56 Division 1; 1956–70 Division 2; 1970–72 Division 1; 1972–73 Division 2; 1973–75 Division 3; 1975–80 Division 4; 1980–83 Division 3; 1983–88 Division 2; 1988–92 Division 3; 1992–95 Division 2; 1995–2001 Division 1; 2001–03 Division 2; 2003–04 Division 3; 2004–12 FL 1; 2012–17 FL C; 2017–19 Premier League; 2019– FL C.

MANAGERS

Fred Walker 1908–10
Richard Pudan 1910–12
Arthur Fairclough 1912–19
Ambrose Langley 1919–21
Herbert Chapman 1921–25
Cecil Potter 1925–26
Jack Chaplin 1926–29
Clem Stephenson 1929–42
Ted Magner 1942–43
David Steele 1943–47
George Stephenson 1947–52
Andy Beattie 1952–56
Bill Shankly 1956–59
Eddie Boot 1960–64
Tom Johnston 1964–68
Ian Greaves 1968–74
Bobby Collins 1974
Tom Johnston 1975–78
(had been General Manager since 1975)
Mike Buxton 1978–86
Steve Smith 1986–87
Malcolm Macdonald 1987–88
Eoin Hand 1988–92
Ian Ross 1992–93
Neil Warnock 1993–95
Brian Horton 1995–97
Peter Jackson 1997–99
Steve Bruce 1999–2000
Lou Macari 2000–02
Mick Wadsworth 2002–03
Peter Jackson 2003–07
Andy Ritchie 2007–08
Stan Ternent 2008
Lee Clark 2008–12
Simon Grayson 2012–13
Mark Robins 2013–14
Chris Powell 2014–15
David Wagner 2015–19
Jan Siewert January 2019–

LATEST SEQUENCES

Longest Sequence of League Wins: 11, 5.4.1920 – 4.9.1920.

Longest Sequence of League Defeats: 8, 2.3.2019 – 26.4.2019.

Longest Sequence of League Draws: 6, 3.3.1987 – 3.4.1987.

Longest Sequence of Unbeaten League Matches: 43, 1.1.2011 – 19.11.2011.

Longest Sequence Without a League Win: 22, 4.12.1971 – 29.4.1972.

Successive Scoring Runs: 27 from 12.3.2005.

Successive Non-scoring Runs: 7 from 14.10.2000.

TEN YEAR LEAGUE RECORD

		P	W	D	L	F	A	Pts	Pos
2009-10	FL 1	46	23	11	12	82	56	80	6
2010-11	FL 1	46	25	12	9	77	48	87	3
2011-12	FL 1	46	21	18	7	79	47	81	4
2012-13	FL C	46	15	13	18	53	73	58	19
2013-14	FL C	46	14	11	21	58	65	53	17
2014-15	FL C	46	13	16	17	58	75	55	16
2015-16	FL C	46	13	12	21	59	70	51	19
2016-17	FL C	46	25	6	15	56	58	81	5
2017-18	PR Lge	38	9	10	19	28	58	37	16
2018-19	PR Lge	38	3	7	28	22	76	16	20

DID YOU KNOW ?

Alex Jackson, one of the Huddersfield Town stars of the inter-war period, was also employed as a departmental manager in a local sports outfitter's shop. In the days of the maximum wage many footballers, including top-class players, took on second jobs to supplement their income.

HUDDERSFIELD TOWN – PREMIER LEAGUE 2018–19 LEAGUE RECORD

Match No.	*Date*	*Venue*	*Opponents*	*Result*		*H/T Score*	*Lg Pos.*	*Goalscorers*	*Attendance*
1	Aug 11	H	Chelsea	L	0-3	0-2	20		24,121
2	19	A	Manchester C	L	1-6	1-3	20	Stankovic 43	54,021
3	25	H	Cardiff C	D	0-0	0-0	18		23,787
4	Sept 1	A	Everton	D	1-1	1-1	17	Billing 34	38,767
5	15	H	Crystal Palace	L	0-1	0-1	17		23,696
6	22	A	Leicester C	L	1-3	1-1	20	Jorgensen 5	31,676
7	29	H	Tottenham H	L	0-2	0-2	20		23,885
8	Oct 6	A	Burnley	D	1-1	0-1	18	Schindler 66	20,533
9	20	H	Liverpool	L	0-1	0-1	19		24,263
10	27	A	Watford	L	0-3	0-2	20		20,457
11	Nov 5	H	Fulham	W	1-0	1-0	18	Fosu-Mensah (og) 29	17,082
12	10	H	West Ham U	D	1-1	1-0	19	Pritchard 6	24,069
13	25	A	Wolverhampton W	W	2-0	1-0	14	Mooy 2 6, 74	30,130
14	Dec 1	H	Brighton & HA	L	1-2	1-1	17	Jorgensen 1	22,973
15	4	A	Bournemouth	L	1-2	1-2	17	Kongolo 38	9980
16	8	A	Arsenal	L	0-1	0-0	18		59,893
17	15	H	Newcastle U	L	0-1	0-0	18		24,036
18	22	H	Southampton	L	1-3	0-2	19	Billing 58	22,384
19	26	A	Manchester U	L	1-3	0-1	20	Jorgensen 88	74,523
20	29	A	Fulham	L	0-1	0-0	20		24,423
21	Jan 2	H	Burnley	L	1-2	1-1	20	Mounie 33	23,715
22	12	A	Cardiff C	D	0-0	0-0	20		30,725
23	20	H	Manchester C	L	0-3	0-1	20		24,190
24	29	H	Everton	L	0-1	0-1	20		23,699
25	Feb 2	A	Chelsea	L	0-5	0-2	20		40,626
26	9	H	Arsenal	L	1-2	0-2	20	Ahearne-Grant 90	24,182
27	23	A	Newcastle U	L	0-2	0-0	20		52,174
28	26	H	Wolverhampton W	W	1-0	0-0	20	Mounie 90	22,714
29	Mar 2	A	Brighton & HA	L	0-1	0-0	20		30,182
30	9	H	Bournemouth	L	0-2	0-1	20		22,304
31	16	A	West Ham U	L	3-4	2-1	20	Bacuna 17, Ahearne-Grant 2 30, 65	59,931
32	30	A	Crystal Palace	L	0-2	0-0	20		25,193
33	Apr 6	H	Leicester C	L	1-4	0-1	20	Mooy (pen) 52	24,146
34	13	A	Tottenham H	L	0-4	0-2	20		58,308
35	20	H	Watford	L	1-2	0-1	20	Ahearne-Grant 90	23,957
36	26	A	Liverpool	L	0-5	0-3	20		53,249
37	May 5	H	Manchester U	D	1-1	0-1	20	Mbenza 60	24,263
38	12	A	Southampton	D	1-1	0-1	20	Pritchard 55	30,367

Final League Position: 20

GOALSCORERS

League (22): Ahearne-Grant 4, Jorgensen 3, Mooy 3 (1 pen), Billing 2, Mounie 2, Pritchard 2, Bacuna 1, Kongolo 1, Mbenza 1, Schindler 1, Stankovic 1, own goal 1.
FA Cup (0).
Carabao Cup (0).

Hamer B 7	Jorgensen M 24	Schindler C 37	Kongolo T 32	Hadergjonaj F 19 + 5	Mooy A 25 + 4	Hogg J 29	Billing P 25 + 2	Lowe C 23 + 6	Pritchard A 26 + 4	Mounie S 19 + 12	Depoitre L 10 + 13	Diakhaby A 6 + 6	Smith T 13 + 2	Stankovic J 9 + 2	Sabiri A 1 + 1	Sobhi R — + 4	van La Parra R 5	Lossl J 30 + 1	Mbenza I 10 + 12	Kachunga E 13 + 7	Durm E 21 + 7	Bacuna J 16 + 5	Williams D 1 + 4	Quaner C — + 2	Puncheon J 5 + 1	Ahearne-Grant K 9 + 4	Duhaney D 1	Rowe A 1 + 1	Daly M — + 2	Coleman J 1	*Match No.*
1	2	3	4	5	6	7	8	9^{1}	10^{2}	11	12	13																			1
1		3	4	9			8	5	6^{1}	11^{3}	12	13	2	7	10^{2}	14															2
1^{2}	3	4	5	2	9	7■	6			11^{1}	14	8^{3}					10	12	13												3
	3	4	5	2^{3}	8		9	6		11^{1}	14	7^{2}					10	1		12	13										4
	2^{3}	3	4	5	6		7	8		10	14	12					11^{2}	1	13	9^{1}											5
	3	4	5^{2}		8		9	6	13		11	12					10	1		7^{1}	2										6
	2	3^{2}	4^{1}	12	6	7	8	9	10^{3}	14	11							1	13		5										7
	3	4		14	8	7	6	5^{3}	9	12	11^{1}						10^{2}	1	13		2										8
	2	3		5^{2}	6	7^{1}	8^{3}	4	10	13	11	14						1	12		9										9
	3	4			9	8	7^{3}	5	10	13	11^{2}					12		1	6^{1}		2	14									10
	2	3	4^{1}	5	9	7	6	8	11^{3}	10^{2}	12							1	13			14									11
	2	3	4	5	6	7	8	9^{3}	10^{1}	11^{2}	14							1	13		12										12
		3	4	5	6	7^{2}	8^{3}		10^{1}	11			2	12				1	13		9		14								13
	2	3	4	5	6^{3}	7^{2}	8		10^{1}	11■	12		13					1			9		14								14
	3	4	5^{1}	2	8	7	6^{2}		9		11				12^{3}	14		1	13		10										15
	3	4	5	13	9	6^{1}		10	8		11		2^{3}					1			14	12	7^{2}								16
	2	3	4^{1}	5		7^{3}	8	9^{2}	10		11					13		1	14		12	6									17
	2	3	4	5			7	8^{2}	9	11								1	10^{3}	13	12	6^{1}		14							18
	3	4	5	6			7	12	9	14	11^{1}							1	10^{3}	8^{2}	2			13							19
	2	3	4	6		7	8	9	10^{1}	11^{2}	13							1		12	5										20
	3	4■	5	2^{2}		6	7	13	9^{1}	11	14							1	10	8	12^{3}										21
	3	4		2		7	8		10^{1}	11^{2}	13							1	12	9	5				6						22
		3	4			8		5	13	12		11^{1}	2					1	10	6		9^{2}			7						23
	3	4	5	2	12	7^{1}		13		10	14	11^{3}						1		9^{2}		6			8						24
		3	4		8		6^{3}	5	14	12		9^{2}	2					1	11^{1}	10		7				13					25
1	3	4	5^{3}		6	7					13	9	2							10^{1}	12	8			11^{2}	14					26
	3	4		12	8	6	13	5		14	11^{1}		2■					1		10		7^{2}			9^{3}						27
		3	4		13	7	8		9^{3}	11				6^{2}				1		14	5	12				10	2^{1}				28
		3	4	14	12	7^{2}	8		9^{1}	11				6^{3}				1		13	5	2				10					29
	3	4			8		7^{3}	12	9	11^{1}				6				1		10^{2}	5	2				13		14			30
			4		7		12	10	9	14			2	3				1			5	6^{1}			13	11^{3}		8^{2}			31
1		3	4		8	7		10^{2}	9^{1}				2	14						12	5	6^{3}	13			11					32
1		3	4		6	7^{3}		9	10^{2}	13			2	8^{1}					12		5	14				11					33
1		3	5	2	13	8		10		12				4^{1}						7	6^{3}	9^{2}	14			11					34
		3	4		10	8^{2}		14		11^{1}			2					1	9^{3}	6	5	7				13			12		35
		3	4			8		12	13	11^{4}			2	6^{3}				1	7^{1}	14	5	9				10					36
		3	4		6	8		5	11			13	12					1	9^{1}		2^{2}	7				10					37
		4	5		6	8			9^{2}	13			2	3					11			7^{1}				10			12	1	38

FA Cup
Third Round | Bristol C | (a) | 0-1

Carabao Cup
Second Round | Stoke C | (a) | 0-2

HULL CITY

FOUNDATION

The enthusiasts who formed Hull City in 1904 were brave men indeed. More than that, they were audacious for they immediately put the club on the map in this Rugby League fortress by obtaining a three-year agreement with the Hull Rugby League club to rent their ground! They had obtained quite a number of conversions to the dribbling code, before the Rugby League forbade the use of any of their club grounds by Association Football clubs. By that time, Hull City were well away, having entered the FA Cup in their initial season and the Football League, Second Division after only a year.

The KCOM Stadium, West Park, Hull, East Yorkshire HU3 6HU.

Telephone: (01482) 504 600.

Ticket Office: (01482) 358 418.

Website: www.hullcitytigers.com

Email: info@hulltigers.com

Ground Capacity: 24,983.

Record Attendance: 55,019 v Manchester U, FA Cup 6th rd, 26 February 1949 (at Boothferry Park); 25,512 v Sunderland, FL C, 28 October 2007 (at KC Stadium).

Pitch Measurements: 105m × 68m (115yd × 74.5yd).

Chairman: Dr Assem Allam.

Vice-Chairman: Ehab Allam.

Manager: Grant McCann.

Assistant Manager: Cliff Byrne.

Colours: Amber shirts with black stripes, black shorts with amber trim, amber socks with black hoops.

Year Formed: 1904.

Turned Professional: 1905.

Club Nickname: 'The Tigers'.

Grounds: 1904, Boulevard Ground (Hull RFC); 1905, Anlaby Road (Hull CC); 1944, Boulevard Ground; 1946, Boothferry Park; 2002, Kingston Communications Stadium; 2016, renamed KCOM stadium.

First Football League Game: 2 September 1905, Division 2, v Barnsley (h) W 4–1 – Spendiff; Langley, Jones; Martin, Robinson, Gordon (2); Rushton, Spence (1), Wilson (1), Howe, Raisbeck.

Record League Victory: 11–1 v Carlisle U, Division 3 (N), 14 January 1939 – Ellis; Woodhead, Dowen; Robinson (1), Blyth, Hardy; Hubbard (2), Richardson (2), Dickinson (2), Davies (2), Cunliffe (2).

Record Cup Victory: 8–2 v Stalybridge Celtic (a), FA Cup 1st rd, 26 November 1932 – Maddison; Goldsmith, Woodhead; Gardner, Hill (1), Denby; Forward (1), Duncan, McNaughton (1), Wainscoat (4), Sargeant (1).

Record Defeat: 0–8 v Wolverhampton W, Division 2, 4 November 1911.

HONOURS

League Champions: Division 3 – 1965–66; Division 3N – 1932–33, 1948–49.
Runners-up: FL C – 2012–13; FL 1 – 2004–05; Division 3 – 1958–59; Third Division – 2003–04; Division 4 – 1982–83.

FA Cup: *Runners-up:* 2014.

League Cup: semi-final – 2017.

League Trophy: *Runners-up:* 1984.

European Competitions
Europa League: 2014–15.

THE SUN FACT FILE

Hull City switched from their established colours of amber and black to play in blue shirts with white collars and cuffs and white shorts for the 1935–36 season, temporarily dropping their nickname of the Tigers. The team had a disastrous campaign, finishing bottom of the old Second Division by a 12-point margin, which led to a return to their traditional colours for 1936–37.

Most League Points (2 for a win): 69, Division 3, 1965–66.

Most League Points (3 for a win): 90, Division 4, 1982–83.

Most League Goals: 109, Division 3, 1965–66.

Highest League Scorer in Season: Bill McNaughton, 39, Division 3 (N), 1932–33.

Most League Goals in Total Aggregate: Chris Chilton, 193, 1960–71.

Most League Goals in One Match: 5, Ken McDonald v Bristol C, Division 2, 17 November 1928; 5, Simon 'Slim' Raleigh v Halifax T, Division 3 (N), 26 December 1930.

Most Capped Player: Theo Whitmore, 28 (105), Jamaica.

Most League Appearances: Andy Davidson, 520, 1952–67.

Youngest League Player: Matthew Edeson, 16 years 63 days v Fulham, 10 October 1992.

Record Transfer Fee Received: £12,000,000 (rising to £17,000,000) from Leicester C for Harry Maguire, June 2017.

Record Transfer Fee Paid: £13,000,000 to Tottenham H for Ryan Mason, August 2016.

Football League Record: 1905 Elected to Division 2; 1930–33 Division 3 (N); 1933–36 Division 2; 1936–49 Division 3 (N); 1949–56 Division 2; 1956–58 Division 3 (N); 1958–59 Division 3; 1959–60 Division 2; 1960–66 Division 3; 1966–78 Division 2; 1978–81 Division 3; 1981–83 Division 4; 1983–85 Division 3; 1985–91 Division 2; 1991–92 Division 3; 1992–96 Division 2; 1996–2004 Division 3; 2004–05 FL 1; 2005–08 FL C; 2008–10 Premier League; 2010–13 FL C; 2013–15 Premier League; 2015–16 FL C; 2016–17 Premier League; 2017– FL C.

LATEST SEQUENCES

Longest Sequence of League Wins: 10, 23.2.1966 – 20.4.1966.

Longest Sequence of League Defeats: 8, 7.4.1934 – 8.9.1934.

Longest Sequence of League Draws: 5, 14.2.2012 – 10.3.2012.

Longest Sequence of Unbeaten League Matches: 19, 13.3.2001 – 22.9.2001.

Longest Sequence Without a League Win: 27, 27.3.1989 – 4.11.1989.

Successive Scoring Runs: 26 from 10.4.1990.

Successive Non-scoring Runs: 6 from 13.11.1920.

MANAGERS

James Ramster 1904–05 *(Secretary-Manager)*
Ambrose Langley 1905–13
Harry Chapman 1913–14
Fred Stringer 1914–16
David Menzies 1916–21
Percy Lewis 1921–23
Bill McCracken 1923–31
Haydn Green 1931–34
John Hill 1934–36
David Menzies 1936
Ernest Blackburn 1936–46
Major Frank Buckley 1946–48
Raich Carter 1948–51
Bob Jackson 1952–55
Bob Brocklebank 1955–61
Cliff Britton 1961–70 *(continued as General Manager to 1971)*
Terry Neill 1970–74
John Kaye 1974–77
Bobby Collins 1977–78
Ken Houghton 1978–79
Mike Smith 1979–82
Bobby Brown 1982
Colin Appleton 1982–84
Brian Horton 1984–88
Eddie Gray 1988–89
Colin Appleton 1989
Stan Ternent 1989–91
Terry Dolan 1991–97
Mark Hateley 1997–98
Warren Joyce 1998–2000
Brian Little 2000–02
Jan Molby 2002
Peter Taylor 2002–06
Phil Parkinson 2006
Phil Brown *(after caretaker role December 2006)* 2007–10
Ian Dowie *(consultant)* 2010
Nigel Pearson 2010–11
Nick Barmby 2011–12
Steve Bruce 2012–16
Mike Phelan 2016–17
Marco Silva 2017
Leonid Slutsky 2017
Nigel Adkins 2017–19
Grant McCann June 2019–

TEN YEAR LEAGUE RECORD

		P	*W*	*D*	*L*	*F*	*A*	*Pts*	*Pos*
2009-10	PR Lge	38	6	12	20	34	75	30	19
2010-11	FL C	46	16	17	13	52	51	65	11
2011-12	FL C	46	19	11	16	47	44	68	8
2012-13	FL C	46	24	7	15	61	52	79	2
2013-14	PR Lge	38	10	7	21	38	53	37	16
2014-15	PR Lge	38	8	11	19	33	51	35	18
2015-16	FL C	46	24	11	11	69	35	83	4
2016-17	PR Lge	38	9	7	22	37	80	34	18
2017-18	FL C	46	11	16	19	70	70	49	18
2018-19	FL C	46	17	11	18	66	68	62	13

DID YOU KNOW ?

Hull City sold 4,533 season tickets for the 1952–53 season, the highest for any club outside the top flight and the fifth highest of any Football League club. Nevertheless, the average home attendance of 25,918 was only fifth best in Division Two.

HULL CITY – SKY BET CHAMPIONSHIP 2018–19 LEAGUE RECORD

Match No.	Date	Venue	Opponents	Result		H/T Score	Lg Pos.	Goalscorers	Attendance
1	Aug 6	H	Aston Villa	L	1-3	1-1	22	Evandro [7]	14,071
2	11	A	Sheffield W	D	1-1	1-0	21	Campbell [36]	23,416
3	18	H	Blackburn R	L	0-1	0-1	22		12,233
4	21	A	Rotherham U	W	3-2	2-1	16	Irvine 2 [28, 47], Campbell [45]	8962
5	25	A	Stoke C	L	0-2	0-1	18		23,311
6	Sept 1	H	Derby Co	L	1-2	0-1	21	Kane [53]	12,285
7	15	H	Ipswich T	W	2-0	1-0	17	Bowen [3], Irvine [89]	11,650
8	18	A	Wigan Ath	L	1-2	1-2	18	Bowen [43]	8848
9	22	A	Reading	L	0-3	0-1	21		12,409
10	29	H	Middlesbrough	D	1-1	0-0	21	Bowen (pen) [69]	13,185
11	Oct 2	H	Leeds U	L	0-1	0-0	21		13,798
12	6	A	Sheffield U	L	0-1	0-0	24		25,360
13	20	H	Preston NE	D	1-1	0-0	23	Bowen (pen) [85]	12,066
14	24	A	Bristol C	L	0-1	0-0	23		19,149
15	27	A	Bolton W	W	1-0	1-0	23	Campbell [7]	13,108
16	Nov 3	H	WBA	W	1-0	1-0	23	Campbell [38]	11,916
17	10	A	Birmingham C	D	3-3	0-2	22	Campbell 2 [50, 60], Grosicki [73]	21,468
18	24	H	Nottingham F	L	0-2	0-0	23		13,364
19	27	H	Norwich C	D	0-0	0-0	22		11,420
20	Dec 1	A	QPR	W	3-2	2-1	19	Bowen 2 [6, 69], Henriksen [22]	13,824
21	8	A	Millwall	D	2-2	1-1	19	Grosicki [6], Henriksen [73]	12,004
22	15	H	Brentford	W	2-0	2-0	17	Campbell 2 [12, 21]	10,530
23	22	H	Swansea C	W	3-2	0-1	16	Bowen 2 [70, 80], Elphick [76]	10,848
24	26	A	Preston NE	W	2-1	1-0	15	Irvine 2 [28, 80]	14,026
25	29	A	Leeds U	W	2-0	1-0	14	Bowen 2 [25, 58]	35,754
26	Jan 1	H	Bolton W	W	6-0	1-0	13	Grosicki 2 [29, 63], Evandro [62], Martin [67], Bowen [76], Dicko [83]	12,418
27	12	H	Sheffield W	W	3-0	1-0	10	Bowen 2 (1 pen) [45, 52 (p)], Campbell [76]	14,102
28	19	A	Aston Villa	D	2-2	2-1	8	Bowen [27], Evandro [37]	33,619
29	26	A	Blackburn R	L	0-3	0-2	12		13,589
30	Feb 2	H	Stoke C	W	2-0	1-0	10	Bowen [44], Grosicki [64]	12,776
31	9	A	Derby Co	L	0-2	0-1	12		28,211
32	12	H	Rotherham U	D	2-2	2-0	12	Bowen [2], Campbell [23]	10,785
33	23	A	Brentford	L	1-5	1-3	13	Campbell [24]	9675
34	26	H	Millwall	W	2-1	2-1	11	Bowen [8], Pugh [42]	10,191
35	Mar 2	H	Birmingham C	W	2-0	1-0	10	Bowen 2 (1 pen) [23, 60 (p)]	12,551
36	9	A	Nottingham F	L	0-3	0-0	11		29,397
37	13	A	Norwich C	L	2-3	1-2	13	Pugh [45], Martin [87]	25,879
38	16	H	QPR	D	2-2	2-0	12	Bowen 2 [7, 44]	11,227
39	30	A	Ipswich T	W	2-0	1-0	12	Grosicki 2 [14, 49]	15,720
40	Apr 6	H	Reading	W	3-1	0-1	11	Grosicki 2 [53, 77], Pugh [65]	11,268
41	10	H	Wigan Ath	W	2-1	0-1	9	Campbell [51], De Wijs [89]	10,827
42	13	A	Middlesbrough	L	0-1	0-1	9		22,427
43	19	A	WBA	L	2-3	0-1	10	Kane 2 [48, 59]	23,501
44	22	H	Sheffield U	L	0-3	0-3	13		14,116
45	27	A	Swansea C	D	2-2	0-1	13	Bowen [77], Dicko [84]	18,192
46	May 5	H	Bristol C	D	1-1	0-0	13	Irvine [55]	12,165

Final League Position: 13

GOALSCORERS

League (66): Bowen 22 (4 pens), Campbell 12, Grosicki 9, Irvine 6, Evandro 3, Kane 3, Pugh 3, Dicko 2, Henriksen 2, Martin 2, De Wijs 1, Elphick 1.
FA Cup (1): Toral 1.
Carabao Cup (1): Toral 1.

Marshall D 43	Liehaj E 35 + 4	Burke R 32 + 2	De Wijs J 30 + 2	Kingsley S 25 + 1	Bowen J 45 + 1	Henriksen M 39	Batty D 22 + 5	Kane T 36 + 3	Evandro G 14 + 9	Campbell F 31 + 8	Milinkovic M — + 8	Dicko N 1 + 15	Keane W 1 + 7	Irvine J 36 + 2	Toral J — + 8	MacDonald A 1	Stewart K 16 + 11	McKenzie R 10 + 8	Elphick T 18	Martin C 15 + 15	Grosicki K 35 + 4	Mazuch O 3 + 3	Fleming B 1 + 3	Pugh M 10 + 4	Ridgewell L 4 + 3	Long G 3 + 1	Sheaf M — + 1	Match No.
1	2	3	4	5	6	7	8	9^1	10^2	11^3	12	13	14															1
1	2	3	4	5	6	8	7^3	9	10^2	11^1		14		12	13													2
1	2		4	5^3	6^2	7		9	10	11^1	13	14		8	12	3												3
1	5	3	4		6	7	8^3	2	10^2	11^1			12	9			13	14										4
1	2	3	4	5	6^1	7	8	9^3	10■	11^2		12	13				14											5
1	2	3	4	5	6	7	8	9^1	10^2	11^3		13	12		14													6
1		2	4	5^1	6	7	8^2	9	10	11^3				13			12		3	14								7
1	2		4^2	5	6	7			14	12		11^1		9			8^3		3	10	13							8
1	2	4		5	6^2	7		9		11				10			8^1		3	13	12							9
1	5	2	4^2	12	10	7		6		13				8					3	11	9^1							10
1	4	2		5	10	7		6		13		14		8^3			12		3	11^1	9^2							11
1	4	2		9	13	7	6	5		11^3		12		8^2					3	10^1	14							12
1	5	2	4		9		7^2	8		12		14		6			13		3	11^1	10^3							13
1	8	2^1	4^2		9		7	5		14		13		6				12	3	10^3	11							14
1	2			5	6^2	9	7^1			11		13		8			14	4	3		10^3	12						15
1	5	2	4^2		6	7	8	14		11^1				9				13	3	12	10^3							16
1	5	2	4		6	7	8^3	14		11^1			13	9					3	12	10^2							17
1	5	2	4		6		7^1	13		10			14	8^3			12		3	11^2	9							18
1	5	4			6	7		2						10			8		3	11	9							19
1	5^2	4^1	13		6	7	8	2		11				10				12	3		9^3	14						20
1			4^2		6	7	8^1	2		11				9			14		3	12	10^3	13	5					21
1				5	6	7	8^3	2		11^2			13	10			12		3		9^1	4	14					22
1			12	5	6		8^2	2	13	11^3				10			7		3	14	9	4^1						23
1	14	13	4	5	6^2	7		2		11^3				10			8		3	12	9^1							24
1	13	3	4	5	6	7	14	2	10^1				11^3		12		8				9^2							25
1	2	3	4	5	6	7	13		10^1			14			12		8^3			11^2	9							26
1		3	4	5	6^1	7		2	10^2	12	14				13		8			11^3	9							27
1	14	3	4^1	5	6^3	7	13	2	10^2								8	12		11	9							28
1	12			5	6	7		2	10^2	13							8	4		11	9^1	3^3		14				29
1	4			5	6^3	7		2		11^2	14			10			8	3		13	9^1			12				30
1	4			5^1	6^3	7		2	12	11				10			8^2	3			9			13	14			31
1	2			5	6	7			10^3	11^1	13			8				3		14	9^2			12	4			32
1^3		13		5	7	6		2	8	11^1	14			9^2				3			10				4	12		33
1	5	3	4		6	7		2			14	12		8						11^2	9^1			10^3	13			34
1	5^2	3	4^1		6	7		2						8				13		11	9			10	12			35
1	5	3	4		6	7		2	12	13				8						11^2	9			10^1				36
1	5	3			6^2	7		2		11^3	12			9			8^1			14	13			10	4			37
1		3		5	6					11^1				8			7	2		12	9			10	4			38
1	5	3^1	4		6		7	2	14	11^2				8				13		12	9^3			10				39
1	5	3	4		6	7		2	13	11^1				8			14			12	9^3			10^2				40
1	5	3	4		6	7^3	12	2^1	13	11				8						14	9			10^2				41
1	5	3	4^3		6	7	14	2^1	13	11				8						12	9			10^2				42
1	5	3^2	4		6	8^1	7^3	2	14	11				10			12	13			9							43
	5		4		6		7	2		11^1		13		8	12			3			9			10^2		1		44
	2		5	6^1	10	4	7					13		9	14		8^2	3			11^3		12			1		45
	5	4			6	3	8			11^1		12		10			7	2^2			9^3		14			1	13	46

FA Cup
Third Round Millwall (a) 1-2

Carabao Cup
First Round Sheffield U (a) 1-1
(Hull C won 5-4 on penalties)
Second Round Derby Co (h) 0-4

IPSWICH TOWN

FOUNDATION

Considering that Ipswich Town only reached the Football League in 1938, many people outside of East Anglia may be surprised to learn that this club was formed at a meeting held in the Town Hall as far back as 1878 when Mr T. C. Cobbold, MP, was voted president. Originally it was the Ipswich Association FC to distinguish it from the older Ipswich Football Club which played rugby. These two amalgamated in 1888 and the handling game was dropped in 1893.

Portman Road, Ipswich, Suffolk IP1 2DA.

Telephone: (01473) 400 500.

Fax: (01473) 400 040.

Ticket Office: (03330) 050 503.

Website: www.itfc.co.uk

Email: enquiries@itfc.co.uk

Ground Capacity: 30,311.

Record Attendance: 38,010 v Leeds U, FA Cup 6th rd, 8 March 1975.

Pitch Measurements: 102.5m × 66m (112yd × 72yd).

Chairman: Marcus Evans.

Director: Mark Andrews.

Manager: Paul Lambert.

Assistant Manager: Stuart Taylor.

Colours: Blue shirts with white sleeves, white shorts with red trim, blue socks with red trim.

Year Formed: 1878.

Turned Professional: 1936.

Previous Name: 1878, Ipswich Association FC; 1888, Ipswich Town.

Club Nicknames: 'The Blues', 'Town', 'The Tractor Boys'.

Grounds: 1878, Broom Hill and Brook's Hall; 1884, Portman Road.

First Football League Game: 27 August 1938, Division 3 (S), v Southend U (h) W 4–2 – Burns; Dale, Parry; Perrett, Fillingham, McLuckie; Williams, Davies (1), Jones (2), Alsop (1), Little.

Record League Victory: 7–0 v Portsmouth, Division 2, 7 November 1964 – Thorburn; Smith, McNeil; Baxter, Bolton, Thompson; Broadfoot (1), Hegan (2), Baker (1), Leadbetter, Brogan (3). 7–0 v Southampton, Division 1, 2 February 1974 – Sivell; Burley, Mills (1), Morris, Hunter, Beattie (1), Hamilton (2), Viljoen, Johnson, Whymark (2), Lambert (1) (Woods). 7–0 v WBA, Division 1, 6 November 1976 – Sivell; Burley, Mills, Talbot, Hunter, Beattie (1), Osborne, Wark (1), Mariner (1) (Bertschin), Whymark (4), Woods.

HONOURS

League Champions: Division 1 – 1961–62; Division 2 – 1960–61, 1967–68, 1991–92; Division 3S – 1953–54, 1956–57.
Runners-up: Division 1 – 1980–81, 1981–82.

FA Cup Winners: 1978.

League Cup: semi-final – 1982, 1985, 2001, 2011.

Texaco Cup Winners: 1973.

European Competitions
European Cup: 1962–63.
UEFA Cup: 1973–74, 1974–75, 1975–76, 1977–78, 1979–80, 1980–81 *(winners)*, 1981–82, 1982–83, 2001–02, 2002–03.
European Cup-Winners' Cup: 1978–79 *(qf)*.

THE SUN FACT FILE

Some of the scenes from the 1979 film *Yesterday's Hero* starring Ian McShane (the son of former professional Harry McShane) were shot at Ipswich Town's Portman Road ground. However, the Football League refused permission for film of the home game with Nottingham Forest on 3 March to be included.

Record Cup Victory: 10–0 v Floriana, European Cup prel. rd, 25 September 1962 – Bailey; Malcolm, Compton; Baxter, Laurel, Elsworthy (1); Stephenson, Moran (2), Crawford (5), Phillips (2), Blackwood.

Record Defeat: 1–10 v Fulham, Division 1, 26 December 1963.

Most League Points (2 for a win): 64, Division 3 (S), 1953–54 and 1955–56.

Most League Points (3 for a win): 87, Division 1, 1999–2000.

Most League Goals: 106, Division 3 (S), 1955–56.

Highest League Scorer in Season: Ted Phillips, 41, Division 3 (S), 1956–57.

Most League Goals in Total Aggregate: Ray Crawford, 204, 1958–63 and 1966–69.

Most League Goals in One Match: 5, Alan Brazil v Southampton, Division 1, 16 February 1981.

Most Capped Player: Allan Hunter, 47 (53), Northern Ireland.

Most League Appearances: Mick Mills, 591, 1966–82.

Youngest League Player: Connor Wickham, 16 years 11 days, v Doncaster R, 11 April 2009.

Record Transfer Fee Received: £8,000,000 (rising to £12,000,000) from Sunderland for Connor Wickham, June 2011.

Record Transfer Fee Paid: £4,800,000 to Sampdoria for Matteo Sereni, August 2001.

Football League Record: 1938 Elected to Division 3 (S); 1954–55 Division 2; 1955–57 Division 3 (S); 1957–61 Division 2; 1961–64 Division 1; 1964–68 Division 2; 1968–86 Division 1; 1986–92 Division 2; 1992–95 Premier League; 1995–2000 Division 1; 2000–02 Premier League; 2002–04 Division 1; 2004–19 FL C; 2019– FL 1.

MANAGERS

Mick O'Brien 1936–37
Scott Duncan 1937–55
(continued as Secretary)
Alf Ramsey 1955–63
Jackie Milburn 1963–64
Bill McGarry 1964–68
Bobby Robson 1969–82
Bobby Ferguson 1982–87
Johnny Duncan 1987–90
John Lyall 1990–94
George Burley 1994–2002
Joe Royle 2002–06
Jim Magilton 2006–09
Roy Keane 2009–11
Paul Jewell 2011–12
Mick McCarthy 2012–18
Paul Hurst 2018
Paul Lambert October 2018–

LATEST SEQUENCES

Longest Sequence of League Wins: 8, 23.9.1953 – 31.10.1953.

Longest Sequence of League Defeats: 10, 4.9.1954 – 16.10.1954.

Longest Sequence of League Draws: 7, 10.11.1990 – 21.12.1990.

Longest Sequence of Unbeaten League Matches: 23, 8.12.1979 – 26.4.1980.

Longest Sequence Without a League Win: 21, 28.8.1963 – 14.12.1963.

Successive Scoring Runs: 31 from 7.3.2004.

Successive Non-scoring Runs: 7 from 28.2.1995.

TEN YEAR LEAGUE RECORD

		P	W	D	L	F	A	Pts	Pos
2009-10	FL C	46	12	20	14	50	61	56	15
2010-11	FL C	46	18	8	20	62	68	62	13
2011-12	FL C	46	17	10	19	69	77	61	15
2012-13	FL C	46	16	12	18	48	61	60	14
2013-14	FL C	46	18	14	14	60	54	68	9
2014-15	FL C	46	22	12	12	72	54	78	6
2015-16	FL C	46	18	15	13	53	51	69	7
2016-17	FL C	46	13	16	17	48	58	55	16
2017-18	FL C	46	17	9	20	57	60	60	12
2018-19	FL C	46	5	16	25	36	77	31	24

DID YOU KNOW?

Mick Stockwell played over 600 games for Ipswich Town between 1985 and 2000, making him the third highest appearance maker in the club's history. He appeared in every single outfield position, completing the set when he featured in the centre of defence at Leeds in January 1994.

IPSWICH TOWN – SKY BET CHAMPIONSHIP 2018–19 LEAGUE RECORD

Match No.	Date	Venue	Opponents	Result		H/T Score	Lg Pos.	Goalscorers	Attendance
1	Aug 4	H	Blackburn R	D	2-2	1-2	7	Edwards [5], Edun [90]	18,940
2	11	A	Rotherham U	L	0-1	0-0	19		9460
3	18	H	Aston Villa	D	1-1	1-1	16	Chalobah [36]	17,824
4	21	A	Derby Co	L	0-2	0-0	20		24,362
5	25	A	Sheffield W	L	1-2	1-1	24	Nsiala [40]	22,499
6	Sept 2	H	Norwich C	D	1-1	0-0	23	Edwards [57]	25,690
7	15	A	Hull C	L	0-2	0-1	24		11,650
8	18	H	Brentford	D	1-1	0-1	24	Jackson [73]	14,897
9	22	H	Bolton W	D	0-0	0-0	23		14,755
10	29	A	Birmingham C	D	2-2	2-0	22	Nolan [26], Pennington [41]	21,612
11	Oct 2	H	Middlesbrough	L	0-2	0-2	23		13,612
12	6	A	Swansea C	W	3-2	2-1	23	Edwards [27], van der Hoorn (og) [31], Chalobah [84]	18,810
13	20	H	QPR	L	0-2	0-2	24		18,345
14	24	A	Leeds U	L	0-2	0-1	24		29,082
15	27	A	Millwall	L	0-3	0-1	24		15,386
16	Nov 3	H	Preston NE	D	1-1	1-0	24	Sears (pen) [45]	15,129
17	10	A	Reading	D	2-2	2-1	24	Edwards [5], Sears [11]	14,952
18	23	H	WBA	L	1-2	0-1	24	Jackson [85]	22,995
19	28	H	Bristol C	L	2-3	1-0	24	Sears 2 [32, 58]	13,726
20	Dec 1	A	Nottingham F	L	0-2	0-2	24		27,873
21	8	A	Stoke C	L	0-2	0-1	24		24,694
22	15	H	Wigan Ath	W	1-0	0-0	24	Sears [67]	14,640
23	22	H	Sheffield U	D	1-1	1-0	24	Harrison [38]	17,942
24	26	A	QPR	L	0-3	0-2	24		14,584
25	29	A	Middlesbrough	L	0-2	0-1	24		23,334
26	Jan 1	H	Millwall	L	2-3	1-0	24	Lankester [2], Jackson [89]	16,957
27	12	H	Rotherham U	W	1-0	1-0	24	Keane [31]	20,893
28	19	A	Blackburn R	L	0-2	0-0	24		12,762
29	26	A	Aston Villa	L	1-2	0-1	24	Sears [76]	33,653
30	Feb 2	H	Sheffield W	L	0-1	0-0	24		16,888
31	10	A	Norwich C	L	0-3	0-1	24		27,040
32	13	H	Derby Co	D	1-1	0-1	24	Nolan [55]	18,604
33	16	H	Stoke C	D	1-1	0-1	24	Keane [90]	15,924
34	23	A	Wigan Ath	D	1-1	1-0	24	Keane (pen) [32]	10,835
35	Mar 2	H	Reading	L	1-2	0-1	24	Edwards [83]	23,009
36	9	A	WBA	D	1-1	0-1	24	Nolan [48]	23,973
37	12	A	Bristol C	D	1-1	0-1	24	Kelly (og) [68]	18,411
38	16	H	Nottingham F	D	1-1	1-1	24	Quaner [5]	16,709
39	30	H	Hull C	L	0-2	0-1	24		15,720
40	Apr 6	A	Bolton W	W	2-1	2-0	24	Quaner 2 [33, 44]	17,811
41	10	A	Brentford	L	0-2	0-2	24		10,039
42	13	H	Birmingham C	D	1-1	0-1	24	Edwards [46]	17,248
43	19	A	Preston NE	L	0-4	0-2	24		12,546
44	22	H	Swansea C	L	0-1	0-0	24		17,247
45	27	A	Sheffield U	L	0-2	0-1	24		30,140
46	May 5	H	Leeds U	W	3-2	1-1	24	Downes [30], Dozzell [47], Quaner [90]	20,895

Final League Position: 24

GOALSCORERS

League (36): Edwards 6, Sears 6 (1 pen), Quaner 4, Jackson 3, Keane 3 (1 pen), Nolan 3, Chalobah 2, Downes 1, Dozzell 1, Edun 1, Harrison 1, Lankester 1, Nsiala 1, Pennington 1, own goals 2.
FA Cup (0).
Carabao Cup (1): Jackson 1.

Bialkowski B 28	Spence J 16 + 1	Donacien J 9 + 1	Chambers L 43	Knudsen J 27 + 1	Skuse C 32 + 2	Chalobah T 35 + 8	Downes F 21 + 8	Edwards G 24 + 9	Harrison E 9 + 7	Sears F 21 + 3	Woolfenden L — + 1	Edun T 3 + 3	Morris B — + 1	Nsiala A 17 + 5	Ward G 11 + 3	Nolan J 23 + 3	Jackson K 14 + 22	Roberts J 6 + 6	Kenlock M 18 + 1	Gerken D 18	Pennington M 30	Graham J 3 + 1	Walters J 2 + 1	Rowe D — + 3	Dozzell A 10 + 9	Lankester J 5 + 6	Bishop T 13 + 5	Collins J 6	Elder C 3 + 1	Keane W 9 + 2	Quaner C 13 + 3	Dawkins S — + 2	Judge A 19	Bree J 13 + 1	Emmanuel J 4	El Mizouni I 1 + 3	Nydam T — + 1	Match No.
1	2^{2}	3	4	5	6	7	8^{1}	9	10	11^{3}	12	13	14																									1
1		2	4	5	6	7		10^{1}	11^{2}			13		3	8^{3}	9	12	14																				2
1		2	4	5	7	6		8	11^{2}			10■		3		9^{1}	12		13																			3
1		2	4	5	8^{2}	6	12	7^{1}	11^{3}					3	10	9	13	14																				4
1		2	4	5		6	12	7	10^{1}	13		8^{2}		3■		9	11																					5
	2		4	5	7^{1}	12		6	14						13	8	11^{3}			1	3	9^{2}	10															6
	2		4	5	7		8^{1}	6^{2}	14							10	12			1	3	9^{3}	11	13														7
	5^{1}	9	3	4	7	8^{2}	14	13	11^{3}						6	12	10			1	2																	8
			4	5	6^{1}	7^{3}		8				12		3	10^{2}	9	11			1	2	14	13															9
		13	4	5	6	7		8^{1}		12				3	10^{2}	9	11			1	2■																	10
		2	4	5	6	7		13		12				3	8	9^{1}	11^{2}			1		10^{3}			14													11
		5^{3}	4	12	6	7	13	8^{2}		11				3	10		14			1	2				9^{1}													12
		5	4		6	7		8^{2}		11				3	10^{1}		13			1	2				9	12												13
1	2		3	5	7^{3}	14	8	13		11^{2}		9^{1}			12	6	10				4																	14
1	12		4	6	8^{1}	3	7	14		11					2		10^{2}				5				9^{3}	13												15
1	2		3	5	6	7	8^{1}	9^{3}		11							12	10^{2}			4			13	14													16
1	2		3	5	7	6	8	9		11^{1}							12	10^{2}			4			13														17
1	2		3	5	7	6	8^{1}	9^{2}		11							14	10^{3}			4					13	12											18
1	2		3	5	7	6	8^{2}	9^{1}	14	11							12	10^{3}			4					13												19
1	2		3	5	7	13				9					8^{3}	14	11^{1}	12			4					10	6^{2}											20
	2		3	5		6	7	12	14	10						9^{2}		11^{1}		1	4				13	8^{3}												21
	2		3	5		6	7^{1}	12		10						9	14	11^{2}		1	4				13	8^{3}												22
	2		3	5		6		7	11^{1}	10					12	8		13		1	4				9^{2}													23
	2		3	5		6	7		11	10					8^{1}	9^{2}		13		1	4					12												24
	2		3			7	8	9		11						6^{2}	10^{1}	12	5	1	4				13													25
	2		3			7^{2}	8		10	11							13		5	1	4				12	9	6^{1}											26
			3		6	7	12			10^{1}				14						1	2					8^{3}		4	5	9	11^{2}	13						27
			3		8	7				9^{1}										1	2					12	13	4	5	11	10^{2}		6					28
1			3		7	6^{1}	8			11							13		5		2							4		10^{2}	12		9					29
1					7	13	8^{1}		14	9				3					5		4						6^{3}			12	10^{2}		11	2				30
1			3	5	7^{1}	6	14		12	9^{3}						8^{2}					4						13			10			11	2				31
1				4		6	8^{1}		14							12			5		3				13		7^{3}			11	10^{2}		9	2				32
1				4		6		13						14		8^{3}	12		5		3						7^{2}			11	10^{1}		9	2				33
1			3	4■		6	14	12								7	13		8		2									10^{1}	11^{3}		9^{2}	5				34
1			2		13	7^{1}		14						12		8			9		4						10	3^{3}			11		6	5^{2}				35
1			3	4	7			9								8	12		5								6^{1}				10^{2}	13	11	2				36
1			3		12	7		9						4		8^{2}	10		5						6^{3}		14						11^{1}		2	13		37
1			3		7^{1}	12		9						14		8	13		5		4						6^{2}				10^{3}		11	2				38
1			3		7^{3}	6		9						4		8^{2}	10^{1}		5						12						13		11	2		14		39
1			3		7	13	12	9^{1}									14		5						6^{2}		8^{3}	4			10		11		2			40
1			3			7^{1}	8							4			12		5						9		6^{3}				10^{2}		11	2		14	13	41
1			3		7			9						13			12		5						6^{2}		8	4^{1}			10		11		2			42
1			3		7	14	8							4			10		5								6^{3}			13			11	12	2^{2}	9^{1}		43
			3			7^{1}	8	9						4			13			1					6^{2}		14		5	10^{3}	12		11	2				44
			3		6	12	9							4			7^{2}		5	1					13		8			11^{1}			10	2				45
1			3■		7	8	6^{1}							4			12		5						9^{2}				13		10		11	2				46

FA Cup
Third Round Accrington S (a) 0-1

Carabao Cup
First Round Exeter C (a) 1-1
(Exeter C won 4-2 on penalties)

LEEDS UNITED

FOUNDATION

Immediately the Leeds City club (founded in 1904) was wound up by the FA in October 1919, following allegations of illegal payments to players, a meeting was called by a Leeds solicitor, Mr Alf Masser, at which Leeds United was formed. They joined the Midland League, playing their first game in that competition in November 1919. It was in this same month that the new club had discussions with the directors of a virtually bankrupt Huddersfield Town who wanted to move to Leeds in an amalgamation. But Huddersfield survived even that crisis.

Elland Road Stadium, Elland Road, Leeds, West Yorkshire LS11 0ES.

Telephone: (0871) 334 1919.

Ticket Office: (0371) 334 1992.

Website: www.leedsunited.com

Email: reception@leedsunited.com

Ground Capacity: 37,890.

Record Attendance: 57,892 v Sunderland, FA Cup 5th rd (replay), 15 March 1967.

Pitch Measurements: 105m × 68m (115yd × 74.5yd).

Chairman: Andrea Radrizzani.

Managing Director: Angus Kinnear.

Head Coach: Marcelo Bielsa.

Assistant Head Coaches: Pablo Quiroga, Diego Flores, Diego Reyes.

Colours: White shirts with blue trim, white shorts with blue trim, white socks with blue trim.

Year Formed: 1919, as Leeds United after disbandment (by FA order) of Leeds City (formed in 1904).

Turned Professional: 1920.

Club Nickname: 'The Whites'.

Ground: 1919, Elland Road.

First Football League Game: 28 August 1920, Division 2, v Port Vale (a) L 0–2 – Down; Duffield, Tillotson; Musgrove, Baker, Walton; Mason, Goldthorpe, Thompson, Lyon, Best.

Record League Victory: 8–0 v Leicester C, Division 1, 7 April 1934 – Moore; George Milburn, Jack Milburn; Edwards, Hart, Copping; Mahon (2), Firth (2), Duggan (2), Furness (2), Cochrane.

HONOURS

League Champions: Division 1 – 1968–69, 1973–74, 1991–92; Division 2 – 1923–24, 1963–64, 1989–90.
Runners-up: Division 1 – 1964–65, 1965–66, 1969–70, 1970–71, 1971–72; Division 2 – 1927–28, 1931–32, 1955–56; FL 1 – 2009–10.

FA Cup Winners: 1972.
Runners-up: 1965, 1970, 1973.

League Cup Winners: 1968.
Runners-up: 1996.

European Competitions
European Cup: 1969–70 *(sf)*, 1974–75 *(runners-up)*.
Champions League: 1992–93, 2000–01 *(sf)*.
Fairs Cup: 1965–66 *(sf)*, 1966–67 *(runners-up)*, 1967–68 *(winners)*, 1968–69 *(qf)*, 1970–71 *(winners)*.
UEFA Cup: 1971–72, 1973–74, 1979–80, 1995–96, 1998–99, 1999–2000 *(sf)*, 2001–02, 2002–03.
European Cup-Winners' Cup: 1972–73 *(runners-up)*.

THE Sun FACT FILE

Following the introduction of the UEFA Cup in the 1971–72 season, Leeds United (as current holders) met Barcelona (first winners) in a match to decide who would retain the Inter-Cities Fairs Cup. United travelled to the Nou Camp for the match which took place on 22 September 1971 but went down to a 2-1 defeat despite Joe Jordan's goal.

Record Cup Victory: 10–0 v Lyn (Oslo), European Cup 1st rd 1st leg, 17 September 1969 – Sprake; Reaney, Cooper, Bremner (2), Charlton, Hunter, Madeley, Clarke (2), Jones (3), Giles (2) (Bates), O'Grady (1).

Record Defeat: 1–8 v Stoke C, Division 1, 27 August 1934.

Most League Points (2 for a win): 67, Division 1, 1968–69.

Most League Points (3 for a win): 86, FL 1, 2009–10.

Most League Goals: 98, Division 2, 1927–28.

Highest League Scorer in Season: John Charles, 42, Division 2, 1953–54.

Most League Goals in Total Aggregate: Peter Lorimer, 168, 1965–79 and 1983–86.

Most League Goals in One Match: 5, Gordon Hodgson v Leicester C, Division 1, 1 October 1938.

Most Capped Player: Lucas Radebe, 58 (70), South Africa.

Most League Appearances: Jack Charlton, 629, 1953–73.

Youngest League Player: Peter Lorimer, 15 years 289 days v Southampton, 29 September 1962.

Record Transfer Fee Received: £30,800,000 from Manchester U for Rio Ferdinand, July 2002.

Record Transfer Fee Paid: £18,000,000 to West Ham U for Rio Ferdinand, November 2000.

Football League Record: 1920 Elected to Division 2; 1924–27 Division 1; 1927–28 Division 2; 1928–31 Division 1; 1931–32 Division 2; 1932–47 Division 1; 1947–56 Division 2; 1956–60 Division 1; 1960–64 Division 2; 1964–82 Division 1; 1982–90 Division 2; 1990–92 Division 1; 1992–2004 Premier League; 2004–07 FL C; 2007–10 FL 1; 2010– FL C.

MANAGERS

Dick Ray 1919–20
Arthur Fairclough 1920–27
Dick Ray 1927–35
Bill Hampson 1935–47
Willis Edwards 1947–48
Major Frank Buckley 1948–53
Raich Carter 1953–58
Bill Lambton 1958–59
Jack Taylor 1959–61
Don Revie OBE 1961–74
Brian Clough 1974
Jimmy Armfield 1974–78
Jock Stein CBE 1978
Jimmy Adamson 1978–80
Allan Clarke 1980–82
Eddie Gray MBE 1982–85
Billy Bremner 1985–88
Howard Wilkinson 1988–96
George Graham 1996–98
David O'Leary 1998–2002
Terry Venables 2002–03
Peter Reid 2003
Eddie Gray *(Caretaker)* 2003–04
Kevin Blackwell 2004–06
Dennis Wise 2006–08
Gary McAllister 2008
Simon Grayson 2008–12
Neil Warnock 2012–13
Brian McDermott 2013–14
Dave Hockaday 2014
Darko Milanic 2014
Neil Redfearn 2014–15
Uwe Rosler 2015
Steve Evans 2015–16
Garry Monk 2016–17
Thomas Christiansen 2017–18
Paul Heckingbottom 2018
Marcelo Bielsa June 2018–

LATEST SEQUENCES

Longest Sequence of League Wins: 9, 18.4.2009 – 5.9.2009.

Longest Sequence of League Defeats: 6, 28.12.2003 – 7.2.2004.

Longest Sequence of League Draws: 5, 2.5.2015 – 22.8.2015.

Longest Sequence of Unbeaten League Matches: 34, 26.10.1968 – 26.8.1969.

Longest Sequence Without a League Win: 17, 1.2.1947 – 26.5.1947.

Successive Scoring Runs: 30 from 27.8.1927.

Successive Non-scoring Runs: 6 from 30.1.1982.

TEN YEAR LEAGUE RECORD

		P	*W*	*D*	*L*	*F*	*A*	*Pts*	*Pos*
2009-10	FL 1	46	25	11	10	77	44	86	2
2010-11	FL C	46	19	15	12	81	70	72	7
2011-12	FL C	46	17	10	19	65	68	61	14
2012-13	FL C	46	17	10	19	57	66	61	13
2013-14	FL C	46	16	9	21	59	67	57	15
2014-15	FL C	46	15	11	20	50	61	56	15
2015-16	FL C	46	14	17	15	50	58	59	13
2016-17	FL C	46	22	9	15	61	47	75	7
2017-18	FL C	46	17	9	20	59	64	60	13
2018-19	FL C	46	25	8	13	73	50	83	3

DID YOU KNOW ?

Following their success in winning the old Second Division title in 1923–24, Leeds United embarked on a short tour of the Netherlands in May 1924. Results included a 4-1 defeat to Ajax, a 3-1 defeat by Bolton Wanderers in Amsterdam and a 2-2 draw with the Dutch national Olympic team.

LEEDS UNITED – SKY BET CHAMPIONSHIP 2018–19 LEAGUE RECORD

Match No.	Date	Venue	Opponents	Result		H/T Score	Lg Pos.	Goalscorers	Attendance
1	Aug 5	H	Stoke C	W	3-1	2-0	2	Klich[15], Hernandez[45], Cooper[57]	34,126
2	11	A	Derby Co	W	4-1	2-1	2	Klich[5], Roofe 2[21, 60], Alioski[64]	27,311
3	18	H	Rotherham U	W	2-0	0-0	2	Ayling[49], Roofe[71]	33,699
4	21	A	Swansea C	D	2-2	1-1	1	Roofe[40], Hernandez[79]	20,860
5	25	A	Norwich C	W	3-0	2-0	1	Klich[21], Alioski[26], Hernandez[67]	25,944
6	31	H	Middlesbrough	D	0-0	0-0	1		35,417
7	Sept 15	A	Millwall	D	1-1	0-0	1	Harrison[89]	17,195
8	18	H	Preston NE	W	3-0	1-0	1	Cooper[37], Roberts 2[74, 82]	27,729
9	22	H	Birmingham C	L	1-2	0-2	1	Alioski[85]	34,800
10	28	A	Sheffield W	D	1-1	0-1	1	Klich[54]	26,717
11	Oct 2	A	Hull C	W	1-0	0-0	1	Roberts[51]	13,798
12	6	H	Brentford	D	1-1	0-0	3	Jansson[88]	31,880
13	20	A	Blackburn R	L	1-2	1-1	4	Klich[45]	20,929
14	24	H	Ipswich T	W	2-0	1-0	1	Roofe[22], Cooper[66]	29,082
15	27	H	Nottingham F	D	1-1	0-1	2	Roofe[82]	34,308
16	Nov 4	A	Wigan Ath	W	2-1	1-1	1	Hernandez[9], Roofe[46]	14,799
17	10	A	WBA	L	1-4	0-0	3	Hernandez[90]	25,661
18	24	H	Bristol C	W	2-0	0-0	3	Roofe[69], Hernandez[86]	34,333
19	27	H	Reading	W	1-0	0-0	2	Dallas[60]	27,806
20	Dec 1	A	Sheffield U	W	1-0	0-0	2	Hernandez[82]	25,794
21	8	H	QPR	W	2-1	1-1	2	Roofe 2 (1 pen)[45, 53 (p)]	33,781
22	15	A	Bolton W	W	1-0	0-0	1	Bamford[66]	17,484
23	23	A	Aston Villa	W	3-2	0-2	1	Clarke[56], Jansson[61], Roofe[90]	41,411
24	26	H	Blackburn R	W	3-2	1-0	1	Williams (og)[33], Roofe 2[90, 90]	34,863
25	29	H	Hull C	L	0-2	0-1	1		35,754
26	Jan 1	A	Nottingham F	L	2-4	0-1	1	Clarke[52], Alioski[64]	29,530
27	11	H	Derby Co	W	2-0	1-0	1	Roofe[20], Harrison[47]	34,668
28	19	A	Stoke C	L	1-2	0-0	1	Alioski[90]	28,586
29	26	A	Rotherham U	W	2-1	0-1	1	Klich 2[51, 86]	11,259
30	Feb 2	H	Norwich C	L	1-3	0-2	2	Bamford[90]	36,524
31	9	A	Middlesbrough	D	1-1	0-0	1	Philips[90]	30,881
32	13	H	Swansea C	W	2-1	2-0	1	Jansson[20], Harrison[34]	34,044
33	23	H	Bolton W	W	2-1	1-1	3	Bamford (pen)[16], Alioski[68]	34,144
34	26	A	QPR	L	0-1	0-0	3		14,763
35	Mar 1	H	WBA	W	4-0	2-0	1	Hernandez[1], Bamford 2[28, 63], Alioski[90]	35,888
36	9	A	Bristol C	W	1-0	1-0	2	Bamford[9]	24,832
37	12	A	Reading	W	3-0	3-0	1	Klich[14], Hernandez 2[22, 43]	17,101
38	16	H	Sheffield U	L	0-1	0-0	3		37,004
39	30	H	Millwall	W	3-2	1-1	2	Hernandez 2[34, 83], Ayling[71]	34,910
40	Apr 6	A	Birmingham C	L	0-1	0-1	3		24,197
41	9	A	Preston NE	W	2-0	0-0	2	Bamford 2[62, 76]	18,019
42	13	H	Sheffield W	W	1-0	0-0	2	Harrison[65]	36,461
43	19	H	Wigan Ath	L	1-2	1-1	3	Bamford[17]	34,758
44	22	A	Brentford	L	0-2	0-1	3		11,580
45	28	H	Aston Villa	D	1-1	0-0	3	Klich[72]	36,786
46	May 5	A	Ipswich T	L	2-3	1-1	3	Klich[45], Dallas[76]	20,895

Final League Position: 3

GOALSCORERS

League (73): Roofe 14 (1 pen), Hernandez 12, Klich 10, Bamford 9 (1 pen), Alioski 7, Harrison 4, Cooper 3, Jansson 3, Roberts 3, Ayling 2, Clarke 2, Dallas 2, Philips 1, own goal 1.
FA Cup (1): Halme 1.
Carabao Cup (2): Bamford 1, Samuel 1.
Championship Play-offs (3): Dallas 2, Roofe 1.

Peacock-Farrell B 28	Ayling L 38	Berardi G 10 + 3	Cooper L 36	Douglas B 21 + 6	Philips K 42	Hernandez P 37 + 2	Samuel S 15 + 4	Klich M 46	Alioski E 44	Roofe K 27 + 5	Dallas S 10 + 16	Baker L 2 + 9	Harrison J 32 + 5	Shackleton J 3 + 16	Bamford P 15 + 7	Jansson P 37 + 2	Roberts T 20 + 8	Forshaw A 19 + 11	Edmondson R — + 1	Clarke J 4 + 18	Pearce T — + 2	Huffer W 1	Halme A 1 + 3	Davis L 1 + 3	Stevens J — + 1	Casilla F 17	Brown I — + 1	Match No.
1	2	3	4	5	6	7	8[2]	9[3]	10[1]	11	12	13	14															1
1	2	3	4	5	6	7	8[1]	9[3]	10	11[2]		14		12	13													2
1	2	3	4	5	7	10	9[2]	6[3]	8	11[1]		12			13	14												3
1	4	3		5	6[3]	7	8	9	10[2]	11[1]		12	13	2	14													4
1	2	4		5	6	7[1]	9[3]	8	10	11[2]		14	13		12	3												5
1	2	3[3]	4	5	6		8	9	10	11[2]	14		7[1]		13	12												6
1	2		4	5	6[2]		8	9[1]	10		13	12	7			3	11[3]	14										7
1	2		4	5	6		8[2]	9[3]	10		12	14	7			3	11[1]	13										8
1	2		4	5[2]	6[1]		9	8[3]	10		12		7			3	11	13	14									9
1	2		4	5	6		8[1]	9	10				7			3	11	12										10
1	5		4	8[1]	2		6[3]	7	11		13		9[2]	14		3	10	12										11
1	2■		4		6		9[1]	8[3]	10		5[2]	14	7			3	11	12		13								12
1		5[1]	4		6	12	9	8	10	7[3]	2[2]			14		3	11			13								13
1	5	2[1]	4		3	9	6[2]	7	8	10	12		11[3]					13			14							14
1	2[1]		4		6[2]	7	14	9	10	11	5					3		8		13	12[3]							15
1			4	8	2	9		6[1]	11	10	5			12		3		7										16
1			4	5[1]	6	7	14	8[3]	10	11[2]	2		13			3	12	9										17
			4	5	6	7	13	9[1]	10[3]	11	2	14	12					8				1	3[2]					18
1			4	5	3	7	13	9[3]	10[2]	11	2	8[1]		14				6		12								19
1			4[1]	8	2	9[2]		7	11[3]	10	5			14		3		6		13			12					20
1				5	4	10[1]	8[2]	9	7	11				2		3		6		13			12					21
1				5	4	7[2]		9	10	11[3]		8[1]		2	13	3		6		12			14					22
1	2				4	9		6	8	11			10[1]	13		3		7		12				5[2]				23
1	2[1]			5	3	9		8	7	11			10[2]	13		4		6		12								24
1	2[1]			5[2]	3	9		8	7	11			10[3]	14		4	13	6		12								25
1	2			5[2]	4■	8		9	10	11			7[1]			3	13	6		12								26
1	2		4			8		9	5	11			10[2]	12		3		6		7[1]				13				27
1	2		4			8		9[2]	5	11			10[1]			3■	12	6		7					13			28
	2		4		3	8[1]		9	5	11			10[3]	13			12	6		7[2]				14		1		29
	2		4	13		10[3]		9	5	11			7[1]		14	3	8[2]	6		12						1		30
	2[1]		4		6	12		9[2]	5	8			7	14	11	3	13			10[3]						1		31
	2		4		6	7[3]		9[2]	5	8			10	13	11[1]	3	12							14		1		32
	2[1]		4		6	7		9	5		12		10	13	11	3	8[2]									1		33
	2[2]		4	12	6[3]	7		9	5[1]		13		10		11	3	8									1	14	34
	2		4		6	7		9	5		12		10[2]	13	11	3	8[1]									1		35
	2	14	4	13	6	7		9[2]	5		12		10[3]		11[1]	3	8									1		36
	2[3]		4	14	6	7		9[2]	5		12		10	13	11	3	8[1]									1		37
	2[1]		4	12	6	7		9[3]	5		14		10[2]		11	3	8			13						1■		38
1	2		4	12	6	7		9[1]	5[3]				10		11	3[2]	8	14		13								39
	2		4		6	7		9[2]	5	13	12		10[1]		11[3]	3	8			14						1		40
	2	12	4		6	7		9	5	14			10[1]		11[2]	3	8[3]	13								1		41
	5	4			3	9		6[3]	8	12	14		11[1]		10[2]	2	7	13								1		42
	2	4			6[1]	7		9[3]	5	12			10		11	3	8[2]	13		14						1		43
	2		4			7		8	5[2]	13	12		10		11	3[1]	9[3]	6		14						1		44
	2	13	4		6	7		9			5[2]		10[1]		11	3	12	8								1		45
	2		4		6	7		9		11	5		10			3		8[1]		12						1		46

FA Cup
Third Round QPR (a) 1-2

Carabao Cup
First Round Bolton W (h) 2-1
Second Round Preston NE (h) 0-2

Championship Play-offs
Semi-Final 1st leg Derby Co (a) 1-0
Semi-Final 2nd leg Derby Co (h) 2-4

LEICESTER CITY

FOUNDATION

In 1884 a number of young footballers, who were mostly old boys of Wyggeston School, held a meeting at a house on the Roman Fosse Way and formed Leicester Fosse FC. They collected 9d (less than 4p) towards the cost of a ball, plus the same amount for membership. Their first professional, Harry Webb from Stafford Rangers, was signed in 1888 for 2s 6d (12p) per week, plus travelling expenses.

King Power Stadium, Filbert Way, Leicester LE2 7FL.

Telephone: (0344) 815 5000.

Fax: (0116) 291 5278.

Ticket Office: (0344) 815 5000 (option 1).

Website: www.lcfc.com

Email: lcfchelp@lcfc.co.uk

Ground Capacity: 32,273.

Record Attendance: 47,298 v Tottenham H, FA Cup 5th rd, 18 February 1928 (at Filbert Street); 32,242 v Sunderland, Premier League, 8 August 2015 (at King Power Stadium).

Pitch Measurements: 105m × 68m (115yd × 74.5yd).

Chairman: Aiyawatt Srivaddhanaprabha.

Chief Executive: Susan Whelan.

Manager: Brendan Rodgers.

Assistant Manager: Chris Davies.

Colours: Bold blue shirts with dark football gold and white trim, bold blue shorts with white trim, bold blue socks with white trim.

Year Formed: 1884.

Turned Professional: 1888.

Previous Name: 1884, Leicester Fosse; 1919, Leicester City.

Club Nickname: 'The Foxes'.

Grounds: 1884, Victoria Park; 1887, Belgrave Road; 1888, Victoria Park; 1891, Filbert Street; 2002, Walkers Stadium (now known as King Power Stadium from 2011).

First Football League Game: 1 September 1894, Division 2, v Grimsby T (a) L 3–4 – Thraves; Smith, Bailey; Seymour, Brown, Henrys; Hill, Hughes, McArthur (1), Skea (2), Priestman.

Record League Victory: 10–0 v Portsmouth, Division 1, 20 October 1928 – McLaren; Black, Brown; Findlay, Carr, Watson; Adcock, Hine (3), Chandler (6), Lochhead, Barry (1).

Record Cup Victory: 8–1 v Coventry C (a), League Cup 5th rd, 1 December 1964 – Banks; Sjoberg, Norman (2); Roberts, King, McDerment; Hodgson (2), Cross, Goodfellow, Gibson (1), Stringfellow (2), (1 og).

Record Defeat: 0–12 (as Leicester Fosse) v Nottingham F, Division 1, 21 April 1909.

HONOURS

League Champions: Premier League – 2015–16; FL C – 2013–14; Division 2 – 1924–25, 1936–37, 1953–54, 1956–57, 1970–71, 1979–80; FL 1 – 2008–09.
Runners-up: Division 1 – 1928–29; First Division – 2002–03; Division 2 – 1907–08.

FA Cup: *Runners-up:* 1949, 1961, 1963, 1969.

League Cup Winners: 1964, 1997, 2000.
Runners-up: 1965, 1999.

European Competitions
UEFA Champions League: 2016–17 (*qf*).
UEFA Cup: 1997–98, 2000–01.
European Cup-Winners' Cup: 1961–62.

THE Sun FACT FILE

The first occasion a match from Leicester City's Filbert Street ground was broadcast live on BBC radio was for the fixture against Newcastle United on 26 November 1927. The programme was scheduled to start at 2.30 with a running commentary from W.H. Bourne. City secured a comfortable 3-0 victory over the Magpies.

Most League Points (2 for a win): 61, Division 2, 1956–57.

Most League Points (3 for a win): 102, FL C, 2013–14.

Most League Goals: 109, Division 2, 1956–57.

Highest League Scorer in Season: Arthur Rowley, 44, Division 2, 1956–57.

Most League Goals in Total Aggregate: Arthur Chandler, 259, 1923–35.

Most League Goals in One Match: 6, John Duncan v Port Vale, Division 2, 25 December 1924; 6, Arthur Chandler v Portsmouth, Division 1, 20 October 1928.

Most Capped Player: Andy King, 50 (includes 3 on loan at Swansea C), Wales.

Most League Appearances: Adam Black, 528, 1920–35.

Youngest League Player: Dave Buchanan, 16 years 192 days v Oldham Ath, 1 January 1979.

Record Transfer Fee Received: £60,000,000 from Manchester C for Riyad Mahrez, July 2018.

Record Transfer Fee Paid: £40,000,000 to Monaco for Youri Tielemans, July 2019.

Football League Record: 1894 Elected to Division 2; 1908–09 Division 1; 1909–25 Division 2; 1925–35 Division 1; 1935–37 Division 2; 1937–39 Division 1; 1946–54 Division 2; 1954–55 Division 1; 1955–57 Division 2; 1957–69 Division 1; 1969–71 Division 2; 1971–78 Division 1; 1978–80 Division 2; 1980–81 Division 1; 1981–83 Division 2; 1983–87 Division 1; 1987–92 Division 2; 1992–94 Division 1; 1994–95 Premier League; 1995–96 Division 1; 1996–2002 Premier League; 2002–03 Division 1; 2003–04 Premier League; 2004–08 FL C; 2008–09 FL 1; 2009–14 FL C; 2014– Premier League.

LATEST SEQUENCES

Longest Sequence of League Wins: 9, 21.12.2013 – 1.2.2014.

Longest Sequence of League Defeats: 8, 17.3.2001 – 28.4.2001.

Longest Sequence of League Draws: 6, 2.10.2004 – 2.11.2004.

Longest Sequence of Unbeaten League Matches: 23, 1.11.2008 – 7.3.2009.

Longest Sequence Without a League Win: 18, 12.4.1975 – 1.11.1975.

Successive Scoring Runs: 32 from 23.11.2013.

Successive Non-scoring Runs: 7 from 21.11.1987.

MANAGERS

Frank Gardner 1884–92
Ernest Marson 1892–94
J. Lee 1894–95
Henry Jackson 1895–97
William Clark 1897–98
George Johnson 1898–1912
Jack Bartlett 1912–14
Louis Ford 1914–15
Harry Linney 1915–19
Peter Hodge 1919–26
Willie Orr 1926–32
Peter Hodge 1932–34
Arthur Lochhead 1934–36
Frank Womack 1936–39
Tom Bromilow 1939–45
Tom Mather 1945–46
John Duncan 1946–49
Norman Bullock 1949–55
David Halliday 1955–58
Matt Gillies 1958–68
Frank O'Farrell 1968–71
Jimmy Bloomfield 1971–77
Frank McLintock 1977–78
Jock Wallace 1978–82
Gordon Milne 1982–86
Bryan Hamilton 1986–87
David Pleat 1987–91
Gordon Lee 1991
Brian Little 1991–94
Mark McGhee 1994–95
Martin O'Neill 1995–2000
Peter Taylor 2000–01
Dave Bassett 2001–02
Micky Adams 2002–04
Craig Levein 2004–06
Robert Kelly 2006–07
Martin Allen 2007
Gary Megson 2007
Ian Holloway 2007–08
Nigel Pearson 2008–10
Paulo Sousa 2010
Sven-Göran Eriksson 2010–11
Nigel Pearson 2011–15
Claudio Ranieri 2015–17
Craig Shakespeare 2017
Claude Puel 2017–19
Brendan Rodgers February 2019–

TEN YEAR LEAGUE RECORD

		P	*W*	*D*	*L*	*F*	*A*	*Pts*	*Pos*
2009-10	FL C	46	21	13	12	61	45	76	5
2010-11	FL C	46	19	10	17	76	71	67	10
2011-12	FL C	46	18	12	16	66	55	66	9
2012-13	FL C	46	19	11	16	71	48	68	6
2013-14	FL C	46	31	9	6	83	43	102	1
2014-15	PR Lge	38	11	8	19	46	55	41	14
2015-16	PR Lge	38	23	12	3	68	36	81	1
2016-17	PR Lge	38	12	8	18	48	63	44	12
2017-18	PR Lge	38	12	11	15	56	60	47	9
2018-19	PR Lge	38	15	7	16	51	48	52	9

DID YOU KNOW ?

Leicester City played a total of 13 League and Cup games on artificial surfaces between 1981 and 1991. They were successful on just one occasion, 27 September 1986, when a goal from Alan Smith secured a 1-0 win over Queens Park Rangers in a First Division fixture.

LEICESTER CITY – PREMIER LEAGUE 2018–19 LEAGUE RECORD

Match No.	*Date*	*Venue*	*Opponents*	*Result*		*H/T Score*	*Lg Pos.*	*Goalscorers*	*Attendance*
1	Aug 10	A	Manchester U	L	1-2	0-1	20	Vardy [90]	74,439
2	18	H	Wolverhampton W	W	2-0	2-0	9	Doherty (og) [29], Maddison [45]	32,043
3	25	A	Southampton	W	2-1	0-0	7	Gray [56], Maguire [90]	29,925
4	Sept 1	H	Liverpool	L	1-2	0-2	8	Ghezzal [63]	32,149
5	15	A	Bournemouth	L	2-4	0-3	10	Maddison (pen) [88], Albrighton [89]	10,543
6	22	H	Huddersfield T	W	3-1	1-1	8	Iheanacho [19], Maddison [66], Vardy [75]	31,676
7	29	A	Newcastle U	W	2-0	1-0	7	Vardy (pen) [30], Maguire [73]	51,523
8	Oct 6	H	Everton	L	1-2	1-1	10	Ricardo Pereira [40]	32,007
9	22	A	Arsenal	L	1-3	1-1	11	Bellerin (og) [31]	59,886
10	27	H	West Ham U	D	1-1	0-1	12	Ndidi [89]	31,848
11	Nov 3	A	Cardiff C	W	1-0	0-0	10	Gray [55]	30,877
12	10	H	Burnley	D	0-0	0-0	10		32,184
13	24	A	Brighton & HA	D	1-1	0-1	10	Vardy (pen) [79]	30,553
14	Dec 1	H	Watford	W	2-0	2-0	8	Vardy (pen) [12], Maddison [23]	31,353
15	5	A	Fulham	D	1-1	0-1	9	Maddison [74]	22,881
16	8	H	Tottenham H	L	0-2	0-1	9		31,957
17	15	A	Crystal Palace	L	0-1	0-1	12		24,738
18	22	A	Chelsea	W	1-0	0-0	9	Vardy [51]	40,558
19	26	H	Manchester C	W	2-1	1-1	7	Albrighton [19], Ricardo Pereira [81]	32,090
20	29	H	Cardiff C	L	0-1	0-0	8		32,047
21	Jan 1	A	Everton	W	1-0	0-0	7	Vardy [58]	39,052
22	12	H	Southampton	L	1-2	0-2	8	Ndidi [58]	31,491
23	19	A	Wolverhampton W	L	3-4	0-2	9	Gray [47], Coady (og) [51], Morgan [87]	31,278
24	30	A	Liverpool	D	1-1	1-1	11	Maguire [45]	53,092
25	Feb 3	H	Manchester U	L	0-1	0-1	11		32,148
26	10	A	Tottenham H	L	1-3	0-1	12	Vardy [76]	44,154
27	23	H	Crystal Palace	L	1-4	0-1	12	Evans [64]	31,778
28	26	H	Brighton & HA	W	2-1	1-0	11	Gray [10], Vardy [63]	30,558
29	Mar 3	A	Watford	L	1-2	0-1	11	Vardy [75]	20,062
30	9	H	Fulham	W	3-1	1-0	10	Tielemans [21], Vardy 2 [78, 86]	32,017
31	16	A	Burnley	W	2-1	1-1	10	Maddison [33], Morgan [90]	20,719
32	30	H	Bournemouth	W	2-0	1-0	8	Morgan [11], Vardy [82]	31,530
33	Apr 6	A	Huddersfield T	W	4-1	1-0	7	Tielemans [24], Vardy 2 (1 pen) [48, 84 (p)], Maddison [79]	24,146
34	12	H	Newcastle U	L	0-1	0-1	7		32,108
35	20	A	West Ham U	D	2-2	0-1	8	Vardy [67], Barnes [90]	59,960
36	28	H	Arsenal	W	3-0	0-0	8	Tielemans [59], Vardy 2 [86, 90]	32,037
37	May 6	A	Manchester C	L	0-1	0-0	9		54,506
38	12	H	Chelsea	D	0-0	0-0	9		32,140

Final League Position: 9

GOALSCORERS

League (51): Vardy 18 (4 pens), Maddison 7 (1 pen), Gray 4, Maguire 3, Morgan 3, Tielemans 3, Albrighton 2, Ndidi 2, Ricardo Pereira 2, Barnes 1, Evans 1, Ghezzal 1, Iheanacho 1, own goals 3.
FA Cup (1): Ghezzal 1.
Carabao Cup (5): Albrighton 1, Fuchs 1, Ghezzal 1, Iborra 1, Iheanacho 1.
Checkatrade Trophy (5): Loft 3, Pascanu 1, Shade 1.

Schmeichel K 38	Amartey D 7 + 2	Morgan W 21 + 1	Maguire H 31	Chilwell B 36	Adrien Silva S 1 + 1	Ndidi O 37 + 1	Ricardo Pereira D 35	Maddison J 35 + 1	Gray D 23 + 11	Iheanacho K 9 + 21	Ghezzal R 8 + 11	Vardy J 30 + 4	Iborra V 3 + 5	Evans J 21 + 3	Mendy N 23 + 8	Albrighton M 18 + 9	Okazaki S 1 + 20	Soyuncu C 4 + 2	Simpson D 3 + 3	Diabate F 1	Fuchs C 2 + 1	Choudhury H 7 + 2	Barnes H 11 + 5	Tielemans Y 13	Match No.
1	2^2	3	4	5	6^1	7	8	9^3	10	11	12	13	14												1
1	12		4	5	14	7	2	9^3	10^1	13		11■		3	6	8^2									2
1	2	3	4	5		7	8	9^1	10^3	11^2	13				6	12	14								3
1	14	3	4	5		7	2	9^3	11^2	12	8				6	10^1	13								4
1		3■	4	5		6	2	9	10^2	12	8^3	11^1		14	7	13									5
1	2		4	5		6		10^1	12	9^2	8^3	11		3	7	13	14								6
1	2	3	4	5		7	8	10^2		9		11^1	13		6	12									7
1	2	3■	4	5		7	8^1	10^3		9^2	13	11			6	12	14								8
1	2		3	8		7	5^1	9^3		10^2	13	11		4	6	12	14								9
1	2		4	5		6		9	13	11^1	8^3	12	7			10	14	3^2							10
1		3	4^3	5		7	2	9^2	10^1			11	14	12	6	8			13						11
1		3		5		7	2		10^1	12	9	11		4^3	6	8^2	13	14							12
1		3		5		12	2	9■	10^2	14		13	6^3	4	7	8	11^1								13
1		3		5		7	2	9	8^3	13		11^1	14	4^2	6	10		12							14
1		3		5		7		9	12	11			13		6^1	8	14	4	2^2	10^3					15
1		3		5		8	2	11	9	10^2	12		7^3	4	6^1	13	14								16
1		3	4			7	2	9^2	10^1	13	12	11			6	8^3	14				5				17
1		3	4	5		8	2	11^1	12	13		10^2			7	9						6			18
1		3	4	5		8	2	11^2	12			10^3			7	9	14		13			6^1			19
1			4	5		7	2	9	10^3	13	12	11^2			6	8^1	14	3							20
1			4	5		8	11		13		9^1	10^2		3	7	12			2			6			21
1		3	4	5		8	2	11	13		14	10			7^1	9^3						6^2	12		22
1		3	4^1	5		7	8	13	9	14		11		12	6				2^2				10^3		23
1			4	5		8	2	9^2	6^1	14		11^3		3	7	10	13					12			24
1			4	5		7	2	9^3	8^2	14	12	11		3	6^1		13						10		25
1			4	5		6	2	9	11^1	13	7^2	12		3			14						10^3	8	26
1			4			7	2	8	12	13	9^1	10		3			14				5		11^3	6^2	27
1			4	5		7	2	8^1	9	13		10^3		3	12		14						11	6^2	28
1		3	4	8		7	5	9	12	14		11^1		2	13								10^2	6^3	29
1			4	5		7	2	9^2	8^3		12	11		3	14		13						10	6^1	30
1		12	4■	5		6	2	9^1	7^2			11		3	14						13		10^3	8	31
1		3		5		6	2	9	7^3	14	13	11^2		4	12								10^1	8	32
1		3		5		6^3	2	9	7	14		11^1					12	4				13	10^2	8	33
1		3	4	5		6^3	2	9	7^2	12		11			13	14							10^1	8	34
1			4	5		7	2	10	9^2	13		11		3	14	6^1							12	8^3	35
1			4	5		6^3	2	10	14			11		3	13	7^1						9^2	12	8	36
1			4	5		8	2	10^2	14	13		11		3		6^3						9	12	7^1	37
1			4	5		6^1	2	10^3				11		3		7^2	12		13			9	14	8	38

FA Cup

Third Round	Newport Co	(a)	1-2

Carabao Cup

Second Round	Fleetwood T	(h)	4-0
Third Round	Wolverhampton W	(a)	0-0
(Leicester C won 3-1 on penalties)			
Fourth Round	Southampton	(h)	0-0
(Leicester C won 6-5 on penalties)			
Quarter-Final	Manchester C	(h)	1-1
(Manchester C won 3-1 on penalties)			

Checkatrade Trophy (Leicester C U21)

Group B (N)	Fleetwood T	(a)	2-2
(Leicester C U21 won 7-6 on penalties)			
Group B (N)	Bury	(a)	1-2
Group B (N)	Rochdale	(a)	2-2
(Leicester C U21 won 4-3 on penalties)			

LEYTON ORIENT

FOUNDATION

There is some doubt about the foundation of Leyton Orient, and, indeed, some confusion with clubs like Leyton and Clapton over their early history. As regards the foundation, the most favoured version is that Leyton Orient was formed originally by members of Homerton Theological College who established Glyn Cricket Club in 1881 and then carried on through the following winter playing football. Eventually many employees of the Orient Shipping Line became involved and so the name Orient was chosen in 1888.

The Breyer Group Stadium, Brisbane Road, Leyton, London E10 5NF.

Telephone: (0208) 926 1111.

Ticket Office: (0208) 926 1010.

Website: www.leytonorient.com

Email: info@leytonorient.net

Ground Capacity: 9,271.

Record Attendance: 34,345 v West Ham U, FA Cup 4th rd, 25 January 1964.

Pitch Measurements: 100.5m × 65m (110yd × 71yd).

Chairman: Nigel Travis.

Chief Executive: Danny Macklin.

Director of Football: Martin Ling.

Interim Head Coach: Ross Embleton.

Interim Assistant Head Coach: Danny Webb.

Colours: Red shirts with white trim, red shorts with white trim, red socks.

Year Formed: 1881. ***Turned Professional:*** 1903.

Previous Names: 1881, Glyn Cricket and Football Club; 1886, Eagle Football Club; 1888, Orient Football Club; 1898, Clapton Orient; 1946, Leyton Orient; 1966, Orient; 1987, Leyton Orient.

Club Nickname: 'The O's'.

Grounds: 1884, Glyn Road; 1896, Whittles Athletic Ground; 1900, Millfields Road; 1930, Lea Bridge Road; 1937, Brisbane Road (renamed Matchroom Stadium; 2018, The Breyer Group Stadium).

First Football League Game: 2 September 1905, Division 2, v Leicester Fosse (a) L 1–2 – Butler; Holmes, Codling; Lamberton, Boden, Boyle; Kingaby (1), Wootten, Leigh, Evenson, Bourne.

Record League Victory: 8–0 v Crystal Palace, Division 3 (S), 12 November 1955 – Welton; Lee, Earl; Blizzard, Aldous, McKnight; White (1), Facey (3), Burgess (2), Heckman, Hartburn (2). 8–0 v Rochdale, Division 4, 20 October 1987 – Wells; Howard, Dickenson (1), Smalley (1), Day, Hull, Hales (2), Castle (Sussex), Shinners (2), Godfrey (Harvey), Comfort (2). 8–0 v Colchester U, Division 4, 15 October 1988 – Wells; Howard, Dickenson, Hales (1p), Day (1), Sitton (1), Baker (1), Ward, Hull (3), Juryeff, Comfort (1). 8–0 v Doncaster R, Division 3, 28 December 1997 – Hyde; Channing, Naylor, Smith (1p), Hicks, Clark, Ling, Roger Joseph, Griffiths (3) (Harris), Richards (2) (Baker (1)), Inglethorpe (1) (Simpson).

HONOURS

League Champions: Division 3 – 1969–70; Division 3S – 1955–56.
Runners-up: Division 2 – 1961–62; Division 3S – 1954–55.

FA Cup: semi-final – 1978.

League Cup: 5th rd – 1963.

THE SUN FACT FILE

Clapton Orient, the O's former name, played their first game on their Brisbane Road ground on the opening day of the 1937–38 season when their Division Three South fixture against Cardiff City attracted a gate of 14,598. Fred Tully gave Orient an early lead only for Cardiff to equalise with the match ending 1-1. The ground was previously the home of amateur club Leyton FC who protested when Leyton Corporation negotiated a lease for the O's to take over as tenants.

Record Cup Victory: 9–2 v Chester, League Cup 3rd rd, 15 October 1962 – Robertson; Charlton, Taylor; Gibbs, Bishop, Lea; Deeley (1), Waites (3), Dunmore (2), Graham (3), Wedge.

Record Defeat: 0–8 v Aston Villa, FA Cup 4th rd, 30 January 1929.

Most League Points (2 for a win): 66, Division 3 (S), 1955–56.

Most League Points (3 for a win): 86, FL 1, 2013–14.

Most League Goals: 106, Division 3 (S), 1955–56.

Highest League Scorer in Season: Tom Johnston, 35, Division 2, 1957–58.

Most League Goals in Total Aggregate: Tom Johnston, 121, 1956–58, 1959–61.

Most League Goals in One Match: 4, Wally Leigh v Bradford C, Division 2, 13 April 1906; 4, Albert Pape v Oldham Ath, Division 2, 1 September 1924; 4, Peter Kitchen v Millwall, Division 3, 21 April 1984.

Most Capped Player: Jobi McAnuff, 23 (32), Jamaica.

Most League Appearances: Peter Allen, 432, 1965–78.

Youngest League Player: Paul Went, 15 years 327 days v Preston NE, 4 September 1965.

Record Transfer Fee Received: £1,000,000 (rising to £1,500,000) from Fulham for Gabriel Zakuani, July 2006.

Record Transfer Fee Paid: £200,000 to Oldham Ath for Liam Kelly, July 2016.

Football League Record: 1905 Elected to Division 2; 1929–56 Division 3 (S); 1956–62 Division 2; 1962–63 Division 1; 1963–66 Division 2; 1966–70 Division 3; 1970–82 Division 2; 1982–85 Division 3; 1985–89 Division 4; 1989–92 Division 3; 1992–95 Division 2; 1995–2004 Division 3; 2004–06 FL 2; 2006–15 FL 1; 2015–17 FL 2; 2017–19 National League; 2019– FL 2.

LATEST SEQUENCES

Longest Sequence of League Wins: 10, 21.1.1956 – 30.3.1956.

Longest Sequence of League Defeats: 9, 1.4.1995 – 6.5.1995.

Longest Sequence of League Draws: 6, 30.11.1974 – 28.12.1974.

Longest Sequence of Unbeaten League Matches: 15, 13.4.2013 – 19.10.2013.

Longest Sequence Without a League Win: 23, 6.10.1962 – 13.4.1963.

Successive Scoring Runs: 22 from 12.3.1927.

Successive Non-scoring Runs: 8 from 19.11.1994.

MANAGERS

Sam Omerod 1905–06
Ike Ivenson 1906
Billy Holmes 1907–22
Peter Proudfoot 1922–29
Arthur Grimsdell 1929–30
Peter Proudfoot 1930–31
Jimmy Seed 1931–33
David Pratt 1933–34
Peter Proudfoot 1935–39
Tom Halsey 1939
Bill Wright 1939–45
Willie Hall 1945
Bill Wright 1945–46
Charlie Hewitt 1946–48
Neil McBain 1948–49
Alec Stock 1949–59
Les Gore 1959–61
Johnny Carey 1961–63
Benny Fenton 1963–64
Dave Sexton 1965
Dick Graham 1966–68
Jimmy Bloomfield 1968–71
George Petchey 1971–77
Jimmy Bloomfield 1977–81
Paul Went 1981
Ken Knighton 1981–83
Frank Clark 1983–91 *(Managing Director)*
Peter Eustace 1991–94
Chris Turner and John Sitton 1994–95
Pat Holland 1995–96
Tommy Taylor 1996–2001
Paul Brush 2001–03
Martin Ling 2003–09
Geraint Williams 2009–10
Russell Slade 2010–14
Kevin Nugent 2014
Mauro Milanese 2014
Fabio Liverani 2014–15
Ian Hendon 2015–16
Kevin Nolan 2016
Andy Hessenthaler 2016
Alberto Cavasin 2016
Andy Edwards 2016–17
Danny Webb 2017
Martin Ling 2017
Omer Riza 2017
Steve Davis 2017
Justin Edinburgh 2017–19
Ross Embleton June 2019– *(interim)*

TEN YEAR LEAGUE RECORD

		P	W	D	L	F	A	Pts	Pos
2009-10	FL 1	46	13	12	21	53	63	51	17
2010-11	FL 1	46	19	13	14	71	62	70	7
2011-12	FL 1	46	13	11	22	48	75	50	20
2012-13	FL 1	46	21	8	17	55	48	71	7
2013-14	FL 1	46	25	11	10	85	45	86	3
2014-15	FL 1	46	12	13	21	59	69	49	23
2015-16	FL 2	46	19	12	15	60	61	69	8
2016-17	FL 2	46	10	6	30	47	87	36	24
2017-18	NL	46	16	12	18	58	56	60	13
2018-19	NL	46	25	14	7	73	35	89	1

DID YOU KNOW ?

Leyton Orient's first game in top-flight football saw them face Arsenal at Brisbane Road in August 1962. The O's, watched by a crowd of 26,300, went two goals down before Derek Gibbs pulled one back late on. The season proved to be Orient's only one in the old First Division and they were relegated after finishing bottom of the table.

LINCOLN CITY

FOUNDATION

The original Lincoln Football Club was established in the early 1860s and was one of the first provisional clubs to affiliate to the Football Association. In their early years, they regularly played matches against the famous Sheffield Football Club and later became known as Lincoln Lindum. The present organisation was formed at a public meeting held in the Monson Arms Hotel in June 1884 and won the Lincolnshire Cup in only their third season. They were founder members of the Midland League in 1889 and that competition's first champions.

Sincil Bank Stadium, Sincil Bank, Lincoln LN5 8LD.

Telephone: (01522) 880 011.

Fax: (01522) 880 020.

Ticket Office: (01522) 880 011.

Website: www.redimps.com

Email: info@lincolncityfc.co.uk

Ground Capacity: 10,049.

Record Attendance: 23,196 v Derby Co, League Cup 4th rd, 15 November 1967.

Pitch Measurements: 100m × 65m (109.5yd × 71yd).

Chairman: Clive Nates.

Chief Executive Officer: Liam Scully.

Manager: Danny Cowley.

Assistant Manager: Nicky Cowley.

Colours: Red and white striped shirts, black shorts with red trim, red socks with white hoops.

Year Formed: 1884.

Turned Professional: 1892.

Ltd Co.: 1895.

Club Nickname: 'The Red Imps'.

Grounds: 1883, John O'Gaunt's; 1894, Sincil Bank.

First Football League Game: 3 September 1892, Division 2, v Sheffield U (a) L 2–4 – William Gresham; Coulton, Neill; Shaw, Mettam, Moore; Smallman, Irving (1), Cameron (1), Kelly, James Gresham.

Record League Victory: 11–1 v Crewe Alex, Division 3 (N), 29 September 1951 – Jones; Green (1p), Varney; Wright, Emery, Grummett (1); Troops (1), Garvey, Graver (6), Whittle (1), Johnson (1).

Record Cup Victory: 8–1 v Bromley, FA Cup 2nd rd, 10 December 1938 – McPhail; Hartshorne, Corbett; Bean, Leach, Whyte (1); Hancock, Wilson (1), Ponting (3), Deacon (1), Clare (2).

Record Defeat: 3–11 v Manchester C, Division 2, 23 March 1895.

Most League Points (2 for a win): 74, Division 4, 1975–76.

HONOURS

League Champions: Division 3 (N) – 1931–32, 1947–48, 1951–52; FL 2 – 2018–19; Division 4 – 1975–76; National League – 1987–88, 2016–17.
Runners-up: Division 3 (N) – 1927–28, 1930–31, 1936–37; Division 4 – 1980–81.

FA Cup: quarter-final – 2017.

League Cup: 4th rd – 1968.

League Trophy Winners: 2018.

THE Sun FACT FILE

Lincoln City did the double over Wigan Borough in 1931–32 only for both results later to be wiped from the record books after their opponents resigned from the Football League as a result of their financial problems. City still went on to win the Third Division North title – the first time they had topped a division since entering the Football League.

Most League Points (3 for a win): 85, FL 2, 2018–19.

Most League Goals: 121, Division 3 (N), 1951–52.

Highest League Scorer in Season: Allan Hall, 41, Division 3 (N), 1931–32.

Most League Goals in Total Aggregate: Andy Graver, 143, 1950–55 and 1958–61.

Most League Goals in One Match: 6, Frank Keetley v Halifax T, Division 3 (N), 16 January 1932; 6, Andy Graver v Crewe Alex, Division 3 (N), 29 September 1951.

Most Capped Player: Gareth McAuley, 5 (80), Northern Ireland.

Most League Appearances: Grant Brown, 407, 1989–2002.

Youngest League Player: Shane Nicholson, 16 years 172 days v Burnley, 22 November 1986.

Record Transfer Fee Received: £750,000 from Liverpool for Jack Hobbs, August 2005.

Record Transfer Fee Paid: £100,000 to Barnet for John Akinde, July 2018.

Football League Record: 1892 Founder member of Division 2. Remained in Division 2 until 1920 when they failed re-election but also missed seasons 1908–09 and 1911–12 when not re-elected. 1921–32 Division 3 (N); 1932–34 Division 2; 1934–48 Division 3 (N); 1948–49 Division 2; 1949–52 Division 3 (N); 1952–61 Division 2; 1961–62 Division 3; 1962–76 Division 4; 1976–79 Division 3; 1979–81 Division 4; 1981–86 Division 3; 1986–87 Division 4; 1987–88 GM Vauxhall Conference; 1988–92 Division 4; 1992–98 Division 3; 1998–99 Division 2; 1999–2004 Division 3; 2004–11 FL 2; 2011–17 Conference National League; 2017–19 FL 2; 2019– FL 1.

LATEST SEQUENCES

Longest Sequence of League Wins: 10, 1.9.1930 – 18.10.1930.

Longest Sequence of League Defeats: 12, 21.9.1896 – 9.1.1897.

Longest Sequence of League Draws: 5, 21.2.1981 – 7.3.1981.

Longest Sequence of Unbeaten League Matches: 19, 29.12.2018 – 13.4.2019.

Longest Sequence Without a League Win: 19, 22.8.1978 – 23.12.1978.

Successive Scoring Runs: 37 from 1.3.1930.

Successive Non-scoring Runs: 5 from 15.11.1913.

MANAGERS

Alf Martin 1896–97
(Secretary/Manager)
David Calderhead 1900–07
John Henry Strawson 1907–14
(had been Secretary)
George Fraser 1919–21
David Calderhead Jnr. 1921–24
Horace Henshall 1924–27
Harry Parkes 1927–36
Joe McClelland 1936–46
Bill Anderson 1946–65
(General Manager to 1966)
Roy Chapman 1965–66
Ron Gray 1966–70
Bert Loxley 1970–71
David Herd 1971–72
Graham Taylor 1972–77
George Kerr 1977–78
Willie Bell 1977–78
Colin Murphy 1978–85
John Pickering 1985
George Kerr 1985–87
Peter Daniel 1987
Colin Murphy 1987–90
Allan Clarke 1990
Steve Thompson 1990–93
Keith Alexander 1993–94
Sam Ellis 1994–95
Steve Wicks *(Head Coach)* 1995
John Beck 1995–98
Shane Westley 1998
John Reames 1998–2000
Phil Stant 2000–01
Alan Buckley 2001–02
Keith Alexander 2002–06
John Schofield 2006–07
Peter Jackson 2007–09
Chris Sutton 2009–10
Steve Tilson 2010–11
David Holdsworth 2011–13
Gary Simpson 2013–14
Chris Moyses 2014–16
Danny Cowley May 2016–

TEN YEAR LEAGUE RECORD

		P	*W*	*D*	*L*	*F*	*A*	*Pts*	*Pos*
2009-10	FL 2	46	13	11	22	42	65	50	20
2010-11	FL 2	46	13	8	25	45	81	47	23
2011-12	Conf	46	13	10	23	56	66	49	17
2012-13	Conf	46	15	11	20	72	86	54	16
2013-14	Conf	46	17	14	15	60	59	65	14
2014-15	Conf	46	16	10	20	62	71	58	15
2015-16	NL	46	16	13	17	69	68	61	13
2016-17	NL	46	30	9	7	83	40	99	1
2017-18	FL 2	46	20	15	11	64	48	75	7
2018-19	FL 2	46	23	16	7	73	43	85	1

DID YOU KNOW ?

Lincoln City were founder members of the Central League when it was formed in 1911, having been voted out of the Football League. After losing their opening game of the season City went on a 23-match unbeaten run. They lost just one more game during the campaign and finished as the first champions of the competition.

LINCOLN CITY – SKY BET LEAGUE TWO 2018–19 LEAGUE RECORD

Match No.	Date	Venue	Opponents	Result		H/T Score	Lg Pos.	Goalscorers	Attendance
1	Aug 4	A	Northampton T	W	1-0	0-0	8	Green [48]	6242
2	11	H	Swindon T	W	4-1	2-1	1	Akinde (pen) [10], Bostwick [29], Toffolo [79], Green [82]	8405
3	18	A	Grimsby T	D	1-1	0-1	1	Akinde (pen) [71]	7201
4	21	H	Bury	W	2-1	0-1	2	Akinde (pen) [75], Frecklington [82]	8016
5	25	H	Notts Co	W	3-1	2-1	1	Frecklington [7], Andrade [33], Anderson [55]	9119
6	Sept 1	A	Exeter C	W	3-0	2-0	1	Frecklington [43], Akinde [45], Brown, T (og) [56]	4067
7	8	H	Crawley T	L	0-1	0-1	1		8321
8	15	A	Macclesfield T	W	2-1	1-0	1	Pett [21], Shackell [87]	2589
9	22	H	Milton Keynes D	W	2-1	0-0	1	McCartan [72], Shackell [90]	9322
10	29	A	Cheltenham T	W	2-0	0-0	1	Alcock (og) [74], McCartan [80]	3202
11	Oct 2	A	Tranmere R	L	0-1	0-0	1		5467
12	6	H	Crewe Alex	W	1-0	0-0	1	Pett [58]	8718
13	13	A	Port Vale	W	6-2	3-0	1	Anderson [3], McCartan [38], Legge (og) [45], Bostwick [48], Wharton [78], Wilson [84]	5137
14	20	H	Cambridge U	D	1-1	1-1	1	Rhead [6]	9108
15	23	H	Carlisle U	D	2-2	2-2	1	O'Connor [13], Andrade [44]	9119
16	27	A	Colchester U	L	0-1	0-1	1		4962
17	Nov 3	H	Forest Green R	W	2-1	1-1	1	Akinde [8], Gordon [72]	8542
18	24	H	Mansfield T	D	1-1	0-0	1	Gordon [85]	9773
19	27	A	Oldham Ath	D	1-1	0-0	2	O'Connor [54]	3597
20	Dec 8	A	Stevenage	W	1-0	1-0	2	Akinde (pen) [11]	3552
21	15	H	Morecambe	W	3-1	3-0	1	Anderson [7], Akinde (pen) [33], Shackell [37]	7975
22	22	H	Newport Co	W	3-2	2-1	1	Akinde [3], Anderson [7], Pett [67]	8632
23	26	A	Crewe Alex	L	1-2	0-0	1	Anderson [90]	4440
24	29	A	Cambridge U	W	2-1	0-1	1	Eardley [70], Akinde [75]	6858
25	Jan 1	H	Port Vale	D	1-1	0-0	1	McCartan [58]	9106
26	12	A	Swindon T	D	2-2	2-0	1	Shackell [39], McCartan [45]	6543
27	19	H	Grimsby T	W	1-0	1-0	1	Toffolo [12]	9650
28	22	A	Yeovil T	W	2-0	2-0	1	Rowe 2 [27, 45]	2486
29	26	A	Bury	D	3-3	2-2	1	Rowe [9], Stokes (og) [27], Akinde (pen) [63]	5169
30	Feb 2	A	Notts Co	D	1-1	1-1	1	Andrade [45]	10,641
31	9	H	Northampton T	D	1-1	1-1	1	Andrade [27]	9352
32	16	H	Stevenage	D	2-2	0-0	1	Andrade 2 [48, 71]	9036
33	23	A	Morecambe	W	2-0	1-0	1	Andrade 2 [10, 57]	2352
34	26	H	Exeter C	D	1-1	0-1	1	Akinde [90]	8589
35	Mar 2	A	Forest Green R	W	2-1	1-1	1	Akinde 2 (1 pen) [13, 79 (p)]	3165
36	8	H	Yeovil T	W	1-0	0-0	1	O'Hara [69]	9014
37	12	H	Oldham Ath	W	2-0	1-0	1	Toffolo [30], Rowe [58]	8454
38	18	A	Mansfield T	D	1-1	0-1	1	Akinde (pen) [75]	7177
39	23	A	Crawley T	W	3-0	1-0	1	Andrade [37], McCartan [76], Bolger [85]	3335
40	30	H	Macclesfield T	D	1-1	1-1	1	Eardley [38]	9567
41	Apr 6	A	Milton Keynes D	W	2-0	1-0	1	Akinde (pen) [34], Andrade [90]	15,851
42	13	H	Cheltenham T	D	1-1	1-0	1	McCartan [18]	9820
43	19	A	Carlisle U	L	0-1	0-0	1		6819
44	22	H	Tranmere R	D	0-0	0-0	1		9658
45	27	A	Newport Co	L	0-1	0-1	1		4605
46	May 4	H	Colchester U	L	0-3	0-3	1		9832

Final League Position: 1

GOALSCORERS

League (73): Akinde 15 (9 pens), Andrade 10, McCartan 7, Anderson 5, Rowe 4, Shackell 4, Frecklington 3, Pett 3, Toffolo 3, Bostwick 2, Eardley 2, Gordon 2, Green 2, O'Connor 2, Bolger 1, O'Hara 1, Rhead 1, Wharton 1, Wilson 1, own goals 4.
FA Cup (6): Akinde 1, Anderson 1, Andrade 1, Bostwick 1, Pett 1, Rhead 1.
Carabao Cup (5): Akinde 1, Green 1 (1 pen), Luque 1, O'Connor 1, Shackell 1.
Checkatrade Trophy (6): Green 3, Anderson 1, McCombe 1, Rhead 1.

Vickers J 18	Wharton S 5+6	Waterfall L 1	Wilson J 4+7	Toffolo H 46	Bostwick M 45	Frecklington L 23+4	Eardley N 43	McCartan S 23+15	Green M 2+17	Akinde J 41+4	Andrade B 39+3	Anderson H 39+4	Rhead M 12+22	O'Connor M 31+8	Pett T 33+11	Shackell J 33+1	Smith G 16	Chapman E 2+3	Luque J — +1	Gordon K — +6	Mensah B — +4	Bolger C 12+5	Rowe D 12+5	Roberts J — +5	O'Hara M 14+3	Angol L — +2	Gilks M 12	Match No.
1	2	3	4	5	6	7	8	9^{3}	10^{1}	11^{2}	12	13	14															1
1	4			5	3	6	2	9^{1}	14	11^{2}	10	8		7^{3}	12	13												2
1			14	5	3	6	2	9^{2}	12	11	10	8^{3}		7^{1}	13	4												3
				5	3	6	2	14	9^{3}	13	11	12	10^{1}		8	4	1	7^{2}										4
				5	3	6	2		13	10^{1}	11^{3}	9		7^{2}	8	4	1	12	14									5
				5	3	6	2			10^{2}	11^{1}	9	12	8^{3}	7	4	1	14		13								6
				5	3	6■	2	12		10	11^{1}	9	14	7^{2}	8^{3}	4	1				13							7
			2	5	4			11^{2}	12	10^{3}	9^{1}	6	13	7	8	3	1				14							8
1				5	3		2	11^{1}	13	10^{2}	9	6^{3}	14	7	8	4					12							9
1				5	3		2	11^{1}	14	10^{2}	9^{3}	8	13	6	7	4					12							10
1				5	3	7	2	11^{1}	13	10^{3}	9	6^{2}	12	14	8	4												11
1				5	3	7	2	11^{2}	13	10^{3}	9	6^{1}	14	8	12	4												12
1	4		12	5	3	8^{3}	2	10^{2}	13		9	6	11^{1}		7			14										13
1	4		12	5	3		2	11^{1}	14	13	9	6^{3}	10^{2}		8			7■										14
1	4		12	5	3		2^{2}	11^{1}	14	13	9	6	10^{3}	8	7													15
1			2	5	3			10^{2}	13	11	9^{1}	6	12	7	8	4												16
1			2	5	3	6^{1}		12	14	11^{2}	10	8^{3}		7	9	4				13								17
1				5	3		2	11^{3}	14	10^{1}	9	6^{2}	13	8	7	4				12								18
1				5	3	13	2	11	14	10^{1}	9	6^{3}	12	8	7^{2}	4												19
	12			5^{3}	3	8	2	13	14	11^{2}	10^{1}	6		9	7	4	1											20
	14		12	5	3	7	2^{3}	11	13	10^{2}		9		8^{1}	6	4	1											21
	14			5	3	7	2	11^{1}		10^{3}	12	6	13	8^{2}	9	4	1											22
1				5	3	8	2	12		11^{1}	9^{2}	10	13	7	6^{3}	4				14								23
	14			5^{1}	4	8	2			10	9^{3}	6	11	12	7^{2}	3	1			13								24
				5	3	7	2	11^{1}		12	9^{3}	6	10^{2}	8	14	4	1			13								25
1	12		14	5	4	7^{1}	2	10^{3}		11^{2}	9■	6		8	13	3■												26
	14			5	3	7	2	11^{2}		10^{3}		6	13	8	9^{1}		1					4	12					27
				5	6	12	2	13		10^{2}		11	14	8^{3}	7	3	1					4	9^{1}					28
				5	7	6	2			11		8		12	10^{2}	4	1					3^{1}	9^{3}	13	14			29
			13	5	3^{2}	7	2	8^{1}		11	10	12		6		4	1						9^{3}			14		30
				5		7^{3}	2			11^{2}	10	8■		6^{1}	12	4	1					3	9		14	13		31
				5	6	7^{1}	2	13		11	10			12	9^{3}	4	1					3	8^{2}		14			32
				5	3		2	12		11^{1}	10^{3}		13	6^{2}	9	4						14	8		7		1	33
				5	3		2	12		11	8		13	6	10^{3}	4						14	9^{2}		7^{1}		1	34
				5	4		2	13		11	8^{1}	10	9^{2}	8^{2}	12	3						14			7		1	35
				5	3		2			11	9	6	10^{3}	7^{1}	14	4^{2}						12	13		8		1	36
				5	4		2			11^{3}	9	6	10^{1}	13	8							3	12	14	7^{2}		1	37
				5	3		2			11^{2}	9	6	13	7^{1}	12							4	10		8		1	38
				5	3		2	12		11^{1}	9^{3}	6	13		7							4	10^{2}	14	8		1	39
				5	4		2	12		11	9	6^{2}	14	13	7							3	10^{1}		8^{3}		1	40
				5	4	12	2	11^{2}		10^{1}	9^{3}	6	13	14	7	3									8		1	41
				5	3	13	2	11^{2}		10	9^{3}	6	14		7^{1}	4							12		8		1	42
				5^{1}	3		2	10^{3}		11	9^{2}	6			7	4■						12	13	14	8		1	43
				5	4		2	14		11	9^{3}	12	10^{2}	7^{1}	13							3	6		8		1	44
1				5	4		2	12		11	13	6^{1}	10^{2}	7^{3}	14							3	9		8			45
1				5	4		2	12		11^{3}	9	6	10^{2}	13	8							3		14	7^{1}			46

FA Cup

First Round	Northampton T	(h)	3-2
Second Round	Carlisle U	(h)	2-0
Third Round	Everton	(a)	1-2

Carabao Cup

First Round	Port Vale	(a)	4-0
Second Round	Blackburn R	(a)	1-4

Checkatrade Trophy

Group H (N)	Mansfield T	(h)	1-2
Group H (N)	Scunthorpe U	(a)	1-1
(Lincoln C won 3-1 on penalties)			
Group H (N)	Wolverhampton W U21	(h)	2-2
(Wolverhampton W U21 won 5-4 on penalties)			
Second Round (N)	Accrington S	(a)	2-2
(Accrington S won 4-2 on penalties)			

LIVERPOOL

FOUNDATION

But for a dispute between Everton FC and their landlord at Anfield in 1892, there may never have been a Liverpool club. This dispute persuaded the majority of Evertonians to quit Anfield for Goodison Park, leaving the landlord, Mr John Houlding, to form a new club. He originally tried to retain the name 'Everton' but when this failed, he founded Liverpool Association FC on 15 March 1892.

Anfield Stadium, Anfield Road, Anfield, Liverpool L4 0TH.

Telephone: (0151) 263 2361.

Fax: (0151) 260 8813.

Ticket Office: (0843) 170 5555.

Website: www.liverpoolfc.com

Email: customerservices@liverpoolfc.com

Ground Capacity: 54,074.

Record Attendance: 61,905 v Wolverhampton W, FA Cup 4th rd, 2 February 1952.

Pitch Measurements: 101m × 68m (110.5yd × 74.5yd).

Chairman: Tom Werner.

Chief Executive: Peter Moore.

Manager: Jürgen Klopp.

Assistant Managers: Peter Krawietz, Pepijn Lijnders.

Colours: Red shirts with white trim, red shorts with white trim, red socks with white trim.

Year Formed: 1892.

Turned Professional: 1892.

Club Nicknames: 'The Reds', 'Pool'.

Ground: 1892, Anfield.

First Football League Game: 2 September 1893, Division 2, v Middlesbrough Ironopolis (a) W 2–0 – McOwen; Hannah, McLean; Henderson, McQue (1), McBride; Gordon, McVean (1), Matt McQueen, Stott, Hugh McQueen.

HONOURS

League Champions: Division 1 – 1900–01, 1905–06, 1921–22, 1922–23, 1946–47, 1963–64, 1965–66, 1972–73, 1975–76, 1976–77, 1978–79, 1979–80, 1981–82, 1982–83, 1983–84, 1985–86, 1987–88, 1989–90; Division 2 – 1893–94, 1895–96, 1904–05, 1961–62.
Runners-up: Premier League – 2001–02, 2008–09, 2013–14, 2018–19; Division 1 – 1898–99, 1909–10, 1968–69, 1973–74, 1974–75, 1977–78, 1984–85, 1986–87, 1988–89, 1990–91.

FA Cup Winners: 1965, 1974, 1986, 1989, 1992, 2001, 2006.
Runners-up: 1914, 1950, 1971, 1977, 1988, 1996, 2012.

League Cup Winners: 1981, 1982, 1983, 1984, 1995, 2001, 2003, 2012.
Runners-up: 1978, 1987, 2005, 2016.

League Super Cup Winners: 1986.

European Competitions

European Cup: 1964–65 *(sf)*, 1966–67, 1973–74, 1976–77 *(winners)*, 1977–78 *(winners)*, 1978–79, 1979–80, 1980–81 *(winners)*, 1981–82 *(qf)*, 1982–83 *(qf)*, 1983–84 *(winners)*, 1984–85 *(runners-up)*.
Champions League: 2001–02 *(qf)*, 2002–03, 2004–05 *(winners)*, 2005–06, 2006–07 *(runners-up)*, 2007–08 *(sf)*, 2008–09 *(qf)*, 2009–10, 2014–15, 2017–18 *(runners-up)*, 2018–19 *(winners)*.
Fairs Cup: 1967–68, 1968–69, 1969–70, 1970–71 *(sf)*.
UEFA Cup: 1972–73 *(winners)*, 1975–76 *(winners)*, 1991–92 *(qf)*, 1995–96, 1997–98, 1998–99, 2000–01 *(winners)*, 2002–03 *(qf)*, 2003–04.
Europa League: 2009–10 *(sf)*, 2010–11, 2012–13, 2014–15, 2015–16 *(runners-up)*.
European Cup-Winners' Cup: 1965–66 *(runners-up)*, 1971–72, 1974–75, 1992–93, 1996–97 *(sf)*.
Super Cup: 1977 *(winners)*, 1978, 1984, 2001 *(winners)*, 2005 *(winners)*.
World Club Championship: 1981, 1984.
FIFA Club World Cup: 2005.

THE Sun FACT FILE

Liverpool's first Football League goal from the penalty spot provided the Reds with the opening goal of their 4-0 win over Northwich Victoria on 3 February 1894. The scorer was Duncan McLean, one of only two players to stay at Anfield following the split with Everton and an ever-present in Division Two matches during the 1893–94 season.

Record League Victory: 10–1 v Rotherham T, Division 2, 18 February 1896 – Storer; Goldie, Wilkie; McCartney, McQue, Holmes; McVean (3), Ross (2), Allan (4), Becton (1), Bradshaw.

Record Cup Victory: 11–0 v Stromsgodset Drammen, ECWC 1st rd 1st leg, 17 September 1974 – Clemence; Smith (1), Lindsay (1p), Thompson (2), Cormack (1), Hughes (1), Boersma (2), Hall, Heighway (1), Kennedy (1), Callaghan (1).

Record Defeat: 1–9 v Birmingham C, Division 2, 11 December 1954.

Most League Points (2 for a win): 68, Division 1, 1978–79.

Most League Points (3 for a win): 97, Premier League, 2018–19.

Most League Goals: 106, Division 2, 1895–96.

Highest League Scorer in Season: Roger Hunt, 41, Division 2, 1961–62.

Most League Goals in Total Aggregate: Roger Hunt, 245, 1959–69.

Most League Goals in One Match: 5, Andy McGuigan v Stoke C, Division 1, 4 January 1902; 5, John Evans v Bristol R, Division 2, 15 September 1954; 5, Ian Rush v Luton T, Division 1, 29 October 1983.

Most Capped Player: Steven Gerrard, 114, England.

Most League Appearances: Ian Callaghan, 640, 1960–78.

Youngest League Player: Jack Robinson, 16 years 250 days v Hull C, 9 May 2010.

Record Transfer Fee Received: £142,000,000 from Barcelona for Phillippe Coutinho, January 2018.

Record Transfer Fee Paid: £75,000,000 to Southampton for Virgil van Dijk, January 2018.

Football League Record: 1893 Elected to Division 2; 1894–95 Division 1; 1895–96 Division 2; 1896–1904 Division 1; 1904–05 Division 2; 1905–54 Division 1; 1954–62 Division 2; 1962–92 Division 1; 1992– Premier League.

MANAGERS

W. E. Barclay 1892–96
Tom Watson 1896–1915
David Ashworth 1920–23
Matt McQueen 1923–28
George Patterson 1928–36
(continued as Secretary)
George Kay 1936–51
Don Welsh 1951–56
Phil Taylor 1956–59
Bill Shankly 1959–74
Bob Paisley 1974–83
Joe Fagan 1983–85
Kenny Dalglish 1985–91
Graeme Souness 1991–94
Roy Evans 1994–98
(then Joint Manager)
Gerard Houllier 1998–2004
Rafael Benitez 2004–10
Roy Hodgson 2010–11
Kenny Dalglish 2011–12
Brendan Rodgers 2012–15
Jürgen Klopp October 2015–

LATEST SEQUENCES

Longest Sequence of League Wins: 12, 21.4.1990 – 6.10.1990.

Longest Sequence of League Defeats: 9, 29.4.1899 – 14.10.1899.

Longest Sequence of League Draws: 6, 19.2.1975 – 19.3.1975.

Longest Sequence of Unbeaten League Matches: 31, 4.5.1987 – 16.3.1988.

Longest Sequence Without a League Win: 14, 12.12.1953 – 20.3.1954.

Successive Scoring Runs: 29 from 27.4.1957.

Successive Non-scoring Runs: 5 from 21.4.2000.

TEN YEAR LEAGUE RECORD

		P	*W*	*D*	*L*	*F*	*A*	*Pts*	*Pos*
2009-10	PR Lge	38	18	9	11	61	35	63	7
2010-11	PR Lge	38	17	7	14	59	44	58	6
2011-12	PR Lge	38	14	10	14	47	40	52	8
2012-13	PR Lge	38	16	13	9	71	43	61	7
2013-14	PR Lge	38	26	6	6	101	50	84	2
2014-15	PR Lge	38	18	8	12	52	48	62	6
2015-16	PR Lge	38	16	12	10	63	50	60	8
2016-17	PR Lge	38	22	10	6	78	42	76	4
2017-18	PR Lge	38	21	12	5	84	38	75	4
2018-19	PR Lge	38	30	7	1	89	22	97	2

DID YOU KNOW ?

Full-back Tom Cooper, who made over 150 first-team appearances for Liverpool between 1934 and 1939, was also a talented golfer. Cooper won the Merseyside Professional Footballers Golf Championship three years in a row: 1936, 1937 and 1938.

LIVERPOOL – PREMIER LEAGUE 2018–19 LEAGUE RECORD

Match No.	Date	Venue	Opponents	Result		H/T Score	Lg Pos.	Goalscorers	Attendance
1	Aug 12	H	West Ham U	W	4-0	2-0	1	Salah [19], Mane 2 [45, 53], Sturridge [88]	53,235
2	20	A	Crystal Palace	W	2-0	1-0	2	Milner (pen) [45], Mane [90]	25,750
3	25	H	Brighton & HA	W	1-0	1-0	1	Salah [23]	53,294
4	Sept 1	A	Leicester C	W	2-1	2-0	1	Mane [10], Firmino [45]	32,149
5	15	A	Tottenham H	W	2-1	1-0	2	Wijnaldum [39], Firmino [54]	80,188
6	22	H	Southampton	W	3-0	3-0	1	Hoedt (og) [10], Matip [21], Salah [45]	50,965
7	29	A	Chelsea	D	1-1	0-1	2	Sturridge [89]	40,625
8	Oct 7	H	Manchester C	D	0-0	0-0	3		52,117
9	20	A	Huddersfield T	W	1-0	1-0	2	Salah [24]	24,263
10	27	H	Cardiff C	W	4-1	1-0	1	Salah [10], Mane 2 [66, 87], Shaqiri [84]	53,373
11	Nov 3	A	Arsenal	D	1-1	0-0	1	Milner [61]	59,993
12	11	H	Fulham	W	2-0	1-0	2	Salah [41], Shaqiri [53]	53,128
13	24	A	Watford	W	3-0	0-0	2	Salah [67], Alexander-Arnold [76], Firmino [89]	20,540
14	Dec 2	H	Everton	W	1-0	0-0	2	Origi [90]	51,756
15	5	A	Burnley	W	3-1	0-0	2	Milner [62], Firmino [69], Shaqiri [90]	21,741
16	8	A	Bournemouth	W	4-0	1-0	1	Salah 3 [25, 48, 77], Cook, S (og) [68]	10,752
17	16	H	Manchester U	W	3-1	1-1	1	Mane [24], Shaqiri 2 [73, 80]	52,908
18	21	A	Wolverhampton W	W	2-0	1-0	1	Salah [18], van Dijk [68]	31,358
19	26	H	Newcastle U	W	4-0	1-0	1	Lovren [11], Salah (pen) [47], Shaqiri [79], Fabinho [85]	53,318
20	29	H	Arsenal	W	5-1	4-1	1	Firmino 3 (1 pen) [14, 16, 65 (p)], Mane [32], Salah (pen) [45]	53,326
21	Jan 3	A	Manchester C	L	1-2	0-1	1	Firmino [64]	54,511
22	12	A	Brighton & HA	W	1-0	0-0	1	Salah (pen) [50]	30,682
23	19	H	Crystal Palace	W	4-3	0-1	1	Salah 2 [46, 75], Firmino [53], Mane [90]	53,171
24	30	H	Leicester C	D	1-1	1-1	1	Mane [3]	53,092
25	Feb 4	A	West Ham U	D	1-1	1-1	1	Mane [22]	59,903
26	9	H	Bournemouth	W	3-0	2-0	1	Mane [24], Wijnaldum [34], Salah [48]	53,178
27	24	A	Manchester U	D	0-0	0-0	1		74,519
28	27	H	Watford	W	5-0	2-0	1	Mane 2 [9, 20], Origi [66], van Dijk 2 [79, 82]	53,316
29	Mar 3	A	Everton	D	0-0	0-0	2		39,335
30	10	H	Burnley	W	4-2	2-1	2	Firmino 2 [19, 67], Mane 2 [29, 90]	53,310
31	17	A	Fulham	W	2-1	1-0	1	Mane [26], Milner (pen) [81]	25,043
32	31	H	Tottenham H	W	2-1	1-0	1	Firmino [16], Alderweireld (og) [90]	53,322
33	Apr 5	A	Southampton	W	3-1	1-1	1	Keita [36], Salah [80], Henderson [86]	31,797
34	14	H	Chelsea	W	2-0	0-0	1	Mane [51], Salah [53]	53,279
35	21	A	Cardiff C	W	2-0	0-0	1	Wijnaldum [57], Milner (pen) [81]	33,082
36	26	H	Huddersfield T	W	5-0	3-0	1	Keita [1], Mane 2 [23, 66], Salah 2 [45, 83]	53,249
37	May 4	A	Newcastle U	W	3-2	2-1	1	van Dijk [13], Salah [28], Origi [86]	52,206
38	12	H	Wolverhampton W	W	2-0	1-0	2	Mane 2 [17, 81]	53,331

Final League Position: 2

GOALSCORERS

League (89): Mane 22, Salah 22 (3 pens), Firmino 12 (1 pen), Shaqiri 6, Milner 5 (3 pens), van Dijk 4, Origi 3, Wijnaldum 3, Keita 2, Sturridge 2, Alexander-Arnold 1, Fabinho 1, Henderson 1, Lovren 1, Matip 1, own goals 3.
FA Cup (1): Origi 1.
Carabao Cup (1): Sturridge 1.
Champions League (24): Salah 5 (2 pens), Firmino 4, Mane 4, Origi 3, Milner 2 (2 pens), van Dijk 2, Wijnaldum 2, Keita 1, Sturridge 1.

Alisson R 38	Alexander-Arnold T 27 + 2	Gomez J 12 + 4	van Dijk V 38	Robertson A 36	Milner J 19 + 12	Wijnaldum G 32 + 3	Keita N 16 + 9	Salah M 37 + 1	Firmino R 31 + 3	Mane S 35 + 1	Henderson J 21 + 11	Shaqiri X 11 + 13	Sturridge D 4 + 14	Lallana A 5 + 8	Matip J 17 + 5	Lovren D 11 + 2	Fabinho H 21 + 7	Moreno A 2	Origi D 4 + 8	Clyne N 1 + 3	Camacho R — + 1	Oxlade-Chamberlain A — + 2	*Match No.*
1	2	3	4	5	6	7	8	9^{2}	10^{3}	11^{1}	12	13	14										1
1	2	3	4	5	6^{2}	7	8^{3}	9	10^{1}	11	12		14	13									2
1	2^{1}	3	4	5	6	7	8^{3}	9	10	11^{2}	12		13		14								3
1	2^{1}	3	4	5	8	6	12	9^{3}	10	11	7^{2}	13			14								4
1	2^{2}	3	4	5	6	7	8^{1}	9	10^{3}	11	12		13		14								5
1	2	13	4^{1}	5	12	6^{3}	14	8	11	10	7	9^{2}			3								6
1	2	3	4	5	8^{1}	6	13	9^{3}	10	11	7^{2}	12	14										7
1		2	4	5	8^{1}	6	12	9	10^{2}	11	7		13			3							8
1		2	4	5	8^{2}	12		9	14		7^{3}	6	10	11^{1}		3	13						9
1	2		4		13	7		11	9^{2}	10		12		8^{1}		3	6	5					10
1	2	3	4	5	8	6		9^{1}	10^{2}	11		12			13		7						11
1	2	3	4	5	13	6^{2}	14	11	9	10	12	8^{3}					7^{1}						12
1	2		4	5	12	7		11^{2}	9^{1}	10	6■	8^{3}			14	3	13						13
1	2	3	4	5		6	12	11^{1}	9^{3}	10		8^{2}	13				7		14				14
1	12	2^{1}	4		9		7	13	14		8	6	11		3			5^{3}	10^{2}				15
1			4	5	2	7	9^{1}	10	11^{2}	12	14	6^{3}		13	3		8						16
1			4	5		7	9^{2}	11	10	6^{1}	13	12				3	8			2			17
1			4	5	2	13	10^{3}	11	9^{2}	8^{1}	6			12		3	7			14			18
1	2		4	5^{3}		6^{2}		11	9^{1}	10	7	8	13			3	12			14			19
1	2		4	5^{2}		6^{3}		11	9	10^{1}	12	8		13		3	7			14			20
1	2		4	5	8^{2}	6^{3}		9	10	11^{1}	7	13	14			3	12						21
1	2		4	5	12	6	14	11^{3}	9	10^{1}	7	8^{2}					3		13				22
1			4	5	2■		10^{3}	11^{2}	9	8	6	12		13	3		7^{1}				14		23
1			4	5		6	7^{1}	11	9^{2}	10	2	8^{3}	14	12	3		13						24
1			4	5	2		8	9	10^{1}	11		12		6^{2}	3		7		13				25
1	12		4	5	2	6^{1}	8	9	10^{3}	11^{2}			14		3		7		13				26
1			4	5	2	8		9^{2}	10^{1}	11	6^{3}	13	12		3		7		14				27
1	2		4	5	6^{1}	8^{3}	14	9		10^{2}	12			13	3		7		11				28
1	2		4	5	13	8^{1}		9	12	10^{2}	6			14	3		7		11^{3}				29
1	2^{1}		4	5		6^{3}	13	9	10	11	12		14	8^{2}	3		7						30
1	2		4	5	13	6		9^{2}	10^{3}	11			14	8^{1}	3		7		12				31
1	2		4	5	8^{1}	6		9^{3}	10	11	7^{2}				3	14	13		12				32
1	2^{1}		4	5	13	6^{3}	8^{2}	9	10	11	12				3	14	7						33
1	2		4	5	13	12	8^{2}	9^{1}	10	11	6^{3}	14			3		7						34
1	2^{2}	14	4	5	13	7	8^{1}	9	10	11	6				3		12^{3}						35
1	2^{1}	14	4	5		7^{2}	8	9		11	6	12	10^{3}			3						13	36
1	2		4	5	14	8^{3}		9^{2}		11	6	12	10			3^{1}	7		13				37
1	2	13	4	5^{1}	12	8^{3}		9		11	6				3		7		10^{2}			14	38

FA Cup

Third Round	Wolverhampton W	(a)	1-2

Carabao Cup

Third Round	Chelsea	(h)	1-2

Champions League

Group C	Paris Saint-Germain	(h)	3-2
Group C	Napoli	(a)	0-1
Group C	Crvena Zvezda	(h)	4-0
Group C	Crvena Zvezda	(a)	0-2
Group C	Paris Saint-Germain	(a)	1-2
Group C	Napoli	(h)	1-0
Round of 16 1st leg	Bayern Munich	(h)	0-0
Round of 16 2nd leg	Bayern Munich	(a)	3-1
Quarter-Final 1st leg	Porto	(h)	2-0
Quarter-Final 2nd leg	Porto	(a)	4-1
Semi-Final 1st leg	Barcelona	(a)	0-3
Semi-Final 2nd leg	Barcelona	(h)	4-0
Final	Tottenham H	(Madrid)	2-0

LUTON TOWN

FOUNDATION

Formed by an amalgamation of two leading local clubs, Wanderers and Excelsior a works team, at a meeting in Luton Town Hall in April 1885. The Wanderers had three months earlier changed their name to Luton Town Wanderers and did not take too kindly to the formation of another Town club but were talked around at this meeting. Wanderers had already appeared in the FA Cup and the new club entered in its inaugural season.

Kenilworth Road Stadium, 1 Maple Road, Luton, Bedfordshire LU4 8AW.

Telephone: (01582) 411 622.

Fax: (01582) 405 070.

Ticket Office: (01582) 416 976.

Website: www.lutontown.co.uk

Email: info@lutontown.co.uk

Ground Capacity: 10,073.

Record Attendance: 30,069 v Blackpool, FA Cup 6th rd replay, 4 March 1959.

Pitch Measurements: 101m × 66m (110.5yd × 72yd).

Chairman: David Wilkinson.

Chief Executive: Gary Sweet.

Manager: Graeme Jones.

Assistant Manager: Gary Brabin.

HONOURS

League Champions: Division 2 – 1981–82; FL 1 – 2004–05, 2018–19; Division 3S – 1936–37; Division 4 – 1967–68; Conference – 2013–14.
Runners-up: FL 2 – 2017–18; Division 2 – 1954–55, 1973–74; Division 3 – 1969–70; Division 3S – 1935–36; Third Division – 2001–02.

FA Cup: *Runners-up:* 1959.

League Cup Winners: 1988.
Runners-up: 1989.

League Trophy Winners: 2009.

Full Members' Cup: *Runners-up:* 1988.

Colours: Orange shirts with black trim, orange shorts, orange socks.

Year Formed: 1885.

Turned Professional: 1890.

Ltd Co.: 1897.

Club Nickname: 'The Hatters'.

Grounds: 1885, Excelsior, Dallow Lane; 1897, Dunstable Road; 1905, Kenilworth Road.

First Football League Game: 4 September 1897, Division 2, v Leicester Fosse (a) D 1–1 – Williams; McCartney, McEwen; Davies, Stewart, Docherty; Gallacher, Coupar, Birch, McInnes, Ekins (1).

Record League Victory: 12–0 v Bristol R, Division 3 (S), 13 April 1936 – Dolman; Mackey, Smith; Finlayson, Nelson, Godfrey; Rich, Martin (1), Payne (10), Roberts (1), Stephenson.

Record Cup Victory: 9–0 v Clapton, FA Cup 1st rd (replay after abandoned game), 30 November 1927 – Abbott; Kingham, Graham; Black, Rennie, Fraser; Pointon, Yardley (4), Reid (2), Woods (1), Dennis (2).

Record Defeat: 0–9 v Small Heath, Division 2, 12 November 1898.

Most League Points (2 for a win): 66, Division 4, 1967–68.

THE Sun FACT FILE

Luton Town won the Soccer Six Championships sponsored by Guinness which took place at the G-Mex Centre in Manchester in December 1990, earning themselves prize money of more than £50,000. They defeated Liverpool 4-0 in the final with goals from Sean Farrell, Lars Elstrup, Julian James and David Preece.

Most League Points (3 for a win): 98, FL 1 2004–05.

Most League Goals: 103, Division 3 (S), 1936–37.

Highest League Scorer in Season: Joe Payne, 55, Division 3 (S), 1936–37.

Most League Goals in Total Aggregate: Gordon Turner, 243, 1949–64.

Most League Goals in One Match: 10, Joe Payne v Bristol R, Division 3 (S), 13 April 1936.

Most Capped Player: Mal Donaghy, 58 (91), Northern Ireland.

Most League Appearances: Bob Morton, 495, 1948–64.

Youngest League Player: Mike O'Hara, 16 years 32 days v Stoke C, 1 October 1960.

Record Transfer Fee Received: £6,000,000 from Leicester C for James Justin, June 2019.

Record Transfer Fee Paid: £850,000 to Odense for Lars Elstrup, August 1989.

Football League Record: 1897 Elected to Division 2; 1900 Failed re-election; 1920 Division 3; 1921–37 Division 3 (S); 1937–55 Division 2; 1955–60 Division 1; 1960–63 Division 2; 1963–65 Division 3; 1965–68 Division 4; 1968–70 Division 3; 1970–74 Division 2; 1974–75 Division 1; 1975–82 Division 2; 1982–96 Division 1; 1996–2001 Division 2; 2001–02 Division 3; 2002–04 Division 2; 2004–05 FL 1; 2005–07 FL C; 2007–08 FL 1; 2008–09 FL 2; 2009–14 Conference Premier; 2014–18 FL 2; 2018–19 FL 1; 2019– FL C.

LATEST SEQUENCES

Longest Sequence of League Wins: 12, 19.2.2002 – 6.4.2002.

Longest Sequence of League Defeats: 8, 11.11.1899 – 6.1.1900.

Longest Sequence of League Draws: 5, 28.8.1971 – 18.9.1971.

Longest Sequence of Unbeaten League Matches: 28, 20.10.2018 – 6.4.2019.

Longest Sequence Without a League Win: 16, 9.9.1964 – 6.11.1964.

Successive Scoring Runs: 25 from 24.10.1931.

Successive Non-scoring Runs: 5 from 10.4.1973.

MANAGERS

Charlie Green 1901–28 *(Secretary-Manager)*
George Thomson 1925
John McCartney 1927–29
George Kay 1929–31
Harold Wightman 1931–35
Ted Liddell 1936–38
Neil McBain 1938–39
George Martin 1939–47
Dally Duncan 1947–58
Syd Owen 1959–60
Sam Bartram 1960–62
Bill Harvey 1962–64
George Martin 1965–66
Allan Brown 1966–68
Alec Stock 1968–72
Harry Haslam 1972–78
David Pleat 1978–86
John Moore 1986–87
Ray Harford 1987–89
Jim Ryan 1990–91
David Pleat 1991–95
Terry Westley 1995
Lennie Lawrence 1995–2000
Ricky Hill 2000
Lil Fuccillo 2000
Joe Kinnear 2001–03
Mike Newell 2003–07
Kevin Blackwell 2007–08
Mick Harford 2008–09
Richard Money 2009–11
Gary Brabin 2011–12
Paul Buckle 2012–13
John Still 2013–15
Nathan Jones 2016–19
Mick Harford 2019 *(caretaker)*
Graeme Jones May 2019–

TEN YEAR LEAGUE RECORD

		P	W	D	L	F	A	Pts	Pos
2009-10	Conf P	44	26	10	8	84	40	88	2
2010-11	Conf P	46	23	15	8	85	37	84	3
2011-12	Conf P	46	22	15	9	78	42	81	5
2012-13	Conf P	46	18	13	15	70	62	67	7
2013-14	Conf P	46	30	11	5	102	35	101	1
2014-15	FL 2	46	19	11	16	54	44	68	8
2015-16	FL 2	46	19	9	18	63	61	66	11
2016-17	FL 2	46	20	17	9	70	43	77	4
2017-18	FL 2	46	25	13	8	94	46	88	2
2018-19	FL 1	46	27	13	6	90	42	94	1

DID YOU KNOW ?

Luton Town's Kenilworth Road ground was a real fortress for The Hatters in the late 1960s. Between April 1967 and December 1970 they played 72 competitive home games and lost just once, against Bradford City in April 1968.

LUTON TOWN – SKY BET LEAGUE ONE 2018–19 LEAGUE RECORD

Match No.	Date	Venue	Opponents	Result		H/T Score	Lg Pos.	Goalscorers	Attendance
1	Aug 4	A	Portsmouth	L	0-1	0-1	20		19,018
2	11	H	Sunderland	D	1-1	0-1	19	Pearson 68	10,059
3	18	A	Peterborough U	L	1-3	0-3	22	Hylton 78	8016
4	21	H	Southend U	W	2-0	2-0	14	Lee 2, Hylton (pen) 33	9086
5	25	H	Shrewsbury T	W	3-2	0-1	10	Grant 51, Stacey 73, Lee 76	8518
6	Sept 1	A	Wycombe W	D	1-1	0-1	9	Pearson 68	6072
7	8	A	Doncaster R	L	1-2	1-1	11	Lee 45	7526
8	15	H	Bristol R	W	1-0	0-0	10	Shinnie 62	8912
9	22	A	Blackpool	D	0-0	0-0	12		4124
10	29	H	Charlton Ath	D	2-2	0-1	12	Cornick 74, Collins 81	9502
11	Oct 2	A	Oxford U	W	2-1	0-0	10	Collins 55, Potts 90	6769
12	6	H	Scunthorpe U	W	3-2	2-1	8	Cornick 10, Lee 26, Justin 85	8682
13	13	A	Barnsley	L	2-3	1-2	10	Collins 2 (1 pen) 45 (p), 86	12,688
14	20	H	Walsall	W	2-0	1-0	7	Rea 20, Grant 55	8953
15	23	H	Accrington S	W	4-1	1-1	6	Hylton 3 5, 54, 70, Shinnie 53	8454
16	27	A	AFC Wimbledon	W	2-0	0-0	5	Ruddock 61, Lee 80	4202
17	Nov 3	A	Rochdale	D	0-0	0-0	5		3689
18	17	H	Plymouth Arg	W	5-1	4-0	5	Collins 3 (1 pen) 12, 45 (p), 77, Lee 23, Justin 29	10,004
19	24	A	Gillingham	W	3-1	1-0	4	Shinnie 25, Lee 2 55, 68	5671
20	27	H	Bradford C	W	4-0	3-0	3	Justin 28, Lee 2 33, 38, Cornick 89	8568
21	Dec 8	H	Fleetwood T	W	2-0	1-0	2	Cornick 11, Morgan (og) 80	8528
22	15	A	Coventry C	W	2-1	1-0	2	Pearson 38, Collins 57	12,559
23	22	H	Burton Alb	W	2-0	1-0	2	Stacey 17, Collins (pen) 73	9538
24	26	A	Scunthorpe U	W	2-0	1-0	2	Shinnie 37, Cornick 50	4050
25	29	A	Walsall	D	2-2	0-1	2	Collins 72, LuaLua 90	5739
26	Jan 1	H	Barnsley	D	0-0	0-0	2		9926
27	12	A	Sunderland	D	1-1	0-1	2	Collins (pen) 67	37,791
28	19	H	Peterborough U	W	4-0	2-0	2	Collins 3 8, 27, 53, Berry 66	10,055
29	26	A	Southend U	W	1-0	1-0	1	Pearson 29	8460
30	29	H	Portsmouth	W	3-2	1-0	1	Collins 2 (1 pen) 39, 77 (p), Moncur 86	10,078
31	Feb 2	A	Shrewsbury T	W	3-0	1-0	1	Collins 2 30, 69, Pearson 53	6859
32	9	H	Wycombe W	W	3-0	1-0	1	Collins 33, Moncur 2 85, 88	10,072
33	16	A	Fleetwood T	W	2-1	1-0	1	Moncur 41, Ruddock 49	3651
34	24	H	Coventry C	D	1-1	1-1	1	Pearson 16	9810
35	Mar 2	H	Rochdale	W	2-0	0-0	1	Hylton 59, Collins 90	9905
36	9	A	Plymouth Arg	D	0-0	0-0	1		11,081
37	12	A	Bradford C	W	1-0	1-0	1	Stacey 16	15,992
38	16	H	Gillingham	D	2-2	1-0	1	Hylton 45, Stacey 67	9963
39	23	H	Doncaster R	W	4-0	1-0	1	Ruddock 33, Hylton 57, LuaLua 82, Berry 90	10,071
40	30	A	Bristol R	W	2-1	2-1	1	Collins 17, Berry 39	9037
41	Apr 6	H	Blackpool	D	2-2	1-1	1	Collins 6, Cummings 86	10,028
42	13	A	Charlton Ath	L	1-3	1-0	1	Cornick 15	16,449
43	20	A	Accrington S	W	3-0	1-0	1	Collins (pen) 24, Ruddock 2 68, 87	3271
44	23	H	AFC Wimbledon	D	2-2	2-1	1	Lee 8, Collins 39	10,070
45	27	A	Burton Alb	L	1-2	1-0	1	Collins 30	4903
46	May 4	H	Oxford U	W	3-1	1-0	1	Moncur 2 3, 73, Lee 53	10,089

Final League Position: 1

GOALSCORERS

League (90): Collins 25 (6 pens), Lee 12, Hylton 8 (1 pen), Cornick 6, Moncur 6, Pearson 6, Ruddock 5, Shinnie 4, Stacey 4, Berry 3, Justin 3, Grant 2, LuaLua 2, Cummings 1, Potts 1, Rea 1, own goal 1.
FA Cup (3): Cornick 2, Shinnie 1.
Carabao Cup (0).
Checkatrade Trophy (7): Grant 2, Jarvis 1, LuaLua 1, Read 1, Sheehan 1 (1 pen), own goal 1.

Stech M 5	Justin J 35 + 8	Pearson M 46	Sheehan A 4 + 13	Potts D 15 + 9	Grant J 13 + 4	McCormack A 17 + 2	Lee E 36 + 2	Ruddock P 46	Collins J 42 + 2	Cornick H 14 + 18	Shinnie A 39 + 2	Jervis J — + 2	Bradley S 44 + 1	Stacey J 45	Hylton D 18 + 7	Rea G 20 + 2	Shea J 41	O'Kane E — + 3	Jarvis A — + 4	LuaLua K 10 + 12	Jones L — + 1	Berry L 12 + 9	Thorne G — + 3	Moncur G 4 + 10	Cummings J — + 5	Connolly A — + 2	Baptiste A — + 2	Match No.
1	2¹	3	4	5	6	7³	8	9	10	11²	12	13	14															1
1		3	4	5	6¹	7	8²	9	11³	12		14		2	10	13												2
1		4³	5	6	14	7²	8	9	11¹		13		3	2	10	12												3
	12	3		5	6²		8¹	9	14	13	10		4	2	11³	7	1											4
	13	4		5	9¹		11	8	12		7		3	2	10²	6	1											5
	2¹	3		6			10	7	11	12	9²		4	8		5	1	13										6
		4		5	8²		10	6	11¹	9			3	2		7	1	12	13									7
	13	3	14	5	8¹		10	6	11		9²		4	2		7	1	12³										8
	13	3		5	8²		10	6	11	12	9¹		4	2		7	1											9
	13	3		5	8²		10	6	11	12	9¹		4	2		7	1											10
	12	3	14	5			10²	8	11	6	9¹		4	2		7³	1			13								11
	12	3	13	5²	8		10¹	6	11	9			4	2		7	1											12
	8	3		5	9³	12		7	10	11¹			4	2	14	6⁷	1			13								13
	12	3		5²	8³			6	11	13	9		4	2	10¹	7	1			14								14
	5	3	14		9¹			8	11	12	6²		4	2	10³	7	1			13								15
	5	3	12				9¹	8	11		6		4	2	10	7	1											16
	5	3	14				9¹	8	11²	12	7³		4	2	10■	6	1			13								17
	5	4			12		10	8	11¹	7²	9³		3	2		6	1		14	13								18
	5	4	12				9¹	8	11	10²	6³		3	2		7	1		13		14							19
	5	4		12	14		11¹	8	10²	7³	9		3	2		6	1		13									20
	5	3		13			9¹	7	10	11³	8²		4	2	12	6	1					14						21
	5	4		13			9	7	10	11²	8¹		3	2	12	6	1											22
	5	4			12		10³	8	11	7¹	9		3	2	13	6²	1					14						23
	5	3			8¹	12	9	6	11	10³	7²		4	2	13		1					14						24
	5	4	14			6	9¹	7	10	11²	8³		3	2	12		1			13								25
	5	4				6	9¹	7	10	12³	8²		3	2	11		1			14		13						26
	5	4				6	9¹	7	11		8		3	2	10■		1					12						27
	5	3²	14			7³		9	10		6¹		4	2			1			11		8	12	13				28
	5	3				6		8	10		7		4	2			1			11¹		9		12				29
	5	3	14	12		6		7	11		8¹		4	2			1			10²		9³		13				30
	5	3		13		6¹		7	10		8		4	2	12		1			11³		9²		14				31
	5	3	14			6		7	11		8³		4	2	10¹		1					9²		12	13			32
	5	4	14			6²	12	7	11		8		3	2	10³		1						13	9¹				33
	5	3				8	12	7	10		6		4	2	11¹		1			13				9²				34
	5	3		12		6	9²	8¹	11		7		4	2	10³		1			13		14						35
	5¹	3		13		6	9	8	11		7		4	2	10²		1			12								36
	5	3		13		6¹	9³	8	10	14	7		4	2	11²		1					12						37
	5	3		12			9²	6	10	14	7		4	2	11¹		1			13		8³						38
	5	3		8²			9	8		13	7		4	2	11³		1			10¹		12			14			39
	5	3					9³	6	10	12	7		4	2			1			11¹		8²	13	14				40
	5	4					9¹	7	10■	13	6		3	2			1			11²		8³		12	14			41
	5	3	13				7¹	11		8²	6■		4	2			1					9³		10	14	12		42
1	8	3	5³				9²	6	10	13			4	2						11¹		7		12			14	43
1	5	4					9¹	7	10	12	6		3	2						11³		8²		13			14	44
	5	4					9³	6	10	13	8		3	2			1			11²		7¹		12	14			45
	5	4				6¹	11³	8	10²	12	7		3	2			1					13		9		14		46

FA Cup

First Round	Wycombe W	(h)	2-0
Second Round	Bury	(a)	1-0
Third Round	Sheffield W	(a)	0-0
Replay	Sheffield W	(h)	0-1

Carabao Cup

First Round	WBA	(a)	0-1

Checkatrade Trophy

Group H (S)	Brighton & HA U21	(h)	2-1
Group H (S)	Milton Keynes D	(h)	3-0
Group H (S)	Peterborough U	(a)	1-2
Second Round (S)	Southend U	(h)	1-1

(Southend U won 4-2 on penalties)

MACCLESFIELD TOWN

FOUNDATION

From the mid-19th century until 1874, Macclesfield Town FC played under rugby rules. In 1891 they moved to the Moss Rose ground and finished champions of the Manchester & District League in 1906 and 1908. By 1911, they had carried off the Cheshire Senior Cup five times. Macclesfield were founder members of the Cheshire County League in 1919.

Moss Rose Stadium, London Road, Macclesfield, Cheshire SK11 7SP.

Telephone: (01625) 264 686.

Fax: (01625) 264 692.

Ticket Office: (01625) 264 686.

Website: www.mtfc.co.uk

Email: reception@mtfc.co.uk

Ground Capacity: 5,911.

Record Attendance: 9,008 v Winsford U, Cheshire Senior Cup 2nd rd, 4 February 1948.

Pitch Measurements: 101m × 67m (110.5yd × 73.5yd).

Director: Amar Alkadhi.

Manager: Sol Campbell.

Assistant Manager: Danny Whitaker.

Colours: Blue shirts with white trim, white shorts with blue trim, blue socks with white trim.

Year Formed: 1874.

Turned Professional: 1886.

Club Nickname: 'The Silkmen'.

Grounds: 1874, Rostron Field; 1891, Moss Rose.

First Football League Game: 9 August 1997, Division 3, v Torquay U (h) W 2–1 – Price; Tinson, Rose, Payne (Edey), Howarth, Sodje (1), Askey, Wood, Landon (1) (Power), Mason, Sorvel.

Record League Victory: 6–0 v Stockport Co, FL 1, 26 December 2005 – Fettis; Harsley, Sandwith, Morley, Swailes (Teague), Navarro, Whitaker (Miles (1)), Bullock (1), Parkin (2), Wijnhard (2) (Townson), McIntyre.

Record Cup Victory: 15–0 v Chester St Mary's, Cheshire Senior Cup 3rd rd, 6 February 1886; 15–0 v Barnton Rovers, Cheshire Senior Cup 1st rd, 12 November 1887.

Record Win: 15–0 v Chester St Marys, Cheshire Senior Cup 2nd rd, 16 February 1886.

HONOURS

League Champions: Vauxhall Conference – 1994–95, 1996–97; National League – 2017–18.
Runners-up: Division 3 – 1997–98.

FA Cup: 4th rd – 2013.

League Cup: 3rd rd – 2019.

FA Trophy Winners: 1969–70, 1995–96.
Runners-up: 1988–89.

THE SUN FACT FILE

Macclesfield Town were founder members of the Northern Premier League when it was established in 1968–69 and became the first champions of the competition, finishing 12 points clear of second-placed Wigan Athletic. The Silkmen finished the season unbeaten at home, winning 17 of their 19 games, and were the only team from the league to reach the second round of the FA Cup.

Record Defeat: 1–13 v Tranmere R reserves, 3 May 1929.

Most League Points (3 for a win): 82, Division 3, 1997–98.

Most League Goals: 66, Division 3, 1999–2000.

Highest League Scorer in Season: Jon Parkin, 22, FL 2, 2004–05.

Most League Goals in Total Aggregate: Matt Tipton, 50, 2002–05; 2006–07; 2009–10.

Most League Goals in One Match: 3, Rickie Lambert v Luton T, Division 3, 24 November 2001; 3, Jonathan Parkin v Notts Co, FL 2, 25 January 2005; 3, Matt Tipton v Rochdale, FL 2, 19 February 2005.

Most Capped Player: George Abbey, 10 (18), Nigeria.

Most League Appearances: Darren Tinson, 263, 1997–2003.

Youngest League Player: Elliott Hewitt, 16 years 342 days v Hereford U, 7 May 2011.

Record Transfer Fee Received: £300,000 from Stockport Co for Rickie Lambert, April 2002.

Record Transfer Fee Paid: £40,000 to Bury for Danny Swailes, January 2005.

Football League Record: 1997 Promoted to Division 3; 1998–99 Division 2; 1999–2004 Division 3; 2004–12 FL 2; 2012–17 National League; 2018– FL2.

MANAGERS

Since 1967
Keith Goalen 1967–68
Frank Beaumont 1968–72
Billy Haydock 1972–74
Eddie Brown 1974
John Collins 1974
Willie Stevenson 1974
John Collins 1975–76
Tony Coleman 1976
John Barnes 1976
Brian Taylor 1976
Dave Connor 1976–78
Derek Partridge 1978
Phil Staley 1978–80
Jimmy Williams 1980–81
Brian Booth 1981–85
Neil Griffiths 1985–86
Roy Campbell 1986
Peter Wragg 1986–93
Sammy McIlroy 1993–2000
Peter Davenport 2000
Gil Prescott 2000–01
David Moss 2001–03
John Askey 2003–04
Brian Horton 2004–06
Paul Ince 2006–07
Ian Brightwell 2007–08
Keith Alexander 2008–10
Gary Simpson 2010–12
Steve King 2012–13
John Askew 2013–18
Mark Yates 2018
Sol Campbell November 2018–

LATEST SEQUENCES

Longest Sequence of League Wins: 6, 25.1.2005 – 26.2.2005.

Longest Sequence of League Defeats: 8, 2.1.2012 – 21.2.2012.

Longest Sequence of League Draws: 5, 25.2.2012 – 10.3.2012.

Longest Sequence of Unbeaten League Matches: 8, 16.10.1999 – 27.11.1999.

Longest Sequence Without a League Win: 36, 2.1.2012 – 12.10.2018 over 2 spells in League.

Successive Scoring Runs: 14 from 11.10.2003.

Successive Non-scoring Runs: 5 from 18.12.1998.

TEN YEAR LEAGUE RECORD

		P	W	D	L	F	A	Pts	Pos
2009-10	FL 2	46	12	18	16	49	58	54	19
2010-11	FL 2	46	14	13	19	59	73	55	15
2011-12	FL 2	46	8	13	25	39	64	37	24
2012-13	Conf	46	17	12	17	65	70	63	11
2013-14	Conf	46	18	7	21	62	63	61	15
2014-15	Conf	46	21	15	10	60	46	78	6
2015-16	NL	46	19	9	18	60	48	66	10
2016-17	NL	46	20	8	18	64	57	68	9
2017-18	NL	46	27	11	8	67	46	92	1
2018-19	FL 2	46	10	14	22	48	74	44	22

DID YOU KNOW ?

Macclesfield Town appointed former England international Paul Ince as manager in October 2006 after the club failed to win any of their first 16 League games. It took Ince four games before he achieved his first victory, a 1-0 defeat of Rochdale. That began a run of six wins in seven games to lift The Silkmen off the bottom of the table.

MACCLESFIELD TOWN – SKY BET LEAGUE TWO 2018–19 LEAGUE RECORD

Match No.	Date	Venue	Opponents	Result		H/T Score	Lg Pos.	Goalscorers	Attendance
1	Aug 4	A	Swindon T	L	2-3	0-0	15	Arthur 2 46, 55	7024
2	11	H	Grimsby T	L	0-2	0-1	23		2589
3	18	A	Oldham Ath	L	1-3	0-1	23	Rose 60	4330
4	21	H	Cheltenham T	D	1-1	1-0	23	Whitaker 19	1496
5	25	H	Mansfield T	D	1-1	0-1	23	Smith 63	2624
6	Sept 1	A	Crewe Alex	L	0-3	0-2	23		3915
7	8	A	Stevenage	L	0-1	0-1	23		2282
8	15	H	Lincoln C	L	1-2	0-1	23	Grimes 83	2589
9	22	A	Morecambe	L	1-2	0-0	24	Whitaker 72	1622
10	29	H	Forest Green R	D	1-1	0-0	24	Wilson 55	1503
11	Oct 2	A	Newport Co	D	3-3	2-1	24	Kelleher 6, Fitzpatrick 2 (2 pens) 11, 82	2624
12	6	H	Notts Co	L	0-1	0-0	24		2381
13	12	A	Tranmere R	L	0-1	0-0	24		6797
14	20	H	Carlisle U	W	2-1	0-0	24	Rose (pen) 79, Vincenti 83	2153
15	23	H	Northampton T	L	0-5	0-4	24		1517
16	27	A	Cambridge U	L	0-1	0-0	24		3946
17	Nov 3	H	Bury	L	1-4	1-3	24	Stephens 30	2485
18	17	A	Milton Keynes D	L	0-2	0-0	24		7087
19	24	H	Yeovil T	W	1-0	0-0	24	Rose (pen) 72	1570
20	27	A	Exeter C	W	1-0	0-0	24	Smith 54	3070
21	Dec 8	A	Colchester U	L	0-1	0-1	24		3099
22	15	H	Crawley T	W	2-0	1-0	24	Durrell 31, Smith 85	1362
23	22	H	Port Vale	D	0-0	0-0	24		3951
24	26	A	Notts Co	W	2-1	1-0	23	Wilson 2 36, 81	6786
25	29	A	Carlisle U	L	1-2	1-1	23	Wilson 2	4884
26	Jan 1	H	Tranmere R	D	1-1	1-1	23	Arthur 41	3398
27	5	H	Swindon T	L	1-2	1-1	23	Marsh 14	1964
28	12	A	Grimsby T	W	2-0	2-0	23	Marsh 26, Wilson 33	4694
29	19	H	Oldham Ath	W	2-1	1-1	23	Smith 45, Wilson 54	3697
30	26	A	Cheltenham T	L	2-3	2-0	23	Rose (pen) 11, Wilson 23	3041
31	Feb 2	A	Mansfield T	L	1-3	1-1	23	Evans 42	5642
32	9	H	Crewe Alex	D	3-3	1-2	23	Wilson 15, Cameron 74, Cole 90	3772
33	16	H	Colchester U	D	1-1	1-0	23	Wilson 44	2092
34	23	A	Crawley T	D	1-1	1-0	23	Smith 40	2190
35	Mar 2	A	Bury	L	0-3	0-1	23		4277
36	9	H	Milton Keynes D	L	1-3	1-1	23	Cameron 19	2017
37	16	A	Yeovil T	W	2-0	2-0	23	Pearson 18, Smith 33	2899
38	23	H	Stevenage	D	2-2	1-1	23	Durrell 42, Whitaker 90	1866
39	30	A	Lincoln C	D	1-1	1-1	24	Wilson 28	9567
40	Apr 6	H	Morecambe	D	1-1	1-1	24	Durrell 33	2072
41	9	H	Exeter C	W	3-2	2-2	22	Smith 30, Rose (pen) 45, Brown, T (og) 85	1588
42	13	A	Forest Green R	L	0-2	0-0	22		2386
43	19	A	Northampton T	L	1-3	1-1	22	Smith 38	4925
44	22	H	Newport Co	D	0-0	0-0	22		2269
45	27	A	Port Vale	W	1-0	0-0	22	Fitzpatrick 66	5414
46	May 4	H	Cambridge U	D	1-1	0-1	22	Durrell 66	3986

Final League Position: 22

GOALSCORERS

League (48): Wilson 10, Smith 8, Rose 5 (4 pens), Durrell 4, Arthur 3, Fitzpatrick 3 (2 pens), Whitaker 3, Cameron 2, Marsh 2, Cole 1, Evans 1, Grimes 1, Kelleher 1, Pearson 1, Stephens 1, Vincenti 1, own goal 1.
FA Cup (1): Stephens 1.
Carabao Cup (4): Grimes 1, Kelleher 1, Smith 1, Whitaker 1.
Checkatrade Trophy (7): Rose 2 (1 pen), Arthur 1, Blissett 1, Stephens 1, Vincenti 1, Wilson 1.

Taylor R 9	Hodgkiss J 17	Fitzpatrick D 40	Kellaher F 41 + 1	Grimes J 13	Rose M 39 + 1	Maycock C 21 + 6	Arthur K 17 + 3	Whitaker D 16 + 6	Marsh T 18 + 7	Smith H 30 + 9	Napa M 8 + 7	Lowe K 11 + 2	Wilson S 21 + 12	Blissett N 11 + 8	Welch-Hayes M 13 + 10	Pearson J 20 + 3	O'Hara K 37	Evans C 10 + 4	Ponticelli J 2 + 1	Vincenti P 9 + 7	Stephens B 18 + 4	Lloyd R 11 + 2	Cameron N 25	Durrell E 16 + 1	Cole R 11 + 7	Ntambwe B 6 + 2	Biabi B 1 + 2	Jules Z 13 + 1	Martis L 1 + 5	Demetriou S 1 + 1	Match No.
1	2	3	4	5	6^{2}	7	8	9	10^{1}	11	12	13																			1
1	2^{3}	5	3	4	8	7^{2}	10	9	6^{1}	11	13		12	14																	2
1		5	3	4	7	6^{2}	10	9		11	8^{3}		13	12	2^{1}	14															3
		5	3	4	7		8^{2}	6		11	13		10^{1}	9	12	2	1														4
		8	3	4		12	7^{2}	6		11	13	2^{1}	9^{3}	10		5	1	14													5
		5	3^{3}	4		6^{2}		9		11	10			12	13	2	1	7	8^{1}	14											6
1		5	13	4	8			7	14	12	9	3		11	6^{3}	2^{1}				10^{2}											7
		5	3	4	7			9	13	11^{1}	8	6	14	12		2^{3}	1			10^{2}											8
		5	3	4	6■	12		7	10^{3}	13	9^{2}			11		2	1	8^{1}		14											9
	2	5	4			8	7	9^{1}	6			3	10	11			1			12											10
	2	5	4			8	7^{3}		9^{1}	12	13	3	11^{2}	10		14	1			6											11
	2	5	4		14	8	7^{3}		9	12	13	3	10	11^{1}			1			6^{2}											12
1	2	5		4	7	6			8^{1}		10^{2}	3	12	11						9	13										13
1	2	5		4	7	8			9^{1}	13	11^{3}	3		10	14					6^{2}	12										14
1	2	5		4	7	8			9	13	11^{2}	3	14	10^{1}						6^{3}	12										15
1	2	5	4		8	7				10		3	12	9^{1}	13					6^{2}	11										16
1	2	5	4		7	8	13			10		3	9^{1}	14						6^{3}	11^{2}	12									17
	2^{3}	5	3		7	14	13	6		10						12	1				8^{2}	11	4	9^{1}							18
		5	4		8			7		10^{1}				12		2	1	14		13	11^{3}	9^{2}	3	6							19
		5	4		9	13		10		11^{2}				12		2	1	7^{3}		14		8^{1}	3	6							20
		5	3		8			7^{2}	12	11				14		2	1			13	10	9^{3}	4	6^{1}							21
		5^{2}	3		7			6		11					13	2	1		12		9	10^{1}	4	8							22
		5	3		7				6	10			12			2	1		11^{1}		9	8	4								23
		5	3		7	14	13		6	10■			11		12	2^{3}	1				9^{2}	8^{1}	4								24
		5	3		6	8	11		7				10		12	2	1					9^{1}	4								25
		5	3	4	6	7	9^{1}		8		13		11		12	2^{2}	1					10									26
	2	5	3		7	8	11^{2}		6				10		12		1			13		9^{1}	4								27
	2		3		8	7	6		9	10			11		5		1						4								28
	2		4		7	8			6	11			10		5		1	9^{1}					3		12						29
	2		4		7	8	9^{2}		6	10^{1}		13	11		5		1	12^{3}					3■		14						30
	2		3		7	8^{3}			6^{2}				10		5		1	9^{1}				14	4		11	12	13				31
	2^{2}		3		7		10^{3}			13			11		5		1	6^{1}					4		9	8		12	14		32
		5	3		7	12	6^{2}			11			10		2		1								9	8^{1}		4	13		33
		5	3		7	8	6^{2}			10			11		2		1							13	9			4^{1}		12	34
		5	3		8	7^{3}	6^{2}			10			11^{1}		2		1				14		4		9		13		12		35
										12						2	1	7			9	8	3	6	13		10^{2}	4	11^{1}	5	36
		9	3		7			13		11						5	1	12			10^{1}		2	6	8^{2}			4			37
		9	4		7^{1}			13		10			12			5	1				11		3	6	8^{2}			2			38
		9	4		7			12	13				10^{1}			5	1				11^{2}		3	6	8^{3}	14		2			39
		9	4		7^{2}			13		12			10^{1}			5	1				11		3	8	6^{3}			2	14		40
		9	3		7^{1}			12		10					13	5^{2}	1				11		2	6	8			4			41
		9	4		7^{2}			12		10			13		5		1				11		3	6	8^{1}			2			42
		8	3					7		11^{1}			14		5^{3}		1				9^{2}		2	10	12	6		4	13		43
		5	3		7^{2}				12	11			10^{1}		2		1	8						6	13	9		4			44
		6	5		8				13	10			14				1	2^{3}			11^{2}		3	7^{1}	12	9		4			45
		6	3		9				13	11			14				1	2^{1}			7^{2}		4	10^{3}	12	8		5			46

FA Cup
First Round Maidstone U (a) 1-2

Carabao Cup
First Round Bradford C (h) 1-1
(Macclesfield T won 4-2 on penalties)
Second Round Walsall (a) 3-3
(Macclesfield T won 3-1 on penalties)
Third Round West Ham U (a) 0-8

Checkatrade Trophy
Group C (N) Blackpool (h) 3-3
(Macclesfield T won 5-3 on penalties)
Group C (N) Accrington S (a) 1-4
Group C (N) WBA U21 (h) 2-1
Second Round (N) Newcastle U U21 (a) 1-1
(Newcastle U U21 won 5-3 on penalties)

MANCHESTER CITY

FOUNDATION

Manchester City was formed as a limited company in 1894 after their predecessors Ardwick had been forced into bankruptcy. However, many historians like to trace the club's lineage as far back as 1880 when St Mark's Church, West Gorton added a football section to their cricket club. They amalgamated with Belle Vue for one season before splitting again under the name Gorton Association FC in 1884–85. In 1887 Gorton AFC turned professional and moved ground to Hyde Road under the new name Ardwick AFC.

Etihad Stadium, Etihad Campus, Manchester M11 3FF.

Telephone: (0161) 444 1894.

Fax: (0161) 438 7999.

Ticket Office: (0161) 444 1894.

Website: www.mancity.com

Email: mancity@mancity.com

Ground Capacity: 55,017.

Record Attendance: 84,569 v Stoke C, FA Cup 6th rd, 3 March 1934 (at Maine Road; British record for any game outside London or Glasgow); 54,693 v Leicester C, Premier League, 6 February 2016 (at Etihad Stadium).

Pitch Measurements: 105m × 68m (115yd × 74.5yd).

Chairman: Khaldoon Al Mubarak.

Chief Executive: Ferran Soriano.

Manager: Pep Guardiola.

Assistant Managers: Mikel Arteta, Rodolfo Borrell, Brian Kidd.

Colours: Field blue shirts with white trim, white shorts with field blue trim, midnight navy socks.

Year Formed: 1887 as Ardwick FC; 1894 as Manchester City.

Turned Professional: 1887 as Ardwick FC.

Previous Names: 1880, St Mark's Church, West Gorton; 1884, Gorton; 1887, Ardwick; 1894, Manchester City.

Club Nicknames: 'The Blues', 'The Citizens'.

Grounds: 1880, Clowes Street; 1881, Kirkmanshulme Cricket Ground; 1882, Queens Road; 1884, Pink Bank Lane; 1887, Hyde Road (1894–1923 as City); 1923, Maine Road; 2003, City of Manchester Stadium (renamed Etihad Stadium 2011).

First Football League Game: 3 September 1892, Division 2, v Bootle (h) W 7–0 – Douglas; McVickers, Robson; Middleton, Russell, Hopkins; Davies (3), Morris (2), Angus (1), Weir (1), Milarvie.

Record League Victory: 10–1 v Huddersfield T, Division 2, 7 November 1987 – Nixon; Gidman, Hinchcliffe, Clements, Lake, Redmond, White (3), Stewart (3), Adcock (3), McNab (1), Simpson.

Record Cup Victory: 10–1 v Swindon T, FA Cup 4th rd, 29 January 1930 – Barber; Felton, McCloy; Barrass, Cowan, Heinemann; Toseland, Marshall (5), Tait (3), Johnson (1), Brook (1).

HONOURS

League Champions: Premier League – 2011–12, 2013–14, 2017–18, 2018–19; Division 1 – 1936–37, 1967–68; First Division – 2001–02; Division 2 – 1898–99, 1902–03, 1909–10, 1927–28, 1946–47, 1965–66.

Runners-up: Premier League – 2012–13, 2014–15; Division 1 – 1903–04, 1920–21, 1976–77; First Division – 1999–2000; Division 2 – 1895–96, 1950–51, 1988–89.

FA Cup Winners: 1904, 1934, 1956, 1969, 2011, 2019.

Runners-up: 1926, 1933, 1955, 1981, 2013.

League Cup Winners: 1970, 1976, 2014, 2016, 2018, 2019.

Runners-up: 1974.

Full Members Cup: *Runners-up:* 1986.

European Competitions

European Cup: 1968–69.

Champions League: 2011–12, 2012–13, 2013–14, 2014–15, 2015–16 *(sf)*, 2016–17, 2017–18 *(qf)*, 2018–19 *(sf)*.

UEFA Cup: 1972–73, 1976–77, 1977–78, 1978–79 *(qf)*, 2003–04, 2008–09 *(qf)*.

Europa League: 2010–11, 2011–12.

European Cup-Winners' Cup: 1969–70 *(winners)*, 1970–71 *(sf)*.

THE Sun FACT FILE

With one game remaining of their First Division fixtures of the 1937–38 season, Manchester City were in 16th place in the table, although only one point separated the bottom seven clubs. City lost their final game at fellow strugglers Huddersfield Town and, with Stoke City, Birmingham, Portsmouth and Grimsby Town all winning on the final day of the season, City found themselves relegated.

Record Defeat: 1–9 v Everton, Division 1, 3 September 1906.
Most League Points (2 for a win): 62, Division 2, 1946–47.
Most League Points (3 for a win): 100, Premier League, 2017–18.
Most League Goals: 108, Division 2, 1926–27, 108, Division 1, 2001–02.
Highest League Scorer in Season: Tommy Johnson, 38, Division 1, 1928–29.
Most League Goals in Total Aggregate: Sergio Aguero, 164, 2011–19.
Most League Goals in One Match: 5, Fred Williams v Darwen, Division 2, 18 February 1899; 5, Tom Browell v Burnley, Division 2, 24 October 1925; 5, Tom Johnson v Everton, Division 1, 15 September 1928; 5, George Smith v Newport Co, Division 2, 14 June 1947; 5, Sergio Aguero v Newcastle U, Premier League, 3 October 2015.
Most Capped Player: David Silva, 87 (125), Spain.
Most League Appearances: Alan Oakes, 564, 1959–76.
Youngest League Player: Glyn Pardoe, 15 years 314 days v Birmingham C, 11 April 1962.
Record Transfer Fee Received: £25,000,000 from Leicester C for Kelechi Iheanacho, August 2017.
Record Transfer Fee Paid: £62,500,000 to Atletico Madrid for Rodrigo Hernández Cascant, July 2019.
Football League Record: 1892 Ardwick elected founder member of Division 2; 1894 Newly-formed Manchester C elected to Division 2; Division 1 1899–1902, 1903–09, 1910–26, 1928–38, 1947–50, 1951–63, 1966–83, 1985–87, 1989–92; Division 2 1902–03, 1909–10, 1926–28, 1938–47, 1950–51, 1963–66, 1983–85, 1987–89; 1992–96 Premier League; 1996–98 Division 1; 1998–99 Division 2; 1999–2000 Division 1; 2000–01 Premier League; 2001–02 Division 1; 2002– Premier League.

LATEST SEQUENCES

Longest Sequence of League Wins: 18, 26.8.2017 – 27.12.2017.
Longest Sequence of League Defeats: 8, 23.8.1995 – 14.10.1995.
Longest Sequence of League Draws: 7, 5.10.2009 – 28.11.2009.
Longest Sequence of Unbeaten League Matches: 30, 8.4.2017 – 2.1.2018.
Longest Sequence Without a League Win: 17, 26.12.1979 – 7.4.1980.
Successive Scoring Runs: 44 from 3.10.1936.
Successive Non-scoring Runs: 6 from 30.1.1971.

MANAGERS

Joshua Parlby 1893–95
(Secretary-Manager)
Sam Omerod 1895–1902
Tom Maley 1902–06
Harry Newbould 1906–12
Ernest Magnall 1912–24
David Ashworth 1924–25
Peter Hodge 1926–32
Wilf Wild 1932–46
(continued as Secretary to 1950)
Sam Cowan 1946–47
John 'Jock' Thomson 1947–50
Leslie McDowall 1950–63
George Poyser 1963 65
Joe Mercer 1965–71
(continued as General Manager to 1972)
Malcolm Allison 1972–73
Johnny Hart 1973
Ron Saunders 1973–74
Tony Book 1974–79
Malcolm Allison 1979–80
John Bond 1980–83
John Benson 1983
Billy McNeill 1983–86
Jimmy Frizzell 1986–87
(continued as General Manager)
Mel Machin 1987–89
Howard Kendall 1989–90
Peter Reid 1990–93
Brian Horton 1993–95
Alan Ball 1995–96
Steve Coppell 1996
Frank Clark 1996–98
Joe Royle 1998–2001
Kevin Keegan 2001–05
Stuart Pearce 2005–07
Sven-Göran Eriksson 2007–08
Mark Hughes 2008–09
Roberto Mancini 2009–13
Manuel Pellegrini 2013–16
Pep Guardiola June 2016–

TEN YEAR LEAGUE RECORD

		P	W	D	L	F	A	Pts	Pos
2009-10	PR Lge	38	18	13	7	73	45	67	5
2010-11	PR Lge	38	21	8	9	60	33	71	3
2011-12	PR Lge	38	28	5	5	93	29	89	1
2012-13	PR Lge	38	23	9	6	66	34	78	2
2013-14	PR Lge	38	27	5	6	102	37	86	1
2014-15	PR Lge	38	24	7	7	83	38	79	2
2015-16	PR Lge	38	19	9	10	71	41	66	4
2016-17	PR Lge	38	23	9	6	80	39	78	3
2017-18	PR Lge	38	32	4	2	106	27	100	1
2018-19	PR Lge	38	32	2	4	95	23	98	1

DID YOU KNOW ?

The big freeze in the winter of 1962–63 meant that Manchester City did not play a home fixture between 15 December and 2 March. City beat Birmingham 2-1 when football resumed but then lost their next six consecutive Football League games, dropping down to 21st place in the table.

MANCHESTER CITY – PREMIER LEAGUE 2018–19 LEAGUE RECORD

Match No.	*Date*	*Venue*	*Opponents*	*Result*		*H/T Score*	*Lg Pos.*	*Goalscorers*	*Attendance*
1	Aug 12	A	Arsenal	W	2-0	1-0	3	Sterling [14], Bernardo Silva [64]	59,934
2	19	H	Huddersfield T	W	6-1	3-1	1	Aguero 3 [25, 35, 75], Gabriel Jesus [31], Silva [48], Kongolo (og) [84]	54,021
3	25	A	Wolverhampton W	D	1-1	0-0	2	Laporte [69]	31,322
4	Sept 1	H	Newcastle U	W	2-1	1-1	3	Sterling [8], Walker [52]	53,946
5	15	H	Fulham	W	3-0	2-0	3	Sane [2], Silva [21], Sterling [47]	53,307
6	22	A	Cardiff C	W	5-0	3-0	2	Aguero [32], Bernardo Silva [35], Gundogan [44], Mahrez 2 [67, 89]	32,321
7	29	H	Brighton & HA	W	2-0	1-0	1	Sterling [29], Aguero [65]	54,152
8	Oct 7	A	Liverpool	D	0-0	0-0	1		52,117
9	20	H	Burnley	W	5-0	1-0	1	Aguero [17], Bernardo Silva [54], Fernandinho [56], Mahrez [83], Sane [90]	54,094
10	29	A	Tottenham H	W	1-0	1-0	1	Mahrez [6]	56,854
11	Nov 4	H	Southampton	W	6-1	4-1	1	Hoedt (og) [6], Aguero [12], Silva [18], Sterling 2 [45, 67], Sane [90]	53,916
12	11	H	Manchester U	W	3-1	1-0	1	Silva [12], Aguero [48], Gundogan [86]	54,316
13	24	A	West Ham U	W	4-0	3-0	1	Silva [11], Sterling [19], Sane 2 [34, 90]	56,886
14	Dec 1	H	Bournemouth	W	3-1	1-1	1	Bernardo Silva [16], Sterling [57], Gundogan [79]	54,409
15	4	A	Watford	W	2-1	1-0	1	Sane [40], Mahrez [51]	20,389
16	8	A	Chelsea	L	0-2	0-1	2		40,571
17	15	H	Everton	W	3-1	1-0	1	Gabriel Jesus 2 [22, 50], Sterling [69]	54,173
18	22	H	Crystal Palace	L	2-3	1-2	2	Gundogan [27], De Bruyne [85]	54,340
19	26	A	Leicester C	L	1-2	1-1	3	Bernardo Silva [14]	32,090
20	30	A	Southampton	W	3-1	3-1	2	Silva [10], Ward-Prowse (og) [45], Aguero [45]	31,381
21	Jan 3	H	Liverpool	W	2-1	1-0	2	Aguero [40], Sane [72]	54,511
22	14	H	Wolverhampton W	W	3-0	2-0	2	Gabriel Jesus 2 (1 pen) [10, 39 (p)], Coady (og) [78]	54,171
23	20	A	Huddersfield T	W	3-0	1-0	2	Danilo [18], Sterling [54], Sane [56]	24,190
24	29	A	Newcastle U	L	1-2	1-0	2	Aguero [1]	50,861
25	Feb 3	H	Arsenal	W	3-1	2-1	2	Aguero 3 [1, 44, 61]	54,483
26	6	A	Everton	W	2-0	1-0	1	Laporte [45], Gabriel Jesus [90]	39,322
27	10	H	Chelsea	W	6-0	4-0	1	Sterling 2 [4, 80], Aguero 3 (1 pen) [13, 19, 56 (p)], Gundogan [25]	54,452
28	27	H	West Ham U	W	1-0	0-0	2	Aguero (pen) [59]	53,528
29	Mar 2	A	Bournemouth	W	1-0	0-0	1	Mahrez [55]	10,699
30	9	H	Watford	W	3-1	0-0	1	Sterling 3 [46, 50, 59]	54,104
31	30	A	Fulham	W	2-0	2-0	1	Bernardo Silva [5], Aguero [27]	25,001
32	Apr 3	H	Cardiff C	W	2-0	2-0	1	De Bruyne [6], Sane [44]	53,559
33	14	A	Crystal Palace	W	3-1	1-0	2	Sterling 2 [15, 63], Gabriel Jesus [90]	25,721
34	20	H	Tottenham H	W	1-0	1-0	1	Foden [5]	54,489
35	24	A	Manchester U	W	2-0	0-0	1	Bernardo Silva [54], Sane [66]	74,431
36	28	A	Burnley	W	1-0	0-0	1	Aguero [63]	21,605
37	May 6	H	Leicester C	W	1-0	0-0	1	Kompany [70]	54,506
38	12	A	Brighton & HA	W	4-1	2-1	1	Aguero [28], Laporte [38], Mahrez [63], Gundogan [72]	30,662

Final League Position: 1

GOALSCORERS

League (95): Aguero 21 (2 pens), Sterling 17, Sane 10, Bernardo Silva 7, Gabriel Jesus 7 (1 pen), Mahrez 7, Gundogan 6, Silva 6, Laporte 3, De Bruyne 2, Danilo 1, Fernandinho 1, Foden 1, Kompany 1, Walker 1, own goals 4.
FA Cup (26): Gabriel Jesus 5, Foden 3, Sterling 3, Aguero 2 (1 pen), Bernardo Silva 2, De Bruyne 2, Mahrez 2, Sane 2, Otamendi 1, Silva 1, own goals 3.
Carabao Cup (16): Gabriel Jesus 5, De Bruyne 2, Diaz 2, Foden 2, Mahrez 2, Aguero 1, Walker 1, Zinchenko 1.
Champions League (30): Aguero 6 (1 pen), Sterling 5, Bernardo Silva 4, Gabriel Jesus 4 (2 pens), Sane 4, Silva 3, Laporte 2, Foden 1, Mahrez 1.
Checkatrade Trophy (13): Braaf 2, Matondo 2, Poveda 2, Richards 2 (1 pen), Bolton 1, Dele-Bashiru 1, Gonzalez 1, Ogunby 1, Zoubdi Touaizi 1 (1 pen).

Ederson 38	Walker K 30 + 3	Stones J 20 + 4	Laporte A 34 + 1	Mendy B 10	Gundogan I 23 + 8	Fernandinho L 27 + 2	Mahrez R 14 + 13	Bernardo Silva M 31 + 5	Sterling R 31 + 3	Aguero S 31 + 2	De Bruyne K 11 + 8	Gabriel Jesus F 8 + 21	Sane L 21 + 10	Kompany V 13 + 4	Silva D 28 + 5	Foden P 3 + 10	Otamendi N 14 + 4	Delph F 8 + 3	Zinchenko A 14	Danilo 9 + 2	Match No.
1	2	3	4	5	6	7	8¹	9	10²	11³	12	13	14								1
1		2	4	9	8³	5	12	6		10¹		11	13	3	7²	14					2
1	2		4	5	8³	7	14	9¹	11²	10		12	13	3	6						3
1	2	3	4	5	13	6	7²	12	9	11		10³		14	8¹						4
1	2		4		13	7	14	6	9²	10³		12	11		8		3	5¹			5
1	2	14	4		8¹	7²	12	6	9	10³			11			13	3	5			6
1	2		4			7	13	6	9	10³		12	11²		8¹	14	3		5		7
1	2	3	4	5		7	8	6	10¹	11²		12	13		9						8
1		2	4	5		7	9	6³		10²	12	13	11	3	8¹	14					9
1	2	3	4	5		7	9³	6	11	10¹	12	14		13	8²						10
1	2	3¹	4	5		7³		6	9	10			11	12	8²	13		14			11
1	2	3	4	5	13	7	9²	6	11	10¹			12		8³	14					12
1	2		4		8¹	7	13		9²	10³		14	11		6	12	3	5			13
1			4		8	7	14	6³	9			10²	11		13		3	12	5¹	2	14
1	2	3	14		12	7	9	6				10¹	11	4²	8³		13	5			15
1	2	3	4		13	7	9³	6	10			12	11²		8¹	14		5			16
1	2		4		8	7	9¹	6	12		13	10	11²				3	5			17
1	2	7	4		6		14	8	9³	12	13	10	11				3²	5¹			18
1		3	4		7		13	8¹	9	10	6²		11		12			5¹		2	19
1	14		4			7¹	9³	6	11	10²		12	13	3	8				5	2	20
1	13	3	5³		12	7		6	9	10			11	4²	8¹		14			2	21
1	2	3	4		13	7		6	9	14	12	10³	11²		8¹					5	22
1	2		4		8³	7¹		13	9	10	6		11²		12		3	14		5	23
1	2	3	4		14	7		12	9	10	6²	13	11¹		8					5³	24
1	2		5		7	3	13	9	11	10²	6¹	12			8		4				25
1	2	3	5		6	7		9	12	10¹	14	13	11³		8²		4				26
1	2	3	4		8	7³	13	9	11	10¹	6²	12			14				5		27
1					7		9¹	13	12	10³	6		11²	3	8	14	4		5	2	28
1	2	3¹			7		12	9	11	10³	6²	14		13	8		4		5		29
1	2				7		9¹	6	11²	10³		13	12	3	8	14	4		5		30
1	2		4		7	13	14	9	11³	10¹	6²	12			8		3		5		31
1	12	3	4			7	9				6	10	11			8			5¹	2	32
1	2	14	4	5	7			12	8	11²	6	13	10³	3	9¹						33
1	2	3	4		7	12		9	11	10³	6²		13		14	8¹			5		34
1	2		4		6²	7³		9	11	10¹		13	12	3	8				5	14	35
1	2	13	4		5			8	7²	11³		12	10¹	3	9		14		6		36
1	2	14	4		7			9	11	10²		13	12	3	8³	6¹			5		37
1	2²		4		7		9	6	10	11	12			3³	8¹		13		5	14	38

FA Cup

Third Round	Rotherham U	(h)	7-0
Fourth Round	Burnley	(h)	5-0
Fifth Round	Newport Co	(a)	4-1
Sixth Round	Swansea C	(a)	3-2
Semi-Final	Brighton & HA	(Wembley)	1-0
Final	Watford	(Wembley)	6-0

Champions League

Group F	Lyon	(h)	1-2
Group F	TSG Hoffenheim	(a)	2-1
Group F	Shakhtar Donetsk	(a)	3-0
Group F	Shakhtar Donetsk	(h)	6-0
Group F	Lyon	(a)	2-2
Group F	TSG Hoffenheim	(h)	2-1
Round of 16 1st leg	Schalke 04	(a)	3-2
Round of 16 2nd leg	Schalke 04	(h)	7-0
Quarter-Final 1st leg	Tottenham H	(a)	0-1
Quarter-Final 2nd leg	Tottenham H	(h)	4-3

Carabao Cup

Third Round	Oxford U	(a)	3-0
Fourth Round	Fulham	(h)	2-0
Quarter-Final	Leicester C	(a)	1-1
(Manchester C won 3-1 on penalties)			
Semi-Final 1st leg	Burton Alb	(h)	9-0
Semi-Final 2nd leg	Burton Alb	(a)	1-0
Final	Chelsea	(Wembley)	0-0
(aet; Manchester C won 4-3 on penalties)			

Checkatrade Trophy (Manchester C U21)

Group D (N)	Shrewsbury T	(a)	1-1
(Shrewsbury T won 3-1 on penalties)			
Group D (N)	Crewe Alex	(a)	4-1
Group D (N)	Tranmere R	(a)	1-0
Second Round (N)	Barnsley	(a)	3-3
(Manchester C U21 won 5-3 on penalties)			
Third Round	Rochdale	(a)	4-2
Quarter-Final	Sunderland	(a)	0-2

MANCHESTER UNITED

FOUNDATION

Manchester United was formed as comparatively recently as 1902 after their predecessors, Newton Heath, went bankrupt. However, it is usual to give the date of the club's foundation as 1878 when the dining room committee of the carriage and waggon works of the Lancashire and Yorkshire Railway Company formed Newton Heath L and YR Cricket and Football Club. They won the Manchester Cup in 1886 and as Newton Heath FC were admitted to the Second Division in 1892.

Old Trafford, Sir Matt Busby Way, Manchester M16 0RA.

Telephone: (0161) 868 8000.

Fax: (0161) 868 8804.

Ticket Office: (0161) 868 8000 (option 1).

Website: www.manutd.co.uk

Email: enquiries@manutd.co.uk

Ground Capacity: 74,879.

Record Attendance: 76,098 v Blackburn R, Premier League, 31 March 2007. 83,260 v Arsenal, First Division, 17 January 1948 (at Maine Road – United shared City's ground after Old Trafford suffered World War II bomb damage).

Ground Record Attendance: 76,962 Wolverhampton W v Grimsby T, FA Cup semi-final, 25 March 1939.

Pitch Measurements: 105m × 68m (115yd × 74.5yd).

Co-Chairmen: Joel Glazer, Avram Glazer.

Chief Executive: Edward Woodward.

Manager: Ole Gunnar Solskjaer.

Assistant Managers: Michael Carrick, Kieran McKenna, Mike Phelan, Mark Dempsey.

Colours: Red shirts with white and black trim, black shorts with white trim, black socks with red and white trim.

Year Formed: 1878 as Newton Heath LYR; 1902, Manchester United.

Turned Professional: 1885.

Previous Name: 1880, Newton Heath; 1902, Manchester United.

Club Nickname: 'Red Devils'.

Grounds: 1880, North Road, Monsall Road; 1893, Bank Street; 1910, Old Trafford (played at Maine Road 1941–49).

HONOURS

League Champions: Premier League – 1992–93, 1993–94, 1995–96, 1996–97, 1998–99, 1999–2000, 2000–01, 2002–03, 2006–07, 2007–08, 2008–09, 2010–11, 2012–13; Division 1 – 1907–08, 1910–11, 1951–52, 1955–56, 1956–57, 1964–65, 1966–67; Division 2 – 1935–36, 1974–75.
Runners-up: Premier League – 1994–95, 1997–98, 2005–06, 2009–10, 2011–12, 2017–18; Division 1 – 1946–47, 1947–48, 1948–49, 1950–51, 1958–59, 1963–64, 1967–68, 1979–80, 1987–88, 1991–92; Division 2 – 1896–97, 1905–06, 1924–25, 1937–38.

FA Cup Winners: 1909, 1948, 1963, 1977, 1983, 1985, 1990, 1994, 1996, 1999, 2004, 2016.
Runners-up: 1957, 1958, 1976, 1979, 1995, 2005, 2007, 2018.

League Cup Winners: 1992, 2006, 2009, 2010, 2017.
Runners-up: 1983, 1991, 1994, 2003.

European Competitions
European Cup: 1956–57 *(sf)*, 1957–58 *(sf)*, 1965–66 *(sf)*, 1967–68 *(winners)*, 1968–69 *(sf)*.
Champions League: 1993–94, 1994–95, 1996–97 *(sf)*, 1997–98 *(qf)*, 1998–99 *(winners)*, 1999–2000 *(qf)*, 2000–01 *(qf)*, 2001–02 *(sf)*, 2002–03 *(qf)*, 2003–04, 2004–05, 2005–06, 2006–07 *(sf)*, 2007–08 *(winners)*, 2008–09 *(runners-up)*, 2009–10 *(qf)*, 2010–11 *(runners-up)*, 2011–12, 2012–13, 2013–14 *(qf)*, 2015–16, 2017–18, 2018–19.
Fairs Cup: 1964–65.
UEFA Cup: 1976–77, 1980–81, 1982–83, 1984–85 *(qf)*, 1992–93, 1995–96.
Europa League: 2011–12, 2015–16, 2016–17 *(winners)*.
European Cup-Winners' Cup: 1963–64 *(qf)*, 1977–78, 1983–84 *(sf)*, 1990–91 *(winners)*. 1991–92.
Super Cup: 1991 *(winners)*, 1999, 2008.
World Club Championship: 1968, 1999 *(winners)*, 2000.
FIFA Club World Cup: 2008 *(winners)*.
NB: In 1958–59 FA refused permission to compete in European Cup.

THE SUN FACT FILE

Eddie McIlvenny, who captained the USA to a sensational victory over England in the 1950 World Cup finals, returned to England and signed for Manchester United shortly afterwards. However, he managed just two first-team appearances for the Red Devils, both at the start of the 1950–51 season, before eventually moving on to sign for League of Ireland club Waterford United.

First Football League Game: 3 September 1892, Division 1, v Blackburn R (a) L 3–4 – Warner; Clements, Brown; Perrins, Stewart, Erentz; Farman (1), Coupar (1), Donaldson (1), Carson, Mathieson.

Record League Victory (as Newton Heath): 10–1 v Wolverhampton W, Division 1, 15 October 1892 – Warner; Mitchell, Clements; Perrins, Stewart (3), Erentz; Farman (1), Hood (1), Donaldson (3), Carson (1), Hendry (1).

Record League Victory (as Manchester U): 9–0 v Ipswich T, Premier League, 4 March 1995 – Schmeichel; Keane (1) (Sharpe), Irwin, Bruce (Butt), Kanchelskis, Pallister, Cole (5), Ince (1), McClair, Hughes (2), Giggs.

Record Cup Victory: 10–0 v RSC Anderlecht, European Cup prel. rd 2nd leg, 26 September 1956 – Wood; Foulkes, Byrne; Colman, Jones, Edwards; Berry (1), Whelan (2), Taylor (3), Viollet (4), Pegg.

Record Defeat: 0–7 v Blackburn R, Division 1, 10 April 1926; 0–7 v Aston Villa, Division 1, 27 December 1930; 0–7 v Wolverhampton W, Division 2, 26 December 1931.

Most League Points (2 for a win): 64, Division 1, 1956–57.

Most League Points (3 for a win): 92, Premier League, 1993–94.

Most League Goals: 103, Division 1, 1956–57 and 1958–59.

Highest League Scorer in Season: Dennis Viollet, 32, 1959–60.

Most League Goals in Total Aggregate: Bobby Charlton, 199, 1956–73.

Most League Goals in One Match: 5, Andy Cole v Ipswich T, Premier League, 3 March 1995; 5, Dimitar Berbatov v Blackburn R, Premier League, 27 November 2010.

Most Capped Player: Bobby Charlton, 106, England.

Most League Appearances: Ryan Giggs, 672, 1991–2014.

Youngest League Player: Jeff Whitefoot, 16 years 105 days v Portsmouth, 15 April 1950.

Record Transfer Fee Received: £80,000,000 from Real Madrid for Cristiano Ronaldo, July 2009.

Record Transfer Fee Paid: £89,300,000 to Juventus for Paul Pogba, August 2016.

Football League Record: 1892 Newton Heath elected to Division 1; 1894–1906 Division 2; 1906–22 Division 1; 1922–25 Division 2; 1925–31 Division 1; 1931–36 Division 2; 1936–37 Division 1; 1937–38 Division 2; 1938–74 Division 1; 1974–75 Division 2; 1975–92 Division 1; 1992– Premier League.

MANAGERS

J. Ernest Mangnall 1903–12
John Bentley 1912–14
John Robson 1914–21
(Secretary-Manager from 1916)
John Chapman 1921–26
Clarence Hilditch 1926–27
Herbert Bamlett 1927–31
Walter Crickmer 1931–32
Scott Duncan 1932–37
Walter Crickmer 1937–45
(Secretary-Manager)
Matt Busby 1945–69
(continued as General Manager then Director)
Wilf McGuinness 1969–70
Sir Matt Busby 1970–71
Frank O'Farrell 1971–72
Tommy Docherty 1972–77
Dave Sexton 1977–81
Ron Atkinson 1981–86
Sir Alex Ferguson 1986–2013
David Moyes 2013–14
Louis van Gaal 2014–16
Jose Mourinho 2016–18
Ole Gunnar Solskjaer December 2018–

LATEST SEQUENCES

Longest Sequence of League Wins: 14, 15.10.1904 – 3.1.1905.

Longest Sequence of League Defeats: 14, 26.4.1930 – 25.10.1930.

Longest Sequence of League Draws: 6, 30.10.1988 – 27.11.1988.

Longest Sequence of Unbeaten League Matches: 29, 11.4.2010 – 1.2.2011.

Longest Sequence Without a League Win: 16, 19.4.1930 – 25.10.1930.

Successive Scoring Runs: 36 from 3.12.2007.

Successive Non-scoring Runs: 5 from 7.2.1981.

TEN YEAR LEAGUE RECORD

		P	*W*	*D*	*L*	*F*	*A*	*Pts*	*Pos*
2009-10	PR Lge	38	27	4	7	86	28	85	2
2010-11	PR Lge	38	23	11	4	78	37	80	1
2011-12	PR Lge	38	28	5	5	89	33	89	2
2012-13	PR Lge	38	28	5	5	86	43	89	1
2013-14	PR Lge	38	19	7	12	64	43	64	7
2014-15	PR Lge	38	20	10	8	62	37	70	4
2015-16	PR Lge	38	19	9	10	49	35	66	5
2016-17	PR Lge	38	18	15	5	54	29	69	6
2017-18	PR Lge	38	25	6	7	68	28	81	2
2018-19	PR Lge	38	19	9	10	65	54	66	6

DID YOU KNOW?

Only six players attached to English clubs have won the Ballon d'Or award made by *France Football* magazine and four of these have been Manchester United players. Winners for the Reds have been Dennis Law (1964), Bobby Charlton (1966), George Best (1968) and Cristiano Ronaldo (2008).

MANCHESTER UNITED – PREMIER LEAGUE 2018–19 LEAGUE RECORD

Match No.	*Date*	*Venue*	*Opponents*	*Result*	*H/T Score*	*Lg Pos.*	*Goalscorers*	*Attendance*
1	Aug 10	H	Leicester C	W 2-1	1-0	1	Pogba (pen) ^{3}, Shaw ^{83}	74,439
2	19	A	Brighton & HA	L 2-3	1-3	10	Lukaku ^{34}, Pogba (pen) ^{90}	30,592
3	27	H	Tottenham H	L 0-3	0-0	13		74,400
4	Sept 2	A	Burnley	W 2-0	2-0	10	Lukaku 2 $^{27, 44}$	21,525
5	15	A	Watford	W 2-1	2-0	8	Lukaku ^{35}, Smalling ^{38}	20,537
6	22	H	Wolverhampton W	D 1-1	1-0	6	Fred ^{18}	74,489
7	29	A	West Ham U	L 1-3	0-2	10	Rashford ^{71}	56,938
8	Oct 6	H	Newcastle U	W 3-2	0-2	8	Mata ^{70}, Martial ^{76}, Sanchez ^{90}	74,519
9	20	A	Chelsea	D 2-2	0-1	9	Martial 2 $^{55, 73}$	40,721
10	28	H	Everton	W 2-1	1-0	8	Pogba ^{27}, Martial ^{49}	74,525
11	Nov 3	A	Bournemouth	W 2-1	1-1	7	Martial ^{35}, Rashford ^{90}	10,792
12	11	A	Manchester C	L 1-3	0-1	8	Martial (pen) ^{58}	54,316
13	24	H	Crystal Palace	D 0-0	0-0	7		74,516
14	Dec 1	A	Southampton	D 2-2	2-2	7	Lukaku ^{33}, Ander Herrera ^{39}	30,187
15	5	H	Arsenal	D 2-2	1-1	8	Martial ^{30}, Lingard ^{69}	74,507
16	8	H	Fulham	W 4-1	3-0	6	Young ^{13}, Mata ^{28}, Lukaku ^{42}, Rashford ^{82}	74,523
17	16	A	Liverpool	L 1-3	1-1	6	Lingard ^{33}	52,908
18	22	A	Cardiff C	W 5-1	3-1	6	Rashford ^{3}, Ander Herrera ^{29}, Martial ^{41}, Lingard 2 (1 pen) $^{57 (p), 90}$	33,028
19	26	H	Huddersfield T	W 3-1	1-0	6	Matic ^{28}, Pogba 2 $^{64, 78}$	74,523
20	30	H	Bournemouth	W 4-1	3-1	6	Pogba 2 $^{5, 33}$, Rashford ^{45}, Lukaku ^{72}	74,556
21	Jan 2	A	Newcastle U	W 2-0	0-0	6	Lukaku ^{64}, Rashford ^{80}	52,217
22	13	A	Tottenham H	W 1-0	1-0	6	Rashford ^{44}	80,062
23	19	H	Brighton & HA	W 2-1	2-0	6	Pogba (pen) ^{27}, Rashford ^{42}	74,532
24	29	H	Burnley	D 2-2	0-0	6	Pogba (pen) ^{87}, Lindelof ^{90}	74,529
25	Feb 3	A	Leicester C	W 1-0	1-0	5	Rashford ^{9}	32,148
26	9	A	Fulham	W 3-0	2-0	4	Pogba 2 (1 pen) $^{14, 65 (p)}$, Martial ^{23}	25,001
27	24	H	Liverpool	D 0-0	0-0	5		74,519
28	27	A	Crystal Palace	W 3-1	1-0	5	Lukaku 2 $^{33, 52}$, Young ^{83}	25,754
29	Mar 2	H	Southampton	W 3-2	0-1	4	Pereira ^{53}, Lukaku 2 $^{59, 88}$	74,459
30	10	A	Arsenal	L 0-2	0-1	5		60,000
31	30	H	Watford	W 2-1	1-0	4	Rashford ^{28}, Martial ^{72}	74,543
32	Apr 2	A	Wolverhampton W	L 1-2	1-1	5	McTominay ^{13}	31,302
33	13	H	West Ham U	W 2-1	1-0	5	Pogba 2 (2 pens) $^{19, 80}$	74,478
34	21	A	Everton	L 0-4	0-2	6		39,395
35	24	H	Manchester C	L 0-2	0-0	6		74,431
36	28	H	Chelsea	D 1-1	1-1	6	Mata ^{11}	74,526
37	May 5	A	Huddersfield T	D 1-1	1-0	6	McTominay ^{8}	24,263
38	12	H	Cardiff C	L 0-2	0-1	6		74,457

Final League Position: 6

GOALSCORERS

League (65): Pogba 13 (7 pens), Lukaku 12, Martial 10 (1 pen), Rashford 10, Lingard 4 (1 pen), Mata 3, Ander Herrera 2, McTominay 2, Young 2, Fred 1, Lindelof 1, Matic 1, Pereira 1, Sanchez 1, Shaw 1, Smalling 1.
FA Cup (8): Ander Herrera 1, Lingard 1, Lukaku 1, Martial 1, Mata 1 (1 pen), Pogba 1, Rashford 1, Sanchez 1.
Carabao Cup (2): Fellaini 1, Mata 1.
Champions League (10): Lukaku 2, Pogba 2 (1 pen), Rashford 2 (1 pen), Fellaini 1, Martial 1, Mata 1, own goal 1.

De Gea D 38	Darmian M 5 + 1	Bailly E 8 + 4	Lindelof V 29 + 1	Shaw L 29	Fred F 13 + 4	Pereira A 6 + 9	Pogba P 34 + 1	Mata J 16 + 6	Rashford M 26 + 7	Sanchez A 9 + 11	Lukaku R 22 + 10	McTominay S 9 + 7	Fellaini M 6 + 8	Young A 28 + 2	Martial A 18 + 9	Lingard J 19 + 8	Ander Herrera A 16 + 6	Smalling C 24	Jones P 15 + 3	Valencia A 5 + 1	Matic N 28	Dalot D 12 + 4	Rojo M 2 + 3	Gomes A — + 2	Garner J — + 1	Chong T — + 2	Greenwood M 1 + 2	*Match No.*
1	2	3	4	5	6^{3}	7	8^{1}	9	10^{2}	11	12	13	14															1
1		3	4	5	6	7^{1}	8	9^{2}	12		10		14	2	11^{3}	13												2
1			13	9	8		6			12	11		14			10	2^{2}	3	4^{3}	5	7^{1}							3
1		14	4	5			6^{2}		12■	11^{3}	10		7			9^{1}	13	3		2	8							4
1		14	4				6			11^{1}	10	13	7	5	12	9^{2}		3		2^{3}	8■							5
1			4	5	8^{3}	14	6	12		11^{2}	10		7		13	9^{1}		3		2								6
1			5^{1}	6	13		9^{3}	14	12		10	3	7	2	11^{2}			4			8							7
1		3^{2}		5			8	12	9^{1}	14	10	6^{3}	13	2	11			4			7							8
1			4	5		13	7	9^{1}	8^{2}	14	11			2	10^{3}		12	3			6							9
1			4	5	6^{1}		8	9^{2}	10^{3}		12			2	11	14	13	3			7							10
1			4	5	6^{1}		8	9^{2}	12	10^{3}				2	11	14	13	3			7							11
1			4	5				14	10^{3}	13	12		7	2	11	9^{2}	6^{1}	3			8							12
1	2		4				8^{3}	9^{1}	12	14	10		13	5	11	6^{2}		3			7							13
1				6^{2}			9		11^{1}		10^{3}	3	7	2	13	14	8		4		5	12						14
1	8	2					14		11		12		13		10^{1}	9^{2}	8	3			7	5	4^{3}					15
1					13			8	10^{2}		11	14		5		9^{1}	6	3^{3}	4		7	2	12					16
1	2	3	4					14	9		11		12	5	13	10^{3}	7^{1}				8	6^{2}						17
1			3	5	12	13	8		10^{1}				14	2	11^{3}	9	6		4		7^{2}							18
1			3	5	6^{2}		9	8^{1}	11					12		10	13		4		7	2^{3}		14				19
1		3■	4	5		13	9		11^{2}		12			2	10^{1}	8	6^{3}		14		7							20
1			3	5			9	8^{2}	11^{1}	13	12				10^{3}	14	6		4	2	7							21
1			3	5			8^{1}		11		12	14		2	10^{3}	9^{2}	7		4		6	13						22
1	14		3				8	12	10^{2}		13			2	11^{3}	9^{1}	6		4		7	5						23
1			3	5		8^{2}	9	7	10	13	11^{1}			2		12			4		6							24
1		3	4	5			8		10^{1}	11^{3}	13			2	12	9^{2}	7		14		6							25
1		14		5			8^{1}	9		12	10	13			11^{3}		6^{2}	3	4		7	2						26
1			4	5		12	8	9^{2}	11	14	10	7		2		13^{3}	6^{1}	3										27
1		13	4	5	8^{3}		6		12	11^{2}	10	7		2				3				9^{1}			14			28
1			4	5	13	6^{1}	8		10^{3}	9^{2}	11	7		2				3				12				14		29
1			4	5	7		9		10		11			2	12			3			8^{2}	6^{1}					13	30
1				5		12	8	9^{3}	10					2	11^{2}	13	6^{1}	3	4		7		14					31
1			4	9	7^{2}	14	8				11^{3}	6		2■	13	10		3	12			5^{1}						32
1					7	13	6	9^{3}	12		11^{1}				10	8		3	4			2	5^{2}				14	33
1			2		8^{1}	14	6		9^{2}		10	12		13	11			3	4^{3}		7	5						34
1	3^{3}		5	6	8	7^{1}	9		10	13	12			2	14	11^{2}		4										35
1		3^{2}	4	5			8	9^{1}	11^{3}	12	10	14		2			6				7		13					36
1			3^{3}	5			8	9	10	11^{2}		6		2			12		4		7^{1}	14				13		37
1						6^{1}	0		11			7		5	12	9		3	4^{3}	14		2^{7}		13			10	38

FA Cup

Third Round	Reading	(h)	2-0
Fourth Round	Arsenal	(a)	3-1
Fifth Round	Chelsea	(a)	2-0
Sixth Round	Wolverhampton W	(a)	1-2

Carabao Cup

Third Round	Derby Co	(h)	2-2

(Derby Co won 8-7 on penalties)

Champions League

Group H	Young Boys	(a)	3-0
Group H	Valencia	(h)	0-0
Group H	Juventus	(h)	0-1
Group H	Juventus	(a)	2-1
Group H	Young Boys	(h)	1-0
Group H	Valencia	(a)	1-2
Round of 16 1st leg	Paris Saint-Germain	(h)	0-2
Round of 16 2nd leg	Paris Saint-Germain	(a)	3-1
Quarter-Final 1st leg	Barcelona	(h)	0-1
Quarter-Final 2nd leg	Barcelona	(a)	0-3

MANSFIELD TOWN

FOUNDATION

The club was formed as Mansfield Wesleyans in 1897, and changed their name to Mansfield Wesley in 1906 and Mansfield Town in 1910. This was after the Mansfield Wesleyan Chapel trustees had requested that the club change its name as 'it has no longer had any connection with either the chapel or school'. The new club participated in the Notts and Derby District League, but in the following season 1911–12 joined the Central Alliance.

One Call Stadium, Quarry Lane, Mansfield, Nottinghamshire NG18 5DA.

Telephone: (01623) 482 482.

Fax: (01623) 482 495.

Ticket Office: (01623) 482 482.

Website: www.mansfieldtown.net

Email: info@mansfieldtown.net

Ground Capacity: 9,186.

Record Attendance: 24,467 v Nottingham F, FA Cup 3rd rd, 10 January 1953.

Pitch Measurements: 100.5m × 64m (110yd × 70yd).

Chairman: John Radford.

Chief Executive: Carolyn Radford.

Manager: John Dempster.

Assistant Manager: Lee Glover.

Colours: Yellow and blue shirts, blue shorts, blue socks.

Year Formed: 1897.

Turned Professional: 1906.

Ltd Co.: 1922.

Previous Name: 1897, Mansfield Wesleyans; 1906, Mansfield Wesley; 1910, Mansfield Town.

Grounds: 1897–99, Westfield Lane; 1899–1901, Ratcliffe Gate; 1901–12, Newgate Lane; 1912–16, Ratcliffe Gate; 1916, Field Mill (renamed One Call Stadium 2012).

Club Nickname: 'The Stags'.

First Football League Game: 29 August 1931, Division 3 (S), v Swindon T (h) W 3–2 – Wilson; Clifford, England; Wake, Davis, Blackburn; Gilhespy, Readman (1), Johnson, Broom (2), Baxter.

Record League Victory: 9–2 v Rotherham U, Division 3 (N), 27 December 1932 – Wilson; Anthony, England; Davies, S. Robinson, Slack; Prior, Broom, Readman (3), Hoyland (3), Bowater (3).

Record Cup Victory: 8–0 v Scarborough (a), FA Cup 1st rd, 22 November 1952 – Bramley; Chessell, Bradley; Field, Plummer, Lewis; Scott, Fox (3), Marron (2), Sid Watson (1), Adam (2).

Record Defeat: 1–8 v Walsall, Division 3 (N), 19 January 1933.

Most League Points (2 for a win): 68, Division 4, 1974–75.

HONOURS

League Champions: Division 3 – 1976–77; Division 4 – 1974–75; Conference – 2012–13.
Runners-up: Division 3N – 1950–51, Third Division – (3rd) 2001–02 *(promoted to Second Division).*

FA Cup: 6th rd – 1969.

League Cup: 5th rd – 1976.

League Trophy Winners: 1987.

THE SUN FACT FILE

Mansfield Town's first overseas fixture came within weeks of the club starting their first season in the Football League. They travelled to The Hague in September 1931 where they faced a Dutch National XI in a game played under floodlights. John Jepson scored both of the Stags' goals in their 2-1 win in front of a 13,000 crowd. Within an hour of the final whistle the Mansfield team set off for home, travelling by boat and train to arrive back at 2pm the following day.

Most League Points (3 for a win): 81, Division 4, 1985–86.

Most League Goals: 108, Division 4, 1962–63.

Highest League Scorer in Season: Ted Harston, 55, Division 3 (N), 1936–37.

Most League Goals in Total Aggregate: Harry Johnson, 104, 1931–36.

Most League Goals in One Match: 7, Ted Harston v Hartlepools U, Division 3N, 23 January 1937.

Most Capped Player: John McClelland, 6 (53), Northern Ireland; Reggie Lambe, 6 (34), Bermuda.

Most League Appearances: Rod Arnold, 440, 1970–83.

Youngest League Player: Cyril Poole, 15 years 351 days v New Brighton, 27 February 1937.

Record Transfer Fee Received: £30,000 (rising to £655,000) from Swindon T for Colin Calderwood, July 1985.

Record Transfer Fee Paid: £150,000 to Peterborough U for Lee Angol, May 2017.

Football League Record: 1931 Elected to Division 3 (S); 1932–37 Division 3 (N); 1937–47 Division 3 (S); 1947–58 Division 3 (N); 1958–60 Division 3; 1960–63 Division 4; 1963–72 Division 3; 1972–75 Division 4; 1975–77 Division 3; 1977–78 Division 2; 1978–80 Division 3; 1980–86 Division 4; 1986–91 Division 3; 1991–92 Division 4; 1992–93 Division 2; 1993–2002 Division 3; 2002–03 Division 2; 2003–04 Division 3; 2004–08 FL 2; 2008–13 Conference Premier; 2013– FL 2.

LATEST SEQUENCES

Longest Sequence of League Wins: 7, 13.9.1991 – 26.10.1991.

Longest Sequence of League Defeats: 7, 18.1.1947 – 15.3.1947.

Longest Sequence of League Draws: 5, 18.10.1986 – 22.11.1986.

Longest Sequence of Unbeaten League Matches: 20, 14.2.1976 – 21.8.1976.

Longest Sequence Without a League Win: 14, 25.3.2000 – 2.9.2000.

Successive Scoring Runs: 27 from 1.10.1962.

Successive Non-scoring Runs: 8 from 25.3.2000.

MANAGERS

John Baynes 1922–25
Ted Davison 1926–28
Jack Hickling 1928–33
Henry Martin 1933–35
Charlie Bell 1935
Harold Wightman 1936
Harold Parkes 1936–38
Jack Poole 1938–44
Lloyd Barke 1944–45
Roy Goodall 1945–49
Freddie Steele 1949–51
George Jobey 1952–53
Stan Mercer 1953–55
Charlie Mitten 1956–58
Sam Weaver 1958–60
Raich Carter 1960–63
Tommy Cummings 1963–67
Tommy Eggleston 1967–70
Jock Basford 1970–71
Danny Williams 1971–74
Dave Smith 1974–76
Peter Morris 1976–78
Billy Bingham 1978–79
Mick Jones 1979–81
Stuart Boam 1981–83
Ian Greaves 1983–89
George Foster 1989–93
Andy King 1993–96
Steve Parkin 1996–99
Billy Dearden 1999–2002
Stuart Watkiss 2002
Keith Curle 2002–04
Carlton Palmer 2004–05
Peter Shirtliff 2005–06
Billy Dearden 2006–08
Paul Holland 2008
Billy McEwan 2008
David Holdsworth 2008–10
Duncan Russell 2010–11
Paul Cox 2011–14
Adam Murray 2014–16
Steve Evans 2016–18
David Flitcroft 2018–19
John Dempster May 2019–

TEN YEAR LEAGUE RECORD

		P	*W*	*D*	*L*	*F*	*A*	*Pts*	*Pos*
2009-10	Conf P	44	17	11	16	69	60	62	9
2010-11	Conf P	46	17	10	19	73	75	61	13
2011-12	Conf P	46	25	14	7	87	48	89	3
2012-13	Conf P	46	30	5	11	92	52	95	1
2013-14	FL 2	46	15	15	16	49	58	60	11
2014-15	FL 2	46	13	9	24	38	62	48	21
2015-16	FL 2	46	17	13	16	61	53	64	12
2016-17	FL 2	46	17	15	14	54	50	66	12
2017-18	FL 2	46	18	18	10	67	52	72	8
2018-19	FL 2	46	20	16	10	69	41	76	4

DID YOU KNOW ?

Iffy Onuora marked his first Football League start for Mansfield Town by scoring a hat-trick in The Stags' 6-2 victory over Lincoln City in March 1995. His three goals came in just seven minutes and his feat remains the quickest hat-trick for Mansfield in a Football League game.

MANSFIELD TOWN – SKY BET LEAGUE TWO 2018–19 LEAGUE RECORD

Match No.	*Date*	*Venue*	*Opponents*	*Result*		*H/T Score*	*Lg Pos.*	*Goalscorers*	*Attendance*
1	Aug 4	H	Newport Co	W	3-0	1-0	3	Walker ^{12}, Khan 2 $^{56, 64}$	4423
2	11	A	Yeovil T	D	2-2	2-2	4	Davies ^{9}, Preston ^{26}	2796
3	18	H	Colchester U	D	1-1	0-0	7	Davies ^{81}	3909
4	21	A	Tranmere R	D	0-0	0-0	9		5466
5	25	A	Macclesfield T	D	1-1	1-0	12	Benning ^{32}	2624
6	Sept 1	H	Carlisle U	W	1-0	0-0	8	Walker (pen) ^{55}	4470
7	15	H	Exeter C	L	1-2	0-1	15	Walker ^{61}	4443
8	22	A	Cambridge U	D	1-1	1-0	16	Rose ^{26}	3909
9	29	H	Northampton T	W	4-0	1-0	14	Elsnik ^{5}, Rose 2 $^{57, 86}$, Hamilton ^{81}	4550
10	Oct 2	H	Oldham Ath	D	0-0	0-0	14		3829
11	6	A	Bury	D	2-2	1-0	14	Rose ^{10}, Preston ^{73}	3880
12	20	A	Swindon T	D	0-0	0-0	13		6208
13	23	A	Morecambe	W	1-0	1-0	11	Bishop ^{36}	1355
14	27	H	Milton Keynes D	D	1-1	1-1	11	Mellis ^{17}	4329
15	30	A	Crewe Alex	W	3-0	2-0	9	Elsnik 2 $^{8, 35}$, Walker ^{61}	2973
16	Nov 3	A	Cheltenham T	D	2-2	1-2	10	Walker 2 $^{7, 90}$	2828
17	6	H	Grimsby T	W	2-1	0-1	7	Walker 2 $^{50, 82}$	4118
18	17	H	Port Vale	W	1-0	1-0	5	Hamilton ^{41}	4316
19	24	A	Lincoln C	D	1-1	0-0	4	Mellis ^{90}	9773
20	Dec 8	H	Notts Co	W	2-0	1-0	5	Hamilton 2 $^{37, 63}$	6604
21	22	A	Stevenage	W	3-1	0-1	5	Sweeney ^{55}, Walker 2 $^{77, 86}$	2761
22	26	H	Bury	W	2-1	0-0	3	Hamilton ^{61}, Walker (pen) ^{79}	4959
23	29	H	Swindon T	D	0-0	0-0	3		5311
24	Jan 1	A	Grimsby T	W	1-0	1-0	3	Bishop ^{21}	5931
25	5	A	Carlisle U	L	2-3	0-2	4	Preston ^{77}, Walker ^{86}	4563
26	12	H	Yeovil T	L	0-1	0-1	5		4374
27	15	H	Crawley T	W	1-0	0-0	3	Walker ^{88}	3739
28	19	A	Colchester U	W	3-2	0-2	3	Ajose ^{51}, Walker ^{64}, Hamilton ^{79}	3546
29	26	H	Tranmere R	W	3-0	1-0	2	Grant 2 $^{22, 68}$, Walker ^{65}	4885
30	29	A	Forest Green R	D	1-1	1-0	2	Grant ^{14}	2428
31	Feb 2	H	Macclesfield T	W	3-1	1-1	2	Grant ^{8}, Pearce ^{56}, Walker ^{89}	5642
32	9	A	Newport Co	L	0-1	0-1	2		3133
33	16	A	Notts Co	L	0-1	0-1	3		12,660
34	23	H	Forest Green R	W	1-0	0-0	3	Walker ^{69}	5256
35	Mar 2	H	Cheltenham T	W	4-2	2-0	3	Hamilton 2 $^{42, 45}$, Atkinson ^{77}, MacDonald ^{90}	5276
36	9	A	Port Vale	L	1-2	0-0	4	Ajose ^{61}	5231
37	12	A	Crawley T	D	0-0	0-0	3		1909
38	18	H	Lincoln C	D	1-1	1-0	3	Pearce ^{4}	7177
39	23	H	Crewe Alex	L	1-2	0-0	4	Pearce ^{90}	4675
40	30	A	Exeter C	W	4-1	2-1	4	Hamilton 2 $^{20, 33}$, Walker 2 (1 pen) $^{57, 74 (p)}$	5017
41	Apr 6	H	Cambridge U	W	1-0	0-0	2	Walker ^{64}	4789
42	13	A	Northampton T	D	1-1	1-0	3	Benning ^{11}	5905
43	19	H	Morecambe	W	4-0	1-0	2	Mellis ^{30}, Pearce ^{70}, Hamilton ^{73}, Benning ^{85}	5177
44	22	A	Oldham Ath	L	2-3	0-1	3	Walker ^{60}, Bishop ^{76}	6179
45	27	H	Stevenage	L	1-2	0-0	3	Walker ^{83}	6390
46	May 4	A	Milton Keynes D	L	0-1	0-1	4		20,718

Final League Position: 4

GOALSCORERS

League (69): Walker 22 (3 pens), Hamilton 11, Grant 4, Pearce 4, Rose 4, Benning 3, Bishop 3, Elsnik 3, Mellis 3, Preston 3, Ajose 2, Davies 2, Khan 2, Atkinson 1, MacDonald 1, Sweeney 1.
FA Cup (1): Hamilton 1.
Carabao Cup (7): Walker 3 (2 pens), Bishop 1, Hamilton 1, Khan 1, Rose 1.
Checkatrade Trophy (7): Butcher 2, Benning 1, Blake 1, Elsnik 1, Mellis 1, Walker 1.
League Two Play-offs (1): Hamilton 1.

Logan C 17	White H 18 + 1	Preston M 38 + 1	Pearce K 46	Hamilton C 46	MacDonald A 13 + 8	Bishop N 43 + 1	Khan O 15 + 7	Benning M 44 + 1	Walker T 43 + 1	Davies C 5 + 9	Butcher C 2 + 10	Mellis J 33 + 8	Graham J — + 8	Sweeney R 37 + 1	Rose D 13 + 21	Olejnik R 17	Atkinson W 4 + 14	Gibbens L 1	Sterling-James O — + 1	Elsnik T 12 + 7	Smith J 12	Grant J 15 + 2	Ajose N 8 + 2	Jones G 12 + 3	Tomlinson W 8 + 4	Turner B 4 + 4	Hakeem Z — + 1	*Match No.*
1	2	3	4	5	6	7	8^1	9	10^2	11^3	12	13	14															1
1	2	3	4	5	7^2	6	9	8	11	10^1	12	13																2
1	2		3	5	6	13	11^2	9	10	12	8^3	7^1		4	14													3
	2		3	5	6	7	9^1	8^2	11	10^3	13			4	14	1	12											4
			3	5	6^2	8	7^3	9	11	10^1		13		4	12	1		2	14									5
	5	3	2	9	6	7	8^2		11	12	13			4	10^1	1												6
	5^1	2	3	9	7	6	10	14	11		8^3			4^2	12	1				13								7
		2	3	5	7	6	9^1	8	10^2				13	4	11	1				12								8
		2	3	5		7	8^1	9	11^2	13	14			4	10	1	12			6^3								9
		2	3	5		6	8^3	9	10^2	13		14		4	11	1	12			7^1								10
		2	3	5		6	7^1	9	10^2		14	13		4	11^3	1	12			8								11
		3	2	9			11^2	8	12		13	7		4	10	1	5■			6^1								12
		2	3	5		7	9^2	8	11^1		13	6^3	14	4	10	1				12								13
		2	3	5^1		7	8^3	9	11^2	13	12	6		4	10	1	14											14
	2	4	3	5		6		9	10^2	13	14	7^3			11^1	1	12			8								15
	2^1	4	3	5		6^2		9	10	12		7			11	1	13			8								16
	12	3^2	4	2		9		6	10	13		7	14	5	11^1	1				8^3								17
	5	2	3	11		7		8	9^1	10^3		6	14	4^2	12	1				13								18
		2	3	11		7^3	12	8^2	9	14		6		4	10	1	5^1			13								19
	5	2	3	11		6^1	12	9	10^2			8		4	13	1	14			7^3								20
1	5	2	3	11		6		9^2	10			8	13	4	12					7^1								21
1	5	2	3	10		7		9	11^2			6^3	14	4	12		13			8^1								22
1	5	2	3	10		7	12	9^1	11			6		4	13					8^2								23
1	5	2	3	10		7		9	11			6		4	8^1					12								24
1	5	2	3	10		7■		9	11			6		4^2	12		13			8^1								25
	5^2	2■	3	11			7^3	9	10			6	13	4	12		8^1			14	1							26
	2		3	5		8		9	10			6		4	12						1	7	11^1					27
	2^3	12	3	5		8		9	10			6		4	13		14				1	7^2	11^1					28
		2	3	5		7^1	13	9	10^2			6		4			12				1	8	11					29
		2	3	5		6		8	10			7		4							1	9	11^1	12				30
		2	3	5^3		7		8	11			6^2		4	12		14				1	9	10^1	13				31
		2	3	5		7		9^2	10			6		4	13^3						1	8	11^1	12	14			32
		2	3	11	13	7	14	9^3	10			6^2									1	8	12	5		4^1		33
		2	3	9		8		4	11■			6									1	10		5	7^1	12		34
			3	8	14	6		4				9		2			12				1	10^2	11^1	5^3	7	13		35
			3	9	14	8	13	4				6^1		2^2			5				1	10	11		7^3	12		36
1			3	9	10^1	7		4	11			6										8		5	12	2		37
1		2	3	10	12	7		8	11			6^1		4								9^2		5	13			38
		2	3	10	13	6	14	9^1	11			7		4							1	8^2	12	5^3				39
1		2	3	11^1	7	6^2		9	10			12												5	8	4	13	40
1		2	3	11	6	7^1		9	10			14		12	13									5^2	8	4^3		41
1		2	3	11	8	7		9	10			12		4	13									5^2	6^1			42
1		2	3	11	12	7^1		8	10^3			6		4	13							9^2		5	14			43
1		2	3	10	12	6		8	11			7		4^1	13							9^2		5				44
1		2	3	11	14	6		9^1	10			7		4	12							13		5^3	8^2			45
1		4^2	3	11	5	7		9^1	10			6		2	13							14			8^3	12		46

FA Cup

First Round	Charlton Ath	(h)	1-1
Replay	Charlton Ath	(a)	0-5

League Two Play-offs

Semi-Final 1st leg	Newport Co	(a)	1-1
Semi-Final 2nd leg	Newport Co	(h)	0-0

(aet; Newport Co won 4-3 on penalties)

Carabao Cup

First Round	Accrington S	(h)	6-1
Second Round	WBA	(a)	1-2

Checkatrade Trophy

Group H (N)	Lincoln C	(a)	2-1
Group H (N)	Wolverhampton W U21	(h)	2-1
Group H (N)	Scunthorpe U	(h)	3-2
Second Round (N)	Bury	(h)	0-1

MIDDLESBROUGH

FOUNDATION

A previous belief that Middlesbrough Football Club was founded at a tripe supper at the Corporation Hotel has proved to be erroneous. In fact, members of Middlesbrough Cricket Club were responsible for forming it at a meeting in the gymnasium of the Albert Park Hotel in 1875.

Riverside Stadium, Middlehaven Way, Middlesbrough TS3 6RS.

Telephone: (01642) 929 420.

Ticket Office: (01642) 929 421.

Website: www.mfc.co.uk

Email: via website.

Ground Capacity: 34,000.

Record Attendance: 53,802 v Newcastle U, Division 1, 27 December 1949 (at Ayresome Park); 34,814 v Newcastle U, Premier League, 5 March 2003 (at Riverside Stadium); 35,000, England v Slovakia, Euro 2004 qualifier, 11 June 2003.

Pitch Measurements: 105m × 68m (115yd × 74.5yd).

Chairman: Steve Gibson.

Chief Executive: Neil Bausor.

Manager: Jonathan Woodgate.

Assistant Manager: Robbie Keane.

Colours: Red shirts with white trim, white shorts with red trim, red socks with white trim.

Year Formed: 1876; re-formed 1986.

Turned Professional: 1889; became amateur 1892, and professional again, 1899.

Club Nickname: 'Boro'.

Grounds: 1877, Old Archery Ground, Albert Park; 1879, Breckon Hill; 1882, Linthorpe Road Ground; 1903, Ayresome Park; 1995, Riverside Stadium.

First Football League Game: 2 September 1899, Division 2, v Lincoln C (a) L 0–3 – Smith; Shaw, Ramsey; Allport, McNally, McCracken; Wanless, Longstaffe, Gettins, Page, Pugh.

Record League Victory: 9–0 v Brighton & HA, Division 2, 23 August 1958 – Taylor; Bilcliff, Robinson; Harris (2p), Phillips, Walley; Day, McLean, Clough (5), Peacock (2), Holliday.

Record Cup Victory: 7–0 v Hereford U, Coca-Cola Cup 2nd rd, 1st leg, 18 September 1996 – Miller; Fleming (1), Branco (1), Whyte, Vickers, Whelan, Emerson (1), Mustoe, Stamp, Juninho, Ravanelli (4).

Record Defeat: 0–9 v Blackburn R, Division 2, 6 November 1954.

HONOURS

League Champions: First Division – 1994–95; Division 2 – 1926–27, 1928–29, 1973–74.
Runners-up: FL C – 2015–16; First Division – 1997–98; Division 2 – 1901–02, 1991–92; Division 3 – 1966–67, 1986–87.

FA Cup: *Runners-up:* 1997.

League Cup Winners: 2004.
Runners-up: 1997, 1998.

Amateur Cup Winners: 1895, 1898.

Anglo-Scottish Cup Winners: 1976.

Full Members' Cup: *Runners-up:* 1990.

European Competitions
UEFA Cup: 2004–05, 2005–06 *(runners-up)*.

THE SUN FACT FILE

Following Middlesbrough's financial crisis in the summer of 1986, the club's Ayresome Park ground was closed by the Official Receiver. Boro opened the 1986–87 season with a 'home' game against Port Vale at Hartlepool, which kicked off at 6.30, shortly after Pools' match with Cardiff City had finished. Just 3,690 fans turned out to watch but shortly afterwards the club was allowed to play matches at their home ground once more.

Most League Points (2 for a win): 65, Division 2, 1973–74.

Most League Points (3 for a win): 94, Division 3, 1986–87.

Most League Goals: 122, Division 2, 1926–27.

Highest League Scorer in Season: George Camsell, 59, Division 2, 1926–27 (Second Division record).

Most League Goals in Total Aggregate: George Camsell, 325, 1925–39.

Most League Goals in One Match: 5, John Wilkie v Gainsborough T, Division 2, 2 March 1901; 5, Andy Wilson v Nottingham F, Division 1, 6 October 1923; 5, George Camsell v Manchester C, Division 2, 25 December 1926; 5, George Camsell v Aston Villa, Division 1, 9 September 1935; 5, Brian Clough v Brighton & HA, Division 2, 22 August 1958.

Most Capped Player: Mark Schwarzer, 52 (109), Australia.

Most League Appearances: Tim Williamson, 563, 1902–23.

Youngest League Player: Luke Williams, 16 years 200 days v Barnsley, 18 December 2009.

Record Transfer Fee Received: £15,000,000 from Burnley for Ben Gibson, August 2018.

Record Transfer Fee Paid: £15,000,000 to Nottingham F for Britt Assombalonga, July 2017.

Football League Record: 1899 Elected to Division 2; 1902–24 Division 1; 1924–27 Division 2; 1927–28 Division 1; 1928–29 Division 2; 1929–54 Division 1; 1954–66 Division 2; 1966–67 Division 3; 1967–74 Division 2; 1974–82 Division 1; 1982–86 Division 2; 1986–87 Division 3; 1987–88 Division 2; 1988–89 Division 1; 1989–92 Division 2; 1992–93 Premier League; 1993–95 Division 1; 1995–97 Premier League; 1997–98 Division 1; 1998–2009 Premier League; 2009–16 FL C; 2016–17 Premier League; 2017– FL C.

MANAGERS

John Robson 1899–1905
Alex Mackie 1905–06
Andy Aitken 1906–09
J. Gunter 1908–10
(Secretary-Manager)
Andy Walker 1910–11
Tom McIntosh 1911–19
Jimmy Howie 1920–23
Herbert Bamlett 1923–26
Peter McWilliam 1927–34
Wilf Gillow 1934–44
David Jack 1944–52
Walter Rowley 1952–54
Bob Dennison 1954–63
Raich Carter 1963–66
Stan Anderson 1966–73
Jack Charlton 1973–77
John Neal 1977–81
Bobby Murdoch 1981–82
Malcolm Allison 1982–84
Willie Maddren 1984–86
Bruce Rioch 1986–90
Colin Todd 1990–91
Lennie Lawrence 1991–94
Bryan Robson 1994–2001
Steve McClaren 2001–06
Gareth Southgate 2006–09
Gordon Strachan 2009–10
Tony Mowbray 2010–13
Aitor Karanka 2013–17
Garry Monk 2017
Tony Pulis 2017–19
Jonathan Woodgate June 2019–

LATEST SEQUENCES

Longest Sequence of League Wins: 9, 16.2.1974 – 6.4.1974.

Longest Sequence of League Defeats: 8, 26.12.1995 – 17.2.1996.

Longest Sequence of League Draws: 8, 3.4.1971 – 1.5.1971.

Longest Sequence of Unbeaten League Matches: 24, 8.9.1973 – 19.1.1974.

Longest Sequence Without a League Win: 19, 3.10.1981 – 6.3.1982.

Successive Scoring Runs: 26 from 21.9.1946.

Successive Non-scoring Runs: 7, 25.1.2014 – 1.3.2014.

TEN YEAR LEAGUE RECORD

		P	*W*	*D*	*L*	*F*	*A*	*Pts*	*Pos*
2009-10	FL C	46	16	14	16	58	50	62	11
2010-11	FL C	46	17	11	18	68	68	62	12
2011-12	FL C	46	18	16	12	52	51	70	7
2012-13	FL C	46	18	5	23	61	70	59	16
2013-14	FL C	46	16	16	14	62	50	64	12
2014-15	FL C	46	25	10	11	68	37	85	4
2015-16	FL C	46	26	11	9	63	31	89	2
2016-17	PR Lge	38	5	13	20	27	53	28	19
2017-18	FL C	46	22	10	14	67	45	76	5
2018-19	FL C	46	20	13	13	49	41	73	7

DID YOU KNOW ?

Former Middlesbrough players Donald McLeod and Henry Carr were both killed in action during 1917. Boro arranged a friendly fixture with Bradford Park Avenue on New Year's Day 1918 to raise funds for their widows and orphans and over 20,000 turned out at Ayresome Park to see the visitors win 2-0.

MIDDLESBROUGH – SKY BET CHAMPIONSHIP 2018–19 LEAGUE RECORD

Match No.	Date	Venue	Opponents	Result		H/T Score	Lg Pos.	Goalscorers	Attendance
1	Aug 4	A	Millwall	D	2-2	0-2	7	Braithwaite 87, Friend 90	15,056
2	7	H	Sheffield U	W	3-0	3-0	1	Braithwaite 7, Flint 18, Downing 25	22,960
3	11	H	Birmingham C	W	1-0	1-0	1	Assombalonga 12	23,748
4	18	A	Bristol C	W	2-0	2-0	1	Braithwaite 13, Assombalonga 32	19,455
5	24	H	WBA	W	1-0	0-0	1	Ayala 90	22,906
6	31	A	Leeds U	D	0-0	0-0	2		35,417
7	Sept 15	A	Norwich C	L	0-1	0-0	4		24,642
8	19	H	Bolton W	W	2-0	1-0	2	Saville 34, Assombalonga 90	21,345
9	22	H	Swansea C	D	0-0	0-0	2		22,881
10	29	A	Hull C	D	1-1	0-0	3	Assombalonga 51	13,185
11	Oct 2	A	Ipswich T	W	2-0	2-0	2	Besic 12, Downing 16	13,612
12	6	H	Nottingham F	L	0-2	0-0	4		24,299
13	19	A	Sheffield W	W	2-1	0-0	1	Besic 49, Assombalonga 55	23,284
14	23	H	Rotherham U	D	0-0	0-0	1		21,235
15	27	H	Derby Co	D	1-1	0-1	3	Bogle (og) 84	22,907
16	Nov 3	A	Stoke C	D	0-0	0-0	3		24,553
17	10	H	Wigan Ath	W	2-0	2-0	2	Hugill 2 (1 pen) 38 (p), 44	22,207
18	24	A	Brentford	W	2-1	0-0	2	Hugill 56, Tavernier 61	9430
19	27	A	Preston NE	D	1-1	0-1	3	Tavernier 46	10,990
20	Dec 1	H	Aston Villa	L	0-3	0-1	3		23,424
21	8	H	Blackburn R	D	1-1	0-1	6	Assombalonga 62	21,985
22	15	A	QPR	L	1-2	0-1	6	Saville 51	14,088
23	22	A	Reading	W	1-0	0-0	4	Friend 77	14,943
24	26	H	Sheffield W	L	0-1	0-1	5		30,341
25	29	H	Ipswich T	W	2-0	1-0	5	Hugill (pen) 37, Tavernier 72	23,334
26	Jan 1	A	Derby Co	D	1-1	0-1	5	Hugill 52	28,123
27	12	A	Birmingham C	W	2-1	1-0	5	Wing 37, Assombalonga 82	21,420
28	19	H	Millwall	D	1-1	0-1	5	Hugill (pen) 90	21,915
29	Feb 2	A	WBA	W	3-2	1-1	5	Saville 17, Assombalonga 2 75, 83	24,863
30	9	H	Leeds U	D	1-1	0-0	5	Wing 47	30,881
31	13	A	Sheffield U	L	0-1	0-0	6		24,805
32	17	A	Blackburn R	W	1-0	1-0	5	Assombalonga 19	13,249
33	23	H	QPR	W	2-0	2-0	5	Howson 2, Fletcher 32	22,338
34	Mar 2	A	Wigan Ath	D	0-0	0-0	5		12,726
35	9	H	Brentford	L	1-2	1-0	5	Fletcher 6	22,069
36	13	H	Preston NE	L	1-2	1-0	5	Fletcher 32	21,088
37	16	A	Aston Villa	L	0-3	0-2	5		36,263
38	30	H	Norwich C	L	0-1	0-0	8		23,795
39	Apr 2	H	Bristol C	L	0-1	0-1	8		21,016
40	6	A	Swansea C	L	1-3	0-2	8	Saville 81	18,171
41	9	A	Bolton W	W	2-0	2-0	7	Fletcher 2 16, 28	12,259
42	13	H	Hull C	W	1-0	1-0	7	Assombalonga 25	22,427
43	19	H	Stoke C	W	1-0	1-0	6	Assombalonga 2	22,890
44	22	A	Nottingham F	L	0-3	0-1	7		27,653
45	27	H	Reading	W	2-1	2-1	7	Wing 31, Assombalonga (pen) 39	22,003
46	May 5	A	Rotherham U	W	2-1	2-0	7	Assombalonga (pen) 28, Mikel 37	11,051

Final League Position: 7

GOALSCORERS

League (49): Assombalonga 14 (2 pens), Hugill 6 (3 pens), Fletcher 5, Saville 4, Braithwaite 3, Tavernier 3, Wing 3, Besic 2, Downing 2, Friend 2, Ayala 1, Flint 1, Howson 1, Mikel 1, own goal 1.
FA Cup (6): Assombalonga 2, Ayala 1, Fletcher 1, Friend 1, Wing 1.
Carabao Cup (8): Fletcher 3, Hugill 1, Johnson 1, Mahmutovic 1, Tavernier 1, Wing 1.
Checkatrade Trophy (2): Hackney 1, Ward 1.

Randolph D 46	Shotton R 33 + 1	Flint A 39	Fry D 33 + 1	Friend G 37 + 1	Clayton A 29 + 7	Leadbitter G 1 + 1	Howson J 44 + 2	Downing S 24 + 14	Assombalonga B 28 + 14	Braithwaite M 12 + 5	Wing L 19 + 9	Tavernier M 2 + 18	Fletcher A 14 + 7	McNair P 7 + 9	Ayala D 32 + 1	Besic M 30 + 7	Hugill J 20 + 17	Saville G 28 + 6	McQueen S 1 + 4	Gestede R 1 + 3	Batth D 8 + 2	van La Parra R — + 3	Mikel J 18	Match No.
1	2	3	4	5	6^{3}	7^{2}	8	9^{1}	10	11	12	13	14											1
1	2	4	3	5	7	14	8^{3}	11	10^{2}	9	6^{1}		13	12										2
1	6	3	2	4	5		8	9	11^{2}	10^{1}	7^{3}	12	13	14										3
1	2	3	4	5	7		8	9^{1}	10^{2}	11^{3}	6	12	13	14										4
1	5	3	4	9	7		6	8^{1}	10^{2}	11^{3}				14	2	12	13							5
1	5	3	4	8	7		10	9	11						2	6								6
1	5	3	4^{2}	8	7^{1}		10	9	11	13					2	6^{3}	14	12						7
1	2	4		5	7		6	9^{3}	13	11^{2}					3	14	10	8^{1}	12					8
1	2	4		5	7		6	9^{2}	10^{1}	11					3	12	13	8^{3}	14					9
1	2	4		5	8^{1}		7	13	10	14					3	12	11^{2}	9	6^{3}					10
1	2	4		5			6	9	12	11^{2}				13	3	8^{3}	10^{1}	7	14					11
1	2	4		5	14		6	9	12	11^{1}					3	8^{2}	10^{3}	7		13				12
1	5	3	4	9	7		6	10^{2}	11^{3}						2	8^{1}	12	13			14			13
1		3		4	7		6	9	11^{2}	10^{1}				5^{3}	2	8	14		12	13				14
1		3	4	8	6		10	9	11^{2}	12				5^{3}	2	7^{1}		13		14				15
1		4	2	5	7		6	9^{1}		11^{2}	13	12				8	10				3			16
1		4	2	5	7		6	9	12	11^{1}	13					8^{2}	10^{3}	14			3			17
1		3	2	5	7		6	9^{1}			13	11^{3}			14	8^{2}	10	12			4			18
1		4	2	6	8		14			13	7^{1}	12			3^{2}		10	9		11^{3}	5			19
1		3	2^{1}	5	6		9	8	14	13		10^{3}		12		7^{2}	11				4			20
1	2	4		5	7^{2}		8	9^{1}	14		12		11^{3}		3	6■	10	13						21
1	2	4		5	7		6^{1}	9^{2}	11		12	13	14		3		10	8^{3}						22
1	2^{2}	4	5	6	9		7		11^{1}		13			12	3	8^{3}	14	10						23
1		3	4^{1}	9	7^{3}		6^{2}	10	11		14	13		5	2	8	12							24
1		3	2	9	13		5	10^{3}			6	12			4^{2}	7^{1}	11	8			14			25
1			2	5	7		8	12	13		9				3	6	11^{2}	10^{1}			4			26
1			2	5	6		8	12	13		9^{1}			14	3	7^{3}	11^{2}	10			4			27
1			2	5	6^{3}		8^{2}	14	13		9				3	7^{1}	11	10			4	12		28
1	2	4	5^{2}	6			12		13		7				3	9^{1}	11	10				14	8^{3}	29
1	5	3	4	8	14		10		13		9^{3}				2	12	11^{2}	7^{1}					6	30
1	5	3^{2}	4	8			10^{1}	12	13		9				2■		11	6^{3}				14	7	31
1	3		2	4^{2}			5	13	11		9		10^{1}	12		7^{3}	14	8					6	32
1	3		4				5	12	10^{3}		6	13	11^{2}		2	8^{1}	14	9					7	33
1	3		4				5	12	10^{3}		9	14	11^{2}		2	7^{1}	13	8					6	34
1	3		4	12			5		11^{1}		9	14	10		2	7^{2}	13	8^{3}					6	35
1	2	3	12	8			5		11		9	14	10^{3}		4■	7^{1}	13						6^{2}	36
1	5^{1}	3	4	8			9	12	13		10^{3}		14		2		11^{2}	7					6	37
1	5^{2}	3	4	8	6^{1}		10	12	11				9		2^{3}	13	14						7	38
1	5^{3}	3	2	4			6	9^{2}	11		12		10			13	14	8^{1}					7	39
1	12	4	2	5^{2}	8^{3}		10	7	14				13		3		11^{1}	6					9	40
1	5	3	4		12		9		11^{2}			13	10		2	6^{1}		8					7	41
1	5	3	4		12		6	13	10			14	11^{1}		2^{3}	8^{2}		9					7	42
1	4	3			6		5	12	11^{2}			13	10^{3}	2		8^{1}	14	9					7	43
1	4	3			6		5	14	11			13	10^{3}	2		8^{1}	12	9^{2}					7	44
1	4	3			12		5		11^{2}		6	13	10^{1}	2		8^{3}	14	9					7	45
1	4	3			13		5	12	11		6^{3}	14	10^{2}	2		8^{1}		9					7	46

FA Cup

Third Round	Peterborough U	(h)	5-0
Fourth Round	Newport Co	(h)	1-1
Replay	Newport Co	(a)	0-2

Carabao Cup

First Round	Notts Co	(h)	3-3
(Middlesbrough won 4-3 on penalties)			
Second Round	Rochdale	(h)	2-1
Third Round	Preston NE	(a)	2-2
(Middlesbrough won 4-3 on penalties)			
Fourth Round	Crystal Palace	(h)	1-0
Quarter-Final	Burton Alb	(h)	0-1

Checkatrade Trophy (Middlesbrough U21)

Group E (N)	Walsall	(a)	1-3
Group E (N)	Port Vale	(a)	0-2
Group E (N)	Burton Alb	(a)	1-0

MILLWALL

FOUNDATION

Formed in 1885 as Millwall Rovers by employees of Morton & Co, a jam and marmalade factory in West Ferry Road. The founders were predominantly Scotsmen. Their first headquarters was The Islanders pub in Tooke Street, Millwall. Their first trophy was the East End Cup in 1887.

The Den, Zampa Road, Bermondsey, London SE16 3LN.

Telephone: (020) 7232 1222.

Ticket Office: (0844) 826 2004.

Website: www.millwallfc.co.uk

Email: questions@millwallplc.com

Ground Capacity: 20,146.

Record Attendance: 48,672 v Derby Co, FA Cup 5th rd, 20 February 1937 (at The Den, Cold Blow Lane); 20,093 v Arsenal, FA Cup 3rd rd, 10 January 1994 (at The Den, Bermondsey).

Pitch Measurements: 106m × 68m (116yd × 74.5yd).

Chairman: John Berylson.

Chief Executive: Steve Kavanagh.

Manager: Neil Harris.

Assistant Manager: Dave Livermore.

Colours: Blue shirts with white sleeves, white shorts with blue trim, blue socks with white hoops.

Year Formed: 1885.

Turned Professional: 1893.

Previous Names: 1885, Millwall Rovers; 1889, Millwall Athletic; 1899, Millwall; 1985, Millwall Football & Athletic Company.

Club Nickname: 'The Lions'.

Grounds: 1885, Glengall Road, Millwall; 1886, Back of 'Lord Nelson'; 1890, East Ferry Road; 1901, North Greenwich; 1910, The Den, Cold Blow Lane; 1993, The Den, Bermondsey.

First Football League Game: 28 August 1920, Division 3, v Bristol R (h) W 2–0 – Lansdale; Fort, Hodge; Voisey (1), Riddell, McAlpine; Waterall, Travers, Broad (1), Sutherland, Dempsey.

Record League Victory: 9–1 v Torquay U, Division 3 (S), 29 August 1927 – Lansdale, Tilling, Hill, Amos, Bryant (3), Graham, Chance, Hawkins (3), Landells (1), Phillips (2), Black. 9–1 v Coventry C, Division 3 (S), 19 November 1927 – Lansdale, Fort, Hill, Amos, Collins (1), Graham, Chance, Landells (4), Cock (2), Phillips (2), Black.

Record Cup Victory: 7–0 v Gateshead, FA Cup 2nd rd, 12 December 1936 – Yuill; Ted Smith, Inns; Brolly, Hancock, Forsyth; Thomas (1), Mangnall (1), Ken Burditt (2), McCartney (2), Thorogood (1).

Record Defeat: 1–9 v Aston Villa, FA Cup 4th rd, 28 January 1946.

Most League Points (2 for a win): 65, Division 3 (S), 1927–28 and Division 3, 1965–66.

HONOURS

League Champions: Division 2 – 1987–88; Second Division – 2000–01; Division 3S – 1927–28, 1937–38; Division 4 – 1961–62.
Runners-up: Division 3 – 1965–66, 1984–85; Division 3S – 1952–53; Division 4 – 1964–65.

FA Cup: *Runners-up:* 2004.

League Cup: 5th rd – 1974, 1977, 1995.

League Trophy: *Runners-up:* 1999.

European Competitions
UEFA Cup: 2004–05.

THE Sun FACT FILE

In 1925 Millwall were the very first winners of the London *Evening News* Cricket Cup for footballers, defeating Fulham in the final which was played at the Army Sports Ground, Leyton. Star of the Lions team was winger Charles Harris who top-scored with 42 runs and added 5 wickets for 33 runs for good measure.

Most League Points (3 for a win): 93, Division 2, 2000–01.

Most League Goals: 127, Division 3 (S), 1927–28.

Highest League Scorer in Season: Richard Parker, 37, Division 3 (S), 1926–27.

Most League Goals in Total Aggregate: Neil Harris, 124, 1995–2004; 2006–11.

Most League Goals in One Match: 5, Richard Parker v Norwich C, Division 3 (S), 28 August 1926.

Most Capped Player: David Forde, 24, Republic of Ireland.

Most League Appearances: Barry Kitchener, 523, 1967–82.

Youngest League Player: Moses Ashikodi, 15 years 240 days v Brighton & HA, 22 February 2003.

Record Transfer Fee Received: £8,000,000 from Middlesbrough for George Saville, January 2019.

Record Transfer Fee Paid: £1,000,000 (rising to £1,500,000) to Sheffield U for Ryan Leonard, August 2018.

Football League Record: 1920 Original Members of Division 3; 1921 Division 3 (S); 1928–34 Division 2; 1934–38 Division 3 (S); 1938–48 Division 2; 1948–58 Division 3 (S); 1958–62 Division 4; 1962–64 Division 3; 1964–65 Division 4; 1965–66 Division 3; 1966–75 Division 2; 1975–76 Division 3; 1976–79 Division 2; 1979–85 Division 3; 1985–88 Division 2; 1988–90 Division 1; 1990–92 Division 2; 1992–96 Division 1; 1996–2001 Division 2; 2001–04 Division 1; 2004–06 FL C; 2006–10 FL 1; 2010–15 FL C; 2015–17 FL 1; 2017– FL C.

LATEST SEQUENCES

Longest Sequence of League Wins: 10, 10.3.1928 – 25.4.1928.

Longest Sequence of League Defeats: 11, 10.4.1929 – 16.9.1929.

Longest Sequence of League Draws: 5, 22.12.1973 – 12.1.1974.

Longest Sequence of Unbeaten League Matches: 19, 22.8.1959 – 31.10.1959.

Longest Sequence Without a League Win: 20, 26.12.1989 – 5.5.1990.

Successive Scoring Runs: 22 from 27.11.1954.

Successive Non-scoring Runs: 6 from 27.4.2013.

MANAGERS

F. B. Kidd 1894–99
(Hon. Treasurer/Manager)
E. R. Stopher 1899–1900
(Hon. Treasurer/Manager)
George Saunders 1900–11
(Hon. Treasurer/Manager)
Herbert Lipsham 1911–19
Robert Hunter 1919–33
Bill McCracken 1933–36
Charlie Hewitt 1936–40
Bill Voisey 1940–44
Jack Cock 1944–48
Charlie Hewitt 1948–56
Ron Gray 1956–57
Jimmy Seed 1958–59
Reg Smith 1959–61
Ron Gray 1961–63
Billy Gray 1963–66
Benny Fenton 1966–74
Gordon Jago 1974–77
George Petchey 1978–80
Peter Anderson 1980–82
George Graham 1982–86
John Docherty 1986–90
Bob Pearson 1990
Bruce Rioch 1990–92
Mick McCarthy 1992–96
Jimmy Nicholl 1996–97
John Docherty 1997
Billy Bonds 1997–98
Keith Stevens 1998–2000
(then Joint Manager)
(*plus* **Alan McLeary** 1999–2000)
Mark McGhee 2000–03
Dennis Wise 2003–05
Steve Claridge 2005
Colin Lee 2005
David Tuttle 2005–06
Nigel Spackman 2006
Willie Donachie 2006–07
Kenny Jackett 2007–13
Steve Lomas 2013
Ian Holloway 2014–15
Neil Harris March 2015–

TEN YEAR LEAGUE RECORD

		P	W	D	L	F	A	Pts	Pos
2009-10	FL 1	46	24	13	9	76	44	85	3
2010-11	FL C	46	18	13	15	62	48	67	9
2011-12	FL C	46	15	12	19	55	57	57	16
2012-13	FL C	46	15	11	20	51	62	56	20
2013-14	FL C	46	11	15	20	46	74	48	19
2014-15	FL C	46	9	14	23	42	76	41	22
2015-16	FL 1	46	24	9	13	73	49	81	4
2016-17	FL 1	46	20	13	13	66	57	73	6
2017-18	FL C	46	19	15	12	56	45	72	8
2018-19	FL C	46	10	14	22	48	64	44	21

DID YOU KNOW ?

For many years the Millwall mascot was a figure dressed in a lion costume who would parade around the pitch before important games. However, in 1957 the club appointed Lenny the Lion, ventriloquist's dummy for children's entertainer Terry Hall and star of BBC's *Lenny the Lion Show*, to the position.

MILLWALL – SKY BET CHAMPIONSHIP 2018–19 LEAGUE RECORD

Match No.	Date	Venue	Opponents	Result	H/T Score	Lg Pos.	Goalscorers	Attendance
1	Aug 4	H	Middlesbrough	D 2-2	2-0	7	O'Brien [12], Gregory [37]	15,056
2	11	A	Blackburn R	D 0-0	0-0	15		13,239
3	18	H	Derby Co	W 2-1	2-0	9	Cooper [7], Williams [20]	13,557
4	22	A	Sheffield W	L 1-2	0-1	14	Tunnicliffe [72]	21,349
5	26	A	Rotherham U	L 0-1	0-1	16		8197
6	Sept 1	H	Swansea C	L 1-2	0-0	16	Wallace, M [62]	12,440
7	15	H	Leeds U	D 1-1	0-0	19	Wallace, J [55]	17,195
8	19	A	QPR	L 0-2	0-2	21		12,398
9	22	A	WBA	L 0-2	0-0	22		23,563
10	29	H	Sheffield U	L 2-3	0-1	23	Cooper [47], Gregory [50]	13,145
11	Oct 3	A	Nottingham F	D 2-2	0-1	22	Williams [75], Gregory [90]	25,753
12	6	H	Aston Villa	W 2-1	1-1	20	Ferguson [26], Elliott [48]	14,491
13	20	A	Reading	L 1-3	1-2	22	Wallace, M [34]	14,532
14	23	H	Wigan Ath	W 2-1	0-1	19	Williams (pen) [60], Morison [82]	11,190
15	27	H	Ipswich T	W 3-0	1-0	18	Gregory 2 [26, 51], Leonard [70]	15,386
16	Nov 3	A	Brentford	L 0-2	0-0	19		9476
17	10	A	Norwich C	L 3-4	1-0	21	Elliott [24], Leonard [81], Wallace, J [83]	26,289
18	24	H	Bolton W	D 1-1	0-1	21	Cooper [82]	12,554
19	28	H	Birmingham C	L 0-2	0-1	21		11,644
20	Dec 2	A	Bristol C	D 1-1	0-0	22	Williams [78]	18,814
21	8	H	Hull C	D 2-2	1-1	21	Gregory [22], O'Brien [54]	12,004
22	15	A	Preston NE	L 2-3	0-2	22	Cooper [61], Gregory [90]	10,924
23	22	A	Stoke C	L 0-1	0-0	22		25,351
24	26	H	Reading	W 1-0	1-0	20	Wallace, J [8]	12,202
25	29	H	Nottingham F	W 1-0	1-0	20	Tunnicliffe [9]	15,273
26	Jan 1	A	Ipswich T	W 3-2	0-1	19	Ferguson (pen) [60], Cooper [68], Elliott [76]	16,957
27	12	H	Blackburn R	L 0-2	0-0	20		13,862
28	19	A	Middlesbrough	D 1-1	1-0	19	Wallace, J [21]	21,915
29	Feb 2	H	Rotherham U	D 0-0	0-0	20		12,084
30	9	A	Swansea C	L 0-1	0-1	20		18,650
31	12	H	Sheffield W	D 0-0	0-0	20		11,828
32	20	A	Derby Co	W 1-0	0-0	19	Wallace, J [72]	24,907
33	23	H	Preston NE	L 1-3	0-3	20	Thompson [67]	13,265
34	26	A	Hull C	L 1-2	1-2	20	Hutchinson [34]	10,191
35	Mar 2	H	Norwich C	L 1-3	1-1	20	Williams [45]	16,748
36	9	A	Bolton W	L 1-2	0-0	21	Gregory [87]	13,035
37	13	A	Birmingham C	W 2-0	2-0	19	Thompson 2 [13, 32]	20,151
38	30	A	Leeds U	L 2-3	1-1	21	Thompson [10], Marshall (pen) [55]	34,910
39	Apr 6	H	WBA	W 2-0	1-0	20	Tunnicliffe [30], Hegazi (og) [66]	15,303
40	10	H	QPR	D 0-0	0-0	19		13,132
41	13	A	Sheffield U	D 1-1	0-0	20	Cooper [90]	26,703
42	19	H	Brentford	D 1-1	1-1	21	Gregory [15]	14,530
43	22	A	Aston Villa	L 0-1	0-1	21		39,839
44	27	H	Stoke C	D 0-0	0-0	21		14,472
45	30	H	Bristol C	L 1-2	1-0	21	Gregory [41]	12,261
46	May 5	A	Wigan Ath	L 0-1	0-1	21		10,859

Final League Position: 21

GOALSCORERS

League (48): Gregory 10, Cooper 6, Wallace J 5, Williams 5 (1 pen), Thompson 4, Elliott 3, Tunnicliffe 3, Ferguson 2 (1 pen), Leonard 2, O'Brien 2, Wallace M 2, Hutchinson 1, Marshall 1 (1 pen), Morison 1, own goal 1.
FA Cup (8): Ferguson 2, Wallace M 2, Cooper 1, Gregory 1, O'Brien 1, Pearce 1.
Carabao Cup (4): Gregory 2, O'Brien 1, Williams 1 (1 pen).

Archer J 24	Romeo M 40 + 1	Hutchinson S 24 + 2	Cooper J 46	Meredith J 33 + 3	Wallace J 41 + 1	Williams S 30 + 1	Saville G 4	O'Brien A 15 + 20	Gregory L 42 + 2	Morison S 15 + 26	Elliott T 16 + 17	Skalak J 4 + 10	Wallace M 19 + 2	Ferguson S 26 + 9	Tunnicliffe R 22 + 4	McLaughlin C 6 + 2	Bradshaw T 2 + 8	Amos B 12	Leonard R 37	Webster B 2 + 2	Karacan J — + 4	Marshall B 13 + 3	Thompson B 12 + 1	Onyedinma F — + 1	Pearce A 11	Martin D 10	Alexander G — + 1	Mitchell B — + 1	*Match No.*
1	2	3	4	5	6	7	8	9^{2}	10^{3}	11^{1}	12	13	14																1
1	2	3	4	5	6^{2}	7	8	9^{1}	10	11		12		13															2
1	2	3	4	5	6^{1}	7	8	9	10^{2}	11				13	12														3
1	2	3	4	5	6		8^{1}	9^{2}	10	11^{3}	14	13			7	12													4
1			4	5	6	7		9^{3}	10^{2}	14	11	12	3		8^{1}	2	13												5
	2^{3}		4	5^{1}	6	8		9^{2}	10	11	14	12	3		7		13	1											6
			4	5	6	8		9	11^{2}	10^{1}	13		3			2	12	1	7										7
			4	5^{1}	6	7		9^{3}	10	12	14	13	3			2	11^{2}	1	8										8
	2		4	5^{3}	6	7		12	13	10	14	9^{1}					11^{2}	1	8	3									9
	2		4	5^{2}	6	7		9^{1}	11	10^{3}	13			12			14	1	8	3									10
	2		4	5^{2}		7		12	10	13	11^{3}	9^{1}	3	9			14	1	8										11
	2		4	5	6	8		13	10	12	11^{2}		3	9^{1}				1	7										12
	2		4	5^{3}	6	8		12	11	13	10^{1}		3	9			14	1	7^{2}										13
	2	14	4	5^{1}	6^{3}	8		12	11	13	10^{2}		3	9				1	7										14
	2	3	4			8		13	11^{3}	12	10^{2}	6^{1}	5	9			14	1	7										15
	2	3	4		13	8			11	12	10^{1}	6^{3}	5^{2}	9			14	1	7										16
		3	4	14	6	8			10^{2}	12	11^{1}		5	9^{3}	13	2		1	7										17
1	13	3	4	5^{2}	6	7		12	11		10^{3}	14		9		2^{1}			8										18
1	2	3^{3}	4	5	6	8		14	10^{2}	11			13	9^{1}	12				7■										19
1	2	3	4	5	6	8^{2}		10^{3}		11^{1}		12		9	7					14	13								20
1	2	3	4	5	6			9^{2}	11	10^{1}	12			13	8				7										21
1	2	3	4	5^{1}	6			9	11	10	13			12	8^{2}				7										22
1	2	3	4	5^{2}	6			13	11	12	10^{3}			9	8				7^{1}		14								23
1	2	3	4	5	6^{2}			13	11	12	10^{1}	14		9^{3}	7				8										24
1	2	3	4	5	6^{2}			12	11^{1}	13	10^{3}			9	7				8		14								25
1	2		4	5^{2}	6^{3}			11		12	10^{1}		3	9	8				7	13	14								26
1	2	3	4	5^{1}	6	14		11^{3}	13	12	10^{2}			9	8				7										27
1	2	3	4		6^{2}	7		14	11^{1}	13			5	12					8			9^{3}	10						28
1	2	3	4		6	7			11	12			5						8			9	10^{1}						29
1	2	3	4		6	8^{1}		14	11	13			5^{3}	12					7			9^{2}	10						30
1	2	3	4		6	8		10^{3}	11^{1}	12			5	14					7			9^{2}		13					31
1	2	3	4		10^{1}	8			11^{2}		12		5	6	13				7			9							32
1	2	3	4		6	8			11	12	10^{2}		5^{1}	13					7^{3}			9	14						33
1		3	4		10			13	11	12	14		5^{1}	6	8				2			9^{3}	7^{2}						34
1	2	3	4	5^{2}	6	8^{1}		12	10	11	13			9									7						35
1	2		4	5^{2}	9	8^{1}			10	13	11			6								12	7		3				36
	2	14	4	13	6^{3}				11^{1}	12				10	9				8			5^{2}	7		3	1			37
	2		4	5^{2}	8			12	11	13	14				7^{3}				8			9	10^{1}		3	1			38
	2		4	5	6^{1}			12	11						7				8			9	10		3	1			39
	2		4	5	6			12	11	13					7^{1}				8			9^{2}	10		3	1			40
	5^{1}		4		10			14	11		13			9	8^{2}	2^{3}			7			12	6		3	1			41
	2		4	5^{1}	8				11		12			10	6				7			13	9^{2}		3	1			42
	2^{2}		4	5^{3}	10			12	11	13	14			9	8^{1}				7			6			3	1			43
	2		4	13	6	8			11	12				5^{2}	10				7			9^{1}			3	1			44
	2		4	5^{1}		8^{2}			10	11	13			9	6	12			7						3	1			45
	2		4	5		7^{1}			10^{3}	11		12		9	6^{2}				8						3	1	13	14	46

FA Cup

Third Round	Hull C	(h)	2-1
Fourth Round	Everton	(h)	3-2
Fifth Round	AFC Wimbledon	(a)	1-0
Sixth Round	Brighton & HA	(h)	2-2

(aet; Brighton & HA won 5-4 on penalties)

Carabao Cup

First Round	Gillingham	(h)	0-0

(Millwall won 3-1 on penalties)

Second Round	Plymouth Arg	(h)	3-2
Third Round	Fulham	(h)	1-3

MILTON KEYNES DONS

FOUNDATION

In July 2004 Wimbledon became MK Dons and relocated to Milton Keynes. In 2007 it recognised itself as a new club with no connection to the old Wimbledon FC. In August of that year the replica trophies and other Wimbledon FC memorabilia were returned to the London Borough of Merton.

Stadiummk, Stadium Way West, Milton Keynes, Buckinghamshire MK1 1ST.

Telephone: (01908) 622 922.

Fax: (01908) 622 933.

Ticket Office: (0333) 200 5343.

Website: www.mkdons.com

Email: info@mkdons.com

Ground Capacity: 30,500.

Record Attendance: 28,127 v Chelsea, FA Cup 4th rd, 31 January 2016.

Pitch Measurements: 105m × 68m (115yd × 74.5yd).

Chairman: Pete Winkelman.

Executive Director: Andrew Cullen.

Manager: Paul Tisdale.

Assistant Manager: Matt Oakley.

Colours: White shirts with gold stripes, white shorts with gold trim, white socks with gold trim.

Year Formed: 2004.

Turned Professional: 2004.

Club Nickname: 'The Dons'.

Grounds: 2004, The National Hockey Stadium; 2007, Stadiummk.

First Football League Game: 7 August 2004, FL 1, v Barnsley (h) D 1–1 – Rachubka; Palmer, Lewington, Harding, Williams, Oyedele, Kamara, Smith, Smart (Herve), McLeod (1) (Hornuss), Small.

Record League Victory: 7–0 v Oldham Ath, FL 1, 20 December 2014 – Martin; Spence, McFadzean, Kay (Baldock), Lewington; Potter (1), Alli (1); Baker C (1), Carruthers (Green), Bowditch (1) (Afobe (1)); Grigg (2).

Record Cup Victory: 6–0 v Nantwich T, FA Cup 1st rd, 12 November 2011 – Martin; Chicksen, Baldock G, Doumbe (1), Flanagan, Williams S, Powell (1) (O'Shea (1), Chadwick (Galloway), Bowditch (2), MacDonald (Williams G (1)), Balanta.

HONOURS

League Champions: FL 2 – 2007–08.
Runners-up: FL 1 – 2014–15.

FA Cup: 5th rd – 2013.

League Cup: 4th rd – 2015.

League Trophy Winners: 2008.

THE SUN FACT FILE

Paul Ince was Milton Keynes Dons' most successful manager to date in his first spell in charge of the club with a win rate of 63 per cent. Ince spent the 2007–08 season as manager, winning the League Two title and the Football League Trophy as well as three divisional Manager of the Month awards before leaving at the end of the campaign to take over at Blackburn Rovers.

Record Defeat: 0–6 v Southampton, Capital One Cup 3rd rd, 23 September 2015.

Most League Points (3 for a win): 97, FL 2, 2007–08.

Most League Goals: 101, FL 1, 2014–15.

Highest League Scorer in Season: Izale McLeod, 21, 2006–07.

Most League Goals in Total Aggregate: Izale McLeod, 62, 2004–07; 2012–14.

Most Capped Player: Lee Hodson, 7 (24), Northern Ireland.

MANAGERS

Stuart Murdock 2004
Danny Wilson 2004–06
Martin Allen 2006–07
Paul Ince 2007–08
Roberto Di Matteo 2008–09
Paul Ince 2009–10
Karl Robinson 2010–16
Robbie Neilson 2016–18
Dan Micciche 2018
Paul Tisdale June 2018–

Most League Goals in One Match: 3, Clive Platt v Barnet, FL 2, 20 January 2007; 3, Mark Wright v Bury, FL 2, 2 February 2008; 3, Aaron Wilbraham v Cheltenham T, FL 1, 31 January 2009; 3, Sam Baldock v Colchester U, FL 1, 12 March 2011; 3, Sam Baldock v Chesterfield, FL 1, 20 August 2012; 3, Dean Bowditch v Bury, FL 1, 22 September 2012; 3, Dele Alli v Notts Co, FL 1, 11 March 2014; 3, Dele Alli v Crewe Alex, FL 1, 20 September 2014; 3, Benik Afobe v Colchester U, FL 1, 29 November 2014; 3, Robert Hall v Leyton Orient, FL 1, 18 April 2015; 3, Ryan Colclough v Fleetwood T, FL 1, 9 September 2016.

Most League Appearances: Dean Lewington, 619, 2004–19.

Youngest League Player: Brendon Galloway, 16 years 42 days v Rochdale, 28 April 2012.

Record Transfer Fee Received: £5,000,000 from Tottenham H for Dele Alli, February 2015.

Record Transfer Fee Paid: £400,000 to Bristol C for Kieran Agard, August 2016.

Football League Record: 2004–06 FL 1; 2006–08 FL 2; 2008–15 FL 1; 2015–16 FL C; 2016–18 FL 1; 2018–19 FL 2; 2019– FL 1.

LATEST SEQUENCES

Longest Sequence of League Wins: 8, 7.9.2007 – 20.10.2007.

Longest Sequence of League Defeats: 6, 2.4.2018 – 28.4.2018.

Longest Sequence of League Draws: 4, 12.2.2013 – 2.3.2013.

Longest Sequence of Unbeaten League Matches: 18, 29.1.2008 – 3.5.2008.

Longest Sequence Without a League Win: 11, 8.3.2016 – 7.5.2016.

Successive Scoring Runs: 18 from 21.8.2018.

Successive Non-scoring Runs: 4, 17.12.2005.

TEN YEAR LEAGUE RECORD

		P	W	D	L	F	A	Pts	Pos
2009-10	FL 1	46	17	9	20	60	68	60	12
2010-11	FL 1	46	23	8	15	67	60	77	5
2011-12	FL 1	46	22	14	10	84	47	80	5
2012-13	FL 1	46	19	13	14	62	45	70	8
2013-14	FL 1	46	17	9	20	63	65	60	10
2014-15	FL 1	46	27	10	9	101	44	91	2
2015-16	FL C	46	9	12	25	39	69	39	23
2016-17	FL 1	46	16	13	17	60	58	61	12
2017-18	FL 1	46	11	12	23	43	69	45	23
2018-19	FL 2	46	23	10	13	71	49	79	3

DID YOU KNOW ?

Luke Chadwick is the only man to win the Milton Keynes Dons Player of the Year award twice. He took the award in both 2009–10 and the following season during a career that saw him make over 200 first team appearances for The Dons.

MILTON KEYNES DONS FC – SKY BET LEAGUE TWO 2018–19 LEAGUE RECORD

Match No.	*Date*	*Venue*	*Opponents*	*Result*		*H/T Score*	*Lg Pos.*	*Goalscorers*	*Attendance*
1	Aug 4	A	Oldham Ath	W	2-1	2-1	7	Agard (pen) [9], Harley [22]	4764
2	11	H	Bury	W	1-0	0-0	3	Cisse [90]	6867
3	18	A	Crewe Alex	D	0-0	0-0	4		3505
4	21	H	Grimsby T	D	1-1	0-1	5	Simpson [46]	6800
5	25	H	Exeter C	W	1-0	0-0	2	Agard (pen) [65]	7672
6	Sept 1	A	Swindon T	D	1-1	1-0	3	Walsh [4]	6620
7	15	H	Forest Green R	D	1-1	1-0	9	Aneke [31]	6638
8	22	A	Lincoln C	L	1-2	0-0	14	Healey [64]	9322
9	25	A	Yeovil T	D	1-1	1-0	11	Agard [45]	2634
10	29	H	Tranmere R	D	1-1	1-1	13	Aneke [45]	7048
11	Oct 2	A	Port Vale	W	2-0	2-0	6	Aneke [23], Agard [31]	3399
12	6	H	Cheltenham T	W	3-0	1-0	4	Aneke [34], Healey [84], Simpson (pen) [90]	6503
13	13	A	Cambridge U	W	1-0	1-0	4	Aneke [29]	5106
14	20	H	Northampton T	W	1-0	1-0	3	Agard [44]	9618
15	23	H	Notts Co	W	2-1	0-1	2	Aneke (pen) [60], Healey [69]	6501
16	27	A	Mansfield T	D	1-1	1-1	2	Houghton [24]	4329
17	Nov 3	A	Crawley T	W	4-0	3-0	2	Healey 2 [7, 45], Agard [18], Aneke [63]	2667
18	17	H	Macclesfield T	W	2-0	0-0	1	Aneke [52], Agard [65]	7087
19	24	A	Stevenage	L	2-3	1-1	2	Healey [29], Agard [68]	3263
20	27	H	Morecambe	W	2-0	0-0	1	Gilbey 2 [58, 84]	5726
21	Dec 8	H	Carlisle U	W	2-0	0-0	1	Houghton [50], Agard [65]	6849
22	22	H	Colchester U	L	0-1	0-1	2		7765
23	26	A	Cheltenham T	L	1-3	1-2	2	Aneke [22]	3266
24	29	A	Northampton T	D	2-2	1-0	2	Gilbey [20], Aneke [69]	6963
25	Jan 1	H	Cambridge U	W	6-0	3-0	2	Healey 2 [5, 63], Agard 2 (1 pen) [7, 76 (p)], Aneke [12], Sow [85]	8128
26	12	A	Bury	L	3-4	2-1	3	Moore-Taylor [9], Lewington [36], Stokes (og) [53]	4072
27	19	H	Crewe Alex	L	0-1	0-1	5		8347
28	26	A	Grimsby T	L	0-1	0-1	6		3862
29	29	H	Oldham Ath	W	2-1	1-0	6	Aneke (pen) [14], Agard (pen) [65]	5950
30	Feb 2	A	Exeter C	L	1-3	0-2	6	Walsh [48]	5766
31	9	H	Swindon T	L	2-3	0-1	8	Hesketh [60], Agard [88]	7864
32	12	A	Newport Co	W	1-0	0-0	4	Aneke [88]	2860
33	16	A	Carlisle U	W	3-2	1-1	4	McGrandles [11], Hesketh [69], Agard [77]	10,459
34	23	H	Newport Co	W	2-0	0-0	4	Cisse [57], Aneke [89]	6984
35	Mar 2	H	Crawley T	W	1-0	1-0	4	Agard [41]	6889
36	9	A	Macclesfield T	W	3-1	1-1	3	Wheeler [44], Brittain [53], Agard [79]	2017
37	12	A	Morecambe	L	2-4	0-2	4	Agard 2 [70, 76]	1460
38	16	H	Stevenage	D	1-1	0-1	3	Aneke [83]	7365
39	23	H	Yeovil T	W	2-0	1-0	3	Harley [13], Aneke [82]	7593
40	30	A	Forest Green R	W	2-1	1-0	2	Agard [38], Martin [87]	3220
41	Apr 6	H	Lincoln C	L	0-2	0-1	3		15,851
42	13	A	Tranmere R	L	1-2	1-1	4	Agard [32]	8357
43	19	A	Notts Co	W	2-1	0-0	3	Wheeler [62], Aneke [85]	7130
44	22	H	Port Vale	D	1-1	0-0	4	Wheeler [52]	8386
45	27	A	Colchester U	L	0-2	0-1	4		5000
46	May 4	H	Mansfield T	W	1-0	1-0	3	Wheeler [2]	20,718

Final League Position: 3

GOALSCORERS

League (71): Agard 20 (4 pens), Aneke 17 (2 pens), Healey 8, Wheeler 4, Gilbey 3, Cisse 2, Harley 2, Hesketh 2, Houghton 2, Simpson 2 (1 pen), Walsh 2, Brittain 1, Lewington 1, Martin 1, McGrandles 1, Moore-Taylor 1, Sow 1, own goal 1.
FA Cup (1): Agard 1.
Carabao Cup (3): Asonganyi 1, Watson 1, own goal 1.
Checkatrade Trophy (5): Aneke 2, Agard 1, Hancox 1, Healey 1.

Nicholls L 40	Brittain C 28 + 3	Moore-Taylor J 22 + 1	Williams G 27 + 3	Lewington D 46	Gilbey A 39	McGrandles C 22 + 3	Houghton J 39 + 5	Pawlett P 3 + 4	Agard K 40 + 3	Harley R 10 + 4	Simpson R 2 + 19	Walsh J 28 + 2	Cisse O 17 + 9	Watson R 13 + 9	Asonganyi D 1 + 2	D'Ath L 3 + 12	Baudry M 4 + 1	Cargill B 28 + 1	Healey R 15 + 3	Aneke C 25 + 12	Sow O 1 + 7	Thomas-Asante B — + 1	Hancox M 1	Martin R 18	Wheeler D 14 + 5	Hesketh J 13 + 3	Walker S — + 7	Moore S 6	Match No.
1	2	3	4	5	6^1	7	8	9^2	10	11	12^3	13	14																1
1	5^3	3	2	8	6		7		10	14	13	4	12	9^1	11^2														2
1	10^3	4	2	5	7^1		6		9			3	8^2	11	12	13	14■												3
1	5	4	2	8	7^2		6		11		12	3	10	9^1				13											4
1	5^1	7	2	9	8^2		6		11		10^3	4	13			14		3	12										5
1	2	7	3	6	8		9		11		10	5						4											6
1	5^1	7	2	9	8		6		11		14	3	12	13				4^2		10^3									7
1	5	3	2	9	8^3		6^2		13			4	10	7					12	11^1	14								8
1	5	3	2	9	7^1		8		10				12	6				4	11										9
1	5^1	3	2	9	6		12		14		13		8^3	7				4	11	10^2									10
1		5	2	6	8		9		11			4		7				3	12	10^1									11
1	14	5	2	6	9		8				12	3		7^1				4	11^3	10^2		13							12
1	12	5	2	6	9^1		8				13	3		7^3		14		4	11	10^2									13
1		3	5	8	7		6		9			2		12				4	11^1	10									14
1	12	3	5	8	7^1		6		9^3		14	2				13		4	11	10^2									15
1		3	5	8	7		6		9			2		12				4	11	10^1									16
1	2^2		5	8	6		7	14	9		13	3				12		4	11^1	10^3									17
1	5	3	2	8	7		6		9^1		14				13	12		4	11^3	10^2									18
1	2	3	5	4	6		7		9		13			12					11	10^2			8^1						19
1		3^2	2	8	6	5	7		9^1		14		12			13		4	11	10^3									20
1			2	9	6	5	3	12	10^1				8	14		7^3		4	11^2		13								21
1			2	9	6	5	3	13	10^3				8^2			7		4	11^1	12	14								22
1			2	9	8	5	3	13	10^1		14		7^3	12		6^2		4		11									23
1		13	2	8	7	5^3	6		11^2		12					14	4	3	9	10^1									24
1			2	8	6^3	5	7^1		9					13		14	3	4	11	10^2	12								25
1		2	5^3	9	6	12	7	8^2	11^1			3				13		4		10	14								26
1		3		8	6	5	7	11^1	9^2	12		2				14		4^3		10	13								27
1		3^2		9	6		7		11^3	14		12		8				4		13	10^1			2	5				28
1				8	7	5	13		9^1	11^3		3		6				4		10^2	14			2	12				29
1				5	10		6^1			9^3		3		7		14		4		11				2	8^2	12	13		30
1				9	6		8^1		11			3		5				4		10				2	12	7^2	13		31
	5			8	9	6			10			3	7					4		13				2^1	11^2	12		1	32
	5			8	10	6			11^1			2	7					4^2		12				3	13	9^3	14	1	33
	2			5	7	8	12		10	14		3	6				4^3			13					9^1	11^2		1	34
	2			5	6	8	12		11			4	7^2							10				3	13	9^1		1	35
	2			5	7	8	12		11			4	6^1							10^2				3	9	13		1	36
	2			5	6	8	3		13		14		7^3							10				4	9^1	11^2	12	1	37
1	5			8	6	13	7		10		14						3^2	4^3		12				2	9^1	11			38
1	3^2			5	6^3	12	7		11	9		4	14							13				2	8^1	10			39
1	3			5		6	8^2		10	7^3	13	4	14							12				2	9^1	11			40
1	2			5^1		6	7^2		10	8		4	13							12				3	9^3	11	14		41
1	2			4		6	7		10	8^1			5							9				3	12	11^2	13		42
1	2		13	5		6	7		11	9^1			4	14						12				3	8^3	10^2			43
1	2		14	5		6	4		10^1	8^3	13		7							12				3	9	11^2			44
1	2^3		13	5		6	4		10	8^2			7							12				3	9^1	11	14		45
1	5		2	8		6	7		10		13	4		12						9^1				3	11^2				46

FA Cup

First Round	Grimsby T	(a)	1-3

Carabao Cup

First Round	Charlton Ath	(h)	3-0
Second Round	Bournemouth	(a)	0-3

Checkatrade Trophy

Group H (S)	Peterborough U	(h)	3-3
(Milton Keynes D won 6-5 on penalties)			
Group H (S)	Luton T	(a)	0-3
Group H (S)	Brighton & HA U21	(h)	2-3

MORECAMBE

FOUNDATION

Several attempts to start a senior football club in a rugby stronghold finally succeeded on 7 May 1920 at the West View Hotel, Morecambe and a team competed in the Lancashire Combination for 1920–21. The club shared with a local cricket club at Woodhill Lane for the first season and a crowd of 3,000 watched the first game. The club moved to Roseberry Park, the name of which was changed to Christie Park after J.B. Christie who as President had purchased the ground.

Globe Arena, Christie Way, Westgate, Morecambe, Lancashire LA4 4TB.

Telephone: (01524) 411 797.

Fax: (01524) 832 230.

Ticket Office: (01524) 411 797.

Website: www.morecambefc.com

Email: office@morecambefc.com

Ground Capacity: 6,476.

Record Attendance: 9,383 v Weymouth, FA Cup 3rd rd, 6 January 1962 (at Christie Park); 5,375 v Newcastle U, League Cup, 28 August 2013 (at Globe Arena).

Pitch Measurements: 103m × 71m (112.5yd × 77.5yd).

Co-Chairmen: Graham Howse, Rod Taylor.

Manager: Jim Bentley.

Assistant Manager: Ken McKenna.

Colours: Red shirts with black sleeves and white trim, black shorts with red trim, black socks with red and white trim.

Year Formed: 1920.

Turned Professional: 1920.

Club Nickname: 'The Shrimps'.

Grounds: 1920, Woodhill Lane; 1921, Christie Park; 2010, Globe Arena.

First Football League game: 11 August 2007, FL 2, v Barnet (h) D 0–0 – Lewis; Yates, Adams, Artell, Bentley, Stanley, Baker (Burns), Sorvel, Twiss (Newby), Curtis, Hunter (Thompson).

HONOURS

League: *Runners-up:* Conference – (3rd) 2006–07 *(promoted via play-offs)*.

FA Cup: 3rd rd – 1962, 2001, 2003.

League Cup: 3rd rd – 2008.

THE Sun FACT FILE

Morecambe had their first experience of play-off football in 2002–03 when they finished second in the Football Conference. The lost on penalties to Dagenham & Redbridge in the semi-final and the following season were also unsuccessful in the play-offs before eventually going up to the Football League thanks to a play-off final victory over Exeter City at Wembley in May 2007.

Record League Victory: 6–0 v Crawley T, FL 2, 10 September 2011 – Roche; Reid, Wilson (pen), McCready, Haining (Parrish), Fenton (1), Drummond, McDonald, Price (Jevons), Carlton (3) (Alessandra), Ellison (1).

Record Cup Victory: 6–2 v Nelson (a), Lancashire Trophy, 27 January 2004.

Record Defeat: 0–7 v Cambridge U, FL 2, 19 April 2016.

Most League Points (3 for a win): 73, FL 2, 2009–10.

Most League Goals: 73, FL 2, 2009–10.

Highest League Scorer in Season: Phil Jevons, 18, 2009–10.

Most League Goals in Total Aggregate: Kevin Ellison, 80, 2011–19.

Most League Goals in One Match: 3, Jon Newby v Rotherham U, FL 2, 29 March 2008.

Most League Appearances: Barry Roche, 420, 2008–19.

Youngest League Player: Aaron McGowan, 16 years 263 days, 20 April 2013.

Record Transfer Fee Received: £225,000 from Stockport Co for Carl Baker, July 2008.

Record Transfer Fee Paid: £50,000 to Southport for Carl Baker, July 2007.

Football League Record: 2006–07 Promoted from Conference; 2007– FL 2.

MANAGERS

Jimmy Milne 1947–48
Albert Dainty 1955–56
Ken Horton 1956–61
Joe Dunn 1961–64
Geoff Twentyman 1964–65
Ken Waterhouse 1965–69
Ronnie Clayton 1969–70
Gerry Irving and Ronnie Mitchell 1970
Ken Waterhouse 1970–72
Dave Roberts 1972–75
Alan Spavin 1975–76
Johnny Johnson 1976–77
Tommy Ferber 1977–78
Mick Hogarth 1978–79
Don Curbage 1979–81
Jim Thompson 1981
Les Rigby 1981–84
Sean Gallagher 1984–85
Joe Wojciechowicz 1985–88
Eric Whalley 1988
Billy Wright 1988–89
Lawrie Milligan 1989
Bryan Griffiths 1989–93
Leighton James 1994
Jim Harvey 1994–2006
Sammy McIlroy 2006–11
Jim Bentley May 2011–

LATEST SEQUENCES

Longest Sequence of League Wins: 7, 31.10.2009 – 12.12.2009.

Longest Sequence of League Defeats: 7, 4.3.2017 – 1.4.2017.

Longest Sequence of League Draws: 5, 3.1.2015 – 31.1.2015.

Longest Sequence of Unbeaten League Matches: 12, 31.1.2009 – 21.3.2009.

Longest Sequence Without a League Win: 13, 20.3.2018 – 18.8.2018.

Successive Scoring Runs: 17 from 13.8.2011.

Successive Non-scoring Runs: 7 from 21.4.2018.

TEN YEAR LEAGUE RECORD

		P	*W*	*D*	*L*	*F*	*A*	*Pts*	*Pos*
2009-10	FL 2	46	20	13	13	73	64	73	4
2010-11	FL 2	46	13	12	21	54	73	51	20
2011-12	FL 2	46	14	14	18	63	57	56	15
2012-13	FL 2	46	15	13	18	55	61	58	16
2013-14	FL 2	46	13	15	18	52	64	54	18
2014-15	FL 2	46	17	12	17	53	52	63	11
2015-16	FL 2	46	12	10	24	69	91	46	21
2016-17	FL 2	46	14	10	22	53	73	52	18
2017-18	FL 2	46	9	19	18	41	56	46	22
2018-19	FL 2	46	14	12	20	54	70	54	18

DID YOU KNOW?

Morecambe won the Lancashire Combination for the second successive season in 1962–63, scoring 153 goals in the process. They won 31 of their 42 games but still only took the title on goal average from Chorley after the teams finished level on 68 points.

MORECAMBE – SKY BET LEAGUE TWO 2018–19 LEAGUE RECORD

Match No.	Date	Venue	Opponents	Result		H/T Score	Lg Pos.	Goalscorers	Attendance
1	Aug 4	A	Crewe Alex	L	0-6	0-2	24		3559
2	11	H	Exeter C	L	0-2	0-1	24		1654
3	18	A	Stevenage	L	0-1	0-1	24		2030
4	21	H	Northampton T	W	1-0	1-0	20	Leitch-Smith 45	1594
5	25	H	Oldham Ath	L	0-2	0-2	22		3050
6	Sept 1	A	Bury	L	2-3	1-2	22	Oates 38, Mandeville 90	3242
7	8	H	Swindon T	L	0-1	0-1	22		1559
8	15	A	Crawley T	L	0-2	0-0	22		1895
9	22	H	Macclesfield T	W	2-1	0-0	21	Leitch-Smith 61, Fleming 77	1622
10	29	A	Grimsby T	W	2-1	0-1	17	Oates 61, Mandeville 65	3972
11	Oct 2	A	Cheltenham T	D	2-2	1-1	18	Cranston 32, Oates 54	2095
12	6	H	Tranmere R	L	3-4	1-2	20	Oates 13, Oliver 73, Leitch-Smith 80	2793
13	13	A	Carlisle U	W	2-0	2-0	17	Leitch-Smith 14, Oliver 26	4569
14	20	H	Colchester U	L	0-1	0-1	18		1839
15	23	H	Mansfield T	L	0-1	0-1	20		1355
16	27	A	Newport Co	D	1-1	0-1	21	Ellison 77	3206
17	Nov 3	H	Yeovil T	W	2-1	1-0	20	Leitch-Smith 23, Oates 48	1406
18	17	A	Forest Green R	W	1-0	0-0	19	Wildig 86	3085
19	24	H	Notts Co	D	1-1	0-0	19	Ellison 88	1658
20	27	A	Milton Keynes D	L	0-2	0-0	20		5726
21	Dec 8	H	Port Vale	D	2-2	2-0	19	Leitch-Smith 27, Oswell 40	1769
22	15	A	Lincoln C	L	1-3	0-3	20	Ellison 80	7975
23	22	H	Cambridge U	W	3-0	0-0	19	Oliver 66, Tutte 87, Ellison 90	1439
24	26	A	Tranmere R	L	1-3	0-3	20	Cranston 66	7483
25	29	A	Colchester U	D	0-0	0-0	20		3653
26	Jan 1	H	Carlisle U	L	0-2	0-1	20		3749
27	5	H	Crewe Alex	D	2-2	0-1	20	Tutte 63, Ellison 84	1662
28	12	A	Exeter C	D	0-0	0-0	21		4113
29	19	H	Stevenage	L	1-2	0-1	22	Ellison 70	1422
30	26	A	Northampton T	D	1-1	0-1	22	Bennett 52	4512
31	Feb 9	H	Bury	L	2-3	0-2	22	Bennett 65, Old 69	2665
32	16	A	Port Vale	W	1-0	0-0	21	Collins 75	4147
33	19	A	Oldham Ath	W	2-1	1-0	20	Cranston 4, Collins 90	4218
34	23	H	Lincoln C	L	0-2	0-1	20		2352
35	Mar 2	A	Yeovil T	L	2-3	1-0	21	Bennett 22, Old 83	2521
36	9	H	Forest Green R	W	3-0	2-0	20	Oates 6, Collins 35, Kenyon 71	1528
37	12	H	Milton Keynes D	W	4-2	2-0	19	Bennett 2 21, 57, Cisse (og) 41, Collins 86	1460
38	16	A	Notts Co	D	0-0	0-0	19		5813
39	23	A	Swindon T	L	0-4	0-2	19		5707
40	30	H	Crawley T	W	1-0	0-0	18	Mandeville 82	2445
41	Apr 6	A	Macclesfield T	D	1-1	1-1	19	Mills 26	2072
42	13	H	Grimsby T	D	1-1	0-0	19	Collins (pen) 80	1897
43	19	A	Mansfield T	L	0-4	0-1	20		5177
44	22	H	Cheltenham T	W	4-0	0-0	18	Oliver 49, Ellison 53, Lavelle 81, Collins 85	3066
45	27	A	Cambridge U	W	2-1	1-0	18	Collins 9, Cranston 87	4083
46	May 4	H	Newport Co	D	1-1	1-0	18	Collins 20	2776

Final League Position: 18

GOALSCORERS

League (54): Collins 8 (1 pen), Ellison 7, Leitch-Smith 6, Oates 6, Bennett 5, Cranston 4, Oliver 4, Mandeville 3, Old 2, Tutte 2, Fleming 1, Kenyon 1, Lavelle 1, Mills 1, Oswell 1, Wildig 1, own goal 1.
FA Cup (0).
Carabao Cup (1): Mandeville 1.
Checkatrade Trophy (3): Oliver 1, Oswell 1, Piggott 1.

Roche B 20	Mills Z 38	Kenyon A 24 + 8	Old S 37 + 2	Cranston J 30 + 5	Fleming A 15 + 4	Tutte A 12 + 6	Oates R 22 + 9	Mandeville L 28 + 14	Ellison K 25 + 18	Oliver V 21 + 9	Oswell J 7 + 10	Wildig A 24 + 2	Sinclair J — + 1	Yarney J 20 + 1	Leitch-Smith A 22 + 3	Jagne L 1 + 1	Conlan L 39 + 1	Mendes Gomes C 7 + 8	Halstead M 26	Piggott J 1 + 5	Lavelle S 31	Hedley B 1	Thompson G 1 + 4	McKay P 2 + 5	Sutton R 14	Bennett R 13 + 3	Mingoia P 14 + 2	Dalby S — + 2	Collins A 11 + 4	Brownsword T — + 1	*Match No.*
1	2	3	4	5	6	7^{1}	8^{3}	9^{2}	10	11	12	13	14																		1
1	2	7^{2}	4	5	6		13	8	10^{3}	11		9^{1}		3	12	14															2
1	2		4		7^{3}	13	12	6	9^{1}	11^{2}	14	8		3	10		5														3
1■	2	13	4		7		9^{3}	6	12		11^{1}	8^{2}		3	10		5	14													4
	2		4		6		10^{2}	8	13	12	11^{1}	7		3	9		5^{3}	14	1												5
1	2		3		6		10^{2}	8	12	13	11^{3}	7		4			5	9^{1}		14											6
1	2		4		6^{3}		10^{2}	8	13	11	14	7		3	9^{1}		5			12											7
1	2		4	5	6			8	10^{2}	12		7		3	9			13		11^{1}											8
1	2	7^{2}			6	12	10^{3}	8	14	13		9^{1}		3	11		5				4										9
1	2		4	13		6	10^{2}	8^{1}		11^{3}	12	7			9		5			14	3										10
1	2		3^{2}	10		13	12	8	14	11				6	9^{3}	7^{1}	5				4										11
1	2					6	8^{2}	10	12	11^{1}	13	7^{3}		3	9		5			14	4										12
1	2			12		7^{3}	9^{2}	6		11	14	8		3	10^{1}		5	13			4										13
1	2			7				8	10	11		6		3	9		5				4										14
1	2			7			12	8	10^{2}	11				3	9		5			13	4	6^{1}									15
1	2	14		7^{2}			10^{1}	9^{3}	13	11	12	6		3	8		5				4										16
	2	13	14	8			9^{3}	6^{2}	12	11		7		3	10^{1}		5		1		4										17
	2	13	3	7		12		9^{2}	10^{3}	11^{1}	14	6			8		5		1		4										18
		6^{3}	4	8		7		10^{1}	13	11	14			2^{2}	9		5		1		3		12								19
		2	4	7		6^{2}		13	10	14	11^{3}			12	9		5		1		3		8^{1}								20
		7	3	6^{3}			12	8	10^{2}	14	11^{1}			2	9		5		1		4		13								21
		6^{1}	4	7			12	8^{3}	10	13	11	14		2	9^{2}		5		1		3										22
		8	3	5		14	6^{1}	12	9	11	10^{2}	7^{3}		2	13				1		4										23
	5	13	4	2		8^{1}	12	9	6^{3}	10		7			11^{2}				1		3		14								24
		8	3	7			11^{3}	6^{2}	13		12			2	10^{1}		5	9	1		4		14								25
	2	6^{1}	3	7		13	9^{3}	14	10	11					12		5	8^{2}	1		4										26
	2	7	4	8		6^{3}	12	9^{1}	11						10^{2}		5	13	1		3			14							27
	5	8	3	6		7^{1}	10^{2}	12	11								9		1		4			13	2						28
	5^{1}	13	4	7		6	10^{2}	9^{3}	11								8		1		3			14	2	12					29
	2	7		5		8	6^{1}	12	9	11									1		4			13	3	10^{2}					30
	2	7	12	8		6^{3}			11								5^{1}	13	1		3^{2}				4	10	9	14			31
	2	7	4	6				13	10^{2}								5	9^{1}	1						3	11	8		12		32
	2	7	4	6			14	12	10^{2}								5	9^{1}	1						3	11^{3}	8		13		33
	2	6	3	7^{1}				12	10^{3}								5	9^{2}	1						4	11	8	14	13		34
	2	8^{2}	3	7			9^{1}	12	13								5	14	1						4	11^{3}	6		10		35
	2	7	4				10^{1}	14	12			8^{2}					5		1					13	3	11^{3}	6		9		36
	2	7	3		13		11^{1}		12			8^{2}					5		1						4	10	6		9		37
	2	6	3	7^{1}	12			13	10								5		1						4	11^{2}	8		9		38
	2	8^{3}	3		12		9^{2}		14			7					5		1		4^{1}					11	6		10	13	39
1	2	7^{3}	3		12		9^{1}	13	14			8					5				4					10^{2}	6		11		40
1	2	13	3	14	7			10^{2}	9			8^{3}					5				4					12	6^{1}		11		41
1	2		4	14	8			10	9^{1}	12		7					5				3					11^{3}	6^{2}		13		42
1	5	7^{1}	2	9	8			6		14							13				4				3^{3}	11	12		10^{2}		43
1	2		4	14	6			12	10^{3}	11^{1}		7					5	13			3						8^{2}		9		44
		13	4	8	9				14	11^{1}							5		1		3			7^{2}	2	12	6		10^{3}		45
			4	10	7			12	14	11^{3}							5	8^{2}	1		3			6^{1}	2		13		9		46

FA Cup

First Round	FC Halifax T	(h)	0-0
Replay	FC Halifax T	(a)	0-1

Carabao Cup

First Round	Preston NE	(a)	1-3

Checkatrade Trophy

Group A (N)	Carlisle U	(a)	2-3
Group A (N)	Stoke C U21	(h)	1-2
Group A (N)	Sunderland	(h)	0-1

NEWCASTLE UNITED

FOUNDATION

In October 1882 a club called Stanley, which had been formed in 1881, changed its name to Newcastle East End to avoid confusion with two other local clubs, Stanley Nops and Stanley Albion. Shortly afterwards another club, Rosewood, merged with them. Newcastle West End had been formed in August 1882 and they played on a pitch which was part of the Town Moor. They moved to Brandling Park in 1885 and St James' Park 1886 (home of Newcastle Rangers). West End went out of existence after a bad run and the remaining committee men invited East End to move to St James' Park. They accepted and, at a meeting in Bath Lane Hall in 1892, changed their name to Newcastle United.

St James' Park, Newcastle-upon-Tyne NE1 4ST.

Telephone: (0844) 372 1892.

Fax: (0191) 201 8600.

Ticket Office: (0844) 372 1892 (option 1).

Website: www.nufc.co.uk

Email: admin@nufc.com

Ground Capacity: 52,354.

Record Attendance: 68,386 v Chelsea, Division 1, 3 September 1930.

Pitch Measurements: 105m × 68m (115yd × 74.5yd).

Managing Director: Lee Charnley.

Head Coach: Steve Bruce.

First-Team Coaches: Steve Agnew, Stephen Clemence.

Colours: Black and white striped shirts, black shorts, white socks with black trim.

Year Formed: 1881.

Turned Professional: 1889.

Previous Names: 1881, Stanley; 1882, Newcastle East End; 1892, Newcastle United.

Club Nickname: 'The Magpies', 'The Toon'.

Grounds: 1881, South Byker; 1886, Chillingham Road, Heaton; 1892, St James' Park.

First Football League Game: 2 September 1893, Division 2, v Royal Arsenal (a) D 2–2 – Ramsay; Jeffery, Miller; Crielly, Graham, McKane; Bowman, Crate (1), Thompson, Sorley (1), Wallace. Graham not Crate scored according to some reports.

Record League Victory: 13–0 v Newport Co, Division 2, 5 October 1946 – Garbutt; Cowell, Graham; Harvey, Brennan, Wright; Milburn (2), Bentley (1), Wayman (4), Shackleton (6), Pearson.

HONOURS

League Champions: Division 1 – 1904–05, 1906–07, 1908–09, 1926–27; FL C – 2009–10, 2016–17; First Division – 1992–93; Division 2 – 1964–65.
Runners-up: Premier League – 1995–96, 1996–97; Division 2 – 1897–98, 1947–48.

FA Cup Winners: 1910, 1924, 1932, 1951, 1952, 1955.
Runners-up: 1905, 1906, 1908, 1911, 1974, 1998, 1999.

League Cup: *Runners-up:* 1976.

Texaco Cup Winners: 1974, 1975.
Anglo-Italian Cup Winners: 1972–73.

European Competitions
Champions League: 1997–98, 2002–03, 2003–04.
Fairs Cup: 1968–69 *(winners)*, 1969–70 *(qf)*, 1970–71.
UEFA Cup: 1977–78, 1994–95, 1996–97 *(qf)*, 1999–2000, 2003–04 *(sf)*, 2004–05 *(qf)*, 2006–07.
Europa League: 2012–13 *(qf)*.
European Cup Winners' Cup: 1998–99.
Intertoto Cup: 2001 *(runners-up)*, 2005, 2006 *(winners)*.

THE Sun FACT FILE

The very first Newcastle United match to be broadcast on radio was the FA Cup fourth-round tie away to Corinthians, which was played at the old Crystal Palace ground on 29 January 1927. The Magpies won 3-1 with goals coming from Tommy McDonald (2) and Bobby McKay. Running commentary was provided by Derek McCulloch with descriptive comments from George Allison.

Record Cup Victory: 9–0 v Southport (at Hillsborough), FA Cup 4th rd, 1 February 1932 – McInroy; Nelson, Fairhurst; McKenzie, Davidson, Weaver (1); Boyd (1), Jimmy Richardson (3), Cape (2), McMenemy (1), Lang (1).

Record Defeat: 0–9 v Burton Wanderers, Division 2, 15 April 1895.

Most League Points (2 for a win): 57, Division 2, 1964–65.

Most League Points (3 for a win): 102, FL C, 2009–10.

Most League Goals: 98, Division 1, 1951–52.

Highest League Scorer in Season: Hughie Gallacher, 36, Division 1, 1926–27.

Most League Goals in Total Aggregate: Jackie Milburn, 177, 1946–57.

Most League Goals in One Match: 6, Len Shackleton v Newport Co, Division 2, 5 October 1946.

Most Capped Player: Shay Given, 82 (134), Republic of Ireland.

Most League Appearances: Jim Lawrence, 432, 1904–22.

Youngest League Player: Steve Watson, 16 years 223 days v Wolverhampton W, 10 November 1990.

Record Transfer Fee Received: £35,000,000 from Liverpool for Andy Carroll, January 2011.

Record Transfer Fee Paid: £20,700,000 to Atlanta United for Miguel Almirón, January 2019.

Football League Record: 1893 Elected to Division 2; 1898–1934 Division 1; 1934–48 Division 2; 1948–61 Division 1; 1961–65 Division 2; 1965–78 Division 1; 1978–84 Division 2; 1984–89 Division 1; 1989–92 Division 2; 1992–93 Division 1; 1993–2009 Premier League; 2009–10 FL C; 2010–16 Premier League; 2016–17 FL C; 2017– Premier League.

MANAGERS

Frank Watt 1895–32 *(Secretary-Manager)*
Andy Cunningham 1930–35
Tom Mather 1935–39
Stan Seymour 1939–47 *(Hon. Manager)*
George Martin 1947–50
Stan Seymour 1950–54 *(Hon. Manager)*
Duggie Livingstone 1954–56
Stan Seymour 1956–58 *(Hon. Manager)*
Charlie Mitten 1958–61
Norman Smith 1961–62
Joe Harvey 1962–75
Gordon Lee 1975–77
Richard Dinnis 1977
Bill McGarry 1977–80
Arthur Cox 1980–84
Jack Charlton 1984
Willie McFaul 1985–88
Jim Smith 1988–91
Ossie Ardiles 1991–92
Kevin Keegan 1992–97
Kenny Dalglish 1997–98
Ruud Gullit 1998–99
Sir Bobby Robson 1999–2004
Graeme Souness 2004–06
Glenn Roeder 2006–07
Sam Allardyce 2007–08
Kevin Keegan 2008
Joe Kinnear 2008–09
Alan Shearer 2009
Chris Hughton 2009–10
Alan Pardew 2010–15
John Carver 2015
Steve McClaren 2015–16
Rafael Benitez 2016–19
Steve Bruce July 2019–

LATEST SEQUENCES

Longest Sequence of League Wins: 13, 25.4.1992 – 18.10.1992.

Longest Sequence of League Defeats: 10, 23.8.1977 – 15.10.1977.

Longest Sequence of League Draws: 4, 15.11.2008 – 6.12.2008.

Longest Sequence of Unbeaten League Matches: 17, 13.2.2010 – 2.5.2010.

Longest Sequence Without a League Win: 21, 14.1.1978 – 23.8.1978.

Successive Scoring Runs: 25 from 15.4.1939.

Successive Non-scoring Runs: 6 from 29.10.1988.

TEN YEAR LEAGUE RECORD

		P	*W*	*D*	*L*	*F*	*A*	*Pts*	*Pos*
2009-10	FL C	46	30	12	4	90	35	102	1
2010-11	PR Lge	38	11	13	14	56	57	46	12
2011-12	PR Lge	38	19	8	11	56	51	65	5
2012-13	PR Lge	38	11	8	19	45	68	41	16
2013-14	PR Lge	38	15	4	19	43	59	49	10
2014-15	PR Lge	38	10	9	19	40	63	39	15
2015-16	PR Lge	38	9	10	19	44	65	37	18
2016-17	FL C	46	29	7	10	85	40	94	1
2017-18	PR Lge	38	12	8	18	39	47	44	10
2018-19	PR Lge	38	12	9	17	42	48	45	13

DID YOU KNOW ?

Sandy Higgins, who made 150 first-team appearances for Newcastle United between 1905 and 1915, was the highest decorated player from among the playing staff from 1914–15 during the First World War. Higgins, who served in the Durham Light Infantry, was awarded the Military Medal for his actions during the German Spring Offensive of 1918.

NEWCASTLE UNITED – PREMIER LEAGUE 2018–19 LEAGUE RECORD

Match No.	Date	Venue	Opponents	Result		H/T Score	Lg Pos.	Goalscorers	Attendance
1	Aug 11	H	Tottenham H	L	1-2	1-2	15	Joselu [11]	51,749
2	18	A	Cardiff C	D	0-0	0-0	12		30,720
3	26	H	Chelsea	L	1-2	0-0	16	Joselu [83]	51,791
4	Sept 1	A	Manchester C	L	1-2	1-1	18	Yedlin [30]	53,946
5	15	H	Arsenal	L	1-2	0-0	18	Clark [90]	52,165
6	22	A	Crystal Palace	D	0-0	0-0	18		25,679
7	29	H	Leicester C	L	0-2	0-1	18		51,523
8	Oct 6	A	Manchester U	L	2-3	2-0	19	Kenedy [7], Muto [10]	74,519
9	20	H	Brighton & HA	L	0-1	0-1	20		50,329
10	27	A	Southampton	D	0-0	0-0	19		30,736
11	Nov 3	H	Watford	W	1-0	0-0	17	Perez [65]	49,157
12	10	H	Bournemouth	W	2-1	2-1	14	Rondon 2 [7, 39]	49,266
13	26	A	Burnley	W	2-1	2-1	13	Mee (og) [4], Clark [23]	20,628
14	Dec 1	H	West Ham U	L	0-3	0-1	15		51,853
15	5	A	Everton	D	1-1	1-1	14	Rondon [19]	39,350
16	9	H	Wolverhampton W	L	1-2	1-1	15	Perez [23]	50,223
17	15	A	Huddersfield T	W	1-0	0-0	14	Rondon [55]	24,036
18	22	H	Fulham	D	0-0	0-0	15		51,237
19	26	A	Liverpool	L	0-4	0-1	15		53,318
20	29	A	Watford	D	1-1	1-0	15	Rondon [29]	20,336
21	Jan 2	H	Manchester U	L	0-2	0-0	15		52,217
22	12	A	Chelsea	L	1-2	1-1	18	Clark [40]	40,491
23	19	H	Cardiff C	W	3-0	1-0	17	Schar 2 [24, 63], Perez [90]	49,864
24	29	H	Manchester C	W	2-1	0-1	14	Rondon [66], Ritchie (pen) [80]	50,861
25	Feb 2	A	Tottenham H	L	0-1	0-0	15		41,219
26	11	A	Wolverhampton W	D	1-1	0-0	16	Hayden [56]	30,687
27	23	H	Huddersfield T	W	2-0	0-0	15	Rondon [46], Perez [52]	52,174
28	26	H	Burnley	W	2-0	2-0	13	Schar [24], Longstaf, Sf [38]	48,323
29	Mar 2	A	West Ham U	L	0-2	0-2	14		59,910
30	9	H	Everton	W	3-2	0-2	13	Rondon [65], Perez 2 [81, 84]	52,242
31	16	A	Bournemouth	D	2-2	1-0	13	Rondon [45], Ritchie [90]	10,625
32	Apr 1	A	Arsenal	L	0-2	0-1	14		59,869
33	6	H	Crystal Palace	L	0-1	0-0	15		51,926
34	12	A	Leicester C	W	1-0	1-0	13	Perez [32]	32,108
35	20	H	Southampton	W	3-1	2-0	12	Perez 3 [27, 31, 86]	52,191
36	27	A	Brighton & HA	D	1-1	1-0	13	Perez [18]	30,587
37	May 4	H	Liverpool	L	2-3	1-2	14	Atsu [20], Rondon [54]	52,206
38	12	A	Fulham	W	4-0	2-0	13	Shelvey [9], Perez [11], Schar [61], Rondon [90]	24,979

Final League Position: 13

GOALSCORERS

League (42): Perez 12, Rondon 11, Schar 4, Clark 3, Joselu 2, Ritchie 2 (1 pen), Atsu 1, Hayden 1, Kenedy 1, Longstaff S 1, Muto 1, Shelvey 1, Yedlin 1, own goal 1.
FA Cup (5): Joselu 1, Longstaff S 1, Perez 1, Ritchie 1 (1 pen), Roberts 1.
Carabao Cup (1): Rondon 1.
Checkatrade Trophy (9): Sorensen 4, Roberts 3 (1 pen), Allan 1, Longstaff M 1.

Dubravka M 38	Yedlin D 28 + 1	Lascelles J 32	Clark C 9 + 2	Dummett P 21 + 5	Ritchie M 35 + 1	Shelvey J 10 + 6	Diame M 24 + 5	Kenedy R 14 + 11	Perez A 34 + 3	Joselu M 5 + 11	Rondon J 30 + 2	Atsu C 15 + 13	Muto Y 5 + 12	Manquillo J 12 + 6	Hayden I 21 + 4	Murphy J 3 + 6	Schar F 22 + 2	Fernandez F 17 + 2	Ki S 14 + 4	Longstaff S 8 + 1	Lejeune F 12	Barreca A — + 1	Almiron M 9 + 1	Match No.
1	2	3	4	5	6¹	7	8	9	10³	11²	12	13	14											1
1		3	4	5	6¹	7	8	9	10³	11			13	2²	12■	14								2
1	2		5	6	7		8		13	12	11³		14			10²	3¹	4	9					3
1	2	3	5¹	6			8	7²	10	13	11³	12				14		4	9					4
1	2	3¹	12	5	6³		8	13	10	11			14		7	9²		4						5
1	2	3		5	6²	8	7	9	10¹	12	11³	13	14					4						6
1	2¹	3	4		6³	8	7	5	10²	11		9	13	14		12								7
1	2	3			6	7	8	9³	10¹	14		13	11²	5		12		4						8
1	2	3		5	6	7	8	9	10	12			11¹					4						9
1	2	3		5	6	7	8¹	9	10²		12	14	11³					4	13					10
1	2	3³		5	6	7²	8	9	12		11		10¹				13	4	14					11
1	2		13	5	6²		8¹	9³	10		11	14			12		3	4	7					12
1	2		5		6		8	7¹	10	12	11²				13		3	4	9					13
1	2				6²	13	7	9³	10¹	14	11	12		5			3	4	8					14
1	2	4					8		12	13	11²	7		6		10¹	3	5	9					15
1	5■	2	4		9		6	14	10	13	11¹	8³		12				3²	7					16
1		3	4	14	13		6	9¹	10		11²	8		5	12		2		7³					17
1	13	4		5	6		9	12	10		11	7¹		2²			3		8					18
1	2	4		5	6¹		8	9²		11			10		7	13		3		12				19
1	2	4		5	6	13	9		7		11	10			8²		12	3¹						20
1	2	4		5	6	12	9¹	13	7³		11	10	14		8		3²							21
1	2¹	4	5		6				7²		11	10		12	9	13				8	3			22
1	2	4			6¹				7		11	10		12	8		3			9	5			23
1	2	4			6			12	7²		11	10¹		13	8		3			9	5			24
1	2	4			6¹			12	7		11	10²			8		3			9	5	13		25
1	5	3			9		13		10¹		11	8³		14	6²		2			7	4		12	26
1	2	4			6¹			12	7	14	11³	13			8		3			9	5		10²	27
1		4		12	6		13		7¹	14	11			2	8		3			9²	5		10³	28
1		4		13	6		12		7		11	14		2	9¹		3²			8³	5		10	29
1	5	3³		12	8²	14		13	9		10				6		2		7¹		4		11	30
1	2			5	6	14	8¹		7³		11	12	13		9			4			3		10²	31
1	2	4		5	6¹		9	13	7³		11		14		8²				12		3		10	32
1	2	4		12	6¹	13			7		11	14			8		3		9²		5³		10	33
1		4		5	6		13		7		11	12		2	8		3		9¹				10²	34
1		4		5	6		14		7		11	12		2	9²		3³	13	8				10¹	35
1				5	6	8²		12	7³		11	10¹	14	2	9		3	4	13					36
1		4		5	6				7		11	10	12	2	8		3¹		9					37
1		4		5¹	6	8	9	14	7		11	10³	12		2²		3	13						38

FA Cup

Third Round	Blackburn R	(h)	1-1
Replay	Blackburn R	(a)	4-2
(aet)			
Fourth Round	Watford	(h)	0-2

Carabao Cup

Second Round	Nottingham F	(a)	1-3

Checkatrade Trophy (Newcastle U U21)

Group G (N)	Doncaster R	(a)	3-1
Group G (N)	Notts Co	(a)	2-0
Group G (N)	Grimsby T	(a)	3-2
Second Round (N)	Macclesfield T	(h)	1-1
(Newcastle U U21 won 5-3 on penalties)			
Third Round	Sunderland	(a)	0-4

NEWPORT COUNTY

FOUNDATION

In 1912 Newport County were formed following a meeting at The Tredegar Arms Hotel. A professional football club had existed in the town called Newport FC, but they ceased to exist in 1907. The first season as Newport County was in the second division of the Southern League. They started life playing at Somerton Park where they remained through their League years. They were elected to the Football League for the beginning of the 1920–21 season as founder members of Division 3. At the end of the 1987–88 season, they were relegated from the Football League and replaced by Lincoln City. On February 27 1989, Newport County went out of business and from the ashes Newport AFC was born. Starting down the pyramid in the Hellenic League, they eventally gained promotion to the Conference in 2011 and were promoted to the Football League after a play-off with Wrexham in 2013.

Rodney Parade, Rodney Road, Newport, South Wales NP19 0UU.

Telephone: (01633) 415 376.

Ticket Office: (01633) 415 374.

Website: www.newport-county.co.uk

Email: office@newport-county.co.uk

Ground Capacity: 8,722.

Record Attendance: 24,268 v Cardiff C, Division 3 (S), 16 October 1937 (Somerton Park); 4,660 v Swansea C, FA Cup 1st rd, 11 November 2006 (Newport Stadium); 9,836 v Tottenham H, FA Cup 4th rd, 27 January 2018 (Rodney Parade).

Pitch Measurements: 100m × 68m (109.5yd × 74.5yd).

Chairmen: Gavin Foxall, Shaun Johnson.

Manager: Michael Flynn.

Assistant Manager: Wayne Hatswell.

Colours: Amber shirts with black trim, black shorts with amber trim, black socks with amber trim.

Year Formed: 1912.

Turned Professional: 1912.

Previous Names: Newport County, 1912; Newport AFC, 1989; Newport County, 1999.

Club Nicknames: 'The Exiles', 'The Ironsides', 'The Port', 'The County'.

Grounds: 1912–89, 1990–92, Somerton Park; 1992–94, Meadow Park Stadium; 1994, Newport Stadium; 2012, Rodney Parade.

First Football League Game: 28 August 1920, Division 3, v Reading (h) L 0–1.

HONOURS

League Champions: Division 3S – 1938–39.
Runners-up: Conference – (3rd) 2012–13 *(promoted via play-offs)*.

FA Cup: 5th rd – 1949, 2019.

League Cup: never past 3rd rd.

Welsh Cup Winners: 1980.
Runners-up: 1963, 1987.

European Competitions
European Cup Winners' Cup: 1980–81 *(qf)*.

THE Sun FACT FILE

Tommy Tynan set a post-war scoring record for Newport County in 1982–83 when he netted 33 goals in League and Cup games. His tally included hat-tricks against Wrexham in the League and Enfield in an FA Cup replay. Tynan went on to become the first player inducted into County's Hall of Fame when it was set up in 2009.

Record League Victory: 10-0 v Merthyr T, Division 3(S), 10 April 1930 – Martin (5), Gittins (2), Thomas (1), Bagley (1), Lawson (1).

Record Cup Victory: 7-0 v Working, FA Cup 1st rd, 24 November 1928 – Young (3), Pugh (2) Gittins (1), Reid (1).

Record Defeat: 0–13 v Newcastle U, Division 2, 5 October 1946.

Most League Points (2 for a win): 61, Division 4, 1979–80.

Most League Points (3 for a win): 78, Division 3, 1982–83.

Most League Goals: 85, Division 4, 1964–65.

Highest League Scorer in Season: Tudor Martin, 34, Division 3 (S), 1929–30.

Most League Goals in Total Aggregate: Reg Parker, 99, 1948–54.

Most League Goals in One Match: 5, Tudor Martin v Merthyr T, Dvision 3 (S), 10 April 1930.

Most Capped Player: Nigel Vaughan, 3 (10), Wales.

Most League Appearances: Len Weare, 527, 1955–70.

Youngest League Player: Regan Poole, 16 years 94 days v Shrewsbury T, 20 September 2014.

Record Transfer Fee Received: £500,000 (rising to £1,000,000) from Peterborough U for Conor Washington, January 2014.

Record Transfer Fee Paid: £80,000 to Swansea C for Alan Waddle, January 1981.

Football League Record: 1920 Original member of Division 3; 1921–31 Division 3 (S) – dropped out of Football League; 1932 Re-elected to Division 3 (S); 1932–39 Division 3 (S); 1946–47 Division 2; 1947–58 Division 3 (S); 1958–62 Division 3; 1962–80 Division 4; 1980–87 Division 3; 1987–88 Division 4 (relegated from Football League); 2011 Promoted to Conference; 2011–13 Conference Premier; 2013– FL 2.

LATEST SEQUENCES

Longest Sequence of League Wins: 4, 21.8.2018 – 8.9.2018.

Longest Sequence of League Defeats: 8, 22.11.2016 – 7.1.2017.

Longest Sequence of League Draws: 4, 31.10.2015 – 24.11.2015.

Longest Sequence of Unbeaten League Matches: 10, 15.3.2019 – 4.5.2019.

Longest Sequence Without a League Win: 12, 15.3.2016 – 6.8.2017.

Successive Scoring Runs: 16 from 11.3.2017.

Successive Non-scoring Runs: 4 from 3.2.2018.

MANAGERS

Davy McDougle 1912–13
(Player-Manager)
Sam Hollis 1913–17
Harry Parkes 1919–22
Jimmy Hindmarsh 1922–35
Louis Page 1935–36
Tom Bromilow 1936–37
Billy McCandless 1937–45
Tom Bromilow 1945–50
Fred Stansfield 1950–53
Billy Lucas 1953–61
Bobby Evans 1961–62
Billy Lucas 1962–67
Leslie Graham 1967–69
Bobby Ferguson 1969–70
(Player Manager)
Billy Lucas 1970–74
Brian Harris 1974–75
Dave Elliott 1975–76
(Player-Manager)
Jimmy Scoular 1976–77
Colin Addison 1977–78
Len Ashurst 1978–82
Colin Addison 1982–85
Bobby Smith 1985–86
John Relish 1986
Jimmy Mullen 1986–87
John Lewis 1987
Brian Eastick 1987–88
David Williams 1988
Eddie May 1988
John Mahoney 1988–89
John Relish 1989–93
Graham Rogers 1993–96
Chris Price 1997
Tim Harris 1997–2002
Peter Nicholas 2002–04
John Cornforth 2004–05
Peter Beadle 2005–08
Dean Holdsworth 2008–11
Anthony Hudson 2011
Justin Edinburgh 2011–15
Jimmy Dack 2015
Terry Butcher 2015
John Sheridan 2015–16
Warren Feeney 2016
Graham Westley 2016–17
Michael Flynn May 2017–

TEN YEAR LEAGUE RECORD

		P	W	D	L	F	A	Pts	Pos
2009-10	Conf S	42	32	7	3	93	26	103	1
2010-11	Conf P	46	18	15	13	78	60	69	9
2011-12	Conf P	46	11	14	21	53	65	47	19
2012-13	Conf P	46	25	10	11	85	60	85	3
2013-14	FL 2	46	14	16	16	56	59	58	14
2014-15	FL 2	46	18	11	17	51	54	65	9
2015-16	FL 2	46	10	13	23	43	64	43	22
2016-17	FL 2	46	12	12	22	51	73	48	22
2017-18	FL 2	46	16	16	14	56	58	64	11
2018-19	FL 2	46	20	11	15	59	59	71	7

DID YOU KNOW ?

Newport County, under their old name of Newport AFC, won 14 consecutive games on their way to the Southern League Midland Division championship in 1994–95. County finished the season 14 points ahead of their nearest rivals Ilkeston Town.

NEWPORT COUNTY – SKY BET LEAGUE TWO 2018–19 LEAGUE RECORD

Match No.	Date	Venue	Opponents	Result		H/T Score	Lg Pos.	Goalscorers	Attendance
1	Aug 4	A	Mansfield T	L	0-3	0-1	22		4423
2	11	H	Crewe Alex	W	1-0	1-0	16	Amond [33]	3243
3	18	A	Exeter C	D	1-1	0-1	18	Harris [81]	4239
4	21	H	Notts Co	W	3-2	2-1	8	Franks [24], Harris [26], Matt [90]	2935
5	25	H	Grimsby T	W	1-0	1-0	5	Dolan [40]	3288
6	Sept 1	A	Port Vale	W	2-1	1-1	2	Bennett [18], Butler [48]	4485
7	8	A	Oldham Ath	W	1-0	0-0	2	Bakinson [69]	4293
8	15	H	Yeovil T	L	0-6	0-3	3		4167
9	22	A	Tranmere R	W	1-0	1-0	3	Franks [5]	5745
10	29	H	Cambridge U	W	4-2	1-2	2	Demetriou (pen) [45], Amond [49], Matt 2 [60, 63]	3104
11	Oct 2	H	Macclesfield T	D	3-3	1-2	3	Butler [29], Demetriou (pen) [59], Matt [90]	2624
12	6	A	Forest Green R	D	1-1	1-1	3	Amond [38]	3081
13	13	H	Stevenage	W	2-1	1-1	3	Dolan [1], Semenyo [90]	3126
14	20	A	Crawley T	L	1-4	0-1	4	Matt [59]	2157
15	23	A	Bury	D	1-1	0-1	4	Matt [56]	3072
16	27	H	Morecambe	D	1-1	1-0	4	Amond [1]	3206
17	Nov 3	A	Carlisle U	L	2-3	1-2	6	Amond [39], Butler [87]	3541
18	17	H	Colchester U	W	2-0	0-0	3	Matt [54], Pring [67]	3512
19	24	A	Cheltenham T	L	1-2	0-2	5	Semenyo [89]	3672
20	27	H	Northampton T	W	3-1	3-1	4	Sheehan [5], Matt [31], Amond [33]	2730
21	Dec 8	A	Swindon T	L	1-2	0-1	6	Amond [47]	6204
22	22	A	Lincoln C	L	2-3	1-2	8	Amond 2 [45, 77]	8632
23	26	H	Forest Green R	L	1-4	1-2	11	Amond (pen) [45]	4203
24	29	H	Crawley T	D	0-0	0-0	10		3166
25	Jan 1	A	Stevenage	L	0-1	0-0	12		2299
26	12	A	Crewe Alex	L	2-3	0-1	13	Semenyo [65], Amond [76]	3104
27	19	H	Exeter C	W	1-0	0-0	13	Matt [71]	3791
28	29	H	Port Vale	D	0-0	0-0	13		2534
29	Feb 2	A	Grimsby T	L	0-3	0-1	14		3712
30	9	H	Mansfield T	W	1-0	1-0	13	Willmott [15]	3133
31	12	H	Milton Keynes D	L	0-1	0-0	15		2860
32	19	A	Notts Co	W	4-1	3-1	15	Franks [9], Matt 2 [15, 33], Amond [47]	6253
33	23	A	Milton Keynes D	L	0-2	0-0	15		6984
34	Mar 2	H	Carlisle U	W	2-0	1-0	12	Azeez [14], Amond [67]	3432
35	9	A	Colchester U	L	0-3	0-2	12		3213
36	12	A	Northampton T	L	0-1	0-0	13		4064
37	15	H	Cheltenham T	W	1-0	0-0	11	Hussey (og) [54]	3192
38	30	A	Yeovil T	W	3-1	0-0	11	Willmott [62], Kennedy [66], Marsh-Brown [90]	3983
39	Apr 6	H	Tranmere R	D	0-0	0-0	13		3170
40	9	H	Swindon T	D	0-0	0-0	13		3314
41	13	A	Cambridge U	W	3-0	2-0	12	Amond [4], Matt [34], McKirdy [90]	4294
42	19	H	Bury	W	3-1	2-1	11	Demetriou 2 [5, 75], Matt [13]	4433
43	22	A	Macclesfield T	D	0-0	0-0	11		2269
44	27	H	Lincoln C	W	1-0	1-0	11	Bennett [7]	4605
45	30	H	Oldham Ath	W	2-0	0-0	7	O'Brien 2 [48, 79]	4642
46	May 4	A	Morecambe	D	1-1	0-1	7	Matt [87]	2776

Final League Position: 7

GOALSCORERS

League (59): Amond 14 (1 pen), Matt 14, Demetriou 4 (2 pens), Butler 3, Franks 3, Semenyo 3, Bennett 2, Dolan 2, Harris 2, O'Brien 2, Willmott 2, Azeez 1, Bakinson 1, Kennedy 1, Marsh-Brown 1, McKirdy 1, Pring 1, Sheehan 1, own goal 1.
FA Cup (12): Amond 5 (1 pen), Matt 3, Butler 1, Dolan 1, Willmott 1, own goal 1.
Carabao Cup (4): Amond 2, Matt 1, Semenyo 1.
Checkatrade Trophy (6): Matt 2, Semenyo 2, Amond 1, Harris 1.
League Two Play-offs (1): Amond 1.

Day J 43	Hornby-Forbes T 13 + 1	Dametriou M 45	Franks F 25	Butler D 45	Crofts A 5 + 4	Bennett S 36 + 2	Dolan M 26 + 6	Marsh-Brown K 3 + 13	Amond P 43 + 2	Matt J 36 + 7	Sheehan J 21 + 12	Semenyo A 12 + 9	Cooper C 4 + 5	Pipe D 16 + 3	Harris M 5 + 11	Bakinson T 26 + 4	O'Brien M 26 + 8	Willmott R 29 + 2	Townsend N 3	Pring C 1 + 6	Labadie J 10 + 3	Poole R 20	Neufville V 1	Kennedy B 7 + 3	McKirdy H 2 + 10	Azeez A 3 + 9	Randall W — + 1	*Match No.*
1	2	3	4	5	6^1	7	8	9^2	10	11^3	12	13	14															1
1		4	2	9	6	3	8		10^2	14	7^3	12	13	5	11^1													2
1		4	2	9		3	8	12	11	10^2	7^3	13		5^1	14	6												3
1	5	4	2	0		3	7^2	12	10	14	9^3		13		11^1	6												4
1	5	4	2	8		3	7^1		10	14	9^2	12	13		11^3	6												5
1		5	3	6		4	7	14	10^1	12	9^2			2	11^3	8	13											6
1		4	2	8		3	7	12	11	10^2	9^1			5		6	13											7
1		4	2	8		3	7	12	10		9^3			5^2	11^1	6	14	13■										8
1	5	3	2	0		7	6^1		10	13	12	11^2				9	4											9
	5	4	2	8		6			10	13	9^3	11^1	12			7	3^2		1	14								10
1	2	4	3	5		7			9	10		11	8^1		12	6												11
1	2	3	4	5		7			9	10^2		11			13	8		6^1		12								12
1	2	4	3	5		7	8		11	10		12		13		6^2		9^1										13
1		4	3■	5		7			8	11^1	9^2	10	6	2	12					13								14
1	5	4		9		7			10	11		12	8^2	2			3	6^1		13								15
1	12	4		5		7^3	8		11	10^1		9		2	14		3^2	6		13								16
1	5^2	3		4			7	14	11	12	8^3	10^1		2	13	6		9										17
1		4	3	5			8^2		9	10		11^3		2	13	7	14	6^1		12								18
1		4	3	5	13				10	9^1		11	8^3	2	14	7	12			6^2								19
1		2	3	9	8				11	10^1	6	12		5		7	4											20
1		4	2	9	7^2	13			10	11	8	12		5^3		6	3^1				14							21
1			3	5		7	6^2		10	9	14	11		2^3	13		4	8^1			12							22
1		4	2	9■		3	6^1		10	11^3		14		5		7	13	12			8^2							23
1	5^1	4	2	9	7^3	3	8^2		10	11					14	13	12	6										24
1	5^3	4	2^1	9		3^2		13	10	11	14				12	8	7	6										25
1	5	4	2	9		3	6^1		10	11	13	8^2				12	14	7^3										26
1		4		9		2			7	11		10				6	3	8				5						27
		2		9		4	12	13	11	10	14					6^2	7	5^3	1		8^1	3						28
		4			14		7	11^2	12	10	13			2		8^1			1		6^3	3	5	9				29
1		2		9		7	12		11	10						6	4	5^1			8	3						30
1		4	3^2	8		7	12	13	10^1	11	14					6		5				2		9^3				31
1		5	4^1	9		7	12		11	10^2	14						3	6			8^3	2			13			32
1		5		6		9	8^1		11^3	10						7^2	4	2				3		13	14	12		33
1		4		5		7	6^2		9	10^1	12						2	8			13	3			14	11^3		34
1		4		8		7			9	10^3						14	2	5			6^2	3			12	11^1	13	35
1		4		9		7^1			10	11	12					8	3^3	5			6^2	2			13	14		36
1		4		8		7			9	11^3	13			12		6^1	3^2	5				2			14	10		37
1		2		8			13	12		10^1	7						3	5			6^3	4		11	9^2	14		38
1		2		8			13	9^2	14	10	7						3	5^3			6	4		11^1		12		39
1		3		5	13			14	10	11^3	8						4	6			7^1	2		9^2		12		40
1		4		8	12	13	6^3		10	11	7^2						3	5				2		9^1	14			41
1		4		8		9	6^1		10^2	11^3	7					14	3	5				2		13	12			42
1		4		9		6^2	7^3	12	11		8						3	5				2		13	10^1	14		43
1		4		9		7	6		10		8						3	5				2		11^1		12		44
1		4		9		8	6^3		11^2	10^1	7			13			2	5				3			14	12		45
1		4		9		8	6^1	14	11	10	7^2						3	5				2^3			13	12		46

FA Cup

First Round	Met Police	(a)	2-0
Second Round	Wrexham	(a)	0-0
Replay	Wrexham	(h)	4-0
Third Round	Leicester C	(h)	2-1
Fourth Round	Middlesbrough	(a)	1-1
Replay	Middlesbrough	(h)	2-0
Fifth Round	Manchester C	(h)	1-4

Carabao Cup

First Round	Cambridge U	(a)	4-1
Second Round	Oxford U	(h)	0-3

Checkatrade Trophy

Group C (S)	Swindon T	(a)	0-1
Group C (S)	Chelsea U21	(h)	3-0
Group C (S)	Plymouth Arg	(h)	2-0
Second Round (S)	Cheltenham T	(a)	1-1

(Cheltenham T won 7-6 on penalties)

League Two Play-offs

Semi-Final 1st leg	Mansfield T	(h)	1-1
Semi-Final 2nd leg	Mansfield T	(a)	0-0

(aet; Newport Co won 4-3 on penalties)

Final (*aet*)	Tranmere R	(Wembley)	0-1

NORTHAMPTON TOWN

FOUNDATION

Formed in 1897 by schoolteachers connected with the Northampton & District Elementary Schools' Association, they survived a financial crisis at the end of their first year when they were £675 in the red and became members of the Midland League – a fast move indeed for a new club. They achieved Southern League membership in 1901.

PTS Academy Stadium, Upton Way, Northampton NN5 5QA.

Telephone: (01604) 683 700.

Fax: (01604) 751 613.

Ticket Office: (01604) 683 777.

Website: www.ntfc.co.uk

Email: wendy.lambell@ntfc.co.uk

Ground Capacity: 7,798.

Record Attendance: 24,523 v Fulham, Division 1, 23 April 1966 (at County Ground); 7,798 v Manchester U, EFL Cup 3rd rd, 21 September 2016 (at Sixfields Stadium).

Pitch Measurements: 106m × 66m (116yd × 72yd).

Chairman: Kelvin Thomas.

Chief Executive: James Whiting.

Manager: Keith Curle.

Assistant Manager: Colin West.

Colours: Claret shirts with white trim, white shorts, white socks.

Year Formed: 1897.

Turned Professional: 1901.

Grounds: 1897, County Ground; 1994, Sixfields Stadium (renamed PTS Academy Stadium 2018).

Club Nickname: 'The Cobblers'.

First Football League Game: 28 August 1920, Division 3, v Grimsby T (a) L 0–2 – Thorpe; Sproston, Hewison; Jobey, Tomkins, Pease; Whitworth, Lockett, Thomas, Freeman, MacKechnie.

Record League Victory: 10–0 v Walsall, Division 3 (S), 5 November 1927 – Hammond; Watson, Jeffs; Allen, Brett, Odell; Daley, Smith (3), Loasby (3), Hoten (1), Wells (3).

Record Cup Victory: 10–0 v Sutton T, FA Cup prel rd, 7 December 1907 – Cooch; Drennan, Lloyd Davies, Tirrell (1), McCartney, Hickleton, Badenock (3), Platt (3), Lowe (1), Chapman (2), McDiarmid.

Record Defeat: 0–11 v Southampton, Southern League, 28 December 1901.

HONOURS

League Champions: Division 3 – 1962–63; FL 2 – 2015–16; Division 4 – 1986–87.
Runners-up: Division 2 – 1964–65; Division 3S – 1927–28, 1949–50; FL 2 – 2005–06; Division 4 – 1975–76.

FA Cup: 5th rd – 1934, 1950, 1970.

League Cup: 5th rd – 1965, 1967.

THE SUN FACT FILE

The legendary Herbert Chapman had his first experience of club management after being appointed by Northampton Town in the summer of 1907. Chapman, who arrived as player-manager, quickly turned around the club's fortunes and in 1908–09 they won the Southern League title for the first time and made a financial profit for only the second time in the club's history. He stayed with the Cobblers for five seasons always achieving a top-ten finish before being appointed manager of Leeds City in the summer of 1912.

Most League Points (2 for a win): 68, Division 4, 1975–76.

Most League Points (3 for a win): 99, Division 4, 1986–87; FL 2, 2015–16.

Most League Goals: 109, Division 3, 1962–63 and Division 3 (S), 1952–53.

Highest League Scorer in Season: Cliff Holton, 36, Division 3, 1961–62.

Most League Goals in Total Aggregate: Jack English, 135, 1947–60.

Most League Goals in One Match: 5, Ralph Hoten v Crystal Palace, Division 3 (S), 27 October 1928.

Most Capped Player: Edwin Lloyd Davies, 12 (16), Wales.

Most League Appearances: Tommy Fowler, 521, 1946–61.

Youngest League Player: Adrian Mann, 16 years 297 days v Bury, 5 May 1984.

Record Transfer Fee Received: £470,000 from Blackburn R for Mark Bunn, September 2008.

Record Transfer Fee Paid: £165,000 to Oldham Ath for Josh Low, July 2003.

Football League Record: 1920 Original Member of Division 3; 1921 Division 3 (S); 1958–61 Division 4; 1961–63 Division 3; 1963–65 Division 2; 1965–66 Division 1; 1966–67 Division 2; 1967–69 Division 3; 1969–76 Division 4; 1976–77 Division 3; 1977–87 Division 4; 1987–90 Division 3; 1990–92 Division 4; 1992–97 Division 3; 1997–99 Division 2; 1999–2000 Division 3; 2000–03 Division 2; 2003–04 Division 3; 2004–06 FL 2; 2006–09 FL 1; 2009–16 FL 2; 2016–18 FL 1; 2018– FL 2.

LATEST SEQUENCES

Longest Sequence of League Wins: 10, 28.12.2015 – 23.2.2016.

Longest Sequence of League Defeats: 8, 26.10.1935 – 21.12.1935.

Longest Sequence of League Draws: 6, 5.2.2011 – 26.2.2011.

Longest Sequence of Unbeaten League Matches: 31, 28.12.2015 – 10.9.2016.

Longest Sequence Without a League Win: 18, 5.2.2011 – 25.4.2011.

Successive Scoring Runs: 28 from 29.8.2015.

Successive Non-scoring Runs: 7 from 7.4.1939.

MANAGERS

Arthur Jones 1897–1907
(Secretary-Manager)
Herbert Chapman 1907–12
Walter Bull 1912–13
Fred Lessons 1913–19
Bob Hewison 1920–25
Jack Tresadern 1925–30
Jack English 1931–35
Syd Puddefoot 1935–37
Warney Cresswell 1937–39
Tom Smith 1939–49
Bob Dennison 1949–54
Dave Smith 1954–59
David Bowen 1959–67
Tony Marchi 1967–68
Ron Flowers 1968–69
Dave Bowen 1969–72
(continued as General Manager and Secretary 1972–85 when joined the board)
Billy Baxter 1972–73
Bill Dodgin Jnr 1973–76
Pat Crerand 1976–77
By committee 1977
Bill Dodgin Jnr 1977
John Petts 1977–78
Mike Keen 1978–79
Clive Walker 1979–80
Bill Dodgin Jnr 1980–82
Clive Walker 1982–84
Tony Barton 1984–85
Graham Carr 1985–90
Theo Foley 1990–92
Phil Chard 1992–93
John Barnwell 1993–94
Ian Atkins 1995–99
Kevin Wilson 1999–2001
Kevan Broadhurst 2001–03
Terry Fenwick 2003
Martin Wilkinson 2003
Colin Calderwood 2003–06
John Gorman 2006
Stuart Gray 2007–09
Ian Sampson 2009–11
Gary Johnson 2011
Aidy Boothroyd 2011–13
Chris Wilder 2014–16
Rob Page 2016–17
Justin Edinburgh 2017
Jimmy Floyd Hasselbaink 2017–18
Dean Austin 2018
Keith Curle October 2018–

TEN YEAR LEAGUE RECORD

		P	W	D	L	F	A	Pts	Pos
2009-10	FL 2	46	18	13	15	62	53	67	11
2010-11	FL 2	46	11	19	16	63	71	52	16
2011-12	FL 2	46	12	12	22	56	79	48	20
2012-13	FL 2	46	21	10	15	64	55	73	6
2013-14	FL 2	46	13	14	19	42	57	53	21
2014-15	FL 2	46	18	7	21	67	62	61	12
2015-16	FL 2	46	29	12	5	82	46	99	1
2016-17	FL 1	46	14	11	21	60	73	53	16
2017-18	FL 1	46	12	11	23	43	77	47	22
2018-19	FL 2	46	14	19	13	64	63	61	15

DID YOU KNOW ?

Northampton Town finished bottom of the Football League in 1993–94 but escaped automatic relegation because the home ground of Conference champions Kidderminster Harriers did not meet the League's minimum capacity requirement. The Cobblers won only nine matches during the season, finishing three points behind second to bottom club Darlington.

NORTHAMPTON TOWN – SKY BET LEAGUE TWO 2018–19 LEAGUE RECORD

Match No.	*Date*	*Venue*	*Opponents*	*Result*		*H/T Score*	*Lg Pos.*	*Goalscorers*	*Attendance*
1	Aug 4	H	Lincoln C	L	0-1	0-0	17		6242
2	11	A	Carlisle U	D	2-2	1-1	17	van Veen [40], Crooks [62]	4521
3	18	H	Cambridge U	D	2-2	0-0	20	van Veen 2 [58, 76]	5047
4	21	A	Morecambe	L	0-1	0-1	21		1594
5	25	A	Colchester U	W	2-1	0-0	16	Crooks [48], Waters [90]	3791
6	Sept 1	H	Tranmere R	D	1-1	0-0	18	Morias [61]	4916
7	8	H	Cheltenham T	L	1-3	0-1	20	van Veen (pen) [62]	4608
8	15	A	Port Vale	L	0-2	0-1	20		4474
9	22	H	Notts Co	D	0-0	0-0	20		4935
10	29	A	Mansfield T	L	0-4	0-1	21		4550
11	Oct 2	H	Bury	D	0-0	0-0	21		4073
12	6	A	Swindon T	D	1-1	0-0	22	O'Toole [60]	6138
13	13	H	Forest Green R	W	2-1	0-1	19	Pierre [63], Williams, A [90]	5073
14	20	A	Milton Keynes D	L	0-1	0-1	19		9618
15	23	A	Macclesfield T	W	5-0	4-0	18	Crooks 3 [23, 33, 43], Powell, D [34], Pierre [90]	1517
16	27	H	Oldham Ath	W	2-1	2-0	18	O'Toole [36], van Veen (pen) [45]	4767
17	Nov 3	H	Crewe Alex	W	2-0	1-0	15	Williams, A [19], Powell, D [81]	5401
18	17	A	Exeter C	D	2-2	1-2	14	Waters [26], Stockley (og) [90]	4332
19	24	H	Grimsby T	D	2-2	1-1	15	Williams, A [4], van Veen [74]	5594
20	27	A	Newport Co	L	1-3	1-3	17	Williams, A [11]	2730
21	Dec 8	A	Crawley T	W	1-0	0-0	14	van Veen (pen) [53]	2389
22	15	H	Stevenage	D	1-1	1-0	14	Bowditch [45]	4756
23	22	A	Yeovil T	D	1-1	0-0	14	Williams, A [88]	3193
24	26	H	Swindon T	D	1-1	1-0	15	Williams, A [6]	5759
25	29	H	Milton Keynes D	D	2-2	0-1	16	Williams, A [78], Morias [90]	6963
26	Jan 1	A	Forest Green R	L	1-2	0-1	16	Foley [50]	2909
27	12	H	Carlisle U	W	3-0	0-0	16	Bridge 2 [48, 62], Morias [72]	4875
28	19	A	Cambridge U	L	2-3	1-1	16	Pierre [27], Morias [48]	4849
29	26	H	Morecambe	D	1-1	1-0	17	Elsnik [22]	4512
30	Feb 2	H	Colchester U	L	0-4	0-1	17		4796
31	5	A	Tranmere R	W	2-1	2-1	16	Hoskins 2 [2, 45]	5098
32	9	A	Lincoln C	D	1-1	1-1	16	Pierre [45]	9352
33	16	H	Crawley T	D	0-0	0-0	16		4581
34	23	A	Stevenage	W	2-1	1-0	16	Powell, J [19], Williams, A [90]	3540
35	Mar 2	A	Crewe Alex	W	2-0	2-0	16	Powell, D [28], O'Toole [32]	4096
36	9	H	Exeter C	W	2-1	1-0	14	Pierre [32], Williams, A [56]	4954
37	12	H	Newport Co	W	1-0	0-0	11	Powell, J [88]	4064
38	16	A	Grimsby T	D	0-0	0-0	11		3890
39	23	A	Cheltenham T	L	1-3	0-2	13	Bowditch [89]	3513
40	30	H	Port Vale	L	1-2	1-1	14	Hoskins [5]	5651
41	Apr 6	A	Notts Co	D	2-2	1-1	14	Powell, D [44], Hoskins [50]	7129
42	13	H	Mansfield T	D	1-1	0-1	15	Foley [69]	5905
43	19	H	Macclesfield T	W	3-1	1-1	15	Bowditch [25], Powell, D [54], Morias [90]	4925
44	22	A	Bury	L	1-3	1-1	15	Williams, A [27]	4407
45	27	H	Yeovil T	D	2-2	0-2	15	Sowunmi (og) [49], Powell, D [55]	4908
46	May 4	A	Oldham Ath	W	5-2	3-1	15	Hoskins [22], Pierre [29], Williams, A 2 [44, 49], Morias [80]	5291

Final League Position: 15

GOALSCORERS

League (64): Williams A 12, van Veen 7 (3 pens), Morias 6, Pierre 6, Powell D 6, Crooks 5, Hoskins 5, Bowditch 3, O'Toole 3, Bridge 2, Foley 2, Powell J 2, Waters 2, Elsnik 1, own goals 2.
FA Cup (2): Bridge 1, van Veen 1.
Carabao Cup (1): Hoskins 1.
Checkatrade Trophy (6): Pierre 2, van Veen 2, Crooks 1, Hoskins 1.

Cornell D 46	Odofin H 10 + 2	Taylor A 32 + 1	Pierre A 41	Buchanan D 37 + 2	Crooks M 19 + 2	McWilliams S 21 + 4	O'Toole J 24 + 7	Powell D 17 + 18	Williams A 26 + 13	Hoskins S 40 + 2	Bridge J 17 + 11	Bowditch D 9 + 11	van Veen K 20 + 5	Waters B 5 + 10	Foley S 33 + 3	Morias J 7 + 12	Facey S 21 + 2	Barnett L 4	Turnbull J 30 + 1	Williams J 6 + 4	Roberts M — + 3	Cox G 4 + 1	Pollock S 4 + 1	Elsnik T 4 + 5	Powell J 6 + 4	Goode C 17	Sordell M 5 + 3	Hughes R 1	Match No.
1	2	3	4	5	6	7^1	8	9^2	10	11	12	13																	1
1	5	4	3	2	8		7^2	11^3	9^1	6		12	10	13	14														2
1	5	4	3	2	8			11^1	9^2	6		13	10		7	12													3
1		3		5	8		14	13	9^1	6		11^3	10		7^2	12	2	4											4
1		3	4	5	7		14		12	6	9^3		10^2	13	8	11^1	2												5
1		3	4	5	8		13			6	9^1		10	12	7	11^2	2												6
1		3	4	5	6	13	9^2	12^3	14	8	10		11		7^1		2												7
1		3	4■	5	8		14		10^1	6	9^2		11	12	7^3		2		13										8
1	2	3		5	6		9			8	12	10^1	11		7			4											9
1	2	3		5			8		12	10	13	9^2	11^1	10	7			4											10
1		2	3		7		9^2	8^1	10^3	11		13	14	12	6		5	4											11
1			4	5	7	8^3	6		11^2	10^1		14	12	13	9		2		3										12
1			4	5^3	7^1		8	14	11	10	13		12	6^2	9		2		3										13
1	2		4	8^3		13	7	14	9^1	11	12		10	5^2	6				3										14
1			3	9	6^3	4	7	11^2	10		5		13	12	8^1				2	14									15
1	12		3	4	8	5	7	13		10	9^1		11^2		6■				2										16
1	2		3	9	6^2	5^1	8	13	10^3	7			11	12					4	14									17
1	2^2	13	4	5		8	7	9	14	6			10^1	11			12		3^3										18
1		2	3	9		5^2	6	13	10^3	7			11		8		12		4^1	14									19
1	2	5	4	3		7	8^3	13	11	9^2			10^1	12	6						14								20
1		3	4	9	12	8		14		11^3		7	10^1		6^2	13	5		2										21
1	14	3^2	4	9	13	8		11^3		12		7^1	10		6		5		2										22
1		4	3	9	8^2	7			12			11	10^3	13	6^1	14	5		2										23
1	5^3	3	4	9^1	6	8		14	11		12	7^2	10		13				2										24
1		3	4		7	8^2		12	11	14	9		10^3	6^1		13	2		5										25
1		3		9	7^3				10^2	8	14	13	12		6	11^1	5		2	4									26
1			4	14		5		12	10^1	9^3	11				7	13	2		3	6		8^2							27
1			3	13		7^2		14	11	5	9					10^3	2		4	6		8^1	12						28
1		3	4					13	12	10	9					11^3	5^2		7	2	14			6	8^1				29
1		3	4			8	6^2	12	13		9					11	5							7		2	10^1		30
1		4	5	6		8^3	12	13		11^1	10					14	2		9						7^2	3			31
1		3	4	8		6^1	10	12		11	9^2					14	5^3		7					13		2			32
1		3	4	8		7	11		13	10^3	9					14					12			6^2	5^1	2			33
1		3	4	9		14	6		13	5	7				12				2^2						10^1	8	11^3		34
1		3	4	5			7^1	6	12	11		13			9				8	14						2^3	10^2		35
1		3	4	5			7^1	6^2	12	11					9				8					14	13	2	10^3		36
1		3	4	5			7^2	10	11^1	6	12				9				8						13	2			37
1		3	4	5			9	10^2	11^1	8	13				7				6							2	12		38
1		3		5			6	14	10	11		13			8					7^1					9^3	2	12	4^2	39
1		3	4	5		7^3	14		10^2	6^1	9	13			8									12		2	11		40
1		3	4	5				11	12	6	10^3	13			7				9^2					8^1		2	14		41
1			4	5^1			14	11^3	10	6					8	12	2		7			13	9^2			3			42
1			3					11	12	5^1		6^2			8	10			4			9^3	7	14	13	2			43
1			4	6^2				11	10	8	13	12			7	14	2^1		5				9^3			3			44
1			4			12		10	11	5	13	8^1			6				3			9^2			7	2			45
1			4			6^1		10^2	11	5					7	13			3	9			8^3	14	12	2			46

FA Cup

First Round	Lincoln C	(a)	2-3

Carabao Cup

First Round	Wycombe W	(a)	1-1

Checkatrade Trophy

Group F (S)	Wycombe W	(h)	0-1
(Wycombe W won 7-6 on penalties)			
Group F (S)	Oxford U	(a)	2-1
Group F (S)	Fulham U21	(h)	2-0
Second Round (S)	Cambridge U	(a)	1-1
(Northampton T won 4-2 on penalties)			
Third Round	Bristol R	(h)	1-2

NORWICH CITY

FOUNDATION

Formed in 1902, largely through the initiative of two local schoolmasters who called a meeting at the Criterion Cafe, they were shocked by an FA Commission which in 1904 declared the club professional and ejected them from the FA Amateur Cup. However, this only served to strengthen their determination. New officials were appointed and a professional club established at a meeting in the Agricultural Hall in March 1905.

Carrow Road, Norwich, Norfolk NR1 1JE.

Telephone: (01603) 760 760.

Fax: (01603) 811 815.

Ticket Office: (01603) 721 902.

Website: www.canaries.co.uk

Email: via website.

Ground Capacity: 27,244.

Record Attendance: 25,037 v Sheffield W, FA Cup 5th rd, 16 February 1935 (at The Nest); 43,984 v Leicester C, FA Cup 6th rd, 30 March 1963 (at Carrow Road).

Pitch Measurements: 105m × 68m (115yd × 74.5yd).

Joint Majority Shareholders: Delia Smith, Michael Wynn-Jones.

Chief Operating Officer: Ben Kensell.

Head Coach: Daniel Farke.

Assistant Head Coach: Edmund Riemer.

Colours: Yellow shirts with green trim, green shorts with yellow trim, yellow socks with green trim.

Year Formed: 1902.

Turned Professional: 1905.

Club Nickname: 'The Canaries'.

Grounds: 1902, Newmarket Road; 1908, The Nest, Rosary Road; 1935, Carrow Road.

First Football League Game: 28 August 1920, Division 3, v Plymouth Arg (a) D 1–1 – Skermer; Gray, Gadsden; Wilkinson, Addy, Martin; Laxton, Kidger, Parker, Whitham (1), Dobson.

Record League Victory: 10–2 v Coventry C, Division 3 (S), 15 March 1930 – Jarvie; Hannah, Graham; Brown, O'Brien, Lochhead (1); Porter (1), Anderson, Hunt (5), Scott (2), Slicer (1).

Record Cup Victory: 8–0 v Sutton U, FA Cup 4th rd, 28 January 1989 – Gunn; Culverhouse, Bowen, Butterworth, Linighan, Townsend (Crook), Gordon, Fleck (3), Allen (4), Phelan, Putney (1).

Record Defeat: 2–10 v Swindon T, Southern League, 5 September 1908.

Most League Points (2 for a win): 64, Division 3 (S), 1950–51.

Most League Points (3 for a win): 95, FL 1, 2009–10.

Most League Goals: 99, Division 3 (S), 1952–53.

HONOURS

League Champions: FL C – 2018–19; First Division – 2003–04; Division 2 – 1971–72, 1985–86; FL 1 – 2009–10; Division 3S – 1933–34.
Runners-up: FL C – 2010–11; Division 3 – 1959–60; Division 3S – 1950–51.

FA Cup: semi-final – 1959, 1989, 1992.

League Cup Winners: 1962, 1985.
Runners-up: 1973, 1975.

European Competitions
UEFA Cup: 1993–94.

THE SUN FACT FILE

Norwich City have worn predominantly yellow and green shirts for almost all of their time in senior football with the exception of a few seasons in the 1920s. The Canaries changed to white shirts with navy blue shorts in 1923 and then for the 1925–26 added yellow and green chevrons at the front and back before switching to yellow and green halves.

Highest League Scorer in Season: Ralph Hunt, 31, Division 3 (S), 1955–56.

Most League Goals in Total Aggregate: Johnny Gavin, 122, 1945–54, 1955–58.

Most League Goals in One Match: 5, Tommy Hunt v Coventry C, Division 3 (S), 15 March 1930; 5, Roy Hollis v Walsall, Division 3 (S), 29 December 1951.

Most Capped Player: Wes Hoolahan, 42 (43), Republic of Ireland.

Most League Appearances: Ron Ashman, 592, 1947–64.

Youngest League Player: Ryan Jarvis, 16 years 282 days v Walsall, 19 April 2003.

Record Transfer Fee Received: £22,000,000 (rising to £24,000,000) from Leicester C for James Maddison, June 2018.

Record Transfer Fee Paid: £8,500,000 to Sporting Lisbon for Ricky van Wolfswinkel, July 2013; £8,500,000 to Everton for Steven Naismith, January 2016.

Football League Record: 1920 Original Member of Division 3; 1921 Division 3 (S): 1934–39 Division 2; 1946–58 Division 3 (S); 1958–60 Division 3; 1960–72 Division 2; 1972–74 Division 1; 1974–75 Division 2; 1975–81 Division 1; 1981–82 Division 2; 1982–85 Division 1; 1985–86 Division 2; 1986–92 Division 1; 1992–95 Premier League; 1995–2004 Division 1; 2004–05 Premier League; 2005–09 FL C; 2009–10 FL 1; 2010–11 FL C; 2011–14 Premier League; 2014–15 FL C; 2015–16 Premier League; 2016–19 FL C; 2019– Premier League.

LATEST SEQUENCES

Longest Sequence of League Wins: 10, 23.11.1985 – 25.1.1986.

Longest Sequence of League Defeats: 7, 1.4.1995 – 6.5.1995.

Longest Sequence of League Draws: 7, 15.1.1994 – 26.2.1994.

Longest Sequence of Unbeaten League Matches: 20, 31.8.1950 – 30.12.1950.

Longest Sequence Without a League Win: 25, 22.9.1956 – 23.2.1957.

Successive Scoring Runs: 27 from 1.12.2018.

Successive Non-scoring Runs: 5 from 18.9.2007.

MANAGERS

John Bowman 1905–07
James McEwen 1907–08
Arthur Turner 1909–10
Bert Stansfield 1910–15
Major Frank Buckley 1919–20
Charles O'Hagan 1920–21
Albert Gosnell 1921–26
Bert Stansfield 1926
Cecil Potter 1926–29
James Kerr 1929–33
Tom Parker 1933–37
Bob Young 1937–39
Jimmy Jewell 1939
Bob Young 1939–45
Duggie Lochhead 1945–46
Cyril Spiers 1946–47
Duggie Lochhead 1947–50
Norman Low 1950–55
Tom Parker 1955–57
Archie Macaulay 1957–61
Willie Reid 1961–62
George Swindin 1962
Ron Ashman 1962–66
Lol Morgan 1966–69
Ron Saunders 1969–73
John Bond 1973–80
Ken Brown 1980–87
Dave Stringer 1987–92
Mike Walker 1992–94
John Deehan 1994–95
Martin O'Neill 1995
Gary Megson 1995–96
Mike Walker 1996–98
Bruce Rioch 1998–2000
Bryan Hamilton 2000
Nigel Worthington 2000–06
Peter Grant 2006–07
Glenn Roeder 2007–09
Bryan Gunn 2009
Paul Lambert 2009–12
Chris Hughton 2012–14
Neil Adams 2014–15
Alex Neil 2015–17
Daniel Farke May 2017–

TEN YEAR LEAGUE RECORD

		P	W	D	L	F	A	Pts	Pos
2009-10	FL 1	46	29	8	9	89	47	95	1
2010-11	FL C	46	23	15	8	83	58	84	2
2011-12	PR Lge	38	12	11	15	52	66	47	12
2012-13	PR Lge	38	10	14	14	41	58	44	11
2013-14	PR Lge	38	8	9	21	28	62	33	18
2014-15	FL C	46	25	11	10	88	48	86	3
2015-16	PR Lge	38	9	7	22	39	67	34	19
2016-17	FL C	46	20	10	16	85	69	70	8
2017-18	FL C	46	15	15	16	49	60	60	14
2018-19	FL C	46	27	13	6	93	57	94	1

DID YOU KNOW ?

Norwich City fans established one of the very first supporters' clubs in the country. The club was formed during 1902–03, the first season of City's existence, and by May 1904 membership had risen from 41 to well over 200.

NORWICH CITY – SKY BET CHAMPIONSHIP 2018–19 LEAGUE RECORD

Match No.	*Date*	*Venue*	*Opponents*	*Result*		*H/T Score*	*Lg Pos.*	*Goalscorers*	*Attendance*
1	Aug 4	A	Birmingham C	D	2-2	0-0	7	Hernandez 2 [83, 90]	22,677
2	11	H	WBA	L	3-4	1-1	17	Rhodes [24], Pukki [70], Hanley [82]	25,144
3	18	A	Sheffield U	L	1-2	1-1	21	Rhodes [26]	23,850
4	22	H	Preston NE	W	2-0	0-0	15	Pukki [80], Tettey [87]	24,936
5	25	H	Leeds U	L	0-3	0-2	17		25,944
6	Sept 2	A	Ipswich T	D	1-1	0-0	17	Leitner [71]	25,690
7	15	H	Middlesbrough	W	1-0	0-0	16	Pukki [58]	24,642
8	19	A	Reading	W	2-1	1-0	12	Pukki [14], Vrancic [73]	12,822
9	22	A	QPR	W	1-0	0-0	11	Pukki [71]	12,843
10	29	H	Wigan Ath	W	1-0	0-0	5	Vrancic (pen) [86]	25,034
11	Oct 3	A	Derby Co	D	1-1	0-0	5	Klose [69]	24,236
12	6	H	Stoke C	L	0-1	0-1	8		24,992
13	20	A	Nottingham F	W	2-1	0-1	6	Klose 2 [60, 84]	29,427
14	23	H	Aston Villa	W	2-1	0-1	4	Rhodes 2 [54, 73]	24,977
15	27	H	Brentford	W	1-0	1-0	4	Emi [34]	25,443
16	Nov 3	A	Sheffield W	W	4-0	0-0	1	Pukki 2 [51, 62], Emi [56], Srbeny [80]	23,425
17	10	H	Millwall	W	4-3	0-1	1	Pukki 2 [49, 90], Leitner [79], Rhodes [90]	26,289
18	24	A	Swansea C	W	4-1	3-1	1	van der Hoorn (og) [16], Emi [24], Stiepermann [37], Pukki [60]	18,780
19	27	A	Hull C	D	0-0	0-0	1		11,420
20	Dec 1	H	Rotherham U	W	3-1	0-1	1	Cantwell [55], Aarons [71], Pukki [84]	25,858
21	8	H	Bolton W	W	3-2	1-0	1	Vrancic [39], Stiepermann [59], Pukki [90]	25,811
22	15	A	Bristol C	D	2-2	1-1	2	Stiepermann [39], Aarons [78]	19,851
23	22	A	Blackburn R	W	1-0	0-0	1	Pukki [86]	14,202
24	26	H	Nottingham F	D	3-3	0-1	2	Vrancic [77], Hernandez 2 [90, 90]	26,933
25	29	H	Derby Co	L	3-4	2-2	2	Godfrey [25], Pukki 2 [31, 81]	26,866
26	Jan 1	A	Brentford	D	1-1	0-1	2	Klose [83]	9524
27	12	A	WBA	D	1-1	0-1	3	Rhodes [83]	26,544
28	18	H	Birmingham C	W	3-1	3-1	2	Pukki [13], Vrancic [22], Trybull [25]	25,932
29	26	H	Sheffield U	D	2-2	1-1	2	Hernandez [11], Pukki [56]	26,844
30	Feb 2	A	Leeds U	W	3-1	2-0	1	Vrancic 2 [5, 78], Pukki [35]	36,524
31	10	H	Ipswich T	W	3-0	1-0	1	Hernandez [2], Pukki 2 [65, 80]	27,040
32	13	A	Preston NE	L	1-3	0-2	2	Pukki [90]	11,280
33	16	A	Bolton W	W	4-0	3-0	1	Pukki 2 [8, 56], Stiepermann [25], Emi [34]	14,006
34	23	H	Bristol C	W	3-2	1-2	1	McLean 2 [36, 66], Godfrey [55]	26,338
35	Mar 2	A	Millwall	W	3-1	1-1	1	Stiepermann [16], Zimmermann [69], Pukki [79]	16,748
36	8	H	Swansea C	W	1-0	0-0	1	Emi [54]	26,360
37	13	H	Hull C	W	3-2	2-1	1	Stiepermann [11], Emi 2 [14, 60]	25,879
38	16	A	Rotherham U	W	2-1	1-0	1	McLean [45], Godfrey [57]	11,026
39	30	A	Middlesbrough	W	1-0	0-0	1	Hernandez [54]	23,795
40	Apr 6	H	QPR	W	4-0	3-0	1	Emi [6], Stiepermann [12], Pukki 2 [38, 85]	26,796
41	10	H	Reading	D	2-2	0-1	1	Godfrey [86], Zimmermann [88]	26,662
42	14	A	Wigan Ath	D	1-1	0-1	1	Pukki [81]	15,655
43	19	H	Sheffield W	D	2-2	1-1	1	Stiepermann [19], Vrancic [90]	26,744
44	22	A	Stoke C	D	2-2	1-0	1	Hernandez [24], Pukki [66]	25,487
45	27	H	Blackburn R	W	2-1	2-1	1	Stiepermann [13], Vrancic [21]	26,848
46	May 5	A	Aston Villa	W	2-1	1-1	1	Pukki [7], Vrancic [86]	41,696

Final League Position: 1

GOALSCORERS

League (93): Pukki 29, Vrancic 10 (1 pen), Stiepermann 9, Emi 8, Hernandez 8, Rhodes 6, Godfrey 4, Klose 4, McLean 3, Aarons 2, Leitner 2, Zimmermann 2, Cantwell 1, Hanley 1, Srbeny 1, Tettey 1, Trybull 1, own goal 1.
FA Cup (0).
Carabao Cup (11): Rhodes 3, Srbeny 2, Aarons 1, Hernandez 1, Pukki 1, Stiepermann 1, Trybull 1, Zimmermann 1.

Krul T 46	Marshall B 4	Hanley G 6 + 3	Klose T 23 + 8	Husband J 1	Tettey A 26 + 4	Pukki T 43	Stiepermann M 39 + 4	Trybull T 22 + 9	Hernandez O 34 + 6	Rhodes J 9 + 27	Leitner M 19 + 10	McLean K 15 + 5	Srbeny D — + 15	Ivo Pinto D 3	Thompson L 1 + 5	Lewis J 42	Godfrey B 26 + 5	Emi B 35 + 3	Zimmermann C 39 + 1	Aarcns M 41	Vrancic M 14 + 22	Cantwell T 18 + 6	Passlack F — + 1	Match No.
1	2	3	4	5^{1}	6	7	8^{3}	9^{2}	10	11	12	13	14											1
1	2	3	4		7	9	14		11	10	6^{2}	8^{1}	12	5^{3}	13									2
1	2	3	4		6^{3}	8^{1}	12	7	10	11	9^{2}		13			5	14							3
1	8^{2}	3	4		6	9		14	10	11	7^{3}			2^{1}		5		12	13					4
1		3	4			8	14	7	10	11^{1}	9^{3}		13	2	6^{2}	5		12						5
1		3	4^{2}		6	9			10	11^{3}	7		14		13	5	12	8^{1}		2				6
1			4		6	11^{1}	9^{3}	13	10	14	7					5		8^{2}	3	2	12			7
1			4		6	11	9^{1}	13		14	7^{2}					5		8^{3}	3	2	12	10		8
1			4		7	11^{1}	9	14		13	6^{3}					5		8^{2}	3	2	12	10		9
1			3		7	11	9			14	6				13	5		10^{3}	4	2^{2}	12	8^{1}		10
1			4		6	11	9^{1}			14	7				13	5		8^{2}	3	2	12	10^{3}		11
1			4		6^{2}	11	9^{3}		13	12	7					5		8^{1}	3	2	14	10		12
1			4		6		9^{2}	14	8^{3}	11	7					5		12	3	2	13	10^{1}		13
1			4				9^{1}	6		11	7				13^{3}	5	14	8^{2}	3	2	12	10		14
1			4		7		9	14	13	11^{1}	6^{3}		12			5		8^{2}	3	2		10		15
1			4		6	11^{3}	13		10		7^{2}		12			5	14	8^{1}	3	2	9			16
1			4		6	11	9^{2}		10	12	7					5^{1}		8	3	2	13			17
1			4		6	11	9		10^{2}	14	7^{3}					5		8^{1}	3	2	13	12		18
1			4		6	11	9^{2}	7^{3}	10^{1}				14			5		8	3	2	12	13		19
1			4		6	11^{2}	9	13		12						5^{3}	14	8	3	2	7^{1}	10		20
1					7	11^{3}	9^{1}		12	13			14			5	4	8^{2}	3	2	6	10		21
1		12			6^{3}	11	9		13	14						5	4	8	3^{2}	2	7	10^{1}		22
1					6	11^{2}	9		12	14	7^{1}					5	4	8^{3}	3	2	13	10		23
1			4		6	11	9		12	13			14			5^{3}	3	8^{1}		2	7	10^{2}		24
1			4		7	11^{1}	9^{2}	12	10	13			14				5		3	2	6^{3}	8		25
1			4		6^{1}	11	9^{2}	12	10	13			14				5		3	2	7	8^{3}		26
1					6	11			10	14		13	12			5^{1}	4	8^{2}	3	2	7	9^{3}		27
1						11^{3}	9	6	10^{2}	13		14				5	4	8^{1}	3	2	7	12		28
1						11	9^{1}	7	10	12						5	4	8^{2}	3	2	6	13		29
1					12	11^{2}	9	7^{1}	10	14		13				5	4	8^{3}	3	2	6			30
1					12	11^{2}	9^{3}	7	10	14						5	4	8	3	2	6^{1}	13		31
1					6	11	9^{1}	7^{3}	10^{2}	12		13				5	4	8	3	2			14	32
1		14				11^{3}	9^{1}	6	10		12	7	13			5^{2}	4	8	3	2				33
1			14			11^{3}	9	6	10^{1}	12		7				5	4	8^{2}	3	2	13			34
1			14			11	9	6	10^{1}		12	7				5^{2}	4	8^{3}	3	2	13			35
1			13			11^{3}	9^{1}	7	10		14	6				5	4	8^{2}	3	2	12			36
1			14			11	9^{3}	6	10^{2}		12	7				5	4	8^{1}	3	2	13			37
1			12			11^{3}	9	6	10^{1}	13		7				5	4	8^{2}	3	2	14			38
1			13			11	9^{1}	6	10^{2}			7				5	4	8	3	2	12			39
1						11^{3}	9^{1}	6^{2}	10	14	13	7				5	4	8	3	2		12		40
1			14			11^{1}	9	7	10	12		6				5^{3}	4		3	2	13	8^{2}		41
1						11	9	6^{3}	10	12	13	7				5^{2}	4		3	2	14	8^{1}		42
1			14			11	9	6^{2}	10^{1}		8	7	13			5^{3}	4		3	2	12			43
1						11	9	7^{1}	10^{2}		13	6				5	4	8	3	2	12			44
1					14	11^{1}	9^{3}		10^{2}	12	13	6				5	4	8	3	2	7			45
1		14			12	11	9^{1}		10^{3}		13	7^{2}				5	4	8	3	2	6			46

FA Cup

Third Round	Portsmouth	(h)	0-1

Carabao Cup

First Round	Stevenage	(h)	3-1
Second Round	Cardiff C	(a)	3-1
Third Round	Wycombe W	(a)	4-3
Fourth Round	Bournemouth	(a)	1-2

NOTTINGHAM FOREST

FOUNDATION

One of the oldest football clubs in the world, Nottingham Forest was formed at a meeting in the Clinton Arms in 1865. Known originally as the Forest Football Club, the game which first drew the founders together was 'shinney', a form of hockey. When they determined to change to football in 1865, one of their first moves was to buy a set of red caps to wear on the field.

The City Ground, Pavilion Road, Nottingham NG2 5FJ.

Telephone: (0115) 982 4444.

Ticket Office: (0115) 982 4388.

Website: www.nottinghamforest.co.uk

Email: enquiries@nottinghamforest.co.uk

Ground Capacity: 30,445.

Record Attendance: 49,946 v Manchester U, Division 1, 28 October 1967.

Pitch Measurements: 102.5m × 67.5m (112yd × 74yd).

Chairman: Nicholas Randall QC.

Chief Executive: Ioannis Vrentzos.

Manager: Sabri Lamouchi.

Assistant Manager: TBC.

Colours: Red shirts with dark red stripes and white trim, white shorts with red trim, red socks with white trim.

Year Formed: 1865.

Turned Professional: 1889.

Previous Name: Forest Football Club.

Club Nickname: 'The Reds'.

Grounds: 1865, Forest Racecourse; 1879, The Meadows; 1880, Trent Bridge Cricket Ground; 1882, Parkside, Lenton; 1885, Gregory, Lenton; 1890, Town Ground; 1898, City Ground.

First Football League Game: 3 September 1892, Division 1, v Everton (a) D 2–2 – Brown; Earp, Scott; Hamilton, Albert Smith, McCracken; McCallum, 'Tich' Smith, Higgins (2), Pike, McInnes.

Record League Victory: 12–0 v Leicester Fosse, Division 1, 12 April 1909 – Iremonger; Dudley, Maltby; Hughes (1), Needham, Armstrong; Hooper (3), Marrison, West (3), Morris (2), Spouncer (3 incl. 1p).

Record Cup Victory: 14–0 v Clapton (away), FA Cup 1st rd, 17 January 1891 – Brown; Earp, Scott; Albert Smith, Russell, Jeacock; McCallum (2), 'Tich' Smith (1), Higgins (5), Lindley (4), Shaw (2).

Record Defeat: 1–9 v Blackburn R, Division 2, 10 April 1937.

Most League Points (2 for a win): 70, Division 3 (S), 1950–51.

Most League Points (3 for a win): 94, Division 1, 1997–98.

Most League Goals: 110, Division 3 (S), 1950–51.

Highest League Scorer in Season: Wally Ardron, 36, Division 3 (S), 1950–51.

HONOURS

League Champions: Division 1 – 1977–78; First Division – 1997–98; Division 2 – 1906–07, 1921–22; Division 3S – 1950–51.
Runners-up: Division 1 – 1966–67, 1978–79; First Division – 1993–94; Division 2 – 1956–57; FL 1 – 2007–08.

FA Cup Winners: 1898, 1959.
Runners-up: 1991.

League Cup Winners: 1978, 1979, 1989, 1990.
Runners-up: 1980, 1992.

Anglo-Scottish Cup Winners: 1977.

Full Members' Cup Winners: 1989, 1992.

European Competitions

European Cup: 1978–79 *(winners)*, 1979–80 *(winners)*, 1980–81.

Fairs Cup: 1961–62, 1967–68.

UEFA Cup: 1983–84 *(sf)*, 1984–85, 1995–96 *(qf)*.

Super Cup: 1979 *(winners)*, 1980.

World Club Championship: 1980.

THE SUN FACT FILE

Nottingham Forest gained an apparently unremarkable 3-0 win away to Chesterfield Town in a wartime regional league match on 26 October 1916. However, despite their resounding victory the Forest players failed to find the net during the game, all three goals being attributed to their opponents.

Most League Goals in Total Aggregate: Grenville Morris, 199, 1898–1913.

Most League Goals in One Match: 4, Enoch West v Sunderland, Division 1, 9 November 1907; 4, Tommy Gibson v Burnley, Division 2, 25 January 1913; 4, Tom Peacock v Port Vale, Division 2, 23 December 1933; 4, Tom Peacock v Barnsley, Division 2, 9 November 1935; 4, Tom Peacock v Port Vale, Division 2, 23 November 1935; 4, Tom Peacock v Doncaster R, Division 2, 26 December 1935; 4, Tommy Capel v Gillingham, Division 3 (S), 18 November 1950; 4, Wally Ardron v Hull C, Division 2, 26 December 1952; 4, Tommy Wilson v Barnsley, Division 2, 9 February 1957; 4, Peter Withe v Ipswich T, Division 1, 4 October 1977; 4, Marlon Harewood v Stoke C, Division 1, 22 February 2003; Gareth McCleary v Leeds U, FL C, 20 March 2012.

Most Capped Player: Stuart Pearce, 76 (78), England.

Most League Appearances: Bob McKinlay, 614, 1951–70.

Youngest League Player: Craig Westcarr, 16 years 257 days v Burnley, 13 October 2001.

Record Transfer Fee Received: £15,000,000 from Middlesbrough for Britt Assombalonga, July 2017.

Record Transfer Fee Paid: £13,200,000 to Benfica for João Carvalho, June 2018.

Football League Record: 1892 Elected to Division 1; 1906–07 Division 2; 1907–11 Division 1; 1911–22 Division 2; 1922–25 Division 1; 1925–49 Division 2; 1949–51 Division 3 (S); 1951–57 Division 2; 1957–72 Division 1; 1972–77 Division 2; 1977–92 Division 1; 1992–93 Premier League; 1993–94 Division 1; 1994–97 Premier League; 1997–98 Division 1; 1998–99 Premier League; 1999–2004 Division 1; 2004–05 FL C; 2005–08 FL 1; 2008– FL C.

LATEST SEQUENCES

Longest Sequence of League Wins: 7, 9.5.1979 – 1.9.1979.

Longest Sequence of League Defeats: 14, 21.3.1913 – 27.9.1913.

Longest Sequence of League Draws: 7, 29.4.1978 – 2.9.1978.

Longest Sequence of Unbeaten League Matches: 42, 26.11.1977 – 25.11.1978.

Longest Sequence Without a League Win: 19, 8.9.1998 – 16.1.1999.

Successive Scoring Runs: 22 from 28.3.1931.

Successive Non-scoring Runs: 7 from 26.11.2011.

MANAGERS

Harry Radford 1889–97 *(Secretary-Manager)*
Harry Haslam 1897–1909 *(Secretary-Manager)*
Fred Earp 1909–12
Bob Masters 1912–25
John Baynes 1925–29
Stan Hardy 1930–31
Noel Watson 1931–36
Harold Wightman 1936–39
Billy Walker 1939–60
Andy Beattie 1960–63
Johnny Carey 1963–68
Matt Gillies 1969–72
Dave Mackay 1972
Allan Brown 1973–75
Brian Clough 1975–93
Frank Clark 1993–96
Stuart Pearce 1996–97
Dave Bassett 1997–99 *(previously General Manager)*
Ron Atkinson 1999
David Platt 1999–2001
Paul Hart 2001–04
Joe Kinnear 2004
Gary Megson 2005–06
Colin Calderwood 2006–08
Billy Davies 2009–11
Steve McClaren 2011
Steve Cotterill 2011–12
Sean O'Driscoll 2012
Alex McLeish 2012–13
Billy Davies 2013–14
Stuart Pearce 2014–15
Dougie Freedman 2015–16
Philippe Montanier 2016–17
Mark Warburton 2017
Aitor Karanka 2018–19
Martin O'Neill 2019
Sabri Lamouchi June 2019–

TEN YEAR LEAGUE RECORD

		P	W	D	L	F	A	Pts	Pos
2009-10	FL C	46	22	13	11	65	40	79	3
2010-11	FL C	46	20	15	11	69	50	75	6
2011-12	FL C	46	14	8	24	48	63	50	19
2012-13	FL C	46	17	16	13	63	59	67	8
2013-14	FL C	46	16	17	13	67	64	65	11
2014-15	FL C	46	15	14	17	71	69	59	14
2015-16	FL C	46	13	16	17	43	47	55	16
2016-17	FL C	46	14	9	23	62	72	51	21
2017-18	FL C	46	15	8	23	51	65	53	17
2018-19	FL C	46	17	15	14	61	54	66	9

DID YOU KNOW ?

It was not until the 1976–77 season that Nottingham Forest introduced an official 'Player of the Year' award voted for by the fans. First winner was 21-year-old Tony Woodcock, with Martin O'Neill in second place and John Robertson third.

NOTTINGHAM FOREST – SKY BET CHAMPIONSHIP 2018–19 LEAGUE RECORD

Match No.	Date	Venue	Opponents	Result		H/T Score	Lg Pos.	Goalscorers	Attendance
1	Aug 4	A	Bristol C	D	1-1	0-1	13	Murphy [46]	22,395
2	7	H	WBA	D	1-1	0-0	10	Guedioura [59]	27,850
3	11	H	Reading	W	1-0	0-0	5	Soudani [68]	27,948
4	18	A	Wigan Ath	D	2-2	1-2	7	Cash [10], Soudani [90]	11,543
5	25	H	Birmingham C	D	2-2	0-1	13	Lolley [75], Murphy [87]	26,799
6	Sept 1	A	Brentford	L	1-2	0-1	14	Cash [62]	10,186
7	15	A	Swansea C	D	0-0	0-0	15		19,522
8	19	H	Sheffield W	W	2-1	1-0	11	Grabban [41], Joao Carvalho [63]	26,252
9	22	H	Rotherham U	W	1-0	0-0	9	Grabban (pen) [86]	27,479
10	29	A	Blackburn R	D	2-2	0-0	11	Grabban 2 (1 pen) [52, 80 (p)]	14,440
11	Oct 3	H	Millwall	D	2-2	1-0	11	Lolley [27], Joao Carvalho [70]	25,753
12	6	A	Middlesbrough	W	2-0	0-0	5	Lolley [49], Grabban [77]	24,299
13	20	H	Norwich C	L	1-2	1-0	9	Grabban [5]	29,427
14	24	A	Bolton W	W	3-0	1-0	7	Lolley [12], Grabban 2 (1 pen) [64, 83 (p)]	13,195
15	27	A	Leeds U	D	1-1	1-0	7	Robinson [11]	34,308
16	Nov 3	H	Sheffield U	W	1-0	0-0	6	Grabban [69]	28,757
17	10	H	Stoke C	D	0-0	0-0	7		28,556
18	24	A	Hull C	W	2-0	0-0	7	Grabban [61], Lolley [64]	13,364
19	28	A	Aston Villa	D	5-5	3-3	6	Grabban 2 [3, 82], Joao Carvalho [6], Cash [22], Lolley [51]	32,868
20	Dec 1	H	Ipswich T	W	2-0	2-0	5	Grabban 2 [9, 38]	27,873
21	8	H	Preston NE	L	0-1	0-0	7		27,777
22	17	A	Derby Co	D	0-0	0-0	7		31,160
23	22	H	QPR	L	0-1	0-1	7		28,177
24	26	A	Norwich C	D	3-3	1-0	10	Cash 2 [45, 74], Robinson [65]	26,933
25	29	A	Millwall	L	0-1	0-1	10		15,273
26	Jan 1	H	Leeds U	W	4-2	1-0	7	Colback 2 [5, 69], Murphy [72], Osborn [76]	29,530
27	12	A	Reading	L	0-2	0-1	9		15,034
28	19	H	Bristol C	L	0-1	0-0	12		28,922
29	26	H	Wigan Ath	W	3-1	1-1	9	Lolley [19], Cash [48], Guedioura [80]	28,848
30	Feb 2	A	Birmingham C	L	0-2	0-1	12		24,235
31	9	H	Brentford	W	2-1	1-0	9	Grabban [16], Wague [79]	27,829
32	12	A	WBA	D	2-2	1-0	9	Johansen (og) [6], Yates [65]	22,691
33	16	A	Preston NE	D	0-0	0-0	8		13,904
34	25	H	Derby Co	W	1-0	1-0	8	Benalouane [2]	29,421
35	Mar 2	A	Stoke C	L	0-2	0-1	9		26,736
36	9	H	Hull C	W	3-0	0-0	8	Joao Carvalho [72], Ansarifard [76], Lolley (pen) [82]	29,397
37	13	H	Aston Villa	L	1-3	1-2	10	Colback [3]	29,224
38	16	A	Ipswich T	D	1-1	1-1	11	Wague [31]	16,709
39	30	H	Swansea C	W	2-1	0-0	9	Murphy [80], Wague [87]	28,469
40	Apr 6	A	Rotherham U	L	1-2	1-1	9	Grabban [28]	11,012
41	9	A	Sheffield W	L	0-3	0-0	10		23,931
42	13	H	Blackburn R	L	1-2	0-1	11	Bennett (og) [52]	27,786
43	19	A	Sheffield U	L	0-2	0-0	13		28,403
44	22	H	Middlesbrough	W	3-0	1-0	11	Lolley 2 (1 pen) [39 (p), 85], Milosevic [64]	27,653
45	27	A	QPR	W	1-0	0-0	10	Ansarifard [55]	15,212
46	May 5	H	Bolton W	W	1-0	1-0	9	Lolley [28]	27,578

Final League Position: 9

GOALSCORERS

League (61): Grabban 16 (3 pens), Lolley 11 (2 pens), Cash 6, Joao Carvalho 4, Murphy 4, Colback 3, Wague 3, Ansarifard 2, Guedioura 2, Robinson 2, Soudani 2, Benalouane 1, Milosevic 1, Osborn 1, Yates 1, own goals 2.
FA Cup (0).
Carabao Cup (9): Cash 2, Murphy 2, Appiah 1, Gil Dias 1, Grabban 1, Lolley 1, Osborn 1.

Pantilimon C 44	Darikwa T 28	Dawson M 8 + 2	Fox D 18	Osborn B 29 + 10	Watson B 14 + 3	Guedioura A 18 + 9	Gil Dias B 10 + 11	Joao Carvalho A 28 + 10	Goncalves D 1 + 6	Murphy D 17 + 11	Grabban L 29 + 10	Lolley J 42 + 4	Tobias Figueiredo P 11 + 2	Colback J 38	Soudani E 1 + 5	Cash M 27 + 9	Robinson J 36 + 2	Byram S 6	Hefele M 13 + 2	Janko S 13 + 2	Bridcutt L — + 1	Yacob C 11 + 5	Ansarifard K 3 + 9	Appiah A 2 + 4	Yates R 15 + 1	Benalouane Y 14	Milosevic A 11 + 1	Leo Bonatini L 2 + 3	Wague M 9 + 2	Pele J 6 + 3	Steele L 2	*Match No.*
1	2	3^{2}	4	5	6	7	8^{3}	9	10	11^{1}	12	13	14																			1
1	2		4	5		6	8^{1}	9^{2}	12		11	10	3	7	13																	2
1	2		4	5		6	8^{1}	9^{2}			11	10^{3}	3	7	13	12	14															3
1	2		4	5	12	6^{2}		9^{1}			11	10^{3}	3	7	13	8	14															4
1			4	13	6^{2}		10	12		11		14	3	7	9^{3}	8	5	2^{1}														5
1	2		4	13	6		8^{1}	9		11^{2}	14	10^{3}		7		12	5		3													6
1			4	10	14	6^{1}	12	13			11	9^{3}		7		8^{2}	5		3	2												7
1			4	10	13	6	12	9^{1}			11	14		7^{2}		8^{3}	5		3	2												8
1			4	10	7	6^{3}	8^{1}	9^{2}			11	12				13	5		3	2	14											9
1			4	13		6	12	9^{2}		14	11^{1}	10		7		8^{3}	5		3	2												10
1		14	4	10^{3}		6	13	9^{1}			11	8^{2}		7		12	5		3	2												11
1	2	3^{1}	4	14	7		8	9^{3}		11^{2}	13	10	12	6			5■															12
1	2		4	5	6		8^{3}	9^{2}	13		11	10^{1}		7	14	12			3													13
1	2	4		14		7	8^{3}	9^{1}			11	10^{2}	3	6	13	12	5															14
1	2	12	4^{1}	13		6	14	9			11	10^{2}	3	7		8^{3}	5															15
1	2	3				7	12	9			11^{1}	10	4			8^{2}	5					6	13									16
1	2	3				6^{2}	13	9^{1}			11	10	4	7		8	5					12										17
1	2	3		12				9			11^{2}	10	4	6		8^{1}	5					7	13									18
1	2	3					13	9^{2}			11^{1}	8	4■	6		10^{3}	5		12			7	14									19
1	2	3^{3}		12		6	8^{2}	9			11^{1}	10		7		14	5		4				13									20
1	2			5			12	9		13	11	10		7^{1}		8^{2}	4		3			6										21
1	2			10				9		12	11^{2}	8^{1}		7		13	4		3	5		6										22
1	2			10^{2}		6		9		12	11	8^{1}	3^{3}	7			4		14	5			13									23
1	2		4				14	9		13	11^{2}	8		6		10^{3}	5^{1}		3	12		7										24
1	2		4			12		9^{2}		11	14	8		7		10^{3}	5		3	13		6^{1}										25
1	2		4	13		12		9		11^{2}		10^{3}		7		8	5		3^{1}			6		14								26
1	2■		4■	10		6^{2}			13	11^{1}	12	9^{3}		7		8	5					3			14							27
1				5		12	13			10	11	6		8		9^{1}	4			2		7^{2}				3						28
1				5	7	6^{2}				10^{1}	12	11		8		9	4			2		13				3						29
1				9	6	8^{3}		14		11^{1}	13	10				7	5			2						3■	4^{2}	12				30
1				5	6				12		11^{1}	10				8^{2}	4			2			14		7		3	9^{3}	13			31
1				10	6					13	11^{2}	8		7			5			2		12			9^{1}	4	3					32
1	2			8				12		10^{1}	11	9		7			5								6	4	3					33
1	2			10^{1}	6^{3}	12				11^{2}		7		9			5								8	4	3	13	14			34
1	2			10	6^{3}	13		12		11		7		9			5^{2}								8^{1}	4	3	14				35
1	2			5				13	14	11^{3}		9^{2}		8									12		7	4	3	10^{1}		6		36
1	2			5		13		9	14	12		10		8									11^{1}		6^{3}	4	3			7^{2}		37
1	2			10^{2}				13		11		9		8		12	5						14		6^{3}	4			3	7^{1}		38
1	2			5	7^{1}			13		14	10^{3}	11		8		9									6^{2}	4			3	12		39
1				5^{3}	7^{1}			14		11	10	9		8		6				2^{2}				13		4			3	12		40
										13	11^{3}	9		7^{2}		8	5	2					14	10^{1}	6	4			3	12	1	41
1				14				13		12	11^{3}	9		5		8	4	2						10^{2}	6^{1}				3	7		42
1										11^{3}	13	6		5		10		2				8^{2}		14	7	3■	12		4	9^{1}		43
1				8		14		10^{2}			12	9				5	4					13	11^{3}		6		3		2	7^{1}		44
1				8		14		10^{1}			12	9				7^{2}	4	5				13	11^{3}		6		3		2			45
				8		13		11^{1}		12	10^{3}	9^{2}				7	4	5						14	6		3		2		1	46

FA Cup

Third Round	Chelsea	(a)	0-2

Carabao Cup

First Round	Bury	(h)	1-1
(Nottingham F won 10-9 on penalties)			
Second Round	Newcastle U	(h)	3-1
Third Round	Stoke C	(h)	3-2
Fourth Round	Burton Alb	(a)	2-3

NOTTS COUNTY

FOUNDATION

According to the official history of Notts County 'the true date of Notts' foundation has to be the meeting at the George Hotel on 7 December 1864'. However, there is documented evidence of continuous play from 1862, when club members played organised matches amongst themselves in The Park in Nottingham. They are the world's oldest professional football club.

Meadow Lane Stadium, Meadow Lane, Nottingham NG2 3HJ.

Telephone: (0115) 952 9000.

Fax: (0115) 955 3994.

Ticket Office: (0115) 955 7210.

Website: www.nottscountyfc.co.uk

Email: office@nottscountyfc.co.uk

Ground Capacity: 19,841.

Record Attendance: 47,310 v York C, FA Cup 6th rd, 12 March 1955.

Pitch Measurements: 100m × 66m (109.5yd × 72yd).

Chairman: Alan Hardy.

Manager: Neal Ardley.

Assistant Manager: Neil Cox.

HONOURS

League Champions: Division 2 – 1896–97, 1913–14, 1922–23; Division 3S – 1930–31, 1949–50; FL 2 – 2009–10; Third Division – 1997–98; Division 4 – 1970–71.
Runners-up: Division 2 – 1894–95, 1980–81; Division 3 – 1972–73; Division 3S – 1936–37; Division 4 – 1959–60.

FA Cup Winners: 1894.
Runners-up: 1891.

League Cup: 5th rd – 1964, 1973, 1976.

Anglo-Italian Cup Winners: 1995.
Runners-up: 1994.

Colours: Black and white striped shirts with yellow trim, black shorts with yellow trim, black socks with yellow trim.

Year Formed: 1862* (*see Foundation*).

Turned Professional: 1885.

Club Nickname: 'The Magpies'.

Grounds: 1862, The Park; 1864, The Meadows; 1877, Beeston Cricket Ground; 1880, Castle Ground; 1883, Trent Bridge; 1910, Meadow Lane.

First Football League Game: 15 September 1888, Football League, v Everton (a) L 1–2 – Holland; Guttridge, McLean; Brown, Warburton, Shelton; Hodder, Harker, Jardine, Albert Moore (1), Wardle.

Record League Victory: 11–1 v Newport Co, Division 3 (S), 15 January 1949 – Smith; Southwell, Purvis; Gannon, Baxter, Adamson; Houghton (1), Sewell (4), Lawton (4), Pimbley, Johnston (2).

Record Cup Victory: 15–0 v Rotherham T (at Trent Bridge), FA Cup 1st rd, 24 October 1885 – Sherwin; Snook, Henry Thomas Moore; Dobson (1), Emmett (1), Chapman; Gunn (1), Albert Moore (2), Jackson (3), Daft (2), Cursham (4), (1 og).

Record Defeat: 1–9 v Blackburn R, Division 1, 16 November 1889. 1–9 v Aston Villa, Division 1, 29 September 1888. 1–9 v Portsmouth, Division 2, 9 April 1927.

Most League Points (2 for a win): 69, Division 4, 1970–71.

Most League Points (3 for a win): 99, Division 3, 1997–98.

THE SUN FACT FILE

Notts County were the last of the 92 Football League clubs to use a substitute following the rule change for the 1965–66 season that allowed one injured player to be replaced. The club finally used a sub on 5 February 1966 when Dennis Shiels replaced Brian Bates in the Fourth Division home game against Lincoln City, which was County's 25th League game of the season. The Magpies used a substitute on only two further occasions in the season.

Most League Goals: 107, Division 4, 1959–60.

Highest League Scorer in Season: Tom Keetley, 39, Division 3 (S), 1930–31.

Most League Goals in Total Aggregate: Les Bradd, 125, 1967–78.

Most League Goals in One Match: 5, Robert Jardine v Burnley, Division 1, 27 October 1888; 5, Daniel Bruce v Port Vale, Division 2, 26 February 1895; 5, Bertie Mills v Barnsley, Division 2, 19 November 1927.

Most Capped Player: Kevin Wilson, 15 (42), Northern Ireland.

Most League Appearances: Albert Iremonger, 564, 1904–26.

Youngest League Player: Tony Bircumshaw, 16 years 54 days v Brentford, 3 April 1961.

Record Transfer Fee Received: £2,500,000 from Derby Co for Craig Short, September 1992.

Record Transfer Fee Paid: £800,000 to Manchester C for Kasper Schmeichel, July 2009.

Football League Record: 1888 Founder Member of the Football League; 1893–97 Division 2; 1897–1913 Division 1; 1913–14 Division 2; 1914–20 Division 1; 1920–23 Division 2; 1923–26 Division 1; 1926–30 Division 2; 1930–31 Division 3 (S); 1931–35 Division 2; 1935–50 Division 3 (S); 1950–58 Division 2; 1958–59 Division 3; 1959–60 Division 4; 1960–64 Division 3; 1964–71 Division 4; 1971–73 Division 3; 1973–81 Division 2; 1981–84 Division 1; 1984–85 Division 2; 1985–90 Division 3; 1990–91 Division 2; 1991–95 Division 1; 1995–97 Division 2; 1997–98 Division 3; 1998–2004 Division 2; 2004–10 FL 2; 2010–15 FL 1; 2015–19 FL 2; 2019– National League.

LATEST SEQUENCES

Longest Sequence of League Wins: 10, 3.12.1997 – 31.1.1998.

Longest Sequence of League Defeats: 10, 12.11.2016 – 7.1.2017.

Longest Sequence of League Draws: 6, 16.8.2008 – 20.9.2008.

Longest Sequence of Unbeaten League Matches: 19, 26.4.1930 – 6.12.1930.

Longest Sequence Without a League Win: 20, 3.12.1996 – 31.3.1997.

Successive Scoring Runs: 35 from 10.10.1959.

Successive Non-scoring Runs: 5 from 15.3.2011.

MANAGERS

Edwin Browne 1883–93; **Tom Featherstone** 1893; **Tom Harris** 1893–1913; **Albert Fisher** 1913–27; **Horace Henshall** 1927–34; **Charlie Jones** 1934; **David Pratt** 1935; **Percy Smith** 1935–36; **Jimmy McMullan** 1936–37; **Harry Parkes** 1938–39; **Tony Towers** 1939–42; **Frank Womack** 1942–43; **Major Frank Buckley** 1944–46; **Arthur Stollery** 1946–49; **Eric Houghton** 1949–53; **George Poyser** 1953–57; **Tommy Lawton** 1957–58; **Frank Hill** 1958–61; **Tim Coleman** 1961–63; **Eddie Lowe** 1963–65; **Tim Coleman** 1965–66; **Jack Burkitt** 1966–67; **Andy Beattie** *(General Manager)* 1967; **Billy Gray** 1967–68; **Jack Wheeler** (*Caretaker Manager*) 1968–69; **Jimmy Sirrel** 1969–75; **Ron Fenton** 1975–77; **Jimmy Sirrel** 1978–82 *(continued as General Manager to 1984)*; **Howard Wilkinson** 1982–83; **Larry Lloyd** 1983–84; **Richie Barker** 1984–85; **Jimmy Sirrel** 1985–87; **John Barnwell** 1987–88; **Neil Warnock** 1989–93; **Mick Walker** 1993–94; **Russell Slade** 1994–95; **Howard Kendall** 1995; **Colin Murphy** 1995–96 *(General Manager)*; **Steve Thompson** 1995–96; **Sam Allardyce** 1997–99; **Gary Brazil** 1999–2000; **Jocky Scott** 2000–01; **Gary Brazil** 2001–02; **Billy Dearden** 2002–04; **Gary Mills** 2004; **Ian Richardson** 2004–05; **Gudjon Thordarson** 2005–06; **Steve Thompson** 2006–07; **Ian McParland** 2007–09; **Hans Backe** 2009; **Sven-Göran Eriksson** 2009–10 *(Director of Football)*; **Steve Cotterill** 2010; **Craig Short** 2010; **Paul Ince** 2010–11; **Martin Allen** 2011–12; **Keith Curle** 2012–13; **Chris Kiwomya** 2013; **Shaun Derry** 2013–15; **Ricardo Moniz** 2015; **Jamie Fullarton** 2016; **Mark Cooper** 2016; **John Sheridan** 2016–17; **Kevin Nolan** 2017–18; **Harry Kewell** 2018; **Neal Ardley** November 2018–

TEN YEAR LEAGUE RECORD

		P	W	D	L	F	A	Pts	Pos
2009-10	FL 2	46	27	12	7	96	31	93	1
2010-11	FL 1	46	14	8	24	46	60	50	19
2011-12	FL 1	46	21	10	15	75	63	73	7
2012-13	FL 1	46	16	17	13	61	49	65	12
2013-14	FL 1	46	15	5	26	64	77	50	20
2014-15	FL 1	46	12	14	20	45	63	50	21
2015-16	FL 2	46	14	9	23	54	83	51	17
2016-17	FL 2	46	16	8	22	54	76	56	16
2017-18	FL 2	46	21	14	11	71	48	77	5
2018-19	FL 2	46	9	14	23	48	84	41	23

DID YOU KNOW ?

In December 1911 Notts County's Meadow Lane ground hosted a rugby league international between England and the Australasian touring team who were a combined Australia and New Zealand side. England won by five points to three in a game that attracted an attendance of just 3,000.

NOTTS COUNTY – SKY BET LEAGUE TWO 2018–19 LEAGUE RECORD

Match No.	*Date*	*Venue*	*Opponents*	*Result*		*H/T Score*	*Lg Pos.*	*Goalscorers*	*Atten-dance*
1	Aug 4	H	Colchester U	D	0-0	0-0	13		7136
2	11	A	Cambridge U	L	2-3	1-0	19	Boldewijn [29], Duffy [78]	4372
3	17	H	Yeovil T	L	0-4	0-2	21		7439
4	21	A	Newport Co	L	2-3	1-2	24	Hemmings [12], Dennis [87]	2935
5	25	A	Lincoln C	L	1-3	1-2	24	Kellett [19]	9119
6	Sept 1	H	Forest Green R	L	1-3	0-1	24	Stead [70]	6049
7	8	A	Exeter C	L	1-5	1-2	24	Boldewijn [43]	3916
8	15	H	Stevenage	D	3-3	2-2	24	Stead (pen) [22], Boldewijn [43], Hemmings [49]	6085
9	22	A	Northampton T	D	0-0	0-0	23		4935
10	29	H	Crewe Alex	W	2-1	1-1	22	Milsom [5], Hewitt [61]	6117
11	Oct 2	H	Crawley T	W	3-1	2-0	20	Hemmings [9], Stead [33], Thomas [87]	5098
12	6	A	Macclesfield T	W	1-0	0-0	17	Stead (pen) [82]	2381
13	20	A	Bury	L	0-4	0-2	21		4103
14	23	A	Milton Keynes D	L	1-2	1-0	22	Alessandra [23]	6501
15	27	H	Swindon T	L	1-2	1-0	22	Hemmings [40]	6114
16	Nov 3	A	Port Vale	D	2-2	1-1	22	Hemmings [22], Ward [87]	4236
17	6	H	Oldham Ath	D	0-0	0-0	22		4487
18	17	H	Cheltenham T	L	0-3	0-1	23		6109
19	24	A	Morecambe	D	1-1	0-0	23	Dennis [52]	1658
20	27	H	Carlisle U	D	1-1	0-0	23	Hewitt [63]	4119
21	Dec 8	A	Mansfield T	L	0-2	0-1	23		6604
22	15	H	Tranmere R	W	3-2	2-1	23	Stead 2 (1 pen) [33, 76 (p)], Hemmings [44]	6535
23	22	A	Grimsby T	L	0-4	0-2	23		4946
24	26	H	Macclesfield T	L	1-2	0-1	24	Hemmings [64]	6786
25	29	H	Bury	D	0-0	0-0	24		7014
26	Jan 1	A	Oldham Ath	L	0-2	0-1	24		4336
27	5	A	Colchester U	D	3-3	3-2	24	Stead [16], Jones [19], Dennis [32]	3181
28	12	H	Cambridge U	L	0-1	0-1	24		15,026
29	19	A	Yeovil T	L	0-2	0-1	24		2716
30	Feb 2	H	Lincoln C	D	1-1	1-1	24	Stead (pen) [2]	10,641
31	9	A	Forest Green R	W	2-1	0-0	24	O'Brien [57], Boldewijn [77]	2871
32	16	H	Mansfield T	W	1-0	1-0	24	Mackail-Smith [19]	12,660
33	19	H	Newport Co	L	1-4	1-3	24	Hemmings [10]	6253
34	23	A	Tranmere R	L	0-1	0-0	24		6559
35	Mar 2	H	Port Vale	D	0-0	0-0	24		7457
36	9	A	Cheltenham T	L	1-4	0-2	24	Hemmings (pen) [69]	3514
37	12	A	Carlisle U	W	3-1	1-0	23	Hemmings 2 (1 pen) [37, 66 (p)], Alessandra [90]	3514
38	16	H	Morecambe	D	0-0	0-0	24		5813
39	23	H	Exeter C	L	0-1	0-0	24		9505
40	30	A	Stevenage	W	3-0	3-0	23	O'Brien [1], Hemmings [21], Boldewijn [45]	2860
41	Apr 6	H	Northampton T	D	2-2	1-1	23	Rose [27], Hemmings [52]	7129
42	13	A	Crewe Alex	L	0-3	0-1	24		4316
43	19	H	Milton Keynes D	L	1-2	0-0	24	Barclay [90]	7130
44	22	A	Crawley T	D	1-1	1-1	24	Mackail-Smith [8]	2800
45	27	H	Grimsby T	W	2-1	0-0	23	Mackail-Smith [48], Clifton (og) [67]	8519
46	May 4	A	Swindon T	L	1-3	0-0	23	Hemmings (pen) [52]	8676

Final League Position: 23

GOALSCORERS

League (48): Hemmings 14 (3 pens), Stead 8 (4 pens), Boldewijn 5, Dennis 3, Mackail-Smith 3, Alessandra 2, Hewitt 2, O'Brien 2, Barclay 1, Duffy 1, Jones 1, Kellett 1, Milsom 1, Rose 1, Thomas 1, Ward 1, own goal 1.
FA Cup (0).
Carabao Cup (3): Stead 2, Crawford 1.
Checkatrade Trophy (5): Dennis 3 (1 pen), Alessandra 1, Boldewijn 1.

Fitzsimons R 28 + 1	Tootle M 22 + 2	Duffy R 17 + 2	Brisley S 17 + 3	Jones D 13	Thomas N 14 + 11	Hewitt E 23 + 2	Vaughan D 18 + 4	Boldewijn E 33 + 3	Stead J 30 + 8	Hemmings K 30 + 6	Dennis K 13 + 11	Alessandra L 17 + 9	Hawkridge T 2 + 2	Husin N 6 + 8	Kellett A 4 + 7	Crawford T 1 + 3	Bird P 8 + 4	Milsom R 37 + 1	Oxlade-Chamberlain C 1 + 1	Ward E 16 + 1	Patching W 3 + 3	Turley J 17 + 1	Evina C 15 + 2	Osbourne S — + 2	Davies K 6 + 1	Etete K — + 4	Barclay B 12 + 1	Schofield R 17	O'Brien J 18	Rose M 17	Stubbs S 17	Doyle M 17	Mackail-Smith C 11 + 5	Gomis V 5 + 5	Palmer A 1	Match No.
1	2	3	4	5	6^3	7	8	9	10^2	11^1	12	13	14																							1
1	2^2	3	4	5	6^1	8	7	9	10^3	11	12			13	14																					2
1		3	4	5	9^2	2	7^1	6	14	11	10^3			8	13	12																				3
1		4	3	5^3	9	2	8^1	6	11^2	10	13			7	14	12																				4
1	2^1	4^2	3			8	14	5		10	11		12	6	9	7^3	13																			5
1			4	5■		3	7	9	12	10	11^3	6^1	2^2	14	13			8																		6
1			3		9^2	8	7	6	12	10	11^3	13						5	2^1	4	14															7
1	12		4		13			6	10	11		9		7^2				8		3		2^1	5													8
1	2					12		6^1	11	10		9		7^2				8		4		3	5	13												9
1	2		13		12	7		6^3	10	11		9^2		14				8^1		3		4	5													10
1	2				12	7		6^1	10	11^2		9^2		13				8■		3		4	5	14												11
1	2		7^3		12	6		10	11	8^1	14	9^2		13						3		4	5													12
1	2				10	7^1	12	6	11	9^2	13	8								4		3	5													13
1	2				13	7	8^2	6	10	11^1		9								4		3■	5		12											14
1	2^2				13	7	12	8	11	9	14	10						6^1		4		3	5^3													15
1	2	14	13			6		8		10^2	11^1	9^3						7		3		4	5			12										16
1		12	3		10	7		6			11^1	9						8		4		2	5													17
1		2	4	9^2	8^3			10			11		5^1		12			7			13	3	14		6											18
1				9	8	2		11^1			10^2			12				7		4	5	3			6	13										19
1			12	5	9^2	7					11			10^1	13			8		4	6	3			2											20
1			3^2	5	9	6	7		10^3	13	14					12		8		4	11^1	2														21
1				5	11	2	6^2		10	9^1	13							8		4		3	12		7											22
1	13			5	11^1	2	6^3		10	9	12			14				8		4		3			7^2											23
1	2		3	5	11	8^2	6^1		10	9^3	14				13			12				4			7■											24
1	5	3	2		13		8		10		11^2			12	7^1		4	6					9													25
1	5^1	3	2		13		8		10^2		11				7^3		4	6	12■				9			14										26
1		3		9	12		8^1		10		11^2	14			7^3		4	6				13	5				2									27
		3			12	5			10		11	7^2					4	8					9^1			13	2	1	6							28
1		3			14	5	8	12	11		13	10^3					4^2	6					9^1				2		7							29
								8	11	12		9^1						5									3	1	6	2	4	7	10^2	13		30
						13		8	11^1	12		14						5									3	1	6	2	4	7	10^2	9^3		31
								9	10^2	12		13						5									3	1	8	2	4	7	6	11^1		32
								9	12	10		6^1						5									3	1	8	2	4	7	13	11^2		33
								9^1	11	10^2		12						5									3	1	8	2	4	7	6	13		34
								9	10	12		13						5									3	1	8	2	4	7	6^1	11^2		35
							13	9	10^2	12								5									3	1	8^1	2	4	7	6	11		36
		3					8	6^1		11		10					12	5										1	7	2	4	9				37
	2	3					8^1	9		10		11^2						5			13							1		6	4	7	12			38
	2	3						10	12	11								5										1	8	6^2	4	7	9^1	13		39
	2	3						9^1	11^3	10^2		14					13	5										1	8	6	4	7	12			40
12	2	3						9^2	10^1	11^3							13	5										1■	8	6	4	7	14			41
	2	4^3						10^2	9^1	11		14						3									13		8	7	5	6	12		1	42
	2							11^2	12	10								5									3	1	8	6^1	4	7	9	13		43
	2							13	11^2								5	10		12							3■	1	8	6	4	7	9^1			44
	2		4						12	11^1							5	6										1	9	7	3	8	10^2	13		45
			2^2				6^1	12	13	11							4	9										1	7	5	3	8	10			46

FA Cup

First Round Barnsley (a) 0-4

Carabao Cup

First Round Middlesbrough (a) 3-3

(Middlesbrough won 4-3 on penalties)

Checkatrade Trophy

Group G (N) Grimsby T (a) 1-2

Group G (N) Newcastle U U21 (h) 0-2

Group G (N) Doncaster R (h) 4-2

Second Round (N) Sunderland (a) 0-2

OLDHAM ATHLETIC

FOUNDATION

It was in 1895 that John Garland, the landlord of the Featherstall and Junction Hotel, decided to form a football club. As Pine Villa they played in the Oldham Junior League. In 1899 the local professional club, Oldham County, went out of existence and one of the liquidators persuaded Pine Villa to take over their ground at Sheepfoot Lane and change their name to Oldham Athletic.

Boundary Park, Furtherwood Road, Oldham, Lancashire OL1 2PB.

Telephone: (0161) 624 4972.

Fax: (0161) 627 5915.

Ticket Office: (0161) 785 5150.

Website: www.oldhamathletic.co.uk

Email: enquiries@oldhamathletic.co.uk

Ground Capacity: 13,560.

Record Attendance: 47,671 v Sheffield W, FA Cup 4th rd, 25 January 1930.

Pitch Measurements: 100m × 68m (109.5yd × 74.5yd).

Chairman: Abdallah Lemsagam.

Head Coach: Laurent Banide.

Assistant Head Coach: Mick Priest.

Colours: Blue shirts with white trim, white shorts with blue trim, blue socks with white trim.

Year Formed: 1895.

Turned Professional: 1899.

Previous Name: 1895, Pine Villa; 1899, Oldham Athletic.

Club Nickname: 'The Latics'.

Grounds: 1895, Sheepfoot Lane; 1900, Hudson Field; 1906, Sheepfoot Lane; 1907, Boundary Park (renamed SportsDirect.com Park 2014, Boundary Park 2018).

First Football League Game: 9 September 1907, Division 2, v Stoke (a) W 3–1 – Hewitson; Hodson, Hamilton; Fay, Walders, Wilson; Ward, Billy Dodds (1), Newton (1), Hancock, Swarbrick (1).

Record League Victory: 11–0 v Southport, Division 4, 26 December 1962 – Bollands; Branagan, Marshall; McCall, Williams, Scott; Ledger (1), Johnstone, Lister (6), Colquhoun (1), Whitaker (3).

Record Cup Victory: 10–1 v Lytham, FA Cup 1st rd, 28 November 1925 – Gray; Wynne, Grundy; Adlam, Heaton, Naylor (1), Douglas, Pynegar (2), Ormston (2), Barnes (3), Watson (2).

Record Defeat: 4–13 v Tranmere R, Division 3 (N), 26 December 1935.

Most League Points (2 for a win): 62, Division 3, 1973–74.

HONOURS

League Champions: Division 2 – 1990–91; Division 3 – 1973–74; Division 3N – 1952–53.
Runners-up: Division 1 – 1914–15; Division 2 – 1909–10; Division 4 – 1962–63.

FA Cup: semi-final – 1913, 1990, 1994.

League Cup: *Runners-up:* 1990.

THE Sun FACT FILE

Oldham Athletic's Boxing Day clash with Blackburn Rovers in 1981 was switched from Ewood Park to the Latics' ground to take advantage of Boundary Park's under-soil heating system. The game was one of only eight fixtures to beat the weather but it was not a good day for the Latics who went down to a 3-0 defeat.

Most League Points (3 for a win): 88, Division 2, 1990–91.

Most League Goals: 95, Division 4, 1962–63.

Highest League Scorer in Season: Tom Davis, 33, Division 3 (N), 1936–37.

Most League Goals in Total Aggregate: Roger Palmer, 141, 1980–94.

Most League Goals in One Match: 7, Eric Gemmell v Chester, Division 3 (N), 19 January 1952.

Most Capped Player: Gunnar Halle, 24 (64), Norway.

Most League Appearances: Ian Wood, 525, 1966–80.

Youngest League Player: Wayne Harrison, 16 years 347 days v Notts Co, 27 October 1984.

Record Transfer Fee Received: £1,700,000 from Aston Villa for Earl Barrett, February 1992.

Record Transfer Fee Paid: £750,000 to Aston Villa for Ian Olney, June 1992.

Football League Record: 1907 Elected to Division 2; 1910–23 Division 1; 1923–35 Division 2; 1935–53 Division 3 (N); 1953–54 Division 2; 1954–58 Division 3 (N); 1958–63 Division 4; 1963–69 Division 3; 1969–71 Division 4; 1971–74 Division 3; 1974–91 Division 2; 1991–92 Division 1; 1992–94 Premier League; 1994–97 Division 1; 1997–2004 Division 2; 2004–18 FL 1; 2018– FL 2.

LATEST SEQUENCES

Longest Sequence of League Wins: 10, 12.1.1974 – 12.3.1974.

Longest Sequence of League Defeats: 8, 15.12.1934 – 2.2.1935.

Longest Sequence of League Draws: 5, 7.4.2018 – 21.4.2018.

Longest Sequence of Unbeaten League Matches: 20, 1.5.1990 – 10.11.1990.

Longest Sequence Without a League Win: 17, 4.9.1920 – 18.12.1920.

Successive Scoring Runs: 25 from 25.8.1962.

Successive Non-scoring Runs: 6 from 12.2.2011.

MANAGERS

David Ashworth 1906–14
Herbert Bamlett 1914–21
Charlie Roberts 1921–22
David Ashworth 1923–24
Bob Mellor 1924–27
Andy Wilson 1927–32
Bob Mellor 1932–33
Jimmy McMullan 1933–34
Bob Mellor 1934–45
(continued as Secretary to 1953)
Frank Womack 1945–47
Billy Wootton 1947–50
George Hardwick 1950–56
Ted Goodier 1956–58
Norman Dodgin 1958–60
Danny McLennan 1960
Jack Rowley 1960–63
Les McDowall 1963–65
Gordon Hurst 1965–66
Jimmy McIlroy 1966–68
Jack Rowley 1968–69
Jimmy Frizzell 1970–82
Joe Royle 1982–94
Graeme Sharp 1994–97
Neil Warnock 1997–98
Andy Ritchie 1998–2001
Mick Wadsworth 2001–02
Iain Dowie 2002–03
Brian Talbot 2004–05
Ronnie Moore 2005–06
John Sheridan 2006–09
Joe Royle 2009
Dave Penney 2009–10
Paul Dickov 2010–13
Lee Johnson 2013–15
Dean Holden 2015
Darren Kelly 2015
David Dunn 2015–16
John Sheridan 2016
Stephen Robinson 2016–17
John Sheridan 2017
Richie Wellens 2017–18
Frankie Bunn 2018
Paul Scholes 2019
Laurent Banide June 2019–

TEN YEAR LEAGUE RECORD

		P	W	D	L	F	A	Pts	Pos
2009-10	FL 1	46	13	13	20	39	57	52	16
2010-11	FL 1	46	13	17	16	53	60	56	17
2011-12	FL 1	46	14	12	20	50	66	54	16
2012-13	FL 1	46	14	9	23	46	59	51	19
2013-14	FL 1	46	14	14	18	50	59	56	15
2014-15	FL 1	46	14	15	17	54	67	57	15
2015-16	FL 1	46	12	18	16	44	58	54	17
2016-17	FL 1	46	12	17	17	31	44	53	17
2017-18	FL 1	46	11	17	18	58	75	50	21
2018-19	FL 2	46	16	14	16	67	60	62	14

DID YOU KNOW ?

Oldham Athletic, already out of the FA Cup, travelled to Belfast on fourth-round day in 1914 to take on Irish League club Distillery in a friendly match. The Latics comfortably won the game 3-0 thanks to a hat-trick from Joseph Walters.

OLDHAM ATHLETIC – SKY BET LEAGUE TWO 2018–19 LEAGUE RECORD

Match No.	Date	Venue	Opponents	Result		H/T Score	Lg Pos.	Goalscorers	Attendance
1	Aug 4	H	Milton Keynes D	L	1-2	1-2	16	Gardner [41]	4764
2	11	A	Forest Green R	D	1-1	0-1	19	Gardner (pen) [78]	2759
3	18	H	Macclesfield T	W	3-1	1-0	12	Surridge [16], Branger [53], Miller [90]	4330
4	21	A	Yeovil T	D	0-0	0-0	13		2904
5	25	A	Morecambe	W	2-0	2-0	8	O'Grady [27], Nepomuceno [29]	3050
6	Sept 1	H	Crawley T	W	2-1	1-1	6	Nepomuceno [8], Surridge [89]	4160
7	8	H	Newport Co	L	0-1	0-0	10		4293
8	15	A	Grimsby T	W	3-0	0-0	6	Surridge 2 [63, 65], Baxter [90]	4746
9	22	H	Colchester U	D	3-3	0-1	6	Surridge 2 [59, 85], Clarke [88]	4017
10	29	A	Swindon T	D	0-0	0-0	6		6181
11	Oct 2	A	Mansfield T	D	0-0	0-0	8		3829
12	6	H	Carlisle U	L	1-3	0-1	12	Miller [69]	4730
13	20	H	Port Vale	L	0-1	0-1	15		4323
14	23	H	Cheltenham T	W	2-0	0-0	12	Benteke [75], Lang [90]	2865
15	27	A	Northampton T	L	1-2	0-2	15	Hunt [72]	4767
16	Nov 3	A	Stevenage	L	2-3	1-1	17	Miller [11], Lang [63]	2583
17	6	A	Notts Co	D	0-0	0-0	15		4487
18	17	H	Cambridge U	W	3-1	0-1	12	Edmundson [61], Lyden [76], Lang [80]	3818
19	24	A	Tranmere R	D	1-1	1-0	13	Branger [40]	7150
20	27	H	Lincoln C	D	1-1	0-0	13	Maouche [49]	3597
21	Dec 8	A	Crewe Alex	W	2-0	2-0	12	Clarke [17], O'Grady [40]	4168
22	15	H	Bury	W	4-2	3-0	10	O'Grady 3 [8, 31, 62], Surridge [10]	5018
23	22	H	Exeter C	L	2-3	1-1	11	Surridge [12], Lang [47]	4079
24	26	A	Carlisle U	L	0-6	0-2	12		5465
25	29	A	Port Vale	W	4-1	1-1	11	Lang [32], Maouche [53], Nepomuceno [86], O'Grady [90]	4435
26	Jan 1	H	Notts Co	W	2-0	1-0	10	Haymer [40], Clarke [47]	4336
27	12	H	Forest Green R	D	0-0	0-0	11		4194
28	19	A	Macclesfield T	L	1-2	1-1	12	Vera (pen) [1]	3697
29	29	A	Milton Keynes D	L	1-2	0-1	14	Haymer [67]	5950
30	Feb 9	A	Crawley T	W	3-0	0-0	14	Branger [74], Dearnley [86], Nepomuceno [90]	2058
31	12	H	Yeovil T	W	4-1	1-0	11	Baxter [45], Lang [51], Maouche [88], Missilou [89]	3868
32	16	H	Crewe Alex	D	1-1	1-0	10	Lang [23]	5288
33	19	H	Morecambe	L	1-2	0-1	11	Baxter [76]	4218
34	23	A	Bury	L	1-3	1-0	13	Lang [8]	7784
35	Mar 2	H	Stevenage	D	1-1	0-0	13	Baxter [47]	3807
36	9	A	Cambridge U	D	1-1	1-0	13	Dunk (og) [12]	4758
37	12	A	Lincoln C	L	0-2	0-1	14		8454
38	30	H	Grimsby T	W	2-0	1-0	15	O'Grady [42], Lang [77]	3998
39	Apr 2	H	Tranmere R	W	2-0	1-0	12	Lang 2 [7, 61]	5143
40	6	A	Colchester U	W	2-0	2-0	11	Iacovitti [6], Lang [12]	3975
41	13	H	Swindon T	D	2-2	1-1	13	Edmundson [7], Branger [70]	4064
42	19	A	Cheltenham T	D	0-0	0-0	13		4022
43	22	H	Mansfield T	W	3-2	1-0	12	Nepomuceno 2 [29, 67], Maouche [56]	6179
44	27	A	Exeter C	L	0-1	0-0	13		5040
45	30	A	Newport Co	L	0-2	0-0	13		4642
46	May 4	H	Northampton T	L	2-5	1-3	14	Branger [11], Lang [64]	5291

Final League Position: 14

GOALSCORERS

League (67): Lang 13, Surridge 8, O'Grady 7, Nepomuceno 6, Branger 5, Baxter 4, Maouche 4, Clarke 3, Miller 3, Edmundson 2, Gardner 2 (1 pen), Haymer 2, Benteke 1, Dearnley 1, Hunt 1, Iacovitti 1, Lyden 1, Missilou 1, Vera 1 (1 pen), own goal 1.
FA Cup (7): Clarke 2, Lang 2, Hunt 1, O'Grady 1, Surridge 1 (1 pen).
Carabao Cup (0).
Checkatrade Trophy (8): Surridge 3, Benteke 1, Clarke 1, Lang 1, Maouche 1, Miller 1.

Iversen D 42	Haymer T 27 + 1	Edmundson S 45	Graham S 4 + 3	Hunt R 32 + 6	Coke G 3 + 1	Gardner D 20	Missilou C 40 + 2	Branger J 29 + 6	Surridge S 10 + 5	Miller I 10 + 6	Nepomuceno G 37 + 5	O'Grady C 28 + 10	Maouche M 26 + 8	Baxter J 13 + 16	Clarke P 42	Taylor A 14 + 1	Lang C 38 + 4	de la Paz Z 3	Benteke J 2 + 7	Dummigan C 3 + 3	Lyden J 6 + 4	Palmer A 1	Robinson H — + 1	Sylla M 7 + 8	Vera U 3 + 2	Stott J 3	Dearnley Z 5 + 4	Afolayan O 4 + 6	Iacovitti A 9	Uche C — + 1	Swaby-Neavin J — + 1	*Match No.*
1	2	3	4	5	6^1	7	8^2	9	10	11^3	12	13	14																			1
1	2	3	4	5	8^1	9	7^2	6			10	11	13	12																		2
1		4	12	2	7	8		6	11^1	13	9^2	10			3	5																3
1		4		2		7	8	6		11^2	9^1	10		12	3	5	13															4
1		4	12	2		7	8^2	6^1			9	10	14	11^3	3	5	13															5
1	14	4	2^3	5		7	8^2	6	12		9	10^1		11	3		13															6
		4		2		6	7^2	8^1	11			10^3	13	12	3	5	9	1	14													7
1		4		2		6	7	8	11^1	14	12	10^3		13	3	5	9^2															8
1		4		2		7	8^3	6	11	14	12	10^2		13	3	5	9^1															9
1		4		2		8	7	6^1		10^3	14	11		12	3	5	9^2			13												10
1		3	12	2		8	7			11^1		10	14	13	4	5	9^2			6^3												11
1		3	5^1	2		9	7^3	12	10	11^2		14		8	4	6	13															12
1	2	4		5		6		8^1			12	10		9	3		11		13		7^2											13
1	2	4		5		7	8			12	9	11^2		10^1	3		6		13													14
1	2	4		5		7^1	8			13	9^2	11^3	10	12	3		6		14													15
1	2^1	4		5		7^3	8			11	9			13	3		6		10^2	14	12											16
1		3		2		7				11^2	9	13		12	4	5	6		10^1		8											17
		4		2		8^1		9	13	10			12		3	5	11			6^2	7	1										18
1		4		2		8	14	9^2	12	10^1	6	13			3	5	11				7^3											19
1		4		2		8^1	7	9^2	13	10■	6		12		3	5	11															20
1		4		5			7^1	12	11		9^2	10	8		3		6			2	13											21
1	2	3		5			7		10		9^1	11	8		4		6				12											22
1	2^3	4		5			7		10	12	9	11^2	8^1		3	14	6				13											23
1		3		2			7	12	10		9	11^1	8		4	5	6															24
1	2	4		5			6	12			11	10	7		3		9^1				8											25
1	2	4					6	5^2	12		11	10^1	7		3		9				8		13									26
1	2	4		12			7	9^1			5	11^2	10	13	3		6							8								27
1	2	4		12			6	10^1			5		9■	13	3		8							7^2	11							28
1	2	4					7	8			5	12	9	13			10^2			14				6^1	11^3	3						29
1	2	3					7^3	6			9		8	13	4		11							14	10^1	5^2	12					30
1	2^1	3		12			7	6			5	14	8	9^3	4		11							13			10^2					31
1		3		2			6	10			5	12	7	9^3	4		8^1		14					13			11^2					32
1		3		2			8	6			9	11^1	13	10	4									7^2	14	5^3	12					33
1		3		2	14		7^1	6			5	13	8^2	10	4		9										11^3	12				34
1	2	3		5			8				9		7	10^1	4		6										11	12				35
1	2	4		5			12	13			9	14	8	7^3	3		6										11^1	10^2				36
1	2	4		5			8				9^1	14	7^2	10■	3		6								13		12	11^3				37
1	2	4					7	6			9^1	11	8		3		10										12		5			38
1	2	4					7	6			9	11^1	8		3		10							12					5			39
1	2	4					7^2	6^1			9	11	8		3		10							13				12	5			40
1	2	4					7	6^2			9	10^3	8^1	12	3		11							13				14	5			41
1	2	4		14			7				9^3		8	6^1	3		10		13					12				11^2	5			42
1	2	3		12			7				9	11	8		4		10							6^1					5			43
	2	4					7^1	12			9	11	8	14	3		6^3	1						10^2				13	5			44
	2	4^2		12			9	6			10		7		3^3		8	1	14					13				11^1	5			45
1	3			2			8	9			5^2	11^3	10				6							7^1				12	4	13	14	46

FA Cup

First Round	Hampton & R	(a)	2-1
Second Round	Maidstone U	(a)	2-0
Third Round	Fulham	(a)	2-1
Fourth Round	Doncaster R	(a)	1-2

Carabao Cup

First Round	Derby Co	(h)	0-2

Checkatrade Trophy

Group F (N)	Barnsley	(h)	1-2
Group F (N)	Bradford C	(a)	4-1
Group F (N)	Everton U21	(h)	3-2
Second Round (N)	Rochdale	(a)	0-2

OXFORD UNITED

FOUNDATION

There had been an Oxford United club around the time of World War I but only in the Oxfordshire Thursday League and there is no connection with the modern club which began as Headington in 1893, adding 'United' a year later. Playing first on Quarry Fields and subsequently Wootten's Fields, they owe much to a Dr Hitchings for their early development.

The Kassam Stadium, Grenoble Road, Oxford OX4 4XP.

Telephone: (01865) 337 500.

Ticket Office: (01865) 337 533.

Website: www.oufc.co.uk

Email: admin@oufc.co.uk

Ground Capacity: 12,573.

Record Attendance: 22,750 v Preston NE, FA Cup 6th rd, 29 February 1964 (at Manor Ground); 12,243 v Leyton Orient, FL 2, 6 May 2006 (at The Kassam Stadium).

Pitch Measurements: 100.5m × 67m (110yd × 73.5yd).

Chairman: Sumrith 'Tiger' Thanakarnjanasuth.

Head Coach: Karl Robinson.

Assistant Head Coach: Derek Fazackerley.

HONOURS

League Champions: Division 2 – 1984–85; Division 3 – 1967–68, 1983–84.

Runners-up: Second Division – 1995–96; FL 2 – 2015–16; Conference – (3rd) 2009–10 *(promoted via play-offs)*.

FA Cup: 6th rd – 1964.

League Cup Winners: 1986.

League Trophy: *Runners-up:* 2016, 2017.

Colours: Yellow shirts with blue trim, yellow shorts with blue trim, yellow socks with blue trim.

Year Formed: 1893.

Turned Professional: 1949.

Previous Names: 1893, Headington; 1894, Headington United; 1960, Oxford United.

Club Nickname: 'The U's'.

Grounds: 1893, Headington Quarry; 1894, Wootten's Fields; 1898, Sandy Lane Ground; 1902, Britannia Field; 1909, Sandy Lane; 1910, Quarry Recreation Ground; 1914, Sandy Lane; 1922, The Paddock Manor Road; 1925, Manor Ground; 2001, The Kassam Stadium.

First Football League Game: 18 August 1962, Division 4, v Barrow (a) L 2–3 – Medlock; Beavon, Quartermain; Ron Atkinson, Kyle, Jones; Knight, Graham Atkinson (1), Houghton (1), Cornwell, Colfar.

Record League Victory: 7–0 v Barrow, Division 4, 19 December 1964 – Fearnley; Beavon, Quartermain; Ron Atkinson (1), Kyle, Jones; Morris, Booth (3), Willey (1), Graham Atkinson (1), Harrington (1).

Record Cup Victory: 9–1 v Dorchester T, FA Cup 1st rd, 11 November 1995 – Whitehead; Wood (2), Mike Ford (1), Smith, Elliott, Gilchrist, Rush (1), Massey (Murphy), Moody (3), Bobby Ford (1), Angel (Beauchamp (1)).

Record Defeat: 0–7 v Sunderland, Division 1, 19 September 1998; 0–7 v Wigan Ath, FL 1, 23 December 2017.

Most League Points (2 for a win): 61, Division 4, 1964–65.

THE Sun FACT FILE

Following their change of name in the summer of 1960 the first game played under the name Oxford United took place on 20 August 1960. Playing at home to Worcester City in a Southern League Premier Division match United won 3-0. New signing Billy Simpson opened the scoring almost straight from the kick-off with Peter Knight and Joe Dickson also finding the net.

Most League Points (3 for a win): 95, Division 3, 1983–84.

Most League Goals: 91, Division 3, 1983–84.

Highest League Scorer in Season: John Aldridge, 30, Division 2, 1984–85.

Most League Goals in Total Aggregate: Graham Atkinson, 77, 1962–73.

Most League Goals in One Match: 4, Tony Jones v Newport Co, Division 4, 22 September 1962; 4, Arthur Longbottom v Darlington, Division 4, 26 October 1963; 4, Richard Hill v Walsall, Division 2, 26 December 1988; 4, John Durnin v Luton T, 14 November 1992; 4, Tom Craddock v Accrington S, FL 2, 20 October 2011.

Most Capped Player: Jim Magilton, 18 (52), Northern Ireland.

Most League Appearances: John Shuker, 478, 1962–77.

Youngest League Player: Jason Seacole, 16 years 149 days v Mansfield T, 7 September 1976.

Record Transfer Fee Received: £3,000,000 from Leeds U for Kemar Roofe, July 2016.

Record Transfer Fee Paid: £470,000 to Aberdeen for Dean Windass, July 1998.

Football League Record: 1962 Elected to Division 4; 1965–68 Division 3; 1968–76 Division 2; 1976–84 Division 3; 1984–85 Division 2; 1985–88 Division 1; 1988–92 Division 2; 1992–94 Division 1; 1994–96 Division 2; 1996–99 Division 1; 1999–2001 Division 2; 2001–04 Division 3; 2004–06 FL 2; 2006–10 Conference; 2010–16 FL 2; 2016– FL 1.

MANAGERS

Harry Thompson 1949–58
(Player-Manager) 1949-51
Arthur Turner 1959–69
(continued as General Manager to 1972)
Ron Saunders 1969
Gerry Summers 1969–75
Mick Brown 1975–79
Bill Asprey 1979–80
Ian Greaves 1980–82
Jim Smith 1982–85
Maurice Evans 1985–88
Mark Lawrenson 1988
Brian Horton 1988–93
Denis Smith 1993–97
Malcolm Crosby 1997–98
Malcolm Shotton 1998–99
Micky Lewis 1999–2000
Denis Smith 2000
David Kemp 2000–01
Mark Wright 2001
Ian Atkins 2001–04
Graham Rix 2004
Ramon Diaz 2004–05
Brian Talbot 2005–06
Darren Patterson 2006
Jim Smith 2006–07
Darren Patterson 2007–08
Chris Wilder 2008–14
Gary Waddock 2014
Michael Appleton 2014–17
Pep Clotet 2017–18
Karl Robinson March 2018–

LATEST SEQUENCES

Longest Sequence of League Wins: 6, 13.4.2013 – 17.8.2013.

Longest Sequence of League Defeats: 8, 18.4.2014 – 23.8.2014.

Longest Sequence of League Draws: 5, 7.10.1978 – 28.10.1978.

Longest Sequence of Unbeaten League Matches: 20, 17.3.1984 – 29.9.1984.

Longest Sequence Without a League Win: 27, 14.11.1987 – 27.8.1988.

Successive Scoring Runs: 17 from 22.4.2006.

Successive Non-scoring Runs: 6 from 26.3.1988.

TEN YEAR LEAGUE RECORD

		P	W	D	L	F	A	Pts	Pos
2009-10	Conf P	44	25	11	8	64	31	86	3
2010-11	FL 2	46	17	12	17	58	60	63	12
2011-12	FL 2	46	17	17	12	59	48	68	9
2012-13	FL 2	46	19	8	19	60	61	65	9
2013-14	FL 2	46	16	14	16	53	50	62	8
2014-15	FL 2	46	15	16	15	50	49	61	13
2015-16	FL 2	46	24	14	8	84	41	86	2
2016-17	FL 1	46	20	9	17	65	52	69	8
2017-18	FL 1	46	15	11	20	61	66	56	16
2018-19	FL 1	46	15	15	16	58	64	60	12

DID YOU KNOW ?

Although in only their second season of Southern League football, Headington United hammered Scottish B Division side St Johnstone by a 7-0 margin in a friendly match played in April 1951. Bill Rowstron and Jimmy Smith netted hat-tricks with a further goal coming from Vic Barney.

OXFORD UNITED – SKY BET LEAGUE ONE 2018–19 LEAGUE RECORD

Match No.	Date	Venue	Opponents	Result		H/T Score	Lg Pos.	Goalscorers	Attendance
1	Aug 4	A	Barnsley	L	0-4	0-2	24		12,820
2	11	H	Fleetwood T	L	0-2	0-1	24		6689
3	18	A	Portsmouth	L	1-4	0-0	24	Whatmough (og) [89]	18,093
4	21	H	Accrington S	L	2-3	1-1	24	Whyte [27], Browne [57]	5748
5	25	H	Burton Alb	W	3-1	1-1	22	Mousinho [18], Henry [50], Holmes [69]	6026
6	Sept 1	A	Sunderland	D	1-1	1-0	22	Holmes [16]	32,193
7	9	H	Coventry C	L	1-2	0-0	23	Obika [86]	7519
8	15	A	Wycombe W	D	0-0	0-0	23		6879
9	22	H	Walsall	L	1-2	0-1	23	Henry [87]	6080
10	29	A	AFC Wimbledon	L	1-2	1-2	23	Brannagan [44]	4068
11	Oct 2	H	Luton T	L	1-2	0-0	23	Holmes [48]	6769
12	6	A	Southend U	D	0-0	0-0	24		6670
13	13	H	Plymouth Arg	W	2-0	1-0	23	Mackie [4], Nelson [74]	7332
14	20	A	Bristol R	D	0-0	0-0	22		8506
15	23	A	Charlton Ath	D	1-1	0-1	21	Whyte [71]	9984
16	27	H	Shrewsbury T	W	3-0	2-0	21	Ruffels [3], Whyte [14], Browne [86]	8697
17	Nov 3	A	Scunthorpe U	D	3-3	1-0	21	Henry [8], Brannagan [50], Nelson [55]	3805
18	17	H	Gillingham	W	1-0	0-0	20	Henry (pen) [59]	6628
19	24	A	Bradford C	L	0-2	0-2	20		19,084
20	27	H	Rochdale	W	4-2	2-1	19	Mackie [11], Henry [14], Browne 2 [52, 78]	5204
21	Dec 8	A	Peterborough U	D	2-2	1-1	19	Henry 2 (1 pen) [42, 88 (p)]	7027
22	15	H	Blackpool	W	2-0	2-0	18	Turton (og) [29], Henry [41]	6003
23	22	A	Doncaster R	D	2-2	0-1	18	Whyte [64], Ruffels [90]	7425
24	26	H	Southend U	L	0-1	0-0	19		8978
25	29	H	Bristol R	L	0-2	0-1	20		8135
26	Jan 1	A	Plymouth Arg	L	0-3	0-2	22		10,223
27	12	A	Fleetwood T	D	2-2	0-2	21	Henry [52], Mackie [64]	2789
28	19	H	Portsmouth	W	2-1	2-0	20	Brannagan [25], Henry [45]	8202
29	29	H	Barnsley	D	2-2	1-0	20	Ruffels [25], Mackie [48]	5794
30	Feb 2	A	Burton Alb	D	0-0	0-0	21		3197
31	9	H	Sunderland	D	1-1	0-1	20	Browne [87]	10,383
32	16	H	Peterborough U	L	0-1	0-0	21		6541
33	19	A	Accrington S	L	2-4	0-1	22	Garbutt [63], Mousinho [89]	2095
34	23	A	Blackpool	W	1-0	1-0	20	Graham [40]	4003
35	Mar 2	H	Scunthorpe U	W	2-1	0-0	19	Sinclair 2 [65, 80]	6237
36	9	A	Gillingham	L	0-1	0-0	21		4991
37	12	A	Rochdale	D	0-0	0-0	21		2331
38	16	H	Bradford C	W	1-0	0-0	19	Mackie [90]	6681
39	23	A	Coventry C	W	1-0	0-0	13	Nelson [57]	14,044
40	30	H	Wycombe W	W	2-1	1-1	12	Sinclair [30], Ruffels [90]	9250
41	Apr 6	A	Walsall	W	3-1	1-1	12	Dickie [21], Garbutt [63], Sinclair [90]	6339
42	13	H	AFC Wimbledon	D	0-0	0-0	12		7678
43	19	H	Charlton Ath	W	2-1	2-1	12	Nelson [18], Garbutt [23]	8680
44	22	A	Shrewsbury T	W	3-2	1-2	11	Whyte 3 [6, 72, 78]	7189
45	27	H	Doncaster R	D	2-2	1-1	11	Browne [13], Henry [49]	9000
46	May 4	A	Luton T	L	1-3	0-1	12	Garbutt [60]	10,089

Final League Position: 12

GOALSCORERS

League (58): Henry 11 (2 pens), Whyte 7, Browne 6, Mackie 5, Garbutt 4, Nelson 4, Ruffels 4, Sinclair 4, Brannagan 3, Holmes 3, Mousinho 2, Dickie 1, Graham 1, Obika 1, own goals 2.
FA Cup (5): Henry 2, Brannagan 1, Browne 1, Mackie 1.
Carabao Cup (5): Whyte 2, Baptiste 1, Browne 1, own goal 1.
Checkatrade Trophy (13): Smith 3, Brannagan 2, Henry 2 (1 pen), Browne 1, Carruthers 1, Holmes 1, McMahon 1, Raglan 1, Spasov 1 (1 pen).

Eastwood S 34	McMahon T 10	Dickie R 36 + 1	Nelson C 46	Garbutt L 18 + 7	Ruffels J 40 + 4	Brannagan C 40 + 1	Mackie J 28 + 14	Henry J 39 + 5	Carruthers S 3 + 7	Obika J 5 + 6	Smith S 5 + 10	Hall R 1 + 3	Whyte G 29 + 7	Shearer S 1	Holmes R 13 + 3	Browne M 25 + 9	Mitchell J 10	Hanson J 22 + 8	Baptiste S 7 + 2	Norman C 6 + 1	Mousinho J 32 + 3	Long S 16 + 2	Bradbury H — + 1	Raglan C — + 1	Little A — + 1	Spasov S — + 1	Graham J 13 + 3	Kashi A 7 + 4	Sinclair J 10 + 6	Sykes M 7 + 2	Smith J — + 1	Stephens J 1 + 1	Jones N 2 + 1	Match No.
1	2	3	4	5	6	7	8^{1}	9^{3}	10^{2}	11	12	13	14																					1
	2	4	3	5	6^{3}	7	9^{1}	13		14	11	8^{2}		1	10	12																		2
	2	3	4	5^{3}	14	8	9	13		12	10^{2}					11	1	6	7^{1}															3
			4		5	6^{2}	13	9^{1}		11	12		8			10	1	7		2	3													4
			3		5	7	12	9			11^{1}		8		13	10^{2}	1	6		2	4													5
			3		5	6	11^{2}	7		13			12		10^{1}	9	1		8	2	4													6
			3	13	5	6	11^{1}	9		12	14				8	10^{3}	1		7^{2}	2	4													7
			3	5	12	6^{3}		9^{2}		11^{1}	14		8		10	13	1		7	2	4													8
		14	3	5	13			9		12	11^{1}		8		10		1	6^{3}	7	2^{2}	4													9
			3	5		6	13	9		11^{2}	14		8^{3}		10		1	7^{1}	12		4	2												10
	2	3	4	5	13	7	12		14	10^{1}			9^{2}		11		1	6^{3}	8■															11
	2	4	3		5	8	10^{1}	6		12			9		11		1				7													12
1	2	3	4		5	6^{3}	11^{1}	9	13		14				10	8^{2}			12		7													13
1	2	3	4		5		10^{2}	6	12		14		9			11^{3}		13	8^{1}		7													14
1	2	3^{2}	4		5	7	11	8	14				13		9^{1}	10^{3}		12			6													15
1	2	4	3		5	8	11^{3}	9^{1}			14		7		10^{2}	12		13			6													16
1	2	3	4		5	8	10	6^{2}					9		11^{1}	13		12			7													17
1		3	4		5	6		9			11^{1}				10^{2}	8		12			7	2	13											18
1		3	4	12	5^{2}	8	10^{3}	6			14		11			9		2		13	7^{1}													19
1		3	4	13	5	7	11	9^{2}					8			10^{1}		2			6	12												20
1		3	4		5	6	10	8					11		12	9		2			7^{1}													21
1		3^{1}	4		5	6	11	9					8^{2}		13	10		2			7			12										22
1		4	3	12	5	8	10^{1}	6					9			11		2			7													23
1		3	4		5	6	11	9			13		8			10^{1}		2			7^{2}				12									24
1		4	3	13	5	6	10	8					9			11					7^{2}	2^{1}				12								25
1		4	3	5^{1}	7	6	10	8					9			11		2			12													26
1		3	4		5	6	12	8					10			11^{2}		2^{1}			7	13					9							27
1		3	4		5	6	11	9					8^{2}			12		2			7						10^{1}	13						28
1		3	4	12	5	6	11	9^{2}					8					2			7						10^{1}	13						29
1		4	3		5	7	12	9	13				8					2			6^{2}						10		11^{1}					30
1		3	4		5	6	11^{3}	9^{1}	14				8			13		2			7^{2}						10		12					31
1		3	4		5	6	12	9^{3}	14				8			13		2			7^{1}						10		11^{2}					32
1			3	12	5	7	10^{3}	13	8^{2}							11^{1}		2			4						9		14	6				33
1		3	4	5	7			9^{2}										13			6	2					8^{3}	12	11^{1}	10	14			34
1		3	4	5^{1}	6		14	9					12			13					7	2					10^{3}		11^{2}	8				35
1		3	4	10^{3}	5		14	9					13								7^{1}	2					8	12	11	6^{2}				36
1		4	3		5	6	10^{2}	8					9			11^{1}						2					12	7	13					37
1		3	4		5	7	13	9^{2}					10			12						2					8^{1}	6	11					38
1		3	4	10	5	7	11^{3}	12								9^{1}					14	2					8^{2}	6	13					39
1		4	3	10^{3}	5	6	13	9^{1}								8^{2}						2					12	7	11	14				40
1		4	3	10	5	7	11^{3}	9^{1}					12			8■					13	2						6■^{2}	14					41
1		4	3	11^{3}	5	8	13	12					9								7^{1}	2					14		10^{2}	6				42
1■		4	3	5	7	6	13	9^{2}										14				2						8^{1}	11	10^{3}		12		43
		4^{2}	3	5		12	10		8^{3}				9					13				2					11^{1}	7■		6		1	14	44
1			4		5	7	14	9^{2}				13	8^{1}			10		6				2							11^{3}	12			3	45
1			4	5^{2}	8	7	11^{3}	10^{1}				14	12			9		6				2							13				3	46

FA Cup

First Round	Forest Green R	(h)	0-0
Replay	Forest Green R	(a)	3-0
Second Round	Plymouth Arg	(a)	2-1
Third Round	Brentford	(a)	0-1

Carabao Cup

First Round	Coventry C	(h)	2-0
Second Round	Newport Co	(a)	3-0
Third Round	Manchester C	(h)	0-3

Checkatrade Trophy

Group F (S)	Fulham U21	(h)	3-0
Group F (S)	Northampton T	(h)	1-2
Group F (S)	Wycombe W	(a)	3-0
Second Round (S)	Tottenham H U21	(h)	3-0
Third Round	Cheltenham T	(a)	1-1
(Oxford U won 4-1 on penalties)			
Quarter-Final	Bury	(a)	2-5

PETERBOROUGH UNITED

FOUNDATION

The old Peterborough & Fletton club, founded in 1923, was suspended by the FA during season 1932–33 and disbanded. Local enthusiasts determined to carry on and in 1934 a new professional club, Peterborough United, was formed and entered the Midland League the following year. Peterborough's first success came in 1939–40, but from 1955–56 to 1959–60 they won five successive titles. During the 1958–59 season they were undefeated in the Midland League. They reached the third round of the FA Cup, won the Northamptonshire Senior Cup, the Maunsell Cup and were runners-up in the East Anglian Cup.

Weston Homes Stadium, London Road, Peterborough PE2 8AL.

Telephone: (01733) 563 947.

Fax: (01733) 344 140.

Ticket Office: (0844) 847 1934.

Website: www.theposh.com

Email: via website.

Ground Capacity: 15,314.

Record Attendance: 30,096 v Swansea T, FA Cup 5th rd, 20 February 1965.

Pitch Measurements: 102.5m × 64m (112yd × 70yd).

Chairman: Darragh MacAnthony.

Chief Executive: Bob Symns.

Manager: Darren Ferguson.

First-Team Coach: Gavin Strachan.

Colours: Blue shirts with white trim, blue shorts with white trim, blue socks.

Year Formed: 1934.

Turned Professional: 1934.

Club Nickname: 'The Posh'.

Ground: 1934, London Road Stadium (renamed ABAX Stadium 2014; Weston Homes Stadium 2019).

First Football League Game: 20 August 1960, Division 4, v Wrexham (h) W 3–0 – Walls; Stafford, Walker; Rayner, Rigby, Norris; Hails, Emery (1), Bly (1), Smith, McNamee (1).

Record League Victory: 9–1 v Barnet (a) Division 3, 5 September 1998 – Griemink; Hooper (1), Drury (Farell), Gill, Bodley, Edwards, Davies, Payne, Grazioli (5), Quinn (2) (Rowe), Houghton (Etherington) (1).

Record Cup Victory: 9–1 v Rushden T, FA Cup 1st qual rd, 6 October 1945 – Hilliard; Bryan, Parrott, Warner, Hobbs, Woods, Polhill (1), Fairchild, Laxton (6), Tasker (1), Rodgers (1); 9–1 v Kingstonian, FA Cup 1st rd, 25 November 1992. Match ordered to be replayed by FA. Peterborough won replay 1–0.

HONOURS

League Champions: Division 4 – 1960–61, 1973–74.
Runners-up: FL 1 – 2008–09; FL 2 – 2007–08.

FA Cup: 6th rd – 1965.

League Cup: semi-final – 1966.

League Trophy Winners: 2014.

THE SUN FACT FILE

After the introduction of the play-off system for the 1986–87 season, automatic promotion from the fourth tier of the Football League was restricted to three clubs. However, Peterborough United finished in fourth place in 1990–91 and were promoted as a restructuring of the competition meant that five teams went up that season.

Record Defeat: 1–8 v Northampton T, FA Cup 2nd rd (2nd replay), 18 December 1946.

Most League Points (2 for a win): 66, Division 4, 1960–61.

Most League Points (3 for a win): 92, FL 2, 2007–08.

Most League Goals: 134, Division 4, 1960–61.

Highest League Scorer in Season: Terry Bly, 52, Division 4, 1960–61.

Most League Goals in Total Aggregate: Jim Hall, 122, 1967–75.

Most League Goals in One Match: 5, Guiliano Grazioli v Barnet, Division 3, 5 September 1998.

Most Capped Player: Gabriel Zakuani, 17 (29), DR Congo.

Most League Appearances: Tommy Robson, 482, 1968–81.

Youngest League Player: Matthew Etherington, 15 years 262 days v Brentford, 3 May 1997.

Record Transfer Fee Received: £5,500,000 from Nottingham F for Britt Assombalonga, August 2014.

Record Transfer Fee Paid: £1,250,000 (in excess of) to Bristol C for Mo Eisa, June 2019.

Football League Record: 1960 Elected to Division 4; 1961–68 Division 3, when they were demoted for financial irregularities; 1968–74 Division 4; 1974–79 Division 3; 1979–91 Division 4; 1991–92 Division 3; 1992–94 Division 1; 1994–97 Division 2; 1997–2000 Division 3; 2000–04 Division 2; 2004–05 FL 1; 2005–08 FL 2; 2008–09 FL 1; 2009–10 FL C; 2010–11 FL 1; 2011–13 FL C; 2013– FL 1.

LATEST SEQUENCES

Longest Sequence of League Wins: 9, 1.2.1992 – 14.3.1992.

Longest Sequence of League Defeats: 8, 16.12.2006 – 27.1.2007.

Longest Sequence of League Draws: 8, 18.12.1971 – 12.2.1972.

Longest Sequence of Unbeaten League Matches: 17, 15.1.2008 – 5.4.2008.

Longest Sequence Without a League Win: 17, 23.9.1978 – 30.12.1978.

Successive Scoring Runs: 33 from 20.9.1960.

Successive Non-scoring Runs: 6 from 13.8.2002.

MANAGERS

Jock Porter 1934–36
Fred Taylor 1936–37
Vic Poulter 1937–38
Sam Haden 1938–48
Jack Blood 1948–50
Bob Gurney 1950–52
Jack Fairbrother 1952–54
George Swindin 1954–58
Jimmy Hagan 1958–62
Jack Fairbrother 1962–64
Gordon Clark 1964–67
Norman Rigby 1967–69
Jim Iley 1969–72
Noel Cantwell 1972–77
John Barnwell 1977–78
Billy Hails 1978–79
Peter Morris 1979–82
Martin Wilkinson 1982–83
John Wile 1983–86
Noel Cantwell 1986–88 *(continued as General Manager)*
Mick Jones 1988–89
Mark Lawrenson 1989–90
Dave Booth 1990–91
Chris Turner 1991–92
Lil Fuccillo 1992–93
Chris Turner 1993–94
John Still 1994–95
Mick Halsall 1995–96
Barry Fry 1996–2005
Mark Wright 2005–06
Steve Bleasdale 2006
Keith Alexander 2006–07
Darren Ferguson 2007–09
Mark Cooper 2009–10
Jim Gannon 2010
Gary Johnson 2010–11
Darren Ferguson 2011–15
Dave Robertson 2015
Graham Westley 2015–16
Grant McCann 2016–18
Steve Evans 2018–19
Darren Ferguson January 2019–

TEN YEAR LEAGUE RECORD

		P	W	D	L	F	A	Pts	Pos
2009-10	FL C	46	8	10	28	46	80	34	24
2010-11	FL 1	46	23	10	13	106	75	79	4
2011-12	FL C	46	13	11	22	67	77	50	18
2012-13	FL C	46	15	9	22	66	75	54	22
2013-14	FL 1	46	23	5	18	72	58	74	6
2014-15	FL 1	46	18	9	19	53	56	63	9
2015-16	FL 1	46	19	6	21	82	73	63	13
2016-17	FL 1	46	17	11	18	62	62	62	11
2017-18	FL 1	46	17	13	16	68	60	64	9
2018-19	FL 1	46	20	12	14	71	62	72	7

DID YOU KNOW?

Peterborough United made a promising start to the 1978–79 season and were unbeaten in their first six League games and fourth in the table. However, a run of 17 games without a win saw them plummet down the table and they were eventually relegated from the Third Division after finishing in 21st position.

PETERBOROUGH UNITED – SKY BET LEAGUE ONE 2018–19 LEAGUE RECORD

Match No.	*Date*	*Venue*	*Opponents*	*Result*		*H/T Score*	*Lg Pos.*	*Goalscorers*	*Attendance*
1	Aug 4	H	Bristol R	W	2-1	2-0	4	Godden [1], O'Hara [26]	6439
2	11	A	Rochdale	W	4-1	3-1	2	Cummings [25], O'Hara 2 [34, 90], Godden [45]	3128
3	18	H	Luton T	W	3-1	3-0	1	Cummings 2 (1 pen) [17 (p), 36], Dembele [19]	8016
4	21	A	Charlton Ath	W	1-0	0-0	1	Cummings (pen) [89]	9762
5	25	A	Plymouth Arg	W	5-1	2-0	1	Godden 2 [8, 90], Dembele [11], Cummings 2 (1 pen) [48, 54 (p)]	9214
6	Sept 1	H	Doncaster R	D	1-1	0-1	1	Tafazolli [58]	7060
7	8	A	Southend U	W	3-2	1-0	1	Godden 2 [32, 57], Toney [87]	6551
8	15	H	Portsmouth	L	1-2	0-0	2	Godden [90]	10,472
9	22	A	Gillingham	W	4-2	1-0	1	Walker [24], Dembele [59], Toney [64], Cooke [87]	4407
10	29	H	Blackpool	D	2-2	1-0	2	Bennett [27], O'Hara [64]	6269
11	Oct 2	A	Sunderland	D	2-2	0-1	2	Ward [74], Toney [84]	28,727
12	6	H	Barnsley	L	0-4	0-2	2		7683
13	13	A	Scunthorpe U	W	2-0	0-0	2	Godden 2 [51, 58]	4566
14	20	H	Accrington S	L	0-1	0-1	2		6141
15	23	H	Fleetwood T	W	1-0	0-0	2	Bennett [52]	5347
16	27	A	Burton Alb	W	2-1	1-0	2	Ward [29], Dembele [58]	3600
17	Nov 3	A	Wycombe W	L	0-1	0-0	3		5225
18	17	H	Bradford C	D	1-1	0-1	4	Toney [61]	8046
19	23	A	Coventry C	D	1-1	0-0	3	Toney [90]	11,719
20	27	H	AFC Wimbledon	W	1-0	0-0	4	Maddison [60]	5064
21	Dec 8	H	Oxford U	D	2-2	1-1	4	Toney [10], Dembele [75]	7027
22	15	A	Shrewsbury T	D	2-2	1-1	4	Godden [12], Bennett [90]	5393
23	22	H	Walsall	D	1-1	0-1	5	Toney [47]	7243
24	26	A	Barnsley	L	0-2	0-1	6		12,843
25	29	A	Accrington S	W	4-0	2-0	5	Toney 3 [19, 41, 85], Bennett [67]	2672
26	Jan 1	H	Scunthorpe U	L	0-2	0-1	7		6974
27	12	H	Rochdale	W	2-1	1-0	6	Tomlin [23], Cooper [84]	6025
28	19	A	Luton T	L	0-4	0-2	6		10,055
29	26	H	Charlton Ath	D	0-0	0-0	6		9002
30	29	A	Bristol R	D	2-2	1-2	6	Toney [37], Ward [90]	6851
31	Feb 2	H	Plymouth Arg	L	0-1	0-0	6		6543
32	9	A	Doncaster R	L	1-3	1-0	7	Cooper [6]	9627
33	16	A	Oxford U	W	1-0	0-0	7	Toney [76]	6541
34	23	H	Shrewsbury T	L	1-2	1-2	7	Naismith [10]	6262
35	Mar 2	H	Wycombe W	W	4-2	3-2	7	Godden 2 [7, 10], Maddison 2 [31, 66]	6484
36	9	A	Bradford C	L	1-3	0-0	7	Maddison (pen) [89]	15,890
37	12	A	AFC Wimbledon	L	0-1	0-0	7		3737
38	16	H	Coventry C	L	1-2	0-1	8	Reed [90]	7084
39	23	H	Southend U	W	2-0	1-0	6	Maddison [41], White [58]	7585
40	Apr 6	H	Gillingham	W	2-0	0-0	7	Maddison (pen) [57], Godden [85]	8331
41	13	A	Blackpool	W	1-0	1-0	7	Maddison [43]	7477
42	19	A	Fleetwood T	D	1-1	0-0	7	Maddison [64]	2774
43	22	H	Sunderland	D	1-1	0-0	7	Godden [90]	11,277
44	27	A	Walsall	L	0-3	0-1	7		5400
45	30	A	Portsmouth	W	3-2	2-1	7	Tomlin [13], Toney 2 [27, 75]	18,396
46	May 4	H	Burton Alb	W	3-1	2-0	7	Ward [19], Toney 2 [35, 88]	9019

Final League Position: 7

GOALSCORERS

League (71): Toney 16, Godden 14, Maddison 8 (2 pens), Cummings 6 (3 pens), Dembele 5, Bennett 4, O'Hara 4, Ward 4, Cooper 2, Tomlin 2, Cooke 1, Naismith 1, Reed 1, Tafazolli 1, Walker 1, White 1.
FA Cup (9): Toney 4, Godden 2, Dembele 1, Maddison 1, Ward 1.
Carabao Cup (0).
Checkatrade Trophy (12): Toney 3, Cummings 2, Godden 2, Cooper 1, Daniel 1, Dembele 1, Maddison 1, Walker 1.

Chapman A 32	Naismith J 42 + 1	Bennett R 36 + 1	Tafazolli R 35 + 2	Daniel C 20	Dembele S 30 + 8	O'Hara M 14 + 8	Woodyard A 41 + 2	Ward J 34 + 9	Godden M 29 + 9	Cummings J 11 + 11	Cooke C 10 + 3	Reed L 19 + 9	Stevens M — + 3	Toney I 31 + 13	Yorwerth J — + 2	Cooper G 4 + 17	Maddison M 31 + 9	Walker J 6 + 6	Lyon D — + 2	Denton T 9 + 1	O'Malley C 14	Lafferty D 18	Dempsey K 6 + 5	Tomlin L 14 + 5	White B 14 + 1	Knight J 6 + 2	Match No.
1	2	3	4	5	6^3	7	8	9	10^2	11^1	12	13	14														1
1	2	3	4	5	6^1	7	8	9	10^2	11^3	13			12	14												2
1	2	4	3	5	6^1	8^3	7	9	10^2	11		13		12		14											3
1	2	4	3	5	6^1	8	7	9^3	10^2	11				13		14	12										4
1	2	3	4	5	6^2	8^3	7	9	10	11^1		14		12			13										5
1	2	4	3	5	9^2	7^1	8	6	10^3	11		14		12			13										6
1	2	9	3	5	11^1	7	4	14	10	6^3				13			12	8^2									7
1	2	4	3	5	9	8^3	7	6^2	10	11^1				12			14	13									8
1	2	4	3^2	5	9	13	7		11^3		14			10	12		6	8^1									9
1	2	3	4	5	9^3	12	8	13	10^1	14				11			6	7^2									10
1	2	3	4	5	9^1	6	7	13	14	11^2	8^3			10			12										11
1	2	3	4	5^2		9	8	10	12			14		11			6^1	7^3	13								12
1	2	3	4	5	9^1	7	8	6	10^2	11^3				12		14		13									13
1	2	3	4	5	9	7^3	8	6^1	11	10^2				13			12	14									14
1	12	4	3	5	10^3	13	8	2				9^2		11		14	6^1	7									15
1	2	4	3		9^3	14	7	6	10^2	13		8		11^1				12		5							16
1	2	3	4		9^1		7	6	10^2	12		8		11			13	14		5^3							17
1	2^2	3	4		12		7	9	10^3	14		8		13			11	6^1		5							18
1	2	3	4		12	8	7	9	11^1	13				10			6^2			5							19
1		4	3	5	9	13	8	2	11^1	12		7		10^2		14	6^3										20
1		3	4	5	9	12	7	2	11^2	13		8^1		10			6										21
1		3	4	5	9^2		7	2	11^1	14		8^3		10		12	6	13									22
	3	4		5	9^1	12	8	2	10^3			7^2	13	11		14	6				1						23
	2^2	3	4	5^1	12	8	7	6	10^3	13				11			9		14		1						24
	2	6	4		10^1	13	7	3	12	14		8		11^3			9^2			5	1						25
	2	3	4^3		9		8	6^2	12	14		7^1		11		13	10			5	1						26
1	3		4		9		13	2^1			7			11		12	6					5	8^3	10^2	14		27
1	2		4■		9^1		14	12			6			11		13	7					5	8^3	10^2	3		28
	2	4			13			14	10^3			7		11		12	6^2				1	5	8	9^1	3		29
	2	4			14		8	13	10^3		6			11			12				1	5	7^1	9^2	3		30
	2	4			10^3		6	7	14		8^2	12		11							1	5^1	13	9■	3		31
	2	4^2	13				6	8^3			7^1	12		11		9	10			5■	1		14		3		32
	2	14	12				6	7						11		8^1	10				1	4^3	9	13	3	5^2	33
	2		4				6^3	7	12			13	14	11■			10			5	1		8^2	9^1	3		34
	2		4				6	7	10		8^1	12				13	9				1	5		11^2	3		35
	2^2		3				6^1	7	11		8			13		12	9				1	5		10	4		36
	2	3■						6	10^2		8^1	7		11			9				1	5	12	13	4		37
	2							7	10		8^1	6		11			9			5^2	1	4	12	13	3		38
1	2		4		12		7	6^2	13			8		10			9^3					5	14	11^1	3		39
1	2	3	4		9		8		12			7^3		11^2		13	6					5		10^1		14	40
1	2	3	4		9^2		8	12				7^3		11		13	6					5		10^1		14	41
1	2	4			9^1		7		14			8		10^2		12	6			13		5		11^3		3	42
1	2	4			8^1		6	12	11			7^2		13		10^3	9					5		14		3	43
1	2	3			8^1		6	13	11			7		12		9^2	10					5^3		14		4	44
1	2		3		12		7	6^1						10			9					5		11	4	8	45
1	2		4		12		7	6						10		13	9^1					5		11^2	3	8	46

FA Cup

First Round	Bromley	(a)	3-1
Second Round	Bradford C	(h)	2-2
Replay	Bradford C	(a)	4-4
(aet; Peterborough U won 3-2 on penalties)			
Third Round	Middlesbrough	(a)	0-5

Carabao Cup

First Round	QPR	(a)	0-2

Checkatrade Trophy

Group H (S)	Milton Keynes D	(a)	3-3
(Milton Keynes D won 6-5 on penalties)			
Group H (S)	Brighton & HA U21	(h)	2-2
(Brighton & HA U21 won 5-4 on penalties)			
Group H (S)	Luton T	(h)	2-1
Second Round (S)	Exeter C	(a)	2-0
Third Round	Chelsea U21	(a)	3-1
Quarter-Final	Portsmouth	(a)	0-1

PLYMOUTH ARGYLE

FOUNDATION

The club was formed in September 1886 as the Argyle Athletic Club by former public and private school pupils who wanted to continue playing the game. The meeting was held in a room above the Borough Arms (a coffee house), Bedford Street, Plymouth. It was common then to choose a local street/terrace as a club name and Argyle or Argyll was a fashionable name throughout the land due to Queen Victoria's great interest in Scotland.

Home Park, Plymouth, Devon PL2 3DQ.

Telephone: (01752) 562 561.

Fax: (01752) 606 167.

Ticket Office: (01752) 907 700.

Website: www.pafc.co.uk

Email: argyle@pafc.co.uk

Ground Capacity: 17,904.

Record Attendance: 43,596 v Aston Villa, Division 2, 10 October 1936.

Pitch Measurements: 103m × 66m (112.5yd × 72yd).

Chairman: Simon Hallett.

Chief Executive: Andrew Parkinson.

Manager: Ryan Lowe.

Assistant Manager: Steven Schumacher.

Colours: Dark green shirts with black stripes, white shorts with dark green trim, white socks with dark green trim.

Year Formed: 1886.

Turned Professional: 1903.

Previous Name: 1886, Argyle Athletic Club; 1903, Plymouth Argyle.

Club Nickname: 'The Pilgrims'.

Ground: 1886, Home Park.

First Football League Game: 28 August 1920, Division 3, v Norwich C (h) D 1–1 – Craig; Russell, Atterbury; Logan, Dickinson, Forbes; Kirkpatrick, Jack, Bowler, Heeps (1), Dixon.

Record League Victory: 8–1 v Millwall, Division 2, 16 January 1932 – Harper; Roberts, Titmuss; Mackay, Pullan, Reed; Grozier, Bowden (2), Vidler (3), Leslie (1), Black (1), (1 og). 8–1 v Hartlepool U (a), Division 2, 7 May 1994 – Nicholls; Patterson (Naylor), Hill, Burrows, Comyn, McCall (1), Barlow, Castle (1), Landon (3), Marshall (1), Dalton (2).

Record Cup Victory: 6–0 v Corby T, FA Cup 3rd rd, 22 January 1966 – Leiper; Book, Baird; Williams, Nelson, Newman; Jones (1), Jackson (1), Bickle (3), Piper (1), Jennings.

HONOURS

League Champions: Second Division – 2003–04; Division 3 – 1958–59; Division 3S – 1929–30, 1951–52; Third Division – 2001–02.
Runners-up: FL 2 – 2016–17; Division 3 – 1974–75, 1985–86; Division 3S – 1921–22, 1922–23, 1923–24, 1924–25, 1925–26, 1926–27.

FA Cup: semi-final – 1984.

League Cup: semi-final – 1965, 1974.

THE Sun FACT FILE

Plymouth Argyle's Home Park was one of a number of Football League grounds to suffer wartime damage. The ground was badly affected by fires that broke out following a German bombing raid in April 1941, leaving the main stand effectively destroyed. Post-war the Ministry of Works initially refused permission to replace it and it was not until 1951 that a new stand appeared.

Record Defeat: 0–9 v Stoke C, Division 2, 17 December 1960.

Most League Points (2 for a win): 68, Division 3 (S), 1929–30.

Most League Points (3 for a win): 102, Division 3, 2001–02.

Most League Goals: 107, Division 3 (S), 1925–26 and 1951–52.

Highest League Scorer in Season: Jack Cock, 32, Division 3 (S), 1926–27.

Most League Goals in Total Aggregate: Sammy Black, 174, 1924–38.

Most League Goals in One Match: 5, Wilf Carter v Charlton Ath, Division 2, 27 December 1960.

Most Capped Player: Moses Russell, 20 (23), Wales.

Most League Appearances: Kevin Hodges, 530, 1978–92.

Youngest League Player: Lee Phillips, 16 years 43 days v Gillingham, 29 October 1996.

Record Transfer Fee Received: £2,000,000 from Hull C for Peter Halmosi, July 2008.

Record Transfer Fee Paid: £500,000 to Cardiff C for Steve MacLean, January 2008.

Football League Record: 1920 Original Member of Division 3; 1921–30 Division 3 (S); 1930–50 Division 2; 1950–52 Division 3 (S); 1952–56 Division 2; 1956–58 Division 3 (S); 1958–59 Division 3; 1959–68 Division 2; 1968–75 Division 3; 1975–77 Division 2; 1977–86 Division 3; 1986–95 Division 2; 1995–96 Division 3; 1996–98 Division 2; 1998–2002 Division 3; 2002–04 Division 2; 2004–10 FL C; 2010–11 FL 1; 2011–17 FL 2; 2017–19 FL 1; 2019– FL 2.

LATEST SEQUENCES

Longest Sequence of League Wins: 9, 8.3.1986 – 12.4.1986.

Longest Sequence of League Defeats: 9, 12.10.1963 – 7.12.1963.

Longest Sequence of League Draws: 5, 26.2.2000 – 14.3.2000.

Longest Sequence of Unbeaten League Matches: 22, 20.4.1929 – 21.12.1929.

Longest Sequence Without a League Win: 13, 1.5.2018 – 2.10.2018.

Successive Scoring Runs: 39 from 15.4.1939.

Successive Non-scoring Runs: 5 from 21.11.2009.

MANAGERS

Frank Brettell 1903–05
Bob Jack 1905–06
Bill Fullerton 1906–07
Bob Jack 1910–38
Jack Tresadern 1938–47
Jimmy Rae 1948–55
Jack Rowley 1955–60
Neil Dougall 1961
Ellis Stuttard 1961–63
Andy Beattie 1963–64
Malcolm Allison 1964–65
Derek Ufton 1965–68
Billy Bingham 1968–70
Ellis Stuttard 1970–72
Tony Waiters 1972–77
Mike Kelly 1977–78
Malcolm Allison 1978–79
Bobby Saxton 1979–81
Bobby Moncur 1981–83
Johnny Hore 1983–84
Dave Smith 1984–88
Ken Brown 1988–90
David Kemp 1990–92
Peter Shilton 1992–95
Steve McCall 1995
Neil Warnock 1995–97
Mick Jones 1997–98
Kevin Hodges 1998–2000
Paul Sturrock 2000–04
Bobby Williamson 2004–05
Tony Pulis 2005–06
Ian Holloway 2006–07
Paul Sturrock 2007–09
Paul Mariner 2009–10
Peter Reid 2010–11
Carl Fletcher 2011–13
John Sheridan 2013–15
Derek Adams 2015–19
Ryan Lowe June 2019–

TEN YEAR LEAGUE RECORD

		P	W	D	L	F	A	Pts	Pos
2009-10	FL C	46	11	8	27	43	68	41	23
2010-11	FL 1	46	15	7	24	51	74	42*	23
2011-12	FL 2	46	10	16	20	47	64	46	21
2012-13	FL 2	46	13	13	20	46	55	52	21
2013-14	FL 2	46	16	12	18	51	58	60	10
2014-15	FL 2	46	20	11	15	55	37	71	7
2015-16	FL 2	46	24	9	13	72	46	81	5
2016-17	FL 2	46	26	9	11	71	46	87	2
2017-18	FL 1	46	19	11	16	58	59	68	7
2018-19	FL 1	46	13	11	22	56	80	50	21

** 10 pts deducted.*

DID YOU KNOW ?

Plymouth Argyle's first set of floodlights were ready for use in September 1952 and were inaugurated with a friendly match with Exeter City on 26 October. Although substantial crowds had turned out for a reserve game under lights, adverse weather on the night kept the attendance down to 2,000 with Argyle winning 3-1.

PLYMOUTH ARGYLE – SKY BET LEAGUE ONE 2018–19 LEAGUE RECORD

Match No.	Date	Venue	Opponents	Result		H/T Score	Lg Pos.	Goalscorers	Attendance
1	Aug 4	A	Walsall	L	1-2	1-1	15	Edwards [40]	5755
2	11	H	Southend U	D	1-1	1-1	16	Carey (pen) [20]	9886
3	18	A	Coventry C	L	0-1	0-1	20		11,453
4	21	H	Wycombe W	D	1-1	1-0	21	Ladapo [4]	9244
5	25	H	Peterborough U	L	1-5	0-2	24	Edwards [90]	9214
6	Sept 1	A	Portsmouth	L	0-3	0-1	24		18,872
7	8	A	Bristol R	D	0-0	0-0	24		9006
8	15	H	Blackpool	L	0-1	0-1	24		8658
9	22	A	Charlton Ath	L	1-2	1-1	24	Carey [9]	10,818
10	29	H	Doncaster R	L	2-3	1-1	24	Lameiras [40], Carey [90]	8532
11	Oct 2	A	Barnsley	D	1-1	1-1	24	Lameiras [39]	10,717
12	6	H	AFC Wimbledon	W	1-0	0-0	23	Ladapo [75]	8542
13	13	A	Oxford U	L	0-2	0-1	24		7332
14	20	H	Burton Alb	L	2-3	2-2	24	Ladapo 2 [9, 35]	8190
15	23	H	Gillingham	W	3-1	2-0	23	Ladapo 2 [22, 34], Lameiras [73]	8754
16	27	A	Scunthorpe U	W	4-1	2-0	22	Ladapo [13], Canavan [45], Grant, J [57], Sarcevic [90]	3508
17	Nov 3	H	Sunderland	L	0-2	0-0	22		12,065
18	17	A	Luton T	L	1-5	0-4	22	Grant, J [89]	10,004
19	24	H	Fleetwood T	W	2-1	0-0	22	Ladapo 2 [72, 81]	8301
20	27	A	Shrewsbury T	L	0-2	0-1	22		5279
21	Dec 8	H	Bradford C	D	3-3	1-2	22	Ladapo 2 [12, 74], Grant, J [50]	9092
22	15	A	Rochdale	W	2-1	0-0	21	Grant, J [73], Perkins (og) [80]	2863
23	22	H	Accrington S	L	0-3	0-0	23		10,193
24	26	A	AFC Wimbledon	L	1-2	1-1	24	Fox [23]	4434
25	29	A	Burton Alb	D	1-1	0-1	24	Lameiras [52]	3577
26	Jan 1	H	Oxford U	W	3-0	2-0	23	Sarcevic [9], Lameiras 2 [41, 67]	10,223
27	12	A	Southend U	W	3-2	1-0	23	Sarcevic [21], Ladapo [49], Lameiras [73]	6851
28	19	H	Coventry C	W	2-1	0-0	21	Lameiras 2 [63, 70]	10,686
29	22	H	Walsall	W	2-1	0-0	17	Edwards [54], Canavan [65]	8446
30	26	A	Wycombe W	L	0-1	0-1	17		5691
31	Feb 2	A	Peterborough U	W	1-0	0-0	16	Lameiras [88]	6543
32	9	H	Portsmouth	D	1-1	0-0	15	Carey [70]	12,052
33	16	A	Bradford C	D	0-0	0-0	15		15,855
34	23	H	Rochdale	W	5-1	1-0	14	Ladapo 2 [26, 75], Edwards [61], Threlkeld [85], Smith-Brown [90]	9360
35	Mar 2	A	Sunderland	L	0-2	0-1	15		32,360
36	9	H	Luton T	D	0-0	0-0	15		11,081
37	12	H	Shrewsbury T	W	2-1	1-0	12	Ladapo [8], Carey (pen) [89]	8572
38	16	A	Fleetwood T	L	0-2	0-0	12		2711
39	23	H	Bristol R	D	2-2	0-0	14	Lameiras [51], Craig (og) [75]	12,003
40	30	A	Blackpool	D	2-2	1-0	14	Ladapo [4], Edwards [73]	8343
41	Apr 6	H	Charlton Ath	L	0-2	0-1	15		10,696
42	13	A	Doncaster R	L	0-2	0-2	18		7795
43	19	A	Gillingham	L	1-3	1-0	19	Ladapo [25]	5987
44	22	H	Barnsley	L	0-3	0-3	20		10,898
45	27	A	Accrington S	L	1-5	0-3	21	Hughes (og) [90]	3134
46	May 4	H	Scunthorpe U	W	3-2	2-1	21	Jones [8], Ladapo [35], Carey [70]	11,907

Final League Position: 21

GOALSCORERS

League (56): Ladapo 18, Lameiras 11, Carey 6 (2 pens), Edwards 5, Grant J 4, Sarcevic 3, Canavan 2, Fox 1, Jones 1, Smith-Brown 1, Threlkeld 1, own goals 3.
FA Cup (2): Lameiras 1, Sarcevic 1.
Carabao Cup (3): Ladapo 1, Ness 1, Songo'o 1.
Checkatrade Trophy (0).

Macey M 33 + 1	Riley J 14 + 4	Edwards R 35 + 1	Wootton S 6 + 3	Smith-Brown A 30 + 1	Grant C 10	Fox D 40 + 3	Ness J 17 + 7	Carey G 42 + 2	Taylor R 6 + 27	Lameiras R 31 + 10	Ladapo F 42 + 3	Sawyer G 29 + 4	Wylde G 1 + 6	Moore T 14	Songo'o Y 38 + 4	Canavan N 30 + 3	Grant J 14 + 3	Sarcevic A 37	O'Keefe S 6 + 5	Grant P 5 + 1	Ainsworth L — + 1	Fletcher A — + 4	Jephcott L 2 + 7	Letheren K 13	Threlkeld O 7 + 5	Anderson P — + 4	Jones L 4 + 5	Cooper M — + 1	Match No.
1	2	3	4	5^{3}	6^{1}	7	8	9	10	11^{2}	12	13	14																1
1		3	4	5^{2}	6	7^{1}	8	9	10	11^{3}	14	12		2	13														2
1			3	5	6^{1}	14	8■	9	13	12	10			2	7^{3}	4	11^{2}												3
1			3	5	6	7^{1}		9^{3}	12		10	14		2	13	4	11^{2}	8											4
1		14	3^{1}	5	10		9	7	12		11	13		2	6^{2}	4^{3}		8											5
1	2	4		5	7^{3}	14	9	13		12	11	3			6^{1}			10	8^{2}										6
1	2^{3}	4	12		10^{1}		9^{2}	7	14		11	5			6	3	13	8											7
1	2	4	12					7	13	14	11^{2}	5			6	3^{1}	10	8	9^{3}										8
1		4	3^{2}	2		14		7		10	11	5^{3}	13		6		9	8^{1}		12									9
1		3		2		6		8		9^{1}	11		5		7^{3}		10^{3}		12	4	13	14							10
1		3		5		8		10		6^{1}	11		12	2	7				9	4									11
1		3		5		7		8		10	11			2	6				9	4									12
1		3^{2}		5^{1}		7		8		10^{3}	11		12	2	6■	14	13		9	4									13
1		3		5		7^{1}	12	9		11^{2}	10		13	2				6	8^{3}	4			14						14
1					5	7^{2}	8	9^{1}		12	10^{3}			2	3	4	11	6	13				14						15
1					5	7^{1}	8	11			10			2	3	4	9	6	12										16
1					5	7^{1}	8	9		12	10			2	3	4	11	6											17
1				5		7	8^{3}	9^{2}	12	14	10^{1}			2	3	4	11	6	13										18
1	13			5		7	8^{1}		12	9^{3}	10^{2}			2	3	4	11	6	14										19
1	14			5		6	9	13	12	7^{2}	11			2^{1}	3	4	10^{3}	8											20
1	2	3^{2}		5		6		8	12	13	11				7	4	10^{1}	9											21
1	2			5		7	13	8	12		9^{2}	3			4		11	6					10^{1}						22
1	2			5		7		9	13	12	11^{1}	3			4		8^{2}	6					10						23
1	2	4		5^{1}		6		8	10	13	11	3			7		12^{2}	9											24
	2^{1}	3		12		8		9^{3}	13	11	10^{2}	5			6	4		7					14	1					25
		3		2		7		8^{3}	12	10^{2}	11^{1}	5	13		6	4		9					14	1					26
		3		2		6		8^{1}	13	10	11^{2}	5			7	4		9					12	1					27
	13	3	12	2		6		8	14	10^{3}	11^{1}	5			7	4^{2}		9						1					28
		3		2		7		8	12	10	11	5			6	4		9^{1}						1					29
		3		2		7^{1}		8	12	10^{2}	11	5			6	4		9					13	1					30
	12	3		2^{2}		6		7	10^{3}	8^{1}	11	5			14	4		9					13	1					31
		3		2		6		8	12	10	11^{1}	5			7	4		9						1					32
		3		2^{1}		7		9	12	10^{2}	11	5			6	4		8						1	13				33
		3		2		7^{3}		8^{1}		10	11	5			6	4^{2}		9						1	12	13	14		34
14		3		8		7		10	12	9^{3}	11	5			6	4								1^{1}	2^{2}	13			35
1	2	3				7	13	8	12	10^{2}	11^{1}	5			6	4									9^{3}	14			36
1	2^{1}	3				7	13	8	14	10^{3}	11	5			6^{2}	4		9							12				37
1	2	4				7^{1}	12	8	13	10^{2}	11	5			6^{3}	3		9									14		38
1	2^{2}	3				7^{1}	9			10	11	5			6	4		8							12		13		39
1	2^{1}	3				6	7	9	14	10	11^{2}	5			13	4		8^{3}							12				40
1		3				7	6^{1}	8	12	10	11	5				4^{2}		9^{3}				14			2		13		41
1		4				7		10	12	9	11	5			6^{2}	3^{1}		8							2		13		42
		3		2^{1}		6	7	10	12	8	11	5				13		9^{2}						1			4		43
		3				6^{2}	14	8	11^{1}	10^{3}		5			7			9				13		1	2	12	4		44
1		3				7^{2}	6^{3}	10	11^{1}	12	13	5			9			8				14			2		4		45
1^{3}		3				6^{1}	13	8		10	11	5			7	14		9^{2}							2		4	12	46

FA Cup

First Round	Stevenage	(h)	1-0
Second Round	Oxford U	(h)	1-2

Carabao Cup

First Round	Bristol C	(a)	1-0
Second Round	Millwall	(a)	2-3

Checkatrade Trophy

Group C (S)	Swindon T	(h)	0-3
Group C (S)	Chelsea U21	(h)	0-5
Group C (S)	Newport Co	(a)	0-2

PORT VALE

FOUNDATION

Port Vale Football Club was formed in 1876 and took its name from the venue of the inaugural meeting at 'Port Vale House' situated in a suburb of Stoke-on-Trent. Upon moving to Burslem in 1884 the club changed its name to 'Burslem Port Vale' and after several seasons in the Midland League became founder members of the Football League Division Two in 1892. The prefix 'Burslem' was dropped from the name as a new ground several miles away was acquired.

Vale Park, Hamil Road, Burslem, Stoke-on-Trent, Staffordshire ST6 1AW.

Telephone: (01782) 655 800.

Ticket Office: (01782) 655 821.

Website: www.port-vale.co.uk

Email: enquiries@port-vale.co.uk

Ground Capacity: 19,052.

Record Attendance: 22,993 v Stoke C, Division 2, 6 March 1920 (at Recreation Ground); 49,768 v Aston Villa, FA Cup 5th rd, 20 February 1960 (at Vale Park).

Pitch Measurements: 104m × 70m (114yd × 76.5yd).

Co-Chair: Kevin Shanahan, Carol Shanahan.

Chief Executive: Colin Garlick.

Manager: John Askey.

Assistant Manager: Dave Kevan.

Colours: White shirts with black and yellow trim, black shorts with yellow trim, black socks with yellow trim.

Year Formed: 1876.

Turned Professional: 1885.

Previous Names: 1876, Port Vale; 1884, Burslem Port Vale; 1909, Port Vale.

Club Nickname: 'Valiants'.

Grounds: 1876, Limekin Lane, Longport; 1881, Westport; 1884, Moorland Road, Burslem; 1886, Athletic Ground, Cobridge; 1913, Recreation Ground, Hanley; 1950, Vale Park.

First Football League Game: 3 September 1892, Division 2, v Small Heath (a) L 1–5 – Frail; Clutton, Elson; Farrington, McCrindle, Delves; Walker, Scarratt, Bliss (1), Jones. (Only 10 men).

Record League Victory: 9–1 v Chesterfield, Division 2, 24 September 1932 – Leckie; Shenton, Poyser; Sherlock, Round, Jones; McGrath, Mills, Littlewood (6), Kirkham (2), Morton (1).

Record Cup Victory: 7–1 v Irthlingborough, FA Cup 1st rd, 12 January 1907 – Matthews; Dunn, Hamilton; Eardley, Baddeley, Holyhead; Carter, Dodds (2), Beats, Mountford (2), Coxon (3).

Record Defeat: 0–10 v Sheffield U, Division 2, 10 December 1892. 0–10 v Notts Co, Division 2, 26 February 1895.

HONOURS

League Champions: Division 3N – 1929–30, 1953–54; Division 4 – 1958–59.
Runners-up: Second Division – 1993–94; Division 3N – 1952–53.

FA Cup: semi-final – 1954.

League Cup: 4th rd – 2007.

League Trophy Winners: 1993, 2001.

Anglo-Italian Cup: *Runners-up:* 1996.

THE Sun FACT FILE

In April 1931 Port Vale played overseas for the first time when they travelled to Holland for two matches. They defeated a Dutch Southern XI 5-1 in a game played on the Philips Electrical Company's ground at Eindhoven. Vale then managed a 2-0 victory over Zwaluwen under floodlights before returning home to play their final League game of the season at home to Bradford City.

Most League Points (2 for a win): 69, Division 3 (N), 1953–54.

Most League Points (3 for a win): 89, Division 2, 1992–93.

Most League Goals: 110, Division 4, 1958–59.

Highest League Scorer in Season: Wilf Kirkham 38, Division 2, 1926–27.

Most League Goals in Total Aggregate: Wilf Kirkham, 153, 1923–29, 1931–33.

Most League Goals in One Match: 6, Stewart Littlewood v Chesterfield, Division 2, 24 September 1922.

Most Capped Player: Chris Birchall, 24 (43), Trinidad & Tobago.

Most League Appearances: Roy Sproson, 760, 1950–72.

Youngest League Player: Malcolm McKenzie, 15 years 347 days v Newport Co, 12 April 1966.

Record Transfer Fee Received: £2,000,000 from Wimbledon for Gareth Ainsworth, October 1998.

Record Transfer Fee Paid: £500,000 to Lincoln C for Gareth Ainsworth, September 1997.

Football League Record: 1892 Original Member of Division 2. Failed re-election in 1896; Re-elected 1898; Resigned 1907; Returned in Oct, 1919, when they took over the fixtures of Leeds City; 1929–30 Division 3 (N); 1930–36 Division 2; 1936–38 Division 3 (N); 1938–52 Division 3 (S); 1952–54 Division 3 (N); 1954–57 Division 2; 1957–58 Division 3 (S); 1958–59 Division 4; 1959–65 Division 3; 1965–70 Division 4; 1970–78 Division 3; 1978–83 Division 4; 1983–84 Division 3; 1984–86 Division 4; 1986–89 Division 3; 1989–94 Division 2; 1994–2000 Division 1; 2000–04 Division 2; 2004–08 FL 1; 2008–13 FL 2; 2013–17 FL 1; 2017– FL 2.

LATEST SEQUENCES

Longest Sequence of League Wins: 8, 8.4.1893 – 30.9.1893.

Longest Sequence of League Defeats: 9, 9.3.1957 – 20.4.1957.

Longest Sequence of League Draws: 6, 26.4.1981 – 12.9.1981.

Longest Sequence of Unbeaten League Matches: 19, 5.5.1969 – 8.11.1969.

Longest Sequence Without a League Win: 17, 7.12.1991 – 21.3.1992.

Successive Scoring Runs: 22 from 12.9.1992.

Successive Non-scoring Runs: 5 from 19.8.2017.

MANAGERS

Sam Gleaves 1896–1905
(Secretary-Manager)
Tom Clare 1905–11
A. S. Walker 1911–12
H. Myatt 1912–14
Tom Holford 1919–24
(continued as Trainer)
Joe Schofield 1924–30
Tom Morgan 1930–32
Tom Holford 1932–35
Warney Cresswell 1936–37
Tom Morgan 1937–38
Billy Frith 1945–46
Gordon Hodgson 1946–51
Ivor Powell 1951
Freddie Steele 1951–57
Norman Low 1957–62
Freddie Steele 1962–65
Jackie Mudie 1965–67
Sir Stanley Matthews
(General Manager) 1965–68
Gordon Lee 1968–74
Roy Sproson 1974–77
Colin Harper 1977
Bobby Smith 1977–78
Dennis Butler 1978–79
Alan Bloor 1979
John McGrath 1980–83
John Rudge 1983–99
Brian Horton 1999–2004
Martin Foyle 2004–07
Lee Sinnott 2007–08
Dean Glover 2008–09
Micky Adams 2009–10
Jim Gannon 2011
Micky Adams 2011–14
Robert Page 2014–16
Bruno Ribeiro 2016
Michael Brown 2017
Neil Aspin 2017–19
John Askey February 2019–

TEN YEAR LEAGUE RECORD

		P	*W*	*D*	*L*	*F*	*A*	*Pts*	*Pos*
2009-10	FL 2	46	17	17	12	61	50	68	10
2010-11	FL 2	46	17	14	15	54	49	65	11
2011-12	FL 2	46	20	9	17	68	60	59*	12
2012-13	FL 2	46	21	15	10	87	52	78	3
2013-14	FL 1	46	18	7	21	59	73	61	9
2014-15	FL 1	46	15	9	22	55	65	54	18
2015-16	FL 1	46	18	11	17	56	58	65	12
2016-17	FL 1	46	12	13	21	45	70	49	21
2017-18	FL 2	46	11	14	21	49	67	47	20
2018-19	FL 2	46	12	13	21	39	55	49	20

**10 pts deducted.*

DID YOU KNOW ?

The inaugural match to open the floodlights at Vale Park in September 1958 saw Port Vale facing West Bromwich Albion, the club which had controversially knocked them out of the 1953–54 FA Cup semi-finals. Vale marked their first home game under lights with a 5-3 victory in front of a crowd of 16,008.

PORT VALE – SKY BET LEAGUE TWO 2018–19 LEAGUE RECORD

Match No.	Date		Venue	Opponents	Result		H/T Score	Lg Pos.	Goalscorers	Attendance
1	Aug	4	H	Cambridge U	W	3-0	1-0	3	Miller [45], Pope 2 (1 pen) [47 (p), 69]	5559
2		11	A	Colchester U	L	0-2	0-2	10		3183
3		18	H	Crawley T	W	1-0	1-0	5	Hannant [20]	4159
4		21	A	Carlisle U	L	1-2	0-1	11	Hannant [88]	3688
5		25	A	Tranmere R	L	0-1	0-0	15		6488
6	Sept	1	H	Newport Co	L	1-2	1-1	19	Pope [27]	4485
7		8	A	Forest Green R	D	1-1	0-1	17	Pope (pen) [73]	2263
8		15	H	Northampton T	W	2-0	1-0	16	Whitfield [24], Oyeleke [69]	4474
9		22	A	Crewe Alex	W	1-0	0-0	12	Legge [75]	6180
10		29	H	Exeter C	D	1-1	0-0	15	Kanu [90]	4615
11	Oct	2	H	Milton Keynes D	L	0-2	0-2	16		3399
12		6	A	Grimsby T	L	0-2	0-1	16		3842
13		13	H	Lincoln C	L	2-6	0-3	16	Conlon [51], Whitfield (pen) [90]	5137
14		20	A	Oldham Ath	W	1-0	1-0	16	Pope (pen) [37]	4323
15		23	A	Stevenage	D	0-0	0-0	16		1943
16		27	H	Bury	W	1-0	0-0	14	Pope [51]	4375
17	Nov	3	H	Notts Co	D	2-2	1-1	13	Hannant [13], Pope [89]	4236
18		17	A	Mansfield T	L	0-1	0-1	16		4316
19		24	H	Swindon T	L	0-1	0-1	17		3877
20		27	A	Yeovil T	W	3-0	2-0	16	Montano 2 [13, 48], Rawlinson [31]	2174
21	Dec	8	A	Morecambe	D	2-2	0-2	15	Kay [83], Pope [87]	1769
22		15	H	Cheltenham T	D	2-2	1-1	15	Montano [13], Kay [90]	3109
23		22	A	Macclesfield T	D	0-0	0-0	15		3951
24		26	H	Grimsby T	L	0-1	0-0	16		5129
25		29	H	Oldham Ath	L	1-4	1-1	17	Whitfield [39]	4435
26	Jan	1	A	Lincoln C	D	1-1	0-0	19	Oyeleke [90]	9106
27		12	H	Colchester U	L	0-3	0-2	19		3636
28		19	A	Crawley T	W	1-0	1-0	18	Miller [27]	2089
29		26	H	Carlisle U	L	0-1	0-0	19		3881
30		29	A	Newport Co	D	0-0	0-0	18		2534
31	Feb	9	A	Cambridge U	L	0-1	0-1	20		4193
32		16	H	Morecambe	L	0-1	0-0	20		4147
33		19	H	Tranmere R	L	1-2	0-1	21	Whitfield [59]	3835
34		23	A	Cheltenham T	L	0-1	0-1	22		3079
35	Mar	2	A	Notts Co	D	0-0	0-0	22		7457
36		9	H	Mansfield T	W	2-1	0-0	21	Miller 2 [50, 52]	5231
37		12	H	Yeovil T	W	3-0	1-0	21	Oyeleke [26], Conlon [62], Montano [84]	3430
38		16	A	Swindon T	D	0-0	0-0	20		6322
39		23	H	Forest Green R	L	0-2	0-0	21		4429
40		30	A	Northampton T	W	2-1	1-1	19	Worrall [44], Pope (pen) [75]	5651
41	Apr	6	H	Crewe Alex	W	1-0	0-0	18	Pope [78]	6823
42		13	A	Exeter C	L	0-2	0-1	18		4013
43		19	H	Stevenage	L	1-4	0-1	19	Montano [67]	4088
44		22	A	Milton Keynes D	D	1-1	0-0	19	Conlon [48]	8386
45		27	H	Macclesfield T	L	0-1	0-0	20		5414
46	May	4	A	Bury	D	1-1	1-1	20	Pope [24]	6719

Final League Position: 20

GOALSCORERS

League (39): Pope 11 (4 pens), Montano 5, Miller 4, Whitfield 4 (1 pen), Conlon 3, Hannant 3, Oyeleke 3, Kay 2, Kanu 1, Legge 1, Rawlinson 1, Worrall 1.
FA Cup (1): Pope 1.
Carabao Cup (0).
Checkatrade Trophy (10): Miller 2, Montano 2, Pope 2, Hannant 1, Pugh 1, Quigley 1, Rawlinson 1.

Brown S 46	Gibbons J 13 + 2	Rawlinson C 28	Smith N 44	Montano C 17 + 12	Worrall D 19 + 6	Joyce L 30 + 7	Oyeleke E 28	Hannant L 42 + 3	Pope T 34 + 4	Miller R 19 + 9	Dodds L 2 + 10	Tonge M — + 1	Legge L 34 + 1	Quigley S 1 + 10	Clark M 39 + 1	Kay A 21 + 6	Hardcastle L 2 + 4	Whitfield B 17 + 13	Conlon T 31 + 3	Kanu I 1 + 2	Vassell T 12 + 3	Pugh D 1	Crookes A 19	Elliott D 1 + 5	Harris M 3 + 3	Howkins K 2 + 1	Calveley M — + 1	Match No.
1	2	3	4	5	6	7	8^{1}	9	10	11^{2}	12	13																1
1	2^{1}	4	3	5	6	8	7	9^{3}	10^{2}	11	12		13	14														2
1	2	4			6^{1}	8	7^{2}	9	10	11^{3}	13		3	14	5	12												3
1		4	2	12	13	5		7	9	11^{2}	10^{3}		3	14	8	6^{1}												4
1		2	8^{2}	5	13	7		9	10	11^{1}			4	12	6	3												5
1	14	4		5^{3}	6	7		9	11	13	10^{1}		3		2		8^{2}	12										6
1		3	4		6^{1}	7	8	5	11	12					2		13	10	9^{2}									7
1		2	3		13	12	7	9	10	11			4		5			6^{2}	8^{1}									8
1		2	3			12	7	9^{3}	10	11^{1}			4	13	5		14	6	8^{2}									9
1		2	3			13	8	9^{1}	11	10^{2}			4		5			6	7	12								10
1		2	4	13		12	8^{2}	9	10	11^{1}			3		5		14	6^{3}	7									11
1		2	4		6^{1}	14		9	10	12			3		5	8^{3}	11^{2}	13	7									12
1		2	4					8		12			3		6^{2}	13		10	7	11	5	9^{1}						13
1	14	4	3			6		11^{1}	10		13		2		5^{2}			9^{3}	7	12	8							14
1		4	3			6		11	10	12			2		5			9^{1}	7		8							15
1		5	4			8^{2}		10	11	7^{1}			3		2	14	12	13	9^{3}		6							16
1		5	4			9		10	11	12	13		3		2			7^{1}	8^{2}		6							17
1		2	4	13		6	$7^{■}$	8	11		12		3		5			9^{1}	10^{2}									18
1		4	3	9^{3}		6^{2}		7	10		12		2	14	5^{1}			11	8		13							19
1		2	3	10^{2}		13	8^{1}	6	11		12		4			7			9		5							20
1	4	2	3	10			8^{1}	6	11					12		7			9		5							21
1		2^{2}	4	10^{1}			9	7	11				3	13	12	6			8		5							22
1			4	7^{1}			8	10	11				3	12	2	6		13	9^{2}		5							23
1			4				8	6	10		13		3	11^{1}	2	7		12	9^{2}		5							24
1			3	6	12		8	9	11				4	13	2	7^{2}		10			5^{1}							25
1	2		3	12		7	8	9	11				4		5	6		10^{1}										26
1	2		3			7^{1}	9	8	11^{3}	12	13		4		5^{2}	6		10			14							27
1	5	2	3			7	9	10^{2}		11^{1}					8	6			13				4	12				28
1	5^{3}	2	3		13	7^{1}	9	10		$11^{■}$					8^{2}	6							4	14	12			29
1	$2^{■}$	4	3			8	11	10^{1}							5	7							6	12	9			30
1	5^{1}	3	2	12		6		11	10						8	7		13					4		9^{2}			31
1	5	2	3	13		8		7	10						9^{1}	6^{3}		14	12				4		11^{2}			32
1	2	3	4	12	13			8^{3}	10	14					6^{1}	7		11^{2}	9				5					33
1	2		4	9^{2}	6^{1}		7^{3}	14	10	13			3			8		11	12				5					34
1			4		9	7	6	11^{1}	10				3		2			12	8				5					35
1			3	14	9	7	8^{2}	11^{1}		10^{3}			4		2	13		12	6				5					36
1			3	12	9	7	6	11^{1}		10^{3}			4		2	14			8^{2}				5		13			37
1			3	12	9	7	6	11		10^{1}			4		2				8				5					38
1			3	11	9^{1}	7	6	12		10			4		2				8^{2}				5		13			39
1			3	13	9	7	6	11^{1}	14	10^{3}			$4^{■}$		2				8^{2}				5			12		40
1			4	11	9^{3}		6^{2}	12	13	10^{1}					2	7		14	8				5			3		41
1			4	11	9	13		6^{2}	12	10^{1}					2	7^{3}		14	8				5			3		42
1			4	10	8	7			11				3		2			9^{2}	6^{1}				5	12			13	43
1			4	8^{1}	10	7		9^{3}	13				3		2	12			6		14		5	11^{2}				44
1			4	11^{1}	9^{2}	7		8	10				3		2			13	6				5	12				45
1			4	12	10^{1}	8		6^{2}	11				3			7		13	9		2		5					46

FA Cup
First Round Sunderland (h) 1-2

Carabao Cup
First Round Lincoln C (h) 0-4

Checkatrade Trophy
Group E (N) Burton Alb (h) 1-0
Group E (N) Middlesbrough U21 (h) 2-0
Group E (N) Walsall (a) 2-1
Second Round (N) Stoke C U21 (h) 4-0
Third Round Shrewsbury T (h) 1-1
(Port Vale won 4-3 on penalties)
Quarter-Final Bristol R (a) 0-3

PORTSMOUTH

FOUNDATION

At a meeting held in his High Street, Portsmouth offices in 1898, solicitor Alderman J. E. Pink and five other business and professional men agreed to buy some ground close to Goldsmith Avenue for £4,950 which they developed into Fratton Park in record breaking time. A team of professionals was signed up by manager Frank Brettell and entry to the Southern League obtained for the new club's September 1899 kick-off.

Fratton Park, Frogmore Road, Portsmouth, Hampshire PO4 8RA.

Telephone: (0345) 646 1898.

Fax: (02392) 734 129.

Ticket Office: (0345) 646 1898.

Website: www.portsmouthfc.co.uk

Email: info@pompeyfc.co.uk

Ground Capacity: 19,669.

Record Attendance: 51,385 v Derby Co, FA Cup 6th rd, 26 February 1949.

Pitch Measurements: 100m × 66m (109.5yd × 72yd).

Chairman: Michael Eisner.

Chief Executive: Mark Catlin.

Manager: Kenny Jackett.

Assistant Manager: Joe Gallen.

Colours: Blue shirts with white trim, white shorts with blue trim, red socks with white trim.

Year Formed: 1898.

Turned Professional: 1898.

Club Nickname: 'Pompey'.

Ground: 1898, Fratton Park.

First Football League Game: 28 August 1920, Division 3, v Swansea T (h) W 3–0 – Robson; Probert, Potts; Abbott, Harwood, Turner; Thompson, Stringfellow (1), Reid (1), James (1), Beedie.

Record League Victory: 9–1 v Notts Co, Division 2, 9 April 1927 – McPhail; Clifford, Ted Smith; Reg Davies (1), Foxall, Moffat; Forward (1), Mackie (2), Haines (3), Watson, Cook (2).

Record Cup Victory: 7–0 v Stockport Co, FA Cup 3rd rd, 8 January 1949 – Butler; Rookes, Ferrier; Scoular, Flewin, Dickinson; Harris (3), Barlow, Clarke (2), Phillips (2), Froggatt.

Record Defeat: 0–10 v Leicester C, Division 1, 20 October 1928.

Most League Points (2 for a win): 65, Division 3, 1961–62.

HONOURS

League Champions: Division 1 – 1948–49, 1949–50; First Division – 2002–03; Division 3 – 1961–62, 1982–83; Division 3S – 1923–24; FL 2 – 2016–17.
Runners-up: Division 2 – 1926–27, 1986–87.

FA Cup Winners: 1939, 2008.
Runners-up: 1929, 1934, 2010.

League Cup: 5th rd – 1961, 1986, 1994, 2005, 2010.

League Trophy Winners: 2019.

European Competitions
UEFA Cup: 2008–09.

THE Sun FACT FILE

Portsmouth played Belgian club RSC Liege in their Festival of Britain fixture that took place at Fratton Park on 9 May 1951. In front of a crowd of 12,280 Pompey ran out 4-1 winners; the first goal came from their own Belgian player, Marcel Gaillard, followed by further strikes from Albert Mundy (2) and Peter Harris.

Most League Points (3 for a win): 98, Division 1, 2002–03.

Most League Goals: 97, Division 1, 2002–03.

Highest League Scorer in Season: Guy Whittingham, 42, Division 1, 1992–93.

Most League Goals in Total Aggregate: Peter Harris, 194, 1946–60.

Most League Goals in One Match: 5, Alf Strange v Gillingham, Division 3, 27 January 1923; 5, Peter Harris v Aston Villa, Division 1, 3 September 1958.

Most Capped Player: Jimmy Dickinson, 48, England.

Most League Appearances: Jimmy Dickinson, 764, 1946–65.

Youngest League Player: Clive Green, 16 years 259 days v Wrexham, 21 August 1976.

Record Transfer Fee Received: £18,800,000 from Real Madrid for Lassana Diarra, January 2009.

Record Transfer Fee Paid: £9,000,000 (rising to £11,000,000) to Liverpool for Peter Crouch, July 2008.

Football League Record: 1920 Original Member of Division 3; 1921 Division 3 (S); 1924–27 Division 2; 1927–59 Division 1; 1959–61 Division 2; 1961–62 Division 3; 1962–76 Division 2; 1976–78 Division 3; 1978–80 Division 4; 1980–83 Division 3; 1983–87 Division 2; 1987–88 Division 1; 1988–92 Division 2; 1992–2003 Division 1; 2003–10 Premier League; 2010–12 FL C; 2012–13 FL 1; 2013–17 FL 2; 2017– FL 1.

LATEST SEQUENCES

Longest Sequence of League Wins: 7, 12.3.2019 – 22.4.2019.

Longest Sequence of League Defeats: 9, 26.12.2012 – 9.2.2013.

Longest Sequence of League Draws: 5, 2.2.2019 – 23.2.2019.

Longest Sequence of Unbeaten League Matches: 15, 18.4.1924 – 18.10.1924.

Longest Sequence Without a League Win: 25, 29.11.1958 – 22.8.1959.

Successive Scoring Runs: 23 from 30.8.1930.

Successive Non-scoring Runs: 6 from 27.12.1993.

MANAGERS

Frank Brettell 1898–1901
Bob Blyth 1901–04
Richard Bonney 1905–08
Bob Brown 1911–20
John McCartney 1920–27
Jack Tinn 1927–47
Bob Jackson 1947–52
Eddie Lever 1952–58
Freddie Cox 1958–61
George Smith 1961–70
Ron Tindall 1970–73
(General Manager to 1974)
John Mortimore 1973–74
Ian St John 1974–77
Jimmy Dickinson 1977–79
Frank Burrows 1979–82
Bobby Campbell 1982–84
Alan Ball 1984–89
John Gregory 1989–90
Frank Burrows 1990–91
Jim Smith 1991–95
Terry Fenwick 1995–98
Alan Ball 1998–99
Tony Pulis 2000
Steve Claridge 2000–01
Graham Rix 2001–02
Harry Redknapp 2002–04
Velimir Zajec 2004–05
Alain Perrin 2005
Harry Redknapp 2005–08
Tony Adams 2008–09
Paul Hart 2009
Avram Grant 2009–10
Steve Cotterill 2010–11
Michael Appleton 2011–12
Guy Whittingham 2012–13
Richie Barker 2013–14
Andy Awford 2014–15
Paul Cook 2015–17
Kenny Jackett June 2017–

TEN YEAR LEAGUE RECORD

		P	W	D	L	F	A	Pts	Pos
2009-10	PR Lge	38	7	7	24	34	66	19*	20
2010-11	FL C	46	15	13	18	53	60	58	16
2011-12	FL C	46	13	11	22	50	59	40†	22
2012-13	FL 1	46	10	12	24	51	69	32†	24
2013-14	FL 2	46	14	17	15	56	66	59	13
2014-15	FL 2	46	14	15	17	52	54	57	16
2015-16	FL 2	46	21	15	10	75	44	78	6
2016-17	FL 2	46	26	9	11	79	40	87	1
2017-18	FL 1	46	20	6	20	57	56	66	8
2018-19	FL 1	46	25	13	8	83	51	88	4

**9 pts deducted; †10 pts deducted.*

DID YOU KNOW ?

Ray Pointer made over 150 appearances for Portsmouth after signing for the club in January 1967. Despite missing the final two months of the 1967–68 campaign after suffering a broken bone in his right leg, he was the first ever recipient of the club's Player of the Season award that season.

PORTSMOUTH – SKY BET LEAGUE ONE 2018–19 LEAGUE RECORD

Match No.	*Date*	*Venue*	*Opponents*	*Result*		*H/T Score*	*Lg Pos.*	*Goalscorers*	*Attendance*
1	Aug 4	H	Luton T	W	1-0	1-0	9	Lowe [16]	19,018
2	11	A	Blackpool	W	2-1	1-0	5	Curtis 2 [9, 59]	4154
3	18	H	Oxford U	W	4-1	0-0	2	Evans [48], Dickie (og) [56], Lowe 2 [65, 90]	18,093
4	21	A	Bristol R	W	2-1	1-0	2	Evans [32], Curtis [87]	9073
5	25	A	Doncaster R	D	0-0	0-0	3		7618
6	Sept 1	H	Plymouth Arg	W	3-0	1-0	2	Curtis 2 [22, 69], Lowe [63]	18,872
7	8	H	Shrewsbury T	D	1-1	0-0	2	Pitman, B (pen) [87]	17,634
8	15	A	Peterborough U	W	2-1	0-0	1	Hawkins [62], Lowe [75]	10,472
9	22	H	Wycombe W	D	2-2	0-1	2	Evans [57], Pitman, B [86]	18,648
10	29	A	Rochdale	W	3-1	1-1	1	Lowe [25], Pitman, B [71], Clarke [81]	3796
11	Oct 2	A	Coventry C	W	1-0	1-0	1	Curtis [45]	11,102
12	6	H	Gillingham	L	0-2	0-2	1		18,158
13	13	A	AFC Wimbledon	W	2-1	2-0	1	Naylor [24], Evans [31]	4569
14	20	H	Fleetwood T	W	1-0	0-0	1	Hawkins [50]	18,046
15	23	H	Burton Alb	D	2-2	1-0	1	Hawkins [36], Clarke [57]	18,200
16	27	A	Accrington S	D	1-1	0-0	1	Hawkins [62]	3558
17	Nov 3	A	Bradford C	W	1-0	1-0	1	Evans [12]	16,393
18	24	A	Scunthorpe U	W	2-1	2-0	1	Naylor [34], Evans [40]	4365
19	27	H	Walsall	W	2-0	1-0	1	Hawkins [25], Curtis [49]	16,794
20	Dec 8	H	Southend U	W	2-0	2-0	1	Turner (og) [11], Lowe [29]	18,062
21	11	H	Charlton Ath	L	1-2	0-2	1	Green [88]	17,891
22	15	A	Barnsley	D	1-1	1-0	1	Evans [43]	12,441
23	22	H	Sunderland	W	3-1	0-0	1	Evans (pen) [48], Curtis [53], Thompson, B [63]	19,402
24	26	A	Gillingham	L	0-2	0-1	1		6940
25	29	A	Fleetwood T	W	5-2	1-2	1	Thompson, B [26], Pitman, B (pen) [57], Walkes [58], Lowe 2 [81, 84]	3494
26	Jan 1	H	AFC Wimbledon	W	2-1	1-0	1	Lowe [8], Curtis [80]	18,732
27	12	H	Blackpool	L	0-1	0-0	1		18,403
28	19	A	Oxford U	L	1-2	0-2	1	Pitman, B [64]	8202
29	29	A	Luton T	L	2-3	0-1	2	Curtis [52], Bogle [79]	10,078
30	Feb 2	H	Doncaster R	D	1-1	0-1	3	Bogle [54]	17,800
31	9	A	Plymouth Arg	D	1-1	0-0	3	Close [56]	12,052
32	16	A	Southend U	D	3-3	3-1	3	Morris [8], Close [20], Hawkins [31]	7300
33	19	H	Bristol R	D	1-1	0-1	4	Clarke, J (og) [58]	17,880
34	23	H	Barnsley	D	0-0	0-0	4		18,624
35	Mar 2	H	Bradford C	W	5-1	2-0	4	Evans (pen) [23], Naylor [41], Lowe [67], Close 2 [70, 87]	17,657
36	9	A	Charlton Ath	L	1-2	1-1	4	Curtis [45]	14,451
37	12	A	Walsall	W	3-2	2-0	4	Pitman, B (pen) [13], Bogle [25], Solomon-Otabor [68]	4097
38	16	H	Scunthorpe U	W	2-0	0-0	4	Bogle [71], Lowe [87]	17,308
39	23	A	Shrewsbury T	W	2-0	1-0	3	Close [40], Pitman, B [79]	8028
40	Apr 6	A	Wycombe W	W	3-2	1-0	4	Lowe [17], Pitman, B 2 [46, 60]	6978
41	13	H	Rochdale	W	4-1	2-0	4	Hawkins [21], Pitman, B (pen) [45], Evans [62], Lowe [79]	18,197
42	19	A	Burton Alb	W	2-1	1-0	4	Close [31], Clarke [90]	4034
43	22	H	Coventry C	W	2-1	0-1	3	Naylor [66], Pitman, B [83]	18,884
44	27	A	Sunderland	D	1-1	1-1	3	Lowe [24]	41,129
45	30	H	Peterborough U	L	2-3	1-2	3	Close [38], Burgess [59]	18,396
46	May 4	H	Accrington S	D	1-1	0-0	4	Close [59]	18,439

Final League Position: 4

GOALSCORERS

League (83): Lowe 15, Curtis 11, Pitman B 11 (4 pens), Evans 10 (2 pens), Close 8, Hawkins 7, Bogle 4, Naylor 4, Clarke 3, Thompson B 2, Burgess 1, Green 1, Morris 1, Solomon-Otabor 1, Walkes 1, own goals 3.
FA Cup (7): Green 2, Hawkins 1, Lowe 1, Thompson B 1, Wheeler 1, own goal 1.
Carabao Cup (1): Burgess 1.
Checkatrade Trophy (18): Evans 3, Green 2, Hawkins 2, Pitman B 2 (1 pen), Wheeler 2, Clarke 1, Close 1, Curtis 1, Dennis 1, Donohue 1, Lowe 1, Thompson N 1.
League One Play-offs (0).

MacGillivray C 46	Thompson N 30 + 1	Whatmough J 26	Clarke M 46	Brown L 44	Lowe J 44 + 1	Naylor T 43	Walkes A 17 + 7	Haunstrup B 2 + 3	Curtis R 36 + 5	Pitman B 16 + 16	Hawkins O 30 + 9	Close B 25 + 9	Burgess C 20 + 5	Evans G 34 + 8	Rose D — + 1	Wheeler D 1 + 10	Thompson B 19 + 4	Green A 2 + 4	Mason J — + 1	Donohue D 5 + 5	Cannon A 1 + 1	Dennis L — + 1	Morris B 5 + 2	Bogle O 7 + 5	Vaughan J 2 + 8	Solomon-Otabor V 5 + 2	*Match No.*
1	2^{2}	3	4	5	6	7	8^{1}	9	10	11^{3}	12	13	14														1
1		3	4	5	9^{1}	7	2		10		11	8^{2}		6	12	13											2
1		3	4	5	9	6	2		11^{1}		10			7		12	8										3
1		3	4	5	10	6	2	13	9^{2}	12	11^{1}			8			7										4
1		3	4	5	8	7	2		10	13	11^{2}	12		9			6^{1}										5
1	14	4^{2}	3	5	9	6	2^{1}		11	12	10^{3}		13	8			7										6
1	2		4	5	8	6				14	11^{1}	13	3	9		12	7^{3}	10^{2}									7
1	2		3	5	8	6		13	10^{1}		11	7^{2}	4	9			12										8
1	2		3	5	8	7			10	12	11^{1}	6	4	9^{2}					13								9
1	2	4	3	5	8	6			10^{3}	11^{2}	14	7		9^{1}		13	12										10
1	2	4	3	5	8	7			10	11^{1}	13	6^{2}		9			12										11
1	2^{1}	4	3	5	8	7			10	11	14	6^{2}		9^{3}		12	13										12
1	2	3	4	5	9	7	14			13	11^{3}	12		8^{2}			6			10^{1}							13
1	2	3	4	5	6	8			11^{1}		10			12			7			9							14
1		3	4	5	8	6	2		10	13	11^{1}			12			9			7^{2}							15
1	2		4	5	8				10	12	11^{1}	7	3	9			6										16
1		4	3	5	8	6	2		10^{2}		11	12		9^{1}		13	7										17
1	2	3	4	5	8^{1}	6			10		11		12	9^{2}		13	7										18
1	2	3	4	5	8	7			10^{2}		11	13		9^{1}		12	6										19
1	2	3	4	5	8	7			10	13	11	12		9^{2}			6^{1}										20
1	2	3	4	5^{2}	8	6			10	12	11^{1}			9			7■	13									21
1	2	3	4	5	8	6	12		10^{1}		11			9			7										22
1	2	3	4	5	8	6			10^{3}	13	11^{1}	12		9^{2}			7	14									23
1	2	3	4	5	8^{1}	6			10^{3}	12	11^{2}			9		13	7	14									24
1		4	3	5^{1}	8	6	2	12	10^{3}	11		9^{2}		13			7	14									25
1		3	4		8	6	2	5	10	13	11^{2}	12	14	9^{3}			7^{1}										26
1		3	4		8	6	2		10	11				7^{2}		13		9^{1}		5	12						27
1		3	4	5	11	7	2		10	13				9^{3}		8^{2}				14	6^{1}	12					28
1		3	4	5	8	6	2		10	11^{2}				9^{1}						13			7	12			29
1	2	3^{3}	4	5	8	6			10			9	12	14						7^{1}				11^{2}	13		30
1	2		4	5	8				10		12	6	3	9									7	11^{1}			31
1			4	5	6^{3}		2		12		11	7	3	13									8	10^{1}	14	9^{2}	32
1			4	5	8^{1}	6	2		10		11^{2}	7	3	9^{3}										12	13	14	33
1			4	5	12	8	2		11			7	3										6	10^{1}	13	9^{2}	34
1	2^{1}		4^{2}	5	8	6	13		10		11^{3}	7	3	9						14					12		35
1	2		4	5	8	6			10	14	11^{1}	7^{3}	3	9^{2}						12					13		36
1	2		4	5	8	6	13			9^{1}		7	3											11^{2}	12	10	37
1	2		4	5	8	6				9^{3}	13	7	3	12						14				11^{1}		10^{2}	38
1	2		4	5	10	6	13			9	12	7	3	8^{1}										11^{2}			39
1	2		4	5	8	6	12		13	9^{1}	11	7	3	10^{2}													40
1	2		4	5	8	6			10^{1}	9^{2}	11^{3}	7	3	12									14	13			41
1	2		4	5	8	6			14	9^{3}	11^{1}	7	3	10^{2}									13	12			42
1	2		4	5	8	6	14		12	9^{1}	11^{2}	7	3	10^{3}											13		43
1	2		4	5	8	6			10^{2}	9	12	7	3	13											11^{1}		44
1	2		4	5	8	6			10^{2}	9	12	7	3												11^{1}	13	45
1			4	5		6	2		12	14	11^{3}	7	3	8^{2}									9^{1}	13		10	46

FA Cup

First Round	Maidenhead U	(a)	4-0
Second Round	Rochdale	(a)	1-0
Third Round	Norwich C	(a)	1-0
Fourth Round	QPR	(h)	1-1
Replay	QPR	(a)	0-2

Checkatrade Trophy

Group A (S)	Gillingham	(h)	4-0
Group A (S)	Crawley T	(a)	1-0
Group A (S)	Tottenham H U21	(h)	3-2
Second Round (S)	Arsenal U21	(h)	2-1
Third Round	Southend U	(a)	2-0
Quarter-Final	Peterborough U	(h)	1-0
Semi-Final	Bury	(a)	3-0
Final	Sunderland	(Wembley)	2-2

(aet; Portsmouth won 5-4 on penalties)

Carabao Cup

First Round	AFC Wimbledon	(h)	1-2

League One Play-offs

Semi-Final 1st leg	Sunderland	(a)	0-1
Semi-Final 2nd leg	Sunderland	(h)	0-0

PRESTON NORTH END

FOUNDATION

North End Cricket and Rugby Club, which was formed in 1863, indulged in most sports before taking up soccer in about 1879. In 1881 they decided to stick to football to the exclusion of other sports and even a 16–0 drubbing by Blackburn Rovers in an invitation game at Deepdale, a few weeks after taking this decision, did not deter them for they immediately became affiliated to the Lancashire FA.

Deepdale Stadium, Sir Tom Finney Way, Deepdale, Preston, Lancashire PR1 6RU.

Telephone: (0344) 856 1964.

Ticket Office: (0344) 856 1966.

Website: www.pnefc.net

Email: enquiries@pne.co.uk

Ground Capacity: 23,404.

Record Attendance: 42,684 v Arsenal, Division 1, 23 April 1938.

Pitch Measurements: 100m × 67m (109.5yd × 73.5yd).

Chairman: Craig Hemmings.

Chief Executive: John Kay.

Manager: Alex Neil.

First-Team Coaches: Steve Thompson, Frankie McAvoy.

Colours: White shirts with blue trim, blue shorts, white socks with blue hoops.

Year Formed: 1880.

Turned Professional: 1885.

Club Nicknames: 'The Lilywhites', 'North End'.

Ground: 1881, Deepdale.

First Football League Game: 8 September 1888, Football League, v Burnley (h) W 5–2 – Trainer; Howarth, Holmes; Robertson, William Graham, Johnny Graham; Gordon (1), Jimmy Ross (2), Goodall, Dewhurst (2), Drummond.

Record League Victory: 10–0 v Stoke, Division 1, 14 September 1889 – Trainer; Howarth, Holmes; Kelso, Russell (1), Johnny Graham; Gordon, Jimmy Ross (2), Nick Ross (3), Thomson (2), Drummond (2).

Record Cup Victory: 26–0 v Hyde, FA Cup 1st rd, 15 October 1887 – Addision; Howarth, Nick Ross; Russell (1), Thomson (5), Johnny Graham (1); Gordon (5), Jimmy Ross (8), John Goodall (1), Dewhurst (3), Drummond (2).

Record Defeat: 0–7 v Nottingham F, Division 2, 9 April 1927; 0–7 v Blackpool, Division 1, 1 May 1948.

Most League Points (2 for a win): 61, Division 3, 1970–71.

Most League Points (3 for a win): 95, Division 2, 1999–2000.

Most League Goals: 100, Division 2, 1927–28 and Division 1, 1957–58.

HONOURS

League Champions: Football League 1888–89, 1889–90; Division 2 – 1903–04, 1912–13, 1950–51; Second Division – 1999–2000; Division 3 – 1970–71; Third Division – 1995–96.
Runners-up: Football League 1890–91, 1891–92; Division 1 – 1892–93, 1905–06, 1952–53, 1957–58; Division 2 – 1914–15, 1933–34; Division 4 – 1986–87.

FA Cup Winners: 1889, 1938.
Runners-up: 1888, 1922, 1937, 1954, 1964.

League Cup: 4th rd – 1963, 1966, 1972, 1981, 2003, 2017.

Double Performed: 1888–89.

THE Sun FACT FILE

Preston North End were a popular team in the immediate post-war period due to the presence of England international Tom Finney in the side. In the 1952–53 season the club had 5,804 season ticket holders, second only to Tottenham Hotspur among the 92 Football League clubs.

Highest League Scorer in Season: Ted Harper, 37, Division 2, 1932–33.

Most League Goals in Total Aggregate: Tom Finney, 187, 1946–60.

Most League Goals in One Match: 4, Jimmy Ross v Stoke, Division 1, 6 October 1888; 4, Nick Ross v Derby Co, Division 1, 11 January 1890; 4, George Drummond v Notts Co, Division 1, 12 December 1891; 4, Frank Becton v Notts Co, Division 1, 31 March 1893; 4, George Harrison v Grimsby T, Division 2, 3 November 1928; 4, Alex Reid v Port Vale, Division 2, 23 February 1929; 4, James McClelland v Reading, Division 2, 6 September 1930; 4, Dick Rowley v Notts Co, Division 2, 16 April 1932; 4, Ted Harper v Burnley, Division 2, 29 August 1932; 4, Ted Harper v Lincoln C, Division 2, 11 March 1933; 4, Charlie Wayman v QPR, Division 2, 25 December 1950; 4, Alex Bruce v Colchester U, Division 3, 28 February 1978; 4, Joe Garner v Crewe Alex, FL 1, 14 March 2015.

Most Capped Player: Tom Finney, 76, England.

Most League Appearances: Alan Kelly, 447, 1961–75.

Youngest League Player: Ethan Walker, 16 years 154 days v Aston Villa, 29 December 2018.

Record Transfer Fee Received: £10,000,000 from West Ham U for Jordan Hugill, January 2018.

Record Transfer Fee Paid: £1,500,000 to Manchester U for David Healy, January 2001.

Football League Record: 1888 Founder Member of League; 1901–04 Division 2; 1904–12 Division 1; 1912–13 Division 2; 1913–14 Division 1; 1914–15 Division 2; 1919–25 Division 1; 1925–34 Division 2; 1934–49 Division 1; 1949–51 Division 2; 1951–61 Division 1; 1961–70 Division 2; 1970–71 Division 3; 1971–74 Division 2; 1974–78 Division 3; 1978–81 Division 2; 1981–85 Division 3; 1985–87 Division 4; 1987–92 Division 3; 1992–93 Division 2; 1993–96 Division 3; 1996–2000 Division 2; 2000–04 Division 1; 2004–11 FL C; 2011–15 FL 1; 2015– FL C.

LATEST SEQUENCES

Longest Sequence of League Wins: 14, 25.12.1950 – 27.3.1951.

Longest Sequence of League Defeats: 8, 22.9.1984 – 27.10.1984.

Longest Sequence of League Draws: 6, 24.2.1979 – 20.3.1979.

Longest Sequence of Unbeaten League Matches: 23, 8.9.1888 – 14.9.1889.

Longest Sequence Without a League Win: 15, 14.4.1923 – 20.10.1923.

Successive Scoring Runs: 30 from 15.11.1952.

Successive Non-scoring Runs: 6 from 19.11.1960.

MANAGERS

Charlie Parker 1906–15
Vincent Hayes 1919–23
Jim Lawrence 1923–25
Frank Richards 1925–27
Alex Gibson 1927–31
Lincoln Hayes 1931–32
Run by committee 1932–36
Tommy Muirhead 1936–37
Run by committee 1937–49
Will Scott 1949–53
Scot Symon 1953–54
Frank Hill 1954–56
Cliff Britton 1956–61
Jimmy Milne 1961–68
Bobby Seith 1968–70
Alan Ball Snr 1970–73
Bobby Charlton 1973–75
Harry Catterick 1975–77
Nobby Stiles 1977–81
Tommy Docherty 1981
Gordon Lee 1981–83
Alan Kelly 1983–85
Tommy Booth 1985–86
Brian Kidd 1986
John McGrath 1986–90
Les Chapman 1990–92
Sam Allardyce 1992 (*Caretaker*)
John Beck 1992–94
Gary Peters 1994–98
David Moyes 1998–2002
Kelham O'Hanlon 2002 (*Caretaker*)
Craig Brown 2002–04
Billy Davies 2004–06
Paul Simpson 2006–07
Alan Irvine 2007–09
Darren Ferguson 2010
Phil Brown 2011
Graham Westley 2012–13
Simon Grayson 2013–17
Alex Neil July 2017–

TEN YEAR LEAGUE RECORD

		P	W	D	L	F	A	Pts	Pos
2009-10	FL C	46	13	15	18	58	73	54	17
2010-11	FL C	46	10	12	24	54	79	42	22
2011-12	FL 1	46	13	15	18	54	68	54	15
2012-13	FL 1	46	14	17	15	54	49	59	14
2013-14	FL 1	46	23	16	7	72	46	85	5
2014-15	FL 1	46	25	14	7	79	40	89	3
2015-16	FL C	46	15	17	14	45	45	62	11
2016-17	FL C	46	16	14	16	64	63	62	11
2017-18	FL C	46	19	16	11	57	46	73	7
2018-19	FL C	46	16	13	17	67	67	61	14

DID YOU KNOW ?

A pre-war Preston North End Supporters' Club had an extremely brief life. Formed early in 1933, it folded at the end of the 1934–35 season. One of the club rules was that members should try to suppress barracking of the players from the terraces.

PRESTON NORTH END – SKY BET CHAMPIONSHIP 2018–19 LEAGUE RECORD

Match No.	Date	Venue	Opponents	Result		H/T Score	Lg Pos.	Goalscorers	Attendance
1	Aug 4	H	QPR	W	1-0	0-0	6	Browne [50]	13,418
2	11	A	Swansea C	L	0-1	0-1	10		19,352
3	18	H	Stoke C	D	2-2	2-1	13	Gallagher (pen) [40], Burke [45]	13,996
4	22	A	Norwich C	L	0-2	0-0	18		24,936
5	25	A	Derby Co	L	0-2	0-1	19		25,257
6	Sept 1	H	Bolton W	D	2-2	2-2	18	Robinson [11], Browne [16]	16,331
7	15	H	Reading	L	2-3	1-1	23	Johnson [31], Robinson [76]	10,849
8	18	A	Leeds U	L	0-3	0-1	23		27,729
9	22	A	Sheffield U	L	2-3	0-1	24	Robinson [80], Johnson [82]	23,857
10	29	H	WBA	L	2-3	0-0	24	Hughes [71], Browne [90]	14,099
11	Oct 2	A	Aston Villa	D	3-3	0-2	24	Johnson (pen) [56], Gallagher [79], Moult [86]	27,331
12	6	H	Wigan Ath	W	4-0	1-0	22	Barkhuizen [17], Robinson 2 [51, 90], Gallagher (pen) [85]	15,280
13	20	A	Hull C	D	1-1	0-0	21	Moult [90]	12,066
14	24	H	Brentford	W	4-3	3-1	19	Browne [5], Robinson 2 [12, 69], Barkhuizen [23]	10,882
15	27	H	Rotherham U	D	1-1	1-0	20	Barkhuizen [40]	11,780
16	Nov 3	A	Ipswich T	D	1-1	0-1	21	Gallagher [73]	15,129
17	10	A	Bristol C	W	1-0	1-0	18	Robinson [35]	19,797
18	24	H	Blackburn R	W	4-1	2-0	16	Barkhuizen [2], Robinson [10], Moult [74], Browne [85]	19,912
19	27	H	Middlesbrough	D	1-1	1-0	15	Browne [43]	10,990
20	Dec 1	A	Birmingham C	L	0-3	0-0	17		20,523
21	8	A	Nottingham F	W	1-0	0-0	15	Moult [56]	27,777
22	15	H	Millwall	W	3-2	2-0	15	Browne [37], Barkhuizen [42], Hughes [81]	10,924
23	22	A	Sheffield W	L	0-1	0-0	15		22,366
24	26	H	Hull C	L	1-2	0-1	17	Browne [47]	14,026
25	29	H	Aston Villa	D	1-1	0-1	17	Nmecha [61]	19,126
26	Jan 1	A	Rotherham U	L	1-2	0-1	17	Nmecha [78]	9077
27	12	H	Swansea C	D	1-1	0-0	18	Johnson (pen) [60]	11,604
28	19	A	QPR	W	4-1	1-0	18	Stockley [14], Storey [68], Browne [82], Potts [87]	13,736
29	26	A	Stoke C	W	2-0	1-0	16	Browne [20], Potts [80]	25,053
30	Feb 1	H	Derby Co	D	0-0	0-0	16		12,124
31	9	A	Bolton W	W	2-1	1-0	14	Browne [40], Barkhuizen [82]	17,381
32	13	H	Norwich C	W	3-1	2-0	13	Davies [2], Gallagher (pen) [24], Maguire [69]	11,280
33	16	H	Nottingham F	D	0-0	0-0	11		13,904
34	23	A	Millwall	W	3-1	3-0	10	Hughes [4], Clarke [16], Maguire [27]	13,265
35	Mar 2	H	Bristol C	D	1-1	1-0	12	Johnson [42]	12,863
36	9	A	Blackburn R	W	1-0	1-0	9	Johnson [8]	21,577
37	13	A	Middlesbrough	W	2-1	0-1	9	Gallagher [63], Stockley [81]	21,088
38	16	H	Birmingham C	W	1-0	0-0	7	Maguire [90]	17,509
39	30	A	Reading	L	1-2	0-2	10	Stockley [90]	16,771
40	Apr 6	H	Sheffield U	L	0-1	0-1	10		18,339
41	9	H	Leeds U	L	0-2	0-0	11		18,019
42	13	A	WBA	L	1-4	0-3	12	Robinson [90]	25,088
43	19	H	Ipswich T	W	4-0	2-0	9	Robinson 2 [6, 22], Nmecha 2 [56, 75]	12,546
44	22	A	Wigan Ath	L	0-2	0-1	12		12,496
45	27	H	Sheffield W	D	3-3	2-0	12	Stockley [9], Lees (og) [36], Browne [62]	15,873
46	May 5	A	Brentford	L	0-3	0-1	14		11,289

Final League Position: 14

GOALSCORERS

League (67): Browne 12, Robinson 12, Barkhuizen 6, Gallagher 6 (3 pens), Johnson 6 (2 pens), Moult 4, Nmecha 4, Stockley 4, Hughes 3, Maguire 3, Potts 2, Burke 1, Clarke 1, Davies 1, Storey 1, own goal 1.
FA Cup (1): Hughes 1.
Carabao Cup (7): Barker 2, Barkhuizen 1, Burke 1, Johnson 1 (1 pen), Moult 1, Robinson 1.

Rudd D 36	Fisher D 32 + 3	Clarke T 21	Davies B 39 + 1	Hughes A 31 + 1	Pearson B 30	Barkhuizen T 26 + 3	Browne A 36 + 2	Harrop J 4 + 4	Robinson C 24 + 3	Moult L 8 + 16	Horgan D — + 1	Gallagher P 30 + 10	Ledson R 14 + 10	Nmecha L 24 + 17	Burke G 6 + 6	Barker B 6 + 10	Huntington P 21 + 1	Johnson D 26 + 9	Earl J 12 + 2	Maxwell C 8	Storey J 27 + 1	Maguire S 21 + 5	Walker E — + 1	O'Reilly A — + 1	Woods C — + 1	Potts B 10	Stockley J 8 + 9	Rafferty J 4 + 2	Ginnelly J — + 5	Ripley C 2	Match No.
1	2	3	4	5	6	7^1	8	9^3	10	11^2	12	13	14																		1
1	2	3	4	5	6	7^2	8	9^3	10			14		11^1	12	13															2
1	2	3	4	5	6	13	9		10	12		7^2	14	11^3	8^1																3
1	2	3		5	8	6^3	7^2	14	9	11^1				10		13	4	12													4
1	2		4	5	6	12		9	10^1	14			7	11^2	8^3	13	3														5
1		2	4	5	6■	13	9		11	14		7^1			8^2	10^3	3	12													6
1	5^1	2	4			9		12	10	11^3		6^2		13	14		3	7	8												7
1	2	3	4			8	6^1	9^2	10	11^3		14		13		12		7	5												8
	2	4	5	6		10^3	8	14	11			7^2	9^1			13	3	12		1											9
	5^1		4	9	7	12	8	14	10^2	13			6			11^3	3			1	2										10
	2^1		4	5	6	10^3	8		9	14		13	7^2	11			3	12		1											11
	2	3	14	5	6	8^1	9		10			13		11^2				7^3		1	4	12									12
	2		4	5			6		12	14		13	7^3	11^1		10		9		1	3	8^4									13
	2		4	5	7	8^3	9		10	13		14		11^1			3	6^2		1		12									14
		2	4	5	6	8^1	9		10	14		13		11^3			3	7^2		1		12									15
		2	4		7	8^3	9^2		10	12		14		13			3	6^1	5	1■		11									16
1		2	4		8	9	12		11			6^1		13			3	7	5			10^2									17
1		2	4		7^1	8	9		10^3	12		6	14	11^2		13	3		5												18
1		2			6	8	9			11^1		7		12		10	4		5		3										19
1	2			12		8	9^2			11		7	6	13	14	10^1	3		5^3		4										20
1		2	4	5		8	6			11^2		7	13	12	14	10^1	3	9^3													21
1		2	4	5	6	8	9^1					7	12	11	13		3	10^2													22
1	2		4	5	7■	10	12			11^1		6^3	13	8^2	14		3	9													23
1	14	2^3	4^2	5		10	9					6	13	11	8^1		3	7			12										24
1	12	2^1		5		10						7^2	6	11	9^3		4	8			3		13	14							25
1		2		5^1		8						10	6	11	9		3	7			4				12						26
1	13	2^3		5	7	10	9										3^2	6^1	12■		4	14				8	11				27
1	2		4	5	7	12	9					6		13							3	10^2				8	11^1				28
1	2		4	5	7	12	9					6^3		14				13			3	10^2				8	11^1				29
1	2		4	5	6	13	9					7^1		12							3	10				8	11^2				30
1	2		4	5	6^1	7	8^3					10^2	13	12				14			3	11				9					31
1	2		4	5	6	8^3	9					7^2		13				12			3	11^1				10	14				32
1	2		4	5	7	8^3	9					6^2		13				14			3	11^1				10	12				33
1		2	4	5	6	7^1	8					10^3	14	12				13			3	11				9^2					34
1	2		4	5		12	9					10^2	6	13				7^3			3	11				8^1	14				35
1	7■		4	5			8					10^1	6	7^2		13		9			3	11^3					12	14			36
1			3	4	7		5^3					8^2		10		13		6	9^1		2	11					14	12			37
1	2		4	5^1	6				12					10		14		7	13		3	9				8^3	11^2				38
1	2		4		6				10^2	14		8		9^1		13^3		7	5		3	11					12				39
1	2		4		7		9		10^2	12		13	6^3	8^1					5		3	11					14				40
1	2		4		7■		9		10^3	12			13	8^1				6	5		3	11^2					14				41
1	2		4				8^3		12			10^1	6	7				9	5		3	13					11^2		14		42
1	5		4						10^2	12		8^1	6	11				7			3	9^3					14	2	13		43
1	5		4						9	13		10	6■	8^2				7			3	11^1						2	12		44
	5		4				9^1		10^3			7		12			14	6			3	8					11	2^2	13	1	45
	5		4				9		10^3	13		7		12				6			3	8^2					11^1	2	14	1	46

FA Cup

Third Round	Doncaster R	(h)	1-3

Carabao Cup

First Round	Morecambe	(h)	3-1
Second Round	Leeds U	(a)	2-0
Third Round	Middlesbrough	(h)	2-2

(Middlesbrough won 4-3 on penalties)

QUEENS PARK RANGERS

FOUNDATION

There is an element of doubt about the date of the foundation of this club, but it is believed that in either 1885 or 1886 it was formed through the amalgamation of Christchurch Rangers and St Jude's Institute FC. The leading light was George Wodehouse, whose family maintained a connection with the club until comparatively recent times. Most of the players came from the Queen's Park district so this name was adopted after a year as St Jude's Institute.

The Kiyan Prince Foundation Stadium, South Africa Road, Shepherds Bush, London W12 7PJ.

Telephone: (020) 8743 0262.

Fax: (020) 8743 1158.

Ticket Office: (08444) 777 007.

Website: www.qpr.co.uk

Email: boxoffice@qpr.co.uk

Ground Capacity: 18,439.

Record Attendance: 41,097 v Leeds U, FA Cup 3rd rd, 9 January 1932 (at White City); 35,353 v Leeds U, Division 1, 27 April 1974 (at Loftus Road).

Pitch Measurements: 100m × 66m (109.5yd × 72yd).

Chairman: Amit Bhatia.

Chief Executive: Lee Hoos.

Manager: Mark Warburton.

Assistant Manager: John Eustace.

Colours: Blue and white hooped shirts with blue and red trim, white shorts with blue and red trim, white socks with blue and red trim.

Year Formed: 1885* (*see Foundation*).

Turned Professional: 1898.

Previous Name: 1885, St Jude's; 1887, Queens Park Rangers. ***Club Nicknames:*** 'Rangers', 'The Hoops', 'R's'.

Grounds: 1885* (*see Foundation*), Welford's Fields; 1888–99, London Scottish Ground, Brondesbury, Home Farm, Kensal Rise Green, Gun Club Wormwood Scrubs, Kilburn Cricket Ground; 1899, Kensal Rise Athletic Ground; 1901, Latimer Road, Notting Hill; 1904, Agricultural Society, Park Royal; 1907, Park Royal Ground; 1917, Loftus Road; 1931, White City; 1933, Loftus Road; 1962, White City; 1963, Loftus Road (renamed The Kiyan Prince Foundation Stadium 2019).

First Football League Game: 28 August 1920, Division 3, v Watford (h) L 1–2 – Price; Blackman, Wingrove; McGovern, Grant, O'Brien; Faulkner, Birch (1), Smith, Gregory, Middlemiss.

Record League Victory: 9–2 v Tranmere R, Division 3, 3 December 1960 – Drinkwater; Woods, Ingham; Keen, Rutter, Angell; Lazarus (2), Bedford (2), Evans (2), Andrews (1), Clark (2).

Record Cup Victory: 8–1 v Bristol R (a), FA Cup 1st rd, 27 November 1937 – Gilfillan; Smith, Jefferson; Lowe, James, March; Cape, Mallett, Cheetham (3), Fitzgerald (3) Bott (2). 8–1 v Crewe Alex, Milk Cup 1st rd, 3 October 1983 – Hucker; Neill, Dawes, Waddock (1), McDonald (1), Fenwick, Micklewhite (1), Stewart (1), Allen (1), Stainrod (3), Gregory.

HONOURS

League Champions: FL C – 2010–11; Division 2 – 1982–83; Division 3 – 1966–67; Division 3S – 1947–48.
Runners-up: Division 1 – 1975–76; Division 2 – 1967–68, 1972–73; Second Division – 2003–04; Division 3S – 1946–47.

FA Cup: *Runners-up:* 1982.

League Cup Winners: 1967.
Runners-up: 1986.

European Competitions
UEFA Cup: 1976–77 (*qf*), 1984–85.

THE Sun FACT FILE

Queens Park Rangers were one of several Football League clubs who entertained their young fans with a live beat music group playing before matches in the mid-1960s. The first band to appear at Loftus Road was the Moments featuring Stevie Marriott who played before the friendly fixture with Hibernian in February 1964. Marriott later found fame as a member of the Small Faces.

Record Defeat: 1–8 v Mansfield T, Division 3, 15 March 1965. 1–8 v Manchester U, Division 1, 19 March 1969.

Most League Points (2 for a win): 67, Division 3, 1966–67.

Most League Points (3 for a win): 88, FL C, 2010–11.

Most League Goals: 111, Division 3, 1961–62.

Highest League Scorer in Season: George Goddard, 37, Division 3 (S), 1929–30.

Most League Goals in Total Aggregate: George Goddard, 174, 1926–34.

Most League Goals in One Match: 4, George Goddard v Merthyr T, Division 3 (S), 9 March 1929; 4, George Goddard v Swindon T, Division 3 (S), 12 April 1930; 4, George Goddard v Exeter C, Division 3 (S), 20 December 1930; 4, George Goddard v Watford, Division 3 (S), 19 September 1931; 4, Tom Cheetham v Aldershot, Division 3 (S), 14 September 1935; 4, Tom Cheetham v Aldershot, Division 3 (S), 12 November 1938.

Most Capped Player: Alan McDonald, 52, Northern Ireland.

Most League Appearances: Tony Ingham, 514, 1950–63.

Youngest League Player: Frank Sibley, 16 years 97 days v Bristol C, 10 March 1964.

Record Transfer Fee Received: £12,000,000 from Anzhi Makhachkala for Chris Samba, July 2013.

Record Transfer Fee Paid: £12,500,000 to Anzhi Makhachkala for Chris Samba, January 2013.

Football League Record: 1920 Original Members of Division 3; 1921–48 Division 3 (S); 1948–52 Division 2; 1952–58 Division 3 (S); 1958–67 Division 3; 1967–68 Division 2; 1968–69 Division 1; 1969–73 Division 2; 1973–79 Division 1; 1979–83 Division 2; 1983–92 Division 1; 1992–96 Premier League; 1996–2001 Division 1; 2001–04 Division 2; 2004–11 FL C; 2011–13 Premier League; 2013–14 FL C; 2014–15 Premier League; 2015– FL C.

LATEST SEQUENCES

Longest Sequence of League Wins: 8, 7.11.1931 – 28.12.1931.

Longest Sequence of League Defeats: 9, 25.2.1969 – 5.4.1969.

Longest Sequence of League Draws: 6, 29.1.2000 – 5.3.2000.

Longest Sequence of Unbeaten League Matches: 20, 11.3.1972 – 23.9.1972.

Longest Sequence Without a League Win: 20, 7.12.1968 – 7.4.1969.

Successive Scoring Runs: 33 from 9.12.1961.

Successive Non-scoring Runs: 6 from 18.3.1939.

MANAGERS

James Cowan 1906–13
Jimmy Howie 1913–20
Ned Liddell 1920–24
Will Wood 1924–25
(had been Secretary since 1903)
Bob Hewison 1925–31
John Bowman 1931
Archie Mitchell 1931–33
Mick O'Brien 1933–35
Billy Birrell 1935–39
Ted Vizard 1939–44
Dave Mangnall 1944–52
Jack Taylor 1952–59
Alec Stock 1959–65
(General Manager to 1968)
Bill Dodgin Jnr 1968
Tommy Docherty 1968
Les Allen 1968–71
Gordon Jago 1971–74
Dave Sexton 1974–77
Frank Sibley 1977–78
Steve Burtenshaw 1978–79
Tommy Docherty 1979–80
Terry Venables 1980–84
Gordon Jago 1984
Alan Mullery 1984
Frank Sibley 1984–85
Jim Smith 1985–88
Trevor Francis 1988–89
Don Howe 1989–91
Gerry Francis 1991–94
Ray Wilkins 1994–96
Stewart Houston 1996–97
Ray Harford 1997–98
Gerry Francis 1998–2001
Ian Holloway 2001–06
Gary Waddock 2006
John Gregory 2006–07
Luigi Di Canio 2007–08
Iain Dowie 2008
Paulo Sousa 2008–09
Jim Magilton 2009
Paul Hart 2009–10
Neil Warnock 2010–12
Mark Hughes 2012
Harry Redknapp 2012–15
Chris Ramsey 2015
Jimmy Floyd Hasselbaink 2015–16
Ian Holloway 2016–18
Steve McClaren 2018–19
Mark Warburton May 2019–

TEN YEAR LEAGUE RECORD

		P	W	D	L	F	A	Pts	Pos
2009-10	FL C	46	14	15	17	58	65	57	13
2010-11	FL C	46	24	16	6	71	32	88	1
2011-12	PR Lge	38	10	7	21	43	66	37	17
2012-13	PR Lge	38	4	13	21	30	60	25	20
2013-14	FL C	46	23	11	12	60	44	80	4
2014-15	PR Lge	38	8	6	24	42	73	30	20
2015-16	FL C	46	14	18	14	54	54	60	12
2016-17	FL C	46	15	8	23	52	66	53	18
2017-18	FL C	46	15	11	20	58	70	56	16
2018-19	FL C	46	14	9	23	53	71	51	19

DID YOU KNOW ?

Queens Park Rangers travelled across the English Channel to make a short European tour in the summer of 1924. After defeating the Netherlands Olympic A team 4-3 in Amsterdam they moved on to Rotterdam to play the Olympic B team, suffering a 1-0 loss.

QUEENS PARK RANGERS – SKY BET CHAMPIONSHIP 2018–19 LEAGUE RECORD

Match No.	*Date*	*Venue*	*Opponents*	*Result*		*H/T Score*	*Lg Pos.*	*Goalscorers*	*Attendance*
1	Aug 4	A	Preston NE	L	0-1	0-0	23		13,418
2	11	H	Sheffield U	L	1-2	1-1	23	Eze [29]	14,128
3	18	A	WBA	L	1-7	1-1	24	Lynch [34]	22,753
4	21	H	Bristol C	L	0-3	0-1	24		11,739
5	25	H	Wigan Ath	W	1-0	1-0	22	Hemed [35]	11,564
6	Sept 1	A	Birmingham C	D	0-0	0-0	22		21,155
7	15	A	Bolton W	W	2-1	1-0	18	Freeman [26], Eze [56]	13,581
8	19	H	Millwall	W	2-0	2-0	16	Luongo [30], Eze [32]	12,398
9	22	H	Norwich C	L	0-1	0-0	16		12,843
10	29	A	Swansea C	L	0-3	0-1	19		18,633
11	Oct 2	A	Reading	W	1-0	0-0	17	Leistner [64]	13,568
12	6	H	Derby Co	D	1-1	0-1	18	Cameron [48]	14,727
13	20	A	Ipswich T	W	2-0	2-0	16	Gerken (og) [13], Hemed (pen) [45]	18,345
14	23	H	Sheffield W	W	3-0	1-0	11	Hemed [35], Freeman [57], Wells [83]	12,534
15	26	H	Aston Villa	W	1-0	1-0	7	Wszolek [38]	16,036
16	Nov 3	A	Blackburn R	L	0-1	0-0	11		13,294
17	10	H	Brentford	W	3-2	0-1	10	Luongo [50], Lynch [58], Wells [60]	17,609
18	24	A	Stoke C	D	2-2	1-1	8	Rangel 2 [7, 78]	24,291
19	27	A	Rotherham U	D	2-2	1-2	8	Wells [12], Freeman [90]	8018
20	Dec 1	H	Hull C	L	2-3	1-2	11	Wszolek [24], Freeman [90]	13,824
21	8	A	Leeds U	L	1-2	1-1	14	Wells [26]	33,781
22	15	H	Middlesbrough	W	2-1	1-0	13	Wszolek [4], Wells [60]	14,088
23	22	A	Nottingham F	W	1-0	1-0	10	Leistner [45]	28,177
24	26	H	Ipswich T	W	3-0	2-0	8	Wszolek [30], Lynch [34], Wells [74]	14,584
25	29	H	Reading	D	0-0	0-0	8		15,721
26	Jan 1	A	Aston Villa	D	2-2	1-1	9	Freeman [41], Eze [57]	37,760
27	12	A	Sheffield U	L	0-1	0-1	11		25,501
28	19	H	Preston NE	L	1-4	0-1	14	Smith [84]	13,736
29	Feb 2	A	Wigan Ath	L	1-2	0-1	14	Samuel [75]	9799
30	9	H	Birmingham C	L	3-4	1-4	15	Smith 2 [45, 48], Cousins [80]	14,234
31	12	A	Bristol C	L	1-2	1-0	16	Smith [45]	19,183
32	19	H	WBA	L	2-3	1-1	18	Freeman [35], Hemed (pen) [75]	12,257
33	23	A	Middlesbrough	L	0-2	0-2	18		22,338
34	26	H	Leeds U	W	1-0	0-0	17	Freeman [49]	14,763
35	Mar 2	A	Brentford	L	0-3	0-0	18		11,771
36	9	H	Stoke C	D	0-0	0-0	18		14,954
37	13	H	Rotherham U	L	1-2	0-0	18	Samuel [85]	10,854
38	16	A	Hull C	D	2-2	0-2	18	Scowen [62], Hemed [84]	11,227
39	30	H	Bolton W	L	1-2	0-1	17	Wells [81]	13,603
40	Apr 6	A	Norwich C	L	0-4	0-3	18		26,796
41	10	A	Millwall	D	0-0	0-0	18		13,132
42	13	H	Swansea C	W	4-0	3-0	17	Furlong [3], Hemed 2 [5, 17], Luongo [54]	13,872
43	19	H	Blackburn R	L	1-2	0-1	17	Smith [90]	13,632
44	22	A	Derby Co	L	0-2	0-0	19		25,986
45	27	H	Nottingham F	L	0-1	0-0	19		15,212
46	May 5	A	Sheffield W	W	2-1	1-0	19	Scowen [28], Smith [90]	26,111

Final League Position: 19

GOALSCORERS

League (53): Freeman 7, Hemed 7 (2 pens), Wells 7, Smith 6, Eze 4, Wszolek 4, Luongo 3, Lynch 3, Leistner 2, Rangel 2, Samuel 2, Scowen 2, Cameron 1, Cousins 1, Furlong 1, own goal 1.
FA Cup (5): Wells 2, Bidwell 1, Oteh 1 (1 pen), Smith 1.
Carabao Cup (5): Wszolek 2, Freeman 1, Samuel 1, Smith 1.

Ingram M 4	Kakay O 3	Leistner T 40 + 3	Lynch J 35	Bidwell J 40	Luongo M 41	Scowen J 23 + 12	Samuel B 9 + 18	Freeman L 43	Eze E 37 + 5	Smith M 7 + 28	Manning R 7 + 2	Smyth P 1 + 2	Sylla I 1 + 2	Washington C 1 + 3	Cousins J 23 + 5	Baptiste A 3 + 1	Wszolek P 29 + 9	Rangel A 20	Lumley J 42	Wells N 32 + 8	Hemed T 16 + 11	Cameron G 17 + 2	Hall G 7 + 5	Furlong D 23 + 2	Chair I — + 4	Oteh A — + 2	Shodipo O 1 + 3	Walker L 1 + 3	Match No.
1	2	3	4	5	6^1	7	8^2	9	10	11^3	12	13	14																1
1	2^2	3	4	5	6	7	12	9	10	13		8^3	11^1	14															2
1	2	3	4^2	5	9	6		10	8^1	11^3				12	7	13	14												3
1		3		5	6^3	7		8	11	13			14	10	12	4	9^2	2^1											4
		3	4	5	6	7		8	11^3	13				12			14	2	1	9^1	10^2								5
		3	4	5	8			9	6	12					7			2	1	10^1	11^2	13							6
		3	4	5	8	13		9^2	6	14					7			2	1	10^3	11^1	12							7
		3	4	5	8	13		9^2	10^3	14					6			2	1	11^1	12	7							8
		3^2	4	5	8	7^3	12	9	6	14					13	2^1			1	11	10								9
			4	5	7			9^3	6^2	12						3	14	2	1	11^1	10	8	13						10
		3	4	5	7	13		9	10^2						6^1		14	2	1	11^3	12	8							11
		3	4	5^3	7			9	10^1	14					6^2		12	2	1	11	13	8							12
		3	4	5	7	13		9	10^1								6	2	1	12	11^2	8							13
		3	4	5	6	13		10^3	9^2						14		8	2	1	12	11^1	7							14
		3	4	5	7	13		10	9^1	14							8	2	1	12	11^3	6^2							15
		3	4	5	7	6^3		10	9^2	12							8	2^1	1	11				13	14				16
		3	4	5	7			9	10						12		6	2	1	11^1		8							17
		3	4	5	7			10	9^1	13					6		8^2	2	1	11^3	12		14						18
		3	4	5	7^3	13		9	10	14							6^2	2	1	11^1	12	8							19
		3	4	5	6		14	10	9	13							8^2	2^3	1	11	12	7^1							20
		3	4	5	6	12	13	10	9^1	14							8^2	2	1	11		7^3							21
		3	4^2	5	7	12		9	10^3	13					8		6		1	11^1				2		14			22
		4		5	8	7		9	10^2	12					2		6		1	11^1			13	3					23
		3	4	5	7	8	14	9^2	10^3								6		1	11^1				2	12	13			24
		3	4	5		8^1		9	10^2	12					7		6		1	11				2	13				25
		3	4	5		8	13	9	10^2	12					7		6^1		1	11^3			14	2					26
		3	4	5		8^2	12	9	10	13					7^3		6^1		1	11				2	14				27
		3	4	5		7	13	9	10^2	12		14			8^1		6^3		1	11				2					28
		3	4	5	8^2	7	12	9	10^3	13	14						6^1		1	11				2					29
		12	4^3	5	8	7^2	9^1	6		11					13		14		1	10			3	2					30
		3		9	6		14	8	13	11^1					7		5		1	10^2	12		4^3	2					31
		3	4	9	7		14	8	12	10^1					6		5^3		1	11^2	13			2					32
		3		5	8		12		10	13	9^1				7		6^3		1	14	11^2		4	2					33
		3		5	8	14	12	9^2	10^1						7		6		1	11^3	13		4	2					34
		3		5	8		12	9	10^1	14					7		6^3		1	11^2	13		4	2					35
		3		5	8	7^3	12	9							2		6^1		1	10^2	11		4	14			13		36
		3	4	5	8		6	9	10^1						7^2		14		1	13	11^3			2			12		37
		3	4	5	8	13	12	9^1	10								6		1	11^3	14	7^2		2					38
		12	4	5	7	8	9	10		13							6	2^3	1	14	11^2		3^1						39
		12	4	5^3		13	14	9	10						7		6^1	2	1	11		8^2		3					40
		3	4		8	6	12	9^2		10	5						13		1	11^1		7		2					41
		4			6	8	10	7^3	14		5				9		12	2^2	1		11^1			3				13	42
			4		6	9	10	7	14	13	5				8^1		2^2		1	12	11^3			3					43
					8	7	6^3	9	13	12	5						2		1	10^2	11^1	4		3				14	44
		3			7	8	9		6^2	13	5								1	14	10^1	4		2			12	11^3	45
		4			8	7	10^2		6	11	5								1			3	13	2			9^1	12	46

FA Cup

Third Round	Leeds U	(h)	2-1
Fourth Round	Portsmouth	(a)	1-1
Replay	Portsmouth	(h)	2-0
Fifth Round	Watford	(h)	0-1

Carabao Cup

First Round	Peterborough U	(h)	2-0
Second Round	Bristol R	(h)	3-1
Third Round	Blackpool	(a)	0-2

READING

FOUNDATION

Reading was formed as far back as 1871 at a public meeting held at the Bridge Street Rooms. They first entered the FA Cup as early as 1877 when they amalgamated with the Reading Hornets. The club was further strengthened in 1889 when Earley FC joined them. They were the first winners of the Berks & Bucks Cup in 1878–79.

Madejski Stadium, Junction 11, M4, Reading, Berkshire RG2 0FL.

Telephone: (0118) 968 1100.

Fax: (0118) 968 1101.

Ticket Office: (0118) 968 1313.

Website: www.readingfc.co.uk

Email: supporterservice@readingfc.co.uk

Ground Capacity: 24,162.

Record Attendance: 33,042 v Brentford, FA Cup 5th rd, 19 February 1927 (at Elm Park); 24,184 v Everton, Premier League, 17 November 2012 (at Madejski Stadium).

Pitch Measurements: 103m × 68m (112.5yd × 74.5yd).

Vice-Chairman: Sir John Madejski.

Chief Executive: Nigel Howe.

Manager: José Gomes.

Assistant Manager: Jorge Mendonça.

Colours: Blue and white hooped shirts, blue shorts with white trim, blue socks with white trim.

Year Formed: 1871.

Turned Professional: 1895.

Club Nickname: 'The Royals'.

Grounds: 1871, Reading Recreation; Reading Cricket Ground; 1882, Coley Park; 1889, Caversham Cricket Ground; 1896, Elm Park; 1998, Madejski Stadium.

First Football League Game: 28 August 1920, Division 3, v Newport Co (a) W 1–0 – Crawford; Smith, Horler; Christie, Mavin, Getgood; Spence, Weston, Yarnell, Bailey (1), Andrews.

Record League Victory: 10–2 v Crystal Palace, Division 3 (S), 4 September 1946 – Groves; Glidden, Gulliver; McKenna, Ratcliffe, Young; Chitty, Maurice Edelston (3), McPhee (4), Barney (1), Deverell (2).

Record Cup Victory: 6–0 v Leyton, FA Cup 2nd rd, 12 December 1925 – Duckworth; Eggo, McConnell; Wilson, Messer, Evans; Smith (2), Braithwaite (1), Davey (1), Tinsley, Robson (2).

Record Defeat: 0–18 v Preston NE, FA Cup 1st rd, 1893–94.

Most League Points (2 for a win): 65, Division 4, 1978–79.

HONOURS

League Champions: FL C – 2005–06, 2011–12; Second Division – 1993–94; Division 3 – 1985–86; Division 3S – 1925–26; Division 4 – 1978–79.
Runners-up: First Division – 1994–95; Second Division – 2001–02; Division 3S – 1931–32, 1934–35, 1948–49, 1951–52.

FA Cup: semi-final – 1927, 2015.

League Cup: 5th rd – 1996, 1998.

Full Members' Cup Winners: 1988.

THE Sun FACT FILE

Reading were one of the very first English clubs to sign up an overseas international player. Attilio Fresia had been capped by Italy against Belgium in May 1913 and after performing well against the Royals later that summer he travelled to England to sign a professional contract.

Most League Points (3 for a win): 106, Championship, 2005–06 (Football League Record).

Most League Goals: 112, Division 3 (S), 1951–52.

Highest League Scorer in Season: Ronnie Blackman, 39, Division 3 (S), 1951–52.

Most League Goals in Total Aggregate: Ronnie Blackman, 158, 1947–54.

Most League Goals in One Match: 6, Arthur Bacon v Stoke C, Division 2, 3 April 1931.

Most Capped Player: Chris Gunter, 58 (95), Wales.

Most League Appearances: Martin Hicks, 500, 1978–91.

Youngest League Player: Peter Castle, 16 years 49 days v Watford, 30 April 2003.

Record Transfer Fee Received: £7,000,000 from TSG 1899 Hoffenheim for Gylfi Sigurdsson, August 2010.

Record Transfer Fee Paid: £6,000,000 (rising to £7,500,000) to Fulham for Sone Aluko, August 2017.

Football League Record: 1920 Original Member of Division 3; 1921–26 Division 3 (S); 1926–31 Division 2; 1931–58 Division 3 (S); 1958–71 Division 3; 1971–76 Division 4; 1976–77 Division 3; 1977–79 Division 4; 1979–83 Division 3; 1983–84 Division 4; 1984–86 Division 3; 1986–88 Division 2; 1988–92 Division 3; 1992–94 Division 2; 1994–98 Division 1; 1998–2002 Division 2; 2002–04 Division 1; 2004–06 FL C; 2006–08 Premier League; 2008–12 FL C; 2012–13 Premier League; 2013– FL C.

LATEST SEQUENCES

Longest Sequence of League Wins: 13, 17.8.1985 – 19.10.1985.

Longest Sequence of League Defeats: 8, 29.12.2007 – 24.2.2008.

Longest Sequence of League Draws: 6, 23.3.2002 – 20.4.2002.

Longest Sequence of Unbeaten League Matches: 33, 9.8.2005 – 14.2.2006.

Longest Sequence Without a League Win: 14, 30.4.1927 – 29.10.1927.

Successive Scoring Runs: 32 from 1.10.1932.

Successive Non-scoring Runs: 6 from 29.3.2008.

MANAGERS

Thomas Sefton 1897–1901
(Secretary-Manager)
James Sharp 1901–02
Harry Matthews 1902–20
Harry Marshall 1920–22
Arthur Chadwick 1923–25
H. S. Bray 1925–26
(Secretary only since 1922 and 1926–35)
Andrew Wylie 1926–31
Joe Smith 1931–35
Billy Butler 1935–39
John Cochrane 1939
Joe Edelston 1939–47
Ted Drake 1947–52
Jack Smith 1952–55
Harry Johnston 1955–63
Roy Bentley 1963–69
Jack Mansell 1969–71
Charlie Hurley 1972–77
Maurice Evans 1977–84
Ian Branfoot 1984–89
Ian Porterfield 1989–91
Mark McGhee 1991–94
Jimmy Quinn and Mick Gooding 1994–97
Terry Bullivant 1997–98
Tommy Burns 1998–99
Alan Pardew 1999–2003
Steve Coppell 2003–09
Brendan Rodgers 2009
Brian McDermott 2009–13
Nigel Adkins 2013–14
Steve Clarke 2014–15
Brian McDermott 2015–16
Jaap Stam 2016–18
Paul Clement 2018
José Gomes December 2018–

TEN YEAR LEAGUE RECORD

		P	W	D	L	F	A	Pts	Pos
2009-10	FL C	46	17	12	17	68	63	63	9
2010-11	FL C	46	20	17	9	77	51	77	5
2011-12	FL C	46	27	8	11	69	41	89	1
2012-13	PR Lge	38	6	10	22	43	73	28	19
2013-14	FL C	46	19	14	13	70	56	71	7
2014-15	FL C	46	13	11	22	48	69	50	19
2015-16	FL C	46	13	13	20	52	59	52	17
2016-17	FL C	46	26	7	13	68	64	85	3
2017-18	FL C	46	10	14	22	48	70	44	20
2018-19	FL C	46	10	17	19	49	66	47	20

DID YOU KNOW ?

Although they were one of the founder members of the Southern League in 1894–95, Reading were an amateur club for the first season and it was only in the summer of 1895 that the decision was made to accept professionalism.

READING – SKY BET CHAMPIONSHIP 2018–19 LEAGUE RECORD

Match No.	*Date*	*Venue*	*Opponents*	*Result*		*H/T Score*	*Lg Pos.*	*Goalscorers*	*Atten-dance*
1	Aug 3	H	Derby Co	L	1-2	0-0	24	Bodvarsson [52]	16,923
2	11	A	Nottingham F	L	0-1	0-0	23		27,948
3	18	H	Bolton W	L	0-1	0-0	23		13,318
4	22	A	Blackburn R	D	2-2	2-0	23	Bodvarsson 2 [12, 25]	11,818
5	25	A	Aston Villa	D	1-1	0-0	23	Baldock (pen) [90]	33,405
6	Sept 1	H	Sheffield W	L	1-2	0-1	23	Moore [64]	14,352
7	15	A	Preston NE	W	3-2	1-1	22	Baldock [23], Tiago Ilori [52], Bacuna [81]	10,849
8	19	H	Norwich C	L	1-2	0-1	22	Bodvarsson [72]	12,822
9	22	H	Hull C	W	3-0	1-0	20	Baldock [4], Bodvarsson [70], Yiadom [81]	12,409
10	29	A	Brentford	D	2-2	1-1	20	Bodvarsson 2 [25, 64]	10,045
11	Oct 2	H	QPR	L	0-1	0-0	20		13,568
12	6	A	WBA	L	1-4	1-0	21	Bacuna [6]	22,865
13	20	H	Millwall	W	3-1	2-1	19	Meite 2 [28, 86], Baldock (pen) [45]	14,532
14	23	A	Birmingham C	L	1-2	0-0	21	Meite [90]	22,126
15	27	A	Swansea C	L	0-2	0-1	22		18,785
16	Nov 3	H	Bristol C	W	3-2	2-2	22	Meite [8], Kelly [45], Bacuna [66]	14,455
17	10	H	Ipswich T	D	2-2	1-2	20	Meite 2 [7, 84]	14,952
18	24	A	Wigan Ath	D	0-0	0-0	20		9211
19	27	A	Leeds U	L	0-1	0-0	20		27,806
20	Dec 1	H	Stoke C	D	2-2	1-0	21	McNulty [42], Barrow [90]	14,414
21	8	H	Sheffield U	L	0-2	0-0	22		12,066
22	15	A	Rotherham U	D	1-1	1-0	21	Baldock [9]	8775
23	22	H	Middlesbrough	L	0-1	0-0	21		14,943
24	26	A	Millwall	L	0-1	0-1	23		12,202
25	29	A	QPR	D	0-0	0-0	23		15,721
26	Jan 1	H	Swansea C	L	1-4	0-3	23	Harriott [77]	15,644
27	12	H	Nottingham F	W	2-0	1-0	22	Swift [23], Robinson (og) [87]	15,034
28	19	A	Derby Co	L	1-2	0-2	22	Aluko [66]	26,404
29	29	A	Bolton W	D	1-1	0-0	22	Nelson Oliveira (pen) [74]	12,195
30	Feb 2	H	Aston Villa	D	0-0	0-0	22		17,458
31	9	A	Sheffield W	D	0-0	0-0	22		23,412
32	13	H	Blackburn R	W	2-1	1-0	21	Swift [45], Nelson Oliveira [86]	11,271
33	16	A	Sheffield U	L	0-4	0-3	21		26,513
34	23	H	Rotherham U	D	1-1	1-0	21	Ejaria [31]	15,958
35	Mar 2	A	Ipswich T	W	2-1	1-0	21	Nelson Oliveira [19], Barrow [90]	23,009
36	9	H	Wigan Ath	W	3-2	1-1	19	Swift [45], Barrow [89], Meite [90]	15,401
37	12	H	Leeds U	L	0-3	0-3	19		17,101
38	16	A	Stoke C	D	0-0	0-0	21		24,368
39	30	H	Preston NE	W	2-1	2-0	19	Meite [30], Barrow [36]	16,771
40	Apr 6	A	Hull C	L	1-3	1-0	21	Baker [16]	11,268
41	10	A	Norwich C	D	2-2	1-0	20	Meite [30], Rinomhota [90]	26,662
42	13	H	Brentford	W	2-1	2-1	19	Meite 2 [8, 15]	16,892
43	19	A	Bristol C	D	1-1	0-0	19	Meite [48]	23,309
44	22	H	WBA	D	0-0	0-0	20		17,255
45	27	A	Middlesbrough	L	1-2	1-2	20	Loader [11]	22,003
46	May 5	H	Birmingham C	D	0-0	0-0	20		17,247

Final League Position: 20

GOALSCORERS

League (49): Meite 12, Bodvarsson 7, Baldock 5 (2 pens), Barrow 4, Bacuna 3, Nelson Oliveira 3 (1 pen), Swift 3, Aluko 1, Baker 1, Ejaria 1, Harriott 1, Kelly 1, Loader 1, McNulty 1, Moore 1, Rinomhota 1, Tiago Ilori 1, Yiadom 1, own goal 1.
FA Cup (0).
Carabao Cup (2): Meite 1, Swift 1.

Mannone V 6	Yiadom A 45	Tiago Ilori A 19	McShane P 4 + 1	Richards O 8 + 2	Meyler D 5	Kelly L 17 + 3	Aluko S 13 + 6	Swift J 28 + 6	Barrow M 25 + 10	Bodvarsson J 9 + 11	Baldock S 15 + 6	Meite Y 31 + 6	Bacuna L 23 + 3	Blackett T 29 + 2	McNulty M 4 + 9	Moore L 38	Popa A — + 1	Sims J 5 + 12	Gunter C 17 + 5	Walker S 7	Rinomhota A 24 + 2	O'Shea J 7 + 2	Ezatolahi S 4	Jaakkola A 15	McCleary G 14 + 17	Loader D 8 + 13	McIntyre T 1 + 1	Osho G 1 + 1 / Howe T — + 1	Harriott C 2 + 10	Ejaria O 16	Baker L 17 + 2	Martinez D 18	Miazga M 18	Nelson Oliveira M 9 + 1	East R 1	Olise M 2 + 2	Barrett J 1 + 1	Match No.
1	2	3	4	5	6¹	7	8	9³	10	11²	12	13	14																									1
1	2	3	4	14	7³	8			9	11	10¹	6	13	5²	12																							2
1	2		3		7³	6		9¹		13	11	8	12	5	10²	4	14																					3
1	2		3			8	9²		13	11	10¹	6³	7	5	14	4		12																				4
1	2	4			8		6³		9²	11¹	10	12	7	5	14	3		13																				5
1	5	3			7³	13	6²		9¹		11	10	8		12	4		14	2																			6
	5	3				7¹	8²	9		12	11	10³	6			4		13	2	1	14																	7
	5	3				7²	8¹	9	12	14	11	10³	6			4		13	2	1																		8
	5	2				8¹		12	13	10	11³		6			4		9	14	1		3■	7²															9
	5	3				14	13	9²	10³	11		8¹	6			4		12	2	1			7															10
	5	3				7²	9³	12	11			10	6		14	4		13	2	1			8¹															11
	6	3				14		9	12			11	7¹	5	10²	4		13	2³	1			8															12
	2	3				7³		9			10¹	11	6	5	14	4			12		13			1	8²													13
	2	3				6	14	8³		10²	12	11	7	5		4		9¹						1	13													14
	2					6	14	8³		12	11	10²	7	5		4		13				3		1	9¹													15
	2					8		13	9²		11	10¹	7	5		4			14	1	6³	3			12													16
	2					8²		13	9		11	10	7	5	14	4					6³	3¹		1	12													17
						6	9²	8				10¹		5	14	4		13	2		7	3		1	11³	12												18
	2	3				7¹		9³				11²	8		14	4		13	5		6			1	12	10												19
	2	3						8²	12		13	14	7	4	11³				5		6			1	9	10¹												20
	2	3					14		12		13		7	4	11³			8²	5		6			1	10¹	9												21
	2							9		12	11¹		7	3				8²	5		6			1	10	13	4											22
	2			5¹				12	10	14	11		7	4				8²			6			1	13	9³		3										23
	2			5				9³	8		12	10¹	7■	4■		3					6			1	13	11²		14										24
	2	3		5			9³	7	10	13		11²						14			6	4		1	8¹	12												25
	2	3		5			9¹	7	10	13		11²									6	4		1	8³	12			14									26
	2	3		5³				9	8	11¹			7			4					6			1	13	14				10²	12							27
	5	3					12	9	8³	11¹			6			4					2			1	14	13				10	7²							28
	5						8	9¹	10				7	13		4			7²		6				12	14						1	3	11³				29
	2			12			13	7				14		5		4					6								8¹	10	9²	1	3	11³				30
	2						11³	6	10	14		12		5		4					7				8¹				13		9²	1	3					31
	2			10		6¹	9²	7		14		12		5		4														8	13	1	3	11³				32
	2			5		7¹		12	10	13		8				4									14					6³	9	1	3	11²				33
	2							8	13			9¹		5		4						12			11³				14	6²	7	1	3	10				34
	2							9	12			8		5		4									10¹	14			13	6³	7	1	3	11²				35
	2							8	11			7		5		4									10²	12			13	9¹	6	1	3					36
	2							9	10³			8		5		4									14	11²			12		6	1	3		7¹	13		37
	2							6³	12			11		5		4			13						10	14			8¹		7	1	3			9²		38
	2		13					9³	11²			8		5		4					6				12				14	10¹	7	1	3					39
	2								10²			8¹		5		4					6				14	12			13	9	7	1	3	11³				40
	3								10¹		14	11		6		5			2³		7				12	13				9	8²	1	4					41
	2								11³			9¹		14		4			5		6				12				13	8	7	1	3	10²				42
	3								11³			10²		6		5			2		7				14		13			9¹	8	1	4	12				43
	2								9			8³		5¹		4			14		6				13	12				10	7	1	3	11²				44
	2										10³					4			5²		6				11¹	9			12	8	7	1	3			13	14	45
	5								12							4			2²		6	13				10		14		8	7	1	3			9³	11¹	46

FA Cup
Third Round — Manchester U — (a) — 0-2

Carabao Cup
First Round — Birmingham C — (h) — 2-0
Second Round — Watford — (h) — 0-2

ROCHDALE

FOUNDATION

Considering the love of rugby in their area, it is not surprising that Rochdale had difficulty in establishing an Association Football club. The earlier Rochdale Town club formed in 1900 went out of existence in 1907 when the present club was immediately established and joined the Manchester League, before graduating to the Lancashire Combination in 1908.

Crown Oil Arena, Sandy Lane, Rochdale, Lancashire OL11 5DR.

Telephone: (0844) 826 1907.

Fax: (01706) 648 466.

Ticket Office: (0844) 826 1907 (option 8).

Website: www.rochdaleafc.co.uk

Email: admin@rochdaleafc.co.uk

Ground Capacity: 7,447.

Record Attendance: 24,231 v Notts Co, FA Cup 2nd rd, 10 December 1949.

Pitch Measurements: 104m × 69.5m (114yd × 76yd).

Chairman: Andrew Kilpatrick.

Chief Executive: David Bottomley.

Manager: Brian Barry-Murphy.

First-Team Coach: Lee Riley.

Colours: Blue shirts with black stripes and white trim, black shorts with white trim, blue socks with white trim.

Year Formed: 1907.

Turned Professional: 1907.

Club Nickname: 'The Dale'.

Ground: 1907, St Clements Playing Fields (renamed Spotland, 1921; renamed Crown Oil Arena, 2016).

First Football League Game: 27 August 1921, Division 3 (N), v Accrington Stanley (h) W 6–3 – Crabtree; Nuttall, Sheehan; Hill, Farrer, Yarwood; Hoad, Sandiford, Dennison (2), Owens (3), Carney (1).

Record League Victory: 8–1 v Chesterfield, Division 3 (N), 18 December 1926 – Hill; Brown, Ward; Hillhouse, Parkes, Braidwood; Hughes, Bertram, Whitehurst (5), Schofield (2), Martin (1).

Record Cup Victory: 8–2 v Crook T, FA Cup 1st rd, 26 November 1927 – Moody; Hopkins, Ward; Braidwood, Parkes, Barker; Tompkinson, Clennell (3) Whitehurst (4), Hall, Martin (1).

Record Defeat: 1–9 v Tranmere R, Division 3 (N), 25 December 1931.

HONOURS

League: *Runners-up:* Division 3N – 1923–24, 1926–27.

FA Cup: 5th rd – 1990, 2003, 2018.

League Cup: *Runners-up:* 1962.

THE Sun FACT FILE

Rochdale are one of the few clubs who have yet to register an average attendance higher than 10,000 in a Football League season. Their best to date was an average of 8,616 recorded in the 1948–49 season when they finished seventh in the old Division Three North.

Most League Points (2 for a win): 62, Division 3 (N), 1923–24.

Most League Points (3 for a win): 82, FL 2, 2009–10.

Most League Goals: 105, Division 3 (N), 1926–27.

Highest League Scorer in Season: Albert Whitehurst, 44, Division 3 (N), 1926–27.

Most League Goals in Total Aggregate: Reg Jenkins, 119, 1964–73.

Most League Goals in One Match: 6, Tommy Tippett v Hartlepools U, Division 3 (N), 21 April 1930.

Most Capped Player: Leo Bertos, 6 (56), New Zealand.

Most League Appearances: Gary Jones, 470, 1998–2001; 2003–12.

Youngest League Player: Zac Hughes, 16 years 105 days v Exeter C, 19 September 1987.

Record Transfer Fee Received: £750,000 (rising to £4,125,000) from Brentford for Scott Hogan, July 2014.

Record Transfer Fee Paid: £150,000 to Stoke C for Paul Connor, March 2001.

Football League Record: 1921 Elected to Division 3 (N); 1958–59 Division 3; 1959–69 Division 4; 1969–74 Division 3; 1974–92 Division 4; 1992–2004 Division 3; 2004–10 FL 2; 2010–12 FL 1; 2012–14 FL 2; 2014– FL 1.

LATEST SEQUENCES

Longest Sequence of League Wins: 8, 29.9.1969 – 3.11.1969.

Longest Sequence of League Defeats: 17, 14.11.1931 – 12.3.1932.

Longest Sequence of League Draws: 6, 17.8.1968 – 14.9.1968.

Longest Sequence of Unbeaten League Matches: 20, 15.9.1923 – 19.1.1924.

Longest Sequence Without a League Win: 28, 14.11.1931 – 29.8.1932.

Successive Scoring Runs: 29 from 10.10.2008.

Successive Non-scoring Runs: 9 from 14.3.1980.

MANAGERS

Billy Bradshaw 1920
Run by committee 1920–22
Tom Wilson 1922–23
Jack Peart 1923–30
Will Cameron 1930–31
Herbert Hopkinson 1932–34
Billy Smith 1934–35
Ernest Nixon 1935–37
Sam Jennings 1937–38
Ted Goodier 1938–52
Jack Warner 1952–53
Harry Catterick 1953–58
Jack Marshall 1958–60
Tony Collins 1960–68
Bob Stokoe 1967–68
Len Richley 1968–70
Dick Conner 1970–73
Walter Joyce 1973–76
Brian Green 1976–77
Mike Ferguson 1977–78
Doug Collins 1979
Bob Stokoe 1979–80
Peter Madden 1980–83
Jimmy Greenhoff 1983–84
Vic Halom 1984–86
Eddie Gray 1986–88
Danny Bergara 1988–89
Terry Dolan 1989–91
Dave Sutton 1991–94
Mick Docherty 1994–96
Graham Barrow 1996–99
Steve Parkin 1999–2001
John Hollins 2001–02
Paul Simpson 2002–03
Alan Buckley 2003
Steve Parkin 2003–06
Keith Hill 2007–11
(Caretaker from December 2006)
Steve Eyre 2011
John Coleman 2012–13
Keith Hill 2013–19
Brian Barry-Murphy April 2019–

TEN YEAR LEAGUE RECORD

		P	W	D	L	F	A	Pts	Pos
2009-10	FL 2	46	25	7	14	82	48	82	3
2010-11	FL 1	46	18	14	14	63	55	68	9
2011-12	FL 1	46	8	14	24	47	81	38	24
2012-13	FL 2	46	16	13	17	68	70	61	12
2013-14	FL 2	46	24	9	13	69	48	81	3
2014-15	FL 1	46	19	6	21	72	66	63	8
2015-16	FL 1	46	19	12	15	68	61	69	10
2016-17	FL 1	46	19	12	15	71	62	69	9
2017-18	FL 1	46	11	18	17	49	57	51	20
2018-19	FL 1	46	15	9	22	54	87	54	16

DID YOU KNOW ?

Calvin Symonds became one of the first black players to appear for Rochdale when he lined up against Barrow in September 1955. He was also one of the first Dale players to produce an autobiography when his book *My Way* was published in Bermuda in 1999.

ROCHDALE – SKY BET LEAGUE ONE 2018–19 LEAGUE RECORD

Match No.	*Date*	*Venue*	*Opponents*	*Result*		*H/T Score*	*Lg Pos.*	*Goalscorers*	*Attendance*
1	Aug 4	A	Burton Alb	W	2-1	2-0	4	Inman 2 [10, 22]	2987
2	11	H	Peterborough U	L	1-4	1-3	14	Henderson (pen) [17]	3128
3	18	A	Fleetwood T	D	2-2	0-1	15	Henderson 2 (1 pen) [50 (p), 90]	3565
4	21	H	Barnsley	L	0-4	0-2	18		4359
5	25	H	Walsall	L	1-2	0-1	19	Camps [79]	3080
6	Sept 1	A	Coventry C	W	1-0	0-0	14	Andrew [47]	9879
7	8	A	Scunthorpe U	D	3-3	0-2	13	Rathbone 2 [52, 66], Gillam [83]	3898
8	15	H	Gillingham	W	3-0	2-0	13	Henderson 3 [9, 18, 64]	2925
9	22	A	Sunderland	L	1-4	0-3	14	Done [71]	28,764
10	29	H	Portsmouth	L	1-3	1-1	17	Wilbraham [4]	3796
11	Oct 2	H	Bristol R	D	0-0	0-0	15		2301
12	6	A	Blackpool	D	2-2	1-2	15	Delaney [9], Andrew [86]	3520
13	13	H	Doncaster R	L	2-3	0-1	16	Henderson (pen) [59], Ntlhe [82]	3600
14	20	A	Bradford C	W	2-0	0-0	16	Henderson 2 (2 pens) [83, 90]	15,875
15	23	A	Wycombe W	L	0-3	0-1	17		3997
16	27	H	Charlton Ath	W	1-0	1-0	14	Henderson [4]	3109
17	Nov 3	H	Luton T	D	0-0	0-0	16		3689
18	17	A	Shrewsbury T	L	2-3	1-1	18	Inman [45], Williams, Jordan LR [58]	5861
19	24	H	Accrington S	W	1-0	0-0	16	Henderson [63]	3497
20	27	A	Oxford U	L	2-4	1-2	17	Henderson [30], Camps [69]	5204
21	Dec 8	A	AFC Wimbledon	D	1-1	1-0	18	Andrew [35]	3988
22	15	H	Plymouth Arg	L	1-2	0-0	19	Inman [76]	2863
23	22	A	Southend U	W	2-1	1-0	17	Williams, Jordan LR [23], Camps [87]	5735
24	26	H	Blackpool	W	2-1	1-1	16	Rathbone [19], Henderson [89]	4006
25	29	H	Bradford C	L	0-4	0-1	16		5673
26	Jan 1	A	Doncaster R	L	0-5	0-3	17		7408
27	5	H	Burton Alb	L	0-4	0-2	18		2666
28	12	A	Peterborough U	L	1-2	0-1	19	Hamilton [90]	6025
29	19	H	Fleetwood T	D	1-1	0-1	19	Henderson [75]	2713
30	26	A	Barnsley	L	1-2	0-0	20	Henderson [49]	11,379
31	Feb 2	A	Walsall	W	2-1	1-1	18	Ebanks-Landell [4], Hamilton [60]	4021
32	9	H	Coventry C	L	0-1	0-0	18		3661
33	19	H	AFC Wimbledon	L	3-4	2-1	20	Ebanks-Landell [2], Hamilton [37], Henderson [81]	2410
34	23	A	Plymouth Arg	L	1-5	0-1	22	Done [48]	9360
35	Mar 2	A	Luton T	L	0-2	0-0	22		9905
36	9	H	Shrewsbury T	W	2-1	1-0	22	Ntlhe [15], McNulty [47]	3217
37	12	H	Oxford U	D	0-0	0-0	22		2331
38	23	H	Scunthorpe U	W	3-1	1-1	22	Wilbraham 2 [14, 60], Ntlhe [51]	3361
39	30	A	Gillingham	D	1-1	1-1	23	Henderson [37]	4686
40	Apr 6	H	Sunderland	L	1-2	1-0	23	Henderson [28]	6546
41	9	A	Accrington S	W	1-0	0-0	19	Rathbone [71]	2824
42	13	A	Portsmouth	L	1-4	0-2	20	Wilbraham [54]	18,197
43	19	H	Wycombe W	W	1-0	0-0	17	Henderson [79]	3711
44	22	A	Bristol R	W	1-0	0-0	14	Hamilton [82]	8516
45	27	H	Southend U	W	1-0	0-0	14	Henderson [53]	5000
46	May 4	A	Charlton Ath	L	0-4	0-3	16		12,705

Final League Position: 16

GOALSCORERS

League (54): Henderson 20 (5 pens), Hamilton 4, Inman 4, Rathbone 4, Wilbraham 4, Andrew 3, Camps 3, Ntlhe 3, Done 2, Ebanks-Landell 2, Jordan LR Williams 2, Delaney 1, Gillam 1, McNulty 1.
FA Cup (2): Henderson 1, own goal 1.
Carabao Cup (3): Rathbone 2, Delaney 1.
Checkatrade Trophy (10): McNulty 2, Adshead 1, Andrew 1, Cannon 1, Clough 1, Dooley 1, Gillam 1, Rafferty 1 (1 pen), Jordan LR Williams 1.

Lillis J 26+1	Rafferty J 26+1	McNulty J 25	McGahey H 21	Done M 27+9	Camps C 40+1	Williams M Jordan 22+6	Perkins D 11+6	Henderson I 45	Wilbraham A 16+7	Inman B 16+13	Thompson J —+1	Delaney R 29+1	Andrew C 13+25	Cannon A 4+8	Ntlhe K 14+5	Rathbone O 26+2	Norman M 6+1	Williams Jordan LR 12+7	Dooley S 16+6	Moore B 7+1	Hart S 11	Clough Z 4+5	Gillam M 6+4	Adshead D 8+2	Randall C 1	Morley A 2+1	Holden R 5+1	Hamilton E 13+1	Ebanks-Landell E 15+1	Matheson L —+3	McLaughlin R 13	Pyke R 3+3	Bunney J 12+4	Lonergan A 7	Keohane J 4+4	Bradley L —+1	*Match No.*
1	2	3	4	5	6^1	7	8	9	10^2	11^3	12	13	14																								1
1	2^1		3^2	5^3	6	7	8	9	10	11		4	12	13	14																						2
1	5^1	3	4	13	12		7	10	11	8^2		2	14		9	6^3																					3
1^2	12	4^3	3	9		7	8	11				5	10	2^1	6		13	14																			4
	2	3	4	9^2	7	6	5^3	11	10	13			12		14	8^1	1																				5
	2		4	9	8	7^2	12	10				3	11	5^3		13	1^1		6	14																	6
	2	4	3		6			11	13				8	7^1		10	1				5	9^2	12														7
1	2		3	13	7			8^2	10			4	9^1			6		12			5		11^3	14													8
1	2		3	14	6			8	10^3			4	9			7^2		12			5		11^1	13													9
1	2	4			7^1		8	9	10			3	13	12		6		11^3			5^2	14															10
13	2	4^3	3			7	6	9		11^1				14		8	1■	12			5		10^2														11
1	2		4			5^1	7	11		8		3	14	13		6^2		12			9	10^3															12
1	5		2			3^1	6^2	10		9			13	12	4	7			14		8^3	11															13
	2		3	9	6	13		10	12			4			5	7^2		11^1	8	1																	14
	2		3	8	9	6^1		11	13	14		4		12	5^2			10^3	7	1																	15
	2		3		7		12	10		9^3		4	13	14		8^2		11^1	6	1	5																16
	2		3	8	7			10		9^2		4	12					11^1	6	1	5	13															17
	2		4	14	7		12	8	13	9^3		3	10				1	11^2	6		5^1																18
1	2		3	5	7	14	13	10		9^2		4	12					11^1	6					8^3													19
1		3	5	14	8	12		10	11^1			4	13			7					6^2			9	2^3												20
1	2		3	5		7	8^3	11		12		4	10	9^1		13							14	6^2													21
1	2			11	7	4	6^1	5		9		3	10	12		8^2							13														22
	2^3			5	6	4	13	11				3	14		12	7^1		9^2		1			10	8													23
	2			5	7	3		11		13		4	14		12	8		9^3		1			10^1	6^2													24
	2			5	7^2	3	14	10		11		4	13		12	8		9^1		1				6^3													25
			4	6	8^2	3		11		12		5	13		2	9	1						14	7^1		10^3											26
1	2			5	7^1	3		8		11		4				6		9					10^2			13	12										27
1	2	4		6	8	3^1		11		14		5^3	13						10^2								7	9	12								28
1	2	3		5^2	7			11		13			10						9^1								6	8	4	12							29
1		3			7^1			10	13	14		4	11^2						6								8	9	2	12	5^3						30
1		4			6	14		10				5	9						7^1								11^3	8	3		2^2	12	13				31
		4^2		14	7			10		12		5	9						6			11^1						8	3		2^3		13	1			32
		4		9	7			11		13			14						6^3									8	3	12	2^2	10^1	5	1			33
				11	6			9		12		4	13						8^2								10^1	7	3■		2		5	1			34
		3		11^1	7	2		10^3		5		4	12					13	6			14						8■					9^2	1			35
		3			8	7		11^3		10^1			13		4	8^2			12			14							2		5		9	1			36
		3		14	7			10	13	9^2					4	8		11^1										6			2^3		5	1	12		37
		3		11^2	6			9	10^3				12		4^1	7			14										2		5		8	1	13		38
1		3		11	7			9^3	10^2				12		4	6^1			14										2		5		8		13		39
1		3		11^1	6			9^2	10^3	14					4	7		13	12										2		5		8				40
1		3		11	6	14		10	9^1						4	7^3												12	2		5		13		8^2		41
1		3		11^2	7	12		9	10	13						8^1						14						6	4		2		5^3				42
1		3		11	6			9^2	10				14		4^1	7													2		5^3	13	8		12		43
1		3		13	6^3	4^1		7	10				14						5^2									11	2			12	9		8		44
1		4		12	8	6^3		11^2	10				14						13									9	3			7^1	5		2		45
1					8	7			13			3	10^3		5^2									6		2		4				11^1	12		9	14	46

FA Cup

First Round	Gateshead	(h)	2-1
Second Round	Portsmouth	(h)	0-1

Carabao Cup

First Round	Grimsby T	(a)	2-0
Second Round	Middlesbrough	(a)	1-2

Checkatrade Trophy

Group B (N)	Bury	(h)	2-1
Group B (N)	Fleetwood T	(a)	2-0
Group B (N)	Leicester C U21	(h)	2-2
(Leicester C U21 won 4-3 on penalties)			
Second Round (N)	Oldham Ath	(h)	2-0
Third Round	Manchester C U21	(h)	2-4

ROTHERHAM UNITED

FOUNDATION

Rotherham were formed in 1870 before becoming Town in the late 1880s. Thornhill United were founded in 1877 and changed their name to Rotherham County in 1905. The Town amalgamated with Rotherham County to form Rotherham United in 1925.

The AESSEAL New York Stadium, New York Way, Rotherham, South Yorkshire S60 1AH.

Telephone: (0170) 9827 760.

Fax: (0170) 9827 774.

Ticket Office: (0170) 982 7768.

Website: www.themillers.co.uk

Email: office@rotherhamunited.net

Ground Capacity: 12,021.

Record Attendance: 25,170 v Sheffield U, Division 2, 13 December 1952 (at Millmoor); 7,082 v Aldershot T, FL 2 Play-offs semi-final 2nd leg, 19 May 2010 (at Don Valley); 11,758 v Sheffield U, FL 1, 7 September 2013 (at New York Stadium).

Pitch Measurements: 102m × 64m (111.5yd × 70yd).

Chairman: Tony Stewart OBE.

Chief Operating Officer: Paul Douglas.

Manager: Paul Warne.

Assistant Manager: Richie Barker.

HONOURS

League Champions: Division 3 – 1980–81; Division 3N – 1950–51; Division 4 – 1988–89.
Runners-up: Second Division – 2000–01; Division 3N – 1946–47, 1947–48, 1948–49; FL 2 – 2012–13; Third Division – 1999–2000; Division 4 – 1991–92.

FA Cup: 5th rd – 1953, 1968.

League Cup: *Runners-up:* 1961.

League Trophy Winners: 1996.

Colours: Red shirts with white sleeves, white shorts with red trim, red socks with white trim.

Year Formed: 1870. ***Turned Professional:*** 1905. ***Club Nickname:*** 'The Millers'.

Previous Names: 1877, Thornhill United; 1905, Rotherham County; 1925, amalgamated with Rotherham Town under Rotherham United.

Grounds: 1870, Red House Ground; 1907, Millmoor; 2008, Don Valley Stadium; 2012, New York Stadium (renamed The AESSEAL New York Stadium, 2014).

First Football League Game: 2 September 1893, Division 2, Rotherham T v Lincoln C (a) D 1–1 – McKay; Thickett, Watson; Barr, Brown, Broadhead; Longden, Cutts, Leatherbarrow, McCormick, Pickering, (1 og). 30 August 1919, Division 2, Rotherham Co v Nottingham F (h) W 2–0 – Branston; Alton, Baines; Bailey, Coe, Stanton; Lee (1), Cawley (1), Glennon, Lees, Lamb.

Record League Victory: 8–0 v Oldham Ath, Division 3 (N), 26 May 1947 – Warnes; Selkirk, Ibbotson; Edwards, Horace Williams, Danny Williams; Wilson (2), Shaw (1), Ardron (3), Guest (1), Hainsworth (1).

Record Cup Victory: 6–0 v Spennymoor U, FA Cup 2nd rd, 17 December 1977 – McAlister; Forrest, Breckin, Womble, Stancliffe, Green, Finney, Phillips (3), Gwyther (2) (Smith), Goodfellow, Crawford (1). 6–0 v Wolverhampton W, FA Cup 1st rd, 16 November 1985 – O'Hanlon; Forrest, Dungworth, Gooding (1), Smith (1), Pickering, Birch (2), Emerson, Tynan (1), Simmons (1), Pugh. 6–0 v King's Lynn, FA Cup 2nd rd, 6 December 1997 – Mimms; Clark, Hurst (Goodwin), Garner (1) (Hudson) (1), Warner (Bass), Richardson (1), Berry (1), Thompson, Druce (1), Glover (1), Roscoe.

Record Defeat: 1–11 v Bradford C, Division 3 (N), 25 August 1928.

THE Sun FACT FILE

The very first game played under the title of Rotherham United was actually a cricket match. United defeated the Rotherham Town Cricket Club by 8 wickets in a benefit match for the Clifton Lane groundsman Albert Denton in August 1925. Future England soccer international Jackie Bestall led the scoring for the winners with a knock of 58.

Most League Points (2 for a win): 71, Division 3 (N), 1950–51.

Most League Points (3 for a win): 91, Division 2, 2000–01.

Most League Goals: 114, Division 3 (N), 1946–47.

Highest League Scorer in Season: Wally Ardron, 38, Division 3 (N), 1946–47.

Most League Goals in Total Aggregate: Gladstone Guest, 130, 1946–56.

Most League Goals in One Match: 4, Roland Bastow v York C, Division 3 (N), 9 November 1935; 4, Roland Bastow v Rochdale, Division 3 (N), 7 March 1936; 4, Wally Ardron v Crewe Alex, Division 3 (N), 5 October 1946; 4, Wally Ardron v Carlisle U, Division 3 (N), 13 September 1947; 4, Wally Ardron v Hartlepools U, Division 3 (N), 13 October 1948; 4, Ian Wilson v Liverpool, Division 2, 2 May 1955; 4, Carl Gilbert v Swansea C, Division 3, 28 September 1971; 4, Carl Airey v Chester, Division 3, 31 August 1987; 4, Shaun Goater v Hartlepool U, Division 3, 9 April 1994; 4, Lee Glover v Hull C, Division 3, 28 December 1997; 4, Darren Byfield v Millwall, Division 1, 10 August 2002; 4, Adam Le Fondre v Cheltenham T, FL 2, 21 August 2010.

Most Capped Player: Kari Arnason, 20 (77), Iceland.

Most League Appearances: Danny Williams, 461, 1946–62.

Youngest League Player: Kevin Eley, 16 years 72 days v Scunthorpe U, 15 May 1984.

Record Transfer Fee Received: £1,600,000 from Cardiff C for Danny Ward, June 2017.

Record Transfer Fee Paid: £500,000 (in excess of) to Plymouth Arg for Freddie Ladapo, June 2019.

Football League Record: 1893 Rotherham Town elected to Division 2; 1896 Failed re-election; 1919 Rotherham County elected to Division 2; 1923–51 Division 3 (N); 1951–68 Division 2; 1968–73 Division 3; 1973–75 Division 4; 1975–81 Division 3; 1981–83 Division 2; 1983–88 Division 3; 1988–89 Division 4; 1989–91 Division 3; 1991–92 Division 4; 1992–97 Division 2; 1997–2000 Division 3; 2000–01 Division 2; 2001–04 Division 1; 2004–05 FL C; 2005–07 FL 1; 2007–13 FL 2; 2013–14 FL 1; 2014–17 FL C; 2017–18 FL 1; 2018–19 FL C; 2019– FL 1.

MANAGERS

Billy Heald 1925–29 *(Secretary only for several years)*
Stanley Davies 1929–30
Billy Heald 1930–33
Reg Freeman 1934–52
Andy Smailes 1952–58
Tom Johnston 1958–62
Danny Williams 1962–65
Jack Mansell 1965–67
Tommy Docherty 1967–68
Jimmy McAnearney 1968–73
Jimmy McGuigan 1973–79
Ian Porterfield 1979–81
Emlyn Hughes 1981–83
George Kerr 1983–85
Norman Hunter 1985–87
Dave Cusack 1987–88
Billy McEwan 1988–91
Phil Henson 1991–94
Archie Gemmill and John McGovern 1994–96
Danny Bergara 1996–97
Ronnie Moore 1997–2005
Mick Harford 2005
Alan Knill 2005–07
Mark Robins 2007–09
Ronnie Moore 2009–11
Andy Scott 2011–12
Steve Evans 2012–15
Neil Redfearn 2015–16
Neil Warnock 2016
Alan Stubbs 2016
Kenny Jackett 2016
Paul Warne November 2016–

LATEST SEQUENCES

Longest Sequence of League Wins: 9, 2.2.1982 – 6.3.1982.

Longest Sequence of League Defeats: 10, 14.2.2017 – 8.4.2017.

Longest Sequence of League Draws: 6, 13.10.1969 – 22.11.1969.

Longest Sequence of Unbeaten League Matches: 18, 13.10.1969 – 7.2.1970.

Longest Sequence Without a League Win: 21, 9.5.2004 – 20.11.2004.

Successive Scoring Runs: 30 from 3.4.1954.

Successive Non-scoring Runs: 6 from 21.8.2004.

TEN YEAR LEAGUE RECORD

		P	*W*	*D*	*L*	*F*	*A*	*Pts*	*Pos*
2009-10	FL 2	46	21	10	15	55	52	73	5
2010-11	FL 2	46	17	15	14	75	60	66	9
2011-12	FL 2	46	18	13	15	67	63	67	10
2012-13	FL 2	46	24	7	15	74	59	79	2
2013-14	FL 1	46	24	14	8	86	58	86	4
2014-15	FL C	46	11	16	19	46	67	46*	21
2015-16	FL C	46	13	10	23	53	71	49	21
2016-17	FL C	46	5	8	33	40	98	23	24
2017-18	FL 1	46	24	7	15	73	53	79	4
2018-19	FL C	46	8	16	22	52	83	40	22

**3 pts deducted.*

DID YOU KNOW ?

Rotherham United followed up their success in winning the Division Three North title in 1950–51 with a five-match tour of Malta. United recorded four victories, including a 14-3 win over Hibernians, but lost 3-1 to a Malta FA team.

ROTHERHAM UNITED – SKY BET CHAMPIONSHIP 2018–19 LEAGUE RECORD

Match No.	Date	Venue	Opponents	Result		H/T Score	Lg Pos.	Goalscorers	Attendance
1	Aug 4	A	Brentford	L	1-5	0-2	24	Vaulks [90]	10,297
2	11	H	Ipswich T	W	1-0	0-0	13	Smith [90]	9460
3	18	A	Leeds U	L	0-2	0-0	15		33,699
4	21	H	Hull C	L	2-3	1-2	17	Wood [16], Proctor [75]	8962
5	26	H	Millwall	W	1-0	1-0	15	Raggett [20]	8197
6	Sept 1	A	Wigan Ath	L	0-1	0-0	15		9584
7	15	H	Derby Co	W	1-0	0-0	14	Manning (pen) [63]	10,707
8	18	A	Aston Villa	L	0-2	0-1	15		27,991
9	22	A	Nottingham F	L	0-1	0-0	19		27,479
10	29	H	Stoke C	D	2-2	0-0	18	Manning (pen) [47], Towell [50]	9706
11	Oct 3	H	Bristol C	D	0-0	0-0	19		8187
12	6	A	Birmingham C	L	1-3	0-2	19	Taylor [77]	19,795
13	20	H	Bolton W	D	1-1	0-0	20	Vaulks [57]	10,011
14	23	A	Middlesbrough	D	0-0	0-0	20		21,235
15	27	A	Preston NE	D	1-1	0-1	21	Smith [55]	11,780
16	Nov 3	H	Swansea C	W	2-1	0-1	18	Manning 2 (2 pens) [79, 87]	9006
17	10	A	Blackburn R	D	1-1	0-0	19	Smith [75]	12,847
18	24	H	Sheffield U	D	2-2	0-1	19	Taylor [66], Proctor [90]	11,607
19	27	H	QPR	D	2-2	2-1	19	Vaulks [6], Robertson [15]	8018
20	Dec 1	A	Norwich C	L	1-3	1-0	20	Towell [11]	25,858
21	8	A	Sheffield W	D	2-2	0-1	20	Smith [46], Towell [55]	24,725
22	15	H	Reading	D	1-1	0-1	20	Mattock [90]	8775
23	22	H	WBA	L	0-4	0-3	20		10,593
24	26	A	Bolton W	L	1-2	1-1	21	Vaulks [37]	15,255
25	29	A	Bristol C	L	0-1	0-0	22		21,207
26	Jan 1	H	Preston NE	W	2-1	1-0	21	Vaulks [45], Smith [76]	9077
27	12	A	Ipswich T	L	0-1	0-1	21		20,893
28	19	H	Brentford	L	2-4	1-1	21	Taylor [20], Konsa (og) [73]	8319
29	26	H	Leeds U	L	1-2	1-0	21	Ajayi [28]	11,259
30	Feb 2	A	Millwall	D	0-0	0-0	21		12,084
31	9	H	Wigan Ath	D	1-1	1-1	21	Robertson [28]	9611
32	12	A	Hull C	D	2-2	0-2	21	Forde [48], McKenzie (og) [55]	10,785
33	16	H	Sheffield W	D	2-2	1-1	22	Taylor [37], Towell [74]	11,736
34	23	A	Reading	D	1-1	0-1	22	Ajayi [79]	15,958
35	Mar 2	H	Blackburn R	W	3-2	1-0	22	Ajayi 2 [2, 83], Williams [57]	9663
36	9	A	Sheffield U	L	0-2	0-1	22		27,402
37	13	A	QPR	W	2-1	0-0	22	Ajayi 2 [71, 90]	10,854
38	16	H	Norwich C	L	1-2	0-1	22	Ajayi [52]	11,026
39	30	A	Derby Co	L	1-6	0-3	22	Wood [53]	27,003
40	Apr 6	H	Nottingham F	W	2-1	1-1	22	Smith [10], Ihiekwe [60]	11,012
41	10	H	Aston Villa	L	1-2	1-0	22	Vaulks (pen) [36]	10,558
42	13	A	Stoke C	D	2-2	0-2	22	Smith [58], Crooks [74]	24,250
43	19	A	Swansea C	L	3-4	2-1	22	Ihiekwe [10], Crooks [38], Vaulks [83]	18,527
44	22	H	Birmingham C	L	1-3	1-0	22	Crooks [22]	10,703
45	27	A	WBA	L	1-2	0-0	22	Robertson [50]	24,534
46	May 5	H	Middlesbrough	L	1-2	0-2	22	Smith (pen) [86]	11,051

Final League Position: 22

GOALSCORERS

League (52): Smith 8 (1 pen), Ajayi 7, Vaulks 7 (1 pen), Manning 4 (4 pens), Taylor 4, Towell 4, Crooks 3, Robertson 3, Ihiekwe 2, Proctor 2, Wood 2, Forde 1, Mattock 1, Raggett 1, Williams 1, own goals 2.
FA Cup (0).
Carabao Cup (4): Proctor 2, Ajayi 1, Vaulks 1.

Rodak M 45	Vyner Z 28 + 3	Ajayi S 46	Wood R 23 + 3	Mattock J 44	Tayler J 30 + 11	Vaulks W 41	Palmer M 8 + 2	Newell J 18 + 13	Ball D 1	Smith M 44 + 1	Vassell K 9 + 14	Wiles B 9 + 11	Williams R 24 + 15	Forde A 17 + 11	Jones B 19 + 2	Raggett S 6 + 1	Manning R 13 + 5	Proctor J 2 + 14	Robertson C 25 + 3	Towell R 28 + 6	Yates J 3 + 4	Crooks M 7 + 9	Ihiekwe M 15	Price L 1	Potter D — + 1	*Match No.*
1	2	3	4	5	6	7	8	9^1	10^2	11^3	12	13	14													1
1	2	3	4	5	6^1	7	8	9^3		11	10^2		12	13	14											2
1	2	8	4^3	5	6	9	7^1			11^3	13		10			3	12	14								3
1	2	3	4	5	6^1	8	7^3	12		11	13		10^2				9	14								4
1	2	7	4	5		6		13		10^1	9^2		11			3	8	12								5
1	2	8	4^1	5	6^2	7				11	13		10			3^3	9	14	12							6
1	2	3	4	5	12	6	14			10^1	11^3		9				8	13		7^2						7
1	2	3	4	5	12	7				10	11^3		9^2	14			8^1	13		6						8
1		3	4	5	14	7	13			12	11		9		2		8^2	10^1		6^3						9
1	12	3	4^1	5	13	7		11^2		10			9		2		8			6						10
1		3		5	6	4	7^1	9^2		11		13	10	12	2		8									11
1	14	3		5	6	4	7^3	9^1		11	12	13	10		2		8^2									12
1	12	3	4	5	6^3	7		13		11	10^2		9		2^1		14			8						13
1	2	3		5		6				11^3	10^2	12	7^1	13			9	14	4	8						14
1	2	3		5	7^3	6		12		11	9^1		10^2				14	13	4	8						15
1	2	3		5	8^1	7		13		11	10^2		9				12	14	4	6^3						16
1	2^2	6	4	5	12			10^1		11	14	13	7^3				9		3	8						17
1	2^1	3		5	10	6		12		11	13		7^2				9^3	14	4	8						18
1	2	3	13	5	10^1	6	9^3	12		11			7^2					14	4	8						19
1	2	3	13	5	12	6		9^3		11			8	7^1				14	4^2	10						20
1	2	3	4	5	10	6				11		12	8	7^1						9						21
1	2	3	4^3	5	9^1	7		14		11			10^2	6				13	12	8						22
1	2	3		5^2	13	6		10^3		11^1			12	7			9	14	4	8						23
1	2	3		5	13	8		9^2		10		14	12	6^1				11^3	4	7						24
1		3		5	7^3	6				11		9^1	10^2	14	2■	12	13		4	8■						25
1		2	4	5	6^2	7	8^1	13		11		10	9	12		3										26
1	2^2	6	14	5	10	8				11		9	12	7^1		3^3			4		13					27
1	2^3	3		5	10	6				11	14	9^1		7^2					4	8	13	12				28
1		6		5	7^2	8				11^3	13			10	2	3			4	9^1	12	14				29
1		7	3	9		6				10	12				5				4	13	11^2	8^1	2			30
1		6	3	5	7^2	8		12		11				10	2				4	13		9^1				31
1	5	7	3^2	9	13	6				10				12					4	8^3	11^1	14	2			32
1		7		5	9^1	6		12		10			13	11^2	2				4	8			3			33
1		6		5	7^3	9		13		11			12	10	2				4	8^2		14	3^1			34
1		6		5	7^2	8				11		13	12	10^1	2				4	9^3		14	3			35
1		6		5	7^2	8■		10^1		11		9	13	12	2^3				4			14	3			36
1	2	6	4	5	7			10^2		11		9^3		13	14					8^1		12	3			37
1	2	6	4^2		13			10		11		8		7^3	5					12	14	9^1	3			38
1	2	6	4		7^2			10				9^3	8	14	5					12	11^1	13	3			39
1		7	4	5^3	9^2	6		11		10		13	14		2^1				12	8			3			40
1	2	6		5	7^1	8		10		11	13	12	14						4	9^2			3^3			41
1	2	6		5	7^1	8		14		11			13	10^2					4	9^3		12	3			42
1	2	6^2		5	10^3	8				11		14	13	7					4	12		9^1	3			43
1		3	4^2	5	12	6		10^3		11	14		7^1	13	2					8		9				44
1		7		5		8^2		9		11	14		13	6^1	2^3				4	12		10	3			45
		7		5				11^3		10	14	8	12	9^1	2				4			6^2	3	1	13	46

FA Cup
Third Round Manchester C (a) 0-7

Carabao Cup
First Round Wigan Ath (h) 3-1
Second Round Everton (a) 1-3

SALFORD CITY

FOUNDATION

The origins of Salford City are obscure, the club having been established as Salford Central in 1940 and remained in minor competitions until 1963 when the name was changed to Salford Amateurs and they entered the Manchester League. In 1980 this club merged with another local club, Anson Villa, and adopted the name Salford. They were members of the Cheshire County League and then the North West Counties League. In 1990 Salford became Salford City and after gaining promotion to the Northern Premier League for 2008-09 they have since made rapid progress to achieve Football League status.

The Peninsula Stadium, Moor Lane, Salford, Greater Manchester M7 3PZ.

Telephone: (0161) 792 6287.

Ticket Office: (0161) 241 9772.

Website: salfordcityfc.co.uk

Email: enquiries@salfordcityfc.co.uk

Ground Capacity: 5,106.

Record Attendance: 4,044 v Wrexham, National League, 1 January 2019.

Chairman: Karen Baird.

President: Dave Russell.

Manager: Graham Alexander.

Assistant Manager: Chris Lucketti.

Colours: Red shirts with white trim, white shorts, white socks.

HONOURS

League Champions: National League North – 2017–18; Northern Premier League Division One North – 2014–15.
Runners-up: North West Counties League Premier Division – 2007–08.
Play-Off Winners: National League – 2018–19 (*promoted to FL 2*); Northern Premier League Premier Division – 2015–16 (*promoted to National League North*).

FA Cup: 2nd rd – 2015–16.

Manchester Premier Cup Winners: 1977–78, 1978–79.
Runners-up: 1989–90, 2001–02, 2012–13.

North West Counties League Challenge Cup Winners: 2005–06.

Lancashire Amateur Cup Winners: 1973, 1975, 1977.

THE Sun FACT FILE

Salford City reached the FA Cup first round proper for the first time in 2015–16 when they were members of the Northern Premier League. They were drawn at home against Notts County and defeated the League Two team 2-0, earning a second-round tie against Hartlepool United. The clubs drew 1-1 but Hartlepool won the replay. All three games were shown live on television.

MANAGERS

Anthony Johnson and Bernard Morley 2015–18
Graham Alexander May 2018–

Year Formed: 1940.

Turned Professional: 2017.

Previous Names: 1940 Salford Central; 1963, Salford Amateurs; 1989, Salford City.

Club Nickname: 'The Ammies'.

Grounds: 1979, Moor Lane (renamed The Peninsula Stadium 2017).

Record National League Victory: 4-0 v Aldershot T, National League, 17 November 2018.

Record Cup Victory: 5–0 v Kennek Ryhope, FA Cup Preliminary rd, 2000–01; 5–0 v Atherton Laburnum R, FA Cup 1st Qualifying rd, 2008–09; 5–0 v Whitby T, FA Cup 1st Qualifying rd, 2015–16.

Record Cup Defeat: 1–7 v St Helen's T, FA Cup prel rd, 2001–02.

Football League Record: 2019 Promoted to FL 2.

TEN YEAR LEAGUE RECORD

		P	*W*	*D*	*L*	*F*	*A*	*Pts*	*Pos*
2009–10	NPL1N	42	16	8	18	63	74	56	11
2010–11	NPL1N	44	17	11	16	68	73	62	12
2011–12	NPL1N	42	14	10	18	69	71	52	13
2012–13	NPL1N	42	11	13	18	65	79	46	16
2013–14	NPL1N	42	15	7	20	68	80	52	12
2014–15	NPL1N	42	30	5	7	92	42	95	1
2015–16	NPLP	46	27	9	10	94	48	90	3
2016–17	NLN	42	22	11	9	79	44	77	4
2017–18	NLN	42	28	7	7	80	45	91	1
2018–19	NL	46	25	10	11	77	45	85	3

DID YOU KNOW ?

Salford City, then known as Salford Amateurs, won the Lancashire Amateur Cup for the first time in the 1972–73 season. They defeated Liverpool County Combination team Langton 3-1 in the final which was played at Old Trafford.

SCUNTHORPE UNITED

FOUNDATION

The year of foundation for Scunthorpe United has often been quoted as 1910, but the club can trace its history back to 1899 when Brumby Hall FC, who played on the Old Showground, consolidated their position by amalgamating with some other clubs and changing their name to Scunthorpe United. The year 1910 was when that club amalgamated with North Lindsey United as Scunthorpe and Lindsey United. The link is Mr W. T. Lockwood whose chairmanship covers both years.

Glanford Park, Jack Brownsword Way, Scunthorpe, North Lincolnshire DN15 8TD.

Telephone: (01724) 840 139.

Fax: (01724) 857 986.

Ticket Office: (01724) 747 670.

Website: www.scunthorpe-united.co.uk

Email: feedback@scunthorpe-united.co.uk

Ground Capacity: 9,088.

Record Attendance: 23,935 v Portsmouth, FA Cup 4th rd, 30 January 1954 (at Old Showground); 9,077 v Manchester U, League Cup 3rd rd, 22 September 2010 (at Glanford Park).

Pitch Measurements: 102.5m × 66m (112yd × 72yd).

Chairman: Peter Swann.

Chief Executive: James Rodwell.

Manager: Paul Hurst.

Assistant Manager: Chris Doig.

Colours: Claret shirts with blue stripes and trim, light blue shorts with claret trim, claret socks with white trim.

Year Formed: 1899.

Turned Professional: 1912.

Previous Names: Amalgamated first with Brumby Hall then North Lindsey United to become Scunthorpe and Lindsey United, 1910; 1958, Scunthorpe United.

Club Nickname: 'The Iron'.

Grounds: 1899, Old Showground; 1988, Glanford Park.

First Football League Game: 19 August 1950, Division 3 (N), v Shrewsbury T (h) D 0–0 – Thompson; Barker, Brownsword; Allen, Taylor, McCormick; Mosby, Payne, Gorin, Rees, Boyes.

Record League Victory: 8–1 v Luton T (h), Division 3, 24 April 1965 – Sidebottom; Horstead, Hemstead; Smith, Neale, Lindsey; Bramley (1), Scott, Thomas (5), Mahy (1), Wilson (1). 8–1 v Torquay U (a), Division 3, 28 October 1995 – Samways; Housham, Wilson, Ford (1), Knill (1), Hope (Nicholson), Thornber, Bullimore (Walsh), McFarlane (4) (Young), Eyre (2), Paterson.

HONOURS

League Champions: FL 1 – 2006–07; Division 3N – 1957–58.
Runners-up: FL 2 – 2004–05, 2013–14.

FA Cup: 5th rd – 1958, 1970.

League Cup: 4th rd – 2010.

League Trophy: *Runners-up:* 2009.

THE Sun FACT FILE

Frank Soo, who was manager of Scunthorpe United between June 1959 and May 1960, was a pioneering figure of Chinese ethnic background in English football. He was both the first player and manager of Chinese descent in the Football League and also the first to appear for England (albeit in a wartime international).

Record Cup Victory: 9–0 v Boston U, FA Cup 1st rd, 21 November 1953 – Malan; Hubbard, Brownsword; Sharpe, White, Bushby; Mosby (1), Haigh (3), Whitfield (2), Gregory (1), Mervyn Jones (2).

Record Defeat: 0–8 v Carlisle U, Division 3 (N), 25 December 1952.

Most League Points (2 for a win): 66, Division 3 (N), 1956–57, 1957–58.

Most League Points (3 for a win): 91, FL 1, 2006–07.

Most League Goals: 88, Division 3 (N), 1957–58.

Highest League Scorer in Season: Barrie Thomas, 31, Division 2, 1961–62.

Most League Goals in Total Aggregate: Steve Cammack, 110, 1979–81, 1981–86.

Most League Goals in One Match: 5, Barrie Thomas v Luton T, Division 3, 24 April 1965.

Most Capped Player: Grant McCann, 12 (40), Northern Ireland.

Most League Appearances: Jack Brownsword, 597, 1950–65.

Youngest League Player: Hakeeb Adelakun, 16 years 201 days v Tranmere R, 29 December 2012.

Record Transfer Fee Received: £2,400,000 from Celtic for Gary Hooper, July 2010.

Record Transfer Fee Paid: £700,000 to Hibernian for Rob Jones, July 2009.

Football League Record: 1950 Elected to Division 3 (N); 1958–64 Division 2; 1964–68 Division 3; 1968–72 Division 4; 1972–73 Division 3; 1973–83 Division 4; 1983–84 Division 3; 1984–92 Division 4; 1992–99 Division 3; 1999–2000 Division 2; 2000–04 Division 3; 2004–05 FL 2; 2005–07 FL 1; 2007–08 FL C; 2008–09 FL 1; 2009–11 FL C; 2011–13 FL 1; 2013–14 FL 2; 2014–19 FL 1; 2019– FL 2.

MANAGERS

Harry Allcock 1915–53
(Secretary-Manager)
Tom Crilly 1936–37
Bernard Harper 1946–48
Leslie Jones 1950–51
Bill Corkhill 1952–56
Ron Suart 1956–58
Tony McShane 1959
Bill Lambton 1959
Frank Soo 1959–60
Dick Duckworth 1960–64
Fred Goodwin 1964–66
Ron Ashman 1967–73
Ron Bradley 1973–74
Dick Rooks 1974–76
Ron Ashman 1976–81
John Duncan 1981–83
Allan Clarke 1983–84
Frank Barlow 1984–87
Mick Buxton 1987–91
Bill Green 1991–93
Richard Money 1993–94
David Moore 1994–96
Mick Buxton 1996–97
Brian Laws 1997–2004; 2004–06
Nigel Adkins 2006–10
Ian Baraclough 2010–11
Alan Knill 2011–12
Brian Laws 2012–13
Russ Wilcox 2013–14
Mark Robins 2014–16
Nick Daws 2016
Graham Alexander 2016–18
Nick Daws 2018
Stuart McCall 2018–19
Paul Hurst May 2019–

LATEST SEQUENCES

Longest Sequence of League Wins: 7, 9.4.2016 – 6.8.2017.

Longest Sequence of League Defeats: 8, 29.11.1997 – 20.1.1998.

Longest Sequence of League Draws: 6, 2.1.1984 – 25.2.1984.

Longest Sequence of Unbeaten League Matches: 28, 23.11.2013 – 21.4.2014.

Longest Sequence Without a League Win: 14, 22.3.1975 – 6.9.1975.

Successive Scoring Runs: 24 from 13.1.2007.

Successive Non-scoring Runs: 7 from 19.4.1975.

TEN YEAR LEAGUE RECORD

		P	*W*	*D*	*L*	*F*	*A*	*Pts*	*Pos*
2009-10	FL C	46	14	10	22	62	84	52	20
2010-11	FL C	46	12	6	28	43	87	42	24
2011-12	FL 1	46	10	22	14	55	59	52	18
2012-13	FL 1	46	13	9	24	49	73	48	21
2013-14	FL 2	46	20	21	5	68	44	81	2
2014-15	FL 1	46	14	14	18	62	75	56	16
2015-16	FL 1	46	21	11	14	60	47	74	7
2016-17	FL 1	46	24	10	12	80	54	82	3
2017-18	FL 1	46	19	17	10	65	50	74	5
2018-19	FL 1	46	12	10	24	53	83	46	23

DID YOU KNOW ?

Despite struggling in the lower half of the Second Division table all season, Scunthorpe United achieved their best-ever average attendance in the 1958–59 term with 12,377. The highest gate that season was 17,488 for the visit of Sheffield Wednesday.

SCUNTHORPE UNITED – SKY BET LEAGUE ONE 2018–19 LEAGUE RECORD

Match No.	Date	Venue	Opponents	Result		H/T Score	Lg Pos.	Goalscorers	Attendance
1	Aug 4	A	Coventry C	W	2-1	0-0	4	Humphrys [68], Dales [81]	12,964
2	11	H	Walsall	D	1-1	0-0	6	Novak [48]	4331
3	19	A	Sunderland	L	0-3	0-3	15		29,876
4	22	H	Fleetwood T	L	0-5	0-4	18		3465
5	25	H	Barnsley	D	2-2	1-0	18	Morris (pen) [9], Burgess [51]	5579
6	Sept 1	A	Accrington S	D	1-1	0-0	18	Lund [80]	2059
7	8	H	Rochdale	D	3-3	2-0	17	Novak [2], Colclough [18], Goode [54]	3898
8	15	A	AFC Wimbledon	W	3-2	2-0	15	Morris 2 [8, 32], Ugbo [52]	3885
9	22	H	Shrewsbury T	W	1-0	0-0	11	Novak [55]	3784
10	29	A	Burton Alb	D	0-0	0-0	10		2797
11	Oct 2	H	Charlton Ath	W	5-3	3-2	9	Goode [3], Borthwick-Jackson 2 [30, 38], Morris (pen) [73], Humphrys [90]	3341
12	6	A	Luton T	L	2-3	1-2	12	Novak [17], Humphrys [90]	8682
13	13	H	Peterborough U	L	0-2	0-0	13		4566
14	20	A	Wycombe W	L	2-3	2-1	15	Colclough [1], Humphrys [7]	4024
15	23	A	Blackpool	L	0-1	0-1	16		2769
16	27	H	Plymouth Arg	L	1-4	0-2	17	Novak [49]	3508
17	Nov 3	H	Oxford U	D	3-3	0-1	19	Clarke [60], Thomas [64], Goode [66]	3665
18	17	A	Bristol R	W	2-1	1-1	17	Novak [15], Lund [78]	8003
19	24	H	Portsmouth	L	1-2	0-2	18	Novak [60]	4365
20	27	A	Southend U	L	0-2	0-1	20		5110
21	Dec 8	H	Gillingham	L	0-2	0-0	20		3054
22	15	A	Doncaster R	L	0-3	0-2	20		7969
23	22	A	Bradford C	L	0-2	0-2	21		16,130
24	26	H	Luton T	L	0-2	0-1	23		4050
25	29	H	Wycombe W	W	1-0	1-0	22	Wootton [8]	3489
26	Jan 1	A	Peterborough U	W	2-0	1-0	21	Novak 2 [5, 57]	6974
27	5	H	Coventry C	W	2-1	0-0	17	Perch [67], Sutton [74]	4692
28	12	A	Walsall	W	2-1	1-0	15	Ojo [12], Novak [68]	3984
29	19	H	Sunderland	D	1-1	0-0	16	Hammill [87]	7263
30	26	A	Fleetwood T	W	1-0	0-0	14	Eastham (og) [76]	2637
31	Feb 2	A	Barnsley	L	0-2	0-2	14		12,150
32	9	H	Accrington S	W	2-0	2-0	13	Wootton [13], van Veen [42]	4824
33	16	A	Gillingham	L	0-1	0-1	14		4170
34	23	H	Doncaster R	D	1-1	0-1	16	Wootton [69]	6255
35	Mar 2	A	Oxford U	L	1-2	0-0	16	Thomas [90]	6237
36	9	H	Bristol R	L	0-1	0-1	18		3877
37	12	H	Southend U	W	4-1	1-1	15	Pearce [23], McMahon [68], Thomas [73], Perch [77]	3233
38	16	A	Portsmouth	L	0-2	0-0	17		17,308
39	23	A	Rochdale	L	1-3	1-1	18	Hallam [16]	3361
40	30	H	AFC Wimbledon	L	1-2	0-2	19	Novak [78]	3955
41	Apr 6	A	Shrewsbury T	D	1-1	1-0	18	Wootton [22]	6419
42	13	H	Burton Alb	L	0-3	0-1	19		3698
43	19	H	Blackpool	D	0-0	0-0	20		3795
44	22	A	Charlton Ath	L	0-4	0-1	21		11,973
45	27	H	Bradford C	L	2-3	0-3	23	Wootton [64], Novak [80]	4528
46	May 4	A	Plymouth Arg	L	2-3	1-2	23	Wootton [42], Morris [60]	11,907

Final League Position: 23

GOALSCORERS

League (53): Novak 12, Wootton 6, Morris 5 (2 pens), Humphrys 4, Goode 3, Thomas 3, Borthwick-Jackson 2, Colclough 2, Lund 2, Perch 2, Burgess 1, Clarke 1, Dales 1, Hallam 1, Hammill 1, McMahon 1, Ojo 1, Pearce 1, Sutton 1, Ugbo 1, van Veen 1, own goal 1.
FA Cup (2): Novak 1, Perch 1.
Carabao Cup (1): Humphrys 1.
Checkatrade Trophy (3): Colclough 1, Dales 1, El-Mhanni 1.

Watson R 5	Clarke J 15	Goode C 21	Burgess C 33 + 3	Borthwick-Jackson C 29	Perch J 39 + 2	Horsfield J 5 + 6	Olomola O 2 + 4	Humphrys S 10 + 6	Dales A 11 + 9	Novak L 39 + 4	Ojo F 37 + 2	Holmes D — + 1	Lund M 16 + 6	Thomas G 28 + 9	Morris J 17 + 2	Colclough R 12 + 5	Butroid L 2 + 4	McArdle R 37 + 1	Flatt J — + 1	Alnwick J 41	Ugbo I 7 + 8	Wootten K 20 + 6	El-Mhanni Y 2 + 3	Lewis C 3 + 12	Sutton L 16 + 2	McMahon T 14	Webster B 8 + 1	Hammill A 10 + 5	van Veen K 6 + 7	McGahey H 8 + 2	Pearce T 9	Hallam J 4 + 3	Match No.
1	2^1	3	4	5	6	7^3	8^2	9	10	11	12	13	14																				1
1	2^1	3	4	5	6	12		8	10^2	11			7^3	9	13	14																	2
1	2	3	4		7			12	8^2	11	13		6^1	9	10^3	14	5																3
1	2		4	5	7^3	14		11^2	8	13	6			9^1	10	12		3															4
1^1	2		4		5	13			8	11	6		7	9^3	10^2	12		3	14														5
	2		4		5			8^2	13	11^1	6		7	9^3	10	12		3		1	14												6
		3	4	5	2	13		12		10^2	7		8^1		9	6				1	11												7
		3	4	5^3	2			14	13	11	7		8		9	6^2	12			1	10^1												8
		3	4	5	2			14	12	10^2	7		8		9	6^3		13		1	11^1												9
		3	4	5	2	13			12	11	8		7^1		9	6				1	10^2												10
	5^1	2	4	8				9	12	10^2	6			13	7	11		3		1													11
	2		3	5				9		11^1	6		7	12	8	10		4		1													12
	2	3	14	5	13			9^3	12	10	7		6^1		8^2	11		4		1													13
	2	3		5	8			10	9^1		7			11		6		4		1	12												14
	2	4	5^1	6	8	12		11	9^2		7^3			13		10		3		1	14												15
	2	4		5	7	8		11^1		12				6		9		3		1	10^2	13											16
	2	3	4	5^1	7	6^2				10			8	11		9	13			1	12												17
		4	13	2	5				6	11	8		7			9^2		3		1	10^1	12											18
		3	4	5^1		7^2		14	11	10	6^3		8	9			13	2		1	12												19
		3	4		5■	7^2			11^3	10				9	8			2		1	6^1	14	12	13									20
		3	4	5	9				13	10			8^2	6^1	7			2		1	12	11											21
	2	3		5	7				8	11^1			6	9^3	10^2			4		1	13	14	12										22
	2	3	12■	5^2	8					11	7			9^3				4^1		1	13	10		14	6								23
		2		4	7			12	13	10^1	8			9				3		1		11	5^2		6								24
			4	5	7				12^2	10	8			9				3		1		11	6^1	13	2								25
		3	2	8	6					11	7			9				4		1		10			5								26
			4	5	7					10^1	8			9				3		1		11		12	6	2							27
			4	5	7^1					10	8		14	9^2				3		1		11^3		13	6	2	12						28
			4	5	6					10	8^2		14	9^1				3		1		11			7^3	2		12	13				29
			4	5^1	6					11	7			8				3		1		10			13	2		9^2		12			30
			6		5^1					10	4		14	11				7		1					12	2	3^3	9^2	13	8			31
			4							10^2	7			9^1				3		1		11		13	6	5			12	2	8		32
			4				12				7			9^2				3		1		11	14		6	5		13	10^3	2	8^1		33
			4		13		12			11	7			9^1				3		1		10			6	5		8^2		2			34
			2		7		9^2			10^3	6			13				4		1		11		12	5^1				14	3	8		35
			4		6^1		14			13	8			12				3		1		11^3			7	2		9^4	10		5		36
			4		6					10	8			9				3		1				12	7^1	2			11		5		37
			4		7		13			10	6			9^2				3		1		11^1		14		5^3		12		2	8		38
			4		6^2					10	8						12	3		1		11			7	2^1		13		5		9	39
			4		6					10	8			9^2						1		13			7^3	2	3	12	11^1		5	14	40
					7					11	8			14				3		1		10		13		2^1	4	9		12	5^2	6^3	41
					8					10	7			13			5	4		1		11^1		12			3	9	14	2^3		6^2	42
					2					13	6				12			3		1		11		14	7^3		4	8	10^2		5	9^1	43
				5	2					11	8		13	10	6^3			3		1				7^1			4	9^2	12			14	44
				5	2					10	8^3		12	14	6			3		1		13		7			4^2	9	11^1				45
				5	2					10			8	14	6			3^3		1		11^2		7^1			4	9	13			12	46

FA Cup

First Round	Burton Alb	(h)	2-1
Second Round	Shrewsbury T	(a)	0-1

Carabao Cup

First Round	Doncaster R	(h)	1-2

Checkatrade Trophy

Group H (N)	Wolverhampton W U21	(h)	0-0
(Scunthorpe U won 4-2 on penalties)			
Group H (N)	Lincoln C	(h)	1-1
(Lincoln C won 3-1 on penalties)			
Group H (N)	Mansfield T	(a)	2-3

SHEFFIELD UNITED

FOUNDATION

In March 1889, Yorkshire County Cricket Club formed Sheffield United six days after an FA Cup semi-final between Preston North End and West Bromwich Albion had finally convinced Charles Stokes, a member of the cricket club, that the formation of a professional football club would prove successful at Bramall Lane. The United's first secretary, Mr J. B. Wostinholm, was also secretary of the cricket club.

Bramall Lane Ground, Cherry Street, Bramall Lane, Sheffield, South Yorkshire S2 4SU.

Telephone: (01142) 537 200.

Ticket Office: (01142) 537 200 (option 1).

Website: www.sufc.co.uk

Email: info@sufc.co.uk

Ground Capacity: 32,702.

Record Attendance: 68,287 v Leeds U, FA Cup 5th rd, 15 February 1936.

Pitch Measurements: 100m × 64m (109.5yd × 70yd).

Chairman: Kevin McCabe.

Chief Executive Officer: Stephen Bettis.

Manager: Chris Wilder.

Assistant Manager: Alan Knill.

Colours: Red and white striped shirts with black trim, black shorts with white trim, white socks with black trim.

Year Formed: 1889.

Turned Professional: 1889.

Club Nickname: 'The Blades'.

Ground: 1889, Bramall Lane.

First Football League Game: 3 September 1892, Division 2, v Lincoln C (h) W 4–2 – Lilley; Witham, Cain; Howell, Hendry, Needham (1); Wallace, Dobson, Hammond (3), Davies, Drummond.

Record League Victory: 10–0 v Burslem Port Vale (a), Division 2, 10 December 1892 – Howlett; Witham, Lilley; Howell, Hendry, Needham; Drummond (1), Wallace (1), Hammond (4), Davies (2), Watson (2). 10-0 v Burnley, Division 1 (h), 19 January 1929.

Record Cup Victory: 6–0 v Leyton Orient (h), FA Cup 1st rd, 6 November 2016 – Ramsdale; Basham (1), O'Connell, Wright, Freeman (1), Coutts (Whiteman), Duffy (Brooks), Fleck, Lafferty, Scougall (1) (Lavery), Chapman (3).

Record Defeat: 0–13 v Bolton W, FA Cup 2nd rd, 1 February 1890.

Most League Points (2 for a win): 60, Division 2, 1952–53.

HONOURS

League Champions: Division 1 – 1897–98; Division 2 – 1952–53; FL 1 – 2016–17; Division 4 – 1981–82.
Runners-up: Division 1 – 1896–97, 1899–1900; FL C – 2005–06, 2018–19; Division 2 – 1892–93, 1938–39, 1960–61, 1970–71, 1989–90; Division 3 – 1988–89.

FA Cup Winners: 1899, 1902, 1915, 1925.
Runners-up: 1901, 1936.

League Cup: semi-final – 2003, 2015.

THE Sun FACT FILE

Although Sheffield United finished in second place in the old Division Two at the end of the 1892–93 season, they did not automatically gain promotion to the top flight. To qualify they had to play First Division club Accrington in a Test Match played at the Nottingham Forest ground. United won 1-0 with a goal from Jack Drummond.

Most League Points (3 for a win): 100, FL 1, 2016–17.

Most League Goals: 102, Division 1, 1925–26.

Highest League Scorer in Season: Jimmy Dunne, 41, Division 1, 1930–31.

Most League Goals in Total Aggregate: Harry Johnson, 201, 1919–30.

Most League Goals in One Match: 5, Harry Hammond v Bootle, Division 2, 26 November 1892; 5, Harry Johnson v West Ham U, Division 1, 26 December 1927.

Most Capped Player: Billy Gillespie, 25, Northern Ireland.

Most League Appearances: Joe Shaw, 632, 1948–66.

Youngest League Player: Louis Reed, 16 years 257 days v Rotherham U, 8 April 2014.

Record Transfer Fee Received: £4,000,000 from Everton for Phil Jagielka, July 2007; £4,000,000 from Tottenham H for Kyle Naughton, July 2009; £4,000,000 from Tottenham H for Kyle Walker, July 2009.

Record Transfer Fee Paid: £6,000,000 to Preston NE for Callum Robinson, July 2019.

Football League Record: 1892 Elected to Division 2; 1893–1934 Division 1; 1934–39 Division 2; 1946–49 Division 1; 1949–53 Division 2; 1953–56 Division 1; 1956–61 Division 2; 1961–68 Division 1; 1968–71 Division 2; 1971–76 Division 1; 1976–79 Division 2; 1979–81 Division 3; 1981–82 Division 4; 1982–84 Division 3; 1984–88 Division 2; 1988–89 Division 3; 1989–90 Division 2; 1990–92 Division 1; 1992–94 Premier League; 1994–2004 Division 1; 2004–06 FL C; 2006–07 Premier League; 2007–11 FL C; 2011–17 FL 1; 2017–19 FL C; 2019– Premier League.

MANAGERS

J. B. Wostinholm 1889–99 *(Secretary-Manager)*
John Nicholson 1899–1932
Ted Davison 1932–52
Reg Freeman 1952–55
Joe Mercer 1955–58
Johnny Harris 1959–68 *(continued as General Manager to 1970)*
Arthur Rowley 1968–69
Johnny Harris *(General Manager resumed Team Manager duties)* 1969–73
Ken Furphy 1973–75
Jimmy Sirrel 1975–77
Harry Haslam 1978–81
Martin Peters 1981
Ian Porterfield 1981–86
Billy McEwan 1986–88
Dave Bassett 1988–95
Howard Kendall 1995–97
Nigel Spackman 1997–98
Steve Bruce 1998–99
Adrian Heath 1999
Neil Warnock 1999–2007
Bryan Robson 2007–08
Kevin Blackwell 2008–10
Gary Speed 2010
Micky Adams 2010–11
Danny Wilson 2011–13
David Weir 2013
Nigel Clough 2013–15
Nigel Adkins 2015–16
Chris Wilder May 2016–

LATEST SEQUENCES

Longest Sequence of League Wins: 8, 28.3.2017 – 5.8.2017.

Longest Sequence of League Defeats: 7, 19.8.1975 – 20.9.1975.

Longest Sequence of League Draws: 6, 6.5.2001 – 8.9.2001.

Longest Sequence of Unbeaten League Matches: 22, 2.9.1899 – 13.1.1900.

Longest Sequence Without a League Win: 19, 27.9.1975 – 7.2.1976.

Successive Scoring Runs: 34 from 30.3.1956.

Successive Non-scoring Runs: 6 from 4.12.1993.

TEN YEAR LEAGUE RECORD

		P	*W*	*D*	*L*	*F*	*A*	*Pts*	*Pos*
2009-10	FL C	46	17	14	15	62	55	65	8
2010-11	FL C	46	11	9	26	44	79	42	23
2011-12	FL 1	46	27	9	10	92	51	90	3
2012-13	FL 1	46	19	18	9	56	42	75	5
2013-14	FL 1	46	18	13	15	48	46	67	7
2014-15	FL 1	46	19	14	13	66	53	71	5
2015-16	FL 1	46	18	12	16	64	59	66	11
2016-17	FL 1	46	30	10	6	92	47	100	1
2017-18	FL C	46	20	9	17	62	55	69	10
2018-19	FL C	46	26	11	9	78	41	89	2

DID YOU KNOW ?

Sheffield United's Bramall Lane ground was damaged by bombing during the Sheffield blitz of December 1940. Part of a stand was destroyed and the bombs left craters on the pitch. As a result United were unable to use the ground until the start of the 1941–42 season, either switching to their opponents' grounds or playing at Hillsborough.

SHEFFIELD UNITED – SKY BET CHAMPIONSHIP 2018–19 LEAGUE RECORD

Match No.	Date	Venue	Opponents	Result	H/T Score	Lg Pos.	Goalscorers	Attendance
1	Aug 4	H	Swansea C	L 1-2	0-0	20	Baldock [62]	24,654
2	7	A	Middlesbrough	L 0-3	0-3	24		22,960
3	11	A	QPR	W 2-1	1-1	12	Sharp [43], McGoldrick (pen) [65]	14,128
4	18	H	Norwich C	W 2-1	1-1	8	Egan [9], Sharp [90]	23,850
5	25	A	Bolton W	W 3-0	2-0	6	Duffy [5], Freeman [22], Fleck [73]	14,848
6	Sept 1	H	Aston Villa	W 4-1	3-0	3	O'Connell [6], Duffy [23], Norwood [41], Sharp [49]	26,030
7	15	A	Bristol C	L 0-1	0-0	5		20,540
8	19	H	Birmingham C	D 0-0	0-0	6		23,525
9	22	H	Preston NE	W 3-2	1-0	4	Sharp [36], Basham [51], McGoldrick [87]	23,857
10	29	A	Millwall	W 3-2	1-0	4	Sharp [40], McGoldrick 2 (1 pen) [79 (p), 88]	13,145
11	Oct 3	A	Blackburn R	W 2-0	0-0	3	Sharp 2 [66, 79]	14,440
12	6	H	Hull C	W 1-0	0-0	1	McGoldrick (pen) [70]	25,360
13	20	A	Derby Co	L 1-2	1-1	2	Basham [41]	27,927
14	23	H	Stoke C	D 1-1	0-0	2	Clarke [70]	24,463
15	27	H	Wigan Ath	W 4-2	2-1	1	Dunkley (og) [23], Sharp 3 [45, 53, 63]	24,429
16	Nov 3	A	Nottingham F	L 0-1	0-0	2		28,757
17	9	H	Sheffield W	D 0-0	0-0	2		30,261
18	24	A	Rotherham U	D 2-2	1-0	5	Duffy [8], Basham [85]	11,607
19	27	A	Brentford	W 3-2	2-1	4	Konsa (og) [10], Norwood [15], Clarke [72]	8903
20	Dec 1	H	Leeds U	L 0-1	0-0	6		25,794
21	8	A	Reading	W 2-0	0-0	3	Sharp [83], Baldock (og) [86]	12,066
22	14	H	WBA	L 1-2	1-1	4	McGoldrick [12]	23,400
23	22	A	Ipswich T	D 1-1	0-1	6	Sharp [47]	17,942
24	26	H	Derby Co	W 3-1	1-0	4	Sharp [41], McGoldrick [64], Clarke [84]	28,974
25	29	H	Blackburn R	W 3-0	0-0	4	Sharp 2 [73, 77], McGoldrick [82]	27,384
26	Jan 1	A	Wigan Ath	W 3-0	1-0	3	McGoldrick [40], Duffy [48], Sharp [54]	13,054
27	12	H	QPR	W 1-0	1-0	2	McGoldrick [37]	25,501
28	19	A	Swansea C	L 0-1	0-0	3		18,673
29	26	A	Norwich C	D 2-2	1-1	3	Sharp 2 (1 pen) [45 (p), 79]	26,844
30	Feb 2	H	Bolton W	W 2-0	0-0	3	McGoldrick [56], Sharp [73]	26,131
31	8	A	Aston Villa	D 3-3	1-0	3	Sharp 3 [11, 53, 62]	34,892
32	13	H	Middlesbrough	W 1-0	0-0	3	Stearman [61]	24,805
33	16	H	Reading	W 4-0	3-0	2	Freeman [1], Madine 2 [16, 44], Fleck [49]	26,513
34	23	A	WBA	W 1-0	1-0	2	Dowell [14]	24,928
35	Mar 4	A	Sheffield W	D 0-0	0-0	3		31,630
36	9	H	Rotherham U	W 2-0	1-0	3	O'Connell [5], Duffy [74]	27,402
37	12	H	Brentford	W 2-0	1-0	3	Norwood (pen) [26], McGoldrick [84]	24,463
38	16	A	Leeds U	W 1-0	0-0	2	Basham [71]	37,004
39	30	H	Bristol C	L 2-3	1-1	3	Sharp [6], Hogan [71]	30,030
40	Apr 6	A	Preston NE	W 1-0	1-0	2	McGoldrick [33]	18,339
41	10	A	Birmingham C	D 1-1	1-1	3	Stevens [38]	22,351
42	13	H	Millwall	D 1-1	0-0	3	Madine [51]	26,703
43	19	H	Nottingham F	W 2-0	0-0	2	Duffy [51], Stevens [85]	28,403
44	22	A	Hull C	W 3-0	3-0	2	McGoldrick 2 [10, 22], Stevens [42]	14,116
45	27	H	Ipswich T	W 2-0	1-0	2	Hogan [24], O'Connell [71]	30,140
46	May 5	A	Stoke C	D 2-2	0-1	2	Dowell [48], Stevens [77]	26,665

Final League Position: 2

GOALSCORERS

League (78): Sharp 23 (1 pen), McGoldrick 15 (3 pens), Duffy 6, Basham 4, Stevens 4, Clarke 3, Madine 3, Norwood 3 (1 pen), O'Connell 3, Dowell 2, Fleck 2, Freeman 2, Hogan 2, Baldock 1, Egan 1, Stearman 1, own goals 3.
FA Cup (0).
Carabao Cup (1): Sharp 1.

Henderson D 46	Basham C 39 + 2	Egan J 44	O'Connell J 41	Baldock G 26 + 1	Lundstram J 5 + 5	Evans L 2	Fleck J 45	Stevens E 45	McGoldrick D 36 + 9	Clarke L 9 + 15	Woodburn B 1 + 6	Sharp B 34 + 6	Duffy M 32 + 4	Leonard R — + 3	Freeman K 20	Stearman R 3 + 13	Norwood O 43	Lafferty D — + 1	Washington C 3 + 12	Johnson M 3 + 8	Coutts P 1 + 12	Cranie M 9 + 6	Dowell K 8 + 8	Madine G 6 + 10	Hogan S 5 + 3	*Match No.*
1	2^{1}	3	4	5	6^{2}	7	8	9	10^{3}	11	12	13	14													1
1	3	4	5	2	7^{2}	8^{1}	9	6	11^{3}	10	12		13	14												2
1	8	3	5				9	6	12^{3}	10	13	11^{2}	7^{1}	14	2	4										3
1	2	3	4				7	8	13	11	9^{3}	10^{2}		12	5^{1}	14	6									4
1	2	3	4				7	8	12	11^{3}	14	10^{2}	9^{1}		5	13	6									5
1	2	3	4		12		7^{3}	8	10			11^{1}	9^{2}		5		6	13	14							6
1	2	3	4		7^{1}			8	10	14		11^{3}	9^{2}		5		6		12	13						7
1	2	3	4	5			7		12	10^{2}	14	13	9^{3}				6		11^{1}	8						8
1	2	3	4				7	8	10^{3}	13		11^{1}	9^{2}		5	14	6			12						9
1	2	3	4				7	8^{2}	11^{3}	13		10	9^{1}		5	14	6			12						10
1	2	3	4				7	8	10^{1}	13		11^{3}	9^{2}		5		6		14		12					11
1	2	3	4				7	8	11^{2}	13		10^{1}	9^{3}		5		6			14	12					12
1	2^{2}	3	4				7	8	11	12		10^{1}	9^{3}		5		6		14		13					13
1	2	3	4				7	8	11^{3}	10			9^{1}		5^{2}	13	6		12		14					14
1	2		4				7	8	11^{2}	10		9^{1}			5	3	6		13		12					15
1		3	4	14			8	9	12	10	13	11			5^{2}		7				6^{1}	2^{3}				16
1	2	3	4				7	8	10^{1}	12		11	9		5		6									17
1	2	3	4				8	9	10^{3}	12		11^{1}	6^{2}		5	13	7			14						18
1	2	3	4		6^{1}		8	9	10^{2}	12		14			5		7		11^{3}		13					19
1	2	3	4	5			7	8^{2}	10			11	9^{1}				6		12	13						20
1	2	3	4	5	6^{1}		8	9	11			13	12				7		10^{2}							21
1	2	3	4	5			7^{2}	8^{1}	10			11	9^{3}				6		13	14	12					22
1	2	3	4	5			7	8	11^{1}	12		10	9				6									23
1	2	3	4	5			8	9	11	12		10	7^{1}				6									24
1	$2^{\blacksquare}$	3	4	5			7	8	10^{2}	13		11^{1}	9^{3}				6		14		12					25
1		3	4	5			7	8	10^{1}	13		11	9^{2}			14	6				12	2^{3}				26
1	2	3	4	5			7	8	10^{1}	13		11^{3}	9^{2}			14	6						12			27
1	2	3	4	5			7^{1}	8	11^{3}	14		10	9^{2}				6						12	13		28
1	2	3	4	5			7	8	12			10^{2}	13				6		14				9^{3}	11^{1}		29
1	2	3	4	5			7	8	10^{1}			11^{3}	9^{2}			12	6						14	13		30
1	2	3	4	5			7	8	12			10^{1}					6		14			13	9^{3}	11^{2}		31
1		3		5^{1}			7	4	11			10^{3}	9^{2}			12	6				14	2	8	13		32
1		3					7	4					9		5^{1}	13	6^{2}			8	12	2	14	10^{3}	11	33
1	14	3^{1}					7	4	10^{2}			11			5	12	6			8		2^{3}	9	13		34
1	2	3	4				8	9	13			11			5		7					12	6^{2}	10^{1}		35
1	2^{1}	3	4	5			7	8	10^{2}				9				6					13		12	11	36
1	2	3	4	5^{1}			7	8	13			14					6					12	9^{2}	$11^{\blacksquare}$	10^{3}	37
1	6^{1}	3	4	5	13		8	9	11^{2}			10					7					2	12			38
1	2	3	4^{1}	5			8	9	10			11					7			13			6^{2}		12	39
1	3	2		5			7	4	11			10^{1}	9^{3}			13	6					12	8^{2}		14	40
1	2	3		5			7	8	11			10	9^{2}				6					4^{1}	13	12		41
1	2^{3}	$3^{\blacksquare}$	4				8	9	11			10^{1}	6^{2}		5		7				14	13		12		42
1			4	5	13		7	8	11				9^{1}			3	6					2^{2}	14	10^{3}	12	43
1	12	3	4	5			7	8	11^{2}				9^{1}				6		14			2		13	10^{3}	44
1	2	3	4	5	14		7	8	11^{2}			12	9^{3}				6							13	10^{1}	45
1	2^{3}	3	4	5	12		7	8	11			10	9^{1}				6^{2}						13	14		46

FA Cup
Third Round Barnet (h) 0-1

Carabao Cup
First Round Hull C (h) 1-1
(Hull C won 5-4 on penalties)

SHEFFIELD WEDNESDAY

FOUNDATION

Sheffield being one of the principal centres of early Association Football, this club was formed as long ago as 1867 by the Sheffield Wednesday Cricket Club (formed 1825) and their colours from the start were blue and white. The inaugural meeting was held at the Adelphi Hotel and the original committee included Charles Stokes who was subsequently a founder member of Sheffield United.

Hillsborough Stadium, Hillsborough, Sheffield, South Yorkshire S6 1SW.

Telephone: (0370) 020 1867.

Fax: (0114) 221 2122.

Ticket Office: (0370) 020 1867 (option 1).

Website: www.swfc.co.uk

Email: footballenquiries@swfc.co.uk

Ground Capacity: 39,732.

Record Attendance: 72,841 v Manchester C, FA Cup 5th rd, 17 February 1934.

Pitch Measurements: 105m × 68m (115yd × 74.5yd).

Chairman: Dejphon Chansiri.

Manager: TBC.

Assistant Manager: TBC.

Colours: Blue and white striped shirts with black trim, black shorts, blue socks with black trim.

Year Formed: 1867 (fifth oldest League club).

Turned Professional: 1887.

Previous Name: The Wednesday until 1929.

Club Nickname: 'The Owls'.

Grounds: 1867, Highfield; 1869, Myrtle Road; 1877, Sheaf House; 1887, Olive Grove; 1899, Owlerton (since 1912 known as Hillsborough). Some games were played at Endcliffe in the 1880s. Until 1895 Bramall Lane was used for some games.

First Football League Game: 3 September 1892, Division 1, v Notts Co (a) W 1–0 – Allan; Tom Brandon (1), Mumford; Hall, Betts, Harry Brandon; Spiksley, Brady, Davis, Bob Brown, Dunlop.

Record League Victory: 9–1 v Birmingham, Division 1, 13 December 1930 – Brown; Walker, Blenkinsop; Strange, Leach, Wilson; Hooper (3), Seed (2), Ball (2), Burgess (1), Rimmer (1).

Record Cup Victory: 12–0 v Halliwell, FA Cup 1st rd, 17 January 1891 – Smith; Thompson, Brayshaw; Harry Brandon (1), Betts, Cawley (2); Winterbottom, Mumford (2), Bob Brandon (1), Woolhouse (5), Ingram (1).

Record Defeat: 0–10 v Aston Villa, Division 1, 5 October 1912.

Most League Points (2 for a win): 62, Division 2, 1958–59.

HONOURS

League Champions: Division 1 – 1902–03, 1903–04, 1928–29, 1929–30; Division 2 – 1899–1900, 1925–26, 1951–52, 1955–56, 1958–59.
Runners-up: Division 1 – 1960–61; Division 2 – 1949–50, 1983–84; FL 1 – 2011–12.

FA Cup Winners: 1896, 1907, 1935.
Runners-up: 1890, 1966, 1993.

League Cup Winners: 1991.
Runners-up: 1993.

European Competitions
Fairs Cup: 1961–62 *(qf)*, 1963–64.
UEFA Cup: 1992–93.
Intertoto Cup: 1995.

THE Sun FACT FILE

Clothing shortages towards the end of the Second World War meant that Sheffield Wednesday were unable to obtain material for their traditional blue and white striped shirts. As a result the Owls turned out in blue and white hoops from December 1945 until the end of the season.

Most League Points (3 for a win): 93, FL 1, 2011–12.

Most League Goals: 106, Division 2, 1958–59.

Highest League Scorer in Season: Derek Dooley, 46, Division 2, 1951–52.

Most League Goals in Total Aggregate: Andrew Wilson, 199, 1900–20.

Most League Goals in One Match: 6, Doug Hunt v Norwich C, Division 2, 19 November 1938.

Most Capped Player: Nigel Worthington, 50 (66), Northern Ireland.

Most League Appearances: Andrew Wilson, 501, 1900–20.

Youngest League Player: Peter Fox, 15 years 269 days v Orient, 31 March 1973.

Record Transfer Fee Received: £3,000,000 from WBA for Chris Brunt, August 2007.

Record Transfer Fee Paid: £10,000,000 to Middlesbrough for Jordan Rhodes, July 2017.

Football League Record: 1892 Elected to Division 1; 1899–1900 Division 2; 1900–20 Division 1; 1920–26 Division 2; 1926–37 Division 1; 1937–50 Division 2; 1950–51 Division 1; 1951–52 Division 2; 1952–55 Division 1; 1955–56 Division 2; 1956–58 Division 1; 1958–59 Division 2; 1959–70 Division 1; 1970–75 Division 2; 1975–80 Division 3; 1980–84 Division 2; 1984–90 Division 1; 1990–91 Division 2; 1991–92 Division 1; 1992–2000 Premier League; 2000–03 Division 1; 2003–04 Division 2; 2004–05 FL 1; 2005–10 FL C; 2010–12 FL 1; 2012– FL C.

MANAGERS

Arthur Dickinson 1891–1920
(Secretary-Manager)
Robert Brown 1920–33
Billy Walker 1933–37
Jimmy McMullan 1937–42
Eric Taylor 1942–58
(continued as General Manager to 1974)
Harry Catterick 1958–61
Vic Buckingham 1961–64
Alan Brown 1964–68
Jack Marshall 1968–69
Danny Williams 1969–71
Derek Dooley 1971–73
Steve Burtenshaw 1974–75
Len Ashurst 1975–77
Jackie Charlton 1977–83
Howard Wilkinson 1983–88
Peter Eustace 1988–89
Ron Atkinson 1989–91
Trevor Francis 1991–95
David Pleat 1995–97
Ron Atkinson 1997–98
Danny Wilson 1998–2000
Peter Shreeves *(Acting)* 2000
Paul Jewell 2000–01
Peter Shreeves 2001
Terry Yorath 2001–02
Chris Turner 2002–04
Paul Sturrock 2004–06
Brian Laws 2006–09
Alan Irvine 2010–11
Gary Megson 2011–12
Dave Jones 2012–13
Stuart Gray 2013–15
Carlos Carvalhal 2015–18
Jos Luhukay 2018
Steve Bruce 2019

LATEST SEQUENCES

Longest Sequence of League Wins: 9, 23.4.1904 – 15.10.1904.

Longest Sequence of League Defeats: 8, 9.9.2000 – 17.10.2000.

Longest Sequence of League Draws: 7, 15.3.2008 – 14.4.2008.

Longest Sequence of Unbeaten League Matches: 19, 10.12.1960 – 8.4.1961.

Longest Sequence Without a League Win: 20, 11.1.1975 – 30.8.1975.

Successive Scoring Runs: 40 from 14.11.1959.

Successive Non-scoring Runs: 8 from 8.3.1975.

TEN YEAR LEAGUE RECORD

		P	*W*	*D*	*L*	*F*	*A*	*Pts*	*Pos*
2009-10	FL C	46	11	14	21	49	69	47	22
2010-11	FL 1	46	16	10	20	67	67	58	15
2011-12	FL 1	46	28	9	9	81	48	93	2
2012-13	FL C	46	16	10	20	53	61	58	18
2013-14	FL C	46	13	14	19	63	65	53	16
2014-15	FL C	46	14	18	14	43	49	60	13
2015-16	FL C	46	19	17	10	66	45	74	6
2016-17	FL C	46	24	9	13	60	45	81	4
2017-18	FL C	46	14	15	17	59	60	57	15
2018-19	FL C	46	16	16	14	60	62	64	12

DID YOU KNOW ?

Sheffield Wednesday officials missed the 1 September deadline for submitting their entry for the FA Cup for the 1886–87 season. As a result the club did not take part and many of the team's star players defected to local rivals Lockwood Brothers.

SHEFFIELD WEDNESDAY – SKY BET CHAMPIONSHIP 2018–19 LEAGUE RECORD

Match No.	*Date*		*Venue*	*Opponents*	*Result*		*H/T Score*	*Lg Pos.*	*Goalscorers*	*Attendance*
1	Aug	4	A	Wigan Ath	L	2-3	1-2	19	Nuhiu [20], Forestieri [67]	14,207
2		11	H	Hull C	D	1-1	0-1	18	Forestieri (pen) [51]	23,416
3		19	A	Brentford	L	0-2	0-1	21		10,134
4		22	H	Millwall	W	2-1	1-0	17	Bannan [16], Lees [46]	21,349
5		25	H	Ipswich T	W	2-1	1-1	14	Lucas Joao 2 [16, 77]	22,499
6	Sept	1	A	Reading	W	2-1	1-0	10	Reach [12], Lucas Joao [46]	14,352
7		15	H	Stoke C	D	2-2	1-2	9	Marco Matias [24], Bannan [82]	24,905
8		19	A	Nottingham F	L	1-2	0-1	12	Fletcher [88]	26,252
9		22	A	Aston Villa	W	2-1	0-0	10	Marco Matias [49], Fletcher [67]	35,572
10		28	H	Leeds U	D	1-1	1-0	9	Reach [45]	26,717
11	Oct	3	H	WBA	D	2-2	2-0	12	Reach [24], Forestieri [41]	22,150
12		7	A	Bristol C	W	2-1	0-0	6	Lucas Joao 2 [64, 66]	20,102
13		19	H	Middlesbrough	L	1-2	0-0	6	Reach [82]	23,284
14		23	A	QPR	L	0-3	0-1	14		12,534
15		27	A	Birmingham C	L	1-3	1-1	15	Fletcher [19]	23,659
16	Nov	3	H	Norwich C	L	0-4	0-0	17		23,425
17		9	A	Sheffield U	D	0-0	0-0	17		30,261
18		24	H	Derby Co	L	1-2	1-2	18	Reach [12]	25,204
19		27	H	Bolton W	W	1-0	0-0	14	Lees [57]	20,861
20	Dec	1	A	Blackburn R	L	2-4	0-1	16	Lucas Joao [62], Bannan [85]	15,154
21		8	H	Rotherham U	D	2-2	1-0	17	Lucas Joao 2 [45, 64]	24,725
22		15	A	Swansea C	L	1-2	0-0	18	Marco Matias [63]	18,692
23		22	H	Preston NE	W	1-0	0-0	17	Hector [62]	22,366
24		26	A	Middlesbrough	W	1-0	1-0	16	Reach [20]	30,341
25		29	A	WBA	D	1-1	1-0	16	Nuhiu [5]	26,548
26	Jan	1	H	Birmingham C	D	1-1	1-0	16	Fletcher [18]	29,462
27		12	A	Hull C	L	0-3	0-1	16		14,102
28		19	H	Wigan Ath	W	1-0	0-0	16	Fletcher [62]	22,323
29	Feb	2	A	Ipswich T	W	1-0	0-0	16	Lucas Joao [90]	16,888
30		9	H	Reading	D	0-0	0-0	16		23,412
31		12	A	Millwall	D	0-0	0-0	15		11,828
32		16	A	Rotherham U	D	2-2	1-1	15	Forestieri [35], Iorfa [90]	11,736
33		23	H	Swansea C	W	3-1	3-0	15	Reach 2 [11, 32], Fletcher [42]	22,935
34		26	H	Brentford	W	2-0	1-0	12	Fletcher 2 [41, 48]	23,094
35	Mar	4	H	Sheffield U	D	0-0	0-0	13		31,630
36		9	A	Derby Co	D	1-1	0-1	13	Iorfa [57]	28,574
37		12	A	Bolton W	W	2-0	1-0	9	Fletcher [44], Aarons [59]	13,624
38		16	H	Blackburn R	W	4-2	1-0	10	Fletcher [10], Nuhiu [60], Iorfa [79], Marco Matias [86]	24,608
39		30	A	Stoke C	D	0-0	0-0	11		26,398
40	Apr	6	H	Aston Villa	L	1-3	1-1	12	Hooper [7]	29,458
41		9	H	Nottingham F	W	3-0	0-0	9	Marco Matias 2 [47, 67], Boyd [58]	23,931
42		13	A	Leeds U	L	0-1	0-0	10		36,461
43		19	A	Norwich C	D	2-2	1-1	11	Forestieri [33], Fletcher [53]	26,744
44		22	H	Bristol C	W	2-0	2-0	9	Bannan [17], Lucas Joao [39]	23,998
45		27	A	Preston NE	D	3-3	0-2	9	Bannan [49], Forestieri [76], Nuhiu [78]	15,873
46	May	5	H	QPR	L	1-2	0-1	12	Hector (pen) [84]	26,111

Final League Position: 12

GOALSCORERS

League (60): Fletcher 11, Lucas Joao 10, Reach 8, Forestieri 6 (1 pen), Marco Matias 6, Bannan 5, Nuhiu 4, Iorfa 3, Hector 2 (1 pen), Lees 2, Aarons 1, Boyd 1, Hooper 1.
FA Cup (1): Nuhiu 1.
Carabao Cup (2): Marco Matias 1, Reach 1.

Dawson C 26	Lees T 42	van Aken J 1	Pudil D 9 + 2	Palmer L 34 + 1	Hutchinson S 22 + 2	Pelupessy J 26 + 7	Bannan B 40 + 1	Reach A 42	Nuhiu A 13 + 21	Forestieri F 15 + 10	Lucas Joao E 18 + 13	Fletcher S 32 + 8	Baker A 11	Fox M 21 + 4	Thorniley J 17 + 3	Marco Matias A 20 + 11	Preston F 1 + 2	Penney M 12 + 4	Boyd G 14 + 6	Onomah J 10 + 5	Hector M 36 + 1	Kirby C — + 1	Westwood K 20	Jones D — + 1	Winnall S 1 + 6	Aarons R 6 + 3	Iorfa D 9 + 3	Lazaar A 3 + 1	Hooper G 4 + 2	Lee K 1 + 1	*Match No.*
1	2	3^{2}	4	5	6	7^{1}	8	9	10■	11	12	13																			1
1	2		4		3	7	8	6		11		10^{1}	5	9^{2}	12	13															2
1	3		4^{3}		6^{1}	8	7		10	11		13	2		5	9^{2}	12	14													3
1	3			2		6	7	9	13	12		11^{1}			4	10^{2}	8^{3}	5	14												4
1	3			2		6	7	9	11	12	10^{1}	13			4	8^{2}		5													5
1	3			2		6	7	9	11	12	10^{1}	13			4	8^{2}		5													6
1	3			2		6^{2}	7	9^{1}	12		10	11			4	8^{3}		5		13	14										7
1	3		13				7	9	11		10^{1}	12	2	5	4^{2}	8				6											8
1	2		4			6	7	9	12		13	10^{2}	5			11^{1}		8			3										9
1	2			12		6	7	9	13	11^{1}	14	10^{2}	5^{3}		4			8			3										10
1	2		4	5		7		9	10^{2}	11	12							8		6^{1}	3	13									11
1	2		4	5		14	7^{3}	9		13	12	10^{1}			8^{2}			11		6	3										12
1	3			2		7	8	9	12		10^{1}	11			4			5			6										13
1			4^{3}			6^{2}	7	8	11		10^{1}	13	2	5	12			14		9	3										14
1	3			2		7	6	8	10		13	11^{2}		5				12		9^{1}	4										15
1	3		4^{2}	2		7	8	9	11^{3}		12	10^{1}			13		14	5		6											16
1	2					5	7	10				11	6	9	4	12		8^{1}			3										17
1	3					7	8	6	12	10	11		2	5^{2}		9^{1}		13			4										18
1	2					6	7	11	12	13	14	10^{2}	5		4	9^{3}		8^{1}			3										19
1	3			2		7	8	9	13	12^{3}	11	10^{1}			5	6^{2}				14	4										20
1	2		12			6^{1}	7	9	11		10		5	8	4^{2}	13					3										21
1	2		3			6		9	11		10	13	5	8^{2}	4	12				7^{1}											22
	3			2	13	7		8	12		11	10^{2}		5		9^{1}			14	6^{3}	4		1								23
	3			2	6^{2}	14	9	8			10^{1}	11		5		7			13	12^{3}	4		1								24
1	3			2	6^{2}	12	8	10^{3}	11^{1}					5		7			9		4			13	14						25
	3			2	6		8	9	12			11^{1}		5		10			7^{2}		4		1		13						26
	3			2	6		8	9	12			11^{2}		5		7^{1}			10		4		1		13						27
	3			2	6		9	8	13		12	11^{2}		5		7^{1}			10		4		1								28
	3			2	7		6	8		9^{3}	13	11^{1}		5					10^{2}	12	4		1			14					29
				2	7		8	6	14	11^{1}	13	10^{3}		5	4				9^{2}		3		1			12					30
				2	7	8^{2}	9	6		13	10^{1}	11		5	4				12		3		1								31
				2	6		7	8		9■	11^{1}	12		5	4^{3}				10^{2}		3		1			13	14				32
	3			2	7	14	8	6			10^{3}	11^{2}				13					4		1			9^{1}	12	5			33
	3			2	7^{3}	13	8	6		10^{1}		11							14		4		1			9	12	5^{2}			34
	3			5	7		8	6	14	10^{2}		11^{1}		13					12		4		1			9	2^{3}				35
	3			5	7		6	8	12			11^{3}		14					9^{2}		4		1		13	10^{1}	2				36
	3			5	7		8	6	10^{2}			11^{1}		14		13					4		1		12	9^{3}	2				37
	3			5	7^{1}	12	8	6	14			11^{3}				13					4		1		10^{2}	9	2				38
	3			5	7		6	8^{1}	13	11^{2}						14			9		4		1		12		2		10^{3}		39
	3			5	7		8^{2}	6		14		10		12		13			9		4		1				2^{1}		11^{3}		40
	3			2		7		8	13		11^{1}	10^{3}		5		6^{2}			9		4		1					14	12		41
	3			2	7		8	6^{2}	14	13		10^{3}		5		12			9		4		1						11^{1}		42
1	3			5	7^{3}	12	13			10^{2}	14	11				6			9	8^{1}	4						2				43
1	3					7	8	6		13	11^{2}					14			9^{3}	12	4						2	5	10^{1}		44
1	3			5		7	8		12	10^{3}	13	11^{1}				6				9^{2}	4						2■			14	45
	3			2	13	7			12	9	10^{2}	11^{3}		5		6					4		1						14	8^{1}	46

FA Cup

Third Round	Luton T	(h)	0-0
Replay	Luton T	(a)	1-0
Fourth Round	Chelsea	(a)	0-3

Carabao Cup

First Round	Sunderland	(a)	2-0
Second Round	Wolverhampton W	(h)	0-2

SHREWSBURY TOWN

FOUNDATION

Shrewsbury School having provided a number of the early England and Wales international players it is not surprising that there was a Town club as early as 1876 which won the Birmingham Senior Cup in 1879. However, the present Shrewsbury Town club was formed in 1886 and won the Welsh FA Cup as early as 1891.

Montgomery Waters Meadow, Oteley Road, Shrewsbury, Shropshire SY2 6ST.

Telephone: (01743) 289 177.

Fax: (01743) 246 942.

Ticket Office: (01743) 273 943.

Website: www.shrewsburytown.com

Email: info@shrewsburytown.co.uk

Ground Capacity: 9,875.

Record Attendance: 18,917 v Walsall, Division 3, 26 April 1961 (at Gay Meadow); 10,210 v Chelsea, League Cup 4th rd, 28 October 2014 (at New Meadow).

Pitch Measurements: 105m × 68.5m (115yd × 75yd).

Chairman: Roland Wycherley.

Chief Executive: Brian Caldwell.

Manager: Sam Ricketts.

Assistant Manager: Graham Barrow.

Colours: Blue and yellow striped shirts, blue shorts with yellow trim, blue socks with yellow and white trim.

Year Formed: 1886.

Turned Professional: 1896.

Club Nicknames: 'Town', 'Blues', 'Salop'. The name 'Salop' is a colloquialism for the county of Shropshire. Since Shrewsbury is the only club in Shropshire, cries of 'Come on Salop' are frequently used!

Grounds: 1886, Old Racecourse Ground; 1889, Ambler's Field; 1893, Sutton Lane; 1895, Barracks Ground; 1910, Gay Meadow; 2007, New Meadow (renamed ProStar Stadium 2008; Greenhous Meadow 2010; Montgomery Waters Meadow 2017).

First Football League Game: 19 August 1950, Division 3 (N), v Scunthorpe U (a) D 0–0 – Egglestone; Fisher, Lewis; Wheatley, Depear, Robinson; Griffin, Hope, Jackson, Brown, Barker.

Record League Victory: 7–0 v Swindon T, Division 3 (S), 6 May 1955 – McBride; Bannister, Skeech; Wallace, Maloney, Candlin; Price, O'Donnell (1), Weigh (4), Russell, McCue (2); 7-0 v Gillingham, FL 2, 13 September 2008 – Daniels; Herd, Tierney, Davies (2), Jackson (1) (Langmead), Coughlan (1), Cansdell-Sherriff (1), Thornton, Hibbert (1) (Hindmarch), Holt (pen), McIntyre (Ashton).

Record Cup Victory: 11–2 v Marine, FA Cup 1st rd, 11 November 1995 – Edwards; Seabury (Dempsey (1)), Withe (1), Evans (1), Whiston (2), Scott (1), Woods, Stevens (1), Spink (3) (Anthrobus), Walton, Berkley, (1 og).

HONOURS

League Champions: Division 3 – 1978–79; Third Division – 1993–94.
Runners-up: FL 2 – 2011–12, 2014–15; Division 4 – 1974–75; Conference – (3rd) 2003–04 *(promoted via play-offs)*.

FA Cup: 6th rd – 1979, 1982.

League Cup: semi-final – 1961.

League Trophy: *Runners-up:* 1996, 2018.

Welsh Cup Winners: 1891, 1938, 1977, 1979, 1984, 1985.
Runners-up: 1931, 1948, 1980.

THE SUN FACT FILE

Shrewsbury Town were the first EFL club to introduce a 'safe standing' or rail seating area at the start of the 2018–19 season. A total of 550 seats were installed at the rear of the South Stand at the Montgomery Waters Meadow Stadium, allowing fans to stand to watch yet ensuring the stadium met all safety regulations.

Record Defeat: 1–8 v Norwich C, Division 3 (S), 13 September 1952; 1–8 v Coventry C, Division 3, 22 October 1963.

Most League Points (2 for a win): 62, Division 4, 1974–75.

Most League Points (3 for a win): 89, FL 2, 2014–15.

Most League Goals: 101, Division 4, 1958–59.

Highest League Scorer in Season: Arthur Rowley, 38, Division 4, 1958–59.

Most League Goals in Total Aggregate: Arthur Rowley, 152, 1958–65 (thus completing his League record of 434 goals).

Most League Goals in One Match: 5, Alf Wood v Blackburn R, Division 3, 2 October 1971.

Most Capped Player: Jimmy McLaughlin, 5 (12), Northern Ireland; Bernard McNally, 5, Northern Ireland.

Most League Appearances: Mickey Brown, 418, 1986–91; 1992–94; 1996–2001.

Youngest League Player: Graham French, 16 years 177 days v Reading, 30 September 1961.

Record Transfer Fee Received: £600,000 (rising to £1,500,000) from Manchester C for Joe Hart, May 2006.

Record Transfer Fee Paid: £200,000 to Tranmere R for Oliver Norburn, August 2018.

Football League Record: 1950 Elected to Division 3 (N); 1951–58 Division 3 (S); 1958–59 Division 4; 1959–74 Division 3; 1974–75 Division 4; 1975–79 Division 3; 1979–89 Division 2; 1989–94 Division 3; 1994–97 Division 2; 1997–2003 Division 3; 2003–04 Conference; 2004–12 FL 2; 2012–14 FL 1; 2014–15 FL 2; 2015– FL 1.

MANAGERS

W. Adams 1905–12
(Secretary-Manager)
A. Weston 1912–34
(Secretary-Manager)
Jack Roscamp 1934–35
Sam Ramsey 1935–36
Ted Bousted 1936–40
Leslie Knighton 1945–49
Harry Chapman 1949–50
Sammy Crooks 1950–54
Walter Rowley 1955–57
Harry Potts 1957–58
Johnny Spuhler 1958
Arthur Rowley 1958–68
Harry Gregg 1968–72
Maurice Evans 1972–73
Alan Durban 1974–78
Richie Barker 1978
Graham Turner 1978–84
Chic Bates 1984–87
Ian McNeill 1987–90
Asa Hartford 1990–91
John Bond 1991–93
Fred Davies 1994–97
(previously Caretaker-Manager 1993–94)
Jake King 1997–99
Kevin Ratcliffe 1999–2003
Jimmy Quinn 2003–04
Gary Peters 2004–08
Paul Simpson 2008–10
Graham Turner 2010–14
Mike Jackson 2014
Micky Mellon 2014–16
Paul Hurst 2016–18
John Askey 2018
Sam Ricketts December 2018–

LATEST SEQUENCES

Longest Sequence of League Wins: 7, 28.10.1995 – 16.12.1995.

Longest Sequence of League Defeats: 11, 9.4.2003 – 14.8.2004. (Spread over 2 periods in Football League. 2003–04 season in Conference.)

Longest Sequence of League Draws: 6, 30.10.1963 – 14.12.1963.

Longest Sequence of Unbeaten League Matches: 16, 30.10.1993 – 26.2.1994.

Longest Sequence Without a League Win: 18, 8.3.2003 – 14.8.2004.

Successive Scoring Runs: 28 from 7.9.1960.

Successive Non-scoring Runs: 6 from 1.1.1991.

TEN YEAR LEAGUE RECORD

		P	*W*	*D*	*L*	*F*	*A*	*Pts*	*Pos*
2009-10	FL 2	46	17	12	17	55	54	63	12
2010-11	FL 2	46	22	13	11	72	49	79	4
2011-12	FL 2	46	26	10	10	66	41	88	2
2012-13	FL 1	46	13	16	17	54	60	55	16
2013-14	FL 1	46	9	15	22	44	65	42	23
2014-15	FL 2	46	27	8	11	67	31	89	2
2015-16	FL 1	46	13	11	22	58	79	50	20
2016-17	FL 1	46	13	12	21	46	63	51	18
2017-18	FL 1	46	25	12	9	60	39	87	3
2018-19	FL 1	46	12	16	18	51	59	52	18

DID YOU KNOW ?

Shrewsbury Town enjoyed their best ever start to a season in 1945–46 when the club resumed activities after a five-year break. Playing in the Midland League, the Shrews went undefeated in their first 19 games and it was not until a 4-3 loss at Boston United on 16 February that they were defeated in a league match.

SHREWSBURY TOWN – SKY BET LEAGUE ONE 2018–19 LEAGUE RECORD

Match No.	*Date*	*Venue*	*Opponents*	*Result*	*H/T Score*	*Lg Pos.*	*Goalscorers*	*Attendance*
1	Aug 4	H	Bradford C	L 0-1	0-1	20		7625
2	11	A	Charlton Ath	L 1-2	0-0	22	John-Lewis [83]	9429
3	18	H	Blackpool	D 0-0	0-0	21		5216
4	21	A	Doncaster R	D 0-0	0-0	22		6943
5	25	A	Luton T	L 2-3	1-0	23	Whalley (pen) [23], Angol [66]	8518
6	Sept 1	H	Bristol R	D 1-1	0-0	23	Leadbitter (og) [73]	5759
7	8	A	Portsmouth	D 1-1	0-0	22	Docherty [74]	17,634
8	15	H	Southend U	W 2-0	2-0	17	Docherty [5], Angol [45]	5651
9	22	A	Scunthorpe U	L 0-1	0-0	20		3784
10	29	H	Gillingham	D 2-2	0-1	19	Angol [59], Norburn [88]	5695
11	Oct 2	A	Walsall	D 0-0	0-0	20		4555
12	6	H	Accrington S	W 1-0	0-0	16	Gilliead [62]	4353
13	13	A	Fleetwood T	L 1-2	0-2	17	Laurent [57]	2983
14	20	H	Sunderland	L 0-2	0-0	18		9007
15	23	H	Barnsley	W 3-1	2-0	18	Docherty [2], Norburn [23], Waterfall [68]	5587
16	27	A	Oxford U	L 0-3	0-2	19		8697
17	Nov 3	A	AFC Wimbledon	W 2-1	0-1	18	Waterfall 2 [57, 89]	4066
18	17	H	Rochdale	W 3-2	1-1	16	Norburn 2 (1 pen) [32 (p), 72], Okenabirhie [65]	5861
19	24	A	Wycombe W	L 2-3	1-2	17	Amadi-Holloway [4], Okenabirhie [73]	4598
20	27	H	Plymouth Arg	W 2-0	1-0	15	Docherty [35], Okenabirhie [68]	5279
21	Dec 8	A	Burton Alb	L 1-2	0-1	17	Okenabirhie [90]	3062
22	15	H	Peterborough U	D 2-2	1-1	17	Docherty [2], Okenabirhie [59]	5393
23	22	H	Coventry C	W 1-0	0-0	15	Amadi-Holloway [49]	8083
24	26	A	Accrington S	L 1-2	0-2	18	Norburn (pen) [52]	3061
25	29	A	Sunderland	D 1-1	1-1	17	Waterfall [30]	33,288
26	Jan 1	H	Fleetwood T	D 0-0	0-0	16		5919
27	12	H	Charlton Ath	L 0-3	0-1	18		5995
28	19	A	Blackpool	D 0-0	0-0	17		3186
29	29	A	Bradford C	L 3-4	1-2	19	Okenabirhie 3 (1 pen) [27, 76, 90 (p)]	14,906
30	Feb 2	H	Luton T	L 0-3	0-1	23		6859
31	9	A	Bristol R	D 1-1	1-0	22	Whalley [36]	8322
32	16	H	Burton Alb	D 1-1	1-1	22	Campbell [8]	6254
33	23	A	Peterborough U	W 2-1	2-1	19	Norburn (pen) [28], Campbell [36]	6262
34	26	H	Doncaster R	W 2-0	2-0	17	Laurent [18], Campbell [35]	5394
35	Mar 2	H	AFC Wimbledon	D 0-0	0-0	17		6166
36	9	A	Rochdale	L 1-2	0-1	20	Docherty [90]	3217
37	12	A	Plymouth Arg	L 1-2	0-1	20	Norburn [60]	8572
38	16	H	Wycombe W	W 2-1	0-0	18	Beckles [87], Norburn (pen) [90]	6001
39	23	H	Portsmouth	L 0-2	0-1	19		8028
40	30	A	Southend U	W 2-0	0-0	15	Okenabirhie [50], Waterfall [69]	6818
41	Apr 6	H	Scunthorpe U	D 1-1	0-1	14	Hammill (og) [84]	6419
42	13	A	Gillingham	W 2-0	0-0	13	Bolton [50], Campbell [61]	4109
43	19	A	Barnsley	L 1-2	1-1	15	Campbell [38]	13,426
44	22	H	Oxford U	L 2-3	2-1	16	Norburn (pen) [17], Docherty [40]	7189
45	28	A	Coventry C	D 1-1	0-1	17	Okenabirhie [78]	13,549
46	May 4	H	Walsall	D 0-0	0-0	18		9635

Final League Position: 18

GOALSCORERS

League (51): Okenabirhie 10 (1 pen), Norburn 9 (5 pens), Docherty 7, Campbell 5, Waterfall 5, Angol 3, Amadi-Holloway 2, Laurent 2, Whalley 2 (1 pen), Beckles 1, Bolton 1, Gilliead 1, John-Lewis 1, own goals 2.
FA Cup (13): Okenabirhie 3 (1 pen), Bolton 2, Docherty 2, Laurent 2, Norburn 2 (1 pen), Holloway 1, Waterfall 1.
Carabao Cup (1): Whalley 1.
Checkatrade Trophy (12): Okenabirhie 3, Gilliead 2, Angol 1, Beckles 1, Docherty 1, Eisa 1, John-Lewis 1, Loft 1, Sears 1.

Coleman J 16	Bolton J 30 + 1	Kennedy K 1	Sadler M 28 + 1	Beckles O 34 + 2	Loft D 1	Colkett C 1	Laurent J 29 + 13	Whalley S 28 + 4	Amadi-Holloway A 17 + 13	Payne S 2 + 4	Grant A 40 + 2	Gilliead A 16 + 11	Okenabirhie F 23 + 15	Haynes R 15 + 1	Waterfall L 44	Docherty G 34 + 7	Norburn O 39 + 2	John-Lewis L 5 + 12	Angol L 10 + 7	Sears R 2 + 3	Emmanuel J 13 + 1	Gnahoua A — + 1	Barnett R — + 1	Eisa A — + 4	Arnold S 23	Edwards D 3 + 3	Smith S — + 3	Vincelot R 1 + 2	Golbourne S 15	Campbell T 13 + 2	Williams R 16	Mitchell J 7 + 2	Match No.
1	2	3	4	5	6^{2}	7^{1}	8	9	10	11^{3}	12	13	14																				1
1	5			4			7^{2}	9	10^{3}		13	11	14	2	3	6	8^{1}	12															2
1	2		3				7	6^{2}	13		9	10	12	5	4	8		11^{1}															3
1	2		3				6	9			8	11		5	4	7		10^{1}	12														4
1	2		3				7	6			9^{2}	10^{1}	12	5	4	8	13		11														5
1			4	5			7	9	12		6^{1}	11			3		8	13	10^{2}	2													6
1			3	5			7^{1}	9	12		6	11			4	13	8	10^{2}			2												7
1			3	5			13	9			6	11			4	7^{1}	8	12	10^{2}		2												8
1			3	5				10	12		8^{2}	6^{1}			4	7	9		11		2	13											9
1			3	5				6	10^{1}		7^{2}	13			4	9	8	12	11		2												10
1			3	5			12	6	11^{1}		8	9^{2}			4		7	13	10		2												11
1			4	5			8	9			6^{1}	11	12		3		7		10		2												12
1			4	5			8^{2}	9	12			11	6^{3}		3	13	7	10^{1}	14		2												13
1			3	5			8^{2}	9^{1}	13		7	11^{3}		12	4	6	14		10		2												14
1	2			4			12				7		11	9^{1}	3	6^{2}	8		10		5		13										15
1	2			4			13		12		7		11	9^{3}	3	8^{2}	6		10^{1}		5			14									16
			4	5			12		10		6	11^{1}	9		3	7	8				2				1								17
			4	5			7		10^{1}		6		11^{2}		3	9	8	12			2			13	1								18
			3	5			8^{2}		10^{1}		6	13	11		4	7^{3}	9	14			2			12	1								19
	2		4	5			8		11^{1}		6	12	10^{3}		3	9	7^{2}	13						14	1								20
	2		4	5			9^{1}	12	10^{3}		6	13	11		3	8^{2}	7	14							1								21
	2		3	5			9^{1}	12^{3}	10^{2}		6		11		4	7	8	13	14						1								22
	2		3				9		11^{2}		6		10^{3}	5^{1}	4	8	7	13		14	12				1								23
	2		3				9^{1}		11^{3}		7^{2}	13	10	5	4	8	6	12	14						1								24
	2		3	14			9^{3}				6	10^{1}	12	5^{2}	4	8	7	11	13						1								25
	2		3				4		10^{2}		7^{1}	12	11	5	9	6	8		13						1								26
	2		3				4		11^{3}		7	12	10	5	9	6^{1}	8^{2}		14						1	13							27
	5		2	4			10^{2}				7	13	11^{1}	9	3	6	8								1		12						28
	5		2^{2}	4			10^{1}	14	12		7		11	9^{3}	3	6	8								1		13						29
	5		4				14	12		13	7		11		3	6	8^{1}								1			2^{2}	9	10^{3}			30
	5		4	3			11	9	13		7		10^{2}			12^{3}	6^{1}								1	14■			8		2		31
	5			4				9		12	7	10^{2}	13		3		6								1				8	11^{1}	2		32
	13			4			11	9^{2}	5^{3}		7		14		3	12	6■								1				8	10^{1}	2		33
	2						6	5^{1}		12	7	14	11^{2}	8	3	9				13					1					10^{3}	4		34
	3						7	2	10				12		5	13	8								1^{1}	9^{2}			6	11^{3}	4	14	35
				4			13	5	12	14			10^{1}	8	3	9	6								1	7^{3}				11^{2}	2		36
				4			6	5^{2}	12	10^{3}	8		13		3	14	7								1				9	11^{1}	2		37
	4			12			9	5	10				13		3^{1}	14	6								1	7^{3}			8	11^{2}	2		38
	4^{1}			5			13	10			7^{3}		11		2	6	8								1^{2}				9	12	3	14	39
	6			3			12	10^{3}	13		5		11^{2}		4	8	7^{1}									14			9		2	1	40
	5^{2}			4				10	12		6^{1}		11		3	9	7												8	13	2	1	41
	5^{2}			4			12	10^{1}			8		14		3	6	7			13									9	11^{3}	2	1	42
				4			13	9			7^{3}		12		3	10^{2}	6			5							14		8	11^{1}	2	1	43
	5			4			12	10			7	14	13		3	9	6^{2}												8^{3}	11^{1}	2	1	44
	5			4			7				6^{1}	11^{2}	13		3	9												12	8	10	2	1	45
	2		12	4			13				8^{1}		11^{2}		5^{3}	9	7											14	6	10	3	1	46

FA Cup

First Round	Salford C	(h)	1-1
Replay	Salford C	(a)	3-1
Second Round	Scunthorpe U	(h)	1-0
Third Round	Stoke C	(h)	1-1
Replay	Stoke C	(a)	3-2
Fourth Round	Wolverhampton W	(h)	2-2
Replay	Wolverhampton W	(a)	2-3

Carabao Cup

First Round	Burton Alb	(h)	1-2

Checkatrade Trophy

Group D (N)	Manchester C U21	(h)	1-1
(Shrewsbury T won 3-1 on penalties)			
Group D (N)	Tranmere R	(h)	6-0
Group D (N)	Crewe Alex	(a)	2-1
Second Round (N)	Walsall	(h)	2-1
Third Round	Port Vale	(a)	1-1
(Port Vale won 4-3 on penalties)			

SOUTHAMPTON

FOUNDATION

The club was formed by members of the St Mary's Church of England Young Men's Association at a meeting of the Y.M.A. in November 1885 and it was named as such. For the sake of brevity this was usually shortened to St Mary's Y.M.A. The rector Canon Albert Basil Orme Wilberforce was elected president. The name was changed to plain St Mary's during 1887–88 and did not become Southampton St Mary's until 1894, the inaugural season in the Southern League.

St Mary's Stadium, Britannia Road, Southampton, Hampshire SO14 5FP.

Telephone: (0845) 688 9448.

Fax: (02380) 727 727.

Ticket Office: (0845) 688 9288.

Website: www.saints.com

Email: sfc@saintsfc.com

Ground Capacity: 32,384.

Record Attendance: 31,044 v Manchester U, Division 1, 8 October 1969 (at The Dell); 32,363 v Coventry C, FL C, 28 April 2012 (at St Mary's).

Pitch Measurements: 105m × 68m (115yd × 74.5yd).

Chairman: Gao Jisheng.

Managing Director: Toby Steele.

Manager: Ralph Hasenhüttl.

Assistant Manager: Danny Röhl.

Colours: Red and white striped shirts with black trim, black shorts with red trim, black socks with red hoops.

Year Formed: 1885. ***Turned Professional:*** 1894.

Previous Names: 1885, St Mary's Young Men's Association; 1887–88, St Mary's; 1894–95 Southampton St Mary's; 1897, Southampton.

Club Nickname: 'Saints'.

Grounds: 1885, 'The Common' (from 1887 also used the County Cricket Ground and Antelope Cricket Ground); 1889, Antelope Cricket Ground; 1896, The County Cricket Ground; 1898, The Dell; 2001, St Mary's.

First Football League Game: 28 August 1920, Division 3, v Gillingham (a) D 1–1 – Allen; Parker, Titmuss; Shelley, Campbell, Turner; Barratt, Dominy (1), Rawlings, Moore, Foxall.

Record League Victory: 8–0 v Sunderland, Premier League, 18 October 2014 – Forster; Clyne, Fonte, Alderweireld, Bertrand; Davis S (Mané), Schneiderlin, Cork (1); Long (Wanyama (1)), Pelle (2) (Mayuka), Tadic (1) (plus 3 Sunderland own goals).

Record Cup Victory: 7–1 v Ipswich T, FA Cup 3rd rd, 7 January 1961 – Reynolds; Davies, Traynor, Conner, Page, Huxford, Paine (1), O'Brien (3 incl. 1p), Reeves, Mulgrew (2), Penk (1).

HONOURS

League Champions: Division 3 – 1959–60; Division 3S – 1921–22.
Runners-up: Division 1 – 1983–84; FL C – 2011–12; Division 2 – 1965–66, 1977–78; FL 1 – 2010–11; Division 3 – 1920–21.

FA Cup Winners: 1976.
Runners-up: 1900, 1902, 2003.

League Cup: *Runners-up:* 1979, 2017.

League Trophy Winners: 2010.

Full Members' Cup: *Runners-up:* 1992.

European Competitions
Fairs Cup: 1969–70.
UEFA Cup: 1971–72, 1981–82, 1982–83, 1984–85, 2003–04.
Europa League: 2015–16, 2016–17.
European Cup-Winners' Cup: 1976–77 *(qf)*.

THE SUN FACT FILE

Local newspaper the *Southern Daily Echo* introduced a Southampton Player of the Year award in 1973–74 with Mick Channon being the first recipient. The club introduced its own award in 2012–13 and in the seven years that have followed the same player has won both awards on six occasions. The exception was in 2015–16 when Shane Long won the *Echo* award and Virgil Van Dijk the club award.

Record Defeat: 0–8 v Tottenham H, Division 2, 28 March 1936; 0–8 v Everton, Division 1, 20 November 1971.

Most League Points (2 for a win): 61, Division 3 (S), 1921–22 and Division 3, 1959–60.

Most League Points (3 for a win): 92, FL 1, 2010–11.

Most League Goals: 112, Division 3 (S), 1957–58.

Highest League Scorer in Season: Derek Reeves, 39, Division 3, 1959–60.

Most League Goals in Total Aggregate: Mike Channon, 185, 1966–77, 1979–82.

Most League Goals in One Match: 5, Charlie Wayman v Leicester C, Division 2, 23 October 1948.

Most Capped Player: Maya Yoshida, 78 (95), Japan.

Most League Appearances: Terry Paine, 713, 1956–74.

Youngest League Player: Theo Walcott, 16 years 143 days v Wolverhampton W, 6 August 2005.

Record Transfer Fee Received: £75,000,000 from Liverpool for Virgil van Dijk, January 2018.

Record Transfer Fee Paid: £19,000,000 to Monaco for Guido Carrillo, January 2018.

Football League Record: 1920 Original Member of Division 3; 1921–22 Division 3 (S); 1922–53 Division 2; 1953–58 Division 3 (S); 1958–60 Division 3; 1960–66 Division 2; 1966–74 Division 1; 1974–78 Division 2; 1978–92 Division 1; 1992–2005 Premier League; 2005–09 FL C; 2009–11 FL 1; 2011–12 FL C; 2012– Premier League.

LATEST SEQUENCES

Longest Sequence of League Wins: 10, 16.4.2011 – 20.8.2011.

Longest Sequence of League Defeats: 5, 16.8.1998 – 12.9.1998.

Longest Sequence of League Draws: 8, 29.8.2005 – 15.10.2005.

Longest Sequence of Unbeaten League Matches: 19, 5.9.1921 – 31.12.1921.

Longest Sequence Without a League Win: 20, 30.8.1969 – 27.12.1969.

Successive Scoring Runs: 28 from 10.2.2008.

Successive Non-scoring Runs: 5 from 22.9.2018.

MANAGERS

Cecil Knight 1894–95
(Secretary-Manager)
Charles Robson 1895–97
Er Arnfield 1897–1911
(Secretary-Manager)
(continued as Secretary)
George Swift 1911–12
Er Arnfield 1912–19
Jimmy McIntyre 1919–24
Arthur Chadwick 1925–31
George Kay 1931–36
George Gross 1936–37
Tom Parker 1937–43
J. R. Sarjantson stepped down from the board to act as Secretary-Manager 1943–47 with the next two listed being Team Managers during this period
Arthur Dominy 1943–46
Bill Dodgin Snr 1946–49
Sid Cann 1949–51
George Roughton 1952–55
Ted Bates 1955–73
Lawrie McMenemy 1973–85
Chris Nicholl 1985–91
Ian Branfoot 1991–94
Alan Ball 1994–95
Dave Merrington 1995–96
Graeme Souness 1996–97
Dave Jones 1997–2000
Glenn Hoddle 2000–01
Stuart Gray 2001
Gordon Strachan 2001–04
Paul Sturrock 2004
Steve Wigley 2004
Harry Redknapp 2004–05
George Burley 2005–08
Nigel Pearson 2008
Jan Poortvliet 2008–09
Mark Wotte 2009
Alan Pardew 2009–10
Nigel Adkins 2010–13
Mauricio Pochettino 2013–14
Ronald Koeman 2014–16
Claude Puel 2016–17
Mauricio Pellegrino 2017–18
Mark Hughes 2018
Ralph Hasenhüttl December 2018–

TEN YEAR LEAGUE RECORD

		P	*W*	*D*	*L*	*F*	*A*	*Pts*	*Pos*
2009-10	FL 1	46	23	14	9	85	47	73*	7
2010-11	FL 1	46	28	8	10	86	38	92	2
2011-12	FL C	46	26	10	10	85	46	88	2
2012-13	PR Lge	38	9	14	15	49	60	41	14
2013-14	PR Lge	38	15	11	12	54	46	56	8
2014-15	PR Lge	38	18	6	14	54	33	60	7
2015-16	PR Lge	38	18	9	11	59	41	63	6
2016-17	PR Lge	38	12	10	16	41	48	46	8
2017-18	PR Lge	38	7	15	16	37	56	36	17
2018-19	PR Lge	38	9	12	17	45	65	39	16

**10 pts deducted.*

DID YOU KNOW ?

Ken Wimshurst was the first player to appear as a substitute for Southampton when he replaced injured goalkeeper John Hollowbread after 28 minutes of the home game with Coventry City on 8 September 1965. Cliff Huxford took over in goal and Saints went on to record a 1-0 victory thanks to Martin Chivers' 61st minute goal.

SOUTHAMPTON – PREMIER LEAGUE 2018–19 LEAGUE RECORD

Match No.	*Date*	*Venue*	*Opponents*	*Result*		*H/T Score*	*Lg Pos.*	*Goalscorers*	*Attendance*
1	Aug 12	H	Burnley	D	0-0	0-0	11		30,784
2	18	A	Everton	L	1-2	0-2	12	Ings [54]	38,601
3	25	H	Leicester C	L	1-2	0-0	16	Bertrand [52]	29,925
4	Sept 1	A	Crystal Palace	W	2-0	0-0	10	Ings [47], Hojbjerg [90]	25,495
5	17	H	Brighton & HA	D	2-2	1-0	13	Hojbjerg [35], Ings (pen) [65]	28,811
6	22	A	Liverpool	L	0-3	0-3	14		50,965
7	29	A	Wolverhampton W	L	0-2	0-0	15		31,147
8	Oct 7	H	Chelsea	L	0-3	0-1	16		30,663
9	20	A	Bournemouth	D	0-0	0-0	16		10,986
10	27	H	Newcastle U	D	0-0	0-0	16		30,736
11	Nov 4	A	Manchester C	L	1-6	1-4	16	Ings (pen) [29]	53,916
12	10	H	Watford	D	1-1	1-0	17	Gabbiadini [20]	28,153
13	24	A	Fulham	L	2-3	1-2	17	Armstrong 2 [18, 53]	24,603
14	Dec 1	H	Manchester U	D	2-2	2-2	18	Armstrong [13], Cedric Soares [20]	30,187
15	5	A	Tottenham H	L	1-3	0-1	18	Austin [90]	33,012
16	8	A	Cardiff C	L	0-1	0-0	19		30,067
17	16	H	Arsenal	W	3-2	2-1	17	Ings 2 [20, 44], Austin [85]	29,497
18	22	A	Huddersfield T	W	3-1	2-0	16	Redmond [15], Ings (pen) [42], Obafemi [71]	22,384
19	27	H	West Ham U	L	1-2	0-0	16	Redmond [50]	31,654
20	30	H	Manchester C	L	1-3	1-3	17	Hojbjerg [37]	31,381
21	Jan 2	A	Chelsea	D	0-0	0-0	18		40,668
22	12	A	Leicester C	W	2-1	2-0	16	Ward-Prowse (pen) [11], Long [45]	31,491
23	19	H	Everton	W	2-1	0-0	15	Ward-Prowse [50], Digne (og) [64]	29,989
24	30	H	Crystal Palace	D	1-1	0-1	16	Ward-Prowse [77]	28,339
25	Feb 2	A	Burnley	D	1-1	0-0	16	Redmond [55]	19,787
26	9	H	Cardiff C	L	1-2	0-0	18	Stephens [90]	31,438
27	24	A	Arsenal	L	0-2	0-2	18		59,877
28	27	H	Fulham	W	2-0	2-0	17	Romeu [23], Ward-Prowse [40]	27,597
29	Mar 2	A	Manchester U	L	2-3	1-0	17	Valery [26], Ward-Prowse [75]	74,459
30	9	H	Tottenham H	W	2-1	0-1	16	Valery [76], Ward-Prowse [81]	31,890
31	30	A	Brighton & HA	W	1-0	0-0	16	Hojbjerg [53]	30,636
32	Apr 5	H	Liverpool	L	1-3	1-1	16	Long [9]	31,797
33	13	H	Wolverhampton W	W	3-1	2-1	16	Redmond 2 [2, 30], Long [71]	31,708
34	20	A	Newcastle U	L	1-3	0-2	16	Lemina [59]	52,191
35	23	A	Watford	D	1-1	1-0	16	Long [1]	19,170
36	27	H	Bournemouth	D	3-3	1-2	16	Long [12], Ward-Prowse [55], Targett [67]	31,310
37	May 4	A	West Ham U	L	0-3	0-1	16		59,961
38	12	H	Huddersfield T	D	1-1	1-0	16	Redmond [41]	30,367

Final League Position: 16

GOALSCORERS

League (45): Ings 7 (3 pens), Ward-Prowse 7 (1 pen), Redmond 6, Long 5, Hojbjerg 4, Armstrong 3, Austin 2, Valery 2, Bertrand 1, Cedric Soares 1, Gabbiadini 1, Lemina 1, Obafemi 1, Romeu 1, Stephens 1, Targett 1, own goal 1.
FA Cup (4): Redmond 3, Armstrong 1.
Carabao Cup (2): Austin 1, Ings 1.
Checkatrade Trophy (2): Barnes 1, Obafemi 1.

McCarthy A 25	Stephens J 19 + 5	Vestergaard J 23	Hoedt W 13	Cedric Soares R 16 + 2	Romeu O 25 + 6	Lemina M 18 + 3	Bertrand R 24	Armstrong S 16 + 13	Redmond N 36 + 2	Austin C 11 + 14	Ings D 23 + 1	Elyounoussi M 8 + 8	Gabbiadini M 4 + 8	Ward-Prowse J 21 + 5	Long S 12 + 14	Hojbjerg P 31	Targett M 13 + 3	Davis S 1 + 2	Bednarek J 24 + 1	Yoshida M 17	Obafemi M 1 + 5	Valery Y 20 + 3	Johnson T — + 1	Ramsey K 1	Gunn A 12	Slattery C 1 + 2	Gallagher S — + 4	Sims J 2 + 5	Forster F 1	Match No.
1	2	3	4	5^2	6	7	8	9^3	10	11^1	12	13	14																	1
1	3		4	2	7^2	8	5	14	9	11^3	10		13	6^1	12															2
1		3	4	2	13	7	5	14	9	12	11^1	6^3			10^2	8■														3
1		3	4	2	14	7	5		9	12	10^1	6^2			11^3	8	13													4
1		3	4	2		7	5		9		11^1	6^3	12	13	10^2	8		14												5
1		3	4	2	6^1	9	5	12	7	14					11^3	8	10^2		13											6
1		3	4	2		7	5	12	9	10^2	11	6^1	13			8														7
1			4	5	12	6	8		10		11		9^2		13	7			2^1	3										8
1	3		4	2		7^3	5	12	9	11^2	10^1	6	14		13	8														9
1	3		4	2	7^1	8	5		6	10^3	11	9^2	12	14	13															10
1	3		4	2		7	5	14	10^3		11^1	13		6^2	9	8					12									11
1			4	2		7	5	9^2	10^3	12	11^1		8	13		6				3	14									12
1			4	2		6		9^1	10	11^2		12	8			7	5			3	13									13
1	2	4		8		7^2		11	9				12			6		13		3	10^1	5								14
1	3			2	14			9^2	10	12		13	11^1	8		7^3	5	6		4										15
1	12	4			7^1	8		10	9	11^3			13	14		6	5		3			2^2								16
1		4			7			10^3	9^1	13	11^2				12	6	8		2	3		5	14							17
1	14	4			6	13		10^1	9		11^2					7	8		2	3	12	5^3								18
1		4			7	6^3		10	9	13	11^2	14			12		8		2	3^1		5								19
1	3				7^3	8^1			12	11^2		10		9	14	6■	5		4			13		2						20
	14	5		6	8			10^3	7^1	13	11^2			9	12				3	4		2			1					21
1	3	4		12	6			10^2	9^3					7	11^1		8		2			5■				13	14			22
1	3	4		12	7			14	10^3		11^2			6	13	8	9^1		2			5								23
1	3	4^2			7			12	10		11	13		8		6^1	9		2			5^3				14				24
1	3	4			7			8^1	10^3	14	11^2			5	12		9		2			13				6				25
1	3	4^1			7		9		11	12		13		8	10^3	6			2			5^2					14			26
	3^1	4			7			10^2	11	12		14		8		6	9		2		13^3	5			1					27
		4			7		9		11	10^1				6	12	8			2	3		5			1					28
		4			7		9	12	10	11^1				6		8			2	3^2		5			1		13			29
		4			6^1		8	14	10	11^2				9	13^3	7			2	3		5			1			12		30
	13				6		5	9^2	11^1		10^3			8		7			3	4		2			1		12	14		31
		4^2			6^3		8	14	10	13				9	11^1	7			2	3		5			1			12		32
	14	4			12		8		10		11^2			6	13	7			2	3		5^1			1			9^3		33
	2^1				6	13	8	12	10		11^2			5	14	7			4	3					1			9^3		34
	4				6^1	13	8	10^3	9					5	11^2	7			2	3		14			1			12		35
	4				7^1		5	13	11	14	10^3			6	9^2	8	12		3			2			1					36
	4				14	7^1	5	6^2	12		11^3	9		13	10	8			3			2							1	37
	4				7^3		5		9	13	11^2			6	10^1	8	12		3			2			1			14		38

FA Cup

Third Round	Derby Co	(a)	2-2
Replay	Derby Co	(h)	2-2

(aet; Derby Co won 5-3 on penalties)

Carabao Cup

Second Round	Brighton & HA	(a)	1-0
Third Round	Everton	(a)	1-1

(Southampton won 4-3 on penalties)

Fourth Round	Leicester C	(a)	0-0

(Leicester C won 6-5 on penalties)

Checkatrade Trophy (Southampton U21)

Group B (S)	Colchester U	(a)	2-0
Group B (S)	Cambridge U	(a)	0-4
Group B (S)	Southend U	(a)	0-3

SOUTHEND UNITED

FOUNDATION

The leading club in Southend around the turn of the 20th century was Southend Athletic, but they were an amateur concern. Southend United was a more ambitious professional club when they were founded in 1906, employing Bob Jack as secretary-manager and immediately joining the Second Division of the Southern League.

Roots Hall Stadium, Victoria Avenue, Southend-on-Sea, Essex SS2 6NQ.

Telephone: (01702) 304 050.

Ticket Office: (08444) 770 077.

Website: www.southendunited.co.uk

Email: info@southend-united.co.uk

Ground Capacity: 12,392.

Record Attendance: 22,862 v Tottenham H, FA Cup 3rd rd replay, 11 January 1936 (at Southend Stadium); 31,090 v Liverpool, FA Cup 3rd rd, 10 January 1979 (at Roots Hall).

Pitch Measurements: 100.5m × 67.5m (110yd × 74yd).

Chairman: Ron Martin.

Manager: Kevin Bond.

Assistant Manager: Gary Waddock.

Colours: Navy blue shirts, navy blue shorts with white trim, white socks.

Year Formed: 1906.

Turned Professional: 1906.

Club Nicknames: 'The Blues', 'The Shrimpers'.

Grounds: 1906, Roots Hall, Prittlewell; 1920, Kursaal; 1934, Southend Stadium; 1955, Roots Hall Football Ground.

First Football League Game: 28 August 1920, Division 3, v Brighton & HA (a) W 2–0 – Capper; Reid, Newton; Wileman, Henderson, Martin; Nicholls, Nuttall, Fairclough (2), Myers, Dorsett.

Record League Victory: 9–2 v Newport Co, Division 3 (S), 5 September 1936 – McKenzie; Nelson, Everest (1); Deacon, Turner, Carr; Bolan, Lane (1), Goddard (4), Dickinson (2), Oswald (1).

Record Cup Victory: 10–1 v Golders Green, FA Cup 1st rd, 24 November 1934 – Moore; Morfitt, Kelly; Mackay, Joe Wilson, Carr (1); Lane (1), Johnson (5), Cheesmuir (2), Deacon (1), Oswald. 10–1 v Brentwood, FA Cup 2nd rd, 7 December 1968 – Roberts; Bentley, Birks; McMillan (1) Beesley, Kurila; Clayton, Chisnall, Moore (4), Best (5), Hamilton. 10–1 v Aldershot, Leyland DAF Cup prel rd, 6 November 1990 – Sansome; Austin, Powell, Cornwell, Prior (1), Tilson (3), Cawley, Butler, Ansah (1), Benjamin (1), Angell (4).

Record Defeat: 1–9 v Brighton & HA, Division 3, 27 November 1965; 0–8 v Crystal Palace, League Cup 2nd rd (1st leg), 25 September 1990.

HONOURS

League Champions: FL 1 – 2005–06; Division 4 – 1980–81.
Runners-up: Division 3 – 1990–91; Division 4 – 1971–72, 1977–78.

FA Cup: 3rd rd – 1921; 5th rd – 1926, 1952, 1976, 1993.

League Cup: quarter-final – 2007.

League Trophy: *Runners-up:* 2004, 2005, 2013.

THE Sun FACT FILE

Southend United defender Tom Wilson was left almost blinded in the left eye after a ball struck him in a reserve team fixture at Leicester in March 1935, which effectively ended his career. Wilson later successfully sued the club under the Workmen's Compensation Act in Southend County Court and they were ordered to pay him a weekly amount of 27s 6d (£1.37).

Most League Points (2 for a win): 67, Division 4, 1980–81.

Most League Points (3 for a win): 85, Division 3, 1990–91.

Most League Goals: 92, Division 3 (S), 1950–51.

Highest League Scorer in Season: Jim Shankly, 31, 1928–29; Sammy McCrory, 1957–58, both in Division 3 (S).

Most League Goals in Total Aggregate: Roy Hollis, 122, 1953–60.

Most League Goals in One Match: 5, Jim Shankly v Merthyr T, Division 3 (S), 1 March 1930.

Most Capped Player: Jason Demetriou, 13 (50), Cyprus.

Most League Appearances: Sandy Anderson, 452, 1950–63.

Youngest League Player: Phil O'Connor, 16 years 76 days v Lincoln C, 26 December 1969.

Record Transfer Fee Received: £2,000,000 (rising to £2,750,000) from Nottingham F for Stan Collymore, June 1993.

Record Transfer Fee Paid: £500,000 to Galatasaray for Mike Marsh, September 1995.

Football League Record: 1920 Original Member of Division 3; 1921–58 Division 3 (S); 1958–66 Division 3; 1966–72 Division 4; 1972–76 Division 3; 1976–78 Division 4; 1978–80 Division 3; 1980–81 Division 4; 1981–84 Division 3; 1984–87 Division 4; 1987–89 Division 3; 1989–90 Division 4; 1990–91 Division 3; 1991–92 Division 2; 1992–97 Division 1; 1997–98 Division 2; 1998–2004 Division 3; 2004–05 FL 2; 2005–06 FL 1; 2006–07 FL C; 2007–10 FL 1; 2010–15 FL 2; 2015– FL 1.

LATEST SEQUENCES

Longest Sequence of League Wins: 8, 29.8.2005 – 9.10.2005.

Longest Sequence of League Defeats: 7, 16.4.2016 – 13.8.2016.

Longest Sequence of League Draws: 6, 30.1.1982 – 19.2.1982.

Longest Sequence of Unbeaten League Matches: 16, 20.2.1932 – 29.8.1932.

Longest Sequence Without a League Win: 17, 26.8.2006 – 2.12.2006.

Successive Scoring Runs: 24 from 23.3.1929.

Successive Non-scoring Runs: 6 from 6.4.1979.

MANAGERS

Bob Jack 1906–10
George Molyneux 1910–11
O. M. Howard 1911–12
Joe Bradshaw 1912–19
Ned Liddell 1919–20
Tom Mather 1920–21
Ted Birnie 1921–34
David Jack 1934–40
Harry Warren 1946–56
Eddie Perry 1956–60
Frank Broome 1960
Ted Fenton 1961–65
Alvan Williams 1965–67
Ernie Shepherd 1967–69
Geoff Hudson 1969–70
Arthur Rowley 1970–76
Dave Smith 1976–83
Peter Morris 1983–84
Bobby Moore 1984–86
Dave Webb 1986–87
Dick Bate 1987
Paul Clark 1987–88
Dave Webb *(General Manager)* 1988–92
Colin Murphy 1992–93
Barry Fry 1993
Peter Taylor 1993–95
Steve Thompson 1995
Ronnie Whelan 1995–97
Alvin Martin 1997–99
Alan Little 1999–2000
David Webb 2000–01
Rob Newman 2001–03
Steve Wignall 2003
Steve Tilson 2003–10
Paul Sturrock 2010–13
Phil Brown 2013–18
Chris Powell 2018–19
Kevin Bond April 2019–

TEN YEAR LEAGUE RECORD

		P	W	D	L	F	A	Pts	Pos
2009-10	FL 1	46	10	13	23	51	72	43	23
2010-11	FL 2	46	16	13	17	62	56	61	13
2011-12	FL 2	46	25	8	13	77	48	83	4
2012-13	FL 2	46	16	13	17	61	55	61	11
2013-14	FL 2	46	19	15	12	56	39	72	5
2014-15	FL 2	46	24	12	10	54	38	84	5
2015-16	FL 1	46	16	11	19	58	64	59	14
2016-17	FL 1	46	20	12	14	70	53	72	7
2017-18	FL 1	46	17	12	17	58	62	63	10
2018-19	FL 1	46	14	8	24	55	68	50	19

DID YOU KNOW ?

A Football Combination fixture between Southend United Reserves and Queens Park Rangers drew an attendance of 3,092 to Roots Hall in November 1967, including over 500 away fans. The attraction was the return from injury of Rangers star Rodney Marsh who scored the only goal of the match five minutes from time.

SOUTHEND UNITED – SKY BET LEAGUE ONE 2018–19 LEAGUE RECORD

Match No.	Date		Venue	Opponents	Result		H/T Score	Lg Pos.	Goalscorers	Attendance
1	Aug	4	H	Doncaster R	L	2-3	0-0	14	Hopper ^{75}, Robinson ^{86}	7147
2		11	A	Plymouth Arg	D	1-1	1-1	15	Demetriou (pen) ^{38}	9886
3		18	H	Bradford C	W	2-0	0-0	8	Hopper ^{52}, Cox ^{56}	6295
4		21	A	Luton T	L	0-2	0-2	13		9086
5		25	A	Bristol R	W	1-0	1-0	11	Hopper ^{40}	8172
6	Sept	1	H	Charlton Ath	L	1-2	0-0	13	Robinson ^{60}	7923
7		8	H	Peterborough U	L	2-3	0-1	15	Hopper ^{63}, McLaughlin ^{75}	6551
8		15	A	Shrewsbury T	L	0-2	0-2	18		5651
9		22	H	Fleetwood T	W	1-0	0-0	16	Cox ^{53}	5712
10		29	A	Wycombe W	W	3-2	1-0	13	Robinson ^{38}, Hopper ^{53}, Cox ^{57}	4784
11	Oct	2	A	Burton Alb	W	2-1	0-1	11	Hopper ^{61}, Cox ^{78}	2149
12		6	H	Oxford U	D	0-0	0-0	11		6670
13		13	A	Gillingham	W	2-0	0-0	9	Cox 2 $^{51, 53}$	5584
14		20	H	Coventry C	L	1-2	0-1	12	Hopper ^{68}	7775
15		23	H	Walsall	W	3-0	1-0	9	Bunn 2 $^{23, 82}$, Dieng ^{76}	5603
16		27	A	Sunderland	L	0-3	0-1	11		30,894
17	Nov	3	A	Barnsley	L	0-1	0-0	12		10,709
18		17	H	Blackpool	L	1-2	0-1	14	Demetriou ^{74}	6882
19		24	A	AFC Wimbledon	L	1-2	1-1	15	Trotter (og) ^{11}	4195
20		27	H	Scunthorpe U	W	2-0	1-0	14	Dieng ^{8}, Mantom ^{80}	5110
21	Dec	8	A	Portsmouth	L	0-2	0-2	15		18,062
22		15	H	Accrington S	W	3-0	2-0	12	Mantom ^{19}, Cox ^{23}, Robinson ^{72}	6286
23		22	H	Rochdale	L	1-2	0-1	13	White ^{81}	5735
24		26	A	Oxford U	W	1-0	0-0	11	Kightly ^{79}	8978
25		29	A	Coventry C	L	0-1	0-0	12		11,395
26	Jan	1	H	Gillingham	W	2-0	1-0	9	Mantom ^{40}, Moore ^{90}	7903
27		12	H	Plymouth Arg	L	2-3	0-1	12	Cox (pen) ^{86}, Kelman ^{90}	6851
28		19	A	Bradford C	W	4-0	2-0	10	Cox ^{2}, Mantom ^{26}, Humphrys 2 $^{54, 73}$	15,517
29		26	H	Luton T	L	0-1	0-1	12		8460
30	Feb	2	H	Bristol R	L	1-2	1-2	12	Cox ^{39}	5982
31		9	A	Charlton Ath	D	1-1	1-0	14	Humphrys ^{22}	12,389
32		12	A	Doncaster R	L	0-3	0-1	14		6557
33		16	H	Portsmouth	D	3-3	1-3	13	Cox 3 (1 pen) $^{36, 78 (p), 87}$	7300
34		23	A	Accrington S	D	1-1	1-0	13	Humphrys ^{20}	2472
35	Mar	2	H	Barnsley	L	0-3	0-0	13		6217
36		9	A	Blackpool	D	2-2	1-1	14	Kiernan ^{20}, Turner ^{48}	15,871
37		12	A	Scunthorpe U	L	1-4	1-1	18	Cox ^{3}	3233
38		16	H	AFC Wimbledon	L	0-1	0-0	20		7570
39		23	A	Peterborough U	L	0-2	0-1	20		7585
40		30	H	Shrewsbury T	L	0-2	0-0	20		6818
41	Apr	6	A	Fleetwood T	D	2-2	1-0	20	Bunn ^{21}, Hyam ^{80}	2761
42		13	H	Wycombe W	L	0-2	0-0	22		7689
43		19	A	Walsall	D	1-1	1-0	22	Cox ^{43}	4624
44		22	H	Burton Alb	W	3-2	1-0	19	Mantom ^{18}, Bunn ^{48}, Dieng ^{77}	6169
45		27	A	Rochdale	L	0-1	0-0	20		5000
46	May	4	H	Sunderland	W	2-1	1-0	19	White ^{43}, Humphrys ^{87}	10,779

Final League Position: 19

GOALSCORERS

League (55): Cox 15 (2 pens), Hopper 7, Humphrys 5, Mantom 5, Bunn 4, Robinson 4, Dieng 3, Demetriou 2 (1 pen), White 2, Hyam 1, Kelman 1, Kiernan 1, Kightly 1, McLaughlin 1, Moore 1, Turner 1, own goal 1.
FA Cup (9): Cox 2, Mantom 2, Bunn 1, Dieng 1, Kightly 1, McLaughlin 1, White 1.
Carabao Cup (2): McCoulsky 2.
Checkatrade Trophy (7): McCoulsky 2, Bunn 1, Bwomono 1, Hutchinson 1, Kyprianou 1, McLaughlin 1.

Oxley M 25	Demetriou J 22 + 2	Lennon H 7 + 2	Turner M 33 + 3	Coker B 16	McLaughlin S 20 + 10	Hyam L 11 + 7	Mantom S 43	Kightly M 15 + 16	Cox S 42 + 3	Hopper T 13 + 1	Robinson T 13 + 11	Barratt S — + 1	Dieng T 38 + 5	White J 31 + 2	Klass M 3 + 7	Hendrie S 13 + 6	Bwomeno E 27 + 3	McCoulsky S — + 15	Bunn H 17 + 7	Stockdale D 3	Moore T 33 + 1	Yearwood D 21 + 6	Kyprianou H 1	Hutchinson I 2 + 6	Bishop N 18	Clifford T — + 1	Kelman C 2 + 8	Hart S 18	Humphrys S 8 + 2	Pitoula-Wabo N — + 2	Kiernan R 10	Acauah E 1 + 2	Match No.
1	2	3	4	5	6^{3}	7	8	9^{2}	10^{1}	11	12	13	14																				1
1	2		3	5	6^{1}		8	9^{2}	10^{3}	11	13		7	4	12	14																	2
1	2		4	5	6		8	9^{2}	10^{1}	11^{3}	12		7	3	13	14																	3
1	9		3	5	6^{1}	12	8		10	11	13		7^{3}	4			2^{2}	14															4
1	6		3	5	7^{2}		8	9^{3}	12	10	11^{1}			4	14	13	2																5
1■	7		4	5	6^{1}		8	9■	13	11^{3}	10^{2}			3			2	14	12														6
			4	5	6^{2}		7		10^{1}	11	12		8	3			2	13	9	1													7
	2			5	6^{2}		8		10^{1}	11	12		7	4				13	9	1	3												8
	6		4	5			7		10	11^{1}	9^{2}		8	2	12			13		1	3												9
1	6		4	5	12		7^{2}	13	11^{1}	10	9^{3}		8	2							3	14											10
1	5		3	9				12	7^{2}	11	10^{3}		6	2	13			14			4	8^{1}											11
1	5		3	9			7	12	10^{1}	11^{2}	14		8	2^{3}				13			4	6											12
1		13	3	9			6		10		11^{2}		7			4	5	12			2	8^{1}											13
1	14		3	9^{3}			7^{2}		11■	13	10^{1}		6			4	5		12		2	8											14
1	2	4^{2}	12	5	6		7	14		11^{1}			8					13	9^{3}		3	10											15
1	2		4	5^{2}	6^{3}		7	14	11				8			12		13	9		3	10^{1}											16
1	2		3				8^{2}	12	10^{1}		13		9	5		6		14	11^{3}		4	7											17
1	2		4■		13		6	9^{3}	10		14		8			5^{1}		12	11		3	7^{2}											18
1	2				14		6		10		11^{2}		8	3		5^{3}		12	13		4	7^{1}	9										19
1	2^{2}				9	6	8	14	10^{1}				7^{3}	3		5	12	13	11		4												20
1			3^{1}		6	9	8^{3}		11		13		7	5		12	2		10^{2}		4	14											21
1					9^{2}	6	8	13	11^{1}		10^{3}		7	4		5	2				3	12		14									22
					9^{2}	6^{1}	8		10		11		7	3		5	2	12			4			13	1								23
			3			12	8	6^{3}	10^{2}		11		7	14		5	2				4	9^{1}			1	13							24
					12		8	9^{2}	11		10		7	4		5^{1}	2		14		3	6^{3}		13	1								25
			3			12	8		13		10■		7	14		5	2		11^{2}		4	6^{1}		9^{3}	1								26
			3				7	12	10				6	4		5	2		9^{2}			8		11^{1}	1		13						27
			4			7	9^{2}		11^{1}		12		8	5			2				3	13			1		14	6	10^{3}				28
			3		13		6^{1}		10				8	2			5				4	7^{2}			1		12	9	11				29
			2^{1}		13		6	12	10				8^{2}	3			5				4	7			1		14	9^{3}	11				30
			13		12		8	7^{1}	11				9	3	14		2				4	6■			1			5^{3}	10^{2}				31
			12		9		7	13	10				8	4^{1}	6^{2}		2				3				1			5	11				32
			3		11		7^{1}	9^{2}	10				6		12		2				4			13	1			5	8^{3}	14			33
		13	3		11^{1}	14	7		10				6		9^{3}		2				4			12	1			5	8^{2}				34
			3		11^{1}		7^{2}	9^{3}	10				8		6		2		12		4	14			1		13	5					35
	12	3	2			8	7^{3}		11^{1}				6				5		14		13				1		10^{2}	9			4		36
	2^{1}	6	4		13	8^{2}	9	14	11				7						10^{3}		3				1			6		12			37
1	2	3^{1}	4		8^{3}	7^{2}		12	11				9						10			14					13	6			5		38
1							8	9^{3}	10^{1}				7				2		12		3	6		14			11^{2}	5			4	13	39
	2					13		8	9				6	4					10^{2}			7^{1}			1		12	5			3	11	40
	2	4				8	7^{3}	9	10				13	5			14		11^{1}						1			6^{2}	12		3		41
	2^{2}	3			13		9	6^{3}	10				8	4			12								1			5	11^{1}		7	14	42
1			5			13	8		10					3		12	2		11^{1}		4	9^{2}					14	6^{3}			7		43
1			2			12	8	14	11				13	4			5		10^{1}		3	6^{3}						9			7^{2}		44
1			2		14	6^{2}	8	13	11				12^{3}	4		9^{1}	5		10		3										7		45
1			3		11		6	12	10				13	2			5				4^{1}	8^{3}						9^{2}	14		7		46

FA Cup

First Round	Crawley T	(h)	1-1
Replay	Crawley T	(a)	6-2
(aet)			
Second Round	Barnsley	(h)	2-4

Carabao Cup

First Round	Brentford	(h)	2-4

Checkatrade Trophy

Group B (S)	Cambridge U	(h)	3-1
Group B (S)	Colchester U	(a)	0-2
Group B (S)	Southampton U21	(h)	3-0
Second Round (S)	Luton T	(a)	1-1
(Southend U won 4-2 on penalties)			
Third Round	Portsmouth	(h)	0-2

STEVENAGE

FOUNDATION

There have been several clubs associated with the town of Stevenage. Stevenage Town was formed in 1884. They absorbed Stevenage Rangers in 1955 and later played at Broadhall Way. The club went into liquidation in 1968 and Stevenage Athletic was formed, but they, too, followed a similar path in 1976. Then Stevenage Borough was founded. The Broadhall Way pitch was dug up and remained unused for three years. Thus the new club started its life in the modest surrounds of the King George V playing fields with a roped-off ground in the Chiltern League. A change of competition followed to the Wallspan Southern Combination and by 1980 the club returned to the council-owned Broadhall Way when "Borough" was added to the name. Entry into the United Counties League was so successful the league and cup were won in the first season. On to the Isthmian League Division Two and the climb up the pyramid continued. In 1995–96 Stevenage Borough won the Conference but was denied a place in the Football League as the ground did not measure up to the competition's standards. Subsequent improvements changed this and the 7,100 capacity venue became one of the best appointed grounds in non-league football. After winning elevation to the Football League the club dropped Borough from its title.

Lamex Stadium, Broadhall Way, Stevenage, Hertfordshire SG2 8RH.

Telephone: (01438) 223 223.

Fax: (01438) 743 666.

Ticket Office: (01438) 223 223.

Website: stevenagefc.com

Email: info@stevenagefc.com

Ground Capacity: 6,722.

Record Attendance: 8,040 v Newcastle U, FA Cup 4th rd, 25 January 1998.

Pitch Measurements: 104m × 64m (114yd × 70yd).

Chairman: Phil Wallace.

Chief Executive Officer: Alex Tunbridge.

Manager: Dino Maamria.

First-Team Coaches: David Oldfield, Mark Sampson.

Colours: White shirts with red and black trim, red shorts with white trim, white socks with red hoops.

Nickname: 'The Boro'.

Previous Name: 1976, Stevenage Borough; 2010, Stevenage.

Grounds: 1976, King George V playing fields; 1980, Broadhall Way (renamed Lamex Stadium 2009).

HONOURS

League Champions: Conference – 1995–96, 2009–10.

FA Cup: 5th rd – 2012.

League Cup: 2nd rd – 2012, 2017.

THE Sun FACT FILE

Stevenage Borough, as the club was then known, entered the Football Conference for the first time in 1994 after winning the Isthmian League the previous season. Their opening Conference game saw them travel to Stafford Rangers where they won 3-0 with Steve Conroy scoring their first goal in the competition.

First Football League Game: 7 August 2010, FL 2, v Macclesfield T (h) D 2–2 – Day; Henry, Laird, Bostwick, Roberts, Foster, Wilson (Sinclair), Byrom, Griffin (1), Winn (Odubade), Vincenti (1) (Beardsley).

Year Formed: 1976.

Turned Professional: 1976.

Record League Victory: 6–0 v Yeovil T, FL 2, 14 April 2012 – Day; Lascelles (1), Laird, Roberts (1), Ashton (1), Shroot (Mousinho), Wilson (Myrie-Williams), Long, Agyemang (1), Reid (Slew), Freeman (2).

Record Victory: 11–1 v British Timken Ath 1980–81.

Record Defeat: 0–8 v Charlton Ath, FL Trophy, 9 October 2018.

Most League Points (3 for a win): 73, FL 1, 2011–12.

Most League Goals: 69, FL 1, 2011–12.

Highest League Scorer in Season: Matthew Godden, 20, FL 2, 2016–17.

Most League Goals in Total Aggregate: Matthew Godden, 30, 2016–18.

Most League Goals in One Match: 3, Chris Holroyd v Hereford U, FL 2, 28 September 2010; 3, Dani Lopez v Sheffield U, FL 1, 16 March 2013; 3, Chris Whelpdale v Morecambe, FL 2, 28 November 2015; 3, Matthew Godden v Newport Co, FL 2, 7 January 2017; 3, Alex Revell v Exeter C, FL 2, 28 April 2018.

Most Capped Player: Marcus Haber, 5 (including 3 on loan at Notts Co) (27), Canada.

Most League Appearances: Ronnie Henry, 230, 2014–19.

Youngest League Player: Liam Smyth, 17 years 47 days v Port Vale, 23 October 2018.

Record Transfer Fee Received: £260,000 from Peterborough U for George Boyd, January 2007.

Record Transfer Fee Paid: £125,000 to Exeter C for James Dunne, May 2012.

Football League Record: 2011 Promoted from Conference Premier; 2010–11 FL 2; 2011–14 FL 1; 2014– FL 2.

MANAGERS

Derek Montgomery 1976–83
Frank Cornwell 1983–87
John Bailey 1987–88
Brian Wilcox 1988–90
Paul Fairclough 1990–98
Richard Hill 1998–2000
Steve Wignall 2000
Paul Fairclough 2000–02
Wayne Turner 2002–03
Graham Westley 2003–06
Mark Stimson 2006–07
Peter Taylor 2007–08
Graham Westley 2008–12
Gary Smith 2012–13
Graham Westley 2013–15
Teddy Sheringham 2015–16
Darren Sarll 2016–18
Dino Maamria March 2018–

LATEST SEQUENCES

Longest Sequence of League Wins: 6, 12.3.2011 – 2.4.2011.

Longest Sequence of League Defeats: 6, 13.4.2013 – 17.8.2013.

Longest Sequence of League Draws: 5, 17.3.2012 – 31.3.2012.

Longest Sequence of Unbeaten League Matches: 17, 9.4.2012 – 6.10.2012.

Longest Sequence Without a League Win: 10, 11.3.2014 – 21.4.2014.

Successive Scoring Runs: 17 from 9.4.2012.

Successive Non-scoring Runs: 4 from 20.2.2016.

TEN YEAR LEAGUE RECORD

		P	W	D	L	F	A	Pts	Pos
2009-10	Conf P	44	30	9	5	79	24	99	1
2010-11	FL 2	46	18	15	13	62	45	69	6
2011-12	FL 1	46	18	19	9	69	44	73	6
2012-13	FL 1	46	15	9	22	47	64	54	18
2013-14	FL 1	46	11	9	26	46	72	42	24
2014-15	FL 2	46	20	12	14	62	54	72	6
2015-16	FL 2	46	11	15	20	52	67	48	18
2016-17	FL 2	46	20	7	19	67	63	67	10
2017-18	FL 2	46	14	13	19	60	65	55	16
2018-19	FL 2	46	20	10	16	59	55	70	10

DID YOU KNOW ?

Mitchell Cole scored a hat-trick in just six minutes for Stevenage after coming on as a substitute in the club's Football Conference match at Eastbourne Borough in March 2010. Stevenage won the game 6-0 and went on to take the title and earn promotion to the Football League.

STEVENAGE – SKY BET LEAGUE TWO 2018–19 LEAGUE RECORD

Match No.	*Date*		*Venue*	*Opponents*	*Result*		*H/T Score*	*Lg Pos.*	*Goalscorers*	*Attendance*
1	Aug	4	H	Tranmere R	D	2-2	2-1	11	Ball [20], Byrom [27]	3315
2		11	A	Crawley T	W	3-1	0-0	6	Reid [48], Revell 2 [88, 90]	2102
3		18	H	Morecambe	W	1-0	1-0	3	Timlin [45]	2030
4		21	A	Forest Green R	D	0-0	0-0	4		1834
5		25	A	Yeovil T	L	0-2	0-2	9		2635
6	Sept	1	H	Cambridge U	L	0-1	0-1	13		2998
7		8	H	Macclesfield T	W	1-0	1-0	11	Newton [41]	2282
8		15	A	Notts Co	D	3-3	2-2	13	Kennedy [38], Revell [45], Newton [73]	6085
9		22	H	Grimsby T	W	1-0	0-0	9	Seddon [83]	2332
10		29	A	Carlisle U	W	1-0	0-0	4	Kennedy [56]	4200
11	Oct	2	A	Exeter C	L	0-1	0-1	7		3671
12		6	H	Colchester U	W	3-1	1-1	5	Guthrie [41], Kennedy (pen) [82], Sonupe [84]	2763
13		13	A	Newport Co	L	1-2	1-1	7	Wildin [45]	3126
14		20	H	Crewe Alex	L	0-1	0-0	10		2164
15		23	H	Port Vale	D	0-0	0-0	10		1943
16		27	A	Cheltenham T	W	2-0	2-0	8	Guthrie [18], Seddon [45]	2382
17	Nov	3	H	Oldham Ath	W	3-2	1-1	7	Byrom [22], Guthrie [68], Newton [81]	2583
18		17	A	Bury	L	0-4	0-0	9		3385
19		24	H	Milton Keynes D	W	3-2	1-1	8	Seddon [21], Cuthbert [84], Kennedy [90]	3263
20		27	A	Swindon T	L	2-3	1-3	9	Cuthbert [14], Reid [78]	5273
21	Dec	8	H	Lincoln C	L	0-1	0-1	10		3552
22		15	A	Northampton T	D	1-1	0-1	11	Kennedy [75]	4756
23		22	H	Mansfield T	L	1-3	1-0	12	Newton [45]	2761
24		26	A	Colchester U	W	2-1	2-0	10	Gilmartin (og) [5], Newton [36]	5032
25		29	A	Crewe Alex	L	0-1	0-1	12		3625
26	Jan	1	H	Newport Co	W	1-0	0-0	11	Revell [85]	2299
27		5	A	Cambridge U	L	0-2	0-2	11		4235
28		12	H	Crawley T	W	2-1	2-1	10	Ball 2 [24, 40]	2347
29		19	A	Morecambe	W	2-1	1-0	9	Kennedy (pen) [25], Wilkinson [90]	1422
30		26	H	Forest Green R	L	0-2	0-1	9		2494
31	Feb	2	H	Yeovil T	W	1-0	0-0	9	Revell [72]	2157
32		9	A	Tranmere R	L	0-2	0-1	9		5283
33		16	A	Lincoln C	D	2-2	0-0	9	Chair 2 [87, 90]	9036
34		23	H	Northampton T	L	1-2	0-1	10	Revell [79]	3540
35	Mar	2	A	Oldham Ath	D	1-1	0-0	11	Guthrie [90]	3807
36		9	H	Bury	L	0-1	0-0	11		3530
37		12	H	Swindon T	W	2-0	1-0	10	Revell [36], Chair [90]	2194
38		16	A	Milton Keynes D	D	1-1	1-0	10	Chair [30]	7365
39		23	A	Macclesfield T	D	2-2	1-1	11	Nugent [44], Newton [52]	1866
40		30	H	Notts Co	L	0-3	0-3	12		2860
41	Apr	6	A	Grimsby T	W	2-0	1-0	12	Guthrie 2 [23, 50]	3689
42		13	H	Carlisle U	W	3-0	1-0	11	Iontton [16], Guthrie 2 (1 pen) [52, 62 (p)]	2770
43		19	A	Port Vale	W	4-1	1-0	10	Sonupe 2 [12, 50], Chair [84], Guthrie [90]	4088
44		22	H	Exeter C	D	1-1	1-1	10	Guthrie [28]	3195
45		27	A	Mansfield T	W	2-1	0-0	10	Guthrie [71], Chair [90]	6390
46	May	4	H	Cheltenham T	W	2-0	0-0	10	Martin [56], Gibson [58]	3071

Final League Position: 10

GOALSCORERS

League (59): Guthrie 11 (1 pen), Revell 7, Chair 6, Kennedy 6 (2 pens), Newton 6, Ball 3, Seddon 3, Sonupe 3, Byrom 2, Cuthbert 2, Reid 2, Gibson 1, Iontton 1, Martin 1, Nugent 1, Timlin 1, Wildin 1, Wilkinson 1, own goal 1.
FA Cup (0).
Carabao Cup (1): Ball 1.
Checkatrade Trophy (5): Guthrie 3 (1 pen), Kennedy 2 (1 pen).

Farman P 33	Wildin L 39	Cuthbert S 46	Nugent B 34	Hunt J 26 + 3	Byrom J 43 + 3	Ball J 12 + 6	Timlin M 40 + 2	Kennedy B 22 + 3	Reid A 1 + 10	Revell A 35 + 5	Ferry J 2 + 10	Newton D 16 + 9	Sonupe E 9 + 23	Henry R 10 + 8	Guthrie K 26 + 8	Wilkinson L 8 + 10	Seddon S 22 + 1	Georgiou A 1	Iontton A 10 + 8	Dieng T 13	Vancooten T 10 + 2	Campbell-Ryce J 11 + 1	Smyth L — + 3	Makasi M 13 + 1	Chair I 16	Gibson J 2 + 4	Adebayo E — + 2	Mckee M 1 + 6	Martin J 5	Match No.
1	2	3	4	5■	6	7³	8²	9	10¹	11	12	13	14																	1
1	5	3	4		6	8²	7		12	11	13	10³	14	2	9¹															2
1	2	3	4	5	6	9²	8	13		10	12		7¹		11															3
1	2	4		5	8	7³	6	9²	13	11	12		14	3	10¹															4
1	2	3		5	8	7²	6■	9³	13	10		14	12	4	11¹															5
1	2	4			8			13		10¹	7	11	12	5	14	3	6³	9²												6
1	2	3	4		7	6	8³	9²		11		10¹	13		14		5		12											7
1	2	3	4²		7	6¹	8	9		10		11	13	12			5													8
	2	3	4	14	8		7	6²		10	13	11³	9¹		12		5			1										9
	2	3	4		8		7	6¹		10	12	11	9²		13		5			1										10
	2■	4	3		7	14	8²	11		10	0³	9¹	12		13		5			1										11
		3	4		8	7²	6	9¹		10³	14	13	12		11		5			1	2									12
	2	3	4		8		7³	9²	14	11	12	10	13				5			1		6¹								13
	2	3	4■	12	7		8	9¹		11			13		10		5			1		6²								14
	2	3			7	12	8			11			9²		10	4	5			1		6¹	13							15
	2	3	4	5	7		8			11	12²				10	13	9			1		6¹								16
	2	3	4²	5³	8		7	13		10		14			11	12	6			1		9¹								17
		3		5	8	6¹	7		14	10	13			2³	11■	4	12			1		9²								18
		3	4	5²	7		8	11³	13	10			12	2		14	6			1		9¹								19
		3		5	8		7	10	12	11			13	2³		4	9¹			1	14	6²								20
	2	3	4		8		7	11		10		12	13				5			1	6¹	9²								21
1	2	4		5¹	6	14	7³	11		10²		13	12	3	9		8													22
1	5²	3		9³	7	8¹		10		12		11	13	2			4		6		14									23
1		4	3	14	8			9²		12		10³		13	11		5		7		2	6¹								24
1		3	4		7¹		8²	6	12■	14		11			10		5		13		2	9³								25
1	2	3	4	5³	6²		12	9¹		13		11		14	10■		8		7											26
1	2	4³	3		6		7	9¹		10		11	13				5		8²			12	14							27
1	2	3³	4	5	8¹	12	7			10²		11				14	9		13					6						28
1	2	3	4¹	5	8	10	7²	9³	12			11				14			13					6						29
1	2	3	4	5	8	11¹	7	9	12	10			13											6²						30
1	2	3	4	5	8²		7			10³				14	11				13					6¹	9	12				31
1	2	3	4■	5	7³		8			11¹					10				12					6²	9	13	14■			32
1	2	3		5	7²	14	9			11			12	8¹		4							13	6³	10					33
1	2	3		5	8¹	14	7			10			13		12	4								6²	11	9³				34
1	2	3		5	6²		7¹			10			14	13	12	4³			8					11	9					35
1	2	3		5	8¹					11²					10	4			7					6³	9	12	14	13		36
1	2	3	4	5	8²		7			11¹				14	10									6³	9	12		13		37
1	2	3	4	5	12		8			11					10²	14			7³					13	9			6¹		38
1	2	4	3	5	7		6			11		12		14	9²	13								10¹	8³					39
1	2	3	4	5	8³		14			10		11¹	12		13				7					6²	9					40
1	5	3	4		7³		6					13	14		10				12		2			9¹	11²				8	41
1	5	3	4		14		6					13	11³		10				7¹		2				9²			12	8	42
1	5	3	4	8³	12		7						9¹		10	14			6²		2				11			13		43
1	2³	4²	5		9¹		7			14			10		11	12					3				8			13	6	44
1	5	3	4		7		6						9¹		11	13					2				10²			12	8	45
1		3	4		7		9						11¹	12	8				13		2				6	5²			10	46

FA Cup
First Round Plymouth Arg (a) 0-1

Carabao Cup
First Round Norwich C (a) 1-3

Checkatrade Trophy
Group G (S) Swansea C U21 (h) 5-0
Group G (S) Charlton Ath (h) 0-8
Group G (S) AFC Wimbledon (a) 0-4

STOKE CITY

FOUNDATION

The date of the formation of this club has long been in doubt. The year 1863 was claimed, but more recent research by local club historian Wade Martin has uncovered nothing earlier than 1868, when a couple of Old Carthusians, who were apprentices at the local works of the old North Staffordshire Railway Company, met with some others from that works, to form Stoke Ramblers. It should also be noted that the old Stoke club went bankrupt in 1908 when a new club was formed.

bet365 Stadium, Stanley Matthews Way, Stoke-on-Trent, Staffordshire ST4 4EG.

Telephone: (01782) 367 598.

Fax: (01782) 592 210.

Ticket Office: (01782) 367 599.

Website: www.stokecityfc.com

Email: info@stokecityfc.com

Ground Capacity: 30,089.

Record Attendance: 51,380 v Arsenal, Division 1, 29 March 1937 (at Victoria Ground); 30,022 v Everton, Premier League, 17 March 2018 (at bet365 Stadium).

Pitch Measurements: 105m × 68m (115yd × 74.5yd).

Chairman: Peter Coates.

Chief Executive: Tony Scholes.

Manager: Nathan Jones.

Assistant Manager: Paul Hart.

Colours: Red and white striped shirts, white shorts with red trim, white socks with red trim.

Year Formed: 1863* (*see Foundation*).

Turned Professional: 1885.

Previous Names: 1868, Stoke Ramblers; 1870, Stoke; 1925, Stoke City.

Club Nickname: 'The Potters'.

Grounds: 1875, Sweeting's Field; 1878, Victoria Ground (previously known as the Athletic Club Ground); 1997, Britannia Stadium (renamed bet365 Stadium, 2016).

First Football League Game: 8 September 1888, Football League, v WBA (h) L 0–2 – Rowley; Clare, Underwood; Ramsey, Shutt, Smith; Sayer, McSkimming, Staton, Edge, Tunnicliffe.

Record League Victory: 10–3 v WBA, Division 1, 4 February 1937 – Doug Westland; Brigham, Harbot; Tutin, Turner (1p), Kirton; Matthews, Antonio (2), Freddie Steele (5), Jimmy Westland, Johnson (2).

Record Cup Victory: 7–1 v Burnley, FA Cup 2nd rd (replay), 20 February 1896 – Clawley; Clare, Eccles; Turner, Grewe, Robertson; Willie Maxwell, Dickson, Alan Maxwell (3), Hyslop (4), Schofield.

Record Defeat: 0–10 v Preston NE, Division 1, 14 September 1889.

Most League Points (2 for a win): 63, Division 3 (N), 1926–27.

HONOURS

League Champions: Division 2 – 1932–33, 1962–63; Second Division – 1992–93; Division 3N – 1926–27.
Runners-up: FL C – 2007–08; Division 2 – 1921–22.

FA Cup: *Runners-up:* 2011.

League Cup Winners: 1972.
Runners-up: 1964.

League Trophy Winners: 1992, 2000.

European Competitions
UEFA Cup: 1972–73, 1974–75.
Europa League: 2011–12.

THE SUN FACT FILE

Stoke City played a prestigious friendly game against Real Madrid at the Victoria Ground in April 1963 in a match to celebrate what was then believed to be the club's centenary. The match attracted a season's best attendance of 44,914 with Dennis Violet and Jimmy McIlroy scoring for the Potters in a 2-2 draw.

Most League Points (3 for a win): 93, Division 2, 1992–93.

Most League Goals: 92, Division 3 (N), 1926–27.

Highest League Scorer in Season: Freddie Steele, 33, Division 1, 1936–37.

Most League Goals in Total Aggregate: Freddie Steele, 142, 1934–49.

Most League Goals in One Match: 7, Neville Coleman v Lincoln C, Division 2, 23 February 1957.

Most Capped Player: Glenn Whelan, 81 (87), Republic of Ireland.

Most League Appearances: Eric Skeels, 507, 1958–76.

Youngest League Player: Peter Bullock, 16 years 163 days v Swansea C, 19 April 1958.

Record Transfer Fee Received: £20,000,000 (rising to £25,000,000) from West Ham U for Marko Arnautovic, July 2017.

Record Transfer Fee Paid: £18,300,000 to Porto for Giannelli Imbula, February 2016.

Football League Record: 1888 Founder Member of Football League; 1890 Not re-elected; 1891 Re-elected; relegated in 1907, and after one year in Division 2, resigned for financial reasons; 1919 re-elected to Division 2; 1922–23 Division 1; 1923–26 Division 2; 1926–27 Division 3 (N); 1927–33 Division 2; 1933–53 Division 1; 1953–63 Division 2; 1963–77 Division 1; 1977–79 Division 2; 1979–85 Division 1; 1985–90 Division 2; 1990–92 Division 3; 1992–93 Division 2; 1993–98 Division 1; 1998–2002 Division 2; 2002–04 Division 1; 2004–08 FL C; 2008–18 Premier League; 2018– FL C.

LATEST SEQUENCES

Longest Sequence of League Wins: 8, 30.3.1895 – 21.9.1895.

Longest Sequence of League Defeats: 11, 6.4.1985 – 17.8.1985.

Longest Sequence of League Draws: 5, 13.5.2012 – 15.9.2012.

Longest Sequence of Unbeaten League Matches: 25, 5.9.1992 – 20.2.1993.

Longest Sequence Without a League Win: 17, 22.4.1989 – 14.10.1989.

Successive Scoring Runs: 21 from 24.12.1921.

Successive Non-scoring Runs: 8 from 29.12.1984.

MANAGERS

Tom Slaney 1874–83 *(Secretary-Manager)*
Walter Cox 1883–84 *(Secretary-Manager)*
Harry Lockett 1884–90
Joseph Bradshaw 1890–92
Arthur Reeves 1892–95
William Rowley 1895–97
H. D. Austerberry 1897–1908
A. J. Barker 1908–14
Peter Hodge 1914–15
Joe Schofield 1915–19
Arthur Shallcross 1919–23
John 'Jock' Rutherford 1923
Tom Mather 1923–35
Bob McGrory 1935–52
Frank Taylor 1952–60
Tony Waddington 1960–77
George Eastham 1977–78
Alan A'Court 1978
Alan Durban 1978–81
Richie Barker 1981–83
Bill Asprey 1984–85
Mick Mills 1985–89
Alan Ball 1989–91
Lou Macari 1991–93
Joe Jordan 1993–94
Lou Macari 1994–97
Chic Bates 1997–98
Chris Kamara 1998
Brian Little 1998–99
Gary Megson 1999
Gudjon Thordarson 1999–2002
Steve Cotterill 2002
Tony Pulis 2002–05
Johan Boskamp 2005–06
Tony Pulis 2006–13
Mark Hughes 2013–18
Paul Lambert 2018
Gary Rowett 2018–19
Nathan Jones January 2019–

TEN YEAR LEAGUE RECORD

		P	W	D	L	F	A	Pts	Pos
2009-10	PR Lge	38	11	14	13	34	48	47	11
2010-11	PR Lge	38	13	7	18	46	48	46	13
2011-12	PR Lge	38	11	12	15	36	53	45	14
2012-13	PR Lge	38	9	15	14	34	45	42	13
2013-14	PR Lge	38	13	11	14	45	52	50	9
2014-15	PR Lge	38	15	9	14	48	45	54	9
2015-16	PR Lge	38	14	9	15	41	55	51	9
2016-17	PR Lge	38	11	11	16	41	56	44	13
2017-18	PR Lge	38	7	12	19	35	68	33	19
2018-19	FL C	46	11	22	13	45	52	55	16

DID YOU KNOW ?

Legendary Stoke City winger Stanley Matthews was the oldest player to have appeared in top-flight football in England. Matthews, who had recently received a knighthood in the New Year's Honours List, was 50 years and five days old when he turned out for the Potters against Fulham on 6 February 1965.

STOKE CITY – SKY BET CHAMPIONSHIP 2018–19 LEAGUE RECORD

Match No.	Date	Venue	Opponents	Result		H/T Score	Lg Pos.	Goalscorers	Attendance
1	Aug 5	A	Leeds U	L	1-3	0-2	23	Afobe (pen) [52]	34,126
2	11	H	Brentford	D	1-1	1-0	21	Afobe [29]	24,806
3	18	A	Preston NE	D	2-2	1-2	18	Pieters [42], Crouch [61]	13,996
4	22	H	Wigan Ath	L	0-3	0-2	22		23,158
5	25	H	Hull C	W	2-0	1-0	16	McClean [9], De Wijs (og) [59]	23,311
6	Sept 1	A	WBA	L	1-2	0-1	17	Pieters [90]	25,183
7	15	A	Sheffield W	D	2-2	2-1	20	Afobe 2 [2, 22]	24,905
8	18	H	Swansea C	W	1-0	0-0	14	Allen [57]	22,078
9	22	H	Blackburn R	L	2-3	0-2	18	Berahino [79], Ince [80]	25,673
10	29	A	Rotherham U	D	2-2	0-0	17	Ince [59], Bojan [85]	9706
11	Oct 2	H	Bolton W	W	2-0	1-0	16	Martins Indi [10], Ince [74]	22,116
12	6	A	Norwich C	W	1-0	1-0	14	Klose (og) [35]	24,992
13	20	H	Birmingham C	L	0-1	0-0	17		28,160
14	23	A	Sheffield U	D	1-1	0-0	17	Allen [88]	24,463
15	27	A	Bristol C	W	1-0	1-0	13	Fletcher [33]	22,456
16	Nov 3	H	Middlesbrough	D	0-0	0-0	15		24,553
17	10	A	Nottingham F	D	0-0	0-0	14		28,556
18	24	H	QPR	D	2-2	1-1	13	Berahino [21], Allen [61]	24,291
19	28	H	Derby Co	W	2-1	1-0	12	Clucas [24], Ince [64]	25,147
20	Dec 1	A	Reading	D	2-2	0-1	12	Afobe [48], Ince [69]	14,414
21	8	H	Ipswich T	W	2-0	1-0	10	Ince [45], Allen [60]	24,694
22	15	A	Aston Villa	D	2-2	0-0	11	Allen [47], Afobe (pen) [78]	36,999
23	22	H	Millwall	W	1-0	0-0	9	Berahino [61]	25,351
24	26	A	Birmingham C	L	0-2	0-1	11		26,344
25	29	A	Bolton W	D	0-0	0-0	12		15,309
26	Jan 1	H	Bristol C	L	0-2	0-1	14		23,912
27	12	A	Brentford	L	1-3	1-2	15	Afobe [23]	9439
28	19	H	Leeds U	W	2-1	0-0	15	Clucas [49], Allen [88]	28,586
29	26	H	Preston NE	L	0-2	0-1	15		25,053
30	Feb 2	A	Hull C	L	0-2	0-1	15		12,776
31	9	H	WBA	L	0-1	0-1	17		26,828
32	13	A	Wigan Ath	D	0-0	0-0	17		9914
33	16	A	Ipswich T	D	1-1	1-0	17	McClean [42]	15,924
34	23	H	Aston Villa	D	1-1	1-0	17	Vokes [5]	27,975
35	Mar 2	H	Nottingham F	W	2-0	1-0	16	Etebo [15], Afobe [74]	26,736
36	9	A	QPR	D	0-0	0-0	16		14,954
37	13	A	Derby Co	D	0-0	0-0	17		25,685
38	16	H	Reading	D	0-0	0-0	16		24,368
39	30	H	Sheffield W	D	0-0	0-0	14		26,398
40	Apr 6	A	Blackburn R	W	1-0	1-0	15	Etebo [14]	17,478
41	9	A	Swansea C	L	1-3	1-2	15	McClean [45]	17,804
42	13	H	Rotherham U	D	2-2	2-0	16	Vokes [27], Clucas [29]	24,250
43	19	A	Middlesbrough	L	0-1	0-1	16		22,890
44	22	H	Norwich C	D	2-2	0-1	16	Williams [47], Edwards [69]	25,487
45	27	A	Millwall	D	0-0	0-0	16		14,472
46	May 5	H	Sheffield U	D	2-2	1-0	16	Vokes [19], Shawcross [69]	26,665

Final League Position: 16

GOALSCORERS

League (45): Afobe 8 (2 pens), Allen 6, Ince 6, Berahino 3, Clucas 3, McClean 3, Vokes 3, Etebo 2, Pieters 2, Bojan 1, Crouch 1, Edwards 1, Fletcher 1, Martins Indi 1, Shawcross 1, Williams 1, own goals 2.
FA Cup (3): Campbell 2, Crouch 1.
Carabao Cup (4): Berahino 2, Afobe 1, own goal 1.
Checkatrade Trophy (3): Campbell 2, Shenton 1.

Butland J 45	Bauer M 6 + 2	Shawcross R 33 + 3	Martins Indi B 36 + 1	Pieters E 21	Allen J 46	Ndiaye P 1	Etebo P 29 + 5	Ince T 36 + 2	Afobe B 32 + 13	McClean J 32 + 10	Bojan K 8 + 13	Fletcher D 4 + 7	Crouch P 2 + 21	Williams A 27 + 6	Edwards T 22 + 5	Berahino S 16 + 7	Diouf M 6 + 8	Martina C 17	Woods R 26 + 1	Adam C 4 + 8	Clucas S 23 + 3	Campbell T 2 + 1	Tymon J 1	Sorenson L — + 1	Batth D 17	Vokes S 10 + 2	Verlinden T 2 + 3	Collins N 1 + 2	Federici A 1	*Match No.*
1	2	3	4	5	6	7^{3}	8^{1}	9	10^{2}	11	12	13	14																	1
1	2	3	4^{3}	5	7		13	8	11	10	9^{2}	6^{1}	14	12																2
1		4		5	7		14	6	11^{1}	9^{2}		8	13	3	2	10^{3}	12													3
1		3		5	8		14	6^{1}	11	9	12	7^{3}	13	4■	2	10^{2}														4
1	14	3	4	5	7		8		12	9	13		11^{1}			10^{2}	6^{3}	2												5
1		3	4	5	7		8^{2}		13	9	14		11			10^{1}	6^{3}	2	12											6
1		3	4	5	8		6^{3}	9	10^{2}		12	13	14				11^{1}	2	7											7
1		3	4	5	9		8	7	11							12	10^{1}	2	6											8
1		3	4^{2}	5	8		6	9	10^{1}		14		13			12	11^{3}	2	7											9
1			4	5	8^{2}		6^{1}	9	10		12		13	3		11^{3}		2	7	14										10
1			4	5	8			9	10^{2}	12	6^{1}	14	13	3		11^{3}		2	7											11
1			4	5	9		8	7^{2}	11^{1}	10^{3}		13		3	14	12		2	6											12
1			4	5	9			7	11^{2}	10^{3}	8^{1}		14	3		13		2	6	12										13
1			4	5^{3}	7			6	11	9	13		12	3	14	10^{2}		2^{1}	8											14
1		14	4	5	8			7	11	13		8^{2}		3	2	10^{1}			6	12^{3}										15
1		3	5		6		8^{1}	9	10^{2}	14	12		13	4	2	11^{3}			7											16
1		4	5		9		8^{2}		11^{3}	7			14	3	2	12	10^{1}		6		13									17
1		3	5		8			7^{2}	13	10^{3}	12		14	4	2	11			6		9^{1}									18
1		3		5	8		6■	9^{3}	13	12				4	14	10^{1}		2	7		11^{2}									19
1		3	4	5^{3}	6			9	10	11^{2}		13		14	12			2	7		8^{1}									20
1		3		5	6			9^{1}	10^{3}	12		14	13	4		11		2	7		8^{2}									21
1		3		5	6			9^{2}	12	11			13	4		10^{1}		2	7		8									22
1		3	13	5^{3}	7			9	12	11			14	4		10^{1}		2	6		8^{2}									23
1		3	5		6			9	13	11			12	4	14	10^{3}		2^{1}	7^{2}		8									24
1		3	5		6		12	9^{3}	10^{1}	11			14	4	2				7		8^{2}	13								25
1		3	5^{2}		6		8	9	10^{3}	11			12	4		13		2	7^{1}		14									26
1		3		5	7		12	9^{3}	10	13			14	4	2	11^{2}			6^{1}		8									27
1	5	3	4		6		8		11	12				2						7	9	10^{1}								28
1	5	3	2		7		6		11^{1}	13			14	4							8	10^{3}	9^{2}	12						29
1			5^{1}		6		8	12	13	10	9^{2}			4	2						7				3	11				30
1		14	4		9		7	8^{3}		11^{1}	12				2	13			6^{2}		5				3	10				31
1	12		4		8		7	9	10^{2}	13					2^{1}				6		5				3	11				32
1		14	4		6		8	9^{1}	12	11^{2}					2				7^{3}	13	5				3	10				33
1			4		7		8	9^{1}	14	11				13	2		12			6^{3}	5				3	10^{2}				34
1		3	5		8		9^{1}	6	11	12	10^{2}				2					13	7				4					35
1		3	5		6			9	10^{1}	11				12	2		13			7^{2}	8■				4					36
1		3	5		8			7	11^{2}	10		14		13	2		12		9^{1}	6^{3}					4					37
1		3	5		7		8	10^{1}	12	6	13				2		14								4	11^{3}	9^{2}			38
1		3	5		7		8	6	11^{2}	9^{1}	10				2		12								4		13			39
1		3^{1}	5		8		7	6^{2}	11	9	10^{3}			13	2						12				4	14				40
1			5■		7		6^{2}		8^{1}	10				4	2■		13			14	9				3	11^{3}		12		41
1		3	5^{3}		7		8		12	6	10^{2}			2						14	9				4	11^{1}	13			42
					8		7		11^{2}	6^{1}				5	2		13				9				4	10	12	3	1	43
1		4			8		7	12	11	6				5	2^{1}						9				3		10^{2}	13		44
1	5	3			8		7	10^{1}	11	9				4							6				2	12				45
1	2	3	5^{3}		6		8	9^{2}	12	11	13								7^{1}	14					4	10				46

FA Cup
Third Round — Shrewsbury T — (a) — 1-1
Replay — Shrewsbury T — (h) — 2-3

Carabao Cup
Second Round — Huddersfield T — (h) — 2-0
Third Round — Nottingham F — (a) — 2-3

Checkatrade Trophy (Stoke C U21)
Group A (N) — Sunderland — (a) — 0-0
(Sunderland won 4-2 on penalties)
Group A (N) — Morecambe — (a) — 2-1
Group A (N) — Carlisle U — (a) — 1-1
(Stoke C U21 won 5-4 on penalties)
Second Round (N) — Port Vale — (a) — 0-4

SUNDERLAND

FOUNDATION

A Scottish schoolmaster named James Allan, working at Hendon Board School, took the initiative in the foundation of Sunderland in 1879 when they were formed as The Sunderland and District Teachers' Association FC at a meeting in the Adults School, Norfolk Street. Due to financial difficulties, they quickly allowed members from outside the teaching profession and so became Sunderland AFC in October 1880.

Stadium of Light, Sunderland, Tyne and Wear SR5 1SU.

Telephone: (0371) 911 1200.

Fax: (0191) 551 5123.

Ticket Office: (0371) 911 1973.

Website: www.safc.com

Email: enquiries@safc.com

Ground Capacity: 48,095.

Record Attendance: 75,118 v Derby Co, FA Cup 6th rd replay, 8 March 1933 (at Roker Park); 48,335 v Liverpool, Premier League, 13 April 2002 (at Stadium of Light).

Pitch Measurements: 105m × 68m (115yd × 74.5yd).

Chairman: Stewart Donald.

Executive Director: Charlie Methven.

Managing Director: Tony Davison.

Manager: Jack Ross.

Assistant Manager: James Fowler.

Colours: Red and white striped shirts, black shorts with red trim, red socks with white trim.

Year Formed: 1879.

Turned Professional: 1886.

Previous Names: 1879, Sunderland and District Teachers AFC; 1880, Sunderland.

Club Nickname: 'The Black Cats'.

Grounds: 1879, Blue House Field, Hendon; 1882, Groves Field, Ashbrooke; 1883, Horatio Street; 1884, Abbs Field, Fulwell; 1886, Newcastle Road; 1898, Roker Park; 1997, Stadium of Light.

First Football League Game: 13 September 1890, Football League, v Burnley (h) L 2–3 – Kirtley; Porteous, Oliver; Wilson, Auld, Gibson; Spence (1), Miller, Campbell (1), Scott, Davy Hannah.

Record League Victory: 9–1 v Newcastle U (a), Division 1, 5 December 1908 – Roose; Forster, Melton; Daykin, Thomson, Low; Mordue (1), Hogg (3), Brown, Holley (3), Bridgett (2).

Record Cup Victory: 11–1 v Fairfield, FA Cup 1st rd, 2 February 1895 – Doig; McNeill, Johnston; Dunlop, McCreadie (1), Wilson; Gillespie (1), Millar (5), Campbell, Jimmy Hannah (3), Scott (1).

HONOURS

League Champions: Division 1 – 1892–93, 1894–95, 1901–02, 1912–13, 1935–36; Football League 1891–92; FL C – 2004–05, 2006–07; First Division – 1995–96, 1998–99; Division 2 – 1975–76; Division 3 – 1987–88.
Runners-up: Division 1 – 1893–94, 1897–98, 1900–01, 1922–23, 1934–35; Division 2 – 1963–64, 1979–80.

FA Cup Winners: 1937, 1973.
Runners-up: 1913, 1992.

League Cup: *Runners-up:* 1985, 2014.

League Trophy: *Runners-up:* 2019.

European Competitions
European Cup-Winners' Cup: 1973–74.

THE SUN FACT FILE

Sunderland were involved in an extraordinary game on the opening day of the 1894–95 season. The scheduled referee arrived late and a local replacement was appointed. After 45 minutes play, with The Black Cats leading Derby County 3-0, the original referee turned up and ordered the match to recommence. Undaunted Sunderland went on to win 8-0, thus making their aggregate over the 135 minutes played as 11-0.

Record Defeat: 0–8 v Sheff Wed, Division 1, 26 December 1911; 0–8 v West Ham U, Division 1, 19 October 1968; 0–8 v Watford, Division 1, 25 September 1982; 0–8 v Southampton, Premier League, 18 October 2014.

Most League Points (2 for a win): 61, Division 2, 1963–64.

Most League Points (3 for a win): 105, Division 1, 1998–99.

Most League Goals: 109, Division 1, 1935–36.

Highest League Scorer in Season: Dave Halliday, 43, Division 1, 1928–29.

Most League Goals in Total Aggregate: Charlie Buchan, 209, 1911–25.

Most League Goals in One Match: 5, Charlie Buchan v Liverpool, Division 1, 7 December 1919; 5, Bobby Gurney v Bolton W, Division 1, 7 December 1935; 5, Dominic Sharkey v Norwich C, Division 2, 20 February 1962.

Most Capped Player: Seb Larsson, 59 (113), Sweden.

Most League Appearances: Jim Montgomery, 537, 1962–77.

Youngest League Player: Derek Forster, 15 years 184 days v Leicester C, 22 August 1964.

Record Transfer Fee Received: £25,000,000 (rising to £30,000,000) from Everton for Jordan Pickford, June 2017.

Record Transfer Fee Paid: £13,800,000 (rising to £17,100,000) to FC Lorient for Didier Ndong, August 2016.

Football League Record: 1890 Elected to Division 1; 1958–64 Division 2; 1964–70 Division 1; 1970–76 Division 2; 1976–77 Division 1; 1977–80 Division 2; 1980–85 Division 1; 1985–87 Division 2; 1987–88 Division 3; 1988–90 Division 2; 1990–91 Division 1; 1991–92 Division 2; 1992–96 Division 1; 1996–97 Premier League; 1997–99 Division 1; 1999–2003 Premier League; 2003–04 Division 1; 2004–05 FL C; 2005–06 Premier League; 2006–07 FL C; 2007–17 Premier League; 2017–18 FL C: 2018– FL 1.

MANAGERS

Tom Watson 1888–96
Bob Campbell 1896–99
Alex Mackie 1899–1905
Bob Kyle 1905–28
Johnny Cochrane 1928–39
Bill Murray 1939–57
Alan Brown 1957–64
George Hardwick 1964–65
Ian McColl 1965–68
Alan Brown 1968–72
Bob Stokoe 1972–76
Jimmy Adamson 1976–78
Ken Knighton 1979–81
Alan Durban 1981–84
Len Ashurst 1984–85
Lawrie McMenemy 1985–87
Denis Smith 1987–91
Malcolm Crosby 1991–93
Terry Butcher 1993
Mick Buxton 1993–95
Peter Reid 1995–2002
Howard Wilkinson 2002–03
Mick McCarthy 2003–06
Niall Quinn 2006
Roy Keane 2006–08
Ricky Sbragia 2008–09
Steve Bruce 2009–11
Martin O'Neill 2011–13
Paolo Di Canio 2013
Gus Poyet 2013–15
Dick Advocaat 2015
Sam Allardyce 2015–16
David Moyes 2016–17
Simon Grayson 2017
Chris Coleman 2017–18
Jack Ross May 2018–

LATEST SEQUENCES

Longest Sequence of League Wins: 13, 14.11.1891 – 2.4.1892.

Longest Sequence of League Defeats: 17, 18.1.2003 – 16.8.2003.

Longest Sequence of League Draws: 6, 26.3.1949 – 19.4.1949.

Longest Sequence of Unbeaten League Matches: 19, 26.12.2018 – 9.4.2019

Longest Sequence Without a League Win: 22, 21.12.2002 – 16.8.2003.

Successive Scoring Runs: 43 from 30.3.2018.

Successive Non-scoring Runs: 10 from 27.11.1976.

TEN YEAR LEAGUE RECORD

		P	*W*	*D*	*L*	*F*	*A*	*Pts*	*Pos*
2009-10	PR Lge	38	11	11	16	48	56	44	13
2010-11	PR Lge	38	12	11	15	45	56	47	10
2011-12	PR Lge	38	11	12	15	45	46	45	13
2012-13	PR Lge	38	9	12	17	41	54	39	17
2013-14	PR Lge	38	10	8	20	41	60	38	14
2014-15	PR Lge	38	7	17	14	31	53	38	16
2015-16	PR Lge	38	9	12	17	48	62	39	17
2016-17	PR Lge	38	6	6	26	29	69	24	20
2017-18	FL C	46	7	16	23	52	80	37	24
2018-19	FL 1	46	22	19	5	80	47	85	5

DID YOU KNOW ?

Sunderland were one of 16 teams participating in the Football League's Mercantile Credit Centenary Festival at Wembley Stadium in April 1988. Matches lasted for 40 minutes and the Black Cats drew their first-round tie with Wigan Athletic 0-0 before going down 2-1 in a penalty shoot-out.

SUNDERLAND – SKY BET LEAGUE ONE 2018–19 LEAGUE RECORD

Match No.	Date		Venue	Opponents	Result		H/T Score	Lg Pos.	Goalscorers	Attendance
1	Aug	4	H	Charlton Ath	W	2-1	0-1	4	Maja [65], Gooch [90]	31,075
2		11	A	Luton T	D	1-1	1-0	6	Maja [45]	10,059
3		19	H	Scunthorpe U	W	3-0	3-0	4	Power [22], Maja [25], Maguire [42]	29,876
4		22	A	Gillingham	W	4-1	3-1	4	Maguire [4], Honeyman [18], Power [20], Maja [59]	8438
5		25	A	AFC Wimbledon	W	2-1	0-1	2	Cattermole 2 [66, 83]	4848
6	Sept	1	H	Oxford U	D	1-1	0-1	4	Wyke [52]	32,193
7		8	H	Fleetwood T	D	1-1	1-1	4	Maja [38]	29,367
8		15	A	Burton Alb	L	1-2	0-2	4	Maguire [54]	4566
9		22	H	Rochdale	W	4-1	3-0	3	Maja 2 [37, 45], Gooch 2 (1 pen) [41 (p), 66]	28,764
10		29	A	Coventry C	D	1-1	0-0	4	Cattermole [49]	16,407
11	Oct	2	H	Peterborough U	D	2-2	1-0	4	Maja [21], Sinclair [79]	28,727
12		6	A	Bradford C	W	2-1	1-0	3	Maja [20], Baldwin [54]	19,487
13		20	A	Shrewsbury T	W	2-0	0-0	3	Beckles (og) [58], O'Nien [84]	9007
14		23	A	Doncaster R	W	1-0	0-0	3	Maguire [47]	11,881
15		27	H	Southend U	W	3-0	1-0	3	Honeyman [29], Maguire [53], McGeady [80]	30,894
16	Nov	3	A	Plymouth Arg	W	2-0	0-0	2	McGeady 2 (1 pen) [53, 78 (p)]	12,065
17		17	H	Wycombe W	D	1-1	0-0	2	Maja [84]	30,727
18		24	A	Walsall	D	2-2	0-0	2	McGeady [62], Gooch [89]	7868
19		27	H	Barnsley	W	4-2	3-1	2	McGeady (pen) [19], Maja [20], Gooch [32], O'Nien [83]	28,514
20	Dec	15	H	Bristol R	W	2-1	1-1	3	Matthews [45], Maja [49]	28,971
21		22	A	Portsmouth	L	1-3	0-0	3	O'Nien [57]	19,402
22		26	H	Bradford C	W	1-0	1-0	3	McGeady [31]	46,039
23		29	H	Shrewsbury T	D	1-1	1-1	3	Maja [44]	33,288
24	Jan	1	A	Blackpool	W	1-0	1-0	3	Maja [23]	10,994
25		5	A	Charlton Ath	D	1-1	1-0	3	O'Nien [2]	16,317
26		12	H	Luton T	D	1-1	1-0	3	Maguire [16]	37,791
27		19	A	Scunthorpe U	D	1-1	0-0	3	Maja [59]	7263
28	Feb	2	H	AFC Wimbledon	W	1-0	0-0	4	McGeady [67]	30,424
29		9	A	Oxford U	D	1-1	1-0	4	Dunne [34]	10,383
30		12	H	Blackpool	D	1-1	0-1	4	Baldwin [75]	27,580
31		15	H	Accrington S	D	2-2	0-1	3	Honeyman [55], McGeady [62]	28,937
32		19	H	Gillingham	W	4-2	2-2	3	Cattermole [4], Flanagan [10], Grigg (pen) [66], McGeady (pen) [77]	28,364
33		23	A	Bristol R	W	2-0	1-0	3	O'Nien [25], McGeady [55]	10,009
34	Mar	2	H	Plymouth Arg	W	2-0	1-0	3	Cattermole [32], Honeyman [87]	32,360
35		9	A	Wycombe W	D	1-1	0-1	3	Watmore [90]	8422
36		12	A	Barnsley	D	0-0	0-0	3		18,282
37		16	H	Walsall	W	2-1	1-1	3	Cattermole [33], Grigg [71]	34,647
38	Apr	3	A	Accrington S	W	3-0	2-0	3	McGeady [4], Grigg [45], Sterling [79]	3802
39		6	A	Rochdale	W	2-1	0-1	3	Wyke [56], Honeyman [89]	6546
40		9	H	Burton Alb	D	1-1	1-1	2	Baldwin [27]	29,513
41		13	H	Coventry C	L	4-5	3-3	3	Honeyman [15], Wyke [41], Grigg [45], Power [69]	36,134
42		19	H	Doncaster R	W	2-0	2-0	3	Morgan [7], Wyke [32]	34,287
43		22	A	Peterborough U	D	1-1	0-0	4	Power [87]	11,277
44		27	H	Portsmouth	D	1-1	1-1	4	Flanagan [9]	41,129
45		30	A	Fleetwood T	L	1-2	1-0	4	Cattermole [29]	4011
46	May	4	A	Southend U	L	1-2	0-1	5	Maguire (pen) [75]	10,779

Final League Position: 5

GOALSCORERS

League (80): Maja 15, McGeady 11 (3 pens), Cattermole 7, Maguire 7 (1 pen), Honeyman 6, Gooch 5 (1 pen), O'Nien 5, Grigg 4 (1 pen), Power 4, Wyke 4, Baldwin 3, Flanagan 2, Dunne 1, Matthews 1, Morgan 1, Sinclair 1, Sterling 1, Watmore 1, own goal 1.
FA Cup (3): Gooch 1, Honeyman 1, McGeady 1.
Carabao Cup (0).
Checkatrade Trophy (16): McGeady 2, Mgunga-Kimpioka 2, Gooch 1, Grigg 1, Honeyman 1, Maguire 1, Maja 1, Morgan 1, Robson 1, Sinclair 1 (1 pen), Watmore 1, Wyke 1, own goals 2.
League One Play-offs (2): Maguire 1, own goal 1.

McLaughlin J 46	Love D 4	Loovens G 11	Ozturk A 7 + 3	Matthews A 20 + 3	O'Nien L 24 + 13	Mumba B 2 + 2	Honeyman G 31 + 4	Gooch L 31 + 8	Maguire C 24 + 9	Maja J 22 + 2	Oviedo B 15 + 8	Sinclair J 7 + 6	Molyneux L — + 2	Baldwin J 34	Power M 29 + 6	Cattermole L 28 + 1	James Reece 23 + 4	McGeouch D 14 + 8	Hume D 6 + 2	Wyke C 14 + 10	Flanagan T 30 + 2	McGeady A 29 + 5	Mgunga-Kimpioka B — + 4	Ruiter R — + 1	Watmore D 3 + 8	Dunne J 12	Leadbitter G 13 + 2	Morgan L 12 + 5	Sterling K — + 8	Grigg W 15 + 3	Match No.
1	2[2]	3	4	5	6[1]	7	8	9	10	11	12	13[3]	14																		1
1		4		2	13	6[3]	7	9[1]	11	10[2]	5		14	3	8	12															2
1		3		2[3]	14	13	9[2]	8	10[1]	11	5			4	7	6	12														3
1	2[2]	3			14		9	8	10[1]	11				4	7[3]	6	5	12	13												4
1	2	3[2]	12				9	8	10	11	14			4	6[3]	7	5[1]	13													5
1	2[1]		3				7	5	10[2]	11[3]	9			4	8■	6	14	13		12											6
1		3		2[3]			9	10	8[1]	11[2]		12		4		6		7	5	13	14										7
1		4[2]		2	14		6	8	12	9	5	11[3]		3		7				10[1]		13									8
1		3					9	8[2]	10[1]	11[3]	14	12		4		6		7	5		2	13									9
1		4[3]		12			10	6	7	11	13			3	14	8		9[2]	5[1]		2										10
1				2					6	10[2]	5■	11[1]		4	8		12	7			3	9	13								11
1			14	2			13		6	11[1]		10[3]		4	8■	7	5	12			3	9[2]									12
1				2	14		13	12	7	11[2]		10[3]		3		8	5	6			4	9[1]									13
1				2	12		9	10[1]	8			11		4		6[2]	5	7			3	13									14
1				2	14		9	10[2]	8	13		11[3]		4		6	5	7[1]			3	12									15
1				2	13	14	6	10[1]	8[2]	11[3]		12		4			5	7			3	9									16
1				2			6	8	9	13	14	11[2]		4	12		5[3]	7[1]			3	10									17
1				2	12		6	8	13	11[2]	10[1]			4	7■		5				3	9									18
1				2	12		7	9[2]	8[1]	11[3]	14	13		4	6		5				3	10									19
1[1]		3		2			9	10[2]	12	11[3]	5			4	7	6						8		13	14						20
1		3■	12		2		9[2]	10	13			14		4	7	6	5					8[1]			11[3]						21
1					2			8[1]	10[2]	11[3]	5			4	6	7		14		13	3	9			12						22
1					2			8[2]	10[3]	11	5[1]			4	7	6	12			13	3	9			14						23
1					2			8	13	10[2]				4	6	7	5	12		11[1]	3	9									24
1					2			8[2]	13	11[1]				4	7		5	6		10	3	9			12						25
1					2			10[1]	9■		13			3	7		5[2]	6		11	4	8	12								26
1					2			6	11[2]	10[1]					8	7	5			12	3	9			13	4					27
1				2	13		9[3]								7		5			11[1]	4	10			14	3	6	8[2]	12		28
1				2	14		9	13						4	7		5			12		10[3]				3	6	8[2]		11[1]	29
1					2		7	8[1]						3			5[2]			12	14	10[3]			9	4	6	13		11	30
1					2		8	7[3]	12					3	14		5			11[2]		9				4	6[1]	13		10	31
1					2		9	12	8[3]						14	6[2]	5	13			3	10				4	7[1]			11	32
1					2		9								14	7	5			13	4	10[1]			8[3]	3	6	12		11[2]	33
1					2		9	14								7	5			13	4	10[3]			12	3	6	8[2]		11[1]	34
1				12	2		9■[3]	14								6	5[2]				3	10			13	4	7	8[1]		11	35
1				5	2			8[1]						3	9[2]	6						10				4	7	12	13	11	36
1				5[2]	2			12						4	9	6[1]			13	14	3	10					7	8[3]		11	37
1					2			6						4	8			7	5	10[2]	3	9[3]					14	12	13	11[1]	38
1					2		12	6[1]			13			4	8			7	5[2]	10	3							9[3]	14	11	39
1					2		6				5			4	12			7[3]		10	3		14				8	9[2]	13	11[1]	40
1					2		6				5			4	7					10	3	12	14				8[1]	9[2]	13	11[3]	41
1			3		2		9	12			5				6[3]	7				11[2]		10[1]				4	14	8		13	42
1			3		2		9[2]	13	14		5				6	7				11		10[1]				4		8[3]		12	43
1			4	14	2[2]		9[3]		12		5				7	6				11	3	10						8[1]		13	44
1			4		2		13	8	9[1]		5				6	7					3							10	12	11[2]	45
1			4	2	12			6[1]	9						7[3]			14	5	11	3						8		13	10[2]	46

FA Cup
First Round — Port Vale — (a) — 2-1
Second Round — Walsall — (a) — 1-1
Replay — Walsall — (h) — 0-1

Carabao Cup
First Round — Sheffield W — (h) — 0-2

Checkatrade Trophy
Group A (N) — Stoke C U21 — (h) — 0-0
(Sunderland won 4-2 on penalties)
Group A (N) — Carlisle U — (h) — 3-1
Group A (N) — Morecambe — (a) — 1-0
Second Round (N) — Notts Co — (h) — 2-0
Third Round — Newcastle U U21 — (h) — 4-0
Quarter-Final — Manchester C U21 — (h) — 2-0
Semi-Final — Bristol R — (a) — 2-0
Final — Portsmouth — (Wembley) — 2-2
(aet; Portsmouth won 5-4 on penalties)

League One Play-offs
Semi-Final 1st leg — Portsmouth — (h) — 1-0
Semi-Final 2nd leg — Portsmouth — (a) — 0-0
Final — Charlton Ath — (Wembley) — 1-2

SWANSEA CITY

FOUNDATION

The earliest Association Football in Wales was played in the northern part of the country and no international took place in the south until 1894, when a local paper still thought it necessary to publish an outline of the rules and an illustration of the pitch markings. There had been an earlier Swansea club, but this has no connection with Swansea Town (now City) formed at a public meeting in June 1912.

Liberty Stadium, Morfa, Landore, Swansea SA1 2FA.

Telephone: (01792) 616 400.

Fax: (01792) 616 606.

Ticket Office: (01792) 616 400.

Website: www.swanseacity.com

Email: info@swanseacityfc.com

Ground Capacity: 21,088.

Record Attendance: 32,796 v Arsenal, FA Cup 4th rd, 17 February 1968 (at Vetch Field); 20,972 v Liverpool, Premier League, 1 May 2016 (at Liberty Stadium).

Pitch Measurements: 105m × 68m (115yd × 74.5yd).

Chairman: Trevor Birch.

Chief Operating Officer: Chris Pearlman.

Head Coach: Steve Cooper.

Assistant Coach: Mike Marsh.

Colours: White shirts with black trim, white shorts with black trim, white socks with black trim.

Year Formed: 1912.

Turned Professional: 1912.

Previous Name: 1912, Swansea Town; 1970, Swansea City.

Club Nicknames: 'The Swans', 'The Jacks'.

Grounds: 1912, Vetch Field; 2005, Liberty Stadium.

First Football League Game: 28 August 1920, Division 3, v Portsmouth (a) L 0–3 – Crumley; Robson, Evans; Smith, Holdsworth, Williams; Hole, Ivor Jones, Edmundson, Rigsby, Spottiswood.

Record League Victory: 8–0 v Hartlepool U, Division 4, 1 April 1978 – Barber; Evans, Bartley, Lally (1) (Morris), May, Bruton, Kevin Moore, Robbie James (3 incl. 1p), Curtis (3), Toshack (1), Chappell.

Record Cup Victory: 12–0 v Sliema W (Malta), ECWC 1st rd 1st leg, 15 September 1982 – Davies; Marustik, Hadziabdic (1), Irwin (1), Kennedy, Rajkovic (1), Loveridge (2) (Leighton James), Robbie James, Charles (2), Stevenson (1), Latchford (1) (Walsh (3)).

Record Defeat: 0–8 v Liverpool, FA Cup 3rd rd, 9 January 1990; 0–8 v Monaco, ECWC, 1st rd 2nd leg, 1 October 1991.

Most League Points (2 for a win): 62, Division 3 (S), 1948–49.

Most League Points (3 for a win): 92, FL 1, 2007–08.

HONOURS

League Champions: FL 1 – 2007–08; Division 3S – 1924–25, 1948–49; Third Division – 1999–2000.

FA Cup: semi-final – 1926, 1964.

League Cup Winners: 2013.

League Trophy Winners: 1994, 2006.

Welsh Cup Winners: 11 times; *Runners-up:* 8 times.

European Competitions
Europa League: 2013–14.
European Cup-Winners' Cup: 1961–62, 1966–67, 1981–82, 1982–83, 1983–84, 1989–90, 1991–92.

THE Sun FACT FILE

When Swansea Town manager Billy McCandless led the team to the Division Three South title in 1948–49 it completed a remarkable personal run of three titles in four consecutive peacetime seasons. Even more remarkable was the fact that he achieved this feat with three different South Wales Football League clubs, having previously gained similar success with Newport County (1938–39) and Cardiff City (1946–47).

Most League Goals: 90, Division 2, 1956–57.

Highest League Scorer in Season: Cyril Pearce, 35, Division 2, 1931–32.

Most League Goals in Total Aggregate: Ivor Allchurch, 166, 1949–58, 1965–68.

Most League Goals in One Match: 5, Jack Fowler v Charlton Ath, Division 3S, 27 December 1924.

Most Capped Player: Ashley Williams, 64 (86), Wales.

Most League Appearances: Wilfred Milne, 587, 1919–37.

Youngest League Player: Nigel Dalling, 15 years 289 days v Southport, 6 December 1974.

Record Transfer Fee Received: £40,000,000 (rising to £45,000,000) from Everton for Gylfi Sigurdsson, August 2017.

Record Transfer Fee Paid: £18,000,000 to West Ham U for André Ayew, January 2018.

Football League Record: 1920 Original Member of Division 3; 1921–25 Division 3 (S); 1925–47 Division 2; 1947–49 Division 3 (S); 1949–65 Division 2; 1965–67 Division 3; 1967–70 Division 4; 1970–73 Division 3; 1973–78 Division 4; 1978–79 Division 3; 1979–81 Division 2; 1981–83 Division 1; 1983–84 Division 2; 1984–86 Division 3; 1986–88 Division 4; 1988–92 Division 3; 1992–96 Division 2; 1996–2000 Division 3; 2000–01 Division 2; 2001–04 Division 3; 2004–05 FL 2; 2005–08 FL 1; 2008–11 FL C; 2011–18 Premier League; 2018– FL C.

LATEST SEQUENCES

Longest Sequence of League Wins: 9, 27.11.1999 – 22.01.2000.

Longest Sequence of League Defeats: 9, 26.1.1991 – 19.3.1991.

Longest Sequence of League Draws: 8, 25.11.2008 – 28.12.2008.

Longest Sequence of Unbeaten League Matches: 19, 19.10.1970 – 9.3.1971.

Longest Sequence Without a League Win: 15, 25.3.1989 – 2.9.1989.

Successive Scoring Runs: 27 from 28.8.1947.

Successive Non-scoring Runs: 6 from 6.2.1996.

MANAGERS

Walter Whittaker 1912–14
William Bartlett 1914–15
Joe Bradshaw 1919–26
Jimmy Thomson 1927–31
Neil Harris 1934–39
Haydn Green 1939–47
Bill McCandless 1947–55
Ron Burgess 1955–58
Trevor Morris 1958–65
Glyn Davies 1965–66
Billy Lucas 1967–69
Roy Bentley 1969–72
Harry Gregg 1972–75
Harry Griffiths 1975–77
John Toshack 1978–83 *(resigned October re-appointed in December)* 1983–84
Colin Appleton 1984
John Bond 1984–85
Tommy Hutchison 1985–86
Terry Yorath 1986–89
Ian Evans 1989–90
Terry Yorath 1990–91
Frank Burrows 1991–95
Bobby Smith 1995
Kevin Cullis 1996
Jan Molby 1996–97
Micky Adams 1997
Alan Cork 1997–98
John Hollins 1998–2001
Colin Addison 2001–02
Nick Cusack 2002
Brian Flynn 2002–04
Kenny Jackett 2004–07
Roberto Martinez 2007–09
Paulo Sousa 2009–10
Brendan Rodgers 2010–12
Michael Laudrup 2012–14
Garry Monk 2014–15
Francesco Guidolin 2016
Bob Bradley 2016
Paul Clement 2017
Carlos Carvalhal 2017–18
Graham Potter 2018–19
Steve Cooper June 2019–

TEN YEAR LEAGUE RECORD

		P	W	D	L	F	A	Pts	Pos
2009-10	FL C	46	17	18	11	40	37	69	7
2010-11	FL C	46	24	8	14	69	42	80	3
2011-12	PR Lge	38	12	11	15	44	51	47	11
2012-13	PR Lge	38	11	13	14	47	51	46	9
2013-14	PR Lge	38	11	9	18	54	54	42	12
2014-15	PR Lge	38	16	8	14	46	49	56	8
2015-16	PR Lge	38	12	11	15	42	52	47	12
2016-17	PR Lge	38	12	5	21	45	70	41	15
2017-18	PR Lge	38	8	9	21	28	56	33	18
2018-19	FL C	46	18	11	17	65	62	65	10

DID YOU KNOW?

Floodlights were installed at the then Swansea Town's Vetch Field ground in time for the start of the 1960–61 season. They were formally opened with a prestigious friendly against Hibernian in September 1960 which resulted in a 4-4 draw.

SWANSEA CITY – SKY BET CHAMPIONSHIP 2018–19 LEAGUE RECORD

Match No.	*Date*		*Venue*	*Opponents*	*Result*		*H/T Score*	*Lg Pos.*	*Goalscorers*	*Attendance*
1	Aug	4	A	Sheffield U	W	2-1	0-0	3	McBurnie [71], Dhanda [85]	24,654
2		11	H	Preston NE	W	1-0	1-0	4	Fulton [32]	19,352
3		17	A	Birmingham C	D	0-0	0-0	2		20,083
4		21	H	Leeds U	D	2-2	1-1	3	McBurnie 2 [24, 51]	20,860
5		25	H	Bristol C	L	0-1	0-1	10		20,522
6	Sept	1	A	Millwall	W	2-1	0-0	6	Naughton [76], McBurnie [85]	12,440
7		15	H	Nottingham F	D	0-0	0-0	6		19,522
8		18	A	Stoke C	L	0-1	0-0	10		22,078
9		22	A	Middlesbrough	D	0-0	0-0	14		22,881
10		29	H	QPR	W	3-0	1-0	7	Baker-Richardson [16], Roberts [76], Fulton [83]	18,633
11	Oct	2	A	Wigan Ath	D	0-0	0-0	6		8964
12		6	H	Ipswich T	L	2-3	1-2	10	Donacien (og) [8], Celina [79]	18,810
13		20	A	Aston Villa	L	0-1	0-1	15		41,326
14		23	H	Blackburn R	W	3-1	0-1	8	Raya (og) [64], Roberts [68], Celina [85]	18,035
15		27	H	Reading	W	2-0	1-0	8	McBurnie 2 (1 pen) [38 (p), 84]	18,785
16	Nov	3	A	Rotherham U	L	1-2	1-0	9	McBurnie [25]	9006
17		10	A	Bolton W	W	1-0	1-0	8	McKay [15]	14,090
18		24	H	Norwich C	L	1-4	1-3	9	James [41]	18,780
19		28	H	WBA	L	1-2	1-2	11	McBurnie [10]	17,865
20	Dec	1	A	Derby Co	L	1-2	0-2	13	Tomori (og) [87]	26,167
21		8	A	Brentford	W	3-2	3-1	12	Routledge [1], Mepham (og) [22], Fer [27]	9442
22		15	H	Sheffield W	W	2-1	0-0	9	Celina [71], Routledge [72]	18,692
23		22	A	Hull C	L	2-3	1-0	12	Bony [3], Celina [88]	10,848
24		26	H	Aston Villa	L	0-1	0-0	12		20,775
25		29	H	Wigan Ath	D	2-2	0-2	13	Burn (og) [59], van der Hoorn [81]	18,591
26	Jan	1	A	Reading	W	4-1	3-0	12	McBurnie 2 (1 pen) [2, 48 (p)], Roberts [30], van der Hoorn [45]	15,644
27		12	A	Preston NE	D	1-1	0-0	13	Baker-Richardson [55]	11,604
28		19	H	Sheffield U	W	1-0	0-0	9	McBurnie [65]	18,673
29		29	H	Birmingham C	D	3-3	1-1	11	James [22], McBurnie 2 [65, 90]	18,194
30	Feb	2	A	Bristol C	L	0-2	0-0	13		23,560
31		9	H	Millwall	W	1-0	1-0	11	Byers [43]	18,650
32		13	A	Leeds U	L	1-2	0-2	12	McBurnie (pen) [87]	34,044
33		23	A	Sheffield W	L	1-3	0-3	12	McBurnie [69]	22,935
34	Mar	2	H	Bolton W	W	2-0	0-0	13	McBurnie [80], Celina [90]	17,880
35		8	A	Norwich C	L	0-1	0-0	14		26,360
36		13	A	WBA	L	0-3	0-1	15		20,282
37		30	A	Nottingham F	L	1-2	0-0	15	Roberts [76]	28,469
38	Apr	2	H	Brentford	W	3-0	2-0	14	Dyer 2 [1, 34], James [78]	17,197
39		6	H	Middlesbrough	W	3-1	2-0	13	Grimes (pen) [34], Routledge [38], Roberts [71]	18,171
40		9	H	Stoke C	W	3-1	2-1	13	James [23], van der Hoorn [40], McBurnie [86]	17,804
41		13	A	QPR	L	0-4	0-3	13		13,872
42		19	H	Rotherham U	W	4-3	1-2	12	McBurnie 2 [36, 79], McKay [50], Byers [69]	18,527
43		22	A	Ipswich T	W	1-0	0-0	10	Routledge [57]	17,247
44		27	H	Hull C	D	2-2	1-0	11	McBurnie 2 [37, 66]	18,192
45	May	1	H	Derby Co	D	1-1	0-1	9	Routledge [66]	18,434
46		5	A	Blackburn R	D	2-2	2-1	10	Baker-Richardson [25], McBurnie [35]	16,227

Final League Position: 10

GOALSCORERS

League (65): McBurnie 22 (3 pens), Celina 5, Roberts 5, Routledge 5, James 4, Baker-Richardson 3, van der Hoorn 3, Byers 2, Dyer 2, Fulton 2, McKay 2, Bony 1, Dhanda 1, Fer 1, Grimes 1 (1 pen), Naughton 1, own goals 5.
FA Cup (13): Celina 3, McBurnie 2, Baker-Richardson 1, Byers 1, Dyer 1, Fulton 1, Grimes 1 (1 pen), James 1, McKay 1, own goal 1.
Carabao Cup (0).
Checkatrade Trophy (3): Garrick 1, Lewis 1, Maric 1.

Nordfeldt K 22	Roberts C 44 + 1	van der Hoorn M 46	Fernandez F 1	Olsson M 13 + 4	Celina B 33 + 5	Fulton J 21 + 12	Carroll T 8 + 4	Asoro J 4 + 10	McBurnie O 37 + 5	McKay B 16 + 14	Montero J — + 12	Grimes M 40 + 5	Dhanda Y 1 + 4	Rodon J 23 + 4	Mulder E 24 + 1	Fer L 15 + 10	James D 28 + 5	Naughton K 31 + 4	Baker-Richardson C 6 + 11	John D 7 + 3	Carter-Vickers C 23 + 7	Dyer N 18 + 4	Byers G 20 + 1	Routledge W 22 + 2	Harries C 2	Bony W 1 + 6	Narsingh L — + 2	Match No.
1	2	3	4	5¹	6	7³	8	9²	10	11	12	13	14															1
1³	2	3		5	7	6	8	9²	10	11¹		13		4	12	14												2
	2	3		5	7	6	8²	9¹	10	11³		14		4	1	13	12											3
	8	3		5¹	9	6	13	14	11	10³	12			4	1	7²		2										4
	2	3		5	6	7	8³	9¹	10²	11	13	12		4	1	14												5
	2	3		5²	9		13		10		14	8		4	1	7¹	6³	12	11■									6
	2	3			11²	7¹		13	10	6		8	9³	4	1			12		5	14							7
	2	3		5				14	13			8	12		1		11³	7			4	6¹	9²	10				8
	2	3		5			12		11	8²		7		4	1		13	6				14	9¹	10³				9
	5	3		14	8²	12	7		11			9		4	1	13		2	10¹				6³					10
1	9	3		12	8	6²	7¹		10	11³		5		4		13		2						14				11
1	7	3¹			9		6	12	11	14		5		4		13	10	2³					8²					12
1	5	3		8	10	6	13		11	9²		14		2		7¹	12								4³			13
1	2	3		5³	11	12	7²		10¹			8				13	9	6	14		4							14
1	8	3		5¹	9	6³			11			7		4		12	10²	2		14	13							15
1	8	3			9	6¹			11	12		5		4		7	10	2²	13									16
	2	3		12	9²	6			11	8³	13	5		4	1	7	10¹									14		17
	8	3		13	9³	6¹			11	14		5		4	1	7²	10	2								12		18
	5¹	3		8	9				10	12	13	7		4	1	6²	11³				2					14		19
	5	3			10	6³			9	14	13	7		4	1	12	11			8²	2¹							20
	12	3		5¹		13			11	9		7		4	1	6		2			14	10²		8³				21
	2	3¹			14				11	9	13	7		4	1	6		5³			12	10²		8				22
	2	3			14				12	9		7		4	1	6	13			5¹		10²		8		11³		23
	2	3			9	6³			10		12	7			1	8¹	11²	5			4	14				13		24
		2			8	6³			10		13	7			1		9	12	11¹		3			5	4²	14		25
	5	3			9	13			11³			7		4	1	6		2	12		14	8¹		10²				26
	5	3			9					14	13	7		4	1	6		2¹	11³			8²		10		12		27
	5	3			9	14			11			7		4¹	1	6	13	2			12	8²		10³				28
	5¹	3			8	12			10	14	13	7			1	6²	11	2			4	9³						29
	2³	3			10	6		12	11	13		7			1				14	5	4	8¹	9²					30
	2	3			8	14			13			7			1		9	12	10²	5³	4		6	11¹				31
	6	3			11	7²		12	13	10³		5			1		9¹	2			4		8				14	32
1	2²	3			10				9	14		8					11	6³	13	5¹	4		7	12				33
1	5¹	3			12	14			11			7					9	2	13		4	8²	6³	10				34
1	2	3			9					12		7					11	5	13	14	4	8²	6³	10¹				35
1	2	3			9					12		7	14				11	5³	13		4	8¹	6	10⁴				36
1	2	3			9				11	12		7					10	5	13		4	8¹	6²					37
1	2	3			9¹	6			13			4					10²	5	12		14	8³	7	11				38
1	2	3³			9			12				7		14			10¹	5			4	8	6	11²			13	39
1	2	3				12		14	9	13		6					10³	5¹			4	8	7	11²				40
1	2	3			13	12			9			7		14			10	5³			4	8²	6¹	11				41
1	2	3				6²			11	8³		7		13			10	5	14		4		12	9¹				42
1	2	3				6¹			10			7		14		13	11²	5			4	12	9	8³				43
1	2	3			13	12			9	14		7					10	5²			4	8³	6¹	11				44
1	2	3				13		14	9	8³		7					10¹	5²		12	4		6	11				45
1	5	2				7		13	9			4	12						10¹	8	3	14	6³	11²				46

FA Cup

Third Round	Aston Villa	(a)	3-0
Fourth Round	Gillingham	(h)	4-1
Fifth Round	Brentford	(h)	4-1
Sixth Round	Manchester C	(h)	2-3

Carabao Cup

Second Round	Crystal Palace	(h)	0-1

Checkatrade Trophy (Swansea C U21)

Group G (S)	Stevenage	(a)	0-5
Group G (S)	AFC Wimbledon	(a)	1-0
Group G (S)	Charlton Ath	(a)	1-0
Second Round (S)	Bristol R	(h)	1-2

SWINDON TOWN

FOUNDATION

It is generally accepted that Swindon Town came into being in 1881, although there is no firm evidence that the club's founder, Rev. William Pitt, captain of the Spartans (an offshoot of a cricket club), changed his club's name to Swindon Town before 1883, when the Spartans amalgamated with St Mark's Young Men's Friendly Society.

The Energy Check County Ground, County Road, Swindon, Wiltshire SN1 2ED.

Telephone: (0330) 002 1879.

Ticket Office: (0330) 002 1879.

Website: www.swindontownfc.co.uk

Email: reception@swindontownfc.co.uk

Ground Capacity: 15,728.

Record Attendance: 32,000 v Arsenal, FA Cup 3rd rd, 15 January 1972.

Pitch Measurements: 100m × 68m (109.5yd × 74.5yd).

Chairman: Lee Power.

Chief Executive: Steve Anderson.

Manager: Richie Wellens.

Assistant Manager: Noel Hunt.

Colours: Red shirts with white trim, red shorts with white trim, red socks with white trim.

Year Formed: 1881* (*see Foundation*).

Turned Professional: 1894.

Club Nickname: 'The Robins'.

Grounds: 1881, The Croft; 1896, County Ground (renamed The Energy Check County Ground 2017).

First Football League Game: 28 August 1920, Division 3, v Luton T (h) W 9–1 – Nash; Kay, Macconachie; Langford, Hawley, Wareing; Jefferson (1), Fleming (4), Rogers, Batty (2), Davies (1), (1 og).

Record League Victory: 9–1 v Luton T, Division 3 (S), 28 August 1920 – Nash; Kay, Macconachie; Langford, Hawley, Wareing; Jefferson (1), Fleming (4), Rogers, Batty (2), Davies (1), (1 og).

Record Cup Victory: 10–1 v Farnham U Breweries (a), FA Cup 1st rd (replay), 28 November 1925 – Nash; Dickenson, Weston, Archer, Bew, Adey; Denyer (2), Wall (1), Richardson (4), Johnson (3), Davies.

Record Defeat: 1–10 v Manchester C, FA Cup 4th rd (replay), 25 January 1930.

Most League Points (2 for a win): 64, Division 3, 1968–69.

HONOURS

League Champions: Second Division – 1995–96; FL 2 – 2011–12; Division 4 – 1985–86.
Runners-up: Division 3 – 1962–63, 1968–69.

FA Cup: semi-final – 1910, 1912.

League Cup Winners: 1969.

League Trophy: *Runners-up:* 2012.

Anglo-Italian Cup Winners: 1970.

THE Sun FACT FILE

Swindon Town finished as champions of the Southern League in 1910–11, giving them the opportunity to play the Football League champions Manchester United for the FA Charity Shield. The game, played at Stamford Bridge in September 1911, attracted a reported attendance of 12,000 who saw United 4-3 up at half-time and go on to win 8-4.

Most League Points (3 for a win): 102, Division 4, 1985–86.

Most League Goals: 100, Division 3 (S), 1926–27.

Highest League Scorer in Season: Harry Morris, 47, Division 3 (S), 1926–27.

Most League Goals in Total Aggregate: Harry Morris, 216, 1926–33.

Most League Goals in One Match: 5, Harry Morris v QPR, Division 3 (S), 18 December 1926; 5, Harry Morris v Norwich C, Division 3 (S), 26 April 1930; 5, Keith East v Mansfield T, Division 3, 20 November 1965.

Most Capped Player: Rod Thomas, 30 (50), Wales.

Most League Appearances: John Trollope, 770, 1960–80.

Youngest League Player: Paul Rideout, 16 years 107 days v Hull C, 29 November 1980.

Record Transfer Fee Received: A combined £4,000,000 from QPR for Ben Gladwin and Massimo Luongo, May 2015.

Record Transfer Fee Paid: £800,000 to West Ham U for Joey Beauchamp, August 1994.

Football League Record: 1920 Original Member of Division 3; 1921–58 Division 3 (S); 1958–63 Division 3; 1963–65 Division 2; 1965–69 Division 3; 1969–74 Division 2; 1974–82 Division 3; 1982–86 Division 4; 1986–87 Division 3; 1987–92 Division 2; 1992–93 Division 1; 1993–94 Premier League; 1994–95 Division 1; 1995–96 Division 2; 1996–2000 Division 1; 2000–04 Division 2; 2004–06 FL 1; 2006–07 FL 2; 2007–11 FL 1; 2011–12 FL 2; 2012–17 FL 1; 2017– FL 2.

MANAGERS

Sam Allen 1902–33
Ted Vizard 1933–39
Neil Harris 1939–41
Louis Page 1945–53
Maurice Lindley 1953–55
Bert Head 1956–65
Danny Williams 1965–69
Fred Ford 1969–71
Dave Mackay 1971–72
Les Allen 1972–74
Danny Williams 1974–78
Bobby Smith 1978–80
John Trollope 1980–83
Ken Beamish 1983–84
Lou Macari 1984–89
Ossie Ardiles 1989–91
Glenn Hoddle 1991–93
John Gorman 1993–94
Steve McMahon 1994–98
Jimmy Quinn 1998–2000
Colin Todd 2000
Andy King 2000–01
Roy Evans 2001
Andy King 2001–05
Iffy Onuora 2005–06
Dennis Wise 2006
Paul Sturrock 2006–07
Maurice Malpas 2008
Danny Wilson 2008–11
Paul Hart 2011
Paolo Di Canio 2011–13
Kevin MacDonald 2013
Mark Cooper 2013–15
Martin Ling 2015
Luke Williams 2015–17
David Flitcroft 2017–18
Phil Brown 2018
Richie Wellens November 2018–

LATEST SEQUENCES

Longest Sequence of League Wins: 10, 31.12.2011 – 28.2.2012.

Longest Sequence of League Defeats: 8, 29.8.2005 – 8.10.2005.

Longest Sequence of League Draws: 6, 22.11.1991 – 28.12.1991.

Longest Sequence of Unbeaten League Matches: 22, 12.1.1986 – 23.8.1986.

Longest Sequence Without a League Win: 19, 30.10.1999 – 4.3.2000.

Successive Scoring Runs: 31 from 17.4.1926.

Successive Non-scoring Runs: 5 from 5.4.1997.

TEN YEAR LEAGUE RECORD

		P	W	D	L	F	A	Pts	Pos
2009-10	FL 1	46	22	16	8	73	57	82	5
2010-11	FL 1	46	9	14	23	50	72	41	24
2011-12	FL 2	46	29	6	11	75	32	93	1
2012-13	FL 1	46	20	14	12	72	39	74	6
2013-14	FL 1	46	19	9	18	63	59	66	8
2014-15	FL 1	46	23	10	13	76	57	79	4
2015-16	FL 1	46	16	11	19	64	71	59	15
2016-17	FL 1	46	11	11	24	44	66	44	22
2017-18	FL 2	46	20	8	18	67	65	68	9
2018-19	FL 2	46	16	16	14	59	56	64	13

DID YOU KNOW ?

Sam Parkin became the first Swindon Town player for over 20 years to score a hat-trick on his debut when he netted all three goals in the Robins' 3-1 win over Barnsley in August 2002. He finished the season as the club's leading scorer with 25 League goals and in the next two seasons achieved 20-goal tallies before moving to Ipswich Town.

SWINDON TOWN – SKY BET LEAGUE TWO 2018–19 LEAGUE RECORD

Match No.	Date	Venue	Opponents	Result		H/T Score	Lg Pos.	Goalscorers	Attendance
1	Aug 4	H	Macclesfield T	W	3-2	0-0	6	Doughty 3 (2 pens) [48, 90 (p), 90 (p)]	7024
2	11	A	Lincoln C	L	1-4	1-2	14	Doughty (pen) [44]	8405
3	18	H	Tranmere R	W	3-2	1-2	6	Adebayo [20], Richards [60], Romanski [73]	6106
4	21	A	Crawley T	D	2-2	2-0	7	Dunne [13], Anderson [37]	2050
5	25	A	Forest Green R	D	1-1	1-1	11	Doughty (pen) [11]	3458
6	Sept 1	H	Milton Keynes D	D	1-1	0-1	12	Adebayo [90]	6620
7	8	A	Morecambe	W	1-0	1-0	7	Adebayo [26]	1559
8	15	H	Bury	L	1-2	0-1	14	Woolfenden [50]	6087
9	22	A	Yeovil T	W	3-0	0-0	8	Alzate [59], Taylor [79], Adebayo [89]	4201
10	29	H	Oldham Ath	D	0-0	0-0	9		6181
11	Oct 2	A	Crewe Alex	L	0-1	0-1	11		2761
12	6	H	Northampton T	D	1-1	0-0	13	Taylor [73]	6138
13	13	A	Exeter C	L	0-2	0-1	13		4506
14	20	H	Mansfield T	D	0-0	0-0	12		6208
15	23	H	Cambridge U	L	0-2	0-2	15		5824
16	27	A	Notts Co	W	2-1	0-1	13	Alzate [65], Turley (og) [80]	6114
17	Nov 3	A	Colchester U	L	0-1	0-1	16		3227
18	17	H	Carlisle U	L	0-4	0-1	18		6722
19	24	A	Port Vale	W	1-0	1-0	14	Adebayo [11]	3877
20	27	H	Stevenage	W	3-2	3-1	12	Pryce 2 [1, 45], Twine [6]	5273
21	Dec 8	H	Newport Co	W	2-1	1-0	11	Doughty [1], Woolery [82]	6204
22	15	A	Grimsby T	L	1-2	1-1	13	Taylor [28]	3809
23	22	H	Cheltenham T	D	0-0	0-0	13		7026
24	26	A	Northampton T	D	1-1	0-1	13	Anderson [63]	5759
25	29	A	Mansfield T	D	0-0	0-0	14		5311
26	Jan 1	H	Exeter C	L	0-2	0-1	14		6755
27	5	A	Macclesfield T	W	2-1	1-1	12	Richards [37], McCourt [90]	1964
28	12	H	Lincoln C	D	2-2	0-2	12	Doughty 2 (1 pen) [55 (p), 88]	6543
29	19	A	Tranmere R	W	2-1	2-0	11	Richards [20], Doughty [36]	5847
30	26	H	Crawley T	L	0-1	0-1	12		6026
31	Feb 9	A	Milton Keynes D	W	3-2	1-0	12	Doughty 2 (1 pen) [34, 73 (p)], Anderson [60]	7864
32	12	H	Forest Green R	W	2-0	2-0	10	Woolery [36], Robinson [44]	6261
33	23	H	Grimsby T	D	1-1	0-0	12	Robinson [74]	6434
34	Mar 2	H	Colchester U	W	3-0	2-0	10	Carroll [39], Woolfenden [41], Bennett [66]	6082
35	9	A	Carlisle U	L	1-2	1-1	10	Bennett [39]	4629
36	12	A	Stevenage	L	0-2	0-1	12		2194
37	16	H	Port Vale	D	0-0	0-0	13		6322
38	23	H	Morecambe	W	4-0	2-0	10	Robinson [10], Woolery [42], Conroy [66], Bennett [81]	5707
39	30	A	Bury	W	3-1	1-1	10	Woolery 2 [25, 57], Robinson [88]	3997
40	Apr 6	H	Yeovil T	D	1-1	1-0	10	Anderson [45]	6645
41	9	A	Newport Co	D	0-0	0-0	10		3314
42	13	A	Oldham Ath	D	2-2	1-1	10	Doughty (pen) [45], Bennett [60]	4064
43	19	A	Cambridge U	D	0-0	0-0	12		4380
44	22	H	Crewe Alex	L	1-2	0-2	14	Doughty (pen) [63]	6107
45	27	A	Cheltenham T	L	2-3	0-3	14	Robinson [84], Richards [90]	4306
46	May 4	H	Notts Co	W	3-1	0-0	13	Woolery [69], Robinson 2 [74, 90]	8676

Final League Position: 13

GOALSCORERS

League (59): Doughty 13 (8 pens), Robinson 7, Woolery 6, Adebayo 5, Anderson 4, Bennett 4, Richards 4, Taylor 3, Alzate 2, Pryce 2, Woolfenden 2, Carroll 1, Conroy 1, Dunne 1, McCourt 1, Romanski 1, Twine 1, own goal 1.
FA Cup (2): Alzate 1, Twine 1.
Carabao Cup (0).
Checkatrade Trophy (4): Anderson 1, Doughty 1 (1 pen), Richards 1, Woolery 1.

Vigouroux L 29	Knoyle K 38 + 4	Lancashire O 15 + 5	Conroy D 26 + 1	McGlashan J 12 + 12	Smith M 8 + 3	Doughty M 26 + 4	Taylor M 29 + 4	Anderson K 36 + 7	Alzate S 15 + 7	Adebayo E 20 + 5	Twine S 7 + 7	McCourt J 17 + 10	Romanski J 3 + 1	Diagouraga T 10 + 2	Richards M 16 + 14	Dunne J 20 + 10	Nelson S 20	Iandolo E 8 + 7	McCormick L 17	Woolfenden L 32	Woolery K 25 + 4	Pryce S 1 + 1	Carroll C 15 + 2	House B 1 + 5	Koiki A 13 + 2	Broadbent T 10 + 2	Rose D 8 + 2	Robinson T 15 + 1	Bennett K 14 + 1	Bancroft J — + 1	McGilp C — + 1	Curran T — + 1	*Match No.*
1	2	3	4	5	6^1	7	8	9	10^2	11	12	13																						1
1	2	3	4	10	8^2	7	5	6	9^1	11	12	13																						2
1	2	3		6	8^3	7	5	10^1	13	11			4	9^2	12	14																		3
1	2	3		6^2	12	7	5	10^1	13	11^3				9■	14	8■	4																		4
1	2	3		9^2	7	6	5	11	8^1	13		12			10^3		4	14																	5
1	2	3		9^1	7^2	6^3	5	11	8	13		12			10		4	14																	6
	2■	12		13		6	5	9^3	8^2	11		7			10^1		3	14	1	4													7
				6			5	13	8	11		7^1	14	12	10	2^3	3	9^2	1	4													8
		4		12	14		5	9	8^2	11		13		7	10^3	6^1	3		1	2													9
		2		12			9■	5	7	10		13		8	11^1	6^2	3		1	4													10
	12	4		13				9	8	11			5	7	10^2	6^3	3	14	1	2^1													11
	2	3		6^1			5	12	9	10	13			7	11^2	8			1	4													12
	5	2	3		8^2		6	9	12	13	10^3			7	11^1				1	4	14												13
1	2	3		12		8	5	6	9	10^2				7^1	11^3		4	14			13												14
1	2	4	3	14		8^2	5	6	9	11^1				7^3	10	12					13												15
1	2	4		9	8	11^1	5	14	13	12		6^3			10^2	7	3																16
1	2	4^1	12	6	8		10	14	13	11		7^2	5^3			9	3																17
1	13		4^3	5	12		9	11	8	10^2	14					7^1	3	6		2													18
1	2	14		13		12	7	9^1	6	10	11^2	8^3					3	5		4													19
1	2	12		13		6	8	9	7^2		11						4	5		3		10^1											20
1	2	13		12		8	7			10	11^1					6	3	5		4	9^2												21
1	2^1			12		8	7		13	10	9^3					6	3	5^2		4	11	14											22
1	2			12		9^1	8		13	10	11^2					7	3	5		4	6												23
1	2		4	10^1		7	6	9^2		12		13				8^3	3	14		5	11												24
1	2		8			6	5	11		9^1		7			12		3			4	10												25
1	2		7			8	5^1	9		10^3	14	6			13		3^2	12		4	11												26
1	2^2		3	14				9			8^1	7			11^3	12		5		4	10		6	13									27
1	2^1		3			12	5^3	9			14	8			10	6^2				4	11		7		13								28
1	13					9^2	14	10				8			11^1	7				3	6		2		5^3	4	12						29
1						8^1		9			12	7^3			10^2	6				4	11		2	14	5	3	13						30
1	2		4			8^2	5^3	10				6				13					11		14		12	3	7^1	9					31
1	2		3			9		10^3				7^2			14	12					8		6		5	4		11^1	13				32
	2		3					10				7^2			13	12			1		8		6		5	4		11	9^1				33
1	5		4					12				6^1		13		8				2	11^3		7			3		10^2	9	14			34
1	5^1		4				14	12				6^2				8				2	11^3		7	13		3		10	9				35
1	13		3				5^2	9						7^1	14	6				2	11^3		12			4		10	8				36
1	2		4					11				13			12					3	9		8		5		6^1	10	7^2				37
	2		3				12	9						13	14			1	4	11^3		8^2		5^1		6	10	7				38
	2		3					9^1						14	12			1	4	11^2		8		5	13	6	10	7^3				39
	2		3			12		11^1										1	4	9		8		5	13	6	10	7^2				40
	2		3			12		8				14			13				1	4	10^2		7^3		5		6^1	11	9				41
	2		3			6^2		11				13				12			1	4	9^3			14	5		7^1	10	8				42
	2		3			6		9^1						14	13			1	4	11			10^2	5		7^3	12	8				43
	5		4			7		11^2						14	8			1	2	12			13	9^1	3		10^3	6				44
	2^1	12	3			8^2	5	13				6			14				1	4	9^3		7					10	11				45
	2		3			6^1	13	11										1		9^3		7^2		5	4		10	8		12	14	46

FA Cup

First Round	York C	(h)	2-1
Second Round	Woking	(h)	0-1

Carabao Cup

First Round	Forest Green R	(h)	0-1

Checkatrade Trophy

Group C (S)	Chelsea U21	(h)	0-4
Group C (S)	Newport Co	(h)	1-0
Group C (S)	Plymouth Arg	(a)	3-0

TOTTENHAM HOTSPUR

FOUNDATION

The Hotspur Football Club was formed from an older cricket club in 1882. Most of the founders were old boys of St John's Presbyterian School and Tottenham Grammar School. The Casey brothers were well to the fore as the family provided the club's first goalposts (painted blue and white) and their first ball. They soon adopted the local YMCA as their meeting place, but after a couple of moves settled at the Red House.

Tottenham Hotspur Stadium, Lilywhite House, 782 High Road, Tottenham, London N17 0BX.

Telephone: (0344) 499 5000.

Fax: (01992) 761 608.

Ticket Office: (0344) 844 0102

Website: www.tottenhamhotspur.com

Email: supporterservices@tottenhamhotspur.com

Ground Capacity: 62,062.

Record Attendance: 75,038 v Sunderland, FA Cup 6th rd, 5 March 1938 (at White Hart Lane); 85,512 v Bayer Leverkusen, UEFA Champions League Group E, 2 November 2016 (at Wembley); 60,124 v Everton, Premier League, 12 May 2019) (at Tottenham Hotspur Stadium).

Pitch Measurements: 105m × 68m (115yd × 74.5yd).

Chairman: Daniel Levy.

Head Coach: Mauricio Pochettino.

Assistant Head Coach: Jesús Pérez.

Colours: White shirts with navy blue trim, navy blue shorts with white trim, white socks with navy blue trim.

Year Formed: 1882. ***Turned Professional:*** 1895.

Previous Names: 1882, Hotspur Football Club; 1884, Tottenham Hotspur.

Club Nickname: 'Spurs'.

Grounds: 1882, Tottenham Marshes; 1888, Northumberland Park; 1899, White Hart Lane; 2018, Tottenham Hotspur Stadium.

First Football League Game: 1 September 1908, Division 2, v Wolverhampton W (h) W 3–0 – Hewitson; Coquet, Burton; Morris (1), Danny Steel, Darnell; Walton, Woodward (2), Macfarlane, Bobby Steel, Middlemiss.

Record League Victory: 9–0 v Bristol R, Division 2, 22 October 1977 – Daines; Naylor, Holmes, Hoddle (1), McAllister, Perryman, Pratt, McNab, Moores (3), Lee (4), Taylor (1).

HONOURS

League Champions: Division 1 – 1950–51, 1960–61; Division 2 – 1919–20, 1949–50.
Runners-up: Premier League – 2016–17; Division 1 – 1921–22, 1951–52, 1956–57, 1962–63; Division 2 – 1908–09, 1932–33.

FA Cup Winners: 1901 (as non-league club), 1921, 1961, 1962, 1967, 1981, 1982, 1991.
Runners-up: 1987.

League Cup Winners: 1971, 1973, 1999, 2008.
Runners-up: 1982, 2002, 2009, 2015.

European Competitions
European Cup: 1961–62 *(sf)*.
Champions League: 2010–11 *(qf)*, 2016–17, 2017–18, 2018–19 *(runners-up)*.
UEFA Cup: 1971–72 *(winners)*, 1972–73 *(sf)*, 1973–74 *(runners-up)*, 1983–84 *(winners)*, 1984–85 *(qf)*, 1999–2000, 2006–07 *(qf)*, 2007–08, 2008–09.
Europa League: 2011–12, 2012–13 *(qf)*, 2013–14, 2014–15, 2015–16, 2016–17.
European Cup-Winners' Cup: 1962–63 *(winners)*, 1963–64, 1967–68, 1981–82 *(sf)*, 1982–83, 1991–92 *(qf)*.
Intertoto Cup: 1995.

THE Sun FACT FILE

Tottenham Hotspur were criticised by the Polish press for what was claimed to be rough tactics, being described as 'no angels' during the club's first ever European tie against Gornik Zabrze in September 1961. This prompted a group of fans to dress up as angels and parade around the pitch before the return leg, and this is widely credited for the introduction of the supporters' anthem 'Glory, Glory, Tottenham Hotspur'.

Record Cup Victory: 13–2 v Crewe Alex, FA Cup 4th rd (replay), 3 February 1960 – Brown; Hills, Henry; Blanchflower, Norman, Mackay; White, Harmer (1), Smith (4), Allen (5), Jones (3 incl. 1p).

Record Defeat: 0–8 v Cologne, UEFA Intertoto Cup, 22 July 1995.

Most League Points (2 for a win): 70, Division 2, 1919–20.

Most League Points (3 for a win): 86, Premier League, 2016–17.

Most League Goals: 115, Division 1, 1960–61.

Highest League Scorer in Season: Jimmy Greaves, 37, Division 1, 1962–63.

Most League Goals in Total Aggregate: Jimmy Greaves, 220, 1961–70.

Most League Goals in One Match: 5, Ted Harper v Reading, Division 2, 30 August 1930; 5, Alf Stokes v Birmingham C, Division 1, 18 September 1957; 5, Bobby Smith v Aston Villa, Division 1, 29 March 1958; 5, Jermain Defoe v Wigan Ath, Premier League, 22 November 2009.

Most Capped Player: Pat Jennings, 74 (119), Northern Ireland; Hugo Lloris, 74 (112), France.

Most League Appearances: Steve Perryman, 655, 1969–86.

Youngest League Player: Ally Dick, 16 years 301 days v Manchester C, 20 February 1982.

Record Transfer Fee Received: £85,300,000 from Real Madrid for Gareth Bale, September 2013.

Record Transfer Fee Paid: £55,500,000 (rising to £63,000,000) to Lyon for Tanguy Ndombele, July 2019.

Football League Record: 1908 Elected to Division 2; 1909–15 Division 1; 1919–20 Division 2; 1920–28 Division 1; 1928–33 Division 2; 1933–35 Division 1; 1935–50 Division 2; 1950–77 Division 1; 1977–78 Division 2; 1978–92 Division 1; 1992– Premier League.

MANAGERS

Frank Brettell 1898–99
John Cameron 1899–1906
Fred Kirkham 1907–08
Peter McWilliam 1912–27
Billy Minter 1927–29
Percy Smith 1930–35
Jack Tresadern 1935–38
Peter McWilliam 1938–42
Arthur Turner 1942–46
Joe Hulme 1946–49
Arthur Rowe 1949–55
Jimmy Anderson 1955–58
Bill Nicholson 1958–74
Terry Neill 1974–76
Keith Burkinshaw 1976–84
Peter Shreeves 1984–86
David Pleat 1986–87
Terry Venables 1987–91
Peter Shreeves 1991–92
Doug Livermore 1992–93
Ossie Ardiles 1993–94
Gerry Francis 1994–97
Christian Gross *(Head Coach)* 1997–98
George Graham 1998–2001
Glenn Hoddle 2001–03
David Pleat (*Caretaker*) 2003–04
Jacques Santini 2004
Martin Jol 2004–07
Juande Ramos 2007–08
Harry Redknapp 2008–12
Andre Villas-Boas 2012–13
Tim Sherwood 2013–14
Mauricio Pochettino May 2014–

LATEST SEQUENCES

Longest Sequence of League Wins: 13, 23.4.1960 – 1.10.1960.

Longest Sequence of League Defeats: 7, 1.1.1994 – 27.2.1994.

Longest Sequence of League Draws: 6, 9.1.1999 – 27.2.1999.

Longest Sequence of Unbeaten League Matches: 22, 31.8.1949 – 31.12.1949.

Longest Sequence Without a League Win: 16, 29.12.1934 – 13.4.1935.

Successive Scoring Runs: 32 from 24.2.1962.

Successive Non-scoring Runs: 6 from 28.12.1985.

TEN YEAR LEAGUE RECORD

		P	*W*	*D*	*L*	*F*	*A*	*Pts*	*Pos*
2009-10	PR Lge	38	21	7	10	67	41	70	4
2010-11	PR Lge	38	16	14	8	55	46	62	5
2011-12	PR Lge	38	20	9	9	66	41	69	4
2012-13	PR Lge	38	21	9	8	66	46	72	5
2013-14	PR Lge	38	21	6	11	55	51	69	6
2014-15	PR Lge	38	19	7	12	58	53	64	5
2015-16	PR Lge	38	19	13	6	69	35	70	3
2016-17	PR Lge	38	26	8	4	86	26	86	2
2017-18	PR Lge	38	23	8	7	74	36	77	3
2018-19	PR Lge	38	23	2	13	67	39	71	4

DID YOU KNOW ?

Although Tottenham Hotspur only had the third highest average attendance from the 92 Football League clubs in 1952–53, they had the most season ticket holders of any club. Their total of 7,328 tickets sold was 1,500 more than any other League club.

TOTTENHAM HOTSPUR – PREMIER LEAGUE 2018–19 LEAGUE RECORD

Match No.	Date	Venue	Opponents	Result		H/T Score	Lg Pos.	Goalscorers	Attendance
1	Aug 11	A	Newcastle U	W	2-1	2-1	5	Vertonghen 8, Alli 18	51,749
2	18	H	Fulham	W	3-1	1-0	2	Lucas Moura 43, Trippier 74, Kane 77	58,297
3	27	A	Manchester U	W	3-0	0-0	2	Kane 50, Lucas Moura 2 52, 84	74,400
4	Sept 2	A	Watford	L	1-2	0-0	5	Doucoure (og) 53	20,141
5	15	H	Liverpool	L	1-2	0-1	6	Lamela 90	80,188
6	22	A	Brighton & HA	W	2-1	1-0	5	Kane (pen) 42, Lamela 76	30,531
7	29	A	Huddersfield T	W	2-0	2-0	4	Kane 2 (1 pen) 25, 34 (p)	23,885
8	Oct 6	H	Cardiff C	W	1-0	1-0	3	Dier 8	43,268
9	20	A	West Ham U	W	1-0	1-0	4	Lamela 44	56,921
10	29	H	Manchester C	L	0-1	0-1	5		56,854
11	Nov 3	A	Wolverhampton W	W	3-2	2-0	4	Lamela 27, Lucas Moura 30, Kane 61	31,185
12	10	A	Crystal Palace	W	1-0	0-0	4	Foyth 66	25,685
13	24	H	Chelsea	W	3-1	2-0	3	Alli 8, Kane 16, Son 54	55,465
14	Dec 2	A	Arsenal	L	2-4	2-1	5	Dier 30, Kane (pen) 34	59,973
15	5	H	Southampton	W	3-1	1-0	3	Kane 9, Lucas Moura 51, Son 55	33,012
16	8	A	Leicester C	W	2-0	1-0	3	Son 45, Alli 58	31,957
17	15	H	Burnley	W	1-0	0-0	3	Eriksen 90	41,645
18	23	A	Everton	W	6-2	3-1	3	Son 2 27, 61, Alli 35, Kane 2 42, 74, Eriksen 48	39,319
19	26	H	Bournemouth	W	5-0	3-0	2	Eriksen 16, Son 2 23, 70, Lucas Moura 35, Kane 61	45,154
20	29	H	Wolverhampton W	L	1-3	1-0	2	Kane 22	46,356
21	Jan 1	A	Cardiff C	W	3-0	3-0	2	Kane 3, Eriksen 12, Son 26	32,485
22	13	H	Manchester U	L	0-1	0-1	3		80,062
23	20	A	Fulham	W	2-1	0-1	3	Alli 51, Winks 90	24,807
24	30	H	Watford	W	2-1	0-1	3	Son 80, Llorente 87	29,164
25	Feb 2	H	Newcastle U	W	1-0	0-0	2	Son 83	41,219
26	10	H	Leicester C	W	3-1	1-0	3	Sanchez 33, Eriksen 63, Son 90	44,154
27	23	A	Burnley	L	1-2	0-0	3	Kane 65	21,338
28	27	A	Chelsea	L	0-2	0-0	3		40,542
29	Mar 2	H	Arsenal	D	1-1	0-1	3	Kane (pen) 74	81,332
30	9	A	Southampton	L	1-2	1-0	3	Kane 26	31,890
31	31	A	Liverpool	L	1-2	0-1	3	Lucas Moura 70	53,322
32	Apr 3	H	Crystal Palace	W	2-0	0-0	3	Son 55, Eriksen 80	59,215
33	13	H	Huddersfield T	W	4-0	2-0	3	Wanyama 24, Lucas Moura 3 27, 87, 90	58,308
34	20	A	Manchester C	L	0-1	0-1	3		54,489
35	23	H	Brighton & HA	W	1-0	0-0	3	Eriksen 88	56,251
36	27	H	West Ham U	L	0-1	0-0	3		60,043
37	May 4	A	Bournemouth	L	0-1	0-0	3		10,630
38	12	H	Everton	D	2-2	1-0	4	Dier 3, Eriksen 75	60,124

Final League Position: 4

GOALSCORERS

League (67): Kane 17 (4 pens), Son 12, Lucas Moura 10, Eriksen 8, Alli 5, Lamela 4, Dier 3, Foyth 1, Llorente 1, Sanchez 1, Trippier 1, Vertonghen 1, Wanyama 1, Winks 1, own goal 1.
FA Cup (7): Llorente 3, Aurier 2, Kane 1, Son 1.
Carabao Cup (9): Son 3, Alli 2 (1 pen), Llorente 2, Kane 1 (1 pen), Lamela 1.
Champions League (20): Kane 5, Lucas Moura 5, Son 4, Eriksen 2, Llorente 2, Lamela 1, Vertonghen 1.
Checkatrade Trophy (7): Brown 1, Duncan 1 (1 pen), Harrison 1, Maghoma 1, Patterson 1, Roles 1, White 1.

Lloris H 33	Aurier S 6 + 2	Sanchez D 22 + 1	Vertonghen J 22	Davies B 20 + 7	Sissoko M 27 + 2	Dier E 18 + 2	Lucas Moura R 25 + 7	Eriksen C 30 + 5	Alli B 22 + 3	Kane H 27 + 1	Dembele M 7 + 3	Son H 23 + 8	Amos L — + 1	Alderweireld T 33 + 1	Trippier K 26 + 1	Lamela E 9 + 10	Winks H 17 + 9	Rose D 20 + 6	Vorm M 2	Llorente F 6 + 14	Wanyama V 4 + 9	Gazzaniga P 3	Foyth J 10 + 2	Skipp O 2 + 6	Walker-Peters K 4 + 2	Nkoudou G — + 1	Janssen V — + 3	Match No.
1	2	3	4	5	6	7^{2}	8^{1}	9	10^{3}	11	12	13	14															1
1		3^{1}	4	8		7^{3}	9	6	10	11^{2}	12			2	5	13	14											2
1	12		4	13		7	10	9	8	11^{3}	6			3	2^{1}		14	5^{2}										3
		3	4	9^{3}			10	7	8	11	5^{1}			2^{2}	6		13	14	1	12								4
			4			7^{2}	10	9		11	6^{3}	13		3	2	12	8^{1}	5	1		14							5
			4			6	10^{1}	9	13	11	7	8^{2}		3	2	12		5				1						6
		3	4^{2}		14	6	9			11	7^{3}	10^{1}		2	5		13	8			12	1						7
1		3		14	6^{2}	8	10			11		9^{1}		4	2	12	7	5^{3}			13							8
1		3		5	6^{2}	7	10	14		11^{1}	12			4	2	9^{3}	8			13								9
1		3		5	8	6^{1}	10^{3}	14	13	11	7^{2}			4	2	9	12											10
1		14		5	8		10^{1}	13		11	7^{2}	12^{3}		4	2	9	6						3					11
1	12			5	6		10^{2}		9	11		13		4	2^{3}	8^{1}	14				7		3					12
1	2			5	7	6		8	9^{1}	10		11^{2}		4		12	13						3					13
1	2		4■	5^{1}	7	6	13	8	9^{3}	11		10^{2}					12	14					3					14
1					12	6	10^{1}	9^{3}	13	11		8		4	2^{2}		7	5					3	14				15
1	2^{2}		4	5	8	6	11^{1}	12	9	13		10^{3}		3			7								14			16
1				4	6		10^{3}	12	9	11		13		3	2	8^{1}		5		14				7^{2}				17
1		3		5	7^{3}		14	8	9^{1}	11		10^{2}		4	2	12	6							13				18
1				13	6		8	9^{1}		11^{3}		10^{2}		4			7	5		14			3	12	2			19
1		3		5	7		12	8	9^{1}	11		10		4	2		6											20
1		3			7			8	9^{1}	11		10^{2}		4	2		6	5		13				12				21
1			4	5	7^{2}			8	9	11		10		3	2	12	6^{1}			13								22
1		3	4			12		6	10^{1}					2	5	9^{2}	7	8		11						13		23
1	5^{1}	3	4^{3}		6^{2}		12	8				11		2	13	14	7	9		10								24
1		4	5		6	14	11^{2}	8				9^{3}		3	2	10^{1}	7	13		12								25
1		3	4		7			9				10		12	2		6	5^{3}		11^{2}	13			8^{1}	14			26
1	5		4		6		14	9		10		11^{2}		3		13	7^{3}	8		12			2^{1}					27
1		3		5	6^{2}		13	9		11		10^{3}		4	2	8^{1}	7	14		12								28
1		3	4		7			9		10		11^{1}		2	5	12		8		13	6^{2}							29
1		3	4	14	7	6	10^{3}	8	9^{1}	11		12						5^{2}		13					2			30
1		3^{3}	4	13	5		11^{2}	7^{1}	8	10		12		2	6			9		14								31
1			4	5	6		13	8	7^{2}	11		9^{1}		3	2		12	10^{3}			14							32
1		3	4^{3}	8	6^{1}		11	9				14						13		10^{2}	7		2	12	5			33
		3	5	6		8^{2}	11	7	9^{1}			10		4^{3}				13		14	12	1	2					34
1			4	13			9^{2}	6	8			11^{3}		3	2			5		10	7^{1}		14				12	35
1		3		5		6	11^{1}	7	9^{2}			10		4				8^{3}		12	14		2				13	36
1		4		14	6^{1}	7^{7}	11	8	9			10■		3^{3}	2			5			12		13■					37
1				5	6	4	10	7	8^{2}					3		9^{3}				11^{1}	12			14	2		13	38

FA Cup

Third Round	Tranmere R	(a)	7-0
Fourth Round	Crystal Palace	(a)	0-2

Carabao Cup

Third Round	Watford	(h)	2-2
(Tottenham H won 4-2 on penalties)			
Fourth Round	West Ham U	(a)	3-1
Quarter-Final	Arsenal	(a)	2-0
Semi-Final 1st leg	Chelsea	(h)	1-0
Semi-Final 2nd leg	Chelsea	(a)	1-2
(Chelsea won 4-2 on penalties)			

Checkatrade Trophy (Tottenham H U21)

Group A (S)	Crawley T	(a)	1-1
(Crawley T won 5-3 on penalties)			
Group A (S)	Gillingham	(a)	4-0
Group A (S)	Portsmouth	(a)	2-3
Second Round (S)	Oxford U	(a)	0-3

Champions League

Group B	Inter Milan	(a)	1-2
Group B	Barcelona	(h)	2-4
Group B	PSV Eindhoven	(a)	2-2
Group B	PSV Eindhoven	(h)	2-1
Group B	Inter Milan	(h)	1-0
Group B	Barcelona	(a)	1-1
Round of 16 1st leg	Borussia Dortmund	(h)	3-0
Round of 16 2nd leg	Borussia Dortmund	(a)	1-0
Quarter-Final 1st leg	Manchester C	(h)	1-0
Quarter-Final 2nd leg	Manchester C	(a)	3-4
Semi-Final 1st leg	Ajax	(h)	0-1
Semi-Final 2nd leg	Ajax	(a)	3-2
Final	Liverpool	(Madrid)	0-2

TRANMERE ROVERS

FOUNDATION

Formed in 1884 as Belmont they adopted their present title the following year and eventually joined their first league, the West Lancashire League, in 1889–90, the same year as their first success in the Wirral Challenge Cup. The club almost folded in 1899–1900 when all the players left en bloc to join a rival club, but they survived the crisis and went from strength to strength, winning the 'Combination' title in 1907–08 and the Lancashire Combination in 1913–14. They joined the Football League in 1921 from the Central League.

Prenton Park, Prenton Road West, Birkenhead, Merseyside CH42 9PY.

Telephone: (0333) 014 4452.

Ticket Office: (0333) 014 4452 (Option 2).

Website: www.tranmererovers.co.uk

Email: customerservice@tranmererovers.co.uk

Ground Capacity: 16,582.

Record Attendance: 24,424 v Stoke C, FA Cup 4th rd, 5 February 1972.

Pitch Measurements: 100m × 64m (109.5yd × 70yd).

Chairman: Mark Palios.

Vice-Chairman: Nicola Palios.

Managing Director: Dawn Tolcher.

Manager: Micky Mellon.

Assistant Manager: Mike Jackson.

HONOURS

League Champions: Division 3 (N) – 1937–38.
Runners-up: Division 4 – 1988–89.

FA Cup: quarter-final – 2000, 2001, 2004.

League Cup: *Runners-up:* 2000.

Welsh Cup Winners: 1935.
Runners-up: 1934.

Leyland DAF Cup Winners: 1990.
Runners-up: 1991.

Colours: White shirts with blue trim, blue shorts with white trim, white socks with blue trim.

Year Formed: 1884.

Turned Professional: 1912.

Previous Name: 1884, Belmont AFC; 1885, Tranmere Rovers.

Club Nickname: 'Rovers'.

Grounds: 1884, Steeles Field; 1887, Ravenshaws Field/Old Prenton Park; 1912, Prenton Park.

First Football League Game: 27 August 1921, Division 3 (N), v Crewe Alex (h) W 4–1 – Bradshaw; Grainger, Stuart (1); Campbell, Milnes (1), Heslop; Moreton, Groves (1), Hyam, Ford (1), Hughes.

Record League Victory: 13–4 v Oldham Ath, Division 3 (N), 26 December 1935 – Gray; Platt, Fairhurst; McLaren, Newton, Spencer; Eden, MacDonald (1), Bell (9), Woodward (2), Urmson (1).

Record Cup Victory: 13–0 v Oswestry U, FA Cup 2nd prel rd, 10 October 1914 – Ashcroft; Stevenson, Bullough, Hancock, Taylor, Holden (1), Moreton (1), Cunningham (2), Smith (5), Leck (3), Gould (1).

THE SUN FACT FILE

Tranmere Rovers' Prenton Park ground staged European football when League of Ireland club Shelbourne faced Rangers in a UEFA Cup first qualifying round first leg tie in July 1998. The game was switched from Dublin because of fears of sectarian violence. The Irish club led 2-0 at half-time but Rangers ran out 5-3 winners and went on to win the second leg 2-0.

Record Defeat: 1–9 v Tottenham H, FA Cup 3rd rd (replay), 14 January 1953.

Most League Points (2 for a win): 60, Division 4, 1964–65.

Most League Points (3 for a win): 80, Division 4, 1988–89; Division 3, 1989–90; Division 2, 2002–03.

Most League Goals: 111, Division 3 (N), 1930–31.

Highest League Scorer in Season: Bunny Bell, 35, Division 3 (N), 1933–34.

Most League Goals in Total Aggregate: Ian Muir, 142, 1985–95.

Most League Goals in One Match: 9, Bunny Bell v Oldham Ath, Division 3 (N), 26 December 1935.

Most Capped Player: John Aldridge, 30 (69), Republic of Ireland.

Most League Appearances: Harold Bell, 595, 1946–64 (incl. League record 401 consecutive appearances).

Youngest League Player: Iain Hume, 16 years 167 days v Swindon T, 15 April 2000.

Record Transfer Fee Received: £2,250,000 from WBA for Jason Koumas, August 2002.

Record Transfer Fee Paid: £450,000 to Aston Villa for Shaun Teale, August 1995.

Football League Record: 1921 Original Member of Division 3 (N): 1938–39 Division 2; 1946–58 Division 3 (N); 1958–61 Division 3; 1961–67 Division 4; 1967–75 Division 3; 1975–76 Division 4; 1976–79 Division 3; 1979–89 Division 4; 1989–91 Division 3; 1991–92 Division 2; 1992–2001 Division 1; 2001–04 Division 2; 2004–14 FL 1; 2014–15 FL 2; 2015–18 National League; 2018–19 FL 2; 2019– FL 1.

MANAGERS

Bert Cooke 1912–35
Jackie Carr 1935–36
Jim Knowles 1936–39
Bill Ridding 1939–45
Ernie Blackburn 1946–55
Noel Kelly 1955–57
Peter Farrell 1957–60
Walter Galbraith 1961
Dave Russell 1961–69
Jackie Wright 1969–72
Ron Yeats 1972–75
John King 1975–80
Bryan Hamilton 1980–85
Frank Worthington 1985–87
Ronnie Moore 1987
John King 1987–96
John Aldridge 1996–2001
Dave Watson 2001–02
Ray Mathias 2002–03
Brian Little 2003–06
Ronnie Moore 2006–09
John Barnes 2009
Les Parry 2009–12
Ronnie Moore 2012–14
Robert Edwards 2014
Micky Adams 2014–15
Gary Brabin 2015–16
Paul Cardin 2016
Micky Mellon October 2016–

LATEST SEQUENCES

Longest Sequence of League Wins: 9, 9.2.1990 – 19.3.1990.

Longest Sequence of League Defeats: 8, 29.10.1938 – 17.12.1938.

Longest Sequence of League Draws: 5, 26.12.1997 – 31.1.1998.

Longest Sequence of Unbeaten League Matches: 18, 16.3.1970 – 4.9.1970.

Longest Sequence Without a League Win: 16, 8.11.1969 – 14.3.1970.

Successive Scoring Runs: 32 from 24.2.1934.

Successive Non-scoring Runs: 7 from 20.12.1997.

TEN YEAR LEAGUE RECORD

		P	W	D	L	F	A	Pts	Pos
2009-10	FL 1	46	14	9	23	45	72	51	19
2010-11	FL 1	46	15	11	20	53	60	56	17
2011-12	FL 1	46	14	14	18	49	53	56	12
2012-13	FL 1	46	19	10	17	58	48	67	11
2013-14	FL 1	46	12	11	23	52	79	47	21
2014-15	FL 2	46	9	12	25	45	67	39	24
2015-16	NL	46	22	12	12	61	44	78	6
2016-17	NL	46	29	8	9	79	39	95	2
2017-18	NL	46	24	10	12	78	46	82	2
2018-19	FL 2	46	20	13	13	63	50	73	6

DID YOU KNOW ?

Tranmere Rovers came close to earning promotion to the Premier League after reaching the play-offs in three consecutive seasons. They lost to Swindon Town in the 1992–93 play-off semi-finals and went out at the same stage in the following two seasons, losing first to Leicester City and then to Reading.

TRANMERE ROVERS – SKY BET LEAGUE TWO 2018–19 LEAGUE RECORD

Match No.	Date	Venue	Opponents	Result		H/T Score	Lg Pos.	Goalscorers	Attendance
1	Aug 4	A	Stevenage	D	2-2	1-2	11	Norwood 2 [33, 55]	3315
2	11	H	Cheltenham T	W	1-0	1-0	8	Norwood [13]	6736
3	18	A	Swindon T	L	2-3	2-1	13	Smith [9], Norwood [13]	6106
4	21	H	Mansfield T	D	0-0	0-0	14		5466
5	25	H	Port Vale	W	1-0	0-0	9	Norwood [77]	6488
6	Sept 1	A	Northampton T	D	1-1	0-0	11	Norwood [51]	4916
7	8	H	Colchester U	D	1-1	1-0	14	Norwood [42]	5885
8	15	A	Carlisle U	W	2-0	0-0	8	Parkes (og) [80], Mullin [86]	5187
9	22	H	Newport Co	L	0-1	0-1	13		5745
10	29	A	Milton Keynes D	D	1-1	1-1	16	Smith [37]	7048
11	Oct 2	H	Lincoln C	W	1-0	0-0	10	Norwood [61]	5467
12	6	A	Morecambe	W	4-3	2-1	7	Banks [28], Gilmour 2 [41, 89], Smith [54]	2793
13	12	H	Macclesfield T	W	1-0	0-0	4	Gilmour [74]	6797
14	20	A	Yeovil T	D	0-0	0-0	6		3007
15	23	A	Forest Green R	L	1-3	0-2	7	Mullin [85]	2181
16	27	H	Crawley T	W	5-1	2-0	7	Jennings [25], Norwood 2 [43, 54], Buxton (pen) [58], Mullin [60]	5445
17	Nov 3	H	Exeter C	W	2-0	1-0	4	Norwood 2 [31, 55]	6209
18	17	A	Crewe Alex	L	2-3	1-1	7	Norwood [36], Mullin [83]	5154
19	24	H	Oldham Ath	D	1-1	0-1	7	Jennings [72]	7150
20	27	A	Grimsby T	L	2-5	1-2	8	Norwood [11], Mullin [65]	3293
21	Dec 8	H	Cambridge U	W	1-0	0-0	7	Norwood [77]	5016
22	15	A	Notts Co	L	2-3	1-2	8	Smith [38], Jennings [58]	6535
23	22	A	Bury	L	1-2	0-0	9	Sutton [90]	4748
24	26	H	Morecambe	W	3-1	3-0	8	Stockton [3], Norwood [29], Harris [45]	7483
25	29	H	Yeovil T	D	0-0	0-0	9		5782
26	Jan 1	A	Macclesfield T	D	1-1	1-1	9	Jennings [32]	3398
27	12	A	Cheltenham T	W	3-1	0-1	9	Norwood [46], Miller [61], Banks [72]	3104
28	19	H	Swindon T	L	1-2	0-2	10	Norwood [52]	5847
29	26	A	Mansfield T	L	0-3	0-1	10		4885
30	Feb 5	H	Northampton T	L	1-2	1-2	10	Norwood [25]	5098
31	9	H	Stevenage	W	2-0	1-0	10	Morris [45], Norwood [79]	5283
32	16	A	Cambridge U	D	0-0	0-0	11		4872
33	19	A	Port Vale	W	2-1	1-0	9	Norwood 2 [10, 56]	3835
34	23	H	Notts Co	W	1-0	0-0	9	Jennings [69]	6559
35	Mar 2	A	Exeter C	W	1-0	1-0	6	Norwood [31]	4855
36	8	H	Crewe Alex	W	1-0	0-0	5	Norwood [72]	7898
37	12	H	Grimsby T	W	4-1	4-1	5	Jennings 2 [18, 44], Monthe [34], Norwood [39]	5269
38	23	A	Colchester U	W	2-0	1-0	5	Norwood [23], Perkins [46]	2800
39	30	H	Carlisle U	W	3-0	1-0	5	Banks [45], Norwood [64], Monthe [82]	8095
40	Apr 2	A	Oldham Ath	L	0-2	0-1	5		5143
41	6	A	Newport Co	D	0-0	0-0	5		3170
42	13	H	Milton Keynes D	W	2-1	1-1	5	Perkins [30], Jennings [62]	8357
43	19	H	Forest Green R	L	0-1	0-0	5		9468
44	22	A	Lincoln C	D	0-0	0-0	6		9658
45	30	H	Bury	D	1-1	1-0	6	Norwood [11]	9145
46	May 4	A	Crawley T	L	1-3	0-2	6	Norwood (pen) [50]	3183

Final League Position: 6

GOALSCORERS

League (63): Norwood 29 (1 pen), Jennings 8, Mullin 5, Smith 4, Banks 3, Gilmour 3, Monthe 2, Perkins 2, Buxton 1 (1 pen), Harris 1, Miller 1, Morris 1, Stockton 1, Sutton 1, own goal 1.
FA Cup (8): Jennings 4, Norwood 2, Mullin 1, Smith 1.
Carabao Cup (1): Cole 1.
Checkatrade Trophy (3): Harris 1, Mullin 1, Stockton 1.
League Two Play-offs (3): Banks 1, Jennings 1, Norwood 1.

Davies S 46	Caprice J 40 + 1	Sutton R 7 + 2	McNulty S 27	Bakayogo Z 20 + 1	Smith J 21 + 14	Harris J 14 + 7	Banks O 30 + 3	Jennings C 43 + 2	Stockton C 13 + 3	Norwood J 45	Tollitt B 1 + 3	Monthe E 42 + 1	Gilmour H 7 + 15	Ellis M 23 + 2	Mottley-Henry D 4 + 8	Mullin P 8 + 14	McCullough L 36	Buxton A 11 + 5	Cole L 3 + 7	Akammadu F — + 1	Ridehalgh L 17 + 1	Perkins D 17	Miller I 2	Pringle B 12 + 1	Nelson S 4 + 3	Morris K 12 + 2	Dagnall C 1 + 4	Gumbs E — + 1	Match No.
1	2	3	4	5	6¹	7	8	9	10	11	12																		1
1	2	4³	3	5	6¹	7	8	9	11²	10	13	12	14																2
1	2¹		3		6²	7■	8	9	11³	10		5	13	4	12	14													3
1	2		3		6¹		7	9	10	11		5		4	12		8												4
1	2		4		9²		8	6	10¹	11		5		3	13	12	7												5
1	2		3	13	6¹		8	9	11²	10		5		4	12		7												6
1	2		3	5	6¹		8	9	11²	10		4			13	12	7												7
1	2		3	5	13		8	9	11²	10		4			6¹	12	7												8
1			3	5	12		8	9³	14	10		4			6¹	11²	7	2	13										9
1			3	5	6²		8	9	11¹	10		4	12		13		7	2											10
1			3	5	9²		8	6	10¹	11■		4	12		13		7	2											11
1			3	5	6³		8	11¹				4	9	14	12	10²	7	2		13									12
1	2		3		10¹		7	9		11		4	8				6	5	12										13
1	2	4	3		9¹	14	6	11		10		5	8³			12	7²		13										14
1	2	4	3		9³	7		11²		10	14	5	6¹			13	8		12										15
1	5		3		13		8	6		11		4	12			10²	7	2	9¹										16
1	2		3		12	14	7²	8		11		4	13			10¹	6	5	9³										17
1	2		3	5	11²		8	9		10		4	7¹			13	6		12										18
1	2		3	5			7	6	12	10		4			9	11¹	8												19
1	2	12	3¹	5³				9		10		4	7		8²	11	6		13		14								20
1	13		3		6¹	7		9	11²	10		4				12	8	2			5								21
1	2	4		5	10	6¹		8		11			12	3		13	7		9²										22
1	2¹	12	4³		14	8		7	13	11		5		3		10²	9				6								23
1	6	5¹				9		7	10²	11		3	13	4		12	8				2								24
1	2	3²	4		12	9		7	10¹	11				5		13	8				6								25
1	6				9¹	8		11		10		4		3			7	2	12		5								26
1	9		2			13	4¹			10		5		7		12	8				3	6	11²						27
1	2		3		14		9	12		11		4		5³			7²	13			6	8	10¹						28
1	2		4¹				8■	10		11		5					7	3			6	9		12					29
1	2				13			11		10		4	14				7²				5	8		9¹	3	6³	12		30
1	2				13			11¹		10		4		12			7				5	8		9	3²	6³	14		31
1	2¹			5	12			11		10		4		3			8	13				7		9²		6			32
1	2			5	13			11		10		3	12	4			7					8		9²		6¹			33
1	2			5	13		12	11		10		3		4³			7¹					8		9²	14	6			34
1	2			5	8²			9		11		4	12	3			6					7		10¹	13				35
1	2			5³	9²		13	11		10		3	14	4			7	12				0		6¹					36
1	2					13	7²	6		11		4	12	3			9				5	8		10¹					37
1	2					13	7¹	6		11		4		3			9				5	8		10²		12			38
1	2				14	12	9³	10		11		3	13	4			7²				5	6				8¹			39
1	2				12	7¹	9	10		11		3		4							5	6				8			40
1	2				10¹		7	9		11		3		4							5	6				8	12		41
1	2					12	7	11		10		4		3							5	8¹		6		9			42
1	2			5		7¹	8	11		10		4		3²		13								9³	12	6	14		43
1	2			5		8	7	9		10		4	13			11¹		14							3²	6		12³	44
1	2¹					7	8	10		11		4				13		12			5			9²	3	6			45
1			3	5	6³		12	13		11	9²	4	7					2				8¹				14	10		46

FA Cup

First Round	Oxford C	(h)	3-3
Replay	Oxford C	(a)	2-0
Second Round	Southport	(h)	1-1
Replay	Southport	(a)	2-0
Third Round	Tottenham H	(h)	0-7

Carabao Cup

First Round	Walsall	(h)	1-3

Checkatrade Trophy

Group D (N)	Crewe Alex	(h)	3-4
Group D (N)	Shrewsbury T	(a)	0-6
Group D (N)	Manchester C U21	(h)	0-1

League Two Play-offs

Semi-Final 1st leg	Forest Green R	(h)	1-0
Semi-Final 2nd leg	Forest Green R	(a)	1-1
Final	Newport Co	(Wembley)	1-0
(*aet*)			

WALSALL

FOUNDATION

Two of the leading clubs around Walsall in the 1880s were Walsall Swifts (formed 1877) and Walsall Town (formed 1879). The Swifts were winners of the Birmingham Senior Cup in 1881, while the Town reached the 4th round (5th round modern equivalent) of the FA Cup in 1883. These clubs amalgamated as Walsall Town Swifts in 1888, becoming simply Walsall in 1895.

Banks's Stadium, Bescot Crescent, Walsall WS1 4SA.
Telephone: (01922) 622 791. ***Fax:*** (01922) 639 202.
Ticket Office: (01922) 651 414/416.
Website: www.saddlers.co.uk
Email: info@walsallfc.co.uk
Ground Capacity: 11,300.
Record Attendance: 25,453 v Newcastle U, Division 2, 29 August 1961 (at Fellows Park); 11,049 v Rotherham U, Division 1, 9 May 2004 (at Bescot Stadium).
Pitch Measurements: 100.5m × 67m (110yd × 73.5yd).
Chairman: Jeff Bonser.
Chief Executive: Stefan Gamble.
Manager: Darrell Clarke.
Assistant Manager: Marcus Stewart.
Colours: Red shirts with white and black trim, red shorts with black trim, red socks with black trim.
Year Formed: 1888.
Turned Professional: 1888.
Previous Names: Walsall Swifts (founded 1877) and Walsall Town (founded 1879) amalgamated in 1888 as Walsall Town Swifts; 1895, Walsall.
Club Nickname: 'The Saddlers'.
Grounds: 1888, Fellows Park; 1990, Bescot Stadium (renamed Banks's Stadium 2007).
First Football League Game: 3 September 1892, Division 2, v Darwen (h) L 1–2 – Hawkins; Withington, Pinches; Robinson, Whitrick, Forsyth; Marshall, Holmes, Turner, Gray (1), Pangbourn.
Record League Victory: 10–0 v Darwen, Division 2, 4 March 1899 – Tennent; Ted Peers (1), Davies; Hickinbotham, Jenkyns, Taggart; Dean (3), Vail (2), Aston (4), Martin, Griffin.
Record Cup Victory: 7–0 v Macclesfield T (a), FA Cup 2nd rd, 6 December 1997 – Walker; Evans, Marsh, Viveash (1), Ryder, Peron, Boli (2 incl. 1p) (Ricketts), Porter (2), Keates, Watson (Platt), Hodge (2 incl. 1p).
Record Defeat: 0–12 v Small Heath, 17 December 1892; 0–12 v Darwen, 26 December 1896, both Division 2.
Most League Points (2 for a win): 65, Division 4, 1959–60.
Most League Points (3 for a win): 89, FL 2, 2006–07.
Most League Goals: 102, Division 4, 1959–60.
Highest League Scorer in Season: Gilbert Alsop, 40, Division 3 (N), 1933–34 and 1934–35.

HONOURS

League Champions: FL 2 – 2006–07; Division 4 – 1959–60.
Runners-up: Second Division – 1998–99; Division 3 – 1960–61; Third Division – 1994–95; Division 4 – 1979–80.
FA Cup: last 16 – 1889; 5th rd – 1939, 1975, 1978, 1987, 2002, 2003.
League Cup: semi-final – 1984.
League Trophy: *Runners-up:* 2015.

THE Sun FACT FILE

While almost every single Football League club was given a 'derby' match for their Football League Jubilee Fund fixtures, Walsall were scheduled to play against Mansfield Town, some 50 miles away and with no obvious local rivalry. The Saddlers won both games, winning 2-1 in 1938–39 and 5-1 the following season.

Most League Goals in Total Aggregate: Tony Richards, 184, 1954–63; Colin Taylor, 184, 1958–63, 1964–68, 1969–73.

Most League Goals in One Match: 5, Gilbert Alsop v Carlisle U, Division 3 (N), 2 February 1935; 5, Bill Evans v Mansfield T, Division 3 (N), 5 October 1935; 5, Johnny Devlin v Torquay U, Division 3 (S), 1 September 1949.

Most Capped Player: Mick Kearns, 15 (18), Republic of Ireland.

Most League Appearances: Colin Harrison, 473, 1964–82.

Youngest League Player: Geoff Morris, 16 years 218 days v Scunthorpe U, 14 September 1965.

Record Transfer Fee Received: £1,500,000 (rising to £5,000,000) from Brentford for Rico Henry, August 2016.

Record Transfer Fee Paid: £300,000 to Anorthosis Famagusta for Andreas Makris, August 2016.

Football League Record: 1892 Elected to Division 2; 1895 Failed re-election; 1896–1901 Division 2; 1901 Failed re-election; 1921 Original Member of Division 3 (N); 1927–31 Division 3 (S); 1931–36 Division 3 (N); 1936–58 Division 3 (S); 1958–60 Division 4; 1960–61 Division 3; 1961–63 Division 2; 1963–79 Division 3; 1979–80 Division 4; 1980–88 Division 3; 1988–89 Division 2; 1989–90 Division 3; 1990–92 Division 4; 1992–95 Division 3; 1995–99 Division 2; 1999–2000 Division 1; 2000–01 Division 2; 2001–04 Division 1; 2004–06 FL 1; 2006–07 FL 2; 2007–19 FL 1; 2019– FL 2.

LATEST SEQUENCES

Longest Sequence of League Wins: 7, 9.4.2005 – 9.8.2005.

Longest Sequence of League Defeats: 15, 29.10.1988 – 4.2.1989.

Longest Sequence of League Draws: 5, 7.5.1988 – 17.9.1988.

Longest Sequence of Unbeaten League Matches: 21, 6.11.1979 – 22.3.1980.

Longest Sequence Without a League Win: 18, 15.10.1988 – 4.2.1989.

Successive Scoring Runs: 27 from 6.11.1979.

Successive Non-scoring Runs: 5 from 10.4.2004.

MANAGERS

H. Smallwood 1888–91 *(Secretary-Manager)*
A. G. Burton 1891–93
J. H. Robinson 1893–95
C. H. Ailso 1895–96 *(Secretary-Manager)*
A. E. Parsloe 1896–97 *(Secretary-Manager)*
L. Ford 1897–98 *(Secretary-Manager)*
G. Hughes 1898–99 *(Secretary-Manager)*
L. Ford 1899–1901 *(Secretary-Manager)*
J. E. Shutt 1908–13 *(Secretary-Manager)*
Haydn Price 1914–20
Joe Burchell 1920–26
David Ashworth 1926–27
Jack Torrance 1927–28
James Kerr 1928–29
Sid Scholey 1929–30
Peter O'Rourke 1930–32
Bill Slade 1932–34
Andy Wilson 1934–37
Tommy Lowes 1937–44
Harry Hibbs 1944–51
Tony McPhee 1951
Brough Fletcher 1952–53
Major Frank Buckley 1953–55
John Love 1955–57
Billy Moore 1957–64
Alf Wood 1964
Reg Shaw 1964–68
Dick Graham 1968
Ron Lewin 1968–69
Billy Moore 1969–72
John Smith 1972–73
Ronnie Allen 1973
Doug Fraser 1973–77
Dave Mackay 1977–78
Alan Ashman 1978
Frank Sibley 1979
Alan Buckley 1979–86
Neil Martin *(Joint Manager with Buckley)* 1981–82
Tommy Coakley 1986–88
John Barnwell 1989–90
Kenny Hibbitt 1990–94
Chris Nicholl 1994–97
Jan Sorensen 1997–98
Ray Graydon 1998–2002
Colin Lee 2002–04
Paul Merson 2004–06
Kevin Broadhurst 2006
Richard Money 2006–08
Jimmy Mullen 2008–09
Chris Hutchings 2009–11
Dean Smith 2011–15
Sean O'Driscoll 2015–16
Jon Whitney 2016–18
Dean Keates 2018–19
Martin O'Connor 2019
Darrell Clarke May 2019–

TEN YEAR LEAGUE RECORD

		P	W	D	L	F	A	Pts	Pos
2009-10	FL 1	46	16	14	16	60	63	62	10
2010-11	FL 1	46	12	12	22	56	75	48	20
2011-12	FL 1	46	10	20	16	51	57	50	19
2012-13	FL 1	46	17	17	12	65	58	68	9
2013-14	FL 1	46	14	16	16	49	49	58	13
2014-15	FL 1	46	14	17	15	50	54	59	14
2015-16	FL 1	46	24	12	10	71	49	84	3
2016-17	FL 1	46	14	16	16	51	58	58	14
2017-18	FL 1	46	13	13	20	53	66	52	19
2018-19	FL 1	46	12	11	23	49	71	47	22

DID YOU KNOW ?

Legendary Walsall forward Gilbert Alsop scored a record 18 hat-tricks in peacetime football for the Saddlers. In a remarkable run-in he netted 16 goals in a run of five games in April 1939, including hat-tricks both home and away against Swindon Town.

WALSALL – SKY BET LEAGUE ONE 2018–19 LEAGUE RECORD

Match No.	*Date*	*Venue*	*Opponents*	*Result*	*H/T Score*	*Lg Pos.*	*Goalscorers*	*Attendance*
1	Aug 4	H	Plymouth Arg	W 2-1	1-1	4	Cook [45], Leahy [64]	5755
2	11	A	Scunthorpe U	D 1-1	0-0	6	Ismail (pen) [64]	4331
3	18	H	Gillingham	W 2-1	2-0	4	Ferrier [12], Osbourne [42]	4361
4	21	A	AFC Wimbledon	W 3-1	1-0	4	Morris [16], Nightingale (og) [70], Cook [79]	3887
5	25	A	Rochdale	W 2-1	1-0	4	Ginnelly [32], Ismail [77]	3080
6	Sept 1	H	Blackpool	D 0-0	0-0	5		4762
7	8	A	Barnsley	D 1-1	0-0	5	Cook [88]	11,468
8	15	H	Doncaster R	L 1-4	1-1	6	Ferrier [17]	4546
9	22	A	Oxford U	W 2-1	1-0	5	Ferrier [24], Ismail [58]	6080
10	29	H	Accrington S	L 0-1	0-1	7		4257
11	Oct 2	H	Shrewsbury T	D 0-0	0-0	7		4555
12	6	A	Bristol R	W 1-0	0-0	5	Morris [90]	7768
13	20	A	Luton T	L 0-2	0-1	8		8953
14	23	A	Southend U	L 0-3	0-1	12		5603
15	27	H	Wycombe W	W 3-2	1-0	9	Cook [36], Osbourne [52], Gape (og) [84]	4265
16	Nov 3	H	Burton Alb	L 1-3	0-2	10	Cook [77]	5297
17	6	H	Charlton Ath	L 0-2	0-1	11		3719
18	17	A	Fleetwood T	D 0-0	0-0	11		3090
19	24	H	Sunderland	D 2-2	0-0	11	Gordon [46], Ginnelly [52]	7868
20	27	A	Portsmouth	L 0-2	0-1	13		16,794
21	Dec 8	H	Coventry C	W 2-1	0-1	10	Leahy 2 (1 pen) [90 (p), 90]	5926
22	15	A	Bradford C	L 0-4	0-1	11		15,314
23	22	A	Peterborough U	D 1-1	1-0	11	Osbourne [45]	7243
24	26	H	Bristol R	L 1-3	1-2	14	Gordon [45]	5069
25	29	H	Luton T	D 2-2	1-0	14	Ferrier (pen) [26], Cook [67]	5739
26	Jan 1	A	Charlton Ath	L 1-2	0-2	15	Cook [47]	10,421
27	12	H	Scunthorpe U	L 1-2	0-1	16	Devlin [53]	3984
28	19	A	Gillingham	W 3-0	2-0	15	Cook 3 [9, 19, 47]	3975
29	22	A	Plymouth Arg	L 1-2	0-0	15	Cook [82]	8446
30	Feb 2	H	Rochdale	L 1-2	1-1	17	Edwards [36]	4021
31	9	A	Blackpool	L 0-2	0-1	17		3252
32	12	H	AFC Wimbledon	L 0-1	0-0	17		3287
33	16	A	Coventry C	L 0-3	0-2	18		10,646
34	23	H	Bradford C	W 3-2	1-1	18	Gordon 2 [42, 62], Edwards [47]	5503
35	Mar 2	A	Burton Alb	D 0-0	0-0	20		3924
36	9	H	Fleetwood T	W 2-0	0-0	16	Ferrier [54], Scarr [67]	4986
37	12	H	Portsmouth	L 2-3	0-2	19	Guthrie 2 [75, 90]	4097
38	16	A	Sunderland	L 1-2	1-1	21	Gordon [4]	34,647
39	23	H	Barnsley	L 0-1	0-0	21		4969
40	30	A	Doncaster R	L 1-3	1-3	21	Gordon [14]	7630
41	Apr 6	H	Oxford U	L 1-3	1-1	22	Cook [26]	6339
42	13	A	Accrington S	L 1-2	1-1	23	Devlin [33]	2662
43	19	H	Southend U	D 1-1	0-1	23	Oteh (pen) [90]	4624
44	22	A	Wycombe W	L 0-1	0-0	23		5595
45	27	H	Peterborough U	W 3-0	1-0	22	Cook [45], Lafferty (og) [57], Gordon [74]	5400
46	May 4	A	Shrewsbury T	D 0-0	0-0	22		9635

Final League Position: 22

GOALSCORERS

League (49): Cook 13, Gordon 7, Ferrier 5 (1 pen), Ismail 3 (1 pen), Leahy 3 (1 pen), Osbourne 3, Devlin 2, Edwards 2, Ginnelly 2, Guthrie 2, Morris 2, Oteh 1 (1 pen), Scarr 1, own goals 3.
FA Cup (7): Cook 3, Devlin 1, Ginnelly 1, Kinsella 1, own goal 1.
Carabao Cup (6): Cook 1, Ferrier 1, Ginnelly 1, Gordon 1, Ismail 1, Morris 1.
Checkatrade Trophy (7): Morris 2, Cook 1, Fitzwater 1, Gordon 1, Johnson 1, Kouhyar 1.

Roberts L 42	Devlin N 42 + 1	Fitzwater J 21	Guthrie J 41 + 1	Leahy L 44	Ismail Z 22 + 10	Dobson G 35 + 4	Chambers A 1	Ginnelly J 18 + 3	Ferrier M 25 + 8	Cook A 34 + 9	Kinsella L 24 + 7	Morris K 11 + 6	Wilson K 5 + 9	Osbourne I 27 + 5	Gordon J 28 + 9	Ronan C 4 + 7	Martin R 8	Edwards J 18 + 2	Johnson C 7	Jarvis M 8 + 1	Mussa O — + 1	Norman C 6 + 3	Laird S 5 + 2	Scarr D 17	Taylor C 5 + 5	Oteh A 4 + 9	Dunn C 4	*Match No.*
1	2	3	4	5	6	7	8¹	9³	10²	11	12	13	14															1
1	2	3	4	5	6	8		9³	11²	10	12		13	7¹	14													2
1	2	3	4	5		8		9	10¹	11		6		7	12													3
1	2	3	4	5		8		9	11	10¹		6²	12	7	13													4
1	2	3	4	5	12■	8		9³	11²	10		6¹	14	7	13													5
1	2	3	4	5	6²	7			11	10¹		9	13	8	12													6
1	2	3	4	5		8		9¹	10	12		13		7	6²	11												7
1	2	3	4	5	13	7		9²	10	11		6³		8¹	14	12												8
1	2	3	4	5	6²	7		9	10	13			12	8	11¹													9
1	2	4	3	5	6	7		9²	11	12	14			10¹	8³	13												10
1	2	3	4	5	6	7		9	11	10	12			8¹														11
1	2	3	4	5	6¹	7		9	10²	11	8	13			12													12
1	2¹	3	4	5	6²	7		0³	11	10	8		13		14	12												13
1		4	3	5		8		10	11	12		7	2	6		9¹												14
1			4	5		9		12	10¹	11		6	2	7		8	3											15
1	12		4	5	13	8		14	11	10		9³	2¹	6²		7	3											16
1	2		4	5	13	8		9¹	11	10	12			7²	6³	14	3											17
1	2		4	5	6	8		9	12	11	7				10¹		3											18
1	2		4	5	6²	7		9	13	10	8	12			11¹		3											19
1	2		4	5		8		9³	11	13	7	14	6²		10¹	12	3											20
1	5	2¹	4	8	13			12	11	10	6			7	9²		3											21
1	2		4	5				9²	13	10	7	6¹	14	8	11³	12	3											22
1	2	4	3	5		12			13	11	7	9	6	8¹	10²													23
1	2	3	4	5	9¹	7			12	10	8	6³			11²	14		13										24
1	2	3	4	5		7			11	10	8		12		9¹			6										25
1	2	3	4	5	13	7			11	10	8	12			9¹			6²										26
1	2		4	5	6				10¹	11	-			7²	12			8	3	9	13							27
1	6		4	5						10	13			7	11²			8	3	9¹		2	12					28
1	6³		4	5	13	12				10	14			7	11			8²	3	9¹		2						29
1	6²		4	5		14			11³	10				8¹				7		9		2		3	12	13		30
1	6²		4		14	8³				10				12				7		9¹		2	5	3	13	11		31
1			4	5	13					11	7			6	9			8²		12		2		3		10¹		32
1	2	4			6					10	8							7		9			5	3	12	11¹		33
1	2		4	5	9¹	14				11■	7			12	8³			6		10²				3		13		34
1	2		4	5	11	9					7				8			6		10				3				35
1	2		4	5³	9	7			10²		6			13	11			8¹				14	12	3				36
1	2		4	5	9²	7			11		6				10			8¹						3	12	13		37
1	2		4	5	11	7				12	6				10			8¹						3	9²	13		38
1	2		4	5	11¹	7			12	13	8			6²	10									3	9			39
1	2		3	5	9³	6			13	12	8			7²	10									4	11¹	14		40
1	2		4	5	6¹	7			12	10				8	11²							13		3	9			41
1	2	6¹	4	5		7				10	9			8²	11■			13						3		12		42
	2			5	9¹	7				10	6							8	4			13		3	11²	12	1	43
	2			9¹	13					12				8	10			7	3			6³	5	4	14	11²	1	44
	5		12	9		7				10³	8			13	11			6²	3				4	2¹		14	1	45
	2			6		7				10	9¹			13	11			8²	5				3	4		12	1	46

FA Cup

First Round	Coventry C	(h)	3-2
Second Round	Sunderland	(h)	1-1
Replay	Sunderland	(a)	1-0
Third Round	Bolton W	(a)	2-5

Carabao Cup

First Round	Tranmere R	(a)	3-1
Second Round	Macclesfield T	(h)	3-3

(Macclesfield T won 3-1 on penalties)

Checkatrade Trophy

Group E (N)	Burton Alb	(a)	2-1
Group E (N)	Middlesbrough U21	(h)	3-1
Group E (N)	Port Vale	(h)	1-2
Second Round (N)	Shrewsbury T	(a)	1-2

WATFORD

FOUNDATION

The club was formed as Watford Rovers in 1881. The name was changed to West Herts in 1893 and then the name Watford was adopted after rival club Watford St Mary's was absorbed in 1898.

Vicarage Road Stadium, Vicarage Road, Watford, Hertfordshire WD18 0ER.

Telephone: (01923) 496 000.

Fax: (01923) 496 001.

Ticket Office: (01923) 223 023.

Website: www.watfordfc.com

Email: yourvoice@watfordfc.com

Ground Capacity: 21,577.

Record Attendance: 34,099 v Manchester U, FA Cup 4th rd (replay), 3 February 1969.

Pitch Measurements: 105m × 68m (115yd × 74.5yd).

Chairman and Chief Executive: Scott Duxbury.

Head Coach: Javi Gracia.

Assistant Head Coaches: Juan Solla, Zigor Aranalde.

Colours: Yellow and black striped shirts, black shorts with yellow trim, black socks with yellow trim.

Year Formed: 1881.

Turned Professional: 1897.

Previous Names: 1881, Watford Rovers; 1893, West Herts; 1898, Watford.

Club Nickname: 'The Hornets'.

Grounds: 1883, Vicarage Meadow, Rose and Crown Meadow; 1889, Colney Butts; 1890, Cassio Road; 1922, Vicarage Road.

First Football League Game: 28 August 1920, Division 3, v QPR (a) W 2–1 – Williams; Horseman, Fred Gregory; Bacon, Toone, Wilkinson; Bassett, Ronald (1), Hoddinott, White (1), Waterall.

Record League Victory: 8–0 v Sunderland, Division 1, 25 September 1982 – Sherwood; Rice, Rostron, Taylor, Terry, Bolton, Callaghan (2), Blissett (4), Jenkins (2), Jackett, Barnes.

Record Cup Victory: 10–1 v Lowestoft T, FA Cup 1st rd, 27 November 1926 – Yates; Prior, Fletcher (1); Frank Smith, Bert Smith, Strain; Stephenson, Warner (3), Edmonds (3), Swan (1), Daniels (1), (1 og).

Record Defeat: 0–10 v Wolverhampton W, FA Cup 1st rd (replay), 24 January 1912.

Most League Points (2 for a win): 71, Division 4, 1977–78.

Most League Points (3 for a win): 89, FL C, 2014–15.

HONOURS

League Champions: Second Division – 1997–98; Division 3 – 1968–69; Division 4 – 1977–78.
Runners-up: Division 1 – 1982–83; FL C – 2014–15; Division 2 – 1981–82; Division 3 – 1978–79.

FA Cup: *Runners-up:* 1984, 2019.

League Cup: semi-final – 1979, 2005.

European Competitions
UEFA Cup: 1983–84.

THE Sun FACT FILE

The Football Combination fixture between Watford Reserves and Mansfield Town Reserves played on 19 December 1959 attracted an attendance of 6,399 to Vicarage Road, almost the same as the previous week's first-team fixture against Workington which drew 7,815. The reason for this was the availability of tickets for the forthcoming FA Cup tie against Birmingham City.

Most League Goals: 92, Division 4, 1959–60.

Highest League Scorer in Season: Cliff Holton, 42, Division 4, 1959–60.

Most League Goals in Total Aggregate: Luther Blissett, 148, 1976–83, 1984–88, 1991–92.

Most League Goals in One Match: 5, Eddie Mummery v Newport Co, Division 3 (S), 5 January 1924.

Most Capped Players: John Barnes, 31 (79), England; Kenny Jackett, 31, Wales.

Most League Appearances: Luther Blissett, 415, 1976–83, 1984–88, 1991–92.

Youngest League Player: Keith Mercer, 16 years 125 days v Tranmere R, 16 February 1973.

Record Transfer Fee Received: £35,000,000 from Everton for Richarlison, July 2018.

Record Transfer Fee Paid: £18,500,000 to Burnley for Andre Gray, August 2017.

Football League Record: 1920 Original Member of Division 3; 1921–58 Division 3 (S); 1958–60 Division 4; 1960–69 Division 3; 1969–72 Division 2; 1972–75 Division 3; 1975–78 Division 4; 1978–79 Division 3; 1979–82 Division 2; 1982–88 Division 1; 1988–92 Division 2; 1992–96 Division 1; 1996–98 Division 2; 1998–99 Division 1; 1999–2000 Premier League; 2000–04 Division 1; 2004–06 FL C; 2006–07 Premier League; 2007–15 FL C; 2015– Premier League.

LATEST SEQUENCES

Longest Sequence of League Wins: 7, 28.8.2000 – 14.10.2000.

Longest Sequence of League Defeats: 9, 26.12.1972 – 27.2.1973.

Longest Sequence of League Draws: 7, 16.2.2008 – 22.3.2008.

Longest Sequence of Unbeaten League Matches: 22, 1.10.1996 – 1.3.1997.

Longest Sequence Without a League Win: 19, 27.11.1971 – 8.4.1972.

Successive Scoring Runs: 22 from 20.8.1985.

Successive Non-scoring Runs: 7 from 18.12.1971.

MANAGERS

John Goodall 1903–10
Harry Kent 1910–26
Fred Pagnam 1926–29
Neil McBain 1929–37
Bill Findlay 1938–47
Jack Bray 1947–48
Eddie Hapgood 1948–50
Ron Gray 1950–51
Haydn Green 1951–52
Len Goulden 1952–55
(General Manager to 1956)
Johnny Paton 1955–56
Neil McBain 1956–59
Ron Burgess 1959–63
Bill McGarry 1963–64
Ken Furphy 1964–71
George Kirby 1971–73
Mike Keen 1973–77
Graham Taylor 1977–87
Dave Bassett 1987–88
Steve Harrison 1988–90
Colin Lee 1990
Steve Perryman 1990–93
Glenn Roeder 1993–96
Graham Taylor 1996
Kenny Jackett 1996–97
Graham Taylor 1997–2001
Gianluca Vialli 2001–02
Ray Lewington 2002–05
Adrian Boothroyd 2005–08
Brendan Rodgers 2008–09
Malky Mackay 2009–11
Sean Dyche 2011–12
Gianfranco Zola 2012–13
Beppe Sannino 2013–14
Oscar Garcia 2014
Billy McKinlay 2014
Slavisa Jokanovic 2014–15
Quique Flores 2015–16
Walter Mazzarri 2016–17
Marco Silva 2017–18
Javi Gracia January 2018–

TEN YEAR LEAGUE RECORD

		P	W	D	L	F	A	Pts	Pos
2009-10	FL C	46	14	12	20	61	68	54	16
2010-11	FL C	46	16	13	17	77	71	61	14
2011-12	FL C	46	16	16	14	56	64	64	11
2012-13	FL C	46	23	8	15	85	58	77	3
2013-14	FL C	46	15	15	16	74	64	60	13
2014-15	FL C	46	27	8	11	91	50	89	2
2015-16	PR Lge	38	12	9	17	40	50	45	13
2016-17	PR Lge	38	11	7	20	40	68	40	17
2017-18	PR Lge	38	11	8	19	44	64	41	14
2018-19	PR Lge	38	14	8	16	52	59	50	11

DID YOU KNOW ?

Watford have gained national and regional honours in indoor five-a-side contests on two occasions. In 1984 they defeated Aston Villa 1-0 to win the *Daily Express* national title while in 1993 they beat Wimbledon 2-1 to secure the London *Evening Standard* prize.

WATFORD – PREMIER LEAGUE 2018–19 LEAGUE RECORD

Match No.	Date	Venue	Opponents	Result	H/T Score	Lg Pos.	Goalscorers	Attendance
1	Aug 11	H	Brighton & HA	W 2-0	1-0	2	Pereyra 2 [35, 54]	20,051
2	19	A	Burnley	W 3-1	1-1	3	Gray [3], Deeney [48], Hughes [51]	18,822
3	26	H	Crystal Palace	W 2-1	0-0	3	Pereyra [53], Holebas [71]	20,014
4	Sept 2	H	Tottenham H	W 2-1	0-0	3	Deeney [69], Cathcart [76]	20,141
5	15	H	Manchester U	L 1-2	0-2	4	Gray [65]	20,537
6	22	A	Fulham	D 1-1	1-0	4	Gray [2]	23,418
7	29	A	Arsenal	L 0-2	0-0	6		60,019
8	Oct 6	H	Bournemouth	L 0-4	0-3	9		20,139
9	20	A	Wolverhampton W	W 2-0	2-0	7	Capoue [20], Pereyra [21]	31,144
10	27	H	Huddersfield T	W 3-0	2-0	7	Pereyra [10], Deulofeu [19], Success [80]	20,457
11	Nov 3	A	Newcastle U	L 0-1	0-0	8		49,157
12	10	A	Southampton	D 1-1	0-1	7	Holebas [82]	28,153
13	24	H	Liverpool	L 0-3	0-0	9		20,540
14	Dec 1	A	Leicester C	L 0-2	0-2	10		31,353
15	4	H	Manchester C	L 1-2	0-1	11	Doucoure [85]	20,389
16	10	A	Everton	D 2-2	0-1	12	Coleman (og) [63], Doucoure [65]	38,400
17	15	H	Cardiff C	W 3-2	1-0	10	Deulofeu [16], Holebas [52], Quina [68]	20,032
18	22	A	West Ham U	W 2-0	1-0	7	Deeney (pen) [30], Deulofeu [87]	56,833
19	26	H	Chelsea	L 1-2	1-1	9	Pereyra [45]	20,415
20	29	H	Newcastle U	D 1-1	0-1	9	Doucoure [82]	20,336
21	Jan 2	A	Bournemouth	D 3-3	3-3	8	Deeney 2 [14, 27], Sema [38]	10,261
22	12	A	Crystal Palace	W 2-1	0-1	7	Cathcart [67], Cleverley [74]	25,010
23	19	H	Burnley	D 0-0	0-0	7		19,510
24	30	A	Tottenham H	L 1-2	1-0	9	Cathcart [38]	29,164
25	Feb 2	A	Brighton & HA	D 0-0	0-0	8		30,414
26	9	H	Everton	W 1-0	0-0	8	Gray [65]	20,333
27	22	A	Cardiff C	W 5-1	1-0	7	Deulofeu 3 [18, 61, 63], Deeney 2 [73, 90]	30,387
28	27	A	Liverpool	L 0-5	0-2	8		53,316
29	Mar 3	H	Leicester C	W 2-1	1-0	8	Deeney [5], Gray [90]	20,062
30	9	A	Manchester C	L 1-3	0-0	8	Deulofeu [66]	54,104
31	30	A	Manchester U	L 1-2	0-1	10	Doucoure [90]	74,543
32	Apr 2	H	Fulham	W 4-1	1-1	8	Doucoure [23], Hughes [63], Deeney [69], Femenia [75]	17,301
33	15	H	Arsenal	L 0-1	0-1	10		20,480
34	20	A	Huddersfield T	W 2-1	1-0	7	Deulofeu 2 [5, 80]	23,957
35	23	H	Southampton	D 1-1	0-1	7	Gray [90]	19,170
36	27	H	Wolverhampton W	L 1-2	0-1	9	Gray [49]	20,323
37	May 5	A	Chelsea	L 0-3	0-0	10		40,650
38	12	H	West Ham U	L 1-4	0-2	11	Deulofeu [46]	20,067

Final League Position: 11

GOALSCORERS

League (52): Deulofeu 10, Deeney 9 (1 pen), Gray 7, Pereyra 6, Doucoure 5, Cathcart 3, Holebas 3, Hughes 2, Capoue 1, Cleverley 1, Femenia 1, Quina 1, Sema 1, Success 1, own goal 1.
FA Cup (10): Capoue 2, Deeney 2 (1 pen), Deulofeu 2, Gray 2, Hughes 1, Success 1.
Carabao Cup (4): Success 2, Capoue 1, Quina 1.

Foster B 38	Janmaat D 17 + 1	Cathcart C 35 + 1	Kabasele C 19 + 2	Holebas J 27 + 1	Doucoure A 34 + 1	Capoue E 33	Hughes W 31 + 1	Pereyra R 33	Gray A 13 + 16	Deeney T 28 + 4	Success I 9 + 21	Sema K 9 + 8	Femenia K 22 + 7	Chalobah N 3 + 6	Mariappa A 20 + 6	Masina A 11 + 3	Navarro M 1 + 1	Deulofeu G 26 + 4	Prodl S — + 1	Wilmot B — + 2	Okaka S — + 2	Quina D 3 + 5	Cleverley T 4 + 9	Britos M 2 + 1	*Match No.*
1	2	3	4	5	6	7	8^{2}	9^{3}	10^{1}	11	12	13	14												1
1	2	3	4	5	6	7	8^{3}	9	11^{1}	10^{2}	14	12	13												2
1	2	3	4	5	6	7	8	9	10^{7}	11^{1}	13	12													3
1	2	3	4	5	6	7	8^{2}	9^{1}	10^{3}	11	12			13	14										4
1	2^{1}	3^{2}	4	5^{3}	6	7	8	9	11	10	14		12			13									5
1	2	3	4	5	6	7	8^{1}	9^{3}	10^{2}	11	13	14	12												6
1		3	4	5	6	7	8	9	10^{2}	11	12		13				2^{1}								7
1		3	4■	5	7	6	8^{1}	9^{3}	11^{7}	10	12		2		13			14							8
1		4			6	7	8	9	12		11^{2}		2		3	5		10^{1}	13^{3}	14					9
1		4^{3}	14		6	7	8	10	13		11^{1}	12	2		3	5		9^{2}							10
1		4		5	6	7	8^{2}	9	12		11^{3}		2	14	3			10^{1}			13				11
1		4		5	6		8^{2}	9^{1}	13	12	11		2	7	3			10							12
1		4			6	7	8^{7}	9	13	11	12		2		3	5		10^{1}							13
1		4		5	6	7■	8^{1}	9^{3}	12	13	11		2	14	3			10^{2}							14
1		4	3	5	9		8^{1}	10	14	11	7^{2}		2	6^{3}				13				12			15
1		4	3	5	6			9		11	10^{2}	8^{3}	2	13	14			12				7^{1}			16
1		4	3	5	6			9		11^{2}	12	8^{3}	2					10^{1}			13	7	14		17
1		4	3	5	6	7		9		11^{1}	13	8^{2}	2		14			10^{3}					12		18
1		4	3^{3}	5	6	7		9		11	14	8^{1}	2		12			10^{2}				13			19
1	2	4		14	13	7	8^{3}	9		12	11				3	5^{2}		10				6^{1}			20
1		4		5	6^{1}	7	13	9		11	14	8^{2}	2		3			10^{3}					12		21
1		4		5	6	7	8^{2}	9^{1}		11		12^{3}	2		3	14		10					13		22
1			4	5		7		9		10	12	8^{1}	2^{2}		3			11					6	13	23
1	2	4		5		7	8	9		11	12				3			10^{2}		13			6^{1}		24
1	2	4		5		7	8		12	11		9^{1}			3			10^{2}				13	6		25
1	2	4		5	6	7	8^{2}		12	11		9^{1}		14	3			10^{3}					13		26
1	2	4			6	7^{3}	8	9^{2}	14	11					3	5		10^{1}				12	13		27
1	2	4			6	7	8	9^{1}	12	10^{3}		14			3	5		11^{2}					13		28
1	2	4		5	6	7	8^{1}	9	12	11					3			10^{2}					13		29
1	2	14	3		7	8			11	12	10^{1}		6^{2}			5		13					9	4^{3}	30
1	2^{1}		3		6	7	8^{2}	9	13	11	14		12			5		10^{3}						4	31
1	13	4		5	6	7^{1}	8	9^{2}	12	11			2		3			10^{3}				14			32
1	2	4	3		8	7	9		11	10■	12	13	6^{1}			5^{2}									33
1		4			6	7	8^{2}		11^{1}		12	9	2	13	3	5	14	10^{3}							34
1	2	4^{2}	3		6	7	8^{1}	9	11		13		12			5		10							35
1		4^{2}	12	5	7	6	8^{1}	9	11		13		2		3			10							36
1		4		5	7		8	9	13	11^{2}	14		2	6^{3}	3			10^{1}					12		37
1		4	3^{3}	5■	6	7	8^{2}	9	12	11			2		14	13		10^{1}							38

FA Cup

Third Round	Woking	(a)	2-0
Fourth Round	Newcastle U	(a)	2-0
Fifth Round	QPR	(a)	1-0
Sixth Round	Crystal Palace	(h)	2-1
Semi-Final (*aet*)	Wolverhampton W	(Wembley)	3-2
Final	Manchester C	(Wembley)	0-6

Carabao Cup

Second Round	Reading	(a)	2-0
Third Round	Tottenham H	(a)	2-2

(Tottenham H won 4-2 on penalties)

WEST BROMWICH ALBION

FOUNDATION

There is a well known story that when employees of Salter's Spring Works in West Bromwich decided to form a football club, they had to send someone to the nearby Association Football stronghold of Wednesbury to purchase a football. A weekly subscription of 2d (less than 1p) was imposed and the name of the new club was West Bromwich Strollers.

The Hawthorns, West Bromwich, West Midlands B71 4LF.

Telephone: (0871) 271 1100.

Fax: (0871) 271 9851.

Ticket Office: (0121) 227 2227.

Website: www.wba.co.uk

Email: enquiries@wbafc.co.uk

Ground Capacity: 26,850.

Record Attendance: 64,815 v Arsenal, FA Cup 6th rd, 6 March 1937.

Pitch Measurements: 105m × 68m (115yd × 74.5yd).

Chairman: Li Piyue.

Chief Executive: Mark Jenkins.

Head Coach: Slaven Bilic.

First-Team Coach: Julian Dicks.

Colours: Navy blue and white striped shirts, white shorts with navy blue trim, navy blue socks with white trim.

Year Formed: 1878.

Turned Professional: 1885.

Previous Name: 1878, West Bromwich Strollers; 1881, West Bromwich Albion.

Club Nicknames: 'The Throstles', 'The Baggies', 'Albion'.

Grounds: 1878, Coopers Hill; 1879, Dartmouth Park; 1881, Bunns Field, Walsall Street; 1882, Four Acres (Dartmouth Cricket Club); 1885, Stoney Lane; 1900, The Hawthorns.

First Football League Game: 8 September 1888, Football League, v Stoke (a) W 2–0 – Roberts; Jack Horton, Green; Ezra Horton, Perry, Bayliss; Bassett, Woodhall (1), Hendry, Pearson, Wilson (1).

Record League Victory: 12–0 v Darwen, Division 1, 4 April 1892 – Reader; Jack Horton, McCulloch; Reynolds (2), Perry, Groves; Bassett (3), McLeod, Nicholls (1), Pearson (4), Geddes (1), (1 og).

Record Cup Victory: 10–1 v Chatham (away), FA Cup 3rd rd, 2 March 1889 – Roberts; Jack Horton, Green; Timmins (1), Charles Perry, Ezra Horton; Bassett (2), Walter Perry (1), Bayliss (2), Pearson, Wilson (3), (1 og).

League Champions: Division 1 – 1919–20; FL C – 2007–08; Division 2 – 1901–02, 1910–11.
Runners-up: Division 1 – 1924–25, 1953–54; FL C – 2009–10; First Division – 2001–02, 2003–04; Division 2 – 1930–31, 1948–49.

FA Cup Winners: 1888, 1892, 1931, 1954, 1968.
Runners-up: 1886, 1887, 1895, 1912, 1935.

League Cup Winners: 1966.
Runners-up: 1967, 1970.

European Competitions
Fairs Cup: 1966–67.
UEFA Cup: 1978–79 *(qf)*, 1979–80, 1981–82.
European Cup-Winners' Cup: 1968–69 *(qf)*.

THE **Sun** FACT FILE

West Bromwich Albion midfield player Asa Hartford was due to sign for Leeds United in November 1971 but the deal was called off after a pre-transfer medical found he had a 'hole in the heart' condition. Despite this, Hartford went on to gain 50 caps for Scotland and continued playing senior football for another 20 years, making a total of over 900 first-team appearances.

Record Defeat: 3–10 v Stoke C, Division 1, 4 February 1937.

Most League Points (2 for a win): 60, Division 1, 1919–20.

Most League Points (3 for a win): 91, FL C, 2009–10.

Most League Goals: 105, Division 2, 1929–30.

Highest League Scorer in Season: William 'Ginger' Richardson, 39, Division 1, 1935–36.

Most League Goals in Total Aggregate: Tony Brown, 218, 1963–79.

Most League Goals in One Match: 6, Jimmy Cookson v Blackpool, Division 2, 17 September 1927.

Most Capped Player: James Morrison, 46, Scotland.

Most League Appearances: Tony Brown, 574, 1963–80.

Youngest League Player: Charlie Wilson, 16 years 73 days v Oldham Ath, 1 October 1921.

Record Transfer Fee Received: £12,000,000 (rising to £15,000,000) from Stoke C for Saido Berahino, January 2017

Record Transfer Fee Paid: £15,000,000 to RB Leipzig for Oliver Burke, August 2017.

Football League Record: 1888 Founder Member of Football League; 1901–02 Division 2; 1902–04 Division 1; 1904–11 Division 2; 1911–27 Division 1; 1927–31 Division 2; 1931–38 Division 1; 1938–49 Division 2; 1949–73 Division 1; 1973–76 Division 2; 1976–86 Division 1; 1986–91 Division 2; 1991–92 Division 3; 1992–93 Division 2; 1993–2002 Division 1; 2002–03 Premier League; 2003–04 Division 1; 2004–06 Premier League; 2006–08 FL C; 2008–09 Premier League; 2009–10 FL C; 2010–18 Premier League; 2018– FL C.

LATEST SEQUENCES

Longest Sequence of League Wins: 11, 5.4.1930 – 8.9.1930.

Longest Sequence of League Defeats: 11, 28.10.1995 – 26.12.1995.

Longest Sequence of League Draws: 5, 30.8.1999 – 3.10.1999.

Longest Sequence of Unbeaten League Matches: 17, 7.9.1957 – 7.12.1957.

Longest Sequence Without a League Win: 20, 27.8.2017 – 2.1.2018.

Successive Scoring Runs: 36 from 26.4.1958.

Successive Non-scoring Runs: 5 from 1.4.2017.

MANAGERS

Louis Ford 1890–92
(Secretary-Manager)
Henry Jackson 1892–94
(Secretary-Manager)
Edward Stephenson 1894–95
(Secretary-Manager)
Clement Keys 1895–96
(Secretary-Manager)
Frank Heaven 1896–1902
(Secretary-Manager)
Fred Everiss 1902–48
Jack Smith 1948–52
Jesse Carver 1952
Vic Buckingham 1953–59
Gordon Clark 1959–61
Archie Macaulay 1961–63
Jimmy Hagan 1963–67
Alan Ashman 1967–71
Don Howe 1971–75
Johnny Giles 1975–77
Ronnie Allen 1977
Ron Atkinson 1978–81
Ronnie Allen 1981–82
Ron Wylie 1982–84
Johnny Giles 1984–85
Nobby Stiles 1985–86
Ron Saunders 1986–87
Ron Atkinson 1987–88
Brian Talbot 1988–91
Bobby Gould 1991–92
Ossie Ardiles 1992–93
Keith Burkinshaw 1993–94
Alan Buckley 1994–97
Ray Harford 1997
Denis Smith 1997–1999
Brian Little 1999–2000
Gary Megson 2000–04
Bryan Robson 2004–06
Tony Mowbray 2006–09
Roberto Di Matteo 2009–11
Roy Hodgson 2011–12
Steve Clarke 2012–13
Pepe Mel 2014
Alan Irvine 2014
Tony Pulis 2015–17
Alan Pardew 2017–18
Darren Moore 2018–19
Slaven Bilic June 2019–

TEN YEAR LEAGUE RECORD

		P	W	D	L	F	A	Pts	Pos
2009-10	FL C	46	26	13	7	89	48	91	2
2010-11	PR Lge	38	12	11	15	56	71	47	11
2011-12	PR Lge	38	13	8	17	45	52	47	10
2012-13	PR Lge	38	14	7	17	53	57	49	8
2013-14	PR Lge	38	7	15	16	43	59	36	17
2014-15	PR Lge	38	11	11	16	38	51	44	13
2015-16	PR Lge	38	10	13	15	34	48	43	14
2016-17	PR Lge	38	12	9	17	43	51	45	10
2017-18	PR Lge	38	6	13	19	31	56	31	20
2018-19	FL C	46	23	11	12	87	62	80	4

DID YOU KNOW?

West Bromwich Albion finished in third position in the old First Division in 1978–79 behind Nottingham Forest and Liverpool. However, the Baggies had three players selected for the PFA team of the season (Derek Statham, Cyrille Regis and Laurie Cunningham), with no other club featuring with more than two players.

WEST BROMWICH ALBION – SKY BET CHAMPIONSHIP 2018–19 LEAGUE RECORD

Match No.	Date	Venue	Opponents	Result		H/T Score	Lg Pos.	Goalscorers	Attendance
1	Aug 4	H	Bolton W	L	1-2	1-1	20	Barnes 45	25,901
2	7	A	Nottingham F	D	1-1	0-0	17	Phillips 87	27,850
3	11	A	Norwich C	W	4-3	1-1	8	Rodriguez 2 (1 pen) 33 (p), 47, Barnes 65, Robson-Kanu 79	25,144
4	18	H	QPR	W	7-1	1-1	3	Phillips 2 29, 88, Gibbs 53, Rodriguez 2 (2 pens) 56, 82, Gayle 67, Robson-Kanu 90	22,753
5	24	A	Middlesbrough	L	0-1	0-0	7		22,906
6	Sept 1	H	Stoke C	W	2-1	1-0	8	Gayle 2 16, 59	25,183
7	14	A	Birmingham C	D	1-1	1-1	5	Phillips 39	22,715
8	18	H	Bristol C	W	4-2	3-0	3	Rodriguez 2 (1 pen) 16 (p), 28, Gayle 24, Barnes 63	22,051
9	22	H	Millwall	W	2-0	0-0	3	Gayle 68, Gibbs 76	23,563
10	29	A	Preston NE	W	3-2	0-0	1	Rodriguez 48, Davies (og) 73, Gayle 88	14,099
11	Oct 3	A	Sheffield W	D	2-2	0-2	4	Pelupessy (og) 85, Barnes 87	22,150
12	6	H	Reading	W	4-1	0-1	2	Gayle 2 49, 65, Barnes 72, Bartley 80	22,865
13	20	A	Wigan Ath	L	0-1	0-0	3		12,739
14	24	H	Derby Co	L	1-4	0-2	4	Rodriguez 83	22,848
15	27	H	Blackburn R	D	1-1	1-0	5	Dawson 40	23,820
16	Nov 3	A	Hull C	L	0-1	0-1	7		11,916
17	10	H	Leeds U	W	4-1	0-0	5	Robson-Kanu 51, Phillips 67, Barnes 82, Gayle 83	25,661
18	23	A	Ipswich T	W	2-1	1-0	2	Rodriguez 26, Barnes 77	22,995
19	28	A	Swansea C	W	2-1	2-1	4	Dawson 13, Hegazi 44	17,865
20	Dec 3	H	Brentford	D	1-1	0-0	3	Barnes 77	20,949
21	7	H	Aston Villa	D	2-2	1-1	3	Gayle 28, Rodriguez 90	26,513
22	14	A	Sheffield U	W	2-1	1-1	3	Barry 41, Gibbs 76	23,400
23	22	A	Rotherham U	W	4-0	3-0	3	Gayle 3 6, 44, 54, Barnes 20	10,593
24	26	H	Wigan Ath	W	2-0	1-0	3	Rodriguez 2 8, 69	25,555
25	29	H	Sheffield W	D	1-1	0-1	3	Brunt 90	26,548
26	Jan 1	A	Blackburn R	L	1-2	0-0	4	Rodriguez (pen) 63	14,258
27	12	H	Norwich C	D	1-1	1-0	4	Gayle 12	26,544
28	21	A	Bolton W	W	2-0	1-0	3	Rodriguez 19, Field 75	14,750
29	Feb 2	H	Middlesbrough	L	2-3	1-1	4	Rodriguez 42, Gayle 63	24,863
30	9	A	Stoke C	W	1-0	1-0	4	Gayle 25	26,828
31	12	H	Nottingham F	D	2-2	0-1	4	Murphy 54, Rodriguez (pen) 89	22,691
32	16	A	Aston Villa	W	2-0	2-0	4	Robson-Kanu 41, Rodriguez 45	39,263
33	19	A	QPR	W	3-2	1-1	4	Montero 5, Murphy 61, Livermore 90	12,257
34	23	H	Sheffield U	L	0-1	0-1	4		24,928
35	Mar 1	A	Leeds U	L	0-4	0-2	4		35,888
36	9	H	Ipswich T	D	1-1	1-0	4	Johansen 4	23,973
37	13	H	Swansea C	W	3-0	1-0	4	Brunt 19, Holgate 54, Rodriguez 85	20,282
38	16	A	Brentford	W	1-0	0-0	4	Edwards 51	11,488
39	29	H	Birmingham C	W	3-2	0-1	4	Gayle 47, Rodriguez (pen) 65, Livermore 74	24,789
40	Apr 6	A	Millwall	L	0-2	0-1	4		15,303
41	9	A	Bristol C	L	2-3	0-3	4	Gayle 47, Rodriguez 74	20,581
42	13	H	Preston NE	W	4-1	3-0	4	Gayle 3 27, 31, 71, Rodriguez 43	25,088
43	19	H	Hull C	W	3-2	1-0	4	Gibbs 42, Gayle 2 62, 85	23,501
44	22	A	Reading	D	0-0	0-0	4		17,255
45	27	H	Rotherham U	W	2-1	0-0	4	Rodriguez (pen) 77, Harper 79	24,534
46	May 5	A	Derby Co	L	1-3	0-1	4	Johansen 47	32,055

Final League Position: 4

GOALSCORERS

League (87): Gayle 23, Rodriguez 22 (8 pens), Barnes 9, Phillips 5, Gibbs 4, Robson-Kanu 4, Brunt 2, Dawson 2, Johansen 2, Livermore 2, Murphy 2, Barry 1, Bartley 1, Edwards 1, Field 1, Harper 1, Hegazi 1, Holgate 1, Montero 1, own goals 2.
FA Cup (2): Bartley 1, Sako 1.
Carabao Cup (3): Burke 1, Edwards 1, Leko 1.
Checkatrade Trophy (4): Azaz 1, Bradley 1, Leko 1, Tulloch 1.
Championship Play-offs (2): Dawson 1, Gayle 1.

Johnstone S 46	Nyom A 2	Bartley K 24 + 4	Hegazi A 38	Gibbs K 35 + 1	Phillips M 23 + 7	Livermore J 36 + 3	Brunt C 22 + 10	Barnes H 26	Rodriguez J 45	Robson-Kanu H 14 + 21	Burke O — + 3	Adarabioyo T 21 + 8	Morrison J 11 + 8	Gayle D 33 + 6	Townsend C 10 + 2	Barry G 15 + 9	Dawson C 40 + 1	Hoolahan W — + 6	Field S 4 + 8	Mears T 4 + 5	Edwards K 3 + 3	Sako B 2 + 3	Harper R 13 + 3	Holgate M 19	Leko J — + 2	Murphy J 8 + 5	Johansen S 11 + 1	Montero J 1 + 3	Match No.
1	2	3	4	5	6	7	8	9^1	10	11	12																		1
1		3	4	5	6	7	8	9	11^1	13		2	10^2	12															2
1	2	3	4	5^1	6	7	8	9^3	10	13			14	11^2	12														3
1		3	4	5	6	7	8^3	9^1	10	13		2	14	11^2		12													4
1		4	3	8	5	6	7	9^2	10	14		2^3	12	11^1			13												5
1		4	3	8	5	6	7	9^1	10	12				11^2		13	2												6
1		4	3		5	6	7^2	9	10^1	12				11	8	13	2												7
1		4	3	8	5	6		9	10^2	13				11^1		7^3	2	12	14										8
1		4	3	8	5^2	6	7	9^1	10			14		11^3			2	13		12									9
1		4	3	8		6	12	9^2	10	13				11^1		7^3	2		14	5									10
1		4	3	8		6	7	9	10^2	14				11^1		12	2	13		5^3									11
1		4	3	8		6^1	13	9^2	10			14		11		7	2			5^3	12								12
1		4	3	8		6■	7	9	10	13		12		11^3			2^1			5^2	14								13
1		4		8^2	5^1		7	9	10	13		3	14	11^3			2		6	12									14
1		4^1			5	6	13	9^2	10	14		2	7		8		3	12				11^3							15
1			3		5^3	6	7^1	11	10		13	4	9^2		8		2		12			14							16
1			4	5^2	8^1	6		9	11	10^3		2	7	12			3			13			14						17
1			4	5	6	7		11	10	9^2		2	8^1	12		13	3												18
1			4	5	6	7		11^2	10	9^1		2	8	12		13	3												19
1			4	5	6	7		9	10	11^1		2	8	12			3												20
1			4	5	6	7^1	12	11	10		13	2^2		9		8	3												21
1			4	5	6	7	12	9^1	10			2		11		8	3												22
1			4	5	6^2	8	12	11	10	14		2	13	9^3		7^1	3												23
1			4	5^1	6	8^2	14	11	9	12		2	13	10^3		7	3												24
1		4		5	13	7	8	11	9■	14		2^3	6^2			12	3					10^1							25
1		4		5	6	12■	13	9	11^3	10		2^1	8^2			7	3	14											26
1			4	5			8		9	10^2				11^1		7	3					12	6	2	13				27
1			4	5			8^3		10	9^1		14		11		7	3		12			13	6^2	2					28
1			4	5		13	14		10	9^2				11		7^1	3		8^3				6	2		12			29
1		14	4	5		6			10					11^1		7	3						13	2		9^2	8^3	12	30
1				5		7^2			10			4		11		12	3	13					6	2		9	8^1		31
1		13	4	5		7			10	9^3						8^1	3		12				6	2		11^2	14		32
1			4	5	14	6			10							13	3		7^2				12	2		9	8^1	11^3	33
1			4^2	5	9^1	8^3			10			13		11		7	3				14		6	2				12	34
1			4			7			10	9^3		5	12	11		8^1	3		13				6^2	2				14	35
1		3			6^3	7			9			4^1	13	10	5		2		14						12	11	8^2		36
1		12	4			8	7		10	13				9	5		3^1			14			6	2^2		11^3			37
1			4			13	7		10	12			6^2	11	5		3				9^1			2			8		38
1		14	4			7	6		9^2	12			8^3	10	5		3				11^1			2		13			39
1			4■			6	7		11^2	9^1		3		10	5					13				2		12	8		40
1		4		14		7			9	13		12		10	5^3		3				11^1		6^2	2			8		41
1		4	3^1	9^2	14	6^3	7		10			12		11	13		2							5			8		42
1		3	4^1	9	13		7			10^3		12		11			2						6^2	5		14	8		43
1		4			12		13		11	10^2		2		14	8		3		7^1				6	5^3		9			44
1		3	4	9	12		7		10^3	14				11			2						6	5^2		13	8^1		45
1		3^2	4	8	12				11	14■				10			2		13				6	5		9^3	7^1		46

FA Cup

Third Round	Wigan Ath	(h)	1-0
Fourth Round	Brighton & HA	(a)	0-0
Replay	Brighton & HA	(h)	1-3
(aet)			

Carabao Cup

First Round	Luton T	(h)	1-0
Second Round	Mansfield T	(h)	2-1
Third Round	Crystal Palace	(h)	0-3

Checkatrade Trophy (WBA U21)

Group C (N)	Blackpool	(a)	2-1
Group C (N)	Accrington S	(a)	1-2
Group C (N)	Macclesfield T	(a)	1-2

Championship Play-offs

Semi-Final 1st leg	Aston Villa	(a)	1-2
Semi-Final 2nd leg	Aston Villa	(h)	1-0

(aet; Aston Villa won 4-3 on penalties)

WEST HAM UNITED

FOUNDATION

Thames Ironworks FC was formed by employees of this famous shipbuilding company in 1895 and entered the FA Cup in their initial season at Chatham and the London League in their second. The committee wanted to introduce professional players, so Thames Ironworks was wound up in June 1900 and relaunched a month later as West Ham United.

London Stadium, Queen Elizabeth Olympic Park, London E20 2ST.

Telephone: (020) 8548 2748.

Fax: (020) 8548 2758.

Ticket Office: (0333) 030 1966.

Website: www.whufc.com

Email: supporterservices@westhamunited.co.uk

Ground Capacity: 60,000.

Record Attendance: 42,322 v Tottenham H, Division 1, 17 October 1970 (at Boleyn Ground); 59,988 v Everton, Premier League, 30 March 2019 (at London Stadium).

Pitch Measurements: 105m × 68m (115yd × 74.5yd).

Joint Chairmen: David Sullivan and David Gold.

Vice-Chairman: Baroness Karren Brady CBE.

Chief Operating Officer: Ben Illingworth.

Manager: Manuel Pellegrini.

Assistant Manager: Rubén Cousillas.

Colours: Claret shirts with sky blue trim, white shorts with claret and sky blue trim, white socks with claret and sky blue trim.

Year Formed: 1895.

Turned Professional: 1900.

Previous Name: 1895, Thames Ironworks FC; 1900, West Ham United.

Club Nicknames: 'The Hammers', 'The Irons'.

Grounds: 1895, Memorial Recreation Ground, Canning Town; 1904, Boleyn Ground; 2016, London Stadium.

First Football League Game: 30 August 1919, Division 2, v Lincoln C (h) D 1–1 – Hufton; Cope, Lee; Lane, Fenwick, McCrae; David Smith, Moyes (1), Puddefoot, Morris, Bradshaw.

Record League Victory: 8–0 v Rotherham U, Division 2, 8 March 1958 – Gregory; Bond, Wright; Malcolm, Brown, Lansdowne; Grice, Smith (2), Keeble (2), Dick (4), Musgrove. 8–0 v Sunderland, Division 1, 19 October 1968 – Ferguson; Bonds, Charles; Peters, Stephenson, Moore (1); Redknapp, Boyce, Brooking (1), Hurst (6), Sissons.

HONOURS

League Champions: Division 2 – 1957–58, 1980–81.
Runners-up: First Division – 1992–93; Division 2 – 1922–23, 1990–91.

FA Cup Winners: 1964, 1975, 1980.
Runners-up: 1923, 2006.

League Cup: *Runners-up:* 1966, 1981.

European Competitions
UEFA Cup: 1999–2000; 2006–07.
Europa League: 2015–16, 2016–17.
European Cup-Winners' Cup: 1964–65 *(winners)*, 1965–66 *(sf)*, 1975–76 *(runners-up)*, 1980–81 *(qf)*.
Intertoto Cup: 1999 *(winners)*.

THE SUN FACT FILE

West Ham United were one of a number of British clubs who travelled to Germany to play exhibition matches against military teams to entertain the troops stationed there. The Hammers drew 2-2 with a Combined Services team at Berlin's Olympic Stadium on 2 October 1945. Both their goals were scored by forward Jackie Wood.

Record Cup Victory: 10–0 v Bury, League Cup 2nd rd (2nd leg), 25 October 1983 – Parkes; Stewart (1), Walford, Bonds (Orr), Martin (1), Devonshire (2), Allen, Cottee (4), Swindlehurst, Brooking (2), Pike.

Record Defeat: 2–8 v Blackburn R, Division 1, 26 December 1963; 0–6 v Oldham Ath, League Cup semi-final (1st leg), 14 February 1990.

Most League Points (2 for a win): 66, Division 2, 1980–81.

Most League Points (3 for a win): 88, Division 1, 1992–93.

Most League Goals: 101, Division 2, 1957–58.

Highest League Scorer in Season: Vic Watson, 42, Division 1, 1929–30.

Most League Goals in Total Aggregate: Vic Watson, 298, 1920–35.

Most League Goals in One Match: 6, Vic Watson v Leeds U, Division 1, 9 February 1929; 6, Geoff Hurst v Sunderland, Division 1, 19 October 1968.

Most Capped Player: Bobby Moore, 108, England.

Most League Appearances: Billy Bonds, 663, 1967–88.

Youngest League Player: Billy Williams, 16 years 221 days v Blackpool, 6 May 1922.

Record Transfer Fee Received: £25,000,000 from Marseille for Dmitri Payet, January 2017.

Record Transfer Fee Paid: £45,000,000 to Eintracht Frankfurt for Sébastien Haller, July 2019.

Football League Record: 1919 Elected to Division 2; 1923–32 Division 1; 1932–58 Division 2; 1958–78 Division 1; 1978–81 Division 2; 1981–89 Division 1; 1989–91 Division 2; 1991–93 Division 1; 1993–2003 Premier League; 2003–04 Division 1; 2004–05 FL C; 2005–11 Premier League; 2011–12 FL C; 2012– Premier League.

MANAGERS

Syd King 1902–32
Charlie Paynter 1932–50
Ted Fenton 1950–61
Ron Greenwood 1961–74
(continued as General Manager to 1977)
John Lyall 1974–89
Lou Macari 1989–90
Billy Bonds 1990–94
Harry Redknapp 1994–2001
Glenn Roeder 2001–03
Alan Pardew 2003–06
Alan Curbishley 2006–08
Gianfranco Zola 2008–10
Avram Grant 2010–11
Sam Allardyce 2011–15
Slaven Bilic 2015–17
David Moyes 2017–18
Manuel Pellegrini May 2018–

LATEST SEQUENCES

Longest Sequence of League Wins: 9, 19.10.1985 – 14.12.1985.

Longest Sequence of League Defeats: 9, 28.3.1932 – 29.8.1932.

Longest Sequence of League Draws: 5, 29.11.2015 – 26.12.2015.

Longest Sequence of Unbeaten League Matches: 27, 27.12.1980 – 10.10.1981.

Longest Sequence Without a League Win: 17, 31.1.1976 – 21.8.1976.

Successive Scoring Runs: 27 from 5.10.1957.

Successive Non-scoring Runs: 5 from 17.9.2006.

TEN YEAR LEAGUE RECORD

		P	W	D	L	F	A	Pts	Pos
2009-10	PR Lge	38	8	11	19	47	66	35	17
2010-11	PR Lge	38	7	12	19	43	70	33	20
2011-12	FL C	46	24	14	8	81	48	86	3
2012-13	PR Lge	38	12	10	16	45	53	46	10
2013-14	PR Lge	38	11	7	20	40	51	40	13
2014-15	PR Lge	38	12	11	15	44	47	47	12
2015-16	PR Lge	38	16	14	8	65	51	62	7
2016-17	PR Lge	38	12	9	17	47	64	45	11
2017-18	PR Lge	38	10	12	16	48	68	42	13
2018-19	PR Lge	38	15	7	16	52	55	52	10

DID YOU KNOW ?

When West Ham played in the European Cup-Winners' Cup in 1965–66 the Supporters' Club produced their own programmes for the three away ties against Olympiakos, Magdeburg and Borussia Dortmund. Just 200 copies were produced for each match and copies were handed out free to the Hammers' travelling supporters.

WEST HAM UNITED – PREMIER LEAGUE 2018–19 LEAGUE RECORD

Match No.	*Date*	*Venue*	*Opponents*	*Result*		*H/T Score*	*Lg Pos.*	*Goalscorers*	*Attendance*
1	Aug 12	A	Liverpool	L	0-4	0-2	20		53,235
2	18	H	Bournemouth	L	1-2	1-0	20	Arnautovic (pen) [33]	56,888
3	25	A	Arsenal	L	1-3	1-1	20	Arnautovic [25]	59,830
4	Sept 1	H	Wolverhampton W	L	0-1	0-0	20		56,947
5	16	A	Everton	W	3-1	2-1	16	Yarmolenko 2 [11, 31], Arnautovic [61]	39,161
6	23	H	Chelsea	D	0-0	0-0	17		56,875
7	29	H	Manchester U	W	3-1	2-0	13	Felipe Anderson [5], Lindelof (og) [43], Arnautovic [74]	56,938
8	Oct 5	A	Brighton & HA	L	0-1	0-1	15		30,544
9	20	H	Tottenham H	L	0-1	0-1	15		56,921
10	27	A	Leicester C	D	1-1	1-0	13	Balbuena [30]	31,848
11	Nov 3	H	Burnley	W	4-2	1-1	13	Arnautovic [10], Felipe Anderson 2 [68, 84], Hernandez [90]	56,862
12	10	A	Huddersfield T	D	1-1	0-1	13	Felipe Anderson [74]	24,069
13	24	H	Manchester C	L	0-4	0-3	13		56,886
14	Dec 1	A	Newcastle U	W	3-0	1-0	13	Hernandez 2 [11, 63], Felipe Anderson [90]	51,853
15	4	H	Cardiff C	W	3-1	0-0	12	Lucas Perez 2 [49, 54], Antonio [61]	56,811
16	8	H	Crystal Palace	W	3-2	0-1	10	Snodgrass [48], Hernandez [62], Felipe Anderson [65]	56,995
17	15	A	Fulham	W	2-0	2-0	9	Snodgrass [17], Antonio [29]	24,081
18	22	H	Watford	L	0-2	0-1	12		56,833
19	27	A	Southampton	W	2-1	0-0	9	Felipe Anderson 2 [53, 59]	31,654
20	30	A	Burnley	L	0-2	0-2	11		20,933
21	Jan 2	H	Brighton & HA	D	2-2	0-0	10	Arnautovic 2 [66, 68]	59,870
22	12	H	Arsenal	W	1-0	0-0	9	Rice [48]	59,946
23	19	A	Bournemouth	L	0-2	0-0	10		10,495
24	29	A	Wolverhampton W	L	0-3	0-0	11		31,122
25	Feb 4	H	Liverpool	D	1-1	1-1	12	Antonio [28]	59,903
26	9	A	Crystal Palace	D	1-1	1-0	10	Noble (pen) [27]	25,552
27	22	H	Fulham	W	3-1	2-1	9	Hernandez [29], Diop [40], Antonio [90]	59,950
28	27	A	Manchester C	L	0-1	0-0	10		53,528
29	Mar 2	H	Newcastle U	W	2-0	2-0	9	Rice [7], Noble (pen) [42]	59,910
30	9	A	Cardiff C	L	0-2	0-1	9		32,458
31	16	H	Huddersfield T	W	4-3	1-2	9	Noble (pen) [15], Ogbonna [75], Hernandez 2 [84, 90]	59,931
32	30	H	Everton	L	0-2	0-2	11		59,988
33	Apr 8	A	Chelsea	L	0-2	0-1	11		40,537
34	13	A	Manchester U	L	1-2	0-1	11	Felipe Anderson [49]	74,478
35	20	H	Leicester C	D	2-2	1-0	11	Antonio [37], Lucas Perez [82]	59,960
36	27	A	Tottenham H	W	1-0	0-0	11	Antonio [67]	60,043
37	May 4	H	Southampton	W	3-0	1-0	11	Arnautovic 2 [16, 69], Fredericks [72]	59,961
38	12	A	Watford	W	4-1	2-0	10	Noble 2 (1 pen) [15, 78 (p)], Lanzini [39], Arnautovic [71]	20,067

Final League Position: 10

GOALSCORERS

League (52): Arnautovic 10 (1 pen), Felipe Anderson 9, Hernandez 7, Antonio 6, Noble 5 (4 pens), Lucas Perez 3, Rice 2, Snodgrass 2, Yarmolenko 2, Balbuena 1, Diop 1, Fredericks 1, Lanzini 1, Ogbonna 1, own goal 1.
FA Cup (4): Arnautovic 1, Carroll 1, Felipe Anderson 1, Lucas Perez 1.
Carabao Cup (12): Diangana 2, Lucas Perez 2, Ogbonna 2, Snodgrass 2, Antonio 1, Diop 1, Fredericks 1, Hernandez 1.
Checkatrade Trophy (0).

Fabianski L 38	Fredericks R 12 + 3	Balbuena F 23	Ogbonna A 20 + 4	Masuaku A 19 + 4	Noble M 29 + 2	Rice D 34	Antonio M 22 + 11	Wilshere J 4 + 4	Felipe Anderson G 36	Arnautovic M 24 + 4	Snodgrass R 25 + 8	Hernandez J 14 + 11	Yarmolenko A 5 + 4	Zabaleta P 23 + 3	Sanchez C 2 + 5	Lucas Perez M 4 + 11	Diop I 33	Cresswell A 18 + 2	Obiang P 12 + 12	Diangana G 6 + 11	Carroll A 3 + 9	Xande Silva N — + 1	Nasri S 3 + 2	Lanzini M 8 + 2	Johnson B 1	*Match No.*
1	2	3	4	5	6	7^{2}	8	9	10^{3}	11^{1}	12	13	14													1
1		3	4	5	7^{1}			8	9	10	6^{3}	11^{2}	12	2	13	14										2
1	2	3		5			9^{2}	8	10	11^{3}	6^{1}	12	14		7	13	4									3
1	2	3					10^{1}	7^{2}	9	11	8^{3}	14	12		6		4	5	13							4
1		3		5	8^{2}	6	12		10	11^{3}	14		7^{1}	2	13		4		9							5
1		4		5	6^{1}	7	10^{3}		11^{2}		13		9	2	14	12	3		8							6
1		3		5	8	6	13		10^{1}	11^{2}	12		7^{3}	2			4		9	14						7
1		3		5	8^{1}	6	12		10	11	14		7^{3}	2		13	4		9^{2}							8
1		3			8^{1}	6	14		10^{2}	11	9	13	7^{3}	2			4	5		12						9
1		3	14	5	8■	6	12		10^{1}		9	11^{2}		2			4	13		7^{3}						10
1		3	14			6	13		10	11^{3}	9	12		2			4	5	8^{1}	7^{2}						11
1	14	3				6	13		10	11	9	12		2^{3}			4	5	8^{2}	7^{1}						12
1		3		5^{3}		7	9		10^{2}	11		13		2		14	4	12	6	8^{1}						13
1		3		12	7^{3}	8		14	9	11^{1}	6	10		2			4	5^{2}	13							14
1			4	5	7	8	2		9	11^{1}	6^{2}	10^{3}				12	3			14	13					15
1		3		5	7	8			9^{3}		6	10^{2}		2		11^{1}	4		14	13	12					16
1		3		5	7^{1}	8	10^{2}		9		6	11^{3}		2			4		12	14	13					17
1		3^{1}	12	5	7^{3}	8	10		9		6	11^{2}		2			4			14	13					18
1			4	14	13	7	2		10		9^{3}					11^{2}	3	5	6	8^{1}	12					19
1			4		7	8	2		9	10^{3}	6^{2}					11^{1}	3	5		13	12	14				20
1			4		14	8	13		9	11	6^{2}			2		12	3	5	7^{3}		10^{1}					21
1			4		6	7	8^{3}		10	11^{2}	12			2			3	5	14		13		9^{1}			22
1			4		6^{2}	7	8		10		12	13		2			3	5		14	11^{3}		9^{1}			23
1			4	5	7^{2}	8	10		9	11^{3}	6^{1}	14		2			3		13		12					24
1	2		4	14	7^{1}	6	8		10^{3}		9	11^{2}					3	5	12		13					25
1	2^{1}		4		8	6	7^{3}		10	12	9	11^{2}		14			3	5	13							26
1	12		4		8	6	7		10^{3}	13	9	11^{2}		2^{1}			3	5						14		27
1	2		4			7	8		10^{1}					13			3		6	14	11		8^{2}	12	5^{3}	28
1	2		4	12	8^{3}	6			10	13	7	11^{1}					3	5^{2}	14					9		29
1	2		4		8^{3}	6	13		10^{1}	12	7	11					3	5					14	9^{2}		30
1			4		8^{3}	6	7^{1}		10	11^{2}		12		2		14	3	5					13	9		31
1			4			7	12			10^{3}	6	13		2		11^{2}	3	5	8^{1}	14				9		32
1	2	3	4		7^{2}	6			10	8	12	11^{1}						5	13					9		33
1	14	3	4	5	8	6	13		7		9	11^{2}		2^{3}						12				10^{1}		34
1		3	4	5	8^{3}	6	7	14	10	11^{2}	9^{1}			2		13			12							35
1	2	3	14	5	8^{3}	6	7		10	11^{1}	9^{2}					13	4		12							36
1	2	3		5	7^{1}		10	12		11					13	14	4		6	8^{3}				9^{2}		37
1	2^{2}	3		5	7	6^{3}	8	13	10	11				12	14		4							9^{1}		38

FA Cup

Third Round	Birmingham C	(h)	2-0
Fourth Round	AFC Wimbledon	(a)	2-4

Carabao Cup

Second Round	AFC Wimbledon	(a)	3-1
Third Round	Macclesfield T	(h)	8-0
Fourth Round	Tottenham H	(h)	1-3

Checkatrade Trophy (West Ham U U21)

Group D (S)	Bristol R	(a)	0-2
Group D (S)	Exeter C	(a)	0-2
Group D (S)	Yeovil T	(a)	0-4

WIGAN ATHLETIC

FOUNDATION

Following the demise of Wigan Borough and their resignation from the Football League in 1931, a public meeting was called in Wigan at the Queen's Hall in May 1932 at which a new club, Wigan Athletic, was founded in the hope of carrying on in the Football League. With this in mind, they bought Springfield Park for £2,250, but failed to gain admission to the Football League until 46 years later.

The DW Stadium, Loire Drive, Newtown, Wigan, Lancashire WN5 0UZ.

Telephone: (01942) 774 000.

Fax: (01942) 770 477.

Ticket Office: (01942) 311 311.

Website: www.wiganathletic.com

Email: feedback@wiganathletic.com

Ground Capacity: 25,146.

Record Attendance: 27,526 v Hereford U, 12 December 1953 (at Springfield Park); 25,133 v Manchester U, Premier League, 11 May 2008 (at DW Stadium).

Pitch Measurements: 105m × 68m (115yd × 74.5yd).

Executive Chairman: Darren Royle.

Chief Executive: Jonathan Jackson.

Manager: Paul Cook.

Assistant Manager: Leam Richardson.

Colours: White shirts with blue panel and green stripes, blue shorts with white trim, blue socks with white and green trim.

Year Formed: 1932.

Turned Professional: 1932.

Club Nickname: 'The Latics'.

Grounds: 1932, Springfield Park; 1999, JJB Stadium (renamed the DW Stadium, 2009).

First Football League Game: 19 August 1978, Division 4, v Hereford U (a) D 0–0 – Brown; Hinnigan, Gore, Gillibrand, Ward, Davids, Corrigan, Purdie, Houghton, Wilkie, Wright.

Record League Victory: 7–0 v Oxford U, FL 1, 23 December 2017 – Walton; Bythe, Dunkley, Burn, Evans, Morsy, Massey (1), Powell (Toney), Jacobs (Robert G), Grigg (3) (Power 2), James.

Record Cup Victory: 6–0 v Carlisle U (a), FA Cup 1st rd, 24 November 1934 – Caunce; Robinson, Talbot; Paterson, Watson, Tufnell; Armes (2), Robson (1), Roberts (2), Felton, Scott (1).

Record Defeat: 1–9 v Tottenham H, Premier League, 22 November 2009; 0–8 v Chelsea, Premier League, 9 May 2010.

Most League Points (2 for a win): 55, Division 4, 1978–79 and 1979–80.

HONOURS

League Champions: FL 1 – 2015–16, 2017–18; Second Division – 2002–03; Third Division – 1996–97.
Runners-up: FL C – 2004–05.

FA Cup Winners: 2013.

League Cup: *Runners-up:* 2006.

League Trophy Winners: 1985, 1999.

European Competitions
Europa League: 2013–14.

THE SUN FACT FILE

Although Wigan Athletic reached the final of the Lancashire and Cheshire Floodlight Cup in 1954–55 it was not until the 1966–67 season that floodlights were installed at the Latics' Springfield Park ground. The lights were used for the first time for a Northern Floodlit League match against Crewe Alexandra on 19 October 1966.

Most League Points (3 for a win): 100, Division 2, 2002–03.

Most League Goals: 89, FL 1, 2017–18.

Highest League Scorer in Season: Graeme Jones, 31, Division 3, 1996–97.

Most League Goals in Total Aggregate: Andy Liddell, 70, 1998–2004.

Most League Goals in One Match: Not more than three goals by one player.

Most Capped Players: Kevin Kilbane, 22 (110), Republic of Ireland; Henri Camara, 22 (99), Senegal.

Most League Appearances: Kevin Langley, 317, 1981–86, 1990–94.

Youngest League Player: Steve Nugent, 16 years 132 days v Leyton Orient, 16 September 1989.

Record Transfer Fee Received: £15,250,000 from Manchester U for Antonio Valencia, June 2009.

Record Transfer Fee Paid: £7,000,000 to Newcastle U for Charles N'Zogbia, January 2009.

Football League Record: 1978 Elected to Division 4; 1982–92 Division 3; 1992–93 Division 2; 1993–97 Division 3; 1997–2003 Division 2; 2003–04 Division 1; 2004–05 FL C; 2005–13 Premier League; 2013–15 FL C; 2015–16 FL 1; 2016–17 FL C; 2017–18 FL 1; 2018– FL C.

LATEST SEQUENCES

Longest Sequence of League Wins: 11, 2.11.2002 – 18.1.2003.

Longest Sequence of League Defeats: 8, 10.9.2011 – 6.11.2011.

Longest Sequence of League Draws: 6, 11.12.2001 – 5.1.2002.

Longest Sequence of Unbeaten League Matches: 25, 8.5.1999 – 3.1.2000.

Longest Sequence Without a League Win: 14, 9.5.1989 – 17.10.1989.

Successive Scoring Runs: 24 from 27.4.1996.

Successive Non-scoring Runs: 4 from 8.12.2018.

MANAGERS

Charlie Spencer 1932–37
Jimmy Milne 1946–47
Bob Pryde 1949–52
Ted Goodier 1952–54
Walter Crook 1954–55
Ron Suart 1955–56
Billy Cooke 1956
Sam Barkas 1957
Trevor Hitchen 1957–58
Malcolm Barrass 1958–59
Jimmy Shirley 1959
Pat Murphy 1959–60
Allenby Chilton 1960
Johnny Ball 1961–63
Allan Brown 1963–66
Alf Craig 1966–67
Harry Leyland 1967–68
Alan Saunders 1968
Ian McNeill 1968–70
Gordon Milne 1970–72
Les Rigby 1972–74
Brian Tiler 1974–76
Ian McNeill 1976–81
Larry Lloyd 1981–83
Harry McNally 1983–85
Bryan Hamilton 1985–86
Ray Mathias 1986–89
Bryan Hamilton 1989–93
Dave Philpotts 1993
Kenny Swain 1993–94
Graham Barrow 1994–95
John Deehan 1995–98
Ray Mathias 1998–99
John Benson 1999–2000
Bruce Rioch 2000–01
Steve Bruce 2001
Paul Jewell 2001–07
Chris Hutchings 2007
Steve Bruce 2007–09
Roberto Martinez 2009–13
Owen Coyle 2013
Uwe Rosler 2013–14
Malky Mackay 2014–15
Gary Caldwell 2015–16
Warren Joyce 2016–17
Paul Cook May 2017–

TEN YEAR LEAGUE RECORD

		P	W	D	L	F	A	Pts	Pos
2009-10	PR Lge	38	9	9	20	37	79	36	16
2010-11	PR Lge	38	9	15	14	40	61	42	16
2011-12	PR Lge	38	11	10	17	42	62	43	15
2012-13	PR Lge	38	9	9	20	47	73	36	18
2013-14	FL C	46	21	10	15	61	48	73	5
2014-15	FL C	46	9	12	25	39	64	39	23
2015-16	FL 1	46	24	15	7	82	45	87	1
2016-17	FL C	46	10	12	24	40	57	42	23
2017-18	FL 1	46	29	11	6	89	29	98	1
2018-19	FL C	46	13	13	20	51	64	52	18

DID YOU KNOW ?

Wigan Athletic played their first competitive game as a Football League club in a League Cup tie at Tranmere Rovers on 12 August 1978. The Latics drew 1-1 at Prenton Park then won the second leg 2-1 in front of a crowd of 8,512 to progress to a second-round tie at Luton Town.

WIGAN ATHLETIC – SKY BET CHAMPIONSHIP 2018–19 LEAGUE RECORD

Match No.	*Date*	*Venue*	*Opponents*	*Result*	*H/T Score*	*Lg Pos.*	*Goalscorers*	*Attendance*
1	Aug 4	H	Sheffield W	W 3-2	2-1	2	Jacobs 2 [11, 26], Powell [60]	14,207
2	11	A	Aston Villa	L 2-3	1-1	9	Powell [41], Connolly [55]	34,331
3	18	H	Nottingham F	D 2-2	2-1	12	Powell [2], Grigg (pen) [30]	11,543
4	22	A	Stoke C	W 3-0	2-0	8	Grigg 2 (1 pen) [27, 57 (p)], Massey [32]	23,158
5	25	A	QPR	L 0-1	0-1	12		11,564
6	Sept 1	H	Rotherham U	W 1-0	0-0	9	Vaughan [73]	9584
7	15	A	Brentford	L 0-2	0-1	11		9951
8	18	H	Hull C	W 2-1	2-1	7	Morsy [21], Windass [37]	8848
9	21	H	Bristol C	W 1-0	0-0	3	Powell [52]	10,192
10	29	A	Norwich C	L 0-1	0-0	8		25,034
11	Oct 2	H	Swansea C	D 0-0	0-0	7		8964
12	6	A	Preston NE	L 0-4	0-1	11		15,280
13	20	H	WBA	W 1-0	0-0	8	Windass [74]	12,739
14	23	A	Millwall	L 1-2	1-0	10	Wallace, J (og) [45]	11,190
15	27	A	Sheffield U	L 2-4	1-2	14	Naismith [39], Garner [69]	24,429
16	Nov 4	H	Leeds U	L 1-2	1-1	16	James [6]	14,799
17	10	A	Middlesbrough	L 0-2	0-2	16		22,207
18	24	H	Reading	D 0-0	0-0	17		9211
19	28	H	Blackburn R	W 3-1	1-0	15	Roberts [37], Vaughan (pen) [54], McManaman [86]	10,777
20	Dec 1	A	Bolton W	D 1-1	1-1	15	Grigg (pen) [25]	15,237
21	8	H	Derby Co	L 0-1	0-1	16		10,768
22	15	A	Ipswich T	L 0-1	0-0	16		14,640
23	22	H	Birmingham C	L 0-3	0-2	19		13,774
24	26	A	WBA	L 0-2	0-1	19		25,555
25	29	A	Swansea C	D 2-2	2-0	19	Garner 2 (1 pen) [10 (p), 34]	18,591
26	Jan 1	H	Sheffield U	L 0-3	0-1	20		13,054
27	12	H	Aston Villa	W 3-0	1-0	19	Roberts [41], Jacobs [79], Garner (pen) [83]	13,882
28	19	A	Sheffield W	L 0-1	0-0	20		22,323
29	26	A	Nottingham F	L 1-3	1-1	20	Windass [33]	28,848
30	Feb 2	H	QPR	W 2-1	1-0	19	Windass [8], Clarke [55]	9799
31	9	A	Rotherham U	D 1-1	1-1	19	Windass [32]	9611
32	13	H	Stoke C	D 0-0	0-0	19		9914
33	23	H	Ipswich T	D 1-1	0-1	19	Garner [90]	10,835
34	Mar 2	H	Middlesbrough	D 0-0	0-0	19		12,726
35	5	A	Derby Co	L 1-2	1-0	19	Massey [25]	23,655
36	9	A	Reading	L 2-3	1-1	20	Powell [20], Garner [64]	15,401
37	12	A	Blackburn R	L 0-3	0-1	20		12,763
38	16	H	Bolton W	W 5-2	1-0	19	Garner [4], Massey [51], Powell [55], Jacobs [69], Clarke [81]	13,664
39	30	H	Brentford	D 0-0	0-0	20		9953
40	Apr 6	A	Bristol C	D 2-2	1-0	19	James [37], Byrne [90]	20,931
41	10	A	Hull C	L 1-2	1-0	21	Powell [41]	10,827
42	14	H	Norwich C	D 1-1	1-0	21	James (pen) [45]	15,655
43	19	A	Leeds U	W 2-1	1-1	20	Massey 2 [44, 62]	34,758
44	22	H	Preston NE	W 2-0	1-0	18	Clarke [11], Evans, L [68]	12,496
45	27	A	Birmingham C	D 1-1	1-1	18	Powell [45]	23,645
46	May 5	H	Millwall	W 1-0	1-0	18	Garner [15]	10,859

Final League Position: 18

GOALSCORERS

League (51): Garner 8 (2 pens), Powell 8, Massey 5, Windass 5, Grigg 4 (3 pens), Jacobs 4, Clarke 3, James 3 (1 pen), Roberts 2, Vaughan 2 (1 pen), Byrne 1, Connolly 1, Evans L 1, McManaman 1, Morsy 1, Naismith 1, own goal 1.
FA Cup (0).
Carabao Cup (1): Vaughan 1.

Walton C 34	James R 44 + 1	Dunkley C 37 + 1	Kipre C 37 + 1	Robinson A 26	Gibson D 11 + 7	Morsy S 40	Massey G 15 + 5	Powell N 25 + 7	Jacobs M 19 + 3	Grigg W 10 + 7	Vaughan J 6 + 13	Power M — + 1	McManaman C 1 + 21	Connolly C 7 + 10	Evans L 31 + 3	Windass J 30 + 9	Byrne N 26 + 4	Roberts G 12 + 4	Garner J 17 + 16	Naismith K 22 + 8	Burn D 13 + 1	Da Silva Lopes L — + 1	Jones J 12	Pilkington A 7 + 3	Fox D 10	Clarke L 9 + 6	Baningime B 1	Olsson J 4 + 2	Gelhardt J — + 1	Weir J — + 1	Jolley C — + 1	*Match No.*
1	2	3	4	5	6^{3}	7	8^{2}	9^{1}	10	11	12	13	14																			1
1	2	3	4	5		7		9^{2}	10	11^{3}	14		8^{1}	6	12	13																2
1	2	3	4	5		7	8^{1}	9^{3}	10	11^{2}	13			12	6		14															3
1	2	3	4	5		7	8	9^{3}	10^{2}	11^{1}			14	12	6	13																4
1	12	3	4	5		7	8^{3}	9		11	13				6	10^{2}	2^{1}	14														5
1	2	3	4	5		7		9^{1}		11^{3}	13		12	8	6	10^{2}			14													6
1	2	3	4	5	12	7■		9^{1}			11^{2}		14	8	6	10^{3}			13													7
1	2	3	4	5	12	7		9^{3}	10	11^{2}	14				6	8^{1}				13												8
1	2	3	4	5	12	6		9^{1}	10^{2}					13	7	8			11^{3}	14												9
1	2	3	4	5	12	7^{3}		9	10	14				13	6^{2}	8			11^{1}													10
1	2	3	4	5	6^{1}			9^{3}	10	12			14	13	7	8			11^{2}													11
1	2	3	4	5	6■	7		9^{1}	8^{3}	11			13			10^{2}			14		12											12
1	2	4	3			8		11^{3}			14			12	7	10	6^{2}	9^{1}		13	5											13
1	2^{2}	4	3			8		12			11^{1}		14	6	7	10^{3}	13			9	5											14
1	2	3		5		7		9^{2}					14	6^{1}		11	8	10^{3}	13	12	4											15
1	2		3	5	7^{1}	8					14		12			10	6		11^{3}	9^{2}	4	13										16
1	2		3	5	8			11^{1}			13		12		7	10^{3}	6	9^{2}		14	4											17
1	2		3		7^{2}	8		11^{1}		13				14		10	6	9^{3}	12	5	4											18
1	2		3			8		10^{3}			11^{2}		13	14	7	12	6	9^{1}		5	4											19
1	2		3			8				11^{3}	13		12		7	10^{1}	6	9^{2}	14	5	4											20
1	2		3		12	8					11^{3}			13	7	10^{2}	6	9^{1}	14	5■	4											21
1	2		3			8				11^{2}	12		14	5	7	10^{3}	6^{1}	9	13		4											22
1	2		3			8	13			12	11^{1}				7	10^{3}	6^{2}	9	14	5	4											23
1	2	4	3			8	6^{3}			14			12	7	13	10^{2}			11^{1}	9	5											24
1	2^{1}	4	3		6^{3}	9	7				13			14	8		12		11^{2}	10	5											25
1	2	4	3		6^{3}	9	7^{2}			14			12		8	13		10	11^{1}	5												26
	2	3	4			7			12		14				8	10	13	9^{1}	11^{3}	5			1	6^{2}								27
	2	3	4			8			12	13			14		7	10		9^{1}	11^{3}	5			1	6^{2}								28
	2	3	4		7^{2}	8			9^{3}		11^{1}		13			10	6	14	12	5			1									29
	7	14	3		13				9						8	10	2		12	5			1	6^{2}	4^{3}	11^{1}						30
	7	3	12				13		9^{1}							10	2			5			1	6	4^{2}	11	8					31
	7	3	4			8	12	13	9							10^{2}	2		14	5			1	6^{1}		11^{3}						32
	2	3^{3}				8		12	9				13		7	10^{2}			14	5			1	6^{1}	4	11						33
	7	3	2			8			12						6	11^{2}	5		14	9^{3}			1	13	4	10^{1}						34
	6	3	4			9	7^{3}	13	10^{2}						8	14	2			12			1		5^{1}	11						35
	7	3		5		8	6^{1}	10^{2}	9							14	2		11^{3}	12			1			13		4				36
	2	3		5		8	6^{1}	10^{3}	9^{2}				12		7	13			11				1			14		4				37
1	6	3	4	5	14	7	8^{1}	9^{3}	10							13	2		11^{2}							12						38
1	6	3		5		7	8^{3}	9	10^{1}				14				2		11^{2}					12	4	13						39
1	6	3	2^{2}	8		7	14	10								9^{1}	5		11^{3}					12	4	13						40
1	2	3		8	6^{1}	7	12	10^{2}							14	11	5		9^{3}						4	13						41
1	6	3		5		7	8^{3}	12							9	13	2			10^{2}					4^{1}	11		14				42
1	6^{2}	3	4■	5		7	8^{3}	13							9		2		14	10						11^{1}		12				43
1	6	3		5		7	8^{1}	12							9		2	13	14	10^{3}					4	11^{2}						44
		3	5^{1}	6	8			7^{2}							9	10^{3}	2		11	12			1					4	13	14		45
1	7^{2}	3	2	5				9					13		6			14	11^{1}	10				8^{3}				4			12	46

FA Cup
Third Round WBA (a) 0-1

Carabao Cup
First Round Rotherham U (a) 1-3

WOLVERHAMPTON WANDERERS

FOUNDATION

Enthusiasts of the game at St Luke's School, Blakenhall formed a club in 1877. In the same neighbourhood a cricket club called Blakenhall Wanderers had a football section. Several St Luke's footballers played cricket for them and shortly before the start of the 1879–80 season the two amalgamated and Wolverhampton Wanderers FC was brought into being.

Molineux Stadium, Waterloo Road, Wolverhampton, West Midlands WV1 4QR.

Telephone: (0371) 222 2220.

Fax: (01902) 687 006.

Ticket Office: (0371) 222 1877.

Website: wolves.co.uk

Email: info@wolves.co.uk

Ground Capacity: 31,700.

Record Attendance: 61,315 v Liverpool, FA Cup 5th rd, 11 February 1939.

Pitch Measurements: 105m × 68m (115yd × 74.5yd).

Executive Chairman: Jeff Shi.

Head Coach: Nuno Espírito Santo.

Assistant Head Coach: Rui Pedro Silva.

Colours: Gold shirts with black trim, black shorts with gold trim, gold socks with black trim.

Year Formed: 1877* (*see Foundation*).

Turned Professional: 1888.

Previous Names: 1879, St Luke's combined with Wanderers Cricket Club to become Wolverhampton Wanderers (1923) Ltd. New limited companies followed in 1982 and 1986 (current).

Club Nickname: 'Wolves'.

Grounds: 1877, Windmill Field; 1879, John Harper's Field; 1881, Dudley Road; 1889, Molineux.

First Football League Game: 8 September 1888, Football League, v Aston Villa (h) D 1–1 – Baynton; Baugh, Mason; Fletcher, Allen, Lowder; Hunter, Cooper, Anderson, White, Cannon, (1 og).

Record League Victory: 10–1 v Leicester C, Division 1, 15 April 1938 – Sidlow; Morris, Dowen; Galley, Cullis, Gardiner; Maguire (1), Horace Wright, Westcott (4), Jones (1), Dorsett (4).

Record Cup Victory: 14–0 v Crosswell's Brewery, FA Cup 2nd rd, 13 November 1886 – Ike Griffiths; Baugh, Mason; Pearson, Allen (1), Lowder; Hunter (4), Knight (2), Brodie (4), Bernie Griffiths (2), Wood. Plus one goal 'scrambled through'.

Record Defeat: 1–10 v Newton Heath, Division 1, 15 October 1892.

HONOURS

League Champions: Division 1 – 1953–54, 1957–58, 1958–59; FL C – 2008–09, 2017–18; Division 2 – 1931–32, 1976–77; FL 1 – 2013–14; Division 3 – 1988–89; Division 3N – 1923–24; Division 4 – 1987–88.
Runners-up: Division 1 – 1937–38, 1938–39, 1949–50, 1954–55, 1959–60; Division 2 – 1966–67, 1982–83.

FA Cup Winners: 1893, 1908, 1949, 1960.
Runners-up: 1889, 1896, 1921, 1939.

League Cup Winners: 1974, 1980.

League Trophy Winners: 1988.

Texaco Cup Winners: 1971.

European Competitions
European Cup: 1958–59, 1959–60 *(qf)*.
UEFA Cup: 1971–72 (*runners-up*), 1973–74, 1974–75, 1980–81.
European Cup-Winners' Cup: 1960–61 *(sf)*.

THE Sun FACT FILE

In the 1912–13 season two church ministers appeared in Football League matches for Wolverhampton Wanderers, believed to have been a unique occurrence. Rev. Kenneth Hunt and Rev. William Jordan were both Oxford University graduates and both had been capped by England at amateur international level.

Most League Points (2 for a win): 64, Division 1, 1957–58.

Most League Points (3 for a win): 103, FL 1, 2013–14.

Most League Goals: 115, Division 2, 1931–32.

Highest League Scorer in Season: Dennis Westcott, 38, Division 1, 1946–47.

Most League Goals in Total Aggregate: Steve Bull, 250, 1986–99.

Most League Goals in One Match: 5, Joe Butcher v Accrington, Division 1, 19 November 1892; 5, Tom Phillipson v Barnsley, Division 2, 26 April 1926; 5, Tom Phillipson v Bradford C, Division 2, 25 December 1926; 5, Billy Hartill v Notts Co, Division 2, 12 October 1929; 5, Billy Hartill v Aston Villa, Division 1, 3 September 1934.

Most Capped Player: Billy Wright, 105, England (70 consecutive).

Most League Appearances: Derek Parkin, 501, 1967–82.

Youngest League Player: Jimmy Mullen, 16 years 43 days v Leeds U, 18 February 1939.

Record Transfer Fee Received: £12,000,000 (rising to £14,000,000) from Sunderland for Steven Fletcher, August 2012.

Record Transfer Fee Paid: £30,000,000 to Benfica for Raúl Jiménez, April 2019.

Football League Record: 1888 Founder Member of Football League: 1906–23 Division 2; 1923–24 Division 3 (N); 1924–32 Division 2; 1932–65 Division 1; 1965–67 Division 2; 1967–76 Division 1; 1976–77 Division 2; 1977–82 Division 1; 1982–83 Division 2; 1983–84 Division 1; 1984–85 Division 2; 1985–86 Division 3; 1986–88 Division 4; 1988–89 Division 3; 1989–92 Division 2; 1992–2003 Division 1; 2003–04 Premier League; 2004–09 FL C; 2009–12 Premier League; 2012–13 FL C; 2013–14 FL 1; 2014–18 FL C; 2018– Premier League.

MANAGERS

George Worrall 1877–85
(Secretary-Manager)
John Addenbrooke 1885–1922
George Jobey 1922–24
Albert Hoskins 1924–26
(had been Secretary since 1922)
Fred Scotchbrook 1926–27
Major Frank Buckley 1927–44
Ted Vizard 1944–48
Stan Cullis 1948–64
Andy Beattie 1964–65
Ronnie Allen 1966–68
Bill McGarry 1968–76
Sammy Chung 1976–78
John Barnwell 1978–81
Ian Greaves 1982
Graham Hawkins 1982–84
Tommy Docherty 1984–85
Bill McGarry 1985
Sammy Chapman 1985–86
Brian Little 1986
Graham Turner 1986–94
Graham Taylor 1994–95
Mark McGhee 1995–98
Colin Lee 1998–2000
Dave Jones 2001–04
Glenn Hoddle 2004–06
Mick McCarthy 2006–12
Stale Solbakken 2012–13
Dean Saunders 2013
Kenny Jackett 2013–16
Walter Zenga 2016
Paul Lambert 2016–17
Nuno Espírito Santo May 2017–

LATEST SEQUENCES

Longest Sequence of League Wins: 9, 11.1.2014 – 11.3.2014.

Longest Sequence of League Defeats: 8, 5.12.1981 – 13.2.1982.

Longest Sequence of League Draws: 6, 22.4.1995 – 20.8.1995.

Longest Sequence of Unbeaten League Matches: 21, 15.1.2005 – 13.8.2005.

Longest Sequence Without a League Win: 19, 1.12.1984 – 6.4.1985.

Successive Scoring Runs: 41 from 20.12.1958.

Successive Non-scoring Runs: 7 from 2.2.1985.

TEN YEAR LEAGUE RECORD

		P	W	D	L	F	A	Pts	Pos
2009-10	PR Lge	38	9	11	18	32	56	38	15
2010-11	PR Lge	38	11	7	20	46	66	40	17
2011-12	PR Lge	38	5	10	23	40	82	25	20
2012-13	FL C	46	14	9	23	55	69	51	23
2013-14	FL 1	46	31	10	5	89	31	103	1
2014-15	FL C	46	22	12	12	70	56	78	7
2015-16	FL C	46	14	16	16	53	58	58	14
2016-17	FL C	46	16	10	20	54	58	58	15
2017-18	FL C	46	30	9	7	82	39	99	1
2018-19	PR Lge	38	16	9	13	47	46	57	7

DID YOU KNOW ?

Wolverhampton Wanderers had a particularly difficult season in 1984–85 when they were relegated from the old Second Division. From 1 December to 6 April they played 19 League matches without a win, scoring just 5 goals and conceding 31.

WOLVERHAMPTON WANDERERS – PREMIER LEAGUE 2018–19 LEAGUE RECORD

Match No.	*Date*	*Venue*	*Opponents*	*Result*		*H/T Score*	*Lg Pos.*	*Goalscorers*	*Attendance*
1	Aug 11	H	Everton	D	2-2	1-1	7	Neves [44], Jimenez [80]	31,231
2	18	A	Leicester C	L	0-2	0-2	14		32,043
3	25	H	Manchester C	D	1-1	0-0	13	Boly [57]	31,322
4	Sept 1	A	West Ham U	W	1-0	0-0	9	Traore [90]	56,947
5	16	H	Burnley	W	1-0	0-0	9	Jimenez [61]	30,406
6	22	A	Manchester U	D	1-1	0-1	10	Joao Moutinho [53]	74,489
7	29	H	Southampton	W	2-0	0-0	8	Ivan Cavaleiro [79], Jonny [87]	31,147
8	Oct 6	A	Crystal Palace	W	1-0	0-0	7	Doherty [56]	25,715
9	20	H	Watford	L	0-2	0-2	8		31,144
10	27	A	Brighton & HA	L	0-1	0-0	9		30,654
11	Nov 3	H	Tottenham H	L	2-3	0-2	11	Neves (pen) [68], Jimenez (pen) [79]	31,185
12	11	A	Arsenal	D	1-1	1-0	11	Ivan Cavaleiro [13]	60,030
13	25	H	Huddersfield T	L	0-2	0-1	11		30,130
14	30	A	Cardiff C	L	1-2	1-0	11	Doherty [18]	30,213
15	Dec 5	H	Chelsea	W	2-1	0-1	12	Jimenez [59], Jota [63]	31,300
16	9	A	Newcastle U	W	2-1	1-1	10	Jota [17], Doherty [90]	50,223
17	15	H	Bournemouth	W	2-0	1-0	7	Jimenez [12], Ivan Cavaleiro [90]	30,997
18	21	H	Liverpool	L	0-2	0-1	7		31,358
19	26	A	Fulham	D	1-1	0-0	10	Saiss [85]	24,382
20	29	A	Tottenham H	W	3-1	0-1	7	Boly [72], Jimenez [83], Helder Costa [87]	46,356
21	Jan 2	H	Crystal Palace	L	0-2	0-0	9		30,666
22	14	A	Manchester C	L	0-3	0-2	11		54,171
23	19	H	Leicester C	W	4-3	2-0	8	Jota 3 [4, 64, 90], Bennett [12]	31,278
24	29	H	West Ham U	W	3-0	0-0	7	Saiss [66], Jimenez 2 [80, 86]	31,122
25	Feb 2	A	Everton	W	3-1	2-1	7	Neves (pen) [7], Jimenez [45], Dendoncker [66]	39,380
26	11	H	Newcastle U	D	1-1	0-0	7	Boly [90]	30,687
27	23	A	Bournemouth	D	1-1	0-1	8	Jimenez (pen) [83]	10,671
28	26	A	Huddersfield T	L	0-1	0-0	8		22,714
29	Mar 2	H	Cardiff C	W	2-0	2-0	7	Jota [16], Jimenez [18]	31,309
30	10	A	Chelsea	D	1-1	0-0	7	Jimenez [56]	40,692
31	30	A	Burnley	L	0-2	0-1	7		20,990
32	Apr 2	H	Manchester U	W	2-1	1-1	7	Jota [25], Smalling (og) [77]	31,302
33	13	A	Southampton	L	1-3	1-2	8	Boly [28]	31,708
34	20	H	Brighton & HA	D	0-0	0-0	9		31,096
35	24	H	Arsenal	W	3-1	3-0	7	Neves [28], Doherty [37], Jota [45]	31,436
36	27	A	Watford	W	2-1	1-0	7	Jimenez [41], Jota [77]	20,323
37	May 4	H	Fulham	W	1-0	0-0	7	Dendoncker [75]	30,456
38	12	A	Liverpool	L	0-2	0-1	7		53,331

Final League Position: 7

GOALSCORERS

League (47): Jimenez 13 (2 pens), Jota 9, Boly 4, Doherty 4, Neves 4 (2 pens), Ivan Cavaleiro 3, Dendoncker 2, Saiss 2, Bennett 1, Helder Costa 1, Joao Moutinho 1, Jonny 1, Traore 1, own goal 1.
FA Cup (12): Doherty 4, Jimenez 4, Ivan Cavaleiro 2, Jota 1, Neves 1.
Carabao Cup (2): Helder Costa 1 (1 pen), Leo Bonatini 1.
Checkatrade Trophy (3): Ashley-Seal 1, Giles 1, Goncalves 1.

Rui Patricio P 37	Bennett R 34	Coady C 38	Boly W 36	Doherty M 35 + 3	Joao Moutinho F 35 + 3	Neves R 34 + 1	Jonny C 32 + 1	Halder Costa W 16 + 9	Jimenez R 36 + 2	Jota D 29 + 4	Leo Bonatini L — + 7	Ruben Vinagre G 7 – 10	White M 5 + 21	Traore A 8 + 21	Saiss R 12 + 7	Ivan Cavaleiro R 6 + 17	Dendoncker L 17 + 2	Ruddy J 1	Norris W — + 1	Kilman M — + 1	Match No.
1	2	3	4	5	6^{3}	7	8^{2}	9^{1}	10	11	12	13	14								1
1	2	3	4	5^{2}	6	7	8	9^{3}	11	10^{1}	12		14	13							2
1	2	3	4	5	6	7	8^{1}	9^{2}	11	10		13		12							3
1	2	3	4	5	6	7	8	9^{2}	11^{3}	10^{1}	13	14		12							4
1	2	3	4	5	6	7	8	9^{3}	11^{1}	10^{2}	13		14	12							5
1	2	3	4	5	6^{3}	7	8	9^{2}	11	10^{1}			14	12	13						6
1	2	3	4	5	6	7	8	9^{2}	11^{3}	10^{1}	14			12		13					7
1	2	3	4	5	6	7	8	9^{2}	10^{3}	11^{1}				14	13	12					8
1	2	3	4	5^{3}	7	6	8^{2}	9	10^{1}	11		12		14		13					9
1	2	3	4	5	7	6	8^{2}	9	11^{1}	12	14			10^{3}		13					10
1	2	3	4	5	6^{3}	7	8	9^{1}	10		12		13	14		11^{2}					11
1	2	3	4	5	6	7	8	9^{1}	10^{3}	12			14	13		11^{2}					12
1	2	3	4	5	6^{3}	7		9^{1}	10	14		8	12	13		11^{2}					13
1		3	4	5	6	7		10^{3}	9	12		8^{2}	13	11^{1}	2	14					14
1	2	3	4	5	6			12	9^{2}	10^{1}		8	11^{3}		7	14	13				15
1	2	3	4	5	14	7		9^{1}	13	11		8	12	10^{2}	6^{3}						16
1	2	3	4	5	6	7	8	12	10^{1}	11^{3}			9^{2}		13	14					17
1	2	3	4	5	9^{3}	7	8^{2}		11			14	12	10^{1}	6	13					18
1	2	3	4	5	6		8^{3}	13	11			14	9^{2}	10^{1}	7	12					19
1	2	3	4	5	13	7	8	12	11				14	9^{2}		10^{3}	6^{1}				20
1	2	3	4	5	6	13	8	9^{2}	10				12	14	7^{1}	11^{3}					21
1	2	3	4■	5	6^{3}	7	9		10^{2}	11^{1}			14	12	13		8				22
1	2	3		12	8^{2}	7	5		10	11		9^{1}	13		4		6				23
1	2	3		5	8^{2}	7	9^{3}		10	11^{1}		14	12		4	13	6				24
1	2	3	4	5	8	7^{2}	9	13	10^{1}	11^{3}				14	12		6				25
1	2	3	4	5^{2}	8	7	9	12	10	11^{1}				14		13	6^{3}				26
1	2	3	4	5	8	7	9		10^{1}	11^{3}				13	14	12	6^{2}				27
1	2	3	4	5	8^{2}	7	9	14	10^{3}	11^{1}			12			13	6				28
	2	3	4	12	13				10	11^{3}		9	8^{2}	5^{1}	7	14	6	1			29
1		3	4	5	8	7	9		10^{1}	11^{2}			12	13	2		6				30
1		3	4	12	8	7	9	14	13	11				5^{3}	2	10^{1}	6^{2}				31
1	2	3	4	5	8	7^{1}	13		10	11^{2}		9^{3}			14	12	6				32
1		3	4	5^{3}	8	7^{2}	9	14	10	11^{1}			13	12	2		6				33
1	2	3	4	5^{2}	8	7	9^{1}		10	11		12	6^{3}	14			13				34
1	2	3	4	5	8^{3}	7	9		10^{1}	11^{2}			14	13		12	6				35
1	2	3	4	5	8	7	9		10^{1}	11^{2}			13			12	6				36
1^{2}	2	3	4^{1}	5	8	7	9^{3}		10	11		14					6		12	13	37
1	2	3	4	5^{2}	8^{3}	7	9^{1}		10	11		14	13	12			6				38

FA Cup

Third Round	Liverpool	(h)	2-1
Fourth Round	Shrewsbury T	(a)	2-2
Replay	Shrewsbury T	(h)	3-2
Fifth Round	Bristol C	(a)	1-0
Sixth Round	Manchester U	(h)	2-1
Semi-Final	Watford	(Wembley)	2-3

(*aet*)

Carabao Cup

Second Round	Sheffield W	(a)	2-0
Third Round	Leicester C	(h)	0-0

(Leicester C won 3-1 on penalties)

Checkatrade Trophy (Wolverhampton W U21)

Group H (N)	Scunthorpe U	(a)	0-0

(Scunthorpe U won 4-2 on penalties)

Group H (N)	Mansfield T	(a)	1-2
Group H (N)	Lincoln C	(a)	2-2

(Wolverhampton W U21 won 5-4 on penalties)

WYCOMBE WANDERERS

FOUNDATION

In 1887 a group of young furniture trade workers called a meeting at the Steam Engine public house with the aim of forming a football club and entering junior football. It is thought that they were named after the famous FA Cup winners, The Wanderers, who had visited the town in 1877 for a tie with the original High Wycombe club. It is also possible that they played informally before their formation, although there is no proof of this.

Adams Park, Hillbottom Road, High Wycombe, Buckinghamshire HP12 4HJ.

Telephone: (01494) 472 100.

Ticket Office: (01494) 441 118.

Website: www.wycombewanderers.co.uk

Email: wwfc@wwfc.com

Ground Capacity: 10,137.

Record Attendance: 15,850 v St Albans C, FA Amateur Cup 4th rd, 25 February 1950 (at Loakes Park); 9,921 v Fulham, FA Cup 3rd rd, 9 January 2002 (at Adams Park).

Pitch Measurements: 100m × 64m (109.5yd × 70yd).

Chairman: Trevor Stroud.

Manager: Gareth Ainsworth.

Assistant Manager: Richard Dobson.

HONOURS

League Champions: Conference – 1992–93.

Runners-up: FL 2 – (3rd) 2008–09, 2010–11 *(promoted to FL 1)*; Conference – 1991–92.

FA Cup: semi-final – 2001.

League Cup: semi-final – 2007.

FA Amateur Cup Winners: 1931.

Colours: Light blue and dark blue quartered shirts, dark blue shorts, dark blue socks with light blue trim.

Year Formed: 1887. ***Turned Professional:*** 1974.

Club Nicknames: 'The Chairboys' (after High Wycombe's tradition of furniture making), 'The Blues'.

Grounds: 1887, The Rye; 1893, Spring Meadow; 1895, Loakes Park; 1899, Daws Hill Park; 1901, Loakes Park; 1990, Adams Park.

First Football League Game: 14 August 1993, Division 3 v Carlisle U (a) D 2–2: Hyde; Cousins, Horton (Langford), Kerr, Crossley, Ryan, Carroll, Stapleton, Thompson, Scott, Guppy (1) (Hutchinson), (1 og).

Record League Victory: 5–0 v Burnley, Division 2, 15 April 1997 – Parkin; Cousins, Bell, Kavanagh, McCarthy, Forsyth, Carroll (2p) (Simpson), Scott (Farrell), Stallard (1), McGavin (1) (Read (1)), Brown.
5–0 v Northampton T, Division 2, 4 January 2003 – Talia; Senda, Ryan, Thomson, McCarthy, Johnson, Bulman, Simpson (1), Faulconbridge (Harris), Dixon (1) (Roberts 3), Brown (Currie).
5–0 v Hartlepool U, FL 1, 25 February 2012 – Bull; McCoy, Basey, Eastmond (Bloomfield), Laing, Doherty (1), Hackett, Lewis, Bevon (2) (Strevons), Hayes (2) (McClure), McNamee.

Record Cup Victory: 5–0 v Hitchin T (a), FA Cup 2nd rd, 3 December 1994 – Hyde; Cousins, Brown, Crossley, Evans, Ryan (1), Carroll, Bell (1), Thompson, Garner (3) (Hemmings), Stapleton (Langford).
5–0 v Chesterfield (a), FA Cup 2nd rd, 3 December 2017 – Blackman; Harriman, Stewart (1), Pierre, Jacobson, Bloomfield (Wood), O'Nien, Gape (Bean), Kashket (3) (Cowan-Hall), Hayes (1), Akinfenwa.

Record Defeat: 0–7 v Shrewsbury T, Johnstone's Paint Trophy, 7 October 2008.

THE SUN FACT FILE

Entering the final game of the 1998–99 season, Wycombe looked odds-on favourites for relegation from the Second Division. As the game progressed results elsewhere seemed to confirm this but Paul Emblen's 83rd minute goal proved the winner at Lincoln City and kept The Chairboys up.

Most League Points (3 for a win): 84, FL 2, 2014–15; 84, FL 2, 2017–18.

Most League Goals: 79, FL 2, 2017–18.

Highest League Scorer in Season: Scott McGleish, 25, 2007–08.

Most League Goals in Total Aggregate: Nathan Tyson, 51, 2004–06, 2017–19.

Most League Goals in One Match: 3, Miquel Desouza v Bradford C, Division 2, 2 September 1995; 3, John Williams v Stockport Co, Division 2, 24 February 1996; 3, Mark Stallard v Walsall, Division 2, 21 October 1997; 3, Sean Devine v Reading, Division 2, 2 October 1999; 3, Sean Divine v Bury, Division 2, 26 February 2000; 3, Stuart Roberts v Northampton T, Division 2, 4 January 2003; 3, Nathan Tyson v Lincoln C, FL 2, 5 March 2005; 3, Nathan Tyson v Kidderminster H, FL 2, 2 April 2005; 3, Nathan Tyson v Stockport Co, FL 2, 10 September 2005; 3, Kevin Betsy v Mansfield T, FL 2, 24 September 2005; 3, Scott McGleish v Mansfield T, FL 2, 8 January 2008; 3, Stuart Beavon v Bury, FL 1, 17 March 2012; 3, Craig Mackail-Smith v Crawley T, FL 2, 18 November 2017.

Most Capped Player: Mark Rogers, 7, Canada; Marvin McCoy, 7 (8), Antigua and Barbuda.

Most League Appearances: Matt Bloomfield, 444, 2003–19.

Youngest League Player: Jordon Ibe, 15 years 311 days v Hartlepool U, 15 October 2011.

Record Transfer Fee Received: £675,000 from Nottingham F for Nathan Tyson, January 2006.

Record Transfer Fee Paid: £200,000 to Barnet for Sean Devine, April 1999; £200,000 to Barnet for Darren Currie, July 2001.

Football League Record: 1993 Promoted to Division 3 from Conference; 1993–94 Division 3; 1994–2004 Division 2; 2004–09 FL 2; 2009–10 FL 1; 2010–11 FL 2; 2011–12 FL 1; 2012–18 FL 2; 2018– FL 1.

MANAGERS

First coach appointed 1951.
Prior to Brian Lee's appointment in 1969 the team was selected by a Match Committee which met every Monday evening.

James McCormack 1951–52
Sid Cann 1952–61
Graham Adams 1961–62
Don Welsh 1962–64
Barry Darvill 1964–68
Brian Lee 1969–76
Ted Powell 1976–77
John Reardon 1977–78
Andy Williams 1978–80
Mike Keen 1980–84
Paul Bence 1984–86
Alan Gane 1986–87
Peter Suddaby 1987–88
Jim Kelman 1988–90
Martin O'Neill 1990–95
Alan Smith 1995–96
John Gregory 1996–98
Neil Smillie 1998–99
Lawrie Sanchez 1999–2003
Tony Adams 2003–04
John Gorman 2004–06
Paul Lambert 2006–08
Peter Taylor 2008–09
Gary Waddock 2009–12
Gareth Ainsworth November 2012–

LATEST SEQUENCES

Longest Sequence of League Wins: 6, 12.11.2016 – 17.12.2016.

Longest Sequence of League Defeats: 6, 18.3.2006 – 17.4.2006.

Longest Sequence of League Draws: 5, 24.1.2004 – 21.2.2004.

Longest Sequence of Unbeaten League Matches: 21, 6.8.2005 – 10.12.2005.

Longest Sequence Without a League Win: 13, 10.1.2004 – 20.3.2004.

Successive Scoring Runs: 16 from 13.9.2014.

Successive Non-scoring Runs: 5 from 15.10.1996.

TEN YEAR LEAGUE RECORD

		P	W	D	L	F	A	Pts	Pos
2009-10	FL 1	46	10	15	21	56	76	45	22
2010-11	FL 2	46	22	14	10	69	50	80	3
2011-12	FL 1	46	11	10	25	65	88	43	21
2012-13	FL 2	46	17	9	20	50	60	60	15
2013-14	FL 2	46	12	14	20	46	54	50	22
2014-15	FL 2	46	23	15	8	67	45	84	4
2015-16	FL 2	46	17	13	16	45	44	64	13
2016-17	FL 2	46	19	12	15	58	53	69	9
2017-18	FL 2	46	24	12	10	79	60	84	3
2018-19	FL 1	46	14	11	21	55	67	53	17

DID YOU KNOW ?

Wycombe Wanderers had the distinction of winning the final two London *Evening Standard* Five-a-Side Championships at Wembley Arena. In May 1994 they beat Wimbledon in the final and 12 months later they defeated Luton Town.

WYCOMBE WANDERERS – SKY BET LEAGUE ONE 2018–19 LEAGUE RECORD

Match No.	Date	Venue	Opponents	Result		H/T Score	Lg Pos.	Goalscorers	Attendance
1	Aug 4	H	Blackpool	D	0-0	0-0	12		5115
2	11	A	Doncaster R	L	0-3	0-0	20		7122
3	18	H	Bristol R	L	1-2	0-2	23	Kashket [82]	4858
4	21	A	Plymouth Arg	D	1-1	0-1	23	Bloomfield [84]	9244
5	25	A	Bradford C	W	2-1	1-0	17	Mackail-Smith [28], Riley (og) [52]	15,563
6	Sept 1	H	Luton T	D	1-1	1-0	16	Jacobson (pen) [15]	6072
7	8	A	Charlton Ath	L	2-3	1-1	18	Williams [7], Cowan-Hall [90]	10,358
8	15	H	Oxford U	D	0-0	0-0	19		6879
9	22	A	Portsmouth	D	2-2	1-0	18	Morris [21], Jacobson (pen) [89]	18,648
10	29	H	Southend U	L	2-3	0-1	20	Mackail-Smith [83], Akinfenwa [86]	4784
11	Oct 2	A	Fleetwood T	D	1-1	0-1	21	Akinfenwa [56]	2304
12	6	H	Burton Alb	W	2-1	2-0	17	Jacobson (pen) [30], Akinfenwa [37]	4022
13	13	A	Coventry C	L	0-1	0-0	18		10,480
14	20	H	Scunthorpe U	W	3-2	1-2	17	Gape [27], Onyedinma [53], Mackail-Smith [90]	4024
15	23	H	Rochdale	W	3-0	1-0	14	Morris [10], Akinfenwa [67], Onyedinma [72]	3997
16	27	A	Walsall	L	2-3	0-1	15	Leahy (og) [80], Samuel [90]	4265
17	Nov 3	H	Peterborough U	W	1-0	0-0	15	Morris [67]	5225
18	17	A	Sunderland	D	1-1	0-0	15	Onyedinma [67]	30,727
19	24	H	Shrewsbury T	W	3-2	2-1	12	El-Abd [11], Jacobson [40], Samuel [71]	4598
20	27	A	Accrington S	W	2-1	0-1	10	Kashket [77], Samuel [90]	1740
21	Dec 8	H	Barnsley	W	1-0	0-0	9	Williams [55]	5225
22	15	A	Gillingham	D	2-2	2-0	9	El-Abd [12], Tyson [17]	4687
23	22	H	AFC Wimbledon	L	1-2	0-1	9	Onyedinma [90]	5814
24	26	A	Burton Alb	L	1-3	1-3	12	Buxton (og) [27]	3679
25	29	A	Scunthorpe U	L	0-1	0-1	13		3489
26	Jan 1	H	Coventry C	L	0-2	0-1	14		6183
27	12	H	Doncaster R	W	3-2	0-0	13	Cowan-Hall 2 [77, 90], Thompson [90]	4747
28	19	A	Bristol R	W	1-0	0-0	11	Jombati [57]	8163
29	26	H	Plymouth Arg	W	1-0	1-0	9	Songo'o (og) [24]	5691
30	29	A	Blackpool	D	2-2	1-0	9	Akinfenwa [12], Jacobson [53]	2388
31	Feb 2	H	Bradford C	D	0-0	0-0	9		4586
32	9	A	Luton T	L	0-3	0-1	10		10,072
33	16	A	Barnsley	L	1-2	0-1	11	Jacobson (pen) [90]	11,821
34	23	H	Gillingham	L	0-1	0-0	12		4879
35	Mar 2	A	Peterborough U	L	2-4	2-3	12	Tafazolli (og) [16], Bloomfield [38]	6484
36	9	H	Sunderland	D	1-1	1-0	12	Samuel [35]	8422
37	12	H	Accrington S	L	1-3	1-1	13	Cowan-Hall [23]	3819
38	16	A	Shrewsbury T	L	1-2	0-0	14	McCarthy [67]	6001
39	30	A	Oxford U	L	1-2	1-1	17	El-Abd [21]	9250
40	Apr 6	H	Portsmouth	L	2-3	0-1	19	Bean [55], Kashket [82]	6978
41	9	H	Charlton Ath	L	0-1	0-1	20		5487
42	13	A	Southend U	W	2-0	0-0	17	Akinfenwa 2 [69, 72]	7689
43	19	A	Rochdale	L	0-1	0-0	18		3711
44	22	H	Walsall	W	1-0	0-0	17	McCarthy [54]	5595
45	27	A	AFC Wimbledon	L	1-2	0-1	18	Samuel [49]	4850
46	May 4	H	Fleetwood T	W	1-0	0-0	17	Jacobson [75]	5575

Final League Position: 17

GOALSCORERS

League (55): Akinfenwa 7, Jacobson 7 (4 pens), Samuel 5, Cowan-Hall 4, Onyedinma 4, El-Abd 3, Kashket 3, Mackail-Smith 3, Morris 3, Bloomfield 2, McCarthy 2, Williams 2, Bean 1, Gape 1, Jombati 1, Thompson 1, Tyson 1, own goals 5.
FA Cup (0).
Carabao Cup (6): Akinfenwa 1, Cowan-Hall 1, Kashket 1, Saunders 1 (1 pen), Stewart 1, Williams 1.
Checkatrade Trophy (3): Kashket 2, Samuel 1.

Allsop R 38	Harriman M 20 + 4	Stewart A 16 + 1	El-Abd A 34	Jacobson J 36	Saunders S 2 + 2	Bean M 7 + 2	Bloomfield M 22 + 6	Williams R 15 + 5	Akinfenwa A 26 + 10	Cowan-Hall P 15 + 18	Freeman N 18 + 9	Mackail-Smith C 13 + 8	Jombati S 31 + 2	Morris B 15 + 4	Gape D 41 + 2	McCarthy J 44	Thompson C 33 + 6	Kashket S 11 + 16	Onyedinma F 16 + 5	Charles D 5	Makabu-Makalamby Y 2 + 1	Samuel A 26 + 4	Ingram M 1	Tyson N 10 + 9	Stockdale D 2	Henderson S 3	Bolton L 4 + 6	Owens C — + 2	Frempah — + 1	Match No.
1	2■	3	4	5	6	7	8	9^3	10^1	11^2	12	13	14																	1
1		3	4	5	6^3	7^2	8	11	10		13	14	2	9^1	12															2
1	2		4	5	14		8^1	11	10		13	9^3			7^2	3	6	12												3
1	5^3	3	4^2	9			8	11^1	14			10	12	6	7	2		13												4
1	5	3		9	14		8^1	11^3	12		13	10^2	4	6	7	2														5
1		3		5			7^1	11^2	9			10^3	2	8	6	4	12	14	13											6
1		4		5				9^3	10^1	14		11^2	3	8	7	2	6	13	12											7
1	12	4^2		5			6	11^1	13	14		10^3	3	8	7	2			9											8
1				5			6^1		10	12			2	8	7	3	13	11^2	9	4										9
1				5			6^3	12	10	13		14	2	8	7	3		9^2	11^1	4										10
1	5						7	9^3	10	12		11^2	2	8^1	6	3	13		14	4										11
1	2			5			7^3	11^2	10^1	12		9		13	6	3	8		14	4										12
1	2		4	5			7^3	9^1	11	14		10^2		12	6	3	8		13											13
1■	2		4	5				13	11	9^1		10^2			8	3	7		6		12									14
1	2		4	5		12			10^1	6	13			8		3	7^2	14	9^3			11								15
1	2		4	5					10	6^1		11^3		8	14	3	7^2	13	9			12								16
1			3	5				11		8^2		12		6	7	2	13		9	4		10^1								17
			4	5				10^3		14		13	3	7	6	2	8		11^2			9^1	1	12						18
			4	5				12		13	6	14	3		7	2	8		11^2			10^1		9^3	1					19
	5		4								6^1	10^2	3	14	7	2	8^3	13	9			11		12	1					20
			4	5				9					3		8	2	7		6			11		10		1				21
			4	5				12					3	6	7	2	8		9			10		11^1		1				22
			4	5				9^1				14	3	12	7^3	2	8	13	6			11^2		10		1				23
1			4	5^1					13			10^3	3	8^2	7	2	6	12	9			14		11						24
1		3	4	5				14	12	13	9				8	2	7	11^3	6^2			10^1								25
1	5	4							12		9^2	14	3		6	2	7	13	10			11^3		8^1						26
1			4	5			6^2		12	11	9		3		7	2	8	13						10^1						27
1			4	5			12		14	6	9^2		3		8	2	7	10^1				11^3		13						28
1			4	5			9^1		10^2	6	11		3		8	2	7					13					12			29
1			4	5			13		11^3	6^2	10^1		3		8	2	7					9		12			14			30
1			4	5		14	6^2			13			3		7	2	8	12				10^3		11			9^1			31
1			3	5			6^2		10	9^1	14		2		7	4	8	13						11^3			12			32
1			3■	5					13	11^1	7^3		2		4	6	9	14				10		12			8^2			33
1		4		5			6^3		10	11^2	13		3		7	2	8	9^1				12		14						34
1		4		5			9^2		11		8		3		6	2	7					10^1		12			13			35
1	13	4		5		8■	6^1			12			3		7	2	14					10		11■			8^3			36
1	5		4				7^2		11	6^3	9		3			2	8^1	12				10					13	14		37
	13	4	3	5		6	14			11^1	12				8	2	7^3				1	10					9^2			38
	12	4	3	5^1		6^2	14		10	13	11				8	2	7^3				1	9								39
1	9	4	3			6^1	7^3		13	11^2	5				8	2	12	14				10								40
1	5		4						10	12	8		3		7	2	6	11^2				9^1							13	41
1	6		3						11^1	12	5		2		8	4	7	9				10								42
1	6	13	3						11	12	5		2		8	4	7	9^2				10^1								43
1	5		4				13		10	14	8^1		3		7^2	2	6	9^3				11		12						44
1	5	3	4				13		10	14	8^2				7^1	2	6	9^3				11		12						45
1	2		3	5		7^3	8		10		14				6	4		11^1				9^2					12	13		46

FA Cup

First Round	Luton T	(a)	0-2

Carabao Cup

First Round	Northampton T	(h)	1-1
(Wycombe W won 7-6 on penalties)			
Second Round	Forest Green R	(h)	2-2
(Wycombe W won 4-3 on penalties)			
Third Round	Norwich C	(h)	3-4

Checkatrade Trophy

Group F (S)	Northampton T	(a)	1-0
Group F (S)	Fulham U21	(h)	2-1
Group F (S)	Oxford U	(h)	0-3

YEOVIL TOWN

FOUNDATION

One of the prime movers of Yeovil football was Ernest J. Sercombe. His association with the club began in 1895 as a playing member of Yeovil Casuals, of which team he became vice-captain and in his last season 1899–1900, he was chosen to play for Somerset against Devon. Upon the reorganisation of the club, he became secretary of the old Yeovil Town FC and with the amalgamation with Petters United in 1914, he continued to serve until his resignation in 1930.

Huish Park, Lufton Way, Yeovil, Somerset BA22 8YF.

Telephone: (01935) 423 662.

Fax: (01935) 847 886.

Ticket Office: (01935) 847 888.

Website: www.ytfc.net

Email: info@ytfc.net

Ground Capacity: 9,565.

Record Attendance: 16,318 v Sunderland, FA Cup 4th rd, 29 January 1949 (at Huish); 9,527 v Leeds U, FL 1, 25 April 2008 (at Huish Park).

Pitch Measurements: 108m × 67m (118yd × 73.5yd).

Chairman: John Fry.

Chief Operating Officer: David Mills.

Manager: Darren Sarll.

Player-Coach: Andrew Crofts.

Colours: Green and white hooped shirts with black trim, white shorts with green trim, white socks with green trim.

Year Formed: 1895.

Turned Professional: 1921.

Previous Names: 1895, Yeovil Casuals; 1907, Yeovil Town; 1915, Yeovil & Petters United; 1946, Yeovil Town.

Club Nickname: 'The Glovers'.

Grounds: 1895, Pen Mill Ground; 1921, Huish; 1990, Huish Park.

First Football League Game: 9 August 2003, Division 3 v Rochdale (a) W 3-1: Weale; Williams (Lindegaard), Crittenden, Lockwood, O'Brien, Pluck (Rodrigues), Gosling (El Kholti), Way, Jackson, Gall (2), Johnson (1).

Record League Victory: 6–0 v Newport Co, FL 2, 15 September 2018 – Baxter; Mugabi, Sowunmi, Warren (Rogers), Dickinson (1), Green (2) (Olomola (1)), Pattison, D'Almeida, Arquin (2), Jaiyesimi (1) (Donnellan), Fisher.

Record Cup Victory: 12–1 v Westbury United, FA Cup 1st qual rd, 1923–24.

HONOURS

League Champions: FL 2 – 2004–05; Conference – 2002–03.
Runners-up: Conference – 2000–01.

FA Cup: 5th rd – 1949.

League Cup: never past 2nd rd.

THE Sun FACT FILE

Yeovil Town, then known as Yeovil & Petters United, reached the first round proper of the FA Cup for the first time in 1924–25. The club won four games before defeating Division Three South club Bournemouth in the final qualifying round. That earned a home tie against Bristol Rovers. The Glovers went out 4-2 in front of a 6,000 crowd but finished with only eight men due to injuries.

Record Defeat: 0–8 v Manchester United, FA Cup 5th rd, 12 February 1949.

Most League Points (3 for a win): 83, FL 2, 2004–05.

Most League Goals: 90, FL 2, 2004–05.

Highest League Scorer in Season: Phil Jevons, 27, 2004–05.

Most League Goals in Total Aggregate: Phil Jevons, 42, 2004–06.

Most League Goals in One Match: 3, Phil Jevons v Oxford U, FL 2, 18 September 2004; 3, Phil Jevons v Chester C, FL 2, 30 October 2004; 3, Phil Jevons v Bristol R, FL 2, 12 February 2005; 3, Arron Davies v Chesterfield, FL 1, 4 March 2006; 3, Jack Compton v AFC Wimbledon, FL 2, 30 January 2016.

Most Capped Players: Joel Grant, 12 (14), Jamaica.

Most League Appearances: Nathan Smith, 260, 2008–11, 2014–18.

Youngest League Player: Devon Arnold, 17 years 38 days v Cheltenham T, 1 January 2019.

Record Transfer Fee Received: A combined £1,000,000 from Nottingham F for Arron Davies and Chris Cohen, July 2007.

Record Transfer Fee Paid: £250,000 to Quilmes for Pablo Bastianini, August 2005.

Football League Record: 2003 Promoted to Division 3 from Conference; 2003–04 Division 3; 2004–05 FL 2; 2005–13 FL 1; 2013–14 FL C; 2014–15 FL 1; 2015–19 FL 2; 2019– National League.

LATEST SEQUENCES

Longest Sequence of League Wins: 8, 29.12.2012 – 16.2.2013.

Longest Sequence of League Defeats: 6, 22.1.2019 – 16.2.2019.

Longest Sequence of League Draws: 3, 22.4.2019 – 4.5.2019.

Longest Sequence of Unbeaten League Matches: 9, 29.12.2012 – 23.2.2013.

Longest Sequence Without a League Win: 16, 26.9.2015 – 28.12.2015.

Successive Scoring Runs: 22 from 30.10.2004.

Successive Non-scoring Runs: 4 from 8.3.2019.

MANAGERS

Jack Gregory 1922–28
Tommy Lawes 1928–29
Dave Pratt 1929–33
Louis Page 1933–35
Dave Halliday 1935–38
Billy Kingdon 1938–46
Alec Stock 1946–49
George Patterson 1949–51
Harry Lowe 1951–53
Ike Clarke 1953–57
Norman Dodgin 1957
Jimmy Baldwin 1957–60
Basil Hayward 1960–64
Glyn Davies 1964–65
Joe McDonald 1965–67
Ron Saunders 1967–69
Mike Hughes 1969–72
Cecil Irwin 1972–75
Stan Harland 1975–81
Barry Lloyd 1978–81
Malcolm Allison 1981
Jimmy Giles 1981–83
Trevor Finnigan and Mike Hughes 1983
Steve Coles 1983–84
Ian McFarlane 1984
Gerry Gow 1984–87
Brian Hall 1987–90
Clive Whitehead 1990–91
Steve Rutter 1991–93
Brian Hall 1994–95
Graham Roberts 1995–98
Colin Lippiatt 1998–99
Steve Thompson 1999–2000
Dave Webb 2000
Gary Johnson 2001–05
Steve Thompson 2005–06
Russell Slade 2006–09
Terry Skiverton 2009–12
Gary Johnson 2012–15
Terry Skiverton 2015
Paul Sturrock 2015
Darren Way 2015–19
Darren Sarll June 2019–

TEN YEAR LEAGUE RECORD

		P	*W*	*D*	*L*	*F*	*A*	*Pts*	*Pos*
2009-10	FL 1	46	13	14	19	55	59	53	15
2010-11	FL 1	46	16	11	19	56	66	59	14
2011-12	FL 1	46	14	12	20	59	80	54	17
2012-13	FL 1	46	23	8	15	71	56	77	4
2013-14	FL C	46	8	13	25	44	75	37	24
2014-15	FL 1	46	10	10	26	36	75	40	24
2015-16	FL 2	46	11	15	20	43	59	48	19
2016-17	FL 2	46	11	17	18	49	64	50	20
2017-18	FL 2	46	12	12	22	59	75	48	19
2018-19	FL 2	46	9	13	24	41	66	40	24

DID YOU KNOW ?

Yeovil Town competed in the Anglo-Italian Cup at the end of the 1976–77 after finishing in seventh place in the Southern League. They won both their home games, defeating Turris and Bari but found it more difficult in Italy, losing 3-1 to Teramo. They needed to win their last game at Parma to reach the final but missed out after the game ended in a goalless draw.

YEOVIL TOWN – SKY BET LEAGUE TWO 2018–19 LEAGUE RECORD

Match No.	*Date*	*Venue*	*Opponents*	*Result*		*H/T Score*	*Lg Pos.*	*Goalscorers*	*Attendance*
1	Aug 4	A	Bury	L	0-1	0-0	17		3151
2	11	H	Mansfield T	D	2-2	2-2	17	Jaiyesimi [6], Arquin [17]	2796
3	17	A	Notts Co	W	4-0	2-0	4	Fisher 3 [34, 36, 72], Arquin [83]	7439
4	21	H	Oldham Ath	D	0-0	0-0	12		2904
5	25	H	Stevenage	W	2-0	2-0	7	Fisher [24], D'Almeida [42]	2635
6	Sept 1	A	Grimsby T	W	1-0	0-0	5	Patrick [78]	4284
7	15	A	Newport Co	W	6-0	3-0	5	Arquin [20], Green 2 [38, 48], Jaiyesimi [45], Olomola [68], Dickinson [76]	4167
8	22	H	Swindon T	L	0-3	0-0	10		4201
9	25	H	Milton Keynes D	D	1-1	0-1	6	Olomola [88]	2634
10	29	A	Crawley T	L	1-3	1-1	12	Dickinson [42]	2142
11	Oct 2	A	Colchester U	L	1-3	0-1	15	James [90]	2435
12	6	H	Exeter C	D	2-2	0-1	15	Green [48], Fisher [61]	4223
13	20	H	Tranmere R	D	0-0	0-0	14		3007
14	23	H	Crewe Alex	D	1-1	1-1	14	Fisher [25]	2397
15	27	A	Carlisle U	W	1-0	0-0	12	James [90]	3928
16	Nov 3	A	Morecambe	L	1-2	0-1	14	Olomola [68]	1406
17	24	A	Macclesfield T	L	0-1	0-0	18		1570
18	27	H	Port Vale	L	0-3	0-2	19		2174
19	Dec 8	H	Forest Green R	L	1-2	0-0	20	Browne [56]	2529
20	15	A	Cambridge U	D	0-0	0-0	19		3807
21	22	H	Northampton T	D	1-1	0-0	20	Arquin [89]	3193
22	26	A	Exeter C	L	1-2	0-1	21	James [53]	5974
23	29	A	Tranmere R	D	0-0	0-0	21		5782
24	Jan 1	H	Cheltenham T	L	1-4	0-2	21	James [47]	2883
25	5	H	Bury	L	0-1	0-1	22		2426
26	12	A	Mansfield T	W	1-0	1-0	22	Green [19]	4374
27	19	H	Notts Co	W	2-0	1-0	20	James [8], Dobre [90]	2716
28	22	H	Lincoln C	L	0-2	0-2	20		2486
29	Feb 2	A	Stevenage	L	0-1	0-0	21		2157
30	5	A	Cheltenham T	L	0-1	0-0	21		2457
31	9	H	Grimsby T	L	1-3	0-2	21	Fisher [90]	2692
32	12	A	Oldham Ath	L	1-4	0-1	21	Mugabi [54]	3868
33	16	A	Forest Green R	L	0-3	0-2	22		2449
34	23	H	Cambridge U	W	1-0	1-0	21	Duffus [25]	2596
35	Mar 2	H	Morecambe	W	3-2	0-1	20	Abrahams 2 [58, 62], Seager [87]	2521
36	8	A	Lincoln C	L	0-1	0-0	20		9014
37	12	A	Port Vale	L	0-3	0-1	22		3430
38	16	H	Macclesfield T	L	0-2	0-2	22		2899
39	23	A	Milton Keynes D	L	0-2	0-1	22		7593
40	30	H	Newport Co	L	1-3	0-0	22	James [73]	3983
41	Apr 6	A	Swindon T	D	1-1	0-1	22	Gafaiti [90]	6645
42	13	H	Crawley T	L	0-1	0-0	23		3232
43	19	A	Crewe Alex	L	0-2	0-1	23		3410
44	22	H	Colchester U	D	1-1	0-0	23	Gray [53]	3370
45	27	A	Northampton T	D	2-2	2-0	24	Abrahams (pen) [18], Gray [24]	4908
46	May 4	H	Carlisle U	D	0-0	0-0	24		3418

Final League Position: 24

GOALSCORERS

League (41): Fisher 7, James 6, Arquin 4, Green 4, Abrahams 3 (1 pen), Olomola 3, Dickinson 2, Gray 2, Jaiyesimi 2, Browne 1, D'Almeida 1, Dobre 1, Duffus 1, Gafaiti 1, Mugabi 1, Patrick 1, Seager 1.
FA Cup (1): Fisher 1.
Carabao Cup (0).
Checkatrade Trophy (4): James 1, Mahmutovic 1, own goals 2.

Baxter N 34	James T 37 + 1	Mugabi B 27 + 5	Donnellan S 10 + 1	Dickinson C 32 + 1	Green J 16 + 3	D'Almeida S 33 + 2	Santos A 15 + 2	Arquin Y 22 + 10	Zoko F 16 + 10	Jaiyesimi D 9	Warren G 24 + 2	Cole R — + 1	Fisher A 26 + 14	Sowunmi O 17	McDonald W 8 + 1	Pattison A 24 + 5	Henry K — + 4	Gray J 19 + 11	Olomola O 10 + 7	Patrick O 1 + 8	Rogers G 2 + 2	Mahmutovic E 3 + 1	Browne R 17 + 11	Nelson S 12	Gafaiti A 21 + 1	Arnold D — + 1	Grant J 8	Dobre M 21	Worthington M 12 + 3	Alcock C 4	Duffus C 9 + 7	Seager R 2 + 9	Abrahams T 11 + 4	Ojo D 4 + 2	Match No.
1	2■	3	4	5	6■	7	8	9^{2}	10^{3}	11^{1}	12	13	14																						1
1		2	4^{1}	5		8	7^{2}	6	10	11^{3}	12			3	9	13	14																		2
1	2			5		7		11		9^{1}	4		10	3	6^{2}	8	13	12																	3
1	2			5	12	7^{2}		6		11	4		10	3	9^{1}	8		13																	4
1	2^{3}	12		5	13	8^{1}		6		11	4		10	3	9^{2}	7		14																	5
1		2		5	9^{1}	8		6		11^{3}	4		10^{2}	3		7		14	12	13															6
1		2	13	5	6^{1}	8		9		10^{2}	4^{3}		11	3		7			12		14														7
1		2		5	6	8		9^{1}		10^{3}			11^{2}	3		7		14	12			4	13												8
1	14	2^{1}	4	5	6	8		9^{3}		11^{2}			12	3		7			10				13												9
1	2		4	5	11^{3}	7		12					13			8^{1}		6	10	14		3	9^{2}												10
1	2	4	3	5	6	7^{1}		9^{2}					10^{3}			8		12	11	13			14												11
1	2	3	4	5	6^{2}	7							10			8		9^{1}	11	13			12												12
1	2	3		5				9			4		10^{2}			7	13	8	11	12			6^{1}												13
1	2	3	4	5		7	14	9					10^{7}			0		0^{4}	11^{1}	13			12												14
1	2	3	4	5		7		14					10^{3}		13	8^{2}		12	9	11^{1}			6												15
1	2	3	4	5		7		10^{2}	13						6	12		8^{3}	11^{1}	14			9												16
	5	3				7		10^{1}	11^{3}		4				9	8	13	6^{2}		14			12	1	2										17
	2	3^{2}		5	14	9^{1}	12		11		4				10	8		7^{3}				13	6	1											18
	5				6	7	8	10^{1}	14		4				9^{3}			13	11^{2}			2	12	1	3										19
	2			5	9^{2}	7	8	10	13		4		12					14	11^{1}				6^{3}	1	3										20
	2			5	6	7	8	13	11^{2}		3		10						12				9^{1}	1	4										21
	2			5	9	7	8	12	10^{2}		3		11						13				6^{1}	1	4										22
	2			5	9	7	8	6	10^{1}		4		11						12					1	3										23
	2			5	9	7	8	6^{2}	11^{3}		3		10^{1}						13				12	1	4	14									24
1	5	3	4	9	6	7	8^{1}	13	11^{2}		2		10					12																	25
1	5	14		8	10	6			11^{2}		2		13					7^{3}					12		3		4	9^{1}							26
1	7	13		5		6		12	10^{2}		4		14					8					9^{1}		3^{3}		2	11							27
1	8	3		5		7		9	10^{2}		4^{3}		13					6^{1}			14						2	11	12						28
1	3	12		5		7^{3}							10					8					9^{1}		4			11	6^{2}	2	13	14			29
	7■			5				13			3		10^{1}					6					9^{2}	1	4			11^{3}	8	2	14		12		30
				5					13		3		10			12		8					6	1	4			11^{1}	7^{3}	2■	14		9^{2}		31
		3		4				11^{1}	9				10			7^{3}		8					12	1	2			5^{2}	6		13		14		32
1		3		5				11^{2}	9^{3}				10^{1}			7		8					12		4			6		2	14	13			33
1		2		13			8	4^{2}					11					14					6		3			9	7		10^{1}		12	5^{3}	34
1	5						8		13				11^{3}	3		12							2		4			9	7^{1}		10^{2}	14	6		35
1	5						9^{3}		17				13	3		8							2		4		7	10			11^{2}	14	6^{1}		36
1	2					12	9^{3}		13					3		8							5^{1}		4		7	10			11^{2}	14	6		37
1	2	13					8^{1}		11				10	4		7^{3}									3		5	9	12			14	6^{2}		38
1	7^{2}	3		5^{1}					10^{3}		4		13					11			9						2	6	8			12		14	39
1	7	3				6^{2}			14		4		10^{1}								9^{3}						2	11	8		13		12	5	40
1	7	2				8^{2}					4		13	3^{1}											12			11	6		10^{3}	14	9	5	41
1	7	2				14					3^{3}		12			13									4			9^{2}	8		11^{1}	10	6	5	42
1	5	2				8^{1}			14				10^{2}	3		7									4■			9	13		12	11	6^{3}		43
1	5	4				7		13					14	3		8^{2}		6					2^{3}					11			10^{1}		9	12	44
1	5	4				7		13	12				14	3		8		6^{2}										11	2		10^{3}		9^{1}		45
	5	4					7^{2}	12					14	3		8		6						1				11	2		10^{1}	13	9^{3}		46

FA Cup

First Round	Stockport Co	(h)	1-3

Carabao Cup

First Round	Aston Villa	(h)	0-1

Checkatrade Trophy

Group D (S)	Exeter C	(h)	0-0
(Exeter C won 5-2 on penalties)			
Group D (S)	Bristol R	(a)	0-2
Group D (S)	West Ham U U21	(h)	4-0

ENGLISH LEAGUE PLAYERS DIRECTORY

Players listed represent those with their clubs during the 2018–19 season.

Players are listed alphabetically on pages 537–543.
The number alongside each player corresponds to the team number heading. (Aarons, Maximillian 58 = team 58 (Norwich C)). Club names in *italic* indicate loans.

ACCRINGTON S (1)

BROWN, Scott (M) **244 13**
H: 5 9 W: 10 02 b.Runcorn 8-5-85
Internationals: England U17, U18, U19.

2001–02	Everton	0	0		
2002–03	Everton	0	0		
2003–04	Everton	0	0		
2004–05	Bristol C	19	0		
2005–06	Bristol C	29	1		
2006–07	Bristol C	15	4	**63**	**5**
2006–07	Cheltenham T	4	0		
2007–08	Cheltenham T	20	0		
2008–09	Port Vale	18	1	**18**	**1**
2009–10	Cheltenham T	1	0	**25**	**0**
2010–11	Morecambe	32	3	**32**	**3**

From Fleetwood T, York C, Macclesfield T, Chester FC, Southport, Grimsby T.

2015–16	Accrington S	13	3		
2016–17	Accrington S	28	0		
2017–18	Accrington S	36	1		
2018–19	Accrington S	29	0	**106**	**4**

CLARK, Jordan (F) **184 19**
H: 6 0 W: 11 07 b.Barnsley 22-9-93

2010–11	Barnsley	4	0		
2011–12	Barnsley	2	0		
2012–13	Barnsley	0	0		
2012–13	*Chesterfield*	2	0	**2**	**0**
2013–14	Barnsley	0	0	**6**	**0**
2013–14	*Scunthorpe U*	1	0	**1**	**0**
2014–15	Shrewsbury T	27	3		
2015–16	Shrewsbury T	20	2	**47**	**5**
2016–17	Accrington S	42	1		
2017–18	Accrington S	43	8		
2018–19	Accrington S	43	5	**128**	**14**

CONNEELY, Seamus (D) **246 12**
H: 5 9 W: 10 10 b.Galway 9-7-88
Internationals: Republic of Ireland U21, U23.

2008	Galway U	20	0		
2009	Galway U	34	2		
2010	Galway U	32	0	**86**	**2**
2010–11	Sheffield U	0	0		
2011–12	Sheffield U	0	0		
2014–15	Accrington S	16	3		
2015–16	Accrington S	46	3		
2016–17	Accrington S	38	1		
2017–18	Accrington S	33	2		
2018–19	Accrington S	27	1	**160**	**10**

EVTIMOV, Dimitar (G) **41 0**
H: 6 3 W: 13 00 b.Plevan 7-9-93
Internationals: Bulgaria U19, U21, Full caps.

2012–13	Nottingham F	0	0		
2013–14	Nottingham F	1	0		
2014–15	Nottingham F	0	0		
2014–15	*Mansfield T*	10	0	**10**	**0**
2015–16	Nottingham F	1	0		
2016–17	Nottingham F	0	0		
2016–17	*Olhanense*	10	0	**10**	**0**
2017–18	Port Vale	1	0	**1**	**0**
2017–18	Nottingham F	0	0		
2018–19	Nottingham F	0	0	**2**	**0**
2018–19	Burton Alb	7	0	**7**	**0**
2018–19	Accrington S	11	0	**11**	**0**

FINLEY, Sam (M) **37 1**
H: 5 7 W: 10 10 b.Liverpool 4-8-92
From Southport, Warrington T, The New Saints, AFC Fylde.

2018–19	Accrington S	37	1	**37**	**1**

GILBOY, Lewis (M) **0 0**

2018–19	Accrington S	0	0		

HUGHES, Mark (D) **457 27**
H: 6 1 W: 13 03 b.Liverpool 9-12-86

2004–05	Everton	0	0		
2005–06	Everton	0	0		
2005–06	*Stockport Co*	3	1	**3**	**1**
2006–07	Everton	1	0	**1**	**0**
2006–07	Northampton T	17	2		
2007–08	Northampton T	35	1		
2008–09	Northampton T	41	1	**93**	**4**
2009–10	Walsall	26	1	**26**	**1**
2010–11	N Queensland F	30	4	**30**	**4**
2011–12	Bury	25	0		
2012–13	Bury	27	0	**52**	**0**
2012–13	*Accrington S*	5	0		
2013–14	Morecambe	44	5		
2014–15	Morecambe	40	3	**84**	**8**
2015–16	Stevenage	20	1	**20**	**1**
2015–16	Accrington S	15	1		
2016–17	Accrington S	36	2		
2017–18	Accrington S	46	4		
2018–19	Accrington S	46	1	**148**	**8**

JOHNSON, Callum (M) **72 1**
b. 23-10-97
From Middlesbrough.

2017–18	Accrington S	31	1		
2018–19	Accrington S	41	0	**72**	**1**

KEE, Billy (F) **379 127**
H: 5 9 W: 11 04 b.Loughborough 1-12-90
Internationals: Northern Ireland U19, U21.

2009–10	Leicester C	0	0		
2009–10	*Accrington S*	37	9		
2010–11	Torquay U	40	9		
2011–12	Torquay U	4	0	**44**	**9**
2011–12	Burton Alb	20	12		
2012–13	Burton Alb	40	13		
2013–14	Burton Alb	37	12		
2014–15	Burton Alb	2	2	**99**	**39**
2014–15	Scunthorpe U	12	0	**12**	**0**
2014–15	*Mansfield T*	13	2	**13**	**2**
2015–16	Accrington S	45	17		
2016–17	Accrington S	39	13		
2017–18	Accrington S	46	25		
2018–19	Accrington S	44	13	**211**	**77**

MANGAN, Andy (F) **137 26**
H: 6 0 W: 11 09 b.Liverpool 30-8-86
Internationals: England C.

2003–04	Blackpool	2	0		
2004–05	Blackpool	0	0	**2**	**0**

From Hyde

2006–07	Accrington S	34	4		
2007–08	Bury	20	4	**20**	**4**
2007–08	*Accrington S*	7	1		

From Forest Green R, Wrexham.

2012–13	Fleetwood T	12	4	**12**	**4**

From Forest Green R.

2014–15	Shrewsbury T	30	8		

From Tranmere R.

2015–16	Shrewsbury T	19	5		
2016–17	Shrewsbury T	10	0	**59**	**13**

From Tranmere R.

2018–19	Accrington S	3	0	**44**	**5**

MAXTED, Jonathan (G) **20 0**
H: 6 0 W: 11 03 b. 26-10-93

2012–13	Doncaster R	0	0		
2013–14	Doncaster R	0	0		
2014–15	Hartlepool U	0	0		
2017–18	Accrington S	1	0		
2018–19	Accrington S	19	0	**20**	**0**

McCONVILLE, Sean (M) **251 51**
H: 5 8 W: 11 07 b.Liverpool 6-3-89

2008–09	Accrington S	5	0		
2009–10	Accrington S	28	1		
2010–11	Accrington S	43	13		
2011–12	Rochdale	4	0	**4**	**0**

From Barrow, Stalybridge Celtic, Chester.

2015–16	Accrington S	42	5		
2016–17	Accrington S	41	5		
2017–18	Accrington S	43	12		
2018–19	Accrington S	45	15	**247**	**51**

MINGOIA, Piero (M) **213 18**
H: 5 6 W: 10 12 b.Enfield 20-10-91

2010–11	Watford	5	0		
2011–12	Watford	0	0		
2011–12	*Brentford*	0	0		
2012–13	Watford	0	0		
2012–13	*Accrington S*	7	1		
2013–14	Watford	0	0	**5**	**0**
2013–14	Accrington S	37	1		
2014–15	Accrington S	36	8		
2015–16	Accrington S	46	3		
2016–17	Cambridge U	40	5		
2017–18	Cambridge U	22	0	**62**	**5**
2018–19	Accrington S	4	0	**130**	**13**
2018–19	*Morecambe*	16	0	**16**	**0**

MOHAMMED, Zehn (D) **0 0**
b. 28-2-00

2017–18	Accrington S	0	0		
2018–19	Accrington S	0	0		

NOLAN, Liam (D) **57 0**
H: 5 9 W: 10 12 b.Liverpool 20-9-94
Internationals: Northern Ireland U21.

2012–13	Crewe Alex	0	0		
2013–14	Crewe Alex	13	0		
2014–15	Crewe Alex	13	0	**26**	**0**
2017–18	Accrington S	29	0		
2018–19	Accrington S	2	0	**31**	**0**

OGLE, Reagan (D) **4 0**
H: 5 8 W: 10 06 b. 29-3-99

2016–17	Accrington S	1	0		
2017–18	Accrington S	3	0		
2018–19	Accrington S	0	0	**4**	**0**

PERRITT, Harry (M) **0 0**

2018–19	Accrington S	0	0		

RODGERS, Harvey (M) **30 1**
H: 5 10 W: 12 06 b.York 20-10-96

2016–17	Hull C	0	0		
2016–17	*Accrington S*	19	1		
2017–18	Fleetwood T	0	0		
2017–18	Accrington S	5	0		
2018–19	Accrington S	6	0	**30**	**1**

SAVIN, Toby (G) **0 0**

2017–18	Accrington S	0	0		
2018–19	Accrington S	0	0		

SCOTT, Andrew (M) **0 0**
b. 19-6-00
Internationals: Northern Ireland U17.
From Maiden C.

2018–19	Accrington S	0	0		

SHAH, Kasom (D) **0 0**
b. 14-2-00

2018–19	Accrington S	0	0		

SIMMONDS, Okera (F) **0 0**
H: 6 2 W: 12 04 b.Manchester 25-12-99
Internationals: England U16.

2018–19	Accrington S	0	0		

SOUSA, Erico (M) **10 0**
b. 12-3-95

2013–14	Barnsley	0	0		

From Hyde U, Celje, Tadcaster Alb.

2017–18	Accrington S	6	0		
2018–19	Accrington S	4	0	**10**	**0**

SYKES, Ross (D) **22 3**
H: 6 5 W: 11 07 b.Burnley 26-3-99

2016–17	Accrington S	0	0		
2017–18	Accrington S	2	0		
2018–19	Accrington S	20	3	**22**	**3**

WARNER, Tony (G) **333 0**
H: 6 4 W: 15 06 b.Liverpool 11-5-74
Internationals: Trinidad & Tobago Full caps.

1993–94	Liverpool	0	0		
1994–95	Liverpool	0	0		
1995–96	Liverpool	0	0		
1996–97	Liverpool	0	0		
1997–98	Liverpool	0	0		
1997–98	*Swindon T*	2	0	**2**	**0**
1998–99	Liverpool	0	0		
1998–99	*Celtic*	3	0	**3**	**0**
1998–99	*Aberdeen*	6	0	**6**	**0**
1999–2000	Millwall	45	0		
2000–01	Millwall	35	0		
2001–02	Millwall	46	0		
2002–03	Millwall	46	0		
2003–04	Millwall	28	0	**200**	**0**

2004–05	Cardiff C	26	0	**26**	**0**
2005–06	Fulham	18	0		
2006–07	Fulham	0	0		
2006–07	*Leeds U*	13	0	**13**	**0**
2006–07	*Norwich C*	13	0	**13**	**0**
2007–08	Fulham	3	0	**21**	**0**
2007–08	*Barnsley*	3	0	**3**	**0**
2008–09	Hull C	0	0		
2008–09	*Leicester C*	4	0	**4**	**0**
2009–10	Hull C	0	0		
2010–11	Scunthorpe U	2	0	**2**	**0**
2010–11	Tranmere R	25	0	**25**	**0**
2012–13	Wellington Phoenix	15	0	**15**	**0**
2013–14	Blackpool	0	0		
2014–15	Accrington S	0	0		
2015–16	Accrington S	0	0		
2018–19	Accrington S	0	0		

WATSON, Niall (M) **2** **0**
b. 15-6-00

2017–18	Accrington S	2	0		
2018–19	Accrington S	0	0	**2**	**0**

WILLIAMS, Danny (M) **113** **4**
H: 5 9 W: 10 12 b.Wigan 25-1-88
From FC United of Manchester, Clitheroe, Kendal T.

2013–14	Inverness CT	20	1		
2014–15	Inverness CT	34	2		
2015–16	Inverness CT	34	1	**88**	**4**
2016–17	Dundee	23	0		
2017–18	Dundee	0	0	**23**	**0**
2017–18	Accrington S	1	0		
2018–19	Accrington S	1	0	**2**	**0**

WILLIAMS, Matty (D) **0** **0**

2018–19	Accrington S	0	0		

WOOD, Will (D) **4** **0**
H: 5 9 W: 10 08 b.Burgess Hill 29-11-96
From Southampton.

2018–19	Accrington S	4	0	**4**	**0**

ZANZALA, Offrande (F) **35** **5**
b. 13-12-97

2015–16	Derby Co	0	0		
2015–16	*Stevenage*	2	0	**2**	**0**
2016–17	Derby Co	0	0		
2017–18	Derby Co	0	0		
2017–18	*Accrington S*	6	1		
2018–19	Accrington S	27	4	**33**	**5**

Players retained or with offer of contract
Esteves, De Sousa Erico Henrique.

Scholars
Bolton, Jack Adam; Bowe, Adam; Cullen, Kane; Ellis, Gabriel David; Evans, Jack Robert Matthew; Feathers, Aspen Shaun; Gilboy, Lewis Anthony; Isherwood, Liam Paul; Kasongo, Guelor Bukomo; Martin, Daniel James; Morris, John-Jo; Nolan, Mitchell Arron; O'Neill, Alex James; Perritt, Harrison Joshua; Ridge, Charles Disney; Savin, Toby; Shah, Kasom; Williams, Matthew Charles.

AFC WIMBLEDON (2)

APPIAH, Kwesi (F) **92** **17**
H: 5 11 W: 12 08 b.Thamesmead 12-8-90
Internationals: Ghana Full caps.

2008–09	Peterborough U	0	0		

From Brackley T, Thurrock, Margate.

2011–12	Crystal Palace	4	0		
2012–13	Crystal Palace	2	0		
2012–13	*Aldershot T*	2	0	**2**	**0**
2012–13	*Yeovil T*	5	0	**5**	**0**
2013–14	Crystal Palace	0	0		
2013–14	*Notts Co*	7	0	**7**	**0**
2013–14	*AFC Wimbledon*	7	3		
2014–15	Crystal Palace	0	0		
2014–15	*Cambridge U*	19	6	**19**	**6**
2014–15	*Reading*	6	1	**6**	**1**
2015–16	Crystal Palace	0	0	**6**	**0**
2017–18	Viking FK	0	0		
2017–18	AFC Wimbledon	14	3		
2018–19	AFC Wimbledon	26	4	**47**	**10**

ASHLEY, Ossama (M) **0** **0**

2017–18	AFC Wimbledon	0	0		
2018–19	AFC Wimbledon	0	0		

BARCHAM, Andy (F) **386** **48**
H: 5 8 W: 11 10 b.Basildon 16-12-86
Internationals: England U16.

2005–06	Tottenham H	0	0		
2006–07	Tottenham H	0	0		
2007–08	Tottenham H	0	0		
2007–08	*Leyton Orient*	25	1	**25**	**1**
2008–09	Tottenham H	0	0		
2008–09	Gillingham	33	6		
2009–10	Gillingham	42	7		
2010–11	Gillingham	24	6	**99**	**19**
2011–12	Scunthorpe U	41	9		
2012–13	Scunthorpe U	34	0	**75**	**9**
2013–14	Portsmouth	26	3		
2014–15	Portsmouth	19	1	**45**	**4**
2015–16	AFC Wimbledon	33	5		
2016–17	AFC Wimbledon	37	5		
2017–18	AFC Wimbledon	45	4		
2018–19	AFC Wimbledon	27	1	**142**	**15**

BUREY, Tyler (F) **3** **0**
b. 9-1-01

2018–19	AFC Wimbledon	3	0	**3**	**0**

CONNOLLY, Dylan (F) **12** **0**
H: 5 9 W: 10 12 b.Dublin 2-5-95
Internationals: Republic of Ireland U17, U21.

2014–15	Ipswich T	0	0		
2015–16	Ipswich T	0	0		

From Bray W, Dundalk.

2018–19	AFC Wimbledon	12	0	**12**	**0**

EGAN, Alfie (M) **12** **0**
b. 3-9-97

2016–17	AFC Wimbledon	9	0		
2017–18	AFC Wimbledon	2	0		
2018–19	AFC Wimbledon	1	0	**12**	**0**

HANSON, James (F) **343** **83**
H: 6 4 W: 12 04 b.Bradford 9-11-87

2009–10	Bradford C	34	12		
2010–11	Bradford C	36	6		
2011–12	Bradford C	39	13		
2012–13	Bradford C	43	10		
2013–14	Bradford C	35	12		
2014–15	Bradford C	38	9		
2015–16	Bradford C	41	11		
2016–17	Bradford C	17	4	**283**	**77**
2016–17	Sheffield U	13	1		
2017–18	Sheffield U	1	0	**14**	**1**
2017–18	*Bury*	17	0	**17**	**0**
2018–19	AFC Wimbledon	29	5	**29**	**5**

HARTIGAN, Anthony (M) **42** **0**
H: 5 10 W: 10 10 b.Kingston upon Thames 27-1-00

2017–18	AFC Wimbledon	11	0		
2018–19	AFC Wimbledon	31	0	**42**	**0**

KALAMBAYI, Paul (D) **17** **0**
b. 28-7-99

2015–16	AFC Wimbledon	0	0		
2016–17	AFC Wimbledon	0	0		
2017–18	AFC Wimbledon	0	0		
2018–19	AFC Wimbledon	17	0	**17**	**0**

McDONALD, Rod (D) **90** **3**
H: 6 3 W: 12 13 b.Crewe 11-4-92

2010–11	Oldham Ath	0	0		

From Colwyn Bay, Nantwich T, Hereford U, AFC Telford U.

2015–16	Northampton T	23	3		
2016–17	Northampton T	7	0	**30**	**3**
2016–17	Coventry C	0	0		
2017–18	Coventry C	37	0	**37**	**0**
2018–19	AFC Wimbledon	23	0	**23**	**0**

McDONNELL, Joe (G) **22** **0**
H: 5 10 W: 9 13 b.Basingstoke 19-5-94

2014–15	AFC Wimbledon	4	0		
2015–16	AFC Wimbledon	0	0		
2016–17	AFC Wimbledon	3	0		
2017–18	AFC Wimbledon	1	0		
2018–19	AFC Wimbledon	14	0	**22**	**0**

NIGHTINGALE, Will (M) **77** **1**
H: 6 1 W: 13 03 b.Wandsworth 2-7-95

2013–14	AFC Wimbledon	0	0		
2014–15	AFC Wimbledon	4	0		
2015–16	AFC Wimbledon	4	0		
2016–17	AFC Wimbledon	12	0		
2017–18	AFC Wimbledon	18	1		
2018–19	AFC Wimbledon	39	0	**77**	**1**

OSHILAJA, Adedeji (D) **155** **9**
H: 5 11 W: 11 10 b.Bermondsey 16-7-93

2012–13	Cardiff C	0	0		
2013–14	Cardiff C	0	0		
2013–14	*Newport Co*	8	0	**8**	**0**
2013–14	*Sheffield W*	2	0	**2**	**0**
2014–15	Cardiff C	0	0		
2014–15	*AFC Wimbledon*	23	1		
2015–16	Cardiff C	0	0		
2015–16	*Gillingham*	22	3		
2016–17	Cardiff C	0	0		
2016–17	*Gillingham*	33	2	**55**	**5**
2017–18	AFC Wimbledon	42	2		
2018–19	AFC Wimbledon	25	1	**90**	**4**

PIGOTT, Joe (F) **155** **37**
H: 6 0 W: 9 05 b.London 24-11-93

2012–13	Charlton Ath	0	0		
2013–14	Charlton Ath	11	0		
2013–14	*Gillingham*	7	1	**7**	**1**
2014–15	Charlton Ath	1	0		
2014–15	*Newport Co*	10	3	**10**	**3**
2014–15	*Southend U*	20	6		
2015–16	Charlton Ath	0	0	**12**	**0**
2015–16	*Southend U*	23	3	**43**	**9**
2015–16	*Luton T*	15	4	**15**	**4**
2016–17	Cambridge U	10	0	**10**	**0**

From Maidstone U.

2017–18	AFC Wimbledon	18	5		
2018–19	AFC Wimbledon	40	15	**58**	**20**

PINNOCK, Mitch (M) **36** **3**
H: 5 10 b. 12-12-94
Internationals: England C.

2012–13	Southend U	2	0		
2013–14	Southend U	0	0	**2**	**0**

From Bromley, Maidstone U, Dover Ath, Kingstonian, Dover Ath.

2018–19	AFC Wimbledon	34	3	**34**	**3**

PURRINGTON, Ben (D) **116** **0**
H: 5 9 W: 11 07 b.Exeter 5-5-96

2013–14	Plymouth Arg	12	0		
2014–15	Plymouth Arg	8	0		
2015–16	Plymouth Arg	13	0		
2016–17	Plymouth Arg	19	0	**52**	**0**
2016–17	Rotherham U	10	0		
2017–18	Rotherham U	10	0	**20**	**0**
2018–19	AFC Wimbledon	26	0	**26**	**0**
2018–19	*Charlton Ath*	18	0	**18**	**0**

RUDONI, Jack (M) **0** **0**

2018–19	AFC Wimbledon	0	0		

SIBBICK, Toby (D) **26** **0**
H: 6 0 W: 10 12 b.Isleworth 23-5-99

2016–17	AFC Wimbledon	2	0		
2017–18	AFC Wimbledon	1	0		
2018–19	AFC Wimbledon	23	0	**26**	**0**

SOARES, Tom (M) **435** **39**
H: 6 0 W: 11 04 b.Reading 10-7-86
Internationals: England U20, U21.

2003–04	Crystal Palace	3	0		
2004–05	Crystal Palace	22	0		
2005–06	Crystal Palace	44	1		
2006–07	Crystal Palace	37	3		
2007–08	Crystal Palace	39	6		
2008–09	Crystal Palace	4	1	**149**	**11**
2008–09	Stoke C	7	0		
2008–09	*Charlton Ath*	11	1	**11**	**1**
2009–10	Stoke C	0	0		
2009–10	*Sheffield W*	25	2	**25**	**2**
2010–11	Stoke C	0	0		
2011–12	Stoke C	0	0	**7**	**0**
2011–12	*Hibernian*	10	2	**10**	**2**
2012–13	Bury	23	2		
2013–14	Bury	30	6		
2014–15	Bury	43	8		
2015–16	Bury	42	4		
2016–17	Bury	26	2	**164**	**22**
2016–17	AFC Wimbledon	15	0		
2017–18	AFC Wimbledon	31	1		
2018–19	AFC Wimbledon	23	0	**69**	**1**

THOMAS, Terell (D) **26** **0**
H: 6 0 b. 13-10-97

2014–15	Charlton Ath	0	0		
2015–16	Charlton Ath	0	0		
2016–17	Charlton Ath	0	0		
2017–18	Wigan Ath	3	0	**3**	**0**
2018–19	AFC Wimbledon	23	0	**23**	**0**

TROTTER, Liam (M) **330** **39**
H: 6 2 W: 12 02 b.Ipswich 24-8-88

2005–06	Ipswich T	1	0		
2006–07	Ipswich T	0	0		
2006–07	*Millwall*	2	0		
2007–08	Ipswich T	7	1		
2008–09	Ipswich T	3	1		
2008–09	*Grimsby T*	15	2	**15**	**2**
2008–09	*Scunthorpe U*	12	1	**12**	**1**
2009–10	Ipswich T	12	0	**23**	**2**
2009–10	*Millwall*	20	1		
2010–11	Millwall	35	7		
2011–12	Millwall	35	7		
2012–13	Millwall	36	6		

2013–14	Millwall	19	3	**147**	**24**
2013–14	*Bolton W*	16	1		
2014–15	Bolton W	14	1		
2015–16	Bolton W	13	1		
2015–16	*Nottingham F*	9	1	**9**	**1**
2016–17	Bolton W	20	2	**63**	**5**
2017–18	AFC Wimbledon	42	3		
2018–19	AFC Wimbledon	19	1	**61**	**4**

TZANEV, Nikola (G) 0 0
Internationals: New Zealand U20, Full caps.
From Brentford.

2016–17	AFC Wimbledon	0	0		
2017–18	AFC Wimbledon	0	0		
2018–19	AFC Wimbledon	0	0		

WAGSTAFF, Scott (M) 293 28
H: 5 10 W: 10 03 b.Maidstone 31-3-90

2007–08	Charlton Ath	2	0		
2008–09	Charlton Ath	2	0		
2008–09	*Bournemouth*	5	0	**5**	**0**
2009–10	Charlton Ath	30	4		
2010–11	Charlton Ath	40	8		
2011–12	Charlton Ath	34	4		
2012–13	Charlton Ath	9	1	**117**	**17**
2012–13	*Leyton Orient*	7	0	**7**	**0**
2013–14	Bristol C	37	5		
2014–15	Bristol C	26	2		
2015–16	Bristol C	9	1	**72**	**8**
2016–17	Gillingham	26	1		
2017–18	Gillingham	31	0	**57**	**1**
2018–19	AFC Wimbledon	35	2	**35**	**2**

WOOD, Tommy (F) 1 0
b. 26-11-98
From Burnley.

2018–19	AFC Wimbledon	1	0	**1**	**0**

WORDSWORTH, Anthony (M) 335 62
H: 6 1 W: 12 00 b.Camden 3-1-89

2007–08	Colchester U	3	0		
2008–09	Colchester U	30	3		
2009–10	Colchester U	41	11		
2010–11	Colchester U	35	5		
2011–12	Colchester U	44	13		
2012–13	Colchester U	24	3	**177**	**35**
2012–13	Ipswich T	7	1		
2013–14	Ipswich T	10	1		
2014–15	Ipswich T	1	0	**18**	**2**
2014–15	*Rotherham U*	6	1	**6**	**1**
2014–15	*Crawley T*	18	4	**18**	**4**
2015–16	Southend U	21	4		
2016–17	Southend U	34	11		
2017–18	Southend U	24	3	**79**	**18**
2018–19	AFC Wimbledon	37	2	**37**	**2**

Players retained or with offer of contract
Collins, Reuben Alexander; Mbiya-Kalambayi, Paul Mbwebwe; McLoughlin, Shane Daniel; Osew, Paul Asiedu; Procter, Archie Mark; Stabana, Kyron Thomas.

Scholars
Assal, Ayoub; Awoyejo, Jamil Tyrique Daniel; Bolton, Elliott James; Burey, Tyler David Sylvester; Currie, Jack Alexander; Fisher, David; Lodge, Francis Donte Antonio; Macnab, Finlay Alexander; Madelin, Jack; Mbele, Richie Bless; Mills, Bobby John Barry; Osu, Olukayode Jacomo Maria; Robinson, Zachary Scott; Weekes, Reece Lee Philip; White, Albert James.

ARSENAL (3)

AUBAMEYANG, Pierre-Emerick (F) 333 177
H: 6 2 W: 11 09 b.Bitam 18-6-89
Internationals: France U21. Gabon U23, Full caps.

2008–09	AC Milan	0	0		
2008–09	*Dijon*	34	8	**34**	**8**
2009–10	AC Milan	0	0		
2009–10	*Lille*	14	2	**14**	**2**
2010–11	AC Milan	0	0		
2010–11	*Monaco*	19	2	**19**	**2**
2010–11	*Saint-Etienne*	17	10		
2011–12	Saint-Etienne	19	6		
2012–13	Saint-Etienne	37	19	**73**	**35**
2013–14	Borussia Dortmund	32	13		
2014–15	Borussia Dortmund	33	16		
2015–16	Borussia Dortmund	31	25		
2016–17	Borussia Dortmund	32	31		
2017–18	Borussia Dortmund	16	13	**144**	**98**
2017–18	Arsenal	13	10		
2018–19	Arsenal	36	22	**49**	**32**

BELLERIN, Hector (D) 151 6
H: 5 10 W: 11 09 b.Barcelona 19-3-95
Internationals: Spain U16, U17, U19, U21, Full caps.

2012–13	Arsenal	0	0		
2013–14	Arsenal	0	0		
2013–14	*Watford*	8	0	**8**	**0**
2014–15	Arsenal	20	2		
2015–16	Arsenal	36	1		
2016–17	Arsenal	33	1		
2017–18	Arsenal	35	2		
2018–19	Arsenal	19	0	**143**	**6**

BIELIK, Krystian (M) 46 3
H: 5 10 W: 11 00 b.Vrinnevi 4-1-98
Internationals: Poland U16, U17, U18, U19, U21.

2014–15	Legia Warsaw	5	0	**5**	**0**
2014–15	Arsenal	0	0		
2015–16	Arsenal	0	0		
2016–17	Arsenal	0	0		
2016–17	*Birmingham C*	10	0	**10**	**0**
2017–18	Arsenal	0	0		
2017–18	*Walsall*	0	0		
2018–19	Arsenal	0	0		
2018–19	*Charlton Ath*	31	3	**31**	**3**

CECH, Petr (G) 571 0
H: 6 5 W: 14 07 b.Plzen 20-5-82
Internationals: Czech Republic U16, U17, U18, U20, U21, Full caps.

1998–99	Viktoria Plzen	0	0		
1999–2000	Chmel	1	0		
2000–01	Chmel	26	0	**27**	**0**
2001–02	Sparta Prague	26	0	**26**	**0**
2002–03	Rennes	37	0		
2003–04	Rennes	38	0	**75**	**0**
2004–05	Chelsea	35	0		
2005–06	Chelsea	34	0		
2006–07	Chelsea	20	0		
2007–08	Chelsea	26	0		
2008–09	Chelsea	35	0		
2009–10	Chelsea	34	0		
2010–11	Chelsea	38	0		
2011–12	Chelsea	34	0		
2012–13	Chelsea	36	0		
2013–14	Chelsea	34	0		
2014–15	Chelsea	7	0	**333**	**0**
2015–16	Arsenal	34	0		
2016–17	Arsenal	35	0		
2017–18	Arsenal	34	0		
2018–19	Arsenal	7	0	**110**	**0**

CHAMBERS, Calum (M) 125 5
H: 6 0 W: 10 05 b.Petersfield 20-1-95
Internationals: England U17, U19, U21, Full caps.

2011–12	Southampton	0	0		
2012–13	Southampton	0	0		
2013–14	Southampton	22	0	**22**	**0**
2014–15	Arsenal	23	1		
2015–16	Arsenal	12	0		
2016–17	Arsenal	1	1		
2016–17	*Middlesbrough*	24	1	**24**	**1**
2017–18	Arsenal	12	0		
2018–19	Arsenal	0	0	**48**	**2**
2018–19	*Fulham*	31	2	**31**	**2**

ELNENY, Mohamed (M) 172 7
H: 5 11 W: 11 00 b.Al-Mahalla Al-Kubra 11-7-92
Internationals: Egypt U20, U23, Full caps.

2010–11	El Mokawloon	21	2		
2011–12	El Mokawloon	14	0	**35**	**2**
2012–13	Basel	15	0		
2013–14	Basel	32	1		
2014–15	Basel	28	2	**75**	**3**
2015–16	Basle	16	2	**16**	**2**
2015–16	Arsenal	11	0		
2016–17	Arsenal	14	0		
2017–18	Arsenal	13	0		
2018–19	Arsenal	8	0	**46**	**0**

GILMOUR, Charlie (M) 0 0
b.Brighton 11-2-99
Internationals: England U16, U17. Scotland U16, U17, U19.

2017–18	Arsenal	0	0		
2018–19	Arsenal	0	0		

GUENDOUZI, Matteo (M) 59 0
H: 5 11 W: 10 10 b.Poissy 14-4-99
Internationals: France U18, U19, U20, U21.

2015–16	Lorient	0	0		
2016–17	Lorient	8	0		
2017–18	Lorient	18	0	**26**	**0**
2018–19	Arsenal	33	0	**33**	**0**

HOLDING, Rob (D) 58 1
b.Tameside 20-9-95
Internationals: England U21.

2014–15	Bolton W	0	0		
2014–15	*Bury*	1	0	**1**	**0**
2015–16	Bolton W	26	1	**26**	**1**
2016–17	Arsenal	9	0		
2017–18	Arsenal	12	0		
2018–19	Arsenal	10	0	**31**	**0**

ILIEV, Dejan (G) 0 0
H: 6 5 b.Strumica 25-2-95
Internationals: Macedonia U17, U19, U21.

2012–13	Arsenal	0	0		
2013–14	Arsenal	0	0		
2014–15	Arsenal	0	0		
2015–16	Arsenal	0	0		
2017–18	Arsenal	0	0		
2018–19	Arsenal	0	0		

IWOBI, Alex (M) 100 11
H: 5 11 W: 11 11 b.Lagos 3-5-96
Internationals: England U16, U17, U18. Nigeria Full caps.

2012–13	Arsenal	0	0		
2013–14	Arsenal	0	0		
2014–15	Arsenal	0	0		
2015–16	Arsenal	13	2		
2016–17	Arsenal	26	3		
2017–18	Arsenal	26	3		
2018–19	Arsenal	35	3	**100**	**11**

JENKINSON, Carl (D) 108 3
H: 6 1 W: 12 02 b.Harlow 8-2-92
Internationals: Finland U19, U21. England U17, U21, Full caps.

2010–11	Charlton Ath	8	0	**8**	**0**
2010–11	Arsenal	0	0		
2011–12	Arsenal	9	0		
2012–13	Arsenal	14	0		
2013–14	Arsenal	14	1		
2014–15	Arsenal	0	0		
2014–15	*West Ham U*	32	0		
2015–16	Arsenal	0	0		
2015–16	*West Ham U*	20	2	**52**	**2**
2016–17	Arsenal	1	0		
2017–18	Arsenal	0	0		
2017–18	*Birmingham C*	7	0	**7**	**0**
2018–19	Arsenal	3	0	**41**	**1**

JOHN-JULES, Tyreece (F) 0 0
H: 6 0 b. 14-2-01
Internationals: England U16, U17, U18.

2018–19	Arsenal	0	0		

KOLASINAC, Sead (D) 145 6
H: 6 0 W: 12 13 b.Karlsruhe 20-6-93
Internationals: Germany U18, U19, U20. Bosnia and Herzegovina Full caps.

2012–13	Schalke 04	16	0		
2013–14	Schalke 04	24	0		
2014–15	Schalke 04	6	0		
2015–16	Schalke 04	23	1		
2016–17	Schalke 04	25	3	**94**	**4**
2017–18	Arsenal	27	2		
2018–19	Arsenal	24	0	**51**	**2**

KOSCIELNY, Laurent (D) 398 31
H: 6 1 W: 11 11 b.Tulle 10-9-85
Internationals: France Full caps.

2004–05	Guingamp	11	0		
2005–06	Guingamp	9	0		
2006–07	Guingamp	21	0	**41**	**0**
2007–08	Tours	33	1		
2008–09	Tours	34	5	**67**	**6**
2009–10	Lorient	35	3	**35**	**3**
2010–11	Arsenal	30	2		
2011–12	Arsenal	33	2		
2012–13	Arsenal	25	2		
2013–14	Arsenal	32	2		
2014–15	Arsenal	27	3		
2015–16	Arsenal	33	4		
2016–17	Arsenal	33	2		
2017–18	Arsenal	25	2		
2018–19	Arsenal	17	3	**255**	**22**

LACAZETTE, Alexandre (F) 270 127
H: 5 9 W: 10 12 b.Lyon 28-5-91
Internationals: France U16, U17, U18, U19, U20, U21, Full caps.

2009–10	Lyon	1	0		
2010–11	Lyon	9	1		
2011–12	Lyon	29	5		
2012–13	Lyon	31	3		
2013–14	Lyon	36	15		
2014–15	Lyon	33	27		
2015–16	Lyon	34	21		

2016–17	Lyon	30	28	**203**	**100**
2017–18	Arsenal	32	14		
2018–19	Arsenal	35	13	**67**	**27**

LENO, Bernd (G) 265 0
H: 6 3 W: 12 06 b.Bietigheim-Bissingen 4-3-92
Internationals: Germany, U17, U18, U19, U21, Full caps.
From Stuttgart.

2011–12	Bayer Leverkusen	33	0		
2012–13	Bayer Leverkusen	32	0		
2013–14	Bayer Leverkusen	34	0		
2014–15	Bayer Leverkusen	34	0		
2015–16	Bayer Leverkusen	33	0		
2016–17	Bayer Leverkusen	34	0		
2017–18	Bayer Leverkusen	33	0	**233**	**0**
2018–19	Arsenal	32	0	**32**	**0**

LICHTSTEINER, Stephan (D) 483 24
H: 5 11 W: 10 12 b.Adligenswil 16-1-84
Internationals: Switzerland U21, Full caps.

2001–02	Grasshopper	1	0		
2002–03	Grasshopper	25	0		
2003–04	Grasshopper	26	2		
2004–05	Grasshopper	27	2	**79**	**4**
2005–06	Lille	31	1		
2006–07	Lille	24	0		
2007–08	Lille	34	4	**89**	**5**
2008–09	Lazio	33	1		
2009–10	Lazio	33	2		
2010–11	Lazio	34	0	**100**	**3**
2011–12	Juventus	35	2		
2012–13	Juventus	28	4		
2013–14	Juventus	27	2		
2014–15	Juventus	32	3		
2015–16	Juventus	26	0		
2016–17	Juventus	26	1		
2017–18	Juventus	27	0	**201**	**12**
2018–19	Arsenal	14	0	**14**	**0**

MACEY, Matt (G) 49 0
H: 6 6 W: 14 05 b.Bristol 9-9-94

2011–12	Bristol R	0	0		
2012–13	Bristol R	0	0		
2013–14	Arsenal	0	0		
2014–15	Arsenal	0	0		
2014–15	*Accrington S*	4	0	**4**	**0**
2015–16	Arsenal	0	0		
2016–17	Arsenal	0	0		
2016–17	*Luton T*	11	0	**11**	**0**
2017–18	Arsenal	0	0		
2018–19	Arsenal	0	0		
2018–19	*Plymouth Arg*	34	0	**34**	**0**

MAITLAND-NILES, Ainsley (F) 63 2
H: 5 10 W: 11 05 b.Goodmayes 29-8-97
Internationals: England U17, U18, U19, U20, U21.

2014–15	Arsenal	1	0		
2015–16	Arsenal	0	0		
2015–16	*Ipswich T*	30	1	**30**	**1**
2016–17	Arsenal	1	0		
2017–18	Arsenal	15	0		
2018–19	Arsenal	16	1	**33**	**1**

MARTINEZ, Damian (G) 57 0
H: 6 3 W: 13 05 b.Mar del Plata 2-9-92
Internationals: Argentina U17, U20.

2010–11	Arsenal	0	0		
2011–12	Arsenal	0	0		
2011–12	*Oxford U*	1	0	**1**	**0**
2012–13	Arsenal	0	0		
2013–14	Arsenal	0	0		
2013–14	*Sheffield W*	11	0	**11**	**0**
2014–15	Arsenal	4	0		
2014–15	*Rotherham U*	8	0	**8**	**0**
2015–16	Arsenal	0	0		
2015–16	*Wolverhampton W*	13	0	**13**	**0**
2016–17	Arsenal	2	0		
2017–18	Arsenal	0	0		
2018–19	Arsenal	0	0	**6**	**0**
2018–19	*Reading*	18	0	**18**	**0**

MAVROPANOS, Konstantinos (D) 23 3
H: 6 4 W: 12 08 b.Athens 11-12-97
Internationals: Greece U21.

2016–17	PAS Giannina	2	0		
2017–18	PAS Giannina	14	3	**16**	**3**
2017–18	Arsenal	3	0		
2018–19	Arsenal	4	0	**7**	**0**

MEDLEY, Zechariah (D) 0 0
b. 7-7-00
Internationals: England U16.

2018–19	Arsenal	0	0		

MKHITARYAN, Henrikh (M) 344 116
H: 5 10 W: 12 00 b.Yerevan 21-1-89
Internationals: Armenia U17, U19, U21, Full caps.

2006	Pyunik	12	1		
2007	Pyunik	24	12		
2008	Pyunik	24	6		
2009	Pyunik	10	11	**70**	**30**
2009–10	Metalurg Donetsk	29	9		
2010–11	Metalurg Donetsk	8	3	**37**	**12**
2010–11	Shakhtar Donetsk	17	3		
2011–12	Shakhtar Donetsk	26	10		
2012–13	Shakhtar Donetsk	29	25	**72**	**38**
2013–14	Borussia Dortmund	31	9		
2014–15	Borussia Dortmund	28	3		
2015–16	Borussia Dortmund	31	11	**90**	**23**
2016–17	Manchester U	24	4		
2017–18	Manchester U	15	1	**39**	**5**
2017–18	Arsenal	11	2		
2018–19	Arsenal	25	6	**36**	**8**

MONREAL, Nacho (D) 357 10
H: 5 10 W: 11 04 b.Pamplona 26-2-86
Internationals: Spain U19, U21, Full caps.

2006–07	Osasuna	11	0		
2007–08	Osasuna	27	0		
2008–09	Osasuna	28	0		
2009–10	Osasuna	31	1		
2010–11	Osasuna	31	1	**128**	**2**
2011–12	Malaga	31	0		
2012–13	Malaga	14	1	**45**	**1**
2012–13	Arsenal	10	1		
2013–14	Arsenal	23	0		
2014–15	Arsenal	28	0		
2015–16	Arsenal	37	0		
2016–17	Arsenal	36	0		
2017–18	Arsenal	28	5		
2018–19	Arsenal	22	1	**184**	**7**

MUSTAFI, Shkodran (D) 198 14
H: 6 0 W: 11 07 b.Bad Hersfeld 17-4-92
Internationals: Germany U16, U17, U18, U19, U20, U21, Full caps.

2009–10	Everton	0	0		
2010–11	Everton	0	0		
2011–12	Everton	0	0		
2011–12	Sampdoria	1	0		
2012–13	Sampdoria	17	0		
2013–14	Sampdoria	33	1	**51**	**1**
2014–15	Valencia	33	4		
2015–16	Valencia	30	2	**63**	**6**
2016–17	Arsenal	26	2		
2017–18	Arsenal	27	3		
2018–19	Arsenal	31	2	**84**	**7**

NKETIAH, Eddie (F) 8 1
b.Lewisham 30-5-99
Internationals: England U18, U19, U20, U21.

2017–18	Arsenal	3	0		
2018–19	Arsenal	5	1	**8**	**1**

OSEI-TUTU, Jordi (D) 0 0
b.Slough 2-10-98

2017–18	Arsenal	0	0		
2018–19	Arsenal	0	0		

OZIL, Mesut (M) 371 64
H: 5 11 W: 11 06 b.Gelsenkirchen 15-10-88
Internationals: Germany U19, U21, Full caps.

2005–06	Schalke 04	0	0		
2006–07	Schalke 04	19	0		
2007–08	Schalke 04	11	0	**30**	**0**
2007–08	Werder Bremen	12	1		
2008–09	Werder Bremen	27	3		
2009–10	Werder Bremen	31	9		
2010–11	Werder Bremen	0	0	**70**	**13**
2010–11	Real Madrid	36	6		
2011–12	Real Madrid	35	4		
2012–13	Real Madrid	32	9		
2013–14	Real Madrid	2	0	**105**	**19**
2013–14	Arsenal	26	5		
2014–15	Arsenal	22	4		
2015–16	Arsenal	35	6		
2016–17	Arsenal	33	8		
2017–18	Arsenal	26	4		
2018–19	Arsenal	24	5	**166**	**32**

PAPASTATHOPOULOS, Sokratis (D) 319 13
H: 6 1 W: 12 13 b.Kalamata 9-6-88
Internationals: Greece U17, U19, U21.

2005–06	AEK Athens	0	0		
2005–06	*Niki Volou*	11	0	**11**	**0**
2006–07	AEK Athens	14	0		
2007–08	AEK Athens	24	1	**38**	**1**
2008–09	Genoa	21	2		
2009–10	Genoa	30	0	**51**	**2**
2010–11	AC Milan	5	0		
2010–11	AC Milan	0	0	**5**	**0**
2012–13	*Werder Bremen*	30	1		
2012–13	Werder Bremen	29	1	**59**	**2**
2013–14	Borussia Dortmund	28	1		
2014–15	Borussia Dortmund	21	1		
2015–16	Borussia Dortmund	25	1		
2016–17	Borussia Dortmund	26	2		
2017–18	Borussia Dortmund	30	2	**130**	**7**
2018–19	Arsenal	25	1	**25**	**1**

PLEGUEZUELO, Julio (D) 25 0
H: 5 9 W: 11 00 b. 26-1-97
Internationals: Spain U16, U17, U18.

2016–17	Arsenal	0	0		
2016–17	*Mallorca*	15	0	**15**	**0**
2017–18	Arsenal	0	0		
2018	*Gimnastic*	10	0	**10**	**0**
2018–19	Arsenal	0	0		

RAMSEY, Aaron (M) 289 42
H: 5 9 W: 10 07 b.Caerphilly 26-12-90
Internationals: Wales U17, U21, Full caps. Great Britain.

2006–07	Cardiff C	1	0		
2007–08	Cardiff C	15	1		
2008–09	Arsenal	9	0		
2009–10	Arsenal	18	3		
2010–11	Arsenal	7	1		
2010–11	*Nottingham F*	5	0	**5**	**0**
2010–11	*Cardiff C*	6	1	**22**	**2**
2011–12	Arsenal	34	2		
2012–13	Arsenal	36	1		
2013–14	Arsenal	23	10		
2014–15	Arsenal	29	6		
2015–16	Arsenal	31	5		
2016–17	Arsenal	23	1		
2017–18	Arsenal	24	7		
2018–19	Arsenal	28	4	**262**	**40**

SAKA, Bukayo (M) 1 0
H: 5 10 b.London 5-9-01
Internationals: England U16, U17, U18, U19.

2018–19	Arsenal	1	0	**1**	**0**

SMITH-ROWE, Emile (M) 3 0
H: 6 0 W: 11 07 b.London 28-6-00
Internationals: England U16, U17, U18, U19.

2017–18	Arsenal	0	0		
2018–19	Arsenal	0	0		
2018–19	*RB Leipzig*	3	0	**3**	**0**

SUAREZ, Denis (M) 114 9
H: 5 11 W: 10 12 b.Tui 6-1-94
Internationals: Spain U16, U17, U18, U19, U20, U21, Full caps.

2011–12	Manchester C	0	0		
2012–13	Manchester C	0	0		
2013–14	Manchester C	0	0		
2013–14	Barcelona	0	0		
2014–15	Barcelona	0	0		
2014–15	*Sevilla*	31	2	**31**	**2**
2015–16	Villareal	33	4	**33**	**4**
2016–17	Barcelona	26	1		
2017–18	Barcelona	18	2		
2018–19	Barcelona	2	0	**46**	**3**

On loan from Barcelona.

2018–19	Arsenal	4	0	**4**	**0**

TORREIRA, Lucas (M) 139 10
H: 5 5 W: 9 06 b.Fray Bentos 11-2-96
Internationals: Uruguay Full caps.

2014–15	Pescara	5	0		
2015–16	Sampdoria	0	0		
2015–16	*Pescara*	29	4	**34**	**4**
2016–17	Sampdoria	35	0		
2017–18	Sampdoria	36	4	**71**	**4**
2018–19	Arsenal	34	2	**34**	**2**

WELBECK, Danny (F) 214 44
H: 6 1 W: 11 07 b.Manchester 26-11-90
Internationals: England U17, U18, U19, U21, Full caps.

2007–08	Manchester U	0	0		
2008–09	Manchester U	3	1		
2009–10	Manchester U	5	0		
2009–10	*Preston NE*	8	2	**8**	**2**
2010–11	Manchester U	0	0		
2010–11	*Sunderland*	26	6	**26**	**6**
2011–12	Manchester U	30	9		
2012–13	Manchester U	27	1		
2013–14	Manchester U	25	9		
2014–15	Manchester U	2	0	**92**	**20**
2014–15	Arsenal	25	4		
2015–16	Arsenal	11	4		
2016–17	Arsenal	16	2		
2017–18	Arsenal	28	5		
2018–19	Arsenal	8	1	**88**	**16**

WILLOCK, Joe (M) **4** **0**
b.Waltham Forest 20-8-99
Internationals: England U16, U19, U20.

2017–18	Arsenal	2	0		
2018–19	Arsenal	2	0	**4**	**0**

XHAKA, Granit (M) **249** **14**
H: 6 0 W: 11 00 b.Gnjilane 27-9-92
Internationals: Switzerland U17, U18, U19, U21, Full caps.

2010–11	Basel	19	1		
2011–12	Basel	23	0	**42**	**1**
2012–13	Borussia M'gladbach	22	1		
2013–14	Borussia M'gladbach	28	0		
2014–15	Borussia M'gladbach	30	2		
2015–16	Borussia M'gladbach	28	3	**108**	**6**
2016–17	Arsenal	32	2		
2017–18	Arsenal	38	1		
2018–19	Arsenal	29	4	**99**	**7**

Players retained or with offer of contract
Amaechi, Xavier Casmier; Asano, Takuma; Ballard, Daniel George; Balogun, Folarin Jerry; Bola, Tolaji; Burton, Robert; Clarke, Harrison Thomas; Coyle, Trae; McEneff, Jordan John; McGuinness, Mark James; Nelson, Reiss; Nwakali, Kelechi; Okonkwo, Arthur; Olayinka, Olujimi James Ayodele; Olowu, Joseph Olugbenga; Omole, Tobi; Ospina, David; Sheaf, Ben; Smith, Matthew Gerrard; Swanson, Zak; Thompson, Dominic; Tormey, Nathan Alexander.

Scholars
Alebiosu, Ryan; Cottrell, Ben; Daley-Campbell, Vontae; Dennis, Matthew; Flaherty, Stanley James; Greenwood, Sam; Hein, Karl Jakob; Lopez Salguero, Joel; Matthews, Alfie; Smith, Tom; Spencer-Adams, Bayli Alexander.

ASTON VILLA (4)

ADOMAH, Albert (F) **486** **80**
H: 6 1 W: 11 08 b.Lambeth 13-12-87
Internationals: Ghana Full caps.

2007–08	Barnet	22	5		
2008–09	Barnet	45	9		
2009–10	Barnet	45	5	**112**	**19**
2010–11	Bristol C	46	5		
2011–12	Bristol C	45	5		
2012–13	Bristol C	40	7	**131**	**17**
2013–14	Middlesbrough	42	12		
2014–15	Middlesbrough	43	5		
2015–16	Middlesbrough	43	6		
2016–17	Middlesbrough	2	0	**130**	**23**
2016–17	Aston Villa	38	3		
2017–18	Aston Villa	39	14		
2018–19	Aston Villa	36	4	**113**	**21**

ANDRE MOREIRA, Campos (G) **50** **0**
H: 6 5 W: 14 02 b.Ribeirao 2-12-95
Internationals: Portugal U19, U20, U21.

2013–14	Ribeirao	16	0	**16**	**0**
2014–15	Atletico Madrid	0	0		
2014–15	*Moreirense*	0	0		
2015–16	Atletico Madrid	0	0		
2015–16	*Uniao Madeira*	19	0	**19**	**0**
2016–17	Atletico Madrid	0	0		
2016–17	*Belenenses*	0	0		
2017–18	Atletico Madrid	0	0		
2017–18	*Belenenses*	10	0	**10**	**0**

On loan from Atletico Madrid.

2018–19	Aston Villa	0	0		
2018–19	*Feirense*	5	0	**5**	**0**

BJARNASON, Birkir (M) **291** **48**
H: 6 0 W: 11 07 b.Akureyri 27-5-88
Internationals: Iceland U17, U19, U21, Full caps.

2004	Por Akureyri	0	0		
2005	KA Akureyri	0	0		
2006	Viking Stavanger	16	1		
2007	Viking Stavanger	6	0		
2008	Viking Stavanger	0	0		
2008	*FK Bodo/Glimt*	22	5	**22**	**5**
2009	Viking Stavanger	30	7		
2010	Viking Stavanger	25	8		
2011	Viking Stavanger	25	0	**102**	**16**
2011–12	Standard Liege	16	0		
2012–13	Standard Liege	0	0	**16**	**0**
2012–13	*Pescara Calcio*	24	2		
2013–14	Pescara Calcio	1	0		
2013–14	Sampdoria	14	0	**14**	**0**
2014–15	Pescara Calcio	35	10	**60**	**12**
2015–16	Basle	29	10		
2016–17	Basle	0	0	**29**	**10**
2016–17	Aston Villa	8	0		
2017–18	Aston Villa	23	3		
2018–19	Aston Villa	17	2	**48**	**5**

BREE, James (D) **85** **0**
H: 5 10 W: 11 09 b.Wakefield 11-10-97

2013–14	Barnsley	1	0		
2014–15	Barnsley	11	0		
2015–16	Barnsley	19	0		
2016–17	Barnsley	19	0	**50**	**0**
2016–17	Aston Villa	7	0		
2017–18	Aston Villa	6	0		
2018–19	Aston Villa	8	0	**21**	**0**
2018–19	*Ipswich T*	14	0	**14**	**0**

BUNN, Mark (G) **172** **0**
H: 6 0 W: 12 02 b.Southgate 16-11-84

2004–05	Northampton T	0	0		
2005–06	Northampton T	0	0		
2006–07	Northampton T	42	0		
2007–08	Northampton T	45	0		
2008–09	Northampton T	3	0	**90**	**0**
2008–09	Blackburn R	0	0		
2008–09	*Leicester C*	3	0	**3**	**0**
2009–10	Blackburn R	0	0		
2009–10	*Sheffield U*	32	0	**32**	**0**
2010–11	Blackburn R	3	0		
2011–12	Blackburn R	3	0		
2012–13	Blackburn R	0	0	**6**	**0**
2012–13	Norwich C	23	0		
2013–14	Norwich C	0	0		
2014–15	Norwich C	0	0	**23**	**0**
2015–16	Aston Villa	10	0		
2016–17	Aston Villa	6	0		
2017–18	Aston Villa	1	0		
2018–19	Aston Villa	1	0	**18**	**0**

CHESTER, James (D) **314** **21**
H: 5 11 W: 11 04 b.Warrington 23-1-89
Internationals: Wales Full caps.

2007–08	Manchester U	0	0		
2008–09	Manchester U	0	0		
2008–09	*Peterborough U*	5	0	**5**	**0**
2009–10	Manchester U	0	0		
2009–10	*Plymouth Arg*	3	0	**3**	**0**
2010–11	Manchester U	0	0		
2010–11	*Carlisle U*	18	2	**18**	**2**
2010–11	Hull C	21	1		
2011–12	Hull C	44	2		
2012–13	Hull C	44	1		
2013–14	Hull C	24	1		
2014–15	Hull C	23	2	**156**	**7**
2015–16	WBA	13	0	**13**	**0**
2016–17	Aston Villa	45	3		
2017–18	Aston Villa	46	4		
2018–19	Aston Villa	28	5	**119**	**12**

DAVIS, Keinan (M) **39** **2**
H: 5 6 W: 10 10 b.Stevenage 13-2-98
Internationals: England U20.

2015–16	Aston Villa	0	0		
2016–17	Aston Villa	6	0		
2017–18	Aston Villa	28	2		
2018–19	Aston Villa	5	0	**39**	**2**

DE LAET, Ritchie (D) **195** **11**
H: 6 1 W: 12 02 b.Antwerp 28-11-88
Internationals: Belgium U21, Full caps.

2007–08	Stoke C	0	0		
2008–09	Stoke C	0	0		
2008–09	Manchester U	1	0		
2009–10	Manchester U	2	0		
2010–11	Manchester U	0	0		
2010–11	*Sheffield U*	6	0	**6**	**0**
2010–11	*Preston NE*	5	0	**5**	**0**
2010–11	*Portsmouth*	22	0	**22**	**0**
2011–12	Manchester U	0	0	**3**	**0**
2011–12	*Norwich C*	6	1	**6**	**1**
2012–13	Leicester C	41	1		
2013–14	Leicester C	36	2		
2014–15	Leicester C	26	0		
2015–16	Leicester C	12	1	**115**	**4**
2015–16	*Middlesbrough*	10	0	**10**	**0**
2016–17	Aston Villa	3	0		
2017–18	Aston Villa	5	0		
2017–18	*Royal Antwerp*	6	0	**6**	**0**
2018–19	Aston Villa	0	0	**8**	**0**
2018–19	*Melbourne City*	14	6	**14**	**6**

DOYLE-HAYES, Jake (M) **6** **0**
b.Ballyjamesduff 30-12-98
Internationals: Republic of Ireland U17, U18, U19.

2017–18	Aston Villa	0	0		
2018–19	Aston Villa	0	0		
2018–19	*Cambridge U*	6	0	**6**	**0**

EL GHAZI, Anwar (F) **140** **30**
H: 6 2 W: 12 00 b.Barendrecht 3-5-95
Internationals: Netherlands U17, U18, U21, Full caps.

2014–15	Ajax	31	9		
2015–16	Ajax	27	11		
2016–17	Ajax	12	0	**70**	**20**
2016–17	Lille	12	1		
2017–18	Lille	27	4	**39**	**5**

On loan from Lille.

2018–19	Aston Villa	31	5	**31**	**5**

ELMOHAMADY, Ahmed (M) **403** **27**
H: 5 11 W: 12 10 b.El Mahalla El-Kubra 9-9-87
Internationals: Egypt Full caps.

2003–04	Ghazi Al-Mehalla	0	0		
2004–05	Ghazi Al-Mehalla	14	4		
2005–06	Ghazi Al-Mehalla	3	0	**17**	**4**
2006–07	ENPPI	12	2		
2007–08	ENPPI	6	1		
2008–09	ENPPI	28	6		
2009–10	ENPPI	12	1	**58**	**10**
2010–11	Sunderland	36	0		
2011–12	Sunderland	18	1		
2012–13	Sunderland	2	0	**56**	**1**
2012–13	*Hull C*	41	3		
2013–14	Hull C	38	2		
2014–15	Hull C	38	2		
2015–16	Hull C	41	3		
2016–17	Hull C	33	0	**191**	**10**
2017–18	Aston Villa	43	0		
2018–19	Aston Villa	38	2	**81**	**2**

ELPHICK, Tommy (M) **346** **14**
H: 5 11 W: 11 07 b.Brighton 7-9-87

2005–06	Brighton & HA	1	0		
2006–07	Brighton & HA	3	0		
2007–08	Brighton & HA	39	2		
2008–09	Brighton & HA	39	1		
2009–10	Brighton & HA	44	3		
2010–11	Brighton & HA	27	1		
2011–12	Brighton & HA	0	0		
2012–13	Brighton & HA	0	0	**153**	**7**
2012–13	Bournemouth	34	2		
2013–14	Bournemouth	38	1		
2014–15	Bournemouth	46	1		
2015–16	Bournemouth	12	1	**130**	**5**
2016–17	Aston Villa	26	0		
2017–18	Aston Villa	4	0		
2017–18	*Reading*	4	0	**4**	**0**
2018–19	Aston Villa	11	1	**41**	**1**
2018–19	*Hull C*	18	1	**18**	**1**

GARDNER, Gary (M) **173** **14**
H: 6 2 W: 12 13 b.Solihull 29-6-92
Internationals: England U17, U19, U20, U21.

2009–10	Aston Villa	0	0		
2010–11	Aston Villa	0	0		
2011–12	Aston Villa	14	0		
2011–12	*Coventry C*	4	1	**4**	**1**
2012–13	Aston Villa	2	0		
2013–14	Aston Villa	0	0		
2013–14	*Sheffield W*	3	0	**3**	**0**
2014–15	Aston Villa	0	0		
2014–15	*Brighton & HA*	17	2	**17**	**2**
2014–15	Nottingham F	18	4		
2015–16	Aston Villa	0	0		
2015–16	*Nottingham F*	20	2	**38**	**6**
2016–17	Aston Villa	26	1		
2017–18	Aston Villa	0	0		
2017–18	*Barnsley*	29	2	**29**	**2**
2018–19	Aston Villa	0	0	**42**	**1**
2018–19	*Birmingham C*	40	2	**40**	**2**

GREALISH, Jack (M) **160** **20**
H: 5 9 W: 10 10 b.Birmingham 10-9-95
Internationals: Republic of Ireland U17, U18, U21. England U21.

2012–13	Aston Villa	0	0		
2013–14	Aston Villa	1	0		
2013–14	*Notts Co*	37	5	**37**	**5**
2014–15	Aston Villa	17	0		
2015–16	Aston Villa	16	1		
2016–17	Aston Villa	31	5		
2017–18	Aston Villa	27	3		
2018–19	Aston Villa	31	6	**123**	**15**

GREEN, Andre (F) **46** **3**
H: 5 11 W: 11 03 b.Solihull 2-5-98
Internationals: England U16, U17, U18, U19, U20.

2014–15	Aston Villa	0	0		
2015–16	Aston Villa	2	0		

2016–17	Aston Villa	15	0		
2017–18	Aston Villa	5	1		
2018–19	Aston Villa	18	1	**40**	**2**
2018–19	*Portsmouth*	6	1	**6**	**1**

HEPBURN-MURPHY, Rushian (F) 29 2
H: 5 8 W: 9 04 b.Birmingham 19-9-98
Internationals: England U16, U17, U18, U19, U20.

2014–15	Aston Villa	1	0		
2015–16	Aston Villa	1	0		
2016–17	Aston Villa	3	0		
2017–18	Aston Villa	3	0		
2018–19	Aston Villa	5	0	**13**	**0**
2018–19	*Cambridge U*	16	2	**16**	**2**

HOGAN, Scott (F) 130 47
H: 5 11 W: 10 01 b.Salford 13-4-92
Internationals: Republic of Ireland Full caps.

2009–10	Rochdale	0	0		
2013–14	Rochdale	33	17	**33**	**17**
2014–15	Brentford	1	0		
2015–16	Brentford	7	7		
2016–17	Brentford	25	14	**33**	**21**
2016–17	Aston Villa	13	1		
2017–18	Aston Villa	37	6		
2018–19	Aston Villa	6	0	**56**	**7**
2018–19	*Sheffield U*	8	2	**8**	**2**

HOURIHANE, Conor (M) 338 63
H: 5 11 W: 9 11 b.Cork 2-2-91
Internationals: Republic of Ireland U19, U21, Full caps.

2008–09	Sunderland	0	0		
2009–10	Sunderland	0	0		
2010–11	Ipswich T	0	0		
2011–12	Plymouth Arg	38	2		
2012–13	Plymouth Arg	42	5		
2013–14	Plymouth Arg	45	8	**125**	**15**
2014–15	Barnsley	46	13		
2015–16	Barnsley	41	10		
2016–17	Barnsley	25	6	**112**	**29**
2016–17	Aston Villa	17	1		
2017–18	Aston Villa	41	11		
2018–19	Aston Villa	43	7	**101**	**19**

HUTTON, Alan (D) 362 6
H: 6 1 W: 11 05 b.Glasgow 30-11-84
Internationals: Scotland U21, Full caps.

2004–05	Rangers	10	0		
2005–06	Rangers	19	0		
2006–07	Rangers	33	1		
2007–08	Rangers	20	0	**82**	**1**
2007–08	Tottenham H	14	0		
2008–09	Tottenham H	8	0		
2009–10	Tottenham H	8	0		
2009–10	*Sunderland*	11	0	**11**	**0**
2010–11	Tottenham H	21	2		
2011–12	Tottenham H	0	0	**51**	**2**
2011–12	Aston Villa	31	0		
2012–13	Aston Villa	0	0		
2012–13	*Nottingham F*	7	0	**7**	**0**
2012–13	*Mallorca*	17	0	**17**	**0**
2013–14	Aston Villa	0	0		
2013–14	*Bolton W*	9	0	**9**	**0**
2014–15	Aston Villa	30	1		
2015–16	Aston Villa	28	0		
2016–17	Aston Villa	34	0		
2017–18	Aston Villa	29	0		
2018–19	Aston Villa	33	2	**185**	**3**

JEDINAK, Mile (M) 430 40
H: 6 2 W: 13 12 b.Sydney 3-8-84
Internationals: Australia U20, Full caps.

2000–01	Sydney U	3	0		
2001–02	Sydney U	7	1		
2002–03	Sydney U	18	2		
2003–04	Varteks	0	0		
2004–05	Sydney U	24	3		
2005–06	Sydney U	30	6	**82**	**12**
2006–07	Central Coast M	8	0		
2007–08	Central Coast M	22	2		
2008–09	Central Coast M	15	6	**45**	**8**
2008–09	Genclerbirligi	15	1		
2009–10	Genclerbirligi	2	0		
2009–10	Antalya	28	5	**28**	**5**
2010–11	Genclerbirligi	21	3	**38**	**4**
2011–12	Crystal Palace	31	1		
2012–13	Crystal Palace	41	3		
2013–14	Crystal Palace	38	1		
2014–15	Crystal Palace	24	5		
2015–16	Crystal Palace	27	0		
2016–17	Crystal Palace	1	0	**162**	**10**
2016–17	Aston Villa	33	0		
2017–18	Aston Villa	25	1		
2018–19	Aston Villa	17	0	**75**	**1**

KALINIC, Lovre (G) 215 0
H: 6 7 W: 12 06 b.Split 3-4-90
Internationals: Croatia U16, U17, U21, Full caps.

2008–09	Hadjuk Split	0	0		
2008–09	*Junak Sinj*	4	0	**4**	**0**
2009–10	Hadjuk Split	0	0		
2009–10	*Novalja*	23	0	**23**	**0**
2010–11	Hadjuk Split	1	0		
2011–12	Hadjuk Split	1	0		
2011–12	*Karlovac*	11	0	**11**	**0**
2012–13	Hadjuk Split	4	0		
2013–14	Hadjuk Split	24	0		
2014–15	Hadjuk Split	28	0		
2015–16	Hadjuk Split	31	0		
2016–17	Hadjuk Split	13	0	**102**	**0**
2016–17	Gent	19	0		
2017–18	Gent	35	0		
2018–19	Gent	14	0	**68**	**0**
2018–19	Aston Villa	7	0	**7**	**0**

KODJIA, Jonathan (F) 253 81
H: 6 2 W: 12 02 b.Saint-Denis 22-10-89
Internationals: Ivory Coast Full caps.

2008–09	Reims	2	0		
2009–10	Reims	0	0		
2010–11	Reims	5	0		
2011–12	Reims	2	0		
2011–12	*Cherbourg*	16	4	**16**	**4**
2012–13	Reims	0	0		
2012–13	*Amiens SC*	34	9	**34**	**9**
2013–14	Reims	0	0	**9**	**0**
2013–14	*Caen*	27	5	**27**	**5**
2014–15	Angers SCO	28	15	**28**	**15**
2015–16	Bristol C	45	19		
2016–17	Bristol C	4	0	**49**	**19**
2016–17	Aston Villa	36	19		
2017–18	Aston Villa	15	1		
2018–19	Aston Villa	39	9	**90**	**29**

LANSBURY, Henri (M) 277 48
H: 6 0 W: 13 06 b.Enfield 12-10-90
Internationals: England U16, U17, U19, U21.

2007–08	Arsenal	0	0		
2008–09	Arsenal	0	0		
2008–09	*Scunthorpe U*	16	4	**16**	**4**
2009–10	Arsenal	1	0		
2009–10	*Watford*	37	5	**37**	**5**
2010–11	Arsenal	0	0		
2010–11	*Norwich C*	23	4	**23**	**4**
2011–12	Arsenal	2	0		
2011–12	*West Ham U*	22	1	**22**	**1**
2012–13	Arsenal	0	0	**3**	**0**
2012–13	Nottingham F	32	5		
2013–14	Nottingham F	29	7		
2014–15	Nottingham F	39	10		
2015–16	Nottingham F	28	4		
2016–17	Nottingham F	17	6	**145**	**32**
2016–17	Aston Villa	18	0		
2017–18	Aston Villa	10	2		
2018–19	Aston Villa	3	0	**31**	**2**

LYDEN, Jordan (M) 14 1
H: 5 10 W: 11 00 b.Perth 30-1-96
Internationals: Australia U20.

2015–16	Aston Villa	4	0		
2016–17	Aston Villa	0	0		
2017–18	Aston Villa	0	0		
2018–19	Aston Villa	0	0	**4**	**0**
2018–19	*Oldham Ath*	10	1	**10**	**1**

McGINN, John (M) 228 22
H: 5 8 W: 10 08 b.Glasgow 18-10-94
Internationals: Scotland U19, U21, Full caps.

2012–13	St Mirren	22	1		
2013–14	St Mirren	35	3		
2014–15	St Mirren	30	0	**87**	**4**
2015–16	Hibernian	36	3		
2016–17	Hibernian	29	4		
2017–18	Hibernian	35	5		
2018–19	Hibernian	1	0	**101**	**12**
2018–19	Aston Villa	40	6	**40**	**6**

McKIRDY, Harry (M) 39 5
H: 5 9 W: 11 00 b.Stoke-on-Trent 29-3-97
From Stoke C.

2016–17	Aston Villa	0	0		
2016–17	*Stevenage*	11	1	**11**	**1**
2017–18	Aston Villa	0	0		
2017–18	*Crewe Alex*	16	3	**16**	**3**
2018–19	Aston Villa	0	0		
2018–19	*Newport Co*	12	1	**12**	**1**

MOONEY, Kelsey (F) 8 1
b. 5-2-99

2018–19	Aston Villa	0	0		
2018–19	*Cheltenham T*	8	1	**8**	**1**

NYLAND, Orjan (G) 188 0
H: 6 4 W: 12 04 b.Volda 10-9-90
Internationals: Norway U18, U21, Full caps.

2011	Hodd	28	0		
2012	Hodd	28	0	**56**	**0**
2013	Molde	20	0		
2014	Molde	28	0		
2015	Molde	13	0	**61**	**0**
2015–16	Ingolstadt	6	0		
2016–17	Ingolstadt	12	0		
2017–18	Ingolstadt	30	0	**48**	**0**
2018–19	Aston Villa	23	0	**23**	**0**

O'HARE, Callum (F) 20 3
b.Solihull 1-5-98
Internationals: England U20.

2016–17	Aston Villa	0	0		
2017–18	Aston Villa	4	0		
2018–19	Aston Villa	0	0	**4**	**0**
2018–19	*Carlisle U*	16	3	**16**	**3**

RAMSEY, Jacob (M) 1 0
b. 28-5-01
Internationals: England U18.

2018–19	Aston Villa	1	0	**1**	**0**

REVAN, Dominic (D) 0 0
b. 19-9-00

2018–19	Aston Villa	0	0		

SARKIC, Matija (G) 0 0
H: 6 4 W: 11 07 b.Podgorica 23-6-97
Internationals: Montenegro U17, U19, U21.

2014–15	Anderlecht	0	0		
2015–16	Aston Villa	0	0		
2016–17	Aston Villa	0	0		
2017–18	Aston Villa	0	0		
2017–18	*Wigan Ath*	0	0		
2018–19	Aston Villa	0	0		

STEER, Jed (G) 111 0
H: 6 2 W: 14 00 b.Norwich 23-9-92
Internationals: England U16, U17, U19.

2009–10	Norwich C	0	0		
2010–11	Norwich C	0	0		
2011–12	Norwich C	0	0		
2011–12	*Yeovil T*	12	0		
2012–13	Cambridge U	0	0		
2012–13	Norwich C	0	0		
2013–14	Aston Villa	0	0		
2014–15	Aston Villa	1	0		
2014–15	*Doncaster R*	13	0	**13**	**0**
2014–15	*Yeovil T*	12	0	**24**	**0**
2015–16	Aston Villa	0	0		
2015–16	*Huddersfield T*	38	0	**38**	**0**
2016–17	Aston Villa	0	0		
2017–18	Aston Villa	0	0		
2018–19	Aston Villa	16	0	**17**	**0**
2018–19	*Charlton Ath*	19	0	**19**	**0**

TAYLOR, Corey (F) 11 0
b.Erdington 23-9-97
Internationals: England U17.

2015–16	Aston Villa	0	0		
2016–17	Aston Villa	1	0		
2017–18	Aston Villa	0	0		
2018–19	Aston Villa	0	0	**1**	**0**
2018–19	*Walsall*	10	0	**10**	**0**

TAYLOR, Neil (D) 260 0
H: 5 9 W: 10 02 b.Ruthin 7-2-89
Internationals: Wales U17, U19, U21, C, Full caps. Great Britain.

2007–08	Wrexham	26	0	**26**	**0**
2010–11	Swansea C	29	0		
2011–12	Swansea C	36	0		
2012–13	Swansea C	6	0		
2013–14	Swansea C	10	0		
2014–15	Swansea C	34	0		
2015–16	Swansea C	34	0		
2016–17	Swansea C	11	0	**160**	**0**
2016–17	Aston Villa	14	0		
2017–18	Aston Villa	29	0		
2018–19	Aston Villa	31	0	**74**	**0**

WHELAN, Glenn (M) 514 19
H: 5 11 W: 12 07 b.Dublin 13-1-84
Internationals: Republic of Ireland U16, U21, B, Full caps.

2000–01	Manchester C	0	0		
2001–02	Manchester C	0	0		
2002–03	Manchester C	0	0		
2003–04	Manchester C	0	0		
2003–04	*Bury*	13	0	**13**	**0**
2004–05	Sheffield W	36	2		
2005–06	Sheffield W	43	1		
2006–07	Sheffield W	38	7		
2007–08	Sheffield W	25	2	**142**	**12**

2007–08	Stoke C	14	1		
2008–09	Stoke C	26	1		
2009–10	Stoke C	33	2		
2010–11	Stoke C	29	0		
2011–12	Stoke C	30	1		
2012–13	Stoke C	32	0		
2013–14	Stoke C	32	0		
2014–15	Stoke C	28	0		
2015–16	Stoke C	37	0		
2016–17	Stoke C	30	0	**291**	**5**
2017–18	Aston Villa	33	1		
2018–19	Aston Villa	35	1	**68**	**2**

Players retained or with offer of contract

Bazeley, Isaiah Robert Graham; Birch, Jack David; Bridge, Mungo Olayipo Oladapo; Brunt, Lewis; Campton-Sturridge, Dj; Clarke, Jack Aidan; Cox, Jordan Raymond; Guilbert, Frederic; Guy, Ben Tyler; Hooper, Anton Abeku; McCormack, Ross; Odutayo, Colin Ladipo; Rowe, Callum Miles; Suliman, Easah Zaheer; Tait, Moran Michael; Tshibola, Aaron; Vassilev, Indiana Denchev; Wright, Tyreik Samuel.

Scholars

Archer, Cameron Desmond; Burton, Bradley; Farr, Charlie Edward James; Ige, Luke; McConnachie, Charlie; Onodi, Akos Sandor; Patterson, Ethan James Alexander; Philogene-Bidace, Jaden; Pressley, Aaron Alex; Sea, Dimitri Disseka; Sinisalo, Viljami Kari Veikko; Sohna, Harrison Sheriff; Sohna, Myles Baboucarr; Walker, Jake.

BARNSLEY (5)

ADEBOYEJO, Victor (F) 40 3
b. 12-1-98

2014–15	Leyton Orient	1	0		
2015–16	Leyton Orient	1	0		
2016–17	Leyton Orient	13	1	**15**	**1**
2017–18	Barnsley	0	0		
2018–19	Barnsley	25	2	**25**	**2**

BAHRE, Mike-Steven (M) 60 2
H: 5 10 W: 11 00 b.Garbsen 10-8-95

2014–15	Hannover 96	0	0		
2015–16	Hannover 96	1	0		
2015–16	*Hallescher*	6	0	**6**	**0**
2016–17	Hannover 96	2	0		
2017–18	*Meppen*	16	1	**16**	**1**
2017–18	Hannover 96	0	0		
2018–19	Hannover 96	0	0	**3**	**0**

On loan from Hannover 96.

2018–19	Barnsley	35	1	**35**	**1**

BIRD, Jared (M) 14 0
H: 5 9 W: 9 11 b.Nottingham 21-8-97
From Derby Co.

2016–17	Barnsley	0	0		
2017–18	Barnsley	3	0		
2017–18	*Yeovil T*	11	0	**11**	**0**
2018–19	Barnsley	0	0	**3**	**0**

BROWN, Jacob (M) 47 8
H: 5 10 W: 9 11 b. 10-4-98

2014–15	Barnsley	0	0		
2015–16	Barnsley	0	0		
2016–17	Barnsley	2	0		
2017–18	Barnsley	0	0		
2017–18	*Chesterfield*	13	0	**13**	**0**
2018–19	Barnsley	32	8	**34**	**8**

CAVARE, Dimitri (D) 73 3
H: 6 1 W: 13 03 b.Pointe-à-Pitre 5-2-95
Internationals: France U20. Guadeloupe Full caps.

2013–14	Lens	1	0		
2014–15	Lens	20	0	**21**	**0**
2015–16	Rennes	0	0		
2016–17	Rennes	2	0		
2017–18	Rennes	0	0	**2**	**0**
2017–18	Barnsley	9	1		
2018–19	Barnsley	41	2	**50**	**3**

DAVIES, Adam (G) 184 0
H: 6 1 W: 11 11 b.Rinteln 17-7-92
Internationals: Wales Full caps.

2009–10	Everton	0	0		
2010–11	Everton	0	0		
2011–12	Everton	0	0		
2013–14	Sheffield W	0	0		
2014–15	Barnsley	23	0		
2015–16	Barnsley	38	0		
2016–17	Barnsley	46	0		
2017–18	Barnsley	35	0		
2018–19	Barnsley	42	0	**184**	**0**

DOUGALL, Kenneth (M) 171 13
H: 6 0 W: 12 06 b.Brisbane 7-5-93
Internationals: Australia U23.

2013–14	Brisbane C	34	10	**34**	**10**
2014–15	Telstar	29	1	**29**	**1**
2015–16	Sparta Rotterdam	32	0		
2016–17	Sparta Rotterdam	20	1		
2017–18	Sparta Rotterdam	29	1	**81**	**2**
2018–19	Barnsley	27	0	**27**	**0**

FEENEY, Kieran (F) 0 0
H: 5 9 b.Blackburn 27-1-01

2018–19	Barnsley	0	0		

FIELDING, Sam (D) 0 0
b.Burton upon Trent 2-11-99
From York C.

2018–19	Barnsley	0	0		

FRYERS, Zeki (D) 65 1
H: 6 0 W: 12 00 b.Manchester 9-9-92
Internationals: England U16, U17, U19.

2011–12	Manchester U	2	0	**2**	**0**
2012–13	Standard Liege	7	0	**7**	**0**
2012–13	Tottenham H	0	0		
2013–14	Tottenham H	7	0	**7**	**0**
2014–15	Crystal Palace	1	0		
2014–15	*Rotherham U*	10	0	**10**	**0**
2014–15	*Ipswich T*	3	0	**3**	**0**
2015–16	Crystal Palace	0	0		
2016–17	Crystal Palace	8	0	**9**	**0**
2017–18	Barnsley	22	1		
2018–19	Barnsley	5	0	**27**	**1**

GREATOREX, Jake (G) 0 0
H: 6 1 b.Pontefract 7-9-99

2018–19	Barnsley	0	0		

GREEN, Jordan (F) 76 7
H: 5 6 W: 10 03 b.London 22-2-95

2015–16	Bournemouth	0	0		
2016–17	Bournemouth	0	0		
2016–17	*Newport Co*	10	0	**10**	**0**
2017–18	Yeovil T	37	2		
2018–19	Yeovil T	19	4	**56**	**6**
2018–19	Barnsley	10	1	**10**	**1**

HEDGES, Ryan (M) 96 8
H: 6 1 W: 10 03 b.Swansea 7-9-95
Internationals: Wales U19, U21, Full caps.

2013–14	Swansea C	0	0		
2014–15	Swansea C	0	0		
2014–15	*Leyton Orient*	17	2	**17**	**2**
2015–16	Swansea C	0	0		
2015–16	*Stevenage*	6	0	**6**	**0**
2016–17	Swansea C	0	0		
2016–17	*Yeovil T*	21	4	**21**	**4**
2016–17	Barnsley	8	0		
2017–18	Barnsley	23	2		
2018–19	Barnsley	21	0	**52**	**2**

HELLIWELL, Jordan (D) 0 0
H: 5 7 b.Wakefield 23-9-01

2018–19	Barnsley	0	0		

JACKSON, Adam (D) 67 4
H: 6 2 W: 12 04 b.Darlington 18-5-94
Internationals: England U16, U17, U18, U19.

2011–12	Middlesbrough	0	0		
2012–13	Middlesbrough	0	0		
2013–14	Middlesbrough	0	0		
2014–15	Middlesbrough	0	0		
2015–16	Middlesbrough	0	0		
2015–16	*Coventry C*	0	0		
2015–16	*Hartlepool U*	29	3	**29**	**3**
2016–17	Barnsley	10	0		
2017–18	Barnsley	22	1		
2018–19	Barnsley	6	0	**38**	**1**

KENDRICK, Henry (G) 0 0
H: 6 3 b.Barnsley 3-12-00

2018–19	Barnsley	0	0		

LINDSAY, Liam (D) 170 10
H: 6 4 W: 12 07 b.Paisley 12-10-95

2012–13	Partick Thistle	1	0		
2013–14	*Alloa Ath*	10	0	**10**	**0**
2013–14	Partick Thistle	1	0		
2014–15	Partick Thistle	1	0		
2014–15	Airdrieonians	13	1	**13**	**1**
2015–16	Partick Thistle	25	1		
2016–17	Partick Thistle	36	6	**64**	**7**
2017–18	Barnsley	42	1		
2018–19	Barnsley	41	1	**83**	**2**

McGEEHAN, Cameron (M) 145 35
H: 5 11 W: 11 03 b.Kingston upon Thames 6-4-95
Internationals: Northern Ireland U17, U19, U21.

2013–14	Norwich C	0	0		
2014–15	Norwich C	0	0		
2014–15	*Luton T*	15	3		
2014–15	*Cambridge U*	4	3	**4**	**3**
2015–16	Luton T	41	12		
2016–17	Luton T	24	10	**80**	**25**
2017–18	Barnsley	9	1		
2017–18	*Scunthorpe U*	13	0	**13**	**0**
2018–19	Barnsley	39	6	**48**	**7**

MILLER, George (F) 87 18
H: 5 10 W: 10 01 b.Bolton 11-8-98

2015–16	Bury	1	0		
2016–17	Bury	28	7		
2017–18	Middlesbrough	0	0		
2017–18	*Bury*	19	8	**48**	**15**
2018–19	Middlesbrough	0	0		
2018–19	*Bradford C*	39	3	**39**	**3**
2018–19	Barnsley	0	0		

MOON, Jasper (M) 0 0
H: 6 1 b.Coventry 24-11-00

2018–19	Barnsley	0	0		

MOORE, Kieffer (F) 143 41
H: 6 5 W: 13 01 b.Torquay 8-8-92
Internationals: England C.
From Truro C, Dorchester T.

2013–14	Yeovil T	20	4		
2014–15	Yeovil T	30	3	**50**	**7**
2015	Viking	9	0	**9**	**0**

From Forest Green R, Torquay U.

2016–17	Ipswich T	11	0		
2017–18	Ipswich T	0	0	**11**	**0**
2017–18	*Rotherham U*	22	13	**22**	**13**
2017–18	Barnsley	20	4		
2018–19	Barnsley	31	17	**51**	**21**

MOTTLEY-HENRY, Dylan (F) 15 0
b. 2-8-97

2014–15	Bradford C	1	0		
2015–16	Bradford C	1	0	**2**	**0**

From Altrincham, Bradford PA, Tranmere R.

2017–18	Barnsley	1	0		
2018–19	Barnsley	0	0	**1**	**0**
2018–19	*Tranmere R*	12	0	**12**	**0**

MOWATT, Alex (D) 204 23
H: 5 10 W: 11 03 b.Doncaster 13-2-95
Internationals: England U19, U20.

2013–14	Leeds U	29	1		
2014–15	Leeds U	38	9		
2015–16	Leeds U	34	2		
2016–17	Leeds U	15	0	**116**	**12**
2016–17	Barnsley	11	1		
2017–18	Barnsley	1	0		
2017–18	*Oxford U*	30	2	**30**	**2**
2018–19	Barnsley	46	8	**58**	**9**

OTIM, Elvis (M) 0 0
b. 25-7-98
From Nottingham F.

2018–19	Barnsley	0	0		

PINILLOS, Daniel (D) 127 2
H: 6 0 W: 11 09 b.Logrono 22-10-92

2013–14	Ourense	21	0	**21**	**0**
2013–14	Cordoba	16	1		
2014–15	Cordoba	12	0		
2015–16	Nottingham F	19	0		
2016–17	Nottingham F	16	1	**35**	**1**
2017–18	Cordoba	0	0	**28**	**1**
2017–18	Barnsley	8	0		
2018–19	Barnsley	35	0	**43**	**0**

PINNOCK, Ethan (D) 58 3
H: 6 4 W: 12 06 b.Lambeth 29-5-93
Internationals: England C.
From Dulwich Hamlet.

2017–18	Barnsley	12	2		
2018–19	Barnsley	46	1	**58**	**3**

SMITH, Will (D) 0 0

2016–17	Barnsley	0	0		
2017–18	Barnsley	0	0		
2018–19	Barnsley	0	0		

STYLES, Callum (F) 48 0
b. 28-3-00

2015–16	Bury	1	0		
2016–17	Bury	13	0		
2017–18	Bury	11	0		
2018–19	Bury	16	0	**41**	**0**
2018–19	Barnsley	7	0	**7**	**0**

THIAM, Mamadou (F) 134 19
H: 6 0 W: 12 13 b.Aubervilliers 20-3-95
Internationals: Senegal U20.

2013–14	Dijon	0	0		
2014–15	Dijon	8	0		
2015–16	Dijon	17	3		
2016–17	Dijon	0	0	**25**	**3**
2016–17	*Clermont*	34	8	**34**	**8**
2017–18	Barnsley	29	1		
2018–19	Barnsley	46	7	**75**	**8**

WALTON, Jack (G) 6 0
H: 6 0 W: 12 02 b.Bury 23-4-98

2014–15	Barnsley	0	0		
2015–16	Barnsley	0	0		
2016–17	Barnsley	0	0		
2017–18	Barnsley	3	0		
2018–19	Barnsley	3	0	**6**	**0**

WILLIAMS, Ben (D) 11 0
H: 5 10 W: 11 00 b. 31-3-99
Internationals: Wales U17.
From Blackburn R.

2017–18	Barnsley	0	0		
2018–19	Barnsley	11	0	**11**	**0**

WILLIAMS, Jordan (D) 20 0
b. 22-10-99
Internationals: England U17, U18.

2017–18	Huddersfield T	0	0		
2017–18	*Bury*	9	0	**9**	**0**
2018–19	Barnsley	11	0	**11**	**0**

WOODROW, Cauley (F) 132 33
H: 6 0 W: 12 04 b.Hemel Hempstead 2-12-94
Internationals: England U17, U20, U21.

2011–12	Fulham	0	0		
2012–13	Fulham	0	0		
2013–14	Fulham	6	1		
2013–14	*Southend U*	19	2	**19**	**2**
2014–15	Fulham	29	3		
2015–16	Fulham	14	4		
2016–17	Fulham	5	0		
2016–17	*Burton Alb*	14	5	**14**	**5**
2017–18	Fulham	0	0	**54**	**8**
2017–18	*Bristol C*	14	2	**14**	**2**
2018–19	Barnsley	31	16	**31**	**16**

Players retained or with offer of contract
Aramburu, Mateo Sebastian; Barnett, Jordan Thomas; Berkovits, Amir; McBeam, Daniel Paul; Palmer, Romal Jordan; Simoes, Inacio Elliot Jorge; Wolfe, Matthew Ryan.

Scholars
Aleksiev, Sezgin Seher; Binns, Bradley; Buckwell, Willard Tommy Lee James; Calligan, William Marcus; Feeney, Kieran Jack, Gagen, Harry; Greenfield, Daniel Christopher James; Helliwell, Jordan Lewis; Kendrick, Henry; Lancaster, William Jack; Moon, Jasper; Olatubosun, Joshua Oluwaferanmi Paul; Pache, Rudi; Rangel, Joao Antonio; Sandhu, Jaydan; Thorpe, Christopher Tevin Johnson; Walmsley, Callum Richard; Winfield, Charlie James.

BIRMINGHAM C (6)

ADAMS, Che (F) 163 45
H: 5 10 W: 10 06 b.Leicester 13-7-96
Internationals: England C, U20.

2014–15	Sheffield U	10	0		
2015–16	Sheffield U	36	11		
2016–17	Sheffield U	1	0	**47**	**11**
2016–17	Birmingham C	40	7		
2017–18	Birmingham C	30	5		
2018–19	Birmingham C	46	22	**116**	**34**

CAMP, Lee (G) 503 0
H: 5 11 W: 11 11 b.Derby 22-8-84
Internationals: England U21. Northern Ireland Full caps.

2002–03	Derby Co	1	0		
2003–04	Derby Co	0	0		
2003–04	*QPR*	12	0		
2004–05	Derby Co	45	0		
2005–06	Derby Co	40	0		
2006–07	Derby Co	3	0	**89**	**0**
2006–07	*Norwich C*	3	0		
2006–07	*QPR*	11	0		
2007–08	QPR	46	0		
2008–09	QPR	4	0	**73**	**0**
2008–09	*Nottingham F*	15	0		
2009–10	Nottingham F	45	0		
2010–11	Nottingham F	46	0		
2011–12	Nottingham F	46	0		
2012–13	Nottingham F	26	0	**178**	**0**
2012–13	Norwich C	3	0	**6**	**0**
2013–14	WBA	0	0		
2013–14	Bournemouth	33	0		
2014–15	Bournemouth	9	0		
2015–16	Bournemouth	0	0	**42**	**0**
2015–16	Rotherham U	41	0		
2016–17	Rotherham U	18	0	**59**	**0**
2017–18	Cardiff C	0	0		
2017–18	*Sunderland*	12	0	**12**	**0**
2018–19	Birmingham C	44	0	**44**	**0**

COLIN, Maxime (D) 266 7
H: 5 11 W: 12 00 b.Arras 15-11-91
Internationals: France U20.

2010–11	Boulogne	26	0		
2011–12	Boulogne	23	0		
2012–13	Boulogne	4	0	**53**	**0**
2012–13	Troyes	18	0		
2013–14	Troyes	35	0		
2014–15	Troyes	2	0	**55**	**0**
2014–15	Anderlecht	17	1		
2015–16	Anderlecht	1	0	**18**	**1**
2015–16	Brentford	21	0		
2016–17	Brentford	38	4		
2017–18	Brentford	3	0	**62**	**4**
2017–18	Birmingham C	35	2		
2018–19	Birmingham C	43	0	**78**	**2**

DACRES-COGLEY, Josh (D) 18 0
H: 5 9 W: 10 10 b.Coventry 12-3-96

2016–17	Birmingham C	14	0		
2017–18	Birmingham C	3	0		
2018–19	Birmingham C	1	0	**18**	**0**

DAVIS, David (M) 260 12
H: 5 8 W: 12 03 b.Smethwick 20-2-91

2009–10	Wolverhampton W	0	0		
2009–10	*Darlington*	5	0	**5**	**0**
2010–11	Wolverhampton W	0	0		
2010–11	*Walsall*	7	0	**7**	**0**
2010–11	*Shrewsbury T*	19	2	**19**	**2**
2011–12	Wolverhampton W	7	0		
2011–12	*Chesterfield*	9	0	**9**	**0**
2012–13	Wolverhampton W	28	0		
2013–14	Wolverhampton W	18	0	**53**	**0**
2014–15	Birmingham C	42	3		
2015–16	Birmingham C	35	1		
2016–17	Birmingham C	41	4		
2017–18	Birmingham C	38	2		
2018–19	Birmingham C	11	0	**167**	**10**

DEAN, Harlee (M) 303 10
H: 6 0 W: 11 10 b.Basingstoke 26-7-91

2008–09	Dagenham & R	0	0		
2009–10	Dagenham & R	1	0	**1**	**0**
2010–11	Southampton	0	0		
2011–12	Southampton	0	0		
2011–12	*Brentford*	26	1		
2012–13	Brentford	44	3		
2013–14	Brentford	32	0		
2014–15	Brentford	35	1		
2015–16	Brentford	42	0		
2016–17	Brentford	42	3		
2017–18	Brentford	3	0	**224**	**8**
2017–18	Birmingham C	34	1		
2018–19	Birmingham C	44	1	**78**	**2**

GARDNER, Craig (M) 327 36
H: 5 10 W: 11 13 b.Solihull 25-11-86
Internationals: England U21.

2004–05	Aston Villa	0	0		
2005–06	Aston Villa	8	0		
2006–07	Aston Villa	13	2		
2007–08	Aston Villa	23	3		
2008–09	Aston Villa	14	0		
2009–10	Aston Villa	1	0	**59**	**5**
2009–10	Birmingham C	13	1		
2010–11	Birmingham C	29	8		
2011–12	Sunderland	30	3		
2012–13	Sunderland	33	6		
2013–14	Sunderland	18	2	**81**	**11**
2014–15	WBA	35	3		
2015–16	WBA	34	3		
2016–17	WBA	9	0	**78**	**6**
2016–17	*Birmingham C*	20	2		
2017–18	Birmingham C	26	2		
2018–19	Birmingham C	21	1	**109**	**14**

GROUNDS, Jonathan (D) 336 11
H: 6 1 W: 13 10 b.Thornaby 2-2-88

2007–08	Middlesbrough	5	0		
2008–09	Middlesbrough	2	0		
2008–09	*Norwich C*	16	3	**16**	**3**
2009–10	Middlesbrough	20	0		
2010–11	Middlesbrough	6	1		
2011–12	Middlesbrough	0	0	**33**	**1**
2011–12	*Chesterfield*	13	0	**13**	**0**
2011–12	*Yeovil T*	14	0	**14**	**0**
2012–13	Oldham Ath	44	1		
2013–14	Oldham Ath	45	2	**89**	**3**
2014–15	Birmingham C	45	1		
2015–16	Birmingham C	45	1		
2016–17	Birmingham C	42	2		
2017–18	Birmingham C	26	0		
2018–19	Birmingham C	0	0	**158**	**4**
2018–19	*Bolton W*	13	0	**13**	**0**

HARDING, Wes (D) 36 0
H: 5 11 W: 12 06 b.Leicester 20-10-96

2017–18	Birmingham C	9	0		
2018–19	Birmingham C	27	0	**36**	**0**

JOTA, Ramallo (M) 201 42
H: 5 11 W: 10 08 b.A Coruna 16-6-91

2010–11	Celta Vigo	4	0		
2011–12	Celta Vigo	0	0		
2012–13	Celta Vigo	0	0		
2013–14	Celta Vigo	0	0	**4**	**0**
2013–14	*Eibar*	35	11		
2014–15	Brentford	42	11		
2015–16	Brentford	5	0		
2015–16	*Eibar*	13	0		
2016–17	Brentford	21	12		
2016–17	*Eibar*	5	0	**53**	**11**
2017–18	Brentford	4	0	**72**	**23**
2017–18	Birmingham C	32	5		
2018–19	Birmingham C	40	3	**72**	**8**

JUTKIEWICZ, Lucas (F) 385 83
H: 6 1 W: 12 11 b.Southampton 20-3-89

2005–06	Swindon T	5	0		
2006–07	Swindon T	33	5	**38**	**5**
2006–07	Everton	0	0		
2007–08	Everton	0	0		
2007–08	*Plymouth Arg*	3	0	**3**	**0**
2008–09	Everton	1	0		
2008–09	*Huddersfield T*	7	0	**7**	**0**
2009–10	Everton	0	0	**1**	**0**
2009–10	*Motherwell*	33	12	**33**	**12**
2010–11	Coventry C	42	9		
2011–12	Coventry C	25	9	**67**	**18**
2011–12	Middlesbrough	19	2		
2012–13	Middlesbrough	24	8		
2013–14	Middlesbrough	22	1	**65**	**11**
2013–14	*Bolton W*	20	7	**20**	**7**
2014–15	Burnley	25	0		
2015–16	Burnley	5	0		
2016–17	Burnley	2	0	**32**	**0**
2016–17	Birmingham C	38	11		
2017–18	Birmingham C	35	5		
2018–19	Birmingham C	46	14	**119**	**30**

KIEFTENBELD, Maikel (M) 367 10
H: 5 10 W: 11 11 b.Lemelerveld 26-6-90
Internationals: Netherlands U21.

2008–09	Go Ahead Eagles	30	1		
2009–10	Go Ahead Eagles	33	2	**63**	**3**
2010–11	Groningen	33	0		
2011–12	Groningen	26	1		
2012–13	Groningen	29	1		
2013–14	Groningen	31	0		
2014–15	Groningen	33	0	**152**	**2**
2015–16	Birmingham C	42	3		
2016–17	Birmingham C	39	1		
2017–18	Birmingham C	35	0		
2018–19	Birmingham C	36	1	**152**	**5**

LAKIN, Charlie (M) 10 0
b.Solihull 8-5-99

2017–18	Birmingham C	0	0		
2018–19	Birmingham C	10	0	**10**	**0**

LUBULA, Beryl (F) 4 0
b. 8-1-98

2017–18	Birmingham C	1	0		
2018–19	Birmingham C	3	0	**4**	**0**

MAGHOMA, Jacques (M) 362 47
H: 5 9 W: 11 06 b.Lubumbashi 23-10-87
Internationals: DR Congo Full caps.

2005–06	Tottenham H	0	0		
2006–07	Tottenham H	0	0		
2007–08	Tottenham H	0	0		
2008–09	Tottenham H	0	0		
2009–10	Burton Alb	35	3		
2010–11	Burton Alb	41	4		
2011–12	Burton Alb	36	4		
2012–13	Burton Alb	43	15	**155**	**26**
2013–14	Sheffield W	25	2		
2014–15	Sheffield W	32	0	**57**	**2**
2015–16	Birmingham C	40	5		
2016–17	Birmingham C	27	3		

2017–18	Birmingham C	41	5		
2018–19	Birmingham C	42	6	**150**	**19**

MORRISON, Michael (D) 399 25
H: 6 0 W: 12 00 b.Bury St Edmunds 3-3-88
Internationals: England C.

2008–09	Leicester C	35	3		
2009–10	Leicester C	31	2		
2010–11	Leicester C	11	0	**77**	**5**
2010–11	Sheffield W	12	0	**12**	**0**
2011–12	Charlton Ath	45	4		
2012–13	Charlton Ath	44	1		
2013–14	Charlton Ath	45	1		
2014–15	Charlton Ath	2	0	**136**	**6**
2014–15	Birmingham C	21	0		
2015–16	Birmingham C	46	3		
2016–17	Birmingham C	31	3		
2017–18	Birmingham C	33	1		
2018–19	Birmingham C	43	7	**174**	**14**

MRBATI, Kerim (F) 151 26
b. 20-5-94
Internationals: Sweden U19, U21, Full caps.

2012	Enkoping	16	2	**16**	**2**
2013	Sirius	23	2		
2014	Sirius	23	3	**46**	**5**
2015	Djurgarden	28	4		
2016	Djurgarden	0	0		
2017	Djurgarden	25	8		
2018	Djurgarden	24	6	**77**	**18**
2018–19	Birmingham C	12	1	**12**	**1**

N'DOYE, Cheick (M) 310 61
H: 6 3 W: 13 12 b.Rufisque 29-3-86
Internationals: Senegal Full caps.

2009–10	Epinal	7	0		
2010–11	Epinal	30	11		
2011–12	Epinal	35	4	**72**	**15**
2012–13	Creteil	34	11		
2013–14	Creteil	36	10		
2014–15	Creteil	37	11	**107**	**32**
2015–16	Angers	32	9		
2016–17	Angers	33	5		
2017–18	Birmingham C	37	0		
2018–19	Birmingham C	2	0	**39**	**0**
2018–19	*Angers*	27	0	**92**	**14**

PEDERSEN, Kristian (D) 158 4
H: 6 2 W: 13 01 b.Ringsted 4-8-94
Internationals: Denmark U21.

2014–15	HB Koge	28	1		
2015–16	HB Koge	30	1	**58**	**2**
2016–17	Union Berlin	29	0		
2017–18	Union Berlin	32	1	**61**	**1**
2018–19	Birmingham C	39	1	**39**	**1**

ROBERTS, Marc (D) 110 6
H: 6 0 W: 12 11 b.Wakefield 26-7-90
Internationals: England C.

2014–15	Barnsley	0	0		
2015–16	Barnsley	32	1		
2016–17	Barnsley	40	4	**72**	**5**
2017–18	Birmingham C	30	1		
2018–19	Birmingham C	8	0	**38**	**1**

SOLOMON-OTABOR, Viv (M) 88 8
H: 5 9 W: 12 02 b.London 2-1-96
From Crystal Palace.

2015–16	Birmingham C	22	1		
2016–17	Birmingham C	3	0		
2016–17	*Bolton W*	4	0	**4**	**0**
2017–18	Birmingham C	0	0		
2017–18	*Blackpool*	44	5	**44**	**5**
2018–19	Birmingham C	8	1	**33**	**2**
2018–19	*Portsmouth*	7	1	**7**	**1**

STOCKDALE, David (G) 342 0
H: 6 3 W: 13 04 b.Leeds 20-9-85
Internationals: England C.

2002–03	York C	1	0		
2003–04	York C	0	0	**1**	**0**
2006–07	Darlington	6	0		
2007–08	Darlington	41	0	**47**	**0**
2008–09	Fulham	0	0		
2008–09	*Rotherham U*	8	0	**8**	**0**
2008–09	*Leicester C*	8	0	**8**	**0**
2009–10	Fulham	1	0		
2009–10	*Plymouth Arg*	21	0	**21**	**0**
2010–11	Fulham	7	0		
2011–12	Fulham	8	0		
2011–12	*Ipswich T*	18	0	**18**	**0**
2012–13	Fulham	2	0		
2012–13	*Hull C*	24	0	**24**	**0**
2013–14	Fulham	21	0	**39**	**0**
2014–15	Brighton & HA	42	0		
2015–16	Brighton & HA	46	0		
2016–17	Brighton & HA	45	0	**133**	**0**
2017–18	Birmingham C	36	0		
2018–19	Southend U	3	0	**3**	**0**
2018–19	Wycombe W	2	0	**2**	**0**
2018–19	Birmingham C	0	0	**36**	**0**
2018–19	*Coventry C*	2	0	**2**	**0**

TRUEMAN, Connal (G) 2 0
H: 6 1 W: 11 10 b.Birmingham 26-3-96

2014–15	Birmingham C	0	0		
2014–15	*Oldham Ath*	0	0		
2015–16	Birmingham C	0	0		
2016–17	Birmingham C	0	0		
2017–18	Birmingham C	0	0		
2018–19	Birmingham C	2	0	**2**	**0**

VASSELL, Isaac (F) 71 11
H: 5 7 W: 11 02 b.Newquay 9-9-93

2011–12	Plymouth Arg	6	0		
2012–13	Plymouth Arg	0	0		
2013–14	Plymouth Arg	0	0	**6**	**0**

From Truro C.

2016–17	Luton T	40	8		
2017–18	Luton T	2	2	**42**	**10**
2017–18	Birmingham C	9	1		
2018–19	Birmingham C	14	0	**23**	**1**

WEAVER, Jake (G) 0 0
b.Redditch 8-5-97

2018–19	Birmingham C	0	0		

Players retained or with offer of contract
Bailey, Odin Ohray; Bajrami, Geraldo; Hutton, Remeao; Keita, Cheick; Lubala, Beryly Logos; Luyambula, Michael Ngemba; McCoy, Oliver John; Mrabti, Abdallah Kerim; O'Keeffe, Corey James John; Ramallo, Jose Ignacio Peleteiro; Redmond, Joseph Patrick; Seddon, Steven Jeffrey; Siviter, Adam; Stirk, Ryan William.

Scholars
Andrews, Joshua Matthew; Baker, George Nicholas John; Boyd-Munce, Caolan Stephen; Bradley-Hurst, Joshua; Brown, Leo Calvin; Burke, Ryan Darren; Campbell, Tate Lucas; Concannon, Jack Paul; Forrest, Benjamin; George, Kai Adan; Gordon, Nico Diago; Hilton, Rhys; Hurst, Kyle Christopher; Jeacock, Zachary Anton John; Kinina, Nicholas Peter; Knight, Kai George; Landers, Lewis; McLean, Ben Neil; Moore, Ryan; Ngandu, Mayuba Christ Cross; Okoro, Chinedu Nicholas; Powell, Lucas Stefan; Roberts, Mitchell; Thompson-Sommers, Kane Angelis; Traore, Oumar.

BLACKBURN R (7)

ARMSTRONG, Adam (F) 176 41
H: 5 8 W: 10 12 b.Newcastle upon Tyne 10-2-97
Internationals: England U16, U17, U18, U19, U20, U21.

2013–14	Newcastle U	4	0		
2014–15	Newcastle U	11	0		
2015–16	Newcastle U	0	0		
2015–16	*Coventry C*	40	20	**40**	**20**
2016–17	Newcastle U	2	0		
2016–17	*Barnsley*	34	6	**34**	**6**
2017–18	Newcastle U	0	0	**17**	**0**
2017–18	*Bolton W*	20	1	**20**	**1**
2017–18	*Blackburn R*	21	9		
2018–19	Blackburn R	44	5	**65**	**14**

BELL, Amari (D) 183 9
H: 5 11 W: 12 00 b.Burton-upon-Trent 5-5-94

2012–13	Birmingham C	0	0		
2013–14	Birmingham C	1	0		
2014–15	Birmingham C	0	0	**1**	**0**
2014–15	*Swindon T*	10	0	**10**	**0**
2014–15	*Gillingham*	7	0	**7**	**0**
2015–16	Fleetwood T	44	0		
2016–17	Fleetwood T	44	2		
2017–18	Fleetwood T	27	4	**115**	**6**
2017–18	Blackburn R	12	0		
2018–19	Blackburn R	38	3	**50**	**3**

BENNETT, Elliott (M) 380 28
H: 5 9 W: 10 11 b.Telford 18-12-88

2006–07	Wolverhampton W	0	0		
2007–08	Wolverhampton W	0	0		
2007–08	*Crewe Alex*	9	1	**9**	**1**
2007–08	*Bury*	19	1		
2008–09	Wolverhampton W	0	0		
2008–09	*Bury*	46	3	**65**	**4**
2009–10	Wolverhampton W	0	0		
2009–10	*Brighton & HA*	43	7		
2010–11	Brighton & HA	46	6		
2011–12	Norwich C	33	1		
2012–13	Norwich C	24	1		
2013–14	Norwich C	2	0		
2014–15	Norwich C	9	0		
2014–15	*Brighton & HA*	7	0	**96**	**13**
2015–16	Norwich C	0	0	**68**	**2**
2015–16	*Bristol C*	15	0	**15**	**0**
2015–16	Blackburn R	21	2		
2016–17	Blackburn R	25	3		
2017–18	Blackburn R	41	2		
2018–19	Blackburn R	40	1	**127**	**8**

BRERETON, Ben (F) 78 9
b.Stoke-on-Trent 18-4-99
Internationals: England U19, U20.
From Stoke C.

2016–17	Nottingham F	18	3		
2017–18	Nottingham F	35	5	**53**	**8**
2018–19	Blackburn R	25	1	**25**	**1**

BUCKLEY, John (M) 2 0
b. 13-10-99

2018–19	Blackburn R	2	0	**2**	**0**

BUTTERWORTH, Daniel (F) 1 0
H: 5 11 W: 10 12 b.Manchester 14-9-94
From Manchester U.

2017–18	Blackburn R	0	0		
2018–19	Blackburn R	1	0	**1**	**0**

CONWAY, Craig (M) 446 45
H: 5 7 W: 10 07 b.Irvine 2-5-85
Internationals: Scotland Full caps.

2002–03	Ayr U	1	0		
2003–04	Ayr U	6	0		
2004–05	Ayr U	23	3		
2005–06	Ayr U	31	4	**61**	**7**
2006–07	Dundee U	30	0		
2007–08	Dundee U	15	1		
2008–09	Dundee U	36	5		
2009–10	Dundee U	33	4		
2010–11	Dundee U	22	3	**136**	**13**
2011–12	Cardiff C	31	3		
2012–13	Cardiff C	27	2		
2013–14	Cardiff C	0	0	**58**	**5**
2013–14	*Brighton & HA*	13	1	**13**	**1**
2013–14	Blackburn R	18	4		
2014–15	Blackburn R	38	3		
2015–16	Blackburn R	35	3		
2016–17	Blackburn R	42	6		
2017–18	Blackburn R	24	2		
2018–19	Blackburn R	21	1	**178**	**19**

DACK, Bradley (M) 244 64
H: 5 9 b.Greenwich 31-12-93

2012–13	Gillingham	16	1		
2013–14	Gillingham	28	3		
2014–15	Gillingham	42	9		
2015–16	Gillingham	40	13		
2016–17	Gillingham	34	5	**160**	**31**
2017–18	Blackburn R	42	18		
2018–19	Blackburn R	42	15	**84**	**33**

DAVENPORT, Jacob (M) 18 1
b.Manchester 28-12-98

2017–18	Manchester C	0	0		
2017–18	*Burton Alb*	17	1	**17**	**1**
2018–19	Blackburn R	1	0	**1**	**0**

EVANS, Corry (M) 269 9
H: 5 8 W: 10 12 b.Belfast 30-7-90
Internationals: Northern Ireland U16, U17, U19, U21, B, Full caps.

2007–08	Manchester U	0	0		
2008–09	Manchester U	0	0		
2009–10	Manchester U	0	0		
2010–11	Manchester U	0	0		
2010–11	*Carlisle U*	1	0	**1**	**0**
2010–11	*Hull C*	18	3		
2011–12	Hull C	43	2		
2012–13	Hull C	32	1		
2013–14	Hull C	0	0	**93**	**6**
2013–14	Blackburn R	21	1		
2014–15	Blackburn R	38	1		
2015–16	Blackburn R	30	1		
2016–17	Blackburn R	19	0		
2017–18	Blackburn R	32	0		
2018–19	Blackburn R	35	0	**175**	**3**

FISHER, Andy (G) 0 0
b. 12-2-98

2016–17	Blackburn R	0	0		
2017–18	Blackburn R	0	0		
2018–19	Blackburn R	0	0		

GRAHAM, Danny (F) **506 149**
H: 5 11 W: 12 05 b.Gateshead 12-8-85
Internationals: England U20.

2003–04	Middlesbrough	0	0		
2003–04	*Darlington*	9	2	**9**	**2**
2004–05	Middlesbrough	11	1		
2005–06	Middlesbrough	3	0		
2005–06	*Derby Co*	14	0	**14**	**0**
2005–06	*Leeds U*	3	0	**3**	**0**
2006–07	Middlesbrough	1	0		
2006–07	*Blackpool*	4	1	**4**	**1**
2006–07	*Carlisle U*	11	7		
2007–08	Carlisle U	45	14		
2008–09	Carlisle U	44	15	**100**	**36**
2009–10	Watford	46	14		
2010–11	Watford	45	23	**91**	**37**
2011–12	Swansea C	36	12		
2012–13	Swansea C	18	3	**54**	**15**
2012–13	Sunderland	13	0		
2013–14	Sunderland	0	0		
2013–14	*Hull C*	18	1	**18**	**1**
2013–14	*Middlesbrough*	18	6	**33**	**7**
2014–15	Sunderland	14	1		
2014–15	*Wolverhampton W*	5	1	**5**	**1**
2015–16	Sunderland	10	0	**37**	**1**
2015–16	*Blackburn R*	18	7		
2016–17	Blackburn R	35	12		
2017–18	Blackburn R	42	14		
2018–19	Blackburn R	43	15	**138**	**48**

GRAYSON, Joe (M) **8 2**
H: 5 10 W: 11 09 b. 26-3-99

2018–19	Blackburn R	0	0		
2018–19	*Grimsby T*	8	2	**8**	**2**

HARDCASTLE, Lewis (M) **6 0**
H: 5 9 W: 12 00 b.Bolton 4-7-98

2017–18	Blackburn R	0	0		
2018–19	Blackburn R	0	0		
2018–19	*Port Vale*	6	0	**6**	**0**

HART, Sam (D) **46 1**
b. 10-9-96

2016–17	Liverpool	0	0		
2016–17	*Port Vale*	11	1		
2017–18	Port Vale	0	0	**11**	**1**
2017–18	Blackburn R	3	0		
2017–18	*Rochdale*	3	0		
2018–19	Blackburn R	0	0	**3**	**0**
2018–19	*Rochdale*	11	0	**14**	**0**
2018–19	*Southend U*	18	0	**18**	**0**

LENIHAN, Darragh (M) **131 4**
H: 5 10 W: 12 00 b.Dublin 16-3-94
Internationals: Republic of Ireland U17, U19, U21, Full caps.

2011–12	Blackburn R	0	0		
2012–13	Blackburn R	0	0		
2013–14	Blackburn R	0	0		
2014–15	Blackburn R	3	0		
2014–15	*Burton Alb*	17	1	**17**	**1**
2015–16	Blackburn R	23	0		
2016–17	Blackburn R	40	0		
2017–18	Blackburn R	14	1		
2018–19	Blackburn R	34	2	**114**	**3**

LEUTWILER, Jayson (G) **127 0**
H: 6 3 W: 12 07 b.Basel 25-4-89
Internationals: Switzerland U16, U17, U18, U19, U20, U21. Canada Full caps.

2012–13	Middlesbrough	0	0		
2013–14	Middlesbrough	3	0	**3**	**0**
2014–15	Shrewsbury T	46	0		
2015–16	Shrewsbury T	29	0		
2016–17	Shrewsbury T	43	0	**118**	**0**
2017–18	Blackburn R	1	0		
2018–19	Blackburn R	5	0	**6**	**0**

MAGLIORE, Tyler (D) **2 0**
b. 21-12-98

2018–19	Blackburn R	2	0	**2**	**0**

MULGREW, Charlie (D) **339 59**
H: 6 3 W: 13 01 b.Glasgow 6-3-86
Internationals: Scotland U21, Full caps.

2002–03	Celtic	0	0		
2003–04	Celtic	0	0		
2004–05	Celtic	0	0		
2005–06	Celtic	0	0		
2005–06	*Dundee U*	13	2	**13**	**2**
2006–07	Wolverhampton W	6	0		
2007–08	*Southend U*	18	1	**18**	**1**
2007–08	Wolverhampton W	0	0	**6**	**0**
2008–09	Aberdeen	35	5		
2009–10	Aberdeen	37	4	**72**	**9**
2010–11	Celtic	23	0		
2011–12	Celtic	30	8		
2012–13	Celtic	30	5		
2013–14	Celtic	28	6		
2014–15	Celtic	10	0		
2015–16	Celtic	11	1	**132**	**20**
2016–17	Blackburn R	28	3		
2017–18	Blackburn R	41	14		
2018–19	Blackburn R	29	10	**98**	**27**

NUTTALL, Joe (F) **41 6**
H: 6 0 W: 11 05 b.Bury 27-1-97

2015–16	Aberdeen	2	0		
2016–17	Aberdeen	0	0	**2**	**0**
2016–17	*Stranraer*	9	2	**9**	**2**
2016–17	*Dumbarton*	2	0	**2**	**0**
2017–18	Blackburn R	13	2		
2018–19	Blackburn R	15	2	**28**	**4**

NYAMBE, Ryan (D) **83 0**
H: 6 0 W: 12 00 b.Katima Mulilo 4-12-97
Internationals: Namibia Full caps.

2014–15	Blackburn R	0	0		
2015–16	Blackburn R	0	0		
2016–17	Blackburn R	25	0		
2017–18	Blackburn R	29	0		
2018–19	Blackburn R	29	0	**83**	**0**

PLATT, Matt (D) **0 0**
b. 3-10-97

2016–17	Blackburn R	0	0		
2017–18	Blackburn R	0	0		
2018–19	Blackburn R	0	0		
2018–19	*Accrington S*	0	0		

RAYA, David (G) **98 0**
H: 6 0 W: 12 08 b.Barcelona 15-9-95

2013–14	Blackburn R	0	0		
2014–15	Blackburn R	2	0		
2015–16	Blackburn R	5	0		
2016–17	Blackburn R	5	0		
2017–18	Blackburn R	45	0		
2018–19	Blackburn R	41	0	**98**	**0**

REED, Harrison (M) **89 4**
H: 5 9 W: 11 09 b.Worthing 27-1-95
Internationals: England U19, U20.

2011–12	Southampton	0	0		
2012–13	Southampton	0	0		
2013–14	Southampton	4	0		
2014–15	Southampton	9	0		
2015–16	Southampton	1	0		
2016–17	Southampton	3	0		
2017–18	Southampton	0	0		
2017–18	*Norwich C*	39	1	**39**	**1**
2018–19	Southampton	0	0	**17**	**0**
2018–19	Blackburn R	33	3	**33**	**3**

RODWELL, Jack (D) **189 12**
H: 6 2 W: 12 08 b.Southport 11-3-91
Internationals: England U16, U17, U19, U21, Full caps.

2007–08	Everton	2	0		
2008–09	Everton	19	0		
2009–10	Everton	26	2		
2010–11	Everton	24	0		
2011–12	Everton	14	2	**85**	**4**
2012–13	Manchester C	11	2		
2013–14	Manchester C	5	0	**16**	**2**
2014–15	Sunderland	23	3		
2015–16	Sunderland	22	1		
2016–17	Sunderland	20	0		
2017–18	Sunderland	2	1	**67**	**5**
2018–19	Blackburn R	21	1	**21**	**1**

ROTHWELL, Joe (M) **109 8**
H: 6 1 W: 12 02 b.Manchester 11-1-95
Internationals: England U16, U17, U19, U20.

2014–15	Manchester U	0	0		
2014–15	*Blackpool*	3	0	**3**	**0**
2015–16	Manchester U	0	0		
2015–16	*Barnsley*	4	0	**4**	**0**
2016–17	Oxford U	33	1		
2017–18	Oxford U	36	5	**69**	**6**
2018–19	Blackburn R	33	2	**33**	**2**

SAMUEL, Dominic (F) **96 20**
H: 6 0 W: 14 00 b.Southwark 1-4-94
Internationals: England U19.

2011–12	Reading	0	0		
2012–13	Reading	1	0		
2012–13	*Colchester U*	2	0	**2**	**0**
2013–14	Reading	0	0		
2013–14	*Dagenham & R*	1	0	**1**	**0**
2014–15	Reading	0	0		
2014–15	*Coventry C*	13	6	**13**	**6**
2015–16	Reading	1	0		
2015–16	*Gillingham*	25	7	**25**	**7**
2016–17	Reading	9	2	**11**	**2**
2016–17	*Ipswich T*	6	0	**6**	**0**
2017–18	Blackburn R	36	5		
2018–19	Blackburn R	2	0	**38**	**5**

SMALLWOOD, Richard (M) **282 9**
H: 5 11 W: 11 05 b.Redcar 29-12-90
Internationals: England U18.

2008–09	Middlesbrough	0	0		
2009–10	Middlesbrough	0	0		
2010–11	Middlesbrough	13	1		
2011–12	Middlesbrough	13	0		
2012–13	Middlesbrough	22	2		
2013–14	Middlesbrough	13	0		
2013–14	*Rotherham U*	18	0		
2014–15	Middlesbrough	0	0	**61**	**3**
2014–15	*Rotherham U*	41	1		
2015–16	Rotherham U	43	1		
2016–17	Scunthorpe U	16	1	**16**	**1**
2016–17	Rotherham U	25	1	**127**	**3**
2017–18	Blackburn R	46	2		
2018–19	Blackburn R	32	0	**78**	**2**

TRAVIS, Lewis (D) **31 1**
b. 16-10-97

2016–17	Blackburn R	0	0		
2017–18	Blackburn R	5	0		
2018–19	Blackburn R	26	1	**31**	**1**

WHARTON, Scott (D) **51 6**
b.Blackburn 3-10-97

2015–16	Blackburn R	0	0		
2016–17	Blackburn R	2	0		
2016–17	*Cambridge U*	9	1	**9**	**1**
2017–18	Blackburn R	0	0		
2017–18	*Lincoln C*	14	2		
2018–19	Blackburn R	0	0	**2**	**0**
2018–19	*Lincoln C*	11	1	**25**	**3**
2018–19	*Bury*	15	2	**15**	**2**

WHITTINGHAM, Peter (M) **507 86**
H: 5 10 W: 9 13 b.Nuneaton 8-9-84
Internationals: England U19, U20, U21.

2002–03	Aston Villa	4	0		
2003–04	Aston Villa	32	0		
2004–05	Aston Villa	13	1		
2004–05	*Burnley*	7	0	**7**	**0**
2005–06	Aston Villa	4	0		
2005–06	*Derby Co*	11	0	**11**	**0**
2006–07	Aston Villa	3	0	**56**	**1**
2006–07	Cardiff C	19	4		
2007–08	Cardiff C	41	5		
2008–09	Cardiff C	33	3		
2009–10	Cardiff C	41	20		
2010–11	Cardiff C	45	11		
2011–12	Cardiff C	46	12		
2012–13	Cardiff C	40	8		
2013–14	Cardiff C	32	3		
2014–15	Cardiff C	43	6		
2015–16	Cardiff C	36	6		
2016–17	Cardiff C	37	7	**413**	**85**
2017–18	Blackburn R	20	0		
2018–19	Blackburn R	0	0	**20**	**0**

WILLIAMS, Derrick (D) **223 6**
H: 5 11 W: 11 11 b.Waterford 17-1-93
Internationals. Republic of Ireland U19, U21, Full caps.

2009–10	Aston Villa	0	0		
2010–11	Aston Villa	0	0		
2011–12	Aston Villa	0	0		
2012–13	Aston Villa	1	0	**1**	**0**
2013–14	Bristol C	43	1		
2014–15	Bristol C	44	2		
2015–16	Bristol C	24	1	**111**	**4**
2016–17	Blackburn R	39	1		
2017–18	Blackburn R	45	1		
2018–19	Blackburn R	27	0	**111**	**2**

Players retained or with offer of contract
Albinson, Charlie; Annesley, Louie John; Barnes, Samuel Peter; Carter, Hayden James; Chapman, Harrison James; Downing, Paul Michael; Doyle, Charley Ian; Doyle, Jack Marc; Gladwin, Ben; Lyons, Brad Joseph; Magloire, Tyler Jordan; Mansell, Lewis David; Mols, Stefan Edouard; Paton, Benjamin Alan; Rankin-Costello, Joseph Scott; Thompson, Lewis; Vale, Jack.

Scholars
Boyomo, Flavien Enzo Thiedort; Brennan, Luke; Burns, Samuel Gordon; Connell, Kyle Edward; Connolly, James Alfred; Durrant, Samuel; Eastham, Jordan James; Jackson, Andrew Ellis; Pike, Daniel Christopher; Saadi, Jalil; Whitehall, Isaac Ben; Wilson, George Chester; Zimba, Chanka Solomon.

BLACKPOOL (8)

ADARKWA, Nana (M) 0 0
b.Newham 24-10-00

2018–19	Blackpool	0	0		

ANDERTON, Nick (D) 36 0
H: 6 2 W: 12 06 b. 22-4-96

2014–15	Preston NE	0	0		
2015–16	Preston NE	0	0		

From Aldershot T, Barrow.

2017–18	Blackpool	4	0		
2018–19	Accrington S	22	0	**22**	**0**
2018–19	Blackpool	10	0	**14**	**0**

AVON, Will (D) 0 0

2018–19	Blackpool	0	0		

BOLA, Marc (D) 66 2
H: 6 1 W: 12 04 b.Greenwich 9-12-97

2016–17	Arsenal	0	0		
2016–17	*Notts Co*	13	0	**13**	**0**
2017–18	Arsenal	0	0		
2017–18	*Bristol R*	18	0	**18**	**0**
2018–19	Blackpool	35	2	**35**	**2**

BONEY, Miles (G) 2 0
H: 5 11 W: 11 09 b.Blackpool 1-2-98

2014–15	Blackpool	0	0		
2015–16	Blackpool	0	0		
2016–17	Blackpool	1	0		
2017–18	Blackpool	0	0		
2018–19	Blackpool	1	0	**2**	**0**

DANIELS, Donervon (D) 127 6
H: 6 1 W: 14 05 b.Montserrat 24-11-93
Internationals: England U20.

2011–12	WBA	0	0		
2012–13	WBA	0	0		
2012–13	*Tranmere R*	13	1	**13**	**1**
2013–14	WBA	0	0		
2013–14	*Gillingham*	3	1	**3**	**1**
2014–15	WBA	0	0		
2014–15	*Blackpool*	19	1		
2014–15	*Aberdeen*	9	0	**9**	**0**
2015–16	Wigan Ath	42	3		
2016–17	Wigan Ath	1	0		
2017–18	Wigan Ath	1	0	**44**	**3**
2017–18	*Rochdale*	15	0	**15**	**0**
2018–19	Blackpool	24	0	**43**	**1**

DAVIES, Steve (F) 326 69
H: 6 0 W: 12 00 b.Liverpool 29-12-87

2005–06	Tranmere R	22	2		
2006–07	Tranmere R	28	1		
2007–08	Tranmere R	10	2	**60**	**5**
2008–09	Derby Co	19	3		
2009–10	Derby Co	18	1		
2010–11	Derby Co	20	5		
2011–12	Derby Co	26	11		
2012–13	Derby Co	0	0	**83**	**20**
2012–13	Bristol C	37	13	**37**	**13**
2013–14	Blackpool	28	3		
2014–15	Blackpool	17	5		
2014–15	*Sheffield U*	13	2	**13**	**2**
2015–16	Bradford C	25	5	**25**	**5**
2016–17	Rochdale	29	9		
2017–18	Rochdale	32	7	**61**	**16**
2018–19	Blackpool	2	0	**47**	**8**

Transferred to Hamilton A January 2019.

DELFOUNESO, Nathan (F) 283 38
H: 6 1 W: 12 04 b.Birmingham 2-2-91
Internationals: England U16, U17, U19, U21.

2007–08	Aston Villa	0	0		
2008–09	Aston Villa	4	0		
2009–10	Aston Villa	9	1		
2010–11	Aston Villa	11	1		
2010–11	*Burnley*	11	1	**11**	**1**
2011–12	Aston Villa	6	0		
2011–12	*Leicester C*	4	0	**4**	**0**
2012–13	Aston Villa	1	0		
2012–13	*Blackpool*	40	6		
2013–14	Aston Villa	0	0	**31**	**2**
2013–14	*Blackpool*	11	0		
2013–14	*Coventry C*	14	3	**14**	**3**
2014–15	Blackpool	38	3		
2015–16	Blackburn R	15	1	**15**	**1**
2015–16	*Bury*	4	0	**4**	**0**
2016–17	Swindon T	18	1	**18**	**1**
2016–17	Blackpool	18	5		
2017–18	Blackpool	40	9		
2018–19	Blackpool	39	7	**186**	**30**

DODOO, Joseph (F) 48 7
H: 6 0 W: 12 08 b.Nottingham 6-1-95
Internationals: England U18.

2013–14	Leicester C	0	0		
2014–15	Leicester C	0	0		
2015–16	Leicester C	1	0	**1**	**0**
2015–16	*Bury*	4	1	**4**	**1**
2016–17	Rangers	20	3		
2017–18	Rangers	0	0		
2017–18	*Charlton Ath*	5	1	**5**	**1**
2018–19	Rangers	0	0	**20**	**3**

On loan from Rangers.

2018–19	Blackpool	18	2	**18**	**2**

FEENEY, Liam (M) 364 26
H: 5 10 W: 12 02 b.Hammersmith 21-1-87

2008–09	Southend U	1	0	**1**	**0**
2008–09	Bournemouth	14	3		
2009–10	Bournemouth	44	5		
2010–11	Bournemouth	46	4		
2011–12	Bournemouth	5	0	**109**	**12**
2011–12	Millwall	34	4		
2012–13	Millwall	22	1		
2013–14	Millwall	17	0	**73**	**5**
2013–14	*Bolton W*	4	0		
2013–14	*Blackburn R*	6	0		
2014–15	Bolton W	41	3		
2015–16	Bolton W	37	5	**82**	**8**
2015–16	*Ipswich T*	9	1	**9**	**1**
2016–17	Blackburn R	34	0		
2017–18	Blackburn R	1	0	**41**	**0**
2017–18	*Cardiff C*	15	0	**15**	**0**
2018–19	Blackpool	34	0	**34**	**0**

GNANDUILLET, Armand (F) 210 38
H: 6 4 W: 13 12 b.Angers 13-2-92
Internationals: Ivory Coast U20.

2012–13	Chesterfield	13	3		
2013–14	Chesterfield	34	5		
2014–15	Chesterfield	26	2		
2014–15	*Tranmere R*	4	2	**4**	**2**
2014–15	*Oxford U*	4	0	**4**	**0**
2015–16	Chesterfield	9	0	**82**	**10**
2015–16	*Stevenage*	14	5	**14**	**5**
2015–16	Leyton Orient	17	4		
2016–17	Leyton Orient	1	0	**18**	**4**
2016–17	Blackpool	19	3		
2017–18	Blackpool	26	4		
2018–19	Blackpool	43	10	**88**	**17**

GUY, Callum (M) 43 0
b. 25-11-96

2015–16	Derby Co	0	0		
2016–17	Derby Co	0	0		
2016–17	*Port Vale*	11	0	**11**	**0**
2017–18	Derby Co	0	0		
2017–18	*Bradford C*	17	0	**17**	**0**
2018–19	Blackpool	15	0	**15**	**0**

HENEGHAN, Ben (D) 83 2
b.Bolton 19-9-93
Internationals: England C.

2016–17	Motherwell	37	0		
2017–18	Motherwell	4	1	**41**	**1**
2017–18	Sheffield U	0	0		
2018–19	Blackpool	42	1	**42**	**1**

HOWARD, Mark (G) 213 0
H: 6 0 W: 11 13 b.Southwark 21-9-86

2005–06	Falkirk	8	0	**8**	**0**
2006–07	Cardiff C	0	0		
2006–07	Swansea C	0	0		
2007–08	St Mirren	10	0		
2008–09	St Mirren	33	0		
2009–10	St Mirren	2	0	**45**	**0**
2010–11	Aberdeen	9	0	**9**	**0**
2011–12	Blackpool	4	0		
2011–12	Sheffield U	0	0		
2012–13	Sheffield U	11	0		
2013–14	Sheffield U	19	0		
2014–15	Sheffield U	35	0		
2015–16	Sheffield U	15	0	**80**	**0**
2016–17	Bolton W	27	0		
2017–18	Bolton W	8	0	**35**	**0**
2018–19	Blackpool	32	0	**36**	**0**

LONG, Chris (F) 115 21
H: 5 7 W: 12 02 b.Huyton 25-2-95
Internationals: England U16, U17, U18, U19, U20.

2013–14	Everton	0	0		
2013–14	*Milton Keynes D*	4	1	**4**	**1**
2014–15	Everton	0	0		
2014–15	*Brentford*	10	4	**10**	**4**
2015–16	Burnley	10	0		
2016–17	Burnley	0	0		
2016–17	*Fleetwood T*	18	4		
2016–17	*Bolton W*	10	1	**10**	**1**
2017–18	Burnley	0	0	**10**	**0**
2017–18	*Northampton T*	38	9	**38**	**9**
2018–19	Fleetwood T	8	0	**26**	**4**
2018–19	Blackpool	17	2	**17**	**2**

MAFOUMBI, Christoffer (G) 37 0
H: 6 5 W: 12 08 b. 3-3-94
Internationals: Congo Full caps.

2011–12	Lens	0	0		
2012–13	Lens	0	0		
2013–14	Lens	0	0		
2014–15	Le Ponet	12	0	**12**	**0**
2015–16	Vereya Stara Zagora	3	0	**3**	**0**
2016–17	Free State Stars	4	0	**4**	**0**
2017–18	Blackpool	4	0		
2018–19	Blackpool	14	0	**18**	**0**

NOTTINGHAM, Michael (D) 29 2
b.Birmingham 14-4-89
Internationals: Saint Kitts and Nevis Full caps.
From Gresley, Solihull Moors, Salford C.

2018–19	Blackpool	29	2	**29**	**2**

O'SULLIVAN, John (M) 125 7
H: 5 11 W: 13 01 b.Birmingham 18-9-93
Internationals: Republic of Ireland U19, U21.

2011–12	Blackburn R	0	0		
2012–13	Blackburn R	1	0		
2013–14	Blackburn R	0	0		
2014–15	Blackburn R	2	0		
2014–15	*Accrington S*	13	4		
2014–15	*Barnsley*	8	0	**8**	**0**
2015–16	Blackburn R	2	0		
2015–16	*Rochdale*	2	0	**2**	**0**
2015–16	*Bury*	19	0	**19**	**0**
2016–17	Blackburn R	0	0	**5**	**0**
2016–17	*Accrington S*	19	1	**32**	**5**
2016–17	Carlisle U	17	1		
2017–18	Carlisle U	18	1	**35**	**2**
2018–19	Blackpool	13	0	**13**	**0**
2018–19	*Dundee*	11	0	**11**	**0**

PRITCHARD, Harry (M) 37 3
b.High Wycombe 14-9-92
From Flackwell Heath, Burnham, Maidenhead U.

2018–19	Blackpool	37	3	**37**	**3**

ROACHE, Rowan (F) 1 0
H: 5 10 W: 11 09 b. 9-2-00
Internationals: Republic of Ireland U16, U17, U18, U19.

2016–17	Blackpool	0	0		
2017–18	Blackpool	1	0		
2018–19	Blackpool	0	0	**1**	**0**
2018–19	*Derby Co*	0	0		

RYAN, James (M) 381 37
H: 5 8 W: 11 08 b.Maghull 6-9-88
Internationals: Republic of Ireland U21.

2006–07	Liverpool	0	0		
2007–08	Liverpool	0	0		
2007–08	*Shrewsbury T*	4	0	**4**	**0**
2008–09	Accrington S	44	10		
2009–10	Accrington S	39	3		
2010–11	Accrington S	46	9	**129**	**22**
2011–12	Scunthorpe U	24	2		
2012–13	Scunthorpe U	45	2	**69**	**4**
2013–14	Chesterfield	39	2		
2014–15	Chesterfield	44	4	**83**	**6**
2015–16	Fleetwood T	43	2		
2016–17	Fleetwood T	16	0	**59**	**2**
2017–18	Blackpool	36	3		
2018–19	Blackpool	1	0	**37**	**3**

SHAW, Nathan (M) 0 0

2018–19	Blackpool	0	0		

SIMS, Jack (G) 0 0
H: 6 2 W: 11 07 b.Southend-on-Sea 10-3-00

2018–19	Blackpool	0	0		

SINCLAIR-SMITH, Finlay (M) 0 0

2017–18	Blackpool	0	0		
2018–19	Blackpool	0	0		

SPEARING, Jay (M) 289 16
H: 5 6 W: 11 01 b.Wallasey 25-11-88

2006–07	Liverpool	0	0		
2007–08	Liverpool	0	0		
2008–09	Liverpool	0	0		
2009–10	Liverpool	3	0		
2009–10	*Leicester C*	7	1	**7**	**1**
2010–11	Liverpool	11	0		
2011–12	Liverpool	16	0		
2012–13	Liverpool	0	0		
2012–13	*Bolton W*	37	2		

2013–14	Liverpool	0	0	**30**	**0**
2013–14	Bolton W	45	2		
2014–15	Bolton W	21	1		
2014–15	*Blackburn R*	15	1	**15**	**1**
2015–16	Bolton W	22	2		
2016–17	Bolton W	37	3		
2017–18	Bolton W	0	0	**162**	**10**
2017–18	Blackpool	33	0		
2018–19	Blackpool	42	4	**75**	**4**

TAYLOR, Chris (M) **392** **41**
H: 5 11 W: 11 00 b.Oldham 20-12-86

2005–06	Oldham Ath	14	0		
2006–07	Oldham Ath	44	4		
2007–08	Oldham Ath	42	5		
2008–09	Oldham Ath	42	10		
2009–10	Oldham Ath	32	1		
2010–11	Oldham Ath	42	11		
2011–12	Oldham Ath	38	2		
2012–13	Millwall	22	3		
2013–14	Blackburn R	34	0		
2014–15	Blackburn R	16	1		
2015–16	Blackburn R	12	0	**62**	**1**
2015–16	*Millwall*	10	3	**32**	**6**
2016–17	Bolton W	16	0		
2016–17	*Oldham Ath*	16	0	**270**	**33**
2017–18	Bolton W	0	0	**16**	**0**
2018–19	Blackpool	12	1	**12**	**1**

THOMPSON, Jordan (M) **87** **5**
H: 5 9 W: 10 03 b.Belfast 3-1-97
Internationals: Northern Ireland U17, U19, U21, Full caps.

2015–16	Rangers	2	0		
2015–16	*Airdrieonians*	7	1	**7**	**1**
2016–17	Rangers	0	0		
2016–17	*Raith R*	29	1	**29**	**1**
2017–18	Rangers	0	0	**2**	**0**
2017–18	*Livingston*	11	0	**11**	**0**
2018–19	Blackpool	38	3	**38**	**3**

TILT, Curtis (D) **79** **5**
H: 6 4 W: 11 11 b. 4-8-91
From Halesowen T, Hednesford T, AFC Telford U, Wrexham.

2017–18	Blackpool	42	1		
2018–19	Blackpool	37	4	**79**	**5**

TURTON, Oliver (D) **243** **6**
H: 5 11 W: 11 11 b.Manchester 6-12-92

2010–11	Crewe Alex	1	0		
2011–12	Crewe Alex	2	0		
2012–13	Crewe Alex	20	0		
2013–14	Crewe Alex	12	1		
2014–15	Crewe Alex	44	1		
2015–16	Crewe Alex	46	1		
2016–17	Crewe Alex	45	1	**170**	**4**
2017–18	Blackpool	41	1		
2018–19	Blackpool	32	1	**73**	**2**

VIRTUE, Matthew (M) **26** **3**
b.Epsom 2-5-97

2017–18	Liverpool	0	0		
2017–18	*Notts Co*	13	0	**13**	**0**
2018–19	Blackpool	13	3	**13**	**3**

Players retained or with offer of contract
Ceesay, Ceesay Yusifu; Feeney-Howard, Liam Michael.

Scholars
Bange, Ewan; Beaumont, Tyrese; Graham, Sean Malachy Robert; Jaaskelainen, Emil Anton; Kellett, Samuel Robert; Maddox, Samuel William; Mandjoba, Andy Kanga Shalom; McGladdery, William; O'Brien, Brendan Sean; Ravenscroft, Hayden James Joseph; Shaw, Nathan Edward; Smith, Ryley; Watkinson, Owen Lewis; Winstanley, Harry George.

BOLTON W (9)

ALNWICK, Ben (G) **239** **0**
H: 6 2 W: 13 12 b.Prudhoe 1-1-87
Internationals: England U16, U17, U18, U19, U21.

2003–04	Sunderland	0	0		
2004–05	Sunderland	3	0		
2005–06	Sunderland	5	0		
2006–07	Sunderland	11	0	**19**	**0**
2006–07	Tottenham H	0	0		
2007–08	Tottenham H	0	0		
2007–08	*Luton T*	4	0	**4**	**0**
2007–08	*Leicester C*	8	0	**8**	**0**
2008–09	Tottenham H	0	0		
2008–09	*Carlisle U*	6	0	**6**	**0**
2009–10	Tottenham H	1	0		
2009–10	*Norwich C*	3	0	**3**	**0**
2010–11	Tottenham H	0	0		
2010–11	*Leeds U*	0	0		
2010–11	*Doncaster R*	0	0		
2011–12	Tottenham H	0	0		
2011–12	*Leyton Orient*	6	0		
2012–13	Tottenham H	0	0	**1**	**0**
2012–13	Barnsley	10	0		
2013–14	Barnsley	0	0	**10**	**0**
2013–14	Charlton Ath	10	0	**10**	**0**
2013–14	Leyton Orient	1	0	**7**	**0**
2014–15	Peterborough U	41	0		
2015–16	Peterborough U	39	0		
2016–17	Peterborough U	4	0	**84**	**0**
2016–17	Bolton W	21	0		
2017–18	Bolton W	39	0		
2018–19	Bolton W	27	0	**87**	**0**

AMEOBI, Sam (F) **188** **14**
H: 6 3 W: 10 04 b.Newcastle upon Tyne 1-5-92
Internationals: Nigeria U20. England U21.

2010–11	Newcastle U	1	0		
2011–12	Newcastle U	10	0		
2012–13	Newcastle U	8	0		
2012–13	*Middlesbrough*	9	1	**9**	**1**
2013–14	Newcastle U	10	0		
2014–15	Newcastle U	25	2		
2015–16	Newcastle U	0	0		
2015–16	*Cardiff C*	36	1	**36**	**1**
2016–17	Newcastle U	4	0	**58**	**2**
2016–17	*Bolton W*	20	2		
2017–18	Bolton W	35	4		
2018–19	Bolton W	30	4	**85**	**10**

BEEVERS, Mark (D) **405** **21**
H: 6 4 W: 13 00 b.Barnsley 21-11-89
Internationals: England U19.

2006–07	Sheffield W	2	0		
2007–08	Sheffield W	28	0		
2008–09	Sheffield W	34	0		
2009–10	Sheffield W	35	0		
2010–11	Sheffield W	28	2		
2011–12	Sheffield W	7	0		
2011–12	*Milton Keynes D*	14	1	**14**	**1**
2012–13	Sheffield W	6	0	**140**	**2**
2012–13	Millwall	35	1		
2013–14	Millwall	28	0		
2014–15	Millwall	25	2		
2015–16	Millwall	42	4	**130**	**7**
2016–17	Bolton W	45	7		
2017–18	Bolton W	44	1		
2018–19	Bolton W	32	3	**121**	**11**

BROCKBANK, Harry (F) **3** **0**
H: 5 11 W: 12 08 b.Bolton 26-9-98

2017–18	Bolton W	0	0		
2018–19	Bolton W	3	0	**3**	**0**

BUCKLEY, Will (F) **298** **44**
H: 6 0 W: 13 00 b.Oldham 12-8-88

2007–08	Rochdale	7	0		
2008–09	Rochdale	37	10		
2009–10	Rochdale	15	3	**59**	**13**
2009–10	Watford	6	1		
2010–11	Watford	33	4	**39**	**5**
2011–12	Brighton & HA	29	8		
2012–13	Brighton & HA	36	8		
2013–14	Brighton & HA	30	3		
2014–15	Brighton & HA	1	0	**96**	**19**
2014–15	Sunderland	22	0		
2015–16	Sunderland	0	0		
2015–16	*Leeds U*	4	0	**4**	**0**
2015–16	*Birmingham C*	10	1	**10**	**1**
2016–17	Sunderland	0	0	**22**	**0**
2016–17	*Sheffield W*	11	0	**11**	**0**
2017–18	Bolton W	24	2		
2018–19	Bolton W	33	4	**57**	**6**

CONNELL, Luca (M) **10** **0**
b.Liverpool 20-4-01
Internationals: Republic of Ireland U17, U18, U19.

2018–19	Bolton W	10	0	**10**	**0**

DARCY, Ronan (M) **1** **0**
b. 20-8-00

2018–19	Bolton W	1	0	**1**	**0**

DONALDSON, Clayton (F) **442** **136**
H: 6 1 W: 11 07 b.Bradford 7-2-84
Internationals: England C. Jamaica Full caps.

2002–03	Hull C	2	0		
2003–04	Hull C	0	0		
2004–05	Hull C	0	0	**2**	**0**

From York C

2007–08	Hibernian	17	5	**17**	**5**
2008–09	Crewe Alex	37	6		
2009–10	Crewe Alex	37	13		
2010–11	Crewe Alex	43	28	**117**	**47**
2011–12	Brentford	46	11		
2012–13	Brentford	44	18		
2013–14	Brentford	46	17	**136**	**46**
2014–15	Birmingham C	46	15		
2015–16	Birmingham C	40	11		
2016–17	Birmingham C	23	6		
2017–18	Birmingham C	4	0	**113**	**32**
2017–18	Sheffield U	26	5	**26**	**5**
2018–19	Bolton W	31	1	**31**	**1**

DYER, Lloyd (M) **493** **65**
H: 5 8 W: 10 03 b.Birmingham 13-9-82

2001–02	WBA	0	0		
2002–03	WBA	0	0		
2003–04	WBA	17	2		
2003–04	*Kidderminster H*	7	1	**7**	**1**
2004–05	WBA	4	0		
2004–05	*Coventry C*	6	0	**6**	**0**
2005–06	WBA	0	0	**21**	**2**
2005–06	*QPR*	15	0	**15**	**0**
2005–06	Millwall	6	0	**6**	**0**
2006–07	Milton Keynes D	41	5		
2007–08	Milton Keynes D	45	11	**86**	**16**
2008–09	Leicester C	44	10		
2009–10	Leicester C	33	3		
2010–11	Leicester C	35	3		
2011–12	Leicester C	36	4		
2012–13	Leicester C	42	3		
2013–14	Leicester C	40	7	**230**	**30**
2014–15	Watford	14	1		
2014–15	*Birmingham C*	18	1	**18**	**1**
2015–16	Watford	0	0	**14**	**1**
2015–16	Burnley	3	0	**3**	**0**
2016–17	Burton Alb	42	7		
2017–18	Burton Alb	38	7	**80**	**14**
2018–19	Bolton W	7	0	**7**	**0**

EARING, Jack (M) **1** **0**
b.Bury 21-1-99

2016–17	Bolton W	0	0		
2017–18	Bolton W	0	0		
2018–19	Bolton W	1	0	**1**	**0**

HALL, Connor (F) **13** **0**
H: 5 11 W: 12 02 b.Slough 18-2-98

2017–18	Bolton W	0	0		
2018–19	Bolton W	0	0		
2018–19	*Accrington S*	13	0	**13**	**0**

HOBBS, Jack (D) **301** **5**
H: 6 3 W: 13 05 b.Portsmouth 18-8-88
Internationals: England U19.

2004–05	Lincoln C	1	0	**1**	**0**
2005–06	Liverpool	0	0		
2006–07	Liverpool	0	0		
2007–08	Liverpool	2	0		
2007–08	*Scunthorpe U*	9	1	**9**	**1**
2008–09	Liverpool	0	0	**2**	**0**
2008–09	Leicester C	44	1		
2009–10	Leicester C	44	0		
2010–11	Leicester C	26	0	**114**	**1**
2010–11	*Hull C*	13	0		
2011–12	Hull C	40	1		
2012–13	Hull C	22	0	**75**	**1**
2013–14	Nottingham F	27	1		
2014–15	Nottingham F	17	0		
2015–16	Nottingham F	20	0		
2016–17	Nottingham F	9	0		
2017–18	Nottingham F	2	0	**75**	**1**
2018–19	Bolton W	25	1	**25**	**1**

JOHNSON, Chiori (D) **0** **0**
b.London 5-10-97

2018–19	Bolton W	0	0		

LE FONDRE, Adam (F) **491** **174**
H: 5 9 W: 11 04 b.Stockport 2-12-86

2004–05	Stockport Co	20	4		
2005–06	Stockport Co	22	6		
2006–07	Stockport Co	21	7	**63**	**17**
2006–07	*Rochdale*	7	4		
2007–08	Rochdale	46	16		
2008–09	Rochdale	44	18		
2009–10	Rochdale	1	0	**98**	**38**
2009–10	Rotherham U	44	25		
2010–11	Rotherham U	45	23		
2011–12	Rotherham U	4	4	**93**	**52**
2011–12	Reading	32	12		
2012–13	Reading	34	12		
2013–14	Reading	38	15	**104**	**39**
2014–15	Cardiff C	23	3		
2014–15	*Bolton W*	17	8		
2015–16	Cardiff C	0	0		

2015–16	*Wolverhampton W*	26	3	**26**	**3**
2016–17	Cardiff C	0	0	**23**	**3**
2016–17	*Wigan Ath*	12	1	**12**	**1**
2016–17	*Bolton W*	19	6		
2017–18	Bolton W	35	7		
2018–19	Bolton W	1	0	**72**	**21**

Transferred to Sydney FC August 2018.

LITTLE, Mark (D) **340** **5**
H: 6 1 W: 12 10 b.Worcester 20-8-88
Internationals: England U19.

2005–06	Wolverhampton W	0	0		
2006–07	Wolverhampton W	26	0		
2007–08	Wolverhampton W	1	0		
2007–08	*Northampton T*	17	0		
2008–09	Wolverhampton W	0	0		
2008–09	*Northampton T*	9	0	**26**	**0**
2009–10	Wolverhampton W	0	0	**27**	**0**
2009–10	*Chesterfield*	12	0	**12**	**0**
2009–10	*Peterborough U*	9	0		
2010–11	Peterborough U	35	0		
2011–12	Peterborough U	35	1		
2012–13	Peterborough U	40	1		
2013–14	Peterborough U	38	1	**157**	**3**
2014–15	Bristol C	37	1		
2015–16	Bristol C	23	0		
2016–17	Bristol C	28	0	**88**	**1**
2017–18	Bolton W	28	1		
2018–19	Bolton W	2	0	**30**	**1**

LOWE, Jason (M) **224** **3**
H: 6 0 W: 12 08 b.Wigan 2-9-91
Internationals: England U20, U21.

2009–10	Blackburn R	0	0		
2010–11	Blackburn R	1	0		
2010–11	*Oldham Ath*	7	2	**7**	**2**
2011–12	Blackburn R	32	0		
2012–13	Blackburn R	36	0		
2013–14	Blackburn R	39	1		
2014–15	Blackburn R	12	0		
2015–16	Blackburn R	10	0		
2016–17	Blackburn R	43	0	**173**	**1**
2017–18	WBA	0	0		
2017–18	Birmingham C	9	0	**9**	**0**
2018–19	Bolton W	35	0	**35**	**0**

MAGENNIS, Josh (F) **324** **52**
H: 6 2 W: 14 07 b.Bangor 15-8-90
Internationals: Northern Ireland U17, U19, U21, Full caps.

2009–10	Cardiff C	9	0	**9**	**0**
2009–10	*Grimsby T*	2	0	**2**	**0**
2010–11	Aberdeen	29	3		
2011–12	Aberdeen	23	1		
2012–13	Aberdeen	35	5		
2013–14	Aberdeen	18	1	**105**	**10**
2013–14	*St Mirren*	13	0	**13**	**0**
2014–15	Kilmarnock	38	8		
2015–16	Kilmarnock	34	10	**72**	**18**
2016–17	Charlton Ath	39	10		
2017–18	Charlton Ath	42	10	**81**	**20**
2018–19	Bolton W	42	4	**42**	**4**

MATTHEWS, Remi (G) **72** **0**
H: 6 0 W: 12 04 b.Gorleston 10-2-94

2014–15	Norwich C	0	0		
2014–15	*Burton Alb*	0	0		
2015–16	Norwich C	0	0		
2015–16	*Burton Alb*	2	0	**2**	**0**
2015–16	*Doncaster R*	9	0	**9**	**0**
2016–17	Norwich C	0	0		
2016–17	*Hamilton A*	17	0	**17**	**0**
2017–18	Norwich C	0	0		
2017–18	*Plymouth Arg*	26	0	**26**	**0**
2018–19	Bolton W	18	0	**18**	**0**

MURPHY, Luke (M) **332** **30**
H: 6 1 W: 11 05 b.Alsager 21-10-89

2008–09	Crewe Alex	9	1		
2009–10	Crewe Alex	32	3		
2010–11	Crewe Alex	39	3		
2011–12	Crewe Alex	42	8		
2012–13	Crewe Alex	39	6	**161**	**21**
2013–14	Leeds U	37	3		
2014–15	Leeds U	30	3		
2015–16	Leeds U	36	1		
2016–17	Leeds U	0	0		
2016–17	*Burton Alb*	19	1		
2017–18	Leeds U	0	0		
2017–18	*Burton Alb*	38	1	**57**	**2**
2018–19	Leeds U	0	0	**103**	**7**
2018–19	Bolton W	11	0	**11**	**0**

MUSCATT, Joe (D) **1** **0**
b. 15-12-97

2018–19	Bolton W	1	0	**1**	**0**

NOONE, Craig (M) **339** **29**
H: 6 3 W: 12 07 b.Kirkby 17-11-87

2008–09	Plymouth Arg	21	1		
2009–10	Plymouth Arg	17	1		
2009–10	*Exeter C*	7	2	**7**	**2**
2010–11	Plymouth Arg	17	3	**55**	**5**
2010–11	Brighton & HA	23	2		
2011–12	Brighton & HA	33	2		
2012–13	Brighton & HA	3	0	**59**	**4**
2012–13	Cardiff C	32	7		
2013–14	Cardiff C	17	1		
2014–15	Cardiff C	37	1		
2015–16	Cardiff C	38	5		
2016–17	Cardiff C	34	2		
2017–18	Cardiff C	0	0	**158**	**16**
2017–18	Bolton W	24	1		
2018–19	Bolton W	36	1	**60**	**2**

O'NEIL, Gary (M) **487** **33**
H: 5 10 W: 11 00 b.Beckenham 18-5-83
Internationals: England U19, U20, U21.

1999–2000	Portsmouth	1	0		
2000–01	Portsmouth	10	1		
2001–02	Portsmouth	33	1		
2002–03	Portsmouth	31	3		
2003–04	Portsmouth	3	2		
2003–04	*Walsall*	7	0	**7**	**0**
2004–05	Portsmouth	24	2		
2004–05	*Cardiff C*	9	1	**9**	**1**
2005–06	Portsmouth	36	6		
2006–07	Portsmouth	35	1		
2007–08	Portsmouth	2	0	**175**	**16**
2007–08	Middlesbrough	26	0		
2008–09	Middlesbrough	29	4		
2009–10	Middlesbrough	36	4		
2010–11	Middlesbrough	18	0	**109**	**8**
2010–11	West Ham U	8	0		
2011–12	West Ham U	16	2		
2012–13	West Ham U	24	1	**48**	**3**
2013–14	QPR	29	1	**29**	**1**
2014–15	Norwich C	21	0		
2015–16	Norwich C	27	0	**48**	**0**
2016–17	Bristol C	29	1		
2017–18	Bristol C	4	0	**33**	**1**
2018–19	Bolton W	29	3	**29**	**3**

OLKOWSKI, Pawel (D) **221** **13**
H: 6 0 W: 12 08 b.Ozimek 13-2-90
Internationals: Poland U19, U21, Full caps.

2010–11	GKS Katowice	31	5	**31**	**5**
2011–12	Gornick Zabrze	29	1		
2012–13	Gornick Zabrze	29	0		
2013–14	Gornick Zabrze	30	3	**88**	**4**
2014–15	FC Koln	27	2		
2015–16	FC Koln	19	0		
2016–17	FC Koln	14	0		
2017–18	FC Koln	5	0	**65**	**2**
2018–19	Bolton W	37	2	**37**	**2**

OZTUMER, Erhun (M) **153** **37**
b.Greenwich 29-5-91

2014–15	Peterborough U	20	1		
2015–16	Peterborough U	30	6	**50**	**7**
2016–17	Walsall	41	15		
2017–18	Walsall	45	15	**86**	**30**
2018–19	Bolton W	17	0	**17**	**0**

PRITCHARD, Joe (M) **4** **0**
H: 5 8 W: 10 06 b.Watford 10-9-96
From Tottenham H.

2018–19	Bolton W	4	0	**4**	**0**

ROBINSON, Antonee (D) **56** **0**
H: 6 0 W: 11 07 b.Milton Keynes 8-8-97
Internationals: USA U18, Full caps.

2015–16	Everton	0	0		
2016–17	Everton	0	0		
2017–18	Everton	0	0		
2017–18	*Bolton W*	30	0		
2018–19	Bolton W	0	0	**30**	**0**
2018–19	*Wigan Ath*	26	0	**26**	**0**

TAYLOR, Andrew (D) **396** **6**
H: 5 10 W: 11 04 b.Hartlepool 1-8-86
Internationals: England U16, U17, U18, U19, U20, U21.

2003–04	Middlesbrough	0	0		
2004–05	Middlesbrough	0	0		
2005–06	Middlesbrough	13	0		
2005–06	*Bradford C*	24	0	**24**	**0**
2006–07	Middlesbrough	34	0		
2007–08	Middlesbrough	19	0		
2008–09	Middlesbrough	26	0		
2009–10	Middlesbrough	12	0		
2010–11	Middlesbrough	21	3	**125**	**3**
2010–11	*Watford*	19	1	**19**	**1**
2011–12	Cardiff C	42	1		
2012–13	Cardiff C	43	0		
2013–14	Cardiff C	18	0	**103**	**1**
2014–15	Wigan Ath	26	1		
2015–16	*Reading*	19	0	**19**	**0**
2016–17	Wigan Ath	0	0	**26**	**1**
2016–17	*Bolton W*	34	0		
2017–18	Bolton W	20	0		
2018–19	Bolton W	26	0	**80**	**0**

TURNER, Jake (G) **0** **0**
b.Wilmslow 25-2-99
Internationals: England U18, U19.

2016–17	Bolton W	0	0		
2017–18	Bolton W	0	0		
2018–19	Bolton W	0	0		

VELA, Joshua (M) **167** **12**
H: 5 11 W: 11 07 b.Salford 14-12-93

2010–11	Bolton W	0	0		
2011–12	Bolton W	3	0		
2012–13	Bolton W	4	0		
2013–14	Bolton W	0	0		
2013–14	*Notts Co*	7	0	**7**	**0**
2014–15	Bolton W	29	0		
2015–16	Bolton W	31	2		
2016–17	Bolton W	46	9		
2017–18	Bolton W	30	1		
2018–19	Bolton W	17	0	**160**	**12**

WHEATER, David (D) **375** **27**
H: 6 5 W: 12 12 b.Redcar 14-2-87
Internationals: England U16, U17, U18, U19, U21.

2004–05	Middlesbrough	0	0		
2005–06	Middlesbrough	6	0		
2005–06	*Doncaster R*	7	1	**7**	**1**
2006–07	Middlesbrough	2	1		
2006–07	*Wolverhampton W*	1	0	**1**	**0**
2006–07	*Darlington*	15	2	**15**	**2**
2007–08	Middlesbrough	34	3		
2008–09	Middlesbrough	32	1		
2009–10	Middlesbrough	42	1		
2010–11	Middlesbrough	24	3	**140**	**9**
2010–11	Bolton W	7	0		
2011–12	Bolton W	24	2		
2012–13	Bolton W	4	0		
2013–14	Bolton W	23	1		
2014–15	Bolton W	17	1		
2015–16	Bolton W	28	1		
2016–17	Bolton W	43	9		
2017–18	Bolton W	33	1		
2018–19	Bolton W	33	0	**212**	**15**

WILLIAMS, Ben (G) **377** **0**
H: 6 0 W: 13 01 b.Manchester 27-8-82

2001–02	Manchester U	0	0		
2002–03	Manchester U	0	0		
2002–03	*Coventry C*	0	0		
2002–03	*Chesterfield*	14	0	**14**	**0**
2003–04	Manchester U	0	0		
2003–04	*Crewe Alex*	10	0		
2004–05	Crewe Alex	23	0		
2005–06	Crewe Alex	17	0		
2006–07	Crewe Alex	39	0		
2007–08	Crewe Alex	46	0	**135**	**0**
2008–09	Carlisle U	31	0	**31**	**0**
2009–10	Colchester U	46	0		
2010–11	Colchester U	33	0		
2011–12	Colchester U	36	0	**115**	**0**
2014–15	Bradford C	14	0		
2015–16	Bradford C	43	0	**57**	**0**
2016–17	Bury	22	0	**22**	**0**
2017–18	Blackpool	3	0	**3**	**0**
2018–19	Bolton W	0	0		

WILSON, Marc (M) **254** **4**
H: 6 2 W: 12 07 b.Lisburn 17-8-87
Internationals: Republic of Ireland U18, U19, U21, Full caps.

2005–06	Portsmouth	0	0		
2005–06	*Yeovil T*	2	0	**2**	**0**
2006–07	Portsmouth	0	0		
2006–07	*Bournemouth*	19	3		
2007–08	Portsmouth	0	0		
2007–08	*Bournemouth*	7	0		
2007–08	*Luton T*	4	0	**4**	**0**
2008–09	Portsmouth	3	0		
2009–10	Portsmouth	28	0		
2010–11	Portsmouth	4	0	**35**	**0**
2010–11	Stoke C	28	1		
2011–12	Stoke C	35	0		
2012–13	Stoke C	19	0		
2013–14	Stoke C	33	0		
2014–15	Stoke C	27	0		
2015–16	Stoke C	4	0	**146**	**1**
2016–17	Bournemouth	0	0	**26**	**3**
2016–17	*WBA*	4	0	**4**	**0**

2017–18	Sunderland	21	0	21	0
2018–19	Bolton W	16	0	16	0

Players retained or with offer of contract
Edwards, Liam John; Politic, Dennis-Dorian; Zouma, Lindsay Yoan.

Scholars
Alexander, Matthew; Argent-Barnes, Matthew; Aspinall, James Alexander; Boon, Jordan Mark; Broughton, Max Alexander; Brown, Edward James; Brown-Sterling, De' Marlio Shakie; Connell, Luca John; Darcy, Ronan Thomas; Edmondson, Myles Gregory; Graham, Sonny; Hartshorne, William Lancaster; James, Callum George Lennon; Jones-Griffiths, Shakeel Tyrik Zane; King-Harmes, Callum; Moulden, Edward James; Navarro, Luca; Osigwe, Kwame Kelechi Okechukwu; Preston, Callum Mark; Richards, D'Neal Demareo; Senior, Adam Nicholas; White, Joseph Anthony.

BOURNEMOUTH (10)

AKE, Nathan (M) **122 10**
H: 5 11 W: 11 01 b.Den Haag 18-2-95
Internationals: Netherlands U15, U16, U17, U19, U21, Full caps.

2012–13	Chelsea	3	0		
2013–14	Chelsea	1	0		
2014–15	Chelsea	1	0		
2014–15	*Reading*	5	0	**5**	**0**
2015–16	Chelsea	0	0		
2015–16	*Watford*	24	1	**24**	**1**
2016–17	Chelsea	2	0	**7**	**0**
2016–17	*Bournemouth*	10	3		
2017–18	Bournemouth	38	2		
2018–19	Bournemouth	38	4	**86**	**9**

ARTER, Harry (M) **262 29**
H: 5 9 W: 11 07 b.Sidcup 28-12-89
Internationals: Republic of Ireland U17, U19, Full caps.

2007–08	Charlton Ath	0	0		
2008–09	Charlton Ath	0	0		
From Woking.					
2010–11	Bournemouth	18	0		
2010–11	*Carlisle U*	5	1	**5**	**1**
2011–12	Bournemouth	34	5		
2012–13	Bournemouth	37	8		
2013–14	Bournemouth	31	3		
2014–15	Bournemouth	43	9		
2015–16	Bournemouth	21	1		
2016–17	Bournemouth	35	1		
2017–18	Bournemouth	13	1		
2018–19	Bournemouth	0	0	**232**	**28**
2018–19	*Cardiff C*	25	0	**25**	**0**

BEGOVIC, Asmir (G) **285 1**
H: 6 5 W: 13 01 b.Trebinje 20-6-87
Internationals: Canada U20. Bosnia & Herzogovina Full caps.

2006–07	Portsmouth	0	0		
2006–07	*Macclesfield T*	3	0	**3**	**0**
2007–08	Portsmouth	0	0		
2007–08	*Bournemouth*	8	0		
2007–08	*Yeovil T*	2	0		
2008–09	Portsmouth	2	0		
2008–09	*Yeovil T*	14	0	**16**	**0**
2009–10	Portsmouth	9	0	**11**	**0**
2009–10	*Ipswich T*	6	0	**6**	**0**
2009–10	Stoke C	4	0		
2010–11	Stoke C	28	0		
2011–12	Stoke C	23	0		
2012–13	Stoke C	38	0		
2013–14	Stoke C	32	1		
2014–15	Stoke C	35	0	**160**	**1**
2015–16	Chelsea	17	0		
2016–17	Chelsea	2	0	**19**	**0**
2017–18	Bournemouth	38	0		
2018–19	Bournemouth	24	0	**70**	**0**

BORUC, Artur (G) **389 0**
H: 6 4 W: 13 08 b.Siedlce 20-2-80
Internationals: Poland Full caps.

2005–06	Celtic	34	0		
2006–07	Celtic	36	0		
2007–08	Celtic	30	0		
2008–09	Celtic	34	0		
2009–10	Celtic	28	0	**162**	**0**
2010–11	Fiorentina	26	0		
2011–12	Fiorentina	36	0	**62**	**0**
2012–13	Southampton	20	0		
2013–14	Southampton	29	0		
2014–15	Southampton	0	0	**49**	**0**
2014–15	*Bournemouth*	37	0		
2015–16	Bournemouth	32	0		
2016–17	Bournemouth	35	0		
2017–18	Bournemouth	0	0		
2018–19	Bournemouth	12	0	**116**	**0**

BROOKS, David (M) **60 10**
b. 8-7-98
Internationals: England U20. Wales U21, Full caps.

2015–16	Sheffield U	0	0		
2016–17	Sheffield U	0	0		
2017–18	Sheffield U	30	3	**30**	**3**
2018–19	Bournemouth	30	7	**30**	**7**

BUTCHER, Matt (M) **34 2**
H: 6 2 W: 12 13 b.Portsmouth 14-5-97
From Poole T.

2015–16	Bournemouth	0	0		
2016–17	Bournemouth	0	0		
2016–17	*Yeovil T*	34	2	**34**	**2**
2017–18	Bournemouth	0	0		
2018–19	Bournemouth	0	0		

COOK, Lewis (M) **128 1**
H: 5 9 W: 11 03 b.York 3-2-97
Internationals: England U16, U17, U18, U19, U20, U21, Full caps.

2014–15	Leeds U	37	0		
2015–16	Leeds U	43	1	**80**	**1**
2016–17	Bournemouth	6	0		
2017–18	Bournemouth	29	0		
2018–19	Bournemouth	13	0	**48**	**0**

COOK, Steve (D) **285 18**
H: 6 1 W: 12 13 b.Hastings 19-4-91

2008–09	Brighton & HA	2	0		
2009–10	Brighton & HA	0	0		
2010–11	Brighton & HA	0	0		
2011–12	Brighton & HA	1	0	**3**	**0**
2011–12	Bournemouth	26	0		
2012–13	Bournemouth	33	1		
2013–14	Bournemouth	38	3		
2014–15	Bournemouth	46	5		
2015–16	Bournemouth	36	4		
2016–17	Bournemouth	38	2		
2017–18	Bournemouth	34	2		
2018–19	Bournemouth	31	1	**282**	**18**

DANIELS, Charlie (M) **402 21**
H: 6 1 W: 12 12 b.Harlow 7-9-86

2005–06	Tottenham H	0	0		
2006–07	Tottenham H	0	0		
2006–07	*Chesterfield*	2	0	**2**	**0**
2007–08	Tottenham H	0	0		
2007–08	*Leyton Orient*	31	2		
2008–09	Tottenham H	0	0		
2008–09	*Gillingham*	5	1	**5**	**1**
2008–09	Leyton Orient	21	2		
2009–10	Leyton Orient	41	0		
2010–11	Leyton Orient	42	0		
2011–12	Leyton Orient	13	0	**148**	**4**
2011–12	Bournemouth	21	2		
2012–13	Bournemouth	34	4		
2013–14	Bournemouth	23	0		
2014–15	Bournemouth	42	1		
2015–16	Bournemouth	37	3		
2016–17	Bournemouth	34	4		
2017–18	Bournemouth	35	1		
2018–19	Bournemouth	21	1	**247**	**16**

DEFOE, Jermain (F) **580 210**
H: 5 7 W: 10 04 b.Beckton 7-10-82
Internationals: England U16, U18, U21, B, Full caps.

1999–2000	West Ham U	0	0		
2000–01	West Ham U	1	0		
2000–01	*Bournemouth*	29	18		
2001–02	West Ham U	35	10		
2002–03	West Ham U	38	8		
2003–04	West Ham U	19	11	**93**	**29**
2003–04	Tottenham H	15	7		
2004–05	Tottenham H	35	13		
2005–06	Tottenham H	36	9		
2006–07	Tottenham H	34	10		
2007–08	Tottenham H	19	4		
2007–08	Portsmouth	12	8		
2008–09	Portsmouth	19	7	**31**	**15**
2008–09	Tottenham H	8	3		
2009–10	Tottenham H	34	18		
2010–11	Tottenham H	22	4		
2011–12	Tottenham H	25	11		
2012–13	Tottenham H	34	11		
2013–14	Tottenham H	14	1	**276**	**91**
2014	Toronto	19	11	**19**	**11**
2014–15	Sunderland	17	4		
2015–16	Sunderland	33	15		
2016–17	Sunderland	37	15	**87**	**34**
2017–18	Bournemouth	24	4		
2018–19	Bournemouth	4	0	**57**	**22**
2018–19	*Rangers*	17	8	**17**	**8**

DOBRE, Mihai (M) **36 2**
b. 30-8-98
Internationals: Romania U17, U21.

2017–18	Bournemouth	0	0		
2017–18	*Bury*	10	0	**10**	**0**
2017–18	*Rochdale*	5	1	**5**	**1**
2018–19	Bournemouth	0	0		
2018–19	*Yeovil T*	21	1	**21**	**1**

FRANCIS, Simon (D) **560 9**
H: 6 0 W: 12 06 b.Nottingham 16-2-85
Internationals: England U18, U20.

2002–03	Bradford C	25	1		
2003–04	Bradford C	30	0	**55**	**1**
2003–04	Sheffield U	5	0		
2004–05	Sheffield U	6	0		
2005–06	Sheffield U	1	0	**12**	**0**
2005–06	*Grimsby T*	5	0	**5**	**0**
2005–06	*Tranmere R*	17	1	**17**	**1**
2006–07	Southend U	40	1		
2007–08	Southend U	27	2		
2008–09	Southend U	45	0		
2009–10	Southend U	45	1	**157**	**4**
2010–11	Charlton Ath	34	0		
2011–12	Charlton Ath	0	0	**34**	**0**
2011–12	Bournemouth	29	0		
2012–13	Bournemouth	42	1		
2013–14	Bournemouth	46	1		
2014–15	Bournemouth	42	1		
2015–16	Bournemouth	38	0		
2016–17	Bournemouth	34	0		
2017–18	Bournemouth	32	0		
2018–19	Bournemouth	17	0	**280**	**3**

FRASER, Ryan (M) **194 23**
H: 5 4 W: 10 13 b.Aberdeen 24-2-94
Internationals: Scotland U19, U21, Full caps.

2010–11	Aberdeen	2	0		
2011–12	Aberdeen	3	0		
2012–13	Aberdeen	16	0	**21**	**0**
2012–13	Bournemouth	5	0		
2013–14	Bournemouth	37	3		
2014–15	Bournemouth	21	1		
2015–16	Bournemouth	0	0		
2015–16	*Ipswich T*	18	4	**18**	**4**
2016–17	Bournemouth	28	3		
2017–18	Bournemouth	26	5		
2018–19	Bournemouth	38	7	**155**	**19**

GOSLING, Dan (M) **214 18**
H: 6 0 W: 11 00 b.Brixham 2-2-90
Internationals: England U17, U18, U19, U21.

2006–07	Plymouth Arg	12	2		
2007–08	Plymouth Arg	10	0	**22**	**2**
2007–08	Everton	0	0		
2008–09	Everton	11	2		
2009–10	Everton	11	2	**22**	**4**
2010–11	Newcastle U	1	0		
2011–12	Newcastle U	12	1		
2012–13	Newcastle U	3	0		
2013–14	Newcastle U	8	0	**24**	**1**
2013–14	*Blackpool*	14	2	**14**	**2**
2014–15	Bournemouth	18	0		
2015–16	Bournemouth	34	3		
2016–17	Bournemouth	27	2		
2017–18	Bournemouth	28	2		
2018–19	Bournemouth	25	2	**132**	**9**

HYNDMAN, Emerson (M) **55 6**
H: 5 7 W: 9 08 b.Dallas 9-4-96
Internationals: USA U17, U20, U23, Full caps.

2013–14	Fulham	0	0		
2014–15	Fulham	9	0		
2015–16	Fulham	16	1	**25**	**1**
2016–17	Bournemouth	0	0		
2016–17	*Rangers*	13	4	**13**	**4**
2017–18	Bournemouth	1	0		
2018–19	Bournemouth	1	0	**2**	**0**
2018–19	*Hibernian*	15	1	**15**	**1**

IBE, Jordan (F) **155 11**
H: 5 9 W: 11 00 b.Southwark 8-12-95
Internationals: England U18, U19, U20, U21.

2011–12	Wycombe W	7	1	**7**	**1**
2011–12	Liverpool	0	0		
2012–13	Liverpool	1	0		
2013–14	Liverpool	1	0		
2013–14	*Birmingham C*	11	1	**11**	**1**
2014–15	Liverpool	12	0		
2014–15	*Derby Co*	20	5	**20**	**5**

2015–16	Liverpool	27	1	**41**	**1**
2016–17	Bournemouth	25	0		
2017–18	Bournemouth	32	2		
2018–19	Bournemouth	19	1	**76**	**3**

KING, Josh (F) 227 48
H: 5 11 W: 11 09 b.Oslo 15-1-92
Internationals: Norway U15, U16, U18, U19, U21, Full caps.

2008–09	Manchester U	0	0		
2009–10	Manchester U	0	0		
2010–11	Manchester U	0	0		
2010–11	*Preston NE*	8	0	**8**	**0**
2011–12	Manchester U	0	0		
2011–12	*Moenchengladbach*	2	0	**2**	**0**
2011–12	*Hull C*	18	1	**18**	**1**
2012–13	Manchester U	0	0		
2012–13	Blackburn R	16	2		
2013–14	Blackburn R	32	2		
2014–15	Blackburn R	16	1	**64**	**5**
2015–16	Bournemouth	31	6		
2016–17	Bournemouth	36	16		
2017–18	Bournemouth	33	8		
2018–19	Bournemouth	35	12	**135**	**42**

LERMA, Jefferson (M) 197 11
H: 5 10 W: 11 00 b.El Cerrito 25-10-94
Internationals: Colombia Full caps.

2013	Atletico Huila	24	0		
2014	Atletico Huila	32	4		
2015	Atletico Huila	22	2	**78**	**6**
2015–16	*Levante*	33	1		
2016–17	Levante	30	2		
2017–18	Levante	26	0	**89**	**3**
2018–19	Bournemouth	30	2	**30**	**2**

MAHONEY, Connor (M) 58 2
H: 5 9 W: 10 08 b.Blackburn 12-2-97
Internationals: England U17, U18, U20.

2013–14	Accrington S	4	0	**4**	**0**
2013–14	Blackburn R	0	0		
2014–15	Blackburn R	0	0		
2015–16	Blackburn R	2	0		
2016–17	Blackburn R	14	0	**16**	**0**
2017–18	Bournemouth	0	0		
2017–18	*Barnsley*	8	0	**8**	**0**
2018–19	Bournemouth	0	0		
2018–19	*Birmingham C*	30	2	**30**	**2**

MEPHAM, Chris (D) 56 1
H: 6 3 W: 11 11 b. 5-11-97
Internationals: Wales U20, U21, Full caps.

2016–17	Brentford	0	0		
2017–18	Brentford	21	1		
2018–19	Brentford	22	0	**43**	**1**
2018–19	Bournemouth	13	0	**13**	**0**

MINGS, Tyrone (D) 89 3
H: 6 3 W: 12 00 b.Bath 19-3-93

2012–13	Ipswich T	1	0		
2013–14	Ipswich T	16	0		
2014–15	Ipswich T	40	1	**57**	**1**
2015–16	Bournemouth	1	0		
2016–17	Bournemouth	7	0		
2017–18	Bournemouth	4	0		
2018–19	Bournemouth	5	0	**17**	**0**
2018–19	*Aston Villa*	15	2	**15**	**2**

MOUSSET, Lys (M) 92 17
H: 6 0 W: 12 08 b.Montvilliers 8-2-96
Internationals: France U20, U21.

2013–14	Le Havre	5	0		
2014–15	Le Havre	1	0		
2015–16	Le Havre	28	14	**34**	**14**
2016–17	Bournemouth	11	0		
2017–18	Bournemouth	23	2		
2018–19	Bournemouth	24	1	**58**	**3**

OFOBORH, Nnamdi (F) 0 0
H: 6 0 W: 12 02 b.Southwark 7-11-99
Internationals: Nigeria U20.

2018–19	Bournemouth	0	0		

PUGH, Marc (M) 426 70
H: 5 11 W: 11 04 b.Bacup 2-4-87

2005–06	Burnley	0	0		
2005–06	Bury	6	1		
2006–07	Bury	35	3	**41**	**4**
2007–08	Shrewsbury T	37	4		
2008–09	Shrewsbury T	7	0	**44**	**4**
2008–09	*Luton T*	4	0	**4**	**0**
2008–09	*Hereford U*	9	1		
2009–10	Hereford U	40	13	**49**	**14**
2010–11	Bournemouth	41	12		
2011–12	Bournemouth	42	8		
2012–13	Bournemouth	40	6		
2013–14	Bournemouth	42	5		
2014–15	Bournemouth	42	9		
2015–16	Bournemouth	26	3		
2016–17	Bournemouth	21	2		
2017–18	Bournemouth	20	0		
2018–19	Bournemouth	0	0	**274**	**45**
2018–19	*Hull C*	14	3	**14**	**3**

RAMSDALE, Aaron (G) 39 0
b. 14-5-98
Internationals: England U18, U19, U20, U21.

2015–16	Sheffield U	0	0		
2016–17	Sheffield U	0	0		
2016–17	Bournemouth	0	0		
2017–18	Bournemouth	0	0		
2017–18	*Chesterfield*	19	0	**19**	**0**
2018–19	Bournemouth	0	0		
2018–19	*AFC Wimbledon*	20	0	**20**	**0**

RICO, Diego (D) 169 8
H: 5 11 W: 11 11 b.Burgos 26-4-93

2011–12	Zaragoza	0	0		
2012–13	Zaragoza	0	0		
2013–14	Zaragoza	30	2		
2014–15	Zaragoza	37	2		
2015–16	Zaragoza	39	1	**106**	**5**
2016–17	Leganes	25	1		
2017–18	Leganes	26	2	**51**	**3**
2018–19	Bournemouth	12	0	**12**	**0**

SIMPSON, Jack (D) 7 0
H: 5 10 W: 13 01 b. 8-1-97
Internationals: England U21.

2015–16	Bournemouth	0	0		
2016–17	Bournemouth	0	0		
2017–18	Bournemouth	1	0		
2018–19	Bournemouth	6	0	**7**	**0**

SMITH, Adam (D) 264 9
H: 5 8 W: 10 07 b.Leytonstone 29-4-91
Internationals: England U16, U17, U19, U20, U21.

2007–08	Tottenham H	0	0		
2008–09	Tottenham H	0	0		
2009–10	Tottenham H	0	0		
2009–10	*Wycombe W*	3	0	**3**	**0**
2009–10	*Torquay U*	16	0	**16**	**0**
2010–11	Tottenham H	0	0		
2010–11	*Bournemouth*	38	1		
2011–12	Tottenham H	1	0		
2011–12	*Milton Keynes D*	17	2	**17**	**2**
2011–12	*Leeds U*	3	0	**3**	**0**
2012–13	Tottenham H	0	0		
2012–13	*Millwall*	25	1	**25**	**1**
2013–14	Tottenham H	0	0	**1**	**0**
2013–14	*Derby Co*	8	0	**8**	**0**
2013–14	Bournemouth	5	0		
2014–15	Bournemouth	29	0		
2015–16	Bournemouth	31	2		
2016–17	Bournemouth	36	1		
2017–18	Bournemouth	27	1		
2018–19	Bournemouth	25	1	**191**	**6**

SOLANKE, Dominic (F) 56 8
H: 6 1 W: 11 11 b.Reading 14-9-97
Internationals: England U16, U17, U18, U19, U20, U21, Full caps.

2014–15	Chelsea	0	0		
2015–16	Chelsea	0	0		
2015–16	*Vitesse*	25	7	**25**	**7**
2016–17	Chelsea	0	0		
2017–18	Liverpool	21	1		
2018–19	Liverpool	0	0	**21**	**1**
2018–19	Bournemouth	10	0	**10**	**0**

STANISLAS, Junior (M) 238 32
H: 6 0 W: 12 00 b.Kidbrooke 26-11-89
Internationals: England U20, U21.

2007–08	West Ham U	0	0		
2008–09	West Ham U	9	2		
2008–09	*Southend U*	6	1	**6**	**1**
2009–10	West Ham U	26	3		
2010–11	West Ham U	6	1		
2011–12	West Ham U	1	0	**42**	**6**
2011–12	Burnley	31	0		
2012–13	Burnley	35	5		
2013–14	Burnley	27	2	**93**	**7**
2014–15	Bournemouth	13	1		
2015–16	Bournemouth	21	3		
2016–17	Bournemouth	21	7		
2017–18	Bournemouth	19	5		
2018–19	Bournemouth	23	2	**97**	**18**

SURMAN, Andrew (M) 409 35
H: 5 10 W: 11 06 b.Johannesburg 20-8-86
Internationals: England U21.

2003–04	Southampton	0	0		
2004–05	Southampton	0	0		
2004–05	*Walsall*	14	2	**14**	**2**
2005–06	Southampton	12	2		
2005–06	*Bournemouth*	24	6		
2006–07	Southampton	37	4		
2007–08	Southampton	40	2		
2008–09	Southampton	44	7		
2009–10	Southampton	0	0	**133**	**15**
2009–10	Wolverhampton W	7	0	**7**	**0**
2010–11	Norwich C	22	3		
2011–12	Norwich C	25	4		
2012–13	Norwich C	4	0		
2013–14	Norwich C	0	0		
2013–14	*Bournemouth*	35	0		
2014–15	Norwich C	1	0	**52**	**7**
2014–15	Bournemouth	41	3		
2015–16	Bournemouth	38	0		
2016–17	Bournemouth	22	0		
2017–18	Bournemouth	25	2		
2018–19	Bournemouth	18	0	**203**	**11**

SURRIDGE, Sam (F) 58 16
b.Wimborne 28-7-98

2015–16	Bournemouth	0	0		
2016–17	Bournemouth	0	0		
2017–18	Bournemouth	0	0		
2017–18	*Yeovil T*	41	8	**41**	**8**
2018–19	Bournemouth	2	0	**2**	**0**
2018–19	*Oldham Ath*	15	8	**15**	**8**

TAYLOR, Kyle (M) 0 0
b. 28-8-99

2017–18	Bournemouth	0	0		
2018–19	Bournemouth	0	0		

TRAVERS, Mark (G) 2 0
H: 6 3 W: 12 13 b. 18-5-99
Internationals: Republic of Ireland U16, U17, U18, U19, U21.
From Shamrock R.

2018–19	Bournemouth	2	0	**2**	**0**

WILSON, Callum (M) 185 75
H: 5 11 W: 10 06 b.Coventry 27-2-92
Internationals: England U21, Full caps.

2009–10	Coventry C	0	0		
2010–11	Coventry C	1	0		
2011–12	Coventry C	0	0		
2012–13	Coventry C	11	1		
2013–14	Coventry C	37	21	**49**	**22**
2014–15	Bournemouth	45	20		
2015–16	Bournemouth	13	5		
2016–17	Bournemouth	20	6		
2017–18	Bournemouth	28	8		
2018–19	Bournemouth	30	14	**136**	**53**

Players retained or with offer of contract
Anthony, Jaidon; Cordner, Tyler Jack; Dennis, William Jonathon; Gillela, Dinesh; Hamilton, Tyrell Anthony; Hobson, Shaun Jermaine; Jordan, Corey; Kilkenny, Gavin; Ndjoli, Mikael Bongili; O'Connell, Keelan; Seaman, Charlie; Sherring, Sam; Vincent, Francis William.

Scholars
Bertrand, Harvey-Joe Edward; Camp, Brennan; Clements, Nathan John; Cope, Jake William; Dinsmore, Thomas Jack; Genesini, Brooklyn David Anthony; Glover, Ryan Michael Scott; Gray, Luke Antony; Hanfrey, Thomas William; Hunt, George Elliott; Ibsen Rossi, Zeno; Kurran-Browne, Connor Chadney; Moriah-Welsh, Nathan Daniel; Murray, Jordan Kenneth; Nippard, Luke Ryan; Oliver, James Robert; Pardoe, Luke Daniel; Parker-Trott, Thomas James; Plain, Cameron Christopher; Saydee, Christian; Scrimshaw, Jake; Torniainen, Jack Maurice; Ward, Calum Brian Joseph.

BRADFORD C (11)

ADAMS, Kielen (F) 0 0

2018–19	Bradford C	0	0		

AKPAN, Hope (M) 221 14
H: 6 0 W: 10 08 b.Liverpool 14-8-91
Internationals: Nigeria Full caps.

2007–08	Everton	0	0		
2008–09	Everton	0	0		
2009–10	Everton	0	0		
2010–11	Everton	0	0		
2010–11	*Hull C*	2	0	**2**	**0**
2011–12	Crawley T	26	1		
2012–13	Crawley T	21	4	**47**	**5**
2012–13	Reading	9	0		
2013–14	Reading	29	1		
2014–15	Reading	20	0	**58**	**1**

2015–16	Blackburn R	35	3		
2016–17	Blackburn R	25	1	**60**	**4**
2017–18	Burton Alb	26	2	**26**	**2**
2018–19	Bradford C	28	2	**28**	**2**

ANDERSON, Jermaine (M) **98 7**
b. 16-5-96
Internationals: England U18, U20.

2012–13	Peterborough U	1	0		
2013–14	Peterborough U	13	0		
2014–15	Peterborough U	24	1		
2015 16	Peterborough U	14	4		
2016–17	Peterborough U	7	0		
2017–18	Peterborough U	17	0		
2018–19	Peterborough U	0	0	**76**	**5**
2018–19	*Doncaster R*	9	1	**9**	**1**
2018–19	Bradford C	13	1	**13**	**1**

BIRCHALL, Matthew (M) **0 0**

2018–19	Bradford C	0	0		

BRUNKER, Kai (F) **26 0**
b. 10-6-94

2015–16	Freiburg	0	0		
2016–17	Freiburg	0	0		
2017–18	Freiburg	0	0		
2017–18	Bradford C	9	0		
2018–19	Bradford C	17	0	**26**	**0**

CADDIS, Paul (D) **308 21**
H: 5 7 W: 10 07 b.Irvine 19-4-88
Internationals: Scotland U19, U21, Full caps.

2007–08	Celtic	2	0		
2008–09	Celtic	5	0		
2008–09	*Dundee U*	11	0	**11**	**0**
2009–10	Celtic	10	0	**17**	**0**
2010–11	Swindon T	38	1		
2011–12	Swindon T	39	4		
2012–13	Swindon T	0	0	**77**	**5**
2012–13	*Birmingham C*	27	0		
2013–14	Birmingham C	38	5		
2014–15	Birmingham C	45	6		
2015–16	Birmingham C	39	4		
2016–17	Birmingham C	0	0	**149**	**15**
2016–17	Bury	13	0	**13**	**0**
2017–18	Blackburn R	14	0	**14**	**0**
2018–19	Bradford C	27	1	**27**	**1**

CHICKSEN, Adam (D) **178 3**
H: 5 8 W: 11 09 b.Milton Keynes 27-9-91
Internationals: Zimbabwe Full caps.

2008–09	Milton Keynes D	1	0		
2009–10	Milton Keynes D	6	0		
2010–11	Milton Keynes D	14	0		
2011–12	Milton Keynes D	20	0		
2011–12	*Leyton Orient*	3	0		
2012–13	Milton Keynes D	32	2		
2013–14	Milton Keynes D	0	0	**73**	**2**
2013–14	Brighton & HA	1	0		
2014–15	Brighton & HA	5	0		
2014–15	*Gillingham*	3	0		
2014–15	*Fleetwood T*	13	0	**13**	**0**
2015–16	Brighton & HA	1	0	**7**	**0**
2015–16	*Leyton Orient*	6	0	**9**	**0**
2015–16	*Gillingham*	6	0	**9**	**0**
2016–17	Charlton Ath	21	1	**21**	**1**
2017–18	Bradford C	18	0		
2018–19	Bradford C	28	0	**46**	**0**

CLARKE, Billy (F) **339 69**
H: 5 7 W: 10 01 b.Cork 13-12-87
Internationals: Republic of Ireland U17, U19, U21.

2004–05	Ipswich T	0	0		
2005–06	Ipswich T	2	0		
2005–06	*Colchester U*	6	0	**6**	**0**
2006–07	Ipswich T	27	3		
2007–08	Ipswich T	20	0		
2007–08	*Falkirk*	8	1	**8**	**1**
2008–09	Ipswich T	0	0	**49**	**3**
2008–09	*Darlington*	20	8	**20**	**8**
2008–09	*Northampton T*	5	3	**5**	**3**
2008–09	*Brentford*	8	6	**8**	**6**
2009–10	Blackpool	18	1		
2010–11	Blackpool	0	0		
2011–12	Blackpool	9	0	**27**	**1**
2011–12	*Sheffield U*	5	1	**5**	**1**
2011–12	Crawley T	17	3		
2012–13	Crawley T	36	10		
2013–14	Crawley T	29	7	**82**	**20**
2014–15	Bradford C	36	13		
2015–16	Bradford C	29	4		
2016–17	Bradford C	33	7		
2017–18	Charlton Ath	17	1		
2018–19	Charlton Ath	0	0	**17**	**1**
2018–19	Bradford C	14	1	**112**	**25**

COLVILLE, Luca (M) **11 1**
H: 6 1 W: 11 00 b.York 17-2-99

2018–19	Bradford C	11	1	**11**	**1**

DEVINE, Daniel (M) **17 0**
H: 5 11 W: 12 00 b.Bradford 4-9-97

2015–16	Bradford C	0	0		
2016–17	Bradford C	11	0		
2017–18	Bradford C	3	0		
2018–19	Bradford C	3	0	**17**	**0**

DOYLE, Eoin (F) **343 109**
H: 6 0 W: 11 07 b.Tallaght 12-3-88

2009	Sligo	15	3		
2010	Sligo	35	6		
2011	Sligo	34	20	**84**	**29**
2011–12	Hibernian	13	1		
2012–13	Hibernian	36	10	**49**	**11**
2013–14	Chesterfield	43	11		
2014–15	Chesterfield	26	21	**69**	**32**
2014–15	Cardiff C	16	5		
2015–16	Cardiff C	0	0	**16**	**5**
2015–16	*Preston NE*	28	4		
2016–17	Preston NE	11	1		
2016–17	*Portsmouth*	12	2	**12**	**2**
2017–18	Preston NE	0	0	**39**	**5**
2017–18	*Oldham Ath*	30	14	**30**	**14**
2018–19	Bradford C	44	11	**44**	**11**

ELLINGTON, Raecce (F) **0 0**

2018–19	Bradford C	0	0		

GOLDTHORP, Eliot (M) **2 0**

2018–19	Bradford C	2	0	**2**	**0**

HENRY, Karl (M) **528 11**
H: 6 0 W: 12 00 b.Wolverhampton 26-11-82
Internationals: England U18, U20.

1999–2000	Stoke C	0	0		
2000–01	Stoke C	0	0		
2001–02	Stoke C	24	0		
2002–03	Stoke C	18	1		
2003–04	Stoke C	20	0		
2003–04	*Cheltenham T*	9	1	**9**	**1**
2004–05	Stoke C	34	0		
2005–06	Stoke C	24	0	**120**	**1**
2006–07	Wolverhampton W	34	3		
2007–08	Wolverhampton W	40	3		
2008–09	Wolverhampton W	43	0		
2009–10	Wolverhampton W	34	0		
2010–11	Wolverhampton W	29	0		
2011–12	Wolverhampton W	31	0		
2012–13	Wolverhampton W	39	0	**250**	**6**
2013–14	QPR	27	1		
2014–15	QPR	33	0		
2015–16	QPR	38	1		
2016–17	QPR	14	0	**112**	**2**
2017–18	Bolton W	33	1	**33**	**1**
2018–19	Bradford C	4	0	**4**	**0**

HUDSON, Ellis (M) **1 0**
b.Bradford 14-2-99

2016–17	Bradford C	1	0		
2017–18	Bradford C	0	0		
2018–19	Bradford C	0	0	**1**	**0**

JONES, Alex (F) **55 15**
b. 28-9-94
From WBA.

2015–16	Birmingham C	0	0		
2016–17	Port Vale	19	9	**19**	**9**
2016–17	Bradford C	15	5		
2017–18	Bradford C	7	0		
2018–19	Bradford C	2	0	**24**	**5**
2018–19	*Cambridge U*	12	1	**12**	**1**

KNIGHT-PERCIVAL, Nathaniel (M) **227 13**
H: 6 0 W: 11 06 b.Cambridge 31-3-87

2012–13	Peterborough U	31	0		
2013–14	Peterborough U	15	1	**46**	**1**
2014–15	Shrewsbury T	28	1		
2015–16	Shrewsbury T	35	5	**63**	**6**
2016–17	Bradford C	42	0		
2017–18	Bradford C	41	4		
2018–19	Bradford C	35	2	**118**	**6**

MALTBY, Jake (M) **0 0**

2017–18	Bradford C	0	0		
2018–19	Bradford C	0	0		

McCARTAN, Shay (M) **173 36**
H: 5 10 W: 11 09 b.Newry 18-5-94
Internationals: Northern Ireland U17, U19, U21, Full caps.

2011–12	Burnley	1	0		
2012–13	Burnley	0	0	**1**	**0**
2013–14	Accrington S	18	1		
2014–15	Accrington S	31	6		
2015–16	Accrington S	27	7		
2016–17	Accrington S	34	11	**110**	**25**
2017–18	Bradford C	24	4		
2018–19	Bradford C	0	0	**24**	**4**
2018–19	*Lincoln C*	38	7	**38**	**7**

McGOWAN, Ryan (D) **264 8**
H: 6 1 W: 11 09 b.Adelaide 15-8-89
Internationals: Australia U17, U20, U23, Full caps.

2007–08	Hearts	1	0		
2008–09	Hearts	0	0		
2009–10	Hearts	0	0		
2009–10	*Ayr U*	28	1	**28**	**1**
2010–11	Hearts	8	0		
2010–11	*Partick Thistle*	8	0	**8**	**0**
2011–12	Hearts	28	2		
2012–13	Hearts	20	0	**57**	**2**
2013	Shandong Luneng	29	1		
2014	Shandong Luneng	17	1	**46**	**2**
2014–15	Dundee U	12	1		
2015–16	Dundee U	22	0	**34**	**1**
2016	Henan Jianye	28	2	**28**	**2**
2017	Guizhou Zhicheng	12	0	**12**	**0**
2017–18	Al-Sharjah	10	0	**10**	**0**
2017–18	Bradford C	3	0		
2018–19	Bradford C	23	0	**26**	**0**
2018–19	*Dundee*	15	0	**15**	**0**

MELLOR, Kelvin (D) **247 15**
H: 5 10 W: 11 09 b.Copenhagen 25-1-91

2007–08	Crewe Alex	0	0		
2008–09	Crewe Alex	0	0		
2009–10	Crewe Alex	0	0		
2010–11	Crewe Alex	1	0		
2011–12	Crewe Alex	12	1		
2012–13	Crewe Alex	35	0		
2013–14	Crewe Alex	28	1	**76**	**2**
2014–15	Plymouth Arg	37	1		
2015–16	Plymouth Arg	41	1	**78**	**2**
2016–17	Blackpool	44	4		
2017–18	Blackpool	29	6	**73**	**10**
2018–19	Bradford C	20	1	**20**	**1**

MILAMBO, Jeremie (D) **0 0**
b. 28-2-01

2018–19	Bradford C	0	0		

O'CONNOR, Anthony (D) **250 15**
H: 6 2 W: 12 06 b.Cork 25-10-92
Internationals: Republic of Ireland U17, U19, U21.

2010–11	Blackburn R	0	0		
2011–12	Blackburn R	0	0		
2012–13	Blackburn R	0	0		
2012–13	*Burton Alb*	46	0		
2013–14	Blackburn R	0	0		
2013–14	*Torquay U*	31	0	**31**	**0**
2014–15	Plymouth Arg	40	3	**40**	**3**
2015–16	Burton Alb	21	1	**67**	**1**
2016–17	Aberdeen	32	3		
2017–18	Aberdeen	38	2	**70**	**5**
2018–19	Bradford C	42	6	**42**	**6**

O'DONNELL, Richard (G) **256 0**
H: 6 2 W: 13 05 b.Sheffield 12-9-88

2007–08	Sheffield W	0	0		
2007–08	*Rotherham U*	0	0		
2007–08	*Oldham Ath*	4	0	**4**	**0**
2008–09	Sheffield W	0	0		
2009–10	Sheffield W	0	0		
2010–11	Sheffield W	9	0		
2011–12	Sheffield W	6	0	**15**	**0**
2011–12	*Macclesfield T*	11	0	**11**	**0**
2012–13	Chesterfield	14	0	**14**	**0**
2013–14	Walsall	46	0		
2014–15	Walsall	44	0	**90**	**0**
2015–16	Wigan Ath	10	0	**10**	**0**
2015–16	Bristol C	21	0		
2016–17	Bristol C	8	0	**29**	**0**
2016–17	Rotherham U	12	0		
2017–18	Rotherham U	10	0	**22**	**0**
2017–18	Northampton T	19	0	**19**	**0**
2018–19	Bradford C	42	0	**42**	**0**

PATRICK, Omari (F) **10 1**
b. 26-5-96
From Kidderminster H.

2018–19	Bradford C	1	0	**1**	**0**
2018–19	*Yeovil T*	9	1	**9**	**1**

POPPLER-ISHERWOOD, Thomas (D) **21 0**
H: 6 5 b. 28-1-98
Internationals: Sweden U16, U17, U18, U19.

2015–16	Bayern Munich	0	0		
2016–17	Bayern Munich	0	0		
2017–18	Bayern Munich	18	0	**18**	**0**
2018–19	Bradford C	3	0	**3**	**0**

Transferred to Ostersund FK January 2019.

POWELL, Reece (F) **0 0**
2017–18 Bradford C 0 0
2018–19 Bradford C 0 0

RICHARDS-EVERTON, Ben (D) **99 3**
H: 6 2 W: 14 00 b.Birmingham 17-10-92
Internationals: England C.
From Hinckley U, Tamworth.
2014–15 Partick Thistle 2 0 **2 0**
2014–15 *Airdrieonians* 18 0 **18 0**
2015–16 Dunfermline Ath 34 2
2016–17 Dunfermline Ath 6 0 **40 2**
2017–18 Accrington S 22 1
2018–19 Accrington S 17 0 **39 1**
2018–19 Bradford C 0 0

RILEY, Joe (D) **8 0**
H: 6 0 W: 11 03 b.Blackpool 6-12-96
2016–17 Manchester U 0 0
2016–17 *Sheffield U* 2 0 **2 0**
2017–18 Manchester U 0 0
2018–19 Bradford C 6 0 **6 0**

ROBINSON, Tyrell (M) **23 3**
b. 16-9-97
From Arsenal.
2017–18 Bradford C 21 3
2018–19 Bradford C 2 0 **23 3**

SCANNELL, Sean (F) **322 20**
H: 5 9 W: 11 07 b.Croydon 19-9-90
Internationals: Republic of Ireland U17, U18, U19, U21, B.
2007–08 Crystal Palace 23 2
2008–09 Crystal Palace 25 2
2009–10 Crystal Palace 26 2
2010–11 Crystal Palace 19 2
2011–12 Crystal Palace 37 4 **130 12**
2012–13 Huddersfield T 34 2
2013–14 Huddersfield T 38 1
2014–15 Huddersfield T 42 4
2015–16 Huddersfield T 29 1
2016–17 Huddersfield T 15 0
2017–18 Burton Alb 18 0 **18 0**
2017–18 Huddersfield T 0 0 **158 8**
2018–19 Bradford C 16 0 **16 0**

SEEDORF, Sherwin (F) **6 0**
b. 17-3-98
From Feyenoord, Nike Academy.
2018–19 Bradford C 6 0 **6 0**

STAUNTON, Reece (D) **1 0**
b. 10-12-01
2017–18 Bradford C 1 0
2018–19 Bradford C 0 0 **1 0**

SYKES-KENWORTHY, George (G) **0 0**
2017–18 Bradford C 0 0
2018–19 Bradford C 0 0

WILSON, Ben (G) **28 0**
H: 6 1 W: 11 09 b.Stanley 9-8-92
2010–11 Sunderland 0 0
2011–12 Sunderland 0 0
2013–14 Accrington S 0 0
2013–14 Cardiff C 0 0
2014–15 Cardiff C 0 0
2015–16 Cardiff C 0 0
2015–16 *AFC Wimbledon* 8 0 **8 0**
2016–17 Cardiff C 3 0
2016–17 *Rochdale* 8 0 **8 0**
2017–18 Cardiff C 0 0 **3 0**
2017–18 *Oldham Ath* 5 0 **5 0**
2018–19 Bradford C 4 0 **4 0**

WOOD, Connor (D) **22 1**
b.Harlow 17-7-96
From Soham Town Rangers, Chesham U.
2017–18 Leicester C 0 0
2018–19 Bradford C 22 1 **22 1**

WRIGHT, Josh (M) **322 19**
H: 6 1 W: 11 07 b.Bethnal Green 6-11-89
Internationals: England U16, U17, U18, U19.
2007–08 Charlton Ath 0 0
2007–08 *Barnet* 32 1 **32 1**
2008–09 Charlton Ath 2 0 **2 0**
2008–09 *Brentford* 5 0 **5 0**
2008–09 *Gillingham* 5 0
2009–10 Scunthorpe U 35 0
2010–11 Scunthorpe U 36 0 **71 0**
2011–12 Millwall 18 1
2012–13 Millwall 24 0
2013–14 Millwall 3 0
2013–14 *Leyton Orient* 2 0
2014–15 Millwall 1 0 **46 1**
2014–15 *Crawley T* 4 0 **4 0**
2014–15 Leyton Orient 29 2 **31 2**
2015–16 Gillingham 41 1
2016–17 Gillingham 41 13
2017–18 Gillingham 3 0 **90 14**
2017–18 Southend U 23 1 **23 1**
2018–19 Bradford C 18 0 **18 0**

Players retained or with offer of contract
Gibson, Jordan Lewis; Reeves, Jake Kenny.

Scholars
Adams, Kielen Marcel; Aitken, Daniel Ross; Birchall, Matthew; Cousin-Dawson, Finn; Darke, Alfie Geoffrey; Drovi, Dyllan Atty Aliby; Ellington, Raeece Abdul-Haq; Farrar, Christian Max; Goldthorp, Eliot James; Kirkpatrick, Oliver James; Maltby, Jake Peter; Milambo, Jeremie Mukanya; Ripley, Wade Owen; Scales, Kian; Shanks, Connor David; Sikora, Jorge Jack Antoni; Smethurst, Hayden; Staunton, Reece Joseph.

BRENTFORD (12)

ARCHIBALD, Theo (M) **30 1**
H: 5 11 W: 9 06 b.Glasgow 5-3-98
Internationals: Scotland U16, U19, U21.
2016–17 Celtic 0 0
2016–17 *Albion R* 14 0 **14 0**
2017–18 Brentford 2 0
2018–19 Forest Green R 14 1 **14 1**
2018–19 Brentford 0 0 **2 0**

BALCOMBE, Ellery (G) **0 0**
b. 15-10-99
Internationals: England U18, U19, U20.
2016–17 Brentford 0 0
2017–18 Brentford 0 0
2018–19 Brentford 0 0

BARBET, Yoann (D) **140 8**
H: 6 2 W: 12 11 b.Talence 10-5-93
Internationals: France U18.
2014–15 Chamois Niortais 33 2 **33 2**
2015–16 Brentford 18 1
2016–17 Brentford 23 1
2017–18 Brentford 34 3
2018–19 Brentford 32 1 **107 6**

BENRAHMA, Said (F) **113 26**
H: 5 8 W: 10 08 b.Toulouse 10-8-95
Internationals: Algeria Full caps.
2013–14 Nice 5 0
2014–15 Nice 3 1
2015–16 Nice 9 2
2015–16 *Angers* 12 1 **12 1**
2016–17 Nice 0 0
2016–17 *Gazelec Ajaccio* 15 3 **15 3**
2017–18 Nice 0 0 **17 3**
2017–18 *Chateauroux* 31 9 **31 9**
2018–19 Brentford 38 10 **38 10**

BENTLEY, Daniel (G) **264 0**
H: 6 2 W: 11 05 b.Wickford 13-7-93
2011–12 Southend U 1 0
2012–13 Southend U 9 0
2013–14 Southend U 46 0
2014–15 Southend U 42 0
2015–16 Southend U 43 0 **141 0**
2016–17 Brentford 45 0
2017–18 Brentford 45 0
2018–19 Brentford 33 0 **123 0**

BONHAM, Jack (G) **85 0**
H: 6 4 W: 14 13 b.Stevenage 14-9-93
Internationals: Republic of Ireland U17.
2010–11 Watford 0 0
2011–12 Watford 0 0
2012–13 Watford 1 0 **1 0**
2013–14 Brentford 1 0
2014–15 Brentford 0 0
2015–16 Brentford 0 0
2016–17 Brentford 1 0
2017–18 Brentford 0 0
2017–18 *Carlisle U* 42 0 **42 0**
2018–19 Brentford 0 0 **2 0**
2018–19 *Bristol R* 40 0 **40 0**

CANOS, Sergi (M) **134 21**
H: 5 8 W: 11 11 b.Nules 2-2-97
Internationals: Spain U16, U17, U19.
2015–16 Liverpool 1 0 **1 0**
2015–16 *Brentford* 38 7
2016–17 Norwich C 3 0 **3 0**
2016–17 Brentford 18 4
2017–18 Brentford 30 3
2018–19 Brentford 44 7 **130 21**

CARROLL, Canice (M) **33 2**
b. 26-1-99
Internationals: Republic of Ireland U17, U18, U19, U20.
2015–16 Oxford U 0 0
2016–17 Oxford U 4 0
2017–18 Oxford U 12 1
2018–19 Oxford U 0 0 **16 1**
2018–19 Brentford 0 0
2018–19 *Swindon T* 17 1 **17 1**

CLARKE, Josh (M) **88 6**
H: 5 8 W: 11 00 b.Waltham Forest 5-7-95
2012–13 Brentford 0 0
2013–14 Brentford 1 0
2014–15 Brentford 0 0
2014–15 *Dagenham & R* 0 0
2014–15 *Stevenage* 1 0 **1 0**
2015–16 Brentford 11 0
2015–16 *Barnet* 10 3 **10 3**
2016–17 Brentford 30 2
2017–18 Brentford 28 1
2018–19 Brentford 1 0 **71 3**
2018–19 *Burton Alb* 6 0 **6 0**

COLE, Reece (M) **24 2**
b. 17-2-98
2015–16 Brentford 0 0
2016–17 Brentford 1 0
2017–18 Brentford 0 0
2017–18 *Newport Co* 4 1 **4 1**
2018–19 Brentford 0 0 **1 0**
2018–19 *Yeovil T* 1 0 **1 0**
2018–19 *Macclesfield T* 18 1 **18 1**

DA SILVA, Josh (M) **17 1**
b. 23-10-98
Internationals: England U19, U20.
2016–17 Arsenal 0 0
2017–18 Arsenal 0 0
2018–19 Brentford 17 1 **17 1**

DALSGAARD, Henrik (F) **270 21**
H: 6 4 W: 12 11 b.Viborg 27-7-89
Internationals: Denmark U20, U21, Full caps.
2008–09 AaB 4 1
2009–10 AaB 25 0
2010–11 AaB 15 1
2011–12 AaB 30 2
2012–13 AaB 31 2
2013–14 AaB 18 2
2014–15 AaB 26 1
2015–16 AaB 17 0 **166 9**
2015–16 Zulte Waregem 19 3
2016–17 Zulte Waregem 16 6 **35 9**
2017–18 Brentford 29 1
2018–19 Brentford 40 2 **69 3**

DANIELS, Luke (G) **211 0**
H: 6 1 W: 12 10 b.Bolton 5-1-88
Internationals: England U18, U19.
2006–07 WBA 0 0
2007–08 *Motherwell* 2 0 **2 0**
2007–08 WBA 0 0
2008–09 WBA 0 0
2008–09 *Shrewsbury T* 38 0 **38 0**
2009–10 WBA 0 0
2009–10 *Tranmere R* 37 0 **37 0**
2010–11 WBA 0 0
2010–11 *Charlton Ath* 0 0
2010–11 *Rochdale* 1 0 **1 0**
2010–11 *Bristol R* 9 0 **9 0**
2011–12 WBA 0 0
2011–12 *Southend U* 9 0 **9 0**
2012–13 WBA 0 0
2013–14 WBA 1 0
2014–15 WBA 0 0 **1 0**
2014–15 Scunthorpe U 23 0
2015–16 Scunthorpe U 39 0
2016–17 Scunthorpe U 39 0 **101 0**
2016–17 Brentford 0 0
2017–18 Brentford 1 0
2018–19 Brentford 12 0 **13 0**

FIELD, Tom (D) **32 1**
H: 5 10 W: 10 13 b.Kingston upon Thames 2-8-85
Internationals: Republic of Ireland U16.
2013–14 Brentford 0 0
2014–15 Brentford 0 0
2015–16 Brentford 1 0
2016–17 Brentford 15 1
2017–18 Bradford C 8 0 **8 0**
2017–18 Brentford 0 0
2018–19 Brentford 1 0 **17 1**
2018–19 *Cheltenham T* 7 0 **7 0**

FINNSSON, Kolbeinn (M) **0 0**
Internationals: Iceland U16, U17, U19, U21, Full caps.
From Groningen.

2018–19	Brentford	0	0		

FORSS, Marcus (F) **6 1**
H: 6 1 b. 18-6-99
Internationals: Finland U17, U18, U19, U21.
From WBA.

2018–19	Brentford	6	1	**6**	**1**

GUNNARSSON, Patrik (G) **1 0**
b. 15-11-00
Internationals: Iceland U17, U18, U19, U21.
From Breidablik.

2018–19	Brentford	1	0	**1**	**0**

HENRY, Rico (D) **80 3**
H: 5 7 W: 10 06 b.Birmingham 8-7-97
Internationals: England U19, U20.

2014–15	Walsall	9	0		
2015–16	Walsall	35	2		
2016–17	Walsall	2	0	**46**	**2**
2016–17	Brentford	12	0		
2017–18	Brentford	8	0		
2018–19	Brentford	14	1	**34**	**1**

JEANVIER, Julian (D) **133 9**
H: 6 0 W: 12 04 b.Clichy 31-3-92
Internationals: Guinea Full caps.

2012–13	Nancy	6	0	**6**	**0**
2013–14	Lille	0	0		
2014–15	Lille	0	0		
2014–15	*Mouscron-Peruwelz*	17	0	**17**	**0**
2015–16	Lille	0	0		
2015–16	*Red Star*	24	2	**24**	**2**
2016–17	Reims	29	3		
2017–18	Reims	33	2	**62**	**5**
2018–19	Brentford	24	2	**24**	**2**

KIRK, Nikolaj (M) **4 0**
H: 5 11 b. 19-3-98
Internationals: Denmark U16, U17, U18.

2018–19	Midtjylland	0	0		

On loan from Midtjylland.

2018–19	Brentford	0	0		
2019	*Stabaek*	4	0	**4**	**0**

KONSA, Ezri (D) **113 1**
H: 6 0 W: 12 02 b. 23-10-97
Internationals: England U20, U21.

2015–16	Charlton Ath	0	0		
2016–17	Charlton Ath	32	0		
2017–18	Charlton Ath	39	0	**71**	**0**
2018–19	Brentford	42	1	**42**	**1**

MACLEOD, Lewis (M) **93 15**
H: 5 9 W: 11 05 b.Law 16-6-94
Internationals: Scotland U16, U17, U18, U19, U21.

2012–13	Rangers	21	3		
2013–14	Rangers	18	5		
2014–15	Rangers	13	3	**52**	**11**
2014–15	Brentford	0	0		
2015–16	Brentford	1	0		
2016–17	Brentford	13	0		
2017–18	Brentford	10	1		
2018–19	Brentford	17	3	**41**	**4**

MARCONDES, Emiliano (M) **137 37**
H: 6 0 W: 11 11 b.Hvidovre 9-3-95
Internationals: Denmark U17, U18, U19, U20, U21.

2012–13	Nordsjaelland	3	0		
2013–14	Nordsjaelland	11	1		
2014–15	Nordsjaelland	24	5		
2015–16	Nordsjaelland	30	2		
2016–17	Nordsjaelland	25	12		
2017–18	Nordsjaelland	19	17	**112**	**37**
2017–18	Brentford	12	0		
2018–19	Brentford	13	0	**25**	**0**

MAUPAY, Neal (F) **172 55**
H: 5 7 W: 10 12 b.Versailles 14-8-96
Internationals: France U16, U17, U19, U21.

2012–13	Nice	15	3		
2013–14	Nice	16	2		
2014–15	Nice	13	1	**44**	**6**
2015–16	Saint-Etienne	15	1		
2016–17	Saint-Etienne	0	0	**15**	**1**
2016–17	*Brest*	28	11	**28**	**11**
2017–18	Brentford	42	12		
2018–19	Brentford	43	25	**85**	**37**

McEACHRAN, Josh (D) **177 1**
H: 5 10 W: 10 03 b.Oxford 1-3-93
Internationals: England U16, U17, U19, U20, U21.

2010–11	Chelsea	9	0		
2011–12	Chelsea	2	0		
2011–12	*Swansea C*	4	0	**4**	**0**
2012–13	Chelsea	0	0		
2012–13	*Middlesbrough*	38	0	**38**	**0**
2013–14	Chelsea	0	0		
2013–14	*Watford*	7	0	**7**	**0**
2013–14	*Wigan Ath*	8	0	**8**	**0**
2014–15	Chelsea	0	0	**11**	**0**
2014–15	*Vitesse*	19	0	**19**	**0**
2015–16	Brentford	14	0		
2016–17	Brentford	27	0		
2017–18	Brentford	25	0		
2018–19	Brentford	24	1	**90**	**1**

MOKOTJO, Kamohelo (M) **254 10**
H: 5 6 W: 9 13 b.Odendaalsrus 11-3-91
Internationals: South Africa U20, U23, Full caps.

2008–09	SuperSport U	1	0		
2009–10	SuperSport U	0	0	**1**	**0**
2009–10	*Excelsior*	25	1	**25**	**1**
2010–11	Feyenoord	14	0		
2011–12	Feyenoord	20	0		
2012–13	Feyenoord	1	0	**35**	**0**
2013–14	PEC Zwolle	27	2		
2014–15	PEC Zwolle	0	0	**27**	**2**
2014–15	FC Twente	33	1		
2015–16	FC Twente	31	1		
2016–17	FC Twente	33	1	**97**	**3**
2017–18	Brentford	35	1		
2018–19	Brentford	34	3	**69**	**4**

ODUBAJO, Moses (M) **210 16**
H: 5 9 W: 11 05 b.Greenwich 28-7-93
Internationals: England U20.

2011–12	Leyton Orient	3	1		
2012–13	Leyton Orient	44	2		
2013–14	Leyton Orient	46	10	**93**	**13**
2014–15	Brentford	45	3		
2015–16	Hull C	42	0		
2016–17	Hull C	0	0		
2017–18	Hull C	0	0	**42**	**0**
2018–19	Brentford	30	0	**75**	**3**

OGBENE, Chiedozie (M) **20 0**
H: 5 9 W: 11 11 b. 1-5-97
From Cork C, Limerick.

2017–18	Brentford	2	0		
2018–19	Brentford	4	0	**6**	**0**
2018–19	*Exeter C*	14	0	**14**	**0**

OKSANEN, Jaako (D) **25 2**
H: 6 0 W: 11 05 b.Helsinki 7-11-00
Internationals: Finland U16, U17, U18, U19, U21.

2016	Klubi 04	1	0		
2017	Klubi 04	22	2	**23**	**2**
2017	HJK Helsinki	1	0	**1**	**0**
2018–19	Brentford	1	0	**1**	**0**

RACIC, Luka (D) **2 0**
b.Greve 8-5-99
Internationals: Denmark U16, U17, U18, U19, U21.

2018–19	Brentford	2	0	**2**	**0**

SAWYERS, Romaine (M) **271 22**
H: 5 9 W: 11 00 b.Birmingham 2-11-91
Internationals: St Kitts and Nevis U23, Full caps.

2009–10	WBA	0	0		
2010–11	WBA	0	0		
2010–11	*Port Vale*	1	0	**1**	**0**
2011–12	WBA	0	0		
2011–12	*Shrewsbury T*	7	0	**7**	**0**
2012–13	WBA	0	0		
2012–13	Walsall	4	0		
2013–14	Walsall	44	6		
2014–15	Walsall	42	4		
2015–16	Walsall	46	6	**136**	**16**
2016–17	Brentford	43	2		
2017–18	Brentford	42	4		
2018–19	Brentford	42	0	**127**	**6**

SORENSEN, Mads (D) **28 1**
H: 6 1 W: 11 07 b. 7-1-99
Internationals: Denmark U18, U19.

2014–15	Horsens	6	0		
2015–16	Horsens	5	0		
2016–17	Horsens	6	0		
2017–18	Horsens	3	1	**20**	**1**
2017–18	Brentford	0	0		
2018–19	Brentford	8	0	**8**	**0**

WATKINS, Ollie (F) **154 41**
H: 5 10 W: 11 00 b.Torbay 30-12-95

2013–14	Exeter C	1	0		
2014–15	Exeter C	2	0		
2015–16	Exeter C	20	8		
2016–17	Exeter C	45	13	**68**	**21**
2017–18	Brentford	45	10		
2018–19	Brentford	41	10	**86**	**20**

YENNARIS, Nico (D) **161 13**
H: 5 7 W: 10 03 b.Leytonstone 23-5-93
Internationals: England U17, U18, U19. China Full caps.

2010–11	Arsenal	0	0		
2011–12	Arsenal	1	0		
2011–12	*Notts Co*	2	0	**2**	**0**
2012–13	Arsenal	0	0		
2013–14	Arsenal	0	0	**1**	**0**
2013–14	*Bournemouth*	0	0		
2013–14	Brentford	8	0		
2014–15	Brentford	1	0		
2014–15	Wycombe W	14	1	**14**	**1**
2015–16	Brentford	31	2		
2016–17	Brentford	46	6		
2017–18	Brentford	41	4		
2018–19	Brentford	17	0	**144**	**12**

Transferred to Beijing Guoan January 2019.

ZAMBUREK, Jan (M) **1 0**
H: 6 0 b. 13-2-01
Internationals: Czech Republic U16, U17, U18.

2018–19	Brentford	1	0	**1**	**0**

Players retained or with offer of contract
Andersson, Simon Leonard; Coote, Alistair Michael; Dasilva, Cole Perry; Dasilva, Pelenda Joshua Tunga; Hammar, Fredrik; Hansen, Emiliano Marcondes; Hardy, Joseph Keith; Majka, Matej; Mitchell, Jonathan; Mogensen, Gustav Busch Trend; Onen, Jayden Roy; Shaibu, Justin Kwabena; Thompson-Brissett, Jaden; Titov, David; Tsaroulla, Nicholas Andrew.

BRIGHTON & HA (13)

ALZATE, Steve (M) **34 3**
H: 5 10 W: 10 03 b.Camden Town 1-9-98

2016–17	Leyton Orient	12	1	**12**	**1**
2017–18	Brighton & HA	0	0		
2018–18	Brighton & HA	0	0		
2018–19	*Swindon T*	22	2	**22**	**2**

ANDONE, Florin (F) **179 60**
H: 6 0 W: 11 07 b.Botosani 5-1-94
Internationals: Romania U19, Full caps.

2012–13	Villarreal	0	0		
2013–14	Villarreal	0	0		
2013–14	*Atletico Baleares*	34	12	**34**	**12**
2014–15	Cordoba	20	5		
2015–16	Cordoba	36	21	**56**	**26**
2016–17	Deportivo la Coruna	37	12		
2017–18	Deportivo la Coruna	29	7	**66**	**19**
2018–19	Brighton & HA	23	3	**23**	**3**

BALOGUN, Leon (D) **115 6**
H: 6 3 W: 12 11 b.Berlin 28-6-88
Internationals: Nigeria Full caps.

2008–09	Hannover 96	1	0		
2009–10	Hannover 96	2	0	**3**	**0**
2010–11	Werder Bremen	3	0		
2011–12	Werder Bremen	0	0	**3**	**0**
2012–13	Fortuna Dusseldorf	17	0		
2013–14	Fortuna Dusseldorf	11	0	**28**	**0**
2014–15	Darmstadt 98	21	4	**21**	**4**
2015–16	Mainz 05	21	1		
2016–17	Mainz 05	17	0		
2017–18	Mainz 05	14	0	**52**	**1**
2018–19	Brighton & HA	8	1	**8**	**1**

BARCLAY, Ben (D) **13 1**
b. 7-10-96

2018–19	Brighton & HA	0	0		
2018–19	*Notts Co*	13	1	**13**	**1**

BERNARDO, Junior (D) **82 2**
H: 6 1 W: 12 00 b.S„o Paulo 14-5-95

2014	Red Bull Brasil	0	0		
2015	Red Bull Brasil	3	0	**3**	**0**
2015–16	Liefering	1	0	**1**	**0**
2015–16	Red Bull Salzburg	13	0		
2016–17	Red Bull Salzburg	3	1	**16**	**1**
2016–17	RB Leipzig	22	0		
2017–18	RB Leipzig	18	1	**40**	**1**
2018–19	Brighton & HA	22	0	**22**	**0**

BISSOUMA, Yves (M) 75 3
H: 5 9 W: 12 04 b.Issia 30-8-96
Internationals: Mali Full caps.

2016–17	Lille	23	1		
2017–18	Lille	24	2	**47**	**3**
2018–19	Brighton & HA	28	0	**28**	**0**

BONG, Gaetan (D) 279 3
H: 6 0 W: 11 09 b.Sakbayeme 25-4-88
Internationals: France U21. Cameroon Full caps.

2005–06	Metz	3	0		
2006–07	Metz	2	0		
2007–08	Metz	11	0		
2008–09	Metz	0	0	**16**	**0**
2008–09	*Tours*	34	0	**34**	**0**
2009–10	Valenciennes	29	2		
2010–11	Valenciennes	22	1		
2011–12	Valenciennes	28	0		
2012–13	Valenciennes	29	0		
2013–14	Valenciennes	1	0	**109**	**3**
2013–14	Olympiacos	19	0	**19**	**0**
2014–15	Wigan Ath	14	0	**14**	**0**
2015–16	Brighton & HA	16	0		
2016–17	Brighton & HA	24	0		
2017–18	Brighton & HA	25	0		
2018–19	Brighton & HA	22	0	**87**	**0**

BURN, Dan (D) 224 9
H: 6 6 W: 13 00 b.Blyth 1-5-92

2009–10	Darlington	4	0	**4**	**0**
2010–11	Fulham	0	0		
2011–12	Fulham	0	0		
2012–13	Fulham	0	0		
2012–13	*Yeovil T*	34	2	**34**	**2**
2013–14	Fulham	9	0		
2013–14	*Birmingham C*	24	0	**24**	**0**
2014–15	Fulham	20	1		
2015–16	Fulham	32	0	**61**	**1**
2016–17	Wigan Ath	42	1		
2017–18	Wigan Ath	45	5		
2018–19	Wigan Ath	14	0	**101**	**6**
2018–19	Brighton & HA	0	0		

BUTTON, David (G) 293 0
H: 6 3 W: 13 00 b.Stevenage 27-2-89
Internationals: England U16, U17, U19, U20.

2005–06	Tottenham H	0	0		
2006–07	Tottenham H	0	0		
2007–08	*Rochdale*	0	0		
2007–08	Tottenham H	0	0		
2008–09	Tottenham H	0	0		
2008–09	*Bournemouth*	4	0	**4**	**0**
2008–09	*Luton T*	0	0		
2008–09	*Dagenham & R*	3	0	**3**	**0**
2009–10	Tottenham H	0	0		
2009–10	*Crewe Alex*	10	0	**10**	**0**
2009–10	*Shrewsbury T*	26	0	**26**	**0**
2010–11	Tottenham H	0	0		
2010–11	*Plymouth Arg*	30	0	**30**	**0**
2011–12	Tottenham H	0	0		
2011–12	*Leyton Orient*	1	0	**1**	**0**
2011–12	*Doncaster R*	7	0	**7**	**0**
2011–12	*Barnsley*	9	0	**9**	**0**
2012–13	Tottenham H	0	0		
2012–13	Charlton Ath	5	0	**5**	**0**
2013–14	Brentford	42	0		
2014–15	Brentford	46	0		
2015–16	Brentford	46	0	**134**	**0**
2016–17	Fulham	40	0		
2017–18	Fulham	20	0	**60**	**0**
2018–19	Brighton & HA	4	0	**4**	**0**

COLLAR, Will (M) 0 0
b.Horsham 14-7-97

2018–19	Brighton & HA	0	0		

CONNOLLY, Aaron (F) 2 0
b. 28-1-00
Internationals: Republic of Ireland U17, U19, U21.

2017–18	Brighton & HA	0	0		
2018–19	Brighton & HA	0	0		
2018–19	*Luton T*	2	0	**2**	**0**

COX, George (M) 5 0
b. 14-1-98

2018–19	Brighton & HA	0	0		
2018–19	*Northampton T*	5	0	**5**	**0**

DUFFY, Shane (D) 227 15
H: 6 4 W: 12 00 b.Derry 1-1-92
Internationals: Northern Ireland U16, U17, U19, U21, B. Republic of Ireland U19, U21, Full caps.

2008–09	Everton	0	0		
2009–10	Everton	0	0		
2010–11	Everton	0	0		
2010–11	*Burnley*	1	0	**1**	**0**
2011–12	Everton	4	0		
2011–12	*Scunthorpe U*	18	2	**18**	**2**
2012–13	Everton	1	0		
2013–14	Everton	0	0		
2013–14	*Yeovil T*	37	1	**37**	**1**
2014–15	Everton	0	0	**5**	**0**
2014–15	Blackburn R	19	1		
2015–16	Blackburn R	41	4		
2016–17	Blackburn R	3	0	**63**	**5**
2016–17	Brighton & HA	31	2		
2017–18	Brighton & HA	37	0		
2018–19	Brighton & HA	35	5	**103**	**7**

DUNK, Lewis (D) 246 13
H: 6 3 W: 12 02 b.Brighton 1-12-91
Internationals: England Full caps.

2009–10	Brighton & HA	1	0		
2010–11	Brighton & HA	5	0		
2011–12	Brighton & HA	31	0		
2012–13	Brighton & HA	8	0		
2013–14	Brighton & HA	6	0		
2013–14	*Bristol C*	2	0	**2**	**0**
2014–15	Brighton & HA	38	5		
2015–16	Brighton & HA	38	3		
2016–17	Brighton & HA	43	2		
2017–18	Brighton & HA	38	1		
2018–19	Brighton & HA	36	2	**244**	**13**

GROSS, Pascal (M) 251 30
H: 5 7 W: 10 06 b.Bad Salzungen 15-6-91
Internationals: Germany U18, U19.

2008–09	1899 Hoffenheim	4	0		
2009–10	1899 Hoffenheim	1	0		
2010–11	1899 Hoffenheim	0	0	**5**	**0**
2010–11	Karlsruher	3	1		
2011–12	Karlsruher	22	2	**25**	**3**
2012–13	Ingolstadt 04	30	2		
2013–14	Ingolstadt 04	29	2		
2014–15	Ingolstadt 04	34	7		
2015–16	Ingolstadt 04	32	1		
2016–17	Ingolstadt 04	33	5	**158**	**17**
2017–18	Brighton & HA	38	7		
2018–19	Brighton & HA	25	3	**63**	**10**

GYOKERES, Viktor (F) 56 20
H: 6 2 W: 13 08 b.Brommapoijkarna 4-6-98
Internationals: Sweden U19, U21, Full caps.

2015	Brommapojkarna	8	0		
2016	Brommapojkarna	19	7		
2017	Brommapojkarna	29	13	**56**	**20**
2017–18	Brighton & HA	0	0		
2018–19	Brighton & HA	0	0		

HALL, Ben (D) 29 1
H: 6 1 W: 12 06 b.Enniskillen 16-1-97
Internationals: Northern Ireland U16, U17, U19, U21.

2015–16	Motherwell	18	1	**18**	**1**
2016–17	Brighton & HA	0	0		
2017–18	Brighton & HA	0	0		
2017–18	*Notts Co*	11	0		
2018–19	Brighton & HA	0	0		
2018–19	*Notts Co*	0	0	**11**	**0**

HEMED, Tomer (F) 376 94
H: 6 0 W: 12 04 b.Haifa 2-5-87
Internationals: Israel U17, U18, U19, U21, Full caps.

2005–06	Maccabi Haifa	3	1		
2006–07	Maccabi Haifa	8	2		
2007–08	Maccabi Haifa	7	0		
2007–08	*Maccabi Herzliya*	17	3	**17**	**3**
2008–09	Maccabi Haifa	0	0		
2008–09	*Bnei Yehuda*	28	1	**28**	**1**
2009–10	Maccabi Haifa	0	0		
2009–10	*Maccabi Ahi Nazareth*	33	9	**33**	**9**
2010–11	Maccabi Haifa	31	13	**49**	**16**
2011–12	Mallorca	29	7		
2012–13	Mallorca	37	11		
2013–14	Mallorca	24	2	**90**	**20**
2014–15	Almeria	35	8	**35**	**8**
2015–16	Brighton & HA	44	17		
2016–17	Brighton & HA	37	11		
2017–18	Brighton & HA	16	2		
2018–19	Brighton & HA	0	0	**97**	**30**
2018–19	*QPR*	27	7	**27**	**7**

IZQUIERDO, Jose (D) 240 65
H: 5 7 W: 11 07 b.Pereira 7-7-92
Internationals: Colombia Full caps.

2010	Deportivo Pereira	9	1		
2011	Deportivo Pereira	21	1		
2012	Deportivo Pereira	24	10		
2013	Deportivo Pereira	15	2	**69**	**14**
2013	Once Caldas	16	3		
2014	Once Caldas	24	9	**40**	**12**
2014–15	Club Brugge	32	13		
2015–16	Club Brugge	24	7		
2016–17	Club Brugge	28	14		
2017–18	Club Brugge	0	0	**84**	**34**
2017–18	Brighton & HA	32	5		
2018–19	Brighton & HA	15	0	**47**	**5**

JAHANBAKHSH, Alireza (M) 215 61
H: 5 11 W: 12 02 b.Jirandeh 11-8-93
Internationals: Iran U20, U23, Full caps.

2010–11	Damash Tehran	12	0	**12**	**0**
2011–12	Damash Gilan	16	2		
2012–13	Damash Gilan	28	8	**44**	**10**
2013–14	NEC	27	5		
2014–15	NEC	28	12	**55**	**17**
2015–16	AZ Alkmaar	23	3		
2016–17	AZ Alkmaar	29	10		
2017–18	AZ Alkmaar	33	21	**85**	**34**
2018–19	Brighton & HA	19	0	**19**	**0**

KAYAL, Beram (M) 261 8
H: 5 10 W: 11 09 b.Jadeidi 2-5-88
Internationals: Israel U17, U18, U19, U21, Full caps.

2008–09	Maccabi Haifa	30	1		
2009–10	Maccabi Haifa	27	1	**57**	**2**
2010–11	Celtic	21	2		
2011–12	Celtic	19	0		
2012–13	Celtic	27	0		
2013–14	Celtic	13	0		
2014–15	Celtic	6	0	**86**	**2**
2014–15	Brighton & HA	18	1		
2015–16	Brighton & HA	43	2		
2016–17	Brighton & HA	20	0		
2017–18	Brighton & HA	19	0		
2018–19	Brighton & HA	18	1	**118**	**4**

KNOCKAERT, Anthony (M) 274 53
H: 5 8 W: 10 11 b.Lille 20-11-91
Internationals: France U20, U21.

2011–12	Guingamp	34	10	**34**	**10**
2012–13	Leicester C	42	8		
2013–14	Leicester C	42	5		
2014–15	Leicester C	9	0	**93**	**13**
2015–16	Standard Liege	20	5	**20**	**5**
2015–16	Brighton & HA	19	5		
2016–17	Brighton & HA	45	15		
2017–18	Brighton & HA	33	3		
2018–19	Brighton & HA	30	2	**127**	**25**

LOCADIA, Jurgen (F) 159 48
H: 6 2 W: 12 04 b.Emmen 7-11-93
Internationals: Netherlands U17, U18, U19, U20, U21.

2011–12	PSV Eindhoven	0	0		
2012–13	PSV Eindhoven	15	6		
2013–14	PSV Eindhoven	31	13		
2014–15	PSV Eindhoven	23	6		
2015–16	PSV Eindhoven	29	8		
2016–17	PSV Eindhoven	14	3		
2017–18	PSV Eindhoven	15	9	**127**	**45**
2017–18	Brighton & HA	6	1		
2018–19	Brighton & HA	26	2	**32**	**3**

MARCH, Solly (M) 146 9
H: 6 1 W: 12 02 b.Lewes 26-7-94
Internationals: England U20, U21.

2012–13	Brighton & HA	0	0		
2013–14	Brighton & HA	23	0		
2014–15	Brighton & HA	11	1		
2015–16	Brighton & HA	16	3		
2016–17	Brighton & HA	25	3		
2017–18	Brighton & HA	36	1		
2018–19	Brighton & HA	35	1	**146**	**9**

MOLUMBY, Jayson (M) 0 0
b. 6-8-99
Internationals: Republic of Ireland U16, U17, U19, U21.

2017–18	Brighton & HA	0	0		
2018–19	Brighton & HA	0	0		

MONTOYA, Martin (D) 140 3
H: 5 9 W: 11 09 b.Barcelona 14-4-91
Internationals: Spain U17, U18, U19, U21, U23.

2008–09	Barcelona	0	0		
2009–10	Barcelona	0	0		
2010–11	Barcelona	2	0		
2011–12	Barcelona	7	0		
2012–13	Barcelona	15	1		
2013–14	Barcelona	13	0		
2014–15	Barcelona	8	0		
2015–16	Barcelona	0	0	**45**	**1**
2015–16	*Inter Milan*	3	0	**3**	**0**
2015–16	*Real Betis*	13	0	**13**	**0**

2016–17	Valencia	29	2		
2017–18	Valencia	25	0	**54**	**2**
2018–19	Brighton & HA	25	0	**25**	**0**

MURRAY, Glenn (F) **478 188**
H: 6 1 W: 12 12 b.Maryport 25-9-83

2005–06	Carlisle U	26	3		
2006–07	Carlisle U	1	0	**27**	**3**
2006–07	*Stockport Co*	11	3	**11**	**3**
2006–07	Rochdale	31	16		
2007–08	Rochdale	23	9	**54**	**25**
2007–08	Brighton & HA	21	9		
2008–09	Brighton & HA	23	11		
2009–10	Brighton & HA	32	12		
2010–11	Brighton & HA	42	22		
2011–12	Crystal Palace	38	6		
2012–13	Crystal Palace	42	30		
2013–14	Crystal Palace	14	1		
2014–15	Crystal Palace	17	7		
2014–15	*Reading*	18	8	**18**	**8**
2015–16	Crystal Palace	2	0	**113**	**44**
2015–16	Bournemouth	19	3	**19**	**3**
2016–17	Brighton & HA	45	23		
2017–18	Brighton & HA	35	12		
2018–19	Brighton & HA	38	13	**236**	**102**

OSTIGARD, Leo (D) **12 0**
Internationals: Norway U16, U17, U18, U19, U20, U21.

2017–18	Molde	1	0	**1**	**0**
2017–18	*Viking*	11	0	**11**	**0**
2018–19	Brighton & HA	0	0		

PROPPER, Davy (M) **274 35**
H: 6 1 W: 11 05 b.Arnhem 2-9-91
Internationals: Netherlands U19, U21, Full caps.

2009–10	Vitesse	11	0		
2010–11	Vitesse	29	3		
2011–12	Vitesse	19	1		
2012–13	Vitesse	14	0		
2013–14	Vitesse	35	7		
2014–15	Vitesse	34	7	**142**	**18**
2015–16	PSV Eindhoven	33	10		
2016–17	PSV Eindhoven	34	6	**67**	**16**
2017–18	PSV	0	0		
2017–18	Brighton & HA	35	0		
2018–19	Brighton & HA	30	1	**65**	**1**

RYAN, Mathew (G) **267 0**
H: 6 0 W: 12 13 b.Plumpton 8-4-82
Internationals: Australia U23, Full caps.

2009	Blacktown C	0	0		
2009–10	Central Coast Mariners	0	0		
2010	Blacktown C	11	0	**11**	**0**
2010–11	Central Coast Mariners	31	0		
2011–12	Central Coast Mariners	24	0		
2012–13	Central Coast Mariners	25	0	**80**	**0**
2013–14	Club Brugge	40	0		
2014–15	Club Brugge	37	0	**77**	**0**
2015–16	Valencia	8	0		
2016–17	Valencia	2	0	**10**	**0**
2016–17	*Genk*	17	0	**17**	**0**
2017–18	Brighton & HA	38	0		
2018–19	Brighton & HA	34	0	**72**	**0**

SALTOR, Bruno (D) **427 7**
H: 5 10 W: 11 10 b.Masnou (Barca) 1-10-80

2001–02	Espanyol	1	0	**1**	**0**
2001–02	*Gimnastic*	12	0	**12**	**0**
2004–05	Lleida	1	1		
2005–06	Lleida	38	0	**39**	**1**
2006–07	Almeria	23	0		
2007–08	Almeria	34	0		
2008–09	Almeria	34	0	**91**	**0**
2009–10	Valencia	26	0		
2010–11	Valencia	19	0		
2011–12	Valencia	14	0	**59**	**0**
2012–13	Brighton & HA	30	1		
2013–14	Brighton & HA	33	1		
2014–15	Brighton & HA	35	3		
2015–16	Brighton & HA	46	1		
2016–17	Brighton & HA	42	0		
2017–18	Brighton & HA	25	0		
2018–19	Brighton & HA	14	0	**225**	**6**

SANCHEZ, Robert (G) **17 0**
b. 18-11-97
From Levante.

2018–19	Brighton & HA	0	0		
2018–19	*Forest Green R*	17	0	**17**	**0**

SANDERS, Max (M) **0 0**
b. 4-1-99
Internationals: England U19.

2017–18	Brighton & HA	0	0		
2018–19	Brighton & HA	0	0		

STEELE, Jason (G) **272 0**
H: 6 2 W: 12 07 b.Newton Aycliffe 18-8-90
Internationals: England U16, U17, U19, U21. Great Britain.

2007–08	Middlesbrough	0	0		
2008–09	Middlesbrough	0	0		
2009–10	Middlesbrough	0	0		
2009–10	*Northampton T*	13	0	**13**	**0**
2010–11	Middlesbrough	35	0		
2011–12	Middlesbrough	34	0		
2012–13	Middlesbrough	46	0		
2013–14	Middlesbrough	16	0		
2014–15	Middlesbrough	0	0	**131**	**0**
2014–15	*Blackburn R*	31	0		
2015–16	Blackburn R	41	0		
2016–17	Blackburn R	41	0	**113**	**0**
2017–18	Sunderland	15	0	**15**	**0**
2018–19	Brighton & HA	0	0		

STEPHENS, Dale (M) **345 37**
H: 5 7 W: 11 04 b.Bolton 12-6-89

2006–07	Bury	3	0		
2007–08	Bury	6	1	**9**	**1**
2008–09	Oldham Ath	0	0		
2009–10	Oldham Ath	26	2		
2009–10	*Rochdale*	6	1	**6**	**1**
2010–11	Oldham Ath	34	9	**60**	**11**
2010–11	*Southampton*	6	0	**6**	**0**
2011–12	Charlton Ath	30	5		
2012–13	Charlton Ath	28	2		
2013–14	Charlton Ath	26	3	**84**	**10**
2013–14	Brighton & HA	14	2		
2014–15	Brighton & HA	16	2		
2015–16	Brighton & HA	45	7		
2016–17	Brighton & HA	39	2		
2017–18	Brighton & HA	36	0		
2018–19	Brighton & HA	30	1	**180**	**14**

SUTTNER, Markus (M) **275 14**
H: 5 10 W: 11 03 b.Hollabrunn 16-4-87
Internationals: Austria U21, Full caps.

2008–09	Austria Vienna	22	0		
2009–10	Austria Vienna	27	0		
2010–11	Austria Vienna	27	2		
2011–12	Austria Vienna	30	1		
2012–13	Austria Vienna	35	3		
2013–14	Austria Vienna	35	2		
2014–15	Austria Vienna	31	1	**207**	**9**
2015–16	Ingolstadt 04	18	0		
2016–17	Ingolstadt 04	31	4	**49**	**4**
2017–18	Brighton & HA	14	0		
2018–19	Brighton & HA	0	0	**14**	**0**
2018–19	*Fortuna Dusseldorf*	5	1	**5**	**1**

TOWELL, Richie (D) **201 53**
H: 5 8 W: 10 06 b.Dublin 17-7-91
Internationals: Republic of Ireland U17, U19, U21.

2010–11	Celtic	1	0		
2011–12	Celtic	0	0		
2011–12	*Hibernian*	16	0		
2012–13	Celtic	0	0	**1**	**0**
2012–13	*Hibernian*	14	1	**30**	**1**
2013	Dundalk	31	7		
2014	Dundalk	33	11		
2015	Dundalk	32	25	**96**	**43**
2015–16	Brighton & HA	0	0		
2016–17	Brighton & HA	1	0		
2017–18	Brighton & HA	0	0		
2017–18	*Rotherham U*	39	5		
2018–19	Brighton & HA	0	0	**1**	**0**
2018–19	*Rotherham U*	34	4	**73**	**9**

WALTON, Christian (G) **110 0**
H: 6 0 W: 11 11 b.Wadebridge 9-11-95
Internationals: England U19, U20, U21.

2011–12	Plymouth Arg	0	0		
2012–13	Plymouth Arg	0	0		
2013–14	Brighton & HA	0	0		
2014–15	Brighton & HA	3	0		
2015–16	Brighton & HA	0	0		
2015–16	*Bury*	4	0	**4**	**0**
2015–16	*Plymouth Arg*	4	0	**4**	**0**
2016–17	Brighton & HA	0	0		
2016–17	*Luton T*	27	0	**27**	**0**
2016–17	*Southend U*	7	0	**7**	**0**
2017–18	Brighton & HA	0	0		
2017–18	*Wigan Ath*	31	0		
2018–19	Brighton & HA	0	0	**3**	**0**
2018–19	*Wigan Ath*	34	0	**65**	**0**

WHITE, Ben (D) **57 2**
b.Poole 8-11-97

2016–17	Brighton & HA	0	0		
2017–18	Brighton & HA	0	0		
2017–18	*Newport Co*	42	1	**42**	**1**
2018–19	Brighton & HA	0	0		
2018–19	*Peterborough U*	15	1	**15**	**1**

Players retained or with offer of contract
Ahannach, Soufyan; Arce Mina, Billy Vladimir; Baluta, Tudor-Cristian; Cashman, Danny Christopher; Cochrane, Alexander William; Cocoracchio, Luca George; Davies, Archie; Davies, Jordan Andrew; Dreyer, Anders Laustrup; Gwargis, Peter; Jenks, Teddy Christopher Graham; Kazukolovas, Kipras; Keto, Hugo Oliver; Leonard, Marc Henry; Lopata, Kacper Mieczyslaw; Mac Allister, Alexis; Mateju, Ales; McGill, Thomas Peter Wayne; Mlakar, Jan; O'Hora, Warren Patrick; Radulovic Samoukovic, Bojan; Rushworth, Carl Andrew; Schelotto, Ezequiel Matias; Shihab, Tareq Shakib; Tau, Percy Muzi; Tilley, James Alexander David.

Scholars
Bentley, George Richard; Clark-Eden, Ben; Longman, Ryan James; Packham, Samuel James; Rees, Roco; Roberts, Haydon; Spong, Jack; Tanimowo, Ayobami Babatunde; Tolaj, Lorent; Tutt, Cameron; Vukoje, Stefan Charles; Weaire, Matthew; Wilson, Benjamin John; Zalewski, Piotr.

BRISTOL C (14)

ADELAKUN, Hakeeb (F) **144 16**
H: 6 3 W: 11 11 b.Hackney 11-6-96

2012–13	Scunthorpe U	2	0		
2013–14	Scunthorpe U	28	2		
2014–15	Scunthorpe U	32	6		
2015–16	Scunthorpe U	21	2		
2016–17	Scunthorpe U	17	2		
2017–18	Scunthorpe U	39	4	**139**	**16**
2018–19	Bristol C	5	0	**5**	**0**

BAKER, Nathan (D) **221 2**
H: 6 2 W: 11 11 b.Worcester 23-4-91
Internationals: England U19, U20, U21.

2008–09	Aston Villa	0	0		
2009–10	Aston Villa	0	0		
2009–10	*Lincoln C*	18	0	**18**	**0**
2010–11	Aston Villa	4	0		
2011–12	Aston Villa	8	0		
2011–12	*Millwall*	6	0	**6**	**0**
2012–13	Aston Villa	26	0		
2013–14	Aston Villa	30	0		
2014–15	Aston Villa	11	0		
2015–16	Aston Villa	0	0		
2015–16	*Bristol C*	36	1		
2016–17	Aston Villa	32	1	**111**	**1**
2017–18	Bristol C	34	0		
2018–19	Bristol C	16	0	**86**	**1**

BAKINSON, Tyreeq (M) **31 1**
H: 6 1 W: 11 00 b.Camden 8-1-98

2015–16	Luton T	1	0		
2016–17	Luton T	0	0		
2017–18	Luton T	0	0	**1**	**0**
2017–18	Bristol C	0	0		
2018–19	Bristol C	0	0		
2018–19	*Newport Co*	30	1	**30**	**1**

BALDWIN, Aden (D) **4 0**
b. 10-6-97

2018–19	Bristol C	0	0		
2018–19	*Cheltenham T*	4	0	**4**	**0**

BROWNHILL, Josh (M) **184 18**
H: 5 10 W: 10 12 b.Warrington 19-12-95

2013–14	Preston NE	24	3		
2014–15	Preston NE	18	2		
2015–16	Preston NE	3	0	**45**	**5**
2015–16	*Barnsley*	22	2	**22**	**2**
2016–17	Bristol C	27	1		
2017–18	Bristol C	45	5		
2018–19	Bristol C	45	5	**117**	**11**

DIEDHIOU, Famara (F) **241 86**
H: 6 4 W: 12 08 b.Saint-Louis 15-12-92
Internationals: Senegal Full caps.

2011–12	Belfort	11	3	**11**	**3**
2012–13	Epinal	30	12	**30**	**12**
2013–14	Ajaccio	33	13	**33**	**13**
2014–15	Sochaux	13	1		
2014–15	*Clermont*	14	2		
2015–16	Sochaux	0	0	**13**	**1**
2015–16	*Clermont*	36	21	**50**	**23**
2016–17	Angers	31	8	**31**	**8**
2017–18	Bristol C	32	13		
2018–19	Bristol C	41	13	**73**	**26**

EISA, Mohamed (F) **50 23**

H: 6 0 W: 11 00 b. 12-7-94

From Dartford, Corinthian, Greenwich Bor.

2017–18	Cheltenham T	45	23	**45**	**23**
2018–19	Bristol C	5	0	**5**	**0**

ELIASSON, Niclas (M) **136 8**

H: 5 9 W: 10 06 b.Varberg 7-12-95

Internationals: Sweden U17, U19, U21.

2012	Falkenberg	0	0		
2013	Falkenberg	29	1	**29**	**1**
2014	AIK Solna	16	1		
2015	AIK Solna	10	0		
2016	AIK Solna	5	0	**31**	**1**
2016	*Norrkoping*	13	1		
2017	Norrkoping	17	3	**30**	**4**
2017–18	IFK Norrkoping	0	0		
2017–18	Bristol C	13	0		
2018–19	Bristol C	33	2	**46**	**2**

FIELDING, Frank (G) **323 0**

H: 5 11 W: 12 00 b.Blackburn 4-4-88

Internationals: England U19, U21.

2006–07	Blackburn R	0	0		
2007–08	Blackburn R	0	0		
2007–08	*Wycombe W*	36	0	**36**	**0**
2008–09	Blackburn R	0	0		
2008–09	*Northampton T*	12	0	**12**	**0**
2008–09	*Rochdale*	23	0		
2009–10	Blackburn R	0	0		
2009–10	*Rochdale*	18	0	**41**	**0**
2010–11	Blackburn R	0	0		
2010–11	Derby Co	16	0		
2011–12	Derby Co	44	0		
2012–13	Derby Co	16	0	**76**	**0**
2013–14	Bristol C	16	0		
2014–15	Bristol C	46	0		
2015–16	Bristol C	21	0		
2016–17	Bristol C	27	0		
2017–18	Bristol C	43	0		
2018–19	Bristol C	5	0	**158**	**0**

HEGELER, Jens (M) **192 12**

H: 6 4 W: 12 08 b.Cologne 22-1-88

Internationals: Germany U21.

2007–08	Bayer Leverkusen	1	0		
2008–09	Bayer Leverkusen	6	2		
2008–09	*Augsburg*	11	0		
2009–10	Bayer Leverkusen	0	0		
2009–10	*Augsburg*	2	2	**13**	**2**
2010–11	Bayer Leverkusen	0	0		
2010–11	*Nurembourg*	34	3		
2011–12	Bayer Leverkusen	0	0		
2011–12	*Nurembourg*	31	1	**65**	**4**
2012–13	Bayer Leverkusen	27	3		
2013–14	Bayer Leverkusen	18	0	**52**	**5**
2014–15	Hertha Berlin	24	1		
2015–16	Hertha Berlin	16	0		
2016–17	Hertha Berlin	6	0	**46**	**1**
2016–17	Bristol C	12	0		
2017–18	Bristol C	4	0		
2018–19	Bristol C	0	0	**16**	**0**

HOLDEN, Rory (F) **6 0**

H: 5 7 W: 10 10 b.Derry 23-8-97

Internationals: Northern Ireland U21.

From Derry C.

2017–18	Bristol C	0	0		
2018–19	Bristol C	0	0		
2018–19	*Rochdale*	6	0	**6**	**0**

HUNT, Jack (D) **296 3**

H: 5 9 W: 11 02 b.Rothwell 6-12-90

2009–10	Huddersfield T	0	0		
2010–11	Huddersfield T	19	1		
2010–11	*Chesterfield*	20	0	**20**	**0**
2011–12	Huddersfield T	43	1		
2012–13	Huddersfield T	40	0		
2013–14	Huddersfield T	2	0	**104**	**2**
2013–14	Crystal Palace	0	0		
2013–14	*Barnsley*	11	0	**11**	**0**
2014–15	Crystal Palace	0	0		
2014–15	*Nottingham F*	17	0	**17**	**0**
2014–15	*Rotherham U*	16	0	**16**	**0**
2015–16	Sheffield W	34	0		
2016–17	Sheffield W	32	0		
2017–18	Sheffield W	29	0	**95**	**0**
2018–19	Bristol C	33	1	**33**	**1**

JANNEH, Saikou (F) **0 0**

From Clevedon T.

2018–19	Bristol C	0	0		

KELLY, Lloyd (D) **43 2**

H: 5 10 W: 11 00 b. 1-10-98

Internationals: England U20, U21.

2016–17	Bristol C	0	0		
2017–18	Bristol C	11	1		
2018–19	Bristol C	32	1	**43**	**2**

MAENPAA, Niki (G) **213 0**

H: 6 3 W: 13 05 b.Espoo 23-1-85

Internationals: Finland U18, U19, U21, Full caps.

2006–07	Den Bosch	27	0		
2007–08	Den Bosch	33	0		
2008–09	Den Bosch	7	0	**67**	**0**
2009–10	Willem II	6	0		
2010–11	Willem II	12	0	**18**	**0**
2011–12	AZ Alkmaar	0	0		
2012–13	VVV-Venlo	33	0		
2013–14	VVV-Venlo	33	0		
2014–15	VVV-Venlo	35	0	**101**	**0**
2015–16	Brighton & HA	0	0		
2016–17	Brighton & HA	1	0		
2017–18	Brighton & HA	0	0	**1**	**0**
2018–19	Bristol C	26	0	**26**	**0**

MARINOVIC, Stefan (G) **107 0**

H: 6 3 W: 14 07 b.Auckland 7-10-91

Internationals: New Zealand U20, Full caps.

2009–10	Wehen Wiesbaden	2	0		
2010–11	Wehen Wiesbaden	0	0		
2011–12	Wehen Wiesbaden	0	0	**2**	**0**
2012–13	Ismaning	1	0	**1**	**0**
2013–14	1860 Munich	1	0	**1**	**0**
2014–15	Unterhaching	9	0		
2015–16	Unterhaching	31	0		
2016–17	Unterhaching	30	0	**70**	**0**
2017	Vancouver Whitecaps	8	0		
2018	Vancouver Whitecaps	24	0	**32**	**0**
2018–19	Bristol C	1	0	**1**	**0**

MORRELL, Joe (M) **39 3**

H: 5 3 W: 11 04 b.Ipswich 3-1-97

Internationals: Wales U17, U19, U21.

2013–14	Bristol C	0	0		
2014–15	Bristol C	0	0		
2015–16	Bristol C	0	0		
2016–17	Bristol C	0	0		
2017–18	Bristol C	0	0		
2017–18	*Cheltenham T*	38	3	**38**	**3**
2018–19	Bristol C	1	0	**1**	**0**

O'DOWDA, Callum (M) **176 17**

H: 5 11 W: 11 11 b.Oxford 23-4-95

Internationals: Republic of Ireland U21, Full caps.

2012–13	Oxford U	0	0		
2013–14	Oxford U	10	0		
2014–15	Oxford U	39	4		
2015–16	Oxford U	38	8	**87**	**12**
2016–17	Bristol C	34	0		
2017–18	Bristol C	24	1		
2018–19	Bristol C	31	4	**89**	**5**

O'LEARY, Max (G) **15 0**

H: 6 1 W: 12 03 b.Bath 10-10-96

2013–14	Bristol C	0	0		
2014–15	Bristol C	0	0		
2015–16	Bristol C	0	0		
2016–17	Bristol C	0	0		
2017–18	Bristol C	0	0		
2018–19	Bristol C	15	0	**15**	**0**

PACK, Marlon (M) **393 26**

H: 6 2 W: 11 09 b.Portsmouth 25-3-91

2008–09	Portsmouth	0	0		
2009–10	Portsmouth	0	0		
2009–10	*Wycombe W*	8	0	**8**	**0**
2009–10	*Dagenham & R*	17	1	**17**	**1**
2010–11	Portsmouth	1	0	**1**	**0**
2010–11	*Cheltenham T*	38	2		
2011–12	Cheltenham T	43	5		
2012–13	Cheltenham T	43	7		
2013–14	Cheltenham T	0	0	**124**	**14**
2013–14	Bristol C	43	0		
2014–15	Bristol C	34	3		
2015–16	Bristol C	45	1		
2016–17	Bristol C	33	2		
2017–18	Bristol C	42	3		
2018–19	Bristol C	46	2	**243**	**11**

PATERSON, Jamie (F) **285 44**

H: 5 9 W: 10 07 b.Coventry 20-12-91

2010–11	Walsall	14	0		
2011–12	Walsall	34	3		
2012–13	Walsall	46	12	**94**	**15**
2013–14	Nottingham F	32	8		
2014–15	Nottingham F	21	1		
2015–16	Nottingham F	1	0	**54**	**9**
2015–16	*Huddersfield T*	34	6	**34**	**6**
2016–17	Bristol C	22	4		
2017–18	Bristol C	41	5		
2018–19	Bristol C	40	5	**103**	**14**

PEARSON, Sam (M) **0 0**

b. 26-10-01

Internationals: Wales U19.

2018–19	Bristol C	0	0		

PISANO, Eros (D) **354 27**

H: 6 1 W: 13 01 b.Butso Arsizio 31-3-87

Internationals: Italy U20.

2004–05	Varese	2	1		
2005–06	Varese	32	2		
2006–07	Varese	22	1		
2007–08	Varese	0	0		
2007–08	*Pisa*	6	0	**6**	**0**
2008–09	Varese	28	3		
2009–10	Varese	32	2		
2010–11	Varese	40	5	**156**	**14**
2011–12	Palermo	28	0		
2012–13	Palermo	11	0		
2012–13	Genoa	10	1	**10**	**1**
2013–14	Palermo	34	2		
2014–15	Palermo	4	0	**77**	**2**
2014–15	*Verona*	15	0		
2015–16	Verona	34	5		
2016–17	Verona	25	3	**74**	**8**
2017–18	Bristol C	16	0		
2018–19	Bristol C	15	2	**31**	**2**

PRING, Cameron (D) **15 1**

b. 22-1-98

2018–19	Bristol C	0	0		
2018–19	*Newport Co*	7	1	**7**	**1**
2018–19	*Cheltenham T*	8	0	**8**	**0**

SEMENYO, Antoine (F) **26 3**

b. 7-1-00

2017–18	Bristol C	1	0		
2018–19	Newport Co	21	3	**21**	**3**
2018–19	Bristol C	4	0	**5**	**0**

SMITH, Jon (M) **40 4**

H: 5 10 W: 10 01 b.Liverpool 27-7-97

2016–17	Bristol C	0	0		
2016–17	*Cheltenham T*	5	0	**5**	**0**
2017–18	Bristol C	0	0		
2018–19	Bristol C	0	0		
2018–19	*Tranmere R*	35	4	**35**	**4**

SMITH, Korey (M) **301 6**

H: 5 9 W: 11 01 b.Hatfield 31-1-91

2008–09	Norwich C	2	0		
2009–10	Norwich C	37	4		
2010–11	Norwich C	28	0		
2011–12	Norwich C	0	0		
2011–12	*Barnsley*	12	0	**12**	**0**
2012–13	Norwich C	0	0	**67**	**4**
2012–13	*Yeovil T*	17	0	**17**	**0**
2012–13	*Oldham Ath*	10	0		
2013–14	Oldham Ath	42	1	**52**	**1**
2014–15	Bristol C	44	0		
2015–16	Bristol C	36	0		
2016–17	Bristol C	23	0		
2017–18	Bristol C	45	1		
2018–19	Bristol C	5	0	**153**	**1**

TAYLOR, Matty (F) **139 50**

H: 5 9 W: 11 05 b. 30-3-90

Internationals: England C.

From Oxford U, North Leigh, Forest Green R.

2015–16	Bristol R	46	27		
2016–17	Bristol R	27	16	**73**	**43**
2016–17	Bristol C	15	2		
2017–18	Bristol C	18	1		
2018–19	Bristol C	33	4	**66**	**7**

WALSH, Liam (M) **33 1**

b. 15-9-97

Internationals: England U16, U18.

2015–16	Everton	0	0		
2015–16	*Yeovil T*	15	1	**15**	**1**
2016–17	Everton	0	0		
2017–18	Everton	0	0		
2017–18	*Birmingham C*	3	0	**3**	**0**
2017–18	Bristol C	6	0		
2018–19	Bristol C	9	0	**15**	**0**

WATKINS, Marley (M) **201 26**

H: 5 10 W: 10 03 b.London 17-10-90

Internationals: Wales Full caps.

2008–09	Cheltenham T	12	0		
2009–10	Cheltenham T	13	1		
2010–11	Cheltenham T	1	0	**26**	**1**

From Bath C, Hereford U

2013–14	Inverness CT	26	1		
2014–15	Inverness CT	33	7	**59**	**8**
2015–16	Barnsley	34	5		
2016–17	Barnsley	42	10	**76**	**15**
2017–18	Norwich C	24	0	**24**	**0**
2018–19	Bristol C	16	2	**16**	**2**

WEBSTER, Adam (D) **162** **9**
H: 6 1 W: 11 11 b.West Wittering 4-1-95
Internationals: England U18, U19.

2011–12	Portsmouth	3	0		
2012–13	Portsmouth	18	0		
2013–14	Portsmouth	4	2		
2014–15	Portsmouth	15	1		
2015–16	Portsmouth	27	2	**67**	**5**
2016–17	Ipswich T	23	1		
2017–18	Ipswich T	28	0	**51**	**1**
2018–19	Bristol C	44	3	**44**	**3**

WEIMANN, Andreas (F) **278** **42**
H: 5 9 W: 11 09 b.Vienna 5-8-91
Internationals: Austria U17, U19, U20, U21, Full caps.

2008–09	Aston Villa	0	0		
2009–10	Aston Villa	0	0		
2010–11	Aston Villa	1	0		
2010–11	*Watford*	18	4		
2011–12	Aston Villa	14	2		
2011–12	*Watford*	3	0	**21**	**4**
2012–13	Aston Villa	30	7		
2013–14	Aston Villa	37	5		
2014–15	Aston Villa	31	3	**113**	**17**
2015–16	Derby Co	30	4		
2016–17	Derby Co	11	0		
2016–17	*Wolverhampton W*	19	2	**19**	**2**
2017–18	Derby Co	40	5	**81**	**9**
2018–19	Bristol C	44	10	**44**	**10**

WOLLACOTT, Jojo (G) **0** **0**
b. 8-9-96

2015–16	Bristol C	0	0		
2016–17	Bristol C	0	0		
2017–18	Bristol C	0	0		
2018–19	Bristol C	0	0		

WRIGHT, Bailey (D) **248** **9**
H: 5 9 W: 13 05 b.Melbourne 28-7-92
Internationals: Australia U17, Full caps.

2010–11	Preston NE	2	0		
2011–12	Preston NE	13	1		
2012–13	Preston NE	38	2		
2013–14	Preston NE	43	4		
2014–15	Preston NE	27	1		
2015–16	Preston NE	38	0		
2016–17	Preston NE	18	0	**179**	**8**
2016–17	Bristol C	21	1		
2017–18	Bristol C	36	0		
2018–19	Bristol C	12	0	**69**	**1**

Players retained or with offer of contract
Andrews, Jake; Dowling, George Philip Denzil; Edwards, Opanin Osafo-Adjei; Harrison, Tom Jack; Hinds, Fredrick Peter; Lemonheigh-Evans, Connor; Moir-Pring, Cameron Lewis; Moore, Taylor David; Morton, James Samuel; Nurse, George Damien; Rees, Ricardo Estaban; Sesay, Alhaji; Vyner, Zachary George Onyego.

Scholars
Bell, Samuel John; Burford, James; Buse, William Jack; Conway, Tommy Daniel John; Day, Marcus Reece; Gould, William James; Hall, Joseph; Harper, Vincent; Low, Joseph David; Owers, Joshua Gary; Pearson, Callum; Pearson, Samuel; Robertson, Lochlan David William; Sainsbury, Aaron James; Smith, Kieran Paul; Smith, Zachary William Pince; Soady, Barnaby James; Spark, Jack Edward Joseph; Taylor, James Edward; Taylor, James John; Towler, Ryley Ben; Webb, Bradley James; Williams, Max James.

BRISTOL R (15)

ANDRE, Alexis (G) **1** **0**
b. 31-5-97

2017–18	Bristol R	1	0		
2018–19	Bristol R	0	0	**1**	**0**

BAGHDADI, Mohammed (D) **3** **0**
H: 5 10 W: 11 03 b. 30-10-96

2013–14	Eintracht Braunschweig	0	0		
2014–15	Eintracht Braunschweig	1	0		
2015–16	Eintracht Braunschweig	0	0		
2016–17	Eintracht Braunschweig	0	0	**1**	**0**
2017–18	Bristol R	2	0		
2018–19	Bristol R	0	0	**2**	**0**

Transferred to Eintracht Norderstedt, January 2019.

BENNETT, Kyle (F) **320** **37**
H: 5 5 W: 9 08 b.Telford 9-9-90
Internationals: England U18.

2007–08	Wolverhampton W	0	0		
2008–09	Wolverhampton W	0	0		
2009–10	Wolverhampton W	0	0		
2010–11	Bury	32	2	**32**	**2**
2011–12	Doncaster R	36	4		
2012–13	Doncaster R	35	3		
2013–14	Doncaster R	3	0		
2013–14	*Crawley T*	4	0	**4**	**0**
2013–14	*Bradford C*	18	1	**18**	**1**
2014–15	Doncaster R	42	8	**116**	**15**
2015–16	Portsmouth	42	6		
2016–17	Portsmouth	39	6		
2017–18	Portsmouth	18	0	**99**	**12**
2017–18	Bristol R	17	3		
2018–19	Bristol R	19	0	**36**	**3**
2018–19	*Swindon T*	15	4	**15**	**4**

CLARKE, James (D) **112** **2**
H: 6 0 W: 13 03 b.Aylesbury 17-11-89
From Watford, Oxford U, Oxford C, Salisbury C, Woking.

2015–16	Bristol R	37	0		
2016–17	Bristol R	22	0		
2017–18	Bristol R	11	0		
2018–19	Bristol R	42	2	**112**	**2**

CLARKE, Ollie (M) **181** **15**
H: 5 11 W: 11 11 b.Bristol 29-6-92

2009–10	Bristol R	0	0		
2010–11	Bristol R	1	0		
2011–12	Bristol R	0	0		
2012–13	Bristol R	5	0		
2013–14	Bristol R	32	2		
2015–16	Bristol R	33	2		
2016–17	Bristol R	30	4		
2017–18	Bristol R	40	1		
2018–19	Bristol R	40	6	**181**	**15**

CLARKE-HARRIS, Jonson (F) **205** **40**
H: 6 0 W: 11 01 b.Leicester 21-7-94

2012–13	Peterborough U	0	0		
2012–13	*Southend U*	3	0	**3**	**0**
2012–13	*Bury*	12	4	**12**	**4**
2013–14	Oldham Ath	40	6		
2014–15	Oldham Ath	5	1	**45**	**7**
2014–15	Rotherham U	15	3		
2014–15	*Milton Keynes D*	5	0	**5**	**0**
2014–15	*Doncaster R*	9	1	**9**	**1**
2015–16	Rotherham U	35	6		
2016–17	Rotherham U	7	0		
2017–18	Rotherham U	14	0	**71**	**9**
2017–18	*Coventry C*	17	3		
2018–19	Coventry C	27	5	**44**	**8**
2018–19	Bristol R	16	11	**16**	**11**

CRAIG, Tony (D) **475** **12**
H: 6 0 W: 10 03 b.Greenwich 20-4-85

2002–03	Millwall	2	1		
2003–04	Millwall	9	0		
2004–05	Millwall	10	0		
2004–05	*Wycombe W*	14	0	**14**	**0**
2005–06	Millwall	28	0		
2006–07	Millwall	30	1		
2007–08	Crystal Palace	13	0	**13**	**0**
2007–08	*Millwall*	5	1		
2008–09	Millwall	44	2		
2009–10	Millwall	30	2		
2010–11	Millwall	24	0		
2011–12	Millwall	23	0		
2011–12	*Leyton Orient*	4	0	**4**	**0**
2012–13	Brentford	44	0		
2013–14	Brentford	44	0		
2014–15	Brentford	23	0	**111**	**0**
2015–16	Millwall	18	1		
2016–17	Millwall	43	1		
2017–18	Millwall	4	0	**270**	**9**
2017–18	Bristol R	17	1		
2018–19	Bristol R	46	2	**63**	**3**

EBBUTT, Cameron (F) **0** **0**

2018–19	Bristol R	0	0		

HARGREAVES, Cameron (D) **0** **0**
From Exeter C.

2017–18	Bristol R	0	0		
2018–19	Bristol R	0	0		

HOLMES-DENNIS, Tareiq (M) **81** **2**
H: 5 9 W: 11 11 b.Farnborough 31-10-95
Internationals: England U18.

2012–13	Charlton Ath	0	0		
2013–14	Charlton Ath	0	0		
2014–15	Charlton Ath	0	0		
2014–15	*Oxford U*	14	0	**14**	**0**
2014–15	*Plymouth Arg*	17	1	**17**	**1**
2015–16	Charlton Ath	11	0		
2015–16	*Oldham Ath*	10	0	**10**	**0**
2016–17	Charlton Ath	1	0	**12**	**0**
2016–17	Huddersfield T	9	0		
2017–18	Huddersfield T	0	0	**9**	**0**
2017–18	*Portsmouth*	1	0	**1**	**0**
2018–19	Bristol R	18	1	**18**	**1**

JONES, Connor (M) **0** **0**

2018–19	Bristol R	0	0		

KELLY, Michael (D) **22** **0**
H: 5 11 b.Kilmarnock 3-11-97
Internationals: Scotland U16, U17.

2017–18	Bristol R	1	0		
2018–19	Bristol R	21	0	**22**	**0**

KILGOUR, Alfie (D) **4** **0**
b. 18-5-98

2015–16	Bristol R	0	0		
2016–17	Bristol R	0	0		
2017–18	Bristol R	0	0		
2018–19	Bristol R	4	0	**4**	**0**

LEADBITTER, Daniel (D) **106** **0**
H: 6 0 W: 11 00 b.Newcastle upon Tyne 17-10-90

2011–12	Torquay U	2	0		
2012–13	Torquay U	13	0	**15**	**0**
2015–16	Bristol R	33	0		
2016–17	Bristol R	30	0		
2017–18	Bristol R	17	0		
2018–19	Bristol R	11	0	**91**	**0**

LINES, Chris (M) **430** **35**
H: 6 2 W: 12 00 b.Bristol 30-11-88

2005–06	Bristol R	4	0		
2006–07	Bristol R	7	0		
2007–08	Bristol R	27	3		
2008–09	Bristol R	45	4		
2009–10	Bristol R	42	10		
2010–11	Bristol R	42	3		
2011–12	Bristol R	1	0		
2011–12	Sheffield W	41	3		
2012–13	Sheffield W	6	0	**47**	**3**
2012–13	*Milton Keynes D*	16	0	**16**	**0**
2013–14	Port Vale	34	1		
2014–15	Port Vale	27	2	**61**	**3**
2015–16	Bristol R	33	0		
2016–17	Bristol R	44	3		
2017–18	Bristol R	42	5		
2018–19	Bristol R	19	1	**306**	**29**

LOCKYER, Tom (D) **211** **5**
H: 6 0 W: 11 05 b.Bristol 30-12-94
Internationals: Wales U21, Full caps.

2012–13	Bristol R	4	0		
2013–14	Bristol R	41	1		
2015–16	Bristol R	43	0		
2016–17	Bristol R	46	0		
2017–18	Bristol R	37	1		
2018–19	Bristol R	40	3	**211**	**5**

MATTHEWS, Sam (M) **16** **0**
b. 1-3-97

2013–14	Bournemouth	0	0		
2014–15	Bournemouth	0	0		
2015–16	Bournemouth	0	0		
2016–17	Bournemouth	0	0		
2017–18	Bournemouth	0	0		

From Braintree T, Eastleigh.

2018–19	Bristol R	16	0	**16**	**0**

MENAYESE, Rollin (D) **17** **0**
H: 6 3 W: 12 08 b. 4-12-97
Internationals: Wales U17.
From Weston-super-Mare.

2017–18	Bristol R	3	0		
2017–18	*Swindon T*	14	0	**14**	**0**
2018–19	Bristol R	0	0	**3**	**0**

MENSAH, Bernard (F) **15** **0**
H: 5 8 W: 9 04 b.Hounslow 29-12-94

2011–12	Watford	0	0		
2012–13	Watford	0	0		
2013–14	Watford	1	0		
2014–15	Watford	1	0		
2015–16	Watford	0	0	**2**	**0**

From Aldershot T.

2017–18	Bristol R	8	0		
2018–19	Bristol R	1	0	**9**	**0**
2018–19	*Lincoln C*	4	0	**4**	**0**

MOORE, Deon (F) **5** **0**
b.Croydon 14-5-99
From Carshalton Ath.

2016–17	Peterborough U	4	0	**4**	**0**

From Mersham.

2018–19	Bristol R	1	0	**1**	**0**

MORGAN, Ben (D) **0 0**

2018–19	Bristol R	0	0		

NICHOLS, Tom (F) **223 45**

H: 5 10 W: 10 10 b.Wellington 1-9-93

2010–11	Exeter C	1	0		
2011–12	Exeter C	7	1		
2012–13	Exeter C	3	0		
2013–14	Exeter C	28	6		
2014–15	Exeter C	36	15		
2015–16	Exeter C	23	10	**98**	**32**
2015–16	Peterborough U	7	1		
2016–17	Peterborough U	43	10	**50**	**11**
2017–18	Bristol R	39	1		
2018–19	Bristol R	36	1	**75**	**2**

OGOGO, Abu (D) **363 22**

H: 5 8 W: 10 02 b.Epsom 3-11-89

2007–08	Arsenal	0	0		
2008–09	Arsenal	0	0		
2008–09	*Barnet*	9	1	**9**	**1**
2009–10	Dagenham & R	30	2		
2010–11	Dagenham & R	33	1		
2011–12	Dagenham & R	40	1		
2012–13	Dagenham & R	46	1		
2013–14	Dagenham & R	44	8		
2014–15	Dagenham & R	32	4	**225**	**17**
2015–16	Shrewsbury T	42	2		
2016–17	Shrewsbury T	26	0		
2017–18	Shrewsbury T	35	2	**103**	**4**
2018–19	Coventry C	10	0	**10**	**0**
2018–19	Bristol R	16	0	**16**	**0**

PARTINGTON, Joe (M) **105 5**

H: 5 11 W: 11 13 b.Portsmouth 1-4-90
Internationals: Wales U17, U19, U21.

2007–08	Bournemouth	6	1		
2008–09	Bournemouth	11	1		
2009–10	Bournemouth	11	0		
2010–11	Bournemouth	5	0		
2011–12	Bournemouth	5	0		
2012–13	Bournemouth	14	0		
2013–14	Bournemouth	0	0		
2014–15	Bournemouth	0	0	**52**	**2**
2016–17	Bristol R	7	0		
2017–18	Bristol R	32	3		
2018–19	Bristol R	14	0	**53**	**3**

PAYNE, Stefan (F) **114 16**

H: 5 10 W: 11 07 b.Lambeth 10-8-91
Internationals: England C.

2009–10	Fulham	0	0		
2010–11	Gillingham	16	0		
2011–12	Gillingham	12	1	**28**	**1**
2011–12	*Aldershot T*	1	0	**1**	**0**

From Sutton U, Macclesfield T, Ebbsfleet U, AFC Hornchurch, Dover Ath.

2015–16	Barnsley	0	0		
2016–17	Barnsley	7	0		
2016–17	*Shrewsbury T*	12	2		
2017–18	Barnsley	2	0	**9**	**0**
2017–18	Shrewsbury T	38	11		
2018–19	Bristol R	20	2	**20**	**2**
2018–19	*Shrewsbury T*	6	0	**56**	**13**

REILLY, Gavin (F) **226 59**

H: 5 9 W: 10 05 b.Dumfries 10-5-93

2010–11	Queen of the South	1	0		
2011–12	Queen of the South	14	2		
2012–13	Queen of the South	30	12		
2013–14	Queen of the South	34	12		
2014–15	Queen of the South	32	13	**111**	**39**
2015–16	Hearts	28	4		
2016–17	Hearts	0	0	**28**	**4**
2016–17	*Dunfermline Ath*	22	1	**22**	**1**
2017–18	St Mirren	35	11	**35**	**11**
2018–19	Bristol R	30	4	**30**	**4**

RODMAN, Alex (F) **194 24**

H: 6 2 W: 12 08 b.Sutton Coldfield 15-2-87
Internationals: England C.

2010–11	Aldershot T	14	5		
2011–12	Aldershot T	18	1		
2012–13	Aldershot T	11	1	**43**	**7**
2012–13	*York C*	18	1	**18**	**1**
2015–16	Newport Co	29	4	**29**	**4**
2016–17	Notts Co	16	1	**16**	**1**
2016–17	Shrewsbury T	20	1		
2017–18	Shrewsbury T	41	5	**61**	**6**
2018–19	Bristol R	27	5	**27**	**5**

RUSSE, Luke (M) **3 0**

b. 19-7-99

2017–18	Bristol R	3	0		
2018–19	Bristol R	0	0	**3**	**0**

SERCOMBE, Liam (M) **392 52**

H: 5 10 W: 10 10 b.Exeter 25-4-90

2008–09	Exeter C	29	2		
2009–10	Exeter C	28	1		
2010–11	Exeter C	42	3		
2011–12	Exeter C	33	7		
2012–13	Exeter C	20	1		
2013–14	Exeter C	44	5		
2014–15	Exeter C	40	4	**236**	**23**
2015–16	Oxford U	45	14		
2016–17	Oxford U	30	3	**75**	**17**
2017–18	Bristol R	42	8		
2018–19	Bristol R	39	4	**81**	**12**

SINCLAIR, Stuart (M) **115 5**

H: 5 7 W: 10 08 b.Houghton Conquest 9-11-87
From Luton T, Cambridge C, Bedford T, Dunstable T, Arlesey T, Salisbury C.

2015–16	Bristol R	30	2		
2016–17	Bristol R	38	1		
2017–18	Bristol R	29	2		
2018–19	Bristol R	18	0	**115**	**5**

SLOCOMBE, Sam (G) **197 0**

H: 6 0 W: 11 11 b.Scunthorpe 5-6-88

2008–09	Scunthorpe U	0	0		
2009–10	Scunthorpe U	1	0		
2010–11	Scunthorpe U	2	0		
2011–12	Scunthorpe U	28	0		
2012–13	Scunthorpe U	29	0		
2013–14	Scunthorpe U	46	0		
2014–15	Scunthorpe U	9	0	**115**	**0**
2015–16	Oxford U	23	0	**23**	**0**
2016–17	Blackpool	34	0	**34**	**0**
2017–18	Bristol R	23	0		
2018–19	Bristol R	2	0	**25**	**0**
2018–19	*Lincoln C*	0	0		

SMITH, Adam (G) **118 0**

H: 5 11 W: 11 00 b.Sunderland 23-11-92

2010–11	Leicester C	0	0		
2011–12	Leicester C	0	0		
2011–12	*Chesterfield*	0	0		
2011–12	*Bristol R*	0	0		
2012–13	Leicester C	0	0		
2013–14	Leicester C	0	0		
2013–14	*Stevenage*	0	0		
2014–15	Leicester C	0	0		
2014–15	*Mansfield T*	4	0	**4**	**0**
2015–16	Northampton T	46	0		
2016–17	Northampton T	40	0	**86**	**0**
2017–18	Bristol R	23	0		
2018–19	Bristol R	5	0	**28**	**0**

UPSON, Edward (M) **320 19**

H: 5 10 W: 11 07 b.Bury St Edmunds 21-11-89
Internationals: England U17, U19.

2006–07	Ipswich T	0	0		
2007–08	Ipswich T	0	0		
2008–09	Ipswich T	0	0		
2009–10	Ipswich T	0	0		
2009–10	*Barnet*	9	1	**9**	**1**
2010–11	Yeovil T	23	0		
2011–12	Yeovil T	41	3		
2012–13	Yeovil T	41	2		
2013–14	Yeovil T	24	4	**129**	**9**
2013–14	Millwall	10	0		
2014–15	Millwall	26	2		
2015–16	Millwall	32	0	**68**	**2**
2016–17	Milton Keynes D	42	3		
2017–18	Milton Keynes D	37	3	**79**	**6**
2018–19	Bristol R	35	1	**35**	**1**

WALKER, Zain (M) **0 0**

From Fulham.

2018–19	Bristol R	0	0		

WARWICK, Harry (F) **0 0**

2018–19	Bristol R	0	0		

WIDDRINGTON, Theo (M) **0 0**

2017–18	Portsmouth	0	0		
2018–19	Bristol R	0	0		

Players retained or with offer of contract
Armstrong, Liam James; Holmes, Dennis Tareiq Marcus; Kavanagh, Rhys Michael.

Scholars
Anderson, Graeme James; Bailey, Joshua Mark; Bremner, James Christopher; Clutton, Lewis David; Crawford, Isaiah Marco; Dillon, Osian Llyr; Fowler, George James; Hoole, Luca Anthony; Hulbert, Oliver George; Isherwood, Scott Benjamin; Mehew, Thomas Samuel James; Noble, Luc Joseph; Paul, Levi Anthony; Phillips, Kieran Lee; Raymond, Mason Stevie-Dean; Sell, Jack Michael Phillip; Thomas-Barker, Harry Craig; Tomlinson, Lucas George; Walker, Zain Alexander; Warwick, Harry Joshua.

BURNLEY (16)

BARDSLEY, Phillip (D) **305 8**

H: 5 11 W: 11 13 b.Salford 28-6-85
Internationals: Scotland Full caps.

2003–04	Manchester U	0	0		
2004–05	Manchester U	0	0		
2005–06	Manchester U	8	0		
2005–06	*Burnley*	6	0		
2006–07	Manchester U	0	0		
2006–07	*Rangers*	5	1	**5**	**1**
2006–07	*Aston Villa*	13	0	**13**	**0**
2007–08	Manchester U	0	0	**8**	**0**
2007–08	*Sheffield U*	16	0	**16**	**0**
2007–08	Sunderland	11	0		
2008–09	Sunderland	28	0		
2009–10	Sunderland	26	0		
2010–11	Sunderland	34	3		
2011–12	Sunderland	31	1		
2012–13	Sunderland	18	1		
2013–14	Sunderland	26	2	**174**	**7**
2014–15	Stoke C	25	0		
2015–16	Stoke C	11	0		
2016–17	Stoke C	15	0	**51**	**0**
2017–18	Burnley	13	0		
2018–19	Burnley	19	0	**38**	**0**

BARNES, Ashley (F) **342 83**

H: 6 0 W: 12 00 b.Bath 30-10-89
Internationals: Austria U20.

2006–07	Plymouth Arg	0	0		
2007–08	Plymouth Arg	0	0		
2008–09	Plymouth Arg	15	1		
2009–10	Plymouth Arg	7	1	**22**	**2**
2009–10	*Torquay U*	6	0	**6**	**0**
2009–10	*Brighton & HA*	8	4		
2010–11	Brighton & HA	42	18		
2011–12	Brighton & HA	43	11		
2012–13	Brighton & HA	34	8		
2013–14	Brighton & HA	22	5	**149**	**46**
2013–14	Burnley	21	3		
2014–15	Burnley	35	5		
2015–16	Burnley	8	0		
2016–17	Burnley	28	6		
2017–18	Burnley	36	9		
2018–19	Burnley	37	12	**165**	**35**

BENSON, Josh (M) **0 0**

H: 5 9 W: 11 03 b. 5-12-99
From Arsenal.

2018–19	Burnley	0	0		

BRADY, Robert (F) **218 19**

H: 5 9 W: 10 12 b.Belfast 14-1-92
Internationals: Republic of Ireland Youth, U21, Full caps.

2008–09	Manchester U	0	0		
2009–10	Manchester U	0	0		
2010–11	Manchester U	0	0		
2011–12	Manchester U	0	0		
2011–12	*Hull C*	39	3		
2012–13	Manchester U	0	0		
2012–13	Hull C	32	4		
2013–14	Hull C	16	3		
2014–15	Hull C	27	0	**114**	**10**
2015–16	Norwich C	36	3		
2016–17	Norwich C	23	4	**59**	**7**
2016–17	Burnley	14	1		
2017–18	Burnley	15	1		
2018–19	Burnley	16	0	**45**	**2**

CORK, Jack (D) **424 13**

H: 6 0 W: 10 12 b.Carshalton 25-6-89
Internationals: England U16, U17, U18, U19, U20, U21, Full caps. Great Britain.

2006–07	Chelsea	0	0		
2006–07	*Bournemouth*	7	0	**7**	**0**
2007–08	Chelsea	0	0		
2007–08	*Scunthorpe U*	34	2	**34**	**2**
2008–09	Chelsea	0	0		
2008–09	*Southampton*	23	0		
2008–09	*Watford*	19	0	**19**	**0**
2009–10	Chelsea	0	0		
2009–10	*Coventry C*	21	0	**21**	**0**
2009–10	*Burnley*	11	1		
2010–11	Chelsea	0	0		
2010–11	*Burnley*	40	3		
2011–12	Southampton	46	0		
2012–13	Southampton	28	0		

2013–14	Southampton	28	0		
2014–15	Southampton	12	2	**137**	**2**
2014–15	Swansea C	15	1		
2015–16	Swansea C	35	1		
2016–17	Swansea C	30	0	**80**	**2**
2017–18	Burnley	38	2		
2018–19	Burnley	37	1	**126**	**7**

CROUCH, Peter (F) 585 141
H: 6 7 W: 13 03 b.Macclesfield 30-1-81
Internationals: England U20, U21, B, Full caps.

1998–99	Tottenham H	0	0		
1999–2000	Tottenham H	0	0		
2000–01	QPR	42	10	**42**	**10**
2001–02	Portsmouth	37	18		
2001–02	Aston Villa	7	2		
2002–03	Aston Villa	14	0		
2003–04	Aston Villa	16	4	**37**	**6**
2003–04	*Norwich C*	15	4	**15**	**4**
2004–05	Southampton	27	12	**27**	**12**
2005–06	Liverpool	32	8		
2006–07	Liverpool	32	9		
2007–08	Liverpool	21	5	**85**	**22**
2008–09	Portsmouth	38	11		
2009–10	Portsmouth	0	0	**75**	**29**
2009–10	Tottenham H	38	8		
2010–11	Tottenham H	34	4		
2011–12	Tottenham H	1	0	**73**	**12**
2011–12	Stoke C	32	10		
2012–13	Stoke C	34	7		
2013–14	Stoke C	34	8		
2014–15	Stoke C	33	8		
2015–16	Stoke C	11	0		
2016–17	Stoke C	27	7		
2017–18	Stoke C	31	5		
2018–19	Stoke C	23	1	**225**	**46**
2018–19	Burnley	6	0	**6**	**0**

DEFOUR, Steven (M) 336 28
H: 5 8 W: 10 03 b.Mechelen 15-4-88
Internationals: Belgium U16, U17, U18, Full caps.

2004–05	Genk	4	0		
2005–06	Genk	26	1	**30**	**1**
2006–07	Standard Liege	29	4		
2007–08	Standard Liege	24	1		
2008–09	Standard Liege	33	4		
2009–10	Standard Liege	13	1		
2010–11	Standard Liege	27	3		
2011–12	Standard Liege	1	0	**127**	**13**
2011–12	Porto	24	1		
2012–13	Porto	25	2		
2013–14	Porto	16	0	**65**	**3**
2014–15	Anderlecht	29	6		
2015–16	Anderlecht	32	2		
2016–17	Anderlecht	2	1	**63**	**9**
2016–17	Burnley	21	1		
2017–18	Burnley	24	1		
2018–19	Burnley	6	0	**51**	**2**

DRISCOLL-GLENNON, Anthony (D) 0 0
b.Bootle 26-11-99

2018–19	Burnley	0	0		

DUNNE, Jimmy (D) 44 3
b.Drogheda 19-10-97
Internationals: Republic of Ireland U21.

2017–18	Burnley	0	0		
2017–18	*Accrington S*	20	0	**20**	**0**
2018–19	Burnley	0	0		
2018–19	*Hearts*	12	2	**12**	**2**
2018–19	*Sunderland*	12	1	**12**	**1**

GIBSON, Ben (D) 227 6
H: 6 1 W: 12 04 b.Nunthorpe 15-1-93
Internationals: England U17, U18, U20, U21.

2010–11	Middlesbrough	1	0		
2011–12	Middlesbrough	0	0		
2011–12	*Plymouth Arg*	13	0	**13**	**0**
2012–13	Middlesbrough	1	0		
2012–13	*Tranmere R*	28	1	**28**	**1**
2013–14	Middlesbrough	31	1		
2014–15	Middlesbrough	36	0		
2015–16	Middlesbrough	33	1		
2016–17	Middlesbrough	38	1		
2017–18	Middlesbrough	45	1	**185**	**4**
2018–19	Burnley	1	1	**1**	**1**

GUDMUNDSSON, Johann Berg (M) 284 31
H: 6 1 W: 12 06 b.Reykjavik 27-10-90
Internationals: Iceland U19, U21, Full caps.

2009–10	AZ	0	0		
2010–11	AZ	23	1		
2011–12	AZ	30	3		
2012–13	AZ	31	2		
2013–14	AZ	35	3	**119**	**9**
2014–15	Charlton Ath	41	10		
2015–16	Charlton Ath	40	6	**81**	**16**
2016–17	Burnley	20	1		
2017–18	Burnley	35	2		
2018–19	Burnley	29	3	**84**	**6**

HART, Joe (G) 439 0
H: 6 3 W: 13 03 b.Shrewsbury 19-4-87
Internationals: England U19, U21, Full caps.

2004–05	Shrewsbury T	6	0		
2005–06	Shrewsbury T	46	0	**52**	**0**
2006–07	Manchester C	1	0		
2006–07	*Tranmere R*	6	0	**6**	**0**
2006–07	*Blackpool*	5	0	**5**	**0**
2007–08	Manchester C	26	0		
2008–09	Manchester C	23	0		
2009–10	Manchester C	0	0		
2009–10	*Birmingham C*	36	0	**36**	**0**
2010–11	Manchester C	38	0		
2011–12	Manchester C	38	0		
2012–13	Manchester C	38	0		
2013–14	Manchester C	31	0		
2014–15	Manchester C	36	0		
2015–16	Manchester C	35	0		
2016–17	Manchester C	0	0		
2016–17	*Torino*	36	0	**36**	**0**
2017–18	Manchester C	0	0	**266**	**0**
2017–18	*West Ham U*	19	0	**19**	**0**
2018–19	Burnley	19	0	**19**	**0**

HEATON, Tom (G) 323 0
H: 6 1 W: 13 12 b.Chester 15-4-86
Internationals: England 16, U17, U18, U19, U21, Full caps.

2003–04	Manchester U	0	0		
2004–05	Manchester U	0	0		
2005–06	Manchester U	0	0		
2005–06	*Swindon T*	14	0	**14**	**0**
2006–07	Manchester U	0	0		
2007–08	Manchester U	0	0		
2008–09	Manchester U	0	0		
2008–09	*Cardiff C*	21	0		
2009–10	Manchester U	0	0		
2009–10	*Rochdale*	12	0	**12**	**0**
2009–10	*Wycombe W*	16	0	**16**	**0**
2010–11	Cardiff C	27	0		
2011–12	Cardiff C	2	0	**50**	**0**
2012–13	Bristol C	43	0	**43**	**0**
2013–14	Burnley	46	0		
2014–15	Burnley	38	0		
2015–16	Burnley	46	0		
2016–17	Burnley	35	0		
2017–18	Burnley	4	0		
2018–19	Burnley	19	0	**188**	**0**

HENDRICK, Jeff (M) 294 29
H: 6 1 W: 11 11 b.Dublin 31-1-92
Internationals: Republic of Ireland U17, U19, U21, Full caps.

2010–11	Derby Co	4	0		
2011–12	Derby Co	42	3		
2012–13	Derby Co	45	6		
2013–14	Derby Co	30	4		
2014–15	Derby Co	41	7		
2015–16	Derby Co	32	2		
2016–17	Derby Co	2	0	**196**	**22**
2016–17	Burnley	32	2		
2017–18	Burnley	34	2		
2018–19	Burnley	32	3	**98**	**7**

KOIKI, Ali (D) 15 0
b. 22-8-99
From Crystal Palace.

2018–19	Burnley	0	0		
2018–19	*Swindon T*	15	0	**15**	**0**

LEGZDINS, Adam (G) 114 0
H: 6 1 W: 14 02 b.Penkridge 28-11-86

2006–07	Birmingham C	0	0		
2007–08	Birmingham C	0	0		
2008–09	Crewe Alex	0	0		
2009–10	Crewe Alex	6	0	**6**	**0**
2010–11	Burton Alb	46	0		
2011–12	Derby Co	4	0		
2011–12	*Burton Alb*	1	0	**47**	**0**
2012–13	Derby Co	31	0		
2013–14	Derby Co	0	0	**35**	**0**
2014–15	Leyton Orient	11	0	**11**	**0**
2015–16	Birmingham C	5	0		
2016–17	Birmingham C	10	0	**15**	**0**
2017–18	Burnley	0	0		
2018–19	Burnley	0	0		

LENNON, Aaron (M) 399 35
H: 5 6 W: 10 03 b.Leeds 16-4-87
Internationals: England U17, U19, U21, B, Full caps.

2003–04	Leeds U	11	0		
2004–05	Leeds U	27	1	**38**	**1**
2005–06	Tottenham H	27	2		
2006–07	Tottenham H	26	3		
2007–08	Tottenham H	29	2		
2008–09	Tottenham H	35	5		
2009–10	Tottenham H	22	3		
2010–11	Tottenham H	34	3		
2011–12	Tottenham H	23	3		
2012–13	Tottenham H	34	4		
2013–14	Tottenham H	27	1		
2014–15	Tottenham H	9	0		
2014–15	*Everton*	14	2		
2015–16	Tottenham H	0	0	**266**	**26**
2015–16	Everton	25	5		
2016–17	Everton	11	0		
2017–18	Everton	15	0	**65**	**7**
2017–18	Burnley	14	0		
2018–19	Burnley	16	1	**30**	**1**

LINDEGAARD, Anders (G) 113 0
H: 6 4 W: 12 08 b.Odense 13-4-84
Internationals: Denmark U19, U20, Full caps.

2003–04	Odense	0	0		
2004–05	Odense	0	0		
2005–06	Odense	0	0		
2006–07	Odense	1	0		
2007–08	Odense	1	0		
2008–09	*Kolding*	10	0	**10**	**0**
2009	*Aalesund*	26	0		
2009	Odense	4	0	**6**	**0**
2010	Aalesund	30	0	**56**	**0**
2010–11	Manchester U	0	0		
2011–12	Manchester U	8	0		
2012–13	Manchester U	10	0		
2013–14	Manchester U	1	0		
2014–15	Manchester U	0	0		
2015–16	Manchester U	0	0	**19**	**0**
2015–16	WBA	0	0		
2015–16	*Preston NE*	14	0		
2016–17	Preston NE	8	0	**22**	**0**
2017–18	Burnley	0	0		
2018–19	Burnley	0	0		

LONG, Kevin (D) 136 7
H: 6 3 W: 13 01 b.Cork 18-8-90
Internationals: Republic of Ireland Full caps.

2009	Cork C	16	0	**16**	**0**
2009–10	Burnley	0	0		
2010–11	Burnley	0	0		
2010–11	*Accrington S*	15	0		
2011–12	Burnley	0	0		
2011–12	*Accrington S*	24	4	**39**	**4**
2011–12	*Rochdale*	16	0	**16**	**0**
2012–13	Burnley	14	0		
2012–13	*Portsmouth*	5	0	**5**	**0**
2013–14	Burnley	7	0		
2014–15	Burnley	1	0		
2015–16	Burnley	0	0		
2015–16	*Barnsley*	11	2	**11**	**2**
2015–16	*Milton Keynes D*	2	0	**2**	**0**
2016–17	Burnley	3	0		
2017–18	Burnley	16	1		
2018–19	Burnley	6	0	**47**	**1**

LOWTON, Matt (M) 265 13
H: 5 11 W: 12 04 b.Chesterfield 9-6-89

2008–09	Sheffield U	0	0		
2009–10	Sheffield U	2	0		
2009–10	*Ferencvaros*	5	0	**5**	**0**
2010–11	Sheffield U	32	4		
2011–12	Sheffield U	44	6	**78**	**10**
2012–13	Aston Villa	37	2		
2013–14	Aston Villa	23	0		
2014–15	Aston Villa	12	0	**72**	**2**
2015–16	Burnley	27	1		
2016–17	Burnley	36	0		
2017–18	Burnley	26	0		
2018–19	Burnley	21	0	**110**	**1**

McNEIL, Dwight (F) 22 3
b. 22-11-99
Internationals: England U20.

2017–18	Burnley	1	0		
2018–19	Burnley	21	3	**22**	**3**

MEE, Ben (D) 283 6
H: 5 11 W: 11 09 b.Sale 21-9-89
Internationals: England U19, U20, U21.

2007–08	Manchester C	0	0		
2008–09	Manchester C	0	0		
2009–10	Manchester C	0	0		

2010–11	Manchester C	0	0		
2010–11	*Leicester C*	15	0	**15**	**0**
2011–12	Manchester C	0	0		
2011–12	Burnley	31	0		
2012–13	Burnley	19	1		
2013–14	Burnley	38	0		
2014–15	Burnley	33	2		
2015–16	Burnley	46	2		
2016–17	Burnley	34	1		
2017–18	Burnley	29	0		
2018–19	Burnley	38	0	**268**	**6**

POPE, Nick (G) 112 0
H: 6 3 W: 11 13 b.Cambridge 19-4-92
Internationals: England Full caps.

2011–12	Charlton Ath	0	0		
2012–13	Charlton Ath	1	0		
2013–14	Charlton Ath	0	0		
2013–14	*York C*	22	0	**22**	**0**
2014–15	Charlton Ath	8	0		
2014–15	*Bury*	22	0	**22**	**0**
2015–16	Charlton Ath	24	0	**33**	**0**
2016–17	Burnley	0	0		
2017–18	Burnley	35	0		
2018–19	Burnley	0	0	**35**	**0**

TARKOWSKI, James (D) 231 12
H: 6 1 W: 12 10 b.Manchester 19-11-92
Internationals: England Full caps.

2010–11	Oldham Ath	9	0		
2011–12	Oldham Ath	16	1		
2012–13	Oldham Ath	21	2		
2013–14	Oldham Ath	26	2	**72**	**5**
2013–14	Brentford	13	2		
2014–15	Brentford	34	1		
2015–16	Brentford	23	1	**70**	**4**
2015–16	Burnley	4	0		
2016–17	Burnley	19	0		
2017–18	Burnley	31	0		
2018–19	Burnley	35	3	**89**	**3**

TAYLOR, Charlie (D) 188 3
H: 5 9 W: 11 00 b.York 18-9-93
Internationals: England U19.

2011–12	Leeds U	2	0		
2011–12	*Bradford C*	3	0	**3**	**0**
2012–13	Leeds U	0	0		
2012–13	*York C*	4	0	**4**	**0**
2012–13	*Inverness CT*	7	0	**7**	**0**
2013–14	Leeds U	0	0		
2013–14	*Fleetwood T*	32	0	**32**	**0**
2014–15	Leeds U	23	2		
2015–16	Leeds U	39	1		
2016–17	Leeds U	29	0	**93**	**3**
2017–18	Burnley	11	0		
2018–19	Burnley	38	0	**49**	**0**

VYDRA, Matej (F) 240 73
H: 5 10 W: 11 09 b.Chotebor 1-5-92
Internationals: Czech Republic U16, U17, U18, U19, U21, Full caps.

2009–10	Banik Ostrava	13	4	**13**	**4**
2010–11	Udinese	2	0		
2011–12	Udinese	0	0		
2011–12	*Club Brugge*	1	0	**1**	**0**
2012–13	Udinese	0	0		
2012–13	*Watford*	41	20		
2013–14	Udinese	0	0		
2013–14	*WBA*	23	3	**23**	**3**
2014–15	Udinese	0	0	**2**	**0**
2014–15	*Watford*	42	16		
2015–16	Watford	0	0		
2015–16	*Reading*	31	3	**31**	**3**
2016–17	Watford	1	0	**84**	**36**
2016–17	Derby Co	33	5		
2017–18	Derby Co	40	21	**73**	**26**
2018–19	Burnley	13	1	**13**	**1**

WALTERS, Jon (F) 495 94
H: 6 0 W: 12 06 b.Birkenhead 20-9-83
Internationals: Republic of Ireland U21, B, Full caps.

2001–02	Bolton W	0	0		
2002–03	Bolton W	4	0		
2002–03	*Hull C*	11	5		
2003–04	Bolton W	0	0	**4**	**0**
2003–04	Crewe Alex	0	0		
2003–04	*Barnsley*	8	0	**8**	**0**
2003–04	Hull C	16	1		
2004–05	Hull C	21	1	**48**	**7**
2004–05	*Scunthorpe U*	3	0	**3**	**0**
2005–06	Wrexham	38	5	**38**	**5**
2006–07	Chester C	26	9	**26**	**9**
2006–07	Ipswich T	16	4		
2007–08	Ipswich T	40	13		
2008–09	Ipswich T	36	5		
2009–10	Ipswich T	43	8		
2010–11	Ipswich T	1	0		
2010–11	Stoke C	36	6		
2011–12	Stoke C	38	7		
2012–13	Stoke C	38	8		
2013–14	Stoke C	32	5		
2014–15	Stoke C	32	8		
2015–16	Stoke C	27	5		
2016–17	Stoke C	23	4	**226**	**43**
2017–18	Burnley	3	0		
2018–19	Burnley	0	0	**3**	**0**
2018–19	*Ipswich T*	3	0	**139**	**30**

WARD, Stephen (D) 439 27
H: 5 11 W: 12 02 b.Dublin 20-8-85
Internationals: Republic of Ireland U20, U21, B, Full caps.

2003	Bohemians	6	0		
2004	Bohemians	16	2		
2005	Bohemians	29	7		
2006	Bohemians	21	2	**72**	**11**
2006–07	Wolverhampton W	18	3		
2007–08	Wolverhampton W	29	0		
2008–09	Wolverhampton W	42	0		
2009–10	Wolverhampton W	22	0		
2010–11	Wolverhampton W	34	1		
2011–12	Wolverhampton W	38	3		
2012–13	Wolverhampton W	39	2		
2013–14	Wolverhampton W	0	0	**222**	**9**
2013–14	*Brighton & HA*	44	4	**44**	**4**
2014–15	Burnley	9	0		
2015–16	Burnley	24	1		
2016–17	Burnley	37	1		
2017–18	Burnley	28	1		
2018–19	Burnley	3	0	**101**	**3**

WELLS, Nahki (F) 287 94
H: 5 7 W: 11 00 b.Bermuda 1-6-90
Internationals: Bermuda Full caps.

2010–11	Carlisle U	3	0	**3**	**0**
2011–12	Bradford C	33	10		
2012–13	Bradford C	39	18		
2013–14	Bradford C	19	14	**91**	**42**
2013–14	Huddersfield T	22	7		
2014–15	Huddersfield T	35	11		
2015–16	Huddersfield T	44	17		
2016–17	Huddersfield T	43	10		
2017–18	Huddersfield T	0	0	**144**	**45**
2017–18	Burnley	9	0		
2018–19	Burnley	0	0	**9**	**0**
2018–19	*QPR*	40	7	**40**	**7**

WESTWOOD, Ashley (M) 337 21
H: 5 10 W: 11 00 b.Nantwich 1-4-90

2008–09	Crewe Alex	2	0		
2009–10	Crewe Alex	36	6		
2010–11	Crewe Alex	46	5		
2011–12	Crewe Alex	41	3		
2012–13	Crewe Alex	3	0	**128**	**14**
2012–13	Aston Villa	30	0		
2013–14	Aston Villa	35	3		
2014–15	Aston Villa	27	0		
2015–16	Aston Villa	32	2		
2016–17	Aston Villa	23	0	**147**	**5**
2016–17	Burnley	9	0		
2017–18	Burnley	19	0		
2018–19	Burnley	34	2	**62**	**2**

WOOD, Chris (F) 324 107
H: 6 3 W: 12 10 b.Auckland 7-12-91
Internationals: New Zealand U17, U23, Full caps.

2008–09	WBA	2	0		
2009–10	WBA	18	1		
2010–11	WBA	1	0		
2010–11	*Barnsley*	7	0	**7**	**0**
2010–11	*Brighton & HA*	29	8	**29**	**8**
2011–12	WBA	0	0		
2011–12	*Birmingham C*	23	9	**23**	**9**
2011–12	*Bristol C*	19	3	**19**	**3**
2012–13	WBA	0	0	**21**	**1**
2012–13	*Millwall*	19	11	**19**	**11**
2012–13	Leicester C	20	9		
2013–14	Leicester C	26	4		
2014–15	Leicester C	7	1	**53**	**14**
2014–15	*Ipswich T*	8	0	**8**	**0**
2015–16	Leeds U	36	13		
2016–17	Leeds U	44	27		
2017–18	Leeds U	3	1	**83**	**41**
2017–18	Burnley	24	10		
2018–19	Burnley	38	10	**62**	**20**

Players retained or with offer of contract
Agyei, Daniel Ebenezer Kwasi; Bayode, Olatunde Tobias; Cropper, Jordan Geoffrey; Goodridge, Mace Lewin; Harker, Robert William; McMahon, George James; N'Guessan, Christian Dashiell; O'Neill, Aiden Connor; Perkins, Teddy Arthur; Steels, Vinnie Barry; Younger, Oliver.

Scholars
Allan, Meredith Dylon Thomas; Allen, Harry George; Calderbank-Park, Kai; Chima, Udoka Godwill; Conley, Joseph Thomas; Conn, Christopher Seamus Michael; Fenlon, Rhys-James Roy; George, Mitchell Colin; Harris, William; Kershaw, Ethan Samuel; Major, Jayden Anthony; Moss, Daniel Thomas; Mupariwa, Terry Tauyanashe; Patterson, Kane Mazo; Pruti, Edon; Rain, Matthew; Taylor, Richard Akinfolarin; Thomas, Bobby Craig; Tucker, Ne'Jai; Wilson, Scott John; Woods, Oscar Gordon; Yari, Kian.

BURTON ALB (17)

AKINS, Lucas (F) 384 65
H: 5 10 W: 11 07 b.Huddersfield 25-2-89

2006–07	Huddersfield T	2	0		
2007–08	Huddersfield T	3	0	**5**	**0**
2008–09	Hamilton A	11	0		
2008–09	*Partick Thistle*	9	1	**9**	**1**
2009–10	Hamilton A	0	0	**11**	**0**
2010–11	Tranmere R	33	2		
2011–12	Tranmere R	44	5	**77**	**7**
2012–13	Stevenage	46	10		
2013–14	Stevenage	31	3	**77**	**13**
2014–15	Burton Alb	35	9		
2015–16	Burton Alb	44	12		
2016–17	Burton Alb	38	5		
2017–18	Burton Alb	42	5		
2018–19	Burton Alb	46	13	**205**	**44**

ALLEN, Jamie (M) 204 19
H: 5 11 W: 11 05 b.Rochdale 29-1-95

2012–13	Rochdale	0	0		
2013–14	Rochdale	25	6		
2014–15	Rochdale	35	0		
2015–16	Rochdale	38	3		
2016–17	Rochdale	31	2		
2017–18	Rochdale	4	0	**133**	**11**
2017–18	Burton Alb	29	1		
2018–19	Burton Alb	42	7	**71**	**8**

BEARDSLEY, Chris (F) 203 21
H: 6 0 W: 12 12 b.Derby 28-2-84

2002–03	Mansfield T	5	0		
2003–04	Mansfield T	15	1		
2004–05	Doncaster R	4	0	**4**	**0**
2004–05	Kidderminster H	25	5	**25**	**5**
2005–06	Mansfield T	3	0		
2006–07	Mansfield T	10	0		

From Rushden & D, York C, Kettering T.

2010–11	Stevenage	23	1		
2011–12	Stevenage	31	7		
2012–13	Preston NE	19	1		
2013–14	Preston NE	0	0	**19**	**1**
2013–14	*Bristol R*	24	1	**24**	**1**
2014–15	Stevenage	29	4	**83**	**12**
2015–16	Mansfield T	14	1	**47**	**2**
2018–19	Burton Alb	1	0	**1**	**0**

BOYCE, Liam (F) 152 62
H: 6 0 W: 13 01 b.Belfast 8-4-91
Internationals: Northern Ireland U19, U21, Full caps.
From Cliftonville.

2014–15	Ross Co	30	10		
2015–16	Ross Co	35	15		
2016–17	Ross Co	34	23	**99**	**48**
2017–18	Burton Alb	16	3		
2018–19	Burton Alb	37	11	**53**	**14**

BRAYFORD, John (D) 377 10
H: 5 8 W: 11 02 b.Stoke 29-12-87
Internationals: England C.

2008–09	Crewe Alex	36	2		
2009–10	Crewe Alex	45	0	**81**	**2**
2010–11	Derby Co	46	1		
2011–12	Derby Co	23	0		
2012–13	Derby Co	40	1	**109**	**2**
2013–14	Cardiff C	0	0		
2013–14	*Sheffield U*	15	1		
2014–15	Cardiff C	26	0	**26**	**0**
2014–15	Sheffield U	22	1		
2015–16	Sheffield U	19	1		
2016–17	Sheffield U	3	0		
2016–17	*Burton Alb*	33	0		
2017–18	Sheffield U	0	0	**59**	**3**
2017–18	Burton Alb	28	0		
2018–19	Burton Alb	41	3	**102**	**3**

BUXTON, Jake (D) **391 17**
H: 6 1 W: 13 05 b.Sutton-in-Ashfield 4-3-85

2002–03	Mansfield T	3	0		
2003–04	Mansfield T	9	1		
2004–05	Mansfield T	30	1		
2005–06	Mansfield T	39	0		
2006–07	Mansfield T	30	1		
2007–08	Mansfield T	40	2		
2008–09	Mansfield T	0	0	**151**	**5**
From Burton Alb.					
2008–09	Derby Co	0	0		
2009–10	Derby Co	19	1		
2010–11	Derby Co	1	0		
2011–12	Derby Co	21	2		
2012–13	Derby Co	31	3		
2013–14	Derby Co	45	2		
2014–15	Derby Co	19	3		
2015–16	Derby Co	3	0	**139**	**11**
2016–17	Wigan Ath	39	1	**39**	**1**
2017–18	Burton Alb	32	0		
2018–19	Burton Alb	30	0	**62**	**0**

BYWATER, Steve (G) **384 0**
H: 6 2 W: 12 10 b.Manchester 7-6-81
Internationals: England U19, U21.

1997–98	Rochdale	0	0		
1998–99	West Ham U	0	0		
1999–2000	West Ham U	4	0		
1999–2000	*Wycombe W*	2	0	**2**	**0**
1999–2000	*Hull C*	4	0	**4**	**0**
2000–01	West Ham U	1	0		
2001–02	West Ham U	0	0		
2001–02	*Wolverhampton W*	0	0		
2001–02	*Cardiff C*	0	0		
2002–03	West Ham U	0	0		
2003–04	West Ham U	17	0		
2004–05	West Ham U	36	0		
2005–06	West Ham U	1	0	**59**	**0**
2005–06	*Coventry C*	14	0	**14**	**0**
2006–07	Derby Co	37	0		
2007–08	Derby Co	18	0		
2007–08	*Ipswich T*	17	0	**17**	**0**
2008–09	Derby Co	31	0		
2009–10	Derby Co	42	0		
2010–11	Derby Co	22	0	**150**	**0**
2010–11	*Cardiff C*	8	0	**8**	**0**
2011–12	Sheffield W	32	0		
2012–13	Sheffield W	0	0	**32**	**0**
2013–14	Millwall	7	0		
2014–15	Millwall	0	0	**7**	**0**
2014–15	*Gillingham*	13	0	**13**	**0**
2014–15	Doncaster R	21	0	**21**	**0**
2015–16	Burton Alb	0	0		
2016–17	Burton Alb	5	0		
2017–18	Burton Alb	44	0		
2018–19	Burton Alb	8	0	**57**	**0**

CAMPBELL, Harry (G) **1 0**
H: 6 1 W: 12 02 b.Blackburn 16-11-95

2015–16	Bolton W	0	0		
2016–17	Burton Alb	0	0		
2017–18	Burton Alb	0	0		
2018–19	Burton Alb	1	0	**1**	**0**

DANIEL, Colin (M) **339 32**
H: 5 11 W: 11 06 b.Eastwood 15-2-88

2006–07	Crewe Alex	0	0		
2007–08	Crewe Alex	1	0		
2008–09	Crewe Alex	13	1	**14**	**1**
2008–09	*Macclesfield T*	8	0		
2009–10	Macclesfield T	38	3		
2010–11	Macclesfield T	43	8		
2011–12	Macclesfield T	36	2	**125**	**13**
2013–14	Mansfield T	28	2		
2014–15	Port Vale	28	4		
2015–16	Port Vale	20	2	**48**	**6**
2015–16	*Mansfield T*	9	2	**37**	**4**
2016–17	Blackpool	34	4		
2017–18	Blackpool	44	4	**78**	**8**
2018–19	Peterborough U	20	0	**20**	**0**
2018–19	Burton Alb	17	0	**17**	**0**

FOX, Ben (M) **28 1**
H: 5 11 W: 12 00 b.Burton upon Trent 1-2-98

2016–17	Burton Alb	1	0		
2017–18	Burton Alb	0	0		
2018–19	Burton Alb	27	1	**28**	**1**

FRASER, Scott (M) **161 20**
H: 6 0 W: 10 12 b.Dundee 30-3-95

2013–14	Dundee U	1	0		
2014–15	Dundee U	0	0		
2014–15	*Airdrieonians*	38	5	**38**	**5**
2015–16	Dundee U	32	1		
2016–17	Dundee U	25	4		
2017–18	Dundee U	23	4	**81**	**9**
2018–19	Burton Alb	42	6	**42**	**6**

HARNESS, Marcus (M) **103 6**
H: 6 0 W: 11 00 b.Coventry 1-8-94

2013–14	Burton Alb	3	0		
2014–15	Burton Alb	18	0		
2015–16	Burton Alb	5	0		
2016–17	Burton Alb	10	0		
2017–18	Burton Alb	0	0		
2017–18	*Port Vale*	35	1	**35**	**1**
2018–19	Burton Alb	32	5	**68**	**5**

HART, Ben (D) **0 0**

2018–19	Burton Alb	0	0		

HAWKINS, Callum (G) **0 0**
b.Rotherham 12-12-99

2018–19	Burton Alb	0	0		

HESKETH, Jake (M) **34 3**
H: 5 6 W: 9 13 b. 27-3-96

2014–15	Southampton	2	0		
2015–16	Southampton	0	0		
2016–17	Southampton	0	0		
2017–18	Southampton	0	0		
2018–19	Southampton	0	0	**2**	**0**
2018–19	Burton Alb	16	1	**16**	**1**
2018–19	*Milton Keynes D*	16	2	**16**	**2**

HODGE, Elliot (M) **3 0**
b. 23-12-95

2017–18	Notts Co	1	0	**1**	**0**
2018–19	Burton Alb	2	0	**2**	**0**

HUTCHINSON, Reece (D) **25 0**
b. 14-4-00

2017–18	Burton Alb	0	0		
2018–19	Burton Alb	25	0	**25**	**0**

McCRORY, Damien (M) **302 11**
H: 6 2 W: 12 10 b.Limerick 22-2-90
Internationals: Republic of Ireland U18, U19.

2008–09	Plymouth Arg	0	0		
2008–09	*Port Vale*	12	0		
2009–10	Plymouth Arg	0	0		
2009–10	*Port Vale*	5	0	**17**	**0**
2009–10	*Grimsby T*	10	0	**10**	**0**
2009–10	Dagenham & R	20	0		
2010–11	Dagenham & R	23	0		
2011–12	Dagenham & R	33	1	**76**	**1**
2012–13	Burton Alb	42	1		
2013–14	Burton Alb	40	1		
2014–15	Burton Alb	34	5		
2015–16	Burton Alb	38	3		
2016–17	Burton Alb	16	0		
2017–18	Burton Alb	11	0		
2017–18	*Portsmouth*	3	0	**3**	**0**
2018–19	Burton Alb	15	0	**196**	**10**

MILLER, Will (M) **47 2**
H: 5 6 W: 10 01 b.London 8-6-96
Internationals: England U18.

2016–17	Tottenham H	0	0		
2016–17	*Burton Alb*	15	1		
2017–18	Burton Alb	10	0		
2018–19	Burton Alb	22	1	**47**	**2**

QUINN, Stephen (M) **398 26**
H: 5 6 W: 9 08 b.Dublin 4-4-86
Internationals: Republic of Ireland U21, Full caps.

2005–06	Sheffield U	0	0		
2005–06	*Milton Keynes D*	15	0	**15**	**0**
2005–06	*Rotherham U*	16	0	**16**	**0**
2006–07	Sheffield U	15	2		
2007–08	Sheffield U	19	2		
2008–09	Sheffield U	43	7		
2009–10	Sheffield U	44	4		
2010–11	Sheffield U	37	1		
2011–12	Sheffield U	45	4		
2012–13	Sheffield U	3	0	**206**	**20**
2012–13	Hull C	42	3		
2013–14	Hull C	15	0		
2014–15	Hull C	28	1	**85**	**4**
2015–16	Reading	27	1		
2016–17	Reading	7	0		
2017–18	Reading	0	0	**34**	**1**
2018–19	Burton Alb	42	1	**42**	**1**

SBARRA, Joe (M) **27 0**
H: 5 10 W: 11 00 b.Lichfield 21-12-98

2016–17	Burton Alb	1	0		
2017–18	Burton Alb	17	0		
2018–19	Burton Alb	9	0	**27**	**0**

SORDELL, Marvin (F) **278 50**
H: 5 9 W: 12 06 b.Pinner 17-2-91
Internationals: England U20, U21. Great Britain.

2009–10	Watford	6	1		
2009–10	*Tranmere R*	8	1	**8**	**1**
2010–11	Watford	43	12		
2011–12	Watford	26	8	**75**	**21**
2011–12	Bolton W	3	0		
2012–13	Bolton W	22	4		
2013–14	Bolton W	0	0	**25**	**4**
2013–14	*Charlton Ath*	31	7	**31**	**7**
2014–15	Burnley	14	0		
2015–16	Burnley	3	0	**17**	**0**
2015–16	Colchester U	21	4	**21**	**4**
2016–17	Coventry C	20	4	**20**	**4**
2016–17	Burton Alb	21	4		
2017–18	Burton Alb	40	3		
2018–19	Burton Alb	12	2	**73**	**9**
2018–19	*Northampton T*	8	0	**8**	**0**

TEMPLETON, David (M) **251 62**
H: 5 8 W: 8 12 b.Glasgow 7-1-89
Internationals: Scotland U19, U21.

2005–06	Stenhousemuir	17	8		
2006–07	Stenhousemuir	13	3	**30**	**11**
2007–08	Hearts	0	0		
2007–08	*Raith R*	15	4	**15**	**4**
2008–09	Hearts	3	0		
2009–10	Hearts	16	2		
2010–11	Hearts	33	7		
2011–12	Hearts	27	1		
2012–13	Hearts	2	1	**81**	**11**
2012–13	Rangers	24	16		
2013–14	Rangers	20	3		
2014–15	Rangers	22	3		
2015–16	Rangers	1	0	**67**	**22**
2016–17	Hamilton A	3	1		
2017–18	Hamilton A	27	8	**30**	**9**
2018–19	Burton Alb	28	5	**28**	**5**

WALLACE, Kieran (M) **37 1**
H: 6 1 W: 11 11 b.Nottingham 26-1-95
Internationals: England U16, U17.

2014–15	Sheffield U	4	0		
2015–16	Sheffield U	11	0		
2016–17	Sheffield U	0	0	**15**	**0**
2016–17	*Fleetwood T*	0	0		
From Matlock T.					
2018–19	Burton Alb	22	1	**22**	**1**

Players retained or with offer of contract
Livesey, Jack Kinloch; Myers-Harness, Marcus Anthony.

Scholars
Armitage, Thomas George; Bromfield, Jack; Carter, Tyo Kaden; Clamp, Kyle John William; Cooke, Daniel Thomas; Fairbrother, Oliver Joe; Ganley, Regan Scott; Gilligan, Ciaran Patrick; Hart, Benjamin Ethan; Hewlett, Thomas Paul; Holmes, Jack Harry; Lal, Rueben Arun; Mallass, Noaman; McDonnell, Cael Liam; Oddy, Charlie Andrew; Shittu, Akinola Emmanuel; Smith, Nathan John; Vale, Ethan Peter William.

BURY (18)

ADAMS, Joe (M) **3 0**
b. 13-2-01
Internationals: Wales U17, U19.

2017–18	Bury	2	0		
2018–19	Bury	1	0	**3**	**0**

ADAMS, Nicky (F) **472 38**
H: 5 10 W: 11 00 b.Bolton 16-10-86
Internationals: Wales U21.

2005–06	Bury	15	1		
2006–07	Bury	19	1		
2007–08	Bury	43	12		
2008–09	Leicester C	12	0		
2008–09	*Rochdale*	14	1		
2009–10	Leicester C	18	0	**30**	**0**
2009–10	*Leyton Orient*	6	0	**6**	**0**
2010–11	Brentford	7	0	**7**	**0**
2010–11	Rochdale	30	0		
2011–12	Rochdale	41	4	**85**	**5**
2012–13	Crawley T	46	8		
2013–14	Crawley T	24	1	**70**	**9**
2013–14	Rotherham U	15	1	**15**	**1**
2013–14	Bury	0	0		
2014–15	Bury	38	1		
2015–16	Northampton T	39	3	**39**	**3**
2016–17	Carlisle U	42	3		

2017–18	Carlisle U	17	0	**59**	**3**
2018–19	Bury	46	2	**161**	**17**

AIMSON, Will (D) **89** **4**
H: 5 10 W: 11 00 b.Christchurch 1-1-94

2013–14	Hull C	0	0		
2014–15	Hull C	0	0		
2014–15	*Tranmere R*	2	0	**2**	**0**
2015–16	Hull C	0	0		
2015–16	Blackpool	15	0		
2016–17	Blackpool	18	0		
2017–18	Blackpool	17	0	**50**	**0**
2018–19	Bury	37	4	**37**	**4**

ALLARDYCE, Sam (D) **0** **0**
b. 1-9-00
From Manchester U.

2018–19	Bury	0	0		

ARCHER, Jordan (F) **160** **0**

2011–12	Tottenham H	0	0		
2012–13	Tottenham H	0	0		
2012–13	*Wycombe W*	27	0	**27**	**0**
2013–14	Tottenham H	0	0		
2014–15	Tottenham H	0	0		
2014–15	*Northampton T*	13	0	**13**	**0**
2014–15	*Millwall*	0	0		
2015–16	Millwall	39	0		
2016–17	Millwall	36	0		
2017–18	Millwall	45	0	**120**	**0**
2018–19	Bury	0	0		

BARJONAS, Jamie (M) **13** **0**
H: 5 8 W: 11 05 b.Glasgow 24-1-99
Internationals: Scotland U15, U16, U17, U19.

2016–17	Rangers	4	0		
2017–18	Rangers	5	0		
2018–19	Rangers	0	0	**9**	**0**

On loan from Rangers.

2018–19	Bury	4	0	**4**	**0**

BECKFORD, Jermaine (F) **359** **135**
H: 6 2 W: 13 02 b.Ealing 9-12-83
Internationals: Jamaica Full caps.

2005–06	Leeds U	5	0		
2006–07	Leeds U	5	0		
2006–07	*Carlisle U*	4	1	**4**	**1**
2006–07	*Scunthorpe U*	18	8	**18**	**8**
2007–08	Leeds U	40	20		
2008–09	Leeds U	34	26		
2009–10	Leeds U	42	25	**126**	**71**
2010–11	Everton	32	8		
2011–12	Everton	2	0	**34**	**8**
2011–12	Leicester C	39	9		
2012–13	Leicester C	4	0	**43**	**9**
2012–13	*Huddersfield T*	21	8	**21**	**8**
2013–14	Bolton W	33	7		
2014–15	Bolton W	13	0	**46**	**7**
2014–15	*Preston NE*	23	12		
2015–16	Preston NE	10	2		
2016–17	Preston NE	18	1	**51**	**15**
2017–18	Bury	15	8		
2018–19	Bury	1	0	**16**	**8**

BROWN, Aaron (F) **0** **0**
Internationals: Northern Ireland U17

2018–19	Bury	0	0		

BUNN, Harry (F) **177** **23**
H: 5 9 W: 11 10 b.Oldham 25-11-92

2010–11	Manchester C	0	0		
2011–12	Manchester C	0	0		
2011–12	*Rochdale*	6	0	**6**	**0**
2011–12	*Preston NE*	1	1	**1**	**1**
2011–12	*Oldham Ath*	11	0	**11**	**0**
2012–13	Manchester C	0	0		
2012–13	*Crewe Alex*	4	0	**4**	**0**
2013–14	Manchester C	0	0		
2013–14	*Sheffield U*	2	0	**2**	**0**
2013–14	*Huddersfield T*	3	0		
2014–15	Manchester C	0	0		
2014–15	*Huddersfield T*	30	9		
2015–16	Huddersfield T	42	6		
2016–17	Huddersfield T	16	0	**91**	**15**
2017–18	Bury	37	3		
2018–19	Bury	1	0	**38**	**3**
2018–19	*Southend U*	24	4	**24**	**4**

COONEY, Ryan (M) **21** **0**
b. 26-2-00

2016–17	Bury	0	0		
2017–18	Bury	12	0		
2018–19	Bury	9	0	**21**	**0**

DANNS, Neil (M) **483** **72**
H: 5 10 W: 10 12 b.Liverpool 23-11-82
Internationals: Guyana Full caps.

2000–01	Blackburn R	0	0		
2001–02	Blackburn R	0	0		
2002–03	Blackburn R	2	0		
2003–04	Blackpool	12	2		
2003–04	Blackburn R	1	0		
2003–04	*Hartlepool U*	9	1	**9**	**1**
2004–05	Blackburn R	0	0	**3**	**0**
2004–05	Colchester U	32	11		
2005–06	Colchester U	41	8	**73**	**19**
2006–07	Birmingham C	29	3		
2007–08	Birmingham C	2	0	**31**	**3**
2007–08	Crystal Palace	4	0		
2008–09	Crystal Palace	20	2		
2009–10	Crystal Palace	42	8		
2010–11	Crystal Palace	37	8	**103**	**18**
2011–12	Leicester C	29	5		
2012–13	Leicester C	1	0		
2012–13	*Bristol C*	9	2	**9**	**2**
2012–13	*Huddersfield T*	17	2	**17**	**2**
2013–14	Leicester C	0	0	**30**	**5**
2013–14	Bolton W	33	6		
2014–15	Bolton W	41	1		
2015–16	Bolton W	32	2	**106**	**9**
2016–17	Bury	18	2		
2016–17	*Blackpool*	13	2	**25**	**4**
2017–18	Bury	25	5		
2018–19	Bury	34	2	**77**	**9**

DAWSON, Stephen (M) **460** **19**
H: 5 9 W: 11 09 b.Dublin 4-12-85
Internationals: Republic of Ireland U21.

2003–04	Leicester C	0	0		
2004–05	Leicester C	0	0		
2005–06	Mansfield T	40	1		
2006–07	Mansfield T	34	1		
2007–08	Mansfield T	43	2	**117**	**4**
2008–09	Bury	43	2		
2009–10	Bury	45	4		
2010–11	Leyton Orient	40	2		
2011–12	Leyton Orient	20	1	**60**	**3**
2011–12	Barnsley	12	0		
2012–13	Barnsley	32	4		
2013–14	Barnsley	37	1	**81**	**5**
2014–15	Rochdale	30	0	**30**	**0**
2015–16	Scunthorpe U	23	0		
2016–17	Scunthorpe U	43	1	**66**	**1**
2016–17	Bury	0	0		
2017–18	Bury	13	0		
2018–19	Bury	5	0	**106**	**6**

EDWARDS, Phil (D) **476** **34**
H: 5 8 W: 11 03 b.Bootle 8-11-85

2005–06	Wigan Ath	0	0		
2006–07	Accrington S	33	1		
2007–08	Accrington S	31	1		
2008–09	Accrington S	46	0		
2009–10	Accrington S	46	8		
2010–11	Accrington S	44	13	**200**	**23**
2011–12	Stevenage	22	0	**22**	**0**
2011–12	*Rochdale*	3	0		
2012–13	Rochdale	44	0	**47**	**0**
2013–14	Burton Alb	41	2		
2014–15	Burton Alb	45	6		
2015–16	Burton Alb	46	0		
2016–17	Burton Alb	0	0	**132**	**8**
2016–17	*Oxford U*	38	3	**38**	**3**
2017–18	Bury	37	0		
2018–19	Bury	0	0	**37**	**0**

HILL, Cameron (M) **0** **0**

2017–18	Bury	0	0		
2018–19	Bury	0	0		

HULME, Callum (M) **1** **0**
b. 10-11-00
From Manchester C.

2016–17	Bury	0	0		
2017–18	Bury	0	0		
2018–19	Bury	1	0	**1**	**0**

MALONEY, Scott (G) **0** **0**

2017–18	Bury	0	0		
2018–19	Bury	0	0		

MAYNARD, Nicky (F) **357** **114**
H: 5 11 W: 11 00 b.Winsford 11-12-86

2005–06	Crewe Alex	1	1		
2006–07	Crewe Alex	31	16		
2007–08	Crewe Alex	27	14	**59**	**31**
2008–09	Bristol C	43	11		
2009–10	Bristol C	42	20		
2010–11	Bristol C	13	6		
2011–12	Bristol C	27	8	**125**	**45**
2011–12	West Ham U	14	2		
2012–13	West Ham U	0	0	**14**	**2**
2012–13	Cardiff C	4	1		
2013–14	Cardiff C	8	0		
2013–14	*Wigan Ath*	16	4	**16**	**4**
2014–15	Cardiff C	10	1	**22**	**2**
2015–16	Milton Keynes D	35	7		
2016–17	Milton Keynes D	31	2	**66**	**9**
2017–18	Aberdeen	18	0	**18**	**0**
2018–19	Bury	37	21	**37**	**21**

MAYOR, Danny (M) **287** **32**
H: 6 0 W: 11 12 b.Leyland 18-10-90

2008–09	Preston NE	0	0		
2008–09	*Tranmere R*	3	0	**3**	**0**
2009–10	Preston NE	7	0		
2010–11	Preston NE	21	0		
2011–12	Preston NE	36	2		
2012–13	Preston NE	0	0	**64**	**2**
2012–13	Sheffield W	8	0		
2012–13	*Southend U*	5	0	**5**	**0**
2013–14	Sheffield W	0	0	**8**	**0**
2013–14	Bury	39	5		
2014–15	Bury	44	8		
2015–16	Bury	44	5		
2016–17	Bury	21	3		
2017–18	Bury	20	1		
2018–19	Bury	39	8	**207**	**30**

McFADZEAN, Callum (D) **86** **2**
b.Sheffield 16-1-94
Internationals: England U16. Scotland U21.

2010–11	Sheffield U	0	0		
2011–12	Sheffield U	0	0		
2012–13	Sheffield U	8	0		
2013–14	Sheffield U	7	0		
2013–14	*Chesterfield*	4	0	**4**	**0**
2013–14	*Burton Alb*	7	1		
2014–15	Sheffield U	0	0		
2014–15	*Burton Alb*	9	1	**16**	**2**
2015–16	Sheffield U	1	0	**16**	**0**
2015–16	*Stevenage*	6	0	**6**	**0**
2016–17	Kilmarnock	4	0	**4**	**0**

From Alfreton T, Guiseley.

2018–19	Bury	40	0	**40**	**0**

MILLER, Tom (D) **94** **7**
H: 5 11 W: 11 07 b.Ely 29-6-90
From Rangers, Dundalk, Newport Co, Lincoln C.

2015–16	Carlisle U	29	5		
2016–17	Carlisle U	41	0		
2017–18	Carlisle U	17	2	**87**	**7**
2018–19	Bury	7	0	**7**	**0**

MOORE, Byron (M) **396** **41**
H: 6 0 W: 10 06 b.Stoke 24-8-88

2006–07	Crewe Alex	0	0		
2007–08	Crewe Alex	33	3		
2008–09	Crewe Alex	36	3		
2009–10	Crewe Alex	32	3		
2010–11	Crewe Alex	38	6		
2011–12	Crewe Alex	42	8		
2012–13	Crewe Alex	41	4		
2013–14	Crewe Alex	40	3	**262**	**30**
2014–15	Port Vale	15	1		
2015–16	Port Vale	36	3	**51**	**4**
2016–17	Bristol R	27	2		
2017–18	Bristol R	20	0	**47**	**2**
2018–19	Bury	36	5	**36**	**5**

MURPHY, Joe (G) **533** **0**
H: 6 2 W: 13 06 b.Dublin 21-8-81
Internationals: Republic of Ireland U21, Full caps.

1999–2000	Tranmere R	21	0		
2000–01	Tranmere R	20	0		
2001–02	Tranmere R	22	0	**63**	**0**
2002–03	WBA	2	0		
2003–04	WBA	3	0		
2004–05	WBA	0	0	**5**	**0**
2004–05	*Walsall*	25	0		
2005–06	Sunderland	0	0		
2005–06	*Walsall*	14	0	**39**	**0**
2006–07	Scunthorpe U	45	0		
2007–08	Scunthorpe U	45	0		
2008–09	Scunthorpe U	42	0		
2009–10	Scunthorpe U	40	0		
2010–11	Scunthorpe U	29	0	**201**	**0**
2011–12	Coventry C	46	0		
2012–13	Coventry C	45	0		
2013–14	Coventry C	46	0	**137**	**0**
2014–15	Huddersfield T	2	0		
2014–15	*Chesterfield*	0	0		
2015–16	Huddersfield T	7	0		
2016–17	Huddersfield T	0	0	**9**	**0**
2016–17	*Bury*	16	0		
2017–18	Bury	17	0		
2018–19	Bury	46	0	**79**	**0**

NYAUPEMBE, Dougie (D) **1** **0**
H: 5 8 W: 10 10 b. 2-10-99

2017–18	Bury	1	0		
2018–19	Bury	0	0	**1**	**0**

O'CONNELL, Eoghan (D) **76** **4**
H: 6 1 W: 12 08 b.Cork 13-8-95
Internationals: Republic of Ireland U19, U21.

2013–14	Celtic	1	0		
2014–15	Celtic	3	0		
2015–16	Celtic	1	0		
2015–16	*Oldham Ath*	2	0	**2**	**0**
2016	*Cork C*	7	1	**7**	**1**
2016–17	Celtic	2	0	**7**	**0**
2016–17	*Walsall*	17	1	**17**	**1**
2017–18	Bury	12	0		
2018–19	Bury	31	2	**43**	**2**

O'SHEA, Jay (M) **388** **82**
H: 5 9 W: 12 00 b.Dun Laoghaire 10-8-88
Internationals: Republic of Ireland U19, U21, U23.

2007	Bray Wanderers	27	4	**27**	**4**
2008	Galway U	29	8		
2009	Galway U	19	3	**48**	**11**
2009–10	Birmingham C	1	0		
2009–10	*Middlesbrough*	2	0	**2**	**0**
2010–11	Birmingham C	0	0	**1**	**0**
2010–11	*Stevenage*	5	0	**5**	**0**
2010–11	*Port Vale*	5	1	**5**	**1**
2011–12	Milton Keynes D	28	5		
2012–13	Milton Keynes D	11	1	**39**	**6**
2012–13	*Chesterfield*	26	7		
2013–14	Chesterfield	40	9		
2014–15	Chesterfield	41	7		
2015–16	Chesterfield	46	9		
2016–17	Chesterfield	27	6	**180**	**38**
2016–17	*Sheffield U*	10	3	**10**	**3**
2017–18	Bury	27	4		
2018–19	Bury	44	15	**71**	**19**

OMOTAYO, Gold (F) **13** **1**
b.Zurich 27-1-94
From Whitehawk.

2018–19	Bury	13	1	**13**	**1**

ROSSITER, Jordan (M) **27** **1**
H: 5 8 W: 10 10 b.Liverpool 24-3-97
Internationals: England U16, U17, U18, U19.

2013–14	Liverpool	0	0		
2014–15	Liverpool	0	0		
2015–16	Liverpool	1	0	**1**	**0**
2016–17	Rangers	4	0		
2017–18	Rangers	2	0		
2018–19	Rangers	4	0	**10**	**0**

On loan from Rangers.

2018–19	Bury	16	1	**16**	**1**

SERIKI, Femi (F) **0** **0**

2018–19	Bury	0	0		

SHOTTON, Saul (D) **4** **0**
H: 6 0 W: 11 11 b. 10-11-00

2017–18	Bury	4	0		
2018–19	Bury	0	0	**4**	**0**

SKINNER, Aaron (D) **0** **0**

2018–19	Bury	0	0		

STOKES, Chris (M) **127** **7**
H: 5 7 W: 10 04 b.Trowbridge 8-3-91
Internationals: England U17, C.

2009–10	Crewe Alex	2	0	**2**	**0**

From Forest Green R.

2014–15	Coventry C	16	1		
2015–16	Coventry C	36	2		
2016–17	Coventry C	7	0		
2017–18	Coventry C	29	0	**88**	**3**
2018–19	Bury	37	4	**37**	**4**

TELFORD, Dominic (F) **71** **10**
H: 5 9 W: 11 05 b.Burnley 5-12-96

2014–15	Blackpool	14	1		
2015–16	Blackpool	0	0	**14**	**1**
2016–17	Stoke C	0	0		
2017–18	Stoke C	0	0		
2017–18	*Bristol R*	19	3	**19**	**3**
2018–19	Bury	38	6	**38**	**6**

THOMPSON, Adam (D) **214** **5**
H: 6 2 W: 12 10 b.Harlow 28-9-92
Internationals: Northern Ireland U17, U19, U21, Full caps.

2010–11	Watford	10	1		
2011–12	Watford	0	0		
2011–12	*Brentford*	20	0	**20**	**0**
2012–13	Watford	4	0		
2012–13	*Wycombe W*	2	0	**2**	**0**
2012–13	*Barnet*	1	0	**1**	**0**
2013–14	Watford	0	0	**14**	**1**
2013–14	Southend U	16	0		
2014–15	Southend U	28	0		
2015–16	Southend U	25	2		
2016–17	Southend U	40	1	**109**	**3**
2017–18	Bury	15	0		
2017–18	*Bradford C*	9	0	**9**	**0**
2018–19	Bury	44	1	**59**	**1**

Players retained or with offer of contract
McFarlane-Archer, Jordan; Moloney, Scott Gavin.

Scholars
Allardyce, Sam Craig; Brown, Aaron Ellis John; Copping, Bobby Joel; Edwards-Williams, Mark Brendan; Erskine, Calum Andrew; Hatton, Jack Andrew; Hill, Cameron Taylor; Holden, James William; Jones, Edward Thomas; Mulgrew, Charlie Dean; Ondoa, Obama Frank Cedric; Shotton, Saul; Skinner, Aaron William.

CAMBRIDGE U (19)

AMOO, David (F) **202** **26**
H: 5 10 W: 12 03 b.Southwark 23-4-91

2007–08	Liverpool	0	0		
2008–09	Liverpool	0	0		
2009–10	Liverpool	0	0		
2010–11	Liverpool	0	0		
2010–11	*Milton Keynes D*	3	0	**3**	**0**
2010–11	*Hull C*	7	1	**7**	**1**
2011–12	Liverpool	0	0		
2011–12	*Bury*	27	4	**27**	**4**
2012–13	Preston NE	17	0	**17**	**0**
2012–13	Tranmere R	11	1		
2013–14	Tranmere R	0	0	**11**	**1**
2013–14	Carlisle U	43	8		
2014–15	Carlisle U	27	5	**70**	**13**
2017–18	Cambridge U	24	2		
2018–19	Cambridge U	43	5	**67**	**7**

BROWN, Jevani (M) **84** **13**
b. 16-10-94
Internationals: Jamaica U17.

2013–14	Peterborough U	0	0		
2014–15	Peterborough U	0	0		
2017–18	Cambridge U	41	6		
2018–19	Cambridge U	43	7	**84**	**13**

CARROLL, Jake (D) **202** **3**
H: 6 0 W: 12 03 b.Dublin 11-1-91
Internationals: Republic of Ireland U18.

2011	St Patricks	7	0		
2012	St Patricks	19	1		
2013	St Patricks	7	0	**33**	**1**
2013–14	Huddersfield T	4	0		
2013–14	*Bury*	6	1	**6**	**1**
2014–15	Huddersfield T	2	0	**6**	**0**
2014–15	*Partick Thistle*	10	0	**10**	**0**
2015–16	Hartlepool U	41	1		
2016–17	Hartlepool U	21	0	**62**	**1**
2016–17	Cambridge U	20	0		
2017–18	Cambridge U	33	0		
2018–19	Cambridge U	32	0	**85**	**0**

CORR, Barry (F) **293** **82**
H: 6 3 W: 12 07 b.Co Wicklow 2-4-85

2001–02	Leeds U	0	0		
2002–03	Leeds U	0	0		
2003–04	Leeds U	0	0		
2004–05	Leeds U	0	0		
2005–06	Sheffield W	16	0		
2006–07	Sheffield W	1	0	**17**	**0**
2006–07	*Bristol C*	3	0	**3**	**0**
2006–07	*Swindon T*	8	3		
2007–08	Swindon T	17	5		
2008–09	Swindon T	11	2	**36**	**10**
2009–10	Exeter C	34	3	**34**	**3**
2010–11	Southend U	41	18		
2011–12	Southend U	0	0		
2012–13	Southend U	32	6		
2013–14	Southend U	43	12		
2014–15	Southend U	39	14	**155**	**50**
2015–16	Cambridge U	22	12		
2016–17	Cambridge U	7	2		
2017–18	Cambridge U	10	4		
2018–19	Cambridge U	9	1	**48**	**19**

DARLING, Harry (D) **15** **0**
H: 5 11 W: 11 11 b. 8-8-99

2016–17	Cambridge U	0	0		
2017–18	Cambridge U	3	0		
2018–19	Cambridge U	12	0	**15**	**0**

DAVIES, Leon (D) **15** **0**
b. 21-11-99

2015–16	Cambridge U	0	0		
2016–17	Cambridge U	5	0		
2017–18	Cambridge U	4	0		
2018–19	Cambridge U	6	0	**15**	**0**

DEEGAN, Gary (M) **359** **19**
H: 5 9 W: 11 11 b.Dublin 28-9-87

2005–06	Shelbourne	0	0		
2006	*Kilkenny City*	18	4	**18**	**4**
2007	Longford Town	30	3	**30**	**3**
2008	Galway U	17	0	**17**	**0**
2008	Bohemians	12	3	**12**	**3**
2009	Bohemains	23	2	**23**	**2**
2009–10	Coventry C	17	2		
2010–11	Coventry C	1	0		
2011–12	Coventry C	24	3	**42**	**5**
2012–13	Hibernian	20	0	**20**	**0**
2013–14	Northampton T	27	1	**27**	**1**
2014–15	Southend U	22	0		
2015–16	Southend U	25	0	**47**	**0**
2016–17	Shrewsbury T	40	0	**40**	**0**
2017–18	Cambridge U	42	0		
2018–19	Cambridge U	41	1	**83**	**1**

DUNK, Harrison (M) **178** **10**
H: 6 0 W: 11 07 b. 25-10-90

2014–15	Cambridge U	32	2		
2015–16	Cambridge U	45	4		
2016–17	Cambridge U	38	2		
2017–18	Cambridge U	37	2		
2018–19	Cambridge U	26	0	**178**	**10**

FORDE, David (G) **509** **0**
H: 6 3 W: 13 06 b.Galway 20-12-79
Internationals: Republic of Ireland Full caps.

2001–02	West Ham U	0	0		
2002–03	West Ham U	0	0		
2003–04	West Ham U	0	0		
2004	Derry C	11	0		
2005	Derry C	33	0		
2006	Derry C	29	0	**73**	**0**
2006–07	Cardiff C	7	0		
2007–08	Cardiff C	0	0	**7**	**0**
2007–08	*Luton T*	5	0	**5**	**0**
2007–08	*Bournemouth*	11	0	**11**	**0**
2008–09	Millwall	46	0		
2009–10	Millwall	46	0		
2010–11	Millwall	46	0		
2011–12	Millwall	27	0		
2012–13	Millwall	40	0		
2013–14	Millwall	40	0		
2014–15	Millwall	46	0		
2015–16	Millwall	8	0		
2016–17	Millwall	0	0	**299**	**0**
2016–17	*Portsmouth*	46	0	**46**	**0**
2017–18	Cambridge U	43	0		
2018–19	Cambridge U	25	0	**68**	**0**

FOY, Matt (F) **0** **0**

2014–15	Cambridge U	0	0		
2015–16	Cambridge U	0	0		
2016–17	Cambridge U	0	0		
2017–18	Cambridge U	0	0		
2018–19	Cambridge U	0	0		

HALLIDAY, Bradley (M) **173** **3**
H: 5 11 W: 10 10 b.Redcar 10-7-95

2013–14	Middlesbrough	0	0		
2014–15	Middlesbrough	0	0		
2014–15	*York C*	24	1	**24**	**1**
2015–16	Middlesbrough	0	0		
2015–16	*Hartlepool U*	6	0	**6**	**0**
2015–16	*Accrington S*	32	0	**32**	**0**
2016–17	Middlesbrough	0	0		
2016–17	Cambridge U	30	1		
2017–18	Cambridge U	43	1		
2018–19	Cambridge U	38	0	**111**	**2**

IBEHRE, Jabo (F) **595** **121**
H: 6 2 W: 13 13 b.Islington 28-1-83

1999–2000	Leyton Orient	3	0		
2000–01	Leyton Orient	5	2		
2001–02	Leyton Orient	28	4		
2002–03	Leyton Orient	25	5		
2003–04	Leyton Orient	35	4		
2004–05	Leyton Orient	19	2		
2005–06	Leyton Orient	33	8		
2006–07	Leyton Orient	30	4		
2007–08	Leyton Orient	31	7	**209**	**36**
2008–09	Walsall	39	10	**39**	**10**
2009–10	Milton Keynes D	10	1		
2009–10	*Southend U*	4	0	**4**	**0**
2009–10	*Stockport Co*	20	5	**20**	**5**
2010–11	Milton Keynes D	42	3		
2011–12	Milton Keynes D	39	8		

2012–13 Milton Keynes D 3 0 **94 12**
2012–13 Colchester U 30 8
2013–14 Colchester U 37 8
2014–15 Colchester U 5 0 **72 16**
2014–15 *Oldham Ath* 11 2 **11 2**
2014–15 *Barnsley* 9 2 **9 2**
2015–16 Carlisle U 36 15
2016–17 Carlisle U 38 12 **74 27**
2017–18 Cambridge U 27 7
2018–19 Cambridge U 36 4 **63 11**

IRON, Finley (G) 0 0
2016–17 Cambridge U 0 0
2017–18 Cambridge U 0 0
2018–19 Cambridge U 0 0

JOHN, Louis (D) 22 0
b. 20-11-92
2013–14 Crawley T 0 0
From Sutton U.
2018–19 Cambridge U 22 0 **22 0**

KNOWLES, Tom (M) 4 1
b. 27-9-98
2017–18 Cambridge U 1 0
2018–19 Cambridge U 3 1 **4 1**

LAMBE, Reggie (M) 245 28
H: 5 7 W: 10 09 b.Bermuda 4-2-91
Internationals: Bermuda Full caps.
2009–10 Ipswich T 0 0
2010–11 Ipswich T 2 0 **2 0**
2010–11 *Bristol R* 7 0 **7 0**
2012 Toronto 27 2
2013 Toronto 27 0 **54 2**
2014 Nykoping 11 1 **11 1**
2014–15 Mansfield T 30 5
2015–16 Mansfield T 37 5 **67 10**
2016–17 Carlisle U 38 6
2017–18 Carlisle U 34 6 **72 12**
2018–19 Cambridge U 32 3 **32 3**

LEWIS, Paul (M) 48 5
H: 6 1 W: 11 00 b. 17-12-94
Internationals: England C.
From Macclesfield T.
2016–17 Cambridge U 13 0
2017–18 Cambridge U 12 1
2018–19 Cambridge U 23 4 **48 5**

MARIS, George (F) 105 19
b.Sheffield 6-3-96
2014–15 Barnsley 2 0
2015–16 Barnsley 1 0 **3 0**
2016–17 Cambridge U 23 4
2017–18 Cambridge U 40 10
2018–19 Cambridge U 39 5 **102 19**

MITOV, Dimitar (G) 24 0
H: 6 2 W: 12 00 b. 22-1-97
Internationals: Bulgaria U16, U17, U19, U21.
2014–15 Charlton Ath 0 0
2015–16 Charlton Ath 0 0
2016–17 Charlton Ath 0 0
2017–18 Cambridge U 3 0
2018–19 Cambridge U 21 0 **24 0**

NEAL, Joe (F) 0 0
2018–19 Cambridge U 0 0

O'NEIL, Liam (M) 140 5
H: 6 0 W: 12 06 b.Cambridge 31-7-93
2011–12 WBA 0 0
2011–12 *VPS* 14 0 **14 0**
2012–13 WBA 0 0
2013–14 WBA 3 0
2014–15 WBA 0 0 **3 0**
2014–15 *Scunthorpe U* 22 2 **22 2**
2015–16 Chesterfield 26 0
2016–17 Chesterfield 17 2 **43 2**
2016–17 Cambridge U 13 1
2017–18 Cambridge U 26 0
2018–19 Cambridge U 19 0 **58 1**

OSAOABE, Emmanuel (M) 61 3
b.Dundalk 1-10-96
2015–16 Gillingham 18 2
2016–17 Gillingham 24 1 **42 3**
2017–18 Cambridge U 4 0
2017–18 *Newport Co* 3 0 **3 0**
2018–19 Cambridge U 12 0 **16 0**

PILKINGTON, Kevin (G) 363 0
H: 6 1 W: 13 08 b.Hitchin 8-3-74
1992–93 Manchester U 0 0
1993–94 Manchester U 0 0
1994–95 Manchester U 1 0
1995–96 Manchester U 3 0
1995–96 *Rochdale* 6 0 **6 0**
1996–97 Manchester U 0 0
1996–97 *Rotherham U* 17 0 **17 0**
1997–98 Manchester U 2 0 **6 0**
1998–99 Port Vale 8 0
1999–2000 Port Vale 15 0 **23 0**
2000–01 Mansfield T 2 0
2001–02 Mansfield T 45 0
2002–03 Mansfield T 32 0
2003–04 Mansfield T 46 0
2004–05 Mansfield T 42 0 **167 0**
2005–06 Notts Co 45 0
2006–07 Notts Co 39 0
2007–08 Notts Co 32 0
2008–09 Notts Co 25 0
From Luton T, Mansfield T.
2012–13 Notts Co 1 0
2013–14 Notts Co 1 0
2014–15 Notts Co 1 0
2015–16 Notts Co 0 0
2016–17 Notts Co 0 0 **144 0**
2018–19 Cambridge U 0 0

SQUIRE, Sam (M) 0 0
2017–18 Cambridge U 0 0
2018–19 Cambridge U 0 0

TAFT, George (D) 122 5
H: 5 9 W: 11 09 b.Leicester 29-7-93
Internationals: England U18, U19.
2010–11 Leicester C 0 0
2011–12 Leicester C 0 0
2012–13 Leicester C 0 0
2013–14 Leicester C 0 0
2013–14 *York C* 3 0 **3 0**
2014–15 Burton Alb 30 1
2015–16 Burton Alb 0 0 **30 1**
2015–16 *Cambridge U* 11 1
2016–17 Mansfield T 13 0
2017–18 Mansfield T 0 0 **13 0**
2017–18 *Cambridge U* 28 1
2018–19 Cambridge U 37 2 **76 4**

TAYLOR, Greg (D) 177 5
H: 6 1 W: 12 02 b.Bedford 15-1-90
Internationals: England C.
2008–09 Northampton T 0 0
2014–15 Cambridge U 43 0
2015–16 Cambridge U 16 0
2016–17 Cambridge U 36 2
2017–18 Cambridge U 43 1
2018–19 Cambridge U 39 2 **177 5**

WORMAN, Ben (M) 1 0
b. 30-8-01
2017–18 Cambridge U 0 0
2018–19 Cambridge U 1 0 **1 0**

Players retained or with offer of contract
Norville-Williams, Jordan Zion Wilford; Thompson-Lambe, Reginald Everard Vibart.

Scholars
Battersby, Jake Anthony; Bennett, Sam; D'Arcy, Blake Lewis; Dearman, Joe Clive; Dickens, Thomas Oliver; Foxall, Craig Thomas; Goode, Samuel Joshua; Gray, Joshua Michael; Hasani, Inglian; Jeche, Joshua Tanatswa; Johnson, Charlie Alexander; Simper, Lewis Matthew; Steel, Harvey James; Toyer, Daniel Charles.

CARDIFF C (20)

BACUNA, Leandro (M) 239 18
H: 6 2 W: 12 00 b.Groningen 21-8-91
Internationals: Netherlands U19, U21. Curacao Full caps.
2009–10 FC Groningen 20 2
2012–13 FC Groningen 33 5 **53 7**
2013–14 Aston Villa 35 5
2014–15 Aston Villa 19 0
2015–16 Aston Villa 31 1
2016–17 Aston Villa 30 1
2017–18 Aston Villa 1 0 **116 7**
2017–18 Reading 33 1
2018–19 Reading 26 3 **59 4**
2018–19 Cardiff C 11 0 **11 0**

BAMBA, Souleymane (D) 346 22
H: 6 3 W: 14 02 b.Ivry-sur-Seine 13-1-85
Internationals: Ivory Coast Full caps.
2004–05 Paris Saint-Germain 1 0
2005–06 Paris Saint-Germain 0 0 **1 0**
2006–07 Dunfermline Ath 23 0
2007–08 Dunfermline Ath 15 0
2008–09 Dunfermline Ath 1 0 **39 0**
2008–09 Hibernian 29 0
2009–10 Hibernian 30 2
2010–11 Hibernian 16 2 **75 4**
2010–11 Leicester C 16 2
2011–12 Leicester C 36 1 **52 3**
2012–13 Trabzonspor 18 0
2013–14 Trabzonspor 9 0 **27 0**
2014–15 Palermo 1 0 **1 0**
2014–15 *Leeds U* 19 1
2015–16 Leeds U 30 4
2016–17 Leeds U 2 0 **51 5**
2016–17 Cardiff C 26 2
2017–18 Cardiff C 46 4
2018–19 Cardiff C 28 4 **100 10**

BENNETT, Joe (D) 251 6
H: 5 10 W: 10 04 b.Rochdale 28-3-90
Internationals: England U19, U20, U21.
2008–09 Middlesbrough 1 0
2009–10 Middlesbrough 12 0
2010–11 Middlesbrough 31 0
2011–12 Middlesbrough 41 1
2012–13 Middlesbrough 0 0 **85 1**
2012–13 Aston Villa 25 0
2013–14 Aston Villa 5 0
2014–15 Brighton & HA 41 1 **41 1**
2015–16 Aston Villa 0 0
2015–16 *Bournemouth* 0 0
2015–16 *Sheffield W* 3 0 **3 0**
2016–17 Aston Villa 0 0 **30 0**
2016–17 Cardiff C 24 3
2017–18 Cardiff C 38 1
2018–19 Cardiff C 30 0 **92 4**

BOGLE, Omar (F) 87 31
H: 6 3 W: 12 08 b.Birmingham 26-7-92
Internationals: England C
From Hinckley U, Solihull Moors.
2016–17 Grimsby T 27 19 **27 19**
2016–17 Wigan Ath 14 3 **14 3**
2017–18 Cardiff C 10 3
2017–18 *Peterborough U* 9 1 **9 1**
2018–19 Cardiff C 0 0 **10 3**
2018–19 *Birmingham C* 15 1 **15 1**
2018–19 *Portsmouth* 12 4 **12 4**

BROWN, Ciaron (D) 5 0
b. 1-1-01
2018–19 Cardiff C 0 0
2018–19 *Livingston* 5 0 **5 0**

CONNOLLY, Matthew (D) 286 13
H: 6 1 W: 11 03 b.Barnet 24-9-87
2005–06 Arsenal 0 0
2006–07 Arsenal 0 0
2006–07 *Bournemouth* 5 1 **5 1**
2007–08 Arsenal 0 0
2007–08 *Colchester U* 16 2 **16 2**
2007–08 QPR 20 0
2008–09 QPR 35 0
2009–10 QPR 19 2
2010–11 QPR 36 0
2011–12 QPR 6 0
2011–12 *Reading* 6 0 **6 0**
2012–13 QPR 0 0 **116 2**
2012–13 Cardiff C 36 5
2013–14 Cardiff C 3 0
2014–15 Cardiff C 23 0
2014–15 *Watford* 6 1 **6 1**
2015–16 Cardiff C 43 1
2016–17 Cardiff C 28 1
2017–18 Cardiff C 4 0
2018–19 Cardiff C 0 0 **137 7**

COXE, Cameron (D) 0 0
b. 18-12-98
Internationals: Wales U17, U19, U20, U21.
2017–18 Cardiff C 0 0
2018–19 Cardiff C 0 0

CUNNINGHAM, Greg (D) 243 8
H: 6 0 W: 11 00 b.Galway 31-1-91
Internationals: Republic of Ireland U17, U21, Full caps.
2008–09 Manchester C 0 0
2009–10 Manchester C 2 0
2010–11 Manchester C 0 0
2010–11 *Leicester C* 13 0 **13 0**
2011–12 Manchester C 0 0
2011–12 *Nottingham F* 27 0 **27 0**
2012–13 Manchester C 0 0 **2 0**
2012–13 Bristol C 30 1
2013–14 Bristol C 37 1
2014–15 Bristol C 24 2 **91 4**
2015–16 Preston NE 43 2
2016–17 Preston NE 40 1
2017–18 Preston NE 20 1 **103 4**
2018–19 Cardiff C 7 0 **7 0**

DAMOUR, Loïc (M) 206 8
H: 5 11 W: 11 09 b.Soissy 8-1-91
Internationals: France U16, U17, U18, U19, U20.

2008–09	Strasbourg	5	0		
2009–10	Strasbourg	5	0		
2010–11	Strasbourg	34	1	**44**	**1**
2011–12	Boulogne	17	0		
2012–13	Boulogne	1	0	**18**	**0**
2012–13	RWDM Brussels	6	0	**6**	**0**
2013–14	White Star Brussels	9	0	**9**	**0**
2014–15	Saint-Raphael	31	3	**31**	**3**
2015–16	Bourg-en-Bresse	33	2		
2016–17	Bourg-en-Bresse	36	2	**69**	**4**
2017–18	Cardiff C	27	0		
2018–19	Cardiff C	2	0	**29**	**0**

ECUELE MANGA, Bruno (D) 325 13
H: 6 2 W: 11 11 b.Libreville 16-7-88
Internationals: Gabon Full caps.

2008–09	Angers	29	1		
2009–10	Angers	28	3	**57**	**4**
2010–11	Lorient	31	1		
2011–12	Lorient	32	2		
2012–13	Lorient	17	0		
2013–14	Lorient	35	1		
2014–15	Lorient	3	0	**118**	**4**
2014–15	Cardiff C	29	3		
2015–16	Cardiff C	24	2		
2016–17	Cardiff C	21	0		
2017–18	Cardiff C	38	0		
2018–19	Cardiff C	38	0	**150**	**5**

ETHERIDGE, Neil (G) 184 0
H: 6 3 W: 14 00 b.Enfield 7-2-90
Internationals: England U16. Philippines Full caps.

2008–09	Fulham	0	0		
2009–10	Fulham	0	0		
2010–11	Fulham	0	0		
2011–12	Fulham	0	0		
2012–13	Fulham	0	0		
2012–13	*Bristol R*	12	0	**12**	**0**
2013–14	Fulham	0	0		
2013–14	*Crewe Alex*	4	0	**4**	**0**
2014–15	Oldham Ath	0	0		
2014–15	Charlton Ath	4	0	**4**	**0**
2015–16	Walsall	40	0		
2016–17	Walsall	41	0	**81**	**0**
2017–18	Cardiff C	45	0		
2018–19	Cardiff C	38	0	**83**	**0**

GUNNARSSON, Aron (M) 394 31
H: 5 9 W: 11 00 b.Akureyri 22-9-89
Internationals: Iceland U17, U19, U21, Full caps.

2007–08	AZ	1	0	**1**	**0**
2008–09	Coventry C	40	1		
2009–10	Coventry C	40	1		
2010–11	Coventry C	42	4	**122**	**6**
2011–12	Cardiff C	42	5		
2012–13	Cardiff C	45	8		
2013–14	Cardiff C	23	1		
2014–15	Cardiff C	45	4		
2015–16	Cardiff C	28	2		
2016–17	Cardiff C	40	3		
2017–18	Cardiff C	20	1		
2018–19	Cardiff C	28	1	**271**	**25**

HARRIS, Kedeem (M) 110 7
H: 5 9 W: 10 08 b.Westminster 8-6-93

2009–10	Wycombe W	2	0		
2010–11	Wycombe W	0	0		
2011–12	Wycombe W	17	0	**19**	**0**
2011–12	Cardiff C	0	0		
2012–13	Cardiff C	0	0		
2013–14	Cardiff C	0	0		
2013–14	*Brentford*	10	1	**10**	**1**
2014–15	Cardiff C	14	1		
2015–16	Cardiff C	3	0		
2015–16	*Barnsley*	11	0	**11**	**0**
2016–17	Cardiff C	37	4		
2017–18	Cardiff C	3	0		
2018–19	Cardiff C	13	1	**70**	**6**

HARRIS, Mark (M) 24 2
b. 29-12-98
Internationals: Wales U17, U19, U20, U21.

2016–17	Cardiff C	2	0		
2017–18	Cardiff C	0	0		
2018–19	Cardiff C	0	0	**2**	**0**
2018–19	*Newport Co*	16	2	**16**	**2**
2018–19	*Port Vale*	6	0	**6**	**0**

HEALEY, Rhys (M) 77 20
H: 5 8 W: 10 10 b.Manchester 6-12-94

2012–13	Cardiff C	0	0		
2013–14	Cardiff C	1	0		
2014–15	Cardiff C	0	0		
2014–15	*Colchester U*	21	4	**21**	**4**
2015–16	Cardiff C	0	0		
2015–16	*Dundee*	7	1	**7**	**1**
2016–17	Newport Co	17	6	**17**	**6**
2016–17	Cardiff C	7	1		
2017–18	Cardiff C	3	0		
2018–19	Milton Keynes D	18	8	**18**	**8**
2018–19	Cardiff C	3	0	**14**	**1**

HOILETT, Junior (M) 337 44
H: 5 8 W: 11 00 b.Ottawa 5-6-90
Internationals: Canada Full caps.

2007–08	Blackburn R	0	0		
2007–08	*Paderborn*	12	1	**12**	**1**
2008–09	Blackburn R	0	0		
2008–09	*St Pauli*	21	6	**21**	**6**
2009–10	Blackburn R	23	0		
2010–11	Blackburn R	24	5		
2011–12	Blackburn R	34	7	**81**	**12**
2012–13	QPR	26	1		
2013–14	QPR	35	4		
2014–15	QPR	22	0		
2015–16	QPR	29	6		
2016–17	QPR	0	0	**112**	**11**
2016–17	Cardiff C	33	2		
2017–18	Cardiff C	46	9		
2018–19	Cardiff C	32	3	**111**	**14**

HUMPHRIES, Lloyd (M) 0 0
b.3-10-01
Internationals: Wales U19.

2018–19	Cardiff C	0	0		

MADINE, Gary (F) 344 74
H: 6 1 W: 12 00 b.Gateshead 24-8-90

2007–08	Carlisle U	11	0		
2008–09	Carlisle U	14	1		
2008–09	*Rochdale*	3	0	**3**	**0**
2009–10	Carlisle U	20	4		
2009–10	*Coventry C*	9	0		
2009–10	*Chesterfield*	4	0	**4**	**0**
2010–11	Carlisle U	21	8		
2010–11	Sheffield W	22	5		
2011–12	Sheffield W	38	18		
2012–13	Sheffield W	30	3		
2013–14	Sheffield W	1	0		
2013–14	*Carlisle U*	5	2	**71**	**15**
2014–15	Sheffield W	10	0	**101**	**26**
2014–15	*Coventry C*	11	3	**20**	**3**
2014–15	*Blackpool*	15	3	**15**	**3**
2015–16	Bolton W	32	5		
2016–17	Bolton W	36	9		
2017–18	Bolton W	28	10	**96**	**24**
2017–18	Cardiff C	13	0		
2018–19	Cardiff C	5	0	**18**	**0**
2018–19	*Sheffield U*	16	3	**16**	**3**

MENDEZ-LAING, Nathaniel (M) 247 36
H: 5 10 W: 11 12 b.Birmingham 15-4-92
Internationals: England U16, U17.

2009–10	Wolverhampton W	0	0		
2010–11	Wolverhampton W	0	0		
2010–11	*Peterborough U*	33	5		
2011–12	Wolverhampton W	0	0		
2011–12	*Sheffield U*	8	1	**8**	**1**
2012–13	Peterborough U	21	3		
2012–13	*Portsmouth*	8	0	**8**	**0**
2013–14	Peterborough U	16	1		
2013–14	*Shrewsbury T*	6	0	**6**	**0**
2014–15	Peterborough U	14	0	**84**	**9**
2014–15	*Cambridge U*	11	1	**11**	**1**
2015–16	Rochdale	33	7		
2016–17	Rochdale	39	8	**72**	**15**
2017–18	Cardiff C	38	6		
2018–19	Cardiff C	20	4	**58**	**10**

MORRISON, Sean (D) 303 32
H: 6 4 W: 14 00 b.Plymouth 8-1-91

2007–08	Swindon T	2	0		
2008–09	Swindon T	20	1		
2009–10	Swindon T	9	1		
2009–10	*Southend U*	8	0	**8**	**0**
2010–11	Swindon T	19	4	**50**	**6**
2010–11	Reading	0	0		
2010–11	*Huddersfield T*	0	0		
2011–12	Reading	0	0		
2011–12	*Huddersfield T*	19	1	**19**	**1**
2012–13	Reading	16	2		
2013–14	Reading	21	1		
2014–15	Reading	1	1	**38**	**4**
2014–15	Cardiff C	41	6		
2015–16	Cardiff C	30	3		
2016–17	Cardiff C	44	4		
2017–18	Cardiff C	39	7		
2018–19	Cardiff C	34	1	**188**	**21**

MURPHY, Brian (G) 160 0
H: 6 0 W: 13 00 b.Waterford 7-5 83
Internationals. Republic of Ireland U16.

2000–01	Manchester C	0	0		
2001–02	Manchester C	0	0		
2002–03	Manchester C	0	0		
2002–03	*Oldham Ath*	0	0		
2002–03	*Peterborough U*	1	0	**1**	**0**

From Waterford

2003–04	Swansea C	11	0		
2004–05	Swansea C	2	0		
2005–06	Swansea C	0	0		
2006–07	Swansea C	0	0	**13**	**0**
2007	Bohemians	29	0		
2008	Bohemians	33	0		
2009	Bohemians	35	0	**97**	**0**
2009–10	Ipswich T	16	0		
2010–11	Ipswich T	4	0		
2011–12	Ipswich T	0	0	**20**	**0**
2011–12	QPR	0	0		
2012–13	QPR	0	0		
2013–14	QPR	2	0		
2014–15	QPR	0	0	**2**	**0**
2015–16	Portsmouth	21	0		
2016–17	Portsmouth	0	0	**21**	**0**
2016–17	Cardiff C	5	0		
2017–18	Cardiff C	1	0		
2018–19	Cardiff C	0	0	**0**	**0**

MURPHY, Josh (F) 166 20
H: 5 8 W: 10 07 b.Wembley 24-2-95
Internationals: England U18, U19, U20.

2012–13	Norwich C	0	0		
2013–14	Norwich C	9	0		
2014–15	Norwich C	13	1		
2014–15	*Wigan Ath*	5	0	**5**	**0**
2015–16	Norwich C	0	0		
2015–16	*Milton Keynes D*	42	5	**42**	**5**
2016–17	Norwich C	27	4		
2017–18	Norwich C	41	7	**90**	**12**
2018–19	Cardiff C	29	3	**29**	**3**

O'KEEFE, Stuart (M) 138 7
H: 5 8 W: 10 00 b.Eye 4-3-91

2008–09	Southend U	3	0		
2009–10	Southend U	7	0		
2010–11	Southend U	0	0	**10**	**0**
2010–11	Crystal Palace	4	0		
2011–12	Crystal Palace	13	0		
2012–13	Crystal Palace	5	0		
2013–14	Crystal Palace	12	1		
2014–15	Crystal Palace	2	0	**36**	**1**
2014–15	*Blackpool*	4	0	**4**	**0**
2014–15	Cardiff C	6	0		
2015–16	Cardiff C	24	2		
2016–17	Cardiff C	8	0		
2016–17	*Milton Keynes D*	18	4	**18**	**4**
2017–18	Cardiff C	0	0		
2017–18	*Portsmouth*	21	0	**21**	**0**
2018–19	Cardiff C	0	0	**38**	**2**
2018–19	*Plymouth Arg*	11	0	**11**	**0**

PATERSON, Callum (D) 196 47
H: 6 0 W: 12 00 b.London 13-10-94
Internationals: Scotland U18, U19, U21, Full caps.

2012–13	Hearts	22	3		
2013–14	Hearts	37	11		
2014–15	Hearts	29	6		
2015–16	Hearts	29	5		
2016–17	Hearts	20	8	**137**	**33**
2017–18	Cardiff C	32	10		
2018–19	Cardiff C	27	4	**59**	**14**

PELTIER, Lee (D) 414 5
H: 5 10 W: 12 00 b.Liverpool 11-12-86
Internationals: England U18.

2004–05	Liverpool	0	0		
2005–06	Liverpool	0	0		
2006–07	Liverpool	0	0		
2006–07	*Hull C*	7	0	**7**	**0**
2007–08	Liverpool	0	0		
2007–08	Yeovil T	34	0		
2008–09	Yeovil T	35	1	**69**	**1**
2009–10	Huddersfield T	42	0		
2010–11	Huddersfield T	38	1		
2011–12	Leicester C	40	2		
2012–13	Leicester C	0	0	**40**	**2**
2012–13	Leeds U	41	0		
2013–14	Leeds U	25	1	**66**	**1**
2013–14	*Nottingham F*	7	0	**7**	**0**
2014–15	Huddersfield T	11	0	**91**	**1**
2014–15	Cardiff C	15	0		
2015–16	Cardiff C	41	0		
2016–17	Cardiff C	28	0		
2017–18	Cardiff C	30	0		
2018–19	Cardiff C	20	0	**134**	**0**

RALLS, Joe (M) 229 20
H: 5 10 W: 11 00 b.Farnborough 13-10-93
Internationals: England U19.

2011–12	Cardiff C	10	1		
2012–13	Cardiff C	4	0		
2013–14	Cardiff C	0	0		
2013–14	*Yeovil T*	37	3	**37**	**3**
2014–15	Cardiff C	28	2		
2015–16	Cardiff C	43	1		
2016–17	Cardiff C	42	6		
2017–18	Cardiff C	37	7		
2018–19	Cardiff C	28	0	**192**	**17**

REID, Bobby (M) 203 34
H: 5 7 W: 10 10 b.Bristol 1-3-93

2010–11	Bristol C	1	0		
2011–12	Bristol C	0	0		
2011–12	*Cheltenham T*	1	0	**1**	**0**
2012–13	Bristol C	4	1		
2012–13	*Oldham Ath*	7	0	**7**	**0**
2013–14	Bristol C	24	1		
2014–15	Bristol C	2	0		
2014–15	*Plymouth Arg*	33	3	**33**	**3**
2015–16	Bristol C	28	2		
2016–17	Bristol C	30	3		
2017–18	Bristol C	46	19	**135**	**26**
2018–19	Cardiff C	27	5	**27**	**5**

RICHARDS, Ashley (M) 131 0
H: 6 1 W: 12 04 b.Swansea 12-4-91
Internationals: Wales U17, U19, U21, Full caps.

2009–10	Swansea C	15	0		
2010–11	Swansea C	6	0		
2011–12	Swansea C	8	0		
2012–13	Swansea C	0	0		
2012–13	*Crystal Palace*	11	0	**11**	**0**
2013–14	Swansea C	0	0		
2013–14	*Huddersfield T*	9	0	**9**	**0**
2014–15	Swansea C	10	0	**39**	**0**
2014–15	*Fulham*	14	0		
2015–16	Fulham	22	0	**36**	**0**
2016–17	Cardiff C	26	0		
2017–18	Cardiff C	6	0		
2018–19	Cardiff C	4	0	**36**	**0**

SMITHIES, Alex (G) 354 0
H: 6 1 W: 10 01 b.Huddersfield 25-3-90
Internationals: England U16, U17, U18, U19.

2006–07	Huddersfield T	0	0		
2007–08	Huddersfield T	2	0		
2008–09	Huddersfield T	27	0		
2009–10	Huddersfield T	46	0		
2010–11	Huddersfield T	22	0		
2011–12	Huddersfield T	13	0		
2012–13	Huddersfield T	46	0		
2013–14	Huddersfield T	46	0		
2014–15	Huddersfield T	44	0		
2015–16	Huddersfield T	1	0	**247**	**0**
2015–16	QPR	18	0		
2016–17	QPR	46	0		
2017–18	QPR	43	0	**107**	**0**
2018–19	Cardiff C	0	0		

TOMLIN, Lee (F) 300 62
H: 5 11 W: 11 09 b.Leicester 12-1-89
Internationals: England C.

2010–11	Peterborough U	37	8		
2011–12	Peterborough U	37	8		
2012–13	Peterborough U	42	11		
2013–14	Peterborough U	19	5		
2013–14	Middlesbrough	14	4		
2014–15	Middlesbrough	42	7	**56**	**11**
2015–16	Bournemouth	6	0	**6**	**0**
2015–16	*Bristol C*	18	6		
2016–17	Bristol C	38	6	**56**	**12**
2017–18	Cardiff C	13	1		
2017–18	*Nottingham F*	15	4	**15**	**4**
2018–19	Cardiff C	0	0	**13**	**1**
2018–19	*Peterborough U*	19	2	**154**	**34**

VICTOR CAMARASA (M) 148 13
H: 6 0 W: 12 00 b.Meliana 28-5-94
Internationals: Spain U21.

2012–13	Levante	0	0		
2013–14	Levante	3	0		
2014–15	Levante	24	2		
2015–16	Levante	34	2		
2016–17	Levante	0	0	**61**	**4**
2016–17	*Alaves*	31	3	**31**	**3**
2017–18	Real Betis	24	1		
2018–19	Real Betis	0	0	**24**	**1**

On loan from Real Betis.

2018–19	Cardiff C	32	5	**32**	**5**

WARD, Danny (M) 282 48
H: 5 11 W: 12 05 b.Bradford 11-12-91

2008–09	Bolton W	0	0		
2009–10	Bolton W	2	0		
2009–10	*Swindon T*	28	7	**28**	**7**
2010–11	Bolton W	0	0	**2**	**0**
2010–11	*Coventry C*	5	0	**5**	**0**
2010–11	*Huddersfield T*	7	3		
2011–12	Huddersfield T	39	4		
2012–13	Huddersfield T	28	2		
2013–14	Huddersfield T	38	10		
2014–15	Huddersfield T	12	0	**124**	**19**
2014–15	*Rotherham U*	16	3		
2015–16	Rotherham U	34	4		
2016–17	Rotherham U	41	10	**91**	**17**
2017–18	Cardiff C	18	4		
2018–19	Cardiff C	14	1	**32**	**5**

ZOHORE, Kenneth (F) 164 39
H: 6 4 W: 12 06 b.Copenhagen 31-1-94
Internationals: Denmark U17, U18, U19, U21.

2009–10	Copenhagen	1	0		
2010–11	Copenhagen	15	1		
2011–12	Copenhagen	0	0	**16**	**1**
2011–12	Fiorentina	0	0		
2012–13	Fiorentina	0	0		
2013–14	Fiorentina	0	0		
2013–14	*Brondby*	25	5	**25**	**5**
2014–15	Fiorentina	0	0		
2014–15	*Gothenburg*	11	2	**11**	**2**
2015–16	Odense BK	16	7	**16**	**7**
2015–16	KV Kortrijk	0	0		
2015–16	*Cardiff C*	12	2		
2016–17	Cardiff C	29	12		
2017–18	Cardiff C	36	9		
2018–19	Cardiff C	19	1	**96**	**24**

Players retained or with offer of contract
Bodenham, Jack Tomas; Burwood, Warren Robert John; Evans, Jacob; Hall, Matthew Raymond; Martin, Daniel John; McKay, Jack; McKay, Paul; Pryce, Ryan; Spence, Sion; Waite, James Tyler; Warnock, William Douglas Neil; Williams, Jack Daniel; Wootton, Laurence Thomas.

Scholars
Bagan, Joel Matthew; Bowen, Sam Lewis; Colwill, Rubin; Davies, Connor William; Davies, Isaak James; Davies, Jac Tomos; Duffey, Jordan James; Evans, Kieron Thomas; Griffiths, Daniel Lawrence; Jones, Trystan Rhys; Parsons, Samuel Steven; Patten, Keenan; Pinchard, Harry Matthew; Ratcliffe, George; Reynolds, Ryan Michael; Sharif, Badedi Adam Mohamed; Smith, Henry William Leonard; Williams-Margetson, Ben.

CARLISLE U (21)

ADEWUSI, Sam (M) 1 0
b. 26-12-99

2018–19	Carlisle U	1	0	**1**	**0**

BENNETT, Richie (F) 75 15
b.Oldham 3-3-91
From Ashton U, Northwich Vic, Barrow.

2017–18	Carlisle U	38	6		
2018–19	Carlisle U	21	4	**59**	**10**
2018–19	*Morecambe*	16	5	**16**	**5**

BIRCH, Charlie (M) 0 0

2018–19	Carlisle U	0	0		

BRANTHWAITE, Jarrad (M) 0 0

2018–19	Carlisle U	0	0		

BROWN, Max (F) 0 0
b.Carlisle --

2018–19	Carlisle U	0	0		

COLLIN, Adam (G) 322 0
H: 6 2 W: 12 00 b.Penrith 9-12-84

2003–04	Newcastle U	0	0		
2003–04	*Oldham Ath*	0	0		

From Workington

2009–10	Carlisle U	29	0		
2010–11	Carlisle U	46	0		
2011–12	Carlisle U	46	0		
2012–13	Carlisle U	12	0		
2013–14	Rotherham U	34	0		
2014–15	Rotherham U	36	0		
2015–16	Rotherham U	1	0	**71**	**0**
2015–16	*Aberdeen*	3	0	**3**	**0**
2016–17	Notts Co	43	0		
2017–18	Notts Co	30	0	**73**	**0**
2018–19	Carlisle U	42	0	**175**	**0**

CULLEN, Mark (F) 182 36
H: 5 9 W: 11 11 b.Ashington 21-4-92

2009–10	Hull C	3	1		
2010–11	Hull C	17	0		
2010–11	*Bradford C*	4	0	**4**	**0**
2011–12	Hull C	4	0		
2011–12	*Bury*	4	0		
2012–13	Hull C	0	0		
2012–13	Hull C	0	0	**24**	**1**
2012–13	*Bury*	10	1	**14**	**1**
2014–15	Luton T	42	13	**42**	**13**
2015–16	Blackpool	41	9		
2016–17	Blackpool	27	9		
2017–18	Blackpool	9	0		
2018–19	Blackpool	12	3	**89**	**21**
2018–19	Carlisle U	9	0	**9**	**0**

DEVITT, Jamie (F) 276 43
H: 5 10 W: 10 05 b.Dublin 6-7-90
Internationals: Republic of Ireland U21.

2007–08	Hull C	0	0		
2008–09	Hull C	0	0		
2009–10	Hull C	0	0		
2009–10	*Darlington*	6	1	**6**	**1**
2009–10	*Shrewsbury T*	9	2	**9**	**2**
2009–10	*Grimsby T*	15	5	**15**	**5**
2010–11	Hull C	16	0		
2011–12	Hull C	0	0		
2011–12	*Bradford C*	7	1	**7**	**1**
2011–12	*Accrington S*	16	2	**16**	**2**
2012–13	Hull C	0	0	**16**	**0**
2012–13	*Rotherham U*	1	0	**1**	**0**
2013–14	Chesterfield	7	0	**7**	**0**
2013–14	*Morecambe*	14	2		
2014–15	Morecambe	36	3		
2015–16	Morecambe	39	6	**89**	**11**
2016–17	Carlisle U	35	0		
2017–18	Carlisle U	40	10		
2018–19	Carlisle U	35	11	**110**	**21**

EGAN, Jack (F) 0 0

2017–18	Carlisle U	0	0		
2018–19	Carlisle U	0	0		

ETUHU, Kelvin (F) 233 11
H: 5 11 W: 11 02 b.Kano 30-5-88

2005–06	Manchester C	0	0		
2006–07	Manchester C	0	0		
2006–07	*Rochdale*	4	2	**4**	**2**
2007–08	Manchester C	6	1		
2007–08	*Leicester C*	4	0	**4**	**0**
2008–09	Manchester C	4	0		
2009–10	Manchester C	0	0		
2009–10	*Cardiff C*	16	0	**16**	**0**
2010–11	Manchester C	0	0	**10**	**1**
2011–12	Kavala	0	0		
2011–12	Portsmouth	13	1		
2012–13	Portsmouth	0	0	**13**	**1**
2012–13	Barnsley	26	0		
2013–14	Barnsley	20	0	**46**	**0**
2014–15	Bury	43	2		
2015–16	Bury	18	0		
2016–17	Bury	20	2	**81**	**4**
2017–18	Carlisle U	20	3		
2018–19	Carlisle U	39	0	**59**	**3**

FRYER, Joe (G) 47 0
b.Chester-le-Street 14-11-95

2016–17	Middlesbrough	0	0		
2016–17	*Hartlepool U*	14	0	**14**	**0**
2017–18	Middlesbrough	0	0		
2017–18	*Stevenage*	28	0	**28**	**0**
2018–19	Carlisle U	5	0	**5**	**0**

GERRARD, Anthony (D) 465 19
H: 6 2 W: 13 07 b.Huyton 6-2-86
Internationals: Republic of Ireland U18.

2004–05	Everton	0	0		
2004–05	*Walsall*	8	0		
2005–06	Walsall	34	0		
2006–07	Walsall	35	1		
2007–08	Walsall	44	3		
2008–09	Walsall	42	3	**163**	**7**
2009–10	Cardiff C	39	2		
2010–11	Cardiff C	0	0		
2010–11	*Hull C*	41	5	**41**	**5**
2011–12	Cardiff C	20	1		
2012–13	Cardiff C	0	0	**59**	**3**
2012–13	Huddersfield T	38	1		
2013–14	Huddersfield T	40	1		
2014–15	Huddersfield T	3	0	**81**	**2**
2014–15	*Oldham Ath*	6	0		
2015–16	Shrewsbury T	11	0	**11**	**0**
2015–16	Oldham Ath	18	0		
2016–17	Oldham Ath	14	0		
2017–18	Oldham Ath	31	2	**69**	**2**
2018–19	Carlisle U	41	0	**41**	**0**

GILLESPHEY, Macaulay (D) 79 2
H: 5 11 W: 11 00 b. 24-11-95

2015–16	Newcastle U	0	0		
2015–16	*Carlisle U*	23	2		
2016–17	Newcastle U	0	0		
2016–17	*Carlisle U*	32	0		
2017–18	Newcastle U	0	0		
2018–19	Carlisle U	24	0	**79**	**2**

GLENDON, George (M) 72 0
H: 5 10 W: 11 00 b.Manchester 3-5-95
Internationals: England U16, U17.

2013–14	Manchester C	0	0		
2014–15	Manchester C	0	0		
2015–16	Manchester C	0	0		
2016–17	Fleetwood T	26	0		
2017–18	Fleetwood T	30	0	**56**	**0**
2018–19	Carlisle U	16	0	**16**	**0**

GNAHOUA, Arthur (F) 13 1
H: 6 2 W: 12 08 b.London 5-4-92
From Stalybridge Celtic, Macclesfield T, Kidderminster H.

2017–18	Shrewsbury T	11	1		
2018–19	Shrewsbury T	1	0	**12**	**1**
2018–19	Carlisle U	1	0	**1**	**0**

GRAINGER, Danny (D) 307 34
H: 5 10 W: 10 10 b.Kettering 28-7-86

2008–09	Dundee U	9	0	**9**	**0**
2009–10	St Johnstone	36	1		
2010–11	St Johnstone	33	2	**69**	**3**
2011–12	Hearts	27	0		
2012–13	Hearts	13	2	**40**	**2**
2013–14	St Mirren	13	0	**13**	**0**
2013–14	Dunfermline Ath	11	2	**11**	**2**
2014–15	Carlisle U	41	3		
2015–16	Carlisle U	36	5		
2016–17	Carlisle U	31	6		
2017–18	Carlisle U	34	8		
2018–19	Carlisle U	23	5	**165**	**27**

GRANT, Peter (M) 111 6
H: 6 2 W: 11 04 b.Peterborough 3-6-91

2012–13	Peterborough U	0	0		
2013–14	Peterborough U	0	0		
2014–15	Falkirk	30	3		
2015–16	Falkirk	23	0		
2016–17	Falkirk	21	1		
2017–18	Falkirk	27	2	**101**	**6**
2018–19	Plymouth Arg	6	0	**6**	**0**
2018–19	Carlisle U	4	0	**4**	**0**

GRAY, Louis (G) 0 0
H: 6 1 W: 11 11 b.Wrexham 11-8-95
From Wrexham.

2017–18	Everton	0	0		
2017 18	*Carlisle U*	0	0		
2018–19	Carlisle U	0	0		

HOPE, Hallam (F) 175 36
H: 5 10 W: 12 00 b.Manchester 17-3-94
Internationals: England U16, U17, U18, U19.

2010–11	Everton	0	0		
2011–12	Everton	0	0		
2013–14	Everton	0	0		
2013–14	*Northampton T*	3	1	**3**	**1**
2013–14	*Bury*	8	5		
2014–15	Everton	0	0		
2014–15	*Sheffield W*	4	0	**4**	**0**
2014–15	Bury	19	0		
2015–16	Bury	6	0		
2015–16	*Carlisle U*	21	4		
2016–17	Bury	33	3	**66**	**8**
2017–18	Carlisle U	41	9		
2018–19	Carlisle U	40	14	**102**	**27**

JONES, Mike (M) 443 36
H: 5 11 W: 12 04 b.Birkenhead 15-8-87

2005–06	Tranmere R	1	0		
2006–07	Tranmere R	0	0		
2006–07	*Shrewsbury T*	13	1	**13**	**1**
2007–08	Tranmere R	9	1	**10**	**1**
2008–09	Bury	46	4		
2009–10	Bury	41	5		
2010–11	Bury	42	8		
2011–12	Bury	24	3	**153**	**20**
2011–12	Sheffield W	10	0		
2012–13	Sheffield W	0	0	**10**	**0**
2012–13	Crawley T	40	1		
2013–14	Crawley T	42	3	**82**	**4**
2014–15	Oldham Ath	45	6		
2015–16	Oldham Ath	35	3	**80**	**9**
2016–17	Carlisle U	28	0		
2017–18	Carlisle U	43	0		
2018–19	Carlisle U	24	1	**95**	**1**

KENNEDY, Jason (M) 412 39
H: 6 1 W: 13 02 b.Stockton 11-9-86

2004–05	Middlesbrough	1	0		
2005–06	Middlesbrough	3	0		
2006–07	Middlesbrough	0	0		
2006–07	*Boston U*	13	1	**13**	**1**
2006–07	*Bury*	12	0	**12**	**0**
2007–08	Middlesbrough	0	0	**4**	**0**
2007–08	*Livingston*	18	2	**18**	**2**
2007–08	*Darlington*	13	2		
2008–09	Darlington	46	5	**59**	**7**
2009–10	Rochdale	42	0		
2010–11	Rochdale	45	4		
2011–12	Rochdale	44	4		
2012–13	Rochdale	46	4		
2013–14	Bradford C	8	1		
2013–14	*Rochdale*	7	0	**184**	**12**
2014–15	Bradford C	20	2	**28**	**3**
2014–15	*Carlisle U*	11	3		
2015–16	Carlisle U	44	2		
2016–17	Carlisle U	27	9		
2017–18	Carlisle U	6	0		
2018–19	Carlisle U	6	0	**94**	**14**

KERR, Keighran (F) 0 0

2018–19	Carlisle U	0	0		

LIDDLE, Gary (D) 528 28
H: 6 1 W: 12 06 b.Middlesbrough 15-6-86

2003–04	Middlesbrough	0	0		
2004–05	Middlesbrough	0	0		
2005–06	Middlesbrough	0	0		
2006 07	Hartlepool U	42	3		
2007–08	Hartlepool U	41	2		
2008–09	Hartlepool U	43	0		
2009–10	Hartlepool U	40	3		
2010–11	Hartlepool U	42	6		
2011–12	Hartlepool U	39	4	**247**	**18**
2012–13	Notts Co	46	0		
2013–14	Notts Co	32	4	**78**	**4**
2014–15	Bradford C	41	1		
2015–16	Bradford C	20	2	**61**	**3**
2015–16	Chesterfield	15	0		
2016–17	Chesterfield	26	1	**41**	**1**
2016–17	Carlisle U	21	1		
2017–18	Carlisle U	41	0		
2018–19	Carlisle U	39	1	**101**	**2**

McCARRON, Liam (M) 16 0
b. 7-3-01

2018–19	Carlisle U	16	0	**16**	**0**

MILLER, Gary (D) 320 5
H: 6 1 W: 11 03 b.Glasgow 15-4-87

2005–06	Livingston	4	0		
2006–07	Livingston	13	0		
2006–07	*Ayr U*	15	1	**15**	**1**
2007–08	Livingston	0	0		
2007–08	*Ross Co*	20	0		
2008–09	Livingston	23	0	**40**	**0**
2009–10	Ross Co	32	0		
2010–11	Ross Co	31	0		
2011–12	Ross Co	36	1	**119**	**1**
2012–13	St Johnstone	17	0		
2013–14	St Johnstone	25	1		
2014–15	St Johnstone	19	0	**61**	**1**
2015–16	Partick Thistle	21	1	**21**	**1**
2016–17	Plymouth Arg	31	0		
2017–18	Plymouth Arg	15	0	**46**	**0**
2018–19	Carlisle U	18	1	**18**	**1**

O'REILLY, Luke (G) 0 0
From Cardiff C, Tottenham H.

2018–19	Carlisle U	0	0		

PARKES, Tom (D) 278 6
H: 6 3 W: 12 05 b.Sutton-in-Ashfield 15-1-92
Internationals: England U17. England C.

2008–09	Leicester C	0	0		
2009–10	Leicester C	0	0		
2009–10	*Burton Alb*	22	1		
2010–11	Leicester C	0	0		
2010–11	*Yeovil T*	1	0	**1**	**0**
2010–11	*Burton Alb*	5	0		
2011–12	Leicester C	0	0		
2011–12	*Burton Alb*	4	0	**31**	**1**
2011–12	*Bristol R*	14	0		
2012–13	Leicester C	0	0		
2012–13	Bristol R	40	1		
2013–14	Bristol R	44	1		
2015–16	Bristol R	31	0	**129**	**2**
2016–17	Leyton Orient	41	1	**41**	**1**
2017–18	Carlisle U	37	1		
2018–19	Carlisle U	39	1	**76**	**2**

SCOUGALL, Stefan (M) 125 10
H: 5 7 W: 8 13 b.Edinburgh 7-12-92
Internationals: Scotland U21.

2013–14	Sheffield U	15	2		
2014–15	Sheffield U	25	1		
2015–16	Sheffield U	11	0		
2015–16	*Fleetwood T*	10	1	**10**	**1**
2016–17	Sheffield U	25	4	**76**	**7**
2017–18	St Johnstone	24	1		
2018–19	St Johnstone	0	0	**24**	**1**
2018–19	Carlisle U	15	1	**15**	**1**

SLATER, Regan (M) 36 2
b. 11-9-99

2016–17	Sheffield U	0	0		
2017–18	Sheffield U	1	0	**1**	**0**
2018–19	Carlisle U	35	2	**35**	**2**

Scholars
Armstrong, Jamie Peter; Barnes, Charlie George; Belchior, Rodrigues Pires Papa; Birch, Charlie Mark; Branthwaite, Jarrad Paul; Brockbank, Liam; Casson, Ceiran; Charters, Taylor Ryan; Dixon, Joshua; Galloway, Josh; Hodgson, Kelly Jay Alexander; Kerr, Keighran Ronnie David; Lightfoot, Robert Liam; McLachlan, Ben Thomas; Soper, Kyle; Ward, Regan; Wilson, Thomas Jackson.

CHARLTON ATH (22)

ANDERSON, Terrique (F) 0 0

2018–19	Charlton Ath	0	0		

ARIBO, Joe (M) 81 14
b.Camberwell 21-7-96
From Staines T.

2015–16	Charlton Ath	0	0		
2016–17	Charlton Ath	19	0		
2017–18	Charlton Ath	26	5		
2018–19	Charlton Ath	36	9	**81**	**14**

BAUER, Patrick (D) 169 10
H: 6 4 W: 13 08 b.Backnang 28-10-92
Internationals: Germany U17, U18, U20.

2010–11	Stuttgart	0	0		
2011–12	Stuttgart	0	0		
2012–13	Stuttgart	0	0		
2013–14	Maritimo	16	0		
2014–15	Maritimo	29	2	**45**	**2**
2015–16	Charlton Ath	19	1		
2016–17	Charlton Ath	36	4		
2017–18	Charlton Ath	34	3		
2018–19	Charlton Ath	35	0	**124**	**8**

BLUMBERG, Ryan (D) 0 0
b.Sydney 1-12-98

2018–19	Charlton Ath	0	0		

CAREY, Luke (M) 0 0

2018–19	Charlton Ath	0	0		

CUMMINGS, Joe (D) 0 0

2016–17	Sheffield U	0	0		
2017–18	Sheffield U	0	0		
2017–18	Charlton Ath	0	0		
2018–19	Charlton Ath	0	0		

DASILVA, Jay (D) 76 0
b. 22-4-98
Internationals: England U16, U17, U18, U19, U20.

2016–17	Chelsea	0	0		
2016–17	*Charlton Ath*	10	0		
2017–18	Chelsea	0	0		
2017–18	*Charlton Ath*	38	0		
2018–19	Charlton Ath	0	0	**48**	**0**
2018–19	*Bristol C*	28	0	**28**	**0**

DEMPSEY, Ben (M) 0 0
b. 25-11-99

2018–19	Charlton Ath	0	0		

DIJKSTEEL, Anfernee (M) 40 1
b. 27-10-96
Internationals: Netherlands U20.

2016–17	Charlton Ath	0	0		
2017–18	Charlton Ath	10	0		
2018–19	Charlton Ath	30	1	**40**	**1**

DOUGHTY, Alfie (M) 0 0

2018–19	Charlton Ath	0	0		

FORSTER-CASKEY, Jake (M) 166 16
H: 5 10 W: 10 00 b.Southend 25-4-94
Internationals: England U16, U17, U18, U20, U21.

2009–10	Brighton & HA	1	0		

2010–11	Brighton & HA	0	0		
2011–12	Brighton & HA	4	1		
2012–13	Brighton & HA	3	0		
2012–13	*Oxford U*	16	3	**16**	**3**
2013–14	Brighton & HA	28	3		
2014–15	Brighton & HA	29	1		
2015–16	Brighton & HA	2	0	**67**	**5**
2015–16	*Milton Keynes D*	20	1	**20**	**1**
2016–17	Charlton Ath	15	2		
2016–17	*Rotherham U*	6	0	**6**	**0**
2017–18	Charlton Ath	41	5		
2018–19	Charlton Ath	1	0	**57**	**7**

FOSU, Tarique (M) **105** **20**
H: 5 7 W: 10 08 b. 5-11-95
Internationals: England U18.

2013–14	Reading	0	0		
2014–15	Reading	1	0		
2015–16	Reading	0	0		
2015–16	*Fleetwood T*	6	1	**6**	**1**
2015–16	*Accrington S*	8	3	**8**	**3**
2016–17	Reading	0	0	**1**	**0**
2016–17	*Colchester U*	33	5	**33**	**5**
2017–18	Charlton Ath	30	9		
2018–19	Charlton Ath	27	2	**57**	**11**

HACKETT-FAIRCHILD, Recco (F) **12** **0**
H: 6 3 W: 11 00 b. 30-6-98
From Norwich C.

2017–18	Charlton Ath	5	0		
2018–19	Charlton Ath	7	0	**12**	**0**

KENNEDY, Mikhail (D) **2** **0**
b. 18-8-96
Internationals: Northern Ireland U17, U19, U21.

2014–15	Charlton Ath	0	0		
2015–16	Charlton Ath	2	0		
2016–17	Charlton Ath	0	0		
2017–18	Charlton Ath	0	0		
2018–19	Charlton Ath	0	0	**2**	**0**

LAPSLIE, George (M) **28** **0**
b. 5-9-97

2016–17	Charlton Ath	0	0		
2017–18	Charlton Ath	1	0		
2018–19	Charlton Ath	27	0	**28**	**0**

MALONEY, Taylor (M) **2** **0**
H: 5 9 W: 10 03 b. 21-1-99

2017–18	Charlton Ath	1	0		
2018–19	Charlton Ath	1	0	**2**	**0**

MARSHALL, Mark (M) **280** **22**
H: 5 7 W: 10 07 b.Jamaica 9-5-86

2008–09	Swindon T	12	0		
2009–10	Swindon T	7	0	**19**	**0**
2009–10	*Hereford U*	8	0	**8**	**0**
2010–11	Barnet	46	6		
2011–12	Barnet	25	1	**71**	**7**
2013–14	Coventry C	14	0	**14**	**0**
2014–15	Port Vale	46	7	**46**	**7**
2015–16	Bradford C	31	0		
2016–17	Bradford C	42	6	**73**	**6**
2017–18	Charlton Ath	27	1		
2018–19	Charlton Ath	22	1	**49**	**2**

MASCOLL, Jamie (M) **0** **0**
From Dulwich Hamlet.

2017–18	Charlton Ath	0	0		
2018–19	Charlton Ath	0	0		

MAYNARD-BREWER, Ashley (G) **0** **0**
b. 25-6-99
Internationals: Australia U23.

2017–18	Charlton Ath	0	0		
2018–19	Charlton Ath	0	0		

MORGAN, Albie (M) **8** **0**
b.Portsmouth 2-2-00

2018–19	Charlton Ath	8	0	**8**	**0**

OCRAN, Wilberforce (F) **0** **0**
b. 24-9-99
From Barnsley.

2018–19	Charlton Ath	0	0		

OSAGHAE, Joseph (G) **0** **0**
b. 20-2-01

2018–19	Charlton Ath	0	0		

PAGE, Lewis (D) **55** **1**
b.London 20-5-96

2014–15	West Ham U	0	0		
2015–16	West Ham U	0	0		
2015–16	*Cambridge U*	6	0	**6**	**0**
2016–17	West Ham U	0	0		
2016–17	*Coventry C*	22	0	**22**	**0**
2016–17	Charlton Ath	8	0		
2017–18	Charlton Ath	8	1		
2018–19	Charlton Ath	11	0	**27**	**1**

PARKER, Josh (F) **178** **31**
H: 5 11 W: 12 00 b.Slough 1-12-90
Internationals: Antigua and Barbuda Full caps.

2009–10	QPR	4	0		
2010–11	QPR	1	0	**5**	**0**
2010–11	*Northampton T*	3	0	**3**	**0**
2010–11	*Wycombe W*	1	0	**1**	**0**
2011–12	Oldham Ath	13	0	**13**	**0**
2011–12	*Dagenham & R*	8	0	**8**	**0**
2012–13	Oxford U	15	0	**15**	**0**
2013–14	Domzale	25	11	**25**	**11**
2014–15	Red Star Belgrade	9	2		
2015–16	Red Star Belgrade	3	2	**12**	**4**
2015–16	*Aberdeen*	7	0	**7**	**0**
2016–17	Gillingham	16	2		
2017–18	Gillingham	42	10		
2018–19	Gillingham	21	4	**79**	**16**
2018–19	Charlton Ath	10	0	**10**	**0**

PEARCE, Jason (D) **425** **20**
H: 5 11 W: 12 00 b.Hillingdon 6-12-87

2006–07	Portsmouth	0	0		
2007–08	Bournemouth	33	1		
2008–09	Bournemouth	44	2		
2009–10	Bournemouth	39	1		
2010–11	Bournemouth	46	3	**162**	**7**
2011–12	Portsmouth	43	2	**43**	**2**
2011–12	Leeds U	0	0		
2012–13	Leeds U	33	0		
2013–14	Leeds U	45	2		
2014–15	Leeds U	21	0	**99**	**2**
2014–15	Wigan Ath	16	2		
2015–16	Wigan Ath	31	2	**47**	**4**
2016–17	Charlton Ath	23	1		
2017–18	Charlton Ath	25	2		
2018–19	Charlton Ath	26	2	**74**	**5**

PHILLIPS, Dillon (M) **35** **0**
H: 6 2 W: 11 11 b. 11-6-95

2012–13	Charlton Ath	0	0		
2013–14	Charlton Ath	0	0		
2014–15	Charlton Ath	0	0		
2015–16	Charlton Ath	0	0		
2016–17	Charlton Ath	8	0		
2017–18	Charlton Ath	0	0		
2018–19	Charlton Ath	27	0	**35**	**0**

PRATLEY, Darren (M) **430** **45**
H: 6 1 W: 10 12 b.Barking 22-4-85

2001–02	Fulham	0	0		
2002–03	Fulham	0	0		
2003–04	Fulham	1	0		
2004–05	Fulham	0	0		
2004–05	*Brentford*	14	1		
2005–06	Fulham	0	0	**1**	**0**
2005–06	*Brentford*	32	4	**46**	**5**
2006–07	Swansea C	28	1		
2007–08	Swansea C	42	5		
2008–09	Swansea C	37	4		
2009–10	Swansea C	36	7		
2010–11	Swansea C	34	9	**177**	**26**
2011–12	Bolton W	25	1		
2012–13	Bolton W	31	2		
2013–14	Bolton W	20	2		
2014–15	Bolton W	22	4		
2015–16	Bolton W	36	1		
2016–17	Bolton W	12	0		
2017–18	Bolton W	32	2	**178**	**12**
2018–19	Charlton Ath	28	2	**28**	**2**

REEVES, Ben (D) **188** **32**
H: 5 10 W: 10 07 b.Verwood 19-11-91
Internationals: Northern Ireland Full caps.

2008–09	Southampton	0	0		
2009–10	Southampton	0	0		
2010–11	Southampton	0	0		
2011–12	Southampton	2	0		
2011–12	*Dagenham & R*	5	0	**5**	**0**
2012–13	Southampton	3	0	**5**	**0**
2012–13	*Southend U*	10	1	**10**	**1**
2013–14	Milton Keynes D	28	7		
2014–15	Milton Keynes D	30	7		
2015–16	Milton Keynes D	18	3		
2016–17	Milton Keynes D	34	7	**110**	**24**
2017–18	Charlton Ath	29	3		
2018–19	Charlton Ath	29	4	**58**	**7**

SARPENG-WIREDU, Brendan (M) **0** **0**
b. 7-11-99

2018–19	Charlton Ath	0	0		

SARR, Naby (D) **76** **3**
H: 6 5 W: 14 11 b.Marseille 13-8-93
Internationals: France U20, U21.

2012–13	Lyon	0	0		
2013–14	Lyon	2	0	**2**	**0**
2014–15	Sporting Lisbon	8	0	**8**	**0**
2015–16	Charlton Ath	12	1		
2017–18	Charlton Ath	18	0		
2018–19	Charlton Ath	36	2	**66**	**3**

SOLLY, Chris (D) **288** **3**
H: 5 8 W: 10 07 b.Rochester 20-1-91
Internationals: England U16, U17.

2008–09	Charlton Ath	1	0		
2009–10	Charlton Ath	9	0		
2010–11	Charlton Ath	14	1		
2011–12	Charlton Ath	44	0		
2012–13	Charlton Ath	45	1		
2013–14	Charlton Ath	12	0		
2014–15	Charlton Ath	38	0		
2015–16	Charlton Ath	34	0		
2016–17	Charlton Ath	27	0		
2017–18	Charlton Ath	27	0		
2018–19	Charlton Ath	37	1	**288**	**3**

STEVENSON, Toby (D) **3** **0**
b.Colchester 22-11-99
From Leyton Orient.

2018–19	Charlton Ath	3	0	**3**	**0**

TAYLOR, Lyle (F) **282** **82**
H: 6 2 W: 12 00 b.Greenwich 29-3-90
Internationals: Montserrat Full caps.

2007–08	Millwall	0	0		
2008–09	Millwall	0	0		
From Concord R					
2010–11	Bournemouth	11	0		
2011–12	Bournemouth	18	0	**29**	**0**
2011–12	*Hereford U*	8	2	**8**	**2**
2013–14	Sheffield U	20	2	**20**	**2**
2013–14	*Partick Thistle*	20	7		
2014–15	Scunthorpe U	18	3	**18**	**3**
2014–15	*Partick Thistle*	15	3	**35**	**10**
2015–16	AFC Wimbledon	42	20		
2016–17	AFC Wimbledon	43	10		
2017–18	AFC Wimbledon	46	14	**131**	**44**
2018–19	Charlton Ath	41	21	**41**	**21**

VETOKELE, Igor (F) **194** **48**
H: 5 8 W: 11 00 b.Ostend 23-3-92
Internationals: Belgium U17, U18, U19, U20, U21. Angola Full caps.

2010–11	Gent	0	0		
2011–12	Cercle Brugge	34	8		
2012–13	Cercle Brugge	4	1	**38**	**9**
2012–13	Copenhagen	15	3		
2013–14	Copenhagen	29	13	**44**	**16**
2014–15	Charlton Ath	41	11		
2015–16	Charlton Ath	16	1		
2016–17	Charlton Ath	0	0		
2016–17	*Zulte Waregem*	15	0	**15**	**0**
2016–17	*Sint-Truidense*	17	8	**17**	**8**
2017–18	Charlton Ath	0	0		
2018–19	Charlton Ath	23	3	**80**	**15**

WILLIAMS, Jon (M) **134** **3**
H: 5 6 W: 10 00 b.Tunbridge Wells 9-10-93
Internationals: Wales U17, U19, U21, Full caps.

2010–11	Crystal Palace	0	0		
2011–12	Crystal Palace	14	0		
2012–13	Crystal Palace	29	0		
2013–14	Crystal Palace	9	0		
2013–14	*Ipswich T*	13	1		
2014–15	Crystal Palace	2	0		
2014–15	*Ipswich T*	7	1		
2015–16	Crystal Palace	1	0		
2015–16	*Nottingham F*	10	0	**10**	**0**
2015–16	*Milton Keynes D*	13	0	**13**	**0**
2016–17	Crystal Palace	0	0		
2016–17	*Ipswich T*	8	0	**28**	**2**
2017–18	Crystal Palace	0	0		
2017–18	*Sunderland*	12	1	**12**	**1**
2018–19	Crystal Palace	0	0	**55**	**0**
2018–19	Charlton Ath	16	0	**16**	**0**

YAO, Kenneth (D) **0** **0**
b. 5-9-98

2018–19	Charlton Ath	0	0		

ZEMURA, Jordan (D) **0** **0**

2018–19	Charlton Ath	0	0		

Players retained or with offer of contract
Aouachria, Wassim Chouaib; Quitirna, Junior Armando; Sarpong, Wiredu Brendan Nana Akwasi.

Scholars
Afrane-Kesey, Richard George Marcel; Aidoo, Kasim Ishmael Amu-Kadar; Albon, Luca James; Allsopp, Edward; Barton, Frederick Joseph Terry; Buhari, Muhammad Ashraf Haroun; French, Billy; Godding, Ryan

Geoffrey; Gody, Naka James; Harvey, Nathan Michael; Isiaka, Kareem; Keefe, Samuel James; Kirunda, Tyrone Rhakeem; Moore, Charlie John; Osaghae, Joseph Etinosa; Powell, Johl Cameron; Vennings, James Frederick.

CHELSEA (23)

ABRAHAM, Tammy (F) 111 53
H: 6 3 W: 12 13 b.London 2-10-97
Internationals: England U18, U19, U21, Full caps.

2015–16	Chelsea	2	0		
2016–17	Chelsea	0	0		
2016–17	*Bristol C*	41	23	**41**	**23**
2017–18	Chelsea	0	0		
2017–18	*Swansea C*	31	5	**31**	**5**
2018–19	Chelsea	0	0	**2**	**0**
2018–19	*Aston Villa*	37	25	**37**	**25**

ALONSO, Marcus (D) 244 27
H: 6 2 W: 13 05 b.Madrid 28-12-90
Internationals: Spain U19, Full caps.

2008–09	RM Castilla	11	0		
2009–10	RM Castilla	28	3	**39**	**3**
2009–10	Real Madrid	1	0	**1**	**0**
2010–11	Bolton W	4	0		
2011–12	Bolton W	5	1		
2012–13	Bolton W	26	4	**35**	**5**
2013–14	Fiorentina	3	0		
2013–14	*Sunderland*	16	0	**16**	**0**
2014–15	Fiorentina	22	1		
2015–16	Fiorentina	31	3		
2016–17	Fiorentina	2	0	**58**	**4**
2016–17	Chelsea	31	6		
2017–18	Chelsea	33	7		
2018–19	Chelsea	31	2	**95**	**15**

AMPADU, Ethan (M) 9 0
b.Exeter 14-9-00
Internationals: England U16, Wales U17, U19, Full caps.

2016–17	Exeter C	8	0	**8**	**0**
2017–18	Chelsea	1	0		
2018–19	Chelsea	0	0	**1**	**0**

ARRIZABALAGA, Kepa (G) 179 0
H: 6 1 W: 12 11 b.Ondorroa 3-10-94
Internationals: Spain U18, U19, U21, Full caps.

2011–12	Basconia	12	0		
2012–13	Basconia	19	0	**31**	**0**
2013–14	Athletic Bilbao	0	0		
2014–15	Athletic Bilbao	0	0		
2014–15	*Ponferradina*	20	0	**20**	**0**
2015–16	Athletic Bilbao	0	0		
2015–16	*Vallodolid*	39	0	**39**	**0**
2016–17	Athletic Bilbao	23	0		
2017–18	Athletic Bilbao	30	0	**53**	**0**
2018–19	Chelsea	36	0	**36**	**0**

AZPILICUETA, Cesar (D) 381 7
H: 5 10 W: 10 13 b.Pamplona 28-8-89
Internationals: Spain U16, U17, U19, U20, U21, U23, Full caps.

2006–07	Osasuna	1	0		
2007–08	Osasuna	29	0		
2008–09	Osasuna	36	0		
2009–10	Osasuna	33	0	**99**	**0**
2010–11	Marseille	15	0		
2011–12	Marseille	30	1		
2012–13	Marseille	2	0	**47**	**1**
2012–13	Chelsea	27	0		
2013–14	Chelsea	29	0		
2014–15	Chelsea	29	0		
2015–16	Chelsea	37	2		
2016–17	Chelsea	38	1		
2017–18	Chelsea	37	2		
2018–19	Chelsea	38	1	**235**	**6**

BAKER, Lewis (M) 122 20
b.Luton 25-4-95
Internationals: England U17, U19, U20, U21.

2012–13	Chelsea	0	0		
2013–14	Chelsea	0	0		
2014–15	Chelsea	0	0		
2014–15	*Sheffield W*	4	0	**4**	**0**
2014–15	*Milton Keynes D*	12	3	**12**	**3**
2015–16	Chelsea	0	0		
2015–16	*Vitesse*	31	5		
2016–17	Chelsea	0	0		
2016–17	*Vitesse*	33	10	**64**	**15**
2017–18	Chelsea	0	0		
2017–18	*Middlesbrough*	12	1	**12**	**1**
2018–19	Chelsea	0	0		
2018–19	*Leeds U*	11	0	**11**	**0**
2018–19	*Reading*	19	1	**19**	**1**

BARKLEY, Ross (M) 196 28
H: 6 2 W: 12 00 b.Liverpool 5-12-93
Internationals: England U16, U17, U19, U20, U21, Full caps.

2010–11	Everton	0	0		
2011–12	Everton	6	0		
2012–13	Everton	7	0		
2012–13	*Sheffield W*	13	4	**13**	**4**
2012–13	*Leeds U*	4	0	**4**	**0**
2013–14	Everton	34	6		
2014–15	Everton	29	2		
2015–16	Everton	38	8		
2016–17	Everton	36	5		
2017–18	Everton	0	0	**150**	**21**
2017–18	Chelsea	2	0		
2018–19	Chelsea	27	3	**29**	**3**

BATSHUAYI, Michy (F) 227 85
H: 5 11 W: 12 04 b.Brussels 2-10-93
Internationals: Belgium U21, Full caps.

2010–11	Standard Liege	2	0		
2011–12	Standard Liege	23	6		
2012–13	Standard Liege	34	12		
2013–14	Standard Liege	38	21	**97**	**39**
2014–15	Marseille	26	9		
2015–16	Marseille	36	17	**62**	**26**
2016–17	Chelsea	20	5		
2017–18	Chelsea	12	2		
2017–18	*Borussia Dortmund*	10	7	**10**	**7**
2018–19	Chelsea	0	0	**32**	**7**
2018–19	*Valencia*	15	1	**15**	**1**
2018–19	*Crystal Palace*	11	5	**11**	**5**

BAXTER, Nathan (G) 34 0
b.London 8-11-98

2018–19	Chelsea	0	0		
2018–19	*Yeovil T*	34	0	**34**	**0**

BLACKMAN, Jamal (G) 85 0
H: 6 6 W: 14 09 b.Croydon 27-10-93
Internationals: England U16, U17, U18, U19.

2011–12	Chelsea	0	0		
2012–13	Chelsea	0	0		
2013–14	Chelsea	0	0		
2014–15	Chelsea	0	0		
2014–15	*Middlesbrough*	0	0		
2015–16	Chelsea	0	0		
2015–16	*Ostersunds FK*	12	0	**12**	**0**
2016–17	Chelsea	0	0		
2016–17	*Wycombe W*	42	0	**42**	**0**
2017–18	Chelsea	0	0		
2017–18	*Sheffield U*	31	0	**31**	**0**
2018–19	Chelsea	0	0		
2018–19	*Leeds U*	0	0		

BROWN, Isaiah (M) 73 8
H: 6 0 W: 10 13 b.Peterborough 7-1-97
Internationals: England U16, U17, U19, U20.

2012–13	WBA	1	0	**1**	**0**
2013–14	Chelsea	0	0		
2014–15	Chelsea	1	0		
2015–16	Chelsea	0	0		
2015–16	*Vitesse*	22	1	**22**	**1**
2016–17	Chelsea	0	0		
2016–17	*Rotherham U*	20	3	**20**	**3**
2016–17	*Huddersfield T*	15	4	**15**	**4**
2017–18	Chelsea	0	0		
2017–18	*Brighton & HA*	13	0	**13**	**0**
2018–19	Chelsea	0	0	**1**	**0**
2018–19	*Leeds U*	1	0	**1**	**0**

BULKA, Marcin (G) 0 0
H: 6 6 W: 13 10 b.Ptock 4-10-99
Internationals: Poland U18, U19, U20, U21.

2018–19	Chelsea	0	0		

CABALLERO, Willy (G) 326 0
H: 6 1 W: 12 08 b.Santa Elena 28-9-81
Internationals: Argentina U21, Full caps.

2001–04	Boca Juniors	15	0	**15**	**0**
2004–08	Elche	67	0		
2008–09	Elche	38	0		
2009–10	Elche	39	0		
2010–11	Elche	22	0	**166**	**0**
2010–11	Malaga	15	0		
2011–12	Malaga	28	0		
2012–13	Malaga	36	0		
2013–14	Malaga	38	0	**117**	**0**
2014–15	Manchester C	2	0		
2015–16	Manchester C	4	0		
2016–17	Manchester C	17	0	**23**	**0**
2017–18	Chelsea	3	0		
2018–19	Chelsea	2	0	**5**	**0**

CAHILL, Gary (D) 392 30
H: 6 2 W: 12 06 b.Dronfield 19-12-85
Internationals: England U20, U21, Full caps.

2003–04	Aston Villa	0	0		
2004–05	Aston Villa	0	0		
2004–05	*Burnley*	27	1	**27**	**1**
2005–06	Aston Villa	7	1		
2006–07	Aston Villa	20	0		
2007–08	Aston Villa	1	0	**28**	**1**
2007–08	*Sheffield U*	16	2	**16**	**2**
2007–08	Bolton W	13	0		
2008–09	Bolton W	33	3		
2009–10	Bolton W	29	5		
2010–11	Bolton W	36	3		
2011–12	Bolton W	19	2	**130**	**13**
2011–12	Chelsea	10	1		
2012–13	Chelsea	26	2		
2013–14	Chelsea	30	1		
2014–15	Chelsea	36	1		
2015–16	Chelsea	23	2		
2016–17	Chelsea	37	6		
2017–18	Chelsea	27	0		
2018–19	Chelsea	2	0	**191**	**13**

CHALOBAH, Trevor (D) 43 2
H: 6 3 b.Freetown 5-7-99
Internationals: England U16, U17, U19, U20, U21.

2017–18	Chelsea	0	0		
2018–19	Chelsea	0	0		
2018–19	*Ipswich T*	43	2	**43**	**2**

CHRISTENSEN, Andreas (D) 98 5
H: 6 2 W: 11 09 b.Allerod 10-4-96
Internationals: Denmark U16, U17, U19, U21, Full caps.

2012–13	Chelsea	0	0		
2013–14	Chelsea	0	0		
2014–15	Chelsea	1	0		
2015–16	Chelsea	0	0		
2015–16	*Borussia M'gladbach*	31	3		
2016–17	Chelsea	0	0		
2016–17	Borussia M'gladbach	31	2	**62**	**5**
2017–18	Chelsea	27	0		
2018–19	Chelsea	8	0	**36**	**0**

COLKETT, Charlie (M) 35 4
H: 5 9 W: 10 03 b.London 4-9-96
Internationals: England U16, U17, U18, U19, U20.

2015–16	Chelsea	0	0		
2016–17	Chelsea	0	0		
2016–17	*Bristol R*	15	3	**15**	**3**
2016–17	*Swindon T*	19	1	**19**	**1**
2017–18	Chelsea	0	0		
2018–19	Chelsea	0	0		
2018–19	*Shrewsbury T*	1	0	**1**	**0**

Transferred to Ostersunds FK January 2019.

COLLINS, Bradley (G) 70 0
H: 6 0 W: 10 12 b. 18-2-97

2017–18	Chelsea	0	0		
2017–18	*Forest Green R*	39	0	**39**	**0**
2018–19	Chelsea	0	0		
2018–19	*Burton Alb*	31	0	**31**	**0**

CUMMING, Jamie (G) 0 0
b.Winchester 4-9-99
Internationals: England U17, U19.

2018–19	Chelsea	0	0		

DRINKWATER, Daniel (M) 276 17
H: 5 10 W: 11 00 b.Manchester 5-3-90
Internationals: England U18, U19, Full caps.

2008–09	Manchester U	0	0		
2009–10	Manchester U	0	0		
2009–10	*Huddersfield T*	33	2	**33**	**2**
2010–11	Manchester U	0	0		
2010–11	*Cardiff C*	9	0	**9**	**0**
2010–11	*Watford*	12	0	**12**	**0**
2011–12	Manchester U	0	0		
2011–12	*Barnsley*	17	1	**17**	**1**
2011–12	Leicester C	19	2		
2012–13	Leicester C	42	1		
2013–14	Leicester C	45	7		
2014–15	Leicester C	23	0		
2015–16	Leicester C	35	2		
2016–17	Leicester C	29	1		
2017–18	Leicester C	0	0	**193**	**13**
2017–18	Chelsea	12	1		
2018–19	Chelsea	0	0	**12**	**1**

EMERSON, dos Santos (D) 76 2
H: 5 9 W: 9 13 b.Santos 13-3-94
Internationals: Brazil U17. Italy Full caps.

2011	Santos	0	0		
2012	Santos	1	0		

2013	Santos	14	1		
2014	Santos	3	0	**18**	**1**
2014–15	*Palermo*	9	0	**9**	**0**
2015–16	Roma	8	1		
2016–17	Roma	25	0		
2017–18	Roma	1	0	**34**	**1**
2017–18	Chelsea	5	0		
2018–19	Chelsea	10	0	**15**	**0**

FABREGAS, Francesc (M) **446 78**
H: 5 11 W: 11 01 b.Arenys de Mar 4-5-87
Internationals: Spain Youth, U21, Full caps.

2003–04	Arsenal	0	0		
2004–05	Arsenal	33	2		
2005–06	Arsenal	35	3		
2006–07	Arsenal	38	2		
2007–08	Arsenal	32	7		
2008–09	Arsenal	22	3		
2009–10	Arsenal	27	15		
2010–11	Arsenal	25	3	**212**	**35**
2011–12	Barcelona	28	9		
2012–13	Barcelona	32	11		
2013–14	Barcelona	36	8	**96**	**28**
2014–15	Chelsea	34	3		
2015–16	Chelsea	37	5		
2016–17	Chelsea	29	5		
2017–18	Chelsea	32	2		
2018–19	Chelsea	6	0	**138**	**15**

Transferred to Monaco January 2019.

GIROUD, Olivier (F) **372 142**
H: 6 3 W: 13 11 b.Chambery 30-9-86
Internationals: France Full caps.

2005–06	Grenoble	3	0		
2006–07	Grenoble	15	2	**18**	**2**
2008–09	Tours	23	8		
2009–10	Tours	38	21	**61**	**29**
2010–11	Montpellier	37	12		
2011–12	Montpellier	36	21	**73**	**33**
2012–13	Arsenal	34	11		
2013–14	Arsenal	36	16		
2014–15	Arsenal	27	14		
2015–16	Arsenal	38	16		
2016–17	Arsenal	29	12		
2017–18	Arsenal	16	4	**180**	**73**
2017–18	Chelsea	13	3		
2018–19	Chelsea	27	2	**40**	**5**

GRANT, Josh (D) **8 0**
b. 11-10-98
Internationals: England U18, U20.

2018–19	Chelsea	0	0		
2018–19	*Yeovil T*	8	0	**8**	**0**

GUEHI, Marc (D) **0 0**
Internationals: England U16, U17, U18, U19, U20.

2018–19	Chelsea	0	0		

HAZARD, Eden (M) **391 121**
H: 5 7 W: 8 11 b.La Louviere 7-1-91
Internationals: Belgium U15, U16, U17, U19, Full caps.

2007–08	Lille	3	0		
2008–09	Lille	30	4		
2009–10	Lille	37	5		
2010–11	Lille	38	7		
2011–12	Lille	38	20	**146**	**36**
2012–13	Chelsea	34	9		
2013–14	Chelsea	35	14		
2014–15	Chelsea	38	14		
2015–16	Chelsea	31	4		
2016–17	Chelsea	36	16		
2017–18	Chelsea	34	12		
2018–19	Chelsea	37	16	**245**	**85**

HECTOR, Michael (D) **267 15**
H: 6 4 W: 12 13 b.Newham 19-7-92
Internationals: Jamaica Full caps.

2009–10	Reading	0	0		
2010–11	Reading	0	0		
2011	*Dundalk*	11	2	**11**	**2**
2011–12	Reading	0	0		
2011–12	*Barnet*	27	2	**27**	**2**
2012–13	Reading	0	0		
2012–13	*Shrewsbury T*	8	0	**8**	**0**
2012–13	*Aldershot T*	8	1	**8**	**1**
2012–13	*Cheltenham T*	18	1	**18**	**1**
2013–14	Reading	9	0		
2013–14	*Aberdeen*	20	1	**20**	**1**
2014–15	Reading	41	3		
2015–16	Chelsea	0	0		
2015–16	*Reading*	30	1	**80**	**4**
2016–17	Chelsea	0	0		
2016–17	*Ein Frankfurt*	22	1	**22**	**1**
2017–18	Chelsea	0	0		
2017–18	*Hull C*	36	1	**36**	**1**
2018–19	Chelsea	0	0		
2018–19	*Sheffield W*	37	2	**37**	**2**

HIGUAIN, Gonzalo (F) **431 242**
H: 6 0 W: 11 11 b.Brest 10-12-87
Internationals: Argentina U23, Full caps.

2004–05	River Plate	4	0		
2005–06	River Plate	14	5		
2006–07	River Plate	17	8	**35**	**13**
2006–07	Real Madrid	19	2		
2007–08	Real Madrid	25	8		
2008–09	Real Madrid	34	22		
2009–10	Real Madrid	32	27		
2010–11	Real Madrid	17	10		
2011–12	Real Madrid	35	22		
2012–13	Real Madrid	28	16	**190**	**107**
2013–14	Napoli	32	17		
2014–15	Napoli	37	18		
2015–16	Napoli	35	36	**104**	**71**
2016–17	Juventus	38	24		
2017–18	Juventus	35	16		
2018–19	Juventus	0	0	**73**	**40**
2018–19	*AC Milan*	15	6	**15**	**6**

On loan from Juventus.

2018–19	Chelsea	14	5	**14**	**5**

HUDSON-ODOI, Callum (M) **12 0**
H: 6 0 b.Wandsworth 7-11-00
Internationals: England U16, U17, U18, U19, Full caps.

2017–18	Chelsea	2	0		
2018–19	Chelsea	10	0	**12**	**0**

JAMES, Reece (D) **45 3**
b.London 8-12-99
Internationals: England U18, U19, U20.

2018–19	Chelsea	0	0		
2018–19	*Wigan Ath*	45	3	**45**	**3**

JORGINHO, Filho Jorge (M) **290 16**
H: 5 11 W: 11 03 b.Imbituba 20-12-91
Internationals: Italy Full caps.

2010–11	Verona	0	0		
2010–11	*Sambonifacese*	31	1	**31**	**1**
2011–12	Verona	30	2		
2012–13	Verona	41	2		
2013–14	Verona	18	7	**89**	**11**
2013–14	Napoli	15	0		
2014–15	Napoli	23	0		
2015–16	Napoli	35	0		
2016–17	Napoli	27	0		
2017–18	Napoli	33	2	**133**	**2**
2018–19	Chelsea	37	2	**37**	**2**

KALAS, Tomas (D) **191 2**
H: 6 0 W: 12 00 b.Olomouc 15-5-93
Internationals: Czech Republic U17, U18, U19, U21, Full caps.

2009–10	Sigma Olomouc	1	0		
2010–11	Chelsea	0	0		
2010–11	*Sigma Olomouc*	4	0	**5**	**0**
2011–12	Chelsea	0	0		
2012–13	Chelsea	0	0		
2012–13	*Vitesse*	34	1	**34**	**1**
2013–14	Chelsea	2	0		
2014–15	Chelsea	0	0		
2014–15	*Cologne*	0	0		
2014–15	*Middlesbrough*	17	0		
2015–16	Chelsea	0	0		
2015–16	*Middlesbrough*	26	0	**43**	**0**
2016–17	Chelsea	0	0		
2016–17	*Fulham*	36	1		
2017–18	Chelsea	0	0		
2017–18	*Fulham*	33	0	**69**	**1**
2018–19	Chelsea	0	0	**2**	**0**
2018–19	*Bristol C*	38	0	**38**	**0**

KANE, Todd (D) **155 10**
H: 5 11 W: 11 00 b.Huntingdon 17-9-93
Internationals: England U19.

2011–12	Chelsea	0	0		
2012–13	Chelsea	0	0		
2012–13	*Preston NE*	3	0	**3**	**0**
2012–13	*Blackburn R*	14	0		
2013–14	Chelsea	0	0		
2013–14	*Blackburn R*	27	2	**41**	**2**
2014–15	Chelsea	0	0		
2014–15	*Bristol C*	5	0	**5**	**0**
2014–15	*Nottingham F*	8	1	**8**	**1**
2015–16	Chelsea	0	0		
2015–16	*NEC*	31	1	**31**	**1**
2016–17	Chelsea	0	0		
2017–18	Chelsea	0	0		
2017–18	*FC Groningen*	11	0	**11**	**0**
2017–18	*Oxford U*	17	3	**17**	**3**
2018–19	Chelsea	0	0		
2018–19	*Hull C*	39	3	**39**	**3**

KANTE, Ngolo (M) **255 14**
H: 5 7 W: 11 00 b.Paris 29-3-91
Internationals: France Full caps.

2011–12	Boulogne	1	0		
2012–13	Boulogne	37	3	**38**	**3**
2013–14	Caen	38	2		
2014–15	Caen	37	2	**75**	**4**
2015–16	Leicester C	37	1	**37**	**1**
2016–17	Chelsea	35	1		
2017–18	Chelsea	34	1		
2018–19	Chelsea	36	4	**105**	**6**

KENEDY, Robert (F) **84 6**
H: 6 0 W: 12 08 b.Santa Rita do Sapucai 8-2-96
Internationals: Brazil U17, U20, U23.

2013	Fluminense	9	0		
2014	Fluminense	20	2		
2015	Fluminense	1	0	**30**	**2**
2015–16	Chelsea	14	1		
2016–17	Chelsea	1	0		
2016–17	*Watford*	1	0	**1**	**0**
2017–18	Chelsea	0	0		
2017–18	*Newcastle U*	13	2		
2018–19	Chelsea	0	0	**15**	**1**
2018–19	*Newcastle U*	25	1	**38**	**3**

KOVACIC, Mateo (M) **228 12**
H: 5 11 W: 11 07 b.Linz 6-5-94
Internationals: Croatia U17, U19, U21, Full caps.

2010–11	Dinamo Zagreb	7	1		
2011–12	Dinamo Zagreb	25	4		
2012–13	Dinamo Zagreb	11	1	**43**	**6**
2012–13	InterMilan	13	0		
2013–14	InterMilan	32	0		
2014–15	InterMilan	35	5	**80**	**5**
2015–16	Real Madrid	25	0		
2016–17	Real Madrid	27	1		
2017–18	Real Madrid	21	0		
2018–19	Real Madrid	0	0	**73**	**1**

On loan from Real Madrid.

2018–19	Chelsea	32	0	**32**	**0**

LOFTUS-CHEEK, Ruben (M) **70 9**
H: 6 4 W: 11 03 b.Lewisham 23-1-96
Internationals: England U16, U17, U19, U21, Full caps.

2012–13	Chelsea	0	0		
2013–14	Chelsea	0	0		
2014–15	Chelsea	3	0		
2015–16	Chelsea	13	1		
2016–17	Chelsea	6	0		
2017–18	Chelsea	0	0		
2017–18	*Crystal Palace*	24	2	**24**	**2**
2018–19	Chelsea	24	6	**46**	**7**

LUIZ, David (D) **268 16**
H: 6 2 W: 13 03 b.Sao Paulo 22-4-87
Internationals: Brazil U20, Full caps.

2005	Vitoria	0	0		
2006	Vitoria	26	1	**26**	**1**
2006–07	Benfica	10	0		
2007–08	Benfica	8	0		
2008–09	Benfica	19	2		
2009–10	Benfica	29	2		
2010–11	Benfica	16	0	**82**	**4**
2010–11	Chelsea	12	2		
2011–12	Chelsea	20	2		
2012–13	Chelsea	30	2		
2013–14	Chelsea	19	0		
2014–15	PSG	0	0		
2016–17	PSG	0	0		
2016–17	Chelsea	33	1		
2017–18	Chelsea	10	1		
2018–19	Chelsea	36	3	**160**	**11**

McEACHRAN, George (M) **0 0**
H: 5 8 b.Oxford 30-8-00
Internationals: England U16, U17, U18, U19.

2018–19	Chelsea	0	0		

MIAZGA, Matt (D) **121 5**
H: 6 4 W: 12 08 b.Clifton, NJ 19-7-95
Internationals: Poland U18. USA U18, U20, U23, Full caps.

2013	New York Red Bulls	1	0		
2014	New York Red Bulls	7	0		
2015	New York Red Bulls	26	1	**34**	**1**
2015–16	Chelsea	2	0		
2016–17	Chelsea	0	0		
2016–17	*Vitesse*	23	0		
2017–18	Chelsea	0	0		
2017–18	*Vitesse*	36	4	**59**	**4**
2018–19	Chelsea	0	0	**2**	**0**
2018–19	*Nantes*	8	0	**8**	**0**
2018–19	*Reading*	18	0	**18**	**0**

MORATA, Alvaro (F) 188 62
H: 6 2 W: 12 08 b.Madrid 23-10-92
Internationals: Spain U17, U18, U19, U21, Full caps.

2010–11	Real Madrid	1	0		
2011–12	Real Madrid	1	0		
2012–13	Real Madrid	12	2		
2013–14	Real Madrid	23	8		
2014–15	Juventus	29	8		
2015–16	Juventus	34	7	**63**	**15**
2016–17	Real Madrid	26	15	**63**	**25**
2017–18	Chelsea	31	11		
2018–19	Chelsea	16	5	**47**	**16**
2018–19	*Atletico Madrid*	15	6	**15**	**6**

MOSES, Victor (M) 292 35
H: 5 10 W: 11 07 b.Lagos 12-12-90
Internationals: England U16, U17, U19, U21. Nigeria Full caps.

2007–08	Crystal Palace	13	3		
2008–09	Crystal Palace	27	2		
2009–10	Crystal Palace	18	6	**58**	**11**
2009–10	Wigan Ath	14	1		
2010–11	Wigan Ath	21	1		
2011–12	Wigan Ath	38	6		
2012–13	Wigan Ath	1	0	**74**	**8**
2012–13	Chelsea	23	1		
2013–14	Chelsea	0	0		
2013–14	*Liverpool*	19	1	**19**	**1**
2014–15	Chelsea	0	0		
2014–15	*Stoke C*	19	3	**19**	**3**
2015–16	Chelsea	0	0		
2015–16	*West Ham U*	21	1	**21**	**1**
2016–17	Chelsea	34	3		
2017–18	Chelsea	28	3		
2018–19	Chelsea	2	0	**87**	**7**
2018–19	*Fenerbahce*	14	4	**14**	**4**

MOUNT, Mason (M) 64 17
H: 5 10 b.Portsmouth 10-1-99
Internationals: England U16, U17, U18, U19, U21.

2017–18	Chelsea	0	0		
2017–18	*Vitesse*	29	9	**29**	**9**
2018–19	Chelsea	0	0		
2018–19	*Derby Co*	35	8	**35**	**8**

PALMER, Kasey (M) 72 9
H: 5 11 W: 10 10 b.London 9-11-96
Internationals: England U17, U18, U20, U21.

2015–16	Chelsea	0	0		
2016–17	Chelsea	0	0		
2016–17	*Huddersfield T*	24	4		
2017–18	Chelsea	0	0		
2017–18	*Huddersfield T*	4	0	**28**	**4**
2017–18	*Derby Co*	15	2	**15**	**2**
2018–19	Chelsea	0	0		
2018–19	*Blackburn R*	14	1	**14**	**1**
2018–19	*Bristol C*	15	2	**15**	**2**

PEDRO, Rodriguez (F) 330 86
H: 5 7 W: 10 01 b.Santa Cruz de Tenerife 28-7-87
Internationals: Spain U21, Full caps.

2007–08	Barcelona	2	0		
2008–09	Barcelona	6	0		
2009–10	Barcelona	34	12		
2010–11	Barcelona	33	13		
2011–12	Barcelona	29	5		
2012–13	Barcelona	28	7		
2013–14	Barcelona	37	15		
2014–15	Barcelona	35	6	**204**	**58**
2015–16	Chelsea	29	7		
2016–17	Chelsea	35	9		
2017–18	Chelsea	31	4		
2018–19	Chelsea	31	8	**126**	**28**

PIAZON, Lucas (M) 119 24
H: 6 0 W: 11 11 b.Curitiba 20-1-94
Internationals: Brazil U17, U20, U23.

2011–12	Chelsea	0	0		
2012–13	Chelsea	1	0		
2012–13	*Malaga*	11	0	**11**	**0**
2013–14	Chelsea	0	0		
2013–14	*Vitesse*	29	11		
2014–15	Chelsea	0	0		
2014–15	Vitesse	0	0	**29**	**11**
2014–15	*Eintracht Frankfurt*	0	0		
2015–16	Chelsea	0	0		
2015–16	*Reading*	23	3	**23**	**3**
2016–17	Chelsea	0	0		
2016–17	*Fulham*	29	5		
2017–18	Chelsea	0	0		
2017–18	*Fulham*	22	5	**51**	**10**
2018–19	Chelsea	0	0	**1**	**0**
2018–19	*Chievo*	4	0	**4**	**0**

RUDIGER, Antonio (D) 182 7
H: 6 3 W: 13 05 b.Berlin 3-3-93
Internationals: Germany U18, U19, U20, U21, Full caps.

2011–12	Stuttgart	1	0		
2012–13	Stuttgart	16	0		
2013–14	Stuttgart	30	2		
2014–15	Stuttgart	19	0	**66**	**2**
2015–16	Roma	30	2		
2016–17	Roma	26	0	**56**	**2**
2017–18	Chelsea	27	2		
2018–19	Chelsea	33	1	**60**	**3**

STERLING, Dujon (D) 38 0
H: 5 11 b.London 3-11-99
Internationals: England U16, U17, U19, U20.

2017–18	Chelsea	0	0		
2018–19	Chelsea	0	0		
2018–19	*Coventry C*	38	0	**38**	**0**

TOMORI, Fikayo (D) 79 1
H: 6 0 W: 11 11 b.Calgary 19-12-97
Internationals: Canada U20. England U19, U20, U21.

2015–16	Chelsea	1	0		
2016–17	Chelsea	0	0		
2016–17	*Brighton & HA*	9	0	**9**	**0**
2017–18	Chelsea	0	0		
2017–18	*Hull C*	25	0	**25**	**0**
2018–19	Chelsea	0	0	**1**	**0**
2018–19	*Derby Co*	44	1	**44**	**1**

UGBO, Ike (F) 46 4
H: 6 1 W: 11 07 b.Lewisham 21-9-98
Internationals: Engalnd U17, U20.

2017–18	Chelsea	0	0		
2017–18	*Barnsley*	16	1	**16**	**1**
2017–18	*Milton Keynes D*	15	2	**15**	**2**
2018–19	Chelsea	0	0		
2018–19	*Scunthorpe U*	15	1	**15**	**1**

WILLIAN, da Silva (M) 334 49
H: 5 9 W: 11 10 b.Ribeirao 9-8-88
Internationals: Brazil U20, Full caps.

2006	Corinthians	5	0		
2007	Corinthians	0	0	**5**	**0**
2008–09	Shakhtar Donetsk	29	5		
2009–10	Shakhtar Donetsk	22	5		
2010–11	Shakhtar Donetsk	28	3		
2011–12	Shakhtar Donetsk	27	5		
2012–13	Shakhtar Donetsk	14	2	**120**	**20**
2012–13	Anzhi Makhachkala	7	1		
2013–14	Anzhi Makhachkala	4	0	**11**	**1**
2013–14	Chelsea	25	4		
2014–15	Chelsea	36	2		
2015–16	Chelsea	35	5		
2016–17	Chelsea	34	8		
2017–18	Chelsea	36	6		
2018–19	Chelsea	32	3	**198**	**28**

ZAPPACOSTA, Davide (M) 207 10
H: 6 1 W: 11 00 b.Sora 11-6-92
Internationals: Italy U21, Full caps.

2009–10	Isola Liri	2	0		
2010–11	Isola Liri	11	1	**13**	**1**
2011–12	Avellino	27	0		
2012–13	Avellino	24	1		
2013–14	Avellino	32	2	**83**	**3**
2014–15	Atalanta	29	3	**29**	**3**
2015–16	Torino	25	1		
2016–17	Torino	29	1		
2017–18	Torino	2	0	**56**	**2**
2017–18	Chelsea	22	1		
2018–19	Chelsea	4	0	**26**	**1**

ZOUMA, Kurt (D) 174 7
H: 6 2 W: 13 04 b.Lyon 27-10-94
Internationals: France U16, U17, U19, U20, U21, Full caps.

2011–12	St Etienne	20	1		
2012–13	St Etienne	18	2		
2013–14	Chelsea	0	0		
2013–14	*St Etienne*	23	0	**61**	**3**
2014–15	Chelsea	15	0		
2015–16	Chelsea	23	1		
2016–17	Chelsea	9	0		
2017–18	Chelsea	0	0		
2017–18	*Stoke C*	34	1	**34**	**1**
2018–19	Chelsea	0	0	**47**	**1**
2018–19	*Everton*	32	2	**32**	**2**

Players retained or with offer of contract
Aina, Temitayo Olufisayo; Angban, Bekanty Victorien; Anjorin, Faustino Adebola Rasheed; Baba, Abdul Rahman; Bakayoko, Tiemoue; Ballo, Thierno Mamadou; Baxter, Nathan; Clarke-Salter, Jake-Liam; Colley, Joseph; Dasilva, Jay Rhys; De Souza, Nathan Allan; Ekwah Elimby, Pierre Emmanuel; Familia-Castillo, Juan Carlos; Gallagher, Conor; Gilmour, Billy Clifford; Lamptey, Tariq; Lavinier, Marcel; Lewis, Marcel; Maatsen, Ian; Maddox, Jacob; McCormick, Luke; Mola, Clinton; Musonda, Charles; Nartey, Richard Nicos Tettey; Nunn, George Johannes; Omeruo, Kenneth; Pantic, Danilo; Pasalic, Mario; Pulisic, Christian Mate; Redan, Daishawn Orpheo Marvin; Russell, Jonathan; Simeu, Dynel Brown Kembo; Tie, Nicolas; Uwakwe, Tariq; Van Ginkel, Marco Wulfert Cornelius; Wakely, Jack; Ziger, Karlo.

Scholars
Aina, Jordan; Askew, Jake; Broja, Armando; Clark, James Robert; Lawrence, Henry; McClelland, Sam; Wady, Ethan James.

CHELTENHAM T (24)

ADDAI, Alex (M) 21 0
b.Stepney 20-12-93

2011–12	Blackpool	0	0		
2012–13	Blackpool	0	0		
2013–14	Blackpool	0	0		

From Carshalton Ath, Whitehawk, Crawley Down Gatwick, Kingstonian, Grays Ath, Wingate & Finchley, Merstham.

2018–19	Cheltenham T	21	0	**21**	**0**

ATANGANA, Nigel (M) 146 4
H: 6 2 W: 11 05 b.Corbeil-Essonnes 9-9-89

2014–15	Portsmouth	30	1		
2015–16	Portsmouth	13	0	**43**	**1**
2015–16	Leyton Orient	16	0		
2016–17	Leyton Orient	29	0	**45**	**0**
2017–18	Cheltenham T	32	1		
2018–19	Cheltenham T	26	2	**58**	**3**

BASFORD, Aaron (F) 0 0

2018–19	Cheltenham T	0	0		

BINGHAM, Rakish (F) 138 21
H: 6 0 W: 12 00 b.Newham 25-10-93

2011–12	Wigan Ath	0	0		
2012–13	Wigan Ath	0	0		
2013–14	Wigan Ath	0	0		
2014–15	Mansfield T	28	6	**28**	**6**
2014–15	*Hartlepool U*	5	1		
2015–16	Hartlepool U	31	4	**36**	**5**
2016–17	Hamilton A	30	5		
2017–18	Hamilton A	32	5		
2018–19	Hamilton A	2	0	**64**	**10**
2018–19	Cheltenham T	10	0	**10**	**0**

BOWER, Matthew (D) 5 0
H: 6 6 W: 11 05 b. 11-12-98

2016–17	Cheltenham T	0	0		
2017–18	Cheltenham T	3	0		
2018–19	Cheltenham T	2	0	**5**	**0**

BOYLE, William (D) 118 11
H: 6 2 W: 11 00 b.Garforth 1-9-95

2014–15	Huddersfield T	1	0		
2015–16	Huddersfield T	1	0		
2015–16	*York C*	12	0	**12**	**0**
2016–17	Huddersfield T	0	0	**2**	**0**
2016–17	*Kilmarnock*	11	0	**11**	**0**
2016–17	Cheltenham T	21	2		
2017–18	Cheltenham T	34	5		
2018–19	Cheltenham T	38	4	**93**	**11**

BRENNAN, Archie (M) 0 0

2018–19	Cheltenham T	0	0		

BROOM, Ryan (M) 48 2
H: 5 10 W: 12 08 b.Newport 4-9-96

2015–16	Bristol R	1	0		
2016–17	Bristol R	5	0		
2017–18	Bristol R	3	0	**9**	**0**
2018–19	Cheltenham T	39	2	**39**	**2**

CLEMENTS, Chris (M) 190 18
H: 5 9 W: 10 04 b.Birmingham 6-2-90

2008–09	Crewe Alex	0	0		
2009	*IBV*	15	1	**15**	**1**
2009–10	Crewe Alex	0	0		
2010–11	Crewe Alex	0	0		
2013–14	Mansfield T	23	1		
2014–15	Mansfield T	34	1		
2015–16	Mansfield T	38	5		
2016–17	Mansfield T	20	3	**115**	**10**
2016–17	Grimsby T	16	4		
2017–18	Grimsby T	0	0	**16**	**4**

2017–18	*Forest Green R*	14	1	**14**	**1**
2018–19	Cheltenham T	30	2	**30**	**2**

DAWSON, Kevin (M) **238** **19**
H: 5 10 W: 12 08 b.Dublin 30-6-90
Internationals: Republic of Ireland U18.

2011	Shelbourne	26	2		
2012	Shelbourne	25	2	**51**	**4**
2012–13	Yeovil T	20	2		
2013–14	Yeovil T	35	1		
2014–15	Yeovil T	17	1		
2015–16	Yeovil T	10	0		
2016–17	Yeovil T	39	2	**121**	**6**
2016–17	Cheltenham T	0	0		
2017–18	Cheltenham T	34	5		
2018–19	Cheltenham T	32	4	**66**	**9**

DEBAYO, Josh (D) **5** **0**
H: 6 0 W: 10 10 b.London 17-10-96

2015–16	Southampton	0	0		
2016–17	Leicester C	0	0		
2018–19	Cheltenham T	5	0	**5**	**0**

DUKU, Immanuelson (F) **11** **1**
b. 28-12-92
From Chesham U, Hemel Hempstead T, Kings Langley, Banbury U, Hayes & Yeading.

2018–19	Cheltenham T	11	1	**11**	**1**

DUNCAN, Camden (D) **0** **0**

2018–19	Cheltenham T	0	0		

FLINDERS, Scott (G) **434** **1**
H: 6 4 W: 13 00 b.Rotherham 12-6-86
Internationals: England U20.

2004–05	Barnsley	11	0		
2005–06	Barnsley	3	0	**14**	**0**
2006–07	Crystal Palace	8	0		
2006–07	*Gillingham*	9	0	**9**	**0**
2006–07	*Brighton & HA*	12	0	**12**	**0**
2007–08	Crystal Palace	0	0		
2007–08	*Yeovil T*	9	0	**9**	**0**
2008–09	Crystal Palace	0	0	**8**	**0**
2009–10	Hartlepool U	46	0		
2010–11	Hartlepool U	26	1		
2011–12	Hartlepool U	45	0		
2012–13	Hartlepool U	46	0		
2013–14	Hartlepool U	43	0		
2014–15	Hartlepool U	46	0	**252**	**1**
2015–16	York C	43	0	**43**	**0**

From Macclesfield T.

2017–18	Cheltenham T	41	0		
2018–19	Cheltenham T	46	0	**87**	**0**

FORSTER, Jordon (D) **126** **8**
b.Edinburgh 23-9-93

2010–11	Hibernian	0	0		
2011–12	Hibernian	0	0		
2011–12	*Berwick R*	10	2	**10**	**2**
2012–13	Hibernian	3	0		
2012–13	*East Fife*	12	0	**12**	**0**
2013–14	Hibernian	26	4		
2014–15	Hibernian	17	1		
2015–16	Hibernian	0	0		
2015–16	*Plymouth Arg*	12	0	**12**	**0**
2016–17	Hibernian	16	0	**62**	**5**
2017–18	Cheltenham T	4	0		
2018–19	Cheltenham T	26	1	**30**	**1**

HANDLEY, Tom (D) **0** **0**

2018–19	Cheltenham T	0	0		

HUSSEY, Chris (D) **253** **6**
H: 5 10 W: 10 03 b.Hammersmith 2-1-89

2009–10	Coventry C	8	0		
2010–11	Coventry C	11	0		
2010–11	*Crewe Alex*	0	0		
2011–12	Coventry C	29	0		
2012–13	Coventry C	10	0	**58**	**0**
2012–13	AFC Wimbledon	19	0		
2013–14	AFC Wimbledon	0	0	**19**	**0**
2013–14	Burton Alb	27	1	**27**	**1**
2013–14	*Bury*	11	2		
2014–15	Bury	38	0		
2015–16	Bury	41	1	**90**	**3**
2016–17	Sheffield U	7	0		
2017–18	Sheffield U	0	0	**7**	**0**
2017–18	*Swindon T*	18	1	**18**	**1**
2018–19	Cheltenham T	34	1	**34**	**1**

LAPWORTH, Freddie (G) **0** **0**

2018–19	Cheltenham T	0	0		

LLOYD, George (M) **14** **3**
H: 5 8 W: 9 13 b. 11-2-00

2017–18	Cheltenham T	7	2		
2018–19	Cheltenham T	7	1	**14**	**3**

LONG, Sean (D) **38** **0**
H: 5 10 W: 11 00 b.Dublin 2-5-95
Internationals: Republic of Ireland U16, U17, U18, U19, U21.

2013–14	Reading	0	0		
2014–15	Reading	0	0		
2015–16	Reading	0	0		
2015–16	*Luton T*	9	0	**9**	**0**
2016–17	Reading	0	0		
2016–17	*Cambridge U*	7	0	**7**	**0**
2017–18	Lincoln C	17	0	**17**	**0**
2018–19	Cheltenham T	5	0	**5**	**0**

LOVETT, Rhys (G) **1** **0**
b. 15-5-97
From Rochdale.

2016–17	Cheltenham T	0	0		
2017–18	Cheltenham T	1	0		
2018–19	Cheltenham T	0	0	**1**	**0**

LUMBOMBO KALALA, Kalvin (M) **7** **0**
H: 6 0 W: 12 08 b.Parigi 1-1-98

2016–17	Carpi	0	0		
2017–18	Carpi	0	0		
2018–19	Cheltenham T	7	0	**7**	**0**

MADDOX, Jacob (M) **38** **1**
b. 3-11-98
Internationals: England U16, U17, U19, U21

2018–19	Cheltenham T	38	1	**38**	**1**

McALINDEN, Liam (F) **123** **16**
H: 6 1 W: 11 10 b.Cannock 26-9-93
Internationals: Northern Ireland U21. Republic of Ireland U21.

2010–11	Wolverhampton W	0	0		
2011–12	Wolverhampton W	0	0		
2012–13	Wolverhampton W	1	0		
2013–14	Wolverhampton W	7	1		
2013–14	*Shrewsbury T*	9	3		
2014–15	Wolverhampton W	6	0		
2014–15	*Fleetwood T*	19	4	**19**	**4**
2015–16	Wolverhampton W	0	0	**14**	**1**
2015–16	*Shrewsbury T*	8	0	**17**	**3**
2015–16	*Crawley T*	6	1	**6**	**1**
2016–17	Exeter C	32	5		
2017–18	Exeter C	29	2	**61**	**7**
2018–19	Cheltenham T	6	0	**6**	**0**

MULLINS, John (D) **461** **26**
H: 5 11 W: 12 07 b.Hampstead 6-11-85

2004–05	Reading	0	0		
2004–05	*Kidderminster H*	21	2	**21**	**2**
2005–06	Reading	0	0		
2006–07	Mansfield T	43	2		
2007–08	Mansfield T	43	2	**86**	**4**
2008–09	Stockport Co	33	3		
2009–10	Stockport Co	36	1	**69**	**4**
2010–11	Rotherham U	35	1		
2011–12	Rotherham U	35	2		
2012–13	Rotherham U	29	4	**99**	**7**
2012–13	*Oxford U*	8	2		
2013–14	Oxford U	35	3		
2014–15	Oxford U	44	2		
2015–16	Oxford U	40	0	**127**	**7**
2016–17	Luton T	23	0		
2017–18	Luton T	17	2	**40**	**2**
2018–19	Cheltenham T	19	0	**19**	**0**

SMITH, Tom (M) **10** **1**
H: 5 10 W: 11 00 b. 25-1-98

2014–15	Swindon T	1	0		
2015–16	Swindon T	1	1		
2016–17	Swindon T	8	0		
2017–18	Swindon T	0	0	**10**	**1**
2018–19	Cheltenham T	0	0		

THOMAS, Conor (M) **167** **8**
H: 6 1 W: 11 05 b.Coventry 29-10-93
Internationals: England U17, U18.

2010–11	*Liverpool*	0	0		
2010–11	Coventry C	0	0		
2011–12	Coventry C	27	1		
2012–13	Coventry C	11	0		
2013–14	Coventry C	43	0		
2014–15	Coventry C	16	0		
2015–16	Coventry C	3	0	**100**	**1**
2016–17	Swindon T	33	1		
2017–18	Swindon T	2	0	**35**	**1**
2018–19	Cheltenham T	32	6	**32**	**6**

TOZER, Ben (D) **302** **11**
H: 6 1 W: 12 11 b.Plymouth 1-3-90

2007–08	Swindon T	2	0	**2**	**0**
2007–08	Newcastle U	0	0		
2008–09	Newcastle U	0	0		
2009–10	Newcastle U	1	0		
2010–11	Newcastle U	0	0	**1**	**0**
2010–11	*Northampton T*	31	3		
2011–12	Northampton T	45	3		
2012–13	Northampton T	46	0		
2013–14	Northampton T	29	0		
2013–14	*Colchester U*	1	0	**1**	**0**
2014–15	Northampton T	22	0	**173**	**6**
2015–16	Yeovil T	26	0	**26**	**0**
2016–17	Newport Co	23	1		
2017–18	Newport Co	39	3	**62**	**4**
2017–18	Cheltenham T	0	0		
2018–19	Cheltenham T	37	1	**37**	**1**

VARNEY, Luke (F) **446** **86**
H: 5 11 W: 11 00 b.Leicester 28-9-82

2002–03	Crewe Alex	0	0		
2003–04	Crewe Alex	8	1		
2004–05	Crewe Alex	26	4		
2005–06	Crewe Alex	27	5		
2006–07	Crewe Alex	34	17	**95**	**27**
2007–08	Charlton Ath	39	8		
2008–09	Charlton Ath	18	2	**57**	**10**
2008–09	*Sheffield W*	4	2		
2008–09	Derby Co	10	1		
2009–10	Derby Co	1	0		
2009–10	*Sheffield W*	39	9	**43**	**11**
2010–11	Derby Co	1	0	**12**	**1**
2010–11	*Blackpool*	30	5	**30**	**5**
2011–12	Portsmouth	30	6	**30**	**6**
2012–13	Leeds U	34	4		
2013–14	Leeds U	11	2	**45**	**6**
2013–14	*Blackburn R*	12	0		
2014–15	Blackburn R	11	0	**23**	**0**
2014–15	*Ipswich T*	10	1		
2015–16	Ipswich T	18	1		
2016–17	Ipswich T	15	3	**43**	**5**
2016–17	Burton Alb	15	1		
2017–18	Burton Alb	18	0	**33**	**1**
2018–19	Cheltenham T	35	14	**35**	**14**

WATERS, Billy (M) **139** **22**
H: 5 9 W: 11 07 b.Epsom 15-10-94

2012–13	Crewe Alex	0	0		
2013–14	Crewe Alex	9	0		
2014–15	Crewe Alex	16	2	**25**	**2**
2016–17	Cheltenham T	46	12		
2017–18	Northampton T	17	0		
2017–18	*Cambridge U*	18	2	**18**	**2**
2018–19	Northampton T	15	2	**32**	**2**
2018–19	Cheltenham T	18	4	**64**	**16**

Scholars
Basford, Aaron John; Bedford, Kian Leslie; Brennan, Archie Noel; Briscoe, Tyreece Morgan Owen; Chamberlain, Thomas Jack; Clift, Finley Lewis; Dawes, William John; Duncan, Camden Lloyd; Gilkes, Joshua Michael; Handley, Thomas Tristan; Horton, Grant Dean; Lapworth, Freddie James; Lawrence, Isaac Anthony; Price, Oliver Stephen; Richards, Ioan; Scott, Miles Norman Daniel; Stanton, Charles Matthew Shayne.

COLCHESTER U (25)

BARNES, Aaron (D) **1** **0**
b. 14-10-96

2016–17	Charlton Ath	1	0		
2017–18	Charlton Ath	0	0	**1**	**0**
2018–19	Colchester U	0	0		

BARNES, Dillon (G) **24** **0**
H: 6 4 W: 11 11 b. 8-4-96
From Bedford T.

2015–16	Colchester U	0	0		
2016–17	Colchester U	0	0		
2017–18	Colchester U	2	0		
2018–19	Colchester U	22	0	**24**	**0**

CHILVERS, Noah (M) **2** **0**
b. 22-2-01

2018–19	Colchester U	2	0	**2**	**0**

CLAMPIN, Ryan (M) **0** **0**
b. 29-1-99

2018–19	Colchester U	0	0		

COMLEY, Brandon (M) **98** **1**
H: 5 11 W: 11 05 b.Islington 18-11-95
Internationals: Montserrat Full caps.

2014–15	QPR	1	0		
2015–16	QPR	0	0		
2015–16	*Carlisle U*	12	0	**12**	**0**
2016–17	QPR	1	0	**2**	**0**
2016–17	*Grimsby T*	33	0		
2017–18	Grimsby T	0	0	**33**	**0**
2017–18	Colchester U	38	1		
2018–19	Colchester U	13	0	**51**	**1**

DICKENSON, Brennan (F) **183 21**
H: 6 0 W: 12 07 b.Ferndown 26-2-93

2012–13	Brighton & HA	0	0		
2012–13	*Chesterfield*	11	1	**11**	**1**
2012–13	*AFC Wimbledon*	7	2	**7**	**2**
2013–14	Brighton & HA	0	0		
2013–14	*Northampton T*	13	1	**13**	**1**
2014–15	Gillingham	34	1		
2015–16	Gillingham	33	1	**67**	**2**
2016–17	Colchester U	36	12		
2017–18	Colchester U	7	0		
2018–19	Colchester U	42	3	**85**	**15**

DUNNE, Louis (M) **2 0**
b.Waltham Forest 7-9-98
Internationals: Republic of Ireland U15, U17, U18.

2015–16	Colchester U	2	0		
2016–17	Colchester U	0	0		
2017–18	Colchester U	0	0		
2018–19	Colchester U	0	0	**2**	**0**

EASTMAN, Tom (D) **303 17**
H: 6 3 W: 13 12 b.Clacton 21-10-91

2009–10	Ipswich T	1	0		
2010–11	Ipswich T	9	0	**10**	**0**
2011–12	Colchester U	25	3		
2011–12	*Crawley T*	6	0	**6**	**0**
2012–13	Colchester U	29	2		
2013–14	Colchester U	36	0		
2014–15	Colchester U	46	1		
2015–16	Colchester U	43	2		
2016–17	Colchester U	35	3		
2017–18	Colchester U	42	3		
2018–19	Colchester U	31	3	**287**	**17**

EISA, Abobaker (M) **23 3**
b. 5-1-96
From Uxbridge, Wealdstone.

2017–18	Shrewsbury T	5	1		
2018–19	Shrewsbury T	4	0	**9**	**1**
2018–19	Colchester U	14	2	**14**	**2**

GILMARTIN, Rene (G) **86 0**
H: 6 5 W: 13 06 b.Dublin 31-5-87
Internationals: Republic of Ireland U19, U21.

2005–06	Walsall	2	0		
2006–07	Walsall	0	0		
2007–08	Walsall	0	0		
2008–09	Walsall	11	0		
2009–10	Walsall	22	0	**35**	**0**
2010–11	Watford	0	0		
2011–12	Watford	2	0		
2011–12	*Yeovil T*	8	0	**8**	**0**
2011–12	*Crawley T*	6	0	**6**	**0**
2012–13	Plymouth Arg	13	0		
2013–14	Plymouth Arg	0	0	**13**	**0**
2014–15	Watford	0	0		
2015–16	Watford	0	0		
2016–17	Watford	0	0	**2**	**0**
2017–18	Colchester U	0	0		
2018–19	Colchester U	22	0	**22**	**0**

GONDOH, Ryan (F) **6 0**
b. 6-6-97
From Barnet, Metropolitan Police, Kingstonian, Carshalton Ath, Maldon & Tiptree.

2017–18	Colchester U	2	0		
2018–19	Colchester U	4	0	**6**	**0**

JACKSON, Ryan (M) **229 7**
H: 5 9 W: 10 03 b.Streatham 31-7-90
Internationals: England C.

2011–12	AFC Wimbledon	7	0	**7**	**0**
2013–14	Newport Co	29	0		
2014–15	Newport Co	34	0	**63**	**0**
2015–16	Gillingham	37	2		
2016–17	Gillingham	34	1	**71**	**3**
2017–18	Colchester U	42	2		
2018–19	Colchester U	46	2	**88**	**4**

JAMES, Cameron (D) **22 0**
H: 6 0 W: 12 00 b.Chelmsford 11-2-98

2015–16	Colchester U	1	0		
2016–17	Colchester U	14	0		
2017–18	Colchester U	7	0		
2018–19	Colchester U	0	0	**22**	**0**

KENSADALE, Ollie (D) **2 0**
b. 20-4-00

2018–19	Colchester U	2	0	**2**	**0**

KENT, Frankie (D) **127 6**
H: 6 2 W: 12 00 b.Romford 21-11-95

2013–14	Colchester U	1	0		
2014–15	Colchester U	10	0		
2015–16	Colchester U	26	0		
2016–17	Colchester U	13	0		
2017–18	Colchester U	37	2		
2018–19	Colchester U	40	4	**127**	**6**

LAPSLIE, Tom (M) **122 3**
H: 5 6 W: 10 12 b.Waltham Forest 5-5-95

2013–14	Colchester U	0	0		
2014–15	Colchester U	11	1		
2015–16	Colchester U	10	1		
2016–17	Colchester U	37	0		
2017–18	Colchester U	29	0		
2018–19	Colchester U	35	1	**122**	**3**

MANDRON, Mikael (F) **110 13**
H: 6 3 W: 12 13 b.Boulogne 11-10-94
Internationals: Scotland U20.

2011–12	Sunderland	0	0		
2012–13	Sunderland	2	0		
2013–14	Sunderland	0	0		
2013–14	*Fleetwood T*	11	1	**11**	**1**
2014–15	Sunderland	1	0		
2014–15	*Shrewsbury T*	3	0	**3**	**0**
2015–16	Sunderland	0	0	**3**	**0**
2015–16	*Hartlepool U*	5	0	**5**	**0**
2016–17	Wigan Ath	3	0	**3**	**0**
2017–18	Colchester U	44	10		
2018–19	Colchester U	41	2	**85**	**12**

MILLER, Todd (M) **1 0**
b. 1-10-02

2018–19	Colchester U	1	0	**1**	**0**

NORRIS, Luke (F) **209 46**
H: 6 1 W: 13 05 b.Stevenage 3-6-93

2011–12	Brentford	1	0		
2012–13	Brentford	0	0		
2013–14	Brentford	1	0	**2**	**0**
2013–14	*Northampton T*	10	4	**10**	**4**
2013–14	*Dagenham & R*	19	4	**19**	**4**
2014–15	Gillingham	37	6		
2015–16	Gillingham	33	8	**70**	**14**
2016–17	Swindon T	39	4		
2017–18	Swindon T	35	13	**74**	**17**
2018–19	Colchester U	34	7	**34**	**7**

NOUBLE, Frank (F) **256 37**
H: 6 3 W: 12 08 b.Lewisham 24-9-91
Internationals: England U17, U19.

2009–10	West Ham U	8	0		
2009–10	*WBA*	3	0	**3**	**0**
2009–10	*Swindon T*	8	0	**8**	**0**
2010–11	West Ham U	2	0		
2010–11	*Swansea C*	6	1	**6**	**1**
2010–11	*Barnsley*	4	0		
2010–11	*Charlton Ath*	9	1	**9**	**1**
2011–12	West Ham U	3	1	**13**	**1**
2011–12	*Gillingham*	13	5		
2011–12	*Barnsley*	6	0	**10**	**0**
2012–13	Wolverhampton W	2	0	**2**	**0**
2012–13	Ipswich T	17	2		
2013–14	Ipswich T	38	2		
2014–15	Ipswich T	1	0	**56**	**4**
2014–15	Coventry C	31	6	**31**	**6**
2016–17	Gillingham	12	1	**25**	**6**
2016–17	Southend U	5	0	**5**	**0**
2017–18	Newport Co	45	9	**45**	**9**
2018–19	Colchester U	43	9	**43**	**9**

OGEDI-UZOKWE, Junior (F) **10 1**
b. 20-3-94
From Maldon & Tiptree

2017–18	Colchester U	9	1		
2018–19	Colchester U	1	0	**10**	**1**

PELL, Harry (M) **216 27**
H: 6 4 W: 13 05 b.Tilbury 21-10-91

2010–11	Bristol R	10	0	**10**	**0**
2010–11	*Hereford U*	7	0		
2011–12	Hereford U	30	3	**37**	**3**
2012–13	AFC Wimbledon	17	2		
2013–14	AFC Wimbledon	33	4		
2014–15	AFC Wimbledon	9	0	**59**	**6**
2016–17	Cheltenham T	42	7		
2017–18	Cheltenham T	37	5	**79**	**12**
2018–19	Colchester U	31	6	**31**	**6**

PROSSER, Luke (D) **240 12**
H: 6 2 W: 12 04 b.Waltham Cross 28-5-88

2005–06	Port Vale	0	0		
2006–07	Port Vale	0	0		
2007–08	Port Vale	5	0		
2008–09	Port Vale	26	1		
2009–10	Port Vale	2	1	**33**	**2**
2010–11	Southend U	17	1		
2011–12	Southend U	21	1		
2012–13	Southend U	25	0		
2013–14	Southend U	25	3		
2014–15	Southend U	30	0		
2015–16	Southend U	13	2	**131**	**7**
2015–16	*Northampton T*	8	0	**8**	**0**
2016–17	Colchester U	14	0		
2017–18	Colchester U	16	1		
2018–19	Colchester U	38	2	**68**	**3**

ROONEY, Paul (D) **0 0**
b.Dublin 22-3-97
From St Patricks Ath, Bohemians.

2016–17	Millwall	0	0		
2017–18	Colchester U	0	0		
2018–19	Colchester U	0	0		

ROSS, Ethan (G) **3 0**
b. 6-3-97
From WBA.

2018–19	Colchester U	3	0	**3**	**0**

SAUNDERS, Sam (M) **292 44**
H: 5 6 W: 11 04 b.Erith 29-8-83

2007–08	Dagenham & R	22	0		
2008–09	Dagenham & R	40	14	**62**	**14**
2009–10	Brentford	26	1		
2010–11	Brentford	21	2		
2011–12	Brentford	37	10		
2012–13	Brentford	31	3		
2013–14	Brentford	17	5		
2014–15	Brentford	5	2		
2014–15	Wycombe W	11	2		
2015–16	Brentford	25	3		
2016–17	Brentford	8	0	**170**	**26**
2016–17	Wycombe W	17	1		
2017–18	Wycombe W	22	1		
2018–19	Wycombe W	4	0	**54**	**4**
2018–19	Colchester U	6	0	**6**	**0**

SENIOR, Courtney (F) **61 10**
b. 30-6-97

2014–15	Wycombe W	1	0	**1**	**0**
2015–16	Brentford	0	0		
2017–18	Colchester U	18	4		
2018–19	Colchester U	42	6	**60**	**10**

STEVENSON, Ben (M) **60 4**
H: 6 0 W: 10 08 b.Leicester 23-3-97

2015–16	Coventry C	0	0		
2016–17	Coventry C	28	2		
2017–18	Coventry C	5	0	**33**	**2**
2017–18	Wolverhampton W	0	0		
2017–18	*Colchester U*	13	2		
2018–19	Wolverhampton W	0	0		
2018–19	Colchester U	14	0	**27**	**2**

SZMIDICS, Sammie (M) **142 35**
H: 5 6 W: 10 01 b.Colchester 24-9-95

2013–14	Colchester U	7	0		
2014–15	Colchester U	31	4		
2015–16	Colchester U	5	0		
2016–17	Colchester U	19	5		
2017–18	Colchester U	37	12		
2018–19	Colchester U	43	14	**142**	**35**

VINCENT-YOUNG, Kane (D) **110 4**
H: 5 11 W: 11 00 b.Camden Town 15-3-96

2014–15	Colchester U	0	0		
2015–16	Colchester U	14	0		
2016–17	Colchester U	18	0		
2017–18	Colchester U	38	1		
2018–19	Colchester U	40	3	**110**	**4**

VOSE, Bailey (G) **0 0**
b. 11-5-98
From Brighton & HA.

2018–19	Colchester U	0	0		

WRIGHT, Diaz (M) **9 0**
b. 22-2-98

2016–17	Colchester U	0	0		
2017–18	Colchester U	0	0		
2018–19	Colchester U	9	0	**9**	**0**

Players retained or with offer of contract
Hyde, Tyrique; Issa, Tariq Ahmed; Kensdale, Oliver James; Kiangebeni, Percy; Ogedi-, Uzokwe Junior Chukwuemka; Szmodics, Samuel Joseph.

Scholars
Ager, Dean Fred; Anderson, Callum George; Chilvers, Noah Christopher; Cornish, Sam David; Coulter, Callum Andrew Charles; Cracknell, William David; Freitas, Gouveia Diogo Manuel; Hallett, Chandler Lewis; Hasanally, Andre Christopher; Hutchinson, Jacob; Jones, Callum Wiiliam Adam; Jopling, Kyle Oliver; Kazeem, Al-Amin Ayomide; Maughn, Maxwell David Thomas; Michaels, Kieran James; Mudd, Reuben Alan; Sims, Oliver James Richard; Stone, Frankie Alfie; Tricker, Matthew James Elliot.

COVENTRY C (26)

ADDAI, Corey (G) 0 0
b. 10-10-97
2015–16 Coventry C 0 0
2016–17 Coventry C 0 0
2017–18 Coventry C 0 0
2018–19 Coventry C 0 0

ALLASSANI, Reise (M) 5 0
b.Wandsworth 3-1-96
Internationals: England U16, U17.
2013–14 Crystal Palace 0 0
2014–15 Crystal Palace 0 0
2015–16 Crystal Palace 0 0
From Dulwich Hamlet.
2018–19 Coventry C 5 0 **5 0**

ANDREU, Tony (M) 248 59
H: 5 10 W: 11 05 b.Cagnes-Sur-Mer 22-5-88
2009–10 Nyon 29 2
2010–11 Nyon 21 2
2011–12 Nyon 27 6 **77 10**
2012–13 Livingston 33 7 **33 7**
2013–14 Hamilton A 35 13
2014–15 Hamilton A 23 12
2014–15 Norwich C 6 0
2015–16 Norwich C 0 0
2015–16 *Rotherham U* 11 2 **11 2**
2016–17 Norwich C 0 0 **6 0**
2016–17 *Dundee U* 31 13 **31 13**
2017–18 Coventry C 5 0
2018–19 Coventry C 10 1 **15 1**
2018–19 *Hamilton A* 17 1 **75 26**

BAKAYOKO, Amadou (F) 124 16
H: 6 4 W: 13 05 b. 1-1-96
2013–14 Walsall 6 0
2014–15 Walsall 7 0
2015–16 Walsall 0 0
2016–17 Walsall 39 4
2017–18 Walsall 41 5 **93 9**
2018–19 Coventry C 31 7 **31 7**

BAYLISS, Tom (M) 62 8
b. 6-4-99
Internationals: England U19.
2017–18 Coventry C 24 5
2018–19 Coventry C 38 3 **62 8**

BIAMOU, Maxime (F) 88 14
b. 13-11-90
2014–15 Villemobmble Sports 15 3 **15 3**
2015–16 Yzeure 30 6 **30 6**
From Sutton U.
2017–18 Coventry C 39 5
2018–19 Coventry C 4 0 **43 5**

BREMANG, David (F) 0 0
2018–19 Coventry C 0 0

BROWN, Junior (D) 220 21
H: 5 9 W: 10 09 b.Crewe 7-5-89
2006–07 Crewe Alex 0 0
2007–08 Crewe Alex 1 0 **1 0**
2012–13 Fleetwood T 43 11
2013–14 Fleetwood T 21 1 **64 12**
2013–14 *Tranmere R* 9 1 **9 1**
2014–15 Oxford U 11 0 **11 0**
2014–15 Mansfield T 24 2 **24 2**
2015–16 Shrewsbury T 31 0
2016–17 Shrewsbury T 43 5
2017–18 Shrewsbury T 15 1 **89 6**
2018–19 Coventry C 22 0 **22 0**

BURGE, Lee (G) 140 0
H: 5 11 W: 11 00 b.Hereford 9-1-93
2011–12 Coventry C 0 0
2012–13 Coventry C 0 0
2013–14 Coventry C 0 0
2014–15 Coventry C 18 0
2015–16 Coventry C 9 0
2016–17 Coventry C 33 0
2017–18 Coventry C 40 0
2018–19 Coventry C 40 0 **140 0**

BURROUGHS, Jack (M) 0 0
Internationals: Scotland U19.
2018–19 Coventry C 0 0

CAMWELL, Chris (D) 1 0
b. 27-10-98
2016–17 Coventry C 1 0
2017–18 Coventry C 0 0
2018–19 Coventry C 0 0 **1 0**

CHAPLIN, Conor (M) 135 30
H: 5 10 W: 10 12 b.Worthing 16-2-97
2014–15 Portsmouth 9 1
2015–16 Portsmouth 30 8
2016–17 Portsmouth 39 8
2017–18 Portsmouth 26 5 **104 22**
2018–19 Coventry C 31 8 **31 8**

DAVIES, Tom (D) 88 1
H: 5 11 W: 11 00 b.Warrington 18-4-92
2014–15 Fleetwood T 0 0
2015–16 Accrington S 32 1 **32 1**
2016–17 Portsmouth 12 0
2017–18 Portsmouth 0 0 **12 0**
2017–18 Coventry C 21 0
2018–19 Coventry C 23 0 **44 0**

DRYSDALE, Declan (D) 0 0
2018–19 Tranmere R 0 0
2018–19 Coventry C 0 0

ECCLES, Josh (D) 0 0
2018–19 Coventry C 0 0

GRIMMER, Jack (M) 134 3
H: 6 0 W: 12 06 b.Aberdeen 25-1-94
Internationals: Scotland U16, U17, U18, U19, U21.
2009–10 Aberdeen 2 0
2010–11 Aberdeen 2 0
2011–12 Aberdeen 0 0 **4 0**
2011–12 Fulham 0 0
2012–13 Fulham 0 0
2013–14 Fulham 0 0
2013–14 *Port Vale* 13 1 **13 1**
2014–15 Fulham 13 0
2014–15 *Shrewsbury T* 6 0
2015–16 Fulham 0 0
2015–16 *Shrewsbury T* 21 1
2016–17 Fulham 0 0 **13 0**
2016–17 *Shrewsbury T* 24 0 **51 1**
2017–18 Coventry C 42 1
2018–19 Coventry C 11 0 **53 1**

HICKMAN, Jak (F) 0 0
b. 11-9-98
2017–18 Coventry C 0 0
2018–19 Coventry C 0 0

HIWULA, Jordy (F) 177 43
H: 5 10 W: 11 12 b.Manchester 24-9-94
Internationals: England U18, U19.
2013–14 Manchester C 0 0
2014–15 Manchester C 0 0
2014–15 *Yeovil T* 8 0 **8 0**
2014–15 *Walsall* 19 9
2015–16 Huddersfield T 0 0
2015–16 *Wigan Ath* 14 2 **14 2**
2015–16 *Walsall* 13 3 **32 12**
2016–17 Huddersfield T 0 0
2016–17 *Bradford C* 41 9 **41 9**
2017–18 Huddersfield T 0 0
2017–18 *Fleetwood T* 43 8 **43 8**
2018–19 Coventry C 39 12 **39 12**

HYAM, Dominic (D) 68 1
H: 6 2 W: 11 00 b.Leuchars 20-12-95
Internationals: Scotland U19, U21.
2014–15 Reading 0 0
2015–16 Reading 0 0
2015–16 *Dagenham & R* 16 0 **16 0**
2016–17 Reading 0 0
2016–17 *Portsmouth* 0 0
2017–18 Coventry C 14 0
2018–19 Coventry C 38 1 **52 1**

JONES, Jodi (F) 102 11
b.London 22-10-97
2014–15 Dagenham & R 8 1
2015–16 Dagenham & R 27 3 **35 4**
2015–16 Coventry C 6 0
2016–17 Coventry C 34 1
2017–18 Coventry C 19 5
2018–19 Coventry C 8 1 **67 7**

KELLY, Liam (M) 283 27
H: 6 2 W: 13 11 b.Milton Keynes 10-2-90
Internationals: Scotland U18, U21, Full caps.
2009–10 Kilmarnock 15 1
2010–11 Kilmarnock 32 7
2011–12 Kilmarnock 34 1
2012–13 Kilmarnock 19 6 **100 15**
2012–13 Bristol C 19 0
2013–14 Bristol C 2 0 **21 0**
2014–15 Oldham Ath 37 1
2015–16 Oldham Ath 41 6 **78 7**
2016–17 Leyton Orient 21 4 **21 4**
2017–18 Coventry C 33 1
2018–19 Coventry C 30 0 **63 1**

MASON, Brandon (M) 28 0
H: 5 9 W: 11 00 b.Westminster 30-9-97
2016–17 Watford 2 0
2017–18 Watford 0 0 **2 0**
2017–18 *Dundee U* 1 0 **1 0**
2018–19 Coventry C 25 0 **25 0**

MAYCOCK, Callum (D) 31 0
b. 23-12-97
2016–17 Coventry C 3 0
2017–18 Coventry C 1 0
2018–19 Coventry C 0 0 **4 0**
2018–19 *Macclesfield T* 27 0 **27 0**

McCALLUM, Sam (D) 7 0
b. 2-9-00
2018–19 Coventry C 7 0 **7 0**

McFADZEAN, Kyle (D) 284 14
H: 6 1 W: 13 04 b.Sheffield 20-2-87
Internationals: England C.
2004–05 Sheffield U 0 0
2005–06 Sheffield U 0 0
2006–07 Sheffield U 0 0
From Alfreton T
2011–12 Crawley T 37 2
2012–13 Crawley T 17 3
2013–14 Crawley T 42 1 **96 6**
2014–15 Milton Keynes D 41 3
2015–16 Milton Keynes D 39 0 **80 3**
2016–17 Burton Alb 31 1
2017–18 Burton Alb 42 0
2018–19 Burton Alb 35 4 **108 5**
2018–19 Coventry C 0 0

NGANDU, Jonny (F) 0 0
2018–19 Coventry C 0 0

O'BRIEN, Liam (G) 66 0
H: 6 1 W: 12 06 b.Ruislip 30-11-91
Internationals: England U19.
2008–09 Portsmouth 0 0
2009–10 Portsmouth 0 0
2010–11 Barnet 8 0
2011–12 Barnet 10 0
2012–13 Barnet 3 0 **21 0**
2013–14 Brentford 0 0
2014–15 Dagenham & R 10 0
2015–16 Dagenham & R 24 0 **34 0**
2016–17 Portsmouth 0 0
2017–18 Coventry C 7 0
2018–19 Coventry C 4 0 **11 0**

PONTICELLI, Jordan (F) 27 3
b. 10-9-98
2017–18 Coventry C 19 3
2018–19 Coventry C 5 0 **24 3**
2018–19 *Macclesfield T* 3 0 **3 0**

SHIPLEY, Jordan (M) 64 7
b. 26-6-97
Internationals: Republic of Ireland U21.
2016–17 Coventry C 1 0
2017–18 Coventry C 30 4
2018–19 Coventry C 33 3 **64 7**

STEDMAN, Billy (M) 0 0
b. 3-11-99
2018–19 Coventry C 0 0

THOMPSON, Jordan (D) 4 0
b. 8-4-99
2016–17 Coventry C 0 0
2017–18 Coventry C 0 0
2018–19 Coventry C 4 0 **4 0**

WAKEFIELD, Charlie (M) 8 0
H: 6 0 W: 11 05 b.Worthing 9-4-98
Internationals: England U16, U17.
2018–19 Chelsea 0 0
2018–19 Coventry C 8 0 **8 0**

WALTERS, Dexter (M) 0 0
2018–19 Coventry C 0 0

WESTBROOKE, Zain (M) 8 0
b. 28-10-96
From Chelsea.
2016–17 Brentford 1 0
2017–18 Brentford 0 0 **1 0**
2017–18 Coventry C 0 0
2018–19 Coventry C 7 0 **7 0**

WILLIAMS, Morgan (D) 1 0
b. 30-8-99
From Mickleover Sports.
2018–19 Coventry C 1 0 **1 0**

WILLIS, Jordan (D) 179 4
H: 5 11 W: 11 00 b.Coventry 24-8-94
Internationals: England U18, U19.

2011–12	Coventry C	3	0		
2012–13	Coventry C	1	0		
2013–14	Coventry C	28	0		
2014–15	Coventry C	34	0		
2015–16	Coventry C	4	0		
2016–17	Coventry C	36	3		
2017–18	Coventry C	35	0		
2018–19	Coventry C	38	1	**179**	**4**

Players retained or with offer of contract
Bosma, Bouwe Jacob; Green, Lewis Craig.

Scholars
Bannatyne-Billson, Thomas David; Burroughs, Jack Stephen; Crowther, Morgan James John Arthur; Endall, Joshua Anthony; Fixter, Dylan George Cobb; Lafferty, Daniel Paul; Lautaru, Costelus; Martin, Callum Paul; Rowe, Blaine Morgan Brian; Rowe, Luke James Albert; Tyler, Cian Lee; White, Lewis George; Whitmore, Aaron Jay.

CRAWLEY T (27)

ALLARAKHIA, Tarryn (M) 5 0
b. 17-10-97
From Leyton Orient, Aveley, Maldon and Tiptree.

2017–18	Colchester U	0	0		
2018–19	Crawley T	5	0	**5**	**0**

BULMAN, Dannie (M) 517 25
H: 5 9 W: 11 12 b.Ashford 24-1-79

1998–99	Wycombe W	11	1		
1999–2000	Wycombe W	29	1		
2000–01	Wycombe W	36	4		
2001–02	Wycombe W	46	5		
2002–03	Wycombe W	42	3		
2003–04	Wycombe W	38	0	**202**	**14**

From Stevenage, Crawley T.

2010–11	Oxford U	5	0	**5**	**0**
2011–12	Crawley T	41	3		
2012–13	Crawley T	36	1		
2013–14	Crawley T	39	0		
2014–15	AFC Wimbledon	41	1		
2015–16	AFC Wimbledon	42	3		
2016–17	AFC Wimbledon	38	0	**121**	**4**
2017–18	Crawley T	37	0		
2018–19	Crawley T	36	3	**189**	**7**

CAMARA, Panutche (F) 75 5
H: 6 1 W: 9 13 b. 28-2-97
From Dulwich Hamlet.

2017–18	Crawley T	30	2		
2018–19	Crawley T	45	3	**75**	**5**

CONNOLLY, Mark (D) 207 10
H: 6 1 W: 12 01 b.Monaghan 16-12-91
Internationals: Republic of Ireland U17, U19, U21.

2009–10	Bolton W	0	0		
2009–10	*St Johnstone*	1	0	**1**	**0**
2010–11	Bolton W	0	0		
2011–12	Bolton W	0	0		
2011–12	*Macclesfield T*	7	0	**7**	**0**
2012–13	Crawley T	33	2		
2013–14	Crawley T	36	1		
2014–15	Kilmarnock	26	2	**26**	**2**
2016–17	Crawley T	41	3		
2017–18	Crawley T	40	2		
2018–19	Crawley T	23	0	**173**	**8**

Transferred to Dundee U January 2019.

DALLISON, Tom (M) 39 0
H: 5 10 W: 14 01 b. 2-2-96

2012–13	Arsenal	0	0		
2013–14	Brighton & HA	0	0		
2014–15	Brighton & HA	0	0		
2015–16	Brighton & HA	0	0		
2015–16	*Crawley T*	1	0		
2016–17	Brighton & HA	0	0		
2016–17	*Cambridge U*	5	0	**5**	**0**
2017–18	Brighton & HA	0	0		
2017–18	*Accrington S*	2	0	**2**	**0**
2018–19	Falkirk	12	0	**12**	**0**
2018–19	Crawley T	19	0	**20**	**0**

DOHERTY, Josh (M) 34 0
H: 5 10 W: 11 00 b.Newtownards 15-3-96
Internationals: Northern Ireland U17, U19, U21.

2013–14	Watford	1	0		
2014–15	Watford	0	0		
2015–16	Watford	0	0	**1**	**0**

From Leyton Orient, Ards.

2017–18	Crawley T	15	0		
2018–19	Crawley T	18	0	**33**	**0**

FRANCOMB, George (D) 266 11
H: 5 11 W: 11 07 b.Hackney 8-9-91

2009–10	Norwich C	2	0		
2010–11	Norwich C	0	0		
2010–11	*Barnet*	13	0	**13**	**0**
2011–12	Norwich C	0	0		
2011–12	*Hibernian*	14	0	**14**	**0**
2012–13	Norwich C	0	0	**2**	**0**
2012–13	*AFC Wimbledon*	15	0		
2013–14	AFC Wimbledon	33	3		
2014–15	AFC Wimbledon	37	3		
2015–16	AFC Wimbledon	40	3		
2016–17	AFC Wimbledon	34	2		
2017–18	AFC Wimbledon	37	0	**196**	**11**
2018–19	Crawley T	41	0	**41**	**0**

GALACH, Brian (F) 1 0
H: 5 9 W: 10 03 b.Waltham Forest 16-5-01
From Leyton Orient, Aldershot T.

2018–19	Crawley T	1	0	**1**	**0**

GERMAN, Ricky (F) 13 0
H: 6 2 W: 12 08 b.Brent 13-1-99

2016–17	Chesterfield	7	0		
2017–18	Chesterfield	2	0	**9**	**0**
2018–19	Crawley T	4	0	**4**	**0**

GREGO-COX, Reece (F) 40 2
H: 5 7 W: 10 03 b.Hammersmith 12-11-96
Internationals: Republic of Ireland U17, U19, U21.

2014–15	QPR	4	0		
2015–16	QPR	0	0		
2016–17	Newport Co	7	0	**7**	**0**
2016–17	QPR	1	0		
2017–18	QPR	0	0	**5**	**0**
2018–19	Crawley T	28	2	**28**	**2**

McNERNEY, Joe (D) 90 6
H: 6 4 W: 13 03 b. 24-1-89
From Woking.

2015–16	Crawley T	11	1		
2016–17	Crawley T	34	3		
2017–18	Crawley T	16	1		
2018–19	Crawley T	29	1	**90**	**6**

MEITE, Ibrahim (F) 22 2
H: 6 1 W: 11 05 b.Wandsworth 1-6-96

2016–17	Cardiff C	1	0		
2017–18	Cardiff C	0	0		
2017–18	*Crawley T*	19	2		
2018–19	Cardiff C	0	0	**1**	**0**
2018–19	Crawley T	2	0	**21**	**2**

MERSIN, Yusuf (G) 10 0
H: 6 5 W: 13 05 b.Greenwich 23-9-94
Internationals: Turkey U16, U17, U18.
From Liverpool, Kasimpasa.

2016–17	Crawley T	8	0		
2017–18	Crawley T	2	0		
2018–19	Crawley T	0	0	**10**	**0**

MILSOM, Robert (M) 227 5
H: 5 10 W: 11 04 b.Redhill 2-1-87

2005–06	Fulham	0	0		
2006–07	Fulham	0	0		
2007–08	Fulham	0	0		
2007–08	*Brentford*	6	0	**6**	**0**
2008–09	Fulham	1	0		
2008–09	*Southend U*	6	0	**6**	**0**
2009–10	Fulham	0	0		
2010	*TPS Turku*	14	0	**14**	**0**
2010–11	Fulham	0	0	**1**	**0**
2010–11	Aberdeen	18	1		
2011–12	Aberdeen	22	1		
2012–13	Aberdeen	13	0	**53**	**2**
2013–14	Rotherham U	27	1		
2014–15	Rotherham U	8	0	**35**	**1**
2014–15	*Bury*	2	0	**2**	**0**
2015–16	Notts Co	14	0		
2016–17	Notts Co	38	0		
2017–18	Notts Co	17	1		
2018–19	Crawley T	3	0	**3**	**0**
2018–19	*Notts Co*	38	1	**107**	**2**

MORAIS, Filipe (M) 364 39
H: 5 9 W: 11 10 b.Lisbon 21-11-85
Internationals: Portugal U21.

2003–04	Chelsea	0	0		
2004–05	Chelsea	0	0		
2005–06	Chelsea	0	0		
2005–06	*Milton Keynes D*	13	0	**13**	**0**
2006–07	Millwall	12	1	**12**	**1**
2006–07	*St Johnstone*	13	1		
2007–08	Hibernian	28	1		
2008–09	Hibernian	2	0	**30**	**1**
2008–09	Inverness CT	12	3	**12**	**3**
2009–10	St Johnstone	30	2	**43**	**3**
2010–11	Oldham Ath	23	3		
2011–12	Oldham Ath	36	5		
2012–13	Oldham Ath	0	0	**59**	**8**
2012–13	Stevenage	28	3		
2013–14	Stevenage	27	4	**55**	**7**
2014–15	Bradford C	30	3		
2015–16	Bradford C	7	1		
2016–17	Bradford C	17	1	**54**	**5**
2016–17	Bolton W	19	2		
2017–18	Bolton W	33	1	**52**	**3**
2018–19	Crawley T	34	8	**34**	**8**

MORRIS, Glenn (G) 322 0
H: 6 0 W: 12 03 b.Woolwich 20-12-83

2001–02	Leyton Orient	2	0		
2002–03	Leyton Orient	23	0		
2003–04	Leyton Orient	27	0		
2004–05	Leyton Orient	12	0		
2005–06	Leyton Orient	4	0		
2006–07	Leyton Orient	3	0		
2007–08	Leyton Orient	16	0		
2008–09	Leyton Orient	26	0		
2009–10	Leyton Orient	11	0	**124**	**0**
2010–11	Southend U	33	0		
2011–12	Southend U	24	0		
2012–13	Southend U	0	0	**57**	**0**
2012–13	Aldershot T	2	0	**2**	**0**
2014–15	Gillingham	10	0		
2015–16	Gillingham	0	0	**10**	**0**
2016–17	Crawley T	39	0		
2017–18	Crawley T	44	0		
2018–19	Crawley T	46	0	**129**	**0**

N'GALA, Bondz (D) 194 7
H: 6 0 W: 12 03 b.Forest Gate 13-9-89

2007–08	West Ham U	0	0		
2008–09	West Ham U	0	0		
2008–09	*Milton Keynes D*	3	0	**3**	**0**
2009–10	West Ham U	0	0		
2009–10	*Scunthorpe U*	2	0	**2**	**0**
2009–10	*Plymouth Arg*	9	0		
2010–11	Plymouth Arg	26	1	**35**	**1**
2011–12	Yeovil T	31	2	**31**	**2**
2012–13	Stevenage	25	0	**25**	**0**
2012–13	*Barnet*	6	0		
2013–14	Portsmouth	27	3	**27**	**3**
2015–16	Barnet	42	1		
2016–17	Barnet	10	0	**58**	**1**

From Eastleigh, Dover Ath, Dagenham & R.

2018–19	Crawley T	13	0	**13**	**0**

NATHANIEL-GEORGE, Ashley (M) 30 6
b. 14-6-95
From Wealdstone, Potters Bar T, Hendon.

2018–19	Crawley T	30	6	**30**	**6**

PALMER, Oliver (F) 221 42
b.London 21-1-92

2013–14	Mansfield T	38	4		
2014–15	Mansfield T	16	1	**54**	**5**
2015–16	Leyton Orient	45	7		
2016–17	Leyton Orient	20	5	**65**	**12**
2016–17	*Luton T*	17	3	**17**	**3**
2017–18	Lincoln C	45	8	**45**	**8**
2018–19	Crawley T	40	14	**40**	**14**

PAYNE, Josh (M) 179 13
H: 6 0 W: 11 09 b.Basingstoke 25-11-90
Internationals: England C.

2008–09	West Ham U	2	0		
2008–09	*Cheltenham T*	11	1	**11**	**1**
2009–10	West Ham U	0	0		
2009–10	*Colchester U*	3	0	**3**	**0**
2009–10	*Wycombe W*	3	1	**3**	**1**
2010–11	West Ham U	0	0	**2**	**0**
2010–11	Doncaster R	0	0		
2010–11	Oxford U	28	1		
2011–12	Oxford U	6	0	**34**	**1**
2011–12	Aldershot T	17	2		
2012–13	Aldershot T	15	1	**32**	**3**
2016–17	Crawley T	32	1		
2017–18	Crawley T	35	5		
2018–19	Crawley T	27	1	**94**	**7**

POLEON, Dominic (F) 206 32
H: 6 3 W: 12 13 b.Newham 7-9-93

2012–13	Leeds U	6	2		
2012–13	*Bury*	7	2	**7**	**2**
2012–13	*Sheffield U*	7	0	**7**	**0**
2013–14	Leeds U	19	1		
2014–15	Leeds U	4	0	**29**	**3**
2014–15	Oldham Ath	35	4		
2015–16	Oldham Ath	25	4	**60**	**8**

2016–17 AFC Wimbledon 41 8 **41 8**
2017–18 Bradford C 32 6 **32 6**
2018–19 Crawley T 30 5 **30 5**

RANDALL, Mark (M) 171 7
H: 6 0 W: 12 12 b.Milton Keynes 28-9-89
Internationals: England U17, U18.
2006–07 Arsenal 0 0
2007–08 Arsenal 1 0
2007–08 *Burnley* 10 0 **10 0**
2008–09 Arsenal 1 0
2009–10 Arsenal 0 0
2009–10 *Milton Keynes D* 16 0
2010–11 Arsenal 0 0 **2 0**
2010–11 *Rotherham U* 10 1 **10 1**
2011–12 Chesterfield 16 1
2012–13 Chesterfield 29 1
2013–14 Chesterfield 0 0 **45 2**
2013–14 Milton Keynes D 4 0
2014–15 Milton Keynes D 9 0
2015–16 Milton Keynes D 0 0 **29 0**
2015–16 Barnet 12 2 **12 2**
2016–17 Newport Co 25 1 **25 1**
2017–18 Crawley T 32 1
2018–19 Crawley T 6 0 **38 1**

SESAY, David (D) 18 0
b. 18-9-98
From Watford.
2018–19 Crawley T 18 0 **18 0**

SMITH, Jimmy (M) 407 47
H: 6 0 W: 10 03 b.Newham 7-1-87
Internationals: England U16, U17, U19.
2004–05 Chelsea 0 0
2005–06 Chelsea 1 0
2006–07 Chelsea 0 0
2006–07 *QPR* 29 6 **29 6**
2007–08 Chelsea 0 0
2007–08 *Norwich C* 9 0 **9 0**
2008–09 Chelsea 0 0 **1 0**
2008–09 *Sheffield W* 12 0 **12 0**
2008–09 *Leyton Orient* 16 0
2009–10 Leyton Orient 40 2
2010–11 Leyton Orient 31 7
2011–12 Leyton Orient 38 6
2012–13 Leyton Orient 35 3
2013–14 Leyton Orient 0 0 **160 18**
2013–14 Stevenage 42 3 **42 3**
2014–15 Crawley T 36 1
2015–16 Crawley T 31 1
2016–17 Crawley T 46 7
2017–18 Crawley T 37 10
2018–19 Crawley T 4 1 **154 20**

YOUNG, Lewis (M) 273 4
H: 5 10 W: 11 02 b.Stevenage 27-9-89
2008–09 Watford 1 0
2009–10 Watford 0 0 **1 0**
2009–10 *Hereford U* 6 0 **6 0**
2010–11 Burton Alb 19 0 **19 0**
2011–12 Northampton T 30 0 **30 0**
2012–13 Yeovil T 15 0
2013–14 Yeovil T 0 0 **15 0**
2013–14 Bury 4 0 **4 0**
2014–15 Crawley T 38 0
2015–16 Crawley T 38 0
2016–17 Crawley T 43 0
2017–18 Crawley T 41 3
2018–19 Crawley T 38 1 **198 4**

Players retained or with offer of contract
Dallison-Lisbon, Thomas Albert; Pereira, Camara Panutche Amadu.

CREWE ALEX (28)

AINLEY, Callum (M) 131 12
H: 5 8 W: 10 01 b.Middlewich 2-11-97
2015–16 Crewe Alex 16 1
2016–17 Crewe Alex 27 1
2017–18 Crewe Alex 45 4
2018–19 Crewe Alex 43 6 **131 12**

BOWERY, Jordan (F) 290 45
H: 6 1 W: 12 00 b.Nottingham 2-7-91
2008–09 Chesterfield 3 0
2009–10 Chesterfield 10 0
2010–11 Chesterfield 27 1
2011–12 Chesterfield 40 8
2012–13 Chesterfield 3 1 **83 10**
2012–13 Aston Villa 10 0
2013–14 Aston Villa 9 0 **19 0**
2013–14 *Doncaster R* 3 0 **3 0**
2014–15 Rotherham U 33 5
2015–16 Rotherham U 7 0 **40 5**
2015–16 *Bradford C* 3 0 **3 0**
2015–16 Oxford U 17 7 **17 7**
2016–17 Leyton Orient 17 1 **17 1**
2016–17 *Crewe Alex* 19 2
2017–18 Crewe Alex 45 12
2018–19 Crewe Alex 44 8 **108 22**

DALE, Owen (F) 20 1
H: 5 9 W: 10 03 b.Warrington 1-11-98
2016–17 Crewe Alex 0 0
2017–18 Crewe Alex 4 0
2018–19 Crewe Alex 16 1 **20 1**

FINNEY, Oliver (M) 19 0
b.Stoke-on-Trent 15-12-97
2015–16 Crewe Alex 0 0
2016–17 Crewe Alex 1 0
2017–18 Crewe Alex 1 0
2018–19 Crewe Alex 17 0 **19 0**

GARRATT, Ben (G) 223 0
H: 6 1 W: 10 06 b.Market Drayton 25-4-94
Internationals: England U17, U18, U19.
2011–12 Crewe Alex 0 0
2012–13 Crewe Alex 1 0
2013–14 Crewe Alex 26 0
2014–15 Crewe Alex 30 0
2015–16 Crewe Alex 46 0
2016–17 Crewe Alex 46 0
2017–18 Crewe Alex 36 0
2018–19 Crewe Alex 38 0 **223 0**

GREEN, Paul (M) 532 45
H: 5 9 W: 10 02 b.Pontefract 10-4-83
Internationals: Republic of Ireland Full caps.
2003–04 Doncaster R 43 8
2004–05 Doncaster R 42 7
2005–06 Doncaster R 34 3
2006–07 Doncaster R 41 2
2007–08 Doncaster R 38 5 **198 25**
2008–09 Derby Co 29 3
2009–10 Derby Co 33 2
2010–11 Derby Co 36 2
2011–12 Derby Co 27 1 **125 8**
2012–13 Leeds U 32 4
2013–14 Leeds U 9 0 **41 4**
2013–14 *Ipswich T* 14 2 **14 2**
2014–15 Rotherham U 37 3
2015–16 Rotherham U 24 0 **61 3**
2016–17 Oldham Ath 41 1
2017–18 Oldham Ath 6 0 **47 1**
2017–18 *Crewe Alex* 20 1
2018–19 Crewe Alex 26 1 **46 2**

HUNT, Nicky (D) 375 3
H: 6 1 W: 13 07 b.Westhoughton 3-9-83
Internationals: England U21.
2000–01 Bolton W 1 0
2001–02 Bolton W 0 0
2002–03 Bolton W 0 0
2003–04 Bolton W 31 1
2004–05 Bolton W 29 0
2005–06 Bolton W 20 0
2006–07 Bolton W 33 0
2007–08 Bolton W 14 0
2008–09 Bolton W 0 0
2008–09 *Birmingham C* 11 0 **11 0**
2009–10 Bolton W 0 0 **128 1**
2009–10 *Derby Co* 21 0 **21 0**
2010–11 Bristol C 7 0
2011–12 Bristol C 0 0 **7 0**
2011–12 Preston NE 17 1 **17 1**
2012–13 Rotherham U 9 0 **9 0**
2012–13 Accrington S 11 0
2013–14 Accrington S 37 0
2014–15 Accrington S 29 0 **77 0**
2015–16 Mansfield T 19 0 **19 0**
2015–16 Leyton Orient 16 0
2016–17 Leyton Orient 35 1 **51 1**
2017–18 Notts Co 13 0 **13 0**
2018–19 Crewe Alex 22 0 **22 0**

JAASKELAINEN, William (G) 4 0
b. 25-7-98
Internationals: Finland U19.
2015–16 Bolton W 0 0
2017–18 Bolton W 0 0
2017–18 Crewe Alex 0 0
2018–19 Crewe Alex 4 0 **4 0**

JOHNSON, Travis (D) 0 0
b. 28-8-00
2018–19 Crewe Alex 0 0

JONES, James (M) 144 17
H: 5 9 W: 10 10 b.Winsford 1-2-96
Internationals: Scotland U19, U21.
2014–15 Crewe Alex 24 1
2015–16 Crewe Alex 31 0
2016–17 Crewe Alex 45 10
2017–18 Crewe Alex 6 1
2018–19 Crewe Alex 38 5 **144 17**

KIRK, Charlie (M) 103 16
H: 5 7 W: 11 00 b.Winsford 24-12-97
2015–16 Crewe Alex 14 0
2016–17 Crewe Alex 22 0
2017–18 Crewe Alex 25 5
2018–19 Crewe Alex 42 11 **103 16**

LOWERY, Tom (M) 53 1
b.Holmes Chapel 31-12-97
2016–17 Crewe Alex 7 0
2017–18 Crewe Alex 31 0
2018–19 Crewe Alex 15 1 **53 1**

LUNDSTRAM, Josh (M) 0 0
2017–18 Crewe Alex 0 0
2018–19 Crewe Alex 0 0

MILLER, Shaun (F) 356 77
H: 5 10 W: 11 08 b.Alsager 25-9-87
2006–07 Crewe Alex 7 3
2007–08 Crewe Alex 15 1
2008–09 Crewe Alex 33 4
2009–10 Crewe Alex 33 7
2010–11 Crewe Alex 42 18
2011–12 Crewe Alex 33 5
2012–13 Sheffield U 15 4
2013–14 Sheffield U 13 0 **28 4**
2013–14 *Shrewsbury T* 8 3 **8 3**
2014–15 Coventry C 12 1 **12 1**
2014–15 *Crawley T* 5 0 **5 0**
2014–15 *York C* 6 0 **6 0**
2015–16 Morecambe 37 15 **37 15**
2016–17 Carlisle U 30 4
2017–18 Carlisle U 23 3 **53 7**
2017–18 *Crewe Alex* 15 6
2018–19 Crewe Alex 29 3 **207 47**

NG, Perry (D) 104 4
H: 5 11 W: 12 02 b.Liverpool 24-6-94
2014–15 Crewe Alex 0 0
2015–16 Crewe Alex 6 0
2016–17 Crewe Alex 16 0
2017–18 Crewe Alex 38 4
2018–19 Crewe Alex 44 0 **104 4**

NICHOLLS, Alex (M) 351 53
H: 5 10 W: 11 00 b.Stourbridge 9-12-87
2005–06 Walsall 8 0
2006–07 Walsall 0 0
2007–08 Walsall 19 2
2008–09 Walsall 45 6
2009–10 Walsall 37 4
2010–11 Walsall 37 5
2011–12 Walsall 45 7 **191 24**
2012–13 Northampton T 15 7
2013–14 Northampton T 0 0
2014–15 Northampton T 6 1 **21 8**
2014–15 *Exeter C* 32 5
2015–16 Exeter C 35 5 **67 10**
2016–17 Barnet 17 2
2016–17 *Dundee U* 9 0 **9 0**
2017–18 Barnet 25 7 **42 9**
2018–19 Crewe Alex 21 2 **21 2**

NOLAN, Eddie (D) 284 4
H: 6 0 W: 13 05 b.Waterford 5-8-88
Internationals: Republic of Ireland U21, B, Full caps.
2005–06 Blackburn R 0 0
2006–07 Blackburn R 0 0
2006–07 *Stockport Co* 4 0 **4 0**
2007–08 Blackburn R 0 0
2007–08 *Hartlepool U* 11 0 **11 0**
2008–09 Blackburn R 0 0
2008–09 Preston NE 21 0
2009–10 Preston NE 19 0
2009–10 *Sheffield W* 14 1 **14 1**
2010–11 Preston NE 0 0 **40 0**
2010–11 Scunthorpe U 35 0
2011–12 Scunthorpe U 30 1
2012–13 Scunthorpe U 12 0
2013–14 Scunthorpe U 39 0
2014–15 Scunthorpe U 6 0 **122 1**
2015–16 York C 15 1 **15 1**
2016–17 Blackpool 3 0 **3 0**
2017–18 Crewe Alex 42 0
2018–19 Crewe Alex 33 1 **75 1**

OFFORD, Luke (M) 0 0
b.Chichester 19-11-99
2017–18 Crewe Alex 0 0
2018–19 Crewe Alex 0 0

PICKERING, Harry (M) **67 3**
H: 6 1 W: 12 04 b. 29-12-98

2017–18	Crewe Alex	35	3		
2018–19	Crewe Alex	32	0	**67**	**3**

PORTER, Chris (F) **498 146**
H: 6 1 W: 12 09 b.Wigan 12-12-83

2002–03	Bury	2	0		
2003–04	Bury	37	9		
2004–05	Bury	32	9	**71**	**18**
2005–06	Oldham Ath	31	7		
2006–07	Oldham Ath	35	21	**66**	**28**
2007–08	Motherwell	37	14		
2008–09	Motherwell	22	9	**59**	**23**
2008–09	Derby Co	5	3		
2009–10	Derby Co	21	4		
2010–11	Derby Co	18	2	**44**	**9**
2011–12	Sheffield U	34	5		
2012–13	Sheffield U	21	3		
2012–13	*Shrewsbury T*	5	1	**5**	**1**
2013–14	Sheffield U	32	7		
2013–14	*Chesterfield*	3	0	**3**	**0**
2014–15	Sheffield U	1	0	**88**	**15**
2014–15	Colchester U	21	7		
2015–16	Colchester U	32	7		
2016–17	Colchester U	38	16	**91**	**30**
2017–18	Crewe Alex	31	9		
2018–19	Crewe Alex	40	13	**71**	**22**

RAY, George (D) **137 5**
H: 5 10 W: 11 03 b.Warrington 13-10-93
Internationals: Wales U21.

2011–12	Crewe Alex	0	0		
2012–13	Crewe Alex	4	0		
2013–14	Crewe Alex	9	0		
2014–15	Crewe Alex	35	2		
2015–16	Crewe Alex	22	0		
2016–17	Crewe Alex	23	1		
2017–18	Crewe Alex	12	0		
2018–19	Crewe Alex	32	2	**137**	**5**

RAYNES, Michael (D) **401 13**
H: 6 4 W: 12 00 b.Wythenshawe 15-10-87

2004–05	Stockport Co	19	0		
2005–06	Stockport Co	25	1		
2006–07	Stockport Co	9	0		
2007–08	Stockport Co	27	0		
2008–09	Stockport Co	35	3		
2009–10	Stockport Co	25	1	**140**	**5**
2009–10	Scunthorpe U	12	0		
2010–11	Scunthorpe U	22	0	**34**	**0**
2011–12	Rotherham U	33	0	**33**	**0**
2012–13	Oxford U	38	1		
2013–14	Oxford U	27	0		
2014–15	Oxford U	4	0	**69**	**1**
2014–15	Mansfield T	10	0	**10**	**0**
2015–16	Carlisle U	40	3		
2016–17	Carlisle U	41	2	**81**	**5**
2017–18	Crewe Alex	29	2		
2018–19	Crewe Alex	5	0	**34**	**2**

REILLY, Lewis (F) **8 0**
b. 7-7-99

2017–18	Crewe Alex	5	0		
2018–19	Crewe Alex	3	0	**8**	**0**

RICHARDS, Dave (G) **15 0**
H: 5 11 W: 11 11 b.Abergavenny 31-12-93

2013–14	Cardiff C	0	0		
2013–14	Bristol C	0	0		
2014–15	Bristol C	0	0		
2015–16	Crewe Alex	0	0		
2016–17	Crewe Alex	0	0		
2017–18	Crewe Alex	11	0		
2018–19	Crewe Alex	4	0	**15**	**0**

SASS-DAVIES, Billy (D) **2 0**
b.Manchester 17-2-00
Internationals: Wales U19.

2017–18	Crewe Alex	0	0		
2018–19	Crewe Alex	2	0	**2**	**0**

STERRY, Jamie (D) **29 0**
H: 5 11 W: 11 00 b.Newcastle upon Tyne 21-11-95

2014–15	Newcastle U	0	0		
2015–16	Newcastle U	1	0		
2016–17	Newcastle U	2	0		
2016–17	*Coventry C*	16	0	**16**	**0**
2017–18	Newcastle U	0	0		
2017–18	*Crewe Alex*	9	0		
2018–19	Newcastle U	0	0	**3**	**0**
2018–19	Crewe Alex	1	0	**10**	**0**

TAYLOR-SINCLAIR, Aaron (D) **245 13**
H: 6 1 W: 11 07 b.Aberdeen 8-4-91

2008–09	Montrose	1	0		
2009–10	Montrose	30	2		
2010–11	Montrose	35	3	**66**	**5**
2011–12	Partick Thistle	30	1		
2012–13	Partick Thistle	28	1		
2013–14	Partick Thistle	36	2	**94**	**4**
2014–15	Wigan Ath	0	0		
2015–16	Doncaster R	43	2		
2016–17	Doncaster R	4	0	**47**	**2**
2017–18	Plymouth Arg	24	0	**24**	**0**
2018–19	Motherwell	6	0	**6**	**0**

On loan from Motherwell.

2018–19	Crewe Alex	8	2	**8**	**2**

WALKER, Brad (M) **135 11**
H: 6 1 W: 12 08 b. 25-4-95

2012–13	Hartlepool U	0	0		
2013–14	Hartlepool U	36	3		
2014–15	Hartlepool U	28	5		
2015–16	Hartlepool U	23	1		
2016–17	Hartlepool U	20	1	**107**	**10**
2017–18	Crewe Alex	27	1		
2018–19	Crewe Alex	1	0	**28**	**1**

WINTLE, Ryan (M) **84 4**
H: 5 5 W: 10 01 b.Newcastle-under-Lyme 13-6-97

2015–16	Crewe Alex	3	0		
2016–17	Crewe Alex	17	1		
2017–18	Crewe Alex	18	2		
2018–19	Crewe Alex	46	1	**84**	**4**

Players retained or with offer of contract
Griffiths, Regan Jon.

Scholars
Adebisi, Rio Adesola Frederick; Allen, Luke; Booth, Samuel James; Djalo, Abdul Karimo; Fenton, Matthew Adam; Goodrich, Jack David; Hartshorn, Ethan James; Heath, Connor John; Linton, Malachi Derek David; Lokko, Daniel Arvin Yaw Senyo; Lomas, Aaron Philip; Odipe, Olaolu Josiah James; Onyeka, Tyreece Obiora; Priestman, Jakob Adam; Robbins, Joseph Aidan Thomas; Walklate, Andrew Lawrence; Woodthorpe, Nathan John Edward; Wrench, Jamie Laurence.

CRYSTAL PALACE (29)

BENTEKE, Christian (F) **305 106**
H: 6 3 W: 13 00 b.Kinshasa 3-12-90
Internationals: Belgium U17, U18, U19, U21, Full caps.

2007–08	Genk	7	0		
2008–09	Genk	3	0		
2008–09	Standard Liege	9	3		
2009–10	*KV Kortrijk*	24	9	**24**	**9**
2010–11	Standard Liege	5	0		
2010–11	*KV Mechelen*	15	5	**15**	**5**
2011–12	Standard Liege	4	0	**18**	**3**
2011–12	Genk	32	16		
2012–13	Genk	5	3	**47**	**19**
2012–13	Aston Villa	34	19		
2013–14	Aston Villa	26	10		
2014–15	Aston Villa	29	13	**89**	**42**
2015–16	Liverpool	29	9	**29**	**9**
2016–17	Crystal Palace	36	15		
2017–18	Crystal Palace	31	3		
2018–19	Crystal Palace	16	1	**83**	**19**

DANN, Scott (D) **387 29**
H: 6 2 W: 12 00 b.Liverpool 14-2-87
Internationals: England U21.

2004–05	Walsall	1	0		
2005–06	Walsall	0	0		
2006–07	Walsall	30	4		
2007–08	Walsall	28	3	**59**	**7**
2007–08	Coventry C	16	0		
2008–09	Coventry C	31	3	**47**	**3**
2009–10	Birmingham C	30	0		
2010–11	Birmingham C	20	2		
2011–12	Birmingham C	0	0	**50**	**2**
2011–12	Blackburn R	27	1		
2012–13	Blackburn R	46	4		
2013–14	Blackburn R	25	0	**98**	**5**
2013–14	Crystal Palace	14	1		
2014–15	Crystal Palace	34	2		
2015–16	Crystal Palace	35	5		
2016–17	Crystal Palace	23	3		
2017–18	Crystal Palace	17	1		
2018–19	Crystal Palace	10	0	**133**	**12**

DREHER, Luke (M) **1 0**
H: 6 1 W: 12 00 b.Epsom 27-11-98

2015–16	Crystal Palace	0	0		
2016–17	Crystal Palace	0	0		
2017–18	Crystal Palace	0	0		
2018–19	Crystal Palace	1	0	**1**	**0**

GUAITA, Vicente (G) **234 0**
H: 6 3 W: 12 08 b.Valencia 18-2-87

2006–07	Valencia	0	0		
2007–08	Valencia	0	0		
2008–09	Valencia	2	0		
2009–10	Valencia	0	0		
2009–10	*Recreativo*	30	0	**30**	**0**
2010–11	Valencia	21	0		
2011–12	Valencia	26	0		
2012–13	Valencia	14	0		
2013–14	Valencia	13	0	**76**	**0**
2014–15	Getafe	29	0		
2015–16	Getafe	38	0		
2016–17	Getafe	8	0		
2017–18	Getafe	33	0	**108**	**0**
2018–19	Crystal Palace	20	0	**20**	**0**

HENNESSEY, Wayne (G) **286 0**
H: 6 0 W: 11 06 b.Anglesey 24-1-87
Internationals: Wales U17, U19, U21, Full caps.

2004–05	Wolverhampton W	0	0		
2005–06	Wolverhampton W	0	0		
2006–07	Wolverhampton W	0	0		
2006–07	*Bristol C*	0	0		
2006–07	*Stockport Co*	15	0	**15**	**0**
2007–08	Wolverhampton W	46	0		
2008–09	Wolverhampton W	35	0		
2009–10	Wolverhampton W	13	0		
2010–11	Wolverhampton W	24	0		
2011–12	Wolverhampton W	34	0		
2012–13	Wolverhampton W	0	0		
2013–14	Wolverhampton W	0	0	**152**	**0**
2013–14	*Yeovil T*	12	0	**12**	**0**
2013–14	Crystal Palace	1	0		
2014–15	Crystal Palace	3	0		
2015–16	Crystal Palace	29	0		
2016–17	Crystal Palace	29	0		
2017–18	Crystal Palace	27	0		
2018–19	Crystal Palace	18	0	**107**	**0**

HENRY, Dion (G) **1 0**
H: 5 11 W: 10 03 b.Ipswich 12-9-97

2014–15	Peterborough U	0	0		
2015–16	Peterborough U	1	0		
2016–17	Peterborough U	0	0	**1**	**0**
2017–18	Crystal Palace	0	0		
2018–19	Crystal Palace	0	0		

INNISS, Ryan (D) **70 0**
H: 6 5 W: 13 02 b.Kent 5-6-95
Internationals: England U16, U17.

2012–13	Crystal Palace	0	0		
2013–14	Crystal Palace	0	0		
2013–14	*Cheltenham T*	2	0	**2**	**0**
2013–14	*Gillingham*	3	0	**3**	**0**
2014–15	Crystal Palace	0	0		
2014–15	*Yeovil T*	6	0	**6**	**0**
2014–15	*Port Vale*	5	0		
2015–16	Crystal Palace	0	0		
2015–16	*Port Vale*	15	0	**20**	**0**
2016–17	Crystal Palace	0	0		
2016–17	*Southend U*	10	0	**10**	**0**
2017–18	Crystal Palace	0	0		
2017–18	*Colchester U*	18	0	**18**	**0**
2018–19	Crystal Palace	0	0		
2018–19	*Dundee*	11	0	**11**	**0**

KAIKAI, Sullay (F) **91 20**
H: 6 0 W: 11 07 b.London 26-8-95

2013–14	Crystal Palace	0	0		
2013–14	*Crawley T*	5	0	**5**	**0**
2014–15	Crystal Palace	0	0		
2014–15	*Cambridge U*	25	5	**25**	**5**
2015–16	Crystal Palace	1	0		
2015–16	*Shrewsbury T*	26	12	**26**	**12**
2016–17	Brentford	18	3	**18**	**3**
2016–17	Crystal Palace	1	0		
2017–18	Crystal Palace	1	0		
2017–18	*Charlton Ath*	14	0	**14**	**0**
2018–19	Crystal Palace	0	0	**3**	**0**

Transferred to NAC Breda January 2019.

KELLY, Martin (D) **141 1**
H: 6 3 W: 12 02 b.Bolton 27-4-90
Internationals: England U19, U20, U21, Full caps.

2007–08	Liverpool	0	0		
2008–09	Liverpool	0	0		
2008–09	*Huddersfield T*	7	1	**7**	**1**
2009–10	Liverpool	1	0		
2010–11	Liverpool	11	0		
2011–12	Liverpool	12	0		
2012–13	Liverpool	4	0		

2013–14	Liverpool	5	0	**33**	**0**
2014–15	Crystal Palace	31	0		
2015–16	Crystal Palace	13	0		
2016–17	Crystal Palace	29	0		
2017–18	Crystal Palace	15	0		
2018–19	Crystal Palace	13	0	**101**	**0**

KIRBY, Nya (M) **11** **1**
H: 5 9 W: 10 06 b.Islington 31-1-00
Internationals: England U16, U17, U18, U19.
From Tottenham H.

2017–18	Crystal Palace	0	0		
2018–19	Crystal Palace	0	0		
2018–19	*Blackpool*	11	1	**11**	**1**

KOUYATE, Cheikhou (M) **349** **19**
H: 6 3 W: 11 11 b.Dakar 21-12-89
Internationals: Senegal U20, Full caps.

2007–08	Brussels	10	0		
2008–09	Brussels	0	0	**10**	**0**
2008–09	*Kortrijk*	26	3	**26**	**3**
2009–10	Anderlecht	21	1		
2010–11	Anderlecht	23	1		
2011–12	Anderlecht	38	0		
2012–13	Anderlecht	33	1		
2013–14	Anderlecht	38	1	**153**	**4**
2014–15	West Ham U	31	4		
2015–16	West Ham U	34	5		
2016–17	West Ham U	31	1		
2017–18	West Ham U	33	2	**129**	**12**
2018–19	Crystal Palace	31	0	**31**	**0**

McARTHUR, James (M) **457** **37**
H: 5 6 W: 9 13 b.Glasgow 7-10-87
Internationals: Scotland U21, Full caps.

2004–05	Hamilton A	6	0		
2005–06	Hamilton A	20	1		
2006–07	Hamilton A	36	1		
2007–08	Hamilton A	34	4		
2008–09	Hamilton A	37	2		
2009–10	Hamilton A	35	1	**168**	**9**
2010–11	Wigan Ath	18	0		
2011–12	Wigan Ath	31	3		
2012–13	Wigan Ath	34	3		
2013–14	Wigan Ath	41	4		
2014–15	Wigan Ath	5	1	**129**	**11**
2014–15	Crystal Palace	32	2		
2015–16	Crystal Palace	28	2		
2016–17	Crystal Palace	29	5		
2017–18	Crystal Palace	33	5		
2018–19	Crystal Palace	38	3	**160**	**17**

McGREGOR, Gio (M) **0** **0**
b.Hammersmith 9-1-99

2018–19	Crystal Palace	0	0		

MEYER, Max (M) **175** **18**
H: 5 7 W: 10 03 b.Oberhausen 18-9-95
Internationals: Germany U16, U17, U19, U21, U23, Full caps.

2012–13	Schalke 04	5	0		
2013–14	Schalke 04	30	6		
2014–15	Schalke 04	28	5		
2015–16	Schalke 04	32	5		
2016–17	Schalke 04	27	1		
2017–18	Schalke 04	24	0	**146**	**17**
2018–19	Crystal Palace	29	1	**29**	**1**

MILIVOJEVIC, Luka (M) **259** **46**
H: 6 0 b.Kragujevac 7-4-91
Internationals: Serbia U21, Full caps.

2007–08	Radnicki Kraguejevac	5	1	**5**	**1**
2008–09	Rad Belgrade	1	0		
2009–10	Rad Belgrade	9	0		
2010–11	Rad Belgrade	26	0		
2011–12	Rad Belgrade	13	3	**49**	**3**
2011–12	Red Star Belgrade	11	1		
2012–13	Red Star Belgrade	25	6	**36**	**7**
2013–14	Anderlecht	16	0		
2014–15	Anderlecht	3	0	**19**	**0**
2014–15	Olympiacos	23	2		
2015–16	Olympiacos	22	3		
2016–17	Olympiacos	17	6	**62**	**11**
2016–17	Crystal Palace	14	2		
2017–18	Crystal Palace	36	10		
2018–19	Crystal Palace	38	12	**88**	**24**

PUNCHEON, Jason (M) **422** **59**
H: 5 9 W: 12 05 b.Croydon 26-6-86

2003–04	Wimbledon	8	0	**8**	**0**
2004–05	Milton Keynes D	25	1		
2005–06	Milton Keynes D	1	0		
2006–07	Barnet	37	5		
2007–08	Barnet	41	10	**78**	**15**
2008–09	Plymouth Arg	6	0		
2008–09	*Milton Keynes D*	27	4		
2009–10	Plymouth Arg	0	0	**6**	**0**
2009–10	*Milton Keynes D*	24	7	**77**	**12**

2009–10	Southampton	19	3		
2010–11	Southampton	15	0		
2010–11	*Millwall*	7	5	**7**	**5**
2010–11	*Blackpool*	11	3	**11**	**3**
2011–12	Southampton	8	0		
2011–12	*QPR*	2	0	**2**	**0**
2012–13	Southampton	32	6		
2013–14	Southampton	0	0	**74**	**9**
2013–14	Crystal Palace	34	7		
2014–15	Crystal Palace	37	6		
2015–16	Crystal Palace	31	2		
2016–17	Crystal Palace	36	0		
2017–18	Crystal Palace	10	0		
2018–19	Crystal Palace	5	0	**153**	**15**
2018–19	*Huddersfield T*	6	0	**6**	**0**

RIEDEWALD, Jairo (D) **75** **2**
H: 6 0 W: 12 06 b.Amsterdam 9-9-96
Internationals: Netherlands U16, U17, U19, U21, Full caps.

2013–14	Ajax	5	2		
2014–15	Ajax	19	0		
2015–16	Ajax	23	0		
2016–17	Ajax	16	0	**63**	**2**
2017–18	Crystal Palace	12	0		
2018–19	Crystal Palace	0	0	**12**	**0**

SAKHO, Mamadou (D) **261** **10**
H: 6 2 W: 12 07 b.Paris 13-2-90
Internationals: France U16, U17, U18, U19, U21, Full caps.

2006–07	Paris St Germain	0	0		
2007–08	Paris St Germain	12	0		
2008–09	Paris St Germain	23	1		
2009–10	Paris St Germain	32	0		
2010–11	Paris St Germain	35	4		
2011–12	Paris St Germain	22	0		
2012–13	Paris St Germain	27	2	**151**	**7**
2013–14	Liverpool	18	1		
2014–15	Liverpool	16	0		
2015–16	Liverpool	22	1		
2016–17	Liverpool	0	0		
2016–17	*Crystal Palace*	8	0		
2017–18	Liverpool	0	0	**56**	**2**
2017–18	Crystal Palace	19	1		
2018–19	Crystal Palace	27	0	**54**	**1**

SAKO, Bakary (M) **340** **64**
H: 5 11 W: 11 12 b.Ivry Sur Seine 26-4-88
Internationals: France U21. Mali U17, Full caps.

2006–07	Chateauroux	17	0		
2007–08	Chateauroux	12	1		
2008–09	Chateauroux	35	9	**64**	**10**
2009–10	St Etienne	30	1		
2010–11	St Etienne	38	7		
2011–12	St Etienne	36	5		
2012–13	St Etienne	2	0	**106**	**13**
2012–13	Wolverhampton W	37	9		
2013–14	Wolverhampton W	40	12		
2014–15	Wolverhampton W	41	15	**118**	**36**
2015–16	Crystal Palace	20	2		
2016–17	Crystal Palace	7	0		
2017–18	Crystal Palace	16	3		
2018–19	WBA	5	0	**5**	**0**
2018–19	Crystal Palace	4	0	**47**	**5**

SCHLUPP, Jeffrey (M) **204** **20**
H: 5 8 W: 11 00 b.Hamburg 23-12-92
Internationals: Ghana Full caps.

2010–11	Leicester C	0	0		
2010–11	*Brentford*	9	6	**9**	**6**
2011–12	Leicester C	21	2		
2012–13	Leicester C	19	3		
2013–14	Leicester C	26	1		
2014–15	Leicester C	32	3		
2015–16	Leicester C	24	1		
2016–17	Leicester C	4	0	**126**	**10**
2016–17	Crystal Palace	15	0		
2017–18	Crystal Palace	24	0		
2018–19	Crystal Palace	30	4	**69**	**4**

SORLOTH, Alexander (F) **124** **32**
H: 6 4 W: 14 02 b.Trondheim 5-12-95
Internationals: Norway U16, U17, U18, U19, U21, Full caps.

2013	Rosenborg	0	0		
2014	Rosenborg	6	0	**6**	**0**
2015	Bodo/Glimt	26	13	**26**	**13**
2015–16	Groningen	13	2		
2016–17	Groningen	25	3	**38**	**5**
2017–18	Midtjylland	19	10	**19**	**10**
2017–18	Crystal Palace	4	0		
2018–19	Crystal Palace	12	0	**16**	**0**
2018–19	*Gent*	19	4	**19**	**4**

SOUARE, Pape (D) **127** **3**
H: 5 10 W: 10 10 b.Mbao 6-6-90
Internationals: Senegal U23, Full caps.

2010–11	Lille	4	0		
2011–12	Lille	7	0		
2012–13	Lille	0	0		
2012–13	*Reims*	23	0	**23**	**0**
2013–14	Lille	33	3		
2014–15	Lille	12	0	**56**	**3**
2014–15	Crystal Palace	9	0		
2015–16	Crystal Palace	34	0		
2016–17	Crystal Palace	3	0		
2017–18	Crystal Palace	1	0		
2018–19	Crystal Palace	1	0	**48**	**0**

SPERONI, Julian (G) **465** **0**
H: 6 0 W: 11 00 b.Buenos Aires 18-5-79
Internationals: Argentina U20, U21.

1999–2000	Platense	2	0		
2000–01	Platense	0	0	**2**	**0**
2001–02	Dundee	17	0		
2002–03	Dundee	38	0		
2003–04	Dundee	37	0	**92**	**0**
2004–05	Crystal Palace	6	0		
2005–06	Crystal Palace	4	0		
2006–07	Crystal Palace	5	0		
2007–08	Crystal Palace	46	0		
2008–09	Crystal Palace	45	0		
2009–10	Crystal Palace	45	0		
2010–11	Crystal Palace	45	0		
2011–12	Crystal Palace	42	0		
2012–13	Crystal Palace	46	0		
2013–14	Crystal Palace	37	0		
2014–15	Crystal Palace	36	0		
2015–16	Crystal Palace	2	0		
2016–17	Crystal Palace	0	0		
2017–18	Crystal Palace	11	0		
2018–19	Crystal Palace	1	0	**371**	**0**

TAVARES, Nikola (D) **0** **0**
Internationals: Croatia U18, U19.

2018–19	Crystal Palace	0	0		

TOMKINS, James (D) **296** **15**
H: 6 3 W: 11 10 b.Basildon 29-3-89
Internationals: England U16, U17, U18, U19, U20, U21. Great Britain.

2005–06	West Ham U	0	0		
2006–07	West Ham U	0	0		
2007–08	West Ham U	6	0		
2008–09	West Ham U	12	1		
2008–09	*Derby Co*	7	0	**7**	**0**
2009–10	West Ham U	23	0		
2010–11	West Ham U	19	1		
2011–12	West Ham U	44	4		
2012–13	West Ham U	26	1		
2013–14	West Ham U	31	0		
2014–15	West Ham U	22	1		
2015–16	West Ham U	25	0	**208**	**8**
2016–17	Crystal Palace	24	3		
2017–18	Crystal Palace	28	3		
2018–19	Crystal Palace	29	1	**81**	**7**

TOWNSEND, Andros (M) **274** **29**
H: 6 0 W: 12 00 b.Chingford 16-7-91
Internationals: England U16, U17, U19, U21, Full caps.

2008–09	Tottenham H	0	0		
2008–09	*Yeovil T*	10	1	**10**	**1**
2009–10	Tottenham H	0	0		
2009–10	*Leyton Orient*	22	2	**22**	**2**
2009–10	*Milton Keynes D*	9	2	**9**	**2**
2010–11	Tottenham H	0	0		
2010–11	*Ipswich T*	13	1	**13**	**1**
2010–11	*Watford*	3	0	**3**	**0**
2010–11	*Millwall*	11	2	**11**	**2**
2011–12	Tottenham H	0	0		
2011–12	*Leeds U*	6	1	**6**	**1**
2011–12	*Birmingham C*	15	0	**15**	**0**
2012–13	Tottenham H	5	0		
2012–13	*QPR*	12	2	**12**	**2**
2013–14	Tottenham H	25	1		
2014–15	Tottenham H	17	2		
2015–16	Tottenham H	3	0	**50**	**3**
2015–16	Newcastle U	13	4	**13**	**4**
2016–17	Crystal Palace	36	3		
2017–18	Crystal Palace	36	2		
2018–19	Crystal Palace	38	6	**110**	**11**

TUPPER, Joe (G) **0** **0**
b. 15-11-97
From Reading.

2018–19	Crystal Palace	0	0		

VAN AANHOLT, Patrick (D) **268 23**
H: 5 9 W: 10 08 b.Den Bosch 3-7-88
Internationals: Netherlands U16, U17, U18, U19, U20, U21, Full caps.

2007–08	Chelsea	0	0		
2008–09	Chelsea	0	0		
2009–10	Chelsea	2	0		
2009–10	*Coventry C*	20	0	**20**	**0**
2009–10	*Newcastle U*	7	0	**7**	**0**
2010–11	Chelsea	0	0		
2010–11	*Leicester C*	12	1	**12**	**1**
2011–12	Chelsea	0	0		
2011–12	*Wigan Ath*	3	0	**3**	**0**
2011–12	*Vitesse*	9	0		
2012–13	Chelsea	0	0		
2012–13	*Vitesse*	31	1		
2013–14	Chelsea	0	0	**2**	**0**
2013–14	*Vitesse*	27	4	**67**	**5**
2014–15	Sunderland	28	0		
2015–16	Sunderland	33	4		
2016–17	Sunderland	21	3	**82**	**7**
2016–17	Crystal Palace	11	2		
2017–18	Crystal Palace	28	5		
2018–19	Crystal Palace	36	3	**75**	**10**

WAN BISSAKA, Aaron (M) **42 0**
b. 26-11-97
Internationals: DR Congo U20. England U20, U21.

2016–17	Crystal Palace	0	0		
2017–18	Crystal Palace	7	0		
2018–19	Crystal Palace	35	0	**42**	**0**

WARD, Joel (D) **302 11**
H: 6 2 W: 11 13 b.Emsworth 29-10-89

2008–09	Portsmouth	0	0		
2008–09	*Bournemouth*	21	1	**21**	**1**
2009–10	Portsmouth	3	0		
2010–11	Portsmouth	42	3		
2011–12	Portsmouth	44	3	**89**	**6**
2012–13	Crystal Palace	25	0		
2013–14	Crystal Palace	36	0		
2014–15	Crystal Palace	37	1		
2015–16	Crystal Palace	30	2		
2016–17	Crystal Palace	38	0		
2017–18	Crystal Palace	19	0		
2018–19	Crystal Palace	7	1	**192**	**4**

WICKHAM, Connor (F) **201 40**
H: 6 0 W: 14 01 b.Hereford 31-3-93
Internationals: England U16, U17, U19, U21.

2008–09	Ipswich T	2	0		
2009–10	Ipswich T	26	4		
2010–11	Ipswich T	37	9	**65**	**13**
2011–12	Sunderland	16	1		
2012–13	Sunderland	12	0		
2012–13	*Sheffield W*	6	1		
2013–14	Sunderland	15	5		
2013–14	*Sheffield W*	11	8	**17**	**9**
2013–14	*Leeds U*	5	0	**5**	**0**
2014–15	Sunderland	36	5	**79**	**11**
2015–16	Crystal Palace	21	5		
2016–17	Crystal Palace	8	2		
2017–18	Crystal Palace	0	0		
2018–19	Crystal Palace	6	0	**35**	**7**

WOODS, Sam (D) **0 0**
b.Bromley 11-9-98

2018–19	Crystal Palace	0	0		

ZAHA, Wilfried (F) **303 45**
H: 5 11 W: 10 05 b.Ivory Coast 10-11-92
Internationals: England U19, U21, Full caps. Ivory Coast Full caps.

2009–10	Crystal Palace	1	0		
2010–11	Crystal Palace	41	1		
2011–12	Crystal Palace	41	6		
2012–13	Crystal Palace	43	6		
2012–13	Manchester U	0	0		
2013–14	Manchester U	2	0	**2**	**0**
2013–14	*Cardiff C*	12	0	**12**	**0**
2014–15	Crystal Palace	31	4		
2015–16	Crystal Palace	34	2		
2016–17	Crystal Palace	35	7		
2017–18	Crystal Palace	29	9		
2018–19	Crystal Palace	34	10	**289**	**45**

Players retained or with offer of contract
Aveiro, Brandon Paulo Vale; Bryon, Lewis; Daly, James Stanley; Eyenga Lokilo, Jason; Flanagan, Kian; Jach, Jaroslaw Przemyslaw; Lumeka, Levi Jeremiah; Mensah, Jacob Kwabena; Mitchell, Tyrick; Webber, Oliver Henry.

Scholars
Addy, Tetteh-Quaye; Ajayi, Joshua; Akrobor-Boateng, David Lionel; Boateng, Malachi; Chamberlin-Gayle, Jashaun Deviente; Donkin, William Rupert James; Gurung, Bivesh; Hanson, Ryan David; Keutcha, Pierrick Brandon; Luthra, Rohan; Malcolm, Joshua; Matthews, Drew; Onoabhagbe, Ehizojie Martins; Parris, Kamari; Robertson, Sean Dominic; Russell, Jacob Lukc; Russell, Jude Thomas; Street, Robert Nicholas; Trehy, Cian; Watson, Courtney Alfie Haynes.

DERBY CO (30)

BENNETT, Mason (F) **99 7**
H: 5 10 W: 10 02 b.Shirebrook 15-7-96
Internationals: England U16, U17, U19.

2011–12	Derby Co	9	0		
2012–13	Derby Co	6	0		
2013–14	Derby Co	13	1		
2013–14	*Chesterfield*	5	0	**5**	**0**
2014–15	Derby Co	2	0		
2014–15	*Bradford C*	11	1	**11**	**1**
2015–16	Derby Co	0	0		
2015–16	*Burton Alb*	16	1	**16**	**1**
2016–17	Derby Co	2	0		
2017–18	Derby Co	3	0		
2017–18	*Notts Co*	2	1	**2**	**1**
2018–19	Derby Co	30	3	**65**	**4**

BIRD, Max (M) **4 0**
H: 6 0 W: 10 10 b.Burton 18-9-00

2017–18	Derby Co	0	0		
2018–19	Derby Co	4	0	**4**	**0**

BOGLE, Jayden (D) **40 2**
b. 27-7-00
Internationals: England U20.
From Stoke C.

2017–18	Derby Co	0	0		
2018–19	Derby Co	40	2	**40**	**2**

BRYSON, Craig (M) **486 62**
H: 5 7 W: 10 00 b.Rutherglen 6-11-86
Internationals: Scotland U21, Full caps.

2003–04	Clyde	0	0		
2004–05	Clyde	28	3		
2005–06	Clyde	33	2		
2006–07	Clyde	34	3	**95**	**8**
2007–08	Kilmarnock	19	4		
2008–09	Kilmarnock	33	2		
2009–10	Kilmarnock	33	4		
2010–11	Kilmarnock	33	2	**118**	**12**
2011–12	Derby Co	44	6		
2012–13	Derby Co	37	5		
2013–14	Derby Co	45	16		
2014–15	Derby Co	38	4		
2015–16	Derby Co	21	3		
2016–17	Derby Co	34	2		
2017–18	Derby Co	4	1		
2017–18	*Cardiff C*	22	2	**22**	**2**
2018–19	Derby Co	28	3	**251**	**40**

BUCHANAN, Lee (D) **0 0**
b. 7-3-01

2018–19	Derby Co	0	0		

BUTTERFIELD, Jacob (D) **303 27**
H: 5 10 W: 11 00 b.Bradford 10-6-90
Internationals: England U21.

2007–08	Barnsley	3	0		
2008–09	Barnsley	3	0		
2009–10	Barnsley	20	1		
2010–11	Barnsley	40	2		
2011–12	Barnsley	24	5	**90**	**8**
2012–13	Norwich C	0	0		
2012–13	*Bolton W*	8	0	**8**	**0**
2012–13	*Crystal Palace*	9	0	**9**	**0**
2013–14	Norwich C	0	0		
2013–14	Middlesbrough	31	3	**31**	**3**
2014–15	Huddersfield T	45	6		
2015–16	Huddersfield T	5	1	**50**	**7**
2015–16	Derby Co	37	7		
2016–17	Derby Co	40	1		
2017–18	Derby Co	3	0		
2017–18	*Sheffield W*	20	0	**20**	**0**
2018–19	Derby Co	0	0	**80**	**8**
2018–19	*Bradford C*	15	1	**15**	**1**

CARSON, Scott (G) **468 0**
H: 6 0 W: 13 06 b.Whitehaven 3-9-85
Internationals: England U18, U21, B, Full caps.

2002–03	Leeds U	0	0		
2003–04	Leeds U	3	0		
2004–05	Leeds U	0	0	**3**	**0**
2004–05	Liverpool	4	0		
2005–06	Liverpool	0	0		
2005–06	*Sheffield W*	9	0	**9**	**0**
2006–07	Liverpool	0	0		
2006–07	*Charlton Ath*	36	0	**36**	**0**
2007–08	Liverpool	0	0	**4**	**0**
2007–08	*Aston Villa*	35	0	**35**	**0**
2008–09	WBA	35	0		
2009–10	WBA	43	0		
2010–11	WBA	32	0	**110**	**0**
2011–12	Bursaspor	34	0		
2012–13	Bursaspor	29	0	**63**	**0**
2013–14	Wigan Ath	16	0		
2014–15	Wigan Ath	34	0	**50**	**0**
2015–16	Derby Co	36	0		
2016–17	Derby Co	46	0		
2017–18	Derby Co	46	0		
2018–19	Derby Co	30	0	**158**	**0**

COLE, Ashley (D) **508 19**
H: 5 8 W: 10 05 b.Stepney 20-12-80
Internationals: England U20, U21, B, Full caps.

1998–99	Arsenal	0	0		
1999–2000	Arsenal	1	0		
1999–2000	*Crystal Palace*	14	1	**14**	**1**
2000–01	Arsenal	17	3		
2001–02	Arsenal	29	2		
2002–03	Arsenal	31	1		
2003–04	Arsenal	32	0		
2004–05	Arsenal	35	2		
2005–06	Arsenal	11	0		
2006–07	Arsenal	0	0	**156**	**8**
2006–07	Chelsea	23	0		
2007–08	Chelsea	27	1		
2008–09	Chelsea	34	1		
2009–10	Chelsea	27	4		
2010–11	Chelsea	38	0		
2011–12	Chelsea	32	0		
2012–13	Chelsea	31	1		
2013–14	Chelsea	17	0	**229**	**7**
2014–15	Roma	11	0	**11**	**0**
2016	LA Galaxy	29	1		
2017	LA Galaxy	29	1	**58**	**2**
2018	L.A Galaxy	31	1	**31**	**1**
2018–19	Derby Co	9	0	**9**	**0**

DAVIES, Curtis (D) **445 23**
H: 6 2 W: 11 13 b.Waltham Forest 15-3-85
Internationals: England U21.

2003–04	Luton T	6	0		
2004–05	Luton T	44	1		
2005–06	Luton T	6	1	**56**	**2**
2005–06	WBA	33	2		
2006–07	WBA	32	0		
2007–08	WBA	0	0	**65**	**2**
2007–08	*Aston Villa*	12	1		
2008–09	Aston Villa	35	1		
2009–10	Aston Villa	2	1		
2010–11	Aston Villa	0	0	**49**	**3**
2010–11	*Leicester C*	12	0	**12**	**0**
2010–11	Birmingham C	6	0		
2011–12	Birmingham C	42	5		
2012–13	Birmingham C	41	6	**89**	**11**
2013–14	Hull C	37	2		
2014–15	Hull C	21	0		
2015–16	Hull C	39	2		
2016–17	Hull C	26	0	**123**	**4**
2017–18	Derby Co	46	1		
2018–19	Derby Co	5	0	**51**	**1**

ELSNIK, Timi (M) **50 7**
H: 5 10 W: 10 03 b.Kidricevo 29-4-98
Internationals: Slovenia U16, U17, U18, U19.

2015–16	Derby Co	0	0		
2016–17	Derby Co	0	0		
2017–18	Derby Co	0	0		
2017–18	*Swindon T*	22	3	**22**	**3**
2018–19	Derby Co	0	0		
2018–19	*Mansfield T*	19	3	**19**	**3**
2018–19	*Northampton T*	9	1	**9**	**1**

EVANS, George (M) **121 8**
H: 6 0 W: 11 12 b.Cheadle 13-12-94
Internationals: England U17, U19, U20.

2012–13	Manchester C	0	0		
2013–14	Manchester C	0	0		
2013–14	*Crewe Alex*	23	1	**23**	**1**
2014–15	Manchester C	0	0		
2014–15	*Scunthorpe U*	16	1	**16**	**1**
2015–16	Manchester C	0	0		
2015–16	*Walsall*	12	3	**12**	**3**
2015–16	Reading	6	0		
2016–17	Reading	35	2		

2017–18 Reading 18 1 **59 3**
2018–19 Derby Co 11 0 **11 0**

FORSYTH, Craig (M) 282 19
H: 6 0 W: 12 00 b.Carnoustie 24-2-89
Internationals: Scotland Full caps.
2006–07 Dundee 1 0
2007–08 Dundee 0 0
2007–08 *Montrose* 9 0 **9 0**
2008–09 Dundee 1 0
2008–09 *Arbroath* 26 2 **26 2**
2009–10 Dundee 24 2
2010–11 Dundee 33 8 **59 10**
2011–12 Watford 20 3
2012–13 Watford 2 0 **22 3**
2012–13 *Bradford C* 7 0 **7 0**
2012–13 *Derby Co* 10 0
2013–14 Derby Co 46 2
2014–15 Derby Co 44 1
2015–16 Derby Co 12 0
2016–17 Derby Co 3 1
2017–18 Derby Co 31 0
2018–19 Derby Co 13 0 **159 4**

HOLMES, Duane (M) 136 13
H: 5 8 W: 10 03 b.Wakefield 6-11-94
Internationals: USA Full caps.
2012–13 Huddersfield T 0 0
2013–14 Huddersfield T 16 0
2013–14 *Yeovil T* 5 0 **5 0**
2014–15 Huddersfield T 0 0
2014–15 *Bury* 6 0 **6 0**
2015–16 Huddersfield T 6 1 **22 1**
2016–17 Scunthorpe U 32 3
2017–18 Scunthorpe U 45 7
2018–19 Scunthorpe U 1 0 **78 10**
2018–19 Derby Co 25 2 **25 2**

HUDDLESTONE, Tom (M) 448 17
H: 6 2 W: 11 02 b.Nottingham 28-12-86
Internationals: England U16, U17, U19, U20, U21, Full caps.
2003–04 Derby Co 43 0
2004–05 Derby Co 45 0
2005–06 Tottenham H 4 0
2005–06 *Wolverhampton W* 13 1 **13 1**
2006–07 Tottenham H 21 1
2007–08 Tottenham H 28 3
2008–09 Tottenham H 22 0
2009–10 Tottenham H 33 2
2010–11 Tottenham H 14 2
2011–12 Tottenham H 2 0
2012–13 Tottenham H 20 0
2013–14 Tottenham H 0 0 **144 8**
2013–14 Hull C 36 3
2014–15 Hull C 31 0
2015–16 Hull C 37 2
2016–17 Hull C 31 1 **135 6**
2017–18 Derby Co 44 2
2018–19 Derby Co 24 0 **156 2**

JOHNSON, Brad (M) 448 62
H: 6 0 W: 12 10 b.Hackney 28-4-87
2004–05 Cambridge U 1 0 **1 0**
2005–06 Northampton T 3 0
2006–07 Northampton T 27 5
2007–08 Northampton T 23 2 **53 7**
2007–08 Leeds U 21 3
2008–09 Leeds U 15 1
2008–09 *Brighton & HA* 10 4 **10 4**
2009–10 Leeds U 36 7
2010–11 Leeds U 45 5 **117 16**
2011–12 Norwich C 28 2
2012–13 Norwich C 37 1
2013–14 Norwich C 32 3
2014–15 Norwich C 41 15
2015–16 Norwich C 4 0 **142 21**
2015–16 Derby Co 31 5
2016–17 Derby Co 33 3
2017–18 Derby Co 33 4
2018–19 Derby Co 28 2 **125 14**

JOZEFZOON, Florian (F) 184 22
H: 5 8 W: 11 00 b.Amsterdam 9-2-91
Internationals: Netherlands U19, U21.
2010–11 Ajax 4 0
2011–12 Ajax 0 0 **4 0**
2011–12 *NAC Breda* 16 0 **16 0**
2012–13 RKC Waalwijk 34 7 **34 7**
2013–14 PSV Eindhoven 16 2
2014–15 PSV Eindhoven 15 2
2015–16 PSV Eindhoven 9 1
2016–17 PSV Eindhoven 5 0 **45 5**
2016–17 Brentford 19 1
2017–18 Brentford 39 7 **58 8**
2018–19 Derby Co 27 2 **27 2**

KEOGH, Richard (D) 541 19
H: 6 0 W: 11 02 b.Harlow 11-8-86
Internationals: Republic of Ireland U21, Full caps.
2004–05 Stoke C 0 0
2005–06 Bristol C 9 1
2005–06 *Wycombe W* 3 0 **3 0**
2006–07 Bristol C 31 2
2007–08 Bristol C 0 0 **40 3**
2007–08 *Huddersfield T* 9 1 **9 1**
2007–08 *Carlisle U* 7 0
2007–08 *Cheltenham T* 10 0 **10 0**
2008–09 Carlisle U 32 1
2009–10 Carlisle U 41 3 **80 4**
2010–11 Coventry C 46 1
2011–12 Coventry C 45 0 **91 1**
2012–13 Derby Co 46 4
2013–14 Derby Co 41 1
2014–15 Derby Co 45 0
2015–16 Derby Co 46 1
2016–17 Derby Co 42 0
2017–18 Derby Co 42 1
2018–19 Derby Co 46 3 **308 10**

KNIGHT, Jason (M) 0 0
b. 13-2-01
Internationals: Republic of Ireland U17, U18, U19.
2018–19 Derby Co 0 0

LAWRENCE, Tom (F) 179 29
H: 5 9 W: 11 11 b.Wrexham 13-1-94
Internationals: Wales U17, U19, U21, Full caps.
2012–13 Manchester U 0 0
2013–14 Manchester U 1 0 **1 0**
2013–14 *Carlisle U* 9 3 **9 3**
2013–14 *Yeovil T* 19 2 **19 2**
2014–15 Leicester C 3 0
2014–15 *Rotherham U* 6 1 **6 1**
2015–16 Leicester C 0 0
2015–16 *Blackburn R* 21 2 **21 2**
2015–16 *Cardiff C* 14 0 **14 0**
2016–17 Leicester C 0 0 **3 0**
2016–17 *Ipswich T* 34 9 **34 9**
2017–18 Derby Co 39 6
2018–19 Derby Co 33 6 **72 12**

LEDLEY, Joe (M) 445 53
H: 6 0 W: 11 06 b.Cardiff 23-1-87
Internationals: Wales U17, U19, U21, Full caps.
2004–05 Cardiff C 28 3
2005–06 Cardiff C 42 3
2006–07 Cardiff C 46 2
2007–08 Cardiff C 41 10
2008–09 Cardiff C 40 4
2009–10 Cardiff C 29 3 **226 25**
2010–11 Celtic 29 2
2011–12 Celtic 32 7
2012–13 Celtic 25 7
2013–14 Celtic 20 4 **106 20**
2013–14 Crystal Palace 14 2
2014–15 Crystal Palace 32 2
2015–16 Crystal Palace 19 1
2016–17 Crystal Palace 18 1 **83 6**
2017–18 Derby Co 26 1
2018–19 Derby Co 4 1 **30 2**

LOWE, Max (D) 57 2
H: 5 9 W: 11 09 b.Birmingham 11-5-97
Internationals: England U16, U17, U18, U20.
2013–14 Derby Co 0 0
2014–15 Derby Co 0 0
2015–16 Derby Co 0 0
2016–17 Derby Co 9 0
2017–18 Derby Co 0 0
2017–18 *Shrewsbury T* 12 0 **12 0**
2018–19 Derby Co 3 0 **12 0**
2018–19 *Aberdeen* 33 2 **33 2**

MACDONALD, Calum (D) 0 0
Internationals: Scotland U21.
2016–17 Derby Co 0 0
2017–18 Derby Co 0 0
2018–19 Derby Co 0 0

MALONE, Scott (D) 285 22
H: 6 2 W: 11 11 b.Rowley Regis 25-3-91
Internationals: England U19.
2008–09 Wolverhampton W 0 0
2008–09 *Ujpest* 7 1 **7 1**
2009–10 Wolverhampton W 0 0
2009–10 *Southend U* 17 0 **17 0**
2010–11 Wolverhampton W 0 0
2010–11 *Burton Alb* 22 1 **22 1**
2011–12 Wolverhampton W 0 0
2011–12 Bournemouth 32 5 **32 5**
2012–13 Millwall 15 1
2013–14 Millwall 33 3
2014–15 Millwall 20 1 **68 5**
2014–15 Cardiff C 13 0
2015–16 Cardiff C 41 2 **54 2**
2016–17 Fulham 36 6 **36 6**
2017–18 Huddersfield T 22 0 **22 0**
2018–19 Derby Co 27 2 **27 2**

MARRIOTT, Jack (F) 168 57
H: 5 8 W: 11 03 b.Beverley 9-9-94
2012–13 Ipswich T 1 0
2013–14 Ipswich T 1 0
2013–14 *Gillingham* 1 0 **1 0**
2014–15 Ipswich T 0 0 **2 0**
2014–15 *Carlisle U* 4 0 **4 0**
2014–15 *Colchester U* 5 1 **5 1**
2015–16 Luton T 40 14
2016–17 Luton T 39 8 **79 22**
2017–18 Peterborough U 44 27 **44 27**
2018–19 Derby Co 33 7 **33 7**

MARTIN, Chris (F) 416 113
H: 6 2 W: 12 06 b.Beccles 4-11-88
Internationals: England U19. Scotland Full caps.
2006–07 Norwich C 18 4
2007–08 Norwich C 7 0
2008–09 Norwich C 0 0
2008–09 *Luton T* 40 11 **40 11**
2009–10 Norwich C 42 17
2010–11 Norwich C 30 4
2011–12 Norwich C 4 0
2011–12 *Crystal Palace* 26 7 **26 7**
2012–13 Norwich C 1 0 **102 25**
2012–13 *Swindon T* 12 1 **12 1**
2012–13 *Derby Co* 13 2
2013–14 Derby Co 44 20
2014–15 Derby Co 35 18
2015–16 Derby Co 45 15
2016–17 Derby Co 5 0
2016–17 *Fulham* 31 10 **31 10**
2017–18 Derby Co 23 1
2017–18 *Reading* 10 1 **10 1**
2018–19 Derby Co 0 0 **165 56**
2018–19 *Hull C* 30 2 **30 2**

MITCHELL, Jonathan (G) 24 0
H: 5 11 W: 13 08 b.Hartlepool 24-11-94
Internationals: England U21.
2014–15 Derby Co 0 0
2015–16 Derby Co 0 0
2015–16 *Luton T* 5 0 **5 0**
2016–17 Derby Co 0 0
2017–18 Derby Co 0 0
2018–19 Derby Co 0 0
2018–19 *Oxford U* 10 0 **10 0**
2018–19 *Shrewsbury T* 9 0 **9 0**

MITCHELL-LAWSON, Jayden (M) 1 0
b. 17-9-99
From Swindon T.
2018–19 Derby Co 1 0 **1 0**

NUGENT, Dave (F) 576 152
H: 5 11 W: 12 13 b.Liverpool 2-5-85
Internationals: England U20, U21, Full caps.
2001–02 Bury 5 0
2002–03 Bury 31 4
2003–04 Bury 26 3
2004–05 Bury 26 11 **88 18**
2004–05 Preston NE 18 8
2005–06 Preston NE 32 10
2006–07 Preston NE 44 15 **94 33**
2007–08 Portsmouth 15 0
2008–09 Portsmouth 16 3
2009–10 Portsmouth 3 0
2009–10 *Burnley* 30 6 **30 6**
2010–11 Portsmouth 44 13 **78 16**
2011–12 Leicester C 42 15
2012–13 Leicester C 42 14
2013–14 Leicester C 46 20
2014–15 Leicester C 29 5 **159 54**
2015–16 Middlesbrough 38 8
2016–17 Middlesbrough 4 0 **42 8**
2016–17 Derby Co 17 6
2017–18 Derby Co 37 9
2018–19 Derby Co 31 2 **85 17**

PEARCE, Alex (D) 324 20
H: 6 0 W: 11 10 b.Wallingford 9-11-88
Internationals: Scotland U19, U21, Full caps.
2006–07 Reading 0 0
2006–07 *Northampton T* 15 1 **15 1**
2007–08 Reading 0 0
2007–08 *Bournemouth* 11 0 **11 0**

2007–08	*Norwich C*	11	0	11	0
2008–09	Reading	16	1		
2008–09	*Southampton*	9	2	9	2
2009–10	Reading	25	4		
2010–11	Reading	21	1		
2011–12	Reading	46	5		
2012–13	Reading	19	0		
2013–14	Reading	45	3		
2014–15	Reading	40	0	212	14
2015–16	Derby Co	0	0		
2015–16	*Bristol C*	7	0	7	0
2016–17	Derby Co	40	2		
2017–18	Derby Co	7	1		
2018–19	Derby Co	1	0	48	3
2018–19	*Millwall*	11	0	11	0

RAVAS, Henrich (G) 0 0
From Boston U.

2018–19	Derby Co	0	0

ROOS, Kelle (G) 65 0
H: 6 4 W: 14 02 b.Rijkevoort 31-5-92

2013–14	Derby Co	0	0		
2014–15	Derby Co	0	0		
2015–16	Derby Co	0	0		
2015–16	*Rotherham U*	4	0	4	0
2015–16	*AFC Wimbledon*	17	0	17	0
2016–17	Derby Co	0	0		
2016–17	*Bristol R*	16	0	16	0
2017–18	Derby Co	0	0		
2017–18	*Port Vale*	8	0	8	0
2017–18	*Plymouth Arg*	4	0	4	0
2018–19	Derby Co	16	0	16	0

THOMAS, Luke (F) 45 4
H: 5 7 W: 10 08 b. 19-2-99

2015–16	Derby Co	0	0		
2016–17	Derby Co	0	0		
2017–18	Derby Co	2	0		
2018–19	Derby Co	0	0	2	0
2018–19	*Coventry C*	43	4	43	4

THORNE, George (M) 108 4
H: 6 2 W: 13 01 b.Chatham 4-1-93
Internationals: England U16, U17, U18, U19.

2009–10	WBA	1	0		
2010–11	WBA	1	0		
2011–12	WBA	3	0		
2011–12	*Portsmouth*	14	0	14	0
2012–13	WBA	5	0		
2012–13	*Peterborough U*	7	1	7	1
2013–14	WBA	0	0	10	0
2013–14	*Watford*	8	0	8	0
2013–14	*Derby Co*	9	1		
2014–15	Derby Co	3	0		
2015–16	Derby Co	34	2		
2017–18	Derby Co	20	0		
2018–19	Derby Co	0	0	66	3
2018–19	*Luton T*	3	0	3	0

WAGHORN, Martyn (F) 310 85
H: 5 9 W: 13 01 b.South Shields 23-1-90
Internationals: England U19, U21.

2007–08	Sunderland	3	0		
2008–09	Sunderland	1	0		
2008–09	*Charlton Ath*	7	1	7	1
2009–10	Sunderland	0	0		
2009–10	*Leicester C*	43	12		
2010–11	Sunderland	2	0	6	0
2010–11	Leicester C	30	4		
2011–12	Leicester C	4	1		
2011–12	*Hull C*	5	1	5	1
2012–13	Leicester C	24	3		
2013–14	Leicester C	2	0	103	20
2013–14	*Millwall*	14	3	14	3
2013–14	Wigan Ath	15	5		
2014–15	Wigan Ath	23	3	38	8
2015–16	Rangers	25	20		
2016–17	Rangers	32	7	57	27
2017–18	Ipswich T	44	16	44	16
2018–19	Derby Co	36	9	36	9

WILSON, Tyree (M) 0 0

2018–19	Derby Co	0	0

WISDOM, Andre (D) 139 0
H: 6 1 W: 12 04 b.Leeds 9-5-93
Internationals: England U16, U17, U19, U21.

2009–10	Liverpool	0	0		
2010–11	Liverpool	0	0		
2011–12	Liverpool	0	0		
2012–13	Liverpool	12	0		
2013–14	Liverpool	2	0		
2013–14	*Derby Co*	34	0		
2014–15	Liverpool	0	0		
2014–15	*WBA*	24	0	24	0
2015–16	Liverpool	0	0		
2015–16	*Norwich C*	10	0	10	0
2016–17	Liverpool	0	0	14	0
2016–17	*Red Bull Salzburg*	16	0	16	0
2017–18	Derby Co	30	0		
2018–19	Derby Co	11	0	75	0

Players retained or with offer of contract
Anya, Ikechi; Babos, Alexander Jon; Barnes, Joshua Edwin; Bateman, Joseph Joshua; Blackman, Nicholas Alexander; Brown, Jordan Brian; Cresswell, Cameron Ian; Dixon, Connor Liam; Gordon, Kellan Sheene; Hunt, Max; McAllister, Kyle; Minkley, Callum; Shonibare, Joshua; Sibley, Louie Joseph; Splatt, Javaun Delmarco; Wassall, Ethan Luca; Whittaker, Morgan Reece; Yates, Matthew Dean.

Scholars
Brown, Archibald Norman; Cashin, Eiran Joe; Charles, Jaden Gary; Ebosele, Festy Oseiwe; Foster-Theniger, Bradley; French, Samuel Nicholas; Greco, Yoann; Halwax, Harry; McDonald, Kornell Mark Marshall; Stretton, Jack Kirk; Thompson, Liam Francis; Wilson, Tyree Benjamin.

DONCASTER R (31)

AMOS, Danny (D) 4 0
H: 5 11 W: 10 10 b.Sheffield 22-12-99
Internationals: Northern Ireland U19, U21.

2016–17	Doncaster R	0	0		
2017–18	Doncaster R	3	0		
2018–19	Doncaster R	1	0	4	0

ANDERSON, Thomas (M) 111 5
H: 6 4 W: 13 01 b.Burnley 2-9-93

2012–13	Burnley	0	0		
2013–14	Burnley	0	0		
2014–15	Burnley	0	0		
2014–15	*Carlisle U*	8	0	8	0
2015–16	Burnley	0	0		
2015–16	*Chesterfield*	18	0		
2016–17	Burnley	0	0		
2016–17	*Chesterfield*	35	2	53	2
2017–18	Burnley	0	0		
2017–18	*Port Vale*	20	0	20	0
2017–18	*Doncaster R*	7	2		
2018–19	Doncaster R	23	1	30	3

ANDREW, Danny (D) 178 8
H: 5 11 W: 11 06 b.Holbeach 23-12-90

2009–10	Peterborough U	2	0	2	0
2009–10	*Cheltenham T*	10	0		
2010–11	Cheltenham T	43	4		
2011–12	Cheltenham T	10	0		
2012–13	Cheltenham T	1	0	64	4

From Gloucester C, Macclesfield T.

2014–15	Fleetwood T	7	0		
2015–16	Fleetwood T	9	0	16	0
2016–17	Grimsby T	46	0	46	0
2017–18	Doncaster R	4	0		
2018–19	Doncaster R	46	4	50	4

BEESTIN, Alfie (F) 34 2
H: 5 10 W: 11 11 b.Leeds 1-10-97

2016–17	Doncaster R	3	0		
2017–18	Doncaster R	26	2		
2018–19	Doncaster R	5	0	34	2

BEN KHEMIS, Issam (F) 6 0
H: 5 9 W: 11 05 b.Paris 10-1-96
Internationals: Tunisia Full caps.

2015–16	Lorient	1	0		
2016–17	Lorient	2	0		
2017–18	Lorient	0	0	3	0
2017–18	Doncaster R	3	0		
2018–19	Doncaster R	0	0	3	0

BLAIR, Matty (M) 243 20
H: 5 10 W: 11 09 b.Coventry 30-11-87
Internationals: England C.

2012–13	York C	44	6	44	6
2013–14	Fleetwood T	24	3		
2013–14	*Northampton T*	3	1	3	1
2014–15	Fleetwood T	8	0	32	3
2014–15	*Cambridge U*	2	0	2	0
2014–15	Mansfield T	3	0		
2015–16	Mansfield T	32	2	35	2
2016–17	Doncaster R	45	3		
2017–18	Doncaster R	40	2		
2018–19	Doncaster R	42	3	127	8

BLANEY, Shane (D) 0 0
H: 6 3 W: 12 06 b.Letterkenny 20-1-99
From Finn Harps.

2018–19	Doncaster R	0	0

BOOCOCK, Rieves (F) 1 0
b.Sheffield 22-9-00

2018–19	Doncaster R	1	0	1	0

BUTLER, Andy (D) 558 49
H: 6 0 W: 13 00 b.Doncaster 4-11-83

2003–04	Scunthorpe U	35	2		
2004–05	Scunthorpe U	37	10		
2005–06	Scunthorpe U	16	1		
2006–07	Scunthorpe U	11	1		
2006–07	*Grimsby T*	4	0	4	0
2007–08	Scunthorpe U	36	2	135	16
2008–09	Huddersfield T	42	4		
2009–10	Huddersfield T	11	0	53	4
2009–10	*Blackpool*	7	0	7	0
2010–11	Walsall	31	4		
2011–12	Walsall	42	5		
2012–13	Walsall	41	3		
2013–14	Walsall	45	2		
2014–15	Sheffield U	0	0		
2014–15	*Walsall*	7	0	166	14
2014–15	Doncaster R	33	3		
2015–16	Doncaster R	40	4		
2016–17	Doncaster R	44	3		
2017–18	Doncaster R	36	4		
2018–19	Doncaster R	40	1	193	15

COPPINGER, James (F) 627 70
H: 5 7 W: 10 03 b.Middlesbrough 10-1-81
Internationals: England U16.

1997–98	Newcastle U	0	0		
1998–99	Newcastle U	0	0		
1999–2000	Newcastle U	0	0		
1999–2000	*Hartlepool U*	10	3		
2000–01	Newcastle U	1	0		
2001–02	Newcastle U	0	0	1	0
2001–02	*Hartlepool U*	14	2	24	5
2002–03	Exeter C	43	5	43	5
2004–05	Doncaster R	31	0		
2005–06	Doncaster R	36	5		
2006–07	Doncaster R	39	4		
2007–08	Doncaster R	39	3		
2008–09	Doncaster R	32	5		
2009–10	Doncaster R	39	4		
2010–11	Doncaster R	40	7		
2011–12	Doncaster R	38	2		
2012–13	Doncaster R	25	2		
2012–13	*Nottingham F*	6	0	6	0
2013–14	Doncaster R	41	4		
2014–15	Doncaster R	34	4		
2015–16	Doncaster R	39	3		
2016–17	Doncaster R	39	10		
2017–18	Doncaster R	38	3		
2018–19	Doncaster R	43	4	553	60

CRAWFORD, Ali (M) 262 34
H: 5 7 W: 9 09 b.Lanark 30-7-91

2009–10	Hamilton A	7	0		
2010–11	Hamilton A	14	0		
2011–12	Hamilton A	19	2		
2012–13	Hamilton A	33	3		
2013–14	Hamilton A	36	2		
2014–15	Hamilton A	38	10		
2015–16	Hamilton A	33	5		
2016–17	Hamilton A	33	8		
2017–18	Hamilton A	14	1	227	31
2018–19	Doncaster R	35	3	35	3

CUMMINGS, Shaun (D) 172 2
H: 6 0 W: 11 10 b.Hammersmith 25-2-89
Internationals: Jamaica Full caps.

2007–08	Chelsea	0	0		
2008–09	Chelsea	0	0		
2008–09	*Milton Keynes D*	32	0	32	0
2009–10	Chelsea	0	0		
2009–10	*WBA*	3	0	3	0
2009–10	Reading	8	0		
2010–11	Reading	10	0		
2011–12	Reading	34	0		
2012–13	Reading	9	0		
2013–14	Reading	11	0		
2014–15	Reading	5	1	77	1
2014–15	Millwall	12	0		
2015–16	Millwall	16	1		
2016–17	Millwall	16	0	44	1
2017–18	Rotherham U	12	0	12	0
2018–19	Doncaster R	4	0	4	0

DOWNING, Paul (D) 274 7
H: 6 1 W: 12 06 b.Taunton 26-10-91

2009–10	WBA	0	0		
2009–10	*Hereford U*	6	0		
2010–11	WBA	0	0		
2010–11	*Hereford U*	0	0	6	0
2010–11	*Swansea C*	0	0		
2011–12	WBA	0	0		

2011–12	*Barnet*	26	0	**26**	**0**
2012–13	Walsall	31	1		
2013–14	Walsall	44	1		
2014–15	Walsall	35	1		
2015–16	Walsall	46	3	**156**	**6**
2016–17	Milton Keynes D	37	0		
2017–18	Milton Keynes D	0	0	**37**	**0**
2017–18	Blackburn R	28	1		
2018–19	Blackburn R	3	0	**31**	**1**
2018–19	Doncaster R	18	0	**18**	**0**

GARRETT, Tyler (D) 24 0
b. 26-10-96

2015–16	Bolton W	3	0	**3**	**0**
2016–17	Doncaster R	2	0		
2017–18	Doncaster R	13	0		
2018–19	Doncaster R	0	0	**15**	**0**
2018–19	*AFC Wimbledon*	6	0	**6**	**0**

GIBBONS, Myron (F) 0 0
b.Doncaster 15-11-00

2018–19	Doncaster R	0	0		

GREAVES, Anthony (M) 0 0
b. 17-11-00

2018–19	Doncaster R	0	0		

HASANI, Lirak (M) 2 0
b.Doncaster 25-6-02

2018–19	Doncaster R	2	0	**2**	**0**

HORTON, Branden (D) 0 0
b. 9-9-00

2017–18	Doncaster R	0	0		
2018–19	Doncaster R	0	0		

JONES, Louis (G) 0 0

2015–16	Doncaster R	0	0		
2016–17	Doncaster R	0	0		
2017–18	Doncaster R	0	0		
2018–19	Doncaster R	0	0		

KIWOMYA, Alex (M) 58 8
H: 5 10 W: 10 08 b.Sheffield 20-5-96
Internationals: England U16, U17, U18, U19.

2014–15	Chelsea	0	0		
2014–15	*Barnsley*	5	0	**5**	**0**
2015–16	Chelsea	0	0		
2015–16	*Fleetwood T*	4	0	**4**	**0**
2016–17	Chelsea	0	0		
2016–17	*Crewe Alex*	34	7	**34**	**7**
2017–18	Doncaster R	12	1		
2018–19	Doncaster R	3	0	**15**	**1**

LAWLOR, Ian (G) 80 0
H: 6 4 W: 12 08 b.Dublin 27-10-94
Internationals: Republic of Ireland U17, U19, U21.

2011–12	Manchester C	0	0		
2012–13	Manchester C	0	0		
2013–14	Manchester C	0	0		
2014–15	Manchester C	0	0		
2015–16	Manchester C	0	0		
2015–16	*Barnet*	5	0	**5**	**0**
2015–16	*Bury*	12	0	**12**	**0**
2016–17	Doncaster R	19	0		
2017–18	Doncaster R	34	0		
2018–19	Doncaster R	10	0	**63**	**0**

LONGBOTTOM, William (F) 4 0
H: 5 9 W: 9 11 b.Leeds 12-12-98

2015–16	Doncaster R	1	0		
2016–17	Doncaster R	3	0		
2017–18	Doncaster R	0	0		
2018–19	Doncaster R	0	0	**4**	**0**

LUND, Mitchell (D) 50 1
H: 6 1 W: 11 11 b.Leeds 27-8-96

2014–15	Doncaster R	4	0		
2015–16	Doncaster R	30	1		
2016–17	Doncaster R	6	0		
2017–18	Doncaster R	0	0		
2017–18	*Morecambe*	10	0	**10**	**0**
2018–19	Doncaster R	0	0	**40**	**1**

MAROSI, Marko (G) 78 0
H: 6 3 W: 12 08 b. 23-10-93
Internationals: Slovakia U21.

2013–14	Wigan Ath	0	0		
2014–15	Doncaster R	3	0		
2015–16	Doncaster R	1	0		
2016–17	Doncaster R	25	0		
2017–18	Doncaster R	13	0		
2018–19	Doncaster R	36	0	**78**	**0**

MARQUIS, John (F) 272 87
H: 6 1 W: 11 03 b.Lewisham 16-5-92

2009–10	Millwall	1	0		
2010–11	Millwall	11	4		
2011–12	Millwall	17	1		
2012–13	Millwall	10	0		
2013–14	Millwall	2	0		
2013–14	*Portsmouth*	5	1	**5**	**1**
2013–14	*Torquay U*	5	3	**5**	**3**
2013–14	*Northampton T*	14	2		
2014–15	Millwall	1	0		
2014–15	*Cheltenham T*	13	1	**13**	**1**
2014–15	*Gillingham*	21	8	**21**	**8**
2015–16	Millwall	10	0	**52**	**5**
2015–16	*Leyton Orient*	13	0	**13**	**0**
2015–16	*Northampton T*	15	6	**29**	**8**
2016–17	Doncaster R	45	26		
2017–18	Doncaster R	45	14		
2018–19	Doncaster R	44	21	**134**	**61**

MASON, Niall (M) 98 3
b. 10-1-97

2015–16	Aston Villa	0	0		
2016–17	Aston Villa	0	0		
2016–17	*Doncaster R*	38	0		
2017–18	Doncaster R	40	3		
2018–19	Doncaster R	20	0	**98**	**3**

MAY, Alfie (F) 77 9
H: 5 9 W: 11 05 b. 2-7-93
From Hythe T.

2016–17	Doncaster R	16	3		
2017–18	Doncaster R	27	4		
2018–19	Doncaster R	34	2	**77**	**9**

McCULLOUGH, Luke (D) 136 0
H: 6 2 W: 12 11 b.Portadown 15-2-94
Internationals: Northern Ireland U16, U17, U19, U20, U21, Full caps.

2012–13	Manchester U	0	0		
2012–13	*Cheltenham T*	1	0	**1**	**0**
2013–14	Doncaster R	14	0		
2014–15	Doncaster R	33	0		
2015–16	Doncaster R	32	0		
2016–17	Doncaster R	7	0		
2017–18	Doncaster R	13	0		
2018–19	Doncaster R	0	0	**99**	**0**
2018–19	*Tranmere R*	36	0	**36**	**0**

MORRIS, James (F) 0 0

2017–18	Doncaster R	0	0		
2018–19	Doncaster R	0	0		

OGLEY, Declan (G) 0 0

2017–18	Doncaster R	0	0		
2018–19	Doncaster R	0	0		

PRIOR, Cody (D) 0 0

2017–18	Doncaster R	0	0		
2018–19	Doncaster R	0	0		

ROWE, Tommy (M) 406 62
H: 5 11 W: 12 11 b.Manchester 1-5-89

2006–07	Stockport Co	4	0		
2007–08	Stockport Co	24	6		
2008–09	Stockport Co	44	7	**72**	**13**
2008–09	Peterborough U	0	0		
2009–10	Peterborough U	32	2		
2010–11	Peterborough U	35	5		
2011–12	Peterborough U	43	4		
2012–13	Peterborough U	31	5		
2013–14	Peterborough U	34	7	**175**	**23**
2014–15	Wolverhampton W	14	0		
2015–16	Wolverhampton W	3	0	**17**	**0**
2015–16	*Scunthorpe U*	14	1	**14**	**1**
2015–16	*Doncaster R*	10	3		
2016–17	Doncaster R	46	13		
2017–18	Doncaster R	40	4		
2018–19	Doncaster R	32	5	**128**	**25**

SADLIER, Kieran (F) 14 3
H: 5 10 W: 10 06 b. 14-9-94
Internationals: Republic of Ireland U17, U19, U21.

2013–14	West Ham U	0	0		
2015–16	Peterborough U	0	0		
2015–16	*FC Halifax T*	0	0		

From Sligo R, Cork C.

2018–19	Doncaster R	14	3	**14**	**3**

TAYLOR, Paul (F) 190 23
H: 5 11 W: 11 02 b.Liverpool 4-11-87

2008–09	Chester C	9	0	**9**	**0**
2009–10	Montegnee	1	0	**1**	**0**
2009–10	*Charleoi*	3	0	**3**	**0**
2010–11	Anderlecht	0	0		
2010–11	Peterborough U	1	0		
2011–12	Peterborough U	44	12		
2012–13	Peterborough U	3	0		
2012–13	Ipswich T	3	0		
2013–14	Ipswich T	18	1		
2013–14	*Peterborough U*	6	0		
2014–15	Ipswich T	0	0	**21**	**1**
2014–15	*Rotherham U*	17	0	**17**	**0**
2014–15	*Blackburn R*	5	0	**5**	**0**
2016–17	Peterborough U	39	3	**93**	**15**
2017–18	Bradford C	27	6	**27**	**6**
2018–19	Doncaster R	14	1	**14**	**1**

WHITEMAN, Ben (M) 113 16
b.Rochdale 17-6-96

2014–15	Sheffield U	0	0		
2015–16	Sheffield U	6	0		
2016–17	Sheffield U	2	0	**8**	**0**
2016–17	*Mansfield T*	23	7	**23**	**7**
2017–18	Doncaster R	42	6		
2018–19	Doncaster R	40	3	**82**	**9**

WRIGHT, Joe (D) 89 2
H: 6 4 W: 12 06 b. 26-2-95
Internationals: Wales U21.

2013–14	Huddersfield T	0	0		
2014–15	Huddersfield T	0	0		
2015–16	Huddersfield T	0	0		
2015–16	*Accrington S*	20	0	**20**	**0**
2016–17	Doncaster R	22	0		
2017–18	Doncaster R	33	0		
2018–19	Doncaster R	14	2	**69**	**2**

Players retained or with offer of contract
McLean, Rian Tyrone; Watters, Max James.

Scholars
Baldock-Smith, Cameron; Barnett, Cameron; Blythe, Benjamin Elliot; Boocock, Rieves; Conradi, Skar Marius; Dimou, Nathan; Foulkes, Cameron; Gibbons, Myron Jordan; Greaves, A.j. Anthony Junior Nelson; Hasani, Lirak; Horton, Branden; McGowan, Will; Ogley, Declan; Smith, Martijn Earl; Walker, Elliott; Watson, Jack Charles.

EVERTON (32)

ANDRE GOMES, Filipe (M) 150 13
H: 6 2 W: 13 01 b.Porto 30-7-93
Internationals: Portugal U17, U28, U19, U20, U21, Full caps.

2012–13	Benfica	7	1		
2013–14	Benfica	7	1	**14**	**2**
2014–15	Valencia	33	4		
2015–16	Valencia	30	3	**63**	**7**
2016–17	Barcelona	30	3		
2017–18	Barcelona	16	0	**46**	**3**

On loan from Barcelona.

2018–19	Everton	27	1	**27**	**1**

BAINES, Leighton (D) 485 33
H: 5 8 W: 11 00 b.Liverpool 11-12-84
Internationals: England U21, Full caps.

2002–03	Wigan Ath	6	0		
2003–04	Wigan Ath	26	0		
2004–05	Wigan Ath	41	1		
2005–06	Wigan Ath	37	0		
2006–07	Wigan Ath	35	3		
2007–08	Wigan Ath	0	0	**145**	**4**
2007–08	Everton	22	0		
2008–09	Everton	31	1		
2009–10	Everton	37	1		
2010–11	Everton	38	5		
2011–12	Everton	33	4		
2012–13	Everton	38	5		
2013–14	Everton	32	5		
2014–15	Everton	31	2		
2015–16	Everton	18	2		
2016–17	Everton	32	2		
2017–18	Everton	22	2		
2018–19	Everton	6	0	**340**	**29**

BANINGIME, Beni (M) 9 0
H: 5 10 W: 11 00 b.Kinshasa 9-9-98

2017–18	Everton	8	0		
2018–19	Everton	0	0	**8**	**0**
2018–19	*Wigan Ath*	1	0	**1**	**0**

BERNARD, Caldeira (M) 192 27
H: 5 4 W: 8 11 b.Belo Horizonte 8-9-92
Internationals: Brazil Full caps.

2011	Atletico Mineiro	23	0		
2012	Atletico Mineiro	36	11		
2013	Atletico Mineiro	3	1	**62**	**12**
2013–14	Shaktar Donetsk	18	2		
2014–15	Shaktar Donetsk	14	0		
2015–16	Shaktar Donetsk	21	2		
2016–17	Shaktar Donetsk	24	4		
2017–18	Shaktar Donetsk	19	6	**96**	**14**
2018–19	Everton	34	1	**34**	**1**

BESIC, Muhamed (M) 139 4
H: 5 10 W: 11 11 b.Berlin 10-9-92
Internationals: Bosnia-Herzegovina U21, Full caps.

2010–11	Hamburg	3	0		
2011–12	Hamburg	0	0		
2012–13	Hamburg	0	0	**3**	**0**
2012–13	Ferencvaros	22	1		
2013–14	Ferencvaros	25	0	**47**	**1**
2014–15	Everton	23	0		
2015–16	Everton	12	0		
2016–17	Everton	0	0		
2017–18	Everton	2	0		
2017–18	*Middlesbrough*	15	1		
2018–19	Everton	0	0	**37**	**0**
2018–19	*Middlesbrough*	37	2	**52**	**3**

BOLASIE, Yannick (M) 316 36
H: 6 2 W: 13 02 b.DR Congo 24-5-89
Internationals: DR Congo Full caps.

2008–09	Plymouth Arg	0	0		
2008–09	*Barnet*	20	3		
2009–10	Plymouth Arg	16	1		
2009–10	*Barnet*	22	2	**42**	**5**
2010–11	Plymouth Arg	35	7	**51**	**8**
2011–12	Bristol C	23	1		
2012–13	Bristol C	0	0	**23**	**1**
2012–13	Crystal Palace	43	3		
2013–14	Crystal Palace	29	0		
2014–15	Crystal Palace	34	4		
2015–16	Crystal Palace	26	5		
2016–17	Crystal Palace	1	0	**133**	**12**
2016–17	Everton	13	1		
2017–18	Everton	16	1		
2018–19	Everton	0	0	**29**	**2**
2018–19	*Aston Villa*	21	2	**21**	**2**
2018–19	*Anderlecht*	17	6	**17**	**6**

BROWNING, Tyias (D) 44 0
H: 5 11 W: 12 00 b.Liverpool 27-5-94
Internationals: England U17, U19, U21.

2011–12	Everton	0	0		
2012–13	Everton	0	0		
2013–14	Everton	0	0		
2013–14	*Wigan Ath*	2	0	**2**	**0**
2014–15	Everton	2	0		
2015–16	Everton	5	0		
2016–17	Everton	0	0		
2016–17	*Preston NE*	8	0	**8**	**0**
2017–18	Everton	0	0		
2017–18	*Sunderland*	27	0	**27**	**0**
2018–19	Everton	0	0	**7**	**0**

Transferred to Guangzhou Evergrande February 2019.

CALVERT-LEWIN, Dominic (M) 109 16
b. 16-3-97
Internationals: England U20, U21.

2013–14	Sheffield U	0	0		
2014–15	Sheffield U	2	0		
2015–16	Sheffield U	9	0		
2015–16	*Northampton T*	20	5	**20**	**5**
2016–17	Sheffield U	0	0	**11**	**0**
2016–17	Everton	11	1		
2017–18	Everton	32	4		
2018–19	Everton	35	6	**78**	**11**

COLEMAN, Seamus (D) 256 21
H: 6 4 W: 10 07 b.Donegal 11-10-88
Internationals: Republic of Ireland U21, U23, Full caps.

2008–09	Everton	0	0		
2009–10	Everton	3	0		
2009–10	*Blackpool*	9	1	**9**	**1**
2010–11	Everton	34	4		
2011–12	Everton	18	0		
2012–13	Everton	26	0		
2013–14	Everton	36	6		
2014–15	Everton	35	3		
2015–16	Everton	28	1		
2016–17	Everton	26	4		
2017–18	Everton	12	0		
2018–19	Everton	29	2	**247**	**20**

CONNOLLY, Callum (D) 88 9
b.Liverpool 23-9-97
Internationals: England U17, U18, U19, U20, U21.

2015–16	Everton	1	0		
2015–16	*Barnsley*	3	0	**3**	**0**
2016–17	Everton	0	0		
2016–17	*Wigan Ath*	17	2		
2017–18	Everton	0	0		
2017–18	*Ipswich T*	34	4	**34**	**4**
2018–19	Everton	0	0	**1**	**0**
2018–19	*Wigan Ath*	17	1	**34**	**3**
2018–19	*Bolton W*	16	2	**16**	**2**

DAVIES, Tom (M) 75 4
b.Liverpool 30-6-98
Internationals: England U16, U17, U18, U19, U21.

2015–16	Everton	2	0		
2016–17	Everton	24	2		
2017–18	Everton	33	2		
2018–19	Everton	16	0	**75**	**4**

DIGNE, Lucas (D) 176 9
H: 5 10 W: 11 11 b.Meaux 20-7-93
Internationals: France U16, U17, U18, U19, U21, Full caps.

2011–12	Lille	16	0		
2012–13	Lille	33	2	**49**	**2**
2013–14	Paris Saint-Germain	15	0		
2014–15	Paris Saint-Germain	15	0		
2014–15	Paris Saint-Germain	0	0	**30**	**0**
2015–16	Roma	33	3	**33**	**3**
2016–17	Barcelona	17	0		
2017–18	Barcelona	12	0	**29**	**0**
2018–19	Everton	35	4	**35**	**4**

EVANS, Antony (M) 26 2
b.Fazakerley 23-9-98

2016–17	Everton	0	0		
2016–17	*Morecambe*	14	2	**14**	**2**
2017–18	Everton	0	0		
2018–19	Everton	0	0		
2018–19	*Blackpool*	12	0	**12**	**0**

GANA, Idrissa (M) 268 8
H: 5 9 W: 11 05 b.Dakar 26-9-89
Internationals: Senegal Full caps.

2010–11	Lille	11	0		
2011–12	Lille	25	0		
2012–13	Lille	29	0		
2013–14	Lille	37	1		
2014–15	Lille	32	4	**134**	**5**
2015–16	Aston Villa	35	0	**35**	**0**
2016–17	Everton	33	1		
2017–18	Everton	33	2		
2018–19	Everton	33	0	**99**	**3**

GARBUTT, Luke (D) 116 9
H: 5 10 W: 11 07 b.Harrogate 21-5-93
Internationals: England U16, U17, U18, U19, U20, U21.

2010–11	Everton	0	0		
2011–12	Everton	0	0		
2011–12	*Cheltenham T*	34	2	**34**	**2**
2012–13	Everton	0	0		
2013–14	Everton	1	0		
2013–14	*Colchester U*	19	2	**19**	**2**
2014–15	Everton	4	0		
2015–16	Everton	0	0		
2015–16	*Fulham*	25	1	**25**	**1**
2016–17	Everton	0	0		
2016–17	*Wigan Ath*	8	0	**8**	**0**
2017–18	Everton	0	0		
2018–19	Everton	0	0	**5**	**0**
2018–19	*Oxford U*	25	4	**25**	**4**

HOLGATE, Mason (D) 77 2
H: 5 11 W: 11 11 b.Doncaster 22-10-96
Internationals: England U20, U21.

2014–15	Barnsley	20	1	**20**	**1**
2015–16	Everton	0	0		
2016–17	Everton	18	0		
2017–18	Everton	15	0		
2018–19	Everton	5	0	**38**	**0**
2018–19	*WBA*	19	1	**19**	**1**

JAGIELKA, Phil (D) 576 32
H: 6 0 W: 13 01 b.Manchester 17-8-82
Internationals: England U20, U21, B, Full caps.

1999–2000	Sheffield U	1	0		
2000–01	Sheffield U	15	0		
2001–02	Sheffield U	23	3		
2002–03	Sheffield U	42	0		
2003–04	Sheffield U	43	3		
2004–05	Sheffield U	46	0		
2005–06	Sheffield U	46	8		
2006–07	Sheffield U	38	4	**254**	**18**
2007–08	Everton	34	1		
2008–09	Everton	34	0		
2009–10	Everton	12	0		
2010–11	Everton	33	1		
2011–12	Everton	30	2		
2012–13	Everton	36	2		
2013–14	Everton	26	0		
2014–15	Everton	37	4		
2015–16	Everton	21	0		
2016–17	Everton	27	3		
2017–18	Everton	25	0		
2018–19	Everton	7	1	**322**	**14**

KEANE, Michael (D) 206 13
H: 5 7 W: 12 13 b.Stockport 11-1-93
Internationals: Republic of Ireland U17, U19. England U19, U20, U21, Full caps.

2011–12	Manchester U	0	0		
2012–13	Manchester U	0	0		
2012–13	*Leicester C*	22	2	**22**	**2**
2013–14	Manchester U	0	0		
2013–14	*Derby Co*	7	0	**7**	**0**
2013–14	*Blackburn R*	13	3	**13**	**3**
2014–15	Manchester U	1	0	**1**	**0**
2014–15	Burnley	21	0		
2015–16	Burnley	44	5		
2016–17	Burnley	35	2	**100**	**7**
2017–18	Everton	30	0		
2018–19	Everton	33	1	**63**	**1**

KENNY, Jonjoe (D) 55 0
H: 5 9 W: 10 08 b.Kirkdale 15-3-97
Internationals: England U16, U17, U18, U19, U20, U21.

2014–15	Everton	0	0		
2015–16	Everton	1	0		
2015–16	*Wigan Ath*	7	0	**7**	**0**
2015–16	*Oxford U*	17	0	**17**	**0**
2016–17	Everton	1	0		
2017–18	Everton	19	0		
2018–19	Everton	10	0	**31**	**0**

LOOKMAN, Ademola (F) 92 16
H: 5 9 b.Wandsworth 18-7-98
Internationals: England U19, U20, U21.

2015–16	Charlton Ath	24	5		
2016–17	Charlton Ath	21	5	**45**	**10**
2016–17	Everton	8	1		
2017–18	Everton	7	0		
2017–18	*RB Leipzig*	11	5	**11**	**5**
2018–19	Everton	21	0	**36**	**1**

MARTINA, Cuco (D) 247 5
H: 6 1 W: 11 05 b.Rotterdam 25-9-89
Internationals: Curacao Full caps.

2008–09	Roosendaal	14	0		
2009–10	Roosendaal	23	1		
2010–11	Roosendaal	32	1	**69**	**2**
2011–12	Waalwijk	23	0		
2012–13	Waalwijk	34	1	**57**	**1**
2013–14	FC Twente	16	1		
2014–15	FC Twente	32	0	**48**	**1**
2015–16	Southampton	15	1		
2016–17	Southampton	9	0	**24**	**1**
2017–18	Everton	21	0		
2018–19	Everton	0	0	**21**	**0**
2018–19	*Stoke C*	17	0	**17**	**0**
2018–19	*Feyenoord*	11	0	**11**	**0**

McCARTHY, James (M) 323 27
H: 5 11 W: 11 05 b.Glasgow 12-11-90
Internationals: Republic of Ireland U17, U18, U19, U21, Full caps.

2006–07	Hamilton A	23	1		
2007–08	Hamilton A	35	7		
2008–09	Hamilton A	37	6	**95**	**14**
2009–10	Wigan Ath	20	1		
2010–11	Wigan Ath	24	3		
2011–12	Wigan Ath	33	0		
2012–13	Wigan Ath	38	3		
2013–14	Wigan Ath	5	0	**120**	**7**
2013–14	Everton	34	1		
2014–15	Everton	28	2		
2015–16	Everton	29	2		
2016–17	Everton	12	1		
2017–18	Everton	4	0		
2018–19	Everton	1	0	**108**	**6**

MINA, Yerry (D) 112 14
H: 6 5 W: 11 11 b.Guachene 23-9-94
Internationals: Colombia U23, Full caps.

2013	Deportivo Pasto	10	1	**10**	**1**
2014	Santa Fe	23	2		
2015	Santa Fe	23	2		
2016	Santa Fe	10	2	**56**	**6**
2016	Palmeiras	13	4		
2017	Palmeiras	15	2	**28**	**6**
2017–18	Barcelona	5	0	**5**	**0**
2018–19	Everton	13	1	**13**	**1**

NIASSE, Oumar (F) 124 36
H: 6 0 b.Ouakam 18-4-90
Internationals: Senegal U23, Full caps.

2013–14	Akhisar Belediyespor	34	12	**34**	**12**
2014–15	Lokomotiv Moscow	13	4		
2015–16	Lokomotiv Moscow	15	8	**28**	**12**
2015–16	Everton	5	0		
2016–17	Everton	0	0		
2016–17	*Hull C*	17	4	**17**	**4**

2017–18	Everton	22	8		
2018–19	Everton	5	0	**32**	**8**
2018–19	*Cardiff C*	13	0	**13**	**0**

PENNINGTON, Matthew (D) 107 4
H: 6 1 W: 12 02 b.Warrington 6-10-94
Internationals: England U19.

2013–14	Everton	0	0		
2013–14	*Tranmere R*	17	2	**17**	**2**
2014–15	Everton	0	0		
2014–15	*Coventry C*	24	0	**24**	**0**
2015–16	Everton	4	0		
2015–16	*Walsall*	5	0	**5**	**0**
2016–17	Everton	3	1		
2017–18	Everton	0	0		
2017–18	*Leeds U*	24	0	**24**	**0**
2018–19	Everton	0	0	**7**	**1**
2018–19	*Ipswich T*	30	1	**30**	**1**

PICKFORD, Jordan (G) 194 0
H: 6 1 b.Washington 7-3-94
Internationals: England U16, U17, U18, U19, U20, U21, Full caps.

2010–11	Sunderland	0	0		
2011–12	Sunderland	0	0		
2012–13	Sunderland	0	0		
2013–14	Sunderland	0	0		
2013–14	*Burton Alb*	12	0	**12**	**0**
2013–14	*Carlisle U*	18	0	**18**	**0**
2014–15	Sunderland	0	0		
2014–15	*Bradford C*	33	0	**33**	**0**
2015–16	Sunderland	2	0		
2015–16	*Preston NE*	24	0	**24**	**0**
2016–17	Sunderland	29	0	**31**	**0**
2017–18	Everton	38	0		
2018–19	Everton	38	0	**76**	**0**

RICHARLISON, de Andrade (F) 139 36
H: 5 10 W: 11 03 b.Nova Venecia 10-5-97
Internationals: Brazil U20, Full caps.

2015	America Mineiro	24	9	**24**	**9**
2016	Fluminense	28	4		
2017	Fluminense	14	5		
2017–18	Fluminense	0	0	**42**	**9**
2017–18	Watford	38	5	**38**	**5**
2018–19	Everton	35	13	**35**	**13**

SANDRO, Ramirez (F) 92 16
H: 5 8 W: 11 03 b.Las Palmas 9-7-95
Internationals: Spain U16, U17, U18, U19, U21.

2014–15	Barcelona	7	2		
2015–16	Barcelona	10	0	**17**	**2**
2016–17	Malaga	30	14	**30**	**14**
2017–18	Everton	8	0		
2017–18	*Sevilla*	13	0	**13**	**0**
2018–19	Everton	0	0	**8**	**0**
2018–19	*Real Sociedad*	24	0	**24**	**0**

SCHNEIDERLIN, Morgan (M) 326 16
H: 5 11 W: 11 11 b.Obernai 8-11-89
Internationals: France U16, U17, U18, U19, U20, U21, Full caps.

2007–08	Strasbourg	5	0	**5**	**0**
2008–09	Southampton	30	0		
2009–10	Southampton	37	1		
2010–11	Southampton	27	0		
2011–12	Southampton	42	2		
2012–13	Southampton	36	5		
2013–14	Southampton	33	2		
2014–15	Southampton	26	4	**231**	**14**
2015–16	Manchester U	29	1		
2016–17	Manchester U	3	0	**32**	**1**
2016–17	Everton	14	1		
2017–18	Everton	30	0		
2018–19	Everton	14	0	**58**	**1**

SIGURDSSON, Gylfi (M) 343 90
H: 6 1 W: 12 02 b.Reykjavik 9-9-89
Internationals: Iceland U17, U18, U19, U21, Full caps.

2007–08	Reading	0	0		
2008–09	Reading	0	0		
2008–09	*Shrewsbury T*	5	1	**5**	**1**
2008–09	*Crewe Alex*	15	3	**15**	**3**
2009–10	Reading	38	16		
2010–11	Reading	4	2	**42**	**18**
2010–11	Hoffenheim	28	9		
2011–12	Hoffenheim	6	0	**34**	**9**
2011–12	*Swansea C*	18	7		
2012–13	Tottenham H	33	3		
2013–14	Tottenham H	25	5	**58**	**8**
2014–15	Swansea C	32	7		
2015–16	Swansea C	36	11		
2016–17	Swansea C	38	9	**124**	**34**
2017–18	Everton	27	4		
2018–19	Everton	38	13	**65**	**17**

STEKELENBURG, Maarten (G) 293 0
H: 6 6 W: 14 05 b.Haarlem 22-9-82
Internationals: Netherlands U21, Full caps.

2001–02	Ajax	0	0		
2002–03	Ajax	9	0		
2003–04	Ajax	10	0		
2004–05	Ajax	11	0		
2005–06	Ajax	27	0		
2006–07	Ajax	32	0		
2007–08	Ajax	31	0		
2008–09	Ajax	12	0		
2009–10	Ajax	33	0		
2010–11	Ajax	26	0	**191**	**0**
2011–12	Roma	29	0		
2012–13	Roma	18	0	**47**	**0**
2013–14	Fulham	19	0		
2014–15	Fulham	0	0		
2014–15	Monaco	0	0		
2015–16	Fulham	0	0	**19**	**0**
2015–16	*Southampton*	17	0	**17**	**0**
2016–17	Everton	19	0		
2017–18	Everton	0	0		
2018–19	Everton	0	0	**19**	**0**

TOSUN, Cenk (M) 245 88
H: 6 0 W: 12 04 b.Wetzlar 7-6-91
Internationals: Germany U16, U18, U19, U21. Turkey U21, Full caps.

2009–10	Eintracht Frankfurt	1	0	**1**	**0**
2010–11	Gaziantepspor	14	10		
2011–12	Gaziantepspor	32	6		
2012–13	Gaziantepspor	32	10		
2013–14	Gaziantepspor	31	13	**109**	**39**
2014–15	Besiktas	18	5		
2015–16	Besiktas	29	8		
2016–17	Besiktas	33	20		
2017–18	Besiktas	16	8	**96**	**41**
2017–18	Everton	14	5		
2018–19	Everton	25	3	**39**	**8**

VIRGINIA, Joao (G) 0 0
H: 6 3 W: 13 01 b.Faro 10-10-99
Internationals: Portugal U16, U17, U18, U19, U20, U21.
From Benfica, Arsenal.

2018–19	Everton	0	0		

WALCOTT, Theo (F) 342 77
H: 5 9 W: 11 01 b.Stanmore 16-3-89
Internationals: England U16, U17, U19, U21, Full caps.

2005–06	Southampton	21	4	**21**	**4**
2005–06	Arsenal	0	0		
2006–07	Arsenal	16	0		
2007–08	Arsenal	25	4		
2008–09	Arsenal	22	2		
2009–10	Arsenal	23	3		
2010–11	Arsenal	28	9		
2011–12	Arsenal	35	8		
2012–13	Arsenal	32	14		
2013–14	Arsenal	13	5		
2014–15	Arsenal	14	5		
2015–16	Arsenal	28	5		
2016–17	Arsenal	28	10		
2017–18	Arsenal	6	0	**270**	**65**
2017–18	Everton	14	3		
2018–19	Everton	37	5	**51**	**8**

WILLIAMS, Ashley (D) 577 20
H: 6 0 W: 11 02 b.Wolverhampton 23-8-84
Internationals: Wales Full caps.

2003–04	Stockport Co	10	0		
2004–05	Stockport Co	44	1		
2005–06	Stockport Co	36	1		
2006–07	Stockport Co	46	1		
2007–08	Stockport Co	26	0	**162**	**3**
2007–08	*Swansea C*	3	0		
2008–09	Swansea C	46	2		
2009–10	Swansea C	46	5		
2010–11	Swansea C	46	3		
2011–12	Swansea C	37	1		
2012–13	Swansea C	37	0		
2013–14	Swansea C	34	1		
2014–15	Swansea C	37	0		
2015–16	Swansea C	36	2	**322**	**14**
2016–17	Everton	36	1		
2017–18	Everton	24	1		
2018–19	Everton	0	0	**60**	**2**
2018–19	*Stoke C*	33	1	**33**	**1**

WILLIAMS, Joe (M) 64 1
H: 5 10 W: 10 06 b.Liverpool 8-12-96
Internationals: England U20.

2014–15	Everton	0	0		
2015–16	Everton	0	0		
2016–17	Everton	0	0		
2017–18	Everton	0	0		
2017–18	*Barnsley*	34	1	**34**	**1**
2018–19	Everton	0	0		
2018–19	*Bolton W*	30	0	**30**	**0**

Players retained or with offer of contract
Adeniran, Dennis Emmanuel Abiodun; Astley, Ryan; Bowler, Joshua Luke; Broadhead, Nathan Paul; Carroll, Bobby Lee; Denny, Alexander; Dowell, Kieran O'Neill; Feeney, Morgan; Foulds, Matthew Colin; Galloway, Brendan Joel Zibusiso; Gibson, Lewis Jack; Gordon, Anthony Michael; Hornby, Fraser; John, Kyle Alex; Mampala, Manasse; Markelo, Nathangelo Alexandro; Mirallas Y Castillo, Kevin Antonio Joel Gislain; Onyekuru, Henry Chukwuemeka; Ouzounidis, Con; Robinson, Antonee; Sambou, Bassala; Simms, Ellis Reco; Tarashaj, Shani; Vlasic, Nikola.

Scholars
Adedoyin, Korede Yemi; Anderson, Joseph William; Anderson Ogbomo, Jonathan Osazee; Barrett, Jack Joseph; Collins, Michael Kieran; Hansen, Nicolas Defreitas; Hosie, Joshua; Hughes, Rhys; Hunt, MacKenzie James; Iversen, Einar Hjellestad; McKeown, Bernard Joshua; Phillips, Kieran James; Quirk, Sebastian Anthony; Richards, Elliot Thomas; Stanley, Kameron Mark James; Thompson, Max; Tyrer, Harry; Warnock, Ethan Daniel; Warren, Tom; Zuk, Pawel Andrzej.

EXETER C (33)

ABRAHAMS, Tristan (F) 40 6
H: 5 9 W: 10 08 b.Lewisham 29-12-98

2016–17	Leyton Orient	9	2	**9**	**2**
2018–19	Exeter C	16	1	**16**	**1**
2018–19	*Yeovil T*	15	3	**15**	**3**

BELSTEN, Joe (D) 0 0

2018–19	Exeter C	0	0		

BOATENG, Hiram (M) 116 3
H: 5 7 W: 11 00 b.Wandsworth 8-1-96

2012–13	Crystal Palace	0	0		
2013–14	Crystal Palace	0	0		
2013–14	*Crawley T*	1	0	**1**	**0**
2014–15	Crystal Palace	0	0		
2015–16	Crystal Palace	1	0		
2015–16	*Plymouth Arg*	24	1	**24**	**1**
2016–17	Crystal Palace	0	0	**1**	**0**
2016–17	*Bristol R*	9	0	**9**	**0**
2016–17	*Northampton T*	16	0	**16**	**0**
2017–18	Exeter C	38	1		
2018–19	Exeter C	27	1	**65**	**2**

BOWMAN, Ryan (F) 136 23
H: 6 2 W: 11 12 b.Carlisle 30-11-91

2009–10	Carlisle U	6	0		
2010–11	Carlisle U	3	0	**9**	**0**
From Darlington, Hereford U					
2013–14	York C	37	8	**37**	**8**
From York C, Gateshead.					
2016–17	Motherwell	24	2		
2017–18	Motherwell	32	7		
2018–19	Motherwell	16	1	**72**	**10**
2018–19	Exeter C	18	5	**18**	**5**

BROWN, Troy (D) 258 15
H: 6 1 W: 12 01 b.Croydon 17-9-90
Internationals: Wales U17, U19, U21.

2009–10	Ipswich T	1	0		
2010–11	Ipswich T	12	0	**13**	**0**
2011–12	Rotherham U	6	1	**6**	**1**
2011–12	*Aldershot T*	17	2		
2012–13	Aldershot T	34	3	**51**	**5**
2013–14	Cheltenham T	39	4		
2014–15	Cheltenham T	43	1	**82**	**5**
2015–16	Exeter C	40	1		
2016–17	Exeter C	30	2		
2017–18	Exeter C	25	1		
2018–19	Exeter C	11	0	**106**	**4**

COLLINS, Archie (M) 26 1
b. 31-8-99

2016–17	Exeter C	0	0		
2017–18	Exeter C	0	0		
2018–19	Exeter C	26	1	**26**	**1**

CROLL, Luke (D) 45 0
H: 6 1 W: 12 08 b.Lambeth 10-1-95

2014–15	Crystal Palace	0	0		
2015–16	Crystal Palace	0	0		

2015–16 *Plymouth Arg* 3 0 **3 0**
2016–17 Crystal Palace 0 0
2016–17 *Exeter C* 19 0
2017–18 Exeter C 10 0
2018–19 Exeter C 13 0 **42 0**

DEAN, Will (M) 0 0
b. 7-8-00
2017–18 Exeter C 0 0
2018–19 Exeter C 0 0

DODD, James (M) 0 0
2018–19 Exeter C 0 0

DYER, Jordan (D) 0 0
2018–19 Exeter C 0 0

FORTE, Jonathan (M) 411 80
H: 6 0 W: 12 02 b.Sheffield 25-7-86
Internationals: England U16, U17, U18. Barbados Full caps.
2003–04 Sheffield U 7 0
2004–05 Sheffield U 22 1
2005–06 Sheffield U 1 0
2005–06 *Doncaster R* 13 4
2005–06 *Rotherham U* 11 4 **11 4**
2006–07 Sheffield U 0 0
2006–07 *Doncaster R* 41 5 **54 9**
2007–08 Scunthorpe U 38 4
2008–09 Scunthorpe U 8 0
2008–09 *Notts Co* 18 8
2009–10 Scunthorpe U 28 2
2010–11 Scunthorpe U 24 3 **98 9**
2010–11 Southampton 10 2
2011–12 Southampton 1 0
2011–12 *Preston NE* 3 0 **3 0**
2011–12 *Notts Co* 10 5
2012–13 Southampton 0 0
2012–13 *Crawley T* 12 3 **12 3**
2012–13 *Sheffield U* 12 1 **42 2**
2013–14 Southampton 0 0 **11 2**
2014–15 Oldham Ath 34 15
2015–16 Oldham Ath 26 3 **60 18**
2016–17 Notts Co 35 8
2017–18 Notts Co 30 7 **93 28**
2018–19 Exeter C 27 5 **27 5**

HAMON, James (G) 27 0
H: 6 1 W: 11 00 b. 1-7-95
2013–14 Exeter C 0 0
2014–15 Exeter C 21 0
2015–16 Exeter C 1 0
2016–17 Exeter C 1 0
2017–18 Exeter C 0 0
2018–19 Exeter C 4 0 **27 0**

HARTRIDGE, Alex (D) 3 0
b. 9-3-99
2017–18 Exeter C 0 0
2018–19 Exeter C 3 0 **3 0**

HOLMES, Lee (M) 329 29
H: 5 8 W: 10 06 b.Mansfield 2-4-87
Internationals: England U16, U17, U19.
2002–03 Derby Co 2 0
2003–04 Derby Co 23 2
2004–05 Derby Co 3 0
2004–05 *Swindon T* 15 1
2005–06 Derby Co 18 0
2006–07 Derby Co 0 0
2006–07 *Bradford C* 16 0 **16 0**
2007–08 Derby Co 0 0 **46 2**
2007–08 *Walsall* 19 4 **19 4**
2008–09 Southampton 11 0
2009–10 Southampton 5 0
2010–11 Southampton 7 0
2011–12 Southampton 6 1 **29 1**
2011–12 *Oxford U* 7 2 **7 2**
2011–12 *Swindon T* 10 1 **25 2**
2012–13 Preston NE 28 3
2013–14 Preston NE 32 3
2014–15 Preston NE 0 0 **60 6**
2014–15 *Portsmouth* 5 0 **5 0**
2014–15 *Exeter C* 8 0
2015–16 Exeter C 37 2
2016–17 Exeter C 16 5
2017–18 Exeter C 27 2
2018–19 Exeter C 34 3 **122 12**

JAY, Matt (D) 42 5
H: 5 10 W: 10 12 b.Torbay 27-2-96
2013–14 Exeter C 2 0
2014–15 Exeter C 3 0
2015–16 Exeter C 0 0
2016–17 Exeter C 2 0
2017–18 Exeter C 17 1
2018–19 Exeter C 18 4 **42 5**

KEY, Josh (M) 0 0
b. 1-11-99
2017–18 Exeter C 0 0
2018–19 Exeter C 0 0

KITE, Harry (M) 0 0
b.Exeter 29-6-00
2017–18 Exeter C 0 0
2018–19 Exeter C 0 0

LAW, Nicky (M) 423 54
H: 5 10 W: 11 07 b.Nottingham 29-3-88
2005–06 Sheffield U 0 0
2006–07 Sheffield U 4 0
2006–07 *Yeovil T* 6 0 **6 0**
2007–08 Sheffield U 1 0
2007–08 *Bradford C* 10 2
2008–09 Sheffield U 0 0 **5 0**
2008–09 *Bradford C* 33 0
2009–10 Rotherham U 42 4
2010–11 Rotherham U 44 4 **86 8**
2011–12 Motherwell 38 4
2012–13 Motherwell 38 6 **76 10**
2013–14 Rangers 32 9
2014–15 Rangers 36 10
2015–16 Rangers 18 1 **86 20**
2016–17 Bradford C 40 4
2017–18 Bradford C 38 0 **121 6**
2018–19 Exeter C 43 10 **43 10**

MARTIN, Aaron (D) 151 9
H: 6 3 W: 11 13 b.Newport (IW) 29-9-89
2009–10 Southampton 2 0
2010–11 Southampton 8 0
2011–12 Southampton 10 1
2012–13 Southampton 0 0
2012–13 *Crystal Palace* 4 0 **4 0**
2012–13 *Coventry C* 12 0
2013–14 Southampton 0 0 **20 1**
2013–14 Birmingham C 8 0 **8 0**
2014–15 Yeovil T 12 3 **12 3**
2014–15 Coventry C 27 0
2015–16 Coventry C 29 2 **68 2**
2016–17 Oxford U 4 0
2017–18 Oxford U 12 0 **16 0**
2018–19 Exeter C 23 3 **23 3**

MARTIN, Lee (M) 330 21
H: 5 10 W: 10 03 b.Taunton 9-2-87
2004–05 Manchester U 0 0
2005–06 Manchester U 0 0
2006–07 Manchester U 0 0
2006–07 *Rangers* 7 0 **7 0**
2006–07 *Stoke C* 13 1 **13 1**
2007–08 Manchester U 0 0
2007–08 *Plymouth Arg* 12 2 **12 2**
2007–08 *Sheffield U* 6 0 **6 0**
2008–09 Manchester U 1 0
2008–09 *Nottingham F* 13 1 **13 1**
2009–10 Manchester U 0 0 **1 0**
2009–10 Ipswich T 16 1
2010–11 Ipswich T 16 0
2010–11 *Charlton Ath* 20 2 **20 2**
2011–12 Ipswich T 34 5
2012–13 Ipswich T 34 0
2013–14 Ipswich T 0 0 **100 6**
2013–14 Millwall 26 1
2014–15 Millwall 27 1
2015–16 Millwall 8 0 **61 2**
2015–16 *Northampton T* 10 0 **10 0**
2016–17 Gillingham 17 0
2017–18 Gillingham 35 6 **52 6**
2018–19 Exeter C 35 1 **35 1**

MOXEY, Dean (D) 330 14
H: 6 2 W: 11 00 b.Exeter 14-1-86
Internationals: England C.
2008–09 Exeter C 43 4
2009–10 Derby Co 30 0
2010–11 Derby Co 22 2 **52 2**
2010–11 Crystal Palace 17 1
2011–12 Crystal Palace 24 0
2012–13 Crystal Palace 30 0
2013–14 Crystal Palace 20 0 **91 1**
2014–15 Bolton W 20 1
2015–16 Bolton W 33 0
2016–17 Bolton W 19 0 **72 1**
2017–18 Exeter C 34 3
2018–19 Exeter C 38 3 **115 10**

NORMAN, Felix (G) 0 0
b. 26-1-00
2018–19 Exeter C 0 0

OATES, Jimmy (D) 0 0
From Hereford U.
2018–19 Exeter C 0 0

PYM, Christy (G) 151 0
H: 6 0 W: 11 09 b.Exeter 24-4-95
Internationals: England U20.
2012–13 Exeter C 0 0
2013–14 Exeter C 9 0
2014–15 Exeter C 25 0
2015–16 Exeter C 0 0
2016–17 Exeter C 28 0
2017–18 Exeter C 46 0
2018–19 Exeter C 43 0 **151 0**

RANDALL, Joel (M) 0 0
b.Salisbury 29-10-99
2017–18 Exeter C 0 0
2018–19 Exeter C 0 0

SPARKES, Jack (M) 3 0
b.Exeter 29-9-00
2017–18 Exeter C 3 0
2018–19 Exeter C 0 0 **3 0**

SWEENEY, Pierce (D) 112 12
H: 5 10 W: 12 07 b.Dublin 11-9-94
Internationals: Republic of Ireland U17, U19, U21.
2012–13 Reading 0 0
2013–14 Reading 0 0
2014–15 Reading 0 0
2015–16 Reading 0 0
2016–17 Exeter C 29 0
2017–18 Exeter C 40 8
2018–19 Exeter C 43 4 **112 12**

TAYLOR, Jake (M) 235 25
H: 5 10 W: 12 01 b.Ascot 1-12-91
Internationals: Wales U17, U19, U21, Full caps.
2010–11 Reading 1 0
2011–12 Reading 0 0
2011–12 *Aldershot T* 3 0 **3 0**
2011–12 *Exeter C* 30 3
2012–13 Reading 0 0
2012–13 *Cheltenham T* 8 1 **8 1**
2012–13 *Crawley T* 4 0 **4 0**
2013–14 Reading 8 0
2014–15 Reading 22 2
2014–15 *Leyton Orient* 3 0 **3 0**
2015–16 Reading 0 0 **31 2**
2015–16 *Motherwell* 7 0 **7 0**
2015–16 Exeter C 16 4
2016–17 Exeter C 43 4
2017–18 Exeter C 44 8
2018–19 Exeter C 46 3 **179 22**

TILLSON, Jordan (D) 122 2
H: 6 0 W: 11 09 b.Bath 5-3-93
2012–13 Exeter C 0 0
2013–14 Exeter C 1 0
2014–15 Exeter C 3 0
2015–16 Exeter C 26 1
2016–17 Exeter C 20 0
2017–18 Exeter C 37 1
2018–19 Exeter C 21 0 **108 2**
2018–19 *Cheltenham T* 14 0 **14 0**

WEALE, Chris (G) 295 1
H: 6 2 W: 13 03 b.Chard 9-2-82
Internationals: England C.
2003–04 Yeovil T 35 0
2004–05 Yeovil T 38 0
2005–06 Yeovil T 25 0
2006–07 Bristol C 1 0
2007–08 Hereford U 1 0
2007–08 Bristol C 3 0
2008–09 Bristol C 5 0 **9 0**
2008–09 *Hereford U* 1 0 **2 0**
2008–09 *Yeovil T* 10 1
2009–10 Leicester C 45 0
2010–11 Leicester C 29 0
2011–12 Leicester C 1 0 **75 0**
2011–12 *Northampton T* 3 0 **3 0**
2012–13 Shrewsbury T 46 0
2013–14 Shrewsbury T 35 0 **81 0**
2014–15 Yeovil T 8 0
2014–15 *Burton Alb* 0 0
2015–16 Yeovil T 9 0
2016–17 Yeovil T 0 0 **125 1**
2016–17 Derby Co 0 0
From Dorchester T.
2018–19 Exeter C 0 0

WILLIAMS, Randell (F) 36 3
H: 6 3 b.London 30-12-96
From Tower Hamlets.
2016–17 Crystal Palace 0 0
2017–18 Watford 0 0
2017–18 *Wycombe W* 6 1

2018–19	Watford	0	0		
2018–19	*Wycombe W*	20	2	**26**	**3**
2018–19	Exeter C	10	0	**10**	**0**

WOODMAN, Craig (D) **540** **7**
H: 5 9 W: 10 11 b.Tiverton 22-12-82

1999–2000	Bristol C	0	0		
2000–01	Bristol C	2	0		
2001–02	Bristol C	6	0		
2002–03	Bristol C	10	0		
2003–04	Bristol C	21	0		
2004–05	Bristol C	3	0		
2004–05	*Mansfield T*	8	1	**8**	**1**
2004–05	*Torquay U*	22	1		
2005–06	Bristol C	37	1		
2005–06	*Torquay U*	2	0	**24**	**1**
2006–07	Bristol C	11	0	**90**	**1**
2007–08	Wycombe W	29	0		
2008–09	Wycombe W	46	1		
2009–10	Wycombe W	44	1	**119**	**2**
2010–11	Brentford	41	1		
2011–12	Brentford	18	0	**59**	**1**
2012–13	Exeter C	44	0		
2013–14	Exeter C	41	1		
2014–15	Exeter C	32	0		
2015–16	Exeter C	25	0		
2016–17	Exeter C	33	0		
2017–18	Exeter C	33	0		
2018–19	Exeter C	32	0	**240**	**1**

Players retained or with offer of contract
Seymour, Benjamin Mark; Smallcombe, Max Frederick.

Scholars
Belsten, Joe; Diabate, Cheick Tiemoko; Lawrence, Charles James; Morison, Louis; Simpson, Theo Jon; Stafford, Jack Elliot; Wilson, Lewis.

FLEETWOOD T (34)

BAGGLEY, Barry (M) **3** **0**
b.Belfast 11-2-02
Internationals: Northern Ireland U17.

2018–19	Fleetwood T	3	0	**3**	**0**

BAINES, Lewis (D) **0** **0**

2017–18	Fleetwood T	0	0		
2018–19	Fleetwood T	0	0		

BIGGINS, Harrison (M) **30** **1**
b. 15-3-96
From Stocksbridge Park Steels.

2017–18	Fleetwood T	7	0		
2018–19	Fleetwood T	23	1	**30**	**1**

BOYLE, Dylan (M) **0** **0**
Internationals: Northern Ireland U17.

2018–19	Fleetwood T	0	0		

BURNS, Wes (F) **170** **22**
H: 5 8 W: 10 10 b.Cardiff 28-12-95
Internationals: Wales U21.

2012–13	Bristol C	6	0		
2013–14	Bristol C	20	1		
2014–15	Bristol C	3	1		
2014–15	*Oxford U*	9	1	**9**	**1**
2014–15	*Cheltenham T*	14	4	**14**	**4**
2015–16	Bristol C	14	1	**43**	**3**
2015–16	*Fleetwood T*	14	5		
2016–17	Fleetwood T	10	0		
2016–17	*Aberdeen*	13	0	**13**	**0**
2017–18	Fleetwood T	28	2		
2018–19	Fleetwood T	39	7	**91**	**14**

CAIRNS, Alex (G) **115** **0**
H: 6 0 W: 11 05 b.Doncaster 4-1-93

2011–12	Leeds U	1	0		
2012–13	Leeds U	0	0		
2013–14	Leeds U	0	0		
2014–15	Leeds U	0	0	**1**	**0**
2015–16	Chesterfield	0	0		
2015–16	Rotherham U	0	0		
2016–17	Fleetwood T	30	0		
2017–18	Fleetwood T	38	0		
2018–19	Fleetwood T	46	0	**114**	**0**

CLARKE, Eddie (D) **2** **0**
b. 29-12-98

2018–19	Fleetwood T	2	0	**2**	**0**

CRELLIN, Billy (G) **0** **0**
Internationals: England U17, U18, U19.

2017–18	Fleetwood T	0	0		
2018–19	Fleetwood T	0	0		

DEMPSEY, Kyle (M) **176** **14**
b.Whitehaven 17-9-95

2013–14	Carlisle U	4	0		
2014–15	Carlisle U	43	10	**47**	**10**
2015–16	Huddersfield T	21	1		
2016–17	Huddersfield T	0	0	**21**	**1**
2016–17	*Fleetwood T*	38	2		
2017–18	Fleetwood T	45	1		
2018–19	Fleetwood T	14	0	**97**	**3**
2018–19	*Peterborough U*	11	0	**11**	**0**

EASTHAM, Ashley (D) **280** **13**
H: 6 3 W: 12 06 b.Preston 22-3-91

2009–10	Blackpool	1	0		
2009–10	*Cheltenham T*	20	0		
2010–11	Blackpool	0	0		
2010–11	*Cheltenham T*	9	0	**29**	**0**
2010–11	*Carlisle U*	0	0		
2011–12	Blackpool	0	0		
2011–12	*Bury*	25	2		
2012–13	Blackpool	0	0	**1**	**0**
2012–13	*Fleetwood T*	1	0		
2012–13	*Notts Co*	4	0	**4**	**0**
2012–13	*Bury*	19	0	**44**	**2**
2013–14	Rochdale	15	0		
2014–15	Rochdale	41	2		
2015–16	Rochdale	20	2	**76**	**4**
2016–17	Fleetwood T	35	2		
2017–18	Fleetwood T	45	3		
2018–19	Fleetwood T	45	2	**126**	**7**

EVANS, Ched (F) **220** **75**
H: 6 0 W: 12 00 b.Rhyl 28-12-88
Internationals: Wales U21, Full caps.

2006–07	Manchester C	0	0		
2007–08	Manchester C	0	0		
2007–08	*Norwich C*	28	10	**28**	**10**
2008–09	Manchester C	16	1	**16**	**1**
2009–10	Sheffield U	33	4		
2010–11	Sheffield U	34	9		
2011–12	Sheffield U	36	29		
2016–17	Chesterfield	25	5	**25**	**5**
2017–18	Sheffield U	9	0	**112**	**42**
2018–19	Fleetwood T	39	17	**39**	**17**

GARNER, Gerard (F) **1** **0**
b.Liverpool 2-11-98

2017–18	Fleetwood	0	0		
2018–19	Fleetwood T	1	0	**1**	**0**

GRANT, Bobby (M) **331** **70**
H: 5 11 W: 12 00 b.Liverpool 1-7-90

2006–07	Accrington S	1	0		
2007–08	Accrington S	7	0		
2008–09	Accrington S	15	1		
2009–10	Accrington S	42	14		
2010–11	Scunthorpe U	27	0		
2010–11	*Rochdale*	6	2		
2011–12	Scunthorpe U	29	7		
2011–12	*Accrington S*	8	3	**73**	**18**
2012–13	Scunthorpe U	3	0	**59**	**7**
2012–13	Rochdale	36	15	**42**	**17**
2013–14	Blackpool	6	0		
2013–14	*Fleetwood T*	1	0		
2014–15	Blackpool	0	0	**6**	**0**
2014–15	*Shrewsbury T*	33	6	**33**	**6**
2015–16	Fleetwood T	38	10		
2016–17	Fleetwood T	46	9		
2017–18	Fleetwood T	29	3		
2018–19	Fleetwood T	4	0	**118**	**22**

HILL, James (D) **2** **0**
b. 10-1-02

2018–19	Fleetwood T	2	0	**2**	**0**

HOLGATE, Harrison (D) **0** **0**

2018–19	Fleetwood T	0	0		

HOLT, Jason (M) **205** **26**
H: 5 5 W: 11 00 b.Edinburgh 19-2-93
Internationals: Scotland U19, U20, U21.

2010–11	Hearts	1	0		
2011–12	Hearts	2	1		
2011–12	*Raith R*	5	1	**5**	**1**
2012–13	Hearts	21	3		
2013–14	Hearts	23	1		
2014–15	Hearts	15	2	**62**	**7**
2014–15	*Sheffield U*	16	5	**16**	**5**
2015–16	Rangers	32	10		
2016–17	Rangers	31	0		
2017–18	Rangers	26	2	**89**	**12**

On loan from Rangers.

2018–19	Fleetwood T	33	1	**33**	**1**

HUNTER, Ashley (F) **167** **31**
H: 5 10 W: 10 08 b.Derby 29-9-93

2014–15	Fleetwood T	12	1		
2015–16	Fleetwood T	24	5		
2016–17	Fleetwood T	44	8		
2017–18	Fleetwood T	44	9		
2018–19	Fleetwood T	43	8	**167**	**31**

JONES, Gethin (D) **51** **0**
H: 5 10 W: 11 09 b.Perth 13-10-95
Internationals: Wales U17, U19, U21.

2014–15	Everton	0	0		
2014–15	*Plymouth Arg*	6	0	**6**	**0**
2015–16	Everton	0	0		
2016–17	Everton	0	0		
2016–17	*Barnsley*	17	0	**17**	**0**
2017–18	Fleetwood T	10	0		
2018–19	Fleetwood T	3	0	**13**	**0**
2018–19	*Mansfield T*	15	0	**15**	**0**

JONES, Paul (G) **281** **0**
H: 6 3 W: 13 00 b.Maidstone 28-6-86

2008–09	Exeter C	46	0		
2009–10	Exeter C	26	0		
2010–11	Exeter C	18	0		
2010–11	*Peterborough U*	1	0		
2011–12	Peterborough U	35	0	**36**	**0**
2012–13	Crawley T	46	0		
2013–14	Crawley T	46	0		
2014–15	Portsmouth	46	0		
2015–16	Portsmouth	9	0	**55**	**0**
2015–16	*Crawley T*	8	0	**100**	**0**
2016–17	Norwich C	0	0		
2017–18	Norwich C	0	0		
2017–18	*Exeter C*	0	0	**90**	**0**
2018–19	Fleetwood T	0	0		

MADDEN, Patrick (F) **374** **117**
H: 6 0 W: 11 13 b.Dublin 4-3-90
Internationals: Republic of Ireland U19, U21, U23, Full caps.

2008	Bohemians	18	4		
2009	Bohemians	2	0		
2009	Shelbourne	13	6	**13**	**6**
2010	Bohemians	34	10	**54**	**14**
2010–11	Carlisle U	13	0		
2011–12	Carlisle U	18	1		
2012–13	Carlisle U	1	1	**32**	**2**
2012–13	*Yeovil T*	35	22		
2013–14	Yeovil T	9	0	**44**	**22**
2013–14	Scunthorpe U	21	5		
2014–15	Scunthorpe U	46	14		
2015–16	Scunthorpe U	46	20		
2016–17	Scunthorpe U	34	11		
2017–18	Scunthorpe U	20	2	**167**	**52**
2017–18	Fleetwood T	20	6		
2018–19	Fleetwood T	44	15	**64**	**21**

MAGUIRE, Joe (D) **32** **1**
H: 5 10 W: 11 00 b.Manchester 18-1-96

2015–16	Liverpool	0	0		
2015–16	*Leyton Orient*	0	0		
2016–17	Liverpool	0	0		
2016–17	Fleetwood T	3	0		
2017–18	Fleetwood T	2	0		
2018–19	Fleetwood T	0	0	**5**	**0**
2018–19	*Crawley T*	27	1	**27**	**1**

MARNEY, Dean (M) **378** **21**
H: 5 10 W: 11 09 b.Barking 31-1-84
Internationals: England U21.

2002–03	Tottenham H	0	0		
2002–03	*Swindon T*	9	0	**9**	**0**
2003–04	Tottenham H	3	0		
2003–04	*QPR*	2	0	**2**	**0**
2004–05	Tottenham H	5	2		
2004–05	*Gillingham*	3	0	**3**	**0**
2005–06	Tottenham H	0	0	**8**	**2**
2005–06	*Norwich C*	13	0	**13**	**0**
2006–07	Hull C	37	2		
2007–08	Hull C	41	6		
2008–09	Hull C	31	0		
2009–10	Hull C	16	1	**125**	**9**
2009–10	Burnley	0	0		
2010–11	Burnley	36	3		
2011–12	Burnley	37	0		
2012–13	Burnley	38	2		
2013–14	Burnley	38	3		
2014–15	Burnley	20	0		
2015–16	Burnley	12	0		
2016–17	Burnley	21	1		
2017–18	Burnley	0	0	**202**	**9**
2018–19	Fleetwood T	16	1	**16**	**1**

McALENY, Conor (F) **110** **24**
H: 5 10 W: 12 05 b.Liverpool 12-8-92

2009–10	Everton	0	0		
2010–11	Everton	0	0		
2011–12	Everton	2	0		
2011–12	*Scunthorpe U*	3	0	**3**	**0**
2012–13	Everton	0	0		

2013–14	Everton	0	0		
2013–14	*Brentford*	4	0	**4**	**0**
2014–15	Everton	0	0		
2014–15	*Cardiff C*	8	2	**8**	**2**
2015–16	Everton	0	0		
2015–16	*Charlton Ath*	8	0	**8**	**0**
2015–16	*Wigan Ath*	13	4	**13**	**4**
2016–17	Everton	0	0	**2**	**0**
2016–17	*Oxford U*	18	10	**18**	**10**
2017–18	Fleetwood T	29	5		
2018–19	Fleetwood T	14	0	**43**	**5**
2018–19	*Kilmarnock*	11	3	**11**	**3**

MOONEY, Dan (F) **1** **0**
b. 3-7-99
Internationals: Wales U19.

2018–19	Fleetwood T	1	0	**1**	**0**

MORGAN, Craig (D) **441** **11**
H: 6 0 W: 11 04 b.Flint 18-6-85
Internationals: Wales U17, U19, U21, Full caps.

2001–02	Wrexham	2	0		
2002–03	Wrexham	6	1		
2003–04	Wrexham	18	0		
2004–05	Wrexham	26	0		
2005–06	Milton Keynes D	40	0		
2006–07	Milton Keynes D	3	0	**43**	**0**
2006–07	*Wrexham*	1	0	**53**	**1**
2006–07	Peterborough U	23	1		
2007–08	Peterborough U	41	2		
2008–09	Peterborough U	27	0		
2009–10	Peterborough U	34	1	**125**	**4**
2010–11	Preston NE	31	2		
2011–12	Preston NE	19	1		
2012–13	Preston NE	0	0	**50**	**3**
2012–13	Rotherham U	21	1		
2013–14	Rotherham U	35	0		
2014–15	Rotherham U	35	0	**91**	**1**
2015–16	Wigan Ath	36	2		
2016–17	Wigan Ath	20	0		
2017–18	Wigan Ath	0	0	**56**	**2**
2018–19	Fleetwood T	23	0	**23**	**0**

NADESAN, Ashley (F) **61** **13**
H: 6 2 W: 11 11 b. 9-9-94

2015–16	Fleetwood T	0	0		
2016–17	Fleetwood T	0	0		
2017–18	Fleetwood T	1	0		
2017–18	*Carlisle U*	15	4		
2018–19	Fleetwood T	20	1	**21**	**1**
2018–19	*Carlisle U*	25	8	**40**	**12**

RYDEL, Ryan (D) **5** **0**
b. 9-2-01

2018–19	Fleetwood T	5	0	**5**	**0**

SHERON, Nathan (D) **26** **0**
b.Whiston 4-10-97

2017–18	Fleetwood T	0	0		
2018–19	Fleetwood T	26	0	**26**	**0**

SMITH, Lawrence (M) **0** **0**

2018–19	Fleetwood T	0	0		

SOUTAR, Harry (D) **26** **2**
H: 6 6 W: 12 08 b.Aberdeen 22-6-98
Internationals: Scotland U17, U19. Australia U23.

2015–16	Dundee U	2	1		
2016–17	Dundee U	0	0	**2**	**1**
2016–17	Stoke C	0	0		
2017–18	Stoke C	0	0		
2017–18	*Ross Co*	13	0	**13**	**0**
2018–19	Stoke C	0	0		
2018–19	Fleetwood T	11	1	**11**	**1**

SOUTHAM, Macauley (M) **1** **0**
b. 2-2-96

2014–15	Cardiff C	0	0		
2015–16	Cardiff C	0	0		

From Barry T.

2018–19	Fleetwood T	1	0	**1**	**0**

SOWERBY, Jack (F) **78** **7**
b. 23-3-95

2014–15	Fleetwood T	0	0		
2015–16	Fleetwood T	8	0		
2016–17	Fleetwood T	8	1		
2017–18	Fleetwood T	22	2		
2018–19	Carlisle U	25	4	**25**	**4**
2018–19	Fleetwood T	15	0	**53**	**3**

SPURR, Tommy (D) **361** **10**
H: 6 1 W: 11 05 b.Leeds 13-9-87

2005–06	Sheffield W	2	0		
2006–07	Sheffield W	36	0		
2007–08	Sheffield W	41	2		
2008–09	Sheffield W	41	2		
2009–10	Sheffield W	46	1		
2010–11	Sheffield W	26	0	**192**	**5**
2011–12	Doncaster R	19	0		
2012–13	Doncaster R	46	1		
2013–14	Doncaster R	0	0	**65**	**1**
2013–14	Blackburn R	43	3		
2014–15	Blackburn R	12	0		
2015–16	Blackburn R	23	0	**78**	**3**
2016–17	Preston NE	17	1		
2017–18	Preston NE	5	0	**22**	**1**
2018–19	Fleetwood T	4	0	**4**	**0**

TAYLOR, Ryan (M) **293** **31**
H: 5 8 W: 10 04 b.Liverpool 19-8-84
Internationals: England U21.

2001–02	Tranmere R	0	0		
2002–03	Tranmere R	25	1		
2003–04	Tranmere R	30	5		
2004–05	Tranmere R	43	8	**98**	**14**
2005–06	Wigan Ath	11	0		
2006–07	Wigan Ath	16	1		
2007–08	Wigan Ath	17	3		
2008–09	Wigan Ath	12	2	**56**	**6**
2008–09	Newcastle U	10	0		
2009–10	Newcastle U	31	4		
2010–11	Newcastle U	5	0		
2011–12	Newcastle U	31	2		
2012–13	Newcastle U	1	0		
2013–14	Newcastle U	0	0		
2014–15	Newcastle U	14	0	**92**	**6**
2015–16	Hull C	4	0	**4**	**0**
2016–17	Port Vale	22	4	**22**	**4**
2017–18	ATK	11	1	**11**	**1**
2018–19	Fleetwood T	10	0	**10**	**0**

WALLACE, James (M) **111** **8**
H: 5 11 W: 12 08 b.Fazackerly 19-12-91
Internationals: England U19, U20.

2008–09	Everton	0	0		
2009–10	Everton	0	0		
2010–11	Everton	0	0		
2010–11	*Stockport Co*	14	1	**14**	**1**
2010–11	*Bury*	0	0		
2011–12	Everton	0	0		
2011–12	*Shrewsbury T*	3	0		
2011–12	*Stevenage*	0	0		
2011–12	*Tranmere R*	18	2		
2012–13	Tranmere R	19	2		
2013–14	Everton	0	0		
2013–14	Tranmere R	18	2	**55**	**6**
2014–15	Sheffield U	10	0		
2015–16	Sheffield U	4	0		
2015–16	*Shrewsbury T*	7	0	**10**	**0**
2016–17	Sheffield U	0	0	**14**	**0**

From Tranmere R.

2018–19	Fleetwood T	18	1	**18**	**1**

WALLACE, Ross (M) **463** **45**
H: 5 6 W: 9 12 b.Dundee 23-5-85
Internationals: Scotland U18, U19, U21, B, Full caps.

2001–02	Celtic	0	0		
2002–03	Celtic	0	0		
2003–04	Celtic	8	1		
2004–05	Celtic	16	0		
2005–06	Celtic	11	0		
2006–07	Celtic	2	0	**37**	**1**
2006–07	Sunderland	32	6		
2007–08	Sunderland	21	2		
2008–09	Sunderland	0	0	**53**	**8**
2008–09	Preston NE	39	5		
2009–10	Preston NE	41	7	**80**	**12**
2010–11	Burnley	40	3		
2011–12	Burnley	44	5		
2012–13	Burnley	36	3		
2013–14	Burnley	14	0		
2014–15	Burnley	15	1	**149**	**12**
2015–16	Sheffield W	40	4		
2016–17	Sheffield W	41	5		
2017–18	Sheffield W	27	2	**108**	**11**
2018–19	Fleetwood T	36	1	**36**	**1**

Players retained or with offer of contract
Fowler, Michael; Saunders, Harvey Read; Southam-Hales, MacAuley Anthony.

Scholars
Bani, Alkeo; Boyle, Dylan Michael; Clayton, Graham Alexander; Cooke, Jamie John; Crowe, Barry Thomas; Goldsborough, Liam Paul; Johnston, Carl Robert; Makepeace, Kian James Blackmore; Mashigo, Katlego Keabetswe; Matete, Jay; McCaragher, Gregory Adam; Morris, Shayden Jermaine; Pengelly, Scott James; Steer, Kai Philip James; Williams, Anthony Joseph.

FOREST GREEN R (35)

BROWN, Reece (M) **99** **13**
H: 5 9 W: 12 04 b.Dudley 3-3-96
Internationals: England U16, U17, U18, U20.

2013–14	Birmingham C	6	0		
2014–15	Birmingham C	1	0		
2014–15	*Notts Co*	3	0	**3**	**0**
2015–16	Birmingham C	1	0		
2016–17	Birmingham C	8	0	**16**	**0**
2016–17	*Chesterfield*	2	0	**2**	**0**
2017–18	Forest Green R	33	2		
2018–19	Forest Green R	45	11	**78**	**13**

CAMPBELL, Tahvon (F) **84** **7**
b. 10-1-97

2015–16	WBA	0	0		
2015–16	*Yeovil T*	17	1		
2016–17	WBA	0	0		
2016–17	*Yeovil T*	19	1	**36**	**2**
2016–17	*Notts Co*	11	0	**11**	**0**
2017–18	WBA	0	0		
2017–18	*Forest Green R*	14	2		
2018–19	Forest Green R	18	3	**32**	**5**
2018–19	*Gillingham*	5	0	**5**	**0**

COLLINS, Lee (D) **373** **8**
H: 6 1 W: 11 10 b.Telford 23-9-83

2006–07	Wolverhampton W	0	0		
2007–08	Wolverhampton W	0	0		
2007–08	*Hereford U*	16	0	**16**	**0**
2008–09	Wolverhampton W	0	0		
2008–09	Port Vale	39	1		
2009–10	Port Vale	45	1		
2010–11	Port Vale	42	2		
2011–12	Port Vale	16	0	**142**	**4**
2011–12	Barnsley	7	0		
2012–13	Barnsley	0	0	**7**	**0**
2012–13	Shrewsbury T	8	0	**8**	**0**
2012–13	Northampton T	15	0		
2013–14	Northampton T	22	1		
2014–15	Northampton T	37	0	**74**	**1**
2015–16	Mansfield T	35	0		
2016–17	Mansfield T	37	0	**72**	**0**
2017–18	Forest Green R	43	2		
2018–19	Forest Green R	11	1	**54**	**3**

COOPER, Charlie (M) **34** **1**
b. 1-5-97
From Birmingham C.

2017–18	Forest Green R	25	1		
2018–19	Forest Green R	0	0	**25**	**1**
2018–19	*Newport Co*	9	0	**9**	**0**

DIGBY, Paul (M) **81** **1**
H: 5 9 W: 10 00 b.Sheffield 2-2-95
Internationals: England U19, U20.

2011–12	Barnsley	4	0		
2012–13	Barnsley	0	0		
2013–14	Barnsley	5	0		
2014–15	Barnsley	11	0		
2015–16	Barnsley	1	0	**21**	**0**
2015–16	*Ipswich T*	4	0		
2016–17	Ipswich T	4	0	**8**	**0**
2016–17	Mansfield T	0	0		
2017–18	Mansfield T	15	0	**15**	**0**
2018–19	Forest Green R	37	1	**37**	**1**

DOIDGE, Christian (F) **130** **45**
H: 6 1 W: 12 02 b.Newport 25-8-92

2014–15	Dagenham & R	11	2		
2015–16	Dagenham & R	35	8	**46**	**10**
2017–18	Forest Green R	42	20		
2018–19	Forest Green R	25	14	**67**	**34**
2018–19	*Bolton W*	17	1	**17**	**1**

GODWIN-MALIFE, Udoka (D) **5** **0**
b. 9-5-00
From Oxford C.

2018–19	Forest Green R	5	0	**5**	**0**

GRUBB, Dayle (M) **49** **8**
H: 6 0 W: 12 13 b. 24-7-91
From Weston-super-Mare

2017–18	Forest Green R	21	5		
2018–19	Forest Green R	28	3	**49**	**8**

GUNNING, Gavin (D) **251** **10**
H: 5 11 W: 13 08 b.Dublin 26-1-91
Internationals: Republic of Ireland U17, U19, U21.

2007–08	Blackburn R	0	0		
2008–09	Blackburn R	0	0		
2009–10	Blackburn R	0	0		
2009–10	*Tranmere R*	6	0	**6**	**0**
2009–10	*Rotherham U*	21	0	**21**	**0**
2010–11	Blackburn R	0	0		

2010–11	*Bury*	2	0	**2**	**0**
2010–11	*Motherwell*	14	0	**14**	**0**
2011–12	Dundee U	31	2		
2012–13	Dundee U	25	3		
2013–14	Dundee U	27	3		
2014–15	Birmingham C	0	0		
2015–16	Oldham Ath	0	0		
2015–16	Dundee U	19	0	**102**	**8**
2016–17	Greenock Morton	10	0	**10**	**0**
2016–17	Grimsby T	14	0	**14**	**0**
2017–18	Port Vale	19	0	**19**	**0**
2017–18	Forest Green R	21	1		
2018–19	Forest Green R	42	1	**63**	**2**

HOLLIS, Haydn (D) **137** **7**
H: 6 4 W: 13 01 b.Selston 14-10-92

2011–12	Notts Co	1	0		
2012–13	Notts Co	6	0		
2013–14	Notts Co	10	4		
2014–15	Notts Co	41	0		
2015–16	Notts Co	29	2		
2016–17	Notts Co	31	1		
2017–18	Notts Co	0	0	**118**	**7**
2017–18	Forest Green R	19	0		
2018–19	Forest Green R	0	0	**19**	**0**

JAMES, Lloyd (M) **354** **14**
H: 5 11 W: 11 01 b.Bristol 16-2-88
Internationals: Wales U17, U19, U21.

2005–06	Southampton	0	0		
2006–07	Southampton	0	0		
2007–08	Southampton	0	0		
2008–09	Southampton	41	0		
2009–10	Southampton	30	2	**71**	**2**
2010–11	Colchester U	28	0		
2011–12	Colchester U	23	1	**51**	**1**
2011–12	*Crawley T*	6	0	**6**	**0**
2012–13	Leyton Orient	28	0		
2013–14	Leyton Orient	42	3		
2014–15	Leyton Orient	13	1		
2015–16	Leyton Orient	25	4	**108**	**8**
2016–17	Exeter C	43	1		
2017–18	Exeter C	40	2	**83**	**3**
2018–19	Forest Green R	35	0	**35**	**0**

McCOULSKY, Shawn (F) **55** **6**
b.Lewisham 6-1-97
From Dulwich Hamlet.

2017–18	Bristol C	0	0		
2017–18	*Newport Co*	27	6	**27**	**6**
2018–19	Bristol C	0	0		
2018–19	*Southend U*	15	0	**15**	**0**
2018–19	Forest Green R	13	0	**13**	**0**

MILLS, Joseph (D) **240** **8**
H: 5 9 W: 11 00 b.Swindon 30-10-89
Internationals: England U17, U18.

2006–07	Southampton	0	0		
2007–08	Southampton	0	0		
2008–09	Southampton	8	0		
2008–09	*Scunthorpe U*	14	0	**14**	**0**
2009–10	Southampton	16	0		
2010–11	Southampton	2	0		
2010–11	*Doncaster R*	18	2	**18**	**2**
2011–12	Southampton	0	0	**26**	**0**
2011–12	Reading	15	0		
2012–13	Reading	0	0	**15**	**0**
2012–13	*Burnley*	10	0		
2013–14	Burnley	0	0	**10**	**0**
2013–14	*Oldham Ath*	11	0		
2013–14	*Shrewsbury T*	13	0	**13**	**0**
2014–15	Oldham Ath	30	0		
2015–16	Oldham Ath	15	1	**56**	**1**
2016–17	Perth Glory	22	1		
2017–18	Perth Glory	22	0	**44**	**1**
2018–19	Forest Green R	44	4	**44**	**4**

MONDAL, Junior (F) **18** **3**
b. 27-3-97
From Spennymoor T, Whitby T.

2018–19	Forest Green R	18	3	**18**	**3**

MONTGOMERY, James (G) **18** **0**
b. 20-4-94
From Gateshead.

2018–19	Forest Green R	18	0	**18**	**0**

MULLINGS, Shamir (F) **7** **1**
H: 6 4 W: 12 08 b. 30-10-93
From Southend U, Bromley, Havant & Waterlooville, Chelmsford C.

2017–18	Forest Green R	7	1		
2018–19	Forest Green R	0	0	**7**	**1**

PEARCE, Isaac (F) **4** **0**
b. 27-10-98

2017–18	Fulham	0	0		
2018–19	Forest Green R	4	0	**4**	**0**

RAWSON, Farrend (D) **102** **3**
H: 6 1 W: 11 07 b.Nottingham 11-7-96

2014–15	Derby Co	0	0		
2014–15	*Rotherham U*	4	0		
2015–16	Derby Co	0	0		
2015–16	*Rotherham U*	16	2	**20**	**2**
2016–17	Derby Co	0	0		
2016–17	*Coventry C*	14	0	**14**	**0**
2017–18	Derby Co	0	0		
2017–18	*Accrington S*	12	0	**12**	**0**
2017–18	Forest Green R	18	1		
2018–19	Forest Green R	38	0	**56**	**1**

REID, Reuben (F) **413** **113**
H: 6 0 W: 12 02 b.Bristol 26-7-88

2005–06	Plymouth Arg	1	0		
2006–07	Plymouth Arg	6	0		
2006–07	*Rochdale*	2	0	**2**	**0**
2006–07	*Torquay U*	7	2	**7**	**2**
2007–08	Plymouth Arg	0	0		
2007–08	*Wycombe W*	11	1	**11**	**1**
2007–08	Brentford	10	1	**10**	**1**
2008–09	Rotherham U	41	18	**41**	**18**
2009–10	WBA	4	0		
2009–10	*Peterborough U*	13	0	**13**	**0**
2010–11	WBA	0	0	**4**	**0**
2010–11	*Walsall*	18	3	**18**	**3**
2010–11	Oldham Ath	19	2		
2011–12	Oldham Ath	20	5	**39**	**7**
2012–13	Yeovil T	19	4	**19**	**4**
2012–13	*Plymouth Arg*	18	2		
2013–14	Plymouth Arg	46	17		
2014–15	Plymouth Arg	42	18		
2015–16	Plymouth Arg	29	7		
2016–17	Plymouth Arg	0	0	**142**	**44**
2016–17	Exeter C	36	13		
2017–18	Exeter C	21	7	**57**	**20**
2017–18	Forest Green R	21	6		
2018–19	Forest Green R	29	7	**50**	**13**

SHEPHARD, Liam (D) **127** **6**
H: 5 10 W: 10 08 b.Rhondda 22-11-94
Internationals: Wales U21.

2013–14	Swansea C	0	0		
2014–15	Swansea C	0	0		
2014–15	*Yeovil T*	20	0		
2015–16	Swansea C	0	0		
2015–16	*Yeovil T*	6	0		
2016–17	Swansea C	0	0		
2016–17	*Yeovil T*	38	1	**64**	**1**
2017–18	Peterborough U	24	0	**24**	**0**
2018–19	Forest Green R	39	5	**39**	**5**

THOMAS, Lewis (G) **0** **0**
Internationals: Wales U17.
From Swansea C.

2018–19	Forest Green R	0	0		

WILLIAMS, George C (F) **89** **7**
H: 5 10 W: 12 04 b.Milton Keynes 7-9-95
Internationals: Wales U17, U19, U21, Full caps.

2012–13	Fulham	0	0		
2013–14	Fulham	0	0		
2014–15	Fulham	14	0		
2014–15	*Milton Keynes D*	4	0		
2015–16	Fulham	1	0		
2015–16	*Gillingham*	10	0	**10**	**0**
2016–17	Fulham	0	0		
2016–17	*Milton Keynes D*	11	0	**15**	**0**
2017–18	Fulham	0	0	**15**	**0**
2017–18	*St Johnstone*	11	0	**11**	**0**
2018–19	Forest Green R	38	7	**38**	**7**

WINCHESTER, Carl (D) **229** **17**
H: 5 10 W: 11 08 b.Belfast 12-4-93
Internationals: Northern Ireland U16, U17, U18, U19, U21, Full caps.

2010–11	Oldham Ath	6	1		
2011–12	Oldham Ath	12	0		
2012–13	Oldham Ath	9	0		
2013–14	Oldham Ath	12	1		
2014–15	Oldham Ath	41	4		
2015–16	Oldham Ath	31	1		
2016–17	Oldham Ath	9	1	**120**	**8**
2016–17	Cheltenham T	20	1		
2017–18	Cheltenham T	44	5	**64**	**6**
2018–19	Forest Green R	45	3	**45**	**3**

Players retained or with offer of contract
McGinley, Nathan.

Scholars
Artwell, Oliver Joseph Robert; Bradshaw, Daniel William; Hendy, Samuel Joseph; Hill, Ethan; Jones, Daniel Owen; Jones, Isaiah Malchai Tayne; Kalnins, Rendijs; Lehmann, Declan; Malshanskyj, Jay Perry; Marsh, Taylor; Ogunleye, Daniel Oluwatomi Emeka; Oladipo, Destiny Olajuwon; Owens, Louis Benjamin; Saunders, Alfie; Spurrier, Lewis Jon James; Turner, William; Youssef, Elias.

FULHAM (36)

ADEBAYO, Elijah (D) **34** **7**
b.Brent 7-1-98

2017–18	Fulham	0	0		
2017–18	*Cheltenham T*	7	2	**7**	**2**
2018–19	Fulham	0	0		
2018–19	*Swindon T*	25	5	**25**	**5**
2018–19	*Stevenage*	2	0	**2**	**0**

AYITE, Floyd (M) **256** **41**
H: 5 9 W: 10 10 b.Bordeaux 15-12-88
Internationals: Togo Full caps.

2008–09	Bordeaux	0	0		
2008–09	*Angers*	33	3	**33**	**3**
2009–10	Bordeaux	0	0		
2009–10	*Nancy*	6	0	**6**	**0**
2010–11	Bordeaux	7	0		
2011–12	Bordeaux	0	0	**7**	**0**
2011–12	Reims	18	3		
2012–13	Reims	23	2		
2013–14	Reims	32	5	**73**	**10**
2014–15	Bastia	30	6		
2015–16	Bastia	32	8	**62**	**14**
2016–17	Fulham	31	9		
2017–18	Fulham	28	4		
2018–19	Fulham	16	1	**75**	**14**

BABEL, Ryan (F) **381** **81**
H: 6 1 W: 12 06 b.Amsterdam 19-12-86
Internationals: Netherlands U17, U19, U20, U21, U23, Full caps.

2003–04	Ajax	1	0		
2004–05	Ajax	20	7		
2005–06	Ajax	25	2		
2006–07	Ajax	27	5		
2007–08	Liverpool	30	4		
2008–09	Liverpool	27	3		
2009–10	Liverpool	25	4		
2010–11	Liverpool	9	1	**91**	**12**
2010–11	Hoffenheim	15	1		
2011–12	Hoffenheim	31	4	**46**	**5**
2012–13	Ajax	16	4	**89**	**18**
2013–14	Kasimpasa	29	5		
2014–15	Kasimpasa	29	9	**58**	**14**
2015–16	Al-Ain	8	1	**8**	**1**
2016–17	Deportivo La Coruna	11	4	**11**	**4**
2016–17	Besiktas	18	5		
2017–18	Besiktas	32	13		
2018–19	Besiktas	12	4	**62**	**22**
2018–19	Fulham	16	5	**16**	**5**

BETTINELLI, Marcus (G) **128** **0**
H: 6 4 W: 12 13 b.Camberwell 24-5-92
Internationals: England U21.

2010–11	Fulham	0	0		
2011–12	Fulham	0	0		
2012–13	Fulham	0	0		
2013–14	Fulham	0	0		
2013–14	*Accrington S*	39	0	**39**	**0**
2014–15	Fulham	39	0		
2015–16	Fulham	11	0		
2016–17	Fulham	6	0		
2017–18	Fulham	26	0		
2018–19	Fulham	7	0	**89**	**0**

BRYAN, Joe (D) **241** **17**
H: 5 7 W: 11 05 b.Bristol 17-9-93

2011–12	Bristol C	1	0		
2012–13	Bristol C	13	0		
2012–13	*Plymouth Arg*	10	1	**10**	**1**
2013–14	Bristol C	21	2		
2014–15	Bristol C	41	6		
2015–16	Bristol C	39	2		
2016–17	Bristol C	44	1		
2017–18	Bristol C	43	5		
2018–19	Bristol C	1	0	**203**	**16**
2018–19	Fulham	28	0	**28**	**0**

CAIRNEY, Tom (M) **295** **36**
H: 6 0 W: 11 05 b.Nottingham 20-1-91
Internationals: Scotland U19, U21, Full caps.

2009–10	Hull C	11	1		
2010–11	Hull C	22	1		
2011–12	Hull C	27	0		
2012–13	Hull C	10	0		
2013–14	Hull C	0	0	**70**	**2**
2013–14	Blackburn R	37	5		
2014–15	Blackburn R	39	3	**76**	**8**
2015–16	Fulham	39	8		

2016 17	Fulham	45	12		
2017–18	Fulham	34	5		
2018–19	Fulham	31	1	**149**	**26**

CHRISTIE, Cyrus (D) 267 5
H: 6 2 W: 12 03 b.Coventry 30-9-92
Internationals. Republic of Ireland Full caps.

2011–12	Coventry C	37	0		
2012–13	Coventry C	31	2		
2013–14	Coventry C	34	0	**102**	**2**
2014–15	Derby Co	38	0		
2015–16	Derby Co	42	1		
2016–17	Derby Co	27	1		
2017–18	Derby Co	0	0	**107**	**2**
2017–18	Middlesbrough	25	1	**25**	**1**
2017–18	Fulham	5	0		
2018–19	Fulham	28	0	**33**	**0**

CISSE, Ibrahima (M) 108 2
H: 6 0 W: 12 02 b.Liege 28-2-94
Internationals: Belgium U17, U18, U19, U21. Guinea Full caps.

2011–12	Standard Liege	0	0		
2012–13	Standard Liege	18	1		
2013–14	Standard Liege	16	0		
2014–15	Mechelen	33	1		
2015–16	Mechelen	15	0	**48**	**1**
2016–17	Standard Liege	17	0	**51**	**1**
2017–18	Fulham	6	0		
2018–19	Fulham	3	0	**9**	**0**

DE LA TORRE, Luca (M) 5 0
H: 5 9 W: 9 13 b.San Diego 23-5-98
Internationals: USA U17, U20, Full caps.

2016–17	Fulham	0	0		
2017–18	Fulham	5	0		
2018–19	Fulham	0	0	**5**	**0**

EDUN, Tayo (D) 8 1
H: 5 9 b.London 14-5-98
Internationals: England U17, U18, U19, U20.

2016–17	Fulham	0	0		
2017–18	Fulham	2	0		
2018–19	Fulham	0	0	**2**	**0**
2018–19	*Ipswich T*	6	1	**6**	**1**

ELLIOTT, Harvey (M) 2 0
b.Esbjerg 4-4-03
Internationals: England U17.

2018–19	Fulham	2	0	**2**	**0**

JOHANSEN, Stefan (F) 274 41
H: 6 0 W: 12 04 b.Vardo 8-1-91
Internationals: Norway U16, U17, U18, U19, U21, U23, Full caps.

2007	Bodo/Glimt	4	0		
2008	Bodo/Glimt	1	0		
2009	Bodo/Glimt	4	0		
2010	Bodo/Glimt	20	0	**29**	**0**
2011	Stromsgodset	13	1		
2012	Stromsgodset	27	3		
2013	Stromsgodset	27	4	**67**	**8**
2013–14	Celtic	16	2		
2014–15	Celtic	34	9		
2015–16	Celtic	23	1	**73**	**12**
2016–17	Fulham	36	11		
2017–18	Fulham	45	8		
2018–19	Fulham	12	0	**93**	**19**
2018–19	*WBA*	12	2	**12**	**2**

KAMARA, Aboubakar (F) 112 26
H: 5 10 W: 12 08 b.Gonesse 7-3-95

2013–14	Monaco	0	0		
2014 15	Monaco	2	0	**2**	**0**
2015–16	Kortrijk	12	0	**12**	**0**
2015–16	Amiens	16	5		
2016–17	Amiens	29	10	**45**	**15**
2017–18	Fulham	30	7		
2018–19	Fulham	13	3	**43**	**10**
2018–19	*Yeni Malatyaspor*	10	1	**10**	**1**

KEBANO, Neeskens (M) 143 28
H: 5 11 W: 11 11 b.Montereau 10-3-92
Internationals: France U17, U18, U19, U20. DR Congo Full caps.

2010–11	Paris Saint-Germain	3	0		
2011–12	Paris Saint-Germain	0	0		
2012–13	Paris Saint-Germain	0	0	**3**	**0**
2012–13	*Caen*	12	1	**12**	**1**
2013–14	Charleroi	26	5		
2014–15	Charleroi	33	12		
2015–16	Charleroi	5	1	**64**	**18**
2016–17	Genk	3	0	**3**	**0**
2016–17	Fulham	28	6		
2017–18	Fulham	26	3		
2018–19	Fulham	7	0	**61**	**9**

LE MARCHAND, Maxime (M) 252 6
H: 5 11 W: 10 10 b.Saint Melo 10-11-89

2009–10	Rennes	0	0		
2009–10	*Le Havre*	27	1		
2010–11	Le Havre	22	0		
2011–12	Le Havre	20	1		
2012–13	Le Havre	28	0		
2013–14	Le Havre	31	2		
2014–15	Le Havre	33	1	**161**	**5**
2015–16	Nice	26	1		
2016–17	Nice	10	0		
2017–18	Nice	29	0	**65**	**1**
2018–19	Fulham	26	0	**26**	**0**

MARKOVIC, Lazar (F) 132 24
H: 5 9 W: 10 03 b.Cacak 2-3-94
Internationals: Serbia U17, U21, Full caps.

2010–11	Partizan Belgrade	1	0		
2011–12	Partizan Belgrade	26	6		
2012–13	Partizan Belgrade	19	7	**46**	**13**
2013–14	Benfica	26	5	**26**	**5**
2014–15	Liverpool	19	2		
2015–16	Liverpool	0	0		
2015–16	*Fenerbahce*	14	0	**14**	**0**
2016–17	Liverpool	0	0		
2016–17	*Sporting Lisbon*	6	1	**6**	**1**
2016–17	*Hull C*	12	2	**12**	**2**
2017–18	Liverpool	0	0		
2017–18	*Anderlecht*	8	1	**8**	**1**
2018–19	Liverpool	0	0	**19**	**2**
2018–19	Fulham	1	0	**1**	**0**

MAWSON, Alfie (D) 174 20
H: 5 8 W: 12 11 b.Hillingdon 19-1-94
Internationals: England U21.

2012–13	Brentford	0	0		
2013–14	Brentford	0	0		
2014–15	Brentford	0	0		
2014–15	*Wycombe W*	45	6	**45**	**6**
2015–16	Barnsley	45	6		
2016–17	Barnsley	4	2	**49**	**8**
2016–17	Swansea C	27	4		
2017–18	Swansea C	38	2	**65**	**6**
2018–19	Fulham	15	0	**15**	**0**

McDONALD, Kevin (M) 455 36
H: 6 2 W: 13 03 b.Carnoustie 4-11-88
Internationals: Scotland U19, U21, Full caps.

2005–06	Dundee	26	3		
2006–07	Dundee	31	2		
2007–08	Dundee	34	9	**91**	**14**
2008–09	Burnley	25	1		
2009–10	Burnley	26	1		
2010–11	Burnley	0	0	**51**	**2**
2010–11	*Scunthorpe U*	5	1	**5**	**1**
2010–11	*Notts Co*	11	0	**11**	**0**
2011–12	Sheffield U	31	3		
2012–13	Sheffield U	45	1		
2013–14	Sheffield U	1	1	**77**	**5**
2013–14	Wolverhampton W	41	5		
2014–15	Wolverhampton W	46	0		
2015–16	Wolverhampton W	33	3	**120**	**8**
2016–17	Fulham	43	3		
2017–18	Fulham	42	3		
2018–19	Fulham	15	0	**100**	**6**

MITROVIC, Aleksandar (F) 241 93
H: 6 2 W: 13 10 b.Smederevo 16-9-94
Internationals: Serbia U19, U21, Full caps.

2011–12	Teleoptik	25	7	**25**	**7**
2012–13	Partizan Belgrade	25	10		
2013–14	Partizan Belgrade	3	3	**28**	**13**
2013–14	Anderlecht	32	16		
2014–15	Anderlecht	37	20	**69**	**36**
2015–16	Newcastle U	34	9		
2016–17	Newcastle U	25	4		
2017–18	Newcastle U	6	1	**65**	**14**
2017–18	*Fulham*	17	12		
2018–19	Fulham	37	11	**54**	**23**

NORDTVEIT, Havard (D) 245 10
H: 6 2 W: 11 10 b.Vats 21-6-90
Internationals: Norway U16, U17, U18, U19, U21, Full caps.

2006	Haugesund	1	0		
2007	Haugesund	9	0	**10**	**0**
2007–08	Arsenal	0	0		
2008–09	Arsenal	0	0		
2008–09	*Salamanca*	3	0	**3**	**0**
2009	*Lillestrom*	17	0	**17**	**0**
2009–10	Arsenal	0	0		
2009–10	*Nuremberg*	19	0	**19**	**0**
2010–11	Arsenal	0	0		
2010–11	Borussia M'gladbach	16	1		
2011–12	Borussia M'gladbach	31	1		
2012–13	Borussia M'gladbach	31	1		
2013–14	Borussia M'gladbach	21	1		
2014–15	Borussia M'gladbach	22	2		
2015–16	Borussia M'gladbach	31	4	**152**	**10**
2015–16	West Ham U	0	0		
2016–17	West Ham U	16	0	**16**	**0**
2017–18	Hoffenheim	15	0		
2018–19	Hoffenheim	8	0	**23**	**0**

On loan from Hoffenhem.

2018–19	Fulham	5	0	**5**	**0**

NORMAN, Magnus (G) 7 0
H: 6 3 W: 12 13 b.Kingston Upon Thames 19-1-97
Internationals: England U16, U18.

2017–18	Fulham	0	0		
2018–19	Fulham	0	0		
2018–19	*Rochdale*	7	0	**7**	**0**

O'RILEY, Matt (M) 0 0
H: 6 2 W: 12 02 b.Hounslow 21-11-00
Internationals: England U16, U18.

2017–18	Fulham	0	0		
2018–19	Fulham	0	0		

ODOI, Dennis (D) 355 11
H: 5 10 W: 11 09 b.Leuven 27-5-88
Internationals: Belgium U20, U21, Full caps.

2006–07	Oud-Heverlee Leuven	3	0		
2007–08	Oud-Heverlee Leuven	21	0		
2008–09	Oud-Heverlee Leuven	33	3	**57**	**3**
2009–10	Sint-Truiden	26	1		
2010–11	Sint-Truiden	33	2	**59**	**3**
2011–12	Anderlecht	19	0		
2012–13	Anderlecht	14	0	**33**	**0**
2013–14	Lokeren	37	1		
2014–15	Lokeren	35	0		
2015–16	Lokeren	35	1	**107**	**2**
2016–17	Fulham	30	2		
2017–18	Fulham	38	1		
2018–19	Fulham	31	0	**99**	**3**

RAMIREZ, Fabricio (G) 169 0
H: 6 1 W: 12 02 b.Las Palmas 31-12-87
Internationals: Spain U20.

2006–07	Deportivo La Coruna	0	0		
2007–08	Deportivo La Coruna	6	0		
2008–09	Deportivo La Coruna	0	0		
2009–10	Valladolid	1	0		
2010–11	Valladolid	0	0	**1**	**0**
2010–11	*Recreativo*	40	0	**40**	**0**
2011–12	Real Betis	15	0		
2012–13	Real Betis	2	0	**17**	**0**
2013–14	Deportivo La Coruna	6	0		
2014–15	Deportivo La Coruna	31	0		
2015–16	Deportivo La Coruna	0	0	**43**	**0**
2016–17	Besiktas	32	0		
2017–18	Besiktas	34	0	**66**	**0**
2018–19	Fulham	2	0	**2**	**0**

REAM, Tim (D) 406 9
H: 6 1 W: 11 05 b.St Louis 5-10-87
Internationals: USA Full caps.

2006	St Louis Billikens	19	0		
2007	St Louis Billikens	19	0		
2008	St Louis Billikens	22	0		
2008	Chicago Fire	12	0		
2009	Chicago Fire	7	0	**19**	**0**
2009	St Louis Billikens	22	6	**82**	**6**
2010	New York RB	30	1		
2011	New York RB	28	0	**58**	**1**
2011–12	Bolton W	13	0		
2012–13	Bolton W	15	0		
2013–14	Bolton W	42	0		
2014–15	Bolton W	44	0	**114**	**0**
2015–16	Fulham	29	0		
2016–17	Fulham	34	1		
2017–18	Fulham	44	1		
2018–19	Fulham	26	0	**133**	**2**

RODAK, Marek (G) 100 0
H: 6 2 W: 10 12 b. 13-12-96
Internationals: Slovakia U17, U19, U21.

2014–15	Fulham	0	0		
2015–16	Fulham	0	0		
2016–17	Fulham	0	0		
2016–17	*Accrington S*	20	0	**20**	**0**
2017–18	Fulham	0	0		
2017–18	*Rotherham U*	35	0		
2018–19	Fulham	0	0		
2018–19	*Rotherham U*	45	0	**80**	**0**

RUI FONTE, Pedro (F) 158 22
H: 6 0 W: 12 13 b.Lisbon 23-3-90
Internationals: Portugal U16, U17, U18, U19, U20, U21.

2008–09	Arsenal	0	0		
2008–09	*Crystal Palace*	10	0	**10**	**0**
2009–10	Setubal	13	0	**13**	**0**

2010–11	Espanyol	11	0		
2011–12	Espanyol	19	1		
2012–13	Espanyol	10	0	**40**	**1**
2013–14	Benfica	0	0		
2014–15	Benfica	0	0		
2014–15	Belenenses	12	2	**12**	**2**
2015–16	Braga	15	4		
2016–17	Braga	22	10		
2017–18	Braga	2	1	**39**	**15**
2017–18	Fulham	27	3		
2018–19	Fulham	0	0	**27**	**3**
2018–19	*Lille*	17	1	**17**	**1**

SCHURRLE, Andre (F) **275** **68**
H: 6 0 W: 11 06 b.Ludwigschafen 6-11-90
Internationals: Germany U19, U20, U21, Full caps.

2009–10	Mainz	33	5		
2010–11	Mainz	33	15	**66**	**20**
2011–12	Bayer Leverkusen	31	7		
2012–13	Bayer Leverkusen	34	11	**65**	**18**
2013–14	Chelsea	30	8		
2014–15	Chelsea	14	3	**44**	**11**
2014–15	Wolfsburg	14	1		
2015–16	Wolfsburg	29	9	**43**	**10**
2016–17	Borussia Dortmund	15	2		
2017–18	Borussia Dortmund	18	1		
2018–19	Borussia Dortmund	0	0	**33**	**3**

On loan from Borussia Dortmund.

2018–19	Fulham	24	6	**24**	**6**

SERGIO RICO, Gonzalez (G) **143** **0**
H: 6 4 W: 13 12 b.Seville 1-9-93
Internationals: Spain Full caps.

2010–11	Sevilla	0	0		
2011–12	Sevilla	0	0		
2012–13	Sevilla	0	0		
2013–14	Sevilla	0	0		
2014–15	Sevilla	21	0		
2015–16	Sevilla	34	0		
2016–17	Sevilla	35	0		
2017–18	Sevilla	24	0		
2018–19	Sevilla	0	0	**114**	**0**

On loan from Sevilla.

2018–19	Fulham	29	0	**29**	**0**

SERI, Jean (M) **189** **15**
H: 5 5 W: 10 08 b.Grand-Bereby 19-7-91
Internationals: Ivory Coast U23, Full caps.

2013–14	Pacos de Ferreira	21	1		
2014–15	Pacos de Ferreira	33	1	**54**	**2**
2015–16	Nice	38	3		
2016–17	Nice	34	7		
2017–18	Nice	31	2	**103**	**12**
2018–19	Fulham	32	1	**32**	**1**

SESSEGNON, Ryan (D) **106** **22**
H: 5 10 W: 11 02 b.Roehampton 18-5-00
Internationals: England U16, U17, U19, U21.

2016–17	Fulham	25	5		
2017–18	Fulham	46	15		
2018–19	Fulham	35	2	**106**	**22**

SESSEGNON, Steven (D) **0** **0**
H: 5 8 W: 10 06 b.Roehampton 18-5-00
Internationals: England U16, U17, U18, U19, U20.

2017–18	Fulham	0	0		
2018–19	Fulham	0	0		

VIETTO, Luciano (F) **181** **40**
H: 5 8 W: 10 10 b.Balnearia 5-12-93
Internationals: Argentina U20.

2011–12	Racing Club	2	0		
2012–13	Racing Club	32	13		
2013–14	Racing Club	35	5	**69**	**18**
2014–15	Villarreal	32	12	**32**	**12**
2015–16	Atletico Madrid	19	1		
2016–17	Atletico Madrid	0	0		
2016–17	*Sevilla*	21	6	**21**	**6**
2017–18	Atletico Madrid	6	0		
2017–18	*Valencia*	14	2	**14**	**2**
2018–19	Atletico Madrid	0	0	**25**	**1**

On loan from Atletico Madrid.

2018–19	Fulham	20	1	**20**	**1**

ZAMBO, Andre-Franck (M) **101** **0**
H: 6 0 W: 11 09 b.Yaounde 16-11-95
Internationals: Cameroon Full caps.

2015–16	Marseille	9	0		
2016–17	Marseille	33	0		
2017–18	Marseille	37	0	**79**	**0**
2018–19	Fulham	22	0	**22**	**0**

Players retained or with offer of contract
Asare, Zico Kukuu; Ashby-Hammond, Luca; Ashby-Hammond, Taye; Bakumo-Abraham, Jason Timiebi; Davis, Benjamin James; Djalo Taritolay, Marcelo-Amado; Fossey, Marlon Joseph; Francois, Tyrese Jay; Frei, Elias; Harris, Jayden John-Lloyd; Hilton, Sonny; Jasper, Sylvester; Jenz, Moritz; Kait, Mattias; Mundle-Smith, Jaydn Josiah; Murphy, Luca Michael; Opoku, Jerome; Santos Clase, Nicolas; Stahl, Toni; Thompson, Cameron Randy; Thorsteinsson, Jon Dagur; Tiehi, Jean-Pierre Alberic; Wickens, George Alexander.

Scholars
Ablade, Terry; Antwi, Cameron Akwasi; Armsworth, Scott David; Carvalho, Fabio; Cover, Tristan; De Havilland, Ryan James; Drameh, Cody Callum Pierre; McAvoy, Connor; Page, Jonathon Charles; Tahir, Showkat Mohamed; Warland, Riley Charles.

GILLINGHAM (37)

BINGHAM, Billy (D) **198** **8**
H: 5 11 W: 11 02 b.Welling 15-7-90

2008–09	Dagenham & R	0	0		
2009–10	Dagenham & R	2	0		
2010–11	Dagenham & R	6	0		
2011–12	Dagenham & R	27	2		
2012–13	Dagenham & R	18	2		
2013–14	Dagenham & R	30	0		
2014–15	Dagenham & R	34	4	**117**	**8**
2015–16	Crewe Alex	21	0		
2016–17	Crewe Alex	30	0	**51**	**0**
2017–18	Gillingham	9	0		
2018–19	Gillingham	21	0	**30**	**0**

BURKE, Graham (F) **70** **5**
H: 5 11 W: 11 11 b.Dublin 21-9-93
Internationals: Republic of Ireland U19, U21, Full caps.

2010–11	Aston Villa	0	0		
2011–12	Aston Villa	0	0		
2012–13	Aston Villa	0	0		
2013–14	Aston Villa	0	0		
2013–14	*Shrewsbury T*	3	0	**3**	**0**
2014–15	Aston Villa	0	0		
2014–15	*Notts Co*	7	1		
2015–16	Notts Co	31	2		
2016–17	Notts Co	5	0	**43**	**3**

From Shamrock R.

2018–19	Preston NE	12	1	**12**	**1**
2018–19	Gillingham	12	1	**12**	**1**

BYRNE, Mark (M) **319** **28**
H: 5 9 W: 11 00 b.Dublin 9-11-88

2006–07	Nottingham F	0	0		
2007–08	Nottingham F	1	0		
2008–09	Nottingham F	1	0		
2009–10	Nottingham F	0	0		
2010–11	Nottingham F	0	0	**2**	**0**
2010–11	*Barnet*	28	6		
2011–12	Barnet	43	5		
2012–13	Barnet	40	3	**111**	**14**
2014–15	Newport Co	42	4		
2015–16	Newport Co	46	2	**88**	**6**
2016–17	Gillingham	31	1		
2017–18	Gillingham	42	3		
2018–19	Gillingham	45	4	**118**	**8**

CAMPBELL, Roman (F) **0** **0**
b.Gravesend --

2018–19	Gillingham	0	0		

CATHERALL, Louie (G) **0** **0**
b. 19-4-00

2018–19	Gillingham	0	0		

CHAPMAN, Ben (M) **0** **0**

2016–17	Gillingham	0	0		
2017–18	Gillingham	0	0		
2018–19	Gillingham	0	0		

CHARLES, Regan (M) **27** **3**
H: 5 9 W: 10 12 b.London 1-3-97
From Arsenal.

2015–16	Charlton Ath	1	0		
2016–17	Charlton Ath	0	0		
2017–18	Charlton Ath	0	0	**1**	**0**
2018–19	Gillingham	26	3	**26**	**3**

DA SILVA LOPES, Leonardo (M) **102** **3**
H: 5 6 W: 9 08 b.Lisbon 30-11-98
Internationals: Portugal U20.

2014–15	Peterborough U	2	0		
2015–16	Peterborough U	8	0		
2016–17	Peterborough U	38	2		
2017–18	Peterborough U	39	0	**87**	**2**
2018–19	Wigan Ath	1	0	**1**	**0**
2018–19	Gillingham	14	1	**14**	**1**

DIVINE, Danny (D) **0** **0**
b. 10-3-00

2018–19	Gillingham	0	0		

EAVES, Tom (M) **216** **58**
H: 6 3 W: 13 07 b.Liverpool 14-1-92

2009–10	Oldham Ath	15	0		
2010–11	Bolton W	0	0		
2010–11	*Oldham Ath*	0	0	**15**	**0**
2011–12	Bolton W	0	0		
2012–13	Bolton W	3	0		
2012–13	*Bristol R*	16	7	**16**	**7**
2012–13	*Shrewsbury T*	10	6		
2013–14	Bolton W	0	0		
2013–14	*Rotherham U*	8	0	**8**	**0**
2013–14	*Shrewsbury T*	25	2	**35**	**8**
2014–15	Bolton W	1	0		
2014–15	*Yeovil T*	5	0		
2014–15	*Bury*	9	1	**9**	**1**
2015–16	Bolton W	0	0	**4**	**0**
2016–17	Yeovil T	40	4	**45**	**4**
2017–18	Gillingham	41	17		
2018–19	Gillingham	43	21	**84**	**38**

EHMER, Max (M) **263** **12**
H: 6 2 W: 11 00 b.Frankfurt 3-2-92

2009–10	QPR	0	0		
2010–11	QPR	0	0		
2010–11	*Yeovil T*	27	0		
2011–12	QPR	0	0		
2011–12	*Yeovil T*	24	0	**51**	**0**
2011–12	*Preston NE*	9	0	**9**	**0**
2012–13	QPR	0	0		
2012–13	*Stevenage*	6	1	**6**	**1**
2013–14	QPR	1	0		
2013–14	*Carlisle U*	12	1	**12**	**1**
2014–15	QPR	0	0	**1**	**0**
2014–15	*Gillingham*	27	1		
2015–16	Gillingham	30	0		
2016–17	Gillingham	45	6		
2017–18	Gillingham	42	2		
2018–19	Gillingham	40	1	**184**	**10**

FULLER, Barry (D) **432** **3**
H: 5 10 W: 11 10 b.Ashford 25-9-84
Internationals: England C.

2004–05	Charlton Ath	0	0		
2005–06	Charlton Ath	0	0		
2005–06	*Barnet*	15	1		

From Stevenage B.

2007–08	Gillingham	10	0		
2008–09	Gillingham	37	0		
2009–10	Gillingham	36	0		
2010–11	Gillingham	42	0		
2011–12	Gillingham	9	0		
2012–13	Gillingham	0	0		
2012–13	Barnet	39	0	**54**	**1**
2013–14	AFC Wimbledon	45	0		
2014–15	AFC Wimbledon	45	1		
2015–16	AFC Wimbledon	45	0		
2016–17	AFC Wimbledon	28	0		
2017–18	AFC Wimbledon	42	0	**205**	**1**
2018–19	Gillingham	39	1	**173**	**1**

GARMSTON, Bradley (D) **97** **2**
H: 5 9 W: 10 12 b.Greenwich 18-1-94
Internationals: Republic of Ireland U17, U9, U21.

2012–13	WBA	0	0		
2012–13	*Colchester U*	13	0	**13**	**0**
2013–14	WBA	0	0		
2014–15	WBA	0	0		
2014–15	*Gillingham*	8	1		
2015–16	Gillingham	33	0		
2016–17	Gillingham	5	0		
2017–18	Gillingham	19	1		
2018–19	Gillingham	19	0	**84**	**2**

HADDLER, Tom (G) **1** **0**
b. 30-7-96

2014–15	Gillingham	0	0		
2015–16	Gillingham	0	0		
2016–17	Gillingham	0	0		
2017–18	Gillingham	1	0		
2018–19	Gillingham	0	0	**1**	**0**

HANLAN, Brandon (F) **66** **11**
H: 6 0 W: 11 07 b.Chelsea 31-5-97

2016–17	Charlton Ath	9	0		
2017–18	Colchester U	18	2	**18**	**2**
2017–18	Charlton Ath	0	0	**9**	**0**
2018–19	Gillingham	39	9	**39**	**9**

HOLY, Tomas (G) **167 0**
H: 6 9 W: 16 05 b.Rychnov nad Kneznou 10-12-91
Internationals: Czech Republic U16, U17, U18.

2010–11	Sparta Prague	0	0		
2011–12	Sparta Prague	0	0		
2012–13	Sparta Prague	0	0		
2013–14	Sparta Prague	0	0		
2013–14	*Vlasim*	9	0	**9**	**0**
2013–14	*Viktoria Zizkov*	14	0		
2014–15	Sparta Prague	0	0		
2014–15	*Viktoria Zizkov*	27	0	**41**	**0**
2015–16	Sparta Prague	0	0		
2015–16	*Zlin*	20	0	**20**	**0**
2016–17	Fastav Zlin	0	0		
2016–17	Gillingham	6	0		
2017–18	Gillingham	45	0		
2018–19	Gillingham	46	0	**97**	**0**

HUCKLE, Ryan (D) **0 0**
b. 18-2-00

2018–19	Gillingham	0	0		

KING, Billy (M) **178 22**
b. 12-5-94
Internationals: Scotland U16, U19, U21.

2012–13	Hearts	8	0		
2013–14	Hearts	32	3		
2014–15	Hearts	31	8		
2015–16	Hearts	15	2		
2015–16	*Rangers*	12	1	**12**	**1**
2016–17	Hearts	0	0	**86**	**13**
2016–17	*Inverness CT*	26	1	**26**	**1**
2017–18	Dundee U	35	5		
2018–19	Dundee U	16	2	**51**	**7**

On loan from Dundee U.

2018–19	Gillingham	3	0	**3**	**0**

LACEY, Alex (D) **105 5**
b.Milton Keynes 31-5-93

2014–15	Luton T	18	0	**18**	**0**
2015–16	Yeovil T	20	0		
2016–17	Yeovil T	40	3	**60**	**3**
2016–17	Gillingham	0	0		
2017–18	Gillingham	11	1		
2018–19	Gillingham	16	1	**27**	**2**

LIST, Elliott (M) **81 7**
b.Camberwell 12-5-97
From Crystal Palace.

2015–16	Gillingham	6	0		
2016–17	Gillingham	15	0		
2017–18	Gillingham	23	2		
2018–19	Gillingham	37	5	**81**	**7**

M'BO, Noel (F) **1 0**
b. 14-3-99

2015–16	Gillingham	0	0		
2016–17	Gillingham	0	0		
2017–18	Gillingham	0	0		
2018–19	Gillingham	1	0	**1**	**0**

NASH, Liam (F) **12 0**
H: 5 9 W: 11 03 b. 9-1-96
From Hullbridge Sports, Billericay T, Aveley, Great Wakering R, Maldon & Tiptree.

2017–18	Gillingham	12	0		
2018–19	Gillingham	0	0	**12**	**0**

NASSERI, David (M) **33 3**
b. 26-7-96

2013–14	Bury	0	0		
2014–15	Birmingham C	0	0		

From Macclesfield T.

2017–18	Syrianska FC	25	2	**25**	**2**
2017–18	Gillingham	4	1		
2018–19	Gillingham	4	0	**8**	**1**

O'MARA, Finn (D) **2 0**
H: 6 0 W: 11 09 b. 2-3-99

2016–17	Gillingham	0	0		
2017–18	Gillingham	2	0		
2018–19	Gillingham	0	0	**2**	**0**

O'NEILL, Luke (D) **150 6**
H: 6 0 W: 11 04 b.Slough 20-8-91
Internationals: England U17.

2009–10	Leicester C	1	0	**1**	**0**
2009–10	*Tranmere R*	4	0	**4**	**0**

From Kettering T, Mansfield T

2012–13	Burnley	1	0		
2013–14	Burnley	0	0		
2013–14	*York C*	15	1	**15**	**1**
2013–14	*Southend U*	1	0		
2014–15	Burnley	0	0	**1**	**0**
2014–15	*Scunthorpe U*	13	0	**13**	**0**
2014–15	*Leyton Orient*	8	0	**8**	**0**
2015–16	Southend U	14	0		
2016–17	Southend U	17	1	**32**	**1**
2017–18	Gillingham	38	1		
2018–19	Gillingham	38	3	**76**	**4**

OLDAKER, Darren (M) **21 0**
b.London 4-1-99

2015–16	Gillingham	0	0		
2016–17	Gillingham	5	0		
2017–18	Gillingham	3	0		
2018–19	Gillingham	13	0	**21**	**0**

PARRETT, Dean (M) **185 19**
H: 5 10 W: 11 04 b.Hampstead 16-11-91
Internationals: England U16, U17, U19, U20.

2008–09	Tottenham H	0	0		
2009–10	Tottenham H	0	0		
2009–10	*Aldershot T*	4	0	**4**	**0**
2010–11	Tottenham H	0	0		
2010–11	*Plymouth Arg*	8	1	**8**	**1**
2010–11	*Charlton Ath*	9	1	**9**	**1**
2011–12	Tottenham H	0	0		
2011–12	*Yeovil T*	10	1	**10**	**1**
2012–13	Tottenham H	0	0		
2012–13	*Swindon T*	3	0	**3**	**0**
2013–14	Stevenage	12	1		
2014–15	Stevenage	30	4		
2015–16	Stevenage	27	3	**69**	**8**
2016–17	AFC Wimbledon	32	5		
2017–18	AFC Wimbledon	23	2	**55**	**7**
2018–19	Gillingham	27	1	**27**	**1**

REES, Josh (M) **19 1**
H: 5 9 W: 11 00 b.Hemel Hempstead 4-10-93
Internationals: England U16, U17, C.

2011–12	Arsenal	0	0		
2013–14	Nottingham F	1	0		
2014–15	Nottingham F	0	0		
2015–16	Nottingham F	0	0	**1**	**0**

From Braintree T, Chelmsford C, Bromley.

2018–19	Gillingham	18	1	**18**	**1**

REILLY, Callum (M) **152 7**
H: 6 1 W: 12 03 b.Warrington 3-10-93
Internationals: Republic of Ireland U21.

2012–13	Birmingham C	18	1		
2013–14	Birmingham C	25	0		
2014–15	Birmingham C	17	1	**60**	**2**
2014–15	*Burton Alb*	2	0		
2015–16	Burton Alb	14	0		
2016–17	Burton Alb	0	0	**16**	**0**
2016–17	*Coventry C*	18	0	**18**	**0**
2017–18	Bury	18	0	**18**	**0**
2017–18	*Gillingham*	15	0		
2018–19	Gillingham	25	5	**40**	**5**

SCARLETT, Miquel (D) **0 0**

2017–18	Gillingham	0	0		
2018–19	Gillingham	0	0		

SIMPSON, Aaron (M) **0 0**

2016–17	Gillingham	0	0		
2017–18	Gillingham	0	0		
2018–19	Gillingham	0	0		

STEVENSON, Bradley (M) **3 0**
b. 12-9-98

2016–17	Gillingham	0	0		
2017–18	Gillingham	0	0		
2018–19	Gillingham	3	0	**3**	**0**

TUCKER, Jack (D) **1 0**
b. 13-11-99

2017–18	Gillingham	1	0		
2018–19	Gillingham	0	0	**1**	**0**

WILKINSON, Conor (F) **107 12**
H: 6 1 W: 12 02 b.Croydon 23-1-95
Internationals: Republic of Ireland U17, U19, U21.

2012–13	Millwall	0	0		
2013–14	Bolton W	0	0		
2013–14	*Torquay U*	3	0	**3**	**0**
2014–15	Bolton W	4	0		
2014–15	*Oldham Ath*	17	3	**17**	**3**
2015–16	Bolton W	0	0		
2015–16	*Barnsley*	8	1	**8**	**1**
2015–16	*Newport Co*	12	1	**12**	**1**
2015–16	*Portsmouth*	1	0	**1**	**0**
2016–17	Bolton W	9	0	**13**	**0**
2016–17	*Chesterfield*	12	4	**12**	**4**
2017–18	Gillingham	34	3		
2018–19	Gillingham	7	0	**41**	**3**

WOODS, Henry (M) **0 0**

2018–19	Gillingham	0	0		

ZAKUANI, Gaby (D) **446 15**
H: 6 1 W: 12 13 b.DR Congo 31-5-86
Internationals: DR Congo Full caps.

2002–03	Leyton Orient	1	0		
2003–04	Leyton Orient	10	2		
2004–05	Leyton Orient	33	0		
2005–06	Leyton Orient	43	1	**87**	**3**
2006–07	Fulham	0	0		
2006–07	*Stoke C*	9	0		
2007–08	Fulham	0	0		
2007–08	*Stoke C*	19	0	**28**	**0**
2008–09	Fulham	0	0		
2008–09	Peterborough U	32	1		
2009–10	Peterborough U	29	0		
2010–11	Peterborough U	30	2		
2011–12	Peterborough U	41	1		
2012–13	Peterborough U	33	1		
2013–14	Peterborough U	15	0		
2013–14	*Kalloni*	15	1	**15**	**1**
2014–15	Peterborough U	22	1		
2015–16	Peterborough U	24	3	**226**	**9**
2016–17	Northampton T	21	2	**21**	**2**
2017–18	Gillingham	40	0		
2018–19	Gillingham	29	0	**69**	**0**

Players retained or with offer of contract
Charles-Cook, Regan Evans; Walsh, Joe Anthony; Wignal List, Elliott Ricardo.

Scholars
Allen, Ben James; Arthurs, Jude Robert; Bancroft, Toby William Day; Blanks, Charlie Benn Devon; Bramble, Thomas-James Everton; Campbell, Roman Cameron; Fernandez, Emmanuel Oluwasegun; Hards, Jay Scott; Laing, Harry Derek; Lamb, Thomas Jay; Morrell, Jack Lawrence; Noyelle, Charles William; Scarlett, Miquel Howard Hugh; Sheminant, George; Witt, James David.

GRIMSBY T (38)

BATTERSBY, Ollie (G) **0 0**

2018–19	Grimsby T	0	0		

BUCKLEY, Brandon (F) **0 0**
b. 21-9-00

2018–19	Grimsby T	0	0		

BURRELL, Rumarn (F) **4 0**
b. 16-12-00

2018–19	Grimsby T	4	0	**4**	**0**

CARDWELL, Harry (F) **35 1**
b. 23-10-96
Internationals: Scotland U19, U21.
From Reading.

2017–18	Grimsby T	16	0		
2018–19	Grimsby T	19	1	**35**	**1**

CLIFTON, Harry (M) **49 2**
H: 5 11 W: 13 12 b. 12-6-98
Internationals: Wales U21.

2016–17	Grimsby T	0	0		
2017–18	Grimsby T	10	0		
2018–19	Grimsby T	39	2	**49**	**2**

COLLINS, Danny (D) **439 18**
H: 6 2 W: 11 13 b.Buckley 6-8-80
Internationals: England C. Wales Full caps.

2004–05	Chester C	12	1	**12**	**1**
2004–05	Sunderland	14	0		
2005–06	Sunderland	23	1		
2006–07	Sunderland	38	0		
2007–08	Sunderland	36	1		
2008–09	Sunderland	35	1		
2009–10	Sunderland	3	0	**149**	**3**
2009–10	Stoke C	25	0		
2010–11	Stoke C	25	0		
2011–12	Stoke C	0	0	**50**	**0**
2011–12	*Ipswich T*	16	3	**16**	**3**
2011–12	*West Ham U*	11	1	**11**	**1**
2012–13	Nottingham F	40	0		
2013–14	Nottingham F	23	1		
2014–15	Nottingham F	8	1	**71**	**2**
2015–16	Rotherham U	24	2		
2016–17	Rotherham U	0	0	**24**	**2**
2016–17	Grimsby T	36	2		
2017–18	Grimsby T	40	4		
2018–19	Grimsby T	30	0	**106**	**6**

COOK, Jordan (F) **176 20**
H: 5 10 W: 10 10 b.Hetton-le-Hole 20-3-90

2007–08	Sunderland	0	0		
2008–09	Sunderland	0	0		
2009–10	Sunderland	0	0		

2009–10	*Darlington*	5	0	**5**	**0**
2010–11	Sunderland	3	0		
2010–11	*Walsall*	8	1		
2011–12	Sunderland	0	0	**3**	**0**
2011–12	*Carlisle U*	14	4	**14**	**4**
2012–13	Charlton Ath	7	0		
2012–13	*Yeovil T*	1	0	**1**	**0**
2013–14	Charlton Ath	3	0	**10**	**0**
2014–15	Walsall	32	5		
2015–16	Walsall	34	3	**74**	**9**
2016–17	Luton T	35	3		
2017–18	Luton T	10	0	**45**	**3**
2018–19	Grimsby T	24	4	**24**	**4**

CURRAN, Jock (M) **0** **0**

2018–19	Grimsby T	0	0		

DAVIS, Harry (D) **245** **21**

H: 6 2 W: 12 04 b.Burnley 24-9-91

2009–10	Crewe Alex	1	0		
2010–11	Crewe Alex	1	0		
2011–12	Crewe Alex	41	5		
2012–13	Crewe Alex	42	1		
2013–14	Crewe Alex	32	3		
2014–15	Crewe Alex	31	1		
2015–16	Crewe Alex	11	1		
2016–17	Crewe Alex	25	1	**184**	**12**
2016–17	*St Mirren*	6	2		
2017–18	St Mirren	20	3	**26**	**5**
2018–19	Grimsby T	35	4	**35**	**4**

DIXON, Paul (D) **387** **6**

H: 5 9 W: 11 01 b.Aberdeen 11-10-86

Internationals: Scotland U21, Full caps.

2005–06	Dundee	29	2		
2006–07	Dundee	33	0		
2007–08	Dundee	30	0	**92**	**2**
2008–09	Dundee U	29	1		
2009–10	Dundee U	25	0		
2010–11	Dundee U	30	0		
2011–12	Dundee U	37	3		
2012–13	Huddersfield T	37	0		
2013–14	Huddersfield T	37	0		
2014–15	Huddersfield T	11	0	**85**	**0**
2014–15	Dundee U	15	0		
2015–16	Dundee U	28	0		
2016–17	Dundee U	17	0	**181**	**4**
2017–18	Grimsby T	26	0		
2018–19	Grimsby T	3	0	**29**	**0**

Transferred to Falkirk January 2019.

FOX, Andrew (D) **62** **1**

b. 15-1-93

2015–16	Peterborough U	18	1	**18**	**1**
2016–17	Stevenage	9	0	**9**	**0**
2017–18	AFC Eskilstuna	13	0	**13**	**0**
2017–18	Grimsby T	10	0		
2018–19	Grimsby T	12	0	**22**	**0**

HALL-JOHNSON, Reece (M) **40** **0**

H: 5 8 W: 10 08 b.Aylesbury 9-5-95

2013–14	Norwich C	0	0		
2014–15	Norwich C	0	0		
2015–16	Norwich C	0	0		

From Maidstone U, Bishop's Stortford, Braintree T.

2017–18	Grimsby T	12	0		
2018–19	Grimsby T	28	0	**40**	**0**

HENDRIE, Luke (M) **117** **2**

b. 27-8-94

Internationals: England U16, U17.

2013–14	Derby Co	0	0		
2014–15	Derby Co	0	0		
2015–16	Burnley	0	0		
2015–16	*Hartlepool U*	3	0	**3**	**0**
2015–16	*York C*	18	0	**18**	**0**
2016–17	Burnley	0	0		
2016–17	*Kilmarnock*	32	0	**32**	**0**
2017–18	Burnley	0	0		
2017–18	*Bradford C*	13	0	**13**	**0**
2017–18	Shrewsbury T	10	0	**10**	**0**
2018–19	Grimsby T	41	2	**41**	**2**

HESSENTHALER, Jake (M) **203** **7**

b.Gravesend 20-4-94

2012–13	Gillingham	0	0		
2013–14	Gillingham	19	1		
2014–15	Gillingham	37	1		
2015–16	Gillingham	38	4		
2016–17	Gillingham	28	1		
2017–18	Gillingham	37	0	**159**	**7**
2018–19	Grimsby T	44	0	**44**	**0**

HOOPER, JJ (F) **110** **17**

H: 6 1 W: 13 01 b.Greenwich 9-10-93

2013–14	Northampton T	3	0		

From Havant & Waterlooville.

2015–16	Port Vale	28	5		
2016–17	Port Vale	23	5	**51**	**10**
2016–17	*Northampton T*	10	0	**13**	**0**
2017–18	Grimsby T	31	6		
2018–19	Grimsby T	15	1	**46**	**7**

McKEOWN, James (G) **125** **0**

H: 6 1 W: 14 00 b.Birmingham 24-7-89

Internationals: Republic of Ireland U19.

2005–06	Walsall	0	0		
2006–07	Walsall	0	0		
2007–08	Peterborough U	1	0		
2008–09	Peterborough U	1	0		
2009–10	Peterborough U	4	0	**6**	**0**
2016–17	Grimsby T	39	0		
2017–18	Grimsby T	37	0		
2018–19	Grimsby T	43	0	**119**	**0**

McPHERSON, Brandon (M) **0** **0**

2018–19	Grimsby T	0	0		

OHMAN, Ludvig (D) **127** **2**

H: 6 2 W: 12 08 b.Umea 9-10-91

Internationals: Sweden U17, U19.

2010	Kalmar	1	0		
2011	Kalmar	0	0		
2012	Kalmar	16	0		
2013	Kalmar	15	0		
2014	Kalmar	6	0		
2015	Kalmar	19	0	**57**	**0**
2016	Nagoya Grampus	9	0	**9**	**0**
2017	Eskilstuna	26	2	**26**	**2**
2018	Brommapojkarna	22	0	**22**	**0**
2018–19	Grimsby T	13	0	**13**	**0**

POLLOCK, Matthew (D) **2** **0**

b. 28-9-01

2018–19	Grimsby T	2	0	**2**	**0**

PRINGLE, Ben (M) **248** **24**

H: 5 8 W: 11 10 b.Whitley Bay 25-7-88

2009–10	Derby Co	5	0		
2010–11	Derby Co	15	0	**20**	**0**
2010–11	*Torquay U*	5	0	**5**	**0**
2011–12	Rotherham U	21	4		
2012–13	Rotherham U	41	7		
2013–14	Rotherham U	45	5		
2014–15	Rotherham U	40	3	**147**	**19**
2015–16	Fulham	15	2	**15**	**2**
2015–16	*Ipswich T*	10	2	**10**	**2**
2016–17	Preston NE	10	0		
2017–18	Preston NE	0	0		
2017–18	*Oldham Ath*	13	1	**13**	**1**
2018–19	Preston NE	0	0	**10**	**0**
2018–19	Grimsby T	15	0	**15**	**0**
2018–19	*Tranmere R*	13	0	**13**	**0**

RING, Sebastian (D) **116** **5**

b. 18-4-95

2013	Orebro SK	0	0		
2013	BK Forward	9	1		
2014	Orebro SK	0	0		
2014	BK Forward	24	2	**33**	**3**
2015	Orebro SK	0	0		
2016	Orebro SK	21	1		
2017	Orebro SK	22	1		
2018	Orebro SK	25	0	**68**	**2**
2018–19	Grimsby T	15	0	**15**	**0**

ROBLES, Louis (F) **40** **6**

b. 11-9-96

2014–15	Wigan Ath	1	0		
2015–16	Wigan Ath	0	0	**1**	**0**
2016–17	Atletico Baleares	5	0	**5**	**0**
2017–18	San Rocque de Lepe	33	6	**33**	**6**
2018–19	Grimsby T	1	0	**1**	**0**

ROSE, Ahkeem (F) **16** **1**

b. 27-11-98

2018–19	Grimsby T	16	1	**16**	**1**

RUSSELL, Sam (G) **10** **0**

H: 6 0 W: 10 12 b.Middlesbrough 4-10-82

From Middlesbrough, Rochdale, Wrexham, Darlington.

2017–18	Forest Green R	5	0	**5**	**0**
2018–19	Grimsby T	5	0	**5**	**0**

THOMAS, Wesley (F) **301** **78**

H: 5 10 W: 11 00 b.Barking 23-1-87

2008–09	Dagenham & R	5	0		
2009–10	Dagenham & R	23	3	**28**	**3**
2010–11	Cheltenham T	41	18	**41**	**18**
2011–12	Crawley T	6	1	**6**	**1**
2011–12	Bournemouth	36	11		
2012–13	Bournemouth	6	0		
2012–13	*Portsmouth*	6	3	**6**	**3**
2012–13	*Blackpool*	9	3	**9**	**3**
2012–13	*Birmingham C*	11	3		
2013–14	Bournemouth	10	0	**52**	**11**
2013–14	Rotherham U	13	5	**13**	**5**
2014–15	Birmingham C	33	4		
2015–16	Birmingham C	0	0	**44**	**7**
2015–16	*Swindon T*	6	2	**6**	**2**
2015–16	*Bradford C*	10	1	**10**	**1**
2016–17	Oxford U	13	3		
2017–18	Oxford U	37	10	**50**	**13**
2018–19	Grimsby T	36	11	**36**	**11**

VERNAM, Charles (F) **57** **5**

b. 8-10-96

2013–14	Derby Co	0	0		
2014–15	Derby Co	0	0		
2015–16	Derby Co	0	0		
2016	*Vestmannaeyjar*	9	1	**9**	**1**
2016–17	Derby Co	0	0		
2016–17	*Coventry C*	4	0	**4**	**0**
2017–18	Derby Co	0	0		
2017–18	*Grimsby T*	9	1		
2018–19	Grimsby T	35	3	**44**	**4**

WELSH, John (M) **355** **17**

H: 5 7 W: 12 02 b.Liverpool 10-1-84

Internationals: England U16, U19, U20, U21.

2000–01	Liverpool	0	0		
2001–02	Liverpool	0	0		
2002–03	Liverpool	0	0		
2003–04	Liverpool	1	0		
2004–05	Liverpool	3	0		
2005–06	Liverpool	0	0	**4**	**0**
2005–06	Hull C	32	2		
2006–07	Hull C	18	1		
2007–08	Hull C	0	0		
2007–08	*Chester C*	6	0	**6**	**0**
2008–09	Hull C	0	0	**50**	**3**
2008–09	*Carlisle U*	4	0	**4**	**0**
2008–09	*Bury*	5	0	**5**	**0**
2009–10	Tranmere R	45	4		
2010–11	Tranmere R	41	4		
2011–12	Tranmere R	44	3	**130**	**11**
2012–13	Preston NE	36	1		
2013–14	Preston NE	36	2		
2014–15	Preston NE	32	0		
2015–16	Preston NE	24	0		
2016–17	Preston NE	6	0		
2017–18	Preston NE	9	0	**143**	**3**
2018–19	Grimsby T	13	0	**13**	**0**

WHITMORE, Alex (D) **89** **2**

H: 5 11 W: 10 10 b.Newcastle upon Tyne 7-9-95

2016–17	Burnley	0	0		
2016–17	*Morecambe*	35	0	**35**	**0**
2017–18	Burnley	0	0		
2017–18	*Bury*	8	0	**8**	**0**
2017–18	Chesterfield	15	1	**15**	**1**
2018–19	Grimsby T	31	1	**31**	**1**

WOOLFORD, Martyn (M) **355** **37**

H: 6 0 W: 11 09 b.Castleford 13-10-85

Internationals: England C.

2008–09	Scunthorpe U	39	4		
2009–10	Scunthorpe U	40	5		
2010–11	Scunthorpe U	24	6	**103**	**15**
2010–11	Bristol C	15	0		
2011–12	Bristol C	25	1		
2012–13	Bristol C	15	3	**55**	**4**
2012–13	Millwall	15	1		
2013–14	Millwall	40	7		
2014–15	Millwall	38	3	**93**	**11**
2015–16	Sheffield U	28	1	**28**	**1**
2016–17	Fleetwood T	10	1	**10**	**1**
2017–18	Grimsby T	31	2		
2018–19	Grimsby T	35	3	**66**	**5**

WRIGHT, Max (M) **2** **0**

b.Grimsby 6-4-98

2016–17	Grimsby T	0	0		
2017–18	Grimsby T	0	0		
2018–19	Grimsby T	2	0	**2**	**0**

Players retained or with offer of contract

Whitehouse, Elliott Mark.

Scholars

Banks, Hugo James; Buckley, Brandon Adam; Burrell, Rumarn Kameron-Scott; Curran, Jock Alan; Derrick, Lewis Jack; Hope, Joseph Alexander; Jamieson, Thomas Andrew; McPherson, Brandon Samuel; Owoeye, Ayodeji Abel Bamidele; Painter, Cameron Nathan; Powles, Emil Kendal; Poynter, Conley Kevin; Richardson, Kyle William; Saunders, Oliver Matthew; Stead, Lennon Oren.

HUDDERSFIELD T (39)

AHEARNE-GRANT, Karlan (F) 111 29
H: 6 0 b.London 19-12-97
Internationals: England U17, U18, U19.

2014–15	Charlton Ath	5	0		
2015–16	Charlton Ath	17	1		
2015–16	*Cambridge U*	3	0	**3**	**0**
2016–17	Charlton Ath	8	0		
2017–18	Charlton Ath	22	1		
2017–18	*Crawley T*	15	9	**15**	**9**
2018–19	Charlton Ath	28	14	**80**	**16**
2018–19	Huddersfield T	13	4	**13**	**4**

BACUNA, Juninho (F) 103 3
H: 6 1 W: 12 04 b.Groningen 7-8-97
Internationals: Netherlands U18, U20, U21.

2014–15	Groningen	11	0		
2015–16	Groningen	14	0		
2016–17	Groningen	24	1		
2017–18	Groningen	33	1	**82**	**2**
2018–19	Huddersfield T	21	1	**21**	**1**

BILLING, Phillip (M) 81 5
H: 6 4 W: 12 08 b. 11-6-96
Internationals: Denmark U19, U21.

2013–14	Huddersfield T	1	0		
2014–15	Huddersfield T	0	0		
2015–16	Huddersfield T	13	1		
2016–17	Huddersfield T	24	2		
2017–18	Huddersfield T	16	0		
2018–19	Huddersfield T	27	2	**81**	**5**

BROWN, Jaden (D) 0 0
Internationals: England U16, U17, U18, U19.
From Tottenham H.

2018–19	Huddersfield T	0	0
2018–19	*Exeter C*	0	0

COLEMAN, Joel (G) 65 0
H: 6 6 W: 12 13 b.Bolton 26-9-95

2013–14	Oldham Ath	0	0		
2014–15	Oldham Ath	11	0		
2015–16	Oldham Ath	32	0	**43**	**0**
2016–17	Huddersfield T	5	0		
2017–18	Huddersfield T	0	0		
2018–19	Huddersfield T	1	0	**6**	**0**
2018–19	*Shrewsbury T*	16	0	**16**	**0**

DALY, Matty (M) 2 0
H: 5 9 b. 10-3-01
Internationals: England U17, U18.

2018–19	Huddersfield T	2	0	**2**	**0**

DEPOITRE, Laurent (F) 230 67
H: 6 3 W: 14 05 b.Tournai 7-12-88
Internationals: Belgium Full caps.

2010–11	Aalst	14	8		
2011–12	Aalst	33	8	**47**	**16**
2012–13	Oostende	34	14		
2013–14	Oostende	28	6	**62**	**20**
2014–15	Gent	29	12		
2015–16	Gent	27	12		
2016–17	Gent	2	0	**58**	**24**
2016–17	Porto	7	1	**7**	**1**
2017–18	Huddersfield T	33	6		
2018–19	Huddersfield T	23	0	**56**	**6**

DIAKHABY, Adama (F) 59 6
H: 6 0 W: 10 03 b.Ajaccio 5-7-96
Internationals: France U21.
From Caen.

2015–16	Rennes	0	0		
2016–17	Rennes	25	4	**25**	**4**
2017–18	Monaco	22	2	**22**	**2**
2018–19	Huddersfield T	12	0	**12**	**0**

DUHANEY, Demeaco (D) 1 0
H: 5 11 W: 11 00 b.Manchester 13-10-98
Internationals: England U18, U20.

2017–18	Manchester C	0	0		
2018–19	Huddersfield T	1	0	**1**	**0**

DURM, Erik (D) 92 2
H: 6 0 W: 10 01 b.Pirmasens 12-5-92
Internationals: Germany U19, U20, U21, Full caps.

2010–11	Mainz	0	0		
2011–12	Mainz	0	0		
2012–13	Borussia Dortmund	0	0		
2013–14	Borussia Dortmund	19	0		
2014–15	Borussia Dortmund	18	1		
2015–16	Borussia Dortmund	14	1		
2016–17	Borussia Dortmund	13	0		
2017–18	Borussia Dortmund	0	0	**64**	**2**
2018–19	Huddersfield T	28	0	**28**	**0**

HADERGJONAJ, Florent (D) 145 2
H: 6 0 W: 11 11 b.Langnau 31-7-94
Internationals: Switzerland U20, U21, Full caps.

2013–14	Young Boys	11	1		
2014–15	Young Boys	26	0		
2015–16	Young Boys	32	0		
2016–17	Young Boys	2	0	**71**	**1**
2016–17	Ingolstadt 04	25	1	**25**	**1**
2017–18	FC Ingolstadt	2	0	**2**	**0**
2017–18	*Huddersfield T*	23	0		
2018–19	Huddersfield T	24	0	**47**	**0**

HAMER, Ben (G) 230 0
H: 5 11 W: 12 04 b.Chard 20-11-87

2006–07	Reading	0	0		
2007–08	Reading	0	0		
2007–08	*Brentford*	20	0		
2008–09	Reading	0	0		
2008–09	*Brentford*	45	0		
2009–10	Reading	0	0		
2010–11	Reading	0	0		
2010–11	*Brentford*	10	0	**75**	**0**
2010–11	*Exeter C*	18	0	**18**	**0**
2011–12	Charlton Ath	41	0		
2012–13	Charlton Ath	41	0		
2013–14	Charlton Ath	32	0	**114**	**0**
2014–15	Leicester C	8	0		
2015–16	Leicester C	0	0		
2015–16	*Bristol C*	4	0	**4**	**0**
2016–17	Leicester C	0	0		
2017–18	Leicester C	4	0	**12**	**0**
2018–19	Huddersfield T	7	0	**7**	**0**

HOGG, Jonathan (M) 285 2
H: 5 7 W: 10 05 b.Middlesbrough 6-12-88

2007–08	Aston Villa	0	0		
2008–09	Aston Villa	0	0		
2009–10	Aston Villa	0	0		
2009–10	*Darlington*	5	1	**5**	**1**
2010–11	Aston Villa	5	0		
2010–11	*Portsmouth*	19	0	**19**	**0**
2011–12	Aston Villa	0	0	**5**	**0**
2011–12	Watford	40	0		
2012–13	Watford	38	0	**78**	**0**
2013–14	Huddersfield T	34	0		
2014–15	Huddersfield T	26	0		
2015–16	Huddersfield T	22	0		
2016–17	Huddersfield T	37	1		
2017–18	Huddersfield T	30	0		
2018–19	Huddersfield T	29	0	**178**	**1**

JORGENSEN, Mathias Zanka (D) 261 15
H: 6 3 W: 12 06 b.Copenhagen 23-4-90
Internationals: Denmark U16, U17, U18, U21, Full caps.

2007–08	Copenhagen	12	1		
2008–09	Copenhagen	20	0		
2009–10	Copenhagen	24	4		
2010–11	Copenhagen	25	1		
2011–12	Copenhagen	11	0		
2012–13	PSV Eindhoven	5	2		
2013–14	PSV Eindhoven	9	0	**14**	**2**
2014–15	Copenhagen	29	1		
2015–16	Copenhagen	31	3		
2016–17	Copenhagen	33	0	**185**	**10**
2017–18	Huddersfield T	38	0		
2018–19	Huddersfield T	24	3	**62**	**3**

KACHUNGA, Elias (F) 190 38
H: 5 9 W: 10 01 b.Cologne 22-4-92
Internationals: Germany U19, U21, DR Congo Full caps.

2009–10	Borussia M'gladbach	0	0		
2010–11	Borussia M'gladbach	2	0		
2011–12	Borussia M'gladbach	0	0		
2011–12	*Osnabruck*	17	10	**17**	**10**
2012–13	Borussia M'gladbach	0	0	**2**	**0**
2012–13	*Hertha Berlin*	2	0	**2**	**0**
2012–13	*Paderborn*	13	3		
2013–14	Paderborn	33	6		
2014–15	Paderborn	32	6	**78**	**15**
2015–16	Ingolstadt	10	0		
2016–17	Ingolstadt	0	0	**10**	**0**
2016–17	*Huddersfield T*	42	12		
2017–18	Huddersfield T	19	1		
2018–19	Huddersfield T	20	0	**81**	**13**

KONGOLO, Terence (D) 154 2
H: 6 0 W: 11 00 b.Rotterdam 14-2-94
Internationals: Netherlands U16, U17, U18, U19, U20, U21, Full caps.

2011–12	Feyenoord	1	0		
2012–13	Feyenoord	5	0		
2013–14	Feyenoord	17	0		
2014–15	Feyenoord	31	0		
2015–16	Feyenoord	29	0		
2016–17	Feyenoord	23	1	**106**	**1**
2017–18	Monaco	3	0	**3**	**0**
2017–18	*Huddersfield T*	13	0		
2018–19	Huddersfield T	32	1	**45**	**1**

LOSSL, Jonas (G) 290 0
H: 6 5 W: 14 00 b.Kolding 1-2-89
Internationals: Denmark U17, U18, U19, U20, U21, Full caps.

2009–10	Midtjylland	12	0		
2010–11	Midtjylland	30	0		
2011–12	Midtjylland	25	0		
2012–13	Midtjylland	27	0		
2013–14	Midtjylland	33	0	**127**	**0**
2014–15	Guingamp	30	0		
2015–16	Guingamp	37	0	**67**	**0**
2016–17	Mainz	27	0		
2017–18	Mainz	0	0	**27**	**0**
2017–18	*Huddersfield T*	38	0		
2018–19	Huddersfield T	31	0	**69**	**0**

LOWE, Chris (D) 283 15
H: 5 7 W: 10 10 b.Plauen 16-4-89

2008–09	Chemnitzer	17	1		
2009–10	Chemnitzer	34	4		
2010–11	Chemnitzer	33	4	**84**	**9**
2011–12	Borussia Dortmund	7	0		
2012–13	Borussia Dortmund	0	0	**7**	**0**
2012–13	Kaiserslauten	14	0		
2013–14	Kaiserslauten	29	1		
2014–15	Kaiserslauten	33	2		
2015–16	Kaiserslauten	23	1	**99**	**4**
2016–17	Huddersfield T	41	2		
2017–18	Huddersfield T	23	0		
2018–19	Huddersfield T	29	0	**93**	**2**

MBENZA, Isaac (F) 145 20
H: 6 2 W: 12 02 b.Saint-Denis 8-3-96
Internationals: Belgium U17, U19, U21.

2014–15	Valenciennes	13	1		
2015–16	Valenciennes	35	6	**48**	**7**
2016–17	Standard Liege	21	1	**21**	**1**
2016–17	Montpellier	16	3		
2017–18	Montpellier	38	8		
2018–19	Montpellier	0	0	**54**	**11**

On loan from Montpellier.

2018–19	Huddersfield T	22	1	**22**	**1**

MOOY, Aaron (M) 233 34
H: 5 9 W: 10 10 b.Sydney 15-9-90
Internationals: Australia U20, U23, Full caps.

2009–10	Bolton W	0	0		
2010–11	St Mirren	13	0		
2011–12	St Mirren	8	1	**21**	**1**
2012–13	Western Sydney W	23	1		
2013–14	Western Sydney W	26	3	**49**	**4**
2014–15	Melbourne C	27	7		
2015–16	Melbourne C	26	11	**53**	**18**
2016–17	Manchester C	0	0		
2016–17	*Huddersfield T*	45	4		
2017–18	Huddersfield T	36	4		
2018–19	Huddersfield T	29	3	**110**	**11**

MOUNIE, Steve (F) 128 34
H: 6 3 W: 12 08 b.Parakou 29-9-94
Internationals: Benin Full caps.

2014–15	Montpellier	0	0		
2015–16	Montpellier	2	0		
2015–16	*Nimes*	32	11	**32**	**11**
2016–17	Montpellier	35	14	**37**	**14**
2017–18	Huddersfield T	28	7		
2018–19	Huddersfield T	31	2	**59**	**9**

O'BRIEN, Lewis (M) 40 4
H: 5 8 W: 9 13 b.Colchester 14-10-98

2017–18	Huddersfield T	0	0		
2018–19	Huddersfield T	0	0		
2018–19	*Bradford C*	40	4	**40**	**4**

PAYNE, Jack (M) 185 30
H: 5 5 W: 9 06 b.Tower Hamlets 25-10-94

2013–14	Southend U	11	0		
2014–15	Southend U	34	6		
2015–16	Southend U	32	9	**77**	**15**
2016–17	Huddersfield T	23	2		
2017–18	Huddersfield T	0	0		
2017–18	*Oxford U*	28	3	**28**	**3**
2017–18	*Blackburn R*	18	1	**18**	**1**
2018–19	Huddersfield T	0	0	**23**	**2**
2018–19	*Bradford C*	39	9	**39**	**9**

PRITCHARD, Alex (M) 173 28
H: 5 7 W: 9 11 b.Grays 3-5-93
Internationals: England U20, U21.

2011–12	Tottenham H	0	0		
2012–13	Tottenham H	0	0		
2012–13	*Peterborough U*	6	0	**6**	**0**

2013–14	Tottenham H	1	0		
2013–14	*Swindon T*	36	6	**36**	**6**
2014–15	Tottenham H	0	0		
2014–15	*Brentford*	45	12	**45**	**12**
2015–16	Tottenham H	1	0	**2**	**0**
2015–16	*WBA*	2	0	**2**	**0**
2016–17	Norwich C	30	6		
2017–18	Norwich C	8	1	**38**	**7**
2017–18	Huddersfield T	14	1		
2018–19	Huddersfield T	30	2	**44**	**3**

PYKE, Rekeil (F) **25** **0**
H: 5 10 W: 10 03 b. 1-9-97

2016–17	Huddersfield T	0	0		
2016–17	*Colchester U*	12	0	**12**	**0**
2017–18	Huddersfield T	0	0		
2017–18	*Port Vale*	7	0	**7**	**0**
2018–19	Huddersfield T	0	0		
2018–19	*Rochdale*	6	0	**6**	**0**

QUANER, Collin (F) **167** **23**
H: 6 3 W: 12 11 b.Dusseldorf 18-6-91
Internationals: Germany U20.
From Fortuna Dusseldorf.

2010–11	Armenia Bielefeld	17	1	**17**	**1**
2011–12	Ingolstadt 04	15	1		
2012–13	Ingolstadt 04	1	0		
2013–14	Ingolstadt 04	11	1	**27**	**2**
2013–14	*Rostock*	7	0	**7**	**0**
2014–15	Aalen	27	6	**27**	**6**
2015–16	Union Berlin	15	1		
2016–17	Union Berlin	14	7	**29**	**8**
2016–17	Huddersfield T	16	2		
2017–18	Huddersfield T	26	0		
2018–19	Huddersfield T	2	0	**44**	**2**
2018–19	*Ipswich T*	16	4	**16**	**4**

ROWE, Aaron (M) **2** **0**
b. 7-9-00

2018–19	Huddersfield T	2	0	**2**	**0**

SABIRI, Abdelhamid (M) **46** **23**
H: 6 0 W: 12 08 b.Goulmima 28-11-96
Internationals: Germany U21.

2015–16	Sportfreunde Siegen3018			**30**	**18**
2016–17	Nuremburg	9	5	**9**	**5**
2017–18	Nurnberg	0	0		
2017–18	Huddersfield T	5	0		
2018–19	Huddersfield T	2	0	**7**	**0**

SCHINDLER, Christopher (D) **270** **7**
H: 6 2 W: 12 02 b.Munich 29-4-90
Internationals: Germany U21.

2009–10	1860 Munich	0	0		
2010–11	1860 Munich	16	1		
2011–12	1860 Munich	30	1		
2012–13	1860 Munich	18	0		
2013–14	1860 Munich	26	0		
2014–15	1860 Munich	29	1		
2015–16	1860 Munich	33	1	**152**	**4**
2016–17	Huddersfield T	44	2		
2017–18	Huddersfield T	37	0		
2018–19	Huddersfield T	37	1	**118**	**3**

SCHOFIELD, Ryan (G) **17** **0**
H: 6 3 W: 11 00 b.Huddersfield 11-12-99
Internationals: England U18, U19, U20.

2018–19	Huddersfield T	0	0		
2018–19	*Notts Co*	17	0	**17**	**0**

SMITH, Tommy (D) **182** **4**
H: 6 1 W: 13 02 b.Warrington 14-4-92

2012–13	Huddersfield T	0	0		
2013–14	Huddersfield T	24	0		
2014–15	Huddersfield T	41	0		
2015–16	Huddersfield T	36	0		
2016–17	Huddersfield T	42	4		
2017–18	Huddersfield T	24	0		
2018–19	Huddersfield T	15	0	**182**	**4**

SOBHI, Ramadan (F) **116** **15**
b.Cairo 27-1-97
Internationals: Egypt U17, U20, U23, Full caps.

2013–14	Al Ahly	3	1		
2014–15	Al Ahly	24	5		
2015–16	Al Ahly	28	5		
2016–17	Stoke C	17	0		
2017–18	Stoke C	24	2	**41**	**2**
2018–19	Huddersfield T	4	0	**4**	**0**
2018–19	*Al Ahly*	16	2	**71**	**13**

STANKOVIC, Jon (M) **36** **1**
H: 6 3 W: 12 04 b.Ljubijana 14-1-96
Internationals: Slovenia U16, U17, U18, U19, U21.

2012–13	Domzale	6	0		
2013–14	Domzale	12	0		
2014–15	Domzale	0	0		
2015–16	Domzale	0	0	**18**	**0**
2016–17	Huddersfield T	7	0		
2017–18	Huddersfield T	0	0		
2018–19	Huddersfield T	11	1	**18**	**1**

VAN LA PARRA, Rajiv (M) **250** **23**
H: 5 11 W: 11 05 b.Rotterdam 4-6-91
Internationals: Netherlands, U17, U19, U21.

2008–09	Caan	2	0		
2009–10	Caan	8	1		
2010–11	Caan	6	0	**16**	**1**
2011–12	Heerenveen	23	4		
2012–13	Heerenveen	31	5		
2013–14	Heerenveen	32	5	**86**	**14**
2014–15	Wolverhampton W	40	1		
2015–16	Wolverhampton W	13	0	**53**	**1**
2015–16	*Brighton & HA*	6	2	**6**	**2**
2015–16	Huddersfield T	8	0		
2016–17	Huddersfield T	40	2		
2017–18	Huddersfield T	33	3		
2018–19	Huddersfield T	5	0	**86**	**5**
2018–19	*Middlesbrough*	3	0	**3**	**0**

WILLIAMS, Daniel (M) **218** **14**
H: 6 0 W: 11 12 b.Karlsruhe 8-3-89
Internationals: USA Full caps.

2009–10	SC Freiburg	5	0		
2010–11	SC Freiburg	7	0		
2011–12	SC Freiburg	1	0	**13**	**0**
2011–12	Hoffenheim	24	0		
2012–13	Hoffenheim	21	1	**45**	**1**
2013–14	Reading	30	3		
2014–15	Reading	25	1		
2015–16	Reading	39	5		
2016–17	Reading	41	4	**135**	**13**
2017–18	Huddersfield T	20	0		
2018–19	Huddersfield T	5	0	**25**	**0**

Players retained or with offer of contract
Chapman, Jacob Anthony; Crichlow-Noble, Romoney; Edmonds-Green, Rarmani River Miguel Joseph; High, Scott John; Marriott, Isaac William; Mewitt, Luke Edward; Obiero, Micah Obonyo Dulo; Tear, Darren Dominic.

Scholars
Alfieri, George Anthony; Annakin, Taylor William Gerald; Austerfield, Joshua James; Bamford, Thomas Samuel; Bell, Thomas James; Bellagambi, Giosue Ebong; Danaher, George Charles; Davison-Hale, Harrison William Roger; Dihby, Mohammed; Dyson, Oliver Jason Lee; Eli, Jordan James Raphael; Elliott, Christopher Tchanga; Gibson, Samuel Joseph; Harratt, Kian Shay; Headley, Jaheim Anthony; Ijiwole, Andrew Jose; Jackson, Ben Joseph; Kherbouche, Nasim; Meeson, Seth David; Mills, Benjamin Peter; Mintus, Darnell Dantae Bowers; O'Malley, Mason Lewis; Olagunju, Mustapha Oluwatosin; Raymond, Dahomey Asher; Sharrock-Peplow, Samuel Jacob; Thompson, Oran James; Thompson, Remi Kai.

HULL C (40)

BATTY, Daniel (D) **28** **0**
b.Featherstone 10-12-97

2016–17	Hull C	0	0		
2017–18	Hull C	1	0		
2018–19	Hull C	27	0	**28**	**0**

BOWEN, Jarrod (F) **95** **36**
b.Leominster 1-1-96

2014–15	Hull C	0	0		
2015–16	Hull C	0	0		
2016–17	Hull C	7	0		
2017–18	Hull C	42	14		
2018–19	Hull C	46	22	**95**	**36**

BURKE, Reece (D) **108** **4**
H: 6 2 W: 12 11 b.London 2-9-96
Internationals: England U18, U19, U20.

2013–14	West Ham U	0	0		
2014–15	West Ham U	5	0		
2015–16	West Ham U	0	0		
2015–16	*Bradford C*	34	2	**34**	**2**
2016–17	West Ham U	0	0		
2016–17	*Wigan Ath*	10	1	**10**	**1**
2017–18	West Ham U	0	0	**5**	**0**
2017–18	*Bolton W*	25	1	**25**	**1**
2018–19	Hull C	34	0	**34**	**0**

CAMPBELL, Frazier (F) **271** **58**
H: 5 11 W: 12 04 b.Huddersfield 13-9-87
Internationals: England U16, U17, U18, U21, Full caps.

2005–06	Manchester U	0	0		
2006–07	Manchester U	0	0		
2007–08	Manchester U	1	0		
2007–08	*Hull C*	34	15		
2008–09	Manchester U	1	0		
2008–09	*Tottenham H*	10	1	**10**	**1**
2009–10	Manchester U	0	0	**2**	**0**
2009–10	Sunderland	31	4		
2010–11	Sunderland	3	0		
2011–12	Sunderland	12	1		
2012–13	Sunderland	12	1	**58**	**6**
2012–13	Cardiff C	12	7		
2013–14	Cardiff C	37	6	**49**	**13**
2014–15	Crystal Palace	20	4		
2015–16	Crystal Palace	11	0		
2016–17	Crystal Palace	12	1	**43**	**5**
2017–18	Hull C	36	6		
2018–19	Hull C	39	12	**109**	**33**

CURRY, Adam (D) **0** **0**
b. 21-5-97
From South Shields.

2016–17	Hull C	0	0		
2017–18	Hull C	0	0		
2018–19	Hull C	0	0		

DE WIJS, Jordy (D) **68** **1**
H: 6 2 W: 13 03 b.Vlijmen 8-1-95
Internationals: Netherlands U17, U18, U20, U21.

2014–15	PSV Eindhoven	0	0		
2015–16	PSV Eindhoven	1	0		
2016–17	PSV Eindhoven	0	0		
2016–17	*Excelsior*	15	0		
2017–18	PSV Eindhoven	1	0	**2**	**0**
2017–18	*Excelsior*	19	0	**34**	**0**
2018–19	Hull C	32	1	**32**	**1**

DICKO, Nouha (M) **227** **63**
H: 5 8 W: 11 00 b.Paris 14-5-92
Internationals: Mali Full caps.

2009–10	Strasbourg B	18	4		
2010–11	Strasbourg B	24	8	**42**	**12**
2010–11	Strasbourg	3	0	**3**	**0**
2011–12	Wigan Ath	0	0		
2011–12	*Blackpool*	10	4		
2012–13	Wigan Ath	0	0		
2012–13	*Blackpool*	22	5	**32**	**9**
2012–13	*Wolverhampton W*	4	1		
2013–14	Wigan Ath	0	0		
2013–14	*Rotherham U*	5	5	**5**	**5**
2013–14	Wolverhampton W	19	12		
2014–15	Wolverhampton W	37	14		
2015–16	Wolverhampton W	5	0		
2016–17	Wolverhampton W	30	3		
2017–18	Wolverhampton W	5	1	**100**	**31**
2017–18	Hull C	29	4		
2018–19	Hull C	16	2	**45**	**6**

EVANDRO, Goebel (M) **302** **47**
H: 5 10 W: 9 11 b.Blumenau 23-8-86
Internationals: Brazil U20.

2005	Atletico Paranaense	28	4		
2006	Atletico Paranaense	16	2		
2007	Atletico Paranaense	15	1		
2008	Atletico Paranaense	0	0		
2008	*Goias*	3	0	**3**	**0**
2008	*Palmeiras*	26	0		
2009	Atletico Paranaense	0	0		
2009	*Palmeiras*	8	2	**34**	**2**
2009	*Atletico Mineiro*	28	3		
2010	Atletico Paranaense	0	0	**59**	**7**
2010	*Atletico Mineiro*	2	0	**30**	**3**
2010	*Vitoria*	7	2	**7**	**2**
2010–11	Red Star Belgrade	9	5		
2011–12	Red Star Belgrade	25	8		
2012–13	Red Star Belgrade	1	0	**35**	**13**
2012–13	Estoril	25	3		
2013–14	Estoril	28	11	**53**	**14**
2014–15	Porto	21	1		
2015–16	Porto	11	1		
2016–17	Porto	7	0	**39**	**2**
2016–17	Hull C	11	0		
2017–18	Hull C	8	1		
2018–19	Hull C	23	3	**42**	**4**

FLEMING, Brandon (D) **4** **0**
b.Dewsbury 3-12-99

2017–18	Hull C	0	0		
2018–19	Hull C	4	0	**4**	**0**

GROSICKI, Kamil (M) **362 65**
H: 5 11 W: 12 04 b.Szczecin 8-6-88
Internationals: Poland U19, U21, Full caps.

2005–06	Pognon Szczecin	2	0		
2006–07	Pognon Szczecin	21	2	**23**	**2**
2007–08	Legia Warsaw	11	1		
2007–08	Sion	8	2	**8**	**2**
2008–09	Legia Warsaw	0	0	**11**	**1**
2008–09	Jagiellonia	13	4		
2009–10	Jagiellonia	30	4		
2010–11	Jagiellonia	15	6	**58**	**14**
2010–11	Sivasspor	17	6		
2011–12	Sivasspor	40	7		
2012–13	Sivasspor	28	2		
2013–14	Sivasspor	5	0	**90**	**15**
2013–14	Rennes	13	0		
2014–15	Rennes	19	0		
2015–16	Rennes	33	9		
2016–17	Rennes	16	4	**81**	**13**
2016–17	Hull C	15	0		
2017–18	Hull C	37	9		
2018–19	Hull C	39	9	**91**	**18**

HENRIKSEN, Markus (M) **271 41**
H: 6 2 W: 13 05 b.Trondheim 25-7-92
Internationals: Norway U16, U17, U18, U19, U21, U23, Full caps.

2009	Rosenborg	3	0		
2010	Rosenborg	28	7		
2011	Rosenborg	29	3		
2012	Rosenborg	18	1	**78**	**11**
2012–13	AZ Alkmaar	29	3		
2013–14	AZ Alkmaar	26	2		
2014–15	AZ Alkmaar	22	7		
2015–16	AZ Alkmaar	28	12		
2016–17	AZ Alkmaar	3	2	**108**	**26**
2016–17	Hull C	15	0		
2017–18	Hull C	31	2		
2018–19	Hull C	39	2	**85**	**4**

IRVINE, Jackson (M) **209 24**
H: 5 10 W: 11 00 b.Melbourne 7-3-93
Internationals: Scotland U19. Australia U20, U23, Full caps.

2012–13	Celtic	1	0		
2013–14	Celtic	0	0		
2013–14	*Kilmarnock*	27	1	**27**	**1**
2014–15	Celtic	0	0	**1**	**0**
2014–15	*Ross Co*	28	2		
2015–16	Ross Co	36	2	**64**	**4**
2016–17	Burton Alb	42	10		
2017–18	Burton Alb	3	1	**45**	**11**
2017–18	Hull C	34	2		
2018–19	Hull C	38	6	**72**	**8**

KEANE, Will (F) **82 8**
H: 6 2 W: 11 05 b.Stockport 11-1-93
Internationals: England U16, U17, U19, U20, U21.

2009–10	Manchester U	0	0		
2010–11	Manchester U	0	0		
2011–12	Manchester U	1	0		
2012–13	Manchester U	0	0		
2013–14	Manchester U	0	0		
2013–14	*Wigan Ath*	4	0	**4**	**0**
2013–14	*QPR*	10	0	**10**	**0**
2014–15	Manchester U	0	0		
2014–15	*Sheffield W*	13	3	**13**	**3**
2015–16	Manchester U	1	0		
2015–16	*Preston NE*	20	1	**20**	**1**
2016–17	Manchester U	0	0	**2**	**0**
2016–17	Hull C	5	0		
2017–18	Hull C	9	1		
2018–19	Hull C	8	0	**22**	**1**
2018–19	*Ipswich T*	11	3	**11**	**3**

KINGSLEY, Stephen (D) **166 1**
H: 5 10 W: 10 09 b.Stirling 23-7-94
Internationals: Scotland U18, U19, U21, Full caps.

2010–11	Falkirk	3	0		
2011–12	Falkirk	15	0		
2012–13	Falkirk	35	0		
2013–14	Falkirk	35	1	**88**	**1**
2014–15	Swansea C	0	0		
2014–15	*Yeovil T*	12	0	**12**	**0**
2015–16	Swansea C	4	0		
2015–16	*Crewe Alex*	12	0	**12**	**0**
2016–17	Swansea C	13	0	**17**	**0**
2017–18	Hull C	11	0		
2018–19	Hull C	26	0	**37**	**0**

LEWIS-POTTER, Keane (F) **0 0**
b. 22-2-01

2018–19	Hull C	0	0		

LICHAJ, Eric (D) **275 6**
H: 5 11 W: 12 07 b.Chicago 17-11-88
Internationals: USA U17, U20, Full caps.

2007–08	Aston Villa	0	0		
2008–09	Aston Villa	0	0		
2009–10	Aston Villa	0	0		
2009–10	*Lincoln C*	6	0	**6**	**0**
2009–10	*Leyton Orient*	9	1	**9**	**1**
2010–11	Aston Villa	5	0		
2010–11	*Leeds U*	16	0	**16**	**0**
2011–12	Aston Villa	10	1		
2012–13	Aston Villa	17	0	**32**	**1**
2013–14	Nottingham F	24	0		
2014–15	Nottingham F	42	0		
2015–16	Nottingham F	43	1		
2016–17	Nottingham F	41	2		
2017–18	Nottingham F	23	1	**173**	**4**
2018–19	Hull C	39	0	**39**	**0**

LONG, George (G) **172 0**
H: 6 0 W: 12 05 b.Sheffield 5-11-93
Internationals: England U18, U20.

2010–11	Sheffield U	1	0		
2011–12	Sheffield U	2	0		
2012–13	Sheffield U	36	0		
2013–14	Sheffield U	27	0		
2014–15	Sheffield U	0	0		
2014–15	*Oxford U*	10	0	**10**	**0**
2014–15	*Motherwell*	13	0	**13**	**0**
2015–16	Sheffield U	31	0		
2016–17	Sheffield U	3	0		
2017–18	Sheffield U	0	0	**100**	**0**
2017–18	*AFC Wimbledon*	45	0	**45**	**0**
2018–19	Hull C	4	0	**4**	**0**

MACDONALD, Angus (D) **83 1**
H: 6 0 W: 11 00 b.Winchester 15-10-92
Internationals: England C, U16, U19.

2011–12	Reading	0	0		
2011–12	*Torquay U*	2	0		
2012–13	Reading	0	0		
2012–13	*AFC Wimbledon*	4	0	**4**	**0**
2012–13	*Torquay U*	14	0	**16**	**0**

From Salisbury C, Torquay U.

2016–17	Barnsley	39	1		
2017–18	Barnsley	11	0	**50**	**1**
2017–18	Hull C	12	0		
2018–19	Hull C	1	0	**13**	**0**

MARSHALL, David (G) **454 0**
H: 6 3 W: 13 04 b.Glasgow 5-3-85
Internationals: Scotland Youth, U21, B, Full caps.

2003–04	Celtic	11	0		
2004–05	Celtic	18	0		
2005–06	Celtic	4	0		
2006–07	Celtic	2	0	**35**	**0**
2006–07	Norwich C	2	0		
2007–08	Norwich C	46	0		
2008–09	Norwich C	46	0	**94**	**0**
2008–09	Cardiff C	0	0		
2009–10	Cardiff C	43	0		
2010–11	Cardiff C	11	0		
2011–12	Cardiff C	45	0		
2012–13	Cardiff C	46	0		
2013–14	Cardiff C	37	0		
2014–15	Cardiff C	38	0		
2015–16	Cardiff C	40	0		
2016–17	Cardiff C	4	0	**264**	**0**
2016–17	Hull C	16	0		
2017–18	Hull C	2	0		
2018–19	Hull C	43	0	**61**	**0**

MAZUCH, Ondrej (D) **192 7**
H: 6 2 W: 13 12 b.Hodonin 15-3-89
Internationals: Czech Republic U16, U17, U19, U20, U21, Full caps.

2006–07	Brno	24	1	**24**	**1**
2007–08	Fiorentina	0	0		
2008–09	Fiorentina	0	0		
2009–10	Fiorentina	0	0		
2009–10	*Anderlecht*	30	4		
2010–11	Anderlecht	35	1	**65**	**5**
2011–12	Dnipro Dnipropetrovsk	10	0		
2012–13	Dnipro Dnipropetrovsk	19	0		
2013–14	Dnipro Dnipropetrovsk	26	0		
2014–15	Dnipro Dnipropetrovsk	10	0	**65**	**0**
2015–16	Sparta Prague	4	0		
2016–17	Sparta Prague	14	1	**18**	**1**
2017–18	Hull C	14	0		
2018–19	Hull C	6	0	**20**	**0**

McKENZIE, Robbie (M) **18 0**
b.Kingston upon Hull 25-9-98

2017–18	Hull C	0	0		
2018–19	Hull C	18	0	**18**	**0**

MILINKOVIC, Manuel David (M) **85 13**
H: 5 10 W: 11 00 b.Antibes 20-5-94

2014–15	Ternana	3	0	**3**	**0**
2015–16	Salernitana	9	0	**9**	**0**
2015–16	Genoa	0	0		
2015–16	*Virtus Lanciano*	7	0	**7**	**0**
2016–17	Genoa	0	0		
2016–17	*Messina*	34	7	**34**	**7**
2017–18	Genoa	0	0		
2017–18	*Hearts*	24	6	**24**	**6**
2018–19	Hull C	8	0	**8**	**0**

RIDGEWELL, Liam (D) **440 24**
H: 5 10 W: 10 03 b.Bexley 21-7-84
Internationals: England U19, U20, U21.

2001–02	Aston Villa	0	0		
2002–03	Aston Villa	0	0		
2002–03	*Bournemouth*	5	0	**5**	**0**
2003–04	Aston Villa	11	0		
2004–05	Aston Villa	15	0		
2005–06	Aston Villa	32	5		
2006–07	Aston Villa	21	1	**79**	**6**
2007–08	Birmingham C	35	1		
2008–09	Birmingham C	36	1		
2009–10	Birmingham C	31	3		
2010–11	Birmingham C	36	4		
2011–12	Birmingham C	14	0	**152**	**9**
2011–12	WBA	13	1		
2012–13	WBA	30	0		
2013–14	WBA	33	1	**76**	**2**
2014	Portland Timbers	15	2		
2014–15	*Wigan Ath*	6	0	**6**	**0**
2015	Portland Timbers	37	1		
2015–16	*Brighton & HA*	5	0	**5**	**0**
2016	Portland Timbers	22	1		
2017	Portland Timbers	17	3		
2018	Portland Timbers	19	0	**110**	**7**
2018–19	Hull C	7	0	**7**	**0**

RITSON, Lewis (D) **0 0**
b.South Shields 1-11-98

2017–18	Hull C	0	0		
2018–19	Hull C	0	0		

SHEAF, Max (M) **1 0**
b.Gravesend 10-3-00

2018–19	Hull C	1	0	**1**	**0**

STEWART, Kevin (D) **75 3**
H: 5 7 W: 11 06 b.Enfield 7-9-93

2012–13	Tottenham H	0	0		
2012–13	*Crewe Alex*	4	0		
2013–14	Crewe Alex	0	0	**4**	**0**
2014–15	Liverpool	0	0		
2014–15	*Cheltenham T*	4	1	**4**	**1**
2014–15	*Burton Alb*	7	2	**7**	**2**
2015–16	Liverpool	7	0		
2015–16	*Swindon T*	5	0	**5**	**0**
2016–17	Liverpool	4	0	**11**	**0**
2017–18	Hull C	17	0		
2018–19	Hull C	27	0	**44**	**0**

TORAL, Jon (M) **117 17**
H: 6 0 W: 12 07 b.Reus 5-2-95

2013–14	Arsenal	0	0		
2014–15	Arsenal	0	0		
2014–15	*Brentford*	34	6	**34**	**6**
2015–16	Arsenal	0	0		
2015–16	*Birmingham C*	36	8	**36**	**8**
2016–17	Arsenal	0	0		
2016–17	*Rangers*	12	2	**12**	**2**
2017–18	Hull C	27	1		
2018–19	Hull C	8	0	**35**	**1**

Players retained or with offer of contract

Andrew, Charlie Alfred; Chadwick, William Anthony; De, Wijs Jordy; Foulkes, Harrison Andrew; Greaves, Jacob John; Hamilton, Tyler Lee; Hickey, Jordan; Jacob, Matthew James; Mannion, William John; Salam, Ahmed Mamdoh Abdel.

Scholars

Adamson, Benjamin Peter; Bayram, Jake Thomas; Best, Thomas Steven Michael; Cartwright, Harvey Jay; Guilfoyle, Robert Patrick; Hawkins, Daniel Thomas; Nicholls, Matthew Jake; Robson, David Leslie; Rouse, Jay; Smith, Andrew John; Taylor, William Leeson; Thompson, Quinn; Wood, Harry.

IPSWICH T (41)

BIALKOWSKI, Bartosz (G) **283** **0**
H: 6 3 W: 12 10 b.Braniewo 6-7-87
Internationals: Poland U20, U21, Full caps.

2004–05	Gornik Zabrze	7	0	**7**	**0**
2005–06	Southampton	5	0		
2006–07	Southampton	8	0		
2007–08	Southampton	1	0		
2008–09	Southampton	0	0		
2009–10	Southampton	7	0		
2009–10	*Barnsley*	2	0	**2**	**0**
2010–11	Southampton	0	0		
2011–12	Southampton	1	0	**22**	**0**
2012–13	Notts Co	40	0		
2013–14	Notts Co	44	0	**84**	**0**
2014–15	Ipswich T	31	0		
2015–16	Ipswich T	20	0		
2016–17	Ipswich T	44	0		
2017–18	Ipswich T	45	0		
2018–19	Ipswich T	28	0	**168**	**0**

BISHOP, Teddy (M) **78** **1**
H: 5 11 W: 10 03 b.Cambridge 15-7-96

2013–14	Ipswich T	0	0		
2014–15	Ipswich T	33	1		
2015–16	Ipswich T	4	0		
2016–17	Ipswich T	19	0		
2017–18	Ipswich T	4	0		
2018–19	Ipswich T	18	0	**78**	**1**

BROWN, Kai (F) **0** **0**
b. 30-4-01

2018–19	Ipswich T	0	0		

CHAMBERS, Luke (D) **635** **33**
H: 6 1 W: 11 13 b.Kettering 29-8-85

2002–03	Northampton T	1	0		
2003–04	Northampton T	24	0		
2004–05	Northampton T	27	0		
2005–06	Northampton T	43	0		
2006–07	Northampton T	29	1	**124**	**1**
2006–07	Nottingham F	14	0		
2007–08	Nottingham F	42	6		
2008–09	Nottingham F	39	2		
2009–10	Nottingham F	23	3		
2010–11	Nottingham F	44	6		
2011–12	Nottingham F	43	0	**205**	**17**
2012–13	Ipswich T	44	3		
2013–14	Ipswich T	46	3		
2014–15	Ipswich T	45	1		
2015–16	Ipswich T	45	3		
2016–17	Ipswich T	46	4		
2017–18	Ipswich T	37	1		
2018–19	Ipswich T	43	0	**306**	**15**

COLLINS, James M (D) **351** **14**
H: 6 2 W: 14 05 b.Newport 23-8-83
Internationals: Wales U19, U20, U21, Full caps.

2000–01	Cardiff C	3	0		
2001–02	Cardiff C	7	1		
2002–03	Cardiff C	2	0		
2003–04	Cardiff C	20	1		
2004–05	Cardiff C	34	1	**66**	**3**
2005–06	West Ham U	14	2		
2006–07	West Ham U	16	0		
2007–08	West Ham U	3	0		
2008–09	West Ham U	18	0		
2009–10	West Ham U	3	0		
2009–10	Aston Villa	27	1		
2010–11	Aston Villa	32	3		
2011–12	Aston Villa	32	1	**91**	**5**
2012–13	West Ham U	29	0		
2013–14	West Ham U	24	1		
2014–15	West Ham U	27	0		
2015–16	West Ham U	19	0		
2016–17	West Ham U	22	2		
2017–18	West Ham U	13	1	**188**	**6**
2018–19	Ipswich T	6	0	**6**	**0**

DAWKINS, Simon (F) **156** **26**
H: 5 10 W: 11 01 b.Edgware 1-12-87
Internationals: Jamaica Full caps.

2005–06	Tottenham H	0	0		
2006–07	Tottenham H	0	0		
2007–08	Tottenham H	0	0		
2008–09	Tottenham H	0	0		
2008–09	*Leyton Orient*	11	0	**11**	**0**
2009–10	Tottenham H	0	0		
2010–11	Tottenham H	0	0		
2011	*San Jose Earthquakes*	26	6		
2011–12	Tottenham H	0	0		
2012	*San Jose Earthquakes*	29	8		
2012–13	Tottenham H	0	0		
2012–13	*Aston Villa*	4	0	**4**	**0**
2013–14	Tottenham H	0	0		
2013–14	Derby Co	26	4		
2014–15	Derby Co	34	3		
2015–16	Derby Co	0	0	**60**	**7**
2016	San Jose Earthquakes	24	5		
2017	San Jose Earthquakes	0	0	**79**	**19**
2018–19	Ipswich T	2	0	**2**	**0**

DONACIEN, Janoi (D) **171** **1**
H: 6 0 W: 11 11 b.St Lucia 3-11-93
Internationals: St Lucia Full caps.

2011–12	Aston Villa	0	0		
2012–13	Aston Villa	0	0		
2013–14	Aston Villa	0	0		
2014–15	Aston Villa	0	0		
2014–15	*Tranmere R*	31	0	**31**	**0**
2015–16	Aston Villa	0	0		
2015–16	*Wycombe W*	2	0	**2**	**0**
2015–16	*Newport Co*	29	0	**29**	**0**
2016–17	Accrington S	35	1		
2017–18	Accrington S	45	0		
2018–19	Ipswich T	10	0	**10**	**0**
2018–19	*Accrington S*	19	0	**99**	**1**

DOWNES, Flynn (M) **49** **1**
H: 5 8 W: 11 00 b. 20-1-99
Internationals: England U19, U20.

2016–17	Ipswich T	0	0		
2017–18	Ipswich T	10	0		
2017–18	*Luton T*	10	0	**10**	**0**
2018–19	Ipswich T	29	1	**39**	**1**

DOZZELL, Andre (M) **28** **2**
b.Ipswich 2-5-99
Internationals: England U16, U17, U18, U19, U20.

2015–16	Ipswich T	2	1		
2016–17	Ipswich T	6	0		
2017–18	Ipswich T	1	0		
2018–19	Ipswich T	19	1	**28**	**2**

EDWARDS, Gwion (M) **196** **31**
H: 5 9 W: 12 00 b.Carmarthen 1-3-93
Internationals: Wales U19, U21.

2011–12	Swansea C	0	0		
2012–13	Swansea C	0	0		
2012–13	*St Johnstone*	6	0		
2013–14	Swansea C	0	0		
2013–14	*St Johnstone*	13	0	**19**	**0**
2013–14	*Crawley T*	6	2		
2014–15	Crawley T	37	4		
2015–16	Crawley T	42	8	**85**	**14**
2016–17	Peterborough U	33	7		
2017–18	Peterborough U	26	4	**59**	**11**
2018–19	Ipswich T	33	6	**33**	**6**

EL MIZOUNI, Idris (M) **4** **0**
b. 26-9-00
Internationals: Tunisia U23, Tunisia Full caps.

2018–19	Ipswich T	4	0	**4**	**0**

EMMANUEL, Josh (D) **70** **0**
H: 5 11 W: 11 00 b.London 18-8-97

2015–16	Ipswich T	4	0		
2015–16	*Crawley T*	2	0	**2**	**0**
2016–17	Ipswich T	15	0		
2017–18	Ipswich T	0	0		
2017–18	*Rotherham U*	31	0	**31**	**0**
2018–19	Ipswich T	4	0	**23**	**0**
2018–19	*Shrewsbury T*	14	0	**14**	**0**

GERKEN, Dean (G) **273** **0**
H: 6 3 W: 12 08 b.Southend 22-5-85

2003–04	Colchester U	1	0		
2004–05	Colchester U	13	0		
2005–06	Colchester U	7	0		
2006–07	Colchester U	27	0		
2007–08	Colchester U	40	0		
2008–09	Colchester U	21	0	**109**	**0**
2008–09	*Darlington*	7	0	**7**	**0**
2009–10	Bristol C	39	0		
2010–11	Bristol C	1	0		
2011–12	Bristol C	10	0		
2012–13	Bristol C	3	0	**53**	**0**
2013–14	Ipswich T	41	0		
2014–15	Ipswich T	16	0		
2015–16	Ipswich T	26	0		
2016–17	Ipswich T	2	0		
2017–18	Ipswich T	1	0		
2018–19	Ipswich T	18	0	**104**	**0**

HARRISON, Ellis (F) **168** **32**
H: 5 11 W: 12 06 b.Newport 1-2-94
Internationals: Wales U21.

2010–11	Bristol R	1	0		
2011–12	Bristol R	0	0		
2012–13	Bristol R	13	3		
2013–14	Bristol R	25	1		
2015–16	Bristol R	30	7		
2015–16	*Hartlepool U*	2	0	**2**	**0**
2016–17	Bristol R	37	8		
2017–18	Bristol R	44	12	**150**	**31**
2018–19	Ipswich T	16	1	**16**	**1**

HUWS, Emyr (M) **94** **10**
H: 5 10 W: 11 07 b.Llanelli 30-9-93
Internationals: Wales U17, U19, U21, Full caps.

2010–11	Manchester C	0	0		
2011–12	Manchester C	0	0		
2012–13	Manchester C	0	0		
2012–13	*Northampton T*	10	0	**10**	**0**
2013–14	Manchester C	0	0		
2013–14	*Birmingham C*	17	2	**17**	**2**
2014–15	Wigan Ath	16	0		
2015–16	Wigan Ath	0	0	**16**	**0**
2015–16	*Huddersfield T*	30	5	**30**	**5**
2016–17	Cardiff C	3	0		
2016–17	*Ipswich T*	13	3		
2017–18	Cardiff C	0	0	**3**	**0**
2017–18	Ipswich T	5	0		
2018–19	Ipswich T	0	0	**18**	**3**

JACKSON, Kayden (F) **101** **20**
H: 5 11 W: 11 07 b.Bradford 22-2-94
Internationals: England C.

2013–14	Swindon T	0	0		
2014–15	Swindon T	0	0		

From Oxford C, Tamworth, Wrexham.

2016–17	Barnsley	0	0		
2016–17	*Grimsby T*	20	1	**20**	**1**
2017–18	Accrington S	44	16		
2018–19	Accrington S	1	0	**45**	**16**
2018–19	Ipswich T	36	3	**36**	**3**

JUDGE, Alan (F) **315** **48**
H: 5 6 W: 11 03 b.Dublin 11-11-88
Internationals: Republic of Ireland U17, U8, U19, U21, U23, Full caps.

2006–07	Blackburn R	0	0		
2007–08	Blackburn R	0	0		
2008–09	Blackburn R	0	0		
2008–09	*Plymouth Arg*	17	2		
2009–10	Blackburn R	0	0		
2009–10	*Plymouth Arg*	37	5	**54**	**7**
2010–11	Blackburn R	0	0		
2010–11	Notts Co	19	1		
2011–12	Notts Co	43	7		
2012–13	Notts Co	39	8	**101**	**16**
2013–14	Blackburn R	11	0	**11**	**0**
2013–14	Brentford	22	7		
2014–15	Brentford	37	3		
2015–16	Brentford	38	14		
2017–18	Brentford	13	0		
2018–19	Brentford	20	1	**130**	**25**
2018–19	Ipswich T	19	0	**19**	**0**

KENLOCK, Myles (D) **55** **0**
H: 6 1 W: 10 08 b.Croydon 29-11-96

2015–16	Ipswich T	2	0		
2016–17	Ipswich T	18	0		
2017–18	Ipswich T	16	0		
2018–19	Ipswich T	19	0	**55**	**0**

KNUDSEN, Jonas (D) **253** **8**
H: 6 1 W: 11 05 b.Esbjerg 16-9-92
Internationals: Denmark U18, U19, U20, U21, Full caps.

2009–10	Esbjerg	7	0		
2010–11	Esberg	5	0	**5**	**0**
2011–12	Esbjerg	0	0		
2012–13	Esbjerg	32	1		
2013–14	Esbjerg	31	1		
2014–15	Esbjerg	28	2		
2015–16	Esbjerg	2	0	**100**	**4**
2015–16	Ipswich T	42	1		
2016–17	Ipswich T	36	2		
2017–18	Ipswich T	42	1		
2018–19	Ipswich T	28	0	**148**	**4**

LANKESTER, Jack (F) **11** **1**
b.Ipswich 19-1-00

2018–19	Ipswich T	11	1	**11**	**1**

McLOUGHLIN, Shane (D) **11** **1**
b.Castleisland 1-3-97
Internationals: Republic of Ireland U16, U18.

2014–15	Ipswich T	0	0		
2015–16	Ipswich T	0	0		
2016–17	Ipswich T	0	0		
2017–18	Ipswich T	1	0		
2018–19	Ipswich T	0	0	**1**	**0**
2018–19	*AFC Wimbledon*	10	1	**10**	**1**

MORRIS, Ben (F) **8 1**
b. 6-6-99
Internationals: England U17, U18, U19.

2016–17	Ipswich T	0	0		
2017–18	Ipswich T	3	0		
2018–19	Ipswich T	1	0	**4**	**0**
2018–19	*Forest Green R*	4	1	**4**	**1**

NDABA, Corrie (D) **0 0**
Internationals: Republic of Ireland U18.

2018–19	Ipswich T	0	0

NOLAN, Jon (M) **99 13**
H: 5 11 W: 11 05 b.Huyton 22-4-92
Internationals: England C.
From Everton, Stockport Co, Lindoln C, Grimsby T.

2016–17	Chesterfield	30	1	**30**	**1**
2017–18	Shrewsbury T	43	9	**43**	**9**
2018–19	Ipswich T	26	3	**26**	**3**

NSIALA, Aristote (D) **154 6**
H: 6 4 W: 14 09 b.DR Congo 25-3-92
Internationals: DR Congo Full caps.

2009–10	Everton	0	0		
2010–11	Everton	0	0		
2010–11	*Macclesfield T*	10	0	**10**	**0**
2011–12	Everton	0	0		
2011–12	*Accrington S*	19	0		
2012–13	Accrington S	17	0		
2013–14	Accrington S	0	0	**36**	**0**
2016–17	Hartlepool U	21	1	**21**	**1**
2016–17	Shrewsbury T	21	1		
2017–18	Shrewsbury T	44	3	**65**	**4**
2018–19	Ipswich T	22	1	**22**	**1**

NYDAM, Tristan (M) **24 0**
H: 5 7 W: 9 06 b. 6-11-99
Internationals: England U18, U19.

2016–17	Ipswich T	0	0		
2017–18	Ipswich T	18	0		
2018–19	Ipswich T	1	0	**19**	**0**
2018–19	*St Johnstone*	5	0	**5**	**0**

ROBERTS, Jordan (M) **93 11**
H: 5 11 W: 12 13 b.Watford 5-1-94
Internationals: England C.

2011–12	Aldershot T	4	0		
2012–13	Aldershot T	5	0	**9**	**0**

From Havant & Waterlooville, Bishops Stortford, Aldershot T.

2015–16	Inverness CT	9	2	**9**	**2**
2016–17	Crawley T	23	3		
2017–18	Crawley T	35	6	**58**	**9**
2018–19	Ipswich T	12	0	**12**	**0**
2018–19	*Lincoln C*	5	0	**5**	**0**

ROWE, Danny (M) **38 5**
H: 6 0 b.Wythenshawe 9-3-92

2016–17	Ipswich T	4	0		
2017–18	Ipswich T	2	0		
2017–18	*Lincoln C*	12	1		
2018–19	Ipswich T	3	0	**9**	**0**
2018–19	*Lincoln C*	17	4	**29**	**5**

SEARS, Freddie (F) **351 63**
H: 5 8 W: 10 01 b.Hornchurch 27-11-89
Internationals: England U19, U20, U21.

2007–08	West Ham U	7	1		
2008–09	West Ham U	17	0		
2009–10	West Ham U	1	0		
2009–10	*Crystal Palace*	18	0	**18**	**0**
2009–10	*Coventry C*	10	0	**10**	**0**
2010–11	West Ham U	11	1		
2010–11	*Scunthorpe U*	9	0	**9**	**0**
2011–12	West Ham U	10	0	**46**	**2**
2011–12	*Colchester U*	11	2		
2012–13	Colchester U	35	7		
2013–14	Colchester U	32	12		
2014–15	Colchester U	24	10	**102**	**31**
2014–15	Ipswich T	21	9		
2015–16	Ipswich T	45	6		
2016–17	Ipswich T	40	7		
2017–18	Ipswich T	36	2		
2018–19	Ipswich T	24	6	**166**	**30**

SKUSE, Cole (M) **514 11**
H: 6 1 W: 11 05 b.Bristol 29-3-86

2004–05	Bristol C	7	0		
2005–06	Bristol C	38	2		
2006–07	Bristol C	42	0		
2007–08	Bristol C	25	0		
2008–09	Bristol C	33	2		
2009–10	Bristol C	43	2		
2010–11	Bristol C	30	1		
2011–12	Bristol C	36	2		
2012–13	Bristol C	25	0	**279**	**9**
2013–14	Ipswich T	43	0		
2014–15	Ipswich T	40	1		
2015–16	Ipswich T	39	0		
2016–17	Ipswich T	40	0		
2017–18	Ipswich T	39	1		
2018–19	Ipswich T	34	0	**235**	**2**

SPENCE, Jordan (D) **235 6**
H: 6 2 W: 12 07 b.Woodford 24-5-90
Internationals: England U16, U17, U18, U19, U21.

2007–08	West Ham U	0	0		
2008–09	West Ham U	0	0		
2008–09	*Leyton Orient*	20	0	**20**	**0**
2009–10	West Ham U	1	0		
2009–10	*Scunthorpe U*	9	0	**9**	**0**
2010–11	West Ham U	2	0		
2010–11	*Bristol C*	11	0		
2011–12	West Ham U	0	0		
2011–12	*Bristol C*	10	0	**21**	**0**
2012–13	West Ham U	4	0		
2013–14	West Ham U	0	0	**7**	**0**
2013–14	*Sheffield W*	4	0	**4**	**0**
2013–14	*Milton Keynes D*	29	2		
2014–15	Milton Keynes D	38	0		
2015–16	Milton Keynes D	33	0		
2016–17	Milton Keynes D	0	0	**100**	**2**
2016–17	Ipswich T	17	0		
2017–18	Ipswich T	40	4		
2018–19	Ipswich T	17	0	**74**	**4**

WARD, Grant (M) **168 11**
H: 5 10 W: 11 07 b.Lewisham 5-12-94

2013–14	Tottenham H	0	0		
2014	*Chicago Fire*	23	1	**23**	**1**
2014–15	Tottenham H	0	0		
2014–15	*Coventry C*	11	0	**11**	**0**
2015–16	Tottenham H	0	0		
2015–16	*Rotherham U*	40	2	**40**	**2**
2016–17	Ipswich T	43	6		
2017–18	Ipswich T	37	2		
2018–19	Ipswich T	14	0	**94**	**8**

WRIGHT, Harry (G) **0 0**
b. 3-11-98

2018–19	Ipswich T	0	0

Players retained or with offer of contract
Clements, Bailey James; Cotter, Barry Noel; Dobra, Armando; Drinan, Aaron John; El Mizouni, Idris; Folami, Gbenga Tai; George-Kenlock, Myles Lewis; McGavin, Brett; Webber, Patrick Damian; Woolfenden, Luke Matthew.

Scholars
Baker, Teddy James; Barley, Henry James Stuart; Brown, Zak William; Crowe, Dylan; Edwards Alley, Jake Vintin; Egan, Toby Joe; Fehrenbach, Louie Oscar; Foudil, Lounes Mohamed; Healy, Matthew James; Henderson, Alexander; Henry, Ashton Donald; Hughes, Thomas; Marshall, Ross Steven; O'Reilly, Connor Anthony; Oppong, Colin; Reed, Lewis John; Ronan, Kian; Ruffles, Dylan Isaac; Simpson, Tyreece Tyson Nesbett; Smith, Thomas Ryan; Vega, Luca; Viral, Allan Miloud Bernard; Ware, Mitchell Vincent.

LEEDS U (42)

ALIOSKI, Ezgjan (M) **223 37**
b.Prilep 12-2-92
Internationals: Macedonia U19, U21, Full caps.

2012–13	Young Boys	0	0		
2012–13	Schaffhausen	10	0		
2013–14	Schaffhausen	26	2		
2014–15	Schaffhausen	35	2		
2015–16	Schaffhausen	16	0	**87**	**4**
2015–16	Lugano	16	3		
2016–17	Lugano	34	16	**50**	**19**
2017–18	Leeds U	42	7		
2018–19	Leeds U	44	7	**86**	**14**

AYLING, Luke (D) **353 8**
H: 5 11 W: 10 08 b.Lambeth 25-8-91

2009–10	Arsenal	0	0		
2009–10	*Yeovil T*	4	0		
2010–11	Yeovil T	37	0		
2011–12	Yeovil T	44	0		
2012–13	Yeovil T	39	0		
2013–14	Yeovil T	42	2	**166**	**2**
2014–15	Bristol C	46	4		
2015–16	Bristol C	33	0		
2016–17	Bristol C	1	0	**80**	**4**
2016–17	Leeds U	42	0		
2017–18	Leeds U	27	0		
2018–19	Leeds U	38	2	**107**	**2**

BAMFORD, Patrick (F) **186 64**
H: 6 1 W: 11 02 b.Newark 5-9-93
Internationals: Republic of Ireland U18. England U18, U19, U21.

2010–11	Nottingham F	0	0		
2011–12	Nottingham F	2	0	**2**	**0**
2011–12	Chelsea	0	0		
2012–13	Chelsea	0	0		
2012–13	*Milton Keynes D*	14	4		
2013–14	Chelsea	0	0		
2013–14	*Milton Keynes D*	23	14	**37**	**18**
2013–14	*Derby Co*	21	8	**21**	**8**
2014–15	Chelsea	0	0		
2014–15	*Middlesbrough*	38	17		
2015–16	Chelsea	0	0		
2015–16	*Crystal Palace*	6	0	**6**	**0**
2015–16	*Norwich C*	7	0	**7**	**0**
2016–17	Chelsea	0	0		
2016–17	*Burnley*	6	0	**6**	**0**
2016–17	*Middlesbrough*	8	1		
2017–18	Middlesbrough	39	11	**85**	**29**
2018–19	Leeds U	22	9	**22**	**9**

BERARDI, Gaetano (D) **260 0**
H: 5 10 W: 11 00 b.Sorengo 21-8-88
Internationals: Switzerland U20, U21, Full caps.

2006–07	Brescia	1	0		
2007–08	Brescia	9	0		
2008–09	Brescia	26	0		
2009–10	Brescia	29	0		
2010–11	Brescia	27	0		
2011–12	Brescia	13	0	**105**	**0**
2011–12	Sampdoria	9	0		
2012–13	Sampdoria	21	0		
2013–14	Sampdoria	5	0	**35**	**0**
2014–15	Leeds U	22	0		
2015–16	Leeds U	28	0		
2016–17	Leeds U	26	0		
2017–18	Leeds U	31	0		
2018–19	Leeds U	13	0	**120**	**0**

BOGUSZ, Mateusz (M) **0 0**
H: 5 9 b.Ruda Slalka 22-8-01
Internationals: Poland U16, U17, U19, U20.

2018–19	Leeds U	0	0

CASILLA, Francisco (G) **258 0**
H: 6 4 W: 13 01 b.Alcocer 2-10-86
Internationals: Spain U19, U21, Full caps.

2004–05	Real Madrid	0	0		
2005–06	Real Madrid	0	0		
2006–07	Real Madrid	0	0		
2007–08	Espanyol	4	0		
2008–09	Cadiz	35	0		
2009–10	Cadiz	31	0	**66**	**0**
2010–11	Cartagena	35	0	**35**	**0**
2011–12	Espanyol	16	0		
2012–13	Espanyol	21	0		
2013–14	Espanyol	37	0		
2014–15	Espanyol	37	0	**115**	**0**
2015–16	Real Madrid	4	0		
2016–17	Real Madrid	11	0		
2017–18	Real Madrid	10	0	**25**	**0**
2018–19	Leeds U	17	0	**17**	**0**

CLARKE, Jack (F) **22 2**
b.York 23-11-00

2017–18	Leeds U	0	0		
2018–19	Leeds U	22	2	**22**	**2**

COOPER, Liam (D) **237 12**
H: 6 2 W: 13 07 b.Hull 30-8-91
Internationals: Scotland U17, U19.

2008–09	Hull C	0	0		
2009–10	Hull C	2	0		
2010–11	Hull C	2	0		
2010–11	*Carlisle U*	6	1	**6**	**1**
2011–12	Hull C	7	0		
2011–12	*Huddersfield T*	4	0	**4**	**0**
2012–13	Hull C	0	0	**11**	**0**
2012–13	Chesterfield	29	2		
2013–14	Chesterfield	41	3		
2014–15	Chesterfield	1	0	**71**	**5**
2014–15	Leeds U	29	1		
2015–16	Leeds U	39	1		
2016–17	Leeds U	11	0		
2017–18	Leeds U	30	1		
2018–19	Leeds U	36	3	**145**	**6**

COYLE, Lewie (M) **98 0**
H: 5 8 W: 10 08 b.Hull 15-10-95

2015–16	Leeds U	11	0
2016–17	Leeds U	4	0

2017–18	Leeds U	0	0		
2017–18	*Fleetwood T*	42	0		
2018–19	Leeds U	0	0	**15**	**0**
2018–19	*Fleetwood T*	41	0	**83**	**0**

DALBY, Sam (F) 18 1
b.Leytonstone 17-1-00

2016–17	Leyton Orient	16	1		
2017–18	Leyton Orient	0	0	**16**	**1**
2018–19	Leeds U	0	0		
2018–19	*Morecambe*	2	0	**2**	**0**

DALLAS, Stuart (M) 227 46
H: 6 0 W: 12 09 b.Cookstown 19-4-91
Internationals: Northern Ireland U21, U23, Full caps.

2010–11	Crusaders	13	16		
2011–12	Crusaders	8	8	**21**	**24**
2012–13	Brentford	7	0		
2013–14	Brentford	18	2		
2013–14	*Northampton T*	12	3	**12**	**3**
2014–15	Brentford	38	6	**63**	**8**
2015–16	Leeds U	45	5		
2016–17	Leeds U	31	2		
2017–18	Leeds U	29	2		
2018–19	Leeds U	26	2	**131**	**11**

DAVIS, Leif (D) 4 0
b.Newcastle-upon-Tyne 12-1-00
From Morecambe.

2018–19	Leeds U	4	0	**4**	**0**

DE BOCK, Laurens (D) 235 3
b. 7-11-92
Internationals: Belgium U16, U17, U18, U19, U21.

2009–10	Lokeren	5	0		
2010–11	Lokeren	25	0		
2011–12	Lokeren	29	1		
2012–13	Lokeren	21	0	**80**	**1**
2012–13	Club Brugge	11	0		
2013–14	Club Brugge	33	0		
2014–15	Club Brugge	36	0		
2015–16	Club Brugge	31	1		
2016–17	Club Brugge	18	0		
2017–18	Club Brugge	6	0	**135**	**1**
2017–18	Leeds U	7	0		
2018–19	Leeds U	0	0	**7**	**0**
2018–19	*Oostende*	13	1	**13**	**1**

DENTON, Tyler (D) 25 0
H: 5 8 W: 10 06 b.Dewsbury 6-9-95
Internationals: England U17.

2016–17	Leeds U	0	0		
2017–18	Leeds U	0	0		
2017–18	*Port Vale*	15	0	**15**	**0**
2018–19	Leeds U	0	0		
2018–19	*Peterborough U*	10	0	**10**	**0**

DIAZ, Hugo (D) 1 0
b. 9-2-97
From Deportivo La Coruna.

2017–18	Leeds U	1	0		
2018–19	Leeds U	0	0	**1**	**0**

DOUGLAS, Barry (D) 284 22
H: 5 9 W: 10 00 b.Glasgow 4-9-89
Internationals: Scotland Full caps.

2008–09	Queen's Park	30	2		
2009–10	Queen's Park	35	8	**65**	**10**
2010–11	Dundee U	23	2		
2011–12	Dundee U	10	1		
2012–13	Dundee U	28	1	**61**	**4**
2013–14	Lech Poznan	18	0		
2014–15	Lech Poznan	27	3		
2015–16	Lech Poznan	13	0	**58**	**3**
2015–16	Konyaspor	12	0		
2016–17	Konyaspor	22	0	**34**	**0**
2017–18	Wolverhampton W	39	5	**39**	**5**
2018–19	Leeds U	27	0	**27**	**0**

EDMONDSON, Ryan (F) 2 0
b. 20-5-01
From Leeds U.

2017–18	Leeds U	1	0		
2018–19	Leeds U	1	0	**2**	**0**

FORSHAW, Adam (M) 240 14
H: 6 1 W: 11 02 b.Liverpool 8-10-91

2009–10	Everton	0	0		
2010–11	Everton	1	0		
2011–12	Everton	0	0	**1**	**0**
2011–12	*Brentford*	7	0		
2012–13	Brentford	43	3		
2013–14	Brentford	39	8	**89**	**11**
2014–15	Wigan Ath	16	1	**16**	**1**
2014–15	Middlesbrough	18	0		
2015–16	Middlesbrough	29	2		
2016–17	Middlesbrough	34	0		
2017–18	Middlesbrough	11	0	**92**	**2**
2017–18	Leeds U	12	0		
2018–19	Leeds U	30	0	**42**	**0**

GOTTS, Robbie (D) 0 0
b.Harrogate 9-11-99

2018–19	Leeds U	0	0		

HALME, Aapo (D) 49 1
b.Helsinki 22-5-98
Internationals: Finland U16, U17, U18, U19, 21.

2014	Honka	1	0	**1**	**0**
2015	Klubi 04	15	1	**15**	**1**
2015	HJK	2	0		
2016	HJK	14	0		
2017	HJK	13	0	**29**	**0**
2018–19	Leeds U	4	0	**4**	**0**

HERNANDEZ, Pablo (M) 377 66
H: 5 8 W: 10 00 b.Castellon 11-4-85
Internationals: Spain Full caps.

2005–06	Valencia	1	0		
2006–07	*Cadiz*	14	4	**14**	**4**
2007–08	Getafe	28	3	**28**	**3**
2008–09	Valencia	21	4		
2009–10	Valencia	33	5		
2010–11	Valencia	26	5		
2011–12	Valencia	30	3	**111**	**17**
2012–13	Swansea C	30	3		
2013–14	Swansea C	27	2	**57**	**5**
2014–15	Al Arabi	13	6		
2014–15	*Al-Nasr*	12	3	**12**	**3**
2015–16	Al Arabi	0	0	**13**	**6**
2015–16	*Rayo Vallecano*	27	3	**27**	**3**
2016–17	Leeds U	35	6		
2017–18	Leeds U	41	7		
2018–19	Leeds U	39	12	**115**	**25**

HUFFER, Will (G) 1 0
b.London 30-10-98
Internationals: England U17, U18.

2018–19	Leeds U	1	0	**1**	**0**

JANSSON, Pontus (D) 238 20
H: 6 3 W: 13 08 b.Arlov 13-2-91
Internationals: Sweden U17, U19, U21, Full caps.

2009	Malmo	2	0		
2009	*IFK Malmo*	9	4	**9**	**4**
2010	Malmo	18	1		
2011	Malmo	15	2		
2012	Malmo	30	1		
2013	Malmo	24	1		
2014	Malmo	9	1	**98**	**6**
2014–15	Torino	9	0		
2015–16	Torino	7	1		
2015–16	Torino	0	0	**16**	**1**
2016–17	*Leeds U*	34	3		
2017–18	Leeds U	42	3		
2018–19	Leeds U	39	3	**115**	**9**

KLICH, Mateusz (M) 212 32
H: 6 0 W: 10 10 b.Tarnow 13-6-90
Internationals: Poland U18, U19, U20, U21, Full caps.

2008–09	Cracovia	8	0		
2009–10	Cracovia	21	1		
2010–11	Cracovia	27	4	**56**	**5**
2011–12	Wolfsburg	0	0		
2012–13	Wolfsburg	0	0		
2012–13	*Zwolle*	13	2		
2013–14	Zwolle	30	4	**43**	**6**
2014–15	Wolfsburg	0	0		
2014–15	Kaiserslautern	5	1		
2015–16	Kaiserslautern	16	3	**21**	**4**
2016–17	FC Twente	29	6	**29**	**6**
2017–18	Leeds U	4	0		
2017–18	*FC Utrecht*	13	1	**13**	**1**
2018–19	Leeds U	46	10	**50**	**10**

McKAY, Paul (M) 7 0
H: 6 3 W: 12 13 b.Glasgow 19-11-96

2014–15	Doncaster R	0	0		
2015–16	Doncaster R	0	0		
2015–16	Leeds U	0	0		
2016–17	Leeds U	0	0		
2017–18	Leeds U	0	0		
2018–19	Leeds U	0	0		
2018–19	*Cardiff C*	0	0		
2018–19	*Morecambe*	7	0	**7**	**0**

MIAZEK, Kamil (G) 4 0
b. 15-8-96
Internationals: Poland U19.
From Feyenoord.

2016–17	Chojniczanka Chojnice	4	0		
2017–18	Chojniczanka Chojnice	0	0	**4**	**0**
2018–19	Leeds U	0	0		

O'CONNOR, Paudie (D) 23 0
b.Limerick 14-7-97
From Limerick.

2017–18	Leeds U	4	0		
2018–19	Leeds U	0	0	**4**	**0**
2018–19	*Blackpool*	10	0	**10**	**0**
2018–19	*Bradford C*	9	0	**9**	**0**

O'KANE, Eunan (M) 279 18
H: 5 8 W: 13 04 b.Derry 10-7-90
Internationals: Northern Ireland U16, U17, U19, U20, U21. Republic of Ireland U21, Full caps.

2007–08	Everton	0	0		
2008–09	Everton	0	0		
2009–10	Coleraine	13	4	**13**	**4**
2009–10	Torquay U	16	1		
2010–11	Torquay U	45	6		
2011–12	Torquay U	45	5		
2012–13	Torquay U	0	0	**106**	**12**
2012–13	Bournemouth	37	1		
2013–14	Bournemouth	37	1		
2014–15	Bournemouth	11	0		
2015–16	Bournemouth	16	0	**101**	**2**
2016–17	Leeds U	24	0		
2017–18	Leeds U	32	0		
2018–19	Leeds U	0	0	**56**	**0**
2018–19	*Luton T*	3	0	**3**	**0**

ODOUR, Clarke (F) 0 0
b. 25-6-99

2018–19	Leeds U	0	0		

PEACOCK-FARRELL, Bailey (G) 40 0
H: 6 2 W: 11 07 b.Darlington 29-10-96
Internationals: Northern Ireland U21, Full caps.

2015–16	Leeds U	1	0		
2016–17	Leeds U	0	0		
2017–18	Leeds U	11	0		
2018–19	Leeds U	28	0	**40**	**0**

PEARCE, Tom (D) 16 2
b.Ormskirk 12-4-98
Internationals: England U20, U21.
From Everton.

2017–18	Leeds U	5	1		
2018–19	Leeds U	2	0	**7**	**1**
2018–19	*Scunthorpe U*	9	1	**9**	**1**

PHILIPS, Kalvin (M) 128 10
H: 5 10 W: 11 05 b.Leeds 2-12-95

2014–15	Leeds U	2	1		
2015–16	Leeds U	10	0		
2016–17	Leeds U	33	1		
2017–18	Leeds U	41	7		
2018–19	Leeds U	42	1	**128**	**10**

REY, Oriol (D) 0 0
b.Barcelona 25-2-98
From Barcelona.

2017–18	Leeds U	0	0		
2018–19	Leeds U	0	0		

ROBERTS, Tyler (F) 73 12
H: 5 11 W: 11 11 b.Gloucester 12-1-98
Internationals: Wales U16, U17, U19, U20, U21, Full caps.

2014–15	WBA	0	0		
2015–16	WBA	1	0		
2016–17	WBA	0	0	**1**	**0**
2016–17	*Oxford U*	14	0	**14**	**0**
2016–17	*Shrewsbury T*	13	4	**13**	**4**
2017–18	Leeds U	0	0		
2017–18	*Walsall*	17	5	**17**	**5**
2018–19	Leeds U	28	3	**28**	**3**

ROOFE, Kemar (M) 183 53
H: 5 10 W: 11 03 b.Walsall 6-1-93

2011–12	WBA	0	0		
2012–13	WBA	0	0		
2012–13	*Northampton T*	6	0	**6**	**0**
2013–14	WBA	0	0		
2013–14	*Cheltenham T*	9	1	**9**	**1**
2014–15	WBA	0	0		
2014–15	*Colchester U*	2	0	**2**	**0**
2014–15	*Oxford U*	16	6		
2015–16	Oxford U	40	18	**56**	**24**
2016–17	Leeds U	42	3		
2017–18	Leeds U	36	11		
2018–19	Leeds U	32	14	**110**	**28**

SAMUEL, Saiz (F) 151 22
H: 5 9 W: 10 10 b.Madrid 22-1-91
Internationals: Spain U19.

2009–10	Real Madrid	0	0		
2010–11	Real Madrid	0	0		
2011–12	Melilla	16	1	**16**	**1**

2011–12	Getafe	1	0		
2012–13	Getafe	0	0		
2013–14	Almeria	0	0		
2014–15	Atletico Madrid	0	0		
2015–16	Atletico Madrid	0	0		
2015–16	*Huesca*	29	3		
2016–17	Huesca	42	12		
2017–18	Huesca	0	0	**71**	**15**
2017–18	Leeds U	34	5		
2018–19	Leeds U	19	0	**53**	**5**
2018–19	*Getafe*	10	1	**11**	**1**

SHACKLETON, Jamie (M) 19 0
b.Leeds 8-10-99
Internationals: England U20.

2018–19	Leeds U	19	0	**19**	**0**

SHAUGHNESSY, Conor (M) 19 0
H: 6 3 W: 11 09 b. 30-6-96
Internationals: Republic of Ireland U16, U17, U18, U21, Full caps.

2017–18	Leeds U	9	0		
2018–19	Leeds U	0	0	**9**	**0**
2018–19	*Hearts*	10	0	**10**	**0**

STEVENS, Jordan (M) 10 0
b. 25-3-00

2017–18	Forest Green R	9	0	**9**	**0**
2017–18	Leeds U	0	0		
2018–19	Leeds U	1	0	**1**	**0**

STRUIJK, Pascal (D) 0 0
Internationals: Netherlands U17.
From Ajax.

2017–18	Leeds U	0	0
2018–19	Leeds U	0	0

TEMENUZHKOV, Kun (F) 0 0
H: 5 5 b.Haskovo 1-2-00
Internationals: Bulgaria U16, U17, U18, U19, U21.
From Barcelona.

2018–19	Leeds U	0	0

WILKS, Mallik (F) 71 17
b.Leeds 15-12-98

2016–17	Leeds U	0	0		
2017–18	Leeds U	0	0		
2017–18	*Accrington S*	19	3	**19**	**3**
2017–18	*Grimsby T*	6	0	**6**	**0**
2018–19	Leeds U	0	0		
2018–19	*Doncaster R*	46	14	**46**	**14**

Players retained or with offer of contract
Anita, Vurnon San Benito; Balboa, Balboa Adrian; Bouy, Ouasim; Casey, Oliver Joseph; Cibicki, Pawel; De, Bock Laurens Henri; Downing, Matthew Christopher; Ekuban, Caleb Ansah; Grot, Jay-Roy Jornell; Hosannah, Bryce Joseph; Ideguchi, Yosuke; Jenkins, Jack; Kamwa, Bobby-Emmanuel; Kitching, Liam James; Machuca, Pindado Alejandro; McCalmont, Alfie John; Mihaylov, Dzhoshkun Temenuzhkov; Nicell, Callum Luke; Oduor, Clarke Sydney Omondi; Phillips, Kalvin Mark; Sacko, Hadi; Saiz, Alonso Samuel; Sarkic, Oliver; Shergill, Joshveer Singh.

Scholars
Burlace, Dane Lee; Cresswell, Charlie Richard; Edris, Niklas Haugland; Gibbon, Cole Jay; Hudson, Theodore Douglas; Huggins, Niall Joseph; Kumwenda, Henri Mwayi; Leak-Blunt, Connor Jay; Lyons, Luke Anthony; Male, Harrison Darren; Odunston, Lucas Thomas; Rae, Joshua Hugh; Rubie, Mason; Stanley, Joseph Thomas; Thornton, Jamie William; Turner, Matthew David.

LEICESTER C (43)

ADRIEN SILVA, Sebastien (M) 237 36
H: 5 9 W: 11 11 b.Angouleme 15-3-89
Internationals: Portugal U16, U17, U18, U19, U21, Full caps.

2007–08	Sporting Lisbon	6	0		
2008–09	Sporting Lisbon	13	0		
2009–10	Sporting Lisbon	13	0		
2010–11	Sporting Lisbon	0	0		
2010–11	*Maccabi Haifa*	6	0	**6**	**0**
2010–11	*Academica*	6	1	**6**	**1**
2011–12	Sporting Lisbon	0	0		
2011–12	*Academica*	28	4	**28**	**4**
2012–13	Sporting Lisbon	19	3		
2013–14	Sporting Lisbon	28	8		
2014–15	Sporting Lisbon	30	8		
2015–16	Sporting Lisbon	29	8		
2016–17	Sporting Lisbon	27	4		
2017–18	Sporting Lisbon	3	0	**168**	**31**
2017–18	Leicester C	12	0		
2018–19	Leicester C	2	0	**14**	**0**
2018–19	*Monaco*	15	0	**15**	**0**

ALBRIGHTON, Marc (M) 240 17
H: 6 2 W: 12 06 b.Tamworth 18-11-89
Internationals: England U20, U21.

2008–09	Aston Villa	0	0		
2009–10	Aston Villa	3	0		
2010–11	Aston Villa	29	5		
2011–12	Aston Villa	26	2		
2012–13	Aston Villa	9	0		
2013–14	Aston Villa	19	0	**86**	**7**
2013–14	*Wigan Ath*	4	0	**4**	**0**
2014–15	Leicester C	18	2		
2015–16	Leicester C	38	2		
2016–17	Leicester C	33	2		
2017–18	Leicester C	34	2		
2018–19	Leicester C	27	2	**150**	**10**

AMARTEY, Daniel (M) 124 4
H: 6 0 W: 12 04 b.Accra 1-12-94
Internationals: Ghana U20, Full caps.

2013	Djurgardens	23	0		
2014	Djurgardens	11	0	**34**	**0**
2014–15	Copenhagen	29	3		
2015–16	Copenhagen	15	0	**44**	**3**
2015–16	Leicester C	5	0		
2016–17	Leicester C	24	1		
2017–18	Leicester C	8	0		
2018–19	Leicester C	9	0	**46**	**1**

BARNES, Harvey (M) 89 21
b. 8-12-97
Internationals: England U18, U20, U21.

2016–17	Leicester C	0	0		
2016–17	*Milton Keynes D*	21	6	**21**	**6**
2017–18	Leicester C	3	0		
2017–18	*Barnsley*	23	5	**23**	**5**
2018–19	Leicester C	16	1	**19**	**1**
2018–19	*WBA*	26	9	**26**	**9**

BENKOVIC, Filip (D) 76 8
H: 6 4 W: 14 05 b.Zagreb 13-7-97
Internationals: Croatia U17, U19, U21, Full caps.

2015–16	Dinamo Zagreb	13	0		
2016–17	Dinamo Zagreb	18	2		
2017–18	Dinamo Zagreb	25	4	**56**	**6**
2018–19	Leicester C	0	0		
2018–19	*Celtic*	20	2	**20**	**2**

CHILWELL, Ben (D) 80 1
H: 5 10 W: 11 03 b.Milton Keynes 21-12-96
Internationals: England U18, U19, U20, U21, Full caps.

2015–16	Leicester C	0	0		
2015–16	*Huddersfield T*	8	0	**8**	**0**
2016–17	Leicester C	12	1		
2017–18	Leicester C	24	0		
2018–19	Leicester C	36	0	**72**	**1**

CHOUDHURY, Hamza (M) 43 0
H: 5 10 W: 10 01 b.Loughborough 1-10-97
Internationals: England U21.

2015–16	Leicester C	0	0		
2015–16	*Burton Alb*	13	0		
2016–17	Leicester C	0	0		
2016–17	*Burton Alb*	13	0	**26**	**0**
2017–18	Leicester C	8	0		
2018–19	Leicester C	9	0	**17**	**0**

DIABATE, Fousseni (M) 32 2
H: 5 9 W: 10 06 b.Aubervilliers 18-10-95
Internationals: Mali U20, U23.
From Rennes, Reims.

2016–17	Guingamp	0	0		
2017–18	Ajaccio GFCO	0	0		
2017–18	Leicester C	14	0		
2018–19	Leicester C	1	0	**15**	**0**
2018–19	*Sivasspor*	17	2	**17**	**2**

ELDER, Callum (D) 81 1
H: 5 11 W: 10 08 b.Sydney 27-1-95
Internationals: Australia U20.

2013–14	Leicester C	0	0		
2014–15	Leicester C	0	0		
2014–15	*Mansfield T*	21	0	**21**	**0**
2015–16	Leicester C	0	0		
2015–16	*Peterborough U*	18	1	**18**	**1**
2016–17	Leicester C	0	0		
2016–17	*Brentford*	6	0	**6**	**0**
2016–17	*Barnsley*	5	0	**5**	**0**
2017–18	Leicester C	0	0		
2017–18	*Wigan Ath*	27	0	**27**	**0**
2018–19	Leicester C	0	0		
2018–19	*Ipswich T*	4	0	**4**	**0**

EVANS, Jonny (D) 291 13
H: 6 2 W: 12 02 b.Belfast 3-1-88
Internationals: Northern Ireland U16, U17, U21, Full caps.

2004–05	Manchester U	0	0		
2005–06	Manchester U	0	0		
2006–07	Manchester U	0	0		
2006–07	*Antwerp*	14	2	**14**	**2**
2006–07	*Sunderland*	18	1		
2007–08	Manchester U	0	0		
2007–08	*Sunderland*	15	0	**33**	**1**
2008–09	Manchester U	17	0		
2009–10	Manchester U	18	0		
2010–11	Manchester U	13	0		
2011–12	Manchester U	29	1		
2012–13	Manchester U	23	3		
2013–14	Manchester U	17	0		
2014–15	Manchester U	14	0		
2015–16	Manchester U	0	0	**131**	**4**
2015–16	WBA	30	1		
2016–17	WBA	31	2		
2017–18	WBA	28	2	**89**	**5**
2018–19	Leicester C	24	1	**24**	**1**

FUCHS, Christian (D) 431 24
H: 6 1 W: 12 08 b.Pitten 7-4-86
Internationals: Austria U17, U19, U21, Full caps.

2002–03	Wiener Neustadt	12	0	**12**	**0**
2003–04	Mattersburg	13	0		
2004–05	Mattersburg	24	2		
2005–06	Mattersburg	35	1		
2006–07	Mattersburg	35	6		
2007–08	Mattersburg	33	3	**140**	**12**
2008–09	Bochum	22	2		
2009–10	Bochum	31	4		
2010–11	Bochum	0	0	**53**	**6**
2010–11	*Mainz 05*	31	0	**31**	**0**
2011–12	Schalke	29	2		
2012–13	Schalke	29	0		
2013–14	Schalke	16	0		
2014–15	Schalke	25	2	**99**	**4**
2015–16	Leicester C	32	0		
2016–17	Leicester C	36	2		
2017–18	Leicester C	25	0		
2018–19	Leicester C	3	0	**96**	**2**

GHEZZAL, Rachid (M) 132 14
H: 6 0 W: 10 03 b.Decines-Charpieu 9-5-92
Internationals: France U20. Algeria Full caps.

2012–13	Lyon	14	1		
2013–14	Lyon	0	0		
2014–15	Lyon	18	0		
2015–16	Lyon	29	8		
2016–17	Lyon	26	2	**87**	**11**
2017–18	Monaco	26	2	**26**	**2**
2018–19	Leicester C	19	1	**19**	**1**

GRAY, Demarai (M) 183 16
H: 5 10 W: 10 04 b.Birmingham 28-6-96
Internationals: England U18, U19, U20, U21.

2013–14	Birmingham C	7	1		
2014–15	Birmingham C	41	6		
2015–16	Birmingham C	24	1	**72**	**8**
2015–16	Leicester C	12	0		
2016–17	Leicester C	30	1		
2017–18	Leicester C	35	3		
2018–19	Leicester C	34	4	**111**	**8**

IBORRA, Vicente (F) 305 35
H: 6 3 W: 12 00 b.Moncada 16-1-88

2007–08	Levante	14	1		
2008–09	Levante	31	2		
2009–10	Levante	36	1		
2010–11	Levante	16	0		
2011–12	Levante	33	0		
2012–13	Levante	35	4	**165**	**8**
2013–14	Sevilla	27	3		
2014–15	Sevilla	26	7		
2015–16	Sevilla	29	7		
2016–17	Sevilla	31	7	**113**	**24**
2017–18	Leicester C	19	3		
2018–19	Leicester C	8	0	**27**	**3**

Transferred to Villarreal January 2019.

IHEANACHO, Kelechi (M) 97 16
H: 6 2 W: 13 08 b.Imo 3-10-96
Internationals: Nigeria U17, U20, Full caps.

2014–15	Manchester C	0	0		
2015–16	Manchester C	26	8		
2016–17	Manchester C	20	4	**46**	**12**
2017–18	Leicester C	21	3		
2018–19	Leicester C	30	1	**51**	**4**

IVERSEN, Daniel (G) **42 0**
b. 19-7-97
Internationals: Denmark U16, U17, U18, U19, U20, U21.

2014–15	Esbjerg	0	0		
2015–16	Esbjerg	0	0		
2015–16	Leicester C	0	0		
2016–17	Leicester C	0	0		
2017–18	Leicester C	0	0		
2018–19	Leicester C	0	0		
2018–19	*Oldham Ath*	42	0	**42**	**0**

JAKUPOVIC, Eldin (G) **161 1**
H: 6 3 W: 13 00 b.Kozarac 2-10-84
Internationals: Bosnia & Herzegovina U21, Switzerland U21, Full caps.

2004–05	Grasshoppers	8	0		
2005–06	FC Thun	23	0	**23**	**0**
2007–08	Grasshoppers	23	1		
2008–09	Grasshoppers	32	0	**63**	**1**
2010–11	Olympiacos Volou	26	0	**26**	**0**
2011–12	Aris Salonika	1	0	**1**	**0**
2012–13	Hull C	5	0		
2013–14	Hull C	1	0		
2013–14	*Leyton Orient*	13	0	**13**	**0**
2014–15	Hull C	3	0		
2015–16	Hull C	2	0		
2016–17	Hull C	22	0	**33**	**0**
2017–18	Leicester C	2	0		
2018–19	Leicester C	0	0	**2**	**0**

JAMES, Matthew (M) **146 7**
H: 6 0 W: 11 12 b.Bacup 22-7-91
Internationals: England U16, U17, U19, U20.

2007–08	Manchester U	0	0		
2008–09	Manchester U	0	0		
2009–10	Manchester U	0	0		
2009–10	*Preston NE*	18	2		
2010–11	Manchester U	0	0		
2010–11	*Preston NE*	10	0	**28**	**2**
2011–12	Manchester U	0	0		
2012–13	Leicester C	24	3		
2013–14	Leicester C	35	1		
2014–15	Leicester C	27	0		
2015–16	Leicester C	0	0		
2016–17	Leicester C	1	0		
2016–17	*Barnsley*	18	1	**18**	**1**
2017–18	Leicester C	13	0		
2018–19	Leicester C	0	0	**100**	**4**

KING, Andy (M) **344 57**
H: 6 0 W: 11 10 b.Barnstaple 29-10-88
Internationals: Wales U19, U21, Full caps.

2007–08	Leicester C	11	1		
2008–09	Leicester C	45	9		
2009–10	Leicester C	43	9		
2010–11	Leicester C	45	15		
2011–12	Leicester C	30	4		
2012–13	Leicester C	42	7		
2013–14	Leicester C	30	4		
2014–15	Leicester C	24	2		
2015–16	Leicester C	25	2		
2016–17	Leicester C	23	1		
2017–18	Leicester C	11	1		
2017–18	*Swansea C*	11	2	**11**	**2**
2018–19	Leicester C	0	0	**329**	**55**
2018–19	*Derby Co*	4	0	**4**	**0**

KNIGHT, Josh (D) **8 0**
b.Leicester 7-9-97

2017–18	Leicester C	0	0		
2018–19	Leicester C	0	0		
2018–19	*Peterborough U*	8	0	**8**	**0**

LESHABELA, Thakgalo (M) **0 0**
b. 18-9-99
Internationals: South Africa U20.

2018–19	Leicester C	0	0		

MADDISON, James (M) **132 29**
H: 5 10 W: 11 07 b.Coventry 23-11-96
Internationals: England U21.

2013–14	Coventry C	0	0		
2014–15	Coventry C	12	2		
2015–16	Norwich C	0	0		
2015–16	*Coventry C*	23	3	**35**	**5**
2016–17	Norwich C	3	1		
2016–17	*Aberdeen*	14	2	**14**	**2**
2017–18	Norwich C	44	14	**47**	**15**
2018–19	Leicester C	36	7	**36**	**7**

MAGUIRE, Harry (D) **273 17**
H: 6 2 W: 12 06 b.Mosborough 5-3-93
Internationals: England U21, Full caps.

2010–11	Sheffield U	5	0		
2011–12	Sheffield U	44	1		
2012–13	Sheffield U	44	3		
2013–14	Sheffield U	41	5	**134**	**9**
2014–15	Hull C	3	0		
2014–15	*Wigan Ath*	16	1	**16**	**1**
2015–16	Hull C	22	0		
2016–17	Hull C	29	2	**54**	**2**
2017–18	Leicester C	38	2		
2018–19	Leicester C	31	3	**69**	**5**

MENDY, Nampalys (D) **233 1**
H: 5 6 W: 10 10 b.La Seyne-sur-Mer 9-6-92
Internationals: France U18, U19, U20, U21.

2010–11	Monaco	14	0		
2011–12	Monaco	28	0		
2012–13	Monaco	32	0	**74**	**0**
2013–14	Nice	36	0		
2014–15	Nice	36	0		
2015–16	Nice	38	1		
2016–17	Leicester C	4	0		
2017–18	Leicester C	0	0		
2017–18	*Nice*	14	0	**124**	**1**
2018–19	Leicester C	31	0	**35**	**0**

MORGAN, Wes (D) **620 24**
H: 6 2 W: 14 00 b.Nottingham 21-1-84
Internationals: Jamaica Full caps.

2002–03	Nottingham F	0	0		
2002–03	*Kidderminster H*	5	1	**5**	**1**
2003–04	Nottingham F	32	2		
2004–05	Nottingham F	43	1		
2005–06	Nottingham F	43	2		
2006–07	Nottingham F	38	0		
2007–08	Nottingham F	42	1		
2008–09	Nottingham F	42	1		
2009–10	Nottingham F	44	3		
2010–11	Nottingham F	46	1		
2011–12	Nottingham F	22	1	**352**	**12**
2011–12	Leicester C	17	0		
2012–13	Leicester C	45	1		
2013–14	Leicester C	45	2		
2014–15	Leicester C	37	2		
2015–16	Leicester C	38	2		
2016–17	Leicester C	27	1		
2017–18	Leicester C	32	0		
2018–19	Leicester C	22	3	**263**	**11**

NDIDI, Onyinye (D) **149 8**
b. 16-12-96
Internationals: Nigeria U20, Full caps.

2014–15	Genk	6	0		
2015–16	Genk	36	4		
2016–17	Genk	19	0	**61**	**4**
2016–17	Leicester C	17	2		
2017–18	Leicester C	33	0		
2018–19	Leicester C	38	2	**88**	**4**

OKAZAKI, Shinji (F) **363 93**
H: 5 9 W: 11 00 b.Hyogo 16-4-86
Internationals: Japan U23, Full caps.

2005	Shimizu S-Pulse	1	0		
2006	Shimizu S-Pulse	7	0		
2007	Shimizu S-Pulse	21	5		
2008	Shimizu S-Pulse	27	10		
2009	Shimizu S-Pulse	34	14		
2010	Shimizu S-Pulse	31	13	**121**	**42**
2010–11	Stuttgart	12	2		
2011–12	Stuttgart	26	7		
2012–13	Stuttgart	25	1	**63**	**10**
2013–14	Mainz 05	33	15		
2014–15	Mainz 05	32	12	**65**	**27**
2015–16	Leicester C	36	5		
2016–17	Leicester C	30	3		
2017–18	Leicester C	27	6		
2018–19	Leicester C	21	0	**114**	**14**

RICARDO PEREIRA, Domingos (D) **161 8**
H: 5 9 W: 11 00 b.Lisbon 6-10-93
Internationals: Portugal U19, U20, U21, Full caps.

2011–12	Vitoria Guimaraes	3	0		
2012–13	Vitoria Guimaraes	27	0	**30**	**0**
2013–14	Porto	14	2		
2014–15	Porto	5	0		
2015–16	Porto	0	0		
2015–16	*Nice*	26	0		
2016–17	Porto	0	0		
2016–17	*Nice*	24	2	**50**	**2**
2017–18	Porto	27	2	**46**	**4**
2018–19	Leicester C	35	2	**35**	**2**

SCHMEICHEL, Kasper (G) **460 0**
H: 6 1 W: 13 00 b.Copenhagen 5-11-86
Internationals: Denmark U19, U20, U21, Full caps.

2003–04	Manchester C	0	0		
2004–05	Manchester C	0	0		
2005–06	Manchester C	0	0		
2005–06	*Darlington*	4	0	**4**	**0**
2005–06	*Bury*	15	0		
2006–07	Manchester C	0	0		
2006–07	*Falkirk*	15	0	**15**	**0**
2006–07	*Bury*	14	0	**29**	**0**
2007–08	Manchester C	7	0		
2007–08	*Cardiff C*	14	0	**14**	**0**
2007–08	*Coventry C*	9	0	**9**	**0**
2008–09	Manchester C	1	0		
2009–10	Manchester C	0	0	**8**	**0**
2009–10	Notts Co	43	0	**43**	**0**
2010–11	Leeds U	37	0	**37**	**0**
2011–12	Leicester C	46	0		
2012–13	Leicester C	46	0		
2013–14	Leicester C	46	0		
2014–15	Leicester C	24	0		
2015–16	Leicester C	38	0		
2016–17	Leicester C	30	0		
2017–18	Leicester C	33	0		
2018–19	Leicester C	38	0	**301**	**0**

SIMPSON, Danny (D) **307 1**
H: 5 9 W: 11 05 b.Eccles 4-1-87

2005–06	Manchester U	0	0		
2006–07	Manchester U	0	0		
2006–07	*Sunderland*	14	0	**14**	**0**
2007–08	Manchester U	3	0		
2007–08	*Ipswich T*	8	0	**8**	**0**
2008–09	Manchester U	0	0		
2008–09	*Blackburn R*	12	0	**12**	**0**
2009–10	Manchester U	0	0	**3**	**0**
2009–10	Newcastle U	39	1		
2010–11	Newcastle U	30	0		
2011–12	Newcastle U	35	0		
2012–13	Newcastle U	19	0	**123**	**1**
2013–14	QPR	33	0		
2014–15	QPR	1	0	**34**	**0**
2014–15	Leicester C	14	0		
2015–16	Leicester C	30	0		
2016–17	Leicester C	35	0		
2017–18	Leicester C	28	0		
2018–19	Leicester C	6	0	**113**	**0**

SOYUNCU, Caglar (D) **90 3**
H: 6 2 W: 12 08 b.Izmir 23-5-96
Internationals: Turkey U18, U19, U20, U21, Full caps.

2014–15	Altinordu	4	0		
2015–16	Altinordu	30	2	**34**	**2**
2016–17	Freiburg	24	0		
2017–18	Freiburg	26	1	**50**	**1**
2018–19	Leicester C	6	0	**6**	**0**

THOMAS, George (M) **84 8**
H: 5 8 W: 12 00 b.Leicester 24-3-97
Internationals: Wales U17, U19, U20, U21, Full caps.

2013–14	Coventry C	1	0		
2014–15	Coventry C	6	0		
2015–16	Coventry C	7	0		
2015–16	*Yeovil T*	5	0	**5**	**0**
2016–17	Coventry C	28	5	**42**	**5**
2017–18	Leicester C	0	0		
2018–19	Leicester C	0	0		
2018–19	*Scunthorpe U*	37	3	**37**	**3**

TIELEMANS, Youri (M) **199 34**
H: 5 9 W: 10 08 b.Sint-Pieters-Leeuw 7-5-97
Internationals: Belgium U16, U21, Full caps.

2013–14	Anderlecht	29	1		
2014–15	Anderlecht	39	6		
2015–16	Anderlecht	34	6		
2016–17	Anderlecht	37	13	**139**	**26**
2017–18	Monaco	27	0		
2018–19	Monaco	20	5	**47**	**5**

On loan from Monaco.

2018–19	Leicester C	13	3	**13**	**3**

VARDY, Jamie (F) **239 100**
H: 5 10 W: 11 12 b.Sheffield 11-1-87
Internationals: England Full caps.

2012–13	Leicester C	26	4		
2013–14	Leicester C	37	16		
2014–15	Leicester C	34	5		
2015–16	Leicester C	36	24		
2016–17	Leicester C	35	13		
2017–18	Leicester C	37	20		
2018–19	Leicester C	34	18	**239**	**100**

WARD, Danny (G) **71 0**
H: 5 11 W: 13 12 b.Wrexham 22-6-93
Internationals: Wales U17, U19, U21, Full caps.

2011–12	Liverpool	0	0		
2012–13	Liverpool	0	0		
2013–14	Liverpool	0	0		
2014–15	Liverpool	0	0		

2014–15	*Morecambe*	5	0	**5**	**0**
2015–16	Liverpool	2	0		
2015–16	*Aberdeen*	21	0	**21**	**0**
2016–17	Liverpool	0	0		
2016–17	*Huddersfield T*	43	0	**43**	**0**
2017–18	Liverpool	0	0	**2**	**0**
2018–19	Leicester C	0	0		

Players retained or with offer of contract
Bolkiah, Faiq Jefri; Davies, Rhys Paul Richard; Dewsbury-Hall, Kiernan; Flynn, Shane Aidan Conor; Hughes, Samuel Joseph; Husek, Lukas; Johansson, Viktor Tobias; Johnson, Darnell Tobias Jack; Kapustka, Bartosz; Kranthove, Justen Shelden; Loft, Ryan; Moore, Elliott Jordan; Muskwe, Admiral Dalindlela; Ndukwu, Layton Julius; Okpoda Eppiah, Joshua Felix; Pascanu, Alexandru Stefan; Shade, Tyrese; Slimani, Islam; Sowah, Kamal; Tavares, Sidnei Wilson Vieira David; Tee, Conor; Uche Rubio, Raul; Ughelumba, Calvin Chinedu; Wright, Callum.

Scholars
Arlott-John, Dempsey Michael Asa; Barrett, Connor; Bollard, Dylan Jack; Bosworth, Oliver Michael; Elewa-Ikpakwu, Edward; Gbadebo, Camron Israel; Gyamfi, Dennis; Gyamfi, Johnson Adu; Heaven, George William; Keaveny, Jozsef Phelim; Leathers, Adam James; Loughlan, Liam; McAteer, Kasey; Murch, Oliver Edward; Myring, Harrison; Sams, Thomas James; Stolarczyk, Jakub.

LINCOLN C (44)

ADEBAYO-SMITH, Jordan (F) **0 0**

2018–19	Lincoln C	0	0		

AKINDE, John (F) **271 83**
H: 6 2 W: 10 01 b.Camberwell 8-7-89

2008–09	Bristol C	7	1		
2008–09	*Wycombe W*	11	7		
2009–10	Bristol C	7	0		
2009–10	*Wycombe W*	6	1	**17**	**8**
2009–10	*Brentford*	2	0	**2**	**0**
2010–11	Bristol C	2	0	**16**	**1**
2010–11	*Bristol R*	14	0	**14**	**0**
2010–11	*Dagenham & R*	9	2		
2011–12	Crawley T	25	1		
2011–12	*Dagenham & R*	5	0	**14**	**2**
2012–13	Crawley T	6	0	**31**	**1**
2012–13	Portsmouth	11	0		
2013–14	Portsmouth	0	0	**11**	**0**
2015–16	Barnet	43	23		
2016–17	Barnet	46	26		
2017–18	Barnet	32	7	**121**	**56**
2018–19	Lincoln C	45	15	**45**	**15**

AKINOLA, Tim (M) **0 0**

2018–19	Lincoln C	0	0		

ANDERSON, Harry (F) **99 11**
H: 5 6 W: 9 11 b. 9-1-97

2014–15	Peterborough U	10	0		
2015–16	Peterborough U	5	0		
2016–17	Peterborough U	1	0	**16**	**0**
2017–18	Lincoln C	40	6		
2018–19	Lincoln C	43	5	**83**	**11**

ANDRADE, Bruno (M) **97 13**
H: 5 9 W: 11 09 b.Aveiro 2-10-93

2010–11	QPR	1	0		
2011–12	QPR	1	0		
2011–12	*Aldershot T*	1	0	**1**	**0**
2012–13	QPR	0	0		
2012–13	*Wycombe W*	23	2	**23**	**2**
2013–14	QPR	0	0		
2013–14	*Stevenage*	13	0		
2014–15	QPR	0	0	**2**	**0**
2014–15	*Stevenage*	16	1	**29**	**1**

From Woking, Boreham Wood.

2018–19	Lincoln C	42	10	**42**	**10**

ANTKOWIAK, Michael (G) **0 0**

2017–18	Lincoln C	0	0		
2018–19	Lincoln C	0	0		

BOLGER, Cian (D) **208 13**
H: 6 4 W: 12 05 b.Co. Kildare 12-3-92
Internationals: Republic of Ireland U19, U21.

2009–10	Leicester C	0	0		
2010–11	Leicester C	0	0		
2010–11	*Bristol R*	6	0		
2011–12	Leicester C	0	0		
2011–12	*Bristol R*	39	2		
2012–13	Leicester C	0	0		
2012–13	*Bristol R*	3	0	**48**	**2**
2012–13	Bolton W	0	0		
2013–14	Bolton W	0	0		
2013–14	*Colchester U*	4	0	**4**	**0**
2013–14	*Southend U*	1	0		
2014–15	Southend U	23	1		
2015–16	Southend U	22	0	**46**	**1**
2015–16	*Bury*	9	0	**9**	**0**
2016–17	Fleetwood T	32	5		
2017–18	Fleetwood T	41	3		
2018–19	Fleetwood T	11	1	**84**	**9**
2018–19	Lincoln C	17	1	**17**	**1**

BOSTWICK, Michael (D) **367 40**
H: 6 4 W: 14 00 b.Eltham 17-5-88
Internationals: England C.

2006–07	Millwall	0	0		

From Rushden & D, Ebbsfleet U

2010–11	Stevenage	41	2		
2011–12	Stevenage	43	7	**84**	**9**
2012–13	Peterborough U	39	5		
2013–14	Peterborough U	42	4		
2014–15	Peterborough U	38	7		
2015–16	Peterborough U	36	4		
2016–17	Peterborough U	39	3	**194**	**23**
2017–18	Lincoln C	44	6		
2018–19	Lincoln C	45	2	**89**	**8**

CHAPMAN, Ellis (M) **5 0**
b.Lincoln 8-1-01
From Leicester C.

2017–18	Lincoln C	0	0		
2018–19	Lincoln C	5	0	**5**	**0**

EARDLEY, Neal (M) **331 15**
H: 5 11 W: 11 10 b.Llandudno 6-11-88
Internationals: Wales U17, U19, U21, Full caps.

2005–06	Oldham Ath	1	0		
2006–07	Oldham Ath	36	2		
2007–08	Oldham Ath	42	6		
2008–09	Oldham Ath	34	2		
2009–10	Oldham Ath	0	0	**113**	**10**
2009–10	Blackpool	24	0		
2010–11	Blackpool	31	1		
2011–12	Blackpool	26	1		
2012–13	Blackpool	23	0	**104**	**2**
2013–14	Birmingham C	5	0		
2014–15	Birmingham C	4	0		
2014–15	*Leyton Orient*	1	0	**1**	**0**
2015–16	Birmingham C	5	0	**14**	**0**
2016–17	Hibernian	2	0	**2**	**0**
2016–17	Northampton T	10	0	**10**	**0**
2017–18	Lincoln C	44	1		
2018–19	Lincoln C	43	2	**87**	**3**

FRECKLINGTON, Lee (M) **427 64**
H: 5 8 W: 11 00 b.Lincoln 8-9-85
Internationals: Republic of Ireland B.

2003–04	Lincoln C	0	0		
2004–05	Lincoln C	3	0		
2005–06	Lincoln C	18	2		
2006–07	Lincoln C	42	8		
2007–08	Lincoln C	34	4		
2008–09	Lincoln C	27	7		
2008–09	Peterborough U	7	0		
2009–10	Peterborough U	35	2		
2010–11	Peterborough U	9	1		
2011–12	Peterborough U	37	5		
2012–13	Peterborough U	5	0	**93**	**8**
2012–13	*Rotherham U*	31	6		
2013–14	Rotherham U	39	10		
2014–15	Rotherham U	29	2		
2015–16	Rotherham U	27	5		
2016–17	Rotherham U	22	1		
2017–18	Rotherham U	19	4	**167**	**28**
2017–18	Lincoln C	16	4		
2018–19	Lincoln C	27	3	**167**	**28**

GILKS, Matthew (G) **430 0**
H: 6 3 W: 13 12 b.Rochdale 4-6-82
Internationals: Scotland Full caps.

2000–01	Rochdale	3	0		
2001–02	Rochdale	19	0		
2002–03	Rochdale	20	0		
2003–04	Rochdale	12	0		
2004–05	Rochdale	30	0		
2005–06	Rochdale	46	0		
2006–07	Rochdale	46	0	**176**	**0**
2007–08	Norwich C	0	0		
2008–09	Blackpool	5	0		
2008–09	*Shrewsbury T*	4	0	**4**	**0**
2009–10	Blackpool	26	0		
2010–11	Blackpool	18	0		
2011–12	Blackpool	42	0		
2012–13	Blackpool	45	0		
2013–14	Blackpool	46	0	**182**	**0**
2014–15	Burnley	0	0		
2015–16	Burnley	0	0		
2016–17	Rangers	0	0		
2016–17	Wigan Ath	14	0	**14**	**0**
2017–18	Scunthorpe U	42	0		
2018–19	Scunthorpe U	0	0	**42**	**0**
2018–19	Lincoln C	12	0	**12**	**0**

GORDON, Kellan (M) **32 5**
b.Burton 25-12-97

2017–18	Derby Co	0	0		
2017–18	*Swindon T*	26	3	**26**	**3**
2018–19	Lincoln C	6	2	**6**	**2**

GREEN, Matt (F) **206 42**
H: 6 0 W: 12 09 b.Bath 2-1-87
Internationals: England C.

2006–07	Cardiff C	6	0		
2007–08	Cardiff C	0	0	**6**	**0**
2007–08	*Darlington*	4	0	**4**	**0**

From Torquay U

2010–11	Oxford U	17	0	**17**	**0**
2010–11	*Cheltenham T*	19	0	**19**	**0**

From Mansfield T

2013–14	Birmingham C	10	1		
2014–15	Birmingham C	0	0	**10**	**1**
2015–16	Mansfield T	44	16		
2016–17	Mansfield T	42	10	**86**	**26**
2017–18	Lincoln C	45	13		
2018–19	Lincoln C	19	2	**64**	**15**

IDEHEN, Duncan (M) **0 0**

2018–19	Lincoln C	0	0		

LUQUE, Juan (F) **1 0**
b. 16-6-92
From Heybridge Swifts.

2018–19	Lincoln C	1	0	**1**	**0**

McCOMBE, Jamie (D) **396 27**
H: 6 5 W: 12 05 b.Scunthorpe 1-1-83

2001–02	Scunthorpe U	17	0		
2002–03	Scunthorpe U	31	1		
2003–04	Scunthorpe U	15	0	**63**	**1**
2003–04	Lincoln C	8	0		
2004–05	Lincoln C	41	3		
2005–06	Lincoln C	38	4		
2006–07	Bristol C	41	4		
2007–08	Bristol C	34	3		
2008–09	Bristol C	28	1		
2009–10	Bristol C	16	1	**119**	**9**
2010–11	Huddersfield T	34	5		
2011–12	Huddersfield T	20	3		
2011–12	*Preston NE*	6	0	**6**	**0**
2012–13	Huddersfield T	0	0	**54**	**8**
2012–13	Doncaster R	33	1		
2013–14	Doncaster R	2	0		
2014–15	Doncaster R	18	1	**53**	**2**
2015–16	Stevenage	14	0	**14**	**0**
2017–18	Lincoln C	0	0		
2018–19	Lincoln C	0	0	**87**	**7**

O'CONNOR, Michael (M) **395 37**
H: 6 1 W: 11 08 b.Belfast 6-10-87
Internationals: Northern Ireland U21, B, Full caps.

2005–06	Crewe Alex	2	0		
2006–07	Crewe Alex	29	0		
2007–08	Crewe Alex	23	0		
2008–09	Crewe Alex	23	3	**77**	**3**
2008–09	*Lincoln C*	10	1		
2009–10	Scunthorpe U	32	2		
2010–11	Scunthorpe U	32	8		
2011–12	Scunthorpe U	33	1	**97**	**11**
2012–13	Rotherham U	35	6		
2013–14	Rotherham U	29	2	**64**	**8**
2014–15	Port Vale	44	6		
2015–16	Port Vale	26	4	**70**	**10**
2016–17	Notts Co	32	2		
2017–18	Notts Co	6	0	**38**	**2**
2018–19	Lincoln C	39	2	**49**	**3**

O'HARA, Mark (M) **177 14**
H: 6 0 W: 11 07 b.Barrhead 12-12-95
Internationals: Scotland U19, U21.

2012–13	Kilmarnock	17	0		
2013–14	Kilmarnock	14	0		
2014–15	Kilmarnock	18	0		
2015–16	Kilmarnock	29	0	**78**	**0**
2016–17	Dundee	28	5		
2017–18	Dundee	32	4	**60**	**9**
2018–19	Peterborough U	22	4	**22**	**4**
2018–19	Lincoln C	17	1	**17**	**1**

PETT, Tom (M) 194 24
H: 5 8 W: 11 00 b. 3-12-91
Internationals: England C.

2014–15	Stevenage	34	7		
2015–16	Stevenage	40	1		
2016–17	Stevenage	40	6		
2017–18	Stevenage	27	6	**141**	**20**
2017–18	Lincoln C	9	1		
2018–19	Lincoln C	44	3	**53**	**4**

RHEAD, Matt (F) 147 18
b.Stoke-on-Trent 31-5-84

2013–14	Mansfield T	40	6		
2014–15	Mansfield T	32	3	**72**	**9**
2017–18	Lincoln C	41	8		
2018–19	Lincoln C	34	1	**75**	**9**

SARTORIUS, Elliot (F) 0 0

2018–19	Lincoln C	0	0		

SHACKELL, Jason (D) 479 17
H: 6 4 W: 13 06 b.Stevenage 27-9-83

2002–03	Norwich C	2	0		
2003–04	Norwich C	6	0		
2004–05	Norwich C	11	0		
2005–06	Norwich C	17	0		
2006–07	Norwich C	43	3		
2007–08	Norwich C	39	0		
2008–09	Norwich C	15	0	**133**	**3**
2008–09	Wolverhampton W	12	0		
2009–10	Wolverhampton W	0	0	**12**	**0**
2009–10	*Doncaster R*	21	1	**21**	**1**
2010–11	Barnsley	44	3		
2011–12	Barnsley	0	0	**44**	**3**
2011–12	Derby Co	46	1		
2012–13	Burnley	44	2		
2013–14	Burnley	46	2		
2014–15	Burnley	38	0	**128**	**4**
2015–16	Derby Co	46	1		
2016–17	Derby Co	8	0		
2017–18	Derby Co	0	0	**100**	**2**
2017–18	*Millwall*	7	0	**7**	**0**
2018–19	Lincoln C	34	4	**34**	**4**

SHAW, Tom (M) 0 0
H: 6 0 W: 11 09 b.Nottingham 1-12-86
Internationals: England C.

2018–19	Lincoln C	0	0		

SMITH, Grant (M) 16 0
b. 20-11-93

2012–13	Brighton & HA	0	0		
2013–14	Brighton & HA	0	0		

From Farnborough, Hayes & Yeading, Bognor Regis T, Boreham Wood.

2018–19	Lincoln C	16	0	**16**	**0**

SMITH, Jon (D) 0 0

2018–19	Lincoln C	0	0		

TOFFOLO, Harry (D) 123 6
H: 6 0 W: 11 03 b. 19-8-95
Internationals: England U18, U19, U20.

2014–15	Norwich C	0	0		
2014–15	*Swindon T*	28	1	**28**	**1**
2015–16	Norwich C	0	0		
2015–16	*Rotherham U*	7	0	**7**	**0**
2015–16	*Peterborough U*	7	0	**7**	**0**
2016–17	Norwich C	0	0		
2016–17	*Scunthorpe U*	22	2	**22**	**2**
2017–18	Norwich C	0	0		
2017–18	*Doncaster R*	13	0	**13**	**0**
2017–18	Millwall	0	0		
2018–19	Lincoln C	46	3	**46**	**3**

VICKERS, Josh (G) 58 0
H: 6 0 W: 11 05 b.Billericay 1-12-95
From Arsenal.

2015–16	Swansea C	0	0		
2016–17	Swansea C	0	0		
2016–17	*Barnet*	23	0	**23**	**0**
2017–18	Lincoln C	17	0		
2018–19	Lincoln C	18	0	**35**	**0**

WATKINS, Kyle (D) 0 0

2018–19	Lincoln C	0	0		

WILSON, James (D) 207 6
H: 6 2 W: 11 05 b.Chepstow 26-2-89
Internationals: Wales U19. U21, Full caps.

2005–06	Bristol C	0	0		
2006–07	Bristol C	0	0		
2007–08	Bristol C	0	0		
2008–09	Bristol C	2	0		
2008–09	*Brentford*	14	0		
2009–10	Bristol C	0	0		
2009–10	*Brentford*	13	0	**27**	**0**
2010–11	Bristol C	2	0		
2011–12	Bristol C	21	0		
2012–13	Bristol C	6	0		
2013–14	Bristol C	0	0	**31**	**0**
2013–14	*Cheltenham T*	4	0	**4**	**0**
2013–14	Oldham Ath	16	1		
2014–15	Oldham Ath	41	1		
2015–16	Oldham Ath	43	0	**100**	**2**
2016–17	Sheffield U	7	1		
2017–18	Sheffield U	0	0	**7**	**1**
2017–18	*Walsall*	19	1	**19**	**1**
2017–18	Lincoln C	8	1		
2018–19	Lincoln C	11	1	**19**	**2**

Scholars
Adebayo-Smith, Adebowale Aderinto Jordan; Bucci, Gianluca Franco; Burns, Joshua James; Cox, Lewis Stephen; Finlay, Tyler James; Flitton, Ryan Bradley; Gee, Max Thomas Samuel; Hart, Charlie; Liversidge, Tobias Alexander; Parsons, Niall Stephen; Smith, Jon Douglas; Watkins, Kyle; West, Charlie Taylor; Woodcock, Joshua Lewis; Woolley, Ross Haigh.

LIVERPOOL (45)

ALEXANDER-ARNOLD, Trent (M) 55 2
b. 7-10-98
Internationals: England U16, U17, U18, U19, U21, Full caps.

2016–17	Liverpool	7	0		
2017–18	Liverpool	19	1		
2018–19	Liverpool	29	1	**55**	**2**

ALISSON, Ramses (G) 119 0
H: 6 4 W: 14 05 b.Novo Hamburgo 2-10-92
Internationals: Brazil U17, U21, Full caps.

2013	Internacional	6	0		
2014	Internacional	11	0		
2015	Internacional	26	0		
2016	Internacional	1	0	**44**	**0**
2016–17	Roma	0	0		
2017–18	Roma	37	0	**37**	**0**
2018–19	Liverpool	38	0	**38**	**0**

BREWSTER, Rhian (F) 0 0
Internationals: England U16 U17, U18.
From Chelsea.

2016–17	Liverpool	0	0		
2017–18	Liverpool	0	0		
2018–19	Liverpool	0	0		

CAMACHO, Rafael (M) 1 0
b. 22-5-00
Internationals: Portugal U16, U17, U18.
From Manchester C.

2017–18	Liverpool	0	0		
2018–19	Liverpool	1	0	**1**	**0**

CHRISTIE-DAVIES, Isaac (M) 0 0
b.Brighton 18-9-97
Internationals: England U16, U17. Wales U21.

2018–19	Liverpool	0	0		

CLYNE, Nathaniel (D) 307 5
H: 5 9 W: 10 07 b.Stockwell 5-4-91
Internationals: England U19, U21, Full caps.

2008–09	Crystal Palace	26	0		
2009–10	Crystal Palace	22	1		
2010–11	Crystal Palace	46	0		
2011–12	Crystal Palace	28	0	**122**	**1**
2012–13	Southampton	34	1		
2013–14	Southampton	25	0		
2014–15	Southampton	35	2	**94**	**3**
2015–16	Liverpool	33	1		
2016–17	Liverpool	37	0		
2017–18	Liverpool	3	0		
2018–19	Liverpool	4	0	**77**	**1**
2018–19	*Bournemouth*	14	0	**14**	**0**

EJARIA, Oviemuno (M) 43 3
H: 6 0 W: 11 11 b.Southwark 18-11-97
Internationals: England U20, U21.
From Arsenal.

2016–17	Liverpool	2	0		
2017–18	Liverpool	0	0		
2017–18	*Sunderland*	11	1	**11**	**1**
2018–19	Liverpool	0	0	**2**	**0**
2018–19	*Rangers*	14	1	**14**	**1**
2018–19	*Reading*	16	1	**16**	**1**

FABINHO, Henrique (M) 196 24
H: 6 2 W: 12 04 b.Campinas 23-10-93
Internationals: Brazil Full caps.
From Fluminese.

2012–13	Rio Ave	0	0		
2012–13	*Real Madrid*	1	0	**1**	**0**
2013–14	Rio Ave	0	0		
2013–14	*Monaco*	26	0		
2014–15	Rio Ave	0	0		
2014–15	*Monaco*	36	1		
2015–16	Monaco	34	6		
2016–17	Monaco	37	9		
2017–18	Monaco	34	7	**167**	**23**
2018–19	Liverpool	28	1	**28**	**1**

FIRMINO, Roberto (M) 315 94
H: 5 11 W: 12 00 b.Maceio 2-10-91
Internationals: Brazil Full caps.

2009	Figueirense	2	0		
2010	Figueirense	36	8	**38**	**8**
2010–11	Hoffenheim	11	3		
2011–12	Hoffenheim	30	7		
2012–13	Hoffenheim	33	5		
2013–14	Hoffenheim	33	16		
2014–15	Hoffenheim	33	7	**140**	**38**
2015–16	Liverpool	31	10		
2016–17	Liverpool	35	11		
2017–18	Liverpool	37	15		
2018–19	Liverpool	34	12	**137**	**48**

GOMEZ, Joseph (D) 65 0
H: 6 2 W: 14 00 b.Catford 23-5-97
Internationals: England U16, U17, U19, U21, Full caps.

2014–15	Charlton Ath	21	0	**21**	**0**
2015–16	Liverpool	5	0		
2016–17	Liverpool	0	0		
2017–18	Liverpool	23	0		
2018–19	Liverpool	16	0	**44**	**0**

GRABARA, Kamil (G) 16 0
H: 6 3 W: 11 11 b.Ruda Slaska 8-1-99
Internationals: Portugal U17, U18, U21.
From Ruch Chorzow.

2016–17	Liverpool	0	0		
2017–18	Liverpool	0	0		
2018–19	Liverpool	0	0		
2018–19	*AGF Aarhus*	16	0	**16**	**0**

HENDERSON, Jordan (M) 320 27
H: 6 0 W: 10 07 b.Sunderland 17-6-90
Internationals: England U19, U20, U21, Full caps.

2008–09	Sunderland	1	0		
2008–09	*Coventry C*	10	1	**10**	**1**
2009–10	Sunderland	33	1		
2010–11	Sunderland	37	3	**71**	**4**
2011–12	Liverpool	37	2		
2012–13	Liverpool	30	5		
2013–14	Liverpool	35	4		
2014–15	Liverpool	37	6		
2015–16	Liverpool	17	2		
2016–17	Liverpool	24	1		
2017–18	Liverpool	27	1		
2018–19	Liverpool	32	1	**239**	**22**

HOEVER, Ki-Jana (D) 0 0
b.Amsterdam 18-1-02
Internationals: Netherlands U16, U17.
From Ajax.

2018–19	Liverpool	0	0		

INGS, Danny (F) 187 55
H: 5 10 W: 11 07 b.Winchester 16-3-92
Internationals: England U21, Full caps.

2009–10	Bournemouth	0	0		
2010–11	Bournemouth	26	7		
2011–12	Bournemouth	1	0	**27**	**7**
2011–12	Burnley	15	3		
2012–13	Burnley	32	3		
2013–14	Burnley	40	21		
2014–15	Burnley	35	11	**122**	**38**
2015–16	Liverpool	6	2		
2016–17	Liverpool	0	0		
2017–18	Liverpool	8	1		
2018–19	Liverpool	0	0	**14**	**3**
2018–19	*Southampton*	24	7	**24**	**7**

JONES, Curtis (M) 0 0
b. 30-1-01
Internationals: England U16, U17, U18.

2017–18	Liverpool	0	0		
2018–19	Liverpool	0	0		

KANE, Herbie (M) 38 4
H: 5 9 W: 10 08 b.Bristol 23-11-98
Internationals: England U16, U17, U18.

2018–19	Liverpool	0	0		
2018–19	*Doncaster R*	38	4	**38**	**4**

KARIUS, Loris (G) 150 0
H: 6 2 W: 11 11 b.Biberach 22-6-93
Internationals: Germany U16, U17, U18, U19, U20, U21.

2009–10	Manchester C	0	0		

2010–11	Manchester C	0	0		
2011–12	Manchester C	0	0		
2012–13	Manchester C	0	0		
2012–13	Mainz 05	1	0		
2013–14	Mainz 05	23	0		
2014–15	Mainz 05	33	0		
2015–16	Mainz 05	34	0	**91**	**0**
2016–17	Liverpool	10	0		
2017–18	Liverpool	19	0		
2018–19	Liverpool	0	0	**29**	**0**
2018–19	*Besiktas*	30	0	**30**	**0**

KEITA, Naby (M) 165 37
H: 5 8 W: 10 01 b.Conakry 10-2-95
Internationals: Guinea Full caps.

2013–14	Istres	23	4	**23**	**4**
2014–15	Red Bull Salzburg	30	5		
2015–16	Red Bull Salzburg	29	12	**59**	**17**
2016–17	RB Leipzig	31	8		
2017–18	RB Leipzig	27	6	**58**	**14**
2018–19	Liverpool	25	2	**25**	**2**

KELLEHER, Caoimhin (G) 0 0
H: 5 11 b.Cork 23-11-98
Internationals: Republic of Ireland U17, U19, U21.

2018–19	Liverpool	0	0		

LALLANA, Adam (M) 351 65
H: 5 8 W: 11 06 b.St Albans 10-5-88
Internationals: England U18, U19, U21, Full caps.

2005–06	Southampton	0	0		
2006–07	Southampton	1	0		
2007–08	Southampton	5	1		
2007–08	*Bournemouth*	3	0	**3**	**0**
2008–09	Southampton	40	1		
2009–10	Southampton	44	15		
2010–11	Southampton	36	8		
2011–12	Southampton	41	11		
2012–13	Southampton	30	3		
2013–14	Southampton	38	9	**235**	**48**
2014–15	Liverpool	27	5		
2015–16	Liverpool	30	4		
2016–17	Liverpool	31	8		
2017–18	Liverpool	12	0		
2018–19	Liverpool	13	0	**113**	**17**

LOVREN, Dejan (D) 311 11
H: 6 2 W: 13 02 b.Karlovac 5-7-89
Internationals: Croatia U17, U18, U19, U20, U21, Full caps.

2005–06	Dinamo Zagreb	1	0		
2006–07	Dinamo Zagreb	0	0		
2006–07	*Inter Zapresic*	21	0		
2007–08	Dinamo Zagreb	0	0		
2007–08	*Inter Zapresic*	29	1	**50**	**1**
2008–09	Dinamo Zagreb	22	1		
2009–10	Dinamo Zagreb	14	0	**37**	**1**
2009–10	Lyon	8	0		
2010–11	Lyon	28	0		
2011–12	Lyon	18	1		
2012–13	Lyon	18	1	**72**	**2**
2013–14	Southampton	31	2	**31**	**2**
2014–15	Liverpool	26	0		
2015–16	Liverpool	24	0		
2016–17	Liverpool	29	2		
2017–18	Liverpool	29	2		
2018–19	Liverpool	13	1	**121**	**5**

MANE, Sadio (F) 244 99
H: 5 9 W: 12 00 b.Sedhiou 10-4-92
Internationals: Senegal U23, Full caps.

2011–12	Metz	19	1		
2012–13	Metz	3	1	**22**	**2**
2012–13	Red Bull Salzburg	26	16		
2013–14	Red Bull Salzburg	33	13		
2014–15	Red Bull Salzburg	4	2	**63**	**31**
2014–15	Southampton	30	10		
2015–16	Southampton	37	11	**67**	**21**
2016–17	Liverpool	27	13		
2017–18	Liverpool	29	10		
2018–19	Liverpool	36	22	**92**	**45**

MATIP, Joel (M) 270 17
H: 6 4 W: 13 01 b.Bochum 8-8-91
Internationals: Cameroon Full caps.

2009–10	Schalke 04	20	3		
2010–11	Schalke 04	26	0		
2011–12	Schalke 04	30	3		
2012–13	Schalke 04	32	0		
2013–14	Schalke 04	31	3		
2014–15	Schalke 04	21	2		
2015–16	Schalke 04	34	3	**194**	**14**
2016–17	Liverpool	29	1		
2017–18	Liverpool	25	1		
2018–19	Liverpool	22	1	**76**	**3**

MIGNOLET, Simon (G) 367 1
H: 6 4 W: 13 10 b.St Truiden 6-3-88
Internationals: Belgium U16, U17, U18, U19, U20, U21, Full caps.

2006–07	St Truiden	2	0		
2007–08	St Truiden	25	0		
2008–09	St Truiden	35	1		
2009–10	St Truiden	37	0		
2010–11	St Truiden	23	0	**122**	**1**
2010–11	Sunderland	23	0		
2011–12	Sunderland	29	0		
2012–13	Sunderland	38	0	**90**	**0**
2013–14	Liverpool	38	0		
2014–15	Liverpool	36	0		
2015–16	Liverpool	34	0		
2016–17	Liverpool	28	0		
2017–18	Liverpool	19	0		
2018–19	Liverpool	0	0	**155**	**0**

MILNER, James (M) 522 55
H: 5 9 W: 11 00 b.Leeds 4-1-86
Internationals: England U16, U17, U19, U20, U21, Full caps.

2002–03	Leeds U	18	2		
2003–04	Leeds U	30	3	**48**	**5**
2003–04	*Swindon T*	6	2	**6**	**2**
2004–05	Newcastle U	25	1		
2005–06	Newcastle U	3	0		
2005–06	*Aston Villa*	27	1		
2006–07	Newcastle U	35	3		
2007–08	Newcastle U	29	2		
2008–09	Newcastle U	2	0	**94**	**6**
2008–09	Aston Villa	36	3		
2009–10	Aston Villa	36	7		
2010–11	Aston Villa	1	1	**100**	**12**
2010–11	Manchester C	32	0		
2011–12	Manchester C	26	3		
2012–13	Manchester C	26	4		
2013–14	Manchester C	31	1		
2014–15	Manchester C	32	5	**147**	**13**
2015–16	Liverpool	28	5		
2016–17	Liverpool	36	7		
2017–18	Liverpool	32	0		
2018–19	Liverpool	31	5	**127**	**17**

MORENO, Alberto (D) 145 6
H: 5 7 W: 10 01 b.Seville 5-7-92
Internationals: Spain U21, Full caps.

2011–12	Sevilla	11	0		
2012–13	Sevilla	15	0		
2013–14	Sevilla	29	3	**55**	**3**
2014–15	Liverpool	28	2		
2015–16	Liverpool	32	1		
2016–17	Liverpool	12	0		
2017–18	Liverpool	16	0		
2018–19	Liverpool	2	0	**90**	**3**

ORIGI, Divock (F) 167 35
H: 6 1 W: 11 11 b.Oostende 18-4-95
Internationals: Belgium U16, U17, U19, U21, Full caps.

2012–13	Lille	10	1		
2013–14	Lille	30	5		
2014–15	Lille	33	8	**73**	**14**
2015–16	Liverpool	16	5		
2016–17	Liverpool	34	7		
2017–18	Liverpool	1	0		
2017–18	*Wolfsburg*	31	6	**31**	**6**
2018–19	Liverpool	12	3	**63**	**15**

OXLADE-CHAMBERLAIN, Alex (M) 202 21
H: 5 11 W: 11 00 b.Portsmouth 15-8-93
Internationals: England U18, U19, U21, Full caps.

2009–10	Southampton	2	0		
2010–11	Southampton	34	9	**36**	**9**
2011–12	Arsenal	16	2		
2012–13	Arsenal	25	1		
2013–14	Arsenal	14	2		
2014–15	Arsenal	23	1		
2015–16	Arsenal	22	1		
2016–17	Arsenal	29	2		
2017–18	Arsenal	3	0	**132**	**9**
2017–18	Liverpool	32	3		
2018–19	Liverpool	2	0	**34**	**3**

RANDALL, Connor (D) 29 0
H: 5 11 W: 12 00 b.Liverpool 21-10-95
Internationals: England U17.

2014–15	Liverpool	0	0		
2014–15	*Shrewsbury T*	1	0	**1**	**0**
2015–16	Liverpool	3	0		
2016–17	Liverpool	0	0		
2017–18	Liverpool	0	0		
2017–18	*Hearts*	24	0	**24**	**0**
2018–19	Liverpool	0	0	**3**	**0**
2018–19	*Rochdale*	1	0	**1**	**0**

ROBERTSON, Andrew (D) 227 9
H: 5 10 W: 10 00 b.Glasgow 11-3-94
Internationals: Scotland U21, Full caps.

2012–13	Queen's Park	34	2	**34**	**2**
2013–14	Dundee U	36	3	**36**	**3**
2014–15	Hull C	24	0		
2015–16	Hull C	42	2		
2016–17	Hull C	33	1	**99**	**3**
2017–18	Liverpool	22	1		
2018–19	Liverpool	36	0	**58**	**1**

SALAH, Mohamed (M) 251 111
H: 5 9 W: 11 04 b.Basion 15-6-92
Internationals: Egypt U20, U23, Full caps.

2010–11	Al-Mokawloon	21	4		
2011–12	Al-Mokawloon	15	7	**36**	**11**
2012–13	Basle	29	5		
2013–14	Basle	18	4	**47**	**9**
2013–14	Chelsea	10	2		
2014–15	Chelsea	3	0		
2014–15	*Fiorentina*	16	6	**16**	**6**
2015–16	Chelsea	0	0	**13**	**2**
2015–16	*Roma*	34	14		
2016–17	Roma	31	15	**65**	**29**
2017–18	Liverpool	36	32		
2018–19	Liverpool	38	22	**74**	**54**

SHAQIRI, Xherdan (M) 267 51
H: 5 7 W: 11 05 b.Gnjilane 10-10-91
Internationals: Switzerland U17, U18, U19, U21, Full caps.

2009–10	Basel	32	4		
2010–11	Basel	29	5		
2011–12	Basel	31	9	**92**	**18**
2012–13	Bayern Munich	26	4		
2013–14	Bayern Munich	17	6		
2014–15	Bayern Munich	9	1	**52**	**11**
2014–15	Inter Milan	15	1	**15**	**1**
2015–16	Stoke C	27	3		
2016–17	Stoke C	21	4		
2017–18	Stoke C	36	8	**84**	**15**
2018–19	Liverpool	24	6	**24**	**6**

STURRIDGE, Daniel (F) 218 76
H: 6 2 W: 12 00 b.Birmingham 1-9-89
Internationals: England U16, U17, U18, U19, U20, U21, Full caps. Great Britain.

2006–07	Manchester C	2	0		
2007–08	Manchester C	3	1		
2008–09	Manchester C	16	4		
2009–10	Manchester C	0	0	**21**	**5**
2009–10	Chelsea	13	1		
2010–11	Chelsea	13	0		
2010–11	*Bolton W*	12	8	**12**	**8**
2011–12	Chelsea	30	11		
2012–13	Chelsea	7	1	**63**	**13**
2012–13	Liverpool	14	10		
2013–14	Liverpool	29	21		
2014–15	Liverpool	12	4		
2015–16	Liverpool	14	8		
2016–17	Liverpool	20	3		
2017–18	Liverpool	9	2		
2017–18	*WBA*	6	0	**6**	**0**
2018–19	Liverpool	18	2	**116**	**50**

VAN DIJK, Virgil (D) 257 24
H: 6 4 W: 14 07 b.Breda 8-7-91
Internationals: Netherlands U19, U21, Full caps.

2010–11	Groningen	5	2		
2011–12	Groningen	23	3		
2012–13	Groningen	34	2	**62**	**7**
2013–14	Celtic	36	5		
2014–15	Celtic	35	4		
2015–16	Celtic	5	0	**76**	**9**
2015–16	Southampton	34	3		
2016–17	Southampton	21	1		
2017–18	Southampton	12	0	**67**	**4**
2017–18	Liverpool	14	0		
2018–19	Liverpool	38	4	**52**	**4**

WHELAN, Corey (D) 23 1
b. 12-12-97
Internationals: Republic of Ireland U17, U21.

2017–18	Liverpool	0	0		
2017–18	*Yeovil T*	7	0	**7**	**0**
2018–19	Liverpool	0	0		
2018–19	*Crewe Alex*	16	1	**16**	**1**

WIJNALDUM, Georginio (M) 362 85
H: 5 8 W: 10 10 b.Rotterdam 11-11-90
Internationals: Netherlands U17, U19, U21, Full caps.

2006–07	Feyenoord	3	0		
2007–08	Feyenoord	10	1		
2008–09	Feyenoord	33	4		

2009–10	Feyenoord	31	4		
2010–11	Feyenoord	34	14	**111**	**23**
2011–12	PSV Eindhoven	32	9		
2012–13	PSV Eindhoven	33	14		
2013–14	PSV Eindhoven	11	4		
2014–15	PSV Eindhoven	33	14	**109**	**41**
2015–16	Newcastle U	38	11	**38**	**11**
2016–17	Liverpool	36	6		
2017–18	Liverpool	33	1		
2018–19	Liverpool	35	3	**104**	**10**

WILSON, Harry (M) **60 22**
H: 5 8 W: 11 00 b.Wrexham 22-3-97
Internationals: Wales U17, U19, U21, Full caps.

2015–16	Liverpool	0	0		
2015–16	*Crewe Alex*	7	0	**7**	**0**
2016–17	Liverpool	0	0		
2017–18	Liverpool	0	0		
2017–18	*Hull C*	13	7	**13**	**7**
2018–19	Liverpool	0	0		
2018–19	*Derby Co*	40	15	**40**	**15**

WOODBURN, Ben (F) **13 0**
H: 5 9 W: 11 05 b.Chester 16-11-99
Internationals: Wales U16, U17, U19, Full caps.

2016–17	Liverpool	5	0		
2017–18	Liverpool	1	0		
2018–19	Liverpool	0	0	**6**	**0**
2018–19	*Sheffield U*	7	0	**7**	**0**

Players retained or with offer of contract
Adekanye, Omobolaji Habeeb; Atherton, Daniel; Awoniyi, Taiwo; Boyes, Morgan; Chirivella Burgos, Pedro; Clayton, Thomas Andrew; Cordoba, Anderson Arroyo; Coyle, Liam; Dixon-Bonner, Elijah Malik; Duncan, Bobby; Gallacher, Tony; George, Shamal; Glatzel, Paul Milton; Grujic, Marko; Jaros , Viteslav; Johnston, George; Kent, Ryan; Larouci, Yasser; Lewis, Adam; Longstaff, Luis James; McKenzie-Lyle, Kai; Millar, Liam; Ojo, Oluwaseyi; Phillips, Nathaniel Harry; Raitanen, Patrik; Rodrigues De Souza, Allan; Walls, Jack; Williams, Neco Shay; Williams, Rhys.

Scholars
Bearne, Jack William Garrad; Beck, Owen Michael; Brookwell, Niall; Cain, Jake Steven; Clarkson, Leighton; Hoever, Ki-jana Delano; O'Rourke, Fidel; Ritaccio, Matteo; Savage, Remmi Eugene; Sharif, Abdulrahman Mohamoud; Tagseth, Edvard Sandvik; Turner, Alex; Varesanovic, Dal; Williams, Ben; Winterbottom, Benjamin Harry.

LUTON T (46)

BERRY, Luke (D) **180 40**
H: 5 10 W: 11 05 b.Bassingbourn 12-7-92

2014–15	Barnsley	31	1	**31**	**1**
2015–16	Cambridge U	46	12		
2016–17	Cambridge U	45	17		
2017–18	Cambridge U	3	0	**94**	**29**
2017–18	Luton T	34	7		
2018–19	Luton T	21	3	**55**	**10**

BRADLEY, Sonny (D) **292 16**
H: 6 0 W: 11 05 b.Hedon 14-6-92

2011–12	Hull C	2	0		
2011–12	*Aldershot T*	14	0		
2012–13	Hull C	0	0	**2**	**0**
2012–13	*Aldershot T*	42	1	**56**	**1**
2013–14	Portsmouth	33	2	**33**	**2**
2014–15	Crawley T	26	1		
2015–16	Crawley T	46	1	**72**	**2**
2016–17	Plymouth Arg	44	7		
2017–18	Plymouth Arg	40	4	**84**	**11**
2018–19	Luton T	45	0	**45**	**0**

COLLINS, James S (F) **384 141**
H: 6 2 W: 13 08 b.Coventry 1-12-90
Internationals: Republic of Ireland U19, U21.

2008–09	Aston Villa	0	0		
2009–10	Aston Villa	0	0		
2009–10	*Darlington*	7	2	**7**	**2**
2010–11	Aston Villa	0	0		
2010–11	*Burton Alb*	10	4	**10**	**4**
2010–11	Shrewsbury T	24	8		
2011–12	Shrewsbury T	42	14		
2012–13	Swindon T	45	15	**45**	**15**
2013–14	Hibernian	36	6	**36**	**6**
2014–15	Shrewsbury T	45	15		
2015–16	Shrewsbury T	23	5	**134**	**42**
2015–16	*Northampton T*	21	8	**21**	**8**
2016–17	Crawley T	45	20	**45**	**20**
2017–18	Luton T	42	19		
2018–19	Luton T	44	25	**86**	**44**

CORNICK, Harry (F) **122 19**
H: 5 11 W: 13 03 b.Poole 6-3-95

2013–14	Bournemouth	0	0		
2014–15	Bournemouth	0	0		
2015–16	Bournemouth	0	0		
2015–16	*Yeovil T*	36	7	**36**	**7**
2016–17	Bournemouth	0	0		
2016–17	*Leyton Orient*	11	1	**11**	**1**
2016–17	*Gillingham*	6	0	**6**	**0**
2017–18	Luton T	37	5		
2018–19	Luton T	32	6	**69**	**11**

GAMBIN, Luke (M) **129 15**
H: 5 6 W: 11 00 b.Surrey 16-3-93
Internationals: Malta Full caps.

2011–12	Barnet	1	0		
2012–13	Barnet	10	2		
2015–16	Barnet	44	4		
2016–17	Barnet	19	4	**74**	**10**
2016–17	Luton T	16	1		
2017–18	Luton T	13	1		
2018–19	Luton T	0	0	**29**	**2**
2018–19	*Crawley T*	26	3	**26**	**3**

GRANT, Jorge (M) **113 27**
H: 5 9 W: 11 07 b.Oxford 26-9-94

2013–14	Nottingham F	0	0		
2014–15	Nottingham F	1	0		
2015–16	Nottingham F	10	0		
2016–17	Nottingham F	6	0		
2016–17	*Notts Co*	17	6		
2017–18	Nottingham F	0	0	**17**	**0**
2017–18	*Notts Co*	45	15	**62**	**21**
2018–19	Luton T	17	2	**17**	**2**
2018–19	*Mansfield T*	17	4	**17**	**4**

HYLTON, Danny (F) **367 111**
H: 6 0 W: 11 13 b.Camden 25-2-89

2008–09	Aldershot T	29	5		
2009–10	Aldershot T	21	3		
2010–11	Aldershot T	33	5		
2011–12	Aldershot T	44	13		
2012–13	Aldershot T	27	4	**154**	**30**
2013–14	Rotherham U	1	0	**1**	**0**
2013–14	*Bury*	7	2	**7**	**2**
2013–14	*AFC Wimbledon*	17	3	**17**	**3**
2014–15	Oxford U	44	14		
2015–16	Oxford U	41	12	**85**	**26**
2016–17	Luton T	39	21		
2017–18	Luton T	39	21		
2018–19	Luton T	25	8	**103**	**50**

ISTED, Harry (G) **0 0**
b. 5-3-97
From Southampton, Stoke C.

2017–18	Luton T	0	0		
2018–19	Luton T	0	0		

JAMES, Jack (F) **0 0**
Internationals: Republic of Ireland U18, U19.

2017–18	Luton T	0	0		
2018–19	Luton T	0	0		

JARVIS, Aaron (F) **17 0**
H: 6 2 W: 12 08 b. 24-1-98
From Basinstoke T.

2017–18	Luton T	1	0		
2018–19	Luton T	4	0	**5**	**0**
2018–19	*Falkirk*	12	0	**12**	**0**

JERVIS, Jake (F) **241 50**
H: 6 3 W: 12 13 b.Birmingham 17-9-91

2009–10	Birmingham C	0	0		
2009–10	*Hereford U*	7	2		
2010–11	Birmingham C	0	0		
2010–11	*Notts Co*	10	0	**10**	**0**
2010–11	*Hereford U*	4	0	**11**	**2**
2011–12	Birmingham C	0	0		
2011–12	*Swindon T*	12	3	**12**	**3**
2011–12	*Preston NE*	5	2	**5**	**2**
2012–13	Birmingham C	2	0	**2**	**0**
2012–13	*Carlisle U*	5	3	**5**	**3**
2012–13	*Tranmere R*	4	1	**4**	**1**
2012–13	*Portsmouth*	3	1		
2012–13	Elazigspor	4	1	**4**	**1**
2013–14	Portsmouth	15	4	**18**	**5**
2014–15	Ross Co	27	4	**27**	**4**
2015–16	Plymouth Arg	42	11		
2016–17	Plymouth Arg	42	12		
2017–18	Plymouth Arg	24	4	**108**	**27**
2017–18	Luton T	10	0		
2018–19	Luton T	2	0	**12**	**0**
2018–19	*AFC Wimbledon*	23	2	**23**	**2**

JONES, Lloyd (D) **62 4**
H: 6 3 W: 11 11 b.Plymouth 7-10-95
Internationals: Wales U17, U19. England U19, U20.

2012–13	Liverpool	0	0		
2013–14	Liverpool	0	0		
2014–15	Liverpool	0	0		
2014–15	*Cheltenham T*	6	0	**6**	**0**
2014–15	*Accrington S*	11	1	**11**	**1**
2015–16	Liverpool	0	0		
2015–16	*Blackpool*	10	0	**10**	**0**
2016–17	Liverpool	0	0		
2016–17	*Swindon T*	24	2	**24**	**2**
2017–18	Liverpool	0	0		
2017–18	Luton T	1	0		
2018–19	Luton T	1	0	**2**	**0**
2018–19	*Plymouth Arg*	9	1	**9**	**1**

JUSTIN, James (F) **90 6**
H: 6 0 W: 11 03 b.Luton 11-7-97
Internationals: England U20.

2015–16	Luton T	1	0		
2016–17	Luton T	29	1		
2017–18	Luton T	17	2		
2018–19	Luton T	43	3	**90**	**6**

LEE, Elliot (F) **112 28**
H: 5 11 W: 11 05 b.Co. Durham 16-12-94

2011–12	West Ham U	0	0		
2012–13	West Ham U	0	0		
2013–14	West Ham U	1	0		
2013–14	*Colchester U*	4	1		
2014–15	West Ham U	1	0		
2014–15	*Southend U*	0	0		
2014–15	*Luton T*	11	3		
2015–16	West Ham U	0	0	**2**	**0**
2015–16	*Blackpool*	4	0	**4**	**0**
2015–16	*Colchester U*	15	2	**19**	**3**
2016–17	Barnsley	6	0	**6**	**0**
2017–18	Luton T	32	10		
2018–19	Luton T	38	12	**81**	**25**

LUALUA, Kazenga (F) **217 20**
H: 5 11 W: 12 00 b.Kinshasa 10-12-90

2007–08	Newcastle U	2	0		
2008–09	Newcastle U	3	0		
2008–09	*Doncaster R*	4	0	**4**	**0**
2009–10	Newcastle U	1	0		
2009–10	*Brighton & HA*	11	0		
2010–11	Newcastle U	2	0		
2010–11	*Brighton & HA*	11	4		
2011–12	Newcastle U	0	0	**8**	**0**
2011–12	Brighton & HA	27	1		
2012–13	Brighton & HA	22	5		
2013–14	Brighton & HA	32	1		
2014–15	Brighton & HA	34	3		
2015–16	Brighton & HA	18	3		
2016–17	Brighton & HA	3	0		
2016–17	*QPR*	11	1		
2017–18	Brighton & HA	0	0	**158**	**17**
2017–18	*QPR*	8	0	**19**	**1**
2017–18	Sunderland	6	0	**6**	**0**
2018–19	Luton T	22	2	**22**	**2**

McCORMACK, Alan (M) **429 26**
H: 5 8 W: 11 00 b.Dublin 10-1-84
Internationals: Republic of Ireland U19.

2002–03	Preston NE	0	0		
2003–04	Preston NE	5	0		
2003–04	*Leyton Orient*	10	0	**10**	**0**
2004–05	Preston NE	3	0		
2004–05	*Southend U*	7	2		
2005–06	Preston NE	0	0		
2005–06	*Motherwell*	24	2	**24**	**2**
2006–07	Preston NE	3	0	**11**	**0**
2006–07	Southend U	22	3		
2007–08	Southend U	42	8		
2008–09	Southend U	34	2		
2009–10	Southend U	41	3	**146**	**18**
2010–11	Charlton Ath	24	1	**24**	**1**
2011–12	Swindon T	40	2		
2012–13	Swindon T	40	0	**80**	**2**
2013–14	Brentford	43	1		
2014–15	Brentford	18	1		
2015–16	Brentford	27	0		
2016–17	Brentford	11	0	**99**	**2**
2017–18	Luton T	16	1		
2018–19	Luton T	19	0	**35**	**1**

MONCUR, George (M) **202 36**
H: 5 9 W: 10 00 b.Swindon 18-8-93
Internationals: England U18.

2010–11	West Ham U	0	0		
2011–12	West Ham U	0	0		
2011–12	*AFC Wimbledon*	20	2	**20**	**2**
2012–13	West Ham U	0	0		

2013–14	West Ham U	0	0		
2013–14	*Partick Thistle*	2	1	**2**	**1**
2014–15	Colchester U	41	8		
2015–16	Colchester U	45	12	**86**	**20**
2016–17	Peterborough U	13	2	**13**	**2**
2016–17	Barnsley	12	2		
2017–18	Barnsley	34	2		
2018–19	Barnsley	21	1	**67**	**5**
2018–19	Luton T	14	6	**14**	**6**

MUSONDA, Frankie (D) **3** **0**
H: 6 0 W: 11 03 b.Bedford 12-12-97

2015–16	Luton T	3	0		
2016–17	Luton T	0	0		
2017–18	Luton T	0	0		
2018–19	Luton T	0	0	**3**	**0**

NEUFVILLE, Josh (M) **0** **0**
b.Luton --

2017–18	Luton T	0	0		
2018–19	Luton T	0	0		

PANTER, Corey (D) **0** **0**

2018–19	Luton T	0	0		

PEARSON, Matthew (D) **161** **17**
H: 6 3 W: 11 05 b.Keighley 3-8-93
Internationals: England U18, C.

2012–13	Rochdale	9	0		
2013–14	Rochdale	0	0	**9**	**0**
2015–16	Accrington S	46	3		
2016–17	Accrington S	43	8	**89**	**11**
2017–18	Barnsley	17	0	**17**	**0**
2018–19	Luton T	46	6	**46**	**6**

PECK, Jake (M) **0** **0**

2017–18	Luton T	0	0		
2018–19	Luton T	0	0		

POTTS, Danny (D) **118** **7**
H: 5 8 W: 11 00 b.Barking 13-4-94
Internationals: USA U20. England U18, U19, U20.

2011–12	West Ham U	3	0		
2012–13	West Ham U	2	0		
2012–13	*Colchester U*	5	0	**5**	**0**
2013–14	West Ham U	0	0		
2013–14	*Portsmouth*	5	0	**5**	**0**
2014–15	West Ham U	0	0	**5**	**0**
2015–16	Luton T	14	0		
2016–17	Luton T	23	0		
2017–18	Luton T	42	6		
2018–19	Luton T	24	1	**103**	**7**

REA, Glen (D) **131** **4**
H: 6 0 W: 11 07 b.Brighton 3-9-94
Internationals: Republic of Ireland U21.

2013–14	Brighton & HA	0	0		
2014–15	Brighton & HA	0	0		
2015–16	Brighton & HA	0	0		
2015–16	*Southend U*	14	0	**14**	**0**
2015–16	*Luton T*	10	0		
2016–17	Luton T	39	2		
2017–18	Luton T	46	1		
2018–19	Luton T	22	1	**117**	**4**

READ, Arthur (M) **0** **0**
H: 5 10 W: 10 01 b.Leighton Buzzard 3-11-99

2018–19	Luton T	0	0		

RICHARDSON, Drew (M) **0** **0**
b.Luton 14-1-01

2017–18	Luton T	0	0		
2018–19	Luton T	0	0		

RUDDOCK, Pelly (M) **153** **12**
H: 5 9 W: 9 13 b.Hendon 17-7-93

2011–12	West Ham U	0	0		
2013–14	West Ham U	0	0		
2014–15	Luton T	16	1		
2015–16	Luton T	21	2		
2016–17	Luton T	42	2		
2017–18	Luton T	28	2		
2018–19	Luton T	46	5	**153**	**12**

SENIOR, Jack (D) **10** **0**
H: 5 8 W: 9 13 b.Halifax 13-1-97

2015–16	Huddersfield T	0	0		
2016–17	Luton T	10	0		
2017–18	Luton T	0	0		
2018–19	Luton T	0	0	**10**	**0**

SHEA, James (G) **145** **0**
H: 5 11 W: 12 00 b.Islington 16-6-91

2009–10	Arsenal	0	0		
2010–11	Arsenal	0	0		
2011–12	Arsenal	0	0		
2011–12	*Dagenham & R*	1	0	**1**	**0**
2012–13	Arsenal	0	0		
2013–14	Arsenal	0	0		
2014–15	AFC Wimbledon	38	0		
2015–16	AFC Wimbledon	21	0		
2016–17	AFC Wimbledon	36	0	**95**	**0**
2017–18	Luton T	8	0		
2018–19	Luton T	41	0	**49**	**0**

SHEEHAN, Alan (D) **376** **24**
H: 5 11 W: 11 02 b.Athlone 14-9-86
Internationals: Republic of Ireland U21.

2004–05	Leicester C	1	0		
2005–06	Leicester C	2	0		
2006–07	Leicester C	0	0		
2006–07	*Mansfield T*	10	0	**10**	**0**
2007–08	Leicester C	20	1	**23**	**1**
2007–08	*Leeds U*	10	1		
2008–09	Leeds U	11	1		
2008–09	*Crewe Alex*	3	0	**3**	**0**
2009–10	Leeds U	0	0	**21**	**2**
2009–10	*Oldham Ath*	8	1	**8**	**1**
2009–10	*Swindon T*	22	1		
2010–11	Swindon T	21	1	**43**	**2**
2011–12	Notts Co	39	2		
2012–13	Notts Co	33	0		
2013–14	Notts Co	42	7		
2014–15	Bradford C	23	1		
2014–15	*Peterborough U*	2	0	**2**	**0**
2015–16	Bradford C	2	0	**25**	**1**
2015–16	*Notts Co*	14	2	**128**	**11**
2015–16	*Luton T*	20	1		
2016–17	Luton T	34	2		
2017–18	Luton T	42	3		
2018–19	Luton T	17	0	**113**	**6**

SHINNIE, Andrew (M) **225** **29**
H: 5 11 W: 10 13 b.Aberdeen 17-7-89
Internationals: Scotland U19, U21, Full caps.

2005–06	Rangers	0	0		
2006–07	Rangers	2	0		
2007–08	Rangers	0	0		
2008–09	Rangers	0	0		
2009–10	Rangers	0	0		
2010–11	Rangers	0	0	**2**	**0**
2011–12	Inverness CT	19	7		
2012–13	Inverness CT	38	12	**57**	**19**
2013–14	Birmingham C	26	2		
2014–15	Birmingham C	27	2		
2015–16	Birmingham C	14	0		
2015–16	*Rotherham U*	3	0	**3**	**0**
2016–17	Birmingham C	0	0	**67**	**4**
2016–17	*Hibernian*	27	1	**27**	**1**
2017–18	Luton T	28	1		
2018–19	Luton T	41	4	**69**	**5**

STACEY, Jack (M) **137** **7**
H: 6 4 W: 13 05 b.Bracknell 6-4-96

2014–15	Reading	6	0		
2015–16	Reading	0	0		
2015–16	*Barnet*	2	0	**2**	**0**
2015–16	*Carlisle U*	9	2	**9**	**2**
2016–17	Reading	0	0	**6**	**0**
2016–17	*Exeter C*	34	0	**34**	**0**
2017–18	Luton T	41	1		
2018–19	Luton T	45	4	**86**	**5**

STECH, Marek (G) **144** **0**
H: 6 3 W: 14 00 b.Prague 28-1-90
Internationals: Czech Republic U17 U21, Full caps.

2008–09	West Ham U	0	0		
2008–09	*Wycombe W*	2	0	**2**	**0**
2009–10	West Ham U	0	0		
2009–10	*Bournemouth*	1	0	**1**	**0**
2010–11	West Ham U	0	0		
2011–12	West Ham U	0	0		
2011–12	*Yeovil T*	5	0		
2011–12	*Leyton Orient*	2	0	**2**	**0**
2012–13	Yeovil T	46	0		
2013–14	Yeovil T	26	0	**77**	**0**
2014–15	Sparta Prague	17	0		
2015–16	Sparta Prague	2	0		
2016–17	Sparta Prague	0	0	**19**	**0**
2017–18	Luton T	38	0		
2018–19	Luton T	5	0	**43**	**0**

TOMLINSON, Connor (F) **0** **0**
b. 12-2-01

2016–17	Luton T	0	0		
2017–18	Luton T	0	0		
2018–19	Luton T	0	0		

Players retained or with offer of contract
Mpanzu, Pelly Ruddock.

Scholars
Beckwith, Samuel Wayne; Boorn, Joshua John Batten; Byron, Toby Joshua Olakunle; Jones, Avan Chima Allan; Kalonda, Jonas; Panter, Corey James Rodney; Parker, Tiernan Christopher Luke; Peck, Jake David; Richardson, Drew Philip; Tomlinson, Connor Alexander; Wilson, Braithwaite Dequane Anthomy.

MACCLESFIELD T (47)

ANDOH, Ebo (M) **49** **2**
b. 1-1-93
Internationals: Ghana U20.

2012–13	AEL Limassol	20	0		
2013–14	AEL Limassol	17	1	**37**	**1**
2014–15	Port Vale	0	0		
2015–16	Port Vale	12	1	**12**	**1**

From Whitehawk, Nuneaton Bor.

2018–19	Macclesfield T	0	0		

ARTHUR, Koby (M) **44** **6**
H: 5 6 W: 10 09 b.Kumasi 3-1-96

2012–13	Birmingham C	2	0		
2013–14	Birmingham C	1	0		
2014–15	Birmingham C	9	0		
2014–15	*Cheltenham T*	7	3		
2015–16	Birmingham C	0	0		
2016–17	Birmingham C	0	0	**12**	**0**
2016–17	*Cheltenham T*	5	0	**12**	**3**
2018–19	Macclesfield T	20	3	**20**	**3**

BLISSETT, Nathan (F) **43** **3**
H: 6 0 W: 12 04 b.West Bromwich 29-6-90
From Kidderminster H.

2015–16	Bristol R	2	0	**2**	**0**
2016–17	Plymouth Arg	9	2		
2017–18	Plymouth Arg	13	1	**22**	**3**
2018–19	Macclesfield T	19	0	**19**	**0**

CAMERON, Nathan (D) **202** **13**
H: 6 2 W: 12 04 b.Birmingham 21-11-91
Internationals: England U20.

2009–10	Coventry C	0	0		
2010–11	Coventry C	25	0		
2011–12	Coventry C	14	0		
2012–13	Coventry C	9	0	**48**	**0**
2012–13	*Northampton T*	3	0	**3**	**0**
2013–14	Bury	27	4		
2014–15	Bury	46	2		
2015–16	Bury	28	3		
2016–17	Bury	4	0		
2017–18	Bury	21	2	**126**	**11**
2018–19	Macclesfield T	25	2	**25**	**2**

DEMETRIOU, Stelios (D) **197** **14**
H: 6 0 W: 11 09 b.Islington 4-10-90
Internationals: Cyprus U21, Full caps.

2009–10	Nikos & Sokatis Erimis	23	2	**23**	**2**
2010–11	Akritas Chlorakas	23	4	**23**	**4**
2011–12	Apollon Limassol	0	0		
2011–12	*Erimis Aradippou*	11	1		
2012–13	Lokomotive Plovdiv	3	0	**3**	**0**
2012–13	Erimis Aradippou	10	0		
2013–14	Erimis Aradippou	25	1		
2014–15	Erimis Aradippou	6	0	**52**	**2**
2015	Akropolis IF	5	0	**5**	**0**
2015–16	Doxa Katokopias	29	2		
2016–17	Doxa Katokopias	17	0	**46**	**2**
2016–17	St Mirren	11	3		
2017–18	St Mirren	23	1	**34**	**4**
2018–19	Ross Co	9	0	**9**	**0**
2018–19	Macclesfield T	2	0	**2**	**0**

DURRELL, Elliott (M) **17** **4**
H: 5 10 W: 11 11 b.Shrewsbury 31-7-89

2018–19	Macclesfield T	17	4	**17**	**4**

EVANS, Callum (D) **19** **1**
H: 5 10 W: 11 05 b.Bristol 11-10-95
From Manchester U.

2015–16	Barnsley	0	0		
2016–17	Barnsley	3	0	**3**	**0**
2017–18	Forest Green R	2	0	**2**	**0**
2018–19	Macclesfield T	14	1	**14**	**1**

FITZPATRICK, David (D) **40** **3**
H: 5 10 W: 11 07 b.Manchester 22-2-90

2018–19	Macclesfield T	40	3	**40**	**3**

GRIMES, Jamie (D) **56** **4**
H: 6 2 W: 12 10 b.Nottingham 22-12-90
From Swansea C, Redditch U, Bedford T, Kidderminster H, Dover Ath.

2017–18	Cheltenham T	43	3	**43**	**3**
2018–19	Macclesfield T	13	1	**13**	**1**

HODGKISS, Jared (D) **39** **0**
H: 5 7 W: 11 05 b.Stafford 15-11-86

2005–06	WBA	1	0		

2006–07 WBA 5 0
2007–08 WBA 4 0
2008–09 WBA 0 0 **10 0**
2008–09 *Aberdeen* 7 0 **7 0**
2008–09 *Northampton T* 5 0 **5 0**
From Forest Green R, Kidderminster H, Torquay U.
2018–19 Macclesfield T 17 0 **17 0**

IDEM, Manny (G) 0 0
2018–19 Aston Villa 0 0
2018–19 Macclesfield T 0 0

JULES, Zak (D) 32 1
b. 2-7-97
Internationals: Scotland U17, U18, U19, U20, U21.
2016–17 Reading 0 0
2016–17 *Motherwell* 10 1 **10 1**
2017–18 Shrewsbury T 0 0
2017–18 *Chesterfield* 6 0 **6 0**
2017–18 *Port Vale* 2 0 **2 0**
2018–19 Macclesfield T 14 0 **14 0**

KELLEHER, Fiacre (D) 42 1
b. 10-3-96
2016–17 Celtic 0 0
2016–17 Peterhead 0 0
2017–18 Oxford U 0 0
2018–19 Macclesfield T 42 1 **42 1**

LLOYD, Ryan (M) 30 0
H: 5 10 W: 10 03 b.Newcastle-u-Lyme 1-2-94
2010–11 Port Vale 1 0
2011–12 Port Vale 2 0
2012–13 Port Vale 6 0
2013–14 Port Vale 3 0
2014–15 Port Vale 0 0
2015–16 Port Vale 5 0
2016–17 Port Vale 0 0 **17 0**
2018–19 Macclesfield T 13 0 **13 0**

LOWE, Keith (D) 313 20
H: 6 2 W: 13 03 b.Wolverhampton 13-9-85
2004–05 Wolverhampton W 11 0
2005–06 Wolverhampton W 3 0
2005–06 *Burnley* 16 0 **16 0**
2005–06 *QPR* 1 0 **1 0**
2005–06 *Swansea C* 4 0 **4 0**
2006–07 Wolverhampton W 0 0
2006–07 *Brighton & HA* 0 0
2006–07 *Cheltenham T* 16 1
2007–08 Wolverhampton W 0 0
2007–08 *Port Vale* 28 3 **28 3**
2008–09 Wolverhampton W 0 0 **14 0**
2009–10 Hereford U 19 1 **19 1**
2010–11 Cheltenham T 36 1
2011–12 Cheltenham T 30 1
2012–13 Cheltenham T 31 4
2013–14 Cheltenham T 13 1 **126 8**
2013–14 York C 30 1
2014–15 York C 46 6
2015–16 York C 16 1 **92 8**
From Kidderminister H.
2018–19 Macclesfield T 13 0 **13 0**

MARSH, Tyrone (F) 32 2
b. 24-12-93
2012–13 Oxford U 2 0
2013–14 Oxford U 5 0 **7 0**
From Ebbsfleet U, Torquay U, Dover Ath.
2018–19 Macclesfield T 25 2 **25 2**

MARTIS, Liandro (F) 6 0
b. 13-11-95
Internationals: Curacao U17, U20, Full caps.
2016–17 Leicester C 0 0
2017–18 Leicester C 0 0
2018–19 Leicester C 0 0
2018–19 Macclesfield T 6 0 **6 0**

NTAMBWE, Brice (M) 89 4
H: 6 1 W: 12 13 b.Brussels 29-4-93
Internationals: Belgium U16, U17, U19, U20, U21.
2011–12 Birmingham C 0 0
2012–13 Mons 6 0
2013–14 Mons 19 0
2014–15 Mons 2 0 **27 0**
2014–15 Lierse 1 0
2015–16 Lierse 0 0
2016–17 Lierse 18 1
2017–18 Lierse 21 1 **40 2**
2017–18 *Oosterwijk* 9 1 **9 1**
2018–19 Partick Thistle 5 1 **5 1**
2018–19 Macclesfield T 8 0 **8 0**

PEARSON, James (D) 41 1
H: 6 1 W: 11 11 b.Sheffield 19-1-93
2013–14 Leicester C 0 0
2013–14 *Carlisle U* 3 0 **3 0**
2014–15 Leicester C 0 0
2014–15 *Peterborough U* 0 0
2015–16 Barnet 15 0
2016–17 Barnet 0 0 **15 0**
2017–18 Coventry C 0 0
2018–19 Macclesfield T 23 1 **23 1**

ROSE, Michael (D) 489 37
H: 5 11 W: 12 04 b.Salford 28-7-82
Internationals: England C.
1999–2000 Manchester U 0 0
2000–01 Manchester U 0 0
2001–02 Manchester U 0 0
From Hereford U
2004–05 Yeovil T 40 1
2005–06 Yeovil T 1 0 **41 1**
2005–06 *Cheltenham T* 3 0 **3 0**
2005–06 *Scunthorpe U* 15 0 **15 0**
2006–07 Stockport Co 25 3
2007–08 Stockport Co 28 3
2008–09 Stockport Co 27 0
2009–10 Stockport Co 24 2 **104 8**
2009–10 *Norwich C* 12 1 **12 1**
2010–11 Swindon T 35 3 **35 3**
2010–11 Colchester U 0 0
2011–12 Colchester U 14 0
2012–13 Colchester U 22 2 **36 2**
2012–13 Rochdale 14 2
2013–14 Rochdale 42 4
2014–15 Rochdale 32 1
2015–16 Rochdale 30 1 **118 8**
2016–17 Morecambe 43 7
2017–18 Morecambe 42 2 **85 9**
2018–19 Macclesfield T 40 5 **40 5**

SIMPSON, Luke (G) 8 0
H: 5 10 W: 12 03 b.Bury 23-9-94
2012–13 Oldham Ath 0 0
2013–14 Oldham Ath 0 0
2014–15 Accrington S 8 0 **8 0**
2015–16 Watford 0 0
From York C.
2018–19 Macclesfield T 0 0

SMITH, Harry (F) 62 11
H: 6 5 b. 18-5-95
From Sittingbourne, Folkestone Invicta.
2016–17 Millwall 9 1
2017–18 Millwall 0 0 **9 1**
2017–18 *Swindon T* 14 2 **14 2**
2018–19 Macclesfield T 39 8 **39 8**

STEPHENS, Ben (M) 22 1
b. 9-8-97
From Oadby T, Kettering T, Stratford T.
2018–19 Macclesfield T 22 1 **22 1**

TAYLOR, Rhys (G) 74 0
H: 6 2 W: 12 08 b.Neath 7-4-90
Internationals: Wales U17, U19, U21.
2007–08 Chelsea 0 0
2008–09 Chelsea 0 0
2009–10 Chelsea 0 0
2010–11 Chelsea 0 0
2010–11 *Crewe Alex* 44 0 **44 0**
2011–12 Chelsea 0 0
2011–12 *Rotherham U* 20 0 **20 0**
2012–13 Chelsea 0 0
2012–13 Preston NE 0 0
2012–13 Macclesfield T 0 0
2015–16 Newport Co 1 0 **1 0**
From AFC Fylde.
2018–19 Macclesfield T 9 0 **9 0**

VINCENTI, Peter (F) 280 46
H: 6 2 W: 11 13 b.St Peter 7-7-86
2007–08 Millwall 0 0
2010–11 Stevenage 5 1 **5 1**
2010–11 Aldershot T 23 6
2011–12 Aldershot T 42 6
2012–13 Aldershot T 39 2 **104 14**
2013–14 Rochdale 42 5
2014–15 Rochdale 37 13
2015–16 Rochdale 38 8
2016–17 Rochdale 14 1 **131 27**
2017–18 Coventry C 24 3 **24 3**
2018–19 Macclesfield T 16 1 **16 1**

WELCH-HAYES, Miles (D) 24 0
b.Oxford 25-10-96
2016–17 Oxford U 1 0 **1 0**
Frm Bath C.
2018–19 Macclesfield T 23 0 **23 0**

WHITAKER, Danny (M) 465 69
H: 5 10 W: 11 00 b.Wilmslow 14-11-80
2000–01 Macclesfield T 0 0
2001–02 Macclesfield T 16 2
2002–03 Macclesfield T 41 10
2003–04 Macclesfield T 36 5
2004–05 Macclesfield T 36 2
2005–06 Macclesfield T 42 4
2006–07 Port Vale 45 7
2007–08 Port Vale 41 7 **86 14**
2008–09 Oldham Ath 39 6
2009–10 Oldham Ath 41 2 **80 8**
2010–11 Chesterfield 46 15
2011–12 Chesterfield 30 5
2012–13 Chesterfield 30 1
2013–14 Chesterfield 0 0 **106 21**
2018–19 Macclesfield T 22 3 **193 26**

WILSON, Scott (F) 33 10
b. 11-1-93
From Bath C, Paulton R, Western-super-Mare, Eastleigh.
2018–19 Macclesfield T 33 10 **33 10**

MANCHESTER C (48)

ADARABIOYO, Tosin (D) 29 0
H: 6 3 b. 24-9-97
Internationals: England U16, U17, U18, U19.
2014–15 Manchester C 0 0
2015–16 Manchester C 0 0
2016–17 Manchester C 0 0
2017–18 Manchester C 0 0
2018–19 Manchester C 0 0
2018–19 *WBA* 29 0 **29 0**

AGUERO, Sergio (F) 468 261
H: 5 8 W: 11 09 b.Buenos Aires 2-6-88
Internationals: Argentina U17, U20, U23, Full caps.
2002–03 Independiente 1 0
2003–04 Independiente 5 0
2004–05 Independiente 12 5
2005–06 Independiente 36 18 **54 23**
2006–07 Atletico Madrid 38 6
2007–08 Atletico Madrid 37 19
2008–09 Atletico Madrid 37 17
2009–10 Atletico Madrid 31 12
2010–11 Atletico Madrid 32 20 **175 74**
2011–12 Manchester C 34 23
2012–13 Manchester C 30 12
2013–14 Manchester C 23 17
2014–15 Manchester C 33 26
2015–16 Manchester C 30 24
2016–17 Manchester C 31 20
2017–18 Manchester C 25 21
2018–19 Manchester C 33 21 **239 164**

BARKER, Brandon (M) 69 5
H: 5 9 W: 10 10 b.Manchester 4-10-96
Internationals: England U18, U19, U20.
2014–15 Manchester C 0 0
2015–16 Manchester C 0 0
2015–16 *Rotherham U* 4 1 **4 1**
2016–17 Manchester C 0 0
2016–17 *NAC Breda* 22 2 **22 2**
2017–18 Manchester C 0 0
2017–18 *Hibernian* 27 2 **27 2**
2018–19 Manchester C 0 0
2018–19 *Preston NE* 16 0 **16 0**

BERNABE, Adrian (M) 0 0
b. 26-5-01
Internationals: Spain U17.
From Espanyol, Barcelona.
2018–19 Manchester C 0 0

BERNARDO SILVA, Mota (M) 173 37
H: 5 8 W: 9 11 b.Lisbon 10-8-94
Internationals: Portugal U19, U21, Full caps.
2013–14 Benfica 1 0 **1 0**
2014–15 Monaco 32 9
2015–16 Monaco 32 7
2016–17 Monaco 37 8 **101 24**
2017–18 Manchester C 35 6
2018–19 Manchester C 36 7 **71 13**

BRAVO, Claudio (G) 417 2
H: 6 0 W: 11 00 b.Viluco 13-4-83
Internationals: Chile U23, Full caps.
2003 Colo Colo 25 1
2004 Colo Colo 18 0
2005 Colo Colo 36 0

2006	Colo Colo	14	0	**93**	**1**
2006–07	Real Sociedad	29	0		
2007–08	Real Sociedad	0	0		
2008–09	Real Sociedad	32	0		
2009–10	Real Sociedad	25	1		
2010–11	Real Sociedad	38	0		
2011–12	Real Sociedad	37	0		
2012–13	Real Sociedad	31	0		
2013–14	Real Sociedad	37	0	**229**	**1**
2014–15	Barcelona	37	0		
2015–16	Barcelona	32	0		
2016–17	Barcelona	1	0	**70**	**0**
2016–17	Manchester C	22	0		
2017–18	Manchester C	3	0		
2018–19	Manchester C	0	0	**25**	**0**

DANILO, da Silva (D) 230 23
H: 6 0 W: 11 07 b.Bicas 15-7-91
Internationals: Brazil U20, U23, Full caps.

2009	America Mineiro	8	0		
2010	America Mineiro	7	0	**15**	**0**
2010	Santos	26	4		
2011	Santos	23	1	**49**	**5**
2011–12	Porto	6	0		
2012–13	Porto	28	2		
2013–14	Porto	28	3		
2014–15	Porto	29	6	**91**	**11**
2015–16	Real Madrid	24	2		
2016–17	Real Madrid	17	1		
2017–18	Real Madrid	0	0	**41**	**3**
2017–18	Manchester C	23	3		
2018–19	Manchester C	11	1	**34**	**4**

DE BRUYNE, Kevin (M) 268 57
H: 5 11 W: 12 00 b.Ghent 28-6-91
Internationals: Belgium U18, U19, U21, Full caps.

2008–09	Genk	2	0		
2009–10	Genk	30	3		
2010–11	Genk	32	5		
2011–12	Genk	15	6	**79**	**14**
2011–12	Chelsea	0	0		
2012–13	Chelsea	0	0		
2012–13	*Werder Bremen*	33	10	**33**	**10**
2013–14	Chelsea	3	0	**3**	**0**
2014–15	Wolfsburg	34	10		
2015–16	Wolfsburg	2	0	**36**	**10**
2015–16	Manchester C	25	7		
2016–17	Manchester C	36	6		
2017–18	Manchester C	37	8		
2018–19	Manchester C	19	2	**117**	**23**

DELPH, Fabian (D) 218 13
H: 5 8 W: 11 00 b.Bradford 21-11-89
Internationals: England U19, U21, Full caps.

2006–07	Leeds U	1	0		
2007–08	Leeds U	1	0		
2008–09	Leeds U	42	6		
2009–10	Aston Villa	8	0		
2010–11	Aston Villa	7	0		
2011–12	Aston Villa	11	0		
2011–12	*Leeds U*	5	0	**49**	**6**
2012–13	Aston Villa	24	0		
2013–14	Aston Villa	34	3		
2014–15	Aston Villa	28	0	**112**	**3**
2015–16	Manchester C	17	2		
2016–17	Manchester C	7	1		
2017–18	Manchester C	22	1		
2018–19	Manchester C	11	0	**57**	**4**

DIAZ, Brahim (M) 5 0
H: 5 7 W: 10 10 b. 3-8-99
Internationals: Spain U17, U19, U21.
From Malaga.

2016–17	Manchester C	0	0		
2017–18	Manchester C	5	0		
2018–19	Manchester C	0	0	**5**	**0**

Transferred to Real Madrid January 2019.

EDERSON, de Moraes (G) 177 0
H: 6 2 W: 13 08 b.Osasco 17-8-93
Internationals: Brazil U23, Full caps.

2011–12	Ribeirao	29	0	**29**	**0**
2012–13	Rio Ave	2	0		
2013–14	Rio Ave	18	0		
2014–15	Rio Ave	17	0	**37**	**0**
2015–16	Benfica	10	0		
2016–17	Benfica	27	0	**37**	**0**
2017–18	Manchester C	36	0		
2018–19	Manchester C	38	0	**74**	**0**

FERNANDINHO, Luis (M) 420 52
H: 5 10 W: 10 09 b.Londrina 4-5-85
Internationals: Brazil Full caps.

2003	Paranaense	29	5		
2004	Paranaense	41	9		
2005	Paranaense	2	0	**72**	**14**
2005–06	Shakhtar Donetsk	22	1		
2006–07	Shakhtar Donetsk	25	1		
2008–09	Shakhtar Donetsk	21	5		
2009–10	Shakhtar Donetsk	24	4		
2010–11	Shakhtar Donetsk	15	3		
2011–12	Shakhtar Donetsk	24	4		
2012–13	Shakhtar Donetsk	23	2	**154**	**20**
2013–14	Manchester C	33	5		
2014–15	Manchester C	33	3		
2015–16	Manchester C	33	2		
2016–17	Manchester C	32	2		
2017–18	Manchester C	34	5		
2018–19	Manchester C	29	1	**194**	**18**

FODEN, Phil (M) 18 1
H: 5 7 W: 11 00 b. 28-5-00
Internationals: England U16, U17, U18, U19, U21.

2016–17	Manchester C	0	0		
2017–18	Manchester C	5	0		
2018–19	Manchester C	13	1	**18**	**1**

GABRIEL JESUS, Fernando (F) 115 43
b. 3-4-97
Internationals: Brazil U20, U23, Full caps.

2015	Palmeiras	20	4		
2016	Palmeiras	27	12		
2016–17	Palmeiras	0	0	**47**	**16**
2016–17	Manchester C	10	7		
2017–18	Manchester C	29	13		
2018–19	Manchester C	29	7	**68**	**27**

GARCIA, Eric (D) 0 0
H: 6 0 b.Barcelona 9-1-01
Internationals: Spain U17.
From Barcelona.

2018–19	Manchester C	0	0		

GOMES, Claudio (M) 0 0
H: 5 11 W: 11 00 b.Argenteuil 23-7-00
Internationals: France U16, U27, U18, U19.

2017–18	Paris Saint-Germain	0	0		
2018–19	Manchester C	0	0		

GRIMSHAW, Daniel (G) 0 0
H: 6 1 W: 12 02 b.Manchester 16-1-98

2018–19	Manchester C	0	0		

GUNDOGAN, Ilkay (M) 224 29
H: 5 11 W: 11 00 b.Gelsenkirchen 24-10-90
Internationals: Germany U18, U19, U20, U21, Full caps.

2008–09	Bochum	0	0		
2008–09	Nuremburg	1	0		
2009–10	Nuremburg	22	1		
2010–11	Nuremburg	25	5	**48**	**6**
2011–12	Borussia Dortmund	28	3		
2012–13	Borussia Dortmund	28	3		
2013–14	Borussia Dortmund	1	0		
2014–15	Borussia Dortmund	23	3		
2015–16	Borussia Dortmund	25	1	**105**	**10**
2016–17	Manchester C	10	3		
2017–18	Manchester C	30	4		
2018–19	Manchester C	31	6	**71**	**13**

HARRISON, Jack (M) 96 18
b.Stoke-on-Trent 20-11-96
Internationals: England U21.

2016	New York C	21	4		
2017	New York C	34	10	**55**	**14**
2017–18	Manchester C	0	0		
2017–18	*Middlesbrough*	4	0	**4**	**0**
2018–19	Manchester C	0	0		
2018–19	*Leeds U*	37	4	**37**	**4**

HUMPHREYS, Cameron (D) 0 0
H: 6 2 b.Manchester 22-7-98
Internationals: England U16, U17, U18, U19.

2015–16	Manchester C	0	0		
2016–17	Manchester C	0	0		
2017–18	Manchester C	0	0		
2018–19	Manchester C	0	0		

KOMPANY, Vincent (D) 355 23
H: 6 3 W: 13 05 b.Brussels 10-4-86
Internationals: Belgium U16, U17, Full caps.

2004–05	Anderlecht	29	2		
2005–06	Anderlecht	32	2	**61**	**4**
2006–07	Hamburg	6	0		
2007–08	Hamburg	22	1		
2008–09	Hamburg	1	0	**29**	**1**
2008–09	Manchester C	34	1		
2009–10	Manchester C	25	2		
2010–11	Manchester C	37	0		
2011–12	Manchester C	31	3		
2012–13	Manchester C	26	1		
2013–14	Manchester C	28	4		
2014–15	Manchester C	25	0		
2015–16	Manchester C	14	2		
2016–17	Manchester C	11	3		
2017–18	Manchester C	17	1		
2018–19	Manchester C	17	1	**265**	**18**

LAPORTE, Aymeric (D) 238 12
H: 6 2 W: 13 05 b.Agen 27-5-94
Internationals: France U17, U18, U19, U21.

2011–12	Basconia	33	2	**33**	**2**
2012–13	Athletic Bilbao	15	0		
2013–14	Athletic Bilbao	35	2		
2014–15	Athletic Bilbao	33	0		
2015–16	Athletic Bilbao	26	3		
2016–17	Athletic Bilbao	33	2		
2017–18	Athletic Bilbao	19	0	**161**	**7**
2017–18	Manchester C	9	0		
2018–19	Manchester C	35	3	**44**	**3**

MAHREZ, Riyad (M) 243 55
H: 5 10 W: 9 10 b.Sarcelles 21-2-91
Internationals: Algeria Full caps.

2011–12	Le Havre	9	0		
2012–13	Le Havre	32	4		
2013–14	Le Havre	17	2	**58**	**6**
2013–14	Leicester C	19	3		
2014–15	Leicester C	30	4		
2015–16	Leicester C	37	17		
2016–17	Leicester C	36	6		
2017–18	Leicester C	36	12	**158**	**42**
2018–19	Manchester C	27	7	**27**	**7**

MENDY, Benjamin (D) 180 2
H: 5 11 W: 11 05 b.Longjumeau 17-7-94
Internationals: France U16, U17, U18, U19, U21, Full caps.

2011–12	Le Havre	29	0		
2012–13	Le Havre	28	0	**57**	**0**
2013–14	Marseille	24	1		
2014–15	Marseille	33	0		
2015–16	Marseille	24	1	**81**	**2**
2016–17	Monaco	25	0	**25**	**0**
2017–18	Manchester C	7	0		
2018–19	Manchester C	10	0	**17**	**0**

MURIC, Arijanet (G) 1 0
H: 6 6 W: 12 11 b.Zurich 7-11-98
Internationals: Montenegro U21. Kosovo Full caps.

2017–18	Manchester C	0	0		
2018–19	Manchester C	0	0		
2018–19	*NAC Breda*	1	0	**1**	**0**

NMECHA, Felix (M) 0 0
b.Hamburg 10-10-00
Internationals: England U16, U18, U19. Germany U18

2018–19	Manchester C	0	0		

NMECHA, Lukas (F) 43 4
H: 6 0 W: 12 08 b.Hamburg 14-12-98
Internationals: England U16, U17, U18, U19, U21.

2017–18	Manchester C	2	0		
2018–19	Manchester C	0	0	**2**	**0**
2018–19	*Preston NE*	41	4	**41**	**4**

OTAMENDI, Nicolas (D) 269 20
H: 5 10 W: 11 09 b.Buenos Aires 12-2-88
Internationals: Argentina Full caps.

2007–08	Velez Sarsfield	1	0		
2008–09	Velez Sarsfield	18	0		
2009–10	Velez Sarsfield	19	1		
2010–11	Velez Sarsfield	2	0	**40**	**1**
2010–11	Porto	15	5		
2011–12	Porto	20	1		
2012–13	Porto	29	1		
2013–14	Porto	13	0	**77**	**7**
2013–14	*Atletico Mineiro*	5	0	**5**	**0**
2014–15	Valencia	35	6	**35**	**6**
2015–16	Manchester C	30	1		
2016–17	Manchester C	30	1		
2017–18	Manchester C	34	4		
2018–19	Manchester C	18	0	**112**	**6**

POVEDA-OCAMPO, Ian (M) 0 0
b.London 9-2-00
Internationals: England U16, U17, U18, U19.
From Chelsea, Arsenal, Barcelona, Brentford.

2018–19	Manchester C	0	0		

RICHARDS, Taylor (M) 0 0
b.London 4-12-00
Internationals: England U17.

2018–19	Manchester C	0	0		

SANDLER, Philippe (D) 30 0
H: 6 2 W: 11 11 b.Amersterdam 10-2-97
Internationals: Netherlands U20.

2016–17	PEC Zwolle	7	0		

2017–18	PEC Zwolle	23	0	**30**	**0**
2018–19	Manchester C	0	0		

SANE, Leroy (M) **136 36**
H: 5 8 W: 9 13 b.Essen 11-1-96
Internationals: Germany U19, U21, Full caps.

2013–14	Schalke 04	1	0		
2014–15	Schalke 04	13	3		
2015–16	Schalke 04	33	8	**47**	**11**
2016–17	Manchester C	26	5		
2017–18	Manchester C	32	10		
2018–19	Manchester C	31	10	**89**	**25**

SILVA, David (F) **484 84**
H: 5 7 W: 10 07 b.Arguineguin 8-1-86
Internationals: Spain U16, U17, U19, U20, U21, Full caps.

2003–04	Mestalla	14	1	**14**	**1**
2004–05	Eibar	35	5	**35**	**5**
2005–06	Celta Vigo	34	3	**34**	**3**
2006–07	Valencia	36	5		
2007–08	Valencia	34	4		
2008–09	Valencia	19	4		
2009–10	Valencia	30	8	**119**	**21**
2010–11	Manchester C	35	4		
2011–12	Manchester C	36	6		
2012–13	Manchester C	32	4		
2013–14	Manchester C	27	7		
2014–15	Manchester C	32	12		
2015–16	Manchester C	24	2		
2016–17	Manchester C	34	4		
2017–18	Manchester C	29	9		
2018–19	Manchester C	33	6	**282**	**54**

STERLING, Raheem (F) **226 66**
H: 5 7 W: 10 00 b.Kingston 8-12-94
Internationals: England U16, U17, U19, U21, Full caps.

2011–12	Liverpool	3	0		
2012–13	Liverpool	24	2		
2013–14	Liverpool	33	9		
2014–15	Liverpool	35	7	**95**	**18**
2015–16	Manchester C	31	6		
2016–17	Manchester C	33	7		
2017–18	Manchester C	33	18		
2018–19	Manchester C	34	17	**131**	**48**

STONES, John (D) **170 1**
H: 6 2 W: 11 00 b.Barnsley 28-5-94
Internationals: England U19, U20, U21, Full caps.

2011–12	Barnsley	2	0		
2012–13	Barnsley	22	0	**24**	**0**
2012–13	Everton	0	0		
2013–14	Everton	21	0		
2014–15	Everton	23	1		
2015–16	Everton	33	0	**77**	**1**
2016–17	Manchester C	27	0		
2017–18	Manchester C	18	0		
2018–19	Manchester C	24	0	**69**	**0**

WALKER, Kyle (D) **320 6**
H: 5 10 W: 11 07 b.Sheffield 28-5-90
Internationals: England U19, U21, Full caps.

2008–09	Sheffield U	2	0		
2008–09	*Northampton T*	9	0	**9**	**0**
2009–10	Tottenham H	2	0		
2009–10	*Sheffield U*	26	0	**28**	**0**
2010–11	Tottenham H	1	0		
2010–11	*QPR*	20	0	**20**	**0**
2010–11	*Aston Villa*	15	1	**15**	**1**
2011–12	Tottenham H	37	2		
2012–13	Tottenham H	36	0		
2013–14	Tottenham H	26	1		
2014–15	Tottenham H	15	0		
2015–16	Tottenham H	33	1		
2016–17	Tottenham H	33	0	**183**	**4**
2017–18	Manchester C	32	0		
2018–19	Manchester C	33	1	**65**	**1**

ZINCHENKO, Alexander (M) **65 2**
H: 5 9 W: 9 08 b.Radomyshi 15-12-96
Internationals: Ukraine U16, U17, U18, U19, U21, Full caps.

2014–15	Ufa	7	0		
2015–16	Ufa	24	2	**31**	**2**
2016–17	Manchester C	0	0		
2016–17	PSV	12	0		
2017–18	PSV	0	0	**12**	**0**
2017–18	Manchester C	8	0		
2018–19	Manchester C	14	0	**22**	**0**

Players retained or with offer of contract
Agyepong, Thomas; Agyiri, Ernest; Amankwah, Yeboah; Ambrose, Thierry; Aminu, Mohammed; Antuna Romero, Carlos Uriel; Arzani, Daniel; Bolton, Luke Philip; Caceres, Anthony; Dele-Bashiru, Oluwafisayo Faruq; Diskerud, Mikkel Morgenstar Palssonn; Doyle, Thomas; Fernandes Cantin, Paolo; Frimpong, Jeremie; Garcia Alonso, Manuel; Garcia Serrano, Aleix; Garre, Benjamin Antonio; Gonzalez, Lorenzo Jose; Herrera Ravelo, Yangel Clemente; Ilic, Luka; Itakura, Kou; Latibeaudiere, Joel Owen; Luiz Soares De Paulo, Douglas; Mangala, Eliaquim; Mari Villar, Pablo; Moreno Duran, Marlos; Moulden, Louie; Ogbeta, Nathanael; Ogunby, Henri William; Palaversa, Ante; Pozo La Rosa, Iker; Roberts, Patrick John Joseph; Rosler, Colin; Ross Palmer Brown, Erik; Scott, Thomas Henry; Simmonds, Keyendrah Qwamalik Tegan; Smith, Matthew Robert; Tanor, Collins; Touaizi Zoubdi, Nabil; Wilson, Tyreke.

Scholars
Bazunu, Gavin Okeroghene; Braaf, Jayden Jezairo; Diounkou Tecagne, Alpha Richard; Fiorini, Lewis; Harwood-Bellis, Taylor; Knight, Ben; McDonald, Rowan Alexander; Palmer, Cole; Robinson, Samson Alfie Philip; Sobowale, Oluwatimilehin; Thomas, Lewis Luka; Wright-Phillips, D'Margio Cameron.

MANCHESTER U (49)

ANDER HERRERA, Aguera (M) **292 24**
H: 6 0 W: 10 10 b.Bilbao 14-8-89
Internationals: Spain U20, U21, U23, Full caps.

2008–09	Real Zaragoza	17	2		
2009–10	Real Zaragoza	30	2		
2010–11	Real Zaragoza	19	1	**66**	**5**
2011–12	Athletic Bilbao	32	1		
2012–13	Althetic Bilbao	29	1	**29**	**1**
2013–14	Athletic Bilbao	33	5	**65**	**6**
2014–15	Manchester U	26	6		
2015–16	Manchester U	27	3		
2016–17	Manchester U	31	1		
2017–18	Manchester U	26	0		
2018–19	Manchester U	22	2	**132**	**12**

BAILLY, Eric (D) **90 1**
H: 6 2 W: 12 02 b.Bingerville 12-4-94
Internationals: Ivory Coast Full caps.

2014–15	Espanyol	5	0	**5**	**0**
2014–15	Villareal	10	0		
2015–16	Villareal	25	0	**35**	**0**
2016–17	Manchester U	25	0		
2017–18	Manchester U	13	1		
2018–19	Manchester U	12	0	**50**	**1**

CHONG, Tahith (F) **2 0**
H: 6 1 W: 11 00 b.Willwmstad 1-12-91
Internationals: Netherlands U16, U17, U19, U20, U21.

2018–19	Manchester U	2	0	**2**	**0**

DALOT, Diogo (D) **22 0**
H: 6 0 W: 11 11 b.Braga 18-3-99
Internationals: Portugal U16, U17, U19, U20, U21.

2016–17	Porto	0	0		
2017–18	Porto	6	0	**6**	**0**
2018–19	Manchester U	16	0	**16**	**0**

DARMIAN, Matteo (D) **230 5**
H: 6 0 W: 11 00 b.Legnano 2-12-89
Internationals: Italy U17, U18, U19, U20, U21, Full caps.

2006–07	AC Milan	1	0		
2007–08	AC Milan	0	0		
2008–09	AC Milan	3	0		
2009–10	AC Milan	0	0	**4**	**0**
2009–10	*Padova*	22	1	**22**	**1**
2010–11	Palermo	11	0	**11**	**0**
2011–12	Torino	33	1		
2012–13	Torino	30	0		
2013–14	Torino	37	0		
2014–15	Torino	33	2	**133**	**3**
2015–16	Manchester U	28	1		
2016–17	Manchester U	18	0		
2017–18	Manchester U	8	0		
2018–19	Manchester U	6	0	**60**	**1**

DE GEA, David (G) **332 0**
H: 6 3 W: 12 13 b.Madrid 7-11-90
Internationals: Spain U15, U17, U19, U20, U21, U23, Full caps.

2009–10	Atletico Madrid	19	0		
2010–11	Atletico Madrid	38	0	**57**	**0**
2011–12	Manchester U	29	0		
2012–13	Manchester U	28	0		
2013–14	Manchester U	37	0		
2014–15	Manchester U	37	0		
2015–16	Manchester U	34	0		
2016–17	Manchester U	35	0		
2017–18	Manchester U	37	0		
2018–19	Manchester U	38	0	**275**	**0**

DEARNLEY, Zachary (M) **9 1**
b. 28-9-98

2016–17	Manchester U	0	0		
2018–19	Manchester U	0	0		
2018–19	*Oldham Ath*	9	1	**9**	**1**

FELLAINI, Marouane (M) **322 43**
H: 6 4 W: 13 05 b.Brussels 22-11-87
Internationals: Belgium U18, U19, U21, Full caps.

2006–07	Standard Liege	29	0		
2007–08	Standard Liege	30	6		
2008–09	Standard Liege	3	0	**62**	**6**
2008–09	Everton	30	8		
2009–10	Everton	23	2		
2010–11	Everton	20	1		
2011–12	Everton	34	3		
2012–13	Everton	31	11		
2013–14	Everton	3	0	**141**	**25**
2013–14	Manchester U	16	0		
2014–15	Manchester U	27	6		
2015–16	Manchester U	18	1		
2016–17	Manchester U	28	1		
2017–18	Manchester U	16	4		
2018–19	Manchester U	14	0	**119**	**12**

Transferred to Shandong Luneng January 2019.

FOSU-MENSAH, Timothy (D) **45 0**
H: 5 10 W: 10 10 b.Amsterdam 3-1-98
Internationals: Netherlands U16, U17, U19, U21, Full caps.

2015–16	Manchester U	8	0		
2016–17	Manchester U	4	0		
2017–18	Manchester U	0	0		
2017–18	*Crystal Palace*	21	0	**21**	**0**
2018–19	Manchester U	0	0	**12**	**0**
2018–19	*Fulham*	12	0	**12**	**0**

FRED, Frederico (M) **151 18**
H: 5 7 W: 10 10 b.Belo Horizonte 5-3-93
Internationals: Brazil U20, Full caps.

2012	Internacional	28	6		
2013	Internacional	5	1	**33**	**7**
2013–14	Shakhtar Donetsk	23	2		
2014–15	Shakhtar Donetsk	22	1		
2015–16	Shakhtar Donetsk	12	2		
2016–17	Shakhtar Donetsk	18	2		
2017–18	Shakhtar Donetsk	26	3	**101**	**10**
2018–19	Manchester U	17	1	**17**	**1**

GARNER, James (M) **1 0**
b.Birkenhead 13-3-01
Internationals: England U17, U18.

2018–19	Manchester U	1	0	**1**	**0**

GOMES, Angel (M) **3 0**
b.Enfield 31-8-00
Internationals: England U16, U17, U18, U19.

2016–17	Manchester U	1	0		
2017–18	Manchester U	0	0		
2018–19	Manchester U	2	0	**3**	**0**

GRANT, Lee (G) **468 0**
H: 6 3 W: 13 01 b.Hemel Hempstead 27-1-83
Internationals: England U16, U17, U18, U19, U21.

2000–01	Derby Co	0	0		
2001–02	Derby Co	0	0		
2002–03	Derby Co	29	0		
2003–04	Derby Co	36	0		
2004–05	Derby Co	2	0		
2005–06	Derby Co	0	0		
2005–06	*Burnley*	1	0		
2005–06	*Oldham Ath*	16	0	**16**	**0**
2006–07	Derby Co	7	0		
2007–08	Sheffield W	44	0		
2008–09	Sheffield W	46	0		
2009–10	Sheffield W	46	0	**136**	**0**
2010–11	Burnley	25	0		
2011–12	Burnley	43	0		
2012–13	Burnley	46	0	**115**	**0**
2013–14	Derby Co	46	0		
2014–15	Derby Co	40	0		
2015–16	Derby Co	10	0		
2016–17	Derby Co	0	0	**170**	**0**
2016–17	*Stoke C*	28	0		
2017–18	Stoke C	3	0	**31**	**0**
2018–19	Manchester U	0	0		

GREENWOOD, Mason (F) **3** **0**
b. 1-10-01
Internationals: England U17, U19.

2018–19	Manchester U	3	0	**3**	**0**

HAMILTON, Ethan (M) **14** **4**
b.Edinburgh 18-10-98
Internationals: Scotland U16, U19.

2017–18	Manchester U	0	0		
2018–19	Manchester U	0	0		
2018–19	*Rochdale*	14	4	**14**	**4**

HENDERSON, Dean (G) **91** **0**
H: 6 3 W: 12 13 b.Whitehaven 12-3-97
Internationals: England U16, U17, U20, U21.

2015–16	Manchester U	0	0		
2016–17	Manchester U	0	0		
2016–17	*Grimsby T*	7	0	**7**	**0**
2017–18	Manchester U	0	0		
2017–18	*Shrewsbury T*	38	0	**38**	**0**
2018–19	Manchester U	0	0		
2018–19	*Sheffield U*	46	0	**46**	**0**

JONES, Phil (D) **198** **2**
H: 5 11 W: 11 02 b.Preston 21-2-92
Internationals: England U19, U21, Full caps.

2009–10	Blackburn R	9	0		
2010–11	Blackburn R	26	0	**35**	**0**
2011–12	Manchester U	29	1		
2012–13	Manchester U	17	0		
2013–14	Manchester U	26	1		
2014–15	Manchester U	22	0		
2015–16	Manchester U	10	0		
2016–17	Manchester U	18	0		
2017–18	Manchester U	23	0		
2018–19	Manchester U	18	0	**163**	**2**

LINDELOF, Victor (D) **145** **3**
H: 6 2 W: 12 11 b.Vasteras 17-7-94
Internationals: Sweden U17, U19, U21, Full caps.

2009	Vasteras	1	0		
2010	Vasteras	9	0		
2011	Vasteras	27	0		
2012	Vasteras	13	0	**50**	**0**
2012–13	Benfica	0	0		
2013–14	Benfica	1	0		
2014–15	Benfica	0	0		
2015–16	Benfica	15	1		
2016–17	Benfica	32	1	**48**	**2**
2017–18	Manchester U	17	0		
2018–19	Manchester U	30	1	**47**	**1**

LINGARD, Jesse (M) **158** **28**
H: 5 3 W: 11 11 b.Warrington 15-12-92
Internationals: England U17, U21, Full caps.

2011–12	Manchester U	0	0		
2012–13	Manchester U	0	0		
2012–13	*Leicester C*	5	0	**5**	**0**
2013–14	Manchester U	0	0		
2013–14	*Birmingham C*	13	6	**13**	**6**
2013–14	*Brighton & HA*	15	3	**15**	**3**
2014–15	Manchester U	1	0		
2014–15	*Derby Co*	14	2	**14**	**2**
2015–16	Manchester U	25	4		
2016–17	Manchester U	25	1		
2017–18	Manchester U	33	8		
2018–19	Manchester U	27	4	**111**	**17**

LUKAKU, Romelu (F) **325** **146**
H: 6 3 W: 13 00 b.Antwerp 13-5-93
Internationals: Belgium U15, U18, U21, Full caps.

2008–09	Anderlecht	1	0		
2009–10	Anderlecht	33	15		
2010–11	Anderlecht	37	16		
2011–12	Anderlecht	2	2	**73**	**33**
2011–12	Chelsea	8	0		
2012–13	Chelsea	0	0		
2012–13	*WBA*	35	17	**35**	**17**
2013–14	Chelsea	2	0	**10**	**0**
2013–14	*Everton*	31	15		
2014–15	Everton	36	10		
2015–16	Everton	37	18		
2016–17	Everton	37	25	**141**	**68**
2017–18	Manchester U	34	16		
2018–19	Manchester U	32	12	**66**	**28**

MARTIAL, Anthony (F) **165** **45**
H: 5 11 W: 12 08 b.Massy 5-12-95
Internationals: France U16, U17, U18, U19, U21, Full caps.

2012–13	Lyon	3	0	**3**	**0**
2013–14	Monaco	11	2		
2014–15	Monaco	35	9		
2015–16	Monaco	3	0	**49**	**11**
2015–16	Manchester U	31	11		
2016–17	Manchester U	25	4		
2017–18	Manchester U	30	9		
2018–19	Manchester U	27	10	**113**	**34**

MATA, Juan (M) **411** **94**
H: 5 7 W: 11 00 b.Ocon de Villafranca 28-4-88
Internationals: Spain U16, U17, U19, U20, U21, U23, Full caps.

2006–07	Real Madrid B	39	10	**39**	**10**
2007–08	Valencia	24	5		
2008–09	Valencia	37	11		
2009–10	Valencia	35	9		
2010–11	Valencia	33	8	**129**	**33**
2011–12	Chelsea	34	6		
2012–13	Chelsea	35	12		
2013–14	Chelsea	13	0	**82**	**18**
2013–14	Manchester U	15	6		
2014–15	Manchester U	33	9		
2015–16	Manchester U	38	6		
2016–17	Manchester U	25	6		
2017–18	Manchester U	28	3		
2018–19	Manchester U	22	3	**161**	**33**

MATIC, Nemanja (M) **353** **18**
H: 6 4 W: 13 02 b.Sabac 1-8-88
Internationals: Serbia U21, Full caps.

2005–06	Jedinstvo	7	0		
2006–07	Jedinstvo	9	0	**16**	**0**
2006–07	Kosice	13	1		
2007–08	Kosice	25	1		
2008–09	Kosice	29	2	**67**	**4**
2009–10	Chelsea	2	0		
2010–11	Chelsea	0	0		
2010–11	*Vitesse*	27	2	**27**	**2**
2011–12	Benfica	16	1		
2012–13	Benfica	26	3		
2013–14	Benfica	14	2	**56**	**6**
2013–14	Chelsea	17	0		
2014–15	Chelsea	36	1		
2015–16	Chelsea	33	2		
2016–17	Chelsea	35	1	**123**	**4**
2017–18	Manchester U	36	1		
2018–19	Manchester U	28	1	**64**	**2**

McTOMINAY, Scott (M) **31** **2**
H: 5 10 W: 10 03 b.Lancaster 8-12-96
Internationals: Scotland Full caps.

2016–17	Manchester U	2	0		
2017–18	Manchester U	13	0		
2018–19	Manchester U	16	2	**31**	**2**

O'HARA, Kieran (G) **42** **0**
b. 22-4-96
Internationals: Republic of Ireland U21.

2015–16	Manchester U	0	0		
2015–16	*Morecambe*	5	0		
2016–17	Morecambe	0	0	**5**	**0**
2016–17	Manchester U	0	0		
2017–18	Manchester U	0	0		
2018–19	Manchester U	0	0		
2018–19	*Macclesfield T*	37	0	**37**	**0**

PEREIRA, Andreas (M) **78** **7**
H: 5 10 W: 10 06 b.Duffel 1-1-96
Internationals: Belgium U16, U17. Brazil U20, U23, Full caps.

2014–15	Manchester U	1	0		
2015–16	Manchester U	4	0		
2016–17	Manchester U	0	0		
2016–17	*Granada*	35	5	**35**	**5**
2017–18	Manchester U	0	0		
2017–18	*Valencia*	23	1	**23**	**1**
2018–19	Manchester U	15	1	**20**	**1**

POGBA, Paul (M) **219** **52**
H: 6 1 W: 12 08 b.Lagny-sur-Marne 15-3-93
Internationals: France U16, U17, U18, U19, U20, Full caps.

2009–10	Manchester U	0	0		
2010–11	Manchester U	0	0		
2011–12	Manchester U	3	0		
2012–13	Juventus	27	5		
2013–14	Juventus	36	7		
2014–15	Juventus	26	8		
2015–16	Juventus	35	8	**124**	**28**
2016–17	Manchester U	30	5		
2017–18	Manchester U	27	6		
2018–19	Manchester U	35	13	**95**	**24**

POOLE, Regan (D) **57** **0**
b.Cardiff 18-6-98
Internationals: Wales U17, U19, U20, U21.

2014–15	Newport Co	11	0		
2015–16	Newport Co	4	0		
2015–16	Manchester U	0	0		
2016–17	Manchester U	0	0		
2017–18	Manchester U	0	0		
2017–18	*Northampton T*	22	0	**22**	**0**
2018–19	Manchester U	0	0		
2018–19	*Newport Co*	20	0	**35**	**0**

RASHFORD, Marcus (F) **111** **27**
H: 5 11 W: 11 00 b.Manchester 31-10-97
Internationals: England U16, U18, U20, U21, Full caps.

2015–16	Manchester U	11	5		
2016–17	Manchester U	32	5		
2017–18	Manchester U	35	7		
2018–19	Manchester U	33	10	**111**	**27**

ROJO, Marcos (D) **173** **9**
H: 6 2 W: 12 06 b.La Plata 20-3-90
Internationals: Argentina Full caps.

2008–09	Estudiantes	6	1		
2009–10	Estudiantes	18	0		
2010–11	Estudiantes	19	2	**43**	**3**
2011–12	Spartak Moscow	8	0	**8**	**0**
2012–13	Sporting Lisbon	24	1		
2013–14	Sporting Lisbon	25	4	**49**	**5**
2014–15	Manchester U	22	0		
2015–16	Manchester U	16	0		
2016–17	Manchester U	21	1		
2017–18	Manchester U	9	0		
2018–19	Manchester U	5	0	**73**	**1**

ROMERO, Sergio (G) **176** **0**
H: 6 4 W: 13 01 b.Yrigoyen 22-2-87
Internationals: Argentina U20, Full caps.

2006–07	Racing Club	5	0	**5**	**0**
2007–08	AZ Alkmaar	12	0		
2008–09	AZ Alkmaar	28	0		
2009–10	AZ Alkmaar	27	0		
2010–11	AZ Alkmaar	23	0		
2011–12	AZ Alkmaar	0	0	**90**	**0**
2011–12	Sampdoria	29	0		
2012–13	Sampdoria	32	0		
2013–14	Sampdoria	0	0		
2013–14	*Monaco*	3	0	**3**	**0**
2014–15	Sampdoria	10	0	**71**	**0**
2015–16	Manchester U	4	0		
2016–17	Manchester U	2	0		
2017–18	Manchester U	1	0		
2018–19	Manchester U	0	0	**7**	**0**

SANCHEZ, Alexis (F) **439** **139**
H: 5 6 W: 11 09 b.Tocopilla 19-12-88
Internationals: Chile U20, Full caps.

2005	Cobreloa	35	3		
2006	Cobreloa	12	6	**47**	**9**
2006–07	Udinese	0	0		
2006–07	*Colo Colo*	32	5	**32**	**5**
2007–08	*River Plate*	23	4	**23**	**4**
2008–09	Udinese	32	3		
2009–10	Udinese	32	5		
2010–11	Udinese	31	12	**95**	**20**
2011–12	Barcelona	25	11		
2012–13	Barcelona	29	8		
2013–14	Barcelona	34	19	**88**	**38**
2014–15	Arsenal	35	16		
2015–16	Arsenal	30	13		
2016–17	Arsenal	38	24		
2017–18	Arsenal	19	7	**122**	**60**
2017–18	Manchester U	12	2		
2018–19	Manchester U	20	1	**32**	**3**

SHAW, Luke (D) **132** **1**
H: 6 1 W: 11 11 b.Kingston 12-7-95
Internationals: England U16, U17, U21, Full caps.

2011–12	Southampton	0	0		
2012–13	Southampton	25	0		
2013–14	Southampton	35	0	**60**	**0**
2014–15	Manchester U	16	0		
2015–16	Manchester U	5	0		
2016–17	Manchester U	11	0		
2017–18	Manchester U	11	0		
2018–19	Manchester U	29	1	**72**	**1**

SMALLING, Chris (D) **219** **12**
H: 6 4 W: 14 02 b.Greenwich 22-11-89
Internationals: England U18, U20, U21, Full caps.

2008–09	Fulham	1	0		
2009–10	Fulham	12	0	**13**	**0**
2010–11	Manchester U	16	0		
2011–12	Manchester U	19	1		
2012–13	Manchester U	15	0		
2013–14	Manchester U	25	1		
2014–15	Manchester U	25	4		
2015–16	Manchester U	35	0		
2016–17	Manchester U	18	1		
2017–18	Manchester U	29	4		
2018–19	Manchester U	24	1	**206**	**12**

TUANZEBE, Axel (D) **35 0**

H: 6 0 W: 11 11 b.Bunia 14-11-97

Internationals: England U19, U20, U21.

2015–16	Manchester U	0	0		
2016–17	Manchester U	4	0		
2017–18	Manchester U	1	0		
2017–18	*Aston Villa*	5	0		
2018–19	Manchester U	0	0	**5**	**0**
2018–19	*Aston Villa*	25	0	**30**	**0**

VALENCIA, Antonio (M) **414 35**

H: 5 10 W: 12 04 b.Lago Agrio 5-8-85

Internationals: Ecuador U20, 21, U23, Full caps.

2002	El Nacional	1	0		
2003	El Nacional	26	2		
2004	El Nacional	42	5		
2005	El Nacional	14	4	**83**	**11**
2005–06	Villarreal	2	0	**2**	**0**
2005–06	*Recreativo*	4	0	**4**	**0**
2006–07	Wigan Ath	22	1		
2007–08	Wigan Ath	31	3		
2008–09	Wigan Ath	31	3	**84**	**7**
2009–10	Manchester U	34	5		
2010–11	Manchester U	10	1		
2011–12	Manchester U	27	4		
2012–13	Manchester U	30	1		
2013–14	Manchester U	29	2		
2014–15	Manchester U	32	0		
2015–16	Manchester U	14	0		
2016–17	Manchester U	28	1		
2017–18	Manchester U	31	3		
2018–19	Manchester U	6	0	**241**	**17**

WILLOCK, Matthew (M) **37 1**

b. 20-8-96

2016–17	Manchester U	0	0		
2017–18	Manchester U	0	0		
2017–18	*Utrecht*	3	0	**3**	**0**
2017–18	*St Johnstone*	11	1	**11**	**1**
2018–19	Manchester U	0	0		
2018–19	*St Mirren*	12	0	**12**	**0**
2018–19	*Crawley T*	11	0	**11**	**0**

YOUNG, Ashley (M) **435 64**

H: 5 10 W: 10 03 b.Stevenage 9-7-85

Internationals: England U21, Full caps.

2002–03	Watford	0	0		
2003–04	Watford	5	3		
2004–05	Watford	34	0		
2005–06	Watford	39	13		
2006–07	Watford	20	3	**98**	**19**
2006–07	Aston Villa	13	2		
2007–08	Aston Villa	37	9		
2008–09	Aston Villa	36	7		
2009–10	Aston Villa	37	5		
2010–11	Aston Villa	34	7	**157**	**30**
2011–12	Manchester U	25	6		
2012–13	Manchester U	19	0		
2013–14	Manchester U	20	2		
2014–15	Manchester U	26	2		
2015–16	Manchester U	18	1		
2016–17	Manchester U	12	0		
2017–18	Manchester U	30	2		
2018–19	Manchester U	30	2	**180**	**15**

Players retained or with offer of contract

Barlow, Aidan Will; Bejger, Lukasz; Bernard, Di'Shon Joel; Borthwick-Jackson, Cameron Jake; Bughail-Mellor, D'Mani Lucell; Burkart, Nishan Connell; Castro Pereira, Joel Dinis; Devine, Reece; Dunne, Max Edward; Ercolani, Luca; Fojticek, Alex; Galbraith, Ethan Stuart William; Kovar, Matej; Laird, Ethan Benjamin; Levitt, Dylan James Christopher; Mastny, Ondrej; McCann, Charlie Liam; McGhee, Dion Alex; Mitchell, Demetri Kareem; O'Connor, Lee Patrick; Puigmal Martinez, Arnau; Ramazani, Largie; Stanley, Connor Scott; Tanner, George; Traore, Aliou Badara; Williams, Brandon Paul Brian; Woolston, Paul Hudson

Scholars

Carney, Jacob Andrew; Denham, Oliver James; Elanga, Anthony David Junior; Haygarth, Maxwell James; Helm, Mark; Hockenhull, Ben; Mengi, Teden Mambuene; Neville, Harvey James; Thompson, James George.

MANSFIELD T (50)

AJOSE, Nicholas (F) **269 81**

H: 5 8 W: 11 00 b.Bury 7-10-91

Internationals: England U16, U17.

2009–10	Manchester U	0	0		
2010–11	Manchester U	0	0		
2010–11	*Bury*	28	13		
2011–12	Peterborough U	2	0		
2011–12	*Scunthorpe U*	7	0	**7**	**0**
2011–12	*Chesterfield*	12	1	**12**	**1**
2012–13	*Crawley T*	19	2	**19**	**2**
2012–13	Peterborough U	0	0		
2012–13	*Bury*	19	4		
2013–14	Peterborough U	22	7	**24**	**7**
2013–14	*Swindon T*	16	6		
2014–15	Leeds U	3	0		
2014–15	*Crewe Alex*	27	8	**27**	**8**
2015–16	Leeds U	0	0	**3**	**0**
2015–16	Swindon T	38	24		
2016–17	Charlton Ath	21	6		
2016–17	*Swindon T*	15	5	**69**	**35**
2017–18	Charlton Ath	12	1		
2017–18	*Bury*	9	1	**56**	**18**
2018–19	Charlton Ath	9	1	**42**	**8**
2018–19	Mansfield T	10	2	**10**	**2**

ATKINSON, Will (M) **348 26**

H: 5 10 W: 10 07 b.Beverley 14-10-88

2006–07	Hull C	0	0		
2007–08	Hull C	0	0		
2007–08	*Port Vale*	4	0	**4**	**0**
2007–08	*Mansfield T*	12	0		
2008–09	Hull C	0	0		
2009–10	Hull C	2	1		
2009–10	*Rochdale*	15	3		
2010–11	Hull C	4	0		
2010–11	*Rotherham U*	3	1	**3**	**1**
2010–11	*Rochdale*	21	2	**36**	**5**
2011–12	Hull C	0	0	**6**	**1**
2011–12	*Plymouth Arg*	22	4	**22**	**4**
2011–12	*Bradford C*	12	1		
2012–13	Bradford C	42	1	**54**	**2**
2013–14	Southend U	45	2		
2014–15	Southend U	36	2		
2015–16	Southend U	36	2		
2016–17	Southend U	37	4	**154**	**10**
2017–18	Mansfield T	39	2		
2018–19	Mansfield T	18	1	**69**	**3**

BENNING, Malvind (D) **204 11**

H: 5 10 W: 12 00 b.Sandwell 2-11-93

2012–13	Walsall	10	0		
2013–14	Walsall	16	2		
2014–15	Walsall	20	0	**46**	**2**
2014–15	*York C*	9	0	**9**	**0**
2015–16	Mansfield T	31	4		
2016–17	Mansfield T	45	1		
2017–18	Mansfield T	28	1		
2018–19	Mansfield T	45	3	**149**	**9**

BIRCUMSHAW, Harry (M) **0 0**

2018–19	Mansfield T	0	0		

BISHOP, Neil (M) **484 29**

H: 6 1 W: 12 10 b.Stockton 7-8-81

Internationals: England C.

2007–08	Barnet	39	2		
2008–09	Barnet	44	1	**83**	**3**
2009–10	Notts Co	43	1		
2010–11	Notts Co	43	1		
2011–12	Notts Co	41	2		
2012–13	Notts Co	41	7	**168**	**11**
2013–14	Blackpool	35	1	**35**	**1**
2014–15	Scunthorpe U	35	4		
2015–16	Scunthorpe U	42	1		
2016–17	Scunthorpe U	42	5		
2017–18	Scunthorpe U	35	1	**154**	**11**
2018–19	Mansfield T	44	3	**44**	**3**

BLAKE, Nyle (F) **0 0**

2018–19	Mansfield T	0	0		

BUTCHER, Calum (D) **123 9**

H: 6 1 W: 13 01 b.Rochford 26-2-91

2007–08	Tottenham H	0	0		
2008–09	Tottenham H	0	0		
2009–10	Tottenham H	0	0		
2009–10	*Barnet*	3	0	**3**	**0**

From Hayes & Yeading.

2013–14	Dundee U	6	0		
2014–15	Dundee U	15	1	**21**	**1**
2015–16	Burton Alb	39	5		
2016–17	Burton Alb	1	0	**40**	**5**
2016–17	Millwall	30	2		
2017–18	Millwall	0	0	**30**	**2**
2017–18	Mansfield T	17	1		
2018–19	Mansfield T	12	0	**29**	**1**

Transferred to Dundee U January 2019.

DAVIES, Craig (F) **455 104**

H: 6 2 W: 13 05 b.Burton-on-Trent 9-1-86

Internationals: Wales U17, U19, U21, Full caps.

2004–05	Oxford U	28	6		
2005–06	Oxford U	20	2	**48**	**8**
2005–06	Verona	0	0		
2006–07	Wolverhampton W	23	0	**23**	**0**
2007–08	Oldham Ath	32	10		
2008–09	Oldham Ath	12	0		
2008–09	*Stockport Co*	9	5	**9**	**5**
2008–09	Brighton & HA	16	1		
2009–10	Brighton & HA	5	0	**21**	**1**
2009–10	*Yeovil T*	4	0	**4**	**0**
2009–10	*Port Vale*	24	7	**24**	**7**
2010–11	Chesterfield	41	23	**41**	**23**
2011–12	Barnsley	40	11		
2012–13	Barnsley	20	8	**60**	**19**
2012–13	Bolton W	18	4		
2013–14	Bolton W	8	0		
2013–14	*Preston NE*	15	5	**15**	**5**
2014–15	Bolton W	27	6	**53**	**10**
2015–16	Wigan Ath	26	2		
2016–17	Wigan Ath	14	1	**40**	**3**
2016–17	Scunthorpe U	19	0	**19**	**0**
2017–18	Oldham Ath	40	11	**84**	**21**
2018–19	Mansfield T	14	2	**14**	**2**

FIELDING, Tom (F) **0 0**

From Leicester C.

2018–19	Mansfield T	0	0		

GIBBENS, Lewis (D) **1 0**

b. 10-11-99

2018–19	Mansfield T	1	0	**1**	**0**

GOODEN, Iyrwah (F) **0 0**

2018–19	Mansfield T	0	0		

GRAHAM, Jordan (F) **8 0**

b.Peterborough 30-12-97

2017–18	Mansfield T	0	0		
2018–19	Mansfield T	8	0	**8**	**0**

HAKEEM, Zayn (M) **2 0**

b. 15-2-99

Internationals: Antigua and Barbuda U20.

2015–16	Mansfield T	1	0		
2016–17	Mansfield T	0	0		
2017–18	Mansfield T	0	0		
2018–19	Mansfield T	1	0	**2**	**0**

HAMILTON, CJ (M) **108 13**

H: 5 7 W: 11 09 b.Harrow 23-3-95

2015–16	Sheffield U	0	0		
2016–17	Mansfield T	29	0		
2017–18	Mansfield T	33	2		
2018–19	Mansfield T	46	11	**108**	**13**

KEAN, Jake (G) **114 0**

H: 6 4 W: 11 13 b.Derby 4-2-91

Internationals: England U20.

2010–11	Blackburn R	0	0		
2010–11	*Hartlepool U*	19	0	**19**	**0**
2011–12	Blackburn R	1	0		
2011–12	*Rochdale*	14	0	**14**	**0**
2012–13	Blackburn R	18	0		
2013–14	Blackburn R	18	0		
2014–15	Blackburn R	0	0	**37**	**0**
2014–15	*Yeovil T*	5	0	**5**	**0**
2014–15	*Oldham Ath*	11	0	**11**	**0**
2015–16	Norwich C	0	0		
2015–16	*Colchester U*	3	0	**3**	**0**
2015–16	*Swindon T*	3	0	**3**	**0**
2016–17	Sheffield W	0	0		
2016–17	*Mansfield T*	19	0		
2017–18	Sheffield W	0	0		
2017–18	*Grimsby T*	3	0	**3**	**0**
2018–19	Mansfield T	0	0	**19**	**0**

KHAN, Otis (M) **94 14**

H: 5 9 W: 11 03 b.Ashton-under-Lyme 5-9-95

2013–14	Sheffield U	2	0		
2014–15	Sheffield U	0	0		
2015–16	Sheffield U	0	0	**2**	**0**
2015–16	Barnsley	3	0	**3**	**0**
2016–17	Yeovil T	29	6		
2017–18	Yeovil T	38	6	**67**	**12**
2018–19	Mansfield T	22	2	**22**	**2**

KNOWLES, Jimmy (F) **0 0**

2018–19	Mansfield T	0	0		

LAW, Jason (F) **0 0**

2015–16	Mansfield T	0	0		

2016–17 Mansfield T 0 0
2017–18 Mansfield T 0 0
2018–19 Mansfield T 0 0

LOGAN, Conrad (G) 239 0
H: 6 2 W: 14 00 b.Letterkenny 18-4-86
2003–04 Leicester C 0 0
2004–05 Leicester C 0 0
2005–06 Leicester C 0 0
2005–06 *Boston U* 13 0 **13 0**
2006–07 Leicester C 18 0
2007–08 Leicester C 0 0
2007–08 *Stockport Co* 34 0
2008–09 Leicester C 0 0
2008–09 *Luton T* 22 0 **22 0**
2008–09 *Stockport Co* 7 0 **41 0**
2009–10 Leicester C 2 0
2010–11 Leicester C 3 0
2010–11 *Bristol R* 16 0 **16 0**
2011–12 Leicester C 0 0
2011–12 *Rotherham U* 19 0 **19 0**
2012–13 Leicester C 0 0
2013–14 Leicester C 0 0
2014–15 Leicester C 0 0 **23 0**
2014–15 *Rochdale* 19 0
2016–17 Rochdale 24 0 **43 0**
2016–17 Mansfield T 0 0
2017–18 Mansfield T 45 0
2018–19 Mansfield T 17 0 **62 0**

MACDONALD, Alex (F) 294 28
H: 5 7 W: 11 04 b.Warrington 14-4-90
Internationals: Scotland U19, U21.
2007–08 Burnley 2 0
2008–09 Burnley 3 0
2009–10 Burnley 0 0
2009–10 *Falkirk* 11 1 **11 1**
2010–11 Burnley 0 0
2010–11 *Inverness CT* 10 1 **10 1**
2011–12 Burnley 5 0
2011–12 *Plymouth Arg* 18 4
2012–13 Burnley 1 0 **11 0**
2012–13 *Plymouth Arg* 16 1 **34 5**
2012–13 *Burton Alb* 15 1
2013–14 Burton Alb 35 0
2014–15 Burton Alb 21 6 **71 7**
2014–15 Oxford U 15 3
2015–16 Oxford U 40 5
2016–17 Oxford U 22 1 **77 9**
2016–17 Mansfield T 18 1
2017–18 Mansfield T 41 3
2018–19 Mansfield T 21 1 **80 5**

MELLIS, Jacob (M) 242 17
H: 5 11 W: 10 11 b.Nottingham 8-1-91
Internationals: England U16, U17, U19.
2009–10 Chelsea 0 0
2009–10 *Southampton* 12 0 **12 0**
2010–11 Chelsea 0 0
2010–11 *Barnsley* 15 2
2012–13 Barnsley 36 6
2013–14 Barnsley 30 2 **81 10**
2014–15 Blackpool 13 0 **13 0**
2014–15 *Oldham Ath* 7 0 **7 0**
2015–16 Bury 23 0
2016–17 Bury 35 3 **58 3**
2017–18 Mansfield T 30 1
2018–19 Mansfield T 41 3 **71 4**

OLEJNIK, Robert (G) 346 0
H: 6 0 W: 15 06 b.Vienna 26-11-86
Internationals: Austria U21.
2004–05 Aston Villa 0 0
2005–06 Aston Villa 0 0
2006–07 Aston Villa 0 0
2006–07 *Lincoln C* 0 0
2007–08 Falkirk 13 0
2008–09 Falkirk 15 0
2009–10 Falkirk 38 0
2010–11 Falkirk 36 0 **102 0**
2011–12 Torquay U 46 0 **46 0**
2012–13 Peterborough U 46 0
2013–14 Peterborough U 42 0
2014–15 Peterborough U 0 0 **88 0**
2014–15 *Scunthorpe U* 13 0 **13 0**
2014–15 *York C* 16 0 **16 0**
2015–16 Exeter C 45 0
2016–17 Exeter C 18 0 **63 0**
2017–18 Mansfield T 1 0
2018–19 Mansfield T 17 0 **18 0**

PEARCE, Krystian (D) 333 22
H: 6 1 W: 13 05 b.Birmingham 5-1-90
Internationals: England U17, U19. Barbados Full caps.
2006–07 Birmingham C 0 0
2007–08 Birmingham C 0 0
2007–08 *Port Vale* 12 0 **12 0**
2007–08 *Notts Co* 8 1
2008–09 Birmingham C 0 0
2008–09 *Scunthorpe U* 39 0 **39 0**
2009–10 Birmingham C 0 0
2009–10 *Peterborough U* 2 0 **2 0**
2009–10 Huddersfield T 1 0 **1 0**
2010–11 Notts Co 27 1
2011–12 Notts Co 27 3
2012–13 Notts Co 2 1 **64 6**
2012–13 *Barnet* 17 1 **17 1**
2013–14 Torquay U 35 4 **35 4**
2015–16 Mansfield T 38 3
2016–17 Mansfield T 41 3
2017–18 Mansfield T 38 1
2018–19 Mansfield T 46 4 **163 11**

PRESTON, Matt (D) 101 8
b. 16-3-95
2013–14 Walsall 0 0
2014–15 Walsall 1 0
2015–16 Walsall 10 2
2016–17 Walsall 30 1
2017–18 Walsall 0 0 **41 3**
2017–18 Swindon T 21 2 **21 2**
2018–19 Mansfield T 39 3 **39 3**

ROSE, Danny (F) 196 46
H: 5 8 W: 9 00 b.Barnsley 10-12-93
2010–11 Barnsley 1 0
2011–12 Barnsley 4 0
2012–13 Barnsley 8 1
2013–14 Barnsley 3 0
2013–14 *Bury* 6 3
2014–15 Barnsley 1 0 **17 1**
2014–15 *Bury* 35 10
2015–16 Bury 28 5 **69 18**
2016–17 Mansfield T 37 9
2017–18 Mansfield T 39 14
2018–19 Mansfield T 34 4 **110 27**

SINCLAIR, Tyrese (F) 0 0
2018–19 Mansfield T 0 0

SMITH, Alistair (M) 0 0
2018–19 Mansfield T 0 0

SMITH, Jordan (G) 57 0
b.Nottingham 8-8-94
Internationals: Costa Rica U17, U20, Full caps.
2013–14 Nottingham F 0 0
2014–15 Nottingham F 0 0
2015–16 Nottingham F 0 0
2016–17 Nottingham F 15 0
2017–18 Nottingham F 29 0
2018–19 Barnsley 1 0 **1 0**
2018–19 Nottingham F 0 0 **44 0**
2018–19 Mansfield T 12 0 **12 0**

STERLING-JAMES, Omari (M) 36 1
b.Birmingham 15-9-93
Internationals: St Kitts and Nevis Full caps.
2014–15 Cheltenham T 22 1 **22 1**
From Gloucester C, Solihull Moors.
2017–18 Mansfield T 13 0
2018–19 Mansfield T 1 0 **14 0**

TOMLINSON, Willem (M) 17 0
H: 5 10 W: 10 03 b.Burnley 27-1-98
2015–16 Blackburn R 0 0
2016–17 Blackburn R 1 0
2017–18 Blackburn R 4 0
2018–19 Blackburn R 0 0 **5 0**
2018–19 Mansfield T 12 0 **12 0**

TURNER, Ben (D) 293 11
H: 6 4 W: 14 04 b.Birmingham 21-1-88
Internationals: England U19.
2005–06 Coventry C 1 0
2006–07 Coventry C 1 0
2006–07 *Peterborough U* 8 0 **8 0**
2006–07 *Oldham Ath* 1 0 **1 0**
2007–08 Coventry C 19 0
2008–09 Coventry C 24 0
2009–10 Coventry C 13 0
2010–11 Coventry C 14 4
2011–12 Cardiff C 37 2
2012–13 Cardiff C 31 1
2013–14 Cardiff C 31 0
2014–15 Cardiff C 11 0
2015–16 Cardiff C 1 0 **111 3**
2015–16 *Coventry C* 5 1 **77 5**
2016–17 Burton Alb 39 1
2017–18 Burton Alb 30 2
2018–19 Burton Alb 19 0 **88 3**
2018–19 Mansfield T 8 0 **8 0**

WALKER, Tyler (F) 102 32
H: 5 10 W: 9 13 b. 17-10-96
Internationals: England U20.
2013–14 Nottingham F 0 0
2014–15 Nottingham F 7 1
2015–16 Nottingham F 14 0
2015–16 *Burton Alb* 6 1 **6 1**
2016–17 Nottingham F 0 0
2016–17 *Stevenage* 8 3 **8 3**
2016–17 *Port Vale* 6 2 **6 2**
2017–18 Nottingham F 12 3 **33 4**
2017–18 *Bolton W* 5 0 **5 0**
2018–19 Mansfield T 44 22 **44 22**

WHITE, Hayden (D) 118 3
H: 6 1 W: 10 10 b.Greenwich 15-4-95
2013–14 Bolton W 2 0
2014–15 Bolton W 3 0
2014–15 *Carlisle U* 8 0 **8 0**
2014–15 *Bury* 2 0 **2 0**
2014–15 *Notts Co* 3 0 **3 0**
2015–16 Bolton W 0 0 **5 0**
2015–16 *Blackpool* 29 1 **29 1**
2016–17 Peterborough U 6 0 **6 0**
2016–17 *Mansfield T* 18 1
2017–18 Mansfield T 28 1
2018–19 Mansfield T 19 0 **65 2**

Players retained or with offer of contract
Sweeney, Ryan Joseph; Ward, Keaton Brodie.

Scholars
Armsden, Jordan David Lee; Boyle, Jamie Matthew; Briggs, Andrew Robert; Cashmore, Kamen Austin; Cornell, Jack Michael; Darby, Kieran Thomas; Fisher, Isaac Raymond; Gledhill, Thomas Henry; King, Larell Parker; Marrs, Keaton Bailey; Molyneaux, Rio Charles; O'Sullivan, Riley-Cole Matthew; Purvin, Daniel James; Sarson, Rhys Malcolm; Saunders, Nathan Anthony; Sinclair, Tyrese; Tague, James Nicholas.

MIDDLESBROUGH (51)

ARMSTRONG, Luke (F) 22 3
b. 2-7-96
2015–16 Cowdenbeath 6 0 **6 0**
From Blyth Spartans
2017–18 Middlesbrough 0 0
2018–19 Middlesbrough 0 0
2018 19 *Accrington S* 16 3 **16 3**

ASSOMBALONGA, Britt (F) 241 97
H: 5 9 W: 11 13 b.Kinshasa 6-12-92
Internationals: DR Congo Full caps.
2010–11 Watford 0 0
2011–12 Watford 4 0
2012–13 Watford 0 0
2012–13 *Southend U* 43 15 **43 15**
2013–14 Watford 0 0 **4 0**
2013–14 Peterborough U 43 23 **43 23**
2014–15 Nottingham F 29 15
2015–16 Nottingham F 4 1
2016–17 Nottingham F 32 14 **65 30**
2017–18 Middlesbrough 44 15
2018–19 Middlesbrough 42 14 **86 29**

AYALA, Daniel (M) 217 21
H: 6 3 W: 13 03 b.Sevilla 7-11-90
Internationals: Spain U21.
2007–08 Liverpool 0 0
2008–09 Liverpool 0 0
2009–10 Liverpool 5 0
2010–11 Liverpool 0 0 **5 0**
2010–11 *Hull C* 12 1 **12 1**
2010–11 *Derby Co* 17 0 **17 0**
2011–12 Norwich C 7 0
2012–13 Norwich C 0 0
2012–13 *Nottingham F* 12 1 **12 1**
2013–14 Norwich C 0 0 **7 0**
2013–14 Middlesbrough 19 3
2014–15 Middlesbrough 30 4
2015–16 Middlesbrough 35 3
2016–17 Middlesbrough 14 1
2017–18 Middlesbrough 33 7
2018–19 Middlesbrough 33 1 **164 19**

BRAHIMI, Bilal (F) 0 0
b.Paris 14-3-00
From Leixoes.
2018–19 Middlesbrough 0 0

BRAITHWAITE, Martin (F) **286 67**
H: 5 11 W: 12 02 b.Esbjerg 5-6-91
Internationals: Denmark U17, U19, U21, Full caps.
2009–10 Esbjerg 10 0
2010–11 Esbjerg 16 0
2011–12 Esbjerg 26 5
2012–13 Esbjerg 33 9
2013–14 Esbjerg 4 3 **89 17**
2013–14 Toulouse 32 7
2014–15 Toulouse 34 6
2015–16 Toulouse 36 11
2016–17 Toulouse 34 11 **136 35**
2017–18 Middlesbrough 19 5
2017–18 *Bordeaux* 14 4 **14 4**
2018–19 Middlesbrough 17 3 **36 8**
2018–19 *Leganes* 11 3 **11 3**

CHAPMAN, Harry (M) **37 3**
H: 5 10 W: 11 00 b.Hartlepool 5-11-97
Internationals: England U18, U20.
2015–16 Middlesbrough 0 0
2015–16 *Barnsley* 11 1 **11 1**
2016–17 Middlesbrough 0 0
2016–17 *Sheffield U* 12 1 **12 1**
2017–18 Middlesbrough 0 0
2017–18 *Blackburn R* 12 1
2018–19 Middlesbrough 0 0
2018–19 *Blackburn R* 2 0 **14 1**

CLAYTON, Adam (M) **359 20**
H: 5 9 W: 11 11 b.Manchester 14-1-89
Internationals: England U20.
2007–08 Manchester C 0 0
2008–09 Manchester C 0 0
2009–10 Manchester C 0 0
2009–10 *Carlisle U* 28 1 **28 1**
2010–11 Leeds U 4 0
2010–11 *Peterborough U* 7 0 **7 0**
2010–11 *Milton Keynes D* 6 1 **6 1**
2011–12 Leeds U 43 6 **47 6**
2012–13 Huddersfield T 43 4
2013–14 Huddersfield T 42 7 **85 11**
2014–15 Middlesbrough 41 0
2015–16 Middlesbrough 43 1
2016–17 Middlesbrough 34 0
2017–18 Middlesbrough 32 0
2018–19 Middlesbrough 36 0 **186 1**

COULSON, Hayden (D) **20 0**
b. 17-6-98
Internationals: England U16, U17, U18, U19.
2018–19 Middlesbrough 0 0
2018–19 *St Mirren* 6 0 **6 0**
2018–19 *Cambridge U* 14 0 **14 0**

DE SART, Julien (M) **95 4**
H: 6 0 W: 10 10 b.Waremme 23-12-94
Internationals: Belgium U16, U17, U18, U19, U21.
2013–14 Standard Liege 24 2
2014–15 Standard Liege 26 1
2015–16 Standard Liege 12 0 **62 3**
2015–16 Middlesbrough 2 0
2016–17 Middlesbrough 0 0
2016–17 *Derby Co* 9 1 **9 1**
2017–18 Middlesbrough 0 0
2017–18 *Zulte-Waregem* 22 0 **22 0**
2018–19 Middlesbrough 0 0 **2 0**
Transferred to Kortrijk, August 2018.

DOWNING, Stewart (M) **538 48**
H: 5 11 W: 10 04 b.Middlesbrough 22-7-84
Internationals: England U21, B, Full caps.
2001–02 Middlesbrough 3 0
2002–03 Middlesbrough 2 0
2003–04 Middlesbrough 20 0
2003–04 *Sunderland* 7 3 **7 3**
2004–05 Middlesbrough 35 5
2005–06 Middlesbrough 12 1
2006–07 Middlesbrough 34 2
2007–08 Middlesbrough 38 9
2008–09 Middlesbrough 37 0
2009–10 Aston Villa 25 2
2010–11 Aston Villa 38 7 **63 9**
2011–12 Liverpool 36 0
2012–13 Liverpool 29 3
2013–14 Liverpool 0 0 **65 3**
2013–14 West Ham U 32 1
2014–15 West Ham U 37 6 **69 7**
2015–16 Middlesbrough 45 3
2016–17 Middlesbrough 30 1
2017–18 Middlesbrough 40 3
2018–19 Middlesbrough 38 2 **334 26**

FLETCHER, Ashley (F) **90 13**
b.Keighley 12-10-95
Internationals: England U20.
2015–16 Manchester U 0 0
2015–16 *Barnsley* 21 5 **21 5**
2016–17 West Ham U 16 0 **16 0**
2017–18 Middlesbrough 16 1
2017–18 *Sunderland* 16 2 **16 2**
2018–19 Middlesbrough 21 5 **37 6**

FLINT, Aiden (D) **312 41**
H: 6 2 W: 12 00 b.Pinxton 11-7-89
Internationals: England C.
2010–11 Swindon T 3 0
2011–12 Swindon T 32 2
2012–13 Swindon T 29 2 **64 4**
2013–14 Bristol C 34 3
2014–15 Bristol C 46 14
2015–16 Bristol C 44 6
2016–17 Bristol C 46 5
2017–18 Bristol C 39 8 **209 36**
2018–19 Middlesbrough 39 1 **39 1**

FRIEND, George (D) **351 12**
H: 6 2 W: 13 01 b.Barnstaple 19-10-87
2008–09 Exeter C 4 0
2008–09 Wolverhampton W 6 0
2009–10 Wolverhampton W 1 0 **7 0**
2009–10 *Millwall* 6 0 **6 0**
2009–10 *Southend U* 6 1 **6 1**
2009–10 *Scunthorpe U* 4 0 **4 0**
2009–10 *Exeter C* 13 1 **17 1**
2010–11 Doncaster R 32 1
2011–12 Doncaster R 27 0
2012–13 Doncaster R 0 0 **59 1**
2012–13 Middlesbrough 34 0
2013–14 Middlesbrough 41 3
2014–15 Middlesbrough 42 1
2015–16 Middlesbrough 40 1
2016–17 Middlesbrough 24 0
2017–18 Middlesbrough 33 2
2018–19 Middlesbrough 38 2 **252 9**

FRY, Dael (D) **64 0**
H: 6 1 W: 11 05 b.Middlesbrough 30-8-97
Internationals: England U17, U18, U19, U20, U21.
2015–16 Middlesbrough 7 0
2016–17 Middlesbrough 0 0
2016–17 *Rotherham U* 10 0 **10 0**
2017–18 Middlesbrough 13 0
2018–19 Middlesbrough 34 0 **54 0**

GESTEDE, Rudy (F) **251 61**
H: 6 4 W: 13 07 b.Nancy 10-10-88
Internationals: France U19. Benin Full caps.
2008–09 Metz 5 0
2009–10 *Cannes* 22 4 **22 4**
2010–11 Metz 11 3 **16 3**
2010–11 Metz B 3 1 **3 1**
2011–12 Cardiff C 25 2
2012–13 Cardiff C 27 5
2013–14 Cardiff C 3 0 **55 7**
2013–14 Blackburn R 27 13
2014–15 Blackburn R 39 20 **66 33**
2015–16 Aston Villa 32 5
2016–17 Aston Villa 18 4 **50 9**
2016–17 Middlesbrough 16 1
2017–18 Middlesbrough 19 3
2018–19 Middlesbrough 4 0 **39 4**

GIBSON, Ciaran (G) **0 0**
2018–19 Middlesbrough 0 0

HOWSON, Jonathan (M) **450 49**
H: 5 11 W: 12 01 b.Morley 21-5-88
Internationals: England U21.
2006–07 Leeds U 9 1
2007–08 Leeds U 26 3
2008–09 Leeds U 40 4
2009–10 Leeds U 45 4
2010–11 Leeds U 46 10
2011–12 Leeds U 19 1 **185 23**
2011–12 Norwich C 11 1
2012–13 Norwich C 30 2
2013–14 Norwich C 27 2
2014–15 Norwich C 34 8
2015–16 Norwich C 36 3
2016–17 Norwich C 38 6 **176 22**
2017–18 Middlesbrough 43 3
2018–19 Middlesbrough 46 1 **89 4**

JOHNSON, Marvin (F) **122 10**
H: 5 10 W: 11 09 b.Birmingham 1-12-90
From Solihull Moors, Kidderminster H.
2014–15 Motherwell 11 0
2015–16 Motherwell 38 5
2016–17 Motherwell 4 1 **53 6**
2016–17 Oxford U 39 3
2017–18 Oxford U 2 0 **41 3**
2017–18 Middlesbrough 17 1
2018–19 Middlesbrough 0 0 **17 1**
2018–19 *Sheffield U* 11 0 **11 0**

KONSTANTOPOULOS, Dimitrios (G) **312 0**
H: 6 4 W: 14 02 b.Kalamata 29-11-78
Internationals: Greece U21, Full caps.
2003–04 Hartlepool U 0 0
2004–05 Hartlepool U 25 0
2005–06 Hartlepool U 46 0
2006–07 Hartlepool U 46 0 **117 0**
2007–08 Coventry C 21 0
2008–09 Coventry C 0 0
2008–09 *Swansea C* 4 0 **4 0**
2008–09 *Cardiff C* 6 0 **6 0**
2009–10 Coventry C 3 0 **24 0**
2010–11 Kerkyra 30 0 **30 0**
2011–12 AEK Athens 9 0
2012–13 AEK Athens 24 0 **33 0**
2013–14 Middlesbrough 12 0
2014–15 Middlesbrough 40 0
2015–16 Middlesbrough 46 0
2016–17 Middlesbrough 0 0
2017–18 Middlesbrough 0 0
2018–19 Middlesbrough 0 0 **98 0**

LIDDLE, Ben (M) **2 0**
b.Durham 21-9-98
2018–19 Middlesbrough 0 0
2018–19 *Forest Green R* 2 0 **2 0**

MAHMUTOVIC, Enes (D) **29 0**
H: 6 3 W: 12 08 b. 22-5-97
Internationals: Luxembourg U21, Full caps.
2014–15 Fola Esch 1 0
2015–16 Fola Esch 2 0
2016–17 Fola Esch 22 0 **25 0**
2017–18 Middlesbrough 0 0
2018–19 Middlesbrough 0 0
2018–19 *Yeovil T* 4 0 **4 0**

MALLEY, Connor (M) **0 0**
b.Newcastle 20-3-00
2018–19 Middlesbrough 0 0

McGINLEY, Nathan (D) **49 0**
b.Middlesbrough 15-9-96
2017–18 Middlesbrough 0 0
2017–18 *Wycombe W* 11 0 **11 0**
2018–19 Middlesbrough 0 0
2018–19 *Forest Green R* 38 0 **38 0**

McNAIR, Paddy (D) **65 5**
H: 5 8 W: 11 05 b.Ballyclare 27-4-95
Internationals: Northern Ireland U16, U17, U19, U21, Full caps.
2011–12 Manchester U 0 0
2012–13 Manchester U 0 0
2013–14 Manchester U 0 0
2014–15 Manchester U 16 0
2015–16 Manchester U 8 0 **24 0**
2016–17 Sunderland 9 0
2017–18 Sunderland 16 5 **25 5**
2018–19 Middlesbrough 16 0 **16 0**

MIKEL, John Obi (M) **304 6**
H: 6 0 W: 13 05 b.Plateau State 22-4-87
Internationals: Nigeria Youth, Full caps.
2005 Lyn 6 1 **6 1**
2006–07 Chelsea 22 0
2007–08 Chelsea 29 0
2008–09 Chelsea 34 0
2009–10 Chelsea 25 0
2010–11 Chelsea 28 0
2011–12 Chelsea 22 0
2012–13 Chelsea 22 0
2013–14 Chelsea 24 1
2014–15 Chelsea 18 0
2015–16 Chelsea 25 0
2016–17 Chelsea 0 0 **249 1**
2017 Tianjin Taida 13 1
2018 Tianjin Taida 18 2 **31 3**
2018–19 Middlesbrough 18 1 **18 1**

O'NEILL, Tyrone (F) **0 0**
b.Middlesbrough 12-10-99
2018–19 Middlesbrough 0 0

RANDOLPH, Darren (G) **366 0**
H: 6 1 W: 12 02 b.Dublin 12-5-87
Internationals: Republic of Ireland U21, B, Full caps.
2004–05 Charlton Ath 0 0
2005–06 Charlton Ath 0 0
2006–07 Charlton Ath 1 0
2006–07 *Gillingham* 3 0 **3 0**

2007–08	Charlton Ath	1	0		
2007–08	*Bury*	14	0	**14**	**0**
2008–09	Charlton Ath	1	0		
2008–09	*Hereford U*	13	0	**13**	**0**
2009–10	Charlton Ath	11	0	**14**	**0**
2010–11	Motherwell	37	0		
2011–12	Motherwell	38	0		
2012–13	Motherwell	36	0	**111**	**0**
2013–14	Birmingham C	46	0		
2014–15	Birmingham C	45	0	**91**	**0**
2015–16	West Ham U	6	0		
2016–17	West Ham U	22	0	**28**	**0**
2017–18	Middlesbrough	46	0		
2018–19	Middlesbrough	46	0	**92**	**0**

SHOTTON, Ryan (D) **262** **13**
H: 6 3 W: 13 05 b.Stoke 30-9-88

2006–07	Stoke C	0	0		
2007–08	Stoke C	0	0		
2008–09	Stoke C	0	0		
2008–09	*Tranmere R*	33	5	**33**	**5**
2009–10	Stoke C	0	0		
2009–10	*Barnsley*	30	0	**30**	**0**
2010–11	Stoke C	2	0		
2011–12	Stoke C	23	1		
2012–13	Stoke C	23	0		
2013–14	Stoke C	0	0	**48**	**1**
2013–14	*Wigan Ath*	9	1	**9**	**1**
2014–15	Derby Co	25	2		
2015–16	Derby Co	6	0	**31**	**2**
2015–16	*Birmingham C*	9	1		
2016–17	Birmingham C	43	2		
2017–18	Birmingham C	1	0	**53**	**3**
2017–18	Middlesbrough	24	1		
2018–19	Middlesbrough	34	0	**58**	**1**

SPENCE, Djed (D) **0** **0**
H: 6 0 W: 11 03 b.London 9-8-00
From Fulham.

2018–19	Middlesbrough	0	0

STUBBS, Sam (D) **22** **0**
b. 20-11-98

2016–17	Wigan Ath	0	0		
2017–18	Wigan Ath	0	0		
2017–18	*Crewe Alex*	5	0	**5**	**0**
2018–19	Middlesbrough	0	0		
2018–19	*Notts Co*	17	0	**17**	**0**

TAVERNIER, Marcus (M) **32** **4**
b.Leeds 22-3-99
Internationals: England U19, U20.

2017–18	Middlesbrough	5	1		
2017–18	*Milton Keynes D*	7	0	**7**	**0**
2018–19	Middlesbrough	20	3	**25**	**4**

WALKER, Stephen (F) **7** **0**
b.Middlesbrough 11-10-00
Internationals: England U17, U18, U19.

2018–19	Middlesbrough	0	0		
2018–19	*Milton Keynes D*	7	0	**7**	**0**

WING, Lewis (M) **48** **6**
b.Durham 23-5-95
From Shildon.

2017–18	Middlesbrough	0	0		
2017–18	*Yeovil T*	20	3	**20**	**3**
2018–19	Middlesbrough	28	3	**28**	**3**

WOOD-GORDON, Nathan (D) **0** **0**
b.Middlesbrough 31-5-02
Internationals: England U16, U17.
From Stockton T.

2018–19	Middlesbrough	0	0

Players retained or with offer of contract
Brynn, Solomon; Curry, Mitchell; Fryer, Joseph Luke; Hemming, Zachary; James, Bradley David; Pears, Aynsley Alan William; Reading, Patrick James; Sanchez, Ayala Daniel; Saville, George Alan; Sylla, Amadou.

Scholars
Balde, Almanzar Alberto; Brahimi, Billal; Charlton, Kieran; Cornet, Isiah Jean-Louis Casimir; Dale, Nathan Alan; Dodds, Daniel; Drummond, Luke Jon; Essien, Harold Jimaimah; Flatters, Harry David; Fletcher, Isaac Andrew; Gibson, Joseph William; Green, Harry Steven; Guru, Nathan; Hackney, Hayden Rhys; Hood, Nicholas Joseph; McGill, Gabriel Edward; Robinson, Jack; Stephenson, Terry Gewelling; Sykes, Cain; Watts, Layton; Wearne, Stephen Christopher; Wilson, Andrew; Wood-Gordon, Nathan Dean Joshua.

MILLWALL (52)

ALEXANDER, George (F) **1** **0**
b. 22-6-01

2018–19	Millwall	1	0	**1**	**0**

AMOS, Ben (G) **167** **0**
H: 6 1 W: 13 00 b.Macclesfield 10-4-90
Internationals: England U16, U17, U18, U19, U20, U21.

2007–08	Manchester U	0	0		
2008–09	Manchester U	0	0		
2009–10	Manchester U	0	0		
2009–10	*Peterborough U*	1	0	**1**	**0**
2010–11	Manchester U	0	0		
2010–11	*Oldham Ath*	16	0	**16**	**0**
2011–12	Manchester U	1	0		
2012–13	Manchester U	0	0		
2012–13	*Hull C*	17	0	**17**	**0**
2013–14	Manchester U	0	0		
2013–14	*Carlisle U*	9	0	**9**	**0**
2014–15	Manchester U	0	0	**1**	**0**
2014–15	*Bolton W*	9	0		
2015–16	Bolton W	40	0		
2016–17	Bolton W	0	0		
2016–17	*Cardiff C*	16	0	**16**	**0**
2017–18	Bolton W	0	0	**49**	**0**
2017–18	*Charlton Ath*	46	0	**46**	**0**
2018–19	Millwall	12	0	**12**	**0**

ARCHER, Jordan (G) **184** **0**
H: 6 1 W: 12 08 b.Walthamstow 12-4-93
Internationals: Scotland U19, U20, U21, Full caps.

2011–12	Tottenham H	0	0		
2012–13	Tottenham H	0	0		
2012–13	*Wycombe W*	27	0	**27**	**0**
2013–14	Tottenham H	0	0		
2014–15	Tottenham H	0	0		
2014–15	*Northampton T*	13	0	**13**	**0**
2014–15	*Millwall*	0	0		
2015–16	Millwall	39	0		
2016–17	Millwall	36	0		
2017–18	Millwall	45	0		
2018–19	Millwall	24	0	**144**	**0**

BRADSHAW, Tom (F) **254** **69**
H: 5 5 W: 11 02 b.Shrewsbury 27-7-92
Internationals: Wales U19, U21, Full caps.

2009–10	Shrewsbury T	6	3		
2010–11	Shrewsbury T	26	6		
2011–12	Shrewsbury T	8	1		
2012–13	Shrewsbury T	21	0		
2013–14	Shrewsbury T	28	7	**89**	**17**
2014–15	Walsall	29	17		
2015–16	Walsall	41	17	**70**	**34**
2016–17	Barnsley	42	8		
2017–18	Barnsley	39	9		
2018–19	Barnsley	4	1	**85**	**18**
2018–19	Millwall	10	0	**10**	**0**

BROWN, James (D) **28** **0**
H: 6 1 W: 12 06 b. 12-1-98

2016–17	Millwall	0	0		
2017–18	Millwall	0	0		
2017–18	*Carlisle U*	27	0	**27**	**0**
2018–19	Millwall	0	0		
2018–19	*Livingston*	1	0	**1**	**0**
2018–19	*Lincoln C*	0	0		

COOPER, Jake (D) **141** **16**
H: 6 4 W: 13 05 b.Bracknell 3-2-95
Internationals: England U18, U19, U20.

2013–14	Reading	0	0		
2014–15	Reading	15	2		
2015–16	Reading	24	2		
2016–17	Reading	3	0	**42**	**4**
2016–17	*Millwall*	15	2		
2017–18	Millwall	38	4		
2018–19	Millwall	46	6	**99**	**12**

DEBRAH, Jesse (F) **0** **0**
H: 6 0 W: 11 07 b. 11-1-00

2018–19	Millwall	0	0

DONOVAN, Harry (M) **0** **0**
From Arsenal.

2016–17	Millwall	0	0
2018–19	Millwall	0	0

ELLIOTT, Tom (F) **245** **38**
H: 6 3 W: 12 00 b.Hunslet 9-11-90
Internationals: England U16, U18.

2006–07	Leeds U	3	0		
2007–08	Leeds U	0	0		
2008–09	Leeds U	0	0		
2008–09	*Macclesfield T*	6	0	**6**	**0**
2009–10	Leeds U	0	0		
2009–10	*Bury*	16	1	**16**	**1**
2010–11	Leeds U	0	0	**3**	**0**
2010–11	*Rotherham U*	6	0	**6**	**0**
2011–12	Hamilton A	7	0	**7**	**0**
2011–12	Stockport Co	42	7	**42**	**7**
2014–15	Cambridge U	30	8	**30**	**8**
2015–16	AFC Wimbledon	39	6		
2016–17	AFC Wimbledon	39	9	**78**	**15**
2017–18	Millwall	24	4		
2018–19	Millwall	33	3	**57**	**7**

FERGUSON, Shane (D) **190** **8**
H: 5 9 W: 10 01 b.Limavady 12-7-91
Internationals: Northern Ireland U17, U19, U21, B, Full caps.

2008–09	Newcastle U	0	0		
2009–10	Newcastle U	0	0		
2010–11	Newcastle U	7	0		
2011–12	Newcastle U	7	0		
2012–13	Newcastle U	9	0		
2012–13	*Birmingham C*	11	1		
2013–14	Newcastle U	0	0		
2013–14	*Birmingham C*	18	0	**29**	**1**
2014–15	Newcastle U	0	0		
2014–15	*Rangers*	0	0		
2015–16	Newcastle U	0	0	**23**	**0**
2015–16	Millwall	39	3		
2016–17	Millwall	40	2		
2017–18	Millwall	24	0		
2018–19	Millwall	35	2	**138**	**7**

GREGORY, Lee (F) **204** **64**
H: 6 2 b.Sheffield 26-8-88

2014–15	Millwall	39	9		
2015–16	Millwall	41	18		
2016–17	Millwall	37	17		
2017–18	Millwall	43	10		
2018–19	Millwall	44	10	**204**	**64**

HANSON, Jethro (M) **0** **0**
H: 5 9 W: 10 08 b. 14-6-00

2018–19	Millwall	0	0

HUTCHINSON, Shaun (D) **243** **14**
H: 6 1 W: 12 04 b.Newcastle upon Tyne 23-11-90

2008–09	Motherwell	1	0		
2009–10	Motherwell	5	3		
2010–11	Motherwell	19	1		
2011–12	Motherwell	30	1		
2012–13	Motherwell	31	1		
2013–14	Motherwell	35	1	**121**	**7**
2014–15	Fulham	25	2		
2015–16	Fulham	9	0	**34**	**2**
2016–17	Millwall	16	2		
2017–18	Millwall	46	2		
2018–19	Millwall	26	1	**88**	**5**

KARACAN, Jem (M) **200** **13**
H: 5 10 W: 11 13 b.Lewisham 21-2-89
Internationals: Turkey U17, U18, U19, U21.

2007–08	Reading	0	0		
2007–08	*Bournemouth*	13	1	**13**	**1**
2007–08	*Millwall*	7	0		
2008–09	Reading	15	1		
2009–10	Reading	27	0		
2010–11	Reading	40	3		
2011–12	Reading	37	3		
2012–13	Reading	21	1		
2013–14	Reading	7	2		
2014–15	Reading	8	1		
2015–16	Reading	0	0	**155**	**11**
2015–16	Galatasaray	0	0		
2016–17	Galatasaray	0	0		
2016–17	Bolton W	5	1		
2017–18	Bolton W	16	0	**21**	**1**
2018–19	Millwall	4	0	**11**	**0**

Transferred to Central Coast Mariners, January 2019.

KING, Tom (G) **41** **0**
H: 6 1 b.Plymouth 9-3-95
Internationals: England U17.

2011–12	Crystal Palace	0	0		
2012–13	Crystal Palace	0	0		
2014–15	Millwall	0	0		
2015–16	Millwall	0	0		
2016–17	Millwall	11	0		
2017–18	Millwall	0	0		
2017–18	*Stevenage*	18	0	**18**	**0**
2018–19	Millwall	0	0	**11**	**0**
2018–19	*AFC Wimbledon*	12	0	**12**	**0**

LEONARD, Ryan (D) **282** **22**
H: 6 0 W: 11 01 b.Plympton 24-5-92

2009–10	Plymouth Arg	1	0		
2010–11	Plymouth Arg	0	0	**1**	**0**

2011–12	Southend U	17	1		
2012–13	Southend U	22	2		
2013–14	Southend U	43	5		
2014–15	Southend U	41	3		
2015–16	Southend U	37	2		
2016–17	Southend U	43	3		
2017–18	Southend U	25	4	**228**	**20**
2017–18	Sheffield U	13	0		
2018–19	Sheffield U	3	0	**16**	**0**
2018–19	Millwall	37	2	**37**	**2**

MARSHALL, Ben (F) 336 39
H: 5 11 W: 11 13 b.Salford 29-3-91
Internationals: England U21.

2009–10	Stoke C	0	0		
2009–10	*Northampton T*	15	2	**15**	**2**
2009–10	*Cheltenham T*	6	2	**6**	**2**
2009–10	*Carlisle U*	20	3		
2010–11	Stoke C	0	0		
2010–11	*Carlisle U*	33	3	**53**	**6**
2011–12	Stoke C	0	0		
2011–12	*Sheffield W*	22	5	**22**	**5**
2011–12	Leicester C	16	3		
2012–13	Leicester C	40	4		
2013–14	Leicester C	0	0	**56**	**7**
2013–14	Blackburn R	18	2		
2014–15	Blackburn R	42	6		
2015–16	Blackburn R	44	2		
2016–17	Blackburn R	22	1	**126**	**11**
2016–17	Wolverhampton W	16	2		
2017–18	Wolverhampton W	6	0	**22**	**2**
2017–18	*Millwall*	16	3		
2018–19	Norwich C	4	0	**4**	**0**
2018–19	Millwall	16	1	**32**	**4**

MARTIN, David E (G) 342 0
H: 6 1 W: 13 04 b.Romford 22-1-86
Internationals: England U16, U17, U18, U19.

2003–04	Wimbledon	2	0	**2**	**0**
2004–05	Milton Keynes D	15	0		
2005–06	Milton Keynes D	0	0		
2005–06	Liverpool	0	0		
2006–07	Liverpool	0	0		
2006–07	*Accrington S*	10	0	**10**	**0**
2007–08	Liverpool	0	0		
2008–09	Liverpool	0	0		
2008–09	*Leicester C*	25	0	**25**	**0**
2009–10	Liverpool	0	0		
2009–10	*Tranmere R*	3	0	**3**	**0**
2009–10	*Leeds U*	0	0		
2009–10	*Derby Co*	2	0	**2**	**0**
2010–11	Milton Keynes D	43	0		
2011–12	Milton Keynes D	46	0		
2012–13	Milton Keynes D	31	0		
2013–14	Milton Keynes D	40	0		
2014–15	Milton Keynes D	39	0		
2015–16	Milton Keynes D	35	0		
2016–17	Milton Keynes D	40	0	**289**	**0**
2017–18	Millwall	1	0		
2018–19	Millwall	10	0	**11**	**0**

McLAUGHLIN, Conor (D) 232 8
H: 6 0 W: 11 02 b.Belfast 26-7-91
Internationals: Northern Ireland U21, Full caps.

2009–10	Preston NE	0	0		
2010–11	Preston NE	7	0		
2011–12	Preston NE	17	0	**24**	**0**
2011–12	*Shrewsbury T*	4	0	**4**	**0**
2012–13	Fleetwood T	19	0		
2013–14	Fleetwood T	35	0		
2014–15	Fleetwood T	39	1		
2015–16	Fleetwood T	37	2		
2016–17	Fleetwood T	42	4	**172**	**7**
2017–18	Millwall	24	1		
2018–19	Millwall	8	0	**32**	**1**

McNAMARA, Danny (D) 0 0
b. 27-12-98

2018–19	Millwall	0	0		

MEREDITH, James (D) 267 4
H: 6 1 W: 11 06 b.Albury, Australia 4-4-88
Internationals: Australia Full caps.

2006–07	Derby Co	0	0		
2006–07	*Chesterfield*	1	0	**1**	**0**
2007–08	Shrewsbury T	3	0	**3**	**0**
From York C					
2012–13	Bradford C	32	1		
2013–14	Bradford C	26	0		
2014–15	Bradford C	40	0		
2015–16	Bradford C	42	1		
2016–17	Bradford C	41	2	**181**	**4**
2017–18	Millwall	46	0		
2018–19	Millwall	36	0	**82**	**0**

MITCHELL, Billy (M) 1 0
b. 7-4-01

2018–19	Millwall	1	0	**1**	**0**

MORISON, Steven (F) 410 93
H: 6 2 W: 13 07 b.Enfield 29-8-83
Internationals: England C. Wales Full caps.

2001–02	Northampton T	1	0		
2002–03	Northampton T	13	1		
2003–04	Northampton T	5	1		
2004–05	Northampton T	4	1	**23**	**3**
From Stevenage B.					
2008–09	Millwall	0	0		
2009–10	Millwall	43	20		
2010–11	Millwall	40	15		
2011–12	Norwich C	34	9		
2012–13	Norwich C	19	1	**53**	**10**
2012–13	Leeds U	15	3		
2013–14	Leeds U	0	0		
2013–14	*Millwall*	41	8		
2014–15	Leeds U	26	2	**41**	**5**
2015–16	Millwall	46	15		
2016–17	Millwall	38	11		
2017–18	Millwall	44	5		
2018–19	Millwall	41	1	**293**	**75**

NELSON, Sid (D) 94 1
H: 6 1 b.London 1-1-96

2013–14	Millwall	0	0		
2014–15	Millwall	14	0		
2015–16	Millwall	9	0		
2016–17	Millwall	3	0		
2016–17	*Newport Co*	14	0	**14**	**0**
2017–18	Millwall	0	0		
2017–18	*Yeovil T*	12	0	**12**	**0**
2017–18	*Chesterfield*	15	1	**15**	**1**
2018–19	Millwall	0	0	**26**	**0**
2018–19	*Swindon T*	20	0	**20**	**0**
2018–19	*Tranmere R*	7	0	**7**	**0**

O'BRIEN, Aiden (F) 182 31
H: 5 8 W: 10 12 b.Islington 4-10-93
Internationals: Republic of Ireland U17, U19, U21, Full caps.

2010–11	Millwall	0	0		
2011–12	Millwall	0	0		
2012–13	Millwall	0	0		
2012–13	*Crawley T*	9	0	**9**	**0**
2013–14	Millwall	0	0		
2013–14	*Torquay U*	3	0	**3**	**0**
2014–15	Millwall	19	2		
2015–16	Millwall	43	10		
2016–17	Millwall	43	13		
2017–18	Millwall	30	4		
2018–19	Millwall	35	2	**170**	**31**

ONYEDINMA, Fred (M) 166 20
H: 6 1 b.London 24-11-96

2013–14	Millwall	4	0		
2014–15	Millwall	2	0		
2014–15	*Wycombe W*	25	8		
2015–16	Millwall	34	4		
2016–17	Millwall	42	3		
2017–18	Millwall	37	1		
2018–19	Millwall	1	0	**120**	**8**
2018–19	*Wycombe W*	21	4	**46**	**12**

ROMEO, Mahlon (M) 119 2
H: 5 10 W: 11 05 b.Westminster 19-9-95
Internationals: Antigua and Barbuda Full caps.

2012–13	Gillingham	1	0		
2013–14	Gillingham	0	0		
2014–15	Gillingham	0	0	**1**	**0**
2015–16	Millwall	18	1		
2016–17	Millwall	32	0		
2017–18	Millwall	27	1		
2018–19	Millwall	41	0	**118**	**2**

SAVILLE, George (M) 194 24
H: 5 9 W: 11 07 b.Camberley 1-6-93
Internationals: Northern Ireland Full caps.

2010–11	Chelsea	0	0		
2011–12	Chelsea	0	0		
2012–13	Chelsea	0	0		
2012–13	*Millwall*	3	0		
2013–14	Chelsea	0	0		
2013–14	*Brentford*	40	3	**40**	**3**
2014–15	Wolverhampton W	7	0		
2014–15	*Bristol C*	7	1	**7**	**1**
2015–16	Wolverhampton W	19	5		
2015–16	*Millwall*	12	0		
2016–17	Wolverhampton W	24	1	**50**	**6**
2017–18	Millwall	44	10		
2018–19	Millwall	4	0	**63**	**10**
2018–19	*Middlesbrough*	34	4	**34**	**4**

SKALAK, Jiri (F) 167 20
H: 5 9 W: 10 10 b.Pardubice 12-3-92
Internationals: Czech Republic U16, U17, U18, U19, U20, U21, Full caps.

2010–11	Sparta Prague	0	0		
2011–12	Sparta Prague	0	0		
2011–12	*MFA Ruzomberok*	27	3	**27**	**3**
2012–13	Sparta Prague	7	0		
2012–13	*1.FC Slovacko*	9	0	**9**	**0**
2013–14	Sparta Prague	3	0		
2013–14	*Zbrojovka Brno*	24	3	**24**	**3**
2014–15	Sparta Prague	0	0	**10**	**0**
2014–15	*Mlada Boleslav*	24	6		
2015–16	Mlada Boleslav	16	6	**40**	**12**
2015–16	Brighton & HA	12	2		
2016–17	Brighton & HA	31	0		
2017–18	Brighton & HA	0	0	**43**	**2**
2018–19	Millwall	14	0	**14**	**0**

THOMPSON, Ben (M) 105 7
H: 5 11 W: 12 04 b. 3-10-95

2014–15	Millwall	0	0		
2015–16	Millwall	28	1		
2016–17	Millwall	38	0		
2017–18	Millwall	3	0		
2018–19	Portsmouth	23	2	**23**	**2**
2018–19	Millwall	13	4	**82**	**5**

TUNNICLIFFE, Ryan (M) 196 8
H: 6 0 W: 14 02 b.Bury 30-12-92
Internationals: England U16, U17.

2009–10	Manchester U	0	0		
2010–11	Manchester U	0	0		
2011–12	Manchester U	0	0		
2011–12	*Peterborough U*	27	0	**27**	**0**
2012–13	Manchester U	0	0		
2012–13	*Barnsley*	2	0	**2**	**0**
2013–14	Manchester U	0	0		
2013–14	*Ipswich T*	27	0	**27**	**0**
2013–14	Fulham	3	0		
2013–14	*Wigan Ath*	5	0		
2014–15	Fulham	22	0		
2014–15	*Blackburn R*	17	1	**17**	**1**
2015–16	Fulham	27	2		
2016–17	Fulham	7	0	**59**	**2**
2016–17	*Wigan Ath*	9	1	**14**	**1**
2017–18	Millwall	24	1		
2018–19	Millwall	26	3	**50**	**4**

WALLACE, Jed (M) 241 42
H: 5 10 W: 10 12 b.Reading 15-12-93
Internationals: England U19.

2011–12	Portsmouth	0	0		
2012–13	Portsmouth	22	6		
2013–14	Portsmouth	44	7		
2014–15	Portsmouth	44	14	**110**	**27**
2015–16	Wolverhampton W	9	0		
2015–16	*Millwall*	12	1		
2016–17	Wolverhampton W	9	0	**18**	**0**
2016–17	*Millwall*	16	3		
2017–18	Millwall	43	6		
2018–19	Millwall	42	5	**113**	**15**

WALLACE, Murray (D) 215 12
H: 6 2 W: 11 07 b.Glasgow 10-1-93
Internationals: Scotland U20, U21.

2011–12	Falkirk	19	2	**19**	**2**
2011–12	Huddersfield T	0	0		
2012–13	Huddersfield T	6	1		
2013–14	Huddersfield T	17	0		
2014–15	Huddersfield T	26	2		
2015–16	Huddersfield T	2	0	**51**	**3**
2015–16	*Scunthorpe U*	33	2		
2016–17	Scunthorpe U	46	2		
2017–18	Scunthorpe U	45	1	**124**	**5**
2018–19	Millwall	21	2	**21**	**2**

WHITE, Lewis (M) 0 0
H: 5 8 W: 10 10 b.London 3-5-99

2018–19	Millwall	0	0		

WILLIAMS, Shaun (M) 389 58
H: 5 9 W: 11 11 b.Dublin 19-10-86
Internationals: Republic of Ireland U21, U23, Full caps.

2007	Drogheda U	0	0		
2007	*Dundalk*	19	9	**19**	**9**
2008	Drogheda U	4	0		
2008	*Finn Harps*	14	2	**14**	**2**
2009	Drogheda U	1	0	**5**	**0**
2009	Sporting Fingal	13	7		
2010	Sporting Fingal	32	5	**45**	**12**
2011–12	Milton Keynes D	39	8		
2012–13	Milton Keynes D	44	3		
2013–14	Milton Keynes D	25	8	**108**	**19**
2013–14	Millwall	17	1		
2014–15	Millwall	38	2		

2015–16	Millwall	33	2		
2016–17	Millwall	44	4		
2017–18	Millwall	35	2		
2018–19	Millwall	31	5	**198**	**16**

Players retained or with offer of contract
Olaofe, Isaac Tanitoluwaloba; Ransom, Harry William Dominique; Sandford, Ryan David Luca; Strachan, Robert Alex.

Scholars
Alexander, George John; Barton, Jay Joseph; Bennett, Benjamin Joseph; Davis, Jayden Kyle Andrew; Duncan, Reuben John; Ezennolim, Chibuike Udogu; Fanshawe, Leighton Nana Kofi; Mitchell, Alexander Paul; Mitchell, Billy James; Muller, Hayden Kai; Munting, Jacob Frederick Neil; O'Brien, Sean Desmond; Skeffington, Samuel; Taylor, Harry Gavin; Tiensia, Junior Yoann Peniel; Topalloj, Besart; West, Lewis Callum; Wright, Joseph Dennis.

MILTON KEYNES D (53)

AGARD, Kieran (F) 306 87
H: 5 10 W: 10 10 b.Newham 10-10-89

2006–07	Everton	0	0		
2007–08	Everton	0	0		
2008–09	Everton	0	0		
2009–10	Everton	1	0		
2010–11	Everton	0	0	**1**	**0**
2010–11	*Kilmarnock*	8	1	**8**	**1**
2010–11	*Peterborough U*	0	0		
2011–12	Yeovil T	29	6	**29**	**6**
2012–13	Rotherham U	30	6		
2013–14	Rotherham U	46	21		
2014–15	Rotherham U	2	0	**78**	**27**
2014–15	Bristol C	39	13		
2015–16	Bristol C	25	2	**64**	**15**
2016–17	Milton Keynes D	42	12		
2017–18	Milton Keynes D	41	6		
2018–19	Milton Keynes D	43	20	**126**	**38**

ANEKE, Chuks (M) 167 52
H: 6 3 W: 13 01 b.Newham 3-7-93
Internationals: England U16, U17, U18, U19.

2010–11	Arsenal	0	0		
2011–12	Arsenal	0	0		
2011–12	*Stevenage*	6	0	**6**	**0**
2011–12	*Preston NE*	7	1	**7**	**1**
2012–13	Arsenal	0	0		
2012–13	*Crewe Alex*	30	6		
2013–14	Arsenal	0	0		
2013–14	*Crewe Alex*	40	15	**70**	**21**
2014–15	Arsenal	0	0		
2014–15	Zulte-Waregem	0	0		
2016–17	Milton Keynes D	15	4		
2017–18	Milton Keynes D	31	9		
2018–19	Milton Keynes D	38	17	**84**	**30**

ASONGANYI, Dylan (F) 3 0
b. 10-12-00

2017–18	Milton Keynes D	0	0		
2018–19	Milton Keynes D	3	0	**3**	**0**

BAUDRY, Mathieu (D) 233 16
H: 6 2 W: 12 08 b.Le Havre 24-2-88

2007–08	Troyes	2	1		
2008–09	Troyes	17	0		
2009–10	Troyes	7	0	**26**	**1**
2010–11	Bournemouth	3	1		
2011–12	Bournemouth	7	0	**10**	**1**
2011–12	*Dagenham & R*	11	0	**11**	**0**
2012–13	Leyton Orient	24	3		
2013–14	Leyton Orient	39	2		
2014–15	Leyton Orient	31	1		
2015–16	Leyton Orient	34	2	**128**	**8**
2016–17	Doncaster R	31	5		
2017–18	Doncaster R	22	1	**53**	**6**
2018–19	Milton Keynes D	5	0	**5**	**0**

BRITTAIN, Callum (F) 66 3
H: 5 10 W: 10 10 b.Bedford 12-3-98
Internationals: England U20.

2015–16	Milton Keynes D	0	0		
2016–17	Milton Keynes D	6	0		
2017–18	Milton Keynes D	29	2		
2018–19	Milton Keynes D	31	1	**66**	**3**

CARGILL, Baily (D) 76 2
H: 6 2 W: 13 10 b.Winchester 13-10-95
Internationals: England U20.

2012–13	Bournemouth	0	0		
2013–14	Bournemouth	0	0		
2013–14	*Torquay U*	5	0	**5**	**0**
2014–15	Bournemouth	0	0		
2015–16	Bournemouth	0	0		
2015–16	*Coventry C*	5	1	**5**	**1**
2016–17	Bournemouth	1	0		
2016–17	*Gillingham*	9	1	**9**	**1**
2017–18	Bournemouth	0	0	**1**	**0**
2017–18	*Fleetwood T*	11	0	**11**	**0**
2017–18	*Partick Thistle*	16	0	**16**	**0**
2018–19	Milton Keynes D	29	0	**29**	**0**

CISSE, Ousseynou (D) 226 9
H: 6 5 W: 13 05 b.Dakar 6-4-91
Internationals: Mali Full caps.

2009–10	Amiens	9	0		
2010–11	Amiens	8	0		
2011–12	Amiens	19	0	**36**	**0**
2012–13	Dijon	24	0		
2013–14	Dijon	36	4		
2014–15	Dijon	35	1	**95**	**5**
2015–16	Rayo Vallecano	0	0		
2015–16	*Waasland-Beveren*	12	1	**12**	**1**
2016–17	Tours	25	1	**25**	**1**
2017–18	Milton Keynes D	32	0		
2018–19	Milton Keynes D	26	2	**58**	**2**

D'ATH, Lawson (M) 161 15
H: 5 9 W: 12 02 b.Witney 24-12-92

2010–11	Reading	0	0		
2011–12	Reading	0	0		
2011–12	*Yeovil T*	14	1	**14**	**1**
2012–13	Reading	0	0		
2012–13	*Cheltenham T*	2	1	**2**	**1**
2012–13	*Exeter C*	8	1	**8**	**1**
2013–14	Reading	0	0		
2013–14	*Dagenham & R*	21	1	**21**	**1**
2014–15	Northampton T	41	7		
2015–16	Northampton T	39	4		
2016–17	Northampton T	1	0	**81**	**11**
2016–17	Luton T	11	0		
2017–18	Luton T	9	0	**20**	**0**
2018–19	Milton Keynes D	15	0	**15**	**0**

GILBEY, Alex (M) 189 15
H: 6 0 W: 11 07 b.Dagenham 9-12-94

2011–12	Colchester U	0	0		
2012–13	Colchester U	3	0		
2013–14	Colchester U	36	1		
2014–15	Colchester U	34	1		
2015–16	Colchester U	37	5	**110**	**7**
2016–17	Wigan Ath	15	2		
2017–18	Wigan Ath	2	0	**17**	**2**
2017–18	Milton Keynes D	23	3		
2018–19	Milton Keynes D	39	3	**62**	**6**

HANCOX, Mitch (D) 49 2
H: 5 10 W: 11 03 b.Solihull 9-11-93

2011–12	Birmingham C	0	0		
2012–13	Birmingham C	19	0		
2013–14	Birmingham C	14	0		
2014–15	Birmingham C	0	0		
2015–16	Birmingham C	0	0	**33**	**0**
2015–16	*Crawley T*	15	2	**15**	**2**

From Macclesfield T.

2018–19	Milton Keynes D	1	0	**1**	**0**

HARLEY, Ryan (M) 283 43
H: 5 11 W: 11 00 b.Bristol 22-1-85

2004–05	Bristol C	2	0		
2005–06	Bristol C	0	0	**2**	**0**
2008–09	Exeter C	31	4		
2009–10	Exeter C	44	10		
2010–11	Exeter C	21	6		
2010–11	Swansea C	0	0		
2010–11	*Exeter C*	21	4		
2011–12	Swansea C	0	0		
2011–12	Brighton & HA	16	2		
2012–13	Brighton & HA	2	0	**18**	**2**
2012–13	*Milton Keynes D*	8	0		
2013–14	Swindon T	21	1		
2014–15	Swindon T	0	0	**21**	**1**
2014–15	Exeter C	25	4		
2015–16	Exeter C	28	4		
2016–17	Exeter C	31	5		
2017–18	Exeter C	19	1	**220**	**38**
2018–19	Milton Keynes D	14	2	**22**	**2**

HOUGHTON, Jordan (M) 134 5
H: 6 2 W: 12 13 b.Chertsey 9-11-95
Internationals: England U16, U17, U20.

2015–16	Chelsea	0	0		
2015–16	*Gillingham*	11	1	**11**	**1**
2015–16	*Plymouth Arg*	10	1	**10**	**1**
2016–17	Chelsea	0	0		
2016–17	*Doncaster R*	32	1		
2017–18	Chelsea	0	0		
2017–18	*Doncaster R*	37	0	**69**	**1**
2018–19	Milton Keynes D	44	2	**44**	**2**

JACKSON, Oran (D) 1 0
b. 16-10-98

2015–16	Milton Keynes D	1	0		
2016–17	Milton Keynes D	0	0		
2017–18	Milton Keynes D	0	0		
2018–19	Milton Keynes D	0	0	**1**	**0**

KASUMU, David (M) 1 0
b. 5-10-99

2015–16	Milton Keynes D	0	0		
2016–17	Milton Keynes D	0	0		
2017–18	Milton Keynes D	1	0		
2018–19	Milton Keynes D	0	0	**1**	**0**

LEWINGTON, Dean (D) 648 22
H: 5 11 W: 11 07 b.Kingston 18-5-84

2002–03	Wimbledon	1	0		
2003–04	Wimbledon	28	1	**29**	**1**
2004–05	Milton Keynes D	43	2		
2005–06	Milton Keynes D	44	1		
2006–07	Milton Keynes D	45	1		
2007–08	Milton Keynes D	45	0		
2008–09	Milton Keynes D	40	2		
2009–10	Milton Keynes D	42	1		
2010–11	Milton Keynes D	42	3		
2011–12	Milton Keynes D	46	3		
2012–13	Milton Keynes D	38	1		
2013–14	Milton Keynes D	43	1		
2014–15	Milton Keynes D	41	3		
2015–16	Milton Keynes D	46	1		
2016–17	Milton Keynes D	36	1		
2017–18	Milton Keynes D	22	0		
2018–19	Milton Keynes D	46	1	**619**	**21**

MARTIN, Russell (M) 497 24
H: 6 0 W: 11 08 b.Brighton 4-1-86
Internationals: Scotland Full caps.

2004–05	Wycombe W	7	0		
2005–06	Wycombe W	23	3		
2006–07	Wycombe W	42	2		
2007–08	Wycombe W	44	0	**116**	**5**
2008–09	Peterborough U	46	1		
2009–10	Peterborough U	10	0	**56**	**1**
2009–10	Norwich C	26	0		
2010–11	Norwich C	46	5		
2011–12	Norwich C	33	2		
2012–13	Norwich C	31	3		
2013–14	Norwich C	31	0		
2014–15	Norwich C	45	2		
2015–16	Norwich C	30	3		
2016–17	Norwich C	37	1		
2017–18	Norwich C	5	0	**284**	**16**
2017–18	*Rangers*	15	1	**15**	**1**
2018–19	Walsall	8	0	**8**	**0**
2018–19	Milton Keynes D	18	1	**18**	**1**

McGRANDLES, Conor (M) 115 8
H: 6 0 W: 10 00 b.Falkirk 24-9-95

2012–13	Falkirk	26	2		
2013–14	Falkirk	36	5		
2014–15	Falkirk	3	0		
2014–15	Norwich C	1	0		
2015–16	Norwich C	0	0	**1**	**0**
2015–16	*Falkirk*	5	0	**70**	**7**
2017–18	Milton Keynes D	19	0		
2018–19	Milton Keynes D	25	1	**44**	**1**

MOORE, Stuart (G) 28 0
H: 6 2 W: 11 05 b.Sandown 8-9-94

2013–14	Reading	0	0		
2014–15	Reading	0	0		
2015–16	Reading	0	0		
2015–16	*Peterborough U*	4	0	**4**	**0**
2016–17	Reading	0	0		
2016–17	*Luton T*	8	0	**8**	**0**
2017–18	Swindon T	10	0	**10**	**0**
2018–19	Milton Keynes D	6	0	**6**	**0**

MOORE-TAYLOR, Jordan (D) 183 11
H: 5 10 W: 13 01 b.Exeter 21-1-94

2012–13	Exeter C	7	0		
2013–14	Exeter C	29	1		
2014–15	Exeter C	26	2		
2015–16	Exeter C	32	0		
2016–17	Exeter C	42	5		
2017–18	Exeter C	24	2	**160**	**10**
2018–19	Milton Keynes D	23	1	**23**	**1**

NESBITT, Aidan (M) 26 2
b. 5-2-97
Internationals: Scotland U17, U19, U20, U21.

2015–16	Celtic	0	0		
2015–16	*Partick Thistle*	7	0	**7**	**0**
2016–17	Celtic	0	0		
2017–18	Celtic	0	0		
2017–18	Milton Keynes D	19	2		
2018–19	Milton Keynes D	0	0	**19**	**2**

Transferred to Dundee U, January 2019.

NICHOLLS, Lee (G) **168** **0**
H: 6 3 W: 13 05 b.Huyton 5-10-92
Internationals: England U19.
2009–10 Wigan Ath 0 0
2010–11 Wigan Ath 0 0
2010–11 *Hartlepool U* 0 0
2010–11 *Shrewsbury T* 0 0
2010–11 *Sheffield W* 0 0
2011–12 Wigan Ath 0 0
2011–12 *Accrington S* 9 0 **9** **0**
2012–13 Wigan Ath 0 0
2012–13 *Northampton T* 46 0 **46** **0**
2013–14 Wigan Ath 6 0
2014–15 Wigan Ath 1 0
2015–16 Wigan Ath 2 0 **9** **0**
2015–16 *Bristol R* 15 0 **15** **0**
2016–17 Milton Keynes D 8 0
2017–18 Milton Keynes D 41 0
2018–19 Milton Keynes D 40 0 **89** **0**

NOMBE, Sam (F) **6** **0**
H: 5 9 W: 11 00 b. 22-10-98
2016–17 Milton Keynes D 0 0
2017–18 Milton Keynes D 6 0
2018–19 Milton Keynes D 0 0 **6** **0**

PATTISON, Charlie (M) **0** **0**
b. 28-12-00
2018–19 Milton Keynes D 0 0

PAWLETT, Peter (M) **212** **19**
H: 5 10 W: 10 10 b.Hedon 3-2-91
Internationals: Scotland U19, U21.
2008–09 Aberdeen 5 0
2009–10 Aberdeen 14 0
2010–11 Aberdeen 13 1
2011–12 Aberdeen 21 0
2012–13 Aberdeen 12 0
2012–13 *St Johnstone* 9 0 **9** **0**
2013–14 Aberdeen 35 5
2014–15 Aberdeen 36 6
2015–16 Aberdeen 18 1
2016–17 Aberdeen 18 3 **172** **16**
2017–18 Milton Keynes D 24 3
2018–19 Milton Keynes D 7 0 **31** **3**
Transferred to Dundee U January 2019.

SIETSMA, Wieger (G) **11** **0**
b. 11-7-95
2015–16 Heerenveen 0 0
2016–17 Heerenveen 0 0
2016–17 *Emmen* 6 0 **6** **0**
2017–18 Milton Keynes D 5 0
2018–19 Milton Keynes D 0 0 **5** **0**

SIMPSON, Robbie (F) **306** **33**
H: 6 1 W: 11 11 b.Poole 15-3-85
2007–08 Coventry C 28 1
2008–09 Coventry C 33 3 **61** **4**
2009–10 Huddersfield T 13 0
2010–11 Huddersfield T 0 0
2010–11 *Brentford* 27 4 **27** **4**
2011–12 Huddersfield T 0 0 **13** **0**
2011–12 Oldham Ath 29 6
2012–13 Oldham Ath 37 2
2013–14 *Oldham Ath* 0 0 **66** **8**
2013–14 Leyton Orient 14 0 **14** **0**
2014–15 Cambridge U 35 8
2015–16 Cambridge U 32 4 **67** **12**
2016–17 Exeter C 26 1
2017–18 Exeter C 11 2 **37** **3**
2018–19 Milton Keynes D 21 2 **21** **2**

SOLE, Liam (M) **0** **0**
2018–19 Milton Keynes D 0 0

SOW, Osman (F) **148** **35**
H: 6 4 b.Stockholm 22-4-90
2011–12 FC Dacia 13 1
2012–13 FC Dacia 8 2 **21** **3**
2013 Syrianska FC 7 2 **7** **2**
2013–14 Crystal Palace 0 0
2014–15 Hearts 22 11
2015–16 Hearts 23 9 **45** **20**
2016 Henen Jianye 30 4 **30** **4**
2016–17 *Emirates* 11 3 **11** **3**
2017–18 Milton Keynes D 19 2
2018–19 Milton Keynes D 8 1 **27** **3**
2018–19 *Dundee U* 7 0 **7** **0**

TAPP, Finn (D) **0** **0**
2016–17 Milton Keynes D 0 0
2017–18 Milton Keynes D 0 0
2018–19 Milton Keynes D 0 0

THOMAS-ASANTE, Brandon (F) **22** **0**
H: 5 11 W: 12 08 b. 29-12-98
2016–17 Milton Keynes D 6 0
2017–18 Milton Keynes D 15 0
2018–19 Milton Keynes D 1 0 **22** **0**

WALSH, Joe (D) **196** **12**
H: 5 11 W: 11 00 b.Cardiff 15-5-92
Internationals: Wales U17, U19, U21.
2010–11 Swansea C 0 0
2011–12 Swansea C 0 0
2012–13 Crawley T 30 2
2013–14 Crawley T 39 5
2014–15 Crawley T 28 1 **97** **8**
2014–15 *Milton Keynes D* 2 0
2015–16 Milton Keynes D 18 1
2016–17 Milton Keynes D 39 1
2017–18 Milton Keynes D 10 0
2018–19 Milton Keynes D 30 2 **99** **4**

WATSON, Ryan (M) **85** **2**
H: 6 1 W: 11 07 b.Crewe 7-7-93
2011–12 Wigan Ath 0 0
2012–13 Wigan Ath 0 0
2012–13 *Accrington S* 0 0
2013–14 Leicester C 0 0
2014–15 Leicester C 0 0
2014–15 *Northampton T* 5 0
2015–16 Leicester C 0 0
2015–16 *Northampton T* 11 0 **16** **0**
2016–17 Barnet 19 1
2017–18 Barnet 28 1 **47** **2**
2018–19 Milton Keynes D 22 0 **22** **0**

WILLIAMS, George B (D) **131** **4**
H: 5 9 W: 11 00 b.Hillingdon 14-4-93
2011–12 Milton Keynes D 2 0
From Worcester C.
2014–15 Barnsley 4 0
2015–16 Barnsley 19 1 **23** **1**
2016–17 Milton Keynes D 33 2
2017–18 Milton Keynes D 43 1
2018–19 Milton Keynes D 30 0 **108** **3**

Scholars
Ackom, Delsin; Bird, Jay; Brennan, Finlay Michael; Freeman, John David; Hourican-Harvey, Jack; Leach, Oliver Henry George; Martin, Recoe Reshan; Pattison, Charlie George; Robinson, Jamie Kyle; Rose, George Brian Alan; Sorinola, Matthew Alexander; Sule, Jamal Oshiomah; Wright, Jenson.

MORECAMBE (54)

BROWNSWORD, Tyler (D) **1** **0**
b. 31-12-99
2017–18 Morecambe 0 0
2018–19 Morecambe 1 0 **1** **0**

CAMPBELL, Adam (F) **130** **11**
H: 5 7 W: 11 07 b.North Shields 1-1-95
Internationals: England U16, U17, U19.
2011–12 Newcastle U 0 0
2012–13 Newcastle U 3 0
2013–14 Newcastle U 0 0
2013–14 *Carlisle U* 1 0
2013–14 *St Mirren* 11 2 **11** **2**
2014–15 Newcastle U 0 0 **3** **0**
2014–15 *Fleetwood T* 2 0 **2** **0**
2014–15 *Hartlepool U* 2 0 **2** **0**
2015–16 Notts Co 44 4
2016–17 Notts Co 29 4 **73** **8**
2017–18 Morecambe 25 1
2018–19 Morecambe 0 0 **25** **1**
2018–19 *Carlisle U* 13 0 **14** **0**

CODJOVI, Amilcar (M) **0** **0**
2018–19 Morecambe 0 0

COLLINS, Aaron (F) **70** **12**
b. 27-5-97
Internationals: Wales U19.
2014–15 Newport Co 2 0
2015–16 Newport Co 18 2
2015–16 Wolverhampton W 0 0
2016–17 Wolverhampton W 0 0
2016–17 *Notts Co* 18 2 **18** **2**
2017–18 Wolverhampton W 0 0
2017–18 *Newport Co* 10 0 **30** **2**
2018–19 Wolverhampton W 0 0
2018–19 *Colchester U* 7 0 **7** **0**
2018–19 Morecambe 15 8 **15** **8**

CONLAN, Luke (D) **107** **0**
H: 5 11 W: 11 05 b.Portaferry 31-10-94
Internationals: Northern Ireland U16, U17, U19, U21.
2011–12 Burnley 0 0
2012–13 Burnley 0 0
2013–14 Burnley 0 0
2014–15 Burnley 0 0
2015–16 Burnley 0 0
2015–16 *St Mirren* 3 0 **3** **0**
2015–16 *Morecambe* 16 0
2016–17 Morecambe 21 0
2017–18 Morecambe 27 0
2018–19 Morecambe 40 0 **104** **0**

CRANSTON, Jordan (D) **104** **4**
H: 5 11 W: 13 01 b.Wednesfield 11-3-93
Internationals: Wales U19.
2012–13 Wolverhampton W 0 0
2013–14 Wolverhampton W 0 0
2014–15 Notts Co 9 0 **9** **0**
2015–16 Cheltenham T 0 0
2016–17 Cheltenham T 38 0
2017–18 Cheltenham T 22 0 **60** **0**
2018–19 Morecambe 35 4 **35** **4**

CUVELIER, Florent (M) **104** **7**
H: 6 0 W: 11 05 b.Brussels 12-9-92
Internationals: Belgium U16, U17, U18, U19, U20, U21.
2009–10 Portsmouth 0 0
2010–11 Stoke C 0 0
2011–12 Stoke C 0 0
2011–12 *Walsall* 18 4
2012–13 Stoke C 0 0
2012–13 *Walsall* 19 2
2012–13 *Peterborough U* 1 0 **1** **0**
2013–14 Stoke C 0 0
2013–14 Sheffield U 7 0
2013–14 *Port Vale* 1 0 **1** **0**
2014–15 Sheffield U 3 0
2014–15 *Burton Alb* 1 1 **1** **1**
2015–16 Sheffield U 9 0 **19** **0**
2016–17 Walsall 22 0
2017–18 Walsall 23 0 **82** **6**
2018–19 Morecambe 0 0

ELLISON, Kevin (M) **632** **128**
H: 6 0 W: 12 00 b.Liverpool 23-2-79
2000–01 Leicester C 1 0
2001–02 Leicester C 0 0 **1** **0**
2001–02 Stockport Co 11 0
2002–03 Stockport Co 23 1
2003–04 Stockport Co 14 1 **48** **2**
2003–04 *Lincoln C* 11 0 **11** **0**
2004–05 Chester C 24 9
2004–05 Hull C 16 1
2005–06 Hull C 23 1 **39** **2**
2006–07 Tranmere R 34 4 **34** **4**
2007–08 Chester C 36 11
2008–09 Chester C 39 8 **99** **28**
2008–09 Rotherham U 0 0
2009–10 Rotherham U 39 8
2010–11 Rotherham U 23 3 **62** **11**
2010–11 *Bradford C* 7 1 **7** **1**
2011–12 Morecambe 34 15
2012–13 Morecambe 40 11
2013–14 Morecambe 42 10
2014–15 Morecambe 43 11
2015–16 Morecambe 44 9
2016–17 Morecambe 45 8
2017–18 Morecambe 40 9
2018–19 Morecambe 43 7 **331** **80**

FLEMING, Andy (M) **269** **19**
H: 6 1 W: 12 00 b.Liverpool 18-2-89
Internationals: England C.
2006–07 Wrexham 2 0
2007–08 Wrexham 4 0 **6** **0**
2010–11 Morecambe 30 2
2011–12 Morecambe 17 2
2012–13 Morecambe 32 5
2013–14 Morecambe 35 2
2014–15 Morecambe 35 2
2015–16 Morecambe 33 3
2016–17 Morecambe 30 2
2017–18 Morecambe 32 0
2018–19 Morecambe 19 1 **263** **19**

HALSTEAD, Mark (G) **49** **0**
H: 6 3 W: 14 00 b.Blackpool 1-9-90
2009–10 Blackpool 0 0
2010–11 Blackpool 1 0
2011–12 Blackpool 0 0
2012–13 Blackpool 2 0
2013–14 Blackpool 0 0 **3** **0**
2014–15 Shrewsbury T 1 0
2015–16 Shrewsbury T 16 0
2016–17 Shrewsbury T 3 0 **20** **0**
From Southport.
2018–19 Morecambe 26 0 **26** **0**

HAWLEY, Kyle (F) 1 0
b. 11-5-00

2016–17	Morecambe	1	0		
2017–18	Morecambe	0	0		
2018–19	Morecambe	0	0	**1**	**0**

HEDLEY, Ben (M) 2 0
b. 18-10-98

2015–16	Morecambe	0	0		
2016–17	Morecambe	1	0		
2017–18	Morecambe	0	0		
2018–19	Morecambe	1	0	**2**	**0**

JAGNE, Lamin (M) 2 0
b. 28-10-97

2018–19	Morecambe	2	0	**2**	**0**

KENYON, Alex (M) 194 7
H: 5 11 W: 11 12 b.Preston 17-7-92

2013–14	Morecambe	39	0		
2014–15	Morecambe	37	3		
2015–16	Morecambe	29	3		
2016–17	Morecambe	19	0		
2017–18	Morecambe	38	0		
2018–19	Morecambe	32	1	**194**	**7**

LAVELLE, Sam (D) 58 2
H: 6 0 W: 12 00 b. 3-10-96
Internationals: Scotland U18, U19.

2017–18	Morecambe	27	1		
2018–19	Morecambe	31	1	**58**	**2**

LEITCH-SMITH, AJ (F) 260 49
H: 5 11 W: 12 04 b.Crewe 6-3-90

2008–09	Crewe Alex	0	0		
2009	*IBV*	18	5	**18**	**5**
2009–10	Crewe Alex	1	0		
2010–11	Crewe Alex	16	5		
2011–12	Crewe Alex	38	8		
2012–13	Crewe Alex	28	4		
2013–14	Crewe Alex	20	2	**103**	**19**
2014–15	Yeovil T	33	2	**33**	**2**
2015–16	Port Vale	37	10	**37**	**10**
2016–17	Shrewsbury T	16	1		
2017–18	Shrewsbury T	0	0	**16**	**1**
2017–18	*Dundee*	28	6	**28**	**6**
2018–19	Morecambe	25	6	**25**	**6**

MANDEVILLE, Liam (F) 98 12
H: 5 11 W: 12 02 b.Lincoln 17-2-97

2014–15	Doncaster R	3	0		
2015–16	Doncaster R	8	1		
2016–17	Doncaster R	21	7		
2017–18	Doncaster R	17	1	**49**	**9**
2017–18	*Colchester U*	7	0	**7**	**0**
2018–19	Morecambe	42	3	**42**	**3**

MENDES GOMES, Carlos (F) 15 0
b. 14-11-98
From Atletico Madrid, West Didsbury & Chorlton.

2018–19	Morecambe	15	0	**15**	**0**

MILLS, Zak (D) 96 1
b. 28-5-92
From Histon, Boston U.

2016–17	Grimsby T	30	0		
2017–18	Grimsby T	28	0	**58**	**0**
2018–19	Morecambe	38	1	**38**	**1**

OATES, Rhys (D) 104 11
H: 6 0 W: 11 09 b.Pontefract 4-12-94

2012–13	Barnsley	0	0		
2013–14	Barnsley	0	0		
2014–15	Barnsley	9	0	**9**	**0**
2015–16	Hartlepool U	38	2		
2016–17	Hartlepool U	26	3	**64**	**5**
2018–19	Morecambe	31	6	**31**	**6**

OLD, Steven (D) 245 17
H: 6 3 W: 13 05 b. 17-2-86
Internationals: New Zealand U17, U20, U23, Full caps.

2005–06	Young Heart	19	1	**19**	**1**
2006–07	Newcastle Jets	9	0	**9**	**0**
2007–08	Wellington Phoenix	12	1	**12**	**1**
2008	Macarthur Rams	4	1	**4**	**1**
2008–09	Kilmarnock	0	0		
2009–10	Kilmarnock	10	0		
2010–11	Kilmarnock	0	0	**10**	**0**
2010–11	*Cowdenbeath*	4	0	**4**	**0**

From Basingstoke T, Sutton U.

2013	Shijiazhuang Yongchang	28	1	**28**	**1**
2014	Ljungskile	22	4		
2015	Ljungskile	24	2	**46**	**6**
2016	GAIS	21	0		
2017	GAIS	12	1	**33**	**1**
2017–18	Morecambe	41	4		
2018–19	Morecambe	39	2	**80**	**6**

OLIVER, Vadaine (F) 184 25
H: 6 2 W: 12 04 b.Sheffield 21-10-91

2010–11	Sheffield W	0	0		
2011–12	Sheffield W	0	0		
2013–14	Crewe Alex	25	2		
2014–15	Crewe Alex	9	1	**34**	**3**
2014–15	*Mansfield T*	30	7	**30**	**7**
2015–16	York C	37	7	**37**	**7**
2016–17	Notts Co	19	1	**19**	**1**
2017–18	Morecambe	34	3		
2018–19	Morecambe	30	4	**64**	**7**

OSWELL, Jason (F) 19 1
b.Northwich 7-10-92

2011–12	Crewe Alex	0	0		
2012–13	Inverness CT	2	0	**2**	**0**

From Rhyl, Airbus UK Broughton, Newtown, Stockport Co.

2018–19	Morecambe	17	1	**17**	**1**

PRICE, Freddie (M) 0 0

2018–19	Morecambe	0	0		

ROCHE, Barry (G) 559 1
H: 6 5 W: 14 08 b.Dublin 6-4-82
Internationals: Republic of Ireland U21.

1999–2000	Nottingham F	0	0		
2000–01	Nottingham F	2	0		
2001–02	Nottingham F	0	0		
2002–03	Nottingham F	1	0		
2003–04	Nottingham F	8	0		
2004–05	Nottingham F	2	0	**13**	**0**
2005–06	Chesterfield	41	0		
2006–07	Chesterfield	40	0		
2007–08	Chesterfield	45	0	**126**	**0**
2008–09	Morecambe	46	0		
2009–10	Morecambe	42	0		
2010–11	Morecambe	42	0		
2011–12	Morecambe	44	0		
2012–13	Morecambe	42	0		
2013–14	Morecambe	45	0		
2014–15	Morecambe	14	0		
2015–16	Morecambe	42	1		
2016–17	Morecambe	41	0		
2017–18	Morecambe	42	0		
2018–19	Morecambe	20	0	**420**	**1**

SINCLAIR, James (F) 127 9
H: 5 8 W: 12 07 b.Newcastle 22-10-87

2005–06	Bolton W	0	0		
2006–07	Bolton W	2	0		
2007–08	Bolton W	0	0		
2008–09	Bolton W	0	0	**2**	**0**

From Gateshead.

2010–11	Sektzia Nes Tzion	3	0	**3**	**0**
2011–12	Polonia Bytom	13	0		
2012–13	Polonia Bytom	3	0	**16**	**0**
2013	Ljungskile	27	3		
2014	Ljungskile	23	3	**50**	**6**
2015	Ostersunds FK	10	0	**10**	**0**
2016	GAIS	19	3		
2017	GAIS	26	0	**45**	**3**
2018–19	Morecambe	1	0	**1**	**0**

SUTTON, Ritchie (D) 104 1
H: 6 0 W: 11 04 b.Stoke-on-Trent 29-4-86

2005–06	Crewe Alex	0	0		

From Stafford R, Northwich Vic, FC Halifax T, Nantwich T

2010–11	Port Vale	11	0	**11**	**0**
2013–14	Mansfield T	36	0		
2014–15	Mansfield T	34	0	**70**	**0**
2018–19	Tranmere R	9	1	**9**	**1**
2018–19	Morecambe	14	0	**14**	**0**

SZCZEPANIAK, Dawid (G) 0 0
From Airbus UK.

2018–19	Morecambe	0	0		

THOMPSON, Gary (M) 407 60
H: 6 0 W: 14 02 b.Kendal 24-11-80

2007–08	Morecambe	40	7		
2008–09	Scunthorpe U	24	3		
2009–10	Scunthorpe U	36	9		
2010–11	Scunthorpe U	12	1		
2011–12	Scunthorpe U	39	7	**111**	**20**
2012–13	Bradford C	41	6		
2013–14	Bradford C	44	2	**85**	**8**
2014–15	Notts Co	41	12	**41**	**12**
2015–16	Wycombe W	43	7		
2016–17	Wycombe W	42	3	**85**	**10**
2017–18	Morecambe	40	3		
2018–19	Morecambe	5	0	**85**	**10**

TUTTE, Andrew (M) 246 23
H: 5 9 W: 10 10 b.Huyton 21-9-90
Internationals: England U19, U20.

2007–08	Manchester C	0	0		
2008–09	Manchester C	0	0		
2009–10	Manchester C	0	0		
2010–11	Manchester C	0	0		
2010–11	*Rochdale*	7	0		
2010–11	*Shrewsbury T*	2	0	**2**	**0**
2010–11	*Yeovil T*	15	2	**15**	**2**
2011–12	Rochdale	40	1		
2012–13	Rochdale	37	7		
2013–14	Rochdale	11	2	**95**	**10**
2013–14	Bury	19	1		
2014–15	Bury	42	3		
2015–16	Bury	22	4		
2016–17	Bury	17	1		
2017–18	Bury	16	0	**116**	**9**
2018–19	Morecambe	18	2	**18**	**2**

WILDIG, Aaron (M) 206 13
H: 5 9 W: 11 02 b.Hereford 15-4-92
Internationals: Wales U16.

2009–10	Cardiff C	11	1		
2010–11	Cardiff C	2	0		
2010–11	*Hamilton A*	3	0	**3**	**0**
2011–12	Cardiff C	0	0	**13**	**1**
2011–12	*Shrewsbury T*	12	2		
2012–13	Shrewsbury T	21	1		
2013–14	Shrewsbury T	30	2		
2014–15	Shrewsbury T	1	0	**64**	**5**
2014–15	*Morecambe*	9	1		
2015–16	Morecambe	32	2		
2016–17	Morecambe	28	2		
2017–18	Morecambe	31	1		
2018–19	Morecambe	26	1	**126**	**7**

Players retained or with offer of contract
Mendes-Gomes, Carlos.

Scholars
Bakare, Ibrahim Akorede Abayomi; Beverley, Jack Andrew; Djau, Codjovi Amilcar Adulai; Dorward, Henry; Edwards, Cole Daniel; Eme, Ezeikel Equiano; Farrington, Callum Sean; Giacomini, Joshua Michael; Herbert, Kai; Jones, Ellis; Jumeau, Olivier Philippe; Mason, Ryan Thomas; Obasoto, Abimbola Emmanuel; Price, Freddie Connor Burrows; Twiname, Toby; Young, Kaleb Harry Peter.

NEWCASTLE U (55)

AARONS, Rolando (M) 54 3
H: 5 9 W: 10 08 b.Kingston 16-11-95
Internationals: England U20.

2014–15	Newcastle U	4	1		
2015–16	Newcastle U	10	1		
2016–17	Newcastle U	4	0		
2017–18	Newcastle U	4	0		
2017–18	*Verona*	11	0	**11**	**0**
2018–19	Newcastle U	0	0	**22**	**2**
2018–19	*Liberec*	12	0	**12**	**0**
2018–19	*Sheffield W*	9	1	**9**	**1**

ALMIRON, Miguel (M) 146 30
H: 5 10 W: 11 00 b.Asuncion 13-11-93
Internationals: Paraguay U17, U20, Full caps.

2013	Cerro Porteno	6	1		
2014	Cerro Porteno	14	0		
2015	Cerro Porteno	19	5	**39**	**6**
2015	Lanus	10	0		
2016	Lanus	25	3	**35**	**3**
2017	Atalanta	30	9		
2018	Atalanta	32	12	**62**	**21**
2018–19	Newcastle U	10	0	**10**	**0**

ATSU, Christian (F) 175 22
H: 5 8 W: 10 09 b.Ada Foah 10-1-92
Internationals: Ghana Full caps.

2010–11	Porto	0	0		
2011–12	Porto	0	0		
2011–12	*Rio Ave*	27	6	**27**	**6**
2012–13	Porto	17	1	**17**	**1**
2013–14	Chelsea	0	0		
2013–14	*Vitesse*	26	5	**26**	**5**
2014–15	Chelsea	0	0		
2014–15	*Everton*	5	0	**5**	**0**
2015–16	Chelsea	0	0		
2015–16	*Bournemouth*	0	0		
2015–16	*Malaga*	12	2	**12**	**2**
2016–17	Chelsea	0	0		
2016–17	*Newcastle U*	32	5		
2017–18	Newcastle U	28	2		
2018–19	Newcastle U	28	1	**88**	**8**

BARLASER, Daniel (M) **43** **1**
H: 6 0 W: 9 11 b.Gateshead 18-1-97
Internationals: Turkey U16, U17. England U18.

2015–16	Newcastle U	0	0		
2016–17	Newcastle U	0	0		
2017–18	Newcastle U	0	0		
2017–18	*Crewe Alex*	4	0	**4**	**0**
2018–19	Newcastle U	0	0		
2018–19	*Accrington S*	39	1	**39**	**1**

BARRECA, Antonio (D) **98** **1**
H: 6 0 W: 11 00 b.Turin 18-3-95
Internationals: Italy U18, U19, U20, U21.

2013–14	Torino	0	0		
2014–15	Torino	0	0		
2014–15	*Cittadella*	38	1	**38**	**1**
2015–16	Torino	0	0		
2015–16	*Cagliari*	15	0	**15**	**0**
2016–17	Torino	28	0		
2017–18	Torino	9	0	**37**	**0**
2018–19	Monaco	7	0	**7**	**0**

On loan from Monaco.

2018–19	Newcastle U	1	0	**1**	**0**

CASS, Lewis (D) **0** **0**
b. 27-2-00

2018–19	Newcastle U	0	0

CHARMAN, Luke (F) **0** **0**
b.Durham 9-12-97

2018–19	Newcastle U	0	0
2018–19	*Accrington S*	0	0

CLARK, Ciaran (D) **199** **15**
H: 6 2 W: 12 00 b.Harrow 26-9-89
Internationals: England U17, U18, U19, U20. Republic of Ireland Full caps.

2008–09	Aston Villa	0	0		
2009–10	Aston Villa	1	0		
2010–11	Aston Villa	19	3		
2011–12	Aston Villa	15	1		
2012–13	Aston Villa	29	1		
2013–14	Aston Villa	27	0		
2014–15	Aston Villa	25	1		
2015–16	Aston Villa	18	1	**134**	**7**
2016–17	Newcastle U	34	3		
2017–18	Newcastle U	20	2		
2018–19	Newcastle U	11	3	**65**	**8**

COLBACK, Jack (M) **312** **17**
H: 5 9 W: 11 05 b.Killingworth 24-10-89
Internationals: England U20.

2007–08	Sunderland	0	0		
2008–09	Sunderland	0	0		
2009–10	Sunderland	1	0		
2009–10	*Ipswich T*	37	4		
2010–11	Sunderland	11	0		
2010–11	*Ipswich T*	13	0	**50**	**4**
2011–12	Sunderland	35	1		
2012–13	Sunderland	35	0		
2013–14	Sunderland	33	3	**115**	**4**
2014–15	Newcastle U	35	4		
2015–16	Newcastle U	29	1		
2016–17	Newcastle U	29	0		
2017–18	Newcastle U	0	0		
2017–18	*Nottingham F*	16	1		
2018–19	Newcastle U	0	0	**93**	**5**
2018–19	*Nottingham F*	38	3	**54**	**4**

DARLOW, Karl (G) **168** **0**
H: 6 1 W: 12 05 b.Northampton 8-10-90

2009–10	Nottingham F	0	0		
2010–11	Nottingham F	1	0		
2011–12	Nottingham F	0	0		
2012–13	Nottingham F	20	0		
2012–13	*Walsall*	9	0	**9**	**0**
2013–14	Nottingham F	43	0		
2014–15	Newcastle U	0	0		
2014–15	*Nottingham F*	42	0	**106**	**0**
2015–16	Newcastle U	9	0		
2016–17	Newcastle U	34	0		
2017–18	Newcastle U	10	0		
2018–19	Newcastle U	0	0	**53**	**0**

DIAME, Mohamed (M) **380** **33**
H: 6 1 W: 11 02 b.Creteil 14-6-87
Internationals: Senegal U23, Full caps.

2006–07	Lens	0	0		
2007–08	Linares	31	1	**31**	**1**
2008–09	Rayo Vallecano	35	2	**35**	**2**
2009–10	Wigan Ath	34	1		
2010–11	Wigan Ath	36	1		
2011–12	Wigan Ath	26	3	**96**	**5**
2012–13	West Ham U	33	3		
2013–14	West Ham U	35	4		
2014–15	West Ham U	3	0	**71**	**7**
2014–15	Hull C	12	4		
2015–16	Hull C	38	9	**50**	**13**
2016–17	Newcastle U	37	3		
2017–18	Newcastle U	31	2		
2018–19	Newcastle U	29	0	**97**	**5**

DUBRAVKA, Martin (G) **253** **0**
H: 6 3 W: 13 01 b.Zilina 15-1-89
Internationals: Slovakia U19, U21, Full caps.

2008–09	Zilina	1	0		
2009–10	Zilina	26	0		
2010–11	Zilina	24	0		
2011–12	Zilina	8	0		
2012–13	Zilina	26	0		
2013–14	Zilina	13	0	**98**	**0**
2013–14	Esbjerg	15	0		
2014–15	Esbjerg	33	0		
2015–16	Esbjerg	18	0	**66**	**0**
2016–17	Slovan Liberec	28	0	**28**	**0**
2017–18	Sparta Prague	11	0	**11**	**0**
2017–18	*Newcastle U*	12	0		
2018–19	Newcastle U	38	0	**50**	**0**

DUMMETT, Paul (D) **187** **4**
H: 5 10 W: 10 02 b.Newcastle 26-9-91
Internationals: Wales U21, Full caps.

2010–11	Newcastle U	0	0		
2011–12	Newcastle U	0	0		
2012–13	Newcastle U	0	0		
2012–13	*St Mirren*	30	2	**30**	**2**
2013–14	Newcastle U	18	1		
2014–15	Newcastle U	25	0		
2015–16	Newcastle U	23	1		
2016–17	Newcastle U	45	0		
2017–18	Newcastle U	20	0		
2018–19	Newcastle U	26	0	**157**	**2**

ELLIOT, Rob (G) **162** **0**
H: 6 3 W: 14 10 b.Chatham 30-4-86
Internationals: Republic of Ireland U19, Full caps.

2004–05	Charlton Ath	0	0		
2004–05	*Notts Co*	4	0	**4**	**0**
2005–06	Charlton Ath	0	0		
2006–07	Charlton Ath	0	0		
2006–07	*Accrington S*	7	0	**7**	**0**
2007–08	Charlton Ath	1	0		
2008–09	Charlton Ath	23	0		
2009–10	Charlton Ath	33	0		
2010–11	Charlton Ath	35	0		
2011–12	Charlton Ath	4	0	**96**	**0**
2011–12	Newcastle U	0	0		
2012–13	Newcastle U	10	0		
2013–14	Newcastle U	2	0		
2014–15	Newcastle U	3	0		
2015–16	Newcastle U	21	0		
2016–17	Newcastle U	3	0		
2017–18	Newcastle U	16	0		
2018–19	Newcastle U	0	0	**55**	**0**

FERNANDEZ, Federico (D) **254** **6**
H: 6 3 W: 13 01 b.Tres Algarrobos 21-2-89
Internationals: Argentina U20, Full caps.

2008–09	Estudiantes	14	2		
2009–10	Estudiantes	12	0		
2010–11	Estudiantes	33	1	**59**	**3**
2011–12	Napoli	16	0		
2012–13	Napoli	2	0		
2012–13	*Getafe*	14	1	**14**	**1**
2013–14	Napoli	26	0	**44**	**0**
2014–15	Swansea C	28	0		
2015–16	Swansea C	32	1		
2016–17	Swansea C	27	0		
2017–18	Swansea C	30	1		
2018–19	Swansea C	1	0	**118**	**2**
2018–19	Newcastle U	19	0	**19**	**0**

GAYLE, Dwight (F) **217** **87**
H: 5 10 W: 11 07 b.Walthamstow 20-10-89

2011–12	Dagenham & R	0	0		
2012–13	Dagenham & R	18	7	**18**	**7**
2012–13	Peterborough U	29	13	**29**	**13**
2013–14	Crystal Palace	23	7		
2014–15	Crystal Palace	25	5		
2015–16	Crystal Palace	16	3	**64**	**15**
2016–17	Newcastle U	32	23		
2017–18	Newcastle U	35	6		
2018–19	Newcastle U	0	0	**67**	**29**
2018–19	*WBA*	39	23	**39**	**23**

GIBSON, Liam (D) **5** **0**
H: 6 1 W: 12 08 b.Stanley 25-4-97

2015–16	Newcastle U	0	0		
2016–17	Newcastle U	0	0		
2017–18	Newcastle U	0	0		
2018–19	Newcastle U	0	0		
2018–19	Accrington S	5	0	**5**	**0**

HARKER, Nathan (G) **0** **0**
b. 5-11-98

2018–19	Newcastle U	0	0

HAYDEN, Isaac (D) **102** **5**
H: 6 2 W: 12 06 b.Chelmsford 22-3-95
Internationals: England U16, U17, U18, U19, U20, U21.

2011–12	Arsenal	0	0		
2012–13	Arsenal	0	0		
2013–14	Arsenal	0	0		
2014–15	Arsenal	0	0		
2015–16	Arsenal	0	0		
2015–16	*Hull C*	18	1	**18**	**1**
2016–17	Newcastle U	33	2		
2017–18	Newcastle U	26	1		
2018–19	Newcastle U	25	1	**84**	**4**

JOSELU, Mato (F) **194** **42**
H: 6 3 W: 12 08 b.Stuttgart, Germany 27-3-90
Internationals: Spain U19, U20, U21.

2008–09	Celta Vigo	2	0		
2009–10	Real Madrid	0	0		
2009–10	*Celta Vigo*	24	4	**26**	**4**
2010–11	Real Madrid	1	1		
2011–12	Real Madrid	0	0	**1**	**1**
2012–13	Hoffenheim	25	5		
2013–14	Hoffenheim	0	0	**25**	**5**
2013–14	*Eintracht Frankfurt*	24	9	**24**	**9**
2014–15	Hannover 96	30	8	**30**	**8**
2015–16	Stoke C	22	4		
2016–17	Stoke C	0	0	**22**	**4**
2016–17	*Deportivo La Coruna*	20	5	**20**	**5**
2017–18	Newcastle U	30	4		
2018–19	Newcastle U	16	2	**46**	**6**

KI, Sung-Yeung (M) **250** **24**
H: 6 2 W: 11 10 b.Gwangju 24-1-89
Internationals: South Korea U17, U20, U23, Full caps.

2009–10	Celtic	10	0		
2010–11	Celtic	26	3		
2011–12	Celtic	30	6	**66**	**9**
2012–13	Swansea C	29	0		
2013–14	Swansea C	1	0		
2013–14	*Sunderland*	27	3	**27**	**3**
2014–15	Swansea C	33	8		
2015–16	Swansea C	28	2		
2016–17	Swansea C	23	0		
2017–18	Swansea C	25	2	**139**	**12**
2018–19	Newcastle U	18	0	**18**	**0**

LASCELLES, Jamaal (D) **191** **12**
H: 6 2 W: 13 01 b.Derby 11-11-93
Internationals: England U18, U19, U20, U21.

2010–11	Nottingham F	0	0		
2011–12	Nottingham F	1	0		
2011–12	*Stevenage*	7	1	**7**	**1**
2012–13	Nottingham F	2	0		
2013–14	Nottingham F	29	2		
2014–15	Newcastle U	0	0		
2014–15	*Nottingham F*	26	1	**58**	**3**
2015–16	Newcastle U	18	2		
2016–17	Newcastle U	43	3		
2017–18	Newcastle U	33	3		
2018–19	Newcastle U	32	0	**126**	**8**

LAZAAR, Achraf (D) **128** **4**
H: 5 8 W: 10 08 b.Casablanca 22-1-92
Internationals: Morocco Full caps.

2011–12	Varese	0	0		
2012–13	Varese	21	0		
2013–14	Varese	17	0	**38**	**0**
2013–14	Palermo	14	0		
2014–15	Palermo	29	2		
2015–16	Palermo	30	1		
2016–17	Palermo	0	0	**73**	**3**
2016–17	Newcastle U	4	0		
2017–18	Newcastle U	0	0		
2017–18	*Benevento*	9	1	**9**	**1**
2018–19	Newcastle U	0	0	**4**	**0**
2018–19	*Sheffield W*	4	0	**4**	**0**

LEJEUNE, Florian (D) **217** **13**
H: 6 2 W: 12 11 b.Paris 20-5-91
Internationals: France U20.

2008–09	Agde	3	2	**3**	**2**
2009–10	Istres	14	0		
2010–11	Istres	28	3	**42**	**3**
2011–12	Villarreal	2	0		
2012–13	Villarreal	3	0	**5**	**0**
2012–13	Brest	10	0		
2013–14	Brest	11	0	**21**	**0**
2014–15	Girona	38	4		
2015–16	Manchester C	0	0		
2015–16	*Girona*	38	3	**76**	**7**

2016–17	Eibar	34	1	**34**	**1**
2017–18	Newcastle U	24	0		
2018–19	Newcastle U	12	0	**36**	**0**

LONGSTAFF, Sean (M) **83 15**
H: 5 11 W: 10 03 b.North Shields 30-10-97

2016–17	Newcastle U	0	0		
2016–17	*Kilmarnock*	16	3		
2016–17	Newcastle U	0	0		
2016–17	*Kilmarnock*	16	3	**32**	**6**
2017–18	Newcastle U	0	0		
2017–18	*Blackpool*	42	8	**42**	**8**
2018–19	Newcastle U	9	1	**9**	**1**

MANQUILLO, Javier (D) **106 1**
H: 5 11 W: 12 04 b.Madrid 5-5-94
Internationals: Spain U16, U17, U18, U19, U20, U21.

2012–13	Atletico Madrid	3	0		
2013–14	Atletico Madrid	3	0		
2014–15	Atletico Madrid	0	0		
2014–15	*Liverpool*	10	0	**10**	**0**
2015–16	Atletico Madrid	0	0		
2015–16	*Marseille*	31	0	**31**	**0**
2016–17	Atletico Madrid	0	0	**6**	**0**
2016–17	*Sunderland*	20	1	**20**	**1**
2017–18	Newcastle U	21	0		
2018–19	Newcastle U	18	0	**39**	**0**

MURPHY, Jacob (M) **160 28**
H: 5 9 W: 11 03 b.Wembley 24-2-95
Internationals: England U18, U19, U20, U21.

2013–14	Norwich C	0	0		
2013–14	*Swindon T*	6	0	**6**	**0**
2013–14	*Southend U*	7	1	**7**	**1**
2014–15	Norwich C	0	0		
2014–15	*Blackpool*	9	2	**9**	**2**
2014–15	*Scunthorpe U*	3	0	**3**	**0**
2014–15	*Colchester U*	11	4	**11**	**4**
2015–16	Norwich C	0	0		
2015–16	*Coventry C*	40	9	**40**	**9**
2016–17	Norwich C	37	9	**37**	**9**
2017–18	Newcastle U	25	1		
2018–19	Newcastle U	9	0	**34**	**1**
2018–19	*WBA*	13	2	**13**	**2**

MUTO, Yoshinori (M) **144 44**
H: 5 10 W: 10 12 b.Tokyo 15-7-92
Internationals: Japan Full caps.

2013	FC Tokyo	1	0		
2014	FC Tokyo	33	13		
2015	FC Tokyo	17	10	**51**	**23**
2015–16	Mainz 05	20	7		
2016–17	Mainz 05	29	5		
2017–18	Mainz 05	27	8	**76**	**20**
2018–19	Newcastle U	17	1	**17**	**1**

PEREZ, Ayoze (F) **225 59**
H: 5 10 W: 10 06 b.Santa Cruz de Tenerife 23-7-93
Internationals: Spain U21.

2012–13	Tenerife	16	1		
2013–14	Tenerife	30	16	**46**	**17**
2014–15	Newcastle U	36	7		
2015–16	Newcastle U	34	6		
2016–17	Newcastle U	36	9		
2017–18	Newcastle U	36	8		
2018–19	Newcastle U	37	12	**179**	**42**

RITCHIE, Matt (M) **410 88**
H: 5 8 W: 11 00 b.Gosport 10-9-89
Internationals: Scotland Full caps.

2008–09	Portsmouth	0	0		
2008–09	*Dagenham & R*	37	11	**37**	**11**
2009–10	Portsmouth	2	0		
2009–10	*Notts Co*	16	3	**16**	**3**
2009–10	*Swindon T*	4	0		
2010–11	Portsmouth	5	0	**7**	**0**
2010–11	Swindon T	36	7		
2011–12	Swindon T	40	10		
2012–13	Swindon T	27	9	**107**	**26**
2012–13	Bournemouth	17	3		
2013–14	Bournemouth	30	9		
2014–15	Bournemouth	46	15		
2015–16	Bournemouth	37	4	**130**	**31**
2016–17	Newcastle U	42	12		
2017–18	Newcastle U	35	3		
2018–19	Newcastle U	36	2	**113**	**17**

ROBERTS, Callum (M) **13 0**
b. 1-4-97
Internationals: England U20.

2014–15	Newcastle U	0	0		
2015–16	Newcastle U	0	0		
2016–17	Newcastle U	0	0		
2016–17	*Kilmarnock*	10	0	**10**	**0**
2018–19	Newcastle U	0	0		
2018–19	*Colchester U*	3	0	**3**	**0**

SCHAR, Fabian (D) **152 16**
H: 6 1 W: 13 05 b.Wil 20-12-91
Internationals: Switzerland U20, U21, U23, Full caps.

2012–13	FC Basel	21	4		
2013–14	FC Basel	22	4		
2014–15	FC Basel	30	1	**73**	**9**
2015–16	1899 Hoffenheim	24	1		
2016–17	1899 Hoffenheim	6	0	**30**	**1**
2017–18	Deportivo La Coruna	25	2	**25**	**2**
2018–19	Newcastle U	24	4	**24**	**4**

SHELVEY, Jonjo (M) **281 32**
H: 6 1 W: 11 02 b.Romford 27-2-92
Internationals: England U16, U17, U19, U21, Full caps.

2007–08	Charlton Ath	2	0		
2008–09	Charlton Ath	16	3		
2009–10	Charlton Ath	24	4	**42**	**7**
2010–11	Liverpool	15	0		
2011–12	Liverpool	13	1		
2011–12	*Blackpool*	10	6	**10**	**6**
2012–13	Liverpool	19	1	**47**	**2**
2013–14	Swansea C	32	6		
2014–15	Swansea C	31	3		
2015–16	Swansea C	16	1	**79**	**10**
2015–16	Newcastle U	15	0		
2016–17	Newcastle U	42	5		
2017–18	Newcastle U	30	1		
2018–19	Newcastle U	16	1	**103**	**7**

SORENSEN, Elias (F) **1 0**
b. 18-9-99
Internationals: Denmark U17, U19, U21.
From HB Koge.

2018–19	Newcastle U	0	0		
2018–19	*Blackpool*	1	0	**1**	**0**

WATTS, Kelland (M) **0 0**
b. 3-11-99
Internationals: England U19.

2018–19	Newcastle U	0	0		

WOODMAN, Freddie (G) **30 0**
H: 6 1 W: 10 12 b.London 4-3-97
Internationals: England U16, U17, U18, U19, U20, U21.

2014–15	Newcastle U	0	0		
2014–15	*Hartlepool U*	0	0		
2015–16	Newcastle U	0	0		
2015–16	*Crawley T*	11	0	**11**	**0**
2016–17	Newcastle U	0	0		
2016–17	*Kilmarnock*	14	0	**14**	**0**
2017–18	Newcastle U	0	0		
2017–18	*Aberdeen*	5	0	**5**	**0**
2018–19	Newcastle U	0	0		

YARNEY, Josef (D) **21 0**
b. 8-10-97
From Everton.

2018–19	Newcastle U	0	0		
2018–19	*Morecambe*	21	0	**21**	**0**

YEDLIN, DeAndre (D) **176 4**
H: 5 9 W: 11 07 b.Seattle 9-7-93
Internationals: USA U20, Full caps.

2013	Seattle Sounders	33	2		
2014	Seattle Sounders	29	0	**62**	**2**
2014–15	Tottenham H	1	0		
2015–16	Tottenham H	0	0	**1**	**0**
2015–16	*Sunderland*	23	0	**23**	**0**
2016–17	Newcastle U	27	1		
2017–18	Newcastle U	34	0		
2018–19	Newcastle U	29	1	**90**	**2**

Players retained or with offer of contract
Allan, Thomas David; Bailey, Owen John Edward; Fernandez Satue, Victor; Longelo-Mbule, Rosaire; McEntee, Oisin Michael; Saivet, Henri; Sangare, Mohammed; Sterry, Jamie Michael; Toure, Fode Yannick; Walters, Oliver Reece; Wilson, Adam Ayiro.

Scholars
Allen, Max; Barrett, Ryan Thomas; Brown, William George; Cole, Thomas Anthony; Ebanks, Tai Graham; Gamblin, Lucas Ralph; Joyce, Samuel Edward; Langley, Daniel David; Madia, Deese Kasinga; Reed, Kain; Rounsfell, George David Alan; Swailes, Jude Christopher; Young, Jack.

NEWPORT CO (56)

AMOND, Padraig (F) **413 113**
H: 5 11 W: 12 05 b.Carlow 15-4-88
Internationals: Republic of Ireland U21.

2006	Shamrock R	10	1		
2007	Shamrock R	6	1		
2007	*Kildare Co*	13	5	**13**	**5**
2008	Shamrock R	26	9		
2009	Shamrock R	20	4	**62**	**15**
2010	Sligo R	27	17	**27**	**17**
2010–11	Pacos	17	0	**17**	**0**
2011–12	Accrington S	42	7		
2012–13	Accrington S	36	9		
2013–14	Accrington S	0	0	**78**	**16**
2013–14	Morecambe	45	11		
2014–15	Morecambe	37	8	**82**	**19**
2016–17	Hartlepool U	46	14	**46**	**14**
2017–18	Newport Co	43	13		
2018–19	Newport Co	45	14	**88**	**27**

AZEEZ, Adebayo (F) **203 22**
H: 6 0 W: 12 07 b.Orpington 8-1-94
Internationals: England U19.

2012–13	Charlton Ath	0	0		
2012–13	*Wycombe W*	4	0	**4**	**0**
2012–13	*Leyton Orient*	1	0	**1**	**0**
2013–14	Charlton Ath	0	0		
2013–14	*Torquay U*	9	2	**9**	**2**
2013–14	*Dagenham & R*	15	3	**15**	**3**
2014–15	AFC Wimbledon	43	5		
2015–16	AFC Wimbledon	42	7	**85**	**12**
2016–17	Partick Thistle	38	2	**38**	**2**
2017–18	Cambridge U	13	0		
2018–19	Cambridge U	26	2	**39**	**2**
2018–19	Newport Co	12	1	**12**	**1**

BENNETT, Scott (D) **266 22**
H: 5 10 W: 12 10 b.Newquay 30-11-90

2008–09	Exeter C	0	0		
2009–10	Exeter C	0	0		
2010–11	Exeter C	1	0		
2011–12	Exeter C	15	3		
2012–13	Exeter C	43	6		
2013–14	Exeter C	45	6		
2014–15	Exeter C	28	3	**132**	**18**
2015–16	Notts Co	6	0	**6**	**0**
2015–16	*Newport Co*	12	0		
2015–16	*York C*	11	0	**11**	**0**
2016–17	Newport Co	39	0		
2017–18	Newport Co	28	2		
2018–19	Newport Co	38	2	**117**	**4**

BUTLER, Dan (D) **177 7**
b.Cowes 26-8-94

2012–13	Portsmouth	17	0		
2013–14	Portsmouth	1	0		
2014–15	Portsmouth	30	0	**48**	**0**
2016–17	Newport Co	40	3		
2017–18	Newport Co	44	1		
2018–19	Newport Co	45	3	**129**	**7**

COLLINS, Lewis (M) **0 0**
b.Newport 9-5-01
Internationals: Wales U17, U19.

2017–18	Newport Co	0	0		
2018–19	Newport Co	0	0		

CROFTS, Andrew (D) **431 36**
H: 5 10 W: 12 09 b.Chatham 29-5-84
Internationals: Wales U19, U21, Full caps.

2000–01	Gillingham	1	0		
2001–02	Gillingham	0	0		
2002–03	Gillingham	0	0		
2003–04	Gillingham	8	0		
2004–05	Gillingham	27	2		
2005–06	Gillingham	45	2		
2006–07	Gillingham	43	8		
2007–08	Gillingham	41	5		
2008–09	Gillingham	9	0		
2008–09	*Peterborough U*	9	0	**9**	**0**
2009–10	Brighton & HA	44	5		
2010–11	Norwich C	44	8		
2011–12	Norwich C	24	0		
2012–13	Norwich C	0	0	**68**	**8**
2012–13	Brighton & HA	24	0		
2013–14	Brighton & HA	23	5		
2014–15	Brighton & HA	7	0		
2015–16	Brighton & HA	17	0	**115**	**10**
2015–16	*Gillingham*	6	0	**180**	**17**
2016–17	Charlton Ath	45	1		
2017–18	Charlton Ath	1	0	**46**	**1**
2017–18	Scunthorpe U	4	0	**4**	**0**
2018–19	Newport Co	9	0	**9**	**0**

DAY, Joe (G) **215** **0**
H: 6 1 W: 12 00 b.Brighton 13-8-90

2011–12	Peterborough U	0	0		
2012–13	Peterborough U	0	0		
2013–14	Peterborough U	4	0		
2014–15	Peterborough U	0	0	**4**	**0**
2014–15	*Newport Co*	36	0		
2015–16	Newport Co	41	0		
2016–17	Newport Co	45	0		
2017–18	Newport Co	46	0		
2018–19	Newport Co	43	0	**211**	**0**

DEMETRIOU, Mickey (D) **166** **18**
b.Durrington 12-3-90
Internationals: England C.

2014–15	Shrewsbury T	42	3		
2015–16	Shrewsbury T	1	0		
2015–16	*Cambridge U*	15	0	**15**	**0**
2016–17	Shrewsbury T	0	0	**43**	**3**
2016–17	Newport Co	17	4		
2017–18	Newport Co	46	7		
2018–19	Newport Co	45	4	**108**	**15**

DOLAN, Matthew (M) **203** **15**
b.Hartlepool 11-2-93

2010–11	Middlesbrough	0	0		
2011–12	Middlesbrough	0	0		
2012–13	Middlesbrough	0	0		
2012–13	*Yeovil T*	8	1		
2013–14	Middlesbrough	0	0		
2013–14	*Hartlepool U*	20	2		
2013–14	*Bradford C*	11	0		
2014–15	Bradford C	13	0	**24**	**0**
2014–15	*Hartlepool U*	2	0	**22**	**2**
2015–16	Yeovil T	39	3		
2016–17	Yeovil T	38	4	**85**	**8**
2017–18	Newport Co	40	3		
2018–19	Newport Co	32	2	**72**	**5**

FLYNN, Michael (M) **333** **42**
H: 5 10 W: 13 04 b.Newport 17-10-80

2002–03	Wigan Ath	17	1		
2003–04	Wigan Ath	8	0		
2004–05	Wigan Ath	13	1	**38**	**2**
2004–05	*Blackpool*	6	0		
2004–05	Gillingham	16	3		
2005–06	Gillingham	36	6		
2006–07	Gillingham	45	10	**97**	**19**
2007–08	Blackpool	28	3	**34**	**3**
2008–09	*Darlington*	0	0		
2008–09	Huddersfield T	25	4	**25**	**4**
2009–10	Bradford C	42	6		
2010–11	Bradford C	19	0		
2011–12	Bradford C	30	4	**91**	**10**
2013–14	Newport Co	32	4		
2014–15	Newport Co	11	0		
2016–17	Newport Co	5	0		
2017–18	Newport Co	0	0		
2018–19	Newport Co	0	0	**48**	**4**

FOULSTON, Jay (D) **0** **0**
b. 27-11-00

2017–18	Newport Co	0	0		
2018–19	Newport Co	0	0		

FRANKS, Fraser (D) **151** **10**
H: 6 0 W: 10 12 b.Hammersmith 22-11-90
Internationals: England C.

2009–10	Brentford	0	0		
2011–12	AFC Wimbledon	4	0	**4**	**0**
2014–15	Luton T	13	0	**13**	**0**
2015–16	Stevenage	38	3		
2016–17	Stevenage	41	3		
2017–18	Stevenage	30	1	**109**	**7**
2018–19	Newport Co	25	3	**25**	**3**

HILLMAN, Thomas (D) **0** **0**
b. 20-11-00

2017–18	Newport Co	0	0		
2018–19	Newport Co	0	0		

HORNBY-FORBES, Tyler (M) **53** **2**
b. 8-3-96

2014–15	Fleetwood T	17	0		
2015–16	Fleetwood T	16	2	**33**	**2**
2016–17	Brighton & HA	0	0		
2017–18	*Accrington S*	6	0	**6**	**0**
2018–19	Newport Co	14	0	**14**	**0**

LABADIE, Joss (M) **260** **35**
H: 5 7 W: 11 02 b.Croydon 31-8-90

2008–09	WBA	0	0		
2008–09	*Shrewsbury T*	1	0		
2009–10	WBA	0	0		
2009–10	*Shrewsbury T*	13	5	**14**	**5**
2009–10	*Cheltenham T*	11	0	**11**	**0**
2009–10	*Tranmere R*	9	3		
2010–11	Tranmere R	34	2		
2011–12	Tranmere R	27	5	**70**	**10**
2012–13	Notts Co	24	2		
2012–13	*Torquay U*	7	4		
2013–14	Notts Co	15	1	**39**	**3**
2013–14	*Torquay U*	10	1	**17**	**5**
2014–15	Dagenham & R	24	2		
2015–16	Dagenham & R	28	4	**52**	**6**
2016–17	Newport Co	19	3		
2017–18	Newport Co	25	3		
2018–19	Newport Co	13	0	**57**	**6**

MARSH-BROWN, Keanu (F) **96** **8**
H: 5 11 W: 12 04 b.Hammersmith 10-8-92
Internationals: England U16, U17, C. Guyana Full caps.

2009–10	Fulham	0	0		
2010–11	Fulham	0	0		
2010–11	*Milton Keynes D*	17	2	**17**	**2**
2010–11	*Dundee U*	1	0		
2011–12	Fulham	0	0		
2011–12	Oldham Ath	11	1	**11**	**1**
2011–12	*Dundee U*	11	0	**12**	**0**
2012–13	Yeovil T	21	1	**21**	**1**
2012–13	Barnet	5	1	**5**	**1**
2017–18	Forest Green R	14	2	**14**	**2**
2018–19	Newport Co	16	1	**16**	**1**

MATT, Jamille (F) **184** **41**
H: 6 1 W: 11 11 b.Walsall 20-10-89

2012–13	Fleetwood T	14	3		
2013–14	Fleetwood T	25	8		
2014–15	Fleetwood T	0	0		
2015–16	Fleetwood T	17	3	**56**	**14**
2015–16	*Stevenage*	8	1	**8**	**1**
2015–16	*Plymouth Arg*	11	5	**11**	**5**
2016–17	Blackpool	32	3		
2017–18	Blackpool	0	0	**32**	**3**
2017–18	*Grimsby T*	34	4	**34**	**4**
2018–19	Newport Co	43	14	**43**	**14**

O'BRIEN, Mark (D) **139** **3**
H: 5 11 W: 12 02 b.Dublin 20-11-92
Internationals: Republic of Ireland U19.

2008–09	Derby Co	1	0		
2009–10	Derby Co	0	0		
2010–11	Derby Co	2	0		
2011–12	Derby Co	20	0		
2012–13	Derby Co	9	0		
2013–14	Derby Co	0	0	**32**	**0**
2014–15	Motherwell	19	0	**19**	**0**
2015–16	Luton T	6	0	**6**	**0**
From Southport.					
2016–17	Newport Co	20	1		
2017–18	Newport Co	28	0		
2018–19	Newport Co	34	2	**82**	**3**

PIPE, David (M) **356** **8**
H: 5 9 W: 12 01 b.Caerphilly 5-11-83
Internationals: Wales U21, Full caps.

2002–03	Coventry C	21	1		
2003–04	Coventry C	0	0	**21**	**1**
2003–04	Notts Co	18	0		
2004–05	Notts Co	41	2		
2005–06	Notts Co	43	2		
2006–07	Notts Co	39	0	**141**	**4**
2007–08	Bristol R	40	2		
2008–09	Bristol R	39	1		
2009–10	Bristol R	7	0	**86**	**3**
2009–10	*Cheltenham T*	8	0	**8**	**0**
2013–14	Newport Co	25	0		
From Forest Green R, Eastleigh.					
2016–17	Newport Co	21	0		
2017–18	Newport Co	35	0		
2018–19	Newport Co	19	0	**100**	**0**

RANDALL, Will (M) **19** **0**
H: 5 11 W: 10 03 b.Swindon 2-5-97

2013–14	Swindon T	1	0		
2014–15	Swindon T	4	0		
2015–16	Swindon T	4	0	**9**	**0**
2015–16	Wolverhampton W	0	0		
2016–17	Wolverhampton W	0	0		
2016–17	*Walsall*	2	0	**2**	**0**
2017–18	Wolverhampton W	0	0		
2017–18	*Forest Green R*	7	0	**7**	**0**
2018–19	Newport Co	1	0	**1**	**0**

SHEEHAN, Josh (M) **92** **10**
H: 6 0 W: 11 11 b.Pembrey 30-3-95
Internationals: Wales U19, U21.

2013–14	Swansea C	0	0		
2014–15	Swansea C	0	0		
2014–15	*Yeovil T*	13	0		
2015–16	Swansea C	0	0		
2015–16	*Yeovil T*	13	2	**26**	**2**
2016–17	Swansea C	0	0		
2016–17	*Newport Co*	20	5		
2017–18	Newport Co	13	2		
2018–19	Newport Co	33	1	**66**	**8**

TAYLOR, Owen (M) **0** **0**
b. 6-3-01

2017–18	Newport Co	0	0		
2018–19	Newport Co	0	0		

TOWNSEND, Nick (G) **19** **0**
H: 5 11 W: 13 11 b.Solihull 1-11-94

2012–13	Birmingham C	0	0		
2013–14	Birmingham C	0	0		
2014–15	Birmingham C	0	0		
2015–16	Barnsley	8	0		
2016–17	Barnsley	0	0		
2017–18	Barnsley	8	0	**16**	**0**
2018–19	Newport Co	3	0	**3**	**0**

WILLMOTT, Robbie (M) **132** **8**
H: 5 9 W: 12 00 b.Harlow 16-5-90
Internationals: England C.

2013–14	Newport Co	46	3		
2014–15	Newport Co	16	1		
2017–18	Newport Co	39	2		
2018–19	Newport Co	31	2	**132**	**8**

Players retained or with offer of contract
Randall-Hurren, William George James; Touray, Momodou.

Scholars
Beckett, Callum Peter; Benham, Dewi Sion Edwyn; Bishop, Liam Lawrence; Collins, Lewis Rhys; Edwards, Owura Nsiah; Evans, Ioan Langdon; George, Ryan James; Hillman, Thomas Patrick; Jefferies, Dominic William; Jones, Callum Oliver; Mayor, Matthew Ryan; Murray, Lucas Elliot; Taylor, Owen Philip; Watts, Elis William; Wright, Thomas Josep.

NORTHAMPTON T (57)

BARNETT, Leon (D) **306** **15**
H: 6 0 W: 12 04 b.Stevenage 30-11-85

2003–04	Luton T	0	0		
2004–05	Luton T	0	0		
2005–06	Luton T	20	0		
2006–07	Luton T	39	3	**59**	**3**
2007–08	WBA	32	3		
2008–09	WBA	11	0		
2009–10	WBA	2	0		
2009–10	*Coventry C*	20	0	**20**	**0**
2010–11	WBA	0	0	**45**	**3**
2010–11	Norwich C	25	1		
2011–12	Norwich C	17	1		
2012–13	Norwich C	8	0		
2012–13	*Cardiff C*	8	0	**8**	**0**
2013–14	Norwich C	0	0	**50**	**2**
2013–14	Wigan Ath	41	4		
2014–15	Wigan Ath	20	0		
2015–16	Wigan Ath	20	1	**81**	**5**
2016–17	Bury	24	1	**24**	**1**
2017–18	Northampton T	15	1		
2018–19	Northampton T	4	0	**19**	**1**

BOWDITCH, Dean (F) **420** **82**
H: 5 11 W: 11 05 b.Bishops Stortford 15-6-86
Internationals: England U16, U17, U19.

2002–03	Ipswich T	5	0		
2003–04	Ipswich T	16	4		
2004–05	Ipswich T	21	3		
2004–05	*Burnley*	10	1	**10**	**1**
2005–06	Ipswich T	21	0		
2005–06	*Wycombe W*	11	1	**11**	**1**
2006–07	Ipswich T	9	1		
2006–07	*Brighton & HA*	3	1		
2007–08	Ipswich T	0	0		
2007–08	*Northampton T*	10	2		
2007–08	*Brighton & HA*	5	0	**8**	**1**
2008–09	Ipswich T	1	0	**73**	**8**
2008–09	*Brentford*	9	2	**9**	**2**
2009–10	Yeovil T	30	10		
2010–11	Yeovil T	41	15	**71**	**25**
2011–12	Milton Keynes D	41	12		
2012–13	Milton Keynes D	39	8		
2013–14	Milton Keynes D	12	1		
2014–15	Milton Keynes D	35	7		
2015–16	Milton Keynes D	37	4		
2016–17	Milton Keynes D	28	5	**192**	**37**
2017–18	Northampton T	11	0		
2017–18	*Stevenage*	5	2	**5**	**2**
2018–19	Northampton T	20	3	**41**	**5**

BRIDGE, Jack (M) **39 2**
H: 5 10 W: 11 07 b. 21-9-95

2013–14	Southend U	0	0		
2014–15	Southend U	0	0		
2015–16	Southend U	2	0		
2016–17	Southend U	4	0		
2017–18	Southend U	1	0	**7**	**0**
2017–18	Northampton T	4	0		
2018–19	Northampton T	28	2	**32**	**2**

BUCHANAN, David (M) **486 3**
H: 5 7 W: 11 03 b.Rochdale 6-5-86
Internationals: Northern Ireland U19, U21.

2004–05	Bury	3	0		
2005–06	Bury	23	0		
2006–07	Bury	41	0		
2007–08	Bury	35	0		
2008–09	Bury	46	0		
2009–10	Bury	38	0	**186**	**0**
2010–11	Hamilton A	28	1	**28**	**1**
2011–12	Tranmere R	41	1	**41**	**1**
2012–13	Preston NE	33	0		
2013–14	Preston NE	19	0		
2014–15	Preston NE	17	0	**69**	**0**
2015–16	Northampton T	46	0		
2016–17	Northampton T	45	0		
2017–18	Northampton T	32	1		
2018–19	Northampton T	39	0	**162**	**1**

BUNNEY, Joe (F) **155 16**
H: 6 1 W: 11 00 b.Manchester 26-9-93

2012–13	Rochdale	1	1		
2013–14	Rochdale	21	3		
2014–15	Rochdale	19	2		
2015–16	Rochdale	32	9		
2016–17	Rochdale	29	1		
2017–18	Rochdale	20	0		
2017–18	Northampton T	12	0		
2018–19	Northampton T	0	0	**12**	**0**
2018–19	*Blackpool*	5	0	**5**	**0**
2018–19	*Rochdale*	16	0	**138**	**16**

CODDINGTON, Luke (G) **1 0**
b.Middlesbrough 6-6-95
Internationals: England U17, U18, U19.

2013–14	Middlesbrough	0	0		
2014–15	Middlesbrough	0	0		
2015–16	Middlesbrough	0	0		
2016–17	Huddersfield T	0	0		
2017–18	Northampton T	1	0		
2018–19	Northampton T	0	0	**1**	**0**

CORNELL, David (G) **102 0**
H: 5 11 W: 11 07 b.Gorseinon 28-3-91
Internationals: Wales U17, U19, U21.

2009–10	Swansea C	0	0		
2010–11	Swansea C	0	0		
2011–12	Swansea C	0	0		
2011–12	*Hereford U*	25	0	**25**	**0**
2012–13	Swansea C	0	0		
2013–14	Swansea C	0	0		
2013–14	*St Mirren*	5	0	**5**	**0**
2014–15	Swansea C	0	0		
2014–15	*Portsmouth*	0	0		
2015–16	Oldham Ath	14	0	**14**	**0**
2016–17	Northampton T	6	0		
2017–18	Northampton T	6	0		
2018–19	Northampton T	46	0	**58**	**0**

DALDY, Jack (F) **0 0**
H: 5 5 b.Kettering 27-9-00

2018–19	Northampton T	0	0		

FACEY, Shay (D) **68 1**
H: 5 10 W: 10 00 b.Manchester 7-1-95
Internationals: England U16, U17, U19, U20.

2013–14	Manchester C	0	0		
2014–15	Manchester C	0	0		
2014–15	New York City	0	0		
2015–16	Manchester C	0	0		
2015–16	*New York City*	22	0	**22**	**0**
2015–16	*Rotherham U*	5	0	**5**	**0**
2016–17	Manchester C	0	0		
2016–17	*Heerenveen*	3	0		
2017–18	Heerenveen	0	0	**3**	**0**
2017–18	Northampton T	15	1		
2018–19	Northampton T	23	0	**38**	**1**

FOLEY, Sam (M) **234 18**
H: 6 0 W: 11 08 b.St Albans 17-10-86

2012–13	Yeovil T	41	5		
2013–14	Yeovil T	7	0		
2013–14	*Shrewsbury T*	9	0	**9**	**0**
2014–15	Yeovil T	40	2	**88**	**7**
2015–16	Port Vale	45	6		
2016–17	Port Vale	32	1	**77**	**7**
2016–17	Northampton T	0	0		
2017–18	Northampton T	24	2		
2018–19	Northampton T	36	2	**60**	**4**

HOSKINS, Sam (F) **181 20**
H: 5 8 W: 10 07 b.Dorchester 4-2-93

2011–12	Southampton	0	0		
2011–12	*Preston NE*	0	0		
2011–12	*Rotherham U*	8	2	**8**	**2**
2012–13	Southampton	0	0		
2012–13	*Stevenage*	14	1	**14**	**1**
2013–14	Yeovil T	19	0		
2014–15	Yeovil T	12	1	**31**	**1**
2015–16	Northampton T	34	6		
2016–17	Northampton T	25	3		
2017–18	Northampton T	27	2		
2018–19	Northampton T	42	5	**128**	**16**

HUGHES, Ryan (D) **1 0**
b. 24-4-01

2018–19	Northampton T	1	0	**1**	**0**

IACIOFANO, Joe (F) **1 0**
b.Northampton 9-9-98

2016–17	Northampton T	1	0		
2017–18	Northampton T	0	0		
2018–19	Northampton T	0	0	**1**	**0**

McWILLIAMS, Cameron (M) **0 0**

2017–18	Northampton T	0	0		
2018–19	Northampton T	0	0		

McWILLIAMS, Shaun (M) **49 0**
b.Northampton 14-8-98

2014–15	Northampton T	0	0		
2015–16	Northampton T	0	0		
2016–17	Northampton T	5	0		
2017–18	Northampton T	19	0		
2018–19	Northampton T	25	0	**49**	**0**

MORIAS, Junior (F) **92 16**
H: 5 8 W: 10 10 b.Kingston 4-7-95

2012–13	Wycombe W	19	0		
2013–14	Wycombe W	9	0		
2014–15	Wycombe W	0	0	**28**	**0**

From Boreham Wood, Whitehawk, St Albans C.

2016–17	Peterborough U	20	4		
2017–18	Peterborough U	25	6	**45**	**10**
2018–19	Northampton T	19	6	**19**	**6**

NEWELL, Jack (M) **0 0**

2018–19	Northampton T	0	0		

O'TOOLE, John (M) **372 62**
H: 6 2 W: 13 07 b.Harrow 30-9-88
Internationals: Republic of Ireland U21.

2007–08	Watford	35	3		
2008–09	Watford	22	7		
2008–09	*Sheffield U*	9	1	**9**	**1**
2009–10	Watford	0	0	**57**	**10**
2009–10	Colchester U	31	2		
2010–11	Colchester U	11	0		
2011–12	Colchester U	15	0		
2012–13	Colchester U	15	0	**72**	**2**
2012–13	*Bristol R*	18	3		
2013–14	Bristol R	41	13	**59**	**16**
2014–15	Northampton T	35	2		
2014–15	*Southend U*	2	0	**2**	**0**
2015–16	Northampton T	38	12		
2016–17	Northampton T	40	10		
2017–18	Northampton T	29	6		
2018–19	Northampton T	31	3	**173**	**33**

ODOFIN, Hakeem (D) **13 0**
b. 13-4-98

2015–16	Barnet	1	0	**1**	**0**
2016–17	Wolverhampton W	0	0		
2017–18	Wolverhampton W	0	0		
2018–19	Northampton T	12	0	**12**	**0**

Transferred to Livingston January 2019.

PIERRE, Aaron (D) **189 15**
H: 6 1 W: 13 12 b.Southall 17-2-93
Internationals: Grenada Full caps.

2011–12	Brentford	0	0		
2012–13	Brentford	0	0		
2013–14	Brentford	0	0		
2013–14	*Wycombe W*	8	1		
2014–15	Wycombe W	42	4		
2015–16	Wycombe W	40	2		
2016–17	Wycombe W	39	2	**129**	**9**
2017–18	Northampton T	19	0		
2018–19	Northampton T	41	6	**60**	**6**

POLLOCK, Scott (M) **5 0**
b. 12-3-01

2018–19	Northampton T	5	0	**5**	**0**

POWELL, Daniel (F) **295 45**
H: 5 11 W: 13 03 b.Luton 12-3-91

2008–09	Milton Keynes D	7	1		
2009–10	Milton Keynes D	2	1		
2010–11	Milton Keynes D	29	9		
2011–12	Milton Keynes D	43	6		
2012–13	Milton Keynes D	34	7		
2013–14	Milton Keynes D	32	1		
2014–15	Milton Keynes D	42	8		
2015–16	Milton Keynes D	22	2		
2016–17	Milton Keynes D	20	2	**231**	**37**
2017–18	Northampton T	29	2		
2018–19	Northampton T	35	6	**64**	**8**

ROBERTS, Morgan (F) **4 0**
b. 22-12-00

2017–18	Northampton T	1	0		
2018–19	Northampton T	3	0	**4**	**0**

TAYLOR, Ash (M) **361 23**
H: 6 0 W: 12 00 b.Bromborough 2-9-90
Internationals: Wales U19, U21.

2008–09	Tranmere R	1	0		
2009–10	Tranmere R	33	1		
2010–11	Tranmere R	26	0		
2011–12	Tranmere R	37	2		
2012–13	Tranmere R	44	2		
2013–14	Tranmere R	42	3	**183**	**8**
2014–15	Aberdeen	32	3		
2015–16	Aberdeen	37	4		
2016–17	Aberdeen	31	2	**100**	**9**
2017–18	Northampton T	45	6		
2018–19	Northampton T	33	0	**78**	**6**

TURNBULL, Jordan (D) **167 1**
H: 6 1 W: 11 05 b.Trowbridge 30-10-94
Internationals: England U19, U20.

2014–15	Southampton	0	0		
2014–15	*Swindon T*	44	1		
2015–16	Southampton	0	0		
2015–16	*Swindon T*	42	0	**86**	**1**
2016–17	Coventry C	36	0		
2017–18	Coventry C	0	0	**36**	**0**
2017–18	*Partick Thistle*	0	0		
2017–18	Northampton T	14	0		
2018–19	Northampton T	31	0	**45**	**0**

WARD, Lewis (G) **12 0**
b. 5-3-97
Internationals: England U16.

2014–15	Reading	0	0		
2015–16	Reading	0	0		
2016–17	Reading	0	0		
2017–18	Reading	0	0		
2018–19	Northampton T	0	0		
2018–19	*Forest Green R*	12	0	**12**	**0**

WHALER, Sean (M) **0 0**

2017–18	Northampton T	0	0		
2018–19	Northampton T	0	0		

WILLIAMS, Andy (F) **456 107**
H: 5 11 W: 11 09 b.Hereford 14-8-86

2006–07	Hereford U	41	8		
2007–08	Bristol R	41	4		
2008–09	Bristol R	4	1		
2008–09	*Hereford U*	26	2	**67**	**10**
2009–10	Bristol R	43	3	**88**	**8**
2010–11	Yeovil T	37	6		
2011–12	Yeovil T	35	16		
2012–13	Swindon T	40	11		
2013–14	Swindon T	3	0		
2013–14	*Yeovil T*	9	0	**81**	**22**
2014–15	Swindon T	46	21	**89**	**32**
2015–16	Doncaster R	46	12		
2016–17	Doncaster R	37	11		
2017–18	Doncaster R	9	0	**92**	**23**
2018–19	Northampton T	39	12	**39**	**12**

WILLIAMS, Jay (D) **10 0**
b. 4-10-00

2018–19	Northampton T	10	0	**10**	**0**

Players retained or with offer of contract
Smith, Harry Roy; Waters, Bill Henry Penna.

Scholars
Ballinger, Jacob Bryan; Chukwuemeka, Chigozier Caleb; Daldy, Jack Ryland; Fowler, Jordan Lee; Gordon-Douglas, Urijah Jesse; Harding, Michael Joshua Francis; Hughes, Ryan Annesley; Jarvis, Joseph; Lashley, Bradley; Newell, Jack Michael; Patching, Lewis John; Pollock, Scott Alexander Gladman; Price, Haydn James; Slinn, Matthew; Smith, Ryan Nathan.

NORWICH C (58)

AARONS, Maximillian (D) 41 2
b.London 4-1-00
Internationals: England U19.
From Luton T.

2018–19	Norwich C	41	2	**41**	**2**

CANTWELL, Todd (M) 34 3
b. 27-2-98
Internationals: England U17.

2017–18	Norwich C	0	0		
2017–18	*Fortuna Sittard*	10	2	**10**	**2**
2018–19	Norwich C	24	1	**24**	**1**

EMI, Buendia (M) 113 17
H: 5 7 W: 11 05 b.Mar del Plata 25-12-96
Internationals: Spain U19. Argentina U20.

2013–14	Getafe	0	0		
2014–15	Getafe	6	0		
2015–16	Getafe	17	1		
2016–17	Getafe	12	2		
2017–18	Getafe	0	0	**35**	**3**
2017–18	*Cultural Leonesa*	40	6	**40**	**6**
2018–19	Norwich C	38	8	**38**	**8**

FAMEWO, Akin (D) 16 0
H: 5 11 W: 10 06 b.Lewisham 9-11-98

2016–17	Luton T	3	0		
2017–18	Luton T	3	0		
2018–19	Luton T	0	0	**6**	**0**
2018–19	*Grimsby T*	10	0	**10**	**0**
2018–19	Norwich C	0	0		

GODFREY, Ben (M) 85 6
H: 6 0 W: 11 09 b.York 15-1-98
Internationals: England U20.

2014–15	York C	0	0		
2015–16	York C	12	1	**12**	**1**
2015–16	Norwich C	0	0		
2016–17	Norwich C	2	0		
2017–18	Norwich C	0	0		
2017–18	*Shrewsbury T*	40	1	**40**	**1**
2018–19	Norwich C	31	4	**33**	**4**

HANLEY, Grant (D) 234 10
H: 6 2 W: 12 00 b.Dumfries 20-11-91
Internationals: Scotland U19, U21, Full caps.

2008–09	Blackburn R	0	0		
2009–10	Blackburn R	1	0		
2010–11	Blackburn R	7	0		
2011–12	Blackburn R	23	1		
2012–13	Blackburn R	39	2		
2013–14	Blackburn R	38	1		
2014–15	Blackburn R	31	1		
2015–16	Blackburn R	44	2	**183**	**7**
2016–17	Newcastle U	10	1		
2017–18	Newcastle U	0	0	**10**	**1**
2017–18	Norwich C	32	1		
2018–19	Norwich C	9	1	**41**	**2**

HERNANDEZ, Onel (M) 131 14
b.Moron 1-2-93
Internationals: Germany U18.

2010–11	Arminia Bielefeld	10	0		
2011–12	Arminia Bielefeld	18	0	**28**	**0**
2012–13	Werder Bremen	0	0		
2013–14	Werder Bremen	0	0		
2013–14	Wolfsburg	0	0		
2014–15	Wolfsburg	0	0		
2015–16	Wolfsburg	0	0		
2016–17	Eintracht Brauschweig	34	5	**34**	**5**
2017–18	Eintracht Brauschweig	17	1	**17**	**1**
2017–18	Norwich C	12	0		
2018–19	Norwich C	40	8	**52**	**8**

HUSBAND, James (D) 148 5
H: 5 10 W: 10 00 b.Leeds 3-1-94

2011–12	Doncaster R	3	0		
2012–13	Doncaster R	33	3		
2013–14	Doncaster R	28	1	**64**	**4**
2014–15	Middlesbrough	3	0		
2014–15	*Fulham*	5	0		
2015–16	Middlesbrough	0	0		
2015–16	*Fulham*	12	0	**17**	**0**
2015–16	*Huddersfield T*	11	0	**11**	**0**
2016–17	Middlesbrough	1	0	**4**	**0**
2017–18	Norwich C	18	0		
2018–19	Norwich C	1	0	**19**	**0**
2018–19	*Fleetwood T*	33	1	**33**	**1**

IVO PINTO, Daniel (D) 232 3
H: 6 0 W: 11 07 b.Lourosa 7-1-90
Internationals: Portugal U16, U17, U18, U19, U21.

2008–09	Porto	0	0		
2009–10	Porto	0	0		
2009–10	*Vicente*	1	0	**1**	**0**
2009–10	*Vitoria Setubal*	2	0	**2**	**0**
2010–11	Porto	0	0		
2010–11	*Covilha*	22	0	**22**	**0**
2011–12	Rio Ave	0	0		
2011–12	*Uniao Leiria*	25	0	**25**	**0**
2012–13	Cluj	27	0	**27**	**0**
2013–14	Dinamo Zagreb	28	0		
2014–15	Dinamo Zagreb	29	0		
2015–16	Dinamo Zagreb	13	0	**70**	**0**
2015–16	Norwich C	10	0		
2016–17	Norwich C	37	1		
2017–18	Norwich C	35	2		
2018–19	Norwich C	3	0	**85**	**3**

JAIYESIMI, Diallang (M) 39 2
b.Southwark 18-3-99
From Dulwich Hamlet.

2017–18	Norwich C	0	0		
2017–18	*Grimsby T*	30	0	**30**	**0**
2018–19	Norwich C	0	0		
2018–19	*Yeovil T*	9	2	**9**	**2**

JARVIS, Matthew (M) 380 36
H: 5 8 W: 11 10 b.Middlesbrough 22-5-86
Internationals: England Full caps.

2003–04	Gillingham	10	0		
2004–05	Gillingham	30	3		
2005–06	Gillingham	35	3		
2006–07	Gillingham	35	6	**110**	**12**
2007–08	Wolverhampton W	26	1		
2008–09	Wolverhampton W	28	3		
2009–10	Wolverhampton W	34	3		
2010–11	Wolverhampton W	37	4		
2011–12	Wolverhampton W	37	8		
2012–13	Wolverhampton W	2	0	**164**	**19**
2012–13	West Ham U	32	2		
2013–14	West Ham U	32	2		
2014–15	West Ham U	11	0		
2015–16	West Ham U	3	0	**78**	**4**
2015–16	Norwich C	19	1		
2016–17	Norwich C	0	0		
2017–18	Norwich C	0	0		
2018–19	Norwich C	0	0	**19**	**1**
2018–19	*Walsall*	9	0	**9**	**0**

KLOSE, Timm (D) 244 19
H: 6 5 W: 13 10 b.Frankfurt am Main 9-5-88
Internationals: Switzerland U21, U23, Full caps.

2009–10	Thun	29	2		
2010–11	Thun	30	3	**59**	**5**
2011–12	Nuremburg	13	0		
2012–13	Nuremburg	32	2	**45**	**2**
2013–14	Wolfsburg	10	0		
2014–15	Wolfsburg	12	1		
2015–16	Wolfsburg	8	1	**30**	**2**
2015–16	Norwich C	10	1		
2016–17	Norwich C	32	1		
2017–18	Norwich C	37	4		
2018–19	Norwich C	31	4	**110**	**10**

KRUL, Tim (G) 255 0
H: 6 2 W: 11 08 b.Den Haag 3-4-88
Internationals: Netherlands U16, U17, U19, U20, U21, Full caps.

2005–06	Newcastle U	0	0		
2006–07	Newcastle U	0	0		
2007–08	*Falkirk*	22	0	**22**	**0**
2007–08	Newcastle U	0	0		
2008–09	Newcastle U	0	0		
2008–09	*Carlisle U*	9	0	**9**	**0**
2009–10	Newcastle U	3	0		
2010–11	Newcastle U	21	0		
2011–12	Newcastle U	38	0		
2012–13	Newcastle U	24	0		
2013–14	Newcastle U	36	0		
2014–15	Newcastle U	30	0		
2015–16	Newcastle U	8	0		
2016–17	Newcastle U	0	0		
2016–17	*Ajax*	0	0		
2016–17	*AZ Alkmaar*	18	0	**18**	**0**
2017–18	Newcastle U	0	0	**160**	**0**
2017–18	Brighton & HA	0	0		
2018–19	Norwich C	46	0	**46**	**0**

LEITNER, Moritz (M) 158 4
H: 5 9 W: 10 03 b.Munich 8-12-92
Internationals: Austria U17. Germany U19, U20, U21.

2010–11	1860 Munich	16	0	**16**	**0**
2010–11	Borussia Dortmund	0	0		
2010–11	*Augsburg*	9	0		
2011–12	Borussia Dortmund	17	0		
2012–13	Borussia Dortmund	25	0		
2013–14	Borussia Dortmund	0	0		
2013–14	*Stuttgart*	21	1		
2014–15	Borussia Dortmund	0	0		
2014–15	*Stuttgart*	19	1	**40**	**2**
2015–16	Borussia Dortmund	8	0	**50**	**0**
2016–17	Lazio	2	0	**2**	**0**
2017–18	Augsburg	0	0	**9**	**0**
2017–18	*Norwich C*	12	0		
2018–19	Norwich C	29	2	**41**	**2**

LEWIS, Jamal (D) 64 0
b. 25-1-98
Internationals: Northern Ireland U19, U21, Full caps.

2017–18	Norwich C	22	0		
2018–19	Norwich C	42	0	**64**	**0**

McGOVERN, Michael (G) 290 0
H: 6 2 W: 13 07 b.Enniskillen 12-7-84
Internationals: Northern Ireland U19, U21, Full caps.

2004–05	Celtic	0	0		
2004–05	*Stranraer*	19	0	**19**	**0**
2005–06	Celtic	0	0		
2006–07	Celtic	0	0		
2006–07	*St Johnstone*	1	0	**1**	**0**
2007–08	Celtic	0	0		
2008–09	Dundee U	0	0		
2009–10	Ross Co	35	0		
2010–11	Ross Co	36	0	**71**	**0**
2011–12	Falkirk	35	0		
2012–13	Falkirk	35	0		
2013–14	Falkirk	34	0	**104**	**0**
2014–15	Hamilton A	38	0		
2015–16	Hamilton A	37	0	**75**	**0**
2016–17	Norwich C	20	0		
2017–18	Norwich C	0	0		
2018–19	Norwich C	0	0	**20**	**0**

McLEAN, Kenny (M) 297 43
H: 6 0 W: 11 00 b.Rutherglen 8-1-92
Internationals: Scotland U19, U21, Full caps.

2009–10	St Mirren	0	0		
2009–10	*Arbroath*	20	1	**20**	**1**
2010–11	St Mirren	19	0		
2011–12	St Mirren	28	4		
2012–13	St Mirren	29	3		
2013–14	St Mirren	30	7		
2014–15	St Mirren	25	7	**131**	**21**
2014–15	Aberdeen	13	0		
2015–16	Aberdeen	38	6		
2016–17	Aberdeen	38	4		
2017–18	Aberdeen	22	3		
2017–18	Norwich C	0	0		
2017–18	*Aberdeen*	15	5	**126**	**18**
2018–19	Norwich C	20	3	**20**	**3**

NELSON OLIVEIRA, Miguel (F) 218 48
H: 6 1 W: 12 13 b.Barcelos 8-8-91
Internationals: Portugal U16, U17, U19, U20, U21, Full caps.

2009–10	Benfica	0	0		
2009–10	*Rio Ave*	10	0	**10**	**0**
2010–11	Benfica	0	0		
2010–11	*Pacos Ferreira*	23	4	**23**	**4**
2011–12	Benfica	12	0		
2012–13	Benfica	0	0		
2012–13	*La Coruna*	30	4	**30**	**4**
2013–14	Benfica	0	0		
2013–14	*Rennes*	30	8	**30**	**8**
2014–15	Benfica	0	0		
2014–15	*Swansea C*	10	1	**10**	**1**
2015–16	Benfica	0	0	**12**	**0**
2015–16	*Nottingham F*	28	9	**28**	**9**
2016–17	Norwich C	28	11		
2017–18	Norwich C	37	8		
2018–19	Norwich C	0	0	**65**	**19**
2018–19	*Reading*	10	3	**10**	**3**

ODUSINA, Timi (D) 0 0
b.Croydon 28-10-99

2018–19	Norwich C	0	0		

OXBOROUGH, Aston (G) 0 0
H: 6 5 b.Great Yarmouth 9-5-98
Internationals: England U16.

2018–19	Norwich C	0	0		

PASSLACK, Felix (D) 17 0
H: 5 7 W: 11 09 b.Bottrop 29-5-98
Internationals: Germany U16, U17, U18, U19, U21.

2015–16	Borussia Dortmund	3	0		
2016–17	Borussia Dortmund	10	0		
2017–18	Borussia Dortmund	1	0		
2017–18	*1899 Hoffenheim*	2	0	**2**	**0**
2018–19	Borussia Dortmund	0	0	**14**	**0**

On loan from Borussia Dortmund.

2018–19	Norwich C	1	0	**1**	**0**

PAYNE, Alfie (M) **0 0**
b.Norwich 7-10-99

2018–19	Norwich C	0	0		

PUKKI, Teemu (F) **291 115**
H: 5 9 W: 10 06 b.Kotka 29-3-90
Internationals: Finland U17, U19, U21, Full caps.

2006	KooTeePee	5	0		
2007	KooTeePee	24	3	**29**	**3**
2008–09	Sevilla	1	0	**1**	**0**
2010	HJK Helsinki	7	2		
2011	HJK Helsinki	18	11	**25**	**13**
2011–12	Schalke 04	19	5		
2012–13	Schalke 04	17	3		
2013–14	Schalke 04	1	0	**37**	**8**
2013–14	Celtic	25	7		
2014–15	Celtic	1	0	**26**	**7**
2014–15	Brondby	27	9		
2015–16	Brondby	33	9		
2016–17	Brondby	34	20		
2017–18	Brondby	36	17	**130**	**55**
2018–19	Norwich C	43	29	**43**	**29**

SRBENY, Dennis (F) **119 40**
b.Berlin 5-5-94

2013–14	Hansa Rostock	2	0		
2014–15	Hansa Rostock	18	1	**20**	**1**
2015–16	BFC Dynamo	22	10		
2016–17	BFC Dynamo	33	18	**55**	**28**
2017–18	Paderborn	15	9	**15**	**9**
2017–18	Norwich C	14	1		
2018–19	Norwich C	15	1	**29**	**2**

STIEPERMANN, Marco (F) **242 30**
H: 5 11 W: 11 11 b.Dortmund 9-2-91
Internationals: Germany U16, U17, U18, U19, U20.

2008–09	Borussia Dortmund	0	0		
2009–10	Borussia Dortmund	3	1		
2010–11	Borussia Dortmund	4	0		
2011–12	Borussia Dortmund	0	0	**7**	**1**
2011–12	*Aachen*	21	2	**21**	**2**
2012–13	Energie Cottbus	27	2		
2013–14	Energie Cottbus	29	5	**56**	**7**
2014–15	Greuther Furth	31	4		
2015–16	Greuther Furth	30	5	**61**	**9**
2016–17	Bochum	31	1	**31**	**1**
2017–18	VfL Bochum	0	0		
2017–18	Norwich C	23	1		
2018–19	Norwich C	43	9	**66**	**10**

TETTEY, Alexander (M) **340 20**
H: 5 11 W: 10 09 b.Accra 4-4-86
Internationals: Norway U18, U19, U21, Full caps.

2004–05	Rosenborg	0	0		
2005–06	Rosenborg	10	1		
2006–07	Rosenborg	21	1		
2007–08	Rosenborg	25	4		
2008–09	Rosenborg	28	6		
2009–10	Rosenborg	1	0	**85**	**12**
2009–10	Rennes	24	0		
2010–11	Rennes	17	1		
2011–12	Rennes	19	1	**60**	**2**
2012–13	Norwich C	27	0		
2013–14	Norwich C	21	1		
2014–15	Norwich C	36	2		
2015–16	Norwich C	23	2		
2016–17	Norwich C	35	0		
2017–18	Norwich C	23	0		
2018–19	Norwich C	30	1	**195**	**6**

THOMPSON, Louis (M) **101 6**
H: 5 11 W: 11 10 b.Bristol 19-12-94
Internationals: Wales U19, U21.

2012–13	Swindon T	4	0		
2013–14	Swindon T	28	2		
2014–15	Norwich C	0	0		
2014–15	*Swindon T*	32	2		
2015–16	Norwich C	0	0		
2015–16	*Swindon T*	28	2	**92**	**6**
2016–17	Norwich C	3	0		
2017–18	Norwich C	0	0		
2018–19	Norwich C	6	0	**9**	**0**

TRYBULL, Tom (M) **127 5**
H: 5 11 W: 11 05 b.Berlin 9-3-93
Internationals: Germany U17, U18, U19, U20.

2010–11	Hansa Rostock	17	0	**17**	**0**
2011–12	Werder Bremen	15	1		
2012–13	Werder Bremen	4	0		
2013–14	Werder Bremen	2	0	**21**	**1**
2013–14	St Pauli	12	0		
2014–15	St Pauli	3	0	**15**	**0**
2015–16	Greuther Furth	0	0		
2016–17	Den Haag	23	1	**23**	**1**
2017–18	Norwich C	20	2		
2018–19	Norwich C	31	1	**51**	**3**

VRANCIC, Mario (M) **230 29**
H: 6 1 W: 12 02 b.Slavonski Brod 23-5-89
Internationals: Germany U17, U19, U20. Bosnia-Herzegovina Full caps.

2006–07	Mainz 05	1	0		
2007–08	Mainz 05	5	0		
2008–09	Mainz 05	3	0		
2009–10	Mainz 05	0	0	**9**	**0**
2009–10	*Rot Weiss Ahlen*	12	0	**12**	**0**
2010–11	Borussia Dortmund	0	0		
2011–12	Borussia Dortmund	0	0		
2012–13	Paderborn	33	5		
2013–14	Paderborn	30	5		
2014–15	Paderborn	30	2	**93**	**12**
2015–16	Darmstadt	22	2		
2016–17	Darmstadt	23	4	**45**	**6**
2017–18	Norwich C	35	1		
2018–19	Norwich C	36	10	**71**	**11**

WILDSCHUT, Yanic (F) **245 30**
H: 6 2 W: 13 08 b.Amsterdam 1-11-91
Internationals: Netherlands U21.

2010–11	Zwolle	33	3	**33**	**3**
2011–12	VVV	29	7		
2012–13	VVV	32	1	**61**	**8**
2013–14	Heerenveen	18	2		
2013–14	*Den Haag*	7	0	**7**	**0**
2014–15	Heerenveen	4	0	**22**	**2**
2014–15	Middlesbrough	11	2		
2015–16	Middlesbrough	1	0	**12**	**2**
2015–16	Wigan Ath	34	7		
2016–17	Wigan Ath	25	4	**59**	**11**
2016–17	Norwich C	9	1		
2017–18	Norwich C	16	1		
2017–18	*Cardiff C*	10	0	**10**	**0**
2018–19	Norwich C	0	0	**25**	**2**
2018–19	*Bolton W*	16	2	**16**	**2**

ZIMMERMANN, Christoph (D) **79 3**
b.Dusseldorf 12-1-93

2011–12	Borussia M'gladbach	0	0		
2012–13	Borussia M'gladbach	0	0		
2013–14	Borussia M'gladbach	0	0		
2014–15	Borussia Dortmund	0	0		
2015–16	Borussia Dortmund	0	0		
2016–17	Borussia Dortmund	0	0		
2017–18	Norwich C	39	1		
2018–19	Norwich C	40	2	**79**	**3**

Players retained or with offer of contract
Ahadme, Yahyai Gassan; Barden, Daniel James; Barkarson, Atli; Coley, Joshua; Enigbokan-Bloomfield, Mason Ozail; Franke, Marcel; Heise, Philip Michael; Hondermarck, William Mbongo Desire; Idah, Adam; Johnson, William; Jones, Ciaren Alexander; Lambert, Kole Martyn; Lomas, Louis James; Marshall, Ben; Martin, Joshua Saul; McCracken, Jon Douglas; Milovanovic, Saul John; Morris, Carlton; Mourgos, Savvas; Power, Simon; Raggett, Sean; Richards, Caleb Joel; Scully, Thomas; Spyrou, Anthony Jeffrey John; Thomas, Jordan James Chattenton; Thorvaldsson, Isak.

Scholars
Ahmadi, Arash; Akycampong-Ekumah, Aaron; Barnes, Finlay; Berkeley, Anthonius James; Dickerson, Ryan James; Dronfield, Zachary Gage; Harsani, Giurgi Joshua Alexander; Hutchinson, Shae Armari Akpojotor; Mehmeti, Anis; Olopade, Denzelle; Omobamidele, Andrew Abiola; Parsons, Connor; Richardson, Matthew David Oscar; Vaughan, Ethen James.

NOTTINGHAM F (59)

AHMEDHODZIC, Anel (D) **1 0**
H: 6 3 W: 12 00 b. 26-3-99
Internationals: Sweden U16, U17, U18, U19.
From Malmo.

2016–17	Nottingham F	1	0		
2018–19	Nottingham F	0	0	**1**	**0**

Transferred to Malmo January 2019.

ANSARIFARD, Karim (F) **285 110**
H: 6 1 W: 12 06 b.Ardabil 3-4-90
Internationals: Iran U17, U20, U23, Full caps.

2007–08	Saipa	18	1		
2008–09	Saipa	14	1		
2009–10	Saipa	31	13		
2010–11	Saipa	29	19		
2011–12	Saipa	31	21	**123**	**55**
2012–13	Persepolis	31	8	**31**	**8**
2013–14	Tractor Sazi	28	14	**28**	**14**
2014–15	Osasuna	16	0	**16**	**0**
2015–16	Panionios	27	8		
2016–17	Panionios	14	5	**41**	**13**
2016–17	Olympiacos	9	1		
2017–18	Olympiacos	25	17	**34**	**18**
2018–19	Nottingham F	12	2	**12**	**2**

APPIAH, Arvin (F) **6 0**
b. 5-1-01
Internationals: England U16, U17, U18, U19.

2018–19	Nottingham F	6	0	**6**	**0**

BENALOUANE, Yohan (D) **190 6**
H: 6 1 W: 12 06 b.Bagnois-sur-Ceze 28-3-87
Internationals: France U21. Tunisia Full caps.

2007–08	St Etienne	6	1		
2008–09	St Etienne	29	1		
2009–10	St Etienne	29	1		
2010–11	St Etienne	1	0	**65**	**3**
2010–11	Cesena	15	0		
2011–12	Cesena	11	0		
2012–13	Cesena	0	0	**26**	**0**
2012–13	*Parma*	21	1		
2013–14	Parma	4	0	**25**	**1**
2013–14	*Atalanta*	17	0		
2014–15	Atalanta	27	1	**44**	**1**
2015–16	Leicester C	4	0		
2015–16	*Fiorentina*	0	0		
2016–17	Leicester C	11	0		
2017–18	Leicester C	1	0		
2018–19	Leicester C	0	0	**16**	**0**
2018–19	Nottingham F	14	1	**14**	**1**

BRIDCUTT, Liam (M) **269 3**
H: 5 9 W: 11 07 b.Reading 8-5-89
Internationals: Scotland Full caps.

2007–08	Chelsea	0	0		
2007–08	*Yeovil T*	9	0	**9**	**0**
2008–09	Chelsea	0	0		
2008–09	*Watford*	6	0	**6**	**0**
2009–10	Chelsea	0	0		
2009–10	*Stockport Co*	15	0	**15**	**0**
2010–11	Chelsea	0	0		
2010–11	Brighton & HA	37	2		
2011–12	Brighton & HA	43	0		
2012–13	Brighton & HA	41	0		
2013–14	Brighton & HA	11	0	**132**	**2**
2013–14	Sunderland	12	0		
2014–15	Sunderland	18	0		
2015–16	Sunderland	0	0	**30**	**0**
2015–16	*Leeds U*	24	0		
2016–17	Leeds U	25	0	**49**	**0**
2017–18	Nottingham F	27	1		
2018–19	Nottingham F	1	0	**28**	**1**

CASH, Matty (M) **99 11**
H: 6 2 W: 10 01 b.Slough 7-8-97

2015–16	Nottingham F	0	0		
2015–16	*Dagenham & R*	12	3	**12**	**3**
2016–17	Nottingham F	28	0		
2017–18	Nottingham F	23	2		
2018–19	Nottingham F	36	6	**87**	**8**

CLOUGH, Zach (F) **104 26**
H: 5 7 b.Manchester 8-3-95

2013–14	Bolton W	0	0		
2014–15	Bolton W	8	5		
2015–16	Bolton W	28	7		
2016–17	Bolton W	23	9		
2016–17	Nottingham F	14	4		
2017–18	Nottingham F	13	0		
2017–18	*Bolton W*	9	1	**68**	**22**
2018–19	Nottingham F	0	0	**27**	**4**
2018–19	*Rochdale*	9	0	**9**	**0**

CROOKES, Adam (D) **19 0**
b.Lincoln 18-11-97

2017–18	Nottingham F	0	0		
2018–19	Nottingham F	0	0		
2018–19	*Lincoln C*	0	0		
2018–19	*Port Vale*	19	0	**19**	**0**

DARIKWA, Tendayi (M) **204 10**
H: 6 2 W: 12 02 b.Nottingham 13-12-91
Internationals: Zimbabwe Full caps.

2010–11	Chesterfield	0	0		
2011–12	Chesterfield	2	0		
2012–13	Chesterfield	36	5		
2013–14	Chesterfield	41	3		
2014–15	Chesterfield	46	1	**125**	**9**
2015–16	Burnley	21	1		
2016–17	Burnley	0	0	**21**	**1**
2017–18	Nottingham F	30	0		
2018–19	Nottingham F	28	0	**58**	**0**

DAWSON, Michael (D) **451** **22**
H: 6 2 W: 12 02 b.Leyburn 18-11-83
Internationals: England U21, B, Full caps.

2000–01	Nottingham F	0	0		
2001–02	Nottingham F	1	0		
2002–03	Nottingham F	38	5		
2003–04	Nottingham F	30	1		
2004–05	Nottingham F	14	1		
2004–05	Tottenham H	5	0		
2005–06	Tottenham H	32	0		
2006–07	Tottenham H	37	1		
2007–08	Tottenham H	27	1		
2008–09	Tottenham H	16	1		
2009–10	Tottenham H	29	2		
2010–11	Tottenham H	24	1		
2011–12	Tottenham H	7	0		
2012–13	Tottenham H	27	1		
2013–14	Tottenham H	32	0	**236**	**7**
2014–15	Hull C	28	1		
2015–16	Hull C	32	1		
2016–17	Hull C	22	3		
2017–18	Hull C	40	3	**122**	**8**
2018–19	Nottingham F	10	0	**93**	**7**

DOWELL, Kieran (F) **56** **11**
H: 5 9 W: 9 04 b.Ormskirk 10-10-97
Internationals: England U16, U17, U18, U20, U21.

2014–15	Everton	0	0		
2015–16	Everton	2	0		
2017–18	Everton	0	0		
2017–18	*Nottingham F*	38	9		
2018–19	Everton	0	0	**2**	**0**
2018–19	Nottingham F	0	0	**38**	**9**
2018–19	*Sheffield U*	16	2	**16**	**2**

EDSER, Toby (M) **0** **0**
From Charlton Ath.

2016–17	Nottingham F	0	0		
2017–18	Nottingham F	0	0		
2018–19	Nottingham F	0	0		
2018–19	*Port Vale*	0	0		

GIL DIAS, Bastiao (M) **105** **14**
H: 6 0 W: 12 04 b.Gafanha da Nazare 28-9-96
Internationals: Portugal U18, U19, U20, U21.

2014–15	Braga	0	0		
2015–16	Monaco	0	0		
2015–16	*Varzim*	15	6	**15**	**6**
2016–17	Monaco	0	0		
2016–17	*Rio Ave*	34	6	**34**	**6**
2017–18	Monaco	1	0		
2017–18	*Fiorentina*	27	2	**27**	**2**
2018–19	Monaco	0	0	**1**	**0**

On loan from Monaco.

2018–19	Nottingham F	21	0	**21**	**0**
2018–19	*Olympiacos*	7	0	**7**	**0**

GOMIS, Virgil (F) **10** **0**
b. 16-4-99

2018–19	Nottingham F	0	0		
2018–19	*Notts Co*	10	0	**10**	**0**

GONCALVES, Diogo (M) **14** **0**
H: 5 10 W: 9 11 b.Almodovar 6-2-97
Internationals: Portugal U16, U17, U18, U19, U20, U21.

2014–15	Benfica	0	0		
2015–16	Benfica	0	0		
2016–17	Benfica	0	0		
2017–18	Benfica	7	0		
2018–19	Benfica	0	0	**7**	**0**

On loan from Benfica.

2018–19	Nottingham F	7	0	**7**	**0**

GRABBAN, Lewis (F) **387** **122**
H: 6 0 W: 11 03 b.Croydon 12-1-88

2005–06	Crystal Palace	0	0		
2006–07	Crystal Palace	8	1		
2006–07	*Oldham Ath*	9	0	**9**	**0**
2007–08	Crystal Palace	2	0	**10**	**1**
2007–08	*Motherwell*	6	0	**6**	**0**
2007–08	Millwall	13	3		
2008–09	Millwall	31	6		
2009–10	Millwall	11	0		
2009–10	*Brentford*	7	2		
2010–11	Millwall	1	0	**56**	**9**
2010–11	Brentford	22	5	**29**	**7**
2011–12	Rotherham U	43	18	**43**	**18**
2012–13	Bournemouth	42	13		
2013–14	Bournemouth	44	22		
2014–15	Norwich C	35	12		
2015–16	Norwich C	6	1	**41**	**13**
2015–16	Bournemouth	15	0		
2016–17	Bournemouth	3	0		
2016–17	*Reading*	16	3	**16**	**3**
2017–18	Bournemouth	0	0	**104**	**35**
2017–18	*Sunderland*	19	12	**19**	**12**
2017–18	*Aston Villa*	15	8	**15**	**8**
2018–19	Nottingham F	39	16	**39**	**16**

GUEDIOURA, Adiene (M) **294** **22**
H: 6 1 W: 12 08 b.La Roche-sur-Yon 12-11-85
Internationals: Algeria Full caps.

2004–05	Sedan	0	0		
2005–06	Noisy-Le-Sec	15	1	**15**	**1**
2006–07	L'Entente	21	3	**21**	**3**
2007–08	Creteil	24	6	**24**	**6**
2008–09	Kortrijk	10	0	**10**	**0**
2008–09	Charleroi	12	0		
2009–10	Charleroi	13	1	**25**	**1**
2009–10	Wolverhampton W	14	1		
2010–11	Wolverhampton W	10	1		
2011–12	Wolverhampton W	10	0	**34**	**2**
2011–12	*Nottingham F*	19	1		
2012–13	Nottingham F	35	3		
2013–14	Nottingham F	5	0		
2013–14	Crystal Palace	8	0		
2014–15	Crystal Palace	7	0		
2014–15	*Watford*	17	3		
2015–16	Crystal Palace	0	0	**15**	**0**
2015–16	Watford	18	0		
2016–17	Watford	12	0	**47**	**3**
2016–17	Middlesbrough	5	0		
2017–18	Middlesbrough	1	0	**6**	**0**
2017–18	Nottingham F	11	0		
2018–19	Nottingham F	27	2	**97**	**6**

HEFELE, Michael (D) **174** **14**
H: 6 4 W: 13 10 b.Pfaffenhofen 1-9-90

2010–11	Unterhaching	27	0		
2011–12	Unterhaching	6	1	**33**	**1**
2012–13	Greuther Furth	1	0		
2013–14	Greuther Furth	2	0	**3**	**0**
2013–14	*Wacker Burghausen*	15	0	**15**	**0**
2014–15	Dynamo Dresden	31	3		
2015–16	Dynamo Dresden	38	7	**69**	**10**
2016–17	Huddersfield T	37	3		
2017–18	Huddersfield T	2	0	**39**	**3**
2018–19	Nottingham F	15	0	**15**	**0**

HENDERSON, Stephen (G) **166** **0**
H: 6 3 W: 11 00 b.Dublin 2-5-88
Internationals: Republic of Ireland U16, U17, U19, U21.

2005–06	Aston Villa	0	0		
2006–07	Aston Villa	0	0		
2007–08	Bristol C	1	0		
2008–09	Bristol C	1	0		
2009–10	Bristol C	3	0		
2009–10	*Aldershot T*	8	0	**8**	**0**
2010–11	Bristol C	0	0	**5**	**0**
2010–11	*Yeovil T*	33	0	**33**	**0**
2011–12	Portsmouth	25	0		
2011–12	*West Ham U*	0	0		
2012–13	West Ham U	0	0		
2012–13	*Ipswich T*	24	0	**24**	**0**
2013–14	West Ham U	0	0		
2013–14	*Bournemouth*	2	0	**2**	**0**
2014–15	Charlton Ath	31	0		
2015–16	Charlton Ath	22	0	**53**	**0**
2016–17	Nottingham F	12	0		
2017–18	Nottingham F	0	0		
2017–18	*Portsmouth*	1	0	**26**	**0**
2018–19	Nottingham F	0	0	**12**	**0**
2018–19	*Wycombe W*	3	0	**3**	**0**

JANKO, Saidy (D) **72** **2**
H: 5 10 W: 11 00 b.Zurich 22-10-95
Internationals: Switzerland U18, U19, U20, U21.

2014–15	Manchester U	0	0		
2014–15	*Bolton W*	10	1	**10**	**1**
2015–16	Celtic	10	0		
2016–17	Celtic	2	0	**12**	**0**
2016–17	*Barnsley*	14	1	**14**	**1**
2017–18	St Etienne	21	0	**21**	**0**
2018–19	Porto	0	0		

On loan from Porto.

2018–19	Nottingham F	15	0	**15**	**0**

JOAO CARVALHO, Antonio (M) **60** **5**
H: 5 8 W: 10 06 b.Castanheira de Pera 9-3-97
Internationals: Portugal U16, U17, U18, U19, U20, U21.

2014–15	Benfica	0	0		
2015–16	Benfica	0	0		
2016–17	Benfica	0	0		
2016–17	*Vitoria Setubal*	15	1	**15**	**1**
2017–18	Benfica	7	0	**7**	**0**
2018–19	Nottingham F	38	4	**38**	**4**

LOLLEY, Joe (F) **148** **23**
H: 5 10 W: 11 05 b.Redditch 25-8-92
Internationals: England C.

2013–14	Huddersfield T	6	1		
2014–15	Huddersfield T	17	2		
2015–16	Huddersfield T	32	4		
2015–16	*Scunthorpe U*	6	0	**6**	**0**
2016–17	Huddersfield T	19	1		
2017–18	Huddersfield T	6	1	**80**	**9**
2017–18	Nottingham F	16	3		
2018–19	Nottingham F	46	11	**62**	**14**

MILOSEVIC, Alexander (D) **178** **15**
H: 6 3 W: 12 13 b.Sundbyburg 30-1-92
Internationals: Serbia U17. Sweden U19, U21, U23, Full caps.

2010	Vasalunds IF	24	5	**24**	**5**
2011	Allsvenskan	29	0		
2012	Allsvenskan	6	1		
2013	Allsvenskan	18	5		
2014	Allsvenskan	27	3	**80**	**9**
2014–15	Besiktas	1	0		
2015–16	Besiktas	1	0		
2015–16	*Hannover 96*	10	0	**10**	**0**
2016–17	Besiktas	0	0		
2016–17	*Darmstadt 98*	18	0	**18**	**0**
2017–18	Besiktas	0	0	**2**	**0**
2017–18	Caykur Rizespor	5	0	**5**	**0**
2018	AIK	27	0	**27**	**0**
2018–19	Nottingham F	12	1	**12**	**1**

MURPHY, Daryl (F) **420** **100**
H: 6 2 W: 13 12 b.Waterford 15-3-83
Internationals: Republic of Ireland U21, Full caps.

2000–01	Luton T	0	0		
2001–02	Luton T	0	0		
2005–06	Sunderland	18	1		
2005–06	*Sheffield W*	4	0	**4**	**0**
2006–07	Sunderland	38	10		
2007–08	Sunderland	28	3		
2008–09	Sunderland	23	0		
2009–10	Sunderland	3	0	**110**	**14**
2009–10	*Ipswich T*	18	6		
2010–11	Celtic	18	3		
2011–12	Ipswich T	33	4		
2012–13	Celtic	1	0	**19**	**3**
2012–13	*Ipswich T*	39	7		
2013–14	Ipswich T	45	13		
2014–15	Ipswich T	44	27		
2015–16	Ipswich T	34	10		
2016–17	Ipswich T	4	0	**217**	**67**
2016–17	Newcastle U	15	5	**15**	**5**
2017–18	Nottingham F	27	7		
2018–19	Nottingham F	28	4	**55**	**11**

OSBORN, Ben (D) **212** **15**
H: 5 9 W: 11 11 b.Derby 5-8-94
Internationals: England U18, U19, U20.

2011–12	Nottingham F	0	0		
2012–13	Nottingham F	0	0		
2013–14	Nottingham F	8	0		
2014–15	Nottingham F	37	3		
2015–16	Nottingham F	36	3		
2016–17	Nottingham F	46	4		
2017–18	Nottingham F	46	4		
2018–19	Nottingham F	39	1	**212**	**15**

PANTILIMON, Costel (G) **219** **0**
H: 6 5 W: 15 02 b.Bacau 1-2-87
Internationals: Romania U17, U19, U21, Full caps.

2005–06	Aerostar Bacau	9	0	**9**	**0**
2006–07	Poli Timisoara	8	0		
2007–08	Poli Timisoara	5	0	**13**	**0**
2008–09	Timisoara	31	0		
2009–10	Timisoara	21	0		
2010–11	Timisoara	28	0	**80**	**0**
2011–12	*Manchester C*	0	0		
2012–13	Manchester C	0	0		
2013–14	Manchester C	7	0	**7**	**0**
2014–15	Sunderland	28	0		
2015–16	Sunderland	17	0	**45**	**0**
2015–16	Watford	0	0		
2016–17	Watford	2	0		
2017–18	Watford	0	0	**2**	**0**
2017–18	*Deportivo La Coruna*	6	0	**6**	**0**
2017–18	*Nottingham F*	13	0		
2018–19	Nottingham F	44	0	**57**	**0**

PELE, Judilson (M) **158** **17**
H: 5 10 W: 11 09 b.Agualva-Cacem 29-9-91
Internationals: Portugal U18, U19, U20, U21. Guinea-Bissau Full caps.

2008–09	Belenenses	3	0		

2009–10	Belenenses	13	0		
2010–11	Belenenses	16	0		
2010–11	Genoa	0	0		
2011–12	AC Milan	0	0		
2012–13	AC Milan	0	0		
2012–13	*Arsenal Kyiv*	5	0	**5**	**0**
2013–14	AC Milan	0	0		
2013–14	*Olhanense*	13	0	**13**	**0**
2014–15	AC Milan	0	0		
2014–15	*Belenenses*	30	6	**62**	**6**
2015–16	Benfica	0	0		
2015–16	*Pacos Ferreira*	29	4	**29**	**4**
2016–17	Benfica	0	0		
2016–17	*Feirense*	1	0	**1**	**0**
2017–18	Rio Ave	31	7	**31**	**7**
2018–19	Monaco	8	0	**8**	**0**

On loan from Monaco.

2018–19	Nottingham F	9	0	**9**	**0**

ROBINSON, Jack (D) 155 4

H: 5 11 W: 10 08 b.Warrington 1-9-93

Internationals: England U16, U17, U18, U19, U21.

2009–10	Liverpool	1	0		
2010–11	Liverpool	2	0		
2011–12	Liverpool	0	0		
2012–13	Liverpool	0	0		
2012–13	*Wolverhampton W*	11	0	**11**	**0**
2013–14	Liverpool	0	0	**3**	**0**
2013–14	*Blackpool*	34	0	**34**	**0**
2014–15	QPR	0	0		
2014–15	*Huddersfield T*	30	0	**30**	**0**
2015–16	QPR	1	0		
2016–17	QPR	7	0		
2017–18	QPR	31	2	**39**	**2**
2018–19	Nottingham F	38	2	**38**	**2**

SOUDANI, El Arabi (F) 291 133

H: 5 10 W: 11 11 b.Chlef 25-11-87

Internationals: Algeria Full caps.

2005–06	ASO Chief	1	0		
2006–07	ASO Chief	15	3		
2007–08	ASO Chief	26	11		
2008–09	ASO Chief	22	4		
2009–10	ASO Chief	27	12		
2010–11	ASO Chief	25	19	**116**	**49**
2011–12	Vitoria de Guimaraes	16	4		
2012–13	Vitoria de Guimaraes	21	9	**37**	**13**
2013–14	Dinamo Zagreb	31	16		
2014–15	Dinamo Zagreb	23	11		
2015–16	Dinamo Zagreb	21	8		
2016–17	Dinamo Zagreb	29	17		
2017–18	Dinamo Zagreb	28	17	**132**	**69**
2018–19	Nottingham F	6	2	**6**	**2**

STEELE, Luke (G) 322 0

H: 6 2 W: 12 00 b.Peterborough 24-9-84

Internationals: England U18, U19, U20.

2001–02	Peterborough U	2	0	**2**	**0**
2001–02	Manchester U	0	0		
2002–03	Manchester U	0	0		
2003–04	Manchester U	0	0		
2004–05	Manchester U	0	0		
2004–05	*Coventry C*	32	0		
2005–06	Manchester U	0	0		
2006–07	WBA	0	0		
2006–07	*Coventry C*	5	0	**37**	**0**
2007–08	WBA	2	0	**2**	**0**
2007–08	*Barnsley*	14	0		
2008–09	Barnsley	10	0		
2009–10	Barnsley	39	0		
2010–11	Barnsley	46	0		
2011–12	Barnsley	36	0		
2012–13	Barnsley	33	0		
2013–14	Barnsley	31	0	**209**	**0**
2014–15	Panathinaikos	29	0		
2015–16	Panathinaikos	28	0		
2016–17	Panathinaikos	8	0		
2017–18	Panathinaikos	0	0	**65**	**0**
2017–18	Bristol C	5	0	**5**	**0**
2018–19	Nottingham F	2	0	**2**	**0**

TACHTSIDIS, Panagiotis (M) 226 11

H: 6 4 W: 13 08 b.Nafplio 15-2-91

Internationals: Greece U17, U19, U21, Full caps.

2007–08	AEK Athens	2	0		
2008–09	AEK Athens	8	1		
2009–10	AEK Athens	9	1	**19**	**2**
2010–11	Genoa	0	0		
2010–11	*Cesena*	0	0		
2010–11	*Grosseto*	8	0	**8**	**0**
2011–12	Genoa	0	0		
2011–12	*Verona*	37	2		
2012–13	Roma	21	1	**21**	**1**
2013–14	Genoa	0	0		
2013–14	Catania	12	0	**12**	**0**
2013–14	*Torino*	11	1		
2014–15	Genoa	0	0		
2014–15	*Verona*	34	3	**71**	**5**
2015–16	Genoa	24	2	**24**	**2**
2016–17	Torino	0	0	**11**	**1**
2016–17	*Galgliari*	26	0	**26**	**0**
2017–18	Olympiacos	17	0	**17**	**0**
2018–19	Nottingham F	0	0		
2018–19	*Lecce*	17	0	**17**	**0**

TOBIAS FIGUEIREDO, Pereira (D) 77 4

H: 6 2 W: 13 03 b.Satao 2-2-94

Internationals: Portugal U17, U18, U19, U20, U21, U23.

2012–13	Sporting Lisbon	0	0		
2013–14	Sporting Lisbon	0	0		
2013–14	*Reus*	13	1	**13**	**1**
2014–15	Sporting Lisbon	14	2		
2015–16	Sporting Lisbon	1	0		
2016–17	Sporting Lisbon	2	0		
2016–17	*Nacional*	22	1	**22**	**1**
2017–18	Sporting Lisbon	0	0		
2017–18	*Nottingham F*	12	0		
2018–19	Sporting Lisbon	0	0	**17**	**2**

On loan from Sporting Lisbon.

2018–19	Nottingham F	13	0	**25**	**0**

WAGUE, Molla (D) 104 10

H: 6 3 W: 13 10 b.Verdon 21-2-91

Internationals: France U19. Mali Full caps.

2011–12	Caen	5	1		
2012–13	Caen	20	2		
2013–14	Caen	24	1	**49**	**4**
2014–15	Granada	0	0		
2014–15	*Udinese*	10	2		
2015–16	Granada	0	0		
2015–16	*Udinese*	21	0		
2016–17	Grananda	0	0		
2016–17	*Udinese*	6	0		
2016–17	*Leicester C*	0	0		
2017–18	Udinese	1	0		
2017–18	*Watford*	6	1	**6**	**1**
2018–19	Udinese	0	0	**38**	**2**

On loan from Udinese.

2018–19	Nottingham F	11	3	**11**	**3**

WARD, Jamie (M) 390 90

H: 5 5 W: 9 04 b.Birmingham 12-5-86

Internationals: Northern Ireland U18, U21, Full caps.

2003–04	Aston Villa	0	0		
2004–05	Aston Villa	0	0		
2005–06	Aston Villa	0	0		
2005–06	*Stockport Co*	9	1	**9**	**1**
2006–07	Torquay U	25	9	**25**	**9**
2006–07	Chesterfield	9	3		
2007–08	Chesterfield	35	12		
2008–09	Chesterfield	23	14	**67**	**29**
2008–09	Sheffield U	16	2		
2009–10	Sheffield U	28	7		
2010–11	Sheffield U	19	0	**63**	**9**
2010–11	Derby Co	13	5		
2011–12	Derby Co	37	4		
2012–13	Derby Co	25	12		
2013–14	Derby Co	38	7		
2014–15	Derby Co	25	6	**138**	**34**
2015–16	Nottingham F	31	2		
2016–17	Nottingham F	18	1		
2016–17	*Burton Alb*	18	4	**18**	**4**
2017–18	Nottingham F	8	0		
2017–18	*Cardiff C*	4	0	**4**	**0**
2018–19	Nottingham F	0	0	**57**	**3**
2018–19	*Charlton Ath*	9	1	**9**	**1**

WATSON, Ben (M) 401 36

H: 5 10 W: 10 11 b.Camberwell 9-7-85

Internationals: England U21.

2002–03	Crystal Palace	5	0		
2003–04	Crystal Palace	16	1		
2004–05	Crystal Palace	21	0		
2005–06	Crystal Palace	42	4		
2006–07	Crystal Palace	25	3		
2007–08	Crystal Palace	42	5		
2008–09	Crystal Palace	18	5	**169**	**18**
2008–09	Wigan Ath	10	2		
2009–10	Wigan Ath	5	1		
2009–10	*QPR*	16	2	**16**	**2**
2009–10	*WBA*	7	1	**7**	**1**
2010–11	Wigan Ath	29	3		
2011–12	Wigan Ath	21	3		
2012–13	Wigan Ath	12	1		
2013–14	Wigan Ath	25	2		
2014–15	Wigan Ath	9	1	**111**	**13**
2014–15	Watford	20	0		
2015–16	Watford	35	2		
2016–17	Watford	4	0		
2017–18	Watford	8	0	**67**	**2**
2017–18	Nottingham F	14	0		
2018–19	Nottingham F	17	0	**31**	**0**

YACOB, Claudio (M) 301 5

H: 5 11 W: 11 06 b.Carcarana 18-7-87

Internationals: Argentina U20, Full caps.

2006–07	Racing Club	12	0		
2007–08	Racing Club	24	0		
2008–09	Racing Club	25	1		
2009–10	Racing Club	26	0		
2010–11	Racing Club	21	2		
2011–12	Racing Club	17	1	**125**	**4**
2012–13	WBA	30	0		
2013–14	WBA	27	1		
2014–15	WBA	20	0		
2015–16	WBA	34	0		
2016–17	WBA	33	0		
2017–18	WBA	16	0		
2018–19	WBA	0	0	**160**	**1**
2018–19	Nottingham F	16	0	**16**	**0**

YATES, Ryan (M) 69 6

b.Nottingham 21-11-97

2016–17	Nottingham F	0	0		
2016–17	*Shrewsbury T*	12	0	**12**	**0**
2017–18	Nottingham F	0	0		
2017–18	*Notts Co*	25	3	**25**	**3**
2017–18	*Scunthorpe U*	16	2	**16**	**2**
2018–19	Nottingham F	16	1	**16**	**1**

Players retained or with offer of contract

Ansari, Fard Karim; Antunes, Carvalho Joao Antonio; Ariyibi, Omogbolahan Gregory; Asare, Keith; Cummings, Jason Steven; Dekel, Daks Ethan; En-Neyah, Yassine; Fornah, Tyrese Momodu; Gallacher, Owen John; Grant, Jorge Edward; Harbottle, Riley-Jay; Hayes, Kieran; Johnson, Brennan Price; Lawrence-Gabriel, Jordan Jay; Pereira, Figueiredo Tobias; Preston, Daniel James; Richardson, Jayden De'Chante; Shelvey, George William; Sjostrom, Milosevic Goran Alexander; Smith, Jordan Clifford; Sodeinde, Victor Adeoluwa; Stewart, Ethan; Taylor, Jake Jon; Vellios, Apostolos; Walker, Tyler J Andrew; Worrall, Joseph Adrian; Wright, Jordan Ian.

Scholars

Ajuchi, Ogunseri Gabriel Onoriode; Andrew, Elliott Nicholas; Barnes, Joshua William; Greenwood, Samuel; Liburd-Hines, Nykah Jarone; Mighten, Alexander Cole; Mutoti, Tawanda Fortune; Ram, Max Benjamin; Sanders, Samuel John; Spooner, Malique Tyrese; Statham, Michael Joseph; Swan, William Jonathan.

NOTTS CO (60)

ALESSANDRA, Lewis (F) 365 54

H: 5 9 W: 11 07 b.Heywood 8-2-89

2007–08	Oldham Ath	15	2		
2008–09	Oldham Ath	32	5		
2009–10	Oldham Ath	1	0		
2010–11	Oldham Ath	19	1	**67**	**8**
2011–12	Morecambe	42	4		
2012–13	Morecambe	40	3	**82**	**7**
2013–14	Plymouth Arg	42	7		
2014–15	Plymouth Arg	44	11	**86**	**18**
2015–16	Rochdale	8	1	**8**	**1**
2015–16	*York C*	11	2	**11**	**2**
2016–17	Hartlepool U	46	9	**46**	**9**
2017–18	Notts Co	39	7		
2018–19	Notts Co	26	2	**65**	**9**

BIRD, Pierce (D) 13 0

H: 6 2 W: 14 00 b. 16-4-99

Internationals: Northern Ireland U21.

From Dunkirk.

2017–18	Notts Co	1	0		
2018–19	Notts Co	12	0	**13**	**0**

BOLDEWIJN, Enzio (F) 262 37

H: 6 1 W: 12 06 b.Almere 17-11-92

2010–11	Utrecht	0	0		
2011–12	Utrecht	11	0	**11**	**0**
2012–13	Den Bosch	31	1	**31**	**1**
2013–14	Almere City	27	2		
2014–15	Almere City	31	7		
2015–16	Almere City	35	7	**93**	**16**
2015–16	Crawley T	0	0		
2016–17	Crawley T	46	5		
2017–18	Crawley T	45	10	**91**	**15**
2018–19	Notts Co	36	5	**36**	**5**

BRISLEY, Shaun (M) 319 13
H: 6 2 W: 12 02 b.Macclesfield 6-5-90
2007–08 Macclesfield T 10 2
2008–09 Macclesfield T 38 0
2009–10 Macclesfield T 33 1
2010–11 Macclesfield T 14 0
2011–12 Macclesfield T 29 3 **124 6**
2011–12 Peterborough U 11 0
2012–13 Peterborough U 28 0
2013–14 Peterborough U 22 0
2014–15 Peterborough U 15 1
2014–15 *Scunthorpe U* 7 0 **7 0**
2015–16 Peterborough U 2 0 **78 1**
2015–16 *Northampton T* 9 1 **9 1**
2015–16 *Leyton Orient* 16 1 **16 1**
2016–17 Carlisle U 28 2 **28 2**
2017–18 Notts Co 37 2
2018–19 Notts Co 20 0 **57 2**

CAMPBELL, Remaye (F) 0 0
2018–19 Notts Co 0 0

CRAWFORD, Tom (M) 4 0
b.Chester 30-5-99
Internationals: England C.
2018–19 Notts Co 4 0 **4 0**

CULVERWELL, Max (G) 0 0
2018–19 Notts Co 0 0

DENNIS, Kristian (F) 119 32
H: 5 11 W: 11 00 b.Macclesfield 12-3-90
2007–08 Macclesfield T 1 0
2008–09 Macclesfield T 3 1
2009–10 Macclesfield T 0 0 **4 1**
From Woodley Sports, Mossley, Curzon Ashton, Stockport Co.
2015–16 Chesterfield 0 0
2016–17 Chesterfield 35 8
2017–18 Chesterfield 43 19 **78 27**
2018–19 Notts Co 24 3 **24 3**
2018–19 *Grimsby T* 13 1 **13 1**

DOYLE, Micky (M) 669 36
H: 5 10 W: 11 00 b.Dublin 8-7-81
Internationals: Republic of Ireland U21, Full caps.
2003–04 Coventry C 40 5
2004–05 Coventry C 44 2
2005–06 Coventry C 44 0
2006–07 Coventry C 40 3
2007–08 Coventry C 42 7
2008–09 Coventry C 37 2
2009–10 Coventry C 0 0
2009–10 *Leeds U* 42 0 **42 0**
2010–11 Coventry C 18 1
2010–11 Sheffield U 16 0
2011–12 Sheffield U 43 3
2012–13 Sheffield U 43 3
2013–14 Sheffield U 43 2
2014–15 Sheffield U 43 1 **188 9**
2015–16 Portsmouth 44 2
2016–17 Portsmouth 46 1 **90 3**
2017–18 Coventry C 44 3
2018–19 Coventry C 23 1 **332 24**
2018–19 Notts Co 17 0 **17 0**

DUFFY, Richard (D) 462 13
H: 5 9 W: 10 03 b.Swansea 30-8-85
Internationals: Wales U17, U19, U21, Full caps.
2002–03 Swansea C 0 0
2003–04 Swansea C 18 1
2003–04 Portsmouth 1 0
2004–05 Portsmouth 0 0
2004–05 *Burnley* 7 1 **7 1**
2004–05 *Coventry C* 14 0
2005–06 Portsmouth 0 0
2005–06 *Coventry C* 32 0
2006–07 Portsmouth 0 0
2006–07 *Coventry C* 13 0
2006–07 *Swansea C* 11 0 **29 1**
2007–08 Portsmouth 0 0
2007–08 *Coventry C* 2 0 **61 0**
2008–09 Portsmouth 0 0 **1 0**
2008–09 Millwall 12 0 **12 0**
2009–10 Exeter C 42 1
2010–11 Exeter C 42 2
2011–12 Exeter C 28 0 **112 3**
2012–13 Port Vale 36 0
2013–14 Port Vale 28 0
2014–15 Port Vale 27 1
2015–16 Port Vale 45 0 **136 1**
2016–17 Notts Co 42 4
2017–18 Notts Co 43 2
2018–19 Notts Co 19 1 **104 7**

DUNNE, Declan (G) 0 0
b. 31-3-00
Internationals: Northern Ireland U19.
2018–19 Notts Co 0 0

ETETE, Kion (F) 4 0
b. 28-11-01
2018–19 Notts Co 4 0 **4 0**

EVINA, Cedric (D) 178 3
H: 5 11 W: 12 08 b.Cameroon 16-11-91
2009–10 Arsenal 0 0
2010–11 Arsenal 0 0
2010–11 Oldham Ath 27 2 **27 2**
2011–12 Charlton Ath 3 0
2012–13 Charlton Ath 12 0
2013–14 Charlton Ath 8 0 **23 0**
2014–15 Doncaster R 19 0
2015–16 Doncaster R 42 1
2016–17 Doncaster R 16 0
2017–18 Doncaster R 0 0 **77 1**
2017–18 *Crawley T* 34 0 **34 0**
2018–19 Notts Co 17 0 **17 0**

FITZSIMONS, Ross (G) 46 0
H: 6 1 W: 11 10 b.Hammersmith 28-5-94
2012–13 Crystal Palace 0 0
2013–14 Crystal Palace 0 0
2014–15 Bolton W 0 0
2015–16 Bolton W 0 0
From Bishop's Stortford, Braintree T, Chelmsford C.
2017–18 Notts Co 17 0
2018–19 Notts Co 29 0 **46 0**

HAWKRIDGE, Terry (M) 96 4
H: 5 9 W: 11 00 b.Nottingham 23-2-90
2013–14 Scunthorpe U 45 1
2014–15 Scunthorpe U 11 0
2014–15 *Mansfield T* 5 0 **5 0**
2015–16 Scunthorpe U 0 0 **56 1**
2015–16 Lincoln C 0 0
2017–18 Notts Co 31 3
2018–19 Notts Co 4 0 **35 3**

HEMMINGS, Kane (F) 177 59
b.Burton 8-4-92
2011–12 Rangers 4 0 **4 0**
From Cowdenbeath.
2014–15 Barnsley 23 3 **23 3**
2015–16 Dundee 37 21 **37 21**
2016–17 Oxford U 40 6
2017–18 Oxford U 0 0 **40 6**
2017–18 *Mansfield T* 37 15 **37 15**
2018–19 Notts Co 36 14 **36 14**

HEWITT, Elliott (D) 212 9
H: 5 11 W: 11 10 b.Rhyl 30-5-94
Internationals: Wales U17, U21.
2010–11 Macclesfield T 1 0
2011–12 Macclesfield T 21 0 **22 0**
2012–13 Ipswich T 7 0
2013–14 Ipswich T 4 0
2013–14 *Gillingham* 20 0 **20 0**
2014–15 Ipswich T 3 0 **14 0**
2014–15 *Colchester U* 21 1 **21 1**
2015–16 Notts Co 38 0
2016–17 Notts Co 29 2
2017–18 Notts Co 43 4
2018–19 Notts Co 25 2 **135 8**

HOWES, Alex (M) 2 0
b. 6-1-00
2016–17 Notts Co 2 0
2017–18 Notts Co 0 0
2018–19 Notts Co 0 0 **2 0**

HUSIN, Noor (M) 37 2
H: 5 10 W: 10 03 b.Mazar-i-Sharif 3-3-97
Internationals: Afganistan Full caps.
2015–16 Reading 0 0
2016–17 Crystal Palace 0 0
2016–17 *Accrington S* 11 1 **11 1**
2017–18 Notts Co 12 1
2018–19 Notts Co 14 0 **26 1**

JONES, Daniel (D) 269 11
H: 6 2 W: 13 00 b.Rowley Regis 14-7-86
2005–06 Wolverhampton W 1 0
2006–07 Wolverhampton W 8 0
2007–08 Wolverhampton W 1 0
2007–08 *Northampton T* 33 3 **33 3**
2008–09 Wolverhampton W 0 0
2008–09 *Oldham Ath* 23 1 **23 1**
2009–10 Wolverhampton W 0 0 **10 0**
2009–10 *Notts Co* 7 0
2009–10 *Bristol R* 17 0 **17 0**
2010–11 Sheffield W 25 0
2011–12 Sheffield W 3 0
2012–13 Sheffield W 9 0 **37 0**
2012–13 Port Vale 16 1
2013–14 Port Vale 20 0 **36 1**
2014–15 Chesterfield 33 0
2015–16 Chesterfield 19 1
2016–17 Chesterfield 14 0 **66 1**
2017–18 Notts Co 27 4
2018–19 Notts Co 13 1 **47 5**

KELLETT, Andy (D) 77 8
H: 5 8 W: 12 06 b.Bolton 10-11-93
2012–13 Bolton W 0 0
2013–14 Bolton W 3 0
2014–15 Bolton W 1 0
2014–15 *Plymouth Arg* 12 1 **12 1**
2014–15 *Manchester U* 0 0
2015–16 Bolton W 0 0 **4 0**
2015–16 Wigan Ath 9 2
2016–17 Wigan Ath 5 0
2017–18 Wigan Ath 0 0 **14 2**
2017–18 *Chesterfield* 36 4 **36 4**
2018–19 Notts Co 11 1 **11 1**

KENNEDY-WILLIAMS, Tyreece (D) 0 0
2018–19 Notts Co 0 0

O'BRIEN, Jim (F) 378 23
H: 6 0 W: 11 11 b.Alexandria 28-9-87
Internationals: Republic of Ireland U19, U21.
2006–07 Celtic 0 0
2006–07 *Dunfermline Ath* 13 1 **13 1**
2007–08 Celtic 1 0 **1 0**
2007–08 *Dundee U* 10 0 **10 0**
2008–09 Motherwell 29 1
2009–10 Motherwell 35 3 **64 4**
2010–11 Barnsley 33 1
2011–12 Barnsley 31 2
2012–13 Barnsley 30 2
2013–14 Barnsley 29 2 **123 7**
2014–15 Coventry C 44 6
2015–16 Coventry C 26 2 **70 8**
2015–16 *Scunthorpe U* 9 1 **9 1**
2016–17 Shrewsbury T 18 0 **18 0**
2016–17 *Ross Co* 16 0
2017–18 Ross Co 25 0
2018–19 Ross Co 0 0 **41 0**
2018–19 Bradford C 11 0 **11 0**
2018–19 Notts Co 18 2 **18 2**

OSBOURNE, Sam (F) 5 0
b. 10-1-99
From Dunkirk.
2016–17 Notts Co 3 0
2017–18 Notts Co 0 0
2018–19 Notts Co 2 0 **5 0**

OXLADE-CHAMBERLAIN, Christian (D) 2 0
b. 24-6-98
2015–16 Portsmouth 0 0
2016–17 Portsmouth 0 0
2017–18 Portsmouth 0 0
2018–19 Notts Co 2 0 **2 0**

PATCHING, William (M) 6 0
H: 6 1 W: 11 00 b.Manchester 18-10-98
From Manchester C.
2018–19 Notts Co 6 0 **6 0**

PINDROCH, Branislav (G) 83 0
b. 30-10-91
2010–11 Dukla 9 0
2011–12 Dukla 0 0 **9 0**
2012–13 Karvina 1 0
2013–14 Karvina 26 0
2014–15 Karvina 17 0
2015–16 Karvina 28 0
2016–17 Karvina 1 0 **73 0**
2017–18 Notts Co 1 0
2018–19 Notts Co 0 0 **1 0**

ROSE, Mitchell (M) 145 16
H: 5 9 W: 12 03 b.Doncaster 4-7-94
2012–13 Rotherham U 5 0
2013–14 Rotherham U 0 0
2014–15 Rotherham U 0 0 **5 0**
2014–15 *Crawley T* 1 0 **1 0**
2015–16 Mansfield T 34 2
2016–17 Mansfield T 18 2 **52 4**
2016–17 Newport Co 12 0 **12 0**
2016–17 Grimsby T 0 0
2017–18 Grimsby T 33 8
2018–19 Grimsby T 25 3 **58 11**
2018–19 Notts Co 17 1 **17 1**

STEAD, Jon (F) 580 135
H: 6 3 W: 13 03 b.Huddersfield 7-4-83
Internationals: England U21.
2001–02 Huddersfield T 0 0

2002–03	Huddersfield T	42	6		
2003–04	Huddersfield T	26	16		
2003–04	Blackburn R	13	6		
2004–05	Blackburn R	29	2	**42**	**8**
2005–06	Sunderland	30	1		
2006–07	Sunderland	5	1	**35**	**2**
2006–07	*Derby Co*	17	3	**17**	**3**
2006–07	Sheffield U	14	5		
2007–08	Sheffield U	24	3		
2008–09	Sheffield U	1	0	**39**	**8**
2008–09	Ipswich T	39	12		
2009–10	Ipswich T	22	6		
2009–10	*Coventry C*	10	2	**10**	**2**
2010–11	Ipswich T	3	1	**64**	**19**
2010–11	Bristol C	27	9		
2011–12	Bristol C	24	6		
2012–13	Bristol C	28	5	**79**	**20**
2013–14	Huddersfield T	12	1		
2013–14	*Oldham Ath*	5	0	**5**	**0**
2013–14	*Bradford C*	8	1		
2014–15	Huddersfield T	7	1	**87**	**24**
2014–15	*Bradford C*	32	6	**40**	**7**
2015–16	Notts Co	43	11		
2016–17	Notts Co	38	14		
2017–18	Notts Co	43	9		
2018–19	Notts Co	38	8	**162**	**42**

TOOTLE, Matt (D) **308** **6**
H: 5 9 W: 11 00 b.Widnes 11-10-90

2009–10	Crewe Alex	28	1		
2010–11	Crewe Alex	39	0		
2011–12	Crewe Alex	37	0		
2012–13	Crewe Alex	37	1		
2013–14	Crewe Alex	43	0		
2014–15	Crewe Alex	15	0	**199**	**2**
2015–16	Shrewsbury T	16	0	**16**	**0**
2016–17	Notts Co	33	2		
2017–18	Notts Co	36	2		
2018–19	Notts Co	24	0	**93**	**4**

TURLEY, Jamie (D) **24** **1**
H: 6 1 W: 12 13 b.Reading 7-4-90
Internationals: England C.

2014–15	Swindon T	0	0		
2015–16	Newport Co	0	0		
2016–17	Newport Co	6	1	**6**	**1**
2018–19	Notts Co	18	0	**18**	**0**

VAUGHAN, David (M) **474** **27**
H: 5 7 W: 11 00 b.Abergele 18-2-83
Internationals: Wales U19, U21, Full caps.

2000–01	Crewe Alex	1	0		
2001–02	Crewe Alex	13	0		
2002–03	Crewe Alex	32	3		
2003–04	Crewe Alex	31	0		
2004–05	Crewe Alex	44	6		
2005–06	Crewe Alex	34	5		
2006–07	Crewe Alex	29	4		
2007–08	Crewe Alex	1	0	**185**	**18**
2007–08	Real Sociedad	7	1	**7**	**1**
2008–09	Blackpool	33	1		
2009–10	Blackpool	41	1		
2010–11	Blackpool	35	2	**109**	**4**
2011–12	Sunderland	22	2		
2012–13	Sunderland	24	1		
2013–14	Sunderland	3	0	**49**	**3**
2013–14	*Nottingham F*	9	0		
2014–15	Nottingham F	13	0		
2015–16	Nottingham F	35	1		
2016–17	Nottingham F	31	0		
2017–18	Nottingham F	14	0	**102**	**1**
2018–19	Notts Co	22	0	**22**	**0**

WARD, Elliot (D) **328** **22**
H: 6 2 W: 13 00 b.Harrow 19-1-85

2001–02	West Ham U	0	0		
2002–03	West Ham U	0	0		
2003–04	West Ham U	0	0		
2004–05	West Ham U	11	0		
2004–05	*Bristol R*	3	0	**3**	**0**
2005–06	West Ham U	4	0	**15**	**0**
2005–06	*Plymouth Arg*	16	1	**16**	**1**
2006–07	Coventry C	39	3		
2007–08	Coventry C	37	6		
2008–09	Coventry C	33	5		
2009–10	Coventry C	8	0	**117**	**14**
2009–10	*Doncaster R*	6	1	**6**	**1**
2009–10	*Preston NE*	4	0	**4**	**0**
2010–11	Norwich C	39	1		
2011–12	Norwich C	12	0		
2012–13	Norwich C	0	0	**51**	**1**
2012–13	*Nottingham F*	31	3	**31**	**3**
2013–14	Bournemouth	23	0		
2014–15	Bournemouth	2	0		
2015–16	Bournemouth	0	0	**25**	**0**
2015–16	*Huddersfield T*	5	0	**5**	**0**
2015–16	Blackburn R	7	1		
2016–17	Blackburn R	6	0		
2017–18	Blackburn R	10	0	**23**	**1**
2017–18	*Milton Keynes D*	15	0	**15**	**0**
2018–19	Notts Co	17	1	**17**	**1**

Players retained or with offer of contract
Dunn, Declan Nicholas; Osborne, Samuel Paul.

Scholars
Altaf, Rasharn Christopher; Betts, Owen Adam; Brooks, Tiernan Jon; Bucalossi, Corey Michael Troy; Bugg, Harry Joseph; Culverwell, Max Edward; Cummings, Kieran Robert; Duncan, Coden; Kennedy-Williams, Tyreece; Marshall, Leo Thomas; Newell, Owen Jay; Ramirez, Inscoe Oscar; Simmons, Mazhi Dereiko Devonne; Wilde, Charlie David Nicholas.

OLDHAM ATH (61)

BAXTER, Jose (F) **186** **42**
H: 5 10 W: 11 07 b.Bootle 7-2-92
Internationals: England U16, U17.

2008–09	Everton	3	0		
2009–10	Everton	2	0		
2010–11	Everton	1	0		
2011–12	Everton	1	0		
2011–12	*Tranmere R*	14	3	**14**	**3**
2012–13	Everton	0	0		
2012–13	Crystal Palace	0	0		
2012–13	Oldham Ath	39	13		
2013–14	Oldham Ath	4	2		
2013–14	Sheffield U	35	6		
2014–15	Sheffield U	34	10		
2015–16	Sheffield U	24	4	**93**	**20**
2016–17	Everton	0	0		
2017–18	Everton	0	0	**7**	**0**
2018–19	Oldham Ath	29	4	**72**	**19**

BENTEKE, Jonathan (F) **52** **5**
b. 28-4-95
From Standard Liege.

2013–14	Vise	20	2	**20**	**2**
2014–15	Zulte-Waregem	6	2		
2015–16	Zulte-Waregem	15	0		
2016–17	Zulte-Waregem	0	0	**21**	**2**
2016–17	Crystal Palace	1	0	**1**	**0**
2017–18	Oldham Ath	1	0		
2018–19	Oldham Ath	9	1	**10**	**1**

BRANGER, Johan (M) **97** **28**
H: 6 0 W: 12 06 b.Sens 5-7-93
Internationals: Gabon Full caps.

2011–12	Auxerre	0	0		
2012–13	Auxerre	0	0		
2013–14	Auxerre	0	0		
2014–15	US Raon-l'Etape	20	8	**20**	**8**
2015–16	FC Sens	16	4		
2016–17	FC Sens	0	0	**16**	**4**
2017–18	FC Dieppe	26	11	**26**	**11**
2018–19	Oldham Ath	35	5	**35**	**5**

CLARKE, Peter (D) **654** **48**
H: 6 0 W: 12 00 b.Southport 3-1-82
Internationals: England U21.

1998–99	Everton	0	0		
1999–2000	Everton	0	0		
2000–01	Everton	1	0		
2001–02	Everton	7	0		
2002–03	Everton	0	0		
2002–03	*Blackpool*	16	3		
2002–03	*Port Vale*	13	1	**13**	**1**
2003–04	Everton	1	0		
2003–04	*Coventry C*	5	0	**5**	**0**
2004–05	Everton	0	0	**9**	**0**
2004–05	Blackpool	38	5		
2005–06	Blackpool	46	6		
2006–07	Southend U	38	2		
2007–08	Southend U	45	4		
2008–09	Southend U	43	4	**126**	**10**
2009–10	Huddersfield T	46	5		
2010–11	Huddersfield T	46	4		
2011–12	Huddersfield T	31	0		
2012–13	Huddersfield T	43	0		
2013–14	Huddersfield T	26	0	**192**	**9**
2014–15	Blackpool	39	2	**139**	**16**
2015–16	Bury	45	1		
2016–17	Oldham Ath	46	5		
2017–18	Oldham Ath	19	2		
2017–18	*Bury*	18	1	**63**	**2**
2018–19	Oldham Ath	42	3	**107**	**10**

COKE, Giles (M) **292** **26**
H: 6 0 W: 11 11 b.Westminster 3-6-86

2004–05	Mansfield T	9	0		
2005–06	Mansfield T	40	4		
2006–07	Mansfield T	21	1	**70**	**5**
2007–08	Northampton T	20	5		
2008–09	Northampton T	32	2	**52**	**7**
2009–10	Motherwell	32	2	**32**	**2**
2010–11	Sheffield W	27	4		
2011–12	Sheffield W	0	0		
2011–12	*Bury*	30	6	**30**	**6**
2012–13	Sheffield W	16	0		
2012–13	*Swindon T*	4	0	**4**	**0**
2013–14	Sheffield W	28	1		
2014–15	Sheffield W	13	1	**84**	**6**
2014–15	*Bolton W*	4	0	**4**	**0**
2015–16	Ipswich T	10	0	**10**	**0**
2017–18	Chesterfield	2	0	**2**	**0**
2018–19	Oldham Ath	4	0	**4**	**0**

DE LA PAZ, Zeus (G) **17** **0**
b. 11-3-95
Internationals: Curacao U20, Full caps.

2013–14	PSV Eindhoven	0	0		
2014–15	PSV Eindhoven	0	0		

From Nuneaton T.

2017	Cincinnati Dutch Lions	14	0	**14**	**0**
2017–18	Oldham Ath	0	0		
2018–19	Oldham Ath	3	0	**3**	**0**

DUMMIGAN, Cameron (D) **74** **3**
H: 5 11 W: 11 00 b.Lurgan 2-6-96
Internationals: Northern Ireland U17, U19, U21.

2013–14	Burnley	0	0		
2014–15	Burnley	0	0		
2015–16	Burnley	0	0		
2015–16	*Oldham Ath*	26	1		
2016–17	Oldham Ath	12	0		
2017–18	Oldham Ath	30	2		
2018–19	Oldham Ath	6	0	**74**	**3**

EDMUNDSON, Sam (D) **65** **3**
H: 6 1 W: 11 11 b.Timperley 15-8-97

2015–16	Oldham Ath	2	0		
2016–17	Oldham Ath	3	0		
2017–18	Oldham Ath	15	1		
2018–19	Oldham Ath	45	2	**65**	**3**

GARDNER, Dan (M) **172** **15**
H: 6 1 W: 12 05 b.Manchester 5-4-90

2009–10	Crewe Alex	2	0	**2**	**0**

From Droylsden, FC Halifax T

2013–14	Chesterfield	16	3		
2014–15	Chesterfield	17	1		
2014–15	*Tranmere R*	4	2	**4**	**2**
2015–16	Chesterfield	30	4		
2015–16	*Bury*	6	0	**6**	**0**
2016–17	Chesterfield	34	2	**97**	**10**
2017–18	Oldham Ath	43	1		
2018–19	Oldham Ath	20	2	**63**	**3**

HAYMER, Tom (D) **35** **3**
b. 16-11-99

2017–18	Oldham Ath	7	1		
2018–19	Oldham Ath	28	2	**35**	**3**

HUNT, Robert (M) **82** **1**
H: 5 7 W: 10 08 b.Dagenham 7-7-95

2013–14	Brighton & HA	0	0		
2014–15	Brighton & HA	0	0		
2015–16	Brighton & HA	0	0		
2016–17	Brighton & HA	1	0	**1**	**0**
2016–17	*Oldham Ath*	10	0		
2017–18	Oldham Ath	33	0		
2018–19	Oldham Ath	38	1	**81**	**1**

IACOVITTI, Alex (D) **33** **2**
b. 2-9-97
Internationals: Scotland U17, U19, U21.

2015–16	Nottingham F	0	0		
2016–17	Nottingham F	2	0		
2016–17	*Mansfield T*	8	0	**8**	**0**
2017–18	Nottingham F	0	0	**2**	**0**
2017–18	*Forest Green R*	14	1	**14**	**1**
2018–19	Oldham Ath	9	1	**9**	**1**

MAOUCHE, Mohamed (M) **97** **8**
b. 22-1-93

2010–11	Saint-Etienne	0	0		
2011–12	Servette	0	0		
2012–13	Servette	0	0		
2013–14	Servette	0	0		
2014–15	Lausanne Sport	16	1	**16**	**1**
2015–16	Tours	15	0		
2016–17	Tours	31	3		
2017–18	Tours	0	0	**46**	**3**
2017–18	Oldham Ath	1	0		
2018–19	Oldham Ath	34	4	**35**	**4**

McFARLANE, Ewan (G) 0 0

2018–19	Oldham Ath	0	0		

MISSILOU, Christopher (M) 112 12
H: 5 11 W: 11 00 b.Auxerre 18-7-92
Internationals: France U18. Congo Full caps.

2009–10	Auxerre	0	0		
2010–11	Auxerre	0	0		
2011–12	Auxerre	1	0		
2012–13	Auxerre	0	0	**1**	**0**
2013–14	Evry	11	1	**11**	**1**
2014–15	Stade Brestpos 29	1	0	**1**	**0**
2015–16	Montceau	12	0		
2016–17	Montceau	24	7	**36**	**7**
2017–18	Entente Sannois	6	0	**6**	**0**
2017–18	Le Puy Foot 43	15	3	**15**	**3**
2018–19	Oldham Ath	42	1	**42**	**1**

NEPOMUCENO, Gevaro (F) 210 16
H: 5 9 W: 10 08 b. 10-11-92
Internationals: Curacao Full caps.

2010–11	Den Bosch	2	0		
2011–12	Den Bosch	13	1	**15**	**1**
2012–13	Fortuna Sittard	17	2		
2013–14	Fortuna Sittard	38	5	**55**	**7**
2014–15	Petrolui Ploiesti	25	1		
2015–16	Petrolui Ploiesti	22	0	**47**	**1**
2015–16	Maritimo Funchal	7	0		
2016–17	Maritimo Funchal	5	0	**12**	**0**
2016–17	*Famalicao*	13	0	**13**	**0**
2017–18	Maritimo	0	0		
2017–18	Oldham Ath	26	1		
2018–19	Oldham Ath	42	6	**68**	**7**

NORMAN, Max (F) 0 0

2018–19	Oldham Ath	0	0		

NORRIS, Harry (D) 0 0

2018–19	Oldham Ath	0	0		

O'GRADY, Chris (F) 499 94
H: 6 3 W: 12 04 b.Nottingham 25-1-86

2002–03	Leicester C	1	0		
2003–04	Leicester C	0	0		
2004–05	Leicester C	0	0		
2004–05	*Notts Co*	9	0	**9**	**0**
2005–06	Leicester C	13	1		
2005–06	*Rushden & D*	22	4	**22**	**4**
2006–07	Leicester C	10	0	**24**	**1**
2006–07	Rotherham U	13	4		
2007–08	Rotherham U	38	9	**51**	**13**
2008–09	Oldham Ath	13	0		
2008–09	*Bury*	6	0	**6**	**0**
2008–09	*Bradford C*	2	0	**2**	**0**
2008–09	*Stockport Co*	18	2	**18**	**2**
2009–10	Rochdale	43	22		
2010–11	Rochdale	46	9		
2011–12	Rochdale	1	0	**90**	**31**
2011–12	Sheffield W	32	5		
2012–13	Sheffield W	21	4	**53**	**9**
2012–13	*Barnsley*	16	5		
2013–14	Barnsley	40	15	**56**	**20**
2014–15	Brighton & HA	28	1		
2014–15	*Sheffield U*	4	1	**4**	**1**
2015–16	Brighton & HA	3	0		
2015–16	*Nottingham F*	21	2	**21**	**2**
2016–17	Brighton & HA	0	0	**31**	**1**
2016–17	*Burton Alb*	26	1	**26**	**1**
2017–18	Chesterfield	35	2	**35**	**2**
2018–19	Oldham Ath	38	7	**51**	**7**

ROBINSON, Harry (M) 1 0
b. 26-9-00
Internationals: Northern Ireland U16, U19.
From Glenavon.

2018–19	Oldham Ath	1	0	**1**	**0**

SEFIL, Sonhy (D) 56 4
b. 16-6-94

2012–13	Sedan	0	0		
2013–14	Auxerre	0	0		
2014–15	Auxerre	6	0		
2015–16	Auxerre	15	3	**21**	**3**
2016–17	Asteras Tripolis	5	0	**5**	**0**
2017–18	Lyon Duchere	30	1	**30**	**1**
2018–19	Oldham Ath	0	0		

SHERIDAN, Jay (D) 0 0

2017–18	Oldham Ath	0	0		
2018–19	Oldham Ath	0	0		

STOTT, Jamie (D) 7 0
b. 22-12-97

2016–17	Oldham Ath	4	0		
2017–18	Oldham Ath	0	0		
2018–19	Oldham Ath	3	0	**7**	**0**

SWABY-NEAVIN, Javid (D) 1 0

2018–19	Oldham Ath	1	0	**1**	**0**

SYLLA, Mohamad (M) 15 0
b. 1-12-93
From Entente SSG.

2018–19	Oldham Ath	15	0	**15**	**0**

TAYLOR, Andy (D) 326 9
H: 5 11 W: 11 07 b.Blackburn 14-3-86
Internationals: England U16, U17, U18, U19, U20.

2004–05	Blackburn R	0	0		
2005–06	Blackburn R	0	0		
2005–06	*QPR*	3	0	**3**	**0**
2005–06	*Blackpool*	3	0		
2006–07	Blackburn R	0	0		
2006–07	*Crewe Alex*	4	0	**4**	**0**
2006–07	*Huddersfield T*	8	0	**8**	**0**
2007–08	Blackburn R	0	0		
2007–08	Tranmere R	30	2		
2008–09	Tranmere R	39	1	**69**	**3**
2009–10	Sheffield U	26	0		
2010–11	Sheffield U	9	0		
2011–12	Sheffield U	4	0		
2012–13	Sheffield U	0	0	**39**	**0**
2012–13	Nottingham F	0	0		
2012–13	Walsall	34	0		
2013–14	Walsall	33	1		
2014–15	Walsall	39	1		
2015–16	Walsall	34	2	**140**	**4**
2016–17	Blackpool	38	2		
2017–18	Blackpool	7	0	**48**	**2**
2018–19	Oldham Ath	15	0	**15**	**0**

UCHE, Chinedy (M) 1 0
b. 1-3-99

2017–18	Oldham Ath	0	0		
2018–19	Oldham Ath	1	0	**1**	**0**

VERA, Urko (F) 235 66
b. 14-5-87

2010–11	Lemona	18	13	**18**	**13**
2010–11	Athletic Club	5	1	**5**	**1**
2011–12	Hercules	33	11	**33**	**11**
2012–13	Ponferradina	14	2	**14**	**2**
2012–13	Alcorcon	9	1	**9**	**1**
2013–14	Eibar	31	5	**31**	**5**
2014–15	Mirandes	38	17		
2015	Jeonbuk Motors	6	0	**6**	**0**
2015–16	Osasuna	19	3	**19**	**3**
2016–17	Huesca	14	1	**14**	**1**
2016–17	Mirandes	16	5	**54**	**22**
2017–18	CFR Cluj	15	5		
2017–18	*Astra*	10	1	**10**	**1**
2018–19	CFR Cluj	2	0	**17**	**5**
2018–19	Oldham Ath	5	1	**5**	**1**

WILLIAMS, Jack (M) 0 0

2018–19	Oldham Ath	0	0		

Players retained or with offer of contract
Branger-Engone, Johan-Okeiths; Hamer, Thomas Philip.

Scholars
Allen, Ellis Frank Fabien; Amankwaa, Samuel Osei; Baldwin, Declan James; Gaskell, Reece; Grundy, Jack William; Hackett, Andrew James; Jones, Taylor Jay; Leech, Charley Jon; McKinney, Lewis Christopher Mark; Norman, Max John; Norris, Harry Robert; Pickford, Ryan Paul; Robinson, Harry David; Scholes-Beard, Ryan Stewart; Sheriff, Kelfala; Swaby-Neavin, Javid Reece; Wych, Kyle Craig.

OXFORD U (62)

BAPTISTE, Shandon (M) 9 0
b. 8-4-98
Internationals: Grenada Full caps.

2017–18	Oxford U	0	0		
2018–19	Oxford U	9	0	**9**	**0**

BRADBURY, Harvey (F) 1 0
b. 29-12-98

2016–17	Portsmouth	0	0		
2017–18	Watford	0	0		
2018–19	Watford	0	0		
2018–19	Oxford U	1	0	**1**	**0**

BRANNAGAN, Cameron (M) 69 3
H: 5 11 W: 11 03 b.Manchester 9-5-96
Internationals: England U18, U20.

2013–14	Liverpool	0	0		
2014–15	Liverpool	0	0		
2015–16	Liverpool	3	0		
2016–17	Liverpool	0	0		
2016–17	*Fleetwood T*	13	0	**13**	**0**
2017–18	Liverpool	0	0	**3**	**0**
2017–18	Oxford U	12	0		
2018–19	Oxford U	41	3	**53**	**3**

DAI, Wai-Tsun (M) 8 0
b. 24-7-99
From Reading.

2017–18	Bury	8	0	**8**	**0**
2018–19	Oxford U	0	0		

DICKIE, Rob (D) 91 4
H: 6 0 W: 11 09 b.Wokingham 3-3-96
Internationals: England U18, U19.

2015–16	Reading	1	0		
2016–17	Reading	0	0		
2016–17	*Cheltenham T*	20	2	**20**	**2**
2017–18	Reading	0	0	**1**	**0**
2017–18	*Lincoln C*	18	0	**18**	**0**
2017–18	Oxford U	15	1		
2018–19	Oxford U	37	1	**52**	**2**

EASTWOOD, Simon (G) 189 0
H: 6 2 W: 10 13 b.Huddersfield 26-6-89
Internationals: England U18, U19.

2005–06	Huddersfield T	0	0		
2006–07	Huddersfield T	0	0		
2007–08	Huddersfield T	0	0		
2008–09	Huddersfield T	1	0		
2009–10	Huddersfield T	0	0	**1**	**0**
2009–10	*Bradford C*	22	0	**22**	**0**
2012–13	Portsmouth	27	0	**27**	**0**
2013–14	Blackburn R	7	0		
2014–15	Blackburn R	6	0		
2015–16	Blackburn R	0	0	**13**	**0**
2016–17	Oxford U	46	0		
2017–18	Oxford U	46	0		
2018–19	Oxford U	34	0	**126**	**0**

HALL, Robert (F) 141 19
H: 6 2 W: 10 05 b.Aylesbury 20-10-93
Internationals: England U16, U17, U18, U19.

2010–11	West Ham U	0	0		
2011–12	West Ham U	3	0		
2011–12	*Oxford U*	13	5		
2011–12	*Milton Keynes D*	2	0		
2012–13	West Ham U	1	0	**4**	**0**
2012–13	*Birmingham C*	13	0	**13**	**0**
2012–13	*Bolton W*	1	0		
2013–14	Bolton W	22	1		
2014–15	Bolton W	9	0		
2014–15	*Milton Keynes D*	7	3		
2015–16	Bolton W	0	0	**32**	**1**
2015–16	*Milton Keynes D*	27	2	**36**	**5**
2016–17	Oxford U	26	6		
2017–18	Oxford U	13	2		
2018–19	Oxford U	4	0	**56**	**13**

HANSON, Jamie (F) 78 1
H: 6 3 W: 12 06 b.Burton-upon-Trent 10-11-95
Internationals: England U20.

2012–13	Derby Co	0	0		
2013–14	Derby Co	0	0		
2014–15	Derby Co	2	1		
2015–16	Derby Co	18	0		
2016–17	Derby Co	5	0		
2016–17	*Wigan Ath*	17	0	**17**	**0**
2017–18	Derby Co	6	0	**31**	**1**
2018–19	Oxford U	30	0	**30**	**0**

HARRIS, Max (G) 0 0
b.Gloucester 14-9-99

2018–19	Oxford U	0	0		

HEAP, Aaron (M) 0 0
b.Oxford 14-5-01
Internationals: Northern Ireland U19.

2018–19	Oxford U	0	0		

HENRY, James (M) 397 66
H: 6 1 W: 11 11 b.Reading 10-6-89
Internationals: Scotland U16, U19. England U18, U19.

2006–07	Reading	0	0		
2006–07	*Nottingham F*	1	0	**1**	**0**
2007–08	Reading	0	0		
2007–08	*Bournemouth*	11	4	**11**	**4**
2007–08	*Norwich C*	3	0	**3**	**0**
2008–09	Reading	7	0		
2008–09	*Millwall*	16	3		
2009–10	Reading	3	0	**10**	**0**
2009–10	*Millwall*	9	5		
2010–11	Millwall	42	5		
2011–12	Millwall	39	0		
2012–13	Millwall	35	5		
2013–14	Millwall	5	0	**146**	**18**
2013–14	Wolverhampton W	32	10		
2014–15	Wolverhampton W	37	5		

2015–16	Wolverhampton W	39	7		
2016–17	Wolverhampton W	2	0	**110**	**22**
2016–17	*Bolton W*	30	1	**30**	**1**
2017–18	Oxford U	42	10		
2018–19	Oxford U	44	11	**86**	**21**

HOPKINS, Albie (M) 0 0

2017–18	Oxford U	0	0		
2018–19	Oxford U	0	0		

JAMES, Owen (F) 1 0

b. 13-10-00

2017–18	Oxford U	1	0		
2018–19	Oxford U	0	0	**1**	**0**

JONES, Nico (D) 3 0

b. 3-2-02

2018–19	Oxford U	3	0	**3**	**0**

KASHI, Ahmed (M) 229 7

H: 5 10 W: 12 00 b.Aubervilliers 18-11-88

Internationals: Algeria Full caps.

2008–09	Chateauroux	21	2		
2009–10	Chateauroux	23	1		
2010–11	Chateauroux	17	1		
2011–12	Chateauroux	24	0	**85**	**4**
2012–13	Metz	25	0		
2013–14	Metz	33	0		
2014–15	Metz	19	1	**77**	**1**
2015–16	Charlton Ath	11	0		
2017–18	Charlton Ath	34	2	**45**	**2**
2018–19	Troyes	11	0	**11**	**0**

On loan from Troyes.

2018–19	Oxford U	11	0	**11**	**0**

LITTLE, Armani (M) 1 0

b. 5-4-97

From Southampton.

2018–19	Oxford U	1	0	**1**	**0**

LOFTHOUSE, Kyran (F) 0 0

b.Oxford 21-10-00

2018–19	Oxford U	0	0		

LONG, Sam (D) 36 1

H: 5 10 W: 11 11 b.Oxford 16-1-95

2012–13	Oxford U	1	0		
2013–14	Oxford U	3	0		
2014–15	Oxford U	10	1		
2015–16	Oxford U	1	0		
2016–17	Oxford U	3	0		
2017–18	Oxford U	0	0		
2018–19	Oxford U	18	0	**36**	**1**

LOPES, Fabio (F) 0 0

From Sporting Lisbon, Bicester T, Brackley T.

2018–19	Oxford U	0	0		

MACKIE, Jamie (F) 371 54

H: 5 8 W: 11 00 b.Dorking 22-9-85

Internationals: Scotland Full caps.

2003–04	Wimbledon	13	0	**13**	**0**
2004–05	Milton Keynes D	3	0	**3**	**0**

From Exeter C

2007–08	Plymouth Arg	13	3		
2008–09	Plymouth Arg	43	5		
2009–10	Plymouth Arg	42	8	**98**	**16**
2010–11	QPR	25	9		
2011–12	QPR	31	7		
2012–13	QPR	29	2		
2013–14	Nottingham F	45	4	**45**	**4**
2014–15	Reading	32	5	**32**	**5**
2015–16	QPR	15	1		
2016–17	QPR	18	1		
2017–18	QPR	20	4	**138**	**24**
2018–19	Oxford U	42	5	**42**	**5**

McMAHON, Tony (D) 382 20

H: 5 10 W: 11 04 b.Bishop Auckland 24-3-86

Internationals: England U16, U17, U19.

2003–04	Middlesbrough	0	0		
2004–05	Middlesbrough	13	0		
2005–06	Middlesbrough	3	0		
2006–07	Middlesbrough	0	0		
2007–08	Middlesbrough	1	0		
2007–08	*Blackpool*	2	0		
2008–09	Middlesbrough	13	0		
2008–09	*Sheffield W*	15	1	**15**	**1**
2009–10	Middlesbrough	21	0		
2010–11	Middlesbrough	34	2		
2011–12	Middlesbrough	34	1	**119**	**3**
2012–13	Sheffield U	38	2		
2013–14	Sheffield U	23	0	**61**	**2**
2013–14	Blackpool	18	0		
2014–15	Blackpool	32	1	**52**	**1**
2014–15	*Bradford C*	8	1		
2015–16	Bradford C	40	4		
2016–17	Bradford C	25	6		
2017–18	Bradford C	38	1	**111**	**12**
2018–19	Oxford U	10	0	**10**	**0**
2018–19	*Scunthorpe U*	14	1	**14**	**1**

MOUSINHO, John (M) 436 23

H: 6 1 W: 12 07 b.Hounslow 30-4-86

2005–06	Brentford	7	0		
2006–07	Brentford	34	0		
2007–08	Brentford	23	2	**64**	**2**
2008–09	Wycombe W	34	2		
2009–10	Wycombe W	39	1	**73**	**3**
2010–11	Stevenage	38	7		
2011–12	Stevenage	19	3		
2012–13	Preston NE	24	1		
2013–14	Preston NE	2	0	**26**	**1**
2013–14	*Gillingham*	4	1	**4**	**1**
2013–14	*Stevenage*	16	1	**73**	**11**
2014–15	Burton Alb	42	2		
2015–16	Burton Alb	46	0		
2016–17	Burton Alb	32	0		
2017–18	Burton Alb	1	0	**121**	**2**
2017–18	Oxford U	40	1		
2018–19	Oxford U	35	2	**75**	**3**

NAPA, Malachi (M) 29 0

b. 26-5-99

From Reading.

2017–18	Oxford U	14	0		
2018–19	Oxford U	0	0	**14**	**0**
2018–19	*Macclesfield T*	15	0	**15**	**0**

NELSON, Curtis (D) 310 15

H: 6 0 W: 11 07 b.Newcastle-under-Lyme 21-5-93

Internationals: England U18.

2010–11	Plymouth Arg	35	0		
2011–12	Plymouth Arg	17	0		
2012–13	Plymouth Arg	27	3		
2013–14	Plymouth Arg	44	1		
2014–15	Plymouth Arg	42	1		
2015–16	Plymouth Arg	46	3	**211**	**8**
2016–17	Oxford U	33	2		
2017–18	Oxford U	20	1		
2018–19	Oxford U	46	4	**99**	**7**

OBIKA, Jonathan (F) 262 54

H: 6 0 W: 12 00 b.Enfield 12-9-90

Internationals: England U19, U20.

2008–09	Tottenham H	0	0		
2008–09	*Yeovil T*	10	4		
2009–10	Tottenham H	0	0		
2009–10	*Yeovil T*	22	6		
2009–10	*Millwall*	12	2	**12**	**2**
2010–11	Tottenham H	0	0		
2010–11	*Crystal Palace*	7	0	**7**	**0**
2010–11	*Peterborough U*	1	1	**1**	**1**
2010–11	*Swindon T*	5	0		
2010–11	*Yeovil T*	11	3		
2011–12	Tottenham H	0	0		
2011–12	*Yeovil T*	27	4	**70**	**17**
2012–13	Tottenham H	0	0		
2012–13	*Charlton Ath*	10	3		
2013–14	Tottenham H	0	0		
2013–14	*Brighton & HA*	5	0	**5**	**0**
2013–14	*Charlton Ath*	12	0	**22**	**3**
2014–15	Tottenham H	0	0		
2014–15	Swindon T	32	8		
2015–16	Swindon T	32	11		
2016–17	Swindon T	30	6	**99**	**25**
2017–18	Oxford U	35	5		
2018–19	Oxford U	11	1	**46**	**6**

RAGLAN, Charlie (D) 92 3

H: 6 0 W: 11 13 b.Wythenshawe 28-4-93

2011–12	Port Vale	0	0		
2012–13	Port Vale	0	0		
2013–14	Port Vale	0	0		
2014–15	Chesterfield	18	1		
2015–16	Chesterfield	27	0		
2016–17	Chesterfield	1	0	**46**	**1**
2016–17	*Oxford U*	16	0		
2017–18	Oxford U	0	0		
2017–18	*Port Vale*	10	0	**10**	**0**
2018–19	Oxford U	1	0	**17**	**0**
2018–19	*Cheltenham T*	19	2	**19**	**2**

RUFFELS, Joshua (M) 181 12

H: 5 10 W: 11 11 b.Oxford 23-10-93

2011–12	Coventry C	1	0		
2012–13	Coventry C	0	0	**1**	**0**
2013–14	Oxford U	29	1		
2014–15	Oxford U	33	0		
2015–16	Oxford U	16	0		
2016–17	Oxford U	20	2		
2017–18	Oxford U	38	5		
2018–19	Oxford U	44	4	**180**	**12**

SHEARER, Scott (G) 336 0

H: 6 3 W: 12 00 b.Glasgow 15-2-81

Internationals: Scotland B.

2000–01	Albion R	3	0		
2001–02	Albion R	10	0		
2002–03	Albion R	36	0	**49**	**0**
2003–04	Coventry C	30	0		
2004–05	Coventry C	8	0	**38**	**0**
2004–05	*Rushden & D*	13	0	**13**	**0**
2005–06	Bristol R	45	0		
2006–07	Bristol R	2	0	**47**	**0**
2006–07	*Shrewsbury T*	20	0	**20**	**0**
2007–08	Wycombe W	5	0		
2008–09	Wycombe W	29	0		
2009–10	Wycombe W	29	0		
2010–11	Wycombe W	0	0	**63**	**0**
2011–12	Crawley T	25	0	**25**	**0**
2012–13	Rotherham U	19	0		
2013–14	Rotherham U	12	0	**31**	**0**
2014–15	Crewe Alex	2	0	**2**	**0**
2014–15	*Burton Alb*	1	0	**1**	**0**
2015–16	Mansfield T	21	0		
2016–17	Mansfield T	25	0	**46**	**0**
2016–17	Oxford U	0	0		
2017–18	Oxford U	0	0		
2018–19	Oxford U	1	0	**1**	**0**

SMITH, Jonte (F) 5 0

H: 6 1 W: 10 12 b.Bermuda 10-7-94

Internationals: Bermuda U17, Full caps.

2012–13	Crawley T	4	0		
2013–14	Crawley T	0	0	**4**	**0**

From PS Kemi, Flekkeroy, Gloucester C, Lewes, Welling U, Lewes.

2018–19	Oxford U	1	0	**1**	**0**

SPASOV, Slavi (F) 1 0

b. 31-12-01

2018–19	Oxford U	1	0	**1**	**0**

STEPHENS, Jack (G) 2 0

b. 2-8-97

2014–15	Oxford U	0	0		
2015–16	Oxford U	0	0		
2016–17	Oxford U	0	0		
2017–18	Oxford U	0	0		
2018–19	Oxford U	2	0	**2**	**0**

SYKES, Mark (M) 9 0

b. 4-8-97

Internationals: Northern Ireland U19, U21.

From Glenavon.

2018–19	Oxford U	9	0	**9**	**0**

WHYTE, Gavin (F) 36 7

b.Belfast 31-1-96

Internationals: Northern Ireland U21, Full caps.

From Crusaders.

2018–19	Oxford U	36	7	**36**	**7**

Players retained or with offer of contract

Elechi, Chickanele Michael; Stevens, Jack Alexander; Verissimo, Lopes Fabio Jardel.

Scholars

Chambers-Parillon, Leon Nelson; Cowan, James Scott; Crooks, Ryan; Edwards, Jordan Stanley Blake; Evans, Max James; Harris, Max James; Jones, Nico Anthony; McCreadie, Aaron; Milton, Viktor Henry; Niblett, Freddie; Sampford, Harry John Martyn; Stevens, Jack Finlay.

PETERBOROUGH U (63)

BASSONG, Sebastien (D) 294 7

H: 6 2 W: 11 07 b.Paris 9-7-86

Internationals: France U21. Cameroon Full caps.

2005–06	Metz	23	0		
2006–07	Metz	37	1		
2007–08	Metz	19	0	**79**	**1**
2008–09	Newcastle U	30	0		
2009–10	Newcastle U	0	0	**30**	**0**
2009–10	Tottenham H	28	1		
2010–11	Tottenham H	12	1		
2011–12	Tottenham H	5	0		
2011–12	*Wolverhampton W*	9	0	**9**	**0**
2012–13	Tottenham H	0	0	**45**	**2**
2012–13	Norwich C	34	3		
2013–14	Norwich C	27	0		
2014–15	Norwich C	18	0		
2014–15	*Watford*	11	0	**11**	**0**
2015–16	Norwich C	32	1		
2016–17	Norwich C	9	0	**120**	**4**
2018–19	Peterborough U	0	0		

BENNETT, Rhys (D) **250** **14**
H: 6 3 W: 12 00 b.Manchester 1-9-91
2011–12 Bolton W 0 0
2011–12 *Falkirk* 19 0 **19** **0**
2012–13 Rochdale 33 2
2013–14 Rochdale 22 0
2014–15 Rochdale 39 2
2015–16 Rochdale 16 2 **110** **6**
2016–17 Mansfield T 46 2
2017–18 Mansfield T 38 2 **84** **4**
2018–19 Peterborough U 37 4 **37** **4**

BUCKLEY-RICKETT, Isaac (M) **17** **0**
H: 5 10 W: 10 10 b. 14-3-98
Internationals: England U18, U19, U20.
2017–18 Manchester C 0 0
2017–18 *FC Twente* 6 0 **6** **0**
2017–18 *Oxford U* 11 0 **11** **0**
2018–19 Peterborough U 0 0

BURROWS, Harrison (M) **0** **0**
2017–18 Peterborough U 0 0
2018–19 Peterborough U 0 0

CHAPMAN, Aaron (G) **100** **0**
H: 6 8 W: 14 07 b.Rotherham 29-5-90
2013–14 Chesterfield 0 0
2014–15 Chesterfield 0 0
2014–15 *Accrington S* 3 0
2015–16 Chesterfield 0 0
2015–16 *Bristol R* 5 0 **5** **0**
2016–17 Accrington S 15 0
2017–18 Accrington S 45 0 **63** **0**
2018–19 Peterborough U 32 0 **32** **0**

COOKE, Callum (F) **61** **7**
H: 5 8 W: 11 05 b.Peterlee 21-2-97
Internationals: England U16, U17, U18.
2016–17 Middlesbrough 0 0
2016–17 *Crewe Alex* 18 4 **18** **4**
2017–18 Middlesbrough 0 0
2017–18 *Blackpool* 30 2 **30** **2**
2018–19 Peterborough U 13 1 **13** **1**

COOPER, George (M) **156** **18**
H: 5 9 W: 11 05 b.Warrington 2-11-96
2014–15 Crewe Alex 22 3
2015–16 Crewe Alex 27 1
2016–17 Crewe Alex 46 9
2017–18 Crewe Alex 27 1 **122** **14**
2017–18 Peterborough U 13 2
2018–19 Peterborough U 21 2 **34** **4**

CUMMINGS, Jason (F) **170** **65**
H: 5 10 W: 10 10 b.Edinburgh 1-8-95
Internationals: Scotland U19, U21, Full caps.
2013–14 Hibernian 16 0
2014–15 Hibernian 33 18
2015–16 Hibernian 33 18
2016–17 Hibernian 32 19 **114** **55**
2017–18 Nottingham F 14 1 **14** **1**
2017–18 *Rangers* 15 2 **15** **2**
2018–19 Peterborough U 22 6 **22** **6**
2018–19 *Luton T* 5 1 **5** **1**

DEMBELE, Siriki (M) **74** **9**
b. 7-9-96
From Dundee U.
2017–18 Grimsby T 36 4 **36** **4**
2018–19 Peterborough U 38 5 **38** **5**

GODDEN, Matthew (F) **132** **44**
H: 6 1 W: 12 03 b.Canterbury 29-7-91
2009–10 Scunthorpe U 0 0
2010–11 Scunthorpe U 5 0
2011–12 Scunthorpe U 1 0
2012–13 Scunthorpe U 8 0
2013–14 Scunthorpe U 4 0
2014–15 Scunthorpe U 0 0 **18** **0**
2016–17 Stevenage 38 20
2017–18 Stevenage 38 10 **76** **30**
2018–19 Peterborough U 38 14 **38** **14**

KANU, Idris (F) **21** **1**
b. 5-12-99
From Aldershot T.
2017–18 Peterborough U 18 0
2018–19 Peterborough U 0 0 **18** **0**
2018–19 *Port Vale* 3 1 **3** **1**

LAFFERTY, Danny (D) **190** **13**
H: 6 0 W: 12 08 b.Derry 1-4-89
Internationals: Northern Ireland U17, U19, U21, B, Full caps.
2009–10 Celtic 0 0
2009–10 *Ayr U* 14 1 **14** **1**
2010 Derry C 12 0
2011 Derry C 34 7 **46** **7**
2011–12 Burnley 5 0
2012–13 Burnley 24 0
2013–14 Burnley 10 0
2014–15 Burnley 1 0
2014–15 *Rotherham U* 11 0 **11** **0**
2015–16 Burnley 0 0
2015–16 *Oldham Ath* 15 1 **15** **1**
2016–17 Burnley 0 0 **40** **0**
2016–17 Sheffield U 37 4
2017–18 Sheffield U 8 0
2018–19 Sheffield U 1 0 **46** **4**
2018–19 Peterborough U 18 0 **18** **0**

LYON, Darren (M) **63** **3**
H: 6 1 W: 12 00 b.Glasgow 8-6-95
From Rangers.
2013–14 Hamilton A 1 0
2014–15 Hamilton A 14 0
2015–16 Hamilton A 13 0
2016–17 Hamilton A 5 1
2017–18 Hamilton A 27 2
2018–19 Hamilton A 1 0 **61** **3**
2018–19 Peterborough U 2 0 **2** **0**

MADDISON, Marcus (M) **190** **43**
H: 5 9 W: 11 03 b.Sedgefield 26-9-93
Internationals: England C.
2014–15 Peterborough U 29 7
2015–16 Peterborough U 39 11
2016–17 Peterborough U 41 9
2017–18 Peterborough U 41 8
2018–19 Peterborough U 40 8 **190** **43**

NAISMITH, Jason (D) **196** **7**
H: 6 1 W: 13 02 b.Paisley 25-6-94
Internationals: Scotland U17, U18, U20, U21.
2011–12 St Mirren 2 0
2012–13 St Mirren 0 0
2012–13 *Greenock Morton* 4 0 **4** **0**
2012–13 *Cowdenbeath* 5 0 **5** **0**
2013–14 St Mirren 27 2
2014–15 St Mirren 38 2
2015–16 St Mirren 5 0
2016–17 St Mirren 21 0 **93** **4**
2016–17 Ross Co 16 0
2017–18 Ross Co 35 2 **51** **2**
2018–19 Peterborough U 43 1 **43** **1**

O'MALLEY, Conor (G) **23** **0**
H: 6 3 W: 13 01 b. 1-8-94
From St Patrick's Ath.
2017–18 Peterborough U 9 0
2018–19 Peterborough U 14 0 **23** **0**

REED, Louis (M) **109** **5**
b. 25-7-97
Internationals: England U18, U19, U20.
2013–14 Sheffield U 1 0
2014–15 Sheffield U 19 0
2015–16 Sheffield U 19 0
2016–17 Sheffield U 0 0
2017–18 Sheffield U 0 0 **39** **0**
2017–18 *Chesterfield* 42 4 **42** **4**
2018–19 Peterborough U 28 1 **28** **1**

STEVENS, Mathew (F) **14** **1**
H: 5 11 W: 11 09 b. 12-2-98
2015–16 Barnet 10 1 **10** **1**
2016–17 Peterborough U 1 0
2017–18 Peterborough U 0 0
2018–19 Peterborough U 3 0 **4** **0**

TAFAZOLLI, Ryan (D) **205** **13**
H: 6 5 W: 12 03 b.Sutton 28-9-91
2010–11 Southampton 0 0
From Salisbury, Cambridge C, Carshalton Ath
2013–14 Mansfield T 24 2
2014–15 Mansfield T 36 1
2015–16 Mansfield T 44 5 **104** **8**
2016–17 Peterborough U 31 3
2017–18 Peterborough U 33 1
2018–19 Peterborough U 37 1 **101** **5**

TONEY, Ivan (F) **188** **52**
H: 5 10 W: 12 00 b.Northampton 16-3-96
2012–13 Northampton T 0 0
2013–14 Northampton T 13 3
2014–15 Northampton T 40 8 **53** **11**
2015–16 Newcastle U 2 0
2015–16 *Barnsley* 15 1 **15** **1**
2016–17 Newcastle U 0 0
2016–17 *Shrewsbury T* 19 6 **19** **6**
2016–17 *Scunthorpe U* 15 6
2017–18 Newcastle U 0 0 **2** **0**
2017–18 *Wigan Ath* 24 4 **24** **4**
2017–18 *Scunthorpe U* 16 8 **31** **14**
2018–19 Peterborough U 44 16 **44** **16**

TYLER, Mark (G) **488** **0**
H: 6 0 W: 12 09 b.Norwich 2-4-77
Internationals: England U18.
1994–95 Peterborough U 5 0
1995–96 Peterborough U 0 0
1996–97 Peterborough U 3 0
1997–98 Peterborough U 46 0
1998–99 Peterborough U 27 0
1999–2000 Peterborough U 32 0
2000–01 Peterborough U 40 0
2001–02 Peterborough U 44 0
2002–03 Peterborough U 29 0
2003–04 Peterborough U 43 0
2004–05 Peterborough U 46 0
2005–06 Peterborough U 40 0
2006–07 Peterborough U 41 0
2007–08 Peterborough U 17 0
2008–09 Peterborough U 0 0
2008–09 *Bury* 11 0 **11** **0**
2014–15 Luton T 31 0
2015–16 Luton T 27 0 **58** **0**
2015–16 *Peterborough U* 3 0
2016–17 Peterborough U 3 0
2017–18 Peterborough U 0 0
2018–19 Peterborough U 0 0 **419** **0**

WARD, Joe (M) **60** **4**
b. 9-4-95
Internationals: England C.
2015–16 Brighton & HA 0 0
2016–17 Brighton & HA 0 0
2017–18 Peterborough U 17 0
2018–19 Peterborough U 43 4 **60** **4**

WOODYARD, Alex (M) **97** **2**
H: 5 9 W: 10 00 b.Gravesend 3-5-93
Internationals: England C.
2010–11 Southend U 3 0
2011–12 Southend U 0 0
2012–13 Southend U 5 0
2013–14 Southend U 0 0 **8** **0**
2017–18 Lincoln C 46 2 **46** **2**
2018–19 Peterborough U 43 0 **43** **0**

YORWERTH, Josh (D) **86** **4**
H: 6 1 W: 11 09 b.Bridgend 1-1-95
Internationals: Wales U17, U19, U21.
2014–15 Cardiff C 0 0
2015–16 Ipswich T 0 0
2015–16 *Crawley T* 24 0
2016–17 Crawley T 21 3
2017–18 Crawley T 39 1 **84** **4**
2018–19 Peterborough U 2 0 **2** **0**

Players retained or with offer of contract
Buckley-Ricketts, Isaac; Cartwright, Samuel Elliott; O'Hara, Mark.

Scholars
Allen, Joshua Henry; Barker, Kyle Lennon; Blackmore, William Oliver; Brookes, Harry; Douglas, Rio Davon; Fosu, Mikkel; Garner, Frazer James; Gurney, Jack Ethan; Horne, Taylor Brian; Jones, Archie Joseph; Rolt, Bradley Jordan Ali; Roudette, Gregory Khaya Matteo; Rudman, Nathan Paul; Ruzvidzo, Shaun; Salmon, Toby Joe; Shackleton, Oliver James; Strachan, Luke Robert.

PLYMOUTH ARG (64)

AINSWORTH, Lionel (F) **254** **35**
H: 5 9 W: 9 10 b.Nottingham 1-10-87
Internationals: England U16, U17, U18, U19.
2005–06 Derby Co 2 0
2006–07 Derby Co 0 0 **2** **0**
2006–07 *Bournemouth* 7 0 **7** **0**
2006–07 *Wycombe W* 7 0 **7** **0**
2007–08 Hereford U 15 4
2007–08 Watford 8 0
2008–09 Watford 7 0 **15** **0**
2008–09 *Hereford U* 7 3 **22** **7**
2008–09 Huddersfield T 14 0
2009–10 Huddersfield T 11 0
2009–10 *Brentford* 9 0 **9** **0**
2010–11 Shrewsbury T 33 9
2010–11 *Huddersfield T* 0 0 **25** **0**
2011–12 Shrewsbury T 21 2 **54** **11**
2011–12 *Burton Alb* 7 0 **7** **0**
2012–13 Rotherham U 16 0
2012–13 *Aldershot T* 7 0 **7** **0**
2013–14 Rotherham U 0 0 **16** **0**
2013–14 *Motherwell* 29 11
2014–15 Motherwell 34 6 **63** **17**

2017–18	Plymouth Arg	19	0		
2018–19	Plymouth Arg	1	0	**20**	**0**

ANDERSON, Paul (M) **329** **32**
H: 5 9 W: 10 04 b.Leicester 23-7-88
Internationals: England U19.

2005–06	Hull C	0	0		
2005–06	Liverpool	0	0		
2006–07	Liverpool	0	0		
2007–08	Liverpool	0	0		
2007–08	*Swansea C*	31	7	**31**	**7**
2008–09	Liverpool	0	0		
2008–09	*Nottingham F*	26	2		
2009–10	Nottingham F	37	4		
2010–11	Nottingham F	36	3		
2011–12	Nottingham F	17	0		
2012–13	Nottingham F	0	0	**116**	**9**
2012–13	Bristol C	29	3	**29**	**3**
2013–14	Ipswich T	31	5		
2014–15	Ipswich T	35	1	**66**	**6**
2015–16	Bradford C	11	0		
2016–17	Bradford C	3	0	**14**	**0**
2016–17	Northampton T	36	6	**36**	**6**
2016–17	Mansfield T	0	0		
2017–18	Mansfield T	33	1		
2018–19	Mansfield T	0	0	**33**	**1**
2018–19	Plymouth Arg	4	0	**4**	**0**

BATTLE, Alex (F) **1** **0**
b. 23-1-99

2017–18	Plymouth Arg	1	0		
2018–19	Plymouth Arg	0	0	**1**	**0**

CANAVAN, Niall (D) **229** **20**
H: 6 3 W: 12 00 b.Guiseley 11-4-91
Internationals: Republic of Ireland U21.

2009–10	Scunthorpe U	7	1		
2010–11	Scunthorpe U	8	0		
2010–11	*Shrewsbury T*	3	0	**3**	**0**
2011–12	Scunthorpe U	12	1		
2012–13	Scunthorpe U	40	6		
2013–14	Scunthorpe U	45	4		
2014–15	Scunthorpe U	32	3		
2015–16	Scunthorpe U	10	0	**154**	**15**
2015–16	*Rochdale*	11	1		
2016–17	Rochdale	25	2		
2017–18	Rochdale	3	0	**39**	**3**
2018–19	Plymouth Arg	33	2	**33**	**2**

CAREY, Graham (M) **333** **60**
H: 6 0 W: 10 03 b.Dublin 20-5-89
Internationals: Republic of Ireland U21.

2008–09	Celtic	0	0		
2009	*Bohemians*	15	2	**15**	**2**
2009–10	Celtic	0	0		
2009–10	*St Mirren*	15	3		
2010–11	Celtic	0	0		
2010–11	*Huddersfield T*	19	2	**19**	**2**
2011–12	St Mirren	29	2		
2012–13	St Mirren	26	1	**70**	**6**
2013–14	Ross Co	36	3		
2014–15	Ross Co	22	2	**58**	**5**
2015–16	Plymouth Arg	39	11		
2016–17	Plymouth Arg	46	14		
2017–18	Plymouth Arg	42	14		
2018–19	Plymouth Arg	44	6	**171**	**45**

COOPER, Michael (G) **2** **0**
b. 8-10-99

2017–18	Plymouth Arg	1	0		
2018–19	Plymouth Arg	1	0	**2**	**0**

DYSON, Calum (F) **16** **4**
b. 19-9-96

2015–16	Everton	0	0		
2016–17	Everton	0	0		
2016–17	*Grimsby T*	16	4	**16**	**4**
2017–18	Everton	0	0		
2018–19	Plymouth Arg	0	0		
2018–19	*Stevenage*	0	0		

EDWARDS, Ryan (D) **221** **9**
b.Liverpool 7-10-93

2011–12	Blackburn R	0	0		
2012–13	Rochdale	26	0	**26**	**0**
2012–13	Blackburn R	0	0		
2012–13	*Fleetwood T*	9	0	**9**	**0**
2013–14	Blackburn R	0	0		
2013–14	*Chesterfield*	5	0	**5**	**0**
2013–14	*Tranmere R*	0	0		
2013–14	*Morecambe*	9	0		
2014–15	Morecambe	31	0		
2015–16	Morecambe	37	0		
2016–17	Morecambe	43	1	**120**	**1**
2017–18	Plymouth Arg	25	3		
2018–19	Plymouth Arg	36	5	**61**	**8**

FLETCHER, Alex (F) **18** **1**
H: 5 10 W: 10 10 b. 9-2-99

2016–17	Plymouth Arg	0	0		
2017–18	Plymouth Arg	14	1		
2018–19	Plymouth Arg	4	0	**18**	**1**

FOX, David (M) **382** **17**
H: 5 9 W: 11 08 b.Leek 13-12-83
Internationals: England U16, U17, U19, U20.

2000–01	Manchester U	0	0		
2001–02	Manchester U	0	0		
2002–03	Manchester U	0	0		
2003–04	Manchester U	0	0		
2004–05	Manchester U	0	0		
2004–05	*Shrewsbury T*	4	1	**4**	**1**
2005–06	Manchester U	0	0		
2005–06	Blackpool	7	1		
2006–07	Blackpool	37	4		
2007–08	Blackpool	28	1		
2008–09	Blackpool	22	0	**94**	**6**
2009–10	Colchester U	18	3		
2010–11	Norwich C	32	1		
2011–12	Norwich C	28	0		
2012–13	Norwich C	2	0		
2013–14	Norwich C	0	0	**62**	**1**
2013–14	*Barnsley*	7	0	**7**	**0**
2014–15	Colchester U	30	2	**48**	**5**
2015–16	Crewe Alex	39	2	**39**	**2**
2016–17	Plymouth Arg	40	0		
2017–18	Plymouth Arg	45	1		
2018–19	Plymouth Arg	43	1	**128**	**2**

GARSIDE, Rio (M) **0** **0**
b.Plymouth 30-7-01

2018–19	Plymouth Arg	0	0		

GOULTY, Aaron (F) **0** **0**
b.Plymouth 24-8-01

2018–19	Plymouth Arg	0	0		

GRANT, Conor (M) **84** **4**
H: 5 9 W: 12 08 b.Fazakerley 18-4-95
Internationals: England U18.

2013–14	Everton	0	0		
2014–15	Everton	0	0		
2014–15	*Motherwell*	11	1	**11**	**1**
2015–16	Everton	0	0		
2015–16	*Doncaster R*	19	2		
2016–17	Everton	0	0		
2016–17	*Ipswich T*	6	0	**6**	**0**
2016–17	*Doncaster R*	21	1	**40**	**3**
2017–18	Everton	0	0		
2017–18	*Crewe Alex*	17	0	**17**	**0**
2018–19	Plymouth Arg	10	0	**10**	**0**

GRANT, Joel (F) **325** **54**
H: 6 0 W: 12 01 b.Acton 26-8-87
Internationals: Jamaica U20, Full caps.

2005–06	Watford	7	0		
2006–07	Watford	0	0	**7**	**0**
From Aldershot T.					
2008–09	Crewe Alex	28	2		
2009–10	Crewe Alex	43	9		
2010–11	Crewe Alex	25	5	**96**	**16**
2011–12	Wycombe W	30	4		
2012–13	Wycombe W	41	10	**71**	**14**
2013–14	Yeovil T	34	3		
2014–15	Yeovil T	21	3	**55**	**6**
2015–16	Exeter C	26	4		
2016–17	Exeter C	20	4	**46**	**8**
2017–18	Plymouth Arg	33	6		
2018–19	Plymouth Arg	17	4	**50**	**10**

JEPHCOTT, Luke (F) **9** **0**
b.Truro 26-1-00
Internationals: Wales U19.

2018–19	Plymouth Arg	9	0	**9**	**0**

LADAPO, Freddie (F) **94** **24**
H: 6 0 W: 12 06 b.Romford 1-2-93

2011–12	Colchester U	0	0		
2012–13	Colchester U	4	0		
2013–14	Colchester U	2	0	**6**	**0**
2015–16	Crystal Palace	0	0		
2016–17	Crystal Palace	0	0		
2016–17	*Oldham Ath*	17	2	**17**	**2**
2016–17	*Shrewsbury T*	15	4	**15**	**4**
2017–18	Crystal Palace	1	0	**1**	**0**
2017–18	Southend U	10	0	**10**	**0**
2018–19	Plymouth Arg	45	18	**45**	**18**

LAMEIRAS, Ruben (M) **142** **20**
H: 5 9 W: 11 00 b.Lisbon 22-12-94

2014–15	Tottenham H	0	0		
2015	*Atvidabergs*	11	0	**11**	**0**
2015–16	Coventry C	29	2		
2016–17	Coventry C	27	1	**56**	**3**
2017–18	Plymouth Arg	34	6		
2018–19	Plymouth Arg	41	11	**75**	**17**

LAW, Ryan (D) **0** **0**

2017–18	Plymouth Arg	0	0		
2018–19	Plymouth Arg	0	0		

LETHEREN, Kyle (G) **86** **0**
H: 6 2 W: 13 00 b.Swansea 26-12-87
Internationals: Wales U21.

2010–11	Kilmarnock	0	0		
2011–12	Kilmarnock	2	0		
2012–13	Kilmarnock	9	0	**11**	**0**
2013–14	Dundee	35	0		
2014–15	Dundee	15	0	**50**	**0**
2015–16	Blackpool	5	0		
2016–17	Blackpool	0	0	**5**	**0**
From York C.					
2017–18	Plymouth Arg	7	0		
2018–19	Plymouth Arg	13	0	**20**	**0**

LOLOS, Klaidi (F) **0** **0**

2017–18	Plymouth Arg	0	0		
2018–19	Plymouth Arg	0	0		

MOORE, Tafari (D) **27** **0**
H: 5 8 b.London 5-7-97
Internationals: England U16, U17, U18, U19, U20.

2015–16	Arsenal	0	0		
2016–17	Arsenal	0	0		
2017–18	Arsenal	0	0		
2017–18	Arsenal	0	0		
2017–18	*Wycombe W*	13	0	**13**	**0**
2018–19	Plymouth Arg	14	0	**14**	**0**

NESS, Jamie (M) **153** **7**
H: 6 2 W: 10 13 b.Irvine 2-3-91
Internationals: Scotland U17, U19, U21.

2010–11	Rangers	11	0		
2011–12	Rangers	5	1	**16**	**1**
2012–13	Stoke C	0	0		
2013–14	Stoke C	0	0		
2013–14	*Leyton Orient*	13	1	**13**	**1**
2014–15	Stoke C	0	0		
2014–15	*Crewe Alex*	34	2	**34**	**2**
2015–16	Scunthorpe U	27	0		
2016–17	Scunthorpe U	12	0	**39**	**0**
2017–18	Plymouth Arg	27	3		
2018–19	Plymouth Arg	24	0	**51**	**3**

PECK, Michael (M) **0** **0**
b.Truro 26-3-01

2018–19	Plymouth Arg	0	0		

PURRINGTON, Tom (M) **0** **0**
b.Exeter 24-10-00

2018–19	Plymouth Arg	0	0		

RANDELL, Adam (M) **0** **0**
b.Plymouth 1-10-00

2018–19	Plymouth Arg	0	0		

RILEY, Joe (D) **135** **4**
H: 6 0 W: 11 02 b.Salford 13-10-91

2011–12	Bolton W	3	0		
2012–13	Bolton W	0	0		
2013–14	Bolton W	0	0		
2014–15	Bolton W	0	0	**3**	**0**
2014–15	*Oxford U*	22	0	**22**	**0**
2014–15	Bury	17	1		
2015–16	Bury	33	1	**50**	**2**
2016–17	Shrewsbury T	32	1		
2017–18	Shrewsbury T	10	1	**42**	**2**
2018–19	Plymouth Arg	18	0	**18**	**0**

ROONEY, Daniel (M) **0** **0**
b. 30-11-98
Internationals: Northern Ireland U17.

2017–18	Plymouth Arg	0	0		
2018–19	Plymouth Arg	0	0		

SARCEVIC, Antoni (M) **226** **27**
H: 5 10 W: 11 00 b.Manchester 13-3-92
Internationals: England C.

2009–10	Crewe Alex	0	0		
2010–11	Crewe Alex	6	1		
2011–12	Crewe Alex	6	0	**12**	**1**
2013–14	Fleetwood T	42	13		
2014–15	Fleetwood T	37	2		
2015–16	Fleetwood T	39	3	**118**	**18**
2016–17	Shrewsbury T	12	0	**12**	**0**
2016–17	Plymouth Arg	17	2		
2017–18	Plymouth Arg	30	3		
2018–19	Plymouth Arg	37	3	**84**	**8**

SAWYER, Gary (D) **370** **7**
H: 6 0 W: 11 08 b.Bideford 5-7-85

2004–05	Plymouth Arg	0	0		
2005–06	Plymouth Arg	0	0		
2006–07	Plymouth Arg	22	0		
2007–08	Plymouth Arg	31	1		

2008–09	Plymouth Arg	13	3		
2009–10	Plymouth Arg	29	1		
2009–10	*Bristol C*	2	0	**2**	**0**
2010–11	Bristol R	37	0		
2011–12	Bristol R	24	0	**61**	**0**
2012–13	Leyton Orient	34	1		
2013–14	Leyton Orient	22	0		
2014–15	Leyton Orient	13	0	**69**	**1**
2015–16	Plymouth Arg	43	0		
2016–17	Plymouth Arg	21	0		
2017–18	Plymouth Arg	46	1		
2018–19	Plymouth Arg	33	0	**238**	**6**

SMITH-BROWN, Ashley (D) 100 3
H: 5 10 W: 10 10 b.Manchester 31-3-96
Internationals: England U16, U17, U18, U19, U20.

2016–17	Manchester C	0	0		
2016–17	*NAC Breda*	29	1		
2016–17	Manchester C	0	0		
2016–17	NAC Breda	29	1	**58**	**2**
2017–18	Manchester C	0	0		
2017–18	*Hearts*	2	0	**2**	**0**
2017–18	*Oxford U*	9	0	**9**	**0**
2018–19	Plymouth Arg	31	1	**31**	**1**

SONGO'O, Yann (D) 156 6
H: 6 0 W: 12 00 b.Yaounde 17-11-91
Internationals: France U16. Cameroon U20.

2011–12	Sabadell	6	0	**6**	**0**
2013	Sporting Kansas C	0	0		
2013	*Orlando C*	12	1	**12**	**1**
2013–14	Blackburn R	0	0		
2013–14	*Ross Co*	17	3	**17**	**3**
2014–15	Blackburn R	0	0		
2016–17	Plymouth Arg	46	2		
2017–18	Plymouth Arg	33	0		
2018–19	Plymouth Arg	42	0	**121**	**2**

TAYLOR, Ryan (F) 348 51
H: 6 2 W: 10 10 b.Rotherham 4-5-88

2005–06	Rotherham U	1	0		
2006–07	Rotherham U	10	0		
2007–08	Rotherham U	35	6		
2008–09	Rotherham U	33	4		
2009–10	Rotherham U	19	0		
2009–10	*Exeter C*	7	0	**7**	**0**
2010–11	Rotherham U	34	11	**132**	**21**
2011–12	Bristol C	7	1		
2012–13	Bristol C	25	1		
2013–14	Bristol C	7	0	**39**	**2**
2013–14	Portsmouth	18	6		
2014–15	Portsmouth	37	9	**55**	**15**
2015–16	Oxford U	22	3		
2016–17	Oxford U	21	1	**43**	**4**
2016–17	Plymouth Arg	18	4		
2017–18	Plymouth Arg	21	5		
2018–19	Plymouth Arg	33	0	**72**	**9**

THRELKELD, Oscar (D) 108 4
H: 6 0 W: 12 04 b.Bolton 15-12-94

2013–14	Bolton W	2	0		
2014–15	Bolton W	4	0		
2015–16	Bolton W	3	0	**9**	**0**
2015–16	*Plymouth Arg*	25	1		
2016–17	Plymouth Arg	36	2		
2017–18	Plymouth Arg	24	0		
2018–19	Waasland-Beveren	2	0	**2**	**0**

On loan from Wassland-Beveren.

2018–19	Plymouth Arg	12	1	**97**	**4**

WOOTTON, Scott (D) 154 3
H: 6 2 W: 13 00 b.Birkenhead 12-9-91
Internationals: England U17.

2009–10	Manchester U	0	0		
2010–11	Manchester U	0	0		
2010–11	*Tranmere R*	7	1	**7**	**1**
2011–12	Manchester U	0	0		
2011–12	*Peterborough U*	11	0		
2011–12	*Nottingham F*	13	0	**13**	**0**
2012–13	Manchester U	0	0		
2012–13	*Peterborough U*	2	1	**13**	**1**
2013–14	Manchester U	0	0		
2013–14	Leeds U	20	0		
2014–15	Leeds U	23	0		
2014–15	*Rotherham U*	7	0	**7**	**0**
2015–16	Leeds U	23	0	**66**	**0**
2016–17	Milton Keynes D	1	1		
2017–18	Milton Keynes D	38	0	**39**	**1**
2018–19	Plymouth Arg	9	0	**9**	**0**

WYLDE, Gregg (M) 196 18
H: 5 9 W: 11 04 b.Kirkintilloch 23-3-91
Internationals: Scotland U17, U19, U21.

2009–10	Rangers	4	0		
2010–11	Rangers	30	0		
2011–12	Rangers	42	4	**76**	**4**
2012–13	Bolton W	0	0		
2012–13	*Bury*	4	0	**4**	**0**
2013–14	Aberdeen	8	1	**8**	**1**
2013–14	St Mirren	17	2	**17**	**2**
2015–16	Plymouth Arg	43	7		
2016–17	Millwall	5	0	**5**	**0**
2016–17	*Northampton T*	12	1	**12**	**1**
2017–18	Plymouth Arg	9	1		
2017–18	*Morecambe*	15	2	**15**	**2**
2018–19	Plymouth Arg	7	0	**59**	**8**

Transferred to Livingston January 2019.

Players retained or with offer of contract
Sangster, Cameron.

Scholars
Boyd, Jude Michael; Burdon, Isaac Lewis; Burn, Andrew; Cleal, Jarvis Jai; Collum, Reuben; Garside, Rio Shawn Terry; Goulty, Aaron Richard; Lolos, Klaidi; Peck, Michael Dennis; Purrington, Tom; Randell, Adam Fletcher; Seery, Joseph Andrew; Tomlinson, Oliver Joseph; Townsend, Harry Robert Peter; Wilson, Rubin James.

PORT VALE (65)

AGHO, Nelson (F) 0 0

2018–19	Port Vale	0	0		

ANGUS, Dior (F) 3 1
H: 6 0 W: 12 00 b. 18-1-94
From Solihull Moors, Kidderminster H, Daventry T, Stratford T, Redditch U.

2017–18	Port Vale	3	1		
2018–19	Port Vale	0	0	**3**	**1**

BARNETT, Tyrone (F) 309 65
H: 6 3 W: 13 05 b.Stevenage 28-10-85

2010–11	Macclesfield T	45	13	**45**	**13**
2011–12	Crawley T	26	14	**26**	**14**
2011–12	Peterborough U	13	4		
2012–13	Peterborough U	18	1		
2012–13	*Ipswich T*	3	0	**3**	**0**
2013–14	Peterborough U	21	6		
2013–14	*Bristol C*	17	1	**17**	**1**
2014–15	Peterborough U	4	0	**56**	**11**
2014–15	*Oxford U*	12	4	**12**	**4**
2014–15	Shrewsbury T	18	4		
2015–16	Shrewsbury T	21	4	**39**	**8**
2015–16	*Southend U*	20	5	**20**	**5**
2016–17	AFC Wimbledon	36	2	**36**	**2**
2017–18	Port Vale	25	1		
2018–19	Port Vale	0	0	**25**	**1**
2018–19	*Cheltenham T*	30	6	**30**	**6**

BROWN, Scott (G) 406 0
H: 6 2 W: 13 01 b.Wolverhampton 26-4-85
From Welshpool T

2003–04	Bristol C	0	0		
2004–05	Cheltenham T	0	0		
2005–06	Cheltenham T	1	0		
2006–07	Cheltenham T	11	0		
2007–08	Cheltenham T	0	0		
2008–09	Cheltenham T	35	0		
2009–10	Cheltenham T	46	0		
2010–11	Cheltenham T	46	0		
2011–12	Cheltenham T	22	0		
2012–13	Cheltenham T	46	0		
2013–14	Cheltenham T	45	0		
2014–15	Aberdeen	25	0		
2015–16	Aberdeen	13	0	**38**	**0**
2016–17	Wycombe W	3	0		
2016–17	*Cheltenham T*	21	0	**273**	**0**
2017–18	Wycombe W	46	0	**49**	**0**
2018–19	Port Vale	46	0	**46**	**0**

CALVELEY, Mike (M) 3 0
H: 5 10 W: 10 10 b. 22-6-99

2017–18	Port Vale	2	0		
2018–19	Port Vale	1	0	**3**	**0**

CLARK, Mitchell (D) 40 0
b.Nuneaton 13-3-99
Internationals: Wales U17, U19.

2017–18	Aston Villa	0	0		
2018–19	Port Vale	40	0	**40**	**0**

CONLON, Tom (M) 96 5
H: 5 8 W: 9 11 b.Stoke-on-Trent 3-2-96

2013–14	Peterborough U	1	0	**1**	**0**
2014–15	Stevenage	13	0		
2015–16	Stevenage	32	2		
2016–17	Stevenage	4	0		
2017–18	Stevenage	12	0	**61**	**2**
2018–19	Port Vale	34	3	**34**	**3**

DANIELS, Brendon (M) 7 0
H: 5 11 W: 11 09 b.Stoke 24-9-93
Internationals: England C.

2011–12	Crewe Alex	0	0		
2012–13	Crewe Alex	7	0		
2013–14	Crewe Alex	0	0	**7**	**0**

From Chester, Tamworth, Harrogate T, Fylde, Alfreton T, Altrincham. On loan from Altrincham.

2018–19	Port Vale	0	0		

DODDS, Louis (M) 413 70
H: 5 10 W: 12 04 b.Sheffield 8-10-86

2005–06	Leicester C	0	0		
2006–07	Leicester C	0	0		
2006–07	*Rochdale*	12	2	**12**	**2**
2007–08	Leicester C	0	0		
2007–08	*Lincoln C*	41	9	**41**	**9**
2008–09	Port Vale	44	7		
2009–10	Port Vale	44	6		
2010–11	Port Vale	33	7		
2011–12	Port Vale	35	8		
2012–13	Port Vale	30	7		
2013–14	Port Vale	29	4		
2014–15	Port Vale	37	4		
2015–16	Port Vale	37	8		
2016–17	Shrewsbury T	38	8		
2017–18	Shrewsbury T	9	0	**47**	**8**
2017–18	Chesterfield	12	0	**12**	**0**
2018–19	Port Vale	12	0	**301**	**51**

ELLIOTT, Daniel (F) 6 0
b. 29-9-95
From San Cristobal.

2018–19	Port Vale	6	0	**6**	**0**

GIBBONS, James (D) 45 0
H: 5 9 W: 9 11 b. 16-3-98

2016–17	Port Vale	0	0		
2017–18	Port Vale	30	0		
2018–19	Port Vale	15	0	**45**	**0**

GREEN-BIRCH, Lucas (M) 0 0
b. 29-1-01

2018–19	Port Vale	0	0		

HANNANT, Luke (M) 63 4
b. 4-11-93
From Dereham T, Team Northumbria, Gateshead.

2017–18	Port Vale	18	1		
2018–19	Port Vale	45	3	**63**	**4**

HORNBY, Sam (G) 11 0
b. 14-2-95

2015–16	Burton Alb	0	0		

From Brackley T, Kidderminster H.

2017–18	Port Vale	11	0		
2018–19	Port Vale	0	0	**11**	**0**

JOYCE, Luke (M) 429 13
H: 5 11 W: 12 03 b.Bolton 9-7-87

2005–06	Wigan Ath	0	0		
2005–06	Carlisle U	0	0		
2006–07	Carlisle U	16	1		
2007–08	Carlisle U	3	1		
2008–09	Carlisle U	7	0		
2009–10	Accrington S	41	1		
2010–11	Accrington S	27	1		
2011–12	Accrington S	43	2		
2012–13	Accrington S	44	0		
2013–14	Accrington S	46	1		
2014–15	Accrington S	45	3	**246**	**8**
2015–16	Carlisle U	37	0		
2016–17	Carlisle U	45	1		
2017–18	Carlisle U	38	2	**146**	**5**
2018–19	Port Vale	37	0	**37**	**0**

KAY, Antony (D) 595 49
H: 5 11 W: 11 08 b.Barnsley 21-10-82
Internationals: England U18.

1999–2000	Barnsley	0	0		
2000–01	Barnsley	7	0		
2001–02	Barnsley	1	0		
2002–03	Barnsley	16	0		
2003–04	Barnsley	43	3		
2004–05	Barnsley	39	6		
2005–06	Barnsley	36	1		
2006–07	Barnsley	32	1	**174**	**11**
2007–08	Tranmere R	38	6		
2008–09	Tranmere R	44	11	**82**	**17**
2009–10	Huddersfield T	40	6		
2010–11	Huddersfield T	27	3		
2011–12	Huddersfield T	28	1		
2012–13	Huddersfield T	0	0	**95**	**10**
2012–13	Milton Keynes D	33	1		
2013–14	Milton Keynes D	30	2		
2014–15	Milton Keynes D	45	1		

2015–16 Milton Keynes D 34 2 **142** **6**
2016–17 Bury 42 0 **42** **0**
2017–18 Port Vale 33 3
2018–19 Port Vale 27 2 **60** **5**

LEGGE, Leon (D) **320** **29**
H: 6 1 W: 11 02 b.Bexhill 1-7-85
2009–10 Brentford 29 2
2010–11 Brentford 30 3
2011–12 Brentford 28 4
2012–13 Brentford 7 0 **94** **9**
2012–13 Gillingham 22 2
2013–14 Gillingham 37 2
2014–15 Gillingham 22 4 **81** **8**
2015–16 Cambridge U 39 3
2016–17 Cambridge U 44 6
2017–18 Cambridge U 27 2 **110** **11**
2018–19 Port Vale 35 1 **35** **1**

MILLER, Ricky (F) **58** **6**
b. 13-3-89
2014–15 Luton T 12 1 **12** **1**
From Dover Ath.
2017–18 Peterborough U 10 0 **10** **0**
2017–18 *Mansfield T* 8 1 **8** **1**
2018–19 Port Vale 28 4 **28** **4**

MONTANO, Cristian (F) **189** **25**
H: 5 11 W: 12 00 b.Cali 11-12-91
2010–11 West Ham U 0 0
2011–12 West Ham U 0 0
2011–12 *Notts Co* 15 4 **15** **4**
2011–12 *Swindon T* 4 1 **4** **1**
2011–12 *Dagenham & R* 10 3 **10** **3**
2011–12 *Oxford U* 9 2 **9** **2**
2012–13 Oldham Ath 30 1
2013–14 Oldham Ath 10 2 **40** **3**
2015–16 Bristol R 27 2
2016–17 Bristol R 25 1 **52** **3**
2017–18 Port Vale 30 4
2018–19 Port Vale 29 5 **59** **9**

OYELEKE, Emmanuel (M) **39** **3**
H: 5 9 W: 11 11 b.Wandsworth 24-12-92
2011–12 Brentford 1 0
2012–13 Brentford 0 0
2012–13 *Northampton T* 2 0 **2** **0**
2013–14 Brentford 0 0
2014–15 Brentford 0 0 **1** **0**
2014–15 Exeter C 0 0
2015–16 Exeter C 8 0 **8** **0**
From Aldershot T.
2018–19 Port Vale 28 3 **28** **3**

POPE, Tom (F) **437** **118**
H: 6 3 W: 11 03 b.Stoke 27-8-85
2005–06 Crewe Alex 0 0
2006–07 Crewe Alex 4 0
2007–08 Crewe Alex 26 7
2008–09 Crewe Alex 26 10 **56** **17**
2009–10 Rotherham U 35 3
2010–11 Rotherham U 18 1 **53** **4**
2010–11 *Port Vale* 13 3
2011–12 Port Vale 41 5
2012–13 Port Vale 46 31
2013–14 Port Vale 43 12
2014–15 Port Vale 33 8
2015–16 Bury 36 6
2016–17 Bury 37 4 **73** **10**
2016–17 Port Vale 0 0
2017–18 Port Vale 41 17
2018–19 Port Vale 38 11 **255** **87**

PUGH, Danny (M) **359** **17**
H: 6 0 W: 12 10 b.Cheadle Hulme 19-10-82
2000–01 Manchester U 0 0
2001–02 Manchester U 0 0
2002–03 Manchester U 1 0
2003–04 Manchester U 0 0 **1** **0**
2004–05 Leeds U 38 5
2005–06 Leeds U 12 0
2006–07 Preston NE 45 4
2007–08 Preston NE 7 0
2007–08 Stoke C 30 0
2008–09 Stoke C 17 0
2009–10 Stoke C 7 1
2010–11 Stoke C 10 0
2010–11 *Preston NE* 5 0 **57** **4**
2011–12 Stoke C 3 0 **67** **1**
2011–12 Leeds U 34 2
2012–13 Leeds U 4 0
2012–13 *Sheffield W* 16 1 **16** **1**
2013–14 Leeds U 20 2 **108** **9**
2014–15 Coventry C 5 0 **5** **0**
2015–16 Bury 39 0 **39** **0**
2016–17 Blackpool 18 0 **18** **0**
2016–17 Port Vale 14 0
2017–18 Port Vale 33 2
2018–19 Port Vale 1 0 **48** **2**

QUIGLEY, Scott (F) **20** **0**
H: 6 4 W: 14 02 b. 2-9-92
From The New Saints.
2017–18 Blackpool 9 0
2018–19 Blackpool 0 0 **9** **0**
2018–19 Port Vale 11 0 **11** **0**

RAWLINSON, Connell (D) **28** **1**
H: 6 4 W: 13 08 b.Chester 22-9-91
Internationals: Wales C.
From Chester C, The New Saints.
2018–19 Port Vale 28 1 **28** **1**

SMITH, Nathan (D) **136** **5**
H: 6 0 W: 11 05 b.Madeley 3-4-96
2013–14 Port Vale 0 0
2014–15 Port Vale 0 0
2015–16 Port Vale 0 0
2016–17 Port Vale 46 4
2017–18 Port Vale 46 1
2018–19 Port Vale 44 0 **136** **5**

TONGE, Michael (M) **478** **34**
H: 6 0 W: 11 10 b.Manchester 7-4-83
Internationals: England U20, U21.
2000–01 Sheffield U 2 0
2001–02 Sheffield U 30 3
2002–03 Sheffield U 44 6
2003–04 Sheffield U 46 4
2004–05 Sheffield U 34 2
2005–06 Sheffield U 30 3
2006–07 Sheffield U 27 2
2007–08 Sheffield U 45 1
2008–09 Sheffield U 4 0 **262** **21**
2008–09 Stoke C 10 0
2009–10 Stoke C 0 0
2009–10 *Preston NE* 7 0
2009–10 *Derby Co* 18 2 **18** **2**
2010–11 Stoke C 2 0
2010–11 *Preston NE* 5 1 **12** **1**
2011–12 Stoke C 0 0
2011–12 *Barnsley* 10 0 **10** **0**
2012–13 Stoke C 0 0 **12** **0**
2012–13 Leeds U 35 4
2013–14 Leeds U 23 0
2014–15 Leeds U 10 0 **68** **4**
2014–15 *Millwall* 6 0 **6** **0**
2015–16 Stevenage 29 2
2016–17 Stevenage 27 1 **56** **3**
2017–18 Port Vale 33 3
2018–19 Port Vale 1 0 **34** **3**

TURNER, Dan (F) **34** **3**
b. 23-6-98
2015–16 Port Vale 1 0
2016–17 Port Vale 16 0
2017–18 Port Vale 17 3
2018–19 Port Vale 0 0 **34** **3**
2018–19 *Falkirk* 0 0

VASSELL, Theo (D) **15** **0**
b. 2-1-97
2014–15 Stoke C 0 0
2015–16 Oldham Ath 0 0
2016–17 Walsall 0 0
From Gateshead.
2018–19 Port Vale 15 0 **15** **0**

WHITFIELD, Ben (M) **101** **10**
H: 5 5 W: 9 11 b. 28-2-96
2013–14 Bournemouth 0 0
2014–15 Bournemouth 0 0
2015–16 Bournemouth 0 0
2016–17 Bournemouth 0 0
2016–17 *Yeovil T* 34 2 **34** **2**
2017–18 Bournemouth 0 0
2017–18 *Port Vale* 37 4
2018–19 Port Vale 30 4 **67** **8**

WORRALL, David (M) **368** **28**
H: 6 0 W: 11 03 b.Manchester 12-6-90
2006–07 Bury 1 0
2007–08 Bury 0 0
2007–08 WBA 0 0
2008–09 *Accrington S* 4 0 **4** **0**
2008–09 *Shrewsbury T* 9 0 **9** **0**
2009–10 WBA 0 0
2009–10 Bury 40 4
2010–11 Bury 40 2
2011–12 Bury 41 3
2012–13 Bury 41 2 **163** **11**
2013–14 Rotherham U 3 1 **3** **1**
2013–14 *Oldham Ath* 18 1 **18** **1**
2014–15 Southend U 38 6
2015–16 Southend U 35 3 **73** **9**
2016–17 Millwall 33 1 **33** **1**
2017–18 Port Vale 40 4
2018–19 Port Vale 25 1 **65** **5**

Players retained or with offer of contract
Campbell, Gordon Ryan Joseph; Trickett-Smith, Daniel Thomas.

Scholars
Beeston, Max Charlie; Berks, Joseph Peter; Blight, Mawgan Anthony; Ede, Joshua Lennon; Green-Birch, Lucas Gabriel; Hallchurch, Alexander George Ewart; Jackson, Finley Thomas; Johnson, Kyle Dean; Stevens, Jack Thomas; Wakefield, Jack James.

PORTSMOUTH (66)

BASS, Alex (G) **1** **0**
H: 6 2 W: 11 00 b.Southampton 1-1-97
2014–15 Portsmouth 0 0
2015–16 Portsmouth 0 0
2016–17 Portsmouth 0 0
2017–18 Portsmouth 1 0
2018–19 Portsmouth 0 0 **1** **0**

BROWN, Lee (M) **287** **19**
H: 6 0 W: 12 06 b.Bromley 10-8-90
Internationals: England C.
2008–09 QPR 0 0
2009–10 QPR 1 0
2010–11 QPR 0 0 **1** **0**
2011–12 Bristol R 42 7
2012–13 Bristol R 39 3
2013–14 Bristol R 41 2
2015–16 Bristol R 46 6
2016–17 Bristol R 41 0
2017–18 Bristol R 33 1 **242** **19**
2018–19 Portsmouth 44 0 **44** **0**

BURGESS, Christian (D) **213** **9**
H: 6 5 W: 13 02 b. 7-10-91
2012–13 Middlesbrough 1 0
2013–14 Middlesbrough 0 0 **1** **0**
2013–14 *Hartlepool U* 41 0 **41** **0**
2014–15 Peterborough U 30 2 **30** **2**
2015–16 Portsmouth 37 2
2016–17 Portsmouth 44 4
2017–18 Portsmouth 35 0
2018–19 Portsmouth 25 1 **141** **7**

CANNON, Andy (M) **103** **4**
H: 5 9 W: 11 09 b.Ashton-under-Lyne 14-3-96
2014–15 Rochdale 18 0
2015–16 Rochdale 25 0
2016–17 Rochdale 25 2
2017–18 Rochdale 21 2
2018–19 Rochdale 12 0 **101** **4**
2018–19 Portsmouth 2 0 **2** **0**

CASEY, Matthew (D) **0** **0**
2017–18 Portsmouth 0 0
2018–19 Portsmouth 0 0

CLARKE, Matthew (M) **154** **7**
H: 5 11 W: 11 00 b.Ipswich 22-9-96
2013–14 Ipswich T 0 0
2014–15 Ipswich T 4 0
2015–16 Ipswich T 0 0 **4** **0**
2015–16 *Portsmouth* 29 1
2016–17 Portsmouth 33 1
2017–18 Portsmouth 42 2
2018–19 Portsmouth 46 3 **150** **7**

CLOSE, Ben (M) **87** **10**
H: 5 9 W: 11 11 b.Portsmouth 8-8-96
2013–14 Portsmouth 0 0
2014–15 Portsmouth 6 0
2015–16 Portsmouth 7 0
2016–17 Portsmouth 0 0
2017–18 Portsmouth 40 2
2018–19 Portsmouth 34 8 **87** **10**

CURTIS, Ronan (F) **41** **11**
H: 6 0 W: 12 02 b.Derry 29-3-96
Internationals: Republic of Ireland U21, Full caps.
2018–19 Portsmouth 41 11 **41** **11**

DENNIS, Louis (F) **9** **0**
H: 6 1 W: 10 12 b.Hendon 9-10-92
2011–12 Dagenham & R 0 0
2012–13 Dagenham & R 6 0
2013–14 Dagenham & R 2 0 **8** **0**
From Bromley.
2018–19 Portsmouth 1 0 **1** **0**

DONOHUE, Dion (M) **98 1**
H: 5 11 W: 10 06 b.Bodedern 26-8-93

2015–16	Chesterfield	17	0		
2016–17	Chesterfield	37	1		
2017–18	Chesterfield	2	0	**56**	**1**
2017–18	Portsmouth	32	0		
2018–19	Portsmouth	10	0	**42**	**0**

DURIN, Petar (G) **0 0**
b. 4-3-01
From Atalanta.

2018–19	Portsmouth	0	0		

EVANS, Gary (F) **454 79**
H: 6 0 W: 12 08 b.Stockport 26-4-88

2007–08	Macclesfield T	42	7		
2008–09	Macclesfield T	40	12	**82**	**19**
2009–10	Bradford C	43	11		
2010–11	Bradford C	36	3	**79**	**14**
2011–12	Rotherham U	32	7		
2012–13	Rotherham U	13	2	**45**	**9**
2012–13	Fleetwood T	16	1		
2013–14	Fleetwood T	34	6		
2014–15	Fleetwood T	43	3	**93**	**10**
2015–16	Portsmouth	40	10		
2016–17	Portsmouth	41	5		
2017–18	Portsmouth	32	2		
2018–19	Portsmouth	42	10	**155**	**27**

FLINT, Josh (M) **0 0**
b.Waterlooville 13-10-00

2018–19	Portsmouth	0	0		

HANCOTT, Joe (D) **0 0**

2017–18	Portsmouth	0	0		
2018–19	Portsmouth	0	0		

HAUNSTRUP, Brandon (D) **22 0**
b. 26-10-96

2015–16	Portsmouth	1	0		
2016–17	Portsmouth	0	0		
2017–18	Portsmouth	16	0		
2018–19	Portsmouth	5	0	**22**	**0**

HAWKINS, Oliver (F) **88 15**
b. 8-4-92
From North Greenford U, Hillingdon Bor, Northwood, Hemel Hempstead T.

2015–16	Dagenham & R	18	1	**18**	**1**
2017–18	Portsmouth	31	7		
2018–19	Portsmouth	39	7	**70**	**14**

ISGROVE, Lloyd (M) **62 2**
H: 5 10 W: 11 05 b.Yeovil 12-1-93
Internationals: Wales U21, Full caps.

2011–12	Southampton	0	0		
2012–13	Southampton	0	0		
2013–14	Southampton	0	0		
2013–14	*Peterborough U*	8	1	**8**	**1**
2014–15	Southampton	1	0		
2014–15	*Sheffield W*	8	0	**8**	**0**
2015–16	Southampton	0	0		
2015–16	*Barnsley*	27	0		
2016–17	Southampton	0	0	**1**	**0**
2017–18	Barnsley	16	1		
2018–19	Barnsley	2	0	**45**	**1**
2018–19	Portsmouth	0	0		

JOHNSTON, Oscar (M) **0 0**
b.Portsmouth 13-1-01

2018–19	Portsmouth	0	0		

LETHBRIDGE, Bradley (F) **0 0**

2017–18	Portsmouth	0	0		
2018–19	Portsmouth	0	0		

LOWE, Jamal (F) **111 25**
H: 6 0 W: 12 06 b.Harrow 21-7-94
Internationals: England C.

2012–13	Barnet	8	0	**8**	**0**

From St Albans C, Hemel Hempstead T, Hampton & Richmond.

2016–17	Portsmouth	14	4		
2017–18	Portsmouth	44	6		
2018–19	Portsmouth	45	15	**103**	**25**

MACGILLIVRAY, Craig (G) **66 0**
H: 6 2 W: 12 04 b.Harrogate 12-1-93

2014–15	Walsall	2	0		
2015–16	Walsall	5	0		
2016–17	Walsall	5	0	**12**	**0**
2017–18	Shrewsbury T	8	0	**8**	**0**
2018–19	Portsmouth	46	0	**46**	**0**

MALONEY, Leon (M) **0 0**
b. 13-5-01

2018–19	Portsmouth	0	0		

MAY, Adam (M) **15 0**
b. 6-12-97

2014–15	Portsmouth	1	0		
2015–16	Portsmouth	1	0		
2016–17	Portsmouth	0	0		
2017–18	Portsmouth	13	0		
2018–19	Portsmouth	0	0	**15**	**0**

McGEE, Luke (G) **83 0**
H: 6 2 W: 12 08 b.Edgware 9-2-95
Internationals: England U17.

2014–15	Tottenham H	0	0		
2015–16	Tottenham H	0	0		
2016–17	Tottenham H	0	0		
2016–17	*Peterborough U*	39	0	**39**	**0**
2017–18	Portsmouth	44	0		
2018–19	Portsmouth	0	0	**44**	**0**

MNOGA, Haji (D) **0 0**
b.Portsmouth 16-4-02
Internationals: England U17.

2018–19	Portsmouth	0	0		

MORRIS, Bryn (M) **74 4**
H: 6 0 W: 11 01 b.Hartlepool 25-4-96
Internationals: England U16, U17, U18, U19, U20.

2012–13	Middlesbrough	1	0		
2013–14	Middlesbrough	1	0		
2014–15	Middlesbrough	0	0		
2014–15	*Burton Alb*	5	0	**5**	**0**
2015–16	Middlesbrough	0	0		
2015–16	*Coventry C*	6	0	**6**	**0**
2015–16	*York C*	3	0	**3**	**0**
2015–16	*Walsall*	1	0	**1**	**0**
2016–17	Middlesbrough	0	0	**2**	**0**
2016–17	*Shrewsbury T*	13	0		
2017–18	Shrewsbury T	18	0		
2018–19	Shrewsbury T	0	0	**31**	**0**
2018–19	*Wycombe W*	19	3	**19**	**3**
2018–19	Portsmouth	7	1	**7**	**1**

NAYLOR, Tom (D) **221 17**
H: 5 11 W: 11 05 b.Sutton-in-Ashfield 28-6-91

2011–12	Derby Co	8	0		
2012–13	Derby Co	0	0		
2012–13	*Bradford C*	5	0	**5**	**0**
2013–14	Derby Co	0	0		
2013–14	*Newport Co*	33	1	**33**	**1**
2014–15	Derby Co	0	0	**8**	**0**
2014–15	*Cambridge U*	8	0	**8**	**0**
2014–15	*Burton Alb*	17	0		
2015–16	Burton Alb	41	6		
2016–17	Burton Alb	33	3		
2017–18	Burton Alb	33	3	**124**	**12**
2018–19	Portsmouth	43	4	**43**	**4**

PITMAN, Brett (F) **479 164**
H: 6 0 W: 11 00 b.Jersey 31-1-88

2005–06	Bournemouth	19	1		
2006–07	Bournemouth	29	5		
2007–08	Bournemouth	39	6		
2008–09	Bournemouth	39	17		
2009–10	Bournemouth	46	26		
2010–11	Bournemouth	2	3		
2010–11	Bristol C	39	13		
2011–12	Bristol C	35	7		
2012–13	Bristol C	3	0	**77**	**20**
2012–13	Bournemouth	26	19		
2013–14	Bournemouth	34	5		
2014–15	Bournemouth	34	13	**268**	**95**
2015–16	Ipswich T	42	10		
2016–17	Ipswich T	22	4	**64**	**14**
2017–18	Portsmouth	38	24		
2018–19	Portsmouth	32	11	**70**	**35**

PITMAN, Leon (G) **0 0**

2018–19	Portsmouth	0	0		

READ, Freddie (M) **0 0**
b.Portsmouth 27-10-00

2018–19	Portsmouth	0	0		

SMITH, Dan (M) **0 0**

2017–18	Portsmouth	0	0		
2018–19	Portsmouth	0	0		

THOMPSON, Nathan (D) **234 4**
H: 5 7 W: 11 02 b.Chester 9-11-90

2009–10	Swindon T	0	0		
2010–11	Swindon T	3	0		
2011–12	Swindon T	5	0		
2012–13	Swindon T	26	0		
2013–14	Swindon T	41	1		
2014–15	Swindon T	35	0		
2015–16	Swindon T	23	1		
2016–17	Swindon T	34	2	**167**	**4**
2017–18	Portsmouth	36	0		
2018–19	Portsmouth	31	0	**67**	**0**

WALKES, Anton (M) **57 4**
b. 8-2-97

2016–17	Tottenham H	0	0		
2017	*Atlanta U*	21	2	**21**	**2**
2017–18	Tottenham H	0	0		
2017–18	*Portsmouth*	12	1		
2018–19	Portsmouth	24	1	**36**	**2**

WHATMOUGH, Jack (D) **86 1**
b.Gosport 19-8-96
Internationals: England U18, U19.

2012–13	Portsmouth	0	0		
2013–14	Portsmouth	12	0		
2014–15	Portsmouth	22	0		
2015–16	Portsmouth	2	0		
2016–17	Portsmouth	10	1		
2017–18	Portsmouth	14	0		
2018–19	Portsmouth	26	0	**86**	**1**

Scholars
Bridgman, Stanley Dean; Bruce, Thomas Douglas; Casey, Matthew Adam; Dandy, Joe Mark James; Flint, Joshua Huchson; Hancott, Joe Mark; Johnston, Oscar William James; Kavanagh, Harry John; Kelly, Liam James; Lethbridge, Bradley Stephen; Maloney, Leon Harry; Mnoga, Haji Suleiman Haji Ali; Pitman, Leon Neil David; Read, Frederick Edward; Robb, Ethan David; Stanley, Alfie Frederick James; Teggart, Eoin James; Whiting, James Christopher John.

PRESTON NE (67)

BARKHUIZEN, Tom (F) **228 48**
H: 5 9 W: 11 00 b.Blackpool 4-7-93

2011–12	Blackpool	0	0		
2011–12	*Hereford U*	38	11	**38**	**11**
2012–13	Blackpool	0	0		
2012–13	*Fleetwood T*	13	1	**13**	**1**
2013–14	Blackpool	14	1		
2014–15	Blackpool	7	0	**21**	**1**
2014–15	*Morecambe*	5	0		
2015–16	Morecambe	40	10		
2016–17	Morecambe	14	5	**59**	**15**
2016–17	Preston NE	17	6		
2017–18	Preston NE	46	8		
2018–19	Preston NE	34	6	**97**	**20**

BAXTER, Jack (M) **0 0**
b.Chorley 27-10-00

2018–19	Preston NE	0	0		

BROWNE, Alan (M) **177 26**
H: 5 8 W: 11 03 b.Cork 15-4-95
Internationals: Republic of Ireland U19, U21, Full caps.

2013–14	Preston NE	8	1		
2014–15	Preston NE	20	3		
2015–16	Preston NE	36	3		
2016–17	Preston NE	31	0		
2017–18	Preston NE	44	7		
2018–19	Preston NE	38	12	**177**	**26**

CLARKE, Tom (D) **313 15**
H: 6 0 W: 11 02 b.Sowerby Bridge 21-12-87
Internationals: England U18, U19.

2004–05	Huddersfield T	12	0		
2005–06	Huddersfield T	17	1		
2006–07	Huddersfield T	9	0		
2007–08	Huddersfield T	3	0		
2008–09	Huddersfield T	15	1		
2008–09	*Bradford C*	6	0	**6**	**0**
2009–10	Huddersfield T	21	0		
2010–11	Huddersfield T	5	1		
2011–12	Huddersfield T	14	0		
2011–12	*Leyton Orient*	10	0	**10**	**0**
2012–13	Huddersfield T	0	0	**96**	**3**
2013–14	Preston NE	42	4		
2014–15	Preston NE	43	1		
2015–16	Preston NE	35	0		
2016–17	Preston NE	42	4		
2017–18	Preston NE	18	2		
2018–19	Preston NE	21	1	**201**	**12**

CROWE, Michael (G) **0 0**
H: 6 2 W: 11 11 b.London 13-11-95
Internationals: Wales U19, U21, Full caps.

2013–14	Ipswich T	0	0		
2014–15	Ipswich T	0	0		
2014–15	Woking	0	0		
2015–16	Ipswich T	0	0		

2015–16	*Stevenage*	0	0		
2016–17	Ipswich T	0	0		
2017–18	Ipswich T	0	0		
2018–19	Preston NE	0	0		

DAVIES, Ben (D) **169 3**
H: 6 1 W: 11 09 b.Barrow 11-8-95

2012–13	Preston NE	3	0		
2013–14	Preston NE	0	0		
2013–14	*York C*	44	0	**44**	**0**
2014–15	Preston NE	4	0		
2014–15	*Tranmere R*	3	0	**3**	**0**
2015–16	Preston NE	0	0		
2015–16	*Newport Co*	19	0	**19**	**0**
2016–17	Preston NE	0	0		
2016–17	*Fleetwood T*	22	1	**22**	**1**
2017–18	Preston NE	34	1		
2018–19	Preston NE	40	1	**81**	**2**

EARL, Joshua (D) **33 0**
b. 24-10-98

2017–18	Preston NE	19	0		
2018–19	Preston NE	14	0	**33**	**0**

FISHER, Darnell (M) **143 1**
H: 5 9 W: 11 00 b.Reading 1-5-94

2012–13	Celtic	0	0		
2013–14	Celtic	12	0		
2014–15	Celtic	5	0		
2015–16	Celtic	0	0	**17**	**0**
2015–16	*St Johnstone*	23	1	**23**	**1**
2016–17	Rotherham U	34	0	**34**	**0**
2017–18	Preston NE	34	0		
2018–19	Preston NE	35	0	**69**	**0**

GALLAGHER, Paul (F) **506 84**
H: 6 1 W: 11 00 b.Glasgow 9-8-84
Internationals: Scotland U21, B, Full caps.

2002–03	Blackburn R	1	0		
2003–04	Blackburn R	26	3		
2004–05	Blackburn R	16	2		
2005–06	Blackburn R	1	0		
2005–06	*Stoke C*	37	11		
2006–07	Blackburn R	16	1		
2007–08	Blackburn R	0	0		
2007–08	*Preston NE*	19	1		
2007–08	*Stoke C*	7	0	**44**	**11**
2008–09	Blackburn R	0	0		
2008–09	*Plymouth Arg*	40	13	**40**	**13**
2009–10	Blackburn R	1	0	**61**	**6**
2009–10	Leicester C	41	7		
2010–11	Leicester C	41	10		
2011–12	Leicester C	28	8		
2012–13	Leicester C	8	0		
2012–13	Sheffield U	6	1	**6**	**1**
2013–14	Leicester C	0	0		
2013–14	*Preston NE*	28	6		
2014–15	Leicester C	0	0	**118**	**25**
2014–15	*Preston NE*	46	7		
2015–16	Preston NE	41	5		
2016–17	Preston NE	31	1		
2017–18	Preston NE	32	2		
2018–19	Preston NE	40	6	**237**	**28**

GINNELLY, Josh (M) **53 4**
b.Coventry 24-3-97

2013–14	Shrewsbury T	0	0		
2014–15	Shrewsbury T	3	0	**3**	**0**
2015–16	Burnley	0	0		
2016–17	Burnley	0	0		
2016–17	*Walsall*	9	0		
2017–18	Burnley	0	0		
2017–18	*Lincoln C*	15	2	**15**	**2**
2018–19	Walsall	21	2	**30**	**2**
2018–19	Preston NE	5	0	**5**	**0**

HARROP, Josh (M) **47 3**
H: 5 9 W: 11 00 b.Stockport 15-12-95
Internationals: England U20.

2016–17	Manchester U	1	1	**1**	**1**
2017–18	Preston NE	38	2		
2018–19	Preston NE	8	0	**46**	**2**

HORGAN, Daryl (M) **40 3**
H: 5 7 W: 10 10 b.Galway 10-8-92
Internationals: Republic of Ireland U19, U21, Full caps.
From Dundalk.

2016–17	Preston NE	19	2		
2017–18	Preston NE	20	1		
2018–19	Preston NE	1	0	**40**	**3**
2018–19	Hibernian	0	0		

Transferred to Hibernian August 2018.

HUDSON, Matthew (G) **1 0**
H: 6 4 b.Southport 29-7-98

2014–15	Preston NE	0	0		
2015–16	Preston NE	1	0		
2016–17	Preston NE	0	0		
2017–18	Preston NE	0	0		
2018–19	Preston NE	0	0	**1**	**0**
2018–19	*Bury*	0	0		

HUGHES, Andrew (D) **181 9**
b.Cardiff 5-6-92

2013–14	Newport Co	26	2		
2014–15	Newport Co	16	1		
2015–16	Newport Co	25	0	**67**	**3**
2016–17	Peterborough U	39	1		
2017–18	Peterborough U	43	2	**82**	**3**
2018–19	Preston NE	32	3	**32**	**3**

HUNTINGTON, Paul (D) **364 22**
H: 6 3 W: 12 08 b.Carlisle 17-9-87
Internationals: England U18.

2005–06	Newcastle U	0	0		
2006–07	Newcastle U	11	1		
2007–08	Newcastle U	0	0	**11**	**1**
2007–08	Leeds U	17	2		
2008–09	Leeds U	4	0		
2009–10	Leeds U	0	0	**21**	**2**
2009–10	Stockport Co	26	0	**26**	**0**
2010–11	Yeovil T	40	5		
2011–12	Yeovil T	37	2	**77**	**7**
2012–13	Preston NE	37	3		
2013–14	Preston NE	23	2		
2014–15	Preston NE	32	5		
2015–16	Preston NE	38	0		
2016–17	Preston NE	33	1		
2017–18	Preston NE	44	1		
2018–19	Preston NE	22	0	**229**	**12**

JOHNSON, Daniel (M) **193 32**
H: 5 8 W: 10 07 b.Kingston, Jamaica 8-10-92

2010–11	Aston Villa	0	0		
2011–12	Aston Villa	0	0		
2012–13	Aston Villa	0	0		
2012–13	*Yeovil T*	5	0	**5**	**0**
2013–14	Aston Villa	0	0		
2014–15	Aston Villa	0	0		
2014–15	*Chesterfield*	11	0	**11**	**0**
2014–15	*Oldham Ath*	6	3	**6**	**3**
2014–15	Preston NE	20	8		
2015–16	Preston NE	43	8		
2016–17	Preston NE	40	4		
2017–18	Preston NE	33	3		
2018–19	Preston NE	35	6	**171**	**29**

LEDSON, Ryan (M) **117 4**
H: 5 9 W: 10 12 b.Liverpool 19-8-97
Internationals: England U16, U17, U18, U19, U20.

2013–14	Everton	0	0		
2014–15	Everton	0	0		
2015–16	Everton	0	0		
2015–16	*Cambridge U*	27	0	**27**	**0**
2016–17	Oxford U	22	1		
2017–18	Oxford U	44	3	**66**	**4**
2018–19	Preston NE	24	0	**24**	**0**

MAGUIRE, Sean (F) **192 73**
H: 5 9 W: 11 10 b.Luton 1-5-94
Internationals: Republic of Ireland U19, U21, Full caps.

2010–11	West Ham U	0	0		
2011	*Waterford U*	8	1		
2011–12	West Ham U	0	0		
2012	*Waterford U*	26	13	**34**	**14**
2012–13	West Ham U	0	0		
2013–14	West Ham U	0	0		
2014	*Sligo R*	18	1	**18**	**1**
2014–15	West Ham U	0	0		
2014–15	*Accrington S*	33	7	**33**	**7**
2015	Dundalk	6	0	**6**	**0**
2016	Cork C	30	18		
2017	Cork C	21	20	**51**	**38**
2017–18	Preston NE	24	10		
2018–19	Preston NE	26	3	**50**	**13**

MAXWELL, Chris (G) **186 0**
H: 6 0 W: 11 07 b.Wrexham 30-7-90
Internationals: Wales U17, U19, U21, U23.

2012–13	Fleetwood T	0	0		
2013–14	Fleetwood T	18	0		
2014–15	Fleetwood T	46	0		
2015–16	Fleetwood T	46	0	**110**	**0**
2016–17	Preston NE	38	0		
2017–18	Preston NE	30	0		
2018–19	Preston NE	8	0	**76**	**0**
2018–19	*Charlton Ath*	0	0		

MOULT, Louis (F) **147 46**
H: 6 0 W: 13 05 b.Stoke 14-5-92

2009–10	Stoke C	1	0		
2010–11	Stoke C	0	0		
2010–11	*Bradford C*	11	1	**11**	**1**
2011–12	Stoke C	0	0		
2011–12	*Accrington S*	4	0	**4**	**0**
2012–13	Stoke C	0	0	**1**	**0**
2012–13	Northampton T	13	1	**13**	**1**

From Nuneaton T, Wrexham.

2015–16	Motherwell	38	15		
2016–17	Motherwell	31	15		
2017–18	Motherwell	15	8	**84**	**38**
2017–18	Preston NE	10	2		
2018–19	Preston NE	24	4	**34**	**6**

O'CONNOR, Kevin (D) **18 0**
b.Enniscorthy 7-5-95
Internationals: Republic of Ireland U17, U21.
From Waterford U, Cork C.

2017–18	Preston NE	8	0		
2017–18	*Fleetwood T*	4	0	**4**	**0**
2018–19	Preston NE	0	0	**8**	**0**
2018–19	*Crewe Alex*	6	0	**6**	**0**

O'REILLY, Adam (M) **1 0**
b. 11-5-01
Internationals: Republic of Ireland U17.

2017–18	Preston NE	0	0		
2018–19	Preston NE	1	0	**1**	**0**

PEARSON, Ben (M) **156 3**
H: 5 5 W: 11 03 b.Oldham 4-1-95
Internationals: England U16, U17, U18, U19, U21, Full caps.

2013–14	Manchester U	0	0		
2014–15	Manchester U	0	0		
2014–15	*Barnsley*	22	1		
2015–16	Manchester U	0	0		
2015–16	*Barnsley*	23	1	**45**	**2**
2015–16	Preston NE	15	0		
2016–17	Preston NE	31	1		
2017–18	Preston NE	35	0		
2018–19	Preston NE	30	0	**111**	**1**

POTTS, Brad (M) **259 36**
H: 6 2 W: 12 09 b.Carlisle 3-7-94
Internationals: England U19.

2012–13	Carlisle U	27	0		
2013–14	Carlisle U	37	2		
2014–15	Carlisle U	39	7	**103**	**9**
2015–16	Blackpool	45	6		
2016–17	Blackpool	42	10	**87**	**16**
2017–18	Barnsley	37	3		
2018–19	Barnsley	22	6	**59**	**9**
2018–19	Preston NE	10	2	**10**	**2**

RAFFERTY, Joe (D) **220 3**
H: 6 0 W: 11 11 b.Liverpool 6-10-93
Internationals: Republic of Ireland U18, U19.

2012–13	Rochdale	21	0		
2013–14	Rochdale	31	0		
2014–15	Rochdale	31	1		
2015–16	Rochdale	31	1		
2016–17	Rochdale	40	0		
2017–18	Rochdale	33	1		
2018–19	Rochdale	27	0	**214**	**3**
2018–19	Preston NE	6	0	**6**	**0**

RIPLEY, Connor (G) **139 0**
H: 5 11 W: 11 13 b.Middlesbrough 13-2-93
Internationals: England U19, U20.

2010–11	Middlesbrough	1	0		
2011–12	Middlesbrough	1	0		
2011–12	*Oxford U*	1	0	**1**	**0**
2012–13	Middlesbrough	0	0		
2013–14	Middlesbrough	0	0		
2013–14	*Bradford C*	0	0		
2014	*Ostersunds*	14	0	**14**	**0**
2014–15	Middlesbrough	0	0		
2015–16	Middlesbrough	0	0		
2015–16	*Motherwell*	36	0	**36**	**0**
2016–17	Middlesbrough	0	0		
2016–17	*Oldham Ath*	46	0	**46**	**0**
2017–18	Middlesbrough	0	0		
2017–18	*Burton Alb*	2	0	**2**	**0**
2017–18	*Bury*	15	0	**15**	**0**
2018–19	Middlesbrough	0	0	**2**	**0**
2018–19	*Accrington S*	21	0	**21**	**0**
2018–19	Preston NE	2	0	**2**	**0**

ROBINSON, Callum (F) **159 35**
H: 5 10 W: 11 11 b.Birmingham 2-2-95
Internationals: England U16, U17, U19, U20. Republic of Ireland Full caps.

2013–14	Aston Villa	4	0		
2014–15	Aston Villa	0	0		
2014–15	*Preston NE*	25	4		
2015–16	Aston Villa	0	0	**4**	**0**
2015–16	*Bristol C*	6	0	**6**	**0**
2015–16	*Preston NE*	14	2		
2016–17	Preston NE	42	10		

2017–18 Preston NE 41 7
2018–19 Preston NE 27 12 **149 35**

RUDD, Declan (G) 171 0
H: 6 3 W: 12 06 b.Diss 16-1-91
Internationals: England U16, U17, U19, U20, U21, Full caps.
2008–09 Norwich C 0 0
2009–10 Norwich C 7 0
2010–11 Norwich C 1 0
2011–12 Norwich C 2 0
2012–13 Norwich C 0 0
2012–13 *Preston NE* 14 0
2013–14 Norwich C 0 0
2013–14 *Preston NE* 46 0
2014–15 Norwich C 0 0
2015–16 Norwich C 11 0
2016–17 Norwich C 0 0 **21 0**
2016–17 *Charlton Ath* 38 0 **38 0**
2017–18 Preston NE 16 0
2018–19 Preston NE 36 0 **112 0**

SIMPSON, Connor (F) 11 1
b.Guisborough 24-1-00
2016–17 Hartlepool U 2 0 **2 0**
2017–18 Preston NE 1 0
2018–19 Preston NE 0 0 **1 0**
2018–19 *Carlisle U* 8 1 **8 1**

STOCKLEY, Jayden (F) 209 66
H: 6 2 W: 12 07 b.Poole 10-10-93
2009–10 Bournemouth 2 0
2010–11 Bournemouth 4 0
2011–12 Bournemouth 10 0
2011–12 *Accrington S* 9 3 **9 3**
2012–13 Bournemouth 0 0
2013–14 Bournemouth 0 0
2013–14 *Leyton Orient* 8 1 **8 1**
2013–14 *Torquay U* 19 1 **19 1**
2014–15 Bournemouth 0 0
2014–15 *Cambridge U* 3 2 **3 2**
2014–15 *Luton T* 13 3 **13 3**
2015–16 Bournemouth 0 0 **16 0**
2015–16 *Portsmouth* 9 2 **9 2**
2015–16 *Exeter C* 22 10
2016–17 Aberdeen 27 5 **27 5**
2017–18 Exeter C 41 19
2018–19 Exeter C 25 16 **88 45**
2018–19 Preston NE 17 4 **17 4**

STOREY, Jordan (D) 41 3
H: 6 2 W: 12 00 b. 2-9-97
2016–17 Exeter C 0 0
2017–18 Exeter C 13 2 **13 2**
2018–19 Preston NE 28 1 **28 1**

WALKER, Ethan (F) 1 0
b. 28-7-02
2018–19 Preston NE 1 0 **1 0**

WOODS, Calum (D) 273 11
H: 5 11 W: 11 07 b.Liverpool 5-2-87
2006–07 Dunfermline Ath 12 0
2007–08 Dunfermline Ath 25 0
2008–09 Dunfermline Ath 30 5
2009–10 Dunfermline Ath 29 2
2010–11 Dunfermline Ath 32 3 **128 10**
2011–12 Huddersfield T 26 0
2012–13 Huddersfield T 27 0
2013–14 Huddersfield T 19 1 **72 1**
2014–15 Preston NE 18 0
2015–16 Preston NE 32 0
2016–17 Preston NE 0 0
2017–18 Preston NE 16 0
2018–19 Preston NE 1 0 **67 0**
2018–19 *Bradford C* 6 0 **6 0**

Players retained or with offer of contract
Bodin, Billy Paul; Burke, Graham Dylan.

Scholars
Armer, Jack; Brannigan, Darren Lee; Corcoran, James Hugh; Cottam, James; Dolan, Tyrhys; Earl, Lewis Robert Ian; Jolly, Jerome Thomas; Lenton, Callum; McFayden, Lincoln Tye; McManus, Brian Frank; Ngongo, Precieux Luz; Nolan, Joseph Edward; Pollard, Joshua Thomas; Potts, Louis John; Simmons, Lewis; Walker, Glenn Ethan; Williams, Tyler Michael.

QPR (68)

BANSAL-McNULTY, Amrit (M) 0 0
b. 16-3-00
2018–19 QPR 0 0

BAPTISTE, Alex (D) 482 24
H: 6 0 W: 11 11 b.Sutton-in-Ashfield 31-1-86
2002–03 Mansfield T 4 0
2003–04 Mansfield T 17 0
2004–05 Mansfield T 41 1
2005–06 Mansfield T 41 1
2006–07 Mansfield T 46 3
2007–08 Mansfield T 25 0 **174 5**
2008–09 Blackpool 21 1
2009–10 Blackpool 42 3
2010–11 Blackpool 21 2
2011–12 Blackpool 43 1
2012–13 Blackpool 43 1 **170 8**
2013–14 Bolton W 39 4
2014–15 Bolton W 0 0 **39 4**
2014–15 *Blackburn R* 32 3 **32 3**
2015–16 Middlesbrough 0 0
2015–16 *Sheffield U* 11 1 **11 1**
2016–17 Middlesbrough 0 0
2016–17 *Preston NE* 24 3 **24 3**
2017–18 QPR 26 0
2018–19 QPR 4 0 **30 0**
2018–19 *Luton T* 2 0 **2 0**

BETTACHE, Faysal (M) 0 0
b.Westminster 7-7-00
2018–19 QPR 0 0

BIDWELL, Jake (D) 312 5
H: 6 0 W: 11 00 b.Southport 21-3-93
Internationals: England U16, U17, U18, U19.
2009–10 Everton 0 0
2010–11 Everton 0 0
2011–12 Everton 0 0
2011–12 *Brentford* 24 0
2012–13 Everton 0 0
2012–13 *Brentford* 40 0
2013–14 Brentford 38 0
2014–15 Brentford 43 0
2015–16 Brentford 45 3 **190 3**
2016–17 QPR 36 0
2017–18 QPR 46 2
2018–19 QPR 40 0 **122 2**

BRZOZOWSKI, Marcin (G) 0 0
b. 29-10-98
Internationals: Poland U19.
2015–16 QPR 0 0
2016–17 QPR 0 0
2017–18 QPR 0 0
2018–19 QPR 0 0

CARLYLE, Nathan (D) 0 0
2018–19 QPR 0 0

CHAIR, Ilias (M) 26 7
b.Lierse 30-10-97
Internationals: Morocco U23.
2015–16 Lierse 2 0
2016–17 Lierse 0 0 **2 0**
2017–18 QPR 4 1
2018–19 QPR 4 0 **8 1**
2018–19 *Stevenage* 16 6 **16 6**

COUSINS, Jordan (D) 186 8
H: 5 10 W: 11 05 b.Greenwich 6-3-94
Internationals: England U16, U17, U18, U20.
2011–12 Charlton Ath 0 0
2012–13 Charlton Ath 0 0
2013–14 Charlton Ath 42 2
2014–15 Charlton Ath 44 3
2015–16 Charlton Ath 39 2 **125 7**
2016–17 QPR 18 0
2017–18 QPR 15 0
2018–19 QPR 28 1 **61 1**

DALLING, Deshane (F) 0 0
b.London 13-8-98
From Huddersfield T.
2018–19 QPR 0 0

DIENG, Timothy (G) 32 0
b. 23-11-94
2010–11 Red Star Zurich 0 0
2011–12 Grasshoppers 0 0
2012–13 Grasshoppers 0 0
2012–13 *Grenchen* 3 0 **3 0**
2013–14 Grasshoppers 0 0
2014–15 Grasshoppers 0 0
2015–16 MSV Duisburg 0 0
2016–17 QPR 0 0
2017–18 QPR 0 0
2018–19 QPR 0 0
2018–19 *Stevenage* 13 0 **13 0**
2018–19 *Dundee* 16 0 **16 0**

EZE, Eberechi (M) 78 11
H: 5 8 W: 10 08 b. 29-6-98
Internationals: England U20.
From Millwall.
2016–17 QPR 0 0
2017–18 Wycombe W 20 5 **20 5**
2017–18 QPR 16 2
2018–19 QPR 42 4 **58 6**

FELIX, Joe (D) 0 0
H: 5 4 W: 9 02 b.London 29-9-99
From Fulham.
2018–19 QPR 0 0

FOX, Charlie (D) 0 0
b.Hammersmith 26-11-98
2018–19 QPR 0 0
2018–19 *Wycombe W* 0 0

FREEMAN, Luke (F) 333 41
H: 6 0 W: 10 00 b.Dartford 22-3-92
Internationals: England U16, U17.
2007–08 Gillingham 1 0 **1 0**
2008–09 Arsenal 0 0
2009–10 Arsenal 0 0
2010–11 Arsenal 0 0
2010–11 *Yeovil T* 13 2 **13 2**
2011–12 Arsenal 0 0
2011–12 Stevenage 26 7
2012–13 Stevenage 39 2
2013–14 Stevenage 45 6 **110 15**
2014–15 Bristol C 46 7
2015–16 Bristol C 41 1
2016–17 Bristol C 18 2 **105 10**
2016–17 QPR 16 2
2017–18 QPR 45 5
2018–19 QPR 43 7 **104 14**

FURLONG, Darnell (D) 119 3
b. 31-10-95
2014–15 QPR 3 0
2015–16 QPR 0 0
2015–16 *Northampton T* 10 0 **10 0**
2015–16 *Cambridge U* 21 0 **21 0**
2016–17 QPR 14 0
2016–17 *Swindon T* 24 2 **24 2**
2017–18 QPR 22 0
2018–19 QPR 25 1 **64 1**

GOSS, Sean (M) 25 2
H: 5 10 W: 11 03 b.Wegberg 1-10-95
2015–16 Manchester U 0 0
2016–17 Manchester U 0 0
2016–17 QPR 6 0
2017–18 QPR 0 0
2017–18 *Rangers* 13 2 **13 2**
2018–19 QPR 0 0 **6 0**
2018–19 *St Johnstone* 6 0 **6 0**

HALL, Grant (D) 136 2
H: 5 9 W: 11 02 b.Brighton 29-10-91
2009–10 Brighton & HA 0 0
2010–11 Brighton & HA 0 0
2011–12 Brighton & HA 1 0 **1 0**
2012–13 Tottenham H 0 0
2013–14 Tottenham H 0 0
2013–14 *Swindon T* 27 0 **27 0**
2014–15 Tottenham H 0 0
2014–15 *Birmingham C* 7 0 **7 0**
2014–15 *Blackpool* 12 1 **12 1**
2015–16 QPR 39 1
2016–17 QPR 34 0
2017–18 QPR 4 0
2018–19 QPR 12 0 **89 1**

HAMALAINEN, Niko (M) 7 0
b.Florida 3-5-97
Internationals: Finland U18, U19, U21, Full caps.
2014–15 QPR 0 0
2015–16 QPR 0 0
2015–16 *Dagenham & R* 1 0 **1 0**
2016–17 QPR 3 0
2017–18 QPR 0 0
2018–19 QPR 0 0 **3 0**
2018–19 *Los Angeles FC* 3 0 **3 0**

INGRAM, Matt (G) 155 0
H: 6 3 W: 12 13 b.Croydon 18-12-93
2011–12 Wycombe W 0 0
2012–13 Wycombe W 8 0
2013–14 Wycombe W 46 0
2014–15 Wycombe W 46 0
2015–16 Wycombe W 24 0
2015–16 QPR 4 0
2016–17 QPR 0 0
2017–18 Northampton T 20 0 **20 0**
2017–18 QPR 2 0

2018–19	Wycombe W	1	0	**125**	**0**
2018–19	QPR	4	0	**10**	**0**

KAKAY, Osman (D) **24** **0**
b.Westminster 25-8-97
Internationals: Sierra Leone Full caps.

2015–16	QPR	0	0		
2015–16	*Livingston*	10	0	**10**	**0**
2016–17	QPR	1	0		
2016–17	Chesterfield	8	0		
2017–18	Chesterfield	0	0	**8**	**0**
2017–18	QPR	2	0		
2018–19	QPR	3	0	**6**	**0**

LEISTNER, Toni (D) **192** **6**
H: 6 3 W: 13 05 b.Dresden 19-8-90

2010–11	Dynamo Dresden	1	0		
2011–12	Dynamo Dresden	3	0		
2012–13	Dynamo Dresden	1	0		
2012–13	*Hallescher*	13	0	**13**	**0**
2013–14	Dynamo Dresden	16	0	**21**	**0**
2014–15	Union Berlin	30	1		
2015–16	Union Berlin	26	1		
2016–17	Union Berlin	30	1		
2017–18	Union Berlin	29	1	**115**	**4**
2018–19	QPR	43	2	**43**	**2**

LUMLEY, Joe (G) **86** **0**
H: 6 3 W: 11 07 b.Harlow 15-2-95

2013–14	QPR	0	0		
2014–15	QPR	0	0		
2014–15	*Accrington S*	5	0	**5**	**0**
2014–15	*Morecambe*	0	0		
2015–16	QPR	1	0		
2015–16	*Stevenage*	0	0		
2016–17	QPR	0	0		
2016–17	*Bristol R*	19	0	**19**	**0**
2017–18	QPR	2	0		
2017–18	*Blackpool*	17	0	**17**	**0**
2018–19	QPR	42	0	**45**	**0**

LUONGO, Massimo (F) **239** **23**
H: 5 8 W: 11 10 b.Sydney 25-9-92
Internationals: Australia U20, Full caps.

2010–11	Tottenham H	0	0		
2011–12	Tottenham H	0	0		
2012–13	Tottenham H	0	0		
2012–13	*Ipswich T*	9	0	**9**	**0**
2012–13	*Swindon T*	7	1		
2013–14	Swindon T	44	6		
2014–15	Swindon T	34	6	**85**	**13**
2015–16	QPR	30	0		
2016–17	QPR	35	1		
2017–18	QPR	39	6		
2018–19	QPR	41	3	**145**	**10**

LYNCH, Joel (D) **371** **20**
H: 6 1 W: 12 10 b.Eastbourne 3-10-87
Internationals: England Youth. Wales Full caps.

2005–06	Brighton & HA	16	1		
2006–07	Brighton & HA	39	0		
2007–08	Brighton & HA	22	1		
2008–09	Brighton & HA	2	0	**79**	**2**
2008–09	*Nottingham F*	23	0		
2009–10	Nottingham F	10	0		
2010–11	Nottingham F	12	0		
2011–12	Nottingham F	35	3	**80**	**3**
2012–13	Huddersfield T	22	1		
2013–14	Huddersfield T	29	2		
2014–15	Huddersfield T	34	3		
2015–16	Huddersfield T	37	2	**122**	**8**
2016–17	QPR	30	3		
2017–18	QPR	25	1		
2018–19	QPR	35	3	**90**	**7**

MANNING, Ryan (F) **64** **7**
H: 5 8 W: 10 06 b.Galway 14-6-96
Internationals: Republic of Ireland U17, U19, U21.
From Galway U.

2016–17	QPR	18	1		
2017–18	QPR	19	2		
2018–19	QPR	9	0	**46**	**3**
2018–19	*Rotherham U*	18	4	**18**	**4**

OMAR, Ali (D) **0** **0**
b. 14-9-99

2018–19	QPR	0	0		

OWENS, Charlie (M) **2** **0**
b. 7-12-97
Internationals: Northern Ireland U19, U21.

2017–18	QPR	0	0		
2018–19	QPR	0	0		
2018–19	*Wycombe W*	2	0	**2**	**0**

PHILLIPS, Giles (D) **0** **0**

2018–19	QPR	0	0		

RANGEL, Angel (D) **382** **13**
H: 5 11 W: 11 09 b.Barcelona 28-10-82

2006–07	Terrassa	34	2	**34**	**2**
2007–08	Swansea C	43	2		
2008–09	Swansea C	40	1		
2009–10	Swansea C	38	0		
2010–11	Swansea C	38	2		
2011–12	Swansea C	34	0		
2012–13	Swansea C	33	3		
2013–14	Swansea C	30	0		
2014–15	Swansea C	27	0		
2015–16	Swansea C	23	0		
2016–17	Swansea C	18	1		
2017–18	Swansea C	4	0	**328**	**9**
2018–19	QPR	20	2	**20**	**2**

SAMUEL, Bright (F) **109** **7**
H: 5 9 W: 11 05 b. 1-2-97

2014–15	Blackpool	6	0		
2015–16	Blackpool	23	0		
2016–17	Blackpool	31	4		
2017–18	Blackpool	4	0	**64**	**4**
2017–18	QPR	18	1		
2018–19	QPR	27	2	**45**	**3**

SCOWEN, Josh (M) **264** **16**
H: 5 10 W: 11 09 b.Cheshunt 28-3-93

2010–11	Wycombe W	2	0		
2011–12	Wycombe W	0	0		
2012–13	Wycombe W	34	1		
2013–14	Wycombe W	37	1		
2014–15	Wycombe W	18	1	**91**	**3**
2014–15	Barnsley	21	4		
2015–16	Barnsley	34	4		
2016–17	Barnsley	41	2	**96**	**10**
2017–18	QPR	42	1		
2018–19	QPR	35	2	**77**	**3**

SCRIVENS, Chay (M) **0** **0**

2018–19	QPR	0	0		

SHODIPO, Olamide (M) **27** **0**
b.Dublin 5-7-97
Internationals: Republic of Ireland U19, U21.

2016–17	QPR	11	0		
2016–17	*Port Vale*	6	0	**6**	**0**
2017–18	QPR	0	0		
2017–18	*Colchester U*	6	0	**6**	**0**
2018–19	QPR	4	0	**15**	**0**

SMITH, Matt (F) **269** **59**
H: 6 6 W: 14 00 b.Birmingham 7-6-89

2011–12	Oldham Ath	28	3		
2011–12	*Macclesfield T*	8	1	**8**	**1**
2012–13	Oldham Ath	34	6	**62**	**9**
2013–14	Leeds U	39	12		
2014–15	Leeds U	3	0	**42**	**12**
2014–15	Fulham	15	5		
2014–15	*Bristol C*	14	7	**14**	**7**
2015–16	Fulham	20	2		
2016–17	Fulham	16	2	**51**	**9**
2016–17	QPR	16	4		
2017–18	QPR	41	11		
2018–19	QPR	35	6	**92**	**21**

SMYTH, Paul (M) **31** **5**
b. 10-9-97
Internationals: Northern Ireland U19, U21, Full caps.

2017–18	Linfield	0	0		
2017–18	QPR	13	2		
2018–19	QPR	3	0	**16**	**2**
2018–19	*Accrington S*	15	3	**15**	**3**

SYLLA, Idrissa (F) **221** **61**
H: 6 2 W: 11 11 b.Conakry 3-12-90
Internationals: Guinea Full caps.

2010–11	Le Mans	0	0		
2010–11	*Bastia*	27	7	**27**	**7**
2011–12	Le Mans	25	9		
2012–13	Le Mans	27	5	**52**	**14**
2013–14	Zulte Waregem	27	9		
2014–15	Zulte Waregem	20	5	**47**	**14**
2014–15	Anderlecht	0	0		
2015–16	Anderlecht	30	7		
2016–17	Anderlecht	4	2	**34**	**9**
2016–17	QPR	32	10		
2017–18	QPR	26	7		
2018–19	QPR	3	0	**61**	**17**

Tansferred to Zulte Waregem January 2019.

WALKER, Lewis (F) **4** **0**
b. 10-5-98

2015–16	Derby Co	0	0		
2016–17	Derby Co	0	0		
2017–18	QPR	0	0		
2018–19	QPR	4	0	**4**	**0**

WHEELER, David (M) **190** **38**
H: 5 11 W: 12 00 b.Brighton 4-10-90
Internationals: England U18.

2013–14	Exeter C	35	3		
2014–15	Exeter C	45	7		
2015–16	Exeter C	31	6		
2016–17	Exeter C	38	17		
2017–18	Exeter C	2	0	**151**	**33**
2017–18	QPR	9	1		
2018–19	Portsmouth	11	0	**11**	**0**
2018–19	QPR	0	0	**9**	**1**
2018–19	*Milton Keynes D*	19	4	**19**	**4**

WSZOLEK, Pawel (M) **216** **19**
H: 6 1 W: 12 04 b.Tczew 30-4-92
Internationals: Poland U17, U18, U19, Full caps.

2010–11	Polonia Warsaw	7	0		
2011–12	Polonia Warsaw	26	2		
2012–13	Polonia Warsaw	27	7	**60**	**9**
2013–14	Sampdoria	19	1		
2014–15	Sampdoria	6	0		
2015–16	Sampdoria	2	0	**27**	**1**
2015–16	*Verona*	26	0		
2016–17	Verona	0	0	**26**	**0**
2016–17	QPR	29	3		
2017–18	QPR	36	2		
2018–19	QPR	38	4	**103**	**9**

Players retained or with offer of contract
Alfa, Odysseus Naphtali; Domi, Franklin; Kefalas, Themistoklis; Osayi, Samuel Bright; Oteh, Aramide Jay; Rowan, Charles Alfred; Wells, Ben Michael.

Scholars
Bansal-Mcnulty, Amrit Padraig Singh; Bettache, Faysal; Bowman, Myles Thomas; Brooks, Marcus Adolphus Lee; Carlyle, Nathan Trevor; De, Silva Dillon Senan; Dickinson, Tyla Dez; Drewe, Aaron Michael; Frailing, Jake Lewis John; Genovesi, Caden Seamus; Gubbins, Joseph Matthew; Kargbo, Hamzad Sayeed; Kendall, Charley George; Mahoney, Murphy Joseph; Mahorn, Trent Reagen; McLeod, Kraig Nathaniel Noel; Mema, Armelindo; Mesias, Aiden Justino Araujo; Middlehurst, Thomas Daniel; Orafu, Nathaniel Ikechukwu; Pitblado, Isaac James Millar; Platt, Mickel Anton; Remy, Shiloh Samuel; Williams-Lowe, Kayden Lavon; Woollard-Innocent, Kai Hamilton.

READING (69)

ALUKO, Sone (M) **329** **49**
H: 5 8 W: 9 10 b.Birmingham 19-2-89
Internationals: England U16, U17, U18, U19. Nigeria U20, Full caps.

2005–06	Birmingham C	0	0		
2006–07	Birmingham C	0	0		
2007–08	Birmingham C	0	0		
2007–08	*Aberdeen*	20	3		
2008–09	Birmingham C	0	0		
2008–09	*Blackpool*	1	0	**1**	**0**
2008–09	Aberdeen	32	2		
2009–10	Aberdeen	22	3		
2010–11	Aberdeen	28	2	**102**	**10**
2011–12	Rangers	21	12	**21**	**12**
2012–13	Hull C	23	8		
2013–14	Hull C	17	1		
2014–15	Hull C	25	1		
2015–16	Hull C	25	3	**90**	**13**
2016–17	Fulham	45	8		
2017–18	Fulham	4	0	**49**	**8**
2017–18	Reading	39	3		
2018–19	Reading	19	1	**58**	**4**
2018–19	*Beijing Renhe*	8	2	**8**	**2**

BALDOCK, Sam (F) **308** **95**
H: 5 7 W: 10 07 b.Buckingham 15-3-89
Internationals: England U20.

2005–06	Milton Keynes D	0	0		
2006–07	Milton Keynes D	1	0		
2007–08	Milton Keynes D	5	0		
2008–09	Milton Keynes D	40	12		
2009–10	Milton Keynes D	20	5		
2010–11	Milton Keynes D	30	12		
2011–12	Milton Keynes D	4	4	**100**	**33**
2011–12	West Ham U	23	5		
2012–13	West Ham U	0	0	**23**	**5**
2012–13	Bristol C	34	10		
2013–14	Bristol C	45	24		
2014–15	Bristol C	4	0	**83**	**34**
2014–15	Brighton & HA	20	3		

2015–16	Brighton & HA	28	4		
2016–17	Brighton & HA	31	11		
2017–18	Brighton & HA	2	0	**81**	**18**
2018–19	Reading	21	5	**21**	**5**

BARRETT, Josh (F) **11** **0**
b. 21-6-98
Internationals: Republic of Ireland U17, U19, U21.

2015–16	Reading	3	0		
2016–17	Reading	0	0		
2017–18	Reading	0	0		
2017–18	*Coventry C*	6	0	**6**	**0**
2018–19	Reading	2	0	**5**	**0**

BARROW, Modou (F) **228** **55**
H: 5 9 W: 9 13 b.Banjul 13-10-92
Internationals: Gambia Full caps.

2010	Mjolby AI	15	6	**15**	**6**
2011	Mjolby Sodra	19	23	**19**	**23**
2012	Norrkping	7	0	**7**	**0**
2013	Varbergs	28	2	**28**	**2**
2014	Ostersunds FK	19	9	**19**	**9**
2014–15	Swansea C	11	0		
2014–15	*Nottingham F*	4	0	**4**	**0**
2015–16	Swansea C	22	1		
2015–16	*Blackburn R*	4	0	**4**	**0**
2016–17	Swansea C	18	0	**51**	**1**
2016–17	*Leeds U*	5	0	**5**	**0**
2017–18	Reading	41	10		
2018–19	Reading	35	4	**76**	**14**

BLACKETT, Tyler (D) **117** **0**
H: 6 1 W: 11 12 b.Manchester 2-4-94
Internationals: England U16, U17, U18, U19, U21.

2012–13	Manchester U	0	0		
2013–14	Manchester U	0	0		
2013–14	*Blackpool*	5	0	**5**	**0**
2013–14	*Birmingham C*	8	0	**8**	**0**
2014–15	Manchester U	11	0		
2015–16	Manchester U	0	0	**11**	**0**
2015–16	*Celtic*	3	0	**3**	**0**
2016–17	Reading	34	0		
2017–18	Reading	25	0		
2018–19	Reading	31	0	**90**	**0**

BODVARSSON, Jon Dadi (F) **271** **52**
H: 6 3 W: 13 05 b.Selfoss 25-5-92
Internationals: Iceland U19, U21, Full caps.

2008	Selfoss	0	0		
2009	Selfoss	16	1		
2010	Selfoss	21	3		
2011	Selfoss	21	7		
2012	Selfoss	22	7	**80**	**18**
2013	Viking	23	1		
2014	Viking	29	5		
2015	Viking	29	9	**81**	**15**
2015–16	Kaiserslautern	15	2	**15**	**2**
2016–17	Wolverhampton W	42	3	**42**	**3**
2017–18	Reading	33	7		
2018–19	Reading	20	7	**53**	**14**

CLEMENT, Pelle (F) **24** **0**
b.Amsterdam 19-5-96
Internationals: Netherlands U21.

2014–15	Ajax	0	0		
2015–16	Ajax	0	0		
2016–17	Ajax	1	0	**1**	**0**
2017–18	Reading	23	0		
2018–19	Reading	0	0	**23**	**0**

Transferred to PEC Zwolle January 2019.

EAST, Ryan (M) **1** **0**
b. 7-8-98

2017–18	Reading	0	0		
2018–19	Reading	1	0	**1**	**0**

EZATOLAHI, Saeid (M) **59** **2**
H: 6 3 W: 12 13 b.Bandar-e Anzali 1-10-96
Internationals: Iran U17, U20, Full caps.

2012–13	Malavan	10	0		
2013–14	Malavan	9	0	**19**	**0**
2014–15	Atletico Madrid	0	0		
2015–16	Rostov	1	0		
2016–17	Rostov	10	1		
2016–17	*Anzhi Makhachkala*	10	0	**10**	**0**
2017–18	Rostov	0	0	**11**	**1**
2017–18	*Amkar Perm*	15	1	**15**	**1**

On loan from Rostov.

2018–19	Reading	4	0	**4**	**0**

GUNTER, Chris (D) **434** **4**
H: 5 11 W: 11 02 b.Newport 21-7-89
Internationals: Wales U17, U19, U21, Full caps.

2006–07	Cardiff C	15	0		
2007–08	Cardiff C	13	0	**28**	**0**
2007–08	Tottenham H	2	0		
2008–09	Tottenham H	3	0	**5**	**0**
2008–09	*Nottingham F*	8	0		
2009–10	Nottingham F	44	1		
2010–11	Nottingham F	43	0		
2011–12	Nottingham F	46	1	**141**	**2**
2012–13	Reading	20	0		
2013–14	Reading	44	0		
2014–15	Reading	38	0		
2015–16	Reading	44	0		
2016–17	Reading	46	1		
2017–18	Reading	46	1		
2018–19	Reading	22	0	**260**	**2**

HARRIOTT, Callum (M) **130** **18**
H: 5 5 W: 10 05 b.Norbury 4-3-94
Internationals: England U19. Guyana Full caps.

2010–11	Charlton Ath	3	0		
2011–12	Charlton Ath	0	0		
2012–13	Charlton Ath	14	2		
2013–14	Charlton Ath	28	5		
2014–15	Charlton Ath	21	1		
2015–16	Charlton Ath	20	3	**86**	**11**
2015–16	*Colchester U*	20	5	**20**	**5**
2016–17	Reading	12	1		
2017–18	Reading	0	0		
2018–19	Reading	12	1	**24**	**2**

HOLMES, Thomas (D) **1** **0**
b. 12-3-00

2017–18	Reading	1	0		
2018–19	Reading	0	0	**1**	**0**

HOUSE, Ben (F) **6** **0**
b. 5-7-99
Internationals: Scotland U20, U21.

2018–19	Reading	0	0		
2018–19	*Swindon T*	6	0	**6**	**0**

HOWE, Teddy (D) **1** **0**
b. 9-10-98

2018–19	Reading	1	0	**1**	**0**

JAAKKOLA, Anssi (G) **138** **0**
H: 6 4 W: 13 12 b.Kemi 13-3-87
Internationals: Finland U21, Full caps.

2005	TP-47	3	0		
2006	TP-47	14	0	**17**	**0**
2006–07	Siena	0	0		
2007–08	Siena	1	0		
2008–09	Siena	0	0		
2008–09	*Colligiana*	7	0	**7**	**0**
2009–10	Siena	0	0	**1**	**0**
2010–11	Slavia Prague	2	0	**2**	**0**
2010–11	Kilmarnock	8	0		
2011–12	Kilmarnock	5	0		
2012–13	Kilmarnock	0	0	**13**	**0**
2013–14	Ajax Cape Town	24	0		
2014–15	Ajax Cape Town	28	0		
2015–16	Ajax Cape Town	26	0	**78**	**0**
2016–17	Reading	0	0		
2017–18	Reading	5	0		
2018–19	Reading	15	0	**20**	**0**

KELLY, Liam (M) **82** **7**
b. 22-11-95
Internationals: Republic of Ireland U19, U21.

2014–15	Reading	0	0		
2015–16	Reading	0	0		
2016–17	Reading	28	1		
2017–18	Reading	34	5		
2018–19	Reading	20	1	**82**	**7**

LEGG, George (G) **3** **0**
b. 30-4-96

2016–17	Reading	0	0		
2017–18	Reading	0	0		
2017–18	*Barnet*	3	0	**3**	**0**
2018–19	Reading	0	0		

LOADER, Danny (F) **21** **1**
b. 28-8-00
Internationals: England U16, U17, U18, U19, U20.
From Wycombe W.

2017–18	Reading	0	0		
2018–19	Reading	21	1	**21**	**1**

MANNONE, Vito (G) **179** **0**
H: 6 0 W: 11 08 b.Milan 2-3-88
Internationals: Italy U21.

2005–06	Arsenal	0	0		
2006–07	Arsenal	0	0		
2006–07	*Barnsley*	2	0	**2**	**0**
2007–08	Arsenal	0	0		
2008–09	Arsenal	1	0		
2009–10	Arsenal	5	0		
2010–11	Arsenal	0	0		
2010–11	*Hull C*	10	0		
2011–12	Arsenal	0	0		
2011–12	*Hull C*	21	0	**31**	**0**
2012–13	Arsenal	9	0	**15**	**0**
2013–14	Sunderland	29	0		
2014–15	Sunderland	10	0		
2015–16	Sunderland	19	0		
2016–17	Sunderland	9	0	**67**	**0**
2017–18	Reading	41	0		
2018–19	Reading	6	0	**47**	**0**
2019	*Minnesota U*	17	0	**17**	**0**

McCLEARY, Garath (M) **334** **35**
H: 5 10 W: 12 06 b.Oxford 15-5-87
Internationals: Jamaica Full caps.

2007–08	Nottingham F	8	1		
2008–09	Nottingham F	39	1		
2009–10	Nottingham F	24	0		
2010–11	Nottingham F	18	2		
2011–12	Nottingham F	22	9	**111**	**13**
2011–12	Reading	0	0		
2012–13	Reading	31	3		
2013–14	Reading	42	5		
2014–15	Reading	26	1		
2015–16	Reading	34	4		
2016–17	Reading	41	9		
2017–18	Reading	18	0		
2018–19	Reading	31	0	**223**	**22**

McINTYRE, Tom (D) **2** **0**
b. 6-11-98
Internationals: Scotland U17, U20, U21.

2018–19	Reading	2	0	**2**	**0**

McNULTY, Marc (M) **257** **89**
H: 5 10 W: 11 00 b.Edinburgh 14-9-92
Internationals: Scotland Full caps.

2009–10	Livingston	9	1		
2010–11	Livingston	5	1		
2011–12	Livingston	30	11		
2012–13	Livingston	26	7		
2013–14	Livingston	35	17	**105**	**37**
2014–15	Sheffield U	31	9		
2015–16	Sheffield U	5	1		
2015–16	*Portsmouth*	27	10	**27**	**10**
2016–17	Sheffield U	4	0	**40**	**10**
2016–17	*Bradford C*	15	1	**15**	**1**
2016–17	Coventry C	0	0		
2017–18	Coventry C	42	23	**42**	**23**
2018–19	Reading	13	1	**13**	**1**
2018–19	*Hibernian*	15	7	**15**	**7**

McSHANE, Paul (D) **334** **14**
H: 6 0 W: 11 05 b.Wicklow 6-1-86
Internationals: Republic of Ireland U21, Full caps.

2002–03	Manchester U	0	0		
2003–04	Manchester U	0	0		
2004–05	Manchester U	0	0		
2004–05	*Walsall*	4	1	**4**	**1**
2005–06	Manchester U	0	0		
2005–06	*Brighton & HA*	38	3	**38**	**3**
2006–07	WBA	32	2	**32**	**2**
2007–08	Sunderland	21	0		
2008–09	Sunderland	3	0		
2008–09	*Hull C*	17	1		
2009–10	Sunderland	0	0	**24**	**0**
2009–10	Hull C	27	0		
2010–11	Hull C	19	0		
2010–11	*Barnsley*	10	1	**10**	**1**
2011–12	Hull C	1	0		
2011–12	*Crystal Palace*	11	0	**11**	**0**
2012–13	Hull C	25	2		
2013–14	Hull C	10	0		
2014–15	Hull C	20	1	**119**	**4**
2015–16	Reading	35	0		
2016–17	Reading	30	3		
2017–18	Reading	26	0		
2018–19	Reading	5	0	**96**	**3**

MEITE, Yakou (M) **74** **16**
H: 6 0 W: 11 05 b.Paris 11-2-96
Internationals: Ivory Coast U17, U20, U23, Full caps.

2015–16	Paris Saint-Germain	1	0	**1**	**0**
2016–17	Reading	14	1		
2017–18	Reading	0	0		
2017–18	*Sochaux*	22	3	**22**	**3**
2018–19	Reading	37	12	**51**	**13**

MEYLER, David (M) **194** **16**
H: 6 3 W: 11 09 b.Cork 29-5-89
Internationals: Republic of Ireland U21, Full caps.

2008	Cork C	2	0	**2**	**0**
2008–09	Sunderland	0	0		
2009–10	Sunderland	10	0		

2010–11	Sunderland	5	0		
2011–12	Sunderland	7	0		
2012–13	Sunderland	3	0	**25**	**0**
2012–13	Hull C	28	5		
2013–14	Hull C	30	2		
2014–15	Hull C	28	1		
2015–16	Hull C	26	2		
2016–17	Hull C	20	1		
2017–18	Hull C	25	5	**157**	**16**
2018–19	Reading	5	0	**5**	**0**
2018–19	*Coventry C*	5	0	**5**	**0**

MOORE, Liam (D) **220** **6**
H: 6 1 W: 13 08 b.Loughborough 31-1-93
Internationals: England U17, U20, U21.

2011–12	Leicester C	2	0		
2011–12	*Bradford C*	17	0	**17**	**0**
2012–13	Leicester C	16	0		
2012–13	*Brentford*	7	0		
2013–14	Leicester C	30	1		
2014–15	Leicester C	11	0		
2014–15	*Brentford*	3	0	**10**	**0**
2015–16	Leicester C	0	0	**59**	**1**
2015–16	*Bristol C*	10	0	**10**	**0**
2016–17	Reading	40	1		
2017–18	Reading	46	3		
2018–19	Reading	38	1	**124**	**5**

O'SHEA, John (D) **501** **15**
H: 6 3 W: 13 07 b.Waterford 30-4-81
Internationals: Republic of Ireland U21, Full caps.

1998–99	Manchester U	0	0		
1999–2000	Manchester U	0	0		
1999–2000	*Bournemouth*	10	1	**10**	**1**
2000–01	Manchester U	0	0		
2001–02	Manchester U	9	0		
2002–03	Manchester U	32	0		
2003–04	Manchester U	33	2		
2004–05	Manchester U	23	2		
2005–06	Manchester U	34	1		
2006–07	Manchester U	32	4		
2007–08	Manchester U	28	0		
2008–09	Manchester U	30	0		
2009–10	Manchester U	15	1		
2010–11	Manchester U	20	0	**256**	**10**
2011–12	Sunderland	29	0		
2012–13	Sunderland	34	2		
2013–14	Sunderland	33	1		
2014–15	Sunderland	37	0		
2015–16	Sunderland	28	0		
2016–17	Sunderland	28	0		
2017–18	Sunderland	37	1	**226**	**4**
2018–19	Reading	9	0	**9**	**0**

OLISE, Michael (M) **4** **0**
b. 12-12 01
Internationals: France U18.

2018–19	Reading	4	0	**4**	**0**

OSHO, Gabriel (D) **2** **0**
b.Reading 14-8-98

2018–19	Reading	2	0	**2**	**0**

POPA, Adrian (F) **308** **40**
H: 5 7 W: 11 00 b.Horezu 24-7-88
Internationals: Romania Full caps.

2006–07	Stiinta Timisoara	3	2		
2007–08	Stiinta Timisoara	25	2		
2008–09	Stiinta Timisoara	0	0	**28**	**4**
2008–09	*Buftea*	11	2	**11**	**2**
2008–09	*Gloria Buzzau*	11	0	**11**	**0**
2009–10	Universitatea Cluj	23	3	**23**	**3**
2010–11	Concordia Chiajna	27	4		
2011–12	Concordia Chiajna	30	3		
2012–13	Concordia Chiajna	4	3	**61**	**10**
2012–13	Steau Bucharest	30	1		
2013–14	Steau Bucharest	28	7		
2014–15	Steau Bucharest	28	5		
2015–16	Steau Bucharest	32	4		
2016–17	Steau Bucharest	19	3	**137**	**20**
2016–17	Reading	8	1		
2017–18	Reading	6	0		
2017–18	*Al-Taawoun*	9	0	**9**	**0**
2018–19	Reading	1	0	**15**	**1**
2018–19	*Ludogorets*	13	0	**13**	**0**

RICHARDS, Omar (D) **23** **2**
H: 6 1 W: 10 12 b. 15-2-98

2017–18	Reading	13	2		
2018–19	Reading	10	0	**23**	**2**

RINOMHOTA, Andy (M) **26** **1**
b. 21-4-97
From AFC Portchester.

2017–18	Reading	0	0		
2018–19	Reading	26	1	**26**	**1**

SMITH, Sam (F) **26** **1**
H: 5 11 W: 11 07 b. 8-3-98

2017–18	Reading	8	1		
2018–19	Reading	0	0	**8**	**1**
2018–19	*Oxford U*	15	0	**15**	**0**
2018–19	*Shrewsbury T*	3	0	**3**	**0**

SWIFT, John (M) **143** **22**
H: 6 0 W: 11 07 b.Portsmouth 23-6-95
Internationals: England U16, U17, U18, U19, U20, U21.

2013–14	Chelsea	1	0		
2014–15	Chelsea	0	0		
2014–15	*Rotherham U*	3	0	**3**	**0**
2014–15	*Swindon T*	18	2	**18**	**2**
2015–16	Chelsea	0	0	**1**	**0**
2015–16	*Brentford*	27	7	**27**	**7**
2016–17	Reading	36	8		
2017–18	Reading	24	2		
2018–19	Reading	34	3	**94**	**13**

TIAGO ILORI, Almeida (D) **74** **2**
H: 6 3 W: 12 07 b.London 26-2-93
Internationals: Portugal U18, U19, U20, U21, U23.

2011–12	Sporting Lisbon	1	0		
2012–13	Sporting Lisbon	11	1	**12**	**1**
2013–14	Liverpool	0	0		
2013–14	*Granada*	9	0	**9**	**0**
2014–15	Liverpool	0	0		
2014–15	Bordeaux	0	0		
2015–16	Liverpool	0	0		
2015–16	*Aston Villa*	0	0		
2016–17	Liverpool	0	0		
2016–17	Reading	5	0		
2017–18	Reading	29	0		
2018–19	Reading	19	1	**53**	**1**

Transferred to Sporting Lisbon January 2019.

WALKER, Sam (G) **266** **0**
H: 6 5 W: 14 00 b.Gravesend 2-10-91

2009–10	Chelsea	0	0		
2010–11	Chelsea	0	0		
2010–11	*Barnet*	7	0	**7**	**0**
2011–12	Chelsea	0	0		
2011–12	*Northampton T*	21	0	**21**	**0**
2011–12	*Yeovil T*	20	0	**20**	**0**
2012–13	Chelsea	0	0		
2012–13	*Bristol R*	11	0	**11**	**0**
2012–13	*Colchester U*	19	0		
2013–14	Colchester U	46	0		
2014–15	Colchester U	45	0		
2015–16	Colchester U	0	0		
2016–17	Colchester U	46	0		
2017–18	Colchester U	44	0	**200**	**0**
2018–19	Reading	7	0	**7**	**0**

WATSON, Tennai (D) **27** **0**
b. 4-3-97

2015–16	Reading	0	0		
2016–17	Reading	3	0		
2017–18	Reading	0	0		
2018–19	Reading	0	0	**3**	**0**
2018–19	*AFC Wimbledon*	24	0	**24**	**0**

YIADOM, Andy (M) **195** **11**
H: 5 11 W: 11 11 b.Camden 9-12-91
Internationals: England C. Ghana Full caps.

2011–12	Barnet	7	1		
2012–13	Barnet	39	3		
2015–16	Barnet	40	6	**86**	**10**
2016–17	Barnsley	32	0		
2017–18	Barnsley	32	0	**64**	**0**
2018–19	Reading	45	1	**45**	**1**

Players retained or with offer of contract
Andresson, Jokull; Burley, Andre Maurice Keith; Coleman, Ethan Jay; Driscoll, Liam Michael-Owen; Frost, Tyler Jayden; Holsgrove, Jordan William; Lawless, Conor Michael John; Liddle, Adam; Medford-Smith, Ramarni Nelson; Nolan, Jack Daniel; Novakovich, Andrija; Obita, Jordan John; Odimayo, Akinwale Joseph; Pendlebury, Oliver Jack; Sidoel, Darren Devlin; Southwood, Luke Kevin; Ward, Lewis Moore.

Scholars
Bristow, Ethan David; Desbois, Adam Jack; Dorsett, Abraham Jeriel Richard; Elva-Fountaine, Marcel Patrick Joshua; Hewitt, Joshua David; Hillson, James Andrew; Kealy, Morgan Terence; Leavy, Kian; Moore, Shamar Andrew; Nditi, Roberto Yohana; Nevers, Thierry Odaine; Obamakinwa, Emmanuel Olorunfemi; Olise, Michael; Pemberton, Jacob; Roberts, Myles Conrad; Saydee, Terrance; Simmo, Khalid Zakaria; Sole, Fabio Calogero Antonio; Stevens, Tommy; Vinagre, Pedrosa Neves Pedro.

ROCHDALE (70)

ADSHEAD, Daniel (M) **11** **0**
H: 5 6 W: 10 03 b. 2-9-01
Internationals: England U18.

2017–18	Rochdale	1	0		
2018–19	Rochdale	10	0	**11**	**0**

ANDREW, Calvin (F) **366** **36**
H: 6 0 W: 12 11 b.Luton 19-12-86

2004–05	Luton T	8	0		
2005–06	Luton T	1	1		
2005–06	*Grimsby T*	8	1	**8**	**1**
2005–06	*Bristol C*	3	0	**3**	**0**
2006–07	Luton T	7	1		
2007–08	Luton T	39	2	**55**	**4**
2008–09	Crystal Palace	7	0		
2008–09	*Brighton & HA*	9	2	**9**	**2**
2009–10	Crystal Palace	27	1		
2010–11	Crystal Palace	13	0		
2010–11	*Millwall*	3	0	**3**	**0**
2010–11	*Swindon T*	10	1	**10**	**1**
2011–12	Crystal Palace	6	0	**53**	**1**
2011–12	*Leyton Orient*	10	0	**10**	**0**
2012–13	Port Vale	22	1		
2013–14	Port Vale	0	0	**22**	**1**
2013–14	Mansfield T	15	1	**15**	**1**
2013–14	York C	8	1	**8**	**1**
2014–15	Rochdale	32	5		
2015–16	Rochdale	30	6		
2016–17	Rochdale	39	7		
2017–18	Rochdale	31	3		
2018–19	Rochdale	38	3	**170**	**24**

BRADLEY, Lewis (M) **1** **0**
b. 29-5-01

2018–19	Rochdale	1	0	**1**	**0**

CAMPS, Callum (M) **173** **19**
b.Stockport 30-11-95
Internationals: Northern Ireland U18, U21.

2012–13	Rochdale	2	0		
2013–14	Rochdale	0	0		
2014–15	Rochdale	12	1		
2015–16	Rochdale	32	5		
2016–17	Rochdale	44	8		
2017–18	Rochdale	42	2		
2018–19	Rochdale	41	3	**173**	**19**

DELANEY, Ryan (D) **78** **9**
H: 6 0 W: 11 05 b.Wexford 6-9-96
Internationals: Republic of Ireland U21.
From Wexford.

2016–17	Burton Alb	0	0		
2017	*Cork C*	30	6	**30**	**6**
2017–18	Rochdale	18	2		
2018–19	Rochdale	30	1	**48**	**3**

DONE, Matt (M) **426** **42**
H: 5 10 W: 10 04 b.Oswestry 22-6-88

2005–06	Wrexham	6	0		
2006–07	Wrexham	34	1		
2007–08	Wrexham	26	0	**66**	**1**
2008–09	Hereford U	36	0		
2009–10	Hereford U	20	0	**56**	**0**
2010–11	Rochdale	33	5		
2011–12	Barnsley	31	4		
2012–13	Barnsley	13	0	**44**	**4**
2012–13	*Hibernian*	7	0	**7**	**0**
2013–14	Rochdale	38	0		
2014–15	Rochdale	23	10		
2014–15	Sheffield U	15	7		
2015–16	Sheffield U	31	4		
2016–17	Sheffield U	31	3	**77**	**14**
2017–18	Rochdale	46	6		
2018–19	Rochdale	36	2	**176**	**23**

DOOLEY, Stephen (M) **22** **0**
H: 5 11 W: 12 08 b.Portstewart 19-10-91
From Coleraine, Derry C, Cork C.

2018–19	Rochdale	22	0	**22**	**0**

DUNNE, Joe (D) **0** **0**

2018–19	Rochdale	0	0		

FINNERTY, James (D) **0** **0**
b.Skryne 1-2-99
Internationals: Republic of Ireland U18, U19.
From Aston Villa.

2018–19	Rochdale	0	0		

GILLAM, Matthew (F) 18 2
H: 5 9 W: 11 07 b. 4-10-98
2016–17 Rochdale 0 0
2017–18 Rochdale 8 1
2018–19 Rochdale 10 1 **18 2**

HAMZAT, Juwon (D) 0 0
b. 3-2-01
2018–19 Rochdale 0 0

HENDERSON, Ian (F) 516 129
H: 5 10 W: 11 06 b.Thetford 25-1-85
Internationals: England U18, U20.
2002–03 Norwich C 20 1
2003–04 Norwich C 19 4
2004–05 Norwich C 3 0
2005–06 Norwich C 24 1
2006–07 Norwich C 2 0 **68 6**
2006–07 *Rotherham U* 18 1 **18 1**
2007–08 Northampton T 23 0
2008–09 Northampton T 3 0 **26 0**
2008–09 Luton T 19 1 **19 1**
2009–10 Colchester U 13 2
2009–10 *Ankaragucu* 2 0 **2 0**
2010–11 Colchester U 36 10
2011–12 Colchester U 46 9
2012–13 Colchester U 22 3 **117 24**
2012–13 Rochdale 12 3
2013–14 Rochdale 45 11
2014–15 Rochdale 44 22
2015–16 Rochdale 39 13
2016–17 Rochdale 42 15
2017–18 Rochdale 39 13
2018–19 Rochdale 45 20 **266 97**

HOPPER, Harrison (M) 0 0
b. 24-12-00
2018–19 Rochdale 0 0

HOTI, Florent (M) 0 0
b. 11-12-00
2018–19 Rochdale 0 0

INMAN, Bradden (M) 194 28
H: 5 9 W: 11 03 b.Adelaide 10-12-91
Internationals: Scotland U19, U21.
2009–10 Newcastle U 0 0
2010–11 Newcastle U 0 0
2011–12 Newcastle U 0 0
2012–13 Newcastle U 0 0
2012–13 *Crewe Alex* 21 5
2013–14 Newcastle U 0 0
2013–14 Crewe Alex 36 4
2014–15 Crewe Alex 21 1
2015–16 Crewe Alex 39 10 **117 20**
2016–17 Peterborough U 11 0
2017–18 Peterborough U 0 0 **11 0**
2017–18 *Rochdale* 37 4
2018–19 Rochdale 29 4 **66 8**

KEOHANE, Jimmy (M) 88 9
H: 5 11 W: 11 05 b.Wexford 22-1-91
Internationals: Republic of Ireland U19.
2010–11 Bristol C 0 0
2011–12 Bristol C 0 0
2011–12 Exeter C 4 0
2012–13 Exeter C 33 3
2013–14 Exeter C 20 3
2014–15 Exeter C 23 3
2015–16 Exeter C 0 0 **80 9**
From Woking, Sligo R, Cork C.
2018–19 Rochdale 8 0 **8 0**

LILLIS, Josh (G) 299 0
H: 6 0 W: 12 08 b.Derby 24-6-87
2006–07 Scunthorpe U 1 0
2007–08 Scunthorpe U 3 0
2008–09 Scunthorpe U 5 0
2008–09 *Notts Co* 5 0 **5 0**
2009–10 Scunthorpe U 8 0
2009–10 *Grimsby T* 4 0 **4 0**
2009–10 *Rochdale* 1 0
2010–11 Scunthorpe U 15 0
2010–11 *Rochdale* 23 0
2011–12 Scunthorpe U 6 0 **38 0**
2012–13 Rochdale 46 0
2013–14 Rochdale 45 0
2014–15 Rochdale 16 0
2015–16 Rochdale 40 0
2016–17 Rochdale 14 0
2017–18 Rochdale 40 0
2018–19 Rochdale 27 0 **252 0**

LONERGAN, Andrew (G) 353 1
H: 6 4 W: 13 02 b.Preston 19-10-83
Internationals: Republic of Ireland U16. England U20.
2000–01 Preston NE 1 0
2001–02 Preston NE 0 0
2002–03 Preston NE 0 0
2002–03 *Darlington* 2 0 **2 0**
2003–04 Preston NE 8 0
2004–05 Preston NE 23 1
2005–06 Preston NE 0 0
2005–06 *Wycombe W* 2 0 **2 0**
2006–07 Preston NE 13 0
2006–07 *Swindon T* 1 0 **1 0**
2007–08 Preston NE 43 0
2008–09 Preston NE 46 0
2009–10 Preston NE 45 0
2010–11 Preston NE 29 0 **208 1**
2011–12 Leeds U 35 0
2012–13 Bolton W 5 0
2013–14 Bolton W 17 0
2014–15 Bolton W 29 0 **51 0**
2015–16 Fulham 29 0 **29 0**
2016–17 Wolverhampton W 11 0
2017–18 Wolverhampton W 0 0 **11 0**
2017–18 Leeds U 7 0 **42 0**
2018–19 Middlesbrough 0 0
2018–19 Rochdale 7 0 **7 0**

MATHESON, Luke (D) 3 0
b.Manchester 3-10-02
Internationals: England U17.
2018–19 Rochdale 3 0 **3 0**

McGAHEY, Harrison (D) 139 0
b.Preston 26-9-95
2013–14 Blackpool 4 0 **4 0**
2014–15 Sheffield U 15 0
2014–15 *Tranmere R* 4 0 **4 0**
2015–16 Sheffield U 7 0 **22 0**
2016–17 Rochdale 36 0
2017–18 Rochdale 42 0
2018–19 Rochdale 21 0 **99 0**
2018–19 *Scunthorpe U* 10 0 **10 0**

McLAUGHLIN, Ryan (D) 84 3
H: 5 9 W: 10 12 b.Belfast 30-9-94
Internationals: Northern Ireland U16, U17, U19, U21, Full caps.
2011–12 Liverpool 0 0
2013–14 Liverpool 0 0
2013–14 *Barnsley* 9 0 **9 0**
2014–15 Liverpool 0 0
2015–16 Liverpool 0 0
2015–16 *Aberdeen* 4 0 **4 0**
2016–17 Oldham Ath 36 2
2017–18 Oldham Ath 16 1 **52 3**
2018–19 Blackpool 6 0 **6 0**
2018–19 Rochdale 13 0 **13 0**

McNULTY, Jim (D) 353 7
H: 6 1 W: 12 00 b.Runcorn 13-2-85
Internationals: Scotland U17, U19.
2006–07 Macclesfield T 15 0
2007–08 Macclesfield T 19 1 **34 1**
2007–08 Stockport Co 11 0
2008–09 Stockport Co 26 1 **37 1**
2008–09 Brighton & HA 5 1
2009–10 Brighton & HA 8 0
2009–10 *Scunthorpe U* 3 0
2010–11 Brighton & HA 0 0 **13 1**
2010–11 *Scunthorpe U* 6 0 **9 0**
2011–12 Barnsley 44 2
2012–13 Barnsley 12 0
2013–14 Barnsley 0 0 **56 2**
2013–14 *Tranmere R* 12 0 **12 0**
2013–14 Bury 21 0
2014–15 Bury 25 0 **46 0**
2015–16 Rochdale 46 0
2016–17 Rochdale 35 0
2017–18 Rochdale 40 1
2018–19 Rochdale 25 1 **146 2**

MOORE, Brendan (G) 14 0
b. 16-4-92
From Fleetwood T, Torquay U.
2017–18 Rochdale 6 0
2018–19 Rochdale 8 0 **14 0**
Transferred to Atalanta U January 2019.

MORLEY, Aaron (M) 5 0
b. 27-2-00
2016–17 Rochdale 2 0
2017–18 Rochdale 0 0
2018–19 Rochdale 3 0 **5 0**

NEILD, James (D) 0 0
b. 18-8-01
2018–19 Rochdale 0 0

NTLHE, Kgosietsile (D) 137 7
H: 5 9 W: 10 05 b.Pretoria 21-2-94
Internationals: South Africa U20, Full caps.
2010–11 Peterborough U 0 0
2011–12 Peterborough U 2 0
2012–13 Peterborough U 12 1
2013–14 Peterborough U 27 2
2014–15 Peterborough U 28 1
2015–16 Peterborough U 7 0
2016–17 Peterborough U 0 0 **76 4**
2016–17 Stevenage 22 0 **22 0**
2017–18 Rochdale 20 0
2018–19 Rochdale 19 3 **39 3**

RATHBONE, Oliver (M) 88 7
H: 5 7 W: 10 06 b.Blackburn 10-10-96
From Manchester U.
2016–17 Rochdale 27 2
2017–18 Rochdale 33 1
2018–19 Rochdale 28 4 **88 7**

TAVARES, Fabio (F) 0 0
b. 22-1-01
2018–19 Rochdale 0 0

THOMPSON, Joe (M) 220 23
H: 6 0 W: 9 07 b.Rochdale 5-3-89
2005–06 Rochdale 1 0
2006–07 Rochdale 13 0
2007–08 Rochdale 11 1
2008–09 Rochdale 30 5
2009–10 Rochdale 36 6
2010–11 Rochdale 32 2
2011–12 Rochdale 17 1
2012–13 Tranmere R 19 1
2012–13 *Rochdale* 7 0
2013–14 Tranmere R 6 2 **25 3**
2014–15 Bury 1 0 **1 0**
2015–16 Carlisle U 15 1 **15 1**
2016–17 Rochdale 21 3
2017–18 Rochdale 10 1
2018–19 Rochdale 1 0 **179 19**

WADE, Bradley (G) 0 0
b.Gloucester 3-7-00
2018–19 Rochdale 0 0

WILBRAHAM, Aaron (F) 581 127
H: 6 3 W: 12 04 b.Knutsford 21-10-79
1997–98 Stockport Co 7 1
1998–99 Stockport Co 26 0
1999–2000 Stockport Co 26 4
2000–01 Stockport Co 36 12
2001–02 Stockport Co 21 3
2002–03 Stockport Co 15 7
2003–04 Stockport Co 41 8 **172 35**
2004–05 Hull C 19 2 **19 2**
2004–05 *Oldham Ath* 4 2 **4 2**
2005–06 Milton Keynes D 31 4
2005–06 *Bradford C* 5 1 **5 1**
2006–07 Milton Keynes D 32 7
2007–08 Milton Keynes D 35 10
2008–09 Milton Keynes D 33 16
2009–10 Milton Keynes D 35 10
2010–11 Milton Keynes D 10 2 **176 49**
2010–11 Norwich C 12 1
2011–12 Norwich C 11 1 **23 2**
2012–13 Crystal Palace 21 0
2013–14 Crystal Palace 4 0 **25 0**
2014–15 Bristol C 37 18
2015–16 Bristol C 43 8
2016–17 Bristol C 31 4 **111 30**
2017–18 Bolton W 23 2 **23 2**
2018–19 Rochdale 23 4 **23 4**

WILLIAMS, Jordan LR (M) 41 2
b.Warrington 13-12-92
2017–18 Rochdale 11 0
2017–18 *Lincoln C* 11 0 **11 0**
2018–19 Rochdale 19 2 **30 2**

WILLIAMS, M Jordan (M) 57 0
H: 6 0 W: 12 02 b.Bangor 6-11-95
Internationals: Wales U21.
2014–15 Liverpool 0 0
2014–15 *Notts Co* 8 0 **8 0**
2015–16 Liverpool 0 0
2015–16 *Swindon T* 9 0
2016–17 Liverpool 0 0
2016–17 *Swindon T* 0 0 **9 0**
2017–18 Liverpool 0 0
2017–18 *Rochdale* 12 0
2018–19 Rochdale 28 0 **40 0**

YONSIAN, Florian (F) 0 0
b. 25-11-00
2018–19 Rochdale 0 0

Scholars
Bradley, Lewis Derek; Dunne, Joseph William; Hamzat, Sikirulahi Adejuwon; Hopper, Harrison George; Hoti, Florent; Kisimba, Musambya Hugue; Martin, Benjamin Alexander; Moreland, Morgan Jake; Neild, James; Phillips, Toby Rae; Piper, Morgan Daniel Allan; Tavares, Desiderio Fabio Andre; White, Louis Vincent; Yonsian, Monimon de Louis-Florian.

ROTHERHAM U (71)

AJAYI, Semi (D) **116 12**
H: 6 4 W: 13 00 b.Croydon 9-11-93
Internationals: Nigeria U20, Full caps.

2012–13	Charlton Ath	0	0		
2013–14	Charlton Ath	0	0		
2014–15	Arsenal	0	0		
2014–15	*Cardiff C*	0	0		
2015–16	Cardiff C	0	0		
2015–16	*AFC Wimbledon*	5	0	**5**	**0**
2015–16	*Crewe Alex*	13	0	**13**	**0**
2016–17	Cardiff C	0	0		
2016–17	*Rotherham U*	17	1		
2017–18	Rotherham U	35	4		
2018–19	Rotherham U	46	7	**98**	**12**

BALL, David (F) **320 68**
H: 6 0 W: 11 08 b.Whitefield 14-12-89

2007–08	Manchester C	0	0		
2008–09	Manchester C	0	0		
2009–10	Manchester C	0	0		
2010–11	Manchester C	0	0		
2010–11	*Swindon T*	18	2	**18**	**2**
2010–11	Peterborough U	19	5		
2011–12	Peterborough U	22	4		
2011–12	*Rochdale*	14	3	**14**	**3**
2012–13	Peterborough U	0	0	**41**	**9**
2012–13	Fleetwood T	34	7		
2013–14	Fleetwood T	30	8		
2014–15	Fleetwood T	32	8		
2015–16	Fleetwood T	37	4		
2016–17	Fleetwood T	46	14	**179**	**41**
2017–18	Rotherham U	32	8		
2018–19	Rotherham U	1	0	**33**	**8**
2018–19	*Bradford C*	35	5	**35**	**5**

BILBOE, Laurence (G) **0 0**
b. 21-2-98

2016–17	Rotherham U	0	0
2017–18	Rotherham U	0	0
2018–19	Rotherham U	0	0

CROOKS, Matt (M) **133 21**
H: 6 0 W: 11 05 b.Leeds 20-1-94

2011–12	Huddersfield T	0	0		
2012–13	Huddersfield T	0	0		
2013–14	Huddersfield T	0	0		
2014–15	Huddersfield T	1	0	**1**	**0**
2014–15	*Hartlepool U*	3	0	**3**	**0**
2014–15	Accrington S	16	0		
2015–16	Accrington S	32	6	**48**	**6**
2016–17	Rangers	2	0	**2**	**0**
2016–17	*Scunthorpe U*	12	3	**12**	**3**
2017–18	Northampton T	30	4		
2018–19	Northampton T	21	5	**51**	**9**
2018–19	Rotherham U	16	3	**16**	**3**

FORDE, Anthony (M) **208 12**
H: 5 9 W: 10 10 b.Limerick 16-11-93
Internationals: Republic of Ireland U19, U21.

2011–12	Wolverhampton W	6	0		
2012–13	Wolverhampton W	12	0		
2012–13	*Scunthorpe U*	8	0	**8**	**0**
2013–14	Wolverhampton W	3	0	**21**	**0**
2014–15	Walsall	37	3		
2015–16	Walsall	41	4	**78**	**7**
2016–17	Rotherham U	32	2		
2017–18	Rotherham U	41	2		
2018–19	Rotherham U	28	1	**101**	**5**

HINDS, Akeem (D) **0 0**

2017–18	Rotherham U	0	0
2018–19	Rotherham U	0	0

IHIEKWE, Michael (D) **117 5**
H: 6 1 W: 12 02 b.Liverpool 20-11-92
Internationals: England C.

2011–12	Wolverhampton W	0	0		
2012–13	Wolverhampton W	0	0		
2013–14	Wolverhampton W	0	0		
2013–14	*Cheltenham T*	13	0	**13**	**0**
2014–15	Tranmere R	38	1	**38**	**1**
2017–18	Rotherham U	31	1		
2018–19	Rotherham U	15	2	**46**	**3**
2018–19	*Accrington S*	20	1	**20**	**1**

JONES, Billy (M) **466 25**
H: 5 11 W: 13 00 b.Shrewsbury 24-3-87
Internationals: England U16, U17, U19, U20.

2003–04	Crewe Alex	27	1		
2004–05	Crewe Alex	20	0		
2005–06	Crewe Alex	44	6		
2006–07	Crewe Alex	41	1	**132**	**8**
2007–08	Preston NE	29	0		
2008–09	Preston NE	44	3		
2009–10	Preston NE	44	4		
2010–11	Preston NE	43	6	**160**	**13**
2011–12	WBA	18	0		
2012–13	WBA	27	1		
2013–14	WBA	21	0	**66**	**1**
2014–15	Sunderland	14	0		
2015–16	Sunderland	24	1		
2016–17	Sunderland	27	1		
2017–18	Sunderland	22	1	**87**	**3**
2018–19	Rotherham U	21	0	**21**	**0**

KAYODE, Joshua (F) **0 0**

2017–18	Rotherham U	0	0
2018–19	Rotherham U	0	0

LEWTHWAITE, Tyrone (F) **0 0**
b. 18-12-00
Internationals: Northern Ireland U19.
From Watford.

2018–19	Rotherham U	0	0

MATTOCK, Joe (D) **337 7**
H: 5 11 W: 12 05 b.Leicester 15-5-90
Internationals: England U17, U19, U21.

2006–07	Leicester C	4	0		
2007–08	Leicester C	31	0		
2008–09	Leicester C	31	1		
2009–10	Leicester C	0	0	**66**	**1**
2009–10	WBA	29	0		
2010–11	WBA	0	0		
2010–11	*Sheffield U*	13	0	**13**	**0**
2011–12	WBA	0	0	**29**	**0**
2011–12	*Portsmouth*	7	0	**7**	**0**
2011–12	*Brighton & HA*	15	1	**15**	**1**
2012–13	Sheffield W	7	0		
2013–14	Sheffield W	23	2		
2014–15	Sheffield W	27	0	**57**	**2**
2015–16	Rotherham U	35	1		
2016–17	Rotherham U	36	0		
2017–18	Rotherham U	35	1		
2018–19	Rotherham U	44	1	**150**	**3**

McGINLEY, Reece (F) **0 0**
Internationals: Northern Ireland U17, U19.

2017–18	Rotherham U	0	0
2018–19	Rotherham U	0	0

NEWELL, Joe (M) **235 17**
H: 5 11 W: 11 02 b.Tamworth 15-3-93

2010–11	Peterborough U	2	0		
2011–12	Peterborough U	14	1		
2012–13	Peterborough U	30	0		
2013–14	Peterborough U	11	0		
2014–15	Peterborough U	39	2	**96**	**3**
2015–16	Rotherham U	35	5		
2016–17	Rotherham U	34	2		
2017–18	Rotherham U	39	7		
2018–19	Rotherham U	31	0	**139**	**14**

ONARIASE, Manny (D) **27 1**
H: 6 1 b. 29-1-95

2014–15	West Ham U	0	0		
2015–16	West Ham U	0	0		
2016–17	Brentford	0	0		
2016–17	*Cheltenham T*	22	1		
2017–18	Rotherham U	0	0		
2017–18	*Cheltenham T*	5	0	**27**	**1**
2018–19	Rotherham U	0	0		

PALMER, Matthew (M) **174 7**
H: 5 10 W: 12 06 b.Derby 1-8-93

2012–13	Burton Alb	2	0		
2013–14	Burton Alb	40	0		
2014–15	Burton Alb	33	4		
2015–16	Burton Alb	14	0		
2015–16	*Oldham Ath*	14	1	**14**	**1**
2016–17	Burton Alb	36	1		
2017–18	Burton Alb	11	1	**136**	**6**
2017–18	Rotherham U	14	0		
2018–19	Rotherham U	10	0	**24**	**0**

POTTER, Darren (M) **410 17**
H: 6 0 W: 10 08 b.Liverpool 21-12-84
Internationals: Republic of Ireland Full caps.

2001–02	Liverpool	0	0		
2002–03	Liverpool	0	0		
2003–04	Liverpool	0	0		
2004–05	Liverpool	2	0		
2005–06	Liverpool	0	0		
2005–06	*Southampton*	10	0	**10**	**0**
2006–07	Liverpool	0	0	**2**	**0**
2006–07	Wolverhampton W	38	0		
2007–08	Wolverhampton W	18	0		
2008–09	Wolverhampton W	0	0	**56**	**0**
2008–09	*Sheffield W*	17	2		
2009–10	Sheffield W	46	3		
2010–11	Sheffield W	33	3	**96**	**8**
2011–12	Milton Keynes D	40	2		
2012–13	Milton Keynes D	46	4		
2013–14	Milton Keynes D	29	0		
2014–15	Milton Keynes D	40	2		
2015–16	Milton Keynes D	37	0		
2016–17	Milton Keynes D	37	1	**229**	**9**
2017–18	Rotherham U	16	0		
2018–19	Rotherham U	1	0	**17**	**0**

PRICE, Lewis (G) **149 0**
H: 6 3 W: 13 05 b.Bournemouth 19-7-84
Internationals: Wales U19, U21, Full caps.

2002–03	Ipswich T	0	0		
2003–04	Ipswich T	1	0		
2004–05	Ipswich T	8	0		
2004–05	*Cambridge U*	6	0	**6**	**0**
2005–06	Ipswich T	25	0		
2006–07	Ipswich T	34	0	**68**	**0**
2007–08	Derby Co	6	0		
2008–09	Derby Co	0	0		
2008–09	*Milton Keynes D*	2	0	**2**	**0**
2008–09	*Luton T*	1	0	**1**	**0**
2009–10	Derby Co	0	0	**6**	**0**
2009–10	*Brentford*	13	0	**13**	**0**
2010–11	Crystal Palace	1	0		
2011–12	Crystal Palace	5	0		
2012–13	Crystal Palace	0	0		
2013–14	Crystal Palace	0	0		
2013–14	*Mansfield T*	5	0	**5**	**0**
2014–15	Crystal Palace	0	0	**6**	**0**
2014–15	*Crawley T*	18	0	**18**	**0**
2015–16	Sheffield W	5	0	**5**	**0**
2016–17	Rotherham U	17	0		
2017–18	Rotherham U	1	0		
2018–19	Rotherham U	1	0	**19**	**0**

PROCTOR, Jamie (F) **248 40**
H: 6 2 W: 12 03 b.Preston 25-3-92

2009–10	Preston NE	1	0		
2010–11	Preston NE	5	1		
2010–11	*Stockport Co*	7	0	**7**	**0**
2011–12	Preston NE	31	3	**37**	**4**
2012–13	Swansea C	0	0		
2012–13	*Shrewsbury T*	2	0	**2**	**0**
2012–13	Crawley T	18	7		
2013–14	Crawley T	44	6	**62**	**13**
2014–15	Fleetwood T	41	8		
2015–16	Fleetwood T	23	4	**64**	**12**
2015–16	Bradford C	18	5	**18**	**5**
2016–17	Bolton W	21	0	**21**	**0**
2016–17	*Carlisle U*	17	4	**17**	**4**
2017–18	Rotherham U	4	0		
2018–19	Rotherham U	16	2	**20**	**2**

RAGGETT, Sean (D) **34 3**
H: 5 11 W: 12 04 b.Gillingham 17-4-93
Internationals: England C.
From Dover Ath.

2017–18	Lincoln C	25	2	**25**	**2**
2017–18	Norwich C	2	0	**2**	**0**
2018–19	Rotherham U	7	1	**7**	**1**

ROBERTSON, Clark (D) **206 7**
H: 6 2 W: 12 00 b.Aberdeen 5-9-93
Internationals: Scotland U19, U21.

2009–10	Aberdeen	3	0		
2010–11	Aberdeen	13	0		
2011–12	Aberdeen	9	0		
2012–13	Aberdeen	23	0		
2013–14	Aberdeen	8	0		
2014–15	Aberdeen	1	0	**57**	**0**
2015–16	Blackpool	38	1		
2016–17	Blackpool	44	0		
2017–18	Blackpool	39	3	**121**	**4**
2018–19	Rotherham U	28	3	**28**	**3**

SMITH, Michael (F) **247 58**
H: 6 4 W: 11 02 b.Wallsend 17-10-91

2011–12	Charlton Ath	0	0		
2011–12	*Accrington S*	6	3	**6**	**3**
2012–13	Charlton Ath	0	0		
2012–13	*Colchester U*	8	1	**8**	**1**
2013–14	Charlton Ath	0	0		
2013–14	*AFC Wimbledon*	23	9	**23**	**9**
2013–14	Swindon T	20	8		

2014–15	Swindon T	40	13		
2015–16	Swindon T	5	0	**65**	**21**
2015–16	*Barnsley*	13	0	**13**	**0**
2015–16	*Portsmouth*	16	4		
2016–17	Portsmouth	18	3	**34**	**7**
2016–17	*Northampton T*	14	2		
2017–18	Northampton T	0	0	**14**	**2**
2017–18	Bury	19	1	**19**	**1**
2017–18	Rotherham U	20	6		
2018–19	Rotherham U	45	8	**65**	**14**

SOUTHERN-COOPER, Jake (M) **0** **0**
b. 1-1-00

2018–19	Rotherham U	0	0		

TAYLOR, Jon (M) **309** **48**
H: 5 11 W: 12 04 b.Liverpool 23-12-89

2009–10	Shrewsbury T	2	0		
2010–11	Shrewsbury T	20	6		
2011–12	Shrewsbury T	33	0		
2012–13	Shrewsbury T	37	7		
2013–14	Shrewsbury T	41	9	**133**	**22**
2014–15	Peterborough U	24	3		
2015–16	Peterborough U	44	11	**68**	**14**
2016–17	Rotherham U	42	4		
2017–18	Rotherham U	25	4		
2018–19	Rotherham U	41	4	**108**	**12**

VASSELL, Kyle (F) **141** **28**
H: 6 0 W: 12 04 b.Milton Keynes 7-2-93
Internationals: Northern Ireland Full caps.

2013–14	Peterborough U	6	0		
2014–15	Peterborough U	17	5		
2014–15	*Oxford U*	6	1	**6**	**1**
2015–16	Peterborough U	5	0	**28**	**5**
2015–16	*Dagenham & R*	8	0	**8**	**0**
2015–16	*Shrewsbury T*	13	0	**13**	**0**
2016–17	Blackpool	34	11		
2017–18	Blackpool	29	11	**63**	**22**
2018–19	Rotherham U	23	0	**23**	**0**

VAULKS, Will (D) **233** **23**
H: 5 11 b.Birkenhead 13-9-93
Internationals: Wales Full caps.

2012–13	Tranmere R	0	0		
2012–13	Falkirk	6	0		
2013–14	Falkirk	33	1		
2014–15	Falkirk	34	3		
2015–16	Falkirk	35	6	**108**	**10**
2016–17	Rotherham U	40	1		
2017–18	Rotherham U	44	5		
2018–19	Rotherham U	41	7	**125**	**13**

VYNER, Zak (D) **72** **1**
H: 5 10 W: 10 10 b.Bath 14-5-97

2015–16	Bristol C	4	0		
2016–17	Bristol C	3	0		
2016–17	*Accrington S*	16	0	**16**	**0**
2017–18	Bristol C	1	0	**8**	**0**
2017–18	*Plymouth Arg*	17	1	**17**	**1**
2018–19	Rotherham U	31	0	**31**	**0**

WILES, Ben (M) **20** **0**
b. 17-4-99

2017–18	Rotherham U	0	0		
2018–19	Rotherham U	20	0	**20**	**0**

WILLIAMS, Ryan (F) **149** **13**
H: 5 11 W: 12 00 b.Perth 28-10-93
Internationals: Australia U20, U23, Full caps.

2011–12	Portsmouth	4	0	**4**	**0**
2011–12	Fulham	0	0		
2012–13	Fulham	0	0		
2013–14	Fulham	0	0		
2013–14	*Oxford U*	36	7	**36**	**7**
2014–15	Fulham	2	0	**2**	**0**
2014–15	*Barnsley*	5	0		
2015–16	Barnsley	5	0		
2016–17	Barnsley	16	1	**26**	**1**
2017–18	Rotherham U	42	4		
2018–19	Rotherham U	39	1	**81**	**5**

WOOD, Richard (D) **440** **27**
H: 6 3 W: 12 13 b.Ossett 5-7-85

2002–03	Sheffield W	3	1		
2003–04	Sheffield W	12	0		
2004–05	Sheffield W	34	1		
2005–06	Sheffield W	30	1		
2006–07	Sheffield W	12	0		
2007–08	Sheffield W	27	2		
2008–09	Sheffield W	42	0		
2009–10	Sheffield W	11	2	**171**	**7**
2009–10	Coventry C	24	3		
2010–11	Coventry C	40	1		
2011–12	Coventry C	17	1		
2012–13	Coventry C	36	3	**117**	**8**
2013–14	Charlton Ath	21	0	**21**	**0**
2014–15	Rotherham U	6	0		
2014–15	*Crawley T*	10	3	**10**	**3**
2015–16	Rotherham U	13	0		
2015–16	*Fleetwood T*	6	0	**6**	**0**
2015–16	*Chesterfield*	5	0	**5**	**0**
2016–17	Rotherham U	29	3		
2017–18	Rotherham U	36	4		
2018–19	Rotherham U	26	2	**110**	**9**

YATES, Jerry (M) **69** **8**
H: 5 9 W: 10 10 b.Doncaster 10-11-96

2014–15	Rotherham U	1	0		
2015–16	Rotherham U	0	0		
2016–17	Rotherham U	21	1		
2017–18	Rotherham U	17	1		
2018–19	Carlisle U	23	6	**23**	**6**
2018–19	Rotherham U	7	0	**46**	**2**

Players retained or with offer of contract
McGinley-Mcfarlane, Reece Thomas; Ogunfaolu-Kayode, Joshua Akinola; Purrington, Ben.

Scholars
Beeden, Harrison Clark; Carlton, Mitchell Liam; Cooper, Jake; Diouf, Moussa; Etia, Jacques Creussier; Evans, Wilfred Peel; Farrar, Charlie Ellis; Gateshill, Robert Steven; Gratton, Jacob George; Hodgkinson, Luke James Miller; Hull, Jake Matthew; Hutchinson, Regan William; Johnson, Alex; Lewthwaite, Tyrone Andrew George; Spence, Joel James; Wenham, Travon Tremayne.

SCUNTHORPE U (72)

ALNWICK, Jak (G) **121** **0**
H: 6 2 W: 12 13 b.Hexham 17-6-93
Internationals: England U17, U18, U19, U20.

2010–11	Newcastle U	0	0		
2011–12	Newcastle U	0	0		
2012–13	Newcastle U	0	0		
2013–14	Newcastle U	0	0		
2014–15	Newcastle U	6	0	**6**	**0**
2014–15	*Bradford C*	1	0	**1**	**0**
2015–16	Port Vale	41	0		
2016–17	Port Vale	26	0	**67**	**0**
2016–17	Rangers	1	0		
2017–18	Rangers	5	0		
2018–19	Rangers	0	0	**6**	**0**

On loan from Rangers.

2018–19	Scunthorpe U	41	0	**41**	**0**

BORTHWICK-JACKSON, Cameron (D) **46** **2**
H: 6 3 W: 13 10 b.Manchester 2-2-97
Internationals: England U16, U17, U19, U20.

2015–16	Manchester U	10	0		
2016–17	Manchester U	0	0		
2016–17	*Wolverhampton W*	6	0	**6**	**0**
2017–18	Manchester U	0	0	**10**	**0**
2017–18	*Leeds U*	1	0	**1**	**0**
2018–19	Scunthorpe U	29	2	**29**	**2**

BURGESS, Cameron (D) **106** **4**
H: 6 4 W: 12 11 b.Aberdeen 21-10-95
Internationals: Scotland U18, U19. Australia U20, U23.

2014–15	Fulham	4	0		
2014–15	*Ross Co*	0	0		
2015–16	Fulham	0	0		
2016–17	Fulham	0	0	**4**	**0**
2016–17	*Oldham Ath*	23	1	**23**	**1**
2016–17	*Bury*	18	0	**18**	**0**
2017–18	Scunthorpe U	25	2		
2018–19	Scunthorpe U	36	1	**61**	**3**

BUTROID, Lewis (D) **13** **0**
H: 5 9 W: 10 08 b. 17-9-98

2016–17	Scunthorpe U	0	0		
2017–18	Scunthorpe U	7	0		
2018–19	Scunthorpe U	6	0	**13**	**0**

CLARKE, Jordan (D) **247** **10**
H: 6 0 W: 11 02 b.Coventry 19-11-91
Internationals: England U19, U20.

2009–10	Coventry C	12	0		
2010–11	Coventry C	21	1		
2011–12	Coventry C	19	1		
2012–13	Coventry C	20	0		
2013–14	Coventry C	41	1		
2014–15	Coventry C	11	1	**124**	**4**
2014–15	*Yeovil T*	5	2	**5**	**2**
2014–15	Scunthorpe U	24	0		
2015–16	Scunthorpe U	33	2		
2016–17	Scunthorpe U	23	1		
2017–18	Scunthorpe U	23	0		
2018–19	Scunthorpe U	15	1	**118**	**4**

COLCLOUGH, Ryan (F) **141** **25**
H: 6 3 W: 13 01 b.Budapest 27-12-94

2012–13	Crewe Alex	18	1		
2013–14	Crewe Alex	8	2		
2014–15	Crewe Alex	7	2		
2015–16	Crewe Alex	27	7	**60**	**12**
2015–16	Wigan Ath	10	2		
2016–17	Wigan Ath	10	0		
2016–17	*Milton Keynes D*	18	5	**18**	**5**
2017–18	Wigan Ath	26	4	**46**	**6**
2018–19	Scunthorpe U	17	2	**17**	**2**

DALES, Andy (M) **30** **1**
b. 13-11-94
Internationals: England C.

2013–14	Derby Co	0	0		

From Mickleover Sports.

2018–19	Scunthorpe U	20	1	**20**	**1**
2018–19	*Dundee*	10	0	**10**	**0**

EL-MHANNI, Yasin (M) **5** **0**
b. 26-10-95
From Farnborough, Lewes.

2016–17	Newcastle U	0	0		
2017–18	Newcastle U	0	0		
2018–19	Scunthorpe U	5	0	**5**	**0**

FLATT, Jonathan (G) **5** **0**
H: 6 1 W: 13 12 b.Wolverhampton 12-9-94

2013–14	Wolverhampton W	0	0		
2014–15	Wolverhampton W	0	0		
2014–15	*Chesterfield*	0	0		
2015–16	Wolverhampton W	0	0		
2015–16	*Cheltenham T*	0	0		
2016–17	Wolverhampton W	0	0		
2017–18	Wolverhampton W	0	0		
2017–18	*Cheltenham T*	4	0	**4**	**0**
2018–19	Scunthorpe U	1	0	**1**	**0**

GOODE, Charlie (D) **81** **5**
b. 3-8-95
Internationals: England C.

2015–16	Scunthorpe U	10	1		
2016–17	Scunthorpe U	20	0		
2017–18	Scunthorpe U	13	1		
2018–19	Scunthorpe U	21	3	**64**	**5**
2018–19	*Northampton T*	17	0	**17**	**0**

HALLAM, Jordan (M) **12** **1**
b. 6-10-98

2016–17	Sheffield U	0	0		

From Southport.

2018	Viking	5	0	**5**	**0**
2018–19	Scunthorpe U	7	1	**7**	**1**

HAMMILL, Adam (M) **379** **33**
H: 5 11 W: 11 07 b.Liverpool 25-1-88
Internationals: England U19, U21.

2005–06	Liverpool	0	0		
2006–07	Liverpool	0	0		
2006–07	*Dunfermline Ath*	13	1	**13**	**1**
2007–08	Liverpool	0	0		
2007–08	*Southampton*	25	0	**25**	**0**
2008–09	Liverpool	0	0		
2008–09	*Blackpool*	22	1	**22**	**1**
2008–09	*Barnsley*	14	1		
2009–10	Barnsley	39	4		
2010–11	Barnsley	25	8		
2010–11	Wolverhampton W	10	0		
2011–12	Wolverhampton W	9	0		
2011–12	*Middlesbrough*	10	0	**10**	**0**
2012–13	Wolverhampton W	4	0	**23**	**0**
2012–13	*Huddersfield T*	16	2		
2013–14	Huddersfield T	44	4		
2014–15	Huddersfield T	5	0		
2014–15	*Rotherham U*	14	0	**14**	**0**
2015–16	Huddersfield T	1	0	**66**	**6**
2015–16	Barnsley	25	4		
2016–17	Barnsley	37	3		
2017–18	Barnsley	38	0	**178**	**20**
2018–19	St Mirren	13	4	**13**	**4**
2018–19	Scunthorpe U	15	1	**15**	**1**

HORNSHAW, George (M) **0** **0**

2017–18	Scunthorpe U	0	0		
2018–19	Scunthorpe U	0	0		

HORSFIELD, James (M) **24** **0**
H: 5 10 W: 11 00 b.Hazel Grove 21-9-95

2015–16	Manchester C	0	0		
2015–16	*Doncaster R*	2	0	**2**	**0**
2018–19	Scunthorpe U	11	0	**11**	**0**
2018–19	*Dundee*	11	0	**11**	**0**

LEWIS, Clayton (M) **55** **13**
H: 5 7 W: 11 05 b. 12-2-97
Internationals: New Zealand U20, Full caps.

2013–14	Team Wellington	0	0		

2014–15	Wanderers	11	3	**11**	**3**
2015–16	Auckland C	12	5		
2016–17	Auckland C	13	5	**25**	**10**
2017–18	Auckland City	0	0		
2017–18	Scunthorpe U	4	0		
2018–19	Scunthorpe U	15	0	**19**	**0**

LUND, Matthew (M) 204 30
H: 6 0 W: 11 13 b.Manchester 21-11-90
Internationals: Northern Ireland U21, Full caps.

2009–10	Stoke C	0	0		
2010–11	Stoke C	0	0		
2010–11	*Hereford U*	2	0	**2**	**0**
2011–12	Stoke C	0	0		
2011–12	*Oldham Ath*	3	0	**3**	**0**
2011–12	*Bristol R*	13	2		
2012–13	Stoke C	0	0		
2012–13	*Bristol R*	18	2	**31**	**4**
2012–13	Southend U	12	1	**12**	**1**
2013–14	Rochdale	40	8		
2014–15	Rochdale	14	2		
2015–16	Rochdale	29	1		
2016–17	Rochdale	29	9	**112**	**20**
2016–17	Burton Alb	0	0		
2017–18	Burton Alb	12	1	**12**	**1**
2017–18	*Bradford C*	10	2	**10**	**2**
2018–19	Scunthorpe U	22	2	**22**	**2**

McARDLE, Rory (D) 459 21
H: 6 1 W: 11 04 b.Doncaster 1-5-87
Internationals: Northern Ireland U21, Full caps.

2005–06	Sheffield W	0	0		
2005–06	*Rochdale*	19	1		
2006–07	Sheffield W	1	0	**1**	**0**
2006–07	Rochdale	25	0		
2007–08	Rochdale	43	3		
2008–09	Rochdale	41	2		
2009–10	Rochdale	20	0	**148**	**6**
2010–11	Aberdeen	28	2		
2011–12	Aberdeen	25	0	**53**	**2**
2012–13	Bradford C	40	2		
2013–14	Bradford C	41	3		
2014–15	Bradford C	43	3		
2015–16	Bradford C	35	3		
2016–17	Bradford C	24	1	**183**	**12**
2017–18	Scunthorpe U	36	1		
2018–19	Scunthorpe U	38	0	**74**	**1**

MORRIS, Josh (M) 215 46
H: 5 9 W: 10 00 b.Preston 30-9-91
Internationals: England U20.

2010–11	Blackburn R	4	0		
2011–12	Blackburn R	2	0		
2011–12	*Yeovil T*	5	0	**5**	**0**
2012–13	Blackburn R	10	0		
2012–13	*Rotherham U*	5	0	**5**	**0**
2013–14	Blackburn R	4	0		
2013–14	*Carlisle U*	6	0	**6**	**0**
2013–14	*Fleetwood T*	14	2		
2014–15	Blackburn R	0	0	**20**	**0**
2014–15	*Fleetwood T*	45	8	**59**	**10**
2015–16	Bradford C	13	1	**13**	**1**
2016–17	Scunthorpe U	44	19		
2017–18	Scunthorpe U	44	11		
2018–19	Scunthorpe U	19	5	**107**	**35**

NOVAK, Lee (F) 344 78
H: 6 0 W: 12 04 b.Newcastle upon Tyne 28-9-88

2008–09	Huddersfield T	0	0		
2009–10	Huddersfield T	37	12		
2010–11	Huddersfield T	31	5		
2011–12	Huddersfield T	41	13		
2012–13	Huddersfield T	35	4	**144**	**34**
2013–14	Birmingham C	38	9		
2014–15	Birmingham C	21	1		
2015–16	Birmingham C	0	0	**59**	**10**
2015–16	*Chesterfield*	35	14	**35**	**14**
2016–17	Charlton Ath	29	2		
2017–18	Charlton Ath	2	0	**31**	**2**
2017–18	Scunthorpe U	32	6		
2018–19	Scunthorpe U	43	12	**75**	**18**

OJO, Funso (M) 223 4
H: 5 10 W: 11 03 b.Antwerp 28-8-91
Internationals: Belgium U16, U17, U20, U21.

2008–09	PSV Eindhoven	1	0		
2009–10	PSV Eindhoven	3	0		
2010–11	PSV Eindhoven	2	0		
2010–11	*VVV Venlo*	8	0	**8**	**0**
2011–12	PSV Eindhoven	5	0	**11**	**0**
2012–13	Beerschott	24	1	**24**	**1**
2013–14	Antwerp	8	0	**8**	**0**
2013–14	Dordrecht	13	0		
2014–15	Dordrecht	19	0	**32**	**0**
2015–16	Willem II	32	0		
2016–17	Willem II	28	0	**60**	**0**
2017–18	Scunthorpe U	41	2		
2018–19	Scunthorpe U	39	1	**80**	**3**

OLOMOLA, Olufela (F) 44 10
H: 5 7 b.London 5-9-97

2015–16	Southampton	0	0		
2016–17	Southampton	0	0		
2017–18	Southampton	0	0		
2017–18	*Yeovil T*	21	7		
2018–19	Scunthorpe U	6	0	**6**	**0**
2018–19	*Yeovil T*	17	3	**38**	**10**

PERCH, James (D) 451 18
H: 5 11 W: 11 05 b.Mansfield 29-9-85

2002–03	Nottingham F	0	0		
2003–04	Nottingham F	0	0		
2004–05	Nottingham F	22	0		
2005–06	Nottingham F	38	3		
2006–07	Nottingham F	46	5		
2007–08	Nottingham F	30	0		
2008–09	Nottingham F	37	3		
2009–10	Nottingham F	17	1	**190**	**12**
2010–11	Newcastle U	13	0		
2011–12	Newcastle U	25	0		
2012–13	Newcastle U	27	1	**65**	**1**
2013–14	Wigan Ath	40	0		
2014–15	Wigan Ath	41	3	**81**	**3**
2015–16	QPR	35	0		
2016–17	QPR	32	0		
2017–18	QPR	7	0	**74**	**0**
2018–19	Scunthorpe U	41	2	**41**	**2**

PUGH, Tom (M) 0 0
b.Doncaster 27-9-00

2018–19	Scunthorpe U	0	0		

SUTTON, Levi (M) 42 1
b. 24-3-96

2014–15	Scunthorpe U	0	0		
2015–16	Scunthorpe U	1	0		
2016–17	Scunthorpe U	8	0		
2017–18	Scunthorpe U	15	0		
2018–19	Scunthorpe U	18	1	**42**	**1**

VAN VEEN, Kevin (F) 203 64
H: 6 1 W: 11 11 b.Eindhoven 1-6-91

2013–14	JVC Cuyk	29	20	**29**	**20**
2014–15	FC Oss	20	16	**20**	**16**
2014–15	Scunthorpe U	20	2		
2015–16	Scunthorpe U	20	2		
2015–16	*Cambuur Leeuwarden*	12	1	**12**	**1**
2016–17	Scunthorpe U	33	10		
2017–18	Scunthorpe U	21	5		
2017–18	Northampton T	10	0		
2018–19	Northampton T	25	7	**35**	**7**
2018–19	Scunthorpe U	13	1	**107**	**20**

WATSON, Rory (G) 9 0
b. 5-2-96

2014–15	Hull C	0	0		
2015–16	Hull C	0	0		
2015–16	*Scunthorpe U*	0	0		
2016–17	Scunthorpe U	0	0		
2017–18	Scunthorpe U	4	0		
2018–19	Scunthorpe U	5	0	**9**	**0**

WEBSTER, Byron (D) 275 20
H: 6 5 W: 12 07 b.Sherburn-in-Elmet 31-3-87

2007–08	Siad Most	23	4		
2008–09	Siad Most	0	0	**23**	**4**
2009–10	Doncaster R	5	0		
2010–11	Doncaster R	7	0	**12**	**0**
2010–11	*Hereford U*	2	0	**2**	**0**
2010–11	*Northampton T*	8	0		
2011–12	Northampton T	13	0	**21**	**0**
2012–13	Yeovil T	44	5		
2013–14	Yeovil T	41	3		
2014–15	Millwall	11	0		
2014–15	*Yeovil T*	14	0	**99**	**8**
2015–16	Millwall	40	6		
2016–17	Millwall	44	2		
2017–18	Millwall	10	0		
2018–19	Millwall	4	0	**109**	**8**
2018–19	Scunthorpe U	9	0	**9**	**0**

WOOTTON, Kyle (M) 85 14
H: 6 2 W: 12 04 b. 11-10-96

2014–15	Scunthorpe U	12	1		
2015–16	Scunthorpe U	20	3		
2016–17	Scunthorpe U	2	1		
2016–17	*Cheltenham T*	16	2	**16**	**2**
2017–18	Stevenage	8	1	**8**	**1**
2017–18	Scunthorpe U	1	0		
2018–19	Scunthorpe U	26	6	**61**	**11**

Players retained or with offer of contract
Bedeau, Jacob; Ben, Elmahanni Yasin; Kelsey, Adam James; McGahey, Harrison; Van Veen, Kevin.

Scholars
Barks, Charles David; Busby, Joe David; Chadli, Luca Charles; Colclough, Liam Thomas; Collins, Louis Michael; Collins, Thomas Ryan; Gallimore, Levi; Harrison, Jack; Jessop, Harry Peter; Kalu, James Emmanuel; Marques, Alves Silva Raynner; Morfoot, Cameron John; Okafor, Miracle Chimeremeze; Pugh, Thomas Edward; Riches, Samuel David; Shrimpton, Finley Thomas; Train, Aidan.

SHEFFIELD U (73)

BALDOCK, George (M) 209 7
H: 5 9 W: 10 07 b.Buckingham 26-1-93

2009–10	Milton Keynes D	1	0		
2010–11	Milton Keynes D	2	0		
2011–12	Milton Keynes D	0	0		
2011–12	*Northampton T*	5	0	**5**	**0**
2012–13	Milton Keynes D	2	0		
2013–14	Milton Keynes D	38	2		
2014–15	Milton Keynes D	9	0		
2014–15	*Oxford U*	12	1		
2015–16	Milton Keynes D	15	0		
2015–16	*Oxford U*	27	2	**39**	**3**
2016–17	Milton Keynes D	37	0	**104**	**2**
2017–18	Sheffield U	34	1		
2018–19	Sheffield U	27	1	**61**	**2**

BASHAM, Chris (M) 327 17
H: 5 11 W: 12 08 b.Hebburn 20-7-88

2007–08	Bolton W	0	0		
2007–08	*Rochdale*	13	0	**13**	**0**
2008–09	Bolton W	11	1		
2009–10	Bolton W	8	0	**19**	**1**
2010–11	Blackpool	2	0		
2011–12	Blackpool	17	2		
2012–13	Blackpool	26	1		
2013–14	Blackpool	40	2	**85**	**5**
2014–15	Sheffield U	37	0		
2015–16	Sheffield U	44	3		
2016–17	Sheffield U	43	2		
2017–18	Sheffield U	45	2		
2018–19	Sheffield U	41	4	**210**	**11**

BRYAN, Kean (M) 44 2
H: 6 1 b.Manchester 1-11-96
Internationals: England U16, U17, U19, U20.

2016–17	Manchester C	0	0		
2016–17	*Bury*	12	0	**12**	**0**
2017–18	Manchester C	0	0		
2017–18	*Oldham Ath*	32	2	**32**	**2**
2018–19	Sheffield U	0	0		

CARRUTHERS, Samir (F) 158 7
H: 5 8 W: 11 00 b.Islington 4-4-93
Internationals: Republic of Ireland U19, U21.

2011–12	Aston Villa	3	0		
2012–13	Aston Villa	0	0		
2013–14	Aston Villa	0	0	**3**	**0**
2013–14	*Milton Keynes D*	23	2		
2014–15	Milton Keynes D	32	3		
2015–16	Milton Keynes D	39	1		
2016–17	Milton Keynes D	23	1	**117**	**6**
2016–17	Sheffield U	14	0		
2017–18	Sheffield U	14	1		
2018–19	Sheffield U	0	0	**28**	**1**
2018–19	*Oxford U*	10	0	**10**	**0**

CLARKE, Leon (F) 456 138
H: 6 2 W: 14 02 b.Birmingham 10-2-85

2003–04	Wolverhampton W	0	0		
2003–04	*Kidderminster H*	4	0	**4**	**0**
2004–05	Wolverhampton W	28	7		
2005–06	Wolverhampton W	24	1		
2005–06	*QPR*	1	0		
2005–06	*Plymouth Arg*	5	0	**5**	**0**
2006–07	Wolverhampton W	22	5		
2006–07	Sheffield W	10	1		
2006–07	*Oldham Ath*	5	3	**5**	**3**
2007–08	Sheffield W	8	3		
2007–08	*Southend U*	16	8	**16**	**8**
2008–09	Sheffield W	29	8		
2009–10	Sheffield W	36	6	**83**	**18**
2010–11	QPR	13	0	**14**	**0**
2010–11	*Preston NE*	6	1	**6**	**1**
2011–12	Swindon T	2	0	**2**	**0**
2011–12	*Chesterfield*	14	9	**14**	**9**
2011–12	Charlton Ath	7	0		

2011–12	*Crawley T*	4	1	**4**	**1**
2012–13	Charlton Ath	0	0	**7**	**0**
2012–13	*Scunthorpe U*	15	11	**15**	**11**
2012–13	Coventry C	12	8		
2013–14	Coventry C	23	15	**35**	**23**
2013–14	Wolverhampton W	13	1		
2014–15	Wolverhampton W	16	2	**103**	**16**
2014–15	*Wigan Ath*	10	1		
2015–16	Bury	32	15	**32**	**15**
2016–17	Sheffield U	23	7		
2017–18	Sheffield U	39	19		
2018–19	Sheffield U	24	3	**86**	**29**
2018–19	*Wigan Ath*	15	3	**25**	**4**

COUTTS, Paul (M) 313 10
H: 5 9 W: 11 11 b.Aberdeen 22-7-88
Internationals: Scotland U21.

2008–09	Peterborough U	37	0		
2009–10	Peterborough U	16	0	**53**	**0**
2009–10	Preston NE	13	1		
2010–11	Preston NE	23	1		
2011–12	Preston NE	41	2	**77**	**4**
2012–13	Derby Co	44	3		
2013–14	Derby Co	8	0		
2014–15	Derby Co	7	0	**59**	**3**
2014–15	Sheffield U	20	0		
2015–16	Sheffield U	32	0		
2016–17	Sheffield U	43	2		
2017–18	Sheffield U	16	1		
2018–19	Sheffield U	13	0	**124**	**3**

CRANIE, Martin (D) 360 2
H: 6 1 W: 12 09 b.Yeovil 23-9-86
Internationals: England U17, U18, U19, U20, U21.

2003–04	Southampton	1	0		
2004–05	Southampton	3	0		
2004–05	*Bournemouth*	3	0	**3**	**0**
2005–06	Southampton	11	0		
2006–07	Southampton	1	0	**16**	**0**
2006–07	*Yeovil T*	12	0	**12**	**0**
2007–08	Portsmouth	2	0		
2007–08	*QPR*	6	0	**6**	**0**
2008–09	Portsmouth	0	0		
2008–09	*Charlton Ath*	19	0	**19**	**0**
2009–10	Portsmouth	0	0	**2**	**0**
2009–10	Coventry C	40	1		
2010–11	Coventry C	36	0		
2011–12	Coventry C	38	0	**114**	**1**
2012–13	Barnsley	36	0		
2013–14	Barnsley	35	0		
2014–15	Barnsley	39	1	**110**	**1**
2015–16	Huddersfield T	37	0		
2016–17	Huddersfield T	14	0		
2017–18	Huddersfield T	3	0	**54**	**0**
2017–18	Middlesbrough	9	0		
2018–19	Middlesbrough	0	0	**9**	**0**
2018–19	Sheffield U	15	0	**15**	**0**

DUFFY, Mark (M) 367 38
H: 5 9 W: 11 05 b.Liverpool 7-10-85

2008–09	Morecambe	9	1		
2009–10	Morecambe	35	4		
2010–11	Morecambe	22	0	**66**	**5**
2010–11	Scunthorpe U	22	1		
2011–12	Scunthorpe U	37	2		
2012–13	Scunthorpe U	43	5	**102**	**8**
2013–14	Doncaster R	36	2	**36**	**2**
2014–15	Birmingham C	4	0		
2014–15	*Chesterfield*	3	0	**3**	**0**
2015–16	Birmingham C	0	0	**4**	**0**
2015–16	*Burton Alb*	45	8	**45**	**8**
2016–17	Sheffield U	39	6		
2017–18	Sheffield U	36	3		
2018–19	Sheffield U	36	6	**111**	**15**

EGAN, John (D) 211 18
H: 6 1 W: 11 11 b.Cork 20-10-92
Internationals: Republic of Ireland U17, U19, U21, Full caps.

2009–10	Sunderland	0	0		
2010–11	Sunderland	0	0		
2011–12	Sunderland	0	0		
2011–12	*Crystal Palace*	1	0	**1**	**0**
2011–12	*Sheffield U*	1	0		
2012–13	Sunderland	0	0		
2012–13	*Bradford C*	4	0	**4**	**0**
2013–14	Sunderland	0	0		
2013–14	*Southend U*	13	1	**13**	**1**
2014–15	Gillingham	45	4		
2015–16	Gillingham	36	6	**81**	**10**
2016–17	Brentford	34	4		
2017–18	Brentford	33	2	**67**	**6**
2018–19	Sheffield U	44	1	**45**	**1**

EVANS, Lee (M) 169 11
H: 6 1 W: 13 12 b.Newport 24-7-94
Internationals: Wales U21, Full caps.

2012–13	Wolverhampton W	0	0		
2013–14	Wolverhampton W	26	2		
2014–15	Wolverhampton W	18	1		
2015–16	Wolverhampton W	0	0		
2015–16	*Bradford C*	35	4	**35**	**4**
2016–17	Wolverhampton W	15	0		
2017–18	Wolverhampton W	0	0	**59**	**3**
2017–18	*Wigan Ath*	20	1		
2017–18	Sheffield U	19	2		
2018–19	Sheffield U	2	0	**21**	**2**
2018–19	*Wigan Ath*	34	1	**54**	**2**

FLECK, John (M) 340 18
H: 5 9 W: 11 05 b.Glasgow 24-8-91
Internationals: Scotland U17, U19, U21.

2007–08	Rangers	1	0		
2008–09	Rangers	8	1		
2009–10	Rangers	15	1		
2010–11	Rangers	13	0		
2011–12	Rangers	4	0	**41**	**2**
2011–12	*Blackpool*	7	0	**7**	**0**
2012–13	Coventry C	35	3		
2013–14	Coventry C	43	1		
2014–15	Coventry C	44	0		
2015–16	Coventry C	40	4	**162**	**8**
2016–17	Sheffield U	44	4		
2017–18	Sheffield U	41	2		
2018–19	Sheffield U	45	2	**130**	**8**

FREEMAN, Kieron (D) 199 15
H: 5 10 W: 12 05 b.Nottingham 21-3-92
Internationals: Wales U17, U19, U21, Full caps.

2010–11	Nottingham F	0	0		
2011–12	Nottingham F	0	0		
2011–12	*Notts Co*	19	1		
2012–13	Derby Co	19	0		
2013–14	Derby Co	6	0		
2013–14	*Notts Co*	16	0	**35**	**1**
2013–14	*Sheffield U*	12	0		
2014–15	Derby Co	0	0	**25**	**0**
2014–15	*Mansfield T*	11	0	**11**	**0**
2014–15	Sheffield U	19	1		
2015–16	Sheffield U	19	0		
2015–16	*Portsmouth*	7	0	**7**	**0**
2016–17	Sheffield U	41	10		
2017–18	Sheffield U	10	1		
2018–19	Sheffield U	20	2	**121**	**14**

GRAHAM, Sam (D) 15 0
b. 13-8-00

2018–19	Sheffield U	0	0		
2018–19	*Oldham Ath*	7	0	**7**	**0**
2018–19	*Central Coast Mariners*	8	0	**8**	**0**

HOLMES, Ricky (M) 272 53
H: 6 2 W: 11 11 b.Southend 19-6-87
Internationals: England C.

2010–11	Barnet	25	2		
2011–12	Barnet	41	8		
2012–13	Barnet	25	5	**91**	**15**
2013–14	Portsmouth	40	2		
2014–15	Portsmouth	13	0	**53**	**2**
2014–15	Northampton T	21	5		
2015–16	Northampton T	28	9	**49**	**14**
2016–17	Charlton Ath	35	13		
2017–18	Charlton Ath	23	6	**58**	**19**
2017–18	Sheffield U	5	0		
2018–19	Sheffield U	0	0	**5**	**0**
2018–19	*Oxford U*	16	3	**16**	**3**
2018–19	*Gillingham*	0	0		

LAVERY, Caolan (F) 133 27
H: 5 11 W: 11 12 b.Red Deer 22-10-92
Internationals: Canada U17. Northern Ireland U19, U21.

2012–13	Sheffield W	0	0		
2012–13	*Southend U*	3	0	**3**	**0**
2013–14	Sheffield W	21	4		
2013–14	*Plymouth Arg*	8	3	**8**	**3**
2014–15	Sheffield W	13	2		
2014–15	*Chesterfield*	8	3	**8**	**3**
2015–16	Sheffield W	0	0	**34**	**6**
2015–16	*Portsmouth*	13	4	**13**	**4**
2016–17	Sheffield U	27	4		
2017–18	Sheffield U	3	0		
2017–18	*Rotherham U*	14	2	**14**	**2**
2018–19	Sheffield U	0	0	**30**	**4**
2018–19	*Bury*	23	5	**23**	**5**

LUNDSTRAM, John (M) 191 9
H: 5 11 W: 11 09 b.Liverpool 18-2-94
Internationals: England U17, U18, U19, U20.

2011–12	Everton	0	0		
2012–13	Everton	0	0		
2012–13	*Doncaster R*	14	0	**14**	**0**
2013–14	Everton	0	0		
2013–14	*Yeovil T*	14	2	**14**	**2**
2013–14	*Leyton Orient*	7	0		
2014–15	Everton	0	0		
2014–15	*Blackpool*	17	0	**17**	**0**
2014–15	*Leyton Orient*	4	0	**11**	**0**
2014–15	*Scunthorpe U*	7	0	**7**	**0**
2015–16	Oxford U	37	3		
2016–17	Oxford U	45	1	**82**	**4**
2017–18	Sheffield U	36	3		
2018–19	Sheffield U	10	0	**46**	**3**

McGOLDRICK, David (F) 383 100
H: 6 1 W: 11 10 b.Nottingham 29-11-87
Internationals: Republic of Ireland Full caps.

2003–04	Notts Co	4	0		
2004–05	Notts Co	0	0		
2005–06	Southampton	1	0		
2005–06	*Notts Co*	6	0	**10**	**0**
2006–07	Southampton	9	0		
2006–07	*Bournemouth*	12	6	**12**	**6**
2007–08	Southampton	8	0		
2007–08	*Port Vale*	17	2	**17**	**2**
2008–09	Southampton	46	12	**64**	**12**
2009–10	Nottingham F	33	3		
2010–11	Nottingham F	21	5		
2011–12	Nottingham F	9	0		
2011–12	*Sheffield W*	4	1	**4**	**1**
2012–13	Nottingham F	0	0	**63**	**8**
2012–13	*Coventry C*	22	16	**22**	**16**
2012–13	*Ipswich T*	13	4		
2013–14	Ipswich T	31	14		
2014–15	Ipswich T	26	7		
2015–16	Ipswich T	24	4		
2016–17	Ipswich T	30	5		
2017–18	Ipswich T	22	6	**146**	**40**
2018–19	Sheffield U	45	15	**45**	**15**

MOORE, Simon (G) 153 0
H: 6 3 W: 12 02 b.Sandown 19-5-90
Internationals: Isle of Wight Full caps.

2009–10	Brentford	1	0		
2010–11	Brentford	10	0		
2011–12	Brentford	10	0		
2012–13	Brentford	43	0	**64**	**0**
2013–14	Cardiff C	0	0		
2013–14	*Bristol C*	11	0	**11**	**0**
2014–15	Cardiff C	10	0		
2015–16	Cardiff C	7	0	**17**	**0**
2016–17	Sheffield U	43	0		
2017–18	Sheffield U	18	0		
2018–19	Sheffield U	0	0	**61**	**0**

NORRINGTON-DAVIES, Rhys (D) 0 0
b. 22-4-99
Internationals: Wales U19, U21.

2017–18	Sheffield U	0	0
2018–19	Sheffield U	0	0

NORWOOD, Oliver (M) 312 23
H: 5 11 W: 11 13 b.Burnley 12-4-91
Internationals: England U16, U17. Northern Ireland U19, U21, B, Full caps.

2009–10	Manchester U	0	0		
2010–11	Manchester U	0	0		
2010–11	*Carlisle U*	6	0	**6**	**0**
2011–12	Manchester U	0	0		
2011–12	*Scunthorpe U*	15	1	**15**	**1**
2011–12	*Coventry C*	18	2	**18**	**2**
2012–13	Huddersfield T	39	3		
2013–14	Huddersfield T	40	5		
2014–15	Huddersfield T	1	0	**80**	**8**
2014–15	Reading	38	1		
2015–16	Reading	43	3	**81**	**4**
2016–17	Brighton & HA	33	0		
2017–18	Brighton & HA	0	0	**33**	**0**
2017–18	*Fulham*	36	5	**36**	**5**
2018–19	Sheffield U	43	3	**43**	**3**

O'CONNELL, Jack (D) 235 13
H: 6 3 W: 13 05 b.Liverpool 29-3-94
Internationals: England U18, U19.

2012–13	Blackburn R	0	0		
2012–13	*Rotherham U*	3	0	**3**	**0**
2012–13	*York C*	18	0	**18**	**0**
2013–14	Blackburn R	0	0		
2013–14	*Rochdale*	38	0		
2014–15	Blackburn R	0	0		
2014–15	*Rochdale*	29	5	**67**	**5**
2014–15	Brentford	0	0		
2015–16	Brentford	16	1	**16**	**1**
2016–17	Sheffield U	44	4		
2017–18	Sheffield U	46	0		
2018–19	Sheffield U	41	3	**131**	**7**

PARKHOUSE, David (F) **0 0**
b. 24-10-99
Internationals: Northern Ireland U17, U21.
From Maiden C.

2018–19	Sheffield U	0	0		

SHARP, Billy (F) **512 227**
H: 5 9 W: 11 00 b.Sheffield 5-2-86

2004–05	Sheffield U	2	0		
2004–05	*Rushden & D*	16	9	**16**	**9**
2005–06	Scunthorpe U	37	23		
2006–07	Scunthorpe U	45	30	**82**	**53**
2007–08	Sheffield U	29	4		
2008–09	Sheffield U	22	4		
2009–10	Sheffield U	0	0		
2009–10	*Doncaster R*	33	15		
2010–11	Doncaster R	29	15		
2011–12	Doncaster R	20	10		
2011–12	Southampton	15	9		
2012–13	Southampton	2	0		
2012–13	*Nottingham F*	39	10	**39**	**10**
2013–14	Southampton	0	0	**17**	**9**
2013–14	*Reading*	10	2	**10**	**2**
2013–14	*Doncaster R*	16	4	**98**	**44**
2014–15	Leeds U	33	5	**33**	**5**
2015–16	Sheffield U	44	21		
2016–17	Sheffield U	46	30		
2017–18	Sheffield U	34	13		
2018–19	Sheffield U	40	23	**217**	**95**

SMITH, Tyler (F) **14 2**
b. 4-12-98

2018–19	Sheffield U	0	0		
2018–19	*Doncaster R*	14	2	**14**	**2**

STEARMAN, Richard (D) **434 15**
H: 6 2 W: 10 08 b.Wolverhampton 19-8-87
Internationals: England U16, U17, U19, U21.

2004–05	Leicester C	8	1		
2005–06	Leicester C	34	3		
2006–07	Leicester C	35	1		
2007–08	Leicester C	39	2	**116**	**7**
2008–09	Wolverhampton W	37	1		
2009–10	Wolverhampton W	16	1		
2010–11	Wolverhampton W	31	0		
2011–12	Wolverhampton W	30	0		
2012–13	Wolverhampton W	12	1		
2012–13	*Ipswich T*	15	0	**15**	**0**
2013–14	Wolverhampton W	40	2		
2014–15	Wolverhampton W	42	0		
2015–16	Wolverhampton W	4	0		
2015–16	Fulham	29	0		
2016–17	Fulham	0	0	**29**	**0**
2016–17	*Wolverhampton W*	18	0	**230**	**5**
2017–18	Sheffield U	28	2		
2018–19	Sheffield U	16	1	**44**	**3**

STEVENS, Enda (D) **311 8**
H: 6 0 W: 12 04 b.Dublin 9-7-90
Internationals: Republic of Ireland U21, Full caps.

2008	UCD	2	0	**2**	**0**
2009	St Patrick's Ath	30	0	**30**	**0**
2010	Shamrock R	18	0		
2011	Shamrock R	27	0	**45**	**0**
2011–12	Aston Villa	0	0		
2012–13	Aston Villa	7	0		
2013–14	Aston Villa	0	0		
2013–14	*Notts Co*	2	0	**2**	**0**
2013–14	*Doncaster R*	13	0		
2014–15	Aston Villa	0	0	**7**	**0**
2014–15	*Northampton T*	4	1	**4**	**1**
2014–15	*Doncaster R*	28	1	**41**	**1**
2015–16	Portsmouth	45	0		
2016–17	Portsmouth	45	1	**90**	**1**
2016–17	Sheffield U	0	0		
2017–18	Sheffield U	45	1		
2018–19	Sheffield U	45	4	**90**	**5**

THOMAS, Nathan (F) **146 23**
H: 5 10 W: 12 08 b.Barwick 27-9-94

2013–14	Plymouth Arg	10	0		
2014–15	Plymouth Arg	9	1	**19**	**1**
2014–15	Motherwell	2	0	**2**	**0**
2015–16	Mansfield T	17	1	**17**	**1**
2015–16	Hartlepool U	22	5		
2016–17	Hartlepool U	33	9	**55**	**14**
2017–18	Sheffield U	1	0		
2017–18	*Shrewsbury T*	11	2	**11**	**2**
2018–19	Sheffield U	0	0	**1**	**0**
2018–19	*Notts Co*	25	1	**25**	**1**
2018–19	*Carlisle U*	16	4	**16**	**4**

WASHINGTON, Conor (F) **213 44**
H: 5 10 W: 11 09 b.Chatham 18-5-92
Internationals: Northern Ireland Full caps.

2013–14	Newport Co	24	4	**24**	**4**
2013–14	Peterborough U	17	4		
2014–15	Peterborough U	40	13		
2015–16	Peterborough U	25	10	**82**	**27**
2015–16	QPR	15	0		
2016–17	QPR	40	7		
2017–18	QPR	33	6		
2018–19	QPR	4	0	**92**	**13**
2018–19	Sheffield U	15	0	**15**	**0**

Players retained or with offer of contract
Doherty, Jordan; Eastwood, Jake; Ferguson, Keenan Tyrone Glendon; Greaves, Oliver James; Heneghan, Benjamin John; Mallon, Stephen Anthony; Sheppeard, Harry; Slater, Regan; Wright, Jake Maxwell; York, Reece Cable; Young, Jake Alan.

Scholars
Ackroyd, Sam Richard; Amissah, Jordan; Belehouan, Seri Jean Leroy; Boyes, Harry; Broadbent, George; Brunt, Zak Rian; Dewhurst, Marcus Robert; Foulstone, Harrison Alan; Gaxha, Leonardo; Gomis, Nicksoen; Gordon, Kyron; Kelly, Jacob Edward; Kelly, Samuel Walter; Neal, Harrison; Ompreon, Samuel; Potts, Reon Ben; Weaver, Thomas; Williams, Tommy John Albert.

SHEFFIELD W (74)

BAKER, Ashley (D) **12 0**
b. 30-10-96
Internationals: Wales U19, U21.

2017–18	Sheffield W	1	0		
2018–19	Sheffield W	11	0	**12**	**0**

BANNAN, Barry (D) **287 12**
H: 5 10 W: 10 08 b.Glasgow 1-12-89
Internationals: Scotland U21, Full caps.

2008–09	Aston Villa	0	0		
2008–09	*Derby Co*	10	1	**10**	**1**
2009–10	Aston Villa	0	0		
2009–10	*Blackpool*	20	1	**20**	**1**
2010–11	Aston Villa	12	0		
2010–11	*Leeds U*	7	0	**7**	**0**
2011–12	Aston Villa	28	1		
2012–13	Aston Villa	24	0		
2013–14	Aston Villa	0	0	**64**	**1**
2013–14	Crystal Palace	15	1		
2014–15	Crystal Palace	7	0		
2014–15	*Bolton W*	16	0	**16**	**0**
2015–16	Crystal Palace	0	0	**22**	**1**
2015–16	Sheffield W	35	2		
2016–17	Sheffield W	43	1		
2017–18	Sheffield W	29	0		
2018–19	Sheffield W	41	5	**148**	**8**

BOYD, George (M) **467 86**
H: 5 10 W: 11 07 b.Chatham 2-10-85
Internationals: Scotland B, Full caps.

2006–07	Peterborough U	20	6		
2007–08	Peterborough U	46	12		
2008–09	Peterborough U	46	9		
2009–10	Peterborough U	32	9		
2009–10	*Nottingham F*	6	1	**6**	**1**
2010–11	Peterborough U	43	15		
2011–12	Peterborough U	45	7		
2012–13	Peterborough U	31	6	**263**	**64**
2012–13	*Hull C*	13	4		
2013–14	Hull C	29	2		
2014–15	Hull C	1	0	**43**	**6**
2014–15	Burnley	35	5		
2015–16	Burnley	44	5		
2016–17	Burnley	36	2	**115**	**12**
2017–18	Sheffield W	20	2		
2018–19	Sheffield W	20	1	**40**	**3**

DAWSON, Cameron (G) **36 0**
H: 6 0 W: 10 12 b.Sheffield 7-7-95
Internationals: England U18, U19.

2013–14	Sheffield W	0	0		
2013–14	*Plymouth Arg*	0	0		
2014–15	Sheffield W	0	0		
2015–16	Sheffield W	0	0		
2016–17	Wycombe W	1	0	**1**	**0**
2016–17	Sheffield W	4	0		
2017–18	Chesterfield	2	0	**2**	**0**
2017–18	Sheffield W	3	0		
2018–19	Sheffield W	26	0	**33**	**0**

FLETCHER, Steven (F) **455 121**
H: 6 1 W: 12 00 b.Shrewsbury 26-3-87
Internationals: Scotland U20, U21, B, Full caps.

2003–04	Hibernian	5	0		
2004–05	Hibernian	20	5		
2005–06	Hibernian	34	8		
2006–07	Hibernian	31	6		
2007–08	Hibernian	32	13		
2008–09	Hibernian	34	11	**156**	**43**
2009–10	Burnley	35	8	**35**	**8**
2010–11	Wolverhampton W	29	10		
2011–12	Wolverhampton W	32	12	**61**	**22**
2012–13	Sunderland	28	11		
2013–14	Sunderland	20	3		
2014–15	Sunderland	30	5		
2015–16	Sunderland	16	4	**94**	**23**
2015–16	*Marseille*	12	2	**12**	**2**
2016–17	Sheffield W	38	10		
2017–18	Sheffield W	19	2		
2018–19	Sheffield W	40	11	**97**	**23**

FORESTIERI, Fernando (F) **282 71**
H: 5 8 W: 10 07 b.Rosario 16-1-90
Internationals: Italy U17, U19, U20, U21.

2006–07	Genoa	1	1	**1**	**1**
2007–08	Siena	17	1		
2008–09	Siena	2	0	**19**	**1**
2008–09	Vicenza	13	5	**13**	**5**
2009–10	Malaga	19	1	**19**	**1**
2010–11	Empoli	17	3	**17**	**3**
2011–12	Bari	27	2	**27**	**2**
2012–13	Udinese	0	0		
2012–13	*Watford*	28	8		
2013–14	Watford	28	7		
2014–15	Watford	24	5	**80**	**20**
2015–16	Sheffield W	36	15		
2016–17	Sheffield W	35	12		
2017–18	Sheffield W	10	5		
2018–19	Sheffield W	25	6	**106**	**38**

FOX, Morgan (D) **173 3**
H: 6 1 W: 12 03 b.Chelmsford 21-9-93
Internationals: Wales U21.

2012–13	Charlton Ath	0	0		
2013–14	Charlton Ath	6	0		
2013–14	*Notts Co*	7	1	**7**	**1**
2014–15	Charlton Ath	31	0		
2015–16	Charlton Ath	42	1		
2016–17	Charlton Ath	24	0	**103**	**1**
2016–17	Sheffield W	10	1		
2017–18	Sheffield W	28	0		
2018–19	Sheffield W	25	0	**63**	**1**

HOOPER, Gary (F) **376 169**
H: 5 9 W: 11 02 b.Loughton 26-1-88

2006–07	Southend U	19	0		
2006–07	*Leyton Orient*	4	2	**4**	**2**
2007–08	Southend U	13	2	**32**	**2**
2007–08	*Hereford U*	19	11	**19**	**11**
2008–09	Scunthorpe U	45	24		
2009–10	Scunthorpe U	35	19	**80**	**43**
2010–11	Celtic	26	20		
2011–12	Celtic	37	24		
2012–13	Celtic	32	19	**95**	**63**
2013–14	Norwich C	32	6		
2014–15	Norwich C	30	12		
2015–16	Norwich C	2	0	**64**	**18**
2015–16	Sheffield W	29	13		
2016–17	Sheffield W	23	6		
2017–18	Sheffield W	24	10		
2018–19	Sheffield W	6	1	**82**	**30**

HUNT, Alex (M) **0 0**
b.Sheffield 29-5-00

2018–19	Sheffield W	0	0		

HUTCHINSON, Sam (M) **135 4**
H: 6 0 W: 11 07 b.Windsor 3-8-89
Internationals: England U18, U19.

2006–07	Chelsea	1	0		
2007–08	Chelsea	0	0		
2008–09	Chelsea	0	0		
2009–10	Chelsea	2	0		
2010–11	Chelsea	0	0		
2011–12	Chelsea	2	0		
2012–13	Chelsea	0	0		
2012–13	*Nottingham F*	9	1	**9**	**1**
2013–14	Chelsea	0	0	**5**	**0**
2013–14	*Vitesse*	1	0	**1**	**0**
2013–14	*Sheffield W*	10	1		
2014–15	Sheffield W	20	0		
2015–16	Sheffield W	25	0		
2016–17	Sheffield W	33	2		
2017–18	Sheffield W	8	0		
2018–19	Sheffield W	24	0	**120**	**3**

IORFA, Dominic (D) **126 4**
H: 6 2 W: 12 04 b.Southend-on-Sea 24-6-95
Internationals: England U18, U20, U21.

2013–14	Wolverhampton W	0	0		

2013–14	*Shrewsbury T*	7	0	7	0
2014–15	Wolverhampton W	20	0		
2015–16	Wolverhampton W	42	0		
2016–17	Wolverhampton W	22	0		
2017–18	Wolverhampton W	0	0		
2017–18	*Ipswich T*	23	1	23	1
2018–19	Wolverhampton W	0	0	84	0
2018–19	Sheffield W	12	3	12	3

JONES, David (M) **371 27**
H: 5 11 W: 10 10 b.Southport 4-11-84
Internationals: England U21.

2003–04	Manchester U	0	0		
2004–05	Manchester U	0	0		
2005–06	Manchester U	0	0		
2005–06	*Preston NE*	24	3	24	3
2005–06	NEC Nijmegen	17	6	17	6
2006–07	Manchester U	0	0		
2006–07	Derby Co	28	6		
2007–08	Derby Co	14	1	42	7
2008–09	Wolverhampton W	34	4		
2009–10	Wolverhampton W	20	1		
2010–11	Wolverhampton W	12	1	66	6
2011–12	Wigan Ath	16	0		
2012–13	Wigan Ath	13	0	29	0
2012–13	*Blackburn R*	12	2	12	2
2013–14	Burnley	46	1		
2014–15	Burnley	36	0		
2015–16	Burnley	41	1		
2016–17	Burnley	1	0	124	2
2016–17	Sheffield W	29	0		
2017–18	Sheffield W	27	1		
2018–19	Sheffield W	1	0	57	1

KIRBY, Connor (M) **2 0**
b. 10-9-98

2017–18	Sheffield W	1	0		
2018–19	Sheffield W	1	0	2	0

LEE, Jack (D) **0 0**
b.Sunderland 19-12-98
From Sunderland.

2018–19	Sheffield W	0	0		

LEE, Kieran (D) **293 25**
H: 6 1 W: 12 00 b.Stalybridge 22-6-88

2006–07	Manchester U	1	0		
2007–08	Manchester U	0	0	1	0
2007–08	*QPR*	7	0	7	0
2008–09	Oldham Ath	7	0		
2009–10	Oldham Ath	24	1		
2010–11	Oldham Ath	43	2		
2011–12	Oldham Ath	43	2	117	5
2012–13	Sheffield W	23	0		
2013–14	Sheffield W	26	1		
2014–15	Sheffield W	33	6		
2015–16	Sheffield W	43	5		
2016–17	Sheffield W	26	5		
2017–18	Sheffield W	15	3		
2018–19	Sheffield W	2	0	168	20

LEES, Tom (D) **391 14**
H: 6 1 W: 12 04 b.Warwick 28-11-90
Internationals: England U21.

2008–09	Leeds U	0	0		
2009–10	Leeds U	0	0		
2009–10	*Accrington S*	39	0	39	0
2010–11	Leeds U	0	0		
2010–11	*Bury*	45	4	45	4
2011–12	Leeds U	42	2		
2012–13	Leeds U	40	1		
2013–14	Leeds U	41	0	123	3
2014–15	Sheffield W	44	0		
2015–16	Sheffield W	34	3		
2016–17	Sheffield W	35	1		
2017–18	Sheffield W	29	1		
2018–19	Sheffield W	42	2	184	7

LUCAS JOAO, Eduardo (F) **198 46**
H: 6 4 W: 12 08 b.Luanda 4-9-93
Internationals: Portugal U20, U21, U23, Full caps.

2012–13	Nacional	0	0		
2012–13	*Mirandela*	27	12	27	12
2013–14	Nacional	16	0		
2014–15	Nacional	30	6	46	6
2015–16	Sheffield W	40	6		
2016–17	Sheffield W	10	0		
2016–17	*Blackburn R*	13	3	13	3
2017–18	Sheffield W	31	9		
2018–19	Sheffield W	31	10	112	25

MARCO MATIAS, Andre (F) **211 41**
H: 5 10 W: 10 08 b.Barreiro 10-5-89
Internationals: Portugal U18, U19, U21.

2008–09	Sporting Lisbon	0	0		
2008–09	*Varzim*	12	0	12	0
2009–10	Sporting Lisbon	0	0		
2009–10	*Fatima*	7	2	7	2
2009–10	*Real Massama*	15	0	15	0
2010–11	Vit Guimaraes	0	0		
2010–11	*Freamunde*	24	5		
2011–12	Vit Guimaraes	0	0		
2011–12	*Freamunde*	19	2	43	7
2012–13	Vit Guimaraes	20	0		
2013–14	Vit Guimaraes	22	6	42	6
2014–15	Nacional	33	17	33	17
2015–16	Sheffield W	17	3		
2016–17	Sheffield W	2	0		
2017–18	Sheffield W	9	0		
2018–19	Sheffield W	31	6	59	9

NIELSEN, Frederik (D) **3 0**
b. 7-2-98
Internationals: Denmark U16, U17, U19.
From Nottingham F.

2017–18	Sheffield W	3	0		
2018–19	Sheffield W	0	0	3	0

NUHIU, Atdhe (F) **337 57**
H: 6 6 W: 13 05 b.Prishtina 29-7-89
Internationals: Austria U19, U20, U21.
Kosovo Full caps.

2008–09	Austria Karnten	16	2		
2009–10	Austria Karnten	3	0	19	2
2009–10	SV Ried	27	6	27	6
2010–11	Rapid Vienna	28	5		
2011–12	Rapid Vienna	31	8	59	13
2012–13	Eskisehirspor	28	2	28	2
2013–14	Sheffield W	38	8		
2014–15	Sheffield W	43	8		
2015–16	Sheffield W	41	3		
2016–17	Sheffield W	20	0		
2017–18	Sheffield W	28	11		
2018–19	Sheffield W	34	4	204	34

O'GRADY, Connor (D) **0 0**
b.Sheffield 5-12-97

2016–17	Sheffield W	0	0		
2017–18	Sheffield W	0	0		
2018–19	Sheffield W	0	0		

PALMER, Liam (M) **236 1**
H: 6 2 W: 12 10 b.Worksop 19-9-91
Internationals: Scotland U19, U21, Full caps.

2010–11	Sheffield W	9	0		
2011–12	Sheffield W	14	1		
2012–13	Sheffield W	0	0		
2012–13	*Tranmere R*	43	0		
2013–14	*Tranmere R*	0	0	43	0
2013–14	Sheffield W	39	0		
2014–15	Sheffield W	35	0		
2015–16	Sheffield W	15	0		
2016–17	Sheffield W	21	0		
2017–18	Sheffield W	25	0		
2018–19	Sheffield W	35	0	193	1

PELUPESSY, Joey (M) **156 3**
H: 5 8 W: 9 13 b.Nijverdal 15-5-93

2012–13	FC Twente	3	0		
2013–14	FC Twente	0	0	3	0
2014–15	Heracles	17	1		
2015–16	Heracles	34	0		
2016–17	Heracles	34	1		
2017–18	Heracles	18	0	103	2
2017–18	Sheffield W	17	1		
2018–19	Sheffield W	33	0	50	1

PENNEY, Matt (D) **19 0**
b.Chesterfield 11-2-98

2016–17	Sheffield W	0	0		
2016–17	*Bradford C*	1	0	1	0
2017–18	Sheffield W	0	0		
2017–18	*Mansfield T*	2	0	2	0
2018–19	Sheffield W	16	0	16	0

PRESTON, Fraser (G) **3 0**
b. 1-10-98
Internationals: Scotland U16, U19.

2017–18	Sheffield W	0	0		
2018–19	Sheffield W	3	0	3	0

PUDIL, Daniel (D) **334 28**
H: 6 1 W: 12 11 b.Prague 27-9-85
Internationals: Czech Republic U19, U21, Full caps.

2003–04	Blsany	2	2	2	2
2005–06	Liberec	3	4		
2006–07	Liberec	3	3	6	7
2007–08	Slavia Prague	16	6	16	6
2008–09	Genk	29	4		
2009–10	Genk	27	1		
2010–11	Genk	32	0		
2011–12	Genk	18	0	106	5
2011–12	Cesena	7	1	7	1
2012–13	Watford	37	1		
2013–14	Watford	37	2		
2014–15	Watford	23	0		
2015–16	Watford	0	0	97	3
2015–16	*Sheffield W*	36	2		
2016–17	Sheffield W	26	2		
2017–18	Sheffield W	27	0		
2018–19	Sheffield W	11	0	100	4

REACH, Adam (M) **265 31**
H: 6 1 W: 11 07 b.Gateshead 3-2-93
Internationals: England U19, U20.

2010–11	Middlesbrough	1	1		
2011–12	Middlesbrough	1	0		
2012–13	Middlesbrough	16	2		
2013–14	Middlesbrough	2	0		
2013–14	*Shrewsbury T*	22	3	22	3
2013–14	*Bradford C*	18	3	18	3
2014–15	Middlesbrough	39	2		
2015–16	Middlesbrough	4	1		
2015–16	*Preston NE*	35	4	35	4
2016–17	Middlesbrough	0	0	63	6
2016–17	Sheffield W	39	3		
2017–18	Sheffield W	46	4		
2018–19	Sheffield W	42	8	127	15

RHODES, Jordan (F) **421 185**
H: 6 1 W: 11 03 b.Oldham 5-2-90
Internationals: Scotland U21, Full caps.

2007–08	Ipswich T	8	1		
2008–09	Ipswich T	2	0	10	1
2008–09	*Rochdale*	5	2	5	2
2008–09	*Brentford*	14	7	14	7
2009–10	Huddersfield T	45	19		
2010–11	Huddersfield T	37	16		
2011–12	Huddersfield T	40	35		
2012–13	Huddersfield T	2	2	124	72
2012–13	Blackburn R	43	27		
2013–14	Blackburn R	46	25		
2014–15	Blackburn R	45	21		
2015–16	Blackburn R	25	10	159	83
2015–16	Middlesbrough	18	6		
2016–17	Middlesbrough	6	0	24	6
2016–17	*Sheffield W*	18	3		
2017–18	Sheffield W	31	5		
2018–19	Sheffield W	0	0	49	8
2018–19	*Norwich C*	36	6	36	6

RICE, Isaac (D) **0 0**
b.Lincoln 30-9-00

2018–19	Sheffield W	0	0		

SHAW, Liam (M) **0 0**
H: 5 10 b. 12-3-01

2018–19	Sheffield W	0	0		

STOBBS, Jack (M) **10 0**
H: 5 11 W: 13 05 b.Leeds 27-2-97

2013–14	Sheffield W	1	0		
2014–15	Sheffield W	0	0		
2015–16	Sheffield W	1	0		
2016–17	Sheffield W	0	0		
2017–18	Port Vale	5	0	5	0
2017–18	Sheffield W	3	0		
2018–19	Sheffield W	0	0	5	0

THORNILEY, Jordan (D) **45 0**
b.Warrington 24-11-96
From Everton.

2016–17	Sheffield W	0	0		
2017–18	Sheffield W	11	0		
2017–18	*Accrington S*	14	0	14	0
2018–19	Sheffield W	20	0	31	0

VAN AKEN, Joost (D) **99 3**
H: 5 10 W: 11 11 b.Haarlem 13-5-94
Internationals: Netherlands U21.

2013–14	Heerenveen	6	2		
2014–15	Heerenveen	30	0		
2015–16	Heerenveen	20	0		
2016–17	Heerenveen	26	1		
2017–18	Heerenveen	2	0	84	3
2017–18	Sheffield W	14	0		
2018–19	Sheffield W	1	0	15	0

WESTWOOD, Keiren (G) **435 0**
H: 6 1 W: 13 10 b.Manchester 23-10-84
Internationals: Republic of Ireland Full caps.

2001–02	Manchester C	0	0		
2002–03	Manchester C	0	0		
2003–04	Manchester C	0	0		
2003–04	*Oldham Ath*	0	0		
2004–05	Manchester C	0	0		
2005–06	Manchester C	0	0		
2005–06	Carlisle U	35	0		
2006–07	Carlisle U	46	0		
2007–08	Carlisle U	46	0	127	0
2008–09	Coventry C	46	0		
2009–10	Coventry C	44	0		

2010–11 Coventry C 41 0 **131 0**
2011–12 Sunderland 9 0
2012–13 Sunderland 0 0
2013–14 Sunderland 10 0 **19 0**
2014–15 Sheffield W 43 0
2015–16 Sheffield W 34 0
2016–17 Sheffield W 43 0
2017–18 Sheffield W 18 0
2018–19 Sheffield W 20 0 **158 0**

WILDSMITH, Joe (G) 38 0
H: 6 0 W: 10 03 b.Sheffield 28-12-95
Internationals: England U20.
2013–14 Sheffield W 0 0
2014–15 Sheffield W 0 0
2014–15 *Barnsley* 2 0 **2 0**
2015–16 Sheffield W 9 0
2016–17 Sheffield W 1 0
2017–18 Sheffield W 26 0
2018–19 Sheffield W 0 0 **36 0**

WINNALL, Sam (F) 215 83
H: 5 9 W: 11 04 b.Wolverhampton 19-1-91
2009–10 Wolverhampton W 0 0
2010–11 Wolverhampton W 0 0
2010–11 *Burton Alb* 19 7 **19 7**
2011–12 Wolverhampton W 0 0
2011–12 *Hereford U* 8 2 **8 2**
2011–12 *Inverness CT* 2 0 **2 0**
2012–13 Wolverhampton W 0 0
2012–13 *Shrewsbury T* 4 0 **4 0**
2013–14 Scunthorpe U 45 23 **45 23**
2014–15 Barnsley 32 9
2015–16 Barnsley 43 21
2016–17 Barnsley 22 11 **97 41**
2016–17 Sheffield W 14 3
2017–18 Sheffield W 2 1
2017–18 *Derby Co* 17 6 **17 6**
2018–19 Sheffield W 7 0 **23 4**

Players retained or with offer of contract
Borukov, Preslav Nikolaev; Brennan, Ciaran Thomas; Dawodu, Joshua; Dos, Santos Joao Lucas Eduardo; Grant, Conor Michael; Hughes, Ben Anthony; Kanteh, Damba Master Omar; Van Aken, Joost Maurits; Waldock, Liam Brian; West, Joseph William.

Scholars
Brandy, L'varn Joseph; Cox, Luke Joseph; Ellery, Johnson Michael Jamie; Eratt-Thompson, Declan Sebastian; Farmer, Lewis J.; Hagan, Charles Junior; Hammoud, Eyad Omar; Jackson, Luke John; Kenyon, Toby James; Marques, O'Brien Jordan; Oliver, Sam David; Reaney, Charlie Alexander; Render, Joshua Ben; Vasalo, Elliott Phillip.

SHREWSBURY T (75)

AGIUS, Sam (G) 0 0
b.Walsall 9-3-02
2018–19 Shrewsbury T 0 0

AMADI-HOLLOWAY, Aaron (D) 153 12
H: 6 2 W: 13 00 b.Newark 21-2-93
Internationals: Wales U17, U19.
2012–13 Bristol C 0 0
2013–14 Bristol C 0 0
2013–14 Newport Co 4 0 **4 0**
2014–15 Wycombe W 29 3
2015–16 Wycombe W 23 3 **52 6**
2015–16 *Oldham Ath* 10 2
2016–17 Fleetwood T 6 0 **6 0**
2016–17 Oldham Ath 15 0
2017–18 Oldham Ath 36 2 **61 4**
2018–19 Shrewsbury T 30 2 **30 2**

ANGOL, Lee (M) 97 24
H: 5 10 W: 11 04 b. 4-8-94
2012–13 Wycombe W 3 0
2013–14 Wycombe W 0 0 **3 0**
2014–15 Luton T 0 0
2015–16 Peterborough U 33 11
2016–17 Peterborough U 13 1 **46 12**
2017–18 Mansfield T 29 9 **29 9**
2018–19 Shrewsbury T 17 3 **17 3**
2018–19 *Lincoln C* 2 0 **2 0**

ARNOLD, Steve (G) 56 0
H: 6 1 W: 13 02 b.Welham Green 22-8-89
Internationals: England C.
2012–13 Stevenage 30 0
2013–14 Stevenage 3 0 **33 0**
From Forest Green R, Dover Ath.
2017–18 Gillingham 0 0
2018–19 Shrewsbury T 23 0 **23 0**

BARNETT, Ryan (M) 1 0
b. 23-9-99
2016–17 Shrewsbury T 0 0
2017–18 Shrewsbury T 0 0
2018–19 Shrewsbury T 1 0 **1 0**

BECKLES, Omar (D) 112 7
H: 6 2 W: 12 04 b.Kettering 25-10-91
From Aldershot T.
2016–17 Accrington S 41 2
2017–18 Accrington S 2 1 **43 3**
2017–18 Shrewsbury T 33 3
2018–19 Shrewsbury T 36 1 **69 4**

BOLTON, James (D) 64 2
H: 5 11 W: 11 11 b.Stone 13-8-94
Internationals: England C.
From Macclesfield T, Halifax T, Gateshead.
2017–18 Shrewsbury T 33 1
2018–19 Shrewsbury T 31 1 **64 2**

CAMPBELL, Tyrese (F) 22 5
b.Derby 16-9-97
Internationals: England U17.
From Manchester C.
2017–18 Stoke C 4 0
2018–19 Stoke C 3 0 **7 0**
2018–19 Shrewsbury T 15 5 **15 5**

CHARLES-COOK, Reice (G) 76 0
H: 6 1 W: 12 08 b.London 8-4-94
2013–14 Bury 2 0 **2 0**
2014–15 Coventry C 0 0
2015–16 Coventry C 37 0
2016–17 Coventry C 15 0 **52 0**
2017–18 Swindon T 22 0 **22 0**
2018–19 Sonderjyske 0 0
2018–19 Shrewsbury T 0 0

COYNE, Danny (G) 441 0
H: 6 0 W: 13 00 b.Prestatyn 27-8-73
Internationals: Wales U21, B, Full caps.
1991–92 Tranmere R 0 0
1992–93 Tranmere R 1 0
1993–94 Tranmere R 5 0
1994–95 Tranmere R 5 0
1995–96 Tranmere R 46 0
1996–97 Tranmere R 21 0
1997–98 Tranmere R 16 0
1998–99 Tranmere R 17 0
1999–2000 Grimsby T 44 0
2000–01 Grimsby T 46 0
2001–02 Grimsby T 45 0
2002–03 Grimsby T 46 0 **181 0**
2003–04 Leicester C 4 0 **4 0**
2004–05 Burnley 20 0
2005–06 Burnley 8 0
2006–07 Burnley 12 0 **40 0**
2007–08 Tranmere R 41 0
2008–09 Tranmere R 39 0 **191 0**
2009–10 Middlesbrough 23 0
2010–11 Middlesbrough 1 0
2011–12 Middlesbrough 1 0 **25 0**
2012–13 Sheffield U 0 0
2013–14 Sheffield U 0 0
2013–14 *Shrewsbury T* 0 0
2014–15 Shrewsbury T 0 0
2017–18 Shrewsbury T 0 0
2018–19 Shrewsbury T 0 0

DOCHERTY, Greg (M) 146 13
H: 5 10 W: 11 05 b.Glasgow 10-9-96
Internationals: Scotland U17, U21.
2013–14 Hamilton A 3 0
2014–15 Hamilton A 7 1
2015–16 Hamilton A 34 1
2016–17 Hamilton A 29 1
2017–18 Hamilton A 21 3 **94 6**
2017–18 Rangers 11 0
2018–19 Rangers 0 0 **11 0**
On loan from Rangers
2018–19 Shrewsbury T 41 7 **41 7**

EDWARDS, Dave (M) 444 60
H: 5 11 W: 11 04 b.Shrewsbury 3-2-86
Internationals: Wales U21, Full caps.
2002–03 Shrewsbury T 1 0
2003–04 Shrewsbury T 0 0
2004–05 Shrewsbury T 27 5
2005–06 Shrewsbury T 30 2
2006–07 Shrewsbury T 45 5
2007–08 Luton T 19 4 **19 4**
2007–08 Wolverhampton W 10 1
2008–09 Wolverhampton W 44 3
2009–10 Wolverhampton W 20 1
2010–11 Wolverhampton W 15 1
2011–12 Wolverhampton W 26 3
2012–13 Wolverhampton W 24 2
2013–14 Wolverhampton W 30 9
2014–15 Wolverhampton W 41 6
2015–16 Wolverhampton W 29 5
2016–17 Wolverhampton W 44 10
2017–18 Wolverhampton W 1 0 **284 41**
2017–18 Reading 32 3
2018–19 Reading 0 0 **32 3**
2018–19 Shrewsbury T 6 0 **109 12**

GILLIEAD, Alex (F) 131 8
H: 6 0 W: 11 00 b.Shotley Bridge 11-2-96
Internationals: England U16, U17, U18, U20.
2014–15 Newcastle U 0 0
2015–16 Newcastle U 0 0
2015–16 *Carlisle U* 35 5 **35 5**
2016–17 Newcastle U 0 0
2016–17 *Luton T* 18 1 **18 1**
2016–17 *Bradford C* 9 0
2017–18 Newcastle U 0 0
2017–18 *Bradford C* 42 1 **51 1**
2018–19 Shrewsbury T 27 1 **27 1**

GOLBOURNE, Scott (M) 376 6
H: 5 8 W: 11 08 b.Bristol 29-2-88
Internationals: England U17, U19.
2004–05 Bristol C 9 0
2005–06 Bristol C 5 0
2005–06 Reading 1 0
2006–07 Reading 0 0
2006–07 *Wycombe W* 34 1 **34 1**
2007–08 Reading 1 0
2007–08 *Bournemouth* 5 0 **5 0**
2008–09 Reading 0 0 **2 0**
2008–09 *Oldham Ath* 8 0 **8 0**
2009–10 Exeter C 34 0
2010–11 Exeter C 44 2
2011–12 Exeter C 26 0 **104 2**
2011–12 Barnsley 12 1
2012–13 Barnsley 31 1
2013–14 Barnsley 4 0 **47 2**
2013–14 Wolverhampton W 40 1
2014–15 Wolverhampton W 27 0
2015–16 Wolverhampton W 20 0 **87 1**
2015–16 Bristol C 16 0
2016–17 Bristol C 19 0
2017–18 Bristol C 0 0 **49 0**
2017–18 *Milton Keynes D* 25 0 **25 0**
2018–19 Shrewsbury T 15 0 **15 0**

GRANT, Anthony (M) 477 15
H: 5 10 W: 11 01 b.Lambeth 4-6-87
Internationals: England U16, U17, U19.
2004–05 Chelsea 1 0
2005–06 Chelsea 0 0
2005–06 *Oldham Ath* 2 0 **2 0**
2006–07 Chelsea 0 0
2006–07 *Wycombe W* 40 0 **40 0**
2007–08 Chelsea 0 0 **1 0**
2007–08 *Luton T* 4 0 **4 0**
2007–08 *Southend U* 10 0
2008–09 Southend U 35 1
2009–10 Southend U 38 0
2010–11 Southend U 43 8
2011–12 Southend U 33 1 **159 10**
2012–13 Stevenage 41 0 **41 0**
2013–14 Crewe Alex 38 2
2014–15 Crewe Alex 43 2 **81 4**
2015–16 Port Vale 38 1
2016–17 Port Vale 20 0 **58 1**
2016–17 Peterborough U 11 0
2017–18 Peterborough U 38 0 **49 0**
2018–19 Shrewsbury T 42 0 **42 0**

GREGORY, Cameron (G) 0 0
2017–18 Shrewsbury T 0 0
2018–19 Shrewsbury T 0 0

HAYNES, Ryan (D) 104 1
H: 5 7 W: 10 10 b.Northampton 27-9-95
2012–13 Coventry C 1 0
2013–14 Coventry C 2 0
2014–15 Coventry C 26 1
2015–16 Coventry C 9 0
2015–16 *Cambridge U* 10 0 **10 0**
2016–17 Coventry C 19 0
2017–18 Coventry C 21 0 **78 1**
2018–19 Shrewsbury T 16 0 **16 0**

JOHN-LEWIS, Lemell (M) 236 23
H: 5 10 W: 11 10 b.Hammersmith 17-5-89
2006–07 Lincoln C 0 0
2007–08 Lincoln C 21 3
2008–09 Lincoln C 27 4
2009–10 Lincoln C 24 1 **72 8**
2010–11 Bury 39 2
2011–12 Bury 28 5

2012–13	Bury	16	2	**83**	**9**
2015–16	Newport Co	28	3		
2016–17	Newport Co	2	0	**30**	**3**
2017–18	Shrewsbury T	34	2		
2018–19	Shrewsbury T	17	1	**51**	**3**

JONES, Sam (M) 58 16
H: 6 2 W: 12 08 b.Doncaster 18-9-91
Internationals: Wales U19.
From Alfreton T, Gateshead.

2016–17	Grimsby T	16	7		
2017–18	Grimsby T	25	6	**41**	**13**
2017–18	Shrewsbury T	5	1		
2018–19	Shrewsbury T	0	0	**5**	**1**
2018–19	*Cheltenham T*	12	2	**12**	**2**

KENNEDY, Kieran (D) 23 0
H: 5 10 W: 11 00 b.Urmston 23-9-93
Internationals: England U19.

2011–12	Manchester C	0	0		
2012–13	Manchester C	0	0		
2013–14	Manchester C	0	0		
2013–14	*Leicester C*	0	0		
2014–15	*Leicester C*	0	0		
2015–16	Motherwell	22	0		
2016–17	Motherwell	0	0	**22**	**0**

From AFC Fylde, Macclesfield T.

2018–19	Shrewsbury T	1	0	**1**	**0**

LAURENT, Josh (M) 96 4
H: 6 0 W: 11 00 b.Leytonstone 6-5-95

2013–14	QPR	0	0		
2014–15	QPR	0	0		
2015–16	Brentford	0	0		
2015–16	*Newport Co*	3	0	**3**	**0**
2015–16	Hartlepool U	3	0		
2016–17	Hartlepool U	25	1	**28**	**1**
2016–17	Wigan Ath	1	0		
2017–18	Wigan Ath	0	0	**1**	**0**
2017–18	*Bury*	22	1	**22**	**1**
2018–19	Shrewsbury T	42	2	**42**	**2**

LEASK, Jack (M) 0 0
b.Shrewsbury 9-4-01

2018–19	Shrewsbury T	0	0		

LOFT, Doug (M) 307 25
H: 6 0 W: 12 01 b.Maidstone 25-12-86

2005–06	Brighton & HA	3	1		
2006–07	Brighton & HA	11	1		
2007–08	Brighton & HA	13	0		
2008–09	Brighton & HA	12	0	**39**	**2**
2008–09	*Dagenham & R*	11	0	**11**	**0**
2009–10	Port Vale	32	3		
2010–11	Port Vale	29	1		
2011–12	Port Vale	44	4		
2012–13	Port Vale	32	1		
2013–14	Port Vale	37	9	**174**	**18**
2014–15	Gillingham	36	1		
2015–16	Gillingham	26	4	**62**	**5**
2016–17	Colchester U	8	0		
2017–18	Colchester U	12	0	**20**	**0**
2018–19	Shrewsbury T	1	0	**1**	**0**

McATEE, John (F) 1 0
b. 23-7-99

2016–17	Shrewsbury T	1	0		
2017–18	Shrewsbury T	0	0		
2018–19	Shrewsbury T	0	0	**1**	**0**

MWANDWE, Lifumpa (F) 0 0
b. 29-12-00

2017–18	Shrewsbury T	0	0		
2018–19	Shrewsbury T	0	0		

NORBURN, Oliver (M) 111 12
H: 6 1 W: 12 13 b.Leicester 26-10-92

2011–12	Leicester C	0	0		
2011–12	*Bristol R*	5	0		
2012–13	Bristol R	35	3		
2013–14	Bristol R	16	0	**56**	**3**
2014–15	Plymouth Arg	14	0	**14**	**0**

From Guiseley, Macclesfield T, Tranmere R.

2018–19	Shrewsbury T	41	9	**41**	**9**

OKENABIRHIE, Fejiri (F) 41 10
H: 5 10 W: 11 09 b. 25-2-96
Internationals: England C.

2013–14	Stevenage	3	0		
2014–15	Stevenage	0	0		
2015–16	Stevenage	0	0	**3**	**0**

From Harrow Bor, Dagenham & R.

2018–19	Shrewsbury T	38	10	**38**	**10**

ROWLAND, James (M) 0 0
b.Walsall 3-12-01
From WBA.

2018–19	Shrewsbury T	0	0		

SADLER, Matthew (D) 439 8
H: 5 11 W: 11 08 b.Birmingham 26-2-85
Internationals: England U17, U18, U19.

2001–02	Birmingham C	0	0		
2002–03	Birmingham C	2	0		
2003–04	Birmingham C	0	0		
2003–04	*Northampton T*	7	0	**7**	**0**
2004–05	Birmingham C	0	0		
2005–06	Birmingham C	8	0		
2006–07	Birmingham C	36	0		
2007–08	Birmingham C	5	0	**51**	**0**
2007–08	Watford	15	0		
2008–09	Watford	15	0		
2009–10	Watford	0	0		
2009–10	*Stockport Co*	20	0	**20**	**0**
2010–11	Watford	0	0	**30**	**0**
2010–11	*Shrewsbury T*	46	0		
2011–12	Walsall	46	1	**46**	**1**
2012–13	Crawley T	46	1		
2013–14	Crawley T	46	1		
2014–15	Rotherham U	0	0		
2014–15	*Crawley T*	10	0	**102**	**2**
2014–15	*Oldham Ath*	8	0	**8**	**0**
2014–15	Shrewsbury T	0	0		
2015–16	Shrewsbury T	24	2		
2016–17	Shrewsbury T	34	2		
2017–18	Shrewsbury T	42	1		
2018–19	Shrewsbury T	29	0	**175**	**5**

SEARS, Ryan (D) 5 0
b. 13-12-98

2016–17	Shrewsbury T	0	0		
2017–18	Shrewsbury T	0	0		
2018–19	Shrewsbury T	5	0	**5**	**0**

SHELIS, Christos (D) 0 0
b. 2-2-00
Internationals: Cyprus U17.

2017–18	Shrewsbury T	0	0		
2018–19	Shrewsbury T	0	0		

TAYLOR, Kian (M) 0 0
H: 5 10 b.Leicester 10-1-01

2018–19	Shrewsbury T	0	0		

TURNER, Jamaine (F) 0 0
b. 24-12-01

2018–19	Shrewsbury T	0	0		

VINCELOT, Romain (M) 369 29
H: 5 9 W: 11 02 b.Poitiers 29-10-85

2004–05	Chamois Niortais	3	0	**3**	**0**
2005–06	Chemois Niortais	28	1		
2006–07	Chemois Niortais	9	0		
2007–08	Chemois Niortais	6	0	**43**	**1**
2008–09	Gueugnon	20	0	**20**	**0**
2009–10	Dagenham & R	9	1		
2010–11	Dagenham & R	46	12	**55**	**13**
2011–12	Brighton & HA	15	1		
2012–13	Brighton & HA	0	0	**15**	**1**
2012–13	*Gillingham*	9	1	**9**	**1**
2012–13	Leyton Orient	15	1		
2013–14	Leyton Orient	39	0		
2014–15	Leyton Orient	27	2	**81**	**3**
2015–16	Coventry C	45	4	**45**	**4**
2016–17	Bradford C	45	2		
2017–18	Bradford C	38	4	**83**	**6**
2018–19	Crawley T	12	0	**12**	**0**
2018–19	Shrewsbury T	3	0	**3**	**0**

WARD, Luke (D) 0 0
b. 25-9-01
From Wolverhampton W.

2018–19	Shrewsbury T	0	0		

WATERFALL, Luke (D) 89 8
H: 6 2 W: 13 02 b.Sheffield 30-7-90

2008–09	Tranmere R	0	0		

From Ilkeston, Gainsborough T

2013–14	Scunthorpe U	9	1		
2014–15	Scunthorpe U	0	0	**9**	**1**
2014–15	*Mansfield T*	5	0	**5**	**0**
2017–18	Lincoln C	30	2		
2018–19	Lincoln C	1	0	**31**	**2**
2018–19	Shrewsbury T	44	5	**44**	**5**

WHALLEY, Shaun (M) 150 22
H: 5 9 W: 10 08 b.Whiston 7-8-87

2014–15	Luton T	18	3	**18**	**3**
2015–16	Shrewsbury T	24	6		
2016–17	Shrewsbury T	32	3		
2017–18	Shrewsbury T	44	8		
2018–19	Shrewsbury T	32	2	**132**	**19**

WILLIAMS, Ro-Shaun (M) 16 0
b. 9-3-98
Internationals: England U17, U18.

2015–16	Manchester U	0	0		
2016–17	Manchester u	0	0		
2017–18	Manchester u	0	0		
2018–19	Manchester U	0	0		
2018–19	Shrewsbury T	16	0	**16**	**0**

Players retained or with offer of contract
Amadi, Holloway Aaron Joshua; Eisa, Abobaker Mamoun; Walker, Bradley Paul.

Scholars
Agius, Samuel Thomas; Atkinson, Jack Edward; Corfield, Reiss Morgan; Davies, Rhys Andrew Melville; Davies, Thomas Iwan; Elmore, Archie Nicholas; Grosvenor, Ryan Christopher; Hartley, Zac Darren; Leask, Jack Nathan; Redding, Lewis William; Rowland, James Thomas; Taylor, Brett Andrew; Taylor, Kian George; Turner, Jamaine Noel; Walker, Daniel Richard; Ward, Luke Allan James.

SOUTHAMPTON (76)

ARMSTRONG, Stuart (M) 254 44
H: 6 0 W: 10 10 b.Inverness 30-3-92
Internationals: Scotland U19, U21, Full caps.

2010–11	Dundee U	12	0		
2011–12	Dundee U	23	1		
2012–13	Dundee U	36	3		
2013–14	Dundee U	36	8		
2014–15	Dundee U	20	6	**127**	**18**
2014–15	Celtic	15	1		
2015–16	Celtic	25	4		
2016–17	Celtic	31	15		
2017–18	Celtic	27	3	**98**	**23**
2018–19	Southampton	29	3	**29**	**3**

AUSTIN, Charlie (F) 289 133
H: 6 2 W: 13 03 b.Hungerford 5-7-89

2009–10	Swindon T	33	19		
2010–11	Swindon T	21	12	**54**	**31**
2010–11	Burnley	4	0		
2011–12	Burnley	41	16		
2012–13	Burnley	37	25	**82**	**41**
2013–14	QPR	31	17		
2014–15	QPR	35	18		
2015–16	QPR	16	10	**82**	**45**
2015–16	Southampton	7	1		
2016–17	Southampton	15	6		
2017–18	Southampton	24	7		
2018–19	Southampton	25	2	**71**	**16**

BARNES, Marcus (F) 8 0
b.Reading 1-12-96

2017–18	Southampton	0	0		
2017–18	*Yeovil T*	8	0	**8**	**0**
2018–19	Southampton	0	0		

BEDNAREK, Jan (D) 78 2
H: 6 2 W: 12 02 b.Slupca 12-4-96
Internationals: Poland U16, U17, U18, U19, U20, U21, Full caps.

2013–14	Lech Poznan	2	0		
2014–15	Lech Poznan	2	0		
2015–16	Lech Poznan	0	0		
2015–16	*Gornik Leczna*	17	0	**17**	**0**
2016–17	Lech Poznan	27	1	**31**	**1**
2017–18	Southampton	5	1		
2018–19	Southampton	25	0	**30**	**1**

BERTRAND, Ryan (D) 342 7
H: 5 10 W: 11 00 b.Southwark 5-8-89
Internationals: England U17, U18, U19, U20, U21, Full caps. Great Britain.

2006–07	Chelsea	0	0		
2006–07	*Bournemouth*	5	0	**5**	**0**
2007–08	Chelsea	0	0		
2007–08	*Oldham Ath*	21	0	**21**	**0**
2007–08	*Norwich C*	18	0		
2008–09	Chelsea	0	0		
2008–09	*Norwich C*	38	0	**56**	**0**
2009–10	Chelsea	0	0		
2009–10	*Reading*	44	1	**44**	**1**
2010–11	Chelsea	1	0		
2010–11	*Nottingham F*	19	0	**19**	**0**
2011–12	Chelsea	7	0		
2012–13	Chelsea	19	0		
2013–14	Chelsea	1	0	**28**	**0**
2013–14	*Aston Villa*	16	0	**16**	**0**
2014–15	Southampton	34	2		
2015–16	Southampton	32	1		
2016–17	Southampton	28	2		
2017–18	Southampton	35	0		
2018–19	Southampton	24	1	**153**	**6**

CEDRIC SOARES, Ricardo (D) 199 3
H: 5 8 W: 10 08 b.Gelsenkirchen, Germany 31-8-91
Internationals: Portugal U16, U17, U18, U19, U20, U21, Full caps.

2010–11	Sporting Lisbon	2	0		
2011–12	Sporting Lisbon	0	0		
2011–12	*Academica*	24	0	**24**	**0**
2012–13	Sporting Lisbon	13	1		
2013–14	Sporting Lisbon	28	1		
2014–15	Sporting Lisbon	24	0	**67**	**2**
2015–16	Southampton	24	0		
2016–17	Southampton	30	0		
2017–18	Southampton	32	0		
2018–19	Southampton	18	1	**104**	**1**
2018–19	*Inter Milan*	4	0	**4**	**0**

DAVIS, Steven (M) 472 35
H: 5 8 W: 11 04 b.Ballymena 1-1-85
Internationals: Northern Ireland U15, U16, U17, U19, U21, U23, Full caps.

2004–05	Aston Villa	28	1		
2005–06	Aston Villa	35	4		
2006–07	Aston Villa	28	0	**91**	**5**
2007–08	Fulham	22	0	**22**	**0**
2007–08	*Rangers*	12	0		
2008–09	Rangers	34	6		
2009–10	Rangers	36	3		
2010–11	Rangers	37	4		
2011–12	Rangers	33	5		
2012–13	Southampton	32	2		
2013–14	Southampton	34	2		
2014–15	Southampton	35	0		
2015–16	Southampton	34	5		
2016–17	Southampton	32	0		
2017–18	Southampton	23	3		
2018–19	Southampton	3	0	**193**	**12**
2018–19	*Rangers*	14	0	**166**	**18**

ELYOUNOUSSI, Mohamed (M) 215 66
H: 5 10 W: 11 00 b.Al Hoceima 4-8-94
Internationals: Norway U17, U18, U19, U21, Full caps.

2011	Sarpsborg 08	9	0		
2012	Sarpsborg 08	26	9		
2013	Sarpsborg 08	29	6	**64**	**15**
2014	Molde	30	13		
2015	Molde	28	12		
2016	Molde	12	5	**70**	**30**
2016–17	FC Basel	32	10		
2017–18	FC Basel	33	11	**65**	**21**
2018–19	Southampton	16	0	**16**	**0**

FLANNIGAN, Jake (M) 0 0
H: 5 11 W: 11 03 b.Southampton 2-2-96

2014–15	Southampton	0	0		
2015–16	Southampton	0	0		
2017–18	Southampton	0	0		
2018–19	Southampton	0	0		
2018–19	*Burton Alb*	0	0		

FORSTER, Fraser (G) 295 0
H: 6 0 W: 12 00 b.Hexham 17-3-88
Internationals: England Full caps.

2007–08	Newcastle U	0	0		
2008–09	Newcastle U	0	0		
2008–09	*Stockport Co*	6	0	**6**	**0**
2009–10	Newcastle U	0	0		
2009–10	*Bristol R*	4	0	**4**	**0**
2009–10	*Norwich C*	38	0	**38**	**0**
2010–11	Newcastle U	0	0		
2010–11	*Celtic*	36	0		
2011–12	Newcastle U	0	0		
2011–12	*Celtic*	33	0		
2012–13	Celtic	34	0		
2013–14	Celtic	37	0	**140**	**0**
2014–15	Southampton	30	0		
2015–16	Southampton	18	0		
2016–17	Southampton	38	0		
2017–18	Southampton	20	0		
2018–19	Southampton	1	0	**107**	**0**

GABBIADINI, Manolo (F) 236 53
H: 5 10 W: 11 03 b.Bergamo 26-11-91
Internationals: Italy U20, U21, Full caps.

2009–10	Atalanta	2	0		
2010–11	Atalanta	0	0		
2010–11	*Cittadella*	27	5	**27**	**5**
2011–12	Atalanta	23	1		
2012–13	Atalanta	0	0	**25**	**1**
2012–13	*Bologna*	30	6	**30**	**6**
2013–14	Sampdoria	34	8		
2014–15	Sampdoria	13	7	**47**	**15**
2014–15	Napoli	20	8		
2015–16	Napoli	23	5		
2016–17	Napoli	13	3	**56**	**16**
2016–17	Southampton	11	4		
2017–18	Southampton	28	5		
2018–19	Southampton	12	1	**51**	**10**

Transferred to Sampdoria January 2019.

GALLAGHER, Sam (F) 111 18
H: 6 4 W: 11 11 b.Crediton 15-9-95
Internationals: Scotland U19, England U19, U20.

2013–14	Southampton	18	1		
2014–15	Southampton	0	0		
2015–16	Southampton	0	0		
2015–16	*Milton Keynes D*	13	0	**13**	**0**
2016–17	Southampton	0	0		
2016–17	*Blackburn R*	43	11	**43**	**11**
2017–18	Southampton	0	0		
2017–18	*Birmingham C*	33	6	**33**	**6**
2018–19	Southampton	4	0	**22**	**1**

GUNN, Angus (G) 58 0
H: 6 0 W: 12 02 b.Norwich 22-1-96
Internationals: England U16, U17, U18, U19, U20, U21.

2013–14	Manchester C	0	0		
2014–15	Manchester C	0	0		
2015–16	Manchester C	0	0		
2016–17	Manchester C	0	0		
2017–18	Manchester C	0	0		
2017–18	*Norwich C*	46	0	**46**	**0**
2018–19	Southampton	12	0	**12**	**0**

HOEDT, Wesley (D) 125 4
H: 6 2 W: 12 02 b.Alkmaar 6-3-94
Internationals: Netherlands U20, U20, Full caps.

2013–14	AZ Alkmaar	2	0		
2014–15	AZ Alkmaar	24	2	**26**	**2**
2015–16	Lazio	25	0		
2016–17	Lazio	23	2		
2017–18	Lazio	0	0	**48**	**2**
2017–18	Southampton	28	0		
2018–19	Southampton	13	0	**41**	**0**
2018–19	*Celta Vigo*	10	0	**10**	**0**

HOJBJERG, Pierre (M) 132 6
H: 6 1 W: 12 11 b. 5-8-95
Internationals: Denmark U16, U17, U19, U21, Full caps.

2012–13	Bayern Munich	2	0		
2013–14	Bayern Munich	7	0		
2014–15	Bayern Munich	8	0		
2014–15	*Augsburg*	16	2	**16**	**2**
2015–16	Bayern Munich	0	0	**17**	**0**
2015–16	*Schalke*	23	0	**23**	**0**
2016–17	Southampton	22	0		
2017–18	Southampton	23	0		
2018–19	Southampton	31	4	**76**	**4**

JOHNSON, Tyreke (M) 1 0
b.Swindon 3-11-98
From Watford, Swindon T.

2018–19	Southampton	1	0	**1**	**0**

JONES, Alfie (D) 14 1
b. 7-10-97

2018–19	Southampton	0	0		
2018–19	*St Mirren*	14	1	**14**	**1**

LEMINA, Mario (M) 130 7
H: 6 0 W: 12 00 b.Libreville 1-9-93
Internationals: France U20, U21. Gabon Full caps.

2012–13	Lorient	10	0		
2013–14	Lorient	4	0	**14**	**0**
2013–14	Marseille	14	0		
2014–15	Marseille	23	2		
2015–16	Marseille	4	0	**41**	**2**
2015–16	Juventus	10	2		
2016–17	Juventus	19	1	**29**	**3**
2017–18	Southampton	25	1		
2018–19	Southampton	21	1	**46**	**2**

LEWIS, Harry (G) 0 0
b. 20-12-97
Internationals: England U18.

2015–16	Shrewsbury T	0	0		
2016–17	Shrewsbury T	0	0		
2016–17	Southampton	0	0		
2017–18	Southampton	0	0		
2018–19	Southampton	0	0		

LONG, Shane (F) 419 92
H: 5 10 W: 11 02 b.Co. Tipperary 22-1-87
Internationals: Republic of Ireland B, U21, Full caps.

2005	Cork C	1	0	**1**	**0**
2005–06	Reading	11	3		
2006–07	Reading	21	2		
2007–08	Reading	29	3		
2008–09	Reading	37	9		
2009–10	Reading	31	6		
2010–11	Reading	44	21		
2011–12	Reading	1	0	**174**	**44**
2011–12	WBA	32	8		
2012–13	WBA	34	8		
2013–14	WBA	15	3	**81**	**19**
2013–14	Hull C	15	4	**15**	**4**
2014–15	Southampton	32	5		
2015–16	Southampton	28	10		
2016–17	Southampton	32	3		
2017–18	Southampton	30	2		
2018–19	Southampton	26	5	**148**	**25**

McCARTHY, Alex (G) 190 0
H: 6 4 W: 11 12 b.Guildford 3-12-89
Internationals: England U21, Full caps.

2008–09	Reading	0	0		
2008–09	*Aldershot T*	4	0	**4**	**0**
2009–10	Reading	0	0		
2009–10	*Yeovil T*	44	0	**44**	**0**
2010–11	Reading	13	0		
2010–11	*Brentford*	3	0	**3**	**0**
2011–12	Reading	0	0		
2011–12	*Leeds U*	6	0	**6**	**0**
2011–12	*Ipswich T*	10	0	**10**	**0**
2012–13	Reading	13	0		
2013–14	Reading	44	0	**70**	**0**
2014–15	QPR	3	0	**3**	**0**
2015–16	Crystal Palace	7	0	**7**	**0**
2016–17	Southampton	0	0		
2017–18	Southampton	18	0		
2018–19	Southampton	25	0	**43**	**0**

McQUEEN, Sam (M) 43 2
H: 5 9 W: 11 00 b.Southampton 6-2-95
Internationals: England U21.

2011–12	Southampton	0	0		
2012–13	Southampton	0	0		
2013–14	Southampton	0	0		
2014–15	Southampton	0	0		
2015–16	Southampton	0	0		
2015–16	*Southend U*	18	2	**18**	**2**
2016–17	Southampton	13	0		
2017–18	Southampton	7	0		
2018–19	Southampton	0	0	**20**	**0**
2018–19	*Middlesbrough*	5	0	**5**	**0**

OBAFEMI, Michael (F) 7 1
H: 5 7 W: 11 03 b.Dublin 6-7-00
Internationals: Republic of Ireland U19, Full caps.
From Leyton Orient.

2017–18	Southampton	1	0		
2018–19	Southampton	6	1	**7**	**1**

RAMSEY, Kayne (D) 1 0
b. 10-10-00
From Chelsea.

2018–19	Southampton	1	0	**1**	**0**

REDMOND, Nathan (M) 280 32
H: 5 8 W: 11 11 b.Birmingham 6-3-94
Internationals: England U16, U17, U18, U19, U20, U21, Full caps.

2011–12	Birmingham C	24	5		
2012–13	Birmingham C	38	2	**62**	**7**
2013–14	Norwich C	34	1		
2014–15	Norwich C	43	4		
2015–16	Norwich C	35	6	**112**	**11**
2016–17	Southampton	37	7		
2017–18	Southampton	31	1		
2018–19	Southampton	38	6	**106**	**14**

ROMEU, Oriol (M) 241 5
H: 6 0 W: 12 06 b.Ulldecona 24-9-91
Internationals: Spain U17, U19, U20, U21, U23.

2008–09	Barcelona B	5	0		
2009–10	Barcelona B	26	0		
2010–11	Barcelona B	18	1	**49**	**1**
2010–11	Barcelona	1	0	**1**	**0**
2011–12	Chelsea	16	0		
2012–13	Chelsea	6	0		
2013–14	Chelsea	0	0		
2013–14	*Valencia*	13	0	**13**	**0**
2014–15	Chelsea	0	0	**22**	**0**
2014–15	*Stuttgart*	27	0	**27**	**0**
2015–16	Southampton	29	1		
2016–17	Southampton	35	1		
2017–18	Southampton	34	1		
2018–19	Southampton	31	1	**129**	**4**

SIMS, Josh (M) 37 0
b. 28-3-97
Internationals: England U17, U18, U20.
From Portsmouth.

2016–17	Southampton	7	0		

2017–18	Southampton	6	0		
2018–19	Southampton	7	0	**20**	**0**
2018–19	*Reading*	17	0	**17**	**0**

SLATTERY, Callum (M) **3** **0**
b. 8-2-99
Internationals: England U16, U17, U20.

2018–19	Southampton	3	0	**3**	**0**

STEPHENS, Jack (D) **132** **4**
H: 6 1 W: 13 03 b.Torpoint 27-1-94
Internationals: England U18, U19, U20, U21.

2010–11	Plymouth Arg	5	0	**5**	**0**
2010–11	Southampton	0	0		
2011–12	Southampton	0	0		
2012–13	Southampton	0	0		
2013–14	Southampton	0	0		
2013–14	*Swindon T*	10	0		
2014–15	Southampton	0	0		
2014–15	*Swindon T*	37	1	**47**	**1**
2015–16	Southampton	0	0		
2015–16	*Middlesbrough*	1	0	**1**	**0**
2015–16	*Coventry C*	16	0	**16**	**0**
2016–17	Southampton	17	0		
2017–18	Southampton	22	2		
2018–19	Southampton	24	1	**63**	**3**

TARGETT, Matt (D) **61** **2**
H: 6 0 W: 12 11 b.Edinburgh 18-9-95
Internationals: Scotland U19, England U19, U20, U21.

2013–14	Southampton	0	0		
2014–15	Southampton	6	0		
2015–16	Southampton	14	0		
2016–17	Southampton	5	0		
2017–18	Southampton	2	0		
2017–18	*Fulham*	18	1	**18**	**1**
2018–19	Southampton	16	1	**43**	**1**

VALERY, Yann (D) **23** **2**
H: 5 11 W: 11 00 b.Champigny-sur-Marne 22-2-99
Internationals: France U17, U18.
From Rennes.

2018–19	Southampton	23	2	**23**	**2**

VESTERGAARD, Jannik (D) **208** **14**
H: 6 6 W: 15 02 b.Copenhagen 3-8-92
Internationals: Denmark U18, U19, U20, U21, Full caps.

2010–11	Hoffenheim	1	0		
2011–12	Hoffenheim	23	2		
2012–13	Hoffenheim	16	0		
2013–14	Hoffenheim	25	1		
2014–15	Hoffenheim	6	1	**71**	**4**
2014–15	Werder Bremen	15	1		
2015–16	Werder Bremen	33	2	**48**	**3**
2016–17	Borussia M'gladbach	34	4		
2017–18	Borussia M'gladbach	32	3	**66**	**7**
2018–19	Southampton	23	0	**23**	**0**

WARD-PROWSE, James (M) **193** **17**
H: 5 8 W: 10 06 b.Portsmouth 1-11-94
Internationals: England U17, U19, U20, U21, Full caps.

2011–12	Southampton	0	0		
2012–13	Southampton	15	0		
2013–14	Southampton	34	0		
2014–15	Southampton	25	1		
2015–16	Southampton	33	2		
2016–17	Southampton	30	4		
2017–18	Southampton	30	3		
2018–19	Southampton	26	7	**193**	**17**

YOSHIDA, Maya (D) **200** **11**
H: 6 2 W: 12 03 b.Nagasaki 24-8-88
Internationals: Japan U23, Full caps.

2010–11	VVV	20	0		
2011–12	VVV	32	5		
2012–13	VVV	2	0	**54**	**5**
2012–13	Southampton	32	0		
2013–14	Southampton	8	1		
2014–15	Southampton	22	1		
2015–16	Southampton	20	1		
2016–17	Southampton	23	1		
2017–18	Southampton	24	2		
2018–19	Southampton	17	0	**146**	**6**

Players retained or with offer of contract
Boufal, Sofiane; Brennan, Sean Anthony; Bycroft, Jack Thomas; Carrillo, Guido Marcelo; Clasie, Jordy; Cull, Alexander; Ferry, William; Freeman, Kieran; Hale, Harlem; Hamblin, Harry Mark; Hansen, Kornelius Normann; Hesketh, Jake Alexander; Klarer, Christoph; Kozak, Simon; Kpohomouh, Pascal; Latham, Kingsley Finn; Ledwidge, Kameron Malcolm; Nlundulu, Dan; O'Connor, Thomas James; O'Driscoll Aaron, ; Reed, Harrison James; Robise, Enzo; Rose, Jack Joseph; Smallbone, William Anthony Patrick; Tchaptchet, Wandja Allan; Tella, Nathan; Vokins, Jake.

Scholars
Agbontohoma, David Osaretim; Bartlett, Daniel Grahame; Braithwaite, Benjamin Smales; Burnett, Ethan Darren; Cluett, Ryan; Davis, Harrison; Defise, Lucas Nsiona K; Fleary, Taymar; Glean, Rio Kamil; Idowu, Roland; Jankewitz, Alexandre Tounde Dimitri; Keogh, Seamas; Morris, James William; Norton, Christian Anthony; Olufunwa, Oludare Samuel Araba; Saunders, Michael; Watts, Caleb Cassius; Watts, Callum Neil.

SOUTHEND U (77)

ACQUAH, Emile (F) **3** **0**
b. 13-7-00

2018–19	Southend U	3	0	**3**	**0**

BA, Amadou (F) **5** **0**
H: 5 9 W: 9 13 b. 15-2-98
From Le Havre.

2017–18	Southend U	5	0		
2018–19	Southend U	0	0	**5**	**0**

BARRATT, Sam (M) **1** **0**
b. 25-8-95
Internationals: England C.
From Bracknell T, Maidenhead U.

2018–19	Southend U	1	0	**1**	**0**

BATLOKWA, Rene (M) **0** **0**
b. 1-12-97

2018–19	Southend U	0	0		

BISHOP, Nathan (G) **19** **0**
H: 6 1 W: 11 05 b. 15-10-99
Internationals: England U20.

2016–17	Southend U	0	0		
2017–18	Southend U	1	0		
2018–19	Southend U	18	0	**19**	**0**

BWOMONO, Elvis (D) **41** **0**
H: 5 9 W: 9 13 b. 29-11-98

2017–18	Southend U	11	0		
2018–19	Southend U	30	0	**41**	**0**

CLIFFORD, Tom (D) **1** **0**
b. 9-2-99

2018–19	Southend U	1	0	**1**	**0**

COKER, Ben (D) **227** **4**
H: 5 11 W: 11 09 b.Hatfield 17-6-89

2010–11	Colchester U	20	0		
2011–12	Colchester U	20	0		
2012–13	Colchester U	1	0	**41**	**0**
2013–14	Southend U	45	2		
2014–15	Southend U	32	1		
2015–16	Southend U	40	1		
2016–17	Southend U	31	0		
2017–18	Southend U	22	0		
2018–19	Southend U	16	0	**186**	**4**

COUTTS, Sonny (D) **0** **0**

2017–18	Southend U	0	0		
2018–19	Southend U	0	0		

COX, Simon (F) **427** **120**
H: 5 10 W: 10 12 b.Reading 28-4-87
Internationals: Republic of Ireland Full caps.

2005–06	Reading	2	0		
2006–07	Reading	0	0		
2006–07	*Brentford*	13	0	**13**	**0**
2006–07	*Northampton T*	8	3	**8**	**3**
2007–08	Reading	0	0		
2007–08	Swindon T	36	15		
2008–09	Swindon T	45	29	**81**	**44**
2009–10	WBA	28	9		
2010–11	WBA	19	1		
2011–12	WBA	18	0		
2012–13	WBA	0	0	**65**	**10**
2012–13	Nottingham F	39	5		
2013–14	Nottingham F	34	8	**73**	**13**
2014–15	Reading	37	8		
2015–16	Reading	13	1	**52**	**9**
2015–16	*Bristol C*	4	0	**4**	**0**
2016–17	Southend U	44	16		
2017–18	Southend U	42	10		
2018–19	Southend U	45	15	**131**	**41**

DEMETRIOU, Jason (D) **394** **29**
H: 5 11 W: 10 08 b.Newham 18-11-87
Internationals: Cyprus Full caps.

2005–06	Leyton Orient	3	0		
2006–07	Leyton Orient	15	2		
2007–08	Leyton Orient	43	3		
2008–09	Leyton Orient	43	4		
2009–10	Leyton Orient	39	1	**143**	**10**
2010–11	AEK Larnaca	15	0		
2011–12	AEK Larnaca	23	1		
2012–13	AEK Larnaca	19	3	**57**	**4**
2013–14	An Famagusta	19	1		
2014–15	An Famagusta	25	0	**44**	**1**
2015–16	Walsall	43	3	**43**	**3**
2016–17	Southend U	41	1		
2017–18	Southend U	42	8		
2018–19	Southend U	24	2	**107**	**11**

DIENG, Timothee (M) **174** **9**
H: 5 11 W: 12 00 b.Grenoble 9-4-92

2011–12	Brest	0	0		
2012–13	Brest	2	0		
2013–14	Brest	4	0	**6**	**0**
2014–15	Oldham Ath	22	0		
2015–16	Oldham Ath	38	1	**60**	**1**
2016–17	Bradford C	39	3		
2017–18	Bradford C	26	2	**65**	**5**
2018–19	Southend U	43	3	**43**	**3**

GARD, Lewis (M) **2** **0**
b. 26-8-99

2017–18	Southend U	2	0		
2018–19	Southend U	0	0	**2**	**0**

HENDRIE, Stephen (D) **146** **1**
H: 5 10 W: 11 00 b.Glasgow 8-1-95
Internationals: Scotland U17, U19, U20, U21.

2010–11	Hamilton A	0	0		
2011–12	Hamilton A	25	0		
2012–13	Hamilton A	23	0		
2013–14	Hamilton A	22	0		
2014–15	Hamilton A	30	0	**100**	**0**
2015–16	West Ham U	0	0		
2015–16	*Southend U*	5	1		
2016–17	West Ham U	0	0		
2016–17	*Blackburn R*	4	0	**4**	**0**
2017–18	Southend U	12	0		
2017–18	*Motherwell*	6	0	**6**	**0**
2018–19	Southend U	19	0	**36**	**1**

HOPPER, Tom (F) **151** **34**
H: 6 1 W: 12 00 b.Boston 14-12-93
Internationals: England U18.

2011–12	Leicester C	0	0		
2012–13	Leicester C	0	0		
2012–13	*Bury*	22	3	**22**	**3**
2013–14	Leicester C	0	0		
2014–15	Leicester C	0	0		
2014–15	*Scunthorpe U*	12	4		
2015–16	Scunthorpe U	34	8		
2016–17	Scunthorpe U	31	5		
2017–18	Scunthorpe U	38	7	**115**	**24**
2018–19	Southend U	14	7	**14**	**7**

HOWARD, Rob (D) **0** **0**
b. 15-9-99
From Arsenal, Colchester U.

2018–19	Southend U	0	0		

HUMPHRYS, Stephen (F) **58** **13**
b.Oldham 15-9-97

2016–17	Fulham	2	0		
2016–17	*Shrewsbury T*	14	2	**14**	**2**
2017–18	Fulham	0	0		
2017–18	*Rochdale*	16	2	**16**	**2**
2018–19	Fulham	0	0	**2**	**0**
2018–19	*Scunthorpe U*	16	4	**16**	**4**
2018–19	Southend U	10	5	**10**	**5**

HUTCHINSON, Isaac (M) **8** **0**
b.Eastbourne 10-4-00
From Brighton & HA.

2018–19	Southend U	8	0	**8**	**0**

HYAM, Luke (M) **154** **4**
H: 5 10 W: 11 05 b.Ipswich 24-10-91

2010–11	Ipswich T	10	0		
2011–12	Ipswich T	8	0		
2012–13	Ipswich T	30	1		
2013–14	Ipswich T	35	1		
2014–15	Ipswich T	16	1		
2015–16	Ipswich T	15	0		
2015–16	*Rotherham U*	5	0	**5**	**0**
2017–18	Ipswich T	17	0	**131**	**3**
2018–19	Southend U	18	1	**18**	**1**

KELMAN, Charlie (F) **10** **1**
b. 2-11-01
Internationals: USA U18.

2018–19	Southend U	10	1	**10**	**1**

KIERNAN, Rob (D) **155** **4**
H: 6 1 W: 11 13 b.Rickmansworth 13-1-91
Internationals: Republic of Ireland U18, U19, U21.

2008–09	Watford	0	0		
2009–10	Watford	0	0		
2009–10	*Kilmarnock*	4	0	**4**	**0**
2010–11	Watford	0	0		
2010–11	*Yeovil T*	3	0	**3**	**0**
2010–11	*Bradford C*	8	0	**8**	**0**
2010–11	*Wycombe W*	2	0	**2**	**0**
2011–12	Wigan Ath	0	0		
2011–12	*Accrington S*	3	0	**3**	**0**
2012–13	Wigan Ath	0	0		
2012–13	*Burton Alb*	6	0	**6**	**0**
2012–13	*Brentford*	8	0	**8**	**0**
2013–14	Wigan Ath	12	1		
2013–14	*Southend U*	12	0		
2014–15	Wigan Ath	17	0	**29**	**1**
2014–15	*Birmingham C*	12	1	**12**	**1**
2015–16	Rangers	33	0		
2016–17	Rangers	24	1	**57**	**1**
2017–18	Southend U	1	0		
2018–19	Southend U	10	1	**23**	**1**

KIGHTLY, Michael (F) **309** **46**
H: 5 10 W: 10 10 b.Basildon 24-1-86
Internationals: England U21.

2002–03	Southend U	1	0		
2003–04	Southend U	11	0		
2004–05	Southend U	1	0		
From Grays Ath.					
2006–07	Wolverhampton W	24	8		
2007–08	Wolverhampton W	21	4		
2008–09	Wolverhampton W	38	8		
2009–10	Wolverhampton W	9	0		
2010–11	Wolverhampton W	4	0		
2011–12	Wolverhampton W	18	3		
2011–12	*Watford*	12	3	**12**	**3**
2012–13	Wolverhampton W	0	0	**114**	**23**
2012–13	Stoke C	22	3		
2013–14	Stoke C	0	0	**22**	**3**
2013–14	*Burnley*	36	5		
2014–15	Burnley	17	1		
2015–16	Burnley	18	0		
2016–17	Burnley	5	0	**76**	**6**
2016–17	*Burton Alb*	12	4	**12**	**4**
2017–18	Southend U	29	6		
2018–19	Southend U	31	1	**73**	**7**

KLASS, Michael (M) **10** **0**
b. 9-2-99
From QPR.

2017–18	Southend U	0	0		
2018–19	Southend U	10	0	**10**	**0**

KYPRIANOU, Harry (D) **17** **1**
b. 16-3-97
Internationals: Cyprus U21.

2013–14	Watford	0	0		
2014–15	Watford	0	0		
2015–16	Watford	0	0		
2015–16	Southend U	0	0		
2016–17	Southend U	3	1		
2017–18	Southend U	13	0		
2018–19	Southend U	1	0	**17**	**1**

LENNON, Harry (M) **52** **4**
H: 6 3 W: 11 11 b.Barking 16-12-94

2012–13	Charlton Ath	0	0		
2013–14	Charlton Ath	2	0		
2014–15	Charlton Ath	0	0		
2014–15	*Cambridge U*	2	0	**2**	**0**
2014–15	*Gillingham*	2	0		
2015–16	Charlton Ath	19	2		
2015–16	*Gillingham*	6	2	**8**	**2**
2016–17	Charlton Ath	2	0		
2017–18	Charlton Ath	10	0	**33**	**2**
2018–19	Southend U	9	0	**9**	**0**

MANTOM, Sam (M) **224** **25**
H: 5 9 W: 11 00 b.Stourbridge 20-2-92
Internationals: England U17.

2010–11	WBA	0	0		
2010–11	*Tranmere R*	2	0	**2**	**0**
2010–11	*Oldham Ath*	4	0	**4**	**0**
2011–12	WBA	0	0		
2011–12	*Walsall*	13	3		
2012–13	WBA	0	0		
2012–13	Walsall	29	2		
2013–14	Walsall	43	5		
2014–15	Walsall	12	0		
2015–16	Walsall	37	8	**134**	**18**
2016–17	Scunthorpe U	26	2		
2017–18	Scunthorpe U	8	0	**34**	**2**
2017–18	*Southend U*	7	0		
2018–19	Southend U	43	5	**50**	**5**

McLAUGHLIN, Stephen (M) **216** **29**
H: 5 9 W: 11 12 b.Derry 14-6-90

2011	Derry C	33	3		
2012	Derry C	24	10	**57**	**13**
2012–13	Nottingham F	0	0		
2013–14	Nottingham F	3	0		
2013–14	*Bristol C*	5	0	**5**	**0**
2014–15	Nottingham F	6	0	**9**	**0**
2014–15	*Notts Co*	13	0	**13**	**0**
2014–15	*Southend U*	6	1		
2015–16	Southend U	17	1		
2016–17	Southend U	34	7		
2017–18	Southend U	45	6		
2018–19	Southend U	30	1	**132**	**16**

MOORE, Taylor (D) **103** **1**
H: 6 0 W: 12 08 b.Walthamstow 12-5-97
Internationals: England U17, U18, U19, U20.
From West Ham U.

2014–15	Lens	4	0		
2015–16	Lens	5	0	**9**	**0**
2016–17	Bristol C	5	0		
2016–17	*Bury*	19	0	**19**	**0**
2017–18	Bristol C	0	0		
2017–18	*Cheltenham T*	36	0	**36**	**0**
2018–19	Bristol C	0	0	**5**	**0**
2018–19	Southend U	34	1	**34**	**1**

OXLEY, Mark (G) **203** **1**
H: 5 11 W: 11 05 b.Aston 2-6-90
Internationals: England U18.

2008–09	Hull C	0	0		
2009–10	Hull C	0	0		
2009–10	*Grimsby T*	3	0	**3**	**0**
2010–11	Hull C	0	0		
2011–12	Hull C	0	0		
2012–13	Hull C	1	0		
2012–13	*Burton Alb*	3	0	**3**	**0**
2013–14	Hull C	0	0		
2013–14	*Oldham Ath*	36	0	**36**	**0**
2014–15	Hull C	0	0	**1**	**0**
2014–15	*Hibernian*	35	1		
2015–16	Hibernian	34	0	**69**	**1**
2016–17	Southend U	20	0		
2017–18	Southend U	46	0		
2018–19	Southend U	25	0	**91**	**0**

PITOULA-WABO, Norman (F) **5** **0**
b. 6-5-98

2017–18	Southend U	3	0		
2018–19	Southend U	2	0	**5**	**0**

SEADEN, Harry (G) **0** **0**
b.Southend-on-Sea 23-4-01
Internationals: England U16, U17.

2018–19	Southend U	0	0		

SMITH, Ted (G) **26** **0**
b.Benfleet 18-1-96
Internationals: England U18, U19, U20.

2012–13	Southend U	0	0		
2013–14	Southend U	0	0		
2014–15	Southend U	4	0		
2015–16	Southend U	3	0		
2016–17	Southend U	19	0		
2017–18	Southend U	0	0		
2018–19	Southend U	0	0	**26**	**0**

TURNER, Michael (D) **447** **29**
H: 6 4 W: 13 05 b.Lewisham 9-11-83

2001–02	Charlton Ath	0	0		
2002–03	Charlton Ath	0	0		
2002–03	*Leyton Orient*	7	1	**7**	**1**
2003–04	Charlton Ath	0	0		
2004–05	Brentford	45	1		
2005–06	Brentford	46	2	**91**	**3**
2006–07	Hull C	43	3		
2007–08	Hull C	44	5		
2008–09	Hull C	38	4		
2009–10	Hull C	4	0	**129**	**12**
2009–10	Sunderland	29	2		
2010–11	Sunderland	15	0		
2011–12	Sunderland	24	0	**68**	**2**
2012–13	Norwich C	26	3		
2013–14	Norwich C	22	0		
2014–15	Norwich C	23	1		
2014–15	*Fulham*	9	1	**9**	**1**
2015–16	Norwich C	0	0		
2015–16	*Sheffield W*	11	1	**11**	**1**
2016–17	Norwich C	0	0	**71**	**4**
2017–18	Southend U	25	4		
2018–19	Southend U	36	1	**61**	**5**

WHITE, John (D) **421** **7**
H: 6 0 W: 12 01 b.Maldon 26-7-86

2004–05	Colchester U	20	0		
2005–06	Colchester U	35	0		
2006–07	Colchester U	16	0		
2007–08	Colchester U	21	0		
2008–09	Colchester U	26	0		
2009–10	Colchester U	39	0		
2009–10	*Southend U*	5	0		
2010–11	Colchester U	22	0		
2011–12	Colchester U	26	0		
2012–13	Colchester U	22	0	**227**	**0**
2013–14	Southend U	41	1		
2014–15	Southend U	42	0		
2015–16	Southend U	29	1		
2016–17	Southend U	13	1		
2017–18	Southend U	31	2		
2018–19	Southend U	33	2	**194**	**7**

YEARWOOD, Dru (M) **52** **0**
H: 5 9 W: 9 13 b. 17-2-00

2017–18	Southend U	25	0		
2018–19	Southend U	27	0	**52**	**0**

Players retained or with offer of contract
Lee-Kelman, Charlie Robert Martin; Phillips, Harry William; Robinson, Theo Larayan Ronaldo.

Scholars
Acquah, Emile; Benton, Jon; Brogan, Samuel William Peter; Chandler, Reiss Billy; Dabbs, Ben Derek Harry; Eastwood, Freddy John; Egbri, Terrell Evieoghene; Humphreys, Daniel; Kinali, Eren; Knock, Samuel David; Marah, Sewa Bockarie; Mitchell-Nelson, Miles Nathaniel; Mpenga, Issa Ali; Pianim, Zak Michael; Rush, Matthew Thomas; Seaden, Harry John; Stewart, O'Shane Christan; Taylor, Callum; Udebhu-Osimeh, Idemudia Mohammed.

STEVENAGE (78)

APPLEYARD, Will (G) **0** **0**
From Crewe Alex.

2018–19	Stevenage	0	0		

BALL, James (M) **18** **3**
b. 1-12-95
From Bolton W, Northwich Vic, Staybridge Celtic, Stockport Co.

2018–19	Stevenage	18	3	**18**	**3**

BYRNE, Oliver (G) **0** **0**
From Manchester U, Cardiff C, Blackburn R.

2018–19	Stevenage	0	0		

BYROM, Joel (M) **240** **16**
H: 6 0 W: 12 04 b.Accrington 14-9-86
Internationals: England C.

2004–05	Blackburn R	0	0		
2005–06	Blackburn R	0	0		
2006–07	Accrington S	1	0	**1**	**0**
From Clitheroe, Southport, Clitheroe, Northwich Vic.					
2010–11	Stevenage	7	0		
2011–12	Stevenage	32	4		
2012–13	Preston NE	22	2		
2013–14	Preston NE	11	2	**33**	**4**
2013–14	*Oldham Ath*	4	0	**4**	**0**
2014–15	Northampton T	39	3		
2015–16	Northampton T	35	2		
2016–17	Northampton T	2	0	**76**	**5**
2016–17	Mansfield T	22	0		
2017–18	Mansfield T	19	1	**41**	**1**
2018–19	Stevenage	46	2	**85**	**6**

CAMPBELL-RYCE, Jamal (M) **491** **41**
H: 5 7 W: 12 03 b.Lambeth 6-4-83
Internationals: Jamaica Full caps.

2002–03	Charlton Ath	1	0		
2002–03	*Leyton Orient*	17	2		
2003–04	Charlton Ath	2	0		
2003–04	*Wimbledon*	4	0	**4**	**0**
2004–05	Charlton Ath	0	0	**3**	**0**
2004–05	*Chesterfield*	14	0		
2004–05	Rotherham U	24	0		
2005–06	Rotherham U	7	0	**31**	**0**
2005–06	*Southend U*	13	0		
2005–06	*Colchester U*	4	0	**4**	**0**
2006–07	Southend U	43	2		
2007–08	Southend U	2	0	**58**	**2**
2007–08	Barnsley	37	3		
2008–09	Barnsley	40	9		
2009–10	Barnsley	13	0	**90**	**12**

2009–10	Bristol C	14	0		
2010–11	Bristol C	31	2		
2011–12	Bristol C	17	0	**62**	**2**
2011–12	*Leyton Orient*	8	1	**25**	**3**
2012–13	Notts Co	37	8		
2013–14	Notts Co	36	3		
2014–15	Sheffield U	19	4		
2014–15	*Notts Co*	4	0	**77**	**11**
2015–16	Sheffield U	18	0	**37**	**4**
2015–16	*Chesterfield*	9	2	**23**	**2**
2016–17	Barnet	32	1		
2017–18	Barnet	24	4	**56**	**5**
2017–18	Carlisle U	9	0	**9**	**0**
2018–19	Stevenage	12	0	**12**	**0**

CUTHBERT, Scott (D) 389 18

H: 6 2 W: 14 00 b.Alexandria 15-6-87

Internationals: Scotland U19, U20, U21, B.

2004–05	Celtic	0	0		
2005–06	Celtic	0	0		
2006–07	Celtic	0	0		
2006–07	*Livingston*	4	1	**4**	**1**
2007–08	Celtic	0	0		
2008–09	Celtic	0	0		
2008–09	*St Mirren*	29	0	**29**	**0**
2009–10	Swindon T	39	3		
2010–11	Swindon T	41	2	**80**	**5**
2011–12	Leyton Orient	33	1		
2012–13	Leyton Orient	18	0		
2013–14	Leyton Orient	44	4		
2014–15	Leyton Orient	38	2	**133**	**7**
2015–16	Luton T	36	0		
2016–17	Luton T	38	1		
2017–18	Luton T	23	2	**97**	**3**
2018–19	Stevenage	46	2	**46**	**2**

FARMAN, Paul (G) 46 0

H: 6 5 W: 14 07 b.North Shields 2-11-89

Internationals: England C.

From Blyth Spartans, Gateshead.

2017–18	Lincoln C	13	0	**13**	**0**
2018–19	Stevenage	33	0	**33**	**0**

FERRY, James (M) 12 0

b. 20-4-97

2015–16	Brentford	0	0		
2015–16	*Wycombe W*	0	0		
2017–18	Stevenage	0	0		
2018–19	Stevenage	12	0	**12**	**0**

GEORGIOU, Andronicos (F) 4 0

b.Enfield 28-10-99

2017–18	Stevenage	3	0		
2018–19	Stevenage	1	0	**4**	**0**

GIBSON, Jordan (F) 22 2

b. 26-2-98

From Rangers.

2017–18	Bradford C	5	1		
2018–19	Bradford C	11	0	**16**	**1**
2018–19	Stevenage	6	1	**6**	**1**

GOULDBOURNE, Marcus (M) 0 0

H: 5 10 W: 9 11 b.Luton 31-12-00

2018–19	Stevenage	0	0		

GUTHRIE, Kurtis (F) 92 24

H: 5 11 W: 11 00 b.Jersey 21-4-93

Internationals: England C.

2011–12	Accrington S	13	0		
2012–13	Accrington S	0	0	**13**	**0**
2012–13	Bath City	0	0		
2012–13	Welling	0	0		
2016–17	Colchester U	33	12		
2017–18	Colchester U	12	1	**45**	**13**
2018–19	Stevenage	34	11	**34**	**11**

HENRY, Ronnie (D) 245 0

H: 5 11 W: 11 10 b.Hemel Hempstead 2-1-84

Internationals: England C.

2002–03	Tottenham H	0	0		
2002–03	*Southend U*	3	0	**3**	**0**
2004	Dublin C	12	0	**12**	**0**
2010–11	Stevenage	42	0		
2011–12	Stevenage	32	0		
2014–15	Stevenage	34	0		
2015–16	Stevenage	31	0		
2016–17	Stevenage	33	0		
2017–18	Stevenage	40	0		
2018–19	Stevenage	18	0	**230**	**0**

HUNT, Johnny (M) 56 1

H: 5 11 W: 10 03 b.Liverpool 23-8-90

Internationals: England C.

2014–15	Cambridge U	9	1	**9**	**1**
2017–18	Mansfield T	18	0	**18**	**0**
2018–19	Stevenage	29	0	**29**	**0**

IONTTON, Arthur (M) 20 1

b.Enfield 16-12-00

2017–18	Stevenage	2	0		
2018–19	Stevenage	18	1	**20**	**1**

KENNEDY, Ben (F) 143 28

H: 5 10 W: 11 00 b. 12-1-97

Internationals: Northern Ireland U17, U19, U21.

2014–15	Stevenage	15	4		
2015–16	Stevenage	22	2		
2016–17	Stevenage	36	8		
2017–18	Stevenage	35	7		
2018–19	Stevenage	25	6	**133**	**27**
2018–19	*Newport Co*	10	1	**10**	**1**

MAKASI, Moses (M) 21 1

H: 5 11 W: 11 05 b. 22-9-95

2016–17	West Ham U	0	0		
2017–18	West Ham U	0	0		
2017–18	*Plymouth Arg*	7	1	**7**	**1**
2018–19	Stevenage	14	0	**14**	**0**

MAKOMA, Donovan (M) 0 0

b.Lille 1-2-99

From Barrow.

2018–19	Stevenage	0	0		

MARTIN, Joe (M) 289 15

H: 6 0 W: 12 13 b.Dagenham 29-11-88

Internationals: England U16, U17.

2005–06	Tottenham H	0	0		
2006–07	Tottenham H	0	0		
2007–08	Tottenham H	0	0		
2007–08	*Blackpool*	1	0		
2008–09	Blackpool	15	0		
2009–10	Blackpool	6	0	**22**	**0**
2010–11	Gillingham	17	1		
2011–12	Gillingham	35	1		
2012–13	Gillingham	38	2		
2013–14	Gillingham	46	2		
2014–15	Gillingham	25	2	**161**	**8**
2015–16	Millwall	29	2		
2016–17	Millwall	23	1	**52**	**3**
2017–18	Stevenage	39	2		
2018–19	Bristol R	10	1	**10**	**1**
2018–19	Stevenage	5	1	**44**	**3**

McKEE, Mark (F) 33 1

b. 1-12-98

Internationals: Northern Ireland U16, U17, U19, U21.

From Cliftonville.

2016–17	Stevenage	2	0		
2017–18	Stevenage	24	1		
2018–19	Stevenage	7	0	**33**	**1**

NEWTON, Danny (F) 70 20

b.Liverpool 18-3-91

From Tamworth.

2017–18	Stevenage	45	14		
2018–19	Stevenage	25	6	**70**	**20**

NUGENT, Ben (D) 162 4

H: 6 1 W: 13 00 b.Street 28-11-93

2012–13	Cardiff C	12	1		
2013–14	Cardiff C	0	0		
2013–14	*Brentford*	0	0		
2013–14	*Peterborough U*	11	0	**11**	**0**
2014–15	Cardiff C	0	0	**12**	**1**
2014–15	*Yeovil T*	23	1	**23**	**1**
2015–16	Crewe Alex	39	1		
2016–17	Crewe Alex	20	0	**59**	**1**
2017–18	Gillingham	23	0	**23**	**0**
2018–19	Stevenage	34	1	**34**	**1**

REID, Alex (F) 11 2

b. 6-9-95

2016–17	Fleetwood T	0	0		
2017–18	Fleetwood T	0	0		
2018–19	Stevenage	11	2	**11**	**2**

REVELL, Alex (F) 517 101

H: 6 3 W: 13 00 b.Cambridge 7-7-83

2000–01	Cambridge U	4	0		
2001–02	Cambridge U	24	2		
2002–03	Cambridge U	9	0		
2003–04	Cambridge U	20	3	**57**	**5**

From Braintree T.

2006–07	Brighton & HA	38	7		
2007–08	Brighton & HA	21	6	**59**	**13**
2007–08	Southend U	8	0		
2008–09	Southend U	23	4		
2009–10	Southend U	3	0	**34**	**4**
2009–10	*Swindon T*	10	2	**10**	**2**
2009–10	Wycombe W	15	6	**15**	**6**
2010–11	Leyton Orient	39	13		
2011–12	Leyton Orient	5	0	**44**	**13**
2011–12	Rotherham U	40	10		
2012–13	Rotherham U	41	6		
2013–14	Rotherham U	45	8		
2014–15	Rotherham U	24	4	**150**	**28**
2014–15	Cardiff C	16	2		
2015–16	Cardiff C	10	0	**26**	**2**
2015–16	*Wigan Ath*	6	1	**6**	**1**
2015–16	Milton Keynes D	17	4	**17**	**4**
2016–17	Northampton T	32	8		
2017–18	Northampton T	15	2	**47**	**10**
2017–18	Stevenage	12	6		
2018–19	Stevenage	40	7	**52**	**13**

SEDDON, Steve (D) 41 6

b.Reading 25-12-97

2017–18	Birmingham C	0	0		
2018–19	Birmingham C	0	0		
2018–19	Stevenage	23	3	**23**	**3**
2018–19	*AFC Wimbledon*	18	3	**18**	**3**

SMYTH, Liam (F) 3 0

b. 6-9-01

Internationals: Northern Ireland U19.

2018–19	Stevenage	3	0	**3**	**0**

SONUPE, Emmanuel (M) 37 3

b.London 21-3-96

Internationals: England U16, U18.

2014–15	Tottenham H	0	0		
2014–15	*St Mirren*	4	0	**4**	**0**
2015–16	Tottenham H	0	0		
2016–17	Northampton T	1	0	**1**	**0**

From Kidderminster H.

2018–19	Stevenage	32	3	**32**	**3**

TIMLIN, Michael (M) 387 20

H: 5 8 W: 11 08 b.New Cross 19-3-85

Internationals: Republic of Ireland U17, U21.

2002–03	Fulham	0	0		
2003–04	Fulham	0	0		
2004–05	Fulham	0	0		
2005–06	Fulham	0	0		
2005–06	*Scunthorpe U*	1	0	**1**	**0**
2005–06	*Doncaster R*	3	0	**3**	**0**
2006–07	Fulham	0	0		
2006–07	*Swindon T*	24	1		
2007–08	Fulham	0	0		
2007–08	*Swindon T*	10	1		
2008–09	Swindon T	41	2		
2009–10	Swindon T	21	0		
2010–11	Swindon T	22	2		
2010–11	*Southend U*	8	1		
2011–12	Swindon T	1	0	**119**	**6**
2011–12	Southend U	39	4		
2012–13	Southend U	25	0		
2013–14	Southend U	36	2		
2014–15	Southend U	32	3		
2015–16	Southend U	21	2		
2016–17	Southend U	27	1		
2017–18	Southend U	34	0	**222**	**13**
2018–19	Stevenage	42	1	**42**	**1**

VANCOOTEN, Terence (D) 34 0

H: 6 1 W: 12 04 b. 29-12-97

Internationals: Guyana Full caps.

2016–17	Reading	0	0		
2017–18	Stevenage	22	0		
2018–19	Stevenage	12	0	**34**	**0**

WILDIN, Luther (M) 39 1

b. 3-12-97

Internationals: Antigua and Barbuda U20, Full caps.

2015–16	Notts Co	0	0		
2016–17	Notts Co	0	0		

From Nuneaton T.

2018–19	Stevenage	39	1	**39**	**1**

WILKINSON, Luke (D) 231 21

H: 6 2 W: 11 09 b.Wells 2-12-92

2009–10	Portsmouth	0	0		
2010–11	Dagenham & R	0	0		
2011–12	Dagenham & R	0	0		
2012–13	Dagenham & R	43	6		
2013–14	Dagenham & R	22	0	**65**	**6**
2014–15	Luton T	42	4		
2015–16	Luton T	20	3	**62**	**7**
2015–16	Stevenage	19	2		
2016–17	Stevenage	40	4		
2017–18	Stevenage	27	1		
2018–19	Stevenage	18	1	**104**	**8**

Players retained or with offer of contract

Appleby, Farman Paul David; James-Wildin, Luther Ash; White, Joseph Frederick.

Scholars

Conteh, Bunja; Draper, Harry; Fernandez, Luis Theo; Field, Paul Michael; Fraser-

Robinson, Cadell Daniel; Gouldbourne, Marcus; Jellis, Jamie Ryan; Krasniqi, Drilon; Leslie, Joe Ryan; Okoye-Ahaneku, Samuel Chukwuemeka; Payne, Harry George; Sackey, Theophilus Eniabasi Sowah; Smith, Jack Justin; Switters, Dylan James Joseph.

STOKE C (79)

ADAM, Charlie (M) 373 71
H: 6 1 W: 12 00 b.Dundee 10-12-85
Internationals: Scotland U21, B, Full caps.

2004–05	Rangers	1	0		
2004–05	*Ross Co*	10	2	**10**	**2**
2005–06	Rangers	1	0		
2005–06	*St Mirren*	29	5	**29**	**5**
2006–07	Rangers	32	11		
2007–08	Rangers	16	2		
2008–09	Rangers	9	0	**59**	**13**
2008–09	Blackpool	13	2		
2009–10	Blackpool	43	16		
2010–11	Blackpool	35	12	**91**	**30**
2011–12	Liverpool	28	2	**28**	**2**
2012–13	Stoke C	27	3		
2013–14	Stoke C	31	7		
2014–15	Stoke C	29	7		
2015–16	Stoke C	22	1		
2016–17	Stoke C	24	1		
2017–18	Stoke C	11	0		
2018–19	Stoke C	12	0	**156**	**19**

AFOBE, Benik (F) 260 65
H: 5 10 W: 11 00 b.Leyton 12-2-93
Internationals: England U16, U17, U19, U21. DR Congo Full caps.

2009–10	Arsenal	0	0		
2010–11	Arsenal	0	0		
2010–11	*Huddersfield T*	28	5	**28**	**5**
2011–12	Arsenal	0	0		
2011–12	*Reading*	3	0	**3**	**0**
2012–13	Arsenal	0	0		
2012–13	*Bolton W*	20	2	**20**	**2**
2012–13	*Millwall*	5	0	**5**	**0**
2013–14	Arsenal	0	0		
2013–14	*Sheffield W*	12	2	**12**	**2**
2014–15	Arsenal	0	0		
2014–15	*Milton Keynes D*	22	10	**22**	**10**
2014–15	Wolverhampton W	21	13		
2015–16	Wolverhampton W	25	9		
2015–16	Bournemouth	15	4		
2016–17	Bournemouth	31	6		
2017–18	Bournemouth	17	0	**63**	**10**
2017–18	*Wolverhampton W*	16	6	**62**	**28**
2018–19	Stoke C	45	8	**45**	**8**

ALLEN, Joe (M) 336 25
H: 5 6 W: 9 10 b.Carmarthen 14-3-90
Internationals: Wales U17, U19, U21, Full caps. Great Britain.

2006–07	Swansea C	1	0		
2007–08	Swansea C	6	0		
2008–09	Swansea C	23	1		
2009–10	Swansea C	21	0		
2010–11	Swansea C	40	2		
2011–12	Swansea C	36	4		
2012–13	Swansea C	0	0	**127**	**7**
2012–13	Liverpool	27	0		
2013–14	Liverpool	24	1		
2014–15	Liverpool	21	1		
2015–16	Liverpool	19	2	**91**	**4**
2016–17	Stoke C	36	6		
2017–18	Stoke C	36	2		
2018–19	Stoke C	46	6	**118**	**14**

BATTH, Danny (D) 294 17
H: 6 3 W: 13 05 b.Brierley Hill 21-9-90

2009–10	Wolverhampton W	0	0		
2009–10	*Colchester U*	17	1	**17**	**1**
2010–11	Wolverhampton W	0	0		
2010–11	*Sheffield U*	1	0	**1**	**0**
2010–11	*Sheffield W*	10	0		
2011–12	Wolverhampton W	0	0		
2011–12	*Sheffield W*	44	2	**54**	**2**
2012–13	Wolverhampton W	12	1		
2013–14	Wolverhampton W	46	2		
2014–15	Wolverhampton W	44	4		
2015–16	Wolverhampton W	38	2		
2016–17	Wolverhampton W	39	4		
2017–18	Wolverhampton W	16	1		
2018–19	Wolverhampton W	0	0	**195**	**14**
2018–19	*Middlesbrough*	10	0	**10**	**0**
2018–19	Stoke C	17	0	**17**	**0**

BAUER, Moritz (D) 153 0
H: 5 11 W: 11 07 b.Veltheim 25-1-92
Internationals: Switzerland U19, U21. Austria Full caps.

2011–12	Grasshopper Zurich	16	0		
2012–13	Grasshopper Zurich	13	0		
2013–14	Grasshopper Zurich	15	0		
2014–15	Grasshopper Zurich	16	0		
2015–16	Grasshopper Zurich	33	0	**93**	**0**
2016–17	Rubin Kazan	21	0	**21**	**0**
2017–18	Rubin Kazan	16	0	**16**	**0**
2017–18	Stoke C	15	0		
2018–19	Stoke C	8	0	**23**	**0**

BERAHINO, Saido (F) 188 38
H: 5 10 W: 11 13 b.Burundi 4-8-93
Internationals: England U16, U17, U18, U19, U20, U21.

2010–11	WBA	0	0		
2011–12	WBA	0	0		
2011–12	*Northampton T*	14	6	**14**	**6**
2011–12	*Brentford*	8	4	**8**	**4**
2012–13	WBA	0	0		
2012–13	*Peterborough U*	10	2	**10**	**2**
2013–14	WBA	32	5		
2014–15	WBA	38	14		
2015–16	WBA	31	4		
2016–17	WBA	4	0	**105**	**23**
2016–17	Stoke C	13	0		
2017–18	Stoke C	15	0		
2018–19	Stoke C	23	3	**51**	**3**

BOJAN, Krkic (F) 278 55
H: 5 8 W: 10 03 b.Linyola 28-8-90
Internationals: Spain U17, U21, Full caps.

2007–08	Barcelona	31	10		
2008–09	Barcelona	23	2		
2009–10	Barcelona	23	8		
2010–11	Barcelona	27	6		
2011–12	Roma	33	7		
2012–13	Roma	0	0	**33**	**7**
2012–13	*AC Milan*	19	3	**19**	**3**
2013–14	Barcelona	0	0	**104**	**26**
2013–14	*Ajax*	24	3	**24**	**3**
2014–15	Stoke C	16	4		
2015–16	Stoke C	27	7		
2016–17	Stoke C	9	3		
2016–17	*Mainz*	11	1	**11**	**1**
2017–18	Stoke C	1	0		
2017–18	*Alaves*	13	0	**13**	**0**
2018–19	Stoke C	21	1	**74**	**15**

BUTLAND, Jack (G) 227 0
H: 6 4 W: 12 00 b.Clevedon 10-3-93
Internationals: England U16, U17, U19, U20, U21, Full caps.

2009–10	Birmingham C	0	0		
2010–11	Birmingham C	0	0		
2011–12	Birmingham C	0	0		
2011–12	*Cheltenham T*	24	0	**24**	**0**
2012–13	Birmingham C	46	0	**46**	**0**
2012–13	Stoke C	0	0		
2013–14	Stoke C	3	0		
2013–14	*Barnsley*	13	0	**13**	**0**
2013–14	*Leeds U*	16	0	**16**	**0**
2014–15	Stoke C	3	0		
2014–15	*Derby Co*	6	0	**6**	**0**
2015–16	Stoke C	31	0		
2016–17	Stoke C	5	0		
2017–18	Stoke C	35	0		
2018–19	Stoke C	45	0	**122**	**0**

CAMERON, Geoff (D) 311 14
H: 6 3 W: 13 02 b.Attleboro 11-7-85
Internationals: USA Full caps.

2008	Houston D	24	1		
2009	Houston D	32	2		
2010	Houston D	16	3		
2011	Houston D	37	5		
2012	Houston D	15	0	**124**	**11**
2012–13	Stoke C	35	0		
2013–14	Stoke C	37	2		
2014–15	Stoke C	27	0		
2015–16	Stoke C	30	0		
2016–17	Stoke C	19	0		
2017–18	Stoke C	20	0		
2018–19	Stoke C	0	0	**168**	**2**
2018–19	*QPR*	19	1	**19**	**1**

CLUCAS, Sam (M) 240 32
H: 5 10 W: 11 08 b.Lincoln 25-9-90
Internationals: England C.

2009–10	Lincoln C	0	0		
2011–12	Hereford U	17	0	**17**	**0**
2013–14	Mansfield T	38	8		
2014–15	Mansfield T	5	0	**43**	**8**
2014–15	Chesterfield	41	9	**41**	**9**
2015–16	Hull C	44	6		
2016–17	Hull C	37	3		
2017–18	Hull C	3	0	**84**	**9**
2017–18	Swansea C	29	3	**29**	**3**
2018–19	Stoke C	26	3	**26**	**3**

COLLINS, Nathan (D) 3 0
b. 30-4-01
Internationals: Republic of Ireland U17.

2018–19	Stoke C	3	0	**3**	**0**

DIOUF, Mame (F) 297 85
H: 6 1 W: 12 00 b.Dakar 16-12-87
Internationals: Senegal Full caps.

2007	Molde	21	9		
2008	Molde	23	7		
2009	Molde	29	16	**73**	**32**
2009–10	Manchester U	5	1		
2010–11	Manchester U	0	0		
2010–11	*Blackburn R*	26	3	**26**	**3**
2011–12	Manchester U	0	0	**5**	**1**
2011–12	Hannover 96	10	6		
2012–13	Hannover 96	28	12		
2013–14	Hannover 96	19	8	**57**	**26**
2014–15	Stoke C	34	11		
2015–16	Stoke C	26	5		
2016–17	Stoke C	27	1		
2017–18	Stoke C	35	6		
2018–19	Stoke C	14	0	**136**	**23**

EDWARDS, Thomas (D) 33 1
b. 22-1-99
Internationals: England U20.

2016–17	Stoke C	0	0		
2017–18	Stoke C	6	0		
2018–19	Stoke C	27	1	**33**	**1**

ETEBO, Peter (F) 93 9
H: 5 8 W: 11 00 b.Lagos 9-11-95
Internationals: Nigeria U23, Full caps.
From Warri Wolves.

2015–16	Feirense	4	1		
2016–17	Feirense	23	2		
2017–18	Feirense	18	4	**45**	**7**
2017–18	*Las Palmas*	14	0	**14**	**0**
2018–19	Stoke C	34	2	**34**	**2**

FEDERICI, Adam (G) 228 1
H: 6 2 W: 14 02 b.Nowra 31-1-85
Internationals: Australia U20, U23, Full caps.

2005–06	Reading	0	0		
2006–07	Reading	2	0		
2007–08	Reading	0	0		
2008–09	Reading	15	1		
2008–09	*Southend U*	10	0	**10**	**0**
2009–10	Reading	46	0		
2010–11	Reading	34	0		
2011–12	Reading	46	0		
2012–13	Reading	21	0		
2013–14	Reading	2	0		
2014–15	Reading	43	0	**209**	**1**
2015–16	Bournemouth	6	0		
2016–17	Bournemouth	2	0		
2017–18	Bournemouth	0	0	**8**	**0**
2017–18	*Nottingham F*	0	0		
2018–19	Stoke C	1	0	**1**	**0**

FLETCHER, Darren (M) 352 24
H: 6 0 W: 11 09 b.Edinburgh 1-2-84
Internationals: Scotland U20, U21, B, Full caps.

2000–01	Manchester U	0	0		
2001–02	Manchester U	0	0		
2002–03	Manchester U	0	0		
2003–04	Manchester U	22	0		
2004–05	Manchester U	18	3		
2005–06	Manchester U	27	1		
2006–07	Manchester U	24	3		
2007–08	Manchester U	16	0		
2008–09	Manchester U	26	3		
2009–10	Manchester U	30	4		
2010–11	Manchester U	26	2		
2011–12	Manchester U	8	1		
2012–13	Manchester U	3	1		
2013–14	Manchester U	12	0		
2014–15	Manchester U	11	0	**223**	**18**
2014–15	WBA	15	1		
2015–16	WBA	38	1		
2016–17	WBA	38	2	**91**	**4**
2017–18	Stoke C	27	1		
2018–19	Stoke C	11	1	**38**	**2**

HAUGAARD, Jakob (G) 57 0
H: 6 6 W: 13 10 b.Sundby 1-5-92
Internationals: Denmark U18, U20.

2010–11	Akademisk BK	14	0	**14**	**0**
2011–12	Midtjylland	0	0		

2012–13	Midtjylland	6	0		
2013–14	Midtjylland	1	0		
2014–15	Midtjylland	23	0	**30**	**0**
2015–16	Stoke C	5	0		
2016–17	Stoke C	0	0		
2016–17	*Wigan Ath*	8	0		
2017–18	Wigan Ath	0	0	**8**	**0**
2017–18	Stoke C	0	0		
2018–19	Stoke C	0	0	**5**	**0**

INCE, Tom (M) 303 79
H: 5 10 W: 10 06 b.Stockport 30-1-92
Internationals: England U17, U19, U21.

2009–10	Liverpool	0	0		
2010–11	Liverpool	0	0		
2010–11	*Notts Co*	6	2	**6**	**2**
2011–12	Blackpool	33	6		
2012–13	Blackpool	44	18		
2013–14	Blackpool	23	7	**100**	**31**
2013–14	*Crystal Palace*	8	1	**8**	**1**
2014–15	Hull C	7	0	**7**	**0**
2014–15	*Nottingham F*	6	0	**6**	**0**
2014–15	*Derby Co*	18	11		
2015–16	Derby Co	42	12		
2016–17	Derby Co	45	14	**105**	**37**
2017–18	Huddersfield T	33	2	**33**	**2**
2018–19	Stoke C	38	6	**38**	**6**

JARVIS, Dan (M) 0 0
b. 3-4-98

2018–19	Stoke C	0	0		

MARTINS INDI, Bruno (D) 238 9
H: 6 1 W: 11 09 b.Barreiro, Portugal 8-2-92
Internationals: Netherlands U17, U19, U21, Full caps.

2010–11	Feyenoord	15	1		
2011–12	Feyenoord	29	1		
2012–13	Feyenoord	32	1		
2013–14	Feyenoord	26	2	**102**	**5**
2014–15	Porto	24	2		
2015–16	Porto	23	0		
2016–17	Porto	0	0	**47**	**2**
2016–17	*Stoke C*	35	1		
2017–18	Stoke C	17	0		
2018–19	Stoke C	37	1	**89**	**2**

McCLEAN, James (M) 346 41
H: 5 11 W: 11 00 b.Derry 22-4-89
Internationals: Northern Ireland U21. Republic of Ireland Full caps.

2009	Derry C	27	1		
2010	Derry C	30	10		
2011	Derry C	16	7	**73**	**18**
2011–12	Sunderland	23	5		
2012–13	Sunderland	36	2		
2013–14	Sunderland	0	0	**59**	**7**
2013–14	Wigan Ath	37	3		
2014–15	Wigan Ath	36	6	**73**	**9**
2015–16	WBA	35	2		
2016–17	WBA	34	1		
2017–18	WBA	30	1	**99**	**4**
2018–19	Stoke C	42	3	**42**	**3**

NDIAYE, Papa Badou (M) 215 51
H: 5 10 W: 10 10 b.Dakar 27-10-90
Internationals: Senegal Full caps.

2012	Bodo/Glimt	29	3		
2013	Bodo/Glimt	27	12		
2014	Bodo/Glimt	30	9		
2015	Bodo/Glimt	16	4	**102**	**28**
2015–16	Osmanlispor	33	11		
2016–17	Osmanlispor	26	6	**59**	**17**
2017–18	Galatasaray	17	1		
2017–18	Stoke C	13	2		
2018–19	Stoke C	1	0	**14**	**2**
2018–19	*Galatasaray*	23	3	**40**	**4**

PIETERS, Erik (D) 349 6
H: 6 0 W: 13 00 b.Tiel 7-8-88
Internationals: Netherlands U17, U19, U21, Full caps.

2006–07	FC Utrecht	20	0		
2007–08	FC Utrecht	31	2	**51**	**2**
2008–09	PSV Eindhoven	17	0		
2009–10	PSV Eindhoven	27	0		
2010–11	PSV Eindhoven	31	0		
2011–12	PSV Eindhoven	16	0		
2012–13	PSV Eindhoven	2	0	**93**	**0**
2013–14	Stoke C	36	1		
2014–15	Stoke C	31	0		
2015–16	Stoke C	35	0		
2016–17	Stoke C	36	0		
2017–18	Stoke C	31	0		
2018–19	Stoke C	21	2	**190**	**3**
2018–19	*Amiens*	15	1	**15**	**1**

SHAWCROSS, Ryan (D) 395 22
H: 6 3 W: 13 13 b.Buckley 4-10-87
Internationals: England U21, Full caps.

2006–07	Manchester U	0	0		
2007–08	Manchester U	0	0		
2007–08	Stoke C	41	7		
2008–09	Stoke C	30	3		
2009–10	Stoke C	28	2		
2010–11	Stoke C	36	1		
2011–12	Stoke C	36	2		
2012–13	Stoke C	37	1		
2013–14	Stoke C	37	1		
2014–15	Stoke C	32	2		
2015–16	Stoke C	20	0		
2016–17	Stoke C	35	1		
2017–18	Stoke C	27	1		
2018–19	Stoke C	36	1	**395**	**22**

SORENSON, Lasse (M) 2 0
b. 21-10-99
From Esbjerg.

2017–18	Stoke C	1	0		
2018–19	Stoke C	1	0	**2**	**0**

SWEENEY, Ryan (D) 90 4
b.Kingston upon Thames 15-4-97
Internationals: Republic of Ireland U19, U21.

2014–15	AFC Wimbledon	3	0		
2015–16	AFC Wimbledon	10	0	**13**	**0**
2016–17	Stoke C	0	0		
2016–17	*Bristol R*	16	0		
2017–18	Stoke C	0	0		
2017–18	*Bristol R*	23	3	**39**	**3**
2018–19	Stoke C	0	0		
2018–19	*Mansfield T*	38	1	**38**	**1**

TYMON, Josh (D) 18 0
b. 22-5-99
Internationals: England U17, U18, U19, U20.

2015–16	Hull C	0	0		
2016–17	Hull C	5	0	**5**	**0**
2017–18	Stoke C	3	0		
2017–18	*Milton Keynes D*	9	0	**9**	**0**
2018–19	Stoke C	1	0	**4**	**0**

VERLINDEN, Thibaud (M) 5 0
b. 9-7-99
Internationals: Belgium U16, U17, U19.
From Club Bruges.

2016–17	Stoke C	0	0		
2017–18	Stoke C	0	0		
2017–18	*St Pauli*	0	0		
2018–19	Stoke C	5	0	**5**	**0**

VOKES, Sam (F) 385 89
H: 6 1 W: 13 10 b.Lymington 21-10-89
Internationals: Wales U21, Full caps.

2006–07	Bournemouth	13	4		
2007–08	Bournemouth	41	12	**54**	**16**
2008–09	Wolverhampton W	36	6		
2009–10	Wolverhampton W	5	0		
2009–10	*Leeds U*	8	1	**8**	**1**
2010–11	Wolverhampton W	2	0		
2010–11	*Bristol C*	1	0	**1**	**0**
2010–11	*Sheffield U*	6	1	**6**	**1**
2010–11	*Norwich C*	4	1	**4**	**1**
2011–12	Wolverhampton W	4	0		
2011–12	*Burnley*	9	2		
2011–12	*Brighton & HA*	14	3	**14**	**3**
2012–13	Wolverhampton W	0	0	**47**	**6**
2012–13	Burnley	46	4		
2013–14	Burnley	39	20		
2014–15	Burnley	15	0		
2015–16	Burnley	43	15		
2016–17	Burnley	37	10		
2017–18	Burnley	30	4		
2018–19	Burnley	20	3	**239**	**58**
2018–19	Stoke C	12	3	**12**	**3**

WOODS, Ryan (M) 240 4
H: 5 8 W: 13 01 b.Norton Canes 13-12-93

2012–13	Shrewsbury T	2	0		
2013–14	Shrewsbury T	41	1		
2014–15	Shrewsbury T	43	0		
2015–16	Shrewsbury T	5	0	**91**	**1**
2015–16	Brentford	41	2		
2016–17	Brentford	42	0		
2017–18	Brentford	39	1		
2018–19	Brentford	0	0	**122**	**3**
2018–19	Stoke C	27	0	**27**	**0**

Players retained or with offer of contract
Balde, Rachid; Bursik, Josef John; Campbell, Tyrese Kai; Corrigan, Ryan Michael; Dunwoody, Jake; Imbula, Wanga Gilbert; Jennings, James Jordan; Kanuric, Adnan; Krkic, Perez Bojan; Kyeremateng, Gabriel; Martins, Indi Rolando Maximiliano; McJannet, Cameron Allan; Ngoy, Bin Cibambi Julien Fontaine; Pemberton, Tre Kingsley; Shenton, Oliver; Sorensen, Lasse; Souttar, Harry; Wimmer, Kevin.

Scholars
Akandji, Mohamed; Broome, Nathan Lee; Butler, James Anthony; Coates, Kieran David Tyler; Doucoure, Ibrahima; Forrester, William; Jarrett, Patrick Daniel; Jones, Reece Edward; Keane, Dillon Patrick; Macari, Lewis Jon; Malone, Daniel Eric; Murphy, Max; O'Driscoll, Varian Ethon Sean; Porter, Adam Matthew; Sanali, Soiyir; Stanton, Ethan Bradley; Toure, Abdoulaye; Wara, Semi Scott.

SUNDERLAND (80)

BAINBRIDGE, Jack (D) 0 0
b.Southport 21-5-98

2018–19	Sunderland	0	0		

BALDWIN, Jack (D) 211 11
H: 6 1 W: 11 00 b.Barking 30-6-93

2011–12	Hartlepool U	17	0		
2012–13	Hartlepool U	32	2		
2013–14	Hartlepool U	28	2	**77**	**4**
2013–14	Peterborough U	11	0		
2014–15	Peterborough U	11	0		
2015–16	Peterborough U	18	1		
2016–17	Peterborough U	27	1		
2017–18	Peterborough U	33	2	**100**	**4**
2018–19	Sunderland	34	3	**34**	**3**

CATTERMOLE, Lee (M) 335 14
H: 5 10 W: 11 13 b.Stockton 21-3-88
Internationals: England U16, U17, U18, U19, U21.

2005–06	Middlesbrough	14	1		
2006–07	Middlesbrough	31	1		
2007–08	Middlesbrough	24	1	**69**	**3**
2008–09	Wigan Ath	33	1		
2009–10	Wigan Ath	0	0	**33**	**1**
2009–10	Sunderland	22	0		
2010–11	Sunderland	23	0		
2011–12	Sunderland	23	0		
2012–13	Sunderland	10	0		
2013–14	Sunderland	24	1		
2014–15	Sunderland	28	1		
2015–16	Sunderland	31	0		
2016–17	Sunderland	8	0		
2017–18	Sunderland	35	1		
2018–19	Sunderland	29	7	**233**	**10**

CONNELLY, Lee (F) 0 0
b. 18-10-99
Internationals: Scotland U16, U17.

2018–19	Sunderland	0	0		

DIAMOND, Jack (F) 0 0
b.Gateshead 12-1-00

2018–19	Sunderland	0	0		

EMBLETON, Elliot (M) 29 3
H: 5 8 W: 10 01 b. 2-4-99
Internationals: England U17, U18, U19, U20.

2016–17	Sunderland	0	0		
2017–18	Sunderland	2	0		
2018–19	Sunderland	0	0	**2**	**0**
2018–19	*Grimsby T*	27	3	**27**	**3**

FLANAGAN, Tom (D) 172 8
H: 6 2 W: 11 05 b.Hammersmith 21-10-91
Internationals: Northern Ireland U21, Full caps.

2009–10	Milton Keynes D	1	0		
2010–11	Milton Keynes D	2	0		
2011–12	Milton Keynes D	21	3		
2012–13	Milton Keynes D	0	0		
2012–13	*Gillingham*	13	1	**13**	**1**
2012–13	*Barnet*	9	0	**9**	**0**
2013–14	Milton Keynes D	7	0		
2013–14	*Stevenage*	2	0	**2**	**0**
2014–15	Milton Keynes D	6	0	**37**	**3**
2014–15	*Plymouth Arg*	4	0	**4**	**0**
2015–16	Burton Alb	18	0		
2016–17	Burton Alb	30	0		
2017–18	Burton Alb	27	2	**75**	**2**
2018–19	Sunderland	32	2	**32**	**2**

GAMBLE, Owen (M) 0 0

2017–18	Sunderland	0	0		
2018–19	Sunderland	0	0		

GOOCH, Lynden (M) 84 6
H: 5 8 W: 10 12 b.Santa Cruz 24-12-95
Internationals: Republic of Ireland U18. USA U20, Full caps.

2015–16	Sunderland	0	0		
2015–16	*Doncaster R*	10	0	**10**	**0**
2016–17	Sunderland	11	0		
2017–18	Sunderland	24	1		
2018–19	Sunderland	39	5	**74**	**6**

GRIGG, Will (M) 328 109
H: 5 11 W: 11 00 b.Solihull 3-7-91
Internationals: Northern Ireland U19, U21, Full caps.

2008–09	Walsall	1	0		
2009–10	Walsall	0	0		
2010–11	Walsall	28	4		
2011–12	Walsall	29	4		
2012–13	Walsall	41	19	**99**	**27**
2013–14	Brentford	34	5		
2014–15	Brentford	0	0	**34**	**5**
2014–15	*Milton Keynes D*	44	20	**44**	**20**
2015–16	Wigan Ath	40	25		
2016–17	Wigan Ath	33	5		
2017–18	Wigan Ath	43	19		
2018–19	Wigan Ath	17	4	**133**	**53**
2018–19	Sunderland	18	4	**18**	**4**

HACKETT, Jake (M) 0 0
b.Durham 10-1-00

2018–19	Sunderland	0	0		

HONEYMAN, George (M) 83 12
H: 5 8 W: 11 05 b.Prudhoe 8-9-94

2014–15	Sunderland	0	0		
2015–16	Sunderland	1	0		
2016–17	Sunderland	5	0		
2017–18	Sunderland	42	6		
2018–19	Sunderland	35	6	**83**	**12**

HUME, Denver (D) 9 0
b. 11-8-96

2017–18	Sunderland	1	0		
2018–19	Sunderland	8	0	**9**	**0**

HUNTER, Jordan (M) 0 0
b.Garstang 6-12-99
From Liverpool.

2018–19	Sunderland	0	0		

JAMES, Reece (D) 89 2
H: 5 6 W: 11 03 b.Bacup 7-11-93

2012–13	Manchester U	0	0		
2013–14	Manchester U	0	0		
2013–14	*Carlisle U*	1	0	**1**	**0**
2014–15	Manchester U	0	0		
2014–15	*Rotherham U*	7	0	**7**	**0**
2014–15	*Huddersfield T*	6	1	**6**	**1**
2015–16	Wigan Ath	26	1		
2016–17	Wigan Ath	0	0		
2017–18	Wigan Ath	22	0	**48**	**1**
2018–19	Sunderland	27	0	**27**	**0**

JOHN LEONARD, Ryan (M) 0 0
b. 16-5-01

2018–19	Sunderland	0	0		

KOKOLO, Williams (D) 0 0
b. 9-6-00
From Monaco.

2018–19	Sunderland	0	0		

LEADBITTER, Grant (M) 459 53
H: 5 9 W: 11 06 b.Chester-le-Street 7-1-86
Internationals: England U16, U17, U19, U20, U21.

2002–03	Sunderland	0	0		
2003–04	Sunderland	0	0		
2004–05	Sunderland	0	0		
2005–06	Sunderland	12	0		
2005–06	*Rotherham U*	5	1	**5**	**1**
2006–07	Sunderland	44	7		
2007–08	Sunderland	31	2		
2008–09	Sunderland	23	2		
2009–10	Sunderland	1	0		
2009–10	Ipswich T	38	3		
2010–11	Ipswich T	44	5		
2011–12	Ipswich T	34	5		
2012–13	Ipswich T	0	0	**116**	**13**
2012–13	Middlesbrough	42	3		
2013–14	Middlesbrough	39	6		
2014–15	Middlesbrough	43	11		
2015–16	Middlesbrough	41	4		
2016–17	Middlesbrough	13	1		
2017–18	Middlesbrough	32	3		
2018–19	Middlesbrough	2	0	**212**	**28**
2018–19	Sunderland	15	0	**126**	**11**

LOOVENS, Glenn (D) 386 14
H: 5 10 W: 11 08 b.Doetrinchem 22-10-83
Internationals: Netherlands U21, Full caps.

2001–02	Feyenoord	8	0		
2002–03	Feyenoord	12	0		
2003–04	Feyenoord	1	0		
2003–04	Excelsior	24	2	**24**	**2**
2004–05	Feyenoord	6	0	**27**	**0**
2004–05	De Graafschap	11	0	**11**	**0**
2005–06	Cardiff C	33	2		
2006–07	Cardiff C	30	1		
2007–08	Cardiff C	36	0		
2008–09	Cardiff C	1	0	**100**	**3**
2008–09	Celtic	17	3		
2009–10	Celtic	20	3		
2010–11	Celtic	13	1		
2011–12	Celtic	11	1	**61**	**8**
2012–13	Real Zaragoza	21	0	**21**	**0**
2013–14	Sheffield W	22	0		
2014–15	Sheffield W	26	0		
2015–16	Sheffield W	31	0		
2016–17	Sheffield W	32	1		
2017–18	Sheffield W	20	0	**131**	**1**
2018–19	Sunderland	11	0	**11**	**0**

LOVE, Donald (D) 35 0
H: 5 10 W: 11 05 b.Rochdale 2-12-94
Internationals: Scotland U17, U19, U21.

2015–16	Manchester U	1	0	**1**	**0**
2015–16	*Wigan Ath*	7	0	**7**	**0**
2016–17	Sunderland	12	0		
2017–18	Sunderland	11	0		
2018–19	Sunderland	4	0	**27**	**0**

MAGUIRE, Chris (F) 379 70
H: 5 7 W: 10 05 b.Bellshill 16-1-89
Internationals: Scotland U16, U19, U21, Full caps.

2005–06	Aberdeen	1	0		
2006–07	Aberdeen	19	1		
2007–08	Aberdeen	28	4		
2008–09	Aberdeen	31	3		
2009–10	Aberdeen	17	1		
2009–10	*Kilmarnock*	14	4	**14**	**4**
2010–11	Aberdeen	35	7	**131**	**16**
2011–12	Derby Co	7	1	**7**	**1**
2011–12	*Portsmouth*	11	3	**11**	**3**
2012–13	Sheffield W	10	1		
2013–14	Sheffield W	27	9		
2013–14	*Coventry C*	3	2	**3**	**2**
2014–15	Sheffield W	42	8	**79**	**18**
2015–16	Rotherham U	14	0	**14**	**0**
2015–16	Oxford U	21	4		
2016–17	Oxford U	42	13	**63**	**17**
2017–18	Bury	24	2	**24**	**2**
2018–19	Sunderland	33	7	**33**	**7**

MAJA, Josh (F) 41 16
H: 5 11 W: 11 09 b. 27-12-98
From Fulham.

2016–17	Sunderland	0	0		
2017–18	Sunderland	17	1		
2018–19	Sunderland	24	15	**41**	**16**

Transferred to Bordeaux January 2019.

MATTHEWS, Adam (D) 220 7
H: 5 10 W: 11 02 b.Swansea 13-1-92
Internationals: Wales U17, U19, U21, Full caps.

2008–09	Cardiff C	0	0		
2009–10	Cardiff C	32	1		
2010–11	Cardiff C	8	0	**40**	**1**
2011–12	Celtic	27	0		
2012–13	Celtic	22	2		
2013–14	Celtic	23	1		
2014–15	Celtic	29	1	**101**	**4**
2015–16	Sunderland	1	0		
2015–16	*Bristol C*	9	0		
2016–17	Sunderland	0	0		
2016–17	*Bristol C*	12	0	**21**	**0**
2017–18	Sunderland	34	1		
2018–19	Sunderland	23	1	**58**	**2**

McGEADY, Aiden (M) 405 70
H: 5 10 W: 11 03 b.Glasgow 4-4-86
Internationals: Republic of Ireland Full caps.

2003–04	Celtic	4	1		
2004–05	Celtic	27	4		
2005–06	Celtic	20	4		
2006–07	Celtic	34	5		
2007–08	Celtic	36	7		
2008–09	Celtic	29	3		
2009–10	Celtic	35	7	**185**	**31**
2010–11	Spartak Moscow	11	2		
2011–12	Spartak Moscow	31	3		
2012–13	Spartak Moscow	17	5		
2013–14	Spartak Moscow	13	1	**72**	**11**
2013–14	Everton	16	0		
2014–15	Everton	16	1		
2015–16	Everton	0	0		
2015–16	*Sheffield W*	13	1	**13**	**1**
2016–17	Everton	0	0	**32**	**1**
2016–17	*Preston NE*	34	8	**34**	**8**
2017–18	Sunderland	35	7		
2018–19	Sunderland	34	11	**69**	**18**

McGEOUCH, Dylan (M) 123 2
H: 5 10 W: 10 11 b.Glasgow 15-1-93
Internationals: Scotland U16, U17, U19, U21, Full caps.

2011–12	Celtic	6	1		
2012–13	Celtic	12	1		
2013–14	Celtic	1	0	**19**	**2**
2013–14	*Coventry C*	8	0	**8**	**0**
2014–15	Hibernian	2	0		
2015–16	Hibernian	19	0		
2016–17	Hibernian	18	0		
2017–18	Hibernian	35	0	**74**	**0**
2018–19	Sunderland	22	0	**22**	**0**

McLAUGHLIN, Jon (G) 337 0
H: 6 2 W: 13 00 b.Edinburgh 9-9-87
Internationals: Scotland Full caps.

2008–09	Bradford C	1	0		
2009–10	Bradford C	7	0		
2010–11	Bradford C	25	0		
2011–12	Bradford C	23	0		
2012–13	Bradford C	23	0		
2013–14	Bradford C	46	0	**125**	**0**
2014–15	Burton Alb	45	0		
2015–16	Burton Alb	45	0		
2016–17	Burton Alb	43	0	**133**	**0**
2017–18	Hearts	33	0	**33**	**0**
2018–19	Sunderland	46	0	**46**	**0**

MGUNGA-KIMPIOKA, Benjamin (M) 4 0
b. 21-2-00
Internationals: Sweden U19, U21.
From IK Sirius.

2018–19	Sunderland	4	0	**4**	**0**

MOLYNEUX, Luke (M) 3 0
b. 29-3-98

2017–18	Sunderland	1	0		
2018–19	Sunderland	2	0	**3**	**0**

MORGAN, Lewis (M) 120 22
H: 5 10 W: 11 11 b.Paisley 30-9-96
Internationals: Scotland U21, Full caps.

2014–15	St Mirren	8	0		
2015–16	St Mirren	18	1		
2016–17	St Mirren	33	6		
2017–18	St Mirren	35	14	**94**	**21**
2017–18	Celtic	0	0		
2018–19	Celtic	9	0	**9**	**0**

On loan from Celtic.

2018–19	Sunderland	17	1	**17**	**1**

MUMBA, Bali (F) 5 0
b. 8-10-01
Internationals: England U16, U17, U18.

2017–18	Sunderland	1	0		
2018–19	Sunderland	4	0	**5**	**0**

NEILL, Daniel (M) 0 0

2018–19	Sunderland	0	0		

O'NIEN, Luke (M) 139 20
b. 21-11-94

2013–14	Watford	1	0		
2014–15	Watford	0	0	**1**	**0**
2015–16	Wycombe W	35	5		
2016–17	Wycombe W	31	3		
2017–18	Wycombe W	35	7	**101**	**15**
2018–19	Sunderland	37	5	**37**	**5**

OVIEDO, Bryan (M) 161 6
H: 5 8 W: 10 13 b.Alajuela 18-2-90
Internationals: Costa Rica U20, Full caps.

2009–10	FC Copenhagen	3	0		
2010–11	FC Copenhagen	1	0		
2010–11	*Nordsjaelland*	14	0	**14**	**0**
2011–12	FC Copenhagen	22	2		
2012–13	FC Copenhagen	4	0	**30**	**2**
2012–13	Everton	15	0		
2013–14	Everton	9	2		
2014–15	Everton	6	0		
2015–16	Everton	14	0		
2016–17	Everton	6	0	**50**	**2**
2016–17	Sunderland	10	0		
2017–18	Sunderland	34	2		
2018–19	Sunderland	23	0	**67**	**2**

OZTURK, Alim (D) 143 8
H: 6 3 W: 13 05 b.Alkmaar 17-11-92
Internationals: Turkey U21.

2010–11	Cambuur	0	0		
2011–12	Cambuur	5	0		
2012–13	Cambuur	8	0	**13**	**0**
2013–14	Trabzonspor	0	0		
2013–14	*1461 Trabzon*	18	2	**18**	**2**
2014–15	Hearts	33	4		
2015–16	Hearts	24	1		
2016–17	Hearts	5	0	**62**	**5**
2016–17	Boluspur	20	1		
2017–18	Boluspur	20	0	**40**	**1**
2018–19	Sunderland	10	0	**10**	**0**

PATTERSON, Anthony (G) 0 0
b. 10-5-00

2018–19	Sunderland	0	0		

POWER, Max (M) 271 27
H: 5 11 W: 11 13 b.Bebington 27-7-93

2010–11	Tranmere R	0	0		
2011–12	Tranmere R	4	0		
2012–13	Tranmere R	27	3		
2013–14	Tranmere R	33	2		
2014–15	Tranmere R	45	7	**109**	**12**
2015–16	Wigan Ath	44	6		
2016–17	Wigan Ath	42	0		
2017–18	Wigan Ath	40	5		
2018–19	Wigan Ath	1	0	**127**	**11**
2018–19	Sunderland	35	4	**35**	**4**

ROBSON, Ethan (M) 22 2
H: 5 8 W: 10 12 b. 25-10-96

2016–17	Sunderland	0	0		
2017–18	Sunderland	9	0		
2018–19	Sunderland	0	0	**9**	**0**
2018–19	*Dundee*	13	2	**13**	**2**

RUITER, Robbin (G) 233 0
H: 6 5 W: 12 04 b.Amsterdam 25-3-87

2009–10	Volendam	21	0		
2010–11	Volendam	24	0		
2011–12	Volendam	25	0	**70**	**0**
2012–13	Utrecht	37	0		
2013–14	Utrecht	30	0		
2014–15	Utrecht	31	0		
2015–16	Utrecht	29	0		
2016–17	Utrecht	15	0	**142**	**0**
2017–18	FC Utrecht	0	0		
2017–18	Sunderland	20	0		
2018–19	Sunderland	1	0	**21**	**0**

STRYJEK, Maksymilian (G) 1 0
H: 6 2 W: 12 11 b.Warsaw 18-7-96
Internationals: Poland U17, U18, U19.

2014–15	Sunderland	0	0		
2015–16	Sunderland	0	0		
2016–17	Sunderland	0	0		
2017–18	Sunderland	0	0		
2017–18	*Accrington S*	1	0	**1**	**0**
2018–19	Sunderland	0	0		

TAYLOR, Brandon (D) 0 0
b.Gateshead 10-5-99

2018–19	Sunderland	0	0		

WATMORE, Duncan (F) 63 5
H: 5 9 W: 11 05 b.Cheadle Hulme 8-3-94
Internationals: England U20, U21.

2013–14	Sunderland	0	0		
2013–14	*Hibernian*	9	1	**9**	**1**
2014–15	Sunderland	0	0		
2015–16	Sunderland	23	3		
2016–17	Sunderland	14	0		
2017–18	Sunderland	6	0		
2018–19	Sunderland	11	1	**54**	**4**

WYKE, Charlie (F) 212 66
b.Middlesbrough 6-12-92

2011–12	Middlesbrough	0	0		
2012–13	Middlesbrough	0	0		
2012–13	*Hartlepool U*	25	2		
2013–14	Middlesbrough	0	0		
2013–14	*AFC Wimbledon*	17	2	**17**	**2**
2014–15	Middlesbrough	0	0		
2014–15	*Hartlepool U*	13	4	**38**	**6**
2014–15	Carlisle U	17	6		
2015–16	Carlisle U	34	12		
2016–17	Carlisle U	26	14	**77**	**32**
2016–17	Bradford C	16	7		
2017–18	Bradford C	40	15	**56**	**22**
2018–19	Sunderland	24	4	**24**	**4**

YOUNG, Jacob (D) 0 0
b.Perth 6-3-00

2018–19	Sunderland	0	0		

Players retained or with offer of contract
Connolly, Jack; Kone, Lamine-Gueye; Mbunga-Kimpioka, Benjamin.

Scholars
Best, Sonny Alexander John; Cameron, Adam Stuart; Compper, Lilyan Christian; Derbali, Rayed; Devine, Harrison James; Edmundsson, Andrias; Evans, Kane; Howard, Tomas David; Kennedy, Sean James; Kiernan, Cole David; Kokolo, Williams Joseph Gabriel; Leonard, Ryan John; Lilley, Joseph Isaac; Miller, Liam Ian; Neil, Daniel; Newman, Jack Callum; Ord, Harry; Patterson, Anthony; Scothern, Thomas; Slack, Connor James; Smith, Thomas.

SWANSEA C (81)

ASORO, Joel (F) 41 3
H: 5 9 W: 11 11 b. 27-4-99
Internationals: Sweden U17, U21.

2016–17	Sunderland	1	0		
2017–18	Sunderland	26	3	**27**	**3**
2018–19	Swansea C	14	0	**14**	**0**

AYEW, Jordan (F) 280 49
H: 6 0 W: 12 11 b.Marseille 11-9-91
Internationals: Ghana U20, Full caps.

2009–10	Marseille	4	1		
2010–11	Marseille	22	2		
2011–12	Marseille	34	3		
2012–13	Marseille	35	7		
2013–14	Marseille	16	1	**111**	**14**
2013–14	*Sochaux*	17	5	**17**	**5**
2014–15	Lorient	31	12	**31**	**12**
2015–16	Aston Villa	30	7		
2016–17	Aston Villa	21	2	**51**	**9**
2016–17	Swansea C	14	1		
2017–18	Swansea C	36	7		
2018–19	Swansea C	0	0	**50**	**8**
2018–19	*Crystal Palace*	20	1	**20**	**1**

BAKER-RICHARDSON, Courtney (F) 17 3
H: 6 1 W: 11 07 b.Coventry 5-12-95

2013–14	Coventry C	0	0		
2014–15	Coventry C	0	0		

From Tamworth, Nuneaton T, Redditch U, Kettering T, Leamington.

2017–18	Swansea C	0	0		
2018–19	Swansea C	17	3	**17**	**3**

BENDA, Steven (G) 0 0
H: 6 4 W: 13 01 b.Stuttgart 1-1-98
From Aalen, Heidenheim, TSV 1860.

2018–19	Swansea C	0	0		

BIABI, Botti (F) 25 3
H: 6 2 W: 12 06 b.London 8-3-96

2013–14	Falkirk	0	0		
2014–15	Falkirk	22	3		
2015–16	Falkirk	0	0	**22**	**3**
2015–16	Swansea C	0	0		
2016–17	Swansea C	0	0		
2017–18	Swansea C	0	0		
2018–19	Swansea C	0	0		
2018–19	*Macclesfield T*	3	0	**3**	**0**

BONY, Wilfried (F) 252 109
H: 6 0 W: 13 11 b.Bingerville 10-12-88
Internationals: Ivory Coast Full caps.

2008–09	Sparta Prague	16	3		
2009–10	Sparta Prague	29	9		
2010–11	Sparta Prague	13	10	**58**	**22**
2010–11	Vitesse	7	3		
2011–12	Vitesse	28	12		
2012–13	Vitesse	30	31	**65**	**46**
2013–14	Swansea C	34	16		
2014–15	Swansea C	20	9		
2014–15	Manchester C	10	2		
2015–16	Manchester C	26	4		
2016–17	Manchester C	0	0	**36**	**6**
2016–17	*Stoke C*	10	2	**10**	**2**
2017–18	Swansea C	15	2		
2018–19	Swansea C	7	1	**76**	**28**
2018–19	*Al Arabi*	7	5	**7**	**5**

BYERS, George (M) 22 2
H: 5 11 W: 11 07 b.Ilford 29-5-96
Internationals: Scotland U16, U17.

2014–15	Watford	1	0		
2015–16	Watford	0	0	**1**	**0**
2017–18	Swansea C	0	0		
2018–19	Swansea C	21	2	**21**	**2**

CARROLL, Tommy (M) 158 3
H: 5 10 W: 10 00 b.Watford 28-5-92
Internationals: England U19, U21.

2010–11	Tottenham H	0	0		
2010–11	*Leyton Orient*	12	0	**12**	**0**
2011–12	Tottenham H	0	0		
2011–12	*Derby Co*	12	1	**12**	**1**
2012–13	Tottenham H	7	0		
2013–14	Tottenham H	0	0		
2013–14	*QPR*	26	0	**26**	**0**
2014–15	Tottenham H	0	0		
2014–15	*Swansea C*	13	0		
2015–16	Tottenham H	19	1		
2016–17	Tottenham H	1	0	**27**	**1**
2016–17	Swansea C	17	1		
2017–18	Swansea C	37	0		
2018–19	Swansea C	12	0	**79**	**1**
2018–19	*Aston Villa*	2	0	**2**	**0**

CARTER-VICKERS, Cameron (D) 64 1
H: 6 1 W: 13 08 b.Westcliff on Sea 31-12-97
Internationals: USA U18, U20, U23, Full caps.

2015–16	Tottenham H	0	0		
2016–17	Tottenham H	0	0		
2017–18	Tottenham H	0	0		
2017–18	*Sheffield U*	17	1	**17**	**1**
2017–18	*Ipswich T*	17	0	**17**	**0**
2018–19	Tottenham H	0	0		
2018–19	Swansea C	30	0	**30**	**0**

CELINA, Bersant (F) 101 17
H: 5 4 W: 9 06 b.Prizren 9-9-96
Internationals: Norway U16, U17. Kosovo Full caps.

2014–15	Manchester C	0	0		
2015–16	Manchester C	1	0		
2016–17	Manchester C	0	0		
2016–17	*FC Twente*	27	5	**27**	**5**
2017–18	Manchester C	0	0	**1**	**0**
2017–18	*Ipswich T*	35	7	**35**	**7**
2018–19	Swansea C	38	5	**38**	**5**

COOPER, Brandon (D) 0 0
b.Bridgend 14-1-00
Internationals: Wales U21.

2018–19	Swansea C	0	0		

CULLEN, Liam (F) 0 0
b.Tenby 23-4-99
Internationals: Wales U16, U17, U19.

2018–19	Swansea C	0	0		

DAVIES, Keston (D) 9 0
H: 6 2 W: 13 01 b. 2-10-96
Internationals: Wales U17, U19, U21.

2017–18	Swansea C	0	0		
2017–18	*Yeovil T*	2	0	**2**	**0**
2018–19	Swansea C	0	0		
2018–19	*Notts Co*	7	0	**7**	**0**

DHANDA, Yan (F) 5 1
H: 5 8 W: 10 03 b.Birmingham 14-12-98
Internationals: England U17.
From Liverpool.

2018–19	Swansea C	5	1	**5**	**1**

DYER, Nathan (M) 368 30
H: 5 5 W: 9 00 b.Trowbridge 29-11-87

2005–06	Southampton	17	0		
2005–06	*Burnley*	5	2	**5**	**2**
2006–07	Southampton	18	0		
2007–08	Southampton	17	1		
2008–09	Southampton	4	0	**56**	**1**
2008–09	*Sheffield U*	7	1	**7**	**1**
2008–09	*Swansea C*	17	2		
2009–10	Swansea C	40	2		
2010–11	Swansea C	46	2		
2011–12	Swansea C	34	5		
2012–13	Swansea C	37	3		
2013–14	Swansea C	27	6		
2014–15	Swansea C	32	3		
2015–16	Swansea C	1	0		
2015–16	*Leicester C*	12	1	**12**	**1**
2016–17	Swansea C	8	0		
2017–18	Swansea C	24	0		
2018–19	Swansea C	22	2	**288**	**25**

FER, Leroy (M) 322 46
H: 6 2 W: 12 05 b.Zortermeer 5-1-90
Internationals: Netherlands U16, U17, U19, U21, Full caps.

2007–08	Feyenoord	13	1		
2008–09	Feyenoord	31	6		
2009–10	Feyenoord	31	2		
2010–11	Feyenoord	23	3		
2011–12	Feyenoord	4	2	**102**	**14**

2011–12	FC Twente	26	8		
2012–13	FC Twente	26	5	**52**	**13**
2013–14	Norwich C	29	3		
2014–15	Norwich C	1	0	**30**	**3**
2014–15	QPR	29	6		
2015–16	QPR	19	2	**48**	**8**
2015–16	*Swansea C*	11	0		
2016–17	Swansea C	34	6		
2017–18	Swansea C	20	1		
2018–19	Swansea C	25	1	**90**	**8**

FULTON, Jay (M) 68 3
H: 5 10 W: 10 08 b.Bolton 4-4-94
Internationals: Scotland U18, U19, U21.

2013–14	Swansea C	2	0		
2014–15	Swansea C	2	0		
2015–16	Swansea C	2	0		
2015–16	*Oldham Ath*	11	0	**11**	**0**
2016–17	Swansea C	11	0		
2017–18	Swansea C	2	0		
2017–18	*Wigan Ath*	5	1	**5**	**1**
2018–19	Swansea C	33	2	**52**	**2**

GRIMES, Matt (M) 171 10
H: 5 10 W: 11 00 b.Exeter 15-7-95
Internationals: England U20, U21.

2013–14	Exeter C	35	1		
2014–15	Exeter C	23	4	**58**	**5**
2014–15	Swansea C	3	0		
2015–16	Swansea C	1	0		
2015–16	*Blackburn R*	13	0	**13**	**0**
2016–17	Swansea C	0	0		
2016–17	*Leeds U*	7	0	**7**	**0**
2017–18	Swansea C	0	0		
2017–18	*Northampton T*	44	4	**44**	**4**
2018–19	Swansea C	45	1	**49**	**1**

HARRIES, Cian (D) 11 0
H: 6 1 W: 12 02 b. 1-4-97
Internationals: Wales U17, U19, U20.

2015–16	Coventry C	1	0		
2016–17	Coventry C	8	0	**9**	**0**
2017–18	Swansea C	0	0		
2018–19	Swansea C	2	0	**2**	**0**

JAMES, Daniel (M) 33 4
b. 10-11-97
Internationals: Wales U17, U19, U20, U21, Full caps.

2015–16	Swansea C	0	0		
2016–17	Swansea C	0	0		
2017–18	Swansea C	0	0		
2017–18	*Shrewsbury T*	0	0		
2018–19	Swansea C	33	4	**33**	**4**

JOHN, Declan (M) 99 3
H: 5 10 W: 11 10 b.Merthyr Tydfil 30-6-95
Internationals: Wales U17, U19, Full caps.

2010–11	Llanelli	1	0	**1**	**0**
2011–12	Afan Lido	5	0	**5**	**0**
2012–13	Cardiff C	0	0		
2013–14	Cardiff C	20	0		
2014–15	Cardiff C	6	0		
2014–15	*Barnsley*	9	0	**9**	**0**
2015–16	Cardiff C	1	0		
2015–16	*Chesterfield*	6	0	**6**	**0**
2016–17	Cardiff C	15	0		
2017–18	Cardiff C	0	0	**42**	**0**
2017–18	Rangers	26	3	**26**	**3**
2018–19	Swansea C	10	0	**10**	**0**

LEWIS, Aaron (D) 7 0
H: 6 0 W: 13 05 b.Swansea 26-6-98

2018–19	Swansea C	0	0		
2018–19	*Doncaster R*	7	0	**7**	**0**

MARIC, Adnan (M) 0 0
H: 5 11 W: 12 00 b.Gothenburg 1-10-96
Internationals: Sweden U17.

2017–18	Swansea C	0	0		
2018–19	Swansea C	0	0		

McBURNIE, Oliver (F) 98 34
H: 6 2 W: 10 04 b.Bradford 6-4-96
Internationals: Scotland U19, U21, Full caps.

2013–14	Bradford C	8	0		
2014–15	Bradford C	7	0	**15**	**0**
2015–16	Swansea C	0	0		
2015–16	*Newport Co*	3	3	**3**	**3**
2015–16	*Bristol R*	5	0	**5**	**0**
2016–17	Swansea C	5	0		
2017–18	Swansea C	11	0		
2017–18	*Barnsley*	17	9	**17**	**9**
2018–19	Swansea C	42	22	**58**	**22**

McKAY, Barrie (M) 200 23
H: 5 9 W: 11 00 b.Paisley 30-12-94
Internationals: Scotland U18, U19, U21, Full caps.

2011–12	Rangers	1	0		
2012–13	Rangers	31	1		
2013–14	Rangers	2	0		
2013–14	*Greenock Morton*	18	3	**18**	**3**
2014–15	Rangers	0	0		
2014–15	*Raith R*	23	1	**23**	**1**
2015–16	Rangers	34	6		
2016–17	Rangers	35	5	**103**	**12**
2017–18	Nottingham F	26	5	**26**	**5**
2018–19	Swansea C	30	2	**30**	**2**

MONTERO, Jefferson (M) 266 35
H: 5 8 W: 11 00 b.Babahoyo 1-9-89
Internationals: Ecuador Full caps.

2007	Emelec	22	2		
2008	Independiente de Valle	25	8		
2008–09	*Dorados*	5	1	**5**	**1**
2009	Independiente de Valle	12	11	**37**	**19**
2010–11	Villareal	9	1		
2010–11	*Levante*	11	0	**11**	**0**
2011–12	Villareal	0	0	**9**	**1**
2011–12	*Real Betis*	32	1	**32**	**1**
2012–13	Morelia	32	4		
2013–14	Morelia	25	5	**57**	**9**
2014–15	Swansea C	30	1		
2015–16	Swansea C	23	0		
2016–17	Swansea C	13	0		
2017–18	Swansea C	0	0		
2017–18	*Getafe*	4	0	**4**	**0**
2017–18	*Emelec*	7	0	**29**	**2**
2018–19	Swansea C	12	0	**78**	**1**
2018–19	*WBA*	4	1	**4**	**1**

MULDER, Erwin (G) 251 0
H: 6 4 W: 13 12 b.Zevenaar 3-3-89
Internationals: Netherlands B, U19, U20, U21.

2007–08	Feyenoord	1	0		
2008–09	Feyenoord	0	0		
2008–09	*Excelsior*	36	0	**36**	**0**
2009–10	Feyenoord	10	0		
2010–11	Feyenoord	17	0		
2011–12	Feyenoord	34	0		
2012–13	Feyenoord	22	0		
2013–14	Feyenoord	32	0		
2014–15	Feyenoord	4	0	**120**	**0**
2015–16	Heerenveen	34	0		
2016–17	Heerenveen	36	0		
2017–18	Heerenveen	0	0	**70**	**0**
2017–18	Swansea C	0	0		
2018–19	Swansea C	25	0	**25**	**0**

NARSINGH, Luciano (F) 210 35
H: 5 10 W: 10 12 b.Amsterdam 13-9-90
Internationals: Netherlands U18, U19, U20, U21, Full caps.

2008–09	Heerenveen	2	0		
2009–10	Heerenveen	2	0		
2010–11	Heerenveen	24	5		
2011–12	Heerenveen	34	8	**62**	**13**
2012–13	PSV Eindhoven	18	6		
2013–14	PSV Eindhoven	20	0		
2014–15	PSV Eindhoven	32	6		
2015–16	PSV Eindhoven	30	8	**100**	**20**
2016–17	PSV	15	1	**15**	**1**
2016–17	Swansea C	13	0		
2017–18	Swansea C	18	1		
2018–19	Swansea C	2	0	**33**	**1**

NAUGHTON, Kyle (M) 318 8
H: 5 11 W: 11 07 b.Sheffield 11-11-88
Internationals: England U21.

2006–07	Sheffield U	0	0		
2007–08	*Gretna*	18	0	**18**	**0**
2007–08	Sheffield U	0	0		
2008–09	Sheffield U	40	1		
2009–10	Sheffield U	0	0	**40**	**1**
2009–10	Tottenham H	1	0		
2009–10	*Middlesbrough*	15	0	**15**	**0**
2010–11	Tottenham H	0	0		
2010–11	*Leicester C*	34	5	**34**	**5**
2011–12	Tottenham H	0	0		
2011–12	*Norwich C*	32	0	**32**	**0**
2012–13	Tottenham H	14	0		
2013–14	Tottenham H	22	0		
2014–15	Tottenham H	5	0	**42**	**0**
2014–15	Swansea C	10	0		
2015–16	Swansea C	27	0		
2016–17	Swansea C	31	1		
2017–18	Swansea C	34	0		
2018–19	Swansea C	35	1	**137**	**2**

NORDFELDT, Kristoffer (G) 239 0
H: 6 3 W: 13 05 b.Stockholm 23-6-89
Internationals: Sweden U19, U21, Full caps.

2006	Brommapojkarna	0	0		
2007	Brommapojkarna	0	0		
2008	Brommapojkarna	29	0		
2009	Brommapojkarna	21	0		
2010	Brommapojkarna	25	0		
2011	Brommapojkarna	28	0	**103**	**0**
2011–12	Heerenveen	6	0		
2012–13	Heerenveen	33	0		
2013–14	Heerenveen	35	0		
2014–15	Heerenveen	38	0	**112**	**0**
2015–16	Swansea C	1	0		
2016–17	Swansea C	1	0		
2017–18	Swansea C	0	0		
2018–19	Swansea C	22	0	**24**	**0**

OLSSON, Martin (D) 304 8
H: 5 7 W: 12 12 b.Gavle 17-5-88
Internationals: Sweden U19, U21, Full caps.

2005–06	Blackburn R	0	0		
2006–07	Blackburn R	0	0		
2007–08	Blackburn R	2	0		
2008–09	Blackburn R	9	0		
2009–10	Blackburn R	21	1		
2010–11	Blackburn R	29	2		
2011–12	Blackburn R	27	0		
2012–13	Blackburn R	29	0	**117**	**3**
2013–14	Norwich C	34	0		
2014–15	Norwich C	42	1		
2015–16	Norwich C	24	1		
2016–17	Norwich C	19	1	**119**	**3**
2016–17	Swansea C	15	2		
2017–18	Swansea C	36	0		
2018–19	Swansea C	17	0	**68**	**2**

REID, Tyler (D) 7 0
b. 2-9-97

2017–18	Swansea C	0	0		
2017–18	*Newport Co*	7	0	**7**	**0**
2018–19	Swansea C	0	0		

ROBERTS, Connor (D) 97 5
H: 5 9 W: 11 03 b.Neath 23-9-95
Internationals: Wales U19, U21, Full caps.

2014–15	Swansea C	0	0		
2015–16	Swansea C	0	0		
2015–16	*Yeovil T*	45	0	**45**	**0**
2016–17	Bristol R	2	0	**2**	**0**
2016–17	Swansea C	0	0		
2017–18	Swansea C	4	0		
2017–18	*Middlesbrough*	1	0	**1**	**0**
2018–19	Swansea C	45	5	**49**	**5**

RODON, Joe (D) 39 0
b.Swansea 22-10-97
Internationals: Wales U20, U21.

2015–16	Swansea C	0	0		
2016–17	Swansea C	0	0		
2017–18	Swansea C	0	0		
2017–18	*Cheltenham T*	12	0	**12**	**0**
2018–19	Swansea C	27	0	**27**	**0**

ROUTLEDGE, Wayne (M) 483 44
H: 5 6 W: 11 02 b.Sidcup 7-1-85
Internationals: England U20, U21.

2001–02	Crystal Palace	2	0		
2002–03	Crystal Palace	26	4		
2003–04	Crystal Palace	44	6		
2004–05	Crystal Palace	38	0	**110**	**10**
2005–06	Tottenham H	3	0		
2005–06	*Portsmouth*	13	0	**13**	**0**
2006–07	Tottenham H	0	0		
2006–07	*Fulham*	24	0	**24**	**0**
2007–08	Tottenham H	2	0	**5**	**0**
2007–08	Aston Villa	1	0		
2008–09	Aston Villa	1	0	**2**	**0**
2008–09	*Cardiff C*	9	2	**9**	**2**
2008–09	QPR	19	1		
2009–10	QPR	25	2		
2009–10	Newcastle U	17	3		
2010–11	Newcastle U	17	0	**34**	**3**
2010–11	*QPR*	20	5	**64**	**8**
2011–12	Swansea C	28	1		
2012–13	Swansea C	36	5		
2013–14	Swansea C	35	2		
2014–15	Swansea C	29	3		
2015–16	Swansea C	28	2		
2016–17	Swansea C	27	3		
2017–18	Swansea C	15	0		
2018–19	Swansea C	24	5	**222**	**21**

VAN DER HOORN, Mike (D) 155 14
H: 6 3 W: 12 11 b.Almere 15-10-92
Internationals: Netherlands U20, U21.

2010–11	Utrecht	1	0		

2011–12	Utrecht	12	2		
2012–13	Utrecht	31	4	**44**	**6**
2013–14	Ajax	3	0		
2014–15	Ajax	15	2		
2015–16	Ajax	15	1	**33**	**3**
2016–17	Swansea C	8	1		
2017–18	Swansea C	24	1		
2018–19	Swansea C	46	3	**78**	**5**

Players retained or with offer of contract

Ayew, Andre Morgan Rami; Berry, Cameron; Bia, Bi Botti Boulenin; Blake, Matthew; Cabango, Benjamin; De Boer, Kees Cornelis Henricus; Dulca, Marco-Alexandru; Evans, Jack Marcus; Evans, Keiran; Garrick, Jordon D'Andre; Gonzalez, Tomas Borja; Gould, Joshua Simon; Govea, Merlin Jordy Jair; Gudjohnsen, Arnor Borg; Paulet, Simon; Price, Thomas Owen; Van Der Hoorn, Mike Adrianus Wilhelmus; Zabret, Gregor.

Scholars

Al-Hamadi, Ali Ibrahim Karim Ali; Bevan, Ryan Peter; Clancy, Charlie Mark Patrick; Davies, Thomas Craig; Erickson, Benjamin James; Evans, Cameron James; Evans, Owen Jarrett; Gibbings, Bradley William; Jones, Jacob Alexander; Jones-Thomas, Mason Jake; McKendry, Luke John; Motruk, Luke Ivan; Owen, Bailey Elis; Reed, Scott Steven Joseph; Reid, Jayden Andrew; Rickard, Jamie William; Rushesha, Tivonge Sacha; Rutter, Alexander; Shepperd, Nathan; Shields, Connor Liam; Thomas, Jake; Walsh, Marc Thomas; Williams, Daniel Patrick; Wynter-Coles, Shaquille Leighton Gaston.

SWINDON T (82)

ANDERSON, Keshi (F) **109 16**

H: 5 9 W: 10 10 b.Luton 15-11-95

2014–15	Crystal Palace	0	0		
2015–16	Crystal Palace	0	0		
2015–16	*Doncaster R*	7	3	**7**	**3**
2016–17	Crystal Palace	0	0		
2016–17	*Bolton W*	8	1	**8**	**1**
2016–17	*Northampton T*	14	3	**14**	**3**
2017–18	Swindon T	37	5		
2018–19	Swindon T	43	4	**80**	**9**

BANCROFT, Jacob (F) **1 0**

b. 9-4-01

2018–19	Swindon T	1	0	**1**	**0**

BROADBENT, Tom (D) **41 0**

H: 6 3 W: 14 02 b. 15-2-92

From Farnborough, Petersfield T, Hayes & Yeading U.

2017–18	Bristol R	22	0		
2018–19	Bristol R	7	0	**29**	**0**
2018–19	Swindon T	12	0	**12**	**0**

CONROY, Dion (D) **48 1**

b.Redhill 11-12-95

From Chelsea.

2016–17	Swindon T	14	0		
2017–18	Swindon T	7	0		
2018–19	Swindon T	27	1	**48**	**1**

CURRAN, Taylor (D) **1 0**

b. 7-7-00

2018–19	Southend U	0	0		
2018–19	Swindon T	1	0	**1**	**0**

DIAGOURAGA, Toumani (M) **413 16**

H: 6 2 W: 11 05 b.Paris 10-6-87

2004–05	Watford	0	0		
2005–06	Watford	1	0		
2005–06	*Swindon T*	8	0		
2006–07	Watford	0	0		
2006–07	*Rotherham U*	7	0	**7**	**0**
2007–08	Watford	0	0	**1**	**0**
2007–08	*Hereford U*	41	2		
2008–09	Hereford U	45	2	**86**	**4**
2009–10	Peterborough U	19	0	**19**	**0**
2009–10	*Brentford*	20	0		
2010–11	Brentford	32	1		
2011–12	Brentford	35	4		
2012–13	Brentford	39	1		
2013–14	Brentford	19	0		
2013–14	*Portsmouth*	8	0	**8**	**0**
2014–15	Brentford	38	0		
2015–16	Brentford	27	0	**210**	**6**
2015–16	Leeds U	17	2		
2016–17	Leeds U	1	0		
2016–17	*Ipswich T*	12	0	**12**	**0**
2017–18	Leeds U	0	0	**18**	**2**
2017–18	Plymouth Arg	15	3	**15**	**3**
2017–18	Fleetwood T	17	1	**17**	**1**
2018–19	Swindon T	12	0	**20**	**0**

DOUGHTY, Michael (M) **181 23**

H: 6 1 W: 12 10 b.Westminster 20-11-92

Internationals: Wales U19, U21.

2010–11	QPR	0	0		
2011–12	QPR	0	0		
2011–12	*Crawley T*	16	0	**16**	**0**
2011–12	*Aldershot T*	5	0	**5**	**0**
2012–13	QPR	0	0		
2012–13	*St Johnstone*	5	0	**5**	**0**
2013–14	QPR	0	0		
2013–14	*Stevenage*	36	2	**36**	**2**
2014–15	QPR	3	0		
2014–15	*Gillingham*	9	0	**9**	**0**
2015–16	QPR	5	0		
2015–16	*Swindon T*	20	5		
2016–17	QPR	4	0	**12**	**0**
2016–17	*Swindon T*	14	2		
2017–18	Peterborough U	34	1	**34**	**1**
2018–19	Swindon T	30	13	**64**	**20**

DUNNE, James (M) **344 15**

H: 5 11 W: 10 12 b.Bromley 18-9-89

2007–08	Arsenal	0	0		
2008–09	Arsenal	0	0		
2008–09	*Nottingham F*	0	0		
2009–10	Exeter C	23	3		
2010–11	Exeter C	42	1		
2011–12	Exeter C	45	2	**110**	**6**
2012–13	Stevenage	42	4		
2013–14	Stevenage	13	1	**55**	**5**
2013–14	*St Johnstone*	13	0	**13**	**0**
2014–15	Portsmouth	36	1		
2015–16	Portsmouth	0	0	**36**	**1**
2015–16	*Dagenham & R*	9	0	**9**	**0**
2015–16	Cambridge U	19	1		
2016–17	Cambridge U	33	1	**52**	**2**
2017–18	Swindon T	39	0		
2018–19	Swindon T	30	1	**69**	**1**

EDWARDS, Jordan (M) **1 0**

b. 26-10-99

2017–18	Swindon T	1	0		
2018–19	Swindon T	0	0	**1**	**0**

HENRY, Will (G) **5 0**

b. 6-7-98

2015–16	Swindon T	2	0		
2016–17	Swindon T	3	0		
2017–18	Swindon T	0	0		
2018–19	Swindon T	0	0	**5**	**0**

IANDOLO, Ellis (M) **49 1**

b. 22-8-97

From Maidstone U.

2015–16	Swindon T	12	0		
2016–17	Swindon T	10	0		
2017–18	Swindon T	12	1		
2018–19	Swindon T	15	0	**49**	**1**

KNOYLE, Kyle (D) **70 0**

H: 5 10 W: 9 13 b.Newham 24-9-96

Internationals: England U18.

2015–16	West Ham U	0	0		
2015–16	*Dundee U*	9	0	**9**	**0**
2016–17	West Ham U	0	0		
2016–17	*Wigan Ath*	1	0	**1**	**0**
2017–18	Swindon T	18	0		
2018–19	Swindon T	42	0	**60**	**0**

LANCASHIRE, Oliver (D) **263 6**

H: 6 1 W: 11 10 b.Basingstoke 13-12-88

2006–07	Southampton	0	0		
2007–08	Southampton	0	0		
2008–09	Southampton	11	0		
2009–10	Southampton	2	0	**13**	**0**
2009–10	*Grimsby T*	25	1	**25**	**1**
2010–11	Walsall	29	0		
2011–12	Walsall	20	1	**49**	**1**
2012–13	Aldershot T	12	0	**12**	**0**
2013–14	Rochdale	38	0		
2014–15	Rochdale	21	0		
2015–16	Rochdale	34	2	**93**	**2**
2016–17	Shrewsbury T	16	1	**16**	**1**
2017–18	Swindon T	35	1		
2018–19	Swindon T	20	0	**55**	**1**

MATTHEWS, Archie (G) **0 0**

2018–19	Swindon T	0	0		

McCORMICK, Luke (G) **200 0**

H: 6 0 W: 13 12 b.Coventry 15-8-83

2012–13	Oxford U	15	0	**15**	**0**
2013–14	Plymouth Arg	27	0		
2014–15	Plymouth Arg	46	0		
2015–16	Plymouth Arg	40	0		
2016–17	Plymouth Arg	46	0		
2017–18	Plymouth Arg	9	0	**168**	**0**
2018–19	Swindon T	17	0	**17**	**0**

McCOURT, Jak (M) **101 7**

H: 5 10 W: 10 10 b.Leicester 6-7-95

2013–14	Leicester C	0	0		
2013–14	*Torquay U*	11	0	**11**	**0**
2014–15	Leicester C	0	0		
2015–16	Leicester C	0	0		
2015–16	*Port Vale*	2	0	**2**	**0**
2015–16	Barnsley	1	0	**1**	**0**
2016–17	Northampton T	26	1	**26**	**1**
2017–18	Chesterfield	34	5	**34**	**5**
2018–19	Swindon T	27	1	**27**	**1**

McGILP, Cameron (M) **2 0**

H: 5 11 b.Glasgow 8-2-98

2016–17	Melbourne Victory	1	0		
2017–18	Melbourne Victory	0	0	**1**	**0**

From Melbourne Victory.

2018–19	Birmingham C	0	0		
2018–19	Swindon T	1	0	**1**	**0**

McGLASHAN, Jermaine (M) **307 26**

H: 5 7 W: 10 00 b.Croydon 14-4-88

2010–11	Aldershot T	38	1		
2011–12	Aldershot T	23	4	**61**	**5**
2011–12	Cheltenham T	16	2		
2012–13	Cheltenham T	45	4		
2013–14	Cheltenham T	43	6	**104**	**12**
2014–15	Gillingham	40	5		
2015–16	Gillingham	17	0	**57**	**5**
2016–17	Southend U	35	3		
2017–18	Southend U	26	1	**61**	**4**
2018–19	Swindon T	24	0	**24**	**0**

PRYCE, Sol (F) **2 2**

b.Chippenham 30-1-00

2018–19	Swindon T	2	2	**2**	**2**

RICHARDS, Marc (F) **584 184**

H: 6 2 W: 12 06 b.Wolverhampton 8-7-82

Internationals: England U18, U20.

1999–2000	Blackburn R	0	0		
2000–01	Blackburn R	0	0		
2001–02	Blackburn R	0	0		
2001–02	*Crewe Alex*	4	0	**4**	**0**
2001–02	*Oldham Ath*	5	0	**5**	**0**
2001–02	*Halifax T*	5	0	**5**	**0**
2002–03	Blackburn R	0	0		
2002–03	*Swansea C*	17	7	**17**	**7**
2003–04	Northampton T	41	8		
2004–05	Northampton T	12	2		
2004–05	*Rochdale*	5	2	**5**	**2**
2005–06	Northampton T	0	0		
2005–06	Barnsley	38	12		
2006–07	Barnsley	31	6	**69**	**18**
2007–08	Port Vale	29	5		
2008–09	Port Vale	30	10		
2009–10	Port Vale	46	20		
2010–11	Port Vale	40	16		
2011–12	Port Vale	36	17	**181**	**68**
2012–13	Chesterfield	34	12		
2013–14	Chesterfield	38	8	**72**	**20**
2013–14	Northampton T	0	0		
2014–15	Northampton T	31	18		
2015–16	Northampton T	31	15		
2016–17	Northampton T	42	10		
2017–18	Northampton T	19	1	**176**	**54**
2017–18	Swindon T	20	11		
2018–19	Swindon T	30	4	**50**	**15**

ROBINSON, Theo (F) **382 88**

H: 5 9 W: 10 03 b.Birmingham 22-1-89

Internationals: Jamaica Full caps.

2005–06	Watford	1	0		
2006–07	Watford	1	0		
2007–08	Watford	0	0		
2007–08	*Hereford U*	43	13	**43**	**13**
2008–09	Watford	3	0	**5**	**0**
2008–09	*Southend U*	21	7		
2009–10	Huddersfield T	37	13		
2010–11	Huddersfield T	1	0		
2010–11	Millwall	11	3		
2010–11	*Derby Co*	13	2		
2011–12	Derby Co	39	10		
2012–13	Derby Co	28	8		
2012–13	*Huddersfield T*	6	0	**44**	**13**
2013–14	Millwall	0	0	**11**	**3**
2013–14	Derby Co	0	0	**80**	**20**
2013–14	Doncaster R	31	5		
2014–15	Doncaster R	32	4	**63**	**9**
2014–15	*Scunthorpe U*	8	3	**8**	**3**
2015–16	Motherwell	10	0	**10**	**0**
2015–16	Port Vale	14	2	**14**	**2**

2016–17	Southend U	18	2		
2017–18	Southend U	25	5		
2018–19	Southend U	24	4	**88**	**18**
2018–19	Swindon T	16	7	**16**	**7**

ROMANSKI, Joe (D) **6** **1**
b.Reading 3-2-00

2017–18	Swindon T	2	0		
2018–19	Swindon T	4	1	**6**	**1**

ROSE, Danny (M) **195** **14**
H: 5 7 W: 10 04 b.Bristol 21-2-88
Internationals: England C.

2006–07	Manchester U	0	0		
2007–08	Manchester U	0	0		
From Oxford U, Newport Co					
2012–13	Fleetwood T	0	0		
2012–13	*Aldershot T*	34	2	**34**	**2**
2013–14	Oxford U	40	4		
2014–15	Oxford U	29	2		
2015–16	Oxford U	13	0	**82**	**6**
2015–16	Northampton T	15	1	**15**	**1**
2016–17	Portsmouth	38	5		
2017–18	Portsmouth	15	0		
2018–19	Portsmouth	1	0	**54**	**5**
2018–19	Swindon T	10	0	**10**	**0**

SMITH, Martin (M) **23** **1**
H: 5 10 W: 11 00 b.Sunderland 25-1-96

2014–15	Sunderland	0	0		
2015–16	Sunderland	0	0		
2015–16	*Carlisle U*	2	0	**2**	**0**
2016–17	Kilmarnock	10	1	**10**	**1**
From Coleraine.					
2018–19	Swindon T	11	0	**11**	**0**

TAYLOR, Matthew (D) **659** **84**
H: 5 11 W: 12 03 b.Oxford 27-11-81
Internationals: England U21, B.

1998–99	Luton T	0	0		
1999–2000	Luton T	41	4		
2000–01	Luton T	45	1		
2001–02	Luton T	43	11	**129**	**16**
2002–03	Portsmouth	35	7		
2003–04	Portsmouth	30	0		
2004–05	Portsmouth	32	1		
2005–06	Portsmouth	34	6		
2006–07	Portsmouth	35	8		
2007–08	Portsmouth	13	1	**179**	**23**
2007–08	Bolton W	16	3		
2008–09	Bolton W	34	10		
2009–10	Bolton W	37	8		
2010–11	Bolton W	36	2	**123**	**23**
2011–12	West Ham U	28	1		
2012–13	West Ham U	28	1		
2013–14	West Ham U	20	0	**76**	**2**
2014–15	Burnley	10	0		
2015–16	Burnley	27	4	**37**	**4**
2016–17	Northampton T	43	7		
2017–18	Northampton T	1	0	**44**	**7**
2017–18	Swindon T	38	6		
2018–19	Swindon T	33	3	**71**	**9**

TWINE, Scott (F) **19** **1**
H: 5 9 W: 10 12 b.Swindon 14-7-99

2015–16	Swindon T	0	0		
2016–17	Swindon T	1	0		
2017–18	Swindon T	4	0		
2018–19	Swindon T	14	1	**19**	**1**

VIGOUROUX, Lawrence (G) **119** **0**
b.London 19-11-93
Internationals: Chile U20.

2012–13	Tottenham H	0	0		
2013–14	Tottenham H	0	0		
2015–16	Swindon T	33	0		
2016–17	Swindon T	43	0		
2017–18	Swindon T	14	0		
2018–19	Swindon T	29	0	**119**	**0**

WOOLERY, Kaiyne (F) **91** **12**
H: 5 10 W: 11 07 b.Hackney 11-1-95

2014–15	Bolton W	1	0		
2014–15	*Notts Co*	5	0	**5**	**0**
2015–16	Bolton W	17	2		
2016–17	Bolton W	1	0	**19**	**2**
2016–17	Wigan Ath	1	0	**1**	**0**
2017–18	Swindon T	37	4		
2018–19	Swindon T	29	6	**66**	**10**

WOOLFENDEN, Luke (D) **35** **2**
b.Ipswich 21-10-98

2017–18	Ipswich T	2	0		
2018–19	Ipswich T	1	0	**3**	**0**
2018–19	*Forest Green R*	0	0		
2018–19	Swindon T	32	2	**32**	**2**

YOUNG, Jordan (F) **5** **1**
b. 31-7-99

2015–16	Swindon T	3	1		
2016–17	Swindon T	2	0		
2017–18	Swindon T	0	0		
2018–19	Swindon T	0	0	**5**	**1**

Scholars
Atik, Teoman Edward; Blackwell, Joe Anthony; Cheshire, Anthony Alexander; Dugan, Elliott Lucas; Dunstan-Digweed, Jay; Giamattei, Massimo William; Graham, Ralph Cornelius; Haines, Luke Ryan; Haynes, Sonny; Holland, Toby Steven; Matthews, Archie Cameron; McLeod, Bancroft Jacob Elijah; Smith, Samuel Luca; Stanley, Harry; Suter, Thomas Raymond; Taylor, Joshua James; Wells, Rhys Jay.

TOTTENHAM H (83)

ALDERWEIRELD, Toby (D) **281** **14**
H: 6 1 W: 11 11 b.Wilrijk 2-3-89
Internationals: Belgium U26, U17, U18, U19, U21, Full caps.

2008–09	Ajax	5	0		
2009–10	Ajax	31	2		
2010–11	Ajax	26	2		
2011–12	Ajax	29	1		
2012–13	Ajax	32	2		
2013–14	Ajax	4	0	**127**	**7**
2013–14	Atletico Madrid	12	1	**12**	**1**
2014–15	Southampton	26	1	**26**	**1**
2015–16	Tottenham H	38	4		
2016–17	Tottenham H	30	1		
2017–18	Tottenham H	14	0		
2018–19	Tottenham H	34	0	**116**	**5**

ALLI, Bamidele (M) **203** **64**
H: 6 1 W: 11 12 b.Watford 11-4-96
Internationals: England U17, U18, U19, U21, Full caps.

2012–13	Milton Keynes D	0	0		
2013–14	Milton Keynes D	33	6		
2014–15	Milton Keynes D	39	16	**72**	**22**
2015–16	Tottenham H	33	10		
2016–17	Tottenham H	37	18		
2017–18	Tottenham H	36	9		
2018–19	Tottenham H	25	5	**131**	**42**

AMOS, Luke (M) **20** **2**
H: 5 10 W: 11 00 b.Hatfield 23-2-97
Internationals: England U18.

2016–17	Tottenham H	0	0		
2016–17	*Southend U*	3	0	**3**	**0**
2017–18	Tottenham H	0	0		
2017–18	*Stevenage*	16	2	**16**	**2**
2018–19	Tottenham H	1	0	**1**	**0**

AURIER, Serge (D) **201** **12**
H: 5 9 W: 11 11 b.Paris 24-12-92
Internationals: Ivory Coast Full caps.

2009–10	Lens	5	0		
2010–11	Lens	26	0		
2011–12	Lens	16	0	**47**	**0**
2011–12	Toulouse	10	1		
2012–13	Toulouse	28	1		
2013–14	Toulouse	34	6		
2014–15	Toulouse	0	0	**72**	**8**
2014–15	Paris Saint-Germain	14	0		
2015–16	Paris Saint-Germain	21	2		
2016–17	Paris Saint-Germain	22	0	**57**	**2**
2017–18	PSG	0	0		
2017–18	Tottenham H	17	2		
2018–19	Tottenham H	8	0	**25**	**2**

DAVIES, Ben (D) **181** **6**
H: 5 7 W: 12 00 b.Neath 24-4-93
Internationals: Wales U19, Full caps.

2011–12	Swansea C	0	0		
2012–13	Swansea C	37	1		
2013–14	Swansea C	34	2	**71**	**3**
2014–15	Tottenham H	14	0		
2015–16	Tottenham H	17	0		
2016–17	Tottenham H	23	1		
2017–18	Tottenham H	29	2		
2018–19	Tottenham H	27	0	**110**	**3**

DEMBELE, Mousa (M) **414** **46**
H: 5 9 W: 10 01 b.Wilrijk 17-7-87
Internationals: Belgium U16, U17, U18, U19, Full caps.

2003–04	Beerschot	1	0		
2004–05	Beerschot	19	1	**20**	**1**
2005–06	Willem II	33	9	**33**	**9**
2006–07	AZ	33	6		
2007–08	AZ	33	4		
2008–09	AZ	23	10		
2009–10	AZ	29	4	**118**	**24**
2010–11	Fulham	24	3		
2011–12	Fulham	36	2		
2012–13	Fulham	2	0	**62**	**5**
2012–13	Tottenham H	30	1		
2013–14	Tottenham H	28	1		
2014–15	Tottenham H	26	1		
2015–16	Tottenham H	29	3		
2016–17	Tottenham H	30	1		
2017–18	Tottenham H	28	0		
2018–19	Tottenham H	10	0	**181**	**7**

Transferred to Guangzhou R&F January 2019.

DIER, Eric (D) **182** **11**
H: 6 3 W: 13 08 b.Cheltenham 15-1-94
Internationals: England U18, U19, U20, U21, Full caps.

2012–13	Sporting Lisbon	14	1		
2013–14	Sporting Lisbon	13	0	**27**	**1**
2014–15	Tottenham H	28	2		
2015–16	Tottenham H	37	3		
2016–17	Tottenham H	36	2		
2017–18	Tottenham H	34	0		
2018–19	Tottenham H	20	3	**155**	**10**

ERIKSEN, Christian (M) **319** **74**
H: 5 9 W: 10 02 b.Middelfart 14-2-92
Internationals: Denmark U17, U18, U19, U21, Full caps.

2009–10	Ajax	15	0		
2010–11	Ajax	28	6		
2011–12	Ajax	33	7		
2012–13	Ajax	33	10		
2013–14	Ajax	4	2	**113**	**25**
2013–14	Tottenham H	25	7		
2014–15	Tottenham H	38	10		
2015–16	Tottenham H	35	6		
2016–17	Tottenham H	36	8		
2017–18	Tottenham H	37	10		
2018–19	Tottenham H	35	8	**206**	**49**

EYOMA, Timothy (D) **0** **0**
H: 6 1 W: 11 11 b.Hackney 29-1-00
Internationals: England U16, U17, U18, U19.

2018–19	Tottenham H	0	0		

FOYTH, Juan (D) **19** **1**
H: 5 10 W: 10 12 b.La Plata 12-1-98
Internationals: Argentina U20, Full caps.

2017	Estudiantes	7	0		
2017–18	Estudiantes	0	0	**7**	**0**
2017–18	Tottenham H	0	0		
2018–19	Tottenham H	12	1	**12**	**1**

GAZZANIGA, Paulo (G) **77** **0**
H: 6 5 W: 14 02 b.Santa Fe 2-1-92
Internationals: Argentina Full caps.

2011–12	Gillingham	20	0	**20**	**0**
2012–13	Southampton	9	0		
2013–14	Southampton	8	0		
2014–15	Southampton	2	0		
2015–16	Southampton	2	0		
2016–17	Southampton	0	0	**21**	**0**
2016–17	*Rayo Vallecano*	32	0	**32**	**0**
2017–18	Tottenham H	1	0		
2018–19	Tottenham H	3	0	**4**	**0**

JANSSEN, Vincent (F) **149** **62**
H: 5 11 W: 12 06 b.Heesch 15-6-94
Internationals: Netherlands U16, U18, U20, U21, Full caps.

2013–14	Almere C	35	10		
2014–15	Almere C	34	19	**69**	**29**
2015–16	AZ Alkmaar	34	27	**34**	**27**
2016–17	Tottenham H	27	2		
2017–18	Tottenham H	1	0		
2017–18	*Fenerbahce*	15	4	**15**	**4**
2018–19	Tottenham H	3	0	**31**	**2**

KANE, Harry (F) **234** **139**
H: 6 0 W: 10 00 b.Chingford 28-7-93
Internationals: England U17, U19, U20, U21, Full caps.

2010–11	Tottenham H	0	0		
2010–11	*Leyton Orient*	18	5	**18**	**5**
2011–12	Tottenham H	0	0		
2011–12	*Millwall*	22	7	**22**	**7**
2012–13	Tottenham H	1	0		
2012–13	*Norwich C*	3	0	**3**	**0**
2012–13	*Leicester C*	13	2	**13**	**2**
2013–14	Tottenham H	10	3		
2014–15	Tottenham H	34	21		
2015–16	Tottenham H	38	25		
2016–17	Tottenham H	30	29		
2017–18	Tottenham H	37	30		
2018–19	Tottenham H	28	17	**178**	**125**

LAMELA, Erik (F) **224 37**
H: 6 0 W: 10 13 b.Buenos Aires 4-3-92
Internationals: Argentina U20, Full caps.

2008–09	River Plate	1	0		
2009–10	River Plate	1	0		
2010–11	River Plate	32	4	**34**	**4**
2011–12	Roma	29	4		
2012–13	Roma	32	15	**61**	**19**
2013–14	Tottenham H	9	0		
2014–15	Tottenham H	33	2		
2015–16	Tottenham H	34	5		
2016–17	Tottenham H	9	1		
2017–18	Tottenham H	25	2		
2018–19	Tottenham H	19	4	**129**	**14**

LLORENTE, Fernando (F) **453 141**
H: 6 4 W: 13 12 b.Pamplona 26-2-85
Internationals: Spain U17, U20, U21, Full caps.

2003–04	Basconia	33	12	**33**	**12**
2004–05	Atletico Bilbao	15	3		
2005–06	Atletico Bilbao	22	2		
2006–07	Atletico Bilbao	23	2		
2007–08	Atletico Bilbao	35	11		
2008–09	Atletico Bilbao	34	14		
2009–10	Atletico Bilbao	37	14		
2010–11	Atletico Bilbao	38	18		
2011–12	Atletico Bilbao	32	17		
2012–13	Atletico Bilbao	26	4	**262**	**85**
2013–14	Juventus	34	16		
2014–15	Juventus	31	7		
2015–16	Juventus	1	0	**66**	**23**
2015–16	Sevilla	23	4	**23**	**4**
2016–17	Swansea C	33	15		
2017–18	Swansea C	0	0	**33**	**15**
2017–18	Tottenham H	16	1		
2018–19	Tottenham H	20	1	**36**	**2**

LLORIS, Hugo (G) **457 0**
H: 6 2 W: 12 03 b.Nice 26-12-86
Internationals: France U18, U19, U20, U21, Full caps.

2005–06	Nice	5	0		
2006–07	Nice	37	0		
2007–08	Nice	30	0	**72**	**0**
2008–09	Lyon	35	0		
2009–10	Lyon	36	0		
2010–11	Lyon	37	0		
2011–12	Lyon	36	0		
2012–13	Lyon	2	0	**146**	**0**
2012–13	Tottenham H	27	0		
2013–14	Tottenham H	37	0		
2014–15	Tottenham H	35	0		
2015–16	Tottenham H	37	0		
2016–17	Tottenham H	34	0		
2017–18	Tottenham H	36	0		
2018–19	Tottenham H	33	0	**239**	**0**

LUCAS MOURA, Rodrigues (M) **265 63**
H: 5 8 W: 10 06 b.Sao Paulo 13-8-92
Internationals: Brazil U20, U23, Full caps.

2010	Sao Paulo	25	4		
2011	Sao Paulo	28	9		
2012	Sao Paulo	21	6	**74**	**19**
2012–13	Paris Saint-Germain	10	0		
2013–14	Paris Saint-Germain	36	5		
2014–15	Paris Saint-Germain	29	7		
2015–16	Paris Saint-Germain	36	9		
2016–17	Paris Saint-Germain	37	12		
2017–18	Paris Saint-Germain	5	1	**153**	**34**
2017–18	Tottenham H	6	0		
2018–19	Tottenham H	32	10	**38**	**10**

MARSH, George (M) **0 0**
b.Penbury 5-11-98

2018–19	Tottenham H	0	0		

NKOUDOU, Georges (M) **83 39**
b. 13-2-95
Internationals: France U17, U19, U20, U21.

2013–14	Nantes	6	1		
2014–15	Nantes	28	16	**34**	**17**
2015–16	Marseilles	28	22	**28**	**22**
2016–17	Marseille	0	0		
2016–17	Tottenham H	8	0		
2017–18	Tottenham H	1	0		
2017–18	*Burnley*	8	0	**8**	**0**
2018–19	Tottenham H	1	0	**10**	**0**
2018–19	*Monaco*	3	0	**3**	**0**

OGILVIE, Connor (D) **107 2**
H: 6 0 W: 12 08 b.Harlow 14-2-96
Internationals: England U16, U17.

2013–14	Tottenham H	0	0		
2014–15	Tottenham H	0	0		
2015–16	Tottenham H	0	0		
2015–16	*Stevenage*	21	1		
2016–17	Tottenham H	0	0		
2016–17	*Stevenage*	18	0	**39**	**1**
2017–18	Tottenham H	0	0		
2017–18	*Gillingham*	37	1		
2018–19	Tottenham H	0	0		
2018–19	*Gillingham*	31	0	**68**	**1**

ONOMAH, Joshua (M) **61 4**
H: 5 11 W: 10 01 b.Enfield 27-4-97
Internationals: England U16, U17, U18, U19, U20, U21.

2013–14	Tottenham H	0	0		
2014–15	Tottenham H	0	0		
2015–16	Tottenham H	8	0		
2016–17	Tottenham H	5	0		
2017–18	Tottenham H	0	0		
2017–18	*Aston Villa*	33	4	**33**	**4**
2018–19	Tottenham H	0	0	**13**	**0**
2018–19	*Sheffield W*	15	0	**15**	**0**

ROSE, Danny (M) **195 9**
H: 5 8 W: 11 11 b.Doncaster 2-6-90
Internationals: England U17, U19, U21, Full caps. Great Britain.

2007–08	Tottenham H	0	0		
2008–09	Tottenham H	0	0		
2008–09	*Watford*	7	0	**7**	**0**
2009–10	Tottenham H	1	1		
2010–11	Tottenham H	4	0		
2010–11	*Bristol C*	17	0	**17**	**0**
2011–12	Tottenham H	11	0		
2012–13	Tottenham H	0	0		
2012–13	*Sunderland*	27	1	**27**	**1**
2013–14	Tottenham H	22	1		
2014–15	Tottenham H	28	3		
2015–16	Tottenham H	24	1		
2016–17	Tottenham H	18	2		
2017–18	Tottenham H	10	0		
2018–19	Tottenham H	26	0	**144**	**8**

SANCHEZ, Davinson (D) **104 7**
H: 6 2 W: 13 01 b.Caloto 12-6-96
Internationals: Columbia U17, U20, U23, Full caps.

2013	Atletico Nacional	2	0		
2014	Atletico Nacional	1	0		
2015	Atletico Nacional	5	0		
2016	Atletico Nacional	10	0	**18**	**0**
2016–17	Ajax	32	6		
2017–18	Ajax	0	0	**32**	**6**
2017–18	Tottenham H	31	0		
2018–19	Tottenham H	23	1	**54**	**1**

SISSOKO, Moussa (M) **395 32**
H: 6 2 W: 13 00 b.Le Blanc Mesnil 16-8-89
Internationals: France U16, U17, U18, U19, U21, Full caps.

2007–08	Toulouse	29	1		
2008–09	Toulouse	35	4		
2009–10	Toulouse	37	7		
2010–11	Toulouse	35	5		
2011–12	Toulouse	35	2		
2012–13	Toulouse	19	1	**190**	**20**
2012–13	Newcastle U	12	3		
2013–14	Newcastle U	35	3		
2014–15	Newcastle U	34	4		
2015–16	Newcastle U	37	1	**118**	**11**
2016–17	Tottenham H	25	0		
2017–18	Tottenham H	33	1		
2018–19	Tottenham H	29	0	**87**	**1**

SKIPP, Oliver (M) **8 0**
H: 5 9 W: 11 00 b.Hatfield 16-9-00
Internationals: England U16, U17, U18.

2018–19	Tottenham H	8	0	**8**	**0**

SON, Heung-Min (M) **265 83**
H: 6 0 W: 12 00 b.Chuncheon 8-7-92
Internationals: South Korea U17, U23, Full caps.

2010–11	Hamburg	13	3		
2011–12	Hamburg	27	5		
2012–13	Hamburg	33	12	**73**	**20**
2013–14	Bayer Leverkusen	31	10		
2014–15	Bayer Leverkusen	30	11		
2015–16	Bayer Leverkusen	1	0	**62**	**21**
2015–16	Tottenham H	28	4		
2016–17	Tottenham H	34	14		
2017–18	Tottenham H	37	12		
2018–19	Tottenham H	31	12	**130**	**42**

STERLING, Kazaiah (F) **8 1**
H: 5 9 W: 11 03 b.Enfield 9-11-98
Internationals: England U17, U18.
From Leyton Orient.

2017–18	Tottenham H	0	0		
2018–19	Tottenham H	0	0		
2018–19	*Sunderland*	8	1	**8**	**1**

TRIPPIER, Keiran (D) **281 8**
H: 5 10 W: 11 00 b.Bury 19-9-90
Internationals: England U18, U19, U20, U21, Full caps.

2007–08	Manchester C	0	0		
2008–09	Manchester C	0	0		
2009–10	Manchester C	0	0		
2009–10	*Barnsley*	3	0		
2010–11	Manchester C	0	0		
2010–11	*Barnsley*	39	2	**42**	**2**
2011–12	Manchester C	0	0		
2011–12	Burnley	46	3		
2012–13	Burnley	45	0		
2013–14	Burnley	41	1		
2014–15	Burnley	38	0	**170**	**4**
2015–16	Tottenham H	6	1		
2016–17	Tottenham H	12	0		
2017–18	Tottenham H	24	0		
2018–19	Tottenham H	27	1	**69**	**2**

VERTONGHEN, Jan (D) **376 31**
H: 6 2 W: 12 05 b.Sint-Niklaas 24-4-87
Internationals: Belgium U16, U21, Full caps.

2006–07	Ajax	3	0		
2006–07	*RKC*	12	3	**12**	**3**
2007–08	Ajax	31	2		
2008–09	Ajax	26	4		
2009–10	Ajax	32	3		
2010–11	Ajax	32	6		
2011–12	Ajax	31	8	**155**	**23**
2012–13	Tottenham H	34	4		
2013–14	Tottenham H	23	0		
2014–15	Tottenham H	32	0		
2015–16	Tottenham H	29	0		
2016–17	Tottenham H	33	0		
2017–18	Tottenham H	36	0		
2018–19	Tottenham H	22	1	**209**	**5**

VORM, Michel (G) **273 0**
H: 6 0 W: 13 03 b.Nieuwegein 20-10-83
Internationals: Netherlands Full caps.

2005–06	Den Bosch	35	0	**35**	**0**
2006–07	Utrecht	33	0		
2007–08	Utrecht	11	0		
2008–09	Utrecht	26	0		
2009–10	Utrecht	33	0		
2010–11	Utrecht	33	0	**136**	**0**
2011–12	Swansea C	37	0		
2012–13	Swansea C	26	0		
2013–14	Swansea C	26	0	**89**	**0**
2014–15	Tottenham H	4	0		
2015–16	Tottenham H	1	0		
2016–17	Tottenham H	5	0		
2017–18	Tottenham H	1	0		
2018–19	Tottenham H	2	0	**13**	**0**

WALKER-PETERS, Kyle (F) **9 0**
H: 5 8 W: 9 13 b.Edmonton 13-4-97
Internationals: England U18, U19, U20, U21.

2015–16	Tottenham H	0	0		
2016–17	Tottenham H	0	0		
2017–18	Tottenham H	3	0		
2018–19	Tottenham H	6	0	**9**	**0**

WANYAMA, Victor (M) **262 22**
H: 6 2 W: 11 12 b.Nairobi 25-6-91
Internationals: Kenya Full caps.

2009–10	Beerschot	19	0		
2010–11	Beerschot	30	2	**49**	**2**
2011–12	Celtic	29	4		
2012–13	Celtic	32	6	**61**	**10**
2013–14	Southampton	23	0		
2014–15	Southampton	32	3		
2015–16	Southampton	30	1	**85**	**4**
2016–17	Tottenham H	36	4		
2017–18	Tottenham H	18	1		
2018–19	Tottenham H	13	1	**67**	**6**

WHITEMAN, Alfie (G) **0 0**
b. 2-10-98
Internationals: England U16, U17, U18, U19.

2016–17	Tottenham H	0	0		
2017–18	Tottenham H	0	0		
2018–19	Tottenham H	0	0		

WINKS, Harry (M) **63 2**
H: 5 10 W: 10 03 b.Hemel Hempstead 2-2-96
Internationals: England U17, U18, U19, U20, U21, Full caps.

2013–14	Tottenham H	0	0		
2014–15	Tottenham H	0	0		
2015–16	Tottenham H	0	0		
2016–17	Tottenham H	21	1		
2017–18	Tottenham H	16	0		
2018–19	Tottenham H	26	1	**63**	**2**

Players retained or with offer of contract
Austin, Brandon Anthony; Bowden, Jamie Patrick; Carter-Vickers, Cameron; Clarke, Rayan Romario; De Bie, Jonathan; Dinzeyi, Jonathan Toko Lema; Edwards, Marcus; Etete, Kion Reece; Georgiou, Anthony Michael; Harrison, Shayon; Hinds, Tariq Devontae Aaron; Lyons-Foster, Brooklyn; Maghoma, Edmond-Paris; Markanday, Dilan Kumar; Mukendi, Jeremie; Oakley-Boothe, Tashan; Okedina, Jubril Adesope; Parrott, Troy Daniel; Patterson, Phoenix MacLaren; Pochettino Grippaldi, Maurizio; Richards, Rodel Kurai; Roles, Jack; Shashoua, Armando; Shashoua, Samuel; Statham, Maxwell Louis; Tainio, Maximus Mikael; Tanganga, Japhet Manzambi; Thorpe, Elliot Morgan; Tracey, Shilow; White, Harvey David.

Scholars
Asante, Enock Amponsah; Bennett, J'Neil Lloyd; Binks, Luis Thomas; Cirkin, Dennis; Cooper, Chay; Fagan-Walcott, Malachi Michael; Kurylowicz, Kacper; Oluwayemi, Oluwaferanmi Joshua.

TRANMERE R (84)

AKAMMADU, Franklyn (F) 6 0
b. 11-8-98
2016–17 Cesena 1 0
2017–18 Cesena 0 0 1 0
2017–18 *Prato* 0 0
2017–18 *Fermana* 4 0 4 0
2018–19 Alessandria 0 0
On loan from Alessandria.
2018–19 Tranmere R 1 0 1 0

BAKAYOGO, Zaoumana (D) 259 6
H: 5 9 W: 10 08 b.Paris 11-8-86
Internationals: Ivory Coast U23.
2006–07 Millwall 5 0
2007–08 Millwall 10 0 15 0
From Alfortville.
2009–10 Tranmere R 29 0
2010–11 Tranmere R 27 1
2011–12 Tranmere R 26 0
2012–13 Tranmere R 46 4
2013–14 Leicester C 0 0
2013–14 *Yeovil T* 1 0 1 0
2015–16 Crewe Alex 22 1
2016–17 Crewe Alex 40 0
2017–18 Crewe Alex 32 0 94 1
2018–19 Tranmere R 21 0 149 5

BANKS, Oliver (D) 175 18
H: 6 3 W: 11 11 b.Rotherham 21-9-92
2010–11 Rotherham U 1 1
2011–12 Rotherham U 0 0 1 1
2013–14 Chesterfield 25 7
2014–15 Chesterfield 24 0
2014–15 *Northampton T* 3 0 3 0
2015–16 Chesterfield 32 2 81 9
2016–17 Oldham Ath 33 2
2017–18 Oldham Ath 7 0 40 2
2017–18 *Swindon T* 17 3 17 3
2018–19 Tranmere R 33 3 33 3

BUXTON, Adam (D) 72 3
H: 6 1 W: 12 10 b.Liverpool 12-5-92
2010–11 Wigan Ath 0 0
2011–12 Wigan Ath 0 0
2012–13 Wigan Ath 0 0
2013–14 Wigan Ath 0 0
2013–14 *Burton Alb* 0 0
2013–14 *Accrington S* 11 0
2014–15 Accrington S 17 1
2015–16 Accrington S 28 1 56 2
2016–17 Portsmouth 0 0
2018–19 Tranmere R 16 1 16 1

CAPRICE, Jake (M) 55 0
H: 5 10 W: 11 07 b.Lambeth 11-11-92
2011–12 Crystal Palace 0 0
2012–13 Blackpool 0 0
2012–13 *Dagenham & R* 8 0 8 0
2013–14 Blackpool 0 0
2013–14 *St Mirren* 6 0 6 0
From Lincoln C, Woking, Leyton Orient.
2018–19 Tranmere R 41 0 41 0

COLE, Larnell (M) 64 4
H: 5 4 W: 12 04 b.Manchester 9-3-93
Internationals: England U19, U20.
2011–12 Manchester U 0 0
2012–13 Manchester U 0 0
2013–14 Manchester U 0 0
2013–14 Fulham 1 0
2013–14 *Milton Keynes D* 3 0 3 0
2014–15 Fulham 0 0
2015–16 Fulham 0 0
2015–16 *Shrewsbury T* 29 3 29 3
2016–17 Fulham 0 0 1 0
2016–17 *Inverness CT* 21 1 21 1
2018–19 Tranmere R 10 0 10 0

DAGNALL, Chris (F) 475 118
H: 5 8 W: 12 03 b.Liverpool 15-4-86
2003–04 Tranmere R 10 1
2004–05 Tranmere R 23 6
2005–06 Tranmere R 6 0
2005–06 Rochdale 21 3
2006–07 Rochdale 37 17
2007–08 Rochdale 14 7
2008–09 Rochdale 40 7
2009–10 Rochdale 45 20 157 54
2010–11 Scunthorpe U 37 5
2011–12 Scunthorpe U 23 4 60 9
2011–12 Barnsley 9 0
2011–12 *Bradford C* 7 1 7 1
2012–13 Barnsley 36 5
2013–14 Barnsley 8 1 53 6
2013–14 *Coventry C* 6 1 6 1
2013–14 Leyton Orient 20 6
2014–15 Leyton Orient 38 11 58 17
2015–16 Kerala Blasters 0 0
2015–16 Hibernian 0 0
2016–17 Crewe Alex 41 14
2017–18 Crewe Alex 32 7 73 21
2018–19 Bury 17 2 17 2
2018–19 Tranmere R 5 0 44 7

DAVIES, Scott (G) 159 0
H: 6 0 W: 10 13 b.Blackpool 27-2-87
2007–08 Morecambe 10 0
2008–09 Morecambe 0 0
2009–10 Morecambe 1 0
2012–13 Fleetwood T 45 0
2013–14 Fleetwood T 28 0
2014–15 Fleetwood T 0 0 73 0
2014–15 *Morecambe* 10 0 21 0
2014–15 *Accrington S* 19 0 19 0
2018–19 Tranmere R 46 0 46 0

DEVINE, Jay (M) 0 0
b. 26-7-99
2018–19 Tranmere R 0 0

ELLIS, Mark (D) 296 19
H: 6 2 W: 12 04 b.Kingsbridge 30-9-88
2007–08 Bolton W 0 0
2009–10 Torquay U 27 3
2010–11 Torquay U 27 2
2011–12 Torquay U 35 3 89 8
2012–13 Crewe Alex 44 5
2013–14 Crewe Alex 37 1 81 6
2014–15 Shrewsbury T 32 2
2015–16 Shrewsbury T 9 1 41 3
2015–16 Carlisle U 30 0
2016–17 Carlisle U 7 0
2017–18 Carlisle U 23 2 60 2
2018–19 Tranmere R 25 0 25 0

GEORGE, Shamal (G) 4 0
b.Wirral 6-1-98
2017–18 Liverpool 0 0
2017–18 *Carlisle U* 4 0 4 0
2018–19 Tranmere R 0 0

GILMOUR, Harvey (M) 22 3
b. 15-12-98
2016–17 Sheffield U 0 0
2018–19 Tranmere R 22 3 22 3

GUMBS, Evan (M) 2 0
H: 5 10 W: 12 00 b.Runcorn 21-7-97
2014–15 Tranmere R 1 0
2018–19 Tranmere R 1 0 2 0

HARRIS, Jay (M) 21 1
H: 5 7 W: 11 07 b.Liverpool 15-4-87
From Accrington S, Chester C, Wrexham.
2018–19 Tranmere R 21 1 21 1

JENNINGS, Connor (F) 61 8
H: 6 0 W: 12 00 b.Manchester 21-1-91
Internationals: England C.
2011–12 Scunthorpe U 4 0
2012–13 Scunthorpe U 12 0
2013–14 Scunthorpe U 0 0 16 0
From Wrexham.
2018–19 Tranmere R 45 8 45 8

LONG, Nick (D) 0 0
2018–19 Tranmere R 0 0

McNULTY, Steve (D) 94 2
H: 6 1 W: 13 11 b.Liverpool 26-9-83
2012–13 Fleetwood T 16 2 16 2
2014–15 Luton T 41 0
2015–16 Luton T 10 0 51 0
2018–19 Tranmere R 27 0 27 0

MILLER, Ishmael (F) 245 43
H: 6 3 W: 14 00 b.Manchester 5-3-87
2005–06 Manchester C 1 0
2006–07 Manchester C 16 0
2007–08 Manchester C 0 0 17 0
2007–08 WBA 34 9
2008–09 WBA 15 3
2009–10 WBA 15 2
2010–11 WBA 6 0 70 14
2010–11 *QPR* 12 1 12 1
2011–12 Nottingham F 21 3
2012–13 Nottingham F 0 0
2012–13 *Middlesbrough* 25 5 25 5
2013–14 Nottingham F 4 0 25 3
2013–14 *Yeovil T* 19 10 19 10
2014–15 Blackpool 22 2 22 2
2014–15 Huddersfield T 16 3
2015–16 Huddersfield T 18 1 34 4
2016–17 Bury 3 0 3 0
2018–19 Oldham Ath 16 3 16 3
2018–19 Tranmere R 2 1 2 1

MONTHE, Emmanuel (D) 56 2
H: 6 0 W: 12 08 b. 26-1-95
2013–14 QPR 0 0
From Southport, Whitehawk, Hayes & Yeading, Havant & Waterford, Bath C.
2017–18 Forest Green R 13 0 13 0
2018–19 Tranmere R 43 2 43 2

MULLIN, Paul (F) 184 36
H: 5 10 W: 11 01 b. 6-11-94
2013–14 Huddersfield T 0 0
2014–15 Morecambe 42 8
2015–16 Morecambe 40 9
2016–17 Morecambe 40 8 122 25
2017–18 Swindon T 40 6 40 6
2018–19 Tranmere R 22 5 22 5

NORWOOD, James (F) 49 29
H: 6 0 W: 12 13 b.Eastbourne 5-9-90
Internationals: England U18, C.
2009–10 Exeter C 3 0
2010–11 Exeter C 1 0 4 0
From Forest Green R.
2018–19 Tranmere R 45 29 45 29

NUGENT, George (M) 0 0
2018–19 Tranmere R 0 0

PASSANT, Bailey (G) 0 0
2018–19 Tranmere R 0 0

PERKINS, David (D) 447 17
H: 5 6 W: 11 06 b.Heysham 21-6-82
Internationals: England C.
2006–07 Rochdale 18 0
2007–08 Rochdale 40 4
2008–09 Colchester U 38 5
2009–10 Colchester U 5 1
2009–10 *Chesterfield* 13 1 13 1
2009–10 *Stockport Co* 22 0 22 0
2010–11 Colchester U 36 1 79 7
2011–12 Barnsley 33 1
2012–13 Barnsley 35 1
2013–14 Barnsley 23 0 91 2
2013–14 Blackpool 20 0
2014–15 Blackpool 45 0 65 0
2015–16 Wigan Ath 45 0
2016–17 Wigan Ath 27 0
2017–18 Wigan Ath 13 1 85 1
2018–19 Rochdale 17 0 75 4
2018–19 Tranmere R 17 2 17 2

PILLING, Luke (G) 0 0
b. 25-7-97
Internationals: Wales U17, U21.
2013–14 Tranmere R 0 0
2014–15 Tranmere R 0 0
2018–19 Tranmere R 0 0

RIDEHALGH, Liam (D) 157 2
H: 5 10 W: 11 05 b.Halifax 20-4-91
2009–10 Huddersfield T 0 0
2010–11 Huddersfield T 20 0
2011–12 Huddersfield T 0 0
2011–12 *Swindon T* 11 0 11 0
2011–12 *Chesterfield* 20 1
2012–13 Huddersfield T 0 0

2012–13 *Chesterfield* 14 0 **34 1**
2012–13 *Rotherham U* 20 0 **20 0**
2013–14 Huddersfield T 0 0 **20 0**
2013–14 *Tranmere R* 36 1
2014–15 Tranmere R 18 0
2018–19 Tranmere R 18 0 **72 1**

SPELLMAN, Carl (M) 0 0
2018–19 Tranmere R 0 0

STOCKTON, Cole (F) 141 27
H: 6 1 W: 11 11 b.Huyton 13-3-94
2011–12 Tranmere R 1 0
2012–13 Tranmere R 31 3
2013–14 Tranmere R 21 2
2014–15 Tranmere R 22 4
2015–16 Tranmere R 0 0
2015–16 *Morecambe* 7 2
2016–17 Tranmere R 0 0
2016–17 *Morecambe* 19 5 **26 7**
2017–18 Hearts 12 9 **12 9**
2017–18 Carlisle U 12 1 **12 1**
2018–19 Tranmere R 16 1 **91 10**

TOLLITT, Ben (M) 16 1
b. 30-11-94
2015–16 Portsmouth 12 1
2016–17 Portsmouth 0 0 **12 1**
2018–19 Tranmere R 4 0 **4 0**

WALKER-RICE, Danny (F) 0 0
2018–19 Tranmere R 0 0

WHARTON, Patrick (G) 0 0
2018–19 Tranmere R 0 0

WILLIAMS, Ryan (F) 82 8
H: 5 8 W: 10 09 b.Birkenhead 8-4-91
2012–13 Morecambe 16 2
2013–14 Morecambe 25 3
2014–15 Morecambe 12 0 **53 5**
2015–16 Brentford 0 0
2015–16 Inverness CT 8 0 **8 0**
2016 Ottawa Fury 4 0
2017 Ottawa Fury 16 3 **20 3**
2018 Paysandu 1 0 **1 0**
2018–19 Tranmere R 0 0

Scholars
Bickerstaffe, Joseph; Blackham, Joe; Burton, Jake Joshua; Corness, Nathan; Hayde, Kyle William; Kerr, Ben; Long, Nicholas; Moreton, Matthew George; Musuamba, Harrison; Nugent, George Thomas; Passant, Bayleigh; Salkeld, James Dillon; Sinnott, Lewis Robert; Spellman, Carl John; Thompson, Bailey Lewis; Walker, Daniel Joseph.

WALSALL (85)

BATES, Alfie (M) 0 0
2018–19 Walsall 0 0

CANDLIN, Mitchell (F) 8 0
H: 6 0 W: 11 09 b. 8-6-00
2016–17 Walsall 5 0
2017–18 Walsall 3 0
2018–19 Walsall 0 0 **8 0**
2018–19 *Blackburn R* 0 0

CHAMBERS, Adam (D) 531 12
H: 5 10 W: 11 12 b.Sandwell 20-11-80
1998–99 WBA 0 0
1999–2000 WBA 0 0
2000–01 WBA 11 1
2001–02 WBA 32 0
2002–03 WBA 13 0
2003–04 WBA 0 0
2003–04 *Sheffield W* 11 0 **11 0**
2004–05 WBA 0 0 **56 1**
2004–05 Kidderminster H 2 0 **2 0**
2006–07 Leyton Orient 38 4
2007–08 Leyton Orient 45 3
2008–09 Leyton Orient 33 1
2009–10 Leyton Orient 29 1
2010–11 Leyton Orient 29 0 **174 9**
2011–12 Walsall 29 2
2012–13 Walsall 37 0
2013–14 Walsall 45 0
2014–15 Walsall 45 0
2015–16 Walsall 45 0
2016–17 Walsall 43 0
2017–18 Walsall 43 0
2018–19 Walsall 1 0 **288 2**

COCKERILL-MOLLETT, Callum (D) 1 0
H: 5 10 W: 11 00 b. 15-1-99
Internationals: Republic of Ireland U17, U19.
2016–17 Walsall 0 0
2017–18 Walsall 1 0
2018–19 Walsall 0 0 **1 0**

COOK, Andy (F) 43 13
H: 6 0 W: 11 03 b.Bishop Auckland 18-10-90
Internationals: England C.
2018–19 Walsall 43 13 **43 13**

DEVLIN, Nicky (D) 263 5
H: 5 10 W: 11 07 b.Glasgow 17-10-93
Internationals: Scotland U19.
2010–11 Dumbarton 23 0
2011–12 Motherwell 0 0
2011–12 *Stenhousemuir* 6 0
2012–13 Motherwell 0 0
2012–13 *Dumbarton* 16 0 **39 0**
2012–13 *Stenhousemuir* 8 0
2013–14 Stenhousemuir 30 0 **44 0**
2014–15 Ayr U 36 2
2015–16 Ayr U 34 1
2016–17 Ayr U 34 0 **104 3**
2017–18 Walsall 33 0
2018–19 Walsall 43 2 **76 2**

DOBSON, George (M) 86 2
H: 6 1 b.Harold Wood 15-11-97
From Arsenal.
2015–16 West Ham U 0 0
2016–17 West Ham U 0 0
2016–17 *Walsall* 21 1
2017–18 Sparta Rotterdam 5 0 **5 0**
2017–18 Walsall 21 1
2018–19 Walsall 39 0 **81 2**

DUNN, Chris (G) 167 0
H: 6 5 W: 13 11 b.Brentwood 23-10-87
2006–07 Northampton T 0 0
2007–08 Northampton T 1 0
2008–09 Northampton T 29 0
2009–10 Northampton T 29 0
2010–11 Northampton T 39 0 **98 0**
2011–12 Coventry C 2 0
2012–13 Coventry C 1 0
2013–14 Coventry C 0 0 **3 0**
2013–14 Yeovil T 8 0 **8 0**
2014–15 Cambridge U 43 0
2015–16 Cambridge U 11 0 **54 0**
From Wrexham.
2018–19 Walsall 4 0 **4 0**

EDWARDS, Joe (D) 258 18
H: 5 8 W: 11 07 b.Gloucester 31-10-90
2009–10 Bristol C 0 0
2010–11 Bristol C 2 0
2011–12 Bristol C 2 0
2011–12 *Yeovil T* 4 1
2012–13 Bristol C 0 0 **4 0**
2012–13 Yeovil T 35 2
2013–14 Yeovil T 46 1
2014–15 Yeovil T 34 0 **119 4**
2015–16 Colchester U 42 2 **42 2**
2016–17 Walsall 43 3
2017–18 Walsall 30 7
2018–19 Walsall 20 2 **93 12**

FERRIER, Morgan (F) 33 5
H: 6 1 W: 12 08 b.London 15-11-94
Internationals: England C.
From Nottingham F, Crystal Palace, Bishop's Stortford, Hemel Hempstead T, Dagenham & R, Boreham Wood.
2018–19 Walsall 33 5 **33 5**

GORDON, Josh (F) 37 7
H: 5 10 W: 11 00 b.Stoke-on-Trent 19-1-95
From Stafford Rangers.
2017–18 Leicester C 0 0
2018–19 Walsall 37 7 **37 7**

GUTHRIE, Jon (D) 210 4
H: 5 10 W: 11 00 b.Devizes 1-2-93
2011–12 Crewe Alex 0 0
2012–13 Crewe Alex 2 0
2013–14 Crewe Alex 23 0
2014–15 Crewe Alex 25 0
2015–16 Crewe Alex 39 1
2016–17 Crewe Alex 33 0 **122 1**
2017–18 Walsall 46 1
2018–19 Walsall 42 2 **88 3**

HAYLES-DOCHERTY, Tobias (F) 1 0
b. 30-1-99
2016–17 Walsall 1 0
2017–18 Walsall 0 0
2018–19 Walsall 0 0 **1 0**

ISMAIL, Zeli (M) 149 15
H: 5 8 W: 11 12 b.Kukes 12-12-93
Internationals: England U16, U17.
2010–11 Wolverhampton W 0 0
2011–12 Wolverhampton W 0 0
2012–13 Wolverhampton W 0 0
2012–13 *Milton Keynes D* 7 0 **7 0**
2013–14 Wolverhampton W 9 0
2013–14 *Burton Alb* 15 3
2014–15 Wolverhampton W 0 0
2014–15 *Notts Co* 14 4 **14 4**
2015–16 Wolverhampton W 0 0 **9 0**
2015–16 *Burton Alb* 3 0 **18 3**
2015–16 *Oxford U* 5 0 **5 0**
2015–16 *Cambridge U* 11 1 **11 1**
2016–17 Bury 16 3
2017–18 Bury 21 0 **37 3**
2017–18 *Walsall* 16 1
2018–19 Walsall 32 3 **48 4**

KINSELLA, Liam (M) 69 1
b.Colchester 23-2-96
Internationals: Republic of Ireland U19, U21.
2013–14 Walsall 0 0
2014–15 Walsall 4 0
2015–16 Walsall 7 1
2016–17 Walsall 8 0
2017–18 Walsall 19 0
2018–19 Walsall 31 0 **69 1**

KOUHYAR, Maz (D) 21 1
H: 5 11 W: 10 12 b. 30-9-97
Internationals: Afghanistan Full caps.
2015–16 Walsall 0 0
2016–17 Walsall 6 0
2017–18 Walsall 15 1
2018–19 Walsall 0 0 **21 1**

LAIRD, Scott (D) 278 24
H: 5 11 W: 11 05 b.Taunton 15-5-88
Internationals: Scotland U16. England C.
2006–07 Plymouth Arg 0 0
2007–08 Plymouth Arg 0 0
2010–11 Stevenage 44 4
2011–12 Stevenage 46 8 **90 12**
2012–13 Preston NE 19 4
2013–14 Preston NE 34 1
2014–15 Preston NE 31 0 **84 5**
2015–16 Scunthorpe U 32 2
2016–17 Scunthorpe U 1 0 **33 2**
2016–17 *Walsall* 28 3
2017–18 Forest Green R 36 2
2018–19 Forest Green R 0 0 **36 2**
2018–19 Walsall 7 0 **35 3**

LEAHY, Luke (M) 217 16
H: 5 10 W: 11 07 b.Coventry 19-11-92
2012–13 Falkirk 8 1
2013–14 Falkirk 19 1
2014–15 Falkirk 33 3
2015–16 Falkirk 36 3
2016–17 Falkirk 31 3 **127 11**
2017–18 Walsall 46 2
2018–19 Walsall 44 3 **90 5**

McSKEANE, Alex (F) 0 0
2018–19 Walsall 0 0

MORRIS, Kieron (M) 157 16
H: 5 10 W: 11 01 b.Hereford 3-6-94
2012–13 Walsall 0 0
2013–14 Walsall 2 0
2014–15 Walsall 14 2
2015–16 Walsall 33 3
2016–17 Walsall 35 5
2017–18 Walsall 42 3
2018–19 Walsall 17 2 **143 15**
2018–19 *Tranmere R* 14 1 **14 1**

MUSSA, Omar (F) 1 0
H: 6 0 W: 12 00 b. 18-11-80
Internationals: Belgium U18.
From Mechelen.
2018–19 Walsall 1 0 **1 0**

NORMAN, Cameron (D) 16 0
H: 6 2 W: 11 09 b.Norwich 12-10-95
From Norwich C, Concord Rangers, Needham Market, King's Lynn T.
2018–19 Oxford U 7 0 **7 0**
2018–19 Walsall 9 0 **9 0**

OSBOURNE, Isaiah (M) 254 7
H: 6 2 W: 12 06 b.Birmingham 5-11-87
Internationals: England U16.
2005–06 Aston Villa 0 0

2006–07	Aston Villa	11	0		
2007–08	Aston Villa	8	0		
2008–09	Aston Villa	0	0		
2008–09	*Nottingham F*	8	0	**8**	**0**
2009–10	Aston Villa	0	0		
2009–10	*Middlesbrough*	9	0	**9**	**0**
2010–11	Aston Villa	0	0	**19**	**0**
2010–11	*Sheffield W*	10	0	**10**	**0**
2011–12	Hibernian	30	1	**30**	**1**
2012–13	Blackpool	28	1		
2013–14	Blackpool	24	1	**52**	**2**
2014–15	Scunthorpe U	28	0	**28**	**0**
2015–16	Walsall	0	0		
2016–17	Walsall	30	1		
2017–18	Forest Green R	36	0	**36**	**0**
2018–19	Walsall	32	3	**62**	**4**

OTEH, Aramide (F) 21 2
b.London 10-9-98
From Tottenham H.

2017–18	QPR	6	1		
2018–19	QPR	2	0	**8**	**1**
2018–19	Walsall	13	1	**13**	**1**

PARKER, Dylan (F) 0 0
From Stratford T.

2018–19	Walsall	0	0		

ROBERTS, Liam (G) 67 0
H: 6 0 W: 12 13 b.Walsall 24-11-94

2012–13	Walsall	0	0		
2013–14	Walsall	0	0		
2014–15	Walsall	0	0		
2015–16	Walsall	1	0		
2017–18	Walsall	24	0		
2018–19	Walsall	42	0	**67**	**0**

SANGHA, Jordan (M) 0 0
b. 4-1-98

2015–16	Walsall	0	0		
2016–17	Walsall	0	0		
2017–18	Walsall	0	0		
2018–19	Walsall	0	0		

SCARR, Dan (D) 39 2
b. 24-12-94
From Reddich U, Stourbridge.

2017–18	Birmingham C	0	0		
2017–18	*Wycombe W*	22	1	**22**	**1**
2018–19	Birmingham C	0	0		
2018–19	Walsall	17	1	**17**	**1**

SLINN, Joe (G) 0 0
b.Stoke-on-Trent 27-12-98

2018–19	Walsall	0	0		

VANN, Daniel (D) 0 0

2016–17	Walsall	0	0		
2017–18	Walsall	0	0		
2018–19	Walsall	0	0		

Scholars
Brown, Joseph Grant; Coogan, Danny Peter; Dawe, Ethan Bradley; Flanagan, Kian Jay; Friel, Benjamin Michael; Leak, Thomas John; Leivesley, Samuel James; Little, Luke Thomas; McSkeane, Alex Martin; Moss, Perry; Nolan, Owen Henry; Perry, Samuel Paul; Petrovics, Alex Arpad; Rogerson, Dominic James Philip; Ruddock, Tyreece; Walton, Jacob William; Walton, Jak James; Willis, Joseph.

WATFORD (86)

BRITOS, Miguel (D) 276 13
H: 6 2 W: 12 13 b.Montevideo 17-7-85

2005–06	Fenix	12	0	**12**	**0**
2006–07	Juventud	33	3	**33**	**3**
2007–08	Montevideo Wanderers	26	1	**26**	**1**
2008–09	Bologna	14	1		
2009–10	Bologna	23	0		
2010–11	Bologna	34	3	**71**	**4**
2011–12	Napoli	11	1		
2012–13	Napoli	22	0		
2013–14	Napoli	16	1		
2014–15	Napoli	19	1	**68**	**3**
2015–16	Watford	24	0		
2016–17	Watford	27	1		
2017–18	Watford	12	1		
2018–19	Watford	3	0	**66**	**2**

CAPOUE, Etienne (M) 324 23
H: 6 2 W: 11 10 b.Niort 11-7-88
Internationals: France U18, U19, U21, Full caps.

2006–07	Toulouse	0	0		
2007–08	Toulouse	5	0		
2008–09	Toulouse	32	1		
2009–10	Toulouse	33	0		
2010–11	Toulouse	37	2		
2011–12	Toulouse	33	3		
2012–13	Toulouse	34	7	**174**	**13**
2013–14	Tottenham H	12	1		
2014–15	Tottenham H	12	0	**24**	**1**
2015–16	Watford	33	0		
2016–17	Watford	37	7		
2017–18	Watford	23	1		
2018–19	Watford	33	1	**126**	**9**

CATHCART, Craig (D) 290 13
H: 6 2 W: 11 06 b.Belfast 6-2-89
Internationals: Northern Ireland U16, U17, U20, U21, Full caps.

2005–06	Manchester U	0	0		
2006–07	Manchester U	0	0		
2007–08	Manchester U	0	0		
2007–08	*Antwerp*	13	2	**13**	**2**
2008–09	Manchester U	0	0		
2008–09	*Plymouth Arg*	31	1	**31**	**1**
2009–10	Manchester U	0	0		
2009–10	*Watford*	12	0		
2010–11	Blackpool	30	1		
2011–12	Blackpool	27	0		
2012–13	Blackpool	25	1		
2013–14	Blackpool	30	1	**112**	**3**
2014–15	Watford	29	3		
2015–16	Watford	35	1		
2016–17	Watford	15	0		
2017–18	Watford	7	0		
2018–19	Watford	36	3	**134**	**7**

CHALOBAH, Nathaniel (D) 118 9
H: 6 1 W: 11 11 b.Sierra Leone 12-12-94
Internationals: England U16, U17, U19, U20, U21, Full caps.

2010–11	Chelsea	0	0		
2011–12	Chelsea	0	0		
2012–13	Chelsea	0	0		
2012–13	*Watford*	38	5		
2013–14	Chelsea	0	0		
2013–14	*Nottingham F*	12	2	**12**	**2**
2013–14	*Middlesbrough*	19	1	**19**	**1**
2014–15	Chelsea	0	0		
2014–15	*Burnley*	4	0	**4**	**0**
2014–15	*Reading*	15	1	**15**	**1**
2015–16	Chelsea	0	0		
2015–16	*Napoli*	5	0	**5**	**0**
2016–17	Chelsea	10	0	**10**	**0**
2017–18	Watford	6	0		
2018–19	Watford	9	0	**53**	**5**

CLEVERLEY, Tom (M) 244 26
H: 5 9 W: 10 07 b.Basingstoke 12-8-89
Internationals: England U20, U21, Full caps. Great Britain.

2007–08	Manchester U	0	0		
2008–09	Manchester U	0	0		
2008–09	*Leicester C*	15	2	**15**	**2**
2009–10	Manchester U	0	0		
2009–10	*Watford*	33	11		
2010–11	Manchester U	0	0		
2010–11	*Wigan Ath*	25	3	**25**	**3**
2011–12	Manchester U	10	0		
2012–13	Manchester U	22	2		
2013–14	Manchester U	22	1		
2014–15	Manchester U	1	0	**55**	**3**
2014–15	*Aston Villa*	31	3	**31**	**3**
2015–16	Everton	22	2		
2016–17	Everton	10	0	**32**	**2**
2016–17	*Watford*	17	0		
2017–18	Watford	23	1		
2018–19	Watford	13	1	**86**	**13**

DAHLBERG, Pontus (G) 39 0
H: 6 4 W: 13 03 b.Alvangen 21-1-99
Internationals: Sweden U17, U19, U21, Full caps.

2015	Gothenburg	0	0		
2016	Gothenburg	0	0		
2017	Gothenburg	29	0		
2018	Gothenburg	10	0	**39**	**0**
2018–19	Watford	0	0		

DEENEY, Troy (F) 464 142
H: 5 11 W: 12 00 b.Solihull 29-6-88

2006–07	Walsall	1	0		
2007–08	Walsall	35	1		
2008–09	Walsall	45	12		
2009–10	Walsall	42	14	**123**	**27**
2010–11	Watford	36	3		
2011–12	Watford	43	11		
2012–13	Watford	40	19		
2013–14	Watford	44	24		
2014–15	Watford	42	21		
2015–16	Watford	38	13		
2016–17	Watford	37	10		
2017–18	Watford	29	5		
2018–19	Watford	32	9	**341**	**115**

DEULOFEU, Gerard (F) 128 21
H: 5 10 W: 11 01 b.Riudarenes 13-3-94
Internationals: Spain U16, U17, U19, U20, U21, Full caps.

2010–11	Barcelona	0	0		
2011–12	Barcelona	1	0		
2012–13	Barcelona	1	0		
2013–14	Barcelona	0	0		
2013–14	*Everton*	25	3		
2015–16	Everton	26	2		
2016–17	Everton	11	0	**62**	**5**
2016–17	*AC Milan*	17	4	**17**	**4**
2017–18	Barcelona	10	1	**12**	**1**
2017–18	*Watford*	7	1		
2018–19	Watford	30	10	**37**	**11**

DOUCOURE, Abdoulaye (M) 182 25
b.Meulan-en-Yvelines 1-1-93
Internationals: France U17, U18, U19, U20, U21.

2012–13	Rennes	4	1		
2013–14	Rennes	20	6		
2014–15	Rennes	35	3		
2015–16	Rennes	16	2	**75**	**12**
2015–16	Watford	0	0		
2015–16	*Granada*	15	0	**15**	**0**
2016–17	Watford	20	1		
2017–18	Watford	37	7		
2018–19	Watford	35	5	**92**	**13**

FEMENIA, Kiko (M) 209 11
H: 5 9 W: 9 11 b.Sanet i Negrals 2-2-91
Internationals: Spain U18, U19, U20.

2007–08	Hercules	1	0		
2008–09	Hercules	1	0		
2009–10	Hercules	35	3		
2010–11	Hercules	34	1	**71**	**4**
2011–12	Barcelona	0	0		
2012–13	Barcelona	0	0		
2013–14	Real Madrid	0	0		
2014–15	Alcorcon	17	0	**17**	**0**
2015–16	Alaves	38	5		
2016–17	Alaves	31	0	**69**	**5**
2017–18	Watford	23	1		
2018–19	Watford	29	1	**52**	**2**

FOLIVI, Michael (F) 12 2
H: 5 11 W: 12 06 b.Brent 25-2-98

2016–17	Watford	1	0		
2016–17	*Coventry C*	1	0	**1**	**0**
2017–18	Watford	0	0		
2018–19	Watford	0	0	**1**	**0**
2018–19	*AFC Wimbledon*	10	2	**10**	**2**

FOSTER, Ben (G) 389 0
H: 6 2 W: 12 08 b.Leamington Spa 3-4-83
Internationals: England Full caps.

2000–01	Stoke C	0	0		
2001–02	Stoke C	0	0		
2002–03	Stoke C	0	0		
2003–04	Stoke C	0	0		
2004–05	Stoke C	0	0		
2004–05	*Kidderminster H*	2	0	**2**	**0**
2004–05	*Wrexham*	17	0	**17**	**0**
2005–06	Manchester U	0	0		
2005–06	*Watford*	44	0		
2006–07	Manchester U	0	0		
2006–07	*Watford*	29	0		
2007–08	Manchester U	1	0		
2008–09	Manchester U	2	0		
2009–10	Manchester U	9	0	**12**	**0**
2010–11	Birmingham C	38	0		
2011–12	Birmingham C	0	0	**38**	**0**
2011–12	*WBA*	37	0		
2012–13	WBA	30	0		
2013–14	WBA	24	0		
2014–15	WBA	28	0		
2015–16	WBA	15	0		
2016–17	WBA	38	0		
2017–18	WBA	37	0	**209**	**0**
2018–19	Watford	38	0	**111**	**0**

GOMES, Heurelho (G) 435 0
H: 6 3 W: 12 13 b.Minas Gerais 15-2-81
Internationals: Brazil U23, Full caps.

2001	Cruzeiro	0	0		
2002	Cruzeiro	14	0		
2003	Cruzeiro	40	0		
2004	Cruzeiro	5	0	**59**	**0**
2004–05	PSV Eindhoven	30	0		
2005–06	PSV Eindhoven	32	0		

2006–07	PSV Eindhoven	32	0		
2007–08	PSV Eindhoven	34	0	**128**	**0**
2008–09	Tottenham H	34	0		
2009–10	Tottenham H	31	0		
2010–11	Tottenham H	30	0		
2011–12	Tottenham H	0	0		
2012–13	Tottenham H	0	0		
2012–13	*Hoffenheim*	9	0	**9**	**0**
2013–14	Tottenham H	0	0	**95**	**0**
2014–15	Watford	44	0		
2015–16	Watford	38	0		
2016–17	Watford	38	0		
2017–18	Watford	24	0		
2018–19	Watford	0	0	**144**	**0**

GRAY, Andre (F) 184 62
H: 5 10 W: 12 06 b.Shrewsbury 26-6-91
Internationals: England C.

2009–10	Shrewsbury T	4	0	**4**	**0**
From Hinckley U, Luton T.					
2014–15	Brentford	45	16		
2015–16	Brentford	2	2	**47**	**18**
2015–16	Burnley	41	23		
2016–17	Burnley	32	9	**73**	**32**
2017–18	Watford	31	5		
2018–19	Watford	29	7	**60**	**12**

HOLEBAS, Jose (M) 325 37
H: 6 0 W: 12 06 b.Aschaffenburg 27-6-84
Internationals: Greece Full caps.

2005–06	Viktoria Kahl	33	15	**33**	**15**
2006–07	1860 Munich	0	0		
2007–08	1860 Munich	19	2		
2008–09	1860 Munich	24	1		
2009–10	1860 Munich	31	4	**74**	**7**
2010–11	Olympiacos	24	1		
2011–12	Olympiacos	23	2		
2012–13	Olympiacos	28	4		
2013–14	Olympiacos	19	2	**94**	**9**
2014–15	Roma	24	1	**24**	**1**
2015–16	Watford	11	0		
2016–17	Watford	33	2		
2017–18	Watford	28	0		
2018–19	Watford	28	3	**100**	**5**

HUGHES, Will (M) 212 13
H: 6 1 W: 11 08 b.Weybridge 7-4-95
Internationals: England U17, U21.

2011–12	Derby Co	3	0		
2012–13	Derby Co	35	2		
2013–14	Derby Co	41	3		
2014–15	Derby Co	42	2		
2015–16	Derby Co	6	0		
2016–17	Derby Co	38	2	**165**	**9**
2017–18	Watford	15	2		
2018–19	Watford	32	2	**47**	**4**

JAKUBIAK, Alex (F) 98 13
H: 5 10 W: 10 06 b.Westminster 27-8-96
Internationals: Scotland U19.

2013–14	Watford	1	0		
2014–15	Watford	0	0		
2014–15	*Oxford U*	9	1	**9**	**1**
2014–15	*Dagenham & R*	23	4	**23**	**4**
2015–16	Watford	0	0		
2016–17	Watford	0	0		
2016–17	*Fleetwood T*	3	0	**3**	**0**
2016–17	*Wycombe W*	10	1	**10**	**1**
2017–18	Watford	0	0		
2017–18	*Falkirk*	14	5	**14**	**5**
2018–19	Watford	0	0	**1**	**0**
2018–19	*Bristol R*	38	2	**38**	**2**

JANMAAT, Daryl (D) 310 20
H: 6 1 W: 12 13 b.Leidschendam 22-7-89
Internationals: Netherlands U20, U21, Full caps.

2007–08	Den Haag	25	2	**25**	**2**
2008–09	Heerenveen	10	0		
2009–10	Heerenveen	28	0		
2010–11	Heerenveen	24	3		
2011–12	Heerenveen	22	2	**84**	**5**
2012–13	Feyenoord	32	3		
2013–14	Feyenoord	30	2	**62**	**5**
2014–15	Newcastle U	37	1		
2015–16	Newcastle U	32	2		
2016–17	Newcastle U	2	0	**71**	**3**
2016–17	Watford	27	2		
2017–18	Watford	23	3		
2018–19	Watford	18	0	**68**	**5**

KABASELE, Christian (D) 215 20
b.Lubumbashi 24-2-91
Internationals: Belgium U19, U20, Full caps.

2008–09	Eupen	3	0		
2009–10	Eupen	1	0		
2010–11	Eupen	3	0		
2010–11	*Mechelen*	4	1	**4**	**1**
2011–12	Ludogorets	11	3	**11**	**3**
2012–13	Eupen	26	4		
2013–14	Eupen	26	2	**59**	**6**
2014–15	Genk	34	2		
2015–16	Genk	42	4	**76**	**6**
2016–17	Watford	16	2		
2017–18	Watford	28	2		
2018–19	Watford	21	0	**65**	**4**

MARIAPPA, Adrian (D) 345 6
H: 5 10 W: 11 12 b.Harrow 3-10-86
Internationals: Jamaica Full caps.

2005–06	Watford	3	0		
2006–07	Watford	19	0		
2007–08	Watford	25	0		
2008–09	Watford	39	1		
2009–10	Watford	46	1		
2010–11	Watford	45	1		
2011–12	Watford	39	1		
2012–13	Reading	29	1		
2013–14	Reading	0	0	**29**	**1**
2013–14	Crystal Palace	24	1		
2014–15	Crystal Palace	12	0		
2015–16	Crystal Palace	3	0	**39**	**1**
2016–17	Watford	7	0		
2017–18	Watford	28	0		
2018–19	Watford	26	0	**277**	**4**

MASINA, Adam (D) 141 4
H: 5 10 W: 10 12 b.Khouribga 2-1-94
Internationals: Italy U21.

2013–14	Bologna	0	0		
2014–15	Bologna	28	1		
2015–16	Bologna	33	2		
2016–17	Bologna	32	1		
2017–18	Bologna	34	0	**127**	**4**
2018–19	Watford	14	0	**14**	**0**

NAVARRO, Marc (D) 33 3
H: 6 2 W: 12 06 b.Barcelona 2-7-85
From Barcelona.

2014–15	Espanyol	0	0		
2015–16	Espanyol	0	0		
2016–17	Espanyol	12	2		
2017–18	Espanyol	19	1	**31**	**3**
2018–19	Watford	2	0	**2**	**0**

OKAKA, Stefano (F) 292 59
H: 6 2 W: 12 04 b.Castiglion del Lago 9-8-89
Internationals: Italy U19, U20, U21, Full caps.

2005–06	Roma	9	0		
2006–07	Roma	6	1		
2007–08	Roma	0	0		
2007–08	*Modena*	33	7	**33**	**7**
2008–09	Roma	8	0		
2008–09	*Brescia*	17	2	**17**	**2**
2009–10	Roma	6	0		
2009–10	*Fulham*	11	2	**11**	**2**
2010–11	Roma	4	0	**33**	**1**
2010–11	*Bari*	10	2	**10**	**2**
2011–12	Parma	14	3		
2012–13	Parma	0	0		
2012–13	*Spezia*	38	7	**38**	**7**
2013–14	Parma	2	0	**16**	**3**
2013–14	Sampdoria	13	5		
2014–15	Sampdoria	32	4	**45**	**9**
2015–16	Anderlecht	37	15	**37**	**15**
2016–17	Watford	19	4		
2017–18	Watford	15	1		
2018–19	Watford	2	0	**36**	**5**
2018–19	*Udinese*	16	6	**16**	**6**

PENARANDA, Adalberto (F) 76 9
b.El Vigia 31-5-97
Internationals: Venezuela U17, U20, Full caps.

2013–14	Dep La Guaira	18	1		
2014–15	Dep La Guaira	19	3	**37**	**4**
2015–16	Udinese	0	0		
2015–16	Watford	0	0		
2015–16	*Granada*	23	5	**23**	**5**
2016–17	Watford	0	0		
2016–17	*Malaga*	3	0		
2017–18	Watford	0	0		
2017–18	*Malaga*	13	0	**16**	**0**
2018–19	Watford	0	0		

PEREYRA, Roberto (M) 253 25
H: 6 2 W: 11 11 b.Argentina 17-1-91
Internationals: Argentina U20, Full caps.

2008–09	River Plate	1	0		
2009–10	River Plate	15	0		
2010–11	River Plate	27	0	**43**	**0**
2011–12	Udinese	11	1		
2012–13	Udinese	37	5		
2013–14	Udinese	36	2		
2014–15	Udinese	0	0	**84**	**8**
2014–15	*Juventus*	35	4		
2015–16	Juventus	13	0	**48**	**4**
2016–17	Watford	13	2		
2017–18	Watford	32	5		
2018–19	Watford	33	6	**78**	**13**

PRODL, Sebastien (D) 268 17
H: 6 4 W: 13 05 b.Graz 21-6-87
Internationals: Austria U19, U20, Full caps.

2006–07	Sturm Graz	16	1		
2007–08	Sturm Graz	27	3	**43**	**4**
2008–09	Werder Bremen	22	0		
2009–10	Werder Bremen	9	1		
2010–11	Werder Bremen	25	1		
2011–12	Werder Bremen	16	2		
2012–13	Werder Bremen	28	1		
2013–14	Werder Bremen	27	2		
2014–15	Werder Bremen	22	3	**149**	**10**
2015–16	Watford	21	2		
2016–17	Watford	33	1		
2017–18	Watford	21	0		
2018–19	Watford	1	0	**76**	**3**

QUINA, Domingos (F) 8 1
b. 18-11-99
Internationals: Portugal U17, U18, U19, U20.

2016–17	West Ham U	0	0		
2017–18	West Ham U	0	0		
2018–19	Watford	8	1	**8**	**1**

SEMA, Ken (M) 157 24
H: 5 10 W: 11 03 b.Norrkoping 30-9-93
Internationals: Sweden U23, Full caps.

2013	IFK Norrkoping	0	0		
2013	*IF Sylvia*	22	4	**22**	**4**
2014	Ljungskile	30	7		
2015	Ljungskile	30	4	**60**	**11**
2016	Ostersunds	23	4		
2017	Ostersunds	24	4		
2018	Ostersunds	11	0	**58**	**8**
2018–19	Watford	17	1	**17**	**1**

SINCLAIR, Jerome (F) 46 5
H: 5 8 W: 12 06 b.Birmingham 20-9-96
Internationals: England U16, U17.

2012–13	Liverpool	0	0		
2013–14	Liverpool	0	0		
2014–15	Liverpool	2	0		
2014–15	*Wigan Ath*	1	0	**1**	**0**
2015–16	Liverpool	0	0	**2**	**0**
2016–17	Watford	5	0		
2016–17	*Birmingham C*	5	0	**5**	**0**
2017–18	Watford	4	0		
2018–19	Watford	0	0	**9**	**0**
2018–19	*Sunderland*	13	1	**13**	**1**
2018–19	*Oxford U*	16	4	**16**	**4**

SUCCESS, Isaac (F) 107 9
H: 6 1 W: 11 03 b. 7-1-96
Internationals: Nigeria U17, U20, Full caps.

2014–15	Granada	19	1		
2015–16	Granada	30	6	**49**	**7**
2016–17	Watford	19	1		
2017–18	Watford	0	0		
2017–18	*Malaga*	9	0	**9**	**0**
2018–19	Watford	30	1	**49**	**2**

WILMOT, Ben (M) 17 0
H: 6 2 W: 12 08 b. 4-11-99
Internationals: England U19, U20.

2016–17	Stevenage	0	0		
2017–18	Stevenage	10	0	**10**	**0**
2018–19	Watford	2	0	**2**	**0**
2018–19	*Udinese*	5	0	**5**	**0**

Players retained or with offer of contract
Alvarado Hoyos, Jamie Alberto; Bachmann, Daniel; Barrozo Rodrigues, Matheus Aias; Becerra Maya, Juan Camillo; Estupinan Tenorio, Pervis Josue; Fobi, Kingsley; Forster, Harry James; Foulquier, Dimitri; Gordon, Lewis; Hernandez Suarez, Juan Camilo; Lukebakio Ngandoli, Dodi; Marreh, Sulayman; Mbaye, Mamadou; McLean Cassidy, Ryan Michael; Mukena, Joy-Richard; Oulare, Mamadou Obbi; Parkes, Adam Darren; Santana Ferreira, Matheus Henrique; Segura Portocarrero, Jorge Andres; Sibo, Kwasi; Stuparevic, Filip; Suarez Charris, Luis Javier; Velasquez Reyes, Williams Daniel; Zeegelaar, Marvin Romeo Kwasie.

Scholars
Adebiyi, Emmanuel; Baptiste, Dante Astor Kareem; Bennetts, Jayden; Hoskins, James

Michael; Hudson, Harry Jonathan; Hutchinson, Dominic Charles; MacLean, Ryan Thomas William; Matthews, James John; McKiernan, John Joshua; Miller, Reece; Mullings, Michael Koray; Phillips, Daniel Shaquille Jabari; Sanders, Kai Sidney; Sankoh, Imaad Suffian Aziz; Sesay, Samuel Santigie; Suckling, Ryan George; Tricker, Ben; White, Harvey Batterson.

WBA (87)

BARRY, Gareth (M) 677 54
H: 5 11 W: 12 06 b.Hastings 23-2-81
Internationals: England B, U21, Full caps.

1997–98	Aston Villa	2	0		
1998–99	Aston Villa	32	2		
1999–2000	Aston Villa	30	1		
2000–01	Aston Villa	30	0		
2001–02	Aston Villa	20	0		
2002–03	Aston Villa	35	3		
2003–04	Aston Villa	36	3		
2004–05	Aston Villa	34	7		
2005–06	Aston Villa	36	3		
2006–07	Aston Villa	35	8		
2007–08	Aston Villa	37	9		
2008–09	Aston Villa	38	5	**365**	**41**
2009–10	Manchester C	34	2		
2010–11	Manchester C	33	2		
2011–12	Manchester C	34	1		
2012–13	Manchester C	31	1		
2013–14	Manchester C	0	0	**132**	**6**
2013–14	*Everton*	32	3		
2014–15	Everton	33	0		
2015–16	Everton	33	0		
2016–17	Everton	33	2	**131**	**5**
2017–18	WBA	25	1		
2018–19	WBA	24	1	**49**	**2**

BARTLEY, Kyle (D) 170 11
H: 5 11 W: 11 00 b.Stockport 22-5-91
Internationals: England U16, U17.

2008–09	Arsenal	0	0		
2009–10	Arsenal	0	0		
2009–10	*Sheffield U*	14	0		
2010–11	Arsenal	0	0		
2010–11	*Sheffield U*	21	0	**35**	**0**
2010–11	*Rangers*	5	1		
2011–12	Arsenal	0	0		
2011–12	*Rangers*	19	0	**24**	**1**
2012–13	Arsenal	0	0		
2012–13	Swansea C	2	0		
2013–14	Swansea C	2	0		
2013–14	*Birmingham C*	17	3	**17**	**3**
2014–15	Swansea C	7	0		
2015–16	Swansea C	5	0		
2016–17	Swansea C	0	0		
2016–17	*Leeds U*	45	6	**45**	**6**
2017–18	Swansea C	5	0	**21**	**0**
2018–19	WBA	28	1	**28**	**1**

BOND, Jonathan (G) 91 0
H: 6 3 W: 13 03 b.Hemel Hempstead 19-5-93
Internationals: Wales U17, U19. England U20, U21.

2010–11	Watford	0	0		
2011–12	Watford	1	0		
2011–12	*Dagenham & R*	5	0	**5**	**0**
2011–12	*Bury*	6	0	**6**	**0**
2012–13	Watford	8	0		
2013–14	Watford	10	0		
2014–15	Watford	3	0	**22**	**0**
2015–16	Reading	14	0		
2016–17	Reading	0	0		
2016–17	*Gillingham*	7	0	**7**	**0**
2017–18	Reading	0	0	**14**	**0**
2017–18	*Peterborough U*	37	0	**37**	**0**
2018–19	WBA	0	0		

BRADLEY, Alex (M) 7 1
b.Worcester 27-1-99
Internationals: Finland U19.

2018–19	WBA	0	0		
2018–19	*Burton Alb*	7	1	**7**	**1**

BRUNT, Chris (M) 515 67
H: 6 1 W: 13 04 b.Belfast 14-12-84
Internationals: Northern Ireland U19, U21, U23, Full caps.

2002–03	Middlesbrough	0	0		
2003–04	Middlesbrough	0	0		
2003–04	Sheffield W	9	2		
2004–05	Sheffield W	42	4		
2005–06	Sheffield W	44	7		
2006–07	Sheffield W	44	11		
2007–08	Sheffield W	1	0	**140**	**24**
2007–08	WBA	34	4		
2008–09	WBA	34	8		
2009–10	WBA	40	13		
2010–11	WBA	34	4		
2011–12	WBA	29	2		
2012–13	WBA	31	2		
2013–14	WBA	28	3		
2014–15	WBA	34	2		
2015–16	WBA	22	0		
2016–17	WBA	31	3		
2017–18	WBA	26	0		
2018–19	WBA	32	2	**375**	**43**

BURKE, Oliver (M) 84 11
H: 5 9 W: 11 11 b.Melton Mowbray 7-4-97
Internationals: Scotland U19, U20, Full caps.

2014–15	Nottingham F	2	0		
2014–15	*Bradford C*	2	0	**2**	**0**
2015–16	Nottingham F	18	2		
2016–17	Nottingham F	5	4	**25**	**6**
2016–17	RB Leipzig	25	1	**25**	**1**
2017–18	WBA	15	0		
2018–19	WBA	3	0	**18**	**0**
2018–19	*Celtic*	14	4	**14**	**4**

DAWSON, Craig (D) 297 37
H: 6 0 W: 12 04 b.Rochdale 6-5-90
Internationals: England U21. Great Britain.

2008–09	Rochdale	0	0		
2009–10	Rochdale	42	9		
2010–11	WBA	0	0		
2010–11	*Rochdale*	45	10	**87**	**19**
2011–12	WBA	8	0		
2012–13	WBA	1	0		
2012–13	*Bolton W*	16	4	**16**	**4**
2013–14	WBA	12	0		
2014–15	WBA	29	2		
2015–16	WBA	38	4		
2016–17	WBA	37	4		
2017–18	WBA	28	2		
2018–19	WBA	41	2	**194**	**14**

EDWARDS, Kyle (M) 29 1
H: 5 8 W: 10 01 b.Dudley 17-2-98
Internationals: England U16, U17, U20.

2015–16	WBA	0	0		
2017–18	WBA	0	0		
2017–18	*Exeter C*	23	0	**23**	**0**
2018–19	WBA	6	1	**6**	**1**

FIELD, Sam (M) 31 2
b. 8-5-98
Internationals: England U18, U19, U20.

2015–16	WBA	1	0		
2016–17	WBA	8	0		
2017–18	WBA	10	1		
2018–19	WBA	12	1	**31**	**2**

FITZWATER, Jack (D) 51 4
H: 6 2 W: 11 00 b.Solihull 23-9-97

2015–16	WBA	0	0		
2015–16	*Chesterfield*	1	0	**1**	**0**
2016–17	WBA	0	0		
2017–18	WBA	0	0		
2017–18	*Forest Green R*	14	1	**14**	**1**
2017–18	*Walsall*	15	3		
2018–19	WBA	0	0		
2018–19	*Walsall*	21	0	**36**	**3**

GIBBS, Kieran (M) 213 6
H: 5 10 W: 10 02 b.Lambeth 26-9-89
Internationals: England U19, U20, U21, Full caps.

2007–08	Arsenal	0	0		
2007–08	*Norwich C*	7	0	**7**	**0**
2008–09	Arsenal	8	0		
2009–10	Arsenal	3	0		
2010–11	Arsenal	7	0		
2011–12	Arsenal	16	1		
2012–13	Arsenal	27	0		
2013–14	Arsenal	28	0		
2014–15	Arsenal	22	0		
2015–16	Arsenal	15	1		
2016–17	Arsenal	11	0		
2017–18	Arsenal	0	0	**137**	**2**
2017–18	WBA	33	0		
2018–19	WBA	36	4	**69**	**4**

HARPER, Rekeem (M) 21 1
H: 6 0 W: 10 01 b. 8-3-00
Internationals: England U17, U19.

2016–17	WBA	0	0		
2017–18	WBA	1	0		
2017–18	*Blackburn R*	4	0	**4**	**0**
2018–19	WBA	16	1	**17**	**1**

HEGAZI, Ahmed (D) 157 3
H: 6 5 W: 11 03 b.Ismalia 25-1-91
Internationals: Egypt U20, U23, Full caps.

2009–10	Ismaily	12	0		
2010–11	Ismaily	7	0		
2011–12	Ismaily	9	0	**28**	**0**
2012–13	Fiorentina	2	0		
2013–14	Fiorentina	1	0		
2014–15	Fiorentina	0	0	**3**	**0**
2014–15	*Perugia*	10	0	**10**	**0**
2015–16	Al Ahly	29	0		
2016–17	Al Ahly	11	0	**40**	**0**
2017–18	WBA	38	2		
2018–19	WBA	38	1	**76**	**3**

HOOLAHAN, Wes (M) 532 69
H: 5 6 W: 10 03 b.Dublin 10-8-83
Internationals: Republic of Ireland U21, B, Full caps.

2001–02	Shelbourne	20	3		
2002–03	Shelbourne	23	0		
2004	Shelbourne	31	2		
2005	Shelbourne	29	4	**103**	**9**
2005–06	Livingston	16	0	**16**	**0**
2006–07	Blackpool	42	8		
2007–08	Blackpool	45	5	**87**	**13**
2008–09	Norwich C	32	2		
2009–10	Norwich C	37	11		
2010–11	Norwich C	41	10		
2011–12	Norwich C	33	4		
2012–13	Norwich C	33	3		
2013–14	Norwich C	16	1		
2014–15	Norwich C	36	4		
2015–16	Norwich C	30	4		
2016–17	Norwich C	33	7		
2017–18	Norwich C	29	1	**320**	**47**
2018–19	WBA	6	0	**6**	**0**

HOWKINS, Kyle (D) 30 0
H: 6 5 W: 12 11 b.Walsall 4-5-96

2015–16	WBA	0	0		
2016–17	WBA	0	0		
2016–17	*Mansfield T*	15	0	**15**	**0**
2017–18	WBA	0	0		
2017–18	*Cambridge U*	2	0	**2**	**0**
2017–18	*Port Vale*	10	0		
2018–19	WBA	0	0		
2018–19	*Port Vale*	3	0	**13**	**0**

JOHNSTONE, Samuel (G) 186 0
H: 6 0 W: 12 10 b.Preston 25-3-93
Internationals: England U16, U17, U19, U20.

2009–10	Manchester U	0	0		
2010–11	Manchester U	0	0		
2011–12	Manchester U	0	0		
2011–12	*Scunthorpe U*	12	0	**12**	**0**
2012–13	Manchester U	0	0		
2012–13	*Walsall*	7	0	**7**	**0**
2013–14	Manchester U	0	0		
2013–14	*Yeovil T*	1	0	**1**	**0**
2013–14	*Doncaster R*	18	0		
2014–15	Manchester U	0	0		
2014–15	*Doncaster R*	10	0	**28**	**0**
2014–15	*Preston NE*	22	0		
2015–16	Manchester U	0	0		
2015–16	*Preston NE*	4	0	**26**	**0**
2016–17	Manchester U	0	0		
2016–17	*Aston Villa*	21	0		
2017–18	Manchester U	0	0		
2017–18	*Aston Villa*	45	0	**66**	**0**
2018–19	WBA	46	0	**46**	**0**

LEKO, Jonathan (M) 27 0
H: 6 0 W: 11 11 b.Kinshasa 24-4-99
Internationals: England U16, U17, U18, U19.

2015–16	WBA	5	0		
2016–17	WBA	9	0		
2017–18	Bristol C	11	0	**11**	**0**
2017–18	WBA	0	0		
2018–19	WBA	2	0	**16**	**0**

LIVERMORE, Jake (M) 298 15
H: 5 9 W: 12 08 b.Enfield 14-11-89
Internationals: England Full caps.

2006–07	Tottenham H	0	0		
2007–08	Tottenham H	0	0		
2007–08	*Milton Keynes D*	5	0	**5**	**0**
2008–09	Tottenham H	0	0		
2008–09	*Crewe Alex*	0	0		
2009–10	Tottenham H	1	0		
2009–10	*Derby Co*	16	1	**16**	**1**
2009–10	*Peterborough U*	9	1	**9**	**1**
2010–11	Tottenham H	0	0		
2010–11	*Ipswich T*	12	0	**12**	**0**
2010–11	*Leeds U*	5	0	**5**	**0**
2011–12	Tottenham H	24	0		

2012–13	Tottenham H	11	0		
2013–14	Tottenham H	0	0	**36**	**0**
2013–14	*Hull C*	36	3		
2014–15	Hull C	35	1		
2015–16	Hull C	34	4		
2016–17	Hull C	21	1	**126**	**9**
2016–17	WBA	16	0		
2017–18	WBA	34	2		
2018–19	WBA	39	2	**89**	**4**

MEARS, Tyrone (D) 346 10
H: 5 11 W: 11 10 b.Stockport 18-2-83
Internationals: Jamaica Full caps.

2000–01	Manchester C	0	0		
2001–02	Manchester C	1	0	**1**	**0**
2002–03	Preston NE	22	1		
2003–04	Preston NE	12	1		
2004–05	Preston NE	4	0		
2005–06	Preston NE	32	2	**70**	**4**
2006–07	West Ham U	5	0	**5**	**0**
2006–07	*Derby Co*	13	1		
2007–08	Derby Co	25	1		
2008–09	Derby Co	3	0	**41**	**2**
2008–09	*Marseille*	4	0	**4**	**0**
2009–10	Burnley	38	0		
2010–11	Burnley	44	1		
2011–12	Burnley	0	0	**82**	**1**
2011–12	Bolton W	1	0		
2012–13	Bolton W	26	0		
2013–14	Bolton W	1	0	**28**	**0**
2015	Seattle Sounders	36	1		
2016	Seattle Sounders	38	0	**74**	**1**
2017	Atalanta U	21	1	**21**	**1**
2018	Minnesota U	11	1	**11**	**1**
2018–19	WBA	9	0	**9**	**0**

MORRISON, James (M) 376 37
H: 5 10 W: 10 06 b.Darlington 25-5-86
Internationals: England U17, U18, U19, U20. Scotland Full caps.

2003–04	Middlesbrough	1	0		
2004–05	Middlesbrough	14	0		
2005–06	Middlesbrough	24	1		
2006–07	Middlesbrough	28	2	**67**	**3**
2007–08	WBA	35	4		
2008–09	WBA	30	3		
2009–10	WBA	11	1		
2010–11	WBA	31	4		
2011–12	WBA	30	5		
2012–13	WBA	35	5		
2013–14	WBA	32	1		
2014–15	WBA	33	2		
2015–16	WBA	18	3		
2016–17	WBA	31	5		
2017–18	WBA	4	1		
2018–19	WBA	19	0	**309**	**34**

MYHILL, Boaz (G) 381 0
H: 6 3 W: 14 06 b.California 9-11-82
Internationals: England U20. Wales Full caps.

2000–01	Aston Villa	0	0		
2001–02	Aston Villa	0	0		
2001–02	*Stoke C*	0	0		
2002–03	Aston Villa	0	0		
2002–03	*Bristol C*	0	0		
2002–03	*Bradford C*	2	0	**2**	**0**
2003–04	Aston Villa	0	0		
2003–04	*Macclesfield T*	15	0	**15**	**0**
2003–04	*Stockport Co*	2	0	**2**	**0**
2003–04	Hull C	23	0		
2004–05	Hull C	45	0		
2005–06	Hull C	45	0		
2006–07	Hull C	46	0		
2007–08	Hull C	43	0		
2008–09	Hull C	28	0		
2009–10	Hull C	27	0	**257**	**0**
2010–11	WBA	6	0		
2011–12	WBA	0	0		
2011–12	*Birmingham C*	42	0	**42**	**0**
2012–13	WBA	8	0		
2013–14	WBA	14	0		
2014–15	WBA	11	0		
2015–16	WBA	23	0		
2016–17	WBA	0	0		
2017–18	WBA	1	0		
2018–19	WBA	0	0	**63**	**0**

NYOM, Allan (D) 323 3
H: 5 7 W: 12 11 b.Neuilly-sur-Seine 10-5-88
Internationals: Cameroon Full caps.

2008–09	Arles-Avignon	37	0	**37**	**0**
2009–10	Udinese	0	0		
2010–11	Udinese	0	0		
2010–11	*Granada*	43	1		
2011–12	Udinese	0	0		
2011–12	*Granada*	32	0		
2012–13	Udinese	0	0		
2012–13	*Granada*	35	0		
2013–14	Udinese	0	0		
2013–14	*Granada*	34	0		
2014–15	Udinese	0	0		
2014–15	*Granada*	34	1	**178**	**2**
2015–16	Watford	32	0		
2016–17	Watford	0	0	**32**	**0**
2016–17	WBA	32	0		
2017–18	WBA	29	0		
2018–19	WBA	2	0	**63**	**0**
2018–19	*Leganes*	13	1	**13**	**1**

O'SHEA, Dara (D) 27 0
b. 4-3-99
Internationals: Republic of Ireland U18, U19.

2018–19	WBA	0	0		
2018–19	*Exeter C*	27	0	**27**	**0**

PALMER, Alex (G) 2 0
b. 10-8-96
Internationals: England U16.

2014–15	WBA	0	0		
2015–16	WBA	0	0		
2016–17	WBA	0	0		
2017–18	WBA	0	0		
2018–19	WBA	0	0		
2018–19	*Oldham Ath*	1	0	**1**	**0**
2018–19	*Notts Co*	1	0	**1**	**0**

PHILLIPS, Matthew (M) 355 50
H: 6 0 W: 12 10 b.Aylesbury 13-3-91
Internationals: England U19, U20. Scotland Full caps.

2007–08	Wycombe W	2	0		
2008–09	Wycombe W	37	3		
2009–10	Wycombe W	36	5		
2010–11	Wycombe W	3	0	**78**	**8**
2010–11	Blackpool	27	1		
2011–12	Blackpool	33	7		
2011–12	*Sheffield U*	6	5	**6**	**5**
2012–13	Blackpool	34	4		
2013–14	Blackpool	0	0	**94**	**12**
2013–14	QPR	21	3		
2014–15	QPR	25	3		
2015–16	QPR	44	8	**90**	**14**
2016–17	WBA	27	4		
2017–18	WBA	30	2		
2018–19	WBA	30	5	**87**	**11**

ROBSON-KANU, Hal (F) 325 42
H: 5 7 W: 11 08 b.Acton 21-5-89
Internationals: England U19, U20. Wales U21, Full caps.

2007–08	Reading	0	0		
2007–08	*Southend U*	8	3		
2008–09	Reading	0	0		
2008–09	*Southend U*	14	2	**22**	**5**
2008–09	*Swindon T*	20	4	**20**	**4**
2009–10	Reading	17	0		
2010–11	Reading	27	5		
2011–12	Reading	36	4		
2012–13	Reading	25	7		
2013–14	Reading	36	4		
2014–15	Reading	29	1		
2015–16	Reading	28	3		
2016–17	Reading	0	0	**198**	**24**
2016–17	WBA	29	3		
2017–18	WBA	21	2		
2018–19	WBA	35	4	**85**	**9**

RODRIGUEZ, Jay (F) 308 90
H: 6 0 W: 12 00 b.Burnley 29-7-89
Internationals: England U21, Full caps.

2007–08	Burnley	1	0		
2007–08	Stirling Alb	11	3	**11**	**3**
2008–09	Burnley	25	2		
2009–10	Burnley	0	0		
2009–10	*Barnsley*	6	1	**6**	**1**
2010–11	Burnley	42	14		
2011–12	Burnley	37	15	**105**	**31**
2012–13	Southampton	35	6		
2013–14	Southampton	33	15		
2014–15	Southampton	0	0		
2015–16	Southampton	12	0		
2016–17	Southampton	24	5	**104**	**26**
2017–18	WBA	37	7		
2018–19	WBA	45	22	**82**	**29**

ROGERS, Morgan (M) 0 0
b.Halesowen 26-7-02
Internationals: England U16, U17.

2018–19	WBA	0	0		

RONDON, Jose Salomon (F) 375 120
H: 6 1 W: 13 08 b.Caracas 16-9-89
Internationals: Venezuela U20, Full caps.

2006–07	Aragua	21	7		
2007–08	Aragua	28	8	**49**	**15**
2008–09	Las Palmas	10	0		
2009–10	Las Palmas	36	12	**46**	**12**
2010–11	Malaga	30	14		
2011–12	Malaga	37	11	**67**	**25**
2012–13	Rubin Kazan	25	7		
2013–14	Rubin Kazan	11	6	**36**	**13**
2013–14	Zenit St Petersburg	10	7		
2014–15	Zenit St Petersburg	26	13		
2015–16	Zenit St Petersburg	1	0	**37**	**20**
2015–16	WBA	34	9		
2016–17	WBA	38	8		
2017–18	WBA	36	7		
2018–19	WBA	0	0	**108**	**24**
2018–19	*Newcastle U*	32	11	**32**	**11**

TOWNSEND, Conor (D) 141 6
H: 5 4 W: 9 11 b.Hessle 4-3-93

2011–12	Hull C	0	0		
2012–13	Hull C	0	0		
2012–13	*Chesterfield*	20	1	**20**	**1**
2013–14	Hull C	0	0		
2013–14	*Carlisle U*	12	0	**12**	**0**
2014–15	Hull C	0	0		
2014–15	*Dundee U*	17	0	**17**	**0**
2014–15	*Scunthorpe U*	6	0		
2015–16	Hull C	0	0		
2015–16	Scunthorpe U	20	1		
2016–17	Scunthorpe U	24	0		
2017–18	Scunthorpe U	30	4	**80**	**5**
2018–19	WBA	12	0	**12**	**0**

TULLOCH, Rayhaan (F) 0 0
b.Birmingham 20-1-01
Internationals: England U16, U17, U18.

2017–18	WBA	0	0		
2018–19	WBA	0	0		

WILSON, Kane (D) 50 1
H: 5 10 W: 11 03 b. 11-3-00
Internationals: England U16, U17.

2016–17	WBA	0	0		
2017–18	WBA	0	0		
2017–18	*Exeter C*	19	1		
2018–19	WBA	0	0		
2018–19	*Walsall*	14	0	**14**	**0**
2018–19	*Exeter C*	17	0	**36**	**1**

Players retained or with offer of contract
Elsayed, Ali Elsayed Ahmed; Ferguson, Nathan; Healy, Kevin; House, Bradley Roy; Melbourne, Max; Morton, Callum Damian Peter; Solanke, Babatomiwa Jonathan; Soule, Jamie.

Scholars
Ashton, Eoin Thomas; Asomugha, Stanley; Azaz, Finn; Brown, Zak; Cann, Ted Barnaby; Chambers, Maurice Jack; Clayton-Phillips, Nicholas; Delaney, Zak; Dyce, Tyrese; Gardner-Hickman, Taylor Edward; Gilbert, Alexander George Henry; Griffiths, Joshua James; Harmon, George; Hill, Carrick Matthew; King, Toby James; Martinez, Pablo Jacob; Meredith, Daniel William; Ojebode, Yusuff Akinola Olatunji; Przybek, Adam; Rogers, Morgan Elliot; Sharpe, Thomas; Smith, Lewis Cameron; Taylor, Peter James; Thorndike, Finley Joseph; Wakeling, Jacob Andrew; White, Aksum; Wilding, Samuel; Williams, Harry William; Williams, Remarl Theo Reshaun.

WEST HAM U (88)

ADRIAN (G) 157 0
H: 6 2 W: 12 00 b.Seville 3-1-87

2008–09	Real Betis	0	0		
2009–10	Real Betis	0	0		
2010–11	Real Betis	0	0		
2011–12	Real Betis	0	0		
2012–13	Real Betis	32	0	**32**	**0**
2013–14	West Ham U	20	0		
2014–15	West Ham U	38	0		
2015–16	West Ham U	32	0		
2016–17	West Ham U	16	0		
2017–18	West Ham U	19	0		
2018–19	West Ham U	0	0	**125**	**0**

AFOLAYAN, Oladapo (F) 10 0
H: 5 11 b. 1-1-97
Internationals: England C.

2018–19	West Ham U	0	0		
2018–19	*Oldham Ath*	10	0	**10**	**0**

ANTONIO, Michael (M) 317 67
H: 6 0 W: 11 11 b.Wandsworth 28-3-90

2008–09	Reading	0	0		
2008–09	*Cheltenham T*	9	0	**9**	**0**
2009–10	Reading	1	0		
2009–10	*Southampton*	28	3	**28**	**3**
2010–11	Reading	21	1		
2011–12	Reading	6	0		
2011–12	*Colchester U*	15	4	**15**	**4**
2011–12	*Sheffield W*	14	5		
2012–13	Reading	0	0	**28**	**1**
2012–13	Sheffield W	37	8		
2013–14	Sheffield W	27	4	**78**	**17**
2014–15	Nottingham F	46	14		
2015–16	Nottingham F	4	2	**50**	**16**
2015–16	West Ham U	26	8		
2016–17	West Ham U	29	9		
2017–18	West Ham U	21	3		
2018–19	West Ham U	33	6	**109**	**26**

ARNAUTOVIC, Marko (F) 303 69
H: 6 4 W: 13 00 b.Floridsdorf 19-4-89
Internationals: Austria U18, U19, U21, Full caps.

2006–07	FC Twente	2	0		
2007–08	FC Twente	14	0		
2008–09	FC Twente	28	12		
2009–10	FC Twente	0	0	**44**	**12**
2009–10	*Inter Milan*	3	0	**3**	**0**
2010–11	Werder Bremen	25	3		
2011–12	Werder Bremen	19	6		
2012–13	Werder Bremen	26	5		
2013–14	Werder Bremen	2	0	**72**	**14**
2013–14	Stoke C	30	4		
2014–15	Stoke C	29	1		
2015–16	Stoke C	34	11		
2016–17	Stoke C	32	6	**125**	**22**
2017–18	West Ham U	31	11		
2018–19	West Ham U	28	10	**59**	**21**

BALBUENA, Fabian (D) 258 15
H: 5 11 W: 11 07 b.Ciudad del Este 23-8-91
Internationals: Paraguay Full caps.

2010	Cerro Porteno	7	0		
2011	Cerro Porteno	28	4		
2012	Cerro Porteno	41	1	**76**	**5**
2013	Rubio Nu	17	1	**17**	**1**
2013	Nacional	14	0		
2014	Nacional	16	1	**30**	**1**
2014	Libertad	16	1		
2015	Libertad	26	2		
2016	Libertad	1	0	**43**	**3**
2016	Corinthians	29	0		
2017	Corinthians	32	4		
2018	Corinthians	8	0	**69**	**4**
2018–19	West Ham U	23	1	**23**	**1**

BROWNE, Marcus (M) 34 6
b. 18-12-97

2015–16	West Ham U	0	0		
2016–17	West Ham U	0	0		
2016–17	*Wigan Ath*	0	0		
2017–18	West Ham U	0	0		
2018–19	West Ham U	0	0		
2018–19	*Oxford U*	34	6	**34**	**6**

BYRAM, Samuel (M) 163 9
H: 5 11 W: 11 04 b.Thurrock 16-9-93

2012–13	Leeds U	44	3		
2013–14	Leeds U	25	0		
2014–15	Leeds U	39	3		
2015–16	Leeds U	22	3	**130**	**9**
2015–16	West Ham U	4	0		
2016–17	West Ham U	18	0		
2017–18	West Ham U	5	0		
2018–19	West Ham U	0	0	**27**	**0**
2018–19	*Nottingham F*	6	0	**6**	**0**

CARROLL, Andy (F) 261 71
H: 6 4 W: 11 00 b.Gateshead 6-1-89
Internationals: England U19, U21, Full caps.

2006–07	Newcastle U	4	0		
2007–08	Newcastle U	4	0		
2007–08	*Preston NE*	11	1	**11**	**1**
2008–09	Newcastle U	14	3		
2009–10	Newcastle U	39	17		
2010–11	Newcastle U	19	11	**80**	**31**
2010–11	Liverpool	7	2		
2011–12	Liverpool	35	4		
2012–13	Liverpool	2	0	**44**	**6**
2012–13	*West Ham U*	24	7		
2013–14	West Ham U	15	2		
2014–15	West Ham U	14	5		
2015–16	West Ham U	27	9		
2016–17	West Ham U	18	7		
2017–18	West Ham U	16	3		
2018–19	West Ham U	12	0	**126**	**33**

COVENTRY, Conor (M) 0 0
b. 25-3-00
Internationals: Republic of Ireland U17, U18, U21.

2018–19	West Ham U	0	0		

CRESSWELL, Aaron (D) 359 16
H: 5 7 W: 10 05 b.Liverpool 15-12-89
Internationals: England Full caps.

2008–09	Tranmere R	13	1		
2009–10	Tranmere R	14	0		
2010–11	Tranmere R	43	4	**70**	**5**
2011–12	Ipswich T	44	1		
2012–13	Ipswich T	46	3		
2013–14	Ipswich T	42	2	**132**	**6**
2014–15	West Ham U	38	2		
2015–16	West Ham U	37	2		
2016–17	West Ham U	26	0		
2017–18	West Ham U	36	1		
2018–19	West Ham U	20	0	**157**	**5**

CULLEN, Josh (M) 99 2
H: 5 8 W: 11 00 b.Southend-on-Sea 4-7-96
Internationals: England U16. Republic of Ireland U19, U21.

2014–15	West Ham U	0	0		
2015–16	West Ham U	1	0		
2015–16	*Bradford C*	15	0		
2016–17	West Ham U	0	0		
2016–17	*Bradford C*	40	1	**55**	**1**
2017–18	West Ham U	2	0		
2017–18	*Bolton W*	12	0	**12**	**0**
2018–19	West Ham U	0	0	**3**	**0**
2018–19	*Charlton Ath*	29	1	**29**	**1**

DIANGANA, Grady (M) 17 0
b. 19-4-98
Internationals: England U20.

2016–17	West Ham U	0	0		
2017–18	West Ham U	0	0		
2018–19	West Ham U	17	0	**17**	**0**

DIOP, Issa (D) 110 6
H: 6 4 W: 13 03 b.Toulouse 9-1-97
Internationals: France U16, U17, U18, U19, U20, U21.

2015–16	Toulouse	21	1		
2016–17	Toulouse	30	2		
2017–18	Toulouse	26	2	**77**	**5**
2018–19	West Ham U	33	1	**33**	**1**

FABIANSKI, Lukasz (G) 272 0
H: 6 3 W: 13 01 b.Costrzyn nad Odra 18-4-85
Internationals: Poland U21, Full caps.

2005–06	Legia	30	0		
2006–07	Legia	23	0	**53**	**0**
2007–08	Arsenal	3	0		
2008–09	Arsenal	6	0		
2009–10	Arsenal	4	0		
2010–11	Arsenal	14	0		
2011–12	Arsenal	0	0		
2012–13	Arsenal	4	0		
2013–14	Arsenal	1	0	**32**	**0**
2014–15	Swansea C	37	0		
2015–16	Swansea C	37	0		
2016–17	Swansea C	37	0		
2017–18	Swansea C	38	0	**149**	**0**
2018–19	West Ham U	38	0	**38**	**0**

FELIPE ANDERSON, Gomes (M) 234 41
H: 5 10 W: 10 12 b.Braslia 15-4-93
Internationals: Brazil U17, U20, U23, Full caps.

2010	Santos	5	0		
2011	Santos	18	1		
2012	Santos	35	6		
2013	Santos	3	0	**61**	**7**
2013–14	Lazio	13	0		
2014–15	Lazio	32	10		
2015–16	Lazio	35	7		
2016–17	Lazio	36	4		
2017–18	Lazio	21	4	**137**	**25**
2018–19	West Ham U	36	9	**36**	**9**

FREDERICKS, Ryan (M) 160 2
H: 5 8 W: 11 10 b.Potters Bar 10-10-92
Internationals: England U19.

2010–11	Tottenham H	0	0		
2011–12	Tottenham H	0	0		
2012–13	Tottenham H	0	0		
2012–13	*Brentford*	4	0	**4**	**0**
2013–14	Tottenham H	0	0		
2013–14	*Millwall*	14	1	**14**	**1**
2014–15	Tottenham H	0	0		
2014–15	*Middlesbrough*	17	0	**17**	**0**
2015–16	Bristol C	4	0	**4**	**0**
2015–16	Fulham	32	0		
2016–17	Fulham	30	0		
2017–18	Fulham	44	0	**106**	**0**
2018–19	West Ham U	15	1	**15**	**1**

HERNANDEZ, Javier (F) 340 124
H: 5 8 W: 9 11 b.Guadalajara 1-6-88
Internationals: Mexico U20, Full caps.

2005–06	Tapatio	11	0		
2006–07	Tapatio	12	3		
2006–07	Guadalajara	7	1		
2007–08	Guadalajara	5	0		
2007–08	Tapatio	15	6		
2008–09	Tapatio	7	2	**45**	**11**
2008–09	Guadalajara	22	4		
2009–10	Guadalajara	28	21	**62**	**26**
2010–11	Manchester U	27	13		
2011–12	Manchester U	28	10		
2012–13	Manchester U	22	10		
2013–14	Manchester U	24	4		
2014–15	Manchester U	1	0		
2014–15	*Real Madrid*	23	7	**23**	**7**
2015–16	Manchester U	1	0	**103**	**37**
2015–16	Bayer Leverkusen	28	17		
2016–17	Bayer Leverkusen	26	11	**54**	**28**
2017–18	West Ham U	28	8		
2018–19	West Ham U	25	7	**53**	**15**

HOLLAND, Nathan (M) 0 0
b. 19-6-98
Internationals: England U16, U17, U18, U19.

2016–17	West Ham U	0	0		
2017–18	West Ham U	0	0		
2018–19	West Ham U	0	0		

HUGILL, Jordan (F) 177 38
H: 6 0 W: 10 01 b.Middlesbrough 4-6-92

2013–14	Port Vale	20	4	**20**	**4**
2014–15	Preston NE	3	0		
2014–15	*Tranmere R*	6	1	**6**	**1**
2014–15	*Hartlepool U*	8	4	**8**	**4**
2015–16	Preston NE	29	3		
2016–17	Preston NE	44	12		
2017–18	Preston NE	27	8	**103**	**23**
2017–18	West Ham U	3	0		
2018–19	West Ham U	0	0	**3**	**0**
2018–19	*Middlesbrough*	37	6	**37**	**6**

JOHNSON, Ben (M) 1 0
b. 21-1-00

2017–18	West Ham U	0	0		
2018–19	West Ham U	1	0	**1**	**0**

LANZINI, Manuel (M) 234 43
H: 5 7 W: 11 00 b.Ituzaingo 15-2-93
Internationals: Argentina U20, Full caps.

2010–11	River Plate	22	0		
2010–11	*Fluminense*	22	2		
2011–12	River Plate	0	0		
2011–12	*Fluminense*	6	1	**28**	**3**
2012–13	River Plate	26	8	**26**	**8**
2013–14	River Plate	36	4	**58**	**4**
2014–15	Al-Jazira	24	8		
2015–16	Al-Jazira	0	0	**24**	**8**
2015–16	*West Ham U*	26	6		
2016–17	West Ham U	35	8		
2017–18	West Ham U	27	5		
2018–19	West Ham U	10	1	**98**	**20**

LUCAS PEREZ, Martinez (F) 209 60
H: 5 11 W: 11 07 b.A Coruna 10-9-88

2009–10	Rayo Vallecano	2	0		
2010–11	Rayo Vallecano	5	1	**7**	**1**
2010–11	Karpaty Lviv	8	0		
2011–12	Karpaty Lviv	26	6		
2012–13	Karpaty Lviv	17	8	**51**	**14**
2012–13	*Dynamo Kyiv*	0	0		
2013–14	PAOK	32	9	**32**	**9**
2014–15	*Deportivo La Coruna*	21	6		
2015–16	Deportivo La Coruna	36	17		
2016–17	Deportivo La Coruna	1	1		
2016–17	Arsenal	11	1		
2017–18	Arsenal	0	0	**11**	**1**
2017–18	*Deportivo La Coruna*	35	8	**93**	**32**
2018–19	West Ham U	15	3	**15**	**3**

MASUAKU, Arthur (D) 141 2
b. 7-11-93
Internationals: France U18, U19. DR Congo Full caps.

2012–13	Valenciennes	0	0		
2013–14	Valenciennes	27	1	**27**	**1**

2014–15	Olympiacos	27	0		
2015–16	Olympiacos	24	1	**51**	**1**
2016–17	West Ham U	13	0		
2017–18	West Ham U	27	0		
2018–19	West Ham U	23	0	**63**	**0**

NASRI, Samir (M) **372 49**
H: 5 9 W: 11 11 b.Marseille 26-6-87
Internationals: France U16, U17, U18, U19, U21, Full caps.

2004–05	Marseille	24	1		
2005–06	Marseille	30	1		
2006–07	Marseille	37	3		
2007–08	Marseille	30	6	**121**	**11**
2008–09	Arsenal	29	6		
2009–10	Arsenal	26	2		
2010–11	Arsenal	30	10		
2011–12	Arsenal	1	0	**86**	**18**
2011–12	Manchester C	30	5		
2012–13	Manchester C	28	2		
2013–14	Manchester C	34	7		
2014–15	Manchester C	24	2		
2015–16	Manchester C	12	2		
2016–17	Manchester C	1	0	**129**	**18**
2016–17	*Sevilla*	23	2	**23**	**2**
2017–18	Antalyaspor	8	0	**8**	**0**
2018–19	West Ham U	5	0	**5**	**0**

NEUFVILLE, Vashon (D) **1 0**
H: 5 8 W: 10 08 b. 18-7-99
Internationals: England U16, U17.

2017–18	West Ham U	0	0		
2018–19	West Ham U	0	0		
2018–19	*Newport Co*	1	0	**1**	**0**

NOBLE, Mark (M) **425 51**
H: 5 11 W: 12 00 b.West Ham 8-5-87
Internationals: England U16, U17, U18, U19, U21.

2004–05	West Ham U	13	0		
2005–06	West Ham U	5	0		
2005–06	*Hull C*	5	0	**5**	**0**
2006–07	West Ham U	10	2		
2006–07	*Ipswich T*	13	1	**13**	**1**
2007–08	West Ham U	31	3		
2008–09	West Ham U	29	3		
2009–10	West Ham U	27	2		
2010–11	West Ham U	26	4		
2011–12	West Ham U	45	8		
2012–13	West Ham U	28	4		
2013–14	West Ham U	38	3		
2014–15	West Ham U	28	2		
2015–16	West Ham U	37	7		
2016–17	West Ham U	30	3		
2017–18	West Ham U	29	4		
2018–19	West Ham U	31	5	**407**	**50**

OBIANG, Pedro (M) **223 7**
H: 6 1 W: 12 13 b.Alcala de Henares 13-5-90
Internationals: Spain U17, U19, U20, U21. Equatorial Guinea Full caps.

2008–09	Sampdoria	0	0		
2009–10	Sampdoria	0	0		
2010–11	Sampdoria	4	0		
2011–12	Sampdoria	33	0		
2012–13	Sampdoria	34	1		
2013–14	Sampdoria	27	0		
2014–15	Sampdoria	34	3	**132**	**4**
2015–16	West Ham U	24	0		
2016–17	West Ham U	22	1		
2017–18	West Ham U	21	2		
2018–19	West Ham U	24	0	**91**	**3**

OGBONNA, Angelo (D) **314 3**
H: 6 2 W: 13 08 b.Cassino 23-5-88
Internationals: Italy U21, Full caps.

2006–07	Torino	4	0		
2007–08	Torino	0	0		
2007–08	*Crotone*	22	0	**22**	**0**
2008–09	Torino	19	0		
2009–10	Torino	28	1		
2010–11	Torino	35	0		
2011–12	Torino	39	0		
2012–13	Torino	22	0	**147**	**1**
2013–14	Juventus	16	0		
2014–15	Juventus	25	0	**41**	**0**
2015–16	West Ham U	28	0		
2016–17	West Ham U	20	0		
2017–18	West Ham U	32	1		
2018–19	West Ham U	24	1	**104**	**2**

POWELL, Joe (F) **10 2**
b. 30-10-98

2018–19	West Ham U	0	0		
2018–19	*Northampton T*	10	2	**10**	**2**

RICE, Declan (M) **61 2**
b. 14-1-99
Internationals: Republic of Ireland U16, U17, U19, U21, Full caps.

2016–17	West Ham U	1	0		
2017–18	West Ham U	26	0		
2018–19	West Ham U	34	2	**61**	**2**

SANCHEZ, Carlos (M) **354 15**
H: 6 0 W: 12 08 b.Quidbo 6-2-86
Internationals: Colombia Full caps.

2005–06	River Plate	14	0		
2006–07	River Plate	26	1	**40**	**1**
2007–08	Valenciennes	34	0		
2008–09	Valenciennes	37	1		
2009–10	Valenciennes	28	5		
2010–11	Valenciennes	28	2		
2011–12	Valenciennes	21	1		
2012–13	Valenciennes	27	2	**175**	**11**
2013–14	Elche	30	0	**30**	**0**
2014–15	Aston Villa	28	1		
2015–16	Aston Villa	20	0		
2016–17	Aston Villa	0	0	**48**	**1**
2016–17	*Fiorentina*	31	1		
2017–18	Fiorentina	9	1	**40**	**2**
2017–18	*Espanyol*	14	0	**14**	**0**
2018–19	West Ham U	7	0	**7**	**0**

SNODGRASS, Robert (M) **459 87**
H: 6 0 W: 12 02 b.Glasgow 7-9-87
Internationals: Scotland U20, U21, Full caps.

2003–04	Livingston	0	0		
2004–05	Livingston	17	2		
2005–06	Livingston	27	4		
2006–07	Livingston	6	0		
2006–07	*Stirling Alb*	12	5	**12**	**5**
2007–08	Livingston	31	9	**81**	**15**
2008–09	Leeds U	42	9		
2009–10	Leeds U	44	7		
2010–11	Leeds U	37	6		
2011–12	Leeds U	43	13	**166**	**35**
2012–13	Norwich C	37	6		
2013–14	Norwich C	30	6	**67**	**12**
2014–15	Hull C	1	0		
2015–16	Hull C	24	4		
2016–17	Hull C	20	7	**45**	**11**
2016–17	West Ham U	15	0		
2017–18	West Ham U	0	0		
2017–18	*Aston Villa*	40	7	**40**	**7**
2018–19	West Ham U	33	2	**48**	**2**

WILSHERE, Jack (M) **174 8**
H: 5 7 W: 11 03 b.Stevenage 1-1-92
Internationals: England U16, U17, U19, U21, Full caps.

2008–09	Arsenal	1	0		
2009–10	Arsenal	1	0		
2009–10	*Bolton W*	14	1	**14**	**1**
2010–11	Arsenal	35	1		
2011–12	Arsenal	0	0		
2012–13	Arsenal	25	0		
2013–14	Arsenal	24	3		
2014–15	Arsenal	14	2		
2015–16	Arsenal	3	0		
2016–17	Arsenal	2	0		
2016–17	*Bournemouth*	27	0	**27**	**0**
2017–18	Arsenal	20	1	**125**	**7**
2018–19	West Ham U	8	0	**8**	**0**

XANDE SILVA, Nascimento (F) **27 1**
b. 16-3-97
Internationals: Portugal U16, U17, U18, U19, U20.

2014–15	Vitoria Guimaraes	1	0		
2015–16	Vitoria Guimaraes	20	1		
2016–17	Vitoria Guimaraes	4	0		
2017–18	Vitoria Guimaraes	1	0	**26**	**1**
2018–19	West Ham U	1	0	**1**	**0**

YARMOLENKO, Andriy (M) **255 104**
H: 6 2 W: 12 00 b.Saint Petersburg 23-10-89
Internationals: Ukraine U19, U21, Full caps.

2007–08	Dynamo Kyiv	1	1		
2008–09	Dynamo Kyiv	10	0		
2009–10	Dynamo Kyiv	28	7		
2010–11	Dynamo Kyiv	26	11		
2011–12	Dynamo Kyiv	28	12		
2012–13	Dynamo Kyiv	27	11		
2013–14	Dynamo Kyiv	26	12		
2014–15	Dynamo Kyiv	26	14		
2015–16	Dynamo Kyiv	23	13		
2016–17	Dynamo Kyiv	28	15		
2017–18	Dynamo Kyiv	5	3	**228**	**99**
2017–18	Borussia Dortmund	18	3	**18**	**3**
2018–19	West Ham U	9	2	**9**	**2**

ZABALETA, Pablo (D) **439 20**
H: 5 8 W: 10 12 b.Buenos Aires 16-1-85
Internationals: Argentina U20, U23, Full caps.

2002–03	San Lorenzo	11	0		
2003–04	San Lorenzo	27	3		
2004–05	San Lorenzo	28	5	**66**	**8**
2005–06	Espanyol	27	2		
2006–07	Espanyol	21	0		
2007–08	Espanyol	32	1	**80**	**3**
2008–09	Manchester C	29	1		
2009–10	Manchester C	27	0		
2010–11	Manchester C	26	2		
2011–12	Manchester C	21	1		
2012–13	Manchester C	30	2		
2013–14	Manchester C	35	1		
2014–15	Manchester C	29	1		
2015–16	Manchester C	13	0		
2016–17	Manchester C	20	1	**230**	**9**
2017–18	West Ham U	37	0		
2018–19	West Ham U	26	0	**63**	**0**

Players retained or with offer of contract
Akinola, Olatunji Oluwasehun; Alese, Ajibola; Anang, Joseph Tetteh; Belic, Kristijan; Da Rosa, Bernardo Costa; Dju, Mesaque Geremias; El Mhassani, Anouar; Fernandes Ribeiro, Edimilson; Haksabanovic, Sead; Hector-Ingram, Jahmal Justin; Kemp, Daniel; Lewis, Alfie; Oxford, Reece Joel; Reid, Winston Wiremu; Samuelsen, Martin; Scully, Anthony Richard; Trott, Nathan Wallace Newman.

Scholars
Adarkwa, Sean Jordan; Appiah-Forson, Keenan; Ashby, Harrison; Barrett, Mason; Caiger, Samuel Alfie; Chesters, Daniel Peter; Dalipi, Kevin; Giddings, Jake Patrick Moy; Greenidge, William Winston; Hannam, Reece Phillip Peter; Jinadu, Daniel Oluwagbolade; Longelo Mbule, Emmanuel; McGeachy, Kyle James; Mingi, Jade Jay; Nebyla, Sebastian; Ngakia, Jeremy; Nsumbu, Samuel; Okotcha, Joshua; Parkes, Veron Brandon; Peake, Lennon; Spyridis, Odysseas; Stroud, Peter Forrest; Watson, Louie Shaun.

WIGAN ATH (89)

BYRNE, Nathan (D) **251 15**
H: 5 10 W: 10 10 b.St Albans 5-6-92

2010–11	Tottenham H	0	0		
2010–11	*Brentford*	11	0	**11**	**0**
2011–12	Tottenham H	0	0		
2011–12	*Bournemouth*	9	0	**9**	**0**
2012–13	Tottenham H	0	0		
2012–13	*Crawley T*	12	1	**12**	**1**
2012–13	*Swindon T*	7	0		
2013–14	Swindon T	36	4		
2014–15	Swindon T	42	3		
2015–16	Swindon T	5	3	**90**	**10**
2015–16	Wolverhampton W	24	2		
2016–17	Wolverhampton W	0	0	**24**	**2**
2016–17	Wigan Ath	14	0		
2016–17	*Charlton Ath*	17	1	**17**	**1**
2017–18	Wigan Ath	44	0		
2018–19	Wigan Ath	30	1	**88**	**1**

COLE, Devante (F) **149 32**
H: 6 1 W: 11 06 b.Alderley Edge 10-5-95
Internationals: England U16, U17, U18, U19.

2013–14	Manchester C	0	0		
2014–15	Manchester C	0	0		
2014–15	*Barnsley*	19	5	**19**	**5**
2014–15	*Milton Keynes D*	15	3	**15**	**3**
2015–16	Bradford C	19	5	**19**	**5**
2015–16	Fleetwood T	14	2		
2016–17	Fleetwood T	35	5		
2017–18	Fleetwood T	28	10	**77**	**17**
2017–18	Wigan Ath	6	0		
2018–19	Wigan Ath	0	0	**6**	**0**
2018–19	*Burton Alb*	13	2	**13**	**2**

DUNKLEY, Cheyenne (D) **159 14**
H: 6 2 W: 13 05 b.Wolverhampton 13-2-92
Internationals: England C.
From Kidderminster H.

2014–15	Oxford U	9	0		
2015–16	Oxford U	29	4		
2016–17	Oxford U	40	3	**78**	**7**
2017–18	Wigan Ath	43	7		
2018–19	Wigan Ath	38	0	**81**	**7**

EVANS, Owen (G) **0 0**
Internationals: Wales U19, U21.
From Hereford U.

2016–17	Wigan Ath	0	0		
2017–18	Wigan Ath	0	0		
2018–19	Wigan Ath	0	0		

FOX, Danny (D) **421 15**
H: 5 11 W: 12 06 b.Winsford 29-5-86
Internationals: England U21. Scotland Full caps.

2004–05	Everton	0	0		
2004–05	*Stranraer*	11	1	**11**	**1**
2005–06	Walsall	33	0		
2006–07	Walsall	44	3		
2007–08	Walsall	22	3	**99**	**6**
2007–08	Coventry C	18	1		
2008–09	Coventry C	39	5		
2009–10	Coventry C	0	0	**57**	**6**
2009–10	Celtic	15	0	**15**	**0**
2009–10	Burnley	14	1		
2010–11	Burnley	35	0		
2011–12	Burnley	1	0	**50**	**1**
2011–12	Southampton	41	0		
2012–13	Southampton	20	1		
2013–14	Southampton	3	0	**64**	**1**
2013–14	Nottingham F	14	0		
2014–15	Nottingham F	27	0		
2015–16	Nottingham F	10	0		
2016–17	Nottingham F	23	0		
2017–18	Nottingham F	23	0		
2018–19	Nottingham F	18	0	**115**	**0**
2018–19	Wigan Ath	10	0	**10**	**0**

GARNER, Joe (F) **396 116**
H: 5 10 W: 11 02 b.Blackburn 12-4-88
Internationals: England U16, U17, U19.

2004–05	Blackburn R	0	0		
2005–06	Blackburn R	0	0		
2006–07	Blackburn R	0	0		
2006–07	*Carlisle U*	18	5		
2007–08	Carlisle U	31	14		
2008–09	Nottingham F	28	7		
2009–10	Nottingham F	18	2		
2010–11	Nottingham F	0	0		
2010–11	*Huddersfield T*	16	0	**16**	**0**
2010–11	*Scunthorpe U*	18	6	**18**	**6**
2011–12	Nottingham F	2	0	**48**	**9**
2011–12	Watford	22	1		
2012–13	Watford	2	0	**24**	**1**
2012–13	*Carlisle U*	16	7	**65**	**26**
2012–13	Preston NE	14	0		
2013–14	Preston NE	35	18		
2014–15	Preston NE	37	25		
2015–16	Preston NE	41	6		
2016–17	Preston NE	2	0	**129**	**49**
2016–17	Rangers	31	7	**31**	**7**
2017–18	Ipswich T	32	10	**32**	**10**
2018–19	Wigan Ath	33	8	**33**	**8**

GELHARDT, Joe (F) **1 0**
b.Liverpool 4-5-02
Internationals: England U16, U17.

2018–19	Wigan Ath	1	0	**1**	**0**

GIBSON, Darron (M) **148 6**
H: 6 0 W: 12 04 b.Derry 25-10-87
Internationals: Republic of Ireland U21, B, Full caps.

2005–06	Manchester U	0	0		
2006–07	Manchester U	0	0		
2007–08	Manchester U	0	0		
2007–08	*Wolverhampton W*	21	1	**21**	**1**
2008–09	Manchester U	3	1		
2009–10	Manchester U	15	2		
2010–11	Manchester U	12	0		
2011–12	Manchester U	1	0	**31**	**3**
2011–12	Everton	11	1		
2012–13	Everton	23	1		
2013–14	Everton	1	0		
2014–15	Everton	9	0		
2015–16	Everton	7	0		
2016–17	Everton	0	0	**51**	**2**
2016–17	Sunderland	12	0		
2017–18	Sunderland	15	0	**27**	**0**
2018–19	Wigan Ath	18	0	**18**	**0**

GOLDEN, Tylor (D) **0 0**
b.Ipswich 8-11-99

2017–18	Wigan Ath	0	0		
2018–19	Wigan Ath	0	0		

JACOBS, Michael (M) **319 51**
H: 5 9 W: 11 08 b.Rothwell 23-3-92

2009–10	Northampton T	0	0		
2010–11	Northampton T	41	5		
2011–12	Northampton T	46	6	**87**	**11**
2012–13	Derby Co	38	2		
2013–14	Derby Co	3	0	**41**	**2**
2013–14	Wolverhampton W	30	8		
2014–15	Wolverhampton W	12	0	**42**	**8**
2014–15	*Blackpool*	5	1	**5**	**1**
2015–16	Wigan Ath	35	10		
2016–17	Wigan Ath	43	3		
2017–18	Wigan Ath	44	12		
2018–19	Wigan Ath	22	4	**144**	**29**

JOLLEY, Charlie (F) **1 0**
b.Liverpool 13-1-01

2018–19	Wigan Ath	1	0	**1**	**0**

JONES, Jamie (G) **282 0**
H: 6 2 W: 14 05 b.Kirkby 18-2-89

2007–08	Everton	0	0		
2008–09	Leyton Orient	20	0		
2009–10	Leyton Orient	36	0		
2010–11	Leyton Orient	35	0		
2011–12	Leyton Orient	6	0		
2012–13	Leyton Orient	26	0		
2013–14	Leyton Orient	28	0	**151**	**0**
2014–15	Preston NE	17	0		
2014–15	*Coventry C*	4	0	**4**	**0**
2014–15	*Rochdale*	13	0	**13**	**0**
2015–16	Preston NE	0	0	**17**	**0**
2015–16	*Colchester U*	17	0	**17**	**0**
2015–16	Stevenage	17	0		
2016–17	Stevenage	36	0	**53**	**0**
2017–18	Wigan Ath	15	0		
2018–19	Wigan Ath	12	0	**27**	**0**

KIPRE, Cedric (D) **74 1**
H: 6 3 W: 12 02 b.Paris 9-12-96
Internationals: Ivory Coast U23.

2014–15	Leicester C	0	0		
2015–16	Leicester C	0	0		
2016–17	Leicester C	0	0		
2017–18	Motherwell	36	1	**36**	**1**
2018–19	Wigan Ath	38	0	**38**	**0**

LANG, Callum (F) **72 23**
H: 5 11 W: 11 00 b. 8-9-98

2016–17	Wigan Ath	0	0		
2017–18	Wigan Ath	0	0		
2017–18	*Morecambe*	30	10	**30**	**10**
2018–19	Wigan Ath	0	0		
2018–19	*Oldham Ath*	42	13	**42**	**13**

LONG, Adam (D) **0 0**
b. 11-11-00

2017–18	Wigan Ath	0	0		
2018–19	Wigan Ath	0	0		

MACDONALD, Shaun (M) **208 11**
H: 6 1 W: 11 04 b.Swansea 17-6-88
Internationals: Wales U19, U21, Full caps.

2005–06	Swansea C	7	0		
2006–07	Swansea C	8	0		
2007–08	Swansea C	1	0		
2008–09	Swansea C	5	0		
2008–09	*Yeovil T*	4	2		
2009–10	Swansea C	3	0		
2009–10	*Yeovil T*	31	3		
2010–11	Swansea C	0	0		
2010–11	*Yeovil T*	26	4	**61**	**9**
2011–12	Swansea C	0	0	**24**	**0**
2011–12	Bournemouth	25	1		
2012–13	Bournemouth	28	0		
2013–14	Bournemouth	23	0		
2014–15	Bournemouth	5	0		
2015–16	Bournemouth	3	0	**84**	**1**
2016–17	Wigan Ath	39	1		
2017–18	Wigan Ath	0	0		
2018–19	Wigan Ath	0	0	**39**	**1**

MASSEY, Gavin (F) **287 42**
H: 5 11 W: 11 06 b.Watford 14-10-92

2009–10	Watford	1	0		
2010–11	Watford	3	0		
2011–12	Watford	3	0		
2011–12	*Yeovil T*	16	3	**16**	**3**
2011–12	*Colchester U*	8	0		
2012–13	Watford	0	0	**7**	**0**
2012–13	Colchester U	40	6		
2013–14	Colchester U	30	3		
2014–15	Colchester U	46	7		
2015–16	Colchester U	42	4	**166**	**20**
2016–17	Leyton Orient	36	8	**36**	**8**
2017–18	Wigan Ath	42	6		
2018–19	Wigan Ath	20	5	**62**	**11**

McMANAMAN, Callum (F) **170 14**
H: 5 9 W: 11 03 b.Huyton 25-4-91
Internationals: England U20.

2008–09	Wigan Ath	1	0		
2009–10	Wigan Ath	0	0		
2010–11	Wigan Ath	3	0		
2011–12	Wigan Ath	2	0		
2011–12	*Blackpool*	14	2	**14**	**2**
2012–13	Wigan Ath	20	2		
2013–14	Wigan Ath	30	3		
2014–15	Wigan Ath	23	5		
2014–15	WBA	8	0		
2015–16	WBA	12	0		
2016–17	WBA	0	0	**20**	**0**
2016–17	*Sheffield W*	11	0	**11**	**0**
2017–18	Sunderland	24	1	**24**	**1**
2018–19	Wigan Ath	22	1	**101**	**11**

MERRIE, Christopher (M) **0 0**
b.Liverpool 2-11-98
From Everton.

2017–18	Wigan Ath	0	0		
2018–19	Wigan Ath	0	0		

MORSY, Sam (M) **296 16**
H: 5 9 W: 12 06 b.Wolverhampton 10-9-91
Internationals: Egypt Full caps.

2009–10	Port Vale	1	0		
2010–11	Port Vale	16	1		
2011–12	Port Vale	26	1		
2012–13	Port Vale	28	2	**71**	**4**
2013–14	Chesterfield	34	1		
2014–15	Chesterfield	39	2		
2015–16	Chesterfield	26	4	**99**	**7**
2015–16	Wigan Ath	16	1		
2016–17	Barnsley	14	0	**14**	**0**
2016–17	Wigan Ath	15	1		
2017–18	Wigan Ath	41	2		
2018–19	Wigan Ath	40	1	**112**	**5**

NAISMITH, Kal (F) **189 33**
H: 5 7 W: 13 02 b.Glasgow 18-2-92
Internationals: Scotland U16, U17.

2013–14	Accrington S	38	10		
2014–15	Accrington S	35	4	**73**	**14**
2015–16	Portsmouth	19	3		
2015–16	*Hartlepool U*	4	0	**4**	**0**
2016–17	Portsmouth	37	13		
2017–18	Portsmouth	26	2	**82**	**18**
2018–19	Wigan Ath	30	1	**30**	**1**

OLSSON, Jonas (D) **440 21**
H: 6 4 W: 12 08 b.Landskrona 10-3-83
Internationals: Sweden U21, Full caps.

2002	Landskrona	0	0		
2003	Landskrona	22	0		
2004	Landskrona	22	1		
2005	Landskrona	12	0	**56**	**1**
2005–06	NEC Nijmegen	34	0		
2006–07	NEC Nijmegen	32	2		
2007–08	NEC Nijmegen	27	3	**93**	**5**
2008–09	WBA	28	2		
2009–10	WBA	43	4		
2010–11	WBA	24	1		
2011–12	WBA	33	2		
2012–13	WBA	36	0		
2013–14	WBA	32	1		
2014–15	WBA	13	1		
2015–16	WBA	28	1		
2016–17	WBA	7	0	**244**	**12**
2017	Djurgarden	22	3		
2018	Djurgarden	19	0	**41**	**3**
2018–19	Wigan Ath	6	0	**6**	**0**

PERRY, Alex (M) **0 0**
b.Liverpool 4-3-98

2016–17	Bolton W	0	0		
2017–18	Bolton W	0	0		
2018–19	Wigan Ath	0	0		

PIGGOTT, Joe (F) **6 0**
b. 23-6-99

2017–18	Dundee U	0	0		
2018–19	Wigan Ath	0	0		
2018–19	*Morecambe*	6	0	**6**	**0**

PILKINGTON, Anthony (M) **355 69**
H: 5 11 W: 12 00 b.Blackburn 3-11-87
Internationals: Republic of Ireland U21, Full caps.

2006–07	Stockport Co	24	5		
2007–08	Stockport Co	29	6		
2008–09	Stockport Co	24	5	**77**	**16**
2008–09	Huddersfield T	16	2		
2009–10	Huddersfield T	43	7		
2010–11	Huddersfield T	31	10	**90**	**19**
2011–12	Norwich C	30	8		
2012–13	Norwich C	30	5		
2013–14	Norwich C	15	1	**75**	**14**
2014–15	Cardiff C	20	1		
2015–16	Cardiff C	41	9		
2016–17	Cardiff C	34	7		
2017–18	Cardiff C	8	3		

2018–19	Cardiff C	0	0	**103**	**20**
2018–19	Wigan Ath	10	0	**10**	**0**

POWELL, Nick (F) 187 51
H: 6 0 W: 10 05 b.Crewe 23-3-94
Internationals: England U16, U17, U18, U19, U21.

2010–11	Crewe Alex	17	0		
2011–12	Crewe Alex	38	14	**55**	**14**
2012–13	Manchester U	2	1		
2013–14	Manchester U	0	0		
2013–14	*Wigan Ath*	31	7		
2014–15	Manchester U	0	0		
2014–15	*Leicester C*	3	0	**3**	**0**
2015–16	Manchester U	1	0	**3**	**1**
2015–16	*Hull C*	3	0	**3**	**0**
2016–17	Wigan Ath	21	6		
2017–18	Wigan Ath	39	15		
2018–19	Wigan Ath	32	8	**123**	**36**

ROBERTS, Gary (F) 464 83
H: 5 10 W: 11 09 b.Chester 18-3-84
Internationals: England C.

2006–07	Accrington S	14	8	**14**	**8**
2006–07	Ipswich T	33	2		
2007–08	Ipswich T	21	1	**54**	**3**
2007–08	*Crewe Alex*	4	0	**4**	**0**
2008–09	Huddersfield T	43	9		
2009–10	Huddersfield T	43	7		
2010–11	Huddersfield T	37	9		
2011–12	Huddersfield T	39	6	**162**	**31**
2012–13	Swindon T	39	4	**39**	**4**
2013–14	Chesterfield	40	11		
2014–15	Chesterfield	34	6	**74**	**17**
2015–16	Portsmouth	33	7		
2016–17	Portsmouth	41	10		
2017–18	Portsmouth	0	0	**74**	**17**
2017–18	Wigan Ath	27	1		
2018–19	Wigan Ath	16	2	**43**	**3**

VAUGHAN, James (F) 293 78
H: 5 11 W: 13 00 b.Birmingham 14-7-88
Internationals: England U17, U19, U21.

2004–05	Everton	2	1		
2005–06	Everton	1	0		
2006–07	Everton	14	4		
2007–08	Everton	8	1		
2008–09	Everton	13	0		
2009–10	Everton	8	1		
2009–10	*Derby Co*	2	0	**2**	**0**
2010–11	Everton	1	0	**47**	**7**
2010–11	*Crystal Palace*	30	9	**30**	**9**
2011–12	Norwich C	5	0		
2012–13	Norwich C	0	0	**5**	**0**
2012–13	*Huddersfield T*	33	14		
2013–14	Huddersfield T	23	10		
2014–15	Huddersfield T	26	7		
2015–16	Huddersfield T	4	0	**86**	**31**
2015–16	*Birmingham C*	15	0	**15**	**0**
2016–17	Bury	37	24	**37**	**24**
2017–18	Sunderland	23	2	**23**	**2**
2017–18	Wigan Ath	19	3		
2018–19	Wigan Ath	19	2	**38**	**5**
2018–19	*Portsmouth*	10	0	**10**	**0**

WALKER, Jamie (M) 199 41
H: 5 9 W: 11 00 b.Edinburgh 25-6-93
Internationals: Scotland U16, U17, U19, U21.

2011–12	Hearts	0	0		
2011–12	*Raith R*	23	3	**23**	**3**
2012–13	Hearts	24	2		
2013–14	Hearts	26	3		
2014–15	Hearts	33	11		
2015–16	Hearts	23	7		
2016–17	Hearts	34	12		
2017–18	Hearts	16	2	**156**	**37**
2017–18	Wigan Ath	8	0		
2018–19	Wigan Ath	0	0	**8**	**0**
2018–19	*Peterborough U*	12	1	**12**	**1**

WEIR, Jensen (M) 1 0
b.Warrington 31-1-02

2017–18	Wigan Ath	0	0		
2018–19	Wigan Ath	1	0	**1**	**0**

WINDASS, Josh (M) 169 39
H: 5 9 W: 10 10 b.Hull 9-1-93

2013–14	Accrington S	10	0		
2014–15	Accrington S	35	6		
2015–16	Accrington S	30	15	**75**	**21**
2016–17	Rangers	21	0		
2017–18	Rangers	33	13		
2018–19	Rangers	1	0	**55**	**13**
2018–19	Wigan Ath	39	5	**39**	**5**

Players retained or with offer of contract
Carroll-Burgess, Luke Eugene; Crankshaw, Oliver Samuel; Da, Silva Lopes Leonardo Adelino; Finley, Sam John; Galvin, Ryan Patrick Francis; Joseph, Kyle Alexander; Obi, Chukwuemeka David.

Scholars
Aasgaard, Thelonious Gerard; Baningime, Divin; Berry-McNally, James Jon; Broe, Oliver Jack; Culshaw, Mitchell Scott; Golden, Tylor Reed; Isherwood, Louis James; Jolley, Harry Thomas; Jones, Bobby; Long, Adam David; Maffeo, Becerra Victor Alfonso; McGaughey, Kain Alex; McGuffie, Will Jared; McWilliam, Joseph Norman; Monaghan, Neil Stephen; O'Neill, Mackenzie David; Roberts, Bradley Ian; Robinson, Luke James; Smith, Scott; Weir, Jensen Guy.

WOLVERHAMPTON W (90)

ASHLEY-SEAL, Benny (F) 0 0
b.Southwark 21-11-98
From Norwich C.

2018–19	Wolverhampton W	0	0		

BENNETT, Ryan (M) 355 16
H: 6 2 W: 11 00 b.Thurrock 6-3-90
Internationals: England U18, U21.

2006–07	Grimsby T	5	0		
2007–08	Grimsby T	40	1		
2008–09	Grimsby T	45	5		
2009–10	Grimsby T	13	0	**103**	**6**
2009–10	Peterborough U	22	1		
2010–11	Peterborough U	34	4		
2011–12	Peterborough U	32	1	**88**	**6**
2011–12	Norwich C	8	0		
2012–13	Norwich C	15	1		
2013–14	Norwich C	16	1		
2014–15	Norwich C	7	0		
2015–16	Norwich C	22	0		
2016–17	Norwich C	33	0	**101**	**2**
2017–18	Wolverhampton W	29	1		
2018–19	Wolverhampton W	34	1	**63**	**2**

BOLY, Willy (D) 198 12
H: 6 1 W: 12 11 b. 3-2-91
Internationals: France U16, U17, U19.

2010–11	Auxerre	8	1		
2011–12	Auxerre	33	1		
2012–13	Auxerre	25	1		
2013–14	Auxerre	30	0		
2014–15	Auxerre	1	0	**97**	**3**
2014–15	Braga	0	0		
2015–16	Braga	22	2		
2016–17	Braga	3	0	**25**	**2**
2016–17	Porto	4	0		
2017–18	Porto	0	0	**4**	**0**
2017–18	*Wolverhampton W*	36	3		
2018–19	Wolverhampton W	36	4	**72**	**7**

COADY, Conor (D) 245 9
H: 6 1 W: 11 05 b.Liverpool 25-2-93
Internationals: England U16, U17, U18, U19, U20.

2010–11	Liverpool	0	0		
2011–12	Liverpool	0	0		
2012–13	Liverpool	1	0		
2013–14	Liverpool	0	0	**1**	**0**
2013–14	*Sheffield U*	39	5	**39**	**5**
2014–15	Huddersfield T	45	3	**45**	**3**
2015–16	Wolverhampton W	37	0		
2016–17	Wolverhampton W	40	0		
2017–18	Wolverhampton W	45	1		
2018–19	Wolverhampton W	38	0	**160**	**1**

DENDONCKER, Leander (M) 144 11
H: 6 2 W: 12 02 b.Passendale 15-4-95
Internationals: Belgium U16, U17, U19, U21, Full caps.

2013–14	Anderlecht	0	0		
2014–15	Anderlecht	26	2		
2015–16	Anderlecht	23	1		
2016–17	Anderlecht	40	5		
2017–18	Anderlecht	36	1	**125**	**9**

On loan from Anderlecht.

2018–19	Wolverhampton W	19	2	**19**	**2**

DOHERTY, Matthew (M) 254 19
H: 6 0 W: 12 08 b.Dublin 17-1-92
Internationals: Republic of Ireland U19, U21, Full caps.

2010–11	Wolverhampton W	0	0		
2011–12	Wolverhampton W	1	0		
2011–12	*Hibernian*	13	2	**13**	**2**
2012–13	Wolverhampton W	13	1		
2012–13	*Bury*	17	1	**17**	**1**
2013–14	Wolverhampton W	18	1		
2014–15	Wolverhampton W	33	0		
2015–16	Wolverhampton W	34	2		
2016–17	Wolverhampton W	42	4		
2017–18	Wolverhampton W	45	4		
2018–19	Wolverhampton W	38	4	**224**	**16**

EBANKS-LANDELL, Ethan (M) 145 14
H: 5 6 W: 11 02 b.Oldbury 16-12-92

2009–10	Wolverhampton W	0	0		
2010–11	Wolverhampton W	0	0		
2011–12	Wolverhampton W	0	0		
2012–13	Wolverhampton W	0	0		
2012–13	*Bury*	24	0	**24**	**0**
2013–14	Wolverhampton W	7	2		
2014–15	Wolverhampton W	14	2		
2015–16	Wolverhampton W	21	1		
2016–17	Wolverhampton W	0	0		
2016–17	*Sheffield U*	34	5	**34**	**5**
2017–18	Wolverhampton W	0	0		
2017–18	*Milton Keynes D*	29	2	**29**	**2**
2018–19	Wolverhampton W	0	0	**42**	**5**
2018–19	*Rochdale*	16	2	**16**	**2**

ENNIS, Niall (F) 1 0
H: 5 10 W: 12 00 b.Wolverhampton 20-5-99
Internationals: England U17, U18, U19.

2017–18	Wolverhampton W	0	0		
2017–18	*Shrewsbury T*	1	0	**1**	**0**
2018–19	Wolverhampton W	0	0		

ENOBAKHARE, Bright (F) 65 7
H: 6 0 W: 12 06 b. 8-2-98

2015–16	Wolverhampton W	7	0		
2016–17	Wolverhampton W	13	0		
2017–18	Wolverhampton W	21	1		
2018–19	Wolverhampton W	0	0	**41**	**1**
2018–19	*Kilmarnock*	6	0	**6**	**0**
2018–19	*Coventry C*	18	6	**18**	**6**

GILES, Ryan (M) 0 0
H: 5 10 W: 11 00 b.Telford 26-1-00

2018–19	Wolverhampton W	0	0		

GONCALVES, Pedro (M) 0 0
H: 5 8 W: 10 03 b.Chaves 28-6-98
From Valencia.

2018–19	Wolverhampton W	0	0		

GRAHAM, Jordan (M) 45 2
H: 6 0 W: 10 10 b.Coventry 5-3-95
Internationals: England U16, U17.

2011–12	Aston Villa	0	0		
2012–13	Aston Villa	0	0		
2013–14	Aston Villa	0	0		
2013–14	*Ipswich T*	2	0		
2013–14	*Bradford C*	1	0	**1**	**0**
2014–15	Wolverhampton W	0	0		
2015–16	Wolverhampton W	11	1		
2015–16	*Oxford U*	5	0		
2016–17	Wolverhampton W	2	0		
2017–18	Wolverhampton W	1	0		
2017–18	*Fulham*	3	0	**3**	**0**
2018–19	Wolverhampton W	0	0	**14**	**1**
2018–19	*Ipswich T*	4	0	**6**	**0**
2018–19	*Oxford U*	16	1	**21**	**1**

HAUSE, Kortney (D) 115 6
H: 6 2 W: 13 03 b.Goodmayes 16-7-95
Internationals: England U20, U21.

2012–13	Wycombe W	9	1		
2013–14	Wycombe W	14	1	**23**	**2**
2013–14	Wolverhampton W	0	0		
2014–15	Wolverhampton W	17	0		
2014–15	*Gillingham*	14	1	**14**	**1**
2015–16	Wolverhampton W	25	0		
2016–17	Wolverhampton W	24	2		
2017–18	Wolverhampton W	1	0		
2018–19	Wolverhampton W	0	0	**67**	**2**
2018–19	*Aston Villa*	11	1	**11**	**1**

HELDER COSTA, Wander (M) 127 19
H: 5 10 W: 11 07 b.Luanda 12-1-94
Internationals: Portugal U16, U17, U18, U19, U20, U21, U23, Full caps.

2013–14	Benfica	0	0		
2014–15	Benfica	0	0		
2014–15	*Deportivo La Coruna*	6	0	**6**	**0**
2015–16	Benfica	0	0		
2015–16	*Monaco*	25	3	**25**	**3**
2016–17	Benfica	0	0		
2016–17	*Wolverhampton W*	35	10		
2017–18	Wolverhampton W	36	5		
2018–19	Wolverhampton W	25	1	**96**	**16**

IVAN CAVALEIRO, Ricardo (M) **150 21**
H: 5 9 W: 11 07 b.Vialonga 18-10-93
Internationals: Portugal U17, U18, U19, U20, U21, Full caps.

2012–13	Benfica	0	0		
2013–14	Benfica	8	0		
2014–15	Benfica	0	0	**8**	**0**
2014–15	*Deportivo La Coruna*	34	3	**34**	**3**
2015–16	Monaco	12	1	**12**	**1**
2016–17	Wolverhampton W	31	5		
2017–18	Wolverhampton W	42	9		
2018–19	Wolverhampton W	23	3	**96**	**17**

JIMENEZ, Raul (F) **214 61**
H: 6 2 W: 12 04 b.Tepeji 5-5-91
Internationals: Mexico U23, Full caps.

2011–12	America	15	2		
2012–13	America	29	11		
2013–14	America	27	12		
2014–15	America	4	4	**75**	**29**
2014–15	Atletico Madrid	21	1	**21**	**1**
2015–16	Benfica	28	5		
2016–17	Benfica	19	7		
2017–18	Benfica	33	6		
2018–19	Benfica	0	0	**80**	**18**

On loan from Benfica.

2018–19	Wolverhampton W	38	13	**38**	**13**

JOAO MOUTINHO, Felipe (M) **442 35**
H: 5 7 W: 9 08 b.Portimao 8-9-86
Internationals: Portugal U17, U18, U19, U21, B, Full caps.

2004–05	Sporting Lisbon	15	0		
2005–06	Sporting Lisbon	34	4		
2006–07	Sporting Lisbon	29	4		
2007–08	Sporting Lisbon	30	5		
2008–09	Sporting Lisbon	27	3		
2009–10	Sporting Lisbon	28	5	**163**	**21**
2010–11	Porto	27	0		
2011–12	Porto	29	3		
2012–13	Porto	27	1	**83**	**4**
2013–14	Monaco	31	1		
2014–15	Monaco	37	4		
2015–16	Monaco	26	1		
2016–17	Monaco	31	2		
2017–18	Monaco	33	1	**158**	**9**
2018–19	Wolverhampton W	38	1	**38**	**1**

JOHN, Cameron (D) **0 0**
b. 24-8-99

2018–19	Wolverhampton W	0	0		

JOHNSON, Connor (D) **7 0**
b.Kettering 10-3-98

2016–17	Wolverhampton W	0	0		
2017–18	Wolverhampton W	0	0		
2018–19	Wolverhampton W	0	0		
2018–19	*Walsall*	7	0	**7**	**0**

JONNY, Castro (D) **216 4**
H: 5 9 W: 11 00 b.Vigo 3-3-94
Internationals: Spain U18, U19, U20, U21, Full caps.

2011–12	Celta Vigo	0	0		
2012–13	Celta Vigo	19	0		
2013–14	Celta Vigo	26	0		
2014–15	Celta Vigo	36	0		
2015–16	Celta Vigo	36	1		
2016–17	Celta Vigo	30	0		
2017–18	Celta Vigo	36	2	**183**	**3**
2018–19	Atletico Madrid	0	0		

On loan from Atletico Madrid.

2018–19	Wolverhampton W	33	1	**33**	**1**

JOTA, Diogo (F) **145 48**
H: 5 10 W: 11 00 b.Massarelos 4-12-96
Internationals: Portugal U19, U21, U23.

2014–15	Pacos Ferreira	10	2		
2015–16	Pacos Ferreira	31	12	**41**	**14**
2016–17	Atletico Madrid	0	0		
2016–17	*Porto*	27	8	**27**	**8**
2017–18	Atletico Madrid	0	0		
2017–18	*Wolverhampton W*	44	17		
2018–19	Wolverhampton W	33	9	**77**	**26**

KILMAN, Max (D) **1 0**
b.London 23-5-97
From Maidenhead U.

2018–19	Wolverhampton W	1	0	**1**	**0**

LEO BONATINI, Lohner (F) **134 45**
b. 28-3-94
Internationals: Brazil U17.

2013	Cruzeiro	0	0		
2013	*Goias*	5	0		
2014	Cruzeiro	0	0		
2014	Goias	1	0	**6**	**0**
2014–15	Estoril	15	4		
2015	Cruzeiro	0	0		
2015–16	Estoril	33	17	**48**	**21**
2016–17	Al Hilal	25	12		
2017–18	Al Hilal	0	0	**25**	**12**
2017–18	*Wolverhampton W*	43	12		
2018–19	Wolverhampton W	7	0	**50**	**12**
2018–19	*Nottingham F*	5	0	**5**	**0**

MASON, Joe (F) **231 52**
H: 5 9 W: 11 11 b.Plymouth 13-5-91
Internationals: Republic of Ireland U18, U19, U21.

2009–10	Plymouth Arg	19	3		
2010–11	Plymouth Arg	34	7	**53**	**10**
2011–12	Cardiff C	39	9		
2012–13	Cardiff C	28	6		
2013–14	Cardiff C	0	0		
2013–14	*Bolton W*	16	6		
2014–15	Cardiff C	7	1		
2014–15	*Bolton W*	12	4	**28**	**10**
2015–16	Cardiff C	23	6	**97**	**22**
2015–16	Wolverhampton W	16	3		
2016–17	Wolverhampton W	19	3		
2017–18	Wolverhampton W	0	0		
2017–18	*Burton Alb*	6	1	**6**	**1**
2018	*Colorado Rapids*	11	3	**11**	**3**
2018–19	Wolverhampton W	0	0	**35**	**6**
2018–19	*Portsmouth*	1	0	**1**	**0**

NEVES, Ruben (M) **136 13**
H: 5 11 W: 12 08 b. 13-3-97
Internationals: Portugal U16, U17, U18, U21, U23, Full caps.

2014–15	Porto	24	1		
2015–16	Porto	22	1		
2016–17	Porto	13	1	**59**	**3**
2017–18	Wolverhampton W	42	6		
2018–19	Wolverhampton W	35	4	**77**	**10**

NORRIS, Will (G) **71 0**
H: 6 5 W: 11 09 b.Royston 12-7-93

2014–15	Cambridge U	3	0		
2015–16	Cambridge U	21	0		
2016–17	Cambridge U	45	0	**69**	**0**
2017–18	Wolverhampton W	1	0		
2018–19	Wolverhampton W	1	0	**2**	**0**

RONAN, Connor (M) **34 0**
H: 5 8 W: 11 00 b.Rochdale 6-3-98
Internationals: England U17. Republic of Ireland U17, U19, U21.

2015–16	Wolverhampton W	0	0		
2016–17	Wolverhampton W	4	0		
2017–18	Wolverhampton W	3	0		
2017–18	*Portsmouth*	16	0	**16**	**0**
2018–19	Wolverhampton W	0	0	**7**	**0**
2018–19	*Walsall*	11	0	**11**	**0**

RUBEN VINAGRE, Goncalo (D) **26 1**
b. 9-4-99
Internationals: Portugal U16, U17, U18, U19, U20, U21.

2016–17	Monaco	0	0		
2017–18	Monaco	0	0		
2017–18	*Wolverhampton W*	9	1		
2018–19	Wolverhampton W	17	0	**26**	**1**

RUDDY, John (G) **415 0**
H: 6 3 W: 12 07 b.St Ives 24-10-86
Internationals: England Full caps.

2003–04	Cambridge U	1	0		
2004–05	Cambridge U	38	0	**39**	**0**
2005–06	Everton	1	0		
2005–06	*Walsall*	5	0	**5**	**0**
2005–06	*Rushden & D*	3	0	**3**	**0**
2005–06	*Chester C*	4	0	**4**	**0**
2006–07	Everton	0	0		
2006–07	*Stockport Co*	11	0		
2006–07	*Wrexham*	5	0	**5**	**0**
2006–07	*Bristol C*	1	0	**1**	**0**
2007–08	Everton	0	0		
2007–08	*Stockport Co*	12	0	**23**	**0**
2008–09	Everton	0	0		
2008–09	*Crewe Alex*	19	0	**19**	**0**
2009–10	Everton	0	0	**1**	**0**
2009–10	*Motherwell*	34	0	**34**	**0**
2010–11	Norwich C	45	0		
2011–12	Norwich C	37	0		
2012–13	Norwich C	15	0		
2013–14	Norwich C	38	0		
2014–15	Norwich C	46	0		
2015–16	Norwich C	27	0		
2016–17	Norwich C	27	0	**235**	**0**
2017–18	Wolverhampton W	45	0		
2018–19	Wolverhampton W	1	0	**46**	**0**

RUI PATRICIO, Pedro (G) **364 0**
H: 6 2 W: 13 03 b.Marrazes 15-2-88
Internationals: Portugal U16, U17, U18, U19, U20, U21, Full caps.

2006–07	Sporting Lisbon	1	0		
2007–08	Sporting Lisbon	20	0		
2008–09	Sporting Lisbon	26	0		
2009–10	Sporting Lisbon	30	0		
2010–11	Sporting Lisbon	30	0		
2011–12	Sporting Lisbon	28	0		
2012–13	Sporting Lisbon	30	0		
2013–14	Sporting Lisbon	30	0		
2014–15	Sporting Lisbon	33	0		
2015–16	Sporting Lisbon	34	0		
2016–17	Sporting Lisbon	31	0		
2017–18	Sporting Lisbon	34	0	**327**	**0**
2018–19	Wolverhampton W	37	0	**37**	**0**

SAISS, Romain (M) **242 16**
H: 6 3 W: 12 00 b.Bourg-de-Peage 26-3-90
Internationals: Morocco Full caps.

2010–11	Valence	13	4	**13**	**4**
2011–12	Clermont	17	1		
2012–13	Clermont	31	0	**48**	**1**
2013–14	Le Havre	27	1		
2014–15	Le Havre	34	2	**61**	**3**
2015–16	Angers	35	2	**35**	**2**
2016–17	Wolverhampton W	24	0		
2017–18	Wolverhampton W	42	4		
2018–19	Wolverhampton W	19	2	**85**	**6**

TRAORE, Adama (F) **102 6**
H: 5 10 W: 12 00 b.L'Hospitalet de Llobregat 25-1-96
Internationals: Spain U16, U17, U19, U21.

2013–14	Barcelona	1	0		
2014–15	Barcelona	0	0	**1**	**0**
2015–16	Aston Villa	10	0		
2016–17	Aston Villa	1	0	**11**	**0**
2016–17	Middlesbrough	27	0		
2017–18	Middlesbrough	34	5	**61**	**5**
2018–19	Wolverhampton W	29	1	**29**	**1**

WATT, Elliot (M) **0 0**
b.Preston 11-3-18
Internationals: Scotland U17, U19, U21.
From Preston NE.

2018–19	Wolverhampton W	0	0		

WHITE, Morgan (M) **46 0**
b. 27-1-00
Internationals: England U16, U17, U18, U19, U21.

2016–17	Wolverhampton W	7	0		
2017–18	Wolverhampton W	13	0		
2018–19	Wolverhampton W	26	0	**46**	**0**

WILSON, Donovan (F) **19 1**
b.Yate 14-3-97

2014–15	Wolverhampton W	0	0		
2015–16	Wolverhampton W	0	0		
2016–17	Wolverhampton W	1	0		
2017–18	Wolverhampton W	0	0		
2017–18	*Port Vale*	8	1	**8**	**1**
2018–19	Wolverhampton W	0	0	**1**	**0**
2018–19	*Exeter C*	10	0	**10**	**0**

Players retained or with offer of contract
Agboola, Michael; Burgoyne, Harry James; Caiado Vaz Dias, Joao; Csoka, Daniel; Deslandes, Sylvain Boris Nabil; Diallo, Sadou; Estrada, Pascal; Francis, Edward Albert; Goncalves Miranda, Roderick Jefferson; He, Zhenyu; Herc, Christian; Joseph, Joseph; Kitolano, John Shuguto; Leak, Ryan David; Mir Vincente, Rafael; Neto Hanne, Boubacar Rafael; Neves Alves, Paulo Manuel; Ofosu-Ayeh, Phil; Otasowie, Ebeguowen; Pardington, James; Perry, Taylor; Rasmussen, Oskar Buur; Richards, Lewis Paul Jimmy; Samuels, Austin; Sanderson, Dion Dannic Leonard; Seedorf, Sherwin; Smith, Jackson; Sondergaard, Andreas; Taylor, Terence; Thompson, Callum Niall; Wang, Jiahao; Yang, Ming-Yang.

Scholars
Abbey, Jediael Yeboah; Berkoe, Kevin; Carty, Conor Thomas; Corbeanu, Theodor Alexander; Crabtree, Aaron; Cundle, Luke James; O'Sullivan, Ray; Parker, Todd William; Townsend, Taylor.

WYCOMBE W (91)

AKINFENWA, Adebayo (F) **588 184**
H: 5 11 W: 13 07 b.Nigeria 10-5-82

2001	Atlantas	19	4		
2002	Atlantas	4	1	**23**	**5**
From Barry T					
2003–04	Boston U	3	0	**3**	**0**
2003–04	Leyton Orient	1	0	**1**	**0**
2003–04	Rushden & D	0	0		
2003–04	Doncaster R	9	4	**9**	**4**
2004–05	Torquay U	37	14	**37**	**14**
2005–06	Swansea C	34	9		
2006–07	Swansea C	25	5		
2007–08	Swansea C	0	0	**59**	**14**
2007–08	Millwall	7	0	**7**	**0**
2007–08	Northampton T	15	7		
2008–09	Northampton T	33	13		
2009–10	Northampton T	40	17		
2010–11	Gillingham	44	11		
2011–12	Northampton T	39	18		
2012–13	Northampton T	41	16	**168**	**71**
2013–14	Gillingham	34	10	**78**	**21**
2014–15	AFC Wimbledon	45	13		
2015–16	AFC Wimbledon	38	6	**83**	**19**
2016–17	Wycombe W	42	12		
2017–18	Wycombe W	42	17		
2018–19	Wycombe W	36	7	**120**	**36**

ALLSOP, Ryan (G) **162 0**
H: 6 2 W: 12 06 b.Birmingham 17-6-92
Internationals: England U17.

2012–13	Leyton Orient	20	0	**20**	**0**
2012–13	Bournemouth	10	0		
2013–14	Bournemouth	12	0		
2014–15	Bournemouth	0	0		
2014–15	*Coventry C*	24	0	**24**	**0**
2015–16	Bournemouth	1	0		
2015–16	*Wycombe W*	18	0		
2015–16	Portsmouth	0	0		
2016–17	Bournemouth	1	0		
2017–18	Bournemouth	0	0	**24**	**0**
2017–18	*Blackpool*	22	0	**22**	**0**
2017–18	*Lincoln C*	16	0	**16**	**0**
2018–19	Wycombe W	38	0	**56**	**0**

BEAN, Marcus (M) **444 28**
H: 5 11 W: 11 06 b.Hammersmith 2-11-84
Internationals: Jamaica Full caps.

2002–03	QPR	7	0		
2003–04	QPR	31	1		
2004–05	QPR	20	1		
2004–05	*Swansea C*	8	0		
2005–06	QPR	9	0	**67**	**2**
2005–06	*Swansea C*	9	1	**17**	**1**
2005–06	Blackpool	17	1		
2006–07	Blackpool	6	0		
2007–08	Blackpool	0	0	**23**	**1**
2007–08	*Rotherham U*	12	1	**12**	**1**
2008–09	Brentford	44	9		
2009–10	Brentford	31	0		
2010–11	Brentford	37	3		
2011–12	Brentford	32	2	**144**	**14**
2012–13	Colchester U	31	0		
2013–14	Colchester U	35	5		
2014–15	Colchester U	3	0	**69**	**5**
2014–15	*Portsmouth*	6	1	**6**	**1**
2014–15	Wycombe W	17	0		
2015–16	Wycombe W	30	0		
2016–17	Wycombe W	19	0		
2017–18	Wycombe W	31	2		
2018–19	Wycombe W	9	1	**106**	**3**

BLOOMFIELD, Matt (M) **444 36**
H: 5 9 W: 11 00 b.Felixstowe 8-2-84
Internationals: England U19.

2001–02	Ipswich T	0	0		
2002–03	Ipswich T	0	0		
2003–04	Ipswich T	0	0		
2003–04	Wycombe W	12	1		
2004–05	Wycombe W	26	2		
2005–06	Wycombe W	39	5		
2006–07	Wycombe W	41	4		
2007–08	Wycombe W	35	4		
2008–09	Wycombe W	20	0		
2009–10	Wycombe W	14	2		
2010–11	Wycombe W	34	3		
2011–12	Wycombe W	31	2		
2012–13	Wycombe W	2	1		
2013–14	Wycombe W	32	0		
2014–15	Wycombe W	33	1		
2015–16	Wycombe W	27	1		
2016–17	Wycombe W	33	5		
2017–18	Wycombe W	37	3		
2018–19	Wycombe W	28	2	**444**	**36**

BOLTON, Luke (F) **10 0**
b.Manchester 7-10-99
Internationals: England U20.

2018–19	Manchester C	0	0		
2018–19	Wycombe W	10	0	**10**	**0**

CHARLES, Darius (M) **260 16**
H: 6 1 W: 13 05 b.Ealing 10-12-87
Internationals: England C.

2004–05	Brentford	1	0		
2005–06	Brentford	2	0		
2006–07	Brentford	17	1		
2007–08	Brentford	17	0	**37**	**1**
From Ebbsfleet U.					
2010–11	Stevenage	28	2		
2011–12	Stevenage	28	4		
2012–13	Stevenage	37	1		
2013–14	Stevenage	22	4		
2014–15	Stevenage	29	2	**144**	**13**
2015–16	Burton Alb	0	0		
2015–16	*AFC Wimbledon*	9	0		
2016–17	AFC Wimbledon	34	2		
2017–18	AFC Wimbledon	31	0	**74**	**2**
2018–19	Wycombe W	5	0	**5**	**0**

COWAN-HALL, Paris (F) **200 30**
H: 5 8 W: 11 08 b.Portsmouth 5-10-90

2008–09	Portsmouth	0	0		
2009–10	Portsmouth	0	0		
2009–10	*Grimsby T*	3	0	**3**	**0**
2010–11	Portsmouth	0	0		
2010–11	Scunthorpe U	1	0	**1**	**0**
2012–13	Plymouth Arg	40	3	**40**	**3**
2013–14	Wycombe W	25	4		
2014–15	Wycombe W	20	6		
2014–15	Millwall	5	0		
2015–16	Millwall	3	0	**8**	**0**
2015–16	*Bristol R*	3	0	**3**	**0**
2015–16	*Wycombe W*	5	1		
2016–17	Wycombe W	28	4		
2017–18	Wycombe W	34	8		
2018–19	Wycombe W	33	4	**145**	**27**

EL-ABD, Adam (D) **459 12**
H: 5 10 W: 13 05 b.Brighton 11-9-84
Internationals: Egypt Full caps.

2003–04	Brighton & HA	11	0		
2004–05	Brighton & HA	16	0		
2005–06	Brighton & HA	29	0		
2006–07	Brighton & HA	42	1		
2007–08	Brighton & HA	35	1		
2008–09	Brighton & HA	31	0		
2009–10	Brighton & HA	35	1		
2010–11	Brighton & HA	37	1		
2011–12	Brighton & HA	23	0		
2012–13	Brighton & HA	32	1		
2013–14	Brighton & HA	9	0	**300**	**5**
2013–14	Bristol C	14	0		
2014–15	Bristol C	2	0		
2014–15	*Bury*	24	1	**24**	**1**
2015–16	Bristol C	0	0	**16**	**0**
2015–16	*Swindon T*	13	0	**13**	**0**
2015–16	*Gillingham*	8	0	**8**	**0**
2016–17	Shrewsbury T	28	2	**28**	**2**
2017–18	Wycombe W	36	1		
2018–19	Wycombe W	34	3	**70**	**4**

FREEMAN, Nick (M) **68 3**
b. 7-11-95
From Histon, Hemel Hempstead T, Biggleswade T.

2016–17	Wycombe W	14	0		
2017–18	Wycombe W	27	3		
2018–19	Wycombe W	27	0	**68**	**3**

FREMPAH, Ben (D) **7 0**
H: 13 01 W: 6 2 b.Sassuolo 3-4-95

2013–14	Leicester C	0	0		
2014–15	Ross Co	6	0	**6**	**0**
From Solihull Moors, Guiseley.					
2018–19	Wycombe W	1	0	**1**	**0**

GAPE, Dominic (M) **111 3**
H: 5 11 W: 10 13 b.Southampton 9-9-94

2012–13	Southampton	0	0		
2013–14	Southampton	0	0		
2014–15	Southampton	1	0		
2015–16	Southampton	0	0		
2016–17	Southampton	0	0	**1**	**0**
2016–17	Wycombe W	32	1		
2017–18	Wycombe W	35	1		
2018–19	Wycombe W	43	1	**110**	**3**

HARRIMAN, Michael (D) **216 10**
H: 5 6 W: 11 10 b.Chichester 23-10-92
Internationals: Republic of Ireland U18, U19, U21.

2010–11	QPR	0	0		
2011–12	QPR	1	0		
2012–13	QPR	1	0		
2012–13	*Wycombe W*	20	0		
2013–14	QPR	0	0		
2013–14	*Gillingham*	34	1	**34**	**1**
2014–15	QPR	0	0	**2**	**0**
2014–15	*Luton T*	35	1	**35**	**1**
2015–16	Wycombe W	45	7		
2016–17	Wycombe W	38	0		
2017–18	Wycombe W	18	1		
2018–19	Wycombe W	24	0	**145**	**8**

JACOBSON, Joe (D) **429 31**
H: 5 11 W: 12 06 b.Cardiff 17-11-86
Internationals: Wales U21.

2005–06	Cardiff C	1	0		
2006–07	Cardiff C	0	0	**1**	**0**
2006–07	*Accrington S*	6	1		
2006–07	*Bristol R*	11	0		
2007–08	Bristol R	40	1		
2008–09	Bristol R	22	0	**73**	**1**
2009–10	Oldham Ath	15	0		
2010–11	Oldham Ath	1	0	**16**	**0**
2010–11	Accrington S	26	2	**32**	**3**
2011–12	Shrewsbury T	39	1		
2012–13	Shrewsbury T	30	2		
2013–14	Shrewsbury T	41	4	**110**	**7**
2014–15	Wycombe W	42	3		
2015–16	Wycombe W	34	1		
2016–17	Wycombe W	39	3		
2017–18	Wycombe W	46	6		
2018–19	Wycombe W	36	7	**197**	**20**

JOMBATI, Sido (D) **263 9**
H: 6 0 W: 11 11 b.Lisbon 20-8-87

2011–12	Cheltenham T	36	2		
2012–13	Cheltenham T	37	1		
2013–14	Cheltenham T	43	1	**116**	**4**
2014–15	Wycombe W	35	0		
2015–16	Wycombe W	34	1		
2016–17	Wycombe W	25	2		
2017–18	Wycombe W	20	1		
2018–19	Wycombe W	33	1	**147**	**5**

KASHKET, Scott (M) **73 15**
H: 5 9 W: 10 06 b.London 6-7-95

2014–15	Leyton Orient	1	0		
2015–16	Leyton Orient	15	1		
2016–17	Leyton Orient	0	0	**16**	**1**
2016–17	Wycombe W	21	10		
2017–18	Wycombe W	9	1		
2018–19	Wycombe W	27	3	**57**	**14**

MACKAIL-SMITH, Craig (F) **428 124**
H: 6 3 W: 12 04 b.Watford 25-2-84
Internationals: England C. Scotland Full caps.

2006–07	Peterborough U	15	8		
2007–08	Peterborough U	36	12		
2008–09	Peterborough U	46	23		
2009–10	Peterborough U	43	10		
2010–11	Peterborough U	45	27		
2011–12	Brighton & HA	45	9		
2012–13	Brighton & HA	29	11		
2013–14	Brighton & HA	5	0		
2014–15	Brighton & HA	30	1	**109**	**21**
2014–15	*Peterborough U*	3	0		
2015–16	Luton T	33	4		
2016–17	Luton T	2	0	**35**	**4**
2016–17	*Peterborough U*	18	5	**206**	**85**
2017–18	Wycombe W	41	8		
2018–19	Wycombe W	21	3	**62**	**11**
2018–19	*Notts Co*	16	3	**16**	**3**

MAKABU-MAKALAMBY, Yves (G) **67 0**
b.Brussels 31-1-86
Internationals: Belguim U23, DR Congo Full caps.

2005–06	Chelsea	0	0		
2005–06	*Watford*	0	0		
2006–07	Chelsea	0	0		
2007–08	Hibernian	29	0		
2008–09	Hibernian	21	0		
2009–10	Hibernian	7	0	**57**	**0**
2010–11	Swansea C	0	0		
2011–12	Mechelen	1	0	**1**	**0**
2013–14	Royal Antwerp	3	0		
2014–15	Royal Antwerp	0	0	**3**	**0**
2014–15	Otelul Galati	2	0		
2017–18	Otelul Galati	0	0	**2**	**0**
2017–18	Wycombe W	1	0		
2018–19	Wycombe W	3	0	**4**	**0**

McCARTHY, Jason (D) **147 9**
H: 6 1 W: 12 08 b.Southampton 7-11-95
2013–14 Southampton 0 0
2014–15 Southampton 1 0
2015–16 Southampton 0 0
2015–16 *Wycombe W* 35 2
2016–17 Southampton 0 0 **1 0**
2016–17 *Walsall* 46 5 **46 5**
2017–18 Barnsley 21 0 **21 0**
2018–19 Wycombe W 44 2 **79 4**

SAMUEL, Alex (F) **96 9**
H: 6 0 W: 11 11 b.Neath 20-9-95
Internationals: Wales U18.
From Aberystwyth T.
2014–15 Swansea C 0 0
2015–16 Swansea C 0 0
2015–16 *Greenock Morton* 26 2 **26 2**
2016–17 Swansea C 0 0
2016–17 *Newport Co* 18 2 **18 2**
2017–18 Stevenage 22 0 **22 0**
2018–19 Wycombe W 30 5 **30 5**

STEWART, Anthony (D) **158 7**
H: 5 10 W: 12 03 b.Brixton 18-9-92
2011–12 Wycombe W 4 0
2012–13 Wycombe W 19 1
2013–14 Wycombe W 33 3
2014–15 Crewe Alex 10 0 **10 0**
2015–16 Wycombe W 27 1
2016–17 Wycombe W 31 1
2017–18 Wycombe W 17 1
2018–19 Wycombe W 17 0 **148 7**

THOMPSON, Curtis (M) **129 3**
H: 5 10 W: 12 06 b.Nottingham 2-9-93
2011–12 Notts Co 0 0
2012–13 Notts Co 2 0
2013–14 Notts Co 11 0
2014–15 Notts Co 31 0
2015–16 Notts Co 26 2
2016–17 Notts Co 13 0
2017–18 Notts Co 0 0 **83 2**
2017–18 *Wycombe W* 7 0
2018–19 Wycombe W 39 1 **46 1**

TYSON, Nathan (F) **521 111**
H: 5 10 W: 10 02 b.Reading 4-5-82
Internationals: England U20.
1999–2000 Reading 1 0
2000–01 Reading 0 0
2001–02 Reading 1 0
2001–02 *Swansea C* 11 1 **11 1**
2001–02 *Cheltenham T* 8 1 **8 1**
2002–03 Reading 23 1
2003–04 Reading 8 0 **33 1**
2003–04 Wycombe W 21 9
2004–05 Wycombe W 42 22
2005–06 Wycombe W 15 11
2005–06 Nottingham F 28 10
2006–07 Nottingham F 24 7
2007–08 Nottingham F 34 9
2008–09 Nottingham F 35 5
2009–10 Nottingham F 33 2
2010–11 Nottingham F 30 2 **184 35**
2011–12 Derby Co 23 0
2012–13 Derby Co 16 4 **39 4**
2012–13 *Millwall* 4 0 **4 0**
2013–14 Blackpool 10 0 **10 0**
2013–14 *Fleetwood T* 4 0 **4 0**
2013–14 *Notts Co* 10 0 **10 0**
2014–15 Doncaster R 39 12
2015–16 Doncaster R 32 6 **71 18**
2016–17 Kilmarnock 17 0 **17 0**
2017–18 Wycombe W 33 8
2018–19 Wycombe W 19 1 **130 51**

YATES, Cameron (G) **0 0**
b.Edinburgh 14-2-99
From Leicester C.
2018–19 Wycombe W 0 0

YEOVIL T (92)

ALCOCK, Craig (D) **305 3**
H: 5 8 W: 11 00 b.Cornwall 8-12-87
2006–07 Yeovil T 1 0
2007–08 Yeovil T 8 0
2008–09 Yeovil T 30 1
2009–10 Yeovil T 42 1
2010–11 Yeovil T 26 1
2011–12 Peterborough U 41 0
2012–13 Peterborough U 27 0
2013–14 Peterborough U 28 0 **96 0**
2014–15 Sheffield U 24 0
2015–16 Sheffield U 3 0 **27 0**
2015–16 Doncaster R 27 0
2016–17 Doncaster R 27 0
2017–18 Doncaster R 9 0 **63 0**
2018–19 Cheltenham T 8 0 **8 0**
2018–19 Yeovil T 4 0 **111 3**

ARNOLD, Devon (F) **1 0**
b. 24-11-01
2018–19 Yeovil T 1 0 **1 0**

ARQUIN, Yoann (F) **236 47**
H: 6 2 W: 13 04 b.Le Havre 15-4-88
Internationals: Martinique Full caps.
2008–09 Quimper 24 9 **24 9**
2010–11 Red Star 93 11 2 **11 2**
2011–12 Hereford U 34 8 **34 8**
2012–13 Notts Co 41 7
2013–14 Notts Co 12 3 **53 10**
2013–14 Ross Co 16 4 **16 4**
2014–15 St Mirren 12 0 **12 0**
2015–16 Trabzon 22 3 **22 3**
2016 Syrianska 13 5 **13 5**
2016–17 Mansfield T 12 2 **12 2**
2017–18 FC Kaisar 7 0 **7 0**
2018–19 Yeovil T 32 4 **32 4**

BROWNE, Rhys (M) **68 5**
H: 5 10 W: 12 08 b.Romford 16-11-95
Internationals: Antigua and Barbuda Full caps.
From Norwich C, Charlton Ath, Aldershot T.
2016–17 Grimsby T 5 0 **5 0**
2017–18 Yeovil T 35 4
2018–19 Yeovil T 28 1 **63 5**

CLARKE, Tyrique (F) **0 0**
2018–19 Yeovil T 0 0

D'ALMEIDA, Sessi (M) **63 1**
H: 5 9 W: 11 09 b.Bordeaux 22-11-95
Internationals: Benin Full caps.
2013–14 Bordeaux 0 0
2014–15 Bordeaux 2 0 **2 0**
2015–16 Paris Saint-Germain 0 0
2016–17 Barnsley 3 0 **3 0**
2017–18 Blackpool 23 0 **23 0**
2018–19 Yeovil T 35 1 **35 1**

DICKINSON, Carl (D) **403 10**
H: 6 1 W: 12 04 b.Swadlincote 31-3-87
2004–05 Stoke C 1 0
2005–06 Stoke C 5 0
2006–07 Stoke C 13 0
2006–07 *Blackpool* 7 0 **7 0**
2007–08 Stoke C 27 0
2008–09 Stoke C 5 0
2008–09 *Leeds U* 7 0 **7 0**
2009–10 Stoke C 0 0
2009–10 *Barnsley* 28 1 **28 1**
2010–11 Stoke C 0 0 **51 0**
2010–11 *Portsmouth* 36 0
2011–12 Watford 39 2
2012–13 Watford 4 0 **43 2**
2012–13 *Portsmouth* 6 0 **42 0**
2012–13 *Coventry C* 6 0 **6 0**
2013–14 Port Vale 40 0
2014–15 Port Vale 43 1
2015–16 Port Vale 44 3 **127 4**
2016–17 Notts Co 34 0
2017–18 Notts Co 25 1 **59 1**
2018–19 Yeovil T 33 2 **33 2**

DONNELLAN, Shaun (D) **32 0**
b. 22-5-97
Internationals: Republic of Ireland U19, U21.
2015–16 WBA 0 0
2016–17 WBA 0 0
2016–17 *Stevenage* 0 0
2017–18 WBA 0 0
2017–18 *Walsall* 10 0 **10 0**
2017–18 Yeovil T 11 0
2018–19 Yeovil T 11 0 **22 0**

DUFFUS, Courtney (F) **25 1**
H: 5 7 W: 12 00 b.Cheltenham 24-10-95
Internationals: Republic of Ireland U21.
2013–14 Everton 0 0
2014–15 Everton 0 0
2014–15 *Bury* 3 0 **3 0**
2015–16 Everton 0 0
2016–17 Everton 0 0
2017–18 Oldham Ath 6 0
2018–19 Oldham Ath 0 0 **6 0**
2018–19 Yeovil T 16 1 **16 1**

FISHER, Alex (F) **188 45**
H: 6 2 W: 12 00 b. 30-6-90
2006–07 Oxford U 0 0
2007–08 Oxford U 10 1
2008–09 Oxford U 3 1 **13 2**
2009–10 Jerez Industrial 0 0
2010–11 Jerez Industrial 21 11 **21 11**
2011–12 Tienen 7 1 **7 1**
2012–13 Racing Mechelen 27 7 **27 7**
2013–14 Heist 2 0 **2 0**
2013–14 Monza 14 2 **14 2**
2014–15 Mansfield T 14 1 **14 1**
2015–16 Inverness CT 1 0
2016–17 Inverness CT 21 8 **22 8**
2017–18 Motherwell 11 0 **11 0**
2017–18 Yeovil T 17 6
2018–19 Yeovil T 40 7 **57 13**

GAFAITI, Adel (D) **51 1**
b.London 13-9-94
Internationals: Algeria U20.
2013–14 Norwich C 0 0
2013–14 *Oldham Ath* 1 0 **1 0**
2014–15 Norwich C 0 0
2015–16 Norwich C 0 0
2016–17 Oran 1 0 **1 0**
2016–17 Noisy-le-Sec 7 0 **7 0**
2017–18 Rodeo 12 0 **12 0**
2017–18 Zirka Kropyvnytskyi 8 0 **8 0**
2018–19 Yeovil T 22 1 **22 1**

GRAY, Jake (F) **108 11**
H: 5 11 W: 11 00 b.Aylesbury 25-12-95
2014–15 Crystal Palace 0 0
2014–15 *Cheltenham T* 4 0 **4 0**
2015–16 Crystal Palace 0 0
2015–16 *Hartlepool U* 29 5 **29 5**
2016–17 Luton T 19 1 **19 1**
2017–18 Yeovil T 26 3
2018–19 Yeovil T 30 2 **56 5**

HENRY, Korrey (F) **4 0**
b. 28-11-99
From West Ham U.
2018–19 Yeovil T 4 0 **4 0**

JAMES, Tom (D) **79 6**
H: 5 11 W: 11 00 b.Leamington Spa 19-11-88
Internationals: Wales U19.
2013–14 Cardiff C 1 0
2014–15 Cardiff C 0 0
2015–16 Cardiff C 0 0
2016–17 Cardiff C 0 0 **1 0**
2016–17 Yeovil T 2 0
2017–18 Yeovil T 38 0
2018–19 Yeovil T 38 6 **78 6**

McDONALD, Wesley (F) **9 0**
H: 5 9 W: 12 02 b.Lambeth 4-5-97
2015–16 Birmingham C 0 0
2016–17 Birmingham C 0 0
2017–18 Birmingham C 0 0
2018–19 Yeovil T 9 0 **9 0**

MUGABI, Bevis (D) **85 4**
H: 6 2 W: 11 11 b.Harrow 1-5-95
Internationals: Uganda Full caps.
From Southampton.
2016–17 Yeovil T 31 1
2017–18 Yeovil T 22 2
2018–19 Yeovil T 32 1 **85 4**

NELSON, Stuart (G) **437 0**
H: 6 1 W: 12 12 b.Stroud 17-9-81
2003–04 Brentford 9 0
2004–05 Brentford 43 0
2005–06 Brentford 45 0
2006–07 Brentford 19 0 **116 0**
2007–08 Leyton Orient 30 0 **30 0**
2008–09 Norwich C 0 0
2010–11 Notts Co 33 0
2011–12 Notts Co 46 0 **79 0**
2012–13 Gillingham 45 0
2013–14 Gillingham 46 0
2014–15 Gillingham 24 0
2015–16 Gillingham 46 0
2016–17 Gillingham 34 0
2017–18 Gillingham 0 0 **195 0**
2017–18 Yeovil T 5 0
2018–19 Yeovil T 12 0 **17 0**

OJO, Daniel (D) **6 0**
b. 17-2-01
2018–19 Yeovil T 6 0 **6 0**

PATTISON, Alex (F) **29 0**
b. 6-9-97
2016–17 Middlesbrough 0 0
2017–18 Middlesbrough 0 0
2018–19 Yeovil T 29 0 **29 0**

PHILLIPS, Steve (G) 510 0
H: 6 1 W: 11 10 b.Bath 6-5-78

1996–97	Bristol C	0	0		
1997–98	Bristol C	0	0		
1998–99	Bristol C	15	0		
1999–2000	Bristol C	21	0		
2000–01	Bristol C	42	0		
2001–02	Bristol C	22	0		
2002–03	Bristol C	46	0		
2003–04	Bristol C	46	0		
2004–05	Bristol C	46	0		
2005–06	Bristol C	19	0	**257**	**0**
2006–07	Bristol R	44	0		
2007–08	Bristol R	46	0		
2008–09	Bristol R	46	0		
2009–10	Bristol R	0	0	**136**	**0**
2009–10	*Shrewsbury T*	11	0	**11**	**0**
2009–10	*Crewe Alex*	28	0		
2010–11	Crewe Alex	3	0		
2011–12	Crewe Alex	46	0		
2012–13	Crewe Alex	20	0		
2013–14	Crewe Alex	9	0		
2014–15	Crewe Alex	0	0	**106**	**0**
2017–18	Yeovil T	0	0		
2018–19	Yeovil T	0	0		

ROGERS, Gabriel (M) 4 0
b. 14-2-00

2018–19	Yeovil T	4	0	**4**	**0**

RYAN JOHN, Alex (M) 0 0

2018–19	Yeovil T	0	0		

SANTOS, Alefe (M) 58 1
H: 5 10 W: 10 06 b.Sao Paulo 28-1-95

2012–13	Bristol R	1	0		
2013	Ponte Preta	0	0		
2013–14	Bristol R	23	1	**24**	**1**
2014–15	Derby Co	0	0		
2014–15	*Notts Co*	3	0	**3**	**0**
2015–16	Derby Co	0	0		
2016–17	Derby Co	0	0		
2017–18	Yeovil T	14	0		
2018–19	Yeovil T	17	0	**31**	**0**

SCOTT, Tommy (G) 0 0
b. 13-9-99

2017–18	Yeovil T	0	0		
2018–19	Yeovil T	0	0		

SEAGER, Ryan (F) 48 6
H: 5 11 W: 11 00 b.Southampton 5-2-96
Internationals: England U17.

2014–15	Southampton	1	0		
2015–16	Southampton	0	0		
2015–16	*Crewe Alex*	4	1	**4**	**1**
2016–17	Southampton	0	0		
2017–18	Southampton	0	0		
2017–18	*Milton Keynes D*	14	1	**14**	**1**
2017–18	*Yeovil T*	7	1		
2018–19	Southampton	0	0	**1**	**0**
2018–19	*Telstar*	11	2	**11**	**2**
2018–19	Yeovil T	11	1	**18**	**2**

SOWUNMI, Omar (D) 69 3
H: 6 6 W: 14 09 b.Colchester 7-11-95

2015–16	Yeovil T	5	1		
2016–17	Yeovil T	11	0		
2017–18	Yeovil T	36	2		
2018–19	Yeovil T	17	0	**69**	**3**

WARREN, Gary (D) 207 13
H: 6 0 W: 11 11 b.Bristol 16-8-84
From Newport Co.

2012–13	Inverness CT	31	5		
2013–14	Inverness CT	34	2		
2014–15	Inverness CT	36	2		
2015–16	Inverness CT	25	0		
2016–17	Inverness CT	33	2		
2017–18	Inverness CT	22	2	**181**	**13**
2018–19	Yeovil T	26	0	**26**	**0**

WORTHINGTON, Matt (M) 40 1
b.Southampton 18-12-97

2016–17	Bournemouth	1	0		
2017–18	Bournemouth	0	0		
2017–18	*Yeovil T*	15	0		
2018–19	Bournemouth	0	0	**1**	**0**
2018–19	*Forest Green R*	9	1	**9**	**1**
2018–19	Yeovil T	15	0	**30**	**0**

ZOKO, Francois (F) 538 100
H: 6 0 W: 11 05 b.Daloa 13-9-83
Internationals: Ivory Coast U20, U23.

2001–02	Nancy	24	3		
2002–03	Nancy	28	2		
2003–04	Nancy	19	3	**71**	**8**
2004–05	Laval	27	7		
2005–06	Laval	33	2	**60**	**9**
2006–07	Mons	23	4		
2007–08	Mons	32	8	**55**	**12**
2008–09	Hacettepe	27	1	**27**	**1**
2009–10	Ostend	11	4	**11**	**4**
2010–11	Carlisle U	44	6		
2011–12	Carlisle U	45	13		
2012–13	Carlisle U	0	0	**89**	**19**
2012–13	Notts Co	38	7		
2013–14	Notts Co	1	0	**39**	**7**
2013–14	Stevenage	33	10	**33**	**10**
2014–15	Blackpool	14	1	**14**	**1**
2014–15	*Bradford C*	16	1	**16**	**1**
2015–16	Yeovil T	25	7		
2016–17	Yeovil T	35	8		
2017–18	Yeovil T	37	13		
2018–19	Yeovil T	26	0	**123**	**28**

Scholars
Arnold, Devon Michael; Calverley, George Alexander; Clarke, Tyrique Simieon Spencer; Dix, Lewis; Fleming, Tai McLean; Haughton, Harry Robert; Hayes, Thomas; John, Alex Ryan; Kowalczyk, Kacper Marian; Neild, Daniel Alexander; Nzembela, Neville Nchang Kabamba; Rose, Declan Arthur; Scott, Tommy; Shako, Nestor Kasende; Sturdy, Archie Tomas Robert.

ENGLISH LEAGUE PLAYERS – INDEX

NATIONAL LIST OF REFEREES FOR SEASON 2019–20

Adcock, James
Atkinson, Martin
Attwell, Stuart
Backhouse, Anthony
Bankes, Peter
Bond, Darren
Boyeson, Carl
Bramall, Tom
Breakspear, Charles
Brooks, John
Busby, John
Coggins, Antony
Coote, David
Coy, Martin
Davies, Andy
Dean, Mike
Donohue, Matthew
Doughty, Leigh
Drysdale, Darren
Duncan, Scott
Edwards, Marc
Eltringham, Geoff
England, Darren
Finnie, Will
Friend, Kevin
Gillett, Jarred
Haines, Andy
Hair, Neil
Handley, Darren
Harrington, Tony
Hicks, Craig
Hooper, Simon
Horwood, Graham
Huxtable, Brett
Ilderton, Eddie
Johnson, Kevin
Jones, Rob
Joyce, Ross
Kavanagh, Christopher
Kettle, Trevor
Kinseley, Nick
Langford, Oliver
Lewis, Rob
Linington, James
Madley, Andy
Marriner, Andre
Marsden, Paul
Martin, Stephen
Mason, Lee
Moss, Jonathan
Nield, Tom
Oldham, James
Oldham, Scott
Oliver, Michael
Pawson, Craig
Pollard, Christopher
Probert, Lee
Purkiss, Sam
Robinson, Tim
Rock, David
Salisbury, Graham
Salisbury, Michael
Sarginson, Chris
Scott, Graham
Simpson, Jeremy
Smith, Josh
Stockbridge, Seb
Stroud, Keith
Swabey, Lee
Taylor, Anthony
Tierney, Paul
Toner, Ben
Ward, Gavin
Webb, David
Whitestone, Dean
Woolmer, Andy
Wright, Peter
Yates, Ollie
Young, Alan

ASSISTANT REFEREES

Amey, Justin
Amphlett, Marvyn
Aspinall, Natalie
Atkin, Robert
Avent, David
Aylott, Andrew
Barnard, Nicholas
Bartlett, Richard
Beck, Simon
Bennett, Simon
Benton, David
Beswick, Gary
Betts, Lee
Bickle, Oliver
Blunden, Darren
Bonneywell, Dan
Bristow, Matthew
Brown, Conor
Brown, Stephen
Burt, Stuart
Butler, Stuart
Byrne, George
Byrne, Helen
Cann, Darren
Cheosiaua, Ravel
Clark, Joe
Clayton, Alan
Clayton, Simon
Cook, Dan
Cook, Daniel
Cooper, Ian
Cooper, Nicholas
Cropp, Barry
Crowhurst, Leigh
Crysell, Adam
Cunliffe, Mark
Da Costa, Anthony
Dabbs, Robert
Dallison, Andrew
Davies, Neil
Denton, Michael
Dermott, Philip
Derrien, Mark
Desborough, Mike
Dudley, Ian
Duncan, Mark
Dwyer, Mark
Eaton, Derek
Farmer, Aaron
Farrell, Conor
Finch, Stephen
Fitch-Jackson, Carl
Flynn, John
Foley, Matt
Ford, Declan
Fox, Andrew
Freeman, Lee
Fyvie, Graeme
Garratt, Andrew
George, Michael
Gill, Bhupinder
Gooch, Peter
Gordon, Barry
Graham, Paul
Gratton, Danny
Greenhalgh, Nick
Griffiths, Mark
Grunnill, Wayne
Hanley, Michael

Harty, Thomas
Hatzidakis, Constantine
Hendley, Andrew
Hilton, Gary
Hobday, Paul
Hodskinson, Paul
Holmes, Adrian
Hopton, Nick
Howick, Kevin
Howson, Akil
Hudson, Shaun
Hunt, David
Hunt, Jonathan
Husband, Christopher
Hussin, Ian
Hyde, Robert
Isherwood, Chris
Jackson, Oliver
Jones, Mark
Jones, Matthew
Kane, Graham
Karaivanov, Hristo
Kelly, Paul
Kendall, Richard
Khan, Abbas
Kidd, Christopher
Kirkup, Peter
Laver, Andrew
Leach, Daniel
Ledger, Scott
Lee, Matthew
Lennard, Harry
Lewis, Sam
Liddle, Geoffrey
Lister, Paul
Long, Simon
Lugg, Nigel
Mackey, Oliver
Mainwaring, James
Marks, Louis
Maskell, Garry
Massey-Ellis, Sian
Matthews, Adam
Mcdonough, Michael
Mcgrath, Matthew
Mellor, Gareth
Merchant, Robert
Meredith, Steven
Moore, Anthony
Morris, Kevin
Morris, Richard
Mulraine, Kevin
Newhouse, Paul
Nunn, Adam
Ogles, Samuel
Parry, Matthew
Pashley, Alix
Perry, Marc
Plane, Steven
Plowright, David
Pottage, Mark
Powell, Christopher
Rashid, Lisa
Read, Gregory
Rees, Paul
Robathan, Daniel
Ross, Alasdair
Rushton, Steven
Russell, Geoffrey
Russell, Mark
Scholes, Mark
Sharp, Neil
Shaw, Simon
Simpson, Joe
Smallwood, Billy
Smart, Edward
Smedley, Ian
Smith, Matthew
Smith, Michael
Smith, Rob
Smith, Wade
Stokes, Joseph
Street, Duncan
Taylor, Craig
Taylor, Grant
Tranter, Adrian
Treleaven, Dean
Vallance, James
Venamore, Lee
Viccars, Gareth
Wade, Christopher
Wade, Stephen
Ward, Christopher
Waters, Adrian
Webb, Michael
West, Richard
Whitaker, Ryan
Wigglesworth, Richard
Wild, Richard
Wilding, Darren
Wilkes, Matthew
Williams, Andrew
Williams, Ollie
Wilson, James
Wilson, Marc
Wood, Timothy
Woodward, Daniel
Woodward, Richard
Yates, Paul

MANAGERS – IN AND OUT 2018–19

AUGUST 2018

6 Gary Bowyer resigns as manager of Blackpool. Assistant manager Terry McPhillips takes temporary charge.
21 Gary Johnson sacked as manager of Cheltenham T. Assistant manager Russell Milton takes temporary charge.
24 Nicky Daws sacked as manager of Scunthorpe U. Assistant manager Andy Dawson takes temporary charge.
26 Kevin Nolan sacked as manager of Notts Co. First-team coaches Steve Chettle and Mark Crossley take temporary charge.
27 Stuart McCall appointed manager of Scunthorpe U.
31 Harry Kewell leaves Crawley T and is appointed manager of Notts Co. Felipe Morais and Jimmy Smith take temporary charge of Crawley T.

SEPTEMBER 2018

3 Michael Collins sacked as manager of Bradford C.
4 David Hopkin appointed manager of Bradford C.
6 Lee Bowyer appointed manager of Charlton Ath after being in temporary charge.
7 Gabriele Cioffi appointed manager of Crawley T.
10 Michael Duff appointed manager of Cheltenham T.
10 Terry McPhillips appointed manager of Blackpool after being in temporary charge.
30 Dean Austin sacked as manager of Northampton T.

OCTOBER 2018

1 Keith Curle appointed manager of Northampton T.
3 Steve Bruce sacked as manager of Aston Villa. Under 23s manager Kevin MacDonald takes temporary charge.
8 Mark Yates sacked as manager of Macclesfield T. Assistant managers Danny Whitaker and Neil Howarth take temporary charge.
10 Dean Smith leaves as manager of Brentford and is appointed manager of Aston Villa.
16 Thomas Frank appointed manager of Brentford.
25 Paul Hurst sacked as manager of Ipswich T. Head of coaching and player development Bryan Klug takes temporary charge.
27 Paul Lambert appointed manager of Ipswich T.

NOVEMBER 2018

11 Phil Brown sacked as manager of Swindon T.
12 Neal Ardley leaves as manager of AFC Wimbledon by mutual consent. First-team coach Simon Bassey takes temporary charge.
12 John Askey sacked as manager of Shrewsbury T. Goalkeeping coach Danny Coyne takes temporary charge.
13 Richie Wellens appointed manager of Swindon T.
13 Harry Kewell sacked as manager of Notts Co. First-team coach Steve Chettle takes temporary charge.
14 Slavisa Jokanovic sacked as manager of Fulham. Claudio Ranieri appointed manager.
21 Martin O'Neill leaves as manager of Republic of Ireland.
23 Neal Ardley appointed manager of Notts Co.
27 Sol Campbell appointed manager of Macclesfield T.

DECEMBER 2018

1 Joe Dunne sacked as manager of Cambridge U. Assistant Mark Bonner takes temporary charge.
3 Mark Hughes sacked as manager of Southampton.
3 Sam Ricketts appointed manager of Shrewsbury T.
4 Wally Downes appointed manager of AFC Wimbledon.
5 Ralph Hasenhuttl appointed manager of Southampton.
6 Paul Clement sacked as manager of Reading. Under-23 manager Scott Marshall takes temporary charge.
13 Darrell Clarke leaves as manager of Bristol R by mutual consent. Coach Graham Coughlan takes temporary charge.
18 Jose Mourinho sacked as manager of Manchester U.
19 Ole Gunnar Solskjaer appointed caretaker manager of Manchester U until end of 2018–19 season.
19 Colin Calderwood appointed manager of Cambridge U.
21 Jos Luhukay sacked as manager of Sheffield W. Coach Lee Bullen takes temporary charge.
22 Jose Gomes appointed manager of Reading.
27 Frankie Bunn sacked as manager of Oldham Ath. Coach Peter Wild takes temporary charge.

JANUARY 2019

2 Steve Bruce appointed manager of Sheffield W to commence 1 February 2019. Bruce's long-term assistants Steve Agnew and Stephen Clemence take temporary charge.
4 John Sheridan resigns as manager of Carlisle U. Assistant manager Tommy Wright and First-team coach Paul Murray take temporary charge.
6 Graham Coughlan appointed manager of Bristol R after being in temporary charge.
8 Gary Rowett sacked as manager of Stoke C.
9 Nathan Jones leaves Luton T to become manager of Stoke C. Mick Harford takes temporary charge of Luton T.
11 Aitor Karanka leaves as manager of Nottingham F. First-team coach Simon Ireland takes temporary charge.

14 David Wagner leaves as manager of Huddersfield T. Coach Mark Hudson takes temporary charge.
15 Martin O'Neill appointed manager of Nottingham F.
16 Steven Pressley appointed manager of Carlisle U.
21 Jan Siewert appointed manager of Huddersfield T.
26 Steve Evans sacked as manager of Peterborough U. Darren Ferguson appointed new manager.
30 Neil Aspin resigns as manager of Port Vale.

FEBRUARY 2019

4 John Askey appointed manager of Port Vale.
11 Paul Scholes appointed manager of Oldham Ath.
24 Claude Puel sacked as manager of Leicester C. First-team coaches Mike Stowell and Adam Sadler take temporary charge.
25 David Hopkin resigns as manager of Bradford C. Assistant manager Anton McElhone and first-team coach Martin Drury take temporary charge.
26 Brendan Rodgers leaves Celtic and is appointed manager of Leicester C. Neil Lennon appointed manager of Celtic.
28 Claudio Ranieri sacked as manager of Fulham. Assistant manager Scott Parker takes temporary charge until the end of the season.

MARCH 2019

4 Keith Hill sacked as manager of Rochdale. First-team coach Brian Barry-Murphy and Academy manager Tony Ellis take temporary charge.
4 Gary Bowyer appointed manager of Bradford C.
9 Darren Moore sacked as manager of WBA. First-team coach James Shan takes temporary charge.
14 Paul Scholes resigns as manager of Oldham Ath.
22 Pete Wild appointed manager of Oldham Ath until the end of the season.
24 Stuart McCall sacked as manager of Scunthorpe U. First-team coach Andy Dawson appointed manager until the end of the season.
24 Darren Way sacked as manager of Yeovil T. First-team coach Neale Marmon appointed caretaker manager until the end of the season.
26 Chris Powell sacked as manager of Southend U. Head of Academy Ricky Duncan takes temporary charge.
28 Ole Gunnar Solskjaer appointed manager of Manchester U after being in temporary charge.

APRIL 2019

1 Steve McClaren sacked as manager of QPR. Assistant manager John Eustace takes temporary charge.
2 Kevin Bond appointed manager of Southend U.
3 Brian Barry-Murphy appointed manager of Rochdale after being in temporary charge.
6 Dean Keates sacked as manager of Walsall. First-team coach Martin O'Connor appointed as manager until the end of the season.
16 Alex McLeish sacked as manager of Scotland.
26 Steve Lovell sacked as manager of Gillingham. First-team coach Mark Patterson takes temporary charge.
28 Derek Adams sacked as manager of Plymouth Arg. First-team coach Kevin Nancekivell takes temporary charge.

MAY 2019

2 Graeme Jones appointed manager of Luton T.
7 Pete Wild leaves as temporary manager of Oldham Ath.
8 Mark Warburton appointed manager of QPR.
10 Scott Parker appointed manager of Fulham after being in temporary charge.
10 Darrell Clarke appointed manager of Walsall.
13 Chris Hughton sacked as manager of Brighton & HA.
13 Paul Hurst appointed manager of Scunthorpe U.
14 David Flitcroft sacked as manager of Mansfield T. John Dempster appointed manager.
17 Tony Pulis leaves as manager of Middlesbrough.
20 Graham Potter leaves Swansea C and is appointed manager of Brighton & HA.
20 Steve Clarke appointed manager of Scotland.
21 Steve Evans appointed manager of Gillingham.

JUNE 2019

5 Ryan Lowe leaves Bury and is appointed manager of Plymouth Arg.
5 Nigel Adkins leaves as manager of Hull City.
11 Laurent Banide appointed manager of Oldham Ath.
13 Slaven Bilic appointed manager of WBA.
13 Steve Cooper appointed manager of Swansea C.
14 Jonathan Woodgate appointed manager of Middlesbrough.
16 Mauricio Sarri leaves as manager of Chelsea and takes over as manager of Juventus.
18 Garry Monk leaves as manager of Birmingham C. Pep Clotet appointed caretaker manager.
21 Grant McCann leaves as manager of Doncaster R and is appointed manager of Hull C.
28 Martin O'Neill sacked as manager of Nottinghham F. Sabri Lamouchi appointed manager.
30 Rafael Benitez leaves as manager of Newcastle U.

JULY 2019

2 Paul Wilkinson appointed manager of Bury.
4 Frank Lampard leaves as manager of Derby Co and is appointed manager of Chelsea.
5 Philip Cocu appointed manager of Derby Co.
5 Terry McPhillips leaves as manager of Blackpool.
6 Simon Grayson appointed manager of Blackpool.

TRANSFERS 2018–19

JUNE 2018	*From*	*To*	*Fee in £*
1 Afobe, Benik	Bournemouth	Wolverhampton W	£10m
21 Aimson, Will	Blackpool	Bury	Free
19 Allsop, Ryan	Bournemouth	Wycombe W	Free
26 Armstrong, Stuart	Celtic	Southampton	£7m
6 Bishop, Neal	Scunthorpe U	Mansfield T	Free
18 Blissett, Nathan	Plymouth Arg	Macclesfield T	Free
7 Borini, Fabio	Sunderland	AC Milan	Undisclosed
12 Bradley, Sonny	Plymouth Arg	Luton T	Free
6 Brown, Junior	Shrewsbury T	Coventry C	Free
11 Brown, Lee	Bristol R	Portsmouth	Free
13 Burke, Graham	Shamrock R	Preston NE	Undisclosed
21 Byrom, Joel	Mansfield T	Stevenage	Free
1 Campbell, Tahvon	WBA	Forest Green R	Free
21 Can, Emre	Liverpool	Juventus	Free
8 Canavan, Niall	Rochdale	Plymouth Arg	Free
28 Caprice, Jake	Leyton Orient	Tranmere R	Free
5 Cazorla, Santi	Arsenal	Villarreal	Free
15 Charles, Darius	AFC Wimbledon	Wycombe W	Free
22 Clark, Max	Hull C	Vitesse Arnhem	Undisclosed
13 Clarke-Harris, Jonson	Rotherham U	Coventry C	Free
22 Cook, Jordan	Luton T	Grimsby T	Free
26 Crofts, Andrew	Scunthorpe U	Newport Co	Free
6 Crowe, Michael	Ipswich T	Preston NE	Free
13 Cunningham, Greg	Preston NE	Cardiff C	Undisclosed
19 Dagnall, Chris	Crewe Alex	Bury	Free
29 Dales, Andy	Mickleover Sports	Scunthorpe U	Undisclosed
29 Davies, Craig	Oldham Ath	Mansfield T	Undisclosed
7 Davis, Harry	St Mirren	Grimsby T	Free
22 Dembele, Siriki	Grimsby T	Peterborough U	Undisclosed
21 Dickinson, Carl	Notts Co	Yeovil T	Free
29 Dieng, Timothee	Bradford C	Southend U	Free
26 Donaldson, Clayton	Sheffield U	Bolton W	Free
7 Donnelly, Liam	Hartlepool U	Motherwell	Undisclosed
19 Dunn, Chris	Wrexham	Walsall	Free
11 Dyson, Callum	Everton	Plymouth Arg	Free
29 Engvall, Gustav	Bristol C	KV Mechelen	Undisclosed
8 Evans, Jonny	WBA	Leicester C	£3.5m
20 Fabianski, Lukasz	Swansea C	West Ham U	£7m
12 Farman, Paul	Lincoln C	Stevenage	Undisclosed
21 Flanagan, Jon	Liverpool	Rangers	Free
28 Flanagan, Tom	Burton Alb	Sunderland	Free
27 Flint, Aden	Bristol C	Middlesbrough	£7m
28 Forbes, Tyles	Brighton & HA	Newport Co	Free
5 Forrester, Chris	Peterborough U	Aberdeen	Undisclosed
26 Forte, Jonathan	Notts Co	Exeter C	Free
5 Francomb, George	AFC Wimbledon	Crawley T	Free
18 Franks, Fraser	Stevenage	Newport Co	Free
5 Fredericks, Ryan	Fulham	West Ham U	Free
21 Funes Mori, Ramiro	Everton	Villarreal	Undisclosed
28 Galach, Brian	Aldershot T	Crawley T	Free
20 Gillesphey, Macaulay	Newcastle U	Carlisle U	Free
5 Gillespie, Mark	Walsall	Motherwell	Free
5 Ginnelly, Josh	Burnley	Walsall	Free
19 Gleeson, Stephen	Ipswich T	Aberdeen	Free
21 Glendon, George	Fleetwood T	Carlisle U	Free
4 Godden, Matt	Stevenage	Peterborough U	Undisclosed
13 Goldson, Connor	Brighton & HA	Rangers	Undisclosed
10 Gollini, Pierluigi	Aston Villa	Atalanta	Undisclosed
11 Gomes, Madger	Leeds U	Sochaux	Undisclosed
25 Gradel, Max	Bournemouth	Toulouse	Undisclosed
7 Grant, Conor	Everton	Plymouth Arg	Free
27 Grant, Peter	Falkirk	Plymouth Arg	Free
22 Grimes, Jamie	Cheltenham T	Macclesfield T	Free
1 Hamer, Ben	Leicester C	Huddersfield T	Free
21 Hancox, Mitch	Macclesfield T	Milton Keynes D	Free
26 Hanson, James	Sheffield U	AFC Wimbledon	Undisclosed
21 Heaton, Josh	Darlington	St Mirren	£75,000
1 Hemmings, Kane	Oxford U	Notts Co	Undisclosed

25 Hessenthaler, Jake	Gillingham	Grimsby T	Free
15 Hopper, Tom	Scunthorpe U	Southend U	Free
21 Hughes, Andrew	Peterborough U	Preston NE	Undisclosed
26 Hunt, Johnny	Mansfield T	Stevenage	Free
26 Ismail, Zeli	Bury	Walsall	Free
25 Kelly, Sam	Grimsby T	Hamilton A	Free
10 Kennedy, Kieran	Macclesfield T	Shrewsbury T	Undisclosed
1 Kerschbaumer, Konstantin	Brentford	FC Ingolstadt	Undisclosed
29 Khan, Otis	Yeovil T	Mansfield T	Undisclosed
22 King, Jeff	Bolton W	St Mirren	Free
15 Knasmullner, Christoph	Barnsley	Rapid Vienna	Undisclosed
12 Konsa, Ezri	Charlton Ath	Brentford	Undisclosed
9 Ladapo, Freddie	Southend U	Plymouth Arg	Free
28 Lambe, Reggie	Carlisle U	Cambridge U	Free
11 Larsson, Seb	Hull C	AIK Solna	Free
22 Lennon, Harry	Charlton Ath	Southend U	Undisclosed
7 Lens, Jeremain	Sunderland	Besiktas	Undisclosed
22 Lichaj, Eric	Nottingham F	Hull C	Undisclosed
26 Long, Sean	Lincoln C	Cheltenham T	Free
5 Lopes, Leo Da Silva	Peterborough U	Wigan Ath	Undisclosed
8 Lowe, Jason	Birmingham C	Bolton W	Free
4 MacGillivray, Craig	Shrewsbury T	Portsmouth	Undisclosed
20 Maddison, James	Norwich C	Leicester C	Undisclosed
20 Magnusson, Hordur	Bristol C	CSKA Moscow	Undisclosed
25 Maguire, Chris	Bury	Sunderland	Free
22 Mantom, Sam	Scunthorpe U	Southend U	Undisclosed
30 Marshall, Ben	Wolverhampton W	Norwich C	Undisclosed
22 Marsh-Brown, Keanu	Forest Green R	Newport Co	Free
20 Matt, Jamille	Blackpool	Newport Co	Free
6 Matthews, Sam	Bournemouth	Bristol R	Free
18 McGlashan, Jermaine	Southend U	Swindon T	Free
25 McGowan, Aaron	Morecambe	Hamilton A	Free
25 McLaughlin, Jon	Hearts	Sunderland	Free
28 McMahon, Tony	Bradford C	Oxford U	Free
26 McNair, Paddy	Sunderland	Middlesbrough	Undisclosed
5 Meyler, David	Hull C	Reading	Free
20 Miller, Gary	Plymouth Arg	Carlisle U	Free
22 Miller, Ricky	Peterborough U	Port Vale	Undisclosed
21 Mills, Zak	Grimsby T	Morecambe	Free
27 Mingoia, Piero	Cambridge U	Accrington S	Free
4 Moore, Byron	Bristol R	Bury	Free
19 Moore-Taylor, Jordan	Exeter C	Milton Keynes D	Free
19 Morgan, Craig	Wigan Ath	Fleetwood T	Free
25 Mullin, Paul	Swindon T	Tranmere R	Undisclosed
27 Muniesa, Marc	Stoke C	Girona	Undisclosed
12 Murphy, Josh	Norwich C	Cardiff C	Undisclosed
12 Naismith, Jason	Ross Co	Peterborough U	Undisclosed
11 Nathaniel-George, Ashley	Hendon	Crawley T	Free
8 Naylor, Tom	Burton Alb	Portsmouth	Free
27 Norris, Luke	Swindon T	Colchester U	Undisclosed
8 Nouble, Frank	Newport Co	Colchester U	Free
21 Oates, Rhys	Hartlepool U	Morecambe	Free
14 O'Connor, Anthony	Aberdeen	Bradford C	Free
20 O'Connor, Michael	Notts Co	Lincoln C	Free
27 O'Donnell, Richard	Northampton T	Bradford C	Free
26 Ogogo, Abu	Shrewsbury T	Coventry C	Free
10 Okenabirhie, Fejiri	Dagenham & R	Shrewsbury T	Undisclosed
6 O'Shea, John	Sunderland	Reading	Free
12 O'Sullivan, John	Carlisle U	Blackpool	Free
27 Oswell, Jason	Stockport Co	Morecambe	Undisclosed
1 Oyeleke, Manny	Aldershot T	Port Vale	Free
13 Oztumer, Erhun	Walsall	Bolton W	Free
21 Ozturk, Alim	Boluspor	Sunderland	Free
27 Palmer, Ollie	Lincoln C	Crawley T	Undisclosed
4 Patching, Will	Manchester C	Notts Co	Free
28 Pearce, Isaac	Fulham	Forest Green R	Free
26 Pearson, Matty	Barnsley	Luton T	Undisclosed
6 Penney, Alex	Peterborough U	Hamilton A	Undisclosed
19 Reed, Louis	Sheffield U	Peterborough U	Undisclosed
12 Rees, Josh	Bromley	Gillingham	Undisclosed
28 Reid, Bobby	Bristol C	Cardiff C	£10m
10 Riley, Joe	Shrewsbury T	Plymouth Arg	Free
28 Roberts, Jordan	Crawley T	Ipswich T	Free

29 Robertson, Clark	Blackpool	Rotherham U	Free
30 Robinson, Jack	QPR	Nottingham F	Free
7 Ross, Ethan	WBA	Colchester U	Free
22 Rothwell, Joe	Oxford U	Blackburn R	Undisclosed
28 Shephard, Liam	Peterborough U	Forest Green R	Undisclosed
1 Shinnie, Andrew	Birmingham C	Luton T	Free
25 Smith, Aaron	Nottingham F	Hamilton A	Free
25 Smith, Grant	Boreham Wood	Lincoln C	Free
1 Smith, Tom	Swindon T	Cheltenham T	Free
26 Smith-Brown, Ashley	Manchester C	Plymouth Arg	Undisclosed
28 Smithies, Alex	QPR	Cardiff C	£3.5m
12 Sobhi, Ramadan	Stoke C	Huddersfield T	£5.7m
13 Sonupe, Emmanuel	Kidderminster H	Stevenage	Undisclosed
22 Stephens, Ben	Stratford	Macclesfield T	Undisclosed
12 Storey, Jordan	Exeter C	Preston NE	Undisclosed
29 Sung-yeung, Ki	Swansea C	Newcastle U	Free
27 Tadic, Dusan	Southampton	Ajax	£10m
13 Taylor, Chris	Bolton W	Blackpool	Free
27 Taylor, Lyle	AFC Wimbledon	Charlton Ath	Free
25 Tesche, Robert	Birmingham C	Bochum	Free
14 Thompson, Jordan	Rangers	Blackpool	Free
11 Timlin, Michael	Southend U	Stevenage	Free
11 Toffolo, Harry	Millwall	Lincoln C	Undisclosed
12 Toffolo, Harry	Millwall	Lincoln C	Free
29 Tutte, Andrew	Bury	Morecambe	Free
28 Vassel, Theo	Gateshead	Port Vale	Free
29 Vassell, Kyle	Blackpool	Rotherham U	Free
20 Wallace, Murray	Scunthorpe U	Millwall	Undisclosed
28 Warren, Gary	Inverness CT	Yeovil T	Undisclosed
15 Watkins, Marley	Norwich C	Bristol C	£1m
20 Watson, Ryan	Barnet	Milton Keynes D	Free
28 Webster, Adam	Ipswich T	Bristol C	Undisclosed
7 Welch-Hayes, Miles	Bath C	Macclesfield T	Undisclosed
25 Welsh, John	Preston NE	Grimsby T	Free
15 Whitehouse, Elliott	Lincoln C	Grimsby T	Free
19 Wiedwald, Felix	Leeds U	Eintracht Frankfurt	Undisclosed
25 Wilbraham, Aaron	Bolton W	Rochdale	Free
12 Williams, George	Fulham	Forest Green R	Free
14 Williams, Jordan	Liverpool	Rochdale	Free
21 Wood, Connor	Leicester City	Bradford C	Undisclosed
27 Wootton, Scott	Milton Keynes D	Plymouth Arg	Free

JULY 2018

2 Adelakun, Hakeeb	Scunthorpe U	Bristol C	Free
6 Akinde, John	Barnet	Lincoln C	Undisclosed
4 Akpan, Hope	Burton Alb	Bradford C	Free
13 Amadi-Holloway, Aaron	Oldham Ath	Shrewsbury T	Undisclosed
25 Amrabat, Nordin	Watford	Al-Nassr	Undisclosed
12 Archer, Jordan	Chester C	Bury	Undisclosed
19 Arnold, Steve	Barrow	Shrewsbury T	Free
14 Asoro, Joel	Sunderland	Swansea C	Undisclosed
18 Bakayogo, Zoumana	Crewe Alex	Tranmere R	Free
30 Baldock, Sam	Brighton & HA	Reading	Undisclosed
28 Baldwin, Jack	Peterborough U	Sunderland	Undisclosed
31 Bamford, Patrick	Middlesbrough	Leeds U	£10m
16 Bartley, Kyle	Swansea C	WBA	Undisclosed
30 Baudry, Mathieu	Doncaster R	Milton Keynes D	Free
17 Blind, Daley	Manchester U	Ajax	£14m
17 Bola, Marc	Arsenal	Blackpool	Free
4 Boldewijn, Enzio	Crawley T	Notts Co	Undisclosed
16 Bond, Jonathan	Reading	WBA	Free
1 Brooks, David	Sheffield U	Bournemouth	Undisclosed
17 Buckley-Ricketts, Isaac	Manchester C	Peterborough U	Undisclosed
10 Burke, Reece	West Ham U	Hull C	Undisclosed
16 Button, David	Fulham	Brighton & HA	Undisclosed
31 Celina, Bersant	Manchester C	Swansea C	Undisclosed
16 Coke, Giles	Chesterfield	Oldham Ath	Free
4 Collin, Adam	Notts Co	Carlisle U	Free
25 Conlon, Tom	Stevenage	Port Vale	Free
30 Cooke, Callum	Middlesbrough	Peterborough U	Undisclosed
3 Cranston, Jordan	Cheltenham T	Morecambe	Free
10 Crawford, Ali	Hamilton A	Doncaster R	Free
13 D'Almeida, Sessi	Blackpool	Yeovil T	Free
2 Davenport, Jacob	Manchester C	Blackburn R	Undisclosed

10 Debayo, Josh	Leicester C	Cheltenham T	Free
18 Diagouraga, Toumani	Fleetwood T	Swindon T	Free
31 Digby, Paul	Mansfield T	Forest Green R	Undisclosed
23 Doughty, Michael	Peterborough U	Swindon T	Free
28 Douglas, Barry	Wolverhampton W	Leeds U	Undisclosed
26 Duku, Manny	Hayes & Yeading U	Cheltenham T	Free
17 Edwards, Gwion	Peterborough U	Ipswich T	Undisclosed
19 Egan, John	Brentford	Sheffield U	Undisclosed
23 Eisa, Mohamed	Cheltenham T	Bristol C	Undisclosed
31 Evans, George	Reading	Derby Co	Undisclosed
18 Fabio	Middlesbrough	Nantes	Undisclosed
3 Federici, Adam	Bournemouth	Stoke C	Undisclosed
1 Felix, Joe	Fulham	QPR	Free
10 Flatt, Jonathan	Wolverhampton W	Scunthorpe U	Free
5 Foster, Ben	WBA	Watford	Undisclosed
5 Fraser, Scott	Dundee U	Burton Alb	Free
2 Fuller, Barry	AFC Wimbledon	Gillingham	Free
10 Gilliead, Alex	Newcastle U	Shrewsbury T	Free
6 Grabban, Lewis	Bournemouth	Nottingham F	Undisclosed
3 Grant, Lee	Stoke C	Manchester U	Undisclosed
26 Green, Robert	Huddersfield T	Chelsea	Free
16 Grego-Cox, Reece	Woking	Crawley T	Free
10 Gunn, Angus	Manchester C	Southampton	£13.5m
26 Guthrie, Kurtis	Colchester U	Stevenage	Free
9 Halstead, Mark	Southport	Morecambe	Free
2 Hanlan, Brandon	Charlton Ath	Gillingham	Free
9 Harley, Ryan	Exeter C	Milton Keynes D	Free
23 Harrison, Ellis	Bristol R	Ipswich T	£750,000
22 Henry, Korrey	West Ham U	Yeovil T	Free
30 Hobbs, Jack	Nottingham F	Bolton W	Free
23 Holmes-Dennis, Tareiq	Huddersfield T	Bristol R	Undisclosed
6 Houghton, Jordan	Chelsea	Milton Keynes D	Free
5 Howard, Mark	Bolton W	Blackpool	Free
6 Hunt, Jack	Sheffield W	Bristol C	Undisclosed
31 Hunt, Nicky	Notts Co	Crewe Alex	Free
2 Hyam, Luke	Ipswich T	Southend U	Free
24 Ince, Tom	Huddersfield T	Stoke C	£10m
4 Inman, Brad	Peterborough U	Rochdale	Free
4 James, Lloyd	Exeter C	Forest Green R	Undisclosed
2 James, Reece	Wigan Ath	Sunderland	Free
3 Johnstone, Sam	Manchester U	WBA	£6.5m
21 Jones, Billy	Sunderland	Rotherham U	Free
21 Jozefzoon, Florian	Brentford	Derby Co	Undisclosed
17 Khazri, Wahbi	Sunderland	Saint Etienne	Undisclosed
27 Klaassen, Davy	Everton	Werder Bremen	Undisclosed
24 Krul, Tim	Brighton & HA	Norwich C	Free
23 Laurent, Josh	Wigan Ath	Shrewsbury T	Undisclosed
2 Law, Nicky	Bradford C	Exeter C	Free
21 Long, Chris	Burnley	Fleetwood T	Free
18 Long, George	Sheffield U	Hull C	Undisclosed
21 Loovens, Glenn	Sheffield W	Sunderland	Free
18 Mackie, Jamie	QPR	Oxford U	Free
30 Magennis, Josh	Charlton Ath	Bolton W	Undisclosed
10 Mahrez, Riyad	Leicester C	Manchester C	£60m
27 Makoma, Donovan	Barrow	Stevenage	Undisclosed
6 Mallan, Stevie	Barnsley	Hibernian	Undisclosed
30 Marney, Dean	Burnley	Fleetwood T	Free
26 Marriott, Jack	Peterborough U	Derby Co	Undisclosed
24 Martin, Lee	Gillingham	Exeter C	Free
6 Mason, Brandon	Watford	Coventry C	Free
23 Mbemba, Chancel	Newcastle U	Porto	£7.14m
28 McAlinden, Liam	Exeter C	Cheltenham T	Free
22 McClean, James	WBA	Stoke C	£5m
17 McCourt, Jak	Chesterfield	Swindon T	Free
2 McGeouch, Dylan	Hibernian	Sunderland	Free
24 McGoldrick, David	Ipswich T	Sheffield U	Free
31 McKay, Barrie	Nottingham F	Swansea C	Undisclosed
17 McLaughlin, Ryan	Oldham Ath	Blackpool	Undisclosed
21 McManaman, Callum	Sunderland	Wigan Ath	Undisclosed
6 McNulty, Marc	Coventry C	Reading	Undisclosed
31 Mellor, Kevin	Blackpool	Bradford C	Free
6 Miller, Tom	Carlisle U	Bury	Free
30 Mitrovic, Aleksandar	Newcastle U	Fulham	Undisclosed

19 Morais, Filipe	Bolton W	Crawley T	Free
13 Morias, Junior	Peterborough U	Northampton T	Undisclosed
6 Nicholls, Alex	Barnet	Crewe Alex	Free
18 Nugent, Ben	Gillingham	Stevenage	Free
24 Oates, Jimmy	Hereford U	Exeter C	Free
9 Odoffin, Hakeem	Wolverhampton W	Northampton T	Free
30 O'Grady, Chris	Chesterfield	Oldham Ath	Free
13 Omotayo, Gold	Unattached	Bury	Free
12 Oniangue, Prince	Wolverhampton W	Caen	Undisclosed
30 O'Nien, Luke	Wycombe W	Sunderland	Undisclosed
18 Oxlade-Chamberlain, Christian	Portsmouth	Notts Co	Free
3 Pantilimon, Costel	Watford	Nottingham F	Undisclosed
5 Poleon, Dominic	Bradford C	Crawley T	Undisclosed
17 Pratley, Darren	Bolton W	Charlton Ath	Free
19 Reid, Alex	Fleetwood T	Stevenage	Undisclosed
3 Reilly, Callum	Bury	Gillingham	Undisclosed
3 Reilly, Gavin	St Mirren	Bristol R	Free
24 Richarlison	Watford	Everton	£35m
2 Rodman, Alex	Shrewsbury T	Bristol R	Free
21 Rose, Michael	Morecambe	Macclesfield T	Free
19 Scannell, Sean	Huddersfield T	Bradford C	Undisclosed
13 Shaqiri, Xherdan	Stoke C	Liverpool	£13m
9 Simpson, Robbie	Exeter C	Milton Keynes D	Free
4 Smith, Harry	Millwall	Macclesfield T	Free
16 Stokes, Chris	Coventry C	Bury	Free
19 Taylor, Andy	Blackpool	Oldham Ath	Free
21 Taylor, Rhys	AFC Fylde	Macclesfield T	Free
10 Taylor, Steven	Peterborough U	Wellington Phoenix	Undisclosed
24 Telford, Dominic	Stoke C	Bury	Free
5 Templeton, David	Hamilton A	Burton Alb	Free
16 Thomas, Terell	Wigan Ath	AFC Wimbledon	Undisclosed
14 Thompson, Curtis	Notts Co	Wycombe W	Free
28 Townsend, Conor	Scunthorpe U	WBA	Undisclosed
6 Vaughan, David	Nottingham F	Notts Co	Free
16 Verheydt, Thomas	Crawley T	Go Ahead Eagles	Undisclosed
24 Vernam, Charles	Derby Co	Grimsby T	Undisclosed
19 Vincelot, Romain	Bradford C	Crawley T	Undisclosed
11 Wagstaff, Scott	Gillingham	AFC Wimbledon	Free
25 Walker, Sam	Colchester U	Reading	Free
18 Walkes, Anton	Tottenham H	Portsmouth	Undisclosed
21 Wallace, James	Tranmere R	Fleetwood T	Free
21 Ward, Danny	Liverpool	Leicester C	£12.5m
3 Weimann, Andreas	Derby Co	Bristol C	Undisclosed
13 Whyte, Gavin	Crusaders	Oxford U	Undisclosed
2 Widdrington, Theo	Portsmouth	Bristol R	Free
2 Williams, Morgan	Mickleover Sports	Coventry C	Undisclosed
9 Wilshere, Jack	Arsenal	West Ham U	Free
28 Wilson, Ben	Cardiff C	Bradford C	Free
24 Wilson, Marc	Sunderland	Bolton W	Free
12 Wordsworth, Anthony	Southend U	AFC Wimbledon	Free
6 Yorwerth, Josh	Crawley T	Peterborough U	Undisclosed
AUGUST 2018			
3 Akpom, Chuba	Arsenal	PAOK Salonika	Undisclosed
1 Allarakhia, Tarryn	Colchester U	Crawley T	Free
9 Amat, Jordi	Swansea C	Rayo Vallecano	£1m
9 Angol, Lee	Mansfield T	Shrewsbury T	Undisclosed
6 Armstrong, Adam	Newcastle U	Blackburn R	Undisclosed
7 Bakayoko, Amadou	Walsall	Coventry C	Undisclosed
9 Bryan, Joe	Bristol C	Fulham	£6m
2 Bryan, Kean	Manchester C	Sheffield U	Free
9 Burn, Dan	Wigan Ath	Brighton & HA	Undisclosed
31 Byrne, Jack	Oldham Ath	Kilmarnock	Free
8 Camp, Lee	Cardiff C	Birmingham C	Free
17 Campbell, Joel	Arsenal	Frosinone	Undisclosed
1 Cargill, Baily	Bournemouth	Milton Keynes D	Free
9 Carroll, Canice	Oxford U	Brentford	Undisclosed
30 Chadli, Nacer	WBA	Monaco	£10m
31 Choupo-Moting, Eric Maxim	Stoke C	Paris Saint-Germain	Free
9 Clucas, Sam	Swansea C	Stoke C	£6m
9 Colclough, Ryan	Wigan Ath	Scunthorpe U	Undisclosed
9 Courtois, Thibaut	Chelsea	Real Madrid	Undisclosed
9 Dai, Tsun	Bury	Oxford U	Undisclosed
9 Daniels, Donervon	Wigan Ath	Blackpool	Free

21 Dasilva, Josh	Arsenal	Brentford	Compensation
9 Djuric, Milan	Bristol C	Salernitana	Undisclosed
1 Doyle, Eoin	Preston NE	Bradford C	Undisclosed
9 Fernandez, Federico	Swansea C	Newcastle U	£6m
3 Ferrier, Morgan	Boreham Wood	Walsall	Undisclosed
9 Garner, Joe	Ipswich T	Wigan Ath	Undisclosed
9 Gerrard, Anthony	Oldham Ath	Carlisle U	Free
5 Gibson, Ben	Middlesbrough	Burnley	£15m
9 Gordon, Josh	Leicester C	Walsall	Undisclosed
2 Grant, Anthony	Peterborough U	Shrewsbury T	Undisclosed
9 Hanson, Jamie	Derby Co	Oxford U	Undisclosed
7 Hart, Joe	Manchester C	Burnley	£3.5m
9 Hefele, Michael	Huddersfield T	Nottingham F	Undisclosed
2 Hiwula, Jordy	Huddersfield T	Coventry C	Undisclosed
10 Hodge, Elliot	Notts Co	Burton Alb	Free
9 Holmes, Duane	Scunthorpe U	Derby Co	Undisclosed
11 Horgan, Daryl	Preston NE	Hibernian	Undisclosed
9 Jackson, Kayden	Accrington S	Ipswich T	Undisclosed
31 Jerome, Cameron	Derby Co	Goztepe	Undisclosed
9 John, Declan	Rangers	Swansea C	Undisclosed
2 Jones, Paul	Norwich C	Fleetwood T	Free
31 Kilgallon, Matt	Bradford C	Hamilton A	Undisclosed
3 Kipre, Cedric	Motherwell	Wigan Ath	£1m
17 Klavan, Ragnar	Liverpool	Cagliari	£2m
1 Kouyate, Cheikhou	West Ham U	Crystal Palace	Undisclosed
17 le Fondre, Adam	Bolton W	Sydney FC	Free
8 Leitch-Smith, A-Jay	Shrewsbury T	Morecambe	Free
2 Lonergan, Andy	Leeds U	Middlesbrough	Free
3 Lund, Matthew	Burton Alb	Scunthorpe U	Undisclosed
9 Luque, Joan	Heybridge Swifts	Lincoln C	Undisclosed
24 Lyon, Darren	Hamilton A	Peterborough U	Free
1 Maenpaa, Niki	Brighton & HA	Bristol C	Free
8 Malone, Scott	Huddersfield T	Derby Co	Undisclosed
3 Mancienne, Michael	Nottingham F	New England Revolution	Free
9 Mangan, Andy	Bala T	Accrington S	Free
12 Matthews, Remi	Norwich C	Bolton W	Undisclosed
2 Mawson, Alfie	Swansea C	Fulham	£20m
9 McCarthy, Jason	Barnsley	Wycombe W	Undisclosed
2 McDonald, Rod	Coventry C	AFC Wimbledon	Undisclosed
3 McDonald, Wes	Birmingham C	Yeovil T	Free
2 McFadzean, Callum	Guiseley	Bury	Free
8 McGinn, John	Hibernian	Aston Villa	Undisclosed
2 Moore, Stuart	Swindon T	Milton Keynes D	Free
2 Murphy, Luke	Leeds U	Bolton W	Free
3 Musa, Ahmed	Leicester C	Al-Nassr	Undisclosed
8 Nolan, Jon	Shrewsbury T	Ipswich T	Undisclosed
9 Norburn, Ollie	Tranmere R	Shrewsbury T	Undisclosed
8 Nsiala, Toto	Shrewsbury T	Ipswich T	Undisclosed
7 Odubajo, Moses	Hull C	Brentford	Free
3 O'Neil, Gary	Bristol C	Bolton W	Free
9 Osbourne, Isaiah	Forest Green R	Walsall	Free
9 Payne, Stefan	Shrewsbury T	Bristol R	Undisclosed
1 Perch, James	QPR	Scunthorpe U	Free
9 Perez, Lucas	Arsenal	West Ham U	Undisclosed
9 Quina, Domingos	West Ham U	Watford	Undisclosed
1 Sesay, David	Watford	Crawley T	Free
9 Shackell, Jason	Derby Co	Lincoln C	Free
2 Simpson, Luke	York C	Macclesfield T	Free
2 Skalak, Jiri	Brighton & HA	Millwall	Undisclosed
1 Steele, Luke	Bristol C	Nottingham F	Free
2 Stockton, Cole	Carlisle U	Tranmere R	Free
6 Styles, Callum	Bury	Barnsley	Undisclosed
9 Toney, Ivan	Newcastle U	Peterborough U	Undisclosed
8 Traore, Adama	Middlesbrough	Wolverhampton W	£18m
12 Ulloa, Leonardo	Leicester C	Pachuca	Undisclosed
1 Vieira, Ronaldo	Leeds U	Sampdoria	Undisclosed
9 Vincenti, Peter	Coventry C	Macclesfield T	Free
7 Vydra, Matej	Derby Co	Burnley	Undisclosed
8 Waghorn, Martyn	Ipswich T	Derby Co	Undisclosed
3 Walters, Dexter	Tamworth	Coventry C	Undisclosed
31 Washington, Conor	QPR	Sheffield U	Free
7 Waterfall, Luke	Lincoln C	Shrewsbury T	Undisclosed
8 Williams, Jordan	Huddersfield T	Barnsley	Undisclosed

9 Windass, Josh	Rangers	Wigan Ath	Undisclosed
1 Wyke, Charlie	Bradford C	Sunderland	Undisclosed
2 Zanzala, Offrande	Derby Co	Accrington S	Undisclosed
DECEMBER 2018			
13 Mondal, Junior	Whitby T	Forest Green R	Free
10 Sadlier, Kieran	Cork C	Doncaster R	Free
JANUARY 2019			
4 Afobe, Benik	Wolverhampton W	Stoke C	Undisclosed
17 Anderson, Jermaine	Peterborough U	Bradford C	Free
31 Azeez, Ade	Cambridge U	Newport Co	Undisclosed
31 Bacuna, Leandro	Reading	Cardiff C	£4m
7 Barnett, Tyrone	Port Vale	Cheltenham T	Free
29 Batth, Danny	Wolverhampton W	Stoke C	£3m
31 Bedeau, Jacob	Aston Villa	Scunthorpe U	Free
18 Benalouane, Yohan	Leicester C	Nottingham F	Undisclosed
31 Bingham, Rakish	Hamilton A	Cheltenham T	Free
31 Blackett-Taylor, Corey	Aston Villa	Walsall	Undisclosed
17 Bolger, Cian	Fleetwood T	Lincoln C	Undisclosed
2 Bowman, Ryan	Motherwell	Exeter C	Undisclosed
3 Bradshaw, Tom	Barnsley	Millwall	Undisclosed
4 Brereton, Ben	Nottingham F	Blackburn R	£7m
18 Broadbent, Tom	Bristol R	Swindon T	Undisclosed
1 Brown, Jaden	Tottenham H	Huddersfield T	Free
30 Bruce, Alex	Wigan Ath	Kilmarnock	Undisclosed
31 Byrne, Oliver	Blackburn R	Stevenage	Undisclosed
2 Cannon, Andy	Rochdale	Portsmouth	Undisclosed
4 Chaplin, Conor	Portsmouth	Coventry C	Undisclosed
28 Chapman, Harry	Middlesbrough	Blackburn R	Undisclosed
31 Clarke, Billy	Charlton Ath	Bradford C	Free
31 Clarke-Harris, Jonson	Coventry C	Bristol R	Undisclosed
3 Clement, Pelle	Reading	PEC Zwolle	Undisclosed
3 Connolly, Dylan	Dundalk	AFC Wimbledon	Undisclosed
12 Crooks, Matt	Northampton T	Rotherham U	Undisclosed
31 Crouch, Peter	Stoke C	Burnley	Undisclosed
24 Curran, Taylor	Southend U	Swindon T	Undisclosed
31 Dagnall, Chris	Bury	Tranmere R	Free
8 Dallison, Tom	Falkirk	Crawley T	Free
21 Daniel, Colin	Peterborough U	Burton Alb	Free
6 Diaz, Brahim	Manchester C	Real Madrid	Undisclosed
3 Donacien, Janoi	Accrington S	Ipswich T	Undisclosed
31 Doyle, Michael	Coventry C	Notts Co	Undisclosed
7 Edwards, Dave	Reading	Shrewsbury T	Free
1 Evans, Lee	Sheffield U	Wigan Ath	Undisclosed
12 Fabregas, Cesc	Chelsea	Monaco	Undisclosed
29 Famewo, Akin	Luton T	Norwich C	Undisclosed
29 Fox, Danny	Nottingham F	Wigan Ath	Undisclosed
12 Gabbiadini, Manolo	Southampton	Sampdoria	Undisclosed
1 German, Ricky	Hendon	Crawley T	Undisclosed
31 Gilks, Matt	Scunthorpe U	Lincoln C	Free
7 Gilmour, Harvey	Sheffield U	Tranmere R	Undisclosed
1 Ginnelly, Josh	Walsall	Preston NE	Undisclosed
21 Gnahoua, Arthur	Shrewsbury T	Carlisle U	Free
24 Godwin-Malife, Udoka	Oxford C	Forest Green R	Undisclosed
30 Grant, Karlan	Charlton Ath	Huddersfield T	Undisclosed
29 Grant, Peter	Plymouth Arg	Carlisle U	Free
18 Green, Jordan	Yeovil T	Barnsley	Undisclosed
25 Hallam, Jordan	Sheffield U	Scunthorpe U	Free
3 Hammill, Adam	St Mirren	Scunthorpe U	Free
12 Hendrie, Luke	Shrewsbury T	Grimsby T	Free
19 Humphrys, Stephen	Fulham	Southend U	Undisclosed
7 Iborra, Vicente	Leicester C	Villarreal	Undisclosed
29 Ilori, Tiago	Reading	Sporting Lisbon	Undisclosed
31 Iorfa, Dominic	Wolverhampton W	Sheffield W	Undisclosed
14 Judge, Alan	Brentford	Ipswich T	Undisclosed
28 Jules, Zak	Shrewsbury T	Macclesfield T	Free
29 Leadbitter, Grant	Middlesbrough	Sunderland	Free
4 Leonard, Ryan	Sheffield U	Millwall	Undisclosed
8 Long, Chris	Fleetwood T	Blackpool	Free
12 Lyons, Brad	Coleraine	Blackburn R	Undisclosed
26 Maja, Josh	Sunderland	Bordeaux	Undisclosed
30 Matondo, Rabbi	Manchester C	Schalke	£9.6m
18 Matthews, Remi	Norwich C	Bolton W	Free
3 McCoulsky, Shawn	Bristol C	Forest Green R	Undisclosed

4 McGahey, Harrison	Rochdale	Scunthorpe U	Undisclosed
31 McGilp, Cameron	Birmingham C	Swindon T	Undisclosed
4 McGinley, Nathan	Middlesbrough	Forest Green R	Undisclosed
23 McLaughlin, Ryan	Blackpool	Rochdale	Undisclosed
31 McLoughlin, Shane	Ipswich T	AFC Wimbledon	Free
22 Mepham, Chris	Brentford	Bournemouth	Undisclosed
31 Miller, George	Middlesbrough	Barnsley	Undisclosed
7 Miller, Ishmael	Oldham Ath	Tranmere R	Free
14 Milsom, Rob	Crawley T	Notts Co	Undisclosed
18 Moncur, George	Barnsley	Luton T	Undisclosed
14 Morris, Bryn	Shrewsbury T	Portsmouth	Undisclosed
31 Mullings, Shamir	Maidstone U	Macclesfield T	Undisclosed
17 Nelson, Andrew	Sunderland	Dundee	Undisclosed
18 Norman, Cameron	Oxford U	Walsall	Undisclosed
4 Norwood, Oliver	Brighton & HA	Sheffield U	Undisclosed
8 O'Brien, Jim	Bradford C	Notts Co	Free
30 Odoffin, Hakeem	Northampton T	Livingston	Undisclosed
31 Ogogo, Abu	Bristol R	Coventry C	Free
31 Parker, Josh	Gillingham	Charlton Ath	Undisclosed
5 Perkins, David	Rochdale	Tranmere R	Undisclosed
10 Pilkington, Anthony	Cardiff C	Wigan Ath	Free
3 Potts, Brad	Barnsley	Preston NE	Undisclosed
2 Power, Max	Wigan Ath	Sunderland	Undisclosed
23 Rafferty, Joe	Rochdale	Preston NE	Undisclosed
9 Ripley, Connor	Middlesbrough	Preston NE	Undisclosed
17 Rose, Danny	Portsmouth	Swindon T	Undisclosed
23 Rose, Michael	Ayr U	Coventry C	Free
29 Rose, Mitch	Grimsby T	Notts Co	Free
27 Sako, Bakary	WBA	Crystal Palace	Free
16 Saunders, Harvey	Darlington	Fleetwood T	Undisclosed
21 Scarr, Dan	Birmingham C	Walsall	Undisclosed
31 Scougall, Stefan	St Johnstone	Carlisle U	Free
29 Seager, Ryan	Southampton	Yeovil T	Free
21 Simoes, Elliot	FC United of Manchester	Barnsley	Undisclosed
4 Solanke, Dominic	Liverpool	Bournemouth	£19m
30 Stevenson, Ben	Wolverhampton W	Colchester U	Free
3 Stockley, Jayden	Exeter C	Preston NE	£750,000
9 Sutton, Ritchie	Tranmere R	Morecambe	Free
29 Sweeney, Ryan	Stoke C	Mansfield T	Free
2 Sykes, Mark	Glenavon	Oxford U	Undisclosed
5 Sylla, Idrissa	QPR	Zulte Waregem	Undisclosed
31 Trickett-Smith, Daniel	Leek T	Port Vale	Undisclosed
2 van Veen, Kevin	Northampton T	Scunthorpe U	Undisclosed
22 Vincelot, Romain	Crawley T	Shrewsbury T	Free
31 Virtue, Matty	Liverpool	Blackpool	Undisclosed
31 Vokes, Sam	Burnley	Stoke C	Undisclosed
31 Wakefield, Charlie	Chelsea	Coventry C	Free
9 Walker, Brad	Crewe Alex	Shrewsbury T	Undisclosed
4 Webster, Byron	Millwall	Scunthorpe U	Free
4 Williams, Jonny	Crystal Palace	Charlton Ath	Undisclosed
18 Williams, Randell	Watford	Exeter C	Free
30 Williams, Ro-Shaun	Manchester U	Shrewsbury T	Free
3 Woodrow, Cauley	Fulham	Barnsley	Undisclosed
23 Woods, Calum	Preston NE	Bradford C	Free
4 Woods, Ryan	Brentford	Stoke C	Undisclosed
18 Worthington, Matt	Bournemouth	Yeovil T	Free
9 Wylde, Gregg	Plymouth Arg	Livingston	Free

FEBRUARY 2019

15 Ambrose, Efe	Hibernian	Derby Co	Free
20 Browning, Tyias	Everton	Guangzhou Evergrande	Undisclosed
9 Collins, Aaron	Wolverhampton W	Morecambe	Free
1 Fellaini, Marouane	Manchester U	Shandong Luneng	Undisclosed
1 Grigg, Will	Wigan Ath	Sunderland	£4m
1 Keohane, Jimmy	Cork C	Rochdale	Free
1 Markovic, Lazar	Liverpool	Fulham	Free
4 Martis, Liandro	Leicester C	Macclesfield T	Free
1 Meite, Ibrahim	Cardiff C	Crawley T	Free
1 Ntambwe, Brice	Partick Thistle	Macclesfield T	Free
1 Simmonds, Okera	Blackburn R	Accrington S	Free
1 Smith, Jonte	Lewes	Oxford U	Undisclosed
3 Southam-Hales, Macaulay	Barry Town	Fleetwood T	Undisclosed
4 Tomlinson, Willem	Blackburn R	Mansfield T	Free
2 Turner, Ben	Burton Alb	Mansfield T	Free
1 Yennaris, Nico	Brentford	Beijing Sinobo Guoan	Undisclosed

APRIL 2019

29 Carroll, Jake	Cambridge U	Motherwell	Free (1/7/19)
4 Jimenez, Raul	Benfica	Wolverhampton W	£30m

MAY 2019

22 Allardyce, Sam	Bury	Oxford U	Free
20 Atangana, Nigel	Cheltenham T	Exeter C	Free
24 Beevers, Mark	Bolton W	Peterborough U	Free (1/7/19)
20 Berkoe, Kevin	Wolverhampton W	Oxford U	Free
26 Blake-Tracy, Frazer	King's Lynn	Peterborough U	Undisclosed
31 Bloomfield, Mason	Norwich C	Crawley T	Loan
27 Boateng, Hiram	Exeter C	Milton Keynes D	Compensation
24 Burgess, Scott	Bury	Port Vale	Free
24 Butler, Andy	Doncaster R	Scunthorpe U	Free (1/7/19)
30 Butler, Dan	Newport Co	Peterborough U	Free
30 Clarke, James	Bristol R	Walsall	Free
14 Cowley, Jason	Bromsgrove Sporting	Stevenage	Undisclosed
31 Crookes, Adam	Nottingham Forest	Port Vale	Free
2 Davis, Steven	Southampton	Rangers	Free
30 Dickenson, Brennan	Colchester U	Milton Keynes D	Free
29 Ebanks-Landell, Ethan	Wolverhampton W	Shrewsbury T	Undisclosed
14 Elliott, Christie	Partick Thistle	Carlisle U	Free
22 Fielding, Jamie	Hastings U	Stevenage	Free
29 French, Tyler	AFC Sudbury	Bradford C	Free
24 Halliday, Brad	Cambridge U	Doncaster R	Free (1/7/19)
28 Hannant, Luke	Port Vale	Cambridge U	Free
24 Holy, Tomas	Gillingham	Ipswich T	Free (1/7/19)
31 Hornby, Sam	Port Vale	Bradford C	Free
28 Howard, Michael	Preston NE	Morecambe	Free
21 Iacovitti, Alex	Nottingham F	Oldham Ath	Free
7 Iredale, Jack	Greenock Morton	Carlisle U	Free
18 Kelly, Lloyd	Bristol C	Bournemouth	£13m
30 Knibbs, Harvey	Aston Villa	Cambridge U	Free
30 Lancashire, Olly	Swindon T	Crewe Alex	Free
15 Lines, Chris	Bristol R	Northampton T	Free (1/7/19)
24 Lossl, Jonas	Huddersfield T	Everton	Free (1/7/19)
24 Lowe, Chris	Huddersfield T	Dynamo Dresden	Undisclosed
22 Marosi, Marko	Doncaster R	Coventry C	Free
13 Martin, Joe	Stevenage	Northampton T	Free (1/7/19)
9 McFadzean, Kyle	Burton Alb	Coventry C	Free (1/7/19)
15 Mellish, Jon	Gateshead	Carlisle U	Free
22 Morris, Carlton	Norwich C	Rotherham U	Loan
31 Nadesan, Ashley	Fleetwood T	Crawley T	Free
23 Ogilvie, Connor	Tottenham H	Gillingham	Undisclosed
21 O'Toole, John-Joe	Northampton T	Burton Alb	Free
27 Parkes, Tom	Carlisle U	Exeter C	Free
10 Pinto, Ivo	Norwich C	Dinamo Zagreb	Free
30 Pritchard, Joe	Bolton W	Accrington S	Free
29 Pym, Christy	Exeter C	Peterborough U	Free
14 Raglan, Charlie	Oxford U	Cheltenham T	Free
16 Richards-Everton, Ben	Accrington S	Bradford C	Free (1/7/19)
8 Shinnie, Graeme	Aberdeen	Derby Co	Free (1/7/19)
21 Sinclair, Stuart	Bristol R	Walsall	Free
17 Smith, Harry	Macclesfield T	Northampton T	Undisclosed
24 Tasdemir, Serhat	AFC Fylde	Peterborough U	Undisclosed
31 Towell, Richie	Brighton & HA	Salford C	Free
31 Udoh, Daniel	AFC Telford	Shrewsbury T	Undisclosed
7 Warburton, Matty	Stockport Co	Northampton T	Free (1/7/19)
23 Wilson, Ben	Bradford C	Coventry C	Free (1/7/19)
28 Yussuf, Adi	Solihull U	Blackpool	Free

THE NEW FOREIGN LEGION 2018–19

JUNE 2018	*From*	*To*	*Fee in £*
20 Bacuna, Juninho	FC Groningen	Huddersfield T	Undisclosed
1 Boly, Willy	Porto	Wolverhampton W	£10m
8 Buendia, Emi	Getafe	Norwich C	Undisclosed
14 Carvalho, Joao	Benfica	Nottingham F	£13.2m
6 Dalot, Diogo	Porto	Manchester U	£19m
11 Deulofeu, Gerard	Barcelona	Watford	£11.5m
23 Dias, Gil Bastiao	Monaco	Nottingham F	Loan
19 Diop, Issa	Toulouse	West Ham U	£22m
29 Elyounoussi, Mohamed	FC Basel	Southampton	£16m
11 Etebo, Oghenekaro	Feirense	Stoke C	£6.35m
21 Fred	Shakhtar Donetsk	Manchester U	£47m
14 Goncalves, Diogo	Benfica	Nottingham F	Loan
8 Guaita, Vicente	Getafe	Crystal Palace	Free
12 Isherwood, Thomas	Bayern Munich II	Bradford C	Undisclosed
12 Jimenez, Raul	Benfica	Wolverhampton W	Loan
8 Kongolo, Terence	Monaco	Huddersfield T	Undisclosed
26 Leitner, Moritz	Augsburg	Norwich C	Undisclosed
19 Leno, Bernd	Bayer Leverkusen	Arsenal	£19.3m
5 Lichtsteiner, Stephan	Juventus	Arsenal	Free
8 Mills, Joseph	Perth Glory	Forest Green R	Free
15 Navarro, Marc	Espanyol	Watford	Undisclosed
18 Patricio, Rui	Sporting Lisbon	Wolverhampton W	Free
25 Pedersen, Kristian	Union Berlin	Birmingham C	Undisclosed
30 Pukki, Teemu	Brondby	Norwich C	Free
4 Robles, Louis	San Roque De Lepe	Grimsby T	Free
29 Soudani, Hillal	Dinamo Zagreb	Nottingham F	Undisclosed
JULY 2018			
19 Alisson	Roma	Liverpool	£66.8m
15 Anderson, Felipe	Lazio	West Ham U	Undisclosed
14 Balbuena, Fabian	Corinthians	West Ham U	Undisclosed
6 Benrahma, Said	Nice	Brentford	Undisclosed
5 Bernardo	RB Leipzig	Brighton & HA	£9m
17 Bissouma, Yves	Lille	Brighton & HA	Undisclosed
3 Branger, Johan	FC Dieppe	Oldham Ath	Free
21 Diakhaby, Adama	Monaco	Huddersfield T	Undisclosed
27 Dougall, Kenny	Sparta Rotterdam	Barnsley	Free
13 Durm, Erik	Borussia Dortmund	Huddersfield T	Undisclosed
24 Fabri	Besiktas	Fulham	£5m
11 Guendouzi, Matteo	Lorient	Arsenal	Undisclosed
17 Horsfield, James	NAC Breda	Scunthorpe U	Free
25 Jahanbakhsh, Alireza	AZ Alkmaar	Brighton & HA	Undisclosed
30 Jeanvier, Julian	Stade de Reims	Brentford	Undisclosed
14 Jorginho	Napoli	Chelsea	Undisclosed
12 le Marchand, Maxime	Nice	Fulham	Undisclosed
1 Leistner, Toni	Union Berlin	QPR	Free
2 Masina, Adam	Bologna	Watford	Undisclosed
9 Milinkovic, David	Genoa	Hull C	Undisclosed
24 Moutinho, Joao	Monaco	Wolverhampton W	£5m
10 Olkowski, Pawel	Cologne	Bolton W	Free
25 Otto, Jonny Castro	Atletico Madrid	Wolverhampton W	Loan
2 Papastathopoulos, Sokratis	Borussia Dortmund	Arsenal	Undisclosed
2 Passlack, Felix	Borussia Dortmund	Norwich C	Loan
24 Rico, Diego	Leganes	Bournemouth	£10.7m
31 Sandler, Philippe	PEC Zwolle	Manchester C	Undisclosed
25 Schurrle, Andre	Borussia Dortmund	Fulham	Loan
5 Sema, Ken	Ostersund	Watford	Undisclosed
12 Seri, Jean Michael	Nice	Fulham	Undisclosed
17 Sidoel, Darren	Ajax	Reading	Undisclosed
21 Tau, Percy	Mamelodi Sundowns	Brighton & HA	Undisclosed
10 Torreira, Lucas	Sampdoria	Arsenal	£26m
13 Vestergaard, Jannik	Borussia Monchengladbach	Southampton	Undisclosed
11 Wijs, Jordy de	PSV Eindhoven	Hull C	Undisclosed
11 Yarmolenko, Andriy	Borussia Dortmund	West Ham U	Undisclosed
AUGUST 2018			
22 Akammadu, Franklyn	US Alessandria	Tranmere R	Loan
9 Anguissa, Andre-Frank Zambo	Marseille	Fulham	£22.3m
8 Arrizabalaga, Kepa	Athletic Bilbao	Chelsea	£71m
9 Arzani, Daniel	Melbourne C	Manchester C	Undisclosed

31 Bahre, Mike-Steven	Hannover 96	Barnsley	Loan
9 Benkovic, Filip	Dinamo Zagreb	Leicester C	Undisclosed
9 Bernard	Shakhtar Donetsk	Everton	Free
9 Camarasa, Victor	Real Betis	Cardiff C	Loan
9 Dendoncker, Leander	Anderlecht	Wolverhampton W	Loan
1 Digne, Lucas	Barcelona	Everton	£18m
22 El Ghazi, Anwar	Lille	Aston Villa	Loan
5 Ghezzal, Rachid	Monaco	Leicester C	Undisclosed
9 Gomes, Andre	Barcelona	Everton	Loan
9 Gwargis, Peter	Jonkopings Sodra	Brighton & HA	Undisclosed
31 Janko, Saidy	Porto	Nottingham F	Loan
9 Kovacic, Mateo	Real Madrid	Chelsea	Loan
7 Lerma, Jefferson	Levante	Bournemouth	£25m
9 Mbenza, Isaac	Montpellier	Huddersfield T	Loan
2 Meyer, Max	Schalke 04	Crystal Palace	Free
9 Mina, Yerry	Barcelona	Everton	£27.19m
9 Montoya, Martin	Valencia	Brighton & HA	Undisclosed
1 Moreira, Andre	Atletico Madrid	Aston Villa	Loan
2 Muto, Yoshinori	Mainz	Newcastle U	Undisclosed
7 Nyland, Orjan	FC Ingolstadt	Aston Villa	Undisclosed
9 Rico, Sergio	Sevilla	Fulham	Loan
9 Sanchez, Carlos	Fiorentina	West Ham U	Undisclosed
7 Scott, Andrew	Maiden City Soccer	Accrington S	Free
9 Soyuncu, Caglar	Freiburg	Leicester C	£19m
4 Vidal, Aleix	Barcelona	Sevilla	£9.35m
9 Vietto, Luciano	Atletico Madrid	Fulham	Loan
NOVEMBER 2018			
3 Ansarifard, Karim	Olympiacos	Nottingham F	Free
DECEMBER 2018			
21 Kalinic, Lovre	Gent	Aston Villa	Undisclosed
JANUARY 2019			
31 Almiron, Miguel	Atlanta	Newcastle U	£20m
15 Babel, Ryan	Besiktas	Fulham	Undisclosed
31 Baluta, Tudor-Cristian	Viitorul Constanta	Brighton & HA	Undisclosed
31 Barreca, Antonio	Monaco	Newcastle U	Loan
17 Casilla, Kiko	Real Madrid	Leeds U	Free
15 Charles-Cook, Reice	Sonderjyske	Shrewsbury T	Free
31 Guilbert, Frederic	Caen	Aston Villa	Undisclosed
31 Heise, Philip	Dynamo Dresden	Norwich C	Undisclosed
23 Higuain, Gonzalo	Juventus	Chelsea	Loan
31 Mlakar, Jan	NK Maribor	Brighton & HA	Undisclosed
2 Mussa, Omar	KV Mechelen	Walsall	Undisclosed
8 Ohman, Ludvig	IF Brommapojkarna	Grimsby T	Undisclosed
31 Otto, Jonny Castro	Atletico Madrid	Wolverhampton W	£15m
31 Palaversa, Ante	Hadjuk Split	Manchester C	£7m
31 Pele	Monaco	Nottingham F	Loan
24 Perri, Lucas	Sao Paulo	Crystal Palace	Loan
2 Pulisic, Christian	Borussia Dortmund	Chelsea	£58m
1 Ring, Sebastian	Orebro	Grimsby T	Free
19 Sala, Emiliano	Nantes	Cardiff C	Undisclosed
30 Suarez, Denis	Barcelona	Arsenal	Loan
5 Sylla, Mohamed	Entente SSG	Oldham Ath	Undisclosed
8 Threlkeld, Oscar	Beveren	Plymouth Arg	Loan
31 Tielemans, Youri	Monaco	Leicester C	Loan
1 Wang, David	FC Jumilla	Wolverhampton W	Undisclosed
FEBRUARY 2019			
1 Olsson, Jonas	Djurgarden	Wigan Ath	Free
1 Wague, Molla	Udinese	Nottingham F	Loan
MAY 2019			
21 Bahre, Mike-Steven	Hannover 96	Barnsley	Undisclosed
31 Mills, Matt	Pune City	Forest Green R	Free
31 Roberto	Espanyol	West Ham U	Free

ENGLISH LEAGUE HONOURS 1888–2019

**Won or placed on goal average (ratio), goal difference or most goals scored. ‡Not promoted after play-offs. No official competition during 1915–19 and 1939–46, regional leagues operated.*

FOOTBALL LEAGUE (1888–89 to 1891–92) – TIER 1

MAXIMUM POINTS: ***a*** **44;** ***b*** **52.**

1	1888–89*a*	Preston NE	40	Aston Villa	29	Wolverhampton W	28
1	1889–90*a*	Preston NE	33	Everton	31	Blackburn R	27
1	1890–91*a*	Everton	29	Preston NE	27	Notts Co	26
1	1891–92*b*	Sunderland	42	Preston NE	37	Bolton W	36

DIVISION 1 (1892–93 to 1991–92)

MAXIMUM POINTS: ***c*** **60;** ***d*** **68;** ***e*** **76;** ***f*** **84;** ***g*** **126;** ***h*** **120;** ***k*** **114.**

1	1892–93*c*	Sunderland	48	Preston NE	37	Everton	36
1	1893–94*c*	Aston Villa	44	Sunderland	38	Derby Co	36
1	1894–95*c*	Sunderland	47	Everton	42	Aston Villa	39
1	1895–96*c*	Aston Villa	45	Derby Co	41	Everton	39
1	1896–97*c*	Aston Villa	47	Sheffield U*	36	Derby Co	36
1	1897–98*c*	Sheffield U	42	Sunderland	37	Wolverhampton W*	35
1	1898–99*d*	Aston Villa	45	Liverpool	43	Burnley	39
1	1899–1900*d*	Aston Villa	50	Sheffield U	48	Sunderland	41
1	1900–01*d*	Liverpool	45	Sunderland	43	Notts Co	40
1	1901–02*d*	Sunderland	44	Everton	41	Newcastle U	37
1	1902–03*d*	The Wednesday	42	Aston Villa*	41	Sunderland	41
1	1903–04*d*	The Wednesday	47	Manchester C	44	Everton	43
1	1904–05*d*	Newcastle U	48	Everton	47	Manchester C	46
1	1905–06*e*	Liverpool	51	Preston NE	47	The Wednesday	44
1	1906–07*e*	Newcastle U	51	Bristol C	48	Everton*	45
1	1907–08*e*	Manchester U	52	Aston Villa*	43	Manchester C	43
1	1908–09*e*	Newcastle U	53	Everton	46	Sunderland	44
1	1909–10*e*	Aston Villa	53	Liverpool	48	Blackburn R*	45
1	1910–11*e*	Manchester U	52	Aston Villa	51	Sunderland*	45
1	1911–12*e*	Blackburn R	49	Everton	46	Newcastle U	44
1	1912–13*e*	Sunderland	54	Aston Villa	50	Sheffield W	49
1	1913–14*e*	Blackburn R	51	Aston Villa	44	Middlesbrough*	43
1	1914–15*e*	Everton	46	Oldham Ath	45	Blackburn R*	43
1	1919–20*f*	WBA	60	Burnley	51	Chelsea	49
1	1920–21*f*	Burnley	59	Manchester C	54	Bolton W	52
1	1921–22*f*	Liverpool	57	Tottenham H	51	Burnley	49
1	1922–23*f*	Liverpool	60	Sunderland	54	Huddersfield T	53
1	1923–24*f*	Huddersfield T*	57	Cardiff C	57	Sunderland	53
1	1924–25*f*	Huddersfield T	58	WBA	56	Bolton W	55
1	1925–26*f*	Huddersfield T	57	Arsenal	52	Sunderland	48
1	1926–27*f*	Newcastle U	56	Huddersfield T	51	Sunderland	49
1	1927–28*f*	Everton	53	Huddersfield T	51	Leicester C	48
1	1928–29*f*	Sheffield W	52	Leicester C	51	Aston Villa	50
1	1929–30*f*	Sheffield W	60	Derby Co	50	Manchester C*	47
1	1930–31*f*	Arsenal	66	Aston Villa	59	Sheffield W	52
1	1931–32*f*	Everton	56	Arsenal	54	Sheffield W	50
1	1932–33*f*	Arsenal	58	Aston Villa	54	Sheffield W	51
1	1933–34*f*	Arsenal	59	Huddersfield T	56	Tottenham H	49
1	1934–35*f*	Arsenal	58	Sunderland	54	Sheffield W	49
1	1935–36*f*	Sunderland	56	Derby Co*	48	Huddersfield T	48
1	1936–37*f*	Manchester C	57	Charlton Ath	54	Arsenal	52
1	1937–38*f*	Arsenal	52	Wolverhampton W	51	Preston NE	49
1	1938–39*f*	Everton	59	Wolverhampton W	55	Charlton Ath	50
1	1946–47*f*	Liverpool	57	Manchester U*	56	Wolverhampton W	56
1	1947–48*f*	Arsenal	59	Manchester U*	52	Burnley	52
1	1948–49*f*	Portsmouth	58	Manchester U*	53	Derby Co	53
1	1949–50*f*	Portsmouth*	53	Wolverhampton W	53	Sunderland	52
1	1950–51*f*	Tottenham H	60	Manchester U	56	Blackpool	50
1	1951–52*f*	Manchester U	57	Tottenham H*	53	Arsenal	53
1	1952–53*f*	Arsenal*	54	Preston NE	54	Wolverhampton W	51
1	1953–54*f*	Wolverhampton W	57	WBA	53	Huddersfield T	51
1	1954–55*f*	Chelsea	52	Wolverhampton W*	48	Portsmouth*	48
1	1955–56*f*	Manchester U	60	Blackpool*	49	Wolverhampton W	49
1	1956–57*f*	Manchester U	64	Tottenham H*	56	Preston NE	56
1	1957–58*f*	Wolverhampton W	64	Preston NE	59	Tottenham H	51
1	1958–59*f*	Wolverhampton W	61	Manchester U	55	Arsenal*	50
1	1959–60*f*	Burnley	55	Wolverhampton W	54	Tottenham H	53
1	1960–61*f*	Tottenham H	66	Sheffield W	58	Wolverhampton W	57
1	1961–62*f*	Ipswich T	56	Burnley	53	Tottenham H	52
1	1962–63*f*	Everton	61	Tottenham H	55	Burnley	54
1	1963–64*f*	Liverpool	57	Manchester U	53	Everton	52
1	1964–65*f*	Manchester U*	61	Leeds U	61	Chelsea	56

1	1965–66*f*	Liverpool	61	Leeds U*	55	Burnley	55
1	1966–67*f*	Manchester U	60	Nottingham F*	56	Tottenham H	56
1	1967–68*f*	Manchester C	58	Manchester U	56	Liverpool	55
1	1968–69*f*	Leeds U	67	Liverpool	61	Everton	57
1	1969–70*f*	Everton	66	Leeds U	57	Chelsea	55
1	1970–71*f*	Arsenal	65	Leeds U	64	Tottenham H*	52
1	1971–72*f*	Derby Co	58	Leeds U*	57	Liverpool*	57
1	1972–73*f*	Liverpool	60	Arsenal	57	Leeds U	53
1	1973–74*f*	Leeds U	62	Liverpool	57	Derby Co	48
1	1974–75*f*	Derby Co	53	Liverpool*	51	Ipswich T	51
1	1975–76*f*	Liverpool	60	QPR	59	Manchester U	56
1	1976–77*f*	Liverpool	57	Manchester C	56	Ipswich T	52
1	1977–78*f*	Nottingham F	64	Liverpool	57	Everton	55
1	1978–79*f*	Liverpool	68	Nottingham F	60	WBA	59
1	1979–80*f*	Liverpool	60	Manchester U	58	Ipswich T	53
1	1980–81*f*	Aston Villa	60	Ipswich T	56	Arsenal	53
1	1981–82*g*	Liverpool	87	Ipswich T	83	Manchester U	78
1	1982–83*g*	Liverpool	82	Watford	71	Manchester U	70
1	1983–84*g*	Liverpool	80	Southampton	77	Nottingham F*	74
1	1984–85*g*	Everton	90	Liverpool*	77	Tottenham H	77
1	1985–86*g*	Liverpool	88	Everton	86	West Ham U	84
1	1986–87*g*	Everton	86	Liverpool	77	Tottenham H	71
1	1987–88*h*	Liverpool	90	Manchester U	81	Nottingham F	73
1	1988–89*k*	Arsenal*	76	Liverpool	76	Nottingham F	64
1	1989–90*k*	Liverpool	79	Aston Villa	70	Tottenham H	63
1	1990–91*k*	Arsenal[1]	83	Liverpool	76	Crystal Palace	69
1	1991–92*g*	Leeds U	82	Manchester U	78	Sheffield W	75

[1] *Arsenal deducted 2pts due to player misconduct in match on 20/10/1990 v Manchester U at Old Trafford.*

PREMIER LEAGUE (1992–93 to 2018–19)

MAXIMUM POINTS: *a* 126; *b* 114.

1	1992–93*a*	Manchester U	84	Aston Villa	74	Norwich C	72
1	1993–94*a*	Manchester U	92	Blackburn R	84	Newcastle U	77
1	1994–95*a*	Blackburn R	89	Manchester U	88	Nottingham F	77
1	1995–96*b*	Manchester U	82	Newcastle U	78	Liverpool	71
1	1996–97*b*	Manchester U	75	Newcastle U*	68	Arsenal*	68
1	1997–98*b*	Arsenal	78	Manchester U	77	Liverpool	65
1	1998–99*b*	Manchester U	79	Arsenal	78	Chelsea	75
1	1999–2000*b*	Manchester U	91	Arsenal	73	Leeds U	69
1	2000–01*b*	Manchester U	80	Arsenal	70	Liverpool	69
1	2001–02*b*	Arsenal	87	Liverpool	80	Manchester U	77
1	2002–03*b*	Manchester U	83	Arsenal	78	Newcastle U	69
1	2003–04*b*	Arsenal	90	Chelsea	79	Manchester U	75
1	2004–05*b*	Chelsea	95	Arsenal	83	Manchester U	77
1	2005–06*b*	Chelsea	91	Manchester U	83	Liverpool	82
1	2006–07*b*	Manchester U	89	Chelsea	83	Liverpool*	68
1	2007–08*b*	Manchester U	87	Chelsea	85	Arsenal	83
1	2008–09*b*	Manchester U	90	Liverpool	86	Chelsea	83
1	2009–10*b*	Chelsea	86	Manchester U	85	Arsenal	75
1	2010–11*b*	Manchester U	80	Chelsea*	71	Manchester C	71
1	2011–12*b*	Manchester C*	89	Manchester U	89	Arsenal	70
1	2012–13*b*	Manchester U	89	Manchester C	78	Chelsea	75
1	2013–14*b*	Manchester C	86	Liverpool	84	Chelsea	82
1	2014–15*b*	Chelsea	87	Manchester C	79	Arsenal	75
1	2015–16*b*	Leicester C	81	Arsenal	71	Tottenham H	70
1	2016–17*b*	Chelsea	93	Tottenham H	86	Manchester C	78
1	2017–18*b*	Manchester C	100	Manchester U	81	Tottenham H	77
1	2018–19*b*	Manchester C	98	Liverpool	97	Chelsea	72

DIVISION 2 (1892–93 to 1991–92) – TIER 2

MAXIMUM POINTS: *a* 44; *b* 56; *c* 60; *d* 68; *e* 76; *f* 84; *g* 126; *h* 132; *k* 138.

2	1892–93*a*	Small Heath	36	Sheffield U	35	Darwen	30
2	1893–94*b*	Liverpool	50	Small Heath	42	Notts Co	39
2	1894–95*c*	Bury	48	Notts Co	39	Newton Heath*	38
2	1895–96*c*	Liverpool*	46	Manchester C	46	Grimsby T*	42
2	1896–97*c*	Notts Co	42	Newton Heath	39	Grimsby T	38
2	1897–98*c*	Burnley	48	Newcastle U	45	Manchester C	39
2	1898–99*d*	Manchester C	52	Glossop NE	46	Leicester Fosse	45
2	1899–1900*d*	The Wednesday	54	Bolton W	52	Small Heath	46
2	1900–01*d*	Grimsby T	49	Small Heath	48	Burnley	44
2	1901–02*d*	WBA	55	Middlesbrough	51	Preston NE*	42
2	1902–03*d*	Manchester C	54	Small Heath	51	Woolwich A	48
2	1903–04*d*	Preston NE	50	Woolwich A	49	Manchester U	48
2	1904–05*d*	Liverpool	58	Bolton W	56	Manchester U	53
2	1905–06*e*	Bristol C	66	Manchester U	62	Chelsea	53
2	1906–07*e*	Nottingham F	60	Chelsea	57	Leicester Fosse	48
2	1907–08*e*	Bradford C	54	Leicester Fosse	52	Oldham Ath	50
2	1908–09*e*	Bolton W	52	Tottenham H*	51	WBA	51
2	1909–10*e*	Manchester C	54	Oldham Ath*	53	Hull C*	53
2	1910–11*e*	WBA	53	Bolton W	51	Chelsea	49

2	1911–12*e*	Derby Co*	54	Chelsea	54	Burnley	52
2	1912–13*e*	Preston NE	53	Burnley	50	Birmingham	46
2	1913–14*e*	Notts Co	53	Bradford PA*	49	Woolwich A	49
2	1914–15*e*	Derby Co	53	Preston NE	50	Barnsley	47
2	1919–20*f*	Tottenham H	70	Huddersfield T	64	Birmingham	56
2	1920–21*f*	Birmingham*	58	Cardiff C	58	Bristol C	51
2	1921–22*f*	Nottingham F	56	Stoke C*	52	Barnsley	52
2	1922–23*f*	Notts Co	53	West Ham U*	51	Leicester C	51
2	1923–24*f*	Leeds U	54	Bury*	51	Derby Co	51
2	1924–25*f*	Leicester C	59	Manchester U	57	Derby Co	55
2	1925–26*f*	Sheffield W	60	Derby Co	57	Chelsea	52
2	1926–27*f*	Middlesbrough	62	Portsmouth*	54	Manchester C	54
2	1927–28*f*	Manchester C	59	Leeds U	57	Chelsea	54
2	1928–29*f*	Middlesbrough	55	Grimsby T	53	Bradford PA*	48
2	1929–30*f*	Blackpool	58	Chelsea	55	Oldham Ath	53
2	1930–31*f*	Everton	61	WBA	54	Tottenham H	51
2	1931–32*f*	Wolverhampton W	56	Leeds U	54	Stoke C	52
2	1932–33*f*	Stoke C	56	Tottenham H	55	Fulham	50
2	1933–34*f*	Grimsby T	59	Preston NE	52	Bolton W*	51
2	1934–35*f*	Brentford	61	Bolton W*	56	West Ham U	56
2	1935–36*f*	Manchester U	56	Charlton Ath	55	Sheffield U*	52
2	1936–37*f*	Leicester C	56	Blackpool	55	Bury	52
2	1937–38*f*	Aston Villa	57	Manchester U*	53	Sheffield U	53
2	1938–39*f*	Blackburn R	55	Sheffield U	54	Sheffield W	53
2	1946–47*f*	Manchester C	62	Burnley	58	Birmingham C	55
2	1947–48*f*	Birmingham C	59	Newcastle U	56	Southampton	52
2	1948–49*f*	Fulham	57	WBA	56	Southampton	55
2	1949–50*f*	Tottenham H	61	Sheffield W*	52	Sheffield U*	52
2	1950–51*f*	Preston NE	57	Manchester C	52	Cardiff C	50
2	1951–52*f*	Sheffield W	53	Cardiff C*	51	Birmingham C	51
2	1952–53*f*	Sheffield U	60	Huddersfield T	58	Luton T	52
2	1953–54*f*	Leicester C*	56	Everton	56	Blackburn R	55
2	1954–55*f*	Birmingham C*	54	Luton T*	54	Rotherham U	54
2	1955–56*f*	Sheffield W	55	Leeds U	52	Liverpool*	48
2	1956–57*f*	Leicester C	61	Nottingham F	54	Liverpool	53
2	1957–58*f*	West Ham U	57	Blackburn R	56	Charlton Ath	55
2	1958–59*f*	Sheffield W	62	Fulham	60	Sheffield U*	53
2	1959–60*f*	Aston Villa	59	Cardiff C	58	Liverpool*	50
2	1960–61*f*	Ipswich T	59	Sheffield U	58	Liverpool	52
2	1961–62*f*	Liverpool	62	Leyton Orient	54	Sunderland	53
2	1962–63*f*	Stoke C	53	Chelsea*	52	Sunderland	52
2	1963–64*f*	Leeds U	63	Sunderland	61	Preston NE	56
2	1964–65*f*	Newcastle U	57	Northampton T	56	Bolton W	50
2	1965–66*f*	Manchester C	59	Southampton	54	Coventry C	53
2	1966–67*f*	Coventry C	59	Wolverhampton W	58	Carlisle U	52
2	1967–68*f*	Ipswich T	59	QPR*	58	Blackpool	58
2	1968–69*f*	Derby Co	63	Crystal Palace	56	Charlton Ath	50
2	1969–70*f*	Huddersfield T	60	Blackpool	53	Leicester C	51
2	1970–71*f*	Leicester C	59	Sheffield U	56	Cardiff C*	53
2	1971–72*f*	Norwich C	57	Birmingham C	56	Millwall	55
2	1972–73*f*	Burnley	62	QPR	61	Aston Villa	50
2	1973–74*f*	Middlesbrough	65	Luton T	50	Carlisle U	49
2	1974–75*f*	Manchester U	61	Aston Villa	58	Norwich C	53
2	1975–76*f*	Sunderland	56	Bristol C*	53	WBA	53
2	1976–77*f*	Wolverhampton W	57	Chelsea	55	Nottingham F	52
2	1977–78*f*	Bolton W	58	Southampton	57	Tottenham H*	56
2	1978–79*f*	Crystal Palace	57	Brighton & HA*	56	Stoke C	56
2	1979–80*f*	Leicester C	55	Sunderland	54	Birmingham C*	53
2	1980–81*f*	West Ham U	66	Notts Co	53	Swansea C*	50
2	1981–82*g*	Luton T	88	Watford	80	Norwich C	71
2	1982–83*g*	QPR	85	Wolverhampton W	75	Leicester C	70
2	1983–84*g*	Chelsea*	88	Sheffield W	88	Newcastle U	80
2	1984–85*g*	Oxford U	84	Birmingham C	82	Manchester C*	74
2	1985–86*g*	Norwich C	84	Charlton Ath	77	Wimbledon	76
2	1986–87*g*	Derby Co	84	Portsmouth	78	Oldham Ath‡	75
2	1987–88*h*	Millwall	82	Aston Villa*	78	Middlesbrough	78
2	1988–89*k*	Chelsea	99	Manchester C	82	Crystal Palace	81
2	1989–90*k*	Leeds U*	85	Sheffield U	85	Newcastle U‡	80
2	1990–91*k*	Oldham Ath	88	West Ham U	87	Sheffield W	82
2	1991–92*k*	Ipswich T	84	Middlesbrough	80	Derby Co	78

FIRST DIVISION (1992–93 to 2003–04)

MAXIMUM POINTS: 138

2	1992–93	Newcastle U	96	West Ham U*	88	Portsmouth‡	88
2	1993–94	Crystal Palace	90	Nottingham F	83	Millwall‡	74
2	1994–95	Middlesbrough	82	Reading‡	79	Bolton W	77
2	1995–96	Sunderland	83	Derby Co	79	Crystal Palace‡	75
2	1996–97	Bolton W	98	Barnsley	80	Wolverhampton W‡	76
2	1997–98	Nottingham F	94	Middlesbrough	91	Sunderland‡	90

2	1998–99	Sunderland	105	Bradford C	87	Ipswich T‡	86
2	1999–2000	Charlton Ath	91	Manchester C	89	Ipswich T	87
2	2000–01	Fulham	101	Blackburn R	91	Bolton W	87
2	2001–02	Manchester C	99	WBA	89	Wolverhampton W‡	86
2	2002–03	Portsmouth	98	Leicester C	92	Sheffield U‡	80
2	2003–04	Norwich C	94	WBA	86	Sunderland‡	79

FOOTBALL LEAGUE CHAMPIONSHIP (2004–05 to 2018–19)

MAXIMUM POINTS: 138

2	2004–05	Sunderland	94	Wigan Ath	87	Ipswich T‡	85
2	2005–06	Reading	106	Sheffield U	90	Watford	81
2	2006–07	Sunderland	88	Birmingham C	86	Derby Co	84
2	2007–08	WBA	81	Stoke C	79	Hull C	75
2	2008–09	Wolverhampton W	90	Birmingham C	83	Sheffield U‡	80
2	2009–10	Newcastle U	102	WBA	91	Nottingham F‡	79
2	2010–11	QPR	88	Norwich C	84	Swansea C*	80
2	2011–12	Reading	89	Southampton	88	West Ham U	86
2	2012–13	Cardiff C	87	Hull C	79	Watford‡	77
2	2013–14	Leicester C	102	Burnley	93	Derby Co‡	85
2	2014–15	Bournemouth	90	Watford	89	Norwich C	86
2	2015–16	Burnley	93	Middlesbrough*	89	Brighton & HA‡	89
2	2016–17	Newcastle U	94	Brighton & HA	93	Reading‡	85
2	2017–18	Wolverhampton W	99	Cardiff C	90	Fulham	88
2	2018–19	Norwich C	94	Sheffield U	89	Leeds U‡	83

DIVISION 3 (1920–1921) – TIER 3

MAXIMUM POINTS: *a* 84.

3	1920–21*a*	Crystal Palace	59	Southampton	54	QPR	53

DIVISION 3—SOUTH (1921–22 to 1957–58)

MAXIMUM POINTS: *a* 84; *b* 92.

3	1921–22*a*	Southampton*	61	Plymouth Arg	61	Portsmouth	53
3	1922–23*a*	Bristol C	59	Plymouth Arg*	53	Swansea T	53
3	1923–24*a*	Portsmouth	59	Plymouth Arg	55	Millwall	54
3	1924–25*a*	Swansea T	57	Plymouth Arg	56	Bristol C	53
3	1925–26*a*	Reading	57	Plymouth Arg	56	Millwall	53
3	1926–27*a*	Bristol C	62	Plymouth Arg	60	Millwall	56
3	1927–28*a*	Millwall	65	Northampton T	55	Plymouth Arg	53
3	1928–29*a*	Charlton Ath*	54	Crystal Palace	54	Northampton T*	52
3	1929–30*a*	Plymouth Arg	68	Brentford	61	QPR	51
3	1930–31*a*	Notts Co	59	Crystal Palace	51	Brentford	50
3	1931–32*a*	Fulham	57	Reading	55	Southend U	53
3	1932–33*a*	Brentford	62	Exeter C	58	Norwich C	57
3	1933–34*a*	Norwich C	61	Coventry C*	54	Reading*	54
3	1934–35*a*	Charlton Ath	61	Reading	53	Coventry C	51
3	1935–36*a*	Coventry C	57	Luton T	56	Reading	54
3	1936–37*a*	Luton T	58	Notts Co	56	Brighton & HA	53
3	1937–38*a*	Millwall	56	Bristol C	55	QPR*	53
3	1938–39*a*	Newport Co	55	Crystal Palace	52	Brighton & HA	49
3	1946–47*a*	Cardiff C	66	QPR	57	Bristol C	51
3	1947–48*a*	QPR	61	Bournemouth	57	Walsall	51
3	1948–49*a*	Swansea T	62	Reading	55	Bournemouth	52
3	1949–50*a*	Notts Co	58	Northampton T*	51	Southend U	51
3	1950–51*b*	Nottingham F	70	Norwich C	64	Reading*	57
3	1951–52*b*	Plymouth Arg	66	Reading*	61	Norwich C	61
3	1952–53*b*	Bristol R	64	Millwall*	62	Northampton T	62
3	1953–54*b*	Ipswich T	64	Brighton & HA	61	Bristol C	56
3	1954–55*b*	Bristol C	70	Leyton Orient	61	Southampton	59
3	1955–56*b*	Leyton Orient	66	Brighton & HA	65	Ipswich T	64
3	1956–57*b*	Ipswich T*	59	Torquay U	59	Colchester U	58
3	1957–58*b*	Brighton & HA	60	Brentford*	58	Plymouth Arg	58

DIVISION 3—NORTH (1921–22 to 1957–58)

MAXIMUM POINTS: *a* 76; *b* 84; *c* 80; *d* 92.

3	1921–22*a*	Stockport Co	56	Darlington*	50	Grimsby T	50
3	1922–23*a*	Nelson	51	Bradford PA	47	Walsall	46
3	1923–24*b*	Wolverhampton W	63	Rochdale	62	Chesterfield	54
3	1924–25*b*	Darlington	58	Nelson*	53	New Brighton	53
3	1925–26*b*	Grimsby T	61	Bradford PA	60	Rochdale	59
3	1926–27*b*	Stoke C	63	Rochdale	58	Bradford PA	55
3	1927–28*b*	Bradford PA	63	Lincoln C	55	Stockport Co	54
3	1928–29*b*	Bradford C	63	Stockport Co	62	Wrexham	52
3	1929–30*b*	Port Vale	67	Stockport Co	63	Darlington*	50
3	1930–31*b*	Chesterfield	58	Lincoln C	57	Wrexham*	54
3	1931–32*c*	Lincoln C*	57	Gateshead	57	Chester	50
3	1932–33*b*	Hull C	59	Wrexham	57	Stockport Co	54
3	1933–34*b*	Barnsley	62	Chesterfield	61	Stockport Co	59

3	1934–35*b*	Doncaster R	57	Halifax T	55	Chester	54
3	1935–36*b*	Chesterfield	60	Chester*	55	Tranmere R	55
3	1936–37*b*	Stockport Co	60	Lincoln C	57	Chester	53
3	1937–38*b*	Tranmere R	56	Doncaster R	54	Hull C	53
3	1938–39*b*	Barnsley	67	Doncaster R	56	Bradford C	52
3	1946–47*b*	Doncaster R	72	Rotherham U	64	Chester	56
3	1947–48*b*	Lincoln C	60	Rotherham U	59	Wrexham	50
3	1948–49*b*	Hull C	65	Rotherham U	62	Doncaster R	50
3	1949–50*b*	Doncaster R	55	Gateshead	53	Rochdale*	51
3	1950–51*d*	Rotherham U	71	Mansfield T	64	Carlisle U	62
3	1951–52*d*	Lincoln C	69	Grimsby T	66	Stockport Co	59
3	1952–53*d*	Oldham Ath	59	Port Vale	58	Wrexham	56
3	1953–54*d*	Port Vale	69	Barnsley	58	Scunthorpe U	57
3	1954–55*d*	Barnsley	65	Accrington S	61	Scunthorpe U*	58
3	1955–56*d*	Grimsby T	68	Derby Co	63	Accrington S	59
3	1956–57*d*	Derby Co	63	Hartlepools U	59	Accrington S*	58
3	1957–58*d*	Scunthorpe U	66	Accrington S	59	Bradford C	57

DIVISION 3 (1958–59 to 1991–92)

MAXIMUM POINTS: 92; 138 FROM 1981–82.

3	1958–59	Plymouth Arg	62	Hull C	61	Brentford*	57
3	1959–60	Southampton	61	Norwich C	59	Shrewsbury T*	52
3	1960–61	Bury	68	Walsall	62	QPR	60
3	1961–62	Portsmouth	65	Grimsby T	62	Bournemouth*	59
3	1962–63	Northampton T	62	Swindon T	58	Port Vale	54
3	1963–64	Coventry C*	60	Crystal Palace	60	Watford	58
3	1964–65	Carlisle U	60	Bristol C*	59	Mansfield T	59
3	1965–66	Hull C	69	Millwall	65	QPR	57
3	1966–67	QPR	67	Middlesbrough	55	Watford	54
3	1967–68	Oxford U	57	Bury	56	Shrewsbury T	55
3	1968–69	Watford*	64	Swindon T	64	Luton T	61
3	1969–70	Orient	62	Luton T	60	Bristol R	56
3	1970–71	Preston NE	61	Fulham	60	Halifax T	56
3	1971–72	Aston Villa	70	Brighton & HA	65	Bournemouth*	62
3	1972–73	Bolton W	61	Notts Co	57	Blackburn R	55
3	1973–74	Oldham Ath	62	Bristol R*	61	York C	61
3	1974–75	Blackburn R	60	Plymouth Arg	59	Charlton Ath	55
3	1975–76	Hereford U	63	Cardiff C	57	Millwall	56
3	1976–77	Mansfield T	64	Brighton & HA	61	Crystal Palace*	59
3	1977–78	Wrexham	61	Cambridge U	58	Preston NE*	56
3	1978–79	Shrewsbury T	61	Watford*	60	Swansea C	60
3	1979–80	Grimsby T	62	Blackburn R	59	Sheffield W	58
3	1980–81	Rotherham U	61	Barnsley*	59	Charlton Ath	59
3	1981–82	Burnley*	80	Carlisle U	80	Fulham	78
3	1982–83	Portsmouth	91	Cardiff C	86	Huddersfield T	82
3	1983–84	Oxford U	95	Wimbledon	87	Sheffield U*	83
3	1984–85	Bradford C	94	Millwall	90	Hull C	87
3	1985–86	Reading	94	Plymouth Arg	87	Derby Co	84
3	1986–87	Bournemouth	97	Middlesbrough	94	Swindon T	87
3	1987–88	Sunderland	93	Brighton & HA	84	Walsall	82
3	1988–89	Wolverhampton W	92	Sheffield U*	84	Port Vale	84
3	1989–90	Bristol R	93	Bristol C	91	Notts Co	87
3	1990–91	Cambridge U	86	Southend U	85	Grimsby T*	83
3	1991–92	Brentford	82	Birmingham C	81	Huddersfield T‡	78

SECOND DIVISION (1992–93 to 2003–04)

MAXIMUM POINTS: 138

3	1992–93	Stoke C	93	Bolton W	90	Port Vale‡	89
3	1993–94	Reading	89	Port Vale	88	Plymouth Arg*‡	85
3	1994–95	Birmingham C	89	Brentford‡	85	Crewe Alex‡	83
3	1995–96	Swindon T	92	Oxford U	83	Blackpool‡	82
3	1996–97	Bury	84	Stockport Co	82	Luton T‡	78
3	1997–98	Watford	88	Bristol C	85	Grimsby T	72
3	1998–99	Fulham	101	Walsall	87	Manchester C	82
3	1999–2000	Preston NE	95	Burnley	88	Gillingham	85
3	2000–01	Millwall	93	Rotherham U	91	Reading‡	86
3	2001–02	Brighton & HA	90	Reading	84	Brentford*‡	83
3	2002–03	Wigan Ath	100	Crewe Alex	86	Bristol C*‡	83
3	2003–04	Plymouth Arg	90	QPR	83	Bristol C‡	82

FOOTBALL LEAGUE ONE (2004–05 to 2018–19)

MAXIMUM POINTS: 138

3	2004–05	Luton T	98	Hull C	86	Tranmere R‡	79
3	2005–06	Southend U	82	Colchester U	79	Brentford‡	76
3	2006–07	Scunthorpe U	91	Bristol C	85	Blackpool	83
3	2007–08	Swansea C	92	Nottingham F	82	Doncaster R*	80
3	2008–09	Leicester C	96	Peterborough U	89	Milton Keynes D‡	87
3	2009–10	Norwich C	95	Leeds U	86	Millwall	85
3	2010–11	Brighton & HA	95	Southampton	92	Huddersfield T‡	87

3	2011–12	Charlton Ath	101	Sheffield W	93	Sheffield U‡	90
3	2012–13	Doncaster R	84	Bournemouth	83	Brentford‡	79
3	2013–14	Wolverhampton W	103	Brentford	94	Leyton Orient‡	86
3	2014–15	Bristol C	99	Milton Keynes D	91	Preston NE	89
3	2015–16	Wigan Ath	87	Burton Alb	85	Walsall‡	84
3	2016–17	Sheffield U	100	Bolton W	86	Scunthorpe U*‡	82
3	2017–18	Wigan Ath	98	Blackburn R	96	Shrewsbury T‡	87
3	2018–19	Luton T	94	Barnsley	91	Charlton Ath*	88

DIVISION 4 (1958–59 to 1991–92) – TIER 4

MAXIMUM POINTS: 92; 138 FROM 1981–82.

4	1958–59	Port Vale	64	Coventry C*	60	York C	60	Shrewsbury T	58
4	1959–60	Walsall	65	Notts Co*	60	Torquay U	60	Watford	57
4	1960–61	Peterborough U	66	Crystal Palace	64	Northampton T*	60	Bradford PA	60
4	1961–62[2]	Millwall	56	Colchester U	55	Wrexham	53	Carlisle U	52
4	1962–63	Brentford	62	Oldham Ath*	59	Crewe Alex	59	Mansfield T*	57
4	1963–64	Gillingham*	60	Carlisle U	60	Workington	59	Exeter C	58
4	1964–65	Brighton & HA	63	Millwall*	62	York C	62	Oxford U	61
4	1965–66	Doncaster R*	59	Darlington	59	Torquay U	58	Colchester U*	56
4	1966–67	Stockport Co	64	Southport*	59	Barrow	59	Tranmere R	58
4	1967–68	Luton T	66	Barnsley	61	Hartlepools U	60	Crewe Alex	58
4	1968–69	Doncaster R	59	Halifax T	57	Rochdale*	56	Bradford C	56
4	1969–70	Chesterfield	64	Wrexham	61	Swansea C	60	Port Vale	59
4	1970–71	Notts Co	69	Bournemouth	60	Oldham Ath	59	York C	56
4	1971–72	Grimsby T	63	Southend U	60	Brentford	59	Scunthorpe U	57
4	1972–73	Southport	62	Hereford U	58	Cambridge U	57	Aldershot*	56
4	1973–74	Peterborough U	65	Gillingham	62	Colchester U	60	Bury	59
4	1974–75	Mansfield T	68	Shrewsbury T	62	Rotherham U	59	Chester*	57
4	1975–76	Lincoln C	74	Northampton T	68	Reading	60	Tranmere R	58
4	1976–77	Cambridge U	65	Exeter C	62	Colchester U*	59	Bradford C	59
4	1977–78	Watford	71	Southend U	60	Swansea C*	56	Brentford	56
4	1978–79	Reading	65	Grimsby T*	61	Wimbledon*	61	Barnsley	61
4	1979–80	Huddersfield T	66	Walsall	64	Newport Co	61	Portsmouth*	60
4	1980–81	Southend U	67	Lincoln C	65	Doncaster R	56	Wimbledon	55
4	1981–82	Sheffield U	96	Bradford C*	91	Wigan Ath	91	Bournemouth	88
4	1982–83	Wimbledon	98	Hull C	90	Port Vale	88	Scunthorpe U	83
4	1983–84	York C	101	Doncaster R	85	Reading*	82	Bristol C	82
4	1984–85	Chesterfield	91	Blackpool	86	Darlington	85	Bury	84
4	1985–86	Swindon T	102	Chester C	84	Mansfield T	81	Port Vale	79
4	1986–87	Northampton T	99	Preston NE	90	Southend U	80	Wolverhampton W‡	79
4	1987–88	Wolverhampton W	90	Cardiff C	85	Bolton W	78	Scunthorpe U*‡	77
4	1988–89	Rotherham U	82	Tranmere R	80	Crewe Alex	78	Scunthorpe U*‡	77
4	1989–90	Exeter C	89	Grimsby T	79	Southend U	75	Stockport Co‡	74
4	1990–91	Darlington	83	Stockport Co*	82	Hartlepool U	82	Peterborough U	80
4	1991–92[3]	Burnley	83	Rotherham U*	77	Mansfield T	77	Blackpool	76

[2]*Maximum points:* 88 owing to Accrington Stanley's resignation.
[3]*Maximum points:* 126 owing to Aldershot being expelled (and only 23 teams started the competition).

THIRD DIVISION (1992–93 to 2003–04)

MAXIMUM POINTS: *a* 126; *b* 138.

4	1992–93*a*	Cardiff C	83	Wrexham	80	Barnet	79	York C	75
4	1993–94*a*	Shrewsbury T	79	Chester C	74	Crewe Alex	73	Wycombe W	70
4	1994–95*a*	Carlisle U	91	Walsall	83	Chesterfield	81	Bury‡	80
4	1995–96*b*	Preston NE	86	Gillingham	83	Bury	79	Plymouth Arg*	78
4	1996–97*b*	Wigan Ath*	87	Fulham	87	Carlisle U	84	Northampton T	72
4	1997–98*b*	Notts Co	99	Macclesfield T	82	Lincoln C	72	Colchester U*	74
4	1998–99*b*	Brentford	85	Cambridge U	81	Cardiff C	80	Scunthorpe U	74
4	1999–2000*b*	Swansea C	85	Rotherham U	84	Northampton T	82	Darlington‡	79
4	2000–01*b*	Brighton & HA	92	Cardiff C	82	Chesterfield[4]	80	Hartlepool U‡	77
4	2001–02*b*	Plymouth Arg	102	Luton T	97	Mansfield T	79	Cheltenham T	78
4	2002–03*b*	Rushden & D	87	Hartlepool U	85	Wrexham	84	Bournemouth	74
4	2003–04*b*	Doncaster R	92	Hull C	88	Torquay U*	81	Huddersfield T	81

[4]*Chesterfield deducted 9pts for irregularities.*

FOOTBALL LEAGUE TWO (2004–05 to 2018–19)

MAXIMUM POINTS: 138

4	2004–05	Yeovil T	83	Scunthorpe U*	80	Swansea C	80	Southend U	80
4	2005–06	Carlisle U	86	Northampton T	83	Leyton Orient	81	Grimsby T‡	78
4	2006–07	Walsall	89	Hartlepool U	88	Swindon T	85	Milton Keynes D‡	84
4	2007–08	Milton Keynes D	97	Peterborough U	92	Hereford U	88	Stockport Co	82
4	2008–09	Brentford	85	Exeter C	79	Wycombe W*	78	Bury‡	78
4	2009–10	Notts Co	93	Bournemouth	83	Rochdale	82	Morecambe*‡	73
4	2010–11	Chesterfield	86	Bury	81	Wycombe W	80	Shrewsbury T‡	79
4	2011–12	Swindon T	93	Shrewsbury T	88	Crawley T	84	Southend U‡	83
4	2012–13	Gillingham	83	Rotherham U	79	Port Vale	78	Burton Alb	76
4	2013–14	Chesterfield	84	Scunthorpe U*	81	Rochdale	81	Fleetwood T	76
4	2014–15	Burton Alb	94	Shrewsbury T	89	Bury	85	Wycombe W*‡	84
4	2015–16	Northampton T	99	Oxford U	86	Bristol R*	85	Accrington S‡	85
4	2016–17	Portsmouth*	87	Plymouth Arg	87	Doncaster R	85	Luton T‡	77
4	2017–18	Accrington S	93	Luton T	88	Wycombe W	84	Exeter C‡	80
4	2018–19	Lincoln C	85	Bury*	79	Milton Keynes D	79	Mansfield T‡	76

LEAGUE TITLE WINS

DIVISION 1 (1888–89 to 1991–92) – TIER 1
Liverpool 18, Arsenal 10, Everton 9, Aston Villa 7, Manchester U 7, Sunderland 6, Newcastle U 4, Sheffield W 4 (2 as The Wednesday), Huddersfield T 3, Leeds U 3, Wolverhampton W 3, Blackburn R 2, Burnley 2, Derby Co 2, Manchester C 2, Portsmouth 2, Preston NE 2, Tottenham H 2, Chelsea 1, Ipswich T 1, Nottingham F 1, Sheffield U 1, WBA 1.

PREMIER LEAGUE (1992–93 to 2018–19) – TIER 1
Manchester U 13, Chelsea 5, Manchester C 4, Arsenal 3, Blackburn R 1, Leicester C 1.

DIVISION 2 (1892–93 TO 1991–92) – TIER 2
Leicester C 6, Manchester C 6, Sheffield W 5 (1 as The Wednesday), Birmingham C 4 (1 as Small Heath), Derby Co 4, Liverpool 4, Ipswich T 3, Leeds U 3, Middlesbrough 3, Notts Co 3, Preston NE 3, Aston Villa 2, Bolton W 2, Burnley 2, Chelsea 2, Grimsby T 2, Manchester U 2, Norwich C 2, Nottingham F 2, Stoke C 2, Tottenham H 2, WBA 2, West Ham U 2, Wolverhampton W 2, Blackburn R 1, Blackpool 1, Bradford C 1, Brentford 1, Bristol C 1, Bury 1, Coventry C 1, Crystal Palace 1, Everton 1, Fulham 1, Huddersfield T 1, Luton T 1, Millwall 1, Newcastle U 1, Oldham Ath 1, Oxford U 1, QPR 1, Sheffield U 1, Sunderland 1.

FIRST DIVISION (1992–93 to 2003–04) – TIER 2
Sunderland 1, Bolton W 1, Charlton Ath 1, Crystal Palace 1, Fulham 1, Manchester C 1, Middlesbrough 1, Newcastle U 1, Norwich C 1, Nottingham F 1, Portsmouth 1.

FOOTBALL LEAGUE CHAMPIONSHIP (2004–05 to 2018–19) – TIER 2
Newcastle U 2, Reading 2, Sunderland 2, Wolverhampton W 2, Bournemouth 1, Burnley 1, Cardiff C 1, Leicester C 1, Norwich C 1, QPR 1, WBA 1,

DIVISION 3—SOUTH (1920–21 to 1957–58) – TIER 3
Bristol C 3, Charlton Ath 2, Ipswich T 2, Millwall 2, Notts Co 2, Plymouth Arg 2, Swansea T 2, Brentford 1, Brighton & HA 1, Bristol R 1, Cardiff C 1, Coventry C 1, Crystal Palace 1, Fulham 1, Leyton Orient 1, Luton T 1, Newport Co 1, Norwich C 1, Nottingham F 1, Portsmouth 1, QPR 1, Reading 1, Southampton 1.

DIVISION 3—NORTH (1921–22 to 1957–58) – TIER 3
Barnsley 3, Doncaster R 3, Lincoln C 3, Chesterfield 2, Grimsby T 2, Hull C 2, Port Vale 2, Stockport Co 2, Bradford C 1, Bradford PA 1, Darlington 1, Derby Co 1, Nelson 1, Oldham Ath 1, Rotherham U 1, Scunthorpe U 1, Stoke C 1, Tranmere R 1, Wolverhampton W 1.

DIVISION 3 (1958–59 to 1991–92) – TIER 3
Oxford U 2, Portsmouth 2, Aston Villa 1, Blackburn R 1, Bolton W 1, Bournemouth 1, Bradford C 1, Brentford 1, Bristol R 1, Burnley 1, Bury 1, Cambridge U 1, Carlisle U 1, Coventry C 1, Grimsby T 1, Hereford U 1, Hull C 1, Mansfield T 1, Northampton T 1, Oldham Ath 1, Orient 1, Plymouth Arg 1, Preston NE 1, QPR 1, Reading 1, Rotherham U 1, Shrewsbury T 1, Southampton 1, Sunderland 1, Watford 1, Wolverhampton W 1, Wrexham 1.

SECOND DIVISION (1992–93 to 2003–04) – TIER 3
Birmingham C 1, Brighton & HA 1, Bury 1, Fulham 1, Millwall 1, Plymouth Arg 1, Preston NE 1, Reading 1, Stoke C 1, Swindon T 1, Watford 1, Wigan Ath 1.

FOOTBALL LEAGUE ONE (2004–05 to 2018–19) – TIER 3
Luton T 2, Wigan Ath 2, Brighton & HA 1, Bristol C 1, Charlton Ath 1, Doncaster R 1, Leicester C 1, Norwich C 1, Scunthorpe U 1, Sheffield U 1, Southend U 1, Swansea C 1, Wolverhampton W 1.

DIVISION 4 (1958–59 to 1991–92) – TIER 4
Chesterfield 2, Doncaster R 2, Peterborough U 2, Brentford 1, Brighton & HA 1, Burnley 1, Cambridge U 1, Darlington 1, Exeter C 1, Gillingham 1, Grimsby T 1, Huddersfield T 1, Lincoln C 1, Luton T 1, Mansfield T 1, Millwall 1, Northampton T 1, Notts Co 1, Port Vale 1, Reading 1, Rotherham U 1, Sheffield U 1, Southend U 1, Southport 1, Stockport Co 1, Swindon T 1, Walsall 1, Watford 1, Wimbledon 1, Wolverhampton W 1, York C 1.

THIRD DIVISION (1992–93 to 2003–04) – TIER 4
Brentford 1, Brighton & HA 1, Cardiff C 1, Carlisle U 1, Doncaster R 1, Notts Co 1, Plymouth Arg 1, Preston NE 1, Rushden & D 1, Shrewsbury T 1, Swansea C 1, Wigan Ath 1.

FOOTBALL LEAGUE TWO (2004–05 to 2018–19) – TIER 4
Chesterfield 2, Accrington S 1, Brentford 1, Burton Alb 1, Carlisle U 1, Gillingham 1, Lincoln C 1, Milton Keynes D 1, Northampton T 1, Notts Co 1, Portsmouth 1, Swindon T 1, Walsall 1, Yeovil T 1.

PROMOTED AFTER PLAY-OFFS

1986–87	Charlton Ath to Division 1; Swindon T to Division 2; Aldershot to Division 3
1987–88	Middlesbrough to Division 1; Walsall to Division 2; Swansea C to Division 3
1988–89	Crystal Palace to Division 1; Port Vale to Division 2; Leyton Orient to Division 3
1989–90	Sunderland to Division 1; Notts Co to Division 2; Cambridge U to Division 3
1990–91	Notts Co to Division 1; Tranmere R to Division 2; Torquay U to Division 3
1991–92	Blackburn R to Premier League; Peterborough U to First Division; Blackpool to Second Division
1992–93	Swindon T to Premier League; WBA to First Division; York C to Second Division
1993–94	Leicester C to Premier League; Burnley to First Division; Wycombe W to Second Division
1994–95	Bolton W to Premier League; Huddersfield T to First Division; Wycome Wanderers to Second Division
1995–96	Leicester C to Premier League; Bradford C to First Division; Plymouth Arg to Second Division
1996–97	Crystal Palace to Premier League; Crewe Alex to First Division; Northampton T to Second Division
1997–98	Charlton Ath to Premier League; Grimsby T to First Division; Colchester U to Second Division
1998–99	Watford to Premier League; Manchester C to First Division; Scunthorpe U to Second Division
1999–2000	Ipswich to Premier League; Gillingham to First Division; Peterborough U to Second Division
2000–01	Bolton W to Premier league; Walsall to First Division; Blackpool to Second Division
2001–02	Birmingham C to Premier League; Stoke C to First Division; Cheltenham T to Second Division
2002–03	Wolverhampton W to Premier League; Cardiff C to First Division; Bournemouth to Second Division
2003–04	Crystal Palace to Premier League; Brighton & HA to First Division; Huddersfield T to Second Division
2004–05	West Ham U to Premier League; Sheffield W to Championship; Southend U to Football League One
2005–06	Watford to Premier League; Barnsley to Championship; Cheltenham T to Football League One
2006–07	Derby Co to Premier League; Blackpool to Championship; Bristol R to Football League One
2007–08	Hull C to Premier League; Doncaster R to Championship; Stockport Co to Football League One
2008–09	Burnley to Premier League; Scunthorpe U to Championship; Gillingham to Football League One
2009–10	Blackpool to Premier League; Millwall to Championship; Dagenham & R to Football League One
2010–11	Swansea C to Premier League; Peterborough U to Championship; Stevenage to Football League One
2011–12	West Ham U to Premier League; Huddersfield T to Championship; Crewe Alex to Football League One
2012–13	Crystal Palace to Premier League; Yeovil T to Championship; Bradford C to Football League One
2013–14	QPR to Premier League; Rotherham U to Championship; Fleetwood T to Football League One
2014–15	Norwich C to Premier League; Preston NE to Championship; Southend U to Football League One
2015–16	Hull C to Premier League; Barnsley to Championship; AFC Wimbledon to Football League One
2016–17	Huddersfield T to Premier League; Millwall to Championship; Blackpool to Football League One
2017–18	Fulham to Premier League; Rotherham U to Championship; Coventry C to Football League One
2018–19	Aston Villa to Premier League; Charlton Ath to Championship; Tranmere R to Football League One

RELEGATED CLUBS

1891–92 League extended. Newton Heath, Sheffield W and Nottingham F admitted. *Second Division formed* including Darwen.
1892–93 In Test matches, Sheffield U and Darwen won promotion in place of Notts Co and Accrington S.
1893–94 In Tests, Liverpool and Small Heath won promotion. Newton Heath and Darwen relegated.
1894–95 After Tests, Bury promoted, Liverpool relegated.
1895–96 After Tests, Liverpool promoted, Small Heath relegated.
1896–97 After Tests, Notts Co promoted, Burnley relegated.
1897–98 Test system abolished after success of Stoke C and Burnley. League extended. Blackburn R and Newcastle U elected to First Division. *Automatic promotion and relegation introduced.*

DIVISION 1 TO DIVISION 2 (1898–99 to 1991–92)

1898–99 Bolton W and Sheffield W
1899–1900 Burnley and Glossop
1900–01 Preston NE and WBA
1901–02 Small Heath and Manchester C
1902–03 Grimsby T and Bolton W
1903–04 Liverpool and WBA
1904–05 League extended. Bury and Notts Co, two bottom clubs in First Division, re-elected.
1905–06 Nottingham F and Wolverhampton W
1906–07 Derby Co and Stoke C
1907–08 Bolton W and Birmingham C
1908–09 Manchester C and Leicester Fosse
1909–10 Bolton W and Chelsea
1910–11 Bristol C and Nottingham F
1911–12 Preston NE and Bury
1912–13 Notts Co and Woolwich Arsenal
1913–14 Preston NE and Derby Co
1914–15 Tottenham H and Chelsea*
1919–20 Notts Co and Sheffield W
1920–21 Derby Co and Bradford PA
1921–22 Bradford C and Manchester U
1922–23 Stoke C and Oldham Ath
1923–24 Chelsea and Middlesbrough
1924–25 Preston NE and Nottingham F
1925–26 Manchester C and Notts Co
1926–27 Leeds U and WBA
1927–28 Tottenham H and Middlesbrough
1928–29 Bury and Cardiff C
1929–30 Burnley and Everton
1930–31 Leeds U and Manchester U
1931–32 Grimsby T and West Ham U
1932–33 Bolton W and Blackpool
1933–34 Newcastle U and Sheffield U
1934–35 Leicester C and Tottenham H
1935–36 Aston Villa and Blackburn R
1936–37 Manchester U and Sheffield W
1937–38 Manchester C and WBA
1938–39 Birmingham C and Leicester C
1946–47 Brentford and Leeds U
1947–48 Blackburn R and Grimsby T
1948–49 Preston NE and Sheffield U
1949–50 Manchester C and Birmingham C
1950–51 Sheffield W and Everton
1951–52 Huddersfield T and Fulham
1952–53 Stoke C and Derby Co
1953–54 Middlesbrough and Liverpool
1954–55 Leicester C and Sheffield W
1955–56 Huddersfield T and Sheffield U
1956–57 Charlton Ath and Cardiff C
1957–58 Sheffield W and Sunderland
1958–59 Portsmouth and Aston Villa
1959–60 Luton T and Leeds U
1960–61 Preston NE and Newcastle U
1961–62 Chelsea and Cardiff C
1962–63 Manchester C and Leyton Orient
1963–64 Bolton W and Ipswich T
1964–65 Wolverhampton W and Birmingham C
1965–66 Northampton T and Blackburn R
1966–67 Aston Villa and Blackpool
1967–68 Fulham and Sheffield U
1968–69 Leicester C and QPR
1969–70 Sunderland and Sheffield W
1970–71 Burnley and Blackpool
1971–72 Huddersfield T and Nottingham F
1972–73 Crystal Palace and WBA
1973–74 Southampton, Manchester U, Norwich C
1974–75 Luton T, Chelsea, Carlisle U
1975–76 Wolverhampton W, Burnley, Sheffield U
1976–77 Sunderland, Stoke C, Tottenham H
1977–78 West Ham U, Newcastle U, Leicester C
1978–79 QPR, Birmingham C, Chelsea
1979–80 Bristol C, Derby Co, Bolton W
1980–81 Norwich C, Leicester C, Crystal Palace
1981–82 Leeds U, Wolverhampton W, Middlesbrough
1982–83 Manchester C, Swansea C, Brighton & HA
1983–84 Birmingham C, Notts Co, Wolverhampton W
1984–85 Norwich C, Sunderland, Stoke C
1985–86 Ipswich T, Birmingham C, WBA
1986–87 Leicester C, Manchester C, Aston Villa
1987–88 Chelsea**, Portsmouth, Watford, Oxford U
1988–89 Middlesbrough, West Ham U, Newcastle U
1989–90 Sheffield W, Charlton Ath, Millwall
1990–91 Sunderland and Derby Co
1991–92 Luton T, Notts Co, West Ham U

***Relegated after play-offs.*

**Subsequently re-elected to Division 1 when League was extended after the War.*

PREMIER LEAGUE TO DIVISION 1 (1992–93 to 2003–04)

1992–93 Crystal Palace, Middlesbrough, Nottingham F
1993–94 Sheffield U, Oldham Ath, Swindon T
1994–95 Crystal Palace, Norwich C, Leicester C, Ipswich T
1995–96 Manchester C, QPR, Bolton W
1996–97 Sunderland, Middlesbrough, Nottingham F
1997–98 Bolton W, Barnsley, Crystal Palace
1998–99 Charlton Ath, Blackburn R, Nottingham F
1999–2000 Wimbledon, Sheffield W, Watford
2000–01 Manchester C, Coventry C, Bradford C
2001–02 Ipswich T, Derby Co, Leicester C
2002–03 West Ham U, WBA, Sunderland
2003–04 Leicester C, Leeds U, Wolverhampton W

PREMIER LEAGUE TO CHAMPIONSHIP (2004–05 to 2018–19)

2004–05 Crystal Palace, Norwich C, Southampton
2005–06 Birmingham C, WBA, Sunderland
2006–07 Sheffield U, Charlton Ath, Watford
2007–08 Reading, Birmingham C, Derby Co
2008–09 Newcastle U, Middlesbrough, WBA
2009–10 Burnley, Hull C, Portsmouth
2010–11 Birmingham C, Blackpool, West Ham U
2011–12 Bolton W, Blackburn R, Wolverhampton W
2012–13 Wigan Ath, Reading, QPR
2013–14 Norwich C, Fulham, Cardiff C
2014–15 Hull C, Burnley, QPR
2015–16 Newcastle U, Norwich C, Aston Villa
2016–17 Hull C, Middlesbrough, Sunderland
2017–18 Swansea C, Stoke C, WBA
2018–19 Cardiff C, Fulham, Huddersfield T

DIVISION 2 TO DIVISION 3 (1920–21 to 1991–92)

1920–21 Stockport Co
1921–22 Bradford PA and Bristol C
1922–23 Rotherham Co and Wolverhampton W
1923–24 Nelson and Bristol C
1924–25 Crystal Palace and Coventry C
1925–26 Stoke C and Stockport Co
1926–27 Darlington and Bradford C
1927–28 Fulham and South Shields
1928–29 Port Vale and Clapton Orient
1929–30 Hull C and Notts Co
1930–31 Reading and Cardiff C
1931–32 Barnsley and Bristol C
1932–33 Chesterfield and Charlton Ath
1933–34 Millwall and Lincoln C
1934–35 Oldham Ath and Notts Co
1935–36 Port Vale and Hull C
1936–37 Doncaster R and Bradford C
1937–38 Barnsley and Stockport Co
1938–39 Norwich C and Tranmere R
1946–47 Swansea T and Newport Co
1947–48 Doncaster R and Millwall
1948–49 Nottingham F and Lincoln C
1949–50 Plymouth Arg and Bradford PA
1950–51 Grimsby T and Chesterfield
1951–52 Coventry C and QPR
1952–53 Southampton and Barnsley
1953–54 Brentford and Oldham Ath
1954–55 Ipswich T and Derby Co
1955–56 Plymouth Arg and Hull C
1956–57 Port Vale and Bury
1957–58 Doncaster R and Notts Co
1958–59 Barnsley and Grimsby T
1959–60 Bristol C and Hull C
1960–61 Lincoln C and Portsmouth
1961–62 Brighton & HA and Bristol R
1962–63 Walsall and Luton T
1963–64 Grimsby T and Scunthorpe U
1964–65 Swindon T and Swansea T
1965–66 Middlesbrough and Leyton Orient
1966–67 Northampton T and Bury
1967–68 Plymouth Arg and Rotherham U
1968–69 Fulham and Bury
1969–70 Preston NE and Aston Villa
1970–71 Blackburn R and Bolton W
1971–72 Charlton Ath and Watford
1972–73 Huddersfield T and Brighton & HA
1973–74 Crystal Palace, Preston NE, Swindon T
1974–75 Millwall, Cardiff C, Sheffield W
1975–76 Oxford U, York C, Portsmouth
1976–77 Carlisle U, Plymouth Arg, Hereford U
1977–78 Blackpool, Mansfield T, Hull C
1978–79 Sheffield U, Millwall, Blackburn R
1979–80 Fulham, Burnley, Charlton Ath
1980–81 Preston NE, Bristol C, Bristol R
1981–82 Cardiff C, Wrexham, Orient
1982–83 Rotherham U, Burnley, Bolton W
1983–84 Derby Co, Swansea C, Cambridge U
1984–85 Notts Co, Cardiff C, Wolverhampton W
1985–86 Carlisle U, Middlesbrough, Fulham
1986–87 Sunderland**, Grimsby T, Brighton & HA
1987–88 Huddersfield T, Reading, Sheffield U**
1988–89 Shrewsbury T, Birmingham C, Walsall
1989–90 Bournemouth, Bradford C, Stoke C
1990–91 WBA and Hull C
1991–92 Plymouth Arg, Brighton & HA, Port Vale

FIRST DIVISION TO SECOND DIVISION (1992–93 to 2003–04)

1992–93 Brentford, Cambridge U, Bristol R
1993–94 Birmingham C, Oxford U, Peterborough U
1994–95 Swindon T, Burnley, Bristol C, Notts Co
1995–96 Millwall, Watford, Luton T
1996–97 Grimsby T, Oldham Ath, Southend U
1997–98 Manchester C, Stoke C, Reading
1998–99 Bury, Oxford U, Bristol C
1999–2000 Walsall, Port Vale, Swindon T
2000–01 Huddersfield T, QPR, Tranmere R
2001–02 Crewe Alex, Barnsley, Stockport Co
2002–03 Sheffield W, Brighton & HA, Grimsby T
2003–04 Walsall, Bradford C, Wimbledon

FOOTBALL LEAGUE CHAMPIONSHIP TO FOOTBALL LEAGUE ONE (2004–05 to 2018–19)

2004–05 Gillingham, Nottingham F, Rotherham U
2005–06 Crewe Alex, Millwall, Brighton & HA
2006–07 Southend U, Luton T, Leeds U
2007–08 Leicester C, Scunthorpe U, Colchester U
2008–09 Norwich C, Southampton, Charlton Ath
2009–10 Sheffield W, Plymouth Arg, Peterborough U
2010–11 Preston NE, Sheffield U, Scunthorpe U
2011–12 Portsmouth, Coventry C, Doncaster R
2012–13 Peterborough U, Wolverhampton W, Bristol C
2013–14 Doncaster R, Barnsley, Yeovil T
2014–15 Millwall, Wigan Ath, Blackpool
2015–16 Charlton Ath, Milton Keynes D, Bolton W
2016–17 Blackburn R, Wigan Ath, Rotherham U
2017–18 Barnsley, Burton Alb, Sunderland
2018–19 Rotherham U, Bolton W, Ipswich T

DIVISION 3 TO DIVISION 4 (1958–59 to 1991–92)

1958–59 Stockport Co, Doncaster R, Notts Co, Rochdale
1959–60 York C, Mansfield T, Wrexham, Accrington S
1960–61 Tranmere R, Bradford C, Colchester U, Chesterfield
1961–62 Torquay U, Lincoln C, Brentford, Newport Co
1962–63 Bradford PA, Brighton & HA, Carlisle U, Halifax T
1963–64 Millwall, Crewe Alex, Wrexham, Notts Co
1964–65 Luton T, Port Vale, Colchester U, Barnsley
1965–66 Southend U, Exeter C, Brentford, York C
1966–67 Swansea T, Darlington, Doncaster R, Workington
1967–68 Grimsby T, Colchester U, Scunthorpe U, Peterborough U (demoted)
1968–69 Northampton T, Hartlepool, Crewe Alex, Oldham Ath
1969–70 Bournemouth, Southport, Barrow, Stockport Co
1970–71 Reading, Bury, Doncaster R, Gillingham
1971–72 Mansfield T, Barnsley, Torquay U, Bradford C
1972–73 Rotherham U, Brentford, Swansea C, Scunthorpe U
1973–74 Cambridge U, Shrewsbury T, Southport, Rochdale
1974–75 Bournemouth, Tranmere R, Watford, Huddersfield T
1975–76 Aldershot, Colchester U, Southend U, Halifax T
1976–77 Reading, Northampton T, Grimsby T, York C
1977–78 Port Vale, Bradford C, Hereford U, Portsmouth
1978–79 Peterborough U, Walsall, Tranmere R, Lincoln C
1979–80 Bury, Southend U, Mansfield T, Wimbledon
1980–81 Sheffield U, Colchester U, Blackpool, Hull C
1981–82 Wimbledon, Swindon T, Bristol C, Chester
1982–83 Reading, Wrexham, Doncaster R, Chesterfield
1983–84 Scunthorpe U, Southend U, Port Vale, Exeter C
1984–85 Burnley, Orient, Preston NE, Cambridge U
1985–86 Lincoln C, Cardiff C, Wolverhampton W, Swansea C
1986–87 Bolton W**, Carlisle U, Darlington, Newport Co
1987–88 Rotherham U**, Grimsby T, York C, Doncaster R
1988–89 Southend U, Chesterfield, Gillingham, Aldershot
1989–90 Cardiff C, Northampton T, Blackpool, Walsall
1990–91 Crewe Alex, Rotherham U, Mansfield T
1991–92 Bury, Shrewsbury T, Torquay U, Darlington

*** Relegated after play-offs.*

SECOND DIVISION TO THIRD DIVISION (1992–93 to 2003–04)

1992–93 Preston NE, Mansfield T, Wigan Ath, Chester C
1993–94 Fulham, Exeter C, Hartlepool U, Barnet
1994–95 Cambridge U, Plymouth Arg, Cardiff C, Chester C, Leyton Orient
1995–96 Carlisle U, Swansea C, Brighton & HA, Hull C
1996–97 Peterborough U, Shrewsbury T, Rotherham U, Notts Co
1997–98 Brentford, Plymouth Arg, Carlisle U, Southend U
1998–99 York C, Northampton T, Lincoln C, Macclesfield T
1999–2000 Cardiff C, Blackpool, Scunthorpe U, Chesterfield
2000–01 Bristol R, Luton T, Swansea C, Oxford U
2001–02 Bournemouth, Bury, Wrexham, Cambridge U
2002–03 Cheltenham T, Huddersfield T, Mansfield T Northampton T
2003–04 Grimsby T, Rushden & D, Notts Co, Wycombe W

FOOTBALL LEAGUE ONE TO FOOTBALL LEAGUE TWO (2004–05 to 2018–19)

2004–05 Torquay U, Wrexham, Peterborough U, Stockport Co
2005–06 Hartlepool U, Milton Keynes D, Swindon T, Walsall
2006–07 Chesterfield, Bradford C, Rotherham U, Brentford
2007–08 Bournemouth, Gillingham, Port Vale, Luton T
2008–09 Northampton T, Crewe Alex, Cheltenham T, Hereford U
2009–10 Gillingham, Wycombe W, Southend U, Stockport Co
2010–11 Dagenham & R, Bristol R, Plymouth Arg, Swindon T
2011–12 Wycombe W, Chesterfield, Exeter C, Rochdale
2012–13 Scunthorpe U, Bury, Hartlepool U, Portsmouth
2013–14 Tranmere R, Carlisle U, Shrewsbury T, Stevenage
2014–15 Notts Co, Crawley T, Leyton Orient, Yeovil T
2015–16 Doncaster R, Blackpool, Colchester U, Crewe Alex
2016–17 Port Vale, Swindon T, Coventry C, Chesterfield
2017–18 Oldham Ath, Northampton T, Milton Keynes D, Bury
2018–19 Plymouth Arg, Walsall, Scunthorpe U, Bradford C

LEAGUE STATUS FROM 1986–87

RELEGATED FROM LEAGUE

1986–87 Lincoln C
1987–88 Newport Co
1988–89 Darlington
1989–90 Colchester U
1990–91 —
1991–92 —
1992–93 Halifax T
1993–94 —
1994–95 —
1995–96 —
1996–97 Hereford U
1997–98 Doncaster R
1998–99 Scarborough
1999–2000 Chester C
2000–01 Barnet
2001–02 Halifax T
2002–03 Shrewsbury T, Exeter C
2003–04 Carlisle U, York C
2004–05 Kidderminster H, Cambridge U
2005–06 Oxford U, Rushden & D
2006–07 Boston U, Torquay U
2007–08 Mansfield T, Wrexham
2008–09 Chester C, Luton T
2009–10 Grimsby T, Darlington
2010–11 Lincoln C, Stockport Co
2011–12 Hereford U, Macclesfield T
2012–13 Barnet, Aldershot T
2013–14 Bristol R, Torquay U
2014–15 Cheltenham T, Tranmere R
2015–16 Dagenham & R, York C
2016–17 Hartlepool U, Leyton Orient
2017–18 Barnet, Chesterfield
2018–19 Notts Co, Yeovil T

PROMOTED TO LEAGUE

1986–87 Scarborough
1987–88 Lincoln C
1988–89 Maidstone U
1989–90 Darlington
1990–91 Barnet
1991–92 Colchester U
1992–93 Wycombe W
1993–94 —
1994–95 —
1995–96 —
1996–97 Macclesfield T
1997–98 Halifax T
1998–99 Cheltenham T
1999–2000 Kidderminster H
2000–01 Rushden & D
2001–02 Boston U
2002–03 Yeovil T, Doncaster R
2003–04 Chester C, Shrewsbury T
2004–05 Barnet, Carlisle U
2005–06 Accrington S, Hereford U
2006–07 Dagenham & R, Morecambe
2007–08 Aldershot T, Exeter C
2008–09 Burton Alb, Torquay U
2009–10 Stevenage B, Oxford U
2010–11 Crawley T, AFC Wimbledon
2011–12 Fleetwood T, York C
2012–13 Mansfield T, Newport Co
2013–14 Luton T, Cambridge U
2014–15 Barnet, Bristol R
2015–16 Cheltenham T, Grimsby T
2016–17 Lincoln C, Forest Green R
2017–18 Macclesfield T, Tranmere R
2018–19 Leyton Orient, Salford C

APPLICATIONS FOR RE-ELECTION

FOURTH DIVISION

Eleven: Hartlepool U.
Seven: Crewe Alex.
Six: Barrow (lost League place to Hereford U 1972), Halifax T, Rochdale, Southport (lost League place to Wigan Ath 1978), York C.
Five: Chester C, Darlington, Lincoln C, Stockport Co, Workington (lost League place to Wimbledon 1977).
Four: Bradford PA (lost League place to Cambridge U 1970), Newport Co, Northampton T.
Three: Doncaster R, Hereford U.
Two: Bradford C, Exeter C, Oldham Ath, Scunthorpe U, Torquay U.
One: Aldershot, Colchester U, Gateshead (lost League place to Peterborough U 1960), Grimsby T, Swansea C, Tranmere R, Wrexham, Blackpool, Cambridge U, Preston NE.

Accrington S resigned and Oxford U were elected 1962.
Port Vale were forced to re-apply following expulsion in 1968.
Aldershot expelled March 1992. Maidstone U resigned August 1992.

THIRD DIVISIONS NORTH & SOUTH

Seven: Walsall.
Six: Exeter C, Halifax T, Newport Co.
Five: Accrington S, Barrow, Gillingham, New Brighton, Southport.
Four: Rochdale, Norwich C.
Three: Crystal Palace, Crewe Alex, Darlington, Hartlepool U, Merthyr T, Swindon T.
Two: Aberdare Ath, Aldershot, Ashington, Bournemouth, Brentford, Chester, Colchester U, Durham C, Millwall, Nelson, QPR, Rotherham U, Southend U, Tranmere R, Watford, Workington.
One: Bradford C, Bradford PA, Brighton & HA, Bristol R, Cardiff C, Carlisle U, Charlton Ath, Gateshead, Grimsby T, Mansfield T, Shrewsbury T, Torquay U, York C.

LEAGUE ATTENDANCES SINCE 1946–47

Season	*Matches*	*Total*	*Div. 1*	*Div. 2*	*Div. 3 (S)*	*Div. 3 (N)*
1946–47	1848	35,604,606	15,005,316	11,071,572	5,664,004	3,863,714
1947–48	1848	40,259,130	16,732,341	12,286,350	6,653,610	4,586,829
1948–49	1848	41,271,414	17,914,667	11,353,237	6,998,429	5,005,081
1949–50	1848	40,517,865	17,278,625	11,694,158	7,104,155	4,440,927
1950–51	2028	39,584,967	16,679,454	10,780,580	7,367,884	4,757,109
1951–52	2028	39,015,866	16,110,322	11,066,189	6,958,927	4,880,428
1952–53	2028	37,149,966	16,050,278	9,686,654	6,704,299	4,708,735
1953–54	2028	36,174,590	16,154,915	9,510,053	6,311,508	4,198,114
1954–55	2028	34,133,103	15,087,221	8,988,794	5,996,017	4,051,071
1955–56	2028	33,150,809	14,108,961	9,080,002	5,692,479	4,269,367
1956–57	2028	32,744,405	13,803,037	8,718,162	5,622,189	4,601,017
1957–58	2028	33,562,208	14,468,652	8,663,712	6,097,183	4,332,661
		Total	*Div. 1*	*Div. 2*	*Div. 3*	*Div. 4*
1958–59	2028	33,610,985	14,727,691	8,641,997	5,946,600	4,276,697
1959–60	2028	32,538,611	14,391,227	8,399,627	5,739,707	4,008,050
1960–61	2028	28,619,754	12,926,948	7,033,936	4,784,256	3,874,614
1961–62	2015	27,979,902	12,061,194	7,453,089	5,199,106	3,266,513
1962–63	2028	28,885,852	12,490,239	7,792,770	5,341,362	3,261,481
1963–64	2028	28,535,022	12,486,626	7,594,158	5,419,157	3,035,081
1964–65	2028	27,641,168	12,708,752	6,984,104	4,436,245	3,512,067
1965–66	2028	27,206,980	12,480,644	6,914,757	4,779,150	3,032,429
1966–67	2028	28,902,596	14,242,957	7,253,819	4,421,172	2,984,648
1967–68	2028	30,107,298	15,289,410	7,450,410	4,013,087	3,354,391
1968–69	2028	29,382,172	14,584,851	7,382,390	4,339,656	3,075,275
1969–70	2028	29,600,972	14,868,754	7,581,728	4,223,761	2,926,729
1970–71	2028	28,194,146	13,954,337	7,098,265	4,377,213	2,764,331
1971–72	2028	28,700,729	14,484,603	6,769,308	4,697,392	2,749,426
1972–73	2028	25,448,642	13,998,154	5,631,730	3,737,252	2,081,506
1973–74	2027	24,982,203	13,070,991	6,326,108	3,421,624	2,163,480
1974–75	2028	25,577,977	12,613,178	6,955,970	4,086,145	1,992,684
1975–76	2028	24,896,053	13,089,861	5,798,405	3,948,449	2,059,338
1976–77	2028	26,182,800	13,647,585	6,250,597	4,152,218	2,132,400
1977–78	2028	25,392,872	13,255,677	6,474,763	3,332,042	2,330,390
1978–79	2028	24,540,627	12,704,549	6,153,223	3,374,558	2,308,297
1979–80	2028	24,623,975	12,163,002	6,112,025	3,999,328	2,349,620
1980–81	2028	21,907,569	11,392,894	5,175,442	3,637,854	1,701,379
1981–82	2028	20,006,961	10,420,793	4,750,463	2,836,915	1,998,790
1982–83	2028	18,766,158	9,295,613	4,974,937	2,943,568	1,552,040
1983–84	2028	18,358,631	8,711,448	5,359,757	2,729,942	1,557,484
1984–85	2028	17,849,835	9,761,404	4,030,823	2,667,008	1,390,600
1985–86	2028	16,488,577	9,037,854	3,551,968	2,490,481	1,408,274
1986–87	2028	17,379,218	9,144,676	4,168,131	2,350,970	1,715,441
1987–88	2030	17,959,732	8,094,571	5,341,599	2,751,275	1,772,287
1988–89	2036	18,464,192	7,809,993	5,887,805	3,035,327	1,791,067
1989–90	2036	19,445,442	7,883,039	6,867,674	2,803,551	1,891,178
1990–91	2036	19,508,202	8,618,709	6,285,068	2,835,759	1,768,666
1991–92	2064*	20,487,273	9,989,160	5,809,787	2,993,352	1,694,974
		Total	*Premier*	*Div. 1*	*Div. 2*	*Div. 3*
1992–93	2028	20,657,327	9,759,809	5,874,017	3,483,073	1,540,428
1993–94	2028	21,683,381	10,644,551	6,487,104	2,972,702	1,579,024
1994–95	2028	21,856,020	11,213,168	6,044,293	3,037,752	1,560,807
1995–96	2036	21,844,416	10,469,107	6,566,349	2,843,652	1,965,308
1996–97	2036	22,783,163	10,804,762	6,931,539	3,195,223	1,851,639
1997–98	2036	24,692,608	11,092,106	8,330,018	3,503,264	1,767,220
1998–99	2036	25,435,542	11,620,326	7,543,369	4,169,697	2,102,150
1999–2000	2036	25,341,090	11,668,497	7,810,208	3,700,433	2,161,952
2000–01	2036	26,030,167	12,472,094	7,909,512	3,488,166	2,160,395
2001–02	2036	27,756,977	13,043,118	8,352,128	3,963,153	2,398,578
2002–03	2036	28,343,386	13,468,965	8,521,017	3,892,469	2,460,935
2003–04	2036	29,197,510	13,303,136	8,772,780	4,146,495	2,975,099
		Total	*Premier*	*Championship*	*League One*	*League Two*
2004–05	2036	29,245,870	12,878,791	9,612,761	4,270,674	2,483,644
2005–06	2036	29,089,084	12,871,643	9,719,204	4,183,011	2,315,226
2006–07	2036	29,541,949	13,058,115	10,057,813	4,135,599	2,290,422
2007–08	2036	29,914,212	13,708,875	9,397,036	4,412,023	2,396,278
2008–09	2036	29,881,966	13,527,815	9,877,552	4,171,834	2,304,765
2009–10	2036	30,057,892	12,977,251	9,909,882	5,043,099	2,127,660
2010–11	2036	29,459,105	13,406,990	9,595,236	4,150,547	2,306,332
2011–12	2036	29,454,401	13,148,465	9,784,100	4,091,897	2,429,939
2012–13	2036	29,225,443	13,653,958	9,662,232	3,485,290	2,423,963
2013–14	2036	29,629,309	13,930,810	9,168,922	4,126,701	2,402,876
2014–15	2036	30,052,575	13,746,753	9,838,940	3,884,414	2,582,468
2015–16	2036	30,207,923	13,852,291	9,705,865	3,955,385	2,694,382
2016–17	2036	31,727,248	13,612,316	11,106,918	4,385,178	2,622,836
2017–18	2036	32,656,695	14,560,349	11,313,826	4,303,525	2,478,995
2018–19	2035	32,911,714	14,515,181	11,119,775	4,811,797	2,464,961

**Figures include matches played by Aldershot.*

Football League official total for their three divisions in 2001–02 was 14,716,162.

ENGLISH LEAGUE ATTENDANCES 2018–19

PREMIER LEAGUE ATTENDANCES

	Average Gate			*Season 2018–19*	
	2017–18	*2018–19*	*+/–%*	*Highest*	*Lowest*
Arsenal	59,323	59,899	+0.97	60,030	59,493
Bournemouth	10,641	10,532	–1.02	10,986	9,980
Brighton & HA	30,403	30,426	+0.08	30,682	29,323
Burnley	20,688	20,534	–0.75	21,741	18,497
Cardiff C	20,164	31,408	+55.76	33,082	29,402
Chelsea	41,282	40,441	–2.04	40,721	38,593
Crystal Palace	25,063	25,455	+1.57	25,789	24,738
Everton	38,797	39,043	+0.63	39,400	38,113
Fulham	19,896	24,371	+22.49	25,401	22,008
Huddersfield T	24,032	23,340	–2.88	24,263	17,082
Leicester C	31,636	31,851	+0.68	32,184	30,558
Liverpool	53,049	52,983	–0.13	53,373	50,965
Manchester C	54,070	54,130	+0.11	54,511	53,307
Manchester U	74,976	74,498	–0.64	74,556	74,400
Newcastle U	51,992	51,121	–1.68	52,242	48,323
Southampton	30,794	30,328	–1.51	31,890	27,597
Tottenham H	68,052	54,216	–20.33	81,332	29,164
Watford	20,231	20,016	–1.06	20,540	17,301
West Ham U	56,885	58,336	+2.55	59,988	56,811
Wolverhampton W	28,298	31,030	+9.66	31,436	30,130

TOTAL ATTENDANCES: 14,515,181 (380 games)
Average 38,317 (–0.31%)
HIGHEST: 81,332 Tottenham H v Arsenal
LOWEST: 9,980 Bournemouth v Huddersfield T
HIGHEST AVERAGE: 74,498 Manchester U
LOWEST AVERAGE: 10,532 Bournemouth

SKY BET ENGLISH FOOTBALL LEAGUE CHAMPIONSHIP ATTENDANCES

	Average Gate			*Season 2018–19*	
	2017–18	*2018–19*	*+/–%*	*Highest*	*Lowest*
Aston Villa	32,097	36,027	+12.24	41,696	27,331
Birmingham C	21,042	22,483	+6.85	26,631	19,795
Blackburn R	12,832	14,550	+13.38	21,577	11,818
Bolton W	15,887	14,636	–7.87	17,811	12,195
Brentford	10,234	10,257	+0.23	12,225	8,903
Bristol C	20,953	21,080	+0.61	25,556	18,411
Derby Co	27,175	26,850	–1.20	32,055	23,580
Hull C	15,622	12,165	–22.13	14,116	10,191
Ipswich T	16,272	17,765	+9.18	25,690	13,612
Leeds U	31,525	34,033	+7.96	37,004	27,729
Middlesbrough	25,544	23,217	–9.11	30,881	21,016
Millwall	13,368	13,636	+2.00	17,195	11,190
Norwich C	25,959	26,014	+0.21	27,040	24,642
Nottingham F	24,680	28,144	+14.03	29,530	25,753
Preston NE	13,774	14,160	+2.80	19,912	10,849
QPR	13,928	13,866	–0.44	17,609	10,854
Reading	16,656	14,991	–10.00	17,458	11,271
Rotherham U	8,514	9,880	+16.05	11,736	8,018
Sheffield U	26,854	26,177	–2.52	30,261	23,400
Sheffield W	25,995	24,429	–6.03	31,630	20,861
Stoke C	29,280	25,200	–13.93	28,586	22,078
Swansea C	20,623	18,737	–9.14	20,860	17,197
WBA	24,520	24,148	–1.52	26,548	20,282
Wigan Ath	9,152	11,663	+27.44	15,655	8,848

TOTAL ATTENDANCES: 11,119,775 (551 games)
Average 20,181 (–1.54%)
HIGHEST: 41,696 Aston Villa v Norwich C
LOWEST: 8,018 Rotherham U v QPR
HIGHEST AVERAGE: 36,027 Aston Villa
LOWEST AVERAGE: 9,880 Rotherham U

Premier League and Football League attendance averages and highest crowd figures for 2018–19 are unofficial.

SKY BET ENGLISH FOOTBALL LEAGUE ONE ATTENDANCES

	Average Gate			*Season 2018–19*	
	2017–18	*2018–19*	*+/–%*	*Highest*	*Lowest*
Accrington S	1,979	2,764	+39.68	4,801	1,732
AFC Wimbledon	4,325	4,297	–0.64	4,850	3,499
Barnsley	13,704	12,527	–8.59	18,282	10,709
Blackpool	4,178	5,517	+32.05	15,871	2,388
Bradford C	19,787	16,130	–18.48	19,487	11,075
Bristol R	8,933	8,320	–6.87	10,009	6,851
Burton Alb	4,645	3,351	–27.85	4,903	2,149
Charlton Ath	11,846	11,827	–0.15	17,267	8,810
Coventry C	9,255	12,363	+33.58	26,741	9,220
Doncaster R	8,213	8,098	–1.40	12,794	6,473
Fleetwood T	3,140	3,165	+0.79	5,035	2,304
Gillingham	5,370	5,050	–5.96	8,438	3,423
Luton T	8,676	9,516	+9.68	10,089	8,454
Oxford U	7,376	7,315	–0.82	10,383	5,204
Peterborough U	5,669	7,365	+29.92	11,277	5,064
Plymouth Arg	10,413	9,852	–5.39	12,065	8,190
Portsmouth	17,917	18,223	+1.71	19,402	16,794
Rochdale	3,471	3,550	+2.27	6,546	2,301
Scunthorpe U	4,364	4,227	–3.14	7,263	3,054
Shrewsbury T	6,249	6,407	+2.53	9,635	4,353
Southend U	7,195	6,932	–3.66	10,779	5,110
Sunderland	27,635	32,157	+16.36	46,039	27,580
Walsall	4,760	4,927	+3.51	7,868	3,287
Wycombe W	4,705	5,329	+13.27	8,422	3,819

TOTAL ATTENDANCES:	4,811,797 (552 games) Average 8,717 (+11.81%)
HIGHEST:	46,039 Sunderland v Bradford C
LOWEST:	1,732 Accrington S v AFC Wimbledon
HIGHEST AVERAGE:	32,157 Sunderland
LOWEST AVERAGE:	2,764 Accrington S

SKY BET ENGLISH FOOTBALL LEAGUE TWO ATTENDANCES

	Average Gate			*Season 2018–19*	
	2017–18	*2018–19*	*+/–%*	*Highest*	*Lowest*
Bury	3,931	4,044	+2.87	7,784	2,779
Cambridge U	4,523	4,338	–4.08	6,858	3,059
Carlisle U	4,609	4,712	+2.25	10,459	3,316
Cheltenham T	3,172	3,134	–1.17	5,125	2,095
Colchester U	3,321	3,522	+6.06	5,032	2,435
Crawley T	2,268	2,290	+0.97	3,335	1,734
Crewe Alex	3,876	3,762	–2.95	6,180	2,569
Exeter C	4,005	4,418	+10.32	5,974	3,070
Forest Green R	2,772	2,701	–2.56	4,537	1,600
Grimsby T	4,658	4,430	–4.88	7,201	3,293
Lincoln C	8,782	9,006	+2.55	9,832	7,975
Macclesfield T	1,839	2,389	+29.89	3,986	1,362
Mansfield T	4,309	4,897	+13.67	7,177	3,739
Milton Keynes D	9,202	8,224	–10.63	20,718	5,726
Morecambe	1,492	2,033	+36.22	3,749	1,355
Newport Co	3,489	3,409	–2.30	4,642	2,534
Northampton T	5,830	5,100	–12.52	6,963	4,064
Notts Co	7,911	7,357	–6.99	15,026	4,119
Oldham Ath	4,442	4,364	–1.76	6,179	2,865
Port Vale	4,583	4,431	–3.32	6,823	3,109
Stevenage	2,611	2,715	+3.99	3,552	1,943
Swindon T	6,380	6,390	+0.16	8,676	5,273
Tranmere R	5,115	6,552	+28.09	9,468	5,016
Yeovil T	2,941	2,953	+0.39	4,223	2,174

TOTAL ATTENDANCES:	2,464,961 (552 games) Average 4,466 (–0.57%)
HIGHEST:	20,718 Milton Keynes D v Mansfield T
LOWEST:	1,355 Morecambe v Mansfield T
HIGHEST AVERAGE:	9,006 Lincoln C
LOWEST AVERAGE:	2,033 Morecambe

LEAGUE CUP FINALS 1961–2019

*Played as a two-leg final until 1966. All subsequent finals played at Wembley except between 2001 and 2007 (inclusive) which were played at Millennium Stadium, Cardiff. *After extra time.*

FOOTBALL LEAGUE CUP

1961	Rotherham U v Aston Villa	2-0
	Aston Villa v Rotherham U	3-0*
	Aston Villa won 3-2 on aggregate.	
1962	Rochdale v Norwich C	0-3
	Norwich C v Rochdale	1-0
	Norwich C won 4-0 on aggregate.	
1963	Birmingham C v Aston Villa	3-1
	Aston Villa v Birmingham C	0-0
	Birmingham C won 3-1 on aggregate.	
1964	Stoke C v Leicester C	1-1
	Leicester C v Stoke C	3-2
	Leicester C won 4-3 on aggregate.	
1965	Chelsea v Leicester C	3-2
	Leicester C v Chelsea	0-0
	Chelsea won 3-2 on aggregate.	
1966	West Ham U v WBA	2-1
	WBA v West Ham U	4-1
	WBA won 5-3 on aggregate.	
1967	QPR v WBA	3-2
1968	Leeds U v Arsenal	1-0
1969	Swindon T v Arsenal	3-1*
1970	Manchester C v WBA	2-1*
1971	Tottenham H v Aston Villa	2-0
1972	Stoke C v Chelsea	2-1
1973	Tottenham H v Norwich C	1-0
1974	Wolverhampton W v Manchester C	2-1
1975	Aston Villa v Norwich C	1-0
1976	Manchester C v Newcastle U	2-1
1977	Aston Villa v Everton	0-0
Replay	Aston Villa v Everton	1-1*
	(at Hillsborough)	
Replay	Aston Villa v Everton	3-2*
	(at Old Trafford)	
1978	Nottingham F v Liverpool	0-0*
Replay	Nottingham F v Liverpool	1-0
	(at Old Trafford)	
1979	Nottingham F v Southampton	3-2
1980	Wolverhampton W v Nottingham F	1-0
1981	Liverpool v West Ham U	1-1*
Replay	Liverpool v West Ham U	2-1
	(at Villa Park)	

MILK CUP

1982	Liverpool v Tottenham H	3-1*
1983	Liverpool v Manchester U	2-1*
1984	Liverpool v Everton	0-0*
Replay	Liverpool v Everton	1-0
	(at Maine Road)	
1985	Norwich C v Sunderland	1-0
1986	Oxford U v QPR	3-0

LITTLEWOODS CUP

1987	Arsenal v Liverpool	2-1
1988	Luton T v Arsenal	3-2
1989	Nottingham F v Luton T	3-1
1990	Nottingham F v Oldham Ath	1-0

RUMBELOWS LEAGUE CUP

1991	Sheffield W v Manchester U	1-0
1992	Manchester U v Nottingham F	1-0

COCA-COLA CUP

1993	Arsenal v Sheffield W	2-1
1994	Aston Villa v Manchester U	3-1
1995	Liverpool v Bolton W	2-1
1996	Aston Villa v Leeds U	3-0
1997	Leicester C v Middlesbrough	1-1*
Replay	Leicester C v Middlesbrough	1-0*
	(at Hillsborough)	
1998	Chelsea v Middlesbrough	2-0*

WORTHINGTON CUP

1999	Tottenham H v Leicester C	1-0
2000	Leicester C v Tranmere R	2-1
2001	Liverpool v Birmingham C	1-1*
	Liverpool won 5-4 on penalties.	
2002	Blackburn R v Tottenham H	2-1
2003	Liverpool v Manchester U	2-0

CARLING CUP

2004	Middlesbrough v Bolton W	2-1
2005	Chelsea v Liverpool	3-2*
2006	Manchester U v Wigan Ath	4-0
2007	Chelsea v Arsenal	2-1
2008	Tottenham H v Chelsea	2-1*
2009	Manchester U v Tottenham H	0-0*
	Manchester U won 4-1 on penalties.	
2010	Manchester U v Aston Villa	2-1
2011	Birmingham C v Arsenal	2-1
2012	Liverpool v Cardiff C	2-2*
	Liverpool won 3-2 on penalties.	

CAPITAL ONE CUP

2013	Swansea C v Bradford C	5-0
2014	Manchester C v Sunderland	3-1
2015	Chelsea v Tottenham H	2-0
2016	Manchester C v Liverpool	1-1*
	Manchester C won 3-1 on penalties.	

EFL CUP

2017	Manchester U v Southampton	3-2

CARABAO CUP

2018	Manchester C v Arsenal	3-0
2019	Manchester C v Chelsea	0-0*
	Manchester C won 4-3 on penalties.	

LEAGUE CUP WINS

Liverpool 8, Manchester C 6, Aston Villa 5, Chelsea 5, Manchester U 5, Nottingham F 4, Tottenham H 4, Leicester C 3, Arsenal 2, Birmingham C 2, Norwich C 2, Wolverhampton W 2, Blackburn R 1, Leeds U 1, Luton T 1, Middlesbrough 1, Oxford U 1, QPR 1, Sheffield W 1, Stoke C 1, Swansea C 1, Swindon T 1, WBA 1.

APPEARANCES IN FINALS

Liverpool 12, Manchester U 9, Arsenal 8, Aston Villa 8, Chelsea 8, Tottenham H 8, Manchester C 7, Nottingham F 6, Leicester C 5, Norwich C 4, Birmingham C 3, Middlesbrough 3, WBA 3, Bolton W 2, Everton 2, Leeds U 2, Luton T 2, QPR 2, Sheffield W 2, Southampton 2, Stoke C 2, Sunderland 2, West Ham U 2, Wolverhampton W 2, Blackburn R 1, Bradford C 1, Cardiff C 1, Newcastle U 1, Oldham Ath 1, Oxford U 1, Rochdale 1, Rotherham U 1, Swansea C 1, Swindon T 1, Tranmere R 1, Wigan Ath 1.

APPEARANCES IN SEMI-FINALS

Liverpool 17, Arsenal 15, Tottenham H 15, Aston Villa 14, Chelsea 14, Manchester U 14, Manchester C 11, West Ham U 9, Blackburn R 6, Nottingham F 6, Birmingham C 5, Everton 5, Leeds U 5, Leicester C 5, Middlesbrough 5, Norwich C 5, Bolton W 4, Burnley 4, Crystal Palace 4, Ipswich T 4, Sheffield W 4, Sunderland 4, WBA 4, Bristol C 3, QPR 3, Southampton 3, Stoke C 3, Swindon T 3, Wolverhampton W 3, Cardiff C 2, Coventry C 2, Derby Co 2, Luton T 2, Oxford U 2, Plymouth Arg 2, Sheffield U 2, Tranmere R 2, Watford 2, Wimbledon 2, Blackpool 1, Bradford C 1, Burton Alb 1, Bury 1, Carlisle U 1, Chester C 1, Huddersfield T 1, Hull C 1, Newcastle U 1, Oldham Ath 1, Peterborough U 1, Rochdale 1, Rotherham U 1, Shrewsbury T 1, Stockport Co 1, Swansea C 1, Walsall 1, Wigan Ath 1, Wycombe W 1.

CARABAO CUP 2018–19

■ *Denotes player sent off.*

FIRST ROUND

Tuesday, 14 August 2018

Blackpool (0) 3 *(Nottingham 50, Pritchard 56, Gnanduillet 80)*

Barnsley (1) 1 *(Moncur 19)* 1937

Blackpool: (442) Howard; Nottingham, Daniels (Bola 82), Tilt, Anderton; O'Sullivan, Spearing, Thompson, Pritchard (O'Connor 75); Cullen (Delfouneso 61), Gnanduillet.
Barnsley: (442) Walton; Dougall (Potts 71), Pinnock, McGeehan (Mowatt 81), Bradshaw; Moncur, Isgrove (Thiam 63), Cavare, Jackson; Pinillos, Adeboyejo.
Referee: Mark Heywood.

Bristol C (0) 0

Plymouth Arg (1) 1 *(Songo'o 27)* 9865

Bristol C: (442) O'Leary; Pisano, Hunt, Dasilva (Webster 60), Kelly; Watkins, Walsh, Smith, O'Dowda; Taylor (Weimann 70), Eisa (Brownhill 88).
Plymouth Arg: (442) Macey; Moore, Wootton, Canavan, Smith-Brown; Grant C (Taylor 84), Songo'o (Fox 78), Ness, Carey; Grant J (Wylde 73), Ladapo.
Referee: Kevin Johnson.

Bristol R (1) 2 *(Bennett 32, Clarke O 84)*

Crawley T (0) 1 *(Connolly 88)* 2336

Bristol R: (4231) Smith; Leadbitter, Craig, Lockyer, Clarke J; Lines, Clarke O; Matthews, Bennett (Upson 80), Rodman (Sercombe 82); Payne.
Crawley T: (442) Mersin; Francomb, Connolly, Vincelot, Doherty; Young, Randall, Milsom (Poleon■ 60), Allarakhia (Bulman 60); Grego-Cox, Camara (Nathaniel-George 81).
Referee: Lee Swabey.

Cambridge U (0) 1 *(Azeez 90 (pen))*

Newport Co (2) 4 *(Amond 18, 22, Matt 49, Semenyo 86)* 1618

Cambridge U: (4231) Mitov; Halliday, Taft, Darling, Carroll; Deegan (Corr 58), O'Neil; Osadebe (Knowles 82), Maris, Lambe (Amoo 58); Azeez.
Newport Co: (352) Townsend; Bennett, Franks, Demetriou; Hornby-Forbes, Bakinson, Sheehan (Marsh-Brown 69), Dolan (Cooper 78), Butler; Amond, Matt (Semenyo 69).
Referee: Andy Davies.

Carlisle U (1) 1 *(Hope 22)*

Blackburn R (4) 5 *(Armstrong 2, 54, Dack 6, 34, Palmer 40)* 3156

Carlisle U: (433) Fryer; Liddle, Parkes, Gerrard (Miller 46), Gillesphey; Etuhu, Devitt, Slater (Bennett 62); Yates, Campbell, Hope.
Blackburn R: (4231) Raya; Nyambe, Lenihan, Mulgrew, Bell; Conway, Travis; Dack, Rothwell (Whittingham 60), Palmer (Samuel 59); Armstrong (Nuttall 62).
Referee: Ross Joyce.

Cheltenham T (1) 2 *(Broom 1, Thomas 71 (pen))*

Colchester U (0) 2 *(Szmodics 79, Norris 80)* 1179

Cheltenham T: (442) Flinders; Forster, Mullins, Boyle, Debayo; Broom, Atangana (Tozer 80), Thomas, Maddox (Smith 74); Addai (Lloyd 76), Lumbombo Kalala.
Colchester U: (442) Barnes D; Jackson, Kent, Eastman, Dickenson; Senior, Comley, Pell, Collins (Szmodics 67); Norris, Mandron (Nouble 67).
Cheltenham T won 6-5 on penalties.
Referee: Christopher Sarginson.

Crewe Alex (1) 1 *(Wintle 32)*

Fleetwood T (0) 1 *(Holt 52)* 1783

Crewe Alex: (442) Richards; Hunt, Ng, Nolan, Pickering; Ainley (Reilly 90), Jones, Wintle, Kirk (Lowery 78); Bowery, Nicholls.
Fleetwood T: (433) Cairns; Coyle, Spurr, Bolger, Jones G; Biggins, Sowerby, Sheron (Holt 46); Burns (Long 83), Madden, McAleny (Hunter 70).
Fleetwood T won 4-3 on penalties.
Referee: Trevor Kettle.

Exeter C (0) 1 *(Brown 64)*

Ipswich T (1) 1 *(Jackson 37)* 3675

Exeter C: (442) Pym; Sweeney, Brown, Martin A, Woodman; Martin L, Taylor, Tillson, Boateng (Sparkes 61); Jay (Collins 51), Stockley (Abrahams 51).
Ipswich T: (451) Bialkowski; Donacien (Spence 46), Nsiala, Chambers, Knudsen; Ward (Rowe 77), Chalobah, Nolan, Edun, Sears (Bishop 66); Jackson.
Exeter C won 4-2 on penalties.
Referee: Brett Huxtable.

Grimsby T (0) 0

Rochdale (1) 2 *(Rathbone 39, 79)* 1781

Grimsby T: (433) McKeown; Davis, Collins, Whitmore, Dixon (Robles 72); Welsh, Woolford, Hessenthaler; Vernam, Cook (Wright 83), Hooper (Rose 83).
Rochdale: (352) Lillis; McGahey, Delaney, McNulty (Camps 90); Rafferty, Cannon (Done 70), Rathbone, Perkins, Ntlhe; Henderson, Andrew (Wilbraham 70).
Referee: Darren England.

Leeds U (2) 2 *(Bamford 27, Samuel 35)*

Bolton W (0) 1 *(Oztumer 52)* 19,617

Leeds U: (4231) Blackman; Shackleton, Ayling, Jansson, Pearce; Baker, Phillips; Harrison, Samuel (Alioski 69), Roberts (Klich 68); Bamford (Roofe 80).
Bolton W: (442) Matthews; Little, Hobbs, Wilson, Grounds (Taylor 74); Donaldson (Noone 57), Vela, O'Neil, Wildschut; Oztumer, Hall (Magennis 65).
Referee: Andy Haines.

Macclesfield T (0) 1 *(Kelleher 60)*

Bradford C (0) 1 *(Colville 62)* 1422

Macclesfield T: (442) Taylor; Welch-Hayes, Kelleher, Grimes, Fitzpatrick; Wilson (Arthur 71), Maycock, Rose, Whitaker; Smith, Napa (Marsh 90).
Bradford C: (4231) Wilson; Riley, O'Connor A, McGowan, Chicksen; Colville (Wright 71), Akpan; Seedorf, Payne, Scannell; Miller (Brunker 70).
Macclesfield T won 4-2 on penalties.
Referee: Jeremy Simpson.

Mansfield T (4) 6 *(Walker 9 (pen), 13 (pen), 45, Khan 16, Rose 66, Hamilton 90)*

Accrington S (1) 1 *(Finley 6)* 1565

Mansfield T: (352) Olejnik; White, Sweeney, Pearce; Hamilton, MacDonald, Mellis, Butcher, Benning (Atkinson 46); Walker (Rose 65), Khan (Sterling-James 60).
Accrington S: (433) Maxted; Rodgers, Hughes, Platt, Wood; Finley, Conneely (Mangan 67), Brown (Nolan 68); Mingoia, Zanzala, McConville (Clark 63).
Referee: Sebastian Stockbridge.

Middlesbrough (2) 3 *(Fletcher 27, 74, Mahmutovic 44)*

Notts Co (2) 3 *(Crawford 20, Stead 34, 63)* 9942

Middlesbrough: (433) Lonergan; Mahmutovic, Fry (Spence 66), Ayala (Wood-Gordon 62), McGinley; McNair, Leadbitter, Tavernier; Chapman (Walker 42), Fletcher, Johnson.
Notts Co: (442) Fitzsimons; Bird, Duffy (Brisley 55), Hewitt, Jones; Hawkridge, Kellett (Campbell 76), Husin (Patching 68), Alessandra; Crawford, Stead.
Middlesbrough won 4-3 on penalties.
Referee: Anthony Backhouse.

Millwall (0) 0

Gillingham (0) 0 4401

Millwall: (442) Amos; McLaughlin, Wallace M, Webster, Meredith (O'Brien 74); Skalak (Wallace J 83), Tunnicliffe, Thompson, Ferguson; Onyedinma (Gregory 74), Elliott.
Gillingham: (442) Holy; O'Neill, Lacey, Ehmer, Garmston (Fuller 74); Byrne, Reilly (Stevenson 64), Charles-Cook, Parker; Eaves (Wilkinson 76), Hanlan.
Millwall won 3-1 on penalties.
Referee: Charles Breakspear.

Milton Keynes D (2) 3 *(Asonganyi 7, Watson 16, Cummings 71 (og))*
Charlton Ath (0) 0 3052
Milton Keynes D: (3412) Nicholls; Williams, Cargill (Jackson 65), Walsh; Kasumu, Brittain (Muirhead 77), Houghton (Moore-Taylor 46), Hancox; Cisse; Watson, Asonganyi.
Charlton Ath: (352) Phillips; Dijksteel (Yao 68), Cummings, Blumberg; Marshall (Doughty 68), Maloney, Dempsey, Morgan (Sarpeng-Wiredu 68), Mascoll; Ajose, Hackett-Fairchild.
Referee: John Busby.

Norwich C (1) 3 *(Stiepermann 27, Zimmermann 83, Pukki 89)*
Stevenage (1) 1 *(Ball 40)* 11,687
Norwich C: (4231) McGovern; Passlack, Zimmermann, Godfrey, Aarons; Thompson, Trybull (McLean 46); Leitner (Hernandez 70), Stiepermann, Cantwell (Pukki 78); Srbeny.
Stevenage: (4231) Dieng; Wildin, Cuthbert, Nugent, Hunt; Timlin (Sonupe 85), Byrom; Reid (Ferry 52), Ball (Makoma 63), Guthrie; Revell.
Referee: Craig Hicks.

Nottingham F (0) 1 *(Cash 90)*
Bury (1) 1 *(O'Connell 2)* 8172
Nottingham F: (4231) Smith■; Byram, Dawson, Hefele, Robinson; Watson, Yates (Osborn 46); Cash, Soudani (Steele 34), Goncalves (Lolley 73); Murphy.
Bury: (532) Murphy; Miller, Aimson, Thompson, O'Connell, McFadzean (Stokes 75); O'Shea, Styles (Moore 81), Dawson; Omotayo, Telford (Bunn 64).
Nottingham F won 10-9 on penalties.
Referee: Scott Duncan.

Oldham Ath (0) 0
Derby Co (1) 2 *(Tomori 36, Mount 70)* 3376
Oldham Ath: (442) Iversen; Haymer, Edmundson, Graham, Hunt; Coke (Missilou 77), Gardner, Branger, Nepomuceno; Benteke (Baxter 57), O'Grady.
Derby Co: (433) Carson; Bogle, Keogh, Tomori, Malone; Mount, Evans, Johnson (Bird 76); Wilson H (Bennett 67), Marriott (Waghorn 82), Jozefzoon.
Referee: Darren Bond.

Oxford U (1) 2 *(Browne 39, Whyte 50)*
Coventry C (0) 0 3551
Oxford U: (4231) Mitchell; Norman, Dickie, Mousinho, Garbutt; Brannagan, Browne (Smith 63); Whyte (Mackie 74), Henry (Lopes 74), Baptiste; Obika.
Coventry C: (442) O'Brien; Grimmer, Davies, Hyam, Brown; Sterling (Clarke-Harris 67), Ogogo, Bayliss, Hiwula (Shipley 78); Biamou, Bakayoko (Ponticelli 46).
Referee: James Linington.

Port Vale (0) 0
Lincoln C (1) 4 *(Shackell 5, Green 48 (pen), O'Connor 80, Akinde 82)* 2440
Port Vale: (442) Brown; Rawlinson, Smith, Legge, Montano (Vassell 85); Worrall (Kanu 75), Kay, Oyeleke, Hannant; Dodds (Quigley 65), Miller.
Lincoln C: (3412) Smith; Wilson, Shackell (O'Connor 73), Wharton; Anderson, Pett, Chapman, Toffolo; McCartan (Andrade 63); Rhead (Akinde 61), Green.
Referee: Rob Lewis.

Portsmouth (0) 1 *(Burgess 49)*
AFC Wimbledon (0) 2 *(Pigott 76, Walkes 88 (og))* 6588
Portsmouth: (4141) McGee; Walkes, Burgess, Clarke, Haunstrup; Naylor; Wheeler (Curtis 80), Evans (Hawkins 67), Close, Lowe; Pitman B (Chaplin 66).
AFC Wimbledon: (442) King; Watson (Sibbick 77), Pinnock (Appiah 66), Garratt, Oshilaja; Hanson, Wagstaff, Soares, Wordsworth; Pigott (Hartigan 89), McDonald.
Referee: Ollie Yates.

Preston NE (2) 3 *(Barker 14, Moult 33, Burke 58)*
Morecambe (1) 1 *(Mandeville 45)* 6077
Preston NE: (4231) Maxwell; Woods (Fisher 39), Storey, Huntington, Earl; Johnson (Nmecha 84), Gallagher; Burke, Ledson, Barker (Harrop 62); Moult.
Morecambe: (4231) Roche; Sinclair, Old, Yarney, Conlan; Kenyon (Leitch-Smith 46), Fleming; Mandeville (Ellison 65), Wildig, Oates (Mendes Gomes 65); Oswell.
Referee: Tom Nield.

QPR (2) 2 *(Freeman 3, Wszolek 6)*
Peterborough U (0) 0 4021
QPR: (4231) Lumley; Kakay, Baptiste, Leistner, Bidwell; Scowen, Cousins; Wszolek, Freeman (Manning 77), Samuel (Eze 67); Washington (Smith 83).
Peterborough U: (4411) Chapman; Naismith, Bennett, Tafazolli, Denton; Dembele, Woodyard, O'Hara, Ward (Cooper 73); Cooke (Cummings 46); Toney (Godden 78).
Referee: Gavin Ward.

Reading (1) 2 *(Meite 11, Swift 72)*
Birmingham C (0) 0 6934
Reading: (442) Walker; Yiadom, Moore, Tiago Ilori, Blackett; Meite (O'Shea 82), Bacuna (Rinomhota 73), Swift, Barrow (Clement 26); Baldock, McNulty.
Birmingham C: (4231) Camp; Harding, Roberts, Scarr, Dacres-Cogley; Kieftenbeld, Gardner G (Lakin 73); Mahoney (Jota 66), Lubula, Solomon-Otabor; Bogle (Adams 66).
Referee: Dean Whitestone.

Rotherham U (2) 3 *(Proctor 37, 64, Ajayi 42)*
Wigan Ath (0) 1 *(Vaughan 74)* 3017
Rotherham U: (442) Price; Vyner, Ajayi (Palmer 69), Raggett, Robertson; Forde, Wiles, Jones, Williams (Taylor 75); Ball, Proctor (Vassell 82).
Wigan Ath: (4411) Jones; Da Silva Lopes, Bruce, Kipre, Naismith; McManaman (Cole 63), MacDonald, Connolly (Weir 90), Walker (Gelhardt 78); Roberts; Vaughan.
Referee: Peter Bankes.

Scunthorpe U (0) 1 *(Humphrys 90)*
Doncaster R (1) 2 *(Wilks 36, Andrew 56)* 3272
Scunthorpe U: (4231) Watson; Clarke, Goode, McArdle, Borthwick-Jackson (Butroid 82); Lund, Perch; Colclough, Thomas, Morris (Horsfield 77); Novak (Humphrys 60).
Doncaster R: (433) Marosi; Mason, Wright, Butler, Andrew; Blair, Kane, Whiteman (McCullough 81); Coppinger (May 73), Marquis, Wilks (Taylor 73).
Referee: Geoff Eltringham.

Sheffield U (0) 1 *(Sharp 75)*
Hull C (1) 1 *(Toral 18)* 6327
Sheffield U: (352) Moore; O'Connell, Egan, Leonard (Basham 60); Freeman, Norwood, Duffy (Sharp 46), Lundstram (Fleck 71), Stevens; Woodburn, Clarke.
Hull C: (352) Marshall; MacDonald, Burke (Kingsley 37), Curry; McKenzie (Grosicki 69), Irvine, Stewart, Toral, Fleming; Keane, Dicko (Milinkovic 66).
Hull C won 5-4 on penalties.
Referee: Martin Coy.

Shrewsbury T (1) 1 *(Whalley 27)*
Burton Alb (1) 2 *(Templeton 45, Akins 64 (pen))* 2708
Shrewsbury T: (433) Coleman; Bolton, Waterfall, Beckles, Haynes; Docherty, Laurent (Angol 81), Norburn (Colkett 31); Whalley, John-Lewis (Okenabirhie 71), Gilliead.
Burton Alb: (433) Bywater; Brayford, McFadzean, Buxton, Turner; Sbarra (Hodge 90), Fox, Fraser (Hutchinson 78); Sordell, Akins, Templeton (Boyce 65).
Referee: Graham Salisbury.

Southend U (0) 2 *(McCoulsky 62, 72)*
Brentford (1) 4 *(Forss 42, Jeanvier 64, Benrahma 67, Mokotjo 85)* 3055
Southend U: (4231) Oxley; Demetriou, White, Kyprianou, Coker; Dieng (Mantom 65), Klass; Robinson, Cox (Ba 87), McLaughlin (Kightly 83); McCoulsky.

Brentford: (4132) Daniels; Clarke, Jeanvier, Sorensen (Mepham 30), Field; Mokotjo; Woods, Yennaris, Benrahma (Canos 80); Forss (Maupay 70), Judge.
Referee: Keith Stroud.

Swindon T (0) 0

Forest Green R (0) 1 *(Campbell 60)* 3451

Swindon T: (442) Vigouroux; Knoyle, Nelson, Lancashire, Romanski; Smith, Doughty, Diagouraga (Alzate 80), Taylor; Anderson (McGlashan 80), Adebayo.
Forest Green R: (442) Montgomery; Shephard, Rawson, Hollis, Laird; Archibald, Collins (James 74), Digby, Grubb (Reid 88); Campbell (Winchester 68), Doidge.
Referee: David Webb.

Tranmere R (0) 1 *(Cole 80)*

Walsall (1) 3 *(Ferrier 29, Ginnelly 64, Ismail 68)* 3817

Tranmere R: (442) George; Caprice, Ellis, Monthe, Bakayogo (McNulty 31); Tollitt (Smith 63), Gilmour, Banks (Harris 71), Cole; Mullin, Stockton.
Walsall: (442) Dunn; Wilson, Fitzwater, Guthrie, Leahy; Ismail (Morris 76), Dobson, Kinsella, Ginnelly; Cook, Ferrier (Gordon 62).
Referee: Michael Salisbury.

WBA (0) 1 *(Burke 62)*

Luton T (0) 0 10,404

WBA: (3511) Myhill; Adarabioyo, Hegazi (Bartley 46), Townsend; Phillips (Edwards 46), Morrison, Field, Harper, Burke; Barnes (Leko 66); Robson-Kanu.
Luton T: (41212) Shea; Stacey, Pearson, Bradley, Justin; Rea (Berry 84); Ruddock, Gambin (Jones 63); Shinnie (Lee 76); Jervis, Cornick.
Referee: Robert Jones.

Wycombe W (0) 1 *(Williams 50)*

Northampton T (0) 1 *(Hoskins 82)* 1999

Wycombe W: (433) Makabu-Makalamby; Harriman, McCarthy, El-Abd, Jombati (Jacobson 35); Thompson, Gape, Bloomfield (Morris 46); Freeman, Mackail-Smith, Williams (Kashket 70).
Northampton T: (442) Ward; Facey, Barnett, Taylor, Turnbull; Bridge, Foley, Crooks, Bowditch; Waters, Morias (Hoskins 73).
Wycombe W won 7-6 on penalties.
Referee: Stephen Martin.

Yeovil T (0) 0

Aston Villa (0) 1 *(Hourihane 77)* 6123

Yeovil T: (442) Baxter; James, Sowunmi, Warren, Dickinson; Arquin, Cole (Pattison 33), D'Almeida, McDonald; Jaiyesimi (Henry 82), Fisher (Rogers 85).
Aston Villa: (4141) Andre Moreira; de Laet, Elphick, Tuanzebe, Taylor; Whelan; Adomah, Hourihane, Doyle-Hayes (Grealish 57), Green (Bree 83); Hepburn-Murphy (Kodjia 58).
Referee: John Brooks.

Thursday, 16 August 2018

Sunderland (0) 0

Sheffield W (1) 2 *(Marco Matias 29, Reach 79)* 13,890

Sunderland: (4411) McLaughlin; Hume, Ozturk, Baldwin, James (Molyneux 80); O'Nien, Cattermole (Maja 66), Power, Embleton (Gooch 61); Honeyman; Maguire.
Sheffield W: (343) Wildsmith; Nielsen, Lees, van Aken (Penney 63); Palmer, Hunt (Kirby 46), Bannan (Lee 86), Boyd; Marco Matias, Fletcher, Reach.
Referee: Ben Toner.

SECOND ROUND

Tuesday, 28 August 2018

AFC Wimbledon (1) 1 *(Pigott 2)*

West Ham U (0) 3 *(Diop 63, Ogbonna 83, Hernandez 90)* 3962

AFC Wimbledon: (442) King; Sibbick, Oshilaja, McDonald■, Garratt; Wagstaff, Trotter, Hartigan, Pinnock (Wordsworth 68); Hanson (Appiah 79), Pigott (Nightingale 26).
West Ham U: (4231) Adrian; Zabaleta, Diop, Ogbonna, Cresswell; Obiang (Felipe Anderson 46), Rice; Yarmolenko (Masuaku 90), Lucas Perez (Antonio 81), Snodgrass; Hernandez.
Referee: Tim Robinson.

Blackburn R (1) 4 *(Nuttall 4, Graham 49, Downing 61, Palmer 77)*

Lincoln C (1) 1 *(Luque 28)* 5211

Blackburn R: (352) Raya; Nyambe, Downing, Grayson; Caddis, Travis (Tomlinson 81), Rothwell (Palmer 60), Conway, Bell; Nuttall, Graham (Butterworth 72).
Lincoln C: (442) Slocombe; Eardley, Shackell, Wilson, Crookes; Anderson, O'Connor (Pett 62), Chapman, Luque (Andrade 63); Green, Rhead (Akinde 63).
Referee: Geoff Eltringham.

Bournemouth (2) 3 *(Mousset 15, Fraser 37, Ibe 90)*

Milton Keynes D (0) 0 9747

Bournemouth: (442) Boruc; Francis, Mings, Simpson, Rico; Ibe, Cook L, Lerma, Fraser (King 65); Mousset (Cook S 69), Defoe (Brooks 86).
Milton Keynes D: (352) Nicholls; Cargill (Nombe 62), Jackson, Moore-Taylor; Williams (Tapp 62), Gilbey, Houghton, Watson, Lewington; Cisse, Healey (Sow 72).
Referee: James Linington.

Brentford (1) 1 *(Jeanvier 40)*

Cheltenham T (0) 0 4384

Brentford: (433) Daniels; Clarke, Jeanvier, Mepham (Barbet 50), Field; Yennaris, Macleod, McEachran; Judge, Forss (Ogbene 75), Benrahma.
Cheltenham T: (451) Flinders; Baldwin (McAlinden 87), Mullins, Boyle, Debayo; Broom, Tozer, Dawson (Jones 52), Thomas, Lloyd; Duku (Addai 65).
Referee: Ross Joyce.

Brighton & HA (0) 0

Southampton (0) 1 *(Austin 88)* 13,651

Brighton & HA: (4411) Button; Barclay, Collar, Bernardo, Suttner; Jahanbakhsh, Kayal (Connolly 90), Bissouma, Gyokeres; Gross (Propper 63); Locadia.
Southampton: (4231) Gunn; Stephens, Yoshida, Bednarek, Targett; Davis, Romeu (Gallagher 70); Ward-Prowse, Armstrong (Redmond 81), Elyounoussi; Gabbiadini (Austin 81).
Referee: Andre Marriner.

Burton Alb (0) 1 *(Boyce 52)*

Aston Villa (0) 0 3411

Burton Alb: (433) Bywater (Campbell 31); Brayford (Sordell 11), McFadzean■, Turner, Hutchinson; Fox, Quinn (Harness 46), Fraser; Akins, Boyce, Templeton.
Aston Villa: (4411) Andre Moreira; Bree, Tuanzebe, Elphick (Elmohamady 69), Taylor; de Laet, Lansbury, Hourihane, Adomah; El Ghazi; Hepburn-Murphy.
Referee: Darren Bond.

Cardiff C (0) 1 *(Ecuele Manga 77)*

Norwich C (1) 3 *(Srbeny 26, 64, Aarons 69)* 6953

Cardiff C: (352) Smithies; Ecuele Manga, Connolly, Peltier; Richards (Ward 59), Victor Camarasa (Zohore 71), Harris K, Damour, Cunningham; Reid, Madine (Paterson 59).
Norwich C: (451) McGovern; Aarons, Passlack, Zimmermann, Stiepermann; Cantwell (Rhodes 90), Trybull (Leitner 67), Godfrey, Tettey, Emi (Marshall 83); Srbeny.
Referee: Andrew Madley.

Doncaster R (1) 1 *(May 23)*

Blackpool (1) 2 *(Nottingham 38, Pritchard 60)* 3188

Doncaster R: (433) Lawlor; Mason, Wright, Anderson T, Andrew; Blair, Whiteman, Rowe (Ben Khemis 74); Anderson J (Kiwomya 61), May, Taylor (Beestin 66).
Blackpool: (433) Howard; Nottingham, O'Connor, Heneghan, Bola; Pritchard (Turton 73), Spearing, Taylor; O'Sullivan, Gnanduillet (Dodoo 85), Feeney (Thompson 66).
Referee: Anthony Backhouse.

Fulham (1) 2 *(Kamara 4, 48)*
Exeter C (0) 0 9333
Fulham: (433) Sergio Rico; Christie, Mawson (Sessegnon S 75), Chambers, Sessegnon R; Zambo, Cisse, Johansen; Kamara, Rui Fonte, Kebano (De La Torre 74).
Exeter C: (343) Pym; O'Shea, Croll, Martin A; Oates, Tillson, Martin L (Boateng 46), Holmes (Sparkes 55); Jay, Abrahams (Taylor 69), Collins.
Referee: Kevin Friend.

Hull C (0) 0
Derby Co (2) 4 *(Waghorn 25, Jozefzoon 39, Fleming 73 (og), Mount 89)* 4666
Hull C: (352) Long; McKenzie, MacDonald, Curry; Kane (Milinkovic 59), Batty (Sheaf 69), Stewart, Toral, Fleming; Keane, Dicko.
Derby Co: (433) Roos; Wisdom, Keogh, Tomori, Malone (Lowe 71); Mount, Huddlestone, Johnson (Bird 80); Marriott (Holmes 71), Waghorn, Jozefzoon.
Referee: Oliver Langford.

Leeds U (0) 0
Preston NE (2) 2 *(Johnson 2 (pen), Barker 45)* 18,652
Leeds U: (4231) Blackman; Dallas, Jansson, Shaughnessy (Samuel 46), Pearce; Phillips, Baker; Roberts (Alioski 60), Shackleton (Klich 46), Harrison; Bamford.
Preston NE: (442) Maxwell; Fisher, Storey, Davies, Earl; Barkhuizen, Johnson (Pearson 71), Ledson■, Barker (Browne 72); Moult (Nmecha 75), Harrop.
Referee: Tony Harrington.

Leicester C (2) 4 *(Fuchs 8, Iborra 39, Iheanacho 46, Ghezzal 71)*
Fleetwood T (0) 0 10,671
Leicester C: (352) Ward; Morgan (Benkovic 62), Evans, Fuchs; Ghezzal (Diabate 76), Adrien Silva, Amartey, Albrighton, Iborra; Okazaki, Iheanacho (Gray 50).
Fleetwood T: (532) Jones P; Jones G, Sheron, Spurr, Dempsey, Bolger; Long (Hill 61), Maguire (Madden 61), Biggins; Grant (Wallace J 67), McAleny.
Referee: Lee Mason.

Middlesbrough (1) 2 *(Johnson 37, Hugill 53)*
Rochdale (0) 1 *(Delaney 83)* 10,344
Middlesbrough: (352) Lonergan; Ayala (Spence 46), Wood-Gordon, McNair; Mahmutovic, Besic (Brahimi 46), Leadbitter, Tavernier, Johnson; Hugill (Chapman 59), Fletcher.
Rochdale: (352) Norman; Delaney, Randall (Rafferty 57), McGahey; Cannon, Williams M, Camps, Inman (Dooley 62), Ntlhe; Andrew, Henderson (Gillam 74).
Referee: Ben Toner.

Newport Co (0) 0
Oxford U (2) 3 *(Demetriou 2 (og), Baptiste 4, Whyte 90)* 2228
Newport Co: (352) Townsend; Franks, Bennett, Demetriou; Hornby-Forbes, Bakinson, Crofts (Sheehan 75), Cooper (Marsh-Brown 61), Butler; Matt (Amond 68), Semenyo.
Oxford U: (4231) Mitchell; Norman, Dickie, Mousinho, Garbutt; Hanson■, Ruffels (Brannagan 75); Baptiste, Obika (Henry 61), Whyte; Smith (Long 82).
Referee: Scott Duncan.

QPR (2) 3 *(Samuel 4, Wszolek 18, Smith 64)*
Bristol R (0) 1 *(Upson 87)* 5007
QPR: (433) Ingram; Kakay, Baptiste, Hall (Owens 65), Hamalainen; Wszolek, Cousins, Chair (Smyth 60); Samuel (Bettache 85), Smith, Washington.
Bristol R: (4231) Smith; Clarke J (Broadbent 57), Lockyer, Craig, Kelly; Clarke O, Upson; Matthews (Reilly 67), Bennett, Rodman; Payne (Nichols 67).
Referee: Charles Breakspear.

Sheffield W (0) 0
Wolverhampton W (0) 2 *(Leo Bonatini 53, Helder Costa 85 (pen))* 13,597
Sheffield W: (352) Wildsmith; Jones (Kirby 86), Fox, Preston (Nuhiu 73); Lee, Nielsen, Baker, Hutchinson, Boyd; Fletcher (Stobbs 74), Forestieri.
Wolverhampton W: (343) Ruddy; Dendoncker, Coady, Hause; Doherty, Watt (Goncalves 62), Saiss, Ruben Vinagre; Traore, Leo Bonatini (Ashley-Seal 80), Gibbs-White (Helder Costa 72).
Referee: Robert Jones.

Stoke C (0) 2 *(Berahino 53, Bacuna 90 (og))*
Huddersfield T (0) 0 7290
Stoke C: (442) Federici; Martina, Williams, Martins Indi, Pieters (Bauer 78); Diouf (Krkic 64), Etebo, Fletcher, McClean; Berahino (Adam 85), Afobe.
Huddersfield T: (4231) Lossl; Smith, Schindler, Stankovic, Durm (Lowe 77); Williams (Mooy 69), Bacuna; Kachunga, Mbenza, Sabiri (Pritchard 46); Depoitre.
Referee: Peter Bankes.

Swansea C (0) 0
Crystal Palace (0) 1 *(Sorloth 70)* 9122
Swansea C: (4231) Nordfeldt; Naughton, Cooper B (Reid 61), Harries, John; Carroll (Asoro 77), Grimes; James, Byers, Dhanda; Baker-Richardson (Cullen 78).
Crystal Palace: (4411) Guaita; Wan Bissaka, Kelly (Ward 62), Riedewald, Schlupp (Townsend 62); Inniss, Kouyate, Meyer, Williams (KaiKai 76); Puncheon; Sorloth.
Referee: John Brooks.

Walsall (1) 3 *(Morris 33, Cook 63, Gordon 64)*
Macclesfield T (2) 3 *(Grimes 10, Smith 25, Whitaker 90)* 2352
Walsall: (442) Dunn; Wilson, Fitzwater, Guthrie, Leahy; Morris, Kinsella, Dobson, Kouhyar; Cook, Gordon (Parker 88).
Macclesfield T: (433) O'Hara; Pearson, Kelleher, Grimes, Fitzpatrick; Evans, Maycock (Welch-Hayes 76), Whitaker; Blissett (Wilson 77), Smith, Napa (Marsh 74).
Macclesfield T won 3-1 on penalties.
Referee: Darren Drysdale.

WBA (1) 2 *(Leko 26, Edwards 75)*
Mansfield T (0) 1 *(Bishop 69)* 10,574
WBA: (532) Myhill; Mears, Adarabioyo, Dawson (Howkins 72), Field, Townsend; Leko (Gayle 77), Barry, Harper; Burke, Edwards (Barnes 77).
Mansfield T: (3412) Olejnik; Sweeney, Pearce, Benning (Graham 85); Atkinson, Bishop, Butcher (MacDonald 53), Hamilton; Khan; Davies (Rose 64), Walker.
Referee: Stephen Martin.

Wycombe W (0) 2 *(Kashket 55, Stewart 74)*
Forest Green R (0) 2 *(Grubb 57, Winchester 86)* 1934
Wycombe W: (433) Allsop; McCarthy, Jombati, Stewart, Jacobson; Thompson, Bean, Saunders; Freeman, Akinfenwa (Samuel 80), Kashket (Cowan-Hall 71).
Forest Green R: (4231) Montgomery; Shephard, Gunning, Digby, Mills; Brown, James (Doidge 61); Grubb, Winchester, Archibald (Williams 72); Reid (Pearce 79).
Wycombe W won 4-3 on penalties.
Referee: Antony Coggins.

Wednesday, 29 August 2018

Everton (1) 3 *(Sigurdsson 28, Calvert-Lewin 61, 87)*
Rotherham U (0) 1 *(Vaulks 86)* 31,972
Everton: (442) Stekelenburg; Kenny, Holgate, Zouma, Digne; Sandro (Schneiderlin 86), Dowell, Davies, Sigurdsson (Walcott 66); Calvert-Lewin, Niasse (Tosun 74).
Rotherham U: (4411) Price; Vyner, Robertson, Raggett, Ajayi; Forde, Palmer, Ball (Vassell 61), Wiles (Vaulks 46); Newell (Taylor 72); Proctor.
Referee: Graham Scott.

Millwall (0) 3 *(Williams 64 (pen), Gregory 83, O'Brien 89)*
Plymouth Arg (1) 2 *(Ness 41, Ladapo 67)* 3645
Millwall: (442) Amos; McLaughlin (O'Brien 77), Ferguson, Romeo, Williams; Webster, Onyedinma (Gregory 68), Elliott, Skalak; Wallace M, Karacan (Wallace J 62).
Plymouth Arg: (4141) Macey; Riley, Edwards, Ness, Sawyer; Songo'o; Sarcevic, O'Keefe (Carey 84), Grant C (Wylde 90), Smith-Brown; Ladapo (Taylor 78).
Referee: Darren England.

Nottingham F (1) 3 *(Murphy 2, Cash 90, Gil Dias 90)*
Newcastle U (0) 1 *(Rondon 90)* 13,942
Nottingham F: (4231) Steele; Byram (Darikwa 39), Hefele, Fox, Robinson; Bridcutt, Watson; Gil Dias, Joao Carvalho (Cash 82), Lolley (Osborn 58); Murphy.
Newcastle U: (4411) Darlow; Sterry, Schar, Fernandez (Perez 69), Clark; Atsu, Longstaff S, Ki, Kenedy; Muto (Murphy 77); Joselu (Rondon 82).
Referee: Jeremy Simpson.

Reading (0) 0
Watford (1) 2 *(Success 37, Quina 62)* 9265
Reading: (343) Walker; Tiago Ilori, O'Shea (Baldock 65), Moore; Gunter, Kelly, Bacuna, Richards (Yiadom 63); Meite, McNulty, Swift (Sims 46).
Watford: (4411) Gomes; Navarro, Mariappa, Prodl, Masina; Femenia, Wilmot, Chalobah (Hughes 86), Sema (Okaka 65); Quina (Doucoure 82); Success.
Referee: Andy Davies.

THIRD ROUND

Tuesday, 25 September 2018

Blackpool (1) 2 *(Gnanduillet 28, Spearing 90)*
QPR (0) 0 1910
Blackpool: (4231) Howard; Nottingham, Heneghan, Tilt, Bola; Spearing, Guy (Turton 77); McLaughlin (O'Sullivan 85), Thompson, Dodoo; Gnanduillet (Delfouneso 83).
QPR: (442) Ingram; Hall, Cousins■, Scowen (Goss 25), Baptiste; Smith, Chair (Smyth 46), Wszolek, Samuel (Oteh 77); Hamalainen, Kakay.
Referee: Tim Robinson.

Bournemouth (1) 3 *(Stanislas 14, Ibe 58 (pen), Wilson 90)*
Blackburn R (0) 2 *(Conway 63, Armstrong 72 (pen))* 9715
Bournemouth: (442) Boruc; Smith, Francis, Simpson, Mings; Stanislas (Pugh 69), Cook L, Lerma, Ibe; Mousset (King 69), Defoe (Wilson 74).
Blackburn R: (541) Raya; Nyambe, Rodwell (Reed 59), Lenihan, Williams■, Bell; Conway, Rothwell, Armstrong, Palmer (Butterworth 64); Brereton (Travis 82).
Referee: Simon Hooper.

Burton Alb (0) 2 *(Boyce 62, Allen 83)*
Burnley (1) 1 *(Long 40)* 2449
Burton Alb: (4231) Evtimov; Akins, Brayford, Turner, McCrory; Allen, Quinn (Fox 69); Hesketh, Templeton (Sordell 81), Fraser (Sbarra 77); Boyce.
Burnley: (442) Heaton; Lowton, Mee, Long, Ward; Gudmundsson, Defour (Hendrick 74), Westwood, McNeil; Wood (Vokes 81), Vydra (Barnes 71).
Referee: Robert Jones.

Manchester U (1) 2 *(Mata 3, Fellaini 90)*
Derby Co (0) 2 *(Wilson H 59, Marriott 85)* 55,227
Manchester U: (4231) Romero■; Dalot, Bailly, Jones, Young; Ander Herrera (Fellaini 63), Matic; Mata (Grant 70), Lingard (Fred 63), Martial; Lukaku.
Derby Co: (4231) Carson; Bogle (Wisdom 86), Keogh, Tomori, Forsyth; Bryson, Johnson; Bennett (Jozefzoon 77), Mount, Wilson H; Nugent (Marriott 79).
Derby Co won 8-7 on penalties. Referee: Stuart Attwell.

Millwall (0) 1 *(Gregory 61)*
Fulham (1) 3 *(Bryan 7, De La Torre 52, Christie 68)* 5839
Millwall: (442) Amos; McLaughlin, Wallace M, Cooper, Ferguson (Wallace J 87); Karacan (Williams 74), Skalak (Romeo 46), Tunnicliffe, O'Brien; Gregory, Elliott.
Fulham: (343) Sergio Rico; Sessegnon S, Ream (Odoi 62), Le Marchand; Christie, McDonald, Zambo, Bryan; De La Torre (O'Riley 85), Kamara, Ayite (Elliott 81).
Referee: Darren Bond.

Oxford U (0) 0
Manchester C (1) 3 *(Gabriel Jesus 36, Mahrez 78, Foden 90)* 11,956
Oxford U: (4231) Mitchell; Long, Nelson, Dickie, Garbutt; Brannagan (Ruffels 55), Baptiste; Whyte, Hanson (Henry 67), Holmes (Smith 77); Obika.
Manchester C: (343) Muric; Kompany, Otamendi, Stones; Danilo, Foden, Silva (Gundogan 63), Zinchenko; Mahrez (Bernabe 86), Gabriel Jesus, Diaz (Sterling 55).
Referee: Roger East.

Preston NE (1) 2 *(Robinson 27, Barkhuizen 66)*
Middlesbrough (1) 2 *(Fletcher 34, Tavernier 69)* 5095
Preston NE: (4231) Maxwell; Clarke, Storey, Huntington, Hughes; Pearson, Browne (Harrop 63); Barkhuizen (Moult 85), Ledson, Barker (Burke 81); Robinson.
Middlesbrough: (442) Konstantopoulos; Batth, McNair, Wood-Gordon (Chapman 72), Fry; Tavernier, Leadbitter, McQueen, Wing; Fletcher, Gestede.
Middlesbrough won 4-3 on penalties.
Referee: Oliver Langford.

WBA (0) 0
Crystal Palace (1) 3 *(Townsend 6, 81, Van Aanholt 76)* 10,818
WBA: (3511) Myhill; Adarabioyo, Hegazi (Howkins 62), Field; Mears (Edwards 63), Hoolahan, Harper, Barry (Brunt 63), Townsend; Morrison; Robson-Kanu.
Crystal Palace: (442) Guaita; Ward, Kelly, Riedewald (Wan Bissaka 22), Van Aanholt (Souare 79); Puncheon, Kouyate, Schlupp, Meyer; Townsend (Ayew 85), Sorloth.
Referee: Peter Bankes.

Wolverhampton W (0) 0
Leicester C (0) 0 21,562
Wolverhampton W: (343) Ruddy; Dendoncker, Coady, Hause; Jonny (Bennett 75), Saiss, Gibbs-White, Ruben Vinagre; Traore, Leo Bonatini (Ashley-Seal 83), Ivan Cavaleiro (Jota 57).
Leicester C: (442) Ward; Ricardo Pereira, Morgan, Evans, Fuchs; Albrighton, Iborra, Adrien Silva (Choudhury 84), Ghezzal; Vardy (Iheanacho 61), Okazaki (Gray 61).
Leicester C won 3-1 on penalties.
Referee: Paul Tierney.

Wycombe W (1) 3 *(Cowan-Hall 17, Saunders 61 (pen), Akinfenwa 75)*
Norwich C (3) 4 *(Rhodes 12, 14, Trybull 41, Rhodes 51)* 3947
Wycombe W: (532) Allsop; Cowan-Hall, McCarthy, Charles (Harriman 62), Jombati, Freeman; Bloomfield (Akinfenwa 62), Saunders, Gape; Mackail-Smith, Samuel (Kashket 82).
Norwich C: (4231) McGovern; Passlack, Zimmermann, Godfrey, Ivo Pinto; Trybull, Thompson (Lewis 76); Emi (Klose 86), Srbeny (Stiepermann 88), Vrancic, Rhodes.
Referee: Jeremy Simpson.

Wednesday, 26 September 2018

Arsenal (2) 3 *(Welbeck 5, 37, Lacazette 90)*
Brentford (0) 1 *(Judge 58)* 49,586
Arsenal: (4231) Leno; Lichtsteiner, Mustafi, Holding, Monreal; Elneny (Ramsey 84), Guendouzi; Mkhitaryan (Torreira 75), Smith-Rowe (Lacazette 64), Iwobi; Welbeck.
Brentford: (433) Daniels; Odubajo (Dalsgaard 64), Jeanvier, Konsa, Barbet; Sawyers, Mokotjo, Yennaris; Judge, Watkins (Benrahma 79), Canos (Maupay 74).
Referee: Mike Dean.

Liverpool (0) 1 *(Sturridge 58)*
Chelsea (0) 2 *(Emerson Palmieri 79, Hazard 85)* 45,503
Liverpool: (433) Mignolet; Clyne, Matip, Lovren, Moreno; Milner (Henderson 60), Fabinho (Salah 87), Keita; Shaqiri, Sturridge, Mane (Firmino 71).
Chelsea: (433) Caballero; Azpilicueta, Cahill, Christensen (Luiz 73), Emerson Palmieri; Barkley, Fabregas, Kovacic (Kante 64); Moses, Morata, Willian (Hazard 56).
Referee: Kevin Friend.

Nottingham F (2) 3 *(Osborn 19, Murphy 40, Lolley 50)*
Stoke C (0) 2 *(Afobe 60, Berahino 83)* 12,915
Nottingham F: (4231) Steele; Darikwa, Tobias Figueiredo, Dawson, Osborn; Watson, Bridcutt; Gil Dias (Cash 72), Goncalves■, Lolley (Fox 84); Murphy (Grabban 56).
Stoke C: (532) Federici; Bauer (Ince 57), Soutar, Williams, Martins Indi, Edwards (Campbell 83); Adam, Krkic, Fletcher; Berahino, Crouch (Afobe 55).
Referee: Darren England.

Tottenham H (0) 2 *(Alli 81 (pen), Lamela 86)*

Watford (0) 2 *(Success 46, Capoue 89)* 23,650

Tottenham H: (4231) Gazzaniga; Aurier, Alderweireld, Sanchez, Davies; Wanyama (Dembele 64), Winks; Sissoko (Son 64), Alli, Lamela; Lucas Moura (Llorente 70).
Watford: (451) Gomes; Navarro (Kabasele■ 77), Cathcart, Mariappa, Masina; Femenia (Hughes 69), Wilmot, Chalobah, Quina, Sema (Capoue 84); Success.
Tottenham H won 4-2 on penalties.
Referee: Lee Mason.

West Ham U (3) 8 *(Antonio 28, Snodgrass 32, 60, Lucas Perez 40, Fredericks 51, Ogbonna 54, Diangana 67, 82)*

Macclesfield T (0) 0 24,833

West Ham U: (433) Adrian; Fredericks, Ogbonna, Diop, Cresswell; Sanchez (Rice 10), Obiang (Coventry 46), Snodgrass; Diangana, Antonio (Powell 62), Lucas Perez.
Macclesfield T: (442) O'Hara; Pearson, Kelleher, Grimes, Fitzpatrick; Maycock, Lowe (Welch-Hayes 68), Whitaker, Napa (Arthur 58); Smith (Blissett 58), Marsh.
Referee: Craig Pawson.

Tuesday, 2 October 2018

Everton (0) 1 *(Walcott 85)*

Southampton (1) 1 *(Ings 44)* 30,545

Everton: (4231) Stekelenburg; Kenny, Keane, Zouma, Baines; Schneiderlin (Walcott 79), Davies; Bernard, Dowell (Niasse 46), Lookman (Richarlison 60); Tosun.
Southampton: (3412) Gunn; Bednarek, Yoshida, Stephens; Cedric Soares, Hojbjerg, Lemina, Targett; Redmond; Ings, Gabbiadini (Davis 73).
Southampton won 4-3 on penalties.
Referee: Chris Kavanagh.

FOURTH ROUND

Tuesday, 30 October 2018

Bournemouth (1) 2 *(Stanislas 39, Cook S 72)*

Norwich C (0) 1 *(Hernandez 70)* 10,331

Bournemouth: (343) Boruc; Francis (Simpson 86), Cook S, Daniels; Pugh, Gosling, Surman, Rico; Stanislas, Defoe (Wilson 71), Ibe (Fraser 61).
Norwich C: (4231) McGovern; Ivo Pinto (Emi 68), Godfrey, Zimmermann, Lewis; Tettey, Trybull (Pukki 82); Passlack (Rhodes 87), Vrancic, Hernandez; Srbeny.
Referee: Lee Mason.

Burton Alb (0) 3 *(Janko 52 (og), Fraser 64, Hesketh 82)*

Nottingham F (0) 2 *(Grabban 70, Appiah 90)* 4284

Burton Alb: (433) Evtimov; Fox, Brayford, McFadzean, Akins; Allen, Quinn, Fraser (Buxton 85); Hesketh (Sbarra 88), Boyce, Templeton (Sordell 70).
Nottingham F: (4231) Steele; Janko (Lolley 69), Hefele, Dawson, Osborn; Bridcutt (Appiah 84), Watson; Cash, Goncalves, Gil Dias; Soudani (Grabban 56).
Referee: John Brooks.

Wednesday, 31 October 2018

Arsenal (1) 2 *(Lichtsteiner 33, Smith-Rowe 50)*

Blackpool (0) 1 *(O'Connor 66)* 48,168

Arsenal: (433) Cech; Lichtsteiner, Mustafi, Pleguezuelo, Jenkinson; Ramsey, Guendouzi■, Smith-Rowe (Iwobi 73); Maitland-Niles (Torreira 60), Welbeck (Aubameyang 76), Mkhitaryan.
Blackpool: (4141) Howard; Nottingham (Pritchard 65), Heneghan, O'Connor■, Bola; Spearing; Thompson, Guy (O'Sullivan 86), Turton, Feeney (Cullen 79); Delfouneso.
Referee: David Coote.

Chelsea (3) 3 *(Tomori 5 (og), Keogh 21 (og), Fabregas 41)*

Derby Co (2) 2 *(Marriott 9, Waghorn 27)* 39,564

Chelsea: (433) Caballero; Zappacosta (Azpilicueta 78), Cahill, Christensen (Luiz 66), Emerson Palmieri; Kante, Fabregas, Kovacic; Loftus-Cheek (Pedro 69), Morata, Willian.
Derby Co: (451) Carson; Bogle, Keogh, Tomori, Malone (Forsyth 82); Waghorn (Bennett 62), Wilson H (Nugent 82), Huddlestone, Mount, Lawrence; Marriott.
Referee: Jonathan Moss.

Middlesbrough (1) 1 *(Wing 45)*

Crystal Palace (0) 0 11,850

Middlesbrough: (3511) Konstantopoulos; Ayala, Batth, Friend; McNair, Wing, Leadbitter, Tavernier, McQueen (Saville 29); Braithwaite (Fletcher 65); Hugill (Gestede 56).
Crystal Palace: (442) Guaita; Wan Bissaka, Kelly, Riedewald, Souare (Woods 79); Townsend, Meyer, Puncheon (KaiKai 84), Schlupp; Sorloth, Ayew (Milivojevic 65).
Referee: Paul Tierney.

West Ham U (0) 1 *(Lucas Perez 71)*

Tottenham H (1) 3 *(Son 16, 54, Llorente 75)* 50,270

West Ham U: (433) Adrian; Fredericks, Diop, Ogbonna, Masuaku; Obiang (Lucas Perez 58), Rice, Felipe Anderson (Snodgrass 46); Diangana, Hernandez (Arnautovic 58), Antonio.
Tottenham H: (4231) Gazzaniga; Aurier, Foyth, Sanchez, Walker-Peters; Winks, Wanyama; Alli (Nkoudou 64), Eriksen (Skipp 84), Son; Llorente (Sissoko 76).
Referee: Stuart Attwell.

Thursday, 1 November 2018

Manchester C (1) 2 *(Diaz 18, 65)*

Fulham (0) 0 35,271

Manchester C: (433) Muric; Danilo, Stones, Kompany, Zinchenko; De Bruyne (Gomes 86), Delph, Foden; Diaz (Mahrez 78), Gabriel Jesus, Sane.
Fulham: (433) Sergio Rico; Fosu-Mensah, Odoi, Ream (Le Marchand 69), Sessegnon R; Cairney, Zambo, Seri; Vietto (Christie 90), Mitrovic, Schurrle (Ayite 81).
Referee: Martin Atkinson.

Tuesday, 27 November 2018

Leicester C (0) 0

Southampton (0) 0 22,150

Leicester C: (442) Ward; Simpson, Soyuncu, Evans, Fuchs; Diabate (Albrighton 78), Adrien Silva (Mendy 61), Ndidi, Gray; Iheanacho (Okazaki 61), Vardy.
Southampton: (352) Gunn; Yoshida, Vestergaard, Stephens; Valery, Hojbjerg, Lemina, Armstrong (Davis 73), Targett (Cedric Soares 61); Redmond, Obafemi (Gabbiadini 90).
Leicester C won 6-5 on penalties.
Referee: Roger East.

QUARTER-FINALS

Tuesday, 18 December 2018

Leicester C (0) 1 *(Albrighton 73)*

Manchester C (1) 1 *(De Bruyne 14)* 24,644

Leicester C: (451) Ward; Simpson, Soyuncu, Maguire, Fuchs; Ghezzal (Maddison 53), Choudhury, Iborra (Albrighton 61), Ndidi, Gray; Iheanacho (Ricardo Pereira 81).
Manchester C: (433) Muric; Walker, Garcia, Otamendi, Zinchenko; De Bruyne (Gundogan 71), Stones, Foden; Mahrez, Aguero (Gabriel Jesus 76), Diaz (Sterling 66).
Manchester C won 3-1 on penalties.
Referee: Lee Mason.

Middlesbrough (0) 0

Burton Alb (0) 1 *(Hesketh 48)* 17,342

Middlesbrough: (433) Randolph; Fry, Flint, Batth, Friend; Wing, Leadbitter, Besic (Tavernier 63); Downing, Hugill (Assombalonga 63), Braithwaite (Fletcher 72).
Burton Alb: (343) Collins; Brayford, Buxton, Turner; Harness, Allen, Quinn, Hutchinson; Hesketh (Fox 81), Akins, Fraser.
Referee: Michael Oliver.

Wednesday, 19 December 2018

Arsenal (0) 0

Tottenham H (1) 2 *(Son 20, Alli 59)* 59,016

Arsenal: (4231) Cech; Maitland-Niles, Papastathopoulos, Xhaka, Monreal; Guendouzi (Nketiah 65), Torreira; Mkhitaryan (Koscielny 46), Ramsey, Iwobi (Lacazette 58); Aubameyang.
Tottenham H: (4231) Gazzaniga; Trippier, Alderweireld, Davies, Rose; Sissoko, Winks; Lucas Moura (Kane 58), Alli, Eriksen; Son (Lamela 79).
Referee: Jonathan Moss.

Chelsea (0) 1 *(Hazard 84)*

Bournemouth (0) 0 40,432

Chelsea: (433) Arrizabalaga; Azpilicueta, Rudiger, Christensen (Luiz 81), Emerson Palmieri; Kovacic, Fabregas, Barkley (Hazard 61); Loftus Cheek, Giroud, Willian (Pedro 55).
Bournemouth: (352) Boruc; Cook S, Simpson, Daniels; Ibe, Stanislas (Fraser 63), Brooks (Defoe 88), Ake, Rico; Wilson, Mousset (King 73).
Referee: Anthony Taylor.

SEMI-FINALS FIRST LEG

Tuesday, 8 January 2019

Tottenham H (1) 1 *(Kane 26 (pen))*

Chelsea (0) 0 44,371

Tottenham H: (41212) Gazzaniga; Trippier, Sanchez, Alderweireld, Rose; Winks (Skipp 90); Sissoko, Eriksen (Llorente 90); Alli; Son (Lamela 79), Kane.
Chelsea: (433) Arrizabalaga; Azpilicueta, Rudiger, Christensen, Alonso; Kante, Jorginho, Barkley (Kovacic 75); Hudson-Odoi (Giroud 79), Hazard, Willian (Pedro 63).
Referee: Michael Oliver.

Wednesday, 9 January 2019

Manchester C (4) 9 *(De Bruyne 5, Gabriel Jesus 30, 34, 57, 65, Zinchenko 37, Foden 62, Walker 70, Mahrez 83)*

Burton Alb (0) 0 32,089

Manchester C: (433) Muric; Walker (Danilo 74), Garcia, Otamendi, Zinchenko; De Bruyne (Foden 58), Gundogan, Silva; Mahrez, Gabriel Jesus, Sane (Bernardo Silva 66).
Burton Alb: (451) Collins; Brayford, Buxton, Turner, Hutchinson; Harness, Fraser (Sbarra 79), Wallace, Allen (Fox 68), Akins; Boyce (Templeton 68).
Referee: Mike Dean.

SEMI-FINALS SECOND LEG

Wednesday, 23 January 2019

Burton Alb (0) 0

Manchester C (1) 1 *(Aguero 26)* 6519

Burton Alb: (4231) Collins; Akins, McFadzean, Turner (Hutchinson 40), McCrory; Quinn (Fox 46), Wallace; Harness, Miller, Templeton; Boyce (Daniel 77).
Manchester C: (433) Muric; Danilo, Sandler, Garcia, Zinchenko (Nmecha 67); Foden, De Bruyne (Mendy 63), Delph; Mahrez, Aguero (Gabriel Jesus 63), Poveda-Ocampo.
Manchester C won 10-0 on aggregate
Referee: Kevin Friend.

Thursday, 24 January 2019

Chelsea (2) 2 *(Kante 27, Hazard 38)*

Tottenham H (0) 1 *(Llorente 50)* 38,610

Chelsea: (433) Arrizabalaga; Azpilicueta, Rudiger, Luiz, Emerson Palmieri; Kante, Jorginho, Barkley (Kovacic 81); Pedro (Willian 76), Giroud, Hazard.
Tottenham H: (41212) Gazzaniga; Aurier, Alderweireld, Vertonghen, Davies (Rose 33); Dier; Sissoko (Sanchez 80), Winks; Eriksen; Llorente (Lucas Moura 68), Lamela.
2-2 on aggregate; Chelsea won 4-2 on penalties.
Referee: Martin Atkinson.

CARABAO CUP FINAL 2019

Sunday, 24 February 2019

(at Wembley Stadium, attendance 81,775)

Chelsea (0) 0 Manchester C (0) 0

Chelsea: (433) Arrizabalaga; Azpilicueta, Rudiger, Luiz, Emerson Palmieri; Kante, Jorginho, Barkley (Loftus-Cheek 89); Pedro (Hudson-Odoi 79), Hazard, Willian (Higuain 95).

Manchester C: (433) Ederson; Walker, Otamendi, Laporte (Kompany 46), Zinchenko; De Bruyne (Sane 86), Fernandinho (Danilo 91), Silva (Gundogan 79); Bernardo Silva, Aguero, Sterling.

aet; Manchester C won 4-3 on penalties.

Referee: Jon Moss.

Raheem Sterling scores the winning penalty for Manchester City in the EFL Cup Final on 24 February. The game against Chelsea finished 0-0 after extra time; City won 4-3 on penalties. (Darren Staples/Sportimage/PA Images)

LEAGUE CUP ATTENDANCES 1960–2019

Season	*Attendances*	*Games*	*Average*
1960–61	1,204,580	112	10,755
1961–62	1,030,534	104	9,909
1962–63	1,029,893	102	10,097
1963–64	945,265	104	9,089
1964–65	962,802	98	9,825
1965–66	1,205,876	106	11,376
1966–67	1,394,553	118	11,818
1967–68	1,671,326	110	15,194
1968–69	2,064,647	118	17,497
1969–70	2,299,819	122	18,851
1970–71	2,035,315	116	17,546
1971–72	2,397,154	123	19,489
1972–73	1,935,474	120	16,129
1973–74	1,722,629	132	13,050
1974–75	1,901,094	127	14,969
1975–76	1,841,735	140	13,155
1976–77	2,236,636	147	15,215
1977–78	2,038,295	148	13,772
1978–79	1,825,643	139	13,134
1979–80	2,322,866	169	13,745
1980–81	2,051,576	161	12,743
1981–82	1,880,682	161	11,681
1982–83	1,679,756	160	10,498
1983–84	1,900,491	168	11,312
1984–85	1,876,429	167	11,236
1985–86	1,579,916	163	9,693
1986–87	1,531,498	157	9,755
1987–88	1,539,253	158	9,742
1988–89	1,552,780	162	9,585
1989–90	1,836,916	168	10,934
1990–91	1,675,496	159	10,538
1991–92	1,622,337	164	9,892
1992–93	1,558,031	161	9,677
1993–94	1,744,120	163	10,700
1994–95	1,530,478	157	9,748
1995–96	1,776,060	162	10,963
1996–97	1,529,321	163	9,382
1997–98	1,484,297	153	9,701
1998–99	1,555,856	153	10,169
1999–2000	1,354,233	153	8,851
2000–01	1,501,304	154	9,749
2001–02	1,076,390	93	11,574
2002–03	1,242,478	92	13,505
2003–04	1,267,729	93	13,631
2004–05	1,313,693	93	14,216
2005–06	1,072,362	93	11,531
2006–07	1,098,403	93	11,811
2007–08	1,332,841	94	14,179
2008–09	1,329,753	93	14,298
2009–10	1,376,405	93	14,800
2010–11	1,197,917	93	12,881
2011–12	1,209,684	93	13,007
2012–13	1,210,031	93	13,011
2013–14	1,362,360	93	14,649
2014–15	1,274,413	93	13,690
2015–16	1,430,554	93	15,382
2016–17	1,462,722	93	15,728
2017–18	1,454,912	93	15,644
2018–19	1,275,575	93	13,716

CARABAO CUP 2018–19

Round	*Aggregate*	*Games*	*Average*
One	178.238	35	5,093
Two	215,101	25	8,604
Three	315,550	16	19,722
Four	221,888	8	27,736
Quarter-finals	141,434	4	35,359
Semi-finals	121,589	4	30,397
Final	81,775	1	81,775
Total	1,275,575	93	13,716

FOOTBALL LEAGUE TROPHY FINALS 1984–2019

The 1984 final was played at Boothferry Park, Hull. All subsequent finals played at Wembley except between 2001 and 2007 (inclusive) which were played at Millennium Stadium, Cardiff.

ASSOCIATE MEMBERS' CUP

1984	Bournemouth v Hull C	2-1

FREIGHT ROVER TROPHY

1985	Wigan Ath v Brentford	3-1
1986	Bristol C v Bolton W	3-0
1987	Mansfield T v Bristol C	1-1*
	Mansfield T won 5-4 on penalties	

SHERPA VANS TROPHY

1988	Wolverhampton W v Burnley	2-0
1989	Bolton W v Torquay U	4-1

LEYLAND DAF CUP

1990	Tranmere R v Bristol R	2-1
1991	Birmingham C v Tranmere R	3-2

AUTOGLASS TROPHY

1992	Stoke C v Stockport Co	1-0
1993	Port Vale v Stockport Co	2-1
1994	Swansea C v Huddersfield T	1-1*
	Swansea C won 3-1 on penalties	

AUTO WINDSCREENS SHIELD

1995	Birmingham C v Carlisle U	1-0*
1996	Rotherham U v Shrewsbury T	2-1
1997	Carlisle U v Colchester U	0-0*
	Carlisle U won 4-3 on penalties	
1998	Grimsby T v Bournemouth	2-1
1999	Wigan Ath v Millwall	1-0
2000	Stoke C v Bristol C	2-1

LDV VANS TROPHY

2001	Port Vale v Brentford	2-1
2002	Blackpool v Cambridge U	4-1
2003	Bristol C v Carlisle U	2-0
2004	Blackpool v Southend U	2-0
2005	Wrexham v Southend U	2-0*

FOOTBALL LEAGUE TROPHY

2006	Swansea C v Carlisle U	2-1

JOHNSTONE'S PAINT TROPHY

2007	Doncaster R v Bristol R	3-2*
2008	Milton Keynes D v Grimsby T	2-0
2009	Luton T v Scunthorpe U	3-2*
2010	Southampton v Carlisle U	4-1
2011	Carlisle U v Brentford	1-0
2012	Chesterfield v Swindon T	2-0
2013	Crewe Alex v Southend U	2-0
2014	Peterborough U v Chesterfield	3-1
2015	Bristol C v Walsall	2-0
2016	Barnsley v Oxford U	3-2

EFL CHECKATRADE TROPHY

2017	Coventry C v Oxford U	2-1
2018	Lincoln C v Shrewsbury T	1-0
2019	Portsmouth v Sunderland	2-2*
	Portsmouth won 5-4 on penalties	

**After extra time.*

FOOTBALL LEAGUE TROPHY WINS

Bristol C 3, Birmingham C 2, Blackpool 2, Carlisle U 2, Port Vale 2, Stoke C 2, Swansea C 2, Wigan Ath 2, Barnsley 1, Bolton W 1, Bournemouth 1, Chesterfield 1, Coventry C 1, Crewe Alex 1, Doncaster R 1, Grimsby T 1, Lincoln C 1, Luton T 1, Mansfield T 1, Milton Keynes D 1, Peterborough U 1, Portsmouth 1, Rotherham U 1, Southampton 1, Tranmere R 1, Wolverhampton W 1, Wrexham 1.

APPEARANCES IN FINALS

Carlisle U 6, Bristol C 5, Brentford 3, Southend U 3, Birmingham C 2, Blackpool 2, Bolton W 2, Bournemouth 2, Bristol R 2, Chesterfield 2, Grimsby T 2, Oxford U 2, Port Vale 2, Shrewsbury T 2, Stockport Co 2, Stoke C 2, Swansea C 2, Tranmere R 2, Wigan Ath 2, Barnsley 1, Burnley 1, Cambridge U 1, Colchester U 1, Coventry C 1, Crewe Alex 1, Doncaster R 1, Huddersfield T 1, Hull C 1, Lincoln C 1, Luton T 1, Mansfield T 1, Millwall 1, Milton Keynes D 1, Peterborough U 1, Portsmouth 1, Rotherham U 1, Scunthorpe U 1, Southampton 1, Sunderland 1, Swindon T 1, Torquay U 1, Walsall 1, Wolverhampton W 1, Wrexham 1.

EFL TROPHY ATTENDANCES 2018–19

Round	*Aggregate*	*Games*	*Average*
One	126,590	96	1,319
Two	37,016	16	2,314
Three	28,241	8	3,530
Quarter-finals	21,246	4	5,312
Semi-finals	10,599	2	5,300
Final	85,021	1	85,021
Total	308,713	127	2,431

EFL CHECKATRADE TROPHY 2018–19

■ *Denotes player sent off.*
In the group stages drawn matches were decided on a penalty shoot-out. Two points were awarded to the team that won on penalties (DW). The team that lost on penalties were awarded one point (DL).

NORTHERN SECTION GROUP A

Tuesday, 4 September 2018

Carlisle U (2) 3 *(Glendon 13, Gillesphey 38, Yates 76)*

Morecambe (2) 2 *(Oliver 6, Piggott 24)* 1213

Carlisle U: (442) Collin; Miller, Liddle, Parkes, Gillesphey; Yates, Devitt, Glendon, Slater; Nadesan (McCarron 83), Bennett.
Morecambe: (433) Halstead (Roche 19); Sinclair, Yarney, Lavelle, Cranston; Fleming, Jagne (Wildig 62), Ellison; Mendes Gomes, Oliver (Oswell 69), Piggott.
Referee: Andy Haines.

Sunderland (0) 0

Stoke C U21 (0) 0 7644

Sunderland: (442) Ruiter; Hume, Ozturk, Flanagan, James; Maguire (Molyneux 78), McGeouch, Robson, O'Nien; Maja (Sinclair 65), Wyke (Mgunga-Kimpioka 75).
Stoke C U21: (433) Gyollai; Bauer, Soutar, Collins, Tymon; Sorensen, Adam (Waddington 66), Shenton; Pemberton (Szerto 86), Campbell, Jarvis.
Sunderland won 4-2 on penalties.
Referee: Martin Coy.

Tuesday, 9 October 2018

Morecambe (1) 1 *(Oswell 26)*

Stoke C U21 (1) 2 *(Shenton 9, Campbell 57)* 512

Morecambe: (4231) Halstead; Conlan, Yarney, Lavelle, Cranston; Hedley, Jagne; Mendes Gomes (Oates 81), Piggott (Leitch-Smith 81), Ellison (Mandeville 24); Oswell.
Stoke C U21: (4231) Haugaard; Thandi, Wara, Soutar (Forrester 31), Niakate; Waddington, Shenton; Jarvis, Pemberton, Tymon; Campbell.
Referee: Anthony Blackhouse.

Sunderland (2) 3 *(Mgunga-Kimpioka 3, Robson 34, Honeyman 63)*

Carlisle U (1) 1 *(Nadesan 22)* 8112

Sunderland: (4231) Ruiter; Matthews, Ozturk, Baldwin, James; McGeouch, Robson (O'Nien 45); Maguire, Honeyman, McGeady (Diamond 79); Mgunga-Kimpioka (Connelly 87).
Carlisle U: (433) Collin; Miller, Liddle, Parkes, Gillesphey; Slater, Glendon (Adewusi 87), Yates; Campbell, Nadesan (Egan 79), McCarron (Jones 56).
Referee: Ben Toner.

Tuesday, 13 November 2018

Carlisle U (1) 1 *(Sowerby 23)*

Stoke C U21 (1) 1 *(Campbell 34)* 882

Carlisle U: (433) Collin; Miller, Liddle, Gillesphey, Grainger; Sowerby, Glendon (Jones 51), Slater (Bennett 70); Yates, Nadesan, Hope (McCarron 83).
Stoke C U21: (451) Gyollai; Thandi, Soutar, Wara, Tymon; Clucas, Dunwoody, Verlinden (Pemberton 59), Shenton, Jarvis; Campbell.
Stoke C U21 won 5-4 on penalties.
Referee: Martin Coy.

Morecambe (0) 0

Sunderland (0) 1 *(Maja 90)* 2377

Morecambe: (4231) Halstead; Cranston, Yarney, Lavelle, Conlan; Cuvelier (Tutte 57), Kenyon; Thompson (Hedley 76), Mendes Gomes (Piggott 68), Ellison; Oswell.
Sunderland: (4312) Ruiter; Hunter (Taylor 61), Ozturk, Loovens, Oviedo; Bainbridge, Power, Hackett (Neill 90); O'Nien; Diamond (Connelly 65), Maja.
Referee: Paul Marsden.

North Group A	P	W	DW	DL	L	F	A	GD	Pts
Sunderland	3	2	1	0	0	4	1	3	8
Stoke C U21	3	1	1	1	0	3	2	1	6
Carlisle U	3	1	0	1	1	5	6	–1	4
Morecambe	3	0	0	0	3	3	6	–3	0

NORTHERN SECTION GROUP B

Tuesday, 4 September 2018

Rochdale (2) 2 *(Clough 16, Gillam 19)*

Bury (0) 1 *(Lavery 70 (pen))* 1582

Rochdale: (41212) Norman; Randall (Matheson 13), McGahey, McNulty, Done; Morley; Adshead (Hoti 79), Rathbone; Clough; Gillam, Jordan LR Williams (Inman 68).
Bury: (352) Hudson; Aimson, Thompson, Edwards (Telford 46); Miller, Moore, Barjonas (Adams N 65), O'Shea, McFadzean; Omotayo (Styles 46), Lavery.
Referee: Carl Boyeson.

Tuesday, 11 September 2018

Fleetwood T (1) 2 *(Long 33, McAleny 49)*

Leicester C U21 (0) 2 *(Loft 81, 90)* 504

Fleetwood T: (442) Jones P; Jones G, Bolger■, Spurr, Clarke; Biggins, Wallace J (Sheron 69), Grant (Garner 79), Dempsey; Long (Boyle 79), McAleny.
Leicester C U21: (442) Johansson; Simpson, Knight, Johnson, Ramsey (Ughelumba 64); Sheriff (Martis 65), Choudhury, Diabate, Dewsbury-Hall; Loft, Uche (Wright 72).
Leicester C U21 won 7-6 on penalties.
Referee: Peter Wright.

Tuesday, 9 October 2018

Fleetwood T (0) 0

Rochdale (1) 2 *(Jordan LR Williams 16, Cannon 47)* 669

Fleetwood T: (442) Crellin; Jones G, Morgan (Eastham 46), Sheron, Clarke; Mooney (Garner 58), Biggins, Holt, Burns (Rydel 75); Long, Dempsey.
Rochdale: (4141) Moore; Matheson, Hart (Clough 55), McGahey, Ntlhe; Dooley; Cannon, Morley, Adshead (Rafferty 45), Done; Jordan LR Williams.
Referee: Ross Joyce.

Tuesday, 16 October 2018

Bury (1) 2 *(Telford 4, 67)*

Leicester C U21 (1) 1 *(Shade 21)* 454

Bury: (352) Hudson; Edwards, Aimson (Thompson 46), Cooney; Nyaupembe, Danns (Adams N 46), Hulme, Barjonas, McFadzean■; Telford (Brown 68), Adams J.
Leicester C U21: (442) Jakupovic; Ramsey (Ughelumba 74), Knight, Johnson, Elder; Shade (Tee 46), Sheriff (Edwards-John 62), Dewsbury-Hall, Leshabela; Loft, Uche.
Referee: Ollie Yates.

Wednesday, 7 November 2018

Rochdale (2) 2 *(Andrew 6, McNulty 17)*

Leicester C U21 (1) 2 *(Pascanu 28, Loft 66)* 615

Rochdale: (433) Norman; Matheson, M Jordan Williams, McNulty, Hamzat (Hopper 74); Hoti, Perkins, Adshead; Clough, Yonsian (Finnerty 84), Andrew (Wilbraham 46).
Leicester C U21: (451) Johansson (Davies 46); Pascanu, Knight, Johnson, Ughelumba; Martis (Russ 63), Sheriff, Leshabela, Dewsbury-Hall, Wright (Thomas 56); Loft.
Leicester C U21 won 4-3 on penalties.
Referee: Thomas Bramall.

Tuesday, 13 November 2018

Bury (3) 3 *(Telford 21 (pen), Dagnall 32, Adams N 37)*

Fleetwood T (1) 1 *(Dempsey 14)* 554

Bury: (352) Hudson; Edwards, Miller, Stokes (Thompson 65); Cooney, Styles, Danns, Barjonas (Hulme 90), Adams N; Dagnall (Moore 73), Telford.
Fleetwood T: (442) Jones P; Jones G (McAleny 46), Taylor, Bolger, Clarke (Baines 45); Biggins, Dempsey, Sheron, Wallace J; Long (Marney 46), Garner.
Referee: Anthony Backhouse.

North Group B	P	W	DW	DL	L	F	A	GD	Pts
Rochdale	3	2	0	1	0	6	3	3	7
Bury	3	2	0	0	1	6	4	2	6
Leicester C U21	3	0	2	0	1	5	6	–1	4
Fleetwood T	3	0	0	1	2	3	7	–4	1

NORTHERN SECTION GROUP C

Tuesday, 4 September 2018

Macclesfield T (2) 3 *(Blissett 14, Rose 35, 78 (pen))*

Blackpool (1) 3 *(Guy 31, O'Sullivan 90, O'Connor 90)* 639

Macclesfield T: (4231) Taylor; Pearson, Lowe, Grimes, Fitzpatrick; Whitaker, Rose; Welch-Hayes, Napa (Wilson 59), Vincenti (Evans 80); Blissett (Smith 69).
Blackpool: (4321) Mafoumbi; McLaughlin (Nottingham 46), Heneghan, O'Connor, Bola; Feeney (Sinclair-Smith 67), Taylor, O'Sullivan; Pritchard, Guy (Turton 77); Gnanduillet.
Macclesfield T won 5-3 on penalties.
Referee: Christopher Sarginson.

Tuesday, 9 October 2018

Accrington S (1) 4 *(Finley 35, Zanzala 63, Fitzpatrick 82 (og), Barlaser 90)*

Macclesfield T (0) 1 *(Vincenti 58)* 900

Accrington S: (442) Maxted; Platt, Sykes, Richards-Everton, Anderton; Mingoia, Finley (Nolan 82), Barlaser, Mangan (Clark 75); Hall, Zanzala (Scott 90).
Macclesfield T: (442) Taylor; Hodgkiss, Lowe, Kelleher, Fitzpatrick; Marsh (Smith 68), Maycock, Rose, Napa; Wilson (Blissett 59), Arthur (Vincenti 42).
Referee: Thomas Bramall.

Blackpool (1) 1 *(Davies 45)*

WBA U21 (1) 2 *(Azaz 3, Bradley 76)* 717

Blackpool: (442) Mafoumbi; McLaughlin, O'Connor, Daniels, Turton; Nottingham, O'Sullivan, Pritchard (Guy 72), Dodoo; Cullen (Gnanduillet 77), Davies (Taylor 64).
WBA U21: (433) Bond; Meredith, Healy, Howkins, Harmon; Tulloch (Clayton-Phillips 78), Wilding, Bradley (Morton 83); Burke, Leko, Azaz.
Referee: Paul Marsden.

Tuesday, 6 November 2018

Accrington S (0) 2 *(Clark 49, Sykes 90)*

WBA U21 (0) 1 *(Leko 62)* 772

Accrington S: (442) Maxted; Platt (Mingoia 74), Richards-Everton, Sykes, Anderton; Charman, McConville, Brown, Clark; Hall, Conneely.
WBA U21: (343) Bond; Ferguson, Howkins, Healy; Clayton-Phillips, Azaz, Meredith, Harmon (Delaney 90); Morton, Leko, Soule (Tulloch 73).
Referee: Peter Wright.

Tuesday, 13 November 2018

Blackpool (2) 3 *(Dodoo 30, 41, Gnanduillet 67)*

Accrington S (1) 2 *(Hall 17, 90 (pen))* 781

Blackpool: (442) Boney; McLaughlin, Daniels, O'Connor, Bunney; Guy (Pritchard 61), O'Sullivan, Feeney, Dodoo (Davies 61); Gnanduillet (Nottingham 87), Taylor.
Accrington S: (442) Maxted; Platt, Sykes, Richards-Everton, Ihiekwe; Clark, Conneely, Brown, Mingoia (Finley 72); Hall, Charman (Scott 88).
Referee: Ollie Yates.

Macclesfield T (2) 2 *(Stephens 19, Arthur 24)*

WBA U21 (1) 1 *(Tulloch 14)* 411

Macclesfield T: (442) O'Hara; Hodgkiss, Kelleher, Pearson, Fitzpatrick; Durrell (Welch-Hayes 69), Maycock, Rose (Evans 59), Arthur; Wilson, Stephens (Smith 59).
WBA U21: (343) Myhill; Ferguson, Howkins, Healy; Meredith, Barry (Soule 46), Azaz, Harmon; Tulloch, Morton, Clayton-Phillips.
Referee: Robert Lewis.

North Group C	P	W	DW	DL	L	F	A	GD	Pts
Accrington S	3	2	0	0	1	8	5	3	6
Macclesfield T	3	1	1	0	1	6	8	–2	5
Blackpool	3	1	0	1	1	7	7	0	4
WBA U21	3	1	0	0	2	4	5	–1	3

NORTHERN SECTION GROUP D

Tuesday, 28 August 2018

Shrewsbury T (0) 1 *(Angol 51)*

Manchester C U21 (0) 1 *(Zoubdi Touaizi 90 (pen))* 1838

Shrewsbury T: (433) Arnold; Bolton (Haynes 81), Waterfall, Kennedy, Beckles; Loft, Norburn, Barnett; Gnahoua (Colkett 86), Angol (John-Lewis 67), Okenabirhie.
Manchester C U21: (433) Muric; Rosler, Humphreys (Latibeaudiere 66), Ogbeta, Wilson (Dionkou 72); Gomes, Bernabe, Dele-Bashiru; Matondo, Zoubdi Touaizi, Garre (Poveda 67).
Shrewsbury T won 3-1 on penalties.
Referee: Paul Marsden.

Tuesday, 4 September 2018

Tranmere R (2) 3 *(Harris 45, Stockton 45, Mullin 46)*

Crewe Alex (1) 4 *(Porter 20, 85, Nicholls 73, Jones 86)* 2174

Tranmere R: (442) George; Buxton (Caprice 77), Ellis, Monthe, Bakayogo; Cole, Gilmour, Harris, Mottley-Henry (Tollitt 63); Mullin (Jennings 81), Stockton.
Crewe Alex: (442) Garratt; O'Connor (Raynes 42), Hunt, Ray, Ng; Nicholls, Lowery (Wintle 59), Jones, Ainley; Porter, Miller (Kirk 50).
Referee: Graham Salisbury.

Tuesday, 25 September 2018

Crewe Alex (0) 1 *(Nicholls 51)*

Manchester C U21 (2) 4 *(Dele-Bashiru 2, Gonzalez 22, Richards 78 (pen), Ogunby 90)* 810

Crewe Alex: (442) Garratt; Whelan, Ray, Ng, O'Connor; Ainley (Nicholls 46), Lowery (Jones 76), Wintle, Finney; Miller (Porter 77), Bowery.
Manchester C U21: (433) Scott; Dionkou, Rosler, Ogbeta, Frimpong (Harwood-Bellis 81); Nmecha (Richards 60), Pozo, Dele-Bashiru; Matondo, Gonzalez (Ogunby 73), Poveda.
Referee: Thomas Bramall.

Tuesday, 9 October 2018

Shrewsbury T (3) 6 *(John-Lewis 11, Docherty 18, Beckles 23, Okenabirhie 56, 74, 90)*

Tranmere R (0) 0 1379

Shrewsbury T: (532) Arnold; Emmanuel (Sears 62), Bolton, Kennedy, Beckles, Haynes; Norburn (Holloway 75), Docherty, Laurent (Barnett 62); John-Lewis, Okenabirhie.
Tranmere R: (4411) Wharton; Caprice (Jennings 76), Sutton, Ellis, Buxton (Monthe 68); Tollitt (Gilmour 46), Williams, Harris, Mottley-Henry; Cole; Akammadu.
Referee: Peter Wright.

Tuesday, 30 October 2018

Tranmere R (0) 0

Manchester C U21 (0) 1 *(Matondo 49)* 747

Tranmere R: (442) George; Buxton (Caprice 61), Ellis, Sutton, Bakayogo; Mottley-Henry, Gilmour, Harris, Tollitt; Smith (Williams 61), Akammadu (Gumbs 81).
Manchester C U21: (433) Grimshaw; Dionkou, Rosler, Humphreys, Ogbeta; Nmecha (Dele-Bashiru 75), Pozo, Bernabe (Richards 86); Matondo, Zoubdi Touaizi, Poveda (Garre 90).
Referee: Paul Marsden.

Tuesday, 13 November 2018

Crewe Alex (0) 1 *(Bowery 79)*

Shrewsbury T (1) 2 *(Eisa 20, Gilliead 63)* 823

Crewe Alex: (433) Garratt; Whelan, Ray, O'Connor (Wintle 58), Pickering; Jones, Nolan, Ng; Bowery, Miller, Nicholls (Ainley 62).
Shrewsbury T: (442) Coleman; Sears, Kennedy, Bolton, Haynes; Eisa (Okenabirhie 90), Loft, Colkett (Rowland 67), Gilliead; John-Lewis, Angol (Gnahoua 76).
Referee: Michael Salisbury.

North Group D	P	W	DW	DL	L	F	A	GD	Pts
Shrewsbury T	3	2	1	0	0	9	2	7	8
Manchester C U21	3	2	0	1	0	6	2	4	7
Crewe Alex	3	1	0	0	2	6	9	–3	3
Tranmere R	3	0	0	0	3	3	11	–8	0

NORTHERN SECTION GROUP E

Tuesday, 4 September 2018

Burton Alb (0) 1 *(Harness 89)*

Walsall (2) 2 *(Morris 9, Gordon 28)* 724

Burton Alb: (433) Campbell; Flannigan (Hodge 59), McFadzean, Turner, Hutchinson; Sbarra, Allen, Hesketh; Akins, Cole (Harness 72), Miller (Sordell 59).
Walsall: (442) Roberts; Devlin, Johnson (Cook 86), Fitzwater, Wilson; Kouhyar, Sangha, Ronan, Morris (Cockerill-Mollett 72); Parker (Hayles-Docherty 72), Gordon.
Referee: Robert Lewis.

Tuesday, 9 October 2018

Port Vale (0) 1 *(Miller 65)*

Burton Alb (0) 0 601

Port Vale: (442) Hornby; Clark, Smith, Rawlinson, Vassell; Worrall (Miller 62), Hardcastle, Joyce, Pugh; Dodds, Kanu.
Burton Alb: (433) Campbell; Akins, Turner, McFadzean, McCrory; Fox, Sbarra (Harness 67), Fraser (Hesketh 77); Sordell (Allen 63), Cole, Miller.
Referee: Robert Lewis.

Walsall (2) 3 *(Fitzwater 26, Kouhyar 31, Cook 89)*

Middlesbrough U21 (0) 1 *(Ward 67)* 702

Walsall: (442) Dunn; Wilson, Fitzwater, Johnson, Leahy; Morris, Ronan, Bates, Kouhyar; Cook, Gordon (Ismail 78).
Middlesbrough U21: (451) Lonergan; Dodds, Hood, Stubbs, Spence D; Ward, Malley, Wing, Liddle, Chapman (Spence K 61); O'Neill.
Referee: John Busby.

Tuesday, 16 October 2018

Port Vale (1) 2 *(Miller 6, Rawlinson 66)*

Middlesbrough U21 (0) 0 554

Port Vale: (532) Hornby; Gibbons (Pugh 46), Rawlinson (Kay 81), Smith, Vassell, Clark; Joyce, Conlon, Hardcastle (Worrall 64); Dodds, Miller.
Middlesbrough U21: (4231) Hemming; Dodds, Stubbs, Guru, Robinson; Liddle (Watts 90), Spence K; Spence D, Malley (Stephenson 76), Ward; O'Neill.
Referee: Matthew Donohue.

Wednesday, 7 November 2018

Burton Alb (0) 0

Middlesbrough U21 (0) 1 *(Hackney 87)* 202

Burton Alb: (433) Evtimov; Miller (Hesketh 82), Buxton, McCrory, Wallace; Sbarra, Fox, Hodge (Boyce 80); Harness, Sordell, Templeton (Allen 67).
Middlesbrough U21: (442) Lonergan; Spence D, Stubbs, Guru, Robinson; Malley, Spence K (Hackney 84), Liddle, Walker (Brahimi 69); Ward, O'Neill.
Referee: Jeremy Simpson.

Tuesday, 13 November 2018

Walsall (1) 1 *(Johnson 45)*

Port Vale (1) 2 *(Quigley 4, Pugh 65)* 878

Walsall: (442) Dunn; Wilson, Fitzwater, Johnson■, Leahy (Devlin 46); Ismail (Kinsella 57), Ronan, Bates, Morris; Ferrier, Gordon (Parker 75).
Port Vale: (433) Hornby; Gibbons, Rawlinson, Vassell, Montano; Hardcastle, Kay (Daniels 65), Conlon (Pugh 46); Kanu (Agho 83), Quigley, Dodds.
Referee: Christopher Sarginson.

North Group E	P	W	DW	DL	L	F	A	GD	Pts
Port Vale	3	3	0	0	0	5	1	4	9
Walsall	3	2	0	0	1	6	4	2	6
Middlesbrough U21	3	1	0	0	2	2	5	–3	3
Burton Alb	3	0	0	0	3	1	4	–3	0

NORTHERN SECTION GROUP F

Tuesday, 4 September 2018

Oldham Ath (1) 1 *(Surridge 31)*

Barnsley (1) 2 *(Adeboyejo 44, Moncur 82)* 1786

Oldham Ath: (4411) de la Paz; Haymer, Edmundson, Graham, Taylor; Lang (Gardner 74), Maouche, Missilou (Baxter 58), Branger; Benteke; Surridge (O'Grady 61).
Barnsley: (433) Walton; Brown, Lindsay (Pinnock 46), Jackson, Williams B; Bahre (Moncur 73), Bird, McGeehan; Williams J, Adeboyejo, Isgrove (Thiam 68).
Referee: Sebastian Stockbridge.

Tuesday, 25 September 2018

Bradford C (0) 1 *(Miller 90)*

Everton U21 (0) 1 *(Sambou 79)* 902

Bradford C: (541) O'Donnell; Scannell (Seedorf 58), O'Connor A, Knight-Percival, Poppler-Isherwood (Payne 81), Wood; Gibson, O'Brien J (Goldthorp 55), O'Brien L, Ball; Miller.
Everton U21: (4411) Virginia; Charsley, Browning, Foulds, Galloway; Bowler (Mampala 75), Markelo, Adeniran, Broadhead (Lavery 89); Evans■; Hornby (Sambou 64).
Bradford C won 6-5 on penalties.
Referee: Paul Marsden.

Tuesday, 9 October 2018

Bradford C (0) 1 *(Brunker 49)*

Oldham Ath (2) 4 *(Lang 10, Maouche 26, Surridge 57, 77)* 1015

Bradford C: (3412) O'Donnell; Poppler-Isherwood, Knight-Percival, Staunton; Seedorf (Riley 77), Payne, Goldthorp, Gibson; Wright (Ellington 86); Ball (Jones 82), Brunker.
Oldham Ath: (4411) de la Paz; Haymer, Edmundson, Lyden (Baxter 46), Taylor (Hunt 30); Lang, Maouche, Clarke, Gardner (Missilou 71); O'Grady; Surridge.
Referee: Sebastian Stockbridge.

Tuesday, 30 October 2018

Oldham Ath (0) 3 *(Clarke 53, Miller 57, Benteke 79)*

Everton U21 (2) 2 *(Markelo 6, Lavery 24)* 1004

Oldham Ath: (442) Iversen; Haymer, Clarke, Edmundson, Taylor; Dummigan, Missilou, Maouche (Gardner 46), Nepomuceno; Lang (Benteke 46), Miller (O'Grady 90).
Everton U21: (442) Hewelt; John, Browning, Feeney, Charsley; Gordon (Bowler 58), Markelo (Simms 75), Adeniran, Broadhead; Sambou, Lavery (Kiersey 58).
Referee: Darren Drysdale.

Tuesday, 6 November 2018

Barnsley (1) 1 *(Hedges 40)*

Everton U21 (0) 1 *(Sambou 53)* 2300

Barnsley: (442) Davies; Williams J, Jackson, Fryers, Williams B; Hedges (Thiam 60), Bird, Moncur, Brown; Woodrow (Isgrove 46), Adeboyejo (Bahre 76).
Everton U21: (442) Hilton; Ouzounidis, Browning, Feeney, Astley; Bowler, Markelo (Mathis 90), Adeniran, Kiersey; Sambou, Mampala (Lavery 86).
Barnsley won 4-2 on penalties.
Referee: Matthew Donohue.

Tuesday, 13 November 2018

Barnsley (1) 2 *(Moncur 28, 64)*

Bradford C (1) 1 *(Ball 8)* 2925

Barnsley: (442) Walton; Williams J, Jackson■, Pinillos, Hedges; Bird, Bahre, Williams B, Moncur (Smith 79); Adeboyejo (Helliwell 87), Brown (Isgrove 73).
Bradford C: (433) O'Donnell; Chicksen, O'Connor A, Devine, Knight-Percival; O'Brien J (O'Brien L 46), Payne, Wright; Seedorf (Wood 55), Brunker (Miller 77), Ball.
Referee: Carl Boyeson.

North Group F	P	W	DW	DL	L	F	A	GD	Pts
Barnsley	3	2	1	0	0	5	3	2	8
Oldham Ath	3	2	0	0	1	8	5	3	6
Everton U21	3	0	0	2	1	4	5	–1	2
Bradford C	3	0	1	0	2	3	7	–4	2

NORTHERN SECTION GROUP G

Tuesday, 4 September 2018

Doncaster R (1) 1 *(Marquis 45)*

Newcastle U U21 (1) 3 *(Allan 14, Roberts 65, Sorensen 86)* 1544

Doncaster R: (433) Marosi; Lund (Mason 32), Anderson T, Butler, Blair; Kane, Rowe (Horton 17), Ben Khemis; Beestin (May 66), Marquis, Wilks.
Newcastle U U21: (4231) Harker; Sterry, Watts, O'Connor, Gibson (Cass 79); Bailey, Nunez-Cumbreras (Wilson 61); Roberts, Longstaff S, Allan (Longstaff M 74); Sorensen.
Referee: Matthew Donohue.

Grimsby T (0) 2 *(Rose M 69 (pen), Hessenthaler 88)*

Notts Co (1) 1 *(Alessandra 12)* 746

Grimsby T: (442) Russell; Hendrie, Whitmore, Famewo, Fox; Thomas, Clifton, Rose M, Vernam (Rose A 84); Robles (Hessenthaler 59), Hooper (Cook 73).
Notts Co: (442) Fitzsimons; Oxlade-Chamberlain, Ward, Brisley, Kellett; Boldewijn, Husin (Hewitt 66), Alessandra, Milsom; Stead, Hemmings (Dennis 61).
Referee: Tom Nield.

Tuesday, 9 October 2018

Doncaster R (1) 2 *(May 23, 57 (pen))*

Grimsby T (0) 0 1420

Doncaster R: (433) Lawlor; Lund, Anderson T, Blaney (Prior 72), Horton; Kane, Anderson J, Crawford; Taylor, May (Morris 84), Beestin (Longbottom 61).
Grimsby T: (4231) Russell; Hall-Johnson, Hessenthaler, Whitmore, Dixon; Welsh, Pringle; Woolford, Vernam (Robles 68), Hooper (Buckley 86); Rose A (Rose M 77).
Referee: Michael Salisbury.

Notts Co (0) 0

Newcastle U U21 (1) 2 *(Roberts 10 (pen), Sorensen 56)* 1139

Notts Co: (4231) Pindroch; Osbourne, Kennedy-Williams (Etete 76), Patching (Campbell 62), Jones; Brisley, Vaughan (Howes 89); Thomas, Husin, Kellett; Dennis.
Newcastle U U21: (442) Harker; Watts, O'Connor, Cass, Gibson; Longstaff S, Roberts, Bailey, Longstaff M (Sangare 85); Sorensen (Wilson 63), Allan (Nunez-Cumbreras 89).
Referee: Alan Young.

Tuesday, 13 November 2018

Grimsby T (1) 2 *(Hooper 9, Cook 53)*

Newcastle U U21 (2) 3 *(Roberts 19, Sorensen 26, Longstaff M 77)* 547

Grimsby T: (442) Russell; Hall-Johnson (Hendrie 86), Whitmore, Dixon, Fox; Hooper, Woolford, Welsh, Cook; Cardwell (Wright 78), Rose A (Robles 65).
Newcastle U U21: (451) Harker; Longstaff M, Watts, O'Connor, Gibson; Allan (Nunez-Cumbreras 86), Bailey, Roberts, Longstaff S, Longelo (Wilson 66); Sorensen (Toure 69).
Referee: Thomas Bramall.

Wednesday, 14 November 2018

Notts Co (3) 4 *(Dennis 15, 40, 63 (pen), Boldewijn 26)*

Doncaster R (0) 2 *(May 50, 70)* 915

Notts Co: (442) Fitzsimons; Hawkridge, Duffy, Brisley, Jones; Patching (Crawford 74), Hewitt, Milsom (Evina 81), Thomas; Boldewijn (Kellett 64), Dennis.
Doncaster R: (433) Lawlor; Cummings (Mason 46), Blaney, Anderson T, Amos; Blair, Anderson J (Wilks 46), Crawford; Longbottom, May, Beestin.
Referee: Andy Haines.

North Group G	P	W	DW	DL	L	F	A	GD	Pts
Newcastle U U21	3	3	0	0	0	8	3	5	9
Notts Co	3	1	0	0	2	5	6	−1	3
Doncaster R	3	1	0	0	2	5	7	−2	3
Grimsby T	3	1	0	0	2	4	6	−2	3

NORTHERN SECTION GROUP H

Tuesday, 4 September 2018

Lincoln C (1) 1 *(Rhead 6)*

Mansfield T (1) 2 *(Butcher 8, Walker 72)* 4205

Lincoln C: (433) Slocombe; Gordon, Bostwick (McCombe 80), Crookes, Toffolo; Luque (O'Connor■ 80), McCartan, Chapman; Mensah (Andrade 67), Rhead, Anderson.
Mansfield T: (352) Logan; White, Preston, Gibbens; Atkinson, MacDonald, Elsnik, Butcher, Benning; Rose (Hamilton 71), Davies (Walker 72).
Referee: Ross Joyce.

Scunthorpe U (0) 0

Wolverhampton W U21 (0) 0 874

Scunthorpe U: (4411) Flatt; Clarke (Perch 46), Goode, Burgess, Borthwick-Jackson; Colclough, Horsfield, Lund, Morris (Hornshaw 77); Dales; Humphrys (Wootton 74).
Wolverhampton W U21: (343) Norris; Molberg, Kilman, John; Buur, Diallo, Goncalves, Giles; Harris-Sealy (Paulinho 87), Ashley-Seal, Ennis.
Scunthorpe U won 4-2 on penalties.
Referee: Thomas Bramall.

Tuesday, 9 October 2018

Mansfield T (1) 2 *(Mellis 4, Benning 47)*

Wolverhampton W U21 (0) 1 *(Goncalves 75)* 1112

Mansfield T: (352) Logan; White, Preston, Pearce; Atkinson, Mellis, Butcher (Khan 79), Elsnik, Benning; Sterling-James (Hamilton 60), Graham (Rose 65).
Wolverhampton W U21: (343) Norris; Iorfa, Kilman, John; Buur, Diallo, Paulinho (Samuels 80), Giles; Goncalves, Ashley-Seal, Ennis.
Referee: Tom Nield.

Scunthorpe U (0) 1 *(Colclough 56)*

Lincoln C (0) 1 *(Anderson 84)* 1878

Scunthorpe U: (4231) Flatt; Sutton, McArdle, Goode, Butroid; Perch, Lund; Colclough (Borthwick-Jackson 68), Lewis (Novak 73), Dales; Humphrys.
Lincoln C: (442) Slocombe; Gordon, Wilson■, Wharton, Crookes; Mensah (Andrade 69), Chapman (Frecklington 90), Pett, Anderson, Green (Akinde 69), Rhead.
Lincoln C won 3-1 on penalties.
Referee: Martin Coy.

Tuesday, 6 November 2018

Lincoln C (2) 2 *(Green 23, 42)*

Wolverhampton W U21 (2) 2 *(Ashley-Seal 39, Giles 45)* 2723

Lincoln C: (442) Slocombe; Gordon, Shackell (Toffolo 46), Wharton, Crookes; Anderson (Andrade 46), Pett, Chapman, Mensah; Rhead, Green (Akinde 81).
Wolverhampton W U21: (3412) Norris; Molberg, Kilman (Buur 33), John; Iorfa, Watt, Diallo, Giles; Goncalves; Ashley-Seal, Ennis.
Wolverhampton W U21 won 5-4 on penalties.
Referee: Trevor Kettle.

Tuesday, 13 November 2018

Mansfield T (1) 3 *(Blake 21, Butcher 53, Elsnik 90)*

Scunthorpe U (0) 2 *(El-Mhanni 73, Dales 89)* 928

Mansfield T: (532) Logan; Blake (Benning 52), Atkinson, Sweeney (Preston 46), Gibbens, Law; Smith, Butcher, Elsnik; Graham, Rose (Fielding 87).
Scunthorpe U: (442) Flatt; Horsfield, McArdle, Burgess, Butroid, El-Mhanni, Ojo, Lewis (Pugh 86), Dales; Wootton, Humphrys.
Referee: Ross Joyce.

North Group H	P	W	DW	DL	L	F	A	GD	Pts
Mansfield T	3	3	0	0	0	7	4	3	9
Lincoln C	3	0	1	1	1	4	5	−1	3
Scunthorpe U	3	0	1	1	1	3	4	−1	3
Wolverhampton W U21	3	0	1	1	1	3	4	−1	3

SOUTHERN SECTION GROUP A

Tuesday, 4 September 2018

Crawley T (0) 1 *(N'Gala 59)*

Tottenham H U21 (0) 1 *(Harrison 49)* 1403

Crawley T: (442) Mersin; Young, McNerney, N'Gala, Maguire; Allarakhia (Palmer 80), Bulman (Sesay 72), Randall, Nathaniel-George (Galach 46); Poleon, Camara.
Tottenham H U21: (3421) Austin; Walcott, Dinzeyi, Binks; Marsh, Brown, Maghoma, Bowden; Roles, Oakley-Boothe; Harrison (Parrott 78).
Crawley T won 5-3 on penalties.
Referee: Tim Robinson.

Portsmouth (2) 4 *(Clarke 41, Close 43, Pitman B 55 (pen), Wheeler 90)*

Gillingham (0) 0 2011

Portsmouth: (4231) McGee; Thompson N, Clarke, Burgess, Haunstrup; Rose, Close; Wheeler, May (Mason 62), Green; Pitman B.
Gillingham: (433) Hadler; O'Neill, Lacey (Scarlett 80), Ogilvie, Simpson; Rees (Chapman 62), Stevenson, Oldaker; List (Nash 65), Wilkinson, Nasseri.
Referee: Alan Young.

Tuesday, 9 October 2018

Crawley T (0) 0

Portsmouth (1) 1 *(Donohue 37)* 1268

Crawley T: (4411) Mersin; Francomb, McNerney, Vincelot, Doherty; Galach (Maguire 58), Bulman, Sesay, Allarakhia; Poleon; Camara (Randall 61).
Portsmouth: (4231) McGee; Mnoga (Naylor 65), Burgess, Walkes, Haunstrup; Close, Rose; Evans (Clarke 46), Dennis, Donohue (Thompson B 64); Mason.
Referee: Gavin Ward.

Gillingham (0) 0

Tottenham H U21 (1) 4 *(Roles 44, Maghoma 57, Brown 82, Duncan 90 (pen))* 308

Gillingham: (41212) Hadler; O'Neill, Ehmer, Tucker, Garmston; Parrett (Reilly 46); Chapman (Byrne 46), Rees; Nasseri; Eaves, List (Hanlan 66).
Tottenham H U21: (532) Whiteman; Hinds (Duncan 86), Marsh, Tanganga, Dinzeyi (Binks 83), Brown; Bowden, Skipp, Maghoma; Roles (Bennett 77), Richards.
Referee: Antony Coggins.

Tuesday, 13 November 2018

Gillingham (0) 2 *(List 57, Stevenson 86)*

Crawley T (1) 1 *(Poleon 18)* 473

Gillingham: (41212) Hadler; Simpson, Lacey, Ogilvie, Garmston; Parrett; Rees, Bingham (Chapman 75); Nasseri (Woods 79); List (Stevenson 65), M'Bo.
Crawley T: (532) Mersin; Francomb, N'Gala, McNerney, Vincelot, Doherty; Allarakhia (Randall 80), Bulman, Nathaniel-George; Grego-Cox, Poleon (Sesay 66).
Referee: Darren Drysdale.

Portsmouth (0) 3 *(Green 50, Evans 69, Hawkins 81)*

Tottenham H U21 (1) 2 *(Patterson 20, White 90)* 3138

Portsmouth: (4231) McGee; Mnoga (Evans 66), Walkes, Burgess, Haunstrup; Close, Rose; Green (Clarke 65), Dennis, Wheeler; Lethbridge (Hawkins 66).
Tottenham H U21: (4231) Whiteman; Lyons-Foster, Marsh, Tanganga, Brown; Bowden (Shashoua 89), White; Duncan (Richards 75), Oakley-Boothe (Parrott 86), Patterson; Sterling.
Referee: Nicholas Kinseley.

South Group A	P	W	DW	DL	L	F	A	GD	Pts
Portsmouth	3	3	0	0	0	8	2	6	9
Tottenham H U21	3	1	0	1	1	7	4	3	4
Gillingham	3	1	0	0	2	2	9	–7	3
Crawley T	3	0	1	0	2	2	4	–2	2

SOUTHERN SECTION GROUP B

Tuesday, 4 September 2018

Colchester U (0) 0

Southampton U21 (1) 2 *(Barnes 26, Obafemi 90)* 532

Colchester U: (4141) Barnes D; Vincent-Young, Eastman, Rooney, Barnes A; Wright; Senior, Collins (Nouble 79), Szmodics (Gondoh 46), Dickenson (Clampin 64); Mandron.
Southampton U21: (4231) Lewis; Johnson, O'Driscoll, O'Connor, Valery; Rowthorn, Slattery; Tella (Afolabi 86), Smallbone, Barnes; Obafemi.
Referee: Charles Breakspear.

Southend U (0) 3 *(McCoulsky 55, 64, Hutchinson 83)*

Cambridge U (0) 1 *(Lambe 52)* 1421

Southend U: (442) Bishop; Bwomono, White, Moore, Hendrie; McLaughlin (Ba 86), Batlokwa, Klass, Bunn (Gard 78); McCoulsky, Cox (Hutchinson 82).
Cambridge U: (4411) Mitov; Davies, Taft, Darling, Taylor (Carroll 46); Lambe, O'Neil, Maris (Lewis 46), Osadebe (Amoo 75); Brown; Azeez.
Referee: Gavin Ward.

Tuesday, 9 October 2018

Cambridge U (2) 4 *(Azeez 16 (pen), 37, 88, Brown 50)*

Southampton U21 (0) 0 469

Cambridge U: (4231) Iron; Halliday (Davies 46), Taft, Darling, Taylor; Deegan, Lewis (O'Neil 58); Amoo (Knowles 73), Brown, Osadebe; Azeez.
Southampton U21: (4231) Lewis; Valery, O'Connor, O'Driscoll, Ramsey; Rowthorn, Hamblin; Tella (Norton 75), Smallbone, Johnson; Barnes.
Referee: Trevor Kettle.

Colchester U (1) 2 *(Kent 39, Collins 49)*

Southend U (0) 0 1516

Colchester U: (3421) Gilmartin; Eastman, Kent, Prosser; Jackson (Vincent-Young 46), Comley, Wright, Dickenson; Szmodics (Senior 59), Collins; Mandron (Norris 84).
Southend U: (442) Bishop; Bwomono, Dieng, Moore, Hendrie; Hutchinson (Yearwood 58), Klass, Batlokwa (Gard 81), McLaughlin; McCoulsky, Robinson (Kightly 58).
Referee: Roger East.

Tuesday, 13 November 2018

Cambridge U (1) 3 *(Azeez 32, 81, Osadebe 90)*

Colchester U (0) 1 *(Pell 90)* 598

Cambridge U: (4132) Mitov; Davies (Halliday 71), John, Darling, Carroll; O'Neil (Maris 46); Osadebe, Lewis, Dunk (Amoo 46); Azeez, Brown.
Colchester U: (3421) Barnes D; Kensadale (Jackson 60), Prosser, Kent; Vincent-Young (Gondoh 71), Pell, Wright, Dickenson; Szmodics (Senior 64), Mandron; Collins.
Referee: Antony Coggins.

Wednesday, 14 November 2018

Southend U (3) 3 *(Bunn 12, Kyprianou 18, Bwomono 24)*

Southampton U21 (0) 0 983

Southend U: (4411) Bishop; Bwomono, White, Moore, Kyprianou; McLaughlin, Hyam (Dieng 73), Yearwood (Demetriou 83), Kightly; Bunn (Kelman 85); McCoulsky.
Southampton U21: (442) Lewis; Valery, Klarer (Ramsey 46), O'Driscoll, Johnson; Smallbone, Slattery, O'Connor, Tella (Hamblin 46); Afolabi, Barnes.
Referee: John Busby.

South Group B	P	W	DW	DL	L	F	A	GD	Pts
Cambridge U	3	2	0	0	1	8	4	4	6
Southend U	3	2	0	0	1	6	3	3	6
Colchester U	3	1	0	0	2	3	4	–1	3
Southampton U21	3	1	0	0	2	2	7	–5	3

SOUTHERN SECTION GROUP C

Tuesday, 7 August 2018

Swindon T (0) 0

Chelsea U21 (2) 4 *(Brown 16, 58, Musonda 30 (pen), Ugbo 89)* 1569

Swindon T: (433) McCormick; Knoyle (Dunne 20), Nelson, Conroy, Romanski; McGlashan (Young 67), McCourt, Diagouraga; Iandolo, Twine, Adebayo.
Chelsea U21: (352) Cumming; Dabo, Colley, Guehi; McEachran (Uwakwe 83), Lamptey, Familio-Castillo, Musonda, McCormick; Ugbo, Brown (Redan 64).
Referee: Brett Huxtable.

Tuesday, 11 September 2018

Swindon T (0) 1 *(Doughty 77 (pen))*

Newport Co (0) 0 1301

Swindon T: (4231) McCormick; Knoyle, Nelson, Woolfenden, Romanski; Dunne, Diagouraga; McGlashan, Anderson (Twine 71), Iandolo (Doughty 72); Adebayo (Alzate 79).
Newport Co: (352) Townsend; Butler, Bennett, O'Brien; Hornby-Forbes, Cooper, Marsh-Brown, Willmott (Bakinson 69), Pring; Matt (Sheehan 69), Semenyo.
Referee: Antony Coggins.

Tuesday, 25 September 2018

Newport Co (1) 3 *(Matt 36, 47, Semenyo 90)*

Chelsea U21 (0) 0 1525

Newport Co: (4231) Townsend; Hornby-Forbes, O'Brien, Foulston (Semenyo 77), Pring; Cooper, Sheehan; Willmott, Collins (Butler 65), Harris; Matt (Amond 88).
Chelsea U21: (3142) Cumming; Grant, Colley, Guehi; McEachran; Nartey, Uwakwe, Gilmour (Gallagher 72), Maatsen (Lamptey 67); Taylor-Crossdale (Brown 64), Redan.
Referee: Kevin Johnson.

Tuesday, 9 October 2018

Plymouth Arg (0) 0

Swindon T (2) 3 *(Richards 16, Anderson 38, Woolery 82)* 1906

Plymouth Arg: (433) Letheren; Moore, Edwards, Grant P, Smith-Brown (Dyson 65); Sarcevic, Ness, Grant C; Grant J (Canavan 65), Fletcher, Lameiras (Wylde 46).
Swindon T: (352) McCormick; Woolfenden, Conroy, Romanski; Knoyle, McCourt, Anderson, Smith, Iandolo; Richards (Woolery 62), Twine.
Referee: Brett Huxtable.

Tuesday, 30 October 2018

Plymouth Arg (0) 0

Chelsea U21 (2) 5 *(Brown 20, Songo'o 37 (og), Taylor-Crossdale 74, Anjorin 86, Redan 89)* 1504

Plymouth Arg: (433) Cooper; Moore, Songo'o, Canavan, Smith-Brown; Sarcevic (Carey 74), Fox (Grant P 60), Ness (Grant C 69); Jephcott, Fletcher, Lameiras.
Chelsea U21: (352) Cumming; Grant, Colley, Nartey; Lamptey, Gallagher, McEachran (Anjorin 71), Gilmour, Fanilia-Castilo; Taylor-Crossdale (Guehi 77), Brown (Redan 60).
Referee: Antony Coggins.

Tuesday, 13 November 2018

Newport Co (2) 2 *(Semenyo 35, Harris 45)*

Plymouth Arg (0) 0 962

Newport Co: (4231) Townsend; Pipe, Franks, O'Brien, Butler; Bakinson (Hillman 77), Bennett (Cooper 28); Willmott (Taylor 85), Sheehan, Semenyo; Harris.
Plymouth Arg: (442) Letheren; Law, Randell, Grant P, Smith-Brown; Ainsworth (Fletcher 78), Peck, O'Keefe (Purrington 81), Wylde; Taylor (Dyson 74), Battle.
Referee: Brett Huxtable.

South Group C	P	W	DW	DL	L	F	A	GD	Pts
Chelsea U21	3	2	0	0	1	9	3	6	6
Newport Co	3	2	0	0	1	5	1	4	6
Swindon T	3	2	0	0	1	4	4	0	6
Plymouth Arg	3	0	0	0	3	0	10	–10	0

SOUTHERN SECTION GROUP D

Tuesday, 4 September 2018

Yeovil T (0) 0

Exeter C (0) 0 1518

Yeovil T: (442) Baxter; Mugabi, Warren, Sowunmi, Dickinson; Green (Jaiyesimi 65), Gray, Santos (Pattison 52), Patrick; Arquin, Olomola.
Exeter C: (433) Hamon; Oates, Croll, O'Shea, Woodman; Tillson, Collins, Boateng (Ogbene 56); Jay, Stockley (Sparkes 66), Martin L (Abrahams 77).
Exeter C won 5-2 on penalties.
Referee: Trevor Kettle.

Tuesday, 18 September 2018

Bristol R (0) 2 *(Jakubiak 57, Lockyer 81)*

West Ham U U21 (0) 0 1021

Bristol R: (442) Bonham; Leadbitter (Partington 46), Lockyer, Broadbent, Kelly; Matthews (Baghdadi 90), Upson, Clarke O, Sinclair (Russe 58); Payne, Jakubiak.
West Ham U U21: (4231) Anang; Johnson, Alese, Oxford, Akinola; Coventry, Lewis (Parkes 83); Diangana, Costa Da Rosa (Adarkwa 61), Powell; Xande Silva.
Referee: Craig Hicks.

Tuesday, 25 September 2018

Exeter C (2) 2 *(Forte 20, 30)*

West Ham U U21 (0) 0 1114

Exeter C: (433) Hamon; Sweeney (Croll 46), O'Shea, Dean, Oates (Sparkes 49); Martin L (Dodd 59), Collins, Ogbene; Jay, Forte, Abrahams.
West Ham U U21: (541) Trott; Johnson, Akinola, Oxford, Alese, Barrett (Hannam 54); Emmanuel, Costa Da Rosa (Nebyla 60), Lewis, Scully (Spyrides 69); Adarkwa.
Referee: Brett Huxtable.

Tuesday, 9 October 2018

Bristol R (0) 2 *(Jakubiak 50, Rodman 85)*

Yeovil T (0) 0 1179

Bristol R: (433) Bonham; Leadbitter, Clarke J, Broadbent, Kelly; Bennett (Nichols 76), Upson, Sercombe; Matthews (Russe 86), Jakubiak (Moore 88), Rodman.
Yeovil T: (442) Baxter; James, Mugabi, Donnellan, Dickinson; Green (Rogers 87), Gray, Pattison, Browne (Patrick 46); Fisher (Arquin 74), Olomola.
Referee: Keith Stroud.

Tuesday, 6 November 2018

Yeovil T (1) 4 *(Johnson 11 (og), Akinola 48 (og), James 65, Mahmutovic 83)*

West Ham U U21 (0) 0 720

Yeovil T: (442) Nelson; James, Donnellan, Mahmutovic, Ojo; Gray, Pattison (Rogers 61), Santos, Patrick; Olomola (McDonald 73), Arquin (Zoko 61).
West Ham U U21: (4411) Trott; Johnson, Alese (Nebyla 75), Pask, Akinola; Kemp, Makasi, Lewis (Ngakia 66), Hector-Ingram (Emmanuel 58); Chesters; Adarkwa.
Referee: Brett Huxtable.

Tuesday, 13 November 2018

Exeter C (0) 2 *(Forte 50, Randall 81)*

Bristol R (0) 0 873

Exeter C: (442) Hamon; Oates, Martin A, O'Shea, Croll (Kite 65); Ogbene (Key 60), Dean, Collins, Jay; Forte (Randall 70), Abrahams.
Bristol R: (442) Smith; Partington, Martin, Menayese, Kelly (Holmes-Dennis 61); Walker (Hargreaves 52), Jones (Widdrington 61), Russe, Matthews; Reilly, Jakubiak.
Referee: Kevin Johnson.

South Group D	P	W	DW	DL	L	F	A	GD	Pts
Exeter C	3	2	1	0	0	4	0	4	8
Bristol R	3	2	0	0	1	4	2	2	6
Yeovil T	3	1	0	1	1	4	2	2	4
West Ham U U21	3	0	0	0	3	0	8	–8	0

SOUTHERN SECTION GROUP E

Tuesday, 4 September 2018

Forest Green R (1) 4 *(Grubb 14, Campbell 48, Williams 85, Pearce 90)*

Cheltenham T (0) 0 1074

Forest Green R: (4231) Montgomery; Shephard (Collins 46), Digby, McGinley, Archibald; Winchester (Brown 64), Worthington; Grubb, Williams, Campbell; Morris (Pearce 69).
Cheltenham T: (442) Lovett; Forster, Mullins, Boyle, Field; Dawson (Atangana 46), Jones (Lumbombo Kalala 79), Clements, Broom; Mooney, Duku (Barnett 57).
Referee: Lee Swabey.

Wednesday, 12 September 2018

Coventry C (0) 0

Arsenal U21 (1) 3 *(Smith-Rowe 4, Nketiah 77, Willock 90)* 2375

Coventry C: (4231) O'Brien; Sterling (Williams 61), Davies, Thompson, Camwell; Kelly (Westbrooke 72), Ogogo; Allassani (Stedman 87), Andreu, Hiwula; Bakayoko.
Arsenal U21: (4231) Iliev; Olowu (Omole 46), Medley, Pleguezuelo (Saka 88), Bola; Gilmour, Willock; Olayinka, Burton (Nketiah 72), Smith-Rowe; John-Jules.
Referee: John Busby.

Tuesday, 9 October 2018

Coventry C (1) 1 *(Hiwula 3)*

Forest Green R (0) 1 *(Pearce 69)* 1341

Coventry C: (4411) O'Brien; Thompson, Williams, Hyam, Mason (Camwell 56); Hiwula, Kelly, Ogogo, Hickman (Burroughs 62); Andreu (Walters 82); Bakayoko.
Forest Green R: (3511) Montgomery; Rawson, Digby (Gunning 56), McGinley; Williams, James (Pearce 57), Collins, Worthington, Archibald; Campbell (Grubb 76); Morris.
Coventry C won 4-2 on penalties.
Referee: Darren Drysdale.

Tuesday, 30 October 2018

Cheltenham T (2) 6 *(Clements 8, Boyle 32, Maddox 48, 51, Mooney 84, Broom 90)*

Arsenal U21 (1) 2 *(John-Jules 35, Gilmour 66 (pen))* 1431

Cheltenham T: (352) Flinders; Forster, Tozer, Boyle; Long (Broom 46), Clements, Maddox (Addai 70), Thomas (Atangana 54), Field; McAlinden, Mooney.
Arsenal U21: (4231) Iliev; Sheaf (Smith 29), Ballard, Medley (Bramall 90), Bola (Zelalem 63); Burton■, Gilmour; Olayinka, Coyle, Saka; John-Jules.
Referee: Tim Robinson.

Wednesday, 7 November 2018

Forest Green R (0) 1 *(Grubb 62)*

Arsenal U21 (2) 3 *(Willock 41 (pen), 43, John-Jules 85)* 1602

Forest Green R: (4231) Montgomery; Archibald, Rawson, Gunning, McGinley; Digby (Brown 66), Worthington; Pearce (Grubb 37), Williams, Reid (Campbell 57); Morris.
Arsenal U21: (433) Iliev; Bramall, Pleguezuelo, Ballard, Bola; Olayinka, Zelalem (Gilmour 46), Willock; Coyle, John-Jules, Saka (Balogun 90).
Referee: Christopher Sarginson.

Tuesday, 13 November 2018

Cheltenham T (1) 2 *(Maddox 35, Boyle 47)*

Coventry C (0) 0 1296

Cheltenham T: (352) Flinders; Forster (Hussey 54), Tozer, Boyle; Broom, Thomas, Maddox (Alcock 54), Atangana, Field; Mooney (Addai 78), Barnett.
Coventry C: (4231) O'Brien; Grimmer, Thompson, Williams, Mason (McCallum 55); Eccles, Bayliss (Burroughs 63); Jones, Ngandu (Hickman 72), Shipley; Bakayoko.
Referee: Craig Hicks.

South Group E	P	W	DW	DL	L	F	A	GD	Pts
Cheltenham T	3	2	0	0	1	8	6	2	6
Arsenal U21	3	2	0	0	1	8	7	1	6
Forest Green R	3	1	0	1	1	6	4	2	4
Coventry C	3	0	1	0	2	1	6	–5	2

SOUTHERN SECTION GROUP F

Tuesday, 4 September 2018

Northampton T (0) 0

Wycombe W (1) 1 *(Kashket 11)* 1053

Northampton T: (4141) Ward; Odofin, Williams J, Barnett, Turnbull; McWilliams S (Whaler 81); Powell D, O'Toole, Bowditch, Waters; Williams A.
Wycombe W: (4321) Makabu-Makalamby; Thompson, Stewart (Jombati 46), Fox, Harriman; Cowan-Hall (Williams 74), Saunders, Freeman; Samuel, Onyedinma (Bean 60); Kashket.
Referee: Darren Drysdale.

Oxford U (1) 3 *(Smith 31, Holmes 58, Spasov 86 (pen))*

Fulham U21 (0) 0 1116

Oxford U: (4231) Mitchell; McMahon, Dickie, Nelson, Garbutt; Brannagan, Ruffels; Holmes (Spasov 63), Lopes, Henry (Long 79); Smith (Obika 64).
Fulham U21: (4411) Stahl■; Drameh, Jenz, Opoku (Mundle-Smith 77), Atkinson; Harris, O'Riley, Davies (Kelly 76), Thompson; Francois; Abraham.
Referee: Craig Hicks.

Tuesday, 18 September 2018

Wycombe W (1) 2 *(Samuel 2, Kashket 90)*

Fulham U21 (0) 1 *(Thompson 54)* 595

Wycombe W: (433) Makabu-Makalamby; Freeman, Jombati (Harriman 66), Charles (Jacobson 66), Thompson; Samuel, Bean, Saunders; Cowan-Hall, Akinfenwa (Bloomfield 66), Kashket.
Fulham U21: (3421) Ashby-Hammond L; Jenz (Carvalho 46), Atkinson, Opoku (Kelly 75); Drameh, Davies, Francois, Mundle-Smith; Harris, Thompson; Abraham (Elliott 46).
Referee: Trevor Kettle.

Tuesday, 9 October 2018

Oxford U (1) 1 *(Henry 24)*

Northampton T (0) 2 *(van Veen 55, Pierre 65)* 929

Oxford U: (433) Eastwood; Long, Dickie, Raglan, Garbutt; Brannagan, Hanson (Obika 74), Baptiste; Henry (Browne 74), Smith, Carruthers (Mousinho 62).
Northampton T: (442) Ward; Facey, Pierre, Turnbull, Buchanan (Bridge 53); O'Toole■, Bowditch, Foley, Powell D (Odofin 80); Waters, van Veen (Williams A 88).
Referee: Kevin Johnson.

Tuesday, 6 November 2018

Northampton T (2) 2 *(Pierre 17, Hoskins 20)*

Fulham U21 (0) 0 1059

Northampton T: (4231) Ward; Odofin, Turnbull, Pierre (McWilliams C 46), Buchanan; McWilliams S (Whaler 83), Williams J; Waters, Hoskins, Powell D; Williams A (Iaciofano 70).
Fulham U21: (4231) Ashby-Hammond T; Sessegnon, Davies, Jenz, Mundle-Smith; De La Torre (Atkinson 46), Francois; Cisse, Thompson, Harris; Santos-Clase (Abraham 62).
Referee: John Busby.

Wycombe W (0) 0

Oxford U (2) 3 *(Brannagan 1, Browne 31, Smith 53)* 1313

Wycombe W: (343) Makabu-Makalamby; Jombati, El-Abd (McCarthy 46), Fox; Freeman, Gape (Morris 46), Bean, Thompson; Onyedinma (Samuel 46), Mackail-Smith, Kashket.
Oxford U: (433) Mitchell; Norman, Dickie, Raglan, Garbutt; Ruffels, Hanson, Brannagan (Heap 86); Whyte, Smith (Bradbury 83), Browne (Long 75).
Referee: Lee Collins.

South Group F	P	W	DW	DL	L	F	A	GD	Pts
Oxford U	3	2	0	0	1	7	2	5	6
Northampton T	3	2	0	0	1	4	2	2	6
Wycombe W	3	2	0	0	1	3	4	–1	6
Fulham U21	3	0	0	0	3	1	7	–6	0

SOUTHERN SECTION GROUP G

Tuesday, 28 August 2018

Stevenage (2) 5 *(Kennedy 44 (pen), 45, Guthrie 69 (pen), 81, 90)*

Swansea C U21 (0) 0 470

Stevenage: (442) Dieng; Vancooten, Wilkinson, Nugent, Timlin; Iontton, Ferry (Makoma 62), Kennedy (Sonupe 66), Campbell-Ryce; Georgiou, Newton (Guthrie 64).
Swansea C U21: (4231) Benda (Gould 86); Dulca, Blake, Lewis J, Davies; Evans C, Blair; De Boer (Garrick 61), Paulet, Cooper O (Price 90); Bia Bi.
Referee: Neil Hair.

Tuesday, 4 September 2018

Charlton Ath (1) 2 *(Sarr 42, Mascoll 84)*

AFC Wimbledon (1) 2 *(Hartigan 27, Soares 49)* 1244

Charlton Ath: (532) Steer; Marshall, Yao, Sarr, Dijksteel, Reeves (Mascoll 57); Lapslie, Maloney, Morgan; Hackett-Fairchild, Vetokele (Ajose 72).
AFC Wimbledon: (442) McDonnell; Sibbick, Thomas (Purrington 90), McDonald, Hanson; Wagstaff, Garratt, Hartigan, Soares (Barcham 68); Jervis (Appiah 78), Pinnock.
AFC Wimbledon won 4-2 on penalties.
Referee: Kevin Johnson.

Tuesday, 18 September 2018

AFC Wimbledon (0) 0

Swansea C U21 (0) 1 *(Lewis A 90)* 306

AFC Wimbledon: (442) McDonnell; Sibbick, Nightingale, McDonald, Garratt; Wagstaff, Hartigan, Soares (Trotter 46), Pinnock; Pigott (Barcham 62), Wood.
Swansea C U21: (532) Benda; Lewis A, Cooper B, Lewis J, Blair, Blake (Jones 46); De Boer, Dulca, Cullen; Paulet (Cooper O 76), Bia Bi.
Referee: Ollie Yates.

Tuesday, 9 October 2018

Stevenage (0) 0

Charlton Ath (3) 8 *(Pratley 25, Stevenson 27, 59, 74 (pen), Ajose 34, Vetokele 48, 57, Lapslie 87)* 793

Stevenage: (451) Appleyard; Iontton, Wilkinson, Vancooten, Hunt; Sonupe (Smyth 57), Makoma, Ball, McKee, Georgiou (Ferry 28); Newton (Reid 46).
Charlton Ath: (532) Phillips; Marshall, Dijksteel, Sarr, Stevenson (Reeves 88), Lapslie; Maloney, Ward (Morgan 60), Pratley; Vetokele, Ajose.
Referee: Lee Swabey.

Tuesday, 6 November 2018

AFC Wimbledon (2) 4 *(Appiah 1, Wordsworth 28, Garratt 68, Egan 79)*

Stevenage (0) 0 304

AFC Wimbledon: (442) King; Watson, Thomas (Oshilaja 69), Kalambayi, Garratt; Wordsworth (Hartigan 69), Trotter, Egan, Burey; Appiah (Pigott 75), Jervis.
Stevenage: (451) Farman; Vancooten, Henry, Wilkinson, Hunt; Sonupe, Kennedy, Timlin (Iontton 64), Ball, Seddon (Revell 53); Newton (Guthrie 64).
Referee: Gavin Ward.

Tuesday, 13 November 2018

Charlton Ath (0) 0

Swansea C U21 (0) 1 *(Maric 54)* 740

Charlton Ath: (41212) Maynard-Brewer; Sarpeng-Wiredu (Anderson 74), Yao, Blumberg, Mascoll; Morgan; Marshall, Fosu; Clarke (Maloney 77); Hackett-Fairchild (Dempsey 41), Ajose.
Swansea C U21: (343) Benda; Harries, Lewis J, Lewis A; Reid, Garrick, Maric, Paulet (Price 75); Cooper O (Evans K 86), Bia Bi (Govea 79), Cullen.
Referee: Charles Breakspear.

South Group G	P	W	DW	DL	L	F	A	GD	Pts
Swansea C U21	3	2	0	0	1	2	5	–3	6
AFC Wimbledon	3	1	1	0	1	6	3	3	5
Charlton Ath	3	1	0	1	1	10	3	7	4
Stevenage	3	1	0	0	2	5	12	–7	3

SOUTHERN SECTION GROUP H

Tuesday, 4 September 2018

Luton T (1) 2 *(Jarvis 5, Grant 79)*

Brighton & HA U21 (0) 1 *(Connolly 86)* 1318

Luton T: (4132) Isted; Justin, Jones, Sheehan, Senior; McCormack (Rea 81); Grant (Neufville 85), O'Kane (Musonda 38), Down; Cornick, Jarvis.
Brighton & HA U21: (4231) Steele; Davies A, White, Kerr, Cochrane; Davies J, Mandroiu; Onen (Barclay 46), Gyokeres, Tilley (Cashman 71); Connolly.
Referee: John Busby.

Milton Keynes D (3) 3 *(Aneke 6, 45, Healey 33)*

Peterborough U (0) 3 *(Cooper 56, Walker 87, Godden 90)* 2404

Milton Keynes D: (3412) Moore; Tapp (Pattison 84), Jackson, Cargill; Brittain, Kasumu (Nesbitt 84), Cisse, Hancox; Watson; Healey, Aneke (Nombe 70).
Peterborough U: (4411) O'Malley; Lyon, Tafazolli, Yorwerth, Denton; Buckley-Rickett (Walker 46), Reed (Godden 82), Cooke (Woodyard 37), Cooper; Maddison; Toney.
Milton Keynes D won 6-5 on penalties.
Referee: Brett Huxtable.

Tuesday, 9 October 2018

Luton T (2) 3 *(Sheehan 17 (pen), LuaLua 29, Grant 60)*

Milton Keynes D (0) 0 875

Luton T: (4312) Isted; Justin, Rea, Sheehan, Senior; Down, McCormack, Grant (Peck 87); Shinnie (Neufville 89); LuaLua (Tomlinson 90), Jarvis.
Milton Keynes D: (352) Moore; Tapp, Jackson, Lewington (Gilbey 46); Brittain, Kasumu, Watson, Cisse (Nesbitt 46), Hancox; Simpson, Aneke (Thomas-Asante 46).
Referee: Craig Hicks.

Peterborough U (1) 2 *(Godden 28, Cummings 52)*

Brighton & HA U21 (0) 2 *(Connolly 71, Davies J 79)* 1872

Peterborough U: (442) Chapman; Naismith, Tafazolli, Bennett, Daniel; Walker (Ward 79), Reed, Cooke, Dembele; Godden, Cummings (Toney 82).
Brighton & HA U21: (4231) Collings; Moore (Davies A 56), White, Ostigard, Barclay; Cox, Tilley (Gwargis 62); Normann, Davies J, Gyokeres; Connolly.
Brighton & HA U21 won 5-4 on penalties.
Referee: Dean Whitestone.

Tuesday, 13 November 2018

Milton Keynes D (2) 2 *(Agard 6, Hancox 41)*

Brighton & HA U21 (1) 3 *(Connolly 23, 69, 76)* 1018

Milton Keynes D: (352) Moore; Williams, Walsh (Brittain 45), Cargill; Watson, McGrandles (Houghton 65), D'Ath (Gilbey 78), Cisse, Hancox; Agard, Simpson.
Brighton & HA U21: (4231) Keto; White, Barclay, O'Hora (Ljubicic 88), Cox; Tilley (Davies A 78), Sanders; Normann, Davies J, Gyokeres; Connolly.
Referee: Roger East.

Peterborough U (2) 2 *(Daniel 19, Toney 36)*

Luton T (0) 1 *(O'Malley 73 (og))* 2017

Peterborough U: (451) O'Malley; Lyon, Bassong, Bennett, Daniel; Maddison (Cooper 90), Reed, Cooke (O'Hara 83), Walker, Dembele (Buckley Rickett 78); Toney.
Luton T: (4312) Stech; Pearson, Jones, Sheehan, James; Down (Justin 83), McCormack, Grant; LuaLua; Jarvis, Cornick (Neufville 89).
Referee: Andy Woolmer.

South Group H	P	W	DW	DL	L	F	A	GD	Pts
Luton T	3	2	0	0	1	6	3	3	6
Peterborough U	3	1	0	2	0	7	6	1	5
Brighton & HA U21	3	1	1	0	1	6	6	0	5
Milton Keynes D	3	0	1	0	2	5	9	–4	2

NORTHERN SECTION SECOND ROUND

Tuesday, 4 December 2018

Accrington S (1) 2 *(Brown 7, Clark 70)*

Lincoln C (1) 2 *(Green 6, McCombe 60)* 746

Accrington S: (442) Maxted; Mingoia (McConville 68), Richards-Everton, Sykes, Anderton; Platt, Conneely (Barlaser 78), Brown, Charman (Clark 63); Hall, Zanzala.
Lincoln C: (442) Slocombe; Eardley (McCombe 46), Adebayo-Smith (Shaw 63), Wharton, Crookes; Gordon, Luque, Chapman, Mensah; Green, Rhead.
Accrington S won 4-2 on penalties.
Referee: Anthony Backhouse.

Barnsley (1) 3 *(Adeboyejo 17, Williams J 61, Lindsay 65)*

Manchester C U21 (1) 3 *(Matondo 45, Poveda 59, 74)* 3070

Barnsley: (442) Davies; Williams J, Pinnock, Lindsay, Pinillos; Potts, Bird (Moore 90), Bahre (Mowatt 61), Thiam; Woodrow (Brown 81), Adeboyejo.
Manchester C U21: (433) Scott; Frimpong, Sandler, Garcia (Rosler 77), Ogbeta; Richards, Pozo, Bernabe (Nmecha 66); Poveda, Bolton (Dele-Bashiru 79), Matondo.
Manchester C U21 won 5-3 on penalties.
Referee: Ollie Yates.

Mansfield T (0) 0

Bury (1) 1 *(Telford 35)* 1029

Mansfield T: (352) Logan; Preston, Pearce (Hamilton 46), Sweeney, White, Mellis, Bishop, Khan (Elsnik 46), Benning; Walker, Rose (Davies 46).
Bury: (352) Hudson; Aimson, Thompson (Lavery 57), Miller; Cooney, Styles, Dawson■, Barjonas, McFadzean (Adams N 46); Dagnall (Omotayo 76), Telford.
Referee: Robert Lewis.

Newcastle U U21 (1) 1 *(Sorensen 23)*

Macclesfield T (0) 1 *(Wilson 84)* 1126

Newcastle U U21: (4231) Harker; Walters, O'Connor, Watts, Gibson; Longstaff M, Bailey; Allan (Longelo 66), Roberts, Wilson (Toure 74); Sorensen (Sangare 80).
Macclesfield T: (442) O'Hara; Pearson (Stephens 76), Lowe, Grimes, Welch-Hayes; Arthur, Napa (Ponticelli 58), Maycock, Evans; Wilson, Blissett (Smith 69).
Newcastle U U21 won 5-3 on penalties.
Referee: Ben Toner.

Port Vale (3) 4 *(Pope 6, Montano 41, 43, Hannant 66)*

Stoke C U21 (0) 0 7940

Port Vale: (4141) Brown; Gibbons, Smith, Rawlinson, Vassell; Kay; Hannant (Kanu 71), Conlon (Miller 81), Oyeleke, Montano (Dodds 60); Pope.

Stoke C U21: (4411) Haugaard; Thandi, Wara, Collins, Tymon (Niakate 46); Verlinden, Sorensen, Waddington (Dunwoody 60), Jarvis (Pemberton 84); Shenton; Campbell.
Referee: Sebastian Stockbridge.

Sunderland (1) 2 *(Jones 22 (og), Sinclair 73 (pen))*
Notts Co (0) 0 8580
Sunderland: (4231) Ruiter; Bainbridge, Ozturk, Loovens, Oviedo; McGeouch, Mumba; O'Nien, Power (Hackett 83), Watmore (Mgunga-Kimpioka 67); Sinclair (Diamond 87).
Notts Co: (451) Fitzsimons; Hawkridge (Husin 63), Duffy, Jones, Brisley; Patching (Kellett 78), Hewitt, Vaughan, Milsom, Thomas; Dennis (Stead 62).
Referee: Graham Salisbury.

Wednesday, 5 December 2018

Shrewsbury T (1) 2 *(Gilliead 24, Loft 72)*
Walsall (0) 1 *(Morris 77)* 1857
Shrewsbury T: (442) Coleman; Emmanuel, Sears, Kennedy, Haynes; Eisa (Mcatee 90), Colkett, Loft, Gilliead (Whalley 62); John-Lewis (Rowland 78), Angol.
Walsall: (352) Dunn; Guthrie, Fitzwater, Martin (Ismail 62); Wilson, Kinsella (Edwards 70), Osbourne (Kouhyar 75), Morris, Leahy; Ronan, Ferrier.
Referee: Peter Wright.

Tuesday, 11 December 2018

Rochdale (0) 2 *(Rafferty 90 (pen), Adshead 90)*
Oldham Ath (0) 0 1854
Rochdale: (433) Norman; Rafferty, Williams M, Delaney, Done; Morley (Adshead 85), Perkins, Rathbone; Inman, Gillam (Yonsian 86), Jordan LR Williams.
Oldham Ath: (442) Iversen; Dummigan (Haymer 29), Clarke, Edmundson, Hunt; Lang, Missilou, Maouche■, Nepomuceno (Branger 87); Surridge, O'Grady (Lyden 54).
Referee: Oliver Langford.

SOUTHERN SECTION SECOND ROUND

Tuesday, 4 December 2018

Cambridge U (1) 1 *(Maris 9)*
Northampton T (0) 1 *(van Veen 89)* 648
Cambridge U: (41212) Mitov; Halliday, Darling, Taylor (Amoo 90), Dunk; Deegan; Lewis (O'Neil 80), Maris; Brown; Lambe, Ibehre (Azeez 80).
Northampton T: (343) Ward; Williams J, Taylor, Turnbull; Facey, McWilliams S, Foley, Buchanan (Roberts 69); Morias (Powell D 68), Williams A (van Veen 68), Waters.
Northampton T won 4-2 on penalties.
Referee: Brett Huxtable.

Chelsea U21 (1) 2 *(Brown 37 (pen), Redan 47)*
AFC Wimbledon (0) 1 *(Wordsworth 69)* 1906
Chelsea U21: (352) Cumming; Guehi, Colley, Nartey; Lamptey (Grant 88), Gallagher, McEachran, Anjorin (McCormick 71), Fanilia-Castilo; Redan, Brown (Gilmour 83).
AFC Wimbledon: (4411) King; Sibbick, Nightingale, Thomas, Garratt; Burey, Hartigan, Trotter (Wordsworth■ 65), Egan (Pinnock 66); Jervis; Hanson (Pigott 57).
Referee: Charles Breakspear.

Cheltenham T (0) 1 *(Addai 68)*
Newport Co (1) 1 *(Amond 17)* 739
Cheltenham T: (352) Flinders; Tozer, Mullins (Forster 72), Boyle; Alcock (Clements 59), Atangana, Addai, Thomas, Field; Jones, Barnett (Mooney 73).
Newport Co: (433) Townsend; Hornby-Forbes (Pipe 66), Franks, Foulston (Demetriou 79), Butler; Cooper (Labadie 70), Sheehan, Pring; Semenyo, Harris, Amond.
Cheltenham T won 7-6 on penalties.
Referee: Lee Collins.

Exeter C (0) 0
Peterborough U (0) 2 *(Toney 67, Cummings 77)* 746
Exeter C: (442) Hamon; Woodman (Sparkes 63), Martin A, Moxey, Oates; Martin L (O'Shea 78), Collins, Dean, Ogbene; Abrahams, Jay (Forte 87).
Peterborough U: (442) O'Malley; Daniel, Tafazolli, Bennett, Ward; Cooper (Walker 87), Reed, Woodyard, Maddison; Toney (O'Hara 90), Cummings (Godden 82).
Referee: Alan Young.

Portsmouth (1) 2 *(Pitman B 10, Green 83)*
Arsenal U21 (0) 1 *(Saka 66)* 3109
Portsmouth: (433) McGee; Walkes, Burgess, Casey, Haunstrup; May, Rose, Read (Mason 59); Green, Pitman B, Dennis.
Arsenal U21: (343) Iliev; Ballard, Koscielny (Tormey 85), Medley; Osei-Tutu, Gilmour, Omole (Coyle 65), Bramall; Saka, John-Jules, Olayinka.
Referee: Thomas Bramall.

Wednesday, 5 December 2018

Luton T (0) 1 *(Read 81)*
Southend U (0) 1 *(McLaughlin 88)* 1545
Luton T: (41212) Stech; Potts, Jones, Musonda, Senior (Justin 87); Sheehan; Read (Ruddock 85), LuaLua; Grant; Jarvis, Hylton.
Southend U: (352) Oxley; White, Turner, Moore; Bwomono, Hyam (Kightly 90), Mantom, Yearwood (Hutchinson 87), Hendrie (McLaughlin 68); McCoulsky, Robinson.
Southend U won 4-2 on penalties.
Referee: Darren Drysdale.

Swansea C U21 (0) 1 *(Garrick 54)*
Bristol R (0) 2 *(Craig 58, Jakubiak 89)* 699
Swansea C U21: (4231) Benda; Reid (Govea 62), Cooper B, Harries, Lewis A; Maric, Paulet (Cullen 90); Asoro (Bia Bi 80), Byers, Dhanda; Garrick.
Bristol R: (433) Bonham; Leadbitter, Clarke J, Craig, Kelly; Upson, Bennett (Matthews 88), Sercombe; Nichols (Reilly 75), Payne (Jakubiak 75), Rodman.
Referee: Christopher Sarginson.

Tuesday, 18 December 2018

Oxford U (2) 3 *(Raglan 12, Smith 16, McMahon 48)*
Tottenham H U21 (0) 0 1422
Oxford U: (4231) Eastwood; McMahon, Raglan, Nelson, Garbutt; Brannagan (Heap 78), Hanson; Whyte (Holmes 59), Henry (Browne 59), Little; Smith.
Tottenham H U21: (4231) Austin; Hinds (Reynolds 85), Marsh, Tanganga, Brown; Bowden (Tracey 73), Roles; Duncan, Oakley-Boothe, Clarke (Thorpe 89); Sterling.
Referee: Kevin Johnson.

NORTHERN SECTION THIRD ROUND

Tuesday, 8 January 2019

Accrington S (2) 2 *(Clark 10, Kee 38)*
Bury (0) 4 *(Telford 55, 74, Maynard 57, Mayor 84)* 1136
Accrington S: (442) Maxted; Mohammed (Mingoia 46), Hughes, Richards-Everton, Wood (Sousa 80); Clark, Conneely, Brown (Finley 71), McConville; Kee, Zanzala.
Bury: (352) Murphy; Thompson, O'Connell, Stokes; Miller, Cooney, O'Shea, Mayor (Adams J 90), McFadzean; Telford (Moore 79), Lavery (Maynard 54).
Referee: Matthew Donohue.

Port Vale (0) 1 *(Pope 83)*
Shrewsbury T (0) 1 *(Sears 63)* 1355
Port Vale: (433) Brown; Gibbons, Rawlinson, Smith, Clark; Oyeleke, Kay, Joyce (Angus 68); Hannant, Pope, Whitfield (Miller 79).
Shrewsbury T: (541) Coleman; Emmanuel (Gilliead 90), Shelis, Kennedy, Beckles, Sears; Eisa, Loft, Rowland (Okenabirhie 90), Barnett; Angol.
Port Vale won 4-3 on penalties.
Referee: Eddie Ilderton.

Rochdale (2) 2 *(McNulty 4, Dooley 29)*
Manchester C U21 (0) 4 *(Bolton 50, Braaf 67, 82, Richards 84)* 2176
Rochdale: (433) Norman; Matheson, M Jordan Williams, McNulty, Ntlhe; Adshead (Yonsian 85), Morley, Rathbone (Inman 61); Dooley (Gillam 65), Holden, Done.
Manchester C U21: (433) Grimshaw; Frimpong, Sandler, Harwood-Bellis, Ogbeta; Richards, Pozo (Gomes 86), Nmecha (Doyle 90); Poveda, Bolton, Garre (Braaf 56).
Referee: Ross Joyce.

Sunderland (0) 4 *(Watts 49 (og), Wyke 52, Maguire 78, Mgunga-Kimpioka 86)*
Newcastle U U21 (0) 0 16,654
Sunderland: (4231) Ruiter; O'Nien, Ozturk, Flanagan, James; Mumba, McGeouch (Hackett 83); Sinclair, Maguire, Watmore (Mgunga-Kimpioka 46); Wyke (Molyneux 77).

Newcastle U U21: (4231) Harker; Walters, Bailey, Watts, Gibson; Longstaff M, Sangare; Allan (Longelo 68), Roberts, Wilson (Nunez-Cumbreras 75); Sorensen (Toure 56).
Referee: Tony Harrington.

SOUTHERN SECTION THIRD ROUND

Tuesday, 8 January 2019

Cheltenham T (0) 1 *(Dawson 64)*

Oxford U (1) 1 *(Brannagan 45)* 1288

Cheltenham T: (352) Flinders; Tozer, Forster (Bower 46), Alcock; Thomas, Dawson, Maddox (Broom 65), Clements, Hussey; Varney (Barnett 65), Addai.
Oxford U: (433) Eastwood; Long (Nelson 80), Raglan, Dickie, Garbutt; Brannagan, Hanson (Mousinho 62), Henry; Whyte, Graham, Browne (Sykes 80).
Oxford U won 4-1 on penalties.
Referee: Ollie Yates.

Northampton T (0) 1 *(Crooks 76)*

Bristol R (1) 2 *(Broadbent 45, Payne 58)* 1312

Northampton T: (352) Cornell; Facey, Taylor (Pierre 71), Turnbull; Williams J, Crooks, Bowditch (Bridge 53), Foley, Buchanan (Powell D 60); Hoskins, Morias.
Bristol R: (4411) Bonham; Partington, Lockyer, Broadbent, Kelly; Sercombe (Nichols 75), Upson, Lines, Rodman (Leadbitter 74); Matthews; Payne (Reilly 83).
Referee: Charles Breakspear.

Southend U (0) 0

Portsmouth (2) 2 *(Dennis 2, Evans 45)* 1649

Southend U: (442) Smith; Bwomono, White, Moore (Hutchinson 60), Hendrie; Kightly (Dieng 46), Hyam, Yearwood, Bunn; Robinson, Cox (McLaughlin 46).
Portsmouth: (4411) Bass; Smith, Burgess, Casey, Haunstrup; Wheeler, Evans, May, Green (Read 46); Dennis; Lethbridge (Maloney 54).
Referee: Craig Hicks.

Wednesday, 9 January 2019

Chelsea U21 (1) 1 *(Nartey 45)*

Peterborough U (0) 3 *(Dembele 65, Toney 72, Maddison 74)* 2671

Chelsea U21: (352) Cumming; Colley, Nartey, Guehi; Grant, Gallagher, McEachran (Redan 76), Gilmour, Fanilia-Castilo; Taylor-Crossdale (Anjorin 62), Ugbo (Brown 85).
Peterborough U: (442) Chapman; Ward, Naismith, Tafazolli, Lafferty (Denton 87); Maddison (Godden 90), Reed, Cooke, Dembele; Toney, Tomlin (Cooper 46).
Referee: John Busby.

QUARTER-FINALS

Tuesday, 22 January 2019

Bristol R (1) 3 *(Clarke O 16, Nichols 62 (pen), Rodman 68)*

Port Vale (0) 0 2016

Bristol R: (442) Bonham; Partington, Lockyer, Craig, Holmes-Dennis; Rodman (Sercombe 70), Lines, Clarke O (Upson 70), Bennett; Nichols, Reilly (Jakubiak 80).
Port Vale: (343) Brown; Vassell (Elliott 46), Smith, Rawlinson; Clark, Kay, Joyce, Hannant (Worrall 66); Oyeleke, Miller (Whitfield 66), Conlon■.
Referee: Matthew Donohue.

Bury (3) 5 *(Telford 16, Thompson 26, Moore 41, Mayor 55, 76)*

Oxford U (1) 2 *(Henry 24 (pen), Carruthers 51)* 1238

Bury: (352) Murphy; Miller, Thompson, Stokes (Adams N 46); Cooney, Danns, Mayor (Hulme 80), O'Connell, McFadzean; Moore (Lavery 61), Telford.
Oxford U: (4231) Eastwood; Hanson, Dickie, Nelson, Ruffels; Brannagan (Carruthers 46), Browne; Kashi, Henry, Graham (Sykes 80); Mackie (Whyte 65).
Referee: Thomas Bramall.

Portsmouth (0) 1 *(Wheeler 85)*

Peterborough U (0) 0 3313

Portsmouth: (4231) MacGillivray; Mnoga (Walkes 58), Casey, Burgess, Haunstrup; Close (Clarke 87), May; Wheeler, Evans, Lowe; Smith (Dennis 59).
Peterborough U: (442) O'Malley; Naismith, Bennett, Tafazolli, Lafferty; Cooper, Cooke, Woodyard (Godden 87), Ward; Toney, Tomlin (Dembele 69).
Referee: Andy Woolmer.

Sunderland (1) 2 *(Watmore 22, Gooch 65)*

Manchester C U21 (0) 0 14,679

Sunderland: (433) Ruiter; Matthews, Ozturk, Baldwin, Oviedo; O'Nien, Cattermole (Robson 76), McGeouch; Maguire, Mgunga-Kimpioka (Connelly 89), Watmore (Gooch 61).
Manchester C U21: (433) Grimshaw; Harwood-Bellis, Frimpong, Ogbeta (Dionkou 46), Dele-Bashiru; Doyle (Bernabe 75), Rosler, Pozo; Garre, Braaf, Zoubdi Touaizi (Knight 78).
Referee: Michael Salisbury.

SEMI-FINALS

Tuesday, 26 February 2019

Bury (0) 0

Portsmouth (0) 3 *(Evans 61, Hawkins 64, Curtis 77)* 3900

Bury: (352) Murphy; Aimson, Thompson, McFadzean (Omotayo 77); Adams N (Cooney 70), Rossiter, O'Shea, Mayor, Moore; Lavery, Maynard (Telford 69).
Portsmouth: (4231) MacGillivray; Thompson N, Clarke, Burgess (Walkes 88), Brown; Naylor, Close; Curtis, Evans, Solomon-Otabor (Lowe 46); Hawkins.
Referee: Ross Joyce.

Tuesday, 5 March 2019

Bristol R (0) 0

Sunderland (1) 2 *(Grigg 44, Morgan 47)* 6699

Bristol R: (442) Bonham; Clarke J, Lockyer, Craig, Holmes-Dennis; Sinclair (Lines 71), Upson, Clarke O (Kelly 71), Sercombe; Nichols (Jakubiak 71), Clarke-Harris.
Sunderland: (4231) McLaughlin; Matthews, Dunne, Flanagan, O'Nien; Leadbitter, Power; McGeady (Watmore 77), Honeyman (Gooch 45), Morgan (McGeouch 84); Grigg.
Referee: Michael Salisbury.

EFL CHECKATRADE TROPHY FINAL 2019

Sunday, 31 March 2019

(at Wembley Stadium, attendance 85,021)

Portsmouth (0) 2 **Sunderland (1) 2**

Portsmouth: (4231) MacGillivray; Thompson N, Burgess, Clarke, Brown; Naylor, Close (Walkes 113); Lowe, Pitman B, Curtis (Evans 56); Bogle (Hawkins 69).
Scorers: Thompson N 82, Lowe 114.

Sunderland: (4231) McLaughlin; O'Nien, Flanagan, Baldwin, James (Hume 88); Cattermole, Leadbitter (Wyke 95); Morgan (Gooch 73), Honeyman, McGeady; Grigg (Power 77).
Scorers: McGeady 38, 119.

aet; Portsmouth won 5-4 on penalties.

Referee: Dean Whitestone.

FA CUP FINALS 1872–2019

VENUES

1872 and 1874–92	Kennington Oval	1895–1914	Crystal Palace
1873	Lillie Bridge	1915	Old Trafford, Manchester
1893	Fallowfield, Manchester	1920–22	Stamford Bridge
1894	Everton	2001–06	Millennium Stadium, Cardiff
1923–2000	Wembley Stadium (old)	2007 to date	Wembley Stadium (new)

THE FA CUP

1872	Wanderers v Royal Engineers	1-0
1873	Wanderers v Oxford University	2-0
1874	Oxford University v Royal Engineers	2-0
1875	Royal Engineers v Old Etonians	1-1*
Replay	Royal Engineers v Old Etonians	2-0
1876	Wanderers v Old Etonians	1-1*
Replay	Wanderers v Old Etonians	3-0
1877	Wanderers v Oxford University	2-1*
1878	Wanderers v Royal Engineers	3-1

Wanderers won the cup outright, but it was restored to the Football Association.

1879	Old Etonians v Clapham R	1-0
1880	Clapham R v Oxford University	1-0
1881	Old Carthusians v Old Etonians	3-0
1882	Old Etonians v Blackburn R	1-0
1883	Blackburn Olympic v Old Etonians	2-1*
1884	Blackburn R v Queen's Park, Glasgow	2-1
1885	Blackburn R v Queen's Park, Glasgow	2-0
1886	Blackburn R v WBA	0-0
Replay	Blackburn R v WBA	2-0
	(at Racecourse Ground, Derby Co)	

A special trophy was awarded to Blackburn R for third consecutive win.

1887	Aston Villa v WBA	2-0
1888	WBA v Preston NE	2-1
1889	Preston NE v Wolverhampton W	3-0
1890	Blackburn R v The Wednesday	6-1
1891	Blackburn R v Notts Co	3-1
1892	WBA v Aston Villa	3-0
1893	Wolverhampton W v Everton	1-0
1894	Notts Co v Bolton W	4-1
1895	Aston Villa v WBA	1-0

FA Cup was stolen from a shop window in Birmingham and never found.

1896	The Wednesday v Wolverhampton W	2-1
1897	Aston Villa v Everton	3-2
1898	Nottingham F v Derby Co	3-1
1899	Sheffield U v Derby Co	4-1
1900	Bury v Southampton	4-0
1901	Tottenham H v Sheffield U	2-2
Replay	Tottenham H v Sheffield U	3-1
	(at Burnden Park, Bolton W)	
1902	Sheffield U v Southampton	1-1
Replay	Sheffield U v Southampton	2-1
1903	Bury v Derby Co	6-0
1904	Manchester C v Bolton W	1-0
1905	Aston Villa v Newcastle U	2-0
1906	Everton v Newcastle U	1-0
1907	The Wednesday v Everton	2-1
1908	Wolverhampton W v Newcastle U	3-1
1909	Manchester U v Bristol C	1-0
1910	Newcastle U v Barnsley	1-1
Replay	Newcastle U v Barnsley	2-0
	(at Goodison Park, Everton)	
1911	Bradford C v Newcastle U	0-0
Replay	Bradford C v Newcastle U	1-0
	(at Old Trafford, Manchester U)	

Trophy was given to Lord Kinnaird – he made nine FA Cup Final appearances – for services to football.

1912	Barnsley v WBA	0-0
Replay	Barnsley v WBA	1-0
	(at Bramall Lane, Sheffield U)	
1913	Aston Villa v Sunderland	1-0
1914	Burnley v Liverpool	1-0
1915	Sheffield U v Chelsea	3-0
1920	Aston Villa v Huddersfield T	1-0*
1921	Tottenham H v Wolverhampton W	1-0
1922	Huddersfield T v Preston NE	1-0
1923	Bolton W v West Ham U	2-0
1924	Newcastle U v Aston Villa	2-0
1925	Sheffield U v Cardiff C	1-0
1926	Bolton W v Manchester C	1-0
1927	Cardiff C v Arsenal	1-0
1928	Blackburn R v Huddersfield T	3-1
1929	Bolton W v Portsmouth	2-0
1930	Arsenal v Huddersfield T	2-0
1931	WBA v Birmingham	2-1
1932	Newcastle U v Arsenal	2-1
1933	Everton v Manchester C	3-0
1934	Manchester C v Portsmouth	2-1
1935	Sheffield W v WBA	4-2
1936	Arsenal v Sheffield U	1-0
1937	Sunderland v Preston NE	3-1
1938	Preston NE v Huddersfield T	1-0*
1939	Portsmouth v Wolverhampton W	4-1
1946	Derby Co v Charlton Ath	4-1*
1947	Charlton Ath v Burnley	1-0*
1948	Manchester U v Blackpool	4-2
1949	Wolverhampton W v Leicester C	3-1
1950	Arsenal v Liverpool	2-0
1951	Newcastle U v Blackpool	2-0
1952	Newcastle U v Arsenal	1-0
1953	Blackpool v Bolton W	4-3
1954	WBA v Preston NE	3-2
1955	Newcastle U v Manchester C	3-1
1956	Manchester C v Birmingham C	3-1
1957	Aston Villa v Manchester U	2-1
1958	Bolton W v Manchester U	2-0
1959	Nottingham F v Luton T	2-1
1960	Wolverhampton W v Blackburn R	3-0
1961	Tottenham H v Leicester C	2-0
1962	Tottenham H v Burnley	3-1
1963	Manchester U v Leicester C	3-1
1964	West Ham U v Preston NE	3-2
1965	Liverpool v Leeds U	2-1*
1966	Everton v Sheffield W	3-2
1967	Tottenham H v Chelsea	2-1
1968	WBA v Everton	1-0*
1969	Manchester C v Leicester C	1-0
1970	Chelsea v Leeds U	2-2*
Replay	Chelsea v Leeds U	2-1
	(at Old Trafford, Manchester U)	
1971	Arsenal v Liverpool	2-1*
1972	Leeds U v Arsenal	1-0
1973	Sunderland v Leeds U	1-0
1974	Liverpool v Newcastle U	3-0
1975	West Ham U v Fulham	2-0
1976	Southampton v Manchester U	1-0
1977	Manchester U v Liverpool	2-1
1978	Ipswich T v Arsenal	1-0
1979	Arsenal v Manchester U	3-2
1980	West Ham U v Arsenal	1-0
1981	Tottenham H v Manchester C	1-1*
Replay	Tottenham H v Manchester C	3-2

1982	Tottenham H v QPR	1-1*
Replay	Tottenham H v QPR	1-0
1983	Manchester U v Brighton & HA	2-2*
Replay	Manchester U v Brighton & HA	4-0
1984	Everton v Watford	2-0
1985	Manchester U v Everton	1-0*
1986	Liverpool v Everton	3-1
1987	Coventry C v Tottenham H	3-2*
1988	Wimbledon v Liverpool	1-0
1989	Liverpool v Everton	3-2*
1990	Manchester U v Crystal Palace	3-3*
Replay	Manchester U v Crystal Palace	1-0
1991	Tottenham H v Nottingham F	2-1*
1992	Liverpool v Sunderland	2-0
1993	Arsenal v Sheffield W	1-1*
Replay	Arsenal v Sheffield W	2-1*
1994	Manchester U v Chelsea	4-0

THE FA CUP SPONSORED BY LITTLEWOODS POOLS

1995	Everton v Manchester U	1-0
1996	Manchester U v Liverpool	1-0
1997	Chelsea v Middlesbrough	2-0
1998	Arsenal v Newcastle U	2-0

THE AXA-SPONSORED FA CUP

1999	Manchester U v Newcastle U	2-0
2000	Chelsea v Aston Villa	1-0
2001	Liverpool v Arsenal	2-1
2002	Arsenal v Chelsea	2-0

THE FA CUP

2003	Arsenal v Southampton	1-0
2004	Manchester U v Millwall	3-0
2005	Arsenal v Manchester U	0-0*
	Arsenal won 5-4 on penalties.	
2006	Liverpool v West Ham U	3-3*
	Liverpool won 3-1 on penalties.	

THE FA CUP SPONSORED BY E.ON

2007	Chelsea v Manchester U	1-0*
2008	Portsmouth v Cardiff C	1-0
2009	Chelsea v Everton	2-1
2010	Chelsea v Portsmouth	1-0
2011	Manchester C v Stoke C	1-0

THE FA CUP WITH BUDWEISER

2012	Chelsea v Liverpool	2-1
2013	Wigan Ath v Manchester C	1-0
2014	Arsenal v Hull C	3-2*

THE FA CUP

2015	Arsenal v Aston Villa	4-0

THE EMIRATES FA CUP

2016	Manchester U v Crystal Palace	2-1*
2017	Arsenal v Chelsea	2-1
2018	Chelsea v Manchester U	1-0
2019	Manchester C v Watford	6-0

**After extra time.*

FA CUP WINS

Arsenal 13, Manchester U 12, Chelsea 8, Tottenham H 8, Aston Villa 7, Liverpool 7, Blackburn R 6, Manchester C 6, Newcastle U 6, Everton 5, The Wanderers 5, WBA 5, Bolton W 4, Sheffield U 4, Wolverhampton W 4, Sheffield W 3, West Ham U 3, Bury 2, Nottingham F 2, Old Etonians 2, Portsmouth 2, Preston NE 2, Sunderland 2, Barnsley 1, Blackburn Olympic 1, Blackpool 1, Bradford C 1, Burnley 1, Cardiff C 1, Charlton Ath 1, Clapham R 1, Coventry C 1, Derby Co 1, Huddersfield T 1, Ipswich T 1, Leeds U 1, Notts Co 1, Old Carthusians 1, Oxford University 1, Royal Engineers 1, Southampton 1, Wigan Ath 1, Wimbledon 1.

APPEARANCES IN FINALS

Arsenal 20, Manchester U 20, Liverpool 14, Chelsea 13, Everton 13, Newcastle U 13, Aston Villa 11, Manchester C 11, WBA 10, Tottenham H 9, Blackburn R 8, Wolverhampton W 8, Bolton W 7, Preston NE 7, Old Etonians 6, Sheffield U 6, Sheffield W 6, Huddersfield T 5, Portsmouth 5, *The Wanderers 5, West Ham U 5, Derby Co 4, Leeds U 4, Leicester C 4, Oxford University 4, Royal Engineers 4, Southampton 4, Sunderland 4, Blackpool 3, Burnley 3, Cardiff C 3, Nottingham F 3, Barnsley 2, Birmingham C 2, *Bury 2, Charlton Ath 2, Clapham R 2, Crystal Palace 2, Notts Co 2, Queen's Park (Glasgow) 2, Watford 2, *Blackburn Olympic 1, *Bradford C 1, Brighton & HA 1, Bristol C 1, *Coventry C 1, Fulham 1, Hull C 1, *Ipswich T 1, Luton T 1, Middlesbrough 1, Millwall 1, *Old Carthusians 1, QPR 1, Stoke C 1, *Wigan Ath 1, *Wimbledon 1.
** Denotes undefeated in final.*

APPEARANCES IN SEMI-FINALS

Arsenal 29, Manchester U 29, Everton 26, Liverpool 24, Chelsea 23, Aston Villa 21, Tottenham H 21, WBA 20, Blackburn R 18, Newcastle U 17, Sheffield W 16, Wolverhampton W 15, Bolton W 14, Manchester C 14, Sheffield U 14, Derby Co 13, Nottingham F 12, Southampton 12, Sunderland 12, Preston NE 10, Birmingham C 9, Burnley 8, Leeds U 8, Huddersfield T 7, Leicester C 7, Portsmouth 7, West Ham U 7, Watford 7, Old Etonians 6, Fulham 6, Oxford University 6, Millwall 5, Notts Co 5, The Wanderers 5, Cardiff C 4, Crystal Palace (professional club) 4, Luton T 4, Queen's Park (Glasgow) 4, Royal Engineers 4, Stoke C 4, Barnsley 3, Blackpool 3, Clapham R 3, Ipswich T 3, Middlesbrough 3, Norwich C 3, Old Carthusians 3, Oldham Ath 3, The Swifts 3, Blackburn Olympic 2, Brighton & HA 2, Bristol C 2, Bury 2, Charlton Ath 2, Grimsby T 2, Hull C 2, Reading 2, Swansea T 2, Swindon T 2, Wigan Ath 2, Wimbledon 2, Bradford C 1, Cambridge University 1, Chesterfield 1, Coventry C 1, Crewe Alex 1, Crystal Palace (amateur club) 1, Darwen 1, Derby Junction 1, Glasgow R 1, Marlow 1, Old Harrovians 1, Orient 1, Plymouth Arg 1, Port Vale 1, QPR 1, Shropshire W 1, Wycombe W 1, York C 1.

FA CUP ATTENDANCES 1969–2019

	1st Round	*2nd Round*	*3rd Round*	*4th Round*	*5th Round*	*6th Round*	*Semi-finals & Final*	*Total*	*No. of matches*	*Average per match*
1969–70	345,229	195,102	925,930	651,374	319,893	198,537	390,700	3,026,765	170	17,805
1970–71	329,687	230,942	956,683	757,852	360,687	304,937	279,644	3,220,432	162	19,879
1971–72	277,726	236,127	986,094	711,399	486,378	230,292	248,546	3,158,562	160	19,741
1972–73	259,432	169,114	938,741	735,825	357,386	241,934	226,543	2,928,975	160	18,306
1973–74	214,236	125,295	840,142	747,909	346,012	233,307	273,051	2,779,952	167	16,646
1974–75	283,956	170,466	914,994	646,434	393,323	268,361	291,369	2,968,903	172	17,261
1975–76	255,533	178,099	867,880	573,843	471,925	206,851	205,810	2,759,941	161	17,142
1976–77	379,230	192,159	942,523	631,265	373,330	205,379	258,216	2,982,102	174	17,139
1977–78	258,248	178,930	881,406	540,164	400,751	137,059	198,020	2,594,578	160	16,216
1978–79	243,773	185,343	880,345	537,748	243,683	263,213	249,897	2,604,002	166	15,687
1979–80	267,121	204,759	804,701	507,725	364,039	157,530	355,541	2,661,416	163	16,328
1980–81	246,824	194,502	832,578	534,402	320,530	288,714	339,250	2,756,800	169	16,312
1981–82	236,220	127,300	513,185	356,987	203,334	124,308	279,621	1,840,955	160	11,506
1982–83	191,312	150,046	670,503	452,688	260,069	193,845	291,162	2,209,625	154	14,348
1983–84	192,276	151,647	625,965	417,298	181,832	185,382	187,000	1,941,400	166	11,695
1984–85	174,604	137,078	616,229	320,772	269,232	148,690	242,754	1,909,359	157	12,162
1985–86	171,142	130,034	486,838	495,526	311,833	184,262	192,316	1,971,951	168	11,738
1986–87	209,290	146,761	593,520	349,342	263,550	119,396	195,533	1,877,400	165	11,378
1987–88	204,411	104,561	720,121	443,133	281,461	119,313	177,585	2,050,585	155	13,229
1988–89	212,775	121,326	690,199	421,255	206,781	176,629	167,353	1,966,318	164	12,173
1989–90	209,542	133,483	683,047	412,483	351,423	123,065	277,420	2,190,463	170	12,885
1990–91	194,195	121,450	594,592	530,279	276,112	124,826	196,434	2,038,518	162	12,583
1991–92	231,940	117,078	586,014	372,576	270,537	155,603	201,592	1,935,340	160	12,095
1992–93	241,968	174,702	612,494	377,211	198,379	149,675	293,241	2,047,670	161	12,718
1993–94	190,683	118,031	691,064	430,234	172,196	134,705	228,233	1,965,146	159	12,359
1994–95	219,511	125,629	640,017	438,596	257,650	159,787	174,059	2,015,249	161	12,517
1995–96	185,538	115,669	748,997	391,218	274,055	174,142	156,500	2,046,199	167	12,252
1996–97	209,521	122,324	651,139	402,293	199,873	67,035	191,813	1,843,998	151	12,211
1997–98	204,803	130,261	629,127	455,557	341,290	192,651	172,007	2,125,696	165	12,883
1998–99	191,954	132,341	609,486	431,613	359,398	181,005	202,150	2,107,947	155	13,599
1999–2000	181,485	127,728	514,030	374,795	182,511	105,443	214,921	1,700,913	158	10,765
2000–01	171,689	122,061	577,204	398,241	256,899	100,663	177,778	1,804,535	151	11,951
2001–02	198,369	119,781	566,284	330,434	249,190	173,757	171,278	1,809,093	148	12,224
2002–03	189,905	104,103	577,494	404,599	242,483	156,244	175,498	1,850,326	150	12,336
2003–04	162,738	117,967	624,732	347,964	292,521	156,780	167,401	1,870,103	149	12,551
2004–05	161,197	98,702	602,152	477,472	339,082	127,914	193,233	1,999,752	146	13,697
2005–06	188,876	107,456	654,570	388,339	286,225	163,449	177,723	1,966,638	160	12,291
2006–07	168,884	113,924	708,628	478,924	340,612	230,064	177,810	2,218,846	158	14,043
2007–08	175,195	99,528	704,300	356,404	276,903	142,780	256,210	2,011,320	152	13,232
2008–09	161,526	96,923	631,070	529,585	297,364	149,566	264,635	2,131,669	163	13,078
2009–10	147,078	100,476	613,113	335,426	288,604	144,918	254,806	1,884,421	151	12,480
2010–11	169,259	101,291	637,202	390,524	284,311	164,092	250,256	1,996,935	150	13,313
2011–12	155,858	92,267	640,700	391,214	250,666	194,971	262,064	1,987,740	151	13,164
2012–13	135,642	115,965	645,676	373,892	288,509	221,216	234,210	2,015,110	156	12,917
2013–14	144,709	75,903	668,242	346,706	254,084	156,630	243,350	1,889,624	149	12,682
2014–15	156,621	111,434	609,368	515,229	208,908	233,341	258,780	2,093,681	153	13,684
2015–16	134,914	94,855	755,187	397,217	235,433	227,262	253,793	2,098,661	149	14,085
2016–17	147,448	97,784	685,467	409,084	212,842	163,620	261,552	1,977,797	156	12,678
2017–18	125,978	87,075	712,036	371,650	210,328	140,641	245,730	1,893,438	149	12,708
2018–19	146,449	92,928	655,501	402,836	146,476	86,028	237,467	1,767,685	150	11,785

THE EMIRATES FA CUP 2018–19

PRELIMINARY AND QUALIFYING ROUNDS

**After extra time.*

EXTRA PRELIMINARY ROUND

Consett v North Shields	2-1
Thackley v Whitley Bay	2-3
Hebburn T v Dunston UTS	2-3
Ashington v Knaresborough T	0-2
Goole v Morpeth T	1-5
Glasshoughton Welfare v Blyth AFC	1-2
Newcastle Benfield v Stockton T	1-1, 3-0
Selby T v Whickham	3-2
Seaham Red Star v Heaton Stannington	1-1, 4-4*
Seaham Red Star won 4-2 on penalties	
Team Northumbria (removed) v Shildon (walkover)	
Northallerton T v Garforth T	0-4
Guisborough T v Newton Aycliffe	3-3, 2-0
Barnoldswick T v Billingham Synthonia	1-1, 4-0
Washington v West Auckland T	0-4
Sunderland RCA v Sunderland Ryhope CW	5-2
Bridlington T v Harrogate Railway Ath	3-0
Penrith v Albion Sports	0-3
Bishop Auckland v Pickering T	0-2
AFC Darwen v Barnton	3-1
Liversedge v Padiham	5-2
City of Liverpool v Silsden AFC	3-1
AFC Liverpool v Ashton Ath	2-2, 1-4
Widnes v Northwich Vic	1-1, 0-1
Burscough v 1874 Northwich	2-2, 3-3*
Burscough won 4-2 on penalties	
Congleton T v Eccleshill U	1-0
Prestwich Heys v Abbey Hey	2-1
West Didsbury & Chorlton v Squires Gate	2-3
Winsford U v Irlam	1-2
Penistone Church v Bootle	2-1
Hemsworth MW v Runcorn T	1-1, 0-1
Hallam v Runcorn Linnets	0-2
Maltby Main v Athersley Recreation	3-0
Parkgate v Sandbach U	2-0
Litherland Remyca v Charnock Richard	4-2
Litherland Remyca removed for fielding an ineligble player. Charnock Richard awarded the tie.	
Maine Road v Handsworth Parramore	0-1
Walsall Wood v Worcester C	1-1, 1-1*
Walsall Wood won 3-2 on penalties	
Highgate U v AFC Wulfrunians	1-0
Boldmere St Michaels v Malvern T	2-2, 2-3
Atherstone T v Hanley T	1-1, 4-1
Stourport Swifts v Shawbury U	2-1
Wednesfield v Rocester	2-1
Coventry U v Rugby T	1-2
Coventry Sphinx v Whitchurch Alport	0-1
Haughmond v Wolverhampton SC	2-0
Racing Club Warwick v Coleshill T	4-3
Romulus v Westfields	6-1
Ellesmere Rangers v Leicester Road	0-1
Sporting Khalsa v Tividale	2-1
Long Eaton U v St Andrews	2-1
Sleaford T v South Normanton Ath	0-1
Heather St Johns v Kimberley MW	3-6
Kirby Muxloe v AFC Mansfield	0-6
Clipstone v Barton T	0-0, 4-3
Lutterworth T v Heanor T	2-1
Hinckley AFC v Anstey Nomads	1-1, 3-4*
(2-2 at the end of normal time)	
Worksop T v Shepshed Dynamo	3-3, 5-4*
(2-2 at the end of normal time)	
Rainworth MW v Dunkirk	2-1
Staveley MW v Boston T	4-2
Teversal v Loughborough University	1-2
Oadby T v Shirebrook T	3-1
Bottesford T v Radford	3-1
Quorn v Belper U	6-1
Leicester Nirvana v Grimsby Bor	0-3
Cogenhoe U v Wisbech T	1-2
Wellingborough Whitworths v Harborough T	0-1
Deeping Rangers v Holbeach U	3-2
Raunds T v Eynesbury R	1-2
Arlesey T v Desborough T	3-4
Thetford T v Fakenham T	1-0
Northampton Sileby Rangers v Ely C	2-0
Godmanchester R v Newport Pagnell T	2-0
Biggleswade U v Wellingborough T	1-1, 1-2
Histon v Peterborough Northern Star	6-1
Daventry T v Potton U	9-2
Biggleswade v Northampton On Chenecks	2-0
Swaffham T v Yaxley	1-3
Rothwell Corinthians v Pinchbeck U	3-0
Hullbridge Sports v Gorleston	2-1
Wroxham v Saffron Walden T	1-1, 2-3*
(2-2 at the end of normal time)	
Great Yarmouth T v Hadleigh U	1-3
Walthamstow v Walsham Le Willows	3-1
Kirkley & Pakefield v FC Clacton	2-2, 2-3
Wodson Park v Hoddesdon T	1-3
Tower Hamlets v Stanway R	0-2
Norwich U v Takeley	1-2
St Margaretsbury v Enfield 1893	2-0
Framlingham T v Whitton U	1-1, 1-3
Southend Manor v FC Romania	1-3
Wivenhoe T v Brantham Ath	0-5
Stowmarket T v Basildon U	0-2
Sporting Bengal U v Ilford	4-3
Haverhill R v Haverhill Bor	2-0
Ipswich W v Baldock T	0-5
Barkingside v Leyton Ath	0-0, 0-3
Cockfosters v Newmarket T	0-2
Woodbridge T v Clapton	2-2, 1-1*
Woodbridge T won 5-4 on penalties	
Burnham Ramblers v West Essex	3-5
Stansted v Sawbridgeworth T	2-1
Redbridge v Long Melford	1-3
Oxhey Jets v Wantage T	3-4
Tuffley R v Colney Heath	1-4
Winslow U v Easington Sports	2-2, 0-2
Harpenden T v Edgware T	1-0
Hadley v Fairford T	2-0
Brackley T Saints v London Colney	1-0
London Lions v Wembley	2-1
Windsor v Highworth T	3-3, 2-1
Bishop's Cleeve v Stotfold	5-2
AFC Hayes v Lydney T	1-2
Flackwell Heath v North Greenford U	0-2
Tring Ath v Berkhamsted	0-2
Southall v Leverstock Green	0-1
Holmer Green v Longlevens	0-1
Ardley U v Shortwood U	7-0
Holyport v Brimscombe & Thrupp	1-2
Abingdon U v Burnham	2-2, 0-2
Crawley Green v Woodley U	7-1
Reading C v Chipping Sodbury T	1-1, 1-2*
(1-1 at the end of normal time)	
Leighton T v Royal Wootton Bassett T	0-1
Arundel v Chertsey T	4-1
Sutton Common R v CB Hounslow U	0-2
Broadbridge Heath v Shoreham	0-2
Langney W v Epsom & Ewell	1-2
Bearsted v Chichester C	2-1
Redhill v Horley T	1-3
AFC Croydon Ath v Rochester U	5-0
Spelthorne Sports v Peacehaven & Telscombe	3-0
Hassocks v Erith T	1-3
Worthing U v Littlehampton T	1-1, 4-2*
(2-2 at the end of normal time)	
Little Common v Bedfont Sports	2-2, 1-2
Crowborough Ath v Hanworth Villa	1-1, 0-2
Raynes Park Vale v Lingfield	3-0
AFC Uckfield T v Glebe	1-0
Abbey Rangers v Newhaven	0-4
Cobham v Sheppey U	1-0
Fisher v Horsham YMCA	1-2
Loxwood v Hollands & Blair	2-1
Sevenoaks T v Lordswood	6-1
Crawley Down Gatwick v Three Bridges	0-1
Eastbourne U v Hackney Wick	0-2
Cray Valley PM v Eastbourne T	3-2
Croydon v Tunbridge Wells	2-2, 3-2*
(2-2 at the end of normal time)	
Erith & Belvedere v Saltdean U	0-0, 0-2

Haywards Heath T v Lancing 0-2
Rushtall v Wick 3-0
East Preston v Balham 0-2
K Sports v Pagham 2-2, 0-2
Deal T v Whitstable T 2-2, 3-4
Broadfields U v Banstead Ath 3-0
Chatham T v Walton & Hersham 3-1
Corinthian v Canterbury C 3-0
Beckenham T v Colliers Wood U 1-1, 2-0*
(0-0 at the end of normal time)
Hamworthy U v Team Solent 3-2
Melksham T v Badshot Lea 4-0
AFC Stoneham v AFC Portchester 0-0, 3-0
Newport (IW) v Amesbury T 3-1
Knaphill v Sholing 0-3
Guildford C v Petersfield T 0-1
Tadley Calleva v Baffins Milton R 1-3
Bemerton Heath Harlequins v Cowes Sports 1-0
Andover New Street v Romsey T 4-0
United Services Portsmouth v Andover T 5-2
Horndean v Godalming T 5-0
Hamble Club v Alresford T 1-1, 2-0
Farnham T v Binfield 1-2
Brockenhurst v Christchurch 2-2, 2-0
Bashley v Bournemouth 0-2
Fareham T v Frimley Green 1-2
Ascot U v Camberley T 2-1
Sandhurst T v Lymington T 1-1, 1-5
Clevedon T v Portland U 1-2
Westbury U v Cribbs 3-0
Hallen v Longwell Green Sports 0-0, 1-0
Wells C v Shaftesbury 2-5
Bodmin T v Keynsham T 4-4, 3-1
Cheddar v Bridgwater T 3-2
Shepton Mallet v Willand R 1-1, 0-3
Bitton v Tavistock 7-0
Buckland Ath v Pewsey Vale 3-0
Bridport v Wellington 0-0, 3-0
Hengrove Ath v Plymouth Parkway 1-5
Saltash U v Odd Down 1-0
Brislington v Cadbury Heath 1-2
Bradford T v Roman Glass St George 5-2

PRELIMINARY ROUND
Knaresborough T v Blyth AFC 5-1
Bridlington T v Garforth T 1-2
Dunston UTS v Pontefract Collieries 4-2
Newcastle Benfield v West Auckland T 1-0
Whitley Bay v Barnoldswick T 6-1
Morpeth T v Marske U 1-0
Consett v Seaham Red Star 5-2
Tadcaster Alb v Shildon 4-1
Clitheroe v Sunderland RCA 6-6, 3-2
Kendal T v Selby T 1-1, 5-4*
(1-1 at the end of normal time)
Pickering T v Colne 0-4
Albion Sports v Guisborough T 2-2, 0-4
Ashton Ath v Skelmersdale U 2-1
Ossett U v Mossley 2-2, 1-1*
Mossley won 4-2 on penalties
Burscough v Northwich Vic 2-0
Atherton Colleries v Colwyn Bay 2-1
Kidsgrove Ath v Ramsbottom U 1-1, 0-0*
Kidsgrove Ath won 3-2 on penalties
Stocksbridge Park Steels v Bamber Bridge 1-3
Prescot Cables v Irlam 1-2
Brighouse T v Parkgate 0-2
Prestwich Heys v Radcliffe 0-2
Droylsden v Squires Gate 4-4, 0-1
Hyde U v Sheffield 5-1
Handsworth Parramore v Congleton T 0-1
Frickley Ath v Liversedge 10-1
Runcorn Linnets v Maltby Main 1-2
Penistone Church v Runcorn T 1-3
Charnock Richard v Leek T 2-2, 2-3
AFC Darwen v Trafford 1-4
City of Liverpool v Glossop North End 1-1, 3-2*
(2-2 at the end of normal time)
Stourport Swifts v Sporting Khalsa 2-1
Sutton Coldfield T v Gresley 3-0
Alvechurch v Bromsgrove Sporting 4-3
Malvern T v Racing Club Warwick 1-2
Bedworth U v Atherstone T 1-3
Romulus v Newcastle T 4-0
Walsall Wood v Whitchurch Alport 2-1
Highgate U v Leicester Road 3-0

Wednesfield v Chasetown 2-2, 1-3
Rugby T v Evesham U 1-0
Haughmond v Market Drayton T 1-1, 1-0
Kimberley MW v Oadby T 0-2
Loughborough Dynamo v Bottesford T 2-4
Staveley MW v Lutterworth T 3-0
Belper T v Lincoln U 2-1
Worksop T v Carlton T 2-1
Loughborough University v Cleethorpes T 3-3, 0-1
AFC Mansfield v Rainworth MW 1-0
Anstey Nomads v Clipstone 4-1
Grimsby Bor v Long Eaton U 1-0
Quorn v South Normanton Ath 3-2
Stamford AFC v Peterborough Sports 1-1, 3-4
Northampton Sileby Rangers v Wisbech T 1-1, 0-0*
Wisbech T won 5-3 on penalties
Deeping Rangers v AFC Rushden & D 1-1, 0-3
Harborough T v Cambridge C 1-2
Corby T v Dunstable T 3-3, 4-0
Biggleswade v Soham T Rangers 3-5
Thetford T v Godmanchester R 0-5
Desborough T v Kempston R 0-3
Bedford T v Dereham T 4-1
Histon v Eynesbury R 1-1, 3-1
Daventry T v Yaxley 7-5
Barton R v Rothwell Corinthians 3-2
Spalding U v Wellingborough T 3-2
Waltham Abbey v Bury T 0-2
Felixstowe & Walton U v Walthamstow 0-1
AFC Sudbury v Mildenhall T 2-0
Heybridge Swifts v West Essex 3-0
Aveley v Potters Bar T 0-2
Hertford T v Tilbury 5-3
Stansted v Takeley 0-1
Long Melford v St Margaretsbury 3-0
Bowers & Pitsea v Barking 1-0
Coggeshall T v Witham T 0-0, 3-1
Haverhill R v Maldon & Tiptree 2-1
Brantham Ath v Welwyn Garden City 1-0
Haringey Bor v Stanway R 1-0
Cheshunt v Canvey Island 1-0
FC Romania v Grays Ath 2-0
Woodbridge T v Hadleigh U 5-1
Basildon U v Whitton U 2-1
Great Wakering R v Leyton Ath 4-1
FC Clacton v Ware 2-4
Newmarket T v Hullbridge Sports 2-1
Saffron Walden T v Hoddesdon T 4-1
Brentwood T v Sporting Bengal U 1-1, 3-1
Romford v Baldock T 3-2
Easington Sports v Chipping Sodbury T 1-2
Northwood v Longlevens 3-1
Ardley U v Burnham 2-4
AFC Dunstable v Swindon Supermarine 0-0, 0-3
Crawley Green v Aylesbury U 2-3
Kidlington v Marlow 0-1
Thame U v Berkhamsted 0-2
Bishop's Cleeve v North Greenford U 5-2
Didcot T v Aylesbury 1-1, 1-0
Brackley T Saints v Hadley 0-0, 0-1
Slimbridge AFC v Wantage T 1-1, 0-1
Chalfont St Peter v London Lions 1-0
Beaconsfield T v Uxbridge 2-0
Colney Heath v Cinderford T 1-3
Harpenden T v Leverstock Green 0-6
Brimscombe & Thrupp v Hayes & Yeading U 0-7
North Leigh v Hanwell T 2-4
Cirencester T v Windsor 5-0
Royal Wootton Bassett T v Lydney T 0-0, 3-5
Tooting & Mitcham U v Horley T 2-1
East Grinstead T v South Park 1-0
Walton Casuals v Shoreham 6-0
Beckenham T v Epsom & Ewell 2-2, 3-0*
(0-0 at the end of normal time)
Three Bridges v Phoenix Sports 2-3
Arundel v Herne Bay 1-7
Sittingbourne v Bearsted 2-0
Newhaven v Pagham 0-2
Cobham v Egham T 1-3
Cray Valley PM v Ashford T (Middlesex) 4-1
Molesey v Lewes 0-0, 1-8
AFC Croydon Ath v Hanworth Villa 1-1, 1-0
Raynes Park Vale v Spelthorne Sports 1-1, 3-4
Carshalton Ath v Horsham 0-1
Ashford U v Horsham YMCA 0-2
AFC Uckfield T v Broadfields U 4-1

Greenwich Bor v Lancing	3-7
Chipstead v Corinthian	0-1
Loxwood v Erith T	1-1, 1-4
Hythe T v Worthing U	3-0
Whyteleafe v Saltdean U	1-1, 2-1
Corinthian Casuals v Croydon	6-0
Ramsgate v Chatham T	2-1
CB Hounslow U v Whitstable T	0-2
Cray W v Rushtall	1-1, 2-2*
Cray W won 4-3 on penalties	
Faversham T v Hackney Wick	4-1
Balham v Thamesmead T	0-2
Hastings U v VCD Ath	3-2
Sevenoaks T v Bedfont Sports	1-0
Thatcham T v Bemerton Heath Harlequins	0-0, 2-3
Salisbury v Hamble Club	6-0
Binfield v Brockenhurst	2-1
Moneyfields v Andover New Street	3-1
Hamworthy U v AFC Totton	1-0
Lymington T v Frimley Green	2-0
Fleet T v Petersfield T	3-1
United Services Portsmouth v Sholing	1-3
AFC Stoneham v Westfield	2-0
Baffins Milton R v Hartley Wintney	1-4
Wimborne T v Newport (IW)	6-0
Melksham T v Blackfield & Langley	1-0
Ascot U v Horndean	1-2
Winchester C v Bournemouth	1-0
Bodmin T v Cadbury Heath	2-2, 1-4
Bideford AFC v Bristol Manor Farm	2-2, 2-4*
(2-2 at the end of normal time)	
Bradford T v Paulton R	0-1
Hallen v Bridport	0-5
Barnstaple T v Shaftesbury	0-1
Plymouth Parkway v Larkhall Ath	1-0
Portland U v Bitton	0-2
Westbury U v Saltash U	3-0
Cheddar v Yate T	0-3
Willand R v Street	1-2
Buckland Ath v Mangotsfield U	2-0

FIRST QUALIFYING ROUND

Radcliffe v Stalybridge Celtic	1-0
Squires Gate v City of Liverpool	1-5
Lancaster C v Trafford	0-2
South Shields v Garforth T	5-1
Warrington T v Burscough	4-0
Runcorn T v Irlam	2-3
Whitley Bay v Whitby T	1-0
Marine v Scarborough Ath	1-1, 3-2
Colne v Hyde U	2-0
Newcastle Benfield v Workington	1-1, 3-5
Dunston UTS v North Ferriby U	4-1
Knaresborough T v Kendal T	7-3
Atherton Colleries v Kidsgrove Ath	1-2
Guisborough T v Farsley Celtic	0-4
Congleton T v Consett	0-1
Witton Alb v Bottesford T	5-0
Clitheroe v Mossley	2-5
Ashton Ath v Morpeth T	1-1, 2-1
Maltby Main v Frickley Ath	1-2
Parkgate v Leek T	2-2, 0-3
Bamber Bridge v Tadcaster Alb	3-1
Basford U v Staveley MW	1-3
Highgate U v Stourbridge	1-2
Cleethorpes T v Walsall Wood	4-1
AFC Mansfield v Stourport Swifts	2-1
Romulus v Belper T	4-0
Nantwich T v Worksop T	5-2
Sutton Coldfield T v Rushall Olympic	2-2, 1-0
Quorn v Atherstone T	0-1
Coalville T v Racing Club Warwick	2-1
Hednesford T v Tamworth	2-0
Grimsby Bor v Stafford Rangers	1-2
Matlock T v Halesowen T	1-2
Barwell v Buxton	2-5
Daventry T v Grantham T	0-1
Mickleover Sports v Haughmond	6-0
Anstey Nomads v Oadby T	2-1
Chasetown v Gainsborough Trinity	1-1, 2-8
Redditch U v Rugby T	2-4
Stratford T v Alvechurch	0-1
Leverstock Green v Hadley	0-0, 1-0
St Neots T v Bishop's Stortford	2-1
Burnham v Bury T	1-0
Cambridge C v Brightlingsea Regent	3-4
Aylesbury U v Marlow	0-0, 1-2*
(1-1 at the end of normal time)	
Heybridge Swifts v Newmarket T	2-0
Hanwell T v Potters Bar T	2-1
Brantham Ath v Spalding U	1-0
Corby T v Hertford T	2-0
AFC Sudbury v Royston T	3-2
Ware v Lowestoft T	0-1
Hendon v Harlow T	1-1, 2-1*
(1-1 at the end of normal time)	
Brentwood T v Haringey Bor	2-3
Haverhill R v Long Melford	0-0, 2-1
AFC Hornchurch v Harrow Bor	1-0
Swindon Supermarine v Woodbridge T	7-1
FC Romania v Soham T Rangers	4-0
Chesham U v Biggleswade T	2-1
Chalfont St Peter v Kempston R	1-1, 2-2*
Kempston R won 4-1 on penalties	
Great Wakering R v Wisbech T	3-1
Romford v Kettering T	1-4
King's Lynn T v Histon	2-2, 7-0
Hayes & Yeading U v AFC Rushden & D	2-1
Northwood v Kings Langley	0-0, 1-3
Coggeshall T v Berkhamsted	1-1, 2-1
Saffron Walden T v St Ives T	0-0, 1-3
Walthamstow v Beaconsfield T	0-2
Wingate & Finchley v Didcot T	0-2
Cheshunt v Leiston	2-2, 2-4
Hitchin T v Godmanchester R	3-1
Bowers & Pitsea v Takeley	5-1
Basildon U v Peterborough Sports	0-2
Barton R v Needham Market	0-4
Enfield T v Bedford T	0-3
Ramsgate v Sevenoaks T	1-1, 3-1
Hastings U v Kingstonian	2-1
Metropolitan Police v Cray W	3-2
Faversham T v Worthing	1-3
Farnborough v Lewes	2-2, 1-1*
Lewes won 4-1 on penalties	
AFC Uckfield T v AFC Croydon Ath	1-0
Fleet T v East Grinstead T	1-2
Phoenix Sports v Lancing	2-2, 3-0
Phoenix Sports removed for fielding an ineligible player. Lancing awarded the tie.	
Merstham v Cray Valley PM	0-0, 3-3*
Cray Valley PM won 4-1 on penalties	
Spelthorne Sports v Erith T	1-5
Hythe T v Tonbridge Angels	0-2
Egham T v Staines T	1-0
Corinthian Casuals v Whyteleafe	0-0, 1-2
Whyteleafe removed for fielding an ineligible player. Corinthian Casuals awarded the tie.	
Margate v Horndean	3-2
Moneyfields v Thamesmead T	1-0
Whitstable T v Bognor Regis T	0-5
Horsham YMCA v Tooting & Mitcham U	1-2
Corinthian v Horsham	1-1, 0-5
Pagham v Whitehawk	0-2
Leatherhead v Herne Bay	2-0
Beckenham T v Walton Casuals	0-0, 0-3
Burgess Hill T v Folkestone Invicta	1-0
Dorking W v Hartley Wintney	2-0
Sittingbourne v Gosport Bor	0-1
Weymouth v Banbury U	1-1, 1-2
Melksham T v Merthyr T	1-4
Bitton v Westbury U	3-0
AFC Stoneham v Cirencester T	0-7
Salisbury v Yate T	1-1, 3-1
Cadbury Heath v Cinderford T	0-1
Binfield v Buckland Ath	3-0
Frome T v Winchester C	1-1, 1-2*
(1-1 at the end of normal time)	
Wimborne T v Dorchester T	1-1, 0-3
Shaftesbury v Poole T	0-1
Sholing v Hamworthy U	0-0, 1-0
Plymouth Parkway v Street	0-0, 4-1
Taunton T v Bemerton Heath Harlequins	7-1
Paulton R v Basingstoke T	1-1, 0-2
Bridport v Tiverton T	0-1
Bishop's Cleeve v Wantage T	0-2
Chipping Sodbury T v Bristol Manor Farm	0-2
Lymington T v Lydney T	2-2, 2-1

SECOND QUALIFYING ROUND

Chester v City of Liverpool	4-0
Ashton U v Trafford	3-0

Radcliffe v Curzon Ashton	1-2
Farsley Celtic AFC v Southport	0-3
Mossley v Kidsgrove Ath	1-2
Staveley MW v Guiseley	0-4
South Shields v Stockport Co	1-2
Knaresborough T v Workington	1-4
Cleethorpes T v Bamber Bridge	3-3, 5-0
York C v Ashton Ath	5-0
Marine v Frickley Ath	1-0
Dunston UTS v Irlam	2-1
FC United of Manchester v Colne	2-0
Nantwich T v Blyth Spartans	3-3, 0-1
Darlington v Bradford (Park Avenue)	0-1
Chorley v Leek T	3-0
Witton Alb v Spennymoor T	2-1
Altrincham v Whitley Bay	5-0
Consett v Warrington T	3-3, 0-2
Sutton Coldfield T v Alfreton T	2-2, 0-3
Boston U v Peterborough Sports	0-2
St Ives T v Grantham T	1-1, 2-0
Kidderminster H v Atherstone T	5-0
Stourbridge v Leamington	3-2
Rugby T v Hednesford T	1-3
St Neots T v Romulus	4-3
Nuneaton Bor v Brackley T	1-1, 0-2
Alvechurch v Corby T	1-4
Kettering T v AFC Mansfield	2-1
Anstey Nomads v Mickleover Sports	1-7
Halesowen T v Gainsborough Trinity	0-3
King's Lynn T v Stafford Rangers	3-1
AFC Telford U v Bedford T	3-1
Buxton v Coalville T	0-0, 1-4
Hampton & Richmond Bor v Burgess Hill T	3-0
Kings Langley v Lewes	1-1, 1-2
Wealdstone v Great Wakering R	2-0
Welling U v Chesham U	2-1
Hendon v Lancing	1-1, 4-0
Woking v Tooting & Mitcham U	4-0
Hanwell T v Lowestoft T	1-0
Egham T v Brightlingsea Regent	3-3, 1-2
Chelmsford C v Worthing	1-2
Concord Rangers v Margate	2-0
Leverstock Green v Dorking W	2-4
Haringey Bor v Erith T	2-1
Leiston v Hastings U	3-4
Coggeshall T v Walton Casuals	2-0
St Albans C v Corinthian Casuals	1-1, 3-0
Bowers & Pitsea v Hemel Hempstead T	1-6
Billericay T v Burnham	4-1
Kempston R v Marlow	1-0
Hitchin T v Didcot T	1-1, 0-0*
Hitchin T won 4-2 on penalties	
Bognor Regis T v AFC Sudbury	1-1, 2-3*
(2-2 at the end of normal time)	
Haverhill R v Leatherhead	0-6
East Thurrock U v Whitehawk	2-3
Brantham Ath v Eastbourne Bor	0-1
Oxford C v Cray Valley PM	5-0
Gosport Bor v Ramsgate	2-3
AFC Hornchurch v East Grinstead T	2-1
AFC Uckfield T v Dartford	1-3
Hayes & Yeading U v Moneyfields	0-1
FC Romania v Beaconsfield T	0-2
Horsham v Heybridge Swifts	4-3
Dulwich Hamlet v Tonbridge Angels	3-1
Metropolitan Police v Needham Market	2-2, 3-2*
(2-2 at the end of normal time)	
Merthyr T v Winchester C	1-4
Lymington T v Torquay U	0-7
Chippenham T v Swindon Supermarine	2-2, 1-0
Bristol Manor Farm v Basingstoke T	5-2
Gloucester C v Plymouth Parkway	3-1
Weston-super-Mare v Salisbury	2-2, 3-2*
(1-1 at the end of normal time)	
Tiverton T v Dorchester T	2-0
Hereford v Truro C	0-0, 4-3*
(3-3 at the end of normal time)	
Poole T v Cinderford T	3-0
Taunton T v Bitton	4-0
Banbury U v Bath C	0-2
Hungerford T v Wantage T	1-1, 2-2*
Hungerford T won 4-1 on penalties	
Binfield v Cirencester T	0-3
Slough T v Sholing	2-2, 3-0*
(0-0 at the end of normal time)	

THIRD QUALIFYING ROUND

Workington v Kidsgrove Ath	0-0, 1-2*
(1-1 at the end of normal time)	
Stockport Co v Corby T	3-0
Mickleover Sports v Alfreton T	1-2
Kettering T v Hednesford T	4-0
Brackley T v Marine	2-3
Peterborough Sports v Chorley	0-3
Altrincham v Bradford (Park Avenue)	4-2
Dunston UTS v Chester	4-3
Stourbridge v Kidderminster H	3-2
FC United of Manchester v Witton Alb	1-2
Cleethorpes T v Guiseley	2-2, 1-2
St Neots T v Coalville T	2-2, 3-3*
St Neots T won 5-3 on penalties	
King's Lynn T v Ashton U	0-1
Curzon Ashton v Southport	1-2
Gainsborough Trinity v Blyth Spartans	1-2
York C v St Ives T	3-0
Warrington T v AFC Telford U	2-1
Tiverton T v Metropolitan Police	3-3, 0-1*
(0-0 at the end of normal time)	
Haringey Bor v AFC Sudbury	2-1
Gloucester C v Dorking W	3-3, 3-0
Leatherhead v Hanwell T	1-1, 0-0*
Leatherhead won 4-2 on penalties	
Eastbourne Bor v Dulwich Hamlet	4-3
Woking v Kempston R	3-2
Taunton T v St Albans C	5-2
Billericay T v Whitehawk	9-1
Hereford v Welling U	0-2
Hitchin T v Hastings U	2-0
Concord Rangers v Beaconsfield T	2-1
Hemel Hempstead T v Ramsgate	5-0
Moneyfields v Worthing	2-3
Bath C v Lewes	3-0
Slough T v Bristol Manor Farm	2-2, 4-0
Hungerford T v Wealdstone	1-2
Hampton & Richmond Bor v AFC Hornchurch	1-0
Chippenham T v Hendon	4-1
Brightlingsea Regent v Torquay U	0-3
Weston-super-Mare v Coggeshall T	1-0
Horsham v Poole T	1-1, 1-2
Oxford C v Dartford	4-1
Winchester C v Cirencester T	3-0

FOURTH QUALIFYING ROUND

Guiseley v Stourbridge	3-1
Warrington T v FC Halifax T	2-2, 0-2
Chorley v Barrow AFC	3-2
Hartlepool U v Kidsgrove Ath	1-0
AFC Fylde v Chesterfield	1-3
Southport v Ashton U	2-1
Blyth Spartans v York C	0-1
Harrogate T v Wrexham	0-0, 0-2
Dunston UTS v Gateshead	0-4
Stockport Co v Altrincham	2-0
Marine v Salford C	1-2
Witton Alb v Solihull Moors	0-2
Alfreton T v St Neots T	4-0
Woking v Welling U	1-0
Hitchin T v Leatherhead	1-1, 2-1*
(1-1 at the end of normal time)	
Chippenham T v Maidenhead U	1-1, 0-1
Eastbourne Bor v Slough T	1-2
Hemel Hempstead T v Oxford C	1-1, 0-5
Weston-super-Mare v Bath C	1-0
Boreham Wood v Dagenham & R	2-2, 1-0
Metropolitan Police v Havant & Waterlooville	1-0
Gloucester C v Bromley	0-1
Aldershot T v Kettering T	2-0
Torquay U v Winchester C	4-1
Billericay T v Taunton T	2-2, 1-0
Eastleigh v Hampton & Richmond Bor	0-1
Wealdstone v Sutton U	1-2
Ebbsfleet U v Worthing	4-0
Maidstone U v Leyton Orient	2-0
Haringey Bor v Poole T	2-1
Barnet v Braintree T	4-2
Concord Rangers v Dover Ath	0-1

THE EMIRATES FA CUP 2018–19

COMPETITION PROPER

■ *Denotes player sent off.*

FIRST ROUND

Friday, 9 November 2018

Haringey Bor (0) 0

AFC Wimbledon (0) 1 *(Pinnock 90)* 2710

Haringey Bor: (4231) Douglas; Olufemi, Richards, Kirby, O'Donoghue; Stone (Rowe 86), Staunton; Barker (McDonald 76), Aresti (Djessi-Sambu 53), Nouble; Ademiluyi.
AFC Wimbledon: (433) McDonnell; Sibbick, Thomas, Oshilaja, Purrington; Wagstaff (Jervis 68), Hartigan (Wordsworth 59), Soares; Pinnock, Pigott, Appiah.
Referee: Michael Salisbury.

Saturday, 10 November 2018

Accrington S (1) 1 *(Barlaser 34)*

Colchester U (0) 0 1267

Accrington S: (442) Ripley; Johnson, Hughes, Ihiekwe, Richards-Everton; McConville, Barlaser, Finley, Clark; Kee, Charman (Mingoia 90).
Colchester U: (4231) Gilmartin (Barnes 30); Jackson, Kent, Eastman (Prosser 3), Vincent-Young; Lapslie, Pell; Senior (Mandron 77), Szmodics, Dickenson; Nouble.
Referee. Martin Coy.

Aldershot T (1) 1 *(Fowler 12)*

Bradford C (0) 1 *(Knight-Percival 71)* 2455

Aldershot T: (442) Mannion; McCoy, Fowler, Osho, Kinsella; Booty (Wanadio 81), McDonnell, Gallagher, Barrett (Howell 58); McClure (Berkeley-Agyepong 76), Rendell.
Bradford C: (4222) O'Donnell; McGowan, O'Connor A, Knight-Percival, Wood; O'Brien L, Akpan (Devine 80); Payne (Wright 75), Ball (O'Brien J 64); Miller, Doyle.
Referee: Paul Marsden.

Barnsley (0) 4 *(Woodrow 48, Fryers 53, Potts 77, Moore 81)*

Notts Co (0) 0 5878

Barnsley: (442) Davies; Cavare (Brown 68), Pinnock, Lindsay, Fryers; Potts, Mowatt (Hedges 77), McGeehan, Thiam; Woodrow (Bahre 68), Moore.
Notts Co: (4411) Fitzsimons; Turley, Brisley, Ward, Evina (Dunne 82); Boldewijn, Milsom, Hewitt, Thomas (Jones 72); Alessandra; Dennis (Etete 72).
Referee: Sebastian Stockbridge.

Bromley (1) 1 *(Johnson R 40)*

Peterborough U (1) 3 *(Godden 45, 56, Ward 84)* 3107

Bromley: (442) Gregory; Wood, Johnson R, Holland, Okoye (Craske 75); Brindley, Porter, Raymond■, Mekki (Goddard 68); Sutherland, Bugiel (Quigley 51).
Peterborough U: (442) Chapman; Naismith, Woodyard, Tafazolli, Bennett; Denton, O'Hara, Cooper (Dembele 74), Ward; Cummings (Toney 86), Godden (Reed 90).
Referee: Kevin Johnson.

Bury (3) 5 *(O'Shea 12, Mayor 18, Moore 36, 64, Telford 90)*

Dover Ath (0) 0 2355

Bury: (532) Murphy; Miller, Aimson, Thompson, Stokes, McFadzean; O'Shea, Mayor (Adams J 74), Danns (Styles 68); Moore (Telford 79), Maynard.
Dover Ath: (442) Walker; Passley, Debayo, Adebowale (Daniel 65), Lokko; Brundle, Diarra, Gomis, Lewis (Nortey 69); Allen, Effiong (Wratten 84).
Referee: Richard Hulme.

Chesterfield (1) 1 *(Maguire 17)*

Billericay T (0) 1 *(Emmanuel 52)* 2952

Chesterfield: (451) Burton; Evans, Hollis, Maguire, Binnom-Williams; Hines, Rowley, Smith J, Weston (Denton 86), Reid (Shaw 66); Fortune (Amantchi 66).
Billericay T: (451) Julian; Kizzi, Doe, Hayles (Inman 35), Kennedy; Emmanuel (O'Hara 70), Deering, Waldren, Lafayette, Howells; Robinson (Jahraldo-Martin 60).
Referee: Martin Woods.

Crewe Alex (0) 0

Carlisle U (0) 1 *(Devitt 90)* 2467

Crewe Alex: (442) Garratt; Hunt, Ray, Nolan, O'Connor; Finney (Ainley 58), Pickering, Ng, Kirk; Nicholls (Miller 75), Porter (Bowery 57).
Carlisle U: (433) Collin; Liddle, Gerrard, Gillesphey, Grainger; Jones (Sowerby 73), Devitt, Slater; Yates, Bennett, Hope (Campbell 81).
Referee: Lee Swabey.

Ebbsfleet U (0) 0

Cheltenham T (0) 0 1624

Ebbsfleet U: (442) Ashmore; Magri, Winfield, Clark, Bush; Payne, Adams (King 60), Coulson (McQueen 79), Weston (Wilson 89); Kedwell, Whitely.
Cheltenham T: (352) Flinders; Forster, Tozer, Mullins (Barnett 22); Broom, Clements, Maddox, Thomas (Atangana 84), Hussey; Mooney (Addai 50), Varney.
Referee: John Busby.

Exeter C (0) 2 *(Tillson 69, Abrahams 90)*

Blackpool (3) 3 *(Dodoo 3, Cullen 19, Pritchard 24)* 3188

Exeter C: (442) Hamon; Sweeney (Oates 73), O'Shea, Croll, Woodman; Collins, Tillson, Taylor, Law; Stockley, Forte (Abrahams 52).
Blackpool: (442) Mafoumbi; McLaughlin (Delfouneso 89), Tilt, Heneghan, Turton; O'Sullivan (Nottingham 74), Thompson, Guy, Pritchard; Cullen (Feeney 67), Dodoo.
Referee: Alan Young.

Gillingham (0) 0

Hartlepool U (0) 0 2224

Gillingham: (3412) Holy; Ehmer, Zakuani, Fuller; O'Neill, Oldaker, Byrne, Ogilvie (Bingham 46); Charles-Cook; Hanlan (List 74), Eaves.
Hartlepool U: (442) Loach; Richardson, Anderson, Magnay, Kitching; Donaldson (Newton 90), Noble, Featherstone, McLaughlin; Dinanga (Muir 77), James (O'Neill 71).
Referee: Brett Huxtable.

Grimsby T (0) 3 *(Embleton 50, Thomas 61, Vernam 73)*

Milton Keynes D (1) 1 *(Agard 23)* 1991

Grimsby T: (4411) McKeown; Hendrie, Davis, Collins, Famewo; Embleton (Woolford 90), Clifton, Hessenthaler, Pringle; Vernam (Welsh 77); Thomas (Cardwell 86).
Milton Keynes D: (343) Nicholls; Brittain, Walsh, Cargill; Williams, Gilbey, Houghton (Cisse 79), Lewington; Agard, Aneke (D'Ath 64), Healey (Simpson 75).
Referee: Carl Boyeson.

Lincoln C (1) 3 *(Anderson 16, Pett 52, Andrade 90)*

Northampton T (0) 2 *(Bridge 55, van Veen 81)* 6012

Lincoln C: (442) Vickers; Wilson, Shackell, Bostwick, Toffolo; Anderson, Pett, O'Connor, Andrade (Wharton 90); McCartan (Green 86), Akinde (Rhead 78).
Northampton T: (442) Cornell; Odofin, Turnbull, Pierre, Buchanan; Hoskins, McWilliams S, O'Toole, Bridge (Powell A 72); Williams D (Morias■ 58), van Veen.
Referee: Graham Salisbury.

Luton T (1) 2 *(Shinnie 41, Cornick 71)*

Wycombe W (0) 0 5343

Luton T: (41212) Shea; Stacey, Bradley, Pearson, Justin; Rea; Cornick, Ruddock; Shinnie (Grant 52); Collins, Lee (LuaLua 86).
Wycombe W: (41212) Allsop; McCarthy, Jombati, El-Abd, Jacobson; Bean (Kashket 85); Gape, Thompson; Cowan-Hall (Williams 69); Samuel (Mackail-Smith 69), Onyedinma.
Referee: Craig Hicks.

Maidenhead U (0) 0

Portsmouth (1) 4 *(Thompson B 43, Hawkins 55, Lowe 60, Wheeler 83)* 3205

Maidenhead U: (4141) Pentney; Clerima, Kilgour, Massey, Steer; Obileye; Odametey, Comley (Owusu 54), Upward (Akintunde 46), Clifton (Bird 67); Kelly.
Portsmouth: (4231) MacGillivray; Thompson N (Burgess 85), Whatmough, Clarke, Brown; Naylor, Thompson B; Lowe (Wheeler 63), Evans (Pitman B 64), Curtis; Hawkins.
Referee: Dean Whitestone.

Maidstone U (0) 2 *(Powell 51, Turgott 69 (pen))*

Macclesfield T (1) 1 *(Stephens 14)* 2169

Maidstone U: (442) Smith; Finney, De Havilland, Walton, McLennan; Paxman (Tajbakhsh 75), Powell (Durojaiye 86), Phillips, Turgott; Romain, Cassidy.
Macclesfield T: (442) O'Hara; Hodgkiss, Kelleher, Grimes, Fitzpatrick; Napa (Blissett 73), Rose, Lloyd (Durrell 81), Vincenti (Welch-Hayes 66); Stephens, Smith.
Referee: Neil Hair.

Metropolitan Police (0) 0

Newport Co (1) 2 *(Amond 41, Matt 48)* 1137

Metropolitan Police: (4411) Williams; Webb, Arthur (Kozakis 82), McLaughlin, Guinness-Walker; Mummery (Hippolyte 59), Birch■, Chislett, Knight (Gilbert 70); Mazzone; Blackmore.
Newport Co: (352) Day; Pipe (O'Brien 52), Franks, Demetriou; Willmott, Bakinson, Dolan, Sheehan (Marsh-Brown 64), Butler; Amond, Matt (Semenyo 83).
Referee: Matthew Donohue.

Morecambe (0) 0

FC Halifax T (0) 0 1736

Morecambe: (4231) Halstead; Mills, Old, Lavelle, Conlan; Wildig, Cranston (Oswell 81); Mandeville (Tutte 55), Leitch-Smith, Oates (Ellison 55); Oliver.
FC Halifax T: (442) Johnson; Hanson, Clarke, Brown, Skarz; Odelusi (Preston 68), Staunton, Maher, Sellers; Southwell (Edwards 83), King.
Referee: Darren Drysdale.

Oxford U (0) 0

Forest Green R (0) 0 3933

Oxford U: (41212) Eastwood; McMahon, Nelson, Dickie, Garbutt (Norman 46); Mousinho (Hanson 63); Brannagan, Henry; Browne; Whyte, Smith (Mackie 63).
Forest Green R: (4231) Montgomery; Winchester, McGinley, Rawson, Archibald; James (Worthington 88), Digby; Campbell (Williams 65), Brown, Grubb; Reid.
Referee: Nicholas Kinseley.

Plymouth Arg (0) 1 *(Lameiras 90)*

Stevenage (0) 0 5719

Plymouth Arg: (433) Macey; Moore, Songo'o, Canavan, Grant C; Sarcevic, Fox, Ness (Lameiras 55); Carey, Ladapo, Grant J.
Stevenage: (442) Dieng; Wildin, Cuthbert, Wilkinson, Hunt; Kennedy (Campbell-Ryce 64), Byrom, Timlin (Sonupe 90), Seddon (Newton 81); Revell, Guthrie.
Referee: Lee Collins.

Rochdale (2) 2 *(Mellish 21 (og), Henderson 23)*

Gateshead (0) 1 *(Mellish 49)* 2415

Rochdale: (433) Moore; Rafferty, McGahey, Delaney, Hart; Dooley, Camps, Done (Andrew 56); Inman (Clough 89), Henderson, Jordan LR Williams (Perkins 75).
Gateshead: (532) Pears; Tinkler, Kerr, Williamson, Mellish, Barrow; Olley, Hunter (Molyneux 65), White; Boden (Rigg 74), Armstrong.
Referee: Peter Wright.

Scunthorpe U (2) 2 *(Perch 16, Novak 33)*

Burton Alb (0) 1 *(Boyce 79)* 2260

Scunthorpe U: (442) Alnwick; Clarke (Horsfield 45), McArdle, Burgess, Butroid; Colclough (Dales 79), Perch, Lund, Thomas (Wootton 76); Novak, Ugbo.
Burton Alb: (433) Collins; Akins, Brayford, McFadzean, McCrory (Templeton 67); Allen, Quinn, Fraser; Hesketh (Sordell 60 (Miller 81)), Cole, Boyce.
Referee: Andy Haines.

Southend U (1) 1 *(Kightly 9)*

Crawley T (0) 1 *(White 85 (og))* 3935

Southend U: (442) Oxley; Demetriou, White, Turner, Hendrie; McLaughlin, Mantom, Dieng, Kightly (Bunn 71); Cox, Robinson (Yearwood 71).
Crawley T: (4141) Morris; Young, Connolly, McNerney, Maguire; Payne; Francomb (Nathaniel-George 57), Morais, Camara, Gambin (Grego-Cox 80); Palmer.
Referee: Scott Oldham.

Southport (1) 2 *(Winnard 29, Gilchrist 70)*

Boreham Wood (0) 0 1460

Southport: (442) Hanford; Richards, Morgan, Edwards, Ogle; Charles (Green 86), Winnard, Wood, Bauress (Homson-Smith 90); Sampson, Gilchrist (Archer 80).
Boreham Wood: (433) Huddart; Woodards (Shaibu 56), Ricketts, Parry, Fyfield; Shakes, Stephens, Murtagh (Smith 81); Thomas, Umerah, Ugwu (Ash 78).
Referee: Marc Edwards.

Sutton U (0) 0

Slough T (0) 0 1830

Sutton U: (442) Butler; Bennett (Bailey 45), Clough, Collins, Thomas; Bolarinwa, Davis, Eastmond, Cadogan; Drinan (Brown W 64), Ayunga (Beckwith 64).
Slough T: (442) Turner; Jackman, Nisbet, Togwell L, Wells; Dobson (Dunn 89), Togwell S, Davies, Harris W; Harris B (Williams 66), Stevens.
Referee: Sam Purkiss.

Swindon T (1) 2 *(Twine 12, Alzate 76)*

York C (1) 1 *(Ferguson 43)* 3744

Swindon T: (352) Vigouroux; Woolfenden, Nelson, Conroy; McGlashan (Knoyle 88), Iandolo, Dunne, Alzate, Anderson; Twine, Adebayo.
York C: (352) Bartlett; Law (Harris 61), Davis, Newton; Dyer (Parkin 80), Hawkins, Griffiths, Moke, Ferguson; Burrow, Bray (Langstaff 80).
Referee: Carl Brook.

Torquay U (0) 0

Woking (0) 1 *(Kretzschmar 48 (pen))* 2419

Torquay U: (442) MacDonald; Wynter, Cameron, Koue Niate, Davis; Andrews (Keating 64), Lemonheigh-Evans, Dickson, Lumbombo Kalala (Koszela 87); Janneh (Williams 82), Reid.
Woking: (442) Ross; Collier, Gerring, Cook, Casey; Kretzschmar, Edser, Hester-Cook (Gayle 82), Little; Loza, Hyde.
Referee: Declan Bourne.

Tranmere R (1) 3 *(Jennings 34, 78, Norwood 89)*

Oxford C (1) 3 *(Tshimanga 39, 66, 82)* 4206

Tranmere R: (4231) Davies; Caprice, McNulty, Monthe, Buxton; Harris (Gilmour 71), Banks; Jennings, Cole (Smith 57), Mullin (Tollitt 46); Norwood.
Oxford C: (433) King; Godwin-Malife, Oastler, Musonda, Jefford; Ashby, Fleet, Wiltshire; Nombe (Jones 90), Tshimanga, McEachran.
Referee: Daniel Middleton.

Walsall (2) 3 *(Cook 12, Ginnelly 28, Devlin 77)*

Coventry C (1) 2 *(Clarke-Harris 33, Thomas 56)* 4760

Walsall: (442) Roberts; Devlin, Martin, Guthrie, Leahy; Ismail, Kinsella, Dobson, Ginnelly (Morris 90); Gordon, Cook.
Coventry C: (433) Burge; Thompson, Willis, Hyam, Mason; Shipley, Doyle, Ogogo (Bayliss 71); Thomas (Jones 71), Clarke-Harris, Hiwula (Chaplin 81).
Referee: Thomas Bramall.

Yeovil T (1) 1 *(Fisher 8)*

Stockport Co (2) 3 *(Warburton 34, Bell 38, Mulhern 62)* 2550

Yeovil T: (442) Baxter; James, Donnellan, Mugabi, Dickinson; McDonald, Pattison, D'Almeida, Gray (Browne 60); Olomola (Patrick 20), Fisher (Zoko 28).
Stockport Co: (4231) Hinchliffe; Minihan, Palmer, Cowan, Duxbury; Keane, Walker; Thomas, Osborne (Downing 87), Warburton (Dimaio 59); Bell (Mulhern 60).
Referee: David Rock.

Sunday, 11 November 2018

Alfreton T (0) 1 *(Sinnott 70)*

Fleetwood T (2) 4 *(Madden 13, 60 (pen), Hunter 20, Garner 90)* 827

Alfreton T: (451) Ramsbottom; Clackstone, Riley, Shiels, Wilde; Bateson (Bacon 88), Sinnott, Hotte, Clarke (Chettle 62), Johnson; Peniket.
Fleetwood T: (442) Cairns; Coyle (Wallace J 60), Eastham, Bolger, Husband; Hunter (Dempsey 81), Sheron, Holt, Wallace R; Burns (Garner 66), Madden.
Referee: Christopher Sarginson.

Barnet (1) 1 *(Robson 16)*

Bristol R (0) 1 *(Lines 66 (pen))* 1705

Barnet: (532) Cousins; Alexander, Reynolds, Robson, Sweeney, Johnson; Taylor J, Adams, Fonguck (Sparkes 69); Duku (Harrison 85), Bettamer (Walker 79).
Bristol R: (532) Smith; Sercombe, Lockyer, Craig, Clarke J, Leadbitter (Bennett 23); Kelly (Lines 46), Sinclair■, Nichols; Clarke O, Payne (Matthews 23).
Referee: Rob Lewis.

Chorley (2) 2 *(O'Keefe 2, Meppen-Walter 43)*

Doncaster R (1) 2 *(Kane 11, 77)* 3239

Chorley: (532) Urwin; Challoner■, Teague, Leather, Meppen-Walter, Blakeman; Glynn (Whitham 74), O'Keefe (Cottrell 28), Newby E; Almond (Anson 64), Carver.
Doncaster R: (433) Lawlor; Mason, Anderson T, Butler, Andrew; Whiteman, Blair (May 46), Kane; Wilks, Marquis, Coppinger.
Referee: Ross Joyce.

Guiseley (2) 4 *(Hatfield 25, Moyo 40, Felix 48, James 55)*

Cambridge U (0) 3 *(Ibehre 65, 90, Maris 89)* 1097

Guiseley: (4411) Green; Moyo, Thornton, Halls, Heaton; Walsh (Walters 54), James, Purver (Harvey 83), Felix; Hatfield; Liburd (Odejayi 68).
Cambridge U: (4411) Forde; Halliday, Taft, Taylor, Carroll; Maris, O'Neil (Amoo 46), Deegan (Lewis 71), Lambe (Azeez 62); Brown; Ibehre.
Referee: Trevor Kettle.

Hitchin T (0) 0

Solihull Moors (0) 2 *(Yussuf 72 (pen), Wright 78)* 3148

Hitchin T: (4411) Johnson; Anderson, Webb, Ferrell, Chesmain; Cain (Smith 87), Spring (Talbot 86), Green, Bickerstaff; Galliford; Forde (Charles 86).
Solihull Moors: (433) Boot; Williams, Daly, Gudger, Reckord; Osborne (Murphy 81), Storer, Carter (Maxwell 75); Thomas (Carline 70), Wright, Yussuf.
Referee: Andrew Miller.

Mansfield T (1) 1 *(Hamilton 45)*

Charlton Ath (0) 1 *(Stevenson 73)* 3240

Mansfield T: (343) Olejnik; Preston, Pearce, Sweeney; White, Bishop, Mellis, Benning (Butcher 78); Walker (Graham 90), Davies (Rose 61), Hamilton.
Charlton Ath: (41212) Phillips; Marshall, Dijksteel, Sarr, Stevenson; Pratley; Lapslie, Maloney (Clarke 69); Ward (Fosu 56); Ajose (Hackett-Fairchild 76), Ahearne-Grant.
Referee: Ollie Yates.

Port Vale (1) 1 *(Pope 35)*

Sunderland (2) 2 *(Honeyman 1, Gooch 19)* 7238

Port Vale: (532) Brown; Clark, Legge, Smith, Rawlinson, Vassell (Oyeleke 30); Hannant, Joyce, Conlon (Montano 71); Whitfield (Miller 80), Pope.
Sunderland: (4231) McLaughlin; Matthews, Flanagan, Baldwin, James; McGeouch, Honeyman; Gooch (O'Nien 81), Maguire (Power 71), McGeady; Sinclair (Maja 64).
Referee: Anthony Backhouse.

Shrewsbury T (1) 1 *(Norburn 25)*

Salford C (1) 1 *(Rooney 27)* 4351

Shrewsbury T: (41212) Arnold; Emmanuel, Waterfall, Sadler, Beckles; Grant; Norburn, Laurent; Docherty; Okenabirhie (Angol 66), Holloway (John-Lewis 90).
Salford C: (442) Neal; Wiseman, Piergianni, Pond, Touray; Politic (Walker 62), Whitehead, Maynard, Lloyd (Hogan 75); Rooney, Gaffney (Rodney 82).
Referee: Ben Toner.

Weston-super-Mare (0) 0

Wrexham (0) 2 *(Summerfield 51, Beavon 81)* 1170

Weston-super-Mare: (442) Purnell; McGrory (Phipps 83), Pope, Bower, Nurse; Swallow (Llewellyn 69), Cane, Diallo, Byrne; Hill, Welch (Lucas 12).
Wrexham: (433) Lainton; Roberts, Pearson, Lawlor, Jennings; Young, Walker (Wright 57), Summerfield; Rutherford, Holroyd (Pyke 67), Beavon (Deverdics 89).
Referee: Leigh Doughty.

Monday, 12 November 2018

Hampton & Richmond Bor (1) 1 *(Dickson 15 (pen))*

Oldham Ath (0) 2 *(Hunt 88, Lang 90)* 2720

Hampton & Richmond Bor: (433) Lovelock; Miller-Rodney, Bray, Mambo, Mavila; MacLaren (Wellard 64), Corcoran, Dundas (Obi 90); Joseph, Dickson (Murrell-Williamson 85), Connors.
Oldham Ath: (442) Iversen; Hunt, Clarke, Edmundson, Taylor; Dummigan, Lyden (Maouche 80), Gardner, Lang; Miller (O'Grady 74), Baxter (Branger 52).
Referee: Tom Nield.

FIRST ROUND REPLAYS

Tuesday, 20 November 2018

Billericay T (0) 1 *(Kizzi 63)*

Chesterfield (1) 3 *(Denton 40, 65, 87)* 2493

Billericay T: (433) Julian; Kizzi, Doe, Inman, Kennedy; Howells, Deering, Waldren (Emmanuel 58); Modeste (Hunte 74), Robinson, Lafayette.
Chesterfield: (4312) Burton; Muggleton, Maguire, Hollis, Binnom-Williams; Weston, Smith J, Rowley (Reid 90); Hines (Kiwomya 68); Denton, Shaw (Amantchi 80).
Referee: John Busby.

Bradford C (0) 1 *(Fowler 101 (og))*

Aldershot T (0) 1 *(Howell 108)* 2248

Bradford C: (3412) O'Donnell; McGowan (Brunker 65), O'Connor A, Knight-Percival; Devine, O'Brien L, O'Brien J, Chicksen (Wood 82); Payne; Ball (Miller 78), Doyle.
Aldershot T: (442) Mannion; Lelan, Osho, Fowler, Kinsella; Bernard (McCoy 83), Gallagher (Howell 95), McDonnell, Booty; Fenelon (McClure 54), Berkeley-Agyepong (Barrett 58).
aet; Bradford C won 4-1 on penalties.
Referee: Graham Salisbury.

Charlton Ath (1) 5 *(Taylor 11, 52, 85, Marshall 81, Ajose 90)*

Mansfield T (0) 0 1910

Charlton Ath: (41212) Phillips; Dijksteel, Bauer (Sarpeng-Wiredu 62), Sarr, Stevenson; Pratley (Marshall 66); Lapslie, Fosu; Clarke (Morgan 74); Taylor, Ajose.
Mansfield T: (532) Olejnik; Atkinson, Preston, Pearce, Sweeney, Benning; Mellis (White 22), Butcher, Elsnik; Rose (Walker 61), Hamilton (Graham 62).
Referee: Kevin Johnson.

Cheltenham T (0) 2 *(Barnett 66, Addai 90)*

Ebbsfleet U (0) 0 1435

Cheltenham T: (352) Flinders; Tozer, Forster, Boyle; Broom, Clements, Thomas (Addai 65), Atangana, Hussey; Barnett, Varney.
Ebbsfleet U: (4411) Ashmore; Magri■, Winfield, King, Bush; Whitely (McQueen 85), Payne, Kedwell, Shields (Graham 61); Coulson (Cheek 70); Drury.
Referee: Christopher Sarginson.

Crawley T (0) 2 *(Palmer 55, 68)*

Southend U (2) 6 *(Cox 17, 92, Bunn 31, White 97, Mantom 106, McLaughlin 114)* 3120

Crawley T: (352) Morris; Connolly, N'Gala, Francomb (Nathaniel-George 46); Young, Gambin (Grego-Cox 83), Payne (Poleon 101), Morais, Doherty; Camara, Palmer.
Southend U: (442) Oxley; Demetriou, White, Moore, Kyprianou; McLaughlin, Dieng, Hyam (Mantom 79), Bunn (Kightly 109); Cox (Hendrie 98), Robinson (McCoulsky 103).
aet.
Referee: Charles Breakspear.

Doncaster R (5) 7 *(May 7, 30, 36, 81, Blair 21, Kane 28, Marquis 85)*

Chorley (0) 0 3048

Doncaster R: (433) Lawlor; Mason, Butler, Anderson T■, Andrew; Whiteman (Rowe 46), Coppinger (Taylor 46), Kane (Crawford 70); May, Marquis, Blair.
Chorley: (352) Urwin; Teague, Leather (Jordan 64), Meppen-Walter; Anson, O'Keefe, Cottrell, Newby A (Whitham 59), Blakeman; Wilson (Noble-Lazarus 71), Almond.
Referee: Darren Drysdale.

FC Halifax T (1) 1 *(King 12)*

Morecambe (0) 0 1218

FC Halifax T: (4231) Johnson; Hanson, Clarke, Brown, Sellers; Staunton, Maher; Preston (Odelusi 90), King, Kosylo; Southwell (Edwards 86).
Morecambe: (4231) Halstead; Mills, Old, Lavelle, Conlan; Wildig (Oswell 76), Cranston (Tutte 56); Mandeville, Leitch-Smith, Oates (Ellison 87); Oliver.
Referee: Martin Coy.

Forest Green R (0) 0

Oxford U (1) 3 *(Henry 36, Mackie 47, Browne 78)* 1614

Forest Green R: (4231) Montgomery; Winchester, Rawson, McGinley, Mills; Digby, James; Reid (Morris 70), Brown (Worthington 79), Archibald (Williams 62); Campbell.
Oxford U: (433) Eastwood; Hanson, Nelson, Dickie, Garbutt; Brannagan, Mousinho, Ruffels; Whyte (Long 72), Mackie (Smith 67), Henry (Browne 67).
Referee: Trevor Kettle.

Oxford C (0) 0

Tranmere R (2) 2 *(Norwood 6, Mullin 30)* 1172

Oxford C: (4231) King; Godwin-Malife (Jones 76), Musonda, Oastler, Jefford; Fleet, Ashby; Nombe, McEachran (Bawling 75), Wiltshire (Oteduko 76); Tshimanga.
Tranmere R: (442) Davies; Caprice, Sutton, Monthe, Bakayogo (Ridehalgh 87); Cole (Mottley-Henry 63), Harris, Gilmour, Jennings; Norwood, Mullin (Stockton 82).
Referee: Craig Hicks.

Slough T (0) 1 *(Dobson 81)*

Sutton U (1) 1 *(Beautyman 9)* 1360

Slough T: (442) Turner; Jackman, Nisbet, Togwell L, Wells; Dobson, Togwell S, Davies (Dunn 75), Harris W (Williams 78); Stevens, Flood (Harris B 70).
Sutton U: (4231) Worner; Bennett, Clough, Collins, Thomas; Brown W (Davis 91 (Cadogan 111)), Taylor J (Bolarinwa 88); Ayunga (Drinan 64), Beckwith, Eastmond; Beautyman.
aet; Slough T won 8-7 on penalties.
Referee: Brett Huxtable.

Wednesday, 21 November 2018

Bristol R (0) 1 *(Nichols 62)*

Barnet (0) 2 *(Robson 75, Harrison 77)* 2740

Bristol R: (433) Smith; Partington (Leadbitter 60), Clarke J, Craig, Kelly (Lockyer 79); Sercombe, Upson, Clarke O (Payne 60); Bennett, Nichols, Rodman.
Barnet: (352) Cousins; Sweeney, Reynolds, Robson; Alexander, Adams, Fonguck (Sparkes 73), Taylor J, Johnson; Duku (Walker 35), Bettamer (Harrison 67).
Referee: Lee Swabey.

Hartlepool U (2) 3 *(Magnay 21, McLaughlin 32, O'Neill 114)*

Gillingham (0) 4 *(Ehmer 50, Eaves 90 (pen), O'Neill 102, List 107)* 1873

Hartlepool U: (442) Loach; Richardson, Davies (Anderson 38), Magnay, Kitching; Donaldson, Featherstone (Muir 97), Noble, McLaughlin; James (Newton 84), Dinanga (O'Neill 67).
Gillingham: (4312) Holy; O'Neill, Ehmer, Zakuani, Fuller (Garmston 73); Byrne, Oldaker, Bingham; Charles-Cook (Rees 64); Eaves (Lacey 118), Hanlan (List 46).
aet.
Referee: Scott Oldham.

Salford C (0) 1 *(Rooney 77)*

Shrewsbury T (1) 3 *(Okenabirhie 33, 90, Docherty 63)* 2432

Salford C: (442) Neal; Wiseman, Pond, Piergianni, Touray; Lloyd (Maynard 64), Whitehead, Walker, Politic (Hogan 64); Rooney, Gaffney.
Shrewsbury T: (41212) Arnold; Emmanuel, Waterfall, Sadler, Beckles; Grant; Norburn (Colkett 78), Docherty (Bolton 88); Laurent; Holloway (John-Lewis 75), Okenabirhie.
Referee: Sebastian Stockbridge.

SECOND ROUND

Friday, 30 November 2018

Solihull Moors (0) 0

Blackpool (0) 0 3005

Solihull Moors: (4132) Boot; Williams, Daly, Gudger, Reckord; Storer; Maxwell (Hylton 64), Carter, Osborne (O'Keeffe 90); Yussuf, Wright (Thomas 79).
Blackpool: (352) Howard; Daniels, Heneghan, Tilt; Nottingham, Spearing, Thompson, Taylor (Pritchard 64), Bola; Gnanduillet, Dodoo (Feeney 83).
Referee: Ross Joyce.

Saturday, 1 December 2018

Accrington S (0) 3 *(Zanzala 49, Kee 66 (pen), Clark 78)*

Cheltenham T (0) 1 *(Addai 73)* 1066

Accrington S: (4411) Ripley; Johnson, Ihiekwe, Hughes, Richards-Everton; Clark, Barlaser, Conneely (Zanzala 46), McConville (Mingoia 87); Finley (Brown 87); Kee.
Cheltenham T: (352) Flinders; Forster, Tozer, Hussey; Broom, Atangana, Thomas, Clements, Maddox (Addai 60); Varney (Barnett 58), Field.
Referee: Andy Haines.

Charlton Ath (0) 0

Doncaster R (0) 2 *(Butler 66, Marquis 77)* 3249

Charlton Ath: (352) Phillips; Dijksteel, Sarr, Stevenson; Marshall, Clarke, Reeves (Morgan 68), Lapslie, Maloney (Sarpeng-Wiredu 79); Hackett-Fairchild, Ajose.
Doncaster R: (442) Lawlor; Mason, Andrew, Butler, Anderson T; Whiteman, Rowe (Crawford 62), Kane, Blair; Marquis (Taylor 79), May (Wilks 62).
Referee: Brett Huxtable.

FC Halifax T (0) 1 *(Hanson 86 (og))*

AFC Wimbledon (1) 3 *(Purrington 42, Wordsworth 73, Pigott 75)* 2044

FC Halifax T: (4231) Johnson; Hanson, Brown, Clarke, Sellers; Maher, Staunton; Preston, King (Leacock-McLeod 62), Kosylo; Southwell (Edwards 76).
AFC Wimbledon: (433) McDonnell; Oshilaja, Nightingale, McDonald, Purrington; Soares (Trotter 63), Hartigan, Wordsworth (Wagstaff 74); Pinnock, Pigott, Jervis (Hanson 74).
Referee: Ben Toner.

Lincoln C (1) 2 *(Rhead 1, Akinde 86)*

Carlisle U (0) 0 6438

Lincoln C: (442) Vickers; Eardley, Bostwick, Shackell, Toffolo; Anderson, Pett, Frecklington (O'Connor 78), Andrade; Green (McCartan 63), Rhead (Akinde 63).
Carlisle U: (532) Collin; Sowerby, Liddle, Gerrard, Gillesphey, Yates (McCarron 46); Etuhu, Jones, Slater (Campbell 73); Hope, Bennett.
Referee: Dean Whitestone.

Maidstone U (0) 0

Oldham Ath (1) 2 *(Clarke 17, O'Grady 84)* 3560

Maidstone U: (442) Smith; Phillips, De Havilland, Finney (Florence 87), McLennan; Paxman, Durojaiye (Muldoon 75), Tajbakhsh, Powell; Cassidy, Romain.
Oldham Ath: (442) Iversen; Dummigan, Clarke, Edmundson, Hunt; Lang, Missilou, Maouche, Nepomuceno; Surridge, O'Grady.
Referee: Alan Young.

Peterborough U (2) 2 *(Toney 29, Dembele 45)*
Bradford C (0) 2 *(Mellor 84, Colville 89)* 3750
Peterborough U: (442) Chapman; Ward, Tafazolli, Bennett, Daniel; Maddison, Reed (O'Hara 86), Woodyard, Dembele (Naismith 79); Godden (Cummings 70), Toney.
Bradford C: (4231) O'Donnell; Caddis, O'Connor A, Mellor, Chicksen; O'Brien J (Colville 64), Henry (Brunker 78); Ball (Miller 64), O'Brien L, Payne; Doyle.
Referee: Trevor Kettle.

Plymouth Arg (0) 1 *(Sarcevic 67)*
Oxford U (0) 2 *(Henry 49, Brannagan 53)* 5984
Plymouth Arg: (433) Macey; Riley, Songo'o, Canavan, Smith-Brown (Lameiras 86); Sarcevic, Fox, Ness (Taylor 73); Carey, Ladapo, Grant J.
Oxford U: (433) Eastwood; Hanson, Dickie, Nelson, Ruffels; Henry, Mousinho, Brannagan; Whyte (Long 90), Mackie, Browne.
Referee: Peter Wright.

Southend U (1) 2 *(Mantom 45, Dieng 84)*
Barnsley (1) 4 *(Moore 41, Woodrow 56, 70, Bahre 90)* 3616
Southend U: (442) Oxley; Bwomono, White, Turner, Hendrie; McLaughlin, Mantom, Yearwood (McCoulsky 76), Kightly (Bunn 76); Dieng, Cox (Robinson 76).
Barnsley: (442) Davies; Brown, Pinnock, Lindsay, Fryers (Pinillos 68); Bahre, McGeehan, Mowatt, Moncur; Moore (Potts 81), Woodrow (Adeboyejo 90).
Referee: Paul Marsden.

Walsall (0) 1 *(Cook 53)*
Sunderland (1) 1 *(McGeady 37)* 3140
Walsall: (433) Roberts; Devlin, Johnson, Guthrie, Leahy; Dobson, Osbourne, Kinsella; Gordon, Cook, Ferrier (Ginnelly 88).
Sunderland: (4231) McLaughlin; Matthews, Flanagan, Baldwin, James; O'Nien, Power; Gooch (Mumba 75), Oviedo (Sinclair 63), McGeady; Maja.
Referee: Carl Boyeson.

Wrexham (0) 0
Newport Co (0) 0 5295
Wrexham: (41212) Lainton; Roberts, Lawlor, Pearson, Carrington; Walker; Wright (Young 63), Summerfield; Rutherford (Jennings 77); Beavon (Fondop-Talom 85), Grant.
Newport Co: (3412) Day; Franks, O'Brien, Demetriou; Pipe, Crofts, Bakinson, Butler; Sheehan; Amond (Harris 90), Matt (Semenyo 75).
Referee: Craig Hicks.

Sunday, 2 December 2018

Barnet (1) 1 *(Sparkes 8)*
Stockport Co (0) 0 2826
Barnet: (532) Cousins; Alexander, Sweeney, Robson, Reynolds, Johnson; Taylor J, Fonguck (Adams 70), Sparkes; Harrison (Duku 81), Walker (Elito 60).
Stockport Co: (4231) Hinchliffe; Minihan (Bell 83), Palmer, Stott, Cowan; Keane (Dimaio 84), Walker; Thomas, Osborne (Warburton 69), Stephenson; Mulhern.
Referee: Scott Oldham.

Bury (0) 0
Luton T (1) 1 *(Cornick 42)* 2977
Bury: (3412) Murphy; Thompson, O'Connell, Stokes (Miller 83); Adams N, O'Shea, Danns (Lavery 74), McFadzean; Mayor; Moore (Telford 57), Maynard.
Luton T: (41212) Shea; Stacey, Bradley, Pearson, Justin; Rea; Shinnie, Ruddock; Lee (Potts 83); Cornick (Hylton 86), Collins.
Referee: Thomas Bramall.

Chesterfield (0) 0
Grimsby T (1) 2 *(Vernam 37, Clifton 70)* 4537
Chesterfield: (4231) Burton; Barry, Evans, Hollis, Binnom-Williams; Weston, Smith J; Shaw (Rowley 77), Hallam (Hines 57), Kiwomya; Denton (Amantchi 56).
Grimsby T: (4231) McKeown; Hendrie, Davis, Collins, Fox; Clifton, Hessenthaler; Vernam (Rose 73), Embleton, Pringle (Cook 86); Thomas (Cardwell 79).
Referee: Michael Salisbury.

Rochdale (0) 0
Portsmouth (0) 1 *(Green 90)* 2555
Rochdale: (41212) Lillis; Rafferty, McGahey, Delaney, Done; M Jordan Williams; Dooley (Cannon 55), Adshead; Henderson; Andrew, Jordan LR Williams.
Portsmouth: (4231) MacGillivray; Thompson N, Whatmough, Clarke, Brown; Thompson B, Close; Lowe (Green 76), Evans (Pitman B 72), Curtis; Hawkins.
Referee: Sebastian Stockbridge.

Shrewsbury T (1) 1 *(Holloway 35)*
Scunthorpe U (0) 0 3427
Shrewsbury T: (433) Arnold; Bolton, Waterfall, Sadler, Beckles; Laurent, Grant, Docherty; Gilliead (John-Lewis 75), Holloway, Okenabirhie (Emmanuel 90).
Scunthorpe U: (442) Alnwick; McArdle, Goode, Burgess, Borthwick-Jackson; Thomas, Lund, Morris, Dales (El-Mhanni 75); Novak, Wootton.
Referee: Neil Hair.

Slough (0) 0
Gillingham (0) 1 *(Oldaker 48)* 2084
Slough: (442) Turner; Jackman, Nisbet (Dunn 81), Togwell L, Wells; Dobson, Davies, Togwell S, Harris W (Soares 87); Flood (Williams 70), Stevens.
Gillingham: (4312) Holy; Fuller (O'Neill 74), Ehmer, Zakuani, Ogilvie; Oldaker, Byrne, Parrett (Garmston 62); List (Charles-Cook 80); Parker, Eaves.
Referee: Christopher Sarginson.

Swindon T (0) 0
Woking (0) 1 *(Hyde 54)* 3654
Swindon T: (442) McCormick; Knoyle, Lancashire, Woolfenden, Iandolo (Taylor 84); Alzate (Anderson 59), Dunne, Doughty, McCourt; Twine, Pryce (Adebayo 59).
Woking: (433) Ross; Collier, Gerring, Cook, Casey; Little, Jolley, Edser; Kretzschmar, Hyde (Luer 78), Loza (Wheeler 87).
Referee: Matthew Donohue.

Tranmere R (1) 1 *(Smith 18)*
Southport (0) 1 *(Bauress 70)* 4701
Tranmere R: (442) Davies; Caprice, McNulty, Monthe, Ridehalgh; Jennings, Harris, Gilmour (Buxton 59), Mottley-Henry (Smith 9); Mullin (Tollitt 46), Norwood.
Southport: (442) Hanford; Richards, Edwards (Parry 90), Astles (Green 71), Winnard; Ogle, Morgan, Wood, Bauress; Charles, Sampson.
Referee: Anthony Backhouse.

Monday, 3 December 2018

Guiseley (1) 1 *(Purver 33)*
Fleetwood T (2) 2 *(Madden 28, Burns 31)* 2324
Guiseley: (541) Green; Halls (Clayton 82), Moyo, Thornton, Cummings, Heaton; Felix (Walsh 73), Purver, James, Hatfield (Walters 73); Liburd.
Fleetwood T: (442) Cairns; Coyle, Morgan, Eastham, Husband; Burns (Biggins 90), Sheron, Marney, McAleny (Hunter 74); Evans, Madden (Bolger 86).
Referee: John Busby.

SECOND ROUND REPLAYS

Tuesday, 11 December 2018

Bradford C (1) 4 *(Miller 22, 72, Ball 53, Caddis 58)*
Peterborough U (3) 4 *(Toney 18, 20, 84, Maddison 45)* 3486
Bradford C: (4231) Wilson; Caddis, O'Connor A, Knight-Percival, Chicksen; Akpan (Henry 70), O'Brien L; Mellor, Payne, Ball (Doyle 87); Miller (Colville 90).
Peterborough U: (442) O'Malley; Ward, Bennett, Tafazolli, Daniel; Maddison, Woodyard, O'Hara (Walker 79), Dembele (Cooper 64); Toney, Cummings (Godden 63).
aet; Peterborough U won 3-2 on penalties.
Referee: Ross Joyce.

Newport Co (0) 4 *(Amond 49, Matt 59, Carrington 65 (og), Butler 90)*

Wrexham (0) 0 4143

Newport Co: (433) Day; Pipe, Butler, Franks, Demetriou (Pring 75); Dolan (Labadie 66), Bennett (Willmott 51), Bakinson; Semenyo, Amond, Matt.
Wrexham: (41212) Lainton; Carrington, Lawlor, Pearson, Jennings; Wright; Summerfield (Deverdics 70), Young■; Rutherford; Beavon (Holroyd 56), Grant (Fondop-Talom 79).
Referee: Kevin Johnson.

Sunderland (0) 0

Walsall (0) 1 *(Kinsella 52)* 8212

Sunderland: (4231) McLaughlin; O'Nien, Flanagan, Baldwin, Oviedo; McGeouch (Cattermole 58), Power; Maguire, Honeyman, Watmore (Mumba 78); Sinclair (Maja 58).
Walsall: (343) Roberts; Devlin, Martin, Guthrie; Kinsella, Morris, Osbourne, Leahy; Gordon, Ferrier, Ginnelly.
Referee: Michael Salisbury.

Monday, 17 December 2018

Southport (0) 0

Tranmere R (2) 2 *(Jennings 14, 43)* 5414

Southport: (451) Hanford; Richards (Archer 80), Winnard, Astles, Ogle; Charles, Wood (Green 63), Edwards (Gilchrist 89), Morgan, Bauress; Sampson.
Tranmere R: (532) Davies; Caprice (Buxton 86), Ellis, McNulty, Monthe, Ridehalgh; Harris, Jennings, Gilmour; Mullin (Stockton 81), Norwood.
Referee: Thomas Bramall.

Tuesday, 18 December 2018

Blackpool (2) 3 *(Gnanduillet 10, Dodoo 19, Spearing 105 (pen))*

Solihull Moors (1) 2 *(Yussuf 33, 51 (pen))* 1441

Blackpool: (352) Howard; Daniels, Heneghan, Tilt; Feeney, Thompson, Spearing, Guy (Pritchard 82), Bola; Dodoo (Delfouneso 29 (O'Sullivan 110)), Gnanduillet.
Solihull Moors: (433) Boot; Williams, Daly, Gudger, Reckord (Carline 95); Osborne, Storer, Carter; Yussuf (Thomas 89), Wright (Maxwell 106), Hylton (Murphy 81).
aet.
Referee: Andy Haines.

THIRD ROUND

Friday, 4 January 2019

Tranmere R (0) 0

Tottenham H (1) 7 *(Aurier 40, 55, Llorente 48, 71, 72, Son 57, Kane 82)* 12,553

Tranmere R: (352) Davies; Ellis, McNulty, Monthe; Caprice, Harris (Banks 58), McCullough, Gilmour, Ridehalgh; Norwood, Jennings (Mullin 83).
Tottenham H: (343) Gazzaniga; Foyth, Sanchez (Eyoma 79), Davies; Aurier, Alli, Skipp, Walker-Peters; Lucas Moura, Llorente (Kane 75), Son (Marsh 65).
Referee: Andre Marriner.

Saturday, 5 January 2019

Accrington S (0) 1 *(Kee 76)*

Ipswich T (0) 0 2869

Accrington S: (442) Ripley; Johnson, Sykes, Hughes, Richards-Everton; Clark, Barlaser, Finley, McConville; Kee, Mangan (Brown 65).
Ipswich T: (442) Bialkowski; Elder, Pennington, Spence, Nsiala; Edwards, Dozzell, Downes (Bishop 47), Nolan (Harrison 80); Sears, Jackson (Keane 66).
Referee: Dean Whitestone.

Aston Villa (0) 0

Swansea C (1) 3 *(Baker-Richardson 2, Dyer 47, Fulton 78)* 30,572

Aston Villa: (433) Kalinic; Bree, Elphick, Hutton, Taylor; O'Hare (Kodjia 55), Whelan (Lansbury 60), McGinn; Adomah, Hogan (Davis 72), El Ghazi.
Swansea C: (4231) Mulder; Naughton, van der Hoorn (Harries 87), Rodon, Roberts; Fer, Grimes; Dyer (James 72), Celina, Routledge; Baker-Richardson (Fulton 71).
Referee: Gavin Ward.

Blackpool (0) 0

Arsenal (2) 3 *(Willock 11, 37, Iwobi 82)* 8955

Blackpool: (433) Howard (Mafoumbi 69); Nottingham, O'Connor, Daniels, Bola; Taylor (Pritchard 62), Spearing, Guy; Delfouneso, Gnanduillet (Davies 83), Feeney.
Arsenal: (4231) Cech; Jenkinson, Lichtsteiner, Papastathopoulos, Kolasinac (Medley 83); Elneny, Ramsey; Maitland-Niles, Willock, Iwobi (Saka 86); Nketiah (Lacazette 64).
Referee: Mike Dean.

Bolton W (0) 5 *(Donaldson 58, Magennis 61, 80, 87, Guthrie 63 (og))*

Walsall (1) 2 *(Cook 19, Beevers 68 (og))* 5506

Bolton W: (442) Alnwick; Olkowski, Wheater, Beevers, Grounds; Murphy (Connell 89), Lowe, Vela (Buckley 46), Wildschut (Donaldson 46); Noone, Magennis.
Walsall: (442) Roberts; Devlin, Martin, Guthrie, Leahy; Ismail (Kouhyar 75), Dobson, Kinsella, Jarvis (Morris 70); Ferrier, Cook.
Referee: Darren England.

Bournemouth (0) 1 *(Pugh 55)*

Brighton & HA (2) 3 *(Knockaert 31, Bissouma 34, Andone 64)* 10,522

Bournemouth: (4411) Boruc; Clyne, Simpson, Cook S, Rico (Daniels 78); Pugh, Taylor (Brooks 46), Surman, Ibe (Stanislas 70); Fraser; Mousset.
Brighton & HA: (433) Steele; Saltor (Montoya 87), Balogun, Duffy, Bong; Kayal, Stephens, Bissouma; Knockaert (Gyokeres 90), Andone, Locadia (March 74).
Referee: Michael Oliver.

Brentford (0) 1 *(Maupay 80 (pen))*

Oxford U (0) 0 6106

Brentford: (343) Daniels; Konsa, Jeanvier, Barbet; Odubajo, McEachran, Da Silva, Henry; Canos (Judge 69), Watkins (Ogbene 90), Benrahma (Maupay 68).
Oxford U: (433) Eastwood; Hanson, Nelson, Dickie, Ruffels; Graham (Norman 88), Mousinho, Henry; Whyte, Mackie (Baptiste 64 (Garbutt 74)), Browne.
Referee: Jeremy Simpson.

Bristol C (0) 1 *(Brownhill 72)*

Huddersfield T (0) 0 12,178

Bristol C: (451) Maenpaa; Hunt, Wright, Webster, Dasilva; Eliasson (Kalas 66), Brownhill, Morrell, Paterson (Taylor 67), O'Dowda; Diedhiou (Weimann 76).
Huddersfield T: (4231) Hamer; Durm, Jorgensen, Stankovic, Lowe; Bacuna (Pritchard 46), Hogg; Kachunga, Puncheon, Diakhaby (Mbenza 73); Depoitre (Mounie 46).
Referee: Peter Bankes.

Burnley (0) 1 *(Wood 90 (pen))*

Barnsley (0) 0 11,053

Burnley: (442) Pope; Tarkowski, Long, Gibson, Ward (Gudmundsson 59); McNeil, Defour (Cork 78), Hendrick, Taylor; Vydra, Vokes (Wood 74).
Barnsley: (4141) Davies; Cavare, Pinnock, Lindsay, Williams B; McGeehan; Hedges (Moore 63), Mowatt, Bahre (Dougall 83), Thiam (Moncur 77); Woodrow.
Referee: Simon Hooper.

Chelsea (0) 2 *(Morata 49, 59)*

Nottingham F (0) 0 40,544

Chelsea: (433) Caballero; Zappacosta, Christensen, Luiz, Emerson Palmieri; Ampadu, Fabregas (Kante 85), Barkley; Loftus-Cheek (Hazard 42), Morata (Azpilicueta 75), Hudson-Odoi.
Nottingham F: (4231) Steele; Darikwa, Yacob, Fox, Janko; Guedioura, Colback; Cash (Lolley 57), Joao Carvalho, Osborn; Murphy.
Referee: Andrew Madley.

Crystal Palace (0) 1 *(Ayew 86)*
Grimsby T (0) 0 19,967
Crystal Palace: (433) Hennessey; Ward, Kelly, Dann, Souare (Kouyate 36); Meyer, Riedewald (Ayew 68), Schlupp; Townsend, Sorloth (Wickham 61), Zaha.
Grimsby T: (433) McKeown; Rose M, Hall-Johnson, Hendrie, Fox■; Embleton, Hessenthaler, Clifton; Woolford (Cook 89), Cardwell, Thomas (Vernam 75).
Referee: Martin Atkinson.

Derby Co (0) 2 *(Marriott 58, Lawrence 61)*
Southampton (1) 2 *(Redmond 4, 48)* 17,095
Derby Co: (433) Roos; Bogle, Keogh, Tomori, Lowe; Bryson, Evans, Bird (Nugent 52); Holmes (Jozefzoon 88), Marriott, Lawrence (Waghorn 81).
Southampton: (442) Gunn; Cedric Soares, Stephens, Vestergaard, Targett; Elyounoussi (Barnes 71), Slattery, Ward-Prowse, Redmond; Austin (Johnson 79), Long.
Referee: Oliver Langford.

Everton (2) 2 *(Lookman 12, Bernard 14)*
Lincoln C (1) 1 *(Bostwick 28)* 37,900
Everton: (4231) Pickford; Kenny, Mina, Zouma, Baines; Davies (Andre Gomes 46), Gueye; Lookman, Sigurdsson (Richarlison 80), Bernard; Calvert-Lewin (Tosun 46).
Lincoln C: (451) Vickers; Eardley, Bostwick, Shackell, Toffolo; Anderson, O'Connor (McCartan 72), Pett (Chapman 78), Frecklington, Andrade; Akinde (Rhead 71).
Referee: John Brooks.

Fleetwood T (0) 2 *(Madden 70, Evans 72 (pen))*
AFC Wimbledon (1) 3 *(Barcham 16, Hartigan 55, Appiah 90)* 2131
Fleetwood T: (442) Cairns; Coyle, Eastham, Morgan, Wallace R; Hunter, Marney (Biggins 57), Wallace J, Burns; Evans, Madden.
AFC Wimbledon: (4141) Ramsdale; Watson, Thomas (Trotter 37), Kalambayi, Purrington; Nightingale; Pinnock, Hartigan, Wordsworth, Barcham (Jervis 81); Appiah.
Referee: Ross Joyce.

Gillingham (0) 1 *(List 81)*
Cardiff C (0) 0 7090
Gillingham: (3412) Holy; Lacey, Zakuani, Ogilvie; O'Neill, Byrne, Reilly, Garmston; Parker; List, Eaves.
Cardiff C: (442) Smithies; Peltier, Morrison, Ecuele Manga, Bennett; Mendez-Laing, Damour (Hoilett 90), Ralls, Harris K (Murphy J 54); Paterson, Reid (Ward 74).
Referee: Tim Robinson.

Manchester U (2) 2 *(Mata 22 (pen), Lukaku 45)*
Reading (0) 0 73,918
Manchester U: (433) Romero; Dalot, Darmian, Jones, Young; McTominay, Andreas Pereira, Fred (Fellaini 62); Mata (Chong 62), Lukaku, Sanchez (Rashford 64).
Reading: (4231) Jaakkola; Yiadom, Tiago Ilori (Aluko 46), Moore, Richards; Rinomhota, Kelly; Harriott (Meite 76), Swift, McCleary (Barrow 61); Loader.
Referee: Stuart Atwell.

Middlesbrough (0) 5 *(Assombalonga 47, 70, Friend 50, Wing 62, Fletcher 87)*
Peterborough U (0) 0 11,647
Middlesbrough: (442) Konstantopoulos; McNair, Fry, Ayala, Friend; Fletcher, Leadbitter, Tavernier (Chapman 75), van La Parra (Wing 46); Gestede (Walker 74), Assombalonga.
Peterborough U: (433) O'Malley; Naismith, Tafazolli, White, Lafferty; O'Hara (Godden 58), Woodyard, Reed (Cooke 75); Ward, Toney, Dembele (Cummings 80).
Referee: James Linington.

Newcastle U (0) 1 *(Ritchie 84 (pen))*
Blackburn R (0) 1 *(Dack 56)* 36,440
Newcastle U: (4411) Woodman; Sterry, Schar, Lejeune, Manquillo; Murphy (Atsu 75), Hayden (Shelvey 57), Longstaff S (Perez 80), Ritchie; Kenedy; Joselu.
Blackburn R: (4231) Raya; Bennett, Lenihan, Mulgrew, Bell; Travis, Evans; Conway, Dack (Williams 85), Armstrong (Reed 70); Graham (Brereton 79).
Referee: Kevin Friend.

Norwich C (0) 0
Portsmouth (0) 1 *(Green 90)* 23,201
Norwich C: (4231) McGovern; Passlack (Hernandez 85), Zimmermann, Hanley■, Godfrey; Trybull, McLean; Cantwell, Srbeny (Pukki 84), Marshall (Klose 78); Rhodes.
Portsmouth: (4231) MacGillivray; Walkes, Whatmough, Clarke, Donohue; Naylor, Thompson B; Lowe, Evans (Green 66), Curtis (Wheeler 90); Pitman B.
Referee: Darren Bond.

Sheffield W (0) 0
Luton T (0) 0 16,974
Sheffield W: (4141) Dawson; Palmer, Lees, Hector, Fox; Hutchinson (Pelupessy 26); Boyd, Reach, Bannan, Marco Matias (Winnall 58); Fletcher (Nuhiu 76).
Luton T: (41212) Shea; Stacey, Pearson, Bradley, Justin; McCormack; Shinnie, Berry (LuaLua 82), Lee (Jarvis 89); Collins (Ruddock 66), Hylton.
Referee: Rob Jones.

Shrewsbury T (1) 1 *(Norburn 45 (pen))*
Stoke C (0) 1 *(Crouch 78)* 7512
Shrewsbury T: (451) Arnold; Bolton, Sadler (Beckles 82), Waterfall, Haynes; Gilliead, Grant, Docherty, Norburn, John-Lewis (Holloway 18 (Angol 84)); Laurent.
Stoke C: (442) Federici; Edwards, Martins Indi, Williams, Pieters; Ince, Clucas, Etebo, McClean (Diouf 74); Afobe (Crouch 74), Berahino (Campbell 74).
Referee: David Webb.

WBA (1) 1 *(Sako 31)*
Wigan Ath (0) 0 15,465
WBA: (433) Bond; Holgate, Adarabioyo, Bartley, Townsend; Brunt, Field, Harper (Morrison 87); Hoolahan (Edwards 72), Sako, Leko (Robson-Kanu 79).
Wigan Ath: (4231) Jones; Byrne, Dunkley, Kipre, Naismith; Evans L, Connolly (Roberts 66); Da Silva Lopes (James 57), Windass, McManaman (MacDonald 77); Grigg.
Referee: Keith Stroud.

West Ham U (1) 2 *(Arnautovic 2, Carroll 90)*
Birmingham C (0) 0 54,840
West Ham U: (4141) Adrian; Antonio, Diop, Ogbonna, Masuaku; Rice; Diangana, Obiang, Nasri (Snodgrass 58), Xande Silva (Felipe Anderson 79); Arnautovic (Carroll 20).
Birmingham C: (442) Camp; Harding, Morrison, Dean, Colin; Mahoney (Solomon-Otabor 73), Gardner G (Gardner C 46), Kieftenbeld, Maghoma; Jutkiewicz, Adams.
Referee: Roger East.

Sunday, 6 January 2019

Fulham (0) 1 *(Odoi 52)*
Oldham Ath (0) 2 *(Surridge 76 (pen), Lang 88)* 16,134
Fulham: (433) Bettinelli; Odoi, Ream, Chambers, Le Marchand; Seri, Cisse, Cairney (Mitrovic 84); Ayite, Kebano (Sessegnon R 74), Vietto.
Oldham Ath: (433) Iversen; Haymer, Clarke, Edmundson, Branger; Missilou, Maouche, Lyden; Lang, O'Grady (Surridge 61), Nepomuceno.
Referee: Anthony Taylor.

Manchester C (3) 7 *(Sterling 12, Foden 43, Ajayi 45 (og), Gabriel Jesus 52, Mahrez 73, Otamendi 78, Sane 85)*
Rotherham U (0) 0 52,708
Manchester C: (433) Ederson; Walker, Stones (Danilo 75), Otamendi, Zinchenko; De Bruyne (Sandler 67), Gundogan, Foden; Mahrez, Gabriel Jesus, Sterling (Sane 57).
Rotherham U: (451) Rodak; Vyner (Wood 89), Ajayi, Robertson, Mattock; Forde, Wiles, Vaulks, Williams (Palmer 90), Taylor (Raggett 74); Smith.
Referee: David Coote.

Millwall (0) 2 *(Ferguson 81, 84)*

Hull C (0) 1 *(Toral 52)* 5307

Millwall: (442) Archer; Romeo, Pearce, Cooper, Wallace M (Williams 63); Wallace J, Tunnicliffe (Morison 63), Leonard, Skalak (Ferguson 64); Elliott, O'Brien.
Hull C: (4231) Long; Kane, Mazuch, McKenzie, Lichaj; Batty, Stewart; Milinkovic, Toral (Sheaf 75), Dicko (Lewis-Potter 81); Martin.
Referee: Andy Woolmer.

Newport Co (1) 2 *(Matt 10, Amond 85 (pen))*

Leicester C (0) 1 *(Ghezzal 82)* 6705

Newport Co: (4231) Day; Hornby-Forbes (Pipe 67), Franks, Demetriou, Neufville; Bennett, Dolan (O'Brien 86); Willmott, Amond, Semenyo; Matt (Bakinson 77).
Leicester C: (4231) Ward; Simpson (Gray 60), Morgan, Evans, Fuchs; Choudhury, James (King 72); Ghezzal, Okazaki (Maddison 46), Albrighton; Iheanacho.
Referee: Chris Kavanagh.

Preston NE (0) 1 *(Hughes 56)*

Doncaster R (1) 3 *(Marquis 5, Anderson T 72, Wilks 87)* 8101

Preston NE: (4231) Crowe; Fisher, Huntington, Storey, Hughes; Gallagher, Ledson (Barker 60); Barkhuizen, Johnson, Burke (Browne 46); Nmecha (Maguire 74).
Doncaster R: (433) Lawlor; Blair, Anderson T, Butler, Andrew; Crawford (Rowe 85), Whiteman, Kane; Wilks (Sadlier 89), Marquis, May (Coppinger 64).
Referee: Andy Davies.

QPR (1) 2 *(Oteh 23 (pen), Bidwell 75)*

Leeds U (1) 1 *(Halme 25)* 11,637

QPR: (4411) Ingram; Kakay, Furlong, Hall, Bidwell; Samuel (Wszolek 86), Cousins, Scowen, Freeman; Eze (Smith 90); Oteh (Chair 83).
Leeds U: (4141) Peacock-Farrell; Shackleton, Ayling, Halme (Pearce 46 (Temenuzhkov 79)), Davis (Odour 87); Forshaw; Clarke, Baker, Roberts, Alioski; Harrison.
Referee: Geoff Eltringham.

Sheffield U (0) 0

Barnet (1) 1 *(Coulthirst 21 (pen))* 9906

Sheffield U: (352) Moore; Cranie, Stearman, Bryan (Basham 74); Freeman, Coutts, Dowell, Lundstram (Sharp 65), Johnson; Washington (Duffy 58), Clarke.
Barnet: (433) Cousins; Alexander, Reynolds, Robson, Johnson; Adams, Taylor J, Sweeney; Elito (Tutonda 80), Coulthirst (Harrison 80), Mason-Clark (Fonguck 58).
Referee: Tony Harrington.

Woking (0) 0

Watford (1) 2 *(Hughes 13, Deeney 74)* 5717

Woking: (4231) Ross; Collier, Gerring, Cook, Casey; Jolley, Taylor (Little 60); Luer (Bradbury 70), Edser (Hodges 69), Loza; Hyde.
Watford: (433) Gomes; Janmaat, Wilmot, Britos, Masina; Cleverley, Chalobah, Quina; Hughes (Navarro 80), Success (Deeney 71), Penaranda (Sema 72).
Referee: Graham Scott.

Monday, 7 January 2019

Wolverhampton W (1) 2 *(Jimenez 38, Neves 55)*

Liverpool (0) 1 *(Origi 51)* 25,849

Wolverhampton W: (3142) Ruddy; Bennett, Coady, Boly; Neves; Jonny (Doherty 75), Joao Moutinho, Dendoncker, Ruben Vinagre; Jimenez (Helder Costa 83), Jota (Ivan Cavaleiro 52).
Liverpool: (442) Mignolet; Camacho, Lovren (Hoever 6), Fabinho, Moreno; Shaqiri, Milner, Keita, Jones (Firmino 70); Sturridge (Salah 70), Origi.
Referee: Paul Tierney.

THIRD ROUND REPLAYS

Tuesday, 15 January 2019

Blackburn R (2) 2 *(Armstrong 33, Lenihan 45)*

Newcastle U (2) 4 *(Longstaff S 1, Roberts 22, Joselu 105, Perez 106)* 14,228

Blackburn R: (343) Raya; Nyambe, Lenihan, Bell; Reed (Dack 78), Travis, Smallwood (Rothwell 103), Bennett; Brereton (Conway 65), Graham, Armstrong (Nuttall 73).
Newcastle U: (4141) Woodman; Sterry, Fernandez, Clark (Lascelles 46 (Hayden 57)), Manquillo; Schar; Murphy, Longstaff S, Roberts (Perez 94), Ritchie (Atsu 109); Joselu.
aet.
Referee: Lee Probert.

Luton T (0) 0

Sheffield W (0) 1 *(Nuhiu 46)* 9259

Luton T: (442) Shea; Justin, Bradley, Pearson, Stacey; Berry (Potts 69), Lee (Jarvis 88), Shinnie, Ruddock; Collins, LuaLua.
Sheffield W: (352) Dawson; Lees, Thorniley, Hector; Palmer, Reach, Bannan, Boyd, Fox; Fletcher (Marco Matias 90), Nuhiu.
Referee: Tim Robinson.

Stoke C (2) 2 *(Campbell 20, 36)*

Shrewsbury T (0) 3 *(Bolton 71, Okenabirhie 77 (pen), Laurent 81)* 10,261

Stoke C: (41212) Federici; Bauer, Williams, Martins Indi, Tymon; Etebo; Adam (Afobe 81), Clucas; Ince; Crouch, Campbell (McClean 72).
Shrewsbury T: (451) Arnold; Bolton, Sadler, Waterfall, Haynes; Holloway (Beckles 46), Docherty, Grant, Gilliead (Angol 90), Okenabirhie (Eisa 87); Laurent.
Referee: Scott Duncan.

Wednesday, 16 January 2019

Southampton (0) 2 *(Armstrong 68, Redmond 70)*

Derby Co (0) 2 *(Wilson H 76, Waghorn 82)* 14,651

Southampton: (3421) Gunn; Ramsey (Targett 110), Stephens, Vestergaard; Cedric Soares, Romeu, Ward-Prowse, Johnson (Redmond 46); Elyounoussi, Armstrong (Slattery 91); Long (Gallagher 73).
Derby Co: (433) Roos; Bogle (Holmes 94), Keogh, Tomori, Malone; Bryson, Huddlestone (Lawrence 80), Mount; Waghorn, Marriott (Nugent 76), Wilson H (Bennett 102).
aet; Derby Co won 5-3 on penalties.
Referee: Anthony Taylor.

FOURTH ROUND

Friday, 25 January 2019

Arsenal (1) 1 *(Aubameyang 43)*

Manchester U (2) 3 *(Sanchez 31, Lingard 33, Martial 82)* 59,571

Arsenal: (4231) Cech; Maitland-Niles, Papastathopoulos (Mustafi 21), Koscielny (Guendouzi 64), Kolasinac; Torreira, Xhaka; Aubameyang, Ramsey, Iwobi (Ozil 64); Lacazette.
Manchester U: (4312) Romero; Young, Bailly, Lindelof, Shaw; Ander Herrera, Matic, Pogba; Lingard (Jones 88); Lukaku (Rashford 72), Sanchez (Martial 72).
Referee: Craig Pawson.

Bristol C (2) 2 *(O'Dowda 8, Eliasson 30)*

Bolton W (1) 1 *(Beevers 6)* 13,747

Bristol C: (4141) Fielding; Wright, Kalas, Baker (Pisano 77), Dasilva (Kelly 83); Pack; Eliasson, Morrell, Palmer (Brownhill 74), O'Dowda; Diedhiou.
Bolton W: (352) Matthews; Beevers, Hobbs, Little; Olkowski, Murphy (O'Neil 76), Lowe, Connell (Donaldson 83), Pritchard (Ameobi 64); Magennis, Noone.
Referee: Stuart Attwell.

Saturday, 26 January 2019

Accrington S (0) 0

Derby Co (0) 1 *(Waghorn 78)* 5397

Accrington S: (3421) Maxted; Sykes, Hughes, Richards-Everton; Johnson (Brown 84), Conneely, Barlaser■, Donacien (Smyth 84); Clark, McConville; Kee.
Derby Co: (433) Roos; Bogle■, Keogh, Tomori, Malone; Wilson H (Jozefzoon 72), Evans, Mount (Bennett 37); Waghorn (Bird 89), Nugent, Holmes.
Referee: Jon Moss.

AFC Wimbledon (2) 4 *(Appiah 34, Wagstaff 41, 46, Sibbick 88)*
West Ham U (0) 2 *(Lucas Perez 57, Felipe Anderson 71)* 4777
AFC Wimbledon: (4231) Ramsdale; Watson, Thomas, Oshilaja, McDonald; Nightingale, Wordsworth; Connolly (Sibbick 86), Wagstaff, Pinnock (Soares 65); Appiah (Jervis 76).
West Ham U: (442) Adrian; Antonio, Diop, Ogbonna, Masuaku; Diangana (Fredericks 46), Noble, Obiang (Felipe Anderson 46), Snodgrass; Hernandez, Carroll (Lucas Perez 46).
Referee: Anthony Taylor.

Brighton & HA (0) 0
WBA (0) 0 20,001
Brighton & HA: (451) Button; Saltor, Duffy, Burn, Montoya; Knockaert, Bissouma, Stephens (Propper 63), Kayal, Locadia (Gyokeres 72); Andone (Murray 83).
WBA: (4312) Bond; Mears, Bartley, Adarabioyo, Townsend; Harper, Field, Edwards; Hoolahan (Tulloch 81); Robson-Kanu, Leko (Holgate 89).
Referee: Lee Mason.

Doncaster R (0) 2 *(Whiteman 68, 90 (pen))*
Oldham Ath (0) 1 *(Clarke 84)* 11,260
Doncaster R: (433) Marosi; Mason, Downing, Anderson T, Andrew; Kane, Whiteman, Coppinger (Blair 63); May (Wright 90), Marquis, Sadlier (Wilks 63).
Oldham Ath: (4411) Iversen; Haymer, Edmundson, Clarke■, Nepomuceno; Branger, Missilou, Sylla, Lang; Baxter (Vera 76); O'Grady.
Referee: Peter Bankes.

Manchester C (1) 5 *(Gabriel Jesus 23, Bernardo Silva 52, De Bruyne 61, Long 73 (og), Aguero 85 (pen))*
Burnley (0) 0 50,121
Manchester C: (433) Ederson; Walker, Stones, Otamendi, Danilo; De Bruyne (Foden 75), Fernandinho (Silva 66), Gundogan; Bernardo Silva, Gabriel Jesus (Aguero 75), Mahrez.
Burnley: (541) Pope; Taylor, Long, Tarkowski, Gibson, Ward; McNeil, Defour (Westwood 77), Hendrick, Brady (Cork 46); Vydra (Wood 62).
Referee: Graham Scott.

Middlesbrough (0) 1 *(Ayala 51)*
Newport Co (0) 1 *(Dolan 90)* 15,794
Middlesbrough: (4141) Randolph; Shotton (McNair 72), Ayala, Flint, Friend; Mikel (Clayton 62); Downing, Wing, Saville, Fletcher (Tavernier 80); Assombalonga.
Newport Co: (4411) Townsend; Poole, O'Brien, Demetriou (Dolan 87), Butler; Willmott, Bennett, Bakinson (Labadie 78), Semenyo; Amond (Sheehan 79); Matt.
Referee: John Brooks.

Millwall (1) 3 *(Gregory 45, Cooper 75, Wallace M 90)*
Everton (1) 2 *(Richarlison 43, Tosun 72)* 16,354
Millwall: (4141) Archer; Romeo, Hutchinson, Cooper, Wallace M; Williams; O'Brien (Skalak 87), Tunnicliffe, Leonard, Ferguson (Morison 89); Gregory (Pearce 90).
Everton: (4231) Pickford; Coleman, Keane, Mina (Zouma 46), Digne; Andre Gomes, Gueye; Lookman (Walcott 79), Sigurdsson, Richarlison; Calvert-Lewin (Tosun 65).
Referee: Michael Oliver.

Newcastle U (0) 0
Watford (0) 2 *(Gray 61, Success 90)* 34,604
Newcastle U: (541) Woodman; Manquillo, Fernandez (Schar 81), Lascelles, Clark, Ritchie (Atsu 73); Murphy (Perez 72), Hayden, Longstaff S, Kenedy; Joselu.
Watford: (4141) Gomes; Janmaat, Cathcart, Britos, Masina; Wilmot; Hughes, Chalobah (Capoue 82), Quina, Success; Gray (Penaranda 68).
Referee: David Coote.

Portsmouth (0) 1 *(Lynch 63 (og))*
QPR (0) 1 *(Wells 74)* 19,378
Portsmouth: (4231) MacGillivray; Walkes, Whatmough, Clarke, Brown; Naylor, Donohue (Close 80); Evans, Dennis, Curtis; Pitman B.
QPR: (442) Lumley; Furlong, Leistner, Lynch, Bidwell; Wszolek (Smith 71), Manning, Scowen, Freeman; Oteh (Samuel 65), Wells (Chair 90).
Referee: Gavin Ward.

Shrewsbury T (0) 2 *(Docherty 47, Waterfall 71)*
Wolverhampton W (0) 2 *(Jimenez 75, Doherty 90)* 9503
Shrewsbury T: (352) Arnold; Beckles, Waterfall, Sadler; Bolton, Docherty (Holloway 90), Grant, Norburn (Vincelot 87), Haynes; Laurent, Okenabirhie (Whalley 81).
Wolverhampton W: (352) Ruddy; Bennett, Coady, Saiss; Doherty, Dendoncker (Jimenez 59), Neves, Gibbs-White (Joao Moutinho 79), Giles (Ivan Cavaleiro 72); Traore, Helder Costa.
Referee: Roger East.

Swansea C (2) 4 *(McBurnie 10, 32, Celina 73, McKay 84)*
Gillingham (0) 1 *(Rees 51)* 15,080
Swansea C: (433) Mulder; Roberts, van der Hoorn, Carter-Vickers, John; Fer (Fulton 82), Celina, Grimes; Baker-Richardson (James 69), McBurnie (Byers 82), McKay.
Gillingham: (3412) Holy; Zakuani, Ehmer, Ogilvie (Parrett 83); O'Neill (Fuller 83), Rees, Byrne, Garmston; Charles-Cook; Eaves, List (Hanlan 71).
Referee: Darren England.

Sunday, 27 January 2019

Chelsea (1) 3 *(Willian 26 (pen), 83, Hudson-Odoi 64)*
Sheffield W (0) 0 37,433
Chelsea: (433) Caballero; Azpilicueta, Rudiger, Christensen, Alonso; Kovacic, Ampadu (Loftus-Cheek 65), Barkley (Jorginho 84); Hudson-Odoi, Higuain (Giroud 82), Willian.
Sheffield W: (451) Westwood; Palmer, Lees, Thorniley, Fox; Reach, Pelupessy (Forestieri 69), Hutchinson, Bannan, Boyd (Nuhiu 75); Fletcher (Lucas Joao 76).
Referee: Andre Marriner.

Crystal Palace (2) 2 *(Wickham 9, Townsend 34 (pen))*
Tottenham H (0) 0 19,491
Crystal Palace: (433) Speroni; Ward, Kelly, Dann, Van Aanholt; Meyer (Milivojevic 79), Kouyate, Schlupp; Townsend (Ayew 88), Wickham (Benteke 70), Zaha.
Tottenham H: (3421) Gazzaniga; Foyth, Sanchez, Vertonghen (Lamela 46); Trippier, Skipp, Dier (Wanyama 63), Walker-Peters; Lucas Moura (Sterling 81), Nkoudou; Llorente.
Referee: Kevin Friend.

Monday, 28 January 2019

Barnet (0) 3 *(Coulthirst 50, 53, Sparkes 75)*
Brentford (1) 3 *(Watkins 40, Maupay 60 (pen), Canos 72)* 6215
Barnet: (433) Huffer; Alexander, Sweeney, Johnson, Tutonda; Taylor J, Robson, Fonguck (Sparkes 70); Mason-Clark, Coulthirst, Elito (Boucaud 90).
Brentford: (343) Daniels; Konsa, Jeanvier, Barbet; Odubajo, Da Silva (Sawyers 61), McEachran, Henry (Dalsgaard 70); Watkins (Benrahma 79), Maupay, Canos.
Referee: Andrew Madley.

FOURTH ROUND REPLAYS

Tuesday, 5 February 2019

Brentford (2) 3 *(Canos 7, Jeanvier 32, Maupay 71)*
Barnet (0) 1 *(Tutonda 74)* 6954
Brentford: (343) Daniels; Sorensen, Konsa, Dalsgaard; Odubajo, McEachran, Sawyers (Da Silva 77), Jeanvier; Canos, Maupay (Ogbene 72), Benrahma (Forss 72).
Barnet: (433) Cousins; Alexander, Sweeney, Johnson (Boucaud 24), Tutonda; Taylor J, Robson, Fonguck (Sparkes 46); Mason-Clark (Akinola 72), Coulthirst, Elito.
Referee: Roger East.

Newport Co (0) 2 *(Willmott 47, Amond 67)*
Middlesbrough (0) 0 6552
Newport Co: (352) Day; Poole, O'Brien, Demetriou; Willmott (Pipe 86), Bennett, Bakinson, Labadie (Dolan 74), Butler; Amond, Matt.
Middlesbrough: (352) Konstantopoulos; Ayala, Flint, Fry; McNair (van La Parra 46), Howson, Clayton, Wing, Friend; Hugill (Gestede 57), Assombalonga (Fletcher 61).
Referee: Stuart Attwell.

QPR (0) 2 *(Wells 70, Smith 77)*
Portsmouth (0) 0 13,115
QPR: (4411) Lumley; Furlong, Hall, Lynch, Bidwell; Samuel (Eze 72), Luongo, Scowen, Freeman; Wells (Manning 82); Smith (Hemed 90).
Portsmouth: (4231) MacGillivray; Walkes, Burgess, Clarke, Brown; Naylor, May (Morris 59); Lowe, Close (Pitman B 74), Dennis (Evans 60); Hawkins.
Referee: David Coote.

Wolverhampton W (2) 3 *(Doherty 2, 45, Ivan Cavaleiro 62)*
Shrewsbury T (2) 2 *(Bolton 11, Laurent 39)* 28,844
Wolverhampton W: (343) Ruddy; Bennett, Coady, Boly; Doherty, Gibbs-White, Saiss, Jonny; Ivan Cavaleiro (Ennis 89), Traore (Jimenez 77), Helder Costa (Joao Moutinho 69).
Shrewsbury T: (532) Arnold; Bolton, Vincelot (Sears 38), Beckles, Waterfall, Haynes; Laurent, Docherty, Norburn; Gilliead (Whalley 66), Okenabirhie (Holloway 78).
Referee: Lee Probert.

Wednesday, 6 February 2019

WBA (0) 1 *(Bartley 77)*
Brighton & HA (0) 3 *(Andone 82, Murray 104, 117)* 8645
WBA: (4312) Bond; Mears, Bartley, Adarabioyo, Townsend; Harper, Livermore (Tulloch 63), Field; Hoolahan (Rogers 82); Robson-Kanu, Rodriguez (Dawson 46 (Hegazi 91)).
Brighton & HA: (4411) Button; Saltor (Bong 106), Balogun, Burn, Bernardo; Knockaert, Bissouma (Propper 88), Kayal, Gyokeres (Locadia 79); Jahanbakhsh (Murray 101); Andone.
aet.
Referee: Paul Tierney.

FIFTH ROUND

Friday, 15 February 2019

QPR (0) 0
Watford (1) 1 *(Capoue 45)* 17,212
QPR: (352) Lumley; Furlong, Leistner, Hall (Samuel 84); Wszolek (Eze 76), Cousins, Luongo, Freeman, Bidwell; Wells (Hemed 71), Smith.
Watford: (4222) Gomes; Janmaat, Kabasele, Britos, Holebas; Cleverley (Quina 84), Capoue; Hughes, Sema (Mariappa 74); Gray (Doucoure 74), Deeney.
Referee: Michael Oliver.

Saturday, 16 February 2019

AFC Wimbledon (0) 0
Millwall (1) 1 *(Wallace M 5)* 4795
AFC Wimbledon: (352) Ramsdale; Oshilaja, Nightingale, McDonald; Sibbick, McLoughlin, Hartigan (Pinnock 63), Wordsworth, Garratt (Barcham 46); Pigott (Connolly 63), Folivi.
Millwall: (442) Archer; Romeo, Pearce, Cooper, Wallace M; Wallace J, Williams, Leonard, Ferguson; O'Brien (Elliott 65), Gregory (Hutchinson 90).
Referee: Jonathan Moss.

Brighton & HA (2) 2 *(Knockaert 33, Locadia 45)*
Derby Co (0) 1 *(Cole 81)* 24,562
Brighton & HA: (433) Button; Saltor, Duffy, Burn, Bernardo; Bissouma (Gross 86), Stephens, Kayal; Knockaert, Locadia (Gyokeres 81), Jahanbakhsh.
Derby Co: (433) Roos; Bogle, Keogh, Tomori, Malone (Cole 46); Bryson, Huddlestone, Wilson H; Waghorn, Nugent (Jozefzoon 73), Holmes (Marriott 46).
Referee: David Coote.

Newport Co (0) 1 *(Amond 88)*
Manchester C (0) 4 *(Sane 51, Foden 75, 89, Mahrez 90)* 9680
Newport Co: (352) Day; Poole, O'Brien, Demetriou; Willmott, Bennett (Franks 86), Bakinson (Sheehan 61), Labadie (Dolan 68), Butler; Matt, Amond.
Manchester C: (433) Ederson; Danilo, Stones, Otamendi, Zinchenko; Foden, Fernandinho (Laporte 79), Silva (Gundogan 82); Mahrez, Gabriel Jesus, Sane.
Referee: Andre Marriner.

Sunday, 17 February 2019

Bristol C (0) 0
Wolverhampton W (1) 1 *(Ivan Cavaleiro 28)* 24,394
Bristol C: (4231) Fielding; Wright, Kalas, Webster, Dasilva; Brownhill, Morrell (Pack 46); Eliasson (Taylor 46), Palmer (Paterson 66), O'Dowda; Diedhiou.
Wolverhampton W: (352) Ruddy; Bennett, Coady, Boly; Doherty (Neves 81), Dendoncker, Saiss, Joao Moutinho, Jonny; Jimenez (Traore 90), Ivan Cavaleiro (Gibbs-White 70).
Referee: Martin Atkinson.

Doncaster R (0) 0
Crystal Palace (2) 2 *(Schlupp 8, Meyer 45)* 14,010
Doncaster R: (4141) Marosi; Blair, Downing, Anderson T, Andrew; Whiteman; May (Boocock 89), Crawford (Rowe 64), Kane, Coppinger (Sadlier 64); Marquis.
Crystal Palace: (433) Hennessey; Ward, Kelly, Dann, Van Aanholt; Meyer, Milivojevic, Schlupp; Townsend (McArthur 80), Batshuayi (Benteke 75), Ayew (Kouyate 60).
Referee: Mike Dean.

Swansea C (0) 4 *(Daniels 49 (og), James 53, Celina 66, Byers 90)*
Brentford (1) 1 *(Watkins 28)* 11,261
Swansea C: (433) Nordfeldt; Roberts (Harries 90), van der Hoorn, Carter-Vickers, Naughton; Fulton, Grimes, Byers; James (Asoro 90), McBurnie (Baker-Richardson 77), Celina.
Brentford: (343) Daniels; Konsa■, Jeanvier, Barbet; Canos (Da Silva 69), Mokotjo (McEachran 78), Sawyers, Odubajo; Watkins, Maupay, Benrahma (Kirk 69).
Referee: Stuart Attwell.

Monday, 18 February 2019

Chelsea (0) 0
Manchester U (2) 2 *(Ander Herrera 31, Pogba 45)* 40,562
Chelsea: (433) Arrizabalaga; Azpilicueta (Zappacosta 82), Rudiger, Luiz, Alonso; Kante, Jorginho, Kovacic (Barkley 71); Pedro (Willian 58), Higuain, Hazard.
Manchester U: (4312) Romero; Young, Smalling, Lindelof, Shaw; Ander Herrera, Matic, Pogba; Mata (Andreas Pereira 76); Rashford (McTominay 90), Lukaku (Sanchez 73).
Referee: Kevin Friend.

SIXTH ROUND

Saturday, 16 March 2019

Swansea C (2) 2 *(Grimes 20 (pen), Celina 29)*
Manchester C (0) 3 *(Bernardo Silva 69, Nordfeldt 78 (og), Aguero 88)* 19,783
Swansea C: (442) Nordfeldt; Roberts, van der Hoorn, Grimes, Carter-Vickers; Dyer (Asoro 61), Fulton (Harries 85), Byers (John 73), James; Routledge, Celina.
Manchester C: (433) Ederson; Walker, Otamendi, Laporte, Delph (Zinchenko 57); Bernardo Silva, Gundogan, Silva; Mahrez (Aguero 64), Gabriel Jesus, Sane (Sterling 57).
Referee: Andre Marriner.

Watford (1) 2 *(Capoue 27, Gray 79)*
Crystal Palace (0) 1 *(Batshuayi 62)* 18,104
Watford: (4222) Gomes; Femenia, Mariappa, Cathcart, Holebas (Masina 46); Doucoure, Capoue; Hughes (Gray 77), Pereyra; Deeney, Deulofeu (Cleverley 89).
Crystal Palace: (4231) Guaita; Wan Bissaka, Tomkins, Kelly, Schlupp; Kouyate, Milivojevic; McArthur (Benteke 84), Meyer, Townsend; Batshuayi.
Referee: Kevin Friend.

Wolverhampton W (0) 2 *(Jimenez 70, Jota 76)*

Manchester U (0) 1 *(Rashford 90)* 31,004

Wolverhampton W: (352) Ruddy; Saiss, Coady, Boly; Doherty, Dendoncker, Neves, Joao Moutinho, Jonny; Jimenez (Helder Costa 90), Jota (Traore 87).
Manchester U: (4312) Romero; Dalot, Smalling, Lindelof, Shaw; Ander Herrera (Andreas Pereira 71), Matic (Mata 86), Pogba; Lingard (McTominay 86); Rashford, Martial.
Referee: Martin Atkinson.

Sunday, 17 March 2019

Millwall (0) 2 *(Pearce 70, O'Brien 79)*

Brighton & HA (0) 2 *(Locadia 88, March 90)* 17,137

Millwall: (451) Martin; Romeo, Pearce, Cooper, Ferguson■; Wallace J (Hutchinson 90), Tunnicliffe, Williams, Leonard, O'Brien (Meredith 85); Gregory (Morison 90).
Brighton & HA: (433) Ryan; Montoya, Duffy, Dunk, Bernardo; Propper, Stephens, Kayal (Izquierdo 73); Knockaert (Locadia 73), Murray, Jahanbakhsh (March 67).
aet; Brighton & HA won 5-4 on penalties.
Referee: Chris Kavanagh.

SEMI-FINALS

Wembley, Saturday, 6 April 2019

Manchester C (1) 1 *(Gabriel Jesus 4)*

Brighton & HA (0) 0 71,521

Manchester C: (433) Ederson; Walker (Danilo 46), Otamendi, Laporte, Mendy (Stones 79); De Bruyne (Fernandinho 65), Gundogan, Silva; Bernardo Silva, Gabriel Jesus, Sterling.
Brighton & HA: (433) Ryan; Montoya, Duffy, Dunk, Bernardo; Propper, Stephens, Bissouma (Locadia 82); Knockaert, Murray (Andone 66), Jahanbakhsh (Izquierdo 70).
Referee: Anthony Taylor.

Wembley, Sunday, 7 April 2019

Watford (0) 3 *(Deulofeu 79, 104, Deeney 90 (pen))*

Wolverhampton W (1) 2 *(Doherty 36, Jimenez 62)* 80,092

Watford: (4312) Gomes; Femenia (Janmaat 108), Mariappa, Cathcart, Holebas (Masina 98); Hughes (Deulofeu 66 (Sema 112)), Capoue, Doucoure; Pereyra; Gray, Deeney.
Wolverhampton W: (352) Ruddy; Saiss, Coady, Boly; Doherty, Dendoncker, Neves (Bennett 86), Joao Moutinho (Traore 102), Jonny (Ruben Vinagre 106); Jimenez, Jota (Ivan Cavaleiro 89).
aet.
Referee: Michael Oliver.

THE EMIRATES FA CUP FINAL 2019

Saturday, 18 May 2019

(at Wembley Stadium, attendance 85,854)

Manchester C (2) 6 Watford (0) 0

Manchester C: (433) Ederson; Walker, Kompany, Laporte, Zinchenko; Bernardo Silva, Gundogan (Sane 73), Silva (Stones 79); Mahrez (De Bruyne 55), Gabriel Jesus, Sterling.
Scorer: Silva 26, Gabriel Jesus 38, 68, De Bruyne 61, Sterling 81, 87.

Watford: (451) Gomes; Femenia, Mariappa, Cathcart, Holebas; Deulofeu (Gray 66), Hughes (Cleverley 73), Capoue, Doucoure, Pereyra (Success 66); Deeney.

Referee: Kevin Friend.

Manchester City's David Silva scores the first goal in a 6-0 romp over Watford in the FA Cup Final on 18 May. (Action Images via Reuters/John Sibley)

NATIONAL LEAGUE 2018–19

(P) Promoted into division at end of 2017–18 season. (R) Relegated into division at end of 2017–18 season.

			Home					*Away*					*Total*						
		P	*W*	*D*	*L*	*F*	*A*	*W*	*D*	*L*	*F*	*A*	*W*	*D*	*L*	*F*	*A*	*GD*	*Pts*
1	Leyton Orient	46	14	6	3	39	15	11	8	4	34	20	25	14	7	73	35	38	89
2	Solihull Moors	46	12	8	3	38	17	13	3	7	35	26	25	11	10	73	43	30	86
3	Salford C (P)¶	46	14	5	4	43	21	11	5	7	34	24	25	10	11	77	45	32	85
4	Wrexham	46	17	3	3	36	13	8	6	9	22	26	25	9	12	58	39	19	84
5	AFC Fylde	46	15	4	4	45	21	7	11	5	27	20	22	15	9	72	41	31	81
6	Harrogate T (P)	46	11	6	6	41	27	10	5	8	37	30	21	11	14	78	57	21	74
7	Eastleigh	46	11	5	7	28	25	11	3	9	34	38	22	8	16	62	63	−1	74
8	Ebbsfleet U	46	10	3	10	32	23	8	10	5	32	27	18	13	15	64	50	14	67
9	Sutton U	46	9	9	5	30	28	8	5	10	25	32	17	14	15	55	60	−5	65
10	Barrow	46	9	6	8	29	28	8	7	8	23	23	17	13	16	52	51	1	64
11	Bromley	46	11	5	7	40	30	5	7	11	28	39	16	12	18	68	69	−1	60
12	Barnet (R)	46	7	8	8	24	26	9	4	10	21	24	16	12	18	45	50	−5	60
13	Dover Ath	46	9	5	9	31	30	7	7	9	27	34	16	12	18	58	64	−6	60
14	Chesterfield (R)	46	8	8	7	28	25	6	9	8	27	28	14	17	15	55	53	2	59
15	FC Halifax T	46	8	11	4	23	13	5	9	9	21	30	13	20	13	44	43	1	59
16	Hartlepool U	46	9	6	8	31	30	6	8	9	25	32	15	14	17	56	62	−6	59
17	Gateshead*	46	9	7	7	25	20	10	2	11	27	28	19	9	18	52	48	4	57
18	Dagenham & R	46	8	8	7	31	29	7	3	13	19	27	15	11	20	50	56	−6	56
19	Maidenhead U	46	9	4	10	27	34	7	2	14	18	36	16	6	24	45	70	−25	54
20	Boreham Wood	46	7	7	9	26	34	5	9	9	27	31	12	16	18	53	65	−12	52
21	Aldershot T†	46	7	6	10	19	26	4	5	14	19	41	11	11	24	38	67	−29	44
22	Braintree T (P)	46	6	3	14	25	44	5	5	13	23	34	11	8	27	48	78	−30	41
23	Havant & Waterlooville (P)	46	7	6	10	37	32	2	7	14	25	52	9	13	24	62	84	−22	40
24	Maidstone U	46	3	4	16	17	39	6	3	14	20	43	9	7	30	37	82	−45	34

**Gateshead deducted 9pts and demoted to National League North for multiple breaches of membership rules.*
†Aldershot T reprieved from relegation. ¶Salford C promoted via play-offs.

NATIONAL LEAGUE PLAY-OFFS 2018–19

▪ *Denotes player sent off.*

NATIONAL LEAGUE PLAY-OFF ELIMINATORS

Thursday 2 May 2019

Wrexham (0) 0

Eastleigh (0) 1 *(Hollands 109)* 6723

Wrexham: Lainton; Roberts, Jennings, Young, Kennedy, Pearson, Summerfield (Rutherford 51), Wright, Holroyd, Beavon (Oswell 71), Grant (McGlashan 100).
Eastleigh: Southwood; Hare (McKnight 79), Green, Johnson, Wynter, Boyce, Jones (Gobern 71), Yeates (Matthews 100), Hollands, McCallum, Williamson (Zebroski 79).
aet.
Referee: Martin Woods.

AFC Fylde (2) 3 *(Croasdale 10, Bond 15, Bradley 23)*

Harrogate T (0) 1 *(Burke 53 (og))* 1560

AFC Fylde: Lynch; Francis-Angol, Byrne, Bond, Burke, Tunnicliffe, Bradley (Odusina 90), Croasdale, Philiskirk (Reid 61), Haughton (Crawford 77), Rowe.
Harrogate T: Belshaw; Senior (Leesley 46), Howe, Burrell, Fallowfield, Kitching, Falkingham, Emmett, Beck, Thewlis (Knowles 67), Muldoon (Thomson 76).
Referee: Peter Gibbons.

NATIONAL LEAGUE PLAY-OFF SEMI-FINALS

Saturday 4 May 2019

Solihull Moors (0) 0

AFC Fylde (1) 1 *(Philliskirk 2)* 3681

Solihull Moors: Boot; Williams, Daly, Gudger, Vaughan (Hylton 56), Carter (Hawkridge 85), Storer, Osbourne, Reckord, Yussuf (Blissett 82), Wright.
AFC Fylde: Lynch; Burke, Byrne, Tunnicliffe, Francis-Angol, Bond, Croasdale, Philliskirk, Reid, Rowe, Bradley (Haughton 71).
Referee: David Rock.

Sunday 5 May 2019

Salford C (1) 1 *(Piergianni 43)*

Eastleigh (0) 1 *(McCallum 57)* 2963

Salford C: Neal; Wiseman (Rodney 120), Maynard, Piergianni, Hogan, Touray, Mafuta (Walker 90), Redmond, Dieseruvwe (Gaffney 115), Rooney, Pond (Whitehead 65).
Eastleigh: Southwood; Hare, Green, Johnson, Boyce, Wynter, Gobern (Miley 112), Hollands (McKnight 120) Williamson (Zebroski 75), McCallum, Yeates (Matthews 87).
aet; Salford C won 4-3 on penalties.
Referee: Leigh Doughty.

NATIONAL LEAGUE PLAY-OFF PROMOTION FINAL

Wembley, Saturday 11 May 2019

Salford C (1) 3 *(Dieseruvwe 15, Piergianni 53, Touray 61)*

AFC Fylde (0) 0 8049

Salford C: Neal; Hogan, Pond, Piergianni, Wiseman, Mafuta (Rodney 55), Maynard, Touray, Whitehead (Shelton 68), Redmond, Dieseruvwe (Gafney 78).
AFC Fylde: Lynch; Burke (Haugton 20), Byrne, Tunnicliffe, Francis-Angol, Bond (Crawford 74), Philliskirk, Croasdale, Reid (Hardy 58), Rowe, Bradley.
Referee: James Oldham.
Salford C promoted to EFL League Two.

NATIONAL LEAGUE PROMOTED TEAMS ROLL CALL 2018–19

LEYTON ORIENT

Player	H	W	DOB
Alabi, James (F)	6 1		08/11/1994
Bonne, Macauley (F)	5 11	12 00	26/10/1995
Brill, Dean (G)	6 2	12 06	02/12/1985
Clay, Craig (M)	5 11	11 07	05/05/1992
Clayden, Charles (F)			
Dayton, James (M)	5 8	10 01	12/12/1988
Ekpiteta, Marvin (D)			
Gorman, Dale (D)	5 11	11 00	28/06/1996
Grainger, Charlie (G)			31/07/1996
Happe, Daniel (D)			
Harrold, Matt (F)	6 1	11 09	25/07/1984
Janata, Arthur (G)			
Judd, Myles (D)	5 10	10 08	26/08/1999
Koroma, Josh (F)	5 10	10 06	08/11/1998
Lawless, Alex (M)	5 11	10 08	05/02/1983
Lee, Charlie (M)	5 9	12 07	05/01/1987
Ling, Sam (D)	5 9	10 01	17/12/1996
McAnuff, Jobi (M)	5 10	11 08	09/11/1981
Sargeant, Sam (G)	6 0	10 08	23/09/1997
Shabani, Brendon (M)			
Simpson, Jay (F)	5 11	13 04	01/12/1988
Sweeney, Jayden (D)			
Turley, Jamie (D)	6 1	12 13	07/04/1990
Widdowson, Joe (D)	6 0	12 00	29/03/1989

SALFORD CITY

Player	H	W	DOB
Adetiloye, Sam (D)			
Askew, Josh (D)			20/02/1998
Crocombe, Max (G)	6 4		12/08/1993
Doyle, Alex (M)			
Dyson, Taylor (M)			
Foulds, Markell (D)			
Gaffney, Rory (F)	6 0	12 04	23/10/1989
Green, Matt (F)	6 0	12 11	02/01/1987
Hogan, Liam (D)	6 0	12 02	08/02/1989
Hornby-Forbes, Tyler (M)	5 11	11 11	08/03/1996
James-Taylor, Douglas (F)			
Jones, James (D)			16/02/1999
Linganzi, Amine (M)	6 1	12 11	16/11/1989
Lloyd, Danny (F)			03/12/1991
Lockett, Brandon (M)			
Mafuta, Gus (M)	5 10	11 03	28/08/1994
Maynard, Lois (D)	6 0	13 08	22/01/1989
Moncrieffe, Kamar (F)			
Neal, Chris (G)	6 1	13 08	23/10/1985
Neave, George (G)			
Ogurindi, Emmanuel (M)			
Piergianni, Carl (D)	6 1	13 05	03/05/1992
Politic, Dennis (M)			
Pond, Nathan (M)	6 3	11 00	05/01/1985
Redmond, Devonte (M)	6 2		19/09/1996
Redshaw, Jack (F)	5 5	10 01	20/11/1990
Rodney, Devante (F)			19/05/1998
Rooney, Adam (F)	5 10	12 03	21/04/1988
Shelton, Mark (M)	6 0	11 00	12/09/1996
Shepherd, William (M)			
Touray, Ibou (D)	5 10	10 10	24/12/1994
Walker, Tom (M)	6 0		12/12/1995
Whitehead, Danny (M)	5 10	10 12	23/10/1993
Wiseman, Scott (D)	6 0	11 05	13/12/1985

NATIONAL LEAGUE ATTENDANCES BY CLUB 2018–19

	Aggregate 2018–19	Average 2018–19	Highest Attendance 2018–19
Leyton Orient	125,227	5,445	8,241 v Braintree T
Wrexham	116,766	5,077	8,283 v Salford C
Chesterfield	103,565	4,503	5,662 v Wrexham
Hartlepool U	71,861	3,124	3,888 v Wrexham
Salford C	57,257	2,489	4,044 v Wrexham
Maidstone U	50,110	2,179	3,087 v Dover Ath
Sutton U	43,941	1,910	3,339 v Leyton Orient
Eastleigh	42,257	1,837	3,323 v FC Halifax T
Aldershot T	40,112	1,744	2,409 v Barnet
AFC Fylde	38,063	1,655	2,941 v Salford C
Harrogate T	36,253	1,576	2,584 v Leyton Orient
FC Halifax T	35,727	1,553	2,577 v Wrexham
Bromley	34,022	1,479	3,047 v Leyton Orient
Ebbsfleet U	33,357	1,450	3,020 v Leyton Orient
Dagenham & R	32,729	1,423	3,694 v Leyton Orient
Barrow	31,637	1,376	3,007 v Hartlepool U
Maidenhead U	31,392	1,365	2,016 v Leyton Orient
Barnet	30,778	1,338	3,648 v Leyton Orient
Havant and W	29,370	1,277	2,058 v Leyton Orient
Solihull Moors	29,295	1,274	3,681 v Leyton Orient
Dover Ath	25,827	1,123	2,270 v Leyton Orient
Gateshead	19,363	842	2,678 v Hartlepool U
Boreham Wood	16,507	718	1,894 v Barnet
Braintree T	15,594	678	2,574 v Leyton Orient

NATIONAL LEAGUE LEADING GOALSCORERS 2018–19

Player	Club	League	FA Cup	FA Trophy	Play-Offs	Total
Danny Rowe	AFC Fylde	27	1	4	0	32
Paul McCallum	Eastleigh	27	0	0	1	28
Macauley Bonne	Leyton Orient	23	0	1	0	24
Adam Rooney	Salford C	21	2	0	0	23
Scott Boden	Chesterfield	21	0	0	0	21
Adi Yussuf	Solihull Moors	14	4	3	0	21
Jack Muldoon	Harrogate T	15	0	2	0	17
Michael Cheek	Ebbsfleet U	16	0	0	0	16
Alfie Rutherford	Havant & Waterlooville	15	0	1	0	16
Blair Turgott	Maidstone U	14	2	0	0	16
Adrian Clifton	Maidenhead U	14	1	0	0	15
JJ Hooper	Bromley	14	0	1	0	15
Jermaine Hylton	Solihull Moors	13	0	2	0	15

NATIONAL LEAGUE NORTH 2018–19

(P) Promoted into division at end of 2017–18 season. (R) Relegated into division at end of 2017–18 season.

			Home					*Away*					*Total*						
		P	*W*	*D*	*L*	*F*	*A*	*W*	*D*	*L*	*F*	*A*	*W*	*D*	*L*	*F*	*A*	*GD*	*Pts*
1	Stockport Co	42	13	5	3	39	18	11	5	5	38	18	24	10	8	77	36	41	82
2	Chorley¶	42	15	3	3	45	15	9	6	6	38	26	24	9	9	83	41	42	81
3	Brackley T	42	14	5	2	44	19	8	6	7	28	21	22	11	9	72	40	32	77
4	Spennymoor T	42	11	6	4	38	25	11	4	6	40	23	22	10	10	78	48	30	76
5	Altrincham (P)	42	9	6	6	39	26	11	5	5	46	30	20	11	11	85	56	29	71
6	Blyth Spartans	42	11	3	7	43	31	9	6	6	31	31	20	9	13	74	62	12	69
7	Bradford (Park Avenue)	42	9	6	6	30	27	9	5	7	41	34	18	11	13	71	61	10	65
8	AFC Telford U	42	11	7	3	33	21	6	7	8	31	34	17	14	11	64	55	9	65
9	Chester FC (R)	42	10	8	3	37	25	6	6	9	23	37	16	14	12	60	62	–2	62
10	Kidderminster H	42	10	3	8	40	33	7	6	8	28	29	17	9	16	68	62	6	60
11	Boston U	42	8	3	10	29	31	9	4	8	33	29	17	7	18	62	60	2	58
12	York C	42	10	4	7	32	27	6	6	9	26	36	16	10	16	58	63	–5	58
13	Leamington	42	8	7	6	30	25	5	8	8	27	35	13	15	14	57	60	–3	54
14	Southport	42	6	9	6	31	29	7	5	9	27	26	13	14	15	58	55	3	53
15	Alfreton T	42	5	7	9	28	39	8	5	8	25	28	13	12	17	53	67	–14	51
16	Darlington 1883	42	7	6	8	25	21	5	8	8	31	41	12	14	16	56	62	–6	50
17	Hereford (P)	42	7	6	8	26	31	4	10	7	21	27	11	16	15	47	58	–11	49
18	Curzon Ashton	42	5	5	11	19	41	8	5	8	25	30	13	10	19	44	71	–27	49
19	Guiseley (R)	42	5	10	6	25	29	4	7	10	21	31	9	17	16	46	60	–14	44
20	Ashton U (P)	42	4	5	12	17	42	5	3	13	26	44	9	8	25	43	86	–43	35
21	FC United of Manchester	42	1	7	13	25	46	7	3	11	24	36	8	10	24	49	82	–33	34
22	Nuneaton Bor	42	1	3	17	16	51	3	4	14	22	45	4	7	31	38	96	–58	19

¶Chorley promoted via play-offs.

NATIONAL LEAGUE NORTH PLAY-OFFS 2018–19

▪ Denotes player sent off.

NATIONAL LEAGUE NORTH PLAY-OFF ELIMINATORS

Wednesday 1 May 2019

Altrincham (1) 2 *(Johnston 35, Hancock 90)*

Blyth Spartans (2) 2 *(Rivers 11, Nicholson 28)* 1698

Altrincham: Thompson; Densmore, Hampson, Jones, Hannigan, Moult, Johnston, Williams (Richman 76), Hulme, Hancock, Ceesay (Poole 62).
Blyth Spartans: Jameson; Nicholson, Liddle, Green (Reid 82), Buddle, Watson, Rivers, Oliver (Laing 83), Maguire (Horner 95), Atkinson, Holmes (Wrightson 67).
aet; Altrincham won 7-6 on penalties.
Referee: James Bell.

Spennymoor T (0) 1 *(Hawkins 75)*

Bradford (Park Avenue) (0) 0 1509

Spennymoor T: Gould; Williams, Harrison, Curtis, Brogan, Chandler, Ramshaw, Thackray (Boyes 54), Hall (Hibbs 71), Hawkins, Taylor.
Bradford (Park Avenue): Andrew; Ross, Lowe, East (Nowakowski 78), Havern, Spencer, Knight, Branson, Beesley, Lewis-Potter (Johnson 67), Clee (Hurst 87).
Referee: Steven Copeland.

NATIONAL LEAGUE NORTH PLAY-OFF SEMI-FINALS

Sunday 5 May 2019

Chorley (0) 1 *(Wilson 82)*

Altrincham (0) 1 *(Hancock 72)* 3446

Chorley: Urwin, Challoner (O'Keefe 79), Blakeman, Teague, Leather, Meppen-Walter, Newby A, Cottrell, Carver (Tuton 109), Wilson, Newby E (Almond 75).
Altrincham: Thompson; Densmore, Hampson, Jones, Hannigan, Moult, Johnston (Harrison 74), Williams (Richman 66), Hulme (Poole 54), Hancock▪, Ceesay (Harrop 94).
aet; Chorley won 3-1 on penalties.
Referee: Elliot Swallow.

Brackley T (0) 0

Spennymoor T (0) 0 1271

Brackley T: Lewis; Myles-Tebbutt (Fairlamb 72), Walker, Byrne, Hall, Dean, Lowe, Murombedzi, Ndlovu, Baker (Sterling-James 110), Walker (Prosser 106).
Spennymoor T: Gould; Williams, Harrison, Curtis, Brogan, Chandler (Anderson 106), Ramshaw, Hibbs (Boyes 91), Hall, Taylor, Hawkins.
aet; Spennymoor U won 5-4 on penalties.
Referee: Lewis Smith.

NATIONAL LEAGUE NORTH PLAY-OFF PROMOTION FINAL

Sunday 12 May 2019

Chorley (0) 1 *(Leather 102)*

Spennymoor T (0) 1 *(Taylor 105)* 3594

Chorley: Urwin; Challoner, Blakeman, Teague, Leather, Meppen-Walter, Newby A, Cottrell (O'Keefe 120), Carver, Wilson (Almond 83), Newby E.
Spennymoor T: Gould; Williams, Brogan, Chandler, Harrison (Anderson 96), Curtis, Hall (Boyes 104), Hibbs (Johnson 65), Taylor, Ramshaw, Hawkins (Atkinson 96).
aet; Chorley won 4-3 on penalties.
Referee: Samuel Barrott.
Chorley promoted to National League.

NATIONAL LEAGUE SOUTH 2018–19

(P) *Promoted into division at end of 2017–18 season.* (R) *Relegated into division at end of 2017–18 season.*

			Home					*Away*					*Total*						
		P	*W*	*D*	*L*	*F*	*A*	*W*	*D*	*L*	*F*	*A*	*W*	*D*	*L*	*F*	*A*	*GD*	*Pts*
1	Torquay U (R)	42	16	2	4	53	23	12	5	4	40	18	27	7	8	93	41	52	88
2	Woking (R)¶	42	12	2	7	38	25	11	7	3	38	24	23	9	10	76	49	27	78
3	Welling U	42	15	4	2	45	22	8	3	10	25	25	23	7	12	70	47	23	76
4	Chelmsford C	42	12	5	4	35	23	9	4	8	33	27	21	9	12	68	50	18	72
5	Bath C	42	12	4	5	33	18	8	7	6	25	18	20	11	11	58	36	22	71
6	Concord Rangers*	42	11	7	3	39	19	9	6	6	30	29	20	13	9	69	48	21	70
7	Wealdstone	42	9	5	7	31	31	9	7	5	31	19	18	12	12	62	50	12	66
8	Billericay T (P)	42	10	3	8	32	33	9	5	7	40	32	19	8	15	72	65	7	65
9	St Albans C	42	12	4	5	34	26	6	6	9	33	38	18	10	14	67	64	3	64
10	Dartford	42	12	6	3	32	21	6	4	11	20	37	18	10	14	52	58	–6	64
11	Slough T (P)	42	9	7	5	26	19	8	5	8	30	31	17	12	13	56	50	6	63
12	Oxford C	42	10	2	9	37	28	7	3	11	27	35	17	5	20	64	63	1	56
13	Chippenham T	42	10	4	7	34	28	6	3	12	23	36	16	7	19	57	64	–7	55
14	Dulwich Hamlet (P)	42	8	4	9	28	31	5	6	10	24	34	13	10	19	52	65	–13	49
15	Hampton & Richmond Bor	42	6	4	11	20	33	7	6	8	29	33	13	10	19	49	66	–17	49
16	Hemel Hempstead T	42	6	7	8	27	36	6	5	10	25	31	12	12	18	52	67	–15	48
17	Gloucester C	42	3	10	8	17	26	9	1	11	18	28	12	11	19	35	54	–19	47
18	Eastbourne Bor	42	6	6	9	33	34	4	6	11	19	31	10	12	20	52	65	–13	42
19	Hungerford T	42	6	6	9	24	31	5	3	13	21	41	11	9	22	45	72	–27	42
20	Truro C	42	5	4	12	30	43	4	8	9	33	44	9	12	21	63	87	–24	39
21	East Thurrock U	42	8	4	9	26	25	2	3	16	16	38	10	7	25	42	63	–21	37
22	Weston-super-Mare	42	2	7	12	19	36	6	4	11	31	44	8	11	23	50	80	–30	35

**Concorde R deducted 3 points for fielding an ineligible player and barred from play-offs.*
¶Woking promoted via play-offs.

NATIONAL LEAGUE SOUTH PLAY-OFFS 2018–19

NATIONAL LEAGUE SOUTH PLAY-OFF ELIMINATOR

Wednesday 1 May 2019

Bath C (0) 1 *(Mann 82)*

Wealdstone (1) 3 *(Sheppard 11, Monakana 63, Pratt 90)* 2201

Bath C: Clarke; Straker, Batten, Artus (Rigg 46 (Pryce 88)), Hinds, Stearn (Mann 70), Cundy, Raynes, Morton, Smith.
Wealdstone: North (Paterson 77); Tyler, Grant, Stevens, Okimo, Poku, Monakana, Smith, Brown (Pratt 67), Green, Sheppard (Mensah 25).
Referee: Matthew Russell.

NATIONAL LEAGUE SOUTH PLAY-OFF SEMI-FINALS

Sunday 5 May 2019

Woking (0) 3 *(Diarra 77, Kretzschmar 86, Hyde 90)*

Wealdstone (2) 2 *(Grant 3, Stevens 19)* 2917

Woking: Ross; Cook, Diarra, Gerring, Casey, Durojaiye (Ferdinand 77), Little, Allassani (Hodges 63), Kretzschmar, Cadogan (Hyde 66), Luer.
Wealdstone: Scott (Paterson 78); Tyler, Grant, Stevens, Okimo, Poku, Monakana, Smith (Mensah 34), Pratt (Brown 85), Green, Sheppard (Mensah 25).
Referee: James Durkin.

Welling U (2) 3 *(Goldberg 25, McDonald 33 (og), Kiernan 90)*

Chelmsford C (1) 2 *(Fenwick 44, Giles 83)* 1912

Welling U: Wilks; Gibbons, Braham-Barrett, Mendy, Acheampong (Hill 46), Audel, Kiernan, Ijaha, Mills, Goldberg (Bettamer 73), McCallum.
Chelmsford C: McDonald; Omozusi, Anderson (Reynolds 53), Spillane, Cascaval, Whelpdale, Porter (Isaac 62), Knott, Wraight, Murphy, Fenwick (Giles 68).
Referee: Name.

NATIONAL LEAGUE SOUTH PLAY-OFF PROMOTION FINAL

Sunday 12 May 2019

Woking (1) 1 *(Little 42)*

Welling U (0) 0 4865

Woking: Ross; Cook, Casey, Ferdinand, Gerring, Diarra, Allassani (Dkurojaiye 86), Little, Cadogan (Hodges 74), Hyde (Bradbury 90), Kretzschmar.
Welling U: Wilks; Gibbons, Braham-Barrett, Mendy (L'Goul 62), Hill, Audel, Kiernan, Ijaha, Mills, Goldberg (Bettamer 70), McCallum.
Referee: Andrew Kitchin.
Woking promoted to National League.

AFC FYLDE

Ground: Mill Farm Sports Village, Coronation Way, Wesham PR4 3JZ.
Tel: (01772) 682 593. *Website:* afcfylde.co.uk *Email:* info@afcfylde.co.uk *Year Formed:* 1988.
Record Attendance: 3,858 v Chorley, National League North, 26 December 2016. *Nickname:* 'The Coasters'.
Manager: Dave Challinor. *Colours:* White shirts, white shorts, white socks.

AFC FYLDE – NATIONAL LEAGUE 2018–19 LEAGUE RECORD

Match No.	*Date*		*Venue*	*Opponents*	*Result*		*H/T Score*	*Lg Pos.*	*Goalscorers*	*Attendance*
1	Aug	4	H	Bromley	W	2-1	1-0	4	Bond [45], Rowe [68]	1227
2		7	A	Wrexham	D	0-0	0-0	7		5777
3		11	A	Havant & W	D	1-1	1-0	7	Rowe (pen) [24]	1182
4		14	H	Solihull Moors	W	3-1	2-0	7	Rowe [4], Bond [19], Toure [67]	1257
5		18	H	Dover Ath	W	4-0	1-0	3	Rowe 2 (1 pen) [41, 85 (p)], Cardle [50], Hardy [90]	1258
6		25	A	Sutton U	D	0-0	0-0	2		1770
7		27	H	Harrogate T	D	0-0	0-0	3		1709
8	Sept	1	A	Ebbsfleet U	W	3-1	0-0	3	Rowe 2 [49, 57], Toure [86]	1395
9		4	H	Salford C	L	0-2	0-1	5		2941
10		8	A	Eastleigh	D	0-0	0-0	7		1750
11		15	H	Aldershot T	W	3-0	2-0	5	Croasdale [43], Tasdemir [45], Cardle [62]	1470
12		22	A	Barnet	D	1-1	1-1	8	Philliskirk [25]	1101
13		25	A	FC Halifax T	D	0-0	0-0	9		1197
14		29	H	Braintree T	W	3-0	1-0	7	Tasdemir [11], Philliskirk [50], Rowe [68]	1535
15	Oct	6	A	Chesterfield	D	0-0	0-0	7		4021
16		13	H	Maidstone U	W	2-0	0-0	6	Byrne [68], Birch [89]	1507
17		27	A	Maidenhead U	W	6-0	2-0	6	Rowe 2 (1 pen) [4, 32 (p)], Toure [55], Tasdemir [75], Philliskirk [86], Bond [88]	1372
18		30	H	Gateshead	W	1-0	0-0	5	Rowe [90]	1470
19	Nov	3	H	Leyton Orient	L	1-3	1-2	6	Rowe [20]	2142
20		17	A	Dagenham & R	L	1-2	1-1	6	Bond [1]	1328
21		24	H	Boreham Wood	W	2-1	0-0	6	Rowe [87], Tasdemir [88]	1345
22		27	A	Hartlepool U	W	2-1	1-0	4	Rowe [44], Gnahoua [74]	1721
23	Dec	1	H	Sutton U	D	2-2	1-0	5	Bond [36], Toure [81]	1401
24		8	A	Dover Ath	L	1-2	1-0	6	Rowe [26]	927
25		22	H	Ebbsfleet U	W	2-0	1-0	5	Croasdale [28], Rowe [80]	1474
26		26	A	Barrow	D	1-1	1-0	5	Bond [38]	1582
27		29	A	Harrogate T	W	2-1	0-0	3	Rowe 2 (1 pen) [47, 90 (p)]	1603
28	Jan	1	H	Barrow	D	0-0	0-0	4		2194
29		5	A	Bromley	L	2-3	1-2	5	Rowe [9], Gnahoua [58]	1102
30		19	H	Wrexham	W	2-0	1-0	4	Hemmings 2 [44, 55]	2912
31		26	A	Solihull Moors	W	2-1	0-0	4	Rowe 2 [52, 74]	1588
32	Feb	9	A	Maidstone U	D	1-1	1-0	4	Davies (og) [28]	2033
33		16	H	Chesterfield	L	0-1	0-1	4		2175
34		19	H	Havant & W	W	6-2	2-1	4	Croasdale [20], Tunnicliffe 2 [45, 69], Rowe [57], Crawford [75], Hemmings [90]	1192
35	Mar	2	H	Maidenhead U	W	2-1	1-1	4	Rowe [31], Crawford [57]	1402
36		9	A	Boreham Wood	D	1-1	1-0	5	Byrne [17]	493
37		12	H	Hartlepool U	W	4-2	1-0	4	Rowe 2 [3, 79], Kerr (og) [56], Walters [90]	1272
38		26	A	Leyton Orient	L	0-2	0-2	5		4696
39		30	A	Aldershot T	D	0-0	0-0	5		1280
40	Apr	2	H	Dagenham & R	D	1-1	1-1	5	Rowe [40]	1275
41		6	H	Eastleigh	W	4-2	1-2	5	Bradley [20], Tunnicliffe [50], Haughton [67], Reid [77]	1525
42		9	A	Gateshead	W	1-0	1-0	4	Haughton [31]	470
43		13	A	Braintree T	L	1-2	0-1	5	Tunnicliffe [85]	331
44		19	H	Barnet	W	1-0	1-0	5	Rowe [21]	1489
45		22	A	Salford C	W	1-0	1-0	4	Reid [31]	3338
46		27	H	FC Halifax T	L	0-2	0-2	5		1891

Final League Position: 5

GOALSCORERS

League (72): Rowe 27 (4 pens), Bond 6, Tasdemir 4, Toure 4, Tunnicliffe 4, Croasdale 3, Hemmings 3, Philliskirk 3, Byrne 2, Cardle 2, Crawford 2, Gnahoua 2, Haughton 2, Reid 2, Birch 1, Bradley 1, Hardy 1, Walters 1, own goals 2.
FA Cup (1): Rowe 1.
FA Trophy (19): Rowe 5 (1 pen), Tasdemir 5, Haughton 2, Tunnicliffe 2, Williams 2, Bond 1, Croasdale 1, Reid 1.
National League Play-Offs (4): Bond 1, Bradley 1, Croasdale 1, Philliskirk 1.

Lynch 45	Francis-Angol 42	Byrne 44	Tunnicliffe 36 + 4	Bond 25 + 9	Hardy 13 + 6	Creasdale 44	Rowe 45	Philliskirk 34 + 5	Cardle 14 + 3	Burke 25 + 2	Tasdemir 5 + 22	Toure 6 + 13	Birch 19 + 7	Kane 6	Hemmings 9 + 18	Kellermann 11 + 2	Brewitt 8 + 8	Williams 2 + 4	Haughton 27 + 3	Gnahoua 7 + 1	Montrose 3 + 2	Enigbokan-Bloomfield — + 1	Bradley 12 + 1	Odusina 6 + 2	Crawford 6 + 2	Walters 3 + 7	Reid 8 + 6	Griffiths 1	Match No.
1	2	3	4	5	6²	7	8	9	10¹	11	12	13																	1
1	3	4	5³	6	7²	8	11	9	10¹	2	13	14	12																2
1	2	3		4	12	5	6	7³	13	8		11¹	10²	9	14														3
1	2	3		6	7¹	8	11	9²	10³	4	13	12	14	5															4
1	2	3		6	7	8	11	9	10²	4¹		13	12	5															5
1	2	3		4	5	6	7		8²	9¹		13	14	10	12	11³													6
1	2	3		4	5²	6	7		8³	9	12	13		10	14	11¹													7
1	2	3	12	4	5²	6	7			8		13		10	9³	11¹	14												8
1	5	3	4	7²	6¹	8	11	14		2		13			10³	9	12												9
1		2	3		12	4	5	6	7³	8	14	13	10		9²	11¹													10
1	2	3	4	12	13	6	11	7	8¹	5³	10²	14				9													11
1	2	3	4	12		5	6	7	8		11²		9		13	10¹													12
1	2	3	5	13		6	11	7	8		10²		4		12	9¹													13
1	2²	3	4	13	14	5	6	7	8³		11¹		9		12	10													14
1	2	3	4			7	11	8	9¹				6		12	10	5²	13											15
1	2	3	4	6²	7¹	8	11	9	10				5		12		13												16
1	2	3	4	6		7	11¹	8	9³		13	10²	5		14				12										17
1	2	3	5	6		7	11	8	12		13	10¹	4²						9										18
1	2	3	4	5		6	7¹	8	12	9³	10²	13			14				11										19
1		2	3	5²		6³	10	7		4	14	11			13	12		8¹	9										20
1	2	3	4			6	10	7¹		5	12	11²			14	13		8³	9										21
1	2	3	4	5		6¹	7	8		9		10³			13		14		11²	12									22
1	2	3	4	6		7	10	8		5³		12			14		13		9²	11¹									23
1	2	3	4			6³	11	7		5		13				8²		14	9	10¹	12								24
1	2	3	13	7		8²	10			4	12						5	14	9³	11¹	6								25
1	2	5		7		8	11			4	12						3	13	6	10²	9¹								26
1	4	5	12	6		7	10	8²		3	13		14				2		9³	11¹									27
1	2	3	4	12		7¹	10	8		5	13				14		6		9²	11³									28
1	4	5	6¹	7³			10	8		3²			14				2		9	11	12	13							29
1		2	5	14		9	10	12					4²		7		13		8³		6¹		3	11					30
1	2	3	4	12		6	11	7							8²		14		9¹				5³	10	13				31
1	2	3	4			5	6	7							8¹				11²				9	10		12	13		32
1	2	3	4			5	6	7¹			14				8³				11				9	10²		13	12		33
1	2	4	6	7		8	11²				12		3		14				10³				5¹		9		13		34
1	3	4	5			6	11				12		2		7¹				9²					13	8		10		35
1	2	3	6	7³		8	11¹	14			13		5						10				4²		9		12		36
1	2	3	4			6	11	7¹			12		5				14		9²						8	13	10³		37
1	2	3	4		5³	6	9	7							12				13				14	8²		10	11¹		38
1	2	3	4	6³	7²	8	11	9					5		13				10¹							14	12		39
1	2²	3	4		7¹	8	11	9		14			6						10³				5			13	12		40
1	2		3	13		7	10	8		4			12				6³		9²				5¹		14		11		41
1	2	3	4	12		8	11²	9			14		6						7³				5			13	10¹		42
1	2	3	4		12	7	10	8²			13		6³						9				5			14	11¹		43
1	4	5	6	7	14	8	11	12		3	13								10¹				2²		9³				44
1	2	3	4	7		8	9³	12		5									13				6	14		10²	11¹		45
			13		2			3		14	12		6		5		8¹		9³					7	4	10²	11	1	46

FA Cup

Fourth Qualifying	Chesterfield	(h)	1-3

FA Trophy

First Round	Stratford T	(h)	5-1
Second Round	Biggleswade T	(h)	1-0
Third Round	Ramsbottom U	(a)	5-5
Replay	Ramsbottom U	(h)	4-1
Fourth Round	Barnet	(h)	0-0

(AFC Fylde won 4-1 on penalties)

Semi-Final 1st Leg	Stockport Co	(h)	0-0
Semi-Final 2nd Leg	Stockport Co	(a)	3-2
Final	Leyton Orient	Wembley	1-0

National League Play-Offs

Eliminator	Harrogate T	(h)	3-1
Semi-Finals	Solihull Moors	(a)	1-0
Final	Salford C	Wembley	0-3

ALDERSHOT TOWN

Ground: The EBB Stadium at the Recreation Ground, High Street, Aldershot, Hampshire GU11 1TW.
Tel: (01252) 320211. *Website:* www.theshots.co.uk *Email:* admin@theshots.co.uk *Year Formed:* 1926.
Record Attendance: 19,138 v Carlisle U, FA Cup 4th rd (replay), 28 January 1970. *Nickname:* 'The Shots'.
Manager: Danny Searle. *Colours:* Red shirts with blue trim, blue shorts with red trim, red socks with blue trim.

ALDERSHOT TOWN – NATIONAL LEAGUE 2018–19 LEAGUE RECORD

Match No.	Date	Venue	Opponents	Result		H/T Score	Lg Pos.	Goalscorers	Attendance
1	Aug 4	H	Barnet	D	0-0	0-0	15		2409
2	7	A	Chesterfield	L	0-3	0-2	20		4930
3	11	A	Solihull Moors	L	0-1	0-0	24		867
4	14	H	Dagenham & R	W	2-1	1-0	17	Rendell 3, Fenelon 54	1917
5	18	H	Harrogate T	L	0-2	0-0	20		1774
6	25	A	Ebbsfleet U	L	1-3	1-1	22	McClure 7	1233
7	27	H	Sutton U	W	2-1	1-0	20	Rendell 45, Berkeley-Agyepong 65	1904
8	Sept 1	A	Wrexham	L	0-2	0-0	20		4648
9	5	A	Havant & W	L	1-2	0-1	21	Rendell 90	1989
10	8	H	Bromley	W	3-2	1-2	18	Rendell 17, Holman 65, Rowe 87	1768
11	15	A	AFC Fylde	L	0-3	0-2	19		1470
12	22	H	Dover Ath	W	2-0	1-0	17	May 2 18, 67	1619
13	25	H	Maidstone U	L	0-1	0-1	19		1619
14	29	A	Hartlepool U	D	1-1	0-1	19	McClure 63	3251
15	Oct 6	H	FC Halifax T	W	3-0	2-0	18	May 8, McDonnell 20, Gallagher 47	1625
16	13	A	Eastleigh	W	2-1	2-1	16	Johnson (og) 36, Rendell 39	2349
17	27	A	Gateshead	L	0-3	0-2	16		703
18	30	H	Boreham Wood	D	1-1	1-0	15	McDonnell 45	1419
19	Nov 3	H	Braintree T	W	1-0	0-0	13	McDonnell 83	1618
20	17	A	Salford C	L	0-4	0-2	15		2875
21	24	H	Barrow	L	0-2	0-1	16		1549
22	27	A	Leyton Orient	D	0-0	0-0	16		4289
23	Dec 1	H	Ebbsfleet U	L	0-2	0-0	17		1663
24	8	A	Harrogate T	L	1-4	1-1	17	McDonnell 14	1362
25	22	H	Wrexham	D	0-0	0-0	18		1866
26	26	A	Maidenhead U	L	3-4	1-1	19	Grant 2 24, 66, McDonnell (pen) 89	1853
27	29	A	Sutton U	L	1-2	1-2	19	Grant 23	2216
28	Jan 1	H	Maidenhead U	D	0-0	0-0	19		2090
29	19	H	Chesterfield	L	0-2	0-1	22		2120
30	26	A	Dagenham & R	D	1-1	0-0	22	Mensah 64	1652
31	Feb 9	H	Eastleigh	L	1-3	0-1	22	Mensah 57	2096
32	12	H	Solihull Moors	L	0-3	0-1	22		1199
33	16	A	FC Halifax T	D	0-0	0-0	22		1650
34	23	A	Braintree T	W	1-0	0-0	22	Grant 64	829
35	Mar 2	H	Gateshead	L	0-2	0-0	22		1885
36	9	A	Barrow	L	1-2	0-1	22	McDonnell 58	1156
37	12	H	Leyton Orient	L	1-2	0-2	22	Rendell (pen) 72	1989
38	16	H	Salford C	L	0-1	0-1	22		1668
39	23	A	Boreham Wood	W	2-0	0-0	22	Goddard 60, Rendell (pen) 80	809
40	26	A	Barnet	L	0-2	0-0	22		1064
41	30	H	AFC Fylde	D	0-0	0-0	22		1280
42	Apr 6	A	Bromley	D	2-2	1-1	22	Grant 25, Howell 51	1521
43	13	H	Hartlepool U	D	1-1	1-0	22	Grant 10	1589
44	19	A	Dover Ath	L	0-1	0-0	22		1348
45	22	H	Havant & W	W	2-0	2-0	21	Mensah 14, McClure 25	1446
46	27	A	Maidstone U	W	2-0	0-0	21	McClure 56, Mensah 86	1929

Final League Position: 21

GOALSCORERS

League (38): Rendell 7 (2 pens), Grant 6, McDonnell 6 (1 pen), McClure 4, Mensah 4, May 3, Berkeley-Agyepong 1, Fenelon 1, Gallagher 1, Goddard 1, Holman 1, Howell 1, Rowe 1, own goal 1.
FA Cup (4): Fowler 1, Howell 1, McDonnell 1, Rendell 1.
FA Trophy (3): Fenelon 1, McDonagh 1, Wanadio 1.

Cole 22	Kinsella 32 + 1	McDonnell 35 + 6	Fowler 19	Fenelon 8 + 10	Bernard 34 + 1	Rowe 6 + 7	Booty 33 + 5	Holman 6 + 7	Berkeley-Agyepong 19 + 8	Smith C 3 + 2	Osborne 5 + 2	Wanadio 16 + 10	Rendell 25 + 5	Gallagher 28 + 8	McClure 18 + 8	Mannion 22	Lelan 18 + 7	Howell 26 + 7	Legg 2	May 11 + 1	McCoy 16	Osho 8	Barrett 3 + 2	Grant 11 + 10	McDonagh 7 + 6	Finney 13 + 2	Goddard 16 + 2	Mensah 16	Menayese 16	Elokobi 12 + 1	Arnold — + 2	*Match No.*
1	2	3	4	5^{1}	6	7	8	9^{3}	10	11^{2}	12	13	14																			1
1	2	6	4	9^{1}	3	12	8	13			5^{3}	14	10	7^{2}	11																	2
	2		3		6^{1}	7	9	10^{3}	11	12	4^{2}	5	13		14	1	8															3
	2	12	3^{1}	10^{2}	5	14	7	9	13			4^{3}	11			1	6	8														4
1	2	13	3	9	4		7^{2}	10^{1}	8			12	11				5	6														5
1	5^{3}	6			2	14		11^{1}	13	4		9	12	8	10^{2}		3	7														6
1	2	7	3	12	5		9^{1}		10			4^{2}	11	13			6	8														7
1	6	7	2	13	3	12	9^{2}	14	10^{1}			5^{3}	11				4	8														8
1	2	3	4	5^{1}	7^{2}	8		13	11			12	6	10			9															9
	3	4^{2}	5			8	14	13	10	12		7^{1}	11	9			2	6^{3}	1													10
	3	6	4		13	8		11	10^{3}	2		14		9	12		5^{2}	7^{1}	1													11
1	2	3	4		8		9^{1}	12	10		5	7		13	6^{3}			14		11^{2}												12
1	2	7	3		5		8	13	9		4^{2}	6			11^{1}		12			10												13
1	5	7	4				8		10^{3}			6^{2}	13	12	11		3	14		9^{1}	2											14
1	2	6	4	12			8	13					11^{3}	7^{2}	10^{1}			14		9	3	5										15
1	5	6^{3}	2	12			8^{2}						11	7^{1}	10		14	13		9	3	4										16
	2	8	5	12			7^{2}					13	11	6^{1}	10	1				9	4	3										17
	2	8	3	9^{1}	4							12	10	6	11^{2}	1	5	13		7												18
	2	3^{1}	4	5^{2}			13					7^{3}	6	8		1	14	12		10	9	11										19
	3	7	4	12			14		6^{3}				10^{2}	8		1	13			9	2	5	11^{1}									20
	4			11^{3}			7^{1}		8					6^{2}	10	1	5	12		14	3	2	9	13								21
	5	6		12	4				14					8	10^{3}	1		7		9^{1}	3	2	13	11^{2}								22
	2	6		12	3							13		8^{2}		1		7		9	4	5	10^{1}	11								23
	2	3^{2}			5		8				14	4		7	12	1	6				9^{3}		13	11^{1}	10							24
	2	9					8				3^{1}	4		7	10^{2}	1	12				5			13	11	6						25
	2	3					8					6		7	5	1	4				9			11		10						26
1	2	8			4		12					3		7	11						5			10^{1}	9	6						27
	2^{1}	7			4		12					3		8	9	1	13				5^{2}			11	10	6						28
		6^{2}			3		9					2		8	14	1	13	7^{1}			4^{3}			12	11	5	10					29
	2	3			5		7					12			13	1	6	4							9	10	11^{1}	8^{2}				30
	2^{2}	6			3		8					14	13	12		1		7^{1}							11^{3}	5	9	10	4			31
		6			3		8						10^{2}	14		1		7^{1}						12	13	5	9^{3}	11	4	2		32
1		13			3		8						10	7^{2}			4^{1}	6						12	14		9	11^{3}	5	2		33
1		12			3		7		13				10■	6			4^{3}	8						11^{2}		14	9^{1}		5	2		34
1				13	2		9		14					8^{3}			3^{1}	7						11^{2}	12		6	10	4	5		35
1		6^{1}		12	3		8		9^{2}					14				7							13	5	10^{3}	11	4	2		36
1		5			3		7^{1}		8^{2}				11		13			6						12			9	10	4	2		37
1		5■			3^{1}		7		8				10	13				6						12			9^{2}	11	4	2		38
					3		7		8^{1}				10^{2}	6	12	1		5						13		14	9	11^{3}	4	2		39
		5^{1}			3^{2}		7		8^{3}				9	14	13	1		6						12			11	10	4	2		40
		12					7		13				9	6^{2}	11^{1}	1		5			3						8	10	4	2		41
		2			5	12			13				4^{2}	6^{1}		1		3^{3}						10	14	9	11	7	8			42
		2^{2}			5	13	6		14				4			1		3						10^{3}	12	9	11^{1}	7	8			43
1	12	5			2^{2}	6			9					7										11		4^{1}	8	10^{3}	3	13	14	44
1	2				5^{2}		8						9		10^{3}			7						13		6	12	11^{1}	4	3	14	45
1	2^{3}	14			7	13	9^{2}						5	8^{1}	6			4									12	10	11	3		46

FA Cup

Fourth Qualifying	Kettering T	(h)	2-0
First Round	Bradford C	(h)	1-1
Replay (aet)	Bradford C	(a)	1-1

(Bradford C won 4-1 on penalties)

FA Trophy

First Round	Bedford T	(h)	3-3
Replay	Bedford T	(a)	0-7

BARNET

Ground: The Hive Stadium, Camrose Avenue, Edgware, London HA8 6AG. *Tel:* (020) 8381 3800.
Website: www.barnetfc.com *Email:* tellus@barnetfc.com *Year Formed:* 1888.
Record Attendance: 11,026 v Wycombe Wanderers, FA Amateur Cup 4th rd, 1951–52. *Nickname:* 'The Bees'.
Manager: Darren Currie. *Colours:* Amber shirts with black trim, black shorts, amber socks.

BARNET – NATIONAL LEAGUE 2018–19 LEAGUE RECORD

Match No.	*Date*	*Venue*	*Opponents*	*Result*	*H/T Score*	*Lg Pos.*	*Goalscorers*	*Atten-dance*
1	Aug 4	A	Aldershot T	D 0-0	0-0	15		2409
2	7	H	Braintree T	D 1-1	0-1	14	Coulthirst [62]	1507
3	11	H	Eastleigh	L 1-2	0-1	17	Adams [90]	1028
4	14	A	Harrogate T	L 0-2	0-2	20		1381
5	18	H	Ebbsfleet U	L 0-3	0-1	22		1217
6	25	A	Chesterfield	W 1-0	0-0	19	Taylor, J [90]	4685
7	27	H	Dagenham & R	W 2-1	1-1	17	Fonguck [41], Barham [63]	1522
8	Sept 1	A	Dover Ath	W 2-1	2-0	13	Barham [4], Harrison [26]	1037
9	4	A	Bromley	W 1-0	1-0	13	Sweeney [21]	1568
10	8	H	Maidenhead U	W 1-0	1-0	9	Walker [3]	1569
11	15	A	Leyton Orient	L 1-3	1-1	11	Fonguck [24]	5607
12	22	H	AFC Fylde	D 1-1	1-1	12	Coulthirst [20]	1101
13	25	H	Havant & W	D 2-2	1-0	12	Coulthirst 2 (1 pen) [13 (p), 81]	965
14	29	A	Wrexham	L 0-1	0-1	13		4727
15	Oct 6	H	Solihull Moors	W 2-0	0-0	11	Fonguck 2 [59, 90]	1054
16	27	A	Barrow	W 2-0	2-0	12	Duku [16], Fonguck [36]	1135
17	30	H	Salford C	L 1-3	1-1	12	Fonguck [43]	1243
18	Nov 3	H	Maidstone U	L 0-2	0-1	12		1424
19	18	A	Hartlepool U	W 3-1	2-1	11	Duku 2 [24, 25], Walker [90]	3545
20	24	H	Gateshead	L 1-2	0-1	11	Taylor, J [57]	940
21	Dec 8	A	Ebbsfleet U	L 0-1	0-0	15		1320
22	22	H	Dover Ath	W 2-0	0-0	14	Taylor, J [56], Vilhete [90]	1011
23	26	A	Boreham Wood	L 0-1	0-0	15		1894
24	29	A	Dagenham & R	W 1-0	1-0	13	Coulthirst [34]	1775
25	Jan 1	H	Boreham Wood	D 1-1	0-0	14	Mason-Clark [68]	2087
26	19	A	Braintree T	L 0-4	0-2	16		700
27	Feb 9	H	Sutton U	L 0-1	0-1	17		1316
28	16	A	Solihull Moors	D 2-2	1-0	19	Fonguck [4], Coulthirst [59]	1747
29	19	A	Sutton U	D 0-0	0-0	17		1917
30	26	H	Chesterfield	L 0-2	0-1	19		902
31	Mar 2	H	Barrow	W 3-1	1-0	17	Johnson [5], Coulthirst [62], Jones (og) [74]	1022
32	5	A	FC Halifax T	L 0-3	0-1	19		1085
33	9	A	Gateshead	L 1-2	1-0	19	Mason-Clark [23]	665
34	12	H	FC Halifax T	D 1-1	1-0	19	Fonguck [24]	702
35	16	H	Hartlepool U	D 0-0	0-0	20		1269
36	19	H	Harrogate T	W 1-0	1-0	17	Tarpey [30]	849
37	23	A	Salford C	D 0-0	0-0	17		2452
38	26	H	Aldershot T	W 2-0	0-0	16	Mason-Clark [46], Coulthirst [85]	1064
39	30	H	Leyton Orient	D 0-0	0-0	16		3648
40	Apr 2	A	Eastleigh	W 3-0	1-0	13	Coulthirst 2 (1 pen) [24, 62 (p)], Mason-Clark [52]	1579
41	6	A	Maidenhead U	W 1-0	1-0	12	Elito [44]	1491
42	9	A	Maidstone U	L 1-2	1-0	12	Elito [1]	1471
43	13	H	Wrexham	L 1-2	0-0	14	Coulthirst [70]	1594
44	19	A	AFC Fylde	L 0-1	0-1	15		1489
45	22	H	Bromley	D 1-1	0-0	14	Coulthirst [71]	1744
46	27	A	Havant & W	W 2-0	0-0	13	Alexander [48], Barham [70]	1003

Final League Position: 13; upgraded to 12 after Gateshead deducted 9pts after the end of the season.

GOALSCORERS

League (45): Coulthirst 12 (2 pens), Fonguck 8, Mason-Clark 4, Barham 3, Duku 3, Taylor J 3, Elito 2, Walker 2, Adams 1, Alexander 1, Harrison 1, Johnson 1, Sweeney 1, Tarpey 1, Vilhete 1, own goal 1.
FA Cup (13): Coulthirst 3 (1 pen), Robson 2, Sparkes 2, Tutonda 2, Alexander 1, Harrison 1, Johnson 1, Taylor J 1.
FA Trophy (10): Coulthirst 5 (1 pen), Mason-Clark 2, Duku 1, Fonguck 1, Robson 1.

Cousins 44	Alexander 42 + 1	Johnson 38	Robson 36 + 5	Adams 26	Harrison 13 + 7	Sparkes 11 + 5	Fonguck 33 + 3	Elito 20 + 5	Walker 10 + 8	Sweeney 41	Taylor J 27 + 3	Coulthirst 27 + 7	Mason-Clark 23 + 15	Kyei 1 + 3	Tutonda 17 + 3	Barham 10 + 11	Payne 1 + 3	Box — + 2	Jules 4	Boucaud 13 + 3	Duku 5 + 1	Reynolds 28 + 2	Tarpey 8 + 7	Bettamer 2 + 1	Vilhete — + 1	Akinola 1 + 13	Matrevics — + 1	Charles 3 + 1	Huffer 2	Taylor H 17 + 1	Santos 3 + 2	Vasiliou — + 3	*Match No.*
1	2	3	4	5	6	7	8^{2}	9^{1}	10^{3}	11	12	13	14																				1
1	2	3	4	6	11	7		8^{2}	10^{1}	9	5	12	13																				2
1	2	3	4	6	11	7^{1}		8^{2}	13	9	5	10	12																				3
1	2	3	4	6	10^{2}	12			13	8	5	11	9	7^{1}																			4
1	2		3	5	11^{3}	6	7	8^{1}	13	9		12	10^{2}		4	14																	5
1	2	3	4	5	6		7			9	13	12	10^{1}		8	11^{2}																	6
1	2	3	4	7	10		8			9	5^{2}	12	13		6	11^{1}																	7
1	2	5	3	7	10		9		12	6	8				4	11^{1}																	8
1	2	3	4	5	6		8^{1}		13	10	7				9■	11^{2}	12																9
1	2	3	4	5	6		8^{2}		9^{1}	10	7		12	13			11^{3}	14															10
1	2	3	5	7			8^{2}		11^{3}	9	6		12	14	4^{1}	10	13																11
1	2		3	4			7		12	9	6^{1}	5	13		8	10^{2}			11														12
1	2		3	7			8		10	9^{1}	4^{2}	11	13		5		14		6	12^{3}													13
1	2		6	7		8	9				3		10^{1}	12	4	11			5														14
1	2		3	7			8		10^{2}	9	4		13		5	12			6		11^{1}												15
1	4	5	6	7			8		10^{3}	9	2				3^{1}	13					11^{2}	12	14										16
1	2	3	4	7			8		10^{2}	9^{1}	5				6	13					11^{3}	12	14										17
1	3	4	7	8			9		10^{1}		6	12	13		2^{2}	14						5	11^{3}										18
1	2	3	5	6	12		8		13	9	7										10^{2}	4		11^{1}									19
1	3	4	6	7^{3}	10	12	8^{2}		11^{1}	9	2										14	5		13									20
1	2^{1}	3	5	6	7^{3}		9	12		10	8	13	14									4		11^{2}									21
1	2	3		6	12		7	8		9	5		10^{2}								11^{1}	4			13								22
1	2	3	6	7	10		8^{2}	13		9	5	11^{1}				12						4											23
1	2	3	6	7	13			8^{3}		9	5	11^{1}	10^{2}		14							4				12							24
1	2	3	5	6	13			9		10	8	7	11^{1}									4^{2}				12							25
1■	2	3	5	7	14			8^{1}	13^{3}	9	6	11	10^{2}									4					12						26
1	2		3		13		14	7		8	4^{2}	11	9^{1}		5					6						12^{3}		10					27
	12		3		14	5	7^{3}	8		10		4^{2}	13		9^{1}							2						11■	1	6			28
		2	4			6^{1}	7	8		9		11	10^{2}			12				13		3							1	5			29
1		2	4^{3}				6	7^{2}		8		10	14			12				13		3				11		9^{1}		5			30
1	2	3	5				7	8^{1}		9		10^{2}	13			11				6		4								12			31
1	2^{3}	3	5				7^{1}	8		9		10			14	11^{2}						4	13			12				6			32
1	2	3				6		8		9		11■	10^{2}							7^{1}		5	13					12		4			33
1	2	3				6^{2}	8	13		9			10^{1}							7		4	11			12				5			34
1	2	3					7			8		10^{2}	9^{1}			13				6		4	11			12				5			35
1	2	3	13			12	7^{3}			8		11	9							6^{1}		4	10^{2}			14				5			36
1	2	3	14			10	13			5		11^{3}	8^{2}							7		4	9^{1}			12				6			37
1	2^{1}	3	13			14	7^{2}	12		8		10	9							6		4	11^{3}							5			38
1	2^{2}	3	12				7	14		8^{3}		11	9							6^{1}		4	10							5	13		39
1	2	3	5			14	7^{1}	8		9^{2}		11	10^{3}									4	12							6	13		40
1	2	3	6					8				11^{3}	9^{2}		12	13						5	10^{1}			14				4	7		41
1	2		4				7^{2}	8^{3}		10		5	11^{1}		9	13						3				12				6		14	42
1		2	5				14	9^{1}		10^{2}	12	6	11^{3}							8		3	13							7	4		43
1	2	3	12					8^{1}		9■	5	11^{2}	10							7^{3}		4	14			13				6			44
1	2	3^{3}				7^{1}	9^{2}				6	11	10					13		8		4				12					5	14	45
1	2	3	5								6	11^{2}	13		8	10^{3}				9^{1}		4				12				7		14	46

FA Cup

Fourth Qualifying	Braintree T	(h)	4-2
First Round	Bristol R	(h)	1-1
Replay	Bristol R	(a)	2-1
Second Round	Stockport Co	(h)	1-0
Third Round	Sheffield U	(a)	1-0
Fourth Round	Brentford	(h)	3-3
Replay	Brentford	(a)	1-3

FA Trophy

First Round	Bath C	(h)	3-2
Second Round	Dorchester T	(h)	2-1
Third Round	Carshalton Ath	(a)	3-3
Replay	Carshalton Ath	(h)	2-1
Fourth Round	AFC Fylde	(a)	0-0

BARROW

Ground: Furness Building Society Stadium, Wilkie Road, Barrow-in-Furness, Cumbria LA14 5UW.
Tel: (01229) 666010. *Website:* www.barrowafc.com *Email:* office@barrowafc.com *Year Formed:* 1901.
Record Attendance: 16,854 v Swansea T, FA Cup 3rd rd, 9 January 1954. *Nickname:* 'The Bluebirds'.
Manager: Ian Evatt. *Colours:* White shirts with blue trim, blue shorts with white trim, white socks with blue trim.

BARROW – NATIONAL LEAGUE 2018–19 LEAGUE RECORD

Match No.	*Date*		*Venue*	*Opponents*	*Result*		*H/T Score*	*Lg Pos.*	*Goalscorers*	*Attendance*
1	Aug	4	H	Havant & W	W	3-0	1-0	1	Hindle 2 [40, 72], Smith [56]	1389
2		7	A	FC Halifax T	L	0-2	0-1	10		1654
3		11	A	Leyton Orient	D	2-2	1-0	8	Hindle [4], Correia [85]	4304
4		14	H	Chesterfield	W	3-2	1-1	8	Hindle [7], Smith 2 [69, 72]	1701
5		18	A	Maidstone U	L	0-1	0-1	11		2003
6		25	H	Braintree T	W	1-0	1-0	8	Rooney [7]	1232
7		27	A	Salford C	L	1-3	1-1	13	Taylor [20]	3012
8	Sept	1	H	Solihull Moors	L	1-2	0-0	15	Smith [90]	1260
9		4	A	Hartlepool U	D	0-0	0-0	15		3361
10		8	H	Dagenham & R	L	0-1	0-0	15		1171
11		15	A	Boreham Wood	D	1-1	0-0	15	Rooney [81]	564
12		22	H	Maidenhead U	W	2-0	1-0	13	Rooney [25], Smith [74]	1520
13		25	H	Gateshead	L	1-2	1-1	15	Smith [25]	1053
14		29	A	Dover Ath	W	2-0	0-0	14	Hindle 2 [69, 83]	814
15	Oct	6	H	Sutton U	W	2-1	2-0	12	Hindle [2], Burgess [42]	1203
16		13	A	Bromley	L	1-2	0-1	13	Sousa [56]	2211
17		27	H	Barnet	L	0-2	0-2	13		1135
18		30	A	Harrogate T	L	2-4	1-0	14	Rooney [32], Smith [77]	1268
19	Nov	3	A	Ebbsfleet U	L	0-1	0-1	17		1277
20		17	H	Eastleigh	L	0-3	0-2	17		1102
21		24	A	Aldershot T	W	2-0	1-0	15	Smith [27], Hindle [84]	1549
22		27	H	Wrexham	D	0-0	0-0	14		851
23	Dec	1	A	Braintree T	W	2-0	1-0	12	Agustien [10], Smith [63]	482
24		8	H	Maidstone U	W	1-0	0-0	12	Smith [62]	804
25		22	A	Solihull Moors	W	1-0	0-0	11	Rooney [74]	958
26		26	H	AFC Fylde	D	1-1	0-1	12	Hindle [75]	1582
27		29	H	Salford C	W	3-2	1-0	11	Blyth 2 (1 pen) [15 (p), 90], Agustien [82]	2311
28	Jan	1	A	AFC Fylde	D	0-0	0-0	11		2194
29		5	A	Havant & W	L	0-2	0-0	11		1074
30		19	H	FC Halifax T	D	0-0	0-0	12		1142
31		26	A	Chesterfield	D	0-0	0-0	11		4626
32	Feb	9	H	Bromley	D	1-1	1-0	11	Angus [16]	1130
33		16	A	Sutton U	W	1-0	0-0	11	Kay [90]	1892
34		23	H	Ebbsfleet U	D	0-0	0-0	12		1058
35	Mar	2	A	Barnet	L	1-3	0-1	12	Jameson [80]	1022
36		5	H	Leyton Orient	L	2-3	0-1	13	Kay [71], Turner [75]	1130
37		9	H	Aldershot T	W	2-1	1-0	11	Angus [32], Rooney (pen) [90]	1156
38		12	A	Wrexham	W	3-1	3-0	11	Jones [3], Blyth [24], Hardcastle [45]	4613
39		16	A	Eastleigh	W	1-0	1-0	11	Hindle [29]	1738
40		23	H	Harrogate T	D	2-2	2-0	11	Hardcastle [19], Rooney (pen) [22]	1934
41		30	H	Boreham Wood	L	1-2	1-2	11	Hindle [37]	1415
42	Apr	6	A	Dagenham & R	D	0-0	0-0	11		2173
43		13	H	Dover Ath	L	2-3	1-0	11	Rooney [44], Hardcastle [67]	1351
44		19	A	Maidenhead U	D	1-1	1-0	11	Hindle [19]	1820
45		22	H	Hartlepool U	W	1-0	1-0	11	Kay [28]	3007
46		27	A	Gateshead	W	2-0	2-0	11	Rooney 2 [8, 22]	798

Final League Position: 11; upgraded to 10 after Gateshead deducted 9pts after the end of the season.

GOALSCORERS

League (52): Hindle 12, Rooney 10 (2 pens), Smith 10, Blyth 3 (1 pen), Hardcastle 3, Kay 3, Agustien 2, Angus 2, Burgess 1, Correia 1, Jameson 1, Jones 1, Sousa 1, Taylor 1, Turner 1.
FA Cup (2): Burgess 1, Smith 1.
FA Trophy (1): own goal 1.

Firth 18	Brown 25 + 5	Jones 41	Granite 29	Wilson 9 + 1	Taylor 43	Rooney 44 + 2	Kay 28 – 13	Hindle 26 + 20	Smith 23	Turner 8 + 3	Burgess 14 + 11	Correia — + 5	Waterston 5 + 2	Elsdon 3 + 2	Barthram 19 + 11	Jameson 21 + 4	Jennings 6 + 8	Molyneux 10 + 5	Blyth 16 + 8	Norrington-Davies 28	Holden 5	Mulholland 1 + 2	Sousa 4 + 1	Dixon 28	Agustien 10	Dyson — + 3	McFarlane 1	Angus 10 + 1	Hird 10 + 1	Hardcastle 14 + 1	Sloan — + 1	Reid — + 3	Philpot 7	*Match No.*
1	2	3	4	5	6	7	8^{2}	9^{1}	10^{3}	11	12	13	14																					1
1	2	3	4	5^{1}	6	7	8	9	10	11^{2}		14		12^{3}	13																			2
1	2	3	4		6	7	8^{2}	9	10^{3}	11^{1}	13	14	12			5																		3
1	2^{1}	3	4		6^{2}	7	8^{3}	9	10		14		11		13	5	12■																	4
1	2	3	4		6	7	12	9	10		8^{3}	14	11^{2}			5^{1}		13																5
1	13	4	5		6	7	8^{1}	9	10		12	14	11^{2}		2^{3}			3																6
1	2	4	5		6	7	8^{1}	9^{2}	10		13		11		12			3																7
1	2	4	5		6	7	12	10	9		8		11^{1}					3																8
1	2	3	5		4	7	8	6	10^{1}		9							11	12															9
1	2	4	5		6	7	9	10^{1}	11		8							3	12															10
1	2	3	5		6	7	8	12	10^{2}		9^{3}					14			13	4	11^{1}													11
1	4	5^{2}			6	9	7^{1}	12	11		8				14	2			13	3	10^{3}													12
1	2^{2}	4			6	7	8^{3}	14	10		9				12	5			13	3	11^{1}													13
1	2	3	5		4	6	7^{1}	12	9^{3}		8				14				13	11	10^{2}													14
1		4	5		6	7^{2}		10	11^{1}		8^{3}						13	3	12	2	9	14												15
1	2	4	5^{1}	13	6	7	12	10	11		8^{2}				14			3^{3}					9											16
1	2^{2}	4		5	6	7	9^{3}	12	10		8				13			14		3			11^{1}											17
1	2	3			8	7	9^{2}	14	11		13					4		6^{1}		5		10^{3}	12											18
	2			3	7	6	9^{1}	11			8					4				5		12	10	1										19
	2	3^{2}	4	5		12	13	14	11	10^{3}	7^{1}									6			9	1	8									20
		2	3	4	7	9^{3}	14	13	10^{2}						6		12		11	5				1	8^{1}									21
	12		4	5^{2}	7	9	13	14	11^{1}						2	6			10	3				1	8^{3}									22
		2	3		7	8^{1}		13	11^{2}		14				4	5	12		10	6				1	9^{3}									23
		5		4	7^{3}	9^{2}		14	11^{1}	13					2	6	12		10	3■				1	8									24
		2	4	7^{1}	3	5		14		8^{3}					9	12			6	10				1	11^{2}	13								25
		4	2		8	7^{1}	14	12		11					5	6			10^{2}	3				1	9^{3}	13								26
		2	3		7	8^{2}	12	11^{1}							5	4			10	6				1	9	13								27
		2	3		7	8^{1}	12	11^{2}			14				5	4	13		10	6				1	9^{3}									28
		2	4		3	5^{3}	14	13							9	7■	12		6^{1}	11				1	10^{2}		8							29
		6	5^{3}		7	8^{1}	13	14			9			4	2				10	3				1				11^{2}	12					30
	14	2			8	12	7^{2}	13		10^{3}				3	5			6■	11^{1}					1				9	4					31
	3	6			7	8^{1}	12	9^{2}						5	2				10					1				11	4	13				32
	7	2			3	5^{1}	8	11			12				10									1				9	4	6^{2}	13			33
	2	3			6	7	8^{1}	11			13				5	4			12					1				10^{2}		9				34
	4	2				6	9^{2}	13		12					5	3	8		11					1				10^{1}		7				35
	2	3				6^{3}	7	12		13	14					4	9	5	11^{1}					1				10^{2}		8				36
	2^{2}	5			7	6	8	14		10^{3}					4	12	13							1				11	3^{1}	9				37
		2			5	6	7^{1}	12							13^{3}	3	9	14	11	4				1				10^{2}		8				38
		2			3	4	6	7^{2}						13		9	10		5^{1}	11				1						8		12		39
		2			5	6	7^{1}	10								3	8	12		4				1						9			11	40
		2			5	6	7^{1}	11							13		9			3				1					4	8		12	10^{2}	41
		2	4		3	7	8^{1}	6^{2}							12					11				1					5	9		13	10	42
		2	4		3	6		5							10					11				1					8	9			7	43
	13		4		3	6	10^{1}	7^{2}								2				11				1				12	9	8			5	44
	2		4		3	6	12	5												11				1				9^{1}	8	10			7	45
	14		3^{3}		6	7	9^{2}	11							2^{1}	12		13		5				1					4	8			10	46

FA Cup
Fourth Qualifying Chorley (a) 2-3

FA Trophy
First Round Halifax T (h) 1-2

BOREHAM WOOD

Ground: Meadow Park, Broughinge Road, Borehamwood, Hertfordshire WD6 5AL. *Tel:* (02089) 535097.
Website: borehamwoodfootballclub.co.uk *Email:* see website. *Year Formed:* 1948.
Record Attendance: 4,030 v Arsenal, Friendly, 13 July 2001. *Nickname:* 'The Wood' *Manager:* Luke Garrard.
Colours: White shirts with black trim, white shorts with black trim, white socks.

BOREHAM WOOD – NATIONAL LEAGUE 2018–19 LEAGUE RECORD

Match No.	Date		Venue	Opponents	Result		H/T Score	Lg Pos.	Goalscorers	Attendance
1	Aug	4	H	Dagenham & R	W	1-0	0-0	6	Balanta 52	833
2		7	A	Havant & W	D	0-0	0-0	8		1348
3		11	A	Wrexham	L	0-3	0-1	11		4356
4		14	H	Gateshead	D	1-1	1-0	12	Stephens 45	608
5		18	A	Leyton Orient	L	0-1	0-0	18		3767
6		25	H	FC Halifax T	W	2-1	0-0	15	Umerah 2 78, 90	572
7		27	A	Maidstone U	W	2-1	0-1	12	Balanta 60, Umerah 85	2035
8	Sept	1	H	Braintree T	D	1-1	1-0	12	Fyfield 35	578
9		4	H	Chesterfield	W	1-0	1-0	10	Fyfield 8	737
10		15	H	Barrow	D	1-1	0-0	12	Murtagh 90	564
11		18	A	Sutton U	W	4-0	3-0	7	Balanta 3, Murtagh 6, Shaibu 23, Umerah 53	1677
12		22	A	Salford C	L	1-3	0-2	10	Umerah 55	2006
13		25	A	Eastleigh	L	0-1	0-0	11		1306
14		29	H	Harrogate T	L	2-4	1-1	12	Ugwu 2 11, 60	566
15	Oct	6	A	Hartlepool U	L	0-2	0-1	14		2988
16		13	H	Maidenhead U	W	3-1	1-0	11	Murtagh 45, Umerah 75, Shaibu 85	684
17		27	H	Bromley	W	2-1	1-1	11	Shaibu 45, Ugwu 60	629
18		30	A	Aldershot T	D	1-1	0-1	11	Stephens 90	1419
19	Nov	3	A	Solihull Moors	D	0-0	0-0	11		803
20		17	H	Ebbsfleet U	D	0-0	0-0	10		724
21		24	A	AFC Fylde	L	1-2	0-0	10	Ugwu 58	1345
22		27	H	Dover Ath	L	0-1	0-0	11		407
23	Dec	8	H	Leyton Orient	W	1-0	1-0	11	Ilesanmi 4	1602
24		18	A	FC Halifax T	D	1-1	1-1	11	Shaibu 4	913
25		22	A	Braintree T	D	1-1	0-1	12	Shaibu 50	371
26		26	H	Barnet	W	1-0	0-0	11	Ash 88	1894
27		29	H	Maidstone U	L	0-1	0-1	12		630
28	Jan	1	A	Barnet	D	1-1	0-0	12	Ash (pen) 85	2087
29		5	A	Dagenham & R	D	4-4	3-3	12	Kanu 14, Shakes 31, Shaibu 35, Ash 87	1043
30		19	H	Havant & W	L	1-3	0-2	14	Kanu 70	511
31		26	A	Gateshead	D	1-1	1-0	14	Shields 43	562
32	Feb	9	A	Maidenhead U	L	0-1	0-0	15		1113
33		16	H	Hartlepool U	L	0-4	0-1	15		679
34		19	H	Wrexham	L	0-2	0-0	16		645
35	Mar	2	A	Bromley	W	2-0	1-0	16	Gabriel 41, Kanu 90	1326
36		9	H	AFC Fylde	D	1-1	0-1	17	Fyfield 57	493
37		12	A	Dover Ath	D	1-1	1-1	16	Shaibu 4	743
38		16	A	Ebbsfleet U	L	2-3	1-2	17	Murtagh 9, Ash 85	1110
39		23	H	Aldershot T	L	0-2	0-0	18		809
40		26	H	Solihull Moors	D	2-2	1-1	20	Gabriel 26, Kanu 88	478
41		30	A	Barrow	W	2-1	2-1	18	Murtagh 19, Shaibu (pen) 34	1415
42	Apr	6	H	Sutton U	L	1-2	1-1	19	Shakes 29	508
43		13	A	Harrogate T	W	1-0	1-0	18	Champion 9	1216
44		19	H	Salford C	L	2-3	1-2	19	Gabriel (pen) 26, Murtagh 70	854
45		22	A	Chesterfield	L	2-3	1-1	19	Murtagh 28, Shaibu (pen) 59	4384
46		27	H	Eastleigh	D	3-3	1-1	20	Gabriel 39, Ash 58, Murtagh 77	502

Final League Position: 20

GOALSCORERS

League (53): Shaibu 9 (2 pens), Murtagh 8, Umerah 6, Ash 5 (1 pen), Gabriel 4 (1 pen), Kanu 4, Ugwu 4, Balanta 3, Fyfield 3, Shakes 2, Stephens 2, Champion 1, Ilesanmi 1, Shields 1.
FA Cup (3): Fyfield 1, Shaibu 1, Umerah 1 (1 pen).
FA Trophy (3): Shaibu 3.
Irn-Bru Cup (0).

Huddart 30	Woodards 25 + 4	Ilesanmi 38 + 5	Ricketts 40	Parry 20 + 6	Stephens 35 + 1	Shakes 39 + 7	Champion 44	Murtagh 43	Ash 6 + 22	Balanta 11	Thomas 12 + 20	Balcombe 8	Shaibu 25 + 15	Umerah 16 + 4	Smith C 8 + 1	Fyfield 41 + 2	Hackett-Fairchild 3 + 1	Ugwu 17 + 3	Smith K 3	Kanu 12 + 6	Shields 7 + 3	Legg 8	Gabriel 10 + 1	Cooper 5	Match No.
1	2	3	4	5	6	7	8	9	10^{1}	11	12														1
	2	3	4	5	6	7	8	9	12	10		1	11^{1}												2
	2^{3}	3	8	4	5	12	6	7	13	9		1	11^{2}	10^{1}	14										3
	4		5^{2}	13	2	6	7	8		9	12	1	10^{1}	11		3									4
	2^{1}	14	5	13	3	6	7	9		11^{3}	12	1		10	8^{2}	4									5
	2^{1}	3	6		4	7	8	9		11	12	1		10		5									6
	2^{1}	12	7		3	5	6	8	13	10	9^{2}	1		11		4									7
		2	5		4	6	7	8		11	10	1	12	9^{1}		3									8
1		2	3	13	4	5	6^{2}	8		11	10^{1}		12	7		9									9
1	12	5	6	2	3	7		8		11			13	10^{2}		4	9^{1}								10
1	2^{2}	13	3	14	4	5	6	7		10^{1}			11	12		8	9^{3}								11
1	2^{2}	3	6		4	7	8	9			12		10^{1}	11		5		13							12
1	2^{2}	12	7^{1}	3	5	6		8			13			11	9	4		10							13
1		2		3	4	5	6	8			12		13	7^{1}	11^{2}	9		10							14
		5		3		6	7	8			10^{1}	1	12	9		4		11	2						15
1		2	7	4		5	6	8			12		13	11^{1}	9^{2}	3		10							16
1	14	4^{3}	5	2		6	7				9		11^{2}	12	8	3	10^{1}	13							17
1	2^{1}		6	3	12	7	8				10		13	9	5^{2}	4		11							18
1	2^{2}		6	3	4	7	8	9^{3}			12		13	10		5	14	11^{1}							19
1	2^{2}	3	6		5	7	8	9	14		13		11^{1}	12		4		10^{3}							20
1	2^{2}	3	6	4		7	8	9			13		12	10^{1}		5		11							21
1	2^{1}	13	5		3	6	7	8	14		9^{3}		11	12		4		10^{2}							22
1		2	3		5	6	7	8	9		10		12			4		11^{1}							23
1		2	5	3	4	6	7	8^{2}			12		11		9^{1}	13		10							24
1		2	5		4	6	7	8	12		9		11^{1}			3		10							25
1	2^{1}	3	6		4	7	8	9	12		13		11^{2}			5		10							26
1		2	3	4^{2}	5	6	7	8	9^{1}		13		12		11^{3}	14		10							27
1	2^{2}	3	4		5	6	7	8	12		13		11			9		10^{1}							28
1	12	2	8		3	5	6	7^{1}	13		14		11			4				9^{2}	10^{3}				29
	2^{1}	3^{2}	6		4	7	8		14		12		11^{3}			5		13		10	9	1			30
		2	5	3		6	7	8			13		12			4		9		10^{2}	11^{1}	1			31
	2	3	4^{2}	5		6	7	8	13				12			9		10^{3}		11^{1}	14	1			32
1		2	3	4		13	5	7	12		9					8				10	11^{1}		6^{2}		33
1		4	5	3		6^{2}	7	8	13		9		12			2				10			11^{1}		34
1		2	5		4	12	6	7	13				11^{1}			3				8	10		9^{2}		35
1		2	5		3	12	6	7	8		13		11^{2}			4				9	10^{1}				36
1		2	3		4	12	5	6	7				11			8				10^{1}	13			9^{2}	37
1	14	2	5■		3	6	7	8^{3}	12				11^{2}			4				10			13	9^{1}	38
	2^{3}	3			4	13	6	7	10^{2}				12			5				11^{1}	14	1	9	8	39
	2^{2}	3	6		5	7	8	9	13				11			4				12		1	10^{1}		40
	2	3		4	5	7	8	9	12				11^{2}			6				13		1	10^{1}		41
		2	5		3	6	7	8	12				10			4				13		1	11^{1}	9^{2}	42
1	4^{1}	5	6^{3}	14	2	7	8	9	12				11^{2}			3				13			10		43
1		5	6	12	2^{3}	7	8	9	13				10^{1}			3			4^{2}	14			11		44
	2	3		4■		13	5	6	14		12		11^{2}			7				9^{1}	10^{3}	1		8	45
1	2	3				4	5	7	12		9^{2}		11^{1}			8			10	13			6		46

FA Cup

Fourth Qualifying	Dagenham & R	(h)	2-2
Replay	Dagenham & R	(a)	1-0
First Round	Southport	(a)	0-2

FA Trophy

First Round *(aet)*	Torquay U	(h)	3-1
Second Round	Blyth Spartans	(a)	0-1

Irn-Bru Cup

Second Round	Dunfermline Ath	(h)	0-0

(Dunfermline Ath won 6-5 on penalties)

BRAINTREE TOWN

Ground: The Cressing Road Stadium, off Clockhouse Way, Braintree, Essex CM7 3DE.
Tel: (01376) 345 617. *Website:* www.braintreetownfc.org.uk *Email:* braintreeTFC@aol.com *Year Formed:* 1898.
Record Attendance: 4,000 v Tottenham H, Friendly, 8 May 1952. *Nickname:* 'The Iron'.
Manager: Glen Driver. *Colours:* Orange shirts with white trim, blue shorts, blue socks.

BRAINTREE TOWN – NATIONAL LEAGUE 2018–19 LEAGUE RECORD

Match No.	*Date*	*Venue*	*Opponents*	*Result*	*H/T Score*	*Lg Pos.*	*Goalscorers*	*Attendance*
1	Aug 4	H	FC Halifax T	L 0-2	0-1	23		621
2	7	A	Barnet	D 1-1	1-0	19	Taylor, J (og) [34]	1507
3	11	A	Chesterfield	L 0-1	0-0	23		4927
4	14	H	Hartlepool U	D 1-1	0-1	21	Bettamer [90]	606
5	18	H	Havant & W	L 3-4	2-2	21	Grant 2 [31, 72], Bettamer [38]	407
6	25	A	Barrow	L 0-1	0-1	23		1232
7	27	H	Maidenhead U	L 0-2	0-2	23		576
8	Sept 1	A	Boreham Wood	D 1-1	0-1	23	Bettamer [48]	578
9	4	A	Dagenham & R	L 0-1	0-0	24		1081
10	8	H	Wrexham	L 0-1	0-0	24		802
11	15	A	Gateshead	W 1-0	0-0	23	Ellul [55]	578
12	22	H	Maidstone U	L 0-1	0-0	23		807
13	25	H	Leyton Orient	L 1-5	1-2	24	Della Verde [23]	2574
14	29	A	AFC Fylde	L 0-3	0-1	24		1535
15	Oct 6	H	Eastleigh	L 1-2	0-2	24	Bettamer [72]	418
16	13	A	Salford C	D 2-2	1-1	24	Bettamer 2 (1 pen) [45 (p), 74]	2710
17	27	H	Dover Ath	W 2-1	1-0	23	Amaluzor [13], Grant (pen) [78]	575
18	30	A	Bromley	W 4-2	2-1	23	Gomis [6], Grant 2 [29, 84], Della Verde [48]	1008
19	Nov 3	A	Aldershot T	L 0-1	0-0	23		1618
20	17	H	Solihull Moors	L 0-3	0-0	23		822
21	24	A	Harrogate T	L 1-3	1-1	24	Amaluzor [26]	1454
22	27	H	Sutton U	D 2-2	1-0	24	Barrington [31], Crook [72]	439
23	Dec 1	H	Barrow	L 0-2	0-1	24		482
24	8	A	Havant & W	L 1-2	0-0	24	Woodford (og) [76]	858
25	22	H	Boreham Wood	D 1-1	1-0	24	Della Verde [30]	371
26	26	A	Ebbsfleet U	L 2-4	1-3	24	Ellul [5], Morton (pen) [48]	1231
27	29	A	Maidenhead U	W 1-0	0-0	24	James [68]	1218
28	Jan 1	H	Ebbsfleet U	L 0-4	0-2	24		752
29	5	A	FC Halifax T	D 0-0	0-0	24		1302
30	19	H	Barnet	W 4-0	2-0	24	Morton 3 (2 pens) [6 (p), 33, 59 (p)], Allen, I [84]	700
31	26	A	Hartlepool U	L 1-2	1-0	24	Amaluzor [39]	2769
32	Feb 9	H	Salford C	W 1-0	0-0	24	Morton [90]	765
33	16	A	Eastleigh	L 1-2	1-2	24	James [42]	2120
34	23	H	Aldershot T	L 0-1	0-0	24		829
35	Mar 2	A	Dover Ath	L 0-3	0-1	24		1053
36	5	H	Chesterfield	L 1-3	0-2	24	Allen, L (pen) [64]	482
37	9	H	Harrogate T	L 0-4	0-3	24		362
38	12	A	Sutton U	W 3-0	0-0	24	Henry [61], Kelly [77], Eyoma [89]	1525
39	16	A	Solihull Moors	L 1-2	1-1	24	Henry [22]	1003
40	23	H	Bromley	L 2-4	0-3	24	Lyons-Foster [54], Sagaf [90]	673
41	30	H	Gateshead	W 2-0	1-0	23	Henry (pen) [44], Cerulli [88]	291
42	Apr 6	A	Wrexham	L 1-3	1-1	23	Henry [41]	4221
43	13	H	AFC Fylde	W 2-1	1-0	23	Sagaf [31], Richards [77]	331
44	19	A	Maidstone U	W 2-0	1-0	23	Sagaf (pen) [2], Henry [85]	1908
45	22	H	Dagenham & R	W 2-0	0-0	23	Cerulli [76], Sagaf [86]	909
46	27	A	Leyton Orient	D 0-0	0-0	22		8241

Final League Position: 22

GOALSCORERS

League (48): Bettamer 6 (1 pen), Grant 5 (1 pen), Henry 5 (1 pen), Morton 5 (3 pens), Sagaf 4 (1 pen), Amaluzor 3, Della Verde 3, Cerulli 2, Ellul 2, James 2, Allen I 1, Allen L 1 (1 pen), Barrington 1, Crook 1, Eyoma 1, Gomis 1, Kelly 1, Lyons-Foster 1, Richards 1, own goals 2.
FA Cup (2): Della Verde 1, Grant 1.
FA Trophy (1): Allen L 1.

Killip 38	Muleba 21 + 1	Webber 6 + 1 / Eleftheriou 18	Durojaiye 7	Clark 8 + 1 / Atkinson 15	Hill 6 + 1	Allen L 21 + 6	Ochieng 3 + 2 / Allen I 10 + 5	Della Verde 17 + 12	Bettamer 14 + 1	Pattisson 9 + 7 / Henry 14 + 1	Rowe 6 + 7	Thompson 5 + 4 / Kelly 6	Grant 8 + 7	Lyons-Foster 39	Ellul 19 / Matsuzaka 9 + 3	Frimpong 1 + 2 / Osborne 1	Rapai 1 + 2	Bettache 1 / Eyoma 6 + 1	Crook 8 + 6	Gabriel 29 + 1 / Gibson — + 2	James 32	Nieskens 8 / Eze — + 2	Sagaf 21 + 6	Amaluzor 19 + 2	Charles — + 2 / Karic 6	Cass 2 + 5	Jones 3 / Cerulli — + 5	Gomis 5 / Smith — + 3	Legg 5	Pitoula-Wabo — + 5 / Temple — + 1	Barrington 7 + 3	Richards 22 + 1	Okosieme 4 + 2	Morton 14	Clayton-Phillips — + 3	Borg 12 + 4	Curran — + 1	Match No.
1	2	3	4	5	6	7³	8¹	9²	10	11	12	13	14																									1
1	2	3	7	4	12	8²		10		9	13	11¹	14	5	6³																							2
1	5	6	7	2	4	13		9²	12	8	11¹	10		3																								3
1	2	3	7¹	4	5³	8		14	11	9	10²			6		12	13																					4
1	2³		6	4	3	8	13	7¹	10	12			11²	5		14		9																				5
1	2		6	4	5	7		14	10	13		11²	9¹	3			12		8³																			6
1			6²	5	4		7	8¹	10	9		14	12	2			11³		13	3																		7
1		2				7		13	10	12				3					8²	4	5	6	9	11¹														8
1		2				3		12	5²		14		13	6³					4¹	7	9	10	8	11														9
1						7¹			10			8²	14	6	3³				12	5	2	4	11	9	13													10
1	2			13				12	9		14		11¹		6³				7	3	5	4	8	10²														11
1	2					13		12	5				6²		3				4	7	9	10	8¹	11														12
1	2			3				9	10		11²				4¹				8³	5	6	7	12	14	13													13
1	2					8		13	10²	9	11³	14	12		4					3	6¹	5	7															14
1	3					8		12	10			9¹	13	4	5					6	2²		7			11												15
1	2					14		7	9	11³			10¹	4	3	6²				5	8			12		13												16
	2					13		3²		14			6¹	4	5					7	9		8	10		12	1	11³										17
	2						14	7		12			9	3	4					5	6²		8	10¹		13	1	11³										18
	2							3¹		12			6	4	5					7	9		8	10²		13	1	11										19
	2					6		8³		7²		13		3	4				12	5			9	10¹				11	1	14								20
	2					7³	9							3	5				14	6				10²		12		11¹	1	13	4	8						21
	2									12				6	3				9²	5		4		11³		10¹			1	13	7	8	14					22
	2	14								9¹					3³				7	5			10²						1	13	4	8	6	11	12			23
	12							8						3	4					5				9					1	13	10²	7	6	11		2¹		24
1								9¹						5	2				12	3	7			11							4	8	13	10		6²		25
1								9¹						5	3				14	4	7		12								11	8²	2³	10	13	6		26
1	2					12		6³						4	5					11	8		14	10¹							13	7		9		3²		27
1	2							9²						5¹						4	7			11							12	8	3	10	13	6³	14	28
1		2		3		8¹		13			12			5						7	4			11							6²	9		10				29
1		2		3		7	12				9²			4						5	6		13	11								8¹		10				30
1		2		5		7		12			9²			3						4	6			11							13	8¹		10				31
1		2		3	·		12			6¹		8		4						5	7			11								9		10				32
1		2		5		13	9³	14		10		7		3						4²	8											6¹		11		12		33
1		2				9	13	7		10¹	12	8²		4	3					5	6													11				34
1		2¹								10		7		5	12	4				6	9		8											11		3		35
1		2		5		9	10¹	14		12	13			4	3						6		8²											11³		7		36
1		2		4		9	10			11		6³		3				12		14	7		8²									13				5¹		37
1		2		11		4²	13			6		8¹		9³	12			5		14	10											7				3		38
1		2		5		8³	10²			11					4			6		12	3	14	13									9				7¹		39
1		2		6		8	10			11				4	12			3			5		13									9²				7¹		40
1		2					10³			11				3	5			8¹			7²		9		4		13	14				6				12		41
1		2		10			11¹			5				7	8²			4					9³		3		13	14				6				12		42
1		2		4			12			11				3	7			6¹					10		5							9				8		43
1		2		4			10			11				7	8						5²		9		3¹		12	13				6						44
1		2		4			5³			11¹				3	10						8²	13	9		7		12			14		6						45
1		2		10¹			11²			4					7		6							9	3	8	13								5	12		46

FA Cup
Fourth Qualifying Barnet (a) 2-4

FA Trophy
First Round Salisbury (a) 1-2

BROMLEY

Ground: The Stadium, Hayes Lane, Bromley BR2 9EF. *Tel:* (02084) 605291. *Website:* bromleyfc.tv
Email: info@bromleyfc.co.uk *Year Formed:* 1892. *Record Attendance:* 10,798 v Nigeria, Friendly, 24 September 1949.
Nickname: 'The Ravens', 'The Lillywhites'. *Manager:* Neil Smith. *Colours:* White shirts with black trim, black shorts with white trim, white socks with black and gold trim.

BROMLEY – NATIONAL LEAGUE 2018–19 LEAGUE RECORD

Match No.	Date	Venue	Opponents	Result		H/T Score	Lg Pos.	Goalscorers	Attendance
1	Aug 4	A	AFC Fylde	L	1-2	0-1	17	Higgs [63]	1227
2	7	H	Dover Ath	D	2-2	1-1	15	Johnson, D [3], Sutherland (pen) [89]	1511
3	11	H	Harrogate T	D	1-1	1-0	15	Porter [12]	1061
4	14	A	Eastleigh	L	0-1	0-1	19		1478
5	18	H	Gateshead	W	1-0	0-0	16	Ogedi-Uzokwe [88]	1078
6	25	A	Wrexham	D	2-2	0-1	17	Sutherland (pen) [69], Summerfield (og) [90]	5714
7	27	H	Havant & W	W	4-0	2-0	14	Bugiel 2 [9, 33], Ogedi-Uzokwe 2 [58, 73]	1413
8	Sept 1	A	Maidenhead U	D	2-2	0-1	14	Porter [90], Sutherland (pen) [90]	1201
9	4	H	Barnet	L	0-1	0-1	16		1568
10	8	A	Aldershot T	L	2-3	2-1	16	Ogedi-Uzokwe [30], Fowler (og) [45]	1768
11	15	H	Salford C	L	0-2	0-1	18		2020
12	22	A	Solihull Moors	L	0-5	0-4	19		648
13	25	A	Ebbsfleet U	W	2-1	2-1	17	Ogedi-Uzokwe [15], Sutherland (pen) [31]	1204
14	29	H	FC Halifax T	D	2-2	1-0	17	Sutherland [14], Porter [81]	1148
15	Oct 6	A	Maidstone U	W	1-0	1-0	16	Ogedi-Uzokwe [11]	2294
16	13	H	Barrow	W	2-1	1-0	15	Bugiel [7], Raymond [75]	2211
17	27	A	Boreham Wood	L	1-2	1-1	15	Bugiel [27]	629
18	30	H	Braintree T	L	2-4	1-2	17	Quigley [18], Bugiel [58]	1008
19	Nov 3	H	Hartlepool U	W	4-0	1-0	14	Sutherland 2 (2 pens) [12, 78], Bugiel [63], Porter [85]	1516
20	17	A	Leyton Orient	L	1-3	1-0	16	Goddard [41]	6058
21	24	H	Dagenham & R	L	0-2	0-1	17		1162
22	27	A	Chesterfield	D	1-1	1-0	18	Porter [35]	3729
23	Dec 8	A	Gateshead	L	0-2	0-1	18		680
24	22	H	Maidenhead U	W	1-0	1-0	17	Holland [41]	1073
25	26	A	Sutton U	L	0-1	0-0	17		2086
26	29	A	Havant & W	W	3-0	1-0	17	Hooper [37], Holland [63], Coulson [86]	1341
27	Jan 1	H	Sutton U	W	2-1	1-1	16	Hooper [33], Goodman [89]	1428
28	5	H	AFC Fylde	W	3-2	2-1	13	Hooper 2 [25, 81], Sutherland (pen) [29]	1102
29	8	H	Wrexham	W	2-0	2-0	11	Okoye [21], Porter [44]	1061
30	19	A	Dover Ath	D	1-1	1-1	11	Mekki [39]	1216
31	26	H	Eastleigh	L	0-1	0-0	12		1381
32	Feb 9	A	Barrow	D	1-1	0-1	12	Hooper [54]	1130
33	16	H	Maidstone U	W	2-0	1-0	12	Hooper 2 [31, 90]	2589
34	23	A	Hartlepool U	W	2-1	2-0	11	Okoye [30], Coulson [45]	2985
35	Mar 2	H	Boreham Wood	L	0-2	0-1	11		1326
36	5	A	Harrogate T	L	0-1	0-0	11		789
37	9	A	Dagenham & R	L	0-3	0-2	14		1186
38	12	H	Chesterfield	D	3-3	0-1	12	Evans (og) [56], Hooper 2 [60, 87]	910
39	23	A	Braintree T	W	4-2	3-0	13	Porter [16], Coulson [21], Raymond [45], Hooper [66]	673
40	30	A	Salford C	L	1-2	0-0	15	Hooper (pen) [85]	2314
41	Apr 2	H	Leyton Orient	W	2-1	0-1	12	Sutherland (pen) [49], Hackett-Fairchild [63]	3047
42	6	H	Aldershot T	D	2-2	1-1	13	Hooper 2 [4, 63]	1521
43	13	A	FC Halifax T	D	2-2	0-1	13	Coulson [55], Brindley [84]	1303
44	19	H	Solihull Moors	L	0-2	0-1	13		1536
45	22	A	Barnet	D	1-1	0-0	13	Higgs [49]	1744
46	27	H	Ebbsfleet U	W	5-1	1-0	12	Porter [21], Sutherland (pen) [51], Brindley [56], Hooper [64], Coulson [90]	1352

Final League Position: 12; upgraded to 11 after Gateshead deducted 9pts after the end of the season.

GOALSCORERS

League (68): Hooper 14 (1 pen), Sutherland 10 (9 pens), Porter 8, Bugiel 6, Ogedi-Uzokwe 6, Coulson 5, Brindley 2, Higgs 2, Holland 2, Okoye 2, Raymond 2, Goddard 1, Goodman 1, Hackett-Fairchild 1, Johnson D 1, Mekki 1, Quigley 1, own goals 3.
FA Cup (2): Johnson R 1, Raymond 1.
FA Trophy (2): Hooper 1, Porter 1.

Gregory 45	Adebayo-Rowling 8 + 2	Johnson D 3 + 3	Sutherland 38 + 3	Johnson R 27 + 6	Holland 36	Raymond 40 + 2	Bugiel 20 + 12	Higgs 15 + 11	Okoye 27 + 10	Porter 42 + 2	Taylor 2 + 10	Ogedi-Uzokwe 17 + 8	Myles-Meekums 3 + 7	Goodman 14 + 8	Goddard 10 + 4	Wood 41	Mekki 11 + 7	De Silva — + 4	Luque 2 + 2	Brindley 32 + 1	Huxter 1	Rooney 5	Quigley 4 + 2	Dunne 2 + 3	Barham 3 + 1	Coulson 24	Hines 1 + 6	Hooper 22	Sarpeng-Wiredu 6 + 5	Lewis — + 4	Philpot — + 3	Hackett-Fairchild 5	Ojemen — + 1	*Match No.*
1	2^1	3	4	5	6	7	8^2	9^3	10	11	12	13	14																					1
1	4	3	5	2	6	8	11	9^3	14	10^2	7^1	13	12																					2
1	5	3	6	2^1	4	7	9		12	8	13	10	11^2																					3
1	4		6	2	5	7	10		3	8	13	11^1	9^2	12																				4
1	2^3	14	7	4		6	10^2	8	3	11		12	13	5	9^1																			5
1	2^1		7	4		8	10^3		3	11	13	12	14	5	9^2	6																		6
1	14	12		3^2		7	10	6	2^3	11	13	9		4	8^1	5																		7
1			12	3		7	10^3	6^2	2	11	13	9	14	4	8^1	5																		8
1	9^1		6^2	3		7		12	2	11	13	10		4	8^3	5	14																	9
1	12			3^2		7		6	2	9	14	11	10^1	4	8^3	5	13																	10
1	2^3		12		3	4	5^1	7		9^2		10		8	13	11	6■	14																11
1		13	6	2	9	7^3	11^1	5^2		8		10		3	12	4			14															12
1			7	12	4	6	9^2	13		8		11	14	2^1		5			10^3	3														13
			6		4		11^3	7	2	8	13	10	12			5^1		14	9^2		1	3												14
1			4	14	5	6		12	2^1	8	10^2	11				9	7^3			13		3												15
1			6		4	7	11^3	14		8^1	13	10			12	5	9^2			2		3												16
1			6		4	7^3	11		14	9^1		10			8^2	5	13			3		2	12											17
1			6		4	7	13		12	8		10^3			9^1	5	14			2		3^2	11											18
1			6	3	4	7	10^2			8		12		13		5	9^1	14		2			11^3											19
1				3	7				5	9		10		13	8	6			12	4			11^2	2^1										20
1			7	2^1	6			14	4	12		9			8^3	5	13			3			11^2		10									21
1			9	4^3	6			8^1	5	10		12		3^2	13	7				2				14	11									22
1			7	4	3	12			6^2	13						5	14			2					10^3	8^1	9	11						23
1			8	13	5	7			14	10^1				2		6	9^3			4					12	3^2		11						24
1			6	4^1	2	7			3	10		11^3				8	13			5			14			9^2	12							25
1			8		5	9			2^1	10^3		13		14		6	7^2			4						3	12	11						26
1			7		3	8			4	10		13		14		5	6^3			2^2						9^1	12	11						27
1			8		5	9	13		2^2	10				14		6	7^1			4						3^3	12	11						28
1			8		5	9	12		4	10						6	7^1			2						3^2	13	11						29
1			7		5	8	12		3	10^3				13		6	9^1	14		2						4^2		11						30
1			7	13	5	8	12			10				3		6	9^1			2^2						4		11						31
1			6		3	7	13		4	10^1						5				2						9^3		11	8^2	12	14			32
1			6		3^2	7	11^1	13	4	9				12		5				2						8^3		10			14			33
1			6	14		7	11^3	12	4	9^2				3		5				2						8		10^1			13			34
1				13		8	11^2	7^3	4	9				3^1		6				2						5		10	12	14				35
1				2		7	10	13	3	8^1						9				4						5^2		11	6	12				36
1			0^2	2		7	10	13	5^1							9				3				12		4		11	8					37
1			8^1	3	6^2	9	13	14								7				2				4		5		11	12			10^3		38
1			12	2	5	7	13			8^1						9				3						4		11^2	6^3	14		10		39
1			8^1	3	4	7	14		12	10^3						5				2						9		11	13			6^2		40
1			8	3	5	7	12		13	9^2						6				2						4		11				10^1		41
1			2^2		3	4	12	14	5	6^1						8				9						10		11	13			7^3		42
1			7^2	3	4	12	13	6	14	9^1						5				2						10		11	8^3					43
1			7	3	4	6		8^2		11						5				2				12		10			9^1				13	44
1			9	3^1	5	8		7	12	10						6				2						4		11						45
1			8	3^1	5	7^2		9	13	10						6				2						4	14	11^3	12					46

FA Cup

Fourth Qualifying	Gloucester C	(a)	1-0
First Round	Peterborough U	(h)	1-3

FA Trophy

First Round	Sutton U	(h)	2-1

(Tie awarded to Sutton U – Bromley removed)

CHESTERFIELD

Ground: The Proact Stadium, 1866 Sheffield Road, Whittington Moor, Chesterfield, Derbyshire S41 8NZ.
Tel: (01246) 269 300. *Website:* www.chesterfield-fc.co.uk *Email:* reception@chesterfield-fc.co.uk
Year Formed: 1866. *Record Attendance:* 30,968 v Newcastle U, Division 2, 7 April 1939 (at Saltergate); 10,089 v Rotherham U, FL 2, 18 March 2011 (at b2net Stadium (now called the Proact Stadium)). *Nickname:* 'The Blues', 'The Spireites'. *Manager:* John Sheridan. *Colours:* Blue shirts with white trim, white shorts with blue trim, blue socks.

CHESTERFIELD – NATIONAL LEAGUE 2018–19 LEAGUE RECORD

Match No.	Date	Venue	Opponents	Result		H/T Score	Lg Pos.	Goalscorers	Attendance
1	Aug 4	A	Ebbsfleet U	W	1-0	0-0	6	Hines (pen) 65	2041
2	7	H	Aldershot T	W	3-0	2-0	1	Carter 2 9, 39, Fortune (pen) 81	4930
3	11	H	Braintree T	W	1-0	0-0	2	Weston 59	4927
4	14	A	Barrow	L	2-3	1-1	5	Hines 14, Evans 50	1701
5	18	A	Salford C	L	2-3	1-1	8	Hines 43, Fortune 59	3595
6	25	H	Barnet	L	0-1	0-0	11		4685
7	27	A	Hartlepool U	L	0-1	0-1	15		3773
8	Sept 1	H	Leyton Orient	L	0-1	0-0	16		4735
9	4	A	Boreham Wood	L	0-1	0-1	17		737
10	8	H	Dover Ath	D	0-0	0-0	17		4303
11	15	A	Dagenham & R	D	1-1	1-0	16	Weston 13	1273
12	22	H	Gateshead	L	0-3	0-2	18		4210
13	25	H	Maidenhead U	L	1-3	0-2	20	Fortune (pen) 67	3681
14	29	A	Maidstone U	D	1-1	0-1	20	Fortune 74	2438
15	Oct 6	H	AFC Fylde	D	0-0	0-0	20		4021
16	13	A	FC Halifax T	D	1-1	0-0	19	Denton 79	2191
17	27	H	Wrexham	D	1-1	0-1	19	Smith, J 90	5662
18	30	A	Sutton U	D	1-1	0-1	19	Smith, J 89	1852
19	Nov 3	A	Harrogate T	D	1-1	0-0	19	Smith, J 57	2291
20	17	H	Havant & W	D	0-0	0-0	19		4082
21	24	A	Eastleigh	D	1-1	1-1	21	Hallam 41	1774
22	27	H	Bromley	D	1-1	0-1	21	Hines (pen) 90	3729
23	Dec 8	H	Salford C	W	2-0	1-0	20	Kiwomya 2 2, 59	5055
24	22	A	Leyton Orient	L	1-3	1-1	20	Kiwomya 35	4755
25	26	H	Solihull Moors	L	0-4	0-2	22		4877
26	29	H	Hartlepool U	D	1-1	0-1	21	Barry 75	4752
27	Jan 1	A	Solihull Moors	D	2-2	0-1	21	Fortune 47, Shaw 68	1375
28	5	H	Ebbsfleet U	D	3-3	0-3	22	Denton 64, Fortune 83, Evans 90	4123
29	19	A	Aldershot T	W	2-0	1-0	21	Evans 2 44, 78	2120
30	26	H	Barrow	D	0-0	0-0	21		4626
31	Feb 9	H	FC Halifax T	W	1-0	0-0	20	Boden (pen) 68	4523
32	16	A	AFC Fylde	W	1-0	1-0	17	Fortune 13	2175
33	23	H	Harrogate T	L	0-1	0-1	19		4661
34	26	A	Barnet	W	2-0	1-0	17	Carter 15, Kiwomya 81	902
35	Mar 2	A	Wrexham	L	0-1	0-0	19		7106
36	5	A	Braintree T	W	3-1	2-0	16	Boden 2 14, 83, Carter 21	482
37	9	H	Eastleigh	L	2-3	1-1	18	Hollis 32, Boden 47	4319
38	12	A	Bromley	D	3-3	1-0	18	Binnom-Williams 44, Boden 82, Rowley 90	910
39	16	A	Havant & W	W	2-1	0-1	16	Evans 52, Boden (pen) 90	1097
40	23	H	Sutton U	W	3-0	1-0	15	Denton 2 28, 55, Boden 48	4311
41	30	H	Dagenham & R	W	2-0	0-0	12	Smith, J 47, Boden 50	4377
42	Apr 6	A	Dover Ath	D	0-0	0-0	14		1348
43	13	H	Maidstone U	W	4-1	1-1	12	Barry 18, Boden 68, Chapman 84, Maguire 90	4592
44	19	A	Gateshead	L	0-1	0-1	12		1208
45	22	H	Boreham Wood	W	3-2	1-1	12	Denton 2 43, 85, Boden (pen) 49	4384
46	27	A	Maidenhead U	L	0-2	0-0	15		1555

Final League Position: 15; upgraded to 14 after Gateshead deducted 9pts after the end of the season.

GOALSCORERS

League (55): Boden 10 (3 pens), Fortune 7 (2 pens), Denton 6, Evans 5, Carter 4, Hines 4 (2 pens), Kiwomya 4, Smith J 4, Barry 2, Weston 2, Binnom-Williams 1, Chapman 1, Hallam 1, Hollis 1, Maguire 1, Rowley 1, Shaw 1.
FA Cup (7): Denton 5 (1 pen), Evans 1, Maguire 1.
FA Trophy (6): Denton 3, Kiwomya 1, Shaw 1, Smith J 1.

Jalal 25	Evans 38 + 1	Smith G 1 + 1	Nelson M 13	Barry 16 + 6	Talbot 13	Weir 24 + 8	Weston 42 + 1	Carter 15 + 5	Hines 13 + 4	Ugwu 6 + 1	Fortune 19 + 9	Maguire 22 + 4	Muggleton 9 + 9	Binnom-Williams 25 + 7	Wedgbury 1 + 2	Shaw 25 + 12	Reid 10 + 15	Burton 19	Rowley 20 + 5	Hollis 35	Amantchi 4 + 7	Denton 20 + 13	Smith J 31 + 1	Kayode — + 3	Kiwomya 8 + 6	Hallam 2 + 1	Beestin 2 + 3	Ofoegbu — + 2	Sharman 2 + 1	Rawson — + 2	Yarney 15	Chapman 13 + 1	Boden 14 + 1	McKay 2 + 2	Anyon 2	Match No.
1	2	3^3	4	5	6	7^1	8	9	10	11^2	12	13	14																							1
1	3		5		7	8	6	9	10^3	11^1	12	4		2^2	13	14																				2
1	4		3	12	7	6^2	8	5	11^3	9^1	10		14	2	13																					3
1	4	12	2		7	8	5	9	11^1		10^2	13		3■	6^3	14																				4
1	2		4^2	13	5	8^3	6	9^1	11		10	3	12			14	7																			5
	8		5	11^3	7	4^1	9		2	12	10	3^2	14				6	1	13																	6
	5^2		4		7	8^3	9		11	10	13		2^1			14	12	1	6	3																7
	4		5		8	6	9		11	10^3	12	3^2	14	2			13	1	7^1																	8
			3	12	10	6^1	8		11		2^3	7		5^2		4	13	1		9	14															9
1	14		3	6	10		8		12	11^1		7^2		5		4	13		2^3	9																10
1	10			13	6	8	4^3		11^1			12	14	3		2^2	9			5		7														11
1			10		6^2	13	4	11	14■					3		2^3	9^1			5		7	8	12												12
1			2		6	8^2	5	9			11^3	4	13	3		14						10	7^1	12												13
	5						7	8^1			13	4	3	2		11^2		1	9			10	6	12												14
	3						6				9^1	2	4	5^2		10	13	1	7		12	11	8													15
	4						6		12		14	2	3	13		10^2	8^3	1	5			11	7		9^1											16
	8^3						10		7			3	9^2	5		12		1	11	6	13	2^1	4		14											17
							3^1		13			10	4	7^3		9	14	1	6	8	12	11^2	2		5											18
	6						4		2^2			10	3	12		7^1	14	1	9	8		13	5		11^3											19
	3						6^2				11^1	4	14	2		10	9^3	1	7	5	13	12	8													20
				6			10					3	13	8		4^1		1	7	5	12	11	9			2^2										21
				5			7^1		9			3	4^3			12	14	1	6	2	13	11^2	8			10										22
	5			2		13	6							4		9		1		3	10^2	11^1	7		8	12										23
	3						7						5^1	2		11		1	13	4	9	10^3	6		8^2		12	14								24
	2		4^1			14	7^3							3		10	8	1	6	5	11^2		9				12	13								25
	4			2			8							3		6	9^3	1	10^2	5	11^1		7				13		12	14						26
	4			2		12	5				11^1			3		6		1		8			9		13		7^2		10^3	14						27
	3			5^2		13	8				11			6		10	14	1■		4		12	7				9^1		2^3							28
1	4			2^1		7	6				10^3			3		11	12		14	5		13	8		9^2											29
1	5			2^2		7	6				10^3			3		11	14		13	4		12	8		9^1											30
1	2					6	5				10^2					9				3		12	7								4	8	11^1	13		31
1	2			12		5	3				8^3					4^2				6		14	7								9	11	10^1	13		32
1						5	3^2	13			8^1	2		14		4^3				6		12	7								9	11	10			33
1	2					5	6	8^1						12			14			4		11^3	7		13						3	9	10^2			34
1	3					8^2	7				10^1			2		13	14			4		12	9								5	6^3	11			35
1	3					7^3	9^2	11^1				14		12		13				4		6	5								2	10	8			36
1	2					8^2	7	5^3			14			13		12				4		10	9								3	6	11^1			37
1	3						6				10^1			2		9^2	14		7	4		12	8^3		13						5		11			38
1	2			6		7^3	9	14			13			12					8^2	4		11^1									3	5	10			39
1	2					12	13	4^2			14	3^1							5	6		8^3	7								9	11	10			40
1	2						6	13				3				12	14		7^3	4		10	9								5	8^1	11^2			41
	3			12		7		8^2			10	5				9^3	6			2		13			14						4			11^1	1	42
	3			2		14	7^1	13				4							8^2	5		10	12								6^3	9	11		1	43
1	3			2		6		5^2			10^3	4^1					9			7		12	8		13							14	11			44
1	3			2		14	4^2	13								12			5	6		8	7^3								9	11	10^1			45
1	2			6		7		8^2								10^1			13	4		12			11						3	5	14	9^3		46

FA Cup

Fourth Qualifying	AFC Fylde	(a)	3-1
First Round	Billericay T	(h)	1-1
Replay	Billericay T	(a)	3-1
Second Round	Grimsby T	(h)	0-2

FA Trophy

First Round	Basford U	(h)	5-1
Second Round	Bedford T	(h)	1-0
Third Round	Brackley T	(h)	0-3

DAGENHAM & REDBRIDGE

Ground: Chigwell Construction Stadium, Victoria Road, Dagenham, Essex RM10 7XL.
Tel: (020) 8592 1549. *Website:* www.daggers.co.uk *Email:* info@daggers.co.uk *Year Formed:* 1992.
Record Attendance: 5,949 v Ipswich T, FA Cup 3rd rd, 5 January 2002. *Nickname:* 'The Daggers'.
Manager: Peter Taylor. *Colours:* Red and blue halved shirts, blue shorts, red socks.

DAGENHAM & REDBRIDGE – NATIONAL LEAGUE 2018–19 LEAGUE RECORD

Match No.	Date	Venue	Opponents	Result		H/T Score	Lg Pos.	Goalscorers	Attendance
1	Aug 4	A	Boreham Wood	L	0-1	0-0	19		833
2	7	H	Maidstone U	L	1-2	0-1	22	Romain 80	1405
3	11	H	Maidenhead U	D	2-2	0-1	19	McQueen 67, Romain 87	1069
4	14	A	Aldershot T	L	1-2	0-1	23	Kandi 73	1917
5	18	A	FC Halifax T	L	1-2	1-1	23	Adeloye 33	1364
6	25	H	Hartlepool U	L	1-2	1-0	24	McQueen 36	1212
7	27	A	Barnet	L	1-2	1-1	24	Romain 1	1522
8	Sept 1	H	Salford C	D	0-0	0-0	24		1114
9	4	H	Braintree T	W	1-0	0-0	22	Kandi (pen) 84	1081
10	8	A	Barrow	W	1-0	0-0	21	Romain 90	1171
11	15	H	Chesterfield	D	1-1	0-1	20	Kandi 79	1273
12	22	A	Eastleigh	L	0-1	0-0	22		1538
13	25	A	Solihull Moors	L	0-2	0-1	22		753
14	29	H	Ebbsfleet U	L	1-3	1-2	22	Mullings 42	1225
15	Oct 6	A	Gateshead	L	0-2	0-2	22		687
16	13	H	Wrexham	L	1-2	1-1	22	Walker (og) 45	1601
17	27	H	Harrogate T	W	2-1	2-0	21	McQueen 2 39, 42	1446
18	30	A	Dover Ath	W	2-0	2-0	20	Adeloye 11, Phipps 44	924
19	Nov 3	A	Sutton U	L	0-1	0-0	22		1909
20	17	H	AFC Fylde	W	2-1	1-1	21	Wilkinson 28, Munns 64	1328
21	24	A	Bromley	W	2-0	1-0	19	Wilkinson 17, Balanta 84	1162
22	27	H	Havant & W	W	3-1	1-0	17	Wilkinson 2 8, 50, Balanta 75	1054
23	Dec 1	A	Hartlepool U	W	2-1	0-1	15	Goodliffe 90, Robinson 90	2030
24	8	H	FC Halifax T	D	1-1	0-0	14	Munns 60	1098
25	22	A	Salford C	W	2-1	1-1	15	Wilkinson 39, Balanta 67	2082
26	26	H	Leyton Orient	W	2-1	0-0	13	McQueen 77, Nunn 87	3694
27	29	H	Barnet	L	0-1	0-1	14		1775
28	Jan 1	A	Leyton Orient	L	0-1	0-1	15		6001
29	5	H	Boreham Wood	D	4-4	3-3	16	Wilkinson 41, Gordon 2 43, 74, Balanta 45	1043
30	19	A	Maidstone U	W	3-0	1-0	13	Smith 22, Wilkinson 73, Reynolds 90	2188
31	26	H	Aldershot T	D	1-1	0-0	13	Wilkinson 49	1652
32	Feb 9	A	Wrexham	L	0-1	0-0	14		5366
33	16	H	Gateshead	L	0-2	0-1	14		1209
34	23	H	Sutton U	W	1-0	0-0	14	Wilkinson 71	1322
35	Mar 2	A	Harrogate T	D	1-1	0-0	14	Wilkinson 90	1262
36	5	A	Maidenhead U	D	1-1	0-0	15	Kandi 85	1156
37	9	H	Bromley	W	3-0	2-0	13	Balanta 3, Wilkinson 14, Kandi 72	1186
38	12	A	Havant & W	L	0-3	0-1	15		713
39	26	H	Dover Ath	L	1-3	0-2	17	Wright 69	1084
40	30	A	Chesterfield	L	0-2	0-0	19		4377
41	Apr 2	A	AFC Fylde	D	1-1	1-1	18	Balanta 18	1275
42	6	H	Barrow	D	0-0	0-0	18		2173
43	13	A	Ebbsfleet U	W	1-0	1-0	17	Adeloye 24	1551
44	19	H	Eastleigh	W	2-0	1-0	16	Harfield 44, Kandi 52	1315
45	22	A	Braintree T	L	0-2	0-0	18		909
46	27	H	Solihull Moors	D	1-1	0-0	18	Wilkinson 46	1370

Final League Position: 18

GOALSCORERS

League (50): Wilkinson 12, Balanta 6, Kandi 6 (1 pen), McQueen 5, Romain 4, Adeloye 3, Gordon 2, Munns 2, Goodliffe 1, Harfield 1, Mullings 1, Nunn 1, Phipps 1, Reynolds 1, Robinson 1, Smith 1, Wright 1, own goal 1.
FA Cup (2): Adeloye 1, Pennell 1.
FA Trophy (1): Balanta 1.

Justham 45	Gordon 31 + 3	Robinson 38 + 1	Donovan 10 + 3	Kandi 14 + 25	Romain 15 + 1	Goodliffe 32 + 1	Phipps 15 + 7	Wright 29 + 5	Hoyte 11 + 4	Harfield 15 + 14	Reynolds 8 + 15	Blanchfield 1 + 4	Davey 10	Adeloye 15 + 12	McQueen 30 + 5	Pennell 18	Leighton 3 + 2	Hyde — + 1	Mullings 3 + 4	Bellamy 1 + 3	Nunn 21	Munns 22 + 4	Onariase 29	Smith 12	Balanta 23	Wilkinson 22 + 1	Clark 20 + 1	Loft 12	Moore 1	Bonds — + 1	Match No.
1	2	3	4	5	6	7■	8^1	9	10	11^2	12	13																			1
1	5	8	7^1	10	11		6^2	4	2	13	9	12	3																		2
1	5	6	7^2	10^3	11			4	2	8	9^1	14	3	12	13																3
1	4	7	8^2	13	9		10^1	2		14	12		5	11	3	6^3															4
1	2	3		7^3	12	8		10	13		11^1		4	9	6	5^2	14														5
1	2^2	3	7^1	12	8	9		11			13		4	10^3	6	5		14													6
1	6	8		12	9	3		5	2	14	10^2		4	13	7^3		11^1														7
1	5	9			10	2		6	12	8	13		4^3	14	7	3^1	11^2														8
1	5	8		13	11	4		7	12	9	6^3			10^1	2^2	3	14														9
1	5	8	7^3	12	11	4^2	14	6	2	9	13			10^1		3															10
1	5	8		7	11	4	14	6	7	9^2	12			10^1	13	3^3															11
1	5	7	8^2	9	11	4	13	6	2^1		12			10^3	14	3															12
1	5	7	8^2	10^1	9	4	13	6	2	12						3	11														13
1	6^2	7	8	12	11	4■		9					5		2	3			10^1	13											14
1		6	7^1	9^3	11			8			12		4		5^2	3			10	14	2	13									15
1	6	9		14	10			4		5^1	13				7^3	3			11	8	2^2	12									16
1		7	13			4	8^2				12			10	5						2	9^1	3	6	11						17
1		6	13			4	7				12			10^1	8	5			14		2	9^3	3		11^2						18
1		7	14			4^1	8				13			10^2	6	5			12		2	9^3	3		11						19
1	13	6		12		4	7							14	8	5					2	9^3	3		10^2	11^1					20
1	13	6		12		4	7							14	8	5					2	9^1	3		10^3	11^2					21
1		7		13		4	8			14					6	5					2^3	9^1	3		10	11^2	12				22
1		6		13		4	7^1			12				14	8	5					2^2	9^3	3		10	11					23
1		7		14		4	8^2			12				13	6						2■	9^1	3		10^3	11	5				24
1	7			13		4	8	12	3						2							9^1	5		10^2	11	6				25
1	6					3	8			12					7						2	9^1	4		10	11	5				26
1	6					3	7^2	8		9^3	12	13							14		2^1		4		10	11	5				27
1	6					3		7	2		12				8				13			9^1	4^2		10	11	5				28
1	6			13		3		7	12	14					8						2^3	9^1	4		10	11^2	5				29
1	7	8		14				13			12				3						2	9^2	5	4	10^3	11^1	6				30
1	13	7		12							10^1				9						2	8^2	4	5		11	3	6			31
1	6	9		12		5^3		7		14	10				13						2		4			11^1	3	8^2			32
1	2	9		12		5^2				13	10				6							8^1	4			11	3	7			33
1	2	9		13		5		12						10^2	6							8	4			11	3	7^1			34
1	2	9		12		5		14		13				10^2	6							8^1	4			11	3	7^3			35
1	2	3		12		13		8		9				7^2	4								10	11		6	5^1				36
1	2			12		3	14	7						13	6							8	4	5	10^1	11^3		9^2			37
1	2^2	3^1		5		7	13	8		9				12	4■							14	10	11	6^3						38
1	2	9		13				12		14											6	8	4	5^1	10	11^2	3	7^3			39
1	2	9		11		3		7		14				13							6^2	12	4		10^3		5	8^1			40
1		9		11			13	7		6				12							2	8^1	4	5	10^2		3				41
1		13		12				7		6											2^2	8^1	4	5	10	11	3	9			42
1		8		9^1				5		6				11^2	13								4	2	10	12	3	7			43
1		7		9				5		8				12									4	2	10^1	11	3	6			44
	5			14		4	7^3		3			8^2	6	11	10					12	2^1	9							1	13	45
1		7		9				5		8													3	2	10	11	4	6			46

FA Cup
Fourth Qualifying Boreham Wood (a) 2-2
Replay Boreham Wood (h) 0-1

FA Trophy
First Round Ebbsfleet U (a) 1-0
Second Round Salford C (a) 0-2

DOVER ATHLETIC

Ground: Crabbie Athletic Ground, Lewisham Road, River, Dover, Kent CT17 0JB. *Tel:* (01304) 822373. *Website:* doverathletic.com *Email:* enquiries@doverathletic.com *Year Formed:* 1894 as Dover FC, reformed as Dover Ath 1983. *Record Attendance:* 7,000 v Folkestone, 13 October 1951 (Dover FC); 5,645 v Crystal Palace, FA Cup 3rd rd, 4 January 2015 (Dover Ath). *Nickname:* 'The Whites'. *Manager:* Andy Hessenthaler. *Colours:* White shirts, black shorts, black socks.

DOVER ATHLETIC – NATIONAL LEAGUE 2018–19 LEAGUE RECORD

Match No.	Date	Venue	Opponents	Result	H/T Score	Lg Pos.	Goalscorers	Attendance
1	Aug 4	H	Wrexham	L 0-1	0-1	19		1359
2	7	A	Bromley	D 2-2	1-1	16	Allen [35], Lokko [72]	1511
3	11	A	Gateshead	L 1-2	1-1	19	Allen [25]	693
4	14	H	Havant & W	W 4-3	1-0	13	Nortey [36], Allen (pen) [67], Brundle [78], Lokko [86]	997
5	18	A	AFC Fylde	L 0-4	0-1	19		1258
6	25	H	Eastleigh	L 1-2	0-2	21	Brundle [65]	844
7	27	A	Leyton Orient	L 0-3	0-0	22		4641
8	Sept 1	H	Barnet	L 1-2	0-2	22	Brundle [65]	1037
9	4	H	Ebbsfleet U	D 1-1	1-1	23	Essam [34]	1127
10	8	A	Chesterfield	D 0-0	0-0	23		4303
11	15	H	Solihull Moors	L 0-2	0-0	24		823
12	22	A	Aldershot T	L 0-2	0-1	24		1619
13	25	A	Sutton U	D 2-2	1-2	23	Brundle (pen) [36], Schmoll [87]	1694
14	29	H	Barrow	L 0-2	0-0	23		814
15	Oct 6	H	Salford C	L 1-4	0-2	23	Gomis [50]	1127
16	13	A	Harrogate T	D 2-2	0-1	23	Effiong 2 [46, 66]	1865
17	27	A	Braintree T	L 1-2	0-1	24	Lokko [68]	575
18	30	H	Dagenham & R	L 0-2	0-2	24		924
19	Nov 3	H	Maidenhead U	W 2-0	1-0	24	Lokko [37], Reason [74]	872
20	17	A	FC Halifax T	L 0-1	0-1	24		1356
21	24	H	Hartlepool U	W 2-1	2-0	23	Gomis [20], Effiong [38]	1027
22	27	A	Boreham Wood	W 1-0	0-0	23	Effiong [56]	407
23	Dec 1	A	Eastleigh	D 2-2	1-1	23	Effiong [21], Reason [56]	1430
24	8	H	AFC Fylde	W 2-1	0-1	21	Effiong 2 [83, 90]	927
25	22	A	Barnet	L 0-2	0-0	21		1011
26	26	H	Maidstone U	W 3-1	0-1	20	Brundle [58], Gomis [75], Effiong [80]	1937
27	29	H	Leyton Orient	D 0-0	0-0	20		2270
28	Jan 1	A	Maidstone U	W 1-0	0-0	18	Allen [86]	3087
29	5	A	Wrexham	W 1-0	0-0	18	Jeffrey [87]	4817
30	19	H	Bromley	D 1-1	1-1	19	Lokko [29]	1216
31	26	A	Havant & W	D 0-0	0-0	19		1024
32	Feb 2	H	Gateshead	L 1-2	1-0	19	Lokko [8]	1037
33	9	H	Harrogate T	L 2-3	0-1	21	Allen [79], Reason [81]	997
34	16	A	Salford C	W 3-1	1-1	20	McNamara [25], Doe [59], Reason [81]	2498
35	23	A	Maidenhead U	L 0-1	0-1	20		1244
36	Mar 2	H	Braintree T	W 3-0	1-0	20	Pavey [18], Reason [57], Brundle [72]	1053
37	9	A	Hartlepool U	L 2-3	2-0	20	Pavey [28], Reason [39]	3431
38	12	H	Boreham Wood	D 1-1	1-1	20	Brundle [11]	743
39	16	H	FC Halifax T	W 2-1	1-0	19	Pavey [25], Jeffrey [61]	897
40	26	A	Dagenham & R	W 3-1	2-0	19	Allen [21], Gomis [28], Pavey [50]	1084
41	30	A	Solihull Moors	D 2-2	2-1	20	Pavey [4], Doe [44]	1338
42	Apr 6	H	Chesterfield	D 0-0	0-0	20		1348
43	13	A	Barrow	W 3-2	0-1	19	Brundle [73], Jeffrey [81], Modeste [90]	1351
44	19	H	Aldershot T	W 1-0	0-0	17	Lewis [88]	1348
45	22	A	Ebbsfleet U	W 1-0	0-0	15	Pavey [51]	1723
46	27	H	Sutton U	W 3-0	1-0	14	Lewis [15], Effiong [76], Passley (pen) [90]	1103

Final League Position: 14; upgraded to 13 after Gateshead deducted 9pts after the end of the season.

GOALSCORERS

League (58): Effiong 9, Brundle 8 (1 pen), Allen 6 (1 pen), Lokko 6, Pavey 6, Reason 6, Gomis 4, Jeffrey 3, Doe 2, Lewis 2, Essam 1, McNamara 1, Modeste 1, Nortey 1, Passley 1 (1 pen), Schmoll 1.
FA Cup (1): Effiong 1.
FA Trophy (4): Pavey 2, Effiong 1, Jeffrey 1.

Walker 36	Nortey 19 + 16	Lokko 39	Essam 18	Schmoll 14	Passley 30 + 1	Brundle 45	Gomis 28	Connors 9 + 1	Effiong 31 + 14	Allen 36 + 5	Daniel 4 + 13	Diarra 7 + 9	Okosieme 4 + 3	Jeffrey 14 + 19	Tajbakhsh 7	Smith G 7	Massanka 1 + 2	Sho-Silva 6 + 2	Smith D 1 + 2	Barry 2 + 1	Fazakerley — + 1	Debayo 15 + 1	Lewis 31	Taylor 24 + 3	Reason 24 + 3	Adebowale 2	Huckle — + 1	Pavey 13 + 11	Modeste 5 + 7	Doe 16 + 3	McNamara 8	Worgan 10	Bedford — + 1	Match No.
1	2	3	4	5	6	7	8^{1}	9	10^{2}	11	12	13																						1
1	6^{2}	3	4	7	2	5	9	8	11^{1}	10	12		13																					2
1	6^{1}	3	4	7	2	5	9	8	11^{3}	10^{2}	12		13	14																				3
1	7	2	3	4	5	6	8^{1}	9	10^{2}	11	13			12																				4
1	6	3	4	7	2	5	9^{2}	8^{3}	11^{1}	10	12	14		13																				5
1	9^{1}	4	5^{3}	10	2	6		3	8^{2}	7	13	14		12	11																			6
1	12	3	4	8	2	7		5	13	11	9			6^{2}	10^{1}																			7
1	9^{1}	2^{3}	3	4	5	6			14	10		12		13	7	8	11^{2}																	8
1	9		3	2	5	6		14	12	10^{2}	13	4			7^{1}	8		11^{3}																9
1	13		3	2	5^{2}	7		6	14	11	12	4		9^{1}	8■			10^{3}																10
1	8		3	2		7			12		11	4	5	9^{1}		6		10^{2}	13															11
1	12		4^{1}	8	2	5				7^{2}	13	3			11	9		6	14	10^{3}														12
1			4	7	2	5			10		13	3	6		9■	8^{1}		12	11^{2}															13
1			4	9	2^{2}	5	11		7^{3}	13	12	3	8			10^{1}		6		14														14
1	2		3			4	10	9	13	14	8^{1}		5			7		11^{3}		6^{2}	12													15
1	12	3	5		2	4	8^{1}		10^{2}	11			13	7■			14					6^{3}	9											16
1	7^{1}	3	4		2	5	8^{3}		6			14					12					10^{2}	9	11	13									17
1		3	4		2	6			10	11	8^{2}	13										5	7	9^{1}	12									18
1	14	3			2	7			11	10^{2}		4										5^{3}	8	9	12	6^{1}	13							19
1	12	3			2	4	6^{1}		11	10		13										5	7	8	9^{2}									20
1	13	5			2	4	6^{3}		11^{2}	9				12				14				3	7	8	10^{1}									21
1	14	4			2	3	7^{2}		10	11^{3}				12								5	6	8^{1}	9			13						22
1		3			2	4	6		11	10				5									7	8	9^{1}			12						23
1	13	4			2	3	6		11	10^{1}				9■									7	5	8^{2}			12						24
1	14	3			2	4	6^{3}		10	9^{2}				8^{1}									7	5				12	11	13				25
1		4			2	3	6		10^{2}	14				11^{3}									7	5	9			13	8^{1}	12				26
1	8^{1}	4				3	6		10					12								2	7		9			11		5				27
1	4^{1}	2				3	9		10	12				14								6^{3}	8		7			11^{2}	13	5				28
1	4	2				3			10	9^{2}				12								7	6		8			11^{1}	13	5				29
1	6	4				2	7■		11^{1}	10^{3}		12		14								5	8	13	9^{2}					3				30
1	11^{3}	4				6			9	10^{1}												5	7	12	8^{2}			13	14	3	2			31
1	7^{1}	4				6			10	11^{2}				14								5	8	12	9			13		3	2^{3}			32
1		2				3			11	10												6^{1}	7	8	9			12	13	5	4^{2}			33
1	14	5					3		9^{1}	10^{3}				12									4	7	8			13	11^{2}	6	2			34
1		2				3	8		5	4		14		12									10	11^{1}				13	7^{2}	9	6^{3}			35
	14	4				2	6		12	10^{2}				13									7	5	9			11^{1}	8^{3}	3		1		36
		2			13	3	5		12	10				9^{1}									6	7	8			11^{2}			4	1		37
	14	4				3	6		12	10^{2}				8^{3}								10	7	5	9^{1}			11			2	1		38
	14	4				3	5		12	8^{2}				10^{1}									6	7	11			9^{3}		13	2	1		39
	14	4			5	2	8^{1}		13	9				12									7	6	11^{2}			10^{3}		3		1		40
		3			2	4	7		14	5^{3}				12									9	10	11^{2}			6^{1}	13	8		1		41
	14	4			2	5	8		11					13									7^{3}	6	9^{2}			10^{1}	12	3		1		42
	7	3			2^{1}	4			5	13				12									9	10	11^{3}			6^{2}	14	8		1		43
	8	4				2			9^{2}	10	13			11								5^{1}	7	6		3		12				1		44
		3			2	5			12	10^{1}				8									7	6	9			11		4		1		45
1		3			2	6			13	10	14			8									7^{2}	5	9^{3}			11^{1}		4			12	46

FA Cup

Fourth Qualifying	Concord Rangers	(a)	1-0
First Round	Bury	(a)	0-5

FA Trophy

First Round	Havant & Waterlooville	(h)	2-2
Replay	Havant & Waterlooville	(a)	1-0
Second Round	Harrogate T	(h)	1-2

EASTLEIGH

Ground: The Silverlake Stadium, Ten Acres, Stoneham Lane, Eastleigh, Hampshire SO50 9HT. *Tel:* (02380) 613361.
Website: eastleighfc.com *Email:* admin@eastleighfc.com *Year Formed:* 1946.
Record Attendance: 5,250 v Bolton W, FA Cup 3rd rd, 9 January 2016. *Nickname:* 'Spitfires'.
Manager: Ben Strevens. *Colours:* Blue shirts with white trim, blue shorts, blue socks.

EASTLEIGH – NATIONAL LEAGUE 2018–19 LEAGUE RECORD

Match No.	*Date*	*Venue*	*Opponents*	*Result*	*H/T Score*	*Lg Pos.*	*Goalscorers*	*Attendance*
1	Aug 4	H	Solihull Moors	L 1-2	0-0	17	McCallum (pen) [77]	1354
2	7	A	Sutton U	L 0-1	0-1	22		1725
3	11	A	Barnet	W 2-1	1-0	14	Green [20], McCallum [64]	1028
4	14	H	Bromley	W 1-0	1-0	11	Yeates [5]	1478
5	18	H	Wrexham	L 1-3	0-2	15	McCallum [68]	1717
6	25	A	Dover Ath	W 2-1	2-0	13	Williamson [19], McCallum [37]	844
7	27	H	Ebbsfleet U	L 0-1	0-1	16		1663
8	Sept 1	A	Harrogate T	L 0-4	0-1	17		1158
9	4	A	Maidenhead U	L 0-2	0-2	18		1212
10	8	H	AFC Fylde	D 0-0	0-0	19		1750
11	15	A	Hartlepool U	D 1-1	0-1	17	McCallum [70]	3302
12	22	H	Dagenham & R	W 1-0	0-0	16	Wynter [89]	1538
13	25	H	Boreham Wood	W 1-0	0-0	14	Yeates [80]	1306
14	29	A	Gateshead	W 1-0	0-0	11	Hare [77]	655
15	Oct 6	A	Braintree T	W 2-1	2-0	10	McCallum [15], Zebroski [37]	418
16	13	H	Aldershot T	L 1-2	1-2	10	McCallum [5]	2349
17	27	A	FC Halifax T	W 1-0	0-0	10	Hare [58]	1343
18	30	H	Leyton Orient	D 1-1	1-0	10	Hare [35]	1938
19	Nov 3	H	Salford C	D 1-1	0-0	10	Williamson [47]	2253
20	17	A	Barrow	W 3-0	2-0	9	McCallum 2 [14, 48], Williamson [43]	1102
21	24	H	Chesterfield	D 1-1	1-1	9	Wynter [11]	1774
22	27	A	Maidstone U	W 3-1	1-0	9	Jones [45], McCallum 2 [60, 85]	1570
23	Dec 1	H	Dover Ath	D 2-2	1-1	9	Williamson [2], McCallum [86]	1430
24	8	A	Wrexham	L 0-2	0-1	9		4105
25	22	H	Harrogate T	W 2-1	1-1	9	Williamson [27], Miley [82]	1622
26	26	A	Havant & W	D 2-2	2-0	9	McCallum 2 [37, 40]	1884
27	29	A	Ebbsfleet U	L 0-3	0-3	10		1305
28	Jan 1	H	Havant & W	W 2-1	0-0	10	Johnson [56], Hare [85]	2104
29	5	A	Solihull Moors	L 1-4	0-2	10	McCallum [53]	829
30	19	H	Sutton U	W 3-2	1-1	10	Boyce [10], Hare [61], Williamson [88]	1872
31	26	A	Bromley	W 1-0	0-0	8	Boyce [88]	1381
32	Feb 9	A	Aldershot T	W 3-1	1-0	9	Hollands [42], McCallum 2 [70, 72]	2096
33	16	H	Braintree T	W 2-1	2-1	8	McCallum 2 [14, 17]	2120
34	23	A	Salford C	W 2-0	1-0	5	McCallum 2 [25, 52]	2329
35	Mar 2	H	FC Halifax T	L 0-1	0-0	7		3323
36	9	A	Chesterfield	W 3-2	1-1	8	McCallum [44], Boyce [59], Jones [83]	4319
37	12	H	Maidstone U	W 2-0	1-0	6	Zebroski [43], Yeates [85]	1642
38	16	H	Barrow	L 0-1	0-1	7		1738
39	30	H	Hartlepool U	W 3-2	2-1	7	Williamson [2], Wynter [14], Hobson [48]	1863
40	Apr 2	H	Barnet	L 0-3	0-1	7		1579
41	6	A	AFC Fylde	L 2-4	2-1	7	Wynter [10], McCallum [15]	1525
42	9	A	Leyton Orient	L 2-3	2-1	7	McCallum 2 [6, 21]	5203
43	13	H	Gateshead	W 1-0	1-0	7	Johnson [15]	1698
44	19	A	Dagenham & R	L 0-2	0-1	7		1315
45	22	H	Maidenhead U	W 2-0	2-0	7	McCallum (pen) [28], Yeates [38]	2146
46	27	A	Boreham Wood	D 3-3	1-1	7	Dennett [30], Gobern [47], McKnight [51]	502

Final League Position: 7

GOALSCORERS

League (62): McCallum 26 (2 pens), Williamson 7, Hare 5, Wynter 4, Yeates 4, Boyce 3, Johnson 2, Jones 2, Zebroski 2, Dennett 1, Gobern 1, Green 1, Hobson 1, Hollands 1, McKnight 1, Miley 1.
FA Cup (0).
FA Trophy (1): Dennett 1.
National League Play-Offs (2): Hollands 1, McCallum 1.

Stack 10	Hare 43	Green 34 + 2	Johnson 33	Boyce 37 + 2	Wynter 42 + 1	Hollands 31 + 3	Gobern 30 + 13	Yeates 42 + 2	Williamson 27 + 9	McCallum 38 + 3	Zebroski 17 + 19	Miley 32 + 10	Constable 2 + 12	Dowling — + 2	Wood — + 1	Jones 27 + 5	Flitney 3	Dennett 3 + 12	Bearwish — + 7	Payne 5	Stryjek 13	Baughan 1 + 1	McKnight 3 + 12	Southwood 20	Hobson 7 + 1	Matthews 6 + 2	Scorey — + 1	Harvey — + 1	*Match No.*
1	2	3	4	5^{3}	6	7	8^{1}	9	10^{2}	11	12	13	14																1
1	5	6	3	2^{2}	4	9^{1}	7	8	10^{3}	11	12	13		14															2
1	2	3	4	6	5	7	8^{1}	13	14	11^{2}	10^{3}	9		12															3
1	3	4	2		5		6	7^{2}	9^{1}	10	11	8	12		13														4
1	2	3	4	12■	8	11^{2}	13	6	10^{3}	5	7^{1}	9	14																5
1	2	3	5		4	13	7	9^{3}	11^{1}	10		8	12			6													6
	2	5		3	4■	8	6^{1}	9		11		7	10				1	12											7
1	2	3	5	4^{2}		9^{1}	6	7		11	10	8				12^{3}		13	14										8
1	2	3	5		8	11	4	6			7	10						9											9
1	2		3		4	6	8^{2}	10		11	12	7	9^{1}			13				5									10
1	2		4		7		3	6		5	12	9				10		8^{1}		11									11
	2	3	5		8		4^{3}	7^{1}		6■	12	9	13			10		14		11^{2}	1								12
	2	3	5	12	6		7^{1}	8^{2}			11	9	13			4^{3}		14		10	1								13
	2	3	5	8	9		4^{3}	6^{2}	13	12	7^{1}	10	14							11	1								14
	2	3	4	5	6	12	7^{2}	8	13	10^{1}	11^{3}	9	14								1								15
		2	3	6^{1}	5^{2}		7	8	12	11	10	9	13			4					1								16
	2	3		4	5	8	9^{1}	6^{3}	11^{2}	10		7				12		13	14		1								17
	2	3		4	5	8	6^{1}	9	10	11	13	7^{2}				12					1								18
	2	3	4	7	5	9		8	11^{2}	10^{1}	12		13			6					1								19
	2		3	6	5	9	13	7^{2}	10^{3}	11^{1}		8				4		12	14		1								20
	2		3	6	7	10	12	5	9^{1}	4		8^{2}				11		13			1								21
	5^{3}			2	3	9	6	8^{2}	11	10^{1}		7	14			4	1	12				13							22
		2	3	4	12	9	6^{2}	7	11^{3}	10		8	14			5^{1}		13			1								23
	2	12	4	3	5	9	7	6	10^{1}	11		8^{2}						13			1								24
	2	3	4	5^{3}	6	8	13	9^{1}	10^{2}	11		12				7					1		14						25
	2	3■	6	5	4	7	14	9^{1}	10^{3}	11^{2}	13	12				8								1					26
	2		3	4^{2}	5		8	9	11^{3}	13	12	10				6		14					7^{1}	1					27
	2		4	7	8		3	6	10^{2}	5		9				11^{1}			13				12	1					28
	2		3	4	5	13	7^{2}	8	10^{3}	11	14	9^{1}				6							12	1					29
	2	3	4	6	7	9	14	8^{3}	10^{1}	11^{2}	12					5							13	1					30
	2	6	3	5	4	8	12	9^{1}	11		10^{2}	13				7								1					31
	2	3	4	6	7	9	13^{3}	8	10^{2}	11^{1}	12	14				5								1					32
	2	3	4^{1}	5	6	9^{2}		8		10^{3}	11	12■				7			14				13	1					33
	2	3		4	5	9	7^{3}	8^{1}		10^{2}	11					6		13	14				12	1					34
	2	3^{2}		4	5	9	7^{1}	8	13	10	11^{3}	12				6							14	1					35
	2			4	5	9	6	7^{1}	12	10^{2}	11^{3}	8				3							13	1	14				36
	2	12	3	4	5	7	8	9^{3}	13	11	10^{2}	6^{1}											14	1					37
	2	3	5	9	10^{2}	11^{3}	4	7	12	6	8^{1}	13											14	1					38
	2	6		5	3	8	14	10^{2}	11		13	12				7^{1}								1	4	9^{3}			39
	2	6		4	5	7■	14	9	11^{1}	12	13	8												1	3^{3}	10^{2}			40
	2	6		4	5		7^{1}	9	11^{3}	10	14	8				12								1	3^{2}	13			41
	2	6		4			12	13	11^{1}	10	14	8^{2}				3							7^{3}	1	5	9			42
	2	3	4	6			13		11^{2}	10^{3}	12	8				7							14	1	5	9^{1}			43
	2	6		4	5			10^{1}	12	11	14	7				8							13	1	3^{2}	9^{3}			44
	2	6	3	4	5	7	12	9^{2}	10^{1}	11	13					8^{3}								1		14			45
					2^{1}	5	6				11	4					1	10^{2}	13			7^{3}	9		3	8	12	14	46

FA Cup
Fourth Qualifying Hampton & Richmond Bor (h) 0-1

FA Trophy
First Round Hemel Hemstead T (a) 1-2

National League Play-Offs
Eliminator Wrexham (a) 1-0
aet
Semi-Finals Salford C (a) 1-1
(aet; Salford C won 4-3 on penalties)

EBBSFLEET UNITED

Ground: The Kuflink Stadium, Stonebridge Road, Northfleet, Kent DA11 9GN.
Tel: (01474) 533 796. *Website:* ebbsfleetunited.co.uk *Email:* info@eufc.co.uk *Year Formed:* 1946 (as Gravesend and Northfleet), 2007 (renamed Ebbsfleet United).
Record Attendance: 12,032 v Sunderland, FA Cup 4th rd, 12 February 1963. *Nickname:* 'The Fleet'.
Manager: Garry Hill. *Colours:* Red shirts with white trim, white shorts, red socks.

EBBSFLEET UNITED – NATIONAL LEAGUE 2018–19 LEAGUE RECORD

Match No.	Date	Venue	Opponents	Result		H/T Score	Lg Pos.	Goalscorers	Attendance
1	Aug 4	H	Chesterfield	L	0-1	0-0	19		2041
2	7	A	Leyton Orient	D	1-1	0-1	18	Whitely [90]	4710
3	11	A	Hartlepool U	W	1-0	0-0	9	Whitely [71]	3182
4	14	H	Sutton U	L	0-1	0-1	15		1506
5	18	A	Barnet	W	3-0	1-0	10	Kedwell [44], Whitely [66], Shields [88]	1217
6	25	H	Aldershot T	W	3-1	1-1	7	Shields 2 [35, 81], Drury [72]	1233
7	27	A	Eastleigh	W	1-0	1-0	6	Kedwell [45]	1663
8	Sept 1	H	AFC Fylde	L	1-3	0-0	9	Whitely [76]	1395
9	4	A	Dover Ath	D	1-1	1-1	11	McQueen [12]	1127
10	8	H	Gateshead	L	0-1	0-1	13		1392
11	15	A	Wrexham	L	1-4	0-4	14	Kedwell [48]	4718
12	22	H	Havant & W	D	1-1	1-1	14	Cheek [27]	1141
13	25	H	Bromley	L	1-2	1-2	16	Powell [45]	1204
14	29	A	Dagenham & R	W	3-1	2-1	15	Bush [4], Kedwell 2 (1 pen) [31, 57 (p)]	1225
15	Oct 6	H	Harrogate T	L	0-2	0-1	15		1169
16	13	A	Solihull Moors	L	1-2	0-1	17	Gudger (og) [59]	1505
17	27	A	Salford C	D	1-1	1-1	17	Whitely [35]	2498
18	30	H	Maidstone U	D	1-1	0-0	16	Clark [57]	2003
19	Nov 3	H	Barrow	W	1-0	1-0	15	Kedwell [35]	1277
20	17	A	Boreham Wood	D	0-0	0-0	14		724
21	24	H	FC Halifax T	W	4-0	2-0	13	Cheek 2 [24, 90], Bush [40], Kedwell (pen) [47]	1104
22	27	A	Maidenhead U	D	1-1	1-0	10	Cheek [14]	1055
23	Dec 1	A	Aldershot T	W	2-0	0-0	10	Cheek [48], Kedwell (pen) [67]	1663
24	8	H	Barnet	W	1-0	0-0	10	Kedwell [84]	1320
25	22	A	AFC Fylde	L	0-2	0-1	10		1474
26	26	H	Braintree T	W	4-2	3-1	10	Kedwell 2 [1, 13], Graham [45], McDonald [63]	1231
27	29	H	Eastleigh	W	3-0	3-0	9	Cheek [2], Kedwell [10], Whitely [37]	1305
28	Jan 1	A	Braintree T	W	4-0	2-0	9	McDonald [3], Cheek 2 (1 pen) [22, 61 (p)], Whitely [79]	752
29	5	A	Chesterfield	D	3-3	3-0	9	Cheek (pen) [21], McDonald [40], Graham [45]	4123
30	19	H	Leyton Orient	W	2-0	1-0	8	King [22], Bush [63]	3020
31	26	A	Sutton U	L	0-1	0-0	10		2108
32	Feb 9	H	Solihull Moors	L	0-1	0-0	10		1325
33	16	A	Harrogate T	W	2-1	1-0	10	Cheek [8], Drury [87]	1488
34	19	H	Hartlepool U	D	0-0	0-0	10		1265
35	23	A	Barrow	D	0-0	0-0	10		1058
36	Mar 2	H	Salford C	L	0-1	0-1	10		1708
37	12	H	Maidenhead U	W	3-0	0-0	10	Whitely [51], Cheek 2 [58, 79]	811
38	16	H	Boreham Wood	W	3-2	2-1	10	King [5], Magri [21], Bush [52]	1110
39	23	A	Maidstone U	W	2-0	1-0	9	Ugwu [20], Cheek [90]	3002
40	26	A	FC Halifax T	D	0-0	0-0	8		1073
41	30	H	Wrexham	W	4-2	3-0	8	Pearson (og) [10], Cheek 2 [40, 44], Ugwu [85]	1523
42	Apr 6	A	Gateshead	D	1-1	0-1	8	Bush [64]	798
43	13	H	Dagenham & R	L	0-1	0-1	8		1551
44	19	A	Havant & W	D	3-3	0-3	8	Kedwell [46], Cheek [51], Magri [57]	1097
45	22	H	Dover Ath	L	0-1	0-0	8		1723
46	27	A	Bromley	L	1-5	0-1	8	Drury [62]	1352

Final League Position: 8

GOALSCORERS

League (64): Cheek 16 (2 pens), Kedwell 13 (3 pens), Whitely 8, Bush 5, Drury 3, McDonald 3, Shields 3, Graham 2, King 2, Magri 2, Ugwu 2, Clark 1, McQueen 1, Powell 1, own goals 2.
FA Cup (4): Coulsdon 2, McQueen 1, Winfield 1.
FA Trophy (0).

Ashmore 45	King 33 + 1	Magri 40 + 3	Bush 39 + 4	Weston 34 + 6	Whitely 31 + 13	Payne 30 + 2	Drury 31 + 5	Adams 29 + 8	Wilson 24 + 3	Kedwell 31 + 11	Cheek 25 + 14	Shields 10 + 7	Powell 7 + 5	McQueen 4 + 7	Coulson 7 + 8	Winfield 21 + 1	Rance 23 + 5	Graham 15 + 10	Clark 9	Allassani 2 + 2	McDonald 5 + 7	Moncur 1 + 3	Ugwu 8	Omar 1 + 1	Miles 1	Achuba — + 1	*Match No.*
1	2	3	4	5	6	7	8^{1}	9^{2}	10^{3}	11	12	13	14														1
1	2	3	4	8^{3}	14		7	6^{1}		9	13	10	5	11^{2}	12												2
1	9	2	3	7	12	14	6	5^{2}		10^{1}	13	8	4	11^{3}													3
1	5	2	3	13	8		7^{2}	14		10	11^{3}	9	6	12		4^{1}											4
1	5	2	13	9^{2}	7^{1}		6	8		11		10	4^{3}		14	3	12										5
1	3	4	13	5	10^{2}		6	8^{3}		11^{1}	14	9			12	2	7										6
1	5	2	14	8^{3}	10^{2}		7	6^{1}		11		9	13		12	3	4										7
1	2	3		8	13		7^{3}	6^{2}		11		9	12	14	10^{1}	4	5										8
1	2	12	3	8	6		14			13	10^{3}	9	7	11^{2}		4^{1}	5										9
1	2	4	3^{3}		6		7		8	10	14	9^{1}		11^{2}	12		5	13									10
1	2	4	12	10	6		7	8^{3}		11^{1}	14				9^{2}		5	13	3								11
1		14	2	9	10			8			11^{3}	12	7^{1}	13		4	6	5^{2}	3■								12
1		2	4	5	10			7		13	11^{1}	12	8^{2}	14		3	6	9^{3}									13
1			2	8	9			7		11^{3}	14		12		13	3	6^{2}	5	4	10^{1}							14
1		12	2	8	9			7^{3}		11	14		13			3	6	5^{2}	4	10^{1}							15
1		3	2		7^{1}	8	9			11	13	12			10	4	6^{2}		5								16
1		3	2	6	9^{2}	7	8			11		12		13	10^{1}	4			5								17
1		3	2	7	10	8		9^{1}		11		12		13	6^{2}	4			5								18
1		3	2	6	9^{1}	7	8^{3}	12	14	11		13			10^{2}	4			5								19
1		3	2		10	8	9			11^{3}	13	7^{2}		14	5^{1}	4			6	12							20
1	5		2	8^{1}	9	6	7^{2}	12	4	11^{3}	10					3		13		14							21
1	4		3	8^{3}	9^{1}	6	7^{2}	12	2	11	10				13	5					14						22
1	5	3	2	8	9^{2}	6		7	4	11	10^{1}				12						13						23
1	4	5	3	8^{1}	9^{3}	6		7	2	11	10^{2}						14	13			12						24
1	5	3	2^{3}		10^{1}	6	8^{2}	7	14	11	13					4		9			12						25
1	12	2	4^{1}	14		8	7	6^{3}	5	11						3^{2}	13	9			10						26
1	4	3	2	7	9^{1}	6	8	13	12	11^{3}	10						5^{2}					14					27
1	2	3	9		12	8^{2}	6	5^{1}	11		7						13	10			4^{3}	14					28
1	5	2	3	12	14	6	8	7^{2}	4	13	10							9^{3}			11^{1}						29
1	4	5	3		12	6	8^{3}	7	2	11	10^{2}						13	9^{1}			14						30
1	4	2	3	14	13	7	6	5	9	11^{2}	10^{1}							8^{3}			12						31
1	5	3	2	14	9	4	8^{3}		6^{2}	11^{1}	13						7■	12■			10						32
1	4	2	3	7	9^{2}	8	6	5	10	13	11^{1}										12						33
1	4	5	3	9	12	6	8		2	13	11^{2}						7				10^{1}						34
1	5	3	2	9	10^{1}	6	8	7	4	12	11																35
1	5	2		9	12	6	8	7^{1}	3	10	11							4									36
1	2	3		5	9	8^{2}		4^{3}	11^{1}	13	6							10				12	7	14			37
1	4	5^{2}	3	12	14	7		8	2		11^{1}					13	6	9^{3}					10				38
1	4	3	2	6	8^{1}	7			9	12	11						5	13					10^{2}				39
1	4	3	2	7^{1}		8	12	6^{2}	9	14	10^{3}						5	13					11				40
1	4	3	2	8	9^{3}	7	12	14	6		11^{2}						5^{1}	13					10				41
1	5	2	4	8	13	9	12	7^{1}		14	10^{3}					3	6^{2}						11				42
1	5	3	2	8	9	7	13		4^{3}	12	11^{2}						6^{1}	14					10				43
1		2	10	8	13	12	7	5^{3}	11^{2}	6	9^{1}					4	3	14									44
1		4	3	9	13	6	7^{1}	14	2	11	12						5	8^{3}					10^{2}				45
		4^{3}	3	9	10		7	14		11	12						5	8				6^{1}		2^{2}	1	13	46

FA Cup
Fourth Qualifying Worthing (h) 4-0
First Round Cheltenham T (h) 0-0
Replay Cheltenham T (a) 0-2

FA Trophy
First Round Dagenham & R (h) 0-1

FC HALIFAX TOWN

Ground: The MBi Shay Stadium, Halifax HX1 2YT. *Tel:* (01422) 341 222.
Website: fchalifaxtown.com *Email:* tonyallan@fchalifaxtown.com *Year Formed:* 1911 (Reformed 2008).
Record Attendance: 36,855 v Tottenham H, FA Cup 5th rd, 15 February 1953. *Nickname:* 'The Shaymen'.
Manager: TBC. *Colours:* Blue shirts with white trim, blue shorts with white trim, blue socks with white trim.

FC HALIFAX TOWN – NATIONAL LEAGUE 2018–19 LEAGUE RECORD

Match No.	Date	Venue	Opponents	Result	H/T Score	Lg Pos.	Goalscorers	Attendance
1	Aug 4	A	Braintree T	W 2-0	1-0	3	Edwards 42, Clarke 65	621
2	7	H	Barrow	W 2-0	1-0	2	Southwell 43, Brown 88	1654
3	11	H	Maidstone U	W 3-0	1-0	1	King 40, Tomlinson 51, Southwell (pen) 70	1534
4	14	A	Salford C	L 1-2	0-1	4	Kosylo 73	2632
5	18	H	Dagenham & R	W 2-1	1-1	2	Kosylo 29, Edwards 59	1364
6	25	A	Boreham Wood	L 1-2	0-0	4	Clarke 70	572
7	27	H	Gateshead	W 1-0	1-0	1	Preston 45	1688
8	Sept 1	A	Sutton U	D 1-1	0-0	4	Southwell 62	1789
9	4	A	Wrexham	D 0-0	0-0	4		5377
10	8	H	Leyton Orient	D 1-1	0-0	5	Southwell (pen) 64	1927
11	15	A	Maidenhead U	L 0-3	0-3	9		1306
12	22	H	Hartlepool U	L 1-2	0-0	11	Hanson 88	2360
13	25	H	AFC Fylde	D 0-0	0-0	10		1197
14	29	A	Bromley	D 2-2	0-1	10	Staunton 60, Preston 90	1148
15	Oct 6	A	Aldershot T	L 0-3	0-2	13		1625
16	13	H	Chesterfield	D 1-1	0-0	14	Kosylo 69	2191
17	27	H	Eastleigh	L 0-1	0-0	14		1343
18	30	A	Solihull Moors	D 0-0	0-0	13		915
19	Nov 3	A	Havant & W	L 1-2	0-0	16	Maher 79	1258
20	17	H	Dover Ath	W 1-0	1-0	12	Kosylo 40	1356
21	24	A	Ebbsfleet U	L 0-4	0-2	14		1104
22	Dec 8	A	Dagenham & R	D 1-1	0-0	16	Clarke 80	1098
23	18	H	Boreham Wood	D 1-1	1-1	16	Southwell 43	913
24	22	H	Sutton U	L 0-1	0-0	16		1319
25	26	A	Harrogate T	W 2-1	0-1	16	Clarke 55, Southwell 88	2310
26	29	A	Gateshead	D 1-1	1-0	16	Preston 1	830
27	Jan 1	H	Harrogate T	D 1-1	0-1	17	Edwards 90	1696
28	5	H	Braintree T	D 0-0	0-0	17		1302
29	19	A	Barrow	D 0-0	0-0	17		1142
30	26	H	Salford C	D 0-0	0-0	16		2115
31	Feb 9	A	Chesterfield	L 0-1	0-0	16		4523
32	16	H	Aldershot T	D 0-0	0-0	18		1650
33	19	A	Maidstone U	W 1-0	0-0	15	Quigley 86	1813
34	23	H	Havant & W	D 0-0	0-0	15		1181
35	Mar 2	A	Eastleigh	W 1-0	0-0	15	Ferry 77	3323
36	5	H	Barnet	W 3-0	1-0	12	Rodney 35, Ferry 60, Duku 73	1085
37	12	A	Barnet	D 1-1	0-1	14	Rodney 72	702
38	16	A	Dover Ath	L 1-2	0-1	14	Kosylo 64	897
39	23	H	Solihull Moors	W 2-0	1-0	14	Duku 14, Rodney 83	1563
40	26	H	Ebbsfleet U	D 0-0	0-0	13		1073
41	30	H	Maidenhead U	L 0-1	0-0	14		1336
42	Apr 6	A	Leyton Orient	D 2-2	2-1	15	Duku 9, Rodney 45	5458
43	13	H	Bromley	D 2-2	1-0	15	Staunton 26, Rodney 75	1303
44	19	A	Hartlepool U	L 1-2	1-1	18	Rodney 14	3018
45	22	H	Wrexham	W 2-1	1-1	16	Quigley 28, Rodney 90	2577
46	27	A	AFC Fylde	W 2-0	2-0	16	Brown 38, Birch (og) 41	1891

Final League Position: 16; upgraded to 15 after 9pts deducation after the end of the season.

GOALSCORERS

League (44): Rodney 7, Southwell 6 (2 pens), Kosylo 5, Clarke 4, Duku 3, Edwards 3, Preston 3, Brown 2, Ferry 2, Quigley 2, Staunton 2, Hanson 1, King 1, Maher 1, Tomlinson 1, own goal 1.
FA Cup (6): Clarke 1, King 1, Kosylo 1, Preston 1, Southwell 1, own goal 1.
FA Trophy (4): Brown 1, Edwards 1, Kosylo 1, Southwell 1.

Johnson 46	Duckworth 18 + 1	Sellers 22 + 1	Clarke 46	Brown 41	Staunton 15 + 4	Southwell 31	Edwards 16 + 17	Tomlinson 12 + 6	Preston 22 + 13	Maher 36 + 3	Kosylo 40 + 2	King 16 + 12	Hanson 28 + 2	Leacock-McLeod 2 + 4	Lenighan 11 + 1	Odelusi 8 + 6	Berrett 26	Skarz 23 + 1	Wootton 2 + 1	Ferry 9 + 1	Quigley 9 + 6	Hardy 5 + 1	Duku 9 + 3	Rodney 12	Gondoh 1 + 4	Freedman — + 1	Match No.
1	2	3	4	5	6	7	8^{1}	9	10^{2}	11	12	13															1
1	4	3^{3}	5	2	6^{2}	9	8	10	11^{1}	7	13	12	14														2
1	3		10	2		5^{2}	9	6	13	4	11^{1}	8	7	12													3
1	2		6	5		9	8	10^{3}	12	3	11^{1}	13	4	14	7^{2}												4
1		3	10	2		5^{1}	9^{3}	6	12	4	11^{2}	14	7		8	13											5
1			2	3		5	6^{1}	7	12		4		11		8		9	10									6
1			2	3		11^{1}	12	8	10		9		5		7		6	4									7
1			4	2		8	12	9^{1}	11		10		5		7		6	3									8
1			2	5		9^{1}	6		11	12	10	13	4		7^{2}		8	3									9
1			2	3		5^{2}	6		9^{1}	12	4		11		7	13	8	10									10
1		13	3	4		11	12		9	6	10		2			8^{1}	7	5^{2}									11
1		2	3	4■		11^{1}	6^{2}		9	12	10■		5		7	13	8										12
1		2	3			10	6		9	4			5	12	7	11^{1}	8										13
1		2	3		12	9^{1}	6		11	4^{2}			5		7	10	8		13								14
1		2	3		14	9	13		11^{3}	5		12	4		7^{1}	10	8		6^{2}								15
1	14		3		5	10^{3}	8			2^{1}	11	13	6		12		7^{2}	4	9								16
1		2	3		4	11	9			5	10	8	7			12		6^{1}									17
1		2	3	4	5	10	11			8	6	7	9														18
1		2	3	4	5^{1}	11	9			6	10	8	7			12											19
1			2	3	4	10^{1}	13		12	5	9	8^{2}	7	14		11^{3}		6									20
1		2	3	4	5	11	12^{2}		10	6	9	8^{1}	7			13											21
1		2	3	4	5■	10^{2}	13		11	7	9		6	8^{1}				12									22
1		2	3	4		9		12	11	5			6	7		10^{1}				8							23
1		2	3	4		6^{2}	13	12	8	10	5		11			7^{1}				9							24
1	3	4	5	6		9		12	11	2	8					10^{1}				7							25
1	2	3	4	5		7	12	8^{1}	9	11	6									10							26
1		2	3	4		6^{1}	12	7	8	10	5		11							9							27
1			2	3		10^{1}	12		9	6	8		4					5		7	11						28
1	2		3	4		11^{1}	13	12	14	5	10	0^{2}					7	6			9^{3}						29
1	2		3	4		7^{1}	13	14	12	9	5	6^{2}					8	11			10^{3}						30
1	2		3	4			12	13	10^{2}	5	9	7^{1}					8	6			11						31
1	2	3	4	5			13	9^{2}	10	6	8						7				11^{1}	12					32
1	2	3	4	5		9^{2}	14	11^{3}	13	6	10						8				12	7^{1}					33
1	2	3	4	6	14		7^{1}		13	5	11						8■			12	10^{3}	9^{2}					34
1	2	3	4	5						6	9	13								8	12	7^{2}	10^{1}	11			35
1	2	3	4	5	14					6	9	13								7^{1}	11^{2}	8^{3}	12	10			36
1	2		3	4					13	5	9^{1}	12	14					6		7		8^{2}	10^{3}	11			37
1	2		3	4						7	5	6					11^{2}	10			9^{1}		12	8	13		38
1	2		4	5	3					6	9^{3}	13					8^{1}	7			12		10^{2}	11	14		39
1	2^{2}		3	4	5				12	6^{1}	9	13					8	7			14		10^{3}	11			40
1			2	4	3^{3}		13		12		9	7	6				8^{1}	5			14		10	11^{2}			41
1			2	3	6						11	7	5				8	4			12		9^{1}	10			42
1			2	3	4						5	6	11				7	10					8^{1}	9	12		43
1			2	3	4						9	7	6^{1}				8	5					10^{2}	11	12	13	44
1			2	3					13	4	10	6					7	5			11^{2}		12	9	8^{1}		45
1			2	3					7	8	4	5					6	11					9	10			46

FA Cup

Fourth Qualifying	Warrington T	(a)	2-2
Replay	Warrington T	(h)	2-0
First Round	Morecambe	(a)	0-0
Replay	Morecambe	(h)	1-0
Second Round	AFC Wimbledon	(h)	1-3

FA Trophy

First Round	Barrow	(a)	2-1
Second Round	Solihull Moors	(h)	2-2
Replay	Solihull Moors	(a)	0-1

GATESHEAD

Ground: Gateshead International Stadium, Neilson Road, Gateshead, Tyne and Wear NE10 0EF.
Tel: (0191) 4783883. *Website:* www.gateshead-fc.com *Email:* info@gateshead-fc.com
Year Formed: 1889 (Reformed 1977). *Record Attendance:* 20,752 v Lincoln C, Division 3N (at Redheugh Park), 25 September 1937. *Nickname:* 'The Tynesiders', 'The Heed'. *Manager:* Mike Williamson.
Colours: White shirts with black trim, black shorts, white socks with black trim.

GATESHEAD – NATIONAL LEAGUE 2018–19 LEAGUE RECORD

Match No.	*Date*		*Venue*	*Opponents*	*Result*		*H/T Score*	*Lg Pos.*	*Goalscorers*	*Attendance*
1	Aug	4	A	Maidenhead U	W	3-1	1-0	2	Olley [17], Boden [48], Armstrong [55]	1264
2		7	H	Salford C	W	2-1	1-1	3	Armstrong 2 (1 pen) [37 (p), 68]	1243
3		11	H	Dover Ath	W	2-1	1-1	3	Tinkler [35], Armstrong [87]	693
4		14	A	Boreham Wood	D	1-1	0-1	2	Rigg [88]	608
5		18	A	Bromley	L	0-1	0-0	5		1078
6		25	H	Leyton Orient	D	1-1	0-0	6	Armstrong [77]	1052
7		27	A	FC Halifax T	L	0-1	0-1	11		1688
8	Sept	1	H	Maidstone U	W	1-0	0-0	8	Boden (pen) [88]	564
9		4	H	Harrogate T	L	2-3	1-1	12	Kerr [35], Rigg [52]	846
10		8	A	Ebbsfleet U	W	1-0	1-0	8	Bush (og) [13]	1392
11		15	H	Braintree T	L	0-1	0-0	10		578
12		22	A	Chesterfield	W	3-0	2-0	9	Boden 2 [18, 68], Rigg [43]	4210
13		25	A	Barrow	W	2-1	1-1	6	Boden [45], Olley [47]	1053
14		29	H	Eastleigh	L	0-1	0-0	9		655
15	Oct	6	H	Dagenham & R	W	2-0	2-0	8	Rigg [18], White [20]	687
16		13	A	Havant & W	W	1-0	0-0	7	Rigg [56]	1250
17		27	H	Aldershot T	W	3-0	2-0	7	Olley [20], Boden [33], White [77]	703
18		30	A	AFC Fylde	L	0-1	0-0	7		1470
19	Nov	3	A	Wrexham	L	1-3	0-1	8	Armstrong [88]	4421
20		17	H	Sutton U	D	0-0	0-0	8		794
21		24	A	Barnet	W	2-1	1-0	7	Boden [20], Armstrong [77]	940
22	Dec	1	A	Leyton Orient	L	0-2	0-0	7		4636
23		8	H	Bromley	W	2-0	1-0	7	Armstrong [16], Kerr [52]	680
24		22	A	Maidstone U	W	3-2	2-0	7	Molyneux 2 [25, 56], Tinkler [33]	2131
25		26	H	Hartlepool U	W	2-1	2-0	7	Armstrong 2 [13, 33]	2678
26		29	H	FC Halifax T	D	1-1	0-1	7	Boden [63]	830
27	Jan	1	A	Hartlepool U	L	1-2	0-1	7	Donaldson (og) [61]	3468
28		5	H	Maidenhead U	L	0-1	0-1	8		581
29		8	H	Solihull Moors	L	1-2	0-1	8	Boden (pen) [56]	519
30		19	A	Salford C	D	1-1	1-1	9	Boden [44]	2055
31		26	H	Boreham Wood	D	1-1	0-1	9	Boden [73]	562
32	Feb	2	A	Dover Ath	W	2-1	0-1	7	Kerr [79], Olley [90]	1037
33		9	H	Havant & W	D	0-0	0-0	8		531
34		16	A	Dagenham & R	W	2-0	1-0	6	Rigg 2 (1 pen) [41 (p), 55]	1209
35		23	H	Wrexham	D	1-1	1-0	8	Rigg [40]	1228
36	Mar	2	A	Aldershot T	W	2-0	0-0	6	Thomson [63], Salkeld [85]	1885
37		9	H	Barnet	W	2-1	0-1	7	Olley [48], White [72]	665
38		12	A	Solihull Moors	L	0-1	0-0	8		924
39		16	A	Sutton U	L	2-4	1-0	8	Olley 2 [44, 46]	1722
40		30	A	Braintree T	L	0-2	0-1	9		291
41	Apr	6	H	Ebbsfleet U	D	1-1	1-0	10	Mellish [4]	798
42		9	H	AFC Fylde	L	0-1	0-1	10		470
43		13	A	Eastleigh	L	0-1	0-1	10		1698
44		19	H	Chesterfield	W	1-0	1-0	9	Rigg (pen) [27]	1208
45		22	A	Harrogate T	L	0-2	0-1	9		1629
46		27	H	Barrow	L	0-2	0-2	9		798

Final League Position: 9; downgraded to 17 after Gateshead deducted 9pts after the end of the season.

GOALSCORERS

League (52): Boden 11 (2 pens), Armstrong 10 (1 pen), Rigg 9 (2 pens), Olley 7, Kerr 3, White 3, Molyneux 2, Tinkler 2, Mellish 1, Salkeld 1, Thomson 1, own goals 2.
FA Cup (5): Boden 1, Mellish 1, Molyneux 1, Olley 1, Rigg 1.
FA Trophy (1): Armstrong 1.

Pears 44	Kerr 35	Tinkler 45	Mellish 45 + 1	Thomson 18 + 7	White 41 + 2	Forbes 14 + 4	Olley 37 + 1	O'Donnell 15 + 8	Boden 27 + 2	Armstrong 16 + 1	Maloney 3 + 8	Hunter 28 + 8	Salkeld 13 + 16	Devitt 14 + 6	Williamson 31	Rigg 37 + 7	Molyneux 11 + 4	Barrow 30	Foden 2	McGeoch — + 4	*Match No.*
1	2	3	4	5	6^{1}	7^{2}	8	9	10^{3}	11	12	13	14								1
1	4	2	8		10		5	9	11	6		3	7^{1}	12							2
1	3	2	8^{3}		7^{2}		9	12	11	10		6	5^{1}	14	4	13					3
1	2	3	5	13	8^{2}		9	7	11	10			6^{1}		4	12					4
1	3	2	4	12	13		7	8	11	9		6	5^{2}			10^{1}					5
1	4	3	5	2^{1}	13		9	6		10	8^{2}	7	12			11					6
1	3	2	9	13	7		5	8	10	11		4^{2}	6^{1}			12					7
1	3	2	4		8	12	7	5■	11			6^{2}	9^{1}	13		10					8
1	3	2	5	12	7	6	8		11				9^{1}	4		10					9
1	3^{1}	2	4	12	8	6	7	5	11					13		10	9^{2}				10
1	3	2	4		8	6	7	5	11				9			10					11
1	3	2	5		7		8	13	10			12	14		4	11^{2}	9^{1}	6^{3}			12
1	3	2	4		6		7	8	11			12				10	9^{1}	5			13
1	3	2	5		7		8		11				12		4	10	9	6^{1}			14
1	2	5	4		6		9		11^{1}			7	12		3	10		8			15
1	2		5		6^{1}	13	9	8^{2}	11			7		12	3	10		4			16
1	5	6	3		8		9		10^{2}	12		7			4	11^{1}	13	2			17
1	5	6	3		9^{2}		8		12	10		7			4	11^{1}	13	2			18
1	4	5	12		8		7		9	10		6^{1}			3	11^{2}	13	2			19
1	3	2	5		7^{2}		9		12	11		8			4	10^{1}	13	6			20
1	3	2^{1}	5	12	7		8		11^{2}	10					4	13	9	6			21
1	3	2	5^{2}		7		9■	13	11	10					4	12	8^{1}	6			22
1	2	5	4		6					11		8			3	10	7	9			23
1	2	3	6^{2}		8			7	11	10^{1}		5		13		12	9	4			24
1	4	2	6		7■			12	11^{2}	10		8			5	13	9	3^{1}			25
	4	2	8					9	10	6		3			5	7	11		1		26
	4	2	8	6				9^{2}	10			3^{1}	12		5	7	11		1	13	27
1	3	7	5	2		9^{1}			10			8	6		4	11				12	28
1	3	2	6		7	9^{1}			10			8	12	5	4	11					29
1	3	2	5		7				10		9	8	12		4	11^{1}		6			30
1	3	2	5		7	13	12		10		9^{2}	8^{1}	6		4	11					31
1	3	2	6	10	7	9	8								4	11		5			32
1	3	5	7	10	9	6	8							4		11		2			33
1	3	2	5	10^{1}	7	9	8^{2}					13	12		4	11		6			34
1	3	2	5	10^{1}	7	9	8^{2}					12	13		4	11		6			35
1		4	6	10^{1}	7	8	9^{2}					13	12	3	5	11		2			36
1		2	5	10	7^{2}	9^{1}	8				13	12		3	4	11		6			37
1		2	5	10^{3}	7		8^{2}	12			14	9^{1}	13	3	4■	11		6			38
1		2	4	10	7		8	6^{2}				9	12	3		11^{1}		5		13	39
1		2	4	9	6		7				12	8^{2}	11	3^{1}		10		5		13	40
1		4	5	10	7	12	8					9^{1}	2	3		11		6			41
1		2	6	10^{2}	7		8	14			13	9^{1}	12	3^{3}	4	11		5			42
1		2	5	10	7	9	8^{2}				12		13	3^{1}	4	11		6			43
1		2	5	10	7	9^{1}	8					12		3	4	11		6			44
1		5	7^{2}	8^{3}	10		9	14			12	6^{1}	13	4	3	11		2			45
1		2	5	13	7■		8	12			14	9^{2}	10^{3}	3^{1}	4	11		6			46

FA Cup

Fourth Qualifying	Dunston UTS	(a)	4-0
First Round	Rochdale	(a)	1-2

FA Trophy

First Round	Salford C	(a)	1-3

HARROGATE TOWN

Ground: CNG Stadium, Wetherby Road, Harrogate HG2 7SA. *Tel:* (01423) 210 600.
Website: harrogatetownafc.com *Email:* enquiries@harrogatetownafc.com *Year Formed:* 1914.
Record Attendance: 4,280 v Harrogate Railway, Whitworth Cup Final, May 1950.
Nickname: 'Town', 'Sulphurites'. *Manager:* Simon Weaver.
Colours: Yellow shirts with black trim, black shorts, yellow socks with black hoops.

HARROGATE TOWN – NATIONAL LEAGUE 2018–19 LEAGUE RECORD

Match No.	Date		Venue	Opponents	Result		H/T Score	Lg Pos.	Goalscorers	Attendance
1	Aug	4	H	Sutton U	D	2-2	0-1	9	Muldoon [60], Langmead [86]	1378
2		7	A	Hartlepool U	D	2-2	0-0	11	Knowles [60], Howe [90]	3623
3		11	A	Bromley	D	1-1	0-1	12	Knowles [73]	1061
4		14	H	Barnet	W	2-0	2-0	9	Emmett [23], Kitching [26]	1381
5		18	A	Aldershot T	W	2-0	0-0	7	Knowles [57], Kinsella (og) [63]	1774
6		25	H	Solihull Moors	W	3-1	1-1	3	Kitching [7], Thomson [75], Howe [78]	1180
7		27	A	AFC Fylde	D	0-0	0-0	4		1709
8	Sept	1	H	Eastleigh	W	4-0	1-0	2	Muldoon 2 [25, 47], Beck 2 [80, 87]	1158
9		4	A	Gateshead	W	3-2	1-1	1	Knowles (pen) [23], Muldoon [56], Williams [85]	846
10		8	H	Havant & W	W	3-2	1-1	1	Howe [12], Knowles [52], Muldoon [57]	1709
11		15	A	Maidstone U	W	2-0	2-0	1	Howe [17], Muldoon [44]	2222
12		22	H	Leyton Orient	L	0-3	0-2	2		2584
13		25	H	Wrexham	D	0-0	0-0	3		2387
14		29	A	Boreham Wood	W	4-2	1-1	3	Thomson [19], Williams [51], Ilesanmi (og) [53], Emmett [74]	566
15	Oct	6	A	Ebbsfleet U	W	2-0	1-0	3	Howe [30], Williams [71]	1169
16		13	H	Dover Ath	D	2-2	1-0	4	Williams [26], Langmead [90]	1865
17		27	A	Dagenham & R	L	1-2	0-2	5	Leesley [83]	1446
18		30	H	Barrow	W	4-2	0-1	4	Jameson (og) [53], Muldoon [56], Falkingham [58], Beck [69]	1268
19	Nov	3	H	Chesterfield	D	1-1	0-0	4	Williams [90]	2291
20		24	H	Braintree T	W	3-1	1-1	4	Muldoon [44], Thomson [64], Woods [90]	1454
21		27	A	Salford C	L	2-3	2-2	5	Muldoon [9], Kitching [25]	1206
22	Dec	1	A	Maidenhead U	W	2-1	1-1	3	Howe [11], Langmead [77]	1090
23		4	A	Solihull Moors	L	0-2	0-1	3		794
24		8	H	Aldershot T	W	4-1	1-1	3	Burrell 3 [32, 54, 70], Muldoon [90]	1362
25		22	A	Eastleigh	L	1-2	1-1	4	Leesley [2]	1622
26		26	H	FC Halifax T	L	1-2	1-0	6	Howe [37]	2310
27		29	H	AFC Fylde	L	1-2	0-0	6	Beck [82]	1603
28	Jan	1	A	FC Halifax T	D	1-1	1-0	6	Thomson [6]	1696
29		5	A	Sutton U	L	1-2	0-1	7	Thomson [60]	1841
30		19	H	Hartlepool U	W	3-1	1-0	6	Kerry [4], Muldoon [50], Beck [68]	2000
31	Feb	9	A	Dover Ath	W	3-2	1-0	7	Beck 2 [6, 84], Thomson [90]	997
32		16	H	Ebbsfleet U	L	1-2	0-1	9	Muldoon [50]	1488
33		23	A	Chesterfield	W	1-0	1-0	7	Burrell [8]	4661
34	Mar	2	H	Dagenham & R	D	1-1	0-0	8	Howe [55]	1262
35		5	H	Bromley	W	1-0	0-0	6	Muldoon (pen) [90]	789
36		9	A	Braintree T	W	4-0	3-0	6	Emmett [1], Beck 2 [10, 56], Thomson [37]	362
37		16	H	Maidenhead U	W	1-0	0-0	6	Beck [53]	1105
38		19	A	Barnet	L	0-1	0-1	6		849
39		23	A	Barrow	D	2-2	0-2	6	Muldoon [47], Howe [69]	1934
40		27	H	Salford C	L	0-1	0-0	6		1700
41		30	H	Maidstone U	D	2-2	1-1	6	Beck [21], Muldoon (pen) [62]	1134
42	Apr	6	A	Havant & W	W	2-1	1-1	6	Woods [42], Thomson [81]	937
43		13	H	Boreham Wood	L	0-1	0-1	6		1216
44		19	A	Leyton Orient	L	0-2	0-1	6		6665
45		22	H	Gateshead	W	2-0	1-0	6	Thewlis [41], Beck [55]	1629
46		27	A	Wrexham	L	1-2	1-1	6	Beck [11]	3690

Final League Position: 6

GOALSCORERS

League (78): Muldoon 15 (2 pens), Beck 13, Howe 9, Thomson 8, Knowles 5 (1 pen), Williams 5, Burrell 4, Emmett 3, Kitching 3, Langmead 3, Leesley 2, Woods 2, Falkingham 1, Kerry 1, Thewlis 1, own goals 3.
FA Cup (0).
FA Trophy (6): Muldoon 2, Kitchin 1, Knowles 1, Thomson 1, own goal 1.
National League Play-Offs (1): Own goal 1.

Belshaw 45	Fallowfield 25	Howe 44 + 1	Burrell 45	Kitching 33	Falkingham 41	Emmett 31 + 2	Thomson 40 + 4	Muldeon 40 + 5	Williams 7 + 27	Knowles 17 + 5	Langmead 34 + 2	Leesley 29 + 6	Kerry 28 + 6	Agnew 7 + 9	Beck 25 + 14	Sutton — + 3	Thewlis 4 + 3	Woods 6 + 10	Senior 3 + 1	Mottley-Henry — + 4	Cracknell 1	Lees 1	*Match No.*
1	2^2	3	4	5	6	7	8	9^1	10	11	12	13											1
1		3	2	5	6	7	8	9^1	10	11	4	12											2
1		2	6	4	5	7	8^2	9^1	10	11	3	12	13										3
1		3	2	5	6	7	8	10^2	13	11^1	4	9		12									4
1		2	5	4	6	7	8^1	10^2	12	11^3	3	9	13	14									5
1		3	4	11	2	6	5	10^2		7^1	9	8		13	12								6
1		3	2	5	6^3		8^2	10	14	11^1	4	9	7	13	12								7
1		3	2	5			8	10^2	13	11^1	4	9^3	7	6	12	14							8
1		3	2	5			8^1	10	13	11^3	4	9	7	6^2	12	14							9
1		3	2	5			8	10^2	13	11^1	4	9	7	6^3	12	14							10
1		3	2	5			8	10^2	13	11^1	4	9	7	6	12								11
1		2	6	4	5		8	9	12	11	3		7		10^1								12
1		3	2	5	6		8^1	10	12	11^2	4	9	7		13								13
1		3	2	5	6	12	8^3	10^2	11		4	9	7^1	14	13								14
1		3	2	5	6	7^1	8	10^2	11		4	9		13	12								15
1		2	5	4	6	7	8	10^1	11^2		3	9			12		13						16
1		2	5	4	6	7	8	12			3	9			11		10^1						17
1	5^3	2	4	3	6	7^2	8	10	13		12	9	14		11^1								18
1	2	4	3	5	6	7	8^2	10^1	12			9	13		11								19
1	2	4	3	5	6	7	8	10^2				9^1	13		11			12					20
1		3	2	5	6	8	7	11^2		13	4				9		10^1	12					21
1	4	3	5		6	7	8^1	10^2		12	2	9			11			13					22
1	2	4	5		3	7	6^2	11^3	14	13	10	9			8^1			12					23
1	2	4	3	5^3	6	7^1	8	10	12	11^2		9	13					14					24
1	2	4	3	5	6	7^2	9		13	11^3		10	8^1		14			12					25
1	5	2	6	3	4	13		11^1	14	10^2		9	7		12			8^3					26
1		2	5	3	6		13	11^1	14	10^3	4	9	7		12			8^2					27
1	2	3	5		7	8	9	12			4	10^1	6		11								28
1	4	2	6		7	9^2	8	13	14		3	11^3	5^1		10			12					29
1	4	3	6	2	5	8^3	7	11^2	14	13			9		10^1			12					30
1	4	12	6	3	5	8	7	11^2	14				9^3		10				2^1	13			31
1	4	2	6	3	5	9	7^2	11^1	13				8		10					12			32
1	2	4	5		3	7^2	6	11^1	13		9		10		8					12			33
1	4	3	6		5	9	7	11^2	13		2		8^1		10					12			34
1	4	2	6		5	8	7	11			3		9		10								35
1	2	4	5		3	7^3	6	11^1	13		9		10	12	8^2			14					36
1	4	2	6		5	8	7	11			3		9		10								37
1	4	3	6		5	8^1	7^2	11			2	12	9		10			13					38
1	4^3	2	6		5	8^1	7^2	11	14		3	13	9		10				12				39
1	2	3	5		7^1	8^2	12	10	13		4	6	9		11								40
1	4	2	6		5		12	11	13		3	10	8	7^2	9^1								41
1		3	4	10	2		5	9			7	6	8^2	12			13	11^1					42
1		4	6	2	5		7^3	11^2	14		3	10		8	13		12	9^1					43
1	2	5	6	11	4	7^3		12		13		14	10		8^2		9		3^1				44
1	5^1	3	7	4	6		13	12					8	14	10		11^2	9^3	2				45
				10			2	8	7		6	4		5	3			11			1	9	46

FA Cup
Fourth Qualifying Wrexham (h) 0-0
Replay Wrexham (a) 0-2

FA Trophy
First Round York C (h) 2-1
Second Round Dover Ath (a) 2-1
Third Round Stockport Co (h) 2-4

National League Play-Offs
Eliminator AFC Fylde (a) 1-3

HARTLEPOOL UNITED

Ground: The Super 6 Stadium, Clarence Road, Hartlepool TS24 8BZ. *Tel:* (01429) 272 584.
Website: www.hartlepoolunited.co.uk *Email:* enquires@hartlepoolunited.co.uk
Year Formed: 1908. *Record Attendance:* 17,426 v Manchester U, FA Cup 3rd rd, 5 January 1957.
Nickname: 'The Pool', 'Monkey Hangers'. *Manager:* Craig Hignett.
Colours: Blue shirts with white stripes, blue shorts with white trim, blue socks with white trim.

HARTLEPOOL UNITED – NATIONAL LEAGUE 2018–19 LEAGUE RECORD

Match No.	Date		Venue	Opponents	Result		H/T Score	Lg Pos.	Goalscorers	Attendance
1	Aug	4	A	Maidstone U	D	1-1	1-1	11	Noble 42	2599
2		7	H	Harrogate T	D	2-2	0-0	12	Muir 53, Cassidy 70	3623
3		11	H	Ebbsfleet U	L	0-1	0-0	16		3182
4		14	A	Braintree T	D	1-1	1-0	18	Muir 25	606
5		18	H	Maidenhead U	W	2-1	0-0	14	James 47, Featherstone 60	2925
6		25	A	Dagenham & R	W	2-1	0-1	12	Woods 48, Noble (pen) 63	1212
7		27	H	Chesterfield	W	1-0	1-0	8	Featherstone 17	3773
8	Sept	1	A	Havant & W	W	2-1	1-0	7	Noble 2 (2 pens) 23, 90	1272
9		4	H	Barrow	D	0-0	0-0	6		3361
10		8	A	Solihull Moors	W	1-0	0-0	4	Noble 58	1311
11		15	H	Eastleigh	D	1-1	1-0	6	Muir 24	3302
12		22	A	FC Halifax T	W	2-1	0-0	5	Noble (pen) 52, Featherstone 64	2360
13		25	A	Salford C	L	0-3	0-0	8		2420
14		29	H	Aldershot T	D	1-1	1-0	8	Muir 33	3251
15	Oct	6	H	Boreham Wood	W	2-0	1-0	6	Davies 2 34, 82	2988
16		13	A	Leyton Orient	D	0-0	0-0	8		6871
17		27	H	Sutton U	L	2-3	0-1	9	Muir 47, Noble 50	2788
18		30	A	Wrexham	L	0-1	0-1	9		4665
19	Nov	3	A	Bromley	L	0-4	0-1	9		1516
20		18	H	Barnet	L	1-3	1-2	12	Kioso 10	3545
21		24	A	Dover Ath	L	1-2	0-2	12	Hawkes 84	1027
22		27	H	AFC Fylde	L	1-2	0-1	13	Noble (pen) 84	1721
23	Dec	1	H	Dagenham & R	L	1-2	1-0	14	Noble (pen) 13	2030
24		8	A	Maidenhead U	W	1-0	1-0	13	Hawkes 17	1157
25		22	H	Havant & W	D	1-1	1-1	13	Noble 18	3024
26		26	A	Gateshead	L	1-2	0-2	14	Noble (pen) 87	2678
27		29	A	Chesterfield	D	1-1	1-0	15	James 45	4752
28	Jan	1	H	Gateshead	W	2-1	1-0	13	Noble (pen) 7, McLaughlin 66	3468
29		5	H	Maidstone U	L	1-2	1-2	14	Cassidy 5	2929
30		19	A	Harrogate T	L	1-3	0-1	15	Kabamba 57	2000
31		26	H	Braintree T	W	2-1	0-1	15	Kabamba 52, Hawkes (pen) 59	2769
32	Feb	9	H	Leyton Orient	D	1-1	1-1	13	Kabamba 45	3297
33		16	A	Boreham Wood	W	4-0	1-0	13	Kabamba 2 7, 88, Hawkes 2 (1 pen) 50, 57 (p)	679
34		19	A	Ebbsfleet U	D	0-0	0-0	13		1265
35		23	H	Bromley	L	1-2	0-2	13	Noble 90	2985
36	Mar	2	A	Sutton U	D	2-2	0-1	13	Kitching 65, James 75	1923
37		9	H	Dover Ath	W	3-2	0-2	12	Hawkes 2 (2 pens) 70, 73, Molyneux 90	3431
38		12	A	AFC Fylde	L	2-4	0-1	13	Donaldson 46, Hawkes 75	1272
39		16	A	Barnet	D	0-0	0-0	12		1269
40		23	H	Wrexham	W	1-0	1-0	12	Hawkes (pen) 24	3888
41		30	A	Eastleigh	L	2-3	1-2	13	Kitching 6, Kabamba 71	1863
42	Apr	6	H	Solihull Moors	L	0-1	0-0	16		2981
43		13	A	Aldershot T	D	1-1	0-1	16	Holohan 80	1589
44		19	H	FC Halifax T	W	2-1	1-1	14	James 32, Molyneux 53	3018
45		22	A	Barrow	L	0-1	0-1	17		3007
46		27	H	Salford C	W	3-2	0-1	17	Featherstone 50, Kabamba 69, James 75	3582

Final League Position: 17; upgraded to 16 after Gateshead deducted 9pts after the end of the season.

GOALSCORERS

League (56): Noble 13 (8 pens), Hawkes 9 (5 pens), Kabamba 7, James 5, Muir 5, Featherstone 4, Cassidy 2, Davies 2, Kitching 2, Molyneux 2, Donaldson 1, Holohan 1, Kioso 1, McLaughlin 1, Woods 1.
FA Cup (4): Magnay 1, McLaughlin 1, Muir 1, O'Neill 1.
FA Trophy (2): Anderson 1, Donaldson 1.

Loach 46	Magnay 29	Davies 12	Kioso 36 + 3	Kitching 34 + 6	Donaldson 43	Noble 37 + 5	Featherstone 41 + 2	Muir 25 + 9	James 40 + 5	Cassidy 5 + 3	Hawkes 16 + 13	Dinanga 2 + 13	Newton 3 + 10	McLaughlin 13 + 11	Richardson 11 + 5	Laing — + 1	Anderson 33 + 3	Woods 8 + 4	O'Neill 2 + 1	Rodgers 4	Hawkins 1 + 3	Raynes 3	Molyneux 12 + 4	Kabamba 17	Amos 6 + 1	Cunningham 5 + 1	Kerr 9	Edgar 9	Holohan 3 + 4	Bale — + 3	Match No.
1	2	3	4	5	6	7	8^{2}	9^{1}	10^{3}	11	12	13	14																		1
1	2	3	4	5	6	8	7^{2}	9^{1}	10	11			13	12																	2
1	2	3^{3}	4^{2}	8		7		9	10	11^{1}		13	14	6	5	12															3
1	4		2	3	7	6^{1}	9	11	10^{2}	13			12	14			5	8^{3}													4
1	3		2	9	5	7	6	10	11^{2}	13				12			4	8^{1}													5
1	4		2	3	6	5	9	7^{2}	11			13		12			10	8^{1}													6
1	3		2	5	6	9	7	11^{2}	10			13		12			4	8^{1}													7
1	3		2	5	6	9^{3}	7	10	11^{1}			13	14	12			4	8^{2}													8
1	3		2	9	5	8	6	11	10					12			4	7^{1}													9
1	5		3	4	7	6	8	11	10					9^{1}			2	12													10
1	3		2	9	5^{2}	8	6	11	10^{3}			14		7^{1}	12		4	13													11
1	4	5^{2}	2	3		7	8	11^{1}	10^{3}		13	14		9	12		6														12
1	6	3		2		7	8	11^{2}	10			12	5^{1}	9			4	13													13
1	5^{3}	4	3	6	2	8	7	10^{1}	11		13			12			14	9^{2}													14
1	4	3	2^{1}	5	6	8	7	10	11					9			12														15
1	5	4	2	3	7	6^{2}	9	10	11^{1}		12	13	14					8^{3}													16
1	5	4	3	6	2	8	7^{2}	11	10			13		9^{1}				12													17
1	3	7■	2		5	4	8^{1}	6^{3}	13		14	11	12	10^{2}			9														18
1	3		2■	5^{3}	6	8	7	10^{2}	13		14	11	12	9			4^{1}														19
1			5	3	9	8	7	12	10			13		6^{1}	2		4		11^{2}												20
1	4		2	6	7		8	13	10^{3}		12	14		9	3^{2}		5		11^{1}												21
1	3			5	8	12	7	14	11		10^{1}		9^{3}	6^{2}	2		4		13												22
1	2		3	4^{1}	6	8	7	10^{3}	11		9^{2}	13	14	12	5																23
1	4		2^{2}	3	6	5	9	7	11		8^{1}			13	12		10														24
1	4	3		5	6	8	7^{2}	11	10^{3}		13		14	9	12					2^{1}											25
1	3	4		2	10	8		11	12		13		6^{1}		7					5	9^{2}										26
1	3			2	5	4	12	6	11		7^{1}				10		9			8											27
1	4		12	5	8	7	6	10	11		9^{1}			13	2^{2}		3														28
1	6^{2}		13	5	8	7		12	11	10	9^{1}				2		4			3											29
1	4^{3}		13	2	6		7^{1}		11^{2}	9	14				5		12					3	8	10							30
1			2	13	8		7		12	14	10				6^{1}		4					3	9	11^{2}	5^{3}						31
1			3		2	12	7		11		8						5^{1}					4	9^{2}	10	6	13					32
1			2	13	4	3^{2}	6	14	11^{3}		5^{1}						7				12			10	9	8					33
1			3	13	2	8	7	14	10^{1}		9^{2}						5						12	11	6^{3}	4					34
1			3	13	2	8	7	10^{1}			9						5				14		12	11	6^{3}	4^{2}					35
1				2	6	7	9		11		8						4						12	10		5^{1}	3				36
1				5^{1}	6	7^{2}	8		10		9						4				14		12	11	13		3	2^{3}			37
1			5^{1}		9	12	8		10		6						4						7	11			3	2			38
1			2		7	6^{1}	12		10		8^{2}						5						9	11			3	4	13		39
1			2	12	8	6^{3}	7		13		9^{2}						5						10	11		3^{1}	4			14	40
1			2	3^{1}	7^{2}	8^{3}	6	14	10		12						5						9	11				4	13		41
1			2	12	6	8^{2}	7		10								5^{1}						9	11			3	4	13		42
1			2	5	7		6	12	10														9^{2}	11			3	4	8^{1}	13	43
1			2		7	12	6		10								5						9^{2}	11			3	4	8^{1}	13	44
1			2		7	12	6	14	10^{1}		13												9	11	5^{2}		3	4	8^{3}		45
1			2^{1}	5	7	8^{2}	6		10		14				13		4						9	11				3^{3}	12		46

FA Cup

Fourth Qualifying	Kidsgrove Ath	(h)	1-0
First Round	Gillingham	(a)	0-0
Replay (aet)	Gillingham	(h)	3-4

FA Trophy

First Round	Leamington	(a)	1-0
Second Round	Telford U	(h)	1-2

HAVANT & WATERLOOVILLE

Ground: West Leigh Park, Martin Road, Havant PO9 5TH. *Tel:* (02392) 787 855.
Website: havantandwaterloovillefc.co.uk *Email:* via website. *Year Formed:* 1998 (merger of Havant Town and Waterlooville). *Record Attendance:* 4,400 v Swansea C, FA Cup 3rd rd replay, 16 January 2008.
Nickname: The 'Hawks'. *Manager:* Paul Doswell.
Colours: White shirts with blue trim, white shorts, white socks.

HAVANT & WATERLOOVILLE – NATIONAL LEAGUE 2018–19 LEAGUE RECORD

Match No.	*Date*		*Venue*	*Opponents*	*Result*		*H/T Score*	*Lg Pos.*	*Goalscorers*	*Attendance*
1	Aug	4	A	Barrow	L	0-3	0-1	24		1389
2		7	H	Boreham Wood	D	0-0	0-0	20		1348
3		11	H	AFC Fylde	D	1-1	0-1	18	Kabamba [48]	1182
4		14	A	Dover Ath	L	3-4	0-1	22	Fogden [48], Pavey [50], Lewis [52]	997
5		18	A	Braintree T	W	4-3	2-2	17	Williams [1], Rose [45], Kabamba [90], Rutherford [90]	407
6		25	H	Salford C	D	1-1	1-1	18	Pavey [22]	1679
7		27	A	Bromley	L	0-4	0-2	21		1413
8	Sept	1	H	Hartlepool U	L	1-2	0-1	21	Woodford [83]	1272
9		5	H	Aldershot T	W	2-1	1-0	18	Lewis [27], Robinson, P [83]	1989
10		8	A	Harrogate T	L	2-3	1-1	20	Kabamba 2 [6, 63]	1709
11		15	H	Sutton U	L	1-2	1-0	21	Kabamba [32]	1273
12		22	A	Ebbsfleet U	D	1-1	1-1	21	Cosgrave [2]	1141
13		25	A	Barnet	D	2-2	0-1	21	Robinson, A 2 [71, 90]	965
14		29	H	Solihull Moors	L	0-1	0-0	21		1115
15	Oct	6	A	Wrexham	L	0-1	0-1	21		4323
16		13	H	Gateshead	L	0-1	0-0	21		1250
17		27	A	Leyton Orient	L	0-4	0-3	22		5043
18		30	H	Maidenhead U	W	7-0	2-0	22	Cordner [8], Williams [41], Rutherford 2 [63, 80], Pavey 2 [64, 66], Bradley [85]	952
19	Nov	3	H	FC Halifax T	W	2-1	0-0	20	Cordner [48], Rutherford [64]	1258
20		17	A	Chesterfield	D	0-0	0-0	20		4082
21		24	H	Maidstone U	W	5-2	2-0	18	Rutherford 3 [11, 63, 85], Ayunga [35], Bradley [54]	1308
22		27	A	Dagenham & R	L	1-3	0-1	19	Ayunga [85]	1054
23	Dec	1	A	Salford C	L	0-3	0-2	19		2181
24		8	H	Braintree T	W	2-1	0-0	19	Rutherford 2 [55, 90]	858
25		22	A	Hartlepool U	D	1-1	1-1	19	Frost [12]	3024
26		26	H	Eastleigh	D	2-2	0-2	18	Robinson, A [80], Strugnell [89]	1884
27		29	H	Bromley	L	0-3	0-1	18		1341
28	Jan	1	A	Eastleigh	L	1-2	0-0	20	Jalloh [82]	2104
29		5	H	Barrow	W	2-0	0-0	19	Lewis [55], Williams [90]	1074
30		19	A	Boreham Wood	W	3-1	2-0	18	Paterson [9], Robinson, A [16], Jalloh [90]	511
31		26	H	Dover Ath	D	0-0	0-0	18		1024
32	Feb	9	A	Gateshead	D	0-0	0-0	18		531
33		16	H	Wrexham	L	2-3	1-0	21	Quigley (pen) [16], Rutherford [69]	1658
34		19	A	AFC Fylde	L	2-6	1-2	21	Paterson (pen) [14], Rutherford [87]	1192
35		23	A	FC Halifax T	D	0-0	0-0	21		1181
36	Mar	2	H	Leyton Orient	L	1-2	0-1	21	Rutherford [67]	2058
37		9	A	Maidstone U	L	0-2	0-2	21		1901
38		12	H	Dagenham & R	W	3-0	1-0	21	Rutherford [3], Harris [74], Lewis [90]	713
39		16	H	Chesterfield	L	1-2	1-0	21	Paul [12]	1097
40		26	A	Maidenhead U	L	1-2	0-0	21	Paterson [89]	1230
41		30	A	Sutton U	D	2-2	1-1	21	Cordner 2 [39, 59]	1816
42	Apr	6	H	Harrogate T	L	1-2	1-1	21	Paterson (pen) [22]	937
43		13	A	Solihull Moors	L	2-3	1-1	21	Quigley [1], Gudger (og) [86]	1179
44		19	H	Ebbsfleet U	D	3-3	3-0	21	Rutherford 2 [22, 44], McNamara [45]	1097
45		22	A	Aldershot T	L	0-2	0-2	22		1446
46		27	H	Barnet	L	0-2	0-0	23		1003

Final League Position: 23

GOALSCORERS

League (62): Rutherford 15, Kabamba 5, Cordner 4, Lewis 4, Paterson 4 (2 pens), Pavey 4, Robinson A 4, Williams 3, Ayunga 2, Bradley 2, Jalloh 2, Quigley 2 (1 pen), Cosgrave 1, Fogden 1, Frost 1, Harris 1, McNamara 1, Paul 1, Robinson P 1, Rose 1, Strugnell 1, Woodford 1, own goal 1.
FA Cup (0).
FA Trophy (2): Kabamba 1, Rutherford 1.

Young 11	Williams 37 + 1	Stock 22 + 1	Harris 24	Fogden 24 + 4	Pavey 13 + 6	Kabamba 24 + 5	Tarbuck 18 + 6	Robinson A 32 + 3	Rose 17 + 6	Robinson P 15 + 1	Lewis 29 + 6	Rutherford 25 + 10	Huggins 8 + 6	Carter 9 + 5	Cosgrave 5 + 10	Strugnell 28 + 5	Woodford 21 + 6	Sekajja 4 + 9	Simpson — + 2	Dudzinski 29	Ridge 2	Cordner 34	Wood 7 + 1	Bradley 4 + 5	Leeflang 3 + 2	Ayunga 4 / McNamara 4	Frost 4 + 3	Paul 12 + 6	Jalloh 3 + 11	Robertson 2	James 6 + 1	Paterson 6 + 6	Quigley 10 + 5	Banjo — + 1	Sarkic 1	Donovan 4	Bilboe 5	Match No.
1	2^{3}	3	4	5	6^{1}	7	8	9^{2}	10	11	12	13	14																									1
1	6^{3}	7^{1}	3	9	10	11^{2}	2	8	5	4		14	13	12																								2
1	2	3	4	5	6^{2}	7^{1}	8	9^{3}	10	11	12			13	14																							3
1	6	7	3	8	12	11^{2}	14	9^{1}	2	4	10			13		5^{3}																						4
1	2	6	3	8	10^{2}	11	7^{1}		5		9	12			13		4																					5
1	2	3	5^{2}	6	8^{3}	9	10^{1}		11	14	7	12				13	4																					6
1	3	12		5	6	7		9^{2}	10	11	13			8^{1}	14	2^{3}	4																					7
1	2^{1}	3	4	5		7	8		10^{3}	11	6^{2}	13		9			12	14																				8
1	3	4^{3}	6	7^{1}	9^{2}	10		12		11	8				14	2	5	13																				9
1	3		5		13	7		10^{1}		11	6		9		8^{2}	2	4		12																			10
1	2	3	5		13	7	14			11	6	12	9^{1}		8^{3}		4	10^{2}																				11
	2	3	5		12	7		13			6^{1}		9		8^{2}		4	14		1	10^{3}	11																12
	2	6	4		10	11	13	14			9		7^{2}				3^{3}	12		1	8^{1}	5																13
	2^{3}		4		6^{1}	7	8	9			5^{2}				14	12	3	10	13	1		11																14
		4	2^{2}		13	9	5	7			10^{3}		6		12	14	3	11^{1}		1		8																15
		5			10	11	6	7	3	4^{2}					13		14	12		1		8	2^{1}	9^{3}														16
		6	4^{3}		13	9	7				8		14		10^{2}	2		11^{1}		1		5	3	12														17
	3^{3}	7			10	11^{1}	6	8		5^{2}		13	12			2				1		9	4	14														18
	3^{2}	6			10^{1}	13	7	8		5		11^{3}			14	2				1		9	4▮	12														19
	5	6			10	13	7^{2}	8		2		11^{3}				4	14			1		3		9^{1}	12													20
	3	8				14					9^{2}	11	12			2	5	13		1		4		7	6^{3}	10^{1}												21
	3^{3}	6				14	12	7^{2}				10			13	2	4			1		5		8	11^{1}	9												22
		7	5			12	6	8			11^{3}	10^{1}				2	4	13		1			3^{2}		14	9												23
	2^{1}	7				9^{2}	6	8		3^{3}		11			14		12			1		5	4	13		10												24
	3	6^{3}	4			9	13	8			11^{1}	10^{2}				2				1		5	14				7	12										25
	3		4^{3}	14		6	12	8			5	13			7^{2}	2				1		9					10	11^{1}										26
	13					10^{1}	6	7	2			11				5				1		4	3^{2}		8^{3}		14	9	12									27
	3			12		6	7	8			5^{1}	9^{3}				2	4			1		10		14			11^{2}		13									28
	3			12		6	7^{1}	8			5	9^{2}				2	4			1		10					11^{3}	13	14									29
	2			5^{2}				7	12		11	10								1		4					13	6^{3}	14	3	8	9^{1}						30
	2			3^{3}				7	12		4	9^{2}								1		10					13	11^{1}	14	6▮	8	5						31
	2			5				6	3		8^{1}	14				13				1		4						7	12		11^{2}	9^{3}	10					32
	2^{2}			5				6	4			10				12		14		1		3						7	11^{1}		9^{3}	13	8					33
	3^{3}		6^{2}	7				8			10	13				2	4			1		5						9^{1}			12	11	14					34
	3			7				6^{3}	4		8	11				2				1		5						13	12		10^{1}	14	9^{2}					35
				5				6	4		7^{2}	10				2	12	14		1		3							11^{1}		9^{3}	13	8					36
				6				7	4		8^{2}	10		14		2	3^{3}			1		5						12	11^{1}			13	9					37
			3^{3}	4				8▮	14		12	9	7	6^{2}		2	13			1		10						11					5^{1}					38
			3	4					12		5	9	8	7^{1}		2				1		10						11^{3}				13	6^{2}	14				39
	3		4	5					14		6	9		8^{3}		2						10							13			12	7^{2}		1	11^{1}		40
	3			5								9		7^{2}		2	4^{1}					10				8		12	14			6^{3}	13			11	1	41
	11		2^{2}						3	4^{3}	14	9										5				7		6	13			10^{1}	12			8	1	42
	3			12				6	7		13	9		5		2						10				8							4^{2}			11^{1}	1	43
	3			5							6	9		7		2	4					10				8		11^{1}					12				1	44
	3			8				6			9^{3}	11	7^{1}	14		2	5			1		4						12	13				10^{2}					45
	3^{1}		5^{2}	6				8^{3}	14			9	13	7		2	4					10						11					12				1	46

FA Cup
Fourth Qualifying Metropolitan Police (a) 0-1

FA Trophy
First Round Dover Ath (a) 2-2
Replay Dover Ath (h) 0-1

LEYTON ORIENT

Ground: The Breyer Group Stadium, Brisbane Road, Leyton, London E10 5NF.
Tel: (0208) 926 1111. *Website:* www.leytonorient.com *Email:* info@leytonorient.net *Year Formed:* 1881.
Record Attendance: 34,345 v West Ham U, FA Cup 4th rd, 25 January 1964. *Nickname:* 'The O's'.
Interim Manager: Ross Embleton. *Colours:* Red shirts with white trim, red shorts with white trim, red socks.

LEYTON ORIENT – NATIONAL LEAGUE 2018–19 LEAGUE RECORD

Match No.	Date		Venue	Opponents	Result		H/T Score	Lg Pos.	Goalscorers	Attendance
1	Aug	4	A	Salford C	D	1-1	0-0	11	Hogan (og) 88	2156
2		7	H	Ebbsfleet U	D	1-1	1-0	13	Brophy 18	4710
3		11	H	Barrow	D	2-2	0-1	13	Bonne 2 55, 80	4304
4		14	A	Maidstone U	W	2-1	2-0	10	Koroma 10, Ekpiteta 35	3037
5		18	H	Boreham Wood	W	1-0	0-0	9	Bonne (pen) 69	3767
6		25	A	Gateshead	D	1-1	0-0	9	Ekpiteta 89	1052
7		27	H	Dover Ath	W	3-0	0-0	5	McAnuff 50, Koroma 81, Harrold 90	4641
8	Sept	1	A	Chesterfield	W	1-0	0-0	5	Dayton 78	4735
9		4	H	Solihull Moors	W	3-0	1-0	2	Lee 45, Bonne 85, Harrold 90	4250
10		8	A	FC Halifax T	D	1-1	0-0	3	Alabi 90	1927
11		15	H	Barnet	W	3-1	1-1	3	Coulson 11, Dayton 68, Bonne 78	5607
12		22	A	Harrogate T	W	3-0	2-0	1	Bonne 23, McAnuff 2 36, 69	2584
13		25	A	Braintree T	W	5-1	2-1	1	Bonne 3 (1 pen) 8 (p), 63, 70, Ekpiteta 41, Koroma 57	2574
14		29	H	Sutton U	L	0-1	0-0	2		5627
15	Oct	6	A	Maidenhead U	W	2-0	2-0	2	Bonne 11, Alabi 30	2016
16		13	H	Hartlepool U	D	0-0	0-0	3		6871
17		27	H	Havant & W	W	4-0	3-0	1	Coulson 13, Lewis (og) 18, Lee 39, Bonne 60	5043
18		30	A	Eastleigh	D	1-1	0-1	3	Bonne 66	1938
19	Nov	3	A	AFC Fylde	W	3-1	2-1	2	Bonne 5, Koroma 2 43, 51	2142
20		17	H	Bromley	W	3-1	0-1	1	McAnuff 56, Koroma 59, Bonne 77	6058
21		24	A	Wrexham	W	2-0	0-0	1	Bonne 86, Brophy 90	6428
22		27	H	Aldershot T	D	0-0	0-0	1		4289
23	Dec	1	H	Gateshead	W	2-0	0-0	1	Koroma 59, Bonne 90	4636
24		8	A	Boreham Wood	L	0-1	0-1	1		1602
25		22	H	Chesterfield	W	3-1	1-1	1	Koroma 8, Ekpiteta 62, Bonne (pen) 85	4755
26		26	A	Dagenham & R	L	1-2	0-0	1	Koroma 73	3694
27		29	A	Dover Ath	D	0-0	0-0	1		2270
28	Jan	1	H	Dagenham & R	W	1-0	1-0	1	Bonne 32	6001
29		5	H	Salford C	L	0-3	0-2	1		6937
30		19	A	Ebbsfleet U	L	0-2	0-1	1		3020
31		26	H	Maidstone U	W	3-0	1-0	1	Maguire-Drew 33, Bonne 2 (1 pen) 56, 90 (p)	5488
32	Feb	9	A	Hartlepool U	D	1-1	1-1	1	McAnuff 22	3297
33		16	H	Maidenhead U	L	0-1	0-0	3		5337
34	Mar	2	A	Havant & W	W	2-1	1-0	3	Maguire-Drew 35, Coulson 73	2058
35		5	A	Barrow	W	3-2	1-0	2	Ling 13, Simpson 47, Maguire-Drew 69	1130
36		9	H	Wrexham	W	1-0	0-0	1	Ekpiteta 72	6643
37		12	A	Aldershot T	W	2-1	2-0	1	Coulson 2 35, 38	1989
38		26	H	AFC Fylde	W	2-0	2-0	1	Ekpiteta 15, Bonne (pen) 24	4696
39		30	A	Barnet	D	0-0	0-0	1		3648
40	Apr	2	A	Bromley	L	1-2	1-0	1	Coulson 45	3047
41		6	H	FC Halifax T	D	2-2	1-2	2	Koroma 45, Harrold 90	5458
42		9	H	Eastleigh	W	3-2	1-2	1	Koroma 10, Bonne 57, Brophy 61	5203
43		13	A	Sutton U	W	2-1	0-0	1	Happe 64, Bonne (pen) 89	3339
44		19	H	Harrogate T	W	2-0	1-0	1	Coulson 2, Harrold 90	6665
45		22	A	Solihull Moors	D	0-0	0-0	1		3681
46		27	H	Braintree T	D	0-0	0-0	1		8241

Final League Position: 1

GOALSCORERS

League (73): Bonne 23 (6 pens), Koroma 11, Coulson 7, Ekpiteta 6, McAnuff 5, Harrold 4, Brophy 3, Maguire-Drew 3, Alabi 2, Dayton 2, Lee 2, Happe 1, Ling 1, Simpson 1, own goals 2.
FA Cup (0).
FA Trophy (11): Harrold 3 (1 pen), Bonne 1, Brophy 1, Clay 1, Coulson 1, Elokobi 1, Gorman 1, Happe 1, Turley 1.

Brill 46	Ling 20 + 2	Coulson 41 + 1	Elokobi 3	Widdowson 44	Koroma 35 + 4	Lawless 7 + 11	Clay 42 + 1	McAnuff 38	Alabi 6 + 20	Bonne 46	Brophy 22 + 15	Dayton 21 + 8	Lee 27 + 8	Ekpiteta 39 + 1	Judd 19	Happe 17 + 3	Gorman 10 + 12	Harrold 3 + 24	Lumeka — + 1	Maguire-Drew 7 + 5	Turley 7 + 3	Simpson 6 + 1	Match No.
1	2^{1}	3	4	5	6^{2}	7^{3}	8	9	10	11	12	13	14										1
1	2	3	4^{3}	5	13	7^{2}	8	6	10	11	9^{1}		14	12									2
1	2	3		5	12		8	6	10^{1}	11	9	13	7^{2}	4									3
1	13	3		2	10	14	6		12	11	8^{1}	7^{3}	9	5	4^{2}								4
1		3^{1}		5	10	14	8	9	13	11		6^{3}	7^{2}	4	2	12							5
1		4		5	11		8	9	13■	10		6^{3}	7^{1}	3	2^{2}		12	14					6
1		3		5	10^{3}	14	8^{1}	9		11		6^{2}	7	4	2		12	13					7
1		3		5	10^{1}		8	9		11		6	7	4	2			12					8
1		3		5	10	12	8	9^{3}		11		6^{1}	7^{2}	4	2			13	14				9
1		3		5	10		8^{1}	9	13	11		6^{2}	7	4	2			12					10
1		3		5	10^{1}		8	6	12	11^{2}		9	7^{3}	4	2		13	14					11
1		3		5	10^{3}		8^{2}	6	12	11^{1}		9	7	4	2		13	14					12
1		3		2	11		7^{2}	6	14	10	13	8^{3}	9^{1}	5	4		12						13
1		3		5	10		8	6	14	11	12	9^{3}	7^{2}	4	2^{1}		13						14
1		3		5			8	6	10^{1}	11	12	9^{2}	7^{3}	4	2		13	14					15
1	12	3		5■	13		8	6	10	11	7^{2}	9^{1}		4	2^{3}			14					16
1	2^{1}	3			10		8	6	14	11	12	9^{3}	7^{2}	4	5		13						17
1		3			10		8	6		11	5	9^{1}	7	4	2			12					18
1		3		5	10		2	6	13	11	12	9^{2}	7^{1}	4			8						19
1		3		5	10		8	7	14	11	13	9^{1}		4^{2}	2	12	6^{3}						20
1		3		5	10		8	6	13	11	12	9^{1}		4	2		7^{2}						21
1		4		3	10		8^{1}	7	13	11	12	9^{2}		5	2		6						22
1	2^{2}	3		5	10	12	8	6	14	11	13	9^{3}		4			7^{1}						23
1	2^{2}	4		3	11	14	8	7	13	10	12	9^{1}		5			6^{3}						24
1	2	3		5	10		6	7	14	11^{1}	9^{2}		8^{3}	4			12	13					25
1	2	3		5	9		7		10^{1}	11	6		8^{2}	4			13	12					26
1	2	4		5	9	12			13	11	6^{2}		7	3			8	10^{1}					27
1	2	3		5	10	12		6		11	9^{1}		8	4			7^{2}	13					28
1	2	3^{3}		5	10	12		9		11	6		8^{2}	4		14	7^{1}			13			29
1	2		4^{2}	5	10	8	12			11	9		7^{3}			3		13		6^{1}	14		30
1	2			5	10^{2}	14	8	9		11	13		7^{3}			3		12		6^{1}	4		31
1				5		13	7	9	12	10	6		8^{1}		2	3		11^{2}			4		32
1	2			5			7	9		10	6		8^{2}			3	14	13		12	4^{1}	11^{3}	33
1	2	4		3			8	7		10			13	6		5		12		9^{1}		11^{2}	34
1	2	4		3			8	7		11	13		14	6		5^{2}				9^{3}	12	10^{1}	35
1	2^{2}	14		3			8	7		10	12			4		6		13		9^{1}	5	11^{3}	36
1	2	4		6			8	7		11	12	13		3		5		10^{1}		9^{2}			37
1		4		6	10^{3}		8	7	13	11	9^{1}	12		3		5	14				2^{2}		38
1		4		6	10^{1}	2^{3}	8	7^{2}		11	9	14	12	3		5						13	39
1		4		6	13	2^{2}	8		12	11	9		7	3■		5						10^{1}	40
1		3		5^{3}	9	2^{1}	8			11	6	12	7^{2}			4		13		14		10	41
1	2^{2}	5		3	10	4^{1}	6			7	9	12		11		8		13					42
1	2^{3}	4		6	10^{2}		8			11	9	12■	14	3		5	7^{1}	13					43
1		3		5	10^{2}		8	6		11	9			2		4		12		7^{1}	13		44
1		4		6	10^{3}		8	7^{1}		11	9		13	3		5		12		14	2^{2}		45
1		4		6	10^{3}		8	7^{2}		11	9^{1}		12	3		5		13		14	2		46

FA Cup

Fourth Qualifying	Maidstone U	(a)	0-2

FA Trophy

First Round	Beaconsfield T	(h)	4-0
Second Round	Wrexham	(a)	1-0
Third Round	Blyth Spartans	(h)	1-0
Fourth Round	Brackley T	(a)	2-1
Semi-Final 1st Leg	AFC Telford U	(h)	1-0
Semi-Final 2nd Leg	AFC Telford U	(a)	2-1
Final	AFC Fylde	Wembley	0-1

MAIDENHEAD UNITED

Ground: York Road, Maidenhead, Berkshire SL6 1SF. *Tel:* (01628) 636 314.
Website: pitchero.com/clubs/maidenheadunited *Email:* social@maidenheadunitedfc.org *Year Formed:* 1870.
Record Attendance: 7,920 v Southall, FA Amateur Cup quarter-final, 7 March 1936. *Nickname:* 'The Magpies'.
Manager: Alan Devonshire. *Colours:* Black and white striped shirts with red trim, black shorts with red trim, white socks with red trim.

MAIDENHEAD UNITED – NATIONAL LEAGUE 2018–19 LEAGUE RECORD

Match No.	*Date*	*Venue*	*Opponents*	*Result*		*H/T Score*	*Lg Pos.*	*Goalscorers*	*Attendance*
1	Aug 4	H	Gateshead	L	1-3	0-1	22	Kerr (og) [90]	1264
2	7	A	Solihull Moors	L	0-1	0-1	24		730
3	11	A	Dagenham & R	D	2-2	1-0	22	Obileye [15], Owusu [81]	1069
4	14	H	Wrexham	L	0-2	0-2	24		1584
5	18	A	Hartlepool U	L	1-2	0-0	24	Massey [80]	2925
6	25	H	Maidstone U	W	3-2	1-1	20	Upward [2], Clifton [77], De Havilland (og) [90]	1339
7	27	A	Braintree T	W	2-0	2-0	18	Clifton [27], Obileye [45]	576
8	Sept 1	H	Bromley	D	2-2	1-0	18	Clifton [33], Kelly [62]	1201
9	4	H	Eastleigh	W	2-0	2-0	14	Kelly 2 [44, 45]	1212
10	8	A	Barnet	L	0-1	0-1	14		1569
11	15	H	FC Halifax T	W	3-0	3-0	13	Kelly 2 [12, 36], Clifton [18]	1306
12	22	A	Barrow	L	0-2	0-1	15		1520
13	25	A	Chesterfield	W	3-1	2-0	13	Alves 2 [8, 45], Upward [69]	3681
14	29	H	Salford C	L	0-3	0-2	16		1726
15	Oct 6	H	Leyton Orient	L	0-2	0-2	17		2016
16	13	A	Boreham Wood	L	1-3	0-1	18	Bird [77]	684
17	27	H	AFC Fylde	L	0-6	0-2	18		1372
18	30	A	Havant & W	L	0-7	0-2	18		952
19	Nov 3	A	Dover Ath	L	0-2	0-1	21		872
20	24	A	Sutton U	W	1-0	0-0	20	Clifton [85]	1606
21	27	H	Ebbsfleet U	D	1-1	0-1	20	Cole, R [73]	1055
22	Dec 1	H	Harrogate T	L	1-2	1-1	20	Clifton [25]	1090
23	8	H	Hartlepool U	L	0-1	0-1	22		1157
24	22	A	Bromley	L	0-1	0-1	22		1073
25	26	H	Aldershot T	W	4-3	1-1	21	Clifton [28], Kelly [51], Odametey [54], Kilgour [62]	1853
26	29	H	Braintree T	L	0-1	0-0	22		1218
27	Jan 1	A	Aldershot T	D	0-0	0-0	22		2090
28	5	A	Gateshead	W	1-0	1-0	20	Clerima [29]	581
29	15	A	Maidstone U	W	4-2	3-1	19	Kilgour [10], Clifton 2 [31, 47], Nombe [41]	1829
30	19	H	Solihull Moors	L	1-2	1-1	20	Clifton (pen) [40]	1180
31	26	A	Wrexham	L	0-1	0-0	20		4323
32	Feb 9	H	Boreham Wood	W	1-0	0-0	19	Akintunde [74]	1113
33	16	A	Leyton Orient	W	1-0	0-0	16	Clifton [53]	5337
34	23	H	Dover Ath	W	1-0	1-0	16	Clifton [13]	1244
35	Mar 2	A	AFC Fylde	L	1-2	1-1	18	Upward [10]	1402
36	5	H	Dagenham & R	D	1-1	0-0	18	Kilgour [90]	1156
37	9	H	Sutton U	W	1-0	0-0	16	Upward [90]	1210
38	12	A	Ebbsfleet U	L	0-3	0-0	17		811
39	16	A	Harrogate T	L	0-1	0-0	18		1105
40	26	H	Havant & W	W	2-1	0-0	18	Upward [62], Clifton [86]	1230
41	30	A	FC Halifax T	W	1-0	0-0	17	Obileye (pen) [72]	1336
42	Apr 6	H	Barnet	L	0-1	0-1	17		1491
43	13	A	Salford C	L	0-3	0-3	20		2419
44	19	H	Barrow	D	1-1	0-1	20	Fondop-Talom [74]	1820
45	22	A	Eastleigh	L	0-2	0-2	20		2146
46	27	H	Chesterfield	W	2-0	0-0	19	Obileye [70], Clifton [77]	1555

Final League Position: 19

GOALSCORERS

League (45): Clifton 14 (1 pen), Kelly 6, Upward 5, Obileye 4 (1 pen), Kilgour 3, Alves 2, Akintunde 1, Bird 1, Clerima 1, Cole R 1, Fondop-Talom 1, Massey 1, Nombe 1, Odametey 1, Owusu 1, own goals 2.
FA Cup (2): Clifton 1, Smith 1.
FA Trophy (1): Owusu 1.

Pentney 45	Clerima 41	Massey 43	Obileye 37	Kilman 1	Mulley 7 + 6	Odametey 38 + 6	Comley 38	Worsfold 19 + 7	Bird 13 + 13	Kelly 22 + 17	Owusu 12 + 12	Clifton 31 + 9	Alves 4 + 9	Steer 36	Smith 7 + 3	Cole C 5 + 4	Sheckelford 2 + 1	Upward 22 + 3	Akintunde 15 + 15	Archer 4 + 4	Hamann 1	Kilgour 17	Nana Ofori-Twumasi 22 + 1	Tarpey 1 + 2	Cole R 1 + 5	Nombe 13 + 1	Fondop-Talom 6 + 5	Gabriel 3 + 2	Match No.
1	2	3	4	5	6^{3}	7	8	9^{1}	10	11^{2}	12	13	14																1
1	2	5	6			7	8^{1}	9	11^{3}	13	4^{2}	14	12	3	10														2
1	2	11■	5		13	4	6	8	7^{2}		10	9		3^{1}	12														3
1	2		3			7	8	9	11	12	5^{2}	10^{1}			6	4	13												4
1	2	11	4		13	3	5	7^{3}	6^{2}	14	10^{1}	12				8		9											5
1	2	3	4		12	6	8^{2}	9^{3}	10^{1}	13		11	14	5				7											6
1	2	10	4		11^{1}	3				6^{2}	13	8^{3}	5		14	7		9	12										7
1	2	3	4		8	6				10^{3}	9^{1}	11^{2}		5		12		7	13	14									8
1	2	3	4		13	6				10^{2}	9^{1}			5	8			7	12	11									9
1	2	9	5		10^{2}	4		13		6	8^{3}		12	3				7	14	11^{1}									10
1	2	3	4■		12	6	7	8		11	13	9^{1}		5^{2}				10^{3}		14									11
1	4	3				6	7	8	14	11	13	9		5^{2}	12	2^{3}		10^{1}											12
1	2	4^{2}	3			12	6	7	13			14	5		9			8	11^{3}	10^{1}									13
1	2		3			7	5^{1}	6		11	14	10	4^{2}		8	12		9^{3}	13										14
1	2	5	4			6	7	8^{1}	10^{3}	11		12	13			3			9^{2}	14									15
1	2	4	5		9^{1}	6		7	14	13				3	8	12			10^{3}	11^{2}									16
1	2	5	4		14	6	7^{1}	8	10^{2}					3	9■			13	11^{3}	12									17
1■	2	6	4		11	7	9	14	13		5^{2}	10^{3}	8^{1}	3		12													18
	2	5	4		9^{1}	6	7		10^{2}	12	13	8	14	3					11^{3}		1								19
1	2^{1}	11	4				6	9	7	8^{2}		13	12	3								5	10						20
1		6	4			8^{1}	9	10		12		7		2								5	3	11^{2}	13				21
1	2	5	4^{2}			14	8		11	12		10^{3}	13	3								7	6		9^{1}				22
1	2	11	4^{1}			14	6■	8^{2}	13	7		10^{3}		3								5	9		12				23
1	2	7	4			8		9^{2}		11		10		3					13			5^{1}	6		12				24
1	2^{1}	7	5			8			14	11^{3}	9	10^{2}		3								4	6	13	12				25
1	2	6	4^{2}			10			14	11^{1}	7^{3}	9	12	3								8	5	13					26
1	2	6				7	8	9^{2}	10	11^{1}				3					13			5	4		12				27
1	2	11	5^{3}			4	7		8^{1}	12		14		3				13	10^{2}			6	9						28
1		10	4■			3	6		14		12	8^{3}		2			7	13	9^{1}			5				11^{2}			29
1		2				6	7		13		12	8		5				9^{2}	11^{1}			3	4			10			30
1		3				9	6		13	12	14	7^{2}		2				8	10^{1}			4	5			11^{3}			31
1		5				6■	7		13	11^{1}		8^{2}		2				9	12			3	4			10			32
1	2	10	4				6			14	13	7^{2}		3				9	8^{3}			5				11^{1}	12		33
1	2	10	4^{3}			12	6					7^{2}		3				9	8			5	14			11^{1}	13		34
1	3	2	5^{2}			13	7			14		8^{1}		4				9	11^{3}			6				10	12		35
1	2	10				4	6^{2}			7^{3}	14	8^{1}		3				9	13			5				11	12		36
1	2	6	5			7	8	13		12				3^{1}				9	10^{2}				4				11■		37
1	2	11	4^{1}			3	5^{2}	14		12	10^{3}	8					7	9					6			13			38
1	2	6	4			14	7^{2}	13		12		8		3				9	10^{1}				5			11^{3}			39
1	2	11	5			4	6		13	12		8^{2}		3				10	9^{1}				7						40
1	2		4			7	8			9^{2}		13		3					12				5			11	10^{1}	6	41
1	2	4				7	8	12	14	9^{1}		6							13				3			11^{2}	10^{3}	5	42
1	6	3	4^{1}			8	7	13		10^{2}		11		5				9^{3}	14				2				12		43
1	2	8				3	4	6^{1}		5^{2}		12							13				7			11	9	10	44
1	2	9				4	5			6^{1}	13	8		3^{3}					14				7			11^{2}	10	12	45
1	2	10	5^{2}			4	6			13	9^{1}	8		3					12				7				11^{3}	14	46

FA Cup

Fourth Qualifying	Chippenham T	(a)	1-1
Replay	Chippenham T	(h)	1-0
First Round	Portsmouth	(h)	0-4

FA Trophy

First Round *(aet)*	Oxford C	(h)	1-2

MAIDSTONE UNITED

Ground: Gallagher Stadium, James Whatman Way, Maidstone ME14 1LQ. *Tel:* (01622) 753817.
Website: www.maidstoneunited.co.uk *Email:* See website. *Year Formed:* 1897 (Reformed 1992).
Record Attendance: 4,101 v Crystal Palace, Friendly, 15 July 2017 (Gallagher Stadium).
Nickname: 'The Stones'. *Manager:* Hakan Hayrettin. *Colours:* Amber shirts with black stripes, black shorts, black socks.

MAIDSTONE UNITED – NATIONAL LEAGUE 2018–19 LEAGUE RECORD

Match No.	Date	Venue	Opponents	Result	H/T Score	Lg Pos.	Goalscorers	Attendance
1	Aug 4	H	Hartlepool U	D 1-1	1-1	11	Turgott (pen) [41]	2599
2	7	A	Dagenham & R	W 2-1	1-0	5	Turgott 2 [41, 51]	1405
3	11	A	FC Halifax T	L 0-3	0-1	10		1534
4	14	H	Leyton Orient	L 1-2	0-2	16	Mullings [80]	3037
5	18	H	Barrow	W 1-0	1-0	13	Mullings [6]	2003
6	25	A	Maidenhead U	L 2-3	1-1	16	Turgott 2 (1 pen) [45, 57 (p)]	1339
7	27	H	Boreham Wood	L 1-2	1-0	19	Paxman [45]	2035
8	Sept 1	A	Gateshead	L 0-1	0-0	19		564
9	4	H	Sutton U	L 0-1	0-1	19		1838
10	8	A	Salford C	L 0-1	0-0	22		2273
11	15	H	Harrogate T	L 0-2	0-2	22		2222
12	22	A	Braintree T	W 1-0	0-0	20	Turgott (pen) [90]	807
13	25	A	Aldershot T	W 1-0	1-0	18	Turgott [25]	1619
14	29	H	Chesterfield	D 1-1	1-0	18	Turgott [31]	2438
15	Oct 6	H	Bromley	L 0-1	0-1	19		2294
16	13	A	AFC Fylde	L 0-2	0-0	20		1507
17	27	H	Solihull Moors	L 1-3	1-2	20	Turgott [9]	2106
18	30	A	Ebbsfleet U	D 1-1	0-0	21	De Havilland [75]	2003
19	Nov 3	A	Barnet	W 2-0	1-0	18	Turgott [28], Omotayo [80]	1424
20	17	H	Wrexham	D 1-1	0-0	18	Walton [64]	2626
21	24	A	Havant & W	L 2-5	0-2	22	Paxman [77], Turgott [78]	1308
22	27	H	Eastleigh	L 1-3	0-1	22	Phillips [89]	1570
23	Dec 8	A	Barrow	L 0-1	0-0	23		804
24	22	H	Gateshead	L 2-3	0-2	23	Cassidy [79], McLennan [82]	2131
25	26	A	Dover Ath	L 1-3	1-0	23	Robinson [7]	1937
26	29	A	Boreham Wood	W 1-0	1-0	23	Cassidy [7]	630
27	Jan 1	H	Dover Ath	L 0-1	0-0	23		3087
28	5	A	Hartlepool U	W 2-1	2-1	23	Powell 2 [4, 40]	2929
29	15	H	Maidenhead U	L 2-4	1-3	23	De Havilland 2 [14, 62]	1829
30	19	H	Dagenham & R	L 0-3	0-1	23		2188
31	26	A	Leyton Orient	L 0-3	0-1	23		5488
32	Feb 9	H	AFC Fylde	D 1-1	0-1	23	Philliskirk (og) [60]	2033
33	16	A	Bromley	L 0-2	0-1	23		2589
34	19	H	FC Halifax T	L 0-1	0-0	23		1813
35	Mar 2	A	Solihull Moors	L 0-5	0-4	23		956
36	9	H	Havant & W	W 2-0	2-0	23	Embery [33], Powell [42]	1901
37	12	A	Eastleigh	L 0-2	0-1	23		1642
38	16	A	Wrexham	L 0-1	0-0	23		3604
39	23	H	Ebbsfleet U	L 0-2	0-1	23		3002
40	30	A	Harrogate T	D 2-2	1-1	24	Amaluzor 2 [45, 52]	1134
41	Apr 6	H	Salford C	L 0-2	0-2	24		2050
42	9	H	Barnet	W 2-1	0-1	23	Amaluzor [46], Swaine [70]	1471
43	13	A	Chesterfield	L 1-4	1-1	24	Turgott [36]	4592
44	19	H	Braintree T	L 0-2	0-1	24		1908
45	22	A	Sutton U	D 2-2	0-1	24	Turgott 2 (2 pens) [53, 90]	1858
46	27	H	Aldershot T	L 0-2	0-0	24		1929

Final League Position: 24

GOALSCORERS

League (37): Turgott 14 (5 pens), Amaluzor 3, De Havilland 3, Powell 3, Cassidy 2, Mullings 2, Paxman 2, Embery 1, McLennan 1, Omotayo 1, Phillips 1, Robinson 1, Swaine 1, Walton 1, own goal 1.
FA Cup (4): Turgott 2 (1 pen), Powell 1, Romain 1.
FA Trophy (9): Phillips 3, De Havilland 2, Cassidy 1, Richards 1, Romain 1, Shields 1.

Henry 6 Worgan 17	Nana Ofori-Twumasi 13 + 1	De Havilland 42	Meredith 3 Finney 20	McLennan 16 + 2	Muldoon 24 + 7	Lewis 13	Phillips 31 + 11	Turgott 31	Loza 7 + 4	Davies 12 Quigley 4 + 7	Paxman 22 + 8	Donnellan S 10 Mullings 8 + 3	Wynter 5 + 3	Amaluzor 10 + 3 Coker 4 + 5	Efete 8	Richards 2 + 3	Walton 24 + 1	Lewington 9 + 1 Durojaiye 3 + 3	Doyle 7	Cassidy 22 + 1	Pitoula-Wabo — + 2	Embery 3 + 7 Wilson 3 + 1	Omotayo 1 + 4	Powell 27 + 2	Romain 15 + 11	Donnellan L — + 1 Smith 5	Swaine 14 + 3	Tajbakhsh 5 + 7	Wishart 18 + 1	Dale — + 1 Shields 3 + 1	Worner 5	Wassmer 6	Robinson 8 + 3	Edobor 3 + 4	Ross 4	Taylor 13 + 2	Philpot — + 1	*Match No.*
1	2	3	4	5	6^{1}	7	8^{2}	9	10	11^{3}	12	13	14																									1
1	2	3^{2}	4	5	6	7	13	9	10	11^{3}	8^{1}	14	12																									2
1	10	4	5^{2}	2	11^{3}	6		7	8^{1}	14	13	9	3	12																								3
1	5	3	4		7^{2}	6	8^{1}	10	11^{3}	9	12	14		13	2																							4
1	4	3			6	7	12	10	13	14	8^{2}	11^{1}	5	9^{3}	2																							5
1	5	3			6^{2}	7		10	12	13	8	11	4	9^{1}	2																							6
1	5	3	4		8^{1}	6	13	10		11	7^{2}		12	9	2																							7
1	3	4	5	6^{3}	7		8	10■	13	14	9^{2}	11		12	2^{1}																							8
1	6	3	5		7	8^{1}	9		10		13	11	4^{2}	12	2																							9
1	3	5	2		7		8		10		9^{1}	11	6^{2}	12	4	13																						10
1	5	3	4	13		8	7			12	9^{1}	11		10^{2}	2		6																					11
1		2	3			4	13	6	11		5^{3}	7^{2}					9	8^{1}	10	12	14																	12
1		2	3			7	12	10^{2}	13		8						5	9^{1}	4	11		6																13
1		2	4			6	8	10		12	9^{2}						7		3	11^{1}	13	5																14
1		3	4		13	5^{1}	12	10		14	6						7^{3}		2	11		8	9^{2}															15
1	5^{3}	2	3		9^{1}		14	10			7						8		4^{2}	11		12	13	6														16
1	2^{3}	3	4	14	7^{2}			10			9						6		5^{1}	11			13	8	12													17
	12	2	4		14		7	9			8						6^{1}		5	11^{2}			13		10	1	3^{3}											18
		3	2	4			6	9			8^{1}						5	12		11			13	7	10^{2}	1												19
		2	3	4	14		6^{1}	9			8^{3}						5	13		11				7^{2}	10	1	12											20
		3	2	5	13			9			8						6^{1}	14		11				7^{2}	10■	1	4^{3}	12										21
		2	3				4	9^{2}								5	8^{1}		10				6	11	1		13	7	12								22
				2	7^{3}		8				14						6^{2}			11					13		4	12	9	5	1	3^{1}	10					23
				2^{3}	6^{1}		7				3^{2}						5			8				13	11		14	12	9	4	1		10					24
				5			2				14						8			11				13	12		3■	7^{3}	9^{2}	6	1	4	10^{1}					25
		3		2	7		8				5^{2}									9				4	13			10^{1}	6■		1	11		12				26
		4		2^{3}	7		8				6^{1}					14				10				5	11			9^{2}			1	3	13	12				27
		3		5	7		2				9													8	13			6^{2}				4	11^{1}	12	1	10		28
		3		5^{2}	7■		2				8													9	13		14	12				4^{3}	11	6	1	10^{1}		29
		2					5^{2}				13						6^{1}							7	9		4	14	11				10^{3}	3	1	8	12	30
		3	2	5			7^{1}										6							8	12		4		10				11		1	9		31
1		3	2^{3}		9^{2}		10			4	13	11					8			7				5^{1}				14	6				12					32
1		3			7^{1}		5			2		4		13						10				8	14			6^{2}	9				11^{3}			12		33
1^{3}		5	2	4			7			6		3^{1}		10				12		11				8	9^{2}								14	13				34
1		3			6		7	10^{1}				2		9^{2}			4					12		8	11	13			5								35
		3			13		6	9		5^{1}		2						1				8^{2}		7	10		4		11						12		36
		3			12		5^{1}	9		4		2		13				1				11^{2}		6	10				8							7		37
		4				7	10		3		2		11^{1}			6	1				12		8					5							9		38
1		3				13	10		4		2		9^{2}			5			11		12		6					8							7^{1}		39
		3				12	10		5		2		9^{2}			6	1		11				7			4		13							8^{1}		40
		3				12	9		2^{1}		5		10^{3}			6^{2}	1		11		13		7	14		4									8		41
		2			12		9	4						5			8^{1}	1		7^{2}				3	13		11		6							10		42
		2				6	9		4				10		13		1				12		5	11^{2}		3		8							7^{1}		43
					6		2	10		3				12		9^{2}	14	1				11^{1}		7^{3}	13		4		5							8		44
1		3			6		12	10		2				9		8^{1}						13		7^{2}	11		4		5								45
		2			7		8	5^{2}						6				1				12		3	4		10			13				11		9^{1}		46

FA Cup

Fourth Qualifying	Leyton Orient	(h)	2-0
First Round	Macclesfield T	(h)	2-1
Second Round	Oldham Ath	(h)	0-2

FA Trophy

First Round	Woking	(a)	1-1
Replay (aet)	Woking	(h)	3-2
Second Round	Oxford C	(h)	1-0
Third Round	Salford C	(a)	1-1
Replay	Salford C	(h)	3-0
Fourth Round	Stockport Co	(h)	0-3

SALFORD CITY

Ground: The Peninsula Stadium, Moor Lane, Salford, Greater Manchester M7 3PZ. *Tel:* (01617) 926 287.
Website: salfordcityfc.co.uk *Email:* enquiries@salfordcityfc.co.uk
Year Formed: 1940 (Salford Central, changing to Salford Amateurs in 1963, and Salford City in 1989).
Record Attendance: 4,044 v Wrexham, National League, 1 January 2019. *Nickname:* 'The Ammies'.
Manager: Graham Alexander. *Colours:* Red shirts with white trim, white shorts, white socks.

SALFORD CITY – NATIONAL LEAGUE 2018–19 LEAGUE RECORD

Match No.	*Date*	*Venue*	*Opponents*	*Result*		*H/T Score*	*Lg Pos.*	*Goalscorers*	*Attendance*
1	Aug 4	H	Leyton Orient	D	1-1	0-0	11	Gaffney [47]	2156
2	7	A	Gateshead	L	1-2	1-1	17	Rooney [11]	1243
3	11	A	Sutton U	L	1-2	1-1	21	Piergianni [20]	1898
4	14	H	FC Halifax T	W	2-1	1-0	14	Rooney 2 [11, 83]	2632
5	18	H	Chesterfield	W	3-2	1-1	12	Rooney [19], Piergianni [56], Whitehead [89]	3595
6	25	A	Havant & W	D	1-1	1-1	14	Rooney [35]	1679
7	27	H	Barrow	W	3-1	1-1	10	Rooney [29], Pond [62], Lloyd (pen) [65]	3012
8	Sept 1	A	Dagenham & R	D	0-0	0-0	11		1114
9	4	A	AFC Fylde	W	2-0	1-0	9	Walker [26], Rooney [69]	2941
10	8	H	Maidstone U	W	1-0	0-0	6	Mullings (og) [47]	2273
11	15	A	Bromley	W	2-0	1-0	4	Gaffney [36], Walker [61]	2020
12	22	H	Boreham Wood	W	3-1	2-0	4	Walker [3], Shelton [21], Gaffney [52]	2006
13	25	H	Hartlepool U	W	3-0	0-0	2	Lloyd [64], Rooney [69], Walker [75]	2420
14	29	A	Maidenhead U	W	3-0	2-0	1	Wiseman [24], Rooney [26], Rodney [90]	1726
15	Oct 6	A	Dover Ath	W	4-1	2-0	1	Rooney 3 [18, 20, 56], Piergianni [66]	1127
16	13	H	Braintree T	D	2-2	1-1	1	Gaffney 2 [1, 90]	2710
17	27	H	Ebbsfleet U	D	1-1	1-1	2	Gaffney [38]	2498
18	30	A	Barnet	W	3-1	1-1	1	Gaffney [45], Walker [47], Shelton [64]	1243
19	Nov 3	A	Eastleigh	D	1-1	0-0	3	Maynard [90]	2253
20	17	H	Aldershot T	W	4-0	2-0	2	Rooney 3 (1 pen) [2, 35, 65 (p)], Gaffney [46]	2875
21	24	A	Solihull Moors	D	0-0	0-0	2		2216
22	27	H	Harrogate T	W	3-2	2-2	2	Whitehead [11], Rooney [44], Gaffney [57]	1206
23	Dec 1	H	Havant & W	W	3-0	2-0	2	Rooney [22], Politic [23], Whitehead [90]	2181
24	8	A	Chesterfield	L	0-2	0-1	2		5055
25	22	H	Dagenham & R	L	1-2	1-1	2	Piergianni [13]	2082
26	26	A	Wrexham	L	1-5	0-3	3	Rooney [90]	8283
27	29	A	Barrow	L	2-3	0-1	4	Green [59], Touray [84]	2311
28	Jan 1	H	Wrexham	W	2-0	1-0	3	Green [23], Gaffney [60]	4044
29	5	A	Leyton Orient	W	3-0	2-0	2	Piergianni 2 [6, 81], Gaffney [8]	6937
30	19	H	Gateshead	D	1-1	1-1	3	Lloyd (pen) [28]	2055
31	26	A	FC Halifax T	D	0-0	0-0	2		2115
32	Feb 9	A	Braintree T	L	0-1	0-0	5		765
33	16	H	Dover Ath	L	1-3	1-1	5	Politic [9]	2498
34	23	H	Eastleigh	L	0-2	0-1	6		2329
35	Mar 2	A	Ebbsfleet U	W	1-0	1-0	5	Piergianni [32]	1708
36	5	H	Sutton U	W	2-0	1-0	5	Dieseruvwe [12], Piergianni [55]	1686
37	9	H	Solihull Moors	W	2-0	0-0	4	Hogan [55], Green [82]	2476
38	16	A	Aldershot T	W	1-0	1-0	4	Redmond [44]	1668
39	23	H	Barnet	D	0-0	0-0	4		2452
40	27	A	Harrogate T	W	1-0	0-0	3	Redmond (pen) [51]	1700
41	30	H	Bromley	W	2-1	0-0	2	Maynard [88], Pond [90]	2314
42	Apr 6	A	Maidstone U	W	2-0	2-0	1	Rooney 2 [13, 42]	2050
43	13	H	Maidenhead U	W	3-0	3-0	2	Dieseruvwe [10], Touray [26], Rooney (pen) [44]	2419
44	19	A	Boreham Wood	W	3-2	2-1	2	Piergianni [6], Hogan [22], Green [88]	854
45	22	H	AFC Fylde	L	0-1	0-1	2		3338
46	27	A	Hartlepool U	L	2-3	1-0	3	Rooney [3], Dieseruvwe [87]	3582

Final League Position: 3

GOALSCORERS

League (77): Rooney 22 (2 pens), Gaffney 11, Piergianni 9, Walker 5, Green 4, Dieseruvwe 3, Lloyd 3 (2 pens), Whitehead 3, Hogan 2, Maynard 2, Politic 2, Pond 2, Redmond 2 (1 pen), Shelton 2, Touray 2, Rodney 1, Wiseman 1, own goal 1.
FA Cup (4): Rooney 2, Gaffney 1, Whitehead 1.
FA Trophy (6): Dieseruvwe 3, Rodney 3.
National League Play-Offs (4): Dieseruvwe 1, Piergianni 2, Touray 1.

Neal 46	Wiseman 46	Touray 45	Hogan 22 + 21	Piergianni 46	Maynard 20 + 9	Rooney 34 + 4	Lloyd 28 + 2	Walker 29 + 10	Whitehead 34 + 4	Gaffney 32 + 11	Haughton 3 + 5	Mafuta 16 + 4	Shelton 13 + 1	Rodney — + 15	Pond 41	Politic 4 + 5	Moncrieffe — + 1	Nolan 5 + 2	Dieseruvwe 11 + 10	Green 15 + 6	Brockbank — + 1	Glynn — + 1	Muscatt 2	Linganzi 3 + 1	Redmond 11 + 2	Match No.
1	2	3	4	5	6	7	8[2]	9[1]	10	11	12	13														1
1	2	3	4[2]	5	7	8		9	10	11	6[1]	12	13													2
1	2	3	5	6	7	8		12	9	11[2]	13	4[3]	10[1]	14												3
1	2	3	13	4	5	9	10[1]	12	7	11	6[2]				8											4
1	2	3	12	4	5	9	10[1]	6[2]	7	11[3]		14		13	8											5
1	2	3	4[1]	5	6	7	8	13	9	11[2]				12	10											6
1	2[1]	3	12	4	13	9	10	6[2]	7	11		5			8											7
1	2	3	14	4	5	9	10■	6[2]	7	11[1]		13[3]		12	8											8
1	2	5	13	4		11		9	7	10[2]	6[1]		8	12	3											9
1	2	3	14	4		10	11[1]	5[3]	6	9[2]	13		7	12	8											10
1	2	3	12	4	13	5	6[2]	7[1]	8	11			9		10											11
1	2	3	14	4	12	10[3]	11[2]	5[1]	6	9			7	13	8											12
1	2	3	12	4	14	10[3]	9[2]	5[1]	6	11			7	13	8											13
1	2	3	14	4	12	11[1]	10[3]	5[2]	6	9			7	13	8											14
1	2	3	12	4		10[3]	11[2]	5[1]	6	9	14		7	13	8											15
1	2	5	13	3		10	9[3]	6	7	11	12		8[1]	14	4[2]											16
1	2	3		4		9	10[2]	5[1]	6	11			7	13	8	12										17
1	2	3	12	4	13	9	10[1]	5[2]	6	11			7		8											18
1	2	3	14	4	13	9	10[1]	5[2]	6	11			7[3]		8	12										19
1	2	3	14	4		11[1]	9	12	7	10[3]			6[2]		5	8	13									20
1	2	3	12	4	5	10	9	6[1]	7	11					8											21
1	2	3	14	4	5[1]	9	10[3]	6[2]	7	11					8	13		12								22
1	2	3	13	4		10[2]	11	6	7	9[1]					8	12		5[3]	14							23
1	2	3[1]	14	4		9	10	6	7	11[2]					8	12		5[3]	13							24
1	2	3	14	4		11	10[2]	5	6	9[3]					8	7[1]			13	12						25
1	2[3]	3	12	5		7	8	9■	10	13		4[1]		14	11[2]					6						26
1	2	3	4	5		10	11[1]		7			6■			8[2]			12	13	9						27
1	2	3	4	5				9	8	10[2]					7			6	12	11[1]	13					28
1	2	3	4	5		13		7	9[1]	11				12	10			8		6[2]						29
1	2	3	5	6		12	10[2]	7		11[3]				14	8[1]			4		9		13				30
1	2	3		4		6	7[2]	8	10	12					11				13	5[1]			9			31
1	2	3	4[3]	5			13	12	7	11					6	9[2]			14	10			8[1]			32
1	2	3		6	12		13	11	7	9					5	8[2]			14	10[1]				4[3]		33
1	2	3	4	5	14		7[2]	8	9	11									12	6[3]				10[1]	13	34
1	2	3	4	5	6					12		9			8				11[1]	10					7	35
1	2	3	5	6	8			13		12		4			11				10[1]	7[2]					9	36
1	2	3	5	6	4					12		7			9				10	11[1]					8	37
1	2	3	4	6	5	13				12		7			9				10[1]	11[2]					8	38
1	2[1]		4	6	8	14		3	12	13		11[3]			5				10	9[2]					7	39
1	5	9	2	4	6					10[1]		7			3				11	12					8	40
1	2	3	5[3]	6	7	8[2]		14		13		4			11				10[1]	12					9	41
1	2	3	5	6	7	8[3]		13	12	14		4[2]			11				10						9[1]	42
1	2	6	3	5	7	11[3]		14	12			9[2]			4				10	13					8[1]	43
1	2	5	4	3		11			12	14		6			8[2]				10[1]	13				9	7[3]	44
1	2[2]	3	4	5	6	10		13		12		7			9				11[3]	14					8[1]	45
1	2	3	4	5[1]	6	10[2]	11		8			7[3]							12	9■				14	13	46

FA Cup

Fourth Qualifying	Marine	(a)	2-1
First Round	Shrewsbury T	(a)	1-1
Replay	Shrewsbury T	(h)	1-3

FA Trophy

First Round	Gateshead	(h)	3-1
Second Round	Dagenham & R	(h)	2-0
Third Round	Maidstone U	(h)	1-1
Replay	Maidstone U	(a)	0-3

National League Play-Offs

Semi-Finals	Eastleigh	(h)	1-1
(aet; Salford C won 4-3 on penalties)			
Final	AFC Fylde	Wembley	3-0

SOLIHULL MOORS

Ground: The Automated Technology Group Stadium, Damson Parkway, Solihull, West Midlands B92 9EJ.
Tel: (0121) 705 6770. *Website:* www.solihullmoorsfc.co.uk *Email:* info@solihullmoorsfc.co.uk *Year Formed:* 2007.
Record Attendance: 3,005 v Blackpool, FA Cup 2nd rd, 30 November 2018. *Nickname:* 'Moors'.
Manager: Tim Flowers. *Colours:* Blue shirts with yellow trim, blue shorts, blue socks with yellow trim.

SOLIHULL MOORS – NATIONAL LEAGUE 2018–19 LEAGUE RECORD

Match No.	*Date*	*Venue*	*Opponents*	*Result*		*H/T Score*	*Lg Pos.*	*Goalscorers*	*Attendance*
1	Aug 4	A	Eastleigh	W	2-1	0-0	4	Yussuf 80, Sweeney 83	1354
2	7	H	Maidenhead U	W	1-0	1-0	4	Yussuf 28	730
3	11	H	Aldershot T	W	1-0	0-0	4	Wright 50	867
4	14	A	AFC Fylde	L	1-3	0-2	6	Maxwell 47	1257
5	18	H	Sutton U	D	2-2	0-1	6	Wright 69, Storer 82	763
6	25	A	Harrogate T	L	1-3	1-1	10	Yussuf 11	1180
7	27	H	Wrexham	W	1-0	0-0	7	Gudger 81	2412
8	Sept 1	A	Barrow	W	2-1	0-0	6	Maxwell 84, Yussuf 89	1260
9	4	A	Leyton Orient	L	0-3	0-1	8		4250
10	8	H	Hartlepool U	L	0-1	0-0	11		1311
11	15	A	Dover Ath	W	2-0	0-0	8	Hylton 72, Wright 79	823
12	22	H	Bromley	W	5-0	4-0	6	Gudger 2, Carter 10, Hylton 19, Wright 45, Osborne 72	648
13	25	H	Dagenham & R	W	2-0	1-0	5	Wright 20, Hylton 89	753
14	29	A	Havant & W	W	1-0	0-0	5	Yussuf 90	1115
15	Oct 6	A	Barnet	L	0-2	0-0	5		1054
16	13	H	Ebbsfleet U	W	2-1	1-0	5	Hylton 18, Maxwell 83	1505
17	27	A	Maidstone U	W	3-1	2-1	4	Wright 2, Yussuf 8, Hylton 75	2106
18	30	H	FC Halifax T	D	0-0	0-0	6		915
19	Nov 3	H	Boreham Wood	D	0-0	0-0	5		803
20	17	A	Braintree T	W	3-0	0-0	4	Wright 46, Yussuf (pen) 53, Stenson 58	822
21	24	H	Salford C	D	0-0	0-0	5		2216
22	Dec 4	H	Harrogate T	W	2-0	1-0	5	Gudger 36, Yussuf (pen) 85	794
23	8	A	Sutton U	D	2-2	1-1	5	Osborne 2 33, 49	1728
24	22	H	Barrow	L	0-1	0-0	6		958
25	26	A	Chesterfield	W	4-0	2-0	4	Blissett 2 4, 29, Gudger 70, Hylton 83	4877
26	29	A	Wrexham	L	0-1	0-0	5		6220
27	Jan 1	H	Chesterfield	D	2-2	1-0	5	Hylton 36, Gudger 49	1375
28	5	H	Eastleigh	W	4-1	2-0	4	Wright 25, Blissett 35, Hylton 2 55, 70	829
29	8	A	Gateshead	W	2-1	1-0	3	Daly 22, Carter 52	519
30	19	A	Maidenhead U	W	2-1	1-1	2	Daly 30, Yussuf 90	1180
31	26	H	AFC Fylde	L	1-2	0-0	3	Osborne 67	1588
32	Feb 9	A	Ebbsfleet U	W	1-0	0-0	2	Yussuf 51	1325
33	12	A	Aldershot T	W	3-0	1-0	1	Blissett 3 14, 73, 90	1199
34	16	H	Barnet	D	2-2	0-1	1	Blissett 73, Storer 90	1747
35	Mar 2	H	Maidstone U	W	5-0	4-0	2	Hylton 3 (1 pen) 9, 26, 33 (p), Carter 14, Yussuf 90	956
36	9	A	Salford C	L	0-2	0-0	3		2476
37	12	H	Gateshead	W	1-0	0-0	2	Blissett 62	924
38	16	H	Braintree T	W	2-1	1-1	2	Daly 38, Yussuf (pen) 77	1003
39	23	A	FC Halifax T	L	0-2	0-1	2		1563
40	26	A	Boreham Wood	D	2-2	1-1	2	Blissett 8, Yussuf 70	478
41	30	H	Dover Ath	D	2-2	1-2	3	Wright 38, Williams 90	1338
42	Apr 6	A	Hartlepool U	W	1-0	0-0	3	Yussuf 58	2981
43	13	H	Havant & W	W	3-2	1-1	3	Williams 24, Gudger 74, Wright 89	1179
44	19	A	Bromley	W	2-0	1-0	3	Osborne 15, Wright 59	1536
45	22	H	Leyton Orient	D	0-0	0-0	3		3681
46	27	A	Dagenham & R	D	1-1	0-0	2	Hylton 55	1370

Final League Position: 2

GOALSCORERS

League (73): Yussuf 14 (3 pens), Hylton 13 (1 pen), Wright 11, Blissett 9, Gudger 6, Osborne 5, Carter 3, Daly 3, Maxwell 3, Storer 2, Williams 2, Stenson 1, Sweeney 1.
FA Cup (6): Yussuf 4 (2 pens), Daly 1, Wright 1.
FA Trophy (10): Yussuf 3 (1 pen), Blisset 2, Hylton 2, Hawkridge 1, Murphy 1, Osbourne 1.
National League Play-Offs (0).

Boot 46	Daly 44	Gudger 38 + 1	Williams 36 + 2	Reckord 41	Storer 41	Osborne 38 + 2	Carter 44	Yussuf 29 + 16	Thomas 5 + 9	Wright 41	Hylton 28 + 14	Carline 11 + 20	Sweeney 1 + 6	Willock — + 1	Maxwell 11 + 22	Murphy — + 5	O'Keeffe 8 + 5	Flowers 4 + 1	Stenson 4 + 13	Blissett 20 + 2	Hawkridge 6 + 5	Vaughan L 9	Sbarra 1 + 5	*Match No.*
1	2	3^{1}	4	5	6	7	8	9	10^{2}	11^{3}	12	13	14											1
1	4		2	3▮	6	7	5^{3}	10^{1}		11	9^{2}	8	12	13	14									2
1	4		2		3	5^{1}	6	7^{2}	12	11	8^{3}	9	14		10	13								3
1	4		2	3	6	5	7^{2}	11		10		9	8^{1}		12	13								4
1	4		2	3	5	6	7	10^{2}		11	12		13		8^{1}		9							5
1	5	12	2	3	4	6	7^{1}	8^{3}		10	9^{2}		14		13		11							6
1	4	5	2	3	7	6	8	9^{2}		11	10^{1}	12					13							7
1	5	6	2	3	4	7^{1}	8^{2}	9		11^{3}	10	14			13	12								8
1	5	6	2	3▮	4	14	7	8^{1}		10^{3}	13	12			9		11^{2}							9
1	3	2	4		6▮	7	8	9^{2}	12	11^{1}	10	5^{3}	14				13							10
1	3	4	2			5^{2}	6	13	9	11	7^{1}	8			10^{3}	14	12							11
1	4	5	2^{2}	3		7	8^{1}	12	10▮	11	9^{3}	14			13		6							12
1	4	5	2	3		6		7^{1}		10	12	8^{2}			9	13	11							13
1	4	5	2	3	6	7^{1}	8	13	10^{3}	11	9^{2}	14					12							14
1	4	5	2	3	6		7	9^{1}	10^{3}	11	12	13			14		8^{2}							15
1	4	5	2	3	6^{2}	12	7	9^{3}	13	11	10^{1}	14			8									16
1	4		2	3		6^{3}	7	9^{2}	13	11	10^{1}				8		14	5	12					17
1	4		2	3	6^{2}	5	7	8	13	11^{3}	9^{1}				14			10	12					18
1	4	5	2	3	6	7^{1}	8	9^{3}	12	10		13			14				11^{2}					19
1	3	4		2	6^{3}	7	8	9^{1}	12	10		14			13		5		11^{2}					20
1	4	5	2	3	6		7	9^{3}	13	10^{1}	12	14			8				11^{2}					21
1	5	6	2	3	4	7	8^{1}	12	14	10	9^{2}				13				11^{3}					22
1	3^{3}	4		2^{1}	7	5	8	9^{2}		11	10	13					6	12	14					23
1	4	5	2	3	6	7	8^{3}	9^{1}		11	10^{2}	14			12				13					24
1	4	5	2	3	6^{2}	7	8	14		11^{3}	12				9				13	10^{1}				25
1	4	5	2	3	6	7	8	13		11^{2}	12				9^{1}				14	10^{3}				26
1	4	5		2	3^{3}	6	7	8^{2}			9	12			14			11^{1}	13	10				27
1	3	4	2	5	6	7^{1}	8	13		11	9^{3}				12				14	10^{2}				28
1	3	5	2	4	6	7^{2}	8	14		11^{1}	9				12				13	10^{3}				29
1	3	2	4	5	6	8	9^{2}	14		11^{1}	12				13					10	7^{3}			30
1	3	4	2	5	6	7	8^{1}	12		11	9^{3}				13					10^{2}	14			31
1	4	5	2	3	7	6	8^{1}	9^{2}		11▮	10^{3}				12▮					14	13			32
1	3	4	13	2	7	6	8	10^{1}			12	14								11	9^{2}	5^{3}		33
1	4	5		2	3	6	7^{2}	8^{1}			9^{3}	14							12	10	13	11		34
1	2	3			6^{2}	5	7	12		11	9^{1}	8			14					10^{3}	13	4		35
1	3	4		2	7	6	8	12		11	9^{1}									10		5		36
1	4	5		2	3	6	7^{2}	13		10^{3}	8^{1}	14			12					9		11		37
1	5	6		2	3		7	12		10^{1}	8^{3}	13			14					9	4^{2}	11		38
1	3	4	14	2^{1}	6		7	13		11^{2}	12	8								10	9^{3}	5▮		39
1	4	5	2	3	6	7^{1}	8	9^{2}			10^{3}								14	11	13		12	40
1	5▮	6	2	3	4	7	8^{3}	14		11^{2}	9^{1}	12								10			13	41
1		5	2	3	4	6^{2}	7	8^{1}		11^{3}	12	9			14					10			13	42
1		5	2	3	4		6	7^{1}		10		8			14				12	9^{3}	11^{2}		13	43
1	5	6	2	3	4	7^{3}	8	9		11^{1}	12	14								10^{2}			13	44
1	3	4	2	5	8	6	9	10^{1}		11^{2}	12									13		7		45
1	3		2								10	6			7			4	12	11^{1}	8	5	9	46

FA Cup

Fourth Qualifying	Witton Alb	(a)	2-0
First Round	Hitchin T	(a)	2-0
Second Round	Blackpool	(h)	0-0
Replay (aet)	Blackpool	(a)	2-3

National League Play-Offs

Semi-Finals	AFC Fylde	(h)	0-1

FA Trophy

First Round	Southport	(a)	1-0
Second Round	FC Halifax T	(a)	2-2
Replay	FC Halifax T	(h)	1-0
Third Round	Hemel Hempstead T	(a)	5-0
Fourth Round	AFC Telford U	(h)	1-2

SUTTON UNITED

Ground: Knights Community Stadium, Gander Green Lane, Sutton, Surrey SM1 2EY. *Tel:* (0208) 644 4440.
Website: www.suttonunited.net *Email:* info@suttonunited.net *Year Formed:* 1898.
Record Attendance: 14,000 v Leeds U, FA Cup 4th rd, 24 January 1970. *Nickname:* 'The U's'.
Manager: Matt Gray. *Colours:* Amber shirts with chocolate trim, amber shorts with chocolate trim, amber socks with chocolate trim.

SUTTON UNITED – NATIONAL LEAGUE 2018–19 LEAGUE RECORD

Match No.	*Date*		*Venue*	*Opponents*	*Result*		*H/T Score*	*Lg Pos.*	*Goalscorers*	*Attendance*
1	Aug	4	A	Harrogate T	D	2-2	1-0	9	Clough [39], Collins (pen) [90]	1378
2		7	H	Eastleigh	W	1-0	1-0	5	Collins (pen) [31]	1725
3		11	H	Salford C	W	2-1	1-1	6	Eastmond [35], Lafayette [63]	1898
4		14	A	Ebbsfleet U	W	1-0	1-0	3	Eastmond [33]	1506
5		18	A	Solihull Moors	D	2-2	1-0	4	Lafayette [25], Wright [76]	763
6		25	H	AFC Fylde	D	0-0	0-0	5		1770
7		27	A	Aldershot T	L	1-2	0-1	9	Lafayette (pen) [90]	1904
8	Sept	1	H	FC Halifax T	D	1-1	0-0	10	Davis [55]	1789
9		4	A	Maidstone U	W	1-0	1-0	7	Lafayette [9]	1838
10		15	A	Havant & W	W	2-1	0-1	7	Wright [60], Beautyman [77]	1273
11		18	H	Boreham Wood	L	0-4	0-3	8		1677
12		22	H	Wrexham	W	3-0	2-0	7	Collins (pen) [15], Cadogan [35], Eastmond [51]	2050
13		25	H	Dover Ath	D	2-2	2-1	7	Eastmond [2], Bailey [18]	1694
14		29	A	Leyton Orient	W	1-0	0-0	6	Ayunga [49]	5627
15	Oct	6	A	Barrow	L	1-2	0-2	9	Thomas [90]	1203
16		27	A	Hartlepool U	W	3-2	1-0	8	Thomas [21], Bolarinwa [63], Eastmond [79]	2788
17		30	H	Chesterfield	D	1-1	1-0	8	Ayunga [37]	1852
18	Nov	3	H	Dagenham & R	W	1-0	0-0	7	Cadogan [56]	1909
19		17	A	Gateshead	D	0-0	0-0	7		794
20		24	H	Maidenhead U	L	0-1	0-0	8		1606
21		27	A	Braintree T	D	2-2	0-1	8	Clough [75], Collins (pen) [86]	439
22	Dec	1	A	AFC Fylde	D	2-2	0-1	8	Pearce [74], Cadogan [88]	1401
23		8	H	Solihull Moors	D	2-2	1-1	8	Brown, W [35], Davis [74]	1728
24		22	A	FC Halifax T	W	1-0	0-0	8	Eastmond [90]	1319
25		26	H	Bromley	W	1-0	0-0	8	Collins [54]	2086
26		29	H	Aldershot T	W	2-1	2-1	8	Beautyman [4], Williams [6]	2216
27	Jan	1	A	Bromley	L	1-2	1-1	8	Davis [11]	1428
28		5	H	Harrogate T	W	2-1	1-0	6	Ayunga [19], Beautyman [82]	1841
29		19	A	Eastleigh	L	2-3	1-1	7	Toure [43], Williams [66]	1872
30		26	H	Ebbsfleet U	W	1-0	0-0	6	Toure [90]	2108
31	Feb	9	A	Barnet	W	1-0	1-0	6	Dobson [36]	1316
32		16	H	Barrow	L	0-1	0-0	7		1892
33		19	H	Barnet	D	0-0	0-0	6		1917
34		23	A	Dagenham & R	L	0-1	0-0	9		1322
35	Mar	2	H	Hartlepool U	D	2-2	1-0	9	Deacon [27], Toure [56]	1923
36		5	A	Salford C	L	0-2	0-1	9		1686
37		9	A	Maidenhead U	L	0-1	0-0	9		1210
38		12	H	Braintree T	L	0-3	0-0	9		1525
39		16	H	Gateshead	W	4-2	0-1	9	Kearney [51], Dobson (pen) [63], Beckwith 2 [86, 89]	1722
40		23	A	Chesterfield	L	0-3	0-1	10		4311
41		30	H	Havant & W	D	2-2	1-1	10	Collins (pen) [5], Beckwith [67]	1816
42	Apr	6	A	Boreham Wood	W	2-1	1-1	9	Beautyman [15], Eastmond [90]	508
43		13	H	Leyton Orient	L	1-2	0-0	9	Ayunga [52]	3339
44		19	A	Wrexham	L	0-1	0-0	10		5264
45		22	H	Maidstone U	D	2-2	1-0	10	Kearney [9], Williams [76]	1858
46		27	A	Dover Ath	L	0-3	0-1	10		1103

Final League Position: 10; upgraded to 9 after Gateshead deducted 9pts after the end of the season.

GOALSCORERS

League (55): Eastmond 7, Collins 6 (5 pens), Ayunga 4, Beautyman 4, Lafayette 4 (1 pen), Beckwith 3, Cadogan 3, Davis 3, Toure 3, Williams 3, Clough 2, Dobson 2 (1 pen), Kearney 2, Thomas 2, Wright 2, Bailey 1, Bolarinwa 1, Brown W 1, Deacon 1, Pearce 1.
FA Cup (3): Beautyman 1, Collins 1 (1 pen), Drinan 1.
FA Trophy (1): Thomas-Asante 1.
Irn-Bru Cup (1): Wright 1.

Butler 29	Bennett 41	Thomas 26 + 3	Clough 22	Collins 30	Bolarinwa 22 + 15	Eastmond 39	Bailey 18 + 5	Beautyman 29 + 4	Taylor 12 + 8	Lafayette 11 + 1	Wright 8 + 5	Drinan 9 + 9	Wishart 10 + 4	Davis 28 + 3	Cadogan 9 + 8	Beckwith 21 + 8	Brown W 9 + 5	Ayunga 20 + 8	Worner 17 + 1	Dundas 3 + 1	Thomas-Asante 6 + 2	McQueen 1 + 7	Pearce 8 + 2	Williams 19 + 3	Toure 18 + 4	Dobson 13 + 5	Deacon 12 + 4	Kearney 5 + 6	Bellikli 2 + 5	Barden 7 + 1	Mason 1 + 1	Lema 1	Match No.
1	2^3	3	4	5	6	7	8	9	10^2	11^1	12	13	14																				1
1	2	3	4	5	6^1	8			14	11	9^3	12	10	7^2	13																		2
1	2	3■	4	5		9			12	7^1	10^3	13	11	6	8^2	14																	3
1	2		3	4	12	7			8^1	10^2		9	11	5	6^3	13	14																4
1	2		3	4	14	7			8^1	10	12	11^3	9	5	6^2	13																	5
1	2		3	4	5	9		14	11	7^1	13	12	10^3	6	8^2																		6
1		2	4	5■	14	7		8	9^3	12	10^2	11^1		6	13	3																	7
1	2		4		5	7			13	9^3	12	11	10	6^1	14	3	8^2																8
1	2		4			7		9	11	5^2	13	14	10	12		3	8^1	6^3															9
1	2	3	5			8	14	9	11^3	7^1	10			6^3	13	4		12															10
1	2		4			7	14	8	11^2	6^1	9	13	10	5^3		3		12															11
1	2	3	4	5^3	12	7	8				10^1	13			6	14	9	11^2															12
1	2	3	4	5^2	6^1	7	8		13		10	14				12	9^3	11															13
1	2	3	5		12	7	8				9^3	11	14	6^1		4	13	10^2															14
1	2	3	4		12			7^1	13	9^3		10	8	5^2	14		6	11															15
1	2	3	4	5	6	9		13				11	12	7^3	8^2		14	10^1															16
1	2	3	4	5	6	10	12					11		7^1	9		13	8^2															17
1	2	3	4^3	5	6^2	8	9					11	14		7	12	13	10^1															18
	2	3	5	6	7^2			9^3	11			12	10^1			4	8	13	1	14													19
1	2^3	3	4	5		8	13	10	11						14		9^2			7^1	6	12											20
1	2^1	3^3	4	5		7	8	13	12						6					10^2	9	11	14										21
1		2	3	4		7	8	13	10					6^3	14		9^1				11^2	12	5										22
1	2			3		6	7		10^1					4	13		8			5	11^2	12	9										23
1	2			3	12	6	7	8^1	14					4				5^3			10^2	13	9	11									24
1	2			3	12	7	8	9						4		13		6^2					10	11	5^1								25
1	2			3	12	6	7	8	14					5				9^2			13		4	11^1	10^3								26
1	2			3^1	12	6	7	8						4^3		13		5			10^2		9	11	14								27
	2				5^3	6	7	8						12		4		10^1	1		13	14	3	9	11^2								28
	2	3			12	6^2	7	8						5^3		4			1			14	13	10	11^1	9							29
	2	3			5^2		7	8						6		4		12	1			13		10^1	11	9							30
	2	13		4	14	6	7^3	8						5^1		3			1					10	11^2	9	12						31
	2			4	13	7		8^2								3		6^3	1				9	10^1	5	11	12	14					32
	2			3	4	7								5				10	1					11^1	9	8	6	12					33
	2			4	12	8								5		3		7	1					10^2	6	11^1	9	13					34
	2^1	3		5	6^2	8		9						7		4		13	1					12	11^3	14	10						35
	2^1	3		5	10	6		8						7^2		4			1					12	11^3	14	9		13				36
		2		4	12	5■	6^3	7						13		3		14	1					10^1	11	9^2	8						37
		2		4	5^1		8	9						6		3		14	1						7^2	13	10	12	11^3				38
	2	3			5			8						6^2		4			1					10^1	13	11	9	7		12			39
	2	3^3			5			7								4		14	1					10^1	12	11	8	6	13	9^2			40
1	2	3■		5		8		9								4		7						11^1	6^3	13	14	12		10^2			41
1	2				4	6		7								3								13	11	10	8^1	5^2	12	9			42
1^2	2				3	6		7										4	12					10	13	11	8	5^1		9			43
	2	12			3	4		5										10^1	1					11	9	6^2	7	13	14	8^3			44
	2^1	12			6	4■		5											1					10	11	7^3	9^2	3	13	8	14		45
		2			5^1		12	6										10	1					11	9	14	13		8^3	7	4^2	3	46

FA Cup

Fourth Qualifying	Wealdstone	(a)	2-1
First Round	Slough T	(h)	0-0
Replay (aet)	Slough T	(a)	1-1

(Slough T won 8-7 on penalties)

FA Trophy

First Round	Bromley	(a)	1-2

(Tie awarded to Sutton U Bromley removed)

Second Round	Spennymoor T	(a)	0-3

Irn-Bru Cup

Second Round	Airdrieonians	(a)	1-0
Third Round	Bohemians	(a)	0-0

(Bohemians won 4-3 on penalties)

WREXHAM

Ground: Racecourse Ground, Mold Road, Wrexham, Wales LL11 2AH. *Tel:* (01978) 891 864.
Website: wrexhamafc.co.uk *Email:* info@wrexhamfc.tv *Year Formed:* 1872.
Record Attendance: 34,445 v Manchester U, FA Cup 4th rd, 26 January 1957. *Nickname:* 'Red Dragons'.
Manager: Bryan Hughes. *Colours:* Red shirts with white trim, white shorts with red trim, red socks with white hoops.

WREXHAM – NATIONAL LEAGUE 2018–19 LEAGUE RECORD

Match No.	*Date*	*Venue*	*Opponents*	*Result*		*H/T Score*	*Lg Pos.*	*Goalscorers*	*Attendance*
1	Aug 4	A	Dover Ath	W	1-0	1-0	6	Fondop-Talom [29]	1359
2	7	H	AFC Fylde	D	0-0	0-0	8		5777
3	11	H	Boreham Wood	W	3-0	1-0	5	Maguire-Drew [25], Pyke [66], Fondop-Talom [84]	4356
4	14	A	Maidenhead U	W	2-0	2-0	1	Fondop-Talom [14], Maguire-Drew [27]	1584
5	18	A	Eastleigh	W	3-1	2-0	1	Smith, M [9], Wynter (og) [13], Fondop-Talom [82]	1717
6	25	H	Bromley	D	2-2	1-0	1	Fondop-Talom [31], Pyke [65]	5714
7	27	A	Solihull Moors	L	0-1	0-0	2		2412
8	Sept 1	H	Aldershot T	W	2-0	0-0	1	Beavon [62], Maguire-Drew [78]	4648
9	4	H	FC Halifax T	D	0-0	0-0	3		5377
10	8	A	Braintree T	W	1-0	0-0	2	Pearson [66]	802
11	15	H	Ebbsfleet U	W	4-1	4-0	2	Holroyd [6], Beavon [12], Pyke [19], Pearson [45]	4718
12	22	A	Sutton U	L	0-3	0-2	3		2050
13	25	A	Harrogate T	D	0-0	0-0	4		2387
14	29	H	Barnet	W	1-0	1-0	4	Beavon [42]	4727
15	Oct 6	H	Havant & W	W	1-0	1-0	4	Pyke [31]	4323
16	13	A	Dagenham & R	W	2-1	1-1	2	Young [43], Summerfield (pen) [67]	1601
17	27	A	Chesterfield	D	1-1	1-0	3	Walker (pen) [20]	5662
18	30	H	Hartlepool U	W	1-0	1-0	2	Young [20]	4665
19	Nov 3	H	Gateshead	W	3-1	1-0	1	Kerr (og) [18], Walker [68], Pyke [90]	4421
20	17	A	Maidstone U	D	1-1	0-0	3	Walker [71]	2626
21	24	H	Leyton Orient	L	0-2	0-0	3		6428
22	27	A	Barrow	D	0-0	0-0	3		851
23	Dec 8	H	Eastleigh	W	2-0	1-0	4	Jennings [2], Grant [58]	4105
24	22	A	Aldershot T	D	0-0	0-0	3		1866
25	26	H	Salford C	W	5-1	3-0	2	Pearson [3], Wright [24], Walker [45], Tollitt [86], Holroyd [90]	8283
26	29	H	Solihull Moors	W	1-0	0-0	2	Rutherford [49]	6220
27	Jan 1	A	Salford C	L	0-2	0-1	2		4044
28	5	H	Dover Ath	L	0-1	0-0	3		4817
29	8	A	Bromley	L	0-2	0-2	4		1061
30	19	A	AFC Fylde	L	0-2	0-1	5		2912
31	26	H	Maidenhead U	W	1-0	0-0	5	Young [65]	4323
32	Feb 9	H	Dagenham & R	W	1-0	0-0	3	Beavon [74]	5366
33	16	A	Havant & W	W	3-2	0-1	2	Pearson [48], Wright [58], Jennings [60]	1658
34	19	A	Boreham Wood	W	2-0	0-0	1	Tollitt 2 [56, 64]	645
35	23	A	Gateshead	D	1-1	0-1	1	Stockton [90]	1228
36	Mar 2	H	Chesterfield	W	1-0	0-0	1	Wright [62]	7106
37	9	A	Leyton Orient	L	0-1	0-0	2		6643
38	12	H	Barrow	L	1-3	0-3	3	Kennedy [77]	4613
39	16	H	Maidstone U	W	1-0	0-0	3	Tollitt [49]	3604
40	23	A	Hartlepool U	L	0-1	0-1	3		3888
41	30	A	Ebbsfleet U	L	2-4	0-3	4	Pearson [82], Beavon [49]	1523
42	Apr 6	H	Braintree T	W	3-1	1-1	4	Grant [18], Pearson [60], Wright [67]	4221
43	13	A	Barnet	W	2-1	0-0	4	Wright [47], McGlashan [86]	1594
44	19	H	Sutton U	W	1-0	0-0	4	Kennedy [78]	5264
45	22	A	FC Halifax T	L	1-2	1-1	5	Holroyd [40]	2577
46	27	H	Harrogate T	W	2-1	1-1	4	Oswell [42], Deverdics [80]	3690

Final League Position: 4

GOALSCORERS

League (58): Pearson 6, Beavon 5, Fondop-Talom 5, Pyke 5, Wright 5, Tollitt 4, Walker 4 (1 pen), Holroyd 3, Maguire-Drew 3, Young 3, Grant 2, Jennings 2, Kennedy 2, Deverdics 1, McGlashan 1, Oswell 1, Rutherford 1, Smith M 1, Stockton 1, Summerfield 1 (1 pen), own goals 2.
FA Cup (4): Beavon 1, Summerfield 1, Wright 1, Young 1.
FA Trophy (3): Fondop-Talum 1, Holroyd 1, Rutherford 1.
National League Play-Offs (0).

Lainton 44	Roberts 31 + 2	Jennings 34 + 3	Smith M 8	Pearson 41	Summerfield 31 + 2	Young 28 + 13	Rutherford 33 + 11	Wright 36 + 7	Beavon 28 + 12	Fondop-Talom 13 + 8	Maguire-Drew 13 + 4	Pyke 14 + 9	Carrington 26 + 4	Holroyd 11 + 15	Deverdics 3 + 9	Tharme 2 + 2	Burgess — + 1	Lawlor 34	Walker 25 + 1	Grant 14 + 2	Tollitt 8 + 5	Oswell 7 + 7	Stockton 1 + 7	Kennedy 10 + 2	Dibble 2	McGlashan 3 + 4	Agustien 3	Spyrou 2 + 1	Sargent 1	Thorn — + 1	*Match No.*
1	2	3	4	5	6	7	8^{3}	9	10^{2}	11^{1}	12	13	14																		1
1	2	5	3	4	6^{2}	9	10	8	12	11^{1}	7^{3}	14	13																		2
1	2^{2}	3	4	5	6	7^{1}	12	9	11^{3}	10	8	14	13																		3
1		2	3	4	5		7	9	13	10^{3}	8^{1}	11^{2}	6	12	14																4
1		2	3	4	5		9^{1}	11	14	6	10^{3}	7^{2}	8	13	12																5
1		2^{3}	3	4	5	14		10	11^{1}	6	8	13	7		9^{2}	12															6
1	2		3^{1}	4	5^{3}	6		8		9^{2}	14	11	7	10		12	13														7
1	2			4	5	12	13	9	10	11	7^{1}	14	6		8^{3}	3^{2}															8
1		5		4	6	13	8^{3}	7	12	10^{1}	11^{2}	9	2	14				3													9
1	2	3		4	5	6^{2}	13	14	10	7^{1}	8	12						11	9^{3}												10
1	2	3		4	5^{3}	13	8	12	10	14		7^{2}		6^{1}				11	9												11
1	2	3		4	5▪	14	6^{3}	13	11^{1}	12		9		10				8	7^{2}												12
1	2			3	4	12	6^{3}	9^{2}	14	11	7^{1}		5	13				10	8												13
1	2			4	5	14	13	8	11	12	7^{1}		6	10^{2}				9	3^{3}												14
1	2			3	4	5	12	13	11^{3}		7^{1}	10	6		14			9	8^{2}												15
1	2			3	4	5	14	12	10^{1}	13	7^{3}	11	6					9^{2}	8												16
1	2	12		3		4	8	10	13	5^{3}		6^{2}	7^{1}	14				11	9												17
1	2	5		4		8	13	6	11^{2}	12	9^{3}	10			14			3	7^{1}												18
1	2	5		4	6	8	9	14	11^{3}			12		10^{1}	13			3	7^{2}												19
1	2	3		4	5	6	7^{3}	8^{2}	14	10^{1}	12	11						9	13												20
1	2	12		3	4	5	8^{1}		10^{3}	13	14	6^{2}	7					11	9												21
1	2	3		4	5	6	12		10^{2}	13		9^{1}						8	7	11											22
1	2^{3}	3	4		5	12	7	8	10^{1}	14			6	13				9		11^{2}											23
1		2		3	4		6^{1}	8	10^{2}				5	12	13			9	7	11											24
1		2		3	4		6^{1}	8	9^{3}				5	13	14			10	7	11^{2}	12										25
1	14	2		3	4^{2}	12	6	8	10^{3}				5					9	7^{1}	11	13										26
1	14	2		3	8	13	9	7^{2}	11^{3}				5^{1}					4	6	10	12										27
1	2	3		4	5	6^{3}	7	13	10^{1}					14				9	8^{2}	11	12										28
1	2	3		4	5	6	7^{2}	8^{3}				14						9		11	12	10^{1}	13								29
1	2			3	4	12	6	8	10^{2}			13	5					9	7^{1}	11^{3}			14								30
1	2	3		4	5^{1}	12	6	8	10^{2}			11^{3}		14				9	7			13									31
1	2	3		4		5^{1}	12	7	13				14					9	6	11^{2}	8		10^{3}								32
1		2		3		4	6	8					5	12				9	7^{1}		10	11^{2}		13							33
1		2				4	6	8					5	13				9	7		11^{2}	10^{1}	12	3							34
		2				4	6	8^{3}					5^{2}	13	12			9	7		10^{1}	11	14	3	1						35
1		2		3		5	7	9	10^{2}					13				6	8		11^{1}	12		4							36
1		2		3		5	6	8	9^{3}									11	7^{1}	12	10^{2}	13	14	4							37
1	2	5				7	12	8	11^{1}					14				4			9	10^{2}	13	3		6^{3}					38
1		2		3		5	7	9	13					6^{2}	8^{1}			11		12	10^{3}			4		14					39
1		2		3		5	6	8	12					11				10						4		7^{2}	9^{1}	13			40
1	2	3		4		14	6	8	13				5					10				12				7^{3}	9^{1}	11^{2}			41
1	2	14		3		4	7	8	9^{1}				6	5				10^{2}		11^{3}		13		12							42
1	2			3	13	5	8^{2}	9	10^{3}				7	6						11^{1}		12		4		14					43
1	2			3	12	5	8^{3}	9	10^{1}				7	6						11^{2}		14		4		13					44
1	2	3		4	6^{2}	7	12	8	13					9^{3}						11		10^{1}		5		14					45
	2	3			4^{2}		7						6		12	10						5^{3}	13		1		11	8^{1}	9	14	46

FA Cup

Fourth Qualifying	Harrogate T	(a)	0-0
Replay	Harrogate T	(h)	2-0
First Round	Weston-super-Mare	(a)	2-0
Second Round	Newport Co	(h)	0-0
Replay	Newport Co	(a)	0-4

FA Trophy

First Round	Boston U	(h)	3-0
Second Round	Leyton Orient	(h)	0-1

National League Play-Offs

Eliminator *(aet)*	Eastleigh	(h)	0-1

SCOTTISH LEAGUE TABLES 2018–19

(P) *Promoted into division at end of 2017–18 season.* (R) *Relegated into division at end of 2017–18 season.*

SPFL LADBROKES PREMIERSHIP 2018–19

			Home					*Away*					*Total*						
		P	*W*	*D*	*L*	*F*	*A*	*W*	*D*	*L*	*F*	*A*	*W*	*D*	*L*	*F*	*A*	*GD*	*Pts*
1	Celtic	38	17	2	0	46	7	10	4	5	31	13	27	6	5	77	20	57	87
2	Rangers	38	14	4	1	45	7	9	5	5	37	20	23	9	6	82	27	55	78
3	Kilmarnock	38	12	2	5	32	14	7	8	4	18	17	19	10	9	50	31	19	67
4	Aberdeen	38	9	4	6	33	27	11	3	5	24	17	20	7	11	57	44	13	67
5	Hibernian	38	6	9	4	28	16	8	3	8	23	23	14	12	12	51	39	12	54
6	Hearts	38	8	4	7	22	18	7	2	10	20	32	15	6	17	42	50	–8	51
7	St Johnstone	38	8	5	6	23	21	7	2	10	15	27	15	7	16	38	48	–10	52
8	Motherwell	38	9	4	6	29	20	6	2	11	17	36	15	6	17	46	56	–10	51
9	Livingston (P)	38	10	2	7	28	17	1	9	9	14	27	11	11	16	42	44	–2	44
10	Hamilton A	38	5	5	9	20	34	4	1	14	8	41	9	6	23	28	75	–47	33
11	St Mirren®	38	5	2	12	15	26	3	6	10	19	40	8	8	22	34	66	–32	32
12	Dundee	38	1	4	14	14	36	4	2	13	17	42	5	6	27	31	78	–47	21

Top 6 teams split after 33 games, teams in the bottom six cannot pass teams in the top six after the split.
®St Mirren not relegated after play-offs.

SPFL LADBROKES CHAMPIONSHIP 2018–19

			Home					*Away*					*Total*						
		P	*W*	*D*	*L*	*F*	*A*	*W*	*D*	*L*	*F*	*A*	*W*	*D*	*L*	*F*	*A*	*GD*	*Pts*
1	Ross Co (R)	36	13	4	1	32	9	8	4	6	31	25	21	8	7	63	34	29	71
2	Dundee U¶	36	11	3	4	29	25	8	5	5	20	15	19	8	9	49	40	9	65
3	Inverness CT	36	5	8	5	22	23	9	6	3	26	17	14	14	8	48	40	8	56
4	Ayr U (P)	36	7	5	6	25	19	8	4	6	25	19	15	9	12	50	38	12	54
5	Greenock Morton	36	6	7	5	21	23	5	6	7	15	22	11	13	12	36	45	–9	46
6	Partick Thistle (R)	36	7	3	8	25	27	5	4	9	18	25	12	7	17	43	52	–9	43
7	Dunfermline Ath	36	5	3	10	13	18	6	5	7	20	22	11	8	17	33	40	–7	41
8	Alloa Ath (P)	36	6	2	10	13	21	4	7	7	26	32	10	9	17	39	53	–14	39
9	Queen of the South®	36	5	7	6	26	22	4	4	10	15	26	9	11	16	41	48	–7	38
10	Falkirk	36	3	7	8	19	27	6	4	8	18	22	9	11	16	37	49	–12	38

¶Dundee U not promoted after play-offs. ®Queen of the South not relegated after play-offs.

SPFL LADBROKES LEAGUE ONE 2018–19

			Home					*Away*					*Total*						
		P	*W*	*D*	*L*	*F*	*A*	*W*	*D*	*L*	*F*	*A*	*W*	*D*	*L*	*F*	*A*	*GD*	*Pts*
1	Arbroath	36	11	4	3	33	21	9	6	3	30	17	20	10	6	63	38	25	70
2	Forfar Ath	36	12	3	3	30	18	7	3	8	24	29	19	6	11	54	47	7	63
3	Raith R¶	36	11	4	3	41	20	5	8	5	34	29	16	12	8	75	49	26	60
4	Montrose (P)	36	9	4	5	29	27	6	2	10	20	23	15	6	15	49	50	–1	51
5	Airdrieonians	36	6	4	8	22	19	8	2	8	29	25	14	6	16	51	44	7	48
6	Dumbarton (R)	36	8	5	5	33	26	4	5	9	27	34	12	10	14	60	60	0	46
7	East Fife	36	6	3	9	25	31	7	4	7	24	25	13	7	16	49	56	–7	46
8	Stranraer	36	6	4	8	24	28	5	5	8	21	29	11	9	16	45	57	–12	42
9	Stenhousemuir (P)®	36	5	4	9	18	29	5	3	10	17	32	10	7	19	35	61	–26	37
10	Brechin C (R)	36	5	6	7	21	28	4	3	11	21	33	9	9	18	42	61	–19	36

¶Raith R not promoted after play-offs. ®Stenhousemuir relegated after play-offs.

SPFL LADBROKES LEAGUE TWO 2018–19

			Home					*Away*					*Total*						
		P	*W*	*D*	*L*	*F*	*A*	*W*	*D*	*L*	*F*	*A*	*W*	*D*	*L*	*F*	*A*	*GD*	*Pts*
1	Peterhead	36	12	4	2	27	12	12	3	3	38	17	24	7	5	65	29	36	79
2	Clyde¶	36	12	3	3	35	18	11	2	5	28	17	23	5	8	63	35	28	74
3	Edinburgh C	36	11	3	4	31	12	9	4	5	27	19	20	7	9	58	31	27	67
4	Annan Ath	36	10	4	4	42	21	10	2	6	28	18	20	6	10	70	39	31	66
5	Stirling Alb	36	8	2	8	19	18	5	6	7	25	27	13	8	15	44	45	–1	47
6	Cowdenbeath	36	8	3	7	28	24	4	4	10	18	22	12	7	17	46	46	0	43
7	Queen's Park (R)	36	7	6	5	24	21	4	4	10	20	26	11	10	15	44	47	–3	43
8	Elgin C	36	7	2	9	27	35	6	2	10	25	32	13	4	19	52	67	–15	43
9	Albion R (R)	36	3	3	12	14	40	4	3	11	18	31	7	6	23	32	71	–39	27
10	Berwick Rangers®	36	3	2	13	13	40	2	2	14	14	51	5	4	27	27	91	–64	19

¶Clyde promoted after play-offs. ®Berwick Rangers relegated after play-offs. Clyde's matches against Albion R (1-0 win) on 16 February 2019 and Queen's Park (1-1 draw) on 23 February 2019 awarded as 0-3 defeats after Clyde fielded an ineligible player.

SCOTTISH LEAGUE ATTENDANCES 2018–19

SPFL LADBROKES PREMIERSHIP ATTENDANCES

	Average Gate			*Season 2018–19*	
	2017–18	*2018–19*	*+/–%*	*Highest*	*Lowest*
Aberdeen	15,775	14,925	–5.39	20,027	12,252
Celtic	57,528	57,778	+0.44	59,143	54,563
Dundee	5,947	6,025	+1.30	8,578	4,426
Hamilton A	3,095	2,829	–8.58	5,827	1,135
Hearts	18,429	17,564	–4.69	19,667	15,147
Hibernian	18,124	17,741	–2.11	20,200	15,096
Kilmarnock	5,391	6,895	+27.90	12,374	4,143
Livingston	1,350	3,664	+171.41	9,246	1,022
Motherwell	5,448	5,448	–0.00	9,545	3,662
Rangers	49,174	49,564	+0.79	50,130	48,729
St Johnstone	3,809	3,891	+2.16	7,086	1,946
St Mirren	4,448	5,352	+20.32	7,288	4,001

SPFL LADBROKES CHAMPIONSHIP ATTENDANCES

	Average Gate			*Season 2018–19*	
	2017–18	*2018–19*	*+/–%*	*Highest*	*Lowest*
Alloa Ath	643	1,179	+83.31	2,116	592
Ayr U	1,589	2,157	+35.80	3,249	1,559
Dundee U	5,505	5,079	–7.75	6,532	4,201
Dunfermline Ath	5,243	5,009	–4.48	6,349	4,347
Falkirk	4,676	4,743	+1.42	6,173	3767
Greenock Morton	1,986	1,943	–2.15	2,757	1,315
Inverness CT	2,395	2,548	+6.40	4,353	1,994
Partick Thistle	4,580	3,043	–33.56	4,438	1,990
Queen of the South	1,457	1,656	+13.60	3,916	727
Ross Co	4,624	3,850	–16.75	6,402	3,065

SPFL LADBROKES LEAGUE ONE ATTENDANCES

	Average Gate			*Season 2018–19*	
	2017–18	*2018–19*	*+/–%*	*Highest*	*Lowest*
Airdrieonians	768	764	–0.64	1,140	590
Arbroath	772	951	+23.05	1,808	532
Brechin C	923	581	–37.07	1,509	355
Dumbarton	832	618	–25.78	756	456
East Fife	683	698	+2.11	1,756	323
Forfar Ath	619	665	+7.57	1,342	459
Montrose	682	789	+15.69	1,666	486
Raith R	1,886	1,556	–17.52	2,833	1,089
Stenhousemuir	444	571	+28.85	797	362
Stranraer	443	339	–23.33	432	219

SPFL LADBROKES LEAGUE TWO ATTENDANCES

	Average Gate			*Season 2018–19*	
	2017–18	*2018–19*	*+/–%*	*Highest*	*Lowest*
Albion R	457	286	–37.33	560	145
Annan Ath	346	398	+14.95	569	317
Berwick Rangers	434	478	+10.14	975	293
Clyde	515	638	+23.80	1,012	408
Cowdenbeath	320	355	+11.01	1,007	250
Edinburgh C	325	401	+23.39	1,057	247
Elgin C	607	623	+2.53	929	485
Peterhead	641	668	+4.19	1,371	522
Queen's Park	688	611	–11.11	1,076	404
Stirling Alb	658	588	–10.61	802	413

ABERDEEN

Year Formed: 1903. *Ground & Address:* Pittodrie Stadium, Pittodrie St, Aberdeen AB24 5QH. *Telephone:* 01224 650400. *Fax:* 01224 644173. *E-mail:* feedback@afc.co.uk *Website:* www.afc.co.uk
Ground Capacity: 20,866 (all seated). *Size of Pitch:* 105m × 66m.
Chairman: Stewart Milne. *Chief Executive:* Duncan Fraser.
Manager: Derek McInnes. *Assistant Manager:* Tony Docherty. *Reserve Team Manager:* Paul Sheerin.
Club Nicknames: 'The Dons'; 'The Reds'; 'The Dandies'.
Record Attendance: 45,061 v Hearts, Scottish Cup 4th rd, 13 March 1954.
Record Transfer Fee received: £1,750,000 for Eoin Jess to Coventry C (February 1996).
Record Transfer Fee paid: £1,000,000 for Paul Bernard from Oldham Ath (September 1995).
Record Victory: 13-0 v Peterhead, Scottish Cup 3rd rd, 10 February 1923.
Record Defeat: 0-9 v Celtic, Premier League, 6 November 2010.
Most Capped Player: Alex McLeish, 77 (Scotland).
Most League Appearances: 556: Willie Miller, 1973-90.
Most League Goals in Season (Individual): 38: Benny Yorston, Division I, 1929-30.
Most Goals Overall (Individual): 199: Joe Harper, 1969-72; 1976-81.

ABERDEEN – SPFL LADBROKES PREMIERSHIP 2018–19 LEAGUE RECORD

Match No.	*Date*	*Venue*	*Opponents*	*Result*	*H/T Score*	*Lg Pos.*	*Goalscorers*	*Attendance*
1	Aug 5	H	Rangers	D 1-1	0-1	6	Anderson ^{90}	19,046
2	11	A	Dundee	W 1-0	0-0	3	Mackay-Steven (pen) ^{75}	7581
3	25	A	Hibernian	D 1-1	1-0	3	Hoban ^{45}	18,583
4	Sept 1	H	Kilmarnock	L 0-2	0-1	8		14,248
5	15	A	St Johnstone	D 1-1	0-1	8	McGinn ^{69}	4880
6	22	H	Motherwell	W 1-0	1-0	5	Wilson ^{6}	14,027
7	29	A	Celtic	L 0-1	0-0	7		59,143
8	Oct 6	H	St Mirren	W 4-1	3-0	6	Cosgrove 2 $^{26, 65}$, McLennan ^{30}, Lowe ^{41}	14,003
9	20	A	Hearts	L 1-2	0-2	7	Mackay-Steven (pen) ^{55}	18,051
10	31	H	Hamilton A	W 3-0	2-0	8	Shinnie ^{8}, Wilson ^{23}, Devlin ^{60}	12,365
11	Nov 4	A	Kilmarnock	W 2-1	0-1	7	Anderson ^{73}, Ferguson ^{87}	5270
12	9	H	Hibernian	W 1-0	1-0	5	Mackay-Steven ^{40}	15,629
13	24	A	Motherwell	L 0-3	0-2	6		5131
14	Dec 5	A	Rangers	W 1-0	1-0	6	McKenna ^{7}	49,711
15	8	H	St Johnstone	L 0-2	0-0	7		13,304
16	11	H	Livingston	W 3-2	1-2	6	McGinn ^{9}, Cosgrove ^{57}, Ferguson ^{90}	12,252
17	15	A	St Mirren	W 2-1	1-1	4	May (pen) ^{30}, Cosgrove ^{61}	4699
18	18	H	Dundee	W 5-1	2-0	4	Cosgrove 2 $^{16, 44}$, Considine ^{50}, McLennan ^{56}, O'Dea (og) ^{73}	13,142
19	22	H	Hearts	W 2-0	1-0	2	Cosgrove 2 (1 pen) $^{2, 69 (p)}$	16,451
20	26	H	Celtic	L 3-4	1-1	4	May (pen) ^{24}, Cosgrove (pen) ^{83}, Ferguson ^{90}	20,027
21	29	A	Livingston	W 2-1	0-0	4	Wilson ^{71}, Lawson (og) ^{85}	5548
22	Jan 23	A	Hamilton A	W 3-0	1-0	4	Cosgrove 2 $^{25, 52}$, Ferguson ^{56}	2104
23	26	H	Kilmarnock	D 0-0	0-0	3		15,560
24	Feb 2	A	Hibernian	W 2-1	2-1	4	Considine ^{12}, Mackay-Steven ^{22}	16,269
25	6	H	Rangers	L 2-4	1-3	3	Cosgrove 2 (1 pen) $^{31, 47 (p)}$	19,190
26	16	H	St Mirren	D 2-2	1-1	3	Ferguson ^{32}, Cosgrove ^{77}	14,701
27	23	A	St Johnstone	W 2-0	1-0	3	Shinnie 2 $^{16, 75}$	5092
28	27	H	Hamilton A	L 0-2	0-1	3		12,468
29	Mar 9	A	Celtic	D 0-0	0-0	3		59,123
30	16	H	Livingston	D 1-1	1-1	3	McGinn ^{30}	14,366
31	30	A	Hearts	L 1-2	1-0	4	McLennan ^{16}	17,880
32	Apr 3	H	Motherwell	W 3-1	1-1	4	Lowe ^{4}, McGinn 2 $^{71, 90}$	13,228
33	6	A	Dundee	W 2-0	0-0	4	Cosgrove 2 (1 pen) $^{59 (p), 77}$	6593
34	20	A	Kilmarnock	W 1-0	0-0	3	McKenna ^{66}	6531
35	28	A	Rangers	L 0-2	0-0	3		49,667
36	May 4	H	Celtic	L 0-3	0-1	4		15,189
37	10	H	Hearts	W 2-1	0-0	3	Ferguson ^{54}, Stewart ^{77}	14,371
38	19	A	Hibernian	W 2-1	1-1	4	Cosgrove ^{43}, Wilson ^{63}	18,631

Final League Position: 4

Honours
League Champions: Division I 1954-55; Premier Division 1979-80, 1983-84, 1984-85.
Runners-up: Premiership 2014-15, 2015-16, 2016-17, 2017-18; Division I 1910-11, 1936-37, 1955-56, 1970-71, 1971-72; Premier Division 1977-78, 1980-81, 1981-82, 1988-89, 1989-90, 1990-91, 1992-93, 1993-94.
Scottish Cup Winners: 1947, 1970, 1982, 1983, 1984, 1986, 1990; *Runners-up:* 1937, 1953, 1954, 1959, 1967, 1978, 1993, 2000, 2017.
League Cup Winners: 1955-56, 1976-77, 1985-86, 1989-90, 1995-96, 2013-14; *Runners-up:* 1946-47, 1978-79, 1979-80, 1987-88, 1988-89, 1992-93, 1999-2000, 2016-17, 2018-19.
Drybrough Cup Winners: 1971, 1980.

European: *European Cup:* 12 matches (1980-81, 1984-85, 1985-86); *Cup Winners' Cup:* 39 matches (1967-68, 1970-71, 1978-79, 1982-83 winners, 1983-84 semi-finals, 1986-87, 1990-91, 1993-94); *UEFA Cup:* 56 matches (*Fairs Cup:* 1968-69. *UEFA Cup:* 1971-72, 1972-73, 1973-74, 1977-78, 1979-80, 1981-82, 1987-88, 1988-89, 1989-90, 1991-92, 1994-95, 1996-97, 2000-01, 2002-03, 2007-08). *Europa League:* 26 matches (2009-10, 2014-15, 2015-16, 2016-17, 2017-18, 2018-19).

Club colours: All: Red with white trim.

Goalscorers: *League (57):* Cosgrove 17 (4 pens), Ferguson 6, McGinn 5, Mackay-Steven 4 (2 pens), Wilson 4, McLennan 3, Shinnie 3, Anderson 2, Considine 2, Lowe 2, May 2 (2 pens), McKenna 2, Devlin 1, Hoban 1, Stewart 1, own goals 2.
William Hill Scottish FA Cup (12): Cosgrove 4 (3 pens), McGinn 3, Considine 1, Lowe 1, McLennan 1, Stewart 1, own goal 1.
Betfred Scottish League Cup (5): Mackay-Steven 2 (1 pen), Ferguson 1, May 1, Shinnie 1.
Irn-Bru Scottish League Challenge (1): Anderson 1. *Europa League: (2):* Ferguson 1, Mackay-Steven 1 (1 pen).

Lewis J 37	Ball D 24 + 7	Devlin M 16 + 6	McKenna S 30	Considine A 33	Gleeson S 7 + 8	Shinnie G 36	Ferguson L 33	McGinn N 22 + 5	Cosgrove S 29 + 6	Mackay-Steven G 19 + 1	Forrester C 1 + 4	May S 21 + 11	Anderson B 1 + 13	Wright S 4 + 9	Hoban T 4 + 1	Ross F 1	Logan S 25 + 1	Wilson J 12 + 12	Lowe M 31 + 2	Campbell D 1 + 7	McLennan C 18 + 3	Stewart G 12 + 3	Cerny T 1 + 1	Ross E — + 4	Halford G — + 2	*Match No.*
1	2	3	4^{2}	5	6^{3}	7	8	9	10^{1}	11	12	13	14													1
1	2	3		4	6^{2}	5	8	7	11^{3}	9	13	10^{1}	12	14												2
1	2	3		5	6^{2}	7	9		14	10		11^{1}			4	8^{3}	12	13								3
1	12	3■		4	7^{2}	6	9	8^{1}	13	10		11^{3}	14				2		5							4
1	14		3	4	7^{3}	6		8	12	10	9^{2}	11^{1}	13				2		5							5
1	7	3	4	5		8		9^{3}	10^{1}	6			12				2	11^{2}	14	13						6
1	7	3	4	5		8		6^{2}	12	9		10^{3}	14				2	11^{1}	13							7
1	6^{3}	3		4	13	8	7		10^{1}	9	12		14				2		5		11^{2}					8
1	6^{1}	3		4		8	7	13	10^{2}	9		14		12			2	11^{3}	5							9
1		3	4			7	6	10		8^{2}		12	14	9^{3}			2	11^{1}	5		13					10
1	6^{1}	3	4			7	9	10^{3}		8		12	13	14			2	11^{2}	5							11
1	14	3	4			8	7	9	13	6^{3}		10^{2}	12				2	11^{1}	5							12
1			3	4		6	9	8^{3}	12	10		7^{2}	14	13			2	11^{1}	5							13
1	6		3	4		7	9	8^{1}	11■			12		13			2		5		10^{2}					14
1	6^{1}		4	3		7	9	13				11	12	10^{3}			2	14	5		8^{2}					15
1	14		4	3		7	6	8^{3}	11			9^{2}	13	10^{1}			2		5		12					16
1	12		3	4		7	6	10	11			9^{2}		13			2		5		8^{1}					17
1	12		4	3		7	6	10^{2}	11^{3}		14	9^{1}					2	13	5		8					18
1			4	3	13	7	6	10	11			9^{3}		14			2		5^{2}	12	8^{1}					19
1	6		4	3		5	7	10^{2}	11			9^{1}		12			2	13			8					20
1	3		4	5	12	8			11			6	10^{1}	7^{2}			2^{3}	13		14	9					21
1	14		3	4	13	7	6^{2}		11^{3}	8		10^{1}		12			2		5			9				22
1			4^{3}	3		8	7	12	11	6^{1}		9^{2}			13		2	14	5			10				23
1^{1}				4	14	8	7		10^{3}	9		11^{2}			3		2	12	5			6	13			24
1			4■	3		7	6	13	11	9					2		5^{1}	12	8^{2}			10				25
1		4		3	12	7	8	6^{2}	11	9					5^{3}			13	2^{1}		14	10				26
1	3	4		5	14	7	8	12	11	9^{2}		13							2		6^{1}	10^{3}				27
1	2^{1}	12	4	3		7	6	10	11			13							5^{2}		8	9				28
1	2		4	3		8	7		10			13						11^{2}	5	12	9^{1}	6^{3}		14		29
1	2	3	4			7	6^{1}	10^{3}	11			9^{2}						14	5	12	8	13				30
1	2	13	4	3		7	6	10	11									12	5		8^{2}	9^{1}				31
1	2	13	4	3		8	7	9	10										5	6^{1}	11^{2}	12				32
1	2		3	4	12	7	6	8^{3}	11			13							5		10^{2}	9^{1}		14		33
1	2	3^{2}	4	5	7	8			11^{1}			10						12	9		6^{3}			13	14	34
1	2	12	4	3■	6^{3}		7		11^{1}			9						10	5	13	8^{2}	14				35
1	6	3	4				7		11^{2}			9					2^{1}	8	5	13		10		14	12^{3}	36
1	7	12	4	3^{1}		9	8		11			13					2	10	5			6^{2}				37
	7^{3}	14	4	3		9	6^{2}		11	13		12					2	8	5		10^{1}		1			38

AIRDRIEONIANS

Year Formed: 2002. *Ground & Address:* The Penny Cars Stadium, New Broomfield, Craigneuk Avenue, Airdrie ML6 8QZ. *Telephone:* (Stadium) 01236 622000. *Fax:* 01236 622001.
E-mail: enquiries@airdriefc.com *Website:* www.airdriefc.com
Ground Capacity: 10,101 (all seated). *Size of Pitch:* 105m × 67m.
Chairman: Martin Ferguson. *Director of Football:* Stuart Millar.
Manager: Ian Murray. *Assistant Manager:* Marc Fitzpatrick.
Club Nickname: 'The Diamonds'.
Record Attendance: 9,044 v Rangers, League 1, 23 August 2013.
Record Victory: 11-0 v Gala Fairydean, Scottish Cup 3rd rd, 19 November 2011.
Record Defeat: 0-7 v Partick Thistle, First Division, 20 October 2012.
Most League Appearances: 222: Paul Lovering, 2004-12.
Most League Goals in Season (Individual): 23: Andy Ryan, 2016-17.
Most Goals Overall (Individual): 43: Bryan Prunty, 2005-08, 2015-16.

AIRDRIEONIANS – SPFL LADBROKES LEAGUE ONE 2018–19 LEAGUE RECORD

Match No.	*Date*	*Venue*	*Opponents*	*Result*	*H/T Score*	*Lg Pos.*	*Goalscorers*	*Attendance*
1	Aug 4	A	Forfar Ath	W 3-1	0-1	2	Conroy ^{80}, McIntosh, L ^{83}, Vitoria ^{86}	652
2	11	H	Montrose	L 0-1	0-0	3		821
3	18	A	Stenhousemuir	W 2-1	1-1	2	Conroy 2 $^{42, 56}$	708
4	25	H	Raith R	L 3-4	2-0	4	Vitoria 2 $^{7, 83}$, Carrick ^{32}	1119
5	Sept 1	H	Stranraer	W 2-0	0-0	3	McIntosh, L ^{52}, Vitoria ^{88}	815
6	15	A	East Fife	L 1-2	0-0	3	Russell ^{74}	625
7	22	H	Dumbarton	D 1-1	0-1	3	Russell ^{70}	777
8	29	A	Arbroath	L 1-3	1-0	4	Vitoria ^{24}	787
9	Oct 6	H	Brechin C	L 1-3	1-1	6	Vitoria ^{15}	717
10	20	A	Montrose	W 3-0	2-0	4	Duffy 2 (1 pen) $^{19 (p), 37}$, Vitoria ^{79}	668
11	27	H	Stenhousemuir	L 0-1	0-0	5		773
12	Nov 3	H	Forfar Ath	L 0-1	0-0	7		645
13	10	A	Stranraer	W 2-1	1-0	6	Gallagher ^{12}, Wilkie ^{47}	326
14	17	H	East Fife	W 4-2	1-2	5	Crighton ^{42}, Duffy 2 (1 pen) $^{61 (p), 86}$, Wilkie ^{72}	818
15	Dec 1	A	Raith R	L 0-2	0-2	5		1567
16	8	A	Dumbarton	D 1-1	1-0	6	McIntosh, L ^{3}	624
17	15	H	Arbroath	L 0-1	0-1	6		611
18	22	A	Brechin C	W 1-0	0-0	6	Duffy (pen) ^{72}	448
19	29	H	Stranraer	W 3-0	2-0	5	McIntosh, L 2 $^{5, 43}$, Duffy ^{85}	725
20	Jan 5	A	East Fife	W 2-1	2-1	5	Wilkie ^{18}, McIntosh, L ^{44}	725
21	12	H	Raith R	D 1-1	1-0	5	McIntosh, L (pen) ^{9}	1140
22	26	A	Stenhousemuir	L 0-1	0-0	5		794
23	Feb 2	H	Dumbarton	D 2-2	1-0	6	Duffy ^{2}, McIntosh, L ^{64}	709
24	9	A	Forfar Ath	L 0-2	0-1	6		538
25	16	H	Brechin C	L 0-1	0-1	6		696
26	23	A	Arbroath	L 2-3	1-1	6	Carrick ^{27}, Duffy ^{52}	840
27	Mar 2	H	Montrose	W 1-0	0-0	6	Duffy ^{47}	638
28	9	A	Raith R	L 0-1	0-0	7		1339
29	23	H	Forfar Ath	W 1-0	1-0	6	Wilkie ^{45}	777
30	30	A	Brechin C	W 3-0	2-0	6	Wilkie ^{29}, Stewart ^{44}, McIntosh, L ^{49}	429
31	Apr 2	A	Dumbarton	D 3-3	2-1	6	Stewart 2 $^{27, 79}$, Duffy ^{32}	691
32	6	H	East Fife	D 0-0	0-0	6		772
33	13	H	Stenhousemuir	L 0-1	0-1	6		600
34	20	A	Montrose	L 1-2	0-1	6	McIntosh, L ^{90}	738
35	27	H	Arbroath	W 3-0	1-0	6	McIntosh, L 2 $^{39, 80}$, McIntosh, S ^{90}	590
36	May 4	A	Stranraer	W 4-1	3-0	5	McIntosh, L 3 $^{9, 43, 55}$, Glass ^{39}	424

Final League Position: 5

Honours
League Champions: Second Division 2003-04.
Runners-up: Second Division 2007-08.
League Challenge Cup Winners: 2008-09; *Runners-up:* 2003-04.

Club colours: Shirt: White with red diamond. Shorts: White with red trim. Socks: White with red trim.

Goalscorers: *League (51):* McIntosh L 15 (1 pen), Duffy 10 (3 pens), Vitoria 7, Wilkie 5, Conroy 3, Stewart 3, Carrick 2, Russell 2, Crighton 1, Gallagher 1, Glass 1, McIntosh S 1.
William Hill Scottish FA Cup (3): Wilkie 2, Duffy 1.
Betfred Scottish League Cup (9): Duffy 3, Crighton 2, Carrick 1, Conroy 1, McIntosh L 1, Vitoria 1.
Irn-Bru Scottish League Challenge (3): Carrick 1, Conroy 1, McIntosh L 1 (1 pen).

Gallacher S 2	Crighton S 36	Page J 13 + 1	Gallagher G 23 + 1	Edwards J 19 + 3	Stewart S 24 + 9	Robertson S 18 + 5	Conroy R 18 + 10	Wilkie K 18 – 8	Duffy D 21 + 11	Carrick D 21 + 4	Vitoria J 12 + 6	McIntosh L 21 + 13	Russell C 1 + 7	Hutton D 28 + 1	MacDonald K 26 + 1	Cairns D 7 + 7	Millar K 27 + 3	O'Neil C 22	MacKenzie B 6	Campbell J 13 + 1	Glass D 9 + 3	McIntosh S 5 – 4	Houston J 3 + 1	Hawkshaw D 3 + 3	*Match No.*
1	2	3	4	5	6^{1}	7	8	9^{3}	10^{2}	11	12	13	14												1
1^{3}	4	3	6	5	2	7	8	9^{1}	10	11^{2}	12	13		14											2
	3	4	14		6	2■	8		10^{2}	9	11	12^{3}	13	1	5	7^{1}									3
	3^{2}	4	7^{1}	12	2		8			9^{3}	11	10	14	1	5	6	13								4
	3	4	8		6	2^{1}	7			11	9	10		1	5		12								5
	3	4	8			2	7^{2}	13	12		9	10	11^{1}	1	5		6								6
	4		6^{2}	12	2	3	7	14		11	9	10^{3}	13	1	5^{1}		8								7
	4			5	6^{3}	3	12	9^{2}	13	10	11		14	1		7^{1}	8	2							8
	3			5	6	4	13	9^{3}	12	10	11		14	1		7^{1}	8	2^{2}							9
	3	4	7^{2}		13	2	6^{1}		10^{3}	11	9	12		1	5	14	8								10
	4	3	7		14	2^{3}	6	12	10^{2}	11	9	13		1	5		8^{1}								11
	3	4	7^{1}		12	2		6^{3}	10	9^{2}	11	13		1	5	14	8								12
	3	4	7		13			6	11^{1}	9^{2}	10^{3}	12			5	14	8	2	1						13
	3	4	6		13		14	9^{1}	11	10^{2}	8^{3}	12		1	5		7	2							14
	3	4^{3}	7		13		12	10^{2}	11^{1}	9	14	6		1	5		8	2							15
	3		7^{1}		6		8		11^{3}	8^{2}	12	10	14		5	13	4	2	1						16
	3		8	9	6			10	13	11^{1}	14	12			5	4^{2}	7^{3}	2	1						17
	3		6	8	5			9^{3}	12	11^{1}	13	10^{2}			4	14	7	2	1						18
	3		7	9	6^{1}	13		11^{3}	12	8^{2}		10			5	14	4	2	1						19
	3	13	7	8	5			11^{3}	14	12		10^{2}			4		6	2	1	9^{1}					20
	3		6	9	5^{2}	12		11^{1}	14	13		10		1	4		7	2		8^{3}					21
	3		9	4^{3}	6		14	12	13	11^{2}		10		1	5		7^{1}	2			8				22
	3		7	14	5	12	8^{3}	13	11^{1}			9		1	4^{2}		6	2			10				23
	3		7		5^{2}	4	8		12	13		9		1			6^{3}	2		10^{1}	11	14			24
	3		6^{1}		13		8		10	12		11		1	4	14		2^{2}		7	9	5^{3}			25
	3		6^{2}		14		8		10	11		13		1	4		12	2		7	9^{3}		5^{1}		26
	3					14	8	12	10	11^{3}		13		1	4			2		7	9^{2}	6	5^{1}		27
	3			8		12	9^{3}	13	11			14		1	4			2^{1}		7	10^{2}	6	5		28
	3			8	5	2	9^{1}	11^{3}	10^{2}			13		1			7	4		6		14		12	29
	3			8	5^{1}	2	12	9^{3}	11^{2}			10		1			7	4		6	13		14		30
	3			8	5	2	12	9^{2}	11^{1}			10		1			7	4		6	13				31
	3			8	5	2	13	9^{2}	11^{1}			10		1			7	4^{3}		6		14		12	32
	3			8^{1}	5	2	14	9^{3}	10			11		1	12		6			7		4^{2}		13	33
	3			5	13	2■	9^{1}	12	10^{3}			11		1	4		6			7	14			8^{2}	34
	2	3		9	5		12					11		1	4	7^{2}	6				10	13		8^{1}	35
	3			9^{1}	5				13			10		1	4	7^{2}	6			12	11	2		8	36

ALBION ROVERS

Year Formed: 1882. *Ground & Address:* Cliftonhill Stadium, Main St, Coatbridge ML5 3RB. *Telephone/Fax:* 01236 606334.
E-mail: secretary@albionroversfc.co.uk *Website:* albionroversfc.co.uk
Ground capacity: 1,572 (seated: 489). *Size of Pitch:* 101m × 66m.
Chairman Eddie Hagerty.
Manager: Kevin Harper. *Assistant Manager:* Joe McLaughlin.
Club Nickname: 'The Wee Rovers'.
Previous Grounds: Cowheath Park, Meadow Park, Whifflet.
Record Attendance: 27,381 v Rangers, Scottish Cup 2nd rd, 8 February 1936.
Record Transfer Fee received: £40,000 from Motherwell for Bruce Cleland (1979).
Record Transfer Fee paid: £7,000 for Gerry McTeague to Stirling Alb, September 1989.
Record Victory: 12-0 v Airdriehill, Scottish Cup 1st rd, 3 September 1887.
Record Defeat: 1-11 v Partick Thistle, League Cup 2nd rd, 11 August 1993.
Most Capped Player: Jock White, 1 (2), Scotland.
Most League Appearances: 399: Murdy Walls, 1921-36.
Most League Goals in Season (Individual): 41: Jim Renwick, Division II, 1932-33.
Most Goals Overall (Individual): 105: Bunty Weir, 1928-31.

ALBION ROVERS – SPFL LADBROKES LEAGUE TWO 2018–19 LEAGUE RECORD

Match No.	*Date*	*Venue*	*Opponents*	*Result*	*H/T Score*	*Lg Pos.*	*Goalscorers*	*Attendance*
1	Aug 4	A	Edinburgh C	L 0-4	0-1	10		303
2	11	H	Peterhead	L 0-4	0-1	10		277
3	18	H	Elgin C	L 0-1	0-0	10		275
4	25	A	Queen's Park	L 0-2	0-2	10		620
5	Sept 1	H	Berwick R	L 3-5	2-2	10	Murdoch[3], McLear[38], Gracie[50]	222
6	15	A	Clyde	L 0-1	0-1	10		708
7	22	A	Cowdenbeath	D 1-1	1-0	10	McLear[25]	348
8	29	H	Stirling Alb	W 3-0	1-0	10	McLear[9], Watters 2[53, 86]	260
9	Oct 6	A	Annan Ath	L 1-3	0-1	10	McLear[59]	369
10	27	H	Queen's Park	L 0-3	0-2	10		390
11	Nov 3	A	Peterhead	L 1-2	0-2	10	Eley[71]	590
12	10	H	Edinburgh C	L 1-2	1-1	10	Escuriola[45]	229
13	17	A	Berwick R	L 0-2	0-1	10		537
14	Dec 1	H	Cowdenbeath	D 1-1	1-1	10	Gallagher (pen)[10]	220
15	8	A	Elgin C	L 2-4	1-2	10	Gracie 2[30, 89]	538
16	22	H	Clyde	L 0-3	0-2	10		320
17	29	H	Annan Ath	D 1-1	0-0	10	Forrester[81]	145
18	Jan 5	A	Queen's Park	D 2-2	2-1	10	Rodgers[15], Fotheringham[19]	642
19	12	H	Peterhead	L 0-2	0-0	10		332
20	26	H	Stirling Alb	L 0-5	0-1	10		293
21	Feb 2	A	Edinburgh C	L 1-3	1-2	10	Newell[19]	331
22	9	H	Elgin C	L 0-3	0-1	10		183
23	12	A	Stirling Alb	L 0-1	0-0	10		461
24	16	A	Clyde	W 3-0	0-1	10	Match awarded to Albion R after Clyde won 1-0.	536
25	19	A	Cowdenbeath	L 0-1	0-0	10		254
26	23	A	Annan Ath	L 0-4	0-3	10		363
27	Mar 2	H	Berwick R	D 1-1	1-0	10	Newell[15]	273
28	9	A	Stirling Alb	W 1-0	1-0	10	Fotheringham[4]	561
29	23	A	Elgin C	W 2-0	2-0	10	Byrne 2[22, 39]	733
30	26	H	Cowdenbeath	W 1-0	1-0	9	Byrne[43]	322
31	30	H	Clyde	L 0-1	0-0	9		560
32	Apr 6	H	Queen's Park	L 0-4	0-1	9		323
33	13	A	Peterhead	D 1-1	0-0	9	Osadolor[90]	715
34	20	H	Edinburgh C	W 3-2	1-1	9	Osadolor 2[9, 77], Phillips[64]	253
35	27	A	Berwick R	W 3-0	2-0	9	Fotheringham 2[24, 50], Phillips (pen)[45]	975
36	May 4	H	Annan Ath	L 0-2	0-0	9		274

Final League Position: 9

Honours

League Champions: Division II 1933-34; Second Division 1988-89; League Two 2014-15.
Runners-up: Division II 1913-14, 1937-38, 1947-48; Third Division 2010-11.
Promoted via play-offs: 2010-11 (to Second Division).
Scottish Cup Runners-up: 1920.

Club colours: Shirt: Yellow with red trim. Shorts: Red. Socks: Red with yellow tops.

Goalscorers: *League (29):* Fotheringham 4, McLear 4, Byrne 3, Gracie 3, Osadolor 3, Newell 2, Phillips 2 (1 pen), Watters 2, Eley 1, Escuriola 1, Forrester 1, Gallagher 1 (1 pen), Murdoch 1, Rodgers 1.
William Hill Scottish FA Cup (0).
Betfred Scottish League Cup (0).
Irn-Bru Scottish League Challenge (1): Cunningham 1.

Hallford G 2	Smith S 6	Wharton B 25 + 1	Murdoch A 9	Forrester S 9 + 3 / Russell M — + 2	McLear L 11 + 3	McGeough P 14 / Tierney R — + 1	Fisher G 10 + 5	Kearney R 5 + 7 / Griffiths R 1	Gracie G 5 + 6	Watson J 12 + 6	Cunningham J 6 + 7	Watters R 5 + 6 / Ward R 1 + 1	Gallagher J 12 + 4	Duncanson L 1 / Reilly A — + 1	Reid A 6 + 2	Eley B 12 + 1 / Morena G 10	Gray S 1	Potts D 4 / Osadolor S 9	Match No.
1	2	3	4	5	6	7	8^{2}	9^{1}	10^{3}	11	12	13	14						1
1		3	4	13	6	8		12	14		10		11^{2}	2^{3}	5	7	9^{1}		2
	7	5	4^{1}		9^{2}	8		2	12		11^{3}		10		14	3		1	3
		4		2		6^{3}	7	14		11	10				12	3■		1	4
		3	2		11	7	8	12	10^{2}	6^{3}	13				5			1	5
		13	3^{3}		6		7		10			12	14		5	4			6
		3		12	10		6			9^{1}	13	11^{2}	7		5	4			7
		4			6^{1}	7	8		13	12	14	9^{3}	11		5	3			8
	11	4			7		9	13	14	6^{1}	12	8^{3}	10^{2}		5	3			9
			4	12	10^{1}	8	/■			6^{2}	11^{3}	13	9			3			10
			4			7			13	6	11^{2}	8^{1}	9			3			11
				3^{2}	13	8	7^{1}	14		6	9^{3}		12			4			12
				3	10	7		9		6^{1}	12	13	8			4		1	13
	2		4	3	10^{1}	7		6^{3}	12	11^{2}	14	13	8						14
	2		4	3	12	7^{1}			11	10^{3}		6^{2}	8						15
	6			3	14	8			10^{3}	13			/			4^{2}			16
		8		4		9^{3}		12		6^{1}		13	7			14			17
		6^{3}		2				5					12						18
		7						12											19
		6								14									20
		6^{2}		12															21
		7^{2}				12													22
				12						14									23
		3																	24
								4		14		12							25
							12			13		11^{3}		14					26
		4														7		11^{1}	27
		3					13									7		10^{3}	28
		3					12									8		10	29
		3					12									8		10	30
		3					12									7^{1}		10	31
		3					6^{4}									7^{1}			32
		3														7^{1}		10	33
		3														8		10^{3}	34
		3														8^{3}		10	35
		3														8^{1}		10	36

McMahon L 6 + 7	Guthrie J 1 + 2	Wilson L 25	Fagan S 24 + 2	Greene M 3 + 3	Morrison P 30	Jones R 2	Escuriola G 9 + 6	Hardie M 14	Byrne D 17	Krones J 7	Reilly B 15 + 3	Fotheringham G 19	Rodgers S 3 / Gordan J — + 6	Daily B — + 1	Clarke R 17	Phillips G 13 + 2	Ross B 5 + 7	Newell G 10 + 1	Match No.
																			1
																			2
6	13																		3
5	9^{1}	8^{2}	13																4
		9^{1}	4	14															5
8		9^{1}	2	11^{2}	1														6
8			2		1														7
10^{2}			2		1														8
			2		1														9
		5	2	14	1														10
		5	2		1	10	12												11
		5	2		1	10	11												12
		5^{2}	2				11												13
		5			1		9												14
14		5		13	1		9												15
		5	12	9^{1}	1			2	11										16
		5^{2}	3	10	1			2	11										17
13			3		1		8^{2}		11	4	7	9	10^{1}	14					18
13			3		1		10^{1}	2	11	4	8	8	9^{1}		5				19
			3		1		9^{3}	2	11■	4	8	7^{2}	10^{1}		5	12	13		20
		10	3		1		9^{1}	2		4	8	7			5		13	11	21
14		9	4		1			2		3^{1}	11	8			5	6^{3}	13	10	22
13		9^{2}	3		1			2	11	4	6	7			5		8^{3}	10^{1}	23
14		9^{2}			1		12	2	10^{1}	4	6^{3}	7			5	13	8	11	24
13			3		1		11^{1}	2			6^{3}	8			5^{2}	9	7	10	25
2		9	3		1						6	8^{1}			5	4	7^{2}	10	26
			3		1		13	2	6^{2}		12	8			5	9		10	27
		4			1			2	6^{1}		12	8	14		5	9		11^{2}	28
		4			1			2	11^{3}		6^{1}	7^{2}	13		5	9	14		29
		4			1			2	11		6^{1}	7			5	9			30
		4			1		13	2	11		6	8			5	9^{2}			31
	14	4	2		1		12		11		8^{3}	10	13		5	9			32
		4	2		1				11		6	8			5	9	12		33
		4	2		1				11^{1}		6^{2}	7	13		5	9	14	12	34
		4	2		1				11		12	7	14		5	9^{1}	13	6^{2}	35
		4	2		1		12		11			7^{2}	13			9	5	6	36

ALLOA ATHLETIC

Year Formed: 1878. *Ground & Address:* Indodrill Stadium, Recreation Park, Clackmannan Rd, Alloa FK10 1RY.
Telephone: 01259 722695. *Fax:* 01259 210886. *E-mail:* fcadmin@alloaathletic.co.uk *Website:* www.alloaathletic.co.uk
Ground Capacity: 3,100 (seated: 919). *Size of Pitch:* 102m × 69m.
Chairman: Mike Mulraney. *Secretary:* Ewen Cameron.
Manager (caretaker): Paddy Connolly.
Club Nicknames: 'The Wasps'; 'The Hornets'.
Previous Grounds: West End Public Park: Gabberston Park; Bellevue Park.
Record Attendance: 15,467 v Celtic, Scottish Cup 5th rd, 5 February 1955.
Record Transfer Fee received: £100,000 for Martin Cameron to Bristol R (July 2000).
Record Transfer Fee paid: £26,000 for Ross Hamilton from Stenhousemuir (July 2000).
Record Victory: 9-0 v Selkirk, Scottish Cup 1st rd, 28 November 2005.
Record Defeat: 0-10 v Dundee, Division II, 8 March 1947; v Third Lanark, League Cup, 8 August 1953.
Most Capped Player: Jock Hepburn, 1, Scotland.
Most League Appearances: 239: Peter Smith 1960-69.
Most League Goals in Season (Individual): 49: 'Wee' Willie Crilley, Division II, 1921-22.
Most Goals Overall (Individual): 91: Willie Irvine, 1996-2001.

ALLOA ATHLETIC – SPFL LADBROKES CHAMPIONSHIP 2018–19 LEAGUE RECORD

Match No.	Date	Venue	Opponents	Result		H/T Score	Lg Pos.	Goalscorers	Attendance
1	Aug 4	A	Ross Co	L	0-1	0-0	8		3065
2	11	H	Greenock Morton	L	0-2	0-1	10		836
3	25	A	Inverness CT	D	2-2	1-1	9	Oakley (og) [33], Flannigan (pen) [87]	2269
4	Sept 1	H	Dundee U	D	1-1	0-0	9	Flannigan [82]	1616
5	15	A	Dunfermline Ath	D	0-0	0-0	9		4568
6	22	H	Ayr U	L	0-2	0-1	9		949
7	29	H	Falkirk	L	0-2	0-1	9		1392
8	Oct 6	A	Queen of the South	D	3-3	3-2	9	Flannigan [3], Hastie [15], Shields [25]	1228
9	20	H	Partick Thistle	W	1-0	0-0	9	Zanatta [50]	1392
10	27	H	Inverness CT	D	0-0	0-0	9		644
11	30	A	Ayr U	L	0-3	0-0	9		1742
12	Nov 3	H	Dunfermline Ath	L	0-1	0-0	9		1169
13	10	A	Greenock Morton	W	2-0	0-0	8	Trouten (pen) [73], Flannigan (pen) [85]	1794
14	20	A	Dundee U	L	2-4	2-3	8	Trouten (pen) [17], Flannigan [38]	4201
15	Dec 1	H	Ross Co	L	0-1	0-0	8		592
16	8	A	Falkirk	D	2-2	1-2	9	Trouten 2 [42, 77]	3907
17	15	A	Partick Thistle	D	2-2	1-2	9	Cawley [24], Zanatta [59]	1990
18	22	H	Queen of the South	W	2-0	0-0	8	Flannigan [63], Zanatta [90]	646
19	29	H	Dundee U	W	2-1	0-0	8	Graham [73], Zanatta [89]	1859
20	Jan 5	A	Dunfermline Ath	D	2-2	0-2	8	Trouten 2 [49, 90]	4723
21	12	H	Greenock Morton	W	2-1	0-1	8	Trouten (pen) [67], Waddell (og) [77]	931
22	26	A	Ross Co	L	0-2	0-1	8		3521
23	Feb 2	H	Ayr U	L	1-3	1-1	8	Trouten [30]	957
24	9	H	Falkirk	L	1-2	1-1	9	Shields [31]	2116
25	16	H	Partick Thistle	L	0-2	0-1	10		1757
26	23	A	Queen of the South	W	2-1	1-0	8	Graham [18], Kirkpatrick [90]	1116
27	Mar 9	H	Dunfermline Ath	L	0-1	0-0	10		1750
28	23	A	Dundee U	L	1-2	1-1	10	Kirkpatrick [6]	4645
29	26	A	Inverness CT	L	2-3	0-2	10	Trouten (pen) [81], Flannigan [90]	2006
30	30	H	Ross Co	W	1-0	1-0	10	Zanatta [33]	697
31	Apr 6	A	Falkirk	W	2-1	1-0	10	Zanatta [38], Kirkpatrick [86]	4170
32	9	A	Greenock Morton	W	2-1	0-0	8	Graham [54], Hamilton [80]	1498
33	13	H	Queen of the South	W	1-0	0-0	6	Hetherington [73]	1086
34	20	A	Partick Thistle	L	1-2	1-0	8	Aitchison [13]	3578
35	27	H	Inverness CT	L	1-2	1-0	9	Trouten (pen) [27]	826
36	May 4	A	Ayr U	D	1-1	1-1	8	Shields [33]	1665

Final League Position: 8

Honours
League Champions: Division II 1921-22; Third Division 1997-98, 2011-12.
Runners-up: Division II 1938-39; Second Division 1976-77, 1981-82, 1984-85, 1988-89, 1999-2000, 2001-02, 2009-10, 2012-13; League One 2016-17.
Promoted via play-offs: 2012-13 (to First Division); 2017-18 (to Championship).
League Challenge Cup Winners: 1999-2000; *Runners-up:* 2001-02, 2014-15.

Club colours: Shirt: Gold and black hoops. Shorts: Black. Socks: Black with gold hoops.

Goalscorers: *League (39):* Trouten 10 (5 pens), Flannigan 7 (2 pens), Zanatta 6, Graham 3, Kirkpatrick 3, Shields 3, Aitchison 1, Cawley 1, Hamilton 1, Hastie 1, Hetherington 1, own goals 2.
William Hill Scottish FA Cup (5): Trouten 2, Cawley 1, Spence 1, Zanatta 1.
Betfred Scottish League Cup (8): Trouten 3 (1 pen), Hastie 2, Spence 2, Cawley 1.
Irn-Bru Scottish League Challenge (8): Trouten 4 (1 pen), Cawley 2, Flannigan 1, Zanatta 1.

Parry N 36	Taggart S 36	Karadachki Z 3	Graham A 36	Dick L 34	Brown A 2 + 12	Robertson J 22 + 4	Hetherington S 29 + 4	Hastie J 14 + 5	Spence G 7 + 6	Trouten A 32 + 2	Peggie R — + 2	Flannigan I 33	Cawley K 22 + 12	Zanatta D 32 + 2	Burt L 3 + 6	Roscoe S 23	Shields C 19 + 11	Aloulou A — + 1	Kirkpatrick J 6 + 11	Hamilton J 1 + 14	Aitchison J 6 + 4	Match No.
1	2	3	4	5	6	7	8	9	10	11^{1}	12											1
1	2	4	3	5	7^{1}		6	10	11	8		9	12									2
1	2	4■	3	5	13		8^{3}	6	11^{1}		12	7	9^{2}	10	14							3
1	2		3	5	13		8	6		7^{3}		10	9^{1}	11^{2}	12	4	14					4
1	2		4	5			6	9	13	10^{1}		8	7^{2}	11^{3}	12	3	14					5
1	2		4	5			7	9^{3}	13	10^{2}		8	6	11^{1}	14	3	12					6
1	2		4	5	12		7^{2}	9^{1}	11^{3}			8	6	13	10	3	14					7
1	2		4	5	13	7		9		14		8	6^{3}	12	10^{1}	3	11^{2}					8
1	2		4	5	14	6	13	12		9^{3}		7	8^{1}	10		3	11^{2}					9
1	2		4	5	13	6	14	12		9^{1}		7	8^{3}	10		3	11^{2}					10
1	2		3	5		8		9^{2}	14	13		7	12	11	10^{3}	4	6^{1}					11
1	2		4	5	12	9	6^{1}	13	11^{2}	8			7^{3}	10		3		14				12
1	2		3	5		6	13	12	11^{1}	9^{2}		7	8	10		4						13
1	2		3	5		7^{1}	9^{2}	10		8		6	12	11		4	13					14
1	2		4	5		7	13	12	11^{2}	10^{3}		8	6^{1}	9		3	14					15
1	2		4	5		8		11^{2}	13	10		7	6^{1}	9		3	12					16
1	2		4	5		13	7	11		10^{1}		8	6^{2}	9		3	12					17
1	2		3		12	9	5	10		8^{2}		7	6^{1}	11	13	4						18
1	2		4	5	13	9	7	11		8^{1}			6^{2}	10		3	12					19
1	2		3	5			6^{1}		14	9		7	12	11	13	4	8^{3}		10^{2}			20
1	2		3	5		13	7		14	10^{3}		8	12	11		4	6^{1}		9^{2}			21
1	2		3	5			7^{1}			8		10	6^{3}	11		4	9^{2}		12	13	14	22
1	2		3	4		5	8^{1}			11^{2}		9		10			7		6	13	12	23
1	2		3			5^{3}	8			10		9	14	11		4	6^{1}		7^{2}	12	13	24
1	2		4	5		14	9^{2}			8^{3}		7	6^{1}	10		3	11		12	13		25
1	2		4	5		14	9			8^{2}		7^{3}	6	10		3	11^{1}		13	12		26
1	2		3	5			7			11^{1}		8	14	9		4	6^{3}		12	10^{2}	13	27
1	2		3	5	14	4	7^{2}			10^{1}		8	12	9			11^{3}		6	13		28
1	2		3	4	13		5			11		8	9^{2}	10			6		7^{1}	12		29
1	2		3	4		5	6			9^{2}		7	12	11			8^{3}		13	14	10^{1}	30
1	4		3	5		2	6			9^{1}		7	12	10			8^{2}		14	13	11^{3}	31
1	4		3	5		2	7			9^{3}		6	12	10			8^{2}		13	14	11^{1}	32
1	4		3	5		2	7			9^{3}		8	6	11^{2}			13		14	12	10^{1}	33
1	4		3	5		2	7			9^{1}		6	14	10			8^{2}		12	13	11^{3}	34
1	4		3	5		2	6			9^{1}		7	8^{3}	10			12		13	14	11^{2}	35
1	3		4	5	13	2	7			9^{1}		6	8	10^{2}			11^{3}		12	14		36

ANNAN ATHLETIC

Year Formed: 1942. *Ground & Address:* Galabank, North Street, Annan DG12 5DQ. *Telephone:* 01461 204108.
E-mail: annanathletic.enquiries@btconnect.com *Website:* www.annanathleticfc.com
Ground capacity: 2,517 (seated: 500). *Size of Pitch:* 100m × 62m.
Chairman: Philip Jones. *Vice-Chairman:* Russell Brown.
Secretary: Alan Irving.
Player/Manager: Peter Murphy.
Assistant Manager: Darren Barr.
Club Nicknames: 'Galabankies'; 'Black and Golds'.
Previous Ground: Mafeking Park.
Record attendance: 2,517, v Rangers, Third Division, 15 September 2012.
Record Victory: 6-0 v Elgin C, Third Division, 7 March 2009.
Record Defeat: 1-8 v Inverness CT, Scottish Cup 3rd rd, 24 January 1998.
Most League Appearances: 285: Peter Watson, 2008-18.
Most League Goals in Season (Individual): 22: Peter Weatherson, 2014-15.
Most Goals Overall (Individual): 56: Peter Weatherson, 2013-17.

ANNAN ATHLETIC – SPFL LADBROKES LEAGUE TWO 2018–19 LEAGUE RECORD

Match No.	*Date*	*Venue*	*Opponents*	*Result*		*H/T Score*	*Lg Pos.*	*Goalscorers*	*Attendance*
1	Aug 4	H	Elgin C	D	1-1	0-0	4	Sonkur [68]	395
2	11	A	Cowdenbeath	W	2-1	1-1	3	Muir [31], Swinglehurst [50]	303
3	18	H	Queen's Park	W	3-1	0-0	2	Muir [46], Sinnamon [49], Smith [52]	420
4	25	A	Berwick Rangers	W	3-0	1-0	2	Smith [8], Muir [61], Wilson [90]	507
5	Sept 1	H	Clyde	L	1-2	1-1	3	Wallace [37]	569
6	15	A	Edinburgh C	L	1-2	0-1	4	Sinnamon [83]	247
7	22	A	Stirling Alb	W	2-1	1-0	4	Horne (og) [12], Wallace [69]	502
8	29	H	Peterhead	L	1-3	0-1	4	Wallace [82]	433
9	Oct 6	H	Albion R	W	3-1	1-0	4	Wallace (pen) [26], Roberts 2 [55, 75]	369
10	27	A	Elgin C	W	1-0	1-0	3	Moxon [38]	533
11	Nov 3	A	Queen's Park	D	0-0	0-0	4		495
12	10	H	Cowdenbeath	L	0-2	0-0	4		374
13	17	H	Stirling Alb	D	2-2	1-0	4	Wallace [20], Sinnamon [70]	399
14	Dec 1	A	Peterhead	L	1-2	0-1	4	Wallace (pen) [80]	577
15	8	H	Edinburgh C	L	1-2	0-1	5	Hooper [64]	317
16	15	A	Clyde	L	0-1	0-0	5		408
17	22	H	Berwick Rangers	W	4-0	1-0	5	Swinglehurst 2 [2, 69], Moxon [46], Smith [55]	373
18	29	A	Albion R	D	1-1	0-0	4	Wilson [86]	145
19	Jan 5	H	Elgin C	W	2-0	1-0	4	Muir 2 [41, 85]	326
20	12	A	Stirling Alb	L	1-2	1-1	4	Muir [33]	617
21	19	A	Edinburgh C	W	2-1	0-1	4	Henderson, B (og) [72], Wilson [47]	285
22	26	H	Peterhead	W	3-0	0-0	4	Wilson [53], Muir 2 [60, 69]	398
23	Feb 9	H	Clyde	D	1-1	0-1	4	Bradley [87]	555
24	16	A	Cowdenbeath	W	4-2	1-2	4	Johnston 2 [15, 87], Smith 2 [56, 90]	255
25	23	H	Albion R	W	4-0	3-0	4	Watson [6], Wallace [16], Swinglehurst [25], Fergusson [87]	363
26	26	A	Berwick Rangers	W	2-1	1-0	4	Muir [26], Bradley [73]	323
27	Mar 2	H	Queen's Park	W	2-1	1-0	4	Wallace 2 [23, 73]	379
28	9	A	Peterhead	L	1-2	1-1	4	Wallace [21]	568
29	16	H	Edinburgh C	W	3-1	1-0	4	Smith (pen) [35], Swinglehurst [58], Nade [73]	341
30	23	A	Clyde	L	1-2	0-0	4	Wallace (pen) [86]	612
31	30	A	Elgin C	W	1-0	1-0	4	Smith [17]	485
32	Apr 6	H	Berwick Rangers	W	6-0	0-0	4	Moxon 2 [46, 65], Wallace (pen) [51], Wilson (og) [71], Johnston [73], Wilson [77]	324
33	13	H	Stirling Alb	D	2-2	0-1	4	Nade [88], Sonkur [90]	468
34	20	A	Queen's Park	W	3-0	0-0	4	Smith 2 [60, 70], Muir [76]	523
35	27	H	Cowdenbeath	W	3-2	2-0	4	Smith 2 [10, 70], Nade [21]	365
36	May 4	A	Albion R	W	2-0	0-0	4	Muir 2 (1 pen) [85 (p), 90]	274

Final League Position: 4

Honours
League Two Runners-up: 2013-14.
League Challenge Cup: Semi-finals: 2009-10, 2011-12.

Club colours: Shirt: Gold with black trim. Shorts: Black. Socks: Gold.

Goalscorers: *League (70):* Muir 12 (1 pen), Wallace 12 (4 pens), Smith 11 (1 pen), Swinglehurst 5, Wilson 5, Moxon 4, Johnston 3, Nade 3, Sinnamon 3, Bradley 2, Roberts 2, Sonkur 2, Fergusson 1, Hooper 1, Watson 1, own goals 3.
William Hill Scottish FA Cup (4): Smith 2 (1 pen), Muir 1, Wilson 1.
Betfred Scottish League Cup (6): Muir 2, Wilson 2, Roberts 1, Smith 1.
Irn-Bru Scottish League Challenge (4): Fergusson 2, Wallace 2.
Play-Offs (5): Johnston 2, Bradley 1, Sonkur 1, Swinglehurst 1.

Mitchell A 25	Hooper S 34	Sonkur A 17 + 3	Swinglehurst S 22	Creaney J 21	Johnston C 30 + 2	Wilson D 33 + 3	Sinnamon R 21 + 2	Smith A 28 + 7	Roberts S 8 + 8	Muir T 24 + 9	Fergusson R 6 + 15	Wright M 2 + 13	Wallace T 28 + 5	Moxon O 29 + 3	Watson P 13 + 2	Jamieson J 8	Bradley K 20 + 6	Strapp L 15 + 5	Nade C 7 + 5	McAdams A 3	Brannan J 2	*Match No.*
1	2	3	4	5	6	7	8	9	10^{1}	11^{2}	12	13										1
1	2	3	4	5	6	7	8	10^{1}	9^{2}	11^{3}	12		13	14								2
1	2	3	4^{3}	5	9	7	8	10	6^{1}	11^{2}	13		12		14							3
1	5	4		2	9	8		11^{2}		10^{1}	13	12	6	7	3							4
	2	4		5	9	8	7	10^{1}		11	12	13	6^{2}		3	1						5
	2	4		5	9	7	6	11^{1}	13	14	10^{3}		12	8^{2}		1	3					6
	2			5	6	7	8	14	10^{2}	11^{3}	12	13	9^{1}	3		1	4					7
	3			5	6^{1}	7	2	13	11^{3}	10^{2}	12	14	9	8		1	4					8
	3	12		5^{3}	6	7	2		11	10		14	9^{1}	8		1	4^{2}	13				9
	3	12	4^{3}			6	2	13	9^{1}	8	11	14	10^{2}	7		1		5				10
	4	3			6^{2}	7	2	13	10	11^{3}	12	14	9^{1}	8		1		5				11
	4	3^{2}			6	7	2	13		10		11	9^{1}	8		1	12	5				12
1	3			5	6^{3}	7	2	13	14	11^{1}	12	10	9^{2}	8			4					13
1	4	3		5^{1}		7	2	10	13	11^{3}		14	9	6^{2}			8	12				14
1	3	4			10	7^{1}	2^{2}	11	13			12	9	8			6	5				15
1	2	8			9	3	7	10^{2}	12^{3}	14		13	11	6^{1}			4	5				16
1	2		3		9	8	7	10^{3}	12	13		14	11^{1}	6^{2}			4	5				17
1	2		4		6^{2}	3	7	11	12		13		10	8^{1}			9	5				18
1	3	12	4	5		8	2	10^{1}	14	9	11^{3}	13		6^{2}			7					19
1	3		4	5	12	7	2	10		9	11^{4}		13	6^{1}			8					20
1	2	8^{1}	4	5	6	3	7	10		11				9	12							21
1	2		4	5	9	7		11		10^{1}	12		6	8	3							22
1	2		4	5	6	7		10^{1}		11^{3}	14		9^{2}	8	3		12		13			23
1	2		4	5^{3}	6	8		11			13		9^{1}	7	3		14	12	10^{2}			24
1	2		4		6^{1}	8^{3}		10		14	13		9	7	3		12	5	11^{2}			25
1	2	3	4			8		9		11	10		6^{1}				7	5	12			26
	2		4		6	7		10		12			9	13	3		8^{1}	5	11^{2}	1		27
	2		4		6	7		11		10^{1}	12		9^{2}	8	3			5	13	1		28
1	2		4		6	7		11		13			12	9^{1}	3		8	5	10^{2}			29
1	2		4		6	8		11		10			9	12	3		7^{1}	5				30
1	2		4	5	9	7^{2}		10		12			6	8	3		13		11^{1}			31
1	2	3	4	5^{3}	6	13		11		14			9	8^{2}			7	12	10^{1}			32
1	2	3	4	5^{2}	6	13		10		11^{3}			9	8^{1}			7	14	12			33
1	2	4		5	6	7^{2}	13	10		11			9^{1}	8			3		12			34
			4		12	7^{2}	14	6		11			9	8^{1}	3		13	5	10^{3}	1	2	35
1		8			9^{1}	13	10	12		14	11		6^{3}	7	3		4^{2}	5			2	36

ARBROATH

Year Formed: 1878. *Ground & Address:* Gayfield Park, Arbroath DD11 1QB. *Telephone:* 01241 872157. *Fax:* 01241 431125. *E-mail:* arbroathfc@outlook.com *Website:* www.arbroathfc.co.uk
Ground Capacity: 6,600 (seated: 861). *Size of Pitch:* 105m × 65m.
Chairman: Mike Caird. *Secretary:* Dr Gary Callon.
Manager: Dick Campbell. *Assistant Manager:* Ian Campbell.
Club Nickname: 'The Red Lichties'.
Previous Ground: Lesser Gayfield.
Record Attendance: 13,510 v Rangers, Scottish Cup 3rd rd, 23 February 1952.
Record Transfer Fee received: £120,000 for Paul Tosh to Dundee (August 1993).
Record Transfer Fee paid: £20,000 for Douglas Robb from Montrose (1981).
Record Victory: 36-0 v Bon Accord, Scottish Cup 1st rd, 12 September 1885.
Record Defeat: 0-8 v Kilmarnock, Division II, 3 January 1949; 1-9 v Celtic, League Cup 3rd rd, 25 August 1993.
Most Capped Player: Ned Doig, 2 (5), Scotland.
Most League Appearances: 445: Tom Cargill, 1966-81.
Most League Goals in Season (Individual): 45: Dave Easson, Division II, 1958-59.
Most Goals Overall (Individual): 120: Jimmy Jack, 1966-71.

ARBROATH – SPFL LADBROKES LEAGUE ONE 2018–19 LEAGUE RECORD

Match No.	Date	Venue	Opponents	Result	H/T Score	Lg Pos.	Goalscorers	Attendance
1	Aug 4	A	Montrose	W 4-0	1-0	1	Wallace 22, Linn 2 (1 pen) 69 (p), 83, Hester 90	1374
2	11	H	Stranraer	W 3-1	1-1	1	Little 10, McKenna 77, Wallace 81	582
3	18	A	Dumbarton	D 1-1	1-0	1	Linn 26	627
4	25	A	East Fife	W 3-0	2-0	1	O'Brien 40, Wallace 45, Denholm 75	639
5	Sept 1	H	Brechin C	D 2-2	2-0	1	Thomson 2, Linn 19	901
6	15	H	Forfar Ath	W 3-1	1-1	1	Linn 3 38, 50, 63	1015
7	22	A	Stenhousemuir	W 2-1	0-1	1	Wallace (pen) 62, McCord 80	585
8	29	H	Airdrieonians	W 3-1	0-1	1	Swankie 51, Hamilton 64, Wallace 85	787
9	Oct 6	A	Raith R	D 1-1	0-0	1	Linn 79	2137
10	20	H	Dumbarton	W 3-1	0-1	1	Wallace 61, Doris 75, Swankie 77	700
11	27	A	Stranraer	W 1-0	1-0	1	Cummins (og) 17	393
12	Nov 3	H	East Fife	W 1-0	0-0	1	McKenna 55	765
13	10	H	Montrose	W 2-0	1-0	1	Denholm 34, Doris 85	1271
14	17	A	Brechin C	W 5-1	1-0	1	Gold 8, Linn 48, McKenna 56, Wallace 65, Thomson 80	847
15	Dec 1	H	Stenhousemuir	W 5-2	2-1	1	Kader 31, Linn 2 36, 52, Hamilton 79, McCord 83	734
16	8	A	Forfar Ath	W 3-2	1-0	1	Linn 3 8, 60, 83	958
17	15	A	Airdrieonians	W 1-0	1-0	1	Little 27	611
18	22	H	Raith R	L 0-2	0-2	1		1808
19	29	A	Montrose	D 1-1	0-0	1	O'Brien 77	1666
20	Jan 5	H	Brechin C	W 1-0	0-0	1	McCord 82	1061
21	12	A	Stenhousemuir	W 4-1	2-1	1	Linn 2 4, 58, Wallace 2 9, 52	760
22	26	H	Forfar Ath	L 0-2	0-1	1		1132
23	Feb 12	H	Stranraer	D 1-1	1-0	1	Linn 26	532
24	16	A	Raith R	W 1-0	1-0	1	Hamilton 27	1937
25	23	H	Airdrieonians	W 3-2	1-1	1	Linn 3 (2 pens) 43, 59 (p), 63 (p)	840
26	26	A	East Fife	D 1-1	1-1	1	Donnelly 25	722
27	Mar 2	A	Dumbarton	L 0-2	0-1	1		700
28	9	H	Stenhousemuir	L 0-2	0-1	1		719
29	16	H	East Fife	W 2-1	1-1	1	McKenna 27, Linn 50	709
30	23	A	Stranraer	D 0-0	0-0	1		432
31	30	A	Forfar Ath	L 1-2	1-1	1	McKenna 19	1342
32	Apr 6	H	Montrose	W 1-0	0-0	1	Little 64	1248
33	13	A	Brechin C	D 1-1	1-1	1	Wallace 5	1509
34	21	H	Raith R	D 2-2	1-1	1	Swankie 30, Wallace 80	932
35	27	A	Airdrieonians	L 0-3	0-1	1		590
36	May 4	H	Dumbarton	D 1-1	0-0	1	McKenna (pen) 62	1373

Final League Position: 1

Honours
League Champions: League One 2018-19. Third Division 2010-11; League Two 2016-17.
Runners-up: Division II 1934-35, 1958-59, 1967-68, 1971-72; Second Division 2000-01; Third Division 1997-98, 2006-07.
Promoted via play-offs: 2007-08 (to Second Division).
Scottish Cup: Semi-finals 1947, Quarter-finals 1993.

Club colours: Shirt: Maroon with white trim. Shorts: Maroon. Socks: Maroon.

Goalscorers: *League (63):* Linn 21 (3 pens), Wallace 11 (1 pen), McKenna 6 (1 pen), Hamilton 3, Little 3, McCord 3, Swankie 3, Denholm 2, Doris 2, O'Brien 2, Thomson 2, Donnelly 1, Gold 1, Hester 1, Kader 1, own goal 1.
William Hill Scottish FA Cup (0).
Betfred Scottish League Cup (9): McKenna 3 (1 pen), Hester 2, Hamilton 1, Linn 1 (1 pen), O'Brien 1, Wallace 1.
Irn-Bru Scottish League Challenge (5): McKenna 2, Denholm 1, Linn 1, O'Brien 1.

Jamieson D 35	Gold D 25 + 5	Little R 36	Hamilton C 34	Kader O 19 + 11	Whatley M 26 + 3	Swankie G 33 + 3	O'Brien T 32	Linn B 31 + 1	McKenna M 29 + 5	Wallace R 24 + 11	Graham F — + 3	Hester K 1 + 2	Denholm D 11 + 19	Thomson J 31 + 1	Smith C 3 + 6	McCord R 2 + 16	Doris S 7 + 13	Donnelly L 9 + 4	Spence G 6 + 5	Bell L 1	Hill D 1	Match No.
1	2³	3	4	5²	6	7	8	9	10¹	11	12	13	14									1
1	6¹	2	4	5³	7	8²	3	9	10	11	14		13	12								2
1	14	3	5	6	7	8¹	4	9³	10²	11		12	13	2								3
1		3	5	6³	7	8	4	9²		11		10¹	13	2	12	14						4
1	14	3	5	6³	7	8	4	9	13	11			12	2²	10¹							5
1	14	3	5	6³	7	10	4	9²	8	11¹			12	2	13							6
1	14	3	5	6¹	8	7	4	9²	11³	10			12	2		13						7
1		4	5	13	8	7¹	3	9	11²	10	14		6³	2		12						8
1		3	5	12	7	8	4	6	10¹	11³			9²	2	13	14						9
1		4	5	14	8	7	3	9³	6¹	10			12	2	11²		13					10
1	6	4	5	14		8	3	9¹	7	11²			12	2	10³		13					11
1	7	3	5	13		8³	4	9¹	10	11			6²	2		14	12					12
1	7	3	5	12	13	8¹	4	9²	10	11			6³	2			14					13
1	7¹	3	5		14	8²	4	9	10³	11			6	2		13	12					14
1	7	3	4	6²	5	8³		9	10	12			13	2		14	11¹					15
1	7	3	5	6³	14	8²	4■	9	10	13			12	2			11¹					16
1	2	4	5	6	8	10		9¹	7²	11³			12	3	13		14					17
1	8	3	5	12	2	7■		9²	6	10¹			14	4	13		11³					18
1	7	3	5	6¹		8	4	9	10³	11²				2	13	14	12					19
1	7	3	5	6¹		8	4	9	10²	12			13	2		14	11³					20
1	7¹	3	5	13		8	4	9	14	11			6²	2		12		10³				21
1	7	3	5			8	4	6	12	10²			9³	2			14	11¹	13			22
1	8	3	5	6³		7¹	4	9	11	13				2		14		12	10²			23
1	6³	3	5	12	7	11	4	9²	8	13			14	2					10¹			24
1	6	3	5		7	8²	4	9¹	10	12			13	2				14	11³			25
1	5²	3		6	8	14	4	9	7³	11¹				2		13		10	12			26
1		3		6²	4	8	5	9	14■				12			7	13	10¹	11³	2		27
1		3	5		7	8	4	9³		12			6	2		14	11¹	10²	13			28
1	6²	3	5	12	7	8¹	4	9	10	14				2				11³	13			29
1	6	3	5	12	7	8	4	9²	10³	13				2		14		11¹				30
1	13	3	5		7	8	4	9¹	6	10²			12	2			11³		14			31
1	8	3	5	6	7	13	4		11²	10³			9¹	2			12	14				32
1	8	3	5	6²	7	12	4		10	11¹			9³	2			13	14				33
1	8	3	5	6	7	11	4		12³	13			9	2¹		14	10²					34
	2	3	5		7	8³	4■		6¹	11			13			12	14	9²	10		1	35
1	2	3	4	9	5	8		14	6	13						7¹	12	11³	10²			36

AYR UNITED

Year Formed: 1910. *Ground & Address:* Somerset Park, Tryfield Place, Ayr KA8 9NB. *Telephone:* 01292 263435. *Fax:* 01292 281314. *E-mail:* info@ayrunitedfc.co.uk *Website:* ayrunitedfc.co.uk
Ground Capacity: 10,185 (seated: 1,597). *Size of Pitch:* 101m × 66m.
Chairman: Lachlan Cameron.
Managing Director: Lewis Grant.
Manager: Ian McCall. *Assistant Manager:* Neil Scally.
Club Nickname: 'The Honest Men'.
Record Attendance: 25,225 v Rangers, Division I, 13 September 1969.
Record Transfer Fee received: £300,000 for Steve Nicol to Liverpool (October 1981).
Record Transfer Fee paid: £90,000 for Mark Campbell from Stranraer (March 1999).
Record Victory: 11-1 v Dumbarton, League Cup, 13 August 1952.
Record Defeat: 0-9 in Division I v Rangers (1929); v Hearts (1931); B Division v Third Lanark (1954).
Most Capped Player: Jim Nisbet, 3, Scotland.
Most League Appearances: 459: John Murphy, 1963-78.
Most League League and Cup Goals in Season (Individual): 66: Jimmy Smith, 1927-28.
Most League and Cup Goals Overall (Individual): 213: Peter Price, 1955-61.

AYR UNITED – SPFL LADBROKES CHAMPIONSHIP 2018–19 LEAGUE RECORD

Match No.	*Date*	*Venue*	*Opponents*	*Result*		*H/T Score*	*Lg Pos.*	*Goalscorers*	*Atten-dance*
1	Aug 4	H	Partick Thistle	W	2-0	2-0	1	Shankland 2 (1 pen) [7 (p), 18]	3249
2	11	A	Inverness CT	D	0-0	0-0	3		2376
3	25	H	Dunfermline Ath	W	4-1	3-0	1	Forrest 2 [5, 37], Shankland [39], Moffat [81]	2597
4	Sept 1	A	Queen of the South	L	0-5	0-4	6		2498
5	15	H	Falkirk	W	3-2	0-2	3	Shankland [48], Geggan [63], Fasan (og) [65]	2250
6	22	A	Alloa Ath	W	2-0	1-0	1	Shankland 2 [23, 65]	949
7	29	A	Greenock Morton	W	5-1	1-1	1	Shankland 2 [19, 75], Moore 2 [73, 81], McDaid [89]	2273
8	Oct 6	H	Dundee U	W	2-0	1-0	1	Shankland [21], McDaid [74]	2621
9	20	A	Ross Co	L	1-2	0-2	2	Shankland [50]	3140
10	27	A	Partick Thistle	W	1-0	0-0	2	Rose [77]	3491
11	30	H	Alloa Ath	W	3-0	0-0	1	Shankland 2 [46, 90], Forrest [81]	1742
12	Nov 3	A	Falkirk	W	1-0	0-0	1	Moore [51]	4310
13	10	H	Queen of the South	D	1-1	0-0	1	Rose [75]	2539
14	17	H	Greenock Morton	D	0-0	0-0	1		2346
15	30	A	Dundee U	W	5-0	2-0	1	Shankland 4 (1 pen) [3, 41, 87 (p), 89], Moffat [78]	6097
16	Dec 15	H	Ross Co	D	3-3	3-1	1	Shankland 2 (1 pen) [21 (p), 25], Geggan [43]	2030
17	22	A	Dunfermline Ath	D	0-0	0-0	2		4916
18	29	A	Queen of the South	D	1-1	1-1	2	Moffat [41]	2349
19	Jan 5	H	Falkirk	L	0-1	0-0	2		2729
20	12	A	Inverness CT	L	0-1	0-0	2		2283
21	25	H	Dundee U	W	1-0	1-0	1	Moore [4]	2232
22	29	H	Inverness CT	L	2-3	0-3	2	McDaid [53], Shankland [85]	1559
23	Feb 2	A	Alloa Ath	W	3-1	1-1	2	Moffat 2 [29, 88], Shankland (pen) [52]	957
24	16	A	Greenock Morton	D	0-0	0-0	2		2335
25	23	H	Dunfermline Ath	L	0-1	0-0	2		2202
26	26	A	Ross Co	L	2-3	0-1	3	Shankland [62], Murdoch [73]	3489
27	Mar 8	A	Falkirk	L	0-2	0-2	3		4344
28	29	A	Dunfermline Ath	W	1-0	1-0	3	McDaid [31]	4671
29	Apr 2	H	Greenock Morton	D	1-1	1-0	3	Shankland (pen) [21]	1802
30	6	H	Inverness CT	L	0-1	0-0	4		1566
31	9	H	Queen of the South	W	1-0	1-0	3	Shankland (pen) [43]	1582
32	12	A	Dundee U	L	1-2	1-0	3	Bell [24]	4392
33	19	H	Ross Co	L	1-3	1-1	3	Miller [12]	1692
34	23	H	Partick Thistle	L	0-1	0-1	3		2429
35	27	A	Partick Thistle	W	2-1	1-1	3	Smith [30], Muirhead [56]	3855
36	May 4	H	Alloa Ath	D	1-1	1-1	4	Shankland [37]	1665

Final League Position: 4

Honours
League Champions: Division II 1911-12, 1912-13, 1927-28, 1936-37, 1958-59, 1965-66; Second Division 1987-88, 1996-97; League One 2017-18.
Runners-up: Division II 1910-11, 1955-56, 1968-69; Second Division 2008-09; League One 2015-16.
Promoted via play-offs: 2008-09 (to First Division); 2010-11 (to First Division); 2015-16 (to Championship).
Scottish Cup: Semi-finals 2002.
League Cup: Runners-up: 2001-02.
League Challenge Cup Runners-up: 1990-91, 1991-92.

Club colours: Shirt: White with black trim. Shorts: Black. Socks: White.

Goalscorers: *League (50):* Shankland 24 (6 pens), Moffat 5, McDaid 4, Moore 4, Forrest 3, Geggan 2, Rose 2, Bell 1, Miller 1, Muirhead 1, Murdoch 1, Smith 1, own goal 1.
William Hill Scottish FA Cup (3): Docherty 1, Moffat 1, Shankland 1.
Betfred Scottish League Cup (15): Shankland 9, Moffat 4, Bell 1, Forrest 1.
Irn-Bru Scottish League Challenge (0).
Play-Offs (2): McCowan 1, Rose 1.

Doohan R 36	Geggan A 22 + 1	Adams J 9 + 4	Rose M 34	Harvie D 31 + 2	Forrest A 10 + 7	Crawford Robert 30 + 3	Murdoch A 33 + 1	McDaid D 20 + 14	Moffat M 29 + 5	Shankland L 29 + 2	McGuffie C — + 9	Docherty R 9 + 10	Ferguson D 1 + 2	Kerr M 18 + 4	Bell S 21 + 5	Smith L 32 + 1	Moore C 8 + 12	Ecrepont F — + 1	Higgins C — + 3	McCowan L 2 + 3	Muirhead A 8 + 1	Miller C 8 + 5	Cadden N 6 + 4	*Match No.*
1	2^{3}	3	4	5	6^{2}	7	8	9^{1}	10	11	12	13	14											1
1	2	3	4	5■	6^{1}	7	9		11^{3}	10		14	12	8^{2}	13									2
1	2	4	3		6^{3}	9^{1}	8	13	10	11	14			7^{2}	12	5								3
1	2	4	3^{3}	5■	6	9	8	14	10^{1}	11				7^{2}	12	13								4
1	2	4	3		6^{3}	9	7^{1}	13	10^{2}	11				8	12	5	14							5
1	2		9		4^{1}	7	6	12	11^{3}	10		13		8^{2}	3	5	14							6
1	6^{2}		4	5		8^{3}	7	9	10^{1}	11	13	14			3	2	12							7
1	6	4		5	9^{2}		7	12	10^{1}	11^{3}		14		8	3	2	13							8
1	6	4	3	5^{3}	14	9	8^{2}	12	10^{1}	11				7		2	13							9
1	2^{1}	3	4	13	12	9^{3}	7^{2}	6		11				8	14	5	10							10
1	8^{2}	14	3	5	9	13	7	6^{3}	10^{1}	11					4	2	12							11
1	6	13	3	5	9^{2}		8	12	14	11^{3}				7^{1}	4	2	10							12
1			4	5	6^{2}	9	8	14	13	11	12			7^{3}	3	2	10^{1}							13
1	2^{3}		4	12	14	9	7	6^{2}	13	10^{1}				8	3	5	11■							14
1	7^{2}		4	5^{1}		9	8	6	10	11	12				3	2		13						15
1	7		4	5		9	8	6^{1}	11^{2}	10					3	2	13		12					16
1	8^{2}		4	5		9	7	6^{1}	10^{3}	11	13	14			3	2	12							17
1			4	5		9	7^{2}	6	11^{1}	10	13	8			3	2	12							18
1			4	5		9	7^{1}	6	11		13	12		8^{2}	3	2	10							19
1	8^{2}		3	5		9		8^{1}	10		12	7	2		4		11^{3}		13	14				20
1			4	5		7	6	9	10	12		8			3	2	11^{1}							21
1			4	5		7^{2}	6	9	11	13		8^{3}			3.	2	10^{1}		12		14			22
1			4	5		13	7	9^{1}	10	11		8				2					3	6^{2}	12	23
1			4	5		8	6	9^{3}	10^{2}	11		7^{1}				2	14				3	12	13	24
1		14	3	5		9^{1}	7	12	10	11					8^{2}	2					4	13	6^{3}	25
1		3	4	5		8	6^{3}	13	10^{2}	11		7^{1}		12		2						9	14	26
1			4	5		9	7^{3}	12	10^{2}	11				8		2				13	3	6^{1}	14	27
1			3	5		8	6	9^{1}	11	10^{2}		13		7	4	2						12		28
1	13		4	5	12	8	6	9^{1}	10^{3}	11				7^{2}	3	2	14							29
1	6^{3}	12	3	5			8^{2}	13	14	10		7			4	2						11	9^{1}	30
1	6^{3}		4	5		8	13	12		10				7	3	2	14					11^{2}	9^{1}	31
1	6^{3}		4	5		7	8	9	10^{1}	11		14		12	3^{2}	2						13		32
1	2^{1}			3	12	8	7	6	10^{3}			13■		14		5					4	11	9^{2}	33
1			3	5	13	8^{2}	6^{1}	12	10					7		2				14	4	9	11^{3}	34
1	6^{2}		4	5		7	8	11	10					13		2				9^{1}	3	12		35
1			4	5	13	12			14	10^{1}		7		8		2^{2}				11	3	6^{3}	9	36

BERWICK RANGERS

Year Formed: 1881. *Ground & Address:* Shielfield Park, Tweedmouth, Berwick-upon-Tweed TD15 2EF. *Telephone:* 01289 307424. *Fax:* 01289 309424. *E-mail:* club@berwickrangers.com *Website:* berwickrangers.com
Ground Capacity: 4,131 (seated: 1,366). *Size of Pitch:* 101m × 64m.
Chairman: John Bell. *Football Secretary:* Dennis McCleary.
Manager: John Brownlie. *Assistant Manager:* Ian Little. *First-Team Coach:* Neil Hastings.
Club Nicknames: 'The Borderers'; 'Black and Gold'; 'The Wee Gers'.
Previous Grounds: Bull Stob Close; Pier Field; Meadow Field; Union Park; Old Shielfield.
Record Transfer Fee received: £80,000 for John Hughes to Swansea C (November 1989).
Record Transfer Fee paid: £27,000 for Sandy Ross from Cowdenbeath (March 1991).
Record Attendance: 13,283 v Rangers, Scottish Cup 1st rd, 28 January 1967.
Record Victory: 8-1 v Forfar Ath, Division II, 25 December 1965; v Vale of Leithen, Scottish Cup, December 1966.
Record Defeat: 1-9 v Hamilton A, First Division, 9 August 1980.
Most League Appearances: 439: Eric Tait, 1970-87.
Most League Goals in Season (Individual): 33: Ken Bowron, Division II, 1963-64.
Most Goals Overall (Individual): 114: Eric Tait, 1970-87.

BERWICK RANGERS – SPFL LADBROKES LEAGUE TWO 2018–19 LEAGUE RECORD

Match No.	*Date*	*Venue*	*Opponents*	*Result*	*H/T Score*	*Lg Pos.*	*Goalscorers*	*Attendance*
1	Aug 4	H	Stirling Alb	W 1-0	0-0	3	Brown [65]	520
2	11	A	Queen's Park	L 0-1	0-1	7		679
3	18	A	Cowdenbeath	L 0-4	0-2	8		314
4	25	H	Annan Ath	L 0-3	0-1	8		507
5	Sept 1	A	Albion R	W 5-3	2-2	7	Phillips [13], Willis (pen) [25], Scott 2 [60, 86], Healy [78]	222
6	15	H	Elgin C	L 0-3	0-3	8		416
7	22	A	Peterhead	L 0-1	0-0	8		546
8	29	H	Clyde	L 2-3	2-0	8	Scott [27], Ogilvie [40]	501
9	Oct 6	A	Edinburgh C	L 0-3	0-1	9		362
10	27	H	Cowdenbeath	L 0-3	-	9		477
11	Nov 3	A	Stirling Alb	L 0-3	0-2	9		514
12	10	A	Elgin C	W 4-2	2-0	9	Willis 2 [26, 78], Hume [33], Barr [68]	549
13	17	H	Albion R	W 2-0	1-0	8	Healy [33], Willis (pen) [66]	537
14	Dec 1	A	Clyde	D 3-3	3-0	9	Barr 2 [18, 36], Willis [45]	578
15	8	H	Peterhead	L 0-5	0-3	9		428
16	22	A	Annan Ath	L 0-4	0-1	9		373
17	29	H	Edinburgh C	D 2-2	0-1	9	Barr [88], Neill [90]	501
18	Jan 5	A	Cowdenbeath	L 0-2	0-1	9		384
19	12	H	Clyde	L 0-3	0-2	9		538
20	19	A	Peterhead	L 0-2	0-0	9		522
21	26	A	Queen's Park	L 1-7	0-3	9	Orru [80]	444
22	Feb 9	H	Stirling Alb	L 1-2	0-1	9	Barr [87]	437
23	23	H	Elgin C	L 0-3	0-0	9		402
24	26	H	Annan Ath	L 1-2	0-1	9	Adamson [78]	323
25	Mar 2	A	Albion R	D 1-1	0-1	9	Adamson [87]	273
26	5	A	Edinburgh C	L 0-1	0-0	9		253
27	9	H	Cowdenbeath	D 1-1	1-1	9	Adamson [24]	409
28	12	H	Queen's Park	L 1-2	1-1	9	Blues [17]	293
29	19	H	Peterhead	W 2-0	2-0	9	Barr [13], Blues [30]	327
30	23	A	Stirling Alb	L 0-1	0-0	9		598
31	30	H	Edinburgh C	L 0-2	0-2	10		468
32	Apr 6	A	Annan Ath	L 0-6	0-0	10		324
33	13	H	Queen's Park	L 0-3	0-2	10		540
34	20	A	Clyde	L 0-5	0-1	10		904
35	27	H	Albion R	L 0-3	0-2	10		975
36	May 4	A	Elgin C	L 0-2	0-0	10		615

Final League Position: 10

Honours
League Champions: Second Division 1978-79; Third Division 2006-07.
Runners-up: Second Division 1993-94; Third Division 1999-2000, 2005-06.
Scottish Cup: Quarter-finals 1953-54, 1979-80.
League Cup: Semi-finals 1963-64.
League Challenge Cup: Quarter-finals 2004-05.

Club colours: Shirt: Black and gold vertical stripes. Shorts: Black. Socks: Black with gold tops.

Goalscorers: *League (27):* Barr 6, Willis 5 (2 pens), Adamson 3, Scott 3, Blues 2, Healy 2, Brown 1, Hume 1, Neill 1, Ogilvie 1, Orru 1, Phillips 1.
William Hill Scottish FA Cup (4): Healy 1, Scott 1, Willis 1, own goal 1.
Betfred Scottish League Cup (0).
Irn-Bru Scottish League Challenge (0).
Play-Offs (0).

Brennan S 23 + 2	Cook J 31 + 1	Wilson R 26	Todd J 7 + 1	Orru J 18 + 3	Lavery D 3 + 1	O'Kane D 23 + 3	Brown R 30	Willis P 16	Healy D 23 + 8	Phillips G 16 + 1	Murrell A 4 + 10	Murphy S 8 + 4	Fleming O 1 + 2	Rose G 5 + 10	Adams A 2	Neill J 8 + 6	Scott C 5 + 2	Ogilvie J 17 + 11	McIlduff A 14 + 3	Hamilton C 2 + 2	Hurst G 5 + 3	Hastings N 1	Murray J — + 3	Hume C 17 + 2	Barr L 22 + 2	Forbes A 21 + 1	Short B — + 1	Allison K 7	See O 1 + 4	Knox M 2 + 3	Valentine E — + 1	Adamson C 9 + 7	Brydon D 7	Aloulou A 7 + 2	Blues C 11 + 2	Goodfellow R 4	*Match No.*
1	2	3	4^{2}	5	6^{3}	7	8	9	10^{1}	11	12	13	14																								1
1	5	3	4	2	9	8^{1}	7	10^{3}	11^{2}	6	13	12		14																							2
1	2	3■	4	13	9	8	6	10	11^{3}	5^{2}	12	7^{1}		14																							3
	5		3^{1}	2	12	7	6	9	11	8	10^{2}		4		1	13																					4
	2	3	4	5		6	7	10^{2}	11	9			13		1	8^{1}	12																				5
1	2	3	4	5^{3}		7	8	6^{1}	11	9	13					12	10^{2}	14																			6
1	4	3				7	2	6	10^{2}	9	13					8	12	11^{1}	5																		7
1	4	3	14			6	2^{1}		11	10						7	8^{3}	9^{2}	5	12	13																8
1	12	4	3^{2}			8	5^{1}	7	10^{3}	6						14	9		2	13	11																9
1		4■		5		7	8	11	12	9^{2}		13				3■	10^{1}	14		2■	6^{3}																10
1	4			5		8	2	7	12	9	13						10^{3}	6			11^{2}	3^{1}	14														11
1	3			5^{3}		6	8^{1}	7	11	10^{2}	14							13	12	2				4	9												12
1	4			5		7		8	11^{1}	9	10^{3}					12		6^{2}					13	3		2	14										13
1	4	3		5		7	6	10	11^{2}	13	12^{3}					8^{1}					14				9	2											14
1		3		5		8^{1}	6		11	9^{2}						7^{3}		13			12		14	4	10	2											15
1	3					8	6			5	11					7^{1}		12			10			4	9	2											16
	4	2		9		6^{3}	8				14					13		10^{1}			11			3^{2}	7	5		1	12								17
	2	3^{1}		9			8■				11^{2}			12		7^{3}		10						4	8	5		1	14	13							18
	4			5				10	11^{2}	9				13		14		7^{3}						3	8	2		1		6^{1}	12						19
	3	4		9^{2}			7^{3}	11	10		12			13				14	8^{1}					2	6	5		1									20
12	2^{2}	3		13			7	11^{3}	10										9					4	8	5		1■		6^{1}		14					21
1		4		8^{2}			6		9									13	5					7^{3}	11	2				14		12	3	10^{1}			22
	5	3					6^{3}		11			13						14	9					4	8^{1}	2		1				12		10^{2}	7		23
12	5						6^{1}		10									9						4	8	2		1^{2}				11	3	13	7		24
1	5						7		10					14				9^{3}	13					4	8	2						12	3	11^{1}	6^{2}		25
1	2	3				8			14			7		11^{2}				9^{3}	5						12							6	4	10^{1}	13		26
1	2	4				13■	6^{1}		11			7^{3}						9	5						8	12						10	3^{2}		14		27
1	4	3					6		11					9^{1}				12	5^{3}					13	8	2						10		14	7^{2}		28
1	3	4					6		12			5						9^{3}						13	8^{1}	2				14		11		10^{2}	7		29
1	3	4				13	2^{2}		12			8^{1}		14				9							10	5						6		11^{3}	7		30
1	3	4				13	2		12			6^{3}		14				9							8	5						11		10^{1}	7^{2}		31
1	2	3				6			13					11^{1}				8	14					7	10^{3}	5						12	4		9^{2}		32
	4	3				6^{2}	5^{3}					8		10				14	9^{1}					2	11				12			13			7	1	33
	4	3		10^{1}		6						7^{2}		11^{3}				14	5						9	2			13			12			8	1	34
	4			13		7^{1}			12^{3}					14				9	5					3	8	2			11^{2}			10			6	1	35
				9		7	8		10					13				11^{1}	5^{2}					4	12	2						6	3			1	36

BRECHIN CITY

Year Formed: 1906. *Ground & Address:* Glebe Park, Trinity Rd, Brechin, Angus DD9 6BJ. *Telephone:* 01356 622856. *Fax:* 01382 206331. *E-mail:* secretary@brechincityfc.com *Website:* www.brechincity.com
Ground Capacity: 4,123 (seated: 1,528). *Size of Pitch:* 101m × 61m.
Chairman: Ken Ferguson. *Vice-Chairman:* Martin Smith. *Secretary:* Grant Hood.
Manager: Barry Smith. *Assistant Manager:* Stevie Campbell.
Club Nicknames: 'The City'; 'The Hedgemen'.
Previous Ground: Nursery Park.
Record Attendance: 8,122 v Aberdeen, Scottish Cup 3rd rd, 3 February 1973.
Record Transfer Fee received: £100,000 for Scott Thomson to Aberdeen (1991) and Chris Templeman to Morton (2004).
Record Transfer Fee paid: £16,000 for Sandy Ross from Berwick Rangers (1991).
Record Victory: 12-1 v Thornhill, Scottish Cup 1st rd, 28 January 1926.
Record Defeat: 0-10 v Airdrieonians, Albion R and Cowdenbeath, all in Division II, 1937-38.
Most League Appearances: 459: David Watt, 1975-89.
Most League Goals in Season (Individual): 26: Ronald McIntosh, Division II, 1959-60.
Most Goals Overall (Individual): 131: Ian Campbell, 1977-85.

BRECHIN CITY – SPFL LADBROKES LEAGUE ONE 2018–19 LEAGUE RECORD

Match No.	Date	Venue	Opponents	Result		H/T Score	Lg Pos.	Goalscorers	Attendance
1	Aug 4	A	Stenhousemuir	L	0-1	0-1	7		484
2	11	H	East Fife	W	1-0	0-0	6	Sinclair 61	414
3	18	A	Montrose	L	1-2	1-2	7	Melingui 35	916
4	25	H	Dumbarton	W	3-2	0-1	5	Melingui 2 60, 90, Tapping, C 77	371
5	Sept 1	A	Arbroath	D	2-2	0-2	4	Jackson 2 50, 55	901
6	15	H	Raith R	D	1-1	0-0	4	Melingui 87	623
7	22	A	Forfar Ath	D	1-1	1-0	5	Hendry 17	635
8	29	H	Stranraer	D	1-1	1-0	5	Tapping, C 31	374
9	Oct 6	A	Airdrieonians	W	3-1	1-1	4	Jackson 2 18, 68, Burns 50	717
10	20	A	East Fife	L	1-3	0-1	5	Tapping, C (pen) 61	639
11	27	H	Montrose	L	1-3	0-0	6	Burns 55	701
12	Nov 3	A	Raith R	L	1-2	0-1	8	Jackson 90	1495
13	10	H	Forfar Ath	W	4-0	3-0	5	Jackson 2 27, 33, Lynas 35, Blues 82	638
14	17	H	Arbroath	L	1-5	0-1	7	McGeever 85	847
15	Dec 1	A	Dumbarton	L	1-4	0-0	9	Sinclair 71	456
16	8	H	Stenhousemuir	L	1-2	1-1	9	Sinclair 43	355
17	22	H	Airdrieonians	L	0-1	0-0	9		448
18	29	A	Forfar Ath	L	0-2	0-1	9		764
19	Jan 5	A	Arbroath	L	0-1	0-0	9		1061
20	12	H	Dumbarton	W	1-0	0-0	9	Tapping, J 90	456
21	26	H	Raith R	W	2-1	0-1	8	Smith 52, Kavanagh 68	601
22	Feb 2	A	Montrose	L	2-5	2-3	8	Smith 13, Toshney 16	693
23	16	A	Airdrieonians	W	1-0	1-0	7	Jackson 16	696
24	23	H	Stranraer	L	1-2	1-1	9	Smith 32	378
25	Mar 2	A	Stenhousemuir	D	1-1	1-0	9	Orsi 8	452
26	5	H	East Fife	D	0-0	0-0	9		402
27	9	H	Forfar Ath	D	2-2	2-1	9	Jackson 12, Hill 30	634
28	23	A	East Fife	W	2-0	1-0	9	Hill 33, Kavanagh 61	544
29	26	A	Stranraer	W	2-0	0-0	8	Jackson 89, Thomson 90	295
30	30	H	Airdrieonians	L	0-3	0-2	8		429
31	Apr 2	H	Montrose	L	0-3	0-2	8		714
32	6	A	Dumbarton	L	1-2	1-2	9	Hill 17	531
33	13	H	Arbroath	D	1-1	1-1	9	Miller 22	1509
34	20	A	Stranraer	L	0-3	0-2	9		374
35	27	A	Raith R	L	2-3	2-2	10	Kavanagh 2 11, 35	1266
36	May 4	H	Stenhousemuir	D	1-1	0-1	10	Jackson 48	565

Final League Position: 10

Honours
League Champions: Second Division 1982-83, 1989-90, 2004-05; Third Division 2001-02; C Division 1953-54.
Runners-up: Second Division 1992-93, 2002-03; Third Division 1995-96.
Promoted via play-offs: 2016-17 (to Championship).
Scottish Cup: Quarter-finals 2011.
League Cup: Semi-finals 1957.
League Challenge Cup Runners-up: 2002-03.

Club colours: Shirt: Red with white trim. Shorts: Red with white trim. Socks: Red.

Goalscorers: *League (42):* Jackson 11, Kavanagh 4, Melingui 4, Hill 3, Sinclair 3, Smith 3, Tapping C 3 (1 pen), Burns 2, Blues 1, Hendry 1, Lynas 1, McGeever 1, Miller 1, Orsi 1, Tapping J 1, Thomson 1, Toshney 1.
William Hill Scottish FA Cup (0).
Betfred Scottish League Cup (3): Melingui 1, Shields 1, Tapping C 1.
Irn-Bru Scottish League Challenge (1): Shields 1.

Brennan C 17	Lynas A 10 + 10	Morena G 12 + 1	Hill D 30	Spark E 21 + 4	Burns S 29 + 1	Henry J 1	Smith E 31 + 1	Sinclair J 16 + 2	Orsi K 26 + 5	Shields D 1 + 2	Jackson A 35 + 1	Melingui B 8 + 10	McGeever R 17 + 3	Tapping C 18	Hendry C 7 + 5	Blues C 3 + 4	McLean P 17 + 2	Tapping J 7 + 1	O'Neil P 14	Robertson S 16	Kavanagh R 11 + 4	Thomson C 13	Toshney L 10 – 1	Tierney R — + 1	Scobbie T 14	Jamieson S 2 + 8	Miller M 5 + 3	Bowman G 5	Match No.
1	2	3^{2}	4	5	6	7^{1}	8	9	10	11	12	13																	1
1	12	7^{3}	4	14	8		2	9^{2}	5	13	10^{1}	11	3	6															2
1	14	6	4	13	5		2	9^{2}	7	12^{3}	10^{1}	11	3	8															3
1		8	4^{1}	12	5		2	9	6		11	10	3	7															4
1	13	8		4	5		2	9^{1}	6		11	10^{2}	3	7	12														5
1	5	8		4			2	9^{1}	6		11	12	3	7	10														6
1	12	7^{2}		4	9		2	8^{1}	5		11	13	3	6	10														7
1		7		4	8		2		5		10	12	3	6	11^{1}	9													8
1	12	7^{1}		4	9		2	13	5		10		3	6	11^{2}	8													9
1	8			2	9		4		5		10	13	3	7	11^{2}	6^{1}	12												10
1		12	4^{1}	5	9		7		6		10^{2}	11	3	8	13		2												11
1	8		4	2	5		6^{1}		10		9	12	3	7	11^{2}	13													12
1	6		4	5	9		2		7		10	11^{1}	3	8		12													13
1	6		4	2	5		8^{2}	13	9		10	11^{1}	3	7		12													14
1	6		4	2	5		3	7	9		11	10		8															15
1	2	7	4	5^{2}	10			9	8		11	13		6			12	3^{1}											16
1	2^{1}	8	3	5	9			10	6		11	13		7^{2}	12			4											17
	2^{1}	8^{2}	3	5	9			10	6		11	13			4	12		7	1										18
			3	5	9		7	10^{2}	6^{1}		11	13			12		2	4	1	8									19
			3	8^{1}	5		9	10^{2}	6		11				13		2	4	1	7	12								20
	12		4		5		8	6	11		10						7		1		9^{1}	2	3						21
	13		4		5		8	6	11		10^{2}						7		1		9^{1}	2	3	12					22
	12		4				8	9^{1}			11		3				2		1	7	6	10			5				23
	12		4				8				11		3				2		1	7	6	10■	9^{1}		5				24
			4				9		6		11		3				2		1	8	10^{1}		7		5	12			25
	13		4				7		6		10						2		1	8	12	9^{1}	3		5	11^{2}			26
			4		12		8^{2}		9^{1}		10						2		1	7	11	6	3		5		13		27
			4		9		8^{2}				10						2		1	7	11^{1}	6	3		5	13	12		28
			3		9^{1}		7		13		10^{2}		14				2		1	8	11^{3}	6	4		5	12			29
			4		9		8		14		10						2		1	7^{3}	12	6^{2}	3		5	11^{1}	13		30
			4	12	9^{1}		8		10		11^{2}		3■				2^{3}		1	7		6	14		5	13			31
			4		10^{1}		8		12		11						2	14		7		6	3^{3}		5	13	9^{2}	1	32
			4^{2}	3	10		8				11		13				2			9	12	6^{1}			5		7	1	33
			4	3	9		7		12		10						2^{2}			8^{1}	11				5	13	6	1	34
			4	2	9^{3}				13		10		12	7^{2}				3^{1}		8	11				5	14	6	1	35
			4	2			13				10			6				3		7^{1}	9^{2}	11			5	12	8	1	36

CELTIC

Year Formed: 1888. *Ground & Address:* Celtic Park, Glasgow G40 3RE. *Telephone:* 0871 226 1888. *Fax:* 0141 551 8106.
E-mail: customerservices@celticfc.co.uk *Website:* www.celticfc.net
Ground Capacity: 60,832 (all seated). *Size of Pitch:* 105m × 68m.
Chairman: Ian Bankier. *Chief Executive:* Peter Lawwell.
Manager: Neil Lennon. *Assistant Manager:* John Kennedy. *First-Team Coach:* Damien Duff.
Club Nicknames: 'The Bhoys'; 'The Hoops'; 'The Celts'.
Record Attendance: 92,000 v Rangers, Division I, 1 January 1938.
Record Transfer Fee received: £19,700,000 for Moussa Dembele to Lyon (August 2018).
Record Transfer Fee paid: £9,000,000 for Odsonne Édouard from Paris Saint-Germain (June 2018).
Record Victory: 11-0 Dundee, Division I, 26 October 1895. *Record Defeat:* 0-8 v Motherwell, Division I, 30 April 1937.
Most Capped Player: Pat Bonner, 80, Republic of Ireland. *Most League Appearances:* 486: Billy McNeill, 1957-75.
Most League Goals in Season (Individual): 50: James McGrory, Division I, 1935-36.
Most League Goals Overall (Individual): 397: James McGrory, 1922-39.

Honours
League Champions: (50 times) Division I 1892-93, 1893-94, 1895-96, 1897-98, 1904-05, 1905-06, 1906-07, 1907-08, 1908-09, 1909-10, 1913-14, 1914-15, 1915-16, 1916-17, 1918-19, 1921-22, 1925-26, 1935-36, 1937-38, 1953-54, 1965-66, 1966-67, 1967-68, 1968-69, 1969-70, 1970-71, 1971-72, 1972-73, 1973-74; Premier Division 1976-77, 1978-79, 1980-81, 1981-82, 1985-86, 1987-88, 1997-98, 2000-01, 2001-02, 2003-04, 2005-06, 2006-07, 2007-08, 2011-12, 2012-13; Premiership 2013-14, 2014-15, 2015-16, 2016-17, 2017-18, 2018-19. *Runners-up:* 31 times.
Scottish Cup Winners: (39 times) 1892, 1899, 1900, 1904, 1907, 1908, 1911, 1912, 1914, 1923, 1925, 1927, 1931, 1933, 1937, 1951, 1954, 1965, 1967, 1969, 1971, 1972, 1974, 1975, 1977, 1980, 1985, 1988, 1989, 1995, 2001, 2004, 2005, 2007, 2011, 2013, 2017, 2018, 2019. *Runners-up:* 18 times.
League Cup Winners: (18 times) 1956-57, 1957-58, 1965-66, 1966-67, 1967-68, 1968-69, 1969-70, 1974-75, 1982-83, 1997-98, 1999-2000, 2000-01, 2005-06, 2008-09, 2014-15, 2016-17, 2017-18, 2018-19. *Runners-up:* 15 times.

CELTIC – SPFL LADBROKES PREMIERSHIP 2018–19 LEAGUE RECORD

Match No.	*Date*	*Venue*	*Opponents*	*Result*		*H/T Score*	*Lg Pos.*	*Goalscorers*	*Attendance*
1	Aug 4	H	Livingston	W	3-1	2-0	2	Rogic ^{8}, Edouard ^{26}, Ntcham (pen) ^{50}	58,778
2	11	A	Hearts	L	0-1	0-0	5		19,113
3	26	H	Hamilton A	W	1-0	0-0	2	Boyata ^{63}	56,044
4	Sept 2	H	Rangers	W	1-0	0-0	2	Ntcham ^{62}	58,865
5	14	A	St Mirren	D	0-0	0-0	2		7288
6	23	A	Kilmarnock	L	1-2	1-0	6	Griffiths ^{34}	10,988
7	29	H	Aberdeen	W	1-0	0-0	4	Sinclair ^{63}	59,143
8	Oct 7	A	St Johnstone	W	6-0	5-0	3	Forrest 4 $^{15, 30, 38, 45}$, Edouard ^{22}, McGregor ^{84}	5993
9	20	H	Hibernian	W	4-2	2-0	2	Rogic ^{8}, Ntcham ^{19}, Edouard 2 $^{70, 88}$	58,452
10	31	A	Dundee	W	5-0	4-0	2	Rogic ^{20}, Sinclair (pen) ^{33}, Forrest ^{38}, Edouard ^{45}, Christie ^{48}	7960
11	Nov 3	H	Hearts	W	5-0	3-0	2	Edouard 2 $^{18, 39}$, Benkovic ^{26}, Forrest ^{65}, Christie (pen) ^{89}	58,831
12	11	A	Livingston	D	0-0	0-0	1		9016
13	24	A	Hamilton A	W	3-0	1-0	1	Christie ^{13}, Martin (og) ^{68}, Griffiths ^{82}	4688
14	Dec 5	A	Motherwell	D	1-1	1-0	3	Christie ^{13}	8433
15	8	H	Kilmarnock	W	5-1	4-0	1	Forrest 2 $^{5, 67}$, Edouard ^{25}, Lustig ^{35}, Christie ^{45}	58,457
16	16	A	Hibernian	L	0-2	0-1	3		18,142
17	19	H	Motherwell	W	3-0	3-0	1	Ralston ^{28}, Sinclair (pen) ^{32}, Johnston ^{45}	54,703
18	22	H	Dundee	W	3-0	1-0	1	Johnston 2 $^{43, 50}$, Benkovic ^{69}	57,234
19	26	A	Aberdeen	W	4-3	1-1	1	Sinclair 3 $^{6, 76, 88}$, Edouard ^{86}	20,027
20	29	A	Rangers	L	0-1	0-1	1		49,863
21	Jan 23	H	St Mirren	W	4-0	2-0	1	Burke 2 $^{11, 55}$, Sinclair (pen) ^{18}, Weah ^{86}	54,821
22	26	H	Hamilton A	W	3-0	1-0	1	McGregor ^{40}, Christie ^{77}, Sinclair ^{87}	58,264
23	30	H	St Johnstone	W	2-0	0-0	1	McGregor ^{53}, Christie ^{55}	54,563
24	Feb 3	A	St Johnstone	W	2-0	0-0	1	Forrest ^{78}, Weah ^{89}	6242
25	6	H	Hibernian	W	2-0	1-0	1	Christie ^{24}, Burke ^{63}	56,730
26	17	A	Kilmarnock	W	1-0	0-0	1	Brown ^{90}	11,916
27	24	H	Motherwell	W	4-1	2-0	1	Sinclair ^{31}, Edouard 2 $^{37, 88}$, Burke ^{90}	58,604
28	27	A	Hearts	W	2-1	1-0	1	Forrest ^{36}, Edouard ^{90}	18,258
29	Mar 9	H	Aberdeen	D	0-0	0-0	1		59,123
30	17	A	Dundee	W	1-0	0-0	1	Edouard ^{90}	7608
31	31	H	Rangers	W	2-1	1-0	1	Edouard ^{27}, Forrest ^{86}	58,773
32	Apr 3	A	St Mirren	W	2-0	1-0	1	Weah ^{15}, Christie ^{85}	6597
33	6	H	Livingston	D	0-0	0-0	1		58,850
34	21	A	Hibernian	D	0-0	0-0	1		19,472
35	27	H	Kilmarnock	W	1-0	0-0	1	Simunovic ^{68}	58,851
36	May 4	A	Aberdeen	W	3-0	1-0	1	Lustig ^{40}, Simunovic ^{53}, Edouard ^{88}	15,189
37	12	A	Rangers	L	0-2	0-1	1		49,844
38	19	H	Hearts	W	2-1	1-1	1	Johnston 2 $^{2, 84}$	58,696

Final League Position: 1

European: *European Cup/Champions League:* 206 matches (1966-67 winners, 1967-68, 1968-69, 1969-70 runners-up, 1970-71, 1971-72, 1972-73, 1973-74 semi-finals, 1974-75, 1977-78, 1979-80, 1981-82, 1982-83, 1986-87, 1988-89, 1998-99, 2001-02, 2002-03, 2003-04, 2004-05, 2005-06, 2006-07, 2007-08, 2008-09, 2009-10, 2010-11, 2012-13, 2013-14, 2014-15, 2015-16, 2016-17, 2017-18, 2018-19). *Cup Winners' Cup:* 38 matches (1963-64 semi-finals, 1965-66 semi-finals, 1975-76, 1980-81, 1984-85, 1985-86, 1989-90, 1995-96). *UEFA Cup:* 75 matches (*Fairs Cup:* 1962-63, 1964-65. *UEFA Cup:* 1976-77, 1983-84, 1987-88, 1991-92, 1992-93, 1993-94, 1996-97, 1997-98, 1998-99, 1999-2000, 2000-01, 2001-02, 2002-03 runners-up, 2003-04 quarter-finals). *Europa League:* 42 matches (2009-10, 2010-11, 2011-12, 2014-15, 2015-16, 2017-18, 2018-19).

Club colours: Shirt: Green and white hoops. Shorts: White. Socks: Green with white hoops.

Goalscorers: *League (77):* Edouard 15, Forrest 11, Christie 9 (1 pen), Sinclair 9 (3 pens), Johnston 5, Burke 4, McGregor 3, Ntcham 3 (1 pen), Rogic 3, Weah 3, Benkovic 2, Griffiths 2, Lustig 2, Simunovic 2, Boyata 1, Brown 1, Ralston 1, own goal 1.
William Hill Scottish FA Cup (15): Sinclair 5, Edouard 3 (2 pens), Forrest 3, Brown 2, Rogic 1, Weah 1.
Betfred Scottish League Cup (8): Christie 2, Griffiths 2, Dembele 1, Forrest 1, Rogic 1, Sinclair 1 (1 pen).
Irn-Bru Scottish League Challenge (0).
Champions League (11): Edouard 3, Dembele 2 (1 pen), Forrest 2, McGregor 2, Ntcham 1, Sinclair 1.
Europa League: (10): Edouard 2, Griffiths 2, Ntcham 2, Ajer 1, McGregor 1, Sinclair 1, Tierney 1.

Gordon C 18	Lustig M 26 + 1	Ajer K 23 + 5	Simunovic J 16 + 2	McGregor C 33 + 2	Brown S 29 + 1	Ntcham J 16 + 4	Forrest J 31 + 2	Rogic T 16 + 5	Hayes J 7 + 9	Edouard O 22 + 10	Tierney K 20 + 1	Griffiths L 6 + 5	Johnston M 7 + 7	Hendry J 3 + 1	Eboue K 1 + 1	Sinclair S 24 + 9	Boyata D 19	Dembele M 1	Christie R 17 + 6	Benkovic F 17 + 3	Mulumbu Y 1	Morgan L — + 9	Arzani D — + 1	Bain S 20	Izaguirre E 13 + 1	Gamboa C 1	Ralston A 3 + 1	Burke O 9 + 5	Weah T 4 + 9	Henderson E 4 + 1	Bitton N 4 + 3	Toljan J 7 + 3	Bayo V — + 1	Dembele K — + 1	*Match No.*
1	2	3	4	5	6	7	8	9^3	10^2	11^1	12	13	14																						1
1	2		3	10	7		12	14	6^1	13	5	11^2		4	8^3	9																			2
1	2	4		7	6	12	5^2	9^3			8	11^1	13				3	10	14																3
1	2	4		10	7	6	8^1	9^3		11^2	5	12				14	3		13																4
1		2		9	6	7■	5	10		11^2	8	12					4		13	3^1															5
1	2			13	6					14	5	11	8^1	4		10^3	3		9		7^2	12													6
1	2			9	6	7^3	8^1	13		10^2	5	11		3		12	4					14													7
1	2		12	10		6	8	7^1		9	5	11^2				13	3			4^3		14													8
1	2			10	7^1	6	5^3	9^2		11	8				13	12	3		14	4															9
1	2	14		7			6	8^2		11^3	5					9	4^1		10	3		12	13												10
1	2^1	12		6			8	9		11^3	5		13			10^2	4		7	3		14													11
		2	4^1		9			6^2	8		11	5					10	3		7	13		12		1											12
1	2			6		8	9^3			10^2	5^1	12				11	3		7	4		14			13										13
1			3	9	6	7^3		14	8^1	13	5	11^2				12			10	4						2									14
1	2		3	6	14	12	7	8^3		11^2		13				10			9^1	4					5										15
1		2	3	9	6	7	8		13	11^2			14			10^1				4		12			5^3										16
1			3	9	6	7	8			11^1			12			10^2				4		13			5		2								17
		12	3^3	6		8	7^1	9	14				11^2			10			13	4				1	5		2								18
1	2	14		10^1	6		8^2	7	12	13						11	3		9	4					5^3										19
1	2^3	12		5	6	7	8			14			11^2			10	3		9	4^1							13								20
	2	3		7	6		8									10			9^2	4				1	5			11^1	12	13					21
	2	3		7	6		12						8^1			10			9^3	4				1	5			13	11^2		14				22
	2	4	3	7	6		8			12						10^3			9^1					1	5			11^2	13		14				23
	2^2	4■	3	7	6		8			13^3						10			9					1	5			11^1	14			12			24
			4	7	6				14				12			10^1	3^3		9					1	5^2			11	8		13	2			25
		4		6	7■		8^3		5	11^1						10	3		9^2					1				12	13			2	14		26
		4					8		13	11	5^2			12		10	3		9^3					1				14		7	6^1	2			27
	14	4			6		8			12	5					10^1	3							1				11	13	9^2	7	2^3			28
		4			7		8			12	5		13			10^2	3							1				11^3	14	9^1	6	2			29
	3	4^3		7	6		8		12	11	5		9^2			10				13				1					14			2^1			30
	2	4		8	6	7^2	9	13	10^1	11	5^3					12	3							1								14			31
	2^1	4	3	9	6	7^3	8			14									12	13				1	5			11	10^2						32
		2	3	9	7		6	8^3	12	11	5								10^1	4^2				1				14	13						33
	2	4	3	9	6	7^3	8^2	12	10^1	11						13								1	5				14						34
	2	4	3	7	6	12	8^1	9^2	13	11						10								1	5										35
	2^1	4	3	7	6		8	9	12	11	5^3					14								1				13	10^2						36
	2^1	4	3	8	6	14		7^2	9	10			5^3			13								1				11				12			37
		3	14	13		7							8			10				4^3				1			2	11^2		9^1	6	5		12	38

CLYDE

Year Formed: 1877. *Ground & Address:* Broadwood Stadium, Cumbernauld, G68 9NE. *Telephone:* 01236 451511. *Fax:* 01236 733490. *E-mail:* info@clydefc.co.uk *Website:* www.clydefc.co.uk
Ground Capacity: 8,086 (all seated). *Size of Pitch:* 100m × 68m.
Chairman: David Dishon. *Vice Chairman:* John Taylor.
Manager: Danny Lennon. *Assistant Manager:* Allan Moore.
Club Nickname: 'The Bully Wee'.
Previous Grounds: Barrowfield Park 1877-98; Shawfield Stadium 1898-1986; Firhill Stadium 1986-91; Douglas Park 1991-94.
Record Attendance: 52,000 v Rangers, Division I, 21 November 1908.
Record Transfer Fee received: £200,000 from Blackburn R for Gordon Greer (May 2001).
Record Transfer Fee paid: £14,000 for Harry Hood from Sunderland (1966).
Record Victory: 11-1 v Cowdenbeath, Division II, 6 October 1951.
Record Defeat: 0-11 v Dumbarton, Scottish Cup 4th rd, 22 November, 1879; v Rangers, Scottish Cup 4th rd, 13 November 1880.
Most Capped Player: Tommy Ring, 12, Scotland.
Most League Appearances: 420: Brian Ahern, 1971-81; 1987-88.
Most League Goals in Season (Individual): 32: Bill Boyd, 1932-33.
Most Goals Overall (Individual): 124: Tommy Ring, 1950-60.

CLYDE – SPFL LADBROKES LEAGUE TWO 2018–19 LEAGUE RECORD

Match No.	Date	Venue	Opponents	Result	H/T Score	Lg Pos.	Goalscorers	Attendance
1	Aug 4	H	Cowdenbeath	W 2-0	2-0	2	McNiff [25], Goodwillie (pen) [28]	569
2	11	A	Stirling Alb	W 3-0	2-0	1	Love 2 [5, 61], Goodwillie [45]	802
3	18	A	Peterhead	L 0-1	0-0	5		671
4	25	H	Edinburgh C	L 0-2	0-0	6		576
5	Sept 1	A	Annan Ath	W 2-1	1-1	4	Goodwillie [10], Love [56]	569
6	15	H	Albion R	W 1-0	1-0	3	McNiff [20]	708
7	22	H	Elgin C	W 4-1	3-1	3	McNiff 2 [16, 40], Goodwillie [37], Belmokhtar [67]	508
8	29	A	Berwick R	W 3-2	0-2	3	Goodwillie [47], Belmokhtar 2 [53, 90]	501
9	Oct 6	A	Queen's Park	L 0-1	0-1	3		1076
10	27	H	Peterhead	L 1-3	0-1	4	Boyle (og) [78]	524
11	Nov 3	A	Edinburgh C	W 1-0	1-0	3	Rankin [34]	376
12	10	H	Stirling Alb	D 1-1	0-0	3	Cogill [90]	541
13	17	A	Elgin C	W 3-1	2-0	3	Goodwillie (pen) [14], Beattie (og) [32], Love [80]	677
14	Dec 1	H	Berwick R	D 3-3	0-3	3	Goodwillie [54], Cogill [64], Rankin [69]	578
15	8	A	Cowdenbeath	D 1-1	1-0	3	Rankin [17]	373
16	15	H	Annan Ath	W 1-0	0-0	3	Rankin [90]	408
17	22	A	Albion R	W 3-0	2-0	3	Goodwillie [9], Rankin [17], Love [82]	320
18	29	H	Queen's Park	W 2-0	2-0	3	Boyle [31], Goodwillie [40]	603
19	Jan 5	A	Peterhead	W 2-1	0-1	3	Love [85], Lamont [86]	754
20	12	A	Berwick R	W 3-0	2-0	3	McStay [9], Goodwillie [36], Rankin [90]	538
21	26	H	Cowdenbeath	W 1-0	0-0	3	Grant [66]	604
22	Feb 9	A	Annan Ath	D 1-1	1-0	3	Syvertsen [25]	555
23	16	H	Albion R	L 0-3	1-0	3	Match awarded to Albion R after Clyde won 1-0.	536
24	23	A	Queen's Park	L 0-3	0-0	3	Match awarded to Queen's Park after 1-1 draw.	977
25	26	A	Stirling Alb	W 1-0	1-0	3	Goodwillie [18]	683
26	Mar 2	H	Edinburgh C	W 1-0	0-0	3	Goodwillie (pen) [50]	844
27	9	A	Elgin C	L 1-2	1-1	3	Rankin [45]	713
28	16	H	Stirling Alb	W 3-1	1-0	3	McStay [18], McNiff [80], Rankin [90]	614
29	19	H	Elgin C	W 2-0	1-0	3	Boyle [14], Rumsby [73]	531
30	23	H	Annan Ath	W 2-1	0-0	3	Lamont [66], McNiff [90]	612
31	30	A	Albion R	W 1-0	0-0	3	McNiff [79]	560
32	Apr 6	H	Peterhead	D 3-3	0-2	3	Goodwillie 2 (1 pen) [47, 72 (p)], Banks [78]	813
33	13	A	Edinburgh C	W 2-1	0-0	2	Love [80], Syvertsen [86]	648
34	20	H	Berwick R	W 5-0	1-0	2	Cuddihy [5], Rumsby [49], Rankin [55], Goodwillie [77], McStay [90]	904
35	27	H	Queen's Park	W 3-0	1-0	2	Goodwillie [33], Love [74], Grant [79]	1012
36	May 4	A	Cowdenbeath	L 1-2	0-1	2	McNiff [57]	1007

Final League Position: 2

Honours
League Champions: Division II 1904-05, 1951-52, 1956-57, 1961-62, 1972-73; Second Division 1977-78, 1981-82, 1992-93, 1999-2000.
Runners-up: Division II 1903-04, 1905-06, 1925-26, 1963-64; First Division 2002-03, 2003-04; League Two 2018-19.
Promoted via play-offs: 2018-19 (to League One).
Scottish Cup Winners: 1939, 1955, 1958; *Runners-up:* 1910, 1912, 1949.
League Cup: Semi-finals 1956, 1957, 1968.
League Challenge Cup Runners-up: 2006-07.

Club colours: Shirt: White with red trim. Shorts: Black. Socks: Black.

Goalscorers: *League (63):* Goodwillie 16 (4 pens), Rankin 9, Love 8, McNiff 8, Belmokhtar 3, McStay 3, Boyle 2, Cogill 2, Grant 2, Lamont 2, Rumsby 2, Syvertsen 2, Banks 1, Cuddihy 1, own goals 2.
William Hill Scottish FA Cup (1): Goodwillie 1.
Betfred Scottish League Cup (5): Goodwillie 3, McNiff 2.
Irn-Bru Scottish League Challenge (1): McStay 1.
Play-Offs (6): Love 2 (1 pen), Syvertsen 2, Goodwillie 1, McNiff 1.

Currie B 36	Cuddihy B 33	Rumsby S 31 + 4	McNiff M 29	Stewart J 11 + 3	Lamont M 29 + 7	McStay C 35	Grant R 36	Rankin J 34 + 1	Goodwillie D 31 + 1	Love A 13 + 11	Boyle J 12 + 13	Cogill D 12 + 2	Nicoll K 17 + 6	Ferns E — + 3	Lyon R — + 15	Belmokhtar A 1 + 11	Lang T 16 + 3	Syvertsen K 10 + 7	Duffie K 4 + 2	Fitzpatrick D 2	Banks S 4 + 8	Hughes K — + 1	Match No.
1	2	3	4	5	6^{1}	7	8	9	10	11^{2}	12	13											1
1	5	2	4	3	13	8^{2}	6^{3}	9	10	11^{1}	14		7	12									2
1	2	3	4	5	12	6^{3}	8^{2}	9	10	11^{1}	14		7	13									3
1	2	3	4		12	6	8	9		11	10^{2}	5^{1}	7	13									4
1	2	3	4		9^{1}	6	5	8	11	10^{2}			7		12	13							5
1	2	3	4		9	8^{3}	5	7	11^{2}	10^{1}	14		6		12	13							6
1	2^{1}	4	3		6	11	5	8^{3}	10	9^{2}			7		13	12	14						7
1	2	3	4		11	6^{2}	8	5^{1}	10	9^{3}	14		7		13	12							8
1	2	3	4	12	5^{2}	6	7	9	11		13		8^{1}		14	10^{3}							9
1		3	4	5^{3}	13	6	8	14	10	9^{2}			7^{1}			12	2■	11					10
1	2	13	4		8^{2}	9	5	7	11			3	6		12			10^{1}					11
1	2	14	3		8^{2}	9^{3}	5^{1}	6	11			4	7		12	13		10					12
1	2		3		8^{2}	9	5	7	11	14		4	6^{3}		12	13		10^{1}					13
1	2	12	4^{2}		11	6	5	8	10		13	3^{3}	7			14		9^{1}					14
1	2	3			11^{1}	6	5	8	10		12	4	7			13		9^{2}					15
1	2	3			9^{2}	10	8	5	11		6^{1}	4	7			13			12				16
1	2	3		5^{2}	9	10	7	8	11^{1}	12	6^{3}	4				14	13						17
1	2	3		5	9^{3}	6	7	8^{2}	10	12	11^{1}	4	13		14								18
1	2	3		5^{2}	9	6	7	8	11	13	10^{1}	4^{3}					12	14					19
1	2	3		5	9^{3}	6	7	8	11^{1}	12	10^{2}		13				4	14					20
1	2	3		5^{1}	11^{2}	6	8	7		12	9^{3}		13		14		4	10					21
1	2	3	5		11^{3}	6	7	8		13	9^{1}		12		14		4	10^{2}					22
1	2	13	5		12	6^{1}	8	9			11	4^{2}	7^{3}				3			10	14		23
1	2	3	5		6	7^{2}	8	9	12		13				14		4			11^{3}	10^{1}		24
1	6	4	5	12	13		7	8	10		11^{1}						3		2		9^{2}		25
1		3	5	11	9	6	8	7	10								4■		2^{1}		12		26
1		4	5	12	11^{3}	6	8	7	10	9^{1}	14	3^{2}							2		13		27
1	2	3	4	5^{3}	9^{2}	6	8	7	10	11^{1}								13	14		12		28
1	2	3	5		12	6	8	9^{2}	10		7^{1}				14		4	13			11^{3}		29
1■	7	3	5		10^{2}	8	6	9	11		14						4		2^{1}		12^{3}	13	30
1	2	3	5		9^{2}	6	7	8	10	12	13						4	11^{1}					31
1	2	4	5		9^{1}	8	6^{3}	7	11	13	10^{2}				14		3				12		32
1	2	4	5		11^{3}	6^{2}	7	8	10	12	14						3	13			9^{1}		33
1	2	3	5		11^{3}	6	8	7^{1}	10	12			13		14		4	9^{2}					34
1	2	3	5		8^{3}	7	6	9^{1}	10	11^{2}			12				4	14			13		35
1	2^{1}	4	5		9	6	8		10	11^{2}		14	7^{3}				3	13			12		36

COWDENBEATH

Year Formed: 1882. *Ground & Address:* Central Park, Cowdenbeath KY4 9QQ. *Telephone:* 01383 610166. *Fax:* 01383 512132.
E-mail: office@cowdenbeathfc.com *Website:* www.cowdenbeathfc.com
Ground Capacity: 4,370 (seated: 1,431). *Size of Pitch:* 95m × 60m.
Chairman: Donald Findlay QC. *Finance Director and Secretary:* David Allan.
Club Nicknames: 'The Blue Brazil'; 'Cowden'; 'The Miners'.
Manager: Gary Bollan. *First-Team Coach:* Ian Flaherty.
Previous Ground: North End Park.
Record Attendance: 25,586 v Rangers, League Cup quarter-final, 21 September 1949.
Record Transfer Fee received: £30,000 for Nicky Henderson to Falkirk (March 1994).
Record Victory: 12-0 v Johnstone, Scottish Cup 1st rd, 21 January 1928.
Record Defeat: 1-11 v Clyde, Division II, 6 October 1951; 0-10 v Hearts, Championship, 28 February 2015.
Most Capped Player: Jim Paterson, 3, Scotland.
Most League and Cup Appearances: 491, Ray Allan 1972-75, 1979-89.
Most League Goals in Season (Individual): 54, Rab Walls, Division II, 1938-39.
Most Goals Overall (Individual): 127, Willie Devlin, 1922-26, 1929-30.

COWDENBEATH – SPFL LADBROKES LEAGUE TWO 2018–19 LEAGUE RECORD

Match No.	Date	Venue	Opponents	Result	H/T Score	Lg Pos.	Goalscorers	Attendance
1	Aug 4	A	Clyde	L 0-2	0-2	9		569
2	11	H	Annan Ath	L 1-2	1-1	8	Sheerin [28]	303
3	18	H	Berwick R	W 4-0	2-0	7	Sheerin [33], Scott [36], Scullion [68], Buchanan [69]	314
4	Sept 1	A	Queen's Park	D 0-0	0-0	8		534
5	15	H	Peterhead	L 2-4	2-1	9	Talbot [10], Buchanan [27]	341
6	22	H	Albion R	D 1-1	0-1	9	Sheerin [82]	348
7	29	A	Edinburgh C	L 0-1	0-0	9		337
8	Oct 6	H	Stirling Alb	W 1-0	1-0	7	Marsh [6]	365
9	13	A	Elgin C	L 1-3	1-1	7	Cox [10]	545
10	27	A	Berwick R	W 3-0	-	7	Swan 2 (1 pen) [29, 36 (p)], Mullen [80]	477
11	Nov 3	H	Elgin C	L 1-2	1-0	7	Malcolm [28]	310
12	10	A	Annan Ath	W 2-0	0-0	7	Kris Renton [67], Skelly [90]	374
13	27	H	Queen's Park	W 2-0	0-0	7	Kris Renton [51], Skelly [82]	275
14	Dec 1	A	Albion R	D 1-1	1-1	6	Skelly (pen) [21]	220
15	8	H	Clyde	D 1-1	0-1	6	Allan [52]	373
16	22	H	Edinburgh C	L 0-2	0-1	6		331
17	29	A	Stirling Alb	L 1-2	1-2	6	Allan [9]	708
18	Jan 5	H	Berwick R	W 2-0	1-0	6	Cox [45], Swan (pen) [61]	384
19	12	A	Elgin C	W 4-1	2-0	5	Cox [17], Kris Renton [38], Allan 2 [46, 69]	575
20	26	A	Clyde	L 0-1	0-0	7		604
21	Feb 9	A	Queen's Park	D 1-1	0-0	7	Henvey [79]	404
22	16	H	Annan Ath	L 2-4	2-1	7	Mullen [11], Kris Renton [34]	255
23	19	H	Albion R	W 1-0	0-0	7	Fraser G (pen) [63]	254
24	23	A	Edinburgh C	L 0-2	0-2	7		351
25	26	A	Peterhead	L 0-1	0-1	7		532
26	Mar 2	H	Stirling Alb	L 1-2	0-1	7	Cox [56]	371
27	5	H	Peterhead	L 1-3	1-2	7	Cox [17]	250
28	9	A	Berwick R	D 1-1	1-1	7	Buchanan [31]	409
29	23	H	Queen's Park	D 0-0	0-0	8		347
30	26	A	Albion R	L 0-1	0-1	8		322
31	30	A	Peterhead	L 1-2	1-1	8	Cox [44]	682
32	Apr 6	H	Edinburgh C	W 4-1	2-0	8	Allan 3 [15, 42, 46], Cox [81]	262
33	13	H	Elgin C	W 2-1	0-1	8	Cox [63], Sheerin [86]	294
34	20	A	Stirling Alb	W 1-0	0-0	7	Cox [57]	507
35	27	A	Annan Ath	L 2-3	0-2	7	Allan 2 [71, 77]	365
36	May 4	H	Clyde	W 2-1	1-0	6	Pyper [38], Miller [64]	1007

Final League Position: 6

Honours
League Champions: Division II 1913-14, 1914-15, 1938-39; Second Division 2011-12; Third Division 2005-06.
Runners-up: Division II 1921-22, 1923-24, 1969-70; Second Division 1991-92; Third Division 2000-01, 2008-09.
Promoted via play-offs: 2009-10 (to First Division).
Scottish Cup: Quarter-finals 1931.
League Cup: Semi-finals 1959, 1970.

Club colours: Shirt: Royal blue with white trim. Shorts: White. Socks: Black with red tops.

Goalscorers: *League (46):* Allan 9, Cox 9, Kris Renton 4, Sheerin 4, Buchanan 3, Skelly 3 (1 pen), Swan 3 (2 pens), Mullen 2, Fraser G 1 (1 pen), Henvey 1, Malcolm 1, Marsh 1, Miller 1, Pyper 1, Scott 1, Scullion 1, Talbot 1.
William Hill Scottish FA Cup (4): Cox 3, Deas 1.
Betfred Scottish League Cup (5): Sheerin 4, Cox 1.
Irn-Bru Scottish League Challenge (1): Sheerin 1.

McGurn D 27 + 1	Mullen F 35	Marsh D 17	Pyper J 19 + 9	Talbot J 10	Cox D 31 + 3	Buchanan R 31 + 1	Malcolm B 25 + 7	Smith B 6 + 1	Sheerin J 9 + 15	Renton Kris 22 + 7	Miller K 28 + 3	Swan H 17 + 6	Gilfillan B 1	Scott M 10 + 3	Scullion P 3 + 1	Skelly J 4 + 8	Deas R 26 + 1	Fraser G 22 + 6	Maley G 1	Kay H — + 1	Allan J 17 + 6	Sneddon K — + 1	Henvey M 2 + 5	Lennox A 8	Todd J 12 + 1	Bollan L 13	Fotheringham M — + 1	*Match No.*
1	2	3	4	5^{1}	6	7	8	9	10	11^{2}	12	13																1
1	2	4			6	8^{1}	5	9	10	13	7	12	3	11^{2}														2
1	2	3	14		12^{3}	6	8	9	10^{1}	13	7■	5		11^{2}	4													3
1	2	4^{2}	12	5	6	7	9	10	11^{1}	13				8	3													4
1	2	4	3	5^{3}	6	7	8	9^{2}	10^{1}	14				11		12	13											5
1	2		4		14	7	9	12	13	10^{3}				11^{1}	3	6^{2}	5	8										6
1	2	4	3		11^{3}	9	13	6^{2}	10	14	7					12	5	8^{1}										7
1	2	3		5	6^{1}	9	7		10^{2}	13	12			11^{3}		14	4	8■										8
1■	5	4	12	2	9	6	8		11^{1}	13	7^{3}			10^{2}	14		3											9
	2	4	3		6^{2}		8		13	10	7^{3}	9		11^{1}		12	5		1	14								10
1	2	4	3		6		8		10^{2}	11		9		7^{1}		12	5	13										11
1	2	4	14	5	6	12	8			10	7^{1}	9^{2}				13	3	11^{3}										12
1		3		5	10^{1}	6	8			11	7	9^{2}				12	4	2			13							13
1	2	3			6^{1}	7■	5		13	10	9					11^{2}	4	8			12							14
1	2	3	14	5	9^{3}		8^{1}			10	7	13				11^{2}	4	6			12							15
1	2	3	13	5■					12	11	8	9^{1}				6^{2}	4	7			10							16
1	2	3	12		6^{2}	9	5^{1}		14	10	7					13	4■	8			11^{3}							17
1	2	4	3		6^{2}	9			13	11	7^{1}	5						10			8	12						18
1	2		4		9^{2}	8				10^{1}	7	5		13			3	6			11		12					19
1	2		4	5	9^{1}	11^{2}	14			10	7			13			3	6			8^{3}		12					20
	2		3		6	7^{3}	12			10^{1}	9	5		14			4	8			11^{2}		13	1				21
13	2		4		10^{3}	8	6			11	9			7^{2}				12			14			1^{1}	3	5■		22
	2				12	9	13			10	6	5					4	8			7^{1}		11^{2}	1	3			23
	2				10■	9	12		14	11^{1}	8	5					4	7^{3}			6^{2}		13	1	3			24
	2		12			10	14			11	7^{3}	9					4	8			6^{1}		13	1	3^{2}	5		25
	2				6	9			13	11	7	5^{1}					3	8			12		10^{2}	1		4		26
	2		12		10	8	7^{3}		14	11		9^{1}					4^{2}	6						1	3	5	13	27
1	2				10	6	12		13		7^{1}	9					3	8			11^{2}				4	5		28
1	2		3		10^{1}	9	8^{2}		13	11	7	5						6			12					4		29
	2		3		9	6	8		13	11^{3}	12	5						7^{1}			10^{2}			1	14	4		30
1	2		3		9	6	8		12		4^{1}						7				10				5	11		31
1	2		7		10^{1}	6	9		13		8						4	12			11^{2}				5	3		32
1	2		8^{1}		11	6	9		13^{3}		7	14					3	12			10^{2}				5	4		33
1	2		4		6	11	9^{1}				7	12					8^{2}	13			10				5	3		34
1	2		4		6	11	9				7						8^{1}	12			10				5	3		35
1	2		3		10	7^{1}	9				8	12						6			11				5	4		36

DUMBARTON

Year Formed: 1872. *Ground:* Dumbarton Football Stadium, Castle Road, Dumbarton G82 1JJ. *Telephone/Fax:* 01389 762569. *E-mail:* office@dumbartonfc.com *Website:* www.dumbartonfootballclub.com
Ground Capacity: total: 2,025 (all seated). *Size of Pitch:* 98m × 67m.
Chairman: John Steele. *Vice-Chairman:* Colin Hosie.
Manager: Jim Duffy. *Assistant Manager:* Craig MacPherson.
Club Nicknames: 'The Sons'; 'Sons of the Rock'.
Previous Grounds: Broadmeadow; Ropework Lane; Townend Ground; Boghead Park; Cliftonhill Stadium.
Record Attendance: 18,000 v Raith R, Scottish Cup, 2 March 1957.
Record Transfer Fee received: £300,000 for Neill Collins to Sunderland (July 2004).
Record Transfer Fee paid: £50,000 for Charlie Gibson from Stirling Alb (1989).
Record Victory: 13-1 v Kirkintilloch Central, Scottish Cup 1st rd, 1 September 1888.
Record Defeat: 1-11 v Albion R, Division II, 30 January 1926: v Ayr U, League Cup, 13 August 1952.
Most Capped Player: James McAulay, 9, Scotland.
Most League Appearances: 298: Andy Jardine, 1957-67.
Most Goals in Season (Individual): 38: Kenny Wilson, Division II, 1971-72. *(League and Cup):* 46 Hughie Gallacher, 1955-56.
Most Goals Overall (Individual): 202: Hughie Gallacher, 1954-62

DUMBARTON – SPFL LADBROKES LEAGUE ONE 2018–19 LEAGUE RECORD

Match No.	Date	Venue	Opponents	Result		H/T Score	Lg Pos.	Goalscorers	Attendance
1	Aug 4	A	East Fife	W	2-0	0-0	3	Dowie 47, Gallagher 61	525
2	11	H	Forfar Ath	L	0-2	0-1	5		575
3	18	H	Arbroath	D	1-1	0-1	5	Forbes 90	627
4	25	A	Brechin C	L	2-3	1-0	8	Barr, B 18, Spencer 56	371
5	Sept 1	A	Stenhousemuir	L	1-2	1-1	9	Barr, B 6	616
6	15	H	Montrose	W	2-1	0-1	6	Dowie 69, Forbes (pen) 71	529
7	22	A	Airdrieonians	D	1-1	1-0	6	Spencer 29	777
8	29	H	Raith R	L	1-5	0-4	8	Gallagher 70	756
9	Oct 6	A	Stranraer	L	2-3	1-2	9	Forbes 12, Thomas 60	305
10	20	A	Arbroath	L	1-3	1-0	9	Russell 15	700
11	27	H	East Fife	W	4-0	2-0	9	Gallagher 7, Barr, B 45, Carswell 51, Thomas 71	713
12	Nov 3	A	Montrose	L	0-1	0-0	10		549
13	10	H	Stenhousemuir	W	2-1	1-1	8	Forbes (pen) 23, Thomas 56	605
14	17	A	Forfar Ath	L	0-3	0-0	9		491
15	Dec 1	H	Brechin C	W	4-1	0-0	8	Gallagher 2 52, 83, Forbes 54, Thomas 69	456
16	8	H	Airdrieonians	D	1-1	0-1	8	Spencer 90	624
17	15	A	Raith R	L	2-4	2-1	8	Forbes 10, Paton 20	1089
18	22	H	Stranraer	L	0-1	0-0	8		686
19	29	A	Stenhousemuir	D	2-2	1-1	8	Forbes 2 45, 90	536
20	Jan 5	H	Forfar Ath	L	2-3	1-3	8	Barr, B 2 18, 85	619
21	12	A	Brechin C	L	0-1	0-0	8		456
22	26	H	Montrose	D	1-1	0-0	9	Melingui 83	521
23	Feb 2	A	Airdrieonians	D	2-2	0-1	9	Barr, B 56, Thomas 86	709
24	16	A	Stranraer	W	3-0	0-0	8	Forbes 56, Thomas 80, Perry 83	327
25	23	A	East Fife	W	4-3	3-0	7	Thomas 3 20, 42, 62, Gallagher 36	571
26	26	H	Raith R	D	2-2	2-1	7	Forbes 27, Carswell 33	507
27	Mar 2	H	Arbroath	W	2-0	1-0	7	Forbes (pen) 30, Thomas 52	700
28	9	A	Montrose	W	3-1	2-0	6	Thomas 2 17, 59, Gallagher 38	574
29	23	A	Raith R	L	1-4	1-3	7	Gallagher 38	1338
30	30	H	Stenhousemuir	L	1-2	0-1	7	Barr, C 85	613
31	Apr 2	H	Airdrieonians	D	3-3	1-2	7	Thomas 21, Gallagher 75, Forbes 82	691
32	6	H	Brechin C	W	2-1	2-1	7	Toshney (og) 36, Gallagher 38	531
33	13	A	Forfar Ath	D	0-0	0-0	7		554
34	20	H	East Fife	W	3-0	2-0	7	Barr, C 20, Thomas 44, Gallagher 66	659
35	27	H	Stranraer	W	2-1	2-0	7	Gallagher 8, Forbes 19	704
36	May 4	A	Arbroath	D	1-1	0-0	6	Gallagher 54	1373

Final League Position: 6

Honours
League Champions: Division I 1890-91 (shared with Rangers), 1891-92; Division II 1910-11, 1971-72; Second Division 1991-92; Third Division 2008-09.
Runners-up: First Division 1983-84; Division II 1907-08; Second Division 1994-95; Third Division 2001-02.
Promoted via play-offs: 2011-12 (Second Division).
Scottish Cup Winners: 1883; *Runners-up:* 1881, 1882, 1887, 1891, 1897.
League Challenge Cup: Runners-up: 2017-18.

Club colours: Shirt: White with yellow and black horizontal stripe. Shorts: Black. Socks: Black with white tops.

Goalscorers: *League (60):* Thomas 14, Forbes 13 (3 pens), Gallagher 13, Barr B 6, Spencer 3, Barr C 2, Carswell 2, Dowie 2, Melingui 1, Paton 1, Perry 1, Russell 1, own goal 1.
William Hill Scottish FA Cup (0).
Betfred Scottish League Cup (3): Barr B 1, Barr C 1, Gallagher 1.
Irn-Bru Scottish League Challenge (2): Paton 1, Russell 1.

Adam G 20	Ballantyne C 30	Dowie A 19	Barr C 14 + 2	Dyer W 14	Hutton K 34 + 1	Carswell S 29 + 2	Gallagher C 27 + 6	Forbes R 32 + 4	Paton M 15 + 9	Loy R 5 + 3	Little A 1 + 5	Thomson R 10 + 10	Barr B 33 + 3	Perry R 10 + 1	Russell I 8 + 8	Spencer B 7 + 10	Allardice S 9 + 3	Aitchison J 4	McGowan J 4	Mutch R 2	Thomas D 26	Smith C 8 + 1	Armour B 3 + 7	Ferguson D 15	van Schaik H 5 + 1	Melingui B 3 + 9	Brennan C 2	McLean B 7	*Match No.*
1	2²	3	4	5	6	7	8³	9¹	10	11	12	13	14																1
1		3	4	5	6	7	8²	9	10	11³		14	12	2¹	13														2
1		4	3¹	5	6	7	12	13	9	10²	14	2	8		11³														3
1		3		5	7	8²	14	12	6¹	11³	2	4	9		10	13													4
1		3		5	6		13	12		11¹		2²	7		9	8	4	10											5
1	2	3		5	12	7³	14	9¹		13		8	11			6	4	10²											6
1	2	3		5	7²	13		9³		14		8¹	11		12	6	4	10											7
		4		5²	8¹		13	10³		14		6	9	2	12	7	3	11	1										8
		4					10²	11¹	12		13	7	9	2	8	6	3			1	5								9
	2	4			7	6		12	13				8¹	3	11²	5	10			1	9								10
	2	3			7³	6	5	9	13		14		8	4	10¹	12					11²	1							11
	2	3			8	7³	6	5	13		14		9²	4	10¹		12				11	1							12
	2				7	13	9	5	6²				12	3	11¹	8	4				10	1							13
	2				8	7	11¹	5	6				9	4		12	3				10	1							14
	2	4		5	7	3	10	8	6¹				9			12			1		11								15
	2	4		5	7	3	10	8	6²				9¹			12	13		1		11								16
	2	3		5	8	4	11	9¹	7				6			12			1		10								17
	2	3		5¹	7	4	11	9	8³			14	6²			12	13				10	1							18
	2	4		5²	7	3	8³	9	13			12	6			14	10¹				11	1							19
	2	3		5²	8¹	4	11	7	6			12	9			13					10	1							20
	5	3			8	4	6	7	2■			10	9			12						1	11¹						21
1¹	5		14		7	4	12	6				8²	9									13	10³	2	3	11			22
1	5				7¹	2³		8	6²			14	9	12							10		13	4	3	11			23
1	5				8	4	7²	9				12	10	6							11			2¹	3	13			24
1	5		12		8	7	11³	6	13				9²	4¹							10		14	2	3				25
	5		4		8	7	10²	6¹	13			12	9³								11			2	3	14	1		26
1	5		4		7	3	6³	8	12			14	9¹								11		10²	2		13			27
1	5		4		7	3	11¹	8	13				9²								10³		14	6		12		2	28
1	5		3		7	4	11	6	8²				9		13						10¹			2		12			29
1	5		4		7		10	8	6²			3	9								11		13	2¹		12			30
1	5		4		7	9	10¹	6					9		13						11			2²		12		3	31
1	5		4		7	8	10¹	6					9								11			2		12		3	32
1	5		3		7		6	8					11								9		12	2		10¹		4	33
1	5		4		8	7	10¹	6				14	9³		12						11²		13	2				3	34
1	5		4		8	7	11¹	6					9²		13						10			2		12		3	35
	5■		4		8¹	7	11	6					9²		13						10		14	2³	12		1	3	36

DUNDEE

Year Formed: 1893. *Ground & Address:* Kilmac Stadium at Dens Park, Sandeman St, Dundee DD3 7JY. *Telephone:* 01382 889966. *Fax:* 01382 832284. *E-mail:* reception@dundeefc.co.uk *Website:* www.dundeefc.co.uk
Ground Capacity: 11,850 (all seated). *Size of Pitch:* 101m × 66m.
Chairman: Tim Keyes. *Managing Director:* John Nelms. *Technical Director:* Gordon Strachan.
Manager: James McPake. *Assistant Manager:* Jimmy Nicholl.
Club Nicknames: 'The Dark Blues'; 'The Dee'.
Previous Ground: Carolina Port 1893-98.
Record Attendance: 43,024 v Rangers, Scottish Cup 2nd rd, 7 February 1953.
Record Transfer Fee received: £1,500,000 for Robert Douglas to Celtic (October 2000).
Record Transfer Fee paid: £600,000 for Fabian Caballero from Sol de América (Paraguay) (July 2000).
Record Victory: 10-0 Division II v Alloa Ath, 9 March 1947 and v Dunfermline Ath, 22 March 1947.
Record Defeat: 0-11 v Celtic, Division I, 26 October 1895.
Most Capped Player: Alex Hamilton, 24, Scotland.
Most League Appearances: 400: Barry Smith, 1995-2006.
Most League Goals in Season (Individual): 52: Alan Gilzean, 1960-64.
Most Goals Overall (Individual): 113: Alan Gilzean 1960-64.

DUNDEE – SPFL LADBROKES PREMIERSHIP 2018–19 LEAGUE RECORD

Match No.	Date	Venue	Opponents	Result		H/T Score	Lg Pos.	Goalscorers	Attendance
1	Aug 4	A	St Mirren	L	1-2	1-1	9	N'Gwatala 12	5470
2	11	H	Aberdeen	L	0-1	0-0	10		7581
3	25	A	St Johnstone	L	0-1	0-0	11		4259
4	Sept 1	H	Motherwell	L	1-3	0-0	12	Kallman 71	5137
5	15	A	Rangers	L	0-4	0-3	12		50,130
6	22	H	Hibernian	L	0-3	0-0	12		6076
7	29	A	Hamilton A	W	2-0	1-0	12	Boyle 38, Madianga 90	1788
8	Oct 6	H	Kilmarnock	L	1-2	1-1	12	Nabi 10	5158
9	20	A	Livingston	L	0-4	0-2	12		2137
10	23	H	Hearts	L	0-3	0-2	12		6112
11	31	H	Celtic	L	0-5	0-4	12		7960
12	Nov 3	A	Motherwell	L	0-1	0-0	12		4129
13	10	H	St Mirren	D	1-1	1-1	12	Miller, K 34	5552
14	24	A	Hibernian	D	2-2	1-2	12	Miller, K 45, McGowan, P 47	16,190
15	Dec 5	H	Hamilton A	W	4-0	1-0	12	Miller, K 3 27, 51, 81, Curran, J 69	4426
16	9	H	Rangers	D	1-1	1-1	11	Miller, K 9	8578
17	15	A	Kilmarnock	L	1-3	0-0	11	Miller, K 90	4668
18	18	A	Aberdeen	L	1-5	0-2	12	Miller, C 68	13,142
19	22	A	Celtic	L	0-3	0-1	12		57,234
20	26	H	Livingston	D	0-0	0-0	12		4905
21	29	H	St Johnstone	L	0-2	0-1	12		6868
22	Jan 23	A	Hearts	W	2-1	1-1	11	Kusunga 24, Nelson 62	15,518
23	26	H	Motherwell	L	0-1	0-0	11		4887
24	Feb 2	A	Hamilton A	D	1-1	0-0	10	Wright 66	2297
25	6	H	Kilmarnock	D	2-2	2-1	10	Nelson 2 8, 20	4694
26	16	A	Livingston	W	2-1	0-1	10	Nelson 54, Wright 83	2321
27	22	H	Hibernian	L	2-4	1-2	10	McGowan, P 35, Woods 79	6450
28	27	A	Rangers	L	0-4	0-3	11		48,859
29	Mar 9	H	Hearts	L	0-1	0-1	11		5667
30	17	H	Celtic	L	0-1	0-0	11		7608
31	30	A	St Mirren	L	1-2	1-1	12	Robson 1	6733
32	Apr 3	A	St Johnstone	L	0-2	0-1	12		3767
33	6	H	Aberdeen	L	0-2	0-0	12		6593
34	20	A	St Johnstone	L	0-2	0-0	12		3946
35	27	A	Motherwell	L	3-4	2-2	12	Woods (pen) 11, Robson 22, Ralph 52	3662
36	May 4	H	Hamilton A	L	0-1	0-0	12		4622
37	11	A	Livingston	W	1-0	1-0	12	Miller, K 11	1374
38	18	H	St Mirren	L	2-3	1-0	12	Kerr 14, Wright 74	5595

Final League Position: 12

Honours
League Champions: Division I 1961-62; First Division 1978-79, 1991-92, 1997-98; Championship 2013-14; Division II 1946-47, 1947-48.
Runners-up: Division I 1902-03, 1906-07, 1908-09, 1948-49; First Division 1980-81, 2007-08, 2009-10, 2011-12.
Scottish Cup Winners: 1910; *Runners-up:* 1925, 1952, 1964, 2003.
League Cup Winners: 1951-52, 1952-53, 1973-74; *Runners-up:* 1967-68, 1980-81, 1995-96.
League Challenge Cup Winners: 1990-91, 2009-10; *Runners-up:* 1994-95.

European: *European Cup:* 8 matches (1962-63 semi-finals). *Cup Winners' Cup:* 2 matches: (1964-65).
UEFA Cup: 22 matches: (*Fairs Cup:* 1967-68 semi-finals, *UEFA Cup:* 1971-72, 1973-74, 1974-75, 2003-04).

Club colours: All: Navy blue.

Goalscorers: *League (31):* Miller K 8, Nelson 4, Wright 3, McGowan P 2, Robson 2, Woods 2 (1 pen), Boyle 1, Curran J 1, Kallman 1, Kerr 1, Kusunga 1, Madianga 1, Miller C 1, N'Gwatala 1, Nabi 1, Ralph 1.
William Hill Scottish FA Cup (1): Curran J 1.
Betfred Scottish League Cup (8): Mendy 2, Moussa 2, Madianga 1, McGowan P 1, Spence 1, Wighton 1.
Irn-Bru Scottish League Challenge (3): Bradbury 1, Jefferies 1, own goal 1.

Hamilton J 17	Curran J 24 + 10	Caulker S 2	Meekings J 4	Kerr C 27 + 1	Spence L 10 + 3	McGowan P 23 + 7	N'Gwatala E 7 + 2	Madianga K 9 + 1 / Robertson F 1	Moussa S 4 + 5	Mendy J 3 + 3 / Mulligan J — + 1	Wighton C — + 3	Kusunga G 22 + 2	Ralph N 26	Nabi A 6 + 7	Kamara G 16 + 1	Kallman B 11 + 7	Miller K 21 + 12	Inniss R 9 + 2	Miller C 15 + 1	Parish E 5	Boyle A 11 + 2	O'Dea D 20 + 1	Henvey M — + 1	Deacon R 1 + 4	Lambert J — + 4	Woods M 22 + 2	Dieng T 16	Dales A 8 + 2	Curran C 11 + 3	Nelson A 9 + 3	Moore C 1 + 2	Horsfield J 10 + 1	Hadenius A 3	McGowan R 15	Robson E 12 + 1	Wright S 11 + 2	O'Sullivan J 6 + 5	Match No.
1	2	3	4	5	6	7^{1}	8	9	10	11	12																											1
1	2		4	13	6^{2}	7	9	8	10	11^{1}	14	3	5^{3}	12																								2
1	2	3	4			6	12	9^{2}	13	11^{3}	14		5	8^{1}	7	10																						3
1	2		3^{1}	5	8	7	14	6^{2}				4		9^{3}		11	10	12	13																			4
	2			5		7	8	6	13			12		14		11^{2}	10■		9^{1}	1	3	4^{3}																5
	12			2		8	9	6^{3}		13				10	7	11^{1}		4	5^{2}	1	3		14															6
				2	8		9	6		12				10^{2}	7	11^{1}		4	5	1	3			13														7
	13			2^{1}	6^{2}		9	8						11	7	12	10	3	5	1	4																	8
				2	7			8^{1}	10					13	6	11^{2}	9	3	5	1	4			12														9
1	6			2	8^{1}		10^{2}	12							7	9	11	3	5			4		13														10
1	9			2	8				12			5			7	10^{1}	11	3^{2}			13	4		6^{3}	14													11
1	7^{2}			2	8	14			11^{3}			5			9		10	12	6		3	4^{1}				13												12
1	6			2		14			13			3	5	12	8	11^{2}	10^{1}		9^{3}			4				7												13
1	8			2	13	9			14			3	5		7		11^{3}		10^{1}			4			12	6^{2}												14
1	6			2	12	10				14		3	5		7		11^{2}		9^{1}			4			13	8^{3}												15
1	6			2	13	10						4	5■		8	12	11^{1}		9		3					7^{2}												16
1	6			2		10^{1}						3		13	7	12	11		9^{2}		5	4				8												17
1	6			2	7^{2}	10						3^{1}	5		13	14	11^{3}		9		12	4				0												18
1	7			2		9							5	10^{2}	6	11^{1}	12	3			4				13	8												19
1	6			2		8							5	12	7	10	11		9^{1}		3	4																20
1	6			2		10							5	13	7^{1}	12	11		9^{2}		3	4				8												21
	6			2		8						3	5			14	13	4								7	1	9^{3}	10^{2}	11^{1}	12							22
	6^{3}			2		8						3	5			14	13	4						12		7	1	9	11^{2}	10^{1}								23
						12						3	5				13									7	1	9^{1}	11^{2}			2	4	6	8^{3}	10	14	24
						12						4	5				13					14				8	1	6	11^{2}	10^{1}		2	7^{3}	3		9		25
	14					12						4	5				13									8	1	6^{2}	10	11^{1}		2	7^{3}	3		9		26
	10					7^{3}						4	5				12									8	1	6^{2}	11^{1}			2		3	13	9	14	27
	6^{2}					10							5				12					4				8	1	9^{1}				2		3	7	11	13	28
	14					13							5				10					4				7	1	6^{2}	11^{1}			2		3	8	9^{3}	12	29
	13											3	6				11^{3}					5				8	1	14	12			2		4	9	10^{2}	7^{1}	30
	12					14						4	5				13									8^{3}	1		11^{1}	10		2		3	7	9^{2}	6	31
	9					10							5				11^{3}					4				8^{1}	1	13	14	12		2^{2}		3	7		6	32
	9			2		10						12	5				14					4^{1}					1		11^{3}	13	8^{2}			3	7		6	33
	12			2		8							5				10^{1}					4				14	1		11	13				3	7	9^{3}	6^{2}	34
	7			2								4	5^{1}				12									6^{3}	1		8	11^{2}	14	13		3	9	10		35
	14			5								3^{3}					13					4				7	1		12	10^{1}		9		2	8	11	6^{2}	36
	14			2		8^{1}						4	6				10^{2}					5				7	1			11^{3}				3	9	12	13	37
1	12			5		9		7^{1}		14		2	8				10^{3}					4■								11^{2}				3	6	13		38

DUNDEE UNITED

Year Formed: 1909 (1923). *Ground & Address:* Tannadice Park, Tannadice St, Dundee DD3 7JW. *Telephone:* 01382 833166. *Fax:* 01382 889398. *E-mail:* admin@dundeeunited.co.uk *Website:* www.dundeeunitedfc.co.uk
Ground Capacity: 14,223 (all seated). *Size of Pitch:* 100m × 66m.
Chairman: Mark Ogren. *Managing Director:* Mal Brannigan.
Head Coach: Robbie Neilson. *Assistant Head Coach:* Gordon Forrest.
Club Nicknames: 'The Terrors'; 'The Arabs'.
Previous Name: Dundee Hibernian (up to 1923).
Record Attendance: 28,000 v Barcelona, Fairs Cup, 16 November 1966.
Record Transfer Fee received: £4,000,000 for Duncan Ferguson from Rangers (July 1993).
Record Transfer Fee paid: £750,000 for Steven Pressley from Coventry C (July 1995).
Record Victory: 14-0 v Nithsdale Wanderers, Scottish Cup 1st rd, 17 January 1931.
Record Defeat: 1-12 v Motherwell, Division II, 23 January 1954.
Most Capped Player: Maurice Malpas, 55, Scotland.
Most League Appearances: 618: Maurice Malpas, 1980-2000.
Most Appearances in European Matches: 76: Dave Narey (record for Scottish player at the time).
Most League Goals in Season (Individual): 40: John Coyle, Division II, 1955-56.
Most Goals Overall (Individual): 199: Peter McKay, 1947-54.

DUNDEE UNITED – SPFL LADBROKES CHAMPIONSHIP 2018–19 LEAGUE RECORD

Match No.	*Date*	*Venue*	*Opponents*	*Result*	*H/T Score*	*Lg Pos.*	*Goalscorers*	*Attendance*
1	Aug 4	H	Dunfermline Ath	L 2-3	1-0	7	Clark [44], Aird [89]	6532
2	11	A	Queen of the South	W 2-1	2-0	5	Stanton [15], Safranko [27]	1960
3	25	H	Partick Thistle	W 3-1	1-0	3	Watson 2 [6, 78], Curran C [86]	5219
4	Sept 1	A	Alloa Ath	D 1-1	0-0	4	Watson [71]	1616
5	15	H	Greenock Morton	D 1-1	0-1	5	Fyvie [90]	4594
6	22	A	Falkirk	W 2-0	0-0	3	Safranko [59], Curran C [86]	4933
7	29	H	Ross Co	L 1-5	1-3	4	Safranko [17]	4446
8	Oct 6	A	Ayr U	L 0-2	0-1	4		2621
9	13	A	Partick Thistle	W 2-1	1-0	4	Aird [45], Safranko [48]	3087
10	20	H	Inverness CT	D 1-1	0-0	4	Safranko [55]	5628
11	27	A	Dunfermline Ath	W 2-0	1-0	3	McMullan [24], King [60]	6349
12	Nov 3	H	Queen of the South	W 2-0	1-0	3	Safranko [3], Doyle (og) [81]	5171
13	10	A	Ross Co	W 1-0	1-0	3	Watson [15]	4565
14	20	H	Alloa Ath	W 4-2	3-2	2	Clark [19], Safranko [21], Aird (pen) [35], Curran C [85]	4201
15	30	H	Ayr U	L 0-5	0-2	3		6097
16	Dec 8	A	Greenock Morton	D 1-1	1-0	3	Frans [31]	1916
17	15	A	Inverness CT	D 1-1	0-1	3	King [76]	2464
18	22	H	Falkirk	W 2-1	1-0	3	Stanton [22], Safranko [53]	5267
19	29	A	Alloa Ath	L 1-2	0-0	3	Booth [60]	1859
20	Jan 5	H	Partick Thistle	D 1-1	0-1	3	Fyvie (pen) [62]	5282
21	12	H	Dunfermline Ath	W 1-0	0-0	3	Clark [81]	5913
22	25	A	Ayr U	L 0-1	0-1	3		2232
23	Feb 2	H	Greenock Morton	W 2-1	2-0	3	Safranko [8], Pawlett [29]	4902
24	16	A	Queen of the South	W 1-0	1-0	3	Clark (pen) [40]	2012
25	23	A	Falkirk	D 1-1	0-0	3	Smith, C [49]	5840
26	26	H	Inverness CT	W 1-0	0-0	2	Clark (pen) [68]	4737
27	Mar 9	A	Partick Thistle	L 1-2	0-1	2	Clark [76]	3173
28	19	H	Ross Co	W 1-0	1-0	2	Butcher [7]	4290
29	23	H	Alloa Ath	W 2-1	1-1	2	Graham (og) [27], Clark [83]	4645
30	26	A	Dunfermline Ath	W 1-0	1-0	2	Pawlett [24]	6096
31	30	H	Queen of the South	L 1-2	0-0	2	Clark [71]	4839
32	Apr 5	A	Ross Co	D 1-1	1-0	2	Safranko [12]	3550
33	12	H	Ayr U	W 2-1	0-1	2	Safranko [63], McMullan [74]	4392
34	20	A	Inverness CT	W 2-0	1-0	2	Safranko [27], McMullan [49]	2971
35	27	H	Falkirk	W 2-0	2-0	2	Bouhenna [15], McMullan [26]	5260
36	May 4	A	Greenock Morton	L 0-1	0-1	2		2244

Final League Position: 2

Honours: *League Champions:* Premier Division 1982-83;. Division II 1924-25, 1928-29.
Runners-up: Division II 1930-31, 1959-60; First Division 1995-96; Championship 2018-19.
Scottish Cup Winners: 1994, 2010; *Runners-up:* 1974, 1981, 1985, 1987, 1988, 1991, 2005, 2014.
League Cup Winners: 1979-80, 1980-81; *Runners-up:* 1981-82, 1984-85, 1997-98, 2007-08, 2014-15.
League Challenge Cup Winners, 2016-17; *Runners-up:* 1995-96.

European: *European Cup:* 8 matches (1983-84, semi-finals). *Cup Winners' Cup:* 10 matches (1974-75, 1988-89, 1994-95). *UEFA Cup:* 86 matches (*Fairs Cup:* 1966-67, 1969-70, 1970-71. *UEFA Cup:* 1975-76, 1977-78, 1978-79, 1979-80, 1980-81, 1981-82, 1982-83, 1984-85, 1985-86, 1986-87 runners-up, 1987-88, 1989-90, 1990-91, 1993-94, 1997-98, 2005-06). *Europa League:* 6 matches (2010-2011, 2011-12, 2012-13).

Club colours: Shirt: Tangerine with black trim. Shorts: Black. Socks: Tangerine.

Goalscorers: *League (49):* Safranko 12, Clark 8 (2 pens), McMullan 4, Watson 4, Aird 3 (1 pen), Curran C 3, Fyvie 2 (1 pen), King 2, Pawlett 2, Stanton 2, Booth 1, Bouhenna 1, Butcher 1, Frans 1, Smith C 1, own goals 2.
William Hill Scottish FA Cup (7): Clark 2 (1 pen), Safranko 2, Booth 1, Harkes 1, King 1.
Betfred Scottish League Cup (6): Clark 3, Barton 1 (1 pen), Frans 1, Glass 1.
Irn-Bru Scottish League Challenge (4): McMullan 2, Chalmers 1, Smith M 1.
Play-Offs (5): Clark 2 (2 pens), McMullan 1, Safranko 1, Sow 1.

Rakovan M 8 + 1	Wardrop S 1	Frans F 20	Edjenguele W 5	Robson J 18 + 1	Stanton S 20 + 5	Rabitsch C 9 + 4	Barton A 5 + 2	Loemba Y 7 + 2	Curran C 8 + 8	Clark N 13 + 12	Aird F 17 + 2	Smith M 4 + 4	McMullan P 27 + 5	Watson P 18 + 5	Safranko P 31 + 2	Murdoch S 12 + 2	Booth C 23 + 3	Glass D — + 2	Bouhenna R 23 + 3	Fyvie F 13 + 4	King B 10 + 6	Siegrist B 27	Nesbitt A 1 + 6	Smith C 6 + 1	Seaman C 9 + 1	Gomis M 2 + 3	Harkes I 10 + 3	Connolly M 9	Reynolds M 12	Butcher C 13	Pawlett P 9 + 2	Sow O 4 + 3	Chalmers L 1 + 1	Laidlaw R 1	Mochrie C — + 1	*Match No.*
1	2	3	4	5^2	6	7^1	8	9	10^3	11	12	13	14																							1
1		3		4	5	6	7	9	12	10^1	8	13		2	11^2																					2
1		4		5		6	7	10	11^2		8^1			3	9	2	12	13																		3
1		4		5		6^1	7	10	11^3		8^2		14	3	9	2	13	12																		4
1		4				6	7^2	5	11^1		9^3		13	2	10		8		3	12	14															5
1		4		5		7		6	10		8		9^1	2	11				3		12															6
1		4		5		7^3		6	11		8^2		9^1	2	10	14■			3	13	12															7
		3			14	8		12		13		6^3	10	2	11		5		4	7^2	9^1	1														8
		4			7		13		14	12	6^2		10	2	11		5		3	8^1	9^3	1														9
		4			7			13		12	6^2		10		11	2	5		3	8	9^1	1														10
		4			6	13			14	12	8^3		9		11^1	2	5		3	7	10^2	1														11
			4		7		14		13	12	6^2		10		11^1	2	5^3		3	8	9	1														12
			4	14	7	12				13	6		10	2^1	11	5			3	8^2	9^3	1														13
			4		7	8^2			14	10	6^3		9^1	2	11	12	5		3		13	1														14
12			4		8				13		6		9	2	11		5		3	7	10^1	1^2														15
1		4			7	13			10		8^2		9^1		11	2	5		3	6	12															16
		4			7	14			13		10^2	8^3	12		11	2	5		3	6^1	9	1														17
		4			7				13		10^3	14	8	12	11^2	2	5		3	6^1	9	1														18
		4			7				10		12		8	3	11	2	5		6		9^1	1														19
		4			6						10^1	8^2	9		11	2	5		3	7	13	1	12													20
		4			7					13		10^1	8^2	14	11	2^3	5		3	6		1	12	9												21
		4			10^1					13			8		11^3		5		3	7^2		1	14	9	2	6■	12									22
										10					11		5			12		1	13	8^1	2		7	3	4	6^3	9^2	14				23
		4		5	14					10			9^3	13	11^1				3			1			2	6	7				8^2	12				24
		3^2		5						9					11^1				12^3			1		10	2	14	7	4		6	8	13				25
				5						9^2			8^3	14	11							1	12		2^1	13	7	3	4	6	10■					26
				5	13					9			8		12							1	10^2	14	2^1		7	3	4	6		11^3				27
				9	8					11			6	2			5		12			1						3^1	4	7	10					28
				9	7^3					11			6	2^1			5		3			1		10^2	14		13		4	8	12					29
				9	12					13			10^3	14	11		6		3			1			2^2		8		4	7	6^1					30
				10	7^1					9			8		11		5		3			1			2^2		13		4	6	12					31
				5						9^2		14	8^1	2	11					12		1				13	7	4	3	6	10^3					32
				10						13			8	2	12		5^2					1					6	3	4	7	9	11^1				33
				5						9^3			8	2	11		12		14			1	13				6	4	3	7^1	10^2					34
				9	12					13			6^1	2	11		5		3			1					8^3		4	7		10^2	14			35
					7					14			12		10		5							9^1	2			3	4	6		11^2	8^3	1	13	36

DUNFERMLINE ATHLETIC

Year Formed: 1885. *Ground & Address:* East End Park, Halbeath Road, Dunfermline KY12 7RB.
Telephone: 01383 724295. *Fax:* 01383 745 959. *E-mail:* enquiries@dafc.co.uk
Website: www.dafc.co.uk
Ground Capacity: 11,380 (all seated). *Size of Pitch:* 105m × 65m.
Chairman: Ross McArthur. *Vice-Chairman:* Billy Braisby.
Head Coach: Stevie Crawford. *First Team Coach:* Callum Davidson.
Club Nickname: 'The Pars'.
Record Attendance: 27,816 v Celtic, Division I, 30 April 1968.
Record Transfer Fee received: £650,000 for Jackie McNamara to Celtic (October 1995).
Record Transfer Fee paid: £540,000 for Istvan Kozma from Bordeaux (September 1989).
Record Victory: 11-2 v Stenhousemuir, Division II, 27 September 1930.
Record Defeat: 1-13 v St. Bernard's, Scottish Cup 1st rd, 15 September 1883.
Most Capped Player: Colin Miller 16 (61), Canada.
Most League Appearances: 497: Norrie McCathie, 1981-96.
Most League Goals in Season (Individual): 53: Bobby Skinner, Division II, 1925-26.
Most Goals Overall (Individual): 212: Charles Dickson, 1954-64.

DUNFERMLINE ATHLETIC – SPFL LADBROKES CHAMPIONSHIP 2018–19 LEAGUE RECORD

Match No.	*Date*	*Venue*	*Opponents*	*Result*		*H/T Score*	*Lg Pos.*	*Goalscorers*	*Attendance*
1	Aug 4	A	Dundee U	W	3-2	0-1	2	Thomson 59, Longridge, J 67, Longridge, L 84	6532
2	11	H	Ross Co	L	1-3	1-2	6	Longridge, L 28	4949
3	25	A	Ayr U	L	1-4	0-3	8	Longridge, J 55	2597
4	Sept 1	H	Inverness CT	L	0-3	0-0	8		5138
5	15	H	Alloa Ath	D	0-0	0-0	8		4568
6	22	A	Greenock Morton	D	1-1	0-0	8	Ryan 68	2084
7	28	H	Partick Thistle	W	1-0	0-0	8	Connolly 69	4740
8	Oct 6	A	Falkirk	W	2-0	1-0	5	Ryan 40, Hippolyte 90	6173
9	20	H	Queen of the South	L	0-1	0-0	7		4443
10	27	H	Dundee U	L	0-2	0-1	7		6349
11	30	A	Inverness CT	D	2-2	2-2	7	Keena 2 10, 29	1994
12	Nov 3	A	Alloa Ath	W	1-0	0-0	7	Longridge, J 69	1169
13	10	H	Falkirk	L	0-1	0-0	7		5762
14	24	A	Ross Co	L	1-2	0-1	7	Longridge, J 74	3121
15	Dec 1	H	Greenock Morton	W	3-0	2-0	7	Keena 3, El Bakhtaoui (pen) 42, Craigen 86	4370
16	8	A	Partick Thistle	L	0-2	0-1	7		2566
17	15	A	Queen of the South	D	0-0	0-0	7		727
18	22	H	Ayr U	D	0-0	0-0	7		4916
19	29	A	Falkirk	W	4-2	2-1	7	Hippolyte 13, Beadling 2 17, 51, Vincent 67	5786
20	Jan 5	H	Alloa Ath	D	2-2	2-0	7	Keena 18, Flannigan (og) 28	4723
21	12	A	Dundee U	L	0-1	0-0	7		5913
22	26	A	Greenock Morton	D	0-0	0-0	7		1907
23	Feb 2	H	Ross Co	L	1-2	1-0	7	Anderson 41	4347
24	16	H	Inverness CT	W	1-0	0-0	7	Thomson 47	4497
25	23	A	Ayr U	W	1-0	0-0	5	Longridge, L (pen) 71	2202
26	26	H	Partick Thistle	W	3-0	0-0	5	Anderson 2 47, 86, Devine 74	4904
27	Mar 2	H	Queen of the South	W	1-0	0-0	4	Blair 74	4708
28	9	A	Alloa Ath	W	1-0	0-0	4	Anderson 53	1750
29	26	H	Dundee U	L	0-1	0-1	5		6096
30	29	H	Ayr U	L	0-1	0-1	5		4671
31	Apr 6	A	Partick Thistle	D	2-2	2-1	5	Beadling 10, Anderson 24	2850
32	9	A	Ross Co	L	0-1	0-0	5		3222
33	13	H	Falkirk	L	0-1	0-0	5		6089
34	20	A	Queen of the South	L	1-2	0-1	5	Longridge, J 90	1704
35	27	H	Greenock Morton	L	0-1	0-0	6		4883
36	May 4	A	Inverness CT	L	0-1	0-1	7		2828

Final League Position: 7

Honours
League Champions: First Division 1988-89, 1995-96, 2010-11; Division II 1925-26; Second Division 1985-86; League One 2015-16.
Runners-up: First Division 1986-87, 1993-94, 1994-95, 1999-2000; Division II 1912-13, 1933-34, 1954-55, 1957-58, 1972-73; Second Division 1978-79; League One 2013-14.
Scottish Cup Winners: 1961, 1968; *Runners-up:* 1965, 2004, 2007.
League Cup Runners-up: 1949-50, 1991-92, 2005-06.
League Challenge Cup Runners-up: 2007-08.

European: *Cup Winners' Cup:* 14 matches (1961-62, 1968-69 semi-finals). *UEFA Cup:* 32 matches (*Fairs Cup:* 1962-63, 1964-65, 1965-66, 1966-67, 1969-70. *UEFA Cup:* 2004-05, 2007-08).

Club colours: Shirt: Black and white stripes. Shorts: Black. Socks: Black.

Goalscorers: *League (33):* Anderson 5, Longridge J 5, Keena 4, Beadling 3, Longridge L 3 (1 pen), Hippolyte 2, Ryan 2, Thomson 2, Blair 1, Connolly 1, Craigen 1, Devine 1, El Bakhtaoui 1 (1 pen), Vincent 1, own goal 1.
William Hill Scottish FA Cup (0).
Betfred Scottish League Cup (14): Hippolyte 4, Ryan 3, El Bakhtaoui 2, Devine 1, Higginbotham 1 (1 pen), Longridge J 1, Longridge L 1, Vincent 1.
Irn-Bru Scottish League Challenge (4): Longridge L 2 (1 pen), Higginbotham 1 (1 pen), Smith 1.

Robinson L 21	Dunnan M 11 + 2	Ashcroft L 36	Devine D 30	Craigen J 31 + 2	Longridge L 19 + 3	Vincent J 25 + 1	Thomson J 24 + 3	Longridge J 32 + 1	El Bakhtaoui F 20 + 7	Hippolyte M 13 + 18	Ryan A 8 + 5	Williamson R 15 + 4	Higginbotham K 15 + 7	Connolly A 9 + 8	Muirhead R 4 + 8	Martin M 8 + 2	Keena A 10 + 2	Beadling T 17 + 2	McCann L — + 6	Smith C 1 + 2	Scully R 14	Anderson B 14	Blair R 12 + 1	Todd Matthew 4 + 4	Martin L 1 + 1	Gill C 1	Morrison S 1	*Match No.*
1	2	3	4^{1}	5	6	7	8	9	10	11	12																	1
1	3	4		6	9	8	7^{3}	5	10	11^{2}	14	2^{1}	12	13														2
1	3	2	4^{1}	6^{3}	9	7		8	10	12	11^{2}	5	14	13														3
1	3	2	4		8	7^{1}	6	9	11	10^{2}		5^{3}	13	14	12													4
1	4	3		2	11^{2}	7	8	5	10	6^{1}	13			12	9													5
1	4	3		2	6	7		5	10	12	11^{1}			9		8												6
1	3	4		2	9	8	12	5	10	13	11^{1}			6^{2}		7												7
1	3	4		2	6	7		5	11	12	10^{1}			9		8												8
1		3	4	2	6	8	14	5	11^{2}	12	10^{3}			9		7^{1}	13											9
1		3	4	6^{2}	9^{1}	8^{3}	14	5	10	11	13	2		12				7										10
1		4	3	2			8	5		9	10			6	12	7	11^{1}											11
1		3	4	2^{1}			6	5	14	11	10	13	12	8^{3}		7	9^{2}											12
1		3	4				7	5	12	9^{1}	11	2	6^{2}	13	14	8	10^{3}											13
1		3	4	14		7^{2}	9	5	11	13		2	6[illegible]		10^{3}	8^{1}	12											14
1		3	4	6		7	8	5	11^{2}	13		2			9^{3}		10^{1}	12	14									15
1		3	4	6^{1}		7^{2}	8	5	11	13		2			9^{3}		10	12	14									16
1		3	4			7	8	5	11^{1}	12		2	9				10	6										17
1		4	3	2		7	9	5	11^{1}	12			6				10	8										18
1		4	3	2		7	9	5	12	11^{3}			6		13	14	10^{1}	8^{2}										19
1		3	4	2^{1}		7	9	5		11		12	6				10	8										20
1		4	3	2		8	9^{3}	5		10			6^{2}	13		14	11^{1}	7		12								21
		4	3	2		7	8	5	11^{2}	12			9		13			6		10^{1}	1							22
		4	3	8^{1}		7	6	5	10^{2}	14		2	9							12	1	11^{3}	13					23
	14	4	3	2	12	6	9	5				13		10^{1}				7			1	11^{2}	8^{3}					24
		4	3	5	12	6	9			13		2		11^{1}				7			1	10^{2}	8					25
		4	3	5	11^{2}		9					2	7^{3}	12	14			6			1	10^{1}	8	13				26
	14	4	3	5	12		9	13				2	7^{1}	11^{2}				6			1	10	8^{3}					27
		3	4	2	11	12	8	5		13			6^{1}					7			1	10^{2}	9					28
		4	3	2	10^{2}		8	5	12	14			6^{3}					7			1	11	9^{1}	13				29
		3	4	12	11	8^{1}	6^{3}	5	13			2	9^{2}					7			1	10		14				30
		3	4	6	9			5	10^{1}	13		12						7	14		1	11^{2}	2	8^{3}				31
		3	4	6	9^{1}			5	12	10^{3}					13			7	14		1	11	2	8^{2}				32
		3	4	6		9		5	11^{2}	13			12		14			8^{3}			1	10	2	7^{1}				33
	4	3		6	9^{3}			5	11^{2}	12		2	13						14		1	10	7	8^{1}				34
	2	4	3^{3}	6	5^{1}	7		9[illegible]	12	11			14								1	10^{2}	8		13			35
	2	4	3	5	8^{3}						13		10^{1}						14			11	7^{2}	12	9	1	6	36

EAST FIFE

Year Formed: 1903. *Ground & Address:* Locality Hub Bayview Stadium, Harbour View, Methil, Fife KY8 3RW. *Telephone:* 01333 426323. *Fax:* 01333 426376. *E-mail:* office@eastfifefc.info. *Website:* www.eastfifefc.info
Ground Capacity: 1,992. *Size of Pitch:* 105m × 65m.
Chairman: Jim Stevenson. *Vice-Chairman:* David Marshall.
Manager: Darren Young. *Assistant Manager:* Tony McMinn.
Club Nickname: 'The Fifers'.
Previous Ground: Bayview Park.
Record Attendance: 22,515 v Raith Rovers, Division I, 2 January 1950 (Bayview Park); 4,700 v Rangers, League One, 26 October 2013 (Bayview Stadium).
Record Transfer Fee received: £150,000 for Paul Hunter from Hull C (March 1990).
Record Transfer Fee paid: £70,000 for John Sludden from Kilmarnock (July 1991).
Record Victory: 13-2 v Edinburgh C, Division II, 11 December 1937.
Record Defeat: 0-9 v Hearts, Division I, 5 October 1957.
Most Capped Player: George Aitken, 5 (8), Scotland.
Most League Appearances: 517: David Clarke, 1968-86.
Most League Goals in Season (Individual): 41: Jock Wood, Division II; 1926-27 and Henry Morris, Division II, 1947-48.
Most Goals Overall (Individual): 225: Phil Weir, 1922-35.

EAST FIFE – SPFL LADBROKES LEAGUE ONE 2018–19 LEAGUE RECORD

Match No.	*Date*	*Venue*	*Opponents*	*Result*		*H/T Score*	*Lg Pos.*	*Goalscorers*	*Attendance*
1	Aug 4	H	Dumbarton	L	0-2	0-0	9		525
2	11	A	Brechin C	L	0-1	0-0	10		414
3	18	A	Raith R	D	2-2	1-1	10	Agnew 2 (1 pen) [27 (p), 65]	2025
4	25	H	Arbroath	L	0-3	0-2	10		639
5	Sept 1	A	Montrose	W	2-0	2-0	10	Davidson [19], Court [27]	569
6	15	H	Airdrieonians	W	2-1	0-0	7	Watt [75], Currie [88]	625
7	22	A	Stranraer	W	2-0	0-0	4	Watson, C [55], Currie [82]	366
8	29	H	Stenhousemuir	W	2-0	1-0	3	Watson, C [37], Currie [90]	545
9	Oct 6	A	Forfar Ath	W	4-0	3-0	3	Smith [10], Agnew 2 [33, 58], Currie [39]	585
10	20	H	Brechin C	W	3-1	1-0	3	Dunsmore [43], Dowds [72], Agnew (pen) [80]	639
11	27	A	Dumbarton	L	0-4	0-2	3		713
12	Nov 3	A	Arbroath	L	0-1	0-0	3		765
13	10	H	Raith R	W	2-1	0-1	3	Smith [76], Dunsmore [90]	1756
14	17	A	Airdrieonians	L	2-4	2-1	3	Smith 2 [10, 35]	818
15	Dec 1	H	Montrose	L	0-2	0-1	3		636
16	8	H	Stranraer	D	3-3	2-0	3	Dunsmore [21], Meggatt [25], Watson, C [54]	482
17	15	A	Stenhousemuir	W	2-0	1-0	3	Smith [21], Dowds [90]	395
18	22	H	Forfar Ath	W	1-0	0-0	3	Agnew [84]	527
19	29	A	Raith R	W	2-1	2-0	3	Dunsmore [12], Currie [44]	2833
20	Jan 5	H	Airdrieonians	L	1-2	1-2	3	Dowds [20]	725
21	12	A	Montrose	W	2-0	2-0	3	Watt 2 [25, 40]	678
22	26	A	Stranraer	W	4-3	0-2	3	Smith [49], Watson, C [70], Dowds 2 [72, 80]	350
23	Feb 23	H	Dumbarton	L	3-4	0-3	4	Slattery [54], Smith [58], Dowds [65]	571
24	26	H	Arbroath	D	1-1	1-1	4	Currie [6]	722
25	Mar 2	A	Forfar Ath	L	0-3	0-3	4		729
26	5	A	Brechin C	D	0-0	0-0	4		402
27	9	H	Stranraer	W	3-1	0-0	4	Slattery [48], Watt [89], Linton [90]	461
28	12	H	Stenhousemuir	D	1-1	0-0	4	Meggatt [90]	323
29	16	A	Arbroath	L	1-2	1-1	4	Dowds [28]	709
30	23	H	Brechin C	L	0-2	0-1	4		544
31	30	H	Raith R	L	1-2	1-0	4	Smith [41]	1592
32	Apr 6	A	Airdrieonians	D	0-0	0-0	4		772
33	13	H	Montrose	L	0-2	0-0	5		652
34	20	A	Dumbarton	L	0-3	0-2	5		659
35	27	A	Stenhousemuir	D	1-1	1-1	5	Dunsmore [32]	742
36	May 4	H	Forfar Ath	L	2-3	1-1	7	Agnew [10], Dunlop [82]	597

Final League Position: 7

Honours
League Champions: Division II 1947-48; Third Division 2007-08; League Two 2015-16.
Runners-up: Division II 1929-30, 1970-71;. Second Division 1983-84, 1995-96; Third Division 2002-03.
Scottish Cup Winners: 1938; *Runners-up:* 1927, 1950.
League Cup Winners: 1947-48, 1949-50, 1953-54.

Club colours: Shirt: Gold and black stripes. Shorts: White. Socks: Black.

Goalscorers: *League (49):* Smith 8, Agnew 7 (2 pens), Dowds 7, Currie 6, Dunsmore 5, Watson C 4, Watt 4, Meggatt 2, Slattery 2, Court 1, Davidson 1, Dunlop 1, Linton 1.
William Hill Scottish FA Cup (4): Agnew 1, Davidson 1, Dowds 1, Watson C 1.
Betfred Scottish League Cup (2): Dowds 1, own goal 1.
Irn-Bru Scottish League Challenge (8): Dowds 3, Agnew 1, Court 1, Currie 1, Smith 1, own goal 1.

Long B 32	Dunsmore A 34	Dunlop R 29 + 2	Watson C 23	Meggatt D 26	Davidson R 33 + 1	Agnew S 29 + 1	Slattery P 29 + 4	McBride S 6 + 6	Smith K 15 + 17	Currie R 7 + 11	Thomson C 3 + 3	Watt L 27 + 3	Court J 17 + 8	Dowds A 25 + 7	Bell K 4 + 12	Kane C 7 + 3	Docherty M 20 + 4	McDowall C 3 + 1	Linton S 5 + 7	Watson B 4 + 8	Murdoch S 5	Higgins C 12	Terry D 1 + 1	Match No.
1	2	3	4	5	6	7	8	9²	10¹	11	12³	13	14											1
1	2²	3	4	5	7	8	6¹	10		11	14	9³		12	13									2
1	2	3	4		8	6³	5	12		13	7	9¹	10	11²	14									3
1	2	3	4		8¹	9	5	13		12	6	7²	10³	11	14									4
1	6	3	2	4	8	7	5	12	13			9²	10³	11¹		14								5
1	6¹	14	2	4	7	8	5		12	13		9	10³	11		3²								6
1	6		2	4	7	8¹	5		12	13		9	11³	10²		3	14							7
1	6²		2	4	7	8	5		12	14		9	10³	11¹		3	13							8
1	6	12	2	4	7	8	5	14	11³	10		9²			13	3¹								9
1	6	3	2	4	7	8	5		12	13		9²	11³	10¹			14							10
1	2³	4	6		9■	8	5³		13		14	7	10	11¹		3	12							11
1		3	2	4		8	5	13	10¹		7²	9	11	12	14		6³							12
1■	6³	3	2	4	7	8			11²			9¹	12	10	13		5	14						13
	6	3	2³	4	7	8	12		9¹	14		13	10	11²			5	1						14
	6	3	2¹		7	8			14	10		9²	11³	13		4	5	1	12					15
	6	3	2	4■	7	8²	13	9	11¹				12	14	10³		5	1						16
1	7	4	2		6	9²	5	8	11³			14		12	10¹		3		13					17
1	6¹	3	2		8	9	5	7²	13	14				11	10³		4		12					18
1	6	3	2	4	8	9¹	7	13	14	11²				10			5³		12					19
1	6³	3	2	4	8	9	5		13	11			14	10¹			7²		12					20
1	6³	3	2	4	8		5		13			10	12	11¹	14		7		9²					21
1		3	2	4	7	10³	9¹		12	13		6		11²		14	8		5					22
1	2			4	7¹		5		9³	13		6		11	10²	3■	8		12	14				23
1	5			4	7		9		12	11¹			10²	13			3		8	6	2			24
1²	5	2		4	13		9		10				14	11³					8	7	6¹	3	12	25
	5	2		4	10		8		13			6	11¹		12		9			7²		3	1	26
1	5	2		4	6	12	9³		14			8	11				7²		13	10¹		3		27
1	5	2		4		6	13		10²			9	11	12			7¹		8³	14		3		28
1	6	3	2³		7	8¹	5		13			9	11²	10	14					12		4		29
1	2	3			6	7	5¹		12	13		9³	10²	11			8			14		4		30
1	5	2		4	6	7²	8		10¹			9	13	11	12							3		31
1	5	2		4	6	7	8		10¹			9		11						12		3		32
1	2			4	6	7	5		10			9		11			8¹			12		3		33
1	2	3		5	7		8¹	10				6²		11	13					12	9	4		34
1	6	3			7	9			10²			8	13■	11			5¹			12	2	4		35
1	6	3			7²	8	14		10¹			9³		11	12	13	5				2	4		36

EDINBURGH CITY

Year formed: 1928 (disbanded 1955, reformed from Postal United in 1986).
Ground & Address: Ainslie Park Stadium, 94 Pilton Drive, Edinburgh EH5 2HF (for 3 seasons from 2017-18 whilst Meadowbank Stadium is redeveloped). *Telephone:* 0845 463 1932.
E-mail: admin@edinburghcityfc.com *Website:* edinburghcityfc.com
Ground Capacity: 3,127 (seated 504). *Size of Pitch:* 96m × 66m
Chairman: Jim Brown. *Director of Football:* Jim Jefferies.
Manager: James McDonaugh. *Coach:* Colin Jack.
Previous name: Postal United.
Club Nickname: 'The Citizens'.
Previous Grounds: City Park 1928-55; Fernieside 1986-95; Meadowbank Stadium 1996-2017.
Record victory: 5-0 v King's Park, Division II (1935-36); 6-1 and 7-2 v Brechin City, Division II (1937-38).
Record defeat: 1-11 v Rangers, Scottish Cup, 19 January 1929.
Most League Appearances: 87: Marc Laird, 2016-19.
Most League Goals in Season (Individual): 30: Blair Henderson, League Two, 2018-19.
Most Goals Overall (Individual): 38: Blair Henderson, 2018-19.

EDINBURGH CITY – SPFL LADBROKES LEAGUE TWO 2018–19 LEAGUE RECORD

Match No.	Date	Venue	Opponents	Result		H/T Score	Lg Pos.	Goalscorers	Attendance
1	Aug 4	H	Albion R	W	4-0	1-0	1	Henderson, B 3 (1 pen) [9 (p), 56, 64], Smith, A [82]	303
2	11	A	Elgin C	L	0-1	0-0	6		612
3	18	H	Stirling Alb	W	3-1	0-0	4	Shepherd (pen) [47], Balatoni [64], Allan (og) [72]	302
4	25	A	Clyde	W	2-0	0-0	3	Shepherd [61], Henderson, B [71]	576
5	Sept 1	A	Peterhead	W	1-0	0-0	1	Henderson, B [52]	560
6	15	H	Annan Ath	W	2-1	1-0	1	Henderson, B 2 [43, 80]	247
7	22	A	Queen's Park	W	2-0	1-0	1	Taylor 2 [39, 59]	487
8	29	H	Cowdenbeath	W	1-0	0-0	1	Balatoni [61]	337
9	Oct 6	H	Berwick Rangers	W	3-0	1-0	1	Laird [29], Henderson, B 2 (1 pen) [48, 70 (p)]	362
10	27	A	Stirling Alb	W	1-0	1-0	1	Thomson [37]	603
11	Nov 3	H	Clyde	L	0-1	0-1	2		376
12	10	A	Albion R	W	2-1	1-1	1	Henderson, B 2 [14, 76]	229
13	Dec 1	H	Queen's Park	W	2-0	2-0	1	Henderson, B [31], Shepherd [33]	358
14	8	A	Annan Ath	W	2-1	1-0	1	Balatoni [41], Henderson, L [56]	317
15	11	H	Peterhead	D	1-1	0-0	1	Henderson, B [68]	455
16	15	H	Elgin C	W	4-1	1-0	1	Henderson, B 3 [21, 79, 87], Smith, A [67]	258
17	22	A	Cowdenbeath	W	2-0	1-0	1	Shepherd [20], Henderson, B [57]	331
18	29	A	Berwick Rangers	D	2-2	1-0	1	Balatoni [31], Henderson, B [54]	501
19	Jan 5	H	Stirling Alb	L	0-1	0-0	1		621
20	12	A	Queen's Park	W	4-0	3-0	1	Galbraith [4], Smith, A [7], Henderson, B 2 [16, 60]	526
21	19	H	Annan Ath	L	1-2	1-0	2	Henderson, B (pen) [40]	285
22	26	A	Elgin C	D	3-3	0-2	1	Smith, A [56], Shepherd [70], Henderson, B [88]	487
23	Feb 2	H	Albion R	W	3-1	2-1	1	Smith, A [25], Breen [33], Henderson, B [57]	331
24	9	A	Peterhead	D	0-0	0-0	1		728
25	23	H	Cowdenbeath	W	2-0	2-0	1	Thomson [15], Henderson, B [28]	351
26	Mar 2	A	Clyde	L	0-1	0-0	2		844
27	5	H	Berwick Rangers	W	1-0	0-0	2	Henderson, B (pen) [62]	253
28	9	H	Queen's Park	W	2-0	1-0	2	Henderson, B [31], Driver [85]	325
29	16	A	Annan Ath	L	1-3	0-1	2	Henderson, B [53]	341
30	23	H	Peterhead	D	0-0	0-0	2		1057
31	30	A	Berwick Rangers	W	2-0	2-0	2	Galbraith [14], Henderson, B [31]	468
32	Apr 6	A	Cowdenbeath	L	1-4	0-2	2	Thomson [52]	262
33	13	H	Clyde	L	1-2	0-0	3	Henderson, B (pen) [47]	648
34	20	A	Albion R	L	2-3	1-1	3	Henderson, B [5], Thomson [47]	253
35	27	H	Elgin C	D	1-1	1-0	3	Walker [25]	354
36	May 4	A	Stirling Alb	D	0-0	0-0	3		543

Final League Position: 3

Honours
League Champions: Scottish Lowland League Champions: 2014-15, 2015-16.
Promoted via play-offs: 2015-16 (to League Two).
League Challenge Cup: Semi-finals 2018-19.

Club colours: Shirt: White. Shorts: Black. Socks: White.

Goalscorers: *League (58):* Henderson B 30 (5 pens), Shepherd 5 (1 pen), Smith A 5, Balatoni 4, Thomson 4, Galbraith 2, Taylor 2, Breen 1, Driver 1, Henderson L 1, Laird 1, Walker 1, own goal 1.
William Hill Scottish FA Cup (3): Henderson B 1, Henderson L 1, McIntyre 1.
Betfred Scottish League Cup (5): Balatoni 1, Henderson B 1, McIntyre 1, Rodger 1, Thomson 1.
Irn-Bru Scottish League Challenge (13): Henderson B 6 (3 pens), Shepherd 3, Smith A 2, Henderson L 1, Walker 1.
Play-Offs (0).

Antell C 36	Thomson C 32 + 1	Balatoni C 35	Rodger G 11 + 8	McIntyre R 35	Black A 28 + 2	Laird M 28 + 1	Smith A 16 + 10	Handling D 9	Taylor G 26 + 6	Henderson B 34 + 1	Stewart K 3 + 5	Dunn J — + 1	Hall C — + 6	Donaldson B 6 + 5	Lumsden R 1 + 3	Henderson L 30	Shepherd S 30 + 4	Watson A 13 + 12	Galbraith D B + 7	Kennedy L — + 2	Breen J 4 + 4	Walker J 8 + 3	Driver C 2 + 5	MacDonald C — + 1	Newman S 1 + 2	Neave R — + 1	*Match No.*
1	2	3	4^{1}	5	6	7	8	9^{3}	10^{2}	11	12	13	14														1
1	2	3		5	6^{1}	7	8	9	11^{3}	10	4^{2}		13	12	14												2
1	2	3		4	5	6^{2}	13	8^{3}	7^{1}	10	12			14		9	11										3
1	2	4		5	8		12	6^{1}	9	11	7			13		3	10^{2}										4
1	2	4		5	8	13	12	6	9^{2}	11	7					3	10^{1}										5
1	2	3		5	7	8	12	6^{2}	9	10	13					4	11^{1}										6
1	2	3		5	7	8	12	6	9^{1}	11^{2}	13					4	10										7
1	2	3		5	7	8	12	6^{2}	9	11	13					4	10^{1}										8
1	5	4		2	8	7	13	9	6^{3}	10^{2}			14			3	11^{1}	12									9
1	2	3	4	5	7		6		9^{2}	10			13			8	11^{1}	12									10
1	2	3	4	5	7		6^{2}		9	11			13			8^{1}	10	12									11
1	2	3	4^{2}	5	12	8	11		13	10						7	9	6^{1}									12
1	2	3	13	5^{1}	7	8	6		9^{2}	11						4	10	12									13
1	2	3	8	5^{1}		7	6		9	10						4	11	12									14
1	2	3	5		7▪	8	6		9^{1}	11						4	10	12									15
1	2	3	4	5		8^{3}	6^{2}		9	10^{1}					14		11	7	12	13							16
1		3	5^{2}	2	13	8	6		9	10				14		4	11^{3}	7^{1}	12								17
1	2	3^{2}	13	5	9^{1}	8	6			10						4	11	7	12								18
1	2	3^{1}	12	5		8	9		13	10			14			4	11^{3}	7^{2}	6								19
1	2	3		5	7	8	6^{2}		9^{3}	10						4^{1}	13	12	11	14							20
1	2	3		5	7	8	13		9^{1}	11						4	10^{2}	12	6^{3}		14						21
1	2	3		5	7		11		9^{2}	10						4	6		12		8^{1}	13					22
1	2	3		5	7	8	10^{3}			11						4	6^{2}	13	14		9^{1}	12					23
1	2	3	14	5	7	8	10^{2}		13	11						4	6		12^{3}		9^{1}						24
1	2	3		5	7	8			9^{1}	10						4	6^{2}	12				11	13				25
1	2	3		5	8	7	12		9^{1}	11						4	6^{2}	14				10^{3}	13				26
1	14	3		5	8	7	12		9^{1}	11				2^{2}		4	6^{3}				13	10					27
1	2	3	12	5	9^{2}	7			10	11^{1}						4^{3}	13	6				8	14				28
1	2	3	4	5	9	7			10^{2}	11					12		8^{1}	6^{3}					13	14			29
1	2	3	14	5	7	8			13	10				9^{3}		4	11^{2}	6^{1}	12								30
1	2	3		5	7	8				11				12		4	10	6^{1}	9^{2}						13		31
1	2	3		5	7^{3}					11				4^{1}		8	10	6	9^{2}		13	12	14				32
1	2	3	14	5	7				13	10						4	11	12	9^{1}		6^{2}	8^{3}					33
1	2	3	13	5					14	10				8		4^{1}	11^{2}	6	9^{3}		12	7					34
1		3	4	5		7			11^{1}	14				2			12	9	8^{2}			6	10^{3}		13		35
1			2	4		6			11^{2}					3	10^{1}		12	5				7	9		8	13	36

ELGIN CITY

Year Formed: 1893. *Ground and Address:* Borough Briggs, Borough Briggs Road, Elgin IV30 1AP.
Telephone: 01343 551114. *Fax:* 01343 547921. *E-mail:* elgincityfc@btconnect.com *Website:* www.elgincity.net
Ground Capacity: 3,927 (seated: 478). *Size of pitch:* 102m × 68m.
Chairman: Graham Tatters. *Secretary:* Keiran Carty.
Manager: Gavin Price. *Assistant Manager:* Keith Gibson.
Previous name: Elgin City United 1900-03.
Club Nicknames: 'City'; 'The Black & Whites'.
Previous Grounds: Association Park 1893-95; Milnfield Park 1895-1909; Station Park 1909-19; Cooper Park 1919-21.
Record Attendance: 12,608 v Arbroath, Scottish Cup, 17 February 1968.
Record Transfer Fee received: £32,000 for Michael Teasdale to Dundee (January 1994).
Record Transfer Fee paid: £10,000 for Russell McBride from Fraserburgh (July 2001).
Record Victory: 18-1 v Brora Rangers, North of Scotland Cup, 6 February 1960.
Record Defeat: 1-14 v Hearts, Scottish Cup, 4 February 1939.
Most League Appearances: 306: Mark Nicholson, 2007-17.
Most League Goals in Season (Individual): 21: Craig Gunn, 2015-16.
Most Goals Overall (Individual): 128: Craig Gunn, 2009-17.

ELGIN CITY – SPFL LADBROKES LEAGUE TWO 2018–19 LEAGUE RECORD

Match No.	Date	Venue	Opponents	Result	H/T Score	Lg Pos.	Goalscorers	Attendance
1	Aug 4	A	Annan Ath	D 1-1	0-0	4	Cameron [85]	395
2	11	H	Edinburgh C	W 1-0	0-0	4	Sutherland, S [60]	612
3	18	A	Albion R	W 1-0	0-0	3	McLeish [57]	275
4	Sept 1	H	Stirling Alb	L 0-3	0-3	6		596
5	15	A	Berwick Rangers	W 3-0	3-0	5	Orru (og) [22], Morrison 2 [24, 45]	416
6	22	A	Clyde	L 1-4	1-3	5	Lowdon [45]	508
7	29	H	Queen's Park	W 2-1	0-1	5	McLeish [60], Sutherland, S (pen) [88]	582
8	Oct 6	A	Peterhead	L 0-3	0-1	5		681
9	13	H	Cowdenbeath	W 3-1	1-1	5	Sutherland, S 2 (1 pen) [25, 75 (p)], McHardy [50]	545
10	27	H	Annan Ath	L 0-1	0-1	5		533
11	Nov 3	A	Cowdenbeath	W 2-1	0-1	5	Morrison [47], Sutherland, S [90]	310
12	10	H	Berwick Rangers	L 2-4	0-2	5	McGovern [64], McHardy [72]	549
13	17	H	Clyde	L 1-3	0-2	5	Sutherland, S [89]	677
14	Dec 1	A	Stirling Alb	L 2-5	2-3	5	Hay [15], Sutherland, S [19]	548
15	8	H	Albion R	W 4-2	2-1	4	Cameron 2 [28, 60], Sutherland, S 2 [44, 56]	538
16	15	A	Edinburgh C	L 1-4	0-1	4	Omar [61]	258
17	22	A	Queen's Park	W 4-0	2-0	4	Sutherland, S 2 (1 pen) [12 (p), 55], Cameron [33], Morrison [61]	455
18	29	H	Peterhead	L 0-3	0-2	5		929
19	Jan 5	A	Annan Ath	L 0-2	0-1	5		326
20	12	H	Cowdenbeath	L 1-4	0-2	6	McHardy [67]	575
21	26	H	Edinburgh C	D 3-3	2-0	6	Hester 2 [29, 32], Bronsky [90]	487
22	Feb 9	A	Albion R	W 3-0	1-0	6	McHardy 3 (1 pen) [30, 51, 83 (p)]	183
23	16	H	Stirling Alb	W 3-2	1-1	6	Cameron 2 [22, 81], Hay [89]	676
24	23	A	Berwick Rangers	W 3-0	0-0	5	Omar [54], McLeish [70], Cameron [72]	402
25	26	H	Queen's Park	D 2-2	0-0	5	Bronsky [82], McHardy [85]	504
26	Mar 2	A	Peterhead	L 0-1	0-1	6		737
27	9	H	Clyde	W 2-1	1-1	5	Maciver 2 [10, 79]	713
28	16	A	Queen's Park	L 1-4	1-1	5	Maciver [10]	543
29	19	A	Clyde	L 0-2	0-1	5		531
30	23	H	Albion R	L 0-2	0-2	6		733
31	30	H	Annan Ath	L 0-1	0-1	6		485
32	Apr 6	A	Stirling Alb	L 1-2	1-1	7	Maciver [39]	413
33	13	A	Cowdenbeath	L 1-2	1-0	7	McLeish [28]	294
34	20	H	Peterhead	L 1-2	1-2	8	Morrison [18]	862
35	27	A	Edinburgh C	D 1-1	0-1	8	Loveland [87]	354
36	May 4	H	Berwick Rangers	W 2-0	0-0	8	Cameron [69], Hester [88]	615

Final League Position: 8

Honours
League Runners-up: League Two 2015-16.
Scottish Cup: Quarter-finals 1968.
Highland League Champions: winners 15 times.

Club colours: Shirt: Black and white stripes. Shorts: Black. Socks: Black.

Goalscorers: *League (52):* Sutherland S 11 (3 pens), Cameron 8, McHardy 7 (1 pen), Morrison 5, Maciver 4, McLeish 4, Hester 3, Bronsky 2, Hay 2, Omar 2, Loveland 1, Lowdon 1, McGovern 1, own goal 1.
William Hill Scottish FA Cup (6): Cameron 1, Hay 1, Loveland 1, McHardy 1, Morrison 1, Omar 1.
Betfred Scottish League Cup (0).
Irn-Bru Scottish League Challenge (1): McHardy 1.

Gourlay K 34	Wilson D 15 + 5	Cooper M 25	McHardy D 31	Omar R 26 + 1	Cameron B 34	Miller S 4 + 5	McGovern J 33	Lowdon J 33	McLeish C 25 + 9	Sutherland S 20 + 1	Beattie C 9 + 6	Taylor M — + 2	Sutherland A 1 + 8	Hay K 5 + 15	Byrne D 2 + 5	Farquhar R 3 + 8	Morrison G 29 + 4	McGowan J 7 + 2	Sopel A — + 4	McHale T 2	Loveland O — + 7	Bronsky S 16 + 1	Roberts S 12 + 2	Hester K 9 + 4	Maciver R 12 + 3	Wilson C 8 + 2	Willis K — + 1	Scott L 1 + 1	*Match No.*
1	2	3	4	5^{3}	6	7^{1}	8	9	10	11^{2}	12	13	14																1
1	2	5	4		6	8^{1}	7	9	10^{2}	11	3	13	12																2
1	4	9	2	7^{2}	6		8	5	11^{3}	10^{1}	3		12	13	14														3
1	2^{1}	5	4		6		7	8	10^{2}	9	3		11^{3}	14		12	13												4
1	2	6^{2}	4	9^{1}	7	12	8	5		10^{3}	3			14		13	11												5
1	5	2	3^{3}	7■	8	10^{1}	9	6	13	12	4						11^{2}	14											6
1	2^{2}	5	4		6	14	7	8	9^{1}	11	3^{3}			13		12	10												7
1		4		12	6	8^{1}	7	5	10	9					13	2^{2}	11^{3}	3	14										8
1		4	3	6^{2}	8		7	2	10^{3}	11				13	14	5^{1}	9		12										9
1		2	4	7	6		3	8	10^{3}	9	13			14	12	5^{1}	11^{2}												10
1	3^{2}	2	4	6^{3}	8		7	5	10^{1}	11	13			12	14		9												11
1		2	4	7^{3}	6		3	8	10	9	12			14	5^{1}	13	11^{2}												12
		2	4	6^{2}	7	12	9■	5	10^{3}	11	3				8^{1}	14	13			1									13
		2	3	7^{3}	8	13		5■	11^{1}	10	4			6^{2}		12	9			1	14								14
1	2		5	8^{3}	7	14	4		10	11	3^{1}			9^{2}		13	6	12											15
1	2^{2}		5	8	7		4		10	11				6^{1}		13	9	3				12							16
1		2	4^{3}	6^{2}	8		7	5	11^{1}	10	13			12			9				14	3							17
1	12	2	4■	9^{2}	7		8	5	11^{1}	10				13			6					3							18
1	4	2			7^{2}		8	5	11■	10	12			9^{1}			6		13			3							19
1	13	2	4	9	8		7	5^{2}		11				6^{1}			10				12	3							20
1		2	4	10	8		6^{1}	5	12	9				14			13					3	7^{2}	11^{3}					21
1		2	3	9	7		8	5	12								6^{2}		14			4	10^{1}	11^{3}	13				22
1	2^{2}		4	9	7		8	5	12					14			6					3	11^{1}	10^{3}	13				23
1	2^{1}		3	9	7^{3}		8	5	13								6					4	11	10^{2}	14	12			24
1	12		3	8^{1}			7	5	10				13				11					4	9		6	2^{2}			25
1	2		3	8			7	5	10^{1}				12				11					4	9		6				26
1		2	4	8	6		7	5	12								10					3	11^{2}		9^{1}	13			27
1		2		9	8		7^{2}	5	12					13			6	4				3	11^{1}	14	10^{3}				28
1	3	2		10	7		6^{1}	5	14					12			8						9^{3}	13	11^{2}	4			29
1		2	4	8	6		7		12				13	14			5^{2}					3	9^{3}	11^{1}	10				30
1	13	3^{2}	4	8^{3}	6		7	5	10								12							11^{1}	9	2	14		31
1			3		8		7	5^{1}	9				12				6	2			13			10^{2}	11	4			32
1			4		7		8	5^{1}	9								6	3			13		12	11^{2}	10	2			33
1			4		8		7	5^{2}	10								9	3^{1}				2	12	13	11	6			34
1			4		8			5	10^{3}				14				11				13	2	3^{2}	12	9	6		7^{1}	35
1	14				7			5	9^{2}								6	3			12	4	8^{3}	11^{1}	10	2		13	36

FALKIRK

Year Formed: 1876. *Ground & Address:* The Falkirk Stadium, 4 Stadium Way, Falkirk FK2 9EE. *Telephone:* 01324 624121. *Fax:* 01324 612418. *Email:* post@falkirkfc.co.uk *Website:* www.falkirkfc.co.uk
Ground Capacity: 8,750 (all seated). *Size of Pitch:* 105m × 68m.
Non-Executive Directors: Gary Deans, Kevin Beattie, Peter Duncan.
Manager: Ray McKinnon. *Assistant Manager:* Darren Taylor.
Club Nickname: 'The Bairns'.
Previous Grounds: Randyford 1876-81; Blinkbonny Grounds 1881-83; Brockville Park 1883-2003.
Record Attendance: 23,100 v Celtic, Scottish Cup 3rd rd, 21 February 1953.
Record Transfer Fee received: £945,000 for Conor McGrandles to Norwich C (August 2014).
Record Transfer Fee paid: £225,000 to Chelsea for Kevin McAllister (August 1991).
Record Victory: 11-1 v Tillicoultry, Scottish Cup 1st rd, 7 Sep 1889.
Record Defeat: 1-11 v Airdrieonians, Division I, 28 April 1951.
Most Capped Player: Alex Parker, 14 (15), Scotland.
Most League Appearances: 451: Tom Ferguson, 1919-32.
Most League Goals in Season (Individual): 43: Evelyn Morrison, Division I, 1928-29.
Most Goals Overall (Individual): 154: Kenneth Dawson, 1934-51.

FALKIRK – SPFL LADBROKES CHAMPIONSHIP 2018–19 LEAGUE RECORD

Match No.	Date	Venue	Opponents	Result	H/T Score	Lg Pos.	Goalscorers	Attendance
1	Aug 4	H	Inverness CT	L 0-1	-	8		4538
2	11	A	Partick Thistle	L 1-2	0-2	9	Greenwood 90	3417
3	25	H	Queen of the South	L 0-3	0-2	10		4026
4	Sept 1	A	Ross Co	L 0-2	0-0	10		3564
5	15	A	Ayr U	L 2-3	2-0	10	Rudden 18, Petravicius 25	2250
6	22	H	Dundee U	L 0-2	0-0	10		4933
7	29	A	Alloa Ath	W 2-0	1-0	10	Rudden 2 26, 69	1392
8	Oct 6	H	Dunfermline Ath	L 0-2	0-1	10		6173
9	20	A	Greenock Morton	L 0-1	0-0	10		2757
10	27	A	Queen of the South	L 0-2	0-0	10		1463
11	30	H	Ross Co	D 1-1	1-0	10	Cowie (og) 25	3767
12	Nov 3	H	Ayr U	L 0-1	0-0	10		4310
13	10	A	Dunfermline Ath	W 1-0	0-0	10	Rudden 71	5762
14	17	H	Partick Thistle	D 1-1	0-0	10	McKee 59	4589
15	Dec 1	A	Inverness CT	W 3-2	2-1	9	Rudden 2 16, 36, Harrison 90	2260
16	8	H	Alloa Ath	D 2-2	2-1	10	Petravicius 7, Paton 28	3907
17	15	H	Greenock Morton	D 0-0	0-0	10		3775
18	22	A	Dundee U	L 1-2	0-1	10	Muirhead (pen) 90	5267
19	29	H	Dunfermline Ath	L 2-4	1-2	10	McKee 2, Harrison 74	5786
20	Jan 5	A	Ayr U	W 1-0	0-0	9	Rudden 56	2729
21	12	A	Partick Thistle	D 1-1	0-0	9	Rudden 76	4438
22	26	H	Inverness CT	D 2-2	1-2	10	Rudden 29, McShane 56	5843
23	Feb 2	H	Queen of the South	W 3-0	1-0	10	Keillor-Dunn 8, Edjenguele 64, Petravicius 77	4538
24	9	A	Alloa Ath	W 2-1	1-1	9	McGhee 20, Waddington 46	2116
25	23	H	Dundee U	D 1-1	0-0	9	McKenna 84	5840
26	Mar 1	A	Greenock Morton	D 1-1	1-1	8	Rudden 40	1838
27	8	H	Ayr U	W 2-0	2-0	8	McGhee 2 27, 40	4344
28	12	A	Ross Co	L 1-2	0-2	8	McShane (pen) 87	3148
29	16	H	Partick Thistle	D 1-1	1-1	8	McShane 45	4896
30	30	A	Inverness CT	D 0-0	0-0	9		2817
31	Apr 2	A	Queen of the South	D 1-1	0-0	8	Keillor-Dunn (pen) 90	1508
32	6	H	Alloa Ath	L 1-2	0-1	9	Rudden 46	4170
33	13	A	Dunfermline Ath	W 1-0	0-0	9	Keillor-Dunn 77	6089
34	20	H	Greenock Morton	L 0-2	0-0	10		5254
35	27	A	Dundee U	L 0-2	0-2	10		5260
36	May 4	H	Ross Co	W 3-2	1-0	10	Rudden 27, McKenna 75, McGhee 77	4682

Final League Position: 10

Honours
League Champions: Division II 1935-36, 1969-70, 1974-75; First Division 1990-91, 1993-94, 2002-03, 2004-05; Second Division 1979-80;
Runners-up: Division I 1907-08, 1909-10; First Division 1985-86, 1988-89, 1997-98, 1998-99; Division II 1904-05, 1951-52, 1960-61; Championship: 2015-16, 2016-17.
Scottish Cup Winners: 1913, 1957; *Runners-up:* 1997, 2009, 2015.
League Cup Runners-up: 1947-48.
League Challenge Cup Winners: 1993-94, 1997-98, 2004-05, 2011-12.

European: *Europa League:* 2 matches (2009-10).

Club colours: All: Navy blue with white trim.

Goalscorers: *League (37):* Rudden 12, McGhee 4, Keillor-Dunn 3 (1 pen), McShane 3 (1 pen), Petravicius 3, Harrison 2, McKee 2, McKenna 2, Edjenguele 1, Greenwood 1, Muirhead 1 (1 pen), Paton 1, Waddington 1, own goal 1.
William Hill Scottish FA Cup (2): McKee 1, Paton 1.
Betfred Scottish League Cup (4): Mackin 2, Lewis 1, Petravicius 1.
Irn-Bru Scottish League Challenge (2): Harrison 1, Lewis 1.

Fasan L 13	Dallison T 10 + 2	Muirhead A 16 + 1	McGhee J 32 + 1	Petravicius D 26 + 2	Paton P 27 + 2	Owen-Evans T 2	Harrison S 14 + 1	Irving A 13 + 6	Lewis D 8 + 8	Haber M 6 + 9 / Laverty A — + 1	Mackin D 1 + 2	Greenwood R — + 3	Sammut R 9 + 3	Russell M 2 + 1	Froxylias D 1 + 3	Kidd L 12 + 4	Brough P 16	Robson T 16 + 5	McKee J 9 + 1	Rudden Z 29 + 2	Buaben P 7	Mitchell D 8 + 1	Dunne C — + 1	Jarvis J — + 1	McKenna C 17	Dixon P 16	Waddington M 8 + 6	MacLean R 8 + 7	McShane I 16	O'Hara K — + 1	Lavery S — + 6	Osman A 15	Keillor-Dunn D 7 + 4	Burgoyne H 15	Edjenguele W 12	Todorov N 1 + 6	Jarvis A 4 + 8	*Match No.*
1	2	3	4	5^{2}	6	7^{1}	8	9	10	11	12	13																										1
1	4	2	5	8^{2}	6		3	9	10		11^{3}	12	7^{1}	13	14																							2
1	3	2	5	12	7	8^{2}	4^{3}	6^{1}	10	11		13		9	14																							3
1	4	3					5	12	11	10^{2}	14		7	9	8^{3}	2	6^{1}	13																				4
1	4	2		9^{3}	8		3	10^{2}	12	13					14	6^{1}	5		7	11																		5
1	4	2		9	8		3	11^{1}	13	10^{3}						12	5	14	6^{2}	7																		6
1	3	2	12	9	7^{1}		4	8	10^{2}	13							5		6	11																		7
1	4	2	8	9			3^{2}	7	11^{1}	13			14				5	12	6^{3}	10																		8
1■	4	2	3	10	6			9^{3}	12				7				5		14	11^{1}	8^{2}	13																9
	3	5	4	6	9			12		11^{2}			8^{1}			13	2			10	7	1																10
		3	2	10^{2}	7			8	12	14			13			5	4	9	6^{1}	11^{3}		1																11
			2	10			3	8	13	12			14			5^{2}	4	9	6^{1}	11	7^{3}	1																12
1	12		3	10	5		2	8								6	4^{1}	9		11	7																	13
1	13		2		6		3	10	11^{2}	12			8^{1}			5	4	9	7																			14
1		7	3	10^{3}	6		2	13	14	12			8^{1}			5	4	9		11^{2}																		15
1		7	4	11	8		2	6^{1}	12	13						5^{2}	3	9		10																		16
		7	4	10	8			12		13			5^{2}			2^{1}	3	9		11	6	1																17
		4	3		8■		14	13	12	11^{2}			9			2^{3}	5	6		10	7^{1}	1																18
		3	2				9	12	11				7^{3}				4^{1}	5	6	10	8^{2}	1	13	14														19
		13	2													5		9	7	11^{3}		1			3	4	6^{1}	8^{2}	10	12	14							20
			3		13											5^{2}		9		11		1			2	4	6^{1}	10	8		14	7^{3}	12					21
			2	10^{2}	14													5		3					4	7	11^{1}	9^{3}	8		13	6	12	1				22
			2	6^{3}	7															11^{1}					4	5	12		8^{2}		13	9	10■	1	3	14		23
			5	11	7															10^{1}					2	9	6^{2}	12	8			4		1	3	13		24
			2	10	6													5		11^{3}					4	3	8^{1}	13	7				9^{2}	1		14	12	25
			2	10	8													12		11^{1}					3	5■		13	7^{2}			6	9^{3}	1	4		14	26
			2	10	8													5		11^{3}					3		13	14	7^{2}			6	9^{1}	1	4		12	27
			2	9^{2}	6															12					3	5	14	10^{1}	8			7		1	4	13	11^{3}	28
			2	9^{3}	6											14				11					3	5		13	7^{2}			8	10^{1}	1	4		12	29
			2	9^{3}	6															11^{1}					3	5		12	7		14	8	10^{2}	1	4		13	30
			2	9	6															12					3	5	11^{3}		7^{2}		14	8	13■	1	4		10^{1}	31
			2	10	8															11					3	5	6^{1}	13	9^{2}			7^{3}		1	4	14	12	32
			5	6^{3}	8															10^{1}					4	2	14	11				9	12	1	3	13	7^{2}	33
			2		6^{2}													14		9					3	5	12	11^{1}	8			7		1	4	10^{3}	13	34
			2	12^{3}												14		5		10					3	4	8^{1}	11^{2}	6			7	9	1			13	35
			5							13								9		10					2	4	12	8^{1}	6			7		1	3		11^{2}	36

FORFAR ATHLETIC

Year Formed: 1885. *Ground & Address:* Station Park, Carseview Road, Forfar DD8 3BT. *Telephone:* 01307 463576. *Fax:* 01307 466956. *E-mail:* david.mcgregor@forfarathletic.co.uk *Website:* www.forfarathletic.co.uk
Ground Capacity: 6,777 (seated: 739). *Size of Pitch:* 103m × 64m.
Chairman: Ross Graham. *Secretary:* David McGregor.
Manager: Jim Weir. *Assistant Manager:* Gary Irvine.
Club Nicknames: 'The Loons'; 'The Sky Blues'.
Record Attendance: 10,780 v Rangers, Scottish Cup 2nd rd, 2 February 1970.
Record Transfer Fee received: £65,000 for David Bingham to Dunfermline Ath (September 1995).
Record Transfer Fee paid: £50,000 for Ian McPhee from Airdrieonians (1991).
Record Victory: 14-1 v Lindertis, Scottish Cup 1st rd, 1 September 1888.
Record Defeat: 2-12 v King's Park, Division II, 2 January 1930.
Most League Appearances: 463: Ian McPhee, 1978-88 and 1991-98.
Most League Goals in Season (Individual): 46: Dave Kilgour, Division II, 1929-30.
Most Goals Overall: 125: John Clark, 1978-91.

FORFAR ATHLETIC – SPFL LADBROKES LEAGUE ONE 2018–19 LEAGUE RECORD

Match No.	Date	Venue	Opponents	Result		H/T Score	Lg Pos.	Goalscorers	Attendance
1	Aug 4	H	Airdrieonians	L	1-3	1-0	8	Hilson 41	652
2	11	A	Dumbarton	W	2-0	1-0	4	Baird 2 27, 70	575
3	18	H	Stranraer	D	0-0	0-0	5		459
4	25	H	Stenhousemuir	W	2-0	2-0	3	Baird 30, MacKintosh 36	467
5	Sept 1	A	Raith R	L	0-4	0-1	5		1447
6	15	A	Arbroath	L	1-3	1-1	8	Cunningham 45	1015
7	22	H	Brechin C	D	1-1	0-1	8	Travis 71	635
8	29	A	Montrose	D	2-2	2-1	7	Bain 16, Hill 27	715
9	Oct 6	H	East Fife	L	0-4	0-3	8		585
10	20	A	Stenhousemuir	W	2-1	2-0	7	Easton 22, Baird 26	442
11	27	H	Raith R	W	3-2	1-2	4	Hilson 15, Easton 67, Hill 81	826
12	Nov 3	A	Airdrieonians	W	1-0	0-0	4	Baird 82	645
13	10	A	Brechin C	L	0-4	0-3	4		638
14	17	H	Dumbarton	W	3-0	0-0	4	Whyte 49, Baird 54, Hill 78	491
15	Dec 1	A	Stranraer	L	1-2	0-1	4	Baird (pen) 80	224
16	8	H	Arbroath	L	2-3	0-1	5	Moore 58, Baird 72	958
17	15	H	Montrose	W	2-1	1-1	4	Hilson 2 37, 80	592
18	22	A	East Fife	L	0-1	0-0	5		527
19	29	H	Brechin C	W	2-0	1-0	4	Baird 19, Hilson (pen) 57	764
20	Jan 5	A	Dumbarton	W	3-2	3-1	4	Hilson 4, Baird 37, Easton 41	619
21	12	H	Stranraer	W	2-1	1-1	4	Hilson 8, Baird 87	533
22	26	A	Arbroath	W	2-0	1-0	4	Coupe 14, Spencer 83	1132
23	Feb 2	A	Raith R	D	1-1	0-1	4	Baird 87	1406
24	9	H	Airdrieonians	W	2-0	1-0	3	Irvine 41, Eckersley 72	538
25	16	A	Montrose	L	0-2	0-1	3		845
26	23	H	Stenhousemuir	W	2-1	0-0	3	Bain 50, Baird 63	492
27	Mar 2	H	East Fife	W	3-0	3-0	2	Hilson 9, Easton 16, Baird 42	729
28	9	A	Brechin C	D	2-2	1-2	3	Easton 45, Spencer 78	634
29	16	H	Raith R	W	2-1	1-0	2	Hilson 2 22, 69	509
30	23	A	Airdrieonians	L	0-1	0-1	3		777
31	30	H	Arbroath	W	2-1	1-1	3	Hilson 37, Moore 89	1342
32	Apr 6	A	Stranraer	L	1-2	1-1	3	Irvine 22	335
33	13	H	Dumbarton	D	0-0	0-0	3		554
34	20	A	Stenhousemuir	W	3-0	2-0	2	Hilson 24, Eckersley 27, Baird (pen) 61	577
35	27	H	Montrose	W	1-0	0-0	2	Baird 76	850
36	May 4	A	East Fife	W	3-2	1-1	2	MacKintosh 37, Easton 55, Hilson 73	597

Final League Position: 2

Honours
League Champions: Second Division 1983-84; Third Division 1994-95; C Division 1948-49.
Runners-up: League One 2018-19; Third Division 1996-97, 2009-10; League Two 2016-17.
Promoted via play-offs: 2009-10 (to Second Division); 2016-17 (to League One).
Scottish Cup: Semi-finals 1982.
League Cup: Semi-finals 1977-78.
League Challenge Cup: Semi-finals 2004-05.

Club colours: Shirt: Sky blue. Shorts: White. Socks: Sky blue.

Goalscorers: *League (54):* Baird 16 (2 pens), Hilson 13 (1 pen), Easton 6, Hill 3, Bain 2, Eckersley 2, Irvine 2, MacKintosh 2, Moore 2, Spencer 2, Coupe 1, Cunningham 1, Travis 1, Whyte 1.
William Hill Scottish FA Cup (2): Baird 1, Moore 1.
Betfred Scottish League Cup (5): Baird 3, Easton 1 (1 pen), Hilson 1.
Irn-Bru Scottish League Challenge (0).
Play-Offs (2): Baird 2.

McCallum M 36	Meechan R 36	Wilson A 8 + 1	Travis M 30	Bain J 31 + 2	Moore L 18 + 11	Reilly T 26 + 2	MacKintosh M 14 + 11	Easton D 26 + 8	Hilson D 33 + 2	Baird J 36	Coupe C 3 + 21	Starkey B — + 2	Whyte D 31 + 1	Fraser G — + 3	Munro A 5 + 2	Malone E 8 + 4	Cunningham R 3 + 7	Aitken M 1 + 10	Hill M 13	Eckersley A 15	Spencer B 10 + 2	Irvine G 12 + 1	Scott C — + 4	Match No.
1	2	3	4	5	6	7	8	9^{1}	10	11^{2}	12	13												1
1	2	3	4	6	9^{1}	7	8	12	10^{2}	11			5	13										2
1	2	3	4	6	9	7^{2}	8	12	10^{1}	11			5	13										3
1	2	4		6	9^{2}	7	8			11	10^{1}	13		12	3	5								4
1	2	3		6	8^{2}	7	9	11^{1}	12	10	13		14		4	5^{3}								5
1	2	4		5	6^{2}	8	7	12	11	10^{3}	14				3		9^{1}	13						6
1	5	2^{1}	3	9		6	8	14	11	10^{2}			4		12		7^{3}	13						7
1	2	12	4	9		7^{2}	14	6^{1}	11	10			5		3^{3}			13	8					8
1	2	3		6			7	9^{1}	12	11^{3}	13		5			4^{2}	14	10	8					9
1	5		4	2	13	6	12	10^{7}	11	9			3				8^{1}		7					10
1	5		4	2	12	7	6	9^{1}	10	11			3						8					11
1	5		4	2	12	7	6^{1}	9^{3}	10	11^{2}	13		3				14		8					12
1	5		4	2	12	8	6^{1}	9	10^{3}	11^{2}	13		3				14		7					13
1	5		4	2	6^{1}	7	14	9^{3}	10	11^{2}	12		3				13		8					14
1	5		4	2	6^{1}	7	13	9^{2}	10^{3}	11	12		3				14		8					15
1	5		4■	2	6	8^{2}		9^{1}	10	11	12		3		13				7					16
1	5			2	6	4	12	9	10	11					3	8			7^{1}					17
1	5			2	6^{1}	4		9	10	11^{2}	12		3			0	13		7					18
1	5		3	6		4	13	9^{1}	10^{2}	11^{3}	12		2			8	14		7					19
1	2		4	6		8	13	9^{2}	10	11^{1}	12		3			5			7					20
1	2		4	9		7	13	6^{1}	10^{2}	11	14		3			8^{3}		12		5				21
1	2		4	9		7^{2}	6	12	11	10^{3}	8^{1}		3			14				5	13■			22
1	2		3	6	14	7	8^{2}	12	10^{3}	11	9^{1}		4							5		13		23
1	2		3	12	8	7	13	11^{2}	9^{3}	10			4							5		6^{1}	14	24
1	2		4		8^{1}	7■		11^{3}	9	10	12		3							5	13	6^{2}	14	25
1	2		4	6	12		13	11^{3}	9	10^{2}			3					14		5	8^{1}	7		26
1	2		4	6	12			9^{2}	10^{3}	11^{1}			3					14		5	8	7	13	27
1	2		4	6^{2}	12	13		9	10	11^{1}			3					14		5	8	7^{3}		28
1	2		4	12	8^{2}			11^{1}	6^{3}	10	13		3					14		5	9	7		29
1	2		4		8	12		11^{1}	6	10^{3}	13		3							5	9	7^{2}	14	30
1	2		4	6^{2}	9				10	11^{1}	12		3			13				5	8	7		31
1	2		4		6	8^{1}	14	13	10	11^{3}	12		3							5	9^{2}	7		32
1	2		4	6^{1}	9^{3}			13	11	10^{2}	12		3					14		5	8	7		33
1	2		3	6	12	7^{1}		8^{2}	10^{3}	11			4			13		14		5	9			34
1	2		3	6^{1}	12			9^{2}	10	11	13		4							5	7	8		35
1	2		4^{3}	6	14		7	9	11^{2}	10^{1}	13		3			12				5		8		36

GREENOCK MORTON

Year Formed: 1874. *Ground & Address:* Cappielow Park, Sinclair St, Greenock PA15 2TU. *Telephone:* 01475 723571. *Fax:* 01475 781084. *E-mail:* admin@gmfc.net *Website:* www.gmfc.net
Ground Capacity: 11,612 (seated: 6,062). *Size of Pitch:* 100m × 65m.
Chairman: Crawford Rae. *Chief Executive:* Dave MacKinnon.
Manager: David Hopkin. *Assistant Manager:* Anton McElhone.
Club Nickname: 'The Ton'.
Previous Grounds: Grant Street 1874; Garvel Park 1875; Cappielow Park 1879; Ladyburn Park 1882; Cappielow Park 1883.
Record Attendance: 23,500 v Celtic, 29 April 1922.
Record Transfer Fee received: £500,000 for Derek Lilley to Leeds U (March 1997).
Record Transfer Fee paid: £250,000 for Janne Lindberg and Marko Rajamäki from MyPa, Finland (November 1994).
Record Victory: 11-0 v Carfin Shamrock, Scottish Cup 4th rd, 13 November 1886.
Record Defeat: 1-10 v Port Glasgow Ath, Division II, 5 May, 1894 and v St Bernards, Division II, 14 October 1933.
Most Capped Player: Jimmy Cowan, 25, Scotland.
Most League Appearances: 534: Derek Collins, 1987-98, 2001-05.
Most League Goals in Season (Individual): 58: Allan McGraw, Division II, 1963-64.
Most Goals Overall (Individual): 136: Andy Ritchie, 1976-83.

GREENOCK MORTON – SPFL LADBROKES CHAMPIONSHIP 2018–19 LEAGUE RECORD

Match No.	Date	Venue	Opponents	Result		H/T Score	Lg Pos.	Goalscorers	Attendance
1	Aug 4	H	Queen of the South	D	2-2	0-0	5	Tidser [47], MacLean [63]	2019
2	11	A	Alloa Ath	W	2-0	1-0	2	Millar 2 [15, 81]	836
3	25	H	Ross Co	W	2-1	0-0	2	Tidser [60], McHugh [77]	1994
4	Sept 1	A	Partick Thistle	L	0-1	0-0	5		3431
5	15	A	Dundee U	D	1-1	1-0	6	Tidser (pen) [11]	4594
6	22	H	Dunfermline Ath	D	1-1	0-0	5	Tiffoney [81]	2084
7	29	H	Ayr U	L	1-5	1-1	6	Telfer [35]	2273
8	Oct 6	A	Inverness CT	D	1-1	1-1	7	Telfer [10]	2186
9	20	H	Falkirk	W	1-0	0-0	6	McHugh [76]	2757
10	27	A	Ross Co	L	0-5	0-2	6		3481
11	30	A	Queen of the South	W	2-1	1-0	6	McHugh [41], Lyon [84]	1174
12	Nov 3	H	Partick Thistle	W	5-1	2-1	4	Oliver [23], McHugh 2 [43, 66], Iredale [54], Tidser [71]	2197
13	10	H	Alloa Ath	L	0-2	0-0	5		1794
14	17	A	Ayr U	D	0-0	0-0	5		2346
15	Dec 1	A	Dunfermline Ath	L	0-3	0-2	6		4370
16	8	H	Dundee U	D	1-1	0-1	6	Buchanan [78]	1916
17	15	A	Falkirk	D	0-0	0-0	6		3775
18	22	H	Inverness CT	L	1-2	0-1	6	Tiffoney [73]	1608
19	29	A	Partick Thistle	W	2-1	1-0	5	Tiffoney [9], Telfer [80]	3074
20	Jan 4	H	Ross Co	W	1-0	0-0	4	Waddell [66]	1537
21	12	A	Alloa Ath	L	1-2	1-0	6	Millar [12]	931
22	26	H	Dunfermline Ath	D	0-0	0-0	6		1907
23	Feb 2	A	Dundee U	L	1-2	0-2	6	McHugh [73]	4902
24	16	H	Ayr U	D	0-0	0-0	6		2335
25	23	A	Inverness CT	L	0-1	0-1	7		2413
26	26	H	Queen of the South	W	1-0	0-0	6	Buchanan [85]	1324
27	Mar 1	H	Falkirk	D	1-1	1-1	6	Kiltie [32]	1838
28	9	A	Ross Co	L	0-2	0-0	6		3110
29	30	H	Partick Thistle	L	0-3	0-3	6		2329
30	Apr 2	A	Ayr U	D	1-1	0-1	6	Kiltie [71]	1802
31	6	A	Queen of the South	D	1-1	0-1	6	Telfer [64]	1442
32	9	H	Alloa Ath	L	1-2	0-0	6	Kiltie (pen) [51]	1498
33	16	H	Inverness CT	D	2-2	2-1	7	Lyon [27], Kiltie (pen) [42]	1315
34	20	A	Falkirk	W	2-0	0-0	6	Kiltie [47], Telfer [54]	5254
35	27	A	Dunfermline Ath	W	1-0	0-0	5	Kiltie (pen) [84]	4883
36	May 4	H	Dundee U	W	1-0	1-0	5	Tidser [19]	2244

Final League Position: 5

Honours
League Champions: First Division 1977-78, 1983-84, 1986-87; Division II 1949-50, 1963-64, 1966-67; Second Division 1994-95, 2006-07; League One 2014–15; Third Division 2002-03.
Runners-up: Division 1 1916-17; First Division 2012-13; Second Division 2005-06;. Division II 1899-1900, 1928-29, 1936-37.
Scottish Cup Winners: 1922; *Runners-up:* 1948.
League Cup Runners-up: 1963-64.
League Challenge Cup Runners-up: 1992-93.

European: *UEFA Cup:* 2 matches (*Fairs Cup:* 1968-69).

Club colours: Shirt: Blue and white hoops. Shorts: White with blue trim. Socks: White with blue tops.

Goalscorers: *League (36):* Kiltie 6 (3 pens), McHugh 6, Telfer 5, Tidser 5 (1 pen), Millar 3, Tiffoney 3, Buchanan 2, Lyon 2, Iredale 1, MacLean 1, Oliver 1, Waddell 1.
William Hill Scottish FA Cup (5): McHugh 2, Millar 1, Thomson R 1, Waddell 1.
Betfred Scottish League Cup (9): Tidser 3 (1 pen), McHugh 2, Armour 1, Bell 1, MacLean 1, Tumilty 1.
Irn-Bru Scottish League Challenge (1): Oliver 1.

Scully R 11 + 1	McKeown R 16	Buchanan G 35	Kilday L 33	Tumilty R 31 + 3	Tidser M 26 + 4	Millar C 26 + 4	McAlister J 33	MacLean R 9 + 7	McHugh B 22 + 7	Telfer C 24 + 5	Bell C — + 1	Oliver G 13 + 5	Waddell K 17 + 6	Iredale J 23 + 5	Johnstone D 3 + 1	Tiffoney S 5 + 6	Armour B — + 1	Lyon R 13 + 6	Gaston D 10	Thomson R 7 + 6	McGrattan L — + 2	Dykes D 4 + 3	McCrorie R 15	Dallas A 5 + 7	Kiltie G 13 + 1	O'Connell K 2 + 4	*Match No.*
1	2	3	4	5	6	7	8	9^2	10	11^1	12	13															1
1	5	4	3	2	8	6	7	10	11^1	9^2		12	13														2
1	5	4	3	2	8	6^2	7	9^3	10			12	14	11^1	13												3
1	5	4	3^1	2	9^2	7	8	6	11				12		10^3	13	14										4
1	5	4	3	2	9	7^3	8	6^2	11	13			12		10^1	14											5
1	5	4	3	2	8		7	6^2	11^1	13		14		9^3	10	12											6
1	5	4	3	2	8^2	6^1	7	13	14	9		10				11^3		12									7
1	5	3	2		9		6	12	13	7		11	4	8^1		10^2											8
1	5	3	2^2	12	8	6	7	11^1	13	9^3		10	4	14													9
1	5	3	2	13	8	6^3	7	11^2	12	9^1		10	4	14													10
		3	2	9	6		7	12	11			10^1	4	5				8	1								11
		3	2	5	8		7		10	6^1		11^2	4	9					1	12	13						12
		3	2^1	5	6		7	8^2	10			11	4	9		13			1	12							13
		3	2	5	8		7	12	10	6^1		11	4	9					1								14
		3	2	5	8^2	6^3	7		11	12			4^1	9		13		14	1	10							15
	5	4	3	2	9	8	6	13	12	7^1						10^2			1	11							16
	5	4^3	3	2	8	9	6	12	10	7^1			13					14	1	11^2							17
	5		3	2	8^1	6	7	14	10	9^3			4			12		13	1	11^7							18
	5	4	3	2		6	7		11	9				13		10^2		8^1	1	12							19
14	9	3	2	5	12	8	7		10	6^2			4	13		11^1			1^3								20
1	9^3	3	4	5	8^1	6	7		11	10^2			2	14						12		13					21
		4	3	2	12	6	8		10	9^2		13		5								7	1	11^1			22
		4	3^2	2	13	6	8^1		10				12	5								7	1	11	9		23
		4				6	2		10	7			3	5				13				8^2	1	9^1	11	12	24
		4		12	13	6	2		10	7^3			3	5				14				8^2	1		11	9^1	25
		3	2	5	8	12	7^3		11^2				4	9				6		13			1	10^1	14		26
		3	4	5^1	8	7							2	9				6		10^2			1	13	11	12	27
		3	4	5	8^2	7				13			2	9				6^1		11			1	12	10		28
		4		5		8	3			7^2			2^1	9				6^3		11		14	1	13	10	12	29
		3	4	5		7	2			8		10^1		9				6		12			1		11		30
		3	4	5		7	2			8		10^1		9				6					1	12	11		31
		3	2	5		7	4			8^2		10^1		9				6					1	12	11	13	32
		3	2	5	7	12	4			8		10^2		9				6					1	13	11^1		33
		3	4	5	8	13	2		14	7^1		10^2		9				6					1	12^3	11		34
		3	2	5	7	12	4		13	6				9				8^2					1	11^1	10		35
		4	3	2	8^3	7			11	12				5				9^1			14	13	1		10	6^2	36

HAMILTON ACADEMICAL

Year Formed: 1874. *Ground:* Hope Stadium, New Douglas Park, Cadzow Avenue, Hamilton ML3 0FT. *Telephone:* 01698 368652. *Fax:* 01698 285422. *E-mail:* office@acciesfc.co.uk *Website:* www.hamiltonacciesfc.co.uk
Ground Capacity: 6,078 (all seated). *Size of Pitch:* 105m × 68m.
Chairman: Allan Maitland. *Vice-Chairman:* Les Gray.
Head Coach: Brian Rice. *First-Team Coach:* Guillaume Beuzelin.
Club Nickname: 'The Accies'.
Previous Grounds: Bent Farm; South Avenue; South Haugh; Douglas Park; Cliftonhill Stadium; Firhill Stadium.
Record Attendance: 28,690 v Hearts, Scottish Cup 3rd rd, 3 March 1937 (at Douglas Park); 5,895 v Rangers, 28 February 2009 (at New Douglas Park).
Record Transfer Fee received: £1,200,000 (rising to £3,200,000) for James McCarthy to Wigan Ath (July 2009).
Record Transfer Fee paid: £180,000 for Tomas Cerny from Sigma Olomouc (July 2009).
Record Victory: 10-2 v Greenock Morton, Scottish Championship, 3 May 2014.
Record Defeat: 1-11 v Hibernian, Division I, 6 November 1965.
Most Capped Player: Colin Miller, 29 (61), Canada, 1988-94.
Most League Appearances: 452: Rikki Ferguson, 1974-88.
Most League Goals in Season (Individual): 35: David Wilson, Division I; 1936-37.
Most Goals Overall (Individual): 246: David Wilson, 1928-39.

HAMILTON ACADEMICAL – SPFL LADBROKES PREMIERSHIP 2018–19 LEAGUE RECORD

Match No.	*Date*	*Venue*	*Opponents*	*Result*		*H/T Score*	*Lg Pos.*	*Goalscorers*	*Attendance*
1	Aug 4	H	Hearts	L	1-4	1-1	12	Miller [17]	3764
2	11	A	Motherwell	W	1-0	0-0	7	Boyd [67]	4807
3	26	A	Celtic	L	0-1	0-0	9		56,044
4	Sept 1	H	St Johnstone	L	1-2	0-2	10	Bingham [69]	1791
5	15	A	Livingston	L	0-1	0-1	11		1342
6	22	H	St Mirren	W	3-0	2-0	9	Brustad [36], Miller 2 (1 pen) [40 (p), 66]	2830
7	29	H	Dundee	L	0-2	0-1	9		1788
8	Oct 6	A	Hibernian	L	0-6	0-3	9		16,857
9	21	H	Rangers	L	1-4	0-1	9	Boyd [80]	5013
10	27	A	Kilmarnock	D	1-1	1-1	9	Imrie [34]	5023
11	31	A	Aberdeen	L	0-3	0-2	10		12,365
12	Nov 3	H	Livingston	W	1-0	0-0	10	Enigbokan-Bloomfield [86]	1459
13	10	A	St Johnstone	L	0-4	0-2	10		2175
14	24	H	Celtic	L	0-3	0-1	10		4688
15	Dec 1	A	St Mirren	W	3-1	2-1	10	Imrie [21], Gordon [42], Keatings [55]	4334
16	5	A	Dundee	L	0-4	0-1	10		4426
17	8	H	Hibernian	L	0-1	0-0	10		2169
18	16	A	Rangers	L	0-1	0-1	10		49,055
19	22	H	Kilmarnock	D	1-1	1-1	10	Miller (pen) [37]	3401
20	26	A	Hearts	L	0-2	0-2	10		16,475
21	29	H	Motherwell	L	1-2	1-1	10	Imrie [17]	3843
22	Jan 23	H	Aberdeen	L	0-3	0-1	10		2104
23	26	A	Celtic	L	0-3	0-1	10		58,264
24	Feb 2	H	Dundee	D	1-1	0-0	11	MacKinnon [90]	2297
25	6	H	St Johnstone	W	2-1	0-0	11	Oakley 2 [68, 79]	1174
26	16	A	Hibernian	L	0-2	0-2	11		16,265
27	24	H	Rangers	L	0-5	0-4	11		5827
28	27	A	Aberdeen	W	2-0	1-0	10	Oakley [34], Miller [59]	12,468
29	Mar 9	A	Motherwell	L	0-3	0-3	10		5248
30	16	H	Hearts	W	1-0	1-0	10	McGowan [36]	2082
31	30	A	Kilmarnock	L	0-5	0-1	10		4762
32	Apr 3	A	Livingston	L	0-2	0-0	10		1022
33	6	H	St Mirren	D	1-1	0-0	10	Davies [63]	3096
34	20	H	Motherwell	D	1-1	0-1	10	Ogboe [84]	2746
35	27	H	Livingston	D	3-3	1-0	10	Oakley [40], Imrie (pen) [47], McGowan [90]	1135
36	May 4	A	Dundee	W	1-0	0-0	10	Andreu (pen) [83]	4622
37	13	A	St Mirren	L	0-2	0-0	10		6421
38	18	H	St Johnstone	W	2-0	1-0	10	Gordon [11], Davies [57]	2553

Final League Position: 10

Honours
League Champions: Division II 1903-04; First Division 1985-86, 1987-88, 2007-08; Third Division 2000-01.
Runners-up: Division II 1952-53, 1964-65; Second Division 1996-97, 2003-04; Championship 2013-14.
Promoted via play-offs: 2013-14 (to Premiership).
Scottish Cup Runners-up: 1911, 1935. *League Cup:* Semi-finalists three times.
League Challenge Cup Winners: 1991-92, 1992-93; *Runners-up:* 2005-06, 2011-12.

Club colours: Shirt: Red and white hoops. Shorts: White. Socks: White.

Goalscorers: *League (28):* Miller 5 (2 pens), Imrie 4 (1 pen), Oakley 4, Boyd 2, Davies 2, Gordon 2, McGowan 2, Andreu 1 (1 pen), Bingham 1, Brustad 1, Enigbokan-Bloomfield 1, Keatings 1, MacKinnon 1, Ogboe 1.
William Hill Scottish FA Cup (0).
Betfred Scottish League Cup (5): Miller 3 (1 pen), Bingham 2.
Irn-Bru Scottish League Challenge (6): Enigbokan-Bloomfield 2, Cunningham 1, Hughes 1, Smith A 1, Smith L 1.

Woods G 32	Penny A 3+5	Gordon Z 35+1	Want S 9+1	McMann S 27+1	MacKinnon D 29	Lyon D 1	Imrie D 22+7	Kelly S 3+3	Miller M 25+6	Bingham R 11+8	Taiwo T 12+4	Cunningham R —+3	Enigbokan-Bloomfield M 1+4	McGowan A 35	Boyd S 10+13	Tshiembe D 15+4	Sowah L 14+4	Kilgallon M 25	Martin S 26+5	Brustad F 11+4	Keatings J 8+9	Smith L —+4	Mucha J 2	Marsden J —+1	Gogic A 12+4	Fulton R 4	Andreu T 15+2	Davies S 5+4	Mimnaugh R 5+3	Oakley G 14+1	McMillan D 4+4	Ogboe M 3+3	*Match No.*
1	2	3	4	5	6	7^3	8^1	9	10	11^2	12	13	14																				1
1	4^3	2	3	5	6			9^1	10^2	11	8	12		7	13	14																	2
1		2	3	4	7		9	13	10^1		8	12		5	11^2	6																	3
1		4	2	9	7		14	13	10	11	6^2			5^1	8	3^3	12																4
1		2		4^1	7		12		8	11					13	5	9^3	3	6	10^2	14												5
1			2	4	7^1		6		9	13	12			5	10	14		3	8^2	11^3													6
1			2	4			9	7^3		12	6^2		14	5	10			3	8	11^1	13												7
1		12	2	4^2			8			10^3	14			5	9	6		3	7^1	11	13												8
1	2	4^2		9	7		8		10^3	12				5	14	3			6	11^1	13												9
1		5			8		9		6	12				2	13■	3		4	7	11^1	10^2												10
1	13	8		5			9■		6	10^2				2		3		4	7^3	11^1	12	14											11
1	13	4							8■	11^2	7^1		14	5	12	2		3	6	10^3	9												12
1		5		13	7		10	12		9			11^1	2	8^2	3		4	6^3	14													13
1		5		9			6		11	10^2	8			2		3^1		4	7	12	13												14
		4^3		9	6		8		7	13				2	12	14		3	5	11^1	10^2		1										15
		3		5	7		9^1		6	12	14			2	13	4			8	11^3	10^2		1										16
1^3		3			7		8		9	11^2	6^1		13	2	14		5	4			10			12									17
1	14	4		6	9		10			7^3	8^2			2	13		5	3^1		12	11												18
1		2	12	9	7^1		8		10		6			5			4^3	3	13	14	11^2												19
1		4	3■	9			8		10^1	13	6			5	14	2^3	12		7	11^2													20
1	12	2		9^3			8		10	14				5^1	7		4^2	3	6		11				13								21
		3		5			9		10^1		7^2			2	12			4	14		13				6	1	8	11^3					22
		3		6			10				7^1			2	11^3		5	4	8		13				12	1	9^2		14				23
1		4		9	7				12					5	10^3			3	8^2						2		6	13		11^1	14		24
1		2			7		8^3		12					5	11^1		4	3	14						6		13	9^2		10			25
1		2			7				8					5			4	3				14			6^2		11^1	12	13	10	9^3		26
1		3			7				9					2			5	4	12						13		6		8^2	11	10^1		27
1	14	3			7^1		12		10					2		4	5		6^3						9		8^2			11	13		28
1		2			6				10^1						13	3	5	4	9		12				7^2		8			11			29
1		4			8		14		10					2		13	5	3	9^3						6		7^2			11^1	12		30
1		4			6				10					5	12		8	3	7						2		9^2			11^1	13		31
1		3		5	6				13					2^1		4			7						12		8^2	14	9	11^3	10		32
1		3		5	8				9^1					2				4	13						7		12	10^2	6^3	11		14	33
1		4		5	6^2		7							2				3	10			14					8	9^3		12	11^1	13	34
		3		5	7^1		8		12					2					6			14			4	1	9	13		11^2		10^3	35
		3		5	7^3		13		12					2			14		6						4	1	8		9	11^2		10^1	36
1		3		5	6		14		13					2			12		8^3						4■		9		7^2	10		11^1	37
1		3	2^3	8	6		13							5			4		7^2								11	9^1	14	10		12	38

HEART OF MIDLOTHIAN

Year Formed: 1874. *Ground & Address:* Tynecastle Stadium, McLeod Street, Edinburgh EH11 2NL. *Telephone:* 0333 043 1874. *Fax:* 0131 200 7222. *E-mail:* supporterservices@homplc.co.uk *Website:* www.heartsfc.co.uk
Ground Capacity: 20,099. *Size of Pitch:* 100m × 64m.
Chief Executive and Chairwoman: Ann Budge.
Director of Football and Manager: Craig Levein. *Assistant Head Coach:* Austin MacPhee.
Club Nicknames: 'Hearts'; 'Jambos'; 'Jam Tarts'.
Previous Grounds: The Meadows 1874; Powderhall 1878; Old Tynecastle 1881 Tynecastle Park; 1886.
Record Attendance: 53,396 v Rangers, Scottish Cup 3rd rd, 13 February 1932 (57,857 v Barcelona, 28 July 2007 at Murrayfield).
Record Transfer Fee received: £9,000,000 for Craig Gordon to Sunderland (August 2008).
Record Transfer Fee paid: £850,000 for Mirsad Beslija from Genk (January 2006).
Record Victory: 15-0 v King's Park, Scottish Cup 2nd rd, 13 February 1937 (21-0 v Anchor, EFA Cup, 30 October 1880).
Record Defeat: 1-8 v Vale of Leven, Scottish Cup 3rd rd, 1883; 0-7 v Celtic, Scottish Cup 4th rd, 1 December 2013.
Most Capped Player: Steven Pressley, 32, Scotland.
Most League Appearances: 515: Gary Mackay, 1980-97.
Most League Goals in Season (Individual): 44: Barney Battles, 1930-31.
Most Goals Overall (Individual): 214: John Robertson, 1983-98.

HEART OF MIDLOTHIAN – SPFL LADBROKES PREMIERSHIP 2018–19 LEAGUE RECORD

Match No.	Date	Venue	Opponents	Result		H/T Score	Lg Pos.	Goalscorers	Attendance
1	Aug 4	A	Hamilton A	W	4-1	1-1	1	Haring 2 [20, 58], Naismith (pen) [49], MacLean [62]	3764
2	11	H	Celtic	W	1-0	0-0	1	Lafferty [56]	19,113
3	25	A	Kilmarnock	W	1-0	0-0	1	Ikpeazu [81]	6239
4	Sept 1	H	St Mirren	W	4-1	4-1	1	Naismith 3 (1 pen) [4 (p), 41, 43], Lee [30]	17,714
5	15	A	Motherwell	W	1-0	1-0	1	Naismith [28]	7218
6	22	H	Livingston	D	0-0	0-0	1		17,798
7	29	H	St Johnstone	W	2-1	1-0	1	Haring [25], Jimmy Dunne [65]	17,240
8	Oct 7	A	Rangers	L	1-3	0-3	1	Jimmy Dunne [67]	49,865
9	20	H	Aberdeen	W	2-1	2-0	1	Djoum [36], Naismith (pen) [43]	18,051
10	23	A	Dundee	W	3-0	2-0	1	Bozanic [2], Naismith [14], MacLean [46]	6112
11	31	H	Hibernian	D	0-0	0-0	1		19,410
12	Nov 3	A	Celtic	L	0-5	0-3	1		58,831
13	10	H	Kilmarnock	L	0-1	0-0	1		17,417
14	24	A	St Mirren	L	0-2	0-0	3		5177
15	Dec 2	H	Rangers	L	1-2	1-2	4	McAuley (og) [27]	19,429
16	5	A	St Johnstone	D	2-2	2-1	4	Djoum [6], Bozanic [41]	3040
17	8	H	Motherwell	W	1-0	1-0	4	Haring [14]	15,915
18	14	A	Livingston	L	0-5	0-0	4		4201
19	22	A	Aberdeen	L	0-2	0-1	5		16,451
20	26	H	Hamilton A	W	2-0	2-0	5	Naismith [18], Djoum [44]	16,475
21	29	A	Hibernian	W	1-0	1-0	5	Lee [28]	20,200
22	Jan 23	H	Dundee	L	1-2	1-1	6	Lee [40]	15,518
23	26	H	St Johnstone	W	2-0	0-0	5	Godinho [52], Morrison [90]	16,672
24	Feb 1	A	Kilmarnock	W	2-1	2-1	5	Clare [38], Naismith [43]	5552
25	6	H	Livingston	D	0-0	0-0	5		15,147
26	17	A	Motherwell	L	1-2	1-1	5	Naismith [37]	5091
27	23	H	St Mirren	D	1-1	0-0	5	Dikamona [56]	16,705
28	27	H	Celtic	L	1-2	0-1	5	Bozanic (pen) [56]	18,258
29	Mar 9	A	Dundee	W	1-0	1-0	5	Clare [15]	5667
30	16	A	Hamilton A	L	0-1	0-1	5		2082
31	30	H	Aberdeen	W	2-1	0-1	5	Clare (pen) [59], Ikpeazu [77]	17,880
32	Apr 3	A	Rangers	L	0-3	0-2	5		49,702
33	6	H	Hibernian	L	1-2	1-1	6	Haring [25]	19,667
34	20	H	Rangers	L	1-3	0-2	6	MacLean [74]	18,212
35	28	A	Hibernian	D	1-1	0-0	6	Ikpeazu [84]	19,395
36	May 4	H	Kilmarnock	L	0-1	0-0	6		17,103
37	10	A	Aberdeen	L	1-2	0-0	6	Burns [65]	14,371
38	19	A	Celtic	L	1-2	1-1	7	Mulraney [18]	58,696

Final League Position: 7

Honours

League Champions: Division I 1894-95, 1896-97, 1957-58, 1959-60; First Division 1979-80; Championship 2014-15.
Runners-up: Division I 1893-94, 1898-99, 1903-04, 1905-06, 1914-15, 1937-38, 1953-54, 1956-57, 1958-59, 1964-65; Premier Division 1985-86, 1987-88, 1991-92, 2005-06; First Division 1977-78, 1982-83.
Scottish Cup Winners: 1891, 1896, 1901, 1906, 1956, 1998, 2006, 2012; *Runners-up:* 1903, 1907, 1968, 1976, 1986, 1996, 2019.
League Cup Winners: 1954-55, 1958-59, 1959-60, 1962-63; *Runners-up:* 1961-62, 1996-97, 2012-13.

European: *European Cup:* 8 matches (1958-59, 1960-61, 2006-07). *Cup Winners' Cup:* 10 matches (1976-77, 1996-97, 1998-99). *UEFA Cup:* 46 matches (*Fairs Cup:* 1961-62, 1963-64, 1965-66. *UEFA Cup:* 1984-85, 1986-87, 1988-89, 1990-91, 1992-93, 1993-94, 2000-01, 2003-04, 2004-05, 2006-07). *Europa League:* 12 matches (2010-11, 2011-12, 2012-13, 2016-17).

Club colours: Shirt: Maroon. Shorts: White with maroon trim. Socks: Maroon.

Goalscorers: *League (42):* Naismith 10 (3 pens), Haring 5, Bozanic 3 (1 pen), Clare 3 (1 pen), Djoum 3, Ikpeazu 3, Lee 3, MacLean 3, Jimmy Dunne 2, Burns 1, Dikamona 1, Godinho 1, Lafferty 1, Morrison 1, Mulraney 1, own goal 1.
William Hill Scottish FA Cup (12): Clare 3 (2 pens), Berra 2, Ikpeazu 2, Edwards 1, Keena 1, MacLean 1, Mitchell 1, Souttar 1.
Betfred Scottish League Cup (18): Naismith 4 (1 pen), Ikpeazu 3, Lee 3, MacLean 3, Haring 2, Smith 2, Garuccio 1.
Irn-Bru Scottish League Challenge (1): Keena 1.

Zlamal Z 29	Hughes A 1+4	Souttar J 23+1	Berra C 25	Garuccio B 13+4	Morrison C 15+10	Haring P 26	Lee O 23+8	Naismith S 19	Ikpeazu U 15+2	MacLean S 17+8	Burns B 3+2	Mulraney J 15+6	Lafferty K 1+1	Smith M 28	Bozanic O 15+10	Cochrane H 6+2	Dunne Jimmy 11	McDonald A —+3	Mitchell D 14+6	Djoum A 30+2	Wighton C 8+9	Dikamona C 12+9	Amankwaa D —+2	Godinho M 11+1	Clare S 23+5	Doyle C 9	Brandon J 5+2	Shaughnessy C 10	Keena A 1+4	Vanecek D 3+2	Smith C 2+1	Edwards R 2+2	Hickey A 1+1	Irving A 1	*Match No.*
1	2	3	4	5^{1}	6^{3}	7	8	9	10^{2}	11	12	13	14																						1
1	12	3	4^{1}	5		8	7	9	11			6^{3}	10^{2}	2	13	14																			2
1		3		5	9	7	6	8	10	12		11^{1}		2^{2}			4	13																	3
1		3		5	12	8	7^{2}	9	11	10^{3}				2			4		6^{1}	13	14														4
1		4			5^{3}	6	7^{2}	10	11^{1}	14				2	13		3		8	9		12													5
1		3		5^{2}	12	8	7^{3}	6		11		14		2			4		9	13	10^{1}														6
1		3			6^{3}	8	7	11		10^{1}				2^{2}	12		4		5	9		13	14												7
1		3		13		8	7^{2}	6	10	11^{3}				2■			4		5^{1}	9	14	12													8
1	13				6		8	10		11^{1}					7		4		5	9		3		2^{2}	12										9
1				13	6		14	10^{1}		11				2	7	8^{2}	4		5^{3}	9	12	3													10
1				5^{1}	6	7	8							2	9^{2}		4		13	10	12	3	14		11^{3}										11
1				12	13	6				11		10^{2}		2		9	4		5^{1}	8	14	3			7^{3}										12
1				5^{2}	6^{3}	7	8			11^{1}				2			4	12	14	9	10	3			13										13
1				5^{1}	9	8	13			11		12		2			3		14	10	6^{3}	4			7^{2}										14
1			4		14	9	13			11				3	8	7^{3}			5	10		12		2^{2}	6^{1}										15
1			4		13	6	8^{2}			14				2	9				5^{1}	7	11	3		12	10^{3}										16
1			4			6	12			10				2	7				8	9		3		5	11^{1}										17
1	12		4	5^{3}	6^{2}	7	14			11				2	8				9	10■		3^{1}			13										18
			4		13	3	6	11^{1}		10				2	8			12	9■					5^{3}	7^{2}	1	14								19
			4	5	6	8^{1}	7	10		11^{2}		13		3	14					9^{3}				2	12	1									20
			4	9		7^{1}	6^{2}	11				13		2	12					8		3		5	10	1									21
		13	4		6^{3}		7			12		14		2					5^{1}	8					9	1		3	10	11^{2}					22
		2	4		13		9	11				8^{3}		3	7				12	6				5^{2}	10^{1}	1				14					23
		2	4		9^{2}		12	10				8^{3}		5^{1}	7				13	6		14			11	1		3							24
		2	4		13		9	11	12			8^{2}		5	7^{3}				14	6					10	1		3^{1}							25
		2	3	12■				10	11			5^{2}			6					7		14		9	8^{3}	1		4^{1}	13						26
1		3	4		14	6^{1}	5^{2}	11	10	12		8			13					7		2^{3}			9										27
1		3	4			7	6	9^{2}	11^{3}						12					8		14		2^{1}	10		5■			13					28
1		3	4	7	5^{1}	8			10						14					9	12	13		2	6^{3}					11^{2}					29
1		3	4	5	6	7			12			9^{1}								8	14				11		2^{3}		13	10^{2}					30
1		3	4			6			10^{1}			8			12					7	11				9		5	2							31
1		2	3			6	14				12				8					7^{3}	10			9^{2}	11^{1}		5	4	13						32
1		3	4		13	7	6		10	14	5	11^{2}		2^{1}						8^{3}					9				12						33
1		3	4				6^{3}		11	12	5	10		2^{2}	7	13				9	8^{1}	14													34
1		2	3						11	13		9		5	14	8^{3}				7					10^{2}			4			6^{1}	12			35
1		3	4				13		11^{3}	10		6		2		8^{2}				7	14				12			5				9^{1}			36
			3							10	5				6	7^{2}					14	2			11	1	9^{1}	4			13	8^{3}	12		37
1	14	3^{3}					8^{1}					9		2^{2}							11				10		13	4			6	12	5	7	38

HIBERNIAN

Year Formed: 1875. *Ground & Address:* Easter Road Stadium, 12 Albion Place, Edinburgh EH7 5QG. *Telephone:* 0131 661 2159. *Fax:* 0131 659 6488. *E-mail:* club@hibernianfc.co.uk *Website:* www.hibernianfc.co.uk
Ground Capacity: 20,421 (all seated). *Size of Pitch:* 105m × 68m.
Chairman: Ronald Gordon. *Chief Executive:* Leean Dempster.
Head Coach: Paul Heckingbottom. *Assistant Head Coach:* Robbie Stockdale.
Club Nickname: 'Hibs'; 'Hibees'.
Previous Grounds: Meadows 1875-78; Powderhall 1878-79; Mayfield 1879-80; First Easter Road 1880-92; Second Easter Road 1892.
Record Attendance: 65,860 v Hearts, Division I, 2 January 1950.
Record Transfer Fee received: £4,400,000 for Scott Brown from Celtic (2007).
Record Transfer Fee paid: £700,000 for Ulises de la Cruz to LDU Quito (2001).
Record Victory: 15-1 v Pebbles Rovers, Scottish Cup 2nd rd, 11 February 1961.
Record Defeat: 0-10 v Rangers, Division I, 24 December 1898.
Most Capped Player: Lawrie Reilly, 38, Scotland.
Most League Appearances: 446: Arthur Duncan, 1969-84.
Most League Goals in Season (Individual): 42: Joe Baker, 1959-60.
Most Goals Overall (Individual): 233: Lawrie Reilly, 1945-58.

HIBERNIAN – SPFL LADBROKES PREMIERSHIP 2018–19 LEAGUE RECORD

Match No.	Date	Venue	Opponents	Result	H/T Score	Lg Pos.	Goalscorers	Attendance
1	Aug 5	H	Motherwell	W 3-0	2-0	2	Mallan [30], Shaw [45], Boyle [51]	17,494
2	12	A	St Johnstone	D 1-1	0-1	2	Shaw [51]	4637
3	25	H	Aberdeen	D 1-1	0-1	2	Maclaren [86]	18,583
4	Sept 1	A	Livingston	L 1-2	0-0	6	Horgan [52]	5305
5	15	H	Kilmarnock	W 3-2	2-2	5	Mallan [12], Gray [23], Kamberi (pen) [78]	17,622
6	22	A	Dundee	W 3-0	0-0	2	Kamberi [51], Boyle [54], Agyepong [88]	6076
7	29	A	St Mirren	W 1-0	1-0	2	Gray [14]	6082
8	Oct 6	H	Hamilton A	W 6-0	3-0	2	Boyle [25], Mallan 2 [34, 71], Hyndman [39], Kilgallon (og) [90], Kamberi [90]	16,857
9	20	A	Celtic	L 2-4	0-2	5	Kamberi [63], Boyle [73]	58,452
10	31	A	Hearts	D 0-0	0-0	5		19,410
11	Nov 3	H	St Johnstone	L 0-1	0-0	6		17,307
12	9	A	Aberdeen	L 0-1	0-1	7		15,629
13	24	H	Dundee	D 2-2	2-1	7	Kusunga (og) [1], Porteous [30]	16,190
14	Dec 1	A	Kilmarnock	L 0-3	0-2	8		6036
15	5	H	St Mirren	D 2-2	0-1	8	Shaw [56], Porteous [73]	15,096
16	8	A	Hamilton A	W 1-0	0-0	8	Shaw [65]	2169
17	16	H	Celtic	W 2-0	1-0	8	Slivka [1], Kamberi [59]	18,142
18	19	H	Rangers	D 0-0	0-0	8		18,662
19	22	H	Livingston	D 1-1	0-0	7	Porteous [80]	17,056
20	26	A	Rangers	D 1-1	0-1	8	McGregor [86]	49,885
21	29	H	Hearts	L 0-1	0-1	8		20,200
22	Jan 23	A	Motherwell	L 0-1	0-1	8		4090
23	27	A	St Mirren	W 3-1	0-1	7	Shaw [61], McGregor [70], Mallan [87]	5650
24	Feb 2	H	Aberdeen	L 1-2	1-2	7	Shaw [9]	16,269
25	6	A	Celtic	L 0-2	0-1	7		56,730
26	16	H	Hamilton A	W 2-0	2-0	7	Kamberi [17], McNulty (pen) [39]	16,265
27	22	A	Dundee	W 4-2	2-1	6	Kamberi [26], McNulty 2 [39, 63], Mallan [66]	6450
28	27	A	St Johnstone	W 2-1	0-1	6	McNulty 2 (1 pen) [65 (p), 84]	4136
29	Mar 8	H	Rangers	D 1-1	0-1	6	Kamberi [76]	20,065
30	16	H	Motherwell	W 2-0	2-0	6	McNulty (pen) [19], Gray [39]	17,184
31	29	A	Livingston	W 2-1	0-0	5	Hanlon [71], Mallan [75]	4774
32	Apr 3	H	Kilmarnock	D 0-0	0-0	6		16,588
33	6	A	Hearts	W 2-1	1-1	5	Horgan 2 [28, 56]	19,667
34	21	H	Celtic	D 0-0	0-0	5		19,472
35	28	H	Hearts	D 1-1	0-0	5	Berra (og) [69]	19,395
36	May 5	A	Rangers	L 0-1	0-1	5		49,662
37	11	A	Kilmarnock	L 0-1	0-1	5		7484
38	19	H	Aberdeen	L 1-2	1-1	5	McNulty [26]	18,631

Final League Position: 5

Honours

League Champions: Division I 1902-03, 1947-48, 1950-51, 1951-52; First Division 1980-81, 1998-99; Championship 2016-17; Division II 1893-94, 1894-95, 1932-33.
Runners-up: Division I 1896-97, 1946-47, 1949-50, 1952-53, 1973-74, 1974-75; Championship 2014-15.
Scottish Cup Winners: 1887, 1902, 2016; *Runners-up:* 1896, 1914, 1923, 1924, 1947, 1958, 1972, 1979, 2001, 2012, 2013.
League Cup Winners: 1972-73, 1991-92, 2006-07; *Runners-up:* 1950-51, 1968-69, 1974-75, 1985-86, 1993-94, 2003-04, 2015-16.
Drybrough Cup Winners: 1972-73, 1973-74.

European: *European Cup:* 6 matches (1955-56 semi-finals). *Cup Winners' Cup:* 6 matches (1972-73). *UEFA Cup:* 64 matches (*Fairs Cup:* 1960-61 semi-finals, 1961-62, 1962-63, 1965-66, 1967-68, 1968-69, 1970-71. *UEFA Cup:* 1973-74, 1974-75, 1975-76, 1976-77, 1978-79, 1989-90, 1992-93, 2001-02, 2005-06. *Europa League:* 10 matches 2010-11, 2013-14, 2018-19).

Club colours: Shirt: Green with white sleeves. Shorts: White. Socks: Green.

Goalscorers: *League (51):* Kamberi 8 (1 pen), Mallan 7, McNulty 7 (3 pens), Shaw 6, Boyle 4, Gray 3, Horgan 3, Porteous 3, McGregor 2, Agyepong 1, Hanlon 1, Hyndman 1, Maclaren 1, Slivka 1, own goals 3.
William Hill Scottish FA Cup (7): Horgan 3, Kamberi 1, Mallan 1 (1 pen), McNulty 1, Slivka 1
Betfred Scottish League Cup (3): Gray 1, Horgan 1, Mallan 1.
Irn-Bru Scottish League Challenge (2): Mackie 1, Murray F 1.
Europa League: (16): Kamberi 4 (1 pen), Mallan 4, Ambrose 2, Gray 2, McGinn 2, Shaw 1, Stevenson 1.

Bogdan A 17+1	Porteous R 16	Ambrose E 21	Hanlon P 26	Gray D 22+2	Mallan S 36+1	Bartley M 7+6	McGinn J 1	Stevenson L 33+1	Boyle M 17+1	Shaw O 11+15	Slivka V 19+10	Maclaren J 6+6	Swanson D —+2	Laidlaw R 1	Whittaker S 12+3	Hyndman E 10+5	Kamberi F 30+3	Horgan D 26+8	Allan L 2+4	Agyepong T 1+8	Milligan M 25+3	Gullan J —+2	Nelom M 2+1	McGregor D 22+2	Mackie S 3+7	Mavrias C 2	Marciano O 20	Omeonga S 11+4	Gauld R 4+1	Bigirimana G —+1	McNulty M 13+2	Johnson D —+1	Murray F 2+4	Spector J —+1	*Match No.*
1	2	3	4	5^{2}	6^{3}	7	8^{1}	9	10	11	12	13	14																						1
	2	3	4		7			9	5	10^{3}		11^{1}	14	1	6	8^{2}	12	13																	2
1	3	2	4	5^{1}	8			7^{2}	11	10		12			6	13		9																	3
1	3	2	4		8^{2}			9	5	14		10^{3}			6	12		7	11^{1}	13															4
1	4	3		2	9			5	10^{2}			14			6^{3}	8^{1}	11	7		12	13														5
1		3	4	2^{3}	8			5	7^{2}	14	9				12		11^{1}	10		13	6														6
1	4	3		2^{2}	8			5		13	14				12	9^{1}	11	10		7^{3}	6														7
1	4	3		2^{3}	9			5	7^{1}		10					8^{2}	11	12			6	13	14												8
1		3			7			5	6		10	13			12	9^{2}	11	8			2^{1}			4											9
1		3			9^{2}	6		5	7^{1}	12	8				2	13	11■				10			4											10
1		3			9	6		5	10	14	13	11			2^{1}	8^{2}		7^{3}			4			12											11
1	4	5			8			9^{3}	7		6^{1}	11^{2}					10	13	12		3			2	14										12
1	3	2	4		8	13		9	5			11^{1}					10	6		12^{3}	7^{2}	14													13
1	2	6	4		8			14	10	13					5^{1}		11	12			7^{2}		9	3^{3}											14
1	4	3			8	7^{1}		5	6	10	13	14					11^{2}	9^{3}			12					2									15
	4	3			9			5	6^{1}	11	7					12	10	13					8^{2}			2	1								16
	4	3			8			5		11^{2}	6^{1}				2	9	10	7	13						12		1								17
12	4	3			6			5	14	11^{2}	7				2	8	10	9^{1}			13						1^{3}								18
1	4	2							5	10^{2}	6	14				8^{1}	12	13	11^{3}		7			3	9										19
1		2	4	14	7			9^{1}	6		5	10^{3}				8^{2}	11	13						3	12										20
1		2	4	13	7					11	6^{1}				5	12	10^{2}	9^{3}	14					3	8										21
	2^{1}		4		9	5^{3}				14	13				6		11	7						3	12		1	8^{2}	10						22
			4	2	9^{1}	6				12	8				5		11	10^{2}						3	14		1	13	7^{3}						23
			4	5	8^{2}	7^{3}		9		11^{1}	6						10				3			2			1		14	12	13				24
			4	2^{2}	13			5		10^{1}	8						11				6			3	7		1		9^{3}		12	14			25
			4	2	8			5		13	7						11^{2}	9^{3}	14		6			3			1	12			10^{1}				26
			4	2	9			5		13	8						11	6^{1}			7			3			1	12			10^{2}				27
			4	2	6^{3}	13		5			8■						11	9^{2}			7			3	14		1	12			10^{1}				28
			4	2	8	12		5									11	7^{1}			6			3■			1	9			10				29
			4	2^{2}	6	13		5			8^{3}						11	7^{1}			3				12		1	9			10		14		30
			4	2	6			5		14	12						10	9^{2}			7			3			1	8^{3}			11^{1}		13		31
			4	2	6			5		13	8^{3}						10^{2}	7^{1}			3			12			1	9			11		14		32
			4	2^{1}	8	12		5			14						10^{3}	7^{2}			6			3			1	9			11			13	33
			4	2	8			5		13	12						11^{1}	7^{3}		14	6^{2}			3			1	9			10				34
			4	2	8			5			12						11^{2}	7^{1}		13	6			3			1	9			10				35
			4	2	7			5									12	8^{2}		13	6^{1}			3			1	10	9^{3}		11		14		36
			4	2	8			5		13							10^{3}	12		14	7			3			1	9^{2}			11^{1}		6		37
			4	2	9	12		5		13	14							7^{1}			6^{3}			3			1	8^{2}			11		10		38

INVERNESS CALEDONIAN THISTLE

Year Formed: 1994. *Ground & Address:* Tulloch Caledonian Stadium, Stadium Road, Inverness IV1 1FF. *Telephone:* 01463 222880. *Fax:* 01463 227479. *E-mail:* info@ictfc.co.uk *Website:* ictfc.co.uk
Ground Capacity: 7,780 (all seated). *Size of Pitch:* 105m × 68m.
Chairman: Graham Rae. *Chief Executive:* Scot Gardiner.
Manager: John Robertson. *Assistant Manager:* Scott Kellacher.
Club Nicknames: 'Caley Thistle'; 'Caley Jags'; 'ICT'.
Record Attendance: 7,753 v Rangers, SPL, 20 January 2008.
Record Transfer Fee received: £400,000 for Marius Niculae to Dinamo Bucharest (July 2008).
Record Transfer Fee paid: £65,000 for John Rankin from Ross Co (July 2006).
Record Victory: 8-1 v Annan Ath, Scottish Cup 3rd rd, 24 January 1998; 7-0 v Ayr U, First Division, 24 April 2010; 7-0 v Arbroath, League Cup Northern Section Group C, 30 July 2016.
Record Defeats: 0-6 v Airdrieonians, First Division, 21 Sep 2000; 0-6 v Celtic, League Cup 3rd rd, 22 Sep 2010; 0-6 v Celtic, Scottish Premiership, 27 April 2014; 0-6 v Celtic, Scottish Cup 5th rd, 11 February 2017.
Most Capped Player: Richard Hastings, 38 (59), Canada.
Most League Appearances: 490: Ross Tokely, 1995-2012.
Most League Goals in Season: 27: Iain Stewart, 1996-97; Denis Wyness, 2002-03.
Most Goals Overall (Individual): 118: Denis Wyness, 2000-03, 2005-08.

INVERNESS CALEDONIAN THISTLE – SPFL LADBROKES CHAMPIONSHIP 2018–19 LEAGUE RECORD

Match No.	*Date*	*Venue*	*Opponents*	*Result*		*H/T Score*	*Lg Pos.*	*Goalscorers*	*Attendance*
1	Aug 4	A	Falkirk	W	1-0	-	3	Oakley 10	4538
2	11	H	Ayr U	D	0-0	0-0	4		2376
3	25	H	Alloa Ath	D	2-2	1-1	5	McKay 10, Welsh (pen) 48	2269
4	Sept 1	A	Dunfermline Ath	W	3-0	0-0	2	Rooney 51, Polworth 72, Oakley 83	5138
5	15	H	Partick Thistle	W	3-2	3-0	1	White 11, Rooney 23, Welsh (pen) 32	2424
6	22	A	Ross Co	D	0-0	0-0	2		6402
7	29	H	Queen of the South	D	0-0	0-0	3		2029
8	Oct 6	H	Greenock Morton	D	1-1	1-1	3	White 45	2186
9	20	A	Dundee U	D	1-1	0-0	3	White 72	5628
10	27	A	Alloa Ath	D	0-0	0-0	5		644
11	30	H	Dunfermline Ath	D	2-2	2-2	4	Calder 20, White 34	1994
12	Nov 3	H	Ross Co	D	2-2	2-2	5	Oakley 19, Rooney 30	4353
13	10	A	Partick Thistle	W	1-0	0-0	4	Walsh 71	2509
14	17	A	Queen of the South	D	3-3	0-1	4	McCart 71, Austin 74, Welsh (pen) 81	1233
15	Dec 1	H	Falkirk	L	2-3	1-2	4	Walsh 6, Oakley 61	2260
16	15	H	Dundee U	D	1-1	1-0	5	Walsh 18	2464
17	22	A	Greenock Morton	W	2-1	1-0	4	Walsh 17, Doran 49	1608
18	29	A	Ross Co	L	1-2	1-1	4	White 31	6313
19	Jan 5	H	Queen of the South	L	1-2	0-0	6	Walsh 69	2225
20	12	H	Ayr U	W	1-0	0-0	5	White 64	2283
21	26	A	Falkirk	D	2-2	2-1	5	Rooney 12, Doran 45	5843
22	29	A	Ayr U	W	3-2	3-0	4	Austin 2 9, 12, Polworth 18	1559
23	Feb 2	H	Partick Thistle	L	1-2	0-2	4	McCauley 77	2171
24	16	A	Dunfermline Ath	L	0-1	0-0	4		4497
25	23	H	Greenock Morton	W	1-0	1-0	4	Tremarco 11	2413
26	26	A	Dundee U	L	0-1	0-0	4		4737
27	Mar 9	A	Queen of the South	W	2-0	2-0	5	Doran 7, McKay 20	1066
28	22	A	Partick Thistle	W	2-1	0-0	4	Doran 65, Walsh 81	2149
29	26	H	Alloa Ath	W	3-2	2-0	3	Doran 29, Welsh (pen) 35, White 61	2006
30	30	H	Falkirk	D	0-0	0-0	4		2817
31	Apr 2	H	Ross Co	L	1-2	1-2	4	Tremarco 24	3795
32	6	A	Ayr U	W	1-0	0-0	3	McKay 66	1566
33	16	A	Greenock Morton	D	2-2	1-2	4	McDonald 18, McCauley 88	1315
34	20	H	Dundee U	L	0-2	0-1	4		2971
35	27	A	Alloa Ath	W	2-1	0-1	4	Rooney 68, Trafford 73	826
36	May 4	H	Dunfermline Ath	W	1-0	1-0	3	Austin 35	2828

Final League Position: 3

Honours
League Champions: First Division 2003-04, 2009-10; Third Division 1996-97.
Runners-up: Second Division 1998-99.
Scottish Cup Winners: 2015; Semi-finals 2003, 2004, 2019.
League Cup Runners-up: 2013-14.
League Challenge Cup Winners: 2003-04, 2017-18; *Runners-up:* 1999-2000, 2009-10.

European: *Europa League:* 4 matches (2015-16).

Club colours: Shirt: Blue and red vertical halves. Shorts: Blue. Socks: Blue with red trim.

Goalscorers: *League (48):* White 7, Walsh 6, Doran 5, Rooney 5, Austin 4, Oakley 4, Welsh 4 (4 pens), McKay 3, McCauley 2, Polworth 2, Tremarco 2, Calder 1, McCart 1, McDonald 1, Trafford 1.
William Hill Scottish FA Cup (17): White 6, Doran 4, Walsh 2, Chalmers 1, McKay 1, Polworth 1, Rooney 1, own goal 1.
Betfred Scottish League Cup (9): Austin 3, Doran 2, Walsh 2, Mackay 1, Oakley 1.
Irn-Bru Scottish League Challenge (1): White 1.
Play-Offs (4): White 2 (1 pen), Donaldson 1, Trafford 1.

Ridgers M 30	Rooney S 28 + 3	McKay B 32 + 1	Donaldson C 28 + 2	Tremarco C 22	Polworth L 34 + 1	Chalmers J 35 + 1	Trafford C 16 + 8	Walsh T 25 + 5	Austin N 9 + 14	Oakley G 10 + 3	Mackay D 1 + 11	Welsh S 26 + 2	White J 26 + 10	Doran A 27 + 6	Calder R 3 + 6	McCart J 22 + 4	Macgregor R — + 5	McHattie K 9 + 1	Mackay C 6	McCauley D 2 + 11	McDonald A 5 + 5	*Match No.*
1	2	3	4	5	6	7	8	9^{3}	10^{1}	11^{2}	12	13	14									1
1	2	3	4	5	7	9	8^{2}	6^{1}	11^{3}	10	13		12	14								2
1	2	3	4	5	6	8		9	11^{3}	10^{2}		7^{1}	12	14	13							3
1	2	3	4	5	8^{1}	6	14	10		12		7	11^{2}	9^{3}	13							4
1	2^{1}	3	4	5	6	7		10		13		8	11^{3}	9^{2}	14	12						5
1	2	3	4	5	10	8		6^{1}			12	7	11	9								6
1	2	3	4	5	10	8		6^{3}	12		14	7	11^{2}	9^{1}	13							7
1	2	3	4	5	9	6^{2}		8	14		12	7	11^{3}	10^{1}	13							8
1	2	3	4■	5	9	7		8^{3}			13	6^{1}	11	12	10^{2}	14						9
1	2	3		5^{3}	9	7		8^{2}	14		13	6	11	10^{1}	12	4						10
1	2	4	3		10^{1}	12	8^{2}	9^{3}	13		6	7	11	14	5							11
1	2^{1}	3	4		10	8		9^{2}		11^{3}	14	7	13	6	5	12						12
1		2	3		9	5	6	8		11^{1}		7	12	10		4						13
1		2	4		9	5	7^{1}	8	13	11^{3}		6	12	10^{2}		3	14					14
1	2	3	4		10	8	13	6		11^{1}		7^{2}	12	9^{3}		5	14					15
1	2	3	4		10	8	13	6		11^{3}		7^{1}	12	9^{2}		5	14					16
1	2	3	4		9	7	13	8		11^{2}		6^{3}	12	10^{1}		5	14					17
1	2■	3	4		9	6		8	12		13	7^{1}	11	10^{2}		5						18
1		2	3	5^{2}	10^{3}	8		6	12			7	11	9^{1}		4	14	13				19
1			3	4	10^{1}	7	13	6			12	8	11	9^{2}		2		5				20
	2	6		5	9	3			10^{2}	12		8	7^{1}	11^{3}		4			1	13	14	21
	2	4		5	6	8	13		10^{3}	11^{2}		7	12			3			1	14	9^{1}	22
	2^{3}	3	13		6	8	12		10^{2}			7	11			4		5	1	14	9^{1}	23
1	2	3		5^{1}		7	6	8	13			14	11	9^{3}		4				10^{2}	12	24
1	2	3	12	5	10^{2}	8	14					7	11	9		4^{3}				13	6^{1}	25
1	2	3	4		6	9^{1}	7^{3}		10		14	8	11	12				5^{2}		13		26
1	13	2	4	5	6	10	8^{1}					9	11	7^{2}		3				12		27
1	13	2	4	5	10	6	8^{1}	12				7	11	9^{2}		3						28
1	2		3		10	6^{1}	8	12	14			7^{2}	11	9^{3}		4		5		13		29
1		9	4	2	6	3^{2}	10	12	13				8^{1}	7		5		11				30
1	13	2^{1}	3	5^{7}	10	8	7■	6^{3}	12				11	9		4					14	31
1	2	12	3^{3}	4	8	7		6^{1}	10^{2}				11	9				5		14	13	32
	2	3			9	7	6^{3}	12	13				11	10^{1}		4		5	1	14	8^{2}	33
	2	3■			10^{3}	8	7	6^{1}	12				11	9^{2}		4		5	1	14	13	34
	2		4	5	9^{1}	3	6	14	12				11	10^{2}		7			1	13	8^{3}	35
1	2	3	4^{3}		13	8	7^{1}	6	10^{2}				11	14		12		5		9		36

KILMARNOCK

Year Formed: 1869. *Ground & Address:* Rugby Park, Kilmarnock KA1 2DP. *Telephone:* 01563 545300. *Fax:* 01563 522181. *E-mail:* info@kilmarnockfc.co.uk *Website:* www.kilmarnockfc.co.uk
Ground Capacity: 18,128 (all seated). *Size of Pitch:* 102m × 67m.
Chief Executive: Kirsten Robertson. *Director:* Billy Bowie.
Manager: Angelo Alessio. *Assistant Manager:* Alex Dyer. *Coach:* Massimo Donati.
Club Nickname: 'Killie'.
Previous Grounds: Rugby Park (Dundonald Road); The Grange; Holm Quarry; Rugby Park 1899.
Record Attendance: 35,995 v Rangers, Scottish Cup Quarter-final, 10 March 1962.
Record Transfer Fee received: £1,900,000 for Steven Naismith to Rangers (2007).
Record Transfer Fee paid: £340,000 for Paul Wright from St Johnstone (1995).
Record Victory: 11-1 v Paisley Academical, Scottish Cup 1st rd, 18 January 1930.
Record Defeat: 1-9 v Celtic, Division I, 13 August 1938.
Most Capped Player: Joe Nibloe, 11, Scotland.
Most League Appearances: 481: Alan Robertson, 1972-88.
Most League Goals in Season (Individual): 34: Harry 'Peerie' Cunningham 1927-28; Andy Kerr 1960-61.
Most Goals Overall (Individual): 148: Willy Culley, 1912-23.

KILMARNOCK – SPFL LADBROKES PREMIERSHIP 2018–19 LEAGUE RECORD

Match No.	Date	Venue	Opponents	Result	H/T Score	Lg Pos.	Goalscorers	Attendance
1	Aug 4	H	St Johnstone	W 2-0	0-0	3	Boyd, S [58], Ndjoli [85]	4644
2	11	A	Livingston	D 0-0	0-0	2		2586
3	25	H	Hearts	L 0-1	0-0	5		6239
4	Sept 1	A	Aberdeen	W 2-0	1-0	2	Brophy [44], Stewart [69]	14,248
5	15	A	Hibernian	L 2-3	2-2	7	Brophy [26], Stewart [44]	17,622
6	23	H	Celtic	W 2-1	0-1	5	Burke [64], Findlay [90]	10,988
7	29	H	Motherwell	W 3-1	2-1	3	Burke [39], Stewart [43], Brophy (pen) [59]	5090
8	Oct 6	A	Dundee	W 2-1	1-1	3	Boyle (og) [17], Brophy (pen) [54]	5158
9	20	A	St Mirren	W 2-1	0-1	3	Power [56], Tshibola [68]	5889
10	27	H	Hamilton A	D 1-1	1-1	2	McKenzie [44]	5023
11	31	A	Rangers	D 1-1	1-1	3	Stewart [15]	49,279
12	Nov 4	H	Aberdeen	L 1-2	1-0	4	Boyd, K (pen) [32]	5270
13	10	A	Hearts	W 1-0	0-0	3	Millen [73]	17,417
14	24	A	St Johnstone	D 0-0	0-0	4		3559
15	Dec 1	H	Hibernian	W 3-0	2-0	2	Brophy 2 (1 pen) [6, 34 (p)], Stewart [90]	6036
16	5	H	Livingston	W 2-0	2-0	1	Stewart 2 [3, 20]	4143
17	8	A	Celtic	L 1-5	0-4	2	Brophy (pen) [52]	58,457
18	15	H	Dundee	W 3-1	0-0	1	Broadfoot [54], Kusunga (og) [66], Stewart [79]	4668
19	22	A	Hamilton A	D 1-1	1-1	4	Brophy [7]	3401
20	26	A	Motherwell	W 1-0	1-0	3	Jones [40]	5426
21	29	H	St Mirren	W 2-1	2-1	3	Findlay [4], Jones [11]	7131
22	Jan 23	H	Rangers	W 2-1	1-1	2	Brophy [22], Jones [66]	12,374
23	26	A	Aberdeen	D 0-0	0-0	2		15,560
24	Feb 1	H	Hearts	L 1-2	1-2	3	Jones (pen) [45]	5552
25	6	A	Dundee	D 2-2	1-2	4	McAleny [18], Burke [54]	4694
26	17	H	Celtic	L 0-1	0-0	4		11,916
27	23	A	Livingston	L 0-1	0-1	4		2569
28	Mar 2	H	Motherwell	D 0-0	0-0	4		6215
29	11	A	St Mirren	W 1-0	0-0	4	Millar [87]	4458
30	16	A	Rangers	D 1-1	1-0	4	McAleny [29]	49,527
31	30	H	Hamilton A	W 5-0	1-0	3	Taylor [5], McAleny [56], Mulumbu [63], Burke [84], Ndjoli [90]	4762
32	Apr 3	A	Hibernian	D 0-0	0-0	3		16,588
33	6	H	St Johnstone	W 2-0	2-0	3	Kane (og) [17], Boyd, K (pen) [43]	4685
34	20	H	Aberdeen	L 0-1	0-0	4		6531
35	27	A	Celtic	L 0-1	0-0	4		58,851
36	May 4	A	Hearts	W 1-0	0-0	3	Findlay [86]	17,103
37	11	H	Hibernian	W 1-0	1-0	3	Brophy (pen) [32]	7484
38	19	H	Rangers	W 2-1	1-0	3	Burke [9], Brophy (pen) [89]	12,248

Final League Position: 3

Honours
League Champions: Division I 1964-65;. Division II 1897-98, 1898-99.
Runners-up: Division I 1959-60, 1960-61, 1962-63, 1963-64; First Division 1975-76, 1978-79, 1981-82, 1992-93; Division II 1953-54, 1973-74; Second Division 1989-90.
Scottish Cup Winners: 1920, 1929, 1997; *Runners-up:* 1898, 1932, 1938, 1957, 1960.
League Cup Winners: 2011-12; *Runners-up:* 1952-53, 1960-61, 1962-63, 2000-01, 2006-07.

European: *European Cup:* 4 matches (1965-66). *Cup Winners' Cup:* 4 matches (1997-98). *UEFA Cup:* 32 matches (*Fairs Cup:* 1964-65, 1966-67 semi-finals, 1969-70, 1970-71. *UEFA Cup:* 1998-99, 1999-2000, 2001-02).

Club colours: Shirt: Blue with white stripes. Shorts: White. Socks: Blue.

Goalscorers: *League (50):* Brophy 11 (6 pens), Stewart 8, Burke 5, Jones 4 (1 pen), Findlay 3, McAleny 3, Boyd K 2 (2 pens), Ndjoli 2, Boyd S 1, Broadfoot 1, McKenzie 1, Millar 1, Millen 1, Mulumbu 1, Power 1, Taylor 1, Tshibola 1, own goals 3.
William Hill Scottish FA Cup (2): Burke 1, Findlay 1.
Betfred Scottish League Cup (10): Boyd K 4 (1 pen), Ndjoli 3, Brophy 1, Erwin 1, own goal 1.
Irn-Bru Scottish League Challenge (1): Thomas 1.

MacDonald J 13	O'Donnell S 36 + 1	Broadfoot K 25 + 2	Boyd S 16 + 1	Taylor G 36	Burke C 30 + 5	Power A 35 + 1	Dicker G 30 + 5	Jones J 25 + 3	Erwin L 1	Boyd K 10 + 9	Ndjoli M 5 + 19	Wilson I — + 6	Brophy E 23 + 6	Kiltie G — + 3	Findlay S 31	Thomas D — + 1	Tshibola A 21 + 6	Stewart G 16	McKenzie R 14 + 10	Byrne J — + 5	Enobakhare B 2 + 4	Bachmann D 25	Millen R 2 + 2	Millar L 2 + 11	McAleny C 6 + 5	Mulumbu Y 9 + 1	Bruce A 3 + 1	Waters C 2	MacKey D — + 1	*Match No.*
1	2	3	4	5	6^2	7	8	9	10^3	11^1	12	13	14																	1
1	2	3	4	5	6^2	7	8	9		11^1	10^3	12	13	14																2
1	2	3		5^2	9	7	8■	11		10^1	6^3	12	13		4	14														3
1	2	3		5	6	8		9^3			13	12	11		4		7^1	10^2	14											4
1	2	3		5^1	6^3	7		9		13			11		4		8	10^2		12	14									5
1	2	3		5	6	7	12	9^2			13		10^1		4		8	11^3	14											6
1	2	3	4	5	6^2	8	12	9^3			14		10^1				7	11			13									7
1	2		4	5	6	7	12	9^1					11^2		3		8^3	10		13	14									8
1	2	3		5	6^1	8	13			12			10^2		4		7	11^3	14		9									9
1	2		3	5		7^3	14			12			11^2		4		8	10	6^1	13	9									10
1	2	3		5	8^1	7	6	10^2			12				4		9	11			13									11
1	2	3		5	8	7^3	6	10		11^1	12			14	4		9^2			13										12
		3		5	6^3	9	8	13		11^2	10^1	14			4		7		12			1	2							13
	2	3	12	5	6	8	7	13		10^3	9^1				4^2			11		14		1								14
	2	3	4	5	13	7	8	9					10^2				12	11	6^1			1								15
	2	3^2	4	5	6	7	8	9			14	13	10^3				12	11^1				1								16
	2		3	5		7	8	10			13		12		4		6^2	11^1	9			1								17
	2	3		5	6^2	7	8	9			12		10^1	13	4			11				1								18
	2		3	5	6^2	7	8	9		12	14		11^1		4		13	10^3				1								19
	2		3	5		7	6	10^2		11^3	14		13		4		9^1	8	12			1								20
	2^2		3	5	9^3	7	0	6			13		11^1		4			10	14			1	12							21
	2	12	3	5	9	8	7	11^2			13		10^1		4		6					1								22
	2		3	5	9^1	8	7	11^2		12■	14		10^3		4		6		13			1								23
	2	14	3	5^1	9^3	8	7	11			10				4		6^2		13			1		12						24
	2	3		5	9	6	7	11^1			14				4		8^2					1		13	10^3	12				25
	2	3■	4	5	6^1	8	7	9					11^3						14			1		13	10^2		12			26
	13		4		12			9		10^3			11		3		7		6			1	2^1	14		8		5^2		27
	2	3			9	8	7	13					12		4		6		11^2			1			10^1			5		28
	2	4		5	6	8	7	9^2					10^1		3		14		11^3			1		12	13					29
	2	3		5	8	7^2	6						11^1		4		13		10			1		14	12	9^3				30
	2	3		5	12		7			10	14				4		6		11^1			1		13	9^3	8^2				31
	2	3		5	13	14	7	9		12					4		11^2		6^1			1			10^3	8				32
	2	3		5	7^1	8	6			11^2	13				4				10^3			1	14	12		9				33
	2	3■		5	9^1	6	7			13			10^2		4■				11■			1		14	12	8^3				34
	2			5	6^3	8	4			14	12		11^2				7		13			1		9^1	10		3			35
	2			5	12	8	7				13		10^3		4		14		9^1			1		11^2		6	3			36
	2			5	9^1	6	7			14			10^3		4^2				11			1		13	12	8	3			37
1^1	2	3		5	9^2	6	7						10		4				11					13	14	8^3			12	38

LIVINGSTON

Year Formed: 1974. *Ground:* Tony Macaroni Arena, Almondvale Stadium, Alderstone Road, Livingston EH54 7DN.
Telephone: 01506 417000. *Fax:* 01506 429948.
E-mail: lfcreception@livingstonfc.co.uk *Website:* livingstonfc.co.uk
Ground Capacity: 9,865 (all seated). *Size of Pitch:* 98m × 69m.
Chairman: Robert Wilson. *Secretary:* Brian Ewing.
Manager: Gary Holt. *Assistant Manager:* David Martindale.
Club Nickname: 'Livi Lions'.
Previous Ground: Meadowbank Stadium (as Meadowbank Thistle).
Record Attendance: 10,024 v Celtic, Premier League, 18 August 2001.
Record Transfer Fee received: £1,000,000 for David Fernandez to Celtic (June 2002).
Record Transfer Fee paid: £120,000 for Wes Hoolahan from Shelbourne (December 2005).
Record Victory: 8-0 v Stranraer, League Cup, 1st rd, 31 July 2012.
Record Defeat: 0-8 v Hamilton A. Division II, 14 December 1974.
Most League Appearances: 446: Walter Boyd, 1979-89.
Most League Goals in Season (Individual): 22: Leigh Griffiths, 2008-09; Iain Russell, 2010-11; Liam Buchanan, 2016-17.
Most Goals Overall (Individual): 64: David Roseburgh, 1986-93.

LIVINGSTON – SPFL LADBROKES PREMIERSHIP 2018–19 LEAGUE RECORD

Match No.	*Date*	*Venue*	*Opponents*	*Result*		*H/T Score*	*Lg Pos.*	*Goalscorers*	*Attendance*
1	Aug 4	A	Celtic	L	1-3	0-2	10	Robinson 90	58,778
2	11	H	Kilmarnock	D	0-0	0-0	9		2586
3	25	A	St Mirren	W	2-0	2-0	6	Hamilton 14, Lithgow 36	4347
4	Sept 1	H	Hibernian	W	2-1	0-0	3	Byrne 58, Pitman 70	5305
5	15	H	Hamilton A	W	1-0	1-0	3	Lawless 3	1342
6	22	A	Hearts	D	0-0	0-0	3		17,798
7	30	H	Rangers	W	1-0	1-0	3	Menga 34	9246
8	Oct 6	A	Motherwell	D	1-1	0-1	4	Jacobs 64	4256
9	20	H	Dundee	W	4-0	2-0	4	Gallagher 18, Halkett 43, Lawless 76, Lithgow 89	2137
10	31	H	St Johnstone	L	0-1	0-1	6		1476
11	Nov 3	A	Hamilton A	L	0-1	0-0	7		1459
12	11	H	Celtic	D	0-0	0-0	7		9016
13	24	A	Rangers	L	0-3	0-1	8		49,448
14	Dec 1	H	Motherwell	W	2-0	1-0	6	Lawless 22, Halkett 83	1982
15	5	A	Kilmarnock	L	0-2	0-2	7		4143
16	8	H	St Mirren	W	3-1	0-1	6	Pitman 50, Hardie 64, Sibbald 88	1727
17	11	A	Aberdeen	L	2-3	2-1	7	Pitman 12, McMillan 33	12,252
18	14	H	Hearts	W	5-0	0-0	5	Halkett (pen) 72, Menga 76, Hardie 2 77, 79, Byrne 86	4201
19	22	A	Hibernian	D	1-1	0-0	6	Hardie 56	17,056
20	26	A	Dundee	D	0-0	0-0	7		4905
21	29	H	Aberdeen	L	1-2	0-0	7	Hardie 89	5548
22	Jan 23	A	St Johnstone	L	0-1	0-0	7		1946
23	27	H	Rangers	L	0-3	0-1	8		9028
24	Feb 2	A	Motherwell	L	0-3	0-3	8		3839
25	6	A	Hearts	D	0-0	0-0	8		15,147
26	16	H	Dundee	L	1-2	1-0	9	Halkett 18	2321
27	23	H	Kilmarnock	W	1-0	1-0	9	Erskine 44	2569
28	Mar 2	A	St Mirren	L	0-1	0-0	9		4014
29	9	H	St Johnstone	W	3-1	1-1	9	Halkett 38, Sibbald 46, Pitman 90	1615
30	16	A	Aberdeen	D	1-1	1-1	8	Sibbald 43	14,366
31	29	H	Hibernian	L	1-2	0-0	9	Hardie (pen) 90	4774
32	Apr 3	H	Hamilton A	W	2-0	0-0	9	Hardie 46, Halkett 79	1022
33	6	A	Celtic	D	0-0	0-0	9		58,850
34	20	H	St Mirren	L	1-3	1-1	9	Robinson 20	2347
35	27	A	Hamilton A	D	3-3	0-1	9	Pitman 2 57, 71, Lawson 67	1135
36	May 4	A	St Johnstone	D	1-1	0-1	9	Halkett 84	2222
37	11	H	Dundee	L	0-1	0-1	9		1374
38	18	A	Motherwell	L	2-3	0-3	9	Tiffoney 2 80, 81	5794

Final League Position: 9

Honours
League Champions: First Division 2000-01; Second Division 1986-87, 1998-99, 2010-11; League One 2016-17; Third Division 1995-96, 2009-10.
Runners-up: Second Division 1982-83; First Division 1987-88; Championship 2017-18.
Promoted via play-offs: 2017-18 (to Premiership).
Scottish Cup: Semi-finals 2001, 2004.
League Cup Winners: 2003-04. Semi-finals 1984-85.
League Challenge Cup Winners: 2014-15; *Runners-up:* 2000-01.

European: *UEFA Cup:* 4 matches (2002-03).

Club colours: All: Amber with black trim.

Goalscorers: *League (42):* Halkett 7 (1 pen), Hardie 7 (1 pen), Pitman 6, Lawless 3, Sibbald 3, Byrne 2, Lithgow 2, Menga 2, Robinson 2, Tiffoney 2, Erskine 1, Gallagher 1, Hamilton 1, Jacobs 1, Lawson 1, McMillan 1.
William Hill Scottish FA Cup (0).
Betfred Scottish League Cup (5): Hamilton 1, McMillan 1, Miller K 1, Miller L 1, Pitman 1.
Irn-Bru Scottish League Challenge (1): Knox 1.

Kelly L 36	Gallagher D 38	Halkett C 34	Saunders S 2 + 1	Brown J 1	Byrne S 29 + 3	Pitman S 38	Robinson S 19 + 7	Kaja E 2 + 4	Miller K 2	Miller L 6 + 3	Lawless S 29 + 6	McMillan J 2 + 5	Hamilton J 2 + 11	Cadden N 4 + 8	Jacobs K 26 + 5	Lithgow A 35	Lamie R 23 + 2	Lawson S 16 + 9	Menga D 20 + 5	Hardie R 13 + 8	Burns B 3 + 5	Sibbald C 16 + 10	van Schaik H — + 1	Erskine C 8 + 2	Wylde G — + 2	Tiffoney S 1 + 7	Odofin H 7 + 6	Brown C 4 + 1	De Vita R — + 3	Stewart R 2	*Match No.*
1	2	3	4	5^{2}	6	7	8	9	10^{3}	11^{1}	12	13	14																		1
1	2	3	4		7	6	8^{1}	5^{2}	10	11^{3}	9		14	12	13																2
1	2	3			7	6	8	13			5^{1}		11^{2}	14	12	4	9	10^{3}													3
1	2	3			7	6	11^{1}	12			5^{3}		14	13	8	4	9		10^{2}												4
1	2	3			7	6	11^{1}				5^{2}				8	4	9	12	10^{3}	13	14										5
1	2	3			7	6	11^{3}				5^{1}	12	14	13	8	4	9		10^{2}												6
1	2	3			7	6	10^{2}				5^{3}				8	4	9	13	11^{1}		12	14									7
1	2	3			6	8	11^{2}				5^{1}		14	12	7	4	9	13	10^{3}												8
1	2	3			7	6	11				5^{1}	13			8^{3}	4	9	12	10^{2}			14									9
1	2	3			7	6	11^{1}	13			5^{3}				8^{2}	4	9		10		12	14									10
1	2	3			8	7		13			12	6^{2}				4	5^{3}	9	11		14	10^{1}									11
1	2	3			7^{3}	6	12				5^{2}				8	4		10	11^{1}		0	13	14								12
1	2	3			0^{3}	9	11^{2}				12		14		7	4	5	8			10^{1}	13									13
1	2	3			7	6	12				5^{2}	13	10^{3}	11^{1}	8	4	9	14													14
1	2	3			7	6					8			5^{1}		4	9	10^{2}	11^{3}	13	14	12									15
1	2	3			7	6					5	12	13		8	4	9^{2}		11^{3}	10^{1}		14									16
1	2	3			8	6	13				12	5	14		7^{1}	4			10^{2}		11^{3}	9									17
1	2^{1}	3	13		7	6	12				5		14	9^{3}	8	4			10^{2}	11											18
1	2	3			6	8	9^{3}			13	5			12	7	4		14	10^{2}	11^{1}											19
1	2	3			6	7				14	5		13■	9	8^{2}	4			10^{3}	11^{1}		12									20
1	2	3			7	6				11^{1}	5^{3}		13	12		4		14	9^{2}	10		8									21
1	4	3			8	7^{3}					5^{1}			14		2	9			10		6		11^{2}	12	13					22
1	2	3			7	6					5				8	4	9^{1}		11^{2}			14		10^{3}	12	13					23
1	3	5			4	7					6^{3}					2		14	13	11		8^{1}		10^{2}		9	12				24
1	2	3			6	7					10				12	4	9	8^{1}		11^{3}		13		14			5^{2}				25
1	2	3			7■	6	11^{1}				14				8	4	9	12		10^{2}				13			5^{3}				26
1	2	3				9	13				10				7	4	5^{1}	6				8^{2}		11^{3}		14		12			27
1	2	3				9^{3}	13				10				7	4		6^{2}		12		8^{1}		11			14	5			28
1	2	3			12	9	8								7	4		6		14		10^{2}		11^{1}			13	5^{3}			29
1	2	3			13	9	8^{1}								7	4		6^{3}		14		10		11^{2}			12	5			30
1	3				14	9	11								7	4	13	6		12		10		8^{1}			2^{3}	5^{2}			31
1	2	3				6	10^{3}				14				7	4	8^{2}	5	12	11^{1}		9							13		32
1	2	3			7	6	13				11				14	4	8^{3}	5	10^{1}			9^{2}					12				33
1	2	3■				6	8				10^{2}				7	4	13	5	14	9^{1}		11^{3}					12				34
1	3					8	9^{2}			13	11				5	4		6	12	10^{1}		7^{3}				14	2				35
	4	3			6^{1}	7				10^{2}	8				12		9	5^{3}	11	14						13	2			1	36
1	2					7				11^{2}	6				8	4	5		10^{3}	13		9				14	3^{1}		12		37
	9				8^{2}	6				11	5					3	4		13	10^{1}		7^{3}				12	2		14	1	38

MONTROSE

Year Formed: 1879. *Ground & Address:* Links Park, Wellington St, Montrose DD10 8QD. *Telephone:* 01674 673200. *Fax:* 01674 677311. *E-mail:* office@montrosefc.co.uk *Website:* www.montrosefc.co.uk
Ground Capacity: total: 4,936, (seated: 1,338). *Size of Pitch:* 100m × 64m.
Chairman: John Crawford. *Secretary:* Brian Petrie.
Manager: Stewart Petrie. *Assistant Manager:* Ross Campbell.
Club Nickname: 'The Gable Endies'.
Record Attendance: 8,983 v Dundee, Scottish Cup 3rd rd, 17 March 1973.
Record Transfer Fee received: £50,000 for Gary Murray to Hibernian (December 1980).
Record Transfer Fee paid: £17,500 for Jim Smith from Airdrieonians (February 1992).
Record Victory: 12-0 v Vale of Leithen, Scottish Cup 2nd rd, 4 January 1975.
Record Defeat: 0-13 v Aberdeen, 17 March 1951.
Most Capped Player: Alexander Keillor, 2 (6), Scotland.
Most League Appearances: 432: David Larter, 1987-98.
Most League Goals in Season (Individual): 28: Brian Third, Division II, 1972-73.
Most Goals Overall (Individual): 126: Bobby Livingstone, 1967-79.

MONTROSE – SPFL LADBROKES LEAGUE ONE 2018–19 LEAGUE RECORD

Match No.	*Date*	*Venue*	*Opponents*	*Result*	*H/T Score*	*Lg Pos.*	*Goalscorers*	*Attendance*
1	Aug 4	H	Arbroath	L 0-4	0-1	10		1374
2	11	A	Airdrieonians	W 1-0	0-0	8	Campbell, R [49]	821
3	18	H	Brechin C	W 2-1	2-1	3	Henderson [4], Campbell, R (pen) [15]	916
4	25	A	Stranraer	L 0-2	0-2	6		360
5	Sept 1	H	East Fife	L 0-2	0-2	7		569
6	15	A	Dumbarton	L 1-2	1-0	10	Johnston [42]	529
7	22	A	Raith R	D 1-1	1-0	9	Webster [28]	1534
8	29	H	Forfar Ath	D 2-2	1-2	9	Webster [30], Cavanagh [75]	715
9	Oct 6	A	Stenhousemuir	L 2-3	1-1	10	Antoniazzi [35], Steeves [89]	362
10	20	H	Airdrieonians	L 0-3	0-2	10		668
11	27	A	Brechin C	W 3-1	0-0	10	Rennie 2 [64, 88], Johnston [71]	701
12	Nov 3	H	Dumbarton	W 1-0	0-0	6	Webster [53]	549
13	10	A	Arbroath	L 0-2	0-1	9		1271
14	17	H	Stranraer	D 1-1	0-0	8	Rennie [58]	532
15	Dec 1	A	East Fife	W 2-0	1-0	7	Henderson [2], Rennie (pen) [69]	636
16	8	H	Raith R	W 3-2	1-1	4	Rennie [10], Johnston [59], Campbell, R [79]	784
17	15	A	Forfar Ath	L 1-2	1-1	5	Rennie (pen) [8]	592
18	22	H	Stenhousemuir	W 3-1	2-0	4	Antoniazzi [10], Henderson [28], Watson [67]	511
19	29	H	Arbroath	D 1-1	0-0	6	Rennie [75]	1666
20	Jan 5	A	Stranraer	W 2-1	2-0	6	Rennie 2 (2 pens) [4, 16]	317
21	12	H	East Fife	L 0-2	0-2	6		678
22	26	A	Dumbarton	D 1-1	0-0	6	Rennie (pen) [89]	521
23	Feb 2	H	Brechin C	W 5-2	3-2	5	Watson 2 [3, 29], Henderson [33], Harrington [73], Johnston [78]	693
24	9	A	Stenhousemuir	L 0-1	0-0	5		409
25	16	H	Forfar Ath	W 2-0	1-0	5	Johnston [21], Rennie (pen) [88]	845
26	23	A	Raith R	L 1-4	0-2	5	Masson [63]	1289
27	Mar 2	A	Airdrieonians	L 0-1	0-0	5		638
28	9	H	Dumbarton	L 1-3	0-2	5	Dillon [51]	574
29	23	H	Stenhousemuir	W 2-0	1-0	5	Masson [12], Rennie [90]	1224
30	30	H	Stranraer	W 3-1	2-0	5	Milne [21], Henderson [35], Watson [55]	486
31	Apr 2	A	Brechin C	W 3-0	2-0	5	Campbell, R 2 (1 pen) [9 (p), 16], Redman [76]	714
32	6	A	Arbroath	L 0-1	0-0	5		1248
33	13	A	East Fife	W 2-0	0-0	4	Watson 2 [68, 90]	652
34	20	H	Airdrieonians	W 2-1	1-0	4	Campbell, R (pen) [41], Masson [67]	738
35	27	A	Forfar Ath	L 0-1	0-0	4		850
36	May 4	H	Raith R	D 1-1	1-1	4	Webster [10]	688

Final League Position: 4

Honours
League Champions: Second Division 1984-85; League Two 2017-18.
Runners-up: Second Division 1990-91; Third Division 1994-95.
Scottish Cup: Quarter-finals 1973, 1976.
League Cup: Semi-finals 1975-76.
League Challenge Cup: Semi-finals 1992-93, 1996-97.

Club colours: Shirt: Blue. Shorts: Blue. Socks: White.

Goalscorers: *League (49):* Rennie 12 (6 pens), Campbell R 6 (3 pens), Watson 6, Henderson 5, Johnston 5, Webster 4, Masson 3, Antoniazzi 2, Cavanagh 1, Dillon 1, Harrington 1, Milne 1, Redman 1, Steeves 1.
William Hill Scottish FA Cup (4): Fotheringham 1, Rennie 1 (1 pen), Steeves 1, Watson 1.
Betfred Scottish League Cup (3): Campbell R 1, Cavanagh 1, Rennie 1.
Irn-Bru Scottish League Challenge (4): Johnston 2, Callaghan 1, Campbell I 1 (1 pen).
Play-Offs (2): Campbell R 2.

Fleming A 29	Allan M 6+3	Dillon S 33+1	Campbell I 30	Masson T 28+5	Redman J 21+5	Cregg P 27+5	Callaghan L 9+11	Steeves A 31+2	Henderson E 19+12	Rennie M 22+11	Webster G 18+7	Antoniazzi C 14+10	Johnston C 16+4	Watson P 18+6	Campbell R 11+9	Harrington R 25	Cavanagh D 3+2	Fotheringham M 1+3	Bolochoweckyj M 14+4	Millar J 7	Skelly J —+1	Milne L 10+3	McLean R 4+2	Terrell R —+1	*Match No.*
1	2	3	4	5	6	7^2	8^1	9	10^3	11	12	13	14												1
1	13	3	4	6	8		12	5	11^1	14	2	9^3		7^2	10										2
1	12	3	4	6		14	8	5	11	13	2^3	9^1		7	10^2										3
1	12	3	4	14		5	7	6	11^1	13			10	8^3		2	9^2								4
1	2	3	4^3	8	6		13	9	14	10		12			11^2	5		7^1							5
1		3	4	8	6^1	7^3	14	9	11^2	12		13	10			5			2■						6
		3	4	7	12	8	9^3	5		10^1	6^2		11	14	13	2				1					7
		3	4	8		7		9		10^1	6	12	11	5^2		2^3	13	14		1					8
		3	5	2		6	13	9		12	7	11^1	10		14		8^2		4^3	1					9
		3	4	6		8		9	13	12	5	11	10^1				7^2		2	1					10
1	3	4		6^1	8	7		5		11	13	9^2	10^3	12	14	2									11
	4	3		6^1	8	7		5	13	11	12	9^3	10^2			2			14	1					12
	4	3		13	7^1	8	9^2	5	11	10	6^3					2		14	12	1					13
	3^3	4		6	8	7		5		10		9^1	11^2	13	14	2			12	1					14
1		3	4	2		7		5	9^2	10^1	13		11	8^3	12	6		14							15
1		3	4	2	12	8	14	5	9^1	11			10^3	7^2	13	6									16
1		3	4		6	7^3		5	9	10^2		12	11^1	8	14	2			13						17
1		3	4	6		7^2	13	5	11^3		12	9^1	10	8		2	14								18
1		3	4	7	12	9		5	10^2	11^3		6^1	13	8■	14	2									19
1		3	4	6	7		8	5	13	10^3	12	14	9^2		11^1	2									20
1		3	4	6^2	7	13	8^1	5	11^3	9		12	10			2					14				21
1		2	4	13		8	14	5	10^2	11	6		12	7^3					3			9^1			22
1		3	4		13	6			11^2	10^1	5		12	7^3		8			2			9	14		23
1		3	4	13		6			12	14	10^2	8^3		7^1		5			2			9	11		24
1		3	4	6	8	7			13	12	5^1		10^3			9			2			14	11^2		25
1		2	4^1	6	8	7^3	14	12	10	11	5			13		9			3^2						26
1		3		6	7	8^3	14	4	12	10^1	5	13							2			9	11^2		27
1		3	4	13		7^1	6^2	5	12	11		10		8	14	2^3						9			28
1		3	4	6	8	14		5	11	12		9^1		7^3	10^2				2			13			29
1		2	4	6	7	13	14	5	9		12			8^2	11^1				3			10^3			30
1		3	4	5^2	6	7		8	10^1	12		14		13	11^3				2			9			31
1		2	4	6	7	12		5	13	11	9^1			8^3	10^2				3			14			32
1			4	6	8	7^3		5	9^1	13	3	14		12	10	2						11^2			33
1		14	4	6	12	7		5	13		2	9^1		8^3	10^2	3						11			34
1			4	7	6^3	8	14	5	12	10^2	2				11^1	3						9	13		35
1		3			7		8	13	12	10	5^2	9^1		6		4^3			2				11	14	36

MOTHERWELL

Year Formed: 1886. *Ground & Address:* Fir Park Stadium, Motherwell ML1 2QN. *Telephone:* 01698 333333. *Fax:* 01698 338001.
E-mail: mfcenquiries@motherwellfc.co.uk *Website:* www.motherwellfc.co.uk
Ground Capacity: 13,742 (all seated). *Size of Pitch:* 105m × 65m.
Chairman: James McMahon. *Chief Executive:* Alan Burrows.
Manager: Steve Robinson. *Assistant Manager:* Keith Lasley.
Club Nicknames: 'The Well'; 'The Steelmen'.
Previous Grounds: The Meadows; Dalziel Park.
Record Attendance: 35,632 v Rangers, Scottish Cup 4th rd replay, 12 March 1952.
Record Transfer Fee received: £1,750,000 for Phil O'Donnell to Celtic (September 1994).
Record Transfer Fee paid: £500,000 for John Spencer from Everton (January 1999).
Record Victory: 12-1 v Dundee U, Division II, 23 January 1954.
Record Defeat: 0-8 v Aberdeen, Premier Division, 26 March 1979.
Most Capped Player: Stephen Craigan, 54, Northern Ireland.
Most League Appearances: 626: Bobby Ferrier, 1918-37.
Most League Goals in Season (Individual): 52: Willie McFadyen, Division I, 1931-32.
Most Goals Overall (Individual): 283: Hugh Ferguson, 1916-25.

MOTHERWELL – SPFL LADBROKES PREMIERSHIP 2018–19 LEAGUE RECORD

Match No.	*Date*	*Venue*	*Opponents*	*Result*	*H/T Score*	*Lg Pos.*	*Goalscorers*	*Attendance*
1	Aug 5	A	Hibernian	L 0-3	0-2	12		17,494
2	11	H	Hamilton A	L 0-1	0-0	12		4807
3	26	H	Rangers	D 3-3	2-3	11	Johnson [3], McHugh [18], Hartley [90]	9545
4	Sept 1	A	Dundee	W 3-1	0-0	9	Johnson [56], Bigirimana [68], Campbell [86]	5137
5	15	H	Hearts	L 0-1	0-1	9		7218
6	22	A	Aberdeen	L 0-1	0-1	10		14,027
7	29	A	Kilmarnock	L 1-3	1-2	10	Main [16]	5090
8	Oct 6	H	Livingston	D 1-1	1-0	10	Bowman [17]	4256
9	20	H	St Johnstone	L 0-1	0-0	10		3752
10	31	A	St Mirren	W 2-0	1-0	9	Turnbull [30], Cadden [47]	4001
11	Nov 3	H	Dundee	W 1-0	0-0	9	Turnbull [69]	4129
12	11	A	Rangers	L 1-7	1-3	9	Main [25]	49,802
13	24	H	Aberdeen	W 3-0	2-0	9	Johnson 2 [25, 30], Turnbull [54]	5131
14	Dec 1	A	Livingston	L 0-2	0-1	9		1982
15	5	H	Celtic	D 1-1	0-1	9	Johnson [88]	8433
16	8	A	Hearts	L 0-1	0-1	9		15,915
17	15	A	St Johnstone	W 2-1	2-0	9	Aldred [2], Johnson [17]	2302
18	19	A	Celtic	L 0-3	0-3	9		54,703
19	22	H	St Mirren	L 0-1	0-0	9		4540
20	26	H	Kilmarnock	L 0-1	0-1	9		5426
21	29	A	Hamilton A	W 2-1	1-1	9	Aldred 2 [21, 77]	3843
22	Jan 23	H	Hibernian	W 1-0	1-0	9	Turnbull [43]	4090
23	26	A	Dundee	W 1-0	0-0	9	Turnbull (pen) [60]	4887
24	Feb 2	H	Livingston	W 3-0	3-0	9	Hastie 2 [6, 21], Main [12]	3839
25	6	A	St Mirren	W 2-1	1-0	8	Hastie [10], Campbell [77]	4383
26	17	H	Hearts	W 2-1	1-1	7	Hastie [13], Turnbull [90]	5091
27	24	A	Celtic	L 1-4	0-2	8	Ariyibi [51]	58,604
28	Mar 2	A	Kilmarnock	D 0-0	0-0	8		6215
29	9	H	Hamilton A	W 3-0	3-0	7	Turnbull 2 (1 pen) [3, 11 (p)], Hastie [37]	5248
30	16	A	Hibernian	L 0-2	0-2	7		17,184
31	30	H	St Johnstone	W 3-0	0-0	7	Frear [70], Turnbull [80], Tait [90]	4083
32	Apr 3	A	Aberdeen	L 1-3	1-1	8	Hastie [36]	13,228
33	7	H	Rangers	L 0-3	0-2	8		9200
34	20	A	Hamilton A	D 1-1	1-0	8	Turnbull [30]	2746
35	27	H	Dundee	W 4-3	2-2	8	Turnbull 2 [12, 90], Scott [24], Ariyibi [50]	3662
36	May 4	H	St Mirren	D 1-1	0-0	8	Turnbull [74]	5274
37	11	A	St Johnstone	L 0-2	0-1	8		3051
38	18	H	Livingston	W 3-2	3-0	8	Donnelly [10], Turnbull 2 (1 pen) [21, 25 (p)]	5794

Final League Position: 8

Honours
League Champions: Division I 1931-32;. First Division 1981-82, 1984-85; Division II 1953-54, 1968-69.
Runners-up: Premier Division 1994-95, 2012-13; Premiership 2013-14; Division I 1926-27, 1929-30, 1932-33, 1933-34; Division II 1894-95, 1902-03.
Scottish Cup: 1952, 1991; *Runners-up:* 1931, 1933, 1939, 1951, 2011, 2018.
League Cup Winners: 1950-51; *Runners-up:* 1954-55, 2004-05, 2017-18.

European: *Champions League:* 2 matches (2012-13). *Cup Winners' Cup:* 2 matches (1991-92). *UEFA Cup:* 8 matches (1994-95, 1995-96, 2008-09). *Europa League:* 18 matches (2009-10, 2010-11, 2012-13, 2013-14, 2014-15).

Club colours: Shirt: Amber with maroon band. Shorts: White. Socks: Amber and maroon bands.

Goalscorers: *League (46):* Turnbull 15 (3 pens), Hastie 6, Johnson 6, Aldred 3, Main 3, Ariyibi 2, Campbell 2, Bigirimana 1, Bowman 1, Cadden 1, Donnelly 1, Frear 1, Hartley 1, McHugh 1, Scott 1, Tait 1.
William Hill Scottish FA Cup (1): Hastie 1.
Betfred Scottish League Cup (14): Frear 3, Main 3 (1 pen), Sammon 3, Johnson 2, Bowman 1, Hartley 1, Tait 1.
Irn-Bru Scottish League Challenge (8): Watson 2, Hastie 1, Livingstone 1, MacDonald 1, Mbulu 1, Turnbull 1, own goal 1.

Carson T 12	McHugh C 20 + 8	Hartley P 14	Donnelly L 6 + 1	Tait R 37 + 1	Cadden C 15 + 5	Grimshaw L 30 + 1	Rose A 10 + 2	Taylor-Sinclair A 5 + 1	Main C 28 + 3	Sammon C 6 + 10	Bigirimana G 12 + 7	Frear E 4 + 18	Johnson D 12 + 10	Aldred T 37	Campbell A 31 + 4	Rodriguez A 16 + 4	Bowman R 7 + 9	Gillespie M 26 + 1	Turnbull D 27 + 3	Duane C 23	Maguire B 1 + 1	Mbulu C 4 + 2	Livingstone A — + 3	Scott J 6 + 6	Ariyibi G 17	Hastie J 12 + 2	McCormack R — + 3	Ferguson R — + 1	Semple J — + 3	Devine D — + 1	Cornelius D — + 1	*Match No.*
1	2	3	4	5	6	7^{3}	8	9^{1}	10^{2}	11	12	13	14																			1
1	3	4		9^{2}	5		7^{1}		10	11	6	13	12	2	8^{3}	14																2
1	3	4		9	5		8^{2}		10	12	6	13	11^{3}	2	7^{1}		14															3
1	3	4		9	5^{1}		8		10^{3}	13	6	12	11^{2}	2	7		14															4
1^{1}	3	4		9	5^{2}		8		10		7	14	11^{3}	2	6		13	12														5
1	3	4^{1}	7^{2}	9	12					10^{3}	8	5	11	2	6		13		14													6
1	3		4^{3}	5^{1}	6	8		9	10	14	7^{2}		13	2			11		12													7
1	7■	4	5	2	6		9^{2}		10^{1}		12		13	3	8		11															8
1		3		12	5^{1}		8	9^{3}	10^{2}			13	14	2	6		11		7	4												9
1	4	2		9	5	6			10^{1}		7^{2}		13	3	12		11		8^{3}		14											10
1	3	4		9	5	6			10^{3}	14	7^{2}		12	2	13		11		8^{1}													11
1	6■	3		5	2	8	12		10		7^{1}			4	13		11^{2}		9^{3}			14										12
		5		6		2			10^{2}	14	8		11^{1}	3	7	12	13	1	9^{3}			4										13
				9		5			10^{3}		6^{1}	13	11	3	7^{2}	12	14	1	8		4	2										14
	8	4^{2}	2^{1}	5		6	12		14	10			11	3	7			1	9				13^{3}									15
	6			5^{3}		2	7^{1}		10		12		11	3		8^{2}	13	1	9	4				14								16
	7			9		5			11^{1}	14			10^{3}	2	6	12	13	1	8^{2}	4		3										17
	4			2		6	9	13	14	11	7^{3}			3	12	8	10^{2}	1		5^{1}												18
	5			9^{2}		6			10	14	12		11	2	7^{1}		13	1	8	4		3^{3}										19
	3^{1}			5		14		9	10■		13	8	11	2	7	6		1		4^{2}		12^{3}										20
		4		2^{2}		6	8	5^{1}		10		9	11	3	7			1	12				13									21
				5		2			10^{1}	13	14			3	7	9		1	8	4					6^{3}	11^{2}	12					22
	14			5		2			11		13	12		3	7	8		1	10^{2}	4					9^{3}	6^{1}						23
				5		2			10^{1}			12		3	6	7		1	8	4				13	11^{2}	9^{3}	14					24
	12			5		2			11			13		3	8	6^{1}		1	9	4					7^{2}	10^{3}	14					25
	13			5		2			10^{1}			12		3	6	7^{3}		1	8	4				14	11^{2}	9						26
	12^{3}		14	5		2				13				3^{2}	6	7		1	8	4				10^{1}	11	9						27
				5		2			10^{1}			12		3	6	7		1	8	4				13	11^{2}	9						28
	13			5		2			10^{3}			12	14	3	6	7^{1}		1	8	4					11	9^{2}						29
				5		2			10^{3}			13	14	3	6^{2}	7		1	8	4				12	11^{1}	9						30
	14			5	13	2			10			12		3	6	7^{2}		1	8	4					11^{3}	9^{1}						31
	7			5	13	2			10			14		3	6^{2}			1^{3}	8	4					11^{1}	9		12				32
				5	12	2			10^{1}			13		3	6	7		1	8	4				14	11^{3}	9^{2}						33
				5	12	2				13		11^{3}		3	6	7		1	8	4				10^{1}	9^{2}	14						34
	13			5	9	2^{1}			12					3	6	7■		1	8	4				10^{3}	11^{2}				14			35
	6			5	7	2^{3}						12		3	8			1	9^{1}	4			14	11	10^{2}				13			36
	6			2	7^{1}	5							12	3	8			1	9	4^{3}				11	10^{2}	13			14			37
	14		4	8^{3}	9	5								3	7			1	6	2^{1}				10	11^{2}					12	13	38

PARTICK THISTLE

Year Formed: 1876. *Ground & Address:* Firhill Stadium, 80 Firhill Rd, Glasgow G20 7AL. *Telephone:* 0141 579 1971. *Fax:* 0141 945 1525. *E-mail:* mail@ptfc.co.uk *Website:* ptfc.co.uk
Ground Capacity: 10,102 (all seated). *Size of Pitch:* 105m × 68m.
Chairman: Jacqui Low. *Chief Executive:* Gerry Britton.
Manager: Gary Caldwell. *Assistant Manager:* Brian Kerr.
Club Nickname: 'The Jags'.
Previous Grounds: Overnewton Park; Jordanvale Park; Muirpark; Inchview; Meadowside Park.
Record Attendance: 49,838 v Rangers, Division I, 18 February 1922. *Ground Record:* 54,728, Scotland v Ireland, 25 February 1928.
Record Transfer Fee received: £350,000 for Liam Lindsay to Barnsley (June 2017); £350,000 for Aidan Fitzpatrick to Norwich C (July 2019).
Record Transfer Fee paid: £85,000 for Andy Murdoch from Celtic (February 1991).
Record Victory: 16-0 v Royal Albert, Scottish Cup 1st rd, 17 January 1931.
Record Defeat: 0-10 v Queen's Park, Scottish Cup 5th rd, 3 December 1881.
Most Capped Player: Alan Rough, 51 (53), Scotland.
Most League Appearances: 410: Alan Rough, 1969-82.
Most League Goals in Season (Individual): 41: Alex Hair, Division I, 1926-27.
Most Goals Overall (Individual): 229: Willie Sharp, 1939-57.

PARTICK THISTLE – SPFL LADBROKES CHAMPIONSHIP 2018–19 LEAGUE RECORD

Match No.	*Date*	*Venue*	*Opponents*	*Result*		*H/T Score*	*Lg Pos.*	*Goalscorers*	*Attendance*
1	Aug 4	A	Ayr U	L	0-2	0-2	10		3249
2	11	H	Falkirk	W	2-1	2-0	7	Penrice 24, Erskine 28	3417
3	25	A	Dundee U	L	1-3	0-1	7	Erskine 90	5219
4	Sept 1	H	Greenock Morton	W	1-0	0-0	7	Erskine 50	3431
5	15	A	Inverness CT	L	2-3	0-3	7	Spittal 82, Doolan 90	2424
6	22	H	Queen of the South	W	3-2	3-2	6	Doolan 32, Spittal 2 38, 41	2710
7	28	A	Dunfermline Ath	L	0-1	0-0	6		4740
8	Oct 6	H	Ross Co	L	0-2	0-1	8		2784
9	13	H	Dundee U	L	1-2	0-1	8	Quitongo 77	3087
10	20	A	Alloa Ath	L	0-1	0-0	8		1392
11	27	H	Ayr U	L	0-1	0-0	8		3491
12	Nov 3	A	Greenock Morton	L	1-5	1-2	8	Ntambwe 16	2197
13	10	H	Inverness CT	L	0-1	0-0	9		2509
14	17	A	Falkirk	D	1-1	0-0	9	Slater 57	4589
15	Dec 1	A	Queen of the South	L	0-1	0-0	10		1508
16	8	H	Dunfermline Ath	W	2-0	1-0	8	Spittal 12, Storey 56	2566
17	15	H	Alloa Ath	D	2-2	2-1	8	Doolan (pen) 18, Spittal 37	1990
18	22	A	Ross Co	L	0-2	0-1	9		3467
19	29	H	Greenock Morton	L	1-2	0-1	9	Slater 60	3074
20	Jan 5	A	Dundee U	D	1-1	1-0	10	Doolan 9	5282
21	12	H	Falkirk	D	1-1	0-0	10	Spittal 61	4438
22	26	H	Queen of the South	W	2-1	1-0	9	Cardle 18, Storey 54	2662
23	Feb 2	A	Inverness CT	W	2-1	2-0	9	Anderson 21, Fitzpatrick 25	2171
24	16	A	Alloa Ath	W	2-0	1-0	8	Spittal 4, McDonald 79	1757
25	23	H	Ross Co	L	2-4	2-0	10	Fitzpatrick 21, Elliot 24	3007
26	26	A	Dunfermline Ath	L	0-3	0-0	10		4904
27	Mar 9	H	Dundee U	W	2-1	1-0	9	McDonald 4, Fitzpatrick 90	3173
28	16	A	Falkirk	D	1-1	1-1	9	McDonald 10	4896
29	22	H	Inverness CT	L	1-2	0-0	9	Bannigan 68	2149
30	30	A	Greenock Morton	W	3-0	3-0	8	Doolan 2 17, 43, Anderson 36	2329
31	Apr 6	H	Dunfermline Ath	D	2-2	1-2	8	Blair (og) 31, McDonald 77	2850
32	13	A	Ross Co	D	0-0	0-0	10		4031
33	20	H	Alloa Ath	W	2-1	0-1	9	Cardle 47, McDonald 66	3578
34	23	A	Ayr U	W	1-0	1-0	6	Gordon 17	2429
35	27	H	Ayr U	L	1-2	1-1	7	Gordon 9	3855
36	May 4	A	Queen of the South	W	3-0	2-0	6	Mansell 14, McDonald 44, Bannigan (pen) 73	3916

Final League Position: 6

Honours

League Champions: First Division 1975-76, 2001-02, 2012-13; Division II 1896-97, 1899-1900, 1970-71; Second Division 2000-01.
Runners-up: First Division 1991-92, 2008-09; Division II 1901-02.
Promoted via play-offs: 2005-06 (to First Division).
Scottish Cup Winners: 1921; *Runners-up:* 1930.
League Cup Winners: 1971-72; *Runners-up:* 1953-54, 1956-57, 1958-59.
League Challenge Cup Runners-up: 2012-13.

European: *Fairs Cup:* 4 matches (1963-64). *UEFA Cup:* 2 matches (1972-73). *Intertoto Cup:* 4 matches (1995-96).

Club colours: Shirt: Red and yellow stripes. Shorts: Black. Socks: Red and yellow hoops.

Goalscorers: *League (43):* Spittal 7, Doolan 6 (1 pen), McDonald 6, Erskine 3, Fitzpatrick 3, Anderson 2, Bannigan 2 (1 pen), Cardle 2, Gordon 2, Slater 2, Storey 2, Elliot 1, Mansell 1, Ntambwe 1, Penrice 1, Quitongo 1, own goal 1.
William Hill Scottish FA Cup (7): Anderson 1, Cardle 1, Elliot 1, Fitzpatrick 1, McDonald 1, Saunders 1, Spittal 1.
Betfred Scottish League Cup (7): Gordon 2, Fitzpatrick 1, Mbuyi-Mutombo 1, Penrice 1, Storer 1, Storey 1.
Irn-Bru Scottish League Challenge (6): Fitzpatrick 2, Mbuyi-Mutombo 2, Melbourne 1, O'Ware 1.

Bell C 12	Melbourne M 2+1	McGinty S 28	O'Ware T 3	Penrice J 36	Spittal B 33+3	Gordon S 9	Slater C 27+3	Storey M 23+7	Erskine C 9+9	Doolan K 24+6	Fitzpatrick A 8+13	Elliot C 33	Storer J 2+2	Wilson C —+2	Mbuyi-Mutombo A 4+5	Keown N 13+1	Ntambwe B 4+1	Bannigan S 26+2	Quitongo J 4+9	Scobbie T 6+1	Sneddon J 13	McCarthy A 1+6	Coulibaly S —+3	Jefferies D 3 – 1	Hazard C 11	Saunders S 10+2	Harkins G 8+5	Cardle J 5+6	Roy A —+4	McMillan J 13	Anderson S 13	McDonald S 10+2	Mansell L 3+5	Match No.
1	2^{1}	3	4	5	6	7	8	9	10	11	12																							1
1		4	3	5	10^{2}	8	6	11	7^{3}	12	13	2	9^{1}	14																				2
1	5	4	3^{1}	6	7		8^{3}	11	13	14		2	9^{2}		10	12																		3
1	13	4		5	8		6	10	9^{1}	11		2				3	7^{2}	12																4
1		4		5	9		8	10^{1}	11	13		2			6^{2}	3	7^{3}	12	14															5
1		4		5	8		7	9	10^{2}	11^{3}		2			12	3	13	6^{1}	14															6
1		4		5	7^{3}		9	10	13	11^{2}		2			14	3		8	12	6^{1}														7
		4		5	8		6	10^{2}	9^{1}	11^{3}	14	2			12	3		7	13		1													8
1		4		5	8^{2}		6	10^{3}	9	11^{1}		2			14	3		7	13			12												9
1		4		5	14		8	9^{2}	10^{3}	11		2				3	7^{1}	0	13				12											10
1		4		5	6		7	9	12			2	14		11^{1}	3		8^{3}	10^{2}				13											11
1		4^{3}		5	7		8	10			13	2	14			3	6^{2}	9	11^{1}			12												12
1		4		5	9		7	6^{1}		11	12	2				3		8	10															13
		4		5	9		7	6^{2}	13	11		2				3		8	10^{1}	12	1													14
		4		5	6			14	8^{2}	11^{1}	9	2			12	3^{3}		7	13	10	1													15
		4		8	6			11^{1}	13	10^{3}		5			9^{2}			7	14	3	1	12		2										16
		4		9	5			11	13	10^{1}	8^{2}	6						7		3	1	12		2										17
		4		5	6		13	10	14	11^{1}	8^{3}	2						7	12	3	1			9^{2}										18
		4		9	6		7	11^{1}	12	10	13	5				2^{2}				3	1	8												19
		4		5	6		9	10^{1}		11		2						8						13	1	3^{2}	7^{3}	12	14					20
		4		5	9^{3}		6	10^{1}	13	11^{2}		2						8							1	3	7	12	14					21
				5	10^{3}		6	12		11^{2}	7	2						8				14			1	3		9^{1}	13	4				22
				9	10		6	11^{2}		14	8^{1}	5						7				13			1	3	12			2	4^{3}			23
				5	10		7			11^{2}	8^{1}	2		14				6							1		9^{3}			4	3	12	13	24
				5	9		6			11^{3}	10	2						7^{1}							1	13	8^{2}		14	3	4	12		25
				9	8		6			10^{3}	12	5											13		1	4^{1}	7			2	3	11^{2}	14	26
				5	9		7	8^{2}			12	2													1	4	14	10^{1}		6	3	11^{3}	13	27
		4		5	10^{1}		7	12			13							6							1	3	14	8^{2}		2		9	11^{3}	28
				9	13		7	12				5^{3}						6			1					4	8^{2}	14		3	2	10	11^{1}	29
				8	9^{1}	6	12			11^{3}	13	5						7^{2}							1	4				2	3	10	14	30
		4		9	6	7^{2}		13		10	14							8							1	2^{1}		12		5^{3}	3	11		31
		4		9	6	7^{1}	8	13		10^{2}	12	2									1									5	3	11		32
		4		8	9	7^{3}	6			11		5^{2}									1					14	13	12		2^{1}	3	10		33
		4		5	13	7		14		12	8^{3}	2						6			1						9	10^{1}			3	11^{2}		34
		4		5	10	9		11^{2}		13	12	2						7			1						6^{3}	8^{1}			3		14	35
		5		6	7^{2}	9^{3}	12					2						8			1						13	14		3	4	11	10^{1}	36

PETERHEAD

Year Formed: 1891. *Ground and Address:* Balmoor Stadium, Balmoor Terrace, Peterhead AB42 1EQ.
Telephone: 01779 478256. *Fax:* 01779 490682. *E-mail:* office@peterheadfc.co.uk *Website:* www.peterheadfc.com
Ground Capacity: 3,150 (seated: 1,000). *Size of Pitch:* 101m × 64m.
Chairman: Rodger Morrison. *Vice-Chairman:* Ian Grant.
Manager: Jim McInally. *Assistant Coach:* David Nicholls.
Club Nickname: 'Blue Toon'.
Previous Ground: Recreation Park.
Record Attendance: 8,643 v Raith R, Scottish Cup 4th rd replay, 25 February 1987 (Recreation Park); 4,855 v Rangers, Third Division, 19 January 2013 (at Balmoor).
Record Victory: 9-0 v Colville Park, Scottish Cup 2nd rd, 14 October 2017.
Record Defeat: 0-13 v Aberdeen, Scottish Cup 3rd rd, 10 February 1923.
Most League Appearances: 275: Martin Bavidge, 2003-13.
Most League Goals in Season (Individual): 32: Rory McAllister, 2013-14.
Most Goals Overall (Individual): 194: Rory McAllister, 2008, 2011-19.

PETERHEAD – SPFL LADBROKES LEAGUE TWO 2018–19 LEAGUE RECORD

Match No.	*Date*	*Venue*	*Opponents*	*Result*		*H/T Score*	*Lg Pos.*	*Goalscorers*	*Attendance*
1	Aug 4	H	Queen's Park	D	1-1	1-1	4	McAllister [25]	552
2	11	A	Albion R	W	4-0	1-0	2	Stevenson [32], Lyle [60], McAllister (pen) [82], Brown, S [90]	277
3	18	H	Clyde	W	1-0	0-0	1	McAllister [53]	671
4	25	A	Stirling Alb	W	2-0	1-0	1	Stevenson [44], McAllister [64]	543
5	Sept 1	H	Edinburgh C	L	0-1	0-0	2		560
6	15	A	Cowdenbeath	W	4-2	1-2	2	Dunlop [14], Lyle [47], McAllister [57], Gibson, W [67]	341
7	22	H	Berwick Rangers	W	1-0	0-0	2	McAllister [73]	546
8	29	A	Annan Ath	W	3-1	1-0	2	Dow [29], McAllister [80], Brown, J [85]	433
9	Oct 6	H	Elgin C	W	3-0	1-0	2	Dow [42], McAllister [52], McLean [86]	681
10	27	A	Clyde	W	3-1	1-0	2	Brown, S [20], Lyle 2 [73, 84]	524
11	Nov 3	H	Albion R	W	2-1	2-0	1	Lyle 2 [5, 16]	590
12	10	A	Queen's Park	L	0-2	0-1	2		475
13	Dec 1	H	Annan Ath	W	2-1	1-0	2	Lyle [2], McLean [84]	577
14	8	A	Berwick Rangers	W	5-0	3-0	2	Leitch [2], McAllister [13], Brown, J [36], McLean [51], Stevenson [78]	428
15	11	A	Edinburgh C	D	1-1	0-0	2	Brown, J [59]	455
16	22	H	Stirling Alb	W	4-1	2-0	2	Leitch [13], McAllister [28], Lyle [55], Eadie [63]	620
17	29	A	Elgin C	W	3-0	2-0	2	Leitch 2 [14, 77], Dow [32]	929
18	Jan 5	H	Clyde	L	1-2	1-0	2	Dow [29]	754
19	12	A	Albion R	W	2-0	0-0	2	Dow [49], McLean [71]	332
20	19	H	Berwick Rangers	W	2-0	0-0	1	McAllister [72], Leitch [90]	522
21	26	A	Annan Ath	L	0-3	0-0	2		398
22	Feb 9	H	Edinburgh C	D	0-0	0-0	2		728
23	16	H	Queen's Park	W	2-1	1-0	2	Sutherland [3], Gibson, W [55]	615
24	23	A	Stirling Alb	W	1-0	1-0	2	McAllister [34]	611
25	26	H	Cowdenbeath	W	1-0	1-0	1	Brown, S [43]	532
26	Mar 2	H	Elgin C	W	1-0	1-0	1	Boyle [8]	737
27	5	A	Cowdenbeath	W	3-1	2-1	1	Sutherland [23], McAllister 2 [35, 81]	250
28	9	H	Annan Ath	W	2-1	1-1	1	Leitch [25], Lyle [71]	568
29	19	A	Berwick Rangers	L	0-2	0-2	1		327
30	23	A	Edinburgh C	D	0-0	0-0	1		1057
31	30	H	Cowdenbeath	W	2-1	1-1	1	McAllister [27], Brown, S [50]	682
32	Apr 6	A	Clyde	D	3-3	2-0	1	Gibson, W [4], Willis [31], Brown, S [52]	813
33	13	H	Albion R	D	1-1	0-0	1	Leitch [64]	715
34	20	A	Elgin C	W	2-1	2-1	1	Wilson, C (og) [2], Leitch [29]	862
35	27	H	Stirling Alb	D	1-1	1-0	1	Leitch [37]	1371
36	May 4	A	Queen's Park	W	2-0	2-0	1	Leitch 2 [26, 44]	964

Final League Position: 1

Honours
League Champions: League Two 2013-14, 2018-19.
Runners up: Third Division 2004-05, 2012-13; League Two 2017-18.
Scottish Cup: Quarter-finals 2001.
League Challenge Cup: Runners up: 2015-16.

Club colours: Shirt: Royal blue with light blue sleeves. Shorts: Royal blue with white trim. Socks: Light blue.

Goalscorers: *League (65):* McAllister 15 (1 pen), Leitch 11, Lyle 9, Brown S 5, Dow 5, McLean 4, Brown J 3, Gibson W 3, Stevenson 3, Sutherland 2, Boyle 1, Dunlop 1, Eadie 1, Willis 1, own goal 1.
William Hill Scottish FA Cup (4): Brown S 1, Lyle 1, McAllister 1, McLean 1.
Betfred Scottish League Cup (0).
Irn-Bru Scottish League Challenge (2): Leitch 1, McLean 1.

Fleming G 36	Home C 4 + 16	Eadie C 16 + 6	Brown J 32 + 3	Stevenson J 31 + 1	McLean R 10 + 11	Brown S 36	Ferry S 26 + 2	Gibson W 32 + 4	Lyle D 18 + 10	McAllister R 30 + 5	Kavanagh R 2 + 14	Norris A — + 5	Macdonald L — + 1	Leitch J 31 + 3	Dunlop M 27	Dow R 28 + 2	Boyle P 25 + 2	Willox R — + 4	Sutherland S 11 + 2	Willis P 1 + 14	Match No.
1	2^{1}	3	4	5	6^{3}	7	8^{2}	9	10	11	12	13	14								1
1	12	4	3	5	11	6	7^{2}	2	9^{3}	10	13	14		8^{1}							2
1	14	3	4	5	10	2	7	6	9^{2}	11^{1}	12	13		8^{3}							3
1	14	4	3	5	11^{3}	6	7	2	9^{2}	10	12	13		8^{1}							4
1	14	3	4	5	10^{2}	6	7	2^{1}	9	11^{3}	12	13		8							5
1		3	5	2	12	8	7	6	11^{2}	10^{1}	14			9	4^{3}	13					6
1			3	5	12	6^{3}	7	2	9^{1}	11^{2}	14			10	4	8	13				7
1		14	3	2	8^{2}	7		6	13	11^{1}	12			10	4^{3}	9	5				8
1			3	2	13	7	6	8	12	11^{1}	14			10^{2}	4	9^{3}	5				9
1		13	3	2	8	7		10	14	11^{1}	9^{2}			6^{3}	4■	12	5				10
1	14	3	4	2	12	6	7	8	9^{3}	11^{2}	13			5^{1}		10					11
1	14	4	3^{1}	2	12	7	5^{3}	6	11	10				8^{2}		9	13				12
1			3	2	11	6^{3}	7	10^{1}	9	12	13			14	4	8^{2}	5				13
1			3	2	11^{1}	7	8	12	14	10	13			6	4	9^{2}	5^{3}				14
1	12		3	2	6	7		5		10^{1}	11			8	4	9					15
1	14	3		2^{1}	13	7	6	5	9^{3}	11	12			10^{2}	4	8					16
1		3	13	2	12	7	6	10^{1}		11^{3}	14			9	4^{2}	8	5				17
1		3	14	2	13	6	7	9	12	11^{1}				10^{3}	4	8^{2}	5				18
1		3	14	2^{3}	13	6	7	12	9	11^{1}				10^{2}	4	8	5				19
1	14	3^{3}	2		13	7	6^{2}	9	11^{1}	12				10	4	8	5				20
1		3^{2}	2	6^{3}	13	7^{1}		9	11	12				10	4	8	5	14			21
1			3	2		7		6^{2}	12	11				10	4	8	5		9^{1}	13	22
1	14		3	2		6		12	11^{3}	10^{2}				9^{1}	4	7	5		8	13	23
1			3	2		6	7	8	13	10^{3}				14	4	9^{2}	5		11^{1}	12	24
1			3	2		7	6	13	12	11^{1}				10^{3}	4	8	5		9^{2}	14	25
1	14		3	2^{2}		7	6^{3}	8	9^{1}	11				12	4	10	5			13	26
1			3	2^{3}		6	12	10	13	11^{2}				8	4	7^{1}	5		9	14	27
1	12	13	3			2	6	7	9^{3}	11^{2}				10	4		5		8^{1}	14	28
1	13		3			6	7^{1}	2	11^{2}					10^{3}	4	9	5	14	8	12	29
1	2	14	3	7^{3}		6		9		10					4	8^{2}	5	13	11^{1}	12	30
1	2	13	3			6		8		11^{2}				10^{1}	4	7	5	14	9^{3}	12	31
1	2^{2}		3	12		6	13	7		14				8	4	9	5		10^{3}	11^{1}	32
1	13		3	2^{3}		7	6	9		12				10^{2}	4	8	5		11^{1}	14	33
1	12	14	3	2^{3}		6	7	8		11^{2}				9	4■	10^{1}	5			13	34
1	14	3	4	2		7	6	9		11^{1}				10^{2}		8^{3}	5		12	13	35
1		4	3	2		6	7	8	12	10^{2}				9^{1}		11^{3}	5		13	14	36

QUEEN OF THE SOUTH

Year Formed: 1919. *Ground & Address:* Palmerston Park, Dumfries DG2 9BA. *Telephone:* 01387 254853.
Fax: 01387 240470. *E-mail:* admin@qosfc.com *Website:* www.qosfc.com
Ground Capacity: 8,690 (seated: 3,377) *Size of Pitch:* 102m × 66m.
Chairman: Billy Hewitson. *Vice-Chairman:* Craig Paterson.
Manager: Allan Johnston. *Assistant Manager:* Sandy Clark. *Coach:* Eddie Warwick.
Club Nickname: 'The Doonhamers'.
Record Attendance: 26,552 v Hearts, Scottish Cup 3rd rd, 23 February 1952.
Record Transfer Fee received: £250,000 for Andy Thomson to Southend U (July 1994).
Record Transfer Fee paid: £30,000 for Jim Butter from Alloa Ath (1995).
Record Victory: 11-1 v Stranraer, Scottish Cup 1st rd, 16 January 1932.
Record Defeat: 2-10 v Dundee, Division I, 1 December 1962.
Most Capped Player: Billy Houliston, 3, Scotland.
Most League Appearances: 731: Allan Ball, 1963-82.
Most League Goals in Season (Individual): 37: Jimmy Gray, Division II, 1927-28.
Most Goals in Season: 43: Stephen Dobbie, 2018-19.
Most Goals Overall (Individual): 251: Jim Patterson, 1949-63.

QUEEN OF THE SOUTH – SPFL LADBROKES CHAMPIONSHIP 2018–19 LEAGUE RECORD

Match No.	*Date*	*Venue*	*Opponents*	*Result*	*H/T Score*	*Lg Pos.*	*Goalscorers*	*Attendance*
1	Aug 4	A	Greenock Morton	D 2-2	0-0	5	Semple [69], Todd [76]	2019
2	11	H	Dundee U	L 1-2	0-2	8	Dobbie [67]	1960
3	25	A	Falkirk	W 3-0	2-0	6	Dobbie 3 [11, 39, 75]	4026
4	Sept 1	H	Ayr U	W 5-0	4-0	3	Dobbie 4 (1 pen) [12, 20 (p), 22, 84], Harkins [37]	2498
5	15	H	Ross Co	D 0-0	0-0	4		1509
6	22	A	Partick Thistle	L 2-3	2-3	7	Dobbie [4], Todd [34]	2710
7	29	A	Inverness CT	D 0-0	0-0	5		2029
8	Oct 6	H	Alloa Ath	D 3-3	2-3	6	Dobbie 3 [36, 43, 70]	1228
9	20	A	Dunfermline Ath	W 1-0	0-0	5	Todd [83]	4443
10	27	H	Falkirk	W 2-0	0-0	4	Doyle [52], Marshall [54]	1463
11	30	H	Greenock Morton	L 1-2	0-1	5	Dobbie [65]	1174
12	Nov 3	A	Dundee U	L 0-2	0-1	6		5171
13	10	A	Ayr U	D 1-1	0-0	6	Murray [81]	2539
14	17	H	Inverness CT	D 3-3	1-0	6	Dykes [31], Dobbie [51], Todd [61]	1233
15	Dec 1	H	Partick Thistle	W 1-0	0-0	5	Dobbie [82]	1508
16	8	A	Ross Co	D 1-1	0-0	4	Stirling [71]	3305
17	15	H	Dunfermline Ath	D 0-0	0-0	4		727
18	22	A	Alloa Ath	L 0-2	0-0	5		646
19	29	H	Ayr U	D 1-1	1-1	6	Todd [29]	2349
20	Jan 5	A	Inverness CT	W 2-1	0-0	5	Mercer [83], Dobbie [84]	2225
21	12	H	Ross Co	W 4-0	2-0	4	Dobbie 2 [12, 77], Doyle [45], Maguire [65]	1386
22	26	A	Partick Thistle	L 1-2	0-1	4	Dobbie (pen) [80]	2662
23	Feb 2	A	Falkirk	L 0-3	0-1	5		4538
24	16	H	Dundee U	L 0-1	0-1	5		2012
25	23	H	Alloa Ath	L 1-2	0-1	6	Jacobs [59]	1116
26	26	A	Greenock Morton	L 0-1	0-0	7		1324
27	Mar 2	A	Dunfermline Ath	L 0-1	0-0	7		4708
28	9	H	Inverness CT	L 0-2	0-2	7		1066
29	30	A	Dundee U	W 2-1	0-0	7	Dobbie (pen) [52], Dykes [57]	4839
30	Apr 2	H	Falkirk	D 1-1	0-0	7	Dobbie (pen) [90]	1508
31	6	H	Greenock Morton	D 1-1	1-0	7	Jacobs [42]	1442
32	9	A	Ayr U	L 0-1	0-1	7		1582
33	13	A	Alloa Ath	L 0-1	0-0	8		1086
34	20	H	Dunfermline Ath	W 2-1	1-0	7	Wilson [44], Todd [52]	1704
35	26	A	Ross Co	L 0-4	0-1	8		4805
36	May 4	H	Partick Thistle	L 0-3	0-2	9		3916

Final League Position: 9

Honours
League Champions: Division II 1950-51; Second Division 2001-02, 2012-13.
Runners-up: Division II 1932-33, 1961-62, 1974-75; Second Division 1980-81, 1985-86; Division Three 1924-25.
Scottish Cup Runners-up: 2007-08.
League Cup: semi-finals 1950-51, 1960-61.
League Challenge Cup Winners: 2002-03, 2012-13; *Runners-up:* 1997-98, 2010-11.

European: *UEFA Cup:* 2 matches (2008-09).

Club colours: Shirt: Royal blue with white trim. Shorts: White. Socks: Royal blue.

Goalscorers: *League (41):* Dobbie 21 (4 pens), Todd 6, Doyle 2, Dykes 2, Jacobs 2, Harkins 1, Maguire 1, Marshall 1, Mercer 1, Murray 1, Semple 1, Stirling 1, Wilson 1.
William Hill Scottish FA Cup (9): Dobbie 7, Dykes 1, Mercer 1.
Betfred Scottish League Cup (14): Dobbie 8 (1 pen), Dykes 3, Harkins 1, Stirling 1, Todd 1.
Irn-Bru Scottish League Challenge (7): Dobbie 4, Dykes 2, Harkins 1.
Play-Offs (9): Dobbie 3, Dykes 2, Murray 2, Doyle 1, own goal 1.

Martin A 27	Marshall J 35	Semple C 15 + 3	Fordyce C 20 + 3	Doyle M 35	Todd J 30	Harkins G 12 + 1	Jacobs K 36	Stirling A 29 + 6	Dykes L 36	Dobbie S 30	Murray C 3 + 18	Bell O 1 + 8	Tremble D — + 1	Mercer S 32	Watson D — + 2	Ivison R — + 2	Frizzell A 2 + 9	Norman David 6 + 4	Leighfield J 7 + 1	Low N 5 + 2	Maguire B 13 + 2	Wilson I 11 + 3	Aird F 3 + 3	McGrath I 2 + 9	Brownlie D 4 + 3	Mehmet D 2	*Match No.*
1	2	3	4	5	6	7^1	8	9^2	10	11	12	13															1
1	5	3	2	4	9^1	7	8	6^2	11	10	12		13														2
1	5	3		4	6^3	8^2	7	9	10	11^1		12		2	13	14											3
1	5	4		3	9	8^2	7	6	11	10^1	12			2		13											4
1	5	4		3	8	9^1	7	6	11	10				2			12										5
1	5	4		3	8	9	7	6^1	11	10				2			12										6
1	5	4		3	8	9^1	7	6^2	11	10				2			12	13									7
1	5	4		3	8	9^1	7	6	11	10				2			12										8
1	5	14	4^3	3	8		7	6^1	11	10		12		2			13	9^2									9
1	2	14	4	3	7		8	9^2	11	10	12	13		5^3				6^1									10
1	5		3	4	9		7^1	6	11	10	12			2				8									11
1	5	12	4	3	9	13	7	6^1	11	10				2^2				8									12
1	5	3	4	2	7^2	9^3	6	12	11	10	13	14						8^1									13
	5	4	3	2	9	8^1	7	6^2	11	10	13							12	1								14
1	5		3	4	8^2	9	7	6^1	10	11^3	14			2			12	13									15
1	5	4	3	8	10^2		7	12	11		13	14		2			6^3	9^1									16
1	5	8	3	4	9	10^2	7		11		13			2			6^1	12									17
1	5	4^1	3	6	10		8	9	11		12	7^2		2			13										18
1	5	4	3	9	8		7	6^2	10	11^1	12			2			13										19
1	5	4	3	9^3	8		7	12	10	11^1				2			13			6^2	14						20
1	5		3	6^2	9^1		7^3	12	10	11	13	14		2						8	4						21
1	5			4	9^1		7	6	10	11	8^2	12		2	13						3						22
1	5		3				7	6	11	10	12			2							4	8^1	9^2	13			23
1	5		12	9			7^2	6^1	11	10				2						8	3[illegible]	4		13			24
1	5		3^1	9			7	6	11	10				2						8^2		4	12	13			25
1	9		3	6			8	12	10	11				5^1							4	7^2	13		2		26
1	4		3	6			8	13	10	11				5							14	7^1	9^3	12	2^2		27
1^2			3	8			7	9	11	10	13			2					12			5^1	6^3	14	4		28
	5			3	7^3		8	6	9	11^2	14			2					1		4	12		10^1	13		29
	5			4	9		7	6	11	10				2					1		3	12		8^1			30
	5			4	9		7^1	6	11	10				2					1		3	8		12			31
	5		13	3	9		7^3	6	10	11^1	14			2					1		4	8^2		12			32
	5			6	9		7^1	11	10					2^2					1		3	8	12	13	4		33
	5		13	3	9		7	6	10		11^1			2^2						14	4^3	8			12	1	34
	5			3	9^2		7	6	10		11^1			2						13	4	8		12		1	35
	5			4	9		7	6^1	10	11^3	14			2					1	8^2	3	13			12		36

QUEEN'S PARK

Year Formed: 1867. *Ground & Address:* Hampden Park, Mount Florida, Glasgow G42 9BA. *Telephone:* 0141 632 1275. *Fax:* 0141 636 1612. *E-mail:* secretary@queensparkfc.co.uk *Website:* queensparkfc.co.uk
Ground Capacity: 51,866 (all seated). *Size of Pitch:* 105m × 68m.
President: Gerry Crawley. *Treasurer:* David Gordon.
Head Coach: Mark Roberts.
Club Nickname: 'The Spiders'.
Previous Grounds: 1st Hampden (Recreation Ground); (Titwood Park was used as an interim measure between 1st & 2nd Hampdens); 2nd Hampden (Cathkin); 3rd Hampden.
Record Attendance: 95,772 v Rangers, Scottish Cup 1st rd, 18 January 1930.
Record for Ground: 149,547 Scotland v England, 1937.
Record Transfer Fees: Not applicable due to amateur status.
Record Victory: 16-0 v St. Peter's, Scottish Cup 1st rd, 12 Sep 1885.
Record Defeat: 0-9 v Motherwell, Division I, 26 April 1930.
Most Capped Player: Walter Arnott, 14, Scotland.
Most League Appearances: 532: Ross Caven, 1982-2002.
Most League Goals in Season (Individual): 30: William Martin, Division I, 1937-38.
Most Goals Overall (Individual): 163: James B. McAlpine, 1919-33.

QUEEN'S PARK – SPFL LADBROKES LEAGUE TWO 2018–19 LEAGUE RECORD

Match No.	*Date*	*Venue*	*Opponents*	*Result*	*H/T Score*	*Lg Pos.*	*Goalscorers*	*Attendance*
1	Aug 4	A	Peterhead	D 1-1	1-1	4	Gibson [7]	552
2	11	H	Berwick R	W 1-0	1-0	4	McKernon (pen) [16]	679
3	18	A	Annan Ath	L 1-3	0-0	6	Osadolor [47]	420
4	25	H	Albion R	W 2-0	2-0	5	Roberts [15], Mortimer [45]	620
5	Sept 1	H	Cowdenbeath	D 0-0	0-0	5		534
6	15	A	Stirling Alb	L 0-1	0-1	6		702
7	22	H	Edinburgh C	L 0-2	0-1	6		487
8	29	A	Elgin C	L 1-2	1-0	6	Peters [12]	582
9	Oct 6	H	Clyde	W 1-0	1-0	6	Peters (pen) [26]	1076
10	27	A	Albion R	W 3-0	2-0	6	Hawke [4], McKernon [15], Osadolor [89]	390
11	Nov 3	H	Annan Ath	D 0-0	0-0	6		495
12	10	H	Peterhead	W 2-0	1-0	6	Summers 2 [26, 51]	475
13	27	A	Cowdenbeath	L 0-2	0-0	6		275
14	Dec 1	A	Edinburgh C	L 0-2	0-2	7		358
15	8	H	Stirling Alb	D 1-1	1-1	7	Hawke [14]	496
16	22	H	Elgin C	L 0-4	0-2	7		455
17	29	A	Clyde	L 0-2	0-2	7		603
18	Jan 5	H	Albion R	D 2-2	1-2	8	McLaren [13], Hawke [69]	642
19	12	H	Edinburgh C	L 0-4	0-3	8		526
20	19	A	Stirling Alb	D 1-1	1-1	8	McLean (pen) [27]	667
21	26	H	Berwick R	W 7-1	3-0	8	McLean 2 (1 pen) [15 (p), 56], Roberts 2 [18, 28], Galt 2 [54, 68], Hawke [73]	444
22	Feb 9	H	Cowdenbeath	D 1-1	0-0	8	McLean (pen) [90]	404
23	16	A	Peterhead	L 1-2	0-1	8	Gibson [49]	615
24	23	H	Clyde	W 3-0	0-0	8	Match awarded to Queen's Park after 1-1 draw.	977
25	26	A	Elgin C	D 2-2	0-0	8	Hawke [51], Moore [66]	504
26	Mar 2	A	Annan Ath	L 1-2	0-1	8	Galt [76]	379
27	9	A	Edinburgh C	L 0-2	0-1	8		325
28	12	A	Berwick R	W 2-1	1-1	7	Moore [35], Hawke [61]	293
29	16	H	Elgin C	W 4-1	1-1	7	Roberts [12], Galt 3 [65, 68, 70]	543
30	23	A	Cowdenbeath	D 0-0	0-0	7		347
31	30	H	Stirling Alb	D 0-0	0-0	7		661
32	Apr 6	A	Albion R	W 4-0	1-0	6	Ruth [14], McLean 2 (2 pens) [69, 71], Summers [90]	323
33	13	A	Berwick R	W 3-0	2-0	6	Moore [21], McLean (pen) [42], Summers [76]	540
34	20	H	Annan Ath	L 0-3	0-0	6		523
35	27	A	Clyde	L 0-3	0-1	6		1012
36	May 4	H	Peterhead	L 0-2	0-2	7		964

Final League Position: 7

Honours
League Champions: Division II 1922-23; B Division 1955-56; Second Division 1980-81; Third Division 1999-2000.
Runners-up: Third Division 2011-12; League Two 2014-15.
Promoted via play-offs: 2006-07 (to Second Division); 2015-16 (to League One).
Scottish Cup Winners: 1874, 1875, 1876, 1880, 1881, 1882, 1884, 1886, 1890, 1893; *Runners-up:* 1892, 1900.
FA Cup Runners-up: 1884, 1885.
FA Charity Shield: 1899 (shared with Aston Villa).

Club colours: Shirt: Black and white thin hoops. Shorts: White. Socks: Black.

Goalscorers: *League (41):* McLean 7 (6 pens), Galt 6, Hawke 6, Roberts 4, Summers 4, Moore 3, Gibson 2, McKernon 2 (1 pen), Osadolor 2, Peters 2 (1 pen), McLaren 1, Mortimer 1, Ruth 1.
William Hill Scottish FA Cup (2): Hawke 1, McLauchlan 1.
Betfred Scottish League Cup (2): Gibson 1, Roberts 1.
Irn-Bru Scottish League Challenge (7): Hawke 3, McLean 2 (1 pen), East 1, Osadolor 1.

Hart J 35	Grant J 18 + 3	McLauchlan G 24 + 1	Gibson S 27	Lachlan G 2	Roberts K 32	McKernon J 30 + 1	Kindlan Dean 3 + 1	Martin A 6 + 4	Osadolor S 8 + 4	Peters J 8 + 4	Mortimer W 17 + 4	Miller A 1 + 3	Sharpe B — + 3	Summers C 29 + 3	McGorry C 16 + 3	MacPherson E — + 3	McLean S 30 + 1	Hawke L 25 + 5	East E 5 + 17	Foy C 1 + 1	Fotheringham G 3 + 2	McLaren D 18 + 1	Moore K 15 + 13	Magee L 9 + 3	Gow A 10 + 8	Mcdougall K 1	Galt D 17	Bradley S — + 5	Ruth M 5 + 2	Main L 1	Black J — + 1	Match No.
1	2	3	4	5	6	7	8	9[1]	10[3]	11[2]	12	13	14																			1
1		4	3	5	9	7	6[2]	8[3]	11[1]		10		13	2	12	14																2
1	2	3	4		9	7	8[1]	14	10[2]		11	5	13			12	6[3]															3
1	2	3	4		8	7		14	10[3]		9[1]			5		12	6	11[2]	13													4
1	2	3[3]	4		6	7		14	10		11			5			8[2]	9[1]	13	12												5
1	2		4		6	8			11[2]	9[1]	10	12		5[3]			13		14	3	7											6
1	2	3	4		9	7			8[1]	12	11			5			10	13			6[2]											7
1	2	3[2]	4		6	7			12	9[3]	11			5			10[1]	8	13			14										8
1	2	3	4		6	7			13	9[2]	8[3]			5			10[1]	11	12				14									9
1	2	4			8[2]	3			14	11[3]				5			9	10	6[1]		13	7	12									10
1	2	3			7	6		14	13	9[1]				5			10[3]	11	8[2]			4	12									11
1	2	3			7	6								5			8[1]	11	10[2]		12	4■	9	13								12
1	2	3			8	6								5			9	10	12		7[1]		11[2]	4	13							13
1	2	3			7	8								5			6[1]	10[2]	9			4■	11	13	12							14
1	2	3■			6	7		10[2]			14			5			8[3]	11	12				13	4	9[1]							15
1	2				6	7	12	8		14	13			5				3[2]	10				11[3]	4	9[1]							16
1	2				6	7			10[1]	11[2]				5	8				12			4	13	3	9							17
	2	3[2]			6[1]	7		10		8				5[3]	13			11				4	14	12	9	1						18
1	2		4[1]			7		10[2]			9	12			6		8	11	13			3	14	5[3]								19
1			8[2]		7	3					2				6		5	10	13			4	12		9		11[1]					20
1		2	4		7	3				13	5[3]			12	6		9	11[1]					14		8[2]		10					21
1		2	4		7	3					5[2]			12	6[3]		8	10[1]	14				13		11		9					22
1		2	4		7	3					5[1]			12	6		8	10					13		11[2]		9					23
1		3	4		6									8	7[1]		5	10	13			2	12		9[2]		11					24
1	12		4[3]		8	7				14				2	6		5[2]	10	13			3	9[1]				11					25
1	12		4		7[3]	8					5[2]			2	6		3	10					9[1]		13		11	14				26
1	12		4		6	2								8[3]	9		5	10[2]				3	13		11■		7[1]	14				27
1			4		7	2								8	6		5	10	12			3	9[1]				11					28
1			4		6	3								8	7		5	10[2]				2	11[3]		14		9[1]	12	13			29
1			4		6	3								8	7		5	10[2]	12			2	11[1]		13		9					30
1		12	4		6	3								8	7[1]		5	10[2]	13			2	9[3]				11		14			31
1		4	5								2			6			7	12				3	11[3]	8	13		9[2]	14	10[1]			32
1		3	4								2			6			8	12				5	10[3]		13		9[1]	14	11[2]	7		33
1		3	4								5[1]			8[2]	12		7	14	13			2	11	6[3]			9		10			34
1		3	4		7	13								8	6[2]		5						9	2[1]			11		10		12	35
1		3	4		7[1]						14			8	6		5	13					9[3]	2	12		11		10[2]			36

RAITH ROVERS

Year Formed: 1883. *Ground & Address:* Stark's Park, Pratt St, Kirkcaldy KY1 1SA. *Telephone:* 01592 263514. *Fax:* 01592 642833. *E-mail:* info@raithrovers.net *Website:* www.raithrovers.net
Ground Capacity: 8,473 (all seated). *Size of Pitch:* 103m × 64m.
Chairman: Bill Clark. *Deputy Chairman:* David Sinton.
Manager: John McGlynn. *Assistant Manager:* Paul Smith.
Club Nickname: 'Rovers'.
Previous Grounds: Robbie's Park.
Record Attendance: 31,306 v Hearts, Scottish Cup 2nd rd, 7 February 1953.
Record Transfer Fee received: £900,000 for Steve McAnespie to Bolton W (September 1995).
Record Transfer Fee paid: £225,000 for Paul Harvey from Airdrieonians (July 1996).
Record Victory: 10-1 v Coldstream, Scottish Cup 2nd rd, 13 February 1954.
Record Defeat: 2-11 v Morton, Division II, 18 March 1936.
Most Capped Player: David Morris, 6, Scotland.
Most League Appearances: 430: Willie McNaught, 1946-51.
Most League Goals in Season (Individual): 38: Norman Haywood, Division II, 1937-38.
Most Goals Overall (Individual): 154: Gordon Dalziel (League), 1987-94.

RAITH ROVERS – SPFL LADBROKES LEAGUE ONE 2018–19 LEAGUE RECORD

Match No.	*Date*	*Venue*	*Opponents*	*Result*	*H/T Score*	*Lg Pos.*	*Goalscorers*	*Attendance*
1	Aug 4	A	Stranraer	D 1-1	1-0	5	Buchanan [29]	424
2	11	H	Stenhousemuir	W 2-0	1-0	2	Nisbet 2 (1 pen) [25 (p), 76]	1415
3	18	H	East Fife	D 2-2	1-1	4	Nisbet 2 (2 pens) [9, 75]	2025
4	25	A	Airdrieonians	W 4-3	0-2	2	Buchanan 2 [56, 87], Nisbet 2 [90, 90]	1119
5	Sept 1	H	Forfar Ath	W 4-0	1-0	2	Nisbet [28], Vaughan 2 [52, 68], Duggan [56]	1447
6	15	A	Brechin C	D 1-1	0-0	2	Nisbet (pen) [65]	623
7	22	H	Montrose	D 1-1	0-1	2	Campbell, I (og) [57]	1534
8	29	A	Dumbarton	W 5-1	4-0	2	Vaughan [1], Flanagan 2 [12, 33], Nisbet [37], Buchanan [87]	756
9	Oct 6	H	Arbroath	D 1-1	0-0	2	Nisbet [87]	2137
10	20	H	Stranraer	W 2-1	2-1	2	Nisbet 2 [5, 39]	1285
11	27	A	Forfar Ath	L 2-3	2-1	2	Matthews [29], Nisbet [33]	826
12	Nov 3	H	Brechin C	W 2-1	1-0	2	Nisbet 2 [41, 90]	1495
13	10	A	East Fife	L 1-2	1-0	2	Buchanan [11]	1756
14	17	A	Stenhousemuir	W 3-1	1-0	2	Armstrong 2 [11, 87], Crane [58]	797
15	Dec 1	H	Airdrieonians	W 2-0	2-0	2	Nisbet [7], Buchanan [31]	1567
16	8	A	Montrose	L 2-3	1-1	2	Armstrong [3], Nisbet [74]	784
17	15	H	Dumbarton	W 4-2	1-2	2	Armstrong [13], Nisbet [63], Murray [88], Vaughan [89]	1089
18	22	A	Arbroath	W 2-0	2-0	2	Armstrong [19], Buchanan [37]	1808
19	29	H	East Fife	L 1-2	0-2	2	Vaughan [84]	2833
20	Jan 5	H	Stenhousemuir	W 5-1	4-1	2	Davidson [18], Gillespie [33], Murray [38], Vaughan [40], Duggan [52]	1398
21	12	A	Airdrieonians	D 1-1	0-1	2	Murray [73]	1140
22	26	A	Brechin C	L 1-2	1-0	2	Nisbet [32]	601
23	Feb 2	H	Forfar Ath	D 1-1	1-0	2	Barjonas [34]	1406
24	16	H	Arbroath	L 0-1	0-1	2		1937
25	23	H	Montrose	W 4-1	2-0	2	Nisbet (pen) [2], Murray [33], Buchanan [55], McGuffie [82]	1289
26	26	A	Dumbarton	D 2-2	1-2	2	Flanagan [19], Nisbet [90]	507
27	Mar 2	A	Stranraer	D 2-2	0-2	3	McGuffie [48], Nisbet (pen) [56]	310
28	9	H	Airdrieonians	W 1-0	0-0	2	Gillespie [74]	1339
29	16	A	Forfar Ath	L 1-2	0-1	3	Nisbet [52]	509
30	23	H	Dumbarton	W 4-1	3-1	2	Matthews [9], Buchanan [26], Nisbet 2 [45, 55]	1338
31	30	A	East Fife	W 2-1	0-1	2	Davidson [87], Nisbet [89]	1592
32	Apr 6	A	Stenhousemuir	D 1-1	0-0	2	Buchanan [90]	784
33	13	H	Stranraer	L 2-3	2-2	2	McKay [4], Barjonas [34]	1204
34	21	A	Arbroath	D 2-2	1-1	3	Nisbet 2 [27, 51]	932
35	27	H	Brechin C	W 3-2	2-2	3	Nisbet 2 [27, 36], Buchanan [68]	1266
36	May 4	A	Montrose	D 1-1	1-1	3	McGuffie [20]	688

Final League Position: 3

Honours
League Champions: First Division 1992-93, 1994-95; Second Division 2002-03, 2008-09; Division II 1907-08, 1909-10 (shared with Leith Ath), 1937-38, 1948-49.
Runners-up: Division II 1908-09, 1926-27, 1966-67;. Second Division 1975-76, 1977-78, 1986-87; League One 2017-18.
Scottish Cup Runners-up: 1913.
League Cup Winners: 1994-95; *Runners-up:* 1948-49.
League Challenge Cup Winners: 2013-14.

European: *UEFA Cup:* 6 matches (1995-96).

Club colours: Shirt: Navy with white trim. Shorts: White with navy trim. Socks: Navy.

Goalscorers: *League (75):* Nisbet 30 (6 pens), Buchanan 11, Vaughan 6, Armstrong 5, Murray 4, Flanagan 3, McGuffie 3, Barjonas 2, Davidson 2, Duggan 2, Gillespie 2, Matthews 2, Crane 1, McKay 1, own goal 1.
William Hill Scottish FA Cup (7): Vaughan 3 (1 pen), Buchanan 1, Flanagan 1, Murray 1, Nisbet 1.
Betfred Scottish League Cup (2): Gillespie 1, Nisbet 1.
Irn-Bru Scottish League Challenge (3): Matthews 1, Nisbet 1, Wedderburn 1.
Play-Offs (4): Nisbet 2 (1 pen), Gullan 1, McKay 1.

Wright K 7	Watson J 8 + 3	McKay D 12 + 3	Benedictus K 25	Murray E 33 + 1	Gillespie G 26 + 1	Matthews R 24 + 7	Wedderburn N 32 + 1	Valentine E 1 + 2	Nisbet K 33 + 1	Buchanan L 25 + 9	Milne L 5 + 9	Flanagan N 23 + 9	Davidson I 29	Duggan C 5 + 9	Vaughan L 7 + 4	Thomson R 22 + 1	Crane C 24	Hendry R 4	Berry J — + 2	Stevenson R 1 + 3	Smith J — + 4	Armstrong D 9	Dingwall T 8 + 1	McGuffie C 5 + 8	Lyness D 7 + 1	Barjonas J 13 + 1	Browne K 1 + 3	Gullan J 7 + 3	Tait D — + 1	*Match No.*
1	2	3	4	5	6	7	8	9^2	10	11^1	12	13																		1
1	2	3	4	5	7	6	8	13	10	11^1	12	9^2																		2
1	2	8	3	5	4	6	7		11	10^1	12	9																		3
1	2	13	4^2	5	7	6^1	8		11	10		9	3■	12																4
1	2	3		5	8	9	4	13	6^2	11		7^1		10	12															5
1	14		3	9^2	8	6	4		5	10^3	13	12	2	11^1	7															6
1^2			3	4	7^3	6^1	8		10	14	5	9	2	13	11	12														7
			4	2			7		6	12	10^3	9^2	3		11	1	5	8^1	13	14										8
			4	2		13	8		11	12	6	9^1	3		10^2	1	5	7												9
	12		4	2■		6	8		10^3	13		11^2	3			1	5	7	14	9^1										10
	2		4			9	8		11	12	6	10	3			1	5	7^1												11
			4	2		7	8		11	10^1	6^2	9	3			1	5			12	13									12
	12		4	2		8	7		10	11^2		6	3^3			1	5			14	13	9^1								13
	2	13	4	5		6			11	9^2	12	10	3			1	7					8^1								14
			4	5	2	7	8		11^2	10	13	9^1	3	12		1					14	6^3								15
			4	5	2	7	8		11	10^1		9	3	12		1						6								16
			4	5	2	7	8		11	10^2		6^1	3	13	12	1						9								17
			4	2	5	8	7		11	10^1	14	6^3	3	13	12	1						9^2								18
			4	5	2	7^3	8		11	10^1	14	6^2	3	13	12	1						9								19
			4	2	7		8^2		11^3	10^1	13	14	3	12	9	1	5					6								20
			4	2	7		8			10^1		12	3	11	9	1	5					6^2	13							21
			4	2	8		7		12			6^2	3	11	10^1	1	5						9	13						22
			4	2	6	13	8		10^2	12			3	11			5						9		1	7^1				23
			4	2	7		8		11^1	13		10^3	3^2				5				14		6	12	1	9				24
				2	7	13	4		10	11^1		9^2	3			1	5						6	12		8^3	14			25
				4	2^1	12	8^3		11	10		6^2	3				5						9	13	1	7	14			26
		3		4	2	7			10	12		13				1	5						9	6^1		8		11^2		27
		3		2	7^2	14	8		11	10^1		12	4			1	5						9^3			6		13		28
		8		4	2	13	7^3		10	11^1			3			1	5						6	14		9^2		12		29
		12		3	2	6	8^1		11	10^2		13	4			1	5							14		7		9^3		30
				3	2	7^1	6		11	10^2		12	4			1	5							13		8		9		31
		4		2	3	13	8		10	12		6				1^1	5							9^2	14	7		11^3		32
		4		2		6	7^2		11	10^1		9^3	3				5							13	1	8	14	12		33
		2	4			6			9	10^1			3	12			5							8	1	7		11		34
		2^2	4	13	14	6^1	12		9	10			3				5							8	1	7^3		11		35
	2	3		4	8	6	7^1					13					5							9^3	1	12	10^2	11	14	36

RANGERS

Year Formed: 1873. *Ground & Address:* Ibrox Stadium, 150 Edmiston Drive, Glasgow G51 2XD.
Telephone: 0871 702 1972. *Fax:* 0870 600 1978. *Website:* rangers.co.uk
Ground Capacity: 51,082 (all seated). *Size of Pitch:* 105m × 68m.
Chairman: Dave King. *Deputy Chairman:* Douglas Park.
Manager: Steven Gerrard. *Assistant Manager:* Gary McAllister.
Club Nickname: 'The Gers'; 'The Teddy Bears'.
Previous Grounds: Flesher's Haugh, Burnbank, Kinning Park, Old Ibrox.
Record Attendance: 118,567 v Celtic, Division I, 2 January 1939.
Record Transfer Fee received: £9,000,000 for Alan Hutton to Tottenham H (January 2008).
Record Transfer Fee paid: £12,000,000 for Tore Andre Flo from Chelsea (November 2000).
Record Victory: 13-0 v Possilpark, Scottish Cup 1st rd, 6 October 1877; v Uddingston, Scottish Cup 3rd rd, 10 November 1877; v Kelvinside Athletic, Scottish Cup 2nd rd, 28 September 1889.
Record Defeat: 1-7 v Celtic, League Cup Final, 19 October 1957.
Most Capped Player: Ally McCoist, 60, Scotland. *Most League Appearances:* 496: John Greig, 1962-78.
Most League Goals in Season (Individual): 44: Sam English, Division I, 1931-32.
Most Goals Overall (Individual): 355: Ally McCoist; 1985-98.

Honours
League Champions: (54 times) Division I 1890-91 (shared with Dumbarton), 1898-99, 1899-1900, 1900-01, 1901-02, 1910-11, 1911-12, 1912-13, 1917-18, 1919-20, 1920-21, 1922-23, 1923-24, 1924-25, 1926-27, 1927-28, 1928-29, 1929-30, 1930-31, 1932-33, 1933-34, 1934-35, 1936-37, 1938-39, 1946-47, 1948-49, 1949-50, 1952-53, 1955-56, 1956-57, 1958-59, 1960-61, 1962-63, 1963-64, 1974-75. Premier Division: 1975-76, 1977-78, 1986-87, 1988-89, 1989-90, 1990-91, 1991-92, 1992-93, 1993-94, 1994-95, 1995-96, 1996-97, 1998-99, 1999-2000, 2002-03, 2004-05, 2008-09, 2009-10, 2010-11. *Runners-up, tier 1:* 31 times. Championship 2015-16. League One 2013-14. Third Division 2012-13.
Scottish Cup Winners: (33 times) 1894, 1897, 1898, 1903, 1928, 1930, 1932, 1934, 1935, 1936, 1948, 1949, 1950, 1953, 1960, 1962, 1963, 1964, 1966, 1973, 1976, 1978, 1979, 1981, 1992, 1993, 1996, 1999, 2000, 2002, 2003, 2008, 2009; *Runners-up:* 18 times.

RANGERS – SPFL LADBROKES PREMIERSHIP 2018–19 LEAGUE RECORD

Match No.	*Date*	*Venue*	*Opponents*	*Result*		*H/T Score*	*Lg Pos.*	*Goalscorers*	*Attendance*
1	Aug 5	A	Aberdeen	D	1-1	1-0	6	Tavernier (pen) [30]	19,046
2	12	H	St Mirren	W	2-0	2-0	3	Morelos [14], Goldson [24]	49,680
3	26	A	Motherwell	D	3-3	3-2	4	Lafferty 2 [15, 38], Ejaria [43]	9545
4	Sept 2	A	Celtic	L	0-1	0-0	7		58,865
5	15	H	Dundee	W	4-0	3-0	4	Coulibaly [4], Kent [14], Tavernier (pen) [45], Middleton [83]	50,130
6	23	H	St Johnstone	W	5-1	2-0	2	Tavernier [9], Morelos [34], Arfield [52], Lafferty [74], Candeias [79]	48,729
7	30	A	Livingston	L	0-1	0-1	6		9246
8	Oct 7	H	Hearts	W	3-1	3-0	6	Kent [3], Morelos [13], Arfield [32]	49,865
9	21	A	Hamilton A	W	4-1	1-0	5	Kent [41], Tavernier 2 (2 pens) [84, 87], Morelos [90]	5013
10	31	H	Kilmarnock	D	1-1	1-1	4	Morelos [9]	49,279
11	Nov 3	A	St Mirren	W	2-0	0-0	3	Candeias [80], Morelos [90]	6033
12	11	H	Motherwell	W	7-1	3-1	3	Arfield 2 [8, 61], Tavernier (pen) [35], Morelos [38], Middleton [59], Grezda 2 [68, 75]	49,802
13	24	H	Livingston	W	3-0	1-0	2	Candeias [20], Morelos [83], Arfield [88]	49,448
14	Dec 2	A	Hearts	W	2-1	2-1	1	Goldson [34], Morelos [41]	19,429
15	5	H	Aberdeen	L	0-1	0-1	2		49,711
16	9	A	Dundee	D	1-1	1-1	2	Halliday [21]	8578
17	16	H	Hamilton A	W	1-0	1-0	1	Candeias [3]	49,055
18	19	A	Hibernian	D	0-0	0-0	2		18,662
19	23	A	St Johnstone	W	2-1	0-1	2	Morelos 2 [65, 88]	7086
20	26	H	Hibernian	D	1-1	1-0	2	Morelos [25]	49,885
21	29	H	Celtic	W	1-0	1-0	2	Jack [30]	49,863
22	Jan 23	A	Kilmarnock	L	1-2	1-1	3	Defoe [12]	12,374
23	27	A	Livingston	W	3-0	1-0	2	Jack [30], Kent [48], Morelos [74]	9028
24	Feb 2	H	St Mirren	W	4-0	1-0	2	Tavernier 2 (2 pens) [3, 55], Defoe (pen) [80], Kent [81]	49,463
25	6	A	Aberdeen	W	4-2	3-1	2	Morelos 2 [20, 38], Tavernier (pen) [43], Defoe [90]	19,190
26	16	H	St Johnstone	D	0-0	0-0	2		49,549
27	24	A	Hamilton A	W	5-0	4-0	2	Jack [16], Defoe [17], Arfield [24], Tavernier (pen) [44], Lafferty [88]	5827
28	27	H	Dundee	W	4-0	3-0	2	Kamara [4], Tavernier [8], Morelos [23], Defoe [89]	48,859
29	Mar 8	A	Hibernian	D	1-1	1-0	2	Candeias [43]	20,065
30	16	H	Kilmarnock	D	1-1	0-1	2	Morelos [64]	49,527
31	31	A	Celtic	L	1-2	0-1	2	Kent [63]	58,773
32	Apr 3	H	Hearts	W	3-0	2-0	2	Defoe [16], Goldson [21], Arfield [48]	49,702
33	7	A	Motherwell	W	3-0	2-0	2	Arfield 3 [22, 39, 60]	9200
34	20	A	Hearts	W	3-1	2-0	2	Defoe [15], Jack [36], Katic [48]	18,212
35	28	H	Aberdeen	W	2-0	0-0	2	Tavernier 2 (2 pens) [48, 80]	49,667
36	May 5	H	Hibernian	W	1-0	1-0	2	Defoe [41]	49,662
37	12	H	Celtic	W	2-0	1-0	2	Tavernier [2], Arfield [63]	49,844
38	19	A	Kilmarnock	L	1-2	0-1	2	Morelos [66]	12,248

Final League Position: 2

League Cup Winners: (27 times) 1946-47, 1948-49, 1960-61, 1961-62, 1963-64, 1964-65, 1970-71, 1975-76, 1977-78, 1978-79, 1981-82, 1983-84, 1984-85, 1986-87, 1987-88, 1988-89, 1990-91, 1992-93, 1993-94, 1996-97, 1998-99, 2001-02, 2002-03, 2004-05, 2007-08, 2009-10, 2010-11; *Runners-up:* 7 times.
League Challenge Cup Winners: 2015-16; *Runners-up:* 2013-14.

European: *European Cup:* 161 matches (1956-57, 1957-58, 1959-60 semi-finals, 1961-62, 1963-64, 1964-65, 1975-76, 1976-77, 1978-79, 1987-88, 1989-90, 1990-91, 1991-92, 1992-93 final pool, 1993-94, 1994-95, 1995-96; 1996-97, 1997-98, 1999-2000, 2000-01, 2001-02, 2003-04, 2004-05, 2005-06, 2007-08, 2008-09, 2009-10, 2010-11, 2011-12).
Cup Winners' Cup: 54 matches (1960-61 runners-up, 1962-63, 1966-67 runners-up, 1969-70, 1971-72 winners, 1973-74, 1977-78, 1979-80, 1981-82, 1983-84).
UEFA Cup: 88 matches (*Fairs Cup:* 1967-68, 1968-69 semi-finals, 1970-71. *UEFA Cup:* 1982-83, 1984-85, 1985-86, 1986-87, 1988-89, 1997-98, 1998-99, 1999-2000, 2000-01, 2001-02, 2002-03, 2004-05, 2006-07, 2007-08 runners-up). *Europa League:* 8 matches (2010-11, 2011-12, 2017-18).

Club colours: Shirt: Royal blue with white trim. Shorts: White with blue trim. Socks: Black with red tops.

Goalscorers: *League (82):* Morelos 18, Tavernier 14 (11 pens), Arfield 11, Defoe 8 (1 pen), Kent 6, Candeias 5, Jack 4, Lafferty 4, Goldson 3, Grezda 2, Middleton 2, Coulibaly 1, Ejaria 1, Halliday 1, Kamara 1, Katic 1.
William Hill Scottish FA Cup (9): Morelos 4, Halliday 2, Coulibaly 1, Lafferty 1, Worrall 1.
Betfred Scottish League Cup (7): Morelos 4, Middleton 2, Katic 1. *Irn-Bru Scottish League Challenge (1):* Rudden 1.
Europa League: (17): Morelos 4, Tavernier 3 (3 pens), Arfield 1, Candeias 1, Coulibaly 1, Ejaria 1, Goldson 1, Katic 1, Lafferty 1, Middleton 1, Murphy 1, own goal 1.

McGregor A 34	Tavernier J 36 + 1	Katic N 16 + 2	Goldson C 34	Flanagan J 14 + 2	Arfield S 28 + 1	Jack R 25 + 4	Coulibaly L 14 + 5	Murphy J 2	Windass J 1	Morelos A 27 + 3	Kent R 25 + 2	Ejaria O 11 + 3	Barisic B 14 + 2	McCrorie Ross 11 + 9	Halliday A 18 + 5	Umar S — + 1	Lafferty K 6 + 15	Middleton G 4 + 11	Wallace L — + 3	Candeias D 26 + 7	Grezda E 7 + 6	Dorrans G — + 1	Worrall J 20 + 2	Rossiter J 2 + 2	Foderingham W 4	McAuley G 6 + 1	Atakayi S — + 1	Davis S 10 + 4	Defoe J 10 + 7	Kamara G 12 + 1	Polster M — + 1	Mebude D — + 1	Firth A — + 1	Match No.
1	2	3	4	5	6	7^{2}	8	9^{1}	10	11■	12	13																						1
1	12	4	3	2			8	10		11^{3}	7^{2}	9	5^{1}	6■	13	14																		2
1	6	4	3	2	12	7				10		8^{3}	5^{2}		9^{1}		11	13	14															3
1	2	3	4		9	6^{1}				11	8^{2}	7	5				10	12		13														4
1	2	4	3		9		8^{1}			11^{2}	10^{3}		5		6		13	12		7	14													5
1	2^{2}	4	3	5	9		8^{1}			11	10^{3}	12		6			14			7		13												6
1	2		3		6		7^{1}			10	12	8	5				11^{2}	13		9			4											7
1	2		3	5	8^{1}	12	6			11	10	9^{2}			13		14			7^{3}			4											8
1	2	4^{1}	3				6			10	11^{2}	8		14	5					9	13		12	7^{3}										9
	2		3	5^{3}	8	12	6^{2}			11	10				9		14	13		7^{1}			4		1									10
1	2		3		8	7				10	9	6^{2}			5					12■	11^{1}		4	13										11
1	2	3^{3}			8	6				11^{2}		9			5		13	10^{1}			7		4			12	14							12
1	2		3	13	9	6	14			12		8^{1}			5^{2}		11^{3}	10		7						4								13
1	2		3		8■	12	7^{2}			10		6		13	5		14			9^{3}	11^{1}					4								14
1	2		4	5^{2}		6	8^{1}			11■		9					12	10		7	13					3								15
1	2		3			7					8^{2}	14	13		5^{1}		10	12		9	11		4	6^{3}										16
1	2		3		8	9							5	6^{2}	13		11	12		7^{1}	10					4								17
1	2		3		9^{1}	6	7			11			5	12				14		8	10^{3}		13			4^{1}								18
1	2		4				9^{1}			11			5^{2}	6	7		14	13	12	8	10^{3}		3											19
1	2	12	3^{1}			9	8^{3}			11				6	5		14	10^{2}		7			4	13										20
1	2		3	13	8^{1}	9	12			11	10			6	5					7^{2}			4											21
1	2				7	6				10	9				5		13			12			4			3		8^{1}	11^{2}					22
1	2	4			8	7				10^{1}	11^{2}		5^{3}	6	14					9			3					13	12					23
1	2	4			6	12				9	11		5	7^{3}			14			13			3					8^{1}	10^{2}					24
1	2	13	4		6^{3}	7	14			10■	11^{1}		5	8						9^{2}			3						12					25
	2		3				14				10		5	6^{1}			13	12		7^{3}			4		1			8^{2}	11	9				26
1	2		3		9^{2}	6	14				10^{1}				5		12			7			4					13	11	8^{3}				27
1	2		3		9^{1}	6				11	10^{3}		5	14						7^{2}			4					12	13	8				28
1	2		4		9^{1}	6				11	10				5					8			3						12	7				29
1	2	4	3				6^{1}			10	11		13		5^{3}					9^{2}	12							8	14	7				30
1	2		3		6^{1}	7^{2}				10■	11			4	8■					9^{3}			5					14	13	12				31
1	2		3	5	8^{2}	7^{1}					10			12			14				13		4					6	11^{3}	9				32
1	2	4	3	5	10^{2}	6								12	14					8	13							9^{1}	11	7^{3}				33
1	2	3	4	5	11	6											13	12		9^{2}								7^{1}	10^{3}	8	14			34
1	2	4	3	5	9	6					10^{3}			12					14	13								8^{2}	11^{1}	7				35
1■	2	4	3	5	9	6				13	11^{1}			14						12								7	10^{2}	8^{3}				36
	2	4	3	5	9^{2}	6				12	10			14						13					1			8^{1}	11^{3}	7				37
			3	2		7				10	11		5		8^{2}					9^{1}			4		1^{3}				13	6		12	14	38

ROSS COUNTY

Year Formed: 1929. *Ground & Address:* The Global Energy Stadium, Victoria Park, Dingwall IV15 9QZ. *Telephone:* 01349 860860. *Fax:* 01349 866277. *E-mail:* info@rosscountyfootballclub.co.uk
Website: www.rosscountyfootballclub.co.uk
Ground Capacity: 6,700 (all seated). *Size of Ground:* 105 × 68m.
Chairman: Roy MacGregor. *Club Secretary:* Fiona MacBean.
Co-managers: Steven Ferguson and Stuart Kettlewell.
Club Nickname: 'The Staggies'.
Record Attendance: 6,110 v Celtic, Premier League, 18 August 2012.
Record Transfer Fee received: £500,000 for Liam Boyce to Burton Albion (June 2017).
Record Transfer Fee paid: £50,000 for Derek Holmes from Hearts (October 1999).
Record Victory: 11-0 v St Cuthbert Wanderers, Scottish Cup 1st rd, 11 December 1993.
Record Defeat: 0-7 v Kilmarnock, Scottish Cup 3rd rd, 17 February 1962.
Most League Appearances: 308: Michael Gardyne, 2006-07, 2008-12, 2014-19.
Most League Goals in Season: 24: Andrew Barrowman, 2007-08.
Most League Goals (Overall): 48: Liam Boyce, 2014-17.

ROSS COUNTY – SPFL LADBROKES CHAMPIONSHIP 2018–19 LEAGUE RECORD

Match No.	Date	Venue	Opponents	Result		H/T Score	Lg Pos.	Goalscorers	Attendance
1	Aug 4	H	Alloa Ath	W	1-0	0-0	3	Fraser 88	3065
2	11	A	Dunfermline Ath	W	3-1	2-1	1	Mullin 25, Gardyne 42, Watson 68	4949
3	25	A	Greenock Morton	L	1-2	0-0	4	Cowie 58	1994
4	Sept 1	H	Falkirk	W	2-0	0-0	1	Lindsay 68, McManus 90	3564
5	15	A	Queen of the South	D	0-0	0-0	2		1509
6	22	H	Inverness CT	D	0-0	0-0	4		6402
7	29	A	Dundee U	W	5-1	3-1	2	McKay 3 11, 29, 51, Kelly, S 42, Mullin 50	4446
8	Oct 6	A	Partick Thistle	W	2-0	1-0	2	Mullin 14, McKay (pen) 56	2784
9	20	H	Ayr U	W	2-1	2-0	1	McKay 23, Mullin 34	3140
10	27	H	Greenock Morton	W	5-0	2-0	1	McKay 3 9, 42, 48, Keillor-Dunn 57, Graham (pen) 90	3481
11	30	A	Falkirk	D	1-1	0-1	2	Vigurs 78	3767
12	Nov 3	A	Inverness CT	D	2-2	2-2	2	Lindsay 17, McKay (og) 43	4353
13	10	H	Dundee U	L	0-1	0-1	2		4565
14	24	H	Dunfermline Ath	W	2-1	1-0	2	McKay 9, Lindsay 60	3121
15	Dec 1	A	Alloa Ath	W	1-0	0-0	2	Watson 90	592
16	8	H	Queen of the South	D	1-1	0-0	2	Mullin 55	3305
17	15	A	Ayr U	D	3-3	1-3	2	Mullin 12, McKay (pen) 48, Cowie 52	2030
18	22	H	Partick Thistle	W	2-0	1-0	1	McKay (pen) 26, Stewart, Ross C 79	3467
19	29	H	Inverness CT	W	2-1	1-1	1	McKay 16, Stewart, Ross C 84	6313
20	Jan 4	A	Greenock Morton	L	0-1	0-0	1		1537
21	12	A	Queen of the South	L	0-4	0-2	1		1386
22	26	H	Alloa Ath	W	2-0	1-0	1	McManus 12, Lindsay 62	3521
23	Feb 2	A	Dunfermline Ath	W	2-1	0-1	1	McKay 52, Gardyne 77	4347
24	23	A	Partick Thistle	W	4-2	0-2	1	Stewart, Ross C 2 47, 74, Lindsay 64, McKay (pen) 79	3007
25	26	H	Ayr U	W	3-2	1-0	1	McKay 3 35, 70, 75	3489
26	Mar 9	H	Greenock Morton	W	2-0	0-0	1	Mullin 55, Graham 78	3110
27	12	H	Falkirk	W	2-1	2-0	1	Graham 12, Watson 22	3148
28	19	A	Dundee U	L	0-1	0-1	1		4290
29	30	A	Alloa Ath	L	0-1	0-1	1		697
30	Apr 2	A	Inverness CT	W	2-1	2-1	1	Mullin 8, Boyle 34	3795
31	5	H	Dundee U	D	1-1	0-1	1	Lindsay 90	3550
32	9	H	Dunfermline Ath	W	1-0	0-0	1	Grivosti 60	3222
33	13	H	Partick Thistle	D	0-0	0-0	1		4031
34	19	A	Ayr U	W	3-1	1-1	1	Graham 3 42, 46, 71	1692
35	26	H	Queen of the South	W	4-0	1-0	1	Stewart, Ross C 29, Graham 2 51, 81, Mullin 54	4805
36	May 4	A	Falkirk	L	2-3	0-1	1	Stewart, Ross C 58, Vigurs 73	4682

Final League Position: 1

Honours
League Champions: First Division 2011-12; Championship 2018-19; Second Division 2007-08; Third Division 1998-99.
Scottish Cup Runners-up: 2010.
League Cup Winners: 2015-16.
League Challenge Cup Winners: 2006-07, 2010-11, 2018-19; *Runners-up:* 2004-05, 2008-09.

Club colours: Shirt: Navy blue and light blue hoops. Shorts: Navy blue. Socks: Navy blue with red tops.

Goalscorers: *League (63):* McKay 17 (4 pens), Mullin 9, Graham 8 (1 pen), Lindsay 6, Ross C Stewart 6, Watson 3, Cowie 2, Gardyne 2, McManus 2, Vigurs 2, Boyle 1, Fraser 1, Grivosti 1, Keillor-Dunn 1, Kelly S 1, own goal 1.
William Hill Scottish FA Cup (6): Graham 2, Ross C Stewart 2, Gardyne 1, Mullin 1.
Betfred Scottish League Cup (8): Mullin 2 (1 pen), Gardyne 1, Lindsay 1, McKay 1, McManus 1, Morris 1, Paton 1.
Irn-Bru Scottish League Challenge (17): Graham 4, Ross C Stewart 3, Keillor-Dunn 2, Lindsay 2, McKay 2, Mullin 2, Armstrong 1, McManus 1.

Fox S 36	Fraser M 26	Watson K 27	Morris C 12	Kelly S 19 + 1	Mullin J 30 + 2	Draper R 23 + 1	Vigurs I 13 + 2	Lindsay J 34 + 1	McKay B 22 + 2	McManus D 12 + 20	Keillor-Dunn D 6 + 5	Graham B 12 + 18	Dow R — + 2	Gardyne M 19 + 6	Dingwall T 1 + 1	Fontaine L 8 + 1	Cowie D 21 + 8	Stewart Ross C 17 + 6	Demetriou S 8 + 1	Grivosti T 12 + 5	Gallagher M — + 2	Wallace J — + 1	Paton H — + 4	van der Weg K 12	Spence L 12 + 3	Semple C 2 + 2	Boyle A 9 + 2	Armstrong D 3 + 3	Munro R — + 1	*Match No.*
1	2	3	4	5	6	7^3	8	9	10^1	11^2	12	13	14																	1
1	2	3	4	5	6^3	7	8	9		11^2	13	12	14	10^1																2
1			3	5	9^3	7^1	8		14	11^2	13	12		10	2	4	6													3
1		4	3		9	7^1	8	13	10^3	12		11^2		5		2	6	14												4
1			3	13	9	4	8	7	12	10^2		11		5^1		2	6^3	14												5
1		2	3	5	12	8^2	13	7	10	14		11^3		9		4	6^1													6
1		2	3	5	6	9	8	7^1	11^3	13	12			10^2		4	14													7
1		2	3	5	8	6■	7^1	9	11^2		10^3	14			12	4	13													8
1		2	3^3	5	6		8^2	10	11		9	14				4^1	7		12	13										9
1		4		5	6	3	8^1	7	11^3	13	10	12					9^2		2		14									10
1		4		5	9	3	7	8	10	13	11^2	12					6^1		2											11
1	2	4		5	7^2	3	6	9	11	12	10^1	13					8^3	14												12
1	2	3		5	6	9	8	7	11	12	10^1	13				4^2														13
1	2	4	3^1		6	12		7	10	9^2	14	13					8	11^3	5											14
1	2	4			7	6		8	11	10^1		12					9^2	13	5	3										15
1	2	4			7	6		8	11	13				12			9^1	10^2	5	3										16
1	2	3			9	6		8	10^1	13				12			7^2	11	5	4										17
1	2	3			7^1	6		8	11^3	13				12			9	10^2	5	4		14								18
1	2	3	4			6		8	11	13		14■		7^1			9^2	10	5^3	12										19
1	2■	4	3^1		12	6		9	11	14				7			8^2	10		5^3			13							20
1		2			9■	3		7	10^1	13				6^2				11		4			12	5	8					21
1	2	3		5^2		8		7	10^3	6		11		14			13							4	9^1	12				22
1	2	3				8		7	10	6^1		11^2		13				14						4	9	5^3	12			23
1	2	3			6^2			7	11^1			13		9			14	10		12				5	8		4^3			24
1	2	3			6^3			7	10^2	13		12		9			14	11^1		4				5	8					25
1	2	3			6			7		10^2		11		9^3			12			4			14	5	8^1			13		26
1	2	3			6^1			9		12		11		10^2			7^3			4■				5	8	14	13			27
1	2	3			6	7^2		9		14		12		10			13	11^1						5	8^3		4			28
1	2^2	3^3			9			6				10		11			8	12		13				5	7^1		4	14		29
1	2			5	6	7^1		8		10		13						11						4	12		3	9^2		30
1	2			5	6			8		10^3		12		14			13	11						4	7^1		3	9^2		31
1	2			5	6			8		13		11^2		9^3			7	10		12				4^1	14		3			32
1	2			5	6			9		13		12		10			8	11^1		4					7^2		3			33
1	2			5	6^1			7^3		12		10^2		9			8	11		3					14		4	13		34
1	2			5	6		14	7		12		10		9		13	8^1	11^3		4							3^2			35
1^3	2			4			7^1	6		5		11						10			14		13		8^2	3		9	12	36

ST JOHNSTONE

Year Formed: 1884. *Ground & Address:* McDiarmid Park, Crieff Road, Perth PH1 2SJ. *Telephone:* 01738 459090. *Fax:* 01738 625 771. *E-mail:* enquiries@perthsaints.co.uk *Website:* perthstjohnstonefc.co.uk
Ground Capacity: 10,673 (all seated). *Size of Pitch:* 105m × 68m.
Chairman: Steve Brown. *Vice-Chairman:* Charlie Fraser.
Manager: Tommy Wright. *Assistant Manager:* Alec Cleland.
Club Nickname: 'Saints'.
Previous Grounds: Recreation Grounds; Muirton Park.
Record Attendance: 29,972 v Dundee, Scottish Cup 2nd rd, 10 February 1951 (Muirton Park): 10,545 v Dundee, Premier Division, 23 May 1999 (McDiarmid Park).
Record Transfer Fee received: £1,750,000 for Callum Davidson to Blackburn R (March 1998).
Record Transfer Fee paid: £400,000 for Billy Dodds from Dundee (January 1994).
Record Victory: 9-0 v Albion R, League Cup, 9 March 1946.
Record Defeat: 1-10 v Third Lanark, Scottish Cup 1st rd, 24 January 1903.
Most Capped Player: Nick Dasovic, 26, Canada.
Most League Appearances: 362: Steven Anderson, 2004-19.
Most League Goals in Season (Individual): 36: Jimmy Benson, Division II, 1931-32.
Most Goals Overall (Individual): 140: John Brogan, 1977-83.

ST JOHNSTONE – SPFL LADBROKES PREMIERSHIP 2018–19 LEAGUE RECORD

Match No.	*Date*	*Venue*	*Opponents*	*Result*		*H/T Score*	*Lg Pos.*	*Goalscorers*	*Attendance*
1	Aug 4	A	Kilmarnock	L	0-2	0-0	11		4644
2	12	H	Hibernian	D	1-1	1-0	10	Watt 22	4637
3	25	H	Dundee	W	1-0	0-0	7	Watt 51	4259
4	Sept 1	A	Hamilton A	W	2-1	2-0	4	Alston 37, McMillan 45	1791
5	15	H	Aberdeen	D	1-1	1-0	6	McMillan 13	4880
6	23	A	Rangers	L	1-5	0-2	8	Alston (pen) 77	48,729
7	29	A	Hearts	L	1-2	0-1	8	Callachan 77	17,240
8	Oct 7	H	Celtic	L	0-6	0-5	8		5993
9	20	A	Motherwell	W	1-0	0-0	8	Kerr 90	3752
10	27	H	St Mirren	W	2-0	0-0	7	Wotherspoon 60, Kennedy 84	2716
11	31	A	Livingston	W	1-0	1-0	7	Kennedy 5	1476
12	Nov 3	A	Hibernian	W	1-0	0-0	5	Shaughnessy 90	17,307
13	10	H	Hamilton A	W	4-0	2-0	4	Davidson 20, Gordon (og) 36, Kennedy 54, Wotherspoon 74	2175
14	24	H	Kilmarnock	D	0-0	0-0	5		3559
15	Dec 5	H	Hearts	D	2-2	1-2	5	Alston 20, Kennedy (pen) 69	3040
16	8	A	Aberdeen	W	2-0	0-0	5	Shaughnessy 71, Alston 74	13,304
17	15	H	Motherwell	L	1-2	0-2	7	Kerr 83	2302
18	23	H	Rangers	L	1-2	1-0	8	Kennedy 45	7086
19	26	A	St Mirren	W	1-0	0-0	6	Watt 89	4891
20	29	A	Dundee	W	2-0	1-0	6	Tanser 1, Craig 58	6868
21	Jan 23	H	Livingston	W	1-0	0-0	5	Davidson 78	1946
22	26	A	Hearts	L	0-2	0-0	6		16,672
23	30	A	Celtic	L	0-2	0-0	6		54,563
24	Feb 3	H	Celtic	L	0-2	0-0	6		6242
25	6	A	Hamilton A	L	1-2	0-0	6	Craig 76	1174
26	16	A	Rangers	D	0-0	0-0	6		49,549
27	23	H	Aberdeen	L	0-2	0-1	7		5092
28	27	H	Hibernian	L	1-2	1-0	7	Kane 15	4136
29	Mar 9	A	Livingston	L	1-3	1-1	8	Shaughnessy 14	1615
30	27	H	St Mirren	W	1-0	1-0	7	Kane 13	2888
31	30	A	Motherwell	L	0-3	0-0	8		4083
32	Apr 3	H	Dundee	W	2-0	1-0	7	Hendry 16, Kennedy 60	3767
33	6	A	Kilmarnock	L	0-2	0-2	7		4685
34	20	H	Dundee	W	2-0	0-0	7	Tanser 54, Hendry 68	3946
35	27	A	St Mirren	D	1-1	0-0	7	Kane 79	5213
36	May 4	H	Livingston	D	1-1	1-0	7	O'Halloran 4	2222
37	11	H	Motherwell	W	2-0	1-0	7	Tanser (pen) 34, Davidson 47	3051
38	18	A	Hamilton A	L	0-2	0-1	7		2553

Final League Position: 7

Honours
League Champions: First Division 1982-83, 1989-90, 1996-97, 2008-09; Division II 1923-24, 1959-60, 1962-63.
Runners-up: Division II 1931-32; First Division 2005-06, 2006-07; Second Division 1987-88.
Scottish Cup Winners: 2014.
League Cup Runners-up: 1969-70, 1998-99.
League Challenge Cup Winners: 2007-08; *Runners-up:* 1996-97.

European: *UEFA Cup:* 10 matches (1971-72, 1999-2000). *Europa League:* 14 matches (2012-13, 2013-14, 2014-15, 2015-16, 2017-18).

Club colours: Shirt: Blue with light blue trim. Shorts: White with blue tartan trim. Socks: White.

Goalscorers: *League (38):* Kennedy 6 (1 pen), Alston 4 (1 pen), Davidson 3, Kane 3, Shaughnessy 3, Tanser 3 (1 pen), Watt 3, Craig 2, Hendry 2, Kerr 2, McMillan 2, Wotherspoon 2, Callachan 1, O'Halloran 1, own goal 1.
William Hill Scottish FA Cup (2): Kerr 1, Watt 1.
Betfred Scottish League Cup (9): Watt 4, Hendry 1, Kennedy 1, McMillan 1, Scougall 1, Wright 1.
Irn-Bru Scottish League Challenge (2): Hendry 2.

Clark Z 34	Comrie A 1	Gordon L 10 + 3	Anderson S 2 + 1	Kerr J 37	Tanser S 37	Wright D 13 + 1	Wotherspoon D 20 + 9	Davidson M 26 + 2	Kennedy M 34 + 2	Watt T 22 + 7	McMillan D 7 + 5	Craig L 33 + 3	Scougall S — + 1	Foster R 37	Alston B 10 + 11	Shaughnessy J 32 + 1	Hendry C 5 + 7	McCann A — + 1	Nydam T 1 + 4	Kane C 14 + 16	Callachan R 17 + 7	Swanson D 6 + 17	O'Halloran M 9 + 5	Goss S 6	Bell C 4	Northcott J — + 1	Easton B 1	Hamilton O — + 1	*Match No.*
1	2	3	4	5^{2}	6	7	8^{1}	9	10^{3}	11	12	13	14																1
1		12	4^{3}	3	5	6^{1}	13	7	10	11^{2}	14	8		2	9														2
1				3	5	6		7^{2}	9	11^{3}	10^{1}	8		2	12	4	13	14											3
1				3	5	6	12		9^{2}	11^{3}	10^{1}	7		2	8	4			13	14									4
1				3	5	6	14		9^{3}	11	10^{1}	8^{2}		2	7	4					12	13							5
1				3	5	6^{1}	10		9	11^{3}		8^{2}		2	7	4			12	14		13							6
1				3	5	6			9^{2}	13	11^{3}	14		2	7^{1}	4				10	8	12							7
1			12	3	5	6	9^{2}				11^{3}	14		2^{1}	7	4				13	8	10■							8
1		4		5	6	7^{3}	14	8	13	10^{1}	11^{2}	9		2		3				12									9
1				3	5	6	9	8	11^{2}	10^{1}		7		2		4			13	12									10
1		4		3	8	14	9^{2}	6	11^{3}	10^{1}		7		5		2				12	13								11
1				4	5	6	13		10^{3}	11^{1}		8		2		3			9^{2}	14	7	12							12
1				4	5	6	9	7	10^{3}	11^{1}	13	8^{2}		2		3			14	12									13
1				3	5	6^{3}	9	7	10^{1}	11^{2}		8		2		4				13	14	12							14
1		12		3	5^{2}		9	7	10	11^{3}	14	8		2	6^{1}	4				13									15
1				3	5		9	7	10	11^{1}		8		2	12	4				13	6^{2}								16
1				4	5		9^{3}	8	11	10	6^{1}	7^{2}		2	14	3				12		13							17
1				3	5		10^{1}	8	11^{2}	12		9		2	7	4					6	13							18
1				4	5		13	7^{2}	6^{1}	10		8		2	9	3				14	12	11^{3}							19
1				4	5		9		6^{1}	11^{7}	12	8		2		3				10	7	13							20
1				3	5		6	8	11^{2}	10^{1}		9		2	13	4				12	7^{3}		14						21
1		2^{2}		3	9			7	10	11^{1}		8		5		4	14				6^{3}	12	13						22
1				3	5		9	7	14	13		8		2	6^{2}	4					12	10^{1}	11^{3}						23
1				3	5		12	7	6^{2}	11				2		4	14				8	10^{1}	13	9^{3}					24
1				3	5		13		11^{1}	10^{2}		9		2	14	4				12	8^{3}		6	7					25
				3	5		7^{2}	8	10^{1}			9		2	12	4				11	14	13		6^{3}	1				26
				3	5		7^{2}	8	10	12		9^{1}		2		4	14			11^{3}		13		6	1				27
				3	5		9^{3}	7	6^{1}	11		8		2^{2}	12	4	14			10		13			1				28
				3	5		8	7^{2}	10^{1}	12				2	14	4				11		9	13	6^{3}	1				29
1		4		2	9			6	11^{1}	12		8		5		3				10	7								30
1				4	5			9	10	14		7^{1}		2		3				11	12	13	8^{3}	6^{2}					31
1				4	5			12	10^{2}			6		2		3	9^{1}			11	7		8			13			32
1		12		3■	5^{1}				9			8		2	14	4	11^{3}			10	7	13	6^{2}						33
1		4			5			12	10^{3}			7		2	13	3	9^{1}			11	6	14	8^{2}						34
1		4		3	5		12	6	10^{1}			7		2			11^{2}			13	9^{3}	14	8						35
1		4		3	5			6	9			8		2			12			10	7^{1}		11						36
1		4		3	5		6	7	9^{3}			8		2^{1}		14	12			10		13	11^{2}						37
1		4		3			6					8		2	13		10^{1}			11	7^{2}	9^{3}	12				5	14	38

ST MIRREN

Year Formed: 1877. *Ground & Address:* The Simple Digital Arena, St Mirren Park, Greenhill Road, Paisley PA3 1RU.
Telephone: 0141 889 2558. *Fax:* 0141 848 6444. *E-mail:* info@stmirren.com *Website:* www.stmirren.com
Ground Capacity: 7,937 (all seated). *Size of Pitch:* 105m × 68m.
Chairman: Gordon Scott. *Chief Executive:* Tony Fitzpatrick.
Manager: Jim Goodwin. *Assistant Manager:* Lee Sharp.
Club Nickname: 'The Buddies'.
Previous Grounds: Shortroods 1877-79, Thistle Park Greenhill 1879-83, Westmarch 1883-94, Love Street 1894-2009.
Record Attendance: 47,438 v Celtic, League Cup, 20 August 1949.
Record Transfer Fee received: £850,000 for Ian Ferguson to Rangers (February 1988).
Record Transfer Fee paid: £400,000 for Thomas Stickroth from Bayer Uerdingen (March 1990).
Record Victory: 15-0 v Glasgow University, Scottish Cup 1st rd, 30 January 1960.
Record Defeat: 0-9 v Rangers, Division I, 4 December 1897.
Most Capped Player: Godmundur Torfason, 29, Iceland.
Most League Appearances: 403: Hugh Murray, 1997-2012.
Most League Goals in Season (Individual): 45: Dunky Walker, Division I, 1921-22.
Most League Goals Overall (Individual): 222: David McCrae, 1923-34.

ST MIRREN – SPFL LADBROKES PREMIERSHIP 2018–19 LEAGUE RECORD

Match No.	Date	Venue	Opponents	Result		H/T Score	Lg Pos.	Goalscorers	Attendance
1	Aug 4	H	Dundee	W	2-1	1-1	7	Mullen 2 [8, 83]	5470
2	12	A	Rangers	L	0-2	0-2	7		49,680
3	25	H	Livingston	L	0-2	0-2	10		4347
4	Sept 1	A	Hearts	L	1-4	1-4	11	Jimmy Dunne (og) [19]	17,714
5	14	H	Celtic	D	0-0	0-0	10		7288
6	22	A	Hamilton A	L	0-3	0-2	11		2830
7	29	H	Hibernian	L	0-1	0-1	11		6082
8	Oct 6	A	Aberdeen	L	1-4	0-3	11	Jackson [76]	14,003
9	20	H	Kilmarnock	L	1-2	1-0	11	Hammill [14]	5889
10	27	A	St Johnstone	L	0-2	0-0	11		2716
11	31	H	Motherwell	L	0-2	0-1	11		4001
12	Nov 3	H	Rangers	L	0-2	0-0	11		6033
13	10	A	Dundee	D	1-1	1-1	11	Jackson (pen) [21]	5552
14	24	H	Hearts	W	2-0	0-0	11	Hammill 2 [46, 55]	5177
15	Dec 1	H	Hamilton A	L	1-3	1-2	11	McGinn, S [45]	4334
16	5	A	Hibernian	D	2-2	1-0	11	Hammill [6], McGinn, P [67]	15,096
17	8	A	Livingston	L	1-3	1-0	11	Jones [36]	1727
18	15	H	Aberdeen	L	1-2	1-1	12	MacPherson [35]	4699
19	22	A	Motherwell	W	1-0	0-0	11	Jackson [68]	4540
20	26	H	St Johnstone	L	0-1	0-0	11		4891
21	29	A	Kilmarnock	L	1-2	1-2	11	Jackson [22]	7131
22	Jan 23	A	Celtic	L	0-4	0-2	12		54,821
23	27	H	Hibernian	L	1-3	1-0	12	Jackson [24]	5650
24	Feb 2	A	Rangers	L	0-4	0-1	12		49,463
25	6	H	Motherwell	L	1-2	0-1	12	McGinn, P [74]	4383
26	16	A	Aberdeen	D	2-2	1-1	12	Nazon (pen) [20], McAllister [61]	14,701
27	23	A	Hearts	D	1-1	0-0	12	Clare (og) [66]	16,705
28	Mar 2	H	Livingston	W	1-0	0-0	12	Flynn [89]	4014
29	11	H	Kilmarnock	L	0-1	0-0	12		4458
30	27	A	St Johnstone	L	0-1	0-1	12		2888
31	30	H	Dundee	W	2-1	1-1	11	Mullen [12], Lyons [57]	6733
32	Apr 3	H	Celtic	L	0-2	0-1	11		6597
33	6	A	Hamilton A	D	1-1	0-0	11	Dreyer (pen) [66]	3096
34	20	A	Livingston	W	3-1	1-1	11	McGinn, P [26], Mullen [78], Jackson [80]	2347
35	27	H	St Johnstone	D	1-1	0-0	11	Mullen [90]	5213
36	May 4	A	Motherwell	D	1-1	0-0	11	Magennis [90]	5274
37	13	H	Hamilton A	W	2-0	0-0	11	McAllister [75], Magennis [90]	6421
38	18	A	Dundee	W	3-2	0-1	11	Cooke 3 [51, 58, 76]	5595

Final League Position: 11

Honours
League Champions: First Division 1976-77, 1999-2000, 2005-06; Division II 1967-68; Championship 2017-18.
Runners-up: First Division 2004-05; Division II 1935-36.
Scottish Cup Winners: 1926, 1959, 1987; *Runners-up:* 1908, 1934, 1962.
League Cup Winners: 2012-13; *Runners-up:* 1955-56, 2009-10.
League Challenge Cup Winners: 2005-06; *Runners-up:* 2016-17.
B&Q Cup Runners-up: 1993-94. *Anglo-Scottish Cup:* 1979-80.

European: *Cup Winners' Cup:* 4 matches (1987-88). *UEFA Cup:* 10 matches (1980-81, 1983-84, 1985-86).

Club colours: Shirt: Black and white stripes. Shorts: Black. Socks: Black with red tops.

Goalscorers: *League (34):* Jackson 6 (1 pen), Mullen 5, Hammill 4, Cooke 3, McGinn P 3, Magennis 2, McAllister 2, Dreyer 1 (1 pen), Flynn 1, Jones 1, Lyons 1, MacPherson 1, McGinn S 1, Nazon 1 (1 pen), own goals 2.
William Hill Scottish FA Cup (4): Cooke 1, Erhahon 1, McAllister 1, Nazon 1.
Betfred Scottish League Cup (8): McGinn S 2, Smith 2, Coulson 1, Kellermann 1, Mullen 1 (1 pen), Stewart 1.
Irn-Bru Scottish League Challenge (7): Jamieson 3, MacPherson 2 (1 pen), Breadner 1, Potter 1.
Play-Offs (1): Mullen 1.

Samson C 13	McGinn P 34 + 1	Baird J 30 + 3	Kpekawa C 4	Coulson H 5 + 1	McGinn S 31 + 3	Willock M 7 + 5	Magennis K 11 + 3	Smith C 9 + 10	Stewart R 1	Mullen D 16 + 7	Flynn R 20 + 6	McShane I 4 + 4	Kellermann J 1 + 2	Brock-Madsen N 3 + 1	Hodson L 19 + 1	Jones A 14	Cooke C 3 + 8	Ferdinand A 18	Edwards R 11 + 3	MacPherson C 10 + 3	Kirkpatrick J — + 2	Jackson S 22 + 8	Jamieson S — + 2	Hammill A 12 + 1	Erhahon E 19 + 1	Rogers D 4 / MacKenzie G 5	Lyness D 4	Breadner C — + 2	Hladky V 17	Popescu M 17	Tansey G 4 + 2	Lyons B 14 + 1	McAllister K 8 + 6	Dreyer A 8 + 2	Nazon D 6 + 4	Muzek M 13 + 1	Corbu L 1 + 2	Match No.
1	2	3	4	5	6	7	8^{1}	9^{3}	10^{2}	11	12	13	14																									1
1	2	3	4	5	7	8^{1}	6	9		10	12	13		11^{2}																								2
1		12	4^{1}	5	8	7^{2}	9	13		11	6			10^{3}	2	3	14																					3
1		4	5	6	8	9^{2}	7	10^{1}		13	12			11	2	3																						4
1	2	4		13	6	14	8	9^{2}		11^{1}	7				5			3^{3}	10	12																		5
1	3			8^{1}	6	14		9^{3}		11^{2}	7			13	5			4	10	2	12																	6
1	2	3			6			9^{1}			7				5			4	10	8		11	12															7
1	2	3			6^{1}			13			7	12			5			4	9	8		11		10^{2}														8
1	2	3			7	8^{2}		14		11	9				5			4^{3}	13	12		10		6^{1}														9
1	2	4			7	8^{1}		12		10^{3}	9	14			5	3			13			11		6^{2}														10
1	2				6	12		9^{2}		13	7■				5	4		3	8			11		10^{1}														11
1	2				7^{3}	6^{1}				9^{2}		8				4	14	3	11	13	12	10			5													12
1	2				12		7	14		13		6^{2}			8	4		3	9			10		11^{1}	5^{3}													13
	2	3			7		10	12		13		8			6	4						11^{1}		9^{2}	5	1												14
	6^{1}	3			7		9			14		8^{2}			2	4	13		12			10■		11^{3}	5	1												15
	2	14			7	13	8^{2}	12^{3}		11^{1}					5	4		3	6					10	9	1												16
	5^{2}	2			7	12		13							6	4		3^{1}	8			11		10	9	1												17
		2			7			12							5	4^{1}		3	8	6		11		10^{2}	9		1	13										18
	7	4			5			13			14				6	2	10^{3}	3	8^{1}			11^{2}		12	9		1											19
	5	2			6			9^{1}			12				7	4		3				11^{2}		10	8		1	13										20
	5	2			6			9^{1}							7	4		3				11	12	10	8		1											21
	2	3			9						10		12^{3}		6^{2}		11^{1}					13			5				1	4	7	8	14					22
	2	3			7																	11			5				1	4	9	8	10	6				23
	5^{2}	2			6													3				10^{1}			9^{3}				1	4	8	7		11	12	13	14	24
	5	2^{3}			7^{1}					14								3				11							1	4	13	6	12	8	10^{2}	9		25
	5	2									8							3^{1}		7		12							1	4	14	10	6		11^{3}	9^{2}	13	26
	5	2									6									8		12			9				1	3	7		10^{1}	13	11^{2}	4		27
	5	2			7					14	8									6^{1}		13			9				1	3			12	11^{3}	10^{2}	4		28
	5	2									8									6^{1}		11			9				1	3		7	10		12	4		29
	5	2									8^{2}									6		11			9■				1	3		7	10^{1}	13	12	4		30
	5	2			14					10^{3}	6^{1}						13					12				4			1	3		7		9	11^{2}	8		31
	14	2			6^{1}								9^{3}				10	3		7		13							1	4		12			11^{2}	8	5	32
	5	2			13					9^{3}	6						14					10^{2}			8				1	3		7^{1}	12	11		4		33
	5	2			7		14			10	6											12			9^{3}	3^{2}			1	4		8^{1}	13	11				34
	5	2^{2}			7		12			11	6											14				3			1	4		8^{3}	13	10^{1}		9		35
	2				6		12			10^{2}	7^{3}						14					11				3^{1}			1	4		8	9		13	5		36
	2	12			7		6			10	13						14					9^{2}				3^{3}			1	4		8^{1}	11			5		37
	2	3			8		6^{1}			10	7				12		13								14				1	4		9^{3}	11			5^{2}		38

STENHOUSEMUIR

Year Formed: 1884. *Ground & Address:* Ochilview Park, Gladstone Rd, Stenhousemuir FK5 4QL. *Telephone:* 01324 562992. *Fax:* 01324 562980. *E-mail:* info@stenhousemuirfc.com *Website:* www.stenhousemuirfc.com
Ground Capacity: 3,776 (seated: 626). *Size of Pitch:* 101m × 66m.
Chairman: Iain McMenemy. *Vice-Chairman:* David Reid. *Secretary/General Manager:* Margaret Kilpatrick.
Manager: Colin McMenamin. *Assistant Manager:* Stuart Balmer.
Club Nickname: 'The Warriors'.
Previous Grounds: Tryst Ground 1884-86; Goschen Park 1886-90.
Record Attendance: 12,500 v East Fife, Scottish Cup quarter-final, 11 March 1950.
Record Transfer Fee received: £70,000 for Euan Donaldson to St Johnstone (May 1995).
Record Transfer Fee paid: £20,000 to Livingston for Ian Little (June 1995); £20,000 to East Fife for Paul Hunter (September 1995).
Record Victory: 9-2 v Dundee U, Division II, 16 April 1937.
Record Defeat: 2-11 v Dunfermline Ath, Division II, 27 September 1930.
Most League Appearances: 434: Jimmy Richardson, 1957-73.
Most League Goals in Season (Individual): 32: Robert Taylor, Division II, 1925-26.

STENHOUSEMUIR – SPFL LADBROKES LEAGUE ONE 2018–19 LEAGUE RECORD

Match No.	*Date*	*Venue*	*Opponents*	*Result*		*H/T Score*	*Lg Pos.*	*Goalscorers*	*Attendance*
1	Aug 4	H	Brechin C	W	1-0	1-0	4	Hill (og) [8]	484
2	11	A	Raith R	L	0-2	0-1	7		1415
3	18	H	Airdrieonians	L	1-2	1-1	8	Crighton (og) [45]	708
4	25	A	Forfar Ath	L	0-2	0-2	9		467
5	Sept 1	H	Dumbarton	W	2-1	1-1	6	Ross [10], Duthie [81]	616
6	15	A	Stranraer	L	0-2	0-1	9		327
7	22	H	Arbroath	L	1-2	1-0	10	McGuigan [24]	585
8	29	A	East Fife	L	0-2	0-1	10		545
9	Oct 6	H	Montrose	W	3-2	1-1	7	Cook [22], McMenamin [50], McGuigan [90]	362
10	20	H	Forfar Ath	L	1-2	0-2	8	Neill [56]	442
11	27	A	Airdrieonians	W	1-0	0-0	8	McGuigan [86]	773
12	Nov 3	H	Stranraer	L	0-2	0-0	9		481
13	10	A	Dumbarton	L	1-2	1-1	10	McGuigan (pen) [33]	605
14	17	H	Raith R	L	1-3	0-1	10	McGuigan [67]	797
15	Dec 1	A	Arbroath	L	2-5	1-2	10	McGuigan 2 [21, 85]	734
16	8	A	Brechin C	W	2-1	1-1	10	McGuigan (pen) [8], Cook [78]	355
17	15	H	East Fife	L	0-2	0-1	10		395
18	22	A	Montrose	L	1-3	0-2	10	McGuigan [81]	511
19	29	H	Dumbarton	D	2-2	1-1	10	Paton [8], McGuigan [54]	536
20	Jan 5	A	Raith R	L	1-5	1-4	10	Ross [25]	1398
21	12	H	Arbroath	L	1-4	1-2	10	McGuigan [40]	760
22	26	H	Airdrieonians	W	1-0	0-0	10	Halleran [74]	794
23	Feb 9	H	Montrose	W	1-0	0-0	9	Hurst [68]	409
24	23	A	Forfar Ath	L	1-2	0-0	10	Hurst [71]	492
25	26	A	Stranraer	D	1-1	1-1	10	Duthie [45]	219
26	Mar 2	H	Brechin C	D	1-1	0-1	10	Cook [52]	452
27	9	A	Arbroath	W	2-0	1-0	10	Marsh [45], McGuigan [56]	719
28	12	A	East Fife	D	1-1	0-0	10	McGuigan [50]	323
29	16	H	Stranraer	L	0-1	0-1	10		362
30	23	A	Montrose	L	0-2	0-1	10		1224
31	30	A	Dumbarton	W	2-1	1-0	10	Marsh [27], McBrearty [72]	613
32	Apr 6	H	Raith R	D	1-1	0-0	10	McGuigan [58]	784
33	13	A	Airdrieonians	W	1-0	1-0	10	McGuigan [5]	600
34	20	H	Forfar Ath	L	0-3	0-2	10		577
35	27	H	East Fife	D	1-1	1-1	9	Donaldson [35]	742
36	May 4	A	Brechin C	D	1-1	1-0	9	McGuigan [24]	565

Final League Position: 9

Honours
League Runners-up: Third Division 1998-99.
Promoted via play-offs: 2008-09 (to Second Division); 2017-18 (to League One).
Scottish Cup: Semi-finals 1902-03. Quarter-finals 1948-49, 1949-50, 1994-95.
League Cup: Quarter-finals 1947-48, 1960-61, 1975-76.
League Challenge Cup Winners: 1995-96.

Club colours: Shirt: Maroon with white trim. Shorts: White. Socks: Maroon.

Goalscorers: *League (35):* McGuigan 16 (2 pens), Cook 3, Duthie 2, Hurst 2, Marsh 2, Ross 2, Donaldson 1, Halleran 1, McBrearty 1, McMenamin 1, Neill 1, Paton 1, own goals 2.
William Hill Scottish FA Cup (6): McBrearty 2, McGuigan 2, Dickson 1, Munro 1.
Betfred Scottish League Cup (4): Dickson 1, Duthie 1, Neill 1, Ross 1.
Irn-Bru Scottish League Challenge (0).
Play-Offs (1): Marsh 1.

Smith G 35	Reid Alan 27 + 2	Neill M 29	Garcia Tena J 11	Donaldson R 31 + 4	Gibbons K 14 + 13	Halleran T 4 + 7	Duthie C 24 + 5	Dickson S 22 + 5	McGuigan M 35	Vaughan B 4 + 13	Lochhead S 1 + 1	McMenamin C 3 + 12	Cook A 23 + 6	Lyon R — + 1	O'Hara K 7 + 8	Ross S 10 + 9	Paton H 10 + 3	Ferry M 28 + 1	McBrearty C 24	McMinn L 1 + 1	Dingwall R 12	Munro A 14	Marsh D 14	Hurst G 13 + 1	Breadner C — + 2	Watters R — + 3	*Match No.*
1	2	3	4	5	6■	7^{2}	8	9	10	11^{1}	12	13															1
1	2^{2}	3	4	5			6	8	10	12	7	11^{1}	9	13													2
1	2	3	4	5^{1}	6^{2}		7^{3}	9	11	13		14	10		8	12											3
1	2^{3}	3	4	5	6^{2}		12	9	11	13		14	10		8^{1}	7											4
1	2	3	4	9	6	13	11	8	10^{2}	12		14			7^{1}	5^{3}											5
1	3^{1}	4	5	6	7^{3}		11	9		10^{2}		14	13		8	2	12										6
1		3	2	4	13		11	8^{2}	10	14			9		12	6^{3}	7	5^{1}									7
1		4	3^{1}	5			11	9^{2}	10	14		12	6		13	2^{3}	7	8									8
1	12	3	4	2	14		6	5	11			10^{1}	9^{3}		13		7^{2}	8									9
1		2	3	4	13		5	8	11	14		10	9^{2}		12	6^{1}		7^{3}									10
1	13	3		4	6^{3}		5^{1}	8	10^{2}			14	9		11		12	7	2								11
1		3		4			5^{2}	7	10	12		14	9■		11	13	8^{3}	6^{1}	2								12
1	2^{3}	4		5	6^{2}		9	8^{1}	10	14					11	13	12	7	3								13
1	2^{1}	4		5	6		9	8^{3}	11	12		14			13		10	7^{2}	3								14
1		3		4	6^{1}	14	11	5	10^{3}				9^{2}		12	13	8	7	2								15
1		4		5	6	14	2	10	11^{2}	13			12			8^{3}	9^{1}	7	3								16
1		3		4	5		10	6^{2}	11	12		13	9				8	7^{1}	2								17
1	2	4		5			11^{3}		10	6^{2}		14	9		13	12	8	7	3^{1}								18
1	2	4		5			12		10^{2}	11^{1}			9		13	8	6	7	3■								19
1^{2}	2		3	5		14	7	8^{3}	11^{1}	13			10			9		6	4■	12							20
	4	3		5			2	6	11			12	10			7		8^{1}		1	9						21
1	2	4^{2}		5		12	11^{1}	9	10							13		7	8		6	3					22
1	2			6	14	11^{2}		8^{1}	10^{3}				9					7	3			4	5	12	13		23
1	5			9^{1}	13		12		10				8					6^{3}	2		7^{2}	3	4	11		14	24
1	2			12			6	13	10				9^{1}					7	3		8^{2}	4	5	11			25
1	2			14	13		6■	12	10^{1}				5^{3}					7	8		9■	3	4	11^{2}			26
1	2	3■			6^{1}	7		13	10				9					12	8^{2}			4	5	11^{3}		14	27
1	2			13	7	9^{2}	6^{1}	12	10				5					8				4	3	11^{3}		14	28
1	2	9^{1}		12	6^{3}	14	13		10				5^{2}					8	7			3	4	11			29
1	2			5	12		6	8	10										7		9^{1}	3	4	11			30
1	5	2		9	12	13			10^{3}							14		6	8		7	4	3^{2}	11^{1}			31
1	2	4		5	13				11				12					8	7		6^{1}	3	9	10^{2}			32
1	5	4		9	12				10^{2}				13			14		7	8		6^{3}	2	3	11^{1}			33
1	5	2^{3}		9	14				10				12					7	8^{1}		6^{2}	3■	4	11	13		34
1	2	3^{1}		5	12		13		10				9			14		8	7		6^{3}		4	11^{2}			35
1	5	2		9	12			14	10				13					7^{1}	8■		6^{2}	3	4	11^{3}			36

STIRLING ALBION

Year Formed: 1945. *Ground & Address:* Forthbank Stadium, Springkerse, Stirling FK7 7UJ. *Telephone:* 01786 450399. *Fax:* 01786 448592. *E-mail:* office@stirlingalbionfc.co.uk *Website:* www.stirlingalbionfc.co.uk
Ground Capacity: 3,808 (seated: 2,508). *Size of Pitch:* 101m × 68m.
Chairman and Operations Director: Stuart Brown.
Manager: Kevin Rutkiewicz. *Assistant Manager:* Martin Hardie.
Club Nickname: 'The Binos'.
Previous Ground: Annfield 1945-92.
Record Attendance: 26,400 v Celtic, Scottish Cup 4th rd, 14 March 1959 (Annfield); 3,808 v Aberdeen, Scottish Cup 4th rd, 15 February 1996 (Forthbank).
Record Transfer Fee received: £90,000 for Stephen Nicholas to Motherwell (March 1999).
Record Transfer Fee paid: £25,000 for Craig Taggart from Falkirk (August 1994).
Record Victory: 20-0 v Selkirk, Scottish Cup 1st rd, 8 December 1984.
Record Defeat: 0-9 v Dundee U, Division I, 30 December 1967; 0-9 v Ross Co, Scottish Cup 5th rd, 6 February 2010.
Most League Appearances: 504: Matt McPhee, 1967-81.
Most League Goals in Season (Individual): 27: Joe Hughes, Division II, 1969-70.
Most Goals Overall (Individual): 129: Billy Steele, 1971-83.

STIRLING ALBION – SPFL LADBROKES LEAGUE TWO 2018–19 LEAGUE RECORD

Match No.	*Date*	*Venue*	*Opponents*	*Result*		*H/T Score*	*Lg Pos.*	*Goalscorers*	*Attendance*
1	Aug 4	A	Berwick R	L	0-1	0-0	8		520
2	11	H	Clyde	L	0-3	0-2	9		802
3	18	A	Edinburgh C	L	1-3	0-0	9	Stewart [54]	302
4	25	H	Peterhead	L	0-2	0-1	9		543
5	Sept 1	A	Elgin C	W	3-0	3-0	9	Thomson [15], MacDonald, P [24], Allan (pen) [34]	596
6	15	H	Queen's Park	W	1-0	1-0	7	McGeachie [12]	702
7	22	H	Annan Ath	L	1-2	0-1	7	Docherty [90]	502
8	29	A	Albion R	L	0-3	0-1	7		260
9	Oct 6	A	Cowdenbeath	L	0-1	0-1	8		365
10	27	H	Edinburgh C	L	0-1	0-1	8		603
11	Nov 3	H	Berwick R	W	3-0	2-0	8	McLaughlin [16], Mackin [26], Jardine [56]	514
12	10	A	Clyde	D	1-1	0-0	8	Jardine [56]	541
13	17	A	Annan Ath	D	2-2	0-1	9	Mackin [53], Docherty [77]	399
14	Dec 1	H	Elgin C	W	5-2	3-2	8	Smith 2 [25, 62], McLaughlin [32], Mackin [45], Docherty [90]	548
15	8	A	Queen's Park	D	1-1	1-1	8	Smith [37]	496
16	22	A	Peterhead	L	1-4	0-2	8	Hughes [87]	620
17	29	H	Cowdenbeath	W	2-1	2-1	8	Mackin (pen) [36], Docherty [45]	708
18	Jan 5	A	Edinburgh C	W	1-0	0-0	7	Smith [51]	621
19	12	H	Annan Ath	W	2-1	1-1	7	MacDonald, P 2 [20, 76]	617
20	19	H	Queen's Park	D	1-1	1-1	6	Smith [9]	667
21	26	A	Albion R	W	5-0	1-0	5	MacDonald, P 3 [38, 52, 56], Smith [64], Mackin (pen) [89]	293
22	Feb 9	A	Berwick R	W	2-1	1-0	5	Mackin (pen) [43], Smith [77]	437
23	12	H	Albion R	W	1-0	0-0	5	Mackin [83]	461
24	16	A	Elgin C	L	2-3	1-1	5	Wright [6], Mackin [58]	676
25	23	H	Peterhead	L	0-1	0-1	6		611
26	26	H	Clyde	L	0-1	0-1	6		683
27	Mar 2	A	Cowdenbeath	W	2-1	1-0	5	Smith [34], MacDonald, P [71]	371
28	9	H	Albion R	L	0-1	0-1	6		561
29	16	A	Clyde	L	1-3	0-1	6	Banner [51]	614
30	23	H	Berwick R	W	1-0	0-0	5	Mackin (pen) [80]	598
31	30	A	Queen's Park	D	0-0	0-0	5		661
32	Apr 6	H	Elgin C	W	2-1	1-1	5	Smith [34], McGregor [89]	413
33	13	A	Annan Ath	D	2-2	1-0	5	Smith 2 (1 pen) [3, 63 (p)]	468
34	20	H	Cowdenbeath	L	0-1	0-0	5		507
35	27	A	Peterhead	D	1-1	0-1	5	MacDonald, P [90]	1371
36	May 4	H	Edinburgh C	D	0-0	0-0	5		543

Final League Position: 5

Honours
League Champions: Division II 1952-53, 1957-58, 1960-61, 1964-65; Second Division 1976-77, 1990-91, 1995-96, 2009-10; Division C 1946-47.
Runners-up: Division II 1948-49, 1950-51; Second Division 2006-07; Third Division 2003-04.
Promoted via play-offs: 2006-07 (to First Division); 2013-14 (to League One).
League Cup: Semi-finals 1961-62.
League Challenge Cup: Semi-finals 1995-96, 1999-2000.

Club colours: Shirt: Red with white sleeves. Shorts: Red with white trim. Socks: Red and white hoops.

Goalscorers: *League (44):* Smith 11 (1 pen), Mackin 9 (4 pens), MacDonald 8, Docherty 4, Jardine 2, McLaughlin 2, Allan 1 (1 pen), Banner 1, Hughes 1, McGeachie 1, McGregor 1, Stewart 1, Thomson 1, Wright 1.
William Hill Scottish FA Cup (1): Docherty 1.
Betfred Scottish League Cup (4): MacDonald P 2, Stewart 2.
Irn-Bru Scottish League Challenge (1): Hamilton 1.

Ferrie C 27	McGeachie R 30 + 2	Marr J 17 + 1	Hamilton L 9 + 4	Allan J 34	Stewart M 4 + 3	Jardine D 33	Docherty D 29 + 3	McLaughlin N 15 + 10	MacDonald P 19 + 8	Fell K 6 + 2	Watson J — + 1	McLaren R 1 + 7	Binnie C 9	Banner K 21 + 8	Robertson W 5	Stowe M — + 1	Kelly M — + 1	Thomson C 17 + 5	Young D — + 1	Barr D 4 + 1	Smith D 20 + 3	Horne E 16	Moon K 5 + 1	Hughes R 23 + 6	Gow A 2	Mackin D 16 + 7	McIndoe M 3	Ashmore M 2 + 4	Thomas A 1 + 1	Wright M 8 + 3	McGregor J 12	McLear L 4 + 6	Glover S 4 + 7	Murray C — + 3	Match No.
1	2	3	4	5	6	7	8	9^1	10	11^2	12	13																							1
	2		3	5	8	7	6^3	11^2	10	13			1	4	9^1	12	14																		2
1	2		3^2	5	11	7	6^1	13	10	14				4	8			9^3	12																3
1	2		3	5	13	8		9^3	11	6^2		14			7^1			10		4	12														4
1	5		2	4		8	6	12	11^1	10		13		3	7^2			9																	5
1	2	3		4	13	9^3	6	14	10	11^1					8^2			5				7	12												6
1	3	4^3		5	12	7	6		10^2	11		14		13				9				2	8^1												7
1	2	12		5	6	8		13	10^1	9^2		14		7				3^3					4	11											8
	3	4		9		6	8	12				11^2	1					5				2	7^1	13	10										9
	2	4		5		8	9	6^1				12	1					14		3			7^2	13	11^3	10									10
	2	4		5		6	8	9					1	12							14	3^1	7^2	13		10	11^3								11
	2	4		5		6	8	9	14				1	13						7^3		3^2		12		11^1	10								12
	3	4		5		6	8	9					1	12						7^1	14	2^3		13		11	10^2								13
	3	4^3		5		6	7	9^2	14				1	2				12		13	11^1			8		10									14
	2	4		5		6^1	8	9	13				1	3				12			11^2			7		10									15
	3	4^1		5		6	8	9^3	13			14	1	12							11	2		7		10^2									16
1	3	4		5^2		6	8	13	9					14				12			11^1	2		7		10^3									17
1	3			5		6	8		10					4				8			11	2		7											18
1	3			5		6	8■	14	10^1					4				9^2			11^3	2		7		13		12							19
1	4			5		7		9^1	10^2					3							11	2		6^3		14		8	12	13					20
1	3			5		6			10^1					13							9	2		7		11		12	8^3	14	4^2				21
1	3			5		6^2	7	12													10^3	2		8		11				9^1	4	13	14		22
1	3			5		6	7	14	10^2												11^1	2		8		13				9^3	4	12			23
1	3			5		6	7^1	9						12								2^3		8		10				11	4^2	14	13		24
1	2	3		5^1		6	12							4				13			11			7^2		10		14		9^3			8		25
1	2	4				6	12		14					3				5			11^2			8^3		10^1				9		13	7		26
1	2	4	14	5		6^2	8		10					3							11■			7^3		12				9^1			13		27
1	4^3	3	12	5		6	8		14					2										7		10		9^1		11^2			13		28
1			12	5^2		6	8^1	10^3	11					2				9				3		7		14				13	4				29
1		4^2	13	5			7	9	11^3					2				10			8			6^1		12					3		14		30
1			4	5			8		10^2					2				9^1			11			7						6^3	3	12	13	14	31
1			4	5			7	9	11^2					2				10^1			8			6							3	12		13	32
1	12		4^1	5		9	7							2				10			8			6							3	11^2	13		33
1	13		4^2	5■		7	6^3	14						2				9			10^1			8		12					3	11			34
1	2					6^1	8^2		14					4				5^3			11			12		10		13			3	9	7		35
1	4			5		7	12		13					2^1							9			8^3		10					3	11^2	6	14	36

STRANRAER

Year Formed: 1870. *Ground & Address:* Stair Park, London Rd, Stranraer DG9 8BS. *Telephone and Fax:* 01776 703271.
E-mail: secretary@stranraerfc.org *Website:* www.stranraerfc.org
Ground Capacity: 4,178 (seated: 1,830). *Size of Pitch:* 103m × 64m.
Chairman: Iain Dougan. *Vice-Chairmen:* Robert Rice and Shaun Niven.
Manager: Stephen Farrell. *Assistant Manager:* Chris Aitken.
Club Nicknames: 'The Blues'; 'The Clayholers'.
Record Attendance: 6,500 v Rangers, Scottish Cup 1st rd, 24 January 1948.
Record Transfer Fee received: £90,000 for Mark Campbell to Ayr U (1999).
Record Transfer Fee paid: £35,000 for Michael Moore from St Johnstone (March 2005).
Record Victory: 9-0 v St Cuthbert Wanderers, Scottish Cup 2nd rd, 23 October 2010; 9-0 v Wigtown & Bladnoch, Scottish Cup 2nd rd, 22 October 2011.
Record Defeat: 1-11 v Queen of the South, Scottish Cup 1st rd, 16 January 1932.
Most League Appearances: 301: Keith Knox, 1986-90; 1999-2001.
Most League Goals in Season (Individual): 27: Derek Frye, 1977-78.
Most Goals Overall (Individual): 136: Jim Campbell, 1965-75.

STRANRAER – SPFL LADBROKES LEAGUE ONE 2018–19 LEAGUE RECORD

Match No.	Date	Venue	Opponents	Result		H/T Score	Lg Pos.	Goalscorers	Attendance
1	Aug 4	H	Raith R	D	1-1	0-1	5	Anderson 53	424
2	11	A	Arbroath	L	1-3	1-1	9	Donnelly 24	582
3	18	A	Forfar Ath	D	0-0	0-0	9		459
4	25	H	Montrose	W	2-0	2-0	7	Brownlie 12, Anderson 17	360
5	Sept 1	A	Airdrieonians	L	0-2	0-0	8		815
6	15	H	Stenhousemuir	W	2-0	1-0	5	Turner 43, Cameron 65	327
7	22	H	East Fife	L	0-2	0-0	7		366
8	29	A	Brechin C	D	1-1	0-1	6	Donnelly 85	374
9	Oct 6	H	Dumbarton	W	3-2	2-1	5	Anderson 9, Brownlie 34, Crossan 65	305
10	20	A	Raith R	L	1-2	1-2	6	Donnelly 28	1285
11	27	H	Arbroath	L	0-1	0-1	7		393
12	Nov 3	A	Stenhousemuir	W	2-0	0-0	5	Anderson 47, Crossan 90	481
13	10	H	Airdrieonians	L	1-2	0-1	7	Turner 61	326
14	17	A	Montrose	D	1-1	0-0	6	Hamill 90	532
15	Dec 1	H	Forfar Ath	W	2-1	1-0	6	Donnelly 42, McManus 55	224
16	8	A	East Fife	D	3-3	0-2	7	Cummins (pen) 61, Cameron 80, McGowan 85	482
17	22	A	Dumbarton	W	1-0	0-0	7	Turner 66	686
18	29	A	Airdrieonians	L	0-3	0-2	7		725
19	Jan 5	H	Montrose	L	1-2	0-2	7	Cameron 57	317
20	12	A	Forfar Ath	L	1-2	1-1	7	Cameron 25	533
21	26	H	East Fife	L	3-4	2-0	7	Anderson 21, Cameron 33, Vitoria 62	350
22	Feb 12	A	Arbroath	D	1-1	0-1	7	Turner 66	532
23	16	H	Dumbarton	L	0-3	0-0	9		327
24	23	A	Brechin C	W	2-1	1-1	8	Cameron 34, Hamill 70	378
25	26	H	Stenhousemuir	D	1-1	1-1	8	Smith, D 45	219
26	Mar 2	H	Raith R	D	2-2	2-0	8	Turner 9, Vitoria 22	310
27	9	A	East Fife	L	1-3	0-0	8	Turner 54	461
28	16	A	Stenhousemuir	W	1-0	1-0	8	Cameron 33	362
29	23	H	Arbroath	D	0-0	0-0	8		432
30	26	H	Brechin C	L	0-2	0-0	9		295
31	30	A	Montrose	L	1-3	0-2	9	McDonald 58	486
32	Apr 6	H	Forfar Ath	W	2-1	1-1	8	Vitoria 1, McManus 71	335
33	13	A	Raith R	W	3-2	2-2	8	Turner 41, Cameron 44, Vitoria 90	1204
34	20	H	Brechin C	W	3-0	2-0	8	Lamont 9, McCann 12, Elliott 90	374
35	27	A	Dumbarton	L	1-2	0-2	8	Cameron 54	704
36	May 4	H	Airdrieonians	L	1-4	0-3	8	Cameron 61	424

Final League Position: 8

Honours
League Champions: Second Division 1993-94, 1997-98; Third Division 2003-04.
Runners-up: Second Division 2004-05; Third Division 2007-08; League One 2014-15.
Promoted via play-offs: 2011-12 (to Second Division).
Scottish Cup: Quarter-finals 2003.
League Cup: Quarter-finals 1968-69.
League Challenge Cup Winners: 1996-97. Semi-finals: 2000-01, 2014-15.

Club colours: Shirt: Blue with white trim. Shorts: White with bluc trim. Socks: Blue with white tops.

Goalscorers: *League (45):* Cameron 10, Turner 7, Anderson 5, Donnelly 4, Vitoria 4, Brownlie 2, Crossan 2, Hamill 2, McManus 2, Cummins 1 (1 pen), Elliott 1, Lamont 1, McCann 1, McDonald 1, McGowan 1, Smith D 1.
William Hill Scottish FA Cup (2): Crossan 1, Smith I 1.
Betfred Scottish League Cup (7): Anderson 2, Cummins 1, Donnelly 1, Layne 1, McGowan 1, Turner 1.
Irn-Bru Scottish League Challenge (0).

Currie M 34	Smith D 32 + 1	McDonald A 26 + 1	Cummins A 25	McGowan C 7 + 1	Hamill J 36	McManus C 33 + 1	Smith I 4 + 8	Donnelly L 16 + 2	Lamont M 12 + 10	Anderson G 24 + 8	Turner K 34 + 1	Ashmore M — + 4	Lidington S — + 1	Elliott C 10 + 8	Brownlie D 27	Layne I 4 + 2	Driver C — + 8	Cameron I 22 + 7	Higgins D 8 + 3	Crossan P 13 + 8	O'Keefe C 2 + 9	Vitoria J 12 + 3	McCann A 13	Avci L 2 + 1	McColm A — + 2	Dunn L — + 1	Baxter J — + 1	*Match No.*
1	2	3	4	5	6	7	8^{3}	9	10^{2}	11^{1}	12	13	14															1
1	2	3	4	5	6^{1}	7^{3}	8^{2}	9	13	11	10	14		12														2
1	5	9	4		2	7	13	11^{1}		8^{2}	6	14		12	3	10^{3}												3
1	2	6	3		4	9	14	10^{3}		8	7^{1}	13		11^{2}	5		12											4
1	8	9■	2	5^{3}	3	6	14	10^{2}	13	11^{1}	7				4		12											5
1	2		3	6	4	8		11^{2}		9^{1}	7				5	10^{3}	14	12	13									6
1	2		5	6	4	8		11^{2}		9^{3}	7			14	3	10^{1}	13	12										7
1	2	6	4		5	8		13		14	9				3	10^{2}		11^{1}	7^{3}	12								8
1	2	6	5		4	7		10^{1}		9^{3}	8				3	12		14	13	11^{2}								9
1	5^{3}	8	2		3	7		9	12	10^{2}	6^{1}				4	13		14		11								10
1	2	6^{2}	5		4		14	8^{3}	12	10^{1}	9				3		13		7	11								11
1	5	9	4		3		14	10^{3}	12	8^{1}	6				2^{2}			13	7	11								12
1	2	6^{2}	5		4	13	14	7	12		9				3			10^{3}	8^{1}	11								13
1	8^{3}	4	3		5	7^{2}	14	10	13		9				2			12	6^{1}	11								14
1	12	5	4		2	7	9^{1}	10^{2}	6^{3}	13	8				3				14	11								15
1		5^{3}	3■	14	2	8	9^{2}	10	6	12	7				4			13		11^{1}								16
1		3		5	2	7	12		6	9^{1}	8						13	10	4	11^{2}								17
1		3		5^{2}	2	8		12	6	10	7						13	11	4	9^{1}								18
1	5		3		2	7		8^{1}	10^{2}	13	9				4		14	11	6^{3}	12								19
1	5	13	4		2	7			6^{2}		8^{1}			12	3			11		9	10							20
1	5		4		2	6^{1}				8	7			13	3			9		11^{2}	12	10						21
1	6^{3}	5	4		2	7			14	9^{1}	8			13	3			11^{2}			12	10						22
1	5^{2}	4■			2	6			14	8	7			13	3			10		11^{1}	12	9^{3}						23
1	5		4		2	6				9	7			10^{1}	3			11				12	8					24
1	5		4		2	7				6^{2}	9			10^{1}	3			11			13	12	8					25
1	5		3		2	7					9			10^{1}	4			11			12	6	8					26
1	5		3		2	7				11^{2}	6			12	4			10		13		9^{1}	8					27
1	4		3		5	6				11	7				2			10			12	9^{1}	8					28
1■	5	4			2	7				6	9				3			11				10^{1}	8	12				29
	5	3			2	7				9^{2}	8				4			11		12	13	10^{1}	6	1				30
	5^{1}	4			2	7			12	6^{2}	9			11	3^{3}			10			14	13	8	1				31
1	5	4			2	3			6^{3}	12	8			9^{1}				11		13	14	10^{2}	7					32
1	5	3			2	4			6^{1}	12	7			9^{2}				11		13		10	8					33
1	5	3			2	4			6^{1}	12	7			9^{2}				11		13		10^{3}	8		14			34
1	5	3			2	4			6	13	7			11^{2}				10		12		9^{1}	8					35
1	5	4			2	3			6^{1}	7				10^{2}				11			9^{3}		8		12	13	14	36

SCOTTISH LEAGUE HONOURS 1890–2019

*=Until 1921–22 season teams were equal if level on points, unless a play-off took place. §Not promoted after play-offs. *Won or placed on goal average (ratio), goal difference or most goals scored (goal average from 1921–22 until 1971–72 when it was replaced by goal difference). No official competition during 1939–46; regional leagues operated.*

DIVISION 1 (1890–91 to 1974–75) – TIER 1

Tier	*Season*	*Max Pts*	*First*	*Pts*	*Second*	*Pts*	*Third*	*Pts*
1	1890–91	36	Dumbarton=	29	Rangers=	29	Celtic	21
	Dumbarton and Rangers held title jointly after indecisive play-off ended 2-2. Celtic deducted 4 points for fielding an ineligible player.							
1	1891–92	44	Dumbarton	37	Celtic	35	Hearts	34
1	1892–93	36	Celtic	29	Rangers	28	St Mirren	20
1	1893–94	36	Celtic	29	Hearts	26	St Bernard's	23
1	1894–95	36	Hearts	31	Celtic	26	Rangers	22
1	1895–96	36	Celtic	30	Rangers	26	Hibernian	24
1	1896–97	36	Hearts	28	Hibernian	26	Rangers	25
1	1897–98	36	Celtic	33	Rangers	29	Hibernian	22
1	1898–99	36	Rangers	36	Hearts	26	Celtic	24
1	1899–1900	36	Rangers	32	Celtic	25	Hibernian	24
1	1900–01	40	Rangers	35	Celtic	29	Hibernian	25
1	1901–02	36	Rangers	28	Celtic	26	Hearts	22
1	1902–03	44	Hibernian	37	Dundee	31	Rangers	29
1	1903–04	52	Third Lanark	43	Hearts	39	Celtic / Rangers=	38
1	1904–05	52	Celtic=	41	Rangers=	41	Third Lanark	35
	Celtic won title after beating Rangers 2-1 in play-off.							
1	1905–06	60	Celtic	49	Hearts	43	Airdrieonians	38
1	1906–07	68	Celtic	55	Dundee	48	Rangers	45
1	1907–08	68	Celtic	55	Falkirk	51	Rangers	50
1	1908–09	68	Celtic	51	Dundee	50	Clyde	48
1	1909–10	68	Celtic	54	Falkirk	52	Rangers	46
1	1910–11	68	Rangers	52	Aberdeen	48	Falkirk	44
1	1911–12	68	Rangers	51	Celtic	45	Clyde	42
1	1912–13	68	Rangers	53	Celtic	49	Hearts / Airdrieonians=	41
1	1913–14	76	Celtic	65	Rangers	59	Hearts / Morton=	54
1	1914–15	76	Celtic	65	Hearts	61	Rangers	50
1	1915–16	76	Celtic	67	Rangers	56	Morton	51
1	1916–17	76	Celtic	64	Morton	54	Rangers	53
1	1917–18	68	Rangers	56	Celtic	55	Kilmarnock / Morton=	43
1	1918–19	68	Celtic	58	Rangers	57	Morton	47
1	1919–20	84	Rangers	71	Celtic	68	Motherwell	57
1	1920–21	84	Rangers	76	Celtic	66	Hearts	50
1	1921–22	84	Celtic	67	Rangers	66	Raith R	51
1	1922–23	76	Rangers	55	Airdrieonians	50	Celtic	46
1	1923–24	76	Rangers	59	Airdrieonians	50	Celtic	46
1	1924–25	76	Rangers	60	Airdrieonians	57	Hibernian	52
1	1925–26	76	Celtic	58	Airdrieonians*	50	Hearts	50
1	1926–27	76	Rangers	56	Motherwell	51	Celtic	49
1	1927–28	76	Rangers	60	Celtic*	55	Motherwell	55
1	1928–29	76	Rangers	67	Celtic	51	Motherwell	50
1	1929–30	76	Rangers	60	Motherwell	55	Aberdeen	53
1	1930–31	76	Rangers	60	Celtic	58	Motherwell	56
1	1931–32	76	Motherwell	66	Rangers	61	Celtic	48
1	1932–33	76	Rangers	62	Motherwell	59	Hearts	50
1	1933–34	76	Rangers	66	Motherwell	62	Celtic	47
1	1934–35	76	Rangers	55	Celtic	52	Hearts	50
1	1935–36	76	Celtic	66	Rangers*	61	Aberdeen	61
1	1936–37	76	Rangers	61	Aberdeen	54	Celtic	52
1	1937–38	76	Celtic	61	Hearts	58	Rangers	49
1	1938–39	76	Rangers	59	Celtic	48	Aberdeen	46
1	1946–47	60	Rangers	46	Hibernian	44	Aberdeen	39
1	1947–48	60	Hibernian	48	Rangers	46	Partick Thistle	36
1	1948–49	60	Rangers	46	Dundee	45	Hibernian	39
1	1949–50	60	Rangers	50	Hibernian	49	Hearts	43
1	1950–51	60	Hibernian	48	Rangers*	38	Dundee	38
1	1951–52	60	Hibernian	45	Rangers	41	East Fife	37
1	1952–53	60	Rangers*	43	Hibernian	43	East Fife	39
1	1953–54	60	Celtic	43	Hearts	38	Partick Thistle	35
1	1954–55	60	Aberdeen	49	Celtic	46	Rangers	41
1	1955–56	68	Rangers	52	Aberdeen	46	Hearts*	45
1	1956–57	68	Rangers	55	Hearts	53	Kilmarnock	42
1	1957–58	68	Hearts	62	Rangers	49	Celtic	46
1	1958–59	68	Rangers	50	Hearts	48	Motherwell	44
1	1959–60	68	Hearts	54	Kilmarnock	50	Rangers*	42
1	1960–61	68	Rangers	51	Kilmarnock	50	Third Lanark	42
1	1961–62	68	Dundee	54	Rangers	51	Celtic	46
1	1962–63	68	Rangers	57	Kilmarnock	48	Partick Thistle	46
1	1963–64	68	Rangers	55	Kilmarnock	49	Celtic*	47
1	1964–65	68	Kilmarnock*	50	Hearts	50	Dunfermline Ath	49
1	1965–66	68	Celtic	57	Rangers	55	Kilmarnock	45

1	1966–67	68	Celtic	58	Rangers	55	Clyde	46
1	1967–68	68	Celtic	63	Rangers	61	Hibernian	45
1	1968–69	68	Celtic	54	Rangers	49	Dunfermline Ath	45
1	1969–70	68	Celtic	57	Rangers	45	Hibernian	44
1	1970–71	68	Celtic	56	Aberdeen	54	St Johnstone	44
1	1971–72	68	Celtic	60	Aberdeen	50	Rangers	44
1	1972–73	68	Celtic	57	Rangers	56	Hibernian	45
1	1973–74	68	Celtic	53	Hibernian	49	Rangers	48
1	1974–75	68	Rangers	56	Hibernian	49	Celtic*	45

PREMIER DIVISION (1975–76 to 1997–98)

1	1975–76	72	Rangers	54	Celtic	48	Hibernian	43
1	1976–77	72	Celtic	55	Rangers	46	Aberdeen	43
1	1977–78	72	Rangers	55	Aberdeen	53	Dundee U	40
1	1978–79	72	Celtic	48	Rangers	45	Dundee U	44
1	1979–80	72	Aberdeen	48	Celtic	47	St Mirren	42
1	1980–81	72	Celtic	56	Aberdeen	49	Rangers*	44
1	1981–82	72	Celtic	55	Aberdeen	53	Rangers	43
1	1982–83	72	Dundee U	56	Celtic*	55	Aberdeen	55
1	1983–84	72	Aberdeen	57	Celtic	50	Dundee U	47
1	1984–85	72	Aberdeen	59	Celtic	52	Dundee U	47
1	1985–86	72	Celtic*	50	Hearts	50	Dundee U	47
1	1986–87	88	Rangers	69	Celtic	63	Dundee U	60
1	1987–88	88	Celtic	72	Hearts	62	Rangers	60
1	1988–89	72	Rangers	56	Aberdeen	50	Celtic	46
1	1989–90	72	Rangers	51	Aberdeen*	44	Hearts	44
1	1990–91	72	Rangers	55	Aberdeen	53	Celtic*	41
1	1991–92	88	Rangers	72	Hearts	63	Celtic	62
1	1992–93	88	Rangers	73	Aberdeen	64	Celtic	60
1	1993–94	88	Rangers	58	Aberdeen	55	Motherwell	54
1	1994–95	108	Rangers	69	Motherwell	54	Hibernian	53
1	1995–96	108	Rangers	87	Celtic	83	Aberdeen*	55
1	1996–97	108	Rangers	80	Celtic	75	Dundee U	60
1	1997–98	108	Celtic	74	Rangers	72	Hearts	67

PREMIER LEAGUE (1998–99 to 2012–13)

1	1998–99	108	Rangers	77	Celtic	71	St Johnstone	57
1	1999–2000	108	Rangers	90	Celtic	69	Hearts	54
1	2000–01	114	Celtic	97	Rangers	82	Hibernian	66
1	2001–02	114	Celtic	103	Rangers	85	Livingston	58
1	2002–03	114	Rangers*	97	Celtic	97	Hearts	63
1	2003–04	114	Celtic	98	Rangers	81	Hearts	68
1	2004–05	114	Rangers	93	Celtic	92	Hibernian*	61
1	2005–06	114	Celtic	91	Hearts	74	Rangers	73
1	2006–07	114	Celtic	84	Rangers	72	Aberdeen	65
1	2007–08	114	Celtic	89	Rangers	86	Motherwell	60
1	2008–09	114	Rangers	86	Celtic	82	Hearts	59
1	2009–10	114	Rangers	87	Celtic	81	Dundee U	63
1	2010–11	114	Rangers	93	Celtic	92	Hearts	63
1	2011–12	114	Celtic	93	Rangers	73	Motherwell	62

Rangers deducted 10 points for entering administration.

1	2012–13	114	Celtic	79	Motherwell	63	St Johnstone	56

SPFL SCOTTISH PREMIERSHIP (2013–14 to 2018–19)

1	2013–14	114	Celtic	99	Motherwell	70	Aberdeen	68
1	2014–15	114	Celtic	92	Aberdeen	75	Inverness CT	65
1	2015–16	114	Celtic	86	Aberdeen	71	Hearts	65
1	2016–17	114	Celtic	106	Aberdeen	76	Rangers	67
1	2017–18	114	Celtic	82	Aberdeen	73	Rangers	70
1	2018–19	114	Celtic	87	Rangers	78	Kilmarnock*	67

DIVISION 2 (1893–93 to 1974–75) – TIER 2

Tier	*Season*	*Max Pts*	*First*	*Pts*	*Second*	*Pts*	*Third*	*Pts*
2	1893–94	36	Hibernian	29	Cowlairs	27	Clyde	24
2	1894–95	36	Hibernian	30	Motherwell	22	Port Glasgow Ath	20
2	1895–96	36	Abercorn	27	Leith Ath	23	Renton / Kilmarnock=	21
2	1896–97	36	Partick Thistle	31	Leith Ath	27	Airdrieonians / Kilmarnock=	21
2	1897–98	36	Kilmarnock	29	Port Glasgow Ath	25	Morton	22
2	1898–99	36	Kilmarnock	32	Leith Ath	27	Port Glasgow Ath	25
2	1899–1900	36	Partick Thistle	29	Morton	28	Port Glasgow Ath	20
2	1900–01	36	St Bernard's	26	Airdrieonians	23	Abercorn	21
2	1901–02	44	Port Glasgow Ath	32	Partick Thistle	30	Motherwell	26
2	1902–03	44	Airdrieonians	35	Motherwell	28	Ayr U / Leith Ath=	27
2	1903–04	44	Hamilton A	37	Clyde	29	Ayr U	28
2	1904–05	44	Clyde	32	Falkirk	28	Hamilton A	27
2	1905–06	44	Leith Ath	34	Clyde	31	Albion R	27
2	1906–07	44	St Bernard's	32	Vale of Leven=	27	Arthurlie=	27
2	1907–08	44	Raith R	30	Dumbarton=	27	Ayr U=	27

Dumbarton deducted 2 points for registration irregularities.

2	1908–09	44	Abercorn	31	Raith R=	28	Vale of Leven=	28
2	1909–10	44	Leith Ath=	33	Raith R=	33	St Bernard's	27

Leith Ath and Raith R held title jointly, no play-off game played.

2	1910–11	44	Dumbarton	31	Ayr U	27	Albion R	25
2	1911–12	44	Ayr U	35	Abercorn	30	Dumbarton	27
2	1912–13	52	Ayr U	34	Dunfermline Ath	33	East Stirling	32
2	1913–14	44	Cowdenbeath	31	Albion R	27	Dunfermline Ath / Dundee U=	26
2	1914–15	52	Cowdenbeath=	37	St Bernard's=	37	Leith Ath=	37

Cowdenbeath won title after a round robin tournament between the three tied clubs.

2	1921–22	76	Alloa Ath	60	Cowdenbeath	47	Armadale	45
2	1922–23	76	Queen's Park	57	Clydebank	50	St Johnstone	48

Clydebank and St Johnstone both deducted 2 points for fielding an ineligible player.

2	1923–24	76	St Johnstone	56	Cowdenbeath	55	Bathgate	44
2	1924–25	76	Dundee U	50	Clydebank	48	Clyde	47
2	1925–26	76	Dunfermline Ath	59	Clyde	53	Ayr U	52
2	1926–27	76	Bo'ness	56	Raith R	49	Clydebank	45
2	1927–28	76	Ayr U	54	Third Lanark	45	King's Park	44
2	1928–29	72	Dundee U	51	Morton	50	Arbroath	47
2	1929–30	76	Leith Ath*	57	East Fife	57	Albion R	54
2	1930–31	76	Third Lanark	61	Dundee U	50	Dunfermline Ath	47
2	1931–32	76	East Stirling*	55	St Johnstone	55	Raith R*	46
2	1932–33	68	Hibernian	54	Queen of the South	49	Dunfermline Ath	47

Armadale and Bo'ness were expelled for failing to meet match guarantees. Their records were expunged.

2	1933–34	68	Albion R	45	Dunfermline Ath*	44	Arbroath	44
2	1934–35	68	Third Lanark	52	Arbroath	50	St Bernard's	47
2	1935–36	68	Falkirk	59	St Mirren	52	Morton	48
2	1936–37	68	Ayr U	54	Morton	51	St Bernard's	48
2	1937–38	68	Raith R	59	Albion R	48	Airdrieonians	47
2	1938–39	68	Cowdenbeath	60	Alloa Ath*	48	East Fife	48
2	1946–47	52	Dundee	45	Airdrieonians	42	East Fife	31
2	1947–48	60	East Fife	53	Albion R	42	Hamilton A	40
2	1948–49	60	Raith R*	42	Stirling Alb	42	Airdrieonians*	41
2	1949–50	60	Morton	47	Airdrieonians	44	Dunfermline Ath*	36
2	1950–51	60	Queen of the South*	45	Stirling Alb	45	Ayr U*	36
2	1951–52	60	Clyde	44	Falkirk	43	Ayr U	39
2	1952–53	60	Stirling Alb	44	Hamilton A	43	Queen's Park	37
2	1953–54	60	Motherwell	45	Kilmarnock	42	Third Lanark*	36
2	1954–55	60	Airdrieonians	46	Dunfermline Ath	42	Hamilton A	39
2	1955–56	72	Queen's Park	54	Ayr U	51	St Johnstone	49
2	1956–57	72	Clyde	64	Third Lanark	51	Cowdenbeath	45
2	1957–58	72	Stirling Alb	55	Dunfermline Ath	53	Arbroath	47
2	1958–59	72	Ayr U	60	Arbroath	51	Stenhousemuir	46
2	1959–60	72	St Johnstone	53	Dundee U	50	Queen of the South	49
2	1960–61	72	Stirling Alb	55	Falkirk	54	Stenhousemuir	50
2	1961–62	72	Clyde	54	Queen of the South	53	Morton	44
2	1962–63	72	St Johnstone	55	East Stirling	49	Morton	48
2	1963–64	72	Morton	67	Clyde	53	Arbroath	46
2	1964–65	72	Stirling Alb	59	Hamilton A	50	Queen of the South	45
2	1965–66	72	Ayr U	53	Airdrieonians	50	Queen of the South	47
2	1966–67	76	Morton	69	Raith R	58	Arbroath	57
2	1967–68	72	St Mirren	62	Arbroath	53	East Fife	49
2	1968–69	72	Motherwell	64	Ayr U	53	East Fife*	48
2	1969–70	72	Falkirk	56	Cowdenbeath	55	Queen of the South	50
2	1970–71	72	Partick Thistle	56	East Fife	51	Arbroath	46
2	1971–72	72	Dumbarton*	52	Arbroath	52	Stirling Alb*	50
2	1972–73	72	Clyde	56	Dumfermline Ath	52	Raith R*	47
2	1973–74	72	Airdrieonians	60	Kilmarnock	58	Hamilton A	55
2	1974–75	76	Falkirk	54	Queen of the South*	53	Montrose	53

Elected to First Division: 1894 Clyde; 1895 Hibernian; 1896 Abercorn; 1897 Partick Thistle; 1899 Kilmarnock; 1900 Morton and Partick Thistle; 1902 Port Glasgow and Partick Thistle; 1903 Airdrieonians and Motherwell; 1905 Falkirk and Aberdeen; 1906 Clyde and Hamilton A; 1910 Raith R; 1913 Ayr U and Dumbarton.

FIRST DIVISION (1975–76 to 2012–13)

2	1975–76	52	Partick Thistle	41	Kilmarnock	35	Montrose	30
2	1976–77	78	St Mirren	62	Clydebank	58	Dundee	51
2	1977–78	78	Morton*	58	Hearts	58	Dundee	57
2	1978–79	78	Dundee	55	Kilmarnock*	54	Clydebank	54
2	1979–80	78	Hearts	53	Airdrieonians	51	Ayr U*	44
2	1980–81	78	Hibernian	57	Dundee	52	St Johnstone	51
2	1981–82	78	Motherwell	61	Kilmarnock	51	Hearts	50
2	1982–83	78	St Johnstone	55	Hearts	54	Clydebank	50
2	1983–84	78	Morton	54	Dumbarton	51	Partick Thistle	46
2	1984–85	78	Motherwell	50	Clydebank	48	Falkirk	45
2	1985–86	78	Hamilton A	56	Falkirk	45	Kilmarnock*	44
2	1986–87	88	Morton	57	Dunfermline Ath	56	Dumbarton	53
2	1987–88	88	Hamilton A	56	Meadowbank Thistle	52	Clydebank	49
2	1988–89	78	Dunfermline Ath	54	Falkirk	52	Clydebank	48
2	1989–90	78	St Johnstone	58	Airdrieonians	54	Clydebank	44
2	1990–91	78	Falkirk	54	Airdrieonians	53	Dundee	52
2	1991–92	88	Dundee	58	Partick Thistle*	57	Hamilton A	57
2	1992–93	88	Raith R	65	Kilmarnock	54	Dunfermline Ath	52

2	1993–94	88	Falkirk	66	Dunfermline Ath	65	Airdrieonians	54
2	1994–95	108	Raith R	69	Dunfermline Ath*	68	Dundee	68
2	1995–96	108	Dunfermline Ath	71	Dundee U*	67	Greenock Morton	67
2	1996–97	108	St Johnstone	80	Airdrieonians	60	Dundee*	58
2	1997–98	108	Dundee	70	Falkirk	65	Raith R*	60
2	1998–99	108	Hibernian	89	Falkirk	66	Ayr U	62
2	1999–2000	108	St Mirren	76	Dunfermline Ath	71	Falkirk	68
2	2000–01	108	Livingston	76	Ayr U	69	Falkirk	56
2	2001–02	108	Partick Thistle	66	Airdrieonians	56	Ayr U*	52
2	2002–03	108	Falkirk	81	Clyde	72	St Johnstone	67
2	2003–04	108	Inverness CT	70	Clyde	69	St Johnstone	57
2	2004–05	108	Falkirk	75	St Mirren*	60	Clyde	60
2	2005–06	108	St Mirren	76	St Johnstone	66	Hamilton A	59
2	2006–07	108	Gretna	66	St Johnstone	65	Dundee*	53
2	2007–08	108	Hamilton A	76	Dundee	69	St Johnstone	58
2	2008–09	108	St Johnstone	65	Partick Thistle	55	Dunfermline Ath	51
2	2009–10	108	Inverness CT	73	Dundee	61	Dunfermline Ath	58
2	2010–11	108	Dunfermline Ath	70	Raith R	60	Falkirk	58
2	2011–12	108	Ross Co	79	Dundee	55	Falkirk	52
2	2012–13	108	Partick Thistle	78	Greenock Morton	67	Falkirk	53

SPFL SCOTTISH CHAMPIONSHIP (2013–14 to 2018–19)

2	2013–14	108	Dundee	69	Hamilton A	67	Falkirk§	66
2	2014–15	108	Hearts	91	Hibernian§	70	Rangers§	67
2	2015–16	108	Rangers	81	Falkirk*§	70	Hibernian§	70
2	2016–17	108	Hibernian	71	Falkirk§	60	Dundee U§	57
2	2017–18	108	St Mirren	74	Livingston	62	Dundee U§	61
2	2018–19	108	Ross Co	71	Dundee U§	65	Inverness CT§	56

SECOND DIVISION (1975–76 to 2012–13) – TIER 3

Tier	*Season*	*Max Pts*	*First*	*Pts*	*Second*	*Pts*	*Third*	*Pts*
3	1975–76	52	Clydebank*	40	Raith R	40	Alloa Ath	35
3	1976–77	78	Stirling Alb	55	Alloa Ath	51	Dunfermline Ath	50
3	1977–78	78	Clyde*	53	Raith R	53	Dunfermline Ath*	48
3	1978–79	78	Berwick Rangers	54	Dunfermline Ath	52	Falkirk	50
3	1979–80	78	Falkirk	50	East Stirling	49	Forfar Ath	46
3	1980–81	78	Queen's Park	50	Queen of the South	46	Cowdenbeath	45
3	1981–82	78	Clyde	59	Alloa Ath*	50	Arbroath	50
3	1982–83	78	Brechin C	55	Meadowbank Thistle	54	Arbroath	49
3	1983–84	78	Forfar Ath	63	East Fife	47	Berwick Rangers	43
3	1984–85	78	Montrose	53	Alloa Ath	50	Dunfermline Ath	49
3	1985–86	78	Dunfermline Ath	57	Queen of the South	55	Meadowbank Thistle	49
3	1986–87	78	Meadowbank Thistle	55	Raith R*	52	Stirling Alb*	52
3	1987–88	78	Ayr U	61	St Johnstone	59	Queen's Park	51
3	1988–89	78	Albion R	50	Alloa Ath	45	Brechin C	43
3	1989–90	78	Brechin C	49	Kilmarnock	48	Stirling Alb	47
3	1990–91	78	Stirling Alb	54	Montrose	46	Cowdenbeath	45
3	1991–92	78	Dumbarton	52	Cowdenbeath	51	Alloa Ath	50
3	1992–93	78	Clyde	54	Brechin C*	53	Stranraer	53
3	1993–94	78	Stranraer	56	Berwick Rangers	48	Stenhousemuir*	47
3	1994–95	108	Greenock Morton	64	Dumbarton	60	Stirling Alb	58
3	1995–96	108	Stirling Alb	81	East Fife	67	Berwick Rangers	60
3	1996–97	108	Ayr U	77	Hamilton A	74	Livingston	64
3	1997–98	108	Stranraer	61	Clydebank	60	Livingston	59
3	1998–99	108	Livingston	77	Inverness CT	72	Clyde	53
3	1999–2000	108	Clyde	65	Alloa Ath	64	Ross Co	62
3	2000–01	108	Partick Thistle	75	Arbroath	58	Berwick Rangers*	54
3	2001–02	108	Queen of the South	67	Alloa Ath	59	Forfar Ath	53
3	2002–03	108	Raith R	59	Brechin C	55	Airdrie U	54
3	2003–04	108	Airdrie U	70	Hamilton A	62	Dumbarton	60
3	2004–05	108	Brechin C	72	Stranraer	63	Greenock Morton	62
3	2005–06	108	Gretna	88	Greenock Morton§	70	Peterhead*§	57
3	2006–07	108	Greenock Morton	77	Stirling Alb	69	Raith R§	62
3	2007–08	108	Ross Co	73	Airdrie U	66	Raith R§	60
3	2008–09	108	Raith R	76	Ayr U	74	Brechin C§	62
3	2009–10	108	Stirling Alb*	65	Alloa Ath§	65	Cowdenbeath	59
3	2010–11	108	Livingston	82	Ayr U*	59	Forfar Ath§	59
3	2011–12	108	Cowdenbeath	71	Arbroath§	63	Dumbarton	58
3	2012–13	108	Queen of the South	92	Alloa Ath	67	Brechin C	61

SPFL SCOTTISH LEAGUE ONE (2013–14 to 2018–19)

3	2013–14	108	Rangers	102	Dunfermline Ath§	63	Stranraer§	51
3	2014–15	108	Greenock Morton	69	Stranraer§	67	Forfar Ath	66
3	2015–16	108	Dunfermline Ath	79	Ayr U	61	Peterhead§	59
3	2016–17	108	Livingston	81	Alloa Ath§	62	Airdrieonians§	52
3	2017–18	108	Ayr U	76	Raith R§	75	Alloa Ath	60
3	2018–19	108	Arbroath	70	Forfar Ath§	63	Raith R§	60

THIRD DIVISION (1994–95 to 2012–13) – TIER 4

Tier	*Season*	*Max Pts*	*First*	*Pts*	*Second*	*Pts*	*Third*	*Pts*
4	1994–95	108	Forfar Ath	80	Montrose	67	Ross Co	60
4	1995–96	108	Livingston	72	Brechin C	63	Inverness CT	57
4	1996–97	108	Inverness CT	76	Forfar Ath*	67	Ross Co	67

4	1997–98	108	Alloa Ath	76	Arbroath	68	Ross Co	67
4	1998–99	108	Ross Co	77	Stenhousemuir	64	Brechin C	59
4	1999–2000	108	Queen's Park	69	Berwick Rangers	66	Forfar Ath	61
4	2000–01	108	Hamilton A*	76	Cowdenbeath	76	Brechin C	72
4	2001–02	108	Brechin C	73	Dumbarton	61	Albion R	59
4	2002–03	108	Greenock Morton	72	East Fife	71	Albion R	70
4	2003–04	108	Stranraer	79	Stirling Alb	77	Gretna	68
4	2004–05	108	Gretna	98	Peterhead	78	Cowdenbeath	51
4	2005–06	108	Cowdenbeath*	76	Berwick Rangers§	76	Stenhousemuir§	73
4	2006–07	108	Berwick Rangers	75	Arbroath§	70	Queen's Park	68
4	2007–08	108	East Fife	88	Stranraer	65	Montrose§	59
4	2008–09	108	Dumbarton	67	Cowdenbeath	63	East Stirling§	61
4	2009–10	108	Livingston	78	Forfar Ath	63	East Stirling§	61
4	2010–11	108	Arbroath	66	Albion R	61	Queen's Park*§	59
4	2011–12	108	Alloa Ath	77	Queen's Park§	63	Stranraer	58
4	2012–13	108	Rangers	83	Peterhead§	59	Queen's Park§	56

SPFL SCOTTISH LEAGUE TWO (2013–14 to 2018–19)

4	2013–14	108	Peterhead	76	Annan Ath§	63	Stirling Alb	57
4	2014–15	108	Albion R	71	Queen's Park§	61	Arbroath§	56
4	2015–16	108	East Fife	62	Elgin C§	59	Clyde§	56
4	2016–17	108	Abroath	66	Forfar Ath	64	Annan Ath§	58
4	2017–18	108	Montrose	77	Peterhead§	76	Stirling Alb§	55
4	2018–19	108	Peterhead	79	Clyde	74	Edinburgh C§	67

RELEGATED CLUBS

RELEGATED FROM DIVISION I (1921–22 to 1973–74)

1921–22 *Dumbarton, Queen's Park, Clydebank
1922–23 Albion R, Alloa Ath
1923–24 Clyde, Clydebank
1924–25 Ayr U, Third Lanark
1925–26 Raith R, Clydebank
1926–27 Morton, Dundee U
1927–28 Bo'ness, Dunfermline Ath
1928–29 Third Lanark, Raith R
1929–30 Dundee U, St Johnstone
1930–31 Hibernian, East Fife
1931–32 Dundee U, Leith Ath
1932–33 Morton, East Stirling
1933–34 Third Lanark, Cowdenbeath
1934–35 St Mirren, Falkirk
1935–36 Airdrieonians, Ayr U
1936–37 Dunfermline Ath, Albion R
1937–38 Dundee, Morton
1938–39 Queen's Park, Raith R
1946–47 Kilmarnock, Hamilton A
1947–48 Airdrieonians, Queen's Park
1948–49 Morton, Albion R
1949–50 Queen of the South, Stirling Alb
1950–51 Clyde, Falkirk
1951–52 Morton, Stirling Alb
1952–53 Motherwell, Third Lanark
1953–54 Airdrieonians, Hamilton A
1954–55 *No clubs relegated as league extended to 18 teams*
1955–56 Clyde, Stirling Alb
1956–57 Dunfermline Ath, Ayr U
1957–58 East Fife, Queen's Park
1958–59 Falkirk, Queen of the South
1959–60 Stirling Alb, Arbroath
1960–61 Clyde, Ayr U
1961–62 St Johnstone, Stirling Alb
1962–63 Clyde, Raith R
1963–64 Queen of the South, East Stirling
1964–65 Airdrieonians, Third Lanark
1965–66 Morton, Hamilton A
1966–67 St Mirren, Ayr U
1967–68 Motherwell, Stirling Alb
1968–69 Falkirk, Arbroath
1969–70 Raith R, Partick Thistle
1970–71 St Mirren, Cowdenbeath
1971–72 Clyde, Dunfermline Ath
1972–73 Kilmarnock, Airdrieonians
1973–74 East Fife, Falkirk

**Season 1921–22 – only 1 club promoted, 3 clubs relegated.*

RELEGATED FROM PREMIER DIVISION (1974–75 to 1997–98)

1974–75 *No relegation due to League reorganisation*
1975–76 Dundee, St Johnstone
1976–77 Hearts, Kilmarnock
1977–78 Ayr U, Clydebank
1978–79 Hearts, Motherwell
1979–80 Dundee, Hibernian
1980–81 Kilmarnock, Hearts
1981–82 Partick Thistle, Airdrieonians
1982–83 Morton, Kilmarnock
1983–84 St Johnstone, Motherwell
1984–85 Dumbarton, Morton
1985–86 *No relegation due to League reorganisation*
1986–87 Clydebank, Hamilton A
1987–88 Falkirk, Dunfermline Ath, Morton
1988–89 Hamilton A
1989–90 Dundee
1990–91 *No clubs relegated*
1991–92 St Mirren, Dunfermline Ath
1992–93 Falkirk, Airdrieonians
1993–94 St Johnstone, Raith R, Dundee
1994–95 Dundee U
1995–96 Partick Thistle, Falkirk
1996–97 Raith R
1997–98 Hibernian

RELEGATED FROM PREMIER LEAGUE (1998–99 to 2012–13)

1998–99 Dunfermline Ath
1999–2000 *No relegation due to League reorganisation*
2000–01 St Mirren
2001–02 St Johnstone
2002–03 *No clubs relegated*
2003–04 Partick Thistle
2005–06 Livingston
2006–07 Dunfermline Ath
2007–08 Gretna
2008–09 Inverness CT
2009–10 Falkirk
2010–11 Hamilton A
2011–12 Dunfermline Ath, Rangers (demoted to Third Division)
2012–13 Dundee

RELEGATED FROM SPFL SCOTTISH PREMIERSHIP (2013–14 to 2018–19)

2013–14 Hibernian, Hearts
2014–15 St Mirren
2015–16 Dundee U
2016–17 Inverness CT
2017–18 Ross Co, Partick Thistle
2018–19 Dundee

RELEGATED FROM FIRST DIVISION (1975–76 to 2012–13)

1975–76 Dunfermline Ath, Clyde
1976–77 Raith R, Falkirk
1977–78 Alloa Ath, East Fife
1978–79 Montrose, Queen of the South
1979–80 Arbroath, Clyde
1980–81 Stirling Alb, Berwick Rangers
1981–82 East Stirling, Queen of the South
1982–83 Dunfermline Ath, Queen's Park
1983–84 Raith R, Alloa Ath
1984–85 Meadowbank Thistle, St Johnstone
1985–86 Ayr U, Alloa Ath
1986–87 Brechin C, Montrose
1987–88 East Fife, Dumbarton
1988–89 Kilmarnock, Queen of the South
1989–90 Albion R, Alloa Ath
1990–91 Clyde, Brechin C
1991–92 Montrose, Forfar Ath
1992–93 Meadowbank Thistle, Cowdenbeath
1993–94 Dumbarton, Stirling Alb, Clyde, Morton, Brechin C
1994–95 Ayr U, Stranraer
1995–96 Hamilton A, Dumbarton
1996–97 Clydebank, East Fife
1997–98 Partick Thistle, Stirling Alb
1998–99 Hamilton A, Stranraer
1999–2000 Clydebank
2000–01 Greenock Morton, Alloa Ath
2001–02 Raith R
2002–03 Alloa Ath, Arbroath
2003–04 Ayr U, Brechin C
2004–05 Partick Thistle, Raith R
2005–06 Stranraer, Brechin C
2006–07 Airdrie U, Ross Co
2007–08 Stirling Alb
2008–09 Livingstone *(for breaching rules)*, Clyde
2009–10 Airdrie U, Ayr U
2010–11 Cowdenbeath, Stirling Alb
2011–12 Ayr U, Queen of the South
2012–13 Dunfermline Ath, Airdrie U

RELEGATED FROM SPFL SCOTTISH CHAMPIONSHIP (2013–14 to 2018–19)

2013–14 Greenock Morton
2014–15 Cowdenbeath
2015–16 Livingston, Alloa Ath
2016–17 Raith R, Ayr U
2017–18 Brechin C, Dumbarton
2018–19 Falkirk

RELEGATED FROM SECOND DIVISION (1993–94 to 2012–13)

1993–94 Alloa Ath, Forfar Ath, East Stirlingshire, Montrose, Queen's Park, Arbroath, Albion R, Cowdenbeath
1994–95 Meadowbank Thistle, Brechin C
1995–96 Forfar Ath, Montrose
1996–97 Dumbarton, Berwick Rangers
1997–98 Stenhousemuir, Brechin C
1998–99 East Fife, Forfar Ath
1999–2000 Hamilton A *(after being deducted 15 points)*
2000–01 Queen's Park, Stirling Alb
2001–02 Greenock Morton
2002–03 Stranraer, Cowdenbeath
2003–04 East Fife, Stenhousemuir
2004–05 Arbroath, Berwick Rangers
2005–06 Dumbarton
2006–07 Stranraer, Forfar Ath
2007–08 Cowdenbeath, Berwick Rangers
2008–09 Queen's Park, Stranraer
2009–10 Arbroath, Clyde
2010–11 Alloa Ath, Peterhead
2011–12 Stirling Alb
2012–13 Albion R

RELEGATED FROM SPFL SCOTTISH LEAGUE ONE (2013–14 to 2018–19)

2013–14 East Fife, Arbroath
2014–15 Stirling Alb
2015–16 Cowdenbeath, Forfar Ath
2016–17 Peterhead, Stenhousmuir
2017–18 Albion R, Queen's Park
2018–19 Stenhousemuir, Brechin C

RELEGATED FROM SPFL SCOTTISH LEAGUE TWO (2015–16 to 2018–19)

2015–16 East Stirlingshire
2016 17 None
2017–18 None
2018–19 Berwick Rangers

SCOTTISH LEAGUE CHAMPIONSHIP WINS

Rangers 54, Celtic 50, Aberdeen 4, Hearts 4, Hibernian 4, Dumbarton 2, Dundee 1, Dundee U 1, Kilmarnock 1, Motherwell 1, Third Lanark 1.

The totals for Rangers and Dumbarton each include the shared championship of 1890–91.

Since the formation of the Scottish Football League in 1890, there have been periodic reorganisations of the leagues to allow for expansion, improve competition and commercial aspects of the game. The table below lists the league names by tier and chronology. This table can be used to assist when studying the records.

Tier	Division	
1	Scottish League Division I	1890–1939
	Scottish League Division A	1946–1956
	Scottish League Division I	1956–1975
	Premier Division	1975–1998
	Scottish Premier League	1998–2013
	SPFL Premiership	2013–
2	Scottish League Division II	1893–1939
	Scottish League Division B	1946–1956
	Scottish League Division II	1956–1975
	First Division	1975–2013
	SPFL Championship	2013–
3	Scottish League Division III	1923–1926
	Scottish League Division C	1946–1949
	Second Division	1975–2013
	SPFL League One	2013–
4	Third Division	1994–2013
	SPFL League Two	2013–

In 2013–14 the SPFL introduced play-offs to determine a second promotion/relegation place for the Premiership, Championship and League One.

The team finishing second bottom of the Premiership plays two legs against the team from the Championship that won the eliminator games played between the teams finishing second, third and fourth.

For both the Championship and League One, the team finishing second bottom joins the teams from second, third and fourth places of the lower league in a play-off series of two-legged semi-finals and finals.

In 2014–15 a play-off was introduced for promotion/relegation from League Two. The team finishing bottom of League Two plays two legs against the victors of the eliminator games between the winners of the Highland and Lowland leagues.

SCOTTISH LEAGUE PLAY-OFFS 2018–19

■ *Denotes player sent off.*

PREMIERSHIP QUARTER-FINAL FIRST LEG

Tuesday, 7 May 2019

Ayr U (0) 1 *(Rose 65)*

Inverness CT (1) 3 *(Trafford 33, White 51, 76 (pen))* 2171

Ayr U: (442) Doohan; Smith, Muirhead, Rose, Harvie; Docherty, Crawford (Kerr 46), Murdoch, McDaid (Forrest 80); Moffat (McCowan 62), Shankland.
Inverness CT: (4411) Ridgers; McKay, McCart, Donaldson, McHattie; Walsh (Rooney 79), Trafford, Chalmers, Doran (McCauley 78); Polworth (McDonald 88); White.
Referee: Alan Muir.

PREMIERSHIP QUARTER-FINAL SECOND LEG

Saturday, 11 May 2019

Inverness CT (0) 1 *(Donaldson 79)*

Ayr U (1) 1 *(McCowan 19)* 2323

Inverness CT: (4411) Ridgers; McKay (Rooney 63), Donaldson, McCart, McHattie; Walsh (McDonald 54), Trafford, Chalmers, Doran; Polworth; White.
Ayr U: (442) Doohan; Smith, Muirhead, Rose, Harvie; Crawford, Murdoch, Kerr (Cadden 83), McDaid (Miller 77); Shankland, McCowan (Moffat 65).
Inverness CT won 4-2 on aggregate.
Referee: Steven McLean.

PREMIERSHIP SEMI-FINAL FIRST LEG

Tuesday, 14 May 2019

Inverness CT (0) 0

Dundee U (0) 1 *(McMullan 78)* 2604

Inverness CT: (343) Ridgers; McKay, Donaldson, McCart; Rooney, Trafford, Chalmers, McHattie; Polworth■, White (Austin 81), Doran (Harper 72).
Dundee U: (4231) Siegrist; Watson, Connolly, Reynolds, Robson; Butcher, Harkes; McMullan (Smith 85), Pawlett, Safranko (Booth 46); Sow (Clark 68).
Referee: Nick Walsh.

PREMIERSHIP SEMI-FINAL SECOND LEG

Friday, 17 May 2019

Dundee U (1) 3 *(Clark 45 (pen), Sow 54, Safranko 80)*

Inverness CT (0) 0 8540

Dundee U: (4231) Siegrist; Watson, Connolly, Reynolds, Robson; Bouhenna, Harkes; McMullan, Clark (Stanton 78), Pawlett (Safranko 63); Sow (Booth 73).
Inverness CT: (343) Ridgers; McKay, Donaldson, McCart; Rooney (Austin 56), Trafford, Chalmers, McHattie; Walsh (Harper 90), White, Doran (McDonald 74).
Dundee U won 4-0 on aggregate.
Referee: Kevin Clancy.

PREMIERSHIP FINAL FIRST LEG

Thursday, 23 May 2019

Dundee U (0) 0

St Mirren (0) 0 11,062

Dundee U: (4231) Siegrist; Watson, Connolly, Reynolds, Robson; Harkes, Bouhenna; McMullan, Clark (Stanton 68), Pawlett (Booth 73); Sow (Safranko 59).
St Mirren: (442) Hladky; McGinn P, MacKenzie, Baird, Popescu; Magennis, Hodson, McGinn S, Flynn; McAllister, Cooke (Mullen 90).
Referee: Bobby Madden.

PREMIERSHIP FINAL SECOND LEG

Sunday, 26 May 2019

St Mirren (1) 1 *(Mullen 26)*

Dundee U (1) 1 *(Clark 23 (pen))* 7732

St Mirren: (343) Hladky; Baird, MacKenzie (Ferdinand 90), Popescu; McGinn P, McGinn S, Magennis (Muzek 86), Hodson; Mullen, Cooke, McAllister (Nazon■ 83).
Dundee U: (4231) Siegrist; Watson, Connolly, Reynolds, Booth; Bouhenna (Butcher 75), Harkes; McMullan, Clark (Sow 69), Robson (Pawlett 55); Safranko.
aet; St Mirren won 2-0 on penalties.
Referee: John Beaton.

CHAMPIONSHIP SEMI-FINALS FIRST LEG

Tuesday, 7 May 2019

Montrose (1) 2 *(Campbell R 43, 69)*

Queen of the South (0) 1 *(Murray 68)* 1124

Montrose: (451) Fleming; Webster, Dillon, Campbell I, Steeves; Henderson (Rennie 63), Masson, Cregg, Harrington, Milne (Redman 78); Campbell R (McLean 73).
Queen of the South: (442) Martin; Mercer (Murray 46), Brownlie, Doyle, Marshall; Todd (Stirling 75), Jacobs, Wilson, Fordyce; Dykes, Aird.
Referee: John McKendrick.

Raith R (1) 2 *(Nisbet 40, Gullan 63)*

Forfar Ath (1) 1 *(Baird 44)* 2007

Raith R: (352) Lyness; Davidson, Benedictus, Murray; McKay, Barjonas (Gillespie 72), Matthews, Wedderburn, Crane; Buchanan (Gullan 46), Nisbet.
Forfar Ath: (442) McCallum; Meechan, Travis, Whyte, Eckersley; Easton (Coupe 72), Irvine, Spencer, Moore (Bain 73); Baird, Hilson (Aitken 85).
Referee: Colin Steven.

CHAMPIONSHIP SEMI-FINALS SECOND LEG

Saturday, 11 May 2019

Forfar Ath (0) 1 *(Baird 55)*

Raith R (0) 1 *(Nisbet 59 (pen))* 2512

Forfar Ath: (442) McCallum; Meechan, Whyte, Travis■, Eckersley (Easton 83); Hilson, Irvine, Bain (Malone 74), Spencer; Baird, Coupe (Moore 68).
Raith R: (352) Lyness; Davidson, Benedictus, Murray; McKay, Matthews, Wedderburn (Gillespie 73), Barjonas (Flanagan 54), Crane; Nisbet, Gullan (Buchanan 90).
Raith R won 3-2 on aggregate.
Referee: Euan Anderson.

Queen of the South (5) 5 *(Dobbie 11, 28, 40, Dykes 23, Doyle 32)*

Montrose (0) 0 2001

Queen of the South: (433) Martin; Mercer, Brownlie, Doyle, Marshall; Jacobs (Maguire 63), Wilson, Todd; Murray, Dykes (Stirling 73), Dobbie (McGrath 54).
Montrose: (532) Fleming; Masson, Webster (Callaghan 64), Dillon, Steeves, Campbell I; Redman, Watson, Campbell R (McLean 46); Rennie (Bolochoweckyj 60), Harrington.
Queen of the South won 6-2 on aggregate.
Referee: Greg Aitken.

CHAMPIONSHIP FINAL FIRST LEG

Wednesday, 15 May 2019

Raith R (0) 1 *(McKay 86)*

Queen of the South (2) 3 *(Dykes 17, Murray 22, Murray 75 (og))* 2471

Raith R: (352) Lyness; Davidson, Benedictus, Murray; McKay, Flanagan (McGuffie 82), Matthews, Wedderburn (Barjonas 70), Crane; Nisbet, Gullan (Duggan 82).
Queen of the South: (433) Martin; Mercer, Doyle, Brownlie, Marshall; Wilson, Jacobs, Todd (Stirling 82); Dykes (McGrath 85), Dobbie (Aird 73), Murray.
Referee: David Munro.

Saturday, 18 May 2019

Queen of the South (0) 0

Raith R (0) 0 2420

Queen of the South: (433) Martin; Doyle, Maguire, Brownlie, Marshall; Wilson, Jacobs, Todd; Dykes, Dobbie, Murray.
Raith R: (352) Lyness; Davidson, Benedictus, Murray; McKay, McGuffie (Gullan 68), Matthews, Barjonas, Crane (Flanagan 47); Nisbet, Duggan (Buchanan 79).
Queen of the South won 3-1 on aggregate.
Referee: Alan Muir.

LEAGUE ONE SEMI-FINALS FIRST LEG

Tuesday, 7 May 2019

Annan Ath (2) 2 *(Johnston 8, Sonkur 39)*

Stenhousemuir (0) 0 637

Annan Ath: (442) Mitchell; Hooper, Sonkur, Swinglehurst, Strapp; Johnston, Wilson, Moxon, Wallace; Smith, Nade (Muir 67).
Stenhousemuir: (442) Smith; Neill, Munro, Marsh, Reid; Dingwall (Watters 76), Gibbons, Dickson, Donaldson; McGuigan, Cook (Duthie 68).
Referee: Steven Reid.

Edinburgh C (0) 0

Clyde (1) 1 *(Syvertsen 15)* 617

Edinburgh C: (442) Antell; Thomson, Balatoni, Donaldson, McIntyre; Watson, Walker, Laird, Breen (Newman 68); Shepherd, Taylor (Driver 85).
Clyde: (4132) Currie; Duffie, Lang, Rumsby, McNiff; Grant (Nicoll 72); McStay, Syvertsen (Banks 80), Lamont (Stewart 88); Goodwillie, Love.
Referee: Barry Cook.

LEAGUE ONE SEMI-FINALS SECOND LEG

Saturday, 11 May 2019

Clyde (1) 3 *(Syvertsen 14, Love 48, Goodwillie 58)*

Edinburgh C (0) 0 1204

Clyde: (4132) Currie; Duffie, Rumsby, Lang, McNiff; Grant (Boyle 69); McStay, Lamont, Love; Goodwillie (Nicoll 69), Syvertsen (Banks 74).
Edinburgh C: (4321) Antell; Thomson, Balatoni, Henderson L, McIntyre; Walker, Laird, Galbraith (Donaldson 54); Watson (Driver 59), Taylor (Breen 71); Shepherd.
Clyde won 4-0 on aggregate.
Referee: Craig Napier.

Stenhousemuir (1) 1 *(Marsh 37)*

Annan Ath (1) 2 *(Bradley 10, Swinglehurst 73)* 794

Stenhousemuir: (442) Smith; Reid, Munro (Neill 68), Marsh, Donaldson; Breadner (Halleran 77), Ferry, Dickson, Cook; Hurst, McGuigan.
Annan Ath: (4231) Mitchell; Brannan (Moxon 65), Sonkur (Watson 89), Swinglehurst, Strapp; Wilson, Bradley; Johnston, Muir, Wallace; Smith (Fergusson 79).
Annan Ath won 4-1 on aggregate.
Referee: David Munro.

LEAGUE ONE FINAL FIRST LEG

Tuesday, 14 May 2019

Annan Ath (1) 1 *(Johnston 22)*

Clyde (0) 0 1006

Annan Ath: (442) Mitchell; Bradley, Sonkur, Swinglehurst, Strapp; Johnston, Wilson, Moxon, Wallace; Nade (Muir 86), Smith.
Clyde: (442) Currie; Duffie, Lang, Rumsby, McNiff; Grant, Nicoll, McStay, Love (Lamont 82); Syvertsen (Boyle 71), Goodwillie.
Referee: Greg Aitken.

LEAGUE ONE FINAL SECOND LEG

Saturday, 18 May 2019

Clyde (0) 2 *(McNiff 60, Love 86 (pen))*

Annan Ath (0) 0 2725

Clyde: (4132) Currie; Cuddihy, Rumsby, Lang, McNiff; Grant; McStay, Lamont (Nicoll 89), Banks (Duffie 90); Goodwillie (Love 68), Syvertsen.
Annan Ath: (442) Mitchell; Hooper, Sonkur, Swinglehurst, Strapp (Creaney 67); Johnston (Muir 90), Wilson, Moxon, Wallace (Bradley 81); Nade, Smith.
Clyde won 2-1 on aggregate.
Referee: Steven Kirkland.

LEAGUE TWO SEMI-FINAL FIRST LEG

Saturday, 27 April 2019

East Kilbride (0) 1 *(Longworth 90)*

Cove Rangers (2) 2 *(Milne H 3, Ross 35)*

East Kilbride: (4411) Muir; Coll, Reid, Howie, Stevenson; Woods (Humphrey 86), Holmes, Bell (Longworth 58), Russell (Winter 46); Brady; Malcolm.
Cove Rangers: (442) McKenzie; Kelly, Milne H, Scully, Ross; Strachan, Yule, Masson (Brown 86), Megginson; Scott (Burnett 58), Park (McManus 78).
Referee: Grant Irvine.

LEAGUE TWO SEMI-FINAL SECOND LEG

Saturday, 4 May 2019

Cove Rangers (2) 3 *(Megginson 29, 42, Masson 80)*

East Kilbride (0) 0

Cove Rangers: (442) McKenzie; Kelly, Milne H, Yule, Ross; Strachan, Scully, Park (Burnett 67), Megginson (Brown 80); Scott■, Masson.
East Kilbride: (4411) Muir; Reid, Coll■, Howie, Proctor; Woods, Holmes, Anderson (Brady 46) Winter; Longworth; Malcolm.
Cove Rangers won 5-1 on aggregate.
Referee: Mike Roncone.

LEAGUE TWO FINAL FIRST LEG

Saturday, 11 May 2019

Cove Rangers (2) 4 *(Burnett 23, Megginson 38, Brown 79, Masson 83)*

Berwick Rangers (0) 0 1914

Cove Rangers: (442) McKenzie; Kelly (Redford 84), Ross, Strachan, Milne; Park, Yule, Scully, Masson; Megginson (MacRae 64), Burnett (Brown 46).
Berwick Rangers: (352) Goodfellow; Hume, Brydon, Wilson (Barr 65); Forbes, Blues, Brown, O'Kane, Orru (Cook 60); Healy, Adamson (McIlduff 46).
Referee: David Lowe.

LEAGUE TWO FINAL SECOND LEG

Saturday, 18 May 2019

Berwick Rangers (0) 0

Cove Rangers (1) 3 *(Masson 8, Brown 47, McManus 75)* 1314

Berwick Rangers: (442) Goodfellow; Brown■, Cook, Hume, McIlduff; O'Kane, Barr, Blues (Aloulou 76), Ogilvie (Forbes 46); See, Rose (Adamson 58).
Cove Rangers: (4411) McKenzie; Kelly, Ross, Strachan, Milne (Watson 84); Park, Yule, Scully, Masson; Brown (Burnett 66); Megginson (McManus 62).
Cove Rangers won 7-0 on aggregate.
Referee: John McKendrick.

SCOTTISH LEAGUE CUP FINALS 1946–2019

SCOTTISH LEAGUE CUP

1946–47	Rangers v Aberdeen	4-0
1947–48	East Fife v Falkirk	0-0*
Replay	East Fife v Falkirk	4-1
1948–49	Rangers v Raith R	2-0
1949–50	East Fife v Dunfermline Ath	3-0
1950–51	Motherwell v Hibernian	3-0
1951–52	Dundee v Rangers	3-2
1952–53	Dundee v Kilmarnock	2-0
1953–54	East Fife v Partick Thistle	3-2
1954–55	Hearts v Motherwell	4-2
1955–56	Aberdeen v St Mirren	2-1
1956–57	Celtic v Partick Thistle	0-0*
Replay	Celtic v Partick Thistle	3-0
1957–58	Celtic v Rangers	7-1
1958–59	Hearts v Partick Thistle	5-1
1959–60	Hearts v Third Lanark	2-1
1960–61	Rangers v Kilmarnock	2-0
1961–62	Rangers v Hearts	1-1*
Replay	Rangers v Hearts	3-1
1962–63	Hearts v Kilmarnock	1-0
1963–64	Rangers v Morton	5-0
1964–65	Rangers v Celtic	2-1
1965–66	Celtic v Rangers	2-1
1966–67	Celtic v Rangers	1-0
1967–68	Celtic v Dundee	5-3
1968–69	Celtic v Hibernian	6-2
1969–70	Celtic v St Johnstone	1-0
1970–71	Rangers v Celtic	1-0
1971–72	Partick Thistle v Celtic	4-1
1972–73	Hibernian v Celtic	2-1
1973–74	Dundee v Celtic	1-0
1974–75	Celtic v Hibernian	6-3
1975–76	Rangers v Celtic	1-0
1976–77	Aberdeen v Celtic	2-1*
1977–78	Rangers v Celtic	2-1*
1978–79	Rangers v Aberdeen	2-1

BELL'S LEAGUE CUP

1979–80	Dundee U v Aberdeen	0-0*
Replay	Dundee U v Aberdeen	3-0
1980–81	Dundee U v Dundee	3-0

SCOTTISH LEAGUE CUP

1981–82	Rangers v Dundee U	2-1
1982–83	Celtic v Rangers	2-1
1983–84	Rangers v Celtic	3-2*

SKOL CUP

1984–85	Rangers v Dundee U	1-0
1985–86	Aberdeen v Hibernian	3-0
1986–87	Rangers v Celtic	2-1
1987–88	Rangers v Aberdeen	3-3*
	Rangers won 5-3 on penalties.	
1988–89	Rangers v Aberdeen	3-2
1989–90	Aberdeen v Rangers	2-1*
1990–91	Rangers v Celtic	2-1*
1991–92	Hibernian v Dunfermline Ath	2-0
1992–93	Rangers v Aberdeen	2-1*

SCOTTISH LEAGUE CUP

1993–94	Rangers v Hibernian	2-1

COCA-COLA CUP

1994–95	Raith R v Celtic	2-2*
	Raith R won 6-5 on penalties.	
1995–96	Aberdeen v Dundee	2-0
1996–97	Rangers v Hearts	4-3
1997–98	Celtic v Dundee U	3-0

SCOTTISH LEAGUE CUP

1998–99	Rangers v St Johnstone	2-1

CIS INSURANCE CUP

1999–2000	Celtic v Aberdeen	2-0
2000–01	Celtic v Kilmarnock	3-0
2001–02	Rangers v Ayr U	4-0
2002–03	Rangers v Celtic	2-1
2003–04	Livingston v Hibernian	2-0
2004–05	Rangers v Motherwell	5-1
2005–06	Celtic v Dunfermline Ath	3-0
2006–07	Hibernian v Kilmarnock	5-1
2007–08	Rangers v Dundee U	2-2*
	Rangers won 3-2 on penalties.	

CO-OPERATIVE INSURANCE CUP

2008–09	Celtic v Rangers	2-0*
2009–10	Rangers v St Mirren	1-0
2010–11	Rangers v Celtic	2-1*

SCOTTISH COMMUNITIES LEAGUE CUP

2011–12	Kilmarnock v Celtic	1-0
2012–13	St Mirren v Hearts	3-2
2013–14	Aberdeen v Inverness CT	0-0*
	Aberdeen won 4-2 on penalties.	

SCOTTISH LEAGUE CUP PRESENTED BY QTS

2014–15	Celtic v Dundee U	2-0
2015–16	Ross Co v Hibernian	2-1

BETFRED SCOTTISH LEAGUE CUP

2016–17	Celtic v Aberdeen	3-0
2017–18	Celtic v Motherwell	2-0
2018–19	Celtic v Aberdeen	1-0

**After extra time.*

SCOTTISH LEAGUE CUP WINS

Rangers 27, Celtic 18, Aberdeen 6, Hearts 4, Dundee 3, East Fife 3, Hibernian 3, Dundee U 2, Kilmarnock 1, Livingston 1, Motherwell 1, Partick Thistle 1, Raith R 1, Ross Co 1, St Mirren 1.

APPEARANCES IN FINALS

Rangers 34, Celtic 33, Aberdeen 15, Hibernian 10, Dundee U 7, Hearts 7, Dundee 6, Kilmarnock 6, Motherwell 4, Partick Thistle 4, Dunfermline Ath 3, East Fife 3, St Mirren 3, Raith R 2, St Johnstone 2, Ayr U 1, Falkirk 1, Inverness CT 1, Livingston 1, Morton 1, Ross Co 1, Third Lanark 1.

BETFRED SCOTTISH LEAGUE CUP 2018–19

▪ *Denotes player sent off.*
PW = Drawn match won on penalties (2pts).
PL = Drawn match lost on penalties (1pt).

FIRST ROUND
NORTHERN SECTION – GROUP A

Saturday, 14 July 2018
Dundee U (0) 1 *(Clark 77)*
Arbroath won 5-3 on penalties.

Ross Co (0) 2 *(McManus 61, Mullin 82)*
Elgin C (0) 0 1270

Tuesday, 17 July 2018
Alloa Ath (4) 4 *(Spence 9, 36, Cawley 10, Trouten 30)*
Arbroath (2) 2 *(Wallace 20, Hester 26)* 302

Ross Co (0) 1 *(Lindsay 85)*
Dundee U (0) 0 1544

Saturday, 21 July 2018
Arbroath (0) 2 *(Hamilton 52, O'Brien 82)*
Elgin C (0) 0 386

Dundee U (1) 1 *(Frans 24)*
Alloa Ath (0) 1 *(Trouten 79 (pen))* 1659
Alloa Ath won 4-3 on penalties.

Tuesday, 24 July 2018
Elgin C (0) 0
Alloa Ath (2) 3 *(Hastie 2, 53, Trouten 11)* 417

Wednesday, 25 July 2018
Arbroath (1) 4 *(McKenna 43 (pen), 59, 72, Hester 83)*
Ross Co (1) 1 *(McKay 23)* 496

Saturday, 28 July 2018
Alloa Ath (0) 0
Ross Co (0) 2 *(Morris 59, Paton 90)* 431

Elgin C (0) 0
Dundee U (0) 4 *(Clark 66, 73, Barton 81 (pen), Glass 90)* 1104

Group A Table	P	W	PW	PL	L	F	A	GD	Pts
Ross Co	4	3	0	0	1	6	4	2	9
Arbroath	4	2	1	0	1	9	6	3	8
Alloa Ath	4	2	1	0	1	8	5	3	8
Dundee U	4	1	0	2	1	6	3	3	5
Elgin C	4	0	0	0	4	0	11	–11	0

NORTHERN SECTION – GROUP B

Saturday, 14 July 2018
Falkirk (0) 0
Montrose (1) 1 *(Rennie 19)* 1730

St Johnstone (0) 0
East Fife (0) 0 1687
St Johnstone won 5-4 on penalties.

Tuesday, 17 July 2018
Falkirk (0) 2 *(Lewis 54, Petravicius 82)*
Forfar Ath (0) 0 1429

Montrose (0) 1 *(Cavanagh 56)*
East Fife (0) 0 466

Saturday, 21 July 2018
Montrose (0) 0
St Johnstone (1) 1 *(Watt 34)* 1160

Sunday, 22 July 2018
East Fife (1) 1 *(Meechan 7 (og))*
Forfar Ath (1) 1 *(Baird 45)* 420
Forfar Ath won 5-4 on penalties.

Tuesday, 24 July 2018
St Johnstone (1) 1 *(Scougall 31)*
Falkirk (0) 0 2379

Wednesday, 25 July 2018
Forfar Ath (2) 3 *(Easton 26 (pen), Baird 28, Hilson 66)*
Montrose (0) 1 *(Campbell R 64)* 658

Saturday, 28 July 2018
East Fife (1) 1 *(Dowds 24)*
Falkirk (0) 2 *(Mackin 49, 63)* 670

Forfar Ath (1) 1 *(Baird 15)*
St Johnstone (1) 3 *(Watt 42, McMillan 51, Kennedy 62)* 1087

Group B Table	P	W	PW	PL	L	F	A	GD	Pts
St Johnstone	4	3	1	0	0	5	1	4	11
Falkirk	4	2	0	0	2	4	3	1	6
Montrose	4	2	0	0	2	3	4	–1	6
Forfar Ath	4	1	1	0	2	5	7	–2	5
East Fife	4	0	0	2	2	2	4	–2	2

NORTHERN SECTION – GROUP C

Saturday, 14 July 2018
Inverness CT (2) 2 *(Austin 30, 41)*
Cove R (0) 0 932

Raith R (0) 0
Cowdenbeath (0) 2 *(Sheerin 53, 86)* 634

Tuesday, 17 July 2018
Cowdenbeath (1) 2 *(Sheerin 24, 81)*
Inverness CT (3) 5 *(Walsh 34, 41, Doran 45, 80, Oakley 73)* 374

Wednesday, 18 July 2018
Cove R (0) 1 *(McManus 75)*
Hearts (1) 2 *(Lee 11, MacLean 57)* 1728

Saturday, 21 July 2018
Cowdenbeath (0) 1 *(Cox 86)*
Cove R (0) 0 320

Raith R (0) 1 *(Nisbet 51)*
Hearts (0) 1 *(Smith 78)* 1452
Hearts won 4-2 on penalties.

Tuesday, 24 July 2018
Hearts (0) 5 *(MacLean 48, Ikpeazu 64, Haring 73, Naismith 75 (pen), Smith 81)*
Cowdenbeath (0) 0 7486

Inverness CT (0) 2 *(Austin 49, Mackay 87)*
Raith R (0) 1 *(Gillespie 61)* 1295

Saturday, 28 July 2018
Cove R (1) 2 *(Park 9, Masson 76)*
Raith R (0) 0 327

Sunday, 29 July 2018
Hearts (3) 5 *(Ikpeazu 29, 33, Garuccio 32, Naismith 64, 81)*
Inverness CT (0) 0 10,030

Group C Table	P	W	PW	PL	L	F	A	GD	PTS
Hearts*	4	3	1	0	0	13	2	11	9
Inverness CT	4	3	0	0	1	9	8	1	9
Cowdenbeath	4	2	0	0	2	5	10	–5	6
Cove Rangers	4	1	0	0	3	3	5	–2	3
Raith R	4	0	0	1	3	2	7	–5	1

**Hearts deducted 2 points for fielding an ineligible player against Cove Rangers 18/7/2018.*

NORTHERN SECTION – GROUP D

Saturday, 14 July 2018

Brechin C (0) 0
Peterhead (0) 0 301
Peterhead won 5-4 on penalties.

Stirling Alb (0) 0
Dundee (1) 4 *(Moussa 39, 57, Mendy 63, Wighton 69)* 1373

Tuesday, 17 July 2018

Dunfermline Ath (1) 3 *(Hippolyte 42, Higginbotham 88 (pen), Ryan 90)*
Peterhead (0) 0 1848

Stirling Alb (1) 1 *(Stewart 44)*
Brechin C (1) 2 *(Melingui 17, Tapping C 84)* 334

Saturday, 21 July 2018

Peterhead (0) 0
Stirling Alb (1) 2 *(MacDonald 9, Stewart 71)* 473

Sunday, 22 July 2018

Dundee (0) 0
Dunfermline Ath (1) 1 *(Longridge J 2)* 2870

Wednesday, 25 July 2018

Brechin C (0) 1 *(Shields 60)*
Dunfermline Ath (4) 7 *(Devine 7, Longridge L 10, El Bakhtaoui 15, 43, Ryan 57, 63, Hippolyte 85)* 658

Peterhead (0) 0
Dundee (0) 2 *(Madianga 49, Mendy 90)* 934

Saturday, 28 July 2018

Dundee (1) 2 *(Spence 11, McGowan P 59)*
Brechin C (0) 0 2058

Dunfermline Ath (0) 3 *(Hippolyte 47, 90, Vincent 56)*
Stirling Alb (1) 1 *(MacDonald P 35)* 2359

Group D Table	P	W	PW	PL	L	F	A	GD	Pts
Dunfermline Ath	4	4	0	0	0	14	2	12	12
Dundee	4	3	0	0	1	8	1	7	9
Brechin C	4	1	0	1	2	3	10	–7	4
Stirling Alb	4	1	0	0	3	4	9	–5	3
Peterhead	4	0	1	0	3	0	7	–7	2

SOUTHERN SECTION – GROUP E

Saturday, 14 July 2018

Ayr U (0) 3 *(Shankland 48, 72, 75)*
Greenock Morton (1) 1 *(Tidser 14)* 1586

Stenhousemuir (0) 0
Partick Thistle (2) 2 *(Gordon 2, 6)* 675

Tuesday, 17 July 2018

Partick Thistle (2) 2 *(Storer 17, Penrice 29)*
Greenock Morton (0) 1 *(Tumilty 74)* 2088

Stenhousemuir (0) 4 *(Neill 54, Duthie 56, Ross 85, Dickson 90)*
Albion R (0) 0 230

Saturday, 21 July 2018

Albion R (0) 0
Ayr U (1) 2 *(Forrest 15, Bell 80)* 519

Greenock Morton (2) 2 *(MacLean 33, McHugh 41)*
Stenhousemuir (0) 0 847

Tuesday, 24 July 2018

Albion R (0) 0
Partick Thistle (0) 2 *(Storey 59, Fitzpatrick 83)* 963

Ayr U (3) 5 *(Shankland 2, 8, 46, Moffat 41, 86)*
Stenhousemuir (0) 0 1227

Saturday, 28 July 2018

Greenock Morton (2) 5 *(McHugh 36, Bell 38, Tidser 74 (pen), 79, Armour 75)*
Albion R (0) 0 758

Partick Thistle (0) 0
Ayr U (1) 2 *(Moffat 6, Shankland 66)* 2871

Group E Table	P	W	PW	PL	L	F	A	GD	Pts
Ayr U	4	4	0	0	0	12	1	11	12
Partick Thistle	4	3	0	0	1	6	3	3	9
Greenock Morton	4	2	0	0	2	9	5	4	6
Stenhousemuir	4	1	0	0	3	4	9	–5	3
Albion R	4	0	0	0	4	0	13	–13	0

SOUTHERN SECTION – GROUP F

Saturday, 14 July 2018

Airdrieonians (0) 1 *(Duffy 53)*
Livingston (2) 2 *(Pitman 24, Miller L 25)* 733

Annan Ath (0) 1 *(Smith 60)*
Hamilton A (0) 0 491

Tuesday, 17 July 2018

Annan Ath (2) 4 *(Muir 30, 42, Wilson 48, Roberts 52)*
Berwick Rangers (0) 0 192

Hamilton A (0) 0
Livingston (0) 0 1012
Livingston won 6-5 on penalties.

Saturday, 21 July 2018

Berwick Rangers (0) 0
Airdrieonians (2) 3 *(Crighton 21, Duffy 36, McIntosh L 75)* 389

Livingston (1) 1 *(Miller K 14)*
Annan Ath (0) 0 678

Tuesday, 24 July 2018

Airdrieonians (1) 4 *(Crighton 38, Conroy 54, Duffy 56, Carrick 88)*
Annan Ath (0) 1 *(Wilson 84)* 461

Berwick Rangers (0) 0
Hamilton A (2) 4 *(Miller 5, 29, 64 (pen), Bingham 87)* 336

Saturday, 28 July 2018

Hamilton A (0) 1 *(Bingham 62)*
Airdrieonians (0) 1 *(Vitoria 83)* 1316
Hamilton A won 3-0 on penalties.

Livingston (1) 2 *(Hamilton 3, McMillan 82)*
Berwick Rangers (0) 0 552

Group F Table	P	W	PW	PL	L	F	A	GD	Pts
Livingston	4	3	1	0	0	5	1	4	11
Airdrieonians	4	2	0	1	1	9	4	5	7
Hamilton A	4	1	1	1	1	5	2	3	6
Annan Ath	4	2	0	0	2	6	5	1	6
Berwick Rangers	4	0	0	0	4	0	10	–10	0

SOUTHERN SECTION – GROUP G

Saturday, 14 July 2018

Clyde (0) 1 *(McNiff 90)*

Edinburgh C (1) 1 *(Balatoni 44)* 407

Edinburgh C won 4-1 on penalties.

Queen of the South (3) 5 *(Harkins 41, Dobbie 42, 87, Dykes 44, Stirling 64)*

Stranraer (2) 3 *(McGowan 4, Donnelly 9, Turner 80)* 803

Tuesday, 17 July 2018

Motherwell (5) 5 *(Frear 8, 24, 28, Tait 18, Main 44)*

Edinburgh C (0) 0 2749

Queen of the South (0) 3 *(Dobbie 47, 49, 78)*

Clyde (0) 0 788

Saturday, 21 July 2018

Edinburgh C (0) 0

Queen of the South (4) 4 *(Dykes 24, Dobbie 26, 38, Todd 34)* 525

Stranraer (0) 1 *(Layne 59)*

Motherwell (1) 1 *(Hartley 38)* 885

Stranraer won 3-2 on penalties.

Tuesday, 24 July 2018

Motherwell (2) 2 *(Sammon 12, 37)*

Queen of the South (0) 0 3337

Stranraer (0) 1 *(Anderson 56)*

Clyde (3) 3 *(Goodwillie 2, 22, McNiff 31)* 382

Saturday, 28 July 2018

Clyde (1) 1 *(Goodwillie 31)*

Motherwell (0) 3 *(Main 76, Johnson 79, Sammon 90)* 1620

Edinburgh C (2) 4 *(McIntyre 7, Rodger 33, Thomson 55, Henderson B 79)*

Stranraer (2) 2 *(Cummins 23, Anderson 35)* 236

Group G Table	*P*	*W*	*PW*	*PL*	*L*	*F*	*A*	*GD*	*Pts*
Motherwell	4	3	0	1	0	11	2	9	10
Queen of the South	4	3	0	0	1	12	5	7	9
Edinburgh C	4	1	1	0	2	5	12	–7	5
Clyde	4	1	0	1	2	5	8	–3	4
Stranraer	4	0	1	0	3	7	13	–6	2

SOUTHERN SECTION – GROUP H

Friday, 13 July 2018

Kilmarnock (0) 0

St Mirren (0) 0 4026

St Mirren won 3-2 on penalties.

Saturday, 14 July 2018

Spartans (0) 0

Dumbarton (0) 0 245

Dumbarton won 4-3 on penalties.

Tuesday, 17 July 2018

Dumbarton (1) 1 *(Gallagher 35)*

Queen's Park (0) 0 425

St Mirren (0) 2 *(McGinn S 59, Mullen 75 (pen))*

Spartans (1) 2 *(Stevens 6, Maxwell 55)* 1430

St Mirren won 5-3 on penalties.

Saturday, 21 July 2018

Dumbarton (1) 2 *(Barr C 41, Barr B 65)*

Kilmarnock (0) 4 *(Ndjoli 48, Boyd K 68, 76, 90)* 1353

Queen's Park (0) 2 *(Gibson 55, Roberts 70)*

Spartans (0) 1 *(Dishington 52)* 508

Tuesday, 24 July 2018

Queen's Park (0) 0

St Mirren (0) 0 1493

St Mirren won 5-4 on penalties.

Spartans (0) 0

Kilmarnock (0) 3 *(Erwin 63, Ndjoli 80, 90)* 1078

Saturday, 28 July 2018

Kilmarnock (0) 2 *(Brophy 62, Boyd K 90 (pen))*

Queen's Park (0) 0 2835

St Mirren (2) 6 *(Coulson 1, Smith 35, 84, Stewart 48, McGinn S 53, Kellermann 82)*

Dumbarton (0) 0 1610

Group H Table	*P*	*W*	*PW*	*PL*	*L*	*F*	*A*	*GD*	*Pts*
Kilmarnock	4	3	0	1	0	9	2	7	10
St Mirren	4	1	3	0	0	8	2	6	9
Dumbarton	4	1	1	0	2	3	10	–7	5
Queen's Park	4	1	0	1	2	2	4	–2	4
Spartans	4	0	0	2	2	3	7	–4	2

Queen of the South, Dundee, St Mirren and Partick Thistle qualified for the Second Round as best runners-up

SECOND ROUND

Saturday, 18 August 2018

Aberdeen (3) 4 *(Mackay-Steven 16, 57 (pen), Shinnie 20, May 26)*

St Mirren (0) 0 9011

Aberdeen: (4132) Lewis; Ball, Devlin, Considine, Shinnie; Gleeson; Wright (Anderson 71), Ferguson, Mackay-Steven; Ross (Forrester 61), May (McLennan 79).
St Mirren: (433) Samson; McGinn P, Baird, Kpekawa (Jones 52), Coulson; Willock, McGinn S, Magennis; Smith (MacPherson 63), Brock-Madsen (Cooke 81), Mullen.
Referee: Steven McLean.

Dundee (0) 0

Ayr U (0) 3 *(Shankland 51, 86, Moffat 89)* 3151

Dundee: (442) Hamilton; Curran J, Meekings, Kusunga■, Ralph; Madianga, Spence (Kamara 78), N'Gwatala, Wighton (Kallman 46); Nabi, Mendy (Moussa■ 62).
Ayr U: (442) Doohan; Geggan, Adams, Rose, Harvie; Forrest (McDaid 74), Crawford (Bell 90), Kerr, Murdoch; Moffat, Shankland (Moore 90).
Referee: John Beaton.

Dunfermline Ath (0) 0

Hearts (0) 1 *(Lee 79)* 8601

Dunfermline Ath: (352) Robinson; Ashcroft, Durnan, Devine; Williamson, Craigen (Ryan 87), Vincent, Longridge L, Longridge J; El Bakhtaoui, Hippolyte (Connolly 81).
Hearts: (442) Zlamal; Smith, Souttar, Hughes (Bozanic 46), Garuccio; Mulraney (Morrison 79), Lee, Haring, Naismith; MacLean, Ikpeazu (Lafferty 70).
Referee: Bobby Madden.

Livingston (0) 0

Motherwell (1) 1 *(Johnson 23)* 1957

Livingston: (352) Kelly; Gallagher, Halkett, Saunders; Kaja (Lamie 46), Pitman, Byrne, Robinson (Cadden 71), Lawless; Miller K, Miller L (Hamilton 55).
Motherwell: (352) Carson; Aldred, McHugh, Hartley (Taylor-Sinclair 66); Tait, Rodriguez (Campbell 61), Rose, Bigirimana, Frear; Main, Johnson (Sammon 75).
Referee: William Collum.

Partick Thistle (0) 1 *(Mbuyi-Mutombo 73)*

Celtic (1) 3 *(Griffiths 18, Dembele 78, Rogic 80)* 6350

Partick Thistle: (4141) Bell; Elliot, O'Ware, McGinty, Melbourne; Penrice; Spittal, Storer (Fitzpatrick 71), Gordon (Slater 37), Mbuyi-Mutombo; Doolan (Erskine 58).
Celtic: (4231) Bain; Gamboa, Hendry, Ajer, Izaguirre; Brown, Ntcham (McGregor 79); Johnston (Forrest 71), Rogic, Sinclair; Griffiths (Dembele 65).
Referee: Craig Thomson.

Queen of the South (1) 2 *(Dykes 45, Dobbie 116 (pen))*

St Johnstone (1) 4 *(Watt 27, 105, Wright 96, Hendry 120)* 1652

Queen of the South: (442) Martin; Mercer, Semple, Fordyce (Bell 5 (Murray 98)), Marshall; Doyle, Jacobs, Harkins, Stirling; Dykes, Dobbie.
St Johnstone: (442) Clark; Foster, Kerr, Shaughnessy, Tanser; Wright (Scougall 106), Davidson, Craig, Alston (McMillan 79); Watt (Hendry 106), Kennedy (McCann 112).
aet.
Referee: Don Robertson.

Sunday, 19 August 2018

Hibernian (1) 3 *(Gray 15, Mallan 70, Horgan 90)*

Ross Co (1) 2 *(Gardyne 10, Mullin 64 (pen))* 7452

Hibernian: (4312) Laidlaw; Gray, Ambrose, Porteous, Stevenson; Martin (Whittaker 46), Mallan, Hyndman (Maclaren 64); Horgan (Hanlon 90); Boyle, Shaw.
Ross Co: (451) Fox; Fraser (Demetriou 73), Morris, Watson, Kelly S; Mullin, Lindsay (Cowie 55), Draper, Vigurs, Gardyne; McManus (Graham 84).
Referee: Kevin Clancy.

Kilmarnock (0) 1 *(Barisic 51 (og))*

Rangers (2) 3 *(Morelos 28, 43, 74)* 12,016

Kilmarnock: (442) Bachmann; O'Donnell, Broadfoot, Boyd S (Ndjoli 81), Taylor; Burke, Dicker, Power (Wilson 81), Jones; Boyd K, Brophy.
Rangers: (433) Foderingham; Tavernier, Goldson, Katic, Barisic; Ejaria, Arfield (McCrorie 79), Halliday; Kent, Morelos (Umar 79), Murphy (Candeias 17).
Referee: Nick Walsh.

QUARTER-FINALS

Tuesday, 25 September 2018

Hibernian (0) 0

Aberdeen (0) 0 11,170

Hibernian: (3142) Bogdan; Ambrose, Porteous, Hanlon (Agyepong 91); Milligan (Whittaker 105); Boyle, Hyndman (Bartley 91), Mallan, Stevenson; Kamberi (Slivka 105), Shaw.
Aberdeen: (442) Lewis; Logan, Devlin, McKenna, Considine; Mackay-Steven, Ball (Anderson 120), Shinnie, Lowe (McGinn 61); Wilson (Forrester 90), Cosgrove (May 79).
aet; Aberdeen won 6-5 on penalties.
Referee: Steven McLean.

Wednesday, 26 September 2018

Hearts (1) 4 *(MacLean 35, Haring 64, Lee 88, Naismith 90)*

Motherwell (1) 2 *(Main 12 (pen), Bowman 80)* 14,377

Hearts: (433) Zlamal; Smith, Souttar, Jimmy Dunne, Mitchell; Lee (Bozanic 90), Djoum, Haring; Morrison (Dikamona 86), MacLean (Amankwaa 90), Naismith.
Motherwell: (352) Carson; Aldred, Donnelly, McHugh; Cadden, Campbell (Johnson 75), Bigirimana (Frear 66), Grimshaw, Tait; Main, Bowman.
Referee: William Collum.

Rangers (2) 4 *(Katic 16, Middleton 31, 70, Morelos 49)*

Ayr U (0) 0 35,042

Rangers: (4141) Foderingham; Flanagan, Katic, Worrall, Halliday; McCrorie (Kelly 69); Kent, Ejaria, Dorrans (Rossiter 56), Middleton; Morelos (Grezda 50).
Ayr U: (4411) Doohan; Smith, Adams, Rose, Harvie; Geggan (Moffat 59), Murdoch (McDaid 65), Kerr, Crawford; Forrest; Shankland (Moore 76).
Referee: Bobby Madden.

St Johnstone (0) 0

Celtic (0) 1 *(Griffiths 83)* 5635

St Johnstone: (4141) Clark; Foster, Kerr, Shaughnessy, Tanser; Callachan; Wright (Swanson 66), Alston, Craig (McMillan 85), Wotherspoon; Watt (Kane 46).
Celtic: (4231) Bain; Lustig, Boyata■, Ajer (Hendry 33), Tierney; Brown, Ntcham; Forrest, Edouard (Morgan 65), McGregor (Rogic 75); Griffiths.
Referee: John Beaton.

SEMI-FINALS

Sunday, 28 October 2018

Aberdeen (0) 1 *(Ferguson 79)*

Rangers (0) 0 46,186

Aberdeen: (4231) Lewis; Logan, Devlin, McKenna, Considine (Lowe 36); Ferguson, Shinnie; McGinn, Wright (May 60), Mackay-Steven; Wilson (Ball 86).
Rangers: (433) McGregor; Tavernier, Goldson, Worrall, Flanagan; Coulibaly, Jack (Middleton 82), Ejaria; Candeias (Arfield 82), Umar, Kent.
Referee: John Beaton.

Hearts (0) 0

Celtic (0) 3 *(Sinclair 53 (pen), Forrest 66, Christie 72)* 61,161

Hearts: (4141) Zlamal; Smith, Dikamona, Dunne, Mitchell; Haring; Djoum, Lee (Clare 76), Bozanic (Morrison 70), Naismith (Amankwaa 8); MacLean.
Celtic: (4231) Bain; Lustig, Benkovic, Ajer (Hendry 80), Tierney; Eboue (Sinclair 26), Ntcham (Christie 46); Forrest, Rogic, McGregor; Edouard.
Referee: William Collum.

BETFRED SCOTTISH LEAGUE CUP FINAL 2018–19

Sunday, 2 December 2018

(at Hampden Park, attendance 50,936)

Celtic (1) 1 **Aberdeen (0) 0**

Celtic: (4141) Bain; Lustig, Boyata (Simunovic 61), Benkovic, Tierney; McGregor; Forrest (Ntcham 86), Rogic (Brown 64), Christie, Sinclair; Edouard.
Scorer: Christie 45.

Aberdeen: (4231) Lewis; Logan, McKenna, Considine, Lowe; Ball, Shinnie; Mackay-Steven (McLennan 45), Ferguson, McGinn (Wilson 70); Cosgrove (Anderson 79).

Referee: Andrew Dallas.

IRN-BRU SCOTTISH LEAGUE CHALLENGE CUP 2018–19

▪ *Denotes player sent off.*

PRELIMINARY ROUND

Sunday, 29 July 2018

BSC Glasgow (0) 0
East Stirling (0) 1 *(Tennant 50 (og))* 142

Wednesday, 1 August 2018

Inverurie Loco Works (1) 2 *(McCabe 37, Smith 68)*
Fraserburgh (1) 2 *(Beagrie 8, Campbell 84)* 399
Inverurie Loco Works won 5-4 on penalties.

FIRST ROUND – NORTH

Tuesday, 14 August 2018

Alloa Ath (2) 3 *(Cawley 40, 45, Flannigan 46)*
Stirling Alb (0) 1 *(Hamilton 55)* 332

Cowdenbeath (1) 1 *(Sheerin 30)*
East Fife (0) 3 *(Goodfellow 68 (og), Dowds 75, Court 90)* 261

Dundee U21 (1) 2 *(Bradbury 22, Jefferies 85)*
Hibernian U21 (1) 2 *(Murray F 25, Mackie 75)* 191
Dundee U21 won 4-3 on penalties.

Hearts U21 (1) 1 *(Keena 44)*
Ross Co (2) 2 *(McKay 4, 30)* 344

Inverness CT (0) 1 *(White 61)*
Dunfermline Ath (1) 2 *(Higginbotham 25 (pen), Smith 87)* 1046

Inverurie Loco Works (0) 0
Formartine United (0) 1 *(Gethins 61)* 399

Peterhead (0) 2 *(McLean 76, Leitch 86)*
Brechin C (1) 1 *(Shields 12)* 496

Raith R (3) 3 *(Wedderburn 16, Matthews 28, Nisbet 30)*
Aberdeen U21 (0) 1 *(Anderson 72)* 479

Wednesday, 15 August 2018

Cove Rangers (1) 2 *(McManus 44, 49)*
Montrose (1) 2 *(Campbell I 34 (pen), Callaghan 69)* 420
Montrose won 4-3 on penalties.

Dundee U (0) 3 *(Chalmers 64, McMullan 78, 90)*
St Johnstone U21 (1) 2 *(Hendry 21, 58)* 700

Elgin C (0) 1 *(McHardy 83)*
Arbroath (0) 1 *(O'Brien 57)* 401
Arbroath won 7-6 on penalties.

Tuesday, 21 August 2018

Livingston U21 (0) 0
Forfar Ath (0) 0 460
Livingston U21 won 5-4 on penalties.

FIRST ROUND – SOUTH

Tuesday, 14 August 2018

Annan Ath (1) 4 *(Wallace 9, 55, Fergusson 67, 81)*
Celtic U21 (0) 0 266

Berwick Rangers (0) 0
Airdrieonians (3) 3 *(Conroy 2, Carrick 19, McIntosh L 22 (pen))* 317

Dumbarton (2) 2 *(Paton 12, Russell 26)*
Greenock Morton (1) 1 *(Oliver 39)* 680

East Stirling (0) 0
Motherwell U21 (3) 3 *(Turnbull 16, Watson 20, Hastie 22)* 163

Edinburgh C (0) 3 *(Shepherd 70, Henderson B 77, 83 (pen))*
Albion R (1) 1 *(Cunningham 15)* 182

Hamilton A U21 (1) 4 *(Enigbokan-Bloomfield 8, 90, Cunningham 62, Hughes 73)*
Clyde (1) 1 *(McStay 9)* 297

Kilmarnock U21 (0) 1 *(Thomas 48)*
St Mirren U21 (1) 2 *(Jamieson 10, MacPherson 55)* 208

Queen's Park (0) 0
Ayr U (0) 0 834
Queen's Park won 4-2 on penalties.

Rangers U21 (0) 1 *(Rudden 90)*
Falkirk (2) 2 *(Lewis 4, Harrison 21)* 636

Stenhousemuir (0) 0
Queen of the South (0) 3 *(Dobbie 59, 66, Dykes 62)* 387

Ryan Christie scores the only goal of the game at Hampden Park as Celtic beat Aberdeen to claim the Scottish League Cup Final on 2nd December. (Jeff Holmes/PA Archive/PA Images)

Stranraer (0) 0
Partick Thistle (3) 5 *(O'Ware 10, Fitzpatrick 34, 90, Mbuyi-Mutombo 36, Melbourne 89)* 480

Wednesday, 15 August 2018
East Kilbride (0) 1 *(McNeil 61)*
Spartans (1) 1 *(Cennerazzo 3)* 207
East Kilbride won 5-4 on penalties.

SECOND ROUND

Thursday, 6 September 2018
Dundee U21 (1) 1 *(Armstrong 43 (og))*
Motherwell U21 (1) 2 *(MacDonald 25, Watson 86)* 208

Saturday, 8 September 2018
Airdrieonians (0) 0
Sutton U (1) 1 *(Wright 21)* 831

Arbroath (1) 3 *(Linn 8, Denholm 71, McKenna 83)*
Annan Ath (0) 0 524

Boreham Wood (0) 0
Dunfermline Ath (0) 0 1001
Dunfermline Ath won 6-5 on penalties.

Coleraine (1) 1 *(Carson 31)*
Formartine U (1) 1 *(MacPhee 20)* 973
Coleraine won 2-1 on penalties.

Dumbarton (0) 0
Montrose (1) 1 *(Johnston 19)* 456

Dundee U (1) 1 *(Smith M 15)*
Alloa Ath (0) 1 *(Trouten 78 (pen))* 1040
Alloa Ath won 5-4 on penalties.

East Fife (0) 2 *(Agnew 51, Currie 74)*
Partick Thistle (1) 1 *(Mbuyi-Mutombo 22)* 932

East Kilbride (0) 2 *(McNeil 72, Malcolm 73)*
Edinburgh C (1) 3 *(Henderson B 36, Smith A 84, 86)* 287

Falkirk (0) 0
Connah's Quay Nomads (0) 1 *(Wilde 46)* 1637

Peterhead (0) 0
Bohemians (0) 1 *(Devaney 63)* 713

Queen of the South (4) 4 *(Dobbie 22, 31, Dykes 25, Harkins 29)*
Crusaders (0) 3 *(Patterson 47, 51 (pen), Heatley 85)* 1204

Ross Co (5) 5 *(Graham 18, 29, 40, 42, Lindsay 37)*
Raith R (0) 0 790

Sligo R (1) 4 *(Drennan 15, 52, 86, Cawley 60)*
Livingston U21 (1) 1 *(Knox 3)* 478

St Mirren U21 (2) 3 *(Jamieson 10, MacPherson 39 (pen), Potter 70)*
Hamilton A U21 (1) 2 *(Smith A 27, Smith L 87)* 316

The New Saints (1) 2 *(Hart 30 (og), Nembhard 90)*
Queen's Park (0) 2 *(Osadolor 89, Hawke 90)* 278
Queen's Park won 4-2 on penalties.

THIRD ROUND

Friday, 12 October 2018
Arbroath (1) 1 *(McKenna 11)*
Edinburgh C (1) 4 *(Henderson B 25 (pen), 68 (pen), Shepherd 56, Henderson L 78)* 506
Arbroath: (442) Hill; Thomson, Little, O'Brien, Hamilton; Gold, Graham (Whatley 64), McCord, Denholm (Linn 64); McKenna, Wallace (Doris 73).
Edinburgh C: (442) Antell; McIntyre, Henderson L, Balatoni, Thomson; Taylor (Stewart 77), Laird, Black, Handling (Smith 56); Henderson B, Shepherd (Hall 85).
Referee: Alan Muir.

Saturday, 13 October 2018
Bohemians (0) 0
Sutton U (0) 0 1130
Bohemians: (4231) Supple; Pender, Cornwall, Byrne, McCourt (Kirk 60); Buckley (Brennan 80), Lunney; Kelly, Stokes, Devaney; Corcoran (Magerusan 72).
Sutton U: (442) Worner; Wishart, Clough, Brown (Davis 55), Thomas; Ayunga (Lafayette 79), Taylor, Eastmond, Bennett; Bolarinwa (Cadogan 78), Drinan.
Bohemians won 4-3 on penalties.
Referee: Mike Roncone.

Connah's Quay Nomads (0) 2 *(Horan 61, Owens 90)*
Coleraine (0) 0 624
Connah's Quay Nomads: (3142) Rushton; Disney, Horan, Holmes; Harrison; Wignall (Bakare 88), Morris, Owen, Poole (Jones 46); Wilde (Wilson 46), Owens.
Coleraine: (433) Johns; Canning, Douglas, O'Donnell■, Mullan; Harkin, Lowry■, Burns; Parkhill (Gawne 71), Bradley (McLaughlin 80), McCauley (Whiteside 87).
Referee: Colin Steven.

Dunfermline Ath (1) 2 *(Longridge L 28, 47 (pen))*
Alloa Ath (1) 2 *(Trouten 8, 70)* 1469
Dunfermline Ath: (442) Robinson; Craigen, Ashcroft, Devine, Longridge J; Longridge L, Martin (Beadling 66), Vincent, Connolly; El Bakhtaoui, Ryan (Hippolyte 69).
Alloa Ath: (442) Parry; Taggart, Dick, Graham, Peggie; Cawley, Robertson, Trouten, Flannigan; Zanatta, Shields (Brown 66).
Alloa Ath won 5-4 on penalties.
Referee: Nick Walsh.

East Fife (1) 2 *(Smith 34, Dowds 78)*
Queen of the South (0) 0 579
East Fife: (442) Long; Watson C, Dunlop, Meggatt, Slattery; Dunsmore, Davidson, Agnew, Watt (Bell 89); Smith (Court 64), Currie (Dowds 75).
Queen of the South: (442) Martin; Mercer (Fordyce 70), Doyle, Semple, Marshall; Frizzell (Bell 61), Jacobs, Todd, Stirling; Dobbie, Dykes.
Referee: Barry Cook.

Motherwell U21 (1) 2 *(McClean 12 (og), Mbulu 71)*
Sligo R (0) 0 950
Motherwell U21: (442) Ferguson; MacDonald, Mbulu, Maguire, Livingstone; Watson, Turnbull, Brown, Hastie; Rehman (Armstrong 67), Scott.
Sligo R: (451) Mahon ; Callan-McFadden, McGinty , McClean (Sharkey 53), Donelon (Cretaro 75); Cawley, McCabe, Twardek, Keaney, McAleer (Morrison 46); Drennan.
Referee: Richard Hulme.

Ross Co (2) 3 *(Stewart 20, Keillor-Dunn 41, 51)*
Montrose (1) 1 *(Johnston 44)* 1122
Ross Co: (451) Fox; Dingwall T (Kelly T 83), Draper, Fontaine, Demetriou; McManus, Lindsay (Wallace 70), Cowie, Vigurs, Keillor-Dunn (Maciver 77); Ross C Stewart.
Montrose: (442) Fleming; Dillon, Bolochoweckyj, Campbell I, Steeves; Redman, Watson (Webster 69), Masson, Cavanagh; Johnston (Campbell R 74), Rennie (Callaghan 69).
Referee: Craig Napier.

St Mirren U21 (1) 2 *(Jamieson 2, Breadner 63)*
Queen's Park (0) 4 *(Hawke 62, McLean 66, 82 (pen), East 80)* 507
St Mirren U21: (4231) Wilson; Cameron, Potter, McBrearty, Miller; Glover, McShane; Henderson (Reilly 79), Kirkpatrick, Breadner; Jamieson.
Queen's Park: (4411) Hart; Grant, McLauchlan, McKernon, Summers; Mortimer (East 54), Roberts, McLaren, McLean; Hawke; Peters (Moore 65).
Referee: Grant Irvine.

QUARTER-FINALS

Friday, 16 November 2018

Queen's Park (0) 1 *(Hawke 64)*

Connah's Quay Nomads (0) 2 *(Horan 81, Wilde 84)* 559

Queen's Park: (4231) Hart; Grant, McLauchlan, McLaren, Summers; McKernon, Roberts; McLean (Mortimer 85), Moore, East (Osadolor 70); Hawke.
Connah's Quay Nomads: (4141) Danby; Holmes, Disney, Horan, Wilson; Harrison; Wignall (Poole 90), Morris, Parker, Bakare (Hughes 64); Wilde.
Referee: David Rock.

Saturday, 17 November 2018

Edinburgh C (1) 2 *(Henderson B 45, Shepherd 57)*

Alloa Ath (2) 2 *(Zanatta 2, Trouten 12)* 478

Edinburgh C: (442) Antell; Thomson, Balatoni, Henderson L, McIntyre; Smith, Black, Laird, Taylor; Shepherd, Henderson B.
Alloa Ath: (4231) Parry; Taggart, Graham, Dick, Peggie (Aloulou 83); Robertson, Flannigan; Cawley (Brown 75), Trouten, Zanatta; Spence (Hetherington 61).
Edinburgh C won 4-3 on penalties.
Referee: Don Robertson.

Motherwell U21 (0) 1 *(Livingstone 53)*

Ross Co (0) 2 *(Ross C Stewart 51, 56)* 1209

Motherwell U21: (4411) Morrison; MacDonald, Mbulu■, Maguire, Livingstone; Watson, Krones, Brown, Hastie (Agyeman 80); Rodriguez; Scott.
Ross Co: (442) Munro; Fraser, Draper, Grivosti, Demetriou (Murray 90); Dingwall T, Lindsay, Cowie, McManus; Ross C Stewart, Graham.
Referee: David Munro.

Saturday, 2 February 2019

Bohemians v East Fife

Match abandoned before kick-off due to frozen pitch. Bohemians withdrew from competition.

SEMI-FINALS

Friday, 15 February 2019

Ross Co (2) 2 *(Armstrong 18, McManus 37)*

East Fife (1) 1 *(Dowds 39)* 1283

Ross Co: (442) Munro; Fraser, Grivosti, Boyle, van der Weg; Mullin, Paton (McKay 83), Draper, Armstrong (Lindsay 73); Ross C Stewart, McManus (Gardyne 79).
East Fife: (451) Long; Dunsmore (Bell 80), Dunlop, Meggatt, Linton; Watson C, Watt (Smith 66), Davidson, Docherty (Currie 74), Slattery; Dowds.
Referee: Alan Newlands.

Saturday, 16 February 2019

Connah's Quay Nomads (1) 1 *(Wilde 18)*

Edinburgh C (1) 1 *(Walker 2)* 1068

Connah's Quay Nomads: (442) Danby; Disney, Barton, Horan, Holmes; Phillips, Harrison, Morris, Bakare; Owens (Hughes 80), Wilde.
Edinburgh C: (442) Antell; Thomson, Balatoni, Henderson L, McIntyre; Shepherd (Driver 108), Laird, Black (Donaldson 110), Walker (Rodger 95); Henderson B, Smith (Taylor 113).
Connah's Quay Nomads won 5-4 on penalties.
Referee: James Oldham.

IRN-BRU SCOTTISH LEAGUE CHALLENGE CUP FINAL 2018–19

Saturday, 23 March 2019

(at Caledonian Stadium, Inverness, attendance 3057)

Connah's Quay Nomads (1) 1 Ross Co (0) 3

Connah's Quay Nomads: (433) Danby; Holmes, Farquharson (Wignall 80), Horan, Barton; Morris (Poole 66), Harrison (Phillips 88), Parker; Bakare, Wilde, Owens.

Scorer: Bakare 21.

Ross Co: (442) Munro; Fraser, Watson, Boyle, van der Weg; McManus (Mullin 66), Lindsay, Cowie (Spence 90), Gardyne (Armstrong 88); Ross C Stewart, Graham.

Scorers: Mullin 75, 79, Lindsay 86.

Referee: Alan Muir.

LEAGUE CHALLENGE FINALS 1990–2019

B&Q CENTENARY CUP

1990–91	Dundee v Ayr U	3-2*

B&Q CUP

1991–92	Hamilton A v Ayr U	1-0
1992–93	Hamilton A v Morton	3-2
1993–94	Falkirk v St Mirren	3-0
1994–95	Airdrieonians v Dundee	3-2*

SCOTTISH LEAGUE CHALLENGE CUP

1995–96	Stenhousemuir v Dundee U	0-0*
	Stenhousemuir won 5-4 on penalties.	
1996–97	Stranraer v St Johnstone	1-0
1997–98	Falkirk v Queen of the South	1-0
1998–99	*No competition.*	
	Suspended due to lack of sponsorship.	

BELL'S CHALLENGE CUP

1999–2000	Alloa Ath v Inverness CT	4-4*
	Alloa Ath won 5-4 on penalties.	
2000–01	Airdrieonians v Livingston	2-2*
	Airdrieonians won 3-2 on penalties.	
2001–02	Airdrieonians v Alloa Ath	2-1

BELL'S CUP

2002–03	Queen of the South v Brechin C	2-0
2003–04	Inverness CT v Airdrie U	2-0
2004–05	Falkirk v Ross Co	2-1
2005–06	St Mirren v Hamilton A	2-1

SCOTTISH LEAGUE CHALLENGE CUP

2006–07	Ross Co v Clyde	1-1*
	Ross Co won 5-4 on penalties.	
2007–08	St Johnstone v Dunfermline Ath	3-2

ALBA CHALLENGE CUP

2008–09	Airdrie U v Ross Co	2-2*
	Airdrie U won 3-2 on penalties.	
2009–10	Dundee v Inverness CT	3-2
2010–11	Ross Co v Queen of the South	2-0

RAMSDENS CUP

2011–12	Falkirk v Hamilton A	1-0
2012–13	Queen of the South v Partick Thistle	1-1*
	Queen of the South won 6-5 on penalties.	
2013–14	Raith R v Rangers	1-0*

PETROFAC TRAINING SCOTTISH LEAGUE CHALLENGE CUP

2014–15	Livingston v Alloa Athletic	4-0
2015–16	Rangers v Peterhead	4-0

IRN-BRU SCOTTISH LEAGUE CHALLENGE CUP

2016–17	Dundee U v St Mirren	2-1
2017–18	Inverness CT v Dumbarton	1-0
2018–19	Ross Co v Connah's Quay Nomads	3-1

**After extra time.*

SCOTTISH CUP FINALS 1874–2019

SCOTTISH FA CUP

1874	Queen's Park v Clydesdale	2-0
1875	Queen's Park v Renton	3-0
1876	Queen's Park v Third Lanark	1-1
Replay	Queen's Park v Third Lanark	2-0
1877	Vale of Leven v Rangers	1-1
Replay	Vale of Leven v Rangers	1-1
2nd Replay	Vale of Leven v Rangers	3-2
1878	Vale of Leven v Third Lanark	1-0
1879	Vale of Leven v Rangers	1-1
	Vale of Leven awarded cup, Rangers failing to appear for replay.	
1880	Queen's Park v Thornliebank	3-0
1881	Queen's Park v Dumbarton	2-1
Replay	Queen's Park v Dumbarton	3-1
	After Dumbarton protested the first game.	
1882	Queen's Park v Dumbarton	2-2
Replay	Queen's Park v Dumbarton	4-1
1883	Dumbarton v Vale of Leven	2-2
Replay	Dumbarton v Vale of Leven	2-1
1884	Queen's Park v Vale of Leven	
	Queen's Park awarded cup, Vale of Leven failing to appear.	
1885	Renton v Vale of Leven	0-0
Replay	Renton v Vale of Leven	3-1
1886	Queen's Park v Renton	3-1
1887	Hibernian v Dumbarton	2-1
1888	Renton v Cambuslang	6-1
1889	Third Lanark v Celtic	3-0
Replay	Third Lanark v Celtic	2-1
	Replay by order of Scottish FA because of playing conditions in first match.	
1890	Queen's Park v Vale of Leven	1-1
Replay	Queen's Park v Vale of Leven	2-1
1891	Hearts v Dumbarton	1-0
1892	Celtic v Queen's Park	1-0
Replay	Celtic v Queen's Park	5-1
	After mutually protested first match.	
1893	Queen's Park v Celtic	0-1
Replay	Queen's Park v Celtic	2-1
	Replay by order of Scottish FA because of playing conditions in first match.	
1894	Rangers v Celtic	3-1
1895	St Bernard's v Renton	2-1
1896	Hearts v Hibernian	3-1
1897	Rangers v Dumbarton	5-1
1898	Rangers v Kilmarnock	2-0
1899	Celtic v Rangers	2-0
1900	Celtic v Queen's Park	4-3
1901	Hearts v Celtic	4-3
1902	Hibernian v Celtic	1-0
1903	Rangers v Hearts	1-1
Replay	Rangers v Hearts	0-0
2nd Replay	Rangers v Hearts	2-0
1904	Celtic v Rangers	3-2
1905	Third Lanark v Rangers	0-0
Replay	Third Lanark v Rangers	3-1
1906	Hearts v Third Lanark	1-0
1907	Celtic v Hearts	3-0
1908	Celtic v St Mirren	5-1
1909	Celtic v Rangers	2-2
Replay	Celtic v Rangers	1-1
	Owing to riot, the cup was withheld.	
1910	Dundee v Clyde	2-2
Replay	Dundee v Clyde	0-0*
2nd Replay	Dundee v Clyde	2-1
1911	Celtic v Hamilton A	0-0
Replay	Celtic v Hamilton A	2-0
1912	Celtic v Clyde	2-0
1913	Falkirk v Raith R	2-0
1914	Celtic v Hibernian	0-0
Replay	Celtic v Hibernian	4-1
1920	Kilmarnock v Albion R	3-2
1921	Partick Thistle v Rangers	1-0
1922	Morton v Rangers	1-0

1923	Celtic v Hibernian	1-0
1924	Airdrieonians v Hibernian	2-0
1925	Celtic v Dundee	2-1
1926	St Mirren v Celtic	2-0
1927	Celtic v East Fife	3-1
1928	Rangers v Celtic	4-0
1929	Kilmarnock v Rangers	2-0
1930	Rangers v Partick Thistle	0-0
Replay	Rangers v Partick Thistle	2-1
1931	Celtic v Motherwell	2-2
Replay	Celtic v Motherwell	4-2
1932	Rangers v Kilmarnock	1-1
Replay	Rangers v Kilmarnock	3-0
1933	Celtic v Motherwell	1-0
1934	Rangers v St Mirren	5-0
1935	Rangers v Hamilton A	2-1
1936	Rangers v Third Lanark	1-0
1937	Celtic v Aberdeen	2-1
1938	East Fife v Kilmarnock	1-1
Replay	East Fife v Kilmarnock	4-2*
1939	Clyde v Motherwell	4-0
1947	Aberdeen v Hibernian	2-1
1948	Rangers v Morton	1-1*
Replay	Rangers v Morton	1-0*
1949	Rangers v Clyde	4-1
1950	Rangers v East Fife	3-0
1951	Celtic v Motherwell	1-0
1952	Motherwell v Dundee	4-0
1953	Rangers v Aberdeen	1-1
Replay	Rangers v Aberdeen	1-0
1954	Celtic v Aberdeen	2-1
1955	Clyde v Celtic	1-1
Replay	Clyde v Celtic	1-0
1956	Hearts v Celtic	3-1
1957	Falkirk v Kilmarnock	1-1
Replay	Falkirk v Kilmarnock	2-1*
1958	Clyde v Hibernian	1-0
1959	St Mirren v Aberdeen	3-1
1960	Rangers v Kilmarnock	2-0
1961	Dunfermline Ath v Celtic	0-0
Replay	Dunfermline Ath v Celtic	2-0
1962	Rangers v St Mirren	2-0
1963	Rangers v Celtic	1-1
Replay	Rangers v Celtic	3-0
1964	Rangers v Dundee	3-1
1965	Celtic v Dunfermline Ath	3-2
1966	Rangers v Celtic	0-0
Replay	Rangers v Celtic	1-0
1967	Celtic v Aberdeen	2-0
1968	Dunfermline Ath v Hearts	3-1
1969	Celtic v Rangers	4-0
1970	Aberdeen v Celtic	3-1
1971	Celtic v Rangers	1-1
Replay	Celtic v Rangers	2-1
1972	Celtic v Hibernian	6-1
1973	Rangers v Celtic	3-2
1974	Celtic v Dundee U	3-0
1975	Celtic v Airdrieonians	3-1
1976	Rangers v Hearts	3-1
1977	Celtic v Rangers	1-0
1978	Rangers v Aberdeen	2-1
1979	Rangers v Hibernian	0-0
Replay	Rangers v Hibernian	0-0*
2nd Replay	Rangers v Hibernian	3-2*
1980	Celtic v Rangers	1-0*
1981	Rangers v Dundee U	0-0*
Replay	Rangers v Dundee U	4-1
1982	Aberdeen v Rangers	4-1*
1983	Aberdeen v Rangers	1-0*
1984	Aberdeen v Celtic	2-1*
1985	Celtic v Dundee U	2-1
1986	Aberdeen v Hearts	3-0
1987	St Mirren v Dundee U	1-0*
1988	Celtic v Dundee U	2-1
1989	Celtic v Rangers	1-0

TENNENTS SCOTTISH CUP

1990	Aberdeen v Celtic	0-0*
	Aberdeen won 9-8 on penalties.	
1991	Motherwell v Dundee U	4-3*
1992	Rangers v Airdrieonians	2-1
1993	Rangers v Aberdeen	2-1
1994	Dundee U v Rangers	1-0
1995	Celtic v Airdrieonians	1-0
1996	Rangers v Hearts	5-1
1997	Kilmarnock v Falkirk	1-0
1998	Hearts v Rangers	2-1
1999	Rangers v Celtic	1-0
2000	Rangers v Aberdeen	4-0
2001	Celtic v Hibernian	3-0
2002	Rangers v Celtic	3-2
2003	Rangers v Dundee	1-0
2004	Celtic v Dunfermline Ath	3-1
2005	Celtic v Dundee U	1-0
2006	Hearts v Gretna	1-1*
	Hearts won 4-2 on penalties.	
2007	Celtic v Dunfermline Ath	1-0

SCOTTISH FA CUP

2008	Rangers v Queen of the South	3-2

HOMECOMING SCOTTISH CUP

2009	Rangers v Falkirk	1-0

ACTIVE NATION SCOTTISH CUP

2010	Dundee U v Ross Co	3-0

SCOTTISH FA CUP

2011	Celtic v Motherwell	3-0

WILLIAM HILL SCOTTISH CUP

2012	Hearts v Hibernian	5-1
2013	Celtic v Hibernian	3-0
2014	St Johnstone v Dundee U	2-0
2015	Inverness CT v Falkirk	2-1
2016	Hibernian v Rangers	3-2
2017	Celtic v Aberdeen	2-1
2018	Celtic v Motherwell	2-0
2019	Celtic v Hearts	2-1

**After extra time.*

SCOTTISH CUP WINS

Celtic 39, Rangers 33, Queen's Park 10, Hearts 8, Aberdeen 7, Clyde 3, Hibernian 3, Kilmarnock 3, St Mirren 3, Vale of Leven 3, Dundee U 2, Dunfermline Ath 2, Falkirk 2, Motherwell 2, Renton 2, Third Lanark 2, Airdrieonians 1, Dumbarton 1, Dundee 1, East Fife 1, Inverness CT 1, Morton 1, Partick Thistle 1, St Bernard's 1, St Johnstone 1.

APPEARANCES IN FINAL

Celtic 58, Rangers 52, Aberdeen 16, Hearts 15, Hibernian 14, Queen's Park 12, Dundee U 10, Kilmarnock 8, Motherwell 8, Vale of Leven 7, Clyde 6, Dumbarton 6, St Mirren 6, Third Lanark 6, Dundee 5, Dunfermline Ath 5, Falkirk 5, Renton 5, Airdrieonians 4, East Fife 3, Hamilton A 2, Morton 2, Partick Thistle 2, Albion R 1, Cambuslang 1, Clydesdale 1, Gretna 1, Inverness CT 1, Queen of the South 1, Raith R 1, Ross Co 1, St Bernard's 1, St Johnstone 1, Thornliebank 1.

WILLIAM HILL SCOTTISH FA CUP 2018–19

■ *Denotes player sent off.*

FIRST PRELIMINARY ROUND

Hawick Royal Albert v Bonnyrigg Rose	0-5
Golspie Sutherland v Burntisland Shipyard	1-4
Auchinleck Talbot v Banks O' Dee	3-1
Coldstream v St Cuthbert W	4-2
Preston Ath v Glasgow University	3-1
Threave R v Beith	0-3
Tynecastle v Shortlees	0-2

Girvan, Linlithgow Rose, Lothian Thistle Hutchison Vale, Newton Stewart, and Wigtown & Bladnoch received a bye to second preliminary round.

SECOND PRELIMINARY ROUND

Preston Ath v Linlithgow Rose	0-2
Girvan v Burntisland Shipyard	0-1
Newton Stewart v Coldstream	0-3
Auchinleck Talbot v Wigtown & Bladnoch	10-0
Bonnyrigg Rose v Shortlees	3-0
Beith v Lothian Thistle Hutchison Vale	3-2

FIRST ROUND

Inverurie Loco Works v Fraserburgh	3-4
Brora v Turriff U	4-3
Burntisland Shipyard v Cumbernauld Colts	1-4
Dalbeattie Star v Kelty Hearts	0-0
Deveronvale v Bonnyrigg Rose	2-1
Edusport Academy v Buckie Thistle	3-1
Forres Mechanics v Civil Service Strollers	2-2
Gala Fairydean v Lossiemouth	6-0
Gretna 2008 v Vale Of Leithen	3-2
Huntly v East Stirling	1-4
Linlithgow Rose v Fort William	3-0
Nairn County v Beith	1-3
Rothes v Clachnacuddin	4-0
Strathspey Thistle v Coldstream	0-2
Whitehill Welfare v Edinburgh C	1-0
Wick Academy v Auchinleck Talbot	1-2
Stirling University v Keith	2-1

FIRST ROUND REPLAYS

Civil Service Strollers v Forres Mechanics	2-1
Kelty Hearts v Dalbeattie Star	3-1

SECOND ROUND

Albion R v Formartine U	0-2
Beith v Linlithgow Rose	4-0
Berwick Rangers v Gretna 2008	3-1
Brora v Coldstream	6-0
Cove R v Auchinleck Talbot	1-1
Cowdenbeath v Clyde	2-1
Cumbernauld Colts v BSC Glasgow	1-4
Deveronvale v Stirling University	1-2
East Kilbride v Spartans	3-1
Edinburgh C v Civil Service Strollers	1-0
Edusport Academy v Fraserburgh	1-2
Elgin C v Whitehill Welfare	2-0
Gala Fairydean v East Stirling	2-0
Peterhead v Kelty Hearts	3-2
Rothes v Annan Ath	0-1
Stirling Alb v Queen's Park	1-2

SECOND ROUND REPLAY

Auchinleck Talbot v Cove R	2-1

THIRD ROUND

Saturday, 24 November 2018

Airdrieonians (2) 3 *(Wilkie 26, 77, Duffy 36)*

Dumbarton (0) 0 592

Airdrieonians: (4231) Hutton; O'Neil, Crighton, Page, MacDonald; Millar, Gallagher (Cairns 71); McIntosh L, Wilkie, Carrick (Russell 82); Duffy (Vitoria 79).
Dumbarton: (433) Smith (McGowan 76); Carswell, Perry, Dowie, Forbes; Hutton, Allardice (Dyer 67), Spencer (Ballantyne 81); Gallagher, Paton, Barr B.
Referee: Steven Kirkland.

Alloa Ath (1) 3 *(Zanatta 31, Spence 59, Trouten 61)*

Brechin C (0) 0 301

Alloa Ath: (442) Parry; Dick, Taggart, Graham, Hetherington; Flannigan (Burt 70), Robertson, Cawley (Shields 70), Trouten; Zanatta (Aloulou 68), Spence.
Brechin C: (451) Brennan; Spark, McGeever, Hill, Burns; Lynas, Smith, Tapping C, Sinclair (Morena 65), Orsi; Jackson.
Referee: Steven Reid.

Arbroath (0) 0

Stranraer (0) 1 *(Smith I 76)* 496

Arbroath: (442) Jamieson; Thomson, Little, O'Brien, Hamilton; Linn, Gold, McCord (Whatley 68), Denholm (Doris 68); Wallace (Kader 68), McKenna.
Stranraer: (352) Currie; Hamill, Brownlie, McDonald; Cummins, McManus (Ashmore 82), Turner, Smith D (Lamont 59), Smith I; Donnelly, Crossan (Driver 90).
Referee: David Dickinson.

Beith (0) 0

Ayr U (0) 3 *(Shankland 64, Docherty 79, Moffat 88)* 1780

Beith: (442) Grindlay; McGlinchey, Docherty N (Docherty R 84), Sheridan, Noble; Christie, Wilson (Haggarty 77), Frize, Bradley (Middleton 85); Milliken, Collins.
Ayr U: (442) Doohan; Smith, Rose, Higgins, Harvie; McDaid (McCowan 84), Bell, Geggan (Docherty 73), Crawford (McGuffie 55); Moffat, Shankland.
Referee: Colin Steven.

Berwick Rangers (0) 1 *(Healy 56)*

East Fife (2) 2 *(Davidson 6, Agnew 11)* 401

Berwick Rangers: (442) Brennan; Hamilton, Wilson, Cook, Orru; Brown (Murrell 74), O'Kane, Neill (Hurst 79), Phillips (Ogilvie 79); Healy, Willis.
East Fife: (442) McDowall; Watson C, Dunlop, Meggatt, Docherty; Dunsmore, Davidson, Agnew, Watt (Linton 79); Currie (Dowds 68), Court (Slattery 86).
Referee: John McKendrick.

Cowdenbeath (1) 1 *(Cox 39)*

Brora (0) 0 432

Cowdenbeath: (4141) McGurn; Mullen, Pyper (Sheerin 61), Deas, Talbot; Marsh; Cox, Miller (Fraser G 82), Malcolm, Buchanan; Kris Renton.
Brora: (442) Malin; Ross (Docherty 71), Williamson, Nicolson, Macdonald; Maclean, Gillespie, Pickles, Brindle (Sutherland 45); MacLeod (Campbell 78), Mackay.
Referee: Duncan Williams.

East Kilbride (0) 1 *(Longworth 90)*

Gala Fairydean (0) 0 180

East Kilbride: (442) McGinley; Reid, Howie, Proctor, Coll; Humphrey (Longworth 69), Holmes, Brady, Winter; Malcolm, Woods.
Gala Fairydean: (442) Martin; Stevenson, Donaldson, Miller, Main; Watson (O'Reily 36), Cunningham, Smith, Baxter; Paton (Morris 71), McKirdy.
Referee: Chris Fordyce.

Forfar Ath (0) 2 *(Baird 75, Moore 85)*

BSC Glasgow (0) 0 385

Forfar Ath: (442) McCallum; Bain, Whyte, Travis, Meechan; Moore, Hill, Reilly, Easton (Coupe 86); Hilson, Baird (MacKintosh 90).
BSC Glasgow: (3421) Marshall; Mitchell, Smith, McMillan; Pignatiello, Hughes, Ballantyne (Irvine 54), Mills; Grehan, Winters; Orr (Taylor 77).
Referee: Grant Irvine.

Fraserburgh (0) 0

Auchinleck Talbot (0) 1 *(Wilson S 59)* 727

Fraserburgh: (433) Leask; Davidson, Hay■, Cowie, Christie; Dickson, Young, Macdonald (Simpson 49); Buchan (Combe 83), Barbour, Johnston (Campbell 55).
Auchinleck Talbot: (442) Leishman; Lyle, McPherson, Armstrong, Pope; Wilson S, McCracken, Glasgow, Hyslop; McIlroy (Samson 62), Wilson G (McDowall 90).
Referee: Peter Stuart.

Greenock Morton (1) 1 *(McHugh 40)*

Peterhead (1) 1 *(Brown S 27)* 958

Greenock Morton: (352) Gaston; Kilday, Buchanan, McKeown; Tumilty, Telfer, McAlister (Millar 46), Tidser, Iredale; McHugh, Oliver (Thomson R 60).
Peterhead: (442) Fleming; Stevenson, Brown J, Dunlop, Boyle; Dow, Brown S, Gibson W, Leitch (Ferry 67); Lyle (McLean 67), McAllister (Kavanagh 75).
Referee: Mike Roncone.

Montrose (0) 0

Annan Ath (0) 0 585

Montrose: (352) Fleming; Bolochoweckyj■, Dillon, Campbell I (Cavanagh 78); Harrington, Masson, Cregg (Watson 81), Callaghan (Rennie 55), Steeves; Antoniazzi, Johnston.
Annan Ath: (442) Mitchell; Sinnamon, Hooper, Moxon, Creaney; Johnston, Sonkur, Wilson, Wallace; Wright (Roberts 78), Fergusson (Smith 53).
Referee: David Lowe.

Queen of the South (3) 4 *(Dobbie 2, 8, Dykes 42, Mercer 67)*

Formartine U (1) 1 *(Wood 28)* 931

Queen of the South: (442) Leighfield; Mercer, Fordyce, Doyle (Semple 76), Marshall; Stirling, Jacobs (Bell 81), Norman (Murray 72), Todd; Dobbie, Dykes.
Formartine U: (451) Main; Crawford (MacPherson 84), Anderson J, Lawrence (Gethins 80), Smith; MacPhee, Anderson S, Rodger, Norris, Greig; Wood (Burnett 81).
Referee: Gavin Ross.

Queen's Park (0) 0

Raith R (2) 3 *(Nisbet 13, Buchanan 24, Flanagan 57)* 679

Queen's Park: (4231) Hart; Grant, McLauchlan (Magee 75), McLaren, Summers; Roberts (Fotheringham 69), McKernon; McLean, Moore (Martin 69), East; Hawke.
Raith R: (442) Thomson; Gillespie (Watson 75), Davidson, Benedictus, Murray; Armstrong, Wedderburn, Matthews, Flanagan; Buchanan (Milne 87), Nisbet (Duggan 81).
Referee: Lloyd Wilson.

Stenhousemuir (2) 4 *(McBrearty 12, 16, Dickson 59, McGuigan 85)*

Falkirk (2) 2 *(Paton 6, McKee 42)* 2050

Stenhousemuir: (352) Smith, McBrearty, Neill, Donaldson; Gibbons, Paton (Reid 90), Ferry, Dickson (Halleran 90), Cook; Duthie, McGuigan (Vaughan 90).
Falkirk: (352) Fasan; McGhee, Muirhead (Dallison 80), Brough; Kidd, McKee, Paton, Irving (Sammut 68), Robson; Petravicius, Lewis.
Referee: Alan Newlands.

Stirling University (0) 0

Elgin C (2) 4 *(Omar 9, Cameron 14, Hay 58, Loveland 80)* 395

Stirling University: (442) Allan; Slattery, Burrows, McGuire (Emmott 66), Mailer; MacEwan (Hall 61), Hunter, Brown (Baber 77), Lyons; Ferris, Bonar.
Elgin C: (442) McHale; Cooper (Loveland 74), McHardy, Beattie, Lowdon; Hay (Wilson D 62), Cameron, Omar (Miller 68), Morrison; Sutherland S, McLeish.
Referee: Barry Cook.

Sunday, 25 November 2018

Edinburgh C (0) 1 *(Henderson L 86)*

Inverness CT (1) 1 *(Rooney 39)* 867

Edinburgh C: (442) Antell; Thomson, Balatoni, Henderson L, McIntyre; Smith A, Black, Laird, Taylor (Watson 70); Shepherd (Rodger 84), Henderson B.
Inverness CT: (442) Ridgers; Rooney (Trafford 74), Donaldson, McKay, McCart; Walsh, Welsh, Chalmers, Polworth; Austin (Oakley 55), White (Mackay 71).
Referee: David Munro.

THIRD ROUND REPLAYS

Tuesday, 27 November 2018

Annan Ath (0) 3 *(Smith 61 (pen), 79, Muir 84)*

Montrose (4) 4 *(Rennie 19 (pen), Fotheringham 23, Watson 25, Steeves 30)* 205

Annan Ath: (442) Mitchell; Hooper, Moxon, Sonkur, Creaney; Johnston (Fergusson 46), Wilson, Sinnamon, Wallace (Bradley 46); Smith, Roberts (Muir 46).
Montrose: (352) Fleming; Steeves, Campbell I, Dillon; Masson, Watson, Cregg (Callaghan 52), Fotheringham (Antoniazzi 68), Harrington; Rennie, Redman (Cavanagh 46).
Referee: David Lowe.

Peterhead (0) 0

Greenock Morton (1) 3 *(Waddell 10, Thomson R 61, Millar 83)* 527

Peterhead: (352) Fleming; Brown J, Dunlop, Eadie (Ferry 63); Stevenson, Brown S, McLean, Leitch (Kavanagh 63), Gibson W; Dow, McAllister.
Greenock Morton: (352) Gaston; Kilday, Buchanan, Waddell; Tumilty, Millar, McAlister, Tidser, Iredale (McKeown 90); McHugh (Armour 90), Thomson R.
Referee: Gavin Ross.

Tuesday, 4 December 2018

Inverness CT (2) 6 *(Walsh 5, 53, White 15, 60, 61, Doran 90)*

Edinburgh C (1) 1 *(Henderson B 7)* 672

Inverness CT: (4411) Ridgers; Rooney, McKay, Donaldson, McCart (Harper 69); Walsh, Trafford, Chalmers, Doran; Polworth (MacGregor 64); White (Austin 78).
Edinburgh C: (442) Antell; Thomson, Balatoni, Henderson L, McIntyre; Smith A (Rodger 64), Black (Watson 49), Laird, Taylor; Shepherd (Hall 80), Henderson B.
Referee: David Munro.

FOURTH ROUND

Saturday, 19 January 2019

Aberdeen (1) 1 *(Lowe 21)*

Stenhousemuir (0) 1 *(McGuigan 71)* 9661

Aberdeen: (4411) Lewis; Logan, Considine, McKenna, Lowe; Mackay-Steven (McLennan 64), Ferguson, Shinnie, McGinn (May 78); Stewart; Cosgrove.
Stenhousemuir: (442) Smith; Munro, Neill, McBrearty, Donaldson; Duthie, Ferry, Dickson, Cook (Reid 47); McGuigan (Vaughan 90), Dingwall (Halleran 89).
Referee: Barry Cook.

Auchinleck Talbot (0) 1 *(McCracken 78)*

Ayr U (0) 0 3100

Auchinleck Talbot: (4141) Leishman; Lyle, McPherson, McCracken, Pope; White; Wilson S (McIlroy 70), Armstrong, Hyslop, Glasgow (Shankland 76); Wilson G (Samson 76).
Ayr U: (442) Doohan; Geggan (Smith 36), Rose, Higgins, Harvie; McDaid, Murdoch (McGuffie 75), Docherty, Crawford; Moffat, Moore (Bell 84).
Referee: Euan Anderson.

Celtic (1) 3 *(Sinclair 37, 56, Weah 83)*

Airdrieonians (0) 0 29,941

Celtic: (4231) Bain; Ralston, Boyata, Benkovic, Izaguirre; Brown (Bitton 82), McGregor; Forrest (Johnston 69), Christie, Sinclair (Weah 69); Burke.
Airdrieonians: (3511) Hutton; O'Neil, Crighton, MacDonald; Stewart (Duffy 76), Campbell (Carrick 59), Gallagher, Millar, Edwards; Wilkie (Glass 53); McIntosh L.
Referee: Andrew Dallas.

Dundee (1) 1 *(Curran J 45)*

Queen of the South (1) 1 *(Dobbie 28)* 2728

Dundee: (442) Dieng; Kerr, Inniss, Kusunga, Ralph; Curran J, Woods, McGowan P, Deacon (Dales 46); Curran C (Nelson 65), Miller K.
Queen of the South: (442) Martin; Mercer, Maguire, Doyle, Marshall; Stirling (Murray 78), Jacobs, Low, Todd; Dykes (Bell 90), Dobbie.
Referee: Kevin Clancy.

East Fife (1) 2 *(Dowds 9, Watson C 75)*

Greenock Morton (1) 1 *(McHugh 7)* 903

East Fife: (451) Long; Watson C, Dunlop, Meggatt, Linton; Watt, Davidson, Docherty (Currie 74), Slattery, Agnew (Kane 84); Dowds (Smith 64).
Greenock Morton: (352) Gaston; Kilday (Oliver 83), Buchanan, Waddell; Tumilty, Dykes (Telfer 77), Millar, Tidser (McAlister 72), Iredale; Thomson R, McHugh.
Referee: Steven Kirkland.

Hibernian (3) 4 *(Kamberi 21, Horgan 25, 53, Mallan 45 (pen))*

Elgin C (0) 0 7082

Hibernian: (4411) Bogdan (Marciano 79); Whittaker, McGregor, Hanlon, Mackie; Gauld (Murray 69), Slivka, Bartley, Mallan; Horgan; Kamberi (Shaw 68).
Elgin C: (451) McHale; Cooper, McHardy, Bronsky, Lowdon; Omar, Cameron, McGovern (Hay 83), Wilson D (McLeish 60), Morrison (Hester 69); Sutherland S.
Referee: Nick Walsh.

Inverness CT (3) 4 *(White 6, Doran 21, Polworth 27, Reid 71 (og))*

East Kilbride (0) 0 1196

Inverness CT: (442) Ridgers; Rooney, McKay, McCart, Tremarco; Polworth, Welsh, Chalmers, Doran (MacGregor 85); White (Austin 62), Oakley (Mackay 70).
East Kilbride: (442) McGinley; Reid, Proctor (Stevenson 49), Howie (Russell 87), Coll; Humphrey (McNeil 71), Brady, Holmes, Andersen; Malcolm, Woods.
Referee: Mike Roncone.

Kilmarnock (1) 2 *(Findlay 19, Burke 78)*

Forfar Ath (0) 0 4376

Kilmarnock: (433) MacDonald; Wilson, Dicker, Findlay, Waters; McKenzie (Burke 65), Tshibola, Power; Kiltie, Boyd K (Boyd S 79), Jones (Ndjoli 65).
Forfar Ath: (442) McCallum; Meechan, Whyte, Travis, Eckersley; Bain, Reilly (Malone 90), MacKintosh, Coupe (Aitken 79); Hilson, Baird.
Referee: Greg Aitken.

Montrose (0) 0

Dundee U (2) 4 *(Safranko 8, Booth 43, King 81, Harkes 90)* 3604

Montrose: (442) Fleming; Harrington, Dillon, Campbell I, Steeves; Webster, Masson, Cregg, Redman (Watson 57); Johnston (Campbell R 56), Rennie (Callaghan 83).
Dundee U: (4231) Siegrist; Watson, Bouhenna, Frans, Booth; Stanton, Gomis; McMullan, Smith C (Harkes 70), Nesbitt (Clark 65); Safranko (King 80).
Referee: David Munro.

Motherwell (0) 1 *(Hastie 90)*

Ross Co (0) 2 *(Graham 52, 60)* 3869

Motherwell: (343) Gillespie; Aldred, Hartley, Dunne; Tait, McHugh (Rodriguez 63), Frear, Turnbull; Ariyibi, McCormack (Main 46), Johnson (Hastie 67).
Ross Co: (4411) Fox; Fraser, Watson, van der Weg, Kelly; Gardyne (McKay 90), Lindsay, Draper, Spence; McManus; Graham (Ross C Stewart 79).
Referee: Steven McLean.

Partick Thistle (1) 4 *(Fitzpatrick 17, Cardle 50, Saunders 74, Spittal 81)*

Stranraer (0) 1 *(Crossan 52)* 2254

Partick Thistle: (4411) Hazard; Elliot, Saunders, McGinty, Penrice; Slater (Harkins 70), Fitzpatrick, Bannigan, Cardle (Coulibaly 85); Spittal; Roy (Doolan 61).
Stranraer: (442) Currie; Hamill, Brownlie, Cummins, Smith D; Lamont (Anderson 70), McManus, Turner, Crossan; Cameron, O'Keefe (Elliott 78).
Referee: Alan Newlands.

Raith R (0) 3 *(Vaughan 69 (pen), 78, 81)*

Dunfermline Ath (0) 0 6013

Raith R: (442) Thomson; Murray, Davidson, Benedictus, Crane; Armstrong (Buchanan 88), Wedderburn, Gillespie, Flanagan (Dingwall 68); Vaughan, Duggan.
Dunfermline Ath: (442) Robinson; Craigen, Devine, Ashcroft■, Longridge J; Thomson, Beadling, Vincent, Higginbotham (Todd 90); Hippolyte (Durnan 57), El Bakhtaoui (Muirhead 71).
Referee: Bobby Madden.

St Johnstone (2) 2 *(Kerr 1, Watt 26)*

Hamilton A (0) 0 2363

St Johnstone: (442) Clark; Foster, Kerr, Shaughnessy, Tanser; Wotherspoon, Callachan, Craig, Kennedy (Swanson 75); Kane, Watt (McMillan 90).
Hamilton A: (352) Fulton; Gordon, Kilgallon, Sowah; McGowan, Gogic (Taiwo 74), Andreu, Imrie, McMann; Miller, Davies (Boyd 69).
Referee: John Beaton.

St Mirren (0) 3 *(Cooke 68, Erhahon 85, McAllister 87)*

Alloa Ath (2) 2 *(Trouten 26, Cawley 34)* 2760

St Mirren: (4411) Hladky; Hodson, Baird, Popescu, Erhahon; McGinn P, McGinn S, Tansey (McAllister 55), Jackson; Flynn (Cooke 39); Lyons■.
Alloa Ath: (4231) Parry; Taggart, Graham, Roscoe, Dick; Hetherington, Robertson; Cawley, Trouten (Brown 71), Shields (Aitchison 83); Zanatta.
Referee: Don Robertson.

Sunday, 20 January 2019

Hearts (0) 1 *(Clare 48)*

Livingston (0) 0 11,077

Hearts: (4411) Doyle; Smith, Shaughnessy, Berra, Garuccio; Morrison (Mulraney 86), Lee, Djoum, Naismith; Clare (Bozanic 80); Vanecek.
Livingston: (532) Kelly; Wylde (Lamie 60), Lithgow, Halkett, Gallagher, Lawless; Pitman, Jacobs, Byrne; Hardie (Erskine 71), Menga (Hamilton 75).
Referee: William Collum.

Wednesday, 30 January 2019

Cowdenbeath (0) 1 *(Cox 47)*

Rangers (3) 3 *(Halliday 12, Coulibaly 26, Lafferty 45)* 4116

Cowdenbeath: (4231) McGurn; Mullen, Pyper, Deas, Talbot (Swan 15); Fraser G, Malcolm (Allan 59); Cox, Miller, Buchanan; Kris Renton (Henvey 59).
Rangers: (41212) Foderingham; Flanagan, McAuley, Katic, Halliday; Coulibaly (Middleton 67); Davis, Jack; Candeias (Houston 86); Lafferty, Defoe.
Referee: Craig Thomson.

FOURTH ROUND REPLAYS

Tuesday, 29 January 2019

Queen of the South (2) 3 *(Dobbie 12, 27, 74)*

Dundee (0) 0 1421

Queen of the South: (442) Martin; Mercer, Fordyce, Maguire, Marshall; Doyle (Murray 37), Jacobs, Low, Stirling; Dobbie (Bell 90), Dykes.
Dundee: (442) Dieng; Kerr, Kusunga, O'Dea, Ralph; Deacon (Lambert 46), Inniss (Moore 31), McGowan P, Dales; Miller K, Curran C (Nelson 75).
Referee: Steven McLean.

Stenhousemuir (0) 1 *(Munro 53)*

Aberdeen (3) 4 *(McGinn 13, Cosgrove 30 (pen), Stewart 38, Donaldson 67 (og))* 2429

Stenhousemuir: (442) Smith; Reid, McBrearty, Munro, Donaldson; Duthie, Ferry, Dickson, Cook; Halleran, McGuigan.
Aberdeen: (442) Lewis; Logan, Considine, Hoban, Lowe; McGinn (Mackay-Steven 77), Ferguson, Shinnie, Wright (Ross 87); Cosgrove (Wilson 84), Stewart.
Referee: Barry Cook.

FIFTH ROUND

Saturday, 9 February 2019

East Fife (0) 0

Partick Thistle (0) 1 *(Anderson 61)* 1724

East Fife: (442) Long; Watson C, Dunlop, Meggatt, Linton (Bell 79); Watt (Court 69), Davidson, Docherty, Slattery; Dowds, Currie (Watson B 83).
Partick Thistle: (352) Hazard; Saunders (Doolan 58), Anderson, McMillan; Elliot, Bannigan, Fitzpatrick (Spittal 60), Slater, Penrice; Harkins, Storey (Mansell 82).
Referee: Don Robertson.

Hibernian (2) 3 *(Horgan 22, Slivka 38, McNulty 58)*

Raith R (0) 1 *(Murray 75)* 9131

Hibernian: (41212) Marciano; Gray, McGregor, Hanlon, Stevenson; Milligan (Whittaker 79); Slivka, Horgan (Omeonga 66); Mallan; Kamberi, McNulty (Shaw 86).
Raith R: (451) Thomson; Murray, Davidson, Benedictus, Crane; Dingwall (Buchanan 86), Gillespie, Wedderburn, Barjonas (Matthews 80), Flanagan; Nisbet (Duggan 68).
Referee: Bobby Madden.

Kilmarnock (0) 0

Rangers (0) 0 11,430

Kilmarnock: (433) Bachmann; O'Donnell, Broadfoot, Boyd S, Taylor; Power (Boyd K 58), Dicker, Mulumbu; Burke (Millar 83), McAleny (McKenzie 75), Jones.
Rangers: (433) McGregor; Tavernier, Goldson, Worrall, Halliday; Arfield (Davis 83), McCrorie, Jack; Candeias, Defoe (Lafferty 86), Kent.
Referee: Alan Muir.

St Mirren (0) 1 *(Nazon 77)*

Dundee U (2) 2 *(Safranko 15, Clark 45)* 3965

St Mirren: (4411) Hladky; McGinn P, Baird, Popescu, Muzek; Lyons, MacPherson (Erhahon 81), Tansey (McAllister 46), Flynn; Dreyer (Jackson 46); Nazon.
Dundee U: (4231) Siegrist; Seaman, Connolly, Reynolds, Robson; Harkes, Butcher■; Pawlett, Smith C (Sow 63), Clark (Gomis 65); Safranko.
Referee: William Collum.

Sunday, 10 February 2019

Aberdeen (0) 4 *(McGinn 47, Considine 63, Cosgrove 67, 73 (pen))*

Queen of the South (0) 1 *(Dobbie 50)* 7857

Aberdeen: (4411) Lewis; Logan (Devlin 74), Hoban, Considine, Lowe; Mackay-Steven (Wilson 79), Ferguson, Shinnie, Stewart; May (McGinn 46); Cosgrove.
Queen of the South: (442) Martin; Mercer (Aird 75), Maguire, Fordyce, Marshall; Stirling, Doyle, Low (McGrath 70), Jacobs; Dobbie, Dykes.
Referee: Euan Anderson.

Celtic (2) 5 *(Sinclair 3, 54, 89, Brown 9, Forrest 52)*

St Johnstone (0) 0 28,404

Celtic: (4231) Bain; Toljan, Boyata, Simunovic (Ajer 46), Hayes; Brown, McGregor; Forrest, Christie (Edouard 62), Sinclair; Burke (Weah 67).
St Johnstone: (4141) Clark; Foster, Kerr, Shaughnessy, Tanser; Goss (Watt 46); Wotherspoon, Davidson (Callachan 67), Craig, Kennedy (Keown 60); Kane.
Referee: Nick Walsh.

Hearts (3) 4 *(Berra 10, Mitchell 31, MacLean 38, Keena 86)*

Auchinleck Talbot (0) 0 14,946

Hearts: (442) Doyle; Smith, Souttar, Berra, Mitchell; Clare (Morrison 46), Lee, Djoum, Naismith (Keena 76); MacLean, Ikpeazu (Vanecek 72).
Auchinleck Talbot: (451) Leishman; Lyle, McPherson, McCracken, Pope; Wilson S, Armstrong, White (Samson 74), Hyslop, Glasgow (Shankland 81); Wilson G (McIlroy 81).
Referee: Kevin Clancy.

Monday, 11 February 2019

Ross Co (0) 2 *(Ross C Stewart 55, Mullin 90)*

Inverness CT (1) 2 *(Doran 13, McKay 65)* 2862

Ross Co: (442) Fox; Fraser, Watson, Boyle, van der Weg; Lindsay (McManus 87), Spence (Mullin 67), Draper, Gardyne; Graham (Ross C Stewart 54), McKay.
Inverness CT: (4411) Ridgers; McKay, Donaldson (Rooney 80), McCart, Tremarco; Walsh (Trafford 85), Welsh, Chalmers, Doran (McCauley 77); Polworth; White.
Referee: John Beaton.

FIFTH ROUND REPLAYS

Tuesday, 19 February 2019

Inverness CT (0) 2 *(White 56, 81)*

Ross Co (1) 2 *(Ross C Stewart 22, Gardyne 67)* 3608

Inverness CT: (4411) Ridgers; McKay, Donaldson, McCart, Tremarco; Walsh (McDonald 15 (McCauley 106)), Chalmers (Austin 76), Welsh, Doran (Trafford 101); Polworth; White.
Ross Co: (4411) Fox; Fraser, Watson, Boyle, van der Weg; Mullin (McManus 78), Draper, Spence (Lindsay 66), Gardyne; McKay (Wallace 112); Ross C Stewart (Graham 100).
aet; Inverness CT won 5-4 on penalties.
Referee: John Beaton.

Wednesday, 20 February 2019

Rangers (2) 5 *(Morelos 7, 45, 78, 83, Halliday 77)*

Kilmarnock (0) 0 37,918

Rangers: (4141) Foderingham; Tavernier, Goldson, Worrall, Barisic (Halliday 74); Jack; Candeias, Kamara (Lafferty 80), Arfield (Davis 73), Kent; Morelos.
Kilmarnock: (41212) Bachmann■; O'Donnell, Bruce (Tshibola 27), Boyd S, Taylor; Mulumbu; Burke, Power; Dicker; McAleny (MacDonald 26), Brophy (Ndjoli 79).
Referee: Alan Muir.

QUARTER-FINALS

Saturday, 2 March 2019

Hibernian (0) 0

Celtic (0) 2 *(Forrest 62, Brown 75)* 15,719

Hibernian: (4132) Marciano; Gray, McGregor, Hanlon, Stevenson; Milligan (Bartley 64); Omeonga (Shaw 76), Slivka, Horgan (Mallan 64); McNulty, Kamberi.
Celtic: (4231) Bain; Lustig, Boyata (Toljan 85), Ajer, Tierney; Bitton, Brown; Forrest, Burke (Henderson 90), Sinclair (Johnston 76); Edouard.
Referee: William Collum.

Sunday, 3 March 2019

Aberdeen (1) 1 *(Cosgrove 11 (pen))*

Rangers (0) 1 *(Worrall 49)* 15,395

Aberdeen: (4231) Lewis; Ball, Considine, McKenna, Lowe; Ferguson, Shinnie; Mackay-Steven (McGinn 16), Stewart, McLennan (Wilson 85); Cosgrove.
Rangers: (4141) McGregor; Tavernier, Goldson, Worrall, Barisic; Jack; Candeias, Kamara, Arfield, Kent; Morelos.
Referee: Kevin Clancy.

Dundee U (0) 1 *(Clark 68 (pen))*

Inverness CT (1) 2 *(Chalmers 19, Doran 90)* 7274

Dundee U: (4231) Siegrist; Seaman, Connolly, Reynolds, Robson; Fyvie (Gomis 64), Harkes; Pawlett, Clark, Smith C (McMullan 53); Safranko.
Inverness CT: (4231) Ridgers; McKay, Donaldson, McCart, Tremarco; Welsh, Trafford (Austin 77); Chalmers, Polworth (Rooney 90), Doran; White.
Referee: Steven McLean.

Monday, 4 March 2019

Partick Thistle (0) 1 *(Elliot 72)*

Hearts (1) 1 *(Berra 12)* 5171

Partick Thistle: (3511) Hazard; McMillan (Storey 75), Anderson, Saunders; Elliot, Slater, Harkins, Spittal (McGinty 87), Penrice; Fitzpatrick (Cardle 70); Mansell.
Hearts: (442) Zlamal; Godinho, Souttar, Berra, Garuccio; Clare, Haring, Bozanic, Djoum; MacLean (Mulraney 81), Ikpeazu.
Referee: Bobby Madden.

QUARTER-FINAL REPLAYS

Tuesday, 12 March 2019

Hearts (2) 2 *(Ikpeazu 24, Clare 35 (pen))*
Partick Thistle (1) 1 *(McDonald 17)* 10,351

Hearts: (442) Zlamal; Godinho, Souttar, Berra, Garuccio; Djoum, Clare, Lee (Haring 66), Mulraney (Morrison 83); Wighton, Ikpeazu.
Partick Thistle: (4231) Hazard; McMillan, Anderson, Saunders, Penrice; Slater, Bannigan; Elliot (Cardle 51), McDonald, Spittal (Fitzpatrick 76); Mansell (Storey 67).
Referee: Bobby Madden.

Rangers (0) 0
Aberdeen (1) 2 *(McGinn 3, McLennan 62)* 47,397

Rangers: (4141) McGregor; Tavernier, Goldson, Worrall, Barisic; Jack; Candeias (Lafferty 66), Kamara (Davis 80), Arfield (Defoe 66), Kent; Morelos.
Aberdeen: (4231) Lewis; Ball, McKenna, Considine, Lowe; Ferguson, Shinnie; McGinn (Devlin 72), Campbell (Gleeson 80), McLennan; May (Wilson 82).
Referee: Kevin Clancy.

SEMI-FINALS

Saturday, 13 April 2019

Hearts (0) 3 *(Ikpeazu 49, Souttar 66, Clare 74 (pen))*
Inverness CT (0) 0 21,011

Hearts: (4132) Zlamal; Smith, Souttar, Berra, Burns; Haring; Lee, Djoum (Bozanic 76), Mulraney (Clare 71); Keena (MacLean 64), Ikpeazu.
Inverness CT: (4231) Ridgers; Rooney, McKay, McCart, Tremarco (McHattie 59); Trafford (Austin 75), Chalmers; Walsh, Polworth, Doran; White (McCauley 83).
Referee: Don Robertson.

Sunday, 14 April 2019

Aberdeen (0) 0
Celtic (1) 3 *(Forrest 45, Edouard 61 (pen), Rogic 69)* 46,773

Aberdeen: (4231) Lewis; Ball■, Considine, McKenna, Lowe; Ferguson■, Campbell; May (Devlin 43), Stewart (Gleeson 70), McLennan; Cosgrove (Wilson 85).
Celtic: (4231) Bain; Lustig, Simunovic, Ajer, Tierney; Brown, McGregor; Forrest (Weah 75), Christie (Rogic 42), Hayes (Sinclair 75); Edouard.
Referee: Craig Thomson.

WILLIAM HILL SCOTTISH CUP FINAL 2019

Saturday, 25 May 2019

(at Hampden Park, attendance 49,434)

Hearts (0) 1 Celtic (0) 2

Hearts: (433) Zlamal; Smith, Souttar, Berra, Hickey; Edwards, Haring (Bozanic 81), Djoum; Clare (Wighton 75), MacLean (Ikpeazu 78), Mulraney.
Scorer: Edwards 52.

Celtic: (4231) Bain; Lustig, Simunovic, Ajer, Hayes (Bitton 89); Brown, McGregor; Forrest, Rogic (Ntcham 70), Johnston (Sinclair 72); Edouard.
Scorers: Edouard 62 (pen), 82.

Referee: William Collum.

Celtic skipper Scott Brown leads the celebrations after his side's 2-1 triumph over Hearts in the Scottish Cup Final on 25 May. (Reuters/Russell Cheyne)

SCOTTISH FOOTBALL PYRAMID 2018–19

BREEDON HIGHLAND LEAGUE

		P	W	D	L	F	A	GD	Pts
1	Cove Rangers	34	30	3	1	100	12	88	93
2	Brora Rangers	34	27	4	3	99	12	87	85
3	Fraserburgh	34	26	1	7	125	37	88	79
4	Formartine U	34	22	6	6	97	37	60	72
5	Inverurie Loco Works	34	20	6	8	96	48	48	66
6	Forres Mechanics	34	21	3	10	79	40	39	66
7	Wick Academy	34	15	7	12	69	54	15	52
8	Buckie Thistle	34	14	7	13	72	54	18	49
9	Huntly	34	14	7	13	57	65	–8	49
10	Rothes*	34	13	8	13	73	57	16	44
11	Nairn Co	34	13	3	18	61	67	–6	42
12	Deveronvale	34	13	2	19	55	65	–10	41
13	Keith	34	10	7	17	62	68	–6	37
14	Strathspey Thistle	34	10	3	21	47	90	–43	33
15	Turriff U	34	9	5	20	74	91	–17	32
16	Clachnacuddin	34	6	6	22	44	79	–35	24
17	Lossiemouth	34	2	2	30	29	139	–110	8
18	Fort William†	34	0	2	32	21	245	–224	–7

**Rothes deducted 3 points for fielding an ineligible player.*

†Fort William deducted 9 points for fielding an ineligible player on 3 occasions.

GEOSONIC LOWLAND LEAGUE

		P	W	D	L	F	A	GD	Pts
1	East Kilbride	28	23	3	2	66	12	54	72
2	BSC Glasgow	28	18	7	3	67	29	38	61
3	Kelty Hearts	28	16	6	6	61	32	29	54
4	Spartans	28	14	9	5	63	31	32	51
5	Civil Service Strollers	28	15	4	9	51	38	13	49
6	East Stirlingshire	28	11	6	11	57	47	10	39
7	Cumbernauld Colts	28	11	6	11	40	47	–7	39
8	Gala Fairydean R	28	10	4	14	43	48	–5	34
9	Edusport Academy	28	9	6	13	43	52	–9	33
10	Stirling University	28	7	10	11	43	50	–7	31
11	Edinburgh University	28	7	9	12	38	54	–16	30
12	Gretna 2008	28	9	2	17	42	67	–25	29
13	Vale of Leithen	28	8	5	15	43	74	–31	29
14	Dalbeattie Star	28	5	7	16	33	63	–30	22
15	Whitehill Welfare	28	2	6	20	24	70	–46	12
16	Selkirk*	0	0	0	0	0	0	0	0

**Selkirk resigned, record expunged.*

CENTRAL TAXIS EAST OF SCOTLAND LEAGUE

		P	W	D	L	F	A	GD	Pts
1	Penicuik Ath	24	20	3	1	92	15	77	63
2	Hill of Beath Hawthorn	24	20	2	2	99	17	82	62
3	Musselburgh Ath	24	17	3	4	74	31	43	54
4	Newtongrange Star	24	14	5	5	79	32	47	47
5	Dunbar U	24	13	4	7	62	34	28	43
6	Leith Ath	24	10	4	10	41	51	–10	34
7	Coldstream*	24	10	3	11	56	51	5	30
8	Easthouses Lily MW	24	9	1	14	41	67	–26	28
9	Oakley U	24	6	5	13	34	50	–16	23
10	Arniston Rangers	24	7	2	15	34	71	–37	23
11	Peebles R	24	6	4	14	40	73	–33	22
12	Hawick Royal Albert	24	4	1	19	21	86	–65	13
13	Tweedmouth Rangers	24	1	1	22	20	115	–95	4

**Coldstream deducted 3 points for fielding an ineligible player.*

SOUTH OF SCOTLAND FOOTBALL LEAGUE

		P	W	D	L	F	A	GD	Pts
1	Stranraer Res	30	29	1	0	131	24	107	88
2	Bonnyton Thistle	30	22	4	4	120	39	81	70
3	Nithsdale W	30	19	3	8	100	72	28	60
4	Abbey Vale	30	17	6	7	100	54	46	57
5	Upper Annandale	30	17	6	7	72	53	19	57
6	Mid-Annandale	30	17	4	9	105	50	49	55
7	Lochar Thistle	30	16	5	9	71	47	24	53
8	Heston R	30	15	3	12	66	48	18	48
9	Threave R	30	14	3	13	79	54	25	45
10	St Cuthbert W	30	13	6	11	79	57	22	45
11	Lochmaben	30	8	5	17	59	87	–28	29
12	Wigtown & Bladnoch	30	8	3	19	48	94	–46	27
13	Newton Stewart	30	6	4	20	38	115	–77	22
14	Creetown	30	4	7	19	36	87	–51	19
15	Dumfries YMCA	30	3	2	25	29	125	–96	11
16	Annan Ath Res	30	0	2	28	26	153	–127	2

MACLEOD & MACCALLUM NORTH CALEDONIAN FOOTBALL LEAGUE

		P	W	D	L	F	A	GD	Pts
1	Golspie Sutherland	16	11	3	2	38	15	23	36
2	Invergordon	16	11	1	4	44	19	25	34
3	Orkney	16	10	3	3	40	19	21	33
4	Alness U	16	8	2	6	42	31	11	26
5	Inverness Ath	16	8	1	7	40	34	6	25
6	St Duthus	16	6	3	7	35	36	–1	21
7	Thurso	16	4	5	7	32	35	–3	17
8	Halkirk U	16	3	2	11	15	43	–28	11
9	Bunillidh Thistle	16	1	0	15	21	75	–54	3

SCOTTISH JUNIOR FOOTBALL ASSOCIATION (SJFA)

MCBOOKIE.COM WEST OF SCOTLAND LEAGUE PREMIERSHIP

			Home					*Away*					*Total*						
		P	*W*	*D*	*L*	*F*	*A*	*W*	*D*	*L*	*F*	*A*	*W*	*D*	*L*	*F*	*A*	*GD*	*Pts*
1	Auchinleck Talbot	30	12	2	1	36	8	15	0	0	46	7	27	2	1	82	15	67	83
2	Hurlford United	30	12	1	2	38	18	10	2	3	41	19	22	3	5	79	37	42	69
3	Pollok	30	7	5	3	26	15	9	3	3	31	17	16	8	6	57	32	25	56
4	Beith Juniors	30	8	2	5	34	25	6	8	1	30	17	14	10	6	64	42	22	52
5	Glenafton Athletic	30	8	4	3	29	25	6	3	6	25	18	14	7	9	54	43	11	49
6	Irvine Meadow XI	30	8	3	4	27	16	6	2	7	20	32	14	5	11	47	48	–1	47
7	Largs Thistle	30	8	6	1	40	15	4	4	7	29	26	12	10	8	69	41	28	46
8	Clydebank	30	6	3	6	33	21	7	1	7	26	26	13	4	13	59	47	12	43
9	Kilwinning Rangers	30	7	1	7	23	21	5	2	8	18	25	12	3	15	41	46	–5	39
10	Cumnock Juniors	30	7	1	7	27	33	3	3	9	19	30	10	4	16	46	63	–17	34
11	Kirkintilloch Rob Roy	30	6	5	4	25	19	2	3	10	16	35	8	8	14	41	54	–13	32
12	Troon	30	5	1	9	19	27	4	4	7	20	26	9	5	16	39	53	–14	32
13	Kilbirnie Ladeside	30	5	2	8	18	28	5	0	10	20	29	10	2	18	38	57	–19	32
14	Renfrew	30	6	3	6	27	31	2	3	10	14	35	8	6	16	41	66	–25	30
15	Petershill	30	3	1	11	10	40	2	2	11	14	40	5	3	22	24	80	–56	15
16	Cambuslang Rangers	30	4	1	10	20	42	1	1	13	15	50	5	2	23	35	92	–57	14

Petershill deducted 3 points for failing to fulfil fixture.
Cambuslang Rangers deducted 3 points for failing to fulfil fixture.

MCBOOKIE.COM NORTH REGION SUPERLEAGUE

			Home					*Away*					*Total*						
		P	*W*	*D*	*L*	*F*	*A*	*W*	*D*	*L*	*F*	*A*	*W*	*D*	*L*	*F*	*A*	*GD*	*Pts*
1	Banks O' Dee	26	12	0	1	58	9	11	2	0	55	11	23	2	1	113	20	93	71
2	Bridge of Don Thistle	26	9	2	2	40	15	8	0	5	32	22	17	2	7	72	37	35	53
3	Montrose Roselea	26	7	4	2	24	11	8	2	3	24	15	15	6	5	48	26	22	51
4	Hermes	26	6	1	6	24	21	8	2	3	25	21	14	3	9	49	42	7	45
5	Culter	26	9	1	3	36	20	4	4	5	22	21	13	5	8	58	41	17	44
6	Maud Juniors	26	8	1	4	31	26	3	1	9	18	38	11	2	13	49	64	–15	35
7	Nairn St Ninian	26	8	1	4	27	21	2	2	9	24	43	10	3	13	51	64	–13	33
8	Dyce Juniors	26	5	5	3	27	18	3	3	7	18	26	8	8	10	45	44	1	32
9	Colony Park	26	7	2	4	26	23	2	2	9	13	32	9	4	13	39	55	–16	31
10	Hall Russell United	26	4	4	5	16	18	3	2	8	15	20	7	6	13	31	38	–7	27
11	Aberdeen East End	26	4	2	7	22	35	3	4	6	12	28	7	6	13	34	63	–29	27
12	Ellon United	26	4	2	7	18	28	3	1	9	23	39	7	3	16	41	67	–26	24
13	Dufftown	26	4	1	8	27	38	3	1	9	16	50	7	2	17	43	88	–45	23
14	Stonehaven Juniors	26	5	2	6	21	27	1	2	10	13	31	6	4	16	34	58	–24	22

MCBOOKIE.COM EAST REGION SUPERLEAGUE

			Home					*Away*					*Total*						
		P	*W*	*D*	*L*	*F*	*A*	*W*	*D*	*L*	*F*	*A*	*W*	*D*	*L*	*F*	*A*	*GD*	*Pts*
1	Lochee United	22	9	2	0	40	10	11	0	0	31	1	20	2	0	71	11	60	62
2	Broughty Athletic	22	9	1	1	28	7	8	1	2	27	14	17	2	3	55	21	34	53
3	Thornton Hibs	22	6	1	4	25	21	6	1	4	26	16	12	2	8	51	37	14	38
4	Whitburn Juniors	22	6	3	2	31	19	5	0	6	27	34	11	3	8	58	53	5	36
5	Tayport	22	8	0	3	27	17	2	3	6	15	20	10	3	9	42	37	5	33
6	Forfar West End	22	5	3	3	19	14	3	2	6	18	22	8	5	9	37	36	1	29
7	Carnoustie Panmure	22	5	3	3	22	18	3	1	7	15	25	8	4	10	37	43	–6	28
8	Kennoway Star Hearts	22	4	0	7	20	19	4	2	5	18	20	8	2	12	38	39	–1	26
9	Kirriemuir Thistle	22	6	0	5	27	27	0	4	7	14	35	6	4	12	41	62	–21	22
10	Fauldhouse United	22	4	2	5	20	20	1	2	8	14	36	5	4	13	34	56	–22	19
11	Downfield Juniors	22	4	1	6	22	26	2	0	9	11	35	6	1	15	33	61	–28	19
12	Glenrothes	22	3	2	6	15	27	0	2	9	9	38	3	4	15	24	65	–41	13

WOMEN'S FOOTBALL 2018–19

FA WOMEN'S SUPER LEAGUE TABLE 2018–19

			Home					Away					Total						
		P	*W*	*D*	*L*	*F*	*A*	*W*	*D*	*L*	*F*	*A*	*W*	*D*	*L*	*F*	*A*	*GD*	*Pts*
1	Arsenal	20	9	0	1	33	8	9	0	1	37	5	18	0	2	70	13	57	54
2	Manchester C	20	7	3	0	25	9	7	2	1	28	8	14	5	1	53	17	36	47
3	Chelsea	20	6	2	2	21	9	6	4	0	25	5	12	6	2	46	14	32	42
4	Birmingham C	20	6	1	3	13	7	7	0	3	16	10	13	1	6	29	17	12	40
5	Reading	20	4	1	5	18	16	4	2	4	15	14	8	3	9	33	30	3	27
6	Bristol C	20	3	3	4	7	11	4	1	5	10	23	7	4	9	17	34	–17	25
7	West Ham U	20	2	1	7	8	18	5	1	4	17	19	7	2	11	25	37	–12	23
8	Liverpool	20	4	0	6	12	21	3	1	6	9	17	7	1	12	21	38	–17	22
9	Brighton & HA	20	2	1	7	5	23	2	3	5	11	15	4	4	12	16	38	–22	16
10	Everton	20	2	2	6	10	22	1	1	8	5	16	3	3	14	15	38	–23	12
11	Yeovil T*	20	1	1	8	4	36	1	0	9	7	24	2	1	17	11	60	–49	–3

**Yeovil T deducted 10 points for entering administration.*

FA WOMEN'S SUPER LEAGUE LEADING GOALSCORERS 2018–19

Player	*Team*	*Goals*
Anna Miedema	Arsenal	21
Nikita Parris	Manchester C	16
Bethany England	Chelsea	12
Georgia Stanway	Manchester C	11
Danielle van de Donk	Arsenal	11
Francesca Kirby	Chelsea	9
Jordan Nobbs	Arsenal	9
Courtney Sweetman-Kirk	Liverpool	9
Fara Williams	Reading	9
Erin Cuthbert	Chelsea	8
Kim Little	Arsenal	8
Brooke Chaplen	Reading	7
Lucy Graham	Bristol C	7
Bethany Mead	Arsenal	7
Jane Ross	West Ham United	7
Alisha Lehmann	West Ham United	6
Ji So Yun	Chelsea	6
Ellen White	Birmingham C	6
Katie McCabe	Arsenal	5
Caroline Weir	Manchester C	5
Rinsola Babajide	Liverpool	4
Ellie Brazil	Brighton & HA	4
Claire Emslie	Manchester C	4
Emma Follis	Birmingham C	4
Inessa Kaagman	Everton	4
Charlie Wellings	Birmingham C	4

FA WOMEN'S CHAMPIONSHIP TABLE 2018–19

			Home					Away					Total						
		P	*W*	*D*	*L*	*F*	*A*	*W*	*D*	*L*	*F*	*A*	*W*	*D*	*L*	*F*	*A*	*GD*	*Pts*
1	Manchester U	20	9	1	0	50	2	9	0	1	48	5	18	1	1	98	7	91	55
2	Tottenham H	20	7	0	3	21	15	8	1	1	23	12	15	1	4	44	27	17	46
3	Charlton Ath	20	7	1	2	24	9	6	1	3	25	12	13	2	5	49	21	28	41
4	Durham	20	5	2	3	17	11	6	4	0	20	5	11	6	3	37	16	21	39
5	Sheffield U	20	6	0	4	23	15	5	1	4	12	16	11	1	8	35	31	4	34
6	Aston Villa	20	3	5	2	13	19	3	3	4	17	20	6	8	6	30	39	–9	26
7	Leicester C	20	3	2	5	16	25	3	1	6	11	19	6	3	11	27	44	–17	21
8	London Bees	20	5	0	5	13	21	2	0	8	10	27	7	0	13	23	48	–25	21
9	Lewes	20	3	1	6	10	18	2	1	7	13	29	5	2	13	23	47	–24	17
10	Crystal Palace	20	2	0	8	7	23	1	2	7	7	21	3	2	15	14	44	–30	11
11	Millwall Lionesses	20	1	2	7	10	32	0	0	10	4	38	1	2	17	14	70	–56	5

FA WOMEN'S CHAMPIONSHIP LEADING GOALSCORERS 2018–19

Player	*Team*	*Goals*
Jessica Sigsworth	Manchester U	17
Rianna Dean	Tottenham H	15
Elizabeta Ejupi	Charlton Ath	14
Lauren James	Manchester U	14
Ella Toone	Manchester U	14
Mollie Green	Manchester U	13
Kit Graham	Charlton Ath	12
Katie Zelem	Manchester U	10
Jodie Hutton	Aston Villa	8
Jade Pennock	Sheffield U	8
Lily Agg	Charlton Ath	7
Elizabeth Hepple	Durham	7
Melissa Johnson	Leicester C	7
Emily Roberts	Durham	7
Angela Addison	Tottenham H	6
Elizabeth Arnot	Manchester U	6
Evie Clarke	Millwall Lionesses	6
Sophie Jones	Sheffield U	6
Zoe Ness	Durham	6
Sarah Wiltshire	Tottenham H	6
Emma Beckett	Tottenham H	5
Includes 4 goals for London Bees		
Rebecca Carter	Lewes	5
Charlie Devlin	Manchester U	5
Kirsty Hanson	Manchester U	5
Ebony Salmon	Sheffield U	5

WOMEN'S CONTINENTAL TYRES LEAGUE CUP 2018–19

PRELIMINARY ROUND

GROUP ONE NORTH TABLE

	P	W	Wp	Lp	L	F	A	GD	Pts
Manchester C	5	4	1	0	0	17	0	17	14
Birmingham C	5	3	0	2	0	10	0	10	11
Bristol C	5	2	1	1	1	10	8	2	9
Sheffield U	5	2	0	0	3	6	13	–7	6
Aston Villa	5	1	0	0	4	4	13	–9	3
Leicester C	5	0	1	0	4	3	16	–13	2

GROUP TWO NORTH TABLE

	P	W	Wp	Lp	L	F	A	GD	Pts
Manchester U	4	3	0	0	1	5	2	3	9
Reading	4	2	0	1	1	9	5	4	7
Everton	4	2	0	0	2	6	7	–1	6
Durham	4	1	0	1	2	5	8	–3	4
Liverpool	4	0	2	0	2	5	8	–3	4

GROUP ONE SOUTH TABLE

	P	W	Wp	Lp	L	F	A	GD	Pts
Chelsea	5	5	0	0	0	25	2	23	15
Brighton & HA	5	3	0	1	1	15	8	7	10
Crystal Palace	5	2	1	0	2	10	12	–2	8
Tottenham H	5	1	1	1	2	9	12	–3	6
London Bees	5	1	1	0	3	9	19	–10	5
Yeovil T	5	0	0	1	4	2	17	–15	1

GROUP TWO SOUTH TABLE

	P	W	Wp	Lp	L	F	A	GD	Pts
Arsenal	4	4	0	0	0	20	2	18	12
West Ham U	4	3	0	0	1	10	4	6	9
Lewes	4	2	0	0	2	8	13	–5	6
Charlton Ath	4	1	0	0	3	4	14	–10	3
Millwall Lionesses	4	0	0	0	4	3	12	–9	0

Drawn games were decided by a penalty shoot-out.
Wp = match won on penalties (2 pts);
Lp = match lost on penalties (1 pt).

KNOCK-OUT ROUNDS

QUARTER-FINALS

Manchester C v Brighton & HA	7-1
Arsenal v Birmingham C	2-1
Chelsea v Reading	4-0
Manchester U v West Ham U	2-0

SEMI-FINALS

Arsenal v Manchester U	2-1
Chelsea v Manchester C	0-2

WOMEN'S CONTINENTAL TYRES LEAGUE CUP FINAL 2019

Bramall Lane, Sheffield, Saturday 23 February 2019

Arsenal (0) 0

Manchester C (0) 0 2421

Arsenal: van Veenendaal; Arnth (Miedema 69), Williamson, Quinn, Veje (Hazard 71), Little, Bloodworth, van de Donk, Evans, Mead, McCabe.
Manchester C: Bardsley; Bonner, Houghton, Beattie, Stokes, Wullaert (Beckie 65), Scott, Walsh, Weir (Emslie 119), Parris (Hemp 105), Stanway.
aet; Manchester C won 4-2 on penalties.
Referee: Lucy Oliver.

FA Women's Super League top scorer Vivianne Miedema battles for Arsenal against Manchester City's Keira Walsh in their WSL clash on 11 May. (John Walton/PA Wire/PA Images)

FA WOMEN'S NATIONAL LEAGUE 2018–19

FA WOMEN'S NATIONAL LEAGUE NORTHERN PREMIER DIVISION 2018–19

			Home					*Away*					*Total*						
		P	*W*	*D*	*L*	*F*	*A*	*W*	*D*	*L*	*F*	*A*	*W*	*D*	*L*	*F*	*A*	*GD*	*Pts*
1	Blackburn R	24	12	0	0	60	7	11	0	1	55	11	23	0	1	115	18	97	69
2	Sunderland	24	9	0	3	52	15	6	3	3	31	21	15	3	6	83	36	47	48
3	Derby Co	24	10	0	2	24	16	5	3	4	30	19	15	3	6	54	35	19	48
4	Huddersfield T	24	9	1	2	51	17	6	1	5	28	23	15	2	7	79	40	39	47
5	Middlesbrough	24	7	3	2	39	19	6	1	5	21	22	13	4	7	60	41	19	43
6	Fylde	24	8	1	3	28	10	5	2	5	20	23	13	3	8	48	33	15	42
7	Stoke C	24	4	5	3	34	25	5	1	6	25	26	9	6	9	59	51	8	33
8	Guiseley Vixens	24	3	2	7	22	26	6	2	4	23	22	9	4	11	45	48	–3	31
9	Nottingham F	24	3	2	7	15	24	4	2	6	14	33	7	4	13	29	57	–28	25
10	Hull C	24	4	2	6	26	30	3	0	9	15	35	7	2	15	41	65	–24	23
11	Sheffield	24	4	1	7	19	24	2	2	8	18	31	6	3	15	37	55	–18	21
12	Doncaster R Belles	24	2	3	7	16	30	2	3	7	16	45	4	6	14	32	75	–43	18
13	Bradford C	24	0	0	12	4	61	0	0	12	8	79	0	0	24	12	140	–128	0

FA WOMEN'S NATIONAL LEAGUE SOUTHERN PREMIER DIVISION 2018–19

			Home					*Away*					*Total*						
		P	*W*	*D*	*L*	*F*	*A*	*W*	*D*	*L*	*F*	*A*	*W*	*D*	*L*	*F*	*A*	*GD*	*Pts*
1	Coventry U	22	9	1	1	47	7	9	2	0	33	7	18	3	1	80	14	66	57
2	Cardiff C	22	9	2	0	31	10	7	0	4	27	16	16	2	4	58	26	32	50
3	Chichester C	22	9	0	2	24	12	6	1	4	24	15	15	1	6	48	27	21	46
4	Oxford U	22	7	0	4	34	15	6	2	3	22	9	13	2	7	56	24	32	41
5	Watford	22	7	0	4	28	25	6	1	4	15	15	13	1	8	43	40	3	40
6	Plymouth Arg	22	5	2	4	23	27	6	0	5	27	27	11	2	9	50	54	–4	35
7	Loughborough Foxes	22	5	2	4	26	12	5	2	4	22	20	10	4	8	48	32	16	34
8	Portsmouth	22	6	0	5	19	16	3	1	7	22	22	9	1	12	41	38	3	28
9	Milton Keynes D	22	3	0	8	15	23	3	1	7	13	29	6	1	15	28	52	–24	19
10	Gillingham	22	3	3	5	14	21	2	1	8	10	33	5	4	13	24	54	–30	19
11	QPR	22	2	3	6	16	31	0	2	9	12	38	2	5	15	28	69	–41	11
12	C&K Basildon	22	0	1	10	5	40	0	1	10	12	51	0	2	20	17	91	–74	2

FA WOMEN'S NATIONAL LEAGUE DIVISION ONE NORTH 2018–19

			Home					*Away*					*Total*						
		P	*W*	*D*	*L*	*F*	*A*	*W*	*D*	*L*	*F*	*A*	*W*	*D*	*L*	*F*	*A*	*GD*	*Pts*
1	Burnley	22	8	1	2	19	8	10	1	0	20	6	18	2	2	39	14	25	56
2	Brighouse T	22	5	4	2	21	14	7	3	1	23	6	12	7	3	44	20	24	43
3	Chester-le-Street T	22	5	1	5	17	15	8	2	1	23	12	13	3	6	40	27	13	42
4	Barnsley	22	7	2	2	23	8	5	3	3	29	26	12	5	5	52	34	18	41
5	Liverpool Feds	22	5	2	4	34	20	5	3	3	23	19	10	5	7	57	39	18	35
6	Leeds U	22	5	2	4	19	13	5	2	4	15	15	10	4	8	34	28	6	34
7	Chorley	22	4	3	4	20	19	4	1	6	13	16	8	4	10	33	35	–2	28
8	Bolton W	22	4	3	4	15	11	3	2	6	9	16	7	5	10	24	27	–3	26
9	Newcastle U	22	4	1	6	15	15	3	3	5	13	16	7	4	11	28	31	–3	25
10	Norton & Stockton Ancients	22	4	2	5	27	30	3	0	8	24	27	7	2	13	51	57	–6	23
11	Morecambe	22	3	2	6	21	27	0	3	8	14	42	3	5	14	35	69	–34	14
12	Crewe Alex	22	1	1	9	11	30	0	1	10	4	41	1	2	19	15	71	–56	5

FA WOMEN'S NATIONAL LEAGUE DIVISION ONE MIDLANDS 2018–19

			Home					*Away*					*Total*						
		P	*W*	*D*	*L*	*F*	*A*	*W*	*D*	*L*	*F*	*A*	*W*	*D*	*L*	*F*	*A*	*GD*	*Pts*
1	WBA	20	10	0	0	42	6	9	0	1	55	9	19	0	1	97	15	82	57
2	Wolverhampton W	20	9	0	1	55	6	8	0	2	43	8	17	0	3	98	14	84	51
3	Birmingham & West Midlands	20	7	1	2	34	12	6	1	3	34	14	13	2	5	68	26	42	41
4	Sporting Khalsa	20	6	1	3	28	23	5	2	3	21	17	11	3	6	49	40	9	36
5	Bedworth U	20	6	1	3	25	21	5	0	5	21	25	11	1	8	46	46	0	34
6	Long Eaton U	20	4	1	5	23	17	5	1	4	25	24	9	2	9	48	41	7	29
7	Nettleham	20	4	0	6	24	24	5	1	4	14	19	9	1	10	38	43	–5	28
8	The New Saints	20	4	0	6	35	24	4	1	5	22	25	8	1	11	57	49	8	25
9	Burton Alb	20	2	2	6	19	34	2	1	7	11	37	4	3	13	30	71	–41	15
10	Solihull Moors	20	1	0	9	7	34	1	0	9	11	54	2	0	18	18	88	–70	6
11	Steel City W	20	0	1	9	5	62	0	0	10	6	65	0	1	19	11	127	–116	1

FA WOMEN'S NATIONAL LEAGUE DIVISION ONE SOUTH-EAST 2018–19

			Home					Away					Total						
		P	W	D	L	F	A	W	D	L	F	A	W	D	L	F	A	GD	Pts
1	Crawley Wasps	22	10	0	1	56	6	9	2	0	32	5	19	2	1	88	11	77	59
2	Billericay T	22	9	1	1	30	12	6	2	3	24	17	15	3	4	54	29	25	48
3	Enfield T	22	6	2	3	24	12	4	3	4	17	17	10	5	7	41	29	12	35
4	Actonians	22	4	3	4	27	24	6	0	5	31	29	10	3	9	58	53	5	33
5	Leyton Orient	22	4	2	5	23	20	5	3	3	16	17	9	5	8	39	37	2	32
6	AFC Wimbledon	22	4	2	5	20	25	5	3	3	16	14	9	5	8	36	39	–3	32
7	Ipswich T	22	3	4	4	20	20	4	3	4	19	22	7	7	8	39	42	–3	28
8	Cambridge U	22	4	2	5	14	13	3	4	4	18	22	7	6	9	32	35	–3	27
9	Stevenage	22	3	1	7	15	21	5	2	4	14	29	8	3	11	29	50	–21	27
10	Norwich C	22	4	3	4	22	20	2	0	9	12	34	6	3	13	34	54	–20	21
11	Denham U	22	0	5	6	6	19	3	2	6	9	34	3	7	12	15	53	–38	16
12	Luton T	22	2	1	8	11	24	1	2	8	8	28	3	3	16	19	52	–33	12

FA WOMEN'S PREMIER LEAGUE DIVISION ONE SOUTH WEST 2017–18

			Home					Away					Total						
		P	W	D	L	F	A	W	D	L	F	A	W	D	L	F	A	GD	Pts
1	Keynsham T	20	9	0	1	59	7	8	2	0	56	8	17	2	1	115	15	100	53
2	Southampton Women	20	7	1	2	33	10	8	0	2	35	6	15	1	4	68	16	52	46
3	Cheltenham T	20	5	4	1	23	12	7	1	2	31	14	12	5	3	54	26	28	41
4	Buckland Ath	19	7	1	1	29	16	5	2	3	33	20	12	3	4	62	36	26	39
5	Chesham U	20	6	2	2	31	13	5	0	5	26	25	11	2	7	57	38	19	35
6	Larkhall Ath	20	6	2	2	27	22	1	4	5	11	21	7	6	7	38	43	–5	27
7	Brislington	20	4	2	4	17	30	2	2	6	22	32	6	4	10	39	62	–23	22
8	Southampton Saints	19	4	0	6	12	25	2	0	7	11	28	6	0	13	23	53	–30	18
9	Swindon T	20	3	1	6	9	29	1	2	7	9	23	4	3	13	18	52	–34	15
10	Maidenhead U	20	1	2	7	10	31	1	0	9	4	40	2	2	16	14	71	–57	8
11	Poole T	20	2	0	8	14	50	0	2	8	7	47	2	2	16	21	97	–76	8

St Nicholas withdrew from the league. Buckland Ath v Southampton Saints postponed.

FA WOMEN'S NATIONAL LEAGUE CUP 2018–19

**After extra time.*

DETERMINING ROUND

Actonians v Oxford U	1-2
Barnsley v Bolton W	3-4
Billericay T v Maidenhead U	10-1
Blackburn R v Liverpool Feds	3-3*
Blackburn R won 5-4 on penalties.	
Buckland Ath v Brislington	3-0
Cambridge U v C & K Basildon	2-0
Chesham U v Enfield T	2-4
Coventry U v Norwich C	7-0
Crawley Wasps v Ipswich T	8-0
Derby Co v Bedworth U	3-1
Doncaster R Belles v Chorley	2-2*
Chorley won 4-3 on penalties.	
Fylde v Burton Alb	9-0
Guiseley Vixens v Chester-le-Street T	4-2
Huddersfield T v Middlesbrough	3-0
Hull C v Bradford C	2-1
Larkhall Ath v Keynsham T	3-2
Long Eaton U v Norton & Stockton Ancients	3-4
Loughborough Foxes v Denham U	4-0
Luton T v Cheltenham T	1-3
Morecambe v Sunderland	0-5
Nettleham v Birmingham & West Midlands	1-2
Plymouth Arg v Milton Keynes D	4-2
Poole T v Watford	1-2
Portsmouth v Chichester C	2-4
QPR v Gillingham	3-1
Solihull v Brighouse T	0-7
Southampton Saints v AFC Wimbledon	0-1
Sporting Khalsa v Leeds U	1-2
Steel City W v Newcastle U	1-6
Stevenage v Cardiff C	1-4
Stoke C v Sheffield	3-0
Swindon T v Leyton Orient	1-5
The New Saints v Nottingham F	0-3
West Bromwich Alb v Burnley	0-3
Wolverhampton W v Crewe Alexandra	1-0
St Nicholas v Southampton Women (walkover)	

FIRST ROUND

AFC Wimbledon v Buckland Ath	4-0
Enfield T v Southampton Women	3-4
Guiseley Vixens v Blackburn R	1-2
Newcastle U v Chorley	1-2*

SECOND ROUND

Billericay T v Chichester C	0-2
Blackburn R v Fylde	3-2
Brighouse T v Leeds U	1-2
Cardiff C v Cheltenham T	5-3
Derby Co v Bolton W	1-2
Huddersfield T v Burnley	1-0
Hull C v Birmingham & West Midlands	2-1*
Larkhall Ath v AFC Wimbledon	2-3*
Nottingham F v Chorley	2-0
Oxford U v Crawley Wasps	1-3*
QPR v Loughborough Foxes	1-3
Stoke C v Norton & Stockton Ancients	3-0
Watford v Coventry U	2-3
Wolverhampton W v Sunderland	1-4
Cambridge U v Leyton Orient	3-0
Southampton Women v Plymouth Arg	1-3

THIRD ROUND

AFC Wimbledon v Cambridge U	2-1
Blackburn R v Sunderland	3-1
Cardiff C v Loughborough Foxes	3-4*
Huddersfield T v Nottingham F	4-1
Stoke C v Leeds U	6-3
Plymouth Arg v Crawley Wasps	3-5*
Bolton W v Hull C	3-1*
Chichester C v Coventry U	0-2

QUARTER-FINALS

Bolton W v Stoke C	1-1*
Bolton W won 5-3 on penalties.	
Loughborough Foxes v AFC Wimbledon	3-0
Coventry U v Crawley Wasps	1-2
Huddersfield T v Blackburn R	1-3

SEMI-FINALS

Blackburn R v Loughborough Foxes	4-0
Crawley Wasps v Bolton W	1-0

FINAL

Burton, Sunday 28 April 2019

Crawley Wasps (0) 0

Blackburn R (1) 3 *(Jordan 8, 81, Flint 52)* 227

Crawley Wasps: Cole; Drury, Gibbs, Green (Flieschman 58), Palmer, Plewa, Rabson, Stevenson (Woolard 89), Stow, Young, Webber (Davis 75).

Blackburn R: Davies; Fenton (Walsh 87), Fletcher, Flint, Gibbons, Holbrook, Jordan, Jukes, Makin (Taylor 67), McDonald, Shepherd.

THE SSE WOMEN'S FA CUP 2018–19

**After extra time.*

PRELIMINARY ROUND

Lumley v Boro Rangers	0-2
Workington Reds v Carlisle U	1-3
Durham Cestria v South Shields	3-0
Altofts v Tingley Ath	0-1*
(0-0 at the end of normal time)	
Rotherham U v Bradford Park Avenue	14-0
Dronfield T v Ossett U	0-8
Hepworth U v Chesterfield	0-4
Bridlington R (walkover) v Leeds Medics & Dentists (withdrawn)	
Manchester Stingers v Merseyrail Bootle	3-1
Tranmere R v Chester	7-0
Wythenshawe Amateurs v Accrington Stanley Community Trust	5-1
FC United of Manchester (walkover) v Blackburn Community Sports Club (withdrawn)	
Bury v Mossley Hill	3-3*
Bury won 3-0 on penalties	
Burscough Dynamo v Fleetwood T Wrens	3-3*
Burscough Dynamo won 3-2 on penalties	
Oadby & Wigston v Sherwood	6-0
Mansfield T v Hykeham Ts	3-2*
(2-2 at the end of normal time)	
Lincoln Moorlands Railway v Loughborough Students	1-3
Leek T v Wyrley	3-0
Goldenhill W v Sutton Coldfield T	0-2*
(0-0 at the end of normal time)	
AFC Telford U v Kidderminster H	0-2
Rugby T v Knowle	2-1
Crusaders v Coundon Court	4-2
Shifnal T v Sedgley & Gornal U	1-0
Droitwich Spa v Stockingford AA Pavilion	1-2
Wymondham T (walkover) v Moulton (withdrawn)	
Newmarket T v Cambridge C	0-2
St Ives T v Corby T	1-0*
(0-0 at the end of normal time)	
Frontiers v Brentwood T	0-4
Beccles T v Chelmsford C	0-1
Colney Heath v Hemel Hempstead T	7-0
Royston T v Hertford T	7-1
QPR Girls (walkover) v Barton U (withdrawn)	
Wantage T v Wycombe W	2-2*
Wycombe W won 3-0 on penalties.	
Brentford v New London Lionesses	1-2
Woodley U (withdrawn) v Abingdon U (walkover)	
Ashford v Eastbourne T	4-3
Regents Park Rangers (walkover) v Carshalton Ath (withdrawn)	
Kent Football U v Herne Bay	8-0
Eastbourne v Aylesford	1-2
Sutton U v AFC Phoenix	1-2
Newhaven v Parkwood Rangers	6-3
Oakwood v Islington Bor	0-4
Saltdean v Steyning T	4-1
London Kent Football U v Tonbridge Angels	11-0
Margate v Thamesview	2-5
Moneyfields v Swindon Spitfires	5-0
(Tie awarded to Swindon Spitfires – Moneyfields removed)	
Winchester C Flyers v Southampton FC Women	0-2
Warsash Wasps v Bournemouth Sports	A-A, 5-1
(First match abandoned due to waterlogged pitch)	
Callington T v Exeter C	2-5
Marine Academy Plymouth v Purnell Sports	8-0
Bideford v Portishead T	0-4
Exeter & Tedburn Rangers (walkover) v Forest Green R (withdrawn)	
Chipping Sodbury T v Downend Flyers	1-2

FIRST ROUND QUALIFYING

South Park Rangers (withdrawn) v Redcar T (walkover)	
Durham Cestria v Alnwick T	1-2
Boro Rangers v Cramlington U	8-1
Washington v Hartlepool U	2-4
Carlisle U v Bishop Auckland	1-2
Penrith v Wallsend Boys Club	5-1
Wakefield v Sheffield Wednesday	0-4
Ossett U v Farsley Celtic	1-2
Tingley Ath v Harrogate T	4-0
Oughtibridge War Memorial (walkover) v Malet Lambert (withdrawn)	
Rotherham U v Bridlington R	1-3
Chesterfield v Yorkshire Amateur	4-0
Warrington Wolverines v Stockport Co	1-4
Wythenshawe Amateurs v Accrington Girls & Ladies	1-3
Manchester Stingers v West Didsbury & Chorlton	2-5
Cammell Laird 1907 v Burscough Dynamo	4-0
Tranmere R v Bury	6-3
FC United of Manchester v Didsbury	6-0
Leicester C Development v Coalville T Ravenettes	15-0
Oadby & Wigston v Mansfield T	4-2
Grimsby Bor v Boston U	1-4
Loughborough Students v Rise Park	5-1
Leicester C v Lutterworth Ath	2-5
Stockingford AA Pavilion v Lye T	2-0
Stourbridge v Solihull U	1-2
St Johns v Sandwell	5-4*
(4-4 at the end of normal time)	
Shifnal T v Leafield Ath	0-7
Leek T v Sutton Coldfield T	1-2
Hereford Lads Club v Kidderminster H	0-9
Rugby T v Shenstone	5-1
Redditch U v Kingfisher	0-3
Crusaders v Solihull Sporting	5-0
Peterborough Northern Star v Northampton T	4-4*
Peterborough Northern Star won 3-1 on penalties	
St Ives T v Peterborough U	1-2
Wymondham T (walkover) v Roade (withdrawn)	
Kettering T v Acle U	1-3
Cambridge C v Riverside	14-0
Histon v Thrapston T	2-1
Leigh Ramblers v Bowers & Pitsea	2-0
Corringham Cosmos (walkover) v Bungay T (withdrawn)	
Brentwood T v Harlow T	1-2
Chelmsford C v AFC Sudbury	0-1
AFC Dunstable v Watford Development	5-0
Bishop's Stortford v Royston T	0-11
Colney Heath v Houghton Ath	2-0
Ashford T (Middlesex) v Wargrave	15-0
New London Lionesses v Hampton & Richmond Bor	4-0
QPR Girls (walkover) v Wealdstone (removed)	
Sandhurst T (withdrawn) v Newbury (walkover)	
Wycombe W v Ascot U	1-3
Abingdon U v Oxford C	1-3
Newhaven v Ashford	2-1
London Kent Football U v Godalming T	1-2
Hassocks v Islington Bor	2-4
Meridian v Worthing	1-4
Regents Park Rangers v Whyteleafe	3-4
Kent Football U v Victoire	8-0
Burgess Hill T v Thamesview	9-2
Abbey Rangers v Saltdean	2-1*
(1-1 at the end of normal time)	
AFC Phoenix v Phoenix Sports	5-0
Aylesford v Fulham	1-3
Basingstoke T v AFC Bournemouth	0-13
Swindon Spitfires v Southampton FC Women	0-6
Shanklin v New Milton T	0-3
Warsash Wasps v Royal Wootton Bassett T	3-1
Alton v Eastleigh	0-2
Frampton Rangers v Feniton	4-3
Exeter C v Frome T	5-0
Ilminster T v Middlezoy R	4-0
Marine Academy Plymouth v Exeter & Tedburn Rangers	13-1
Portishead T v Downend Flyers	2-1
St Agnes v Keynsham T Development	1-3
Torquay U v Weston-super-Mare	1-2

SECOND ROUND QUALIFYING

Steel C W v Chester-le-Street T	1-8
Cammell Laird 1907 v Crewe Alex	1-3
Morecambe v Norton & Stockton Ancients	1-5
Redcar T v Sheffield Wednesday	6-2
Bishop Auckland v Stockport Co	0-8

Tingley Ath v West Didsbury & Chorlton	0-5
Bridlington R v Accrington Girls & Ladies	4-1
Brighouse T v Penrith	5-0
Oughtibridge War Memorial v FC United of Manchester	0-4
Bolton W v Hartlepool U	3-0
Barnsley v Newcastle U	2-3*
(2-2 at the end of normal time)	
Tranmere R v Boro Rangers	0-1
Burnley v Liverpool Marshalls Feds	3-2
Alnwick T v Leeds U	2-3
Chorley v Farsley Celtic	5-0
Oadby & Wigston v Sutton Coldfield T	2-0
Crusaders v Sporting Khalsa	0-2
Rugby T v West Bromwich Alb	0-10
Long Eaton U v The New Saints	7-1
Chesterfield v Burton Alb	1-0
Leicester C Development v Solihull U	6-3
St Johns v Kidderminster H	1-4
Wolverhampton W v Kingfisher	6-0
Bedworth U v Birmingham & West Midlands	0-2
Leafield Ath v Lutterworth Ath	0-0*
Leafield Ath won 4-2 on penalties	
Stockingford AA Pavilion v Nettleham	1-2
Solihull Moors v Loughborough Students	3-2*
(2-2 at the end of normal time)	
Billericay T v Colney Heath	9-1
Wymondham T v Corringham Cosmos	17-1
AFC Sudbury v Acle U	0-7
Chesham U v Peterborough U	5-0
Histon v Leigh Ramblers	3-2
Cambridge C v Leyton Orient	5-4
Luton T v AFC Dunstable	7-0
Enfield T v Actonians	2-1
Boston U v Norwich C	3-11
New London Lionesses v Ipswich T	2-2*
New London Lionesses won 4-2 on penalties	
Peterborough Northern Star v Stevenage	1-5
QPR Girls v Royston T	5-1
Cambridge U v Harlow T	6-0
Worthing v Islington Bor	1-5
Denham U v Crawley Wasps	1-3
AFC Wimbledon v AFC Phoenix	1-0
Oxford C v Fulham	4-3
Newhaven v Newbury	3-1
Kent Football U v Burgess Hill T	9-0
Godalming T v Abbey Rangers	4-2
Whyteleafe v Maidenhead U	2-0
Ashford T (Middlesex) v Ascot U	11-2
Buckland Ath v Ilminster T	4-0
Southampton FC Women v New Milton T	5-0
Poole T v Frampton Rangers	3-1
St Nicholas (withdrawn) v Eastleigh (walkover)	
Larkhall Ath v Weston-super-Mare	7-2
Swindon T v Keynsham T	0-8
Cheltenham T v Brislington	4-1
Southampton Saints v Warsash Wasps	3-0
AFC Bournemouth v Portishead T	4-1
Southampton Women's v Marine Academy Plymouth	1-2
Exeter C v Keynsham T Development	8-1

THIRD ROUND QUALIFYING

West Didsbury & Chorlton v Bolton W	0-4
Leeds U v Boro Rangers	8-0
Norton & Stockton Ancients v Redcar T	3-1
FC United of Manchester v Bridlington R	13-0
Chorley v Crewe Alex	2-1
Chesterfield v Stockport Co	0-6
Brighouse T v Burnley	3-1
Newcastle U v Chester-le-Street T	0-2
Sporting Khalsa v Long Eaton U	1-6
Kidderminster H v Solihull Moors	2-1
Leicester C Development v Oadby & Wigston	2-1
Birmingham & West Midlands v Wolverhampton W	0-2
Leafield Ath v West Bromwich Alb	1-2
Nettleham v Histon	9-0
Norwich C v Enfield T	4-0
Acle U v Cambridge C	0-1
Cambridge U v Stevenage	2-2*
Cambridge U won 4-2 on penalties	
Wymondham T v Billericay T	3-4
Chesham U v Crawley Wasps	0-3
Islington Bor v New London Lionesses	1-2*
(1-1 at the end of normal time)	
Ashford T (Middlesex) v Kent Football U	3-4
AFC Wimbledon v Godalming T	4-0
Whyteleafe v QPR Girls	1-2
Luton T v Oxford C	5-2
Newhaven v AFC Bournemouth	0-8
Buckland Ath v Marine Academy Plymouth	2-0
Eastleigh v Poole T	1-2
Keynsham T v Southampton Saints	6-0
Southampton FC Women v Larkhall Ath	4-1
Cheltenham T v Exeter C	1-0

FIRST ROUND

FC United of Manchester v Chester-le-Street T	0-5
Chorley v Stockport Co	1-2
Leeds U v Brighouse T	1-0
Norton & Stockton Ancients v Bolton W	0-1
Nettleham v Long Eaton U	2-3
Kidderminster H v Wolverhampton W	1-6
West Bromwich Alb v Leicester C Development	2-1
Cambridge C v Cambridge U	0-2
Norwich C v Billericay T	2-3*
(2-2 at the end of normal time)	
Luton T v Kent Football U	1-1*
Luton T won 3-1 on penalties	
New London Lionesses v AFC Wimbledon	3-3*
AFC Wimbledon won 4-3 on penalties	
Crawley Wasps v QPR Girls	6-0
Buckland Ath v Cheltenham T	2-0
Keynsham T v AFC Bournemouth	8-1
Poole T v Southampton FC Women	0-3

SECOND ROUND

Sheffield v Nottingham Forest	2-3
Long Eaton U v Hull C	0-5
Leeds U v Doncaster R Belles	4-3*
(3-3 at the end of normal time)	
Huddersfield T v Bradford C	7-1
Sunderland v Fylde	1-3
Chester-le-Street T v Stoke C	0-2
Middlesbrough v Stockport Co	1-0
Bolton W v West Bromwich Alb	2-2*
Bolton W won 5-4 on penalties	
Guiseley Vixens v Derby Co	0-2
Wolverhampton W v Blackburn R	0-4
Keynsham T v C&K Basildon	8-3
Loughborough Foxes v Gillingham	3-1*
(1-1 at the end of normal time)	
Billericay T v Luton T	3-1*
(1-1 at the end of normal time)	
Milton Keynes Dons v Southampton FC Women	4-0
AFC Wimbledon v Portsmouth	2-0
Oxford U v Cambridge U	4-0
Watford v Buckland Ath	1-0
Coventry U v Plymouth Argyle	2-1
Crawley Wasps v Chichester C	2-0
Cardiff C v Queens Park Rangers	4-0

THIRD ROUND

Cardiff C v Bolton W	2-0
Derby Co v Stoke C	1-2
Huddersfield T v Leeds U	4-1
Middlesbrough v Watford	2-7
Billericay T v Loughborough Foxes	3-4
Hull C v AFC Wimbledon	0-3
Coventry U v Crawley Wasps	1-2
Nottingham Forest v Milton Keynes Dons	0-1
Oxford U v Blackburn R	1-2
Keynsham T v Fylde	2-1

FOURTH ROUND

Loughborough Foxes v Sheffield U	0-2
Charlton Ath v Huddersfield T	3-3*
Huddersfield T won 5-4 on penalties	
Brighton & Hove Alb v Manchester U	0-2

West Ham U v Blackburn R	3-1
Stoke C v Aston Villa	1-2
Manchester C v Watford	3-0
Yeovil T v Birmingham C	1-3
AFC Wimbledon v Bristol C	0-3
Crystal Palace v Tottenham H	0-3
Millwall Lionesses v Lewes	1-0
Durham v Cardiff C	5-1
Everton v Chelsea	0-2
Crawley Wasps v Arsenal	0-4
Leicester C v London Bees	0-2
Reading v Keynsham T	13-0
Liverpool v Milton Keynes Dons	6-0

FIFTH ROUND

Liverpool v Millwall Lionesses	2-0
Bristol C v Durham	0-2
Reading v Birmingham C	2-1
Chelsea v Arsenal	3-0
Manchester U v London Bees	3-0
West Ham U v Huddersfield T	8-1
Aston Villa v Sheffield U	3-3*
Aston Villa won 5-3 on penalties	
Tottenham H v Manchester C	0-3

QUARTER-FINALS

Durham v Chelsea	0-1
Reading v Manchester U	3-2*
(0-0 at the end of normal time)	
Aston Villa v West Ham U	0-1
Manchester C v Liverpool	3-0

SEMI-FINALS

Manchester C v Chelsea	1-0
Reading v West Ham U	1-1*
West Ham U won 4-3 on penalties	

SSE WOMEN'S FA CUP FINAL 2019

Wembley, Saturday 4 May 2019

Manchester C (0) 3 *(Walsh 52, Stanway 81, Hemp 88)*

West Ham U (0) 0 43,264

Manchester C: Bardsley; McManus, Houghton, Beattie, Stokes, Scott, Walsh, Wullaert, Weir (Emslie 85), Parris (Hemp 82), Stanway.

West Ham U: Moorhouse; Simon (Kmita 89), Flaherty, Hendrix, Rafferty (Visalli 62), Percival, Lehmann, Longhurst, So-Hyun, Leon, Ross (Kiernan 65).

Referee: Abigail Byrne.

UEFA WOMEN'S CHAMPIONS LEAGUE 2018–19

▪*Denotes player sent off.*

QUALIFYING ROUND

GROUP 1 (NORTHERN IRELAND)

Ajax v Wexford Youths	4-1
Thor/KA v Linfield	2-0
Ajax v Linfield	2-0
Wexford Youths v Thor/KA	0-3
Linfield v Wexford Youths	2-3
Thor/KA v Ajax	0-0

Group 1	P	W	D	L	F	A	GD	Pts
Ajax	3	2	1	0	6	1	5	7
Thor/KA	3	2	1	0	5	0	5	7
Wexford Youths	3	1	0	2	4	9	–5	3
Linfield	3	0	0	3	2	7	–5	0

GROUP 2 (SLOVENIA)

Minsk v Olimpija Ljubljana	6-0
Somatio Barcelona v Slovan Bratislava	2-0
Minsk v Slovan Bratislava	1-0
Olimpija Ljubljana v Somatio Barcelona	0-6
Slovan Bratislava v Olimpija Ljubljana	1-0
Somatio Barcelona v Minsk	2-0

Group 2	P	W	D	L	F	A	GD	Pts
Somatio Barcelona	3	3	0	0	10	0	10	9
Minsk	3	2	0	1	7	2	5	6
Slovan Bratislava	3	1	0	2	1	3	–2	3
Olimpija Ljubljana	3	0	0	3	0	13	–13	0

GROUP 3 (SCOTLAND)

Glasgow C v Anderlecht	1-2
Gornik Leczna v Martve	12-0
Glasgow C v Martve	7-0
Anderlecht v Gornik Leczna	0-1
Martve v Anderlecht	0-10
Gornik Leczna v Glasgow C	0-2

Group 3	P	W	D	L	F	A	GD	Pts
Glasgow C	3	2	0	1	10	2	8	6
Anderlecht	3	2	0	1	12	2	10	6
Gornik Leczna	3	2	0	1	13	2	11	6
Martve	3	0	0	3	0	29	–29	0

GROUP 4 (HUNGARY)

MTK Hungaria v KFF Mitrovica	6-1
Slavia Prague v Atasehir	7-2
Slavia Prague v KFF Mitrovica	4-0
Atasehir v MTK Hungaria	2-2
KFF Mitrovica v Atasehir	1-6
MTK Hungaria v Slavia Prague	1-4

Group 4	P	W	D	L	F	A	GD	Pts
Slavia Prague	3	3	0	0	15	3	12	9
MTK Hungaria	3	1	1	1	9	7	2	4
Atasehir Belediyespor	3	1	1	1	10	10	0	4
Mitrovica	3	0	0	3	2	16	–14	0

GROUP 5 (MONTENEGRO)

FC Basel v Breznica	4-0
Spartak Subotica v Qiryat Gat	1-0
Qiryat Gat v FC Basel	0-3
Spartak Subotica v Breznica	4-0
Breznica v Qiryat Gat	4-4
FC Basel v Spartak Subotica	0-5

Group 5	P	W	D	L	F	A	GD	Pts
Spartak Subotica	3	3	0	0	10	0	10	9
FC Basel	3	2	0	1	7	5	2	6
Qiryat Gat	3	0	1	2	4	8	–4	1
Breznica Pljevlja	3	0	1	2	4	12	–8	1

GROUP 6 (UKRAINE)

Olimpia Cluj v Cardiff Met	3-2
Kharkiv v Birkirkara	8-0
Olimpia Cluj v Birkirkara	6-1
Cardiff Met v Kharkiv	2-5
Birkirkara v Cardiff Met	2-2
Kharkiv v Olimpia Cluj	3-1

Group 6	P	W	D	L	F	A	GD	Pts
Kharkiv	3	3	0	0	16	3	13	9
Olimpia Cluj	3	2	0	1	10	6	4	6
Cardiff Met	3	0	1	2	6	10	–4	1
Birkirkara	3	0	1	2	3	16	–13	1

GROUP 7 (LATVIA)

BIIK-Kazygurt v Akadimia Elpides Karditsas	2-1
Landhaus Wien v Rigas	2-1
Akadimia Elpides Karditsas v Landhaus Wien	3-1
BIIK-Kazygurt v Rigas	5-0
Rigas v Akadimia Elpides Karditsas	1-2
Landhaus Wien v BIIK-Kazygurt	0-2

Group 7	P	W	D	L	F	A	GD	Pts
BIIK-Kazygurt	3	3	0	0	9	1	8	9
Akadimia Elpides Karditsas	3	2	0	1	6	4	2	6
Landhaus Wien	3	1	0	2	3	6	–3	3
Rigas	3	0	0	3	2	9	–7	0

GROUP 8 (BOSNIA-HERZEGOVINA)

Parnu v Anenii Noi	2-0
Sarajevo v Vllaznia	5-0
Vllaznia v Parnu	3-1
Sarajevo v Anenii Noi	5-0
Anenii Noi v Vllaznia	1-4
Parnu v Sarajevo	1-2

Group 8	P	W	D	L	F	A	GD	Pts
Sarajevo	3	3	0	0	12	1	11	9
Vllaznia	3	2	0	1	7	7	0	6
Parnu	3	1	0	2	4	5	–1	3
Anenii Noi	3	0	0	3	1	11	–10	0

GROUP 9 (LITHUANIA)

NSA Sofia v EBS/Skala	3-0
Gintra Universitetas v Honka	1-1
Honka v NSA Sofia	5-0
Gintra Universitetas v EBS Skala	7-0
EBS/Skala v Honka	0-7
NSA Sofia v Gintra Universitetas	0-9

Group 9	P	W	D	L	F	A	GD	Pts
Gintra Universitetas	3	2	1	0	17	1	16	7
Honka	3	2	1	0	13	1	12	7
NSA Sofia	3	1	0	2	3	14	–11	3
EBS/Skala	3	0	0	3	0	17	–17	0

GROUP 10 (CROATIA)

Avaldsnes v Sporting Lisbon	3-2
Osijek v Dragon	13-0
Avaldsnes v Dragon	3-0
Sporting Lisbon v Osijek	3-0
Dragon v Sporting Lisbon	0-4
Osijek v Avaldsnes	2-2

Group 10	P	W	D	L	F	A	GD	Pts
Avaldsnes	3	2	1	0	8	4	4	7
Sporting Lisbon	3	2	0	1	9	3	6	6
Osijek	3	1	1	1	15	5	10	4
Dragon	3	0	0	3	0	20	–20	0

ROUND OF 32 FIRST LEG

BIIK-Kazygurt v Barcelona	3-1
Ryazan-VDV v Rosengard	0-1
Somatio Barcelona v Glasgow C	0-2
Sarajevo v Chelsea	0-5
Spartak Subotica v Bayern Munich	0-7
Kharkiv v Linkoping	1-6
Avaldsnes v Lyon	0-2
Honka v Zurich	0-1
Thor/KA v Wolfsburg	0-1
Ajax v Sparta Prague	2-0
Fiorentina v Fortuna	2-0
St Polten v Paris Saint-Germain	1-4
Juventus v Brondby	2-2
Gintra Universitetas v Slavia Prague	0-3
LSK Kvinner v Zvezda 2005	3-0
Atletico Madrid v Manchester C	1-1

ROUND OF 32 SECOND LEG

		(agg)
Linkoping v Kharkiv	4-0	10-1
Barcelona v BIIK-Kazygurt	3-0	4-3
Wolfsburg v Thor/KA	2-0	3-0
Brondby v Juventus	1-0	3-2
Sparta Prague v Ajax	1-2	1-4
Bayern Munich v Spartak Subotica	4-0	11-0
Rosengard v Ryazan-VDV	2-0	3-0
Fortuna v Fiorentina	0-2	0-4
Manchester C v Atletico Madrid	0-2	1-3
Chelsea v Sarajevo	6-0	11-0
Zvezda 2005 v LSK Kvinner	0-1	0-4
Slavia Prague v Gintra Universitetas	4-0	7-0
Lyon v Avaldsnes	5-0	7-0
Paris Saint-Germain v St Polten	2-0	6-1
Zurich v Honka	5-1	6-1
Glasgow C v Somatio Barcelona	0-1	2-1

ROUND OF 16 FIRST LEG

LSK Kvinner v Brondby	1-1
Linkoping v Paris	0-2
Barcelona v Glasgow C	5-0
Ajax v Lyon	0-4
Wolfsburg v Atletico Madrid	4-0
Zurich v Bayern Munich	0-2
Chelsea v Fiorentina	1-0
Rosengard v Slavia Prague	2-3

ROUND OF 16 SECOND LEG

		(agg)
Brondby v LSK Kvinner	0-2	1-3
Lyon v Ajax	9-0	13-0
Bayern Munich v Zurich	3-0	5-0
Fiorentina v Chelsea	0-6	0-7
Paris Saint-Germain v Linkoping	3-2	5-2
Atletico Madrid v Wolfsburg	0-6	0-10
Slavia Prague v Rosengard	0-0	3-2
Glasgow C v Barcelona	0-3	0-8

QUARTER-FINALS FIRST LEG

Slavia Prague v Bayern Munich	1-1
Barcelona v LSK Kvinner	3-0
Lyon v Wolfsburg	2-1
Chelsea v Paris Saint-Germain	2-0

QUARTER-FINALS SECOND LEG

		(agg)
Bayern Munich v Slavia Prague	5-1	6-2
LSK Kvinner v Barcelona	0-1	0-4
Wolfsburg v Lyon	2-4	3-6
Paris Saint-Germain v Chelsea	2-1	2-3

SEMI-FINALS FIRST LEG

Lyon v Chelsea	2-1
Bayern Munich v Barcelona	0-1

SEMI-FINALS SECOND LEG

		(agg)
Chelsea v Lyon	1-1	2-3
Barcelona v Bayern Munich	1-0	2-0

UEFA WOMEN'S CHAMPIONS LEAGUE FINAL 2019

Budapest, Saturday 18 May 2019

Lyon (4) 4 *(Marozsan 5, Hegerberg 14, 19, 30)*

Barcelona (0) 1 *(Oshoala 89)* 19,487

Lyon: Bouhaddi; Bronze, Renard, Bathy, Majri, Fishlock (Kumagai 72), Henry, Marozsan, van de Sanden (Cascarino 63), Hegerberg, Le Sommer (Bacha 82).
Barcelona: Panos; Torrejon, Pereira (Van de Gragt 81), Leon, Ouahabi, Losada, Bonmati (Alves 69), Alexia, Mariona, Martens, Duggan (Oshoala 69).
Referee: Anastasia Pustovoitova (Russia).

FIFA WOMEN'S WORLD CUP 2019

QUALIFYING – EUROPE

GROUP 1

Kazakhstan v Wales	0-1
England v Russia	6-0
Kazakhstan v Bosnia-Herzegovina	0-2
Russia v Wales	0-0
Wales v Kazakhstan	1-0
England v Bosnia-Herzegovina	4-0
Bosnia-Herzegovina v Wales	0-1
England v Kazakhstan	5-0
Bosnia-Herzegovina v Russia	1-6
England v Wales	0-0
Kazakhstan v Russia	0-3
Bosnia-Herzegovina v England	0-2
Wales v Bosnia-Herzegovina	1-0
Russia v England	1-3
Bosnia-Herzegovina v Kazakhstan	0-2
Wales v Russia	3-0
Russia v Kazakhstan	3-0
Wales v England	0-3
Russia v Bosnia and Herzegovina	3-0
Kazakhstan v England	0-6

Group 1 Table	P	W	D	L	F	A	GD	Pts
England	8	7	1	0	29	1	28	22
Wales	8	5	2	1	7	3	4	17
Russia	8	4	1	3	16	13	3	13
Bosnia-Herzegovina	8	1	0	7	3	19	–16	3
Kazakhstan	8	1	0	7	2	21	–19	3

GROUP 2

Albania v Switzerland	1-4
Poland v Belarus	4-1
Belarus v Albania	1-0
Switzerland v Poland	2-1
Belarus v Scotland	1-2
Scotland v Albania	5-0
Albania v Poland	1-4
Switzerland v Belarus	3-0
Switzerland v Albania	5-1
Switzerland v Scotland	1-0
Poland v Albania	1-1
Albania v Belarus	1-0
Scotland v Poland	3-0
Scotland v Belarus	2-1
Poland v Scotland	2-3
Belarus v Switzerland	0-5
Scotland v Switzerland	2-1
Belarus v Poland	1-4
Poland v Switzerland	0-0
Albania v Scotland	1-2

Group 2 Table	P	W	D	L	F	A	GD	Pts
Scotland	8	7	0	1	19	7	12	21
Switzerland	8	6	1	1	21	5	16	19
Poland	8	3	2	3	16	12	4	11
Albania	8	1	1	6	6	22	–16	4
Belarus	8	1	0	7	5	21	–16	3

GROUP 3

Norway v Northern Ireland	4-1
Norway v Slovakia	6-1
Northern Ireland v Republic of Ireland	0-2
Slovakia v Republic of Ireland	0-2
Netherlands v Norway	1-0
Slovakia v Netherlands	0-5
Slovakia v Northern Ireland	1-3
Netherlands v Republic of Ireland	0-0
Republic of Ireland v Slovakia	2-1
Netherlands v Northern Ireland	7-0
Republic of Ireland v Netherlands	0-2
Northern Ireland v Norway	0-3
Republic of Ireland v Norway	0-2
Northern Ireland v Netherlands	0-5
Norway v Republic of Ireland	1-0
Netherlands v Slovakia	1-0
Republic of Ireland v Northern Ireland	4-0
Slovakia v Norway	0-4
Norway v Netherlands	2-1
Northern Ireland v Slovakia	0-1

Group 3 Table	P	W	D	L	F	A	GD	Pts
Norway	8	7	0	1	22	4	18	21
Netherlands	8	6	1	1	22	2	20	19
Republic of Ireland	8	4	1	3	10	6	4	13
Northern Ireland	8	1	0	7	4	27	–23	3
Slovakia	8	1	0	7	4	23	–19	3

GROUP 4

Ukraine v Croatia	1-1
Hungary v Denmark	1-6
Croatia v Sweden	0-2
Hungary v Croatia	2-2
Sweden v Denmark	3-0
Match awarded 3-0 to Sweden after game was cancelled.	
Croatia v Denmark	0-4
Sweden v Hungary	5-0
Hungary v Ukraine	0-1
Croatia v Ukraine	0-3
Hungary v Sweden	1-4
Croatia v Hungary	1-3
Denmark v Ukraine	1-0
Sweden v Croatia	4-0
Ukraine v Denmark	1-5
Denmark v Hungary	5-1
Ukraine v Sweden	1-0
Sweden v Ukraine	3-0
Denmark v Croatia	1-1
Denmark v Sweden	0-1
Ukraine v Hungary	2-0

Group 4 Table	P	W	D	L	F	A	GD	Pts
Sweden	8	7	0	1	22	2	20	21
Denmark	8	5	1	2	22	8	14	16
Ukraine	8	4	1	3	9	10	–1	13
Hungary	8	1	1	6	8	26	–18	4
Croatia	8	0	3	5	5	20	–15	3

GROUP 5

Faroe Islands v Czech Republic	0-8
Germany v Slovenia	6-0
Iceland v Faroe Islands	8-0
Czech Republic v Germany	0-1
Germany v Iceland	2-3
Slovenia v Czech Republic	0-4
Germany v Faroe Islands	11-0
Czech Republic v Iceland	1-1
Slovenia v Faroe Islands	5-0
Slovenia v Iceland	0-2
Germany v Czech Republic	4-0
Slovenia v Germany	0-4
Faroe Islands v Iceland	0-5
Faroe Islands v Slovenia	0-4
Iceland v Slovenia	2-0
Czech Republic v Faroe Islands	4-1
Czech Republic v Slovenia	2-0
Iceland v Germany	0-2
Iceland v Czech Republic	1-1
Faroe Islands v Germany	0-8

Group 5 Table	P	W	D	L	F	A	GD	Pts
Germany	8	7	0	1	38	3	35	21
Iceland	8	5	2	1	22	6	16	17
Czech Republic	8	4	2	2	20	8	12	14
Slovenia	8	2	0	6	9	20	–11	6
Faroe Islands	8	0	0	8	1	53	–52	0

GROUP 6

Italy v Moldova	5-0
Romania v Italy	0-1
Belgium v Moldova	12-0
Belgium v Romania	3-2
Italy v Romania	3-0
Portugal v Belgium	0-1
Portugal v Moldova	8-0
Romania v Moldova	3-1
Portugal v Italy	0-1
Moldova v Italy	1-3
Belgium v Portugal	1-1
Italy v Belgium	2-1
Moldova v Romania	0-0
Italy v Portugal	3-0
Moldova v Belgium	0-7
Romania v Portugal	1-1
Moldova v Portugal	0-7
Romania v Belgium	0-1
Belgium v Italy	2-1
Portugal v Romania	5-1

Group 6 Table	P	W	D	L	F	A	GD	Pts
Italy	8	7	0	1	19	4	15	21
Belgium	8	6	1	1	28	6	22	19
Portugal	8	3	2	3	22	8	14	11
Romania	8	1	2	5	7	15	–8	5
Moldova	8	0	1	7	2	45	–43	1

GROUP 7

Serbia v Austria	0-4
Serbia v Israel	2-0
Finland v Serbia	1-0
Israel v Spain	0-6
Austria v Israel	2-0
Serbia v Spain	1-2
Finland v Israel	4-0
Spain v Austria	4-0
Israel v Finland	0-0
Austria v Serbia	1-1
Finland v Spain	0-2
Israel v Serbia	0-1
Austria v Spain	0-1
Spain v Israel	2-0
Finland v Austria	0-2
Serbia v Finland	0-2
Israel v Austria	0-6
Spain v Finland	5-1
Austria v Finland	4-1
Spain v Serbia	3-0

Group 7 Table	P	W	D	L	F	A	GD	Pts
Spain	8	8	0	0	25	2	23	24
Austria	8	5	1	2	19	7	12	16
Finland	8	3	1	4	9	13	–4	10
Serbia	8	2	1	5	5	13	–8	7
Israel	8	0	1	7	0	23	–23	1

FIFA WOMEN'S WORLD CUP 2019

Finals in France

GROUP A

France v Korea Republic	4-0
Norway v Nigeria	3-0
Nigeria v Korea Republic	2-0
France v Norway	2-1
Nigeria v France	0-1
Korea Republic v Norway	1-2

Group A Table	P	W	D	L	F	A	GD	Pts
France	3	3	0	0	7	1	6	9
Norway	3	2	0	1	6	3	3	6
Nigeria	3	1	0	2	2	4	–2	3
Korea Republic	3	0	0	3	1	8	–7	0

GROUP B

Germany v China PR	1-0
Spain v South Africa	3-1
Germany v Spain	1-0
South Africa v China PR	0-1
South Africa v Germany	0-4
China PR v Spain	0-0

Group B Table	P	W	D	L	F	A	GD	Pts
Germany	3	3	0	0	6	0	6	9
Spain	3	1	1	1	3	2	1	4
China PR	3	1	1	1	1	1	0	4
South Africa	3	0	0	3	1	8	–7	0

GROUP C

Australia v Italy	1-2
Brazil v Jamaica	3-0
Australia v Brazil	3-2
Jamaica v Italy	0-5
Jamaica v Australia	1-4
Italy v Brazil	0-1

Group C Table	P	W	D	L	F	A	GD	Pts
Italy	3	2	0	1	7	2	5	6
Australia	3	2	0	1	8	5	3	6
Brazil	3	2	0	1	6	3	3	6
Jamaica	3	0	0	3	1	12	–11	0

GROUP D

England v Scotland	2-1
Argentina v Japan	0-0
Japan v Scotland	2-1
England v Argentina	1-0
Japan v England	0-2
Scotland v Argentina	3-3

Group D Table	P	W	D	L	F	A	GD	Pts
England	3	3	0	0	5	1	4	9
Japan	3	1	1	1	2	3	–1	4
Argentina	3	0	2	1	3	4	–1	2
Scotland	3	0	1	2	5	7	–2	1

GROUP E

Canada v Cameroon	1-0
New Zealand v Netherlands	0-1
Netherlands v Cameroon	3-1
Canada v New Zealand	2-0
Netherlands v Canada	2-1
Cameroon v New Zealand	2-1

Group E Table	P	W	D	L	F	A	GD	Pts
Netherlands	3	3	0	0	6	2	4	9
Canada	3	2	0	1	4	2	2	6
Cameroon	3	1	0	2	3	5	–2	3
New Zealand	3	0	0	3	1	5	–4	0

GROUP F

Chile v Sweden	0-2
USA v Thailand	13-0
Sweden v Thailand	5-1
USA v Chile	3-0
Sweden v USA	0-2
Thailand v Chile	0-2

Group F Table	P	W	D	L	F	A	GD	Pts
USA	3	3	0	0	18	0	18	9
Sweden	3	2	0	1	7	3	4	6
Chile	3	1	0	2	2	5	–3	3
Thailand	3	0	0	3	1	20	–19	0

ROUND OF 16

Germany v Nigeria	3-0
Norway v Australia	1-1
(aet; Norway won 4-1 on penalties)	
England v Cameroon	3-0
France v Brazil	2-1
(aet)	
Spain v USA	1-2
Sweden v Canada	1-0
Italy v China PR	2-0
Netherlands v Japan	2-1

QUARTER-FINALS

Norway v England	0-3
France v USA	1-2
Italy v Netherlands	0-2
Germany v Sweden	1-2

SEMI-FINALS

England v USA	1-2
Netherlands v Sweden	1-0
(aet)	

THIRD PLACE PLAY-OFF

England v Sweden	1-2

FIFA WOMEN'S WORLD CUP FINAL 2019

Lyon, Sunday 7 July 2019

USA (0) 2 *(Rapinoe 61 (pen), Lavelle 69)*

Netherlands (0) 0 57,900

USA: Naeher; Mewis, Sauerbrunn, O'Hara (Krieger 46), Dahlkemper, Ertz, Morgan, Rapinoe (Press 79), Lavelle, Heath (Lloyd 87), Dunn.

Netherlands: van Veenendaal; van Lunteren, van der Gragt, Dekker (van de Sanden 73), Spitse, Miedema, van de Donk, Martens (Roord 70), Groenen, Bloodworth, Beerensteyn.

Referee: Stephanie Frappart (France).

ENGLAND WOMEN'S INTERNATIONALS 2018–19

▪ *Denotes player sent off.*

2019 FIFA WORLD CUP QUALIFYING GROUP 1

Newport, Friday 31 August 2018

Wales (0) 0

England (0) 3 *(Duggan 57, Scott 60, Parris 69)* 5053

England: Bardsley; Bronze, Houghton, Bright, Greenwood, Scott (Walsh 83), Nobbs, Parris, Kirby (Daly 88), Duggan, Taylor (Christiansen 78).

Pavlodar, Tuesday 4 September 2018

Kazakhstan (0) 0

England (2) 6 *(Mead 9 (pen), 82, Daly 35, Christiansen 54, Staniforth 66, Bronze 87)*

England: Earps (Telford 67); Blundell, Williamson, McManus, George, Staniforth, Walsh (Bronze 62), Christiansen, Bruton, Daly (Duggan 67), Mead.

WOMEN'S WORLD CUP 2019 FRANCE – GROUP D

Nice, Sunday 9 June 2019

England (2) 2 *(Parris 14 (pen), White 40)*

Scotland (0) 1 *(Emslie 79)* 13,188

England: Bardsley; Bronze, Houghton, Bright (McManus 55), Greenwood, Walsh, Scott, Parris, Kirby (Stanway 82), Mead (Carney 71), White.
Scotland: Alexander; Howard (Arthur 74), Corsie, Beattie, Docherty (Smith 55), Evans, Murray C (Arnott 87), Little, Weir, Emslie, Cuthbert.

Le Havre, Friday 14 June 2019

England (0) 1 *(Taylor 62)* **Argentina (0) 0** 20,294

England: Telford; Bronze, Houghton, McManus, Greenwood, Moore, Parris (Daly 87), Scott, Kirby (Carney 89), Mead (Stanway 81), Taylor.

Nice, Wednesday 19 June 2019

Japan (0) 0

England (1) 2 *(White 14, 84)* 14,319

England: Bardsley; Bronze, Houghton, Bright, Stokes, Scott, Walsh (Moore 72), Stanway (Carney 74), Daly, White, Duggan (Parris 83).

ROUND OF 16

Valenciennes, Sunday 23 June 2019

England (2) 3 *(Houghton 15, White 45, Greenwood 58)*

Cameroon (0) 0 20,148

England: Bardsley; Bronze, Houghton, Bright, Greenwood, Walsh, Scott (Staniforth 78), Kirby, Parris (Williamson 84), White (Taylor 64), Duggan.

QUARTER-FINALS

Le Havre, Thursday 27 June 2019

Norway (0) 0

England (2) 3 *(Scott 3, White 40, Bronze 57)* 21,111

England: Bardsley; Bronze, Walsh, Houghton, Bright, Parris (Daly 88), Scott, Kirby (Stanway 74), Duggan (Mead 54), Stokes, White.

SEMI-FINALS

Lyon, Tuesday 2 July 2019

England (1) 1 *(White 19)*

USA (2) 2 *(Press 10, Morgan 31)* 53,512

England: Telford; Bronze, Houghton, Bright▪, Walsh (Moore 71), Parris, Scott, Stokes, Daly (Stanway 89), White, Mead (Kirby 58).

3RD PLACE PLAY-OFF

Nice, Saturday 6 July 2019

England (1) 1 *(Kirby 31)*

Sweden (2) 2 *(Asllani 11, Jakobsson 22)* 20,316

England: Telford; Bronze, Greenwood, Houghton, Parris (Carney 74), Scott, Kirby, McManus (Daly 83), Moore, White, Mead (Taylor 50).

FRIENDLIES

Meadow Lane, Nottingham, Saturday 6 October 2018

England (1) 1 *(Kirby 2)* **Brazil (0) 0** 7864

England: Telford; Bronze, Houghton, Bright, Greenwood, Nobbs (Williams 70), Christiansen, Parris (Staniforth 75), Kirby (Lawley 75), Duggan (Mead 61), Daly.

Craven Cottage, London, Tuesday 9 October 2018

England (1) 1 *(Kirby 21)*

Australia (0) 1 *(Polkinghorne 84)*

England: Earps; Bronze, Houghton, McManus (Williamson 86), Greenwood, Nobbs, Walsh, Mead (Parris 63), Staniforth (Daly 63), Duggan, Kirby (Williams 76).

Vienna, Thursday 8 November 2018

Austria (0) 0

England (1) 3 *(Ubogagu 26, Stanway 72, Daly 81)*

England: Earps (Roebuck 79); Blundell, Williamson, McManus, George, Carney, Staniforth, Stanway, Lawley (Parris 65), Duggan (Kelly 79), Ubogagu (Daly 59).

Rotherham, Sunday 11 November 2018

England (0) 0 **Sweden (2) 2** *(Jacobsson 20, 32)* 9161

England: Telford; Bronze, Houghton, Bright, Greenwood, Christiansen (Stanway 73), Nobbs, Scott (Staniforth 83), Parris, Daly (Lawley 73), Mead (Duggan 46).

Manchester City Academy Stadium, Friday 5 April 2019

England (0) 0 **Canada (0) 1** *(Sinclair 81)*

England: Bardsley; Daly (Scott 73), Houghton, McManus, Stokes, Bronze, Walsh, Parris, Taylor (White 73), Duggan (Stanway 84), Carney (Mead 64).

Swindon, Tuesday 9 April 2019

England (0) 2 *(Mead 36, White 46)*

Spain (0) 1 *(Bonmati 67)*

England: Roebuck (Earps 46); Daly (Bonner 68), Bright, Williamson, Greenwood, Moore (Staniforth 54), Scott, Stanway (Walsh 68), Mead (Parris 84), White, Duggan (Ubogagu 54).

Walsall, Saturday 25 May 2019

England (1) 2 *(Parris 45, Scott 59)* **Denmark (0) 0**

England: Bardsley; Daly, Williamson, Bright, Stokes, Scott, Moore, Stanway (Kirby 61), Parris (Carney 61), White, Mead (Staniforth 80).

Brighton, Saturday 1 June 2019

England (0) 0 **New Zealand (0) 1** *(Gregorius 50)* 20,076

England: Telford; Bronze, Houghton, McManus, Greenwood, Staniforth (Scott 68), Walsh (Stanway 89), Parris (Mead 68), Kirby, Duggan (Carney 54), Taylor (White 75).

SHEBELIEVES CUP 2019

Philadelphia, Wednesday 27 February 2019

England (0) 2 *(White 49, Mead 75)*

Brazil (1) 1 *(Silva 16 (pen))* 5954

England: Telford; Bronze, Houghton, McManus, Greenwood, Walsh, Kirby (Staniforth 87), Christiansen (Daly 66), Parris, White (Duggan 76), Carney (Mead 66).

Nashville, Saturday 2 March 2019

USA (1) 2 *(Rapinoe 33, Heath 67)*

England (1) 2 *(Houghton 36, Parris 52)* 22,125

England: Bardsley; Daly, Houghton, McManus, Stokes, Parris (Taylor 88), Bronze, Walsh, Duggan, Kirby (Mead 73), White (Stanway 80).

Tampa, Tuesday 5 March 2019

Japan (0) 0

England (3) 2 *(Staniforth 12, Carney 23, Mead 30)* 8580

England: Telford; Bronze, Houghton, Williamson, Greenwood, Walsh (Bonner 60), Mead (Ubogagu 66), Staniforth (Kirby 81), Christiansen (Stanway 39), Carney (Duggan 66), Taylor (White 51).
England win the SheBelievesCup.

ENGLAND WOMEN'S INTERNATIONAL MATCHES 1972–2019

Note: In the results that follow, WC = World Cup; EC = European (UEFA) Championships; M = Mundialito; CC = Cyprus Cup; AC = Algarve Cup. * = After extra time. Games were organised by the Women's Football Association from 1971 to 1992 and the Football Association from 1993 to date. **Bold type** indicates matches played in season 2018–19.

v ARGENTINA

WC2007	17 Sept	Chengdu	6-1
WC2019	**14 June**	**Le Havre**	**1-0**

v AUSTRALIA

2003	3 Sept	Burnley	1-0
CC2015	6 Mar	Nicosia	3-0
2015	27 Oct	Yongchuan	1-0
2018	**9 Oct**	**London**	**1-1**

v AUSTRIA

WC2005	1 Sept	Amstetten	4-1
WC2006	20 Apr	Gillingham	4-0
WC2010	25 Mar	Shepherd's Bush	3-0
WC2010	21 Aug	Krems	4-0
2017	10 Apr	Milton Keynes	3-0
2018	**8 Nov**	**Vienna**	**3-0**

v BELARUS

EC2007	27 Oct	Walsall	4-0
EC2008	8 May	Minsk	6-1
WC2013	21 Sept	Bournemouth	6-0
WC2014	14 June	Minsk	3-0

v BELGIUM

1978	31 Oct	Southampton	3-0
1980	1 May	Ostende	1-2
M1984	20 Aug	Jesolo	1-1
M1984	25 Aug	Caorle	2-1
1989	14 May	Epinal	2-0
EC1990	17 Mar	Ypres	3-0
EC1990	7 Apr	Sheffield	1-0
EC1993	6 Nov	Koksijde	3-0
EC1994	13 Mar	Nottingham	6-0
EC2016	8 Apr	Rotherham	1-1
EC2016	20 Sept	Leuven	2-0

v BOSNIA-HERZEGOVINA

EC2015	29 Nov	Bristol	1-0
EC2016	12 Apr	Zenica	1-0
WC2017	24 Nov	Walsall	4-0
WC2018	10 Apr	Zenica	2-0

v BRAZIL

2018	**6 Oct**	**Nottingham**	**1-0**
2019	**27 Feb**	**Philadelphia**	**2-1**

v CAMEROON

WC2019	**23 June**	**Valenciennes**	**3-0**

v CANADA

WC1995	6 June	Helsingborg	3-2
2003	19 May	Montreal	0-4
2003	22 May	Ottawa	0-4
CC2009	12 Mar	Nicosia	3-1
CC2010	27 Feb	Nicosia	0-1
CC2011	7 Mar	Nicosia	0-2
CC2013	13 Mar	Nicosia	1-0
2013	7 Apr	Rotherham	1-0
CC2014	10 Mar	Nicosia	2-0
CC2015	11 Mar	Larnaca	1-0
2015	29 May	Hamilton	0-1
WC2015	27 June	Vancouver	2-1
2019	**5 Apr**	**Manchester**	**0-1**

v CHINA PR

AC2005	15 Mar	Guia	0-0*
2007	26 Jan	Guangzhou	0-2
2015	9 Apr	Manchester	2-1
2015	23 Oct	Yongchuan	1-2

v COLOMBIA

WC2015	17 June	Montreal	2-1

v CROATIA

EC1995	19 Nov	Charlton	5-0
EC1996	18 Apr	Osijek	2-0
EC2012	31 Mar	Vrbovec	6-0
EC2012	19 Sept	Walsall	3-0

v CZECH REPUBLIC

2005	26 May	Walsall	4-1
EC2008	20 Mar	Doncaster	0-0
EC2008	28 Sept	Prague	5-1

v DENMARK

1979	19 May	Hvidovre	1-3
1979	13 Sept	Hull	2-2
1981	9 Sept	Tokyo	0-1
EC1984	8 Apr	Crewe	2-1
EC1984	28 Apr	Hjorring	1-0
M1985	19 Aug	Caorle	0-1
EC1987	8 Nov	Blackburn	2-1
EC1988	8 May	Herning	0-2
1991	28 June	Nordby	0-0
1991	30 June	Nordby	3-3
1999	22 Aug	Odense	1-0
2001	23 Aug	Northampton	0-3
2004	19 Feb	Portsmouth	2-0
EC2005	8 June	Blackburn	1-2
2009	22 July	Swindon	1-0
2017	1 July	Copenhagen	2-1
2019	**25 May**	**Walsall**	**2-0**

v ESTONIA

2015	21 Sept	Tallinn	8-0
EC2016	15 Sept	Nottingham	5-0

v FINLAND

1979	19 July	Sorrento	3-1
EC1987	25 Oct	Kirkkonummi	2-1
EC1988	4 Sept	Millwall	1-1
EC1989	1 Oct	Brentford	0-0
EC1990	29 Sept	Tampere	0-0
2000	28 Sept	Leyton	2-1
EC2005	5 June	Manchester	3-2
2009	9 Feb	Larnaca	2-2
2009	11 Feb	Larnaca	4-1
EC2009	3 Sept	Turku	3-2
CC2012	28 Feb	Nicosia	3-1
CC2014	7 Mar	Larnaca	3-0
CC2015	4 Mar	Larnaca	3-1

v FRANCE

1973	22 Apr	Brion	3-0
1974	7 Nov	Wimbledon	2-0
1977	26 Feb	Longjumeau	0-0
M1988	22 July	Riva del Garda	1-1
1998	15 Feb	Alencon	2-3
1999	15 Sept	Yeovil	0-1
2000	16 Aug	Marseilles	0-1
WC2002	17 Oct	Crystal Palace	0-1
WC2002	16 Nov	St Etienne	0-1
WC2006	26 Mar	Blackburn	0-0
WC2006	30 Sept	Rennes	1-1
CC2009	7 Mar	Paralimni	2-2
WC2011	9 July	Leverkusen	1-1*
CC2012	4 Mar	Paralimni	0-3
2012	20 Oct	Paris	2-2
EC2013	18 July	Linkoping	0-3
CC2014	12 Mar	Nicosia	0-2
WC2015	9 June	Moncton	0-1
2016	9 Mar	Boca Raton	0-0
2016	21 Oct	Doncaster	0-0
2017	1 Mar	Pennsylvania	1-2
2017	30 July	Deventer	1-0
2017	20 Oct	Valenciennes	0-1
2018	1 Mar	Columbus	4-1

v GERMANY

EC1990	25 Nov	High Wycombe	1-4
EC1990	16 Dec	Bochum	0-2
EC1994	11 Dec	Watford	1-4
EC1995	23 Feb	Bochum	1-2
WC1995	13 June	Vasteras	0-3
1997	27 Feb	Preston	4-6
WC1997	25 Sept	Dessau	0-3

wc1998	8 Mar	Millwall	0-1
EC2001	30 June	Jena	0-3
wc2001	27 Sept	Kassel	1-3
wc2002	19 May	Crystal Palace	0-1
2003	11 Sept	Darmstadt	0-4
2006	25 Oct	Aalen	1-5
2007	30 Jan	Guangzhou	0-0
wc2007	14 Sept	Shanghai	0-0
2008	17 July	Unterhaching	0-3
EC2009	10 Sept	Helsinki	2-6
2014	23 Nov	Wembley	0-3
wc2015	4 July	Vancouver	1-0*
2015	26 Nov	Duisburg	0-0
2016	6 Mar	Nashville	1-2
2017	7 Mar	Washington	0-1
2018	4 Mar	New Jersey	2-2

v HUNGARY

wc2005	27 Oct	Tapolca	13-0
wc2006	11 May	Southampton	2-0

v ICELAND

EC1992	17 May	Yeovil	4-0
EC1992	19 July	Kopavogur	2-1
EC1994	8 Oct	Reykjavik	2-1
EC1994	30 Oct	Brighton	2-1
wc2002	16 Sept	Reykjavik	2-2
wc2002	22 Sept	Birmingham	1-0
2004	14 May	Peterborough	1-0
2006	9 Mar	Norwich	1-0
2007	17 May	Southend	4-0
2009	16 July	Colchester	0-2

v ITALY

1976	2 June	Rome	0-2
1976	4 June	Cesena	1-2
1977	15 Nov	Wimbledon	1-0
1979	25 July	Naples	1-3
1982	11 June	Pescara	0-2
M1984	24 Aug	Jesolo	1-1
M1985	20 Aug	Caorle	1-1
M1985	25 Aug	Caorle	3-2
EC1987	13 June	Drammen	1-2
M1988	30 July	Arco di Trento	2-1
1989	1 Nov	High Wycombe	1-1
1990	18 Aug	Wembley	1-4
EC1992	17 Oct	Solofra	2-3
EC1992	7 Nov	Rotherham	0-3
1995	25 Jan	Florence	1-1
EC1995	1 Nov	Sunderland	1-1
EC1996	16 Mar	Cosenza	1-2
1997	23 Apr	Turin	0-2
1998	21 Apr	West Bromwich	1-2
1999	26 May	Bologna	1-4
2003	25 Feb	Viareggio	0-1
2005	17 Feb	Milton Keynes	4-1
EC2009	25 Aug	Lahti	1-2
CC2010	3 Mar	Nicosia	3-2
CC2011	2 Mar	Larnaca	2-0
CC2012	6 Mar	Paralimni	1-3
CC2013	6 Mar	Nicosia	4-2
EC2014	5 Mar	Larnaca	2-0
2017	7 Apr	Port Vale	1-1

v JAPAN

1981	6 Sept	Kobe	4-0
wc2007	11 Sept	Shanghai	2-2
wc2011	5 July	Augsburg	2-0
2013	26 June	Burton	1-1
wc2015	1 July	Edmonton	1-2
2019	**5 Mar**	**Tampa**	**3-0**
wc2019	**19 June**	**Nice**	**2-0**

v KAZAKHSTAN

wc2017	28 Nov	Colchester	5-0
wc2018	**4 Sept**	**Pavlodar**	**6-0**

v KOREA REPUBLIC

2010	19 Oct	Suwon	0-0
CC2011	9 Mar	Larnaca	2-0

v MALTA

wc2009	25 Oct	Blackpool	8-0
wc2010	20 May	Ta'Qali	6-0

v MEXICO

AC2005	13 Mar	Lagos	5-0
wc2011	27 June	Wolfsburg	1-1
wc2015	13 June	Moncton	2-1

v MONTENEGRO

wc2014	5 Apr	Brighton	9-0
wc2014	17 Sept	Petrovac	10-0

v NETHERLANDS

1973	9 Nov	Reading	1-0
1974	31 May	Groningen	0-3
1976	2 May	Blackpool	2-0
1978	30 Sept	Vlissingen	1-3
1989	13 May	Epinal	0-0
wc1997	30 Oct	West Ham	1-0
wc1998	23 May	Waalwijk	1-2
wc2001	4 Nov	Grimsby	0-0
wc2002	23 Mar	Den Haag	4-1
2004	18 Sept	Heerhugowaard	2-1
2004	22 Sept	Tuitjenhoorn	1-0
wc2005	17 Nov	Zwolle	1-0
wc2006	31 Aug	Charlton	4-0
2007	14 Mar	Swindon	0-1
EC2009	6 Sept	Tampere	2-1*
EC2011	27 Oct	Zwolle	0-0
EC2012	17 June	Salford	1-0
CC2015	9 Mar	Nicosia	1-1
2016	29 Nov	Tilburg	1-0
2017	3 Aug	Enschede	0-3

v NEW ZEALAND

2010	21 Oct	Suwon	0-0
wc2011	1 July	Dresden	2-1
CC2013	11 Mar	Larnaca	3-1
2019	**1 June**	**Brighton**	**0-1**

v NIGERIA

wc1995	10 June	Karlstad	3-2
2002	23 July	Norwich	0-1
2004	22 Apr	Reading	0-3

v NORTHERN IRELAND

1973	7 Sept	Bath	5-1
EC1982	19 Sept	Crewe	7-1
EC1983	14 May	Belfast	4-0
EC1985	25 May	Antrim	8-1
EC1986	16 Mar	Blackburn	10-0
1987	11 Apr	Leeds	6-0
AC2005	9 Mar	Paderne	4-0
EC2007	13 May	Gillingham	4-0
EC2008	6 Mar	Lurgan	2-0

v NORWAY

1981	25 Oct	Cambridge	0-3
EC1988	21 Aug	Kleppe	0-2
EC1988	18 Sept	Blackburn	1-3
EC1990	27 May	Kleppe	0-2
EC1990	2 Sept	Old Trafford	0-0
wc1995	8 June	Karlstad	3-2
1997	8 June	Lillestrom	0-4
wc1998	14 May	Oldham	1-2
wc1998	15 Aug	Lillestrom	0-2
EC2000	7 Mar	Norwich	0-3
EC2000	4 June	Moss	0-8
AC2002	1 Mar	Albufeira	1-3
2005	6 May	Barnsley	1-0
2008	14 Feb	Larnaca	2-1
2009	23 Apr	Shrewsbury	3-0
2014	17 Jan	La Manga	1-1
wc2015	22 June	Ottawa	2-1
2017	22 Jan	La Manga	0-1
wc2019	**27 June**	**Le Havre**	**3-0**

v PORTUGAL

EC1996	11 Feb	Benavente	5-0
EC1996	19 May	Brentford	3-0
EC2000	20 Feb	Barnsley	2-0
EC2000	22 Apr	Sacavem	2-2
wc2001	24 Nov	Gafanha da Nazare	1-1
wc2002	24 Feb	Portsmouth	3-0
AC2005	11 Mar	Faro	4-0
2017	27 July	Tilburg	2-1

v REPUBLIC OF IRELAND

1978	2 May	Exeter	6-1
1981	2 May	Dublin	5-0
EC1982	7 Nov	Dublin	1-0
EC1983	11 Sept	Reading	6-0
EC1985	22 Sept	Cork	6-0
EC1986	27 Apr	Reading	4-0
1987	29 Mar	Dublin	1-0

v ROMANIA

EC1998	12 Sept	Campina	4-1
EC1998	11 Oct	High Wycombe	2-1

v RUSSIA

EC2001	24 June	Jena	1-1
2003	21 Oct	Moscow	2-2
2004	19 Aug	Bristol	1-2
2007	8 Mar	Milton Keynes	6-0
EC2009	28 Aug	Helsinki	3-2
EC2013	15 July	Linkoping	1-1
wc2017	19 Sept	Tranmere	6-0
wc2018	8 June	Moscow	3-1

v SCOTLAND

1972	18 Nov	Greenock	3-2
1973	23 June	Nuneaton	8-0
1976	23 May	Enfield	5-1
1977	29 May	Dundee	1-2
EC1982	3 Oct	Dumbarton	4-0
EC1983	22 May	Leeds	2-0
EC1985	17 Mar	Preston	4-0
EC1986	12 Oct	Kirkcaldy	3-1
1989	30 Apr	Kirkcaldy	3-0
1990	6 May	Paisley	4-0
1990	12 May	Wembley	4-0
1991	20 Apr	High Wycombe	5-0
EC1992	17 Apr	Walsall	1-0
EC1992	23 Aug	Perth	2-0
1997	9 Mar	Sheffield	6-0
1997	23 Aug	Livingston	4-0
2001	27 May	Bolton	1-0
AC2002	7 Mar	Quarteira	4-1
2003	13 Nov	Preston	5-0
2005	21 Apr	Tranmere	2-1
2007	11 Mar	High Wycombe	1-0
cc2009	10 Mar	Larnaca	3-0
cc2011	4 Mar	Nicosia	0-2
cc2013	8 Mar	Larnaca	4-4
EC2017	19 July	Utrecht	6-0
wc2019	**9 June**	**Nice**	**2-1**

v SERBIA

EC2011	17 Sept	Belgrade	2-2
EC2011	23 Nov	Doncaster	2-0
EC2016	4 June	Wycombe	7-0
EC2016	7 June	Stara Pazova	7-0

v SLOVENIA

EC1993	25 Sept	Ljubljana	10-0
EC1994	17 Apr	Brentford	10-0
EC2011	22 Sept	Swindon	4-0
EC2012	21 June	Velenje	4-0

v SOUTH AFRICA

cc2009	5 Mar	Larnaca	6-0
cc2010	24 Feb	Larnaca	1-0

v SPAIN

EC1993	19 Dec	Osuna	0-0
EC1994	20 Feb	Bradford	0-0
EC1996	8 Sept	Montilla	1-2
EC1996	29 Sept	Tranmere	1-1
2001	22 Mar	Luton	4-2
EC2007	25 Nov	Shrewsbury	1-0
EC2008	2 Oct	Zamora	2-2
wc2010	1 Apr	Millwall	1-0
wc2010	19 June	Aranda de Duero	2-2
EC2013	12 July	Linkoping	2-3
2016	25 Oct	Guadalajara	2-1
EC2017	23 July	Breda	2-0
2019	**9 Apr**	**Swindon**	**2-1**

v SWEDEN

1975	15 June	Gothenburg	0-2
1975	7 Sept	Wimbledon	1-3
1979	27 July	Scafati	0-0*
1980	17 Sept	Leicester	1-1
1982	26 May	Kinna	1-1
1983	30 Oct	Charlton	2-2
EC1984	12 May	Gothenburg	0-1
EC1984	27 May	Luton	1-0
EC1987	11 June	Moss	2-3*
1989	23 May	Wembley	0-2
1995	13 May	Halmstad	0-4
1998	26 July	Dagenham	0-1
EC2001	27 June	Jena	0-4
2002	25 Jan	La Manga	0-5
AC2002	5 Mar	Lagos	3-6
EC2005	11 June	Blackburn	0-1
2006	7 Feb	Larnaca	0-0
2006	9 Feb	Achna	1-1
2008	12 Feb	Larnaca	0-2
EC2009	31 Aug	Turku	1-1
2011	17 May	Oxford	2-0
2013	4 July	Ljungskile	1-4
2014	3 Aug	Hartlepool	4-0
2017	24 Jan	La Manga	0-0
2018	**11 Nov**	**Rotherham**	**0-2**
wc2019	**6 July**	**Nice**	**1-2**

v SWITZERLAND

1975	19 Apr	Basel	3-1
1977	28 Apr	Hull	9-1
1979	23 July	Sorrento	2-0
EC1999	16 Oct	Zofingen	3-0
EC2000	13 May	Bristol	1-0
cc2010	1 Mar	Nicosia	2-2
wc2010	12 Sept	Shrewsbury	2-0
wc2010	16 Sept	Wohlen	3-2
cc2012	1 Mar	Larnaca	1-0
2017	10 June	Biel	4-0

v TURKEY

wc2009	26 Nov	Izmir	3-0
wc2010	29 July	Walsall	3-0
wc2013	26 Sept	Portsmouth	8-0
wc2013	31 Oct	Adana	4-0

v UKRAINE

EC2000	30 Oct	Kiev	2-1
EC2000	28 Nov	Leyton	2-0
wc2014	8 May	Shrewsbury	4-0
wc2014	19 June	Lviv	2-1

v USA

M1985	23 Aug	Caorle	3-1
M1988	27 July	Riva del Garda	2-0
1990	9 Aug	Blaine	0-3
1991	25 May	Hirson	1-3
1997	9 May	San Jose	0-5
1997	11 May	Portland	0-6
AC2002	3 Mar	Ferreiras	0-2
2003	17 May	Birmingham (Alabama)	0-6
2007	28 Jan	Guangzhou	1-1
wc2007	22 Sept	Tianjin	0-3
2011	2 Apr	Leyton	2-1
2015	13 Feb	Milton Keynes	0-1
2016	4 Mar	Tampa	0-1
2017	4 Mar	New Jersey	1-0
2018	8 Mar	Orlando	0-1
2019	**2 Mar**	**Nashville**	**2-2**
wc2019	**2 July**	**Lyon**	**1-2**

v USSR

1990	11 Aug	Blaine	1-1
1991	20 July	Dmitrov	2-1
1991	21 July	Kashira	2-0
1991	7 Sept	Southampton	2-0
1991	8 Sept	Brighton	1-3

v WALES

1974	17 Mar	Slough	5-0
1976	22 May	Bedford	4-0
1976	17 Oct	Ebbw Vale	2-1
1977	18 Sept	Warminster	5-0
1980	1 June	Warminster	6-1
1985	17 Aug	Ramsey (Isle of Man)	6-0
wc2013	26 Oct	Millwall	2-0
wc2014	21 Aug	Cardiff	4-0
wc2018	6 Apr	Southampton	0-0
wc2018	**31 Aug**	**Newport**	**3-0**

v WEST GERMANY

M1984	22 Aug	Jesolo	0-2
1990	5 Aug	Blaine	1-3

OTHER MATCHES

v ITALY B

1984	27 Aug	Monfalcone	3-1
M1988	20 July	Riva del Garda	3-0

v USA B

1990	7 Aug	Blaine	1-0

WELSH FOOTBALL 2018–19

JD WELSH PREMIER LEAGUE 2018–19

			Home					Away					Total						
		P	*W*	*D*	*L*	*F*	*A*	*W*	*D*	*L*	*F*	*A*	*W*	*D*	*L*	*F*	*A*	*GD*	*Pts*
1	The New Saints	32	12	3	1	57	8	11	2	3	42	8	23	5	4	99	16	83	74
2	Connah's Quay Nomads	32	12	2	2	43	14	7	3	6	33	19	19	5	8	76	33	43	62
3	Barry Town U	32	11	1	4	31	22	6	4	6	23	29	17	5	10	54	51	3	56
4	Caernarfon T	32	9	3	4	26	17	4	4	8	19	30	13	7	12	45	47	−2	46
5	Newtown	32	9	4	3	33	21	4	3	9	20	35	13	7	12	53	56	−3	46
6	Bala T	32	8	2	6	27	33	5	3	8	28	30	13	5	14	55	63	−8	44
7	Cardiff Metropolitan Univ	32	11	1	4	32	13	5	2	9	21	27	16	3	13	53	40	13	51
8	Aberystwyth T	32	7	4	5	20	24	6	1	9	24	37	13	5	14	44	61	−17	44
9	Carmarthen T*	32	9	2	5	33	22	3	4	9	16	31	12	6	14	49	53	4	39
10	Cefn Druids	32	5	6	5	25	24	5	3	8	18	25	10	9	13	43	49	6	39
11	Llandudno	32	3	3	10	16	33	2	4	10	17	32	5	7	20	33	65	32	22
12	Llanelli T	32	2	3	11	14	47	2	1	13	17	54	4	4	24	31	101	70	16

Top 6 teams split after 22 games.

PREVIOUS WELSH LEAGUE WINNERS

1993	Cwmbran Town	2000	TNS	2007	TNS	2014	The New Saints
1994	Bangor City	2001	Barry Town	2008	Llanelli	2015	The New Saints
1995	Bangor City	2002	Barry Town	2009	Rhyl	2016	The New Saints
1996	Barry Town	2003	Barry Town	2010	The New Saints	2017	The New Saints
1997	Barry Town	2004	Rhyl	2011	Bangor C	2018	The New Saints
1998	Barry Town	2005	TNS	2012	The New Saints	2019	The New Saints
1999	Barry Town	2006	TNS	2013	The New Saints		

NATHANIEL CAR SALES WELSH LEAGUE 2018–19

			Home					Away					Total						
		P	*W*	*D*	*L*	*F*	*A*	*W*	*D*	*L*	*F*	*A*	*W*	*D*	*L*	*F*	*A*	*GD*	*Pts*
1	Penybont	30	13	2	0	40	13	12	3	0	41	9	25	5	0	81	22	59	80
2	Cambrian & Clydach Vale	30	9	3	3	29	16	9	3	3	29	16	18	6	6	58	32	26	60
3	Haverfordwest Co	30	11	2	2	41	13	5	4	6	28	21	16	6	8	69	34	35	54
4	Afan Lido	30	5	4	6	27	30	10	2	3	41	29	15	6	9	68	59	9	51
5	Goytre U	30	7	4	4	25	20	8	1	6	27	19	15	5	10	52	39	13	50
6	Cwmamman U	30	8	2	5	31	34	6	6	3	24	21	14	8	8	55	55	0	50
7	Llantwit Major	30	7	3	5	21	18	7	3	5	25	19	14	6	10	46	37	9	48
8	Briton Ferry Llansawel	30	5	5	5	23	23	7	1	7	21	27	12	6	12	44	50	−6	42
9	Ammanford	30	7	3	5	34	25	3	3	9	17	32	10	6	14	51	57	−6	36
10	Cwmbran Celtic	30	7	2	6	35	28	3	4	8	14	29	10	6	14	49	57	−8	36
11	Pontypridd T	30	5	3	7	22	26	4	3	8	30	40	9	6	15	52	66	−14	33
12	Undy Ath	30	5	2	8	22	31	3	5	7	29	33	8	7	15	51	64	−13	31
13	Port Talbot T	30	5	4	6	25	25	1	7	7	14	25	6	11	13	39	50	−11	29
14	Taff's Well	30	2	3	10	12	32	5	1	9	21	30	7	4	19	33	62	−29	25
15	Goytre	30	4	4	7	19	30	2	2	11	20	35	6	6	18	39	65	−26	24
16	Ton Pentre	30	2	3	10	20	35	4	1	10	18	41	6	4	20	38	76	−38	22

HUWS GRAY CYMRU ALLIANCE LEAGUE 2018–19

			Home					Away					Total						
		P	*W*	*D*	*L*	*F*	*A*	*W*	*D*	*L*	*F*	*A*	*W*	*D*	*L*	*F*	*A*	*GD*	*Pts*
1	Airbus UK Broughton	30	13	1	1	41	10	11	3	1	34	10	24	4	2	75	20	55	76
2	Flint Town U	30	10	5	0	31	11	7	2	6	21	20	17	7	6	52	31	21	58
3	Porthmadog	30	9	2	4	36	17	8	4	3	24	15	17	6	7	60	32	28	57
4	Bangor C	30	8	1	6	39	27	8	2	5	29	21	16	3	11	68	48	20	51
5	Rhyl	30	10	0	5	31	22	6	3	6	24	22	16	3	11	55	44	11	51
6	Guilsfield	30	6	4	5	20	15	7	2	6	23	30	13	6	11	43	45	−2	45
7	Ruthin T	30	8	1	6	27	21	5	3	7	19	26	13	4	13	46	47	−1	43
8	Buckley T	30	6	2	7	24	23	6	4	5	27	27	12	6	12	51	50	1	42
9	Prestatyn T	30	7	4	4	33	23	4	2	9	19	26	11	6	13	52	49	3	39
10	Gresford Ath	30	4	8	3	22	18	6	1	8	20	28	10	9	11	42	46	−4	39
11	Conwy Bor	30	5	6	4	24	18	4	3	8	22	24	9	9	12	46	42	4	36
12	Llanrhaeadr YM	30	6	1	8	16	26	4	1	10	18	45	10	2	18	34	71	−37	32
13	Penrhyncoch	30	4	3	8	14	18	3	6	6	21	26	7	9	14	35	44	−9	30
14	Holywell T	30	5	2	8	19	26	3	4	8	19	32	8	6	16	38	58	−20	30
15	Denbigh T	30	5	1	9	24	31	4	1	10	13	34	9	2	19	37	65	−28	29
16	Holyhead Hotspur	30	3	2	10	19	37	2	2	11	10	34	5	4	21	29	71	−42	19

JD WELSH FA CUP 2018–19

**After extra time.*

QUALIFYING ROUND 1

Penycae v Offa Athletic	6-2
Newport Corinthians v Cardiff Draconians	1-4
Rhydymwyn v Llangollen Town	4-3*
Aber Valley v Canton Liberal	3-2
Rhosllanerchrugog v Rhos Aelwyd	0-4
Llansantffraid Village v Builth Wells	1-3
Ynysddu Welfare v Machen	2-1
Castell Alun Colts v Llay Welfare	0-5
Abermule v Rhayader Town	3-2
Chepstow Town v Fairwater	6-0
Cefn Mawr Rangers v Coedpoeth United	1-5
Montgomery Town v Machynlleth	2-3
Mynydd Isa Spartans v Brymbo	1-4
Four Crosses v Waterloo Rovers	5-0
Brecon Corries v Clwb Cymric	2-0
Plas Madoc v New Brighton Villa	1-2
Borth United v Presteigne St Andrews	2-0
Merthyr Saints v Treowen Stars	2-2*
Merthyr Saints won 6-5 on penalties.	
Rogerstone v Sully Sports	1-5
Dolgellau Athletic Amateur v Churchstoke	5-2
Cornelly United v Trebanog	3-2
Wattsville v Cardiff Corinthians	6-1
Prestatyn Sports v Pentraeth	2-0
Baglan Dragons v Penrhiwceiber Constitutional Athletic	1-2
Newport Civil Service v Pontlottyn	9-1
Amlwch Town v Llandudno Amateurs	0-6
Pencoed Athletic Amateur v AFC Porth	3-0
Trethomas Bluebirds v St Albans	3-1*
Bodedern v Aberffraw	1-2
Porthcawl Town Athletic v Trefelin BGC	0-4
Blaenrhondda v Penrhiwceiber Rangers	2-2*
Blaenrhondda won 7-6 on penalties.	
Treforest v Panteg	0-3
Dyffryn Nantlle Vale v Gaerwen	2-0
Tredegar Town v Cwmbran Town	3-3*
Cwmbran Town won 7-6 on penalties.	
Glantraeth v Penmaenmawr Phoenix	4-6
Newcastle Emlyn v Glynneath Town	1-4
Penydarren Boys & Girls v Blaenavon Blues	7-4
Holyhead Town v Menai Bridge Tigers	3-2
Caerau v Pontyclun	1-1*
Pontyclun won 10-9 on penalties.	
Treharris Western Athletic v Aberystwyth Exiles	8-1
Pwllheli v CPD Llannefydd	3-3*
Pwllheli won 5-3 on penalties.	
Penlan v Ferndale BC	8-2
Pill YMCA v Ely Rangers	4-3
Trearddur Bay United (resigned) v Meliden (walkover)	
Newport City v Brecon Northcote	5-0
Ynysgerwn v Cefn Cribwr	2-3

QUALIFYING ROUND 2

Cardiff Draconians v Sully Sports	3-4*
Newport City v Pencoed Athletic Amateur	0-3
Rhos Aelwyd v Brymbo	3-4
Llandudno Albion v Llanrug United	3-1
Brecon Corries v Abermule	2-0
Risca United v Treharris Western Athletic	2-3
Cefn Cribwr v Pontyclun	2-4*
Aberffraw v Rhostyllen	0-0*
Rhostyllen won 4-3 on penalties.	
Llandrindod Wells v Four Crosses	4-2
Panteg v Penrhiwceiber Constitutional Athletic	3-2
Penrhyndeudraeth v Coedpoeth United	1-4
Caersws v Tywyn Bryncrug	8-0
STM Sports v Glynneath Town	12-0
Llanrwst United v Brickfield Rangers	0-5
Machynlleth v Dolgellau Athletic Amateur	1-2
Cwmbran Town v Newport Civil Service	2-0
Llay Welfare v Nomads Of Connah's Quay	3-0
Radnor Valley v Carno	4-0
AFC Llwydcoed v Blaenrhondda	1-2
Cornelly United v Chepstow Town	4-3*
Meliden v Penycae	1-2
Llanfair United v Aberaeron	5-2
Holyhead Town v Llanberis	4-3
Bow Street v Borth United	1-2
Croesyceiliog v Ynysddu Welfare	2-3*
Greenfield v Llandudno Amateurs	2-5
Welshpool Town v Llanidloes Town	3-3*
Llanidloes Town won 5-4 on penalties.	
Swansea University v Abergavenny Town	5-0
Cefn Albion v Queens Park	3-2
Berriew v Builth Wells	5-2*
Caerau Ely v Trethomas Bluebirds	2-1
Llanuwchllyn v Hawarden Rangers	1-4
Prestatyn Sports v Pwllheli	3-4*
Aber Valley v Trefelin BGC	1-2
Penmaenmawr Phoenix v New Brighton Villa	3-3*
New Brighton Villa won 4-2 on penalties.	
Llangefni Town v Saltney Town	4-0
Aberbargoed Buds v Bridgend Street	1-1*
Aberbargoed Buds won 5-3 on penalties.	
Lex XI v Corwen	0-4
St Asaph City v Barmouth & Dyffryn United	3-1
Caldicot Town v Merthyr Saints	2-0
Monmouth Town v Wattsville	4-2
Mold Alexandra v Chirk AAA	2-0*
West End v Aberdare Town	5-2
Dinas Powys v Pill YMCA	2-2*
Dinas Powys won 4-3 on penalties.	
Dyffryn Nantlle Vale v Mynydd Llandegai	2-2*
Dyffryn Nantlle Vale won 5-4 on penalties.	
Pontardawe Town v Penlan	2-2*
Penlan won 4-3 on penalties.	
Penydarren BGC v Garden Village	0-3
Llandyrnog United v Rhydymwyn	2-2*
Rhydymwyn won 3-2 on penalties.	

ROUND 1

Llandudno Amateurs v Dyffryn Nantlle Vale	2-4*
Guilsfield v Rhostyllen	2-0
Cambrian & Clydach Vale v Port Talbot Town	5-0
Radnor Valley v Goytre	1-2
Buckley Town v Brymbo	3-1
Llanrhaeadr Ym Mochnant v Flint Town United	1-2
Llanidloes Town v Pontypridd Town	1-2
Berriew v Penrhyncoch	2-2*
Berriew won 5-4 on penalties.	
Coedpoeth United v Ruthin Town	2-3
Treharris Western Athletic v Cornelly United	3-2
Caersws v Holywell Town	3-2*
Pwllheli v Porthmadog	0-3
Undy Athletic v Monmouth Town	3-4
Llay Welfare v Rhydymwyn	2-0
Hawarden Rangers v Llanfair United	2-3
Cwmbran Town v Afan Lido	3-2
Denbigh Town v Holyhead Town	9-3
Ton Pentre v Pencoed Athletic Amateur	3-1
Sully Sports v Brecon Corries	3-1
Holyhead Hotspur v Corwen	4-2
Pontyclun v Llantwit Major	3-1
Cwmamman United v Dinas Powys	4-0
Penycae v Airbus UK Broughton	0-4
Trefelin BGC v Swansea University	1-2
West End v Caldicot Town	0-6
Bangor City v Mold Alexandra	4-2
Ynysddu Welfare v Taffs Well	2-1
Garden Village v Blaenrhondda	1-2
Panteg v Penybont	1-3
Conwy Borough v Rhyl	1-2
Cwmbran Celtic v Ammanford	3-0
Gresford Athletic v Brickfield Rangers	4-3*
Llangefni Town v Borth United	2-0
STM Sports v Haverfordwest County	1-2
Prestatyn Town v New Brighton Villa	5-1
Llandrindod Wells v Aberbargoed Buds	1-1*
Aberbargoed Buds won 4-3 on penalties.	
Briton Ferry Llansawel v Caerau Ely	1-0
Llandudno Albion v St Asaph City	3-4*

Penlan v Goytre United	0-1
Cefn Albion v Dolgellau Athletic Amateur	7-1

ROUND 2

Aberbargoed Buds v Penybont	0-2
Cwmamman United v Blaenrhondda	2-1
Holyhead Hotspur v Ruthin Town	3-1
Llangefni Town v St Asaph City	5-1
Prestatyn Town v Berriew	6-3
Rhyl v Caersws	3-1
Goytre United v Pontyclun	1-0
Haverfordwest County v Swansea University	4-3
Airbus UK Broughton v Llay Welfare	9-1
Pontypridd Town v Goytre	6-3
Bangor City v Cefn Albion	6-1
Buckley Town v Denbigh Town	1-3
Flint Town United v Gresford Athletic	3-2
Guilsfield v Dyffryn Nantlle Vale	4-3
Llanfair United v Porthmadog	1-4
Cwmbran Town v Ton Pentre	1-2
Monmouth Town v Ynysddu Welfare	1-3
Treharris Western Athletic v Briton Ferry Llansawel	3-4
Sully Sports v Cwmbran Celtic	1-3
Caldicot Town v Cambrian & Clydach Vale	2-3

ROUND 3

Flint Town United v Bala Town	0-3
Goytre United v Carmarthen Town	0-3
Denbigh Town v Cambrian & Clydach Vale	1-2
Guilsfield v Connah's Quay Nomads	2-4*
Llangefni Town v Llanelli	1-0
Newtown v Rhyl	1-2
Haverfordwest County v Pontypridd Town	3-0
Ynysddu Welfare v Cefn Druids	1-3
Briton Ferry Llansawel v Llandudno	2-3
Ton Pentre v Cardiff Metropolitan	1-4
Airbus UK Broughton v Porthmadog	1-1*
Airbus UK Broughton won 4-2 on penalties.	
Cwmbran Celtic v The New Saints	0-3
Cwmamman United v Aberystwyth Town	3-4
Bangor City v Holyhead Hotspur	4-1
Prestatyn Town v Caernarfon Town	0-3
Barry Town United v Penybont	4-1*

ROUND 4

Bangor City v Caernarfon Town	1-2
Carmarthen Town v Connah's Quay Nomads	1-3
Haverfordwest County v Bala Town	0-4*
Barry Town United v Cefn Druids	3-2
Airbus UK Broughton v The New Saints	2-5
Cambrian & Clydach Vale v Rhyl	2-2*
Cambrian & Clydach Vale won 3-1 on penalties.	
Aberystwyth Town v Cardiff Metropolitan	1-3
Llangefni Town v Llandudno	1-3

QUARTER-FINALS

Barry Town United v Cambrian & Clydach Vale	3-2
Bala Town v Cardiff Metropolitan	0-1*
Llandudno v The New Saints	1-8
Caernarfon Town v Connah's Quay Nomads	1-2

SEMI-FINALS

Cardiff Metropolitan v Connah's Quay Nomads	0-3
The New Saints v Barry Town U	2-0

JD WELSH FA CUP FINAL 2019

The Rock, Cefn Druids, Sunday 5 May 2019

Connah's Quay Nomads (0) 0

The New Saints (2) 3 *(Draper 7, Brobbel 33, 62)* 1256

Connah's Quay Nomads: Danby; Disney, Horan, Harrison, Morris, Wilde, Poole, Holmes, Owen (Barton 87), Bakare (Wignall 46), Insall (Owens 69).
The New Saints: Harrison, Marriott (Nembhard 60), Hudson, Bodenham, Routledge, Brobbel, Draper (Ebbe 81), Redmond, Cieslewicz, Mullan, Lewis (Spender 74).
Referee: David Morgan.

PREVIOUS WELSH CUP WINNERS

1878	Wrexham	1911	Wrexham	1954	Flint Town United	1987	Merthyr Tydfil
1879	Newtown White Star	1912	Cardiff City	1955	Barry Town	1988	Cardiff City
1880	Druids	1913	Swansea Town	1956	Cardiff City	1989	Swansea City
1881	Druids	1914	Wrexham	1957	Wrexham	1990	Hereford United
1882	Druids	1915	Wrexham	1958	Wrexham	1991	Swansea City
1883	Wrexham	1920	Cardiff City	1959	Cardiff City	1992	Cardiff City
1884	Oswestry White Stars	1921	Wrexham	1960	Wrexham	1993	Cardiff City
1885	Druids	1922	Cardiff City	1961	Swansea Town	1994	Barry Town
1886	Druids	1923	Cardiff City	1962	Bangor City	1995	Wrexham
1887	Chirk	1924	Wrexham	1963	Borough United	1996	TNS
1888	Chirk	1925	Wrexham	1964	Cardiff City	1997	Barry Town
1889	Bangor	1926	Ebbw Vale	1965	Cardiff City	1998	Bangor City
1890	Chirk	1927	Cardiff City	1966	Swansea Town	1999	Inter Cable-Tel
1891	Shrewsbury Town	1928	Cardiff City	1967	Cardiff City	2000	Bangor City
1892	Chirk	1929	Connah's Quay	1968	Cardiff City	2001	Barry Town
1893	Wrexham	1930	Cardiff City	1969	Cardiff City	2002	Barry Town
1894	Chirk	1931	Wrexham	1970	Cardiff City	2003	Barry Town
1895	Newtown	1932	Swansea Town	1971	Cardiff City	2004	Rhyl
1896	Bangor	1933	Chester	1972	Wrexham	2005	TNS
1897	Wrexham	1934	Bristol City	1973	Cardiff City	2006	Rhyl
1898	Druids	1935	Tranmere Rovers	1974	Cardiff City	2007	Carmarthen Town
1899	Druids	1936	Crewe Alexandra	1975	Wrexham	2008	Bangor City
1900	Aberystwyth Town	1937	Crewe Alexandra	1976	Cardiff City	2009	Bangor City
1901	Oswestry United	1938	Shrewsbury Town	1977	Shrewsbury Town	2010	Bangor City
1902	Wellington Town	1939	South Liverpool	1978	Wrexham	2011	Llanelli
1903	Wrexham	1940	Wellington Town	1979	Shrewsbury Town	2012	The New Saints
1904	Druids	1947	Chester	1980	Newport County	2013	Prestatyn Town
1905	Wrexham	1948	Lovell's Athletic	1981	Swansea City	2014	The New Saints
1906	Wellington Town	1949	Merthyr Tydfil	1982	Swansea City	2015	The New Saints
1907	Oswestry United	1950	Swansea Town	1983	Swansea City	2016	The New Saints
1908	Chester	1951	Merthyr Tydfil	1984	Shrewsbury Town	2017	Bala Town
1909	Wrexham	1952	Rhyl	1985	Shrewsbury Town	2018	Connah's Quay N
1910	Wrexham	1953	Rhyl	1986	Wrexham	2019	The New Saints

NATHANIEL MG WELSH LEAGUE CUP 2018–19

**After extra time.*

ROUND 1

Bala T v Guilsfield	3-0
Bangor C v Llandudno	0-1
Cambrian & Clydach Vale v Barry Town U	0-0
Cambrian & Clydach Vale won 3-1 on penalties.	
Carmarthen T v Goytre (Gwent)	5-0
Cefn Druids v Airbus UK Broughton	3-4*
(2-2 at the end of normal time)	
Denbigh T v Prestatyn T	2-3
Flint Town U v Holywell T	3-2*
(1-1 at the end of normal time)	
Goytre U v Afan Lido	3-1
Haverfordwest Co v Llanelli T	3-0
Penybont v Ton Pentre	3-1
Rhyl v Caernarfon T	4-2
Welshpool T v Aberystwyth T	1-3

ROUND 2

Prestatyn T v The New Saints	0-5
Connah's Quay Nomads v Airbus UK Broughton	5-1
Flint Town U v Bala T	1-6
Rhyl v Llandudno	3-5
Cambrian & Clydach Vale v Aberystwyth T	3-1
Cardiff Metropolitan v Carmarthen T	3-1
Haverfordwest Co v Goytre U	6-2
Newtown v Penybont	1-0

QUARTER-FINALS

Bala T v Connah's Quay Nomads	0-1
Cambrian & Clydach Vale v Newtown	1-0
Cardiff Metropolitan v Haverfordwest Co	6-0
Llandudno v The New Saints	0-5

SEMI-FINALS

Connah's Quay Nomads v Cardiff Metropolitan	0-1
Cambrian & Clydach Vale v The New Saints	2-1

NATHANIEL MG WELSH LEAGUE CUP FINAL 2019

Barry, Saturday 19 January 2019

Cardiff Metropolitan (1) 2 *(Roscrow 40, 90)*

Cambrian & Clydach Vale (0) 0 1503

Cardiff Metropolitan: Lang; McCarthy, Lewis, Woolridge, Rees, Edwards, Corsby (Phillips 78), Evans W, Baker. Roscrow, Evans E.

Cambrian & Clydach Vale: Bradley; Crutch, Coles, Evans, Jones K (Jones M 83), Keetch, French (Strinati 59), Shepherd, Thomas, Reed, Jones S (Edwards 78).

Referee: Rob Jenkins.

THE FAW TROPHY 2018–19

**After extra time.*

ROUND 3

Greenfield v Dyffryn Nantlle Vale	2-2*
Dyffryn Nantlle Vale won 3-2 on penalties.	
Cornelly U v Penydarren BGC	0-2
Brymbo v Y Felinheli	7-2
Cefn Cribwr v Wattsville	3-0
Offa Ath v Nomads Of Connah's Quay	1-3
Garden Village v Hakin U	6-0
Glan Conwy v Llandudno Alb	3-2
Baglan Dragons v STM Sports	0-3
Lex XI v Llanrug U	1-6
Ynystawe Ath v Llanidloes T	1-0
Aberbargoed Buds v Pontardawe T	0-2
Bodedern v Llandyrnog U	6-0
Rhydymwyn v Prestatyn Sports	3-0
Newport Civil Service v Chepstow T	5-3
Llansantffraid Village v Mynydd Llandegai	2-3
Penlan v Ynyshir Albs	0-2
Plas Madoc v St Asaph City	4-1
Pontlottyn v Grange Alb	2-2*
Grange Alb won 4-1 on penalties.	
Caersws v Llanfair U	1-2
Glantraeth v Chirk AAA	0-5
Churchstoke v Bow Street	1-2
Pwllheli v Llanberis	2-1
Four Crosses v Machynlleth	5-0
Carno v Berriew	0-2
Saltney T v Cefn Alb	0-6
Merthyr Saints v Swansea University	0-4
Llangefni T v Penycae	6-0
Trebanog v Ynysddu Welfare	1-2
Rhos Aelwyd v Rhostyllen	2-1
Abertillery Bluebirds v Cardiff Draconians	2-0
Corwen v Hawarden Rangers	4-1
Abercarn U v Maltsters Sports	0-2

ROUND 4

Corwen v Glan Conwy	4-0
Four Crosses v Rhos Aelwyd	3-1
Llangefni T v Brymbo	1-0
Llanrug U v Llanfair U	4-2
Plas Madoc v Mynydd Llandegai	5-2
Pwllheli v Dyffryn Nantlle Vale	3-2
Abertillery Bluebirds v Pontardawe T	3-5*
Maltsters Sports v Bow Street	0-1
Newport Civil Service v Grange Alb	0-3
Penydarren BGC v Ynystawe Ath	7-1
STM Sports v Cefn Cribwr	8-2
Swansea University v Garden Village	4-1
Ynysddu Welfare v Ynyshir Albs	0-2
Berriew v Rhydymwyn	2-0
Bodedern v Chirk AAA	1-0
Cefn Alb v Nomads Of Connah's Quay	6-2

ROUND 5

Corwen v Pwllheli	6-1
Llanrug U v Llangefni T	0-4
Grange Alb v Penydarren BGC	1-4
Pontardawe T v Swansea University	3-2
STM Sports v Ynyshir Albs	3-0
Cefn Alb v Bow Street	3-0
Plas Madoc v Berriew	3-2
Bodedern v Four Crosses	2-1

QUARTER-FINALS

Llangefni T v Bodedern	0-1
STM Sports v Penydarren BGC	2-1
Plas Madoc v Pontardawe T	2-4
Corwen v Cefn Alb	3-5

SEMI-FINALS

Pontardawe T v Bodedern	4-0
Cefn Alb v STM Sports	3-1*

FAW TROPHY FINAL 2018–19

Aberystwyth, Saturday 13 April 2019

Pontardawe T (0) 0

Cefn Alb (X) 4 *(Williams N 4, Kendrick 9, Morris 29, Foulkes 90)*

Pontardawe T: Reeves; Aylward, Evans C, Georgievsky, Davies, Dorward, Rees, Griffiths, Taylor. Briggs.
Substitutes: Grey, Carroll, Doyle, Blizzard, Schofield.
Cefn Alb: Roberts; Williams N, Jordan Jones, Nic Jones, Griffiths, Gibbins, James Jones, Cox, Kendrick, Morris, Williams A.
Substitutes: Davies O, Foulkes, Davies Z, Richards, Woodall.
Referee: Mark Petch.

NORTHERN IRISH FOOTBALL 2018–19

NIFL DANSKE BANK PREMIERSHIP 2018–19

			Home					*Away*					*Total*						
		P	*W*	*D*	*L*	*F*	*A*	*W*	*D*	*L*	*F*	*A*	*W*	*D*	*L*	*F*	*A*	*GD*	*Pts*
1	Linfield	38	13	4	2	44	17	13	3	3	33	10	26	7	5	77	27	50	85
2	Ballymena U	38	14	3	3	46	22	10	3	5	37	25	24	6	8	83	47	36	78
3	Glenavon	38	11	5	4	39	22	9	5	4	35	24	20	10	8	74	46	28	70
4	Crusaders	38	11	2	3	33	20	9	3	10	35	35	20	5	13	68	55	13	65
5	Cliftonville	38	14	3	3	44	24	5	1	12	26	42	19	4	15	70	66	4	61
6	Coleraine	38	7	6	5	27	24	8	5	7	32	31	15	11	12	59	55	4	56
7	Glentoran	38	7	4	7	31	25	6	6	8	27	28	13	10	15	58	53	5	49
8	Institute	38	8	2	9	27	33	5	3	11	23	39	13	5	20	50	72	–22	44
9	Dungannon Swifts	38	8	4	7	23	30	3	5	11	21	35	11	9	18	44	65	–21	42
10	Warrenpoint T	38	5	4	11	28	47	5	5	8	23	32	10	9	19	51	79	–28	39
11	Ards	38	4	5	10	19	27	2	4	13	12	36	6	9	23	31	63	–32	27
12	Newry C	38	4	3	13	15	29	2	2	14	16	39	6	5	27	31	68	–37	23

Top 6 teams split after 33 games. Linfield qualify for Champions League first qualifying round.
Ballymena U and Cliftonville (via Play-offs) qualify for Europa League preliminary round.
Europa League play-off final: Cliftonville 2 Glentoran 0 (aet).
Relegation/promotion play-off: Ards 1 Carrick Rangers 3 (on aggregate). Ards relegated to NIFL Championship.

LEADING GOALSCORERS (League goals only)

20	Joe Gormley	Cliftonville
19	Michael McCrudden	Institute
17	Andrew Waterworth	Linfield
16	Cathair Friel	Ballymena U
15	Stephen Murray	Glenavon
14	Paul Heatley	Crusaders
13	Ryan Curran	Cliftonville
13	Robbie McDaid	Glentoran
12	Rory Donnelly	Cliftonville
12	Paul McElroy	Dungannon Swifts
12	Andrew Mitchell	Glenavon
11	Jamie McGonigle	Coleraine
11	Curtis Allen	Glentoran
10	Daniel Hughes	Dungannon Swifts
10	Jordan Stewart	Linfield
10	Andy McGrory	Ballymena U
10	Michael O'Connor	Linfield
10	Darren Murray	Glentoran
10	Adam Lecky	Ballymena U
10	Rory Patterson	Crusaders
9	Jimmy Callacher	Linfield
9	David Cushley	Crusaders

IRISH LEAGUE CHAMPIONSHIP WINNERS

1891	Linfield	1914	Linfield	1949	Linfield	1973	Crusaders	1997	Crusaders
1892	Linfield	1915	Belfast Celtic	1950	Linfield	1974	Coleraine	1998	Cliftonville
1893	Linfield	1920	Belfast Celtic	1951	Glentoran	1975	Linfield	1999	Glentoran
1894	Glentoran	1921	Glentoran	1952	Glenavon	1976	Crusaders	2000	Linfield
1895	Linfield	1922	Linfield	1953	Glentoran	1977	Glentoran	2001	Linfield
1896	Distillery	1923	Linfield	1954	Linfield	1978	Linfield	2002	Portadown
1897	Glentoran	1924	Queen's Island	1955	Linfield	1979	Linfield	2003	Glentoran
1898	Linfield	1925	Glentoran	1956	Linfield	1980	Linfield	2004	Linfield
1899	Distillery	1926	Belfast Celtic	1957	Glentoran	1981	Glentoran	2005	Glentoran
1900	Belfast Celtic	1927	Belfast Celtic	1958	Ards	1982	Linfield	2006	Linfield
1901	Distillery	1928	Belfast Celtic	1959	Linfield	1983	Linfield	2007	Linfield
1902	Linfield	1929	Belfast Celtic	1960	Glenavon	1984	Linfield	2008	Linfield
1903	Distillery	1930	Linfield	1961	Linfield	1985	Linfield	2009	Glentoran
1904	Linfield	1931	Glentoran	1962	Linfield	1986	Linfield	2010	Linfield
1905	Glentoran	1932	Linfield	1963	Distillery	1987	Linfield	2011	Linfield
1906	Cliftonville/	1933	Belfast Celtic	1964	Glentoran	1988	Glentoran	2012	Linfield
	Distillery (shared)	1934	Linfield	1965	Derry City	1989	Linfield	2013	Cliftonville
1907	Linfield	1935	Linfield	1966	Linfield	1990	Portadown	2014	Cliftonville
1908	Linfield	1936	Belfast Celtic	1967	Glentoran	1991	Portadown	2015	Crusaders
1909	Linfield	1937	Belfast Celtic	1968	Glentoran	1992	Glentoran	2016	Crusaders
1910	Cliftonville	1938	Belfast Celtic	1969	Linfield	1993	Linfield	2017	Linfield
1911	Linfield	1939	Belfast Celtic	1970	Glentoran	1994	Linfield	2018	Crusaders
1912	Glentoran	1940	Belfast Celtic	1971	Linfield	1995	Crusaders	2019	Linfield
1913	Glentoran	1948	Belfast Celtic	1972	Glentoran	1996	Portadown		

NIFL BLUEFIN SPORT CHAMPIONSHIP 2018–19

		Home						Away					Total						
		P	*W*	*D*	*L*	*F*	*A*	*W*	*D*	*L*	*F*	*A*	*W*	*D*	*L*	*F*	*A*	*GD*	*Pts*
1	Larne	32	15	1	0	51	5	11	2	3	36	14	26	3	3	87	19	68	81
2	Carrick Rangers	32	12	1	3	37	21	8	3	5	22	21	20	4	8	59	42	17	64
3	Portadown	32	10	2	4	34	27	5	4	7	25	28	15	6	11	59	55	4	51
4	Dundela	32	6	4	6	33	33	7	3	6	34	27	13	7	12	67	60	7	46
5	Ballinamallard U	32	8	1	7	23	19	4	2	10	16	32	12	3	17	39	51	–12	39
6	H&W Welders	32	5	2	9	19	31	6	0	10	26	37	11	2	19	45	68	–23	35
7	Loughgall	32	5	6	5	32	25	6	3	7	28	27	11	9	12	60	52	8	42
8	Dergview	32	6	1	9	21	23	7	2	7	30	28	13	3	16	51	51	0	42
9	Ballyclare Comrades	32	5	5	6	26	33	6	2	8	32	35	11	7	14	58	68	–10	40
10	Knockbreda	32	5	4	7	26	33	5	3	8	19	30	10	7	15	45	63	–18	37
11	PSNI	32	5	2	9	20	33	4	5	7	28	39	9	7	16	48	72	–24	34
12	Limavady U	32	2	4	10	23	35	6	4	6	22	27	8	8	16	45	62	–17	32

Top 6 teams split after 22 games. Pre Promotion play-off: Carrick Rangers 2 Portadown 0.
NIFL Championship relegation/promotion play-off: Ards 1 Carrick Rangers 3 (on aggregate).
Carrick Rangers promoted to NIFL Premiership.

NIFL CHAMPIONSHIP WINNERS

1996	Coleraine	2004	Loughgall	2012	Ballinamallard U
1997	Ballymena United	2005	Armagh City	2013	Ards
1998	Newry Town	2006	Crusaders	2014	Institute
1999	Distillery	2007	Institute	2015	Carrick Rangers
2000	Omagh Town	2008	Loughgall	2016	Ards
2001	Ards	2009	Portadown	2017	Warrenpoint T
2002	Lisburn Distillery	2010	Loughgall	2018	Institute
2003	Dungannon Swifts	2011	Carrick Rangers	2019	Larne

NIFL BLUEFIN SPORT PREMIER INTERMEDIATE LEAGUE 2018–19

		Home						Away					Total						
		P	*W*	*D*	*L*	*F*	*A*	*W*	*D*	*L*	*F*	*A*	*W*	*D*	*L*	*F*	*A*	*GD*	*Pts*
1	Queen's University	22	10	0	1	32	6	8	2	1	23	10	18	2	2	55	16	39	56
2	Annagh U	22	8	0	3	35	15	5	5	1	20	11	13	5	4	55	26	29	44
3	Tobermore U	22	6	1	4	26	18	7	1	3	22	14	13	2	7	48	32	16	41
4	Lisburn Distillery	22	4	4	3	22	17	6	2	3	19	20	10	6	6	41	37	4	36
5	Banbridge T	22	4	5	2	16	11	5	1	5	21	16	9	6	7	37	27	10	33
6	Portstewart	22	4	4	3	11	9	5	1	5	17	19	9	5	8	28	28	0	32
7	Newington YC	22	5	0	6	18	18	3	5	3	13	17	8	5	9	31	35	–4	29
8	Moyola Park	22	6	1	4	24	15	2	2	7	12	24	8	3	11	36	39	–3	27
9	Dollingstown	22	1	3	7	18	26	4	2	5	17	22	5	5	12	35	48	–13	20
10	Armagh C	22	2	2	7	10	20	3	3	5	14	24	5	5	12	24	44	–20	20
11	Lurgan Celtic	22	1	3	7	10	23	4	1	6	13	25	5	4	13	23	48	–25	19
12	Sport & Leisure Swifts	22	2	2	7	18	27	2	0	9	14	38	4	2	16	32	65	–33	14

Top 6 teams split after 22 games. NIFL Championship relegation/promotion play-off: Dergview 4 Queen's University 1 (on aggregate). Queen's University not promoted.

IFA DEVELOPMENT LEAGUES 2018–19

PREMIERSHIP DEVELOPMENT LEAGUE

	P	*W*	*D*	*L*	*F*	*A*	*GD*	*Pts*
Linfield Swifts	33	24	6	3	108	39	69	78
Glentoran II	33	20	5	8	102	57	45	65
Institute	33	19	3	11	86	54	32	60
Cliftonville Olympic	33	18	3	12	92	62	30	57
Coleraine	33	17	3	13	72	71	1	54
Glenavon	33	16	5	12	83	63	20	53
Crusaders	33	15	2	16	78	72	6	47
Dungannon Swifts	33	12	4	17	75	87	–12	40
Ballymena U	33	10	2	21	44	97	–53	32
Newry C	33	9	4	20	57	91	–34	31
Warrenpoint T	33	8	5	20	52	96	–44	29
Ards II	33	7	4	22	42	102	–60	25

CHAMPIONSHIP/PIL DEVELOPMENT

	P	*W*	*D*	*L*	*F*	*A*	*GD*	*Pts*
Portadown	22	16	1	5	82	30	52	49
Ballinamallard U	22	14	1	7	75	45	30	43
H&W Welders	22	14	1	7	73	44	29	43
Carrick Rangers	22	12	1	9	64	44	20	37
Newington	22	12	1	9	52	39	13	37
Loughgall	22	11	2	9	54	57	–3	35
Knockbreda	22	11	0	11	52	44	8	33
Ballyclare Comrades	22	10	1	11	48	59	–11	31
Dundela	22	8	1	13	39	66	–27	25
PSNI Olympic	22	8	1	13	40	73	–33	25
Larne Olympic	22	7	2	13	36	53	–17	23
Moyola Park Olympic	22	3	0	19	32	93	–61	9

ACADEMY LEAGUE U18

	P	*W*	*D*	*L*	*F*	*A*	*GD*	*Pts*
Linfield Rangers	22	15	4	3	59	29	30	49
Ards	22	15	4	3	57	30	27	49
Dungannon Swifts	22	13	5	4	63	27	36	44
Cliftonville Strollers	22	12	3	7	54	32	22	39
Warrenpoint Town	22	9	3	10	42	52	–10	30
Glentoran Colts	22	8	5	9	43	41	2	29
Crusaders	22	7	6	9	38	37	1	27
Glenavon	22	7	5	10	48	58	–10	26
Carrick Rangers	22	8	2	12	28	41	–13	26
Coleraine	22	7	2	13	40	58	–18	23
Ballymena U	22	7	1	14	43	63	–20	22
Ballinamallard U	22	3	2	17	25	72	–47	11

TENNENT'S IRISH FA CUP 2018–19

**After extra time.*

FIRST ROUND

Valley Rangers v Tandragee R	3-2
Albert Foundry v Aquinas	4-3
Ardstraw v Dromore Amateurs	7-0
Ballymacash Rangers v Kilmore Recreation	1-3
Ballynahinch U v Groomsport	3-2
Banbridge Rangers v Sirocco Works	2-0
Bangor Amateurs v Newcastle	3-2
Brantwood v Orangefield Old Boys	4-2
Broomhedge Maghaberry v Ballynahinch Olympic	1-12
Comber Recreation v Immaculata	1-0
Cookstown Youth v Islandmagee	1-6
Crumlin U v Bangor Swifts	2-1
Desertmartin v Ballynure Old Boys	2-2*
Desertmartin won 7-6 on penalties	
Dungiven Celtic v Iveagh U	5-2
Dunloy v Hanover	2-0
Dunmurry Young Men v Rathfriland Rangers	4-5
Fivemiletown U v Bloomfield	7-0
Glebe Rangers v Bangor	1-2
Grove U v Chimney Corner	5-2
Holywood v Newbuildings U	1-2
Killyleagh YC v Markethill Swifts	5-3
Lisburn Rangers v Dromara Village	2-1
Lower Maze v Trojans	2-3
Malachians v Maiden C	2-9
Mossley v Dunmurry Recreation	3-4
Newtowne v 18th Newtownabbey Old Boys	6-3
Oxford Sunnyside v Bryansburn Rangers	6-3
Oxford United Stars v Wakehurst	0-1
Rosario YC v Ballymoney U	1-2
Saintfield U v Laurelvale	1-3
Seapatrick v Coagh U	1-6
Silverwood v Shorts	1-8
St James' Swifts v Sofia Farmer	2-1
St Luke's v Larne Tech Old Boys	0-2
Strabane Ath v Derriaghy Cricket Club	2-1
Suffolk v Colin Valley	1-1*
Colin Valley won 4-3 on penalties	
Tullycarnet v Tullyvallen	4-3
Woodvale v St Patrick's Young Men	2-3

SECOND ROUND

Newington v Valley Rangers	3-1
Ballymoney U v Strabane Ath	1-5
Banbridge T v Rathfriland Rangers	3-1
Bangor v Banbridge Rangers	2-0
Bangor Amateurs v Tullycarnet	0-1
Brantwood v Laurelvale	2-1
Colin Valley v Shorts	3-4
Comber Rec v Lisburn Rangers	4-1
Crewe U v Moyola Park	2-1
Crumlin U v Moneyslane	5-1
Downshire Young Men v Drumaness Mills	0-4
Dundonald v Larne Tech Old Boys	0-3
Dunloy v Armagh C	2-0
Dunmurry Recreation v Dungiven Celtic	1-4
Grove U v Abbey Villa	3-4*
Islandmagee v Albert Foundry	2-1
Killyleagh YC v Crumlin Star	2-3
Kilmore Recreation v Sport & Leisure Swifts	1-2
Lisburn Distillery v Wellington Recreation	2-0
Lurgan Celtic (bye) v St Patrick's Young Men	
Lurgan T v Desertmartin	4-1
Maiden C v Trojans	3-1
Newbuildings U v Ards Rangers	2-0
Newtowne v Ballynahinch Olympic	0-0*
Newtowne won 5-3 on penalties	
Oxford Sunnyside v Portstewart (bye)	
Queen's University v Dollingstown	4-3
Rosemount Recreation v Annagh U	2-1
Seagoe v Ballynahinch U	4-3
Shankill U v 1st Bangor Old Boys	2-1
St. James' Swifts v Coagh U	4-2
Tobermore U v Ardstraw	5-3
Wakehurst v Fivemiletown U	2-3

THIRD ROUND

Crewe U v Sport & Leisure Swifts	1-0
Crumlin Star v Bangor	5-3
Crumlin U v Islandmagee	1-3
Drumaness Mills v Comber Recreation	1-2
Fivemiletown U v Tullycarnet	1-2
Larne Tech Old Boys v Dungiven Celtic	2-1
Lurgan Celtic v Portstewart	2-3
Lurgan T v Dunloy	1-2
Newtowne v Rosemount Recreation	1-1*
Rosemount Recreation won 5-3 on penalties	
Queen's University v Tobermore U	6-3
Seagoe v Maiden C	1-4
Shankill U v Lisburn Distillery	2-4
Shorts v Abbey Villa	1-3
St James' Swifts v Newbuildings U	2-0
Strabane Ath v Banbridge T	2-0
Brantwood v Newington	2-3

FOURTH ROUND

Crewe U v Crumlin Star	1-2
Dunloy v Larne Tech Old Boys	0-2
Lisburn Distillery v Comber Recreation	4-3*
Maiden C v Portstewart	1-0
Queen's University v Newington	4-1
Rosemount Recreation v Islandmagee	3-1
Strabane Ath v St James' Swifts	2-0
Tullycarnet v Abbey Villa	3-4

FIFTH ROUND

Ards v Carrick Rangers	0-1
Ballinamallard U v PSNI	5-1
Cliftonville v Dungannon Swifts	0-1
Coleraine v H&W Welders	2-0
Crusaders v Glentoran	4-1
Dergview v Maiden C	3-2
Dundela v Ballymena U	1-3
Glenavon v Rosemount Recreation	5-0
Institute v Warrenpoint T	0-2
Knockbreda v Strabane Ath	1-2
Larne v Newry C	2-1
Limavady U v Larne Tech Old Boys	0-2
Linfield v Ballyclare Comrades	1-0
Loughgall v Crumlin Star	1-4
Portadown v Abbey Villa	5-1
Queen's University v Lisburn Distillery	6-0

SIXTH ROUND

Ballinamallard U v Carrick Rangers	1-0
Ballymena U v Portadown	4-1
Coleraine v Dergview	3-0
Glenavon v Dungannon Swifts	0-1
Larne v Crumlin Star	3-1
Larne Tech Old Boys v Strabane Ath	3-1
Linfield v Crusaders	1-2*
Warrenpoint T v Queen's University	2-0

QUARTER FINALS

Larne v Coleraine	3-5*
Crusaders v Ballymena U	3-0
Dungannon Swifts v Ballinamallard U	2-2*
Ballinamallard U won 3-2 on penalties	
Warrenpoint T v Larne Tech Old Boys	3-1

SEMI FINALS

Ballinamallard U v Warrenpoint T	0-0*
Ballinamallard U won 5-4 on penalties	
Coleraine v Crusaders	0-2

TENNENT'S IRISH FA CUP FINAL 2019

Windsor Park, Belfast, Saturday 4 May 2019

Crusaders (1) 3 (*Owens J 6, Lowry 47, Clarke 53***)**

Ballinamallard U (0) 0

Ballinamallard U: Connolly; Taheny, Smyth, Clarke, Arkinson, Campbell, McCartney (Hume 68), Kelly (Warrington 80), Cashel, O'Reilly, McBrien (McManus 59).

Crusaders: Doherty H; Burns, Coates, Lowry, Ward, Cushley (Clarke 52), Caddell, Forsythe, Ruddy, Owens J (Patterson 87), Heatley.

Referee: Ian McNabb.

IRISH CUP FINALS (from 1946–47)

1946–47 Belfast Celtic 1, Glentoran 0
1947–48 Linfield 3, Coleraine 0
1948–49 Derry City 3, Glentoran 1
1949–50 Linfield 2, Distillery 1
1950–51 Glentoran 3, Ballymena U 1
1951–52 Ards 1, Glentoran 0
1952–53 Linfield 5, Coleraine 0
1953–54 Derry City 1, Glentoran 0
1954–55 Dundela 3, Glenavon 0
1955–56 Distillery 1, Glentoran 0
1956–57 Glenavon 2, Derry City 0
1957–58 Ballymena U 2, Linfield 0
1958–59 Glenavon 2, Ballymena U 0
1959–60 Linfield 5, Ards 1
1960–61 Glenavon 5, Linfield 1
1961–62 Linfield 4, Portadown 0
1962–63 Linfield 2, Distillery 1
1963–64 Derry City 2, Glentoran 0
1964–65 Coleraine 2, Glenavon 1
1965–66 Glentoran 2, Linfield 0
1966–67 Crusaders 3, Glentoran 1
1967–68 Crusaders 2, Linfield 0
1968–69 Ards 4, Distillery 2
1969–70 Linfield 2, Ballymena U 1
1970–71 Distillery 3, Derry City
1971–72 Coleraine 2, Portadown 1
1972–73 Glentoran 3, Linfield 2
1973–74 Ards 2, Ballymena U 1
1974–75 Coleraine 1:0:1, Linfield 1:0:0
1975–76 Carrick Rangers 2, Linfield 1
1976–77 Coleraine 4, Linfield 1
1977–78 Linfield 3, Ballymena U 1
1978–79 Cliftonville 3, Portadown 2
1979–80 Linfield 2, Crusaders 0
1980–81 Ballymena U 1, Glenavon 0
1981–82 Linfield 2, Coleraine 1
1982–83 Glentoran 1:2, Linfield 1:1
1983–84 Ballymena U 4, Carrick Rangers 1
1984–85 Glentoran 1:1, Linfield 1:0
1985–86 Glentoran 2, Coleraine 1
1986–87 Glentoran 1, Larne 0
1987–88 Glentoran 1, Glenavon 0
1988–89 Ballymena U 1, Larne 0
1989–90 Glentoran 3, Portadown 0
1990–91 Portadown 2, Glenavon 1
1991–92 Glenavon 2, Linfield 1
1992–93 Bangor 1:1:1, Ards 1:1:0
1993–94 Linfield 2, Bangor 0
1994–95 Linfield 3, Carrick Rangers 1
1995–96 Glentoran 1, Glenavon 0
1996–97 Glenavon 1, Cliftonville 0
1997–98 Glentoran 1, Glenavon 0
1998–99 *Portadown awarded trophy after Cliftonville were eliminated for using an ineligible player in semi-final.*
1999–2000 Glentoran 1, Portadown 0
2000–01 Glentoran 1, Linfield 0
2001–02 Linfield 2, Portadown 1
2002–03 Coleraine 1, Glentoran 0
2003–04 Glentoran 1, Coleraine 0
2004–05 Portadown 5, Larne 1
2005–06 Linfield 2, Glentoran 1
2006–07 Linfield 2, Dungannon Swifts 2
(aet; Linfield won 3-2 on penalties).
2007–08 Linfield 2, Coleraine 1
2008–09 Crusaders 1, Cliftonville 0
2009–10 Linfield 2, Portadown 1
2010–11 Linfield 2, Crusaders 1
2011–12 Linfield 4, Crusaders 1
2012–13 Glentoran 3, Cliftonville 1
2013–14 Glenavon 2, Balymena U 1
2014–15 Glentoran 1, Portadown 0
2015–16 Glenavon 2, Linfield 0
2016–17 Linfield 3, Coleraine 0
2017–18 Coleraine 3, Cliftonville 1
2018–19 Crusaders 3, Ballinamallard U 0

BETMCLEAN LEAGUE CUP 2018–19

**After extra time.*

FIRST ROUND

Dundela v Knockbreda	1-3
Lurgan Celtic v Armagh C	4-0
PSNI v Banbridge T	1-0
Queen's University v Lisburn Distillery	3-4

SECOND ROUND

Annagh U v Warrenpoint T	1-3
Ards v Newington YC	3-2
Ballinamallard U v Lurgan Celtic	4-1
Ballymena U v Dollingstown	5-1
Carrick Rangers v Sport & Leisure Swifts	6-0
Cliftonville v Lisburn Distillery	5-1
Coleraine v Ballyclare Comrades	2-1
Crusaders v PSNI	4-1
Dungannon Swifts v Limavady U	2-1*
Glenavon v Dergview	0-1
Glentoran v Larne	3-2*
Institute v Loughgall	5-1
Linfield v Moyola Park	8-0
Newry C v Knockbreda	1-0
Portadown v Tobermore U	3-0*
H&W Welders v Portstewart	3-3*
H&W Welders won 4-2 on penalties.	

THIRD ROUND

Ballymena U v H&W Welders	1-0
Cliftonville v Carrick Rangers	3-2
Crusaders v Ballinamallard U	2-1
Dergview v Ards	1-4
Warrenpoint T v Dungannon Swifts	2-3*
Glentoran v Coleraine	3-3*
Glentoran won 3-2 on penalties.	
Linfield v Institute	5-0
Newry C v Portadown	1-1*
Portadown won 4-1 on penalties.	

QUARTER-FINALS

Ards v Ballymena U	0-1
Glentoran v Crusaders	2-4
Cliftonville v Dungannon Swifts	1-1*
Dungannon Swifts won 3-2 on penalties.	
Portadown v Linfield	1-2

SEMI-FINALS

Crusaders v Ballymena U	0-1
Dungannon Swifts v Linfield	0-1*

BETMCLEAN LEAGUE CUP FINAL 2019

Belfast, Saturday16 February 2019

Ballymena U (0) 0

Linfield (1) 1 *(Waterworth 15)*

Ballymena U: Glendinning; Addis, Friel, Knowles (Kane 46), McCullough, McGrory (Shevlin 83), Balmer, Winchester (McMurray 74), Ervin, Lecky, Millar.
Linfield: Deane; Robinson, Callacher, Waterworth, Stewart (O'Connor 67), Millar, Clarke, McClean, Mulgrew, Quinn, Casement.
Referee: Andrew Davey

ROLL OF HONOUR SEASON 2018–19

Competition	*Winner*	*Runner-up*
NIFL Danske Bank Premiership	Linfield	Ballymena U
Tennent's Irish FA Cup	Crusaders	Ballinamallard U
NIFL Championship	Larne	Carrick Rangers
NIFL Premier Intermediate	Queen's University	Annagh U
BetMcLean Northern Ireland League Cup	Linfield	Ballymena U
County Antrim Shield	Crusaders	Linfield
Steel & Sons Cup	East Belfast	Sirocco Works
Co Antrim Junior Shield	Willowbank	Ballycastle U
Irish Junior Cup	Enniskillen Rangers	Tummery Ath
Mid Ulster Cup (Senior)	Glenaven	Warrenpoint T
Harry Cavan Youth Cup	Linfield Rangers	St Oliver Plunkett
George Wilson Memorial Cup	Knockbreda	Crusaders
North West Senior Cup	Limvardy	Institute
The Fermanagh Mulhern Cup	Tummery Ath	NFC Kesh
Intermediate Cup	Crumlin Star	Queen's University

NORTHERN IRELAND FOOTBALL WRITERS ASSOCIATION AWARDS 2018–19

BETMCLEAN MANAGER OF THE YEAR
David Healy (Linfield)

DANSKE BANK UK PLAYER OF THE YEAR
Jimmy Callacher (Linfield)

DREAM SPANISH HOMES YOUNG PLAYER OF THE YEAR
Kofi Balmer (Ballymena U)

SODEXO CHAMPIONSHIP PLAYER OF THE YEAR
Martin Donnelly (Larne)

BELLEEK PREMIER INTERMEDIATE PLAYER OF THE YEAR
Ryan McCready (Queen's University)

REAVY SOLICITORS INTERNATIONAL PERSONALITY OF THE YEAR
Craig Cathcart (Watford)

JIMMY DUBOIS NON-SENIOR TEAM OF THE YEAR
Crumlin Star

MERIT AWARD
Brian Montgomery

GOLDEN BOOT
Joe Gormley (Cliftonville) and Andrew Waterworth (Linfield)

JORDAN'S GIFT GOAL OF THE SEASON 2018–19
Michael McLellan of Ards v Solitude, Danske Bank Premiership, 29 September 2018

ELECTRIC IRELAND WOMEN'S PERSONALITY OF THE YEAR
Billie Simpson (Cliftonville)

DR MALCOLM BRODIE HALL OF FAME
George Best

UHLSPORT PREMIERSHIP TEAM OF THE YEAR
Jonathan Tuffey (Glenavon)
Chris Casement (Linfield)
Jimmy Callacher (Linfield)
Joshua Robinson (Linfield)
Niall Quinn (Linfield)
Jordan Stewart (Linfield)
Jamie Mulgrew (Linfield)
Jordan Forsythe (Crusaders)
Paul Heatley (Crusaders)
Andrew Waterworth (Linfield)
Adam Lecky (Ballymena U)

BELLEEK NIFWA PREMIERSHIP PLAYER OF THE MONTH 2018-19

Month	*Player*	*Team*
August	Michael McCrudden	Institute
September	Joe Gormley	Cliftonville
October	Andy Hall	Glenavon
November	Paul Heatly	Crusaders
December	Michael McCrudden	Institute
January	Jimmy Callagher	Linfield
February	Joshua Robinson	Linfield
March	David Cushley	Crusaders
April	Sam Johnston	Ards

@BET_MCLEAN NIFWA MANAGER OF THE MONTH 2018-19

Month	*Manager*	*Team*
August	David Healey	Linfield
September	Gary Hamilton	Glenavon
October	Gary Hamilton	Glenavon
November	David Jeffrey	Ballymena U
December	David Jeffrey	Ballymena U
January	David Healey	Linfield
February	David Healey	Linfield
March	Stephen Baxter	Crusaders
April	Gary Hamilton	Glenavon

BELLEEK NIFWA CHAMPIONSHIP 1 PLAYER OF THE MONTH 2018-19

Month	*Player*	*Team*
August	Martin Donnelly	Larne
September	Jordan Hughes	Dundela
October	Jordan Hughes	Dundela
November	Jeff Hughes	Larne
December	Ryan Campbell	Ballinamallard U
January	David McDaid	Larne
February	Caolan Loughran	Carrick Rangers
March	John Connolly	Ballinamallard U
April	David McDaid	Larne

EUROPEAN CUP FINALS

EUROPEAN CUP FINALS 1956–1992

Year	Winners v Runners-up		Venue	Attendance	Referee
1956	Real Madrid v Reims	4-3	Paris	38,239	A. Ellis (England)
1957	Real Madrid v Fiorentina	2-0	Madrid	124,000	L. Horn (Netherlands)
1958	Real Madrid v AC Milan	3-2*	Brussels	67,000	A. Alsteen (Belgium)
1959	Real Madrid v Reims	2-0	Stuttgart	72,000	A. Dutsch (West Germany)
1960	Real Madrid v Eintracht Frankfurt	7-3	Glasgow	127,621	J. Mowat (Scotland)
1961	Benfica v Barcelona	3-2	Berne	26,732	G. Dienst (Switzerland)
1962	Benfica v Real Madrid	5-3	Amsterdam	61,257	L. Horn (Netherlands)
1963	AC Milan v Benfica	2-1	Wembley	45,715	A. Holland (England)
1964	Internazionale v Real Madrid	3-1	Vienna	71,333	J. Stoll (Austria)
1965	Internazionale v Benfica	1-0	Milan	89,000	G. Dienst (Switzerland)
1966	Real Madrid v Partizan Belgrade	2-1	Brussels	46,745	R. Kreitlein (West Germany)
1967	Celtic v Internazionale	2-1	Lisbon	45,000	K. Tschenscher (West Germany)
1968	Manchester U v Benfica	4-1*	Wembley	92,225	C. Lo Bello (Italy)
1969	AC Milan v Ajax	4-1	Madrid	31,782	J. Ortiz de Mendibil (Spain)
1970	Feyenoord v Celtic	2-1*	Milan	53,187	C. Lo Bello (Italy)
1971	Ajax v Panathinaikos	2-0	Wembley	90,000	J. Taylor (England)
1972	Ajax v Internazionale	2-0	Rotterdam	61,354	R. Helies (France)
1973	Ajax v Juventus	1-0	Belgrade	89,484	M. Guglovic (Yugoslavia)
1974	Bayern Munich v Atletico Madrid	1-1	Brussels	48,722	V. Loraux (Belgium)
Replay	Bayern Munich v Atletico Madrid	4-0	Brussels	23,325	A. Delcourt (Belgium)
1975	Bayern Munich v Leeds U	2-0	Paris	48,374	M. Kitabdjian (France)
1976	Bayern Munich v Saint-Etienne	1-0	Glasgow	54,864	K. Palotai (Hungary)
1977	Liverpool v Moenchengladbach	3-1	Rome	52,078	R. Wurtz (France)
1978	Liverpool v Club Brugge	1-0	Wembley	92,500	C. Corver (Netherlands)
1979	Nottingham F v Malmo	1-0	Munich	57,500	E. Linemayr (Austria)
1980	Nottingham F v Hamburger SV	1-0	Madrid	51,000	A. Garrido (Portugal)
1981	Liverpool v Real Madrid	1-0	Paris	48,360	K. Palotai (Hungary)
1982	Aston Villa v Bayern Munich	1-0	Rotterdam	46,000	G. Konrath (France)
1983	Hamburg v Juventus	1-0	Athens	73,500	N. Rainea (Romania)
1984	Liverpool v Roma	1-1*	Rome	69,693	E. Fredriksson (Sweden)
	(Liverpool won 4-2 on penalties)				
1985	Juventus v Liverpool	1-0	Brussels	58,000	A. Daina (Switzerland)
1986	Steaua Bucharest v Barcelona	0-0*	Seville	70,000	M. Vautrot (France)
	(Steaua won 2-0 on penalties)				
1987	FC Porto v Bayern Munich	2-1	Vienna	57,500	A. Ponnet (Belgium)
1988	PSV Eindhoven v Benfica	0-0*	Stuttgart	68,000	L. Agnolin (Italy)
	(PSV won 6-5 on penalties)				
1989	AC Milan v Steaua Bucharest	4-0	Barcelona	97,000	K.-H. Tritschler (West Germany)
1990	AC Milan v Benfica	1-0	Vienna	57,500	H. Kohl (Austria)
1991	Crvena Zvezda v Olympique Marseille	0-0*	Bari	56,000	T. Lanese (Italy)
	(Crvena Zvezda won 5-3 on penalties)				
1992	Barcelona v Sampdoria	1-0*	Wembley	70,827	A. Schmidhuber (Germany)

UEFA CHAMPIONS LEAGUE FINALS 1993–2019

1993	Marseille† v AC Milan	1-0	Munich	64,400	K. Rothlisberger (Switzerland)
1994	AC Milan v Barcelona	4-0	Athens	70,000	P. Don (England)
1995	Ajax v AC Milan	1-0	Vienna	49,730	I. Craciunescu (Romania)
1996	Juventus v Ajax	1-1*	Rome	70,000	M. D. Vega (Spain)
	(Juventus won 4-2 on penalties)				
1997	Borussia Dortmund v Juventus	3-1	Munich	59,000	S. Puhl (Hungary)
1998	Real Madrid v Juventus	1-0	Amsterdam	48,500	H. Krug (Germany)
1999	Manchester U v Bayern Munich	2-1	Barcelona	90,245	P. Collina (Italy)
2000	Real Madrid v Valencia	3-0	Paris	80,000	S. Braschi (Italy)
2001	Bayern Munich v Valencia	1-1*	Milan	79,000	D. Jol (Netherlands)
	(Bayern Munich won 5-4 on penalties)				
2002	Real Madrid v Leverkusen	2-1	Glasgow	50,499	U. Meier (Switzerland)
2003	AC Milan v Juventus	0-0*	Manchester	62,315	M. Merk (Germany)
	(AC Milan won 3-2 on penalties)				
2004	FC Porto v Monaco	3-0	Gelsenkirchen	53,053	K. M. Nielsen (Denmark)
2005	Liverpool v AC Milan	3-3*	Istanbul	65,000	M. M. González (Spain)
	(Liverpool won 3-2 on penalties)				
2006	Barcelona v Arsenal	2-1	Paris	79,610	T. Hauge (Norway)
2007	AC Milan v Liverpool	2-1	Athens	74,000	H. Fandel (Germany)
2008	Manchester U v Chelsea	1-1*	Moscow	67,310	L. Michel (Slovakia)
	(Manchester U won 6-5 on penalties)				
2009	Barcelona v Manchester U	2-0	Rome	62,467	M. Busacca (Switzerland)
2010	Internazionale v Bayern Munich	2-0	Madrid	73,490	H. Webb (England)
2011	Barcelona v Manchester U	3-1	Wembley	87,695	V. Kassai (Hungary)
2012	Chelsea v Bayern Munich	1-1*	Munich	62,500	P. Proença (Portugal)
	(Chelsea won 4-3 on penalties)				
2013	Bayern Munich v Borussia Dortmund	2-1	Wembley	86,298	N. Rizzoli (Italy)
2014	Real Madrid v Atletico Madrid	4-1*	Lisbon	60,000	B. Kuipers (Netherlands)
2015	Barcelona v Juventus	3-1	Berlin	70,442	C. Cakir (Turkey)
2016	Real Madrid v Atletico Madrid	1-1*	Milan	71,942	M. Clattenburg (England)
	(Real Madrid won 5-3 on penalties)				
2017	Real Madrid v Juventus	4-1	Cardiff	65,842	F. Brych (Germany)
2018	Real Madrid v Liverpool	3-1	Kiev	61,561	M. Mazic (Serbia)
2019	Liverpool v Tottenham H	2-0	Madrid	63,272	D. Skomina (Slovenia)

*†Subsequently stripped of title. *After extra time.*

UEFA CHAMPIONS LEAGUE 2018–19

▪ *Denotes player sent off.*

PRELIMINARY ROUND

Tuesday, 26 June 2018

La Fiorita (0) 0

Lincoln Red Imps (1) 2 *(Hernandez 2, Moreno 51)* 840

La Fiorita: (442) Vivan; Gasperoni, Olivi, Di Maio, Mezzadri; Rinaldi (Selva 75), Loiodice (Righi 69), Tommasi, Amati; Buonocunto (Cattelan 89), Olcese.
Lincoln Red Imps: (433) Soler; Garcia, Oliver (Garro 74), Lopes, Chipolina; Montesinos, Moreno (Casciaro R 69), Calderon; Hernandez, Ortiz (Casciaro L 61), Gamiz.

Santa Coloma (0) 0

Drita (0) 2 *(Shabani X 99, Gerbeshi 105 (pen))* 288

Santa Coloma: (433) Casals; San Nicolas, Lima, Ramos, Cistero (Conde 84); Perez, Rebes, Rodriguez (Mercade 86); Torres, Riera (Sanchez Soto 62), Aranda (Faure 105).
Drita: (4231) Rexhepi; Kukar, Limani, Gerbeshi, Leci; Musaj (Shala 98), Shabani B; Shabani X, Krasniqi, Neziraj (Haliti 112); Kryeziu (Livoreka 85).
aet.

Friday, 29 June 2018

Lincoln Red Imps (0) 1 *(Corral 61)*

Drita (1) 4 *(Leci 2, 105 (pen), Neziraj 120, Shabani X 120)* 468

Lincoln Red Imps: (433) Soler; Oliver, Montesinos (Dos Santos 46), Lopes▪, Chipolina (Garcia 105); Moreno, Calderon (Corral 46), Hernandez; Gamiz, Ortiz (Aranda 71), Casciaro L.
Drita: (442) Rexhepi; Kukar, Limani, Gerbeshi▪, Leci; Krasniqi (Haliti 120), Shabani B, Musaj (Shala 68), Shabani X (Ruhani 120); Kryeziu (Livoreka 73), Neziraj.
aet.

FIRST QUALIFYING ROUND FIRST LEG

Tuesday, 10 July 2018

Alashkert (0) 0

Celtic (1) 3 *(Edouard 45, Forrest 81, McGregor 90)* 4948

Alashkert: (451) Cancarevic; Artak Yedigaryan, Voskanyan, Praznovsky, Daghbashyan; Dashyan, Arthur Yedigaryan (Manasyan 82), Grigoryan, Sekulic, Reis De Jesus (Simonyan 85); Nenadovic (Romero 54).
Celtic: (433) Gordon; Hendry, Simunovic, Ajer, Tierney; McGregor, Brown, Ntcham (Eboue 68); Forrest, Dembele (Sinclair 68), Edouard (Morgan 77).

Cork City (0) 0

Legia Warsaw (0) 1 *(Kucharczyk 79)* 5795

Cork City: (433) Cherrie; McCarthy (Beattie 61), Delaney, McLaughlin, Griffin; Morrissey (Cummins 52), Buckley, McCormack; McNamee (Sadlier 82), Sheppard, Keohane.
Legia Warsaw: (352) Malarz; Remy, Astiz, Wieteska; Vesovic, Cafu, Maczynski, Szymanski (Nagy 76), Kucharczyk; Hamalainen (Kulenovic 82), Kante (Hlousek 76).

F91 Dudelange (0) 1 *(Melisse 58)*

Vidi (1) 1 *(Huszti 42)* 1057

F91 Dudelange: (442) Joubert; Jordanov, Schnell, Prempeh, Melisse; Sinani, Kruska, Cruz (Stumpf 46 (Yeye 74)), Couturier; Stolz (Ibrahimovic 90), Turpel.
Vidi: (4312) Kovacsik; Nego, Vinicius, Fiola, Stopira; Huszti (Scepovic S 79), Hadzic, Patkai; Kovacs; Lazovic, Scepovic M.

Drita (0) 0

Malmo (2) 3 *(Strandberg 13, Traustason 39, Rosenberg 82)* 9780

Drita: (442) Rexhepi; Kukar, Limani, Leci (Haliti 83), Shala; Musaj (Kryeziu 76), Shabani B, Krasniqi, Shabani X; Haxhimusa (Livoreka 54), Neziraj.
Malmo: (442) Dahlin; Larsson, Nielsen, Bengtsson, Safari (Brorsson 64); Traustason, Lewicki, Bachirou, Rieks; Rosenberg (Innocent 84), Strandberg (Jeremejeff 61).

Flora Tallinn (0) 1 *(Sappinen 73 (pen))*

Hapoel Beer Sheva (2) 4 *(Sahar 18, Tzedek 36 (pen), Maman 53, Ezra 85)* 1106

Flora Tallinn: (4231) Toom; Kams, Vihmann, Lorenz, Saliste (Aloe 57); Dmitrijev, Ainsalu; Alliku, Beglarishvili (Poom 71), Liivak (Gussev 66); Sappinen.
Hapoel Beer Sheva: (451) Goresh; Bitton B, Tzedek, Taha, Biton; Ezra, Einbinder, Kabha (Broun 48), Maman (Zrihen 61), Melikson; Sahar (Pekhart 79).

Shkendija (2) 5 *(Emini 14, Ibraimi 38, 53, 60, 66)*

The New Saints (0) 0 2700

Shkendija: (433) Zahov; Bejtulai, Musliu, Adili, Murati; Alimi, Taipi (Zejnulai 81), Radeski; Emini (Selmani 83), Junior, Ibraimi (Shefiti 75).
The New Saints: (4321) Harrison; Spender (Lewis 73), Hudson, Cabango, Marriott; Ebbe (Byrne 65), Holland, Brobbel; Routledge, Redmond (Edwards 68); Mullan.

Torpedo Kutaisi (1) 2 *(Kimadze 24, Kukhianidze 63 (pen))*

Sheriff (1) 1 *(Badibanga 14)* 7251

Torpedo Kutaisi: (4411) Kvaskhvadze; Gegetchkori, Kobakhidze (Khurtsilava 82), Azatskiy, Marin; Dolidze (Daffe 62), Hlinka, Tsintsadze, Kimadze (Tughushi 77); Kukhianidze; Kutalia.
Sheriff: (4231) Mikulic; Susic, Kovacevic, Kulusic, Cristiano; Palic, Kendysh; Rodrigues (Boicuic 78), Kapic (Santos Oliveira 67), Badibanga; Kamara.

Vikingur (0) 1 *(Vatnhamar G 51)*

HJK Helsinki (2) 2 *(Dahlstrom 9, Gregersen 29 (og))* 300

Vikingur: (4411) Rasmussen; Lervig E, Gregersen, Cascaval, Jacobsen; Hansen (Lokin 74), Djurhuus (Nieblas 59), Vatnhamar G (Lervig H 89), Djordjevic; Vatnhamar S; Lawal.
HJK Helsinki: (4231) Rudakov; Peiponen, Obilor, Patronen, Rafinha; Annan, Dahlstrom (Vesiaho 54); Riski (Vertainen 80), Yaghoubi, Mensah; Klauss.

Wednesday, 11 July 2018

Astana (1) 1 *(Murtazayev 29 (pen))*

Sutjeska (0) 0 20,500

Astana: (4231) Eric; Rukavina, Postnikov, Anicic, Shomko; Maevskiy, Kleinheisler; Tomasov, Muzhikov (Zainutdinov 90), Murtazayev (Stanojevic 86); Despotovic (Shchetkin 73).
Sutjeska: (4231) Giljen; Milos Vucic, Cicmil, Nedic, Bulatovic; Loncar, Stefanovic; Marko Vucic (Grivic 90), Cetkovic (Vukovic 78), Merdovic; Kordic (Bozovic 85).

Kukesi (0) 0

Valletta (0) 0 350

Kukesi: (433) Frasheri; William, Shameti, Qaqi, Rrumbullaku; Musolli, Shkodra (Spehar 80), Dzaria; Cyrbja, Plaku (Harba 75), Zguro (Ethemi 58).
Valletta: (433) Bonello; Pena, Borg S, Camilleri, Zerafa; Santiago, Muscat (Gill 70), Saleh (Borg J 90); Alba (Nwoko 77), Fontanella, Piciollo.

Ludogorets Razgrad (2) 7 *(Marcelinho 25, 66, Burns 40 (og), Keseru 53, Swierczok 73, 78, 80)*

Crusaders (0) 0 4597

Ludogorets Razgrad: (433) Renan; Cicinho, Moti, Forster, Natanael; Dyakov, Marcelinho, Campanharo (Sasha 64); Wanderson (Lukoki 77), Keseru (Swierczok 68), Misidjan.
Crusaders: (433) O'Neill; Forsyth, Burns, Beverland, Brown; Snoddy, Caddell (Owens K 59), Lowry; Heatley (Glackin 75), Carvill (Clarke 75), Owens J.

Olimpija Ljubljana (0) 0

Qarabag (0) 1 *(Guerrier 79)* 5248

Olimpija Ljubljana: (451) Ivacic; Bagnack, Gajic, Zarifovic, Stiglec; Avramovski (Boateng 88), Putincanin, Tomic, Kronaveter (Brkic 81), Savic (Crnic 71); Abass■.
Qarabag: (433) Vagner; Medvedev, Huseynov B, Rzezniczak, Guerrier; Diniyev (Slachev 46), Garayev■, Ozobic (Quintana 63); Michel, Zoubir (Sadygov 90), Madatov.

Spartak Trnava (0) 1 *(Jirka 79)*

Zrinjski Mostar (0) 0 0

Spartak Trnava: (433) Chudy; Kadlec, Godal, Hladik, Conka; Rada, Grendel (Jarovic 79), Gressak; Jirka, Egho (Miesenboeck 86), Chanturishvili■.
Zrinjski Mostar: (4231) Brkic; Galic, Jakovljevic, Barisic, Stojkic; Rustemovic, Cirjak■; Filipovic (Bencun 89), Bilbja, Todorovic (Pezer 72); Acimovic (Jovic 68).
Behind closed doors.

Spartaks Jurmala (0) 0

Crvena Zvezda (0) 0 2563

Spartaks Jurmala: (433) Nerugals; Freimanis, Kosoric, Oss, Slampe; Maleev, Vitor Faiska, Dmitriev (Mihadjuks 76); Visnakovs, Svarups (Ezequiel Aguirre 66), Kobzar (Davydov 60).
Crvena Zvezda: (4321) Borjan; Stojkovic, Savic, Babic, Rodic; Milic (Ebecilio 46), Krsticic, Jovicic; Ben, Radonjic (Jevtovic 82); Stojiljkovic (Pavkov 17).

Suduva (3) 3 *(Cicilia 9, 13, 19)*

APOEL (0) 1 *(Caju 90)* 3378

Suduva: (532) Kardum; Svrljuga, Leimonas, Jankauskas, Zivanovic, Slavickas; Acevedo (Finkler 58), Matulevicius, Verbickas (Dybal 83); Topcagic (Vezevicius 30), Cicilia.
APOEL: (4231) Waterman; Milanov (Leo Natel 62), Merkis, Tavares, Caju; Morais, Vieira de Souza; Al-Taamari, De Vincenti, Sallai; Guilherme Dellatorre.

Valur (0) 1 *(Sigurbjornsson 84)*

Rosenborg (0) 0 1088

Valur: (352) Einarsson; Saevarsson, Eiriksson, Sigurbjornsson; Geirsson, Finsen (Lydsson 74), Sigurdsson H, Sigurdsson K, Larusson; Thomsen (Halldorsson 85), Pedersen.
Rosenborg: (433) Hansen; Hedenstadt (Lundemo 41), Reginiussen, Hovland, Reitan; Jensen, Trondsen, Meling; Levi, Bendtner, Botheim (Soderlund 64).

FIRST QUALIFYING ROUND SECOND LEG

Tuesday, 17 July 2018

APOEL (1) 1 *(Pote 20)*

Suduva (0) 0 12,149

APOEL: (433) Waterman; Milanov, Carlao, Tavares, Ioannou (Leo Natel 77); Vieira de Souza, Morais, Efrem (Aloneftis 77); Al-Taamari (Sallai 66), Pote, Guilherme Dellatorre.
Suduva: (532) Kardum; Svrljuga, Leimonas, Jankauskas, Zivanovic, Slavickas; Acevedo (Vezevicius 75), Matulevicius, Verbickas; Topcagic (Kasparavicius 54), Cicilia (Finkler 90).

Crusaders (0) 0

Ludogorets Razgrad (1) 2 *(Brown 11 (og), Swierczok 65)* 1116

Crusaders: (451) O'Neill; Burns, Beverland, Owens K, Brown; Forsyth, Carvill, Lowry (Caddell 67), Snoddy, Clarke (Glackin 81); Owens J (Cushley 32).
Ludogorets Razgrad: (433) Broun; Cicinho (Panov 61), Terziev, Moti, Natanael (Nedyalkov 70); Sasha, Marcelinho, Dyakov; Lukoki, Swierczok (Bakalov 79), Joao Paulo.

Crvena Zvezda (0) 2 *(Ben 78, Krsticic 81)*

Spartaks Jurmala (0) 0 23,868

Crvena Zvezda: (433) Borjan; Stojkovic, Savic, Degenek, Rodic; Krsticic, Ebecilio (Meleg 72), Jovicic; Milic (Pavkov 60), Ben, Radonjic (Jovancic 85).
Spartaks Jurmala: (433) Nerugals; Freimanis, Oss, Kosoric, Slampe; Dmitriev (Smith 83), Maleev, Vitor Faiska; Kobzar, Svarups (Ezequiel Aguirre 56), Visnakovs (Davydov 49).

Hapoel Beer Sheva (2) 3 *(Ezra 15, Maman 27, Melikson 48)*

Flora Tallinn (0) 1 *(Alliku 86)* 11,850

Hapoel Beer Sheva: (4231) Anestis; Bitton B, Taha, Tzedek (Bitton A 74), Biton; Cetout, Ogu (Einbinder 57); Ezra, Maman (Zrihan 67), Melikson; Sahar.
Flora Tallinn: (4411) Toom; Kams, Vihmann, Lorenz, Aloe; Alliku, Dmitrijev, Ainsalu (Slein 57), Liivak (Gussev 46); Poom; Sappinen.

HJK Helsinki (3) 3 *(Klauss 1, Mensah 10, Yaghoubi 19)*

Vikingur (1) 1 *(Vatnhamar G 21)* 5125

HJK Helsinki: (4231) Rudakov; Rafinha, Obilor, Patronen, O'Shaughnessy; Annan, Dahlstrom (Ollikainen 84); Riski, Yaghoubi, Mensah (Banza 72); Klauss (Valencic 67).
Vikingur: (4411) Rasmussen; Lervig E, Gregersen, Cascaval (Hansen 67), Jacobsen; Vatnhamar G, Nieblas, Djurhuus (Lokin 59), Djordjevic; Vatnhamar S; Lawal (Olsen 72).

Legia Warsaw (1) 3 *(Kante 27, Radovic 73 (pen), Lopez 89)*

Cork City (0) 0 14,576

Legia Warsaw: (352) Malarz; Remy, Astiz, Wieteska (Antolic 69); Vesovic, Cafu, Maczynski, Kucharczyk (Hlousek 46), Nagy; Kante (Lopez 64), Radovic.
Cork City: (433) Cherrie; Beattie (Kane 79), Delaney, McLaughlin, Griffin; Buckley (Sadlier 79), McCormack, Keohane; Sheppard, Cummins (O'Hanlon 79), McNamee.

Malmo (0) 2 *(Strandberg 55, Larsson 60)*

Drita (0) 0 10,623

Malmo: (442) Dahlin; Larsson, Brorsson, Bengtsson (Safari 64), Nielsen; Lewicki, Bachirou (Innocent 71), Adrian, Rieks (Binaku 58); Strandberg, Jeremejeff.
Drita: (442) Bakaj; Kukar, Limani, Leci, Shala; Musaj (Livoreka 88), Shabani B, Krasniqi (Haxhimusa 62), Shabani X; Kryeziu (Mustafa 72), Neziraj.

The New Saints (3) 4 *(Ebbe 15, Redmond 30, Cabango 35, Byrne 90)*

Shkendija (0) 0 756

The New Saints: (4231) Harrison; Lewis, Hudson, Cabango, Marriott; Routledge, Holland (Byrne 88); Mullan, Edwards, Redmond (Cieslewicz 83); Ebbe (Draper 56).
Shkendija: (4231) Zahov; Bejtulai, Musliu, Adili, Wakili; Zejnulai (Cheshmedjiev 88), Alimi; Todorovski (Radeski 46), Emini, Junior; Shefiti (Ibraimi 46).

Valletta (0) 1 *(Santiago 67)*

Kukesi (0) 1 *(Dzaria 84)* 1307

Valletta: (433) Bonello; Pena, Borg S, Camilleri, Zerafa (Nwoko 86); Alba (Gavrila 90), Muscat, Santiago; Saleh (Gill 83), Fontanella, Piciollo.
Kukesi: (433) Frasheri; William, Shameti, Alla, Rrumbullaku; Musolli, Dzaria, Shkodra (Harba 57); Cyrbja (Ethemi 65), Plaku, Zguro■ (Spehar 57).
Kukesi won on away goals rule.

Vidi (1) 2 *(Lazovic 18, Scepovic M 58)*

F91 Dudelange (0) 1 *(Couturier 54)* 2514

Vidi: (433) Kovacsik; Nego, Vinicius, Fiola, Stopira; Huszti (Nikolov 63), Juhasz, Patkai; Lazovic (Varga 84), Hadzic, Scepovic M (Kovacs 89).
F91 Dudelange: (442) Joubert; Jordanov, Schnell, Prempeh, Melisse■; Sinani (Yeye 76), Cruz, Kruska (Perez 83), Couturier; Turpel, Stolz (Ibrahimovic 69).

Wednesday, 18 July 2018

Celtic (3) 3 *(Dembele 8, 19 (pen), Forrest 35)*

Alashkert (0) 0 59,047

Celtic: (442) Gordon; Hendry, Ajer, Simunovic■, Forrest (Johnston 76); Brown, Tierney, Ntcham, McGregor; Dembele (Christie 66), Edouard (Sinclair 64).
Alashkert: (442) Cancarevic; Dashyan, Voskanyan, Praznovsky, Daghbashyan; Grigoryan, Sekulic (Simonyan 63), Arthur Yedigaryan, Reis De Jesus (Romero 82); Nenadovic (Manasyan 46), Artak Yedigaryan.

Qarabag (0) 0

Olimpija Ljubljana (0) 0 21,520

Qarabag: (4231) Vagner; Medvedev, Rzezniczak, Guseynov, Guerrier; Slachev, Diniyev; Quintana (Ozobic 42), Michel, Zoubir; Madatov (Agolli 90).
Olimpija Ljubljana: (4141) Ivacic; Bagnack (Ilic 74), Zarifovic, Gajic■, Stiglec; Tomic; Boateng, Putincanin, Avramovski, Savic (Crnic 46); Kronaveter (Miskic 72).

Rosenborg (0) 3 *(Bendtner 55 (pen), 90 (pen), Trondsen 72)*

Valur (0) 1 *(Sigurdsson K 85 (pen))* 10,604

Rosenborg: (433) Hansen; Hedenstadt, Reginiussen, Hovland, Meling; Trondsen, Lundemo (Vilhjalmsson 86), Jensen; Helland, Bendtner, Levi (Soderlund 82).
Valur: (352) Einarsson; Sigurbjornsson (Lydsson 74), Saevarsson, Eiriksson; Geirsson, Finsen (Ingvarsson 75), Sigurdsson K, Sigurdsson H, Larusson; Thomsen, Pedersen■ (Jonsson 89).

Sheriff (2) 3 *(Badibanga 9, Santos Oliveira 40, 55)*

Torpedo Kutaisi (0) 0 574

Sheriff: (433) Mikulic; Susic, Posmac, Kulusic, Cristiano; Kendysh (Anton 75), Kapic (Rodrigues 73), Palic; Santos Oliveira (Kovacevic 89), Kamara, Badibanga.
Torpedo Kutaisi: (4231) Kvaskhvadze; Kobakhidze, Khurtsilava, Marin, Azatskiy; Hlinka, Tabatadze; Gegetchkori (Daffe 46), Kukhianidze (Tughushi 57), Kimadze; Kutalia (Kapanadze 68).

Sutjeska (0) 0

Astana (1) 2 *(Despotovic 38, Muzhikov 65)* 3200

Sutjeska: (4231) Giljen; Nedic, Cetkovic, Loncar, Bulatovic; Merdovic, Stefanovic (Bubanja 61); Marko Vucic (Denkovic 54), Milos Vucic, Kordic (Grbovic 71); Cicmil.
Astana: (4231) Eric; Rukavina, Anicic, Kleinheisler (Richard 81), Muzhikov; Despotovic (Shchetkin 79), Tomasov; Maevskiy, Postnikov, Murtazayev (Zainutdinov 85); Shomko.

Zrinjski Mostar (0) 1 *(Todorovic 58)*

Spartak Trnava (1) 1 *(Godal 15)* 5100

Zrinjski Mostar: (4231) Brkic; Galic, Jakovljevic, Barisic, Stojkic; Rustemovic (Bencun 54), Hairlahovic (Pezer 81); Filipovic, Bilbja, Todorovic; Acimovic (Jovic 75).
Spartak Trnava: (433) Chudy; Toth (Miesenboeck 17), Hladik, Godal, Conka; Kadlec, Grendel (Oravec 78), Rada; Jirka, Gressak, Egho (Jarovic 81).

SECOND QUALIFYING ROUND FIRST LEG

Tuesday, 24 July 2018

Astana (1) 2 *(Kleinheisler 31, 90)*

Midtjylland (0) 1 *(Wikheim 51)* 23,010

Astana: (4411) Eric; Rukavina, Postnikov, Anicic, Shomko; Tomasov, Kleinheisler, Maevskiy, Pedro Henrique (Janga 85); Muzhikov (Richard 76); Murtazayev (Shchetkin 46).
Midtjylland: (343) Hansen J; Hansen K (Korcsmar 77), Sanneh, Sviatchenko; Poulsen, Sparv, Munksgaard, Dal Hende; Okosun (Onyeka 68), Onuachu, Wikheim (George 85).

CFR Cluj (0) 0

Malmo (1) 1 *(Strandberg 45)* 6950

CFR Cluj: (4141) Arlauskis; Manea, Vinicius, Muresan, Camora; Hoban (Males 60); Deac (Paun 79), Djokovic (Ionita 46), Culio, Omrani; Tucudean.
Malmo: (442) Dahlin; Larsson (Vindheim 89), Nielsen, Bengtsson, Safari; Traustason (Adrian 89), Lewicki, Christensen, Rieks; Rosenberg, Strandberg (Antonsson 86).

Crvena Zvezda (2) 3 *(Ebecilio 23, Radonjic 35, 58)*

Suduva (0) 0 23,218

Crvena Zvezda: (4321) Borjan; Stojkovic, Savic, Degenek, Rodic; Jovicic, Ebecilio (Jevtovic 64), Krsticic (Jovancic 37); Milic, Radonjic (Gobeljic 78); Ben.
Suduva: (532) Kardum; Svrljuga, Leimonas, Jankauskas, Zivanovic, Slavickas; Acevedo, Matulevicius (Gajduchik 80), Verbickas; Topcagic (Vezevicius 8), Cicilia.

Dinamo Zagreb (2) 5 *(Hajrovic 22, Orsic 28, Ademi 51, 62, Hodzic 82)*

Hapoel Beer Sheva (0) 0 9099

Dinamo Zagreb: (4141) Zagorac; Stojanovic, Dilaver, Theophile-Catherine, Leovac; Ademi; Hajrovic (Fiolic 85), Olmo, Gojak, Orsic (Situm 74); Budimir (Hodzic 70).
Hapoel Beer Sheva: (451) Anestis; Bitton B, Taha, Tzedek, Biton; Ezra (Nwakaeme 54), Cetout (Maman 46), Ogu, Einbinder (Ben Basat 73), Melikson; Sahar.

Legia Warsaw (0) 0

Spartak Trnava (1) 2 *(Grendel 16, Vlasko 90)* 15,527

Legia Warsaw: (352) Malarz; Astiz, Philipps (Hamalainen 69), Hlousek; Szymanski (Radovic 63), Maczynski (Wieteska 17), Vesovic, Cafu, Antolic; Lopez, Kante.
Spartak Trnava: (352) Chudy; Toth, Godal, Gressak; Kadlec, Sloboda (Hladik 86), Grendel (Miesenboeck 64), Rada, Conka; Jirka, Egho (Vlasko 90).

PAOK (1) 2 *(Canas 32, Prijovic 80)*

FC Basel (0) 1 *(Ajeti 82)* 24,670

PAOK: (4231) Paschalakis; Leo Matos, Varela, Crespo, Vieirinha; Canas, Mauricio; Leo Jaba (El Kaddouri 72), Pelkas, Limnios (Shakhov 90); Prijovic (Warda 83).
FC Basel: (343) Omlin; Suchy, Frei, Balanta; Petretta (Kaiser 44), Die, Zuffi, Riveros; Oberlin (Kalulu 62), Ajeti (Bua 90), Stocker.

Shkendija (1) 1 *(Ibraimi 24)*

Sheriff (0) 0 3696

Shkendija: (4231) Zahov; Bejtulai, Musliu, Adili, Murati; Totre (Taipi 76), Alimi; Selmani (Shefiti 65), Emini (Cheshmedjiev 86), Junior; Ibraimi.
Sheriff: (433) Mikulic; Susic, Posmac, Kulusic, Cristiano; Kendysh, Kapic (Rodrigues 80), Palic; Santos Oliveira (Oancea 88), Kamara (Boicuic 73), Badibanga.

Wednesday, 25 July 2018

Ajax (1) 2 *(Ziyech 15, Schone 57)*

Sturm Graz (0) 0 53,106

Ajax: (433) Onana; Mazraoui, de Ligt, De Jong, Tagliafico; van de Beek, Schone (Tadic 66), Eiting (Blind 84); Neres, Huntelaar (Sierhuis 87), Ziyech.
Sturm Graz: (541) Siebenhandl; Koch, Spendlhofer, Avlonitis, Maresic, Filipe Ferreira (Lovric 46); Hierlander, Zulj, Lackner, Grozurek (Huspek 76); Eze (Hosiner 58).

BATE Borisov (0) 0

HJK Helsinki (0) 0 11,567

BATE Borisov: (451) Scherbitski; Rios, Filipovic, Filipenko, Volodjko; Skavysh (Hleb 65), Baha, Dragun, Ivanic, Stasevich; Signevich.
HJK Helsinki: (451) Rudakov; Rafinha, Obilor, Patronen, O'Shaughnessy; Riski (Alho 70), Annan, Yaghoubi, Dahlstrom, Mensah (Sumusalo 89); Klauss (Chrisantus 85).

Celtic (1) 3 *(Edouard 43, 75, Ntcham 46)*

Rosenborg (1) 1 *(Meling 16)* 50,000

Celtic: (433) Gordon; Gamboa, Hendry, Ajer, Tierney; McGregor, Brown, Ntcham (Rogic 76); Forrest, Edouard, Sinclair.
Rosenborg: (433) Hansen; Hedenstadt, Reginiussen, Hovland, Meling; Jensen, Lundemo (Soderlund 61), Trondsen; Helland (Gersbach 72), Bendtner, Levi.

Kukesi (0) 0
Qarabag (0) 0 700
Kukesi: (532) Frasheri; William, Alla, Shameti, Malikji, Rrumbullaku; Cyrbja (Ethemi 90), Dzaria, Qaqi; Musolli, Plaku (Harba 76).
Qarabag: (4231) Vagner; Medvedev, Huseynov B, Sadygov, Agolli; Slachev, Garayev; Guerrier (Huseynov A 89), Michel, Ozobic; Madatov.

Ludogorets Razgrad (0) 0
Vidi (0) 0 5000
Ludogorets Razgrad: (4231) Renan; Cicinho, Forster, Moti, Natanael; Dyakov, Sasha (Campanharo 61); Wanderson, Marcelinho, Misidjan (Lukoki 84); Keseru (Swierczok 60).
Vidi: (4312) Kovacsik; Fiola, Vinicius, Juhasz, Stopira; Varga, Nikolov (Lazovic 71), Nego; Kovacs (Patkai 68); Huszti, Scepovic M (Scepovic S 80).

SECOND QUALIFYING ROUND SECOND LEG

Tuesday, 31 July 2018

Hapoel Beer Sheva (2) 2 *(Ogu 14, Stojanovic 34 (og))*
Dinamo Zagreb (0) 2 *(Budimir 49, Hajrovic 54)* 10,181
Hapoel Beer Sheva: (442) Goresh; Bitton B, Tzedek, Nwakaeme, Einbinder; Biton, Ohayon, Melikson, Ben Basat (Sahar 76); Maman (Ezra 72), Ogu.
Dinamo Zagreb: (442) Zagorac; Ademi, Olmo (Sunjic 78), Hajrovic (Fiolic 82), Budimir (Gavranovic 56); Gojak, Leovac, Theophile-Catherine, Stojanovic; Dilaver, Orsic.

Sheriff (0) 0
Shkendija (0) 0 6319
Sheriff: (442) Pascenco; Santos Oliveira (Balima 69), Cristiano, Palic, Kovacevic; Badibanga (Rodrigues 56), Kamara, Susic, Kendysh; Kapic (Boicuic 78), Posmac.
Shkendija: (442) Zahov; Bejtulai, Alimi, Musliu, Ibraimi; Totre (Taipi 84), Selmani (Cheshmedjiev 90), Murati, Junior; Emini (Nafiu 67), Adili.

Spartak Trnava (0) 0
Legia Warsaw (0) 1 *(Astiz 63)* 17,204
Spartak Trnava: (352) Chudy; Conka, Egho (Hladik 90), Godal; Grendel (Miesenboeck 70), Gressak, Jirka, Kadlec, Rada; Sloboda (Vlasko 76), Toth.
Legia Warsaw: (451) Malarz; Antolic■, Astiz, Hlousek, Kante; Kucharczyk, Maczynski (Hamalainen 80), Pazdan (Lopez 53), Radovic (Cafu 46), Vesovic; Wieteska.

Wednesday, 1 August 2018

FC Basel (0) 0
PAOK (1) 3 *(Varela 7, Prijovic 52, El Kaddouri 60)* 14,328
FC Basel: (4231) Omlin; Widmer, Cumart, Suchy, Balanta; Die, Zuffi; Bua, Kalulu (Oberlin 84), Stocker (Campo 46); Ajeti (van Wolfswinkel 73).
PAOK: (4231) Paschalakis; Leo Matos, Varela, Crespo, Vieirinha; Canas (Shakhov 82), Mauricio; Limnios, Pelkas (Warda 85), El Kaddouri (Leo Jaba 74); Prijovic.

HJK Helsinki (1) 1 *(Yaghoubi 28)*
BATE Borisov (2) 2 *(Rafinha 21 (og), Stasevich 24)* 10,210
HJK Helsinki: (4141) Rudakov; Rafinha, Obilor, Patronen, Sumusalo; Annan; Riski (Alho 69), Dahlstrom (Vertainen 74), Yaghoubi, Mensah; Klauss.
BATE Borisov: (433) Scherbitski; Rios, Filipovic, Filipenko, Volodjko; Baha (Berezkin 77), Yablonskiy, Dragun; Ivanic (Skavysh 67), Signevich, Stasevich (Tuominem 87).

Malmo (0) 1 *(Traustason 55)*
CFR Cluj (1) 1 *(Djokovic 36)* 18,153
Malmo: (442) Dahlin; Larsson (Vindheim 81), Nielsen, Bengtsson, Safari; Traustason (Lewicki 73), Bachirou, Christensen, Rieks; Strandberg (Antonsson 61), Rosenberg.
CFR Cluj: (433) Arlauskis; Manea, Vinicius, Muresan, Camora; Djokovic (Bordeianu 58), Culio■, Hoban (De Luca 64); Deac (Mailat 43), Tucudean, Omrani.

Midtjylland (0) 0
Astana (0) 0 8731
Midtjylland: (343) Hansen J; Hansen K, Sanneh, Sviatchenko (Okosun 76); Munksgaard, Poulsen, Sparv (Mabil 59), Dal Hende; Onyeka (Duelund 71), Onuachu, Wikheim.
Astana: (4411) Eric; Rukavina, Postnikov, Anicic, Shomko; Tomasov, Maevskiy, Kleinheisler (Logvinenko 90), Pedro Henrique (Murtazayev 78); Muzhikov; Kabananga (Shchetkin 62).

Qarabag (1) 3 *(Quintana 24 (pen), 57 (pen), Delarge 89)*
Kukesi (0) 0 25,030
Qarabag: (4411) Vagner; Medvedev, Huseynov B, Sadygov (Rzezniczak 77), Guerrier; Zoubir, Slachev, Garayev, Quintana (Delarge 60); Michel; Emeghara (Madatov 66).
Kukesi: (343) Frasheri; Qaqi, Shameti, Alla■; Malikji, Musolli (Shkodra 84), Dzaria, Rrumbullaku; Cyrbja (Spehar 46), Plaku (Reginaldo 46), William.

Rosenborg (0) 0
Celtic (0) 0 14,263
Rosenborg: (433) Hansen; Hedenstadt, Hovland, Reginiussen, Meling; Jensen, Lundemo (Botheim 90), Trondsen (Vilhjalmsson 75); Helland (Levi 58), Bendtner, Soderlund.
Celtic: (451) Gordon; Gamboa, Hendry, Ajer, Tierney (Lustig 85); Forrest (Rogic 63), McGregor, Brown, Ntcham, Sinclair; Edouard (Christie 72).

Sturm Graz (0) 1 *(Onana 89 (og))*
Ajax (1) 3 *(Huntelaar 39, 77, Tadic 48)* 15,172
Sturm Graz: (442) Siebenhandl; Lackner (Obermair 59), Lovric, Zulj, Hosiner (Pink 46); Filipe Ferreira, Spendlhofer, Hierlander, Koch; Maresic, Eze (Huspek 66).
Ajax: (433) Onana; de Ligt, Neres, Huntelaar, Ziyech; Tadic (van de Beek 67), Mazraoui, Eiting (Wober 75); Schone, De Jong, Tagliafico (Blind 5).

Suduva (0) 0
Crvena Zvezda (2) 2 *(Ben 8, Radonjic 38)* 4020
Suduva: (532) Kardum; Jankauskas, Svrljuga, Zivanovic (Gajduchik 68), Matulevicius (Acevedo 77), Leimonas; Slavickas, Verbickas, Finkler; Vezevicius (Kasparavicius 60), Cicilia.
Crvena Zvezda: (4231) Borjan; Rodic (Gobeljic 66), Savic, Krsticic, Jovicic; Degenek, Radonjic; Srnic (Ebecilio 76), Stojiljkovic, Ben; Milic (Stojkovic 60).

Vidi (1) 1 *(Hadzic 45)*
Ludogorets Razgrad (0) 0 2878
Vidi: (442) Kovacsik; Fiola, Vinicius, Stopira, Nego; Juhasz, Hadzic (Nikolov 89), Huszti, Varga; Scepovic M (Scepovic S 75), Kovacs (Patkai 90).
Ludogorets Razgrad: (433) Renan; Cicinho, Terziev, Moti, Natanael; Campanharo (Goralski 46), Dyakov, Marcelinho; Wanderson (Joao Paulo 74), Swierczok (Keseru 67), Misidjan■.

THIRD QUALIFYING ROUND FIRST LEG

Tuesday, 7 August 2018

Astana (0) 0
Dinamo Zagreb (1) 2 *(Budimir 39, Olmo 84)* 26,500
Astana: (4141) Eric; Rukavina, Postnikov, Anicic, Shomko; Maevskiy; Tomasov (Murtazayev 80), Kleinheisler, Muzhikov (Richard 46), Pedro Henrique; Kabananga (Janga 63).
Dinamo Zagreb: (4141) Zagorac; Stojanovic, Theophile-Catherine, Dilaver, Leovac; Ademi (Sunjic 63); Hajrovic (Kadzior 82), Gojak, Olmo, Orsic; Budimir (Gavranovic 46).

Benfica (0) 1 *(Cervi 69)*

Fenerbahce (0) 0 57,878

Benfica: (433) Vlachodimos; Andre Almeida, Dias, Jardel, Grimaldo; Pizzi, Fejsa, Fernandes; Salvio (Zivkovic 75), Ferreyra (Castillo 63), Cervi.
Fenerbahce: (4231) Demirel; Isla, Neustadter, Skrtel, Kaldirim; Elmas, Topal; Dirar (Alici 86), Giuliano, Valbuena (Ekici 61); Potuk (Soldado 74).

Crvena Zvezda (1) 1 *(Ben 23 (pen))*

Spartak Trnava (1) 1 *(Grendel 25)* 37,112

Crvena Zvezda: (433) Borjan; Stojiljkovic (Milic 53 (Srnic 73)), Savic, Degenek, Rodic; Jovicic, Ebecilio (Simic 80), Krsticic; Ben, Radonjic, Stojkovic.
Spartak Trnava: (451) Chudy; Kadlec, Toth, Godal, Conka; Jirka, Sloboda, Grendel (Miesenboeck 89), Gressak, Rada (Hladik 90); Bakos (Egho 75).

Malmo (0) 1 *(Christensen 62)*

Vidi (0) 1 *(Nego 71)* 17,209

Malmo: (442) Dahlin; Larsson, Nielsen, Bengtsson (Brorsson 31), Safari; Traustason (Lewicki 46), Bachirou, Christensen, Rieks; Antonsson (Gall 80), Rosenberg.
Vidi: (433) Kovacsik; Fiola, Vinicius, Juhasz, Stopira; Hadzic, Nikolov, Nego; Lazovic (Scepovic S 89), Kovacs (Patkai 78), Scepovic M (Varga 82).

Qarabag (0) 0

BATE Borisov (1) 1 *(Dragun 36)* 29,000

Qarabag: (4231) Halldorsson; Medvedev, Huseynov B, Sadygov, Guerrier; Slachev (Ozobic 80), Garayev; Delarge (Madatov 67), Michel, Zoubir; Emeghara.
BATE Borisov: (433) Scherbitski; Rios, Filipovic, Filipenko, Volodjko; Baha, Yablonskiy, Dragun (Berezkin 76); Ivanic (Skavysh 62), Signevich, Stasevich (Hleb 85).

Slavia Prague (0) 1 *(Husbauer 90 (pen))*

Dynamo Kyiv (0) 1 *(Verbic 82)* 19,370

Slavia Prague: (4231) Kolar; Coufal, Ngadeu Ngadjui, Deli, Boril; Soucek, Husbauer; Stoch, Sykora (Olayinka 86), Zmrhal (Baluta 80); Skoda (Tecl 60).
Dynamo Kyiv: (433) Boyko; Kedziora, Burda, Kadar, Morozyuk; Sydorchuk, Garmash, Buyalsky (Shepelev 68); Verbic, Besyedin, Tsygankov (Andrievsky 90).

Standard Liege (0) 2 *(Carcela-Gonzalez 67, Emond 90 (pen))*

Ajax (2) 2 *(Huntelaar 19, Tadic 34)* 20,355

Standard Liege: (433) Ochoa; Cavanda, Luyindama, Laifis, Fai; Marin, Agbo, Bastien (Cimirot 76); M'Poku (Djenepo 85), Orlando Sa (Emond 66), Carcela-Gonzalez.
Ajax: (433) Onana; Mazraoui, de Ligt, De Jong (van de Beek 79), Tagliafico; Schone (Eiting 89), Ziyech (Labyad 73), Blind; Neres, Huntelaar, Tadic.

Wednesday, 8 August 2018

Celtic (1) 1 *(McGregor 17)*

AEK Athens (1) 1 *(Klonaridis 44)* 54,370

Celtic: (442) Gordon; Lustig (Sinclair 77), Hendry, Ajer, Tierney; Brown, Ntcham, Forrest, Rogic (Griffiths 64); McGregor, Edouard.
AEK Athens: (4231) Barkas; Bakakis, Oikonomou, Lampropoulos, Helder Lopes; Galanopoulos■, Andre Simoes; Bakasetas (Alef 66), Klonaridis (Rodrigo Galo 80), Boye; Livaja (Ponce 77).

PAOK (3) 3 *(Prijovic 29 (pen), Limnios 37, Pelkas 44)*

Spartak Moscow (2) 2 *(Popov 7, Promes 17)* 24,463

PAOK: (442) Paschalakis; Leo Matos, Varela, Khacheridi, Crespo; El Kaddouri (Warda 61), Mauricio (Shakhov 85), Pelkas, Canas; Prijovic, Limnios (Leo Jaba 80).
Spartak Moscow: (442) Maksimenko; Lomovitskiy, Eshchenko, Bocchetti (Rasskazov 90), Gigot; Promes, Fernando, Kombarov, Zobnin; Popov (Timofeev 65), Luiz Adriano (Ze Luis 78).

Red Bull Salzburg (2) 3 *(Dabbur 16 (pen), 45, Samassekou 82 (pen))*

Shkendija (0) 0 10,050

Red Bull Salzburg: (442) Stankovic; Ramalho, Lainer, Ulmer, Pongracic; Yabo (Minamino 73), Samassekou, Junuzovic■, Schlager (Mwepu 83); Wolf, Dabbur (Daka 90).
Shkendija: (442) Zahov; Bejtulai, Adili, Musliu, Murati (Mici 76); Alimi, Ibraimi, Totre, Nafiu; Selmani (Emini 62), Junior (Shefiti 90).

THIRD QUALIFYING ROUND SECOND LEG

Tuesday, 14 August 2018

AEK Athens (1) 2 *(Rodrigo Galo 6, Livaja 50)*

Celtic (0) 1 *(Sinclair 78)* 32,300

AEK Athens: (4411) Barkas; Bakakis, Oikonomou, Lampropoulos, Hult; Rodrigo Galo (Albanis 82), Alef, Andre Simoes, Bakasetas (Cosic 90); Klonaridis (Mandalos 72); Livaja.
Celtic: (532) Gordon; Forrest, Lustig (Dembele 60), Hendry, Simunovic, Tierney; McGregor, Brown, Ntcham; Griffiths, Rogic (Sinclair 76).

Ajax (2) 3 *(Huntelaar 30, de Ligt 34, Neres 47)*

Standard Liege (0) 0 51,841

Ajax: (433) Onana; Mazraoui (Nissen 76), de Ligt, Blind, Tagliafico; De Jong, Schone, Ziyech (Labyad 90); Tadic, Huntelaar, Neres (van de Beek 82).
Standard Liege: (433) Ochoa; Cavanda (Pocognoli 66), Luyindama, Laifis, Fai; Marin, Agbo, Carcela-Gonzalez; Bastien (Cimirot 54), Emond (Orlando Sa 78), M'Poku.

BATE Borisov (1) 1 *(Ivanic 21)*

Qarabag (0) 1 *(Michel 54)* 12,489

BATE Borisov: (433) Scherbitski; Rios, Filipovic, Filipenko, Volodjko; Baha (Hleb 70), Yablonskiy, Dragun; Ivanic (Skavysh 78), Stasevich, Signevich.
Qarabag: (4231) Halldorsson; Medvedev (Delarge 85), Huseynov B, Sadygov, Guerrier; Slachev (Ozobic 77), Garayev; Madatov, Michel, Zoubir; Emeghara■.

Dinamo Zagreb (0) 1 *(Gavranovic 74)*

Astana (0) 0 11,903

Dinamo Zagreb: (4141) Zagorac; Stojanovic, Theophile-Catherine, Dilaver, Leovac; Ademi; Hajrovic, Gojak (Sunjic 70), Olmo, Orsic (Peric 83); Budimir (Gavranovic 56).
Astana: (4411) Eric; Rukavina, Postnikov, Maliy, Shomko; Tomasov, Maevskiy, Richard (Muzhikov 78), Pedro Henrique; Kleinheisler (Shchetkin 78); Janga (Kabananga 78).

Dynamo Kyiv (1) 2 *(Verbic 11, Besyedin 74)*

Slavia Prague (0) 0 39,318

Dynamo Kyiv: (433) Boyko; Kedziora, Burda (Shabanov 75), Kadar, Pivaric; Sydorchuk, Shepelev (Buyalsky 88), Garmash; Tsygankov (Morozyuk 90), Besyedin, Verbic.
Slavia Prague: (4231) Kolar; Coufal, Deli, Ngadeu Ngadjui, Boril; Soucek, Husbauer (Frydrych 85); Stoch, Sykora, Zmrhal (Baluta 68); Tecl (Skoda 75).

Fenerbahce (1) 1 *(Potuk 45)*

Benfica (1) 1 *(Fernandes 26)* 42,245

Fenerbahce: (433) Demirel; Isla (Ozbayrakli 79), Neustadter, Skrtel, Kaldirim; Elmas, Topal (Alici 65), Valbuena (Soldado 65); Potuk, Giuliano, Ayew.
Benfica: (433) Vlachodimos; Andre Almeida, Dias, Jardel, Grimaldo; Pizzi, Fejsa, Fernandes; Salvio (Semedo 72), Castillo (Ferreyra 34), Cervi.

Shkendija (0) 0

Red Bull Salzburg (0) 1 *(Minamino 90)* 3213

Shkendija: (4231) Zahov; Bejtulai, Musliu, Adili (Selmani 71), Mici; Alimi, Totre; Nafiu (Bojku 46), Emini (Shefiti 86), Junior; Ibraimi.
Red Bull Salzburg: (442) Stankovic; Lainer, Ramalho, Pongracic, Ulmer; Schlager (Leitgeb 89), Samassekou, Wolf, Haidara; Yabo (Minamino 67), Dabbur (Daka 76).

Spartak Moscow (0) 0

PAOK (0) 0 40,385

Spartak Moscow: (433) Maksimenko; Eshchenko, Gigot, Dzhikija, Kombarov (Melgarejo 76); Glushakov, Fernando (Samedov 62), Zobnin; Tashaev (Ze Luis 46), Promes, Luiz Adriano■.
PAOK: (433) Paschalakis; Leo Matos, Varela, Crespo, Vieirinha (Khacheridi 64); Mauricio, Canas, Pelkas (Shakhov 78); Limnios, Prijovic, El Kaddouri (Warda 46).

Spartak Trnava (1) 1 *(Bakos 6)*

Crvena Zvezda (1) 2 *(Ben 7, Radonjic 98)* 18,032

Spartak Trnava: (451) Chudy; Kadlec, Toth, Godal, Conka (Hladik 106); Jirka, Grendel, Sloboda, Gressak, Rada (Dangubic 100); Bakos.
Crvena Zvezda: (4231) Borjan; Stojiljkovic (Pavkov 75), Savic, Degenek, Rodic; Jovancic (Gobeljic 101), Krsticic; Ben, Simic (Jovicic 85), Radonjic (Babic 107); Stojkovic.
aet.

Vidi (0) 0

Malmo (0) 0 3432

Vidi: (442) Kovacsik; Fiola, Juhasz, Vinicius, Stopira; Nego, Hadzic, Nikolov (Patkai 85), Kovacs (Huszti 89); Lazovic (Tamas 90), Scepovic M.
Malmo: (442) Dahlin; Larsson (Vindheim 75), Brorsson, Nielsen, Lewicki; Bachirou, Innocent (Gall 79), Christensen, Rieks; Rosenberg, Strandberg (Antonsson 70).
Vidi won on away goals.

PLAY-OFF ROUND FIRST LEG

Tuesday, 21 August 2018

BATE Borisov (1) 2 *(Tuominem 9, Hleb 88)*

PSV Eindhoven (1) 3 *(Pereiro 35 (pen), Lozano 61, Malen 89)* 9284

BATE Borisov: (433) Scherbitski; Rios, Milunovic, Filipenko, Filipovic; Baha, Yablonskiy, Dragun (Hleb 65); Ivanic (Volkov 81), Tuominem (Skavysh 60), Stasevich.
PSV Eindhoven: (433) Zoet; Dumfries, Schwaab, Viergever, Tasende; Rosario (Isimat-Mirin 90), Hendrix, Pereiro; Lozano (Malen 86), de Jong, Bergwijn.

Benfica (1) 1 *(Pizzi 45 (pen))*

PAOK (0) 1 *(Warda 76)* 44,084

Benfica: (433) Vlachodimos; Andre Almeida, Dias, Jardel, Grimaldo; Pizzi (Joao Felix 79), Fejsa, Fernandes; Zivkovic (Rafa Silva 64), Ferreyra, Cervi (Seferovic 79).
PAOK: (433) Paschalakis; Leo Matos, Varela, Crespo, Vieirinha; Mauricio, Canas, Pelkas; Leo Jaba (Shakhov 81), Prijovic (Akpom 87), Limnios (Warda 52).

Crvena Zvezda (0) 0

Red Bull Salzburg (0) 0 0

Crvena Zvezda: (4231) Borjan; Stojiljkovic (Jovancic 79), Savic, Degenek, Rodic; Jovicic, Krsticic; Cafu, Ben, Radonjic; Stojkovic.
Red Bull Salzburg: (442) Stankovic; Lainer, Ramalho, Pongracic, Ulmer; Haidara, Samassekou, Wolf (Minamino 87), Junuzovic (Schlager 46); Yabo (Daka 79), Dabbur.
Behind closed doors.

Wednesday, 22 August 2018

Ajax (3) 3 *(van de Beek 2, Ziyech 35, Tadic 43)*

Dynamo Kyiv (1) 1 *(Kedziora 15)* 52,706

Ajax: (433) Onana; Mazraoui, de Ligt, Blind, Tagliafico; van de Beek (de Wit 87), Schone, De Jong; Ziyech, Huntelaar, Tadic.
Dynamo Kyiv: (433) Boyko; Kedziora, Burda, Kadar, Pivaric; Garmash (Shepelev 46), Sydorchuk (Tche Tche 77), Buyalsky; Tsygankov, Besyedin, Verbic.

Vidi (0) 1 *(Lazovic 68)*

AEK Athens (1) 2 *(Klonaridis 35, Bakasetas 49)* 10,681

Vidi: (433) Kovacsik; Fiola, Juhasz, Vinicius, Stopira; Nego, Hadzic, Nikolov (Scepovic M 54); Kovacs, Lazovic, Huszti■.
AEK Athens: (4231) Barkas; Bakakis, Oikonomou, Lampropoulos, Hult; Galanopoulos (Alef 66), Andre Simoes; Bakasetas■, Klonaridis (Helder Lopes 82), Mandalos; Livaja (Ponce 86).

Young Boys (1) 1 *(Mbabu 2)*

Dinamo Zagreb (1) 1 *(Orsic 40)* 21,463

Young Boys: (442) von Ballmoos; Mbabu, Wuthrich, von Bergen, Benito; Fassnacht (Aebischer 70), Sow, Sanogo, Sulejmani; Ngamaleu (Nsame 81), Hoarau.
Dinamo Zagreb: (4141) Zagorac; Stojanovic, Theophile-Catherine, Dilaver, Leovac; Ademi; Hajrovic (Kadzior 83), Olmo (Sunjic 86), Gojak, Orsic; Gavranovic (Budimir 74).

PLAY-OFF ROUND SECOND LEG

Tuesday, 28 August 2018

AEK Athens (0) 1 *(Mandalos 48 (pen))*

Vidi (0) 1 *(Nego 57)* 29,774

AEK Athens: (4231) Barkas; Bakakis, Oikonomou, Lampropoulos, Hult; Galanopoulos, Andre Simoes; Mandalos (Cosic 89), Klonaridis (Ponce 62), Helder Lopes■; Livaja (Alef 84).
Vidi: (433) Kovacsik; Fiola, Juhasz, Vinicius, Stopira; Nego, Hadzic, Nikolov (Patkai 46); Lazovic, Kovacs, Scepovic M.

Dinamo Zagreb (1) 1 *(Hajrovic 7)*

Young Boys (0) 2 *(Hoarau 64 (pen), 66)* 28,137

Dinamo Zagreb: (4141) Zagorac; Stojanovic, Theophile-Catherine, Dilaver, Leovac (Budimir 74); Ademi (Sunjic 31); Hajrovic, Gojak, Olmo, Orsic (Kadzior 82); Gavranovic.
Young Boys: (442) Ballmoos; Mbabu, Wuthrich, von Bergen, Benito; Fassnacht (Bertone 83), Sanogo, Sow, Sulejmani (Assale 55); Ngamaleu (Aebischer 90), Hoarau.

Dynamo Kyiv (0) 0

Ajax (0) 0 40,131

Dynamo Kyiv: (433) Boyko; Kedziora, Burda, Kadar, Pivaric; Shepelev (Garmash 46), Sydorchuk (Shaparenko 64), Buyalsky (Rusyn 85); Tsygankov, Supriaga, Verbic.
Ajax: (433) Onana; Mazraoui, de Ligt, Blind, Wober (Eiting 79); van de Beek (de Wit 84), Schone, De Jong; Ziyech, Huntelaar, Tadic.

Wednesday, 29 August 2018

PAOK (1) 1 *(Prijovic 13)*

Benfica (3) 4 *(Jardel 20, Salvio 26 (pen), 50 (pen), Pizzi 39)* 26,725

PAOK: (442) Paschalakis; Leo Matos■, Varela, Vieirinha, Crespo; El Kaddouri (Akpom 76), Mauricio, Pelkas, Canas (Shakhov 63); Limnios (Warda 46), Prijovic.
Benfica: (352) Vlachodimos; Grimaldo, Jardel, Fejsa; Dias, Cervi, Andre Almeida, Fernandes, Seferovic (Joao Felix 85); Salvio (Semedo 63), Pizzi (Zivkovic 76).

PSV Eindhoven (2) 3 *(Bergwijn 14, de Jong 36, Lozano 62)*

BATE Borisov (0) 0 34,200

PSV Eindhoven: (433) Zoet; Dumfries, Schwaab, Viergever (Isimat-Mirin 71), Tasende; Hendrix, Pereiro, Rosario (Ramselaar 74); Bergwijn (Malen 79), de Jong, Lozano.
BATE Borisov: (433) Scherbitski; Rios, Milunovic, Filipenko, Filipovic; Baha, Dragun (Berezkin 76), Hleb (Ivanic 30); Stasevich, Tuominem (Signevich 51), Volodjko.

Red Bull Salzburg (1) 2 *(Dabbur 45, 48 (pen))*

Crvena Zvezda (0) 2 *(Ben 65, Degenek 66)* 26,500

Red Bull Salzburg: (442) Stankovic; Lainer, Ramalho, Pongracic, Ulmer; Haidara, Wolf, Samassekou, Schlager (Prevljak 83); Daka (Yabo 69), Dabbur.
Crvena Zvezda: (4231) Borjan; Stojiljkovic, Savic, Degenek, Rodic; Milic (Pavkov 49), Jovicic; Krsticic, Radonjic (Gobeljic 82), Simic (Jovancic 37); Ben.
Crvena Zvezda won on away goals.

GROUP STAGE

GROUP A

Tuesday, 18 September 2018

Club Brugge (0) 0

Borussia Dortmund (0) 1 *(Pulisic 85)* 25,181

Club Brugge: (442) Letica; Poulain, Rits, Mitrovic, Denswil; Vlietinck (Cools 57), Vormer, Groeneveld (Bonaventure 75), Vanaken; Wesley, Vossen (Openda 82).
Borussia Dortmund: (4411) Burki; Piszczek, Akanji, Diallo, Schmelzer; Sancho (Pulisic 69), Weigl (Dahoud 84), Witsel, Reus; Gotze (Kagawa 62); Wolf.

Monaco (1) 1 *(Grandsir 18)*

Atletico Madrid (2) 2 *(Costa 31, Gimenez 45)* 10,575

Monaco: (433) Benaglio; Sidibe, Glik, Jemerson, Henrichs; N'Doram, Tielemans, Aholou (Traore Diarra 69); Grandsir (Sylla 77), Falcao, Chadli (Mboula 58).
Atletico Madrid: (442) Oblak; Juanfran, Godin, Gimenez, Lucas; Correa (Lemar 70), Rodri, Saul, Koke; Costa, Griezmann.

Wednesday, 3 October 2018

Atletico Madrid (1) 3 *(Griezmann 28, 67, Koke 90)*

Club Brugge (1) 1 *(Groeneveld 39)* 55,742

Atletico Madrid: (442) Oblak; Arias, Godin, Gimenez (Filipe Luis 46), Lucas; Lemar, Thomas (Correa 63), Saul, Koke; Griezmann, Costa (Rodri 69).
Club Brugge: (352) Letica; Poulain, Mechele, Denswil; Vlietinck (Mata 56), Vormer, Vanaken, Rits (Openda 75), Groeneveld; Wesley, Schrijvers (Nakamba 56).

Borussia Dortmund (0) 3 *(Bruun Larsen 51, Alcacer 72, Reus 90)*

Monaco (0) 0 66,099

Borussia Dortmund: (4231) Burki; Piszczek, Akanji, Zagadou, Diallo; Witsel, Delaney (Weigl 65); Wolf (Bruun Larsen 46), Reus, Sancho (Philipp 83); Alcacer.
Monaco: (433) Benaglio (Subasic 44); Raggi, Glik, Jemerson, Henrichs; Tielemans, Aholou, Golovin (Chadli 77); Sidibe, Falcao, Sylla.

Wednesday, 24 October 2018

Borussia Dortmund (1) 4 *(Witsel 38, Guerreiro 73, 89, Sancho 83)*

Atletico Madrid (0) 0 66,099

Borussia Dortmund: (4411) Burki; Piszczek, Diallo, Zagadou, Hakimi; Pulisic (Sancho 79), Delaney (Dahoud 35), Witsel, Bruun Larsen (Guerreiro 62); Gotze; Reus.
Atletico Madrid: (442) Oblak; Juanfran, Godin, Lucas, Filipe Luis; Lemar, Koke, Thomas (Rodri 46), Saul (Correa 69); Costa, Griezmann.

Club Brugge (1) 1 *(Wesley 39)*

Monaco (1) 1 *(Sylla 32)* 23,957

Club Brugge: (352) Letica; Poulain, Mechele, Denswil; Vlietinck (Mata 82), Vormer, Nakamba, Vanaken, Bonaventure (Diatta 90); Rezaei (Openda 79), Wesley.
Monaco: (343) Badiashile L; Raggi, Glik, Jemerson; Sidibe (Henrichs 64), Ait Bennasser, Tielemans, Chadli; Jovetic (Diop 12 (Aholou 72)), Sylla, Golovin.

Tuesday, 6 November 2018

Atletico Madrid (1) 2 *(Saul 33, Griezmann 80)*

Borussia Dortmund (0) 0 61,023

Atletico Madrid: (442) Oblak; Juanfran, Gimenez (Montero 46), Lucas, Filipe Luis; Saul, Rodri, Thomas, Correa (Vitolo 81); Griezmann, Kalinic (Gelson Martins 62).
Borussia Dortmund: (4411) Burki; Piszczek, Akanji, Toprak, Hakimi; Pulisic (Guerreiro 59), Witsel, Delaney, Sancho (Bruun Larsen 79); Reus; Alcacer (Gotze 74).

Monaco (0) 0

Club Brugge (3) 4 *(Vanaken 12, 17 (pen), Wesley 24, Vormer 85)* 8347

Monaco: (433) Benaglio; Sidibe, Glik (Toure 76), Jemerson, Barreca; Tielemans, Ait Bennasser (Massengo 68), Chadli; Sylla, Falcao (Gouano 61), Diop.
Club Brugge: (352) Horvath; Poulain, Mechele, Denswil; Mata (Vlietinck 77), Vormer, Nakamba, Rits, Diatta (Cools 6); Wesley (Rezaei 72), Vanaken.

Wednesday, 28 November 2018

Atletico Madrid (2) 2 *(Badiashile B 2 (og), Griezmann 24)*

Monaco (0) 0 56,314

Atletico Madrid: (442) Oblak; Arias, Savic■, Lucas, Filipe Luis; Koke (Vitolo 46), Rodri, Thomas, Lemar (Kalinic 63); Correa (Saul 69), Griezmann.
Monaco: (532) Benaglio; Biancone, Raggi, Jemerson, Badiashile B, Chadli (Diop 63); Massengo, Tielemans, Golovin (Thuram 63); Grandsir, Sylla (Falcao 55).

Borussia Dortmund (0) 0

Club Brugge (0) 0 66,099

Borussia Dortmund: (4231) Burki; Piszczek, Akanji, Diallo (Hakimi 80), Zagadou; Pulisic, Witsel (Delaney 89); Dahoud, Guerreiro (Sancho 73), Reus; Alcacer.
Club Brugge: (352) Horvath; Poulain, Mechele, Denswil; Mata, Vormer (Decarli 90), Nakamba, Bonaventure (Rits 76), Amrabat; Wesley (Openda 90), Vanaken.

Tuesday, 11 December 2018

Club Brugge (0) 0

Atletico Madrid (0) 0 25,645

Club Brugge: (352) Horvath; Poulain, Mechele, Denswil; Vormer, Amrabat, Nakamba, Vanaken (Rits 90), Ngonge (Luan Peres 69); Wesley, Openda (Schrijvers 74).
Atletico Madrid: (442) Oblak; Arias, Godin, Montero, Saul; Lemar (Vitolo 60), Rodri, Thomas (Kalinic 68), Koke; Griezmann, Gelson Martins (Correa 60).

Monaco (0) 0

Borussia Dortmund (1) 2 *(Guerreiro 15, 88)* 8731

Monaco: (4411) Benaglio; Biancone (Serrano 78), Glik, Badiashile B, Raggi; Henrichs, Tielemans, Ait Bennasser, Massengo (Thuram 69); Diop; Falcao (Sylla 65).
Borussia Dortmund: (4411) Hitz; Hakimi, Toprak, Diallo, Schmelzer; Pulisic, Weigl, Dahoud (Wolf 76), Guerreiro (Gomez 90); Gotze; Philipp (Alcacer 79).

Group A Table	P	W	D	L	F	A	GD	Pts
Borussia Dortmund	6	4	1	1	10	2	8	13
Atletico Madrid	6	4	1	1	9	6	3	13
Club Brugge	6	1	3	2	6	5	1	6
Monaco	6	0	1	5	2	14	–12	1

GROUP B

Tuesday, 18 September 2018

Barcelona (1) 4 *(Messi 31, 77, 87, Dembele 74)*

PSV Eindhoven (0) 0 73,462

Barcelona: (433) ter Stegen; Sergi Roberto, Pique, Umtiti■, Jordi Alba; Rakitic (Vidal 85), Busquets, Coutinho (Lenglet 81); Messi, Suarez L, Dembele (Arthur 83).
PSV Eindhoven: (433) Zoet; Dumfries, Schwaab, Viergever (Isimat-Mirin 66), Tasende; Rosario (Gutierrez 82), Pereiro, Hendrix; Bergwijn (Malen 78), de Jong, Lozano.

Internazionale (0) 2 *(Icardi 86, Vecino 90)*

Tottenham H (0) 1 *(Eriksen 53)* 64,123

Internazionale: (4231) Handanovic; Skriniar, de Vrij, Miranda, Asamoah; Vecino, Brozovic; Politano (Balde 72), Nainggolan (Valero 89), Perisic (Candreva 64); Icardi.
Tottenham H: (433) Vorm; Aurier, Sanchez, Vertonghen, Davies; Dembele, Dier, Eriksen; Kane (Rose 89), Lamela (Winks 72), Son (Lucas Moura 63).

Wednesday, 3 October 2018

PSV Eindhoven (1) 1 *(Rosario 27)*

Internazionale (1) 2 *(Nainggolan 44, Icardi 60)* 34,750

PSV Eindhoven: (433) Zoet; Dumfries, Schwaab, Viergever, Tasende; Rosario, Pereiro (Malen 75), Hendrix; Lozano, de Jong, Bergwijn.
Internazionale: (4411) Handanovic; D'Ambrosio, Skriniar, de Vrij, Asamoah; Politano (Candreva 90), Vecino, Brozovic, Perisic; Nainggolan (Valero 86); Icardi.

Tottenham H (0) 2 *(Kane 52, Lamela 66)*

Barcelona (2) 4 *(Coutinho 2, Rakitic 28, Messi 56, 90)* 82,137

Tottenham H: (4231) Lloris; Trippier, Alderweireld, Sanchez, Davies; Winks, Wanyama (Dier 57); Lucas Moura, Lamela (Llorente 79), Son (Sissoko 67); Kane.
Barcelona: (433) ter Stegen; Nelson Semedo, Pique, Lenglet, Jordi Alba; Arthur (Vidal 87), Busquets (Vermaelen 90), Rakitic; Messi, Suarez L, Coutinho (Rafinha 83).

Wednesday, 24 October 2018

Barcelona (1) 2 *(Rafinha 32, Jordi Alba 83)*

Internazionale (0) 0 86,290

Barcelona: (433) ter Stegen; Sergi Roberto, Pique, Lenglet, Jordi Alba; Rakitic, Busquets, Arthur (Vidal 77); Rafinha (Nelson Semedo 72), Suarez L, Coutinho (Munir 88).
Internazionale: (4231) Handanovic; D'Ambrosio, Skriniar, Miranda, Asamoah; Vecino, Brozovic; Candreva (Politano 46), Valero (Martinez 63), Perisic (Balde 76); Icardi.

PSV Eindhoven (1) 2 *(Lozano 30, de Jong 87)*

Tottenham H (1) 2 *(Lucas Moura 39, Kane 55)* 35,000

PSV Eindhoven: (433) Zoet; Dumfries, Schwaab, Viergever, Angelino; Rosario, Pereiro (Gakpo 83), Hendrix; Lozano, de Jong, Malen.
Tottenham H: (4231) Lloris■; Trippier, Alderweireld, Sanchez, Davies; Dembele (Winks 74), Dier; Lucas Moura (Lamela 64), Eriksen, Son (Vorm 81); Kane.

Tuesday, 6 November 2018

Internazionale (0) 1 *(Icardi 87)*

Barcelona (0) 1 *(Malcom 83)* 70,915

Internazionale: (4231) Handanovic; Vrsaljko, de Vrij, Skriniar, Asamoah; Vecino, Brozovic (Martinez 85); Politano (Candreva 81), Nainggolan (Valero 63), Perisic; Icardi.
Barcelona: (433) ter Stegen; Sergi Roberto, Pique, Lenglet, Jordi Alba; Rakitic, Busquets, Arthur (Vidal 73); Dembele (Malcom 81), Suarez L, Coutinho.

Tottenham H (0) 2 *(Kane 78, 89)*

PSV Eindhoven (1) 1 *(de Jong 2)* 46,588

Tottenham H: (433) Gazzaniga; Aurier (Trippier 75), Alderweireld, Sanchez, Davies; Winks, Alli, Eriksen; Lucas Moura (Lamela 62), Kane, Son (Llorente 75).
PSV Eindhoven: (433) Zoet; Dumfries, Schwaab, Viergever, Angelino; Rosario, Pereiro (Malen 72), Hendrix; Lozano, de Jong (Sainsbury 80), Bergwijn (Gutierrez 86).

Wednesday, 28 November 2018

PSV Eindhoven (0) 1 *(de Jong 83)*

Barcelona (0) 2 *(Messi 61, Pique 70)* 34,600

PSV Eindhoven: (4231) Zoet; Dumfries, Schwaab, Viergever, Angelino; Rosario, Hendrix (Gutierrez 71); Lozano, Pereiro (Malen 71), Bergwijn (Romero 79); de Jong.
Barcelona: (433) ter Stegen; Nelson Semedo, Pique, Lenglet, Jordi Alba; Rakitic, Busquets, Vidal; Dembele (Suarez D 80), Messi, Coutinho (Malcom 69).

Tottenham H (0) 1 *(Eriksen 80)*

Internazionale (0) 0 57,132

Tottenham H: (4411) Lloris; Aurier, Vertonghen, Alderweireld, Davies; Lucas Moura (Son 62), Sissoko, Winks (Dier 87), Lamela (Eriksen 70); Alli; Kane.
Internazionale: (4231) Handanovic; D'Ambrosio, de Vrij (Miranda 82), Skriniar, Asamoah; Vecino, Brozovic; Politano (Balde 83), Nainggolan (Valero 44), Perisic; Icardi.

Tuesday, 11 December 2018

Barcelona (1) 1 *(Dembele 7)*

Tottenham H (0) 1 *(Lucas Moura 85)* 69,961

Barcelona: (433) Cillessen; Nelson Semedo, Lenglet, Vermaelen, Miranda; Arthur, Alena, Rakitic (Busquets 46); Dembele (Suarez D 76), Munir (Messi 63), Coutinho.
Tottenham H: (4411) Lloris; Walker-Peters (Lamela 61), Alderweireld, Vertonghen, Rose; Eriksen, Sissoko, Winks (Llorente 83), Son (Lucas Moura 71); Alli; Kane.

Internazionale (0) 1 *(Icardi 73)*

PSV Eindhoven (1) 1 *(Lozano 13)* 62,533

Internazionale: (451) Handanovic; D'Ambrosio, de Vrij, Skriniar, Asamoah (Martinez 69); Politano (Vrsaljko 83), Candreva (Balde 56), Brozovic, Valero, Perisic; Icardi.
PSV Eindhoven: (433) Zoet; Dumfries, Sainsbury, Viergever, Angelino; Hendrix, Gutierrez (Sadilek 65), Rosario; Bergwijn (Malen 71), de Jong, Lozano (Pereiro 90).

Group B Table	*P*	*W*	*D*	*L*	*F*	*A*	*GD*	*Pts*
Barcelona	6	4	2	0	14	5	9	14
Tottenham H	6	2	2	2	9	10	–1	8
Internazionale	6	2	2	2	6	7	–1	8
PSV Eindhoven	6	0	2	4	6	13	–7	2

GROUP C

Tuesday, 18 September 2018

Crvena Zvezda (0) 0

Napoli (0) 0 49,112

Crvena Zvezda: (4411) Borjan; Stojkovic, Degenek, Savic, Rodic; Ben, Jovicic (Jovancic 56), Krsticic, Marin (Simic 86); Causic; Boakye (Pavkov 81).
Napoli: (433) Ospina; Hysaj, Albiol, Koulibaly, Rui; Allan (Mertens 61), Fabian, Zielinski (Hamsik 75); Callejon (Ounas 75), Milik, Insigne.

Liverpool (2) 3 *(Sturridge 30, Milner 36 (pen), Firmino 90)*

Paris Saint-Germain (1) 2 *(Meunier 40, Mbappe-Lottin 83)* 52,478

Liverpool: (433) Alisson; Alexander-Arnold, Gomez, van Dijk, Robertson; Milner, Wijnaldum, Henderson; Salah (Shaqiri 85), Sturridge (Firmino 71), Mane (Fabinho 90).
Paris Saint-Germain: (433) Areola; Meunier, Kimpembe, Thiago Silva, Bernat; Rabiot, Marquinhos, Di Maria (Choupo-Moting 80); Mbappe-Lottin, Cavani (Draxler 80), Neymar.

Wednesday, 3 October 2018

Napoli (0) 1 *(Insigne 90)*

Liverpool (0) 0 37,057

Napoli: (433) Ospina; Maksimovic, Albiol, Koulibaly, Rui; Allan, Hamsik (Zielinski 81), Fabian (Verdi 68); Callejon, Milik (Mertens 68), Insigne.
Liverpool: (433) Alisson; Alexander-Arnold, Gomez, van Dijk, Robertson; Milner (Fabinho 76), Wijnaldum, Keita (Henderson 19); Salah, Firmino, Mane (Sturridge 88).

Paris Saint-Germain (4) 6 *(Neymar 20, 22, 81, Cavani 37, Di Maria 42, Mbappe-Lottin 70)*

Crvena Zvezda (0) 1 *(Marin 74)* 39,979

Paris Saint-Germain: (4231) Areola; Meunier, Kimpembe, Thiago Silva (Kehrer 76), Bernat; Verratti, Rabiot; Mbappe-Lottin (Choupo-Moting 76), Neymar (Draxler 82), Di Maria; Cavani.
Crvena Zvezda: (4231) Borjan; Stojkovic, Savic (Babic 46), Degenek, Rodic; Jovicic, Krsticic; Marin, Causic, Simic (Pavkov 46); Ben (Ebecilio 73).

Wednesday, 24 October 2018

Liverpool (2) 4 *(Firmino 20, Salah 45, 51 (pen), Mane 80)*

Crvena Zvezda (0) 0 53,024

Liverpool: (433) Alisson; Alexander-Arnold, Gomez, van Dijk, Robertson (Moreno 82); Shaqiri (Lallana 68), Fabinho, Wijnaldum; Salah (Sturridge 73), Firmino, Mane.
Crvena Zvezda: (4411) Borjan; Stojkovic, Babic, Degenek, Gobeljic; Srnic, Krsticic, Jovicic (Causic 75), Ben (Simic 81); Ebecilio (Jovancic 64); Boakye.

Paris Saint-Germain (0) 2 *(Rui 61 (og), Di Maria 90)*

Napoli (1) 2 *(Insigne 29, Mertens 77)* 46,274

Paris Saint-Germain: (4231) Areola; Meunier, Kimpembe, Marquinhos, Bernat (Kehrer 46); Verratti (Diaby 83), Rabiot; Mbappe-Lottin, Neymar, Di Maria; Cavani (Draxler 76).
Napoli: (433) Ospina; Maksimovic, Albiol, Koulibaly, Rui; Allan, Hamsik, Fabian; Callejon (Rog 87), Mertens (Milik 84), Insigne (Zielinski 53).

Tuesday, 6 November 2018

Crvena Zvezda (2) 2 *(Pavkov 22, 29)*

Liverpool (0) 0 51,318

Crvena Zvezda: (4231) Borjan; Stojkovic (Gobeljic 59), Savic, Degenek, Rodic; Krsticic (Jovicic 73), Jovancic; Srnic, Marin (Causic 64), Ben; Pavkov.
Liverpool: (433) Alisson; Alexander-Arnold (Gomez 46), Matip, van Dijk, Robertson; Milner, Wijnaldum, Lallana (Origi 79); Salah, Sturridge (Firmino 46), Mane.

Napoli (0) 1 *(Insigne 63 (pen))*

Paris Saint-Germain (1) 1 *(Bernat 45)* 55,489

Napoli: (433) Ospina; Maksimovic (Hysaj 76), Albiol, Koulibaly, Rui; Allan, Hamsik, Fabian (Zielinski 70); Callejon, Mertens (Ounas 82), Insigne.
Paris Saint-Germain: (442) Buffon; Kehrer (Choupo-Moting 90), Thiago Silva, Marquinhos, Bernat; Meunier (Kimpembe 73), Draxler, Verratti, Di Maria (Cavani 76); Mbappe-Lottin, Neymar.

Wednesday, 28 November 2018

Napoli (2) 3 *(Hamsik 11, Mertens 33, 52)*

Crvena Zvezda (0) 1 *(Ben 57)* 44,470

Napoli: (433) Ospina; Maksimovic, Albiol (Hysaj 46), Koulibaly, Rui; Allan, Hamsik, Fabian; Callejon (Rog 86), Mertens, Insigne (Zielinski 77).
Crvena Zvezda: (4231) Borjan; Simic (Ebecilio 77), Babic, Degenek, Rodic; Gobeljic, Krsticic; Ben, Marin, Srnic (Jovancic 64); Stojiljkovic (Joveljic 46).

Paris Saint-Germain (2) 2 *(Bernat 13, Neymar 37)*

Liverpool (1) 1 *(Milner 45 (pen))* 46,880

Paris Saint-Germain: (4411) Buffon; Kehrer, Thiago Silva, Kimpembe, Bernat; Mbappe-Lottin (Rabiot 84), Verratti, Marquinhos, Di Maria (Dani Alves 65); Neymar; Cavani (Choupo-Moting 65).
Liverpool: (433) Alisson; Gomez, Lovren, van Dijk, Robertson; Milner (Shaqiri 77), Henderson, Wijnaldum (Keita 66); Salah, Firmino (Sturridge 71), Mane.

Tuesday, 11 December 2018

Crvena Zvezda (0) 1 *(Gobeljic 56)*

Paris Saint-Germain (2) 4 *(Cavani 9, Neymar 40, Marquinhos 74, Mbappe-Lottin 90)* 48,357

Crvena Zvezda: (4411) Borjan; Stojkovic, Gobeljic, Degenek, Rodic; Ben, Jovancic, Causic, Simic (Ebecilio 72); Marin (Joveljic 86); Pavkov (Boakye 72).
Paris Saint-Germain: (4411) Buffon; Kehrer, Thiago Silva, Kimpembe, Bernat; Mbappe-Lottin, Verratti (Rabiot 83), Marquinhos, Di Maria (Draxler 88); Neymar; Cavani.

Liverpool (1) 1 *(Salah 34)*

Napoli (0) 0 52,015

Liverpool: (433) Alisson; Alexander-Arnold (Lovren 90), Matip, van Dijk, Robertson; Wijnaldum, Henderson, Milner (Fabinho 84); Salah, Firmino (Keita 79), Mane.
Napoli: (433) Ospina; Maksimovic, Albiol, Koulibaly, Rui (Ghoulam 70); Allan, Hamsik, Fabian (Zielinski 62); Callejon, Mertens (Milik 67), Insigne.

Group C Table	P	W	D	L	F	A	GD	Pts
Paris Saint-Germain	6	3	2	1	17	9	8	11
Liverpool	6	3	0	3	9	7	2	9
Napoli	6	2	3	1	7	5	2	9
Crvena Zvezda	6	1	1	4	5	17	–12	4

GROUP D

Tuesday, 18 September 2018

Galatasaray (1) 3 *(Rodrigues 9, Derdiyok 67, Inan 90 (pen))*

Lokomotiv Moscow (0) 0 43,542

Galatasaray: (433) Muslera; Linnes, Donk, Aziz, Nagatomo; N'Diaye■, Fernando, Belhanda (Maicon 72); Akbaba, Derdiyok (Onyekuru 81), Rodrigues (Inan 90).
Lokomotiv Moscow: (451) Guilherme; Ignatiev (Eder 69), Kvirkvelia, Corluka, Idowu; Fernandes, Howedes, Denisov, Krychowiak, Aleksey Miranchuk (Anton Miranchuk 86); Farfan.

Schalke 04 (0) 1 *(Embolo 64)*

Porto (0) 1 *(Otavio 75 (pen))* 45,755

Schalke 04: (343) Fahrmann; Sane, Naldo, Nastasic; Caligiuri, Serdar (Harit 84), Bentaleb, McKennie; Schopf, Embolo (Burgstaller 71), Uth (Konoplyanka 66).
Porto: (442) Casillas; Maxi Pereira, Felipe, Eder Militao, Alex Telles; Otavio (Hernani 90), Danilo Pereira, Herrera, Brahimi (Sergio Oliveira 82); Aboubakar (Corona 60), Marega.

Wednesday, 3 October 2018

Lokomotiv Moscow (0) 0

Schalke 04 (0) 1 *(McKennie 88)* 21,471

Lokomotiv Moscow: (451) Guilherme; Ignatiev, Howedes, Kvirkvelia, Idowu; Anton Miranchuk (Denisov 72), Fernandes, Krychowiak, Barinov, Aleksey Miranchuk (Zhemaletdinov 83); Eder.
Schalke 04: (343) Fahrmann; McKennie, Sane, Naldo; Caligiuri, Rudy (Bentaleb 55), Mascarell (Serdar 46), Mendyl; Uth, Embolo (Burgstaller 72), Konoplyanka.

Porto (0) 1 *(Marega 49)*

Galatasaray (0) 0 42,711

Porto: (433) Casillas; Maxi Pereira, Felipe, Eder Militao, Alex Telles; Otavio (Andre Pereira 80), Danilo Pereira, Herrera (Sergio Oliveira 88); Corona (Torres 68), Marega, Brahimi.
Galatasaray: (433) Muslera; Linnes, Maicon, Aziz, Nagatomo; Fernando (Akgun 86), Donk (Inan 68), Belhanda (Feghouli 74); Onyekuru, Gumus, Rodrigues.

Wednesday, 24 October 2018

Galatasaray (0) 0

Schalke 04 (0) 0 46,667

Galatasaray: (433) Muslera; Linnes, Maicon, Kabak, Nagatomo (Bayram 81); Belhanda, Donk, N'Diaye; Gumus (Inan 61), Derdiyok (Celik 69), Rodrigues.
Schalke 04: (4231) Nubel; Caligiuri, Sane, Nastasic, Mendyl; Rudy, Stambouli; Uth (Burgstaller 90), Serdar, Konoplyanka (Skrzybski 77); Embolo (McKennie 82).

Lokomotiv Moscow (1) 1 *(Anton Miranchuk 38)*

Porto (2) 3 *(Marega 26 (pen), Herrera 35, Corona 47)* 16,034

Lokomotiv Moscow: (352) Guilherme; Ignatiev, Kvirkvelia■, Howedes; Anton Miranchuk, Denisov, Krychowiak, Barinov, Fernandes (Zhemaletdinov 66); Eder (Lysov 81), Aleksey Miranchuk.
Porto: (4321) Casillas; Maxi Pereira, Eder Militao, Felipe, Alex Telles; Torres (Bazoer 83), Danilo Pereira, Herrera; Corona (Andre Pereira 69), Brahimi (Adrian 82); Marega.

Tuesday, 6 November 2018

Porto (2) 4 *(Herrera 2, Marega 43, Corona 67, Otavio 90)*

Lokomotiv Moscow (0) 1 *(Farfan 59)* 34,616

Porto: (433) Casillas; Maxi Pereira, Eder Militao, Felipe, Alex Telles; Torres (Sergio Oliveira 84), Danilo Pereira, Herrera; Corona (Hernani 77), Marega, Brahimi (Otavio 69).
Lokomotiv Moscow: (4411) Guilherme; Ignatiev, Howedes, Corluka, Idowu; Anton Miranchuk, Denisov, Krychowiak, Fernandes (Farfan 46); Aleksey Miranchuk; Eder (Smolov 71).

Schalke 04 (1) 2 *(Burgstaller 4, Uth 57)*

Galatasaray (0) 0 54,740

Schalke 04: (532) Nubel; Caligiuri, Stambouli, Sane, Nastasic, Schopf; Harit (McKennie 56), Rudy (Serdar 76), Uth (Bentaleb 63); Embolo, Burgstaller.
Galatasaray: (433) Muslera; Linnes (Bayram 46), Kabak, Aziz, Mariano; Belhanda, Donk, N'Diaye; Onyekuru, Gumus (Celik 72), Rodrigues (Inan 62).

Wednesday, 28 November 2018

Lokomotiv Moscow (1) 2 *(Donk 43 (og), Ignatiev 54)*

Galatasaray (0) 0 14,037

Lokomotiv Moscow: (4231) Guilherme; Ignatiev, Kvirkvelia, Corluka, Rybus; Krychowiak, Denisov; Anton Miranchuk, Aleksey Miranchuk (Barinov 78), Farfan (Rotenberg 90); Smolov (Eder 88).
Galatasaray: (433) Muslera; Linnes (Mariano 88), Kabak, Aziz, Nagatomo; N'Diaye (Inan 68), Donk, Fernando (Feghouli 59); Onyekuru, Derdiyok, Rodrigues.

Porto (0) 3 *(Eder Militao 52, Corona 56, Marega 90)*

Schalke 04 (0) 1 *(Bentaleb 89 (pen))* 41,603

Porto: (433) Casillas; Alex Telles, Felipe, Eder Militao, Maxi Pereira; Torres, Danilo Pereira, Herrera (Hernani 85); Corona (Otavio 79), Marega, Brahimi (Adrian 73).
Schalke 04: (4231) Fahrmann; Caligiuri (Schopf 62), Naldo, Nastasic, Mendyl; Mascarell, Stambouli (Rudy 71); Skrzybski (Harit 46), Bentaleb, Konoplyanka; Di Santo.

Tuesday, 11 December 2018

Galatasaray (1) 2 *(Feghouli 45 (pen), Derdiyok 65)*

Porto (2) 3 *(Felipe 17, Marega 42 (pen), Sergio Oliveira 57)* 33,972

Galatasaray: (451) Muslera; Mariano, Maicon, Kabak, Nagatomo; Feghouli (Celik 89), Fernando, Donk (Onyekuru 46), N'Diaye, Rodrigues; Derdiyok.
Porto: (433) Casillas; Maxi Pereira, Felipe, Diogo Leite, Alex Telles; Herrera, Danilo Pereira, Sergio Oliveira (Awaziem 82); Adrian (Andre Pereira 72), Marega, Hernani (Jorge 72).

Schalke 04 (0) 1 *(Schopf 90)*

Lokomotiv Moscow (0) 0 48,883

Schalke 04: (4132) Fahrmann; Goller (Harit 58), Naldo, Nastasic, Mendyl (Baba 16); Stambouli; Schopf, Serdar, Mascarell; Teuchert (Kutucu 72), Konoplyanka.
Lokomotiv Moscow: (442) Guilherme; Ignatiev, Kvirkvelia, Howedes, Rybus; Barinov, Krychowiak, Denisov, Aleksey Miranchuk; Eder (Anton Miranchuk 46), Farfan (Smolov 80).

Group D Table	P	W	D	L	F	A	GD	Pts
Porto	6	5	1	0	15	6	9	16
Schalke 04	6	3	2	1	6	4	2	11
Galatasaray	6	1	1	4	5	8	–3	4
Lokomotiv Moscow	6	1	0	5	4	12	–8	3

GROUP E

Wednesday, 19 September 2018

Ajax (0) 3 *(Tagliafico 46, 90, van de Beek 77)*

AEK Athens (0) 0 52,285

Ajax: (433) Onana; Mazraoui, De Jong, Blind, Tagliafico; Ziyech, Schone, Eiting; Neres (Dolberg 78), Huntelaar (van de Beek 62), Tadic.
AEK Athens: (4231) Barkas; Cosic, Lampropoulos, Oikonomou, Hult; Galanopoulos (Alef 61), Andre Simoes; Bakakis (Gianniotas 70), Klonaridis, Mandalos; Ponce (Giakoumakis 81).

Benfica (0) 0

Bayern Munich (1) 2 *(Lewandowski 10, Sanches 54)* 60,274

Benfica: (433) Vlachodimos; Andre Almeida, Dias, Jardel, Grimaldo; Fernandes (Zivkovic 75), Fejsa, Pizzi (Rafa Silva 62); Salvio (Pires 62), Seferovic, Cervi.
Bayern Munich: (4231) Neuer; Kimmich, Boateng, Hummels, Alaba; Javi Martinez (Muller 88), Sanches; Robben, Rodriguez (Goretzka 78), Ribery (Gnabry 62); Lewandowski.

Tuesday, 2 October 2018

AEK Athens (0) 2 *(Klonaridis 53, 64)*

Benfica (2) 3 *(Seferovic 6, Grimaldo 15, Semedo 74)* 31,154

AEK Athens: (4231) Barkas; Bakakis, Oikonomou (Cosic 68), Chygrynskiy, Hult; Galanopoulos, Andre Simoes (Rodrigo Galo 80); Bakasetas, Klonaridis, Mandalos; Ponce (Giakoumakis 60).
Benfica: (433) Vlachodimos; Andre Almeida, Dias■, Conti, Grimaldo; Pizzi (Semedo 62), Fejsa, Fernandes; Salvio (Lema 46), Seferovic, Rafa Silva (Cervi 83).

Bayern Munich (1) 1 *(Hummels 4)*

Ajax (1) 1 *(Mazraoui 22)* 70,000

Bayern Munich: (433) Neuer; Kimmich, Boateng, Hummels (Sule 90), Alaba; Muller, Javi Martinez, Thiago; Robben (Rodriguez 62), Lewandowski, Ribery (Gnabry 74).
Ajax: (433) Onana; Mazraoui, de Ligt, Wober, Tagliafico; van de Beek (de Wit 75), Schone, Blind; Ziyech, Tadic, Neres (Dolberg 85).

Tuesday, 23 October 2018

AEK Athens (0) 0

Bayern Munich (0) 2 *(Javi Martinez 61, Lewandowski 63)* 61,221

AEK Athens: (4231) Barkas; Bakakis, Lampropoulos, Chygrynskiy, Hult; Galanopoulos (Rodrigo Galo 84), Andre Simoes; Bakasetas, Klonaridis (Boye 65), Mandalos (Alef 75); Ponce.
Bayern Munich: (433) Neuer; Kimmich, Sule, Hummels, Rafinha; Rodriguez (Goretzka 63), Javi Martinez, Thiago; Robben, Lewandowski (Wagner 84), Gnabry (Muller 74).

Ajax (0) 1 *(Mazraoui 90)*

Benfica (0) 0 52,489

Ajax: (433) Onana; Mazraoui, de Ligt, Blind, Tagliafico; van de Beek (Neres 88), Schone, De Jong; Ziyech, Dolberg, Tadic.
Benfica: (433) Vlachodimos; Andre Almeida, Conti, Jardel, Grimaldo; Pizzi (Pires 79), Fejsa, Fernandes; Salvio, Seferovic, Rafa Silva (Cervi 90).

Wednesday, 7 November 2018

Bayern Munich (1) 2 *(Lewandowski 31 (pen), 71)*

AEK Athens (0) 0 70,000

Bayern Munich: (433) Neuer; Kimmich, Boateng, Hummels, Alaba; Muller, Javi Martinez, Goretzka; Gnabry (Sanches 87), Lewandowski (Wagner 90), Ribery (Rafinha 84).
AEK Athens: (532) Barkas; Bakakis, Lampropoulos, Chygrynskiy, Cosic, Hult; Galanopoulos (Rodrigo Galo 78), Andre Simoes, Alef (Moran 67); Ponce, Mandalos (Boye 79).

Benfica (1) 1 *(Jonas 29)*

Ajax (0) 1 *(Tadic 61)* 51,328

Benfica: (433) Vlachodimos; Andre Almeida, Dias, Jardel, Grimaldo; Fernandes (Pizzi 75), Fejsa, Pires; Salvio (Rafa Silva 48), Jonas (Seferovic 55), Cervi.
Ajax: (433) Onana; Mazraoui, de Ligt, Blind, Tagliafico; De Jong (Wober 86), Schone, van de Beek; Neres (Dolberg 74), Tadic, Ziyech.

Tuesday, 27 November 2018

AEK Athens (0) 0

Ajax (0) 2 *(Tadic 68 (pen), 72)* 25,756

AEK Athens: (4231) Barkas; Bakakis, Oikonomou, Chygrynskiy, Hult; Galanopoulos, Alef; Rodrigo Galo (Boye 75), Livaja■, Mandalos (Klonaridis 78); Ponce (Giakoumakis 82).
Ajax: (433) Onana; Mazraoui (Kristensen 81), de Ligt, Blind, Wober; van de Beek (Labyad 86), Schone, De Jong; Neres, Dolberg (Huntelaar 62), Tadic.

Bayern Munich (3) 5 *(Robben 13, 30, Lewandowski 36, 51, Ribery 76)*

Benfica (0) 1 *(Fernandes 46)* 70,000

Bayern Munich: (433) Neuer; Rafinha, Boateng, Sule, Alaba; Muller (Jeong 81), Kimmich, Goretzka; Robben (Sanches 72), Lewandowski, Ribery (Wagner 77).
Benfica: (433) Vlachodimos; Andre Almeida, Conti, Dias, Grimaldo; Pizzi (Fernandes 46), Fejsa (Semedo 76), Pires; Rafa Silva, Jonas (Seferovic 59), Cervi.

Wednesday, 12 December 2018

Ajax (0) 3 *(Tadic 61, 82 (pen), Tagliafico 90)*

Bayern Munich (1) 3 *(Lewandowski 13, 87 (pen), Coman 90)* 52,244

Ajax: (433) Onana; Mazraoui, de Ligt, Wober■, Tagliafico; De Jong, Blind, van de Beek (Dolberg 78); Ziyech, Tadic, Neres (Huntelaar 89).
Bayern Munich: (4231) Neuer; Rafinha, Boateng, Sule, Alaba; Kimmich, Goretzka (Sanches 89); Gnabry (Thiago 62), Muller■, Ribery (Coman 71); Lewandowski.

Benfica (0) 1 *(Grimaldo 88)*

AEK Athens (0) 0 33,633

Benfica: (433) Vlachodimos; Andre Almeida, Dias, Jardel, Grimaldo; Pizzi (Cervi 59), Semedo, Fernandes; Rafa Silva (Zivkovic 35), Seferovic, Joao Felix (Castillo 76).
AEK Athens: (433) Barkas; Bakakis, Oikonomou, Chygrynskiy, Hult; Galanopoulos■, Cosic, Moran (Rodrigo Galo 77); Klonaridis (Gianniotas 61), Ponce, Boye (Mandalos 67).

Group E Table	P	W	D	L	F	A	GD	Pts
Bayern Munich	6	4	2	0	15	5	10	14
Ajax	6	3	3	0	11	5	6	12
Benfica	6	2	1	3	6	11	–5	7
AEK Athens	6	0	0	6	2	13	–11	0

GROUP F

Wednesday, 19 September 2018

Manchester C (0) 1 *(Bernardo Silva 67)*

Lyon (2) 2 *(Cornet 26, Fekir 43)* 40,111

Manchester C: (433) Ederson; Walker, Stones, Laporte, Delph; Gundogan (Sane 55), Fernandinho, Silva; Bernardo Silva, Gabriel Jesus (Aguero 62), Sterling (Mahrez 75).
Lyon: (4411) Lopes; Da Silva (Dubois 76), Marcelo, Denayer, Mendy; Cornet (Traore 90), Ndombele, Cheikh, Aouar; Fekir (Tousart 78); Depay.

Shakhtar Donetsk (1) 2 *(Ismaily 27, Maycon 81)*

TSG Hoffenheim (2) 2 *(Grillitsch 6, Nordtveit 38)* 28,336

Shakhtar Donetsk: (4231) Pyatov; Butko, Khocholava, Rakitskiy, Ismaily; Stepanenko, Alan Patrick (Maycon 76); Marlos, Taison, Bolbat (Kovalenko 56); Moraes.
TSG Hoffenheim: (343) Baumann; Nordtveit, Vogt, Posch; Kaderabek, Grillitsch, Schulz, Bittencourt (Demirbay 63); Szalai (Zuber 75), Joelinton, Kramaric (Nelson 85).

Tuesday, 2 October 2018

Lyon (0) 2 *(Dembele 70, Dubois 72)*

Shakhtar Donetsk (1) 2 *(Moraes 44, 55)* 0

Lyon: (442) Lopes; Dubois, Marcelo, Denayer, Mendy; Traore (Depay 63), Tousart, Ndombele (Cheikh 87), Aouar; Dembele (Cornet 81), Fekir.
Shakhtar Donetsk: (4411) Pyatov; Matviyenko, Kryvtsov, Rakitskiy, Ismaily; Marlos (Fernando 90), Maycon, Stepanenko, Taison; Alan Patrick (Kovalenko 75); Moraes (Kayode 82).
Behind closed doors.

TSG Hoffenheim (1) 1 *(Belfodil 1)*

Manchester C (1) 2 *(Aguero 8, Silva 87)* 24,851

TSG Hoffenheim: (352) Baumann; Akpoguma, Hoogma, Posch; Kaderabek, Grillitsch (Bittencourt 82), Brenet, Szalai (Kramaric 53), Demirbay (Hack 89); Belfodil, Joelinton.
Manchester C: (433) Ederson; Walker, Kompany, Laporte, Otamendi (Stones 64); Gundogan (Bernardo Silva 68), Fernandinho, Silva; Sane, Aguero, Sterling (Mahrez 75).

Tuesday, 23 October 2018

TSG Hoffenheim (1) 3 *(Kramaric 32, 47, Joelinton 90)*

Lyon (1) 3 *(Traore 26, Ndombele 59, Depay 67)* 24,144

TSG Hoffenheim: (3331) Baumann; Akpoguma, Vogt, Bicakcic (Nelson 73); Kaderabek, Grillitsch, Schulz; Szalai (Joelinton 61), Demirbay, Belfodil (Zuber 80); Kramaric.
Lyon: (433) Lopes; Tete, Marcelo, Denayer, Mendy; Ndombele, Tousart, Aouar; Traore (Cheikh 90), Depay (Dembele 81), Terrier (Ferri 82).

Shakhtar Donetsk (0) 0

Manchester C (2) 3 *(Silva 30, Laporte 35, Bernardo Silva 70)* 37,106

Shakhtar Donetsk: (4411) Pyatov; Matviyenko, Kryvtsov, Rakitskiy, Ismaily; Wellington Nem (Bolbat 69), Stepanenko, Maycon, Fernando (Dentinho 84); Kovalenko (Alan Patrick 61); Moraes.
Manchester C: (433) Ederson; Stones (Walker 80), Otamendi, Laporte, Mendy; Silva, Fernandinho, De Bruyne (Bernardo Silva 69); Sterling, Gabriel Jesus (Foden 88), Mahrez.

Wednesday, 7 November 2018

Lyon (2) 2 *(Fekir 19, Ndombele 28)*

TSG Hoffenheim (0) 2 *(Kramaric 65, Kaderabek 90)* 53,850

Lyon: (532) Lopes; Da Silva, Marcelo, Morel, Denayer, Mendy; Ndombele (Cheikh 88), Tousart, Aouar; Depay (Traore 87), Fekir (Dembele 74).
TSG Hoffenheim: (343) Baumann; Nuhu■, Vogt, Bicakcic; Grillitsch (Nelson 57), Demirbay (Nordtveit 79), Kaderabek, Schulz; Belfodil (Szalai 67), Joelinton, Kramaric.

Manchester C (2) 6 *(Silva 13, Gabriel Jesus 24 (pen), 72 (pen), 90, Sterling 48, Mahrez 84)*

Shakhtar Donetsk (0) 0 52,286

Manchester C: (433) Ederson; Walker (Danilo 61), Stones, Laporte, Zinchenko; Bernardo Silva, Fernandinho (Delph 76), Silva (Gundogan 72); Mahrez, Gabriel Jesus, Sterling.
Shakhtar Donetsk: (4231) Pyatov; Matviyenko, Kryvtsov, Rakitskiy, Ismaily; Stepanenko, Maycon (Alan Patrick 77); Taison (Wellington Nem 77), Kovalenko, Bolbat; Moraes (Kayode 63).

Tuesday, 27 November 2018

Lyon (0) 2 *(Cornet 55, 81)*

Manchester C (0) 2 *(Laporte 63, Aguero 83)* 56,039

Lyon: (343) Lopes; Denayer, Marcelo, Marcal; Da Silva (Tete 73), Ndombele, Aouar, Mendy; Cornet (Terrier 89), Depay, Fekir (Traore 84).
Manchester C: (433) Ederson; Walker, Stones, Laporte, Zinchenko; Mahrez, Fernandinho, Silva; Sane (Delph 71), Aguero (Foden 90), Sterling.

TSG Hoffenheim (2) 2 *(Kramaric 17, Zuber 40)*

Shakhtar Donetsk (2) 3 *(Ismaily 14, Taison 15, 90)* 22,920

TSG Hoffenheim: (532) Baumann; Bicakcic, Vogt, Schulz (Grifo 85), Kaderabek, Nordtveit (Grillitsch 84); Zuber (Nelson 77), Demirbay, Kramaric; Belfodil, Szalai■.
Shakhtar Donetsk: (4411) Pyatov; Matviyenko, Khocholava, Kryvtsov, Ismaily; Maycon, Stepanenko (Alan Patrick 76), Danchenko (Butko 90), Kovalenko (Dentinho 84); Taison; Moraes.

Wednesday, 12 December 2018

Manchester C (1) 2 *(Sane 45, 61)*

TSG Hoffenheim (1) 1 *(Kramaric 16 (pen))* 50,411

Manchester C: (433) Ederson; Stones (Walker 46), Otamendi, Laporte, Zinchenko (Delph 63); Bernardo Silva (Kompany 85), Gundogan, Foden, Sterling, Gabriel Jesus, Sane.
TSG Hoffenheim: (352) Baumann; Brenet (Nelson 46), Nuhu, Hubner; Kaderabek, Grillitsch, Geiger (Amiri 63), Bittencourt (Belfodil 70), Schulz; Joelinton, Kramaric.

Shakhtar Donetsk (1) 1 *(Moraes 22)*

Lyon (0) 1 *(Fekir 65)* 38,916

Shakhtar Donetsk: (4411) Pyatov; Matviyenko, Kryvtsov, Khocholava (Butko 46), Ismaily; Marlos (Bolbat 87), Maycon, Stepanenko, Taison; Kovalenko (Kayode 84); Moraes.
Lyon: (433) Lopes; Denayer, Marcelo, Marcal, Tete; Tousart, Aouar, Mendy; Traore (Ndombele 72), Fekir (Dubois 88), Depay (Dembele 81).

Group F Table	P	W	D	L	F	A	GD	Pts
Manchester C	6	4	1	1	16	6	10	13
Lyon	6	1	5	0	12	11	1	8
Shakhtar Donetsk	6	1	3	2	8	16	–8	6
TSG Hoffenheim	6	0	3	3	11	14	–3	3

GROUP G

Wednesday, 19 September 2018

Real Madrid (1) 3 *(Isco 45, Bale 58, Mariano 90)*

Roma (0) 0 69,251

Real Madrid: (433) Navas; Carvajal, Sergio Ramos, Varane, Marcelo; Kroos, Casemiro, Modric (Ceballos 85); Bale (Mariano 73), Benzema (Asensio 62), Isco.
Roma: (433) Olsen; Florenzi, Manolas, Fazio, Kolarov; Zaniolo (Lorenzo Pellegrini 54), De Rossi, Nzonzi (Schick 69); Under, Dzeko, El Shaarawy (Perotti 62).

Viktoria Plzen (2) 2 *(Krmencik 29, 41)*

CSKA Moscow (0) 2 *(Chalov 49, Vlasic 90 (pen))* 11,312

Viktoria Plzen: (4231) Kozacik; Reznik, Pernica, Hubnik, Limbersky; Horava (Hejda 89), Hrosovsky; Kopic, Kolar (Cermak 64), Kovarik (Reznicek 74); Krmencik.
CSKA Moscow: (352) Akinfeev; Becao, Chernov, Nababkin; Fernandes, Vlasic, Oblyakov, Dzagoev (Zhamaletdinov 74), Efremov (Akhmetov 46); Bijol, Chalov (Sigurdsson 81).

Tuesday, 2 October 2018

CSKA Moscow (1) 1 *(Vlasic 2)*

Real Madrid (0) 0 71,811

CSKA Moscow: (4231) Akinfeev■; Fernandes, Becao, Chernov, Nababkin; Bijol, Akhmetov; Vlasic, Dzagoev (Efremov 65), Oblyakov (Kymats 90); Chalov (Sigurdsson 78).
Real Madrid: (433) Navas; Carvajal (Odriozola 43), Varane, Nacho, Reguilon; Kroos, Casemiro (Modric 57), Ceballos; Lucas (Mariano 58), Benzema, Asensio.

Roma (2) 5 *(Dzeko 3, 40, 90, Under 64, Kluivert 74)*

Viktoria Plzen (0) 0 41,243

Roma: (4411) Olsen; Florenzi, Fazio, Juan Jesus, Kolarov (Luca Pellegrini 75); Under (Zaniolo 74), Cristante, Nzonzi, Kluivert; Lorenzo Pellegrini (Schick 74); Dzeko.
Viktoria Plzen: (4411) Kozacik; Reznik, Hejda, Hubnik, Limbersky; Zeman (Ekpai 71), Prochazka, Hrosovsky, Kovarik; Horava (Kolar 64); Krmencik (Reznicek 78).

Tuesday, 23 October 2018

Real Madrid (1) 2 *(Benzema 11, Marcelo 55)*

Viktoria Plzen (0) 1 *(Hrosovsky 78)* 67,356

Real Madrid: (433) Navas; Lucas, Sergio Ramos, Nacho, Marcelo; Modric, Casemiro, Kroos; Bale (Asensio 75), Benzema (Mariano 88), Isco (Valverde 54).
Viktoria Plzen: (4411) Hruska; Reznik, Hejda, Hubnik, Limbersky; Havel (Ekpai 76), Prochazka (Horava 65), Hrosovsky, Petrzela (Reznicek 86); Cermak; Krmencik.

Roma (2) 3 *(Dzeko 30, 43, Under 50)*

CSKA Moscow (0) 0 46,005

Roma: (4231) Olsen; Florenzi, Manolas, Fazio, Santon; De Rossi (Schick 81), Nzonzi; Under (Kolarov 73), Lorenzo Pellegrini (Cristante 68), El Shaarawy; Dzeko.
CSKA Moscow: (541) Pomazun; Fernandes, Magnusson, Rodrigo Nascimento, Chernov (Khosonov 57), Nababkin; Oblyakov (Dzagoev 57), Sigurdsson, Akhmetov, Vlasic; Chalov (Nishimura 90).

Wednesday, 7 November 2018

CSKA Moscow (0) 1 *(Sigurdsson 51)*

Roma (1) 2 *(Manolas 4, Lorenzo Pellegrini 59)* 64,454

CSKA Moscow: (433) Akinfeev; Fernandes (Schennikov 12), Becao, Magnusson■, Nababkin; Akhmetov (Khosonov 76), Bijol, Oblyakov; Vlasic, Chalov, Sigurdsson (Chernov 63).
Roma: (4231) Olsen; Santon, Manolas, Fazio, Kolarov; Nzonzi, Cristante; Florenzi (Juan Jesus 88), Lorenzo Pellegrini (Zaniolo 82), Kluivert (Under 70); Dzeko.

Viktoria Plzen (0) 0

Real Madrid (4) 5 *(Benzema 20, 37, Casemiro 23, Bale 39, Kroos 67)* 11,483

Viktoria Plzen: (4231) Hruska; Reznik, Hejda, Hubnik, Limbersky; Prochazka, Hrosovsky; Havel (Petrzela 38), Cermak (Horava 61), Kopic; Chory (Reznicek 79).
Real Madrid: (433) Courtois; Odriozola, Sergio Ramos (Sanchez 59), Nacho, Reguilon; Kroos (Isco 73), Casemiro, Ceballos; Lucas, Benzema (Vinicius Junior 62), Bale.

Tuesday, 27 November 2018

CSKA Moscow (1) 1 *(Vlasic 10 (pen))*

Viktoria Plzen (0) 2 *(Prochazka 56, Hejda 81)* 52,892

CSKA Moscow: (3421) Akinfeev; Nababkin, Becao, Chernov; Fernandes, Vlasic, Bistrovic, Schennikov (Efremov 46); Sigurdsson, Oblyakov (Kuchaev 72); Chalov (Zhamaletdinov 80).
Viktoria Plzen: (4231) Hruska; Reznik, Hejda, Hubnik, Limbersky (Kopic 46); Prochazka, Hrosovsky; Petrzela (Havel 70), Cermak, Kovarik; Chory (Reznicek 80).

Roma (0) 0

Real Madrid (0) 2 *(Bale 47, Lucas 59)* 59,124

Roma: (4231) Olsen; Florenzi, Manolas, Fazio, Kolarov; Under, Nzonzi (Coric 64); Cristante, El Shaarawy (Kluivert 22), Zaniolo (Karsdorp 69); Schick.
Real Madrid: (433) Courtois; Carvajal, Varane, Sergio Ramos, Marcelo; Kroos, Llorente, Modric (Valverde 80); Lucas, Benzema (Mariano 77), Bale (Asensio 84).

Wednesday, 12 December 2018

Real Madrid (0) 0

CSKA Moscow (2) 3 *(Chalov 37, Schennikov 43, Sigurdsson 73)* 51,636

Real Madrid: (433) Courtois; Odriozola, Vallejo, Sanchez, Marcelo (Carvajal 75); Isco, Llorente (Kroos 58), Valverde; Asensio, Benzema (Bale 46), Vinicius Junior.
CSKA Moscow: (532) Akinfeev; Fernandes, Nababkin, Becao, Magnusson, Schennikov; Vlasic, Bistrovic, Oblyakov (Kuchaev 88); Chalov (Hernandez 84), Sigurdsson (Nishimura 90).

Viktoria Plzen (0) 2 *(Kovarik 62, Chory 72)*

Roma (0) 1 *(Under 67)* 11,217

Viktoria Plzen: (4231) Hruska; Havel, Hejda, Hubnik, Limbersky; Prochazka, Hrosovsky; Kopic (Petrzela 71), Cermak (Horava 81), Kovarik; Chory (Reznicek 86).
Roma: (4231) Mirante; Santon (Florenzi 75), Marcano, Manolas, Kolarov; Cristante, Nzonzi (Luca Pellegrini■ 80); Under, Kluivert, Pastore (Zaniolo 59); Schick.

Group G Table	P	W	D	L	F	A	GD	Pts
Real Madrid	6	4	0	2	12	5	7	12
Roma	6	3	0	3	11	8	3	9
Viktoria Plzen	6	2	1	3	7	16	–9	7
CSKA Moscow	6	2	1	3	8	9	–1	7

GROUP H

Wednesday, 19 September 2018

Valencia (0) 0

Juventus (1) 2 *(Pjanic 45 (pen), 50 (pen))* 46,067

Valencia: (442) Neto; Ruben Vezo (Cheryshev 56), Gabriel, Murillo, Gaya; Carlos Soler, Parejo, Wass, Goncalo Guedes (Piccini 70); Rodrigo, Batshuayi (Gameiro 70).
Juventus: (433) Szczesny; Joao Cancelo, Bonucci, Chiellini, Alex Sandro; Khedira (Can 23), Pjanic (Douglas Costa 66 (Rugani 89)), Matuidi; Bernardeschi, Mandzukic, Ronaldo■.

Young Boys (0) 0

Manchester U (2) 3 *(Pogba 35, 44 (pen), Martial 66)* 31,120

Young Boys: (442) Ballmoos; Mbabu, Camara, von Bergen, Benito; Fassnacht (Ngamaleu 65), Sow (Aebischer 58), Sanogo, Sulejmani; Hoarau (Nsame 75), Assale.
Manchester U: (433) de Gea; Dalot, Smalling, Lindelof, Shaw; Fred (Fellaini 69), Matic, Pogba (Andreas Pereira 75); Martial, Lukaku, Rashford (Mata 69).

Tuesday, 2 October 2018

Juventus (2) 3 *(Dybala 5, 34, 69)*

Young Boys (0) 0 40,961

Juventus: (352) Szczesny; Barzagli, Bonucci, Benatia; Cuadrado, Pjanic (Khedira 70), Bernardeschi, Matuidi (Can 46), Alex Sandro; Dybala, Mandzukic (Kean 78).
Young Boys: (451) von Ballmoos; Schick, Camara■, von Bergen, Benito; Fassnacht (Assale 70), Sow, Sanogo (Lauper 46), Bertone, Sulejmani (Ngamaleu 70); Hoarau.

Manchester U (0) 0

Valencia (0) 0 73,569

Manchester U: (433) de Gea; Valencia, Bailly, Smalling, Shaw; Fellaini, Matic, Pogba; Rashford, Lukaku, Sanchez (Martial 76).
Valencia: (442) Neto; Piccini, Garay, Gabriel, Gaya; Coquelin (Carlos Soler 79), Parejo, Kondogbia, Goncalo Guedes (Cheryshev 83); Batshuayi (Gameiro 73), Rodrigo.

Tuesday, 23 October 2018

Manchester U (0) 0

Juventus (1) 1 *(Dybala 18)* 73,946

Manchester U: (4231) de Gea; Young, Lindelof, Smalling, Shaw; Pogba, Matic; Rashford, Mata, Martial; Lukaku.
Juventus: (433) Szczesny; Joao Cancelo (Douglas Costa 87), Bonucci, Chiellini, Alex Sandro; Bentancur, Pjanic, Matuidi; Cuadrado (Barzagli 81), Dybala (Bernardeschi 78), Ronaldo.

Young Boys (0) 1 *(Hoarau 55 (pen))*

Valencia (1) 1 *(Batshuayi 26)* 31,120

Young Boys: (442) Wolfli; Mbabu, Lauper, von Bergen, Benito; Sulejmani (Ngamaleu 74), Sow, Sanogo, Fassnacht (Bertone 84); Assale, Hoarau (Nsame 79).
Valencia: (442) Neto; Piccini, Gabriel, Diakhaby, Gaya; Carlos Soler, Parejo, Kondogbia (Coquelin 70), Torres (Gameiro 67); Rodrigo, Batshuayi.

Wednesday, 7 November 2018

Juventus (0) 1 *(Ronaldo 65)*

Manchester U (0) 2 *(Mata 86, Alex Sandro 90 (og))* 41,470

Juventus: (433) Szczesny; De Sciglio (Barzagli 82), Bonucci, Chiellini, Alex Sandro; Khedira (Matuidi 61), Pjanic, Bentancur; Cuadrado (Mandzukic 90), Dybala, Ronaldo.
Manchester U: (433) de Gea; Young, Lindelof, Smalling, Shaw; Ander Herrera (Mata 79), Matic, Pogba; Lingard (Rashford 70), Sanchez (Fellaini 79), Martial.

Valencia (2) 3 *(Santi Mina 14, 42, Carlos Soler 56)*

Young Boys (1) 1 *(Assale 37)* 36,480

Valencia: (442) Neto; Wass, Garay, Gabriel, Gaya; Carlos Soler, Coquelin, Kondogbia (Ruben Vezo 87), Goncalo Guedes (Torres 75); Rodrigo, Santi Mina (Gameiro 68).
Young Boys: (442) von Ballmoos; Mbabu, Lauper, von Bergen, Benito; Fassnacht (Nsame 60), Sow, Sanogo■, Ngamaleu (Sulejmani 47); Hoarau (Aebischer 75), Assale.

Tuesday, 27 November 2018

Juventus (0) 1 *(Mandzukic 59)*

Valencia (0) 0 39,070

Juventus: (433) Szczesny; Joao Cancelo, Bonucci, Chiellini, Alex Sandro (Cuadrado 46); Bentancur, Pjanic, Matuidi; Mandzukic, Dybala (Douglas Costa 79), Ronaldo.
Valencia: (442) Neto; Wass, Gabriel, Diakhaby, Gaya; Coquelin, Kondogbia (Carlos Soler 72), Parejo, Goncalo Guedes; Rodrigo (Gameiro 46), Santi Mina (Batshuayi 67).

Manchester U (0) 1 *(Fellaini 90)*

Young Boys (0) 0 72,876

Manchester U: (433) de Gea; Valencia (Mata 72), Jones, Smalling, Shaw; Fellaini, Matic, Fred (Pogba 65); Lingard (Lukaku 64), Rashford, Martial.
Young Boys: (451) Ballmoos; Mbabu, Camara, von Bergen (Garcia 46), Benito; Sulejmani (Fassnacht 66), Sow, Lauper, Aebischer, Assale; Nsame (Ngamaleu 83).

Wednesday, 12 December 2018

Valencia (1) 2 *(Carlos Soler 17, Jones 47 (og))*

Manchester U (0) 1 *(Rashford 87)* 36,544

Valencia: (442) Jaume; Piccini, Ruben Vezo, Diakhaby, Toni Lato (Garay 50); Carlos Soler, Parejo, Kondogbia, Cheryshev (Torres 65); Batshuayi, Santi Mina (Rodrigo 68).
Manchester U: (4411) Romero; Valencia, Jones, Bailly, Rojo (Young 46); Andreas Pereira, Fellaini, Pogba, Fred (Rashford 57); Mata; Lukaku (Lingard 69).

Young Boys (1) 2 *(Hoarau 30 (pen), 68)*

Juventus (0) 1 *(Dybala 80)* 30,114

Young Boys: (433) Wolfli; Mbabu, Camara, Benito, Garcia; Sow (Wuthrich 90), Lauper, Aebischer; Ngamaleu (Schick 84), Hoarau, Fassnacht (Bertone 80).
Juventus: (442) Szczesny; De Sciglio (Dybala 72), Rugani, Bonucci, Cuadrado (Alex Sandro 22); Douglas Costa, Bentancur, Pjanic (Can 65), Bernardeschi; Mandzukic, Ronaldo.

Group H Table	*P*	*W*	*D*	*L*	*F*	*A*	*GD*	*Pts*
Juventus	6	4	0	2	9	4	5	12
Manchester U	6	3	1	2	7	4	3	10
Valencia	6	2	2	2	6	6	0	8
Young Boys	6	1	1	4	4	12	–8	4

KNOCK-OUT STAGE

ROUND OF 16 FIRST LEG

Tuesday, 12 February 2019

Manchester U (0) 0

Paris Saint-Germain (0) 2 *(Kimpembe 53, Mbappe-Lottin 60)* 74,054

Manchester U: (433) de Gea; Young, Bailly, Lindelof, Shaw; Ander Herrera, Matic, Pogba■; Lingard (Sanchez 45), Martial (Mata 46), Rashford (Lukaku 84).
Paris Saint-Germain: (4231) Buffon; Kehrer, Thiago Silva, Kimpembe, Bernat; Verratti (Paredes 75), Marquinhos; Dani Alves, Draxler, Di Maria (Dagba 81); Mbappe-Lottin.

Roma (0) 2 *(Zaniolo 70, 76)*

Porto (0) 1 *(Adrian 79)* 51,727

Roma: (433) Mirante; Florenzi, Manolas, Fazio, Kolarov; Lorenzo Pellegrini (Nzonzi 83), De Rossi, Cristante; Zaniolo (Santon 87), Dzeko, El Shaarawy (Kluivert 89).
Porto: (433) Casillas; Eder Militao, Felipe, Pepe, Alex Telles; Herrera, Danilo Pereira, Fernando (Andre Pereira 76); Otavio (Hernani 84), Tiquinho Soares, Brahimi (Adrian 68).

Wednesday, 13 February 2019

Ajax (0) 1 *(Ziyech 75)*

Real Madrid (0) 2 *(Benzema 60, Asensio 87)* 52,286

Ajax: (433) Onana; Mazraoui, de Ligt, Blind, Tagliafico; de Jong, Schone (Dolberg 73), van de Beek; Ziyech, Tadic, Neres.
Real Madrid: (433) Courtois; Carvajal, Nacho, Sergio Ramos, Reguilon; Kroos, Casemiro, Modric; Bale (Lucas 61), Benzema (Asensio 73), Vinicius Junior (Mariano 81).

Tottenham H (0) 3 *(Son 47, Vertonghen 83, Llorente 86)*

Borussia Dortmund (0) 0 71,214

Tottenham H: (532) Lloris; Aurier, Sanchez, Foyth, Alderweireld, Vertonghen; Sissoko (Wanyama 90), Winks, Eriksen; Son (Lamela 89), Lucas Moura (Llorente 85).
Borussia Dortmund: (4231) Burki; Hakimi, Zagadou (Schmelzer 77), Toprak, Diallo; Witsel, Delaney; Sancho (Guerreiro 88), Dahoud, Pulisic (Bruun Larsen 88); Gotze.

Tuesday, 19 February 2019

Liverpool (0) 0

Bayern Munich (0) 0 52,250

Liverpool: (433) Alisson; Alexander-Arnold, Matip, Fabinho, Robertson; Wijnaldum, Henderson, Keita (Milner 76); Salah, Firmino (Origi 76), Mane.
Bayern Munich: (433) Neuer; Kimmich, Sule, Hummels, Alaba; Thiago, Javi Martinez, Rodriguez (Sanches 88); Gnabry (Rafinha 90), Lewandowski, Coman (Ribery 82).

Lyon (0) 0

Barcelona (0) 0 57,889

Lyon: (4411) Lopes; Dubois, Marcelo, Denayer, Mendy; Traore (Tousart 68), Ndombele (Cheikh 84), Aouar, Terrier (Cornet 75); Depay; Dembele.
Barcelona: (433) ter Stegen; Nelson Semedo, Pique, Lenglet, Jordi Alba; Sergi Roberto (Vidal 81), Busquets, Rakitic; Messi, Suarez L, Dembele (Coutinho 67).

Wednesday, 20 February 2019

Atletico Madrid (0) 2 *(Gimenez 78, Godin 83)*

Juventus (0) 0 67,193

Atletico Madrid: (442) Oblak; Juanfran, Gimenez, Godin, Filipe Luis; Koke (Correa 66), Thomas (Lemar 61), Rodri, Saul; Griezmann, Costa (Morata 57).
Juventus: (4312) Szczesny; De Sciglio, Bonucci, Chiellini, Alex Sandro; Bentancur, Pjanic (Can 72), Matuidi (Joao Cancelo 85); Dybala (Bernardeschi 80); Mandzukic, Ronaldo.

Schalke 04 (2) 2 *(Bentaleb 38 (pen), 45 (pen))*

Manchester C (1) 3 *(Aguero 18, Sane 85, Sterling 90)* 54,417

Schalke 04: (532) Fahrmann; Caligiuri, Bruma, Sane, Nastasic, Oczipka; Serdar, Bentaleb, McKennie (Skrzybski 77); Uth (Harit 87), Mendyl (Burgstaller 65).
Manchester C: (433) Ederson; Walker, Fernandinho, Otamendi■, Laporte; De Bruyne (Zinchenko 87), Gundogan, Silva (Kompany 69); Sterling, Aguero (Sane 78), Bernardo Silva.

ROUND OF 16 SECOND LEG

Tuesday, 5 March 2019

Borussia Dortmund (0) 0

Tottenham H (0) 1 *(Kane 49)* 66,099

Borussia Dortmund: (451) Burki; Wolf (Bruun Larsen 62), Akanji, Weigl, Diallo; Sancho, Reus (Delaney 74), Witsel, Gotze, Guerreiro (Pulisic 62); Alcacer.
Tottenham H: (532) Lloris; Aurier, Alderweireld, Sanchez, Vertonghen, Davies; Winks (Dier 55), Eriksen (Rose 82), Sissoko; Son (Lamela 70), Kane.

Real Madrid (0) 1 *(Asensio 70)*

Ajax (2) 4 *(Ziyech 7, Neres 18, Tadic 62, Schone 72)* 77,013

Real Madrid: (433) Courtois; Carvajal, Nacho■, Varane, Reguilon; Kroos, Casemiro (Valverde 87), Modric; Lucas (Bale 29), Benzema, Vinicius Junior (Asensio 35).
Ajax: (433) Onana; Mazraoui (Veltman 80), de Ligt, Blind, Tagliafico; van de Beek, Schone (de Wit 73), de Jong; Ziyech, Tadic, Neres (Dolberg 74).

Wednesday, 6 March 2019

Paris Saint-Germain (1) 1 *(Bernat 12)*

Manchester U (2) 3 *(Lukaku 2, 30, Rashford 90 (pen))* 47,441

Paris Saint-Germain: (4231) Buffon; Kehrer (Paredes 70), Thiago Silva, Kimpembe, Bernat; Verratti, Marquinhos; Dani Alves (Cavani 90), Draxler (Meunier 70), Di Maria; Mbappe-Lottin.
Manchester U: (352) de Gea; Bailly (Dalot 35), Smalling, Lindelof; Young (Greenwood 87), Andreas Pereira (Chong 80), Fred, McTominay, Shaw; Lukaku, Rashford.
Manchester U won on away goals.

Porto (1) 3 *(Tiquinho Soares 26, Marega 53, Alex Telles 117 (pen))*

Roma (1) 1 *(De Rossi 37 (pen))* 49,029

Porto: (442) Casillas; Eder Militao (Maxi Pereira 103), Felipe, Pepe, Alex Telles; Otavio (Hernani 93), Herrera, Danilo Pereira, Corona (Brahimi 69); Marega, Tiquinho Soares (Fernando 78).
Roma: (3421) Olsen; Marcano (Cristante 76), Manolas, Juan Jesus; Karsdorp (Florenzi 55), Nzonzi, De Rossi (Lorenzo Pellegrini 45 (Schick 96)), Kolarov; Zaniolo, Perotti; Dzeko.
aet.

Tuesday, 12 March 2019

Juventus (1) 3 *(Ronaldo 27, 48, 86 (pen))*

Atletico Madrid (0) 0 40,884

Juventus: (433) Szczesny; Joao Cancelo, Bonucci, Chiellini, Spinazzola (Dybala 67); Can, Pjanic, Matuidi; Bernardeschi, Mandzukic (Kean 80), Ronaldo.
Atletico Madrid: (451) Oblak; Arias (Vitolo 77), Godin, Gimenez, Juanfran; Griezmann, Saul, Rodri, Koke, Lemar (Correa 57); Morata.

Manchester C (3) 7 *(Aguero 35 (pen), 38, Sane 42, Sterling 56, Bernardo Silva 71, Foden 78, Gabriel Jesus 84)*

Schalke 04 (0) 0 51,518

Manchester C: (433) Ederson; Danilo, Walker, Laporte (Delph 72), Zinchenko; Bernardo Silva, Gundogan, Silva (Foden 64); Sterling, Aguero (Gabriel Jesus 64), Sane.
Schalke 04: (4141) Fahrmann; Bruma, Stambouli, Sane, Oczipka; Serdar; McKennie (Mendyl 74), Konoplyanka, Bentaleb, Burgstaller (Teuchert 79); Embolo (Skrzybski 69).

Wednesday, 13 March 2019

Barcelona (2) 5 *(Messi 17 (pen), 78, Coutinho 31, Pique 81, Dembele 86)*

Lyon (0) 1 *(Tousart 58)* 92,346

Barcelona: (433) ter Stegen; Sergi Roberto (Nelson Semedo 83), Pique, Lenglet, Jordi Alba; Arthur (Vidal 74), Busquets, Rakitic; Messi, Suarez L, Coutinho (Dembele 70).
Lyon: (4312) Lopes (Gorgelin 34); Dubois, Denayer, Marcelo, Mendy (Cornet 77); Ndombele, Tousart, Marcal; Fekir; Dembele, Depay (Traore 73).

Bayern Munich (1) 1 *(Matip 39 (og))*

Liverpool (1) 3 *(Mane 26, 84, van Dijk 69)* 68,145

Bayern Munich: (433) Neuer; Rafinha, Sule, Hummels, Alaba; Javi Martinez (Goretzka 72), Rodriguez (Sanches 79), Thiago; Gnabry, Lewandowski, Ribery (Coman 61).
Liverpool: (433) Alisson; Alexander-Arnold, Matip, van Dijk, Robertson; Milner (Lallana 87), Henderson (Fabinho 13), Wijnaldum; Salah, Firmino (Origi 83), Mane.

QUARTER-FINALS FIRST LEG

Tuesday, 9 April 2019

Liverpool (2) 2 *(Keita 5, Firmino 26)*

Porto (0) 0 52,465

Liverpool: (433) Alisson; Alexander-Arnold, Lovren, van Dijk, Milner; Henderson, Fabinho, Keita; Salah, Firmino (Sturridge 81), Mane (Origi 73).
Porto: (442) Casillas; Maxi Pereira (Fernando 77), Felipe, Eder Militao, Alex Telles; Corona, Danilo Pereira, Torres (Costa 73), Otavio; Marega, Tiquinho Soares (Brahimi 62).

Tottenham H (0) 1 *(Son 78)*

Manchester C (0) 0 60,044

Tottenham H: (4231) Lloris; Trippier, Alderweireld, Vertonghen, Rose; Sissoko, Winks (Wanyama 81); Alli (Llorente 87), Eriksen, Son; Kane (Lucas Moura 58).
Manchester C: (433) Ederson; Walker, Otamendi, Laporte, Delph; Gundogan, Fernandinho, Silva (De Bruyne 89); Mahrez (Sane 89), Aguero (Gabriel Jesus 71), Sterling.

Wednesday, 10 April 2019

Ajax (0) 1 *(Neres 46)*

Juventus (1) 1 *(Ronaldo 45)* 50,390

Ajax: (4231) Onana; Veltman, de Ligt, Blind, Tagliafico; Schone (Ekkelenkamp 75), de Jong; Ziyech, van de Beek, Neres; Tadic.
Juventus: (433) Szczesny; Joao Cancelo, Bonucci, Rugani, Alex Sandro; Bentancur, Pjanic, Matuidi (Dybala 75); Bernardeschi (Khedira 90), Mandzukic (Douglas Costa 60), Ronaldo.

Manchester U (0) 0

Barcelona (1) 1 *(Shaw 12 (og))* 74,093

Manchester U: (433) de Gea; Young, Smalling, Lindelof, Shaw; Fred, McTominay, Pogba; Dalot (Lingard 74), Lukaku (Martial 68), Rashford (Andreas Pereira 85).
Barcelona: (433) ter Stegen; Nelson Semedo, Pique, Lenglet, Jordi Alba; Arthur (Sergi Roberto 65), Busquets (Alena 90), Rakitic; Messi, Suarez L, Coutinho (Vidal 65).

QUARTER-FINALS SECOND LEG

Tuesday, 16 April 2019

Barcelona (2) 3 *(Messi 16, 20, Coutinho 61)*

Manchester U (0) 0 96,708

Barcelona: (433) ter Stegen; Sergi Roberto (Nelson Semedo 71), Pique, Lenglet, Jordi Alba; Rakitic, Busquets, Arthur (Vidal 75); Messi, Suarez L, Coutinho (Dembele 81).
Manchester U: (433) de Gea; Jones, Lindelof, Smalling, Young; McTominay, Fred, Pogba; Lingard (Sanchez 79), Rashford (Lukaku 73), Martial (Dalot 65).

Juventus (1) 1 *(Ronaldo 28)*

Ajax (1) 2 *(van de Beek 34, de Ligt 67)* 41,445

Juventus: (433) Szczesny; De Sciglio (Joao Cancelo 64), Rugani, Bonucci, Alex Sandro; Can, Pjanic, Matuidi; Bernardeschi (Bentancur 81), Dybala (Kean 46), Ronaldo.
Ajax: (4231) Onana; Veltman, de Ligt, Blind, Mazraoui (Sinkgraven 11 (Magallan 82)); Schone, de Jong; Ziyech (Huntelaar 88), van de Beek, Neres; Tadic.

Wednesday, 17 April 2019

Manchester C (3) 4 *(Sterling 4, 21, Bernardo Silva 11, Aguero 59)*

Tottenham H (2) 3 *(Son 7, 10, Llorente 73)* 53,348

Manchester C: (433) Ederson; Walker, Kompany, Laporte, Mendy (Sane 83); De Bruyne, Gundogan, Silva (Fernandinho 62); Sterling, Aguero, Bernardo Silva.
Tottenham H: (4231) Lloris; Trippier, Alderweireld, Vertonghen, Rose (Sanchez 90); Sissoko (Llorente 41), Wanyama; Alli, Eriksen, Lucas Moura (Davies 81); Son.
Tottenham H won on away goals.

Porto (0) 1 *(Eder Militao 68)*

Liverpool (1) 4 *(Mane 26, Salah 65, Firmino 77, van Dijk 84)* 49,117

Porto: (433) Casillas; Eder Militao, Pepe, Felipe, Alex Telles; Otavio (Tiquinho Soares 46), Danilo Pereira, Herrera; Corona (Fernando 78), Marega, Brahimi (Costa 81).
Liverpool: (433) Alisson; Alexander-Arnold (Gomez 66), Matip, van Dijk, Robertson (Henderson 71); Wijnaldum, Fabinho, Milner; Salah, Origi (Firmino 46), Mane.

Mohamed Salah of Liverpool opens the scoring from the penalty spot in the Champions League Final on 1st June. Liverpool beat Tottenham Hotspur 2-0 in Madrid. (Reuters/Toby Melville)

SEMI-FINALS FIRST LEG

Tuesday, 30 April 2019

Tottenham H (0) 0

Ajax (1) 1 *(van de Beek 15)* 60,243

Tottenham H: (343) Lloris; Alderweireld, Sanchez, Vertonghen (Sissoko 39); Trippier (Foyth 79), Eriksen, Wanyama, Rose (Davies 79); Alli, Llorente, Lucas Moura.
Ajax: (433) Onana; Veltman, de Ligt, Blind, Tagliafico; van de Beek, Schone (Mazraoui 64), de Jong; Ziyech (Huntelaar 87), Tadic, Neres.

Wednesday, 1 May 2019

Barcelona (1) 3 *(Suarez L 26, Messi 75, 82)*

Liverpool (0) 0 98,299

Barcelona: (433) ter Stegen; Sergi Roberto (Alena 90), Pique, Lenglet, Jordi Alba; Rakitic, Busquets, Vidal; Messi, Suarez L (Dembele 90), Coutinho (Nelson Semedo 60).
Liverpool: (433) Alisson; Gomez, Matip, van Dijk, Robertson; Milner (Origi 85), Fabinho, Keita (Henderson 24); Salah, Mane, Wijnaldum (Firmino 78).

SEMI-FINALS SECOND LEG

Tuesday, 7 May 2019

Liverpool (1) 4 *(Origi 7, 79, Wijnaldum 54, 56)*

Barcelona (0) 0 55,212

Liverpool: (433) Alisson; Alexander-Arnold, Matip, van Dijk, Robertson (Wijnaldum 46); Henderson, Fabinho, Milner; Shaqiri (Sturridge 90), Mane, Origi (Gomez 85).
Barcelona: (433) ter Stegen; Sergi Roberto, Pique, Lenglet, Jordi Alba; Vidal (Arthur 74), Busquets, Rakitic (Malcom 80); Messi, Suarez L, Coutinho (Nelson Semedo 60).

Wednesday, 8 May 2019

Ajax (2) 2 *(de Ligt 5, Ziyech 36)*

Tottenham H (0) 3 *(Lucas Moura 55, 59, 90)* 52,641

Ajax: (433) Onana; Mazraoui, de Ligt, Blind, Tagliafico; Schone (Veltman 60), van de Beek (Magallan 89), de Jong; Ziyech, Tadic, Dolberg (Sinkgraven 67).
Tottenham H: (4312) Lloris; Trippier (Lamela 81), Alderweireld, Vertonghen, Rose (Davies 82); Sissoko, Wanyama (Llorente 46), Alli; Eriksen; Lucas Moura, Son.

CHAMPIONS LEAGUE FINAL 2019

Saturday, 1 June 2019

(in Madrid, attendance 63,272)

Tottenham H (0) 0 **Liverpool (1) 2** *(Salah 2 (pen), Origi 87)*

Tottenham H: (4231) Lloris; Trippier, Alderweireld, Vertonghen, Rose; Sissoko (Dier 74), Winks (Lucas Moura 65); Alli (Llorente 82), Eriksen, Son; Kane.

Liverpool: (433) Alisson; Alexander-Arnold, Matip, van Dijk, Robertson; Henderson, Fabinho, Wijnaldum (Milner 62); Salah, Firmino (Origi 58), Mane (Gomez 90).

Referee: Damir Skomina.

UEFA CHAMPIONS LEAGUE 2019–20

PARTICIPATING CLUBS

The list below is provisional and is subject to pending legal proceedings and final confirmation from UEFA.

GROUP STAGE

Atalanta
Atletico Madrid
Barcelona
Bayer Leverkusen
Bayern Munich
Benfica
Borussia Dortmund
Chelsea
Galatasaray
Genk
Inter Milan
Juventus
Lille
Liverpool
Lokomotiv Moscow
Lyon
Manchester C
Napoli
Paris Saint-Germain
RB Leipzig
Real Madrid
Red Bull Salzburg
Shakhtar Donetsk
Tottenham H
Valencia
Zenit Saint Petersburg
Plus six play-off winners.

PLAY-OFF ROUND – CHAMPIONS ROUTE

Slavia Prague
Young Boys
Plus six third qualifying round winners (champions route).

PLAY-OFF ROUND – LEAGUE ROUTE

Four third qualifying round winners (league route).

THIRD QUALIFYING ROUND – CHAMPIONS ROUTE

Ajax
PAOK
Plus ten second qualifying round winners (champions route).

THIRD QUALIFYING ROUND – LEAGUE ROUTE

Club Brugge
Dynamo Kyiv
Istanbul Basaksehir
Krasnodar
LASK Linz
Porto
Plus two second qualifying round winners (league route).

SECOND QUALIFYING ROUND – CHAMPIONS ROUTE

APOEL
Dinamo Zagreb
FC Copenhagen
Maccabi Tel Aviv
Plus 16 first qualifying round winners.

SECOND QUALIFYING ROUND – LEAGUE ROUTE

FC Basel
Olympiacos
PSV Eindhoven
Viktoria Plzen

FIRST QUALIFYING ROUND

AIK
Ararat-Armenia
Astana
BATE Borisov
Celtic
CFR Cluj
Dundalk
F91 Dudelange
Ferencvaros
HB Trrshavn
HJK Helsinki
Linfield
Ludogorets Razgrad
Maribor
Nomme Kalju
Partizani
Piast Gliwice
Qarabag
Red Star Belgrade
Riga FC
Rosenborg
Saburtalo Tbilisi
Sarajevo
Sheriff Tiraspol
Shkendija
Slovan Bratislava
Suduva
Sutjeska Niksic
The New Saints
Valletta
Valur
Plus the preliminary round winner.

PRELIMINARY ROUND

FC Santa Coloma
Feronikeli
Lincoln Red Imps
Tre Penne

EUROPEAN CUP-WINNERS' CUP FINALS 1961–99

Year	Winners v Runners-up		Venue	Attendance	Referee
1961	1st Leg Fiorentina v Rangers	2-0	Glasgow	80,000	C. E. Steiner (Austria)
	2nd Leg Fiorentina v Rangers	2-1	Florence	50,000	V. Hernadi (Hungary)
1962	Atletico Madrid v Fiorentina	1-1	Glasgow	27,389	T. Wharton (Scotland)
Replay	Atletico Madrid v Fiorentina	3-0	Stuttgart	38,000	K. Tschenscher (West Germany)
1963	Tottenham Hotspur v Atletico Madrid	5-1	Rotterdam	49,000	A. van Leuwen (Netherlands)
1964	Sporting Lisbon v MTK Budapest	3-3*	Brussels	3,208	L. van Nuffel (Belgium)
Replay	Sporting Lisbon v MTK Budapest	1-0	Antwerp	13,924	G. Versyp (Belgium)
1965	West Ham U v Munich 1860	2-0	Wembley	7,974	I. Zsolt (Hungary)
1966	Borussia Dortmund v Liverpool	2-1*	Glasgow	41,657	P. Schwinte (France)
1967	Bayern Munich v Rangers	1-0*	Nuremberg	69,480	C. Lo Bello (Italy)
1968	AC Milan v Hamburg	2-0	Rotterdam	53,000	J. Ortiz de Mendibil (Spain)
1969	Slovan Bratislava v Barcelona	3-2	Basel	19,000	L. van Ravens (Netherlands)
1970	Manchester C v Gornik Zabrze	2-1	Vienna	7,968	P. Schiller (Austria)
1971	Chelsea v Real Madrid	1-1*	Athens	45,000	R. Scheurer (Switzerland)
Replay	Chelsea v Real Madrid	2-1*	Athens	19,917	R. Scheurer (Switzerland)
1972	Rangers v Dynamo Moscow	3-2	Barcelona	24,701	J. Ortiz de Mendibil (Spain)
1973	AC Milan v Leeds U	1-0	Salonika	40,154	C. Mihas (Greece)
1974	Magdeburg v AC Milan	2-0	Rotterdam	4,641	A. van Gemert (Netherlands)
1975	Dynamo Kyiv v Ferencvaros	3-0	Basle	13,000	R. Davidson (Scotland)
1976	Anderlecht v West Ham U	4-2	Brussels	51,296	R. Wurtz (France)
1977	Hamburger SV v Anderlecht	2-0	Amsterdam	66,000	P. Partridge (England)
1978	Anderlecht v Austria/WAC	4-0	Paris	48,679	H. Adlinger (West Germany)
1979	Barcelona v Fortuna Dusseldorf	4-3*	Basel	58,000	K. Palotai (Hungary)
1980	Valencia v Arsenal	0-0*	Brussels	40,000	V. Christov (Czechoslovakia)
	(Valencia won 5-4 on penalties)				
1981	Dinamo Tbilisi v Carl Zeiss Jena	2-1	Dusseldorf	4,750	R. Lattanzi (Italy)
1982	Barcelona v Standard Liege	2-1	Barcelona	80,000	W. Eschweiler (West Germany)
1983	Aberdeen v Real Madrid	2-1*	Gothenburg	17,804	G. Menegali (Italy)
1984	Juventus v Porto	2-1	Basel	55,000	A. Prokop (Egypt)
1985	Everton v Rapid Vienna	3-1	Rotterdam	38,500	P. Casarin (Italy)
1986	Dynamo Kyiv v Atletico Madrid	3-0	Lyon	50,000	F. Wohrer (Austria)
1987	Ajax v Lokomotiv Leipzig	1-0	Athens	35,107	L. Agnolin (Italy)
1988	Mechelen v Ajax	1-0	Strasbourg	39,446	D. Pauly (West Germany)
1989	Barcelona v Sampdoria	2-0	Berne	42,707	G. Courtney (England)
1990	Sampdoria v Anderlecht	2-0*	Gothenburg	20,103	B. Galler (Switzerland)
1991	Manchester U v Barcelona	2-1	Rotterdam	43,500	B. Karlsson (Sweden)
1992	Werder Bremen v Monaco	2-0	Lisbon	16,000	P. D'Elia (Italy)
1993	Parma v Antwerp	3-1	Wembley	37,393	K.-J. Assenmacher (Germany)
1994	Arsenal v Parma	1-0	Copenhagen	33,765	V. Krondl (Czech Republic)
1995	Real Zaragoza v Arsenal	2-1	Paris	42,424	P. Ceccarini (Italy)
1996	Paris Saint-Germain v Rapid Vienna	1-0	Brussels	37,000	P. Pairetto (Italy)
1997	Barcelona v Paris Saint-Germain	1-0	Rotterdam	52,000	M. Merk (Germany)
1998	Chelsea v VfB Stuttgart	1-0	Stockholm	30,216	S. Braschi (Italy)
1999	Lazio v Mallorca	2-1	Birmingham	33,021	G. Benko (Austria)

INTER-CITIES FAIRS CUP FINALS 1958–71

Year	1st Leg		Attendance	2nd Leg	Attendance	Agg	Winner
1958	London XI v Barcelona	2-2	45,466	0-6	70,000	2-8	Barcelona
1960	Birmingham C v Barcelona	0-0	40,524	1-4	70,000	1-4	Barcelona
1961	Birmingham C v Roma	2-2	21,005	0-2	60,000	2-4	Roma
1962	Valencia v Barcelona	6-2	65,000	1-1	60,000	7-3	Valencia
1963	Dinamo Zagreb v Valencia	1-2	40,000	0-2	55,000	1-4	Valencia
1964	Real Zaragoza v Valencia	2-1	50,000	(in Barcelona, one match only)			Real Zaragoza
1965	Ferencvaros v Juventus	1-0	25,000	(in Turin, one match only)			Ferencvaros
1966	Barcelona v Real Zaragoza	0-1	70,000	4-2*	70,000	4-3	Barcelona
1967	Dinamo Zagreb v Leeds U	2-0	40,000	0-0	35,604	2-0	Dynamo Zagreb
1968	Leeds U v Ferencvaros	1-0	25,368	0-0	70,000	1-0	Leeds U
1969	Newcastle U v Ujpest Dozsa	3-0	60,000	3-2	37,000	6-2	Newcastle U
1970	Anderlecht v Arsenal	3-1	37,000	0-3	51,612	3-4	Arsenal
1971	Juventus v Leeds U	0-0	*(abandoned 51 minutes)*		42,000		
	Juventus v Leeds U	2-2	42,000	1-1	42,483	3-3	Leeds U
	Leeds U won on away goals rule.						

Trophy Play-Off – *between first and last winners to decide who would have possession of the original trophy*

1971	Barcelona v Leeds U	2-1	50,000	(in Barcelona, one match only)

**After extra time.*

UEFA CUP FINALS 1972–97

Year	1st Leg		Attendance	2nd Leg	Attendance	Agg	Winner
1972	Wolverhampton W v Tottenham H	1-2	38,562	1-1	54,303	2-3	Tottenham H
1973	Liverpool v Moenchengladbach	0-0	*(abandoned after 27 minutes)*		44,967		
	Liverpool v Moenchengladbach	3-0	41,169	0-2	35,000	3-2	Liverpool
1974	Tottenham H v Feyenoord	2-2	46,281	0-2	59,317	2-4	Feyenoord
1975	Moenchengladbach v FC Twente	0-0	42,368	5-1	21,767	5-1	Moenchengladbach
1976	Liverpool v Club Brugge	3-2	49,981	1-1	29,423	4-3	Liverpool
1977	Juventus v Athletic Bilbao	1-0	66,000	1-2	39,700	2-2	Juventus
	Juventus won on away goals rule.						
1978	Bastia v PSV Eindhoven	0-0	8,006	0-3	28,000	0-3	PSV Eindhoven
1979	RS Belgrade v Moenchengladbach	1-1	65,000	0-1	45,000	1-2	Moenchengladbach
1980	Moenchengladbach v E. Frankfurt	3-2	25,000	0-1	59,000	3-3	E. Frankfurt
	Eintracht Frankfurt won on away goals rule.						
1981	Ipswich T v AZ 67 Alkmaar	3-0	27,532	2-4	22,291	5-4	Ipswich T
1982	IFK Gothenburg v Hamburger SV	1-0	42,548	3-0	57,312	4-0	IFK Gothenburg
1983	Anderlecht v Benfica	1-0	55,000	1-1	70,000	2-1	Anderlecht
1984	Anderlecht v Tottenham H	1-1	33,000	1-1*	46,258	2-2	Tottenham H
	Tottenham H won 4-3 on penalties.						
1985	Videoton v Real Madrid	0-3	30,000	1-0	80,000	1-3	Real Madrid
1986	Real Madrid v Cologne	5-1	60,000	0-2	22,000	5-3	Real Madrid
1987	IFK Gothenburg v Dundee U	1-0	48,614	1-1	20,900	2-1	IFK Gothenburg
1988	Espanol v Bayer Leverkusen	3-0	31,180	0-3*	21,600	3-3	Bayer Leverkusen
	Bayer Leverkusen won 3-2 on penalties.						
1989	Napoli v VfB Stuttgart	2-1	81,093	3-3	64,000	5-4	Napoli
1990	Juventus v Fiorentina	3-1	47,519	0-0	30,999	3-1	Juventus
1991	Internazionale v Roma	2-0	68,887	0-1	70,901	2-1	Internazionale
1992	Torino v Ajax	2-2	65,377	0-0	40,000	2-2	Ajax
	Ajax won on away goals rule.						
1993	Borussia Dortmund v Juventus	1-3	37,000	0-3	62,781	1-6	Juventus
1994	Salzburg v Internazionale	0-1	43,000	0-1	80,345	0-2	Internazionale
1995	Parma v Juventus	1-0	22,057	1-1	80,000	2-1	Parma
1996	Bayern Munich v Bordeaux	2-0	63,000	3-1	30,000	5-1	Bayern Munich
1997	Schalke 04 v Internazionale	1-0	57,000	0-1*	81,675	1-1	Schalke 04
	Schalke 04 won 4-1 on penalties.						

UEFA CUP FINALS 1998–2009

Year	Winners v Runners-up		Venue	Attendance	Referee
1998	Internazionale v Lazio	3-0	Paris	44,412	A. L. Nieto (Spain)
1999	Parma v Olympique Marseille	3-0	Moscow	61,000	H. Dallas (Scotland)
2000	Galatasaray v Arsenal	0-0*	Copenhagen	38,919	A. L. Nieto (Spain)
	Galatasaray won 4-1 on penalties.				
2001	Liverpool v Alaves	5-4*	Dortmund	48,050	G. Veissiere (France)
	Liverpool won on sudden death 'golden goal'.				
2002	Feyenoord v Borussia Dortmund	3-2	Rotterdam	45,611	V. M. M. Pereira (Portugal)
2003	FC Porto v Celtic	3-2*	Seville	52,140	L. Michel (Slovakia)
2004	Valencia v Olympique Marseille	2-0	Gothenburg	39,000	P. Collina (Italy)
2005	CSKA Moscow v Sporting Lisbon	3-1	Lisbon	47,085	G. Poll (England)
2006	Sevilla v Middlesbrough	4-0	Eindhoven	32,100	H. Fandel (Germany)
2007	Sevilla v Espanyol	2-2*	Glasgow	47,602	M. Busacca (Switzerland)
	Sevilla won 3-1 on penalties.				
2008	Zenit St Petersburg v Rangers	2-0	Manchester	43,878	P. Fröjdfeldt (Sweden)
2009	Shakhtar Donetsk v Werder Bremen	2-1*	Istanbul	37,357	L. M. Chantalejo (Spain)

UEFA EUROPA LEAGUE FINALS 2010–19

Year	Winners v Runners-up		Venue	Attendance	Referee
2010	Atletico Madrid v Fulham	2-1*	Hamburg	49,000	N. Rizzoli (Italy)
2011	FC Porto v Braga	1-0	Dublin	45,391	V. Carballo (Spain)
2012	Atletico Madrid v Athletic Bilbao	3-0	Bucharest	52,347	W. Stark (Germany)
2013	Chelsea v Benfica	2-1	Amsterdam	46,163	B. Kuipers (Netherlands)
2014	Sevilla v Benfica	0-0*	Turin	33,120	F. Brych (Germany)
	Sevilla won 4-2 on penalties.				
2015	Sevilla v Dnipro Dnipropetrovsk	3-2	Warsaw	45,000	M. Atkinson (England)
2016	Sevilla v Liverpool	3-1	Basel	34,429	J. Eriksson (Sweden)
2017	Manchester U v Ajax	2-0	Stockholm	46,961	D. Skomina (Slovenia)
2018	Atletico Madrid v Marseille	3-0	Lyon	55,768	B. Kuipers (Netherlands)
2019	Chelsea v Arsenal	4-1	Baku	51,370	G. Rocchi (Italy)

**After extra time.*

UEFA EUROPA LEAGUE 2018–19

▪ *Denotes player sent off.*

PRELIMINARY ROUND FIRST LEG

AEK Larnaca v Lincoln Red Imps	5-0
Sant Julia v Gzira U	0-2
B36 Torshavn v St Joseph's	1-1
Birkirkara v KI Klaksvik	1-1
Cefn Druids v Trakai	1-1
Europa v Prishtina	1-1
Tre Fiori v Bala Town	3-0
Engordany v Folgore Falciano	2-1

Thursday, 28 June 2018

Cefn Druids (0) 1 *(Davies 48)*

Trakai (0) 1 *(Kazlauskas 86)* 742

Cefn Druids: (4141) Jones; Ashton, Peate, Simpson, Arsan; Owen; Piskorski, Evans, Kershaw, Mudimu (Hajdari 76); Davies.
Trakai: (433) Svedkauskas; Borovskis, Janusevskis, Osipov, Silenas; Jeriomenko, Ntika Bondombe (Baniulis 71), Vorobjovas (Masenzovas 56); Cyzas (Mukanya 63), Otstavnov, Kazlauskas.

Tre Fiori (3) 3 *(Miley 7 (og), Procacci 32, Vassallo 36)*

Bala Town (0) 0 542

Tre Fiori: (433) Pizzolato; Bologna, Ghetti, Filippi, Andreini; Procacci▪, Teodorani (Della Valle 84), Gasperoni (Pasolini 76); Tamagnini, Vassallo (Sossio 87), Succi.
Bala Town: (433) Morris; Burns, Miley (Hayes 79), Stuart J Jones, Smith S; Burke, Venables, Pearson; Smith K (Horwood 69), Mangan, Tames (Sheridan 54).

PRELIMINARY ROUND SECOND LEG

Bala Town v Tre Fiori	1-0
Folgore Falciano v Engordany	1-1
(Engordany won 3-2 on aggregate.)	
Gzira U v Sant Julia	2-1
KI Klaksvik v Birkirkara	2-1
Prishtina v Europa	5-0
St Joseph's v B36 Torshavn	1-1
(aet; B36 Torshavn won 4-2 on penalties.)	
Trakai v Cefn Druids	1-0

Thursday, 5 July 2018

Bala Town (0) 1 *(Burke 77)*

Tre Fiori (0) 0 610

Bala Town: (433) Morris; Burns (Stuart W Jones 88), Stuart J Jones, Miley, Smith S; Smith K (Horwood 67), Pearson, Burke; Sheridan, Mangan (Tames 54), Venables.
Tre Fiori: (433) Pizzolato; Bologna, Ghetti, Filippi (Caforio 82), Andreini; Pasolini, Acquarelli, Tamagnini; Teodorani (Matteoni S 90), Vassallo, Succi (Magnani 71).

Trakai (1) 1 *(Bilyaletdinov 29 (pen))*

Cefn Druids (0) 0 850

Trakai: (433) Svedkauskas; Borovskis, Jeriomenko, Osipov, Silenas; Marazas, Ntika Bondombe, Bilyaletdinov (Mukanya 73); Masenzovas, Baniulis (Cyzas 25), Kazlauskas.
Cefn Druids: (532) Jones; Ashton, Peate, Owen (Taylor 69), Simpson (Morris 86), Arsan; Piskorski, Mudimu, Kershaw; Evans, Davies.

FIRST QUALIFYING ROUND FIRST LEG

Samtredia v Tobol	0-1
Banants v FK Sarajevo	1-2
Fola Esch v Prishtina	0-0
Glenavon v Molde	2-1
KI Klaksvik v Zalgiris Vilnius	1-2
Rabotnicki v Budapest Honved	2-1
Vaduz v Levski Sofia	1-0
Anorthosis Famagusta v Laci	2-1
B36 Torshavn v UFK Titograd Podgorica	0-0
Balzan v Inter Baku	4-1
Buducnost Podgorica v Trencin	0-2
Chikhura Sachkhere v Beitar Jerusalem	0-0
Cliftonville v Nordsjaelland	0-1
Connah's Quay Nomads v Shakhtyor Soligorsk	1-3
CSKA Sofia v Riga FC	1-0
DAC Dunajska Streda v Dinamo Tbilisi	1-1
Derry C v Dinamo Minsk	0-2
Ferencvaros v Maccabi Tel Aviv	1-1
FK Liepaja v Hacken	0-3
Gabala v Progres Niederkorn	0-2
Gornik Zabrze v Zaria Balti	1-0
Hibernian v NSI Runavik	6-1
IBV Vestmannaeyjar v Sarpsborg 08	0-4
Ilves v Slavia Sofia	0-1
KuPS v FC Copenhagen	0-1
Lahti v Hafnarfjordur	0-3
Lech Poznan v Gandzasar Kapan	2-0
Levadia Tallinn v Dundalk	0-1
Milsami v Slovan Bratislava	2-4
Narva Trans v Zeljeznicar	0-2
Neftchi v Ujpesti	3-1
Partizani Tirana v Maribor	0-1
Petrocub Hincesti v Osijek	1-1
Pyunik v Vardar	1-0
Racing Luxembourg v Viitorul Constanta	0-2
Radnicki Nis v Gzira U	4-0
Rangers v Shkupi	2-0
Rudar Pljevlja v Partizan Belgrade	0-3
Rudar Velenje v Tre Fiori	7-0
Shamrock R v AIK Solna	0-1
Siroki Brijeg v Domzale	2-2
Spartak v Coleraine	1-1
Stjarnan v Nomme Kalju	3-0
Stumbras v Apollon Limassol	1-0
Trakai v Irtysh	0-0
Engordany v Kairat	0-3
Ventspils v Luftetari Gijrokaster	5-0

Wednesday, 11 July 2018

Glenavon (1) 2 *(Marshall 37, Daniels 60)*

Molde (1) 1 *(Hestad 36)* 631

Glenavon: (442) Tuffey; Marshall, Marron, Doyle, Muir; Hall, Sykes, Grace, Daniels (Jenkins 90); Murray (King 90), Donnelly (Norton 72).
Molde: (433) Linde; Remmer, Forren, Gabrielsen, Haugen; Hussain (Chukwu 60), Sarr, Aursnes; Hestad, Haland (Svendsen 81), Strand (Brustad 71).

Thursday, 12 July 2018

Cliftonville (0) 0

Nordsjaelland (1) 1 *(Skov Olsen 19)* 1170

Cliftonville: (433) Neeson; McGovern (Catney 62), Harney, Breen, Ives; Curran C, McMenamin (Garrett 74), Bagnall; Gormley, Donnelly R, Curran R.
Nordsjaelland: (442) Larsen; Hansen, Nelsson, Skovgaard, Bartolec; Rygaard (Jakobsen 87), Jensen, Pedersen, Damsgaard; Donyoh (Frese 71), Skov Olsen (Rasmussen 57).

Connah's Quay Nomads (0) 1 *(Morris 89 (pen))*

Shakhtyor Soligorsk (2) 3 *(Ebong 20, Bakaj 34, Shlbun 75)* 577

Connah's Quay Nomads: (4141) Danby; Holmes, Disney, Horan, Wilson; Parker (Poole 66); Wignall (Woolfe 86), Morris, Owen (Edwards 80), Bakare; Owens.
Shakhtyor Soligorsk: (4231) Klimovich; Burko, Kuzmenok, Rybak, Shlbun; Szoke, Selyava; Kovalev (Soiri 80), Canas (Simunovic 83), Ebong; Bakaj (Laptev 73).

Derry C (0) 0

Dinamo Minsk (1) 2 *(Galovic 2, Khvashchinski 64)* 1467

Derry C: (433) Doherty G; McDonagh, Seaborne, Cole, McDermott▪; Shiels, Rory Hale (Ronan Hale 6), McEneff; Splaine, Fisk (Peers 78), Roy (Patterson 60).
Dinamo Minsk: (4231) Gorbunov; Zhavnerchik, Shvetsov, Galovic, Ostroukh (Begunov 77); Kaplenko (Ivanov 29), Yahaya; Khvashchinski (Solovei 66), Nikolic, Gurenko; Saroka.

Hibernian (4) 6 *(Kamberi 3 (pen), 21, 48, Shaw 29, Mallan 43, 84)*

NSI Runavik (0) 1 *(Knudsen 53)* 12,501

Hibernian: (442) Bogdan; Ambrose, McGregor (Swanson 61), Hanlon, Stevenson; Whittaker, Mallan, Slivka, Boyle; Shaw (Bartley 82), Kamberi (Murray 52).

NSI Runavik: (4231) Thomsen; Bardar Hansen, Davidsen (Benjaminsen J 71), Joensen, Hansen E■; Benjaminsen F, Betuel Hansen (Olsen M 40); Knudsen, Justinussen, Frederiksberg (Langgaard 79); Olsen K.

Levadia Tallinn (0) 0

Dundalk (0) 1 *(Connolly 53)* 1343

Levadia Tallinn: (442) Lepmets; Jurgenson, Dudarev, Podholjuzin, Kruglov; Gando (Marin 57), Tkachuk, Peetson (Svraka 67), Kharin (Roosnupp 76); Depelko, Andreev.
Dundalk: (442) Rogers; Gannon, Gartland, Hoare, Massey; McGrath (Adorjan 81), Benson, Shields, Connolly (Mountney 88); Duffy (Murray 90), Hoban.

Rangers (1) 2 *(Murphy 23, Tavernier 90 (pen))*

Shkupi (0) 0 49,309

Rangers: (433) McGregor; Tavernier, Goldson, Katic, Flanagan; Candeias (Jack 56), McCrorie, Arfield (Ejaria 67); Windass (Middleton 79), Morelos, Murphy.
Shkupi: (4231) Zendeli; Adem, Tipuric, Bajrami (Bilali 46), Ndong (Krivanjeva 90); Vujcic, Broja; Stojkoski, Muarem, Ljamcevski (Shabani 60); Ilijoski.

Shamrock R (0) 0

AIK Solna (0) 1 *(Sundgren 74)* 2817

Shamrock R: (433) Bazunu; Boyle, Grace, O'Brien (Lopes 83), Kavanagh; Bone, Bolger G (Bolger A 77), Finn; Carr (Greene 75), Coustrain, Watts.
AIK Solna: (442) Linner; Adu, Milosevic, Karlsson, Jansson; Sundgren, Yasin (Avdic 78), Olsson, Hauksson; Elyounoussi (Silva Rojas 90), Goitom.

Spartak (0) 1 *(Savkovic 90 (pen))*

Coleraine (1) 1 *(McCauley 23)* 976

Spartak: (3511) Peric; Milosevic (Torbica 80), Calasan, Kerkez; Vukcevic, Shimura, Marcic, Cecaric (Duricin 46), Glavcic; Savkovic; Djenic (Afum 36).
Coleraine: (433) Johns; Mullan, McConaghie, O'Donnell, Traynor; Lowry, Lyons (Kirk 90), McCauley (Harkin 82); Parkhill, Bradley (McGonigle 70), Burns.

FIRST QUALIFYING ROUND SECOND LEG

Budapest Honved v Rabotnicki	4-0
Levski Sofia v Vaduz	3-2
(Vaduz won on away goals.)	
Shkupi v Rangers	0-0
Zeljeznicar v Narva Trans	3-1
AIK Solna v Shamrock R	1-1
(aet.)	
Apollon Limassol v Stumbras	2-0
Beitar Jerusalem v Chikhura Sachkhere	1-2
Coleraine v Spartak	0-2
Dinamo Minsk v Derry C	1-2
Dinamo Tbilisi v DAC Dunajska Streda	1-2
Domzale v Siroki Brijeg	1-1
(Domzale won on away goals.)	
Dundalk v Levadia Tallinn	2-1
FK Sarajevo v Banants	3-0
FC Copenhagen v KuPS	1-1
Gandzasar Kapan v Lech Poznan	2-1
Gzira U v Radnicki Nis	0-1
Hacken v FK Liepaja	1-2
Hafnarfjordur v Lahti	0-0
Inter Baku v Balzan	2-1
Irtysh v Trakai	0-1
Kairat v Engordany	7-1
Laci v Anorthosis Famagusta	1-0
Luftetari Girokaster v Ventspils	3-3
Maccabi Tel Aviv v Ferencvaros	1-0
Maribor v Partizani Tirana	2-0
Molde v Glenavon	5-1
Nomme Kalju v Stjarnan	1-0
Nordsjaelland v Cliftonville	2-1
NSI Runavik v Hibernian	4-6
OFK Titograd Podgorica v B36 Torshavn	1-2
Osijek v Petrocub Hincesti	2-1
Partizan Belgrade v Rudar Pljevlja	3-0
Prishtina v Fola Esch	0-0
(aet; Fola Esch won 5-4 on penalties.)	
Progres Niederkorn v Gabala	0-1
Riga FC v CSKA Sofia	1-0
(aet; CSKA Sofia won 5-3 on penalties.)	
Sarpsborg 08 v IBV Vestmannaeyjar	2-0
Shakhtyor Soligorsk v Connah's Quay Nomads	2-0
Slavia Sofia v Ilves	2-1
Slovan Bratislava v Milsami	5-0
Tobol v Samtredia	2-0
Tre Fiori v Rudar Velenje	0-3
Trencin v Buducnost Podgorica	1-1
Ujpesti v Neftchi	4-0
Vardar v Pyunik	0-2
Viitorul Constanta v Racing Luxembourg	0-0
Zaria Balti v Gornik Zabrze	1-1
Zalgiris Vilnius v KI Klaksvik	1-1

Tuesday, 17 July 2018

Shkupi (0) 0

Rangers (0) 0 4750

Shkupi: (4231) Zendeli; Adem, Tipuric, Bilali, Krivanjeva; Vujcic (Muharem 76), Broja; Muarem (Ismaili 90), Stojkoski, Ndong (Shabani 37); Ilijoski.
Rangers: (433) McGregor; Tavernier, Goldson, Katic, Flanagan; Candeias (Ejaria 71), McCrorie, Jack; Windass (Middleton 64), Morelos, Murphy (Halliday 90).

Thursday, 19 July 2018

AIK Solna (0) 1 *(Stefanelli 94)*

Shamrock R (1) 1 *(Carr 19)* 8115

AIK Solna: (352) Linner; Milosevic, Karlsson, Jansson; Sundgren, Yasin, Adu, Avdic (Olsson 62), Lindkvist (Stefanelli 83); Silva Rojas (Goitom 62), Elyounoussi (Hauksson 109).
Shamrock R: (541) Bazunu; Boyle, O'Brien, Lopes, Grace, Kavanagh; Coustrain (Greene 67), Watts (McAlister 93), Bone (Bolger G 84), Finn; Carr (Bolger A 67).

Coleraine (0) 0

Spartak (1) 2 *(Savkovic 33, Cecaric 90)* 1602

Coleraine: (433) Johns; Mullan (McLaughlin 85), McConaghie, O'Donnell, Traynor; Parkhill (Harkin 60), Lyons, Lowry; Burns (McGonigle 59), Bradley, McCauley.
Spartak: (4231) Peric; Dunderski, Calasan, Kerkez, Vukcevic; Jocic, Shimura (Torbica 66); Duricin, Glavcic (Marcic 75), Savkovic; Afum (Cecaric 83).

Dinamo Minsk (1) 1 *(Sachivko 28)*

Derry C (1) 2 *(Roy 7, Ronan Hale 75)* 13,750

Dinamo Minsk: (442) Ignatovich; Begunov, Zhavnerchik, Shvetsov, Sachivko; Nikolic, Yahaya, Bykov, Gurenko (Ostroukh 84); Solovei (Khvashchinski 68), Saroka (Ivanov 63).
Derry C: (442) Doherty G; Peers, Shiels (Ronan Hale 72), Cole, Seaborne; Splaine, McEneff, McDonagh, Rory Hale; Fisk (Doherty B 89), Roy.

Dundalk (2) 2 *(Hoban 31, Duffy 33)*

Levadia Tallinn (1) 1 *(Depelko 42)* 3000

Dundalk: (442) Rogers; Gannon, Gartland, Hoare, Massey; Connolly (Adorjan 61), Benson, Shields, McGrath; Hoban (Kelly 90), Duffy (Chvedukas 83).
Levadia Tallinn: (442) Lepmets; Jurgenson (Peetson 87), Dudarev, Podholjuzin, Kruglov; Gando (Roosnupp 64), Tkachuk, Svraka, Kharin (Nesterov 80); Depelko, Andreev.

Molde (2) 5 *(Hussain 28 (pen), Hestad 34, 59, 90, Sarr 90)*

Glenavon (0) 1 *(Forren 62 (og))* 5150

Molde: (433) Linde; Remmer, Gabrielsen (Gregersen 46), Forren, Haugen; Hestad, Sarr, Hussain; Mostrom (Aursnes 74), Brustad (Wadji 61), Chukwu.
Glenavon: (442) Taylor; King, Marron, Doyle, Muir; Hall (Jenkins 84), Sykes, Grace, Daniels (O'Mahony 90); Murray, Donnelly (Norton 46).

Nordsjaelland (0) 2 *(Donyoh 58, Harney 83 (og))*

Cliftonville (1) 1 *(Gormley 6 (pen))* 1592

Nordsjaelland: (4312) Larsen; Strunck, Tranberg (Rygaard 67), Jenssen, Antwi; Christensen, Nelsson, Damgaard; Aaquist (Skov Olsen 66); Baden Frederiksen, Sadiq (Donyoh 46).
Cliftonville: (541) Neeson; Bagnall, McGovern, Harney, Breen, Ives; Donnelly J (McMenamin 73), Curran C (Garrett 84), Curran R (McDonald 64), Donnelly R; Gormley.

NSI Runavik (3) 4 *(Ambrose 1 (og), Olsen K 6, 35, 57)*

Hibernian (3) 6 *(McGinn 10, Stevenson 16, Gray 45, Ambrose 50, Mallan 70, 77)* 587

NSI Runavik: (433) Thomsen; Bardar Hansen, Joensen, Langgaard, Hentze; Olsen M (Betuel Hansen 71), Benjaminsen F, Justinussen; Benjaminsen J (Mortensen M 88), Olsen K (Mortensen J 74), Knudsen.
Hibernian: (442) Bogdan; Gray, Ambrose, Porteous, Stevenson; Whittaker (Slivka 77), McGinn, Bartley (Gullan 88), Mallan; Shaw (Swanson 78), Kamberi.

Shakhtyor Soligorsk (1) 2 *(Bakaj 24 (pen), Laptev 82)*

Connah's Quay Nomads (0) 0 2700

Shakhtyor Soligorsk: (4231) Klimovich; Shlbun, Kuzmenok (Bordachev 45), Rybak, Matsveychyk; Selyava, Szoke; Kovalev, Canas, Ebong (Soiri 83); Bakaj (Laptev 65).
Connah's Quay Nomads: (451) Danby; Holmes, Disney, Horan (Spittle 46), Wilson; Wignall, Owen (Edwards 53), Parker (Poole 66), Morris, Bakare; Owens■.

SECOND QUALIFYING ROUND FIRST LEG

Aberdeen v Burnley	1-1
APOEL v Flora Tallinn	5-0
Atalanta v FK Sarajevo	2-2
B36 Torshavn v Besiktas	0-2
Balzan v Slovan Bratislava	2-1
Budapest Honved v Progres Niederkorn	1-0
Chikhura Sachkhere v Maribor	0-0
CSKA Sofia v Admira Wacker Modling	3-0
DAC Dunajska Streda v Dinamo Minsk	1-3
Dinamo Brest v Atromitos	4-3
Djurgarden v Mariupol	1-1
Dundalk v AEK Larnaca	0-0
F91 Dudelange v Drita	2-1
FC Santa Coloma v Valur	1-0
Genk v Fola Esch	5-0
Gornik Zabrze v Trencin	0-1
Hajduk Split v Slavia Sofia	1-0
Hapoel Haifa v Hafnarfjordur	1-1
Hibernian v Asteras Tripolis	3-2
Jagiellonia Bialystock v Rio Ave	1-0
Kairat v AZ Alkmaar	2-0
LASK Linz v Lillestrom	4-0
Maccabi Tel Aviv v Radnicki Nis	2-0
Molde v Laci	3-0
Nordsjaelland v AIK Solna	1-0
Olimpija Ljubljana v Crusaders	5-1
Osijek v Rangers	0-1
Partizan Belgrade v Trakai	1-0
RB Leipzig v Hacken	4-0
Rudar Velenje v FCSB	0-2
Sevilla v Ujpesti	4-0
Shakhtyor Soligorsk v Lech Poznan	1-1
Spartak Subotica v Sparta Prague	2-0
Spartaks Jurmala v La Fiorita	6-0
St Gallen v Sarpsborg 08	2-1
Stjarnan v FC Copenhagen	0-2
Sutjeska v Alashkert	0-1
The New Saints v Lincoln Red Imps	2-1
Tobol v Pyunik	2-1
Torpedo Kutaisi v Vikingur	3-0
Ufa v Domzale	0-0
Ventspils v Bordeaux	0-1
Viitorul Constanta v Vitesse	2-2
Zalgiris Vilnius v Vaduz	1-0
Zeljeznicar Sarajevo v Apollon Limassol	1-2
Zrinjski Mostar v Valletta	1-1

Thursday, 26 July 2018

Aberdeen (1) 1 *(Mackay-Steven 19 (pen))*

Burnley (0) 1 *(Vokes 80)* 20,313

Aberdeen: (433) Lewis; Logan, Devlin, McKenna, Hoban; Ferguson (Gleeson 57), Shinnie, Ball; Mackay-Steven, Cosgrove (May 76), McGinn (Wright 79).
Burnley: (4141) Pope (Lindegaard 14); Lowton, Tarkowski, Mee, Ward; Cork; Gudmundsson, Hendrick (Vokes 67), Westwood, Lennon; Wood.

Dundalk (0) 0

AEK Larnaca (0) 0 3000

Dundalk: (442) Rogers; Cleary, Hoare, Gartland, Massey (Jarvis 80); Connolly (Murray 84), Benson, Shields, McGrath (McEleney 67); Hoban, Duffy.
AEK Larnaca: (352) Tono; Silva, Truyols, Mikel Gonzalez; Acoran, Jorge (Cases 83), Tomas (Tete 62), Hevel, Ioannou; Trickovski, Giannou (Roushias 90).

Hibernian (0) 3 *(Ambrose 64, Gray 77, Kamberi 90)*

Asteras Tripolis (2) 2 *(Kyriakopoulos 12, 35)* 14,148

Hibernian: (442) Bogdan; Ambrose, McGregor, Hanlon (Porteous 90), Stevenson; Whittaker (Gray 46), Slivka, McGinn, Mallan; Boyle, Kamberi.
Asteras Tripolis: (4231) Athanasiadis; Kotsiras, Pasalidis■, Triantafyllopoulos, Kyriakopoulos; Iglesias, Bellocq (Rolle 56 (Martinez 77)); Kaltzas, Munafo, Tsilianidis (Christopoulos 87); Manias.

Olimpija Ljubljana (1) 5 *(Boateng 30, 68, Crnic 56, 75, Kadric 90)*

Crusaders (0) 1 *(Forsyth 73)* 2980

Olimpija Ljubljana: (4141) Ivacic; Bagnack, Zarifovic, Ilic, Stiglec; Tomic (Suljic 64); Avramovski (Savic 79), Kapun, Miskic, Crnic; Boateng (Kadric 86).
Crusaders: (442) O'Neill; Burns, Coates, Beverland, Ward; Snoddy, Carvill, Caddell (Brown 82), Lowry (Clarke 73); Forsyth, Cushley (Heatley 59).

Osijek (0) 0

Rangers (1) 1 *(Morelos 18)* 7112

Osijek: (442) Malenica; Sorsa (Bockaj 46), Loncar, Skoric, Barisic; Grgic, Mudrazija, Pusic (Hajradinovic 80); Mioc (Lepa 61); Henty, Maric.
Rangers: (4231) McGregor; Tavernier, Katic, Goldson, Flanagan; Jack, Coulibaly; Kent, Ejaria (McCrorie 78), Murphy (Windass 68); Morelos (Middleton 90).

The New Saints (1) 2 *(Ebbe 6, Hudson 83)*

Lincoln Red Imps (1) 1 *(Chipolina 31)* 632

The New Saints: (4231) Harrison; Lewis, Hudson, Cabango, Marriott; Routledge, Holland; Mullan, Edwards, Redmond (Cieslewicz 88); Ebbe (Draper 40).
Lincoln Red Imps: (433) Soler; Garcia, Casciaro R, Oliver (Annesley 65), Chipolina (Dos Santos 84); Moreno, Montesinos, Hernandez; Garro, Aranda (Ortiz 64), Gamiz.

SECOND QUALIFYING ROUND SECOND LEG

Pyunik v Tobol	1-0
(Pyunik won on away goals.)	
Fola Esch v Genk	1-4
Admira Wacker Modling v CSKA Sofia	1-3
AEK Larnaca v Dundalk	4-0
AIK Solna v Nordsjaelland	0-1
Alashkert v Sutjeska	0-0
Apollon Limassol v Zeljeznicar Sarajevo	3-1
Asteras Tripolis v Hibernian	1-1
Atromitos v Dinamo Brest	1-1
AZ Alkmaar v Kairat	2-1
Besiktas v B36 Torshavn	6-0
Bordeaux v Ventspils	2-1
Burnley v Aberdeen	3-1
(aet.)	
Crusaders v Olimpija Ljubljana	1-1
Dinamo Minsk v DAC Dunajska Streda	4-1
Domzale v Ufa	1-1
(Ufa won on away goals.)	
Drita v F91 Dudelange	1-1
FC Copenhagen v Stjarnan	5-0
FCSB v Rudar Velenje	4-0
FK Sarajevo v Atalanta	0-8
Flora Tallinn v APOEL	2-0
Hacken v RB Leipzig	1-1
Hafnarfjordur v Hapoel Haifa	0-1
La Fiorita v Spartaks Jurmala	0-3
Laci v Molde	0-2
Lech Poznan v Shakhtyor Soligorsk	3-1
(aet.)	
Lillestrom v LASK Linz	1-2
Lincoln Red Imps v The New Saints	1-1
Maribor v Chikhura Sachkhere	2-0
Mariupol v Djurgarden	2-1
(aet.)	
Progres Niederkorn v Budapest Honved	2-0
Radnicki Nis v Maccabi Tel Aviv	2-2
Rangers v Osijek	1-1
Rio Ave v Jagiellonia Bialystock	4-4
Sarpsborg 08 v St Gallen	1-0
(Sarpsborg won on away goals.)	
Slavia Sofia v Hajduk Split	2-3
Slovan Bratislava v Balzan	3-1
Sparta Prague v Spartak Subotical	2-1
Trakai v Partizan Belgrade	1-1
Trencin v Gornik Zabrze	4-1
Ujpesti v Sevilla	1-3
Vaduz v Zalgiris Vilnius	1-1
Valletta v Zrinjski Mostar	1-2

Valur v FC Santa Coloma 3-0
Vikingur v Torpedo Kutaisi 0-4
Vitesse v Viitorul Constanta 3-1

Tuesday, 31 July 2018

AEK Larnaca (3) 4 *(Trickovski 13, 38, Tete 21, Tomas 87)*
Dundalk (0) 0 3991
AEK Larnaca: (4141) Tono; Silva, Truyols, Mikel Gonzalez, Ioannou; Jorge (Cases 70); Acoran (Tomas 87), Trickovski, Hevel, Tete (Konstantinou 81); Giannou.
Dundalk: (442) Rogers; Cleary (Gannon 46), Hoare, Gartland, Jarvis; Connolly (McEleney 46), Benson, Shields, McGrath (Massey 64); Hoban, Duffy.

Asteras Tripolis (0) 1 *(Tsilianidis 56)*
Hibernian (1) 1 *(McGinn 44)* 3870
Asteras Tripolis: (4231) Athanasiadis; Kotsiras, Triantafyllopoulos, Valiente (Salas 90), Kyriakopoulos; Iglesias, Bellocq (Douvikas 57); Kaltzas (Rolle 78), Munafo, Tsilianidis; Manias■.
Hibernian: (352) Bogdan; Ambrose, McGregor (Whittaker 78), Hanlon; Gray, Slivka (Bartley 88), Stevenson, Mallan (Porteous 90), McGinn; Boyle, Kamberi.

Burnley (1) 3 *(Wood 6, Cork 101, Barnes 114 (pen))*
Aberdeen (1) 1 *(Ferguson 27)* 17,404
Burnley: (442) Lindegaard; Lowton, Mee, Tarkowski, Ward (Taylor 91); Gudmundsson, Westwood (Hendrick 106), Cork, Lennon (McNeil 86); Wood (Barnes 46), Vokes.
Aberdeen: (433) Lewis; Logan, Devlin, McKenna, Considine; Hoban (Ball 88), Ferguson (Forrester 106), Shinnie; Mackay-Steven, Cosgrove (May 100), McGinn (Wright 80).
aet.

Crusaders (1) 1 *(Heatley 41)*
Olimpija Ljubljana (1) 1 *(Kapun 15)* 1080
Crusaders: (451) O'Neill; Burns, Coates, Owens K (Cushley 61), Brown; Forsyth, Caddell, Snoddy, Ward, Heatley (Clarke 73); Carvill (Lowry 90).
Olimpija Ljubljana: (451) Vidmar; Ilic, Zarifovic, Maksimenko, Stiglec; Savic, Kapun, Tomic, Kronaveter, Crnic (Turkus 90); Kadric (Boateng 46).

Lincoln Red Imps (1) 1 *(Montesinos 41)*
The New Saints (0) 1 *(Ebbe 82)* 546
Lincoln Red Imps: (433) Soler; Dos Santos, Casciaro R, Lopes, Chipolina; Montesinos (Sergeant 81), Hernandez, Gamiz; Casciaro L, Ortiz (Calderon 75), Garro (Corral 46).
The New Saints: (433) Harrison; Lewis, Hudson, Cabango, Marriott; Edwards, Holland (Draper 79), Routledge; Mullan, Byrne (Ebbe 46), Redmond (Cieslewicz 68).

Rangers (0) 1 *(Katic 53)*
Osijek (0) 1 *(Barisic 89)* 48,202
Rangers: (4411) McGregor; Tavernier, Katic, Goldson, Flanagan; Kent, Jack, Coulibaly (Arfield 75), Candeias (Windass 85); Ejaria (Halliday 90); Morelos.
Osijek: (4231) Malenica; Grgic, Tomelin, Skoric, Barisic; Mioc (Pilj 80), Mudrazija; Henty, Hajradinovic, Bockaj (Sorsa 66); Maric (Strkalj 66).

THIRD QUALIFYING ROUND FIRST LEG

Pyunik v Maccabi Tel Aviv 0-0
Alashkert v CFR Cluj 0-2
Apollon Limassol v Dinamo Brest 4-0
Besiktas v LASK Linz 1-0
Cork C v Rosenborg 0-2
CSKA Sofia v FC Copenhagen 1-2
Dinamo Minsk v Zenit St Petersburg 4-0
Genk v Lech Poznan 2-0
Hajduk Split v FCSB 0-0
Hapoel Beer Sheva v APOEL 2-2
Hapoel Haifa v Atalanta 1-4
Hibernian v Molde 0-0
Istanbul Basaksehir v Burnley 0-0
Jagiellonia Bialystock v Gent 0-1
Legia Warsaw v F91 Dudelange 1-2
Ludogorets Razgrad v Zrinjski Mostar 1-0
Mariupol v Bordeaux 1-3
Nordsjaelland v Partizan Belgrade 1-2
Olimpija Ljubljana v HJK Helsinki 3-0
Olympiacos v Luzern 4-0
Rangers v Maribor 3-1
RB Leipzig v Universitatea Craiova 3-1
Sarpsborg 08 v Rijeka 1-1
Sevilla v Zalgiris Vilnius 1-0
Sheriff v Valur 1-0
Sigma Olomouc v Kairat 2-0
Slovan Bratislava v Rapid Vienna 2-1
Spartak Subotica v Brondby 0-2
Spartaks Jurmala v Suduva 0-1
Sturm Graz v AEK Larnaca 0-2
The New Saints v Midtjylland 0-2
Torpedo Kutaisi v Kukesi 5-2
Trencin v Feyenoord 4-0
Ufa v Progres Niederkorn 2-1
Vitesse v FC Basel 0-1
Zorya Luhansk v Braga 1-1

Thursday, 9 August 2018

Cork C (0) 0 Rosenborg (2) 2 *(Levi 22, 44)* 5488
Cork C: (433) McNulty; Beattie, Delaney, McLaughlin, Griffin; Buckley, McCormack (Morrissey 61), Keohane; McNamee, Cummins, Sheppard (Coughlan 72).
Rosenborg: (433) Hansen; Hedenstadt, Hovland, Reginiussen, Meling; Lundemo, Jensen, Trondsen (Skarsem 86); Levi, Soderlund (Botheim 77), Bendtner.

Hibernian (0) 0 Molde (0) 0 16,339
Hibernian: (352) Laidlaw; Ambrose, Porteous, Hanlon; Gray, Mallan, Bartley (Hyndman 81), Slivka, Stevenson; Boyle (Maclaren 90), Kamberi (Shaw 81).
Molde: (442) Linde; Gabrielsen, Forren, Sarr, Haugen; Eikrem (James 62), Gregersen, Hussain, Strand; Chukwu (Mostrom 72), Hestad (Cibicki 90).

Istanbul Basaksehir (0) 0 Burnley (0) 0 4503
Istanbul Basaksehir: (4231) Gunok; Junior Caicara, da Costa, Epureanu, Clichy; Tekdemir, Emre; Visca, Kahveci (Jojic 58), Elia (Frei 84); Bajic (Napoleoni 89).
Burnley: (433) Hart; Taylor, Mee, Tarkowski, Bardsley; Westwood, Hendrick, Cork; Barnes (Lennon 77), Walters, Gudmundsson (Vokes 62).

Rangers (1) 3 *(Morelos 6, Tavernier 50 (pen), Coulibaly 86)*
Maribor (1) 1 *(Bajde 40)* 48,001
Rangers: (433) McGregor; Tavernier, Katic, Goldson, Flanagan; Arfield, Ejaria (Murphy 78), Coulibaly; Candeias, Morelos (Umar 88), Kent (McCrorie 87).
Maribor: (442) Handanovic; Klinar, Ivkovic, Suler, Viler; Bajde (Mesanovic 62), Vrhovec, Dervisevic, Pihler; Tavares (Vrsic 79), Zahovic.

The New Saints (0) 0
Midtjylland (2) 2 *(Onuachu 9, 27)* 863
The New Saints: (433) Harrison; Spender, Hudson, Cabango, Marriott; Edwards, Holland (Byrne 79), Routledge; Mullan, Ebbe (Cieslewicz 69), Redmond (Nembhard 84).
Midtjylland: (343) Hansen J; Hansen K, Sanneh, Nicolaisen; Munksgaard, Poulsen, Duelund, Dal Hende (Andersson 61); Mabil (Okosun 61), Onuachu (George 79), Wikheim.

THIRD QUALIFYING ROUND SECOND LEG

AEK Larnaca v Sturm Graz 5-0
APOEL v Hapoel Beer Sheva 3-1
Atalanta v Hapoel Haifa 2-0
Bordeaux v Mariupol 2-1
Braga v Zorya Luhansk 2-2
(Zorya Luhansk won on away goals.)
Brondby v Spartak Subotica 2-1
Burnley v Istanbul Basaksehir 1-0
(aet.)
CFR Cluj v Alashkert 5-0
Dinamo Brest v Apollon Limassol 1-0
F91 Dudelange v Legia Warsaw 2-2
FC Basel v Vitesse 1-0
FCBS v Hajduk Split 2-1
FC Copenhagen v CSKA Sofia 2-1
Feyenoord v Trencin 1-1
Suduva v Spartaks Jurmala 0-0
Gent v Jagiellonia Bialystock 3-1
HJK Helsinki v Olimpija Ljubljana 1-4
Kairat v Sigma Olomouc 1-2
Kukesi v Torpedo Kutaisi 2-0
LASK Linz v Besiktas 2-1
(Besiktas won on away goals.)
Lech Poznan v Genk 1-2
Luzern v Olympiacos 1-3
Maccabi Tel Aviv v Pyunik 2-1

Maribor v Rangers	0-0
Midtjylland v The New Saints	3-1
Molde v Hibernian	3-0
Partizan Belgrade v Nordsjaelland	3-2
Progres Niederkorn v Ufa	2-2
Rapid Vienna v Slovan Bratislava	4-0
Rijeka v Sarpsborg 08	0-1
Rosenborg v Cork C	3-0
Valur v Sheriff *(Sheriff won on away goals.)*	2-1
Universitatea Craiova v RB Leipzig	1-1
Zalgiris Vilnius v Sevilla	0-5
Zenit St Petersburg v Dinamo Minsk *(aet.)*	8-1
Zrinjski Mostar v Ludogorets Razgrad	1-1

Thursday, 16 August 2018

Burnley (0) 1 *(Cork 96)*

Istanbul Basaksehir (0) 0 16,583

Burnley: (4312) Hart; Bardsley, Gibson, Long, Taylor; Lennon (Gudmundsson 58), Westwood (Cork 83), Ward; Hendrick; Barnes (Tarkowski 120), Vokes (Wood 83).
Istanbul Basaksehir: (433) Gunok; Junior Caicara, da Costa, Epureanu, Clichy; Tekdemir (Inler 93), Kahveci (Jojic 110), Emre; Visca, Bajic (Adebayor 67), Frei (Napoleoni 101).
aet.

Maribor (0) 0 Rangers (0) 0 11,166

Maribor: (442) Handanovic; Klinar (Pihler 52), Ivkovic, Suler, Viler; Hotic, Vrhovec, Dervisevic (Vrsic 73), Mesanovic (Mlakar 80); Zahovic, Tavares.
Rangers: (4231) McGregor; Tavernier, Goldson, Katic, Halliday; Jack, Ejaria (Kent 68); Candeias, Arfield, Murphy (McCrorie 76); Morelos.

Midtjylland (1) 3 *(George 16, Okosun 62, 80)*

The New Saints (1) 1 *(Ebbe 22)* 4368

Midtjylland: (343) Hansen J; Hansen K, Korcsmar, Andersson; Nicolaisen, Poulsen, Mabil (Kraev 73), Thychosen; George, Onuachu (Baidoo 84), Onyeka (Okosun 61).
The New Saints: (433) Harrison; Spender, Hudson, Cabango, Marriott; Edwards, Holland (Byrne 79), Routledge; Mullan, Ebbe (Draper 73), Redmond (Cieslewicz 70).

Molde (1) 3 *(Haland 35, 82, Aursnes 66)*

Hibernian (0) 0 5554

Molde: (451) Linde; Gregersen (Strand 71), Gabrielsen, Forren, Remmer; Hestad, Hussain, Haugen, Aursnes, Cibicki (Eikrem 57); Haland (James 83).
Hibernian: (4411) Bogdan; Ambrose, Porteous, Hanlon, Stevenson (Gray 88); Mallan, Bartley (Hyndman 40), Slivka, Boyle; Maclaren (Shaw 76); Kamberi.

Rosenborg (2) 3 *(Serbecic 26, Soderlund 34, Trondsen 58)*

Cork C (0) 0 8028

Rosenborg: (433) Hansen; Hedenstadt (Reitan 74), Serbecic, Reginiussen, Meling; Lundemo, Jensen, Trondsen (Konradsen 60); Levi (Helland 60), Soderlund, Bendtner.
Cork C: (433) McNulty; Beattie, Delaney, McLaughlin, Griffin; Morrissey (McNamee 46), Buckley (Dunleavy 75), McCormack; Keohane, Sheppard (Coughlan 72), Sadlier.

PLAY-OFF ROUND FIRST LEG

APOEL v Astana	1-0
Atalanta v FC Copenhagen	0-0
F91 Dudelange v CFR Cluj	2-0
FC Basel v Apollon Limassol	3-2
Genk v Brondby	5-2
Gent v Bordeaux	0-0
Malmo v Midtjylland	2-2
Olimpija Ljubljana v Spartak Trnava	0-2
Olympiacos v Burnley	3-1
Partizan Belgrade v Besiktas	1-1
Rangers v Ufa	1-0
Rapid Vienna v FCBS	3-1
Rosenborg v Shkendija	3-1
Sarpsborg 08 v Maccabi Tel Aviv	3-1
Sheriff v Qarabag	1-0
Sigma Olomouc v Sevilla	0-1
Suduva v Celtic	1-1
Torpedo Kutaisi v Ludogorets Razgrad	0-1
Trencin v AEK Larnaca	1-1
Zenit St Petersburg v Molde	3-1
Zorya Luhansk v RB Leipzig	0-0

Thursday, 23 August 2018

Olympiacos (1) 3 *(Fortounis 19, 60 (pen), Bouchalakis 49)*

Burnley (1) 1 *(Wood 33 (pen))* 25,010

Olympiacos: (4231) Gianniotis; Elabdellaoui, Roderick Miranda, Vukovic, Tsimikas; Christodoulopoulos (Ansarifard 84), Bouchalakis; Camara, Daniel Podence, Fortounis (Fetfatzidis 88); Guerrero.
Burnley: (442) Heaton; Bardsley, Long, Gibson■, Ward (Lennon 66); Taylor, Hendrick, Cork, Gudmundsson (Vokes 76); Barnes, Wood (Tarkowski 62).

Rangers (1) 1 *(Goldson 42)*

Ufa (0) 0 49,338

Rangers: (4411) McGregor; Tavernier, Goldson, Katic, Flanagan; Candeias (Lafferty 69), Jack, Ejaria, Kent (Middleton 76); Arfield; Morelos.
Ufa: (433) Belenov; Zhivoglyadov, Tabidze, Nedelcearu, Alikin; Salatic, Zaseev (Vanek 85), Jokic; Paurevic, Igboun (Krotov 90), Oblyakov (Carp 83).

Suduva (1) 1 *(Verbickas 13)*

Celtic (1) 1 *(Ntcham 3)* 5100

Suduva: (532) Kardum; Svrljuga, Gajduchik, Jankauskas, Leimonas, Slavickas; Finkler (Offenbacher 46), Cadjenovic, Verbickas (Matulevicius 90); Cicilia, Vezevicius (Kasparavicius 60).
Celtic: (352) Gordon; Gamboa (Izaguirre 66), Ajer, Simunovic (Lustig 52); Forrest, Brown, Tierney, McGregor, Ntcham; Johnston (Griffiths 66), Dembele.

PLAY-OFF ROUND SECOND LEG

AEK Larnaca v Trencin	3-0
Apollon Limassol v FC Basel	1-0
(Apollon Limassol won on away goals.)	
Astana v APOEL	1-0
(aet; Astana won 2-1 on penalties.)	
Besiktas v Partizan Belgrade	3-0
Bordeaux v Gent	2-0
Brondby v Genk	2-4
Burnley v Olympiacos	1-1
Celtic v Suduva	3-0
CFR Cluj v F91 Dudelange	2-3
FC Copenhagen v Atalanta	0-0
(aet; FC Copenhagen won 4-3 on penalties.)	
FCSB v Rapid Vienna	2-1
Ludogorets Razgrad v Torpedo Kutaisi	4-0
Maccabi Tel Aviv v Sarpsborg 08	2-1
Midtjylland v Malmo	0-2
Molde v Zenit St Petersburg	2-1
Qarabag v Sheriff	3-0
RB Leipzig v Zorya Luhansk	3-2
Sevilla v Sigma Olomouc	3-0
Shkendija v Rosenborg	0-2
Spartak Trnava v Olimpija Ljubljana	1-1
Ufa v Rangers	1-1

Thursday, 30 August 2018

Burnley (0) 1 *(Vydra 86)*

Olympiacos (0) 1 *(Daniel Podence 83)* 15,234

Burnley: (442) Heaton; Bardsley, Mee, Long, Taylor; McNeil (Wood 75), Westwood, Hendrick, Lennon (Cork 75); Barnes (Vydra 65), Vokes.
Olympiacos: (4231) Gianniotis; Elabdellaoui, Roderick Miranda, Vukovic, Tsimikas; Bouchalakis, Camara; Christodoulopoulos, Fortounis (Torosidis 88), Guerrero (Kouka 71); Daniel Podence (Cisse 90).

Celtic (1) 3 *(Griffiths 27, McGregor 53, Ajer 61)*

FK Suduva (0) 0 44,639

Celtic: (433) Gordon; Lustig, Boyata, Ajer, Tierney (Izaguirre 69); McGregor, Brown, Ntcham; Johnston (Hayes 78), Griffiths (Christie 65), Sinclair.
Suduva: (532) Kardum; Svrljuga, Gajduchik, Jankauskas, Zivanovic, Slavickas; Acevedo, Cadjenovic (Leimonas 56), Offenbacher (Verbickas 79); Cicilia, Gotal (Kasparavicius 73).

Ufa (1) 1 *(Sysuev 32)*

Rangers (1) 1 *(Ejaria 9)* 13,186

Ufa: (433) Belenov; Zhivoglyadov, Tabidze, Nedelcearu, Alikin (Oblyakov 52); Paurevic, Salatic (Krotov 76), Jokic; Vanek, Sysuev, Igboun.
Rangers: (4231) McGregor; Goldson, Tavernier, Katic, Flanagan■; Ejaria, Jack; Candeias (Lafferty 46), Arfield (Halliday 69), Kent; Morelos■.

GROUP STAGE

GROUP A

Thursday, 20 September 2018

AEK Larnaca (0) 0

FC Zurich (0) 1 *(Kololli 61 (pen))* 3173

AEK Larnaca: (451) Tono; Silva (Gbayara 79), Mojsov, Mikel Gonzalez, Ioannou; Acoran, Hevel, Jorge (Garcia 83), Trickovski, Tete (Taulemesse 64); Giannou.
FC Zurich: (4411) Brecher; Ruegg, Bangura, Maxso, Jagne■; Khelifi (Winter 90), Palsson, Kryeziu H, Kololli; Marchesano (Nef 86); Odey (Ceesay 75).

Ludogorets Razgrad (2) 2 *(Keseru 8, Marcelinho 31)*

Bayer Leverkusen (1) 3 *(Havertz 38, 69, Thelin 63)* 8240

Ludogorets Razgrad: (433) Renan; Cicinho, Moti, Nedyalkov, Natanael; Dyakov (Goralski 77), Campanharo, Marcelinho (Junior Brandao 82); Lukoki, Keseru, Wanderson.
Bayer Leverkusen: (4231) Hradecky; Weiser, Tah, Dragovic, Wendell; Bender L (Bailey 73), Kohr; Brandt, Havertz, Paulinho (Volland 46); Thelin (Alario 90).

Thursday, 4 October 2018

Bayer Leverkusen (1) 4 *(Havertz 44, Alario 50, 88, Brandt 90)*

AEK Larnaca (1) 2 *(Trickovski 25, Raspas 90)* 23,354

Bayer Leverkusen: (4411) Hradecky; Weiser, Dragovic, Bender S, Wendell; Bellarabi, Kohr (Jedvaj 83), Bender L, Bailey (Alario 47); Havertz (Brandt 71); Volland.
AEK Larnaca: (4141) Tono; Silva, Mikel Gonzalez, Mojsov, Truyols; Acoran; Trickovski, Cases (Gbayara 82), Hevel, Tomas (Tete 67); Giannou (Raspas 89).

FC Zurich (0) 1 *(Palsson 85)*

Ludogorets Razgrad (0) 0 7092

FC Zurich: (3412) Brecher; Nef, Bangura, Maxso; Ruegg, Palsson, Kryeziu H, Kololli; Domgjoni; Odey (Ceesay 82), Schonbachler (Rodriguez 71).
Ludogorets Razgrad: (433) Renan; Cicinho, Moti, Nedyalkov, Natanael; Campanharo, Marcelinho (Mahlangu 79), Dyakov (Goralski 70); Lukoki, Junior Brandao (Swierczok 71), Wanderson.

Thursday, 25 October 2018

AEK Larnaca (1) 1 *(Jorge 25 (pen))*

Ludogorets Razgrad (1) 1 *(Lukoki 7)* 2631

AEK Larnaca: (343) Tono; Silva, Truyols (Acoran 72), Catala; Jorge, Tete (Gbayara 83), Trickovski, Hevel; Mikel Gonzalez, Ioannou, Giannou (Taulemesse 63).
Ludogorets Razgrad: (433) Renan; Nedyalkov, Cicinho, Natanael, Campanharo (Goralski 63); Dyakov (Mahlangu 81), Keseru (Swierczok 84), Moti; Marcelinho, Wanderson, Lukoki.

FC Zurich (1) 3 *(Marchesano 44, Domgjoni 59, Odey 78)*

Bayer Leverkusen (0) 2 *(Bellarabi 50, 54)* 12,427

FC Zurich: (4231) Brecher; Ruegg, Bangura, Maxso, Jagne; Domgjoni, Kryeziu H; Winter (Khelifi 57), Marchesano (Nef 89), Kololli (Rodriguez 79); Odey.
Bayer Leverkusen: (433) Hradecky; Jedvaj, Dragovic (Weiser 46), Bender S, Wendell; Bellarabi, Bender L, Kohr; Havertz, Bailey (Brandt 79), Thelin (Volland 46).

Thursday, 8 November 2018

Bayer Leverkusen (0) 1 *(Jedvaj 60)*

FC Zurich (0) 0 16,000

Bayer Leverkusen: (451) Hradecky; Weiser, Jedvaj, Dragovic, Wendell (Bender L 74); Brandt (Thelin 62), Aranguiz (Paulinho 62), Kohr, Baumgartlinger, Bailey; Alario.
FC Zurich: (4231) Brecher; Ruegg, Nef, Maxso, Bangura; Domgjoni, Kryeziu H; Khelifi (Palsson 55), Marchesano (Ceesay 69), Kololli; Odey.

Ludogorets Razgrad (0) 0

AEK Larnaca (0) 0 4520

Ludogorets Razgrad: (433) Renan; Cicinho, Moti, Nedyalkov, Natanael; Campanharo, Dyakov (Sasha 66), Marcelinho; Lukoki (Joao Paulo 86), Keseru (Swierczok 76), Wanderson.
AEK Larnaca: (4231) Tono; Silva, Catala, Mikel Gonzalez, Ioannou; Garcia, Hevel; Acoran (Taulemesse 81), Trickovski (Konstantinou 87), Gbayara (Tete 71); Giannou.

Thursday, 29 November 2018

Bayer Leverkusen (0) 1 *(Weiser 85)*

Ludogorets Razgrad (0) 1 *(Marcelinho 69)* 16,066

Bayer Leverkusen: (433) Ozcan; Weiser, Retsos (Baumgartlinger 34), Dragovic, Wendell; Paulinho, Aranguiz (Bender L 63), Bailey; Thelin, Schreck (Havertz 73), Alario.
Ludogorets Razgrad: (451) Renan; Cicinho, Moti, Terziev, Forster; Joao Paulo (Marcelinho 63), Goralski, Sasha (Bakalov 89), Dyakov, Wanderson; Swierczok (Nedyalkov 82).

FC Zurich (0) 1 *(Khelifi 74)*

AEK Larnaca (1) 2 *(Giannou 38, Trickovski 85)* 6107

FC Zurich: (4231) Brecher; Dixon, Nef, Bangura, Kryeziu M; Palsson, Domgjoni (Sohm 88); Khelifi, Marchesano (Krasniqi 46), Rodriguez (Winter 73); Odey.
AEK Larnaca: (442) Tono; Silva, Truyols, Mikel Gonzalez, Ioannou; Acoran (Gbayara 79), Garcia, Jorge (Tomas 84), Hevel; Taulemesse (Trickovski 65), Giannou.

Thursday, 13 December 2018

AEK Larnaca (1) 1 *(Catala 27)*

Bayer Leverkusen (2) 5 *(Kohr 28, 68, Alario 41 (pen), 87, Paulinho 78)* 3000

AEK Larnaca: (4231) Christodoulou; Silva, Truyols, Catala, Ioannou; Garcia, Cases (Hevel 46); Acoran, Tomas, Tete (Trickovski 58); Giannou (Konstantinou 84).
Bayer Leverkusen: (442) Kirschbaum; Weiser, Baumgartlinger, Dragovic, Wendell (Bednarczyk 82); Brandt (Bailey 46), Schreck, Kohr, Paulinho; Alario (Stanilewicz 88), Thelin.

Ludogorets Razgrad (1) 1 *(Swierczok 45)*

FC Zurich (1) 1 *(Odey 21)* 2150

Ludogorets Razgrad: (343) Broun; Terziev, Forster, Nedyalkov; Cicinho, Dyakov (Sasha 82), Goralski, Natanael; Marcelinho, Wanderson (Bakalov 87), Swierczok (Keseru 72).
FC Zurich: (442) Vanins; Dixon (Krasniqi 46), Bangura, Kryeziu M, Guenouche; Khelifi, Palsson, Domgjoni, Kololli (Rodriguez 76); Winter, Odey (Nef 90).

Group A Table	P	W	D	L	F	A	GD	Pts
Bayer Leverkusen	6	4	1	1	16	9	7	13
FC Zurich	6	3	1	2	7	6	1	10
AEK Larnaca	6	1	2	3	6	12	–6	5
Ludogorets Razgrad	6	0	4	2	5	7	–2	4

GROUP B

Thursday, 20 September 2018

Celtic (0) 1 *(Griffiths 87)*

Rosenborg (0) 0 47,287

Celtic: (4141) Gordon; Lustig, Boyata, Benkovic, Tierney; Rogic (Sinclair 57); Brown, Forrest (Johnston 58), McGregor, Ntcham; Edouard (Griffiths 76).
Rosenborg: (433) Hansen; Hedenstadt, Hovland, Reginiussen, Meling; Denic, Jensen, Konradsen (Lundemo 45); de Lanlay (Trondsen 69), Soderlund (Levi 78), Jebali.

RB Leipzig (0) 2 *(Laimer 70, Poulsen 82)*

Red Bull Salzburg (2) 3 *(Dabbur 20, Haidara 22, Gulbrandsen 89)* 24,057

RB Leipzig: (442) Mvogo; Laimer, Upamecano, Konate, Mukiele (Halstenberg 46); Kampl, Ilsanker, Matheus Cunha, Sabitzer; Augustin (Poulsen 46), Bruma (Demme 46).
Red Bull Salzburg: (442) Walke; Lainer, Ramalho, Pongracic, Ulmer; Haidara, Wolf, Samassekou, Schlager (Junuzovic 86); Yabo (Minamino 71), Dabbur (Gulbrandsen 83).

Thursday, 4 October 2018

Red Bull Salzburg (0) 3 *(Dabbur 55, 73 (pen), Minamino 61)*

Celtic (1) 1 *(Edouard 2)* 24,500

Red Bull Salzburg: (442) Walke; Lainer, Ramalho, Pongracic, Ulmer; Haidara, Samassekou, Wolf (Gulbrandsen 79), Schlager; Dabbur (Yabo 85), Minamino (Junuzovic 71).
Celtic: (442) Gordon; Lustig, Boyata, Hendry, Tierney; Forrest■, Mulumbu (Christie 78), Ntcham, McGregor; Griffiths (Sinclair 60), Edouard (Morgan 82).

Rosenborg (0) 1 *(Jebali 79)*

RB Leipzig (1) 3 *(Augustin 12, Konate 54, Matheus Cunha 61)* 11,484

Rosenborg: (433) Hansen; Hedenstadt (Reitan 62), Hovland, Reginiussen, Gersbach; Jensen, Konradsen, Denic (Vilhjalmsson 77); Levi, Soderlund, de Lanlay (Jebali 68).
RB Leipzig: (442) Mvogo; Mukiele (Sabitzer 82), Konate, Orban, Halstenberg (Saracchi 74); Laimer, Ilsanker, Demme (Klostermann 64), Bruma; Augustin, Matheus Cunha.

Thursday, 25 October 2018

RB Leipzig (2) 2 *(Matheus Cunha 31, Bruma 35)*

Celtic (0) 0 38,126

RB Leipzig: (433) Mvogo; Klostermann, Orban, Upamecano, Saracchi; Sabitzer (Ilsanker 61), Laimer, Kampl (Majetschak 83); Augustin (Poulsen 90), Matheus Cunha, Bruma.
Celtic: (442) Gordon; Gamboa (Lustig 46), Boyata, Simunovic (Hendry 74), Tierney; McGregor, Ntcham, Eboue, Morgan (Sinclair 71); Edouard, Christie.

Red Bull Salzburg (1) 3 *(Dabbur 34, 59 (pen), Wolf 53)*

Rosenborg (0) 0 20,639

Red Bull Salzburg: (442) Walke; Lainer, Ramalho, Pongracic, Ulmer; Haidara, Samassekou (Schlager 75), Wolf (Minamino 82), Junuzovic; Dabbur (Prevljak 72), Gulbrandsen.
Rosenborg: (433) Hansen; Hedenstadt, Serbecic, Hovland, Gersbach; Jensen (Denic 71), Lundemo, Konradsen; Levi, Bendtner (Vilhjalmsson 56), de Lanlay (Adegbenro 66).

Thursday, 8 November 2018

Celtic (1) 2 *(Tierney 11, Edouard 79)*

RB Leipzig (0) 1 *(Augustin 78)* 56,027

Celtic: (4312) Gordon; Lustig, Benkovic, Boyata, Tierney; Rogic, McGregor, Forrest (Mulumbu 83); Christie; Sinclair (Ajer 89), Edouard.
RB Leipzig: (433) Mvogo; Mukiele (Demme 70), Orban, Upamecano, Saracchi (Halstenberg 16); Laimer, Ilsanker (Kampl 46), Sabitzer; Augustin, Bruma, Matheus Cunha.

Rosenborg (0) 2 *(Adegbenro 52, Jensen 62)*

Red Bull Salzburg (4) 5 *(Minamino 6, 20, 45, Gulbrandsen 37, Hovland 57 (og))* 12,386

Rosenborg: (433) Hansen; Reitan, Serbecic, Hovland, Meling; Konradsen, Jensen, Denic (Vilhjalmsson 85); Adegbenro (Levi 75), Soderlund (Lundemo 46), Bendtner.
Red Bull Salzburg: (442) Walke; Lainer, Ramalho, Onguene, Ulmer; Haidara, Samassekou, Minamino (Wolf 77), Schlager (Leitgeb 89); Gulbrandsen (Prevljak 85), Dabbur.

Thursday, 29 November 2018

Red Bull Salzburg (0) 1 *(Gulbrandsen 74)*

RB Leipzig (0) 0 29,520

Red Bull Salzburg: (442) Walke; Lainer, Ramalho, Pongracic, Ulmer; Schlager, Wolf (Daka 86), Samassekou, Junuzovic; Dabbur (Prevljak 90), Gulbrandsen (Minamino 76).
RB Leipzig: (433) Mvogo; Mukiele (Klostermann 70), Orban, Upamecano, Saracchi (Halstenberg 78); Laimer, Ilsanker, Bruma; Matheus Cunha, Augustin (Poulsen 62), Werner.

Rosenborg (0) 0

Celtic (1) 1 *(Sinclair 42)* 14,061

Rosenborg: (433) Hansen; Hedenstadt, Hovland, Reginiussen, Meling; Jensen, Trondsen (Vilhjalmsson 65), Konradsen (Denic 45); de Lanlay, Bendtner, Adegbenro (Levi 77).
Celtic: (4411) Gordon; Lustig (Gamboa 65), Benkovic, Boyata, Tierney; Forrest (Brown 76), McGregor, Rogic, Sinclair; Christie; Edouard (Griffiths 65).

Thursday, 13 December 2018

Celtic (0) 1 *(Ntcham 90)*

Red Bull Salzburg (0) 2 *(Dabbur 67, Gulbrandsen 77)* 57,578

Celtic: (4411) Gordon; Lustig (Ajer 21), Benkovic, Simunovic, Tierney; Forrest, McGregor, Rogic, Sinclair (Brown 46); Christie (Ntcham 58); Edouard.
Red Bull Salzburg: (442) Walke; Lainer, Ramalho, Onguene, Ulmer; Mwepu (Leitgeb 80), Samassekou, Wolf, Junuzovic; Minamino (Gulbrandsen 74), Dabbur (Prevljak 90).

RB Leipzig (0) 1 *(Matheus Cunha 47)*

Rosenborg (0) 1 *(Reginiussen 86)* 16,957

RB Leipzig: (433) Mvogo; Mukiele (Klostermann 81), Orban, Konate, Saracchi; Laimer, Kampl (Sabitzer 69), Ilsanker; Bruma, Augustin (Poulsen 46), Matheus Cunha.
Rosenborg: (433) Hansen; Reitan, Hovland, Reginiussen, Meling; Jensen, Konradsen, Trondsen (Denic 75); Jebali (Helland 67), Vilhjalmsson (Botheim 83), Adegbenro.

Group B Table	P	W	D	L	F	A	GD	Pts
Red Bull Salzburg	6	6	0	0	17	6	11	18
Celtic	6	3	0	3	6	8	–2	9
RB Leipzig	6	2	1	3	9	8	1	7
Rosenborg	6	0	1	5	4	14	–10	1

GROUP C

Thursday, 20 September 2018

FC Copenhagen (0) 1 *(Sotiriou 63)*

Zenit St Petersburg (1) 1 *(Mak 44)* 19,005

FC Copenhagen: (442) Joronen; Ankersen, Vavro, Bjelland, Boilesen; Skov, Zeca, Thomsen (Jensen 60), Fischer (Papagiannopoulos 90); Sotiriou (Gregus 77), N'Doye.
Zenit St Petersburg: (4231) Lunev; Smolnikov, Ivanovic, Neto, Aniukov; Paredes, Kuzyaev (Zabolotny 89); Mak (Marchisio 58), Erokhin, Driussi (Shatov 79); Dzyuba.

Slavia Prague (1) 1 *(Zmrhal 35)*

Bordeaux (0) 0 16,548

Slavia Prague: (4231) Kolar; Coufal, Kudela, Ngadeu Ngadjui, Boril; Soucek, Husbauer; Stoch (Baluta 79), Traore (Matousek 90), Zmrhal (Frydrych 83); Tecl.
Bordeaux: (433) Costil; Sabaly, Pablo Castro, Kounde, Palencia; Tchouameni, Sankhare (Cornelius 70), Plasil (Otavio 85); Kalu, Briand, Kamano (Karamoh 60).

Thursday, 4 October 2018

Bordeaux (0) 1 *(Sankhare 84)*

FC Copenhagen (1) 2 *(Sotiriou 42, Skov 90)* 11,860

Bordeaux: (433) Costil; Palencia, Kounde, Pablo Castro, Poundje; Lerager (Tchouameni 78), Sankhare, Otavio; Kalu, Briand (Cornelius 62), Kamano (Karamoh 62).
FC Copenhagen: (442) Andersen; Ankersen, Papagiannopoulos (Vavro 88), Bjelland, Boilesen; Zeca■, Gregus, Kvist (Skov 59), Thomsen (Jensen 70); Sotiriou, N'Doye.

Zenit St Petersburg (0) 1 *(Kokorin 80)*

Slavia Prague (0) 0 45,408

Zenit St Petersburg: (433) Lunev; Aniukov, Ivanovic, Neto, Nabiullin (Zabolotny 90); Erokhin, Paredes, Kranevitter; Mak (Kuzyaev 64), Dzyuba, Driussi (Kokorin 63).
Slavia Prague: (4231) Kolar; Coufal (Frydrych 83), Kudela, Ngadeu Ngadjui, Boril; Husbauer, Soucek; Stoch, Traore (Deli 89), Zmrhal; Matousek (Baluta 53).

Thursday, 25 October 2018

FC Copenhagen (0) 0

Slavia Prague (0) 1 *(Matousek 46)* 20,672

FC Copenhagen: (442) Andersen; Ankersen, Papagiannopoulos, Bjelland, Bengtsson; Skov (Kodro 84), Jensen (Vavro 84), Gregus, Fischer (Holse 71); Sotiriou, N'Doye.
Slavia Prague: (4141) Kolar; Coufal, Kudela, Ngadeu Ngadjui, Boril; Soucek; Stoch (Frydrych 85), Husbauer (Deli 90), Traore, Zmrhal; Matousek (Tecl 72).

Zenit St Petersburg (1) 2 *(Dzyuba 41, Kuzyaev 85)*

Bordeaux (1) 1 *(Briand 26)* 45,723

Zenit St Petersburg: (433) Lunev; Mammana, Ivanovic, Luis Neto, Nabiullin; Erokhin, Paredes, Kuzyaev; Mak (Shatov 75), Dzyuba (Zabolotny 87), Driussi (Ozdoev 89).
Bordeaux: (442) Costil; Lewczuk, Kounde, Pablo Castro, Poundje; Kalu, Tchouameni, Otavio, Sankhare; Karamoh (Youssef 67), Briand (De Preville 78).

Thursday, 8 November 2018

Bordeaux (1) 1 *(Kamano 35 (pen))*

Zenit St Petersburg (0) 1 *(Zabolotny 72)* 8907

Bordeaux: (433) Costil; Sabaly, Jovanovic, Pablo Castro, Poundje; Lerager, Sankhare, Plasil (De Preville 83); Kalu, Cornelius (Briand 46), Kamano (Karamoh 66).
Zenit St Petersburg: (532) Lunev; Aniukov (Mak 61), Neto, Mevlja, Mammana, Nabiullin; Marchisio, Paredes, Erokhin (Kuzyaev 64); Zabolotny, Driussi (Shatov 78).

Slavia Prague (0) 0

FC Copenhagen (0) 0 18,702

Slavia Prague: (4231) Kolar; Frydrych, Ngadeu Ngadjui, Deli, Boril; Soucek, Traore; Stoch, Sykora (Baluta 80), Zmrhal (Skoda 79); Olayinka.
FC Copenhagen: (442) Andersen; Ankersen, Vavro, Bjelland, Boilesen (Bengtsson 35); Skov (Thomsen 64), Gregus, Zeca, Jensen (Wind 79); Sotiriou, N'Doye.

Thursday, 29 November 2018

Bordeaux (0) 2 *(De Preville 49, Kounde 90)*

Slavia Prague (0) 0 6311

Bordeaux: (433) Costil; Sabaly, Kounde, Pablo Castro, Palencia; Youssef (Sankhare 75), Tchouameni, Lerager; Kalu (Karamoh 81), Cornelius, De Preville (Kamano 70).
Slavia Prague: (4231) Kolar; Coufal, Ngadeu Ngadjui, Deli, Boril; Soucek, Traore (Sykora 46); Stoch (Skoda 77), Husbauer, Zmrhal; Matousek (Olayinka 51).

Zenit St Petersburg (0) 1 *(Mak 59)*

FC Copenhagen (0) 0 45,199

Zenit St Petersburg: (352) Lunev; Aniukov, Ivanovic, Mevlja; Kuzyaev, Erokhin (Marchisio 74), Paredes, Hernani (Ozdoev 88), Mak; Driussi (Zabolotny 61), Dzyuba.
FC Copenhagen: (442) Andersen; Ankersen, Vavro (Papagiannopoulos 54), Bjelland, Bengtsson; Skov (Wind 78), Gregus, Zeca, Holse (Jensen 60); Sotiriou, N'Doye.

Thursday, 13 December 2018

FC Copenhagen (0) 0

Bordeaux (0) 1 *(Briand 73)* 18,209

FC Copenhagen: (442) Andersen; Ankersen, Vavro, Bjelland (Papagiannopoulos 7), Boilesen (Bengtsson 62); Skov, Jensen (Gregus 73), Zeca, Thomsen; Sotiriou, N'Doye.
Bordeaux: (433) Costil; Sabaly, Pablo Castro, Kounde, Poundje; Plasil, Otavio, Lerager; Briand, Cornelius (Karamoh 60), De Preville (Kamano 60).

Slavia Prague (2) 2 *(Zmrhal 32, Stoch 41)*

Zenit St Petersburg (0) 0 17,748

Slavia Prague: (4231) Kolar; Coufal, Kudela, Ngadeu Ngadjui, Zeleny (Baluta 90); Husbauer, Soucek; Stoch (Frydrych 90), Olayinka, Zmrhal; Skoda (Traore 84).
Zenit St Petersburg: (442) Kerzhakov; Mammana, Neto, Mevlja, Nabiullin (Driussi 46); Smolnikov, Marchisio, Kranevitter, Hernani; Zabolotny (Mak 46), Shatov (Kuzyaev 73).

Group C Table	P	W	D	L	F	A	GD	Pts
Zenit St Petersburg	6	3	2	1	6	5	1	11
Slavia Prague	6	3	1	2	4	3	1	10
Bordeaux	6	2	1	3	6	6	0	7
FC Copenhagen	6	1	2	3	3	5	–2	5

GROUP D

Thursday, 20 September 2018

Dinamo Zagreb (2) 4 *(Sunjic 16, Hajrovic 27, 57, Olmo 60)*

Fenerbahce (0) 1 *(Neustadter 47)* 17,303

Dinamo Zagreb: (343) Livakovic; Theophile-Catherine, Dilaver, Rrahmani; Stojanovic, Sunjic, Gojak, Hajrovic (Doumbia 82); Orsic (Kadzior 79), Gavranovic (Budimir 86), Olmo.
Fenerbahce: (4231) Tekin; Ozbayrakli, Neustadter, Reyes, Koybasi; Topal, Elmas; Potuk (Slimani 81), Benzia (Jailson 65), Chahechouhe (Alici 65); Frey.

Spartak Trnava (0) 1 *(Oravec 79)*

Anderlecht (0) 0 17,114

Spartak Trnava: (4231) Chudy; Kadlec, Toth, Godal, Conka (Kulhanek 52); Oravec, Rada; Jirka (Malecki 65), Grendel, Chanturishvili; Bakos (Janso 87).
Anderlecht: (442) Didillon; Najar (Saief 65), Vranjes, Sanneh, Milic; Musona (Makarenko 84), Kums, Trebel, Amuzu; Santini, Dimata (Gerkens 84).

Thursday, 4 October 2018

Anderlecht (0) 0

Dinamo Zagreb (1) 2 *(Hajrovic 19 (pen), Gojak 68)* 12,137

Anderlecht: (442) Didillon; Najar (Saief 66), Vranjes■, Sanneh, Milic; Bakkali (Morioka 89), Makarenko, Trebel, Amuzu; Santini, Dimata (Lawrence 85).
Dinamo Zagreb: (433) Livakovic; Stojanovic, Theophile-Catherine■, Dilaver (Peric 46), Rrahmani; Gojak, Ademi, Olmo; Hajrovic (Sunjic 76), Petkovic, Orsic (Gavranovic 90).

Fenerbahce (0) 2 *(Slimani 53, 70)*

Spartak Trnava (0) 0 29,622

Fenerbahce: (4231) Tekin; Isla, Skrtel, Neustadter, Kaldirim; Reyes (Koybasi 76), Jailson; Ayew (Valbuena 76), Elmas, Frey; Slimani (Topal 88).
Spartak Trnava: (4411) Chudy; Kadlec, Toth, Godal (Hladik 67), Oravec; Jirka (Miesenboeck 82), Gressak, Rada, Grendel (Ghorbani 68); Chanturishvili; Bakos.

Thursday, 25 October 2018

Anderlecht (1) 2 *(Bakkali 35, 50)*

Fenerbahce (0) 2 *(Frey 53, Kaldirim 57)* 13,292

Anderlecht: (442) Didillon; Saelemaekers (Najar 86), Bornauw, Sanneh, Lawrence; Gerkens (Dauda 86), Kums, Trebel, Saief; Bakkali, Santini.
Fenerbahce: (442) Tekin; Isla, Neustadter, Skrtel, Kaldirim; Benzia (Guctekin 73), Jailson, Reyes, Elmas (Potuk 86); Frey, Slimani (Ayew 73).

Spartak Trnava (1) 1 *(Ghorbani 32)*

Dinamo Zagreb (0) 2 *(Gavranovic 64, Orsic 77)* 0

Spartak Trnava: (4231) Chudy; Oravec, Toth, Godal, Conka; Gressak, Rada (Skhirtladze 82); Jirka (Malecki 70), Grendel, Chanturishvili; Ghorbani.
Dinamo Zagreb: (433) Livakovic; Stojanovic, Leskovic, Peric, Rrahmani; Gojak, Ademi, Olmo (Sunjic 86); Hajrovic (Kadzior 73), Gavranovic (Petkovic 87), Orsic.
Behind closed doors.

Thursday, 8 November 2018

Dinamo Zagreb (2) 3 *(Gojak 22, Kadlec 36 (og), Orsic 79)*

Spartak Trnava (0) 1 *(Chanturishvili 63)* 18,154

Dinamo Zagreb: (4231) Livakovic; Stojanovic, Theophile-Catherine, Peric, Rrahmani; Gojak, Ademi; Hajrovic, Olmo (Budimir 89), Orsic (Sunjic 81); Gavranovic (Petkovic 76).
Spartak Trnava: (4231) Chudy; Kadlec (Dangubic 86), Toth, Godal, Conka; Gressak, Rada; Jirka, Skhirtladze (Kulhanek 82), Chanturishvili; Ghorbani (Malecki 70).

Fenerbahce (0) 2 *(Valbuena 71, Frey 74)*
Anderlecht (0) 0 32,789
Fenerbahce: (433) Tekin; Ozbayrakli, Neustadter, Skrtel, Kaldirim; Elmas, Jailson (Isla 88), Valbuena (Koybasi 82); Ayew, Slimani, Frey.
Anderlecht: (442) Didillon; Saelemaekers (Najar 77), Vranjes, Bornauw (Sanneh 45), Milic; Gerkens, Kums, Trebel (Sambi Lokonga 77), Makarenko; Bakkali■, Dimata.

Thursday, 29 November 2018

Anderlecht (0) 0
Spartak Trnava (0) 0 8063
Anderlecht: (442) Didillon; Appiah, Bornauw, Sanneh, Lawrence; Musona (Amuzu 81), Makarenko (Sambi Lokonga 82), Kayembe, Saief; Morioka (Verschaeren 81), Dauda.
Spartak Trnava: (4231) Chudy; Oravec, Toth, Gressak, Chanturishvili; Skhirtladze, Cherednychenko; Jirka, Grendel (Miesenboeck 90), Malecki (Janso 90); Bakos (Ghorbani 59).

Fenerbahce (0) 0
Dinamo Zagreb (0) 0 24,776
Fenerbahce: (451) Tekin; Isla, Neustadter, Skrtel, Kaldirim; Alici, Jailson, Elmas, Benzia, Valbuena; Frey.
Dinamo Zagreb: (433) Livakovic; Stojanovic, Theophile-Catherine, Dilaver, Rrahmani; Gojak, Ademi, Olmo; Hajrovic (Kadzior 90), Gavranovic (Petkovic 62), Orsic (Sunjic 64).

Thursday, 13 December 2018

Dinamo Zagreb (0) 0
Anderlecht (0) 0 12,170
Dinamo Zagreb: (433) Livakovic; Stojanovic, Theophile-Catherine, Dilaver, Leovac (Rrahmani 46); Gojak, Sunjic, Olmo; Hajrovic, Gavranovic (Petkovic 64), Orsic (Situm 89).
Anderlecht: (442) Boeckx; Appiah, Bornauw (Delcroix 63), Sanneh, Milic (Saelemaekers 71); Gerkens, Kayembe, Morioka, Saief (Amuzu 69); Bakkali, Santini.

Spartak Trnava (1) 1 *(Yilmaz 41)*
Fenerbahce (0) 0 11,413
Spartak Trnava: (3511) Chudy; Toth (Kulhanek 64), Godal, Oravec; Jirka, Gressak, Vlasko, Grendel (Miesenboeck 81), Chanturishvili; Yilmaz; Bakos (Ghorbani 75).
Fenerbahce: (433) Tekin; Ozbayrakli, Guveli (Yilmaz 82), Skrtel, Reyes; Isla, Jailson, Koybasi; Alici, Slimani, Capkan (Caki 73).

Group D Table	P	W	D	L	F	A	GD	Pts
Dinamo Zagreb	6	4	2	0	11	3	8	14
Fenerbahce	6	2	2	2	7	7	0	8
Spartak Trnava	6	2	1	3	4	7	–3	7
Anderlecht	6	0	3	3	2	7	–5	3

GROUP E

Thursday, 20 September 2018

Arsenal (1) 4 *(Aubameyang 32, 56, Welbeck 48, Ozil 74)*
Vorskla Poltava (0) 2 *(Chesnakov 77, Sharpar 90)* 59,039
Arsenal: (433) Leno; Lichtsteiner, Holding, Papastathopoulos, Monreal; Torreira (Guendouzi 57), Mkhitaryan, Elneny; Iwobi (Smith-Rowe 70), Aubameyang (Ozil 57), Welbeck.
Vorskla Poltava: (4411) Shust; Perduta, Dallku, Chesnakov, Artur; Kobakhidze (Sergiychuk 78), Kravchenko (Sklyar 70), Sharpar, Rebenok; Kulach (Nicolas Careca 75); Kolomoets.

Sporting Lisbon (0) 2 *(Raphinha 54, Cabral 88)*
Qarabag (0) 0 30,098
Sporting Lisbon: (4141) Salin; Ristovski, Coates, Mathieu (Andre Pinto 75), Acuna; Nani (Cabral 87); Bruno Fernandes, Battaglia, Gudelj, Raphinha; Montero (Diaby 90).
Qarabag: (4321) Vagner; Medvedev (Huseynov A 62), Rzezniczak, Huseynov B, Guerrier, Dinlyev (Michel 57), Garayev, Zoubir (Abdullayev 68); Ozobic, Madatov; Emeghara.

Thursday, 4 October 2018

Qarabag (0) 0
Arsenal (1) 3 *(Papastathopoulos 4, Smith-Rowe 53, Guendouzi 79)* 63,412
Qarabag: (4231) Vagner; Medvedev, Huseynov B, Rzezniczak, Agolli; Michel, Garayev (Slachev 84); Madatov (Delarge 61), Ozobic (Abdullayev 67), Zoubir; Emeghara.
Arsenal: (343) Leno; Holding, Papastathopoulos, Monreal (Torreira 46); Lichtsteiner, Elneny, Guendouzi, Kolasinac; Smith-Rowe (Ozil 65), Welbeck, Iwobi (Lacazette 71).

Vorskla Poltava (1) 1 *(Kulach 10)*
Sporting Lisbon (0) 2 *(Montero 90, Cabral 90)* 10,082
Vorskla Poltava: (4411) Shust; Perduta, Dallku, Chesnakov, Artur; Kulach (Sergiychuk 62), Sklyar, Sharpar, Rebenok; Kravchenko (Habelok 83); Kolomoets.
Sporting Lisbon: (451) Salin; Bruno Gaspar, Coates, Andre Pinto, Jefferson; Nani, Bruno Fernandes, Petrovic (Cabral 70), Acuna, Carlos Mane (Montero 58); Diaby (Raphinha 70).

Thursday, 25 October 2018

Qarabag (0) 0
Vorskla Poltava (0) 1 *(Kulach 48)* 22,450
Qarabag: (4411) Vagner; Medvedev, Rzezniczak, Sadygov, Guerrier; Abdullayev (Delarge 69), Michel, Garayev, Zoubir; Slachev (Ozobic 58); Emeghara (Madatov 58).
Vorskla Poltava: (4411) Shust; Perduta, Dallku, Chesnakov, Sapai; Yakubu (Nicolas Careca 47), Sklyar, Sharpar, Rebenok; Kulach (Sergiychuk 77 (Chyzhov 90)); Kolomoets.

Sporting Lisbon (0) 0
Arsenal (0) 1 *(Welbeck 77)* 40,784
Sporting Lisbon: (433) Ribeiro; Ristovski (Bruno Gaspar 46), Andre Pinto, Coates, Acuna; Battaglia, Petrovic, Gudelj (Cabral 71); Nani (Diaby 86), Montero, Bruno Fernandes.
Arsenal: (433) Leno; Lichtsteiner, Papastathopoulos, Holding, Xhaka; Elneny (Torreira 58), Guendouzi, Ramsey; Mkhitaryan, Aubameyang (Iwobi 86), Welbeck (Lacazette 81).

Thursday, 8 November 2018

Arsenal (0) 0
Sporting Lisbon (0) 0 59,758
Arsenal: (4231) Cech; Jenkinson (Kolasinac 60), Papastathopoulos, Holding, Lichtsteiner (Maitland-Niles 73); Guendouzi, Ramsey; Smith-Rowe, Mkhitaryan, Iwobi; Welbeck (Aubameyang 30).
Sporting Lisbon: (442) Ribeiro; Bruno Gaspar, Coates, Mathieu■, Acuna; Nani, Gudelj, Luis (Petrovic 84), Bruno Fernandes; Diaby (Cabral 82), Montero (Dost 68).

Vorskla Poltava (0) 0
Qarabag (1) 1 *(Abdullayev 13 (pen))* 5479
Vorskla Poltava: (4411) Shust; Perduta, Chesnakov, Chyzhov, Artur; Yakubu (Nicolas Careca 55), Sklyar, Sharpar, Rebenok; Kulach; Kolomoets.
Qarabag: (433) Halldorsson; Medvedev, Rzezniczak, Sadygov, Guerrier; Michel, Garayev, Slachev; Delarge (Ozobic 79), Abdullayev, Zoubir (Madatov 71).

Thursday, 29 November 2018

Qarabag (1) 1 *(Zoubir 14)*
Sporting Lisbon (3) 6 *(Dost 5 (pen), Bruno Fernandes 20, 75, Nani 33, Diaby 65, 82)* 5416
Qarabag: (433) Halldorsson; Medvedev, Rzezniczak, Sadygov, Guerrier; Slachev (Ozobic 70), Garayev, Michel; Madatov, Abdullayev (Delarge 82), Zoubir.
Sporting Lisbon: (442) Ribeiro; Bruno Gaspar (Correia 73), Andre Pinto, Coates, Jefferson; Nani (Carlos Mane 79), Wendel, Gudelj, Bruno Fernandes; Dost (Cabral 71), Diaby.

Vorskla Poltava (0) 0

Arsenal (3) 3 *(Smith-Rowe 11, Ramsey 27 (pen), Willock 41)* 7751

Vorskla Poltava: (4411) Shust; Perduta, Dallku, Chesnakov, Artur; Sapai (Nicolas Careca 36), Sklyar, Sharpar, Rebenok (Sakiv 85); Kulach (Kane 71); Kolomoets.
Arsenal: (433) Cech; Lichtsteiner, Jenkinson, Holding (Medley 60), Maitland-Niles; Guendouzi (Gilmour 76), Ramsey (Saka 68), Elneny; Willock, Nketiah, Smith-Rowe.

Thursday, 13 December 2018

Arsenal (1) 1 *(Lacazette 16)*

Qarabag (0) 0 58,101

Arsenal: (4231) Martinez; Jenkinson, Papastathopoulos, Koscielny (Monreal 72), Maitland-Niles; Elneny, Willock; Nketiah, Ozil (Gilmour 83), Saka; Lacazette (Medley 63).
Qarabag: (532) Vagner; Medvedev, Rzezniczak (Ozobic 85), Sadygov, Huseynov B, Guerrier; Slachev, Garayev, Michel (Abdullayev 61); Madatov (Quintana 74), Zoubir.

Sporting Lisbon (3) 3 *(Montero 18, Luis 35, Dallku 45 (og))*

Vorskla Poltava (0) 0 25,504

Sporting Lisbon: (451) Salin; Ristovski (Correia 63), Coates, Andre Pinto, Acuna; Carlos Mane, Luis, Petrovic, Bruno Fernandes (Paz 73), Cabral; Montero (Marques 59).
Vorskla Poltava: (4411) Tkachenko; Perduta, Dallku (Kolomoets 46), Chyzhov, Sakiv; Rebenok, Sklyar, Chesnakov, Artur (Kane 77); Habelok; Nicolas Careca (Sergiychuk 67).

Group E Table	P	W	D	L	F	A	GD	Pts
Arsenal	6	5	1	0	12	2	10	16
Sporting Lisbon	6	4	1	1	13	3	10	13
Vorskla Poltava	6	1	0	5	4	13	–9	3
Qarabag	6	1	0	5	2	13	–11	3

GROUP F

Thursday, 20 September 2018

F91 Dudelange (0) 0

AC Milan (0) 1 *(Higuain 59)* 7983

F91 Dudelange: (442) Frising; Malget (Jordanov 84), Schnell, Prempeh, El Hriti (Melisse 80); Stolz, Couturier, Cruz (Stumpf 74), Kruska; Turpel, Sinani.
AC Milan: (433) Reina; Abate, Caldara, Romagnoli, Laxalt; Bertolacci (Kessie 70), Mauri (Calhanoglu 80), Bakayoko; Borini (Halilovic 87), Higuain, Castillejo.

Olympiacos (0) 0

Real Betis (0) 0 28,650

Olympiacos: (4231) Gianniotis; Elabdellaoui, Meriah, Vukovic, Tsimikas■; Bouchalakis (Natcho 36), Camara; Fetfatzidis (Christodoulopoulos 71), Fortounis, Daniel Podence (Torosidis 80); Kouka.
Real Betis: (343) Robles; Mandi, Javi Garcia, Sidnei; Tello, Guardado, Lo Celso (Inui 83), Barragan; Joaquin (Sanabria 80), Moron, Leon (Canales 72).

Thursday, 4 October 2018

AC Milan (0) 3 *(Cutrone 70, 79, Higuain 76)*

Olympiacos (1) 1 *(Guerrero 14)* 22,294

AC Milan: (433) Reina; Calabria, Zapata, Romagnoli, Rodriguez; Biglia, Bakayoko, Bonaventura (Calhanoglu 54); Suso (Borini 80), Higuain, Castillejo (Cutrone 54).
Olympiacos: (4231) Jose Sa; Torosidis (Meriah 77), Roderick Miranda, Cisse, Koutris; Natcho, Guilherme; Fetfatzidis, Toure (Fortounis 82), Nahuel (Daniel Podence 71); Guerrero.

Real Betis (0) 3 *(Sanabria 56, Lo Celso 80, Tello 88)*

F91 Dudelange (0) 0 40,133

Real Betis: (352) Robles; Bartra, Javi Garcia, Sidnei; Barragan, Guardado (Lo Celso 61), William Carvalho, Inui (Joaquin 71), Tello; Sanabria, Leon (Kaptoum 82).
F91 Dudelange: (433) Frising; Jordanov, Schnell, Prempeh, El Hriti; Couturier, Kruska, Melisse (Stumpf 66); Stolz (Kenia 76), Turpel, Sinani (Pokar 82).

Thursday, 25 October 2018

AC Milan (0) 1 *(Cutrone 83)*

Real Betis (1) 2 *(Sanabria 30, Lo Celso 55)* 22,405

AC Milan: (433) Reina; Calabria, Romagnoli, Zapata, Laxalt; Bakayoko (Cutrone 46), Biglia (Bertolacci 80), Bonaventura; Castillejo■, Higuain, Borini (Suso 46).
Real Betis: (352) Pau Lopez; Mandi, Bartra, Sidnei; Barragan, Lo Celso, William Carvalho (Feddal 90), Canales, Firpo; Leon (Tello 66), Sanabria (Moron 78).

F91 Dudelange (0) 0

Olympiacos (0) 2 *(Torosidis 66, Jordanov 81 (og))* 7500

F91 Dudelange: (442) Bonnefoi; Jordanov, Schnell, Prempeh, Bisevac; Couturier, Cruz (Sinani 51), Kruska, El Hriti (Kenia 74); Stolz (Melisse 65), Turpel.
Olympiacos: (4231) Jose Sa; Torosidis (Elabdellaoui 69), Cisse, Vukovic, Koutris; Camara, Bouchalakis; Leiva (Natcho 78), Fortounis, Daniel Podence; Guerrero (Christodoulopoulos 18).

Thursday, 8 November 2018

Olympiacos (4) 5 *(Torosidis 6, Fortounis 15, 36, Christodoulopoulos 26, Kouka 71)*

F91 Dudelange (0) 1 *(Sinani 69)* 24,032

Olympiacos: (451) Jose Sa; Torosidis, Roderick Miranda, Cisse, Tsimikas; Daniel Podence, Natcho (Toure 61), Fortounis (Kouka 56), Camara, Leiva (Fetfatzidis 33); Christodoulopoulos.
F91 Dudelange: (442) Bonnefoi; Jordanov, Schnell, Prempeh, Melisse; Stolz (Stumpf 84), Bisevac, Kruska (Jensen 61), Couturier; Turpel (Perez 73), Sinani.

Real Betis (1) 1 *(Lo Celso 12)*

AC Milan (0) 1 *(Suso 62)* 45,647

Real Betis: (352) Pau Lopez; Mandi, Bartra, Feddal; Tello, Lo Celso, William Carvalho, Canales, Firpo; Joaquin (Guardado 67), Sanabria (Moron 74).
AC Milan: (352) Reina; Musacchio (Romagnoli 82), Zapata, Rodriguez; Borini, Kessie, Bakayoko, Calhanoglu (Bertolacci 89), Laxalt (Abate 76); Suso, Cutrone.

Thursday, 29 November 2018

AC Milan (1) 5 *(Cutrone 21, Cruz 66 (og), Calhanoglu 70, Schnell 77 (og), Borini 80)*

F91 Dudelange (1) 2 *(Stolz 39, Turpel 49)* 15,521

AC Milan: (433) Reina; Calabria, Simic, Zapata, Laxalt; Bakayoko, Bertolacci (Mauri 58), Halilovic (Suso 51); Calhanoglu, Cutrone (Borini 81), Higuain.
F91 Dudelange: (3511) Bonnefoi; Schnell, Cruz (Pokar 75), Prempeh; Jordanov, Kruska, Couturier, Melisse, Sinani (Perez 87); Turpel; Stolz (Kenia 80).

Real Betis (1) 1 *(Canales 39)*

Olympiacos (0) 0 37,722

Real Betis: (352) Robles; Mandi, Bartra (Javi Garcia 73), Sidnei; Tello (Barragan 84), Canales, William Carvalho, Lo Celso, Firpo; Sanabria, Leon (Inui 62).
Olympiacos: (433) Jose Sa; Elabdellaoui, Cisse, Vukovic, Tsimikas; Guilherme (Natcho 81), Bouchalakis (Guerrero 58), Camara; Daniel Podence, Fortounis, Leiva (Vrousai 72).

Thursday, 13 December 2018

F91 Dudelange (0) 0

Real Betis (0) 0 4931

F91 Dudelange: (442) Bonnefoi; Jordanov, Schnell, Prempeh, El Hriti; Stolz, Cruz, Kenia (Malget 71), Couturier (Melisse 82); Turpel, Sinani (Jensen 88).
Real Betis: (352) Robles; Sidnei, Javi Garcia, Feddal; Guerrero, Kaptoum, William Carvalho (Bartra 74), Inui, Tello; Joaquin (Boudebouz 75), Moron (Leon 69).

Olympiacos (0) 3 *(Cisse 60, Zapata 70 (og), Fortounis 81 (pen))*

AC Milan (0) 1 *(Zapata 72)* 31,010

Olympiacos: (4231) Jose Sa; Elabdellaoui, Cisse (Bouchalakis 85), Vukovic, Koutris; Camara (Torosidis 79), Guilherme; Fetfatzidis (Natcho 69), Fortounis, Daniel Podence; Guerrero.
AC Milan: (433) Reina; Calabria, Abate, Zapata, Rodriguez (Halilovic 85); Kessie, Bakayoko, Calhanoglu; Castillejo, Higuain, Cutrone (Laxalt 78).

Group F Table	*P*	*W*	*D*	*L*	*F*	*A*	*GD*	*Pts*
Real Betis	6	3	3	0	7	2	5	12
Olympiacos	6	3	1	2	11	6	5	10
AC Milan	6	3	1	2	12	9	3	10
F91 Dudelange	6	0	1	5	3	16	–13	1

GROUP G

Thursday, 20 September 2018

Rapid Vienna (0) 2 *(Timofeev 51 (og), Murg 68)*

Spartak Moscow (0) 0 21,400

Rapid Vienna: (4411) Strebinger; Potzmann, Sonnleitner, Barac, Muldur; Murg, Ljubicic, Schwab, Ivan (Berisha 76); Knasmullner (Martic 86); Alar (Pavlovic 71).
Spartak Moscow: (433) Maksimenko; Rasskazov, Bocchetti, Dzhikija, Melgarejo; Timofeev (Ignatov 82), Fernando, Zobnin; Lomovitskiy (Samedov 73), Ze Luis, Pedro Rocha (Popov 73).

Villarreal (1) 2 *(Bacca 1, Gerard 69)*

Rangers (0) 2 *(Arfield 67, Lafferty 76)* 15,982

Villarreal: (442) Fernandez; Miguelon, Bonera, Victor Ruiz, Pedraza; Sansone (Chukwueze 79), Fornals, Funes Mori (Gerard 66), Cazorla, Toko Ekambi (Trigueros 60), Bacca.
Rangers: (433) McGregor; Tavernier, Worrall, Goldson, Barisic (Dorrans 85); Coulibaly (Middleton 70), Halliday, Arfield; Candeias (McCrorie 77), Kent, Lafferty.

Thursday, 4 October 2018

Rangers (1) 3 *(Morelos 44, 90, Tavernier 84 (pen))*

Rapid Vienna (1) 1 *(Berisha 42)* 47,534

Rangers: (433) McGregor; Tavernier, Worrall, Goldson, Flanagan; Arfield, Coulibaly, Ejaria; Kent (Halliday 90), Morelos (Middleton 90), Candeias.
Rapid Vienna: (4141) Strebinger; Muldur, Barac (Dibon 33), Sonnleitner, Potzmann; Schwab; Ivan (Alar 58), Murg, Ljubicic, Berisha (Bolingoli Mbombo 72); Pavlovic.

Spartak Moscow (1) 3 *(Ze Luis 34 (pen), 82, Melgarejo 85)*

Villarreal (1) 3 *(Toko Ekambi 13, Fornals 49, Cazorla 90 (pen))* 21,264

Spartak Moscow: (433) Maksimenko; Rasskazov, Bocchetti, Dzhikija, Kombarov (Timofeev 90); Ignatov (Hanni 69), Fernando, Zobnin; Lomovitskiy (Tashaev 80), Ze Luis, Melgarejo.
Villarreal: (442) Fernandez; Mario, Bonera, Victor Ruiz, Pedraza; Chukwueze (Cazorla 71), Trigueros, Funes Mori, Sansone (Gerard 61); Fornals, Toko Ekambi (Layun 77).

Thursday, 25 October 2018

Rangers (0) 0

Spartak Moscow (0) 0 49,068

Rangers: (433) McGregor; Tavernier, Worrall, Goldson, Flanagan; Ejaria, Jack (Grezda 68), Coulibaly; Candeias (Middleton 86), Morelos, Kent.
Spartak Moscow: (433) Maksimenko; Rasskazov, Bocchetti, Dzhikija, Melgarejo; Ignatov (Popov 84), Fernando, Zobnin; Lomovitskiy (Eremenko 46), Ze Luis, Tashaev (Hanni 46).

Villarreal (3) 5 *(Fornals 26, Toko Ekambi 30, Barac 45 (og), Raba 63, Gerard 85)*

Rapid Vienna (0) 0 14,558

Villarreal: (4231) Fernandez; Miguelon, Alvaro, Funes Mori, Jaume■; Caseres (Cazorla 79), Trigueros; Layun, Fornals (Chukwueze 65), Raba (Gerard 71); Toko Ekambi.
Rapid Vienna: (4141) Strebinger; Muldur, Sonnleitner, Barac, Bolingoli Mbombo; Ljubicic; Potzmann (Ivan 46), Murg (Knasmullner 78), Schwab, Berisha (Thurnwald 59); Alar.

Thursday, 8 November 2018

Rapid Vienna (0) 0

Villarreal (0) 0 22,100

Rapid Vienna: (4411) Strebinger; Muldur, Sonnleitner, Dibon (Bolingoli Mbombo 75), Potzmann; Berisha, Ljubicic, Schwab, Ivan; Murg (Knasmullner 46); Pavlovic (Martic 90).
Villarreal: (352) Fernandez; Mario, Bonera (Funes Mori 46), Victor Ruiz; Layun (Toko Ekambi 61), Raba (Fornals 76), Caseres, Cazorla, Pedraza; Gerard, Sansone.

Spartak Moscow (2) 4 *(Melgarejo 22, Goldson 35 (og), Luiz Adriano 58, Hanni 59)*

Rangers (3) 3 *(Eremenko 5 (og), Candeias 27, Middleton 41)* 22,296

Spartak Moscow: (433) Maksimenko; Rasskazov, Kutepov, Bocchetti, Melgarejo; Eremenko (Glushakov 60), Fernando, Zobnin; Popov (Timofeev 71), Luiz Adriano (Ze Luis 81), Hanni.
Rangers: (433) McGregor; Tavernier, Katic, Goldson, Flanagan (Halliday 82); Coulibaly (Grezda 82), Ejaria (McAuley 90), Arfield; Candeias, Morelos, Middleton.

Thursday, 29 November 2018

Rangers (0) 0

Villarreal (0) 0 50,171

Rangers: (433) McGregor; Tavernier, Worrall, Goldson, Flanagan; Coulibaly (McCrorie 90), Jack, Arfield; Candeias■, Morelos (Lafferty 78), Middleton.
Villarreal: (4231) Fernandez; Mario, Alvaro, Funes Mori, Jaume; Caseres, Morlanes; Trigueros (Cazorla 62), Fornals (Chukwueze 73), Toko Ekambi; Bacca (Gerard 62).

Spartak Moscow (1) 1 *(Ze Luis 20)*

Rapid Vienna (0) 2 *(Muldur 80, Schobesberger 90)* 20,739

Spartak Moscow: (442) Rebrov; Eshchenko, Kutepov, Dzhikija, Kombarov; Melgarejo (Popov 81), Glushakov, Timofeev, Hanni (Samedov 71); Luiz Adriano, Ze Luis.
Rapid Vienna: (4231) Strebinger; Muldur, Barac, Hofmann, Potzmann; Martic, Ljubicic (Schwab 65); Berisha (Thurnwald 80), Knasmullner, Bolingoli Mbombo; Alar (Schobesberger 65).

Thursday, 13 December 2018

Rapid Vienna (0) 1 *(Ljubicic 84)*

Rangers (0) 0 23,850

Rapid Vienna: (4231) Strebinger; Muldur, Hofmann, Barac, Auer; Schwab, Martic (Ljubicic 78); Ivan (Schobesberger 62), Murg (Knasmullner 46), Bolingoli Mbombo; Berisha.
Rangers: (4411) McGregor; Tavernier, McAuley, Goldson, Barisic; Jack (Lafferty 79), McCrorie, Arfield, Coulibaly (Grezda 71); Middleton; Morelos.

Villarreal (1) 2 *(Chukwueze 11, Toko Ekambi 48)*

Spartak Moscow (0) 0 12,903

Villarreal: (4312) Fernandez; Mario, Alvaro, Victor Ruiz, Jaume■; Javi Fuego, Caseres, Fornals; Chukwueze (Cazorla 80); Gerard (Pedraza 76), Toko Ekambi (Bacca 72).
Spartak Moscow: (442) Maksimenko; Rasskazov, Kutepov, Dzhikija, Melgarejo; Lomovitskiy (Tashaev 55), Popov, Glushakov, Hanni (Pedro Rocha 67); Luiz Adriano (Ananidze 74), Ze Luis.

Group G Table	*P*	*W*	*D*	*L*	*F*	*A*	*GD*	*Pts*
Villarreal	6	2	4	0	12	5	7	10
Rapid Vienna	6	3	1	2	6	9	–3	10
Rangers	6	1	3	2	8	8	0	6
Spartak Moscow	6	1	2	3	8	12	–4	5

GROUP H

Thursday, 20 September 2018

Lazio (1) 2 *(Luis Alberto 14, Immobile 84 (pen))*

Apollon Limassol (0) 1 *(Zelaya 87)* 11,898

Lazio: (352) Proto; Bastos, Acerbi, Caceres; Basta, Murgia, Badelj (Lucas 61), Milinkovic-Savic (Lulic 73), Durmisi; Caicedo, Luis Alberto (Immobile 61).
Apollon Limassol: (4231) Vale; Joao Pedro, Yuste, Roberge, Vasiliou; Sachetti, Kyriakou (Markovic 46); Schembri, Pereyra (Zelaya 69), Papoulis; Maglica (Carayol 46).

Marseille (1) 1 *(Ocampos 3)*

Eintracht Frankfurt (0) 2 *(Torro 52, Jovic 89)* 0

Marseille: (442) Pele; Sarr, Rami (Gustavo 8), Caleta-Car, Kamara; Thauvin (Mitroglou 83), Lopez, Strootman, Ocampos (Radonjic 72); Germain, Payet.
Eintracht Frankfurt: (442) Trapp; Da Costa, Abraham, Ndicka, Willems■; de Guzman (Falette 62), Torro, Hasebe, Kostic; Gacinovic (Muller 46), Haller (Jovic 74).
Behind closed doors.

Thursday, 4 October 2018

Apollon Limassol (0) 2 *(Markovic 74, Zelaya 90)*

Marseille (0) 2 *(Payet 53, Gustavo 67)* 3039

Apollon Limassol: (4231) Vale; Joao Pedro, Yuste (Markovic 11), Roberge, Soumah; Bru, Sachetti; Sardinero (Papoulis 56), Pereyra, Carayol (Maglica 65); Zelaya.
Marseille: (442) Pele; Sakai (Sarr 46), Kamara, Caleta-Car, Amavi; Lopez, Strootman, Gustavo (Sertic 76), Radonjic; Payet, Mitroglou (Germain 46).

Eintracht Frankfurt (2) 4 *(Da Costa 4, 90, Kostic 28, Jovic 52)*

Lazio (1) 1 *(Parolo 23)* 47,000

Eintracht Frankfurt: (442) Trapp; Da Costa, Hasebe, Russ, Falette; Gacinovic, de Guzman (Stendera 87), Torro, Kostic (Tawatha 78); Haller, Jovic (Rebic 67).
Lazio: (352) Proto; Felipe, Acerbi, Wallace Santos; Basta■, Parolo, Lucas (Luis Alberto 76), Milinkovic-Savic (Berisha 64), Durmisi (Lulic 17); Correa■, Immobile.

Thursday, 25 October 2018

Eintracht Frankfurt (2) 2 *(Kostic 13, Haller 32)*

Apollon Limassol (0) 0 47,000

Eintracht Frankfurt: (4231) Ronnow; Da Costa (Willems 56), Abraham (Russ 67), N'Dicka, Kostic; Hasebe, Fernandes; Gacinovic, de Guzman, Rebic (Jovic 82); Haller.
Apollon Limassol: (4231) Vale; Joao Pedro, Kyriakou, Roberge, Vasiliou; Markovic, Sachetti; Pereyra (Zelaya 46), Papoulis, Carayol (Schembri 46); Maglica (Stylianou 67).

Marseille (0) 1 *(Payet 86)*

Lazio (1) 3 *(Wallace Santos 10, Caicedo 59, Marusic 90)* 31,930

Marseille: (4231) Mandanda; Sakai, Rami, Kamara, Amavi (Sarr 80); Gustavo, Strootman; Sanson (N'Jie 66), Payet, Ocampos; Mitroglou (Germain 66).
Lazio: (352) Strakosha; Wallace Santos, Acerbi, Radu; Caceres, Parolo, Lucas (Marusic 47), Milinkovic-Savic, Lulic (Berisha 62); Immobile, Caicedo (Cataldi 74).

Thursday, 8 November 2018

Apollon Limassol (0) 2 *(Zelaya 71, 90 (pen))*

Eintracht Frankfurt (1) 3 *(Jovic 17, Haller 55, Gacinovic 58)* 8000

Apollon Limassol: (4231) Kissas; Stylianou, Ouedraogo, Roberge, Vasiliou (Joao Pedro 61); Kyriakou, Sachetti; Sardinero, Alex, Schembri (Faupala 68); Maglica (Zelaya 46).
Eintracht Frankfurt: (442) Trapp; Da Costa, Abraham, N'Dicka, Willems; Stendera■, Fernandes (de Guzman 78), Hasebe, Gacinovic; Haller (Rebic 66), Jovic (Muller 86).

Lazio (1) 2 *(Parolo 45, Correa 55)*

Marseille (0) 1 *(Thauvin 60)* 14,705

Lazio: (352) Strakosha; Wallace Santos (Bastos 57), Felipe, Acerbi; Marusic, Parolo, Cataldi, Berisha (Milinkovic-Savic 70), Durmisi; Immobile, Correa (Luis Alberto 81).
Marseille: (541) Pele; Sakai, Rami (Sarr 79), Gustavo, Caleta-Car, Ocampos; Thauvin (Mitroglou 82), Sanson (Payet 69), Strootman, Lopez; N'Jie.

Thursday, 29 November 2018

Apollon Limassol (1) 2 *(Faupala 31, Markovic 82)*

Lazio (0) 0 1131

Apollon Limassol: (4231) Vale; Joao Pedro, Roberge, Ouedraogo, Soumah; Spoljaric, Sachetti; Sardinero (Zelaya 78), Markovic, Schembri (Papoulis 66); Faupala (Maglica 65).
Lazio: (352) Proto; Bastos (Lulic 60), Felipe, Acerbi; Caceres, Murgia (Rossi 60), Cataldi, Berisha, Durmisi; Correa, Caicedo (Armini 85).

Eintracht Frankfurt (2) 4 *(Jovic 2, 67, Gustavo 17 (og), Sarr 62 (og))*

Marseille (0) 0 47,000

Eintracht Frankfurt: (532) Trapp; Da Costa, Russ, Fernandes, Willems, Tawatha (Kostic 64); Hasebe, Gacinovic, Falette; Jovic (Muller 80), Haller (Rebic 72).
Marseille: (442) Pele; Hubocan, Kamara, Caleta-Car, Amavi (Rocchia 79); Sarr, Lopez (Rolando 61), Gustavo, Radonjic; Mitroglou, Germain (Chabrolle 64).

Thursday, 13 December 2018

Lazio (0) 1 *(Correa 56)*

Eintracht Frankfurt (0) 2 *(Gacinovic 65, Haller 71)* 18,252

Lazio: (352) Proto; Bastos, Felipe, Acerbi; Caceres (Lulic 74), Murgia, Cataldi, Berisha (Rossi 75), Durmisi; Luis Alberto, Correa.
Eintracht Frankfurt: (4411) Ronnow; Da Costa, Russ, Falette, Willems; Muller (Jovic 79), Fernandes, Hasebe (N'Dicka 32), Tawatha; Gacinovic (Stendera 88); Haller.

Marseille (1) 1 *(Thauvin 11)*

Apollon Limassol (2) 3 *(Maglica 8 (pen), 30, Stylianou 56)* 9274

Marseille: (433) Escales; Sakai, Rami, Caleta-Car, Kamara■; Lopez, Strootman (Sarr 58), Gustavo; Thauvin (Radonjic 62), Ocampos■, Payet (N'Jie 75).
Apollon Limassol: (343) Vale; Kyriakou, Roberge, Ouedraogo; Stylianou, Alex, Bru (Papoulis 46), Vasiliou; Sardinero, Maglica (Soumah 71), Schembri (Faupala 59).

Group H Table	*P*	*W*	*D*	*L*	*F*	*A*	*GD*	*Pts*
Eintracht Frankfurt	6	6	0	0	17	5	12	18
Lazio	6	3	0	3	9	11	−2	9
Apollon Limassol	6	2	1	3	10	10	0	7
Marseille	6	0	1	5	6	16	−10	1

GROUP I

Thursday, 20 September 2018

Besiktas (0) 3 *(Babel 51, Roco 69, Lens 82)*

Sarpsborg 08 (0) 1 *(Zachariassen 90)* 24,955

Besiktas: (433) Karius; Gonul (Uysal 86), Pepe, Roco, Erkin; Ljajic (Arslan 78), Medel, Ozyakup; Lens, Larin, Tore (Babel 46).
Sarpsborg 08: (442) Vasyutin; Askar, Horn, Tamm, Thomassen; Halvorsen (Singh 72), Nielsen (Vetti 87), Zachariassen, Heintz; Muhammed (Larsen J 81), Mortensen.

Genk (1) 2 *(Trossard 37, Samatta 71)*

Malmo (0) 0 11,590

Genk: (433) Vukovic; Maehle, Dewaest, Aidoo, Uronen; Pozuelo (Seck 76), Malinovsky, Berge; Trossard, Samatta (Ingvartsen 86), Ndongala (Paintsil 72).
Malmo: (442) Dahlin; Vindheim, Nielsen, Bengtsson, Safari (Binaku 80); Christiansen (Gall 86), Bachirou, Lewicki, Rieks; Rosenberg, Antonsson (Traustason 55).

Thursday, 4 October 2018

Malmo (0) 2 *(Erkin 53 (og), Rosenberg 76 (pen))*

Besiktas (0) 0 17,174

Malmo: (442) Dahlin; Vindheim, Nielsen (Brorsson 90), Bengtsson, Safari; Christiansen (Innocent 72), Bachirou, Lewicki, Rieks; Rosenberg, Traustason (Antonsson 85).
Besiktas: (433) Karius; Gonul (Ozyakup 82), Pepe, Vida, Erkin; Medel, Ljajic (Quaresma 69), Uysal; Tore (Babel 59), Vagner Love, Lens.

Sarpsborg 08 (1) 3 *(Mortensen 5, 63, Zachariassen 54)*

Genk (0) 1 *(Trossard 49)* 7885

Sarpsborg 08: (442) Vasyutin; Tveita, Jorgensen, Tamm, Thomassen; Halvorsen (Heintz 73), Nielsen, Zachariassen, Askar; Muhammed (Singh 82), Mortensen.
Genk: (4321) Vukovic; Maehle, Dewaest, Lucumi, Nastic (Uronen 46); Berge, Pozuelo, Trossard; Malinovsky (Heynen 66), Ndongala (Paintsil 46); Samatta.

Thursday, 25 October 2018

Besiktas (0) 2 *(Vagner Love 74, 86)*

Genk (1) 4 *(Samatta 23, 70, Ndongala 81, Piotrowski 83)* 25,209

Besiktas: (433) Karius; Gonul, Vida, Uysal, Erkin (Pektemek 85); Arslan (Roco 27), Medel, Ozyakup; Quaresma, Larin (Vagner Love 46), Lens.
Genk: (433) Vukovic; Maehle, Dewaest, Lucumi, Uronen; Pozuelo (Seck 80), Malinovsky, Heynen; Paintsil (Piotrowski 75), Samatta (Gano 87), Ndongala.

Sarpsborg 08 (0) 1 *(Halvorsen 87)*

Malmo (0) 1 *(Vindheim 79)* 8022

Sarpsborg 08: (442) Vasyutin; Tveita, Horn, Tamm, Thomassen; Halvorsen, Nielsen (Singh 87), Zachariassen, Askar (Larsen J 85); Muhammed (Heintz 77), Mortensen.
Malmo: (442) Dahlin; Vindheim, Nielsen, Bengtsson (Brorsson 57), Safari; Christiansen (Innocent 83), Bachirou, Lewicki (Antonsson 65), Rieks; Rosenberg, Traustason.

Thursday, 8 November 2018

Genk (0) 1 *(Berge 87)*

Besiktas (1) 1 *(Quaresma 16)* 14,292

Genk: (433) Vukovic; Maehle, Dewaest, Aidoo, Uronen; Malinovsky (Berge 60), Pozuelo, Heynen; Paintsil (Fiolic 66), Samatta, Ndongala (Ingvartsen 89).
Besiktas: (433) Zengin; Tokoz (Ljajic 73), Pepe, Vida, Erkin; Uysal, Ozyakup (Vagner Love 90), Medel; Quaresma, Babel, Lens (Pektemek 11).

Malmo (0) 1 *(Antonsson 67)*

Sarpsborg 08 (0) 1 *(Mortensen 63)* 17,601

Malmo: (442) Dahlin; Vindheim (Larsson 61), Nielsen, Bengtsson, Safari (Gall 85); Traustason, Bachirou, Christiansen, Rieks; Rosenberg, Antonsson (Strandberg 78).
Sarpsborg 08: (442) Vasyutin; Tveita, Horn, Tamm, Thomassen; Halvorsen, Nielsen, Vetti (Jorgensen 90), Askar; Muhammed (Heintz 73), Mortensen.

Thursday, 29 November 2018

Malmo (0) 2 *(Lewicki 65, Antonsson 67)*

Genk (1) 2 *(Pozuelo 42, Paintsil 53)* 16,117

Malmo: (433) Dahlin; Vindheim, Nielsen, Bengtsson, Safari (Brorsson 81); Christiansen (Gall 81), Bachirou, Lewicki; Rieks, Rosenberg, Traustason (Antonsson 54).
Genk: (433) Vukovic; Maehle, Dewaest, Aidoo, Uronen; Malinovsky, Berge, Pozuelo (Heynen 86); Trossard, Samatta (Gano 72), Paintsil (Ndongala 54).

Sarpsborg 08 (2) 2 *(Muhammed 1, Heintz 6)*

Besiktas (0) 3 *(Lens 63, 90, Vagner Love 66)* 8022

Sarpsborg 08: (442) Vasyutin; Tveita, Horn, Tamm (Jorgensen 50), Thomassen; Halvorsen, Nielsen, Zachariassen, Heintz (Askar 69); Muhammed (Larsen J 85), Mortensen.
Besiktas: (433) Karius; Tokoz, Uysal, Vida, Erkin; Adriano (Aksoy 78), Ljajic, Ozyakup; Lens (Secgin 90), Larin (Vagner Love 58), Pektemek.

Thursday, 13 December 2018

Besiktas (0) 0

Malmo (0) 1 *(Antonsson 51)* 24,955

Besiktas: (433) Karius; Tokoz, Uysal, Vida, Adriano; Ljajic, Medel, Ozyakup (Tore 60); Quaresma■, Vagner Love (Larin 72), Pektemek (Aksoy 78).
Malmo: (442) Dahlin; Vindheim, Nielsen, Bengtsson, Safari (Brorsson 55); Traustason (Christiansen 75), Bachirou, Lewicki, Rieks (Larsson 80); Antonsson, Rosenberg.

Genk (2) 4 *(Gano 2, Paintsil 5, Berge 64, Aidoo 68)*

Sarpsborg 08 (0) 0 12,240

Genk: (433) Vukovic; Maehle, Dewaest, Aidoo, Uronen (Nastic 74); Pozuelo (Malinovsky 66), Seck, Berge; Trossard (Ndongala 80), Gano, Paintsil.
Sarpsborg 08: (442) Vasyutin; Tveita, Horn, Tamm, Thomassen (Askar 56); Halvorsen (Larsen K 82), Nielsen, Zachariassen, Heintz; Muhammed (Larsen J 62), Mortensen.

Group I Table	P	W	D	L	F	A	GD	Pts
Genk	6	3	2	1	14	8	6	11
Malmo	6	2	3	1	7	6	1	9
Besiktas	6	2	1	3	9	11	–2	7
Sarpsborg 08	6	1	2	3	8	13	–5	5

GROUP J

Thursday, 20 September 2018

Akhisarspor (0) 0

Krasnodar (1) 1 *(Claesson 26)* 6555

Akhisarspor: (4231) Ozturk; Vrsajevic, Osmanpasa, Yumlu, Keles (Ayik 80); Serginho, Sissoko; Regattin (Manu 60), Josue (Kisa 60), Vural; Seleznyov.
Krasnodar: (433) Kritsyuk; Stotskiy, Martynovich, Spajic, Ramirez; Gazinsky, Kabore, Mamaev (Pereyra 69); Wanderson (Cueva 79), Ari (Petrov 84), Claesson.

Sevilla (2) 5 *(Banega 9, 75 (pen), Vazquez 42, Ben Yedder 49, 71)*

Standard Liege (1) 1 *(Djenepo 39)* 30,003

Sevilla: (352) Vaclik; Carrico, Kjaer, Sergi Gomez; Jesus Navas (Nolito 81), Banega, Amadou (Roque 15), Vazquez (Sarabia 75), Guilherme Arana; Promes, Ben Yedder.
Standard Liege: (4141) Ochoa; Cavanda, Luyindama, Laifis, Fai; Vanheusden; Cimirot, Djenepo (Lestienne 62), Marin, Orlando Sa (Emond 63); Carcela-Gonzalez (Agbo 78).

Thursday, 4 October 2018

Krasnodar (0) 2 *(Pereyra 72, Okriashvili 88)*

Sevilla (1) 1 *(Kabore 43 (og))* 31,346

Krasnodar: (433) Kritsyuk; Petrov, Martynovich, Spajic, Ramirez; Gazinsky, Kabore (Pereyra 69), Mamaev (Suleymanov 73); Wanderson (Okriashvili 84), Cueva, Claesson.
Sevilla: (352) Vaclik; Sergi Gomez, Kjaer, Gnagnon; Jesus Navas, Nolito (Vazquez 76), Banega, Roque, Guilherme Arana; Muriel (Andre Silva 61), Promes (Ben Yedder 76).

Standard Liege (2) 2 *(Emond 17, Djenepo 40)*

Akhisarspor (1) 1 *(Ayik 32)* 8233

Standard Liege: (433) Ochoa; Cavanda, Luyindama, Laifis, Pocognoli; Cimirot, Marin, Agbo (M'Poku 75); Djenepo, Emond (Orlando Sa 83), Carcela-Gonzalez.
Akhisarspor: (4231) Ozturk; Miguel Lopes, Yumlu■, Osmanpasa, Vural; Kisa (Sissoko 41), Ceviker; Helder Barbosa, Josue, Ayik (Regattin 72); Seleznyov (Manu 80).

Thursday, 25 October 2018

Sevilla (3) 6 *(Roque 7, Sarabia 9 (pen), Lukac 35 (og), Muriel 50, Promes 60, Mercado 67)*

Akhisarspor (0) 0 29,720

Sevilla: (352) Vaclik; Mercado, Carrico (Amadou 59), Sergi Gomez; Jesus Navas (Nolito 54), Sarabia (Guilherme Arana 53), Roque, Vazquez, Aleix Vidal; Muriel, Promes.
Akhisarspor: (433) Lukac; Miguel Lopes, Osmanpasa, Nounkeu, Keles (Helder Barbosa 46); Ceviker, Sissoko, Josue (Ataseven 77); Regattin, Seleznyov (Ayik 62), Vural.

Standard Liege (0) 2 *(Emond 47, Laifis 90)*

Krasnodar (1) 1 *(Ari 39)* 20,400

Standard Liege: (433) Ochoa; Cavanda, Luyindama, Laifis, Fai (Lestienne 78); Cimirot, Agbo (Djenepo 46), Pocognoli; Marin, Emond (Bastien 84), Carcela-Gonzalez.

Krasnodar: (433) Sinitsyn; Petrov, Martynovich, Spajic, Ramirez; Gazinsky, Kabore, Pereyra (Cueva 76); Wanderson (Suleymanov 80), Ari (Ignatyev 76), Claesson.

Thursday, 8 November 2018

Akhisarspor (0) 2 *(Manu 52, Ayik 78)*

Sevilla (2) 3 *(Nolito 12, Muriel 38, Banega 87 (pen))* 6430

Akhisarspor: (433) Lukac; Vrsajevic, Miguel Lopes, Osmanpasa (Keles 46), Vural; Ataseven (Ayik 72), Ceviker, Sissoko; Helder Barbosa (Kisa 89), Manu, Josue.
Sevilla: (352) Vaclik; Sergi Gomez■, Amadou, Gnagnon; Aleix Vidal, Vazquez, Banega, Nolito (Roque 64), Escudero; Muriel (Sarabia 74), Promes (Carrico 90).

Krasnodar (0) 2 *(Suleymanov 79, Wanderson 82)*

Standard Liege (1) 1 *(Carcela-Gonzalez 19)* 21,526

Krasnodar: (433) Safonov; Petrov, Martynovich, Spajic, Stotskiy; Gazinsky, Kabore (Suleymanov 73), Cueva (Pereyra 46); Wanderson, Ari, Claesson (Ignatyev 65).
Standard Liege: (433) Ochoa; Fai, Luyindama, Vanheusden, Laifis; Marin (M'Poku 89), Cimirot, Lestienne (Bastien 84); Djenepo (Orlando Sa 89), Emond, Carcela-Gonzalez.

Thursday, 29 November 2018

Krasnodar (0) 2 *(Gazinsky 49, Ari 57)*

Akhisarspor (1) 1 *(Serginho 24)* 11,008

Krasnodar: (433) Safonov; Petrov, Martynovich, Spajic, Ramirez; Gazinsky, Kabore, Cueva (Suleymanov 70); Wanderson, Ari (Pereyra 72), Stotskiy (Ignatyev 46).
Akhisarspor: (433) Lukac; Miguel Lopes, Osmanpasa, Sissoko, Vural; Vrsajevic, Ceviker (Ataseven 72), Serginho (Keles 84); Regattin, Manu (Ayik 42), Helder Barbosa.

Standard Liege (0) 1 *(Djenepo 62)*

Sevilla (0) 0 12,882

Standard Liege: (433) Ochoa; Fai, Luyindama, Vanheusden, Laifis; Bastien, Cimirot, M'Poku (Marin 43); Djenepo, Emond (Orlando Sa 65), Carcela-Gonzalez (Lestienne 85).
Sevilla: (352) Vaclik; Mercado, Kjaer, Carrico; Aleix Vidal (Sarabia■ 51), Banega, Roque, Vazquez (Andre Silva 77), Guilherme Arana (Muriel 85); Ben Yedder, Promes.

Thursday, 13 December 2018

Akhisarspor (0) 0

Standard Liege (0) 0 2674

Akhisarspor: (433) Lukac; Vrsajevic, Osmanpasa, Sissoko, Keles; Serginho (Ataseven 17), Ceviker, Josue; Regattin (Ayik 72), Manu, Helder Barbosa (Kisa 90).
Standard Liege: (442) Ochoa; Fai, Luyindama, Vanheusden, Kosanovic; Marin, Agbo (M'Poku 61), Carcela-Gonzalez, Bastien (Oulare 83); Orlando Sa (Emond 83), Lestienne.

Sevilla (2) 3 *(Ben Yedder 5, 10, Banega 49 (pen))*

Krasnodar (0) 0 34,144

Sevilla: (352) Vaclik; Mercado, Carrico, Sergi Gomez; Promes, Roque, Banega (Amadou 69), Vazquez, Escudero; Ben Yedder (Jesus Navas 72), Andre Silva (Muriel 77).
Krasnodar: (433) Kritsyuk; Petrov, Martynovich, Fjoluson, Ramirez■; Gazinsky, Kabore, Pereyra (Stotskiy 52); Wanderson (Shishkin 77), Ignatyev, Claesson (Cueva 60).

Group J Table	P	W	D	L	F	A	GD	Pts
Sevilla	6	4	0	2	18	6	12	12
Krasnodar	6	4	0	2	8	8	0	12
Standard Liege	6	3	1	2	7	9	–2	10
Akhisarspor	6	0	1	5	4	14	–10	1

GROUP K

Thursday, 20 September 2018

Dynamo Kyiv (2) 2 *(Tsygankov 12, Garmash 45)*

Astana (1) 2 *(Anicic 21, Murtazayev 90)* 21,783

Dynamo Kyiv: (4231) Boyko; Kedziora, Kadar, Burda, Pivaric; Sydorchuk, Buyalsky (Shepelev 90); Tsygankov (Morozyuk 90), Garmash (Duelund 79), Verbic; Rusyn.
Astana: (442) Eric; Rukavina, Postnikov, Anicic, Shomko; Tomasov (Murtazayev 90), Maevskiy, Kleinheisler, Pedro Henrique; Kabananga (Janga 83), Richard (Muzhikov 81).

Rennes (1) 2 *(Sarr 30, Ben Arfa 90 (pen))*

Jablonec (0) 1 *(Travnik 53)* 20,628

Rennes: (433) Koubek; Traore, Mexer, Da Silva, Bensebaini; Grenier, Gelin (Ben Arfa 65), Andre; Del Castillo (Niang 61), Siebatcheu, Sarr (Bourigeaud 76).
Jablonec: (4141) Hruby; Holes, Hovorka, Lischka, Hanousek; Hubschman; Masopust (Kubista 77), Travnik, Povazanec, Jovovic (Brecka 87); Dolezal (Chramosta 46).

Thursday, 4 October 2018

Astana (0) 2 *(Zainuinov 64, Tomasov 90)*

Rennes (0) 0 25,302

Astana: (442) Eric; Rukavina, Postnikov, Anicic, Shomko; Tomasov, Zainuinov (Logvinenko 75), Maevskiy, Pedro Henrique; Richard (Muzhikov 62), Kabananga (Janga 71).
Rennes: (433) Diallo; Zeffane, Gelin, Da Silva, Baal (Bensebaini 28); Andre, Poha (Johansson 77), Grenier; Bourigeaud, Niang, Lea Siliki (Del Castillo 68).

Jablonec (1) 2 *(Hovorka 33, Travnik 81)*

Dynamo Kyiv (2) 2 *(Tsygankov 8, Garmash 14)* 5077

Jablonec: (451) Hruby; Holes, Hovorka, Lischka, Hanousek; Masopust (Kubista 85), Travnik, Hubschman, Povazanec, Jovovic (Sobol 90); Chramosta (Ikaunieks 77).
Dynamo Kyiv: (442) Boyko; Kedziora, Burda, Kadar, Pivaric; Morozyuk, Sydorchuk, Buyalsky (Shepelev 79), Tsygankov; Garmash, Besyedin.

Thursday, 25 October 2018

Jablonec (1) 1 *(Povazanec 4)*

Astana (1) 1 *(Pedro Henrique 11)* 4909

Jablonec: (4141) Hruby; Holes, Hovorka, Lischka, Hanousek; Hubschman; Masopust, Povazanec, Travnik, Jovovic (Acosta 87); Chramosta (Ikaunieks 56 (Kubista 90)).
Astana: (442) Eric; Rukavina, Postnikov, Anicic, Zainuinov; Tomasov, Kleinheisler, Maevskiy, Pedro Henrique (Muzhikov 46); Richard (Murtazayev 89), Kabananga (Janga 74).

Rennes (1) 1 *(Grenier 41)*

Dynamo Kyiv (1) 2 *(Kedziora 21, Buyalsky 89)* 28,001

Rennes: (442) Diallo; Traore, Da Silva, Gelin, Bensebaini; Grenier, Johansson (Lea Siliki 90), Andre, Del Castillo (Bourigeaud 61); Sarr, Niang (Ben Arfa 74).
Dynamo Kyiv: (4231) Boyko; Kedziora, Burda, Kadar, Mykolenko; Shepelev■, Buyalsky; Morozyuk (Tche Tche 82), Garmash (Sydorchuk 68), Sidcley; Verbic (Supriaga 74).

Thursday, 8 November 2018

Astana (1) 2 *(Pedro Henrique 18, Postnikov 88)*

Jablonec (1) 1 *(Zainuinov 41 (og))* 20,092

Astana: (433) Eric; Rukavina, Postnikov, Anicic, Zainuinov; Tomasov, Maevskiy, Kleinheisler; Pedro Henrique (Murtazayev 79), Kabananga (Janga 61), Richard (Muzhikov 71).
Jablonec: (4141) Hruby; Holes, Hovorka, Lischka, Hanousek; Hubschman; Jovovic (Kubista 89), Povazanec, Travnik, Sobol (Kratochvil 72); Dolezal.

Dynamo Kyiv (1) 3 *(Verbic 13, Mykolenko 68, Shaparenko 72)*

Rennes (0) 1 *(Siebatcheu 89)* 24,402

Dynamo Kyiv: (451) Boyko; Kedziora, Burda, Kadar, Mykolenko; Tsygankov, Shaparenko (Duelund 90), Tche Tche (Sydorchuk 82), Buyalsky, Sidcley; Verbic (Supriaga 90).
Rennes: (442) Koubek; Traore (Niang 46), Da Silva, Nyamsi (Gelin 74), Bensebaini; Zeffane, Poha, Lea Siliki, Bourigeaud; Ben Arfa, Sarr (Siebatcheu 71).

Thursday, 29 November 2018

Astana (0) 0

Dynamo Kyiv (1) 1 *(Verbic 29)* 26,508

Astana: (442) Eric; Rukavina, Postnikov, Anicic, Zainuinov (Shomko 75); Tomasov, Maevskiy, Kleinheisler, Murtazayev; Kabananga (Janga 62), Richard (Muzhikov 58).
Dynamo Kyiv: (4231) Boyko; Kedziora, Burda, Kadar, Mykolenko; Tche Tche, Shepelev; Tsygankov (Morozyuk 83), Shaparenko (Garmash 64), Sidcley; Verbic (Sydorchuk 76).

Jablonec (0) 0

Rennes (0) 1 *(Grenier 55)* 4712

Jablonec: (4141) Hruby; Holes, Hovorka, Lischka, Hanousek; Hubschman (Chramosta 82); Travnik, Kubista, Povazanec, Sobol (Kratochvil 63); Dolezal.
Rennes: (3511) Koubek; Zeffane, Mexer, Da Silva; Traore, Bourigeaud (Niang 63), Johansson, Andre, Lea Siliki; Grenier (Ben Arfa 77); Sarr (Hunou 89).

Thursday, 13 December 2018

Dynamo Kyiv (0) 0

Jablonec (1) 1 *(Dolezal 10)* 11,300

Dynamo Kyiv: (4231) Bushchan; Kedziora, Burda, Kadar, Mykolenko; Sydorchuk, Shepelev; Tsygankov, Shaparenko (Tsitaishvili 60), Verbic; Besyedin (Duelund 66 (Andrievsky 75)).
Jablonec: (4411) Hruby; Holes, Hovorka, Lischka, Hanousek; Travnik, Kratochvil (Brecka 89), Hubschman, Jovovic (Sobol 79); Chramosta (Acosta 70); Dolezal.

Rennes (0) 2 *(Sarr 68, 73)*

Astana (0) 0 24,535

Rennes: (433) Diallo; Traore, Mexer, Da Silva, Bensebaini; Bourigeaud (Niang 82), Grenier, Andre; Sarr, Siebatcheu (Johansson 74), Ben Arfa (Hunou 90).
Astana: (442) Eric; Rukavina, Postnikov, Anicic, Zainuinov; Tomasov, Maevskiy, Kleinheisler (Shomko 86), Pedro Henrique (Murtazayev 81); Kabananga, Richard (Beysebekov 46).

Group K Table	P	W	D	L	F	A	GD	Pts
Dynamo Kyiv	6	3	2	1	10	7	3	11
Rennes	6	3	0	3	7	8	–1	9
Astana	6	2	2	2	7	7	0	8
Jablonec	6	1	2	3	6	8	–2	5

GROUP L

Thursday, 20 September 2018

PAOK (0) 0

Chelsea (1) 1 *(Willian 7)* 24,310

PAOK: (4231) Paschalakis; Vieirinha, Khacheridi, Varela, Tosca; Mauricio, Wernbloom; Leo Jaba (Biseswar 82), Shakhov (Prijovic 69), El Kaddouri; Pelkas (Warda 62).
Chelsea: (4312) Arrizabalaga; Zappacosta, Rudiger, Christensen, Alonso (Azpilicueta 65); Kante, Jorginho (Fabregas 65), Willian; Barkley; Pedro, Morata (Giroud 80).

Vidi (0) 0

BATE Borisov (1) 2 *(Tuominem 27, Filipenko 85)* 14,726

Vidi: (4321) Tujvel; Fiola (Hodzic 64), Juhasz, Vinicius, Stopira; Nego, Hadzic, Nikolov (Berecz 78); Kovacs, Scepovic M; Milanov (Hangya 75).
BATE Borisov: (433) Scherbitski; Polyakov, Milunovic, Filipenko, Filipovic■; Baha, Yablonskiy, Dragun; Ivanic (Gordeichuk 66), Tuominem (Skavysh 61), Stasevich (Volodjko 88).

Thursday, 4 October 2018

BATE Borisov (0) 1 *(Crespo 61 (og))*

PAOK (3) 4 *(Prijovic 6, Leo Jaba 11, 17, Pelkas 73)* 10,527

BATE Borisov: (433) Scherbitski; Rios, Polyakov, Filipenko, Volodjko; Baha, Yablonskiy, Dragun (Hleb 72); Ivanic, Tuominem (Skavysh 59), Stasevich (Gordeichuk 77).
PAOK: (4231) Paschalakis; Leo Matos, Varela, Crespo, Tosca; Canas, Mauricio; Limnios (Biseswar 70), Pelkas, Leo Jaba (Vieirinha 85); Prijovic (Akpom 76).

Chelsea (0) 1 *(Morata 70)*

Vidi (0) 0 39,925

Chelsea: (442) Arrizabalaga; Zappacosta, Cahill, Christensen, Emerson Palmieri; Kovacic, Fabregas, Loftus-Cheek (Barkley 65), Pedro (Hazard 54); Morata, Willian (Moses 73).
Vidi: (433) Tujvel; Fiola, Vinicius, Juhasz, Stopira; Hadzic (Patkai 82), Nego, Huszti (Kovacs 77); Scepovic M, Milanov (Hodzic 82), Nikolov.

Thursday, 25 October 2018

Chelsea (2) 3 *(Loftus-Cheek 2, 8, 54)*

BATE Borisov (0) 1 *(Rios 80)* 39,799

Chelsea: (433) Arrizabalaga; Zappacosta, Christensen, Cahill, Emerson Palmieri; Loftus-Cheek, Fabregas, Kovacic (Kante 78); Willian (Moses 57), Giroud, Pedro (Hudson-Odoi 60).
BATE Borisov: (433) Scherbitski; Rios, Filipovic, Filipenko, Volodjko; Baha (Yablonskiy 76), Dragun, Hleb (Ivanic 59); Skavysh, Signevich (Tuominem 71), Stasevich.

PAOK (0) 0

Vidi (2) 2 *(Huszti 12, Stopira 45)* 15,118

PAOK: (4231) Paschalakis; Leo Matos, Varela, Crespo, Tosca; Shakhov (Prijovic 52), Canas; Limnios (Warda 46), Pelkas, El Kaddouri; Karelis (Biseswar 66).
Vidi: (532) Kovacsik; Fiola, Juhasz, Nego, Vinicius, Stopira; Patkai, Hadzic, Milanov (Nikolov 79); Scepovic M (Hodzic 65), Huszti (Kovacs 73).

Thursday, 8 November 2018

BATE Borisov (0) 0

Chelsea (0) 1 *(Giroud 53)* 13,141

BATE Borisov: (433) Scherbitski; Rios, Volkov, Filipenko, Filipovic; Baha, Dragun, Hleb (Berezkin 81); Skavysh (Moukam 76), Signevich (Tuominem 72), Stasevich.
Chelsea: (433) Arrizabalaga; Zappacosta, Christensen, Cahill, Emerson Palmieri; Barkley, Jorginho, Loftus-Cheek (Kovacic 64); Pedro (Hudson-Odoi 86), Giroud, Hazard (Willian 62).

Vidi (0) 1 *(Milanov 49)*

PAOK (0) 0 17,208

Vidi: (4321) Kovacsik; Fiola, Juhasz, Vinicius, Stopira; Nego, Hadzic, Patkai; Milanov (Nikolov 57), Huszti (Kovacs 66); Scepovic M (Hodzic 77).
PAOK: (4231) Paschalakis; Leo Matos, Varela, Crespo, Tosca; Shakhov, Wernbloom; Limnios (Biseswar 59), El Kaddouri (Akpom 63), Leo Jaba (Warda 70); Prijovic.

Thursday, 29 November 2018

BATE Borisov (1) 2 *(Signevich 22, Ivanic 85)*

Vidi (0) 0 4600

BATE Borisov: (433) Scherbitski; Rios, Volkov, Filipenko (Polyakov 46), Filipovic; Baha, Dragun, Ivanic; Hleb (Skavysh 65), Signevich, Stasevich (Gordeichuk 89).
Vidi: (442) Kovacsik; Juhasz, Stopira, Fiola, Vinicius; Nego (Kovacs 67), Hadzic, Patkai (Hodzic 64), Milanov; Huszti (Nikolov 74), Scepovic M.

Chelsea (2) 4 *(Giroud 27, 37, Hudson-Odoi 60, Morata 78)*

PAOK (0) 0 33,933

Chelsea: (532) Arrizabalaga; Zappacosta (Ampadu 63), Christensen, Cahill, Emerson Palmieri, Barkley; Fabregas, Loftus-Cheek, Pedro (Willian 66); Giroud (Morata 74), Hudson-Odoi.
PAOK: (4231) Paschalakis; Leo Matos, Khacheridi■, Crespo, Vieirinha; Mauricio (Pelkas 80), Wernbloom; Leo Jaba, Shakhov, El Kaddouri (Varela 75); Prijovic (Warda 46).

Thursday, 13 December 2018

PAOK (0) 1 *(Prijovic 59)*

BATE Borisov (3) 3 *(Skavysh 18, Signevich 42 (pen), 45)* 13,483

PAOK: (4231) Paschalakis; Leo Matos, Varela, Crespo, Vieirinha (Tosca 46); Mauricio, Canas; Leo Jaba, Pelkas (Akpom 55), Limnios (Warda 46); Prijovic.
BATE Borisov: (433) Scherbitski; Rios, Volkov, Polyakov, Filipovic; Baha, Dragun (Yablonskiy 87), Ivanic; Skavysh (Gordeichuk 82), Signevich■, Stasevich.

Vidi (1) 2 *(Ampadu 32 (og), Nego 56)*

Chelsea (1) 2 *(Willian 30, Giroud 75)* 19,242

Vidi: (433) Kovacsik; Fiola, Juhasz, Vinicius, Stopira; Nego, Hadzic (Patkai 85), Nikolov; Milanov (Kovacs 80), Scepovic M, Huszti (Hodzic 80).
Chelsea: (433) Caballero; Zappacosta, Christensen, Ampadu, Emerson Palmieri; Barkley, Fabregas, Loftus-Cheek; Willian (Pedro 55), Morata (Giroud 45), Hudson-Odoi.

Group L Table	P	W	D	L	F	A	GD	Pts
Chelsea	6	5	1	0	12	3	9	16
BATE Borisov	6	3	0	3	9	9	0	9
Vidi	6	2	1	3	5	7	–2	7
PAOK	6	1	0	5	5	12	–7	3

KNOCK-OUT STAGE

ROUND OF 32 FIRST LEG

Tuesday, 12 February 2019

Fenerbahce (1) 1 *(Slimani 21)*

Zenit St Petersburg (0) 0 36,572

Fenerbahce: (433) Tekin; Isla, Skrtel, Ciftpinar, Kaldirim; Elmas (Ayew 72), Topal, Jailson; Moses (Potuk 84), Slimani, Valbuena (Neustadter 90).
Zenit St Petersburg: (433) Lunev; Aniukov, Ivanovic, Rakitskiy, Nabiullin (Smolnikov 61); Hernani, Kranevitter, Barrios; Driussi (Azmoun 76), Dzyuba, Mak (Marchisio 85).
Referee: Ruddy Buquet.

Thursday, 14 February 2019

BATE Borisov (1) 1 *(Dragun 45)*

Arsenal (0) 0 12,527

BATE Borisov: (433) Scherbitski; Rios, Volkov, Filipenko, Filipovic; Baha, Dragun, Hleb (Berezkin 57); Milic (Dubajic 69), Skavysh (Moukam 80), Stasevich.
Arsenal: (343) Cech; Mustafi, Koscielny, Monreal; Maitland-Niles (Aubameyang 68), Xhaka (Torreira 69), Guendouzi, Kolasinac (Suarez 74); Mkhitaryan, Lacazette■, Iwobi.
Referee: Srdjan Jovanovic.

Celtic (0) 0

Valencia (1) 2 *(Cheryshev 42, Sobrino 49)* 57,430

Celtic: (4411) Bain; Toljan, Boyata, Simunovic, Izaguirre; Forrest, McGregor, Brown, Sinclair (Weah 58); Christie (Edouard 59); Burke.
Valencia: (442) Neto; Piccini (Gameiro 78), Garay, Diakhaby, Toni Lato; Carlos Soler, Parejo (Coquelin 46), Kondogbia, Wass; Sobrino, Cheryshev (Goncalo Guedes 63).
Referee: Ovidiu Alin Hategan.

Club Brugge (0) 2 *(Denswil 64, Wesley 81)*

Red Bull Salzburg (1) 1 *(Junuzovic 17)* 17,000

Club Brugge: (352) Horvath; Amrabat (Poulain 46), Mechele, Denswil; Cools (Diatta 46), Vormer, Rits, Vanaken, Bonaventure; Wesley, Schrijvers (Openda 78).
Red Bull Salzburg: (442) Walke; Lainer, Ramalho, Pongracic, Ulmer; Schlager (Mwepu 76), Samassekou, Wolf (Daka 89), Junuzovic; Gulbrandsen (Minamino 85), Dabbur.
Referee: Georgi Kabakov.

FC Zurich (0) 1 *(Kololli 83 (pen))*

Napoli (2) 3 *(Insigne 12, Callejon 21, Zielinski 77)* 24,000

FC Zurich: (343) Brecher; Nef, Bangura, Maxso; Untersee, Kryeziu H, Domgjoni (Marchesano 46), Kharabadze; Winter (Ceesay 67), Odey (Khelifi 80), Kololli.
Napoli: (442) Meret; Malcuit, Maksimovic, Koulibaly, Ghoulam (Luperto 76); Callejon, Allan (Diawara 59), Fabian, Zielinski; Milik, Insigne (Ounas 68).
Referee: Milorad Mazic.

Galatasaray (0) 1 *(Luyindama 54)*

Benfica (1) 2 *(Salvio 27 (pen), Seferovic 64)* 42,722

Galatasaray: (433) Muslera; Linnes (Mariano 73), Luyindama, Marcao, Nagatomo; Belhanda, Fernando, Ndiaye (Gumus 73); Feghouli, Diagne, Onyekuru.
Benfica: (442) Vlachodimos; Corchia, Dias, Ferro, Yuri Ribeiro; Salvio (Pires 48), Fernandes (Samaris 87), Florentino, Cervi (Krovinovic 80); Joao Felix, Seferovic.
Referee: Jesus Gil Manzano.

Krasnodar (0) 0

Bayer Leverkusen (0) 0 34,827

Krasnodar: (433) Kritsyuk; Petrov, Martynovich, Spajic, Stotskiy; Olsson (Suleymanov 70), Kabore, Pereyra (Golubev 80); Wanderson, Ignatyev, Claesson.
Bayer Leverkusen: (433) Hradecky; Weiser, Tah, Bender S (Dragovic 83), Wendell; Havertz, Aranguiz, Brandt; Bellarabi, Volland, Bailey (Alario 80).
Referee: Davide Massa.

Lazio (0) 0

Sevilla (1) 1 *(Ben Yedder 22)* 19,766

Lazio: (352) Strakosha; Bastos (Felipe 57), Acerbi, Radu; Marusic, Parolo (Cataldi 46), Lucas, Luis Alberto (Durmisi 44), Lulic; Caicedo, Correa.
Sevilla: (352) Vaclik; Mercado, Kjaer, Sergi Gomez; Jesus Navas, Sarabia (Amadou 83), Banega, Vazquez, Escudero (Promes 75); Andre Silva, Ben Yedder (Munir 71).
Referee: Slavko Vincic.

Malmo (0) 1 *(Christiansen 80)*

Chelsea (1) 2 *(Barkley 30, Giroud 58)* 20,312

Malmo: (442) Dahlin; Vindheim, Nielsen, Bengtsson, Safari; Traustason (Lewicki 70), Christiansen (Gall 81), Bachirou, Rieks; Antonsson (Strandberg 70), Rosenberg.
Chelsea: (433) Arrizabalaga; Azpilicueta, Luiz, Christensen, Emerson Palmieri; Barkley, Jorginho (Kante 74), Kovacic; Willian (Hazard 71), Giroud, Pedro (Hudson-Odoi 84).
Referee: Aleksei Kulbakov.

Olympiacos (2) 2 *(Kouka 9, Gil Dias 40)*

Dynamo Kyiv (1) 2 *(Buyalsky 28, Verbic 90)* 31,020

Olympiacos: (4231) Jose Sa; Meriah, Cisse, Vukovic, Tsimikas; Guilherme, Camara; Gil Dias (Masouras 86), Fortounis (Natcho 68), Daniel Podence (Christodoulopoulos 81); Kouka.
Dynamo Kyiv: (433) Boyko; Kedziora, Burda, Shabanov, Mykolenko; Shepelev, Shaparenko (Harmash 82), Buyalsky; Verbic, Sol (Rusyn 82), Tsygankov.
Referee: Craig Pawson.

Rapid Vienna (0) 0

Internazionale (1) 1 *(Martinez 39 (pen))* 23,850

Rapid Vienna: (4231) Strebinger; Potzmann, Sonnleitner, Hofmann, Bolingoli Mbombo; Grahovac (Knasmullner 64), Ljubicic; Thurnwald (Schobesberger 52), Schwab, Ivan; Berisha (Murg 82).
Internazionale: (4231) Handanovic; Cedric, de Vrij, Miranda, Asamoah; Vecino, Valero; Politano (Candreva 78), Nainggolan (D'Ambrosio 82), Perisic; Martinez.
Referee: Tobias Stieler.

Rennes (3) 3 *(Hunou 2, Javi Garcia 11 (og), Ben Arfa 45 (pen))*

Real Betis (1) 3 *(Lo Celso 32, Sidnei 62, Lainez 90)* 28,656

Rennes: (442) Koubek; Traore, Mexer, Da Silva, Zeffane; Hunou (Bensebaini 80), Andre, Grenier (Gelin 70), Sarr (Bourigeaud 49); Ben Arfa, Niang.
Real Betis: (3511) Robles; Mandi, Javi Garcia, Sidnei; Joaquin (Barragan 83), Canales, William Carvalho, Guardado, Firpo (Lainez 27); Lo Celso; Moron (Jese 73).
Referee: Tasos Sidiropoulos.

Shakhtar Donetsk (1) 2 *(Marlos 10 (pen), Taison 67)*

Eintracht Frankfurt (1) 2 *(Hinteregger 7, Kostic 50)* 13,059

Shakhtar Donetsk: (4231) Pyatov; Butko, Kryvtsov, Khocholava, Ismaily; Stepanenko■, Alan Patrick; Marlos (Solomon 69), Kovalenko (Malyshev 81), Taison; Moraes (Bolbat 90).
Eintracht Frankfurt: (442) Trapp; Da Costa, Hasebe, Hinteregger, Ndicka; Gacinovic, Fernandes (de Guzman 82), Rode (Willems 46), Kostic; Jovic, Rebic.
Referee: Anthony Taylor.

Slavia Prague (0) 0

Genk (0) 0 18,125

Slavia Prague: (4231) Kolar; Coufal, Kudela, Ngadeu Ngadjui, Boril; Soucek, Sevcik; Stoch, Husbauer (Kral 76), Zmrhal (Olayinka 61); Skoda (van Buren 76).
Genk: (433) Vukovic; Maehle, Dewaest, Aidoo, De Norre; Heynen, Malinovsky, Fiolic (Pozuelo 56); Trossard (Piotrowski 87), Samatta, Ndongala (Paintsil 69).
Referee: Andris Treimanis.

Sporting Lisbon (0) 0

Villarreal (1) 1 *(Pedraza 3)* 27,134

Sporting Lisbon: (433) Salin; Bruno Gaspar (Ristovski 27), Coates, Andre Pinto, Acuna■; Luis M, Petrovic (Wendel 70), Bruno Fernandes; Dost, Raphinha, Cabral (Luiz Phellype 69).
Villarreal: (433) Fernandez; Mario, Alvaro, Victor Ruiz, Pedraza; Trigueros (Caseres 63), Javi Fuego, Funes Mori; Chukwueze (Raba 74), Bacca, Fornals (Iborra 80).
Referee: Clement Turpin.

Viktoria Plzen (0) 2 *(Pernica 54, 83)*

Dinamo Zagreb (1) 1 *(Olmo 41)* 9731

Viktoria Plzen: (4231) Kozacik; Havel, Pernica, Hubnik, Kovarik; Horava, Hrosovsky; Ekpai (Petrzela 70), Cermak (Prochazka 46), Kayamba; Beauguel (Chory 82).
Dinamo Zagreb: (433) Livakovic; Stojanovic, Theophile-Catherine, Dilaver, Leovac; Gojak, Ademi, Olmo; Situm (Moro 64), Petkovic, Orsic (Atiemwen 76).
Referee: Serdar Gozubuyuk.

ROUND OF 32 SECOND LEG

Wednesday, 20 February 2019

Sevilla (1) 2 *(Ben Yedder 20, Sarabia 78)*

Lazio (0) 0 34,521

Sevilla: (532) Vaclik; Mercado, Kjaer, Sergi Gomez, Jesus Navas, Vazquez■; Roque (Rog 81), Sarabia, Escudero (Promes 6); Andre Silva (Amadou 63), Ben Yedder.
Lazio: (532) Strakosha; Patric Gil (Correa 48), Acerbi, Radu, Marusic■, Milinkovic-Savic (Romulo 56); Badelj (Durmisi 76), Cataldi, Lulic; Immobile, Caicedo.
Referee: Anthony Taylor.

Thursday, 21 February 2019

Arsenal (2) 3 *(Volkov 4 (og), Mustafi 39, Papastathopoulos 60)*

BATE Borisov (0) 0 58,812

Arsenal: (4231) Cech; Lichtsteiner, Mustafi, Koscielny (Papastathopoulos 56), Monreal; Guendouzi (Torreira 63), Xhaka; Mkhitaryan (Suarez 78), Ozil, Iwobi; Aubameyang.
BATE Borisov: (4231) Scherbitski; Rios, Volkov, Filipenko, Filipovic; Simovic, Dragun (Berezkin 64); Milic, Baha (Hleb 58), Stasevich; Skavysh (Dubajic 72).
Referee: Alberto Undiano Mallenco.

Bayer Leverkusen (0) 1 *(Aranguiz 87)*

Krasnodar (0) 1 *(Suleymanov 84)* 16,084

Bayer Leverkusen: (4141) Hradecky; Weiser, Dragovic (Thelin 86), Tah, Wendell; Aranguiz; Volland, Havertz (Baumgartlinger 66), Brandt, Bailey; Alario.
Krasnodar: (433) Safonov; Petrov, Martynovich, Spajic, Ramirez; Olsson (Gazinsky 60), Kabore, Pereyra; Wanderson, Ignatyev (Suleymanov 70), Claesson (Stotskiy 77).
Referee: Gediminas Mazeika.
Krasnodar won on away goals.

Benfica (0) 0

Galatasaray (0) 0 49,545

Benfica: (442) Vlachodimos; Andre Almeida, Dias, Ferro, Grimaldo; Pizzi (Pires 83), Fernandes, Florentino, Cervi (Rafa Silva 58); Joao Felix (Jonas 75), Seferovic.
Galatasaray: (4231) Muslera; Mariano, Luyindama, Marcao, Nagatomo; Donk (Gumus 78), Ndiaye; Feghouli (Akbaba 83), Belhanda, Onyekuru (Akgun 83); Diagne.
Referee: Ovidiu Alin Hategan.

Chelsea (0) 3 *(Giroud 55, Barkley 74, Hudson-Odoi 84)*

Malmo (0) 0 39,813

Chelsea: (433) Caballero; Azpilicueta (Ampadu 79), Rudiger, Christensen, Emerson Palmieri; Kante (Loftus-Cheek 75), Barkley (Jorginho 76), Kovacic; Willian, Giroud, Hudson-Odoi.
Malmo: (442) Dahlin; Vindheim, Nielsen, Bengtsson■, Safari; Traustason (Gall 72), Christiansen (Lewicki 72), Bachirou, Rieks; Antonsson, Rosenberg (Strandberg 62).
Referee: Orel Grinfeld.

Dinamo Zagreb (2) 3 *(Orsic 15, Dilaver 34, Petkovic 73)*

Viktoria Plzen (0) 0 25,860

Dinamo Zagreb: (4231) Livakovic; Moharrami, Theophile-Catherine, Dilaver, Leovac; Ademi, Sunjic; Hajrovic (Moro 68), Olmo, Orsic (Gojak 89); Petkovic (Andric 90).
Viktoria Plzen: (4231) Kozacik; Havel (Reznik 74), Pernica, Limbersky■, Kovarik; Prochazka, Hrosovsky; Kayamba, Horava (Bakos 57), Petrzela; Beauguel (Chory 67).
Referee: Istvan Kovacs.

Dynamo Kyiv (1) 1 *(Sol 32)*

Olympiacos (0) 0 48,902

Dynamo Kyiv: (433) Boyko; Kedziora, Burda, Shabanov, Mykolenko; Buyalsky, Shaparenko (Harmash 76), Shepelev; Tsygankov, Sol (Rusyn 90), Verbic (Smirniy 90).
Olympiacos: (4231) Jose Sa; Torosidis, Meriah, Cisse, Tsimikas; Guilherme, Bouchalakis (Natcho 65); Gil Dias (Masouras 46), Fortounis (Guerrero 65), Daniel Podence; Kouka.
Referee: Ivan Kruzliak.

Eintracht Frankfurt (2) 4 *(Jovic 23, Haller 27 (pen), 80, Rebic 88)*

Shakhtar Donetsk (0) 1 *(Moraes 64)* 47,000

Eintracht Frankfurt: (3412) Trapp; Abraham, Hinteregger, Ndicka; Da Costa, Hasebe, Rode (Willems 73), Kostic; Gacinovic (de Guzman 90); Haller, Jovic (Rebic 71).
Shakhtar Donetsk: (4231) Pyatov; Butko (Bolbat 66), Khocholava, Matviyenko, Ismaily; Kovalenko (Kayode 80), Alan Patrick; Marlos, Taison, Solomon (Maycon 46); Moraes.
Referee: Antonio Miguel Mateu Lahoz.

Genk (1) 1 *(Trossard 10)*

Slavia Prague (1) 4 *(Coufal 23, Traore 54, Skoda 64, 69)* 13,688

Genk: (433) Vukovic (Jackers 56); Maehle, Dewaest, Lucumi, De Norre (Uronen 56); Malinovsky, Pozuelo, Heynen (Wouters 30); Trossard, Samatta, Ito.
Slavia Prague: (4231) Kolar; Coufal, Kudela, Deli, Boril; Soucek, Traore (Stoch 63); Masopust (Olayinka 66), Kral, Zmrhal; Skoda (van Buren 75).
Referee: Boddy Madden.

Internazionale (2) 4 *(Vecino 11, Ranocchia 18, Perisic 80, Politano 87)*

Rapid Vienna (0) 0 32,158

Internazionale: (433) Handanovic; Cedric, Ranocchia, Skriniar (Miranda 77), Asamoah; Vecino, Brozovic (Valero 61), Nainggolan; Candreva, Martinez (Politano 66), Perisic.
Rapid Vienna: (4231) Strebinger; Potzmann, Sonnleitner, Hofmann, Bolingoli Mbombo (Schobesberger 75); Ljubicic, Grahovac; Murg, Knasmullner (Schwab 63), Ivan (Muldur 63); Pavlovic.
Referee: Artur Soraes Dias.

Napoli (1) 2 *(Verdi 43, Ounas 75)*
FC Zurich (0) 0 17,597
Napoli: (442) Meret; Hysaj, Chiriches (Luperto 56), Koulibaly, Ghoulam; Ounas (Milik 77), Diawara, Zielinski (Allan 66), Verdi; Mertens, Insigne.
FC Zurich: (442) Brecher; Winter, Bangura, Kryeziu M, Kololli (Kharabadze 82); Khelifi, Sohm, Domgjoni, Schonbachler (Krasniqi 64); Odey (Zumberi 60), Ceesay.
Referee: Tasos Sidiropoulos.

Real Betis (1) 1 *(Lo Celso 41)*
Rennes (2) 3 *(Bensebaini 22, Hunou 30, Niang 90)* 43,623
Real Betis: (343) Robles; Mandi, Bartra, Sidnei; Joaquin (Emerson 88), William Carvalho, Canales, Guardado (Lainez 77); Lo Celso, Moron, Jese (Leon 69).
Rennes: (442) Koubek; Traore, Mexer, Da Silva, Bensebaini (Zeffane 77); Niang, Grenier, Bourigeaud (Gelin 75), Sarr; Hunou (Del Castillo 83), Ben Arfa.
Referee: Viktor Kassai.

Red Bull Salzburg (3) 4 *(Schlager 17, Daka 29, 43, Dabbur 90)*
Club Brugge (0) 0 24,717
Red Bull Salzburg: (442) Walke; Lainer, Pongracic (Vallci 77), Onguene, Ulmer; Schlager, Wolf (Minamino 63), Samassekou, Junuzovic (Mwepu 71); Daka, Dabbur.
Club Brugge: (352) Horvath; Poulain, Mechele, Denswil; Amrabat (Diatta 63), Vormer, Rits, Vanaken, Bonaventure; Wesley (Vossen 83), Schrijvers (Openda 69).
Referee: Daniel Siebert.

Valencia (0) 1 *(Gameiro 70)*
Celtic (0) 0 36,619
Valencia: (442) Neto; Wass (Lee 75), Garay (Coquelin 22), Diakhaby, Toni Lato; Torres, Carlos Soler, Parejo, Goncalo Guedes; Sobrino (Gameiro 68), Santi Mina.
Celtic: (541) Bain; Toljan■, Boyata, Ajer, Simunovic, Hayes; Forrest (Edouard 63), Brown, McGregor, Christie; Burke (Johnston 73).
Referee: Deniz Aytekin.

Villarreal (0) 1 *(Fornals 80)*
Sporting Lisbon (1) 1 *(Bruno Fernandes 45)* 14,098
Villarreal: (433) Fernandez; Miguelon (Cazorla 71), Mario, Victor Ruiz, Pedraza; Trigueros, Javi Fuego (Iborra 63), Funes Mori; Raba (Toko Ekambi 58), Gerard, Fornals.
Sporting Lisbon: (433) Salin; Borja, Coates, Jefferson■, Tiago Ilori; Wendel, Gudelj, Ristovski (Luiz Phellype 83); Bruno Fernandes, Dost, Diaby (Raphinha 78).
Referee: Pavel Kralovec.

Zenit St Petersburg (2) 3 *(Ozdoev 4, Azmoun 37, 76)*
Fenerbahce (1) 1 *(Topal 43)* 50,448
Zenit St Petersburg: (433) Lunev; Smolnikov, Ivanovic, Rakitskiy, Aniukov; Barrios, Hernani (Mak 56), Ozdoev; Azmoun (Zabolotny 79), Dzyuba (Musaev 88), Driussi.
Fenerbahce: (433) Tekin; Ozbayrakli, Ciftpinar, Skrtel, Kaldirim (Koybasi 67); Jailson (Slimani 80), Topal, Elmas; Moses, Ayew, Potuk (Arslan 46).
Referee: Michael Oliver.

ROUND OF 16 FIRST LEG

Thursday, 7 March 2019

Chelsea (1) 3 *(Pedro 17, Willian 65, Hudson-Odoi 90)*
Dynamo Kyiv (0) 0 37,280
Chelsea: (433) Arrizabalaga; Zappacosta, Luiz, Christensen, Alonso; Barkley (Loftus-Cheek 62), Jorginho (Kante 62), Kovacic; Willian (Hudson-Odoi 78), Giroud, Pedro.
Dynamo Kyiv: (4231) Boyko; Kedziora, Burda, Shabanov, Mykolenko; Sydorchuk, Shepelev; Tsygankov, Shaparenko, Buyalsky (Sidcley 71); Rusyn (Harmash 66).
Referee: Slavko Vincic.

Dinamo Zagreb (1) 1 *(Petkovic 38 (pen))*
Benfica (0) 0 29,704
Dinamo Zagreb: (4231) Livakovic; Stojanovic, Theophile-Catherine, Dilaver, Leovac; Sunjic, Gojak (Moro 78); Orsic, Olmo, Kadzior (Situm 84); Petkovic (Gavranovic 88).
Benfica: (442) Vlachodimos; Corchia, Dias, Ferro, Grimaldo; Fernandes (Zivkovic 70), Florentino (Rafa Silva 58), Pires, Krovinovic; Seferovic (Cervi 35), Joao Felix.
Referee: Michael Oliver.

Eintracht Frankfurt (0) 0
Internazionale (0) 0 48,000
Eintracht Frankfurt: (532) Trapp; Da Costa, Hasebe, Hinteregger, Ndicka, Kostic; Rode (Willems 77), Gacinovic, Fernandes; Haller (Paciencia 80), Jovic.
Internazionale: (433) Handanovic; D'Ambrosio, de Vrij, Skriniar, Asamoah; Vecino, Brozovic, Valero (Cedric 79); Politano, Martinez, Perisic (Candreva 58).
Referee: William Collum.

Napoli (2) 3 *(Milik 10, Fabian 18, Onguene 58 (og))*
Red Bull Salzburg (0) 0 32,579
Napoli: (442) Meret; Hysaj, Maksimovic, Koulibaly, Rui; Callejon, Allan, Fabian, Zielinski (Diawara 66); Milik (Ounas 81), Mertens (Insigne 71).
Red Bull Salzburg: (442) Walke; Lainer, Ramalho, Onguene, Ulmer; Schlager, Wolf, Samassekou, Junuzovic (Mwepu 62); Daka (Gulbrandsen 61), Dabbur (Minamino 76).
Referee: Aleksei Kulbakov.

Rennes (1) 3 *(Bourigeaud 43, Monreal 65 (og), Sarr 88)*
Arsenal (1) 1 *(Iwobi 4)* 29,100
Rennes: (442) Koubek; Zeffane, Da Silva, Mexer, Bensebaini; Bourigeaud (Lea Siliki 73), Andre, Grenier (Gelin 90), Sarr; Hunou, Ben Arfa.
Arsenal: (4231) Cech; Mustafi, Papastathopoulos■, Koscielny, Monreal; Torreira, Xhaka; Mkhitaryan, Ozil (Ramsey 69), Iwobi (Guendouzi 52); Aubameyang (Kolasinac 79).
Referee: Ivan Kruzliak.

Sevilla (2) 2 *(Ben Yedder 1, Munir 28)*
Slavia Prague (2) 2 *(Stoch 25, Kral 39)* 30,698
Sevilla: (352) Vaclik (Soriano 45); Mercado, Kjaer, Sergi Gomez; Jesus Navas, Sarabia, Banega (Promes 76), Rog, Wober (Roque 46); Ben Yedder, Munir.
Slavia Prague: (451) Kolar; Coufal, Deli, Kudela, Boril; Stoch, Kral (Ngadeu Ngadjui 79), Traore, Soucek, Zmrhal (Skoda 72); Masopust (Olayinka 60).
Referee: Ruddy Buquet.

Valencia (2) 2 *(Rodrigo 12, 24)*
Krasnodar (0) 1 *(Claesson 63)* 36,274
Valencia: (442) Neto; Piccini, Gabriel, Diakhaby, Toni Lato; Carlos Soler, Coquelin, Parejo, Goncalo Guedes (Cheryshev 70); Rodrigo (Santi Mina 62), Gameiro (Sobrino 78).
Krasnodar: (433) Safonov; Petrov, Martynovich, Spajic, Ramirez; Gazinsky (Golubev 89), Kabore, Olsson; Wanderson (Suleymanov 80), Claesson, Stotskiy (Ari 55).
Referee: Orel Grinfeld.

Zenit St Petersburg (1) 1 *(Azmoun 35)*
Villarreal (1) 3 *(Iborra 34, Gerard 64, Morlanes 71)* 51,826
Zenit St Petersburg: (442) Lunev; Smolnikov, Ivanovic, Rakitskiy, Kuzyaev; Mak (Shatov 72), Ozdoev (Zabolotny 88), Barrios, Driussi; Dzyuba, Azmoun (Hernani 75).
Villarreal: (4141) Fernandez; Miguelon, Alvaro, Victor Ruiz, Jaume; Funes Mori; Chukwueze, Morlanes (Caseres 72), Iborra, Fornals (Cazorla 78); Gerard (Bacca 85).
Referee: Gianluca Rocchi.

ROUND OF 16 SECOND LEG

Thursday, 14 March 2019

Arsenal (2) 3 *(Aubameyang 5, 72, Maitland-Niles 15)*
Rennes (0) 0 59,453
Arsenal: (4231) Cech; Mustafi, Koscielny, Monreal, Kolasinac; Ramsey (Torreira 87), Xhaka; Maitland-Niles, Ozil (Mkhitaryan 69), Aubameyang; Lacazette (Iwobi 70).
Rennes: (442) Koubek; Traore, Da Silva, Mexer, Bensebaini; Bourigeaud, Andre (Lea Siliki 78), Grenier (Hunou 70), Sarr; Ben Arfa, Niang.
Referee: Andris Treimanis.

Benfica (0) 3 *(Jonas 71, Ferro 94, Grimaldo 105)*

Dinamo Zagreb (0) 0 47,808

Benfica: (442) Vlachodimos; Andre Almeida, Dias, Ferro, Yuri Ribeiro (Grimaldo 46); Pizzi (Fernandes 119), Fejsa, Pires, Zivkovic (Jonas 46); Neves Filipe (Joao Felix 62), Rafa Silva.
Dinamo Zagreb: (433) Livakovic; Stojanovic■, Theophile-Catherine, Dilaver, Rrahmani; Gojak (Atiemwen 97), Moro, Olmo; Kadzior (Situm 75), Petkovic (Gavranovic 86), Orsic (Peric 109).
aet. Referee: Deniz Aytekin.

Dynamo Kyiv (0) 0

Chelsea (3) 5 *(Giroud 5, 33, 59, Alonso 45, Hudson-Odoi 78)* 64,830

Dynamo Kyiv: (4231) Boyko; Kedziora, Burda, Kadar, Mykolenko; Sydorchuk (Tche Tche 65), Shepelev (Andrievsky 87); Tsygankov, Shaparenko, Sidcley (Smirniy 81); Harmash.
Chelsea: (433) Arrizabalaga; Zappacosta (Azpilicueta 69), Rudiger, Christensen, Alonso; Kante (Jorginho 65), Kovacic, Loftus-Cheek; Hudson-Odoi, Giroud, Willian (Pedro 74).
Referee: Tobias Stieler.

Internazionale (0) 0

Eintracht Frankfurt (1) 1 *(Jovic 6)* 49,866

Internazionale: (433) Handanovic; D'Ambrosio, de Vrij, Skriniar, Cedric (Ranocchia 62); Candreva, Vecino, Valero (Esposito 73); Politano (Merola 80), Balde, Perisic.
Eintracht Frankfurt: (442) Trapp; Da Costa, Hasebe, Hinteregger, Ndicka; Gacinovic (de Guzman 59), Rode (Paciencia 89), Willems (Stendera 73), Kostic; Haller, Jovic.
Referee: Ovidiu Alin Hategan.

Krasnodar (0) 1 *(Suleymanov 85)*

Valencia (0) 1 *(Goncalo Guedes 90)* 35,074

Krasnodar: (433) Safonov; Petrov (Suleymanov 75), Spajic, Fjoluson, Ramirez; Olsson, Gazinsky, Pereyra (Taranov 90); Wanderson, Ari (Stotskiy 30), Claesson.
Valencia: (442) Neto; Wass, Gabriel, Diakhaby, Gaya; Carlos Soler (Gameiro 88), Coquelin, Kondogbia, Cheryshev; Sobrino (Rodrigo 58), Santi Mina (Goncalo Guedes 70).
Referee: Anthony Taylor.

Red Bull Salzburg (1) 3 *(Dabbur 25, Gulbrandsen 65, Leitgeb 90)*

Napoli (1) 1 *(Milik 14)* 29,520

Red Bull Salzburg: (442) Walke; Lainer, Ramalho, Onguene, Ulmer; Mwepu (Gulbrandsen 59), Samassekou, Wolf, Szoboszlai (Leitgeb 74); Minamino (Haland 86), Dabbur.
Napoli: (442) Meret; Hysaj, Chiriches (Malcuit 78), Luperto, Rui; Callejon, Allan, Fabian, Zielinski (Diawara 74); Milik, Mertens (Younes 88).
Referee: Carlos Del Cerro.

Slavia Prague (1) 4 *(Ngadeu Ngadjui 15, Soucek 47 (pen), van Buren 102, Olayinka 120)*

Sevilla (1) 3 *(Ben Yedder 44 (pen), Munir 54, Vazquez 98)* 19,020

Slavia Prague: (4231) Kolar; Kudela, Ngadeu Ngadjui, Deli, Boril; Soucek, Kral (Frydrych 106); Masopust (Zmrhal 90), Traore, Stoch (van Buren 92); Skoda (Olayinka 76).
Sevilla: (3142) Vaclik; Carrico, Kjaer, Sergi Gomez; Roque (Gonalons 74); Jesus Navas, Sarabia (Andre Silva 80), Banega, Promes; Ben Yedder (Rog 104), Munir (Vazquez 90).
aet.
Referee: Aleksei Kulbakov.

Villarreal (1) 2 *(Gerard 29, Bacca 47)*

Zenit St Petersburg (0) 1 *(Ivanovic 90)* 14,027

Villarreal: (433) Fernandez; Mario, Alvaro, Victor Ruiz, Jaume; Iborra (Cazorla 70), Funes Mori (Miguelon 77), Caseres (Morlanes 46); Fornals, Gerard, Bacca.
Zenit St Petersburg: (433) Lunev (Kerzhakov 64); Smolnikov, Ivanovic, Mammana, Rakitskiy; Hernani, Barrios (Kranevitter 46), Ozdoev; Shatov, Azmoun (Mak 70), Driussi.
Referee: Artur Soraes Dias.

QUARTER-FINALS FIRST LEG

Thursday, 11 April 2019

Arsenal (2) 2 *(Ramsey 15, Koulibaly 25 (og))*

Napoli (0) 0 59,738

Arsenal: (3412) Cech; Papastathopoulos, Koscielny, Monreal; Maitland-Niles, Torreira (Elneny 77), Ramsey, Kolasinac; Ozil (Mkhitaryan 67); Lacazette (Iwobi 67), Aubameyang.
Napoli: (442) Meret; Hysaj, Maksimovic, Koulibaly, Rui; Callejon, Allan, Fabian (Ounas 83), Zielinski; Insigne (Younes 83), Mertens (Milik 65).
Referee: Alberto Undiano Mallenco.

Benfica (2) 4 *(Joao Felix 21 (pen), 43, 54, Dias 50)*

Eintracht Frankfurt (1) 2 *(Jovic 40, Paciencia 72)* 54,175

Benfica: (442) Vlachodimos; Corchia (Pizzi 66), Dias, Jardel, Grimaldo; Fernandes, Samaris (Zivkovic 85), Fejsa, Cervi; Rafa Silva (Seferovic 60), Joao Felix.
Eintracht Frankfurt: (442) Trapp; Hasebe, Abraham, Hinteregger, Ndicka■; Da Costa, Rode (Gacinovic 85), Fernandes, Kostic; Rebic (Paciencia 68), Jovic (de Guzman 60).
Referee: Anthony Taylor.

Slavia Prague (0) 0

Chelsea (0) 1 *(Alonso 86)* 17,484

Slavia Prague: (4231) Kolar; Coufal, Ngadeu Ngadjui, Deli, Boril; Traore, Kral; Masopust (Husbauer 74), Sevcik, Stoch (Zmrhal 64); Olayinka (van Buren 82).
Chelsea: (433) Arrizabalaga; Azpilicueta, Christensen, Rudiger, Alonso; Barkley (Loftus-Cheek 75), Jorginho, Kovacic (Kante 68); Pedro (Hazard 58), Giroud, Willian.
Referee: Felix Zwayer.

Villarreal (1) 1 *(Cazorla 36 (pen))*

Valencia (1) 3 *(Goncalo Guedes 6, 90, Wass 90)* 17,605

Villarreal: (532) Fernandez; Fornals, Mario (Pedraza 80), Alvaro, Victor Ruiz, Quintilla; Caseres (Morlanes 72), Cazorla, Iborra (Bacca 67); Chukwueze, Gerard.
Valencia: (442) Neto; Roncaglia (Piccini 58), Garay, Gabriel, Gaya; Torres (Coquelin 61), Parejo, Wass, Goncalo Guedes; Rodrigo, Gameiro (Cheryshev 68).
Referee: Michael Oliver.

QUARTER-FINALS SECOND LEG

Thursday, 18 April 2019

Chelsea (4) 4 *(Pedro 5, 27, Deli 10 (og), Giroud 17)*

Slavia Prague (1) 3 *(Soucek 26, Sevcik 51, 54)* 38,326

Chelsea: (433) Arrizabalaga; Azpilicueta, Christensen, Luiz, Emerson Palmieri; Kante, Kovacic, Barkley (Jorginho 70); Pedro (Hudson-Odoi 86), Giroud, Hazard (Willian 65).
Slavia Prague: (4231) Kolar; Kudela, Ngadeu Ngadjui, Deli, Boril; Kral, Soucek; Sevcik (Stoch 78), Traore, Zmrhal (Skoda 85); Masopust (Olayinka 52).
Referee: Damir Skomina.

Eintracht Frankfurt (1) 2 *(Kostic 37, Rode 67)*

Benfica (0) 0 48,000

Eintracht Frankfurt: (523) Trapp; Da Costa, Hasebe, Abraham, Falette (Willems 90), Kostic; Fernandes, Rode (Torro 86); Jovic (Paciencia 76), Gacinovic, Rebic.
Benfica: (442) Vlachodimos; Andre Almeida (Jonas 79), Jardel, Dias, Grimaldo; Fernandes, Samaris (Pizzi 70), Fejsa, Rafa Silva (Salvio 72); Joao Felix, Seferovic.
Referee: Daniele Orsato.
Eintract Frankfurt won on away goals.

Napoli (0) 0

Arsenal (1) 1 *(Lacazette 36)* 39,438

Napoli: (442) Meret; Maksimovic (Mertens 46), Chiriches, Koulibaly, Ghoulam (Rui 71); Callejon, Allan, Fabian, Zielinski; Milik, Insigne (Younes 61).
Arsenal: (3412) Cech; Papastathopoulos, Koscielny, Monreal; Maitland-Niles, Torreira, Xhaka (Elneny 61), Kolasinac; Ramsey (Mkhitaryan 34); Lacazette (Iwobi 68), Aubameyang.
Referee: Ovidiu Alin Hategan.

Valencia (1) 2 *(Toni Lato 13, Parejo 53)*
Villarreal (0) 0 26,403
Valencia: (442) Neto; Wass, Roncaglia, Diakhaby, Toni Lato; Torres, Carlos Soler (Gabriel 45), Parejo (Coquelin 62), Goncalo Guedes (Lee 68); Gameiro, Santi Mina.
Villarreal: (442) Fernandez; Ratiu, Funes Mori, Victor Ruiz, Jaume; Morlanes, Trigueros (Javi Fuego 73), Caseres (Fornals 64), Pedraza; Raba (Chukwueze 45), Gerard.
Referee: William Collum.

SEMI-FINALS FIRST LEG

Thursday, 2 May 2019

Arsenal (2) 3 *(Lacazette 18, 26, Aubameyang 90)*
Valencia (1) 1 *(Diakhaby 11)* 48,000
Arsenal: (4231) Cech; Mustafi, Papastathopoulos, Koscielny (Monreal 82), Kolasinac; Guendouzi (Torreira 58), Xhaka; Maitland-Niles, Ozil (Mkhitaryan 75), Aubameyang; Lacazette.
Valencia: (541) Neto; Piccini, Garay, Gabriel, Diakhaby, Gaya; Carlos Soler (Wass 71), Parejo, Roncaglia, Goncalo Guedes (Gameiro 71); Rodrigo (Santi Mina 89).
Referee: Clement Turpin.

Eintracht Frankfurt (1) 1 *(Jovic 23)*
Chelsea (1) 1 *(Pedro 45)* 55,000
Eintracht Frankfurt: (532) Trapp; Da Costa, Abraham, Hasebe, Hinteregger, Falette; Rode, Fernandes (Paciencia 72), Gacinovic (Willems 90); Jovic, Kostic.
Chelsea: (433) Arrizabalaga; Azpilicueta, Luiz, Christensen, Emerson Palmieri; Jorginho, Kante, Loftus-Cheek (Kovacic 82); Pedro, Giroud, Willian (Hazard 61).
Referee: Carlos Del Cerro.

SEMI-FINALS SECOND LEG

Thursday, 9 May 2019

Chelsea (1) 1 *(Loftus-Cheek 28)*
Eintracht Frankfurt (0) 1 *(Jovic 49)* 40,853
Chelsea: (433) Arrizabalaga; Azpilicueta, Christensen (Zappacosta 74), Luiz, Emerson Palmieri; Loftus-Cheek (Barkley 85), Jorginho, Kovacic; Willian (Pedro 62), Giroud (Higuain 96), Hazard.
Eintracht Frankfurt: (4231) Trapp; Da Costa, Abraham, Hinteregger, Falette; Hasebe, Rode (de Guzman 70); Rebic (Haller 90), Gacinovic (Paciencia 118), Kostic; Jovic.
aet; Chelsea won 4-3 on penalties.
Referee: Ovidiu Alin Hategan.

Valencia (1) 2 *(Gameiro 11, 58)*
Arsenal (1) 4 *(Aubameyang 17, 69, 88, Lacazette 50)* 46,000
Valencia: (442) Neto; Piccini (Carlos Soler 56), Garay, Gabriel, Gaya; Wass, Parejo, Coquelin, Goncalo Guedes (Torres 72); Rodrigo (Santi Mina 71), Gameiro.
Arsenal: (343) Cech; Monreal, Papastathopoulos, Koscielny; Maitland-Niles, Xhaka, Torreira (Guendouzi 79), Kolasinac (Mustafi 71); Lacazette, Ozil (Mkhitaryan 62), Aubameyang.
Referee: Danny Makkelie.

EUROPA LEAGUE FINAL 2019

Wednesday, 29 May 2019

(in Baku, attendance 51,370)

Chelsea (0) 4 Arsenal (0) 1

Chelsea: (433) Arrizabalaga; Azpilicueta, Christensen, Luiz, Emerson Palmieri; Kante, Jorginho, Kovacic (Barkley 76); Pedro (Willian 71), Giroud, Hazard (Zappacosta 89).
Scorers: Giroud 49, Pedro 60, Hazard 65 (pen), 72.

Arsenal: (3412) Cech; Papastathopoulos, Koscielny, Monreal (Guendouzi 66); Maitland-Niles, Torreira (Iwobi 66), Xhaka, Kolasinac; Ozil (Willock 78); Lacazette, Aubameyang.
Scorer: Iwobi 69.

Referee: Gianluca Rocchi.

In his last game for Chelsea, Eden Hazard fittingly scores in their 4-1 rout of Arsenal in the Europa League Final in Baku on 29 May. (REUTERS/Phil Noble)

UEFA EUROPA LEAGUE 2019–20

PARTICIPATING CLUBS
The list below is provisional and is subject to pending legal proceedings and final confirmation from UEFA.

GROUP STAGE
Arsenal
Besiktas
Borussia Moenchengladbach
CSKA Moscow
Getafe
KV Mechelen*
Lazio
Lugano
Manchester U
Milan
Oleksandriya
Rennes
Saint-Etienne
Sevilla
Sporting Lisbon
Wolfsberger
Wolfsburg
Plus four losing teams from the UEFA Champions League play-offs (champions route).
Plus two losing teams from the UEFA Champions League play-offs (league route).
Plus four losing teams from UEFA Champions League third qualifying round (league route).
Plus eight winning teams from the UEFA Europa League play-offs (champions route).
Plus 13 winning teams from the UEFA Europa League play-offs (main route).

PLAY-OFF ROUND – CHAMPIONS ROUTE
Ten winning teams from UEFA Europa League third qualifying round (champions route).
Six losing teams from UEFA Champions League third qualifying round (champions route).

PLAY-OFF ROUND – MAIN ROUTE
26 winning teams from UEFA Europa League third qualifying round (main route).

THIRD QUALIFYING ROUND – CHAMPIONS ROUTE
Ten teams eliminated from UEFA Champions League second qualifying round (champions route).
Nine winning teams from UEFA Europa League second qualifying round (champions route).
One team given a bye from UEFA Europa League second qualifying round (champions route).

THIRD QUALIFYING ROUND – MAIN ROUTE
AEK Athens
Austria Vienna
Bnei Yehuda
Braga
Feyenoord
Mariupol
Midtjylland
Rijeka
Sparta Prague
Spartak Moscow
Standard Liege*
Thun
Trabzonspor
Plus two losing teams from UEFA Champions League second qualifying round (league route).
Plus 37 winning teams from the UEFA Europa League second qualifying round (main route).

SECOND QUALIFYING ROUND – CHAMPIONS ROUTE
16 teams eliminated from UEFA Champions League first qualifying round.
Three losing teams from UEFA Champions League preliminary round.

SECOND QUALIFYING ROUND – MAIN ROUTE
AEL Limassol
Antwerp*/Gent*
Aris
Arsenal Tula
Atromitos
AZ Alkmaar
BK Hacken
Eintracht Frankfurt
Esbjerg
Espanyol
Gabala
Jablonec
Lechia Gdansk
Lokomotiv Plovdiv
Luzern
Mlada Boleslav
Osijek
Partizan Belgrade
Roma
Strasbourg
Sturm Graz
Utrecht
Viitorul Constanta
Vitoria de Guimaraes
Wolverhampton Wanderers
Yeni Malatyaspor
Zorya Luhansk
Plus 47 winning teams from the UEFA Europa League first qualifying round.

FIRST QUALIFYING ROUND
Aberdeen
AEK Larnaca
Akademija Pandev
Alashkert
Apollon Limassol
B36 Torshavn
Balzan
Banants
Brann
Breidablik
Brondby
Buducnost Podgorica
Chikhura Sachkhere
Connah's Quay Nomads
Cork City
Cracovia
Crusaders
CSKA Sofia
Cukaricki
DAC Dunajska Streda
Debrecen
Dinamo Minsk
Dinamo Tbilisi
Domzale
FCI Levadia
FCSB
Fehervár
Flora
Fola Esch
Gzira United
Hajduk Split
Hapoel Be'er Sheva
Haugesund
Hibernians
Honved
IFK Norrkoping
Inter Turku
Jeunesse Esch
Kairat
Kauno Zalgiris
Kilmarnock
KR Reykjavik
Kukesi
KuPS Kuopio
Laci
Legia Warsaw
Levski Sofia
Liepaja
Maccabi Haifa
Makedonija GjP
Malmo
Milsami Orhei
Molde
Mura
Narva Trans
Neftci Baku
Olimpija Ljubljana
Ordabasy
Petrocub Hincesti
Pyunik
Radnicki Nis
Radnik Bijeljina
Rangers
RFS
Riteriai
RoPS
Ruzomberok
Sabail
Shakhtyor Soligorsk
Shamrock Rovers
Shkupi
Siroki Brijeg
Spartak Trnava
Speranta Nisporeni
St Patrick's Athletic
Stjarnan
Teuta
Titograd
Tobol
Torpedo Kutaisi
Universitatea Craiova
Vaduz
Ventspils
Vitebsk
Zalgiris Vilnius
Zeta
Zrinjski Mostar
Plus seven winning teams from the UEFA Europa League preliminary round.

PRELIMINARY ROUND
Ballymena United
Barry Town United
Cardiff Metropolitan University
Cliftonville
Engordany
Europa
KI Klaksvik
La Fiorita
NSI Runavik
Prishtina
Progres Niederkorn
Sant Julia
St Joseph's
Tre Fiori
**Pending result of appeal by KV Mechelen to being expelled from European competitions by Belgian FA.*

BRITISH AND IRISH CLUBS IN EUROPE

SUMMARY OF APPEARANCES

EUROPEAN CUP AND CHAMPIONS LEAGUE (1955–2019)

(Winners in brackets) (SE = seasons entered).

ENGLAND	*SE*	*P*	*W*	*D*	*L*	*F*	*A*
Manchester U (3)	28	279	154	66	59	506	264
Liverpool (6)	23	209	117	46	46	393	184
Arsenal	21	201	101	43	57	332	218
Chelsea (1)	15	160	80	46	34	274	142
Manchester C	9	72	34	14	24	138	96
Leeds U	4	40	22	6	12	76	41
Tottenham H	5	47	22	9	16	90	65
Nottingham F (2)	3	20	12	4	4	32	14
Newcastle U	3	24	11	3	10	33	33
Everton	3	10	2	5	3	14	10
Aston Villa (1)	2	15	9	3	3	24	10
Derby Co	2	12	6	2	4	18	12
Wolverhampton W	2	8	2	2	4	12	16
Leicester C	1	10	5	2	3	11	10
Ipswich T	1	4	3	0	1	16	5
Burnley	1	4	2	0	2	8	8
Blackburn R	1	6	1	1	4	5	8

SCOTLAND							
Celtic (1)	33	206	96	35	75	308	243
Rangers	30	161	62	40	59	232	218
Aberdeen	3	12	5	4	3	14	12
Hearts	3	8	2	1	5	8	16
Dundee U	1	8	5	1	2	14	5
Dundee	1	8	5	0	3	20	14
Hibernian	1	6	3	1	2	9	5
Kilmarnock	1	4	1	2	1	4	7
Motherwell	1	2	0	0	2	0	5

WALES							
The New Saints	12	32	8	4	20	33	58
Barry T	6	14	4	1	9	11	38
Rhyl	2	4	0	0	4	1	19
Cwmbran T	1	2	1	0	1	4	4
Llanelli	1	2	1	0	1	1	4
Bangor C	1	2	0	0	2	0	13

NORTHERN IRELAND							
Linfield	28	67	7	23	37	56	118
Glentoran	12	28	3	7	18	20	59
Crusaders	6	14	1	2	11	7	52
Portadown	3	6	0	1	5	3	24
Cliftonville	3	6	0	1	5	1	20
Glenavon	1	2	0	1	1	0	3
Lisburn Distillery	1	2	0	1	1	3	8
Ards	1	2	0	0	2	3	10
Coleraine	1	2	0	0	2	1	11

REPUBLIC OF IRELAND							
Dundalk	10	28	4	9	15	23	53
Shamrock R	9	20	1	6	13	9	33
Shelbourne	6	20	4	8	8	21	31
Bohemians	6	18	4	4	10	13	29
Waterford U	6	14	3	0	11	15	47
Derry C	4	9	1	1	7	9	26
St Patrick's Ath	4	8	0	3	5	2	23
Cork C	3	10	2	1	7	7	16
Dublin C	3	6	1	0	5	3	25
Athlone T	2	4	0	2	2	7	14
Sligo R	2	4	0	0	4	0	9
Limerick	2	4	0	0	4	4	16
Drogheda U	1	4	2	1	1	6	5
Cork Hibernians	1	2	0	0	2	1	7
Cork Celtic	1	2	0	0	2	1	7

UEFA CUP AND EUROPA LEAGUE 1971–2019

ENGLAND	*SE*	*P*	*W*	*D*	*L*	*F*	*A*
Tottenham H (2)	15	140	78	36	26	278	121
Liverpool (3)	14	124	66	34	24	186	94
Aston Villa	13	56	24	14	18	77	60
Ipswich T (1)	10	52	30	10	12	98	53
Everton	9	52	27	8	17	87	64
Manchester U (1)	9	43	18	14	11	57	37
Newcastle U	8	72	42	17	13	123	60
Arsenal	8	54	31	8	15	105	57
Manchester C	8	52	28	13	11	84	51
Leeds U	8	46	20	10	16	66	48
Southampton	7	22	6	9	7	23	20
Blackburn R	6	22	7	8	7	27	26
Chelsea (2)	5	32	22	5	5	64	30
Wolverhampton W	4	20	13	3	4	41	23
West Ham U	4	16	6	3	7	19	16
Fulham	3	39	21	10	8	64	31
Nottingham F	3	20	10	5	5	18	16
Stoke C	3	16	8	4	4	21	16
WBA	3	12	5	2	5	15	13
Middlesbrough	2	25	13	4	8	36	24
QPR	2	12	8	1	3	39	18
Bolton W	2	18	6	10	2	18	14
Derby Co	2	10	5	2	3	32	17
Leicester C	2	4	0	1	3	3	8
Birmingham C	1	8	4	2	2	11	8
Burnley	1	6	2	3	1	7	6
Norwich C	1	6	2	2	2	6	4
Portsmouth	1	6	2	2	2	11	10
Sheffield W	1	4	2	1	1	13	7
Hull C	1	4	2	1	1	4	3
Watford	1	6	2	1	3	10	12
Wigan Ath	1	6	1	2	3	6	7
Millwall	1	2	0	1	1	2	4

SCOTLAND							
Celtic	21	111	45	26	40	166	127
Aberdeen	21	78	24	26	28	98	101
Dundee U	19	82	33	25	24	134	89
Rangers	18	92	37	30	25	117	90
Hearts	14	50	21	10	19	61	62
Hibernian	13	40	15	11	14	57	63
Motherwell	8	26	8	2	16	33	34
St Johnstone	7	24	7	7	10	25	30
Dundee	4	14	6	0	8	24	24
Kilmarnock	3	12	4	2	6	7	14
St Mirren	3	10	2	3	5	9	12
Dunfermline Ath	2	4	0	2	2	4	6
Raith R	1	6	2	1	3	10	8
Livingston	1	4	1	2	1	7	9
Falkirk	1	2	1	0	1	1	2
Inverness CT	1	2	0	1	1	0	1
Gretna	1	2	0	1	1	3	7
Queen of the South	1	2	0	0	2	2	4
Partick Thistle	1	2	0	0	2	0	4

WALES							
Bangor C	10	22	2	2	18	10	61
The New Saints	9	22	2	3	17	16	56
Llanelli	5	12	3	3	6	12	24
Bala T	5	10	3	0	7	7	19
Rhyl	3	8	2	1	5	9	12
Connah's Quay Nomads	3	8	2	1	5	4	11
Newtown	3	8	2	1	5	6	21
UWIC Inter Cardiff	3	6	1	0	5	1	18
Air UK Broughton	3	6	0	4	2	6	9
Cwmbran T	3	6	0	0	6	0	21
Barry T	2	8	2	2	4	10	16
Carmarthen T	2	6	1	0	5	8	21
Cefn Druids	2	4	0	2	2	1	7
Swansea C	1	12	4	4	4	17	10
Prestatyn T	1	4	1	0	3	3	11
Afan Lido	1	2	0	1	1	1	2
Haverfordwest Co	1	2	0	0	2	1	4
Neath	1	2	0	0	2	1	6
Port Talbot T	1	2	0	0	2	1	7
Llandudno T	1	2	0	0	2	0	6
Aberystwith T	1	2	0	0	2	0	9

NORTHERN IRELAND							
Glentoran	18	40	3	8	29	22	97
Linfield	12	34	9	8	17	37	63
Portadown	11	28	3	7	18	16	62

Crusaders	10	22	4	4	14	21	54
Glenavon	9	20	2	2	16	10	49
Coleraine	9	18	1	5	12	9	46
Cliftonville	6	16	3	3	10	10	31
Ballymena U	2	4	1	0	3	2	9
Dungannon Swifts	1	2	1	0	1	1	4
Ards	1	2	1	0	1	4	8
Bangor	1	2	0	0	2	0	6
Lisburn Distillery	1	2	0	0	2	1	11
REPUBLIC OF IRELAND							
Bohemians	14	30	3	9	18	16	56
St Patrick's Ath	10	38	10	7	21	34	57
Cork C	10	30	6	7	17	21	43
Derry C	9	26	7	5	14	30	45
Shamrock R	9	32	7	5	20	27	57
Dundalk	8	26	7	4	15	20	48
Shelbourne	6	12	0	2	10	8	28
Drogheda U	4	12	3	4	5	10	24
Sligo R	4	10	2	4	4	11	13
Longford T	3	6	1	1	4	6	12
Finn Harps	3	6	0	0	6	3	33
Athlone T	1	4	1	2	1	4	5
University College Dublin	1	4	1	0	3	3	8
Limerick	1	2	0	1	1	1	4
Sporting Fingal	1	2	0	0	2	4	6
Galway U	1	2	0	0	2	2	8
Bray W	1	2	0	0	2	0	8

EUROPEAN CUP WINNERS' CUP 1960–1999

ENGLAND	*SE*	*P*	*W*	*D*	*L*	*F*	*A*
Tottenham H (1)	6	33	20	5	8	65	34
Chelsea (2)	5	39	23	10	6	81	28
Liverpool	5	29	16	5	8	57	29
Manchester U (1)	5	31	16	9	6	55	35
West Ham U (1)	4	30	15	6	9	58	42
Arsenal (1)	3	27	15	10	2	48	20
Everton (1)	3	17	11	4	2	25	9
Manchester C (1)	2	18	11	2	5	32	13
Ipswich T	1	6	3	2	1	6	3
Leeds U	1	9	5	3	1	13	3
Leicester C	1	4	2	1	1	8	5
Newcastle U	1	2	1	0	1	2	2
Southampton	1	6	4	0	2	16	8
Sunderland	1	4	3	0	1	5	3
WBA	1	6	2	2	2	8	5
Wolverhampton W	1	4	1	1	2	6	5
SCOTLAND							
Rangers (1)	10	54	27	11	16	100	62
Aberdeen (1)	8	39	22	5	12	79	37
Celtic	8	38	21	4	13	75	37
Dundee U	3	10	3	3	4	9	10
Hearts	3	10	3	3	4	16	14
Dunfermline Ath	2	14	7	2	5	34	14
Airdrieonians	1	2	0	0	2	1	3
Dundee	1	2	0	1	1	3	4
Hibernian	1	6	3	1	2	19	10
Kilmarnock	1	4	1	2	1	5	6
Motherwell	1	2	1	0	1	3	3
St Mirren	1	4	1	2	1	1	2
WALES							
Cardiff C	14	49	16	14	19	67	61
Wrexham	8	28	10	8	10	34	35
Swansea C	7	18	3	4	11	32	37
Bangor C	3	9	1	2	6	5	12
Barry T	1	2	0	0	2	0	7
Borough U	1	4	1	1	2	2	4
Cwmbran T	1	2	0	0	2	2	12
Merthyr Tydfil	1	2	1	0	1	2	3
Newport Co	1	6	2	3	1	12	3
The New Saints (Llansantfraid)	1	2	0	1	1	1	6
NORTHERN IRELAND							
Glentoran	9	22	3	7	12	18	46
Glenavon	5	10	1	3	6	11	25
Ballymena U	4	8	0	0	8	1	25
Coleraine	4	8	0	1	7	7	34
Crusaders	3	6	0	2	4	5	18
Derry C	3	6	1	1	4	1	11
Linfield	3	6	2	0	4	6	11
Ards	2	4	0	1	3	2	17
Bangor	2	4	0	1	3	2	8
Carrick Rangers	1	4	1	0	3	7	12
Cliftonville	1	2	0	0	2	0	8
Distillery	1	2	0	0	2	1	7
Portadown	1	2	1	0	1	4	7
REPUBLIC OF IRELAND							
Shamrock R	6	16	5	2	9	19	27
Shelbourne	4	10	1	1	8	9	20
Bohemians	3	8	2	2	4	6	13
Dundalk	3	8	2	1	5	7	14
Limerick U	3	6	0	1	5	2	11
Waterford U	3	8	1	1	6	6	14
Cork C	2	4	1	0	3	2	9
Cork Hibernians	2	6	2	1	3	7	8
Galway U	2	4	0	0	4	2	11
Sligo R	2	6	1	1	4	5	11
Bray W	1	2	0	1	1	1	3
Cork Celtic	1	2	0	1	1	1	3
Finn Harps	1	2	0	1	1	2	4
Home Farm	1	2	0	1	1	1	7
St Patrick's Ath	1	2	0	0	2	1	8
University College Dublin	1	2	0	1	1	0	1

INTER-CITIES FAIRS CUP 1955–1970

ENGLAND	*SE*	*P*	*W*	*D*	*L*	*F*	*A*
Leeds U (2)	5	53	28	17	8	92	40
Birmingham C	4	25	14	6	5	51	38
Liverpool	4	22	12	4	6	46	15
Arsenal (1)	3	24	12	5	7	46	19
Chelsea	3	20	10	5	5	33	24
Everton	3	12	7	2	3	22	15
Newcastle U (1)	3	24	13	6	5	37	21
Nottingham F	2	6	3	0	3	8	9
Sheffield W	2	10	5	0	5	25	18
Burnley	1	8	4	3	1	16	5
Coventry C	1	4	3	0	1	9	8
London XI	1	8	4	1	3	14	13
Manchester U	1	11	6	3	2	29	10
Southampton	1	6	2	3	1	11	6
WBA	1	4	1	1	2	7	9
SCOTLAND							
Hibernian	7	36	18	5	13	66	60
Dunfermline Ath	5	28	16	3	9	49	31
Kilmarnock	4	20	8	3	9	34	32
Dundee U	3	10	5	1	4	11	12
Hearts	3	12	4	4	4	20	20
Rangers	3	18	8	4	6	27	17
Celtic	2	6	1	3	2	9	10
Aberdeen	1	4	2	1	1	4	4
Dundee	1	8	5	1	2	14	6
Morton	1	2	0	0	2	3	9
Partick Thistle	1	4	3	0	1	10	7
NORTHERN IRELAND							
Glentoran	4	8	1	1	6	7	22
Coleraine	2	8	2	1	5	15	23
Linfield	2	4	1	0	3	3	11
REPUBLIC OF IRELAND							
Drumcondra	2	6	2	0	4	8	19
Dundalk	2	6	1	1	4	4	25
Shamrock R	2	4	0	2	2	4	6
Cork Hibernians	1	2	0	0	2	1	6
Shelbourne	1	5	1	2	2	3	4
St Patrick's Ath	1	2	0	0	2	4	9

FIFA CLUB WORLD CUP 2018

Formerly known as the FIFA Club World Championship, this tournament is played annually between the champion clubs from all 6 continental confederations, although since 2007 the champions of Oceania must play a qualifying play-off against the champion club of the host country.

(Finals in United Arab Emirates)

■*Denotes player sent off.*

Wednesday 12 December 2018

Al-Ain (1) 3 *(Shiotani 45, Doumbia 49, Berg 85)*

Team Wellington (3) 3 *(Barcia 11, Clapham 15, Ilich 44)* 15,279

Al-Ain: Khalid Eisa; Mohamed Ahmad, Ismail Ahmed, Mohanad Salem (Bandar Al Ahbabi 38), Shiotani, Ahmed Barman (Rayan Yaslem 118), Mohamed Abdulrahman■, Doumbia (Diaky 63), Hussein Elshahat, Caio, Jamal Maroof (Berg 78).
Team Wellington: Basalaj; Gulley, Hilliar, Schrijvers, Barcia, Ilich, Cameron (Molloy 57 (Allen 120)), Sinclair (Kilkolly 80), Clapham (Hailemariam 74), Bevin, Watson.
Referee: Ryuji Sato (Japan).
aet; Al-Ain won 4-3 on penalties.

QUARTER FINALS

Saturday 15 December 2018

Kashima Antlers (0) 3 *(Nagaki 49, Serginho 69 (pen), Abe 84)*

Guadalajara (1) 2 *(Zaldivar 3, Hugo Leonardo 90 (og))* 3,997

Kashima Antlers: Kwoun; Uchida, Jung, Shoji, Yamamoto, Endo (Nishi 87), Nagaki, Hugo Leonardo, Leandro (Abe 46), Serginho, Doi (Anzai 80).
Guadalajara: Gudino; Van Rankin, Pereira, Marin, Ponce, Brizuela, Lopez (Sandoval 71), Perez, Pineda (Godinez 85), Pulido, Zaldivar.
Referee: Jair Marrufo (USA).

Saturday 15 December 2018

Esperance de Tunis (0) 0

Al-Ain (2) 3 *(Mohamed Ahmed 2, Hussain Elshahat 16, Bandar Al Ahbabi 60)* 21,333

Esperance de Tunis: Ben Cherifia; Derbali, Dhaouadi, Chemmam (Machani 70), Ben Mohamed, Coulibaly, Chaaleli (Meskini 46), Badri, Kom (Rjaibi 64), Belaili, Khenissi.
Al-Ain: Khalid Eisa; Bandar Al Ahbabi (Berg 80), Ismail Ahmed, Mohamed Ahmad, Shiotani, Ahmed Barman, Rayan Yaslem (Amer Abdulrahman 67), Mohamed Fayez, Doumbia (Yahir Nader 85), Hussein Elshahat, Caio.
Referee: Jair Marrufo (USA).

MATCH FOR FIFTH PLACE

Tuesday 18 December 2018

Esperance de Tunis (1) 1 *(Belaili 38 (pen))*

Guadalajara (1) 1 *(Sandoval 5 (pen))* 5,883

Esperance de Tunis: Jeridi; Derbali, Dhaouadi, Chammam, Rebai■, Coulibaly, Kom (Machani 90), Badri■, Belaili, Ben Mohammed (Bguir 90), Mejri (Khenissi 90).
Guadalajara: Gudino (Jimenez 90); Van Rankin, Pereira, Marin, Ponce, Brizuela, Perez, Sandoval (Pineda 65), Cervantes (Salcido 46), Godinez, Zaldivar.
Referee: Matthew Conger (New Zealand).
Esperance de Tunis won 6-5 on penalties.

SEMI-FINALS

Tuesday 18 December 2018

River Plate (2) 2 *(Borre 11, 16)*

Al-Ain (1) 2 *(Berg 3, Caio 51)* 21,383

River Plate: Armani, Montiel, Maidana, Pinola, Casco, Fernandez (Quintero 55), Ponzio (De La Cruz 87), Palacios (Perez 55), Martinez (Scocco 91), Borre, Pratto.
Al-Ain: Khalid Eisa, Mohamed Ahmad, Ismail Ahmed, Mohammed Fayez, Shiotani, Ahmed Barman (Amer Abdulrahman 82), Mohamed Abdulrahman (Rayan Yaslem 64), Doumbia (Yahia Nader 107), Hussein Elshahat, Caio, Berg (Bandar Al Ahbabi 75).
Referee: Gianluca Rocchi (Italy).
aet; Al-Ain won 5-4 on penalties.

Wednesday 19 December 2018

Kashima Antlers (0) 1 *(Doi 78)*

Real Madrid (1) 3 *(Bale 44, 53, 55)* 30,554

Kashima Antlers: Kwoun, Nishi (Anzai 56), Jung, Shoji, Yamamoto, Endo (Leandro 81), Nagaki (Uchida 46), Hugo Leonardo, Abe, Serginho, Doi.
Real Madrid: Courtois, Carvajal, Varane, Ramos, Marcelo, Modric, Llorente, Kroos, Vazquez (Isco 68), Benzema, Bale (Asensio 60 (Casemiro 74)).
Referee: Wilton Sampaio (Brazil).

MATCH FOR THIRD PLACE

Kashima Antlers (0) 0

River Plate (1) 4 *(Zuculini 24, Martinez Quarta 73, 90, Borre 89 (pen))* 13,550

Kashima Antlers: Kwoun (Sogahata 23), Uchida (Ogasawara 76), Jung, Inukai, Anzai, Endo (Nishi 65), Nagaki, Hugo Leonardo, Abe, Serginho, Doi.
River Plate: Lux, Moreira (Fernandez 46), Martinez Quarta, Pinola, Casco, Mayada, Zuculini, Palacios (Quintero 46), De La Cruz (Martinez 69), Borre, Alvarez.
Referee: Gianluca Rocchi (Italy).

FIFA CLUB WORLD CUP FINAL 2018

Abu Dhabi, Saturday 22 December 2018

Real Madrid (1) 4 *(Modric 14, Llorente 60, Ramos 79, Nader 90 (og))*

Al-Ain (0) 1 *(Shiotani 86)* 40,696

Real Madrid: Courtois, Carvajal, Varane, Ramos, Marcelo, Modric, Llorente (Casemiro 82), Kroos (Ceballos 70), Vazquez (Vinicius 84), Benzema, Bale.
Al-Ain: Khalid Eisa, Mohamed Ahmad (Bandar Al Ahbabi 64), Ismail Ahmed, Mohammed Fayez, Shiotani, Rayan Yaslem, Mohamed Abdulrahman (Amer Abdulrahman 67), Doumbia, Hussein Elshahat, Caio, Berg (Yahia Nader 75).
Referee: Jair Marrufo (USA).

PREVIOUS FINALS

2000 Corinthians beat Vasco da Gama 4-3 on penalties after 0-0 draw
2001–04 Not contested
2005 Sao Paulo beat Liverpool 1-0
2006 Internacional beat Barcelona 1-0
2007 AC Milan beat Boca Juniors 4-2
2008 Manchester U beat Liga De Quito 1-0
2009 Barcelona beat Estudiantes 2-1
2010 Internazionale beat TP Mazembe Englebert 3-0
2011 Barcelona beat Santos 4-0
2012 Corinthians beat Chelsea 1-0
2013 Bayern Munich beat Raja Casablanca 2-0
2014 Real Madrid beat San Lorenzo 2-0
2015 Barcelona beat River Plate 3-0
2016 Real Madrid beat Kashima Antlers 4-2 (*aet.*)
2017 Real Madrid beat Gremio 1-0
2018 Real Madrid beat Al-Ain 4-1

WORLD CLUB CHAMPIONSHIP

Played annually up to 1974 and intermittently since then between the winners of the European Cup and the winners of the South American Champions Cup – known as the Copa Libertadores. In 1980 the winners were decided by one match arranged in Tokyo in February 1981 which remained the venue until 2004, when the match was superseded by the FIFA Club World Championship. AC Milan replaced Marseille who had been stripped of their European Cup title in 1993.

1960 Real Madrid beat Penarol 0-0, 5-1
1961 Penarol beat Benfica 0-1, 5-0, 2-1
1962 Santos beat Benfica 3-2, 5-2
1963 Santos beat AC Milan 2-4, 4-2, 1-0
1964 Inter-Milan beat Independiente 0-1, 2-0, 1-0
1965 Inter-Milan beat Independiente 3-0, 0-0
1966 Penarol beat Real Madrid 2-0, 2-0
1967 Racing Club beat Celtic 0-1, 2-1, 1-0
1968 Estudiantes beat Manchester United 1-0, 1-1
1969 AC Milan beat Estudiantes 3-0, 1-2
1970 Feyenoord beat Estudiantes 2-2, 1-0
1971 Nacional beat Panathinaikos* 1-1, 2-1
1972 Ajax beat Independiente 1-1, 3-0
1973 Independiente beat Juventus* 1-0
1974 Atlético Madrid* beat Independiente 0-1, 2-0
1975 Independiente and Bayern Munich could not agree dates; no matches.
1976 Bayern Munich beat Cruzeiro 2-0, 0-0
1977 Boca Juniors beat Borussia Moenchengladbach* 2-2, 3-0
1978 Not contested
1979 Olimpia beat Malmö* 1-0, 2-1
1980 Nacional beat Nottingham Forest 1-0
1981 Flamengo beat Liverpool 3-0
1982 Penarol beat Aston Villa 2-0
1983 Gremio Porto Alegre beat SV Hamburg 2-1
1984 Independiente beat Liverpool 1-0
1985 Juventus beat Argentinos Juniors 4-2 on penalties after 2-2 draw
1986 River Plate beat Steaua Bucharest 1-0
1987 FC Porto beat Penarol 2-1 after extra time
1988 Nacional (Uru) beat PSV Eindhoven 7-6 on penalties after 1-1 draw
1989 AC Milan beat Atletico Nacional (Col) 1-0 after extra time
1990 AC Milan beat Olimpia 3-0
1991 Crvena Zvezda beat Colo Colo 3-0
1992 Sao Paulo beat Barcelona 2-1
1993 Sao Paulo beat AC Milan 3-2
1994 Velez Sarsfield beat AC Milan 2-0
1995 Ajax beat Gremio Porto Alegre 4-3 on penalties after 0-0 draw
1996 Juventus beat River Plate 1-0
1997 Borussia Dortmund beat Cruzeiro 2-0
1998 Real Madrid beat Vasco da Gama 2-1
1999 Manchester U beat Palmeiras 1-0
2000 Boca Juniors beat Real Madrid 2-1
2001 Bayern Munich beat Boca Juniors 1-0 after extra time
2002 Real Madrid beat Olimpia 2-0
2003 Boca Juniors beat AC Milan 3-1 on penalties after 1-1 draw
2004 Porto beat Once Caldas 8-7 on penalties after 0-0 draw

**European Cup runners-up; winners declined to take part.*

EUROPEAN SUPER CUP 2018

Played annually between the winners of the European Champions' Cup and the European Cup-Winners' Cup (UEFA Cup from 2000; UEFA Europa League from 2010). AC Milan replaced Marseille in 1993–94.

Tallinn, Wednesday 15 August 2018, attendance 12,424

Atletico Madrid (1) 4 *(Costa 1, 79, Saul 98, Koke 104)*

Real Madrid (1) 2 *(Benzema 27, Ramos 63 (pen))*

Atletico Madrid: Oblak; Juanfran, Savic, Godin, Lucas, Lemar (Partey 90), Rodri (Vitolo 71), Saul, Koke, Costa (Gimenez 109), Greizmann (Correa 57).

Real Madrid: Navas; Carvajal, Ramos, Varane, Marcelo, Kroos (Mayoral 102), Casemiro (Ceballos 76), Isco (Vasquez 83), Bale, Benzema, Asensio (Modric 57).
aet.
Referee: Szymon Marciniak (Poland).

PREVIOUS MATCHES

1972 Ajax beat Rangers 3-1, 3-2
1973 Ajax beat AC Milan 0-1, 6-0
1974 Not contested
1975 Dynamo Kyiv beat Bayern Munich 1-0, 2-0
1976 Anderlecht beat Bayern Munich 4-1, 1-2
1977 Liverpool beat Hamburg 1-1, 6-0
1978 Anderlecht beat Liverpool 3-1, 1-2
1979 Nottingham F beat Barcelona 1-0, 1-1
1980 Valencia beat Nottingham F 1-0, 1-2
1981 Not contested
1982 Aston Villa beat Barcelona 0-1, 3-0
1983 Aberdeen beat Hamburg 0-0, 2-0
1984 Juventus beat Liverpool 2-0
1985 Juventus v Everton not contested due to UEFA ban on English clubs
1986 Steaua Bucharest beat Dynamo Kyiv 1-0
1987 FC Porto beat Ajax 1-0, 1-0
1988 KV Mechelen beat PSV Eindhoven 3-0, 0-1
1989 AC Milan beat Barcelona 1-1, 1-0
1990 AC Milan beat Sampdoria 1-1, 2-0
1991 Manchester U beat Crvena Zvezda 1-0
1992 Barcelona beat Werder Bremen 1-1, 2-1
1993 Parma beat AC Milan 0-1, 2-0
1994 AC Milan beat Arsenal 0-0, 2-0
1995 Ajax beat Zaragoza 1-1, 4-0
1996 Juventus beat Paris Saint-Germain 6-1, 3-1
1997 Barcelona beat Borussia Dortmund 2-0, 1-1
1998 Chelsea beat Real Madrid 1-0
1999 Lazio beat Manchester U 1-0
2000 Galatasaray beat Real Madrid 2-1
2001 Liverpool beat Bayern Munich 3-2
2002 Real Madrid beat Feyenoord 3-1
2003 AC Milan beat Porto 1-0
2004 Valencia beat Porto 2-1
2005 Liverpool beat CSKA Moscow 3-1
2006 Sevilla beat Barcelona 3-0
2007 AC Milan beat Sevilla 3-1
2008 Zenit beat Manchester U 2-1
2009 Barcelona beat Shakhtar Donetsk 1-0
2010 Atletico Madrid beat Internazionale 2-0
2011 Barcelona beat Porto 2-0
2012 Atletico Madrid beat Chelsea 4-1
2013 Bayern Munch beat Chelsea 5-4 on penalties after 2-2 draw
2014 Real Madrid beat Sevilla 2-0
2015 Barcelona beat Sevilla 5-4
2016 Real Madrid beat Sevilla 3-2
2017 Real Madrid beat Manchester U 2-1
2018 Atletico Madrid beat Real Madrid 4-2 after extra time

INTERNATIONAL DIRECTORY

The directory provides the latest available information on international and club football in the 211 national associations in the six Confederations of FIFA, the world governing body. This includes addresses, foundation dates and team colours. FIFA-recognised internationals played in season 2018–19 (i.e. *16 July 2018 to 14 July 2019*) are listed as well as league and cup champions at club level. In Europe, the latest league tables, cup winners and top scorers for the 55 UEFA nations are given, together with all-time league and cup honours. (Key to table symbols used: * team relegated, *+ team relegated after play-offs, + team not relegated after play-offs.)

The four home nations, England, Scotland, Northern Ireland and Wales, are dealt with elsewhere in the Yearbook; but basic details appear in this directory. Gozo is included here for its close links with Maltese football. Northern Cyprus is not a member of FIFA or UEFA and is the subject of an international territorial dispute. Kosovo was granted full membership of both FIFA and UEFA in May 2016 and entered World Cup 2018 qualification in September 2016, followed by participation in the 2018–19 UEFA Nations League and Euro 2020 qualifying. FYR Macedonia's results are now credited to North Macedonia, its new name from February 2019. Swaziland was renamed Eswatini in April 2018.

There are currently 12 associate members and others who have affiliation to their confederations. The associate members are: AFC: Northern Mariana Islands; CAF: Reunion, Zanzibar; CONCACAF: Bonaire, French Guiana, Guadeloupe, Martinique, Saint-Martin, Sint Maarten; OFC: Kiribati, Niue, Tuvalu. Matches between full members and associate members are indicated with †.

EUROPE (UEFA)

ALBANIA

Football Association of Albania, Rruga e Elbasanit, 1000 Tirana.
Founded: 1930. *FIFA:* 1932; *UEFA:* 1954. *National Colours:* Red shirts with white trim, black shorts, red socks.

International matches 2018–19

Israel (h) 1-0, Scotland (a) 0-2, Jordan (h) 0-0, Israel (a) 0-2, Scotland (h) 0-4, Wales (h) 1-0, Turkey (h) 0-2, Andorra (a) 3-0, Iceland (a) 0-1, Moldova (h) 2-0.

League Championship wins (1930–37; 1945–2019)

KF Tirana 24 (formerly SK Tirana; includes 17 Nentori 8); Dinamo Tirana 18; Partizani Tirana 16; Vllaznia Shkoder 9; Skenderbeu Korce 8; Elbasani 2 (incl. Labinoti 1); Flamurtari Vlore 1; Teuta Durres 1; Kukesi 1.

Cup wins (1948–2019)

KF Tirana 16 (formerly SK Tirana; includes 17 Nentori 8); Partizani Tirana 15; Dinamo Tirana 13; Vllaznia 6; Flamurtari Vlore 4; Teuta Durres3; Elbasani 2 (incl. Labinoti 1); Besa 2; Laci 2; Kukesi 2; Apolonia Fier 1; Skenderbeu Korce 1.

Albanian Superliga 2018–19

	P	*W*	*D*	*L*	*F*	*A*	*GD*	*Pts*
Partizani Tirana	36	20	10	6	45	22	23	70
Kukesi	36	17	8	11	42	29	13	59
Teuta	36	15	12	9	43	36	7	57
Skenderbeu	36	17	4	15	45	30	15	55
Flamurtari	36	15	9	12	35	32	3	54
Laci	36	12	13	11	33	30	3	49
KF Tirana	36	12	11	13	44	35	9	47
Luftetari	36	13	8	15	37	39	–2	47
Kastrioti Kruje*†	36	12	6	18	35	53	–18	42
Kamza*	36	4	5	27	13	66	–53	17

† Kastrioti Kruje demoted following a violent assault on a referee.
Top scorer: Reginaldo (Kukesi) 13.
Cup Final: Kukesi 2, KF Tirana 1.

ANDORRA

Federacio Andorrana de Futbol, Avda Carlemany 67, 3er Pis, Apartado postal 65, Escaldes-Engordany.
Founded: 1994. *FIFA:* 1996; *UEFA:* 1996. *National Colours:* All red.

International matches 2018–19

UAE (n) 0-0, Latvia (a) 0-0, Kazakhstan (h) 1-1, Georgia (a) 0-3, Kazakhstan (a) 0-4, Georgia (h) 1-1, Latvia (h) 0-0, Iceland (h) 0-2, Albania (h) 0-3, Moldova (a) 0-1, France (h) 0-4.

League Championship wins (1996–2019)

FC Santa Coloma 13; Principat 3; Encamp 2; Sant Julia 2; Ranger's 2; Lusitanos 2; Constel-lacio Esportiva 1.

Cup wins (1991, 1994–2019)

FC Santa Coloma 10*; Principat 6*; Sant Julia 5; UE Santa Coloma 3; Constel-lacio Esportiva 1; Lusitanos 1; Engordany 1.
* *Includes one unofficial title.*

Andorran Primera Divisio Qualifying Table 2018–19

	P	*W*	*D*	*L*	*F*	*A*	*GD*	*Pts*
Sant Julia	21	13	6	2	42	16	26	45
FC Santa Coloma	21	12	7	2	32	12	20	43
Inter Club d'Escaldes	21	12	4	5	30	21	9	40
Engordany	21	8	7	6	26	24	2	31
Ordino	21	7	2	12	27	32	–5	23
UE Santa Coloma	21	5	6	10	25	29	–4	21
Lusitanos	21	5	4	12	21	38	–17	19
Encamp	21	2	4	15	16	47	–31	10

Championship Round 2018–19

	P	*W*	*D*	*L*	*F*	*A*	*GD*	*Pts*
FC Santa Coloma	27	15	9	3	41	18	23	54
Sant Julia	27	15	8	4	52	26	26	53
Inter Club d'Escaldes	27	15	6	6	39	27	12	51
Engordany	27	8	9	10	30	34	–4	33

Relegation Round 2018–19

	P	*W*	*D*	*L*	*F*	*A*	*GD*	*Pts*
Ordino	27	10	3	14	34	39	–5	33
UE Santa Coloma	27	8	8	11	33	32	1	32
Lusitanos*+	27	5	6	16	22	46	–24	21
Encamp*	27	5	5	17	24	53	–29	20

Top scorer: Pi (FC Santa Coloma) 10.
Cup Final: Engordany 2, FC Santa Coloma 0.

ARMENIA

Football Federation of Armenia, Khanjyan Street 27, 0010 Yerevan.
Founded: 1992. *FIFA:* 1992; *UEFA:* 1993. *National Colours:* Red shirts with white trim, red shorts, red socks.

International matches 2018–19

Liechtenstein (h) 2-1, North Macedonia (a) 0-2, Gibraltar (h) 0-1, North Macedonia (h) 4-0, Gibraltar (a) 6-2, Liechtenstein (a) 2-2, Bosnia-Herzegovina (a) 1-2, Finland (h) 0-2, Liechtenstein (h) 3-0, Greece (a) 3-2.

League Championship wins (1992–2019)

Pyunik 14 (incl. Homenetmen 1*); Shirak 4*; Araks 2 (incl. Tsement 1); Alashkert 3; Ararat Yerevan 1; FK Yerevan 1; Ulisses 1; Banants 1; Ararat-Armenia 1.
* *Includes one unofficial shared title.*

Cup wins (1992–2019)

Pyunik (incl. Homenetmen 1) 8; Mika 6; Ararat Yerevan 5; Banants 3; Tsement 2; Shirak 2; Gandzasar Kapan 1; Alashkert 1.
See also Russia section for Armenian club honours in Soviet era 1936–91.

Armenian Premier League 2018–19

	P	*W*	*D*	*L*	*F*	*A*	*GD*	*Pts*
Ararat-Armenia	32	18	7	7	53	28	25	61
Pyunik	32	18	6	8	46	32	14	60
Banants	32	14	10	8	43	35	8	52
Alashkert	32	15	6	11	37	27	10	51
Lori	32	11	11	10	42	40	2	44
Gandzasar Kapan	32	10	8	14	38	33	5	38
Shirak	32	7	15	10	26	30	–4	36
Artsakh	32	6	10	16	25	49	–24	28
Ararat Yerevan	32	5	7	20	24	60	–36	22

Top scorer: Desire (Lori) 17.
Cup Final: Alashkert 1, Lori 0.

AUSTRIA

Oesterreichischer Fussball-Bund, Ernst-Happel Stadion, Sektor A/F, Meiereistrasse 7, Wien 1021.

Founded: 1904. *FIFA:* 1905; *UEFA:* 1954. *National Colours:* Red shirts, white shorts, red socks.

International matches 2018–19

Sweden (h) 2-0, Bosnia-Herzegovina (a) 0-1, Northern Ireland (h) 1-0, Denmark (a) 0-2, Bosnia-Herzegovina (h) 0-0, Northern Ireland (a) 2-1, Poland (h) 0-1, Israel (a) 2-4. Slovenia (h) 1-0, North Macedonia (a) 4-1.

League Championship wins (1912–2019)

Rapid Vienna 32; Austria Vienna (formerly Amateure) 24; Red Bull Salzburg 13 (incl. Austria Salzburg 3); Wacker Innsbruck 10 (incl. Swarovski Tirol 2, Tirol Innsbruck 3); Admira Vienna (now Admira Wacker Modling) 9 (incl. Wacker Vienna 1); First Vienna 6; Wiener Sportklub 3; Sturm Graz 3; WAF 1; WAC 1; Floridsdorfer 1; Hakoah 1; LASK Linz 1; Voest Linz 1; GAK Graz 1.

Cup wins (1919–2019)

Austria Vienna (formerly Amateure) 27; Rapid Vienna 14; Wacker Innsbruck 7 (incl. Swarovski Tirol 1); Admira Vienna (now Admira Wacker Modling) 6 (incl. Wacker Vienna 1); Red Bull Salzburg 6; Sturm Graz 5; GAK Graz 4; First Vienna 3; WAC 2; Ried 2; WAF 1; Wiener Sportklub 1; Linz ASK 1; Kremser 1; Stockerau 1; Karnten 1; Horn 1; Pasching 1.

Austrian Bundesliga Qualifying Table 2018–19

	P	*W*	*D*	*L*	*F*	*A*	*GD*	*Pts*
Red Bull Salzburg	22	17	4	1	51	18	33	55
LASK Linz	22	13	7	2	40	19	21	46
Sturm Graz	22	7	10	5	26	23	3	31
Wolfsberger	22	7	9	6	32	31	1	30
Austria Vienna	22	9	3	10	29	28	1	30
St Polten	22	8	6	8	26	29	–3	30
Mattersburg	22	8	5	9	28	36	–8	29
Rapid Vienna	22	7	6	9	26	29	–3	27
Hartberg	22	7	5	10	35	45	–10	26
Admira Wacker Modling	22	5	6	11	26	42	–16	21
Rheindorf Altach	22	4	6	12	30	32	–2	18
Wacker Innsbruck	22	4	5	13	17	34	–17	17

Championship Round 2018–19

	P	*W*	*D*	*L*	*F*	*A*	*GD*	*Pts*
Red Bull Salzburg	32	25	5	2	79	27	52	52
LASK Linz	32	18	9	5	59	31	28	40
Wolfsberger	32	12	10	10	47	47	0	31
Austria Vienna	32	12	6	14	45	48	–3	27
Sturm Graz	32	10	10	12	37	40	–3	24
St Polten	32	9	9	14	32	50	–18	21

Relegation Round 2018–19

	P	*W*	*D*	*L*	*F*	*A*	*GD*	*Pts*
Rapid Vienna	32	13	7	12	48	44	4	32
Mattersburg	32	12	7	13	41	48	–7	28
Rheindorf Altach	32	9	10	13	48	44	4	28
Admira Wacker Modling	32	8	9	15	42	62	–20	22
Hartberg	32	10	5	17	48	66	–18	22
Wacker Innsbruck*	32	8	5	19	32	51	–19	20

Top scorer: Dabour (Red Bull Salzburg) 20.
Cup Final: Red Bull Salzburg 2, Rapid Vienna 0.

AZERBAIJAN

Association of Football Federations of Azerbaijan, 2208 Nobel prospekti, 1025 Baku.
Founded: 1992. *FIFA:* 1994; *UEFA:* 1994. *National Colours:* All red.

International matches 2018–19

Kosovo (h) 0-0, Malta (a) 1-1, Faeroe Islands (a) 3-0, Malta (h) 1-1, Faeroe Islands (h) 2-0, Kosovo (a) 0-4, Croatia (a) 1-2, Lithuania (h) 0-0, Hungary (h) 1-3, Slovakia (h) 1-5.

League Championship wins (1992–2019)

Neftchi 8; Qarabag 7; Kapaz 3; Shamkir 3*; FK Baku 2; Inter Baku (now Keshla) 2; Turan 1; Khazar Lankaran 1.
* *Includes one unofficial title.*

Cup wins (1992–2019)

Neftchi 7*; Qarabag 6; Kapaz 4; FK Baku 3; Khazar Lankaran 3; Inshatchi 1; Shafa 1; Keshla (formerly Inter Baku) 1; Gabala 1.
* *Includes one unofficial title.*

Azerbaijani Premyer Liqası 2018–19

	P	*W*	*D*	*L*	*F*	*A*	*GD*	*Pts*
Qarabag	28	20	6	2	65	21	44	66
Neftchi	28	17	7	4	52	26	26	58
Sabail	28	12	5	11	34	37	–3	41
Gabala	28	9	9	10	31	33	–2	36
Zira	28	8	7	13	30	40	–10	31
Sumqayit	28	8	5	15	24	42	–18	29
Sabah	28	7	6	15	20	41	–21	27
Keshla*	28	6	5	17	29	45	–16	23

Top scorer: Madatov (Gabala) 16.
Cup Final: Gabala 1, Sumqayit 0.

BELARUS

Belarus Football Federation, Prospekt Pobeditelei 20/3, 220020 Minsk.
Founded: 1989. *FIFA:* 1992; *UEFA:* 1993. *National Colours:* All red with white trim.

International matches 2018–19

San Marino (h) 5-0, Moldova (a) 0-0, Luxembourg (h) 1-0, Moldova (h) 0-0, Luxembourg (a) 2-0, San Marino (a) 2-0, Netherlands (a) 0-4, Northern Ireland (a) 1-2, Germany (h) 0-2, Northern Ireland (h) 0-1.

League Championship wins (1992–2018)

BATE Borisov 15; Dinamo Minsk 7; Slavia Mozyr (incl. MPKC 1) 2; Dnepr Mogilev 1; Belshina Bobruisk 1; Gomel 1; Shakhtyor Soligorsk 1.

Cup wins (1992–2019)

Dinamo Minsk 3; Belshina Bobruisk 3; Shakhtyor Soligorsk 3; BATE Borisov 3; Dinamo Brest 3; Slavia Mozyr (incl. MPKC 1) 2; Gomel 2; MTZ-RIPA 2; Naftan Novopolotsk 2; Neman Grodno 1; Dinamo 93 Minsk 1; Lokomotiv 96 1; FC Minsk 1; Torpedo-BelAZ Zhodino 1.
See also Russia section for Belarusian club honours in Soviet era 1936–91.

Belarusian Vysheyshaya Liga 2018

	P	*W*	*D*	*L*	*F*	*A*	*GD*	*Pts*
BATE Borisov	30	23	4	3	55	24	31	73
Shakhtyor Soligorsk	30	19	7	4	45	14	31	64
Dinamo Minsk	30	18	9	3	41	17	24	63
Vitebsk	30	19	5	6	47	20	27	62
Torpedo-BelAZ Zhodino	30	16	7	7	36	18	18	55
Dinamo Brest	30	14	10	6	52	30	22	52
Neman Grodno	30	12	7	11	31	32	–1	43
Slutsk	30	11	3	16	26	36	–10	36
Gorodeya	30	9	7	14	31	33	–2	34
Isloch Minsk Raion	30	8	9	13	20	37	–17	33
Minsk	30	7	9	14	34	42	–8	30
Gomel	30	7	7	16	16	36	–20	28
Luch Minsk	30	4	12	14	24	44	–20	24
Tarpeda	30	6	6	18	20	41	–21	24
Smolevichy-STI*	30	5	9	16	21	39	–18	24
Dnepr Mogilev*	30	3	7	20	17	53	–36	16

Top scorer: Savitski (Dinamo Brest) 15.
Cup Final: Shakhtyor Soligorsk 2, Vitebsk 0.

BELGIUM

Union Royale Belge des Societes de Football-Association, 145 Avenue Houba de Strooper, B-1020 Bruxelles.
Founded: 1895. *FIFA:* 1904; *UEFA:* 1954. *National Colours:* All red.

International matches 2018–19

Scotland (a) 4-0, Iceland (a) 3-0, Switzerland (h) 2-1, Netherlands (h) 1-1, Iceland (h) 2-0, Switzerland (h) 2-5, Russia (h) 3-1, Cyprus (a) 2-0, Kazakhstan (h) 3-0, Scotland (h) 3-0.

League Championship wins (1896–2019)

Anderlecht 34; Club Brugge 15; Union St Gilloise 11; Standard Liege 10; Beerschot VAC (became Germinal) 7; RC Brussels 6; RFC Liege 5; Daring Brussels 5; Antwerp 4; Lierse 4; Mechelen 4; Genk 4; Cercle Brugge 3; Beveren 2; RWD Molenbeek 1; Gent 1.

Cup wins (1912–14; 1927; 1935; 1954–2019)

Club Brugge 11; Anderlecht 9; Standard Liege 8; Genk 4; Gent 3; Union Saint-Gilloise 2; Antwerp 2; Cercle Brugge 2; Lierse 2; Beerschot VAC (became Germinal) 2; Beveren 2; Waterschei (became Racing Genk) 2; Mechelen 2; Beerschot Antwerpen Club (incl. Germinal Ekeren) 2; Zulte Waregem 2; Lokeren 2; Racing 1; Daring 1; Tournai 1; KFC Waregem 1; RFC Liege 1; Westerlo 1; La Louviere 1.

Belgian First Division A Qualifying Table 2018–19

	P	*W*	*D*	*L*	*F*	*A*	*GD*	*Pts*
Genk	30	18	9	3	63	31	32	63
Club Brugge	30	16	8	6	64	32	32	56
Standard Liege	30	15	8	7	49	35	14	53
Anderlecht	30	15	6	9	49	34	15	51
Gent	30	15	5	10	53	45	8	50
Antwerp	30	14	7	9	39	34	5	49

	P	W	D	L	F	A	GD	Pts
Sint-Truiden	30	12	11	7	47	36	11	47
Kortrijk	30	12	7	11	44	42	2	43
Sporting Charleroi	30	12	6	12	43	43	0	42
Royal Excel Mouscron	30	11	7	12	33	33	0	40
Zulte Waregem	30	8	9	13	49	60	–11	33
Eupen	30	10	2	18	34	57	–23	32
Cercle Brugge	30	7	7	16	35	59	–24	28
Oostende	30	6	9	15	29	52	–23	27
Waasland-Beveren	30	5	12	13	37	50	–13	27
Lokeren*	30	5	5	20	28	53	–25	20

NB: Points earned in Qualifying phase are halved and rounded up at start of Championship Play-off phase.

Championship Play-offs 2018–19

	P	W	D	L	F	A	GD	Pts
Genk	10	6	2	2	19	8	11	52
Club Brugge	10	7	1	2	19	11	8	50
Standard Liege	10	4	1	5	17	16	1	40
Antwerp†	10	4	2	4	12	16	–4	39
Gent	10	3	1	6	10	15	–5	35
Anderlecht	10	1	3	6	8	19	–11	32

† *Qualified for Europa League play-off final.*

Europa League Play-offs 2018–19
Group A

	P	W	D	L	F	A	GD	Pts
Sporting Charleroi	10	7	1	2	20	7	13	22
Sint-Truiden	10	4	5	1	16	13	3	17
Westerlo†	10	3	3	4	13	12	1	12
Oostende	10	3	3	4	12	15	–3	12
Eupen	10	3	2	5	9	15	–6	11
Beerschot Wilrijk†	10	2	2	6	11	19	–8	8

Group B

	P	W	D	L	F	A	GD	Pts
Kortrijk	10	8	0	2	26	12	14	24
Union SG†	10	6	2	2	24	14	10	20
Waasland-Beveren	10	4	1	5	17	24	–7	13
Zulte Waregem	10	3	4	3	22	22	0	13
Royal Excel Mouscron	10	2	2	6	19	22	–3	8
Cercle Brugge	10	2	1	7	16	30	–14	7

† *Qualified for play-offs from First Division B.*

Semi-final
Sporting Charleroi 2, Kortrijk 1

Final
Antwerp 3, Sporting Charleroi 2
Top scorer: Harbaoui (Zulte Waregem) 25.
Cup Final: Mechelen 2, Gent 1.

BOSNIA-HERZEGOVINA

Football Federation of Bosnia & Herzegovina, Ferhadija 30, 71000 Sarajevo.
Founded: 1992. *FIFA:* 1996; *UEFA:* 1998. *National Colours:* Blue shirts, blue shorts, blue socks with white tops.

International matches 2018–19
Northern Ireland (a) 2-1, Austria (h) 1-0, Turkey (a) 0-0, Northern Ireland (h) 2-0, Austria (a) 0-0, Spain (a) 0-1, Armenia (h) 2-1, Greece (h) 2-2, Finland (a) 0-2, Italy (a) 1-2.

League Championship wins (1998–2019)
Zeljeznicar 6; Zrinjski Mostar 6; FK Sarajevo 4; Siroki Brijeg 2; Brotnjo 1; Leotar 1; Modrica 1; Borac Banja Luka 1.

Cup wins (1998; 2000–19)
FK Sarajevo 6; Zeljeznicar 6; Siroki Brijeg 3; Modrica 1; Orasje 1; Zrinjski Mostar 1; Slavija 1; Borac Banja Luka 1; Olimpic Sarajevo 1; Radnik Bijeljina 1.
See also Serbia section for Bosnian-Herzogovinian club honours in Yugoslav Republic era 1947–91.

Bosnian-Herzegovinian Premijer Liga 2018–19

	P	W	D	L	F	A	GD	Pts
FK Sarajevo	33	21	7	5	68	20	48	70
Zrinjski Mostar	33	19	8	6	46	22	24	65
Siroki Brijeg	33	13	15	5	37	23	14	54
Zeljeznicar	33	14	8	11	43	32	11	50
Radnik Bijeljina	33	10	14	9	29	26	3	44
Mladost Doboj Kakanj	33	12	7	14	36	45	–9	43
Celik Zenica	33	11	10	12	30	49	–19	43
Sloboda Tuzla	33	10	8	15	22	31	–9	38
Zvijezda 09	33	9	11	13	33	45	–12	38
Tuzla City	33	9	9	15	32	44	–12	36
Krupa na Vrbasu*	33	8	9	16	40	48	–8	33
GOSK Gabela*	33	5	8	20	23	54	–31	23

Top scorer: Krpic (Zeljeznicar) 16.
Cup Final: FK Sarajevo 3, 0, Siroki Brijeg 0, 1 (agg. 3-1).

BULGARIA

Bulgarian Football Union, 26 Tzar Ivan Assen II Str., 1124 Sofia.
Founded: 1923. *FIFA:* 1992; *UEFA:* 1954. *National Colours:* White shirts, green shorts, red socks.

International matches 2018–19
Slovenia (a) 2-1, Norway (h) 1-0, Cyprus (h) 2-1, Norway (a) 0-1, Cyprus (a) 1-1, Slovenia (h) 1-1, Montenegro (h) 1-1, Kosovo (a) 1-1, Czech Republic (a) 1-2, Kosovo (h) 2-3.

League Championship wins (1925–2019)
CSKA Sofia 31; Levski Sofia 26; Ludogorets Razgrad 8; Slavia Sofia 7; Lokomotiv Sofia 4; Litex Lovech 4; Vladislav Varna (now Cherno More Varna) 3; Botev Plovdiv (includes Trakija) 2; Athletic Slava 1923 1; Sokol Varna (now Spartak Varna) 1; Sportklub Sofia (now Septemvri Sofia) 1; Ticha Varna (now Cherno More Varna) 1; Spartak Plovdiv 1; Beroe Stara Zagora 1; Etar 1; Lokomotiv Plovdiv 1.

Cup wins (1946–2019)
Levski Sofia (incl. Vitosha 1) 24; CSKA Sofia (incl. Sredets 3) 20; Slavia Sofia 8; Lokomotiv Sofia 4; Litex Lovech 4; Botev Plovdiv (includes Trakija) 3; Beroe Stara Zagora 2; Ludogorets Razgrad 2; Spartak Plovdiv 1; Septemvri Sofia 1; Spartak Sofia 1; Marek Dupnitsa 1; Sliven 1; Cherno More Varna 1; Lokomotiv Plovdiv 1.

Bulgarian First League Qualifying Table 2018–19

	P	W	D	L	F	A	GD	Pts
Ludogorets Razgrad	26	19	5	2	53	14	39	62
CSKA Sofia	26	18	3	5	47	14	33	57
Levski Sofia	26	17	3	6	51	24	27	54
Botev Plovdiv	26	13	6	7	39	21	18	45
Cherno More	26	12	6	8	36	34	2	42
Beroe	26	12	6	8	32	23	9	42
Etar	26	12	4	10	30	27	3	40
Lokomotiv Plovdiv	26	10	5	11	32	28	4	35
Slavia Sofia	26	9	6	11	28	31	–3	33
Botev Vratsa	26	9	4	13	29	40	–11	31
Vitosha Bistritsa	26	7	4	15	17	39	–22	25
Septemvri Sofia	26	6	3	17	23	52	–29	21
Dunav Ruse 2010	26	5	5	16	25	47	–22	20
Vereya	26	0	6	20	12	60	–48	6

Championship Round 2018–19

	P	W	D	L	F	A	GD	Pts
Ludogorets Razgrad	36	23	10	3	67	19	48	79
CSKA Sofia	36	24	6	6	57	17	40	78
Levski Sofia†	36	20	6	10	64	37	27	66
Beroe	36	16	10	10	42	30	12	58
Cherno More	36	15	7	14	44	51	–7	52
Botev Plovdiv	36	14	8	14	44	36	8	50

† *Qualified for Europa League play-off final.*

Relegation Round 2018–19
Group A

	P	W	D	L	F	A	GD	Pts
Etar	32	15	6	11	39	31	8	51
Botev Vratsa	32	13	6	13	49	44	5	45
Vitosha Bistritsa	32	10	4	18	26	49	–23	34
Vereya*	32	0	6	26	13	81	–68	6

Group B

	P	W	D	L	F	A	GD	Pts
Slavia Sofia	32	10	9	13	37	42	–5	39
Lokomotiv Plovdiv	32	10	8	14	37	37	0	38
Septemvri Sofia*+	32	9	6	17	32	58	–26	33
Dunav Ruse 2010+	32	7	8	17	36	55	–19	29

Vereya demoted for match fixing.

Europa League Play-offs
Quarter-finals
Etar 2, 1, Lokomotiv Plovdiv 0, 0 (agg. 3-0)
Slavia Sofia 0, 1, Botev Vratsa 0, 0 (agg. 1-0)
Semi-finals
Etar 0, 2, Slavia Sofia 1, 0 (agg. 2-1)
Final
Levski Sofia 1, Etar 0
Top scorer: Kostov (Levski Sofia) 24.
Cup Final: Lokomotiv Plovdiv 1, Botev Plovdiv 0.

CHANNEL ISLANDS

Guernsey

League Championship wins (1894–2019)
Northerners 32; Guernsey Rangers 17; Vale Recreation 15; St Martin's 14; Sylvans 10; Belgrave Wanderers 8; 2nd Bn Manchesters 3; Guernsey Rovers 2; 2nd Bn Royal

Irish Regt 2; 2nd Bn Wiltshires 2; 10th Comp W Div Royal Artillery 1; 2nd Bn Leicesters 1; 2nd Bn PA Somerset Light Infantry 1; 2nd Middlesex Regt 1; Athletics 1; Band Comp 2nd Bn Royal Fusiliers 1; G&H Comp Royal Fusiliers 1; Grange 1; Yorkshire Regt (Green Howards).

Guernsey Priaulx League 2018–19

	P	*W*	*D*	*L*	*F*	*A*	*GD*	*Pts*
St Martin's	24	17	5	2	66	18	48	56
Alderney	24	16	5	3	50	24	26	53
Guernsey Rovers	24	15	6	3	74	23	51	51
Northerners	24	14	5	5	74	33	41	47
Guernsey Rangers	24	9	1	14	38	69	–31	28
Manzur	24	7	4	13	45	58	–13	25
Vale Recreation	24	5	6	13	42	54	–12	21
Sylvans	24	6	3	15	28	63	–35	21
Belgrave Wanderers	24	1	1	22	25	100	–75	4

Top scorers (joint): Hale (St Martin's), Jardin (Manzur) 8.

Jersey

League Championship wins (1904–2019)

Jersey Wanderers 20; First Tower United 19; St Paul's 20; Jersey Scottish 11; Beeches Old Boys 5; Magpies 4; 2nd Bn King's Own Regt 3; Oaklands 3; St Peter 3; 1st Batt Devon Regt 2; 1st Bn East Surrey Regt 2; Georgetown 2; Mechanics 2; YMCA 2; 2nd Bn East Surrey Regt 1; 20th Comp Royal Garrison Artillery 1; National Rovers 1; Sporting Academics 1; Trinity 1.

Jersey Football Combination 2018–19

	P	*W*	*D*	*L*	*F*	*A*	*GD*	*Pts*
St Paul's	18	17	0	1	61	13	48	51
St Peter	18	14	1	3	61	24	37	43
Jersey Wanderers	18	10	1	7	46	37	9	31
St Clement	18	5	4	9	28	39	–11	19
St Ouen	18	5	1	12	18	44	–26	16
Rozel Rovers	18	3	3	12	26	64	–38	12
Trinity	18	3	2	13	26	45	–19	11

Top scorer: Lester (St Paul's) 15.

Upton Park Trophy 2019 (For Guernsey & Jersey League Champions)

St Paul's (Jersey) 3, St Martin's (Guernsey) 0.

Upton Park Trophy wins (1907–2019)

Northerners 17 (incl. 1 shared); First Tower United 12; St Paul's 12; Jersey Wanderers 11 (incl. 1 shared); St Martin's 11; Jersey Scottish 6; Guernsey Rangers 5; Vale Recreation 4; Belgrave Wanderers 4; Beeches Old Boys 3; Old St Paul's 3; Magpies 3; Sylvans 3; St Peter 2; Jersey Mechanics 1; Jersey YMCA 1; National Rovers 1; Sporting Academics 1; Trinity 1.

CROATIA

Croatian Football Federation, Vukovarska 269A, 10000 Zagreb.
Founded: 1912. *FIFA:* 1992; *UEFA:* 1993. *National Colours:* Red and white check shirts, white shorts, blue socks.

International matches 2018–19

Portugal (a) 1-1, Spain (a) 0-6, England (h) 0-0, Jordan (h) 2-1, Spain (h) 3-2, England (a) 1-2, Azerbaijan (h) 2-1, Hungary (a) 1-2, Wales (h) 2-1, Tunisia (h) 1-2.

League Championship wins (1992–2019)

Dinamo Zagreb (incl. Croatia Zagreb 3) 20; Hajduk Split 6; NK Zagreb 1; Rijeka 1.

Cup wins (1992–2019)

Dinamo Zagreb (incl. Croatia Zagreb 4) 15; Hajduk Split 6; Rijeka 5; Inter Zapresic 1; Osijek 1.
See also Serbia section for Croatian club honours in Yugoslav Republic era 1947–92.

Croatian Prva HNL 2018–19

	P	*W*	*D*	*L*	*F*	*A*	*GD*	*Pts*
Dinamo Zagreb	36	29	5	2	74	20	54	92
Rijeka	36	19	10	7	70	36	34	67
Osijek	36	18	8	10	61	36	25	62
Hajduk Split	36	17	11	8	59	39	20	62
Gorica	36	17	8	11	57	46	11	59
Lokomotiva Zagreb	36	13	10	13	51	43	8	49
Slaven Koprivnica	36	7	16	13	41	53	–12	37
Inter Zapresic	36	9	4	23	40	84	–44	31
Istra 1961+	36	6	7	23	31	73	–42	25
Rudes*	36	3	5	28	26	80	–54	14

Top scorer: Caktas (Hajduk Split) 19.
Cup Final: Rijeka 3, Dinamo Zagreb 1.

CYPRUS

Cyprus Football Association, 10 Achaion Street, 2413 Engomi, PO Box 25071, 1306 Nicosia.
Founded: 1934. *FIFA:* 1948; *UEFA:* 1962. *National Colours:* All blue with white trim.

International matches 2018–19

Norway (a) 0-2, Slovenia (h) 2-1, Bulgaria (a) 1-2, Slovenia (a) 1-1, Bulgaria (h) 1-1, Norway (h) 0-2, San Marino (h) 5-0, Belgium (h) 0-2, Scotland (a) 1-2, Russia (a) 0-1.

League Championship wins (1935–2019)

APOEL 28; Omonia 20; Anorthosis 13; AEL Limassol 6; EPA Larnaca 3; Olympiakos Nicosia 3; Apollon Limassol 3; Pezoporikos Larnaca 2; Trust 1; Cetinkaya 1.

Cup wins (1935–2019)

APOEL 21; Omonia 14; Anorthosis 10; Apollon Limassol 9; AEL Limassol 7; EPA Larnaca 5; Trust 3; Cetinkaya 2; AEK Larnaca 2; Pezoporikos Larnaca 1; Olympiakos Nicosia 1; Nea Salamis Famagusta 1; APOP Kinyras 1.

Cypriot First Division Qualifying Table 2018–19

	P	*W*	*D*	*L*	*F*	*A*	*GD*	*Pts*
APOEL	22	15	4	3	45	20	25	49
Apollon Limassol	22	14	5	3	50	17	33	47
AEL Limassol	22	14	3	5	35	25	10	45
AEK Larnaca	22	11	6	5	37	16	21	39
Omonia	22	9	4	9	25	24	1	31
Nea Salamis Famagusta	22	9	4	9	28	30	–2	31
Anorthosis Famagusta	22	9	7	6	27	26	1	28
Paphos	22	7	6	9	24	36	–12	21
Doxa Katokopia	22	5	5	12	28	39	–11	20
Enosis	22	4	5	13	17	38	–21	17
Alki Oroklini	22	4	5	13	19	43	–24	17
Ermis	22	2	4	16	19	40	–21	10

Championship Round 2018–19

	P	*W*	*D*	*L*	*F*	*A*	*GD*	*Pts*
APOEL	32	21	7	4	66	25	41	70
AEK Larnaca	32	18	8	6	51	23	28	62
Apollon Limassol	32	17	7	8	64	32	32	58
AEL Limassol	32	17	4	11	49	47	2	55
Nea Salamis Famagusta	32	12	8	12	41	47	–6	44
Omonia	32	10	6	16	36	45	–9	36

Relegation Round 2018–19

	P	*W*	*D*	*L*	*F*	*A*	*GD*	*Pts*
Anorthosis Famagusta	32	12	11	9	42	41	1	41
Paphos	32	12	8	12	39	50	–11	38
Doxa Katokopia	32	9	8	15	47	50	–3	35
Enosis	32	9	8	15	35	51	–16	35
Alki Oroklini*	32	10	5	17	35	58	–23	35
Ermis*	32	3	4	25	29	65	–36	13

Top scorer: Trichkovski (AEK Larnaca) 15.
Cup Final: AEL Limassol 2, APOEL 0.

CZECH REPUBLIC

Fotbalova Asociace Ceske Republiky, Diskarska 2431/4, PO Box 11, Praha 6 16017.
Founded: 1901. *FIFA:* 1907; *UEFA:* 1954. *National Colours:* All red.

International matches 2018–19

Ukraine (h) 1-2, Russia (a) 1-5, Slovakia (a) 2-1, Ukraine (a) 0-1, Poland (a) 1-0, Slovakia (h) 1-0, England (a) 0-5, Brazil (h) 1-3, Bulgaria (h) 2-1, Montenegro (a) 3-0.

League Championship wins – Czechoslovakia (1925–93)

Sparta Prague 21; Slavia Prague 13; Dukla Prague (prev. UDA, now Marila Pribram) 11; Slovan Bratislava (formerly NV Bratislava) 8; Spartak Trnava 5; Banik Ostrava 3; Viktoria Zizkov 1; Inter Bratislava 1; Spartak Hradec Kralove 1; Zbrojovka Brno 1; Bohemians 1; Vitkovice 1.

Cup wins – Czechoslovakia (1961–93)

Dukla Prague 8; Sparta Prague 8; Slovan Bratislava 5; Spartak Trnava 4; Banik Ostrava 3; Lokomotiva Kosice 2; TJ Gottwaldov 1; DAC 1904 Dunajska Streda 1; 1.FC Kosice 1.

League Championship wins – Czech Republic (1994–2019)

Sparta Prague 12; Slavia Prague 5; Viktoria Plzen 5; Slovan Liberec 3; Banik Ostrava 1.

Cup wins – Czech Republic (1994–2019)

Sparta Prague 6; Slavia Prague 5; Viktoria Zizkov 2; Jablonec 2; Slovan Liberec 2; Teplice 2; Mlada Boleslav

2; Hradec Kralove (formerly Spartak) 1; Banik Ostrava 1; Viktoria Plzen 1; Sigma Olomouc 1; Fastav Zlin 1.

Czech First League Qualifying Table 2018–19

	P	W	D	L	F	A	GD	Pts
Slavia Prague	30	23	3	4	72	23	49	72
Viktoria Plzen	30	21	5	4	47	27	20	68
Sparta Prague	30	17	6	7	52	27	25	57
Jablonec	30	15	6	9	53	26	27	51
Banik Ostrava	30	13	6	11	38	36	2	45
Slovan Liberec	30	11	9	10	33	28	5	42
Mlada Boleslav	30	11	9	10	52	44	8	42
Sigma Olomouc	30	12	4	14	37	43	–6	40
Fastav Zlin	30	12	3	15	32	40	–8	39
Teplice	30	10	6	14	32	42	–10	36
Bohemians 1905	30	8	10	12	29	37	–8	34
Slovacko	30	10	4	16	32	45	–13	34
Opava	30	9	6	15	39	49	–10	33
Pribram	30	8	7	15	33	63	–30	31
Karvina	30	8	5	17	39	53	–14	29
Dukla Prague	30	5	5	20	25	62	–37	20

Championship Round 2018–19

	P	W	D	L	F	A	GD	Pts
Slavia Prague	35	26	5	4	79	26	53	83
Viktoria Plzen	35	24	6	5	57	32	25	78
Sparta Prague	35	20	6	9	59	33	26	66
Jablonec	35	17	6	12	58	32	26	57
Banik Ostrava†	35	13	8	14	39	43	–4	47
Slovan Liberec	35	12	10	13	34	32	2	46

† *Qualified for Europa League play-off final.*

Relegation Round 2018–19

	P	W	D	L	F	A	GD	Pts
Slovacko	35	13	6	16	43	47	–4	45
Opava	35	12	7	16	47	57	–10	43
Bohemians 1905	35	9	13	13	33	43	–10	40
Pribram+	35	11	7	17	43	73	–30	40
Karvina+	35	9	5	21	42	58	–16	32
Dukla Prague*	35	5	7	23	30	72	–42	22

Europa League Play-offs

First Round

Fastav Zlin 1, 2, Sigma Olomouc 0, 3 (agg. 3-3; Fastav Zlin won on away goals)
Teplice 0, 1, Mlada Boleslav 8, 1 (agg. 1-9)

Second Round

Fastav Zlin 3, 0, Mlada Boleslav 1, 3 (agg. 3-4)

Final

Mlada Boleslav 1, Banik Ostrava 0
Top scorer: Komlichenko (Mlada Boleslav) 29.
Cup Final: Slavia Prague 2, Banik Ostrava 0.

DENMARK

Dansk Boldspil-Union, Idraettens Hus, DBU Alle 1, DK-2605, Brondby.
Founded: 1889. *FIFA:* 1904; *UEFA:* 1954. *National Colours:* Red shirts, white shorts, red socks.

International matches 2018–19

Slovakia (h) 0-3, Wales (h) 2-0, Republic of Ireland (a) 0-0, Austria (h) 2-0, Wales (a) 2-1, Republic of Ireland (h) 0-0, Kosovo (a) 2-2, Switzerland (a) 3-3, Republic of Ireland (h) 1-1, Georgia (h) 5-1.

League Championship wins (1913–2019)

KB Copenhagen 15; FC Copenhagen 13; Brondby 10; B 93 Copenhagen 9; AB (Akademisk) 9; B 1903 Copenhagen 7; Frem 6; AGF Aarhus 5; Vejle 5; Esbjerg 5; AaB Aalborg 4; Hvidovre 3; OB Odense 3; Koge 2; B 1909 Odense 2; Lyngby 2; Midtjylland 2; Silkeborg 1; Herfolge 1; Nordsjaelland 1.

Cup wins (1955–2019)

AGF Aarhus 9; FC Copenhagen 8; Vejle 6; Brondby 7; OB Odense 5; Esbjerg 3; AaB Aalborg 3; Randers Freja 3; Lyngby 3; Frem 2; B 1909 Odense 2; B 1903 Copenhagen 2; Nordsjaelland 2; B 1913 Odense 1; KB Copenhagen 1; Vanlose 1; Hvidovre 1; B 93 Copenhagen 1; AB (Akademisk) 1; Viborg 1; Silkeborg 1; Randers 1; Midtjylland 1.

Danish Superliga Qualifying Table 2018–19

	P	W	D	L	F	A	GD	Pts
FC Copenhagen	26	19	4	3	65	23	42	61
Midtjylland	26	18	6	2	62	26	36	60
OB Odense	26	12	6	8	35	31	4	42
Brondby	26	11	5	10	44	40	4	38
Esbjerg	26	11	5	10	32	35	–3	38
Nordsjaelland	26	9	9	8	42	39	3	36
AaB Aalborg	26	9	9	8	38	35	3	36
Randers	26	9	7	10	29	34	–5	34
AGF Aarhus	26	7	10	9	31	34	–3	31
Horsens	26	8	7	11	31	45	–14	31
SonderjyskE	26	7	7	12	30	37	–7	28
Vendsyssel	26	5	7	14	24	41	–17	22
Hobro	26	5	6	15	22	45	–23	21
Vejle	26	4	8	14	22	42	–20	20

Championship Round 2018–19

	P	W	D	L	F	A	GD	Pts
FC Copenhagen	36	26	4	6	86	37	49	82
Midtjylland	36	21	8	7	76	43	33	71
Esbjerg	36	16	8	12	45	47	–2	56
Brondby†	36	15	7	14	60	52	8	52
OB Odense	36	14	10	12	48	48	0	52
Nordsjaelland	36	10	14	12	52	54	–2	44

† *Qualified for Europa League play-off match.*

Relegation Round 2018–19

Group 1

	P	W	D	L	F	A	GD	Pts
AGF Aarhus	32	12	11	9	46	40	6	47
SonderjyskE	32	9	8	15	37	45	–8	35
Horsens+	32	8	9	15	32	55	–23	33
Vejle*+	32	6	10	16	34	53	–19	28

Group 2

	P	W	D	L	F	A	GD	Pts
Randers	32	12	9	11	35	39	–4	45
AaB Aalborg	32	10	12	10	44	41	3	42
Vendsyssel*+	32	6	11	15	32	49	–17	29
Hobro+	32	6	9	17	31	55	–24	27

Europa League Play-offs

Semi-finals

SonderjyskE 1, 3, Randers 1, 4 (agg. 4-5)
AaB Aalborg 0, 0, AGF Aarhus 1, 2 (agg. 0-3)

Final

Randers 2, 1, AGF Aarhus 1, 1 (agg. 3-2)

Europa League Play-off match

Brondby 4, Randers 2
Top scorer: Skov (FC Copenhagen) 29.
Cup Final: Midtjylland 1, Brondby 1.
aet; Midtjylland won 4-3 on penalties.

ENGLAND

The Football Association, Wembley Stadium, PO Box 1966, London SW1P 9EQ.
Founded: 1863. *FIFA:* 1905; *UEFA:* 1954. *National Colours:* White shirts with light blue trim, white shorts, red socks.

ESTONIA

Eesti Jalgpalli Liit, A. Le Coq Arena, Asula 4c, 11312 Tallinn.
Founded: 1921. *FIFA:* 1923; *UEFA:* 1992. *National Colours:* Blue shirts, black shorts, white socks.

International matches 2018–19

Greece (h) 0-1, Finland (a) 0-1, Finland (h) 0-1, Hungary (h) 3-3, Hungary (a) 0-2,Greece (a) 1-0, Northern Ireland (a) 0-2, Gibraltar (a) 1-0, Northern Ireland (h) 1-2, Germany (a) 0-8.

League Championship wins (1921–40; 1992–2018)

Flora 11; Sport 9; FCI Levadia (formerly Levadia Maardu) 9; Estonia 5; Sillamae Kalev 2; Tallinna JK 2; Norma 2; Lantana (formerly Nikol) 2; Nomme Kalju 2; Olimpia Tartu 1; TVMK Tallinn 1; FCI Tallinn 1.

Cup wins (1993–2019)

FCI Levadia (incl. Levadia Maardu 2) 9; Flora 7; Tallinna Sadam 2; Narva Trans 2; TVMK Tallinn 2; Lantana (formerly Nikol) 1; Norma 1; Levadia Tallinn (pre-2004) 1; Nomme Kalju 1; FCI Tallinn 1.

Estonian Meistriliiga 2018

	P	W	D	L	F	A	GD	Pts
Nomme Kalju	36	25	11	0	114	32	82	86
FCI Levadia	36	26	6	4	109	26	83	84
Flora	36	25	8	3	116	32	84	83
Narva Trans	36	18	7	11	76	57	19	61
Paide Linnameeskond	36	14	9	13	64	74	–10	51
Tammeka Tartu	36	14	7	15	56	58	–2	49
Viljandi Tulevik	36	8	5	23	37	100	–63	29
Tallinna Kalev	36	7	7	22	54	68	–14	28
Kuressaare+	36	6	3	27	34	115	–81	21
Vaprus*	36	2	7	27	25	123	–98	13

Top scorer: Liliu (Nomme Kalju) 31.
Cup Final: Narva Trans 2, Nomme Kalju 1 *aet*.

FAROE ISLANDS

Fotboltssamband Foroya, Gundadalur, PO Box 3028, 110 Torshavn.
Founded: 1979. *FIFA:* 1988; *UEFA:* 1990. *National Colours:* White shirts with blue trim, white shorts, white socks.

International matches 2018–19
Malta (h) 3-1, Kosovo (a) 0-2, Azerbaijan (h) 0-3, Kosovo (h) 1-1, Azerbaijan (a) 0-2, Malta (a) 1-1, Malta (a) 1-2, Romania (a) 1-4, Spain (h) 1-4, Norway (h) 0-2.

League Championship wins (1942–2018)
HB Torshavn 23; KI Klaksvik 17; B36 Torshavn 11; TB Tvoroyri (includes FC Suduroy and Royn) 7; GI Gota 6; B68 Toftir 3; EB/Streymur 2; Vikingur 2; SI Sorvagur 1; IF Fuglafjordur 1; B71 Sandur 1; VB Vagur 1; NSI Runavik 1.

Cup wins (1955–2018)
HB Torshavn 26; B36 Torshavn 6; KI Klaksvik 6; GI Gota 6; TB Tvoroyri (includes FC Suduroy and Royn) 5; Vikingur 5; EB/Streymur 4; NSI Runavik 3; VB Vagur 1; B71 Sandur 1.

Faroese Premier League 2018

	P	W	D	L	F	A	GD	Pts
HB Torshavn	27	24	1	2	58	18	40	73
NSI Runavik	27	17	4	6	64	25	39	55
B36 Torshavn	27	16	5	6	58	33	25	53
KI Klaksvik	27	16	3	8	48	25	23	51
Vikingur	27	11	6	10	39	37	2	39
Skala	27	8	5	14	31	42	–11	29
TB Tvoroyri	27	8	4	15	27	42	–15	28
EB/Streymur	27	4	9	14	30	53	–23	21
Argja Boltfelag	27	5	3	19	16	55	–39	18
07 Vestur*	27	5	2	20	30	71	–41	17

Top scorer: Justinussen (HB Torshavn) 20.
Cup Final: B36 Torshavn 2, HB Torshavn 2.
aet; B36 Torshavn won 5-4 on penalties.

FINLAND

Suomen Palloliitto Finlands Bollfoerbund, Urheilukatu 5, PO Box 191, 00251 Helsinki.
Founded: 1907. *FIFA:* 1908; *UEFA:* 1954. *National Colours:* White shirts with blue trim, white shorts, white socks.

International matches 2018–19
Hungary (h) 1-0, Estonia (h) 1-0, Estonia (a) 1-0, Greece (h) 2-0, Greece (a) 0-1, Hungary (a) 0-2, Italy (a) 0-2, Armenia (a) 2-0, Bosnia-Herzegovina (h) 2-0, Liechtenstein (a) 2-0.

League Championship wins (1908–2018)
HJK Helsinki 29; HPS Helsinki 9; Haka Valkeakoski 9; TPS Turku 8; HIFK Helsinki 7; KuPS Kuopio 5; Kuusysi Lahti 5; KIF Helsinki 4; AIFK Turku 3; VIFK Vaasa 3; Reipas Lahti 3; Tampere United 3; VPS Vaasa 2; KTP Kotka 2; OPS Oulu 2; Jazz Pori 2; Unitas Helsinki 1; PUS Helsinki 1; Sudet Viipuri 1; HT Helsinki 1; Ilves-Kissat 1; Pyrkiva Turku 1; KPV Kokkola 1; Ilves Tampere 1; TPV Tampere 1; MyPa Anjalankoski (renamed MYPA-47) 1; Inter Turku 1; SJK Seinajoki 1; IFK Mariehamn 1.

Cup wins (1955–2019)
HJK Helsinki 13; Haka Valkeakoski 12; Reipas Lahti 7; KTP Kotka 4; Ilves Tampere 3; TPS Turku 3; MyPa Anjalankoski (renamed MYPA-47) 3; KuPS Kuopio 2; Mikkeli 2; Kuusysi Lahti 2; RoPS Rovaniemi 2; Inter Turku 2; Pallo-Pojat 1; Drott (renamed Jaro) 1; HPS Helsinki 1; AIFK Turku 1; Jokerit (formerly PK-35) 1; Atlantis 1; Tampere United 1; FC FC Honka 1; IFK Mariehamn 1; SJK Seinajoki 1.

Finnish Veikkausliiga 2018

	P	W	D	L	F	A	GD	Pts
HJK Helsinki	33	24	6	3	61	19	42	78
RoPS Rovaniemi	33	18	8	7	42	25	17	62
KuPS Kuopio	33	17	7	9	56	37	19	58
Honka	33	15	13	5	51	33	18	58
Ilves	33	14	7	12	45	41	4	49
VPS Vaasa	33	10	11	12	37	43	–6	41
Inter Turku	33	10	10	13	37	44	–7	40
Lahti	33	9	13	11	30	38	–8	40
SJK Seinajoki	33	8	8	17	28	37	–9	32
IFK Mariehamn	33	8	7	18	37	59	–22	31
TPS Turku*+	33	7	8	18	37	55	–18	29
PS Kemi*	33	6	6	21	29	59	–30	24

Top scorer: Klauss (HJK Helsinki) 21.
Cup Final: Ilves 2, IFK Mariehamn 0.

FRANCE

Federation Francaise de Football, 87 Boulevard de Grenelle, 75738 Paris Cedex 15.
Founded: 1919. *FIFA:* 1904; *UEFA:* 1954. *National Colours:* Blue shirts, white shorts, red socks.

International matches 2018–19
Germany (a) 0-0, Netherlands (h) 2-1, Iceland (h) 2-2, Germany (h) 2-1, Netherlands (a) 0-2, Uruguay (h) 1-0, Moldova (a) 4-1, Iceland (h) 4-0, Bolivia (h) 2-0, Turkey (a) 0-2, Andorra (a) 4-0.

League Championship wins (1933–2019)
Saint-Etienne 10; Olympique Marseille 9; AS Monaco 8; Nantes 8; Paris Saint-Germain 8; Olympique Lyonnais 7; Stade de Reims 6; Bordeaux 6; Lille OSC (includes Olympique Lillois) 4; OGC Nice 4; FC Sete 2; Sochaux 2; Racing Club Paris 1; Roubaix-Tourcoing 1; Strasbourg 1; Auxerre 1; Lens 1; Montpellier 1.

Cup wins (1918–2019)
Paris Saint-Germain 12; Olympique Marseille 10; Lille OSC 6; Saint-Etienne 6; Red Star 5; Racing Club Paris 5; AS Monaco 5; Olympique Lyonnais 5; Bordeaux 4; Auxerre 4; Strasbourg 3; OGC Nice 3; Stade Rennais 3; Nantes 3; CAS Genereaux 2; Montpellier 2; FC Sete 2; Sochaux 2; Stade de Reims 2; Sedan 2; Metz 2; Guingamp 2; Olympique de Pantin 1; CA Paris 1; Club Français 1; AS Cannes 1; Excelsior Roubaix 1; EF Nancy-Lorraine 1; Toulouse 1; Le Havre 1; AS Nancy 1; Bastia 1; Lorient 1.

French Ligue 1 2018–19

	P	W	D	L	F	A	GD	Pts
Paris Saint-Germain	38	29	4	5	105	35	70	91
Lille OSC	38	22	9	7	68	33	35	75
Olympique Lyonnais	38	21	9	8	70	47	23	72
Saint-Etienne	38	19	9	10	59	41	18	66
Olympique Marseille	38	18	7	13	60	52	8	61
Montpellier	38	15	14	9	53	42	11	59
Nice	38	15	11	12	30	35	–5	56
Reims	38	13	16	9	39	42	–3	55
Nimes	38	15	8	15	57	58	–1	53
Rennes	38	13	13	12	55	52	3	52
Strasbourg	38	11	16	11	58	48	10	49
Nantes	38	13	9	16	48	48	0	48
Angers	38	10	16	12	44	49	–5	46
Bordeaux	38	10	11	17	34	42	–8	41
Amiens	38	9	11	18	31	52	–21	38
Toulouse	38	8	14	16	35	57	–22	38
AS Monaco	38	8	12	18	38	57	–19	36
Dijon+	38	9	7	22	31	60	–29	34
Caen*	38	7	12	19	29	54	–25	33
Guingamp*	38	5	12	21	28	68	–40	27

Top scorer: Mbappe (Paris Saint-Germain) 33.
Cup Final: Rennes 2, Paris Saint-Germain 2.
aet; Rennes won 6-5 on penalties.

GEORGIA

Georgian Football Federation, 76A Chavchavadze Avenue, 0179 Tbilisi.
Founded: 1990. *FIFA:* 1992; *UEFA:* 1992. *National Colours:* All white with red trim.

International matches 2018–19
Kazakhstan (a) 2-0, Latvia (h) 1-0, Andorra (h) 3-0, Latvia (a) 3-0, Andorra (a) 1-1, Kazakhstan (h) 2-1, Switzerland (h) 0-2, Republic of Ireland (a) 0-1, Gibraltar (h) 3-0, Denmark (a) 1-5.

League Championship wins (1990–2018)
Dinamo Tbilisi 16; Torpedo Kutaisi 4; WIT Georgia 2; Metalurgi Rustavi (formerly Olimpi) 2; Zestafoni 2; Sioni Bolnisi 1; Dila Gori 1; Samtredia 1; Saburtalo 1.

Cup wins (1990–2018)
Dinamo Tbilisi 13; Torpedo Kutaisi 4; Lokomotivi Tbilisi 3; Ameri Tbilisi 2; Guria Lanchkhuti 1; Dinamo Batumi 1; Zestafoni 1; WIT Georgia 1; Gagra 1; Dila Gori 1; Chikhura Sachkhere 1.
See also Russia section for Georgian club honours in Soviet era 1936–91.

Georgian Erovnuli Liga 2018

	P	W	D	L	F	A	GD	Pts
Saburtalo	36	24	7	5	64	29	35	79
Dinamo Tbilisi	36	21	6	9	73	38	35	69
Torpedo Kutaisi	36	20	9	7	66	25	41	69
Chikhura Sachkhere	36	19	7	10	54	33	21	64
Dila Gori	36	17	12	7	60	40	20	63
Lokomotivi Tbilisi	36	12	8	16	43	55	–12	44
Rustavi	36	8	13	15	33	44	–11	37
Sioni+	36	8	7	21	39	65	–26	31
Samtredia*+	36	4	9	23	28	81	–53	21
Kolkheti Poti*	36	4	8	24	26	76	–50	14

Top scorers (joint): Gabedava (Dinamo Tbilisi), Zivzivadze (Chikhura Sachkhere) 22.
Cup Final: Gagra 2, Torpedo Kutaisi 2.
aet; Torpedo Kutaisi won 4-2 on penalties.

GERMANY

Deutscher Fussball-Bund, Hermann-Neuberger-Haus, Otto-Fleck-Schneise 6, 60528 Frankfurt Am Main.
Founded: 1900. *FIFA:* 1904; *UEFA:* 1954. *National Colours:* White shirts with red and black trim, white shorts, white socks with red tops.

International matches 2018–19

France (h) 0-0, Peru (h) 2-1, Netherlands (a) 0-3, France (a) 1-2, Russia (h) 3-0, Netherlands (h) 2-2, Serbia (h) 1-1, Netherlands (a) 3-2, Belarus (a) 2-0, Estonia (h) 8-0.

League Championship wins (1903–2019)

Bayern Munich 29; 1.FC Nuremberg 9; Borussia Dortmund 8; Schalke 04 7; Hamburger SV 6; VfB Stuttgart 5; Borussia Moenchengladbach 5; 1.FC Kaiserslautern 4; Werder Bremen 4; 1.FC Lokomotive Leipzig 3; SpVgg Greuther Furth 3; 1.FC Cologne 3; Viktoria Berlin 2; Hertha Berlin 2; Hannover 96 2; Dresden SC 2; Union Berlin 1; Freiburger FC 1; Phoenix Karlsruhe 1; Karlsruher FV 1; Holstein Kiel 1; Fortuna Dusseldorf 1; Rapid Vienna 1; VfR Mannheim 1; Rot-Weiss Essen 1; Eintracht Frankfurt 1; Munich 1860 1; Eintracht Braunschweig 1; VfL Wolfsburg 1.

Cup wins (1935–2019)

Bayern Munich 19; Werder Bremen 6; Schalke 04 5; Eintracht Frankfurt 5; 1.FC Nuremberg 4; Borussia Dortmund 4; 1.FC Cologne 4; VfB Stuttgart 3; Borussia Moenchengladbach 3; Hamburger SV 3; Dresden SC 2; Munich 1860 2; Karlsruhe SC 2; Fortuna Dusseldorf 2; 1.FC Kaiserslautern 2; 1.FC Lokomotive Leipzig 1; Rapid Vienna 1; First Vienna 1; Rot-Weiss Essen 1; SW Essen 1; Kickers Offenbach 1; Bayer Uerdingen 1; Hannover 96 1; Bayer Leverkusen 1; VfLWolfsburg 1.

German Bundesliga 2018–19

	P	W	D	L	F	A	GD	Pts
Bayern Munich	34	24	6	4	88	32	56	78
Borussia Dortmund	34	23	7	4	81	44	37	76
RB Leipzig	34	19	9	6	63	29	34	66
Bayer Leverkusen	34	18	4	12	69	52	17	58
Borussia M'gladbach	34	16	7	11	55	42	13	55
Wolfsburg	34	16	7	11	62	50	12	55
Eintracht Frankfurt	34	15	9	10	60	48	12	54
Werder Bremen	34	14	11	9	58	49	9	53
TSG Hoffenheim	34	13	12	9	70	52	18	51
Fortuna Dusseldorf	34	13	5	16	49	65	–16	44
Hertha Berlin	34	11	10	13	49	57	–8	43
Mainz 05	34	12	7	15	46	57	–11	43
Freiburg	34	8	12	14	46	61	–15	36
Schalke 04	34	8	9	17	37	55	–18	33
Augsburg	34	8	8	18	51	71	–20	32
Stuttgart*+	34	7	7	20	32	70	–38	28
Hannover 96*	34	5	6	23	31	71	–40	21
1.FC Nuremberg*	34	3	10	21	26	68	–42	19

Top scorer: Lewandowski (Bayern Munich) 22.
Cup Final: Bayern Munich 3, RB Leipzig 0.

GIBRALTAR

Gibraltar Football Association, Bayside Sports Complex, PO Box 513, Gibraltar GX11 1AA.
Founded: 1895. *UEFA:* 2013. *National Colours:* Red shirts with white trim, red shorts, red socks.

International matches 2018–19

North Macedonia (h) 0-2, Liechtenstein (a) 0-2, Armenia (a) 1-0, Liechtenstein (h) 2-1, Armenia (h) 2-6, North Macedonia (a) 0-4, Republic of Ireland (h) 0-1, Estonia (h) 0-1, Greece (a) 0-3, Republic of Ireland (a) 0-2.

League Championship wins (1896–2019)

Lincoln Red Imps 24 (incl. Newcastle United 5; 1 title shared); Prince of Wales 19; Glacis United 17 (incl. 1 shared); Britannia (now Britannia XI) 14; Gibraltar United 11; Europa 7; Manchester United (now Manchester 62) 7; St Theresa's 3; Chief Construction 2; Jubilee 2; Exiles 2; South United 2; Gibraltar FC 2; Albion 1; Athletic 1; Royal Sovereign 1; Commander of the Yard 1; St Joseph's 1.

Cup wins (1895–2019)

Lincoln Red Imps (incl. Newcastle United 4) 17; St Joseph's 9; Europa 8; Glacis United 5; Britannia (now Britannia XI) 3; Gibraltar United 3; Manchester United (now Manchester 62) 3; Gibraltar FC 1; HMS Hood 1; 2nd Bn The King's Regt 1; AARA 1; RAF New Camp 1; 4th Bn Royal Scots 1; Prince of Wales 1; Manchester United Reserves 1; 2nd Bn Royal Green Jackets 1; RAF Gibraltar 1; St Theresa's 1.

Gibraltarian Premier Division 2018–19

	P	W	D	L	F	A	GD	Pts
Lincoln Red Imps	27	21	3	3	84	19	65	66
Europa	27	20	4	3	84	20	64	64
St Joseph's	27	17	4	6	69	29	40	55
Mons Calpe	27	15	4	8	63	29	34	49
Gibraltar Phoenix	27	13	4	10	42	34	8	43
Gibraltar United	27	11	6	10	48	37	11	39
Lynx	27	8	7	12	29	45	–16	31
Glacis United	27	7	3	17	28	58	–30	24
Lions Gibraltar	27	3	0	24	17	77	–60	9
Boca Juniors*	27	2	1	24	13	129	–116	7

Top scorer: Boro (St Joseph's) 21.
Cup Final: Europa 3, Gibraltar United 0.

GOZO

Gozo Football Association, GFA Headquarters, Mgarr Road, Xewkija, XWK 9014, Malta. (Not a member of FIFA or UEFA.)
Founded: 1936.

League Championship wins (1938–2019)

Victoria Hotspurs 13; Nadur Youngsters 11; Sannat Lions 10; Xewkija Tigers 8; Ghajnsielem 7; Xaghra United 6 (incl. Xaghra Blue Stars 1, Xaghra Young Stars 1); Salesian Youths (renamed Oratory Youths) 6; Victoria Athletics 4; Victoria Stars 1; Victoria City 1; Calypcians 1; Victoria United (renamed Victoria Wanderers) 1; Kercem Ajax 1; Zebbug Rovers 1.

Cup wins (1972–2019)

Xewkija Tigers 11; Sannat Lions 9; Nadur Youngsters 8; Ghajnsielem 6; Xaghra United 4; Victoria Hotspurs 2; Kercem Ajax 2; Calypsians 1; Calypsians Bosco Youths 1; Qala St Joseph 1; Victoria Wanderers 1.

Gozitan L-Ewwel Divizjoni 2018–19

	P	W	D	L	F	A	GD	Pts
Victoria Hotspurs	21	19	1	1	68	22	46	58
Nadur Youngsters	21	15	4	2	72	25	47	49
Xewkija Tigers	21	8	3	10	57	45	12	27
Ghajnsielem	21	7	5	9	41	52	–11	26
Victoria Wanderers	21	6	3	12	29	44	–15	21
Kercem Ajax	21	5	6	10	26	44	–18	21
Gharb Rangers+	21	4	6	11	32	50	–18	18
Munxar Falcons*	21	5	2	14	30	73	–43	17

Top scorer: Da Silva (Victoria Hotspurs) 30.
Cup Final: Victoria Hotspurs 3, Nadur Youngsters 2 *aet.*

GREECE

Hellenic Football Federation, Parko Goudi, PO Box 14161, 11510 Athens.
Founded: 1926. *FIFA:* 1927; *UEFA:* 1954. *National Colours:* All white.

International matches 2018–19

Estonia (a) 1-0, Hungary (a) 1-2, Hungary (h) 1-0, Finland (a) 0-2, Finland (h) 1-0, Estonia (h) 0-1, Liechtenstein (a) 2-0, Bosnia-Herzegovina (a) 2-2, Turkey (a) 1-2, Italy (h) 0-3, Armenia (h) 2-3.

League Championship wins (1927–2019)

Olympiacos 44; Panathinaikos 20; AEK Athens 12; Aris Salonika 3; PAOK 3; Larissa 1.

Cup wins (1932–2019)

Olympiacos 27; Panathinaikos 18; AEK Athens 15; PAOK 7; Panionios 2; Larissa 2; Ethnikos 1; Aris Salonika 1; Iraklis 1; Kastoria 1; OFI Crete 1.

Greek Super League 2018–19

	P	W	D	L	F	A	GD	Pts
PAOK (–2)	30	26	4	0	66	14	52	80
Olympiacos	30	24	3	3	71	17	54	75
AEK Athens (–3)	30	18	6	6	50	19	31	57
Atromitos	30	15	7	8	41	28	13	52
Aris	30	15	4	11	46	33	13	49
Panionios	30	11	5	14	27	45	–18	38
Lamia	30	9	10	11	28	37	–9	37
Panathinaikos† (–11)	30	13	8	9	38	30	8	36
Panaitolikos†	30	10	6	14	34	48	–14	36
Larissa	30	8	10	12	26	34	–8	34
Asteras Tripolis	30	8	9	13	25	30	–5	33
Xanthi†	30	7	11	12	22	34	–12	32
OFI Crete†+	30	7	11	12	30	42	–12	32
PAS Giannina*	30	7	6	17	19	38	–19	27
Levadiakos*	30	5	6	19	15	45	–30	21
Apollon Smirnis*	30	2	4	24	11	55	–44	10

† *Final position decided on head-to-head points.*
Top scorer: Koulouris (Atromitos) 19.
Cup Final: PAOK 1, AEK Athens 0.

HUNGARY

Magyar Labdarugo Szovetseg, Kanai ut 2. D, 1112 Budapest.
Founded: 1901. *FIFA:* 1907; *UEFA:* 1954. *National Colours:* Red shirts, white shorts, green socks.

International matches 2018–19
Finland (a) 0-1, Greece (h) 2-1, Greece (a) 0-1, Estonia (a) 3-3, Estonia (h) 2-0, Finland (h) 2-0, Slovakia (a) 0-2, Croatia (h) 2-1, Azerbaijan (a) 3-1, Wales (h) 1-0.

League Championship wins (1901–2019)
Ferencvaros 30; MTK Budapest 23; Ujpest 20; Budapest Honved 14 (incl. Kispest Honved); Debrecen 7; Vasas 6; Csepel 4; Gyor 4; Videoton (renamed Fehervar) 3; Budapesti TC 2; Nagyvarad 1; Vac 1; Dunaferr (renamed Dunaujvaros) 1; Zalaegerszeg 1.

Cup wins (1910–2019)
Ferencvaros 23; MTK Budapest 12; Ujpest 10; Budapest Honved 7 (inc. Kispest Honved); Debrecen 6; Vasas 4; Gyor 4; Diosgyor 2; Fehervar (incl. Videoton 1, Vidi 1) 2; Bocskai 1; III Keruleti TUE 1; Soroksar 1; Szolnoki MAV 1; Siofoki Banyasz 1; Bekescsaba 1; Pecsi 1; Sopron 1; Kecskemet 1.
Cup not regularly held until 1964.

Hungarian Nemzeti Bajnoksag I 2018–19

	P	*W*	*D*	*L*	*F*	*A*	*GD*	*Pts*
Ferencvaros	33	23	5	5	72	27	45	74
Videoton	33	18	7	8	53	37	16	61
Debrecen	33	14	9	10	44	39	5	51
Budapest Honved	33	13	10	10	46	38	8	49
Ujpest	33	12	12	9	38	28	10	48
Mezokovesd-Zsory	33	12	8	13	45	40	5	44
Puskas Akademia	33	11	7	15	36	45	–9	40
Paksi SE	33	9	12	12	33	46	–13	39
Varda SE	33	10	8	15	36	48	–12	38
Diosgyor	33	10	8	15	36	57	–21	38
MTK Budapest*	33	10	4	19	42	56	–14	34
Szombathelyi Haladas*	33	8	6	19	31	51	–20	30

Top scorers (joint): Holender (Budapest Honved), Lanzafame (Ferencvaros) 16.
Cup Final: Fehervar 2, Budapest Honved 1.

ICELAND

Knattspyrnusamband Islands, Laugardal, 104 Reykjavik.
Founded: 1947. *FIFA:* 1947; *UEFA:* 1954. *National Colours:* All blue.

International matches 2018–19
Switzerland (a) 0-6, Belgium (h) 0-3, France (a) 2-2, Switzerland (h) 1-2, Belgium (a) 0-2, Qatar (n) 2-2, Andorra (a) 2-0, France (a) 0-4, Albania (h) 1-0, Turkey (h) 2-1.

League Championship wins (1912–2018)
KR Reykjavik 26; Valur 22; Fram 18; IA Akranes 18; FH Hafnarfjordur 8; Vikingur 5; IBK Keflavik 4; IBV Vestmannaeyjar 3; KA Akureyri 1; Breidablik 1; Stjarnan 1.

Cup wins (1960–2018)
KR Reykjavik 14; Valur 11; IA Akranes 9; Fram 8; IBV Vestmannaeyjar 5; IBK Keflavik 4; Fylkir 2; FH Hafnarfjordur 2; IBA Akureyri 1; Vikingur 1; Breidablik 1; Stjarnan 1.

Icelandic Urvalsdeild karla 2018

	P	*W*	*D*	*L*	*F*	*A*	*GD*	*Pts*
Valur	22	13	7	2	50	24	26	46
Breidablik	22	13	5	4	39	17	22	44
Stjarnan	22	11	7	4	45	26	19	40
KR Reykjavik	22	10	7	5	36	25	11	37
FH Hafnarfjordur	22	10	7	5	36	28	8	37
IBV Vestmannaeyjar	22	8	5	9	29	31	–2	29
KA	22	7	7	8	36	34	2	28
Fylkir	22	7	5	10	31	37	–6	26
Vikingur Reykjavik	22	6	7	9	29	38	–9	25
Grindavik	22	7	4	11	26	37	–11	25
Fjolnir*	22	4	7	11	22	44	–22	19
Keflavik*	22	0	4	18	11	49	–38	4

Top scorer: Peddersen (Valur) 17.
Cup Final: Stjarnan 0, Breidablik 0.
aet; Stjarnan won 4-1 on penalties.

ISRAEL

Israel Football Association, Ramat Gan Stadium, 299 Aba Hilell Street, PO Box 3591, Ramat Gan 52134.
Founded: 1928. *FIFA:* 1929; *UEFA:* 1994. *National Colours:* Blue shirts with white trim, blue shorts, blue socks.

International matches 2018–19
Albania (a) 0-1, Northern Ireland (a) 0-3, Scotland (h) 2-1, Albania (h) 2-0, Guatemala (h) 7-0, Scotland (h) 2-3, Slovenia (h) 1-1, Austria (h) 4-2, Latvia (a) 3-0, Poland (a) 0-4.

League Championship wins (1932–2019)
Maccabi Tel Aviv 22; Hapoel Tel Aviv 14 (incl. 1 shared); Maccabi Haifa 12; Hapoel Petah Tikva 6; Beitar Jerusalem 6; Maccabi Netanya 5; Hapoel Be'er Sheva 5; Hakoah Ramat Gan 2; British Police 1; Beitar Tel Aviv 1 (shared); Hapoel Ramat Gan 1; Hapoel Kfar Saba 1; Bnei Yehuda 1; Hapoel Haifa 1; Ironi Kiryat Shmona 1.

Cup wins (1928–2019)
Maccabi Tel Aviv 23; Hapoel Tel Aviv 15; Beitar Jerusalem 7; Maccabi Haifa 6; Hapoel Haifa 4; Bnei Yehuda 4; Hapoel Kfar Saba 3; Maccabi Petah Tikva 2; Beitar Tel Aviv 2; Hapoel Petah Tikva 2; Hakoah Amidar Ramat Gan 2; Hapoel Ramat Gan 2; Maccabi Hashmonai Jerusalem 1; British Police 1; Hapoel Jerusalem 1; Maccabi Netanya 1; Hapoel Yehud 1; Hapoel Lod 1; Hapoel Be'er Sheba 1; Bnei Sakhnin 1; Ironi Kiryat Shmona 1.

Israeli Premier League Qualifying Table 2018–19

	P	*W*	*D*	*L*	*F*	*A*	*GD*	*Pts*
Maccabi Tel Aviv	26	20	6	0	57	12	45	66
Maccabi Haifa	26	12	8	6	34	27	7	44
Maccabi Netanya	26	12	7	7	34	29	5	43
Hapoel Be'er Sheva	26	10	9	7	36	32	4	39
Bnei Yehuda	26	10	7	9	39	25	14	37
Hapoel Hadera	26	9	6	11	30	41	–11	33
Hapoel Haifa	26	7	11	8	42	37	5	32
Hapoel Tel Aviv	26	6	13	7	26	23	3	31
Ironi Kiryat Shmona	26	7	9	10	25	28	–3	30
Hapoel Ra'anana	26	6	12	8	20	30	–10	30
Beitar Jerusalem	26	7	8	11	32	37	–5	29
Maccabi Petah Tikva	26	6	10	10	26	40	–14	28
Ashdod	26	5	7	14	20	42	–22	22
Bnei Sakhnin	26	4	9	13	21	39	–18	21

Championship Round 2018–19

	P	*W*	*D*	*L*	*F*	*A*	*GD*	*Pts*
Maccabi Tel Aviv	36	27	8	1	77	17	60	89
Maccabi Haifa	36	16	10	10	46	41	5	58
Hapoel Be'er Sheva	36	15	10	11	48	46	2	55
Maccabi Netanya	36	15	8	13	45	47	–2	53
Bnei Yehuda	36	14	9	13	56	41	15	51
Hapoel Hadera	36	12	6	18	43	59	–16	42

Relegation Round 2018–19

	P	*W*	*D*	*L*	*F*	*A*	*GD*	*Pts*
Beitar Jerusalem	33	11	10	12	43	43	0	43
Hapoel Tel Aviv	33	9	15	9	40	30	10	42
Hapoel Ra'anana	33	8	15	10	29	38	–9	39
Ironi Kiryat Shmona	33	9	11	13	34	35	–1	38
Hapoel Haifa	33	8	13	12	44	47	–3	37
Ashdod	33	10	7	16	34	54	–20	37
Maccabi Petah Tikva*	33	8	12	13	33	51	–18	36
Bnei Sakhnin*	33	5	12	16	27	50	–23	27

Top scorer: Saha (Hapoel Be'er Sheva) 15.
Cup Final: Maccabi Netanya 1, Bnei Yehuda 1.
aet; Bnei Yehuda won 5-4 on penalties.

ITALY

Federazione Italiana Giuoco Calcio, Via Gregorio Allegri 14, 00198 Roma.
Founded: 1898. *FIFA:* 1905; *UEFA:* 1954. *National Colours:* Blue shirts, white shorts, blue socks with white tops.

International matches 2018–19
Poland (h) 1-1, Portugal (a) 0-1, Ukraine (h) 1-1, Poland (a) 1-0, Portugal (h) 0-0, USA (h) 1-0, Finland (h) 2-0, Liechtenstein (h) 6-0, Greece (a) 3-0, Bosnia-Herzegovina (h) 2-1.

League Championship wins (1898–2019)
Juventus 35 (excludes two titles revoked); AC Milan 18; Internazionale 18 (includes one title awarded); Genoa 9; Pro Vercelli 7; Bologna 7; Torino 7 (excludes one title revoked); Roma 3; Fiorentina 2; Lazio 2; Napoli 2; Casale 1; Novese 1; Cagliari 1; Hellas Verona 1; Sampdoria 1.

Cup wins (1928–2019)
Juventus 13; Roma 9; Internazionale 7; Lazio 7; Fiorentina 6; Torino 5; Napoli 5; AC Milan 5; Sampdoria 4; Parma 3; Bologna 2; Vado 1; Genoa 1; Venezia 1; Atalanta 1; Vicenza 1.

Italian Serie A 2018–19

	P	*W*	*D*	*L*	*F*	*A*	*GD*	*Pts*
Juventus	38	28	6	4	70	30	40	90
Napoli	38	24	7	7	74	36	38	79
Atalanta	38	20	9	9	77	46	31	69
Internazionale	38	20	9	9	57	33	24	69
AC Milan	38	19	11	8	55	36	19	68
Roma	38	18	12	8	66	48	18	66
Torino	38	16	15	7	52	37	15	63
Lazio	38	17	8	13	56	46	10	59
Sampdoria	38	15	8	15	60	51	9	53
Bologna	38	11	11	16	48	56	–8	44
Sassuolo	38	9	16	13	53	60	–7	43
Udinese	38	11	10	17	39	53	–14	43
SPAL 2013	38	11	9	18	44	56	–12	42
Parma	38	10	11	17	41	61	–20	41
Cagliari	38	10	11	17	36	54	–18	41
Fiorentina	38	8	17	13	47	45	2	41
Genoa	38	8	14	16	39	57	–18	38
Empoli*	38	10	8	20	51	70	–19	38
Frosinone*	38	5	10	23	29	69	–40	25
Chievo*	38	2	14	22	25	75	–50	17

Top scorer: Quagliarella (Sampdoria) 26.
Cup Final: Lazio 2, Atalanta 0.

KAZAKHSTAN

Football Federation of Kazakhstan, 29 Syganak Street, 9th floor, 010000 Astana.
Founded: 1914. *FIFA:* 1994; *UEFA:* 2002. *National Colours:* All yellow.

International matches 2018–19
Georgia (h) 0-2, Andorra (a) 1-1, Latvia (a) 1-1, Andorra (h) 4-0, Latvia (h) 1-1, Georgia (a) 1-2, Moldova (n) 1-0, Scotland (h) 3-0, Russia (h) 0-4, Belgium (a) 0-3, San Marino (h) 4-0.

League Championship wins (1992–2018)
Irtysh Pavlodar (includes Ansat) 5; Aktobe 5; Astana 5; Yelimay (renamed Spartak Semey) 3; FC Astana-64 (includes Zhenis) 3; Kairat 2; Shakhter Karagandy 2; Taraz 1; Tobol 1.

Cup wins (1992–2018)
Kairat 9; FC Astana-64 (incl. Zhenis) 3; Astana (incl. Lokomotiv) 3; Dostyk 1; Vostok 1; Yelimay (renamed Spartak Semey) 1; Irtysh Pavlodar 1; Kaisar 1; Taraz 1; Almaty 1; Tobol 1; Aktobe 1; Atirau 1; Ordabasy 1; Shakhter Karagandy 1.

Kazakh Premer Ligasy 2018

	P	*W*	*D*	*L*	*F*	*A*	*GD*	*Pts*
Astana	33	24	5	4	66	22	44	77
Kairat	33	19	5	9	60	33	27	62
Tobol	33	15	8	10	36	30	6	53
Ordabasy	33	13	7	13	38	44	–6	46
Kaisar	33	11	12	10	35	31	4	45
Zhetysu	33	11	10	12	36	40	–4	43
Aktobe (–6)	33	13	9	11	51	47	4	42
Shakhter Karagandy	33	8	12	13	29	36	–7	36
Atyrau	33	9	9	15	34	47	–13	36
Irtysh Pavlodar+	33	10	5	18	28	45	–17	35
Kyzyl-Zhar*	33	10	5	18	27	48	–21	35
Akzhayik*	33	7	9	17	31	48	–17	30

Top scorer: Pizzelli (Aktobe) 18.
Cup Final: Kairat 1, Atyrau 0.

KOSOVO

Football Federation of Kosovo, Rruga Agim Ramadani 45, Prishtina, Kosovo 10000. *Founded:* 1946. *FIFA:* 2016; *UEFA:* 2016. *National Colours:* All blue.

International matches 2018–19
Azerbaijan (a) 0-0, Faroe Islands (h) 2-0, Malta (h) 3-1, Faroe Islands (a) 1-1, Malta (a) 5-0, Azerbaijan (h) 4-0, Denmark (h) 2-2, Bulgaria (h) 1-1, Montenegro (a) 1-1, Bulgaria (a) 3-2.

League Championship wins (1945–97; 1999–2019)
Prishtina 14; Vellaznimi 9; KF Trepca 7; Liria 5; Buduqnosti 4; Rudari 3; Red Star 3; Besa Peje 3; Feronikeli 3; Jedinstvo 2; Kosova Prishtina 2; Slloga 2; Obiliqi 2; Fushe-Kosova 2; Drita 2; Proletari 1; KXEK Kosova 1; Rudniku 1; KNI Ramiz Sadiku 1; Dukagjini 1; Besiana 1; Hysi 1; Vushtrria 1; Trepca'89 1.

Cup wins (1992–2019)
Prishtina 5; Liria 3; Besa Peje 3; Feronikeli 3; Flamurtari 2; KF Trepca 1; KF 2 Korriku 1; Gjilani 1; Drita 1; Besiana 1; KEK-u 1; Kosova Prishtina 1; Vellaznimi 1; Hysi 1; Trepca'89 1.

Kosovar Superliga 2018–19

	P	*W*	*D*	*L*	*F*	*A*	*GD*	*Pts*
Feronikeli	33	25	5	3	64	14	50	80
Prishtina	33	23	6	4	49	12	37	75
Llapi	33	22	3	8	54	24	30	69
Drita	33	14	6	13	47	39	8	48
Ferizaj	33	14	4	15	39	41	–2	46
Flamurtari	33	12	9	12	33	39	–6	45
Drenica Skenderaj	33	11	10	12	41	34	7	43
Ballkani	33	12	7	14	35	36	–1	43
Trepca'89+	33	11	9	13	40	45	–5	42
Gjilani+	33	10	8	15	28	37	–9	38
Liria Prizren*	33	8	4	21	31	60	–29	28
KEK-u*	33	0	1	32	24	104	–80	1

Top scorer: Rexha (Feronikeli) 21.
Cup Final: Feronikeli 5, Trepca'89 1.

LATVIA

Latvijas Futbola Federacija, Olympic Sports Centre, Grostonas Street 6B, 1013 Riga.
Founded: 1921. *FIFA:* 1922; *UEFA:* 1992. *National Colours:* All carmine red.

International matches 2018–19
Andorra (h) 0-0, Georgia (a) 0-1, Kazakhstan (h) 1-1, Georgia (h) 0-3, Kazakhstan (a) 1-1, Andorra (a) 0-0, North Macedonia (a) 1-3, Poland (a) 0-2, Israel (h) 0-3, Slovenia (h) 0-5.

League Championship wins (1922–2018)
Skonto Riga 15; ASK Riga (incl. AVN 2) 11; Sarkanais Metalurgs Liepaja 9; RFK Riga 8; Olympija Liepaya 7; VEF Riga 6; Ventspils 6; Energija Riga (incl. ESR Riga 2) 4; Elektrons Riga (incl. Alfa 1) 4; Torpedo Riga 3; Keisermezhs Riga 2; Khimikis Daugavpils 2; RAF Yelgava 2; Daugava Liepaja 2; Liepajas Metalurgs 2; Spartaks Jurmala 2; Dinamo Riga 1; Zhmilyeva Team 1; Darba Rezervi 1; RER Riga 1; Starts Brotseni 1; Venta Ventspils 1; Jumieks Riga 1; Gauja Valmiera 1; Daugava Daugavpils 1; FK Liepaja 1; Riga FC 1.

Cup wins (1937–2018)
Skonto Riga 8; ASK Riga 7 (includes AVN 3); Elektrons Riga 7; Ventspils 7; Sarkanais Metalurgs Liepaja 4; Jelgava 4; VEF Riga 3; Tseltnieks Riga 3; RAF Yelgava 3; RFK Riga 2; Daugava Liepaja 2; Starts Brotseni 2; Selmash Liepaya 2; Yurnieks Riga 2; Khimikis Daugavpils 2; Rigas Vilki 1; Dinamo Liepaya 1; Dinamo Riga 1; RER Riga 1; Voulkan Kouldiga 1; Baltika Liepaja 1; Venta Ventspils 1; Pilots Riga 1; Lielupe Yurmala 1; Energija Riga (formerly ESR Riga) 1; Torpedo Riga 1; Daugava SKIF Riga 1; Tseltnieks Daugavpils 1; Olympija Riga 1; FK Riga 1; Liepajas Metalurgs 1; Daugava Daugavpils 1; FK Liepaja 1; Riga FC 1.

Latvian Virsliga 2018

	P	*W*	*D*	*L*	*F*	*A*	*GD*	*Pts*
Riga FC	28	20	4	4	45	16	29	64
Ventspils	28	18	6	4	54	22	32	60
Rigas FS	28	18	1	9	57	23	34	55
FK Liepaja	28	15	6	7	46	25	21	51
Spartaks Jurmala	28	12	6	10	48	37	11	42
Jelgava	28	6	3	19	19	48	–29	21
Metta/LU+	28	5	4	19	24	52	–28	19
Valmiera†	28	2	2	24	22	92	–70	8

† *Valmiera were reprieved from relegation due to league expansion.*
Top scorer: Lemacic (Riga FC) 15.
Cup Final: Riga FC 0, Ventspils 0.
aet; Riga FC won 5-4 on penalties.

LIECHTENSTEIN

Liechtensteiner Fussballverband, Landstrasse 149, 9494 Schaan.
Founded: 1934. *FIFA:* 1974; *UEFA:* 1974. *National Colours:* Blue shirts, red shorts, blue socks.

International matches 2018–19
Armenia (a) 1-2, Gibraltar (h) 2-0, North Macedonia (a) 1-4, Gibraltar (a) 1-2, North Macedonia (h) 0-2, Armenia (h) 2-2, Greece (h) 0-2, Italy (a) 0-6, Armenia (a) 0-3, Finland (h) 0-2.
Liechtenstein has no national league. Teams compete in Swiss regional leagues.

Cup wins (1937–2019)
Vaduz 47; FC Balzers 11; FC Triesen 8; USV Eschen/Mauren 5; FC Schaan 3.
Cup Final: Vaduz 3, FC Ruggell 2.

LITHUANIA

Lietuvos Futbolo Federacija, Stadiono g. 2, 02106 Vilnius.
Founded: 1922. *FIFA:* 1923; *UEFA:* 1992. *National Colours:* Yellow shirts, green shorts, yellow socks.

International matches 2018–19

Serbia (h) 0-1, Montenegro (a) 0-2, Romania (h) 1-2, Montenegro (h) 1-4, Romania (a) 0-3, Serbia (a) 1-4, Luxembourg (a) 1-2, Azerbaijan (a) 0-0, Luxembourg (h) 1-1, Serbia (a) 1-4.

League Championship wins (1990–2018)

FBK Kaunas 8 (incl. Zalgiris Kaunas 1); Zalgiris Vilnius 7; Ekranas 7; Inkaras Kaunas 2; Kareda 2; Suduva 2; Sirijus Klaipeda 1; Mazeikiai 1.

Cup wins (1990–2018)

Zalgiris Vilnius 12; Ekranas 4; FBK Kaunas 4; Kareda 2; Atlantas 2; Suduva 2; Sirijus Klaipeda 1; Lietuvos Makabi Vilnius (renamed Neris Vilnius) 1; Inkaras Kaunas 1; Stumbras 1.

Lithuanian A Lyga Qualifying Table 2018

	P	*W*	*D*	*L*	*F*	*A*	*GD*	*Pts*
Suduva	28	21	4	3	59	16	43	67
Zalgiris Vilnius	28	19	5	4	60	20	40	62
Stumbras	28	13	6	9	36	25	11	45
Riteriai	28	11	9	8	37	26	11	42
Kauno Zalgiris	28	10	5	13	22	31	–9	35
Atlantas	28	6	5	17	26	55	–29	23
Palanga	28	5	5	18	17	58	–41	20
Jonava	28	4	7	17	24	50	–26	19

Championship Round 2018

	P	*W*	*D*	*L*	*F*	*A*	*GD*	*Pts*
Suduva	33	24	5	4	72	20	52	77
Zalgiris Vilnius	33	23	6	4	70	23	47	75
Riteriai	33	14	9	10	46	29	17	51
Stumbras	33	15	6	12	45	35	10	51
Kauno Zalgiris+	33	11	6	16	29	41	–12	39
Atlantas*	33	6	6	21	28	75	–47	24

Top scorer: Antal (Zalgiris Vilnius) 23.
Cup Final: Zalgiris Vilnius 3, Stumbras 0.

LUXEMBOURG

Federation Luxembourgeoise de Football, BP 5 Rue de Limpach, 3932 Mondercange.
Founded: 1908. *FIFA:* 1910; *UEFA:* 1954. *National Colours:* White shirts with blue trim, white shorts, white socks.

International matches 2018–19

Moldova (h) 4-0, San Marino (a) 3-0, Belarus (a) 0-1, San Marino (h) 3-0, Belarus (h) 0-2, Moldova (a) 1-1, Lithuania (h) 2-1, Ukraine (h) 1-2, Madagascar (h) 3-3, Lithuania (a) 1-1, Ukraine (a) 0-1.

League Championship wins (1910–2019)

Jeunesse Esch 28; F91 Dudelange 15; Spora Luxembourg 11; Stade Dudelange 10; Fola Esch 7; Red Boys Differdange 6; Union Luxembourg 6; Avenir Beggen 6; US Hollerich-Bonnevoie 5; Progres NiederKorn 3; Aris Bonnevoie 3; Sporting Club 2; Racing Club 1; National Schifflange 1; Grevenmacher 1.

Cup wins (1922–2019)

Red Boys Differdange 15; Jeunesse Esch 13; Union Luxembourg 10; Spora Luxembourg 8; Avenir Beggen 7; F91 Dudelange 8; Progres NiederKorn 4; Stade Dudelange 4; Grevenmacher 4; Differdange 03 4; Fola Esch 3; Alliance Dudelange 2; US Rumelange 2; Racing Club 1; US Dudelange 1; SC Tetange 1; National Schifflange 1; Aris Bonnevoie 1; Jeunesse Hautcharage 1; Swift Hesperange 1; Etzella Ettelbruck 1; CS Petange 1; Racing 1.

Luxembourg Nationaldivisioun 2018–19

	P	*W*	*D*	*L*	*F*	*A*	*GD*	*Pts*
F91 Dudelange	26	18	5	3	72	33	39	59
Fola Esch	26	15	5	6	65	28	37	50
Jeunesse Esch	26	14	6	6	46	30	16	48
Progres Niederkorn	26	13	5	8	45	35	10	44
Differdange 03	26	13	5	8	35	33	2	44
Racing	26	11	6	9	42	31	11	39
UNA Strassen	26	12	3	11	46	43	3	39
UT Petange	26	11	4	11	38	43	–5	37
Mondorf-les-Bains	26	10	5	11	39	39	0	35
Etzella Ettelbruck	26	7	7	12	31	44	–13	28
Victoria Rosport	26	7	7	12	33	49	–16	28
Hostert+	26	7	4	15	37	58	–21	25
RM Hamm Benfica*	26	5	4	17	29	50	–21	19
Rumelange*	26	4	4	18	34	76	–42	16

Top scorer: Hadji (Fola Esch) 23.
Cup Final: F91 Dudelange 5, Etzella Ettelbruck 0.

MALTA

Malta Football Association, Millennium Stand, Floor 2, National Stadium, Ta'Qali ATD4000.
Founded: 1900. *FIFA:* 1959; *UEFA:* 1960. *National Colours:* Red shirts, white shorts, red socks.

International matches 2018–19

Faroe Islands (a) 1-3, Azerbaijan (h) 1-1, Kosovo (a) 1-3, Azerbaijan (a) 1-1, Kosovo (h) 0-5, Faroe Islands (h) 1-1, Faroe Islands (h) 2-1, Spain (h) 0-2, Sweden (a) 0-3, Romania (h) 0-4.

League Championship wins (1910–2019)

Sliema Wanderers 26; Floriana 25; Valletta 25; Hibernians 12; Hamrun Spartans 7; Birkirkara 4; Rabat Ajax 2; St George's 1; KOMR 1; Marsaxlokk 1.

Cup wins (1935–2019)

Sliema Wanderers 21; Floriana 20; Valletta 14; Hibernians 10; Hamrun Spartans 6; Birkirkara 5; Melita 1; Gzira United 1; Zurrieq 1; Rabat Ajax 1; Balzan 1.

Maltese Premier League 2018–19

	P	*W*	*D*	*L*	*F*	*A*	*GD*	*Pts*
Valletta	26	18	4	4	61	18	43	58
Hibernians	26	18	4	4	54	27	27	58
Gzira United	26	13	11	2	42	21	21	50
Hamrun Spartans	26	12	10	4	35	20	15	46
Sliema Wanderers	26	13	6	7	37	26	11	45
Balzan	26	12	7	7	41	31	10	43
Birkirkara	26	12	3	11	33	26	7	39
Floriana	26	9	5	12	28	25	3	32
Mosta	26	7	8	11	30	45	–15	29
Senglea Athletic	26	7	5	14	33	46	–13	26
Tarxien Rainbows	26	8	2	16	29	58	–29	26
St Andrews*+	26	7	3	16	25	45	–20	24
Qormi*	26	6	2	18	25	51	–26	20
Pieta Hotspurs*	26	3	4	19	25	59	–34	13

Championship Play-off

Valletta 2, Hibernians 2
aet; Valletta won 4-2 on penalties.
Top scorer: Taylon (Hibernians) 18.
Cup Final: Balzan 2, Valletta 2
aet; Balzan won 4-2 on penalties.

MOLDOVA

Federatia Moldoveneasca de Fotbal, Str. Tricolorului 39, 2012 Chisinau.
Founded: 1990. *FIFA:* 1994; *UEFA:* 1993. *National Colours:* All blue.

International matches 2018–19

Luxembourg (a) 0-4, Belarus (h) 0-0, San Marino (h) 2-0, Belarus (a) 0-0, San Marino (a) 1-0, Luxembourg (h) 1-1, Kazakhstan (a) 1-1, France (h) 1-4, Turkey (a) 0-4, Andorra (h) 1-0, Albania (a) 0-2.

League Championship wins (1992–2018)

Sheriff 17; Zimbru Chisinau 8; Constructorul 1; Dacia Chisinau 1; Milsami Orhei 1.

Cup wins (1992–2019)

Sheriff 10; Zimbru Chisinau 6; Tiligul-Tiras 3; Tiraspol 3 (incl. Constructorul 2); Comrat 1; Nistru Otaci 1; Iskra-Stal 1; Milsami Orhei 1; Zaria Balti 1.

Moldovan Divizia Nationala 2018

	P	*W*	*D*	*L*	*F*	*A*	*GD*	*Pts*
Sheriff	28	19	6	3	58	14	44	63
Milsami Orhei	28	13	6	9	36	24	12	45
Petrocub Hincesti	28	12	9	7	38	28	10	45
Speranta Nisporeni	28	9	11	8	27	26	1	38
Zimbru Chisinau	28	9	9	10	28	37	–9	36
Dinamo-Auto	28	7	7	14	25	43	–18	28
Sfîntul Gheorghe	28	6	8	14	30	50	–20	26
Zaria Balti*	28	4	10	14	26	46	–20	22

Top scorer: Ambros (Petrocub Hincesti) 12.
Cup Final: Sheriff 1, Sfîntul Gheorghe 0 *aet.*

MONTENEGRO

Fudbalski Savez Crne Gore, Ulica 19. Decembar 13, PO Box 275, 81000 Podgorica.
Founded: 1931 *FIFA:* 2007; *UEFA:* 2007. *National Colours:* All red with gold trim.

International matches 2018–19

Romania (a) 0-0, Lithuania (h) 2-0, Serbia (h) 0-2, Lithuania (a) 4-1, Serbia (a) 1-2, Romania (h) 0-1, Bulgaria (a) 1-1, England (h) 1-5, Kosovo (h) 1-1, Czech Republic (a) 0-3.

League Championship wins (2006–19)
Sutjeska 4; Buducnost Podgorica 3; Mogren 2; Rudar Pljevlja 2; Zeta 1; Mladost Podgorica 1 (renamed OFK Titograd).

Cup wins (2006–19)
Rudar Pljevlja 4; Buducnost Podgorica 2; Mladost Podgorica (renamed OFK Titograd) 2; Mogren 1; Petrovac 1; Celik 1; Lovcen 1: Sutjeska 1.

Montenegrin Prva CFL 2018–19

	P	*W*	*D*	*L*	*F*	*A*	*GD*	*Pts*
Sutjeska	36	21	11	4	58	21	37	74
Buducnost Podgorica	36	17	14	5	56	25	31	65
Zeta	36	16	13	7	36	21	15	61
OFK Titograd	36	16	9	11	47	41	6	57
Iskra	36	13	11	12	46	39	7	50
Grbalj	36	11	15	10	45	36	9	48
Petrovac	36	13	8	15	40	45	–5	47
Rudar Pljevlja+	36	8	17	11	35	44	–9	41
Lovcen*+	36	5	11	20	29	65	–36	26
Mornar*	36	1	9	26	17	72	–55	12

Top scorer: Krstovic (Zeta) 17.
Cup Final: Buducnost Podgorica 4, Lovcen 0.

NETHERLANDS

Koninklijke Nederlandse Voetbalbond, Woudenbergseweg 56–58, Postbus 515, 3700 AM Zeist.
Founded: 1889. *FIFA:* 1904; *UEFA:* 1954. *National Colours:* Orange shirts, white shorts, orange socks.

International matches 2018–19
Peru (h) 2-1, France (a) 1-2, Germany (h) 3-0, Belgium (a) 1-1, France (h) 2-0, Germany (h) 2-2, Belarus (a) 4-0, Germany (h) 2-3, England (n) 3-1, Portugal (a) 0-1.

League Championship wins (1889–2019)
Ajax 34; PSV Eindhoven 24; Feyenoord 15; HVV The Hague 10; Sparta Rotterdam 6; RAP Amsterdam 5; Go Ahead Eagles Deventer 4; HFC Haarlem 3; HBS Craeyenhout 3; Willem II Tilburg 3; RCH Heemstede 2; Heracles 2; ADO Den Haag 2; AZ 67 Alkmaar 2; VV Concordia 1; Quick Den Haag 1; Be Quick Groningen 1; NAC Breda 1; SC Enschede 1; Volewijckers Amsterdam 1; HFC Haarlem 1; BVV Den Bosch 1; Schiedam 1; Limburgia 1; EVV Eindhoven 1; SVV Rapid JC Den Heerlen (renamed Roda JC Kerkrade) 1; VV DOS (renamed FC Utrecht) 1; DWS Amsterdam 1; FC Twente 1.

Cup wins (1899–2019)
Ajax 19; Feyenoord 13; PSV Eindhoven 9; Quick The Hague 4; AZ 67 Alkmaar 4; HFC Haarlem 3; Sparta Rotterdam 3; FC Twente 3; FC Utrecht 3; Haarlem 2; VOC 2; HBS Craeyenhout 2; DFC 2; RCH Haarlem 2; Wageningen 2; Willem II Tilburg 2; Fortuna 54 2; FC Den Haag (includes ADO) 2; Roda JC 2; RAP Amsterdam 1; Velocitas Breda 1; HVV Den Haag 1; Concordia Delft 1; CVV 1; Schoten 1; ZFC Zaandam 1; Longa 1; VUC 1; Velocitas Groningen 1; Roermond 1; FC Eindhoven 1; VSV 1; Quick 1888 Nijmegen 1; VVV Groningen 1; NAC Breda 1; Heerenveen 1; PEC Zwolle 1; FC Groningen 1; Vitesse 1.

Dutch Eredivisie 2018–19

	P	*W*	*D*	*L*	*F*	*A*	*GD*	*Pts*
Ajax	34	28	2	4	119	32	87	86
PSV Eindhoven	34	26	5	3	98	26	72	83
Feyenoord	34	20	5	9	75	41	34	65
AZ Alkmaar	34	17	7	10	64	43	21	58
Vitesse	34	14	11	9	70	51	19	53
Utrecht	34	15	8	11	60	51	9	53
Heracles Almelo	34	15	3	16	61	68	–7	48
FC Groningen	34	13	6	15	39	41	–2	45
ADO Den Haag	34	12	9	13	58	63	–5	45
Willem II Tilburg	34	13	5	16	58	72	–14	44
Heerenveen	34	10	11	13	64	73	–9	41
VVV Venlo	34	11	8	15	47	63	–16	41
PEC Zwolle	34	11	6	17	44	57	–13	39
Emmen	34	10	8	16	41	72	–31	38
Fortuna Sittard	34	9	7	18	50	80	–30	34
Excelsior*+	34	9	6	19	46	79	–33	33
De Graafschap*+	34	8	5	21	38	75	–37	29
NAC Breda*	34	5	8	21	29	74	–45	23

Europa League Play-offs
Semi-finals
Utrecht 2, 3, Heracles Almelo 0, 0 (agg. 5-0)
Vitesse 1, 3, FC Groningen 2, 1 (agg. 4-3)
Final
Utrecht 1, 2, Vitesse 1, 0 (agg. 3-1)

Top scorer: De Jong (PSV) 21.
Cup Final: Ajax 4, Willem II Tilburg 0.

NORTHERN CYPRUS

Cyprus Turkish Football Federation, 7 Memduh Asaf Street, 107 Koskluciftlik, Lefkosa. (Not a member of FIFA or UEFA.)
Founded: 1955; *National Colours:* Red shirts with white trim, red shorts, red socks.

League Championship wins (1956–63; 1969–74; 1976–2019)
Cetinkaya 14; Magusa Turk Gucu 9; Yenicami Agdelen 9; Gonyeli 9; Dogan Turk Birligi 7; Baf Ulku Yurdu 4; Kucuk Kaymakli 4; Akincilar 1; Binatli 1.

Cup wins (1956–2019)
Cetinkaya 17; Gonyeli 8; Yenicami Agdelen 7; Kucuk Kaymakli 7; Magusa Turk Gucu 6; Turk Ocagi Limasol 5; Lefke 2; Dogan Turk Birligi 2; Genclik Gucu 1; Yalova 1; Binatli 1; Cihangir 1.

Northern Cyprus Super Lig 2018–19

	P	*W*	*D*	*L*	*F*	*A*	*GD*	*Pts*
Magusa Turk Gucu (–1)	30	24	3	3	91	30	61	74
Yenicami Agdelen	30	23	5	2	93	36	57	74
Dogan Turk Birligi	30	18	2	10	59	41	18	56
Alsancak Yesilova	30	16	5	9	59	44	15	53
Cetinkaya	30	14	7	9	46	38	8	49
Turk Ocagi Limasol	30	14	5	11	54	45	9	47
Lefke	30	14	4	12	54	46	8	46
Gonyeli	30	14	3	13	50	46	4	45
Cihangir	30	11	6	13	52	63	–11	39
Genclik Gucu	30	10	6	14	59	68	–9	36
Ulku Yurdu+	30	10	6	14	52	59	–7	36
Kucuk Kaymakli+	30	8	9	13	44	69	–25	33
Binatli+	30	8	5	17	39	65	–26	29
Esentepe*+	30	9	2	19	39	66	–27	29
Larnaca Gencler Birligi*	30	3	9	18	30	71	–41	18
Girne Halk Evi*	30	4	3	23	39	73	–34	15

Top scorer: Ebuka Okoye (Yenicami Agdelen) 30.
Cup Final: Magusa Turk Gucu 2, Yenicami Agdelen 1.

NORTHERN IRELAND

Irish Football Association, 20 Windsor Avenue, Belfast BT9 6EG.
Founded: 1880. *FIFA:* 1911; *UEFA:* 1954. *National Colours:* Green shirts, white shorts, green socks.

NORTH MACEDONIA

Football Federation of North Macedonia, 8-ma Udarna Brigada 31-A, PO Box 84, 1000 Skopje.
Founded: 1948. *FIFA:* 1994; *UEFA:* 1994. *National Colours:* All red.

International matches 2018–19
Gibraltar (a) 2-0, Armenia (h) 2-0, Liechtenstein (h) 4-1, Armenia (a) 0-4, Liechtenstein (a) 2-0, Gibraltar (h) 4-0, Latvia (h) 3-1, Slovenia (a) 1-1, Poland (h) 0-1, Austria (h) 1-4.

League Championship wins (1992–2019)
Vardar 10*; Rabotnicki 4; Sileks 3; Sloga Jugomagnat 3; Shkendija 3; Pobeda 2; Makedonija GjP 1; Renova 1.
** Vardar also won 1 League Championship (1986–87) in Yugoslav Republic era, later controversially annulled.*

Cup wins (1992–2019)
Vardar 5*; Rabotnicki 4; Sloga Jugomagnat 3; Sileks 2; Pelister 2; Teteks 2; Shkendija 2; Pobeda 1; Cementarnica 55 1; Bashkimi 1; Makedonija GjP 1; Metalurg 1; Renova 1; Akademija Pandev 1.
** Vardar also won 1 Cup (1961) in Yugoslav Republic era.*

North Macedonian Prva Liga Table 2018–19

	P	*W*	*D*	*L*	*F*	*A*	*GD*	*Pts*
Shkendija	36	24	7	5	80	29	51	79
Vardar	36	17	13	6	45	23	22	64
Akademija Pandev	36	17	7	12	45	35	10	58
Shkupi	36	13	9	14	40	42	–2	48
Makedonija GjP†	36	12	11	13	45	50	–5	47
Renova†	36	12	11	13	53	49	4	47
Rabotnicki	36	13	7	16	43	49	–6	46
Sileks+	36	11	11	14	27	39	–12	44
Belasica*	36	9	11	16	37	49	–12	38
Pobeda*	36	6	5	25	26	76	–50	23

† Final position decided on head-to-head goals scored.
Top scorer: Stojanovski (Renova) 18.
Cup Final: Makedonija GjP 2, Akademija Pandev 2.
aet; Akademija Pandev won 4-2 on penalties.

NORWAY

Norges Fotballforbund, Ullevaal Stadion, Serviceboks 1, 0840 Oslo.
Founded: 1902. *FIFA:* 1908; *UEFA:* 1954. *National Colours:* Red shirts, white shorts, red socks.

International matches 2018–19
Cyprus (h) 2-0, Bulgaria (a) 0-1, Slovenia (h) 1-0, Bulgaria (h) 1-0, Slovenia (a) 1-1, Cyprus (a) 2-0, Spain (a) 1-2, Sweden (h) 3-3, Romania (h) 2-2, Faroe Islands (a) 2-0.

League Championship wins (1938–2018)
Rosenborg 25; Fredrikstad 9; Viking Stavanger 8; Lillestrom 5; Valerenga 5; Larvik Turn 3; Brann 3; Molde 3; Lyn Oslo 2; Stromsgodset 2; IK Start 2; Freidig 1; Fram 1; Skeid 1; Moss 1; Stabaek 1.

Cup wins (1902–2018)
Odd Grenland 12; Rosenborg 12; Fredrikstad 11; Lyn Oslo 8; Skeid 8; Sarpsborg 6; Brann 6; Lillestrom 6; Viking Stavanger 5; Stromsgodset 5; Orn-Horten 4; Valerenga 4; Molde 4; Frigg 3; Mjondalen 3; Mercantile 2; Bodo/Glimt 2; Tromso 2; Aalesund 2; Grane Nordstrand 1; Kvik Halden 1; Sparta 1; Gjovik/Lyn 1; Moss 1; Bryne 1; Stabaek 1; Hodd 1.
(Known as the Norwegian Championship for HM The King's Trophy.)

Norwegian Eliteserien 2018

	P	*W*	*D*	*L*	*F*	*A*	*GD*	*Pts*
Rosenborg	30	19	7	4	51	24	27	64
Molde	30	18	5	7	63	36	27	59
Brann	30	17	7	6	45	31	14	58
Haugesund	30	16	5	9	45	33	12	53
Kristiansund	30	13	7	10	46	41	5	46
Valerenga	30	11	9	10	39	44	–5	42
Ranheim	30	12	6	12	43	50	–7	42
Sarpsborg 08	30	11	8	11	46	39	7	41
Odd	30	11	7	12	39	38	1	40
Tromso	30	11	3	16	41	48	–7	36
Bodo/Glimt	30	6	14	10	32	35	–3	32
Lillestrom	30	7	11	12	34	44	–10	32
Stromsgodset	30	7	10	13	46	48	–2	31
Stabaek*+	30	6	11	13	37	50	–13	29
Start*	30	8	5	17	30	54	–24	29
Sandefjord*	30	4	11	15	35	57	–22	23

Top scorer: Boli (Stabaek) 17.
Cup Final: Rosenborg 4, Stromsgodset 1.

POLAND

Polski Zwiazek Pilki Noznej, ul. Bitwy Warszawskiej 1920r. 7, 02-366 Warszawa.
Founded: 1919. *FIFA:* 1923; *UEFA:* 1954. *National Colours:* White shirts with red vertical band, red shorts, white socks.

International matches 2018–19
Italy (a) 1-1, Republic of Ireland (h) 1-1, Portugal (h) 2-3, Italy (h) 0-1, Czech Republic (h) 0-1, Portugal (h) 1-1, Austria (a) 1-0, Latvia (h) 2-0, North Macedonia (a) 1-0, Israel (h) 4-0.

League Championship wins (1921–2018)
Ruch Chorzow 14; Gornik Zabrze 14; Wisla Krakow 13; Legia Warsaw 13; Lech Poznan 7; Cracovia 5; Pogon Lwow 4; Widzew Lodz 4; Warta Poznan 2; Polonia Warsaw 2; Polonia Bytom 2; LKS Lodz 2; Stal Mielec 2; Slask Wroclaw 2; Zaglebie Lubin 2; Garbarnia Krakow 1; Szombierki Bytom 1; Piast Gliwice 1.

Cup wins (1926; 1951–2019)
Legia Warsaw 19; Gornik Zabrze 6; Lech Poznan 5; Wisla Krakow 4; Zaglebie Sosnowiec 4; Ruch Chorzow 3; GKS Katowice 3; Amica Wronki 3; Polonia Warsaw 2; Slask Wroclaw 2; Arka Gdynia 2; Lechia Gdansk 2; Dyskobolia Grodzisk 2; Gwardia Warsaw 1; LKS Lodz 1; Stal Rzeszow 1; Widzew Lodz 1; Miedz Legnica 1; Wisla Plock 1; Jagiellonia Bialystok 1; Zawisza Bydgoszcz 1.

Polish Ekstraklasa Qualifying Table 2018–19

	P	*W*	*D*	*L*	*F*	*A*	*GD*	*Pts*
Lechia Gdansk	30	17	9	4	45	25	20	60
Legia Warsaw	30	18	6	6	48	31	17	60
Piast Gliwice	30	15	8	7	47	31	16	53
Cracovia Krakow	30	14	6	10	39	34	5	48
Zaglebie Lubin	30	14	5	11	48	38	10	47
Jagiellonia Bialystok	30	13	8	9	45	41	4	47
Pogon Szczecin	30	12	7	11	44	42	2	43
Lech Poznan	30	13	4	13	41	40	1	43
Wisla Krakow	30	12	6	12	55	48	7	42
Korona Kielce	30	10	10	10	35	44	–9	40
Miedz Legnica	30	8	8	14	30	52	–22	32
Gornik Zabrze	30	7	10	13	36	49	–13	31
Slask Wroclaw	30	8	7	15	35	37	–2	31
Wisla Plock	30	7	9	14	40	49	–9	30
Arka Gdynia	30	6	11	13	39	44	–5	29
Zaglebie Sosnowiec	30	6	6	18	41	63	–22	24

Championship Round 2018–19

	P	*W*	*D*	*L*	*F*	*A*	*GD*	*Pts*
Piast Gliwice	37	21	9	7	57	33	24	72
Legia Warsaw	37	20	8	9	55	38	17	68
Lechia Gdansk	37	19	10	8	54	38	16	67
Cracovia Krakow	37	17	6	14	45	43	2	57
Jagiellonia Bialystok	37	16	9	12	55	52	3	57
Zaglebie Lubin	37	15	8	14	57	48	9	53
Pogon Szczecin	37	14	10	13	57	54	3	52
Lech Poznan	37	15	7	15	49	48	1	52

Relegation Round 2018–19

	P	*W*	*D*	*L*	*F*	*A*	*GD*	*Pts*
Wisla Krakow	37	14	7	16	67	63	4	49
Korona Kielce	37	12	11	14	42	54	–12	47
Gornik Zabrze	37	12	10	15	48	53	–5	46
Slask Wroclaw	37	12	8	17	49	45	4	44
Arka Gdynia	37	10	12	15	49	51	–2	42
Wisla Plock	37	10	11	16	50	58	–8	41
Miedz Legnica*	37	10	10	17	40	65	–25	40
Zaglebie Sosnowiec*	37	7	8	22	49	80	–31	29

Top scorer: Angulo (Gornik Zabrze) 24.
Cup Final: Lechia Gdansk 1, Jagiellonia Bialystok 0.

PORTUGAL

Federacao Portuguesa de Futebol, Rua Alexandre Herculano No. 58, Apartado postal 24013, Lisboa 1250-012.
Founded: 1914. *FIFA:* 1923; *UEFA:* 1954. *National Colours:* Carmine shirts with , red shorts, red and green socks.

International matches 2018–19
Croatia (h) 1-1, Italy (h) 1-0, Poland (a) 3-2, Scotland (a) 3-1, Italy (a) 0-0, Poland (h) 1-1, Ukraine (h) 0-0, Serbia (h) 1-1, Switzerland (h) 3-1, Netherlands (h) 1-0.

League Championship wins (1935–2019)
Benfica 37; Porto 28; Sporting Lisbon 18; Belenenses 1; Boavista 1.

Cup wins (1939–2019)
Benfica 26; Sporting Lisbon 17; Porto 16; Boavista 5; Belenenses 3; Vitoria de Setubal 3; Academica de Coimbra 2; Braga 2; Leixoes 1; Estrela da Amadora 1; Beira-Mar 1; Vitoria de Guimaraes 1; Desportivo das Aves 1.

Portuguese Primeira Liga 2018–19

	P	*W*	*D*	*L*	*F*	*A*	*GD*	*Pts*
Benfica	34	28	3	3	103	31	72	87
Porto	34	27	4	3	74	20	54	85
Sporting Lisbon	34	23	5	6	72	33	39	74
Braga	34	21	4	9	56	37	19	67
Vitoria Guimaraes	34	15	7	12	46	34	12	52
Moreirense	34	16	4	14	39	44	–5	52
Rio Ave	34	12	9	13	50	52	–2	45
Boavista	34	13	5	16	34	40	–6	44
Belenenses	34	10	13	11	42	51	–9	43
Santa Clara	34	11	9	14	43	45	–2	42
Maritimo	34	12	3	19	26	44	–18	39
Portimonense	34	11	6	17	44	59	–15	39
Vitoria Setubal	34	8	12	14	28	39	–11	36
Desportivo Aves	34	10	6	18	35	49	–14	36
Tondela	34	9	8	17	40	54	–14	35
Chaves*	34	8	8	18	34	57	–23	32
Nacional*	34	7	7	20	33	73	–40	28
Feirense*	34	3	11	20	27	64	–37	20

Top scorer: Seferovic (Benfica) 23.
Cup Final: Sporting Lisbon 2, Porto 2.
aet; Sporting Lisbon won 4-2 on penalties.

REPUBLIC OF IRELAND

Football Association of Ireland (Cumann Peile na hEireann), National Sports Campus, Abbotstown, Dublin 15.
Founded: 1921. *FIFA:* 1923; *UEFA:* 1954. *National Colours:* Green shirts, green shorts, green socks with white tops.

League Championship wins (1922–2018)
Shamrock Rovers 17; Shelbourne 13; Dundalk 13; Bohemians 11; St Patrick's Athletic 8; Waterford United 6; Cork United 5; Drumcondra 5; Sligo Rovers 3; Cork

City 3; St James's Gate 2; Cork Athletic 2; Limerick 2; Athlone Town 2; Derry City 2; Dolphin 1; Cork Hibernians 1; Cork Celtic 1; Drogheda United 1.

Cup wins (1922–2018)
Shamrock Rovers 24; Dundalk 11; Bohemians 7; Shelbourne 7; Drumcondra 5; Sligo Rovers 5; Derry City 5; Cork City 4; St Patrick's Athletic 3; St James's Gate 2; Cork (incl. Fordsons 1) 2; Waterford United 2; Cork United 2; Cork Athletic 2; Limerick 2; Cork Hibernians 2; Bray Wanderers 2; Longford Town 2; Alton United 1; Athlone Town 1; Transport 1; Finn Harps 1; Home Farm 1; UC Dublin 1; Galway United 1; Drogheda United 1; Sporting Fingal 1.

League of Ireland Premier Division 2018

	P	*W*	*D*	*L*	*F*	*A*	*GD*	*Pts*
Dundalk	36	27	6	3	85	20	65	87
Cork City	36	24	5	7	71	27	44	77
Shamrock Rovers	36	18	8	10	57	27	30	62
Waterford	36	18	5	13	52	44	8	59
St Patrick's Athletic	36	15	5	16	51	47	4	50
Bohemians	36	13	9	14	52	45	7	48
Sligo Rovers	36	12	6	18	38	50	–12	42
Derry City	36	13	3	20	47	70	–23	42
Limerick*+	36	7	6	23	25	75	–50	27
Bray Wanderers*	36	5	3	28	23	96	–73	18

Top scorer: Hoban (Dundalk) 29.
Cup Final: Dundalk 2, Cork City 1.

ROMANIA

Federatia Romana de Fotbal, House of Football, Str. Sergent Serbanica Vasile 12, 22186 Bucuresti.
Founded: 1909. *FIFA:* 1923; *UEFA:* 1954. *National Colours:* All yellow.

International matches 2018–19
Montenegro (h) 0-0, Serbia (a) 2-2, Lithuania (a) 2-1, Serbia (h) 0-0, Lithuania (h) 3-0, Montenegro (a) 1-0, Sweden (a) 1-2, Faroe Islands (h) 4-1, Norway (a) 2-2, Malta (a) 4-0.

League Championship wins (1910–2019)
Steaua Bucharest (renamed FCSB) 26; Dinamo Bucharest 18; Venus Bucharest 8; Chinezul Timisoara 6; UTA Arad 6; CFR Cluj 5; Petrolul Ploiesti 4; Ripensia Timisoara 4; Universitatea Craiova 4; Rapid Bucharest 3; Olimpia Bucharest 2; United Ploiesti 2 (incl. Prahova Ploiesti 1); Colentina Bucharest 2; Arges Pitesti 2; Romano-Americana Bucharest 1; Coltea Brasov 1; Metalochimia Resita 1; Unirea Tricolor 1; CA Oradea 1; Unirea Urziceni 1; Otelul Galati 1; Astra Giurgiu 1; Viitorul Constanta 1.

Cup wins (1934–2019)
Steaua Bucharest (renamed FCSB) 23; Rapid Bucharest 13; Dinamo Bucharest 13; Universitatea Craiova 6; CFR Cluj 4; Petrolul Ploiesti 3; Ripensia Timisoara 2; UTA Arad 2; Politehnica Timisoara 2; CFR Turnu Severin 1; Metalochimia Resita 1; Universitatea Cluj (includes Stiinta) 1; Progresul Oradea (formerly ICO) 1; Progresul Bucharest 1; Ariesul Turda 1; Chimia Ramnicu Vilcea 1; Jiul Petrosani 1; FCU Craiova 1948 1; Gloria Bistrita 1; Astra Giurgiu 1; Voluntari 1; Viitorul Constanta 1.

Romanian Liga 1 Qualifying Table 2018–19

	P	*W*	*D*	*L*	*F*	*A*	*GD*	*Pts*
CFR Cluj	26	15	9	2	39	16	23	54
FCSB	26	14	7	5	49	29	20	49
Universitatea Craiova	26	13	6	7	43	24	19	45
Astra Giurgiu	26	11	9	6	36	23	13	42
Viitorul Constanta	26	11	5	10	26	27	–1	38
Sepsi	26	10	7	9	32	25	7	37
Botosani	26	9	9	8	31	33	–2	36
Politehnica Iasi	26	10	4	12	28	38	–10	34
Dinamo Bucharest	26	8	8	10	29	37	–8	32
Hermannstadt	26	9	5	12	25	28	–3	32
Gaz Metan Medias	26	7	10	9	25	32	–7	31
Dunarea Calarasi	26	4	12	10	16	25	–9	24
Voluntari	26	4	9	13	30	46	–16	21
Concordia Chiajna	26	4	6	16	19	45	–26	18

NB: Points earned in Qualifying phase are halved and rounded up at start of Championship and Relegation Play-off phase.

Championship Round 2018–19

	P	*W*	*D*	*L*	*F*	*A*	*GD*	*Pts*
CFR Cluj	10	7	2	1	15	4	11	50
FCSB	10	7	2	1	18	6	12	48
Viitorul	10	6	2	2	18	10	8	39
Universitatea Craiova	10	4	1	5	8	10	–2	36
Astra Giurgiu	10	2	0	8	6	20	–14	27
Sepsi	10	0	1	9	5	20	–15	20

Relegation Round 2018–19

	P	*W*	*D*	*L*	*F*	*A*	*GD*	*Pts*
Gaz Metan Media	14	10	2	2	25	9	16	48
Botosani	14	8	2	4	18	9	9	44
Bucharest	14	8	3	3	16	7	9	43
Politehnica Iasi	14	3	5	6	12	18	–6	31
Voluntari	14	5	5	4	14	16	–2	31
Hermannstadt+	14	2	5	7	9	19	–10	27
Dunarea Calarasi*	14	3	4	7	8	18	–10	25
Concordia Chiajna*	14	2	4	8	17	23	–6	19

Top scorer: Tucudean (CFR Cluj) 18.
Cup Final: Viitorul Constanta 2, Astra Giurgiu 1 *aet.*

RUSSIA

Russian Football Union, Ulitsa Narodnaya 7, 115 172 Moscow.
Founded: 1912. *FIFA:* 1912; *UEFA:* 1954. *National Colours:* All brick red.

International matches 2018–19
Turkey (a) 2-1, Czech Republic (h) 5-1, Sweden (h) 0-0, Turkey (h) 2-0, Germany (a) 0-3, Sweden (a) 0-2, Belgium (a) 1-3, Kazakhstan (a) 4-0, San Marino (h) 9-0, Cyprus (h) 1-0.

USSR League Championship wins (1936–91)
Dynamo Kyiv 13; Spartak Moscow 12; Dynamo Moscow 11; CSKA Moscow 7; Torpedo Moscow 3; Dinamo Tbilisi 2; Dnepr Dnepropetrovsk 2; Zorya Voroshilovgrad 1; Ararat Yerevan 1; Dynamo Minsk 1; Zenit Leningrad 1.

Russian League Championship wins (1992–2019)
Spartak Moscow 10; CSKA Moscow 6; Zenit St Petersburg 5; Lokomotiv Moscow 3; Rubin Kazan 2; Spartak Vladikavkaz (formerly Alania) 1.

USSR Cup wins (1936–91)
Spartak Moscow 10; Dynamo Kyiv 9; Dynamo Moscow 6; Torpedo Moscow 6; CSKA Moscow 5; Shakhtar Donetsk 4; Lokomotiv Moscow 2; Ararat Yerevan 2; Dinamo Tbilisi 2; Zenit Leningrad 1; Karpaty Lvov 1; SKA Rostov-on-Don 1; Metalist Kharkov 1; Dnepr Dnepropetrovsk 1.

Russian Cup wins (1992–2019)
Lokomotiv Moscow 8; CSKA Moscow 7; Spartak Moscow 3; Zenit St Petersburg 3; Torpedo Moscow 1; Dynamo Moscow 1; Terek Grozny (renamed Akhmat Grozny) 1; Rubin Kazan 1; Rostov 1; Tosno 1.

Russian Premier Liga 2018–19

	P	*W*	*D*	*L*	*F*	*A*	*GD*	*Pts*
Zenit St Petersburg	30	20	4	6	57	29	28	64
Lokomotiv Moscow	30	16	8	6	45	28	17	56
Krasnodar	30	16	8	6	55	23	32	56
CSKA Moscow	30	14	9	7	46	23	23	51
Spartak Moscow	30	14	7	9	36	31	5	49
Arsenal Tula	30	12	10	8	40	33	7	46
Orenburg	30	12	7	11	39	34	5	43
Akhmat Grozny	30	11	9	10	28	30	–2	42
Rostov	30	10	11	9	25	23	2	41
Ural Yekaterinburg	30	10	8	12	33	45	–12	38
Rubin Kazan	30	7	15	8	24	30	–6	36
Dinamo Moscow	30	6	15	9	28	28	0	33
Krylya Sovetov+	30	8	4	18	25	46	–21	28
Ufa+	30	5	11	14	24	34	–10	26
Anzhi*	30	5	6	19	13	50	–37	21
Yenisey Krasnoyarsk*	30	4	8	18	24	55	–31	20

Top scorer: Chalov (CSKA Moscow) 15.
Cup Final: Lokomotiv Moscow 1, Ural Yekaterinburg 0.

SAN MARINO

Federazione Sammarinese Giuoco Calcio, Strada di Montecchio 17, 47890 San Marino.
Founded: 1931. *FIFA:* 1988; *UEFA:* 1988. *National Colours:* Cobalt blue shirts with white trim, white shorts, cobalt blue socks.

International matches 2018–19
Belarus (a) 0-5, Luxembourg (h) 0-3, Moldova (a) 0-2, Luxembourg (a) 0-3, Moldova (h) 0-1, Belarus (h) 0-2, Cyprus (a) 0-3, Scotland (h) 0-2, Russia (a) 0-9, Kazakhstan (a) 0-4.

League Championship wins (1986–2019)
Tre Fiori 7; La Fiorita 5; Domagnano 4; Folgore Falciano 4; Tre Penne 4; Faetano 3; Murata 3; Montevito 1; Libertas 1; Cosmos 1; Pennarossa 1.

Cup wins (1937–2019)
Libertas 11; Domagnano 8; Tre Fiori 7; Tre Penne 6; Juvenes 5; La Fiorita 5; Cosmos 4; Faetano 3; Murata 3;

Dogana 2; Pennarossa 2; Juvenes/Dogana 2; Folgore Falciano 1.

Campionato Sammarinese 2018–19

First Phase Group A

	P	*W*	*D*	*L*	*F*	*A*	*GD*	*Pts*
Tre Fiori	7	6	0	1	21	8	13	18
Folgore Falciano	7	5	1	1	18	5	13	16
Pennarossa	7	4	0	3	9	11	–2	12
Murata	7	3	2	2	11	12	–1	11
Juvenes/Dogana	7	3	1	3	12	11	1	10
Tre Penne	7	3	0	4	19	9	10	9
San Giovanni	7	0	3	4	2	16	–14	3
Virtus	7	0	1	6	4	24	–20	1

First Phase Group B

	P	*W*	*D*	*L*	*F*	*A*	*GD*	*Pts*
La Fiorita	6	5	1	0	14	4	10	16
Domagnano	6	4	1	1	8	3	5	13
Fiorentino	6	3	3	0	11	6	5	12
Libertas	6	2	2	2	9	11	–2	8
Cailungo	6	2	0	4	7	9	–2	6
Cosmos	6	1	1	4	9	14	–5	4
Faetano	6	0	0	6	2	13	–11	0

Top four in each group qualify for Group 1 in Second Phase; remainder to Group 2.

Second Phase Group 1

	P	*W*	*D*	*L*	*F*	*A*	*GD*	*Pts*
La Fiorita	14	12	1	1	48	10	38	37
Tre Fiori	14	6	4	4	32	23	9	22
Folgore Falciano	14	6	4	4	23	20	3	22
Libertas	14	3	6	5	23	23	0	15
Fiorentino	14	3	6	5	20	24	–4	15
Murata	14	4	3	7	12	30	–18	15
Pennarossa	14	4	2	8	13	27	–14	14
Domagnano	14	3	4	7	21	35	–14	13

Second Phase Group 2

	P	*W*	*D*	*L*	*F*	*A*	*GD*	*Pts*
Tre Penne	12	11	1	0	34	6	28	34
Juvenes/Dogana	12	6	4	2	27	14	13	22
Cosmos	12	5	3	4	13	14	–1	18
Faetano	12	5	2	5	24	17	7	17
Cailungo	12	4	5	3	18	21	–3	17
San Giovanni	12	2	2	8	6	22	–16	8
Virtus	12	0	1	11	9	37	–28	1

Top six in Group 1 and Group 2 winner qualify for Play-offs, plus winner of second/third play-off: Juvenes/Dogana 3, Cosmos 1.

5th to 8th Place

Semi-finals: Juvenes/Dogana 4, Murata 0; Fiorentino 0, Folgore Falciano 4
7th place: Murata 3, Fiorentino 0
5th place: Juvenes/Dogana 1, Murata 0

Final Stage

Quarter-finals

La Fiorita 1, 0, Juvenes/Dogana 0, 0 (agg. 6-0)
Libertas 1, 4, Murata 0, 0 (agg. 5-0)
Tre Fiori 2, 1, Fiorentino 1, 0 (agg. 3-1)
Tre Penne 1, 1, Folgore Falciano 0, 1 (agg. 2-1)

Semi-finals

La Fiorita 1, 4, Libertas 0, 0 (agg. 5-0)
Tre Fiori 0, 1, Tre Penne 1, 2 (agg. 1-3)

3rd Place

Libertas 1, Tre Fiori 3

Final

La Fiorita 1, Tre Penne 3
Top scorer: Campagno (Tre Fiori) 22.
Cup Final: Tre Fiori 1, Folgore Falciano 0.

SCOTLAND

Scottish Football Association, Hampden Park, Glasgow G42 9AY.
Founded: 1873. *FIFA:* 1910; *UEFA:* 1954. *National Colours:* Dark blue shirts, dark blue shorts, red socks.

SERBIA

Football Association of Serbia, Terazije 35, PO Box 263, 11000 Beograd.
Founded: 1919. *FIFA:* 1921; *UEFA:* 1954. *National Colours:* Red shirts, blue shorts, white socks.

International matches 2018–19

Lithuania (a) 1-0, Romania (h) 2-2, Montenegro (a) 2-0, Romania (a) 0-0, Montenegro (h) 2-1, Lithuania (h) 4-1, Germany (a) 1-1, Portugal (a) 1-1, Ukraine (h) 0-5, Lithuania (h) 4-1.

Yugoslav League Championship wins (1923–41; 1947–91)

Crvena Zvezda (Red Star Belgrade) 19; Partizan Belgrade 11*; Hajduk Split 9; Gradjanski Zagreb 5; BSK Belgrade (renamed OFK) 5; Dinamo Zagreb 4; Jugoslavija Belgrade 2; Concordia Zagreb 2; Vojvodina Novi Sad 2; FC Sarajevo 2; HASK Zagreb 1; Zeljeznicar 1.
* *Total includes 1 League Championship (1986–87) originally awarded to Macedonian club Vardar.*

Serbian League Championship wins (1992–2019)

Partizan Belgrade 16; Crvena Zvezda (Red Star Belgrade) 10; Obilic 1.

Yugoslav Cup wins (1923–41; 1947–91)

Crvena Zvezda (Red Star Belgrade) 12; Hajduk Split 9; Dinamo Zagreb 7; Partizan Belgrade 6; OFK Belgrade (incl. BSK 3) 5; Rijeka 2; Velez Mostar 2; HASK Zagreb 1; Jugoslavija Belgrade 1; Vardar Skopje 1; Borac Banjaluka 1.

Serbian and Serbia-Montenegro Cup wins (1992–2019)

Crvena Zvezda (Red Star Belgrade) 12; Partizan Belgrade 10; Rijeka 2; Sartid 1; Zeleznik 1; Jagodina 1; Vojvodina 1; Cukaricki 1.

Serbian SuperLiga Qualifying Table 2018–19

	P	*W*	*D*	*L*	*F*	*A*	*GD*	*Pts*
Crvena Zvezda	30	27	3	0	80	16	64	84
Radnicki Nis	30	23	6	1	58	17	41	75
Partizan Belgrade	30	15	9	6	45	20	25	54
Cukaricki	30	15	9	6	48	25	23	54
Mladost Lucani	30	13	7	10	39	29	10	46
Napredak Krusevac	30	10	11	9	32	35	–3	41
Vojvodina	30	10	9	11	24	26	–2	39
Proleter Novi Sad	30	9	11	10	31	29	2	38
Spartak Subotica	30	10	8	12	32	40	–8	38
Radnik Surdulica	30	11	5	14	25	35	–10	38
Vozdovac	30	11	4	15	28	37	–9	37
Macva Sabac	30	8	8	14	16	26	–10	32
Backa Palanka	30	6	7	17	26	54	–28	25
Rad	30	4	9	17	16	39	–23	21
Dinamo Vranje	30	5	5	20	18	62	–44	20
Zemun	30	3	9	18	19	47	–28	18

NB: Points earned in Qualifying phase are halved and rounded up at start of Championship and Relegation Play-off phase.

Championship Round 2018–19

	P	*W*	*D*	*L*	*F*	*A*	*GD*	*Pts*
Crvena Zvezda	37	33	3	1	97	20	77	60
Radnicki Nis	37	25	10	2	71	30	41	48
Partizan Belgrade	37	20	9	8	58	28	30	42
Cukaricki	37	18	12	7	63	36	27	39
Mladost Lucani	37	16	9	12	49	37	12	34
Napredak Krusevac	37	12	12	13	46	50	–4	28
Vojvodina†	37	10	11	16	27	43	–16	22
Proleter Novi Sad†	37	10	11	16	34	41	–7	22

† *Vojvodina finished ahead of Proleter on regular season points.*

Relegation Round 2018–19

	P	*W*	*D*	*L*	*F*	*A*	*GD*	*Pts*
Radnik Surdulica	37	13	8	16	38	45	–7	28
Spartak Subotica	37	12	10	15	41	49	–8	27
Vozdovac	37	12	7	18	36	48	–12	25
Macva Sabac	37	10	11	16	24	38	–14	25
Rad	37	7	12	18	22	44	–22	23
Dinamo Vranje*+	37	9	6	22	24	67	–43	23
Zemun*	37	6	12	19	36	53	–17	21
Backa Palanka*	37	7	9	21	31	68	–37	18

Top scorer: Haskic (Radnicki Nis) 24.
Cup Final: Partizan Belgrade 1, Crvena Zvezda 0.

SLOVAKIA

Slovensky Futbalovy Zvaz, Trnavska cesta 100, 821 01 Bratislava.
Founded: 1938. *FIFA:* 1994; *UEFA:* 1993. *National Colours:* White shirts with blue trim, white shorts, white socks.

International matches 2018–19

Denmark (h) 3-0, Ukraine (a) 0-1, Czech Republic (h) 1-2, Sweden (a) 1-1, Ukraine (h) 4-1, Czech Republic (a) 0-1, Hungary (h) 2-0, Wales (a) 0-1, Jordan (h) 5-1, Azerbaijan (a) 5-1.

League Championship wins (1939–44; 1994–2019)

Slovan Bratislava (incl. 4 as SK Bratislava) 13; Zilina 7;

Kosice 2; Inter Bratislava 2; Artmedia Petrzalka 2; Trencin 2; Sparta Povazska Bystrica 1; OAP Bratislava 1; Ruzomberok 1; Spartak Trnava 1.
See also Czech Republic section for Slovak club honours in Czechoslovak era 1925–93.

Cup wins (1961; 1969–93; 1993–2019)
Slovan Bratislava 15; Spartak Trnava 6; Inter Bratislava 6; VSS Kosice 5; Lokomotiva Kosice 3; Trencin 3; Zilina 2; Artmedia Petrzalka 2; Dukla Banska Bystrica 2; DAC Dunajska Streda 1; Tatran Presov 1; Chemlon Humenne 1; Koba Senec 1; Matador Puchov 1; Ruzomberok 1; ViOn Zlate Moravce 1.

Slovak Super Liga Qualifying Table 2018–19

	P	W	D	L	F	A	GD	Pts
Slovan Bratislava	22	18	4	0	53	18	35	58
Zilina	22	13	5	4	39	23	16	44
DAC Dunajska Streda	22	13	5	4	42	27	15	44
Ruzomberok	22	9	9	4	34	20	14	36
Zemplin Michalovce	22	9	5	8	29	33	–4	32
Sere	22	9	4	9	27	29	–2	31
Nitra	22	7	5	10	27	30	–3	26
Spartak Trnava	22	7	4	11	28	28	0	25
Trencin	22	6	4	12	30	40	–10	22
Zeleziarne Podbrezova	22	6	3	13	22	35	–13	21
Senica	22	3	6	13	20	43	–23	15
ViOn Zlate Moravce	22	4	2	16	19	44	–25	14

Championship Round 2018–19

	P	W	D	L	F	A	GD	Pts
Slovan Bratislava	32	25	5	2	84	33	51	80
DAC Dunajska Streda	32	19	6	7	63	37	26	63
Ruzomberok	32	15	11	6	50	31	19	56
Zilina	32	16	6	10	56	44	12	54
Zemplin Michalovce	32	11	7	14	39	58	–19	40
Sere	32	11	5	16	39	54	–15	38

Relegation Round 2018–19

	P	W	D	L	F	A	GD	Pts
Spartak Trnava	32	10	8	14	35	35	0	38
Senica	32	10	7	15	42	53	–11	37
Nitra	32	8	10	14	42	48	–6	34
ViOn Zlate Moravce	32	10	4	18	33	55	–22	34
Trencin+	32	8	7	17	41	56	–15	31
Zeleziarne Podbrezova*	32	7	8	17	28	48	–20	29

Top scorer: Sporar (Slovan Bratislava) 29.
Cup Final: Spartak Trnava 3, Zilina 3.
aet; Spartak Trnava won 4-1 on penalties.

SLOVENIA

Nogometna Zveza Slovenije, Brnciceva 41g, PP 3986, 1001 Ljubljana.
Founded: 1920. *FIFA:* 1992; *UEFA:* 1992. *National Colours:* White shirts with blue trim, white shorts, white socks.

International matches 2018–19
Bulgaria (h) 1-2, Cyprus (a) 1-2, Norway (a) 0-1, Cyprus (h) 1-1, Norway (h) 1-1, Bulgaria (a) 1-1, Israel (a) 1-1, North Macedonia (h) 1-1, Austria (a) 0-1, Latvia (a) 5-0.

League Championship wins (1991–2019)
Maribor 15; Olimpija (pre-2005) 4; Gorica 4; Domzale 2; Olimpija Ljubljana 2; Koper 1.

Cup wins (1991–2019)
Maribor 9; Olimpija (pre-2005) 4; Gorica 3; Koper 3; Interblock 2; Domzale 2; Olimpija Ljubljana 2; Mura (pre-2004) 1; Rudar Velenje 1; Celje 1.

Slovenian PrvaLiga 2018–19

	P	W	D	L	F	A	GD	Pts
Maribor	36	23	9	4	82	34	48	78
Olimpija Ljubljana	36	20	9	7	73	47	26	69
Domzale	36	18	9	9	76	47	29	63
Mura	36	13	13	10	53	37	16	52
Celje	36	12	13	11	45	51	–6	49
Aluminij	36	14	6	16	50	53	–3	48
Rudar Velenje	36	12	7	17	50	73	–23	43
Triglav	36	10	7	19	51	83	–32	37
Gorica*+	36	7	10	19	44	63	–19	31
Krsko*	36	5	9	22	29	65	–36	24

Top scorer: Zahovic (Maribor) 18.
Cup Final: Olimpija Ljubljana 2, Maribor 1.

SPAIN

Real Federacion Espanola de Futbol, Calle Ramon y Cajal s/n, Apartado postale 385, 28230 Las Rozas, Madrid.
Founded: 1913. *FIFA:* 1913; *UEFA:* 1954. *National Colours:* All red with yellow trim.

International matches 2018–19
England (a) 2-1, Croatia (h) 6-0, Wales (a) 4-1, England (h) 2-3, Croatia (a) 2-3, Bosnia-Herzegovina (h) 1-0, Norway (h) 2-1, Malta (a) 2-0, Faroe Islands (a) 4-1, Sweden (h) 3-0.

League Championship wins (1929–36; 1940–2019)
Real Madrid 33; Barcelona 26; Atletico Madrid 10; Athletic Bilbao 8; Valencia 6; Real Sociedad 2; Real Betis 1; Sevilla 1; Deportivo La Coruna 1.

Cup wins (1903–2019)
Barcelona 30; Athletic Bilbao (includes Vizcaya Bilbao 1) 23; Real Madrid 19; Atletico Madrid 10; Valencia 8; Real Zaragoza 6; Sevilla 5; Espanyol 4; Real Union de Irun 3; Real Sociedad (includes Ciclista) 2; Real Betis 2; Deportivo La Coruna 2; Racing de Irun 1; Arenas 1; Mallorca 1.

Spanish La Liga 2018–19

	P	W	D	L	F	A	GD	Pts
Barcelona	38	26	9	3	90	36	54	87
Atletico Madrid	38	22	10	6	55	29	26	76
Real Madrid	38	21	5	12	63	46	17	68
Valencia	38	15	16	7	51	35	16	61
Getafe†	38	15	14	9	48	35	13	59
Sevilla†	38	17	8	13	62	47	15	59
Espanyol	38	14	11	13	48	50	–2	53
Athletic Bilbao	38	13	14	11	41	45	–4	53
Real Sociedad	38	13	11	14	45	46	–1	50
Real Betis	38	14	8	16	44	52	–8	50
Alaves	38	13	11	14	39	50	–11	50
Eibar	38	11	14	13	46	50	–4	47
Leganes	38	11	12	15	37	43	–6	45
Villarreal	38	10	14	14	49	52	–3	44
Levante	38	11	11	16	59	66	–7	44
Real Valladolid†	38	10	11	17	32	51	–19	41
Celta Vigo†	38	10	11	17	53	62	–9	41
Girona*	38	9	10	19	37	53	–16	37
Huesca*	38	7	12	19	43	65	–22	33
Rayo Vallecano*	38	8	8	22	41	70	–29	32

† Final position decided on head-to-head points.
Top scorer: Messi (Barcelona) 36.
Cup Final: Valencia 2, Barcelona 1.

SWEDEN

Svenska Fotbollfoerbundet, Evenemangsgatan 31, PO Box 1216, SE-171 23 Solna.
Founded: 1904. *FIFA:* 1904; *UEFA:* 1954. *National Colours:* Yellow shirts with blue trim, blue shorts, yellow socks.

International matches 2018–19
Austria (a) 0-2, Turkey (h) 2-3, Russia (a) 0-0, Slovakia (h) 1-1, Turkey (a) 1-0, Russia (h) 2-0, Romania (h) 2-1, Norway (a) 3-3, Malta (h) 3-0, Spain (n) 0-3.

League Championship wins (1896–2018)
Malmo 20; IFK Gothenburg 18; IFK Norrkoping 13; Orgryte 12; AIK Solna 12; Djurgarden 11; IF Elfsborg 6; Helsingborg 5; GAIS Gothenburg 4; Oster Vaxjo 4; Halmstad 4; Atvidaberg 2; Gothenburg IF 1; IFK Eskilstuna 1; Fassbergs 1; IF Gavic Brynas 1; IK Sleipner 1; Hammarby 1; Kalmar 1.
(Played in cup format from 1896–1925.)

Cup wins (1941–2019)
Malmo 14; AIK Solna 8; IFK Gothenburg 7; IFK Norrkoping 6; Helsingborg 5; Djurgarden 5; Kalmar 3; IF Elfsborg 3; Atvidaberg 2; Hacken 2; GAIS Gothenburg 1; IF Raa 1; Landskrona 1; Oster Vaxjo 1; Degerfors 1; Halmstad 1; Orgryte 1; Ostersund 1.

Allsvenskan 2018

	P	W	D	L	F	A	GD	Pts
AIK	30	19	10	1	50	16	34	67
IFK Norrkoping	30	19	8	3	51	27	24	65
Malmo	30	17	7	6	57	29	28	58
Hammarby	30	17	7	6	56	35	21	58
Hacken	30	16	5	9	58	27	31	53
Ostersund	30	15	4	11	51	39	12	49
Djurgaarden	30	13	9	8	40	31	9	48
GIF Sundsvall	30	12	8	10	47	35	12	44
Orebro	30	9	8	13	34	40	–6	35
Kalmar	30	9	7	14	27	35	–8	34
IFK Gothenburg	30	9	4	17	38	53	–15	31
Elfsborg	30	7	9	14	29	41	–12	30
Sirius	30	8	6	16	37	61	–24	30
Brommapojkarna*+	30	8	2	20	25	64	–39	26
Dalkurd*	30	6	6	18	30	57	–27	24
Trelleborg*	30	3	6	21	24	64	–40	15

Top scorer: Paulinho (Hacken) 20.
Cup Final: Hacken 3, Eskilstuna 0.

SWITZERLAND

Schweizerisher Fussballverband, Worbstrasse 48, Postfach 3000, Bern 15.
Founded: 1895. *FIFA:* 1904; *UEFA:* 1954. *National Colours:* Red shirts, white shorts, red socks.

International matches 2018–19
Iceland (h) 6-0, England (a) 0-1, Belgium (a) 1-2, Iceland (a) 2-1, Qatar (h) 0-1, Belgium (h) 5-2, Georgia (a) 2-0, Denmark (h) 3-3, Portugal (a) 1-3, England (n) 0-0 (5-6p).

League Championship wins (1897–2019)
Grasshoppers 27; FC Basel 20; Servette 17; Young Boys 13; FC Zurich 12; Lausanne-Sport 7; Winterthur 3; Aarau 3; Lugano 3; La Chaux-de-Fonds 3; St Gallen 2; Neuchatel Xamax 2; Sion 2; Anglo-American Club 1; Brühl 1; Cantonal-Neuchatel 1; Etoile La Chaux-de-Fonds 1; Biel-Bienne 1; Bellinzona 1; Luzern 1.

Cup wins (1926–2019)
Grasshoppers 19; FC Basel 13; Sion 13; FC Zurich 10; Lausanne-Sport 9; Servette 7; Young Boys 6; La Chaux-de-Fonds 6; Lugano 3; Luzern 2; Urania Geneva 1; Young Fellows Zurich 1; FC Grenchen 1; St Gallen 1; Aarau 1; Wil 1.

Swiss Super League 2018–19

	P	*W*	*D*	*L*	*F*	*A*	*GD*	*Pts*
Young Boys	36	29	4	3	99	36	63	91
FC Basel	36	20	11	5	71	46	25	71
Lugano	36	10	16	10	50	49	1	46
Thun	36	12	10	14	57	58	–1	46
Luzern	36	14	4	18	56	61	–5	46
St Gallen	36	13	7	16	49	58	–9	46
Zurich	36	11	11	14	43	52	–9	44
Sion	36	12	7	17	50	55	–5	43
Neuchatel Xamax+	36	9	10	17	44	65	–21	37
Grasshoppers*	36	5	10	21	32	71	–39	25

Top scorer: Hoarau (Young Boys) 24.
Cup Final: FC Basel 2, Thun 1.

TURKEY

Turkiye Futbol Federasyonu, Hasan Dogan Milli Takimlar, Kamp ve Egitim Tesisleri, Riva, Beykoz, Istanbul.
Founded: 1923. *FIFA:* 1923; *UEFA:* 1962. *National Colours:* All red.

International matches 2018–19
Russia (h) 1-2, Sweden (a) 3-2, Bosnia-Herzegovina (h) 0-0, Russia (a) 0-2, Sweden (h) 0-1, Ukraine (h) 0-0, Albania (a) 2-0, Moldova (h) 4-0, Greece (h) 2-1, Uzbekistan (h) 2-0, France (h) 2-0, Iceland (a) 1-2.

League Championship wins (1959–2019)
Galatasaray 22; Fenerbahce 19; Besiktas 13; Trabzonspor 6; Bursaspor 1.

Cup wins (1963–2019)
Galatasaray 18; Besiktas 9; Trabzonspor 8; Fenerbahce 6; Altay Izmir 2; Goztepe Izmir 2; Ankaragucu 2; Genclerbirligi 2; Kocaelispor 2; Eskisehirspor 1; Bursaspor 1; Sakaryaspor 1; Kayseri 1; Konyaspor 1; Akhisar Belediyespor 1.

Turkish Super Lig 2018–19

	P	*W*	*D*	*L*	*F*	*A*	*GD*	*Pts*
Galatasaray	34	20	9	5	72	36	36	69
Istanbul Basaksehir	34	19	10	5	49	22	27	67
Besiktas	34	19	8	7	72	46	26	65
Trabzonspor	34	18	9	7	64	46	18	63
Yeni Yeni Malatyaspor	34	13	8	13	47	46	1	47
Fenerbahce	34	11	13	10	44	44	0	46
Antalyaspor	34	13	6	15	39	55	–16	45
Konyaspor	34	9	17	8	40	38	2	44
Alanyaspor	34	12	8	14	37	43	–6	44
Kayserispor	34	10	11	13	35	50	–15	41
Rizespor	34	9	14	11	48	50	–2	41
Sivasspor	34	10	11	13	49	54	–5	41
Ankaragucu	34	11	7	16	38	53	–15	40
Kasimpasa	34	11	6	17	53	62	–9	39
Goztepe	34	11	5	18	37	42	–5	38
Bursaspor*	34	7	16	11	28	37	–9	37
BB Erzurumspor*	34	8	11	15	36	43	–7	35
Akhisar Belediyespor*	34	6	9	19	33	54	–21	27

Top scorer: Diagne (Galatasaray, incl. 20 for Kasimpasa) 30.
Cup Final: Galatasaray 3, Akhisarspor 1.

UKRAINE

Football Federation of Ukraine, Provulok Laboratornyi 7-A, PO Box 55, 01133 Kyiv.
Founded: 1991. *FIFA:* 1992; *UEFA:* 1992. *National Colours:* All yellow with blue trim.

International matches 2018–19
Czech Republic (a) 2-1, Slovakia (h) 1-0, Italy (a) 1-1, Czech Republic (h) 1-0, Slovakia (a) 1-4, Turkey (a) 0-0, Portugal (a) 0-0, Luxembourg (a) 2-1, Serbia (h) 5-0, Luxembourg (h) 1-0.

League Championship wins (1992–2019)
Dynamo Kyiv 15; Shakhtar Donetsk 12; Tavriya Simferopol 1.

Cup wins (1992–2019)
Shakhtar Donetsk 13; Dynamo Kyiv 11; Chornomorets Odesa 2; Vorskla Poltava 1; Tavriya Simferopol 1.
See also Russia section for Ukrainian club honours in Soviet era 1936–91.

Ukrainian Premier League Qualifying Table 2018–19

	P	*W*	*D*	*L*	*F*	*A*	*GD*	*Pts*
Shakhtar Donetsk	22	18	3	1	52	9	43	57
Dynamo Kyiv	22	16	2	4	40	11	29	50
Oleksandria	22	12	5	5	31	19	12	41
Zorya Luhansk	22	8	8	6	28	20	8	32
Lviv	22	7	9	6	19	20	–1	30
Mariupol	22	8	6	8	24	33	–9	30
Vorskla Poltava	22	9	2	11	18	28	–10	29
Desna Chernihiv	22	8	4	10	23	24	–1	28
Karpaty Lviv	22	5	6	11	26	37	–11	21
Olimpik Donetsk	22	4	8	10	25	33	–8	20
Chornomorets Odesa	22	4	4	14	12	34	–22	16
Arsenal Kyiv	22	3	3	16	12	42	–30	12

Championship Round 2018–19

	P	*W*	*D*	*L*	*F*	*A*	*GD*	*Pts*
Shakhtar Donetsk	32	26	5	1	73	11	62	83
Dynamo Kyiv	32	22	6	4	54	18	36	72
Oleksandria	32	14	7	11	39	34	5	49
Mariupol†	32	12	7	13	36	47	–11	43
Zorya Luhansk†	32	11	10	11	39	34	5	43
Lviv	32	8	10	14	25	40	–15	34

† *Final position decided on head-to-head points.*

Relegation Round 2018–19

	P	*W*	*D*	*L*	*F*	*A*	*GD*	*Pts*
Vorskla Poltava	32	12	6	14	31	43	–12	42
Desna	32	12	5	15	35	41	–6	41
Olimpik Donetsk	32	7	13	12	41	48	–7	34
Karpaty Lviv+	32	8	9	15	44	53	–9	33
Chornomorets Odesa*+	32	8	7	17	31	49	–18	31
Arsenal Kyiv*	32	7	5	20	26	56	–30	26

Top scorer: Junior Moraes (Shakhtar Donetsk) 19.
Cup Final: Shakhtar Donetsk 4, Inhulets Petrove 0.

WALES

Football Association of Wales, 11/12 Neptune Court, Vanguard Way, Cardiff CF24 5PJ.
Founded: 1876. *FIFA:* 1910; *UEFA:* 1954. *National Colours:* All red with green trim.

SOUTH AMERICA (CONMEBOL)

ARGENTINA

Asociacion del Futbol Argentina, Viamonte 1366/76, Buenos Aires 1053.
Founded: 1893. *FIFA:* 1912; *CONMEBOL:* 1916. *National Colours:* Light blue and white striped shirts, black shorts, white socks.
International matches 2018–19
Guatemala (n) 3-0, Colombia (n) 0-0, Iraq (n) 4-0, Brazil (n) 0-1, Mexico (h) 2-0, Mexico (h) 2-0, Venezuela (n) 1-3, Morocco (a) 1-0, Nicaragua (h) 5-1, Colombia (n) 0-2, Paraguay (n) 1-1, Qatar (n) 2-0, Venezuela (n) 2-0, Brazil (a) 0-2, Chile (n) 2-1.
League champions 2018–19: Racing Club. *Cup winners 2018:* Rosario Central.

BOLIVIA

Federacion Boliviana de Futbol, Avenida Libertador Bolivar 1168, Casilla 484, Cochabamba.
Founded: 1925. *FIFA:* 1926; *CONMEBOL:* 1926. *National Colours:* Green shirts, green shorts, red socks.
International matches 2018–19
Saudi Arabia (a) 2-2, Myanmar (a) 3-0, Iran (a) 1-2, UAE (a) 0-0, Iraq (n) 0-0, Nicaragua (h) 2-2, Korea Republic (a) 0-1, Japan (a) 0-1, France (a) 0-2, Brazil (a) 0-3, Peru (n) 1-3, Venezuela (n) 1-3.

League champions 2018–19: Wilstermann (Apertura 2018); San Jose (Clausura 2018); Bolivar (Apertura 2019). *Cup winners:* No competition.

BRAZIL

Confederacao Brasileira de Futebol, Avenida Luis Carlos Prestes 130, Barra da Tijuca, Rio de Janeiro 22775-055.
Founded: 1914. *FIFA:* 1923; *CONMEBOL:* 1916. *National Colours:* Yellow shirts with green collar and cuffs, blue shorts, white socks.
International matches 2018–19
USA (a) 2-0, El Salvador (n) 5-0, Saudi Arabia (a) 2-0, Argentina (n) 1-0, Uruguay (n) 1-0, Cameroon (n) 1-0, Panama (n) 1-1, Czech Republic (a) 3-1, Qatar (h) 2-0, Honduras (h) 7-0, Bolivia (h) 3-0, Venezuela (h) 0-0, Peru (h) 5-0, Paraguay (h) 0-0 (4-3p), Argentina (h) 2-0, Peru (h) 3-1.
League champions 2018: Palmeiras. *Cup winners 2018:* Cruzeiro.

CHILE

Federacion de Futbol de Chile, Avenida Quilin 5635, Comuna Penalolen, Casilla 3733, Santiago de Chile.
Founded: 1895. *FIFA:* 1913; *CONMEBOL:* 1916. *National Colours:* Red shirts, blue shorts, blue socks.
International matches 2018–19
Korea Republic (a) 0-0, Peru (n) 0-3, Mexico (a) 1-0, Costa Rica (h) 2-3, Honduras (h) 4-1, Mexico (n) 1-3, USA (a) 1-1, Haiti (h) 2-1, Japan (n) 4-0, Ecuador (n) 2-1, Uruguay (n) 0-1, Colombia (n) 0-0 (5-4p), Peru (n) 0-3, Argentina (n) 1-2.
League champions 2018: Universidad Catolica. *Cup winners 2018:* Palestino.

COLOMBIA

Federacion Colombiana de Futbol, Avenida 32 No. 16–22, Bogota.
Founded: 1924. *FIFA:* 1936; *CONMEBOL:* 1936. *National Colours:* Yellow shirts with blue trim, black shorts, red socks with yellow trim.
International matches 2018–19
Venezuela (n) 2-1, Argentina (n) 0-0, USA (a) 4-2, Costa Rica (n) 3-1, Japan (a) 1-0, Korea Republic (a) 1-2, Panama (h) 3-0, Peru (a) 3-0, Argentina (n) 2-0, Qatar (n) 1-0, Paraguay (n) 1-0, Chile (n) 0-0 (4-5p).
League champions 2018: Deportes Tolima (Apertura); Junior (Finalizacion). *2019:* Junior (Apertura). *Cup winners 2018:* Atletico Nacional.

ECUADOR

Federacion Ecuatoriana del Futbol, Avenida Las Aguas y Calle Alianza, PO Box 09-01-7447, Guayaquil 593.
Founded: 1925. *FIFA:* 1927; *CONMEBOL:* 1927. *National Colours:* Yellow shirts, black shorts, white socks.
International matches 2018–19
Jamaica (n) 2-0, Guatemala (n) 2-0, Qatar (a) 3-4, Oman (n) 0-0, Peru (a) 2-0, Panama (a) 2-1, USA (a) 0-1, Honduras (n) 0-0, Venezuela (n) 1-1, Mexico (n) 2-3, Uruguay (n) 0-4, Chile (n) 1-2, Japan (n) 1-1.
League champions 2018: LDA Quito. *Cup winners:* Inaugural competition still being played.

PARAGUAY

Asociacion Paraguaya de Futbol, Calle Mayor Martinez 1393, Asuncion.
Founded: 1906. *FIFA:* 1925; *CONMEBOL:* 1921. *National Colours:* Red and white striped shirts, blue shorts, white socks with red trim.
International matches 2018–19
South Africa (a) 1-1, Peru (n) 0-1, Mexico (n) 2-4, Honduras (h) 1-1, Guatemala (h) 2-0, Qatar (n) 2-2, Argentina (n) 1-1, Colombia (n) 0-1, Brazil (a) 0-0 (4-3p).
League champions 2018: Olimpia (Apertura); Olimpia (Clausura). *2019:* Olimpia (Apertura). *Cup winners 2018:* Guarani.

PERU

Federacion Peruana de Futbol, Avenida Aviacion 2085, San Luis, Lima 30.
Founded: 1922. *FIFA:* 1924; *CONMEBOL:* 1925. *National Colours:* White shirts with red sash, white shorts, white socks.
International matches 2018–19
Netherlands (a) 1-2, Germany (a) 1-2, Chile (n) 3-0, USA (n) 1-1, Ecuador (h) 0-2, Costa Rica (h) 2-3, Paraguay (n) 1-0, El Salvador (n) 0-2, Costa Rica (h) 1-0, Colombia (h) 0-3, Venezuela (n) 0-0, Bolivia (n) 3-1, Brazil (a) 0-5, Chile (n) 3-0, Uruguay (n) 0-0 (5-4p), Chile (n) 3-0, Brazil (a) 1-3.
League champions 2017: Sporting Cristal. *Cup winners 2019:* Inaugural competition still being played.

URUGUAY

Asociacion Uruguaya de Futbol, Guayabo 1531, Montevideo 11200.
Founded: 1900. *FIFA:* 1923; *CONMEBOL:* 1916. *National Colours:* Sky blue shirts, black shorts, black socks with sky blue tops.
International matches 2018–19
Mexico (n) 4-1, Korea Republic (a) 1-2, Japan (a) 3-4, Brazil (n) 0-1, France (a) 0-1, Uzbekistan (n) 3-0, Thailand (n) 4-0, Panama (h) 3-0, Ecuador (n) 4-0, Japan (n) 2-2, Chile (n) 1-0, Peru (n) 0-0 (4-5p).
League champions 2018: Penarol. *Cup winners:* No competition.

VENEZUELA

Federacion Venezolana de Futbol, Avenida Santos Erminy 1ra Calle las Delicias, Torre Mega II, P.H.B. Sabana Grande, 1050 Caracas.
Founded: 1926. *FIFA:* 1952; *CONMEBOL:* 1952. *National Colours:* All burgundy.
International matches 2018–19
Colombia (n) 1-2, Panama (a) 2-0, UAE (n) 2-0, Japan (a) 1-1, Iran (n) 1-1, Argentina (n) 3-1, Ecuador (n) 1-1, Mexico (n) 1-3, USA (a) 3-0, Peru (n) 0-0, Brazil (a) 0-0, Bolivia (n) 3-1, Argentina (n) 0-2.
League champions 2018: Zamora. *Cup winners 2018:* Zulia.

ASIA (AFC)

AFGHANISTAN

Afghanistan Football Federation, PO Box 128, Kabul.
Founded: 1933. *FIFA:* 1948; *AFC:* 1954. *National Colours:* Red shirts, black shorts with green trim, red socks.
International matches 2018–19
Turkmenistan (n) 0-2, Oman (n) 0-5, Malaysia (a) 1-2.
League champions 2018: Toofan Harirod. Cup winners: No competition.

AUSTRALIA

Football Federation Australia Ltd, Locked Bag A4071, Sydney South, NSW 1235.
Founded: 1961. *FIFA:* 1963; *AFC:* 2006. *National Colours:* All gold.
International matches 2018–19
Kuwait (a) 4-0, Korea Republic (h) 1-1, Lebanon (h) 3-0, Jordan (n) 0-1, Palestine (n) 3-0, Syria (n) 3-2, Uzbekistan (n) 0-0 (4-2p), UAE (a) 0-1, Korea Republic (a) 0-1.
League champions 2018–19: Perth Glory. *Grand Final winners 2019:* Sydney FC. *Cup winners 2018:* Adelaide United.

BAHRAIN

Bahrain Football Association, PO Box 5464, Building 315, Road 2407, Block 934, East Riffa.
Founded: 1957. *FIFA:* 1968; *AFC:* 1969. *National Colours:* All red with gold trim.
International matches 2018–19
Philippines (h) 1-1, China PR (h) 0-0, Syria (h) 0-1, Myanmar (h) 4-1, Oman (a) 1-2, Tajikistan (h) 5-0, Lebanon (h) 1-0, Korea DPR (h) 4-0, UAE (a) 1-1, Thailand (n) 0-1, India (n) 1-0, Korea Republic (n) 1-2.
League champions 2018–19: Riffa. *Cup winners 2018–19:* Riffa.

BANGLADESH

Bangladesh Football Federation, BFF House, Motijheel Commercial Area, Dhaka 1000.
Founded: 1972. *FIFA:* 1976; *AFC:* 1974. *National Colours:* Green shirts with red trim, white shorts, green socks.
International matches 2018–19
Sri Lanka (a) 0-1, Bhutan (h) 2-0, Pakistan (h) 1-0, Nepal (h) 0-2, Laos (h) 1-0, Philippines (n) 0-1, Palestine (n) 0-2, Cambodia (a) 1-0, Laos (a) 1-0, Laos (h) 0-0.
League champions 2018–19: Bashundhara Kings. *Cup winners 2018:* Dhaka Abahani.

BHUTAN

Bhutan Football Federation, PO Box 365, Changiiji, Thimphu 11001.
Founded: 1983. *FIFA:* 2000; *AFC:* 2000. *National Colours:* Orange shirts with yellow trim, orange shorts, orange socks.
International matches 2018–19
Bangladesh (a) 0-2, Nepal (n) 0-4, Pakistan (n) 0-3, Guam (h) 1-0, Guam (a) 0-5.
League champions 2018: Transport United. *Cup winners:* No competition.

BRUNEI

National Football Association of Brunei Darussalam, NFABD House, Jalan Pusat Persidangan, Bandar Seri Begawan BB4313.

Founded: 1959. *FIFA:* 1972; *AFC:* 1969. *National Colours:* Yellow shirts with black trim, yellow shorts with black trim, yellow socks.
International matches 2018–19
Timor-Leste (n) 1-3, Timor-Leste (n) 1-0, Mongolia (a) 0-2, Mongolia (h) 2-1.
League champions 2018–19: MS ABDB. *Cup winners 2018–19:* Kota Rangers.

CAMBODIA

Football Federation of Cambodia, National Football Centre, Road Kabsrov Sangkat Samrongkrom, Khan Dangkor, Phnom Penh 2327 PPT3.
Founded: 1933. *FIFA:* 1954; *AFC:* 1954. *National Colours:* All blue with red trim.
International matches 2018–19
Malaysia (h) 1-3, Timor-Leste (h) 2-2, Singapore (h) 1-2, Malaysia (h) 0-1, Myanmar (a) 1-4, Laos (h) 3-1, Vietnam (a) 0-3, Bangladesh (h) 0-1, Pakistan (h) 2-0, Pakistan (a) 2-1*.
* *Match played in Qatar.*
League champions 2018: Nagaworld. *Cup winners 2018:* National Defense Ministry.

CHINA PR

Football Association of the People's Republic of China, Building A, Dongjiudasha Mansion, Xizhaosi Street, Dongcheng, Beijing 100061.
Founded: 1924. *FIFA:* 1931, rejoined 1980; *AFC:* 1974. *National Colours:* Red shirts with yellow trim, white shorts, red socks with yellow trim.
International matches 2018–19
Qatar (a) 0-1, Bahrain (a) 0-0, India (h) 0-0, Syria (h) 2-0, Palestine (h) 1-1, Kyrgyzstan (n) 2-1, Philippines (n) 3-0, Korea Republic (n) 0-2, Thailand (n) 2-1, Iran (n) 0-3, Thailand (h) 0-1, Uzbekistan (h) 0-1, Philippines (h) 2-0, Tajikistan (h) 1-0.
League champions 2018: Shanghai SIPG. *Cup winners 2018:* Beijing Guoan.

CHINESE TAIPEI

Chinese Taipei Football Association, Room 210, 2F, 55 Chang Chi Street, Tatung, Taipei 10363.
Founded: 1936. *FIFA:* 1954; *AFC:* 1954. *National Colours:* All blue with red and white trim.
International matches 2018–19
Malaysia (h) 2-0, Hong Kong (h) 1-2, Mongolia (h) 2-1, Korea DPR (h) 0-2, Myanmar (a) 0-0, Solomon Islands (h) 0-1, Nepal (h) 1-1, Hong Kong (a) 2-0.
League champions 2018: Tatung. *Cup winners:* No competition.

GUAM

Guam Football Association, PO Box 20008, Barrigada, Guam 96921.
Founded: 1975. *FIFA:* 1996; *AFC:* 1996. *National Colours:* All dark blue with white trim.
International matches 2018–19
Northern Mariana Islands† (n) 4-0, Macao (n) 0-2, Mongolia (a) 1-1, Bhutan (a) 0-1, Bhutan (h) 5-0.
League champions 2018–19: Rovers. *Cup winners 2019:* Bank of Guam Strykers.

HONG KONG

Hong Kong Football Association Ltd, 55 Fat Kwong Street, Ho Man Tin, Kowloon, Hong Kong.
Founded: 1914. *FIFA:* 1954; *AFC:* 1954. *National Colours:* Red shirts, red shorts, white socks with red trim.
International matches 2018–19
Thailand (h) 0-1, Indonesia (a) 1-1, Chinese Taipei (a) 2-1, Korea DPR (n) 0-0, Mongolia (n) 5-1, Chinese Taipei (h) 0-2.
League champions 2018–19: Tai Po. *Cup winners 2018–19:* Kitchee.

INDIA

All India Football Federation, Football House, Sector 19, Phase 1 Dwarka, New Delhi 110075.
Founded: 1937. *FIFA:* 1948; *AFC:* 1954. *National Colours:* Blue shirts with orange trim, blue shorts, blue socks.
International matches 2018–19
Sri Lanka (n) 2-0, Maldives (n) 2-0, Pakistan (n) 3-1, Maldives (n) 1-2, China PR (a) 0-0, Jordan (a) 1-2, Oman (n) 0-0, Thailand (n) 4-1, UAE (a) 0-2, Bahrain (n) 0-1, Curacao (n) 1-3, Thailand (a) 1-0, Tajikistan (h) 2-4, Korea Republic (h) 2-5.
League champions 2018–19: Chennai City. *Cup winners 2019:* Goa.

INDONESIA

Football Association of Indonesia, Gelora Bung Karno Pintu X–XI, PO Box 2305, Senayan, Jakarta 10023.
Founded: 1930. *FIFA:* 1952; *AFC:* 1954. *National Colours:* All red.
International matches 2018–19
Mauritius (h) 1-0, Myanmar (h) 3-0, Hong Kong (h) 1-1, Singapore (a) 0-1, Timor-Leste (h) 3-1, Thailand (a) 2-4, Philippines (h) 0-0, Myanmar (a) 2-0, Jordan (a) 1-4, Vanuatu (h) 6-0.
League champions 2018: Persija. *Cup winners 2018–19:* Resumed competition still being played.

IRAN

Football Federation IR Iran, No. 4 Third St., Seoul Avenue, Tehran 19958-73591.
Founded: 1920. *FIFA:* 1948; *AFC:* 1954. *National Colours:* All white with red trim.
International matches 2018–19
Uzbekistan (a) 1-0, Bolivia (h) 2-1, Trinidad & Tobago (h) 1-0, Venezuela (n) 1-1, Yemen (n) 5-0, Vietnam (n) 2-0, Iraq (n) 0-0, Oman (n) 2-0, China PR (n) 3-0, Japan (n) 0-3, Syria (h) 5-0, Korea Republic (a) 1-1.
League champions 2018–19: Persepolis. *Cup winners 2018–19:* Persepolis.

IRAQ

Iraq Football Association, Al-Shaab Stadium, PO Box 484, Baghdad.
Founded: 1948. *FIFA:* 1950; *AFC:* 1970. *National Colours:* White shirts with green trim, white shorts, white socks.
International matches 2018–19
Palestine (a) 3-0, Kuwait (a) 2-2, Argentina (n) 0-4, Saudi Arabia (a) 1-1, Bolivia (n) 0-0, Palestine (n) 1-0, Vietnam (n) 3-2, Yemen (n) 3-0, Iran (n) 0-0, Qatar (n) 0-1, Syria (h) 1-0, Jordan (h) 3-2, Tunisia (a) 0-2.
League champions 2017–18: Al-Zawra'a; *2018–19:* Al-Shorta. *Cup winners 2018–19:* Competition still being played.

JAPAN

Japan Football Association, JFA House, Football Ave., Bunkyo-ku, Tokyo 113-8311.
Founded: 1921. *FIFA:* 1929, rejoined 1950; *AFC:* 1954. *National Colours:* Blue shirts, black shorts, blue socks.
International matches 2018–19
Costa Rica (h) 3-0, Panama (h) 3-0, Uruguay (h) 4-3, Venezuela (h) 1-1, Kyrgyzstan (h) 4-0, Turkmenistan (n) 3-2, Oman (n) 1-0, Uzbekistan (n) 2-1, Saudi Arabia (n) 1-0, Vietnam (n) 1-0, Iran (n) 3-0, Qatar (n) 1-3, Colombia (h) 0-1, Bolivia (h) 1-0, Trinidad & Tobago (h) 0-0, El Salvador (h) 2-0, Chile (n) 0-4, Uruguay (n) 2-2, Ecuador (n) 1-1.
League champions 2018: Kawasaki Frontale. *Cup winners 2018:* Urawa Red Diamonds.

JORDAN

Jordan Football Association, PO Box 962024, Al-Hussein Youth City, Amman 11196.
Founded: 1949. *FIFA:* 1956; *AFC:* 1970. *National Colours:* All white with red trim.
International matches 2018–19
Lebanon (h) 0-1, Oman (h) 0-0, Albania (a) 0-0, Croatia (a) 1-2, India (h) 2-1, Saudi Arabia (h) 1-1, Kyrgyzstan (n) 0-1, Australia (n) 1-0, Syria (n) 2-0, Palestine (n) 0-0, Vietnam (n) 1-1 (2-4p), Syria (n) 0-1, Iraq (a) 2-3, Slovakia (a) 1-5, Indonesia (h) 4-1.
League champions 2018–19: Al-Faisaly. *Cup winners 2018–19:* Al-Faisaly.

KOREA DPR

DPR Korea Football Association, Kumsongdong, Kwangbok Street, Mangyongdae, PO Box 818, Pyongyang.
Founded: 1945. *FIFA:* 1958; *AFC:* 1974. *National Colours:* All red with white trim.
International matches 2018–19
Uzbekistan (a) 0-2, Mongolia (n) 4-1, Hong Kong (n) 0-0, Chinese Taipei (a) 2-0, Vietnam (a) 1-1, Bahrain (a) 0-4, Saudi Arabia (n) 0-4, Qatar (n) 0-6, Lebanon (n) 1-4, Uzbekistan (a) 0-4, Syria (n) 2-5, India (a) 2-5.
League champions 2017–18: April 25. *Cup winners 2019:* Kigwancha.

KOREA REPUBLIC

Korea Football Association, KFA House 21, Gyeonghuigung-gil 46, Jongno-Gu, Seoul 110-062.
Founded: 1933, 1948. *FIFA:* 1948; *AFC:* 1954. *National Colours:* Red shirts, black shorts, red socks.
International matches 2018–19
Costa Rica (h) 2-0, Chile (h) 0-0, Uruguay (h) 2-1, Panama (h) 2-2, Australia (a) 1-1, Uzbekistan (n) 4-0, Saudi Arabia (n) 0-0, Philippines (n) 1-0, Kyrgyzstan (n) 1-0, China PR (n) 2-0, Bahrain (n) 2-1, Qatar (n) 0-1, Bolivia (n) 1-0, Colombia (n) 2-1, Australia (a) 1-0, Iran (n) 1-1.
League champions 2018: Jeonbuk Hyundai Motors. *Cup winners 2018:* Daegu.

KUWAIT

Kuwait Football Association, Block 5, Street 101, Building 141A, Jabriya, PO Box Hawalli 4020, Kuwait 32071.
Founded: 1952. *FIFA:* 1964; *AFC:* 1964. *National Colours:* All blue with white trim.
International matches 2018–19
Iraq (h) 2-2, Lebanon (h) 1-0, Australia (h) 0-4, Syria (h) 1-2, Nepal (h) 0-0.
League champions 2018–19: Al-Kuwait. *Cup winners 2019:* Al-Kuwait.

KYRGYZSTAN

Football Federation of Kyrgyz Republic, Mederova Street 1 'B', PO Box 1484, Bishkek 720082.
Founded: 1992. *FIFA:* 1994; *AFC:* 1994. *National Colours:* All red.
International matches 2018–19
Palestine (h) 1-1, Syria (h) 2-1, Malaysia (a) 1-0, Japan (a) 0-4, Jordan (n) 1-0, China PR (n) 1-2, Korea Republic (n) 0-1, Philippines (n) 3-1, UAE (a) 2-3. Palestine (h) 2-2.
League champions 2018: Dordoi. *Cup winners 2017:* Dordoi; *2018:* Dordoi.

LAOS

Lao Football Federation, FIFA Training Centre, Ban Houayhong, Chanthabuly, PO Box 1800, Vientiane 856-21.
Founded: 1951. *FIFA:* 1952; *AFC:* 1968. *National Colours:* All red.
International matches 2018–19
UAE (n) 0-3, Bangladesh (a) 0-1, Philippines (n) 1-3, Mongolia (h) 1-4, Vietnam (h) 0-3, Malaysia (a) 1-3, Myanmar (h) 1-3, Cambodia (a) 1-3, Sri Lanka (h) 2-1, Sri Lanka (h) 2-2, Bangladesh (h) 0-1, Bangladesh (a) 0-0.
League champions 2018: Lao Toyota. *Cup winners 2019:* Resumed competition still being played.

LEBANON

Association Libanaise de Football, Verdun Street, Bristol Radwan Centre, PO Box 4732, Beirut.
Founded: 1933. *FIFA:* 1936; *AFC:* 1964. *National Colours:* All red with white trim.
International matches 2018–19
Jordan (a) 1-0, Oman (n) 0-0, Kuwait (a) 0-1, Uzbekistan (n) 0-0, Australia (a) 0-3, Bahrain (a) 0-1, Qatar (n) 0-2, Saudi Arabia (n) 0-2, Korea DPR (n) 4-1.
League champions 2018–19: Al-Ahed. *Cup winners 2018–19:* Al-Ahed.

MACAO

Associacao de Futebol de Macao, Avenida Wai Leong, Taipa University of Science and Technology, Football Field Block 1, Taipa.
Founded: 1939. *FIFA:* 1978; *AFC:* 1978. *National Colours:* All green with white trim.
International matches 2018–19
Solomon Islands (h) 1-4, Mongolia (a) 1-4, Guam (n) 2-0, Northern Mariana Islands† (n) 1-1, Sri Lanka (h) 1-0*, Sri Lanka (a) 0-3‡.
** Match played in China PR. ‡Walkover; match awarded 3-0 to Sri Lanka.*
League champions 2019: Chao Pak Kei. *Cup winners 2018:* Chao Pak Kei.

MALAYSIA

Football Association of Malaysia, 3rd Floor, Wisma FAM, Jalan SS5A/9, Kelana Jaya, Petaling Jaya 47301, Selangor Darul Ehsan.
Founded: 1933. *FIFA:* 1954; *AFC:* 1954. *National Colours:* Yellow shirts, black shorts, yellow socks with black trim.
International matches 2018–19
Chinese Taipei (a) 0-2, Cambodia (a) 3-1, Sri Lanka (a) 4-1, Kyrgyzstan (h) 0-1, Maldives (h) 3-0, Cambodia (a) 1-0, Laos (h) 3-1, Vietnam (a) 0-2, Myanmar (h) 3-0, Thailand (h) 0-0, Thailand (a) 2-2, Vietnam (h) 2-2, Vietnam (a) 0-1, Singapore (h) 0-1, Afghanistan (a) 2-1, Nepal (h) 2-0, Timor-Leste (n) 7-1, Timor-Leste (n) 5-1.
League champions 2018: Johor Darul Ta'zim. *Cup winners 2019:* Competition still being played.

MALDIVES

Football Association of Maldives, FAM House, Ujaalahingun, Male 20388.
Founded: 1982. *FIFA:* 1986; *AFC:* 1984. *National Colours:* Red shirts with white trim, white shorts, red socks with white tops.
International matches 2018–19
Sri Lanka (n) 0-0, India (n) 0-2, Nepal (n) 3-0, India (n) 2-1, Malaysia (a) 0-3.
League champions 2018: TC Sports Club. *Cup winners 2017:* New Radiant; *2018:* Not held.

MONGOLIA

Mongolian Football Federation, PO Box 259, 15th Khoroo, Khan-Uul, Ulaanbaatar 210646.
Founded: 1959. *FIFA:* 1998; *AFC:* 1998. *National Colours:* Blue shirts with white sleeves, blue shorts, blue socks.
International matches 2018–19
Macao (h) 4-1, Northern Mariana Islands† (h) 9-0, Guam (h) 1-1, Singapore (a) 0-2, Laos (a) 4-1, Korea DPR (n) 1-4, Chinese Taipei (a) 1-2, Hong Kong (n) 1-5, Brunei (h) 2-0, Brunei (a) 1-2.
League champions 2018: Erchim. *Cup winners 2018:* Athletic 220.

MYANMAR

Myanmar Football Federation, National Football Training Centre, Waizayanta Road, Thuwunna, Thingankyun Township, Yangon 11070.
Founded: 1947. *FIFA:* 1948; *AFC:* 1954. *National Colours:* All red.
International matches 2018–19
Indonesia (a) 0-3, Bolivia (h) 0-3, Bahrain (a) 1-4, Cambodia (h) 4-1, Laos (a) 3-1, Vietnam (h) 0-0, Malaysia (a) 0-3, Chinese Taipei (h) 0-0, Indonesia (h) 0-2, Singapore (a) 2-1.
League champions 2018: Yangon United. *Cup winners 2018:* Yangon United.

NEPAL

All Nepal Football Association, ANFA House, Satdobato, Lalitpur-17, PO Box 12582, Kathmandu.
Founded: 1951. *FIFA:* 1972; *AFC:* 1954. *National Colours:* All red with white trim.
International matches 2018–19
Pakistan (n) 1-2, Bhutan (n) 4-0, Bangladesh (a) 2-0, Maldives (n) 0-3, Tajikistan (n) 2-0, Palestine (n) 0-1, Kuwait (a) 0-0, Malaysia (a) 0-2, Chinese Taipei (a) 1-1.
League champions 2018–19: Manang Marshyangdi Club. *Cup winners 2019:* Three Star Club.

OMAN

Oman Football Association, Seeb Sports Stadium, PO Box 3462, 112 Ruwi, Muscat.
Founded: 1978. *FIFA:* 1980; *AFC:* 1980. *National Colours:* All yellow with black trim.
International matches 2018–19
Lebanon (n) 0-0, Jordan (a) 0-0, Philippines (n) 1-1, Ecuador (n) 0-0, Syria (h) 1-1, Bahrain (h) 2-1, Tajikistan (h) 2-1, Tajikistan (h) 1-0, India (n) 0-0, Uzbekistan (n) 1-2, Japan (n) 0-1, Turkmenistan (n) 3-1, Iran (n) 0-2, Afghanistan (n) 5-0, Singapore (n) 1-1 (5-4p).
League champions 2018–19: Dhofar. *Cup winners 2018–19:* Sur.

PAKISTAN

Pakistan Football Federation, PFF Football House, Ferozepur Road, Lahore 54600, Punjab.
Founded: 1947. *FIFA:* 1948; *AFC:* 1954. *National Colours:* All white with green trim.
International matches 2018–19
Nepal (n) 2-1, Bangladesh (a) 0-1, Bhutan (n) 3-0, India (n) 1-3, Palestine (a) 1-2, Cambodia (a) 0-2, Cambodia (n) 1-2.
League champions 2018–19: Khan Research Laboratories. *Cup winners 2018:* Pakistan Air Force.

PALESTINE

Palestinian Football Association, Nr. Faisal Al-Husseini Stadium, PO Box 4373, Jerusalem-al-Ram.
Founded: 1928. *FIFA:* 1998; *AFC:* 1998. *National Colours:* All red with white trim.
International matches 2018–19
Iraq (h) 0-3, Kyrgyzstan (a) 1-1, Qatar (a) 0-3, Tajikistan (n) 2-0, Nepal (n) 1-0, Bangladesh (a) 2-0, Tajikistan (n) 0-0 (4-3p), Pakistan (h) 2-1, China PR (a) 1-1, Iraq (n) 0-1, Syria (n) 0-0, Australia (n) 0-3, Jordan (n) 0-0, Kyrgyzstan (a) 1-1.
League champions 2018–19: Hilal Al-Quds. *Cup winners 2018–19:* Competition still being played.

PHILIPPINES

Philippine Football Federation, 27 Danny Floro–corner Capt. Henry Javier Streets, Oranbo, Pasig City 1600.
Founded: 1907. *FIFA:* 1930; *AFC:* 1954. *National Colours:* All white with grey trim.
International matches 2018–19
Bahrain (a) 1-1, Laos (n) 3-1, Bangladesh (a) 1-0, Tajikistan (n) 0-2, Oman (n) 1-1, Singapore (h) 1-0, Timor-Leste (n) 3-2, Thailand (h) 1-1, Indonesia (a) 0-0, Vietnam (a) 1-2, Vietnam (n) 2-4, Korea Republic (n) 0-1, China PR (n) 0-3, Kyrgyzstan (n) 1-3, China PR (a) 0-2.
League champions 2018: Ceres Negros. *Cup winners 2018:* Kaya-Iloilo.

QATAR

Qatar Football Association, 28th Floor, Al Bidda Tower, Corniche Street, West Bay, PO Box 5333, Doha.
Founded: 1960. *FIFA:* 1972; *AFC:* 1974. *National Colours:* All burgundy.
International matches 2018–19
China PR (h) 1-0, Palestine (h) 3-0, Ecuador (h) 4-3, Uzbekistan (a) 0-2, Switzerland (a) 1-0, Iceland (n) 2-2, Lebanon (n) 2-0, Korea DPR (n) 6-0, Saudi Arabia (n) 2-0, Iraq (n) 1-0, Korea Republic (n) 1-0, UAE (a) 4-0, Japan (n) 3-1, Brazil (a) 0-2, Paraguay (n) 2-2, Colombia (n) 0-1, Argentina (n) 0-2.
League champions 2018–19: Al-Sadd. *Cup winners 2019:* Al-Duhail.

SAUDI ARABIA

Saudi Arabian Football Federation, Al Mather Quarter, Prince Faisal Bin Fahad Street, PO Box 5844, Riyadh 11432.
Founded: 1956. *FIFA:* 1956; *AFC:* 1972. *National Colours:* White shirts with green trim, white shorts, white socks.
International matches 2018–19
Bolivia (h) 2-2, Brazil (h) 0-2, Iraq (h) 1-1, Yemen (h) 1-0, Jordan (h) 1-1, Korea Republic (n) 0-0, Korea DPR (n) 4-0, Lebanon (n) 2-0, Qatar (n) 0-2, Japan (n) 0-1, UAE (a) 1-2, Equatorial Guinea (h) 3-2.
League champions 2018–19: Al-Nassr. *Cup winners 2019:* Al-Taawoun.

SINGAPORE

Football Association of Singapore, Jalan Besar Stadium, 100 Tyrwhitt Road, Singapore 207542.
Founded: 1892. *FIFA:* 1956; *AFC:* 1954. *National Colours:* All red.
International matches 2018–19
Mauritius (h) 1-1, Fiji (h) 2-0, Mongolia (h) 2-0, Cambodia (a) 2-1, Indonesia (h) 1-0, Philippines (a) 0-1, Timor-Leste (h) 6-1, Thailand (a) 0-3, Malaysia (a) 1-0, Oman (n) 1-1 (4-5p), Solomon Islands (h) 4-3, Myanmar (h) 1-2.
League champions 2018: Albirex Niigata (S). *Cup winners 2018:* Albirex Niigata (S).

SRI LANKA

Football Federation of Sri Lanka, 100/9 Independence Avenue, Colombo 07.
Founded: 1939. *FIFA:* 1952; *AFC:* 1954. *National Colours:* All yellow with red trim.
International matches 2018–19
Bangladesh (a) 1-0, India (n) 0-2, Maldives (n) 0-0, Malaysia (h) 1-4, Laos (a) 1-2, Laos (a) 2-2, Macao (a) 0-1*, Macao (h) 3-0‡.
** Match played in China PR. ‡Walkover; match awarded 3-0 to Sri Lanka.*
League champions 2018–19: Defenders (formerly Army). *Cup winners 2018:* Army.

SYRIA

Syrian Arab Federation for Football, Al Faihaa Sports Complex, PO Box 421, Damascus.
Founded: 1936. *FIFA:* 1937; *AFC:* 1970. *National Colours:* All red with white trim.
International matches 2018–19
Uzbekistan (a) 1-1, Kyrgyzstan (a) 1-2, Bahrain (a) 1-0, China PR (a) 0-2, Oman (a) 1-1, Kuwait (a) 2-1, Yemen (n) 1-0, Palestine (n) 0-0, Jordan (n) 0-2, Australia (n) 2-3, Iraq (a) 0-1, Jordan (n) 1-0, UAE (a) 0-0, Iran (a) 0-5, Uzbekistan (a) 0-2, Korea DPR (n) 5-2, Tajikistan (n) 0-2.
League champions 2018–19: Al-Jaish. *Cup winners 2018:* Al-Jaish; *2018–19:* Al-Wathba.

TAJIKISTAN

Tajikistan Football Federation, 14/3 Ayni Street, Dushanbe 734 025.
Founded: 1936. *FIFA:* 1994; *AFC:* 1994. *National Colours:* All red with green trim.
International matches 2018–19
Nepal (n) 2-0, Palestine (n) 0-2, Philippines (n) 2-0, Palestine (n) 0-2, Oman (a) 1-2, Oman (a) 0-1, Bahrain (a) 0-5, China PR (a) 0-1, India (a) 1-1, Syria (n) 2-0.
League champions 2018: Istiklol. *Cup winners 2018:* Istiklol.

THAILAND

Football Association of Thailand, National Stadium, Gate 3, Rama 1 Road, Patumwan, Bangkok 10330.
Founded: 1916. *FIFA:* 1925; *AFC:* 1954. *National Colours:* All black with red trim.
International matches 2018–19
Hong Kong (a) 1-0, Trinidad & Tobago (h) 1-0, Timor-Leste (h) 7-0, Indonesia (h) 4-2, Philippines (a) 1-1, Singapore (h) 3-0, Malaysia (a) 0-0, Malaysia (h) 2-2, India (n) 1-4, Bahrain (a) 1-0, UAE (n) 1-1, China PR (n) 1-2, China PR (a) 1-0, Uruguay (n) 0-4, Vietnam (h) 0-1, India (h) 0-1.
League champions 2018: Buriram United. *Cup winners 2018:* Chiangrai United.

TIMOR-LESTE

Federacao Futebol de Timor-Leste, Campo Democracia, Avenida Bairo Formosa, Dili.
Founded: 2002. *FIFA:* 2005; *AFC:* 2005. *National Colours:* Red shirts with black trim, white shorts, black and red socks.
International matches 2018–19
Brunei (n) 3-1, Brunei (n) 0-1, Cambodia (a) 2-2, Thailand (h) 0-7*, Indonesia (a) 1-3, Philippines (h) 2-3**, Singapore (a) 1-6, Malaysia (a) 1-7, Malaysia (h) 1-5**.
** Match played in Thailand. **Match played in Malaysia.*
League champions 2018: Boavista. *Cup winners 2018:* Atletico Ultramar.

TURKMENISTAN

Football Federation of Turkmenistan, Stadium Kopetdag, 245 A. Niyazov Street, Ashgabat 744 001.
Founded: 1992. *FIFA:* 1994; *AFC:* 1994. *National Colours:* All green.
International matches 2018–19
Afghanistan (n) 2-0, Japan (n) 2-3, Uzbekistan (n) 0-4, Oman (n) 1-3.
League champions 2018: Altyn Asyr. *Cup winners 2018:* Kopetdag.

UNITED ARAB EMIRATES (UAE)

United Arab Emirates Football Association, Zayed Sports City, PO Box 916, Abu Dhabi.
Founded: 1971. *FIFA:* 1974; *AFC:* 1974. *National Colours:* All white with red trim.
International matches
Andorra (n) 0-0, Trinidad & Tobago (n) 0-2, Laos (n) 3-0, Honduras (n) 1-1, Venezuela (n) 0-2, Bolivia (h) 0-0, Yemen (h) 2-0, Bahrain (h) 1-1, India (h) 2-0, Thailand (h) 1-1, Kyrgyzstan (h) 3-2, Australia (h) 1-0, Qatar (h) 0-4, Saudi Arabia (h) 2-1, Syria (h) 0-0.
League champions 2018–19: Sharjah. *Cup winners 2018–19:* Shabab Al-Ahli.

UZBEKISTAN

Uzbekistan Football Federation, Massiv Almazar Furkat Street 15/1, Tashkent 700 003.
Founded: 1946. *FIFA:* 1994; *AFC:* 1994. *National Colours:* All white with blue trim.
International matches 2018–19
Syria (h) 1-1, Iran (h) 0-1, Korea DPR (h) 2-0, Qatar (h) 2-0, Lebanon (n) 0-0, Korea Republic (n) 0-4, Oman (n) 2-1, Turkmenistan (n) 4-0, Japan (n) 1-2, Australia (n) 0-0 (2-4p), Uruguay (n) 0-3, China PR (n) 1-0, Turkey (a) 0-2, Korea DPR (h) 4-0, Syria (h) 2-0.
League champions 2018: Lokomotiv Tashkent. *Cup winners 2018:* AGMK.

VIETNAM

Vietnam Football Federation, Le Quang Dao Street, Phu Do Ward, Nam Tu Liem District, Hanoi 844.
Founded: 1960 (NV). *FIFA:* 1952 (SV), 1964 (NV); *AFC:* 1954 (SV), 1978 (SRV). *National Colours:* All red.
International matches 2018–19
Laos (a) 3-0, Malaysia (h) 2-0, Myanmar (a) 0-0, Cambodia (h) 3-0, Philippines (a) 2-1, Philippines (h) 2-1, Malaysia (a) 2-2, Malaysia (h) 1-0, Korea DPR (h) 1-1, Philippines (n) 4-2, Iraq (n) 2-3, Iran (n) 0-2, Yemen (n) 2-0, Jordan (n) 1-1 (4-2p), Japan (n) 0-1, Thailand (a) 1-0, Curacao (n) 1-1 (4-5p).
League champions 2018: Ha Noi. *Cup winners 2018:* Becamex Binh Duong.

YEMEN

Yemen Football Association, Quarter of Sport Al Jeraf (Ali Mohsen Al-Muraisi Stadium), PO Box 908, Al-Thawra City, Sana'a.
Founded: 1940 (SY), 1962 (NY). *FIFA:* 1967 (SY), 1980 (NY); *AFC:* 1972 (SY), 1980 (NY). *National Colours:* Red shirts, white shorts, black socks.
International matches 2018–19
Saudi Arabia (a) 0-1, UAE (a) 0-2, Syria (n) 0-1, Iran (n) 0-5, Iraq (n) 0-3, Vietnam (n) 0-2.
No club competitions since January 2015 due to civil war.

NORTH AND CENTRAL AMERICA AND CARIBBEAN (CONCACAF)

ANGUILLA

Anguilla Football Association, 2 Queen Elizabeth Avenue, PO Box 1318, The Valley, AI-2640.
Founded: 1990. *FIFA:* 1996; *CONCACAF:* 1996. *National Colours:* Orange shirts with black trim, orange shorts with black trim, white socks.
International matches 2018–19
French Guiana† (h) 0-5, Nicaragua* (n) 0-6, Bahamas (a) 1-1, US Virgin Islands (h) 0-3.
* *Match played in Costa Rica.*
League champions 2018: Kicks United. *Cup winners:* No competition.

ANTIGUA & BARBUDA

Antigua & Barbuda Football Association, Ground Floor, Sydney Walling Stand, Antigua Recreation Ground, PO Box 773, St John's.
Founded: 1928. *FIFA:* 1970; *CONCACAF:* 1972. *National Colours:* All yellow with black trim.
International matches 2018–19
St Lucia (h) 0-3, Bahamas (a) 6-0, Martinique† (a) 2-4, Curacao (h) 0-2.
League champions 2018–19: Liberta. *Cup winners:* No competition.

ARUBA

Arubaanse Voetbal Bond, Technical Centre Angel Botta, Shaba 24, PO Box 376, Noord.
Founded: 1932. *FIFA:* 1988; *CONCACAF:* 1986. *National Colours:* Yellow shirts with sky blue sleeves, yellow shorts, yellow socks.
International matches 2018–19
Bermuda (h) 3-1*, Guadeloupe† (a) 0-0, Montserrat (h) 0-2*, St Lucia (a) 0-0‡.
* *Match played in Curacao.* ‡ *Match played in Antigua & Barbuda.*
League champions 2018–19: Racing Club Aruba. *Cup winners 2019:* Dakota.

BAHAMAS

Bahamas Football Association, Rosetta Street, PO Box N-8434, Nassau, NP.
Founded: 1967. *FIFA:* 1968; *CONCACAF:* 1981. *National Colours:* Yellow shirts, black shorts, yellow socks.
International matches 2018–19
Belize (a) 0-4, Antigua & Barbuda (h) 0-6, Anguilla (h) 1-1, Turks & Caicos Islands (h) 6-1, Dominica (a) 0-4.
League champions 2018–19: Dynamos. *Cup winners:* No competition since 2016.

BARBADOS

Barbados Football Association, Bottom Floor, ABC Marble Complex, PO Box 1362, Fontabelle, St Michael.
Founded: 1910. *FIFA:* 1968; *CONCACAF:* 1967. *National Colours:* Gold shirts with royal blue sleeves, gold shorts, gold socks.
International matches 2018–19
Belize (a) 0-1, Jamaica (h) 2-2, Cuba (h) 0-0, Cuba (h) 0-2, Guyana (a) 0-3*, El Salvador (a) 0-3, US Virgin Islands (h) 3-0, Nicaragua (h) 0-1.
* *Match awarded 3-0 to Guyana; Barbados fielded ineligible players.*
League champions 2018–19: Barbados Defence Force. *Cup winners 2018:* Paradise.

BELIZE

Football Federation of Belize, 26 Hummingbird Highway, Belmopan, PO Box 1742, Belize City.
Founded: 1980. *FIFA:* 1986; *CONCACAF:* 1986. *National Colours:* Blue shirts with white trim, blue shorts, blue socks.
International matches 2018–19
Barbados (h) 1-0, Bahamas (h) 4-0, Montserrat (a) 0-1, Puerto Rico (h) 1-0, Guyana (a) 1-2.
League champions 2018–19: Verdes (Opening); San Pedro Pirates (Closing). *Cup winners:* No competition.

BERMUDA

Bermuda Football Association, 48 Cedar Avenue, PO Box HM 745, Hamilton HM11.
Founded: 1928. *FIFA:* 1962; *CONCACAF:* 1967. *National Colours:* All red.
International matches 2018–19
Aruba (a) 1-3*, Sint Maarten† (h) 12-0, El Salvador (h) 1-0, Cuba (a) 0-5, Dominican Republic (a) 3-1, Guyana (h) 1-0, Haiti (n) 1-2, Costa Rica (n) 1-2, Nicaragua (n) 2-0.
* *Match played in Curacao.*
League champions 2018–19: PHC Zebras. *Cup winners 2017–18:* Robin Hood.

BRITISH VIRGIN ISLANDS

British Virgin Islands Football Association, Botanic Station, PO Box 4269, Road Town, Tortola VG 1110.
Founded: 1974. *FIFA:* 1996; *CONCACAF:* 1996. *National Colours:* Green shirts with gold and white trim, green shorts, gold socks.
International matches 2018–19
Martinique† (a) 0-4, Suriname (a) 0-5, Bonaire† (h) 1-2*, Turks & Caicos Islands (h) 2-2*.
* *Match played in Anguilla.*
League champions 2018: One Love United. *Cup winners:* No competition.

CANADA

Canadian Soccer Association, Place Soccer Canada, 237 Metcalfe Street, Ottawa, Ontario K2P 1R2.
Founded: 1912. *FIFA:* 1912; *CONCACAF:* 1961. *National Colours:* All red.
International matches 2018–19
US Virgin Islands (a) 8-0*, Dominica (a) 5-0, St Kitts & Nevis (a) 1-0, French Guiana† (h) 4-1, Martinique† (n) 4-0, Mexico (n) 1-3, Cuba (n) 7-0, Haiti (n) 2-3.
* *Match played in USA.*
Canadian teams compete in MLS and NASL. League champions 2019: Cavalry (Spring). *Cup winners 2018:* Toronto FC.

CAYMAN ISLANDS

Cayman Islands Football Association, PO Box 178, Poindexter Road, Prospect, George Town, Grand Cayman KY1-1104.
Founded: 1966. *FIFA:* 1992; *CONCACAF:* 1990. *National Colours:* Red shirts with white sleeves, red shorts, red socks with white tops.
International matches 2018–19
Jamaica (a) 0-4, Dominican Republic (a) 0-3, St Lucia (h) 0-0, Montserrat (h) 1-2.
League champions 2018–19: Scholars International. *Cup winners:* Not contested since 2017.

COSTA RICA

Federacion Costarricense de Futbol, 600 mts sur del Cruce de la Panasonic, San Rafael de Alajuela, Radial a Santa Ana, San Jose 670-1000.
Founded: 1921. *FIFA:* 1927; *CONCACAF:* 1961. *National Colours:* Red shirts, blue shorts, white socks.
International matches 2018–19
Korea Republic (a) 0-2, Japan (a) 0-3, Mexico (h) 2-3, Colombia (n) 1-3, Chile (a) 3-2, Peru (a) 3-2, USA (a) 0-2, Guatemala (a) 0-1, Jamaica (h) 1-0, Peru (a) 0-1, Nicaragua (h) 4-0, Bermuda (n) 2-1, Haiti (n) 1-2, Mexico (n) 1-1 (4-5p).
League champions 2018–19: Herediano (Apertura); San Carlos (Clausura). *Cup winners:* No competition.

CUBA

Asociacion de Futbol de Cuba, Estadio Pedro Marrero Escuela Nacional de Futbol – Mario Lopez, Avenida 41 no. 44 y 46, La Habana.
Founded: 1924. *FIFA:* 1932; *CONCACAF:* 1961. *National Colours:* All red.
International matches 2018–19
Guatemala (a) 0-3, Guatemala (a) 0-1, Barbados (a) 0-0, Barbados (a) 2-0, Turks & Caicos Islands (h) 11-0, Grenada (a) 2-0, Dominican Republic (h) 1-0, Bermuda (h) 5-0, Haiti (a) 1-2, Mexico (n) 0-7, Martinique† (n) 0-3, Canada (n) 0-7.
League champions 2019: Santiago de Cuba. *Cup winners:* No competition.

CURACAO

Curacao Football Federation, Bonamweg 49, PO Box 341, Willemstad.
Founded: 1921 (Netherlands Antilles), 2010. *FIFA:* 1932, 2010; *CONCACAF:* 1961, 2010. *National Colours:* All white.
International matches 2018–19
Grenada (h) 10-0, US Virgin Islands (a) 5-0*, Guadeloupe† (h) 6-0, Antigua & Barbuda (a) 1-2, India (n) 3-1, Vietnam (n) 1-1 (5-4p), El Salvador (n) 0-1, Honduras (n) 1-0, Jamaica (n) 1-1, USA (a) 0-1.
* *Match played in USA.*
League champions 2017–18: Jong Holland. *Cup winners:* No competition.

DOMINICA

Dominica Football Association, Patrick John Football House, Bath Estate, PO Box 1080, Roseau.
Founded: 1970. *FIFA:* 1994; *CONCACAF:* 1994. *National Colours:* All emerald green.

International matches 2018–19
Suriname (h) 0-0*, Canada (A) 0-5, Sint Maarten† (a) 2-0‡, Bahamas (h) 4-0.
* *Match played in Guadeloupe.* ‡ *Match played in Anguilla.*
League champions 2018–19: South East. *Cup winners:* No competition.

DOMINICAN REPUBLIC

Federacion Dominicana de Futbol, Centro Olimpico Juan Pablo Duarte, Apartado Postal 1953, Santo Domingo.
Founded: 1953. *FIFA:* 1958; *CONCACAF:* 1964. *National Colours:* All blue.
International matches 2018–19
Bonaire† (h) 5-0*, Cayman Islands (h) 3-0, Cuba (a) 0-1, Bermuda (h) 1-3.
* *Match played in Curacao.*
League champions 2018: Cibao. *Cup winners:* No competition.

EL SALVADOR

Federacion Salvadorena de Futbol, Avenida Jose Matias Delgado, Frente al Centro Espanol Colonia Escalon, Zona 10, San Salvador 1029.
Founded: 1935. *FIFA:* 1938; *CONCACAF:* 1961. *National Colours:* All blue.
International matches 2018–19
Montserrat (a) 2-1, Brazil (n) 0-5, Barbados (h) 3-0, Bermuda (a) 0-1, Haiti (h) 1-0, Guatemala (n) 3-1, Jamaica (h) 2-0, Peru (n) 2-0, Haiti (n) 1-0, Japan (a) 0-2, Curacao (n) 1-0, Jamaica (n) 0-0, Honduras (n) 0-4.
League champions 2018–19: Santa Tecla (Apertura); CD Aguila (Clausura). *Cup winner:* No competition.

GRENADA

Grenada Football Association, National Stadium, PO Box 326, St George's.
Founded: 1924. *FIFA:* 1978; *CONCACAF:* 1969. *National Colours:* All green.
International matches 2018–19
Jamaica (h) 1-5, Curacao (a) 0-10, Cuba (h) 0-1, Saint-Martin† (a) 0-1*, Puerto Rico (a) 2-0.
* *Match played in Anguilla.*
League champions 2018–19: Paradise. *Cup winners:* Not contested since 2017.

GUATEMALA

Federacion Nacional de Futbol de Guatemala, 2a Calle 15-57, Zona 15, Boulevard Vista Hermosa, Guatemala City 01015.
Founded: 1919. *FIFA:* 1946; *CONCACAF:* 1961. *National Colours:* White shirts with blue sash, white shorts, white socks.
International matches 2018–19
Cuba (h) 3-0, Cuba (h) 1-0, Argentina (n) 0-3, Ecuador (n) 0-2, Israel (a) 0-7, El Salvador (n) 1-3, Costa Rica (h) 1-0, Paraguay (a) 0-2.
League champions 2018–19: Guastatoya (Apertura); Antigua GFC (Clausura). *Cup winners:* No competition.

GUYANA

Guyana Football Federation, Lot 17, Dadanawa Street Section 'K', Campbellville, PO Box 10727, Georgetown.
Founded: 1902. *FIFA:* 1970; *CONCACAF:* 1961. *National Colours:* All yellow with black, green and red trim.
International matches 2018–19
Barbados (h) 3-0*, Turks & Caicos Islands (a) 8-0, French Guiana† (a) 1-2, Belize (h) 2-1, Bermuda (a) 0-1, Haiti (n) 1-3, USA (a) 0-4, Panama (n) 2-4, Trinidad & Tobago (n) 1-1.
* *Match awarded 3-0 to Guyana; Barbados fielded ineligible players.*
League champions 2017–18: Fruta Conquerors; *2019:* Fruta Conquerors. *Cup winners:* Not contested since 2015.

HAITI

Federation Haitienne de Football, Stade Sylvio Cator, Rue Oswald Durand, Port-au-Prince.
Founded: 1904. *FIFA:* 1933; *CONCACAF:* 1961. *National Colours:* Blue shirts with red trim, blue shorts, blue socks with red tops.
International matches 2018–19
Sint Maarten† (h) 13-0, St Lucia (a) 2-1*, Nicaragua (a) 2-0, El Salvador (a) 0-1, Cuba (h) 2-1, El Salvador (n) 0-1, Chile (a) 1-2, Guyana (n) 3-1, Bermuda (n) 2-1, Nicaragua (n) 2-0, Costa Rica (n) 2-1, Canada (n) 3-2, Mexico (h) 0-1.
* *Match played in Martinique.*
League champions 2018: AS Capoise (Ouverture); Don Bosco (Cloture). *Cup winners:* No competition.

HONDURAS

Federacion Nacional Autonoma de Futbol de Honduras, Colonia Florencia Norte, Edificio Plaza America Ave. Roble, 1 y 2 Nivle, PO Box 827, Tegucigalpa 504.
Founded: 1935. *FIFA:* 1946; *CONCACAF:* 1961. *National Colours:* All white.
International matches 2018–19
UAE (n) 1-1, Panama (h) 1-0, Chile (a) 1-4, Ecuador (n) 0-0, Paraguay (a) 1-1, Brazil (a) 0-7, Jamaica (a) 2-3, Curacao (n) 0-1, El Salvador (n) 4-0.
League champions 2018–19: Motagua (Apertura); Motagua (Clausura). *Cup winners 2018:* Platense.

JAMAICA

Jamaica Football Federation Ltd, 20 St Lucia Crescent, Kingston 5.
Founded: 1910. *FIFA:* 1962; *CONCACAF:* 1963. *National Colours:* Gold shirts, black shorts, gold socks.
International matches 2018–19
Grenada (a) 5-1, Barbados (a) 2-2, Ecuador (a) 0-2, Cayman Islands (h) 4-0, Bonaire† (a) 6-0*, Suriname (h) 2-1, El Salvador (n) 0-2, Costa Rica (a) 0-1, USA (a) 1-0, Honduras (h) 3-2, El Salvador (n) 0-0, Curacao (n) 1-1, Panama (n) 1-0, USA (a) 1-3.
* *Match played in Curacao.*
League champions 2018–19: Portmore United. *Cup winners:* Not contested since 2014.

MEXICO

Federacion Mexicana de Futbol Asociacion, A.C., Colima No. 373, Colonia Roma, Delegacion Cuauhtemoc, Mexico DF 06700.
Founded: 1927. *FIFA:* 1929; *CONCACAF:* 1961. *National Colours:* All black with white trim.
International matches 2018–19
Uruguay (n) 1-4, USA (a) 0-1, Costa Rica (h) 3-2, Chile (h) 0-1, Argentina (a) 0-2, Argentina (a) 0-2, Chile (n) 3-1, Paraguay (n) 4-2, Venezuela (n) 3-1, Ecuador (n) 3-2, Cuba (n) 7-0, Canada (n) 3-1, Martinique† (n) 3-2, Costa Rica (n) 1-1 (5-4p), Haiti (n) 1-0, USA (n) 1-0.
League champions 2018–19: America (Apertura); Tigres UANL (Clausura). *Cup winners 2018–19:* Cruz Azul (Apertura); America (Clausura).

MONTSERRAT

Montserrat Football Association Inc., PO Box 505, Blakes, Montserrat.
Founded: 1994. *FIFA:* 1996; *CONCACAF:* 1996. *National Colours:* White shirts with green hoops, white shorts, white socks.
International matches 2018–19
El Salvador (h) 1-2, Belize (h) 1-0, Aruba (a) 2-0*, Cayman Islands (a) 2-1.
* *Match played in Curacao.*
League champions: Not contested since 2016.

NICARAGUA

Federacion Nicaraguense de Futbol, Porton Principal del Hospital Bautista 1 Cuadra Abajo, 1 Cuadra al Sur y 1/2 Cuadra Abajo, Apartado Postal 976, Managua.
Founded: 1931. *FIFA:* 1950; *CONCACAF:* 1961. *National Colours:* All blue with white trim.
International matches 2018–19
St Vincent/Grenadines (a) 2-0, Anguilla* (h) 6-0, Haiti (h) 0-2, Bolivia (a) 2-2, Barbados (a) 1-0, Argentina (a) 1-5, Costa Rica (a) 0-4, Haiti (n) 0-2, Bermuda (n) 0-2.
* *Match played in Costa Rica.*
League champions 2018–19: Managua (Apertura); Real Esteli (Clausura). *Cup winners:* No competition.

PANAMA

Federacion Panamena de Futbol, Ciudad Deportiva Irving Saladino, Corregimiento de Juan Diaz, Apartado Postal 0827-00391, Zona 8, Panama City.
Founded: 1937. *FIFA:* 1938; *CONCACAF:* 1961. *National Colours:* All red.
International matches 2018–19
Venezuela (h) 0-2, Japan (a) 0-3, Korea Republic (a) 2-2, Honduras (a) 0-1, Ecuador (h) 1-2, USA (a) 0-3, Brazil (n) 1-1, Colombia (a) 0-3, Uruguay (a) 0-3, Trinidad & Tobago (n) 2-0, Guyana (n) 4-2, USA (a) 0-1, Jamaica (n) 0-1.
League champions 2018–19: Tauro (Apertura); CAI de La Chorrera (Clausura). *Cup winners:* No competition.

PUERTO RICO

Federacion Puertorriquena de Futbol, PO Box 367567, San Juan 00936.
Founded: 1940. *FIFA:* 1960; *CONCACAF:* 1961. *National Colours:* Red and white striped shirts with blue trim, blue shorts, red socks.
International matches 2018–19
St Kitts & Nevis (a) 0-1, Martinique† (h) 0-1, Belize (a) 0-1, Grenada (h) 0-2.
League champions 2018–19: Metropolitan FA. *Cup winners:* No competition.

ST KITTS & NEVIS

St Kitts & Nevis Football Association, PO Box 465, Lozack Road, Basseterre.
Founded: 1932. *FIFA:* 1992; *CONCACAF:* 1992. *National Colours:* All red.
International matches 2018–19
Puerto Rico (h) 1-0, Saint-Martin† (a) 10-0*, Canada (h) 0-1, Suriname (a) 0-2.
* *Match played in Anguilla.*
League champions 2017–18: Village Superstars. *Cup winners 2017–18:* Cayon Rockets; *2018–19:* Newtown United.

ST LUCIA

St Lucia National Football Association, Barnard Hill, PO Box 255, Castries.
Founded: 1979. *FIFA:* 1988; *CONCACAF:* 1986. *National Colours:* Sky blue shirts with yellow stripes, sky blue shorts, sky blue socks.
International matches 2018–19
Antigua & Barbuda (a) 3-0, Haiti (h) 1-2*, Cayman Islands (a) 0-0, Aruba (h) 3-2**.
* *Match played in Martinique.* ** *Match played in Antigua & Barbuda.*
League champions 2019: Platinum. *Cup winners:* Not contested since 2013.

ST VINCENT & THE GRENADINES

St Vincent & the Grenadines Football Federation, PO Box 1278, Nichols Building (2nd Floor), Bentinck Square, Victoria Park, Kingstown.
Founded: 1979. *FIFA:* 1988; *CONCACAF:* 1986. *National Colours:* Yellow shirts, blue shorts, blue socks.
International matches 2018–19
Nicaragua (h) 0-2, French Guiana† (a) 1-0, Turks & Caicos Islands (a) 2-3, Bonaire† (h) 2-1.
League champions 2018–19: BESCO Pastures. *Cup winners:* No competition.

SURINAME

Surinaamse Voetbal Bond, Letitia Vriesdelaan 7, PO Box 1223, Paramaribo.
Founded: 1920. *FIFA:* 1929; *CONCACAF:* 1961. *National Colours:* White shirts, white shorts, white socks with green tops.
International matches 2018–19
Dominica (a) 0-0*, British Virgin Islands (h) 5-0, Jamaica (a) 1-2, St Kitts & Nevis (h) 2-0.
* *Match played in Guadeloupe.*
League champions 2017–18: Robinhood. *Cup winners 2018:* Robinhood.

TRINIDAD & TOBAGO

Trinidad & Tobago Football Association, 24–26 Dundonald Street, PO Box 400, Port of Spain.
Founded: 1908. *FIFA:* 1964; *CONCACAF:* 1962. *National Colours:* Red shirts with black trim, black shorts with red trim, red socks.
International matches 2018–19
UAE (n) 2-0, Thailand (a) 0-1, Iran (a) 0-1, Wales (a) 0-1, Japan (a) 0-0, Panama (n) 0-2, USA (a) 0-6, Guyana (n) 1-1.
League champions 2018: W Connection. *Cup winners:* Not contested since 2017.

TURKS & CAICOS ISLANDS

Turks & Caicos Islands Football Association, TCIFA National Academy, Venetian Road, PO Box 626, Providenciales.
Founded: 1996. *FIFA:* 1998; *CONCACAF:* 1996. *National Colours:* All black with white trim.
International matches 2018–19
Cuba (a) 0-11, Guyana (h) 0-8, St Vincent/Grenadines (h) 3-2, Bahamas (a) 1-6, British Virgin Islands (a) 2-2*.
* *Match played in Anguilla.*
League champions 2018: Academy Jaguars; *2019:* Academy Jaguars. *Cup winners:* No competition.

UNITED STATES OF AMERICA (USA)

US Soccer Federation, US Soccer House, 1801 S. Prairie Avenue, Chicago, IL 60616.
Founded: 1913. *FIFA:* 1914; *CONCACAF:* 1961. *National Colours:* White shirts with red and blue trim, white shorts, white socks.
International matches 2018–19
Brazil (h) 0-2, Mexico (h) 1-0, Colombia (h) 2-4, Peru (h) 1-1, England (a) 0-3, Italy (n) 0-1, Panama (h) 3-0, Costa Rica (h) 2-0, Ecuador (h) 1-0, Chile (h) 1-1, Jamaica (h) 0-1, Venezuela (h) 0-3, Guyana (h) 4-0, Trinidad & Tobago (h) 6-0, Panama (h) 1-0, Curacao (h) 1-0, Jamaica (h) 3-1, Mexico (h) 0-1.
League champions 2018: Atlanta United. (N.B. Teams from USA and Canada compete in MLS.) *Cup winners 2018:* Houston Dynamo.

US VIRGIN ISLANDS

USVI Soccer Federation Inc., 498D Strawberry, PO Box 2346, Christiansted, St Croix 00851.
Founded: 1987. *FIFA:* 1998; *CONCACAF:* 1987. *National Colours:* All royal blue with gold trim.
International matches 2018–19
Canada (h) 0-8*, Curacao (h) 0-5*, Barbados (a) 0-3, Anguilla (a) 3-0.
* *Match played in USA.*
League champions 2018–19: Helenites. *Cup winners:* No competition.

OCEANIA (OFC)

AMERICAN SAMOA

Football Federation American Samoa, PO Box 982 413, Pago Pago AS 96799.
Founded: 1984. *FIFA:* 1998; *OFC:* 1998. *National Colours:* All blue with white trim.
International matches 2018–19
New Caledonia (n) 0-5, Fiji (n) 0-9, Tuvalu† (n) 1-1.
League champions 2018: Pago Youth. *Cup winners:* Not contested since 2014.

COOK ISLANDS

Cook Islands Football Association, Matavera Main Road, PO Box 29, Avarua, Rarotonga.
Founded: 1971. *FIFA:* 1994; *OFC:* 1994. *National Colours:* All green with white trim.
International matches 2018–19
None played.
League champions 2018: Tupapa Maraerenga. *Cup winners 2018:* Tupapa Maraerenga.

FIJI

Fiji Football Association, PO Box 2514, Government Buildings, Suva.
Founded: 1938. *FIFA:* 1964; *OFC:* 1966. *National Colours:* White shirts, black shorts, white socks.
International matches 2018–19
Solomon Islands (h) 1-1, Singapore (a) 0-2, New Caledonia (h) 3-0, Mauritius (h) 1-0, Tahiti (n) 1-1, Vanuatu (a) 0-0, Tahiti (n) 2-1, American Samoa (n) 9-0, New Caledonia (n) 0-1.
League champions 2018: Lautoka. *Cup winners 2018:* Ba.

NEW CALEDONIA

Federation Caledonienne de Football, 7 bis, Rue Suffren Quartien latin, BP 560, Noumea 99845.
Founded: 1928. *FIFA:* 2004; *OFC:* 2004. *National Colours:* All red with white trim.
International matches 2018–19
Vanuatu (a) 2-2, Fiji (a) 0-3, American Samoa (n) 5-0, Solomon Islands (n) 2-0, Fiji (n) 1-0.
League champions 2018: Magenta. *Cup winners 2018:* Magenta.

NEW ZEALAND

New Zealand Football, PO Box 301-043, Albany, Auckland.
Founded: 1891. *FIFA:* 1948; *OFC:* 1966. *National Colours:* All white.
International matches 2018–19
Tonga (n) 2-3, Samoa (a) 5-1, Vanuatu (n) 0-0.
League champions 2018–19: Eastern Suburbs. *Cup winners 2018:* Birkenhead United.

PAPUA NEW GUINEA

Papua New Guinea Football Association, PO Box 957, Lae 411, Morobe Province.
Founded: 1962. *FIFA:* 1966; *OFC:* 1966. *National Colours:* All red with white trim.
International matches 2018–19
Samoa (a) 6-0, Vanuatu (n) 2-0.
League champions 2019: Toti City. *Cup winners:* No competition.

SAMOA

Football Federation Samoa, PO Box 1682, Tuanimato, Apia.
Founded: 1968. *FIFA:* 1986; *OFC:* 1986. *National Colours:* Blue shirts, white shorts, blue socks.
International matches 2018–19
Papua New Guinea (h) 0-6, New Zealand (h) 1-5, Tonga (n) 2-0.
League champions 2018: Kiwi. *Cup winners:* Not contested since 2014.

SOLOMON ISLANDS

Solomon Islands Football Federation, Allan Boso Complex, Panatina Academy, PO Box 584, Honiara.

Founded: 1978. *FIFA:* 1988; *OFC:* 1988. *National Colours:* Gold shirts, blue shorts, white socks.
International matches 2018–19
Macao (a) 4-1, Fiji (a) 1-1, Vanuatu (h) 3-1, Chinese Taipei (a) 1-0, Singapore (a) 3-4, Tuvalu† (n) 13-0, New Caledonia (n) 0-2, Tahiti (n) 0-3.
League champions 2018: Solomon Warriors. *Cup winners:* No competition.

TAHITI

Federation Tahitienne de Football, Rue Gerald Coppenrath, Complexe de Fautaua, PO Box 50358, Pirae 98716.
Founded: 1989. *FIFA:* 1990; *OFC:* 1990. *National Colours:* All red.
International matches 2018–19
Fiji (n) 1-1, Fiji (n) 1-2, Tuvalu† (n) 7-0, Solomon Islands (n) 3-0.
League champions 2018–19: Venus. *Cup winners 2018:* Dragon.

TONGA

Tonga Football Association, Loto-Tonga Soka Centre, Valungafulu Road, Atele, PO Box 852, Nuku'alofa.
Founded: 1965. *FIFA:* 1994; *OFC:* 1994. *National Colours:* All red.
International matches 2018–19
New Zealand (n) 3-2, Samoa (a) 0-2.
League champions 2018: Loto Ha'apai United. *Cup winners:* Not contested since 2003.

VANUATU

Vanuatu Football Federation, VFF House, Lini Highway, PO Box 266, Port Vila.
Founded: 1934. *FIFA:* 1988; *OFC:* 1988. *National Colours:* Gold shirts with black trim, black shorts, gold socks with black tops.
International matches 2018–19
New Caledonia (a) 2-2, Solomon Islands (a) 1-3, Fiji (n) 0-0, Indonesia (a) 0-6, Papua New Guinea (h) 0-2, New Zealand (h) 0-0.
League champions 2018–19: Tafea. *Grand Final winners:* Galaxy.

AFRICA (CAF)

ALGERIA

Federation Algerienne De Football, Chemin Ahmed Ouaked, BP 39, Dely-Ibrahim, Algiers 16000.
Founded: 1962. *FIFA:* 1963; *CAF:* 1964. *National Colours:* All white.
International matches 2018–19
Gambia (a) 1-1, Benin (h) 2-0, Benin (a) 0-1, Togo (a) 4-1, Gambia (h) 1-1, Tunisia (h) 1-0, Burundi (n) 1-1, Kenya (n) 2-0, Senegal (n) 1-0, Tanzania (n) 3-0, Guinea (n) 3-0, Ivory Coast (n) 1-1 (4-3p), Nigeria (n) 2-1.
League champions 2018–19: USM Alger. *Cup winners 2018–19:* CR Belouizdad.

ANGOLA

Federacao Angolana de Futetbol, Senado de Compl. da Cidadela Desportiva, BP 3449, Luanda.
Founded: 1979. *FIFA:* 1980; *CAF:* 1980. *National Colours:* Red shirts with yellow trim, black shorts, red socks.
International matches 2018–19
Botswana (h) 1-0, Mauritania (h) 4-1, Mauritania (a) 0-1, Burkina Faso (h) 2-1, Botswana (a) 1-0, Guinea-Bissau (n) 2-0, Tunisia (n) 1-1, Mauritania (n) 0-0, Mali (n) 0-1.
League champions 2018–19: Primeiro de Agosto. *Cup winners 2019:* Primeiro de Agosto.

BENIN

Federation Beninoise de Football, Rue du boulevard Djassain, BP 112, 3-eme Arrondissement de Porto-Novo 01.
Founded: 1962. *FIFA:* 1962; *CAF:* 1962. *National Colours:* All yellow with red and green trim.
International matches 2018–19
Togo (a) 0-0, Algeria (a) 0-2, Algeria (h) 1-0, Gambia (a) 1–3, Togo (h) 2-1, Guinea (n) 1-0, Mauritania (n) 3-1, Ghana (n) 2-2, Guinea-Bissau (n) 0-0, Cameroon (n) 0-0, Morocco (n) 1-1 (4-1p), Senegal (n) 0-1.
League champions 2018–19: Buffles du Borgou. *Cup winners 2019:* ESAE.

BOTSWANA

Botswana Football Association, PO Box 1396, Gaborone.
Founded: 1970. *FIFA:* 1978; *CAF:* 1976. *National Colours:* Blue shirts with black sleeves, blue shorts, blue socks with black trim.
International matches 2018–19
Angola (a) 0-1, Burkina Faso (a) 0-3, Burkina Faso (h) 0-0, Mauritania (a) 1-2, Angola (h) 0-1, Seychelles (h) 2-0, Seychelles (a) 3-1, South Africa (a) 2-2 (5-4p), Lesotho (n) 2-1, Zambia (n) 0-1.
League champions 2018–19: Township Rollers. *Cup winners:* Resumed competition still being played.

BURKINA FASO

Federation Burkinabe de Foot-Ball, Centre Technique National Ouaga 2000, BP 57, Ouagadougou 01.
Founded: 1960. *FIFA:* 1964; *CAF:* 1964. *National Colours:* Green shirts with red sleeves, green shorts, green socks.
International matches 2018–19
Mauritania (a) 0-2, Botswana (h) 3-0, Botswana (a) 0-0, Angola (a) 1-2, Mauritania (h) 1-0, DR Congo (n) 2-1.
League champions 2018–19: Rahimo. *Cup winners 2019:* Rahimo.

BURUNDI

Federation de Football du Burundi, Avenue Muyinga, BP 3426, Bujumbura.
Founded: 1948. *FIFA:* 1972; *CAF:* 1972. *National Colours:* Red shirts, white shorts, green socks.
International matches 2018–19
Ethiopia (a) 1-1, Gabon (a) 1-1, Mali (a) 0-0, Mali (h) 1-1, South Sudan (a) 5-2, Gabon (h) 1-1, Algeria (n) 1-1, Tunisia (a) 1-2, Nigeria (n) 0-1, Madagascar (n) 0-1, Guinea (n) 0-2.
League champions 2018–19: Aigle Noir. *Cup winners 2019:* Aigle Noir.

CAMEROON

Federation Camerounaise de Football, Avenue du 27 aout 1940, Tsinga-Yaounde, BP 1116, Yaounde.
Founded: 1959. *FIFA:* 1962; *CAF:* 1963. *National Colours:* Green shirts, red shorts, yellow socks.
International matches 2018–19
Comoros (a) 1-1, Malawi (h) 1-0, Malawi (a) 0-0, Morocco (a) 0-2, Brazil (n) 1-0, Comoros (h) 3-0, Zambia (n) 2-1, Mali (n) 1-1, Guinea-Bissau (n) 2-1, Ghana (n) 0-0, Benin (n) 0-0, Nigeria (n) 2-3.
League champions 2018: Coton Sport; *2019:* UMS de Loum. *Cup winners 2018:* Eding Sport; *2019:* Stade Renard de Melong.

CAPE VERDE ISLANDS

Federacao Caboverdiana de Futebol, Praia Cabo Verde, FCF CX, PO Box 234, Praia.
Founded: 1982. *FIFA:* 1986; *CAF:* 2000. *National Colours:* All blue with white trim.
International matches 2018–19
Lesotho (a) 1-1, Tanzania (h) 3-0, Tanzania (a) 0-2, Uganda (a) 0-1, Lesotho (h) 0-0.
League champions 2019: CS Mindelense. *Cup winners 2019:* Santo Crucifixo.

CENTRAL AFRICAN REPUBLIC

Federation Centrafricaine de Football, Avenue des Martyrs, BP 344, Bangui.
Founded: 1961. *FIFA:* 1964; *CAF:* 1965. *National Colours:* All white with blue trim.
International matches 2018–19
Guinea (a) 0-1, Ivory Coast (a) 0-4, Ivory Coast (h) 0-0, Rwanda (a) 2-2, Guinea (h) 0-0.
League champions 2018–19: Tempete Mocaf. *Cup winners:* Not contested since 2017.

CHAD

Federation Tchadienne de Football, BP 886, N'Djamena.
Founded: 1962. *FIFA:* 1964; *CAF:* 1964. *National Colours:* Blue shirts, yellow shorts, red socks.
International matches 2018–19
None played.
League champions 2018: Elect-Sport; *2019:* Elect-Sport. *Cup winners:* Not contested since 2015.

COMOROS

Federation Comorienne de Football, Route d'Itsandra, BP 798, Moroni.
Founded: 1979. *FIFA:* 2005; *CAF:* 2003. *National Colours:* Green shirts with white trim, green shorts, green socks.
International matches 2018–19
Cameroon (h) 1-1, Morocco (a) 0-1, Morocco (h) 2-2, Malawi (h) 2-1, Cameroon (a) 0-3, Eswatini (n) 2-2, Mauritius (n) 2-1, Zimbabwe (n) 0-2, Malawi (n) 1-2, Ivory Coast (n) 1-3.
League champions 2018: Volcan Club de Moroni; *2019:* Fomboni. *Cup winners 2018:* Miracle Club.

CONGO

Federation Congolaise de Football, 80 Rue Eugene Etienne, Centre Ville, BP Box 11, Brazzaville 00 242.
Founded: 1962. *FIFA:* 1964; *CAF:* 1965. *National Colours:* All red with white trim.

International matches 2018–19
Zimbabwe (h) 1-1, Liberia (h) 3-1, Liberia (a) 1-2, DR Congo (h) 1-1, Zimbabwe (a) 0-2.
League champions 2018: AS Otoho; *2018–19:* AS Otoho. *Cup winners 2018:* Diables Noirs.

DR CONGO

Federation Congolaise de Football-Association, 31 Avenue de la Justice Kinshasa-Gombe, BP 1284, Kinshasa 1.
Founded: 1919. *FIFA:* 1964; *CAF:* 1964. *National Colours:* Blue shirts with red sleeves, red shorts, blue socks.
International matches 2018–19
Liberia (a) 1-1, Zimbabwe (h) 1-2, Zimbabwe (a) 1-1, Congo (a) 1-1, Liberia (h) 1-0, Burkina Faso (n) 0-0, Kenya (n) 1-1, Uganda (n) 0-2, Egypt (n) 0-2, Zimbabwe (n) 4-0, Madagascar (n) 2-2 (2-4p).
League champions 2017–18: AS Vita Club; *2018–19:* TP Mazembe. *Cup winners 2018:* AS Nyuki; *2019:* AS Maniema Union.

DJIBOUTI

Federation Djiboutienne de Football, Centre Technique National, BP 2694, Ville de Djibouti.
Founded: 1979. *FIFA:* 1994; *CAF:* 1994. *National Colours:* All sky blue.
International matches 2018–19
None played.
League champions 2018–19: AS Port. *Cup winners 2018:* AS Ali Sabieh/Djibouti Telecom.

EGYPT

Egyptian Football Association, 5 Gabalaya Street, Gezira El Borg Post Office, Cairo.
Founded: 1921. *FIFA:* 1923; *CAF:* 1957. *National Colours:* Red shirts, white shorts, black socks.
International matches 2018–19
Niger (h) 6-0, Eswatini (h) 4-1, Eswatini (a) 2-0, Tunisia (h) 3-2, Niger (a) 1-1, Nigeria (a) 0-1, Tanzania (h) 1-0, Guinea (h) 3-1, Zimbabwe (h) 1-0, DR Congo (h) 2-0, Uganda (h) 2-0, South Africa (h) 0-1.
League champions 2018–19: Al-Ahly. *Cup winners 2018–19:* Competition still being played.

EQUATORIAL GUINEA

Federacion Ecuatoguineana de Futbol, Avenida de Hassan II, Apartado de correo 1017, Malabo.
Founded: 1957. *FIFA:* 1986; *CAF:* 1986. *National Colours:* All red with white trim.
International matches 2018–19
Sudan (h) 1-0, Madagascar (h) 0-1, Madagascar (a) 0-1, Senegal (h) 0-1, Sudan (a) 4-1, Saudi Arabia (a) 2-3.
League champions 2018–19: Cano Sport. *Cup winners 2018:* Not contested. *2019:* Akonangui.

ERITREA

Eritrean National Football Federation, Sematat Avenue 29–31, PO Box 3665, Asmara.
Founded: 1996. *FIFA:* 1998; *CAF:* 1998. *National Colours:* White shirts with red trim, white shorts with red trim, blue socks.
International matches 2018–19
None played.
No senior club competitions since 2014.

ESWATINI (SWAZILAND)

Eswatini Football Association, Sigwaca House, Plot 582, Sheffield Road, PO Box 641, Mbabane H100.
Founded: 1968. *FIFA:* 1978; *CAF:* 1976. *National Colours:* Blue shirts with yellow trim, blue shorts, yellow socks.
International matches 2018–19
Tunisia (h) 0-2, Egypt (a) 1-4, Egypt (h) 0-2, Niger (h) 1-2, Tunisia (a) 0-4, Malawi (h) 0-0, Malawi (a) 1-1, Mauritius (n) 2-2, Comoros (n) 2-2.
League champions 2018–19: Green Mamba. *Cup winners 2019:* Young Buffaloes.

ETHIOPIA

Ethiopia Football Federation, Addis Ababa Stadium, PO Box 1080, Addis Ababa.
Founded: 1943. *FIFA:* 1952; *CAF:* 1957. *National Colours:* Green shirts with yellow trim, green shorts with yellow trim, red socks.
International matches 2018–19
Burundi (h) 1-1, Kenya (h) 0-0, Kenya (a) 0-3, Ghana (h) 0-2.
League champions 2017–18: Jimma Aba Jifar. *2018–19:* Mekelle 70 Enderta. *Cup winners 2018:* Mekelakeya.

GABON

Federation Gabonaise de Football, BP 181, Libreville.
Founded: 1962. *FIFA:* 1966; *CAF:* 1967. *National Colours:* Yellow shirts, blue shorts with yellow trim, blue socks with yellow tops.
International matches 2018–19
Burundi (h) 1-1, Zambia (h) 0-1, South Sudan (h) 3-0, South Sudan (a) 1-0, Mali (h) 0-1, Burundi (a) 1-1.
League champions 2018–19: Cercle Mberie Sportif. *Cup winners:* Not contested since 2016.

GAMBIA

Gambia Football Association, Kafining Layout, Bakau, PO Box 523, Banjul.
Founded: 1952. *FIFA:* 1968; *CAF:* 1966. *National Colours:* Red shirts with green and blue trim, red shorts, red socks.
International matches 2018–19
Algeria (h) 1-1, Togo (a) 1-1, Togo (h) 0-1, Benin (h) 3-1, Algeria (a) 1-1, Morocco (a) 1-0.
League champions 2018–19: Brikama United. *Cup winners 2019:* Real Banjul.

GHANA

Ghana Football Association, General Secretariat, South East Ridge, PO Box AN 19338, Accra. *(GFA dissolved June 2018.)*
Founded: 1957. *FIFA:* 1958; *CAF:* 1958. *National Colours:* Red shirts with yellow sleeves, red shorts, red socks.
International matches 2018–19
Kenya (a) 0-1, Ethiopia (a) 2-0, Kenya (h) 1-0, South Africa (n) 0-0, Benin (n) 2-2, Cameroon (n) 0-0, Guinea-Bissau (n) 2-0, Tunisia (n) 1-1 (4-5p).
League champions 2018: Competition abandoned. *Special competition 2019:* Asante Kotoko. *Cup winners 2018:* Competition abandoned.

GUINEA

Federation Guineenne de Football, Annexe 1 du Palais du Peuple, PO Box 3645, Conakry.
Founded: 1960. *FIFA:* 1962; *CAF:* 1963. *National Colours:* Red shirts, yellow shorts, green socks.
International matches 2018–19
Central African Republic (h) 1-0, Rwanda (h) 2-0, Rwanda (a) 1-1, Ivory Coast (h) 1-1, Central African Republic (a) 0-0, Benin (n) 0-1, Egypt (a) 1-3, Madagascar (n) 2-2, Nigeria (n) 0-1, Burundi (n) 2-0, Algeria (n) 0-3.
League champions 2018–19: Horoya. *Cup winners 2018:* Horoya. *2019:* Horoya.

GUINEA-BISSAU

Federacao de Futebol da Guine-Bissau, Alto Bandim (Nova Sede), BP 375, Bissau 1035.
Founded: 1974. *FIFA:* 1986; *CAF:* 1986. *National Colours:* All red with green trim.
International matches 2018–19
Mozambique (a) 2-2, Zambia (a) 1-2, Zambia (h) 2-1, Namibia (a) 0-0, Mozambique (h) 2-2, Angola (n) 0-2, Cameroon (n) 0-2, Benin (n) 0-0, Ghana (n) 0-2.
League champions 2018–19: Uniao Desportiva Internacional de Bissau. *Cup winners 2019:* Competition still being played.

IVORY COAST

Federation Ivoirienne de Football, Treichville Avenue 1, 01, BP 1202, Abidjan 01.
Founded: 1960. *FIFA:* 1964; *CAF:* 1960. *National Colours:* All orange.
International matches 2018–19
Rwanda (a) 2-1, Central African Republic (h) 4-0, Central African Republic (a) 0-0, Guinea (a) 1-1, Rwanda (h) 3-0, Liberia (h) 1-0, Comoros (n) 3-1, Uganda (n) 0-1, Zambia (n) 4-1, South Africa (n) 1-0, Morocco (n) 0-1, Namibia (n) 4-1, Mali (n) 1-0, Algeria (n) 1-1 (3-4p).
League champions 2018–19: SO Armée. *Cup winners 2018:* ASEC Mimosas. *2019:* FC San Pedro.

KENYA

Football Kenya Federation, Nyayo Sports Complex, Kasarani, PO Box 12705, 00400 Nairobi.
Founded: 1960 (KFF); 2011 (FKF). *FIFA:* 1960 (2012); *CAF:* 1968 (2012). *National Colours:* All red.
International matches 2018–19
Ghana (h) 1-0, Malawi (h) 1-0, Ethiopia (a) 0-0, Ethiopia (h) 3-0, Ghana (a) 0-1, Madagascar (n) 1-0, DR Congo (n) 1-1, Algeria (n) 0-2, Tanzania (n) 3-2, Senegal (n) 0-3.
League champions 2018: Gor Mahia. *2018–19:* Gor Mahia. *Cup winners 2018:* Kariobangi Sharks. *2019:* Bandari.

LESOTHO

Lesotho Football Association, Bambatha Tsita Sports Arena, Old Polo Ground, PO Box 1879, Maseru 100.
Founded: 1932. *FIFA:* 1964; *CAF:* 1964. *National Colours:* Green shirts with blue and white trim, green shorts, green socks.

International matches 2018–19
Cape Verde Islands (h) 1-1, Uganda (a) 0-3, Uganda (h) 0-2, Tanzania (h) 1-0, Cape Verde Islands (a) 0-0, Uganda (n) 0-0 (3-2p), Botswana (n) 1-2, Zimbabwe (n) 2-2 (4-5p).
League champions 2018–19: Matlama. *Cup winners:* Not contested since 2017.

LIBERIA

Liberia Football Association, Professional Building, Benson Street, PO Box 10-1066, Monrovia 1000.
Founded: 1936. *FIFA:* 1964; *CAF:* 1960. *National Colours:* Blue shirts with white trim, white shorts, red socks.
International matches 2018–19
Sierra Leone (h) 0-0, DR Congo (h) 1-1, Congo (a) 1-3, Congo (h) 2-1, Zimbabwe (h) 1-0, DR Congo (a) 0-1, Ivory Coast (a) 0-1.
League champions 2018: Barrack Young Controllers; *2019:* LPRC Oilers. *Cup winners 2018:* Barrack Young Controllers; *2019:* LISCR.

LIBYA

Libyan Football Federation, General Sports Federation Building, Sports City, Goriji, PO Box 5137, Tripoli.
Founded: 1962. *FIFA:* 1964; *CAF:* 1965. *National Colours:* Red shirts, black shorts, black socks.
International matches 2018–19
South Africa (a) 0-0, Nigeria (a) 0-4, Nigeria (h) 2-3*, Seychelles (a) 8-1, South Africa (h) 1-2*.
* *Match played in Tunisia.*
League champions 2018–19: Competition cancelled. *Cup winners 2017:* Not contested; *2018:* Al-Ittihad.

MADAGASCAR

Federation Malagasy de Football, 29 Rue de Russie Isoraka, PO Box 4409, Antananarivo 101.
Founded: 1961. *FIFA:* 1964; *CAF:* 1963. *National Colours:* All green with white trim.
International matches 2018–19
Senegal (h) 2-2, Equatorial Guinea (a) 1-0, Equatorial Guinea (h) 1-0, Sudan (h) 1-3, Senegal (a) 0-2, Luxembourg (a) 3-3, Kenya (n) 0-1, Mauritania (n) 1-3, Guinea (n) 2-2, Burundi (n) 1-0, Nigeria (n) 2-0, DR Congo (n) 2-2 (4-2p), Tunisia (n) 0-3.
League champions 2018: CNaPS Sport; *2019:* Fosa Juniors. *Cup winners 2018:* AS St-Michel; *2019:* Fosa Juniors.

MALAWI

Football Association of Malawi, Chiwembe Technical Centre, Off Chiwembe Road, PO Box 51657, Limbe.
Founded: 1966. *FIFA:* 1968; *CAF:* 1968. *National Colours:* All red.
International matches 2018–19
Morocco (a) 0-3, Kenya (a) 0-1, Cameroon (a) 0-1, Cameroon (h) 0-0, Comoros (a) 1-2, Morocco (h) 0-0, Eswatini (a) 0-0, Eswatini (h) 1-1, Seychelles (n) 3-0, Namibia (n) 2-1, Mozambique (n) 1-1, Zambia (n) 2-2 (2-4p), Comoros (n) 2-1, South Africa (a) 0-0 (4-5p).
League champions 2018: Nyasa Big Bullets. *Cup winners:* Not contested since 2015.

MALI

Federation Malienne de Football, Avenue du Mali, Hamdallaye ACI 2000, BP 1020, Bamako 0000.
Founded: 1960. *FIFA:* 1964; *CAF:* 1963. *National Colours:* All yellow with green and red trim.
International matches 2018–19
South Sudan (a) 3-0, Burundi (h) 0-0, Burundi (a) 1-1, Gabon (a) 1-0, South Sudan (h) 3-0, Senegal (a) 1-2, Cameroon (n) 1-1, Mauritania (n) 4-1, Tunisia (n) 1-1, Angola (h) 1-0, Ivory Coast (n) 0-1.
League champions: Not contested since 2017. *Cup winners 2018:* Stade Malien.

MAURITANIA

Federation de Foot-Ball de la Rep. Islamique de Mauritanie, Route de l'Espoire, BP 566, Nouakchott.
Founded: 1961. *FIFA:* 1970; *CAF:* 1968. *National Colours:* Green shirts, yellow shorts, red socks.
International matches 2018–19
Burkina Faso (h) 2-0, Angola (a) 1-4, Angola (h) 1-0, Botswana (h) 2-1, Burkina Faso (h) 0-1, Madagascar (n) 3-1, Benin (n) 1-3, Mali (n) 1-4, Angola (n) 0-0, Tunisia (h) 0-0.
League champions 2018–19: FC Nouadhibou. *Cup winners 2018:* FC Nouadhibou; *2019:* ASC SNIM.

MAURITIUS

Mauritius Football Association, Sepp Blatter House, Trianon.
Founded: 1952. *FIFA:* 1964; *CAF:* 1963. *National Colours:* All white with red trim.
International matches 2018–19
Singapore (a) 1-1, Indonesia (a) 0-1, Fiji (a) 0-1, Eswatini (n) 2-2, Comoros (n) 1-2.
League champions 2018–19: Pamplemousses. *Cup winners 2018:* Pamplemousses; *2019:* Roche-Bois Bolton City.

MOROCCO

Federation Royale Marocaine de Football, 51 bis, Avenue Ibn Sina, Agdal BP 51, Rabat 10 000.
Founded: 1955. *FIFA:* 1960; *CAF:* 1959. *National Colours:* Red shirts with white trim, green shorts, red socks with white tops.
International matches 2018–19
Malawi (h) 3-0, Comoros (h) 1- 0, Comoros (a) 2-2, Cameroon (h) 2-0, Tunisia (a) 1-0, Malawi (a) 0-0, Argentina (h) 0-1, Gambia (h) 0-1, Zambia (h) 2-3, Namibia (n) 1-0, Ivory Coast (n) 1-0, South Africa (n) 1-0, Benin (n) 1-1 (1-4p).
League champions 2018–19: WAC Casablanca. *Cup winners 2018:* RS Berkane.

MOZAMBIQUE

Federacao Mocambicana de Futebol, Avenida Samora Machel 11, Caixa Postal 1467, Maputo.
Founded: 1976. *FIFA:* 1980; *CAF:* 1980. *National Colours:* Red shirts, black shorts, red socks with black tops.
International matches 2018–19
Guinea-Bissau (h) 2-2, Namibia (h) 1-2, Namibia (a) 0-1, Zambia (h) 1-0, Guinea-Bissau (h) 2-2, Namibia (n) 1-2, Seychelles (n) 0-0, Malawi (h) 1-1.
League champions 2018: UD Songo. *Cup winners 2018:* Costa do Sol.

NAMIBIA

Namibia Football Association, Richard Kamuhuka Str., Soccer House, Katutura, PO Box 1345, Windhoek 9000.
Founded: 1990. *FIFA:* 1992; *CAF:* 1992. *National Colours:* All blue.
International matches 2018–19
Zambia (h) 1-1, Mozambique (a) 2-1, Mozambique (h) 1-0, Guinea-Bissau (h) 0-0, Zambia (a) 1-4, Mozambique (n) 2-1, Malawi (n) 1-2, Seychelles (n) 3-0, Morocco (n) 0-1, South Africa (n) 0-1, Ivory Coast (n) 1-4, South Africa (n) 2-1,
League champions 2018–19: Black Africa. *Cup winners 2018:* African Stars.

NIGER

Federation Nigerienne de Football, Avenue Francois Mitterand, BP 10299, Niamey.
Founded: 1961. *FIFA:* 1964; *CAF:* 1964. *National Colours:* Orange shirts, white shorts, green socks.
International matches 2018–19
Egypt (a) 0-6, Tunisia (a) 0-1, Tunisia (h) 1-2, Eswatini (a) 2-1, Egypt (h) 1-1.
League champions 2018–19: AS SONIDEP. *Cup winners 2018:* AS Garde Nationale; *2019:* AS SONIDEP.

NIGERIA

Nigeria Football Federation, Plot 2033, Olusegun Obasanjo Way, Zone 7, Wuse Abuja, PO Box 5101 Garki, Abuja.
Founded: 1945. *FIFA:* 1960; *CAF:* 1960. *National Colours:* Green shirts with white trim, white shorts, green socks.
International matches 2018–19
Seychelles (a) 3-0, Libya (h) 4-0, Libya (a) 3-2*, South Africa (a) 1-1, Uganda (h) 0-0, Seychelles (h) 3-1, Egypt (h) 1-0, Zimbabwe (h) 0-0, Burundi (n) 1-0, Guinea (n) 1-0, Madagascar (n) 0-2, Cameroon (n) 3-2, South Africa (n) 2-1, Algeria (n) 1-2.
* *Match played in Tunisia.*
League champions 2018: Competition abandoned; *2019:* Enyimba. *Cup winners 2017:* Akwa United; *2018:* Enugu Rangers.

RWANDA

Federation Rwandaise de Football Association, BP 2000, Kigali.
Founded: 1972. *FIFA:* 1978; *CAF:* 1976. *National Colours:* Yellow shirts with green trim, yellow shorts, green socks with yellow tops.
International matches 2018–19
Ivory Coast (h) 1-2, Guinea (a) 0-2, Guinea (h) 1-1, Central African Republic (h) 2-2, Ivory Coast (a) 0-3.
League champions 2018–19: Rayon Sports. *Cup winners 2018:* Mukare Victory Sports; *2019:* AS Kigali.

SAO TOME & PRINCIPE

Federacao Santomense de Futebol, Rua Ex-Joao de Deus No. QXXIII-426/26, BP 440, Sao Tome.
Founded: 1975. *FIFA:* 1986; *CAF:* 1986. *National Colours:* All yellow.

International matches 2018–19
None played.
League champions 2018: UDRA. *Cup winners 2018:* FC Porto Real.

SENEGAL

Federation Senegalaise de Football, VDN Ouest-Foire en face du Cicesi, BP 13021, Dakar.
Founded: 1960. *FIFA:* 1964; *CAF:* 1964. *National Colours:* All white with green trim.
International matches 2018–19
Madagascar (a) 2-2, Sudan (h) 3-0, Sudan (a) 1-0, Equatorial Guinea (a) 1-0, Madagascar (h) 2-0, Mali (h) 2-1, Tanzania (n) 2-0, Algeria (n) 0-1, Kenya (n) 3-0, Uganda (n) 1-0, Benin (n) 1-0, Tunisia (n) 1-0.
League champions 2018–19: Generation Foot. *Cup winners 2018:* Generation Foot; *2019:* Tuengueth.

SEYCHELLES

Seychelles Football Federation, Maison Football, Roche Caiman, PO Box 843, Mahé.
Founded: 1979. *FIFA:* 1986; *CAF:* 1986. *National Colours:* All red with white trim.
International matches 2018–19
Nigeria (h) 0-3, South Africa (a) 0-6, South Africa (h) 0-0, Libya (h) 1-8, Nigeria (a) 1-3, Botswana (a) 0-2, Botswana (h) 1-3, Malawi (n) 0-3, Mozambique (n) 0-0, Namibia (n) 0-3.
League champions 2018: Cote d'Or. *Cup winners 2018–19:* Saint Louis Suns United.

SIERRA LEONE

Sierra Leone Football Association, 21 Battery Street, Kingtom, PO Box 672, Freetown.
Founded: 1960. *FIFA:* 1960; *CAF:* 1960. *National Colours:* All blue. *(FIFA membership suspended in October 2018 due to alleged government interference.)*
International matches 2018–19
Liberia (a) 0-0.
League champions 2014–18: Not contested. *2019:* East End Lions. *Cup winners:* Not contested since 2016.

SOMALIA

Somali Football Federation, Mogadishu BN 03040 (DHL only).
Founded: 1951. *FIFA:* 1962; *CAF:* 1968. *National Colours:* All sky blue with white trim.
International matches 2018–19
None played.
League champions 2019: Dekedda. *Cup winners 2018:* Benaadir.

SOUTH AFRICA

South African Football Association, 76 Nasrec Road, Nasrec, Johannesburg 2000.
Founded: 1991. *FIFA:* 1992; *CAF:* 1992. *National Colours:* Yellow shirts with green trim, green shorts, yellow socks.
International matches 2018–19
Libya (h) 0-0, Seychelles (h) 6-0, Seychelles (a) 0-0, Nigeria (h) 1-1, Paraguay (n) 1-1, Libya (a) 2-1*, Botswana (h) 2-2 (4-5p), Uganda (h) 1-1 (4-2p), Malawi (h) 0-0 (5-4p), Ghana (n) 0-0, Ivory Coast (n) 0-1, Namibia (n) 1-0, Morocco (n) 0-1, Egypt (a) 1-0, Nigeria (a) 1-2.
** Match played in Tunisia.*
League champions 2018–19: Mamelodi Sundowns. *Cup winners 2018–19:* TS Galaxy.

SOUTH SUDAN

South Sudan Football Association, Juba National Stadium, Hai Himra, Talata, Juba.
Founded: 2011. *FIFA:* 2012; *CAF:* 2012. *National Colours:* White shirts with blue and red sash, white shorts, white socks.
International matches 2018–19
Mali (h) 0-3, Gabon (a) 0-3, Gabon (h) 0-1, Burundi (h) 2-5, Mali (a) 0-3.
League champions 2018: Al-Hilal Wau; *2019:* Atlabara. *Cup winners 2018:* Al-Merikh. *2019:* Amarat United.

SUDAN

Sudan Football Association, Baladia Street, PO Box 437, 11111 Khartoum.
Founded: 1936. *FIFA:* 1948; *CAF:* 1957. *National Colours:* All red with white trim.
International matches 2018–19
Equatorial Guinea (a) 0-1, Senegal (a) 0-3, Senegal (h) 0-1, Madagascar (a) 3-1, Equatorial Guinea (h) 1-4.
League champions 2018: Al-Hilal Omdurman. *2018–19:* Al-Merrikh. *Cup winners 2018:* Al-Merrikh.

TANZANIA

Tanzania Football Federation, Karume Memorial Stadium, Uhuru/Shauri Moyo Road, PO Box 1574, Ilala/Dar Es Salaam.
Founded: 1930. *FIFA:* 1964; *CAF:* 1964. *National Colours:* Blue shirts, white shorts, blue socks.
International matches 2018–19
Uganda (a) 0-0, Cape Verde Islands (a) 0-3, Cape Verde Islands (h) 2-0, Lesotho (a) 0-1, Uganda (h) 3-0, Egypt (a) 0-1, Senegal (n) 0-2, Kenya (n) 2-3, Algeria (n) 0-3.
League champions 2018–19: Simba. *Cup winners 2018–19:* Azam.

TOGO

Federation Togolaise de Football, Route de Kegoue, BP 05, Lome.
Founded: 1960. *FIFA:* 1964; *CAF:* 1964. *National Colours:* All yellow.
International matches 2018–19
Benin (h) 0-0, Gambia (h) 1-1, Gambia (a) 1-0, Algeria (h) 1-4, Benin (a) 1-2.
League champions 2018–19: ASC Kara. *Cup winners 2019:* Not contested.

TUNISIA

Federation Tunisienne de Football, Stade Annexe d'El Menzah, Cite Olympique, El Menzah 1003.
Founded: 1957. *FIFA:* 1960; *CAF:* 1960. *National Colours:* All white with red trim.
International matches 2018–19
Eswatini (a) 2-0, Niger (h) 1-0, Niger (a) 2-1, Egypt (a) 2-3, Morocco (h) 0-1, Eswatini (h) 4-0, Algeria (a) 0-1, Iraq (h) 2-0, Croatia (a) 2-1, Burundi (h) 2-1, Angola (n) 1-1, Mali (n) 1-1, Mauritania (n) 0-0, Ghana (n) 1-1 (5-4p), Madagascar (n) 3-0, Senegal (n) 0-1.
League champions 2018–19: Esperance de Tunis. *Cup winners 2018–19:* Competition still being played.

UGANDA

Federation of Uganda Football Associations, FUFA House, Plot No. 879, Wakaliga Road, Mengo, PO Box 22518, Kampala.
Founded: 1924. *FIFA:* 1960; *CAF:* 1960. *National Colours:* Red shirts with yellow and black trim, white shorts, red socks.
International matches 2018–19
Tanzania (h) 0-0, Lesotho (h) 3-0, Lesotho (a) 2-0, Cape Verde Islands (h) 1-0, Nigeria (a) 0-0, Tanzania (a) 0-3, Lesotho (n) 0-0 (2-3p), South Africa (n) 1-1 (2-4p), Ivory Coast (n) 1-0, DR Congo (n) 2-0, Zimbabwe (n) 1-1, Egypt (a) 0-2, Senegal (n) 0-1.
League champions 2018–19: KCCA. *Cup winners 2019:* Proline.

ZAMBIA

Football Association of Zambia, Football House, Alick Nkhata Road, Long Acres, PO Box 34751, Lusaka.
Founded: 1929. *FIFA:* 1964; *CAF:* 1964. *National Colours:* All green.
International matches 2018–19
Namibia (a) 1-1, Gabon (a) 1-0, Guinea-Bissau (h) 2-1, Guinea-Bissau (a) 1-2, Mozambique (a) 0-1, Namibia (h) 4-1, Malawi (n) 2-2 (4-2p), Zimbabwe (h) 0-0 (4-2p), Botswana (n) 1-0, Cameroon (n) 1-2, Morocco (a) 3-2, Ivory Coast (n) 1-4.
League champions 2018: ZESCO United; *2019:* ZESCO United. *Cup winners:* Not contested since 2007.

ZIMBABWE

Zimbabwe Football Association, ZIFA House, 53 Livingston Avenue, PO Box CY 114, Causeway, Harare.
Founded: 1965. *FIFA:* 1965; *CAF:* 1980. *National Colours:* All gold with white trim.
International matches 2018–19
Congo (a) 1-1, DR Congo (a) 2-1, DR Congo (h) 1-1, Liberia (a) 0-1, Congo (h) 2-0, Comoros (n) 2-0, Zambia (n) 0-0 (2-4p), Lesotho (n) 2-2 (5-4p), Nigeria (a) 0-0, Egypt (a) 0-1, Uganda (n) 1-1, DR Congo (n) 0-4.
League champions 2018: FC Platinum. *Cup winners 2018:* Triangle United.

UEFA NATIONS LEAGUE 2018–19

▪ *Denotes player sent off.*

LEAGUE A – GROUP 1

Thursday, 6 September 2018

Germany (0) 0

France (0) 0 67,485

Germany: (4231) Neuer; Ginter, Boateng, Hummels, Rudiger; Kimmich, Kroos; Muller, Goretzka (Gundogan 66), Werner; Reus (Sane 83).
France: (4411) Areola; Pavard, Varane, Umtiti, Lucas; Mbappe-Lottin, Pogba, Kante, Matuidi (Tolisso 85); Griezmann (Fekir 80); Giroud (Dembele 66).

Sunday, 9 September 2018

France (1) 2 *(Mbappe-Lottin 13, Giroud 75)*

Netherlands (0) 1 *(Babel 67)* 76,452

France: (4231) Areola; Pavard, Varane, Umtiti, Lucas (Mendy B 62); Pogba, Kante; Mbappe-Lottin, Griezmann (Nzonzi 81), Matuidi; Giroud (Dembele 88).
Netherlands: (343) Cillessen; de Ligt, van Dijk, Blind; Tete (Janmaat 82), Propper, Babel (de Jong L 88), de Jong F; Promes (Vormer 76), Depay, Wijnaldum.

Saturday, 13 October 2018

Netherlands (1) 3 *(van Dijk 30, Depay 87, Wijnaldum 90)*

Germany (0) 0 52,536

Netherlands: (433) Cillessen; Dumfries, de Ligt, van Dijk, Blind; de Roon, de Jong F (Ake 77), Wijnaldum; Bergwijn (Groeneveld 68), Depay, Babel (Promes 68).
Germany: (4141) Neuer; Ginter, Boateng, Hummels, Hector; Kimmich; Muller (Sane 57), Can (Draxler 57), Kroos, Werner; Uth (Brandt 68).

Tuesday, 16 October 2018

France (0) 2 *(Griezmann 62, 80 (pen))*

Germany (1) 1 *(Kroos 14 (pen))* 75,000

France: (4231) Lloris; Pavard, Varane, Kimpembe, Lucas; Kante (Nzonzi 90), Pogba; Mbappe-Lottin (Dembele 86), Griezmann (Ndombele 90), Matuidi; Giroud.
Germany: (442) Neuer; Ginter (Brandt 83), Sule, Hummels, Schulz; Kehrer, Kimmich, Kroos, Sane (Draxler 75); Werner, Gnabry (Muller 88).

Friday, 16 November 2018

Netherlands (1) 2 *(Wijnaldum 44, Depay 90 (pen))*

France (0) 0 48,000

Netherlands: (433) Cillessen; Dumfries, de Ligt, van Dijk, Blind; de Roon, de Jong F, Wijnaldum (Vilhena 89); Bergwijn (Promes 85), Depay, Babel (Ake 90).
France: (4231) Lloris; Pavard, Varane, Kimpembe, Digne; Kante, Nzonzi (Ndombele 81); Mbappe-Lottin, Griezmann, Matuidi (Sissoko 65); Giroud (Dembele 65).

Monday, 19 November 2018

Germany (2) 2 *(Werner 9, Sane 19)*

Netherlands (0) 2 *(Promes 84, van Dijk 90)* 42,186

Germany: (343) Neuer; Sule, Hummels, Rudiger; Kehrer, Kroos, Kimmich, Schulz; Sane (Goretzka 80), Werner (Reus 63), Gnabry (Muller 66).
Netherlands: (433) Cillessen; Tete, de Ligt, van Dijk, Blind; de Roon, de Jong F, Wijnaldum (Vilhena 59); Promes, Depay, Babel (Dilrosun 45 (De Jong L 65)).

League A Group 1	P	W	D	L	F	A	GD	Pts
Netherlands	4	2	1	1	8	4	4	7
France	4	2	1	1	4	4	0	7
Germany	4	0	2	2	3	7	–4	2

LEAGUE A – GROUP 2

Saturday, 8 September 2018

Switzerland (2) 6 *(Zuber 13, Zakaria 23, Shaqiri 53, Seferovic 67, Ajeti 71, Mehmedi 82)*

Iceland (0) 0 14,912

Switzerland: (4231) Sommer; Mbabu, Akanji, Embolo (Ajeti 65), Seferovic (Mehmedi 72); Xhaka, Rodriguez; Zuber (Sow 79), Zakaria, Schar; Shaqiri.
Iceland: (442) Hannes Halldorsson; Saevarsson, Palsson, Ingason, Sigurdsson R; Bjarnason B (Bjarnason E 65), Sigurdsson G, Sigurdarson (Kjartansson 60), Gislason (Sigurjonsson 74); Bodvarsson, Skulason A.

Tuesday, 11 September 2018

Iceland (0) 0

Belgium (2) 3 *(Hazard E 29 (pen), Lukaku 31, 81)* 9710

Iceland: (4411) Hannes Halldorsson; Saevarsson, Sigurdsson R, Ingason, Magnusson; Sigurjonsson, Bjarnason B, Hallfredsson (Traustason 84), Skulason A (Palsson 80); Sigurdsson G; Bodvarsson (Sigthorsson 70).
Belgium: (343) Courtois; Alderweireld, Kompany, Vertonghen; Meunier, Tielemans (Dembele 80), Witsel, Carrasco (Chadli 70); Mertens, Lukaku, Hazard E (Hazard T 89).

Friday, 12 October 2018

Belgium (0) 2 *(Lukaku 58, 84)*

Switzerland (0) 1 *(Gavranovic 76)* 39,049

Belgium: (343) Courtois; Alderweireld, Kompany, Vermaelen (Boyata 73); Meunier, Tielemans, Witsel, Carrasco (Chadli 76); Mertens (Hazard T 90), Lukaku, Hazard E.
Switzerland: (4411) Sommer; Lang, Elvedi, Schar, Rodriguez; Freuler (Fassnacht 87), Xhaka, Zakaria (Fernandes E 83), Zuber; Shaqiri; Seferovic (Gavranovic 69).

Monday, 15 October 2018

Iceland (0) 1 *(Finnbogason A 81)*

Switzerland (0) 2 *(Seferovic 52, Lang 68)* 8663

Iceland: (442) Hannes Halldorsson; Arnason, Bjarnason B, Eyjolfsson, Finnbogason A; Gudmundsson J, Magnusson, Sigurdsson G, Sigurdsson R (Gudmundsson A 84); Sigurjonsson, Traustason (Gislason 68).
Switzerland: (442) Elvedi; Gavranovic (Fernandes E 69), Lang, Moubandje, Mvogo; Schar, Seferovic (Ajeti 90), Shaqiri, Xhaka; Zakaria, Zuber (Fassnacht 88).

Thursday, 15 November 2018

Belgium (0) 2 *(Batshuayi 65, 81)*

Iceland (0) 0 28,891

Belgium: (3421) Courtois; Alderweireld, Kompany (Denayer 84), Boyata; Meunier, Tielemans, Witsel, Hazard T; Hazard E (Vanaken 75), Mertens (Januzaj 75); Batshuayi.
Iceland: (4411) Hannes Halldorsson; Ingason, Fjoluson, Arnason, Magnusson; Sigurdsson A (Sigthorsson 64), Palsson, Gunnarsson, Skulason A; Gudmundsson A (Thorsteinsson 87); Finnbogason A.

Sunday, 18 November 2018

Switzerland (3) 5 *(Rodriguez 26 (pen), Seferovic 31, 44, 84, Elvedi 62)*

Belgium (2) 2 *(Hazard T 2, 17)* 39,049

Switzerland: (4411) Sommer; Mbabu, Elvedi, Klose, Rodriguez; Fernandes E, Xhaka, Freuler (Zakaria 79), Zuber (Benito 87); Shaqiri; Seferovic (Ajeti 90).
Belgium: (343) Courtois; Alderweireld, Kompany, Boyata; Meunier (Origi 90), Tielemans, Witsel, Chadli (Batshuayi 65); Hazard T, Mertens, Hazard E.

League A Group 2	P	W	D	L	F	A	GD	Pts
Switzerland	4	3	0	1	14	5	9	9
Belgium	4	3	0	1	9	6	3	9
Iceland	4	0	0	4	1	13	–12	0

LEAGUE A – GROUP 3

Friday, 7 September 2018

Italy (0) 1 *(Jorginho 78 (pen))*

Poland (1) 1 *(Zielinski 40)* 24,000

Italy: (433) Donnarumma; Balotelli (Belotti 61), Bernardeschi, Biraghi, Bonucci; Chiellini, Gagliardini, Insigne (Chiesa 71); Jorginho, Pellegrini (Bonaventura 46), Zappacosta.
Poland: (442) Fabianski; Bednarek, Bereszynski, Blaszczykowski (Piatek 80), Glik; Klich (Szymanski 55), Krychowiak, Kurzawa, Lewandowski; Reca, Zielinski (Linetty 66).

Monday, 10 September 2018

Portugal (0) 1 *(Andre Silva 48)*

Italy (0) 0 52,635

Portugal: (433) Rui Patricio; Joao Cancelo, Pepe, Dias, Mario Rui; Pizzi (Sanches 74), Neves, William Carvalho (Sergio Oliveira 86); Bruma (Gelson Martins 77), Andre Silva, Bernardo Silva.
Italy: (433) Donnarumma; Lazzari, Caldara, Romagnoli, Criscito (Emerson Palmieri 74); Cristante (Belotti 79), Jorginho, Bonaventura; Zaza, Immobile (Berardi 59), Chiesa.

Thursday, 11 October 2018

Poland (1) 2 *(Piatek 19, Blaszczykowski 77)*

Portugal (2) 3 *(Andre Silva 32, Glik 43 (og), Bernardo Silva 52)* 48,783

Poland: (442) Fabianski; Bereszynski (Kedziora 46), Glik, Bednarek, Jedrzejczyk; Zielinski, Krychowiak, Klich (Blaszczykowski 63), Kurzawa (Grosicki 64); Lewandowski, Piatek.
Portugal: (433) Rui Patricio; Joao Cancelo, Pepe, Dias, Mario Rui; Neves, William Carvalho, Pizzi (Sanches 74); Rafa Silva (Danilo Pereira 85), Andre Silva, Bernardo Silva (Bruno Fernandes 90).

Sunday, 14 October 2018

Poland (0) 0

Italy (0) 1 *(Biraghi 90)* 41,692

Poland: (4312) Szczesny; Bereszynski, Glik, Bednarek, Reca (Jedrzejczyk 87); Szymanski (Grosicki 46), Goralski, Linetty (Blaszczykowski 46); Zielinski; Lewandowski, Milik.
Italy: (433) Donnarumma; Florenzi (Piccini 83), Bonucci, Chiellini, Biraghi; Verratti, Jorginho, Barella; Bernardeschi (Lasagna 81), Insigne, Chiesa.

Saturday, 17 November 2018

Italy (0) 0

Portugal (0) 0 73,000

Italy: (433) Donnarumma; Florenzi, Bonucci, Chiellini, Biraghi; Verratti (Pellegrini 81), Jorginho, Barella; Chiesa (Berardi 87), Immobile (Lasagna 74), Insigne.
Portugal: (433) Rui Patricio; Joao Cancelo, Dias, Fonte, Mario Rui; Pizzi (Joao Mario 68), William Carvalho, Neves; Bruma (Guerreiro 85), Andre Silva (Danilo Pereira 90), Bernardo Silva.

Tuesday, 20 November 2018

Portugal (1) 1 *(Andre Silva 34)*

Poland (0) 1 *(Milik 66 (pen))* 29,917

Portugal: (442) Beto; Joao Cancelo, Pepe, Dias, Rodrigues; Sanches, Danilo Pereira■, William Carvalho, Guerreiro (Joao Mario 61); Andre Silva (Eder 87), Rafa Silva (Bruma 70).
Poland: (4231) Szczesny; Kedziora, Cionek, Bednarek, Bereszynski; Klich (Goralski 75), Krychowiak; Grosicki (Kadzior 79), Zielinski (Szymanski 90), Frankowski; Milik.

League A Group 3	P	W	D	L	F	A	GD	Pts
Portugal	4	2	2	0	5	3	2	8
Italy	4	1	2	1	2	2	0	5
Poland	4	0	2	2	4	6	–2	2

LEAGUE A – GROUP 4

Saturday, 8 September 2018

England (1) 1 *(Rashford 11)*

Spain (2) 2 *(Saul 13, Rodrigo 32)* 26,900

England: (352) Pickford; Maguire, Stones, Gomez; Trippier, Henderson (Dier 64), Alli, Lingard, Shaw (Rose 53); Rashford (Welbeck 90), Kane.
Spain: (433) de Gea; Carvajal, Nacho, Sergio Ramos, Alonso (Martinez 87); Thiago (Sergi Roberto 80), Busquets, Saul; Rodrigo, Aspas (Asensio 68), Isco.

Tuesday, 11 September 2018

Spain (3) 6 *(Saul 24, Asensio 33, Kalinic L 35 (og), Rodrigo 49, Sergio Ramos 57, Isco 70)*

Croatia (0) 0 26,900

Spain: (433) de Gea; Carvajal (Azpilicueta 75), Nacho, Sergio Ramos, Gaya; Saul (Thiago 65), Busquets (Rodri 59), Ceballos; Asensio, Rodrigo, Isco.
Croatia: (4231) Kalinic L; Vrsaljko (Rog 20), Mitrovic, Vida, Pivaric; Rakitic, Brozovic (Pjaca 62); Kovacic, Modric, Perisic; Santini (Livaja 71).

Friday, 12 October 2018

Croatia (0) 0

England (0) 0 *(Behind closed doors)* 0

Croatia: (4231) Livakovic; Jedvaj, Lovren, Vida, Pivaric; Kovacic (Badelj 73), Rakitic; Kramaric, Modric, Perisic (Pjaca 68); Rebic (Livaja 80).
England: (352) Pickford; Walker, Stones, Maguire; Sterling (Sancho 77), Henderson, Dier, Barkley, Chilwell; Rashford, Kane.

Monday, 15 October 2018

Spain (0) 2 *(Alcacer 58, Sergio Ramos 90)*

England (3) 3 *(Sterling 16, 38, Rashford 29)* 50,355

Spain: (433) de Gea; Jonny, Nacho, Sergio Ramos, Alonso; Thiago, Busquets, Saul (Alcacer 56); Aspas (Ceballos 57), Rodrigo (Morata 73), Asensio.
England: (41212) Pickford; Trippier (Alexander-Arnold 85), Maguire, Gomez, Chilwell; Dier; Barkley (Walker 76), Winks (Chalobah 90); Sterling; Rashford, Kane.

Thursday, 15 November 2018

Croatia (0) 3 *(Kramaric 54, Jedvaj 69, 90)*

Spain (0) 2 *(Ceballos 56, Sergio Ramos 78 (pen))* 33,018

Croatia: (4231) Kalinic L; Vrsaljko, Lovren, Vida, Jedvaj; Rakitic (Vlasic 67), Brozovic; Rebic (Brekalo 73), Modric, Perisic; Kramaric (Pjaca 89).
Spain: (433) de Gea; Sergi Roberto, Sergio Ramos, Martinez, Jordi Alba; Saul (Suso 74), Busquets, Ceballos; Rodrigo (Asensio 61), Aspas (Morata 64), Isco.

Sunday, 18 November 2018

England (0) 2 *(Lingard 78, Kane 85)*

Croatia (0) 1 *(Kramaric 57)* 78,221

England: (4411) Pickford; Walker, Gomez, Stones, Chilwell; Rashford (Sancho 73), Dier, Delph (Lingard 73), Sterling; Barkley (Alli 63); Kane.
Croatia: (4231) Kalinic L; Vrsaljko (Milic 26), Lovren, Vida, Jedvaj; Modric, Brozovic; Rebic (Brekalo 46), Vlasic (Rog 79), Perisic; Kramaric.

League A Group 4	P	W	D	L	F	A	GD	Pts
England	4	2	1	1	6	5	1	7
Spain	4	2	0	2	12	7	5	6
Croatia	4	1	1	2	4	10	–6	4

LEAGUE B – GROUP 1

Thursday, 6 September 2018

Czech Republic (1) 1 *(Schick 4)*

Ukraine (1) 2 *(Konoplyanka 45, Zinchenko 90)* 7974

Czech Republic: (532) Vaclik; Kaderabek, Kalas, Gebre Selassie, Brabec, Boril; Soucek, Sykora (Horava 90), Husbauer; Schick (Tecl 83), Krmencik (Zmrhal 46).
Ukraine: (4411) Pyatov; Karavayev, Rakitskiy, Kryvtsov, Matviyenko; Yarmolenko (Zinchenko 66), Malinovsky, Stepanenko, Konoplyanka (Tsygankov 77); Marlos; Yaremchuk (Seleznyov 85).

Sunday, 9 September 2018

Ukraine (0) 1 *(Yarmolenko 80 (pen))*

Slovakia (0) 0 *(Behind closed doors)* 0

Ukraine: (4141) Pyatov; Karavayev, Rakitskiy, Burda, Matviyenko; Stepanenko (Sydorchuk 86); Yarmolenko, Yaremchuk, Malinovsky (Zinchenko 71), Konoplyanka (Tsygankov 78); Marlos.
Slovakia: (4231) Dubravka; Satka, Skrtel, Skriniar, Hubocan; Kucka (Gregus 78), Lobotka; Mak, Hamsik, Weiss (Rusnak 70); Nemec (Duda 65).

Saturday, 13 October 2018

Slovakia (0) 1 *(Hamsik 62)*

Czech Republic (0) 2 *(Krmencik 52, Schick 76)* 17,251

Slovakia: (4231) Dubravka; Pekarik (Sabo 46), Skriniar, Skrtel, Hubocan (Hancko 80); Lobotka, Hamsik; Kucka (Weiss 54), Duda, Mak; Nemec.
Czech Republic: (4231) Vaclik; Kaderabek (Novak 63), Celustka, Brabec, Gebre Selassie; Soucek, Pavelka; Vydra (Jankto 89), Dockal, Zmrhal; Krmencik (Schick 73).

Tuesday, 16 October 2018

Ukraine (1) 1 *(Malinovsky 43)*

Czech Republic (0) 0 32,000

Ukraine: (451) Pyatov; Karavayev, Burda, Rakitskiy, Matviyenko; Yarmolenko, Marlos, Stepanenko, Malinovsky (Zinchenko 86), Konoplyanka (Tsygankov 70); Yaremchuk.
Czech Republic: (451) Pavlenka; Gebre Selassie, Celustka, Brabec, Novak; Vydra (Zmrhal 67), Pavelka, Dockal, Barak, Jankto (Sural 80); Schick (Krmencik 72).

Friday, 16 November 2018

Slovakia (2) 4 *(Rusnak 6, Kucka 26, Zrelak 52, Mak 61)*

Ukraine (0) 1 *(Konoplyanka 47)* 9764

Slovakia: (4141) Dubravka; Pekarik, Skrtel, Skriniar, Hancko; Gregus; Rusnak, Kucka (Bero 30), Hamsik, Mak (Stoch 69); Zrelak (Duris 82).
Ukraine: (4312) Boyko; Karavayev, Burda, Kryvtsov (Plastun 14), Matviyenko; Zinchenko, Stepanenko, Malinovsky; Konoplyanka (Shaparenko 65); Tsygankov, Boryachuk (Kovalenko 62).

Monday, 19 November 2018

Czech Republic (1) 1 *(Schick 32)*

Slovakia (0) 0 16,623

Czech Republic: (4141) Vaclik; Kaderabek, Celustka, Kalas, Novak; Soucek; Vydra (Selassie 64), Dockal, Pavelka, Jankto (Krejci 76); Schick (Dolezal 82).
Slovakia: (433) Dubravka; Pekarik, Skrtel, Skriniar, Hancko; Bero, Gregus (Duda 58), Hamsik; Rusnak (Mak 58), Zrelak (Nemec 79), Stoch.

League B Group 1	*P*	*W*	*D*	*L*	*F*	*A*	*GD*	*Pts*
Ukraine	4	3	0	1	5	5	0	9
Czech Republic	4	2	0	2	4	4	0	6
Slovakia	4	1	0	3	5	5	0	3

LEAGUE B – GROUP 2

Friday, 7 September 2018

Turkey (1) 1 *(Aziz 41)*

Russia (1) 2 *(Cheryshev 13, Dzyuba 49)* 29,702

Turkey: (4231) Kirintili; Aziz (Ayhan 46), Calhanoglu, Ali Kaldirim, Ozbayrakli; Soyuncu, Topal (Malli 71); Tosun, Under, Yazici (Ozyakup 57); Yokuslu.
Russia: (4321) Lunev; Cheryshev (Ionov 79), Dzhikija, Dzyuba, Erokhin; Fernandes, Gazinsky, Kudryashov (Rausch 82); Kuzyaev (Mogilevets 73), Neustadter; Zobnin.

Monday, 10 September 2018

Sweden (1) 2 *(Thelin 35, Claesson 49)*

Turkey (0) 3 *(Calhanoglu 51, Akbaba 88, 90)* 21,832

Sweden: (442) Olsen; Lustig (Krafth 78), Jansson, Lindelof, Augustinsson; Durmaz (Rohden 71), Seb Larsson, Ekdal (Hiljemark 56), Claesson; Thelin, Berg.
Turkey: (4231) Bolat; Celik, Ayhan, Soyuncu, Bayram; Topal (Akbaba 62), Yokuslu; Under (Gurler 77), Ozyakup, Calhanoglu (Malli 86); Tosun.

Thursday, 11 October 2018

Russia (0) 0

Sweden (0) 0 31,698

Russia: (4231) Guilherme; Fernandes, Neustadter, Dzhikija, Rausch; Zobnin, Gazinsky; Ionov (Kuzyaev 76), Golovin, Cheryshev (Zabolotny 87); Dzyuba.
Sweden: (442) Olsen; Lustig, Lindelof, Granqvist, Augustinsson; Claesson, Seb Larsson, Svensson, Forsberg; Thelin (Guidetti 71), Berg (Andersson S 82).

Sunday, 14 October 2018

Russia (1) 2 *(Neustadter 20, Cheryshev 78)*

Turkey (0) 0 38,288

Russia: (4231) Guilherme; Fernandes, Neustadter, Dzhikija, Kudryashov; Gazinsky, Zobnin; Ionov (Kambolov 82), Golovin (Poloz 90), Kuzyaev (Cheryshev 71); Dzyuba.
Turkey: (4231) Bolat; Celik, Aziz, Soyuncu, Ali Kaldirim (Bayram 75); Tekdemir (Ozcan 62), Yokuslu; Under, Ozyakup (Malli 84), Calhanoglu; Tosun.

Saturday, 17 November 2018

Turkey (0) 0

Sweden (0) 1 *(Granqvist 71 (pen))* 42,000

Turkey: (4141) Bolat; Celik, Ayhan, Soyuncu, Ali Kaldirim (Bayram 87); Yokuslu; Under, Tekdemir (Kahveci 72), Malli (Ozyakup 83), Calhanoglu; Tosun.
Sweden: (4222) Olsen; Lustig, Granqvist, Lindelof (Helander 46), Augustinsson; Johansson, Ekdal (Svensson 81); Seb Larsson, Olsson M; Claesson (Thelin 90), Berg.

Tuesday, 20 November 2018

Sweden (1) 2 *(Lindelof 41, Berg 72)*

Russia (0) 0 20,223

Sweden: (4411) Olsen; Lustig, Granqvist, Lindelof, Augustinsson; Seb Larsson, Johansson, Olsson K (Guidetti 89), Olsson M (Thelin 70); Claesson (Svensson 80); Berg.
Russia: (4231) Lunev; Ignatiev, Neustadter, Dzhikija, Nababkin; Kuzyaev, Gazinsky; Ionov (Zabolotny 69), Poloz (Kambolov 46), Erokhin (Ari 77); Dzyuba.

League B Group 2	*P*	*W*	*D*	*L*	*F*	*A*	*GD*	*Pts*
Sweden	4	2	1	1	5	3	2	7
Russia	4	2	1	1	4	3	1	7
Turkey	4	1	0	3	4	7	3	3

LEAGUE B – GROUP 3

Saturday, 8 September 2018

Northern Ireland (0) 1 *(Grigg 90)*

Bosnia-Herzegovina (1) 2 *(Duljevic 37, Saric 64)* 16,942

Northern Ireland: (433) Peacock-Farrell; McLaughlin C (Boyce 69), Evans J, Cathcart, Lewis; Norwood, Davis, Saville; McGinn (Ward 76), Lafferty (Grigg 69), Dallas.
Bosnia-Herzegovina: (433) Sehic; Besic, Sunjic, Zukanovic, Civic (Zakaric 76); Saric (Krunic 67), Cimirot, Pjanic (Bajic 83); Visca, Dzeko, Duljevic.

Tuesday, 11 September 2018

Bosnia-Herzegovina (0) 1 *(Dzeko 78)*

Austria (0) 0 10,000

Bosnia-Herzegovina: (433) Sehic; Todorovic D, Sunjic, Zukanovic, Civic; Saric, Besic, Pjanic (Krunic 89); Visca (Zakaric 87), Dzeko, Duljevic (Bajic 90).
Austria: (352) Lindner; Ilsanker (Schaub 86), Prodl, Hinteregger; Lainer, Lazaro, Zulj, Grillitsch (Burgstaller 81), Alaba; Gregoritsch (Sabitzer 72), Arnautovic.

Friday, 12 October 2018

Austria (0) 1 *(Arnautovic 71)*

Northern Ireland (0) 0 22,300

Austria: (442) Lindner; Lainer, Prodl, Hinteregger, Ulmer; Lazaro (Dragovic 90), Ilsanker, Zulj, Sabitzer (Schopf 75); Burgstaller (Kainz 82), Arnautovic.
Northern Ireland: (433) Peacock-Farrell; McNair, Cathcart, Evans J, Lewis; Norwood, Davis, Saville (Vassell 76); Dallas, Magennis (Grigg 79), Ferguson (Evans C 55).

Monday, 15 October 2018

Bosnia-Herzegovina (1) 2 *(Dzeko 27, 73)*

Northern Ireland (0) 0 11,050

Bosnia-Herzegovina: (433) Sehic; Vranjes, Sunjic, Zukanovic, Civic; Besic (Cimirot 89), Pjanic, Saric; Visca (Milosevic 88), Dzeko, Duljevic (Zakaric 74).
Northern Ireland: (433) Peacock-Farrell; McNair (Vassell 71), Cathcart, Evans J, Lewis; Norwood (Whyte 58), Davis, Saville; Evans C, Boyce (Magennis 80), Dallas.

Thursday, 15 November 2018

Austria (0) 0

Bosnia-Herzegovina (0) 0 37,200

Austria: (4231) Lindner; Lainer, Dragovic, Hinteregger, Alaba; Zulj (Janko 82), Baumgartlinger; Lazaro, Kainz (Schlager 46), Schopf (Gregoritsch 67); Arnautovic.
Bosnia-Herzegovina: (433) Sehic; Vranjes, Sunjic, Zukanovic, Civic; Saric, Pjanic (Gojak 87), Besic; Visca, Dzeko, Duljevic (Krunic 79).

Sunday, 18 November 2018

Northern Ireland (0) 1 *(Evans C 57)*

Austria (0) 2 *(Schlager 49, Lazaro 90)* 17,895

Northern Ireland: (433) Carson; Smith, McAuley, Evans J, Dallas; Evans C (McNair 88), Davis, Saville; McGinn (Whyte 74), Boyce (Lafferty 74), Jones.
Austria: (4231) Lindner; Lainer, Dragovic, Hinteregger, Ulmer; Ilsanker (Zulj 46), Baumgartlinger; Lazaro, Schlager, Alaba; Gregoritsch (Arnautovic 71).

League B Group 3	P	W	D	L	F	A	GD	Pts
Bosnia-Herzegovina	4	3	1	0	5	1	4	10
Austria	4	2	1	1	3	2	1	7
Northern Ireland	4	0	0	4	2	7	–5	0

LEAGUE B – GROUP 4

Thursday, 6 September 2018

Wales (3) 4 *(Lawrence T 6, Bale 17, Ramsey 37, Roberts C 55)*

Republic of Ireland (0) 1 *(Williams S 66)* 25,657

Wales: (4231) Hennessey; Roberts C, Williams A, Mepham, Davies B (Dummett 81); Ampadu (Smith 67), Allen; Lawrence T, Ramsey, Brooks; Bale (Roberts T 75).
Republic of Ireland: (442) Randolph; Coleman, Duffy, Clark, Ward (Stevens 60); Christie, Hendrick, Hourihane (Williams S 56), O'Dowda; Robinson (Horgan 77), Walters.

Sunday, 9 September 2018

Denmark (1) 2 *(Eriksen 32, 63 (pen))*

Wales (0) 0 17,506

Denmark: (433) Schmeichel; Dalsgaard, Jorgensen M, Kjaer, Larsen; Eriksen, Schone, Delaney; Poulsen (Cornelius 86), Braithwaite, Sisto (Fischer 46).
Wales: (4231) Hennessey; Gunter, Chester, Mepham, Davies B; Allen, Ampadu (Roberts T 71); Lawrence T (Woodburn 79), Ramsey, Roberts C (Brooks 59); Bale.

Saturday, 13 October 2018

Republic of Ireland (0) 0

Denmark (0) 0 41,220

Republic of Ireland: (532) Randolph; Christie, Keogh, Duffy, Long K, Doherty; Hendrick, O'Dowda (Stevens 46), Arter (Robinson 65); Long S (O'Brien 83), McClean.
Denmark: (442) Schmeichel; Dalsgaard, Kjaer, Jorgensen M, Larsen; Braithwaite, Schone, Delaney, Sisto; Dolberg (Christensen A 79), Poulsen.

Tuesday, 16 October 2018

Republic of Ireland (0) 0

Wales (0) 1 *(Wilson 58)* 38,321

Republic of Ireland: (352) Randolph; Keogh, Duffy, Long K (Hogan 76); Doherty, Christie, Arter, Hendrick, McClean; Robinson (Maguire 60), O'Brien (Long S 55).
Wales: (4231) Hennessey; Roberts C, Chester, Williams A, Davies B; Smith (Thomas 75), Allen; Wilson (Gunter 84), Brooks (King 87), Lawrence T; Roberts T.

Friday, 16 November 2018

Wales (0) 1 *(Bale 89)*

Denmark (1) 2 *(Jorgensen N 42, Braithwaite 88)* 32,354

Wales: (4411) Hennessey; Roberts C, Williams A, Chester (Ampadu 49), Dummett (Gunter 38); Brooks, Ramsey, Allen, Lawrence T; Bale; Roberts T (Wilson 68).
Denmark: (442) Schmeichel; Dalsgaard, Christensen A, Jorgensen M, Larsen; Eriksen, Schone (Lerager 79), Delaney, Braithwaite; Jorgensen N (Dolberg 70), Poulsen.

Monday, 19 November 2018

Denmark (0) 0

Republic of Ireland (0) 0 11,130

Denmark: (433) Ronnow; Ankersen, Jorgensen M, Bjelland, Knudsen; Schone, Hojbjerg, Eriksen (Lerager 46); Poulsen (Gytkjaer 64), Jorgensen N, Braithwaite (Cornelius 78).
Republic of Ireland: (532) Randolph; Coleman, Keogh, Duffy, Long K, Stevens; Christie, Hendrick, Brady (Robinson 65); O'Dowda (Obafemi 80), O'Brien (Curtis 64).

League B Group 4	P	W	D	L	F	A	GD	Pts
Denmark	4	2	2	0	4	1	3	8
Wales	4	2	0	2	6	5	1	6
Republic of Ireland	4	0	2	2	1	5	–4	2

LEAGUE C – GROUP 1

Friday, 7 September 2018

Albania (0) 1 *(Xhaka 55)*

Israel (0) 0 4126

Albania: (4231) Strakosha; Hysaj, Gjimshiti, Veseli (Mavraj 84), Binaku; Basha, Xhaka; Gavazaj (Prenga S 71), Memushaj, Hyka; Guri (Balaj 46).
Israel: (352) Haimov; Kapiloto (Micha 79), Habashi, Yeini; Dasa, Peretz, Natcho, Kayal (Solomon 71), Tawatha; Zahavi (Hemed 47), Dabour.

Monday, 10 September 2018

Scotland (0) 2 *(Djimsiti 47 (og), Naismith 68)*

Albania (0) 0 17,455

Scotland: (532) McGregor A; O'Donnell, Souttar, Mulgrew, Tierney, Robertson; McGinn, McDonald (Armstrong 46), McGregor C (McTominay 79); Russell (Griffiths 70), Naismith.
Albania: (442) Strakosha; Hysaj, Veseli (Mihaj 90), Djimsiti, Binaku; Lilaj, Xhaka, Memushaj, Ndoj (Manaj 66); Balaj, Gavazaj (Prenga H 46).

Thursday, 11 October 2018

Israel (0) 2 *(Peretz 52, Tierney 76 (og))*

Scotland (1) 1 *(Mulgrew 25 (pen))* 10,234

Israel: (3412) Harush; Yeini, Tibi, Ben Haroush; Dasa, Peretz, Kayal (Einbinder 82), Tawatha (Atar 77); Natcho; Dabour, Sahar (Saba 45).
Scotland: (3412) McGregor A; Mulgrew, Souttar■, Robertson; O'Donnell, McDonald, McGinn, Tierney; McGregor C; Russell (Forrest 67), Naismith (McBurnie 76).

Sunday, 14 October 2018

Israel (1) 2 *(Hemed 8, Saba 83)*

Albania (0) 0 14,950

Israel: (532) Harush; Dasa, Yeini, Tibi (Tzedek 46), Ben Haroush, Tawatha (Habashi 77); Peretz, Natcho, Kayal; Dabour, Hemed (Saba 66).
Albania: (352) Strakosha; Hysaj, Djimsiti, Mavraj; Basha (Lilaj 46), Uzuni, Memushaj, Xhaka, Binaku; Balaj (Vrioni 73), Grezda.

Saturday, 17 November 2018

Albania (0) 0

Scotland (2) 4 *(Fraser 14, Fletcher 45 (pen), Forrest 55, 67)* 8632

Albania: (352) Berisha; Mavraj■, Djimsiti (Dermaku 53), Veseli; Binaku, Memushaj, Xhaka, Kace (Ismajli 27), Uzuni; Grezda, Manaj (Balaj 62).
Scotland: (4141) McGregor A; Paterson, Bates, McKenna, Robertson; Armstrong (McTominay 61); Forrest, Christie, McGregor C, Fraser (Russell 72); Fletcher (Phillips 68).

Tuesday, 20 November 2018

Scotland (2) 3 *(Forrest 34, 43, 64)*

Israel (1) 2 *(Kayal 9, Zahavi 75)* 21,281

Scotland: (4411) McGregor A; Paterson, Bates, McKenna, Robertson; Forrest, McGregor C, Armstrong (Phillips 76), Fraser; Christie (Shinnie 76); Fletcher (McTominay 87).
Israel: (532) Harush; Dasa, Yeini, Taha (Cohen A 67), Ben Haroush, Tawatha (Hemed 85); Peretz (Saba 73), Natcho, Kayal; Dabbur, Zahavi.

League C Group 1	P	W	D	L	F	A	GD	Pts
Scotland	4	3	0	1	10	4	6	9
Israel	4	2	0	2	6	5	1	6
Albania	4	1	0	3	1	8	–7	3

LEAGUE C – GROUP 2

Saturday, 8 September 2018

Estonia (0) 0

Greece (1) 1 *(Fortounis 14)* 5567

Estonia: (541) Aksalu; Kams, Baranov, Vihmann, Mets, Pikk; Ojamaa (Tamm 80), Artjom Dmitrijev, Vassiljev, Luts (Puri 86); Anier (Zenjov 63).
Greece: (4231) Barkas; Torosidis, Manolas, Papastathopoulos, Lykogiannis; Kourbelis, Bouchalakis (Tziolis 78); Mandalos, Fortounis, Pelkas (Koulouris 90); Mitroglou (Bakasetas 50).

Finland (1) 1 *(Pukki 7)* **Hungary (0) 0** 10,220
Finland: (442) Hradecky; Raitala, Toivio, Arajuuri, Uronen (Granlund 45); Lod, Kauko, Schuller (Sparv 63), Soiri (Taylor 85); Tuominen, Pukki.
Hungary: (352) Gulacsi; Fiola, Lang, Kadar; Lovrencsics, Kleinheisler, Kovacs (Kalmar 61), Patkai, Sallai (Eppel 72); Stieber (Varga R 54), Szalai.

Tuesday, 11 September 2018

Finland (1) 1 *(Pukki 12)* **Estonia (0) 0** 4632
Finland: (442) Hradecky; Granlund (Vaisanen S 76), Arajuuri, Toivio, Raitala; Soiri, Sparv, Schuller, Lod (Karjalainen 87); Pukki (Kauko 90), Tuominen.
Estonia: (541) Aksalu; Teniste, Tamm, Mets, Klavan, Kallaste; Ojamaa, Vassiljev, Artjom Dmitrijev (Antonov 77), Luts (Anier 77); Zenjov (Purje 86).

Hungary (2) 2 *(Sallai 15, Kleinheisler 43)*
Greece (1) 1 *(Manolas 18) (Behind closed doors)* 120
Hungary: (433) Gulacsi; Bese, Lang, Kadar, Fiola; Kleinheisler, Nagy A, Kovacs (Patkai 81); Varga R (Lovrencsics 62), Szalai (Eppel 69), Sallai.
Greece: (4231) Barkas; Torosidis, Manolas (Oikonomou 52), Papastathopoulos, Tzavelas (Mitroglou 46); Kourbelis, Bouchalakis; Christodoulopoulos, Fortounis, Pelkas; Donis (Lykogiannis 46).

Friday, 12 October 2018

Estonia (0) 0 **Finland (0) 1** *(Pukki 90)* 8087
Estonia: (541) Aksalu; Teniste, Baranov, Artjom Dmitrijev, Tamm, Kallaste; Zenjov (Luts 60), Vassiljev (Kaljumae 88), Puri, Ojamaa; Sappinen (Purje 71).
Finland: (442) Hradecky; Raitala, Toivio, Arajuuri, Uronen; Lod, Sparv, Schuller (Kamara 72), Soiri (Forsell 61); Tuominen (Markkanen 88), Pukki.

Greece (0) 1 *(Mitroglou 65)* **Hungary (0) 0** 9040
Greece: (4231) Barkas; Bakakis, Papastathopoulos, Manolas, Tsimikas; Zeca, Kourbelis (Tziolis 46); Bakasetas, Fortounis, Pelkas (Christodoulopoulos 85); Mitroglou (Bouchalakis 90).
Hungary: (433) Gulacsi; Bese (Nemeth 75), Orban, Kadar, Fiola; Kleinheisler, Nagy A, Kalmar (Kovacs 55); Varga R (Nagy D 68), Szalai, Sallai.

Monday, 15 October 2018

Estonia (1) 3 *(Luts 20, Patkai 70 (og), Anier 79)*
Hungary (1) 3 *(Nagy D 24, Szalai 54, 81)* 3043
Estonia: (541) Aksalu (Lepmets 43); Teniste, Baranov, Mets, Tamm, Pikk; Luts, Antonov, Vassiljev, Ojamaa; Anier (Purje 90).
Hungary: (352) Gulacsi; Barath, Orban, Kadar; Lovrencsics (Bese 80), Nagy D (Eppel 75), Kovacs, Kleinheisler (Patkai 68), Nagy A; Sallai, Szalai.

Finland (0) 2 *(Soiri 46, Kamara 89)*
Greece (0) 0 10,107
Finland: (442) Hradecky; Raitala, Toivio, Arajuuri, Uronen; Lod, Kamara, Sparv, Soiri (Pirinen 86); Tuominen (Karjalainen 90), Pukki (Skrabb 12).
Greece: (4231) Barkas; Bakakis, Papastathopoulos (Tzavelas 46), Manolas, Tsimikas; Zeca, Tziolis; Bakasetas (Christodoulopoulos 55), Fortounis, Pelkas (Koulouris 73); Mitroglou.

Thursday, 15 November 2018

Greece (1) 1 *(Granlund 25 (og))* **Finland (0) 0** 6376
Greece: (4231) Vlachodimos; Torosidis, Papastathopoulos, Manolas (Siovas 28), Koutris; Zeca, Kourbelis; Pelkas (Bakasetas 84), Fortounis, Mantalos; Mitroglou (Koulouris 69).
Finland: (442) Hradecky; Granlund, Toivio, Arajuuri, Uronen; Lod, Kamara, Kauko, Soiri (Jensen 74); Tuominen (Pirinen 83), Pukki (Lam 90).

Hungary (1) 2 *(Orban 8, Szalai 69)* **Estonia (0) 0** 7775
Hungary: (4231) Dibusz; Barath, Orban, Kadar, Korhut; Nagy A, Patkai; Kalmar (Kleinheisler 84), Kovacs, Nagy D (Dzsudzsak 65); Szalai (Bode 76).
Estonia: (4231) Aksalu; Teniste, Vihmann, Tamm, Pikk; Artjom Dmitrijev, Antonov; Ojamaa (Zenjov 60), Vassiljev (Purje 82); Luts (Puri 77), Anier.

Sunday, 18 November 2018

Greece (0) 0
Estonia (1) 1 *(Lampropoulos 44 (og))* 5567
Greece: (4231) Barkas; Bakakis (Torosidis 46), Papastathopoulos, Lampropoulos, Giannoulis; Samaris, Zeca; Bakasetas, Bouchalakis (Mantalos 71), Masouras (Fortounis 57); Karelis.
Estonia: (5221) Lepmets; Kams, Baranov, Vihmann, Tamm, Kallaste; Artjom Dmitrijev, Lepistu (Antonov 68); Zenjov (Pikk 81), Luts; Sappinen (Ojamaa 86).

Hungary (2) 2 *(Szalai 29, Nagy A 37)*
Finland (0) 0 10,220
Hungary: (5311) Gulacsi; Lovrencsics, Barath (Lang 52), Orban, Kadar (Vinicius 46), Korhut (Holender 54); Kleinheisler, Nagy A, Kalmar; Dzsudzsak; Szalai.
Finland: (442) Joronen; Granlund (Toivio 46), Arajuuri, Vaisanen, Uronen; Lod, Kamara, Lam (Kauko 60), Taylor (Forsell 74); Tuominen, Pukki.

League C Group 2	*P*	*W*	*D*	*L*	*F*	*A*	*GD*	*Pts*
Finland	6	4	0	2	5	3	2	12
Hungary	6	3	1	2	9	6	3	10
Greece	6	3	0	3	4	5	–1	9
Estonia	6	1	1	4	4	8	–4	4

LEAGUE C – GROUP 3

Thursday, 6 September 2018

Norway (2) 2 *(Johansen 20, 42)*
Cyprus (0) 0 6572
Norway: (442) Jarstein; Elabdellaoui, Nordtveit, Ajer, Meling; Johansen (Fossum 71), Berge (Selnaes 69), Henriksen, Elyounoussi M; King (Elyounoussi T 89), Johnsen.
Cyprus: (433) Pardo; Demetriou J, Laifis, Merkis, Vasiliou (Efrem 46); Kousoulos, Artymatas, Margaca (Ioannou N 82); Papoulis, Sotiriou, Kyriakou (Kastanos 77).

Slovenia (1) 1 *(Zajc 40)*
Bulgaria (1) 2 *(Kraev 3, 59)* 5100
Slovenia: (4231) Belec; Skubic, Aljaz Struna, Mevlja, Jokic; Kurtic, Krhin (Bezjak 66); Kampl (Dervisevic 83), Zajc, Verbic; Sporar (Matavz 73).
Bulgaria: (352) Iliev; Chorbadzhiyski, Bodurov, Bozhikov (Lyaskov 46); Bandalovski, Slavchev, Kostadinov, Nedelev (Goranov 82), Despodov; Popov I, Kraev (Raynov 72).

Sunday, 9 September 2018

Bulgaria (0) 1 *(Vasilev 59)*
Norway (0) 0 7100
Bulgaria: (352) Iliev; Popov S, Chorbadzhiyski, Bodurov; Bandalovski, Ivanov, Kostadinov, Raynov (Vasilev 50), Despodov (Goranov 73); Popov I, Kraev (Malinov 82).
Norway: (442) Jarstein; Elabdellaoui, Nordtveit■, Ajer, Meling; Johansen (Fossum 62), Berge (Selnaes 78), Henriksen, Elyounoussi M; King, Johnsen (Sorloth 46).

Cyprus (0) 2 *(Sotiriou 69, Stojanovic 89 (og))*
Slovenia (0) 1 *(Beric 54)* 1115
Cyprus: (424) Panagi; Demetriou J, Kousoulos, Laifis, Ioannou N (Margaca 67); Kyriakou, Artymatas; Papoulis, Kastanos (Roushias 60), Sotiriou, Efrem (Merkis 90).
Slovenia: (442) Belec; Stojanovic, Blazic, Mevlja, Jokic; Crnigoj, Dervisevic, Kurtic (Stulac 76), Verbic (Bezjak 46); Zajc, Beric (Sporar 83).

Saturday, 13 October 2018

Bulgaria (0) 2 *(Despodov 59, Nedelev 68)*
Cyprus (1) 1 *(Kastanos 41)* 10,000
Bulgaria: (442) Iliev; Popov S, Nedyalkov, Bodurov, Zanev; Nedelev, Kostadinov, Slavchev, Despodov (Bozhikov 74); Popov I (Vasilev 83), Kraev (Milanov 57).
Cyprus: (433) Panagi, Demetriou J, Merkis, Laifis, Ioannou N (Christofi 72); Kousoulos, Kastanos (Margaca 65), Artymatas; Papoulis (Roushias 75), Sotiriou, Avraam.

Norway (1) 1 *(Selnaes 45)*
Slovenia (0) 0 14,712
Norway: (433) Jarstein; Elabdellaoui, Rosted, Hovland, Aleesami; Johansen (Fossum 80), Selnaes, Henriksen; Elyounoussi T (Johnsen 75), King, Elyounoussi M (Linnes 90).
Slovenia: (442) Belec; Skubic, Mevlja, Krajnc (Mitrovic 9), Jokic; Crnigoj (Ilicic 61), Krhin, Stulac (Bijol 46), Zajć; Bezjak, Sporar.

Tuesday, 16 October 2018

Norway (1) 1 *(Elyounoussi M 31)*
Bulgaria (0) 0 9523
Norway: (433) Jarstein; Elabdellaoui, Nordtveit, Rosted, Aleesami; Johansen (Fossum 78), Selnaes, Henriksen; Elyounoussi M, King, Elyounoussi T.
Bulgaria: (442) Iliev; Bozhikov, Bodurov, Chorbadzhiyski (Vasilev 49), Zanev; Bandalovski, Kostadinov (Kraev 78), Slavchev (Malinov 58), Nedelev; Despodov, Popov I.

Slovenia (0) 1 *(Skubic 83)* **Cyprus (1) 1** *(Papoulis 37)* 5318
Slovenia: (4231) Belec; Skubic, Mitrovic, Mevlja, Jokic (Balkovec 58); Crnigoj, Krhin (Zahovic 75); Ilicic■, Zajc, Bezjak (Dervisevic 46); Beric.
Cyprus: (433) Panagi; Demetriou J■, Merkis, Sielis, Vasiliou (Ioannou N 90); Artymatas, Kastanos■, Kousoulos; Papoulis (Avraam 73), Sotiriou, Margaca (Christofi 87).

Friday, 16 November 2018

Slovenia (1) 1 *(Verbic 9)*
Norway (0) 1 *(Johnsen 86)* 10,254
Slovenia: (442) Belec; Skubic, Aljaz Struna, Mevlja, Andraz Struna; Crnigoj (Bezjak 58), Rotman, Dervisevic, Verbic; Sporar (Bijol 84), Zajc (Beric 70).
Norway: (442) Jarstein; Elabdellaoui, Nordtveit, Rosted, Aleesami; Johansen (Odegaard 57), Selnaes, Henriksen, Elyounoussi M; Elyounoussi T (Johnsen 63), Kamara (Sorloth 75).

Cyprus (1) 1 *(Zachariou 24)*
Bulgaria (0) 1 *(Dimitrov 89 (pen))* 3844
Cyprus: (433) Panagi; Kousoulos, Merkis, Laifis, Margaca; Zachariou (Roushias 67), Kyriakou, Artymatas; Avraam (Ioannou N 59), Makris, Efrem (Papafotis 78).
Bulgaria: (442) Petkov; Popov S, Bozhikov, Bodurov, Nedyalkov; Nedelev, Kostadinov, Slavchev (Kostov 82), Ivanov (Dimitrov 56); Popov I, Kraev (Delev 56).

Monday, 19 November 2018

Bulgaria (0) 1 *(Ivanov 68)* **Slovenia (0) 1** *(Zajc 75)* 3092
Bulgaria: (433) Petkov; Popov S, Bodurov, Bozhikov, Nedyalkov; Kostadinov, Slavchev, Dimitrov (Ivanov 64); Delev (Zanev 72), Popov I, Kostov (Vasilev 59).
Slovenia: (442) Belec; Skubic, Blazic, Mevlja, Andraz Struna; Ilicic, Dervisevic (Bijol 57), Rotman, Verbic (Pozeg 72); Bezjak, Zajc (Stulac 87).

Cyprus (0) 0 **Norway (1) 2** *(Kamara 36, 48)* 1513
Cyprus: (442) Panagi; Kousoulos, Merkis, Laifis, Ioannou N; Kyriakou (Fylaktou 78), Artymatas, Sielis■, Avraam (Efrem 61); Kastanos, Zachariou (Makris 84).
Norway: (442) Jarstein; Elabdellaoui, Nordtveit, Rosted, Meling; Fossum (Odegaard 45), Selnaes, Henriksen, Elyounoussi M■; Kamara (Berge 90), Elyounoussi T (Sorloth 71).

League C Group 3	P	W	D	L	F	A	GD	Pts
Norway	6	4	1	1	7	2	5	13
Bulgaria	6	3	2	1	7	5	2	11
Cyprus	6	1	2	3	5	9	–4	5
Slovenia	6	0	3	3	5	8	–3	3

LEAGUE C – GROUP 4

Friday, 7 September 2018

Lithuania (0) 0 **Serbia (1) 1** *(Tadic 38 (pen))* 4378
Lithuania: (541) Setkus; Baravykas, Zulpa, Jankauskas, Klimavicius, Vaitkunas; Slivka, Verbickas (Sernas 72), Kuklys (Vorobjovas 46), Novikovas; Cernych.
Serbia: (4231) Dmitrovic; Rukavina, Veljkovic, Milenkovic, Rodic (Kolarov 77); Zivkovic, Tadic; Matic (Lukic 82), Kostic (Radonjic 90), Mitrovic; Nemanja Maksimovic.

Romania (0) 0
Montenegro (0) 0 *(Behind closed doors)* 0
Romania: (4231) Tatarusanu; Benzar, Chiriches (Balasa 31), Sapunaru, Bancu; Pintilii (Anton 73), Stanciu; Chipciu, Maxim, Mitrita (Budescu 67); Keseru.
Montenegro: (4231) Petkovic; Stojkovic, Savic, Simic, Tomasevic; Scekic (Kosovic 74), Vukcevic; Boljevic (Beciraj 80), Ivanic, Jovetic; Mugosa■.

Monday, 10 September 2018

Montenegro (2) 2 *(Savic 34 (pen), Jankovic 35)*
Lithuania (0) 0 5239
Montenegro: (4231) Petkovic; Stojkovic, Savic (Kopitovic 80), Simic, Tomasevic; Kosovic, Vukcevic (Scekic 72); Jankovic (Boljevic 87), Ivanic, Jovovic; Beciraj.
Lithuania: (4231) Setkus; Lasickas (Sernas 62), Leimonas (Kuklys 46), Klimavicius, Vaitkunas; Verbickas (Borovskij 46), Zulpa; Slivka, Vorobjovas, Novikovas; Cernych.

Serbia (1) 2 *(Mitrovic 26, 63)*
Romania (0) 2 *(Stanciu 48 (pen), Tucudean 68)* 15,496
Serbia: (4231) Dmitrovic; Rukavina, Spajic, Veljkovic, Kolarov; Nemanja Maksimovic, Lukic (Matic 71); Ljajic (Prijovic 77), Milinkovic-Savic (Kostic 63), Tadic; Mitrovic.
Romania: (433) Tatarusanu; Manea, Balasa, Sapunaru, Bancu; Marin, Anton, Chipciu (Rotariu 90); Stanciu, Tucudean (Keseru 82), Dragus (Mitrita 60).

Thursday, 11 October 2018

Lithuania (0) 1 *(Zulpa 90)*
Romania (1) 2 *(Chipciu 13, Maxim 90)* 2279
Lithuania: (433) Setkus; Baravykas, Jankauskas, Klimavicius, Slavickas; Zulpa, Vorobjovas (Valskis 63), Slivka; Novikovas, Cernych (Petravicius 87), Sernas (Kuklys 63).
Romania: (4231) Tatarusanu; Manea, Tamas, Sapunaru, Bancu; Anton, Marin; Chipciu, Stanciu (Rotariu 87), Mitrita (Maxim 78); Tucudean (Keseru 71).

Montenegro (0) 0
Serbia (1) 2 *(Mitrovic 18 (pen), 82)* 9394
Montenegro: (4231) Petkovic; Stojkovic (Jankovic 46), Simic, Tomasevic, Vesovic; Scekic (Ivanic 73), Vukcevic; Marusic, Jovetic, Jovovic; Beciraj (Mugosa 80).
Serbia: (4231) Dmitrovic; Rukavina, Milenkovic, Veljkovic, Rodic; Nemanja Maksimovic, Lukic (Jovicic 72); Gacinovic (Milinkovic-Savic 79), Tadic, Zivkovic; Mitrovic (Radonjic 90).

Sunday, 14 October 2018

Lithuania (0) 1 *(Baravykas 88)*
Montenegro (3) 4 *(Mugosa 10, 45 (pen), Kopitovic 35, Zoric 86)* 1515
Lithuania: (4321) Setkus; Baravykas, Janusevskij, Klimavicius, Borovskij; Vorobjovas (Kuklys 46), Zulpa, Slivka; Cernych (Petravicius 49), Novikovas; Valskis (Kazlauskas 79).
Montenegro: (4231) Petkovic; Stojkovic (Radunovic 87), Kopitovic, Simic, Tomasevic; Kosovic, Scekic; Vesovic (Zoric 56), Ivanic, Jovovic (Beciraj 72); Mugosa.

Romania (0) 0 **Serbia (0) 0** 48,513
Romania: (4231) Tatarusanu; Manea, Tamas■, Sapunaru, Tosca; Baluta A, Marin; Maxim (Rotariu 70), Stanciu, Grigore (Nedelcearu 45); Tucudean (Keseru 80).
Serbia: (4231) Rajkovic; Rukavina, Milenkovic, Veljkovic, Rodic (Miletic 77); Lukic, Nemanja Maksimovic; Gacinovic (Milinkovic-Savic 63), Tadic, Radonjic; Mitrovic.

Saturday, 17 November 2018

Romania (1) 3 *(Puscas 7, Keseru 47, Stanciu 65)*
Lithuania (0) 0 *(Behind closed doors)* 34
Romania: (4231) Tatarusanu; Benzar, Sapunaru, Moti, Bancu; Stanciu (Cicaldau 72), Anton; Chipciu (Deac 64), Keseru (Hagi 68), Maxim; Puscas.
Lithuania: (4231) Setkus; Vaitkunas, Girdvainis, Zulpa, Baravykas; Simkus (Slivka 65), Vorobjovas; Petravicius (Kazlauskas 80), Sirgedas, Novikovas■; Cernych (Sernas 73).

Serbia (2) 2 *(Ljajic 30, Mitrovic 32)*

Montenegro (0) 1 *(Mugosa 70)* 15,416

Serbia: (4231) Rajkovic; Rukavina, Milenkovic, Veljkovic, Kolarov; Matic, Nemanja Maksimovic; Gacinovic (Lukic 71), Tadic, Ljajic (Radonjic 90); Mitrovic (Jovic 83).
Montenegro: (4231) Petkovic; Marusic, Kopitovic, Simic, Vesovic; Scekic (Boljevic 46), Kosovic; Jankovic (Djordjevic 82), Ivanic, Jovovic; Mugosa.

Tuesday, 20 November 2018

Montenegro (0) 0

Romania (1) 1 *(Tucudean 44)* 3574

Montenegro: (442) Petkovic; Marusic (Klimenta 87), Kopitovic, Simic, Vesovic; Jankovic (Djordjevic 81), Ivanic, Kosovic, Jovovic; Beciraj (Boljevic 64), Mugosa.
Romania: (4231) Tatarusanu; Manea, Sapunaru, Moti, Tosca; Anton, Stanciu; Chipciu (Deac 82), Keseru (Baluta C 88), Maxim; Tucudean (Puscas 74).

Serbia (0) 4 *(Zulpa 51 (og), Mitrovic 58, Prijovic 71, Ljajic 74)*

Lithuania (0) 1 *(Petravicius 64)* 2088

Serbia: (4231) Rajkovic; Rukavina, Milenkovic, Veljkovic, Rodic; Nemanja Maksimovic, Lukic (Fejsa 77); Zivkovic, Ljajic (Aleksic 82), Gacinovic (Prijovic 46); Mitrovic.
Lithuania: (4141) Setkus; Baravykas, Janusevskij, Girdvainis, Slavickas; Zulpa (Jankauskas 87); Petravicius, Vorobjovas (Matulevicius 69), Sirgedas, Kazlauskas (Sernas 59); Cernych.

League C Group 4	P	W	D	L	F	A	GD	Pts
Serbia	6	4	2	0	11	4	7	14
Romania	6	3	3	0	8	3	5	12
Montenegro	6	2	1	3	7	6	1	7
Lithuania	6	0	0	6	3	16	–13	0

LEAGUE D – GROUP 1

Thursday, 6 September 2018

Kazakhstan (0) 0

Georgia (0) 2 *(Chakvetadze 69, Maliy 74 (og))* 28,736

Kazakhstan: (451) Eric; Beysebekov, Postnikov, Maliy, Shomko; Zhukov, Islamkhan (Zainutdinov 81), Kuat (Turysbek 76), Muzhikov, Murtazaev (Seidakhmet 88); Schetkin.
Georgia: (433) Loria; Kakabadze, Kvirkvelia, Kashia, Navalovski; Kvekveskiri, Merebashvili, Kankava; Qazaishvili (Khocholava 84), Kvilitaia (Gvilia 65), Chakvetadze (Okriashvili 75).

Latvia (0) 0

Andorra (0) 0 4803

Latvia: (442) Vanins; Gabovs, Dubra, Jagodinskis, Solovjovs (Karasausks 76); Kluskins, Fertovs, Rakels, Lukjanovs; Sabala (Gutkovskis 84), Ikaunieks D (Uldrikis 61).
Andorra: (4231) Gomes; Jesus Rubio, Lima, Llovera, San Nicolas; Rebes, Vales; Clemente (Rodrigues 81), Vieira (Garcia E 90), Cervos; Martinez C (Alaez 71).

Sunday, 9 September 2018

Georgia (0) 1 *(Okriashvili 77 (pen))*

Latvia (0) 0 45,716

Georgia: (4231) Loria; Kakabadze, Kvirkvelia, Kashia, Navalovski; Kvekveskiri, Kankava; Okriashvili (Gvilia 80), Qazaishvili (Khocholava 90), Chakvetadze (Papunashvili 85); Katcharava.
Latvia: (4231) Vanins; Gabovs, Dubra, Jagodinskis, Maksimenko; Fertovs, Isajevs; Lukjanovs (Rakels 80), Rugins (Savalnieks 78), Karasausks; Gutkovskis (Sabala 72).

Monday, 10 September 2018

Andorra (0) 1 *(Alaez 86)*

Kazakhstan (0) 1 *(Logvinenko 68)* 1235

Andorra: (4231) Gomes; Jesus Rubio (Gomez 80), Llovera, Lima, San Nicolas (Jordi Rubio 83); Rebes, Vales; Clemente (Alaez 69), Vieira, Cervos; Martinez C.
Kazakhstan: (451) Eric; Beysebekov (Seidakhmet 90), Postnikov, Logvinenko, Shomko; Tunggyshbayev (Zainutdinov 66), Islamkhan, Kuat, Muzhikov■, Murtazaev (Turysbek 59); Schetkin.

Saturday, 13 October 2018

Georgia (1) 3 *(Qazaishvili 33, 84, Kankava 90)*

Andorra (0) 0 35,214

Georgia: (4231) Loria; Kakabadze, Kverkvelia, Kashia, Navalovski; Kvekveskiri, Kankava; Chakvetadze (Tchanturishvili 90), Kiteishvili (Ananidze 68), Qazaishvili; Katcharava (Gvilia 81).
Andorra: (442) Gomes; Jesus Rubio (Jordi Rubio 88), Llovera (Garcia E 45), Lima, San Nicolas; Rodrigues, Rebes (Pujol 78), Vales, Cervos; Vieira■, Martinez C.

Latvia (1) 1 *(Karasausks 40)*

Kazakhstan (1) 1 *(Zainutdinov 16)* 4878

Latvia: (442) Vanins; Savalnieks, Dubra, Jagodinskis, Maksimenko; Lukjanovs, Isajevs (Fertovs 27), Rugins (Ciganiks 67), Karasausks (Gutkovskis 73); Sabala, Rakels.
Kazakhstan: (4141) Eric; Beysebekov, Postnikov, Maliy, Shomko; Kuat; Zhukov, Islamkhan (Fedin 75), Zainutdinov (Seidakhmet 65), Murtazaev (Turysbek 82); Schetkin.

Tuesday, 16 October 2018

Kazakhstan (2) 4 *(Seidakhmet 21, Turysbek 39, Gomes 61 (og), Murtazaev 74)*

Andorra (0) 0 19,854

Kazakhstan: (442) Eric; Beysebekov, Postnikov, Logvinenko, Suyumbayev (Vorogovskiy 82); Seidakhmet (Fedin 77), Zhukov, Muzhikov, Islamkhan; Zainutdinov (Murtazaev 70), Turysbek.
Andorra: (442) Gomes; Jesus Rubio (Garcia M 84), Llovera, Lima, San Nicolas; Rodrigues, Rebes, Vales (Moreno 79), Cervos; Pujol (Ferre 89), Alaez■.

Latvia (0) 0

Georgia (2) 3 *(Kankava 8, Gvilia 29, Chakvetadze 61)* 3185

Latvia: (4312) Vanins; Zulevs, Jagodinskis, Dubra, Maksimenko; Fertovs (Isajevs 46), Tarasovs, Ciganiks; Rakels; Karasausks (Ikaunieks D 70), Gutkovskis (Sabala 70).
Georgia: (4411) Loria; Dvali, Kashia, Khocholava, Kakabadze; Chakvetadze (Zarandia 89), Kvekveskiri, Kankava (Aburjania 34), Merebashvili (Jigauri 80); Gvilia; Qazaishvili.

Thursday, 15 November 2018

Kazakhstan (1) 1 *(Suyumbayev 37)*

Latvia (0) 1 *(Rakels 48)* 21,463

Kazakhstan: (442) Eric; Beysebekov, Maliy, Logvinenko, Suyumbayev; Murtazaev (Fedin 80), Zhukov, Muzhikov, Islamkhan; Zainutdinov (Tunggyshbayev 87), Turysbek (Schetkin 74).
Latvia: (4231) Vanins; Gabovs, Dubra, Jagodinskis, Maksimenko; Isajevs, Tarasovs; Ciganiks (Savalnieks 46), Rakels, Karasausks (Rugins 62); Sabala (Ikaunieks D 72).

Andorra (0) 1 *(Martinez C 63)*

Georgia (1) 1 *(Chakvetadze 9)* 1311

Andorra: (442) Gomes; Jesus Rubio, Llovera, Lima, San Nicolas; Martinez C (Garcia E 90), Vales, Rebes, Cervos (Jordi Rubio 88); Fernandez (Rodriguez 81), Martinez A.
Georgia: (4141) Loria; Kakabadze, Khocholava, Tabidze, Navalovski; Kvekveskiri; Arabuli (Katcharava 78), Kiteishvili (Chanturishvili 78), Gvilia (Zarandia 87), Chakvetadze; Kazaishvili.

Monday, 19 November 2018

Andorra (0) 0

Latvia (0) 0 1021

Andorra: (442) Gomes; San Nicolas, Llovera, Lima, Garcia M (Fernandez 79); Cervos, Vales, Rodriguez (Martinez A 73), Moreno (Sanchez J 88); Martinez C, Alaez.
Latvia: (442) Vanins; Savalnieks, Dubra, Jagodinskis, Maksimenko; Rakels, Isajevs, Ciganiks, Karasausks (Tarasovs 61); Sabala■, Ikaunieks D (Uldrikis 75).

Georgia (0) 2 *(Merebashvili 59, Chakvetadze 84)*

Kazakhstan (0) 1 *(Omirtayev 90)* 52,220

Georgia: (4231) Loria; Kakabadze (Khocholava 86), Kverkvelia, Kashia, Dvali; Kankava, Kvekveskiri; Merebashvili, Gvilia (Katcharava 75), Chakvetadze (Aburjania 90); Qazaishvili.
Kazakhstan: (4411) Nepohodov; Beysebekov, Maliy, Logvinenko, Suyumbayev; Fedin (Turysbek 83), Kuat, Muzhikov, Murtazaev (Omirtayev 90); Zainutdinov; Schetkin (Pertsukh 74).

League D Group 1	P	W	D	L	F	A	GD	Pts
Georgia	6	5	1	0	12	2	10	16
Kazakhstan	6	1	3	2	8	7	1	6
Latvia	6	0	4	2	2	6	–4	4
Andorra	6	0	4	2	2	9	–7	4

LEAGUE D – GROUP 2

Saturday, 8 September 2018

Belarus (2) 5 *(Stasevich 4, Dragun 26, 87, Saroka 67 (pen), Kovalev 90)*

San Marino (0) 0 13,634

Belarus: (451) Chernik; Shitov, Martynovich, Politevich, Stasevich (Kovalev 75); Volodko, Maewski, Bressan, Dragun, Nekhaychik (Balanovich 67); Laptev (Saroka 56).
San Marino: (352) Benedettini; Cesarini (Rinaldi 81), Simoncini, Biordi; Manuel Battistini, Lunadei, Giardi, Gasperoni (Hirsch 63), Palazzi; Berardi F, Vitaioli M (Tomassini 62).

Luxembourg (1) 4 *(Malget 34, Thill O 59, Sinani 75, Martins Pereira 83)*

Moldova (0) 0 2956

Luxembourg: (4141) Moris; Jans, Chanot, Malget, Carlson; Martins Pereira; Sinani, Gerson, Thill O (Mutsch 78), Rodrigues (Da Mota Alves 55); Turpel (Joachim 59).
Moldova: (4231) Koselev; Graur, Posmac, Epureanu, Reabciuk; Carp (Cojocari 77), Gatcan; Antoniuc, Cociuc, Dedov (Platica 63); Ginsari (Nicolaescu 62).

Tuesday, 11 September 2018

Moldova (0) 0

Belarus (0) 0 4942

Moldova: (4231) Koselev; Graur, Posmac, Epureanu, Reabciuk; Carp (Cociuc 63), Gatcan; Ginsari, Ionita, Antoniuc (Platica 86); Nicolaescu (Damascan 67).
Belarus: (433) Chernik; Shitov, Martynovich, Politevich, Volodko; Dragun, Bressan (Kendysh 77), Maewski; Nekhaychik (Balanovich 72), Laptev (Saroka 59), Stasevich.

San Marino (0) 0

Luxembourg (2) 3 *(Chanot 9, Joachim 45, Sinani 52)* 794

San Marino: (343) Benedettini; Brolli, Simoncini, Palazzi; Manuel Battistini, Golinucci E (Lunadei 88), Giardi, Grandoni; Berardi (Tomassini 72), Vitaioli M, Rinaldi.
Luxembourg: (433) Moris; Jans, Chanot (Janisch 70), Martins Pereira, Carlson; Thill O (Thill V 46), Philipps, Barreiro (Mutsch 46); Sinani, Joachim, Da Mota Alves.

Friday, 12 October 2018

Belarus (1) 1 *(Saroka 43)*

Luxembourg (0) 0 14,122

Belarus: (352) Gorbunov; Polyakov, Martynovich, Sivakov; Nekhaychik, Dragun (Korzun 81), Maewski, Stasevich, Volodko; Saroka (Laptev 87), Putsila (Kendysh 76).
Luxembourg: (343) Moris; Chanot, Philipps, Malget (Mahmutovic 46); Jans, Martins Pereira, Thill O (Rodrigues 57), Carlson; Turpel (Da Mota Alves 73), Joachim, Sinani.

Moldova (1) 2 *(Ginsari 31, 67)*

San Marino (0) 0 5242

Moldova: (343) Koselev; Posmac, Carp, Epureanu; Antoniuc, Ionita, Gatcan, Reabciuk (Dedov 46); Ginsari (Sandu 79), Damascan (Boiciuc 54), Cociuc.
San Marino: (433) Benedettini; Manuel Battistini, Brolli, Vitaioli F, Grandoni; Gasperoni, Golinucci E (Golinucci A 84), Mularoni; Hirsch (Tomassini 71), Giardi (Palazzi 46), Vitaioli M.

Monday, 15 October 2018

Belarus (0) 0

Moldova (0) 0 10,870

Belarus: (532) Gorbunov; Polyakov, Maewski, Martynovich, Sivakov, Rios; Kislyak (Dragun 69), Stasevich, Kendysh (Putsila 77); Saroka (Signevich 61), Kovalev.
Moldova: (4231) Koselev; Jardan, Posmac, Epureanu, Reabciuk; Gatcan, Carp; Ginsari (Dedov 78), Ionita, Antoniuc (Sandu 65); Damascan (Boiciuc 72).

Luxembourg (1) 3 *(Turpel 4, Sinani 65, Thill V 73)*

San Marino (0) 0 2876

Luxembourg: (442) Schon; Jans (Bohnert 69), Chanot, Martins Pereira, Janisch; Thill O, Barreiro (Da Mota Alves 67), Philipps, Sinani; Thill V, Turpel (Deville 76).
San Marino: (433) Benedettini; Cesarini, Vitaioli F, Simoncini, Grandoni (Palazzi 76); Gasperoni■, Golinucci E (Golinucci A 85), Giardi; Mularoni, Vitaioli M, Tomassini (Lunadei 61).

Thursday, 15 November 2018

San Marino (0) 0

Moldova (0) 1 *(Damascan 78)* 700

San Marino: (352) Benedettini; Manuel Battistini, Vitaioli F, Simoncini; Palazzi, Grandoni (Hirsch 87); Lunadei (Golinucci A 76), Golinucci E, Mularoni; Vitaioli M (Tomassini 81), Nanni.
Moldova: (3241) Koselev; Posmac, Epureanu, Reabciuk; Gatcan, Carp; Antoniuc (Dedov 66), Cociuc (Sandu 60), Ionita, Ginsari; Nicolaescu (Damascan 46).

Luxembourg (0) 0

Belarus (1) 2 *(Dragun 37, 54)* 4533

Luxembourg: (5221) Moris; Jans, Philipps, Chanot, Gerson (Bensi 46), Janisch; Martins Pereira, Sinani; Thill O, Turpel (Da Mota 67); Joachim.
Belarus: (4231) Gorbunov; Shitov, Martynovich, Sivakov, Volodko; Dragun, Maewski; Stasevich, Hleb (Putilo 74), Savitski (Balanovich 74); Saroka (Signevich 85).

Sunday, 18 November 2018

Moldova (0) 1 *(Ginsari 58 (pen))*

Luxembourg (0) 1 *(Bensi 70)* 4642

Moldova: (4222) Koselev; Jardan, Posmac, Epureanu, Reabciuk; Gatcan (Cebotaru 83), Carp; Antoniuc, Ginsari (Dedov 82); Damascan (Nicolaescu 71), Ionita.
Luxembourg: (4123) Moris; Jans, Chanot, Mahmutovic, Carlson; Philipps (Thill O 31); Bohnert (Sinani 59), Barreiro; Bensi (Turpel 82), Joachim, Da Mota Alves.

San Marino (0) 0

Belarus (1) 2 *(Dragun 8, Saroka 52)* 736

San Marino: (433) Benedettini; Michael Battistini, Vitaioli F, Simoncini, Palazzi; Gasperoni (Tomassini 61), Golinucci E, Golinucci A; Hirsch (Cesarini 89), Nanni (Giardi 62), Rinaldi.
Belarus: (4141) Chernik; Shitov, Politevich, Martynovich, Polyakov; Maewski (Kislyak 79); Savitski (Skavysh 65), Dragun, Hleb (Putilo 69), Stasevich; Saroka.

League D Group 2	P	W	D	L	F	A	GD	Pts
Belarus	6	4	2	0	10	0	10	14
Luxembourg	6	3	1	2	11	4	7	10
Moldova	6	2	3	1	4	5	–1	9
San Marino	6	0	0	6	0	16	–16	0

LEAGUE D – GROUP 3

Friday, 7 September 2018

Azerbaijan (0) 0

Kosovo (0) 0 19,500

Azerbaijan: (4231) Agayev K; Pashaev, Medvedev, Guseynov, Abbasov U; Richard, Garayev; Madatov, Makhmudov (Nazarov 66), Gurbanov R (Khalilzadze 61); Sheydaev (Aliyev 74).
Kosovo: (4231) Ujkani; Vojvoda, Rrahmani, Aliti, Paqarada; Kryeziu, Shala; Zhegrova (Rashani 63), Celina (Avdijaj 69), Zeneli (Voca 84); Muriqi.

Faroe Islands (2) 3 *(Edmundsson 31, Joensen R 38, Hansson 52)*

Malta (1) 1 *(Mifsud 42)* 3234

Faroe Islands: (4411) Nielsen; Vatnhamar G, Gregersen, Nattestad, Davidsen V; Vatnhamar S (Baldvinsson 90), Joensen R, Hansson, Rolantsson (Bartalsstovu 81); Hendriksson (Justinussen F 86); Edmundsson.
Malta: (352) Hogg; Borg S, Agius, Muscat Z (Farrugia 73); Mbong, Effiong (Cohen 84), Muscat R (Pisani 60), Fenech P, Zerafa; Mifsud, Schembri.

Monday, 10 September 2018

Kosovo (0) 2 *(Zeneli 50, Nuhiu 55)*

Faroe Islands (0) 0 12,677

Kosovo: (4231) Ujkani; Vojvoda, Rrahmani, Aliti, Kololli; Shala, Kryeziu; Rashica (Zhegrova 78), Avdijaj (Halimi 68), Zeneli; Nuhiu (Muriqi 84).
Faroe Islands: (4411) Nielsen; Vatnhamar G, Gregersen, Nattestad, Davidsen V; Bartalsstovu (Baldvinsson 79), Hansson, Joensen R, Rolantsson (Olsen K 89); Hendriksson (Vatnhamar S 62); Edmundsson.

Malta (1) 1 *(Agius 10 (pen))*

Azerbaijan (1) 1 *(Khalilzadze 26)* 4500

Malta: (541) Hogg; Mbong, Borg S, Agius (Apap 51), Camilleri, Zerafa; Mifsud, Fenech P, Fenech R (Briffa 64), Schembri; Farrugia (Effiong 77).
Azerbaijan: (4231) Agayev K; Pashaev (Abbasov U 34), Medvedev, Huseynov B, Khalilzadze; Richard, Garayev; Madatov, Makhmudov (Imamverdiyev 56), Nazarov; Aliyev (Sheydaev 68).

Thursday, 11 October 2018

Faroe Islands (0) 0

Azerbaijan (1) 3 *(Richard 28, 85 (pen), Nazarov 67)* 2820

Faroe Islands: (4231) Nielsen; Rolantsson, Gregersen, Faero, Davidsen V; Hansson (Vatnsdal 78), Joensen R; Edmundsson, Hendriksson, Bartalsstovu (Baldvinsson 74); Justinussen F (Olsen K 78).
Azerbaijan: (4231) Agayev K; Medvedev, Mammadov R, Huseynov B, Pashaev; Garayev, Richard (Makhmudov 87); Madatov, Nazarov (Imamverdiyev 88), Abdullayev (Gurbanov 83); Dadashov.

Kosovo (1) 3 *(Kololli 30, 81, Muriqi 68)*

Malta (0) 1 *(Agius 51)* 12,420

Kosovo: (4231) Ujkani; Vojvoda, Rrahmani, Aliti, Kololli; Kryeziu, Shala; Zhegrova, Berisha (Halimi 74), Zeneli (Rashica 76); Muriqi (Kastrati 83).
Malta: (3421) Hogg; Borg S, Agius, Apap; Mbong, Fenech P (Briffa 60), Muscat R (Pisani 83), Failla; Mifsud■, Corbalan; Schembri (Effiong 64).

Sunday, 14 October 2018

Azerbaijan (0) 1 *(Abdullayev 53)*

Malta (1) 1 *(Muscat R 37)* 16,200

Azerbaijan: (4411) Agayev K; Medvedev, Mammadov R (Khalilzadze 46), Huseynov B, Pashaev; Madatov (Imamverdiyev 77), Garayev, Richard, Abdullayev; Nazarov; Dadashov.
Malta: (343) Hogg; Borg S, Agius, Camilleri; Mbong, Muscat R (Briffa 70), Fenech P, Zerafa; Corbalan, Schembri (Farrugia 86), Effiong (Grech 82).

Faroe Islands (0) 1 *(Joensen R 50)*

Kosovo (1) 1 *(Rashica 9)* 2300

Faroe Islands: (4411) Nielsen; Baldvinsson, Gregersen, Nattestad, Davidsen V; Rolantsson, Faero, Hansson, Joensen R; Hendriksson (Vatnsdal 83); Edmundsson (Olsen K 68).
Kosovo: (4231) Ujkani; Vojvoda, Rrahmani, Dallku, Aliti; Voca (Halimi 54), Shala; Zhegrova (Zeneli 74), Berisha, Rashica (Muriqi 90); Nuhiu.

Saturday, 17 November 2018

Azerbaijan (2) 2 *(Nazarov 18, Madatov 28)*

Faroe Islands (0) 0 12,653

Azerbaijan: (4231) Agayev K (Agayev S 46), Pashaev (Mammadov R 71), Medvedev, Huseynov B, Khalilzadze; Garayev, Almeida; Madatov, Nazarov, Abdullayev; Dadasov (Abbasov M 78).
Faroe Islands: (4222) Nielsen; Baldvinsson, Gregersen, Nattestad, Davidsen V (Bartalsstovu 46); Faero (Frederiksberg 73), Hansson; Rolantsson, Vatnhamar S; Hendriksson, Olsen K (Thomsen 63).

Malta (0) 0

Kosovo (1) 5 *(Muriqi 15, Kololli 70, Avdijaj 78, 80, Rashica 86)* 2115

Malta: (541) Hogg; Mbong, Muscat Z, Caruana J, Camilleri, Zerafa; Corbalan (Effiong 65), Muscat R (Mifsud 65), Briffa (Fenech P 74), Gambin; Schembri.
Kosovo: (4231) Ujkani; Vojvoda, Rrahmani, Aliti, Kololli; Shala, Kryeziu; Rashica, Berisha (Halimi 61), Zeneli (Avdijaj 71); Muriqi (Demhasaj 83).

Tuesday, 20 November 2018

Kosovo (1) 4 *(Zeneli 2, 50, Rrahmani 61, Zeneli 76)*

Azerbaijan (0) 0 12,532

Kosovo: (4231) Muric; Vojvoda, Rrahmani, Aliti, Kololli; Shala, Kryeziu; Rashica (Zhegrova 74), Berisha (Halimi 85), Zeneli; Muriqi (Nuhiu 69).
Azerbaijan: (4231) Agayev S; Pashaev, Medvedev, Huseynov B, Khalilzadze; Garayev, Almeida; Madatov (Abbasov M 63), Nazarov, Abdullayev (Gurbanov R 71); Dadasov (Ismayilov 46).

Malta (1) 1 *(Corbalan 4)*

Faroe Islands (1) 1 *(Joensen R 3)* 2152

Malta: (343) Hogg; Muscat Z (Caruana J 66), Agius, Borg S; Mbong, Muscat R, Fenech P, Failla (Nwoko 79); Corbalan (Zerafa 77), Schembri, Mifsud.
Faroe Islands: (4222) Nielsen; Rolantsson, Gregersen, Nattestad (Faero 83), Davidsen V; Vatnsdal, Hendriksson; Vatnhamar S (Bartalsstovu 67), Joensen R; Thomsen (Olsen K 74), Hansson.

League D Group 3	P	W	D	L	F	A	GD	Pts
Kosovo	6	4	2	0	15	2	13	14
Azerbaijan	6	2	3	1	7	6	1	9
Faroe Islands	6	1	2	3	5	10	–5	5
Malta	6	0	3	3	5	14	–9	3

LEAGUE D – GROUP 4

Thursday, 6 September 2018

Armenia (1) 2 *(Pizzelli 31, Barseghyan 76)*

Liechtenstein (1) 1 *(Wolfinger 33)* 5132

Armenia: (4231) Airapetyan; Hambardzumyan, Calisir, Haroyan, Manucharyan (Edigaryan 42); Malakyan G, Ozbiliz (Ghazaryan 83); Mkhitaryan, Yagan (Barseghyan 55), Pizzelli; Beglaryan.
Liechtenstein: (4141) Buchel B; Rechsteiner (Yildiz 80), Kaufmann, Wieser, Goppel; Polverino■; Wolfinger (Meier 81), Hasler, Sele A, Salanovic; Erne (Kuhne 48).

Gibraltar (0) 0

North Macedonia (2) 2 *(Trickovski 19, Alioski 35)* 1850

Gibraltar: (433) Goldwin; Barnett, Olivero, Anthony Hernandez, Chipolina J; Pons (Garro 75), Sergeant, Walker; De Barr (Styche 80), Bardon, Casciaro L (Garcia 90).
North Macedonia: (3412) Dimitrievski; Ristovski, Musliu, Ristevski; Trajkovski (Elmas 68), Nikolov, Spirovski, Alioski; Bardhi (Bejtulai 85); Pandev (Nestorovski 46), Trickovski.

Sunday, 9 September 2018

North Macedonia (1) 2 *(Alioski 13, Pandev 59)*

Armenia (0) 0 4730

North Macedonia: (433) Dimitrievski; Ristovski, Musliu, Bejtulai, Ristevski; Spirovski, Bardhi (Nikolov 74), Elmas; Trickovski (Trajkovski 56), Pandev (Nestorovski 69), Alioski.
Armenia: (4231) Airapetyan; Hambardzumyan, Calisir, Haroyan, Ishkhanyan; Malakyan G (Ozbiliz 68), Mkrtchyan; Barseghyan (Sarkisov 77), Mkhitaryan, Ghazaryan; Adamyan (Pizzelli 46).

Liechtenstein (1) 2 *(Salanovic 32, Wieser 72)*

Gibraltar (0) 0 1110

Liechtenstein: (4141) Buchel B; Quintans, Kaufmann, Wieser, Goppel; Sele A; Salanovic, Meier (Kieber 89), Hasler, Wolfinger (Kuhne 74); Gubser (Yildiz 82).

Gibraltar: (433) Goldwin; De Barr (Styche 71), Barnett, Pons (Garro 46), Sergeant; Walker, Casciaro L, Chipolina J; Anthony Hernandez, Bardon, Olivero.

Saturday, 13 October 2018

Armenia (0) 0

Gibraltar (0) 1 *(Chipolina J 50)* 14,986

Armenia: (4231) Airapetyan; Hambardzumyan, Haroyan, Mkoyan, Hovhannisyan K; Malakyan G (Pizzelli 46), Grigoryan; Barseghyan (Sarkisov 60), Mkhitaryan, Ghazaryan; Movsisyan (Adamyan 69).
Gibraltar: (433) Goldwin; Sergeant, Chipolina R, Chipolina J, Olivero; Pons (Annesley 90), Bardon, Andrew Hernandez (Britto 85); Coombes (Styche 70), Casciaro L, Walker.

North Macedonia (3) 4 *(Trajkovski 10, 30, Pandev 36, Alioski 67)*

Liechtenstein (1) 1 *(Yildiz 37)* 8100

North Macedonia: (442) Dimitrievski; Bejtulai (Ristevski 77), Musliu, Zajkov, Alioski; Trajkovski, Bardhi, Elmas, Hasani; Pandev (Nikolov 68), Nestorovski (Spirovski 83).
Liechtenstein: (4141) Buchel B; Rechsteiner, Kaufmann, Wieser, Goppel; Polverino; Wolfinger (Kieber 79), Sele A (Gubser 29), Marcel Buchel (Erne 72), Yildiz; Hasler.

Tuesday, 16 October 2018

Armenia (1) 4 *(Pizzelli 12, Movsisyan 67, Ghazaryan 81, Mkhitaryan 90)*

North Macedonia (0) 0 14,986

Armenia: (4231) Airapetyan; Hovhannisyan K, Haroyan, Khachaturov, Daghbashyan; Mkhitaryan, Hovsepyan (Mkrtchyan 83); Adamyan, Pizzelli (Grigoryan 22), Ghazaryan; Movsisyan (Barseghyan 74).
North Macedonia: (4411) Dimitrievski; Ristovski, Musliu, Zajkov (Hasani 76), Ristevski; Trajkovski, Spirovski (Elmas■ 57), Ademi, Alioski; Bardhi (Nestorovski 64); Pandev.

Gibraltar (0) 2 *(Cabrera 61, Chipolina J 66)*

Liechtenstein (1) 1 *(Salanovic 15)* 2000

Gibraltar: (433) Goldwin; Chipolina R, Pons, Cabrera (De Barr 90), Casciaro L; Chipolina J, Olivero, Sergeant; Walker, Bardon, Andrew Hernandez (Coombes 46 (Casciaro K 75)).
Liechtenstein: (532) Buchel B; Eberle, Kaufmann, Polverino (Erne 83), Wieser (Malin 46), Goppel; Meier, Hasler, Marcel Buchel (Wolfinger 67); Gubser, Salanovic.

Friday, 16 November 2018

Gibraltar (1) 2 *(De Barr 10, Priestley 78)*

Armenia (1) 6 *(Movsisyan 27, 48, 52, 54, Kartashyan 66, Karapetian 90)* 1955

Gibraltar: (433) Goldwin; Olivero, Walker, Chipolina R, Casciaro L; Bardon, De Barr, Sergeant; Chipolina J (Mouelhi 83), Pons (Priestly 71), Anthony Hernandez (Andrew Hernandez 72).
Armenia: (4213) Airapetyan; Hovhannisyan K, Haroyan, Kartashyan, Daghbashyan; Grigoryan, Hovsepyan (Malakyan G 62); Mkhitaryan; Adamyan (Malakyan E 73), Movsisyan (Karapetyan 70), Ghazaryan.

Liechtenstein (0) 0

North Macedonia (0) 2 *(Bardhi 53, Nestorovski 90)* 2100

Liechtenstein: (541) Buchel B; Brandle (Erne 76), Quintans (Eberle 76), Wieser■, Rechsteiner, Goppel; Hasler, Sele A (Martin Buchel 76), Polverino, Salanovic; Meier.
North Macedonia: (343) Dimitrievski; Bejtulai, Musliu, Ristevski; Trajkovski, Nikolov, Bardi, Hasani (Velkoski 77); Trickovski (Spirovski 77 (Tosevski 85)), Nestorovski, Pandev.

Monday, 19 November 2018

North Macedonia (1) 4 *(Bardhi 27, Nestorovski 67, 80, Trajkovski 90)*

Gibraltar (0) 0 2152

North Macedonia: (4222) Dimitrievski; Bejtulai, Musliu, Ristevski, Alioski; Nikolov, Bardi; Trajkovski, Elmas (Ademi 73); Nestorovski (Velkoski 82), Trickovski (Hasani 59).
Gibraltar: (433) Cafer; De Barr (Priestley 81), Bardon, Andrew Hernandez, Walker; Chipolina R, Mouelhi, Olivero; Sergeant, Annesley (Barnett 88), Casciaro L (Anthony Hernandez 79).

Liechtenstein (1) 2 *(Marcel Buchel 44, Hasler 47)*

Armenia (1) 2 *(Adamyan 9, Karapetian 85)* 1166

Liechtenstein: (3421) Buchel B; Rechsteiner, Quintans (Eberle 83), Hofer; Meier, Sele A (Martin Buchel 57 (Brandle 62)), Polverino, Goppel; Hasler, Marcel Buchel; Salanovic.
Armenia: (4231) Avagyan; Hambartsumyan (Arakeyan 88), Haroyan, Khachaturov, Daghbashyan; Grigoryan, Hovsepyan (Karapetyan 72); Adamyan, Mkhitaryan, Ghazaryan; Movsisyan.

League D Group 4	*P*	*W*	*D*	*L*	*F*	*A*	*GD*	*Pts*
North Macedonia	6	5	0	1	14	5	9	15
Armenia	6	3	1	2	14	8	6	10
Gibraltar	6	2	0	4	5	15	–10	6
Liechtenstein	6	1	1	4	7	12	–5	4

UEFA NATIONS LEAGUE FINALS IN PORTUGAL

SEMI-FINALS

Porto, Wednesday, 5 June 2019

Portugal (1) 3 *(Ronaldo 25, 88, 90)*

Switzerland (0) 1 *(Rodriguez 57 (pen))* 42,415

Portugal: (442) Rui Patricio; Nelson Semedo, Pepe (Fonte 63), Dias, Guerreiro; Bruno Fernandes (Joao Moutinho 90), William Carvalho, Neves, Bernardo Silva; Joao Felix (Goncalo Guedes 70), Ronaldo.
Switzerland: (4411) Sommer; Mbabu, Schar, Akanji, Rodriguez; Zakaria (Fernandes 71), Xhaka, Freuler (Drmic 89), Zuber (Steffen 83); Shaqiri; Seferovic.

Guimaraes, Thursday, 6 June 2019

Netherlands (0) 3 *(de Ligt 73, Walker 98 (og), Promes 114)*

England (1) 1 *(Rashford 32 (pen))* 25,711

Netherlands: (433) Cillessen; Dumfries, de Ligt, van Dijk, Blind; de Roon (van de Beek 68), de Jong F (Strootman 114), Wijnaldum; Bergwijn (Propper 91), Depay, Babel (Promes 68).
England: (433) Pickford; Walker, Stones, Maguire, Chilwell; Rice (Alli 106), Delph (Henderson 77), Barkley; Sancho (Lingard 61), Rashford (Kane 46), Sterling.
aet.

THIRD-PLACE PLAY-OFF

Guimaraes, Sunday, 9 June 2019

Switzerland (0) 0

England (0) 0 15,742

Switzerland: (343) Sommer; Schar, Akanji, Elvedi; Mbabu, Xhaka, Freuler, Rodriguez (Drmic 87); Shaqiri (Zuber 65), Seferovic (Okafor 113), Fernandes (Zakaria 60).
England: (4231) Pickford; Alexander-Arnold, Gomez, Maguire, Rose (Walker 70); Dier, Delph (Barkley 106); Lingard (Sancho 106), Alli, Sterling; Kane (Wilson 75).
aet; England won 6-5 on penalties.

FINAL

Porto, Sunday, 9 June 2019

Portugal (0) 1 *(Goncalo Guedes 60)*

Netherlands (0) 0 43,199

Portugal: (433) Rui Patricio; Nelson Semedo, Dias, Fonte, Guerreiro; Danilo Pereira, William Carvalho (Neves 90), Bruno Fernandes (Joao Moutinho 81); Ronaldo, Goncalo Guedes (Rafa Silva 75), Bernardo Silva.
Netherlands: (433) Cillessen; Dumfries, de Ligt, van Dijk, Blind; de Roon (de Jong L 81), de Jong F, Wijnaldum; Bergwijn (van de Beek 59), Depay, Babel (Promes 46).

EURO 2020 QUALIFYING

GROUP A

Friday, 22 March 2019

Bulgaria (0) 1 *(Nedelev 82 (pen))*

Montenegro (0) 1 *(Mugosa 50)* 5652

Bulgaria: (4231) Mihailov; Popov S, Bozhikov, Bodurov, Zanev; Kostadinov, Chochev (Slavchev 69); Ivanov (Kostov 51), Nedelev, Delev (Minchev 82); Popov I.
Montenegro: (4231) Petkovic; Marusic, Simic, Tomasevic, Stojkovic; Ivanic, Vukcevic; Jankovic (Boljevic 64), Mugosa (Kosovic 89), Vesovic (Jovovic 78); Beciraj.

England (2) 5 *(Sterling 24, 62, 68, Kane 45 (pen), Kalas 84 (og))*

Czech Republic (0) 0 82,575

England: (433) Pickford; Walker, Keane, Maguire, Chilwell; Alli (Rice 63), Dier (Barkley 17), Henderson; Sancho, Kane, Sterling (Hudson-Odoi 70).
Czech Republic: (4231) Pavlenka; Kaderabek, Celustka, Kalas, Novak; Soucek, Pavelka; Gebre Selassie, Darida (Masopust 67), Jankto (Vydra 46); Schick (Skoda 82).

Monday, 25 March 2019

Kosovo (0) 1 *(Zeneli 61)*

Bulgaria (1) 1 *(Bozhikov 39)* 12,580

Kosovo: (4231) Muric; Vojvoda, Rrahmani, Aliti, Kololli (Paqarada 78); Kryeziu, Shala (Zhegrova 59); Rashica, Celina (Halimi 58), Zeneli; Muriqi.
Bulgaria: (442) Mihailov; Popov S, Bodurov, Bozhikov, Nedyalkov; Malinov (Minchev 75), Kostadinov (Antov 79), Nedelev, Slavchev; Popov I, Delev (Zanev 68).

Montenegro (1) 1 *(Vesovic 17)*

England (2) 5 *(Keane 30, Barkley 39, 59, Kane 71, Sterling 81)* 8329

Montenegro: (442) Petkovic; Stojkovic, Savic, Simic (Jovetic 74), Tomasevic; Marusic, Ivanic, Vukcevic, Vesovic (Boljevic 70); Beciraj (Jankovic 61), Mugosa.
England: (433) Pickford; Walker, Maguire, Keane, Rose; Barkley (Ward-Prowse 82), Rice, Alli (Henderson 64); Sterling, Kane (Wilson 82), Hudson-Odoi.

Friday, 7 June 2019

Czech Republic (1) 2 *(Schick 19, 50)*

Bulgaria (1) 1 *(Isa 3)* 13,482

Czech Republic: (4231) Vaclik; Kaderabek, Celustka, Suchy, Novak; Pavelka, Soucek; Masopust (Kopic 65), Kral, Jankto (Krejci 83); Schick (Dolezal 79).
Bulgaria: (442) Mihailov; Popov S, Dimitrov, Bozhikov, Nedyalkov; Minchev (Despodov 46), Malinov (Karabelyov 63), Sarmov, Nedelev (Chunchukov 82); Isa, Popov I.

Montenegro (0) 1 *(Mugosa 69)*

Kosovo (1) 1 *(Rashica 25)* 0

Montenegro: (4231) Mijatovic; Marusic, Vujacic, Simic, Tomasevic (Boljevic 71); Scekic (Bakic 59), Kosovic; Jankovic (Jovovic 85), Mugosa, Vesovic; Beciraj.
Kosovo: (4231) Muric; Vojvoda, Rrahmani, Aliti, Paqarada (Kololli 69); Halimi, Voca; Rashica, Celina (Rashani 78), Zeneli (Zhegrova 39); Muriqi.
Behind closed doors.

Monday, 10 June 2019

Bulgaria (1) 2 *(Popov I 43, Dimitrov 55)*

Kosovo (1) 3 *(Rashica 14, Muriqi 64, Rashani 90)* 4994

Bulgaria: (442) Mihailov; Popov S, Bozhikov (Dimitrov 46), Goranov, Nedyalkov; Ivanov, Kostadinov, Nedelev (Iliev 69), Despodov; Popov I, Isa (Chunchukov 79).
Kosovo: (4231) Muric; Vojvoda (Hadergjonaj 62), Rrahmani, Aliti, Kololli; Halimi, Voca (Raskaj 62); Zhegrova (Rashani 76), Celina, Rashica; Muriqi.

Czech Republic (1) 3 *(Jankto 19, Kopitovic 49 (og), Schick 82 (pen))*

Montenegro (0) 0 11,565

Czech Republic: (4231) Vaclik; Kaderabek, Celustka, Suchy, Novak; Soucek, Pavelka; Masopust (Kopic 39), Kral, Jankto (Krejci 74); Schick (Kozak 88).
Montenegro: (4231) Mijatovic; Marusic (Jankovic 60), Vujacic, Kopitovic, Radunovic; Kosovic, Vukcevic (Savicevic 67); Vesovic, Bakic, Jovovic; Mugosa (Beciraj 85).

Group A Table	P	W	D	L	F	A	GD	Pts
England	2	2	0	0	10	1	9	6
Czech Republic	3	2	0	1	5	6	–1	6
Kosovo	3	1	2	0	5	4	1	5
Montenegro	4	0	2	2	3	10	–7	2
Bulgaria	4	0	2	2	5	7	–2	2

GROUP B

Friday, 22 March 2019

Luxembourg (1) 2 *(Barreiro 45, Rodrigues 55)*

Lithuania (1) 1 *(Cernych 14)* 3353

Luxembourg: (3412) Moris; Chanot, Gerson, Carlson; Jans, Barreiro (Sinani 67), Martins Pereira, Da Mota Alves (Bensi 59); Thill O; Rodrigues, Thill V (Turpel 78).
Lithuania: (4231) Setkus; Baravykas, Klimavicius, Jankauskas, Slavickas; Slivka, Kuklys; Petravicius (Valskis 61), Novikovas (Zulpa 56), Mikoliunas (Marazas 76); Cernych.

Portugal (0) 0

Ukraine (0) 0 58,355

Portugal: (433) Rui Patricio; Joao Cancelo, Pepe, Dias, Guerreiro; Neves (Rafa Silva 62), William Carvalho, Joao Moutinho (Joao Mario 87); Bernardo Silva, Andre Silva (Dyego Sousa 73), Ronaldo.
Ukraine: (4141) Pyatov; Karavayev, Kryvtsov, Matviyenko, Mykolenko; Stepanenko; Marlos (Tsygankov 66), Malinovsky, Zinchenko, Konoplyanka (Buyalsky 87); Yaremchuk (Moraes 76).

Monday, 25 March 2019

Luxembourg (1) 1 *(Turpel 34)*

Ukraine (1) 2 *(Tsygankov 40, Rodrigues 90 (og))* 4653

Luxembourg: (442) Moris; Jans, Chanot, Malget, Carlson; Rodrigues, Barreiro, Martins Pereira, Thill O (Mutsch 90); Turpel, Thill V (Bensi 74).
Ukraine: (4141) Pyatov; Butko (Karavayev 79 (Buyalsky 87)), Burda, Matviyenko, Mykolenko; Zinchenko; Tsygankov, Malinovsky, Moraes, Konoplyanka; Bezus (Yaremchuk 64).

Portugal (1) 1 *(Danilo Pereira 42)*

Serbia (1) 1 *(Tadic 7 (pen))* 50,342

Portugal: (433) Rui Patricio; Joao Cancelo, Pepe, Dias, Guerreiro; William Carvalho, Danilo Pereira, Rafa Silva (Goncalo Guedes 84); Ronaldo (Pizzi 31), Dyego Sousa (Andre Silva 57), Bernardo Silva.
Serbia: (4231) Dmitrovic; Rukavina, Milenkovic, Spajic, Mladenovic; Gacinovic (Radonjic 21), Maksimovic; Lazovic (Zivkovic 69), Tadic, Ljajic (Milinkovic-Savic 87); Mitrovic.

Friday, 7 June 2019

Lithuania (0) 1 *(Novikovas 74)*

Luxembourg (1) 1 *(Rodrigues 21)* 3263

Lithuania: (4231) Bartkus; Mikoliunas■, Klimavicius, Palionis, Andriuskevicius; Slivka, Vorobjovas■; Cernych (Kazlauskas 89), Golubickas (Simkus 52), Novikovas; Valskis (Laukzemis 55).
Luxembourg: (442) Moris; Jans, Selimovic, Gerson, Carlson (Malget 61); Thill O (Sinani 80), Martins Pereira, Barreiro, Thill V; Rodrigues, Turpel (Bensi 67).

Ukraine (2) 5 *(Tsygankov 27, 28, Konoplyanka 46, 75, Yaremchuk 59)*

Serbia (0) 0 34,700

Ukraine: (4231) Pyatov; Karavayev, Kryvtsov, Matviyenko, Mykolenko; Malinovsky, Stepanenko (Shepelev 72); Tsygankov, Zinchenko, Konoplyanka (Kovalenko 76); Yaremchuk (Kravets 67).
Serbia: (352) Dmitrovic; Milenkovic, Spajic, Kolarov; Gacinovic, Ljajic (Fejsa 60), Tadic, Maksimovic, Kostic; Jovic (Lazovic 71), Prijovic (Mitrovic 53).

Monday, 10 June 2019

Serbia (3) 4 *(Mitrovic 20, 34, Jovic 35, Ljajic 90)*

Lithuania (0) 1 *(Novikovas 71 (pen))* 52

Serbia: (4231) Dmitrovic; Rukavina, Spajic, Milenkovic, Kolarov; Maksimovic, Lukic; Jovic (Katai 87), Tadic (Ljajic 81), Kostic (Zivkovic 71); Mitrovic.
Lithuania: (343) Bartkus; Klimavicius, Jankauskas (Chvedukas 46), Palionis; Baravykas, Simkus, Slivka, Andriuskevicius; Cernych (Petravicius 68), Laukzemis (Valskis 77), Novikovas.
Behind closed doors.

Ukraine (1) 1 *(Yaremchuk 6)*

Luxembourg (0) 0 34,700

Ukraine: (4231) Pyatov; Karavayev, Kryvtsov, Matviyenko, Mykolenko; Stepanenko, Malinovsky; Tsygankov (Sobol 87), Zinchenko, Konoplyanka (Kovalenko 79); Yaremchuk.
Luxembourg: (3412) Moris; Chanot, Martins Pereira, Gerson; Jans, Thill O (Turpel 77), Barreiro, Da Graca; Thill V; Rodrigues, Da Mota Alves (Bensi 52).

Group B Table	P	W	D	L	F	A	GD	Pts
Ukraine	4	3	1	0	8	1	7	10
Luxembourg	4	1	1	2	4	5	–1	4
Serbia	3	1	1	1	5	7	–2	4
Portugal	2	0	2	0	1	1	0	2
Lithuania	3	0	1	2	3	7	–4	1

GROUP C

Thursday, 21 March 2019

Holland (2) 4 *(Depay 1, Wijnaldum 21, Depay 55 (pen), van Dijk 86)*

Belarus (0) 0 38,604

Holland: (433) Cillessen; Dumfries (Tete 68), de Ligt, van Dijk, Blind; Wijnaldum, de Roon (Propper 46), de Jong F; Bergwijn, Depay, Babel (Promes 59).
Belarus: (4411) Gorbunov; Shitov, Martynovich, Sivakov, Polyakov; Kovalev (Savitskiy 78), Maewski, Dragun (Laptev 86), Stasevich; Putsila; Signevich (Saroka 62).

Northern Ireland (0) 2 *(McGinn 56, Davis 75 (pen))*

Estonia (0) 0 18,176

Northern Ireland: (433) Peacock-Farrell; Dallas, Cathcart, Evans J, Lewis; McNair, Davis, Saville; McGinn (McLaughlin C 84), Lafferty (Magennis 76), Jones (Ferguson 81).
Estonia: (541) Lepmets; Kams, Baranov, Tamm, Vihmann, Pikk; Artjom Dmitrijev (Sappinen 84), Mets, Kait, Ojamaa (Vassiljev 68); Anier (Zenjov 76).

Sunday, 24 March 2019

Holland (0) 2 *(de Ligt 48, Depay 63)*

Germany (2) 3 *(Sane 15, Gnabry 34, Schulz 90)* 51,694

Holland: (433) Cillessen; Dumfries, de Ligt, van Dijk, Blind; Wijnaldum, de Roon (de Jong L 90), de Jong F; Promes, Depay, Babel (Bergwijn 46).
Germany: (3412) Neuer; Sule, Ginter, Rudiger; Kehrer, Kroos, Kimmich, Schulz; Goretzka (Gundogan 70); Gnabry (Reus 88), Sane.

Northern Ireland (1) 2 *(Evans J 30, Magennis 87)*

Belarus (1) 1 *(Stasevich 33)* 18,188

Northern Ireland: (433) Peacock-Farrell; Dallas, Cathcart, Evans J, Lewis; McNair, Davis, Saville; McGinn (Magennis 68), Lafferty (Boyce 79), Jones (Ferguson 85).
Belarus: (433) Klimovich; Shitov (Polyakov 73), Sivakov, Martynovich, Valadzko; Maewski, Hleb (Putsila 66), Dragun; Savitskiy (Nekhaychik 85), Laptev, Stasevich.

Saturday, 8 June 2019

Belarus (0) 0

Germany (1) 2 *(Sane 13, Reus 62)* 12,510

Belarus: (4231) Gutor; Shitov, Naumov, Martynovich, Palyakow; Gromyko (Korzun 56), Dragun; Kovalev (Gordeichuk 69), Maewski, Valadzko; Laptev (Skavysh 64).
Germany: (4411) Neuer; Tah, Ginter, Sule, Schulz; Gnabry (Draxler 71), Klostermann, Gundogan (Goretzka 81), Sane; Kimmich; Reus (Brandt 76).

Estonia (1) 1 *(Vassiljev 25)*

Northern Ireland (0) 2 *(Washington 77, Magennis 80)* 8378

Estonia: (4141) Lepmets; Sinyavskiy, Mets, Vihmann, Pikk; Artjom Dmitrijev; Teniste (Kams 85), Vassiljev, Kait (Tamm 84), Sappinen (Sorga 61); Zenjov.
Northern Ireland: (433) Peacock-Farrell; Smith (Jones 64), Cathcart, Evans J, Lewis; McNair, Davis, Saville (Magennis 69); Whyte, Boyce (Washington 46), Dallas.

Tuesday, 11 June 2019

Belarus (0) 0

Northern Ireland (0) 1 *(McNair 86)* 5250

Belarus: (532) Gutor; Shitov (Veretilo 71), Naumov, Martynovich, Palyakow, Nekhaychik; Korzun (Kislyak 46), Maewski, Stasevich; Kovalev, Shikavka (Laptev 58).
Northern Ireland: (451) Peacock-Farrell; Smith, Cathcart, Evans J, Lewis; Magennis (Dallas 56), McNair, Davis, Evans C (Saville 69), Jones; Washington (Lafferty 72).

Germany (5) 8 *(Reus 10, 37, Gnabry 17, 62, Goretzka 20, Gundogan 26 (pen), Werner 79, Sane 88)*

Estonia (0) 0 26,050

Germany: (451) Neuer; Kehrer, Ginter, Sule, Schulz (Halstenberg 46); Reus (Werner 65), Gundogan (Draxler 53), Kimmich, Goretzka, Sane; Gnabry.
Estonia: (541) Lepmets; Kams, Mets, Tamm, Vihmann, Pikk; Teniste, Vassiljev (Kreida 82), Artjom Dmitrijev (Kait 59), Puri; Zenjov (Ojamaa 71).

Group C Table	P	W	D	L	F	A	GD	Pts
Northern Ireland	4	4	0	0	7	2	5	12
Germany	3	3	0	0	13	2	11	9
Netherlands	2	1	0	1	6	3	3	3
Belarus	4	0	0	4	1	9	–8	0
Estonia	3	0	0	3	1	12	–11	0

GROUP D

Saturday, 23 March 2019

Georgia (0) 0

Switzerland (0) 2 *(Zuber 57, Zakaria 80)* 49,207

Georgia: (4141) Loria; Kakabadze, Khocholava, Kashia, Tabidze (Kverkvelia 61); Kvekveskiri; Qazaishvili, Kankava, Gvilia, Ananidze (Katcharava 83); Kvilitaia (Lobjanidze S 73).
Switzerland: (4411) Sommer; Lichtsteiner, Schar, Akanji, Rodriguez; Embolo (Steffen 84), Zakaria, Xhaka, Freuler (Sow 89); Zuber; Gavranovic (Ajeti 60).

Gibraltar (0) 0

Rep of Ireland (0) 1 *(Hendrick 49)* 2000

Gibraltar: (442) Goldwin; Sergeant, Annesley (Priestley 64), Chipolina R, Chipolina J; Anthony Hernandez (Pons 77), Bardon, Walker, Olivero; De Barr, Casciaro L.
Rep of Ireland: (442) Randolph; Coleman, Duffy, Keogh, Stevens; McClean, Hendrick, Doherty (Brady 56), Hourihane; McGoldrick, Maguire (Arter 72).

Tuesday, 26 March 2019

Rep of Ireland (1) 1 *(Hourihane 36)*

Georgia (0) 0 40,317

Rep of Ireland: (433) Randolph; Coleman, Duffy, Keogh, Stevens; Hourihane, Hendrick, Whelan; Brady (O'Brien 74), McGoldrick (Doherty 81), McClean.
Georgia: (451) Loria; Kakabadze (Okriashvili 85), Khocholava (Kharabadze 65), Kverkvelia, Kashia; Kiteishvili, Kvekveskiri, Kankava, Gvilia, Arveladze (Qazaishvili 72); Kvilitaia.

Switzerland (1) 3 *(Freuler 19, Xhaka 66, Embolo 76)*

Denmark (0) 3 *(Jorgensen M 84, Gytkjaer 88, Dalsgaard 90)* 18,352

Switzerland: (433) Sommer; Mbabu, Elvedi, Akanji, Rodriguez (Benito 46); Zakaria, Xhaka (Sow 79), Freuler; Embolo, Ajeti (Mehmedi 71), Zuber.
Denmark: (433) Schmeichel; Dalsgaard, Kjaer, Jorgensen M, Larsen; Schone (Hojbjerg 70), Eriksen, Delaney; Poulsen, Jorgensen N (Gytkjaer 70), Braithwaite.

Friday, 7 June 2019

Denmark (0) 1 *(Hojbjerg 76)*

Rep of Ireland (0) 1 *(Duffy 85)* 34,610

Denmark: (4312) Schmeichel; Dalsgaard, Christensen A, Kjaer, Larsen; Poulsen, Delaney, Schone (Hojbjerg 72); Eriksen; Jorgensen N, Braithwaite (Dolberg 64).
Rep of Ireland: (451) Randolph; Coleman, Duffy, Keogh, Stevens; Brady (Judge 66), Hourihane (Hogan 82), Whelan, Hendrick, McClean; McGoldrick (Robinson 87).

Georgia (1) 3 *(Gvilia 30, Papunashvili 59, Arveladze 76 (pen))*

Gibraltar (0) 0 18,631

Georgia: (4231) Loria; Kakabadze, Kashia, Grigalava, Kharabadze; Kvekveskiri, Kankava (Mchedlidze 78); Merebashvili (Kiteishvili 72), Gvilia, Kvaratskhelia (Papunashvili 47); Arveladze.
Gibraltar: (532) Goldwin; Sergeant, Chipolina J, Chipolina R, Annesley (Barnett 86), Olivero; De Barr, Bardon (Coombes 77), Anthony Hernandez; Walker, Casciaro L (Pons 65).

Monday, 10 June 2019

Denmark (2) 5 *(Dolberg 13, 63, Eriksen 30 (pen), Poulsen 73, Braithwaite 90)*

Georgia (1) 1 *(Lobjanidze S 25)* 15,387

Denmark: (433) Schmeichel; Ankersen, Kjaer (Jorgensen M 36), Christensen A, Larsen; Hojbjerg, Eriksen, Delaney; Poulsen (Braithwaite 75), Skov (Wass 62), Dolberg.
Georgia: (4231) Loria; Kakabadze, Kashia, Grigalava, Navalovski; Kankava, Kvekveskiri; Parunashvili (Papunashvili 58), Kiteishvili (Lobjanidze E 75), Gvilia; Lobjanidze S.

Rep of Ireland (1) 2 *(Chipolina J 29 (og), Brady 90)*

Gibraltar (0) 0 36,281

Rep of Ireland: (442) Randolph; Coleman, Duffy, Keogh, Stevens; Robinson (Brady 73), Hourihane, Hendrick, McClean; Hogan (Maguire 66), McGoldrick.
Gibraltar: (532) Goldwin; Sergeant, Chipolina J, Chipolina R, Annesley, Olivero; De Barr, Andrew Hernandez (Jolley 75), Pons (Britto 64); Walker, Casciaro L (Bardon 10).

Group D Table	P	W	D	L	F	A	GD	Pts
Republic of Ireland	4	3	1	0	5	1	4	10
Denmark	3	1	2	0	9	5	4	5
Switzerland	2	1	1	0	5	3	2	4
Georgia	4	1	0	3	4	8	–4	3
Gibraltar	3	0	0	3	0	6	–6	0

GROUP E

Thursday, 21 March 2019

Croatia (1) 2 *(Barisic 43, Kramaric 79)*

Azerbaijan (1) 1 *(Sheydayev 19)* 23,146

Croatia: (4231) Kalinic L; Brekalo, Caleta-Car, Vida, Barisic; Modric (Badelj 90), Kovacic (Vlasic 73); Rakitic, Kramaric, Petkovic (Rebic 69); Perisic.
Azerbaijan: (4141) Agayev S; Medvedev, Mammadov R, Huseynov R, Rahimov; Garayev (Dadasov 88); Madatov, Eddy, Richard (Makhmudov 72), Nazarov (Abdullayev 58); Sheydayev.

Slovakia (1) 2 *(Duda 42, Rusnak 85)*

Hungary (0) 0 14,235

Slovakia: (4231) Dubravka; Pekarik, Vavro, Skriniar, Hancko; Kucka, Lobotka; Hamsik, Duda (Safranko 87), Rusnak (Mihalik 90); Mak (Stoch 79).
Hungary: (4231) Gulacsi; Orban, Lang (Holender 81), Kadar, Korhut; Lovrencsics, Nagy A; Kalmar (Dzsudzsak 61), Kleinheisler (Szoboszlai 54), Kovacs; Szalai.

Sunday, 24 March 2019

Hungary (1) 2 *(Szalai 34, Patkai 76)*

Croatia (1) 1 *(Rebic 13)* 19,400

Hungary: (4231) Gulacsi; Lovrencsics, Barath, Orban, Kadar; Nagy A, Patkai; Dzsudzsak (Bese 84), Szoboszlai (Kalmar 65), Nagy D (Varga R 40); Szalai.
Croatia: (4231) Kalinic L; Jedvaj (Petkovic 77), Lovren, Vida, Barisic (Leovac 29); Modric, Brozovic; Rebic (Brekalo 67), Rakitic, Perisic; Kramaric.

Wales (1) 1 *(James 5)*

Slovakia (0) 0 31,617

Wales: (4231) Hennessey; Roberts C, Mepham, Lawrence J, Davies B; Allen, Smith; Wilson (Vaulks 86), Brooks (Roberts T 60), James (Williams A 72); Bale.
Slovakia: (433) Dubravka; Pekarik (Safranko 90), Vavro, Skriniar, Hancko; Kucka, Lobotka, Hamsik; Rusnak, Duda (Duris 65), Mak (Stoch 69).

Saturday, 8 June 2019

Azerbaijan (0) 1 *(Madatov 69)*

Hungary (1) 3 *(Orban 18, 53, Holman 71)* 10,450

Azerbaijan: (433) Agayev S; Medvedev, Huseynov B, Mammadov R, Krivotsyuk; Richard, Garayev, Nazarov (Dadasov 86); Madatov (Abdullayev 74), Dadashov (Ramazanov 59), Sheydayev.
Hungary: (4231) Gulacsi; Lovrencsics, Orban, Barath, Korhut; Nagy A, Kleinheisler (Patkai 72); Dzsudzsak (Nemeth 86), Szoboszlai (Holman 57), Nagy D; Szalai.

Croatia (1) 2 *(Lawrence J 17 (og), Perisic 48)*

Wales (0) 1 *(Brooks 77)* 17,061

Croatia: (4231) Livakovic; Jedvaj, Lovren, Vida, Barisic; Modric, Brozovic; Brekalo (Pasalic 66), Kovacic (Badelj 76), Perisic (Skoric 90); Kramaric.
Wales: (4411) Hennessey; Roberts C, Mepham, Lawrence J, Davies B; Wilson, Allen, Smith (Brooks 65), James (Matondo 80); Vaulks (Ampadu 66); Bale.

Tuesday, 11 June 2019

Azerbaijan (1) 1 *(Sheydayev 29)*

Slovakia (3) 5 *(Lobotka 8, Kucka 27, Hamsik 30, 57, Hancko 85)* 8200

Azerbaijan: (433) Agayev S; Medvedev, Huseynov B, Krivotsyuk, Rahimov; Richard, Garayev, Eyubov (Makhmudov 79); Abdullayev (Dadashov 89), Sheydayev, Ramazanov (Madatov 61).
Slovakia: (433) Dubravka; Pekarik, Vavro, Skriniar, Hancko; Kucka, Lobotka (Gregus 84), Hamsik (Haraslin 86); Rusnak, Bozenik (Duda 71), Mak.

Hungary (0) 1 *(Patkai 80)*

Wales (0) 0 18,350

Hungary: (4231) Gulacsi; Lovrencsics, Barath, Orban, Korhut; Nagy A, Patkai; Dzsudzsak (Kleinheisler 69), Szoboszlai (Bese 83), Holender (Varga 58); Szalai.
Wales: (4231) Hennessey; Gunter, Williams A, Lawrence J, Davies B; Allen, Ampadu (Smith 54); Lawrence T (Vokes 79), Brooks (Wilson 73), James; Bale.

Group E Table	P	W	D	L	F	A	GD	Pts
Hungary	4	3	0	1	6	4	2	9
Slovakia	3	2	0	1	7	2	5	6
Croatia	3	2	0	1	5	4	1	6
Wales	3	1	0	2	2	3	–1	3
Azerbaijan	3	0	0	3	3	10	–7	0

GROUP F

Saturday, 23 March 2019

Malta (1) 2 *(Nwoko 13, Borg 77 (pen))*

Faroe Islands (0) 1 *(Thomsen 90)* 7531

Malta: (433) Bonello; Borg S, Caruana J, Agius■, Mbong; Muscat R (Mintoff 84), Guillaumier, Fenech P; Corbalan (Muscat Z 63), Nwoko, Mifsud (Zerafa 71).
Faroe Islands: (4411) Nielsen; Rolantsson, Gregersen, Faero, Davidsen V; Vatnhamar S (Bartalsstovu 68), Baldvinsson (Frederiksberg 79), Hansson, Joensen R (Olsen K 72); Hendriksson; Thomsen.

Spain (1) 2 *(Rodrigo 16, Sergio Ramos 71 (pen))*

Norway (0) 1 *(King 65 (pen))* 39,752

Spain: (433) de Gea; Jesus Navas, Sergio Ramos, Martinez, Jordi Alba; Parejo (Rodri 77), Busquets, Ceballos (Canales 74); Rodrigo, Morata (Mata 89), Asensio.
Norway: (442) Jarstein; Elabdellaoui, Nordtveit, Ajer, Aleesami; Odegaard (Elyounoussi M 56), Henriksen, Selnaes, Johansen (Kamara 77); King, Elyounoussi T (Johnsen 55).

Sweden (2) 2 *(Quaison 33, Claesson 40)*

Romania (0) 1 *(Keseru 58)* 30,115

Sweden: (442) Olsen; Lustig (Krafth 24), Helander, Granqvist, Augustinsson; Forsberg (Svensson 67), Seb Larsson, Olsson, Claesson; Quaison (Isak 88), Berg.
Romania: (4231) Tatarusanu; Manea, Sapunaru, Grigore, Bancu; Marin, Baluta T (Ivan 78); Mitrita (Keseru 46), Stanciu, Chipciu; Puscas (Hagi 64).

Tuesday, 26 March 2019

Malta (0) 0

Spain (1) 2 *(Morata 31, 73)* 16,542

Malta: (541) Bonello; Mbong (Muscat R 65), Muscat Z, Caruana J (Micallef 85), Borg S, Zerafa; Mintoff (Mifsud 69), Fenech P, Guillaumier, Corbalan; Nwoko.
Spain: (433) Arrizabalaga; Sergi Roberto, Sergio Ramos, Hermoso, Gaya; Canales, Rodri, Saul (Jesus Navas 65); Asensio, Morata (Rodrigo 78), Bernat (Muniain 56).

Norway (1) 3 *(Johnsen 41, King 59, Kamara 90)*

Sweden (0) 3 *(Claesson 70, Nordtveit 86 (og), Quaison 90)* 23,459

Norway: (442) Jarstein; Elabdellaoui, Nordtveit, Ajer, Aleesami; Odegaard, Selnaes, Henriksen, Elyounoussi M (Kamara 72); Johnsen (Sorloth 88), King.
Sweden: (442) Olsen; Krafth, Helander, Granqvist, Augustinsson; Seb Larsson (Isak 62), Ekdal (Svensson 66), Olsson K (Andersson 90), Claesson; Quaison, Berg.

Romania (3) 4 *(Deac 26, Keseru 29, 33, Puscas 63)*

Faroe Islands (1) 1 *(Davidsen 40 (pen))* 10,502

Romania: (442) Tatarusanu; Benzar (Hagi 46), Grigore, Moti, Bancu; Deac, Stanciu (Man 77), Marin, Chipciu; Puscas, Keseru (Cicaldau 69).
Faroe Islands: (4411) Nielsen; Rolantsson, Gregersen, Faero, Davidsen; Bartalsstovu (Frederiksberg 66), Hendriksson, Vatnsdal (Baldvinsson 29), Joensen; Hansson (Vatnhamar 77); Olsen K.

Friday, 7 June 2019

Faroe Islands (1) 1 *(Olsen K 30)*

Spain (3) 4 *(Sergio Ramos 6, Jesus Navas 19, Gestsson 34 (og), Gaya 71)* 3226

Faroe Islands: (433) Gestsson; Rolantsson, Faero, Gregersen, Davidsen; Hansson, Vatnsdal (Baldvinsson 74), Hendriksson; Vatnhamar, Olsen K (Johannesen 68), Frederiksberg (Olsen M 86).
Spain: (433) Arrizabalaga; Jesus Navas, Hermoso, Sergio Ramos (Llorente 46), Gaya; Sergi Roberto, Rodri, Cazorla; Aspas (Asensio 56), Morata, Isco (Fabian 74).

Norway (0) 2 *(Elyounoussi T 56, Odegaard 70)*

Romania (0) 2 *(Keseru 77, 90)* 17,664

Norway: (442) Grytebust; Elabdellaoui, Nordtveit, Ajer, Aleesami; Odegaard, Selnaes, Berge, Henriksen; Elyounoussi T (Kamara 84), King.
Romania: (4231) Tatarusanu; Chipciu, Sapunaru, Grigore, Tosca; Anton, Stanciu (Maxim 72); Deac, Keseru, Grozav (Hagi 60); Puscas (Tucudean 60).

Sweden (1) 3 *(Quaison 2, Claesson 50, Isak 81)*

Malta (0) 0 26,421

Sweden: (4411) Olsen; Lustig, Jansson, Helander, Augustinsson; Forsberg, Olsson K, Ekdal (Larsson 76), Claesson; Quaison (Guidetti 84); Berg (Isak 68).
Malta: (4312) Bonello; Muscat Z, Borg S (Apap 80), Agius, Mbong; Corbalan, Muscat R, Gambin; Grech (Fenech P 64); Effiong, Montebello (Nwoko 71).

Monday, 10 June 2019

Faroe Islands (0) 0

Norway (0) 2 *(Johnsen 49, 83)* 3083

Faroe Islands: (433) Gestsson; Rolantsson, Gregersen, Faero, Davidsen V; Hansson, Baldvinsson, Hendriksson; Vatnhamar S (Frederiksberg 68), Olsen K (Johannesen 88), Joensen R (Vatnsdal 85).
Norway: (442) Hansen; Elabdellaoui, Nordtveit, Ajer, Aleesami; Odegaard, Berge, Selnaes (Midtsjoe 80), Henriksen (Johansen 71); Johnsen, Elyounoussi T (Kamara 58).

Malta (0) 0

Romania (3) 4 *(Puscas 8, 29, Chipciu 34, Man 90)* 6471

Malta: (442) Bonello; Muscat Z, Agius, Borg S, Zerafa; Muscat R, Fenech P (Grech 59), Mbong, Corbalan (Montebello 84); Effiong, Gambin (Mifsud 68).
Romania: (442) Tatarusanu; Chipciu■, Cristea, Nedelcearu (Sapunaru 35), Bancu; Hagi, Marin, Baluta, Maxim (Rotariu 74); Puscas, Keseru (Man 64).

Spain (0) 3 *(Sergio Ramos 64 (pen), Morata 85 (pen), Oyarzabal 87)*

Sweden (0) 0 72,205

Spain: (433) Arrizabalaga; Carvajal, Sergio Ramos, Martinez (Llorente 88), Jordi Alba; Parejo, Busquets, Fabian; Asensio (Morata 65), Rodrigo (Oyarzabal 71), Isco.
Sweden: (442) Olsen; Lustig, Helander, Augustinsson, Jansson; Seb Larsson (Isak 82), Ekdal (Olsson K 86), Forsberg, Claesson (Johansson 27); Quaison, Berg.

Group F Table	*P*	*W*	*D*	*L*	*F*	*A*	*GD*	*Pts*
Spain	4	4	0	0	11	2	9	12
Sweden	4	2	1	1	8	7	1	7
Romania	4	2	1	1	11	5	6	7
Norway	4	1	2	1	8	7	1	5
Malta	4	1	0	3	2	10	–8	3
Faroe Islands	4	0	0	4	3	12	–9	0

GROUP G

Thursday, 21 March 2019

Austria (0) 0

Poland (0) 1 *(Piatek 68)* 40,400

Austria: (4231) Lindner; Lainer, Dragovic, Hinteregger, Wober; Grillitsch (Onisiwo 84), Baumgartlinger; Lazaro (Janko 81), Sabitzer, Alaba; Arnautovic.
Poland: (442) Szczesny; Kedziora, Glik, Bednarek, Bereszynski; Grosicki (Pazdan 90), Krychowiak, Klich, Zielinski (Piatek 59); Lewandowski, Milik (Frankowski 46).

Israel (0) 1 *(Zahavi 55)*

Slovenia (0) 1 *(Sporar 48)* 12,430

Israel: (532) Harush; Dasa, Taha, Yeini, Ben Haroush, Tawatha (Cohen Y 77); Kayal (Solomon 62), Peretz, Natcho (Cohen A 79); Zahavi, Dabbur.
Slovenia: (433) Oblak; Stojanovic, Struna, Mevlja, Jokic; Zajc (Crnigoj 62), Krhin, Kurtic; Ilicic, Sporar (Bohar 84), Verbic (Bijol 89).

North Macedonia (2) 3 *(Alioski 11, Elmas 29, 90)*

Latvia (0) 1 *(Velkovski 87 (og))* 7043

North Macedonia: (442) Dimitrievski; Ristovski, Musliu, Velkovski, Alioski; Trajkovski (Markoski 83), Bardhi, Nikolov, Hasani (Elmas 23); Nestorovski, Pandev (Ristevski 71).
Latvia: (442) Vanins (Steinbors 33); Gabovs, Dubra, Oss, Maksimenko; Tarasovs, Isajevs, Ciganiks■, Rakels; Karasausks (Tobers 68), Sabala (Uldrikis 80).

Sunday, 24 March 2019

Israel (2) 4 *(Zahavi 34, 45, 55, Dabbur 66)*

Austria (1) 2 *(Arnautovic 8, 75)* 16,180

Israel: (532) Harush; Dasa, Dgani, Yeini, Taha (Habashi 77), Ben Haroush; Kayal (Cohen A 72), Peretz, Natcho; Dabbur (Hemed 80), Zahavi.
Austria: (4231) Lindner; Ulmer, Dragovic, Hinteregger, Wober (Janko 60); Schlager (Onisiwo 60), Baumgartlinger; Lazaro, Sabitzer, Zulj (Kainz 85); Arnautovic.

Poland (0) 2 *(Lewandowski 76, Glik 84)*

Latvia (0) 0 51,112

Poland: (442) Szczesny; Kedziora, Glik, Pazdan, Reca; Grosicki (Frankowski 83), Krychowiak, Klich (Blaszczykowski 62), Zielinski; Lewandowski, Piatek (Milik 87).
Latvia: (442) Steinbors; Dubra, Oss, Maksimenko, Laizans; Rakels, Isajevs, Karasausks (Tobers 86), Ikaunieks; Gutkovskis (Uldrikis 70), Savalnieks (Gabovs 80).

Slovenia (1) 1 *(Zajc 34)*

North Macedonia (0) 1 *(Bardhi 47)* 9872

Slovenia: (433) Oblak; Stojanovic, Struna, Mevlja, Jokic; Zajc (Zahovic 90), Krhin, Kurtic; Ilicic, Sporar (Beric 71), Verbic (Crnigoj 83).
North Macedonia: (442) Dimitrievski; Bejtulai, Velkoski, Musliu, Alioski (Ristevski 90); Ristovski, Bardhi, Nikolov, Elmas; Pandev (Trajkovski 76), Nestorovski (Markoski 88).

Friday, 7 June 2019

Austria (0) 1 *(Burgstaller 74)*

Slovenia (0) 0 19,200

Austria: (4141) Lindner; Lainer, Dragovic, Hinteregger, Ulmer; Laimer (Ilsanker 82); Lazaro, Sabitzer (Burgstaller 71), Schlager, Alaba (Kainz 90); Arnautovic.
Slovenia: (433) Oblak; Stojanovic, Mevlja, Struna, Jokic; Kurtic, Bijol (Popovic 63), Zajc (Bohar 69); Ilicic, Sporar, Crnigoj (Beric 78).

Latvia (0) 0

Israel (1) 3 *(Zahavi 10, 60, 81)* 5508

Latvia: (4231) Steinbors; Savalnieks, Dubra, Oss, Maksimenko; Tobers, Laizans (Rugins 79); Rakels, Karasausks (Kamess 67), Ikaunieks (Ciganiks 57); Gutkovskis.
Israel: (532) Harush; Dasa, Taha, Bitton, Yeini, Ben Haroush (Cohen A 81); Peretz, Natcho, Kayal (Glazer 73); Saba (Sahar 66), Zahavi.

North Macedonia (0) 0

Poland (0) 1 *(Piatek 46)* 25,000

North Macedonia: (352) Dimitrievski; Bejtulai, Velkovski, Musliu■; Ristovski (Ademi 76), Bardhi, Nikolov (Trajkovski 62), Elmas, Alioski; Pandev (Hasani 84), Nestorovski.
Poland: (4231) Fabianski; Kedziora, Bednarek, Glik, Bereszynski; Klich (Goralski 90), Krychowiak; Frankowski (Piatek 46), Zielinski, Grosicki (Rybus 69); Lewandowski.

Monday, 10 June 2019

Latvia (0) 0

Slovenia (4) 5 *(Crnigoj 24, 27, Ilicic 29 (pen), 44, Zajc 47)* 4011

Latvia: (532) Steinbors; Solovjovs, Dubra, Maksimenko (Jagodinskis 16), Oss, Savalnieks; Kamess, Tobers (Rugins 69), Laizans; Rakels (Ontuzans 78), Gutkovskis.
Slovenia: (433) Oblak; Stojanovic, Struna, Mevlja, Jokic; Zajc (Bijol 63), Popovic (Zahovic 77), Kurtic; Crnigoj (Majer 83), Beric, Ilicic.

North Macedonia (1) 1 *(Hinteregger 18 (og))*

Austria (1) 4 *(Lazaro 39, Arnautovic 62 (pen), 82, Bejtulai 87 (og))* 10,501

North Macedonia: (442) Dimitrievski; Ristovski, Bejtulai, Velkovski, Alioski; Nikolov (Hasani 67), Bardhi, Ademi, Elmas (Ristevski 55); Pandev, Nestorovski (Radeski 56).
Austria: (433) Lindner; Lainer, Dragovic (Posch 46), Hinteregger, Ulmer; Laimer, Ilsanker, Schlager; Lazaro, Arnautovic (Burgstaller 88), Sabitzer (Schaub 90).

Poland (1) 4 *(Piatek 35, Lewandowski 56 (pen), Grosicki 59, Kadzior 84)*

Israel (0) 0 57,229

Poland: (442) Fabianski; Kedziora, Bednarek, Glik, Bereszynski; Zielinski, Klich (Goralski 75), Krychowiak, Grosicki (Kadzior 77); Piatek (Milik 73), Lewandowski.
Israel: (4411) Harush; Dasa, Taha, Yeini, Ben Haroush; Bitton (Elhamed 82), Natcho, Kayal (Cohen Y 57), Peretz; Solomon (Saba 72); Zahavi.

Group G Table	P	W	D	L	F	A	GD	Pts
Poland	4	4	0	0	8	0	8	12
Israel	4	2	1	1	8	7	1	7
Austria	4	2	0	2	7	6	1	6
Slovenia	4	1	2	1	7	3	4	5
North Macedonia	4	1	1	2	5	7	−2	4
Latvia	4	0	0	4	1	13	−12	0

GROUP H

Friday, 22 March 2019

Albania (0) 0

Turkey (1) 2 *(Yilmaz 21, Calhanoglu 55)* 11,730

Albania: (3412) Berisha; Veseli, Ismajli, Gjimshiti; Hysaj, Abrashi, Xhaka, Balliu (Sadiku 58); Memushaj; Balaj (Grezda 58), Uzuni.
Turkey: (343) Gunok; Ali Kaldirim, Gonul (Celik 46), Demiral; Tekdemir, Ayhan, Belozoglu (Tokoz 65), Yokuslu; Calhanoglu, Tosun, Yilmaz (Turuc 88).

Andorra (0) 0

Iceland (1) 2 *(Bjarnason B 22, Kjartansson 80)* 1854

Andorra: (442) Gomes; Jesus Rubio (Sanchez J 87), Llovera, Lima, San Nicolas; Martinez A (Alaez 71), Rebes, Vales, Cervos; Martinez C (Clemente 81), Vieira.
Iceland: (4411) Halldorsson; Saevarsson, Arnason, Sigurdsson R, Skulason A; Gudmundsson J (Traustason 83), Gunnarsson (Sigurdarson 63), Bjarnason B, Sigurdsson A; Sigurdsson G; Finnbogason A (Kjartansson 70).

Moldova (0) 1 *(Ambros 89)*

France (3) 4 *(Griezmann 24, Varane 27, Giroud 36, Mbappe-Lottin 87)* 10,042

Moldova: (4231) Koselev; Jardan, Posmac, Carp, Reabciuk; Cebotaru, Ionita; Antoniuc (Ambros 73), Cociuc (Rozgoniuc 46), Ginsari; Nicolaescu (Damascan 59).
France: (451) Lloris; Pavard, Varane, Umtiti, Kurzawa; Mbappe-Lottin, Griezmann (Thauvin 73), Pogba, Kante, Matuidi (Lemar 73); Giroud (Fekir 81).

Monday, 25 March 2019

Andorra (0) 0

Albania (1) 3 *(Sadiku 21, Balaj 87, Abrashi 90)* 1373

Andorra: (442) Gomes; Jesus Rubio, Llovera, Lima, San Nicolas; Rodriguez, Rebes, Vales (Pujol 84), Sanchez J (Cervos 67); Martinez C (Alaez 73), Ferre.
Albania: (442) Berisha; Aliji, Gjimshiti, Ismajli, Hysaj; Grezda (Balaj 70), Kace, Basha (Memushaj 87), Xhaka (Abrashi 67); Uzuni, Sadiku.

France (1) 4 *(Umtiti 12, Giroud 68, Mbappe-Lottin 78, Griezmann 84)*

Iceland (0) 0 64,538

France: (4231) Lloris; Pavard, Varane, Umtiti, Kurzawa (Kimpembe 85); Pogba, Kante (Lemar 80); Mbappe-Lottin, Griezmann, Matuidi; Giroud (Sissoko 89).
Iceland: (532) Halldorsson; Saevarsson (Skulason A 84), Ingason, Arnason, Sigurdsson R, Magnusson; Sigurjonsson (Traustason 57), Gunnarsson, Bjarnason B; Sigurdsson G, Gudmundsson A (Finnbogason A 62).

Turkey (2) 4 *(Ali Kaldirim 24, Tosun 26, 54, Ayhan 70)*

Moldova (0) 0 29,456

Turkey: (433) Gunok; Celik, Demiral, Ayhan, Ali Kaldirim; Tokoz (Belozoglu 84), Tekdemir, Turuc (Karaca 78); Tosun, Yilmaz, Calhanoglu (Yazici 66).
Moldova: (4321) Koselev; Jardan, Rozgoniuc, Posmac, Reabciuk; Ionita, Carp (Turcan 46), Cebotaru; Graur, Ginsari (Antoniuc 73); Ambros (Nicolaescu 57).

Saturday, 8 June 2019

Iceland (1) 1 *(Gudmundsson J 22)*

Albania (0) 0 8968

Iceland: (4411) Halldorsson; Hermannsson, Arnason, Sigurdsson R, Skulason A; Gudmundsson J (Traustason 56), Gunnarsson, Bjarnason B, Sigurjonsson (Sigurdsson A 81); Sigurdsson G; Kjartansson (Sigthorsson 63).
Albania: (433) Berisha; Hysaj, Dermaku, Ismajli, Veseli; Abrashi, Xhaka (Ndoj 71), Basha (Kace 67); Cikalleshi (Sadiku 79), Balaj, Lenjani.

Moldova (1) 1 *(Armas 8)*

Andorra (0) 0 6712

Moldova: (4231) Koselev; Jardan, Efros, Armas, Reabciuk; Ionita■, Carp; Antoniuc (Cociuc 64), Suvorov (Cebotaru 50), Ginsari; Damascan (Boiciuc 81).
Andorra: (442) Gomes; Jesus Rubio (Martinez A 72), Llovera, Lima, San Nicolas; Clemente, Rebes (Moreno 69), Vales, Cervos; Vieira, Alaez (Sanchez A 82).

Turkey (2) 2 *(Ayhan 30, Under 40)*

France (0) 0 36,783

Turkey: (4231) Gunok; Celik, Ayhan, Demiral, Ali Kaldirim; Tekdemir, Tokoz (Omur 90); Under (Yazici 84), Kahveci (Tufan 79), Karaman; Yilmaz.
France: (433) Lloris; Pavard, Varane, Umtiti, Digne (Mendy 46); Sissoko, Matuidi (Coman 46), Pogba; Mbappe-Lottin, Giroud (Ben Yedder 72), Griezmann.

Tuesday, 11 June 2019

Albania (0) 2 *(Cikalleshi 66, Ramadani 90)*

Moldova (0) 0 5004

Albania: (433) Berisha; Hysaj, Ismajli, Mavraj, Veseli; Kace (Qose 84), Ramadani, Lenjani (Roshi 59); Abrashi, Uzuni, Sadiku (Cikalleshi 58).
Moldova: (3421) Koselev; Jardan (Graur 76), Efros, Armas; Antoniuc, Cebotaru, Carp, Reabciuk; Suvorov (Cociuc 74), Ginsari; Damascan (Boiciuc 70).

Andorra (0) 0

France (3) 4 *(Mbappe-Lottin 11, Ben Yedder 30, Thauvin 45, Zouma 60)* 3187

Andorra: (442) Gomes; Jesus Rubio, Llovera, Lima, San Nicolas; Martinez A (Jordi Rubio 58), Rebes, Vales, Cervos (Rodriguez 80); Alaez (Sanchez J 84), Vieira.
France: (4411) Lloris; Dubois, Zouma, Lenglet, Mendy; Ben Yedder (Giroud 72), Ndombele (Sissoko 64), Pogba, Mbappe-Lottin; Griezmann; Thauvin (Lemar 81).

Iceland (2) 2 *(Sigurdsson R 21, 32)*

Turkey (1) 1 *(Tokoz 40)* 9680

Iceland: (4411) Halldorsson; Hermannsson, Arnason, Sigurdsson R, Skulason A (Magnusson 69); Gudmundsson J (Traustason 79), Hallfredsson, Gunnarsson, Bjarnason B; Sigurdsson G; Bodvarsson (Sigthorsson 63).
Turkey: (4231) Gunok; Celik, Demiral, Ayhan, Ali Kaldirim; Tokoz (Yalcin 85), Tufan; Calhanoglu, Kahveci (Omur 63), Karaman (Yazici 46); Yilmaz.

Group H Table	P	W	D	L	F	A	GD	Pts
France	4	3	0	1	12	3	9	9
Turkey	4	3	0	1	9	2	7	9
Iceland	4	3	0	1	5	5	0	9
Albania	4	2	0	2	5	3	2	6
Moldova	4	1	0	3	2	10	–8	3
Andorra	4	0	0	4	0	10	–10	0

GROUP I

Thursday, 21 March 2019

Belgium (2) 3 *(Tielemans 14, Hazard E 45 (pen), 88)*

Russia (1) 1 *(Cheryshev 16)* 34,245

Belgium: (343) Courtois; Alderweireld, Boyata, Vertonghen; Castagne, Tielemans, Dendoncker, Hazard T (Chadli 84); Mertens, Batshuayi, Hazard E.
Russia: (541) Marinato; Fernandes, Nababkin, Dzhikija, Kudryashov, Zhirkov; Akhmetov, Golovin■, Kuzyaev (Anton Miranchuk 25), Cheryshev (Chalov 65); Dzyuba (Smolov 77).

Cyprus (4) 5 *(Sotiriou 19 (pen), 23 (pen), Kousoulos 26, Efrem 31, Laifis 56)*

San Marino (0) 0 3175

Cyprus: (442) Panagi; Demetriou J (Merkis 65), Kousoulos, Laifis, Ioannou N; Efrem, Papoulis (Spoljaric 53), Artymatas, Georgiou; Mitidis, Sotiriou (Makris 27).
San Marino: (532) Benedettini; Manuel Battistini, Cevoli, Simoncini, Palazzi, Rinaldi (Hirsch 46); Giardi (Lunadei 74), Golinucci E, Mularoni; Berardi F, Nanni (Vitaioli M 46).

Kazakhstan (2) 3 *(Pertsukh 6, Vorogovskiy 10, Zainutdinov 51)*

Scotland (0) 0 27,641

Kazakhstan: (532) Nepogodov; Vorogovskiy, Maliy, Postnikov, Yerlanov (Akhmetov 81), Suyumbayev; Pertsukh, Kuat, Merkel; Zainutdinov (Muzhikov 84), Murtazaev (Turysbek 68).
Scotland: (433) Bain; Palmer, Bates, McKenna, Shinnie; Armstrong, McGinn (McTominay 69), McGregor C; Forrest (McNulty 81), McBurnie (Russell 61), Burke.

Sunday, 24 March 2019

Cyprus (0) 0

Belgium (2) 2 *(Hazard E 10, Batshuayi 18)* 8728

Cyprus: (442) Pardo; Kousoulos, Junior (Georgiou 46), Merkis, Laifis; Papoulis, Margaca, Artymatas, Ioannou N; Antoniou (Makris 81), Efrem (Spoljaric 75).
Belgium: (343) Courtois; Alderweireld, Vermaelen, Vertonghen; Castagne, Tielemans, Dendoncker, Hazard T (Carrasco 68); Mertens (Januzaj 56), Batshuayi (Praet 89), Hazard E.

Kazakhstan (0) 0

Russia (2) 4 *(Cheryshev 19, 45, Dzyuba 52, Beysebekov 63 (og))* 29,582

Kazakhstan: (532) Nepogodov; Beysebekov, Akhmetov, Maliy, Logvinenko (Vorogovskiy 33), Suyumbayev; Merkel, Kuat, Pertsukh (Zhukov 85); Zainutdinov, Murtazaev (Turysbek 59).
Russia: (451) Marinato; Fernandes, Semenov, Dzhikija, Kudryashov; Ionov (Ignatiev 61), Akhmetov (Aleksey Miranchuk 72), Gazinsky, Ozdoev, Cheryshev; Dzyuba (Chalov 82).

San Marino (0) 0

Scotland (1) 2 *(McLean 4, Russell 74)* 4077

San Marino: (433) Benedettini; Manuel Battistini, Simoncini (Lunadei 86), Cevoli, Palazzi; Mularoni, Golinucci E, Golinucci A; Berardi F, Vitaioli M (Nanni 60), Hirsch (Grandoni 77).
Scotland: (442) Bain; O'Donnell, Bates, McKenna, Robertson; McLean, Armstrong (Forrest 71), McGregor C (McTominay 57), Paterson (McNulty 37); Fraser, Russell.

Saturday, 8 June 2019

Belgium (2) 3 *(Mertens 11, Castagne 14, Lukaku 50)*

Kazakhstan (0) 0 37,155

Belgium: (343) Courtois; Alderweireld, Kompany (Vermaelen 78), Vertonghen; Castagne, Witsel, De Bruyne (Tielemans 67), Hazard T; Mertens, Lukaku (Batshuayi 72), Hazard E.
Kazakhstan: (451) Nepogodov; Marochkin, Maliy, Erlanov, Beysebekov; Zhukov, Kuat (Tagybergen 78), Fedin (Aimbetov 66), Pertsukh, Vorogovskiy; Zhanglyshbay (Islamkhan 46).

Russia (4) 9 *(Cevoli 26 (og), Dzyuba 31 (pen), 73, 76, 88, Kudryashov 36, Anton Miranchuk 41, Smolov 77, 83)*

San Marino (0) 0 42,241

Russia: (433) Marinato; Fernandes, Semenov, Dzhikija, Kudryashov; Zobnin (Barinov 72), Ozdoev, Anton Miranchuk (Smolov 60); Golovin, Dzyuba, Aleksey Miranchuk (Ionov 60).
San Marino: (4231) Benedettini; Manuel Battistini, Cevoli, Vitaioli F, Grandoni; Golinucci E, Golinucci A (Lunadei 64); Palazzi (Censoni 50), Rinaldi (Tomassini 56), Mularoni; Vitaioli M.

Scotland (0) 2 *(Robertson 61, Burke 89)*

Cyprus (0) 1 *(Kousoulos 87)* 31,277

Scotland: (433) Marshall; O'Donnell, Mulgrew, McKenna, Robertson; McGinn (McTominay 79), McLean, McGregor C (Armstrong 87); Forrest, Brophy (Burke 73), Fraser.
Cyprus: (433) Pardo; Kousoulos, Ioannou N, Laifis, Margaca; Spoljaric (Kosti 70), Artymatas, Makris (Pittas 80); Efrem, Sotiriou, Ioannou M (Georgiou 66).

Tuesday, 11 June 2019

Belgium (1) 3 *(Lukaku 45, 57, De Bruyne 90)*

Scotland (0) 0 32,482

Belgium: (343) Courtois; Alderweireld, Kompany (Vermaelen 90), Vertonghen; Meunier, Tielemans (Mertens 78), Witsel, Hazard T (Carrasco 90); De Bruyne, Lukaku, Hazard E.
Scotland: (4231) Marshall; O'Donnell, Mulgrew, McKenna, Taylor; McTominay, McLean; Russell (Forrest 67), Armstrong (Fraser 32), McGregor C; Burke.

Kazakhstan (1) 4 *(Kuat 45, Fedin 61, Suyumbayev 65, Islamkhan 79)*

San Marino (0) 0 18,652

Kazakhstan: (532) Nepogodov; Vorogovskiy, Erlanov, Maliy, Shomko, Suyumbayev; Tagybergen, Kuat (Pertsukh 84), Islamkhan; Aimbetov (Fedin 58), Turysbek (Zhanglyshbay 69).
San Marino: (4312) Benedettini; Cesarini (Manuel Battistini 76), Vitaioli F, Brolli, Grandoni; Lunadei, Censoni, Mularoni; Michael Battistini (Golinucci E 46); Nanni, Vitaioli M (Berardi M 83).

Russia (1) 1 *(Ionov 38)*

Cyprus (0) 0 42,228

Russia: (433) Marinato; Fernandes, Dzhikija, Semenov, Kudryashov; Ozdoev, Zobnin (Barinov 78), Golovin; Anton Miranchuk (Aleksey Miranchuk 64), Dzyuba, Ionov (Akhmetov 90).
Cyprus: (433) Pardo; Makris (Spoljaric 81), Kousoulos, Laifis, Ioannou N; Artymatas, Kosti, Margaca; Georgiou (Efrem 45), Sotiriou, Avraam (Pittas 71).

Group I Table	P	W	D	L	F	A	GD	Pts
Belgium	4	4	0	0	11	1	10	12
Russia	4	3	0	1	15	3	12	9
Kazakhstan	4	2	0	2	7	7	0	6
Scotland	4	2	0	2	4	7	–3	6
Cyprus	4	1	0	3	6	5	1	3
San Marino	4	0	0	4	0	20	–20	0

GROUP J

Saturday, 23 March 2019

Bosnia-Herzegovina (1) 2 *(Krunic 33, Milosevic 80)*

Armenia (0) 1 *(Mkhitaryan 90 (pen))* 10,000

Bosnia-Herzegovina: (433) Sehic; Todorovic D, Bicakcic, Zukanovic, Civic; Pjanic, Besic, Krunic (Gojak 82); Visca, Dzeko (Koljic 87), Zakaric (Milosevic 64).
Armenia: (4231) Airapetyan; Hovhannisyan K, Haroyan, Calisir, Daghbashyan; Grigoryan, Mkrtchyan; Adamyan (Babayan 67), Mkhitaryan, Ghazaryan (Ozbiliz 81); Karapetyan (Briasco 67).

Italy (1) 2 *(Barella 7, Kean 74)*

Finland (0) 0 24,000

Italy: (433) Donnarumma; Piccini, Bonucci, Chiellini, Biraghi (Spinazzola 90); Barella, Jorginho, Verratti (Zaniolo 85); Kean, Immobile (Quagliarella 79), Bernardeschi.
Finland: (532) Hradecky; Granlund (Soiri 90), Toivio, Vaisanen S, Arajuuri, Pirinen; Lod, Sparv, Kamara; Hamalainen (Lappalainen 70), Pukki (Karjalainen 83).

Liechtenstein (0) 0

Greece (1) 2 *(Fortounis 45, Donis 80)* 2711

Liechtenstein: (451) Buchel B; Wolfinger, Kaufmann, Rechsteiner, Goppel; Hasler (Frick N 86), Martin Buchel (Sele A 67), Wieser, Polverino, Salanovic; Gubser (Yildiz 76).
Greece: (433) Vlachodimos; Bakakis, Siovas, Kourbelis, Koutris; Zeca, Fortounis (Koulouris 83), Samaris; Masouras, Mitroglou (Donis 23), Bakasetas (Kolovos 71).

Tuesday, 26 March 2019

Armenia (0) 0

Finland (1) 2 *(Jensen 14, Soiri 78)* 12,900

Armenia: (4231) Airapetyan; Hovhannisyan K, Haroyan, Calisir, Daghbashyan; Mkhitaryan, Grigoryan; Ozbiliz (Barseghyan 67), Ghazaryan, Babayan (Avetisyan 74); Briasco (Karapetyan 59).
Finland: (532) Hradecky; Jensen (Schuller 69), Toivio, Granlund, Arajuuri, Pirinen; Lod (Taylor 87), Sparv, Kamara; Hamalainen (Soiri 57), Pukki.

Bosnia-Herzegovina (2) 2 *(Visca 10, Pjanic 15)*

Greece (0) 2 *(Fortounis 64 (pen), Kolovos 85)* 10,500

Bosnia-Herzegovina: (433) Sehic; Bicakcic, Sunjic, Zukanovic, Kolasinac; Pjanic■, Besic, Cimirot (Krunic 90); Visca, Dzeko (Gojak 89), Duljevic (Milosevic 80).
Greece: (433) Vlachodimos; Bakakis (Koulouris 79), Papastathopoulos, Siovas, Koutris; Kourbelis (Kolovos 66), Zeca, Bouchalakis (Masouras 46); Fortounis, Donis, Samaris.

Italy (4) 6 *(Sensi 17, Verratti 32, Quagliarella 35 (pen), 45 (pen), Kean 70, Pavoletti 77)*

Liechtenstein (0) 0 19,834

Italy: (433) Sirigu; Mancini, Bonucci (Izzo 79), Romagnoli, Spinazzola; Sensi, Jorginho (Zaniolo 57), Verratti; Politano, Quagliarella (Pavoletti 72), Kean.
Liechtenstein: (442) Buchel B; Wolfinger, Kaufmann■, Hofer, Goppel; Sele A (Malin 46), Polverino, Wieser, Kuhne (Meier 68); Hasler, Salanovic (Martin Buchel 82).

Saturday, 8 June 2019

Armenia (2) 3 *(Ghazaryan 2, Karapetyan 18, Barseghyan 90)*

Liechtenstein (0) 0 9200

Armenia: (433) Airapetyan; Hambardzumyan, Haroyan, Voskanyan, Hovhannisyan K; Mkrtchyan (Grigoryan 76), Mkhitaryan, Avetisyan (Hovsepyan 78); Barseghyan, Karapetyan (Babayan 72), Ghazaryan.
Liechtenstein: (442) Hobi; Wolfinger (Brandle 85), Malin, Hofer, Goppel; Hasler, Sele A (Meier 81), Polverino, Salanovic; Frick Y (Kuhne 46), Marcel Buchel.

Finland (0) 2 *(Pukki 56, 68)*

Bosnia-Herzegovina (0) 0 16,103

Finland: (442) Hradecky; Granlund (Raitala 37), Toivio, Arajuuri, Uronen; Skrabb (Schuller 84), Sparv, Kamara, Forsell (Lappalainen 63); Pukki, Lod.
Bosnia-Herzegovina: (433) Sehic; Bicakcic, Sunjic, Zukanovic, Civic; Besic (Gojak 79), Cimirot, Saric; Visca, Dzeko, Duljevic (Bajic 69).

Greece (0) 0

Italy (3) 3 *(Barella 23, Insigne 30, Bonucci 33)* 19,828

Greece: (3412) Barkas; Papastathopoulos, Manolas, Siovas; Kourbelis (Siopis 46), Samaris (Bakasetas 77), Zeca, Fortounis; Stafylidis; Kolovos (Mavrias 46), Masouras.
Italy: (433) Sirigu; Florenzi, Bonucci, Chiellini, Emerson Palmieri (De Sciglio 68); Barella, Jorginho, Verratti (Pellegrini 81); Chiesa, Belotti (Bernardeschi 84), Insigne.

Tuesday, 11 June 2019

Greece (0) 2 *(Zeca 54, Fortounis 87)*

Armenia (2) 3 *(Karapetyan 8, Ghazaryan 33, Barseghyan 74)* 7011

Greece: (433) Vlachodimos; Mavrias (Kotsiras 17), Papastathopoulos, Siovas, Koutris; Zeca, Fortounis, Samaris (Siopis 75); Masouras, Koulouris, Pelkas (Kolovos 68).
Armenia: (433) Airapetyan; Hambardzumyan, Haroyan, Ishkhanyan, Hovhannisyan K; Mkrtchyan (Hovsepyan 56), Mkhitaryan, Grigoryan; Barseghyan, Karapetyan (Babayan 71), Ghazaryan (Avetisyan 83).

Italy (0) 2 *(Insigne 49, Verratti 86)*

Bosnia-Herzegovina (1) 1 *(Dzeko 32)* 29,100

Italy: (433) Sirigu; Mancini (De Sciglio 66), Bonucci, Chiellini, Emerson Palmieri; Barella, Jorginho, Verratti; Bernardeschi (Belotti 81), Quagliarella (Chiesa 46), Insigne.
Bosnia-Herzegovina: (433) Sehic; Todorovic D, Bicakcic, Zukanovic, Civic (Nastic 70); Besic, Pjanic, Saric; Visca, Dzeko, Gojak (Cimirot 80).

Liechtenstein (0) 0

Finland (1) 2 *(Pukki 37, Kallman 57)* 2160

Liechtenstein: (4141) Hobi; Wolfinger (Brandle 77), Kaufmann, Hofer, Rechsteiner; Wieser (Polverino 46); Sele A, Hasler, Marcel Buchel (Martin Buchel 54), Kuhne; Salanovic.
Finland: (442) Hradecky; Raitala (Vaisanen L 87), Toivio, Arajuuri, Uronen; Lod, Sparv (Schuller 61), Kamara, Lappalainen (Soiri 74); Kallman, Pukki.

Group J Table	P	W	D	L	F	A	GD	Pts
Italy	4	4	0	0	13	1	12	12
Finland	4	3	0	1	6	2	4	9
Armenia	4	2	0	2	7	6	1	6
Greece	4	1	1	2	6	8	–2	4
Bosnia-Herzegovina	4	1	1	2	5	7	–2	4
Liechtenstein	4	0	0	4	0	13	–13	0

THE WORLD CUP 1930–2018

Year	Winners v Runners-up		Venue	Attendance	Referee
1930	Uruguay v Argentina *Winning Coach:* Alberto Suppici	4-2	Montevideo	68,346	J. Langenus (Belgium)
1934	Italy v Czechoslovakia *Winning Coach:* Vittorio Pozzo	2-1*	Rome	55,000	I. Eklind (Sweden)
1938	Italy v Hungary *Winning Coach:* Vittorio Pozzo	4-2	Paris	45,000	G. Capdeville (France)
1950	Uruguay v Brazil *Winning Coach:* Juan Lopez	2-1	Rio de Janeiro	173,850	G. Reader (England)
1954	West Germany v Hungary *Winning Coach:* Sepp Herberger	3-2	Berne	62,500	W. Ling (England)
1958	Brazil v Sweden *Winning Coach:* Vicente Feola	5-2	Stockholm	49,737	M. Guigue (France)
1962	Brazil v Czechoslovakia *Winning Coach:* Aymore Moreira	3-1	Santiago	68,679	N. Latychev (USSR)
1966	England v West Germany *Winning Coach:* Alf Ramsey	4-2*	Wembley	96,924	G. Dienst (Sweden)
1970	Brazil v Italy *Winning Coach:* Mario Zagallo	4-1	Mexico City	107,412	R. Glockner (East Germany)
1974	West Germany v Netherlands *Winning Coach:* Helmut Schon	2-1	Munich	78,200	J. Taylor (England)
1978	Argentina v Netherlands *Winning Coach:* Cesar Luis Menotti	3-1*	Buenos Aires	71,483	S. Gonella (Italy)
1982	Italy v West Germany *Winning Coach:* Enzo Bearzot	3-1	Madrid	90,000	A. C. Coelho (Brazil)
1986	Argentina v West Germany *Winning Coach:* Carlos Bilardo	3-2	Mexico City	114,600	R. A. Filho (Brazil)
1990	West Germany v Argentina *Winning Coach:* Franz Beckenbauer	1-0	Rome	73,603	E. C. Mendez (Mexico)
1994	Brazil v Italy *Brazil won 3-2 on penalties.* *Winning Coach:* Carlos Alberto Parreira	0-0*	Los Angeles	94,194	S. Puhl (Hungary)
1998	France v Brazil *Winning Coach:* Aime Jacquet	3-0	Paris	80,000	S. Belqola (Morocco)
2002	Brazil v Germany *Winning Coach:* Luiz Felipe Scolari	2-0	Yokohama	69,029	P. Collina (Italy)
2006	Italy v France *Italy won 5-3 on penalties.* *Winning Coach:* Marcello Lippi	1-1*	Berlin	69,000	H. Elizondo (Argentina)
2010	Spain v Netherlands *Winning Coach:* Vicente del Bosque	1-0	Johannesburg	84,490	H. Webb (England)
2014	Germany v Argentina *Winning Coach:* Joachim Low	1-0*	Rio de Janeiro	74,738	N. Rizzoli (Italy)
2018	France v Croatia *Winning Coach:* Didier Deschamps	4-2	Moscow	78,011	N. Pitana (Argentina)

*(*After extra time)*

GOALSCORING AND ATTENDANCES IN WORLD CUP FINAL ROUNDS

Year	*Venue*	*Games*	*Goals (av)*	*Attendance (av)*
1930	Uruguay	18	70 (3.9)	590,549 (32,808)
1934	Italy	17	70 (4.1)	363,000 (21,352)
1938	France	18	84 (4.7)	375,700 (20,872)
1950	Brazil	22	88 (4.0)	1,045,246 (47,511)
1954	Switzerland	26	140 (5.4)	768,607 (29,562)
1958	Sweden	35	126 (3.6)	819,810 (23,423)
1962	Chile	32	89 (2.8)	893,172 (27,912)
1966	England	32	89 (2.8)	1,563,135 (48,848)
1970	Mexico	32	95 (3.0)	1,603,975 (50,124)
1974	West Germany	38	97 (2.6)	1,865,753 (49,098)
1978	Argentina	38	102 (2.7)	1,545,791 (40,678)
1982	Spain	52	146 (2.8)	2,109,723 (40,571)
1986	Mexico	52	132 (2.5)	2,394,031 (46,039)
1990	Italy	52	115 (2.2)	2,516,215 (48,388)
1994	USA	52	141 (2.7)	3,587,538 (68,991)
1998	France	64	171 (2.7)	2,785,100 (43,517)
2002	Japan/S. Korea	64	161 (2.5)	2,705,197 (42,268)
2006	Germany	64	147 (2.3)	3,359,439 (52,491)
2010	South Africa	64	145 (2.3)	3,178,856 (49,669)
2014	Brazil	64	171 (2.7)	3,367,727 (52,621)
2018	Russia	64	169 (2.6)	3,031,768 (47,371)
Total		900	2548 (2.8)	40,470,332 (44,967)

LEADING GOALSCORERS

Year	*Player*	*Goals*
1930	Guillermo Stabile (Argentina)	8
1934	Oldrich Nejedly (Czechoslovakia)	5
1938	Leonidas da Silva (Brazil)	7
1950	Ademir (Brazil)	8
1954	Sandor Kocsis (Hungary)	11
1958	Just Fontaine (France)	13
1962	Valentin Ivanov (USSR), Leonel Sanchez (Chile), Garrincha (Brazil), Vava (Brazil), Florian Albert (Hungary), Drazen Jerkovic (Yugoslavia)	4
1966	Eusebio (Portugal)	9
1970	Gerd Muller (West Germany)	10
1974	Grzegorz Lato (Poland)	7
1978	Mario Kempes (Argentina)	6
1982	Paolo Rossi (Italy)	6
1986	Gary Lineker (England)	6
1990	Salvatore Schillaci (Italy)	6
1994	Oleg Salenko (Russia) Hristo Stoichkov (Bulgaria)	6
1998	Davor Suker (Croatia)	6
2002	Ronaldo (Brazil)	8
2006	Miroslav Klose (Germany)	5
2010	Thomas Muller (Germany), David Villa (Spain), Wesley Sneijder (Netherlands), Diego Forlan (Uruguay)	5
2014	James Rodriguez (Colombia)	6
2018	Harry Kane (England)	6

EUROPEAN FOOTBALL CHAMPIONSHIP 1960–2016

(formerly EUROPEAN NATIONS' CUP)

Year	Winners v Runners-up		Venue	Attendance	Referee
1960	USSR v Yugoslavia	2-1*	Paris	17,966	A. E. Ellis (England)
	Winning Coach: Gavriil Kachalin				
1964	Spain v USSR	2-1	Madrid	79,115	A. E. Ellis (England)
	Winning Coach: Jose Villalonga				
1968	Italy v Yugoslavia	1-1	Rome	68,817	G. Dienst (Switzerland)
Replay	Italy v Yugoslavia	2-0	Rome	32,866	J. M. O. de Mendibil (Spain)
	Winning Coach: Ferruccio Valcareggi				
1972	West Germany v USSR	3-0	Brussels	43,066	F. Marschall (Austria)
	Winning Coach: Helmut Schon				
1976	Czechoslovakia v West Germany	2-2	Belgrade	30,790	S. Gonella (Italy)
	Czechoslovakia won 5-3 on penalties.				
	Winning Coach: Vaclav Jezek				
1980	West Germany v Belgium	2-1	Rome	47,860	N. Rainea (Romania)
	Winning Coach: Jupp Derwall				
1984	France v Spain	2-0	Paris	47,368	V. Christov (Slovakia)
	Winning Coach: Michel Hidalgo				
1988	Netherlands v USSR	2-0	Munich	62,770	M. Vautrot (France)
	Winning Coach: Rinus Michels				
1992	Denmark v Germany	2-0	Gothenburg	37,800	B. Galler (Switzerland)
	Winning Coach: Richard Moller Nielsen				
1996	Germany v Czech Republic	2-1*	Wembley	73,611	P. Pairetto (Italy)
	Germany won on sudden death 'golden goal'.				
	Winning Coach: Berti Vogts				
2000	France v Italy	2-1*	Rotterdam	48,200	A. Frisk (Sweden)
	France won on sudden death 'golden goal'.				
	Winning Coach: Roger Lemerre				
2004	Greece v Portugal	1-0	Lisbon	62,865	M. Merk (Germany)
	Winning Coach: Otto Rehhagel				
2008	Spain v Germany	1-0	Vienna	51,428	R. Rosetti (Italy)
	Winning Coach: Luis Aragones				
2012	Spain v Italy	4-0	Kiev	63,170	P. Proenca (Portugal)
	Winning Coach: Vicente del Bosque				
2016	Portugal v France	1-0*	Paris	75,868	M. Clattenburg (England)
	Winning Coach: Fernando Santos				

(**After extra time*)

OLYMPIC FOOTBALL PAST MEDALLISTS 1896–2016

* No official tournament. ** No official tournament but gold medal later awarded by IOC.

1896 Athens*
1 Denmark
2 Greece

1900 Paris*
1 Great Britain
2 France

1904 St Louis**
1 Canada
2 USA

1908 London
1 Great Britain
2 Denmark
3 Netherlands

1912 Stockholm
1 England
2 Denmark
3 Netherlands

1920 Antwerp
1 Belgium
2 Spain
3 Netherlands

1924 Paris
1 Uruguay
2 Switzerland
3 Sweden

1928 Amsterdam
1 Uruguay
2 Argentina
3 Italy

1932 Los Angeles
no tournament

1936 Berlin
1 Italy
2 Austria
3 Norway

1948 London
1 Sweden
2 Yugoslavia
3 Denmark

1952 Helsinki
1 Hungary
2 Yugoslavia
3 Sweden

1956 Melbourne
1 USSR
2 Yugoslavia
3 Bulgaria

1960 Rome
1 Yugoslavia
2 Denmark
3 Hungary

1964 Tokyo
1 Hungary
2 Czechoslovakia
3 East Germany

1968 Mexico City
1 Hungary
2 Bulgaria
3 Japan

1972 Munich
1 Poland
2 Hungary
3 E Germany/USSR

1976 Montreal
1 East Germany
2 Poland
3 USSR

1980 Moscow
1 Czechoslovakia
2 East Germany
3 USSR

1984 Los Angeles
1 France
2 Brazil
3 Yugoslavia

1988 Seoul
1 USSR
2 Brazil
3 West Germany

1992 Barcelona
1 Spain
2 Poland
3 Ghana

1996 Atlanta
1 Nigeria
2 Argentina
3 Brazil

2000 Sydney
1 Cameroon
2 Spain
3 Chile

2004 Athens
1 Argentina
2 Paraguay
3 Italy

2008 Beijing
1 Argentina
2 Nigeria
3 Brazil

2012 London
1 Mexico
2 Brazil
3 South Korea

2016 Rio
1 Brazil
2 Germany
3 Nigeria

BRITISH AND IRISH INTERNATIONAL RESULTS 1872–2019

Note: In the results that follow, WC = World Cup, EC = European Championship, NL = Nations League UI = Umbro International Trophy. TF = Tournoi de France. NC = Nations Cup. Northern Ireland played as Ireland before 1921. *After extra time.

Bold type indicates matches played in season 2018–19.

ENGLAND v SCOTLAND

Played: 114; England won 48, Scotland won 41, Drawn 25. Goals: England 203, Scotland 174.

			E	S
1872	30 Nov	Glasgow	0	0
1873	8 Mar	Kennington Oval	4	2
1874	7 Mar	Glasgow	1	2
1875	6 Mar	Kennington Oval	2	2
1876	4 Mar	Glasgow	0	3
1877	3 Mar	Kennington Oval	1	3
1878	2 Mar	Glasgow	2	7
1879	5 Apr	Kennington Oval	5	4
1880	13 Mar	Glasgow	4	5
1881	12 Mar	Kennington Oval	1	6
1882	11 Mar	Glasgow	1	5
1883	10 Mar	Sheffield	2	3
1884	15 Mar	Glasgow	0	1
1885	21 Mar	Kennington Oval	1	1
1886	31 Mar	Glasgow	1	1
1887	19 Mar	Blackburn	2	3
1888	17 Mar	Glasgow	5	0
1889	13 Apr	Kennington Oval	2	3
1890	5 Apr	Glasgow	1	1
1891	6 Apr	Blackburn	2	1
1892	2 Apr	Glasgow	4	1
1893	1 Apr	Richmond	5	2
1894	7 Apr	Glasgow	2	2
1895	6 Apr	Everton	3	0
1896	4 Apr	Glasgow	1	2
1897	3 Apr	Crystal Palace	1	2
1898	2 Apr	Glasgow	3	1
1899	8 Apr	Aston Villa	2	1
1900	7 Apr	Glasgow	1	4
1901	30 Mar	Crystal Palace	2	2
1902	3 Mar	Aston Villa	2	2
1903	4 Apr	Sheffield	1	2
1904	9 Apr	Glasgow	1	0
1905	1 Apr	Crystal Palace	1	0
1906	7 Apr	Glasgow	1	2
1907	6 Apr	Newcastle	1	1
1908	4 Apr	Glasgow	1	1
1909	3 Apr	Crystal Palace	2	0
1910	2 Apr	Glasgow	0	2
1911	1 Apr	Everton	1	1
1912	23 Mar	Glasgow	1	1
1913	5 Apr	Chelsea	1	0
1914	14 Apr	Glasgow	1	3
1920	10 Apr	Sheffield	5	4
1921	9 Apr	Glasgow	0	3
1922	8 Apr	Aston Villa	0	1
1923	14 Apr	Glasgow	2	2
1924	12 Apr	Wembley	1	1
1925	4 Apr	Glasgow	0	2
1926	17 Apr	Manchester	0	1
1927	2 Apr	Glasgow	2	1
1928	31 Mar	Wembley	1	5
1929	13 Apr	Glasgow	0	1
1930	5 Apr	Wembley	5	2
1931	28 Mar	Glasgow	0	2
1932	9 Apr	Wembley	3	0
1933	1 Apr	Glasgow	1	2
1934	14 Apr	Wembley	3	0
1935	6 Apr	Glasgow	0	2
1936	4 Apr	Wembley	1	1
1937	17 Apr	Glasgow	1	3
1938	9 Apr	Wembley	0	1
1939	15 Apr	Glasgow	2	1
1947	12 Apr	Wembley	1	1
1948	10 Apr	Glasgow	2	0
1949	9 Apr	Wembley	1	3
WC1950	15 Apr	Glasgow	1	0
1951	14 Apr	Wembley	2	3
1952	5 Apr	Glasgow	2	1
1953	18 Apr	Wembley	2	2
WC1954	3 Apr	Glasgow	4	2
1955	2 Apr	Wembley	7	2
1956	14 Apr	Glasgow	1	1
1957	6 Apr	Wembley	2	1
1958	19 Apr	Glasgow	4	0
1959	11 Apr	Wembley	1	0
1960	9 Apr	Glasgow	1	1
1961	15 Apr	Wembley	9	3
1962	14 Apr	Glasgow	0	2
1963	6 Apr	Wembley	1	2
1964	11 Apr	Glasgow	0	1
1965	10 Apr	Wembley	2	2
1966	2 Apr	Glasgow	4	3
EC1967	15 Apr	Wembley	2	3
EC1968	24 Jan	Glasgow	1	1
1969	10 May	Wembley	4	1
1970	25 Apr	Glasgow	0	0
1971	22 May	Wembley	3	1
1972	27 May	Glasgow	1	0
1973	14 Feb	Glasgow	5	0
1973	19 May	Wembley	1	0
1974	18 May	Glasgow	0	2
1975	24 May	Wembley	5	1
1976	15 May	Glasgow	1	2
1977	4 June	Wembley	1	2
1978	20 May	Glasgow	1	0
1979	26 May	Wembley	3	1
1980	24 May	Glasgow	2	0
1981	23 May	Wembley	0	1
1982	29 May	Glasgow	1	0
1983	1 June	Wembley	2	0
1984	26 May	Glasgow	1	1
1985	25 May	Glasgow	0	1
1986	23 Apr	Wembley	2	1
1987	23 May	Glasgow	0	0
1988	21 May	Wembley	1	0
1989	27 May	Glasgow	2	0
EC1996	15 June	Wembley	2	0
EC1999	13 Nov	Glasgow	2	0
EC1999	17 Nov	Wembley	0	1
2013	14 Aug	Wembley	3	2
2014	18 Nov	Glasgow	3	1
WC2016	11 Nov	Wembley	3	0
WC2017	10 June	Glasgow	2	2

ENGLAND v WALES

Played: 102; England won 67, Wales won 14, Drawn 21. Goals: England 247, Wales 91.

			E	W
1879	18 Jan	Kennington Oval	2	1
1880	15 Mar	Wrexham	3	2
1881	26 Feb	Blackburn	0	1
1882	13 Mar	Wrexham	3	5
1883	3 Feb	Kennington Oval	5	0
1884	17 Mar	Wrexham	4	0
1885	14 Mar	Blackburn	1	1
1886	29 Mar	Wrexham	3	1
1887	26 Feb	Kennington Oval	4	0
1888	4 Feb	Crewe	5	1
1889	23 Feb	Stoke	4	1
1890	15 Mar	Wrexham	3	1
1891	7 May	Sunderland	4	1
1892	5 Mar	Wrexham	2	0
1893	13 Mar	Stoke	6	0
1894	12 Mar	Wrexham	5	1

			E	W
1895	18 Mar	Queen's Club, Kensington	1	1
1896	16 Mar	Cardiff	9	1
1897	29 Mar	Sheffield	4	0
1898	28 Mar	Wrexham	3	0
1899	20 Mar	Bristol	4	0
1900	26 Mar	Cardiff	1	1
1901	18 Mar	Newcastle	6	0
1902	3 Mar	Wrexham	0	0
1903	2 Mar	Portsmouth	2	1
1904	29 Feb	Wrexham	2	2
1905	27 Mar	Liverpool	3	1
1906	19 Mar	Cardiff	1	0
1907	18 Mar	Fulham	1	1
1908	16 Mar	Wrexham	7	1
1909	15 Mar	Nottingham	2	0
1910	14 Mar	Cardiff	1	0
1911	13 Mar	Millwall	3	0
1912	11 Mar	Wrexham	2	0
1913	17 Mar	Bristol	4	3
1914	16 Mar	Cardiff	2	0
1920	15 Mar	Highbury	1	2
1921	14 Mar	Cardiff	0	0
1922	13 Mar	Liverpool	1	0
1923	5 Mar	Cardiff	2	2
1924	3 Mar	Blackburn	1	2
1925	28 Feb	Swansea	2	1
1926	1 Mar	Crystal Palace	1	3
1927	12 Feb	Wrexham	3	3
1927	28 Nov	Burnley	1	2
1928	17 Nov	Swansea	3	2
1929	20 Nov	Chelsea	6	0
1930	22 Nov	Wrexham	4	0
1931	18 Nov	Liverpool	3	1
1932	16 Nov	Wrexham	0	0
1933	15 Nov	Newcastle	1	2
1934	29 Sept	Cardiff	4	0
1936	5 Feb	Wolverhampton	1	2
1936	17 Oct	Cardiff	1	2
1937	17 Nov	Middlesbrough	2	1
1938	22 Oct	Cardiff	2	4
1946	13 Nov	Manchester	3	0
1947	18 Oct	Cardiff	3	0
1948	10 Nov	Aston Villa	1	0
WC1949	15 Oct	Cardiff	4	1
1950	15 Nov	Sunderland	4	2
1951	20 Oct	Cardiff	1	1
1952	12 Nov	Wembley	5	2
WC1953	10 Oct	Cardiff	4	1
1954	10 Nov	Wembley	3	2
1955	27 Oct	Cardiff	1	2
1956	14 Nov	Wembley	3	1
1957	19 Oct	Cardiff	4	0
1958	26 Nov	Aston Villa	2	2
1959	17 Oct	Cardiff	1	1
1960	23 Nov	Wembley	5	1
1961	14 Oct	Cardiff	1	1
1962	21 Oct	Wembley	4	0
1963	12 Oct	Cardiff	4	0
1964	18 Nov	Wembley	2	1
1965	2 Oct	Cardiff	0	0
EC1966	16 Nov	Wembley	5	1
EC1967	21 Oct	Cardiff	3	0
1969	7 May	Wembley	2	1
1970	18 Apr	Cardiff	1	1
1971	19 May	Wembley	0	0
1972	20 May	Cardiff	3	0
WC1972	15 Nov	Cardiff	1	0
WC1973	24 Jan	Wembley	1	1
1973	15 May	Wembley	3	0
1974	11 May	Cardiff	2	0
1975	21 May	Wembley	2	2
1976	24 Mar	Wrexham	2	1
1976	8 May	Cardiff	1	0
1977	31 May	Wembley	0	1
1978	3 May	Cardiff	3	1
1979	23 May	Wembley	0	0
1980	17 May	Wrexham	1	4
1981	20 May	Wembley	0	0
1982	27 Apr	Cardiff	1	0
1983	23 Feb	Wembley	2	1
1984	2 May	Wrexham	0	1
WC2004	9 Oct	Old Trafford	2	0
WC2005	3 Sept	Cardiff	1	0
EC2011	26 Mar	Cardiff	2	0
EC2011	6 Sept	Wembley	1	0
EC2016	16 June	Lens	2	1

ENGLAND v NORTHERN IRELAND

Played: 98; England won 75, Northern Ireland won 7, Drawn 16. Goals: England 323, Northern Ireland 81.

			E	NI
1882	18 Feb	Belfast	13	0
1883	24 Feb	Liverpool	7	0
1884	23 Feb	Belfast	8	1
1885	28 Feb	Manchester	4	0
1886	13 Mar	Belfast	6	1
1887	5 Feb	Sheffield	7	0
1888	31 Mar	Belfast	5	1
1889	2 Mar	Everton	6	1
1890	15 Mar	Belfast	9	1
1891	7 Mar	Wolverhampton	6	1
1892	5 Mar	Belfast	2	0
1893	25 Feb	Birmingham	6	1
1894	3 Mar	Belfast	2	2
1895	9 Mar	Derby	9	0
1896	7 Mar	Belfast	2	0
1897	20 Feb	Nottingham	6	0
1898	5 Mar	Belfast	3	2
1899	18 Feb	Sunderland	13	2
1900	17 Mar	Dublin	2	0
1901	9 Mar	Southampton	3	0
1902	22 Mar	Belfast	1	0
1903	14 Feb	Wolverhampton	4	0
1904	12 Mar	Belfast	3	1
1905	25 Feb	Middlesbrough	1	1
1906	17 Feb	Belfast	5	0
1907	16 Feb	Everton	1	0
1908	15 Feb	Belfast	3	1
1909	13 Feb	Bradford	4	0
1910	12 Feb	Belfast	1	1
1911	11 Feb	Derby	2	1
1912	10 Feb	Dublin	6	1
1913	15 Feb	Belfast	1	2
1914	14 Feb	Middlesbrough	0	3
1919	25 Oct	Belfast	1	1
1920	23 Oct	Sunderland	2	0
1921	22 Oct	Belfast	1	1
1922	21 Oct	West Bromwich	2	0
1923	20 Oct	Belfast	1	2
1924	22 Oct	Everton	3	1
1925	24 Oct	Belfast	0	0
1926	20 Oct	Liverpool	3	3
1927	22 Oct	Belfast	0	2
1928	22 Oct	Everton	2	1
1929	19 Oct	Belfast	3	0
1930	20 Oct	Sheffield	5	1
1931	17 Oct	Belfast	6	2
1932	17 Oct	Blackpool	1	0
1933	14 Oct	Belfast	3	0
1935	6 Feb	Everton	2	1
1935	19 Oct	Belfast	3	1
1936	18 Nov	Stoke	3	1
1937	23 Oct	Belfast	5	1
1938	16 Nov	Manchester	7	0
1946	28 Sept	Belfast	7	2
1947	5 Nov	Everton	2	2
1948	9 Oct	Belfast	6	2
WC1949	16 Nov	Manchester	9	2
1950	7 Oct	Belfast	4	1
1951	14 Nov	Aston Villa	2	0
1952	4 Oct	Belfast	2	2
WC1953	11 Nov	Everton	3	1
1954	2 Oct	Belfast	2	0
1955	2 Nov	Wembley	3	0
1956	10 Oct	Belfast	1	1

			E	*NI*
1957	6 Nov	Wembley	2	3
1958	4 Oct	Belfast	3	3
1959	18 Nov	Wembley	2	1
1960	8 Oct	Belfast	5	2
1961	22 Nov	Wembley	1	1
1962	20 Oct	Belfast	3	1
1963	20 Nov	Wembley	8	3
1964	3 Oct	Belfast	4	3
1965	10 Nov	Wembley	2	1
EC1966	20 Oct	Belfast	2	0
EC1967	22 Nov	Wembley	2	0
1969	3 May	Belfast	3	1
1970	21 Apr	Wembley	3	1
1971	15 May	Belfast	1	0
1972	23 May	Wembley	0	1
1973	12 May	Everton	2	1
1974	15 May	Wembley	1	0
1975	17 May	Belfast	0	0
1976	11 May	Wembley	4	0
1977	28 May	Belfast	2	1
1978	16 May	Wembley	1	0
EC1979	7 Feb	Wembley	4	0
1979	19 May	Belfast	2	0
EC1979	17 Oct	Belfast	5	1
1980	20 May	Wembley	1	1
1982	23 Feb	Wembley	4	0
1983	28 May	Belfast	0	0
1984	24 Apr	Wembley	1	0
WC1985	27 Feb	Belfast	1	0
WC1985	13 Nov	Wembley	0	0
EC1986	15 Oct	Wembley	3	0
EC1987	1 Apr	Belfast	2	0
WC2005	26 Mar	Old Trafford	4	0
WC2005	7 Sept	Belfast	0	1

SCOTLAND v WALES

Played: 107; Scotland won 61, Wales won 23, Drawn 23. Goals: Scotland 243, Wales 124.

			S	*W*
1876	25 Mar	Glasgow	4	0
1877	5 Mar	Wrexham	2	0
1878	23 Mar	Glasgow	9	0
1879	7 Apr	Wrexham	3	0
1880	3 Apr	Glasgow	5	1
1881	14 Mar	Wrexham	5	1
1882	25 Mar	Glasgow	5	0
1883	12 Mar	Wrexham	3	0
1884	29 Mar	Glasgow	4	1
1885	23 Mar	Wrexham	8	1
1886	10 Apr	Glasgow	4	1
1887	21 Mar	Wrexham	2	0
1888	10 Mar	Easter Road	5	1
1889	15 Apr	Wrexham	0	0
1890	22 Mar	Paisley	5	0
1891	21 Mar	Wrexham	4	3
1892	26 Mar	Tynecastle	6	1
1893	18 Mar	Wrexham	8	0
1894	24 Mar	Kilmarnock	5	2
1895	23 Mar	Wrexham	2	2
1896	21 Mar	Dundee	4	0
1897	20 Mar	Wrexham	2	2
1898	19 Mar	Motherwell	5	2
1899	18 Mar	Wrexham	6	0
1900	3 Feb	Aberdeen	5	2
1901	2 Mar	Wrexham	1	1
1902	15 Mar	Greenock	5	1
1903	9 Mar	Cardiff	1	0
1904	12 Mar	Dundee	1	1
1905	6 Mar	Wrexham	1	3
1906	3 Mar	Tynecastle	0	2
1907	4 Mar	Wrexham	0	1
1908	7 Mar	Dundee	2	1
1909	1 Mar	Wrexham	2	3
1910	5 Mar	Kilmarnock	1	0
1911	6 Mar	Cardiff	2	2
1912	2 Mar	Tynecastle	1	0
1913	3 Mar	Wrexham	0	0
1914	28 Feb	Glasgow	0	0
1920	26 Feb	Cardiff	1	1
1921	12 Feb	Aberdeen	2	1
1922	4 Feb	Wrexham	1	2
1923	17 Mar	Paisley	2	0
1924	16 Feb	Cardiff	0	2
1925	14 Feb	Tynecastle	3	1
1925	31 Oct	Cardiff	3	0
1926	30 Oct	Glasgow	3	0
1927	29 Oct	Wrexham	2	2
1928	27 Oct	Glasgow	4	2
1929	26 Oct	Cardiff	4	2
1930	25 Oct	Glasgow	1	1
1931	31 Oct	Wrexham	3	2
1932	26 Oct	Tynecastle	2	5
1933	4 Oct	Cardiff	2	3
1934	21 Nov	Aberdeen	3	2
1935	5 Oct	Cardiff	1	1
1936	2 Dec	Dundee	1	2
1937	30 Oct	Cardiff	1	2
1938	9 Nov	Tynecastle	3	2
1946	19 Oct	Wrexham	1	3
1947	12 Nov	Glasgow	1	2
1948	23 Oct	Cardiff	3	1
WC1949	9 Nov	Glasgow	2	0
1950	21 Oct	Cardiff	3	1
1951	14 Nov	Glasgow	0	1
1952	18 Oct	Cardiff	2	1
WC1953	4 Nov	Glasgow	3	3
1954	16 Oct	Cardiff	1	0
1955	9 Nov	Glasgow	2	0
1956	20 Oct	Cardiff	2	2
1957	13 Nov	Glasgow	1	1
1958	18 Oct	Cardiff	3	0
1959	4 Nov	Glasgow	1	1
1960	20 Oct	Cardiff	0	2
1961	8 Nov	Glasgow	2	0
1962	20 Oct	Cardiff	3	2
1963	20 Nov	Glasgow	2	1
1964	3 Oct	Cardiff	2	3
EC1965	24 Nov	Glasgow	4	1
EC1966	22 Oct	Cardiff	1	1
1967	22 Nov	Glasgow	3	2
1969	3 May	Wrexham	5	3
1970	22 Apr	Glasgow	0	0
1971	15 May	Cardiff	0	0
1972	24 May	Glasgow	1	0
1973	12 May	Wrexham	2	0
1974	14 May	Glasgow	2	0
1975	17 May	Cardiff	2	2
1976	6 May	Glasgow	3	1
WC1976	17 Nov	Glasgow	1	0
1977	28 May	Wrexham	0	0
WC1977	12 Oct	Liverpool	2	0
1978	17 May	Glasgow	1	1
1979	19 May	Cardiff	0	3
1980	21 May	Glasgow	1	0
1981	16 May	Swansea	0	2
1982	24 May	Glasgow	1	0
1983	28 May	Cardiff	2	0
1984	28 Feb	Glasgow	2	1
WC1985	27 Mar	Glasgow	0	1
WC1985	10 Sept	Cardiff	1	1
1997	27 May	Kilmarnock	0	1
2004	18 Feb	Cardiff	0	4
2009	14 Nov	Cardiff	0	3
NC2011	25 May	Dublin	3	1
WC2012	12 Oct	Cardiff	1	2
WC2013	22 Mar	Glasgow	1	2

SCOTLAND v NORTHERN IRELAND

Played: 96; Scotland won 64, Northern Ireland won 15, Drawn 17. Goals: Scotland 261, Northern Ireland 81.

			S	NI
1884	26 Jan	Belfast	5	0
1885	14 Mar	Glasgow	8	2
1886	20 Mar	Belfast	7	2
1887	19 Feb	Glasgow	4	1
1888	24 Mar	Belfast	10	2
1889	9 Mar	Glasgow	7	0
1890	29 Mar	Belfast	4	1
1891	28 Mar	Glasgow	2	1
1892	19 Mar	Belfast	3	2
1893	25 Mar	Glasgow	6	1
1894	31 Mar	Belfast	2	1
1895	30 Mar	Glasgow	3	1
1896	28 Mar	Belfast	3	3
1897	27 Mar	Glasgow	5	1
1898	26 Mar	Belfast	3	0
1899	25 Mar	Glasgow	9	1
1900	3 Mar	Belfast	3	0
1901	23 Feb	Glasgow	11	0
1902	1 Mar	Belfast	5	1
1902	9 Aug	Belfast	3	0
1903	21 Mar	Glasgow	0	2
1904	26 Mar	Dublin	1	1
1905	18 Mar	Glasgow	4	0
1906	17 Mar	Dublin	1	0
1907	16 Mar	Glasgow	3	0
1908	14 Mar	Dublin	5	0
1909	15 Mar	Glasgow	5	0
1910	19 Mar	Belfast	0	1
1911	18 Mar	Glasgow	2	0
1912	16 Mar	Belfast	4	1
1913	15 Mar	Dublin	2	1
1914	14 Mar	Belfast	1	1
1920	13 Mar	Glasgow	3	0
1921	26 Feb	Belfast	2	0
1922	4 Mar	Glasgow	2	1
1923	3 Mar	Belfast	1	0
1924	1 Mar	Glasgow	2	0
1925	28 Feb	Belfast	3	0
1926	27 Feb	Glasgow	4	0
1927	26 Feb	Belfast	2	0
1928	25 Feb	Glasgow	0	1
1929	23 Feb	Belfast	7	3
1930	22 Feb	Glasgow	3	1
1931	21 Feb	Belfast	0	0
1931	19 Sept	Glasgow	3	1
1932	12 Sept	Belfast	4	0
1933	16 Sept	Glasgow	1	2
1934	20 Oct	Belfast	1	2
1935	13 Nov	Tynecastle	2	1
1936	31 Oct	Belfast	3	1
1937	10 Nov	Aberdeen	1	1
1938	8 Oct	Belfast	2	0
1946	27 Nov	Glasgow	0	0
1947	4 Oct	Belfast	0	2
1948	17 Nov	Glasgow	3	2
wc1949	1 Oct	Belfast	8	2
1950	1 Nov	Glasgow	6	1
1951	6 Oct	Belfast	3	0
1952	5 Nov	Glasgow	1	1
wc1953	3 Oct	Belfast	3	1
1954	3 Nov	Glasgow	2	2
1955	8 Oct	Belfast	1	2
1956	7 Nov	Glasgow	1	0
1957	5 Oct	Belfast	1	1
1958	5 Nov	Glasgow	2	2
1959	3 Oct	Belfast	4	0
1960	9 Nov	Glasgow	5	2
1961	7 Oct	Belfast	6	1
1962	7 Nov	Glasgow	5	1
1963	12 Oct	Belfast	1	2
1964	25 Nov	Glasgow	3	2
1965	2 Oct	Belfast	2	3
1966	16 Nov	Glasgow	2	1
1967	21 Oct	Belfast	0	1
1969	6 May	Glasgow	1	1
1970	18 Apr	Belfast	1	0
1971	18 May	Glasgow	0	1
1972	20 May	Glasgow	2	0
1973	16 May	Glasgow	1	2
1974	11 May	Glasgow	0	1
1975	20 May	Glasgow	3	0
1976	8 May	Glasgow	3	0
1977	1 June	Glasgow	3	0
1978	13 May	Glasgow	1	1
1979	22 May	Glasgow	1	0
1980	17 May	Belfast	0	1
wc1981	25 Mar	Glasgow	1	1
1981	19 May	Glasgow	2	0
wc1981	14 Oct	Belfast	0	0
1982	28 Apr	Belfast	1	1
1983	24 May	Glasgow	0	0
1983	13 Dec	Belfast	0	2
1992	19 Feb	Glasgow	1	0
2008	20 Aug	Glasgow	0	0
NC2011	9 Feb	Dublin	3	0
2015	25 Mar	Glasgow	1	0

WALES v NORTHERN IRELAND

Played: 96; Wales won 45, Northern Ireland won 27, Drawn 24. Goals: Wales 191, Northern Ireland 132.

			W	NI
1882	25 Feb	Wrexham	7	1
1883	17 Mar	Belfast	1	1
1884	9 Feb	Wrexham	6	0
1885	11 Apr	Belfast	8	2
1886	27 Feb	Wrexham	5	0
1887	12 Mar	Belfast	1	4
1888	3 Mar	Wrexham	11	0
1889	27 Apr	Belfast	3	1
1890	8 Feb	Shrewsbury	5	2
1891	7 Feb	Belfast	2	7
1892	27 Feb	Bangor	1	1
1893	8 Apr	Belfast	3	4
1894	24 Feb	Swansea	4	1
1895	16 Mar	Belfast	2	2
1896	29 Feb	Wrexham	6	1
1897	6 Mar	Belfast	3	4
1898	19 Feb	Llandudno	0	1
1899	4 Mar	Belfast	0	1
1900	24 Feb	Llandudno	2	0
1901	23 Mar	Belfast	1	0
1902	22 Mar	Cardiff	0	3
1903	28 Mar	Belfast	0	2
1904	21 Mar	Bangor	0	1
1905	18 Apr	Belfast	2	2
1906	2 Apr	Wrexham	4	4
1907	23 Feb	Belfast	3	2
1908	11 Apr	Aberdare	0	1
1909	20 Mar	Belfast	3	2
1910	11 Apr	Wrexham	4	1
1911	28 Jan	Belfast	2	1
1912	13 Apr	Cardiff	2	3
1913	18 Jan	Belfast	1	0
1914	19 Jan	Wrexham	1	2
1920	14 Feb	Belfast	2	2
1921	9 Apr	Swansea	2	1
1922	4 Apr	Belfast	1	1
1923	14 Apr	Wrexham	0	3
1924	15 Mar	Belfast	1	0
1925	18 Apr	Wrexham	0	0
1926	13 Feb	Belfast	0	3
1927	9 Apr	Cardiff	2	2
1928	4 Feb	Belfast	2	1
1929	2 Feb	Wrexham	2	2
1930	1 Feb	Belfast	0	7
1931	22 Apr	Wrexham	3	2
1931	5 Dec	Belfast	0	4
1932	7 Dec	Wrexham	4	1
1933	4 Nov	Belfast	1	1

			W	NI
1935	27 Mar	Wrexham	3	1
1936	11 Mar	Belfast	2	3
1937	17 Mar	Wrexham	4	1
1938	16 Mar	Belfast	0	1
1939	15 Mar	Wrexham	3	1
1947	16 Apr	Belfast	1	2
1948	10 Mar	Wrexham	2	0
1949	9 Mar	Belfast	2	0
WC1950	8 Mar	Wrexham	0	0
1951	7 Mar	Belfast	2	1
1952	19 Mar	Swansea	3	0
1953	15 Apr	Belfast	3	2
WC1954	31 Mar	Wrexham	1	2
1955	20 Apr	Belfast	3	2
1956	11 Apr	Cardiff	1	1
1957	10 Apr	Belfast	0	0
1958	16 Apr	Cardiff	1	1
1959	22 Apr	Belfast	1	4
1960	6 Apr	Wrexham	3	2
1961	12 Apr	Belfast	5	1
1962	11 Apr	Cardiff	4	0
1963	3 Apr	Belfast	4	1
1964	15 Apr	Swansea	2	3
1965	31 Mar	Belfast	5	0
1966	30 Mar	Cardiff	1	4
EC1967	12 Apr	Belfast	0	0
EC1968	28 Feb	Wrexham	2	0
1969	10 May	Belfast	0	0
1970	25 Apr	Swansea	1	0
1971	22 May	Belfast	0	1
1972	27 May	Wrexham	0	0
1973	19 May	Everton	0	1
1974	18 May	Wrexham	1	0
1975	23 May	Belfast	0	1
1976	14 May	Swansea	1	0
1977	3 June	Belfast	1	1
1978	19 May	Wrexham	1	0
1979	25 May	Belfast	1	1
1980	23 May	Cardiff	0	1
1982	27 May	Wrexham	3	0
1983	31 May	Belfast	1	0
1984	22 May	Swansea	1	1
WC2004	8 Sept	Cardiff	2	2
WC2005	8 Oct	Belfast	3	2
2007	6 Feb	Belfast	0	0
NC2011	27 May	Dublin	2	0
2016	24 Mar	Cardiff	1	1
EC2016	25 June	Paris	1	0

OTHER BRITISH INTERNATIONAL RESULTS 1908–2019

ENGLAND

v ALBANIA

			E	A
WC1989	8 Mar	Tirana	2	0
WC1989	26 Apr	Wembley	5	0
WC2001	28 Mar	Tirana	3	1
WC2001	5 Sept	Newcastle	2	0

v ALGERIA

			E	A
WC2010	18 June	Cape Town	0	0

v ANDORRA

			E	A
EC2006	2 Sept	Old Trafford	5	0
EC2007	28 Mar	Barcelona	3	0
WC2008	6 Sept	Barcelona	2	0
WC2009	10 June	Wembley	6	0

v ARGENTINA

			E	A
1951	9 May	Wembley	2	1
1953	17 May	Buenos Aires	0	0
(abandoned after 21 mins)				
WC1962	2 June	Rancagua	3	1
1964	6 June	Rio de Janeiro	0	1
WC1966	23 July	Wembley	1	0
1974	22 May	Wembley	2	2
1977	12 June	Buenos Aires	1	1
1980	13 May	Wembley	3	1
WC1986	22 June	Mexico City	1	2
1991	25 May	Wembley	2	2
WC1998	30 June	St Etienne	2	2
2000	23 Feb	Wembley	0	0
WC2002	7 June	Sapporo	1	0
2005	12 Nov	Geneva	3	2

v AUSTRALIA

			E	A
1980	31 May	Sydney	2	1
1983	11 June	Sydney	0	0
1983	15 June	Brisbane	1	0
1983	18 June	Melbourne	1	1
1991	1 June	Sydney	1	0
2003	12 Feb	West Ham	1	3
2016	27 May	Sunderland	2	1

v AUSTRIA

			E	A
1908	6 June	Vienna	6	1
1908	8 June	Vienna	11	1
1909	1 June	Vienna	8	1
1930	14 May	Vienna	0	0
1932	7 Dec	Chelsea	4	3
1936	6 May	Vienna	1	2
1951	28 Nov	Wembley	2	2
1952	25 May	Vienna	3	2
WC1958	15 June	Boras	2	2
1961	27 May	Vienna	1	3
1962	4 Apr	Wembley	3	1
1965	20 Oct	Wembley	2	3
1967	27 May	Vienna	1	0
1973	26 Sept	Wembley	7	0
1979	13 June	Vienna	3	4
WC2004	4 Sept	Vienna	2	2
WC2005	8 Oct	Old Trafford	1	0
2007	16 Nov	Vienna	1	0

v AZERBAIJAN

			E	A
WC2004	13 Oct	Baku	1	0
WC2005	30 Mar	Newcastle	2	0

v BELARUS

			E	B
WC2008	15 Oct	Minsk	3	1
WC2009	14 Oct	Wembley	3	0

v BELGIUM

			E	B
1921	21 May	Brussels	2	0
1923	19 Mar	Highbury	6	1
1923	1 Nov	Antwerp	2	2
1924	8 Dec	West Bromwich	4	0
1926	24 May	Antwerp	5	3
1927	11 May	Brussels	9	1
1928	19 May	Antwerp	3	1
1929	11 May	Brussels	5	1
1931	16 May	Brussels	4	1
1936	9 May	Brussels	2	3
1947	21 Sept	Brussels	5	2
1950	18 May	Brussels	4	1
1952	26 Nov	Wembley	5	0
WC1954	17 June	Basle	4	4*
1964	21 Oct	Wembley	2	2
1970	25 Feb	Brussels	3	1
EC1980	12 June	Turin	1	1
WC1990	27 June	Bologna	1	0*
1998	29 May	Casablanca	0	0
1999	10 Oct	Sunderland	2	1
2012	2 June	Wembley	1	0
WC2018	28 June	Kaliningrad	0	1
WC2018	14 July	St Petersburg	0	2

v BOHEMIA

			E	B
1908	13 June	Prague	4	0

v BRAZIL

			E	B
1956	9 May	Wembley	4	2
WC1958	11 June	Gothenburg	0	0
1959	13 May	Rio de Janeiro	0	2
WC1962	10 June	Vina del Mar	1	3
1963	8 May	Wembley	1	1
1964	30 May	Rio de Janeiro	1	5
1969	12 June	Rio de Janeiro	1	2
WC1970	7 June	Guadalajara	0	1
1976	23 May	Los Angeles	0	1

				E	*B*
	1977	8 June	Rio de Janeiro	0	0
	1978	19 Apr	Wembley	1	1
	1981	12 May	Wembley	0	1
	1984	10 June	Rio de Janeiro	2	0
	1987	19 May	Wembley	1	1
	1990	28 Mar	Wembley	1	0
	1992	17 May	Wembley	1	1
	1993	13 June	Washington	1	1
UI	1995	11 June	Wembley	1	3
TF	1997	10 June	Paris	0	1
	2000	27 May	Wembley	1	1
WC	2002	21 June	Shizuoka	1	2
	2007	1 June	Wembley	1	1
	2009	14 Nov	Doha	0	1
	2013	6 Feb	Wembley	2	1
	2013	2 June	Rio de Janeiro	2	2
	2017	14 Nov	Wembley	0	0

v BULGARIA

				E	*B*
WC	1962	7 June	Rancagua	0	0
	1968	11 Dec	Wembley	1	1
	1974	1 June	Sofia	1	0
EC	1979	6 June	Sofia	3	0
EC	1979	22 Nov	Wembley	2	0
	1996	27 Mar	Wembley	1	0
EC	1998	10 Oct	Wembley	0	0
EC	1999	9 June	Sofia	1	1
EC	2010	3 Sept	Wembley	4	0
EC	2011	2 Sept	Sofia	3	0

v CAMEROON

				E	*C*
WC	1990	1 July	Naples	3	2*
	1991	6 Feb	Wembley	2	0
	1997	15 Nov	Wembley	2	0
	2002	26 May	Kobe	2	2

v CANADA

				E	*C*
	1986	24 May	Burnaby	1	0

v CHILE

				E	*C*
WC	1950	25 June	Rio de Janeiro	2	0
	1953	24 May	Santiago	2	1
	1984	17 June	Santiago	0	0
	1989	23 May	Wembley	0	0
	1998	11 Feb	Wembley	0	2
	2013	15 Nov	Wembley	0	2

v CHINA PR

				E	*CPR*
	1996	23 May	Beijing	3	0

v CIS

				E	*C*
	1992	29 Apr	Moscow	2	2

v COLOMBIA

				E	*C*
	1970	20 May	Bogota	4	0
	1988	24 May	Wembley	1	1
	1995	6 Sept	Wembley	0	0
WC	1998	26 June	Lens	2	0
	2005	31 May	New Jersey	3	2
WC	2018	3 July	Moscow	1	1

v COSTA RICA

				E	*C*
WC	2014	26 June	Belo Horizonte	0	0
	2018	7 June	Leeds	2	0

v CROATIA

				E	*C*
	1996	24 Apr	Wembley	0	0
	2003	20 Aug	Ipswich	3	1
EC	2004	21 June	Lisbon	4	2
EC	2006	11 Oct	Zagreb	0	2
EC	2007	21 Nov	Wembley	2	3
WC	2008	10 Sept	Zagreb	4	1
WC	2009	9 Sept	Wembley	5	1
WC	2018	11 July	Moscow	1	2
NL	**2018**	**12 Oct**	**Rijeka**	**0**	**0**
NL	**2018**	**18 Nov**	**Wembley**	**2**	**1**

v CYPRUS

				E	*C*
EC	1975	16 Apr	Wembley	5	0
EC	1975	11 May	Limassol	1	0

v CZECHOSLOVAKIA

				E	*C*
	1934	16 May	Prague	1	2
	1937	1 Dec	Tottenham	5	4
	1963	29 May	Bratislava	4	2
	1966	2 Nov	Wembley	0	0
WC	1970	11 June	Guadalajara	1	0
	1973	27 May	Prague	1	1
EC	1974	30 Oct	Wembley	3	0
EC	1975	30 Oct	Bratislava	1	2
	1978	29 Nov	Wembley	1	0
WC	1982	20 June	Bilbao	2	0
	1990	25 Apr	Wembley	4	2
	1992	25 Mar	Prague	2	2

v CZECH REPUBLIC

				E	*C*
	1998	18 Nov	Wembley	2	0
	2008	20 Aug	Wembley	2	2
EC	**2019**	**22 Mar**	**Wembley**	**5**	**0**

v DENMARK

				E	*D*
	1948	26 Sept	Copenhagen	0	0
	1955	2 Oct	Copenhagen	5	1
WC	1956	5 Dec	Wolverhampton	5	2
WC	1957	15 May	Copenhagen	4	1
	1966	3 July	Copenhagen	2	0
EC	1978	20 Sept	Copenhagen	4	3
EC	1979	12 Sept	Wembley	1	0
EC	1982	22 Sept	Copenhagen	2	2
EC	1983	21 Sept	Wembley	0	1
	1988	14 Sept	Wembley	1	0
	1989	7 June	Copenhagen	1	1
	1990	15 May	Wembley	1	0
EC	1992	11 June	Malmo	0	0
	1994	9 Mar	Wembley	1	0
WC	2002	15 June	Niigata	3	0
	2003	16 Nov	Old Trafford	2	3
	2005	17 Aug	Copenhagen	1	4
	2011	9 Feb	Copenhagen	2	1
	2014	5 Mar	Wembley	1	0

v ECUADOR

				E	*Ec*
	1970	24 May	Quito	2	0
WC	2006	25 June	Stuttgart	1	0
	2014	4 June	Miami	2	2

v EGYPT

				E	*Eg*
	1986	29 Jan	Cairo	4	0
WC	1990	21 June	Cagliari	1	0
	2010	3 Mar	Wembley	3	1

v ESTONIA

				E	*Es*
EC	2007	6 June	Tallinn	3	0
EC	2007	13 Oct	Wembley	3	0
EC	2014	12 Oct	Tallinn	1	0
EC	2015	9 Oct	Wembley	2	0

v FIFA

				E	*FIFA*
	1938	26 Oct	Highbury	3	0
	1953	21 Oct	Wembley	4	4
	1963	23 Oct	Wembley	2	1

v FINLAND

				E	*F*
	1937	20 May	Helsinki	8	0
	1956	20 May	Helsinki	5	1
	1966	26 June	Helsinki	3	0
WC	1976	13 June	Helsinki	4	1
WC	1976	13 Oct	Wembley	2	1
	1982	3 June	Helsinki	4	1
WC	1984	17 Oct	Wembley	5	0
WC	1985	22 May	Helsinki	1	1
	1992	3 June	Helsinki	2	1
WC	2000	11 Oct	Helsinki	0	0
WC	2001	24 Mar	Liverpool	2	1

v FRANCE

				E	*F*
	1923	10 May	Paris	4	1
	1924	17 May	Paris	3	1
	1925	21 May	Paris	3	2
	1927	26 May	Paris	6	0
	1928	17 May	Paris	5	1
	1929	9 May	Paris	4	1
	1931	14 May	Paris	2	5
	1933	6 Dec	Tottenham	4	1
	1938	26 May	Paris	4	2
	1947	3 May	Highbury	3	0
	1949	22 May	Paris	3	1
	1951	3 Oct	Highbury	2	2
	1955	15 May	Paris	0	1
	1957	27 Nov	Wembley	4	0
EC	1962	3 Oct	Sheffield	1	1
EC	1963	27 Feb	Paris	2	5
WC	1966	20 July	Wembley	2	0
	1969	12 Mar	Wembley	5	0

			E	*F*
wc1982	16 June	Bilbao	3	1
1984	29 Feb	Paris	0	2
1992	19 Feb	Wembley	2	0
ec1992	14 June	Malmo	0	0
tf1997	7 June	Montpellier	1	0
1999	10 Feb	Wembley	0	2
2000	2 Sept	Paris	1	1
ec2004	13 June	Lisbon	1	2
2008	26 Mar	Paris	0	1
2010	17 Nov	Wembley	1	2
ec2012	11 June	Donetsk	1	1
2015	17 Nov	Wembley	2	0
2017	13 June	Paris	2	3

v GEORGIA

			E	*G*
wc1996	9 Nov	Tbilisi	2	0
wc1997	30 Apr	Wembley	2	0

v GERMANY

			E	*G*
1930	10 May	Berlin	3	3
1935	4 Dec	Tottenham	3	0
1938	14 May	Berlin	6	3
1991	11 Sept	Wembley	0	1
1993	19 June	Detroit	1	2
ec1996	26 June	Wembley	1	1*
ec2000	17 June	Charleroi	1	0
wc2000	7 Oct	Wembley	0	1
wc2001	1 Sept	Munich	5	1
2007	22 Aug	Wembley	1	2
2008	19 Nov	Berlin	2	1
wc2010	27 June	Bloemfontein	1	4
2013	19 Nov	Wembley	0	1
2016	26 Mar	Berlin	3	2
2017	22 Mar	Dortmund	0	1
2017	10 Nov	Wembley	0	0

v EAST GERMANY

			E	*EG*
1963	2 June	Leipzig	2	1
1970	25 Nov	Wembley	3	1
1974	29 May	Leipzig	1	1
1984	12 Sept	Wembley	1	0

v WEST GERMANY

			E	*WG*
1954	1 Dec	Wembley	3	1
1956	26 May	Berlin	3	1
1965	12 May	Nuremberg	1	0
1966	23 Feb	Wembley	1	0
wc1966	30 July	Wembley	4	2*
1968	1 June	Hanover	0	1
wc1970	14 June	Leon	2	3*
ec1972	29 Apr	Wembley	1	3
ec1972	13 May	Berlin	0	0
1975	12 Mar	Wembley	2	0
1978	22 Feb	Munich	1	2
wc1982	29 June	Madrid	0	0
1982	13 Oct	Wembley	1	2
1985	12 June	Mexico City	3	0
1987	9 Sept	Dusseldorf	1	3
wc1990	4 July	Turin	1	1*

v GHANA

			E	*G*
2011	29 Mar	Wembley	1	1

v GREECE

			E	*G*
ec1971	21 Apr	Wembley	3	0
ec1971	1 Dec	Piraeus	2	0
ec1982	17 Nov	Salonika	3	0
ec1983	30 Mar	Wembley	0	0
1989	8 Feb	Athens	2	1
1994	17 May	Wembley	5	0
wc2001	6 June	Athens	2	0
wc2001	6 Oct	Old Trafford	2	2
2006	16 Aug	Old Trafford	4	0

v HONDURAS

			E	*H*
2014	7 June	Miami	0	0

v HUNGARY

			E	*H*
1908	10 June	Budapest	7	0
1909	29 May	Budapest	4	2
1909	31 May	Budapest	8	2
1934	10 May	Budapest	1	2
1936	2 Dec	Highbury	6	2
1953	25 Nov	Wembley	3	6
1954	23 May	Budapest	1	7
1960	22 May	Budapest	0	2
wc1962	31 May	Rancagua	1	2
1965	5 May	Wembley	1	0
1978	24 May	Wembley	4	1
wc1981	6 June	Budapest	3	1
wc1982	18 Nov	Wembley	1	0
ec1983	27 Apr	Wembley	2	0
ec1983	12 Oct	Budapest	3	0
1988	27 Apr	Budapest	0	0
1990	12 Sept	Wembley	1	0
1992	12 May	Budapest	1	0
1996	18 May	Wembley	3	0
1999	28 Apr	Budapest	1	1
2006	30 May	Old Trafford	3	1
2010	11 Aug	Wembley	2	1

v ICELAND

			E	*I*
1982	2 June	Reykjavik	1	1
2004	5 June	City of Manchester	6	1
ec2016	27 June	Nice	1	2

v ISRAEL

			E	*I*
1986	26 Feb	Ramat Gan	2	1
1988	17 Feb	Tel Aviv	0	0
ec2007	24 Mar	Tel Aviv	0	0
ec2007	8 Sept	Wembley	3	0

v ITALY

			E	*I*
1933	13 May	Rome	1	1
1934	14 Nov	Highbury	3	2
1939	13 May	Milan	2	2
1948	16 May	Turin	4	0
1949	30 Nov	Tottenham	2	0
1952	18 May	Florence	1	1
1959	6 May	Wembley	2	2
1961	24 May	Rome	3	2
1973	14 June	Turin	0	2
1973	14 Nov	Wembley	0	1
1976	28 May	New York	3	2
wc1976	17 Nov	Rome	0	2
wc1977	16 Nov	Wembley	2	0
ec1980	15 June	Turin	0	1
1985	6 June	Mexico City	1	2
1989	15 Nov	Wembley	0	0
wc1990	7 July	Bari	1	2
wc1997	12 Feb	Wembley	0	1
tf1997	4 June	Nantes	2	0
wc1997	11 Oct	Rome	0	0
2000	15 Nov	Turin	0	1
2002	27 Mar	Leeds	1	2
ec2012	24 June	Kiev	0	0
2012	15 Aug	Berne	2	1
wc2014	14 June	Manaus	1	2
2015	31 Mar	Turin	1	1
2018	27 Mar	Wembley	1	1

v JAMAICA

			E	*J*
2006	3 June	Old Trafford	6	0

v JAPAN

			E	*J*
ui1995	3 June	Wembley	2	1
2004	1 June	City of Manchester	1	1
2010	30 May	Graz	2	1

v KAZAKHSTAN

			E	*K*
wc2008	11 Oct	Wembley	5	1
wc2009	6 June	Almaty	4	0

v KOREA REPUBLIC

			E	*KR*
2002	21 May	Seoguipo	1	1

v KUWAIT

			E	*K*
wc1982	25 June	Bilbao	1	0

v LIECHTENSTEIN

			E	*L*
ec2003	29 Mar	Vaduz	2	0
ec2003	10 Sept	Old Trafford	2	0

v LITHUANIA

			E	*L*
ec2015	27 Mar	Wembley	4	0
ec2015	12 Oct	Vilnius	3	0
wc2017	26 Mar	Wembley	2	0
wc2017	8 Oct	Vilnius	1	0

v LUXEMBOURG

			E	*L*
1927	21 May	Esch-sur-Alzette	5	2
wc1960	19 Oct	Luxembourg	9	0
wc1961	28 Sept	Highbury	4	1
wc1977	30 Mar	Wembley	5	0
wc1977	12 Oct	Luxembourg	2	0

			E	*L*
EC1982	15 Dec	Wembley	9	0
EC1983	16 Nov	Luxembourg	4	0
EC1998	14 Oct	Luxembourg	3	0
EC1999	4 Sept	Wembley	6	0
EC2006	7 Oct	Old Trafford	0	0

		v MALAYSIA	*E*	*M*
1991	12 June	Kuala Lumpur	4	2

		v MALTA	*E*	*M*
EC1971	3 Feb	Valletta	1	0
EC1971	12 May	Wembley	5	0
2000	3 June	Valletta	2	1
WC2016	8 Oct	Wembley	2	0
WC2017	1 Sept	Ta'Qali	4	0

		v MEXICO	*E*	*M*
1959	24 May	Mexico City	1	2
1961	10 May	Wembley	8	0
WC1966	16 July	Wembley	2	0
1969	1 June	Mexico City	0	0
1985	9 June	Mexico City	0	1
1986	17 May	Los Angeles	3	0
1997	29 Mar	Wembley	2	0
2001	25 May	Derby	4	0
2010	24 May	Wembley	3	1

		v MOLDOVA	*E*	*M*
WC1996	1 Sept	Chisinau	3	0
WC1997	10 Sept	Wembley	4	0
WC2012	7 Sept	Chisinau	5	0
WC2013	6 Sept	Wembley	4	0

		v MONTENEGRO	*E*	*M*
EC1989	8 Mar	Tirana	2	0
2010	12 Oct	Wembley	0	0
EC2011	7 Oct	Podgorica	2	2
WC2013	26 Mar	Podgorica	1	1
WC2013	11 Oct	Wembley	4	1
EC2019	**25 Mar**	**Podgorica**	**5**	**1**

		v MOROCCO	*E*	*M*
WC1986	6 June	Monterrey	0	0
1998	27 May	Casablanca	1	0

		v NETHERLANDS	*E*	*N*
1935	18 May	Amsterdam	1	0
1946	27 Nov	Huddersfield	8	2
1964	9 Dec	Amsterdam	1	1
1969	5 Nov	Amsterdam	1	0
1970	14 June	Wembley	0	0
1977	9 Feb	Wembley	0	2
1982	25 May	Wembley	2	0
1988	23 Mar	Wembley	2	2
EC1988	15 June	Dusseldorf	1	3
WC1990	16 June	Cagliari	0	0
2005	9 Feb	Villa Park	0	0
WC1993	28 Apr	Wembley	2	2
WC1993	13 Oct	Rotterdam	0	2
EC1996	18 June	Wembley	4	1
2001	15 Aug	Tottenham	0	2
2002	13 Feb	Amsterdam	1	1
2006	15 Nov	Amsterdam	1	1
2009	12 Aug	Amsterdam	2	2
2012	29 Feb	Wembley	2	3
2016	29 Mar	Wembley	1	2
2018	23 Mar	Amsterdam	1	0
NL2019	**6 June**	**Guimaraes**	**1**	**3**

		v NEW ZEALAND	*E*	*NZ*
1991	3 June	Auckland	1	0
1991	8 June	Wellington	2	0

		v NIGERIA	*E*	*N*
1994	16 Nov	Wembley	1	0
WC2002	12 June	Osaka	0	0
2018	2 June	Wembley	2	1

		v NORTH MACEDONIA	*E*	*M*
EC2002	16 Oct	Southampton	2	2
EC2003	6 Sept	Skopje	2	1
EC2006	6 Sept	Skopje	1	0

		v NORWAY	*E*	*N*
1937	14 May	Oslo	6	0
1938	9 Nov	Newcastle	4	0
1949	18 May	Oslo	4	1
1966	29 June	Oslo	6	1
WC1980	10 Sept	Wembley	4	0
WC1981	9 Sept	Oslo	1	2
WC1992	14 Oct	Wembley	1	1
WC1993	2 June	Oslo	0	2
1994	22 May	Wembley	0	0
1995	11 Oct	Oslo	0	0
2012	26 May	Oslo	1	0
2014	3 Sept	Wembley	1	0

		v PANAMA	*E*	*P*
WC2018	24 June	Nizhny Novgorod	6	1

		v PARAGUAY	*E*	*P*
WC1986	18 June	Mexico City	3	0
2002	17 Apr	Liverpool	4	0
WC2006	10 June	Frankfurt	1	0

		v PERU	*E*	*P*
1959	17 May	Lima	1	4
1962	20 May	Lima	4	0
2014	30 May	Wembley	3	0

		v POLAND	*E*	*P*
1966	5 Jan	Everton	1	1
1966	5 July	Chorzow	1	0
WC1973	6 June	Chorzow	0	2
WC1973	17 Oct	Wembley	1	1
WC1986	11 June	Monterrey	3	0
WC1989	3 June	Wembley	3	0
WC1989	11 Oct	Katowice	0	0
EC1990	17 Oct	Wembley	2	0
EC1991	13 Nov	Poznan	1	1
WC1993	29 May	Katowice	1	1
WC1993	8 Sept	Wembley	3	0
WC1996	9 Oct	Wembley	2	1
WC1997	31 May	Katowice	2	0
EC1999	27 Mar	Wembley	3	1
EC1999	8 Sept	Warsaw	0	0
WC2004	8 Sept	Katowice	2	1
WC2005	12 Oct	Old Trafford	2	1
WC2012	17 Oct	Warsaw	1	1
WC2013	15 Oct	Wembley	2	0

		v PORTUGAL	*E*	*P*
1947	25 May	Lisbon	10	0
1950	14 May	Lisbon	5	3
1951	19 May	Everton	5	2
1955	22 May	Oporto	1	3
1958	7 May	Wembley	2	1
WC1961	21 May	Lisbon	1	1
WC1961	25 Oct	Wembley	2	0
1964	17 May	Lisbon	4	3
1964	4 June	São Paulo	1	1
WC1966	26 July	Wembley	2	1
1969	10 Dec	Wembley	1	0
1974	3 Apr	Lisbon	0	0
EC1974	20 Nov	Wembley	0	0
EC1975	19 Nov	Lisbon	1	1
WC1986	3 June	Monterrey	0	1
1995	12 Dec	Wembley	1	1
1998	22 Apr	Wembley	3	0
EC2000	12 June	Eindhoven	2	3
2002	7 Sept	Villa Park	1	1
2004	18 Feb	Faro	1	1
EC2004	24 June	Lisbon	2	2*
WC2006	1 July	Gelsenkirchen	0	0
2016	2 June	Wembley	1	0

		v REPUBLIC OF IRELAND	*E*	*RI*
1946	30 Sept	Dublin	1	0
1949	21 Sept	Everton	0	2
WC1957	8 May	Wembley	5	1
WC1957	19 May	Dublin	1	1
1964	24 May	Dublin	3	1
1976	8 Sept	Wembley	1	1
EC1978	25 Oct	Dublin	1	1
EC1980	6 Feb	Wembley	2	0
1985	26 Mar	Wembley	2	1
EC1988	12 June	Stuttgart	0	1
WC1990	11 June	Cagliari	1	1
EC1990	14 Nov	Dublin	1	1
EC1991	27 Mar	Wembley	1	1
1995	15 Feb	Dublin	0	1
(abandoned after 27 mins)				
2013	29 May	Wembley	1	1
2015	7 June	Dublin	0	0

		v ROMANIA	*E*	*R*
1939	24 May	Bucharest	2	0
1968	6 Nov	Bucharest	0	0
1969	15 Jan	Wembley	1	1
wc1970	2 June	Guadalajara	1	0
wc1980	15 Oct	Bucharest	1	2
wc1981	29 April	Wembley	0	0
wc1985	1 May	Bucharest	0	0
wc1985	11 Sept	Wembley	1	1
1994	12 Oct	Wembley	1	1
wc1998	22 June	Toulouse	1	2
EC2000	20 June	Charleroi	2	3

		v RUSSIA	*E*	*R*
EC2007	12 Sept	Wembley	3	0
EC2007	17 Oct	Moscow	1	2
EC2016	11 June	Marseille	1	1

		v SAN MARINO	*E*	*SM*
wc1992	17 Feb	Wembley	6	0
wc1993	17 Nov	Bologna	7	1
wc2012	12 Oct	Wembley	5	0
wc2013	22 Mar	Serravalle	8	0
EC2014	9 Oct	Wembley	5	0
EC2015	5 Sept	Serravalle	6	0

		v SAUDI ARABIA	*E*	*SA*
1988	16 Nov	Riyadh	1	1
1998	23 May	Wembley	0	0

		v SERBIA-MONTENEGRO	*E*	*SM*
2003	3 June	Leicester	2	1

		v SLOVAKIA	*E*	*S*
EC2002	12 Oct	Bratislava	2	1
EC2003	11 June	Middlesbrough	2	1
2009	28 Mar	Wembley	4	0
EC2016	20 June	Lille	0	0
wc2016	4 Sept	Trnava	1	0
wc2017	4 Sept	Wembley	2	1

		v SLOVENIA	*E*	*S*
2009	5 Sept	Wembley	2	1
wc2010	23 June	Port Elizabeth	1	0
EC2014	15 Nov	Wembley	3	1
EC2015	14 June	Ljubljana	3	2
wc2016	11 Oct	Ljubljana	0	0
wc2017	5 Oct	Wembley	1	0

		v SOUTH AFRICA	*E*	*SA*
1997	24 May	Old Trafford	2	1
2003	22 May	Durban	2	1

		v SPAIN	*E*	*S*
1929	15 May	Madrid	3	4
1931	9 Dec	Highbury	7	1
wc1950	2 July	Rio de Janeiro	0	1
1955	18 May	Madrid	1	1
1955	30 Nov	Wembley	4	1
1960	15 May	Madrid	0	3
1960	26 Oct	Wembley	4	2
1965	8 Dec	Madrid	2	0
1967	24 May	Wembley	2	0
EC1968	3 Apr	Wembley	1	0
EC1968	8 May	Madrid	2	1
1980	26 Mar	Barcelona	2	0
EC1980	18 June	Naples	2	1
1981	25 Mar	Wembley	1	2
wc1982	5 July	Madrid	0	0
1987	18 Feb	Madrid	4	2
1992	9 Sept	Santander	0	1
EC 1996	22 June	Wembley	0	0
2001	28 Feb	Villa Park	3	0
2004	17 Nov	Madrid	0	1
2007	7 Feb	Old Trafford	0	1
2009	11 Feb	Seville	0	2
2011	12 Nov	Wembley	1	0
2015	13 Nov	Alicante	0	2
2016	15 Nov	Wembley	2	2
NL2018	**8 Sept**	**Wembley**	**1**	**2**
NL2018	**15 Oct**	**Seville**	**3**	**2**

		v SWEDEN	*E*	*S*
1923	21 May	Stockholm	4	2
1923	24 May	Stockholm	3	1
1937	17 May	Stockholm	4	0
1947	19 Nov	Highbury	4	2
1949	13 May	Stockholm	1	3
1956	16 May	Stockholm	0	0
1959	28 Oct	Wembley	2	3
1965	16 May	Gothenburg	2	1
1968	22 May	Wembley	3	1
1979	10 June	Stockholm	0	0
1986	10 Sept	Stockholm	0	1
wc1988	19 Oct	Wembley	0	0
wc1989	6 Sept	Stockholm	0	0
EC1992	17 June	Stockholm	1	2
UI1995	8 June	Leeds	3	3
EC1998	5 Sept	Stockholm	1	2
EC1999	5 June	Wembley	0	0
2001	10 Nov	Old Trafford	1	1
wc2002	2 June	Saitama	1	1
2004	31 Mar	Gothenburg	0	1
wc2006	20 June	Cologne	2	2
2011	15 Nov	Wembley	1	0
EC2012	15 June	Kiev	3	2
2012	14 Nov	Stockholm	2	4
wc2018	7 July	Samara	2	0

		v SWITZERLAND	*E*	*S*
1933	20 May	Berne	4	0
1938	21 May	Zurich	1	2
1947	18 May	Zurich	0	1
1948	2 Dec	Highbury	6	0
1952	28 May	Zurich	3	0
wc1954	20 June	Berne	2	0
1962	9 May	Wembley	3	1
1963	5 June	Basle	8	1
EC1971	13 Oct	Basle	3	2
EC1971	10 Nov	Wembley	1	1
1975	3 Sept	Basle	2	1
1977	7 Sept	Wembley	0	0
wc1980	19 Nov	Wembley	2	1
wc1981	30 May	Basle	1	2
1988	28 May	Lausanne	1	0
1995	15 Nov	Wembley	3	1
EC1996	8 June	Wembley	1	1
1998	25 Mar	Berne	1	1
EC2004	17 June	Coimbra	3	0
2008	6 Feb	Wembley	2	1
EC1989	8 Mar	Tirana	2	0
EC2010	7 Sept	Basle	3	1
EC2011	4 June	Wembley	2	2
EC2014	8 Sept	Basle	2	0
EC2015	8 Sept	Wembley	2	0
2018	**11 Sept**	**Leicester**	**1**	**0**
NL2019	**9 June**	**Guimaraes**	**0**	**0**

		v TRINIDAD & TOBAGO	*E*	*TT*
wc2006	15 June	Nuremberg	2	0
2008	2 June	Port of Spain	3	0

		v TUNISIA	*E*	*T*
1990	2 June	Tunis	1	1
wc1998	15 June	Marseilles	2	0
wc2018	18 June	Volgograd	2	1

		v TURKEY	*E*	*T*
wc1984	14 Nov	Istanbul	8	0
wc1985	16 Oct	Wembley	5	0
EC1987	29 Apr	Izmir	0	0
EC1987	14 Oct	Wembley	8	0
EC1991	1 May	Izmir	1	0
EC1991	16 Oct	Wembley	1	0
wc1992	18 Nov	Wembley	4	0
wc1993	31 Mar	Izmir	2	0
EC2003	2 Apr	Sunderland	2	0
EC2003	11 Oct	Istanbul	0	0
2016	22 May	Etihad Stadium	2	1

		v UKRAINE	*E*	*U*
2000	31 May	Wembley	2	0
2004	18 Aug	Newcastle	3	0
wc2009	1 Apr	Wembley	2	1
wc2009	10 Oct	Dnepr	0	1
EC2012	19 June	Donetsk	1	0
wc2012	11 Sept	Wembley	1	1
wc2013	10 Sept	Kiev	0	0

		v URUGUAY	*E*	*U*
1953	31 May	Montevideo	1	2
wc1954	26 June	Basle	2	4
1964	6 May	Wembley	2	1
wc1966	11 July	Wembley	0	0

			E	*U*
1969	8 June	Montevideo	2	1
1977	15 June	Montevideo	0	0
1984	13 June	Montevideo	0	2
1990	22 May	Wembley	1	2
1995	29 Mar	Wembley	0	0
2006	1 Mar	Liverpool	2	1
WC2014	19 June	Sao Paulo	1	2

		v USA	*E*	*USA*
WC1950	29 June	Belo Horizonte	0	1
1953	8 June	New York	6	3
1959	28 May	Los Angeles	8	1
1964	27 May	New York	10	0
1985	16 June	Los Angeles	5	0
1993	9 June	Foxboro	0	2
1994	7 Sept	Wembley	2	0
2005	28 May	Chicago	2	1
2008	28 May	Wembley	2	0
WC2010	12 June	Rustenburg	1	1
2018	**15 Nov**	**Wembley**	**3**	**0**

		v USSR	*E*	*USSR*
1958	18 May	Moscow	1	1
WC1958	8 June	Gothenburg	2	2
WC1958	17 June	Gothenburg	0	1
1958	22 Oct	Wembley	5	0
1967	6 Dec	Wembley	2	2
EC1968	8 June	Rome	2	0
1973	10 June	Moscow	2	1
1984	2 June	Wembley	0	2
1986	26 Mar	Tbilisi	1	0
EC1988	18 June	Frankfurt	1	3
1991	21 May	Wembley	3	1

		v YUGOSLAVIA	*E*	*Y*
1939	18 May	Belgrade	1	2
1950	22 Nov	Highbury	2	2
1954	16 May	Belgrade	0	1
1956	28 Nov	Wembley	3	0
1958	11 May	Belgrade	0	5
1960	11 May	Wembley	3	3
1965	9 May	Belgrade	1	1
1966	4 May	Wembley	2	0
EC1968	5 June	Florence	0	1
1972	11 Oct	Wembley	1	1
1974	5 June	Belgrade	2	2
EC1986	12 Nov	Wembley	2	0
EC1987	11 Nov	Belgrade	4	1
1989	13 Dec	Wembley	2	1

SCOTLAND

		v ALBANIA	*S*	*A*
NL2018	**10 Sept**	**Glasgow**	**2**	**0**
NL2018	**17 Nov**	**Shkoder**	**4**	**0**

		v ARGENTINA	*S*	*A*
1977	18 June	Buenos Aires	1	1
1979	2 June	Glasgow	1	3
1990	28 Mar	Glasgow	1	0
2008	19 Nov	Glasgow	0	1

		v AUSTRALIA	*S*	*A*
WC1985	20 Nov	Glasgow	2	0
WC1985	4 Dec	Melbourne	0	0
1996	27 Mar	Glasgow	1	0
2000	15 Nov	Glasgow	0	2
2012	15 Aug	Easter Road	3	1

		v AUSTRIA	*S*	*A*
1931	16 May	Vienna	0	5
1933	29 Nov	Glasgow	2	2
1937	9 May	Vienna	1	1
1950	13 Dec	Glasgow	0	1
1951	27 May	Vienna	0	4
WC1954	16 June	Zurich	0	1
1955	19 May	Vienna	4	1
1956	2 May	Glasgow	1	1
1960	29 May	Vienna	1	4
1963	8 May	Glasgow	4	1
(*abandoned after 79 mins*)				
WC1968	6 Nov	Glasgow	2	1
WC1969	5 Nov	Vienna	0	2
EC1978	20 Sept	Vienna	2	3
EC1979	17 Oct	Glasgow	1	1
1994	20 Apr	Vienna	2	1
WC1996	31 Aug	Vienna	0	0
WC1997	2 Apr	Celtic Park	2	0
2003	30 Apr	Glasgow	0	2
2005	17 Aug	Graz	2	2
2007	30 May	Vienna	1	0

		v BELARUS	*S*	*B*
WC1997	8 June	Minsk	1	0
WC1997	7 Sept	Aberdeen	4	1
WC2005	8 June	Minsk	0	0
WC2005	8 Oct	Glasgow	0	1

		v BELGIUM	*S*	*B*
1946	23 Jan	Glasgow	2	2
1947	18 May	Brussels	1	2
1948	28 Apr	Glasgow	2	0
1951	20 May	Brussels	5	0
EC1971	3 Feb	Liege	0	3
EC1971	10 Nov	Aberdeen	1	0
1974	1 June	Brussels	1	2
EC1979	21 Nov	Brussels	0	2
EC1979	19 Dec	Glasgow	1	3
EC1982	15 Dec	Brussels	2	3
EC1983	12 Oct	Glasgow	1	1
EC1987	1 Apr	Brussels	1	4
EC1987	14 Oct	Glasgow	2	0
WC2001	24 Mar	Glasgow	2	2
WC2001	5 Sept	Brussels	0	2
WC2012	16 Oct	Brussels	0	2
WC2013	6 Sept	Glasgow	0	2
2018	**7 Sept**	**Glasgow**	**0**	**4**
EC2019	**11 June**	**Brussels**	**0**	**3**

		v BOSNIA-HERZEGOVINA	*S*	*BH*
EC1999	4 Sept	Sarajevo	2	1
EC1999	5 Oct	Ibrox	1	0

		v BRAZIL	*S*	*B*
1966	25 June	Glasgow	1	1
1972	5 July	Rio de Janeiro	0	1
1973	30 June	Glasgow	0	1
WC1974	18 June	Frankfurt	0	0
1977	23 June	Rio de Janeiro	0	2
WC1982	18 June	Seville	1	4
1987	26 May	Glasgow	0	2
WC1990	20 June	Turin	0	1
WC1998	10 June	St Denis	1	2
2011	27 Mar	Emirates	0	2

		v BULGARIA	*S*	*B*
1978	22 Feb	Glasgow	2	1
EC1986	10 Sept	Glasgow	0	0
EC1987	11 Nov	Sofia	1	0
EC1990	14 Nov	Sofia	1	1
EC1991	27 Mar	Glasgow	1	1
2006	11 May	Kobe	5	1

		v CANADA	*S*	*C*
1983	12 June	Vancouver	2	0
1983	16 June	Edmonton	3	0
1983	20 June	Toronto	2	0
1992	21 May	Toronto	3	1
2002	15 Oct	Easter Road	3	1
2017	22 Mar	Easter Road	1	1

		v CHILE	*S*	*C*
1977	15 June	Santiago	4	2
1989	30 May	Glasgow	2	0

		v CIS	*S*	*C*
EC1992	18 June	Norrkoping	3	0

		v COLOMBIA	*S*	*C*
1988	17 May	Glasgow	0	0
1996	29 May	Miami	0	1
1998	23 May	New York	2	2

v COSTA RICA			*S*	*CR*
wc1990	11 June	Genoa	0	1
2018	23 Mar	Glasgow	0	1

v CROATIA			*S*	*C*
wc2000	11 Oct	Zagreb	1	1
wc2001	1 Sept	Glasgow	0	0
2008	26 Mar	Glasgow	1	1
wc2013	7 June	Zagreb	1	0
wc2013	15 Oct	Glasgow	2	0

v CYPRUS			*S*	*C*
wc1968	11 Dec	Nicosia	5	0
wc1969	17 May	Glasgow	8	0
wc1989	8 Feb	Limassol	3	2
wc1989	26 Apr	Glasgow	2	1
2011	11 Nov	Larnaca	2	1
EC2019	**8 June**	**Glasgow**	**2**	**1**

v CZECHOSLOVAKIA			*S*	*C*
1937	15 May	Prague	3	1
1937	8 Dec	Glasgow	5	0
wc1961	14 May	Bratislava	0	4
wc1961	26 Sept	Glasgow	3	2
wc1961	29 Nov	Brussels	2	4*
1972	2 July	Porto Alegre	0	0
wc1973	26 Sept	Glasgow	2	1
wc1973	17 Oct	Bratislava	0	1
wc1976	13 Oct	Prague	0	2
wc1977	21 Sept	Glasgow	3	1

v CZECH REPUBLIC			*S*	*C*
EC1999	31 Mar	Glasgow	1	2
EC1999	9 June	Prague	2	3
2008	30 May	Prague	1	3
2010	3 Mar	Glasgow	1	0
EC2010	8 Oct	Prague	0	1
EC2011	3 Sept	Glasgow	2	2
2016	24 Mar	Prague	1	0

v DENMARK			*S*	*D*
1951	12 May	Glasgow	3	1
1952	25 May	Copenhagen	2	1
1968	16 Oct	Copenhagen	1	0
EC1970	11 Nov	Glasgow	1	0
EC1971	9 June	Copenhagen	0	1
wc1972	18 Oct	Copenhagen	4	1
wc1972	15 Nov	Glasgow	2	0
EC1975	3 Sept	Copenhagen	1	0
EC1975	29 Oct	Glasgow	3	1
wc1986	4 June	Nezahualcoyotl	0	1
1996	24 Apr	Copenhagen	0	2
1998	25 Mar	Ibrox	0	1
2002	21 Aug	Glasgow	0	1
2004	28 Apr	Copenhagen	0	1
2011	10 Aug	Glasgow	2	1
2016	29 Mar	Glasgow	1	0

v ECUADOR			*S*	*E*
1995	24 May	Toyama	2	1

v EGYPT			*S*	*E*
1990	16 May	Aberdeen	1	3

v ESTONIA			*S*	*E*
wc1993	19 May	Tallinn	3	0
wc1993	2 June	Aberdeen	3	1
wc1997	11 Feb	Monaco	0	0
wc1997	29 Mar	Kilmarnock	2	0
EC1998	10 Oct	Tynecastle	3	2
EC1999	8 Sept	Tallinn	0	0
2004	27 May	Tallinn	1	0
2013	6 Feb	Aberdeen	1	0

v FAROE ISLANDS			*S*	*F*
EC1994	12 Oct	Glasgow	5	1
EC1995	7 June	Toftir	2	0
EC1998	14 Oct	Aberdeen	2	1
EC1999	5 June	Toftir	1	1
EC2002	7 Sept	Toftir	2	2
EC2003	6 Sept	Glasgow	3	1
EC2006	2 Sept	Celtic Park	6	0
EC2007	6 June	Toftir	2	0
2010	16 Nov	Aberdeen	3	0

v FINLAND			*S*	*F*
1954	25 May	Helsinki	2	1
wc1964	21 Oct	Glasgow	3	1
wc1965	27 May	Helsinki	2	1
1976	8 Sept	Glasgow	6	0
1992	25 Mar	Glasgow	1	1
EC1994	7 Sept	Helsinki	2	0
EC1995	6 Sept	Glasgow	1	0
1998	22 Apr	Easter Road	1	1

v FRANCE			*S*	*F*
1930	18 May	Paris	2	0
1932	8 May	Paris	3	1
1948	23 May	Paris	0	3
1949	27 Apr	Glasgow	2	0
1950	27 May	Paris	1	0
1951	16 May	Glasgow	1	0
wc1958	15 June	Orebro	1	2
1984	1 June	Marseilles	0	2
wc1989	8 Mar	Glasgow	2	0
wc1989	11 Oct	Paris	0	3
1997	12 Nov	St Etienne	1	2
2000	29 Mar	Glasgow	0	2
2002	27 Mar	Paris	0	5
EC2006	7 Oct	Glasgow	1	0
EC2007	12 Sept	Paris	1	0
2016	4 June	Metz	0	3

v GEORGIA			*S*	*G*
EC2007	24 Mar	Glasgow	2	1
EC2007	17 Oct	Tbilisi	0	2
EC2014	11 Oct	Ibrox	1	0
EC2015	4 Sept	Tblisi	0	1

v GERMANY			*S*	*G*
1929	1 June	Berlin	1	1
1936	14 Oct	Glasgow	2	0
EC1992	15 June	Norrkoping	0	2
1993	24 Mar	Glasgow	0	1
1999	28 Apr	Bremen	1	0
EC2003	7 June	Glasgow	1	1
EC2003	10 Sept	Dortmund	1	2
EC2014	7 Sept	Dortmund	1	2
EC2015	7 Sept	Glasgow	2	3

v EAST GERMANY			*S*	*EG*
1974	30 Oct	Glasgow	3	0
1977	7 Sept	East Berlin	0	1
EC1982	13 Oct	Glasgow	2	0
EC1983	16 Nov	Halle	1	2
1985	16 Oct	Glasgow	0	0
1990	25 Apr	Glasgow	0	1

v WEST GERMANY			*S*	*WG*
1957	22 May	Stuttgart	3	1
1959	6 May	Glasgow	3	2
1964	12 May	Hanover	2	2
wc1969	16 Apr	Glasgow	1	1
wc1969	22 Oct	Hamburg	2	3
1973	14 Nov	Glasgow	1	1
1974	27 Mar	Frankfurt	1	2
wc1986	8 June	Queretaro	1	2

v GIBRALTAR			*S*	*G*
EC2015	29 Mar	Hampden	6	1
EC2015	11 Oct	Faro	6	0

v GREECE			*S*	*G*
EC1994	18 Dec	Athens	0	1
EC1995	16 Aug	Glasgow	1	0

v HONG KONG XI			*S*	*HK*
†2002	23 May	Hong Kong	4	0

†match not recognised by FIFA

v HUNGARY			*S*	*H*
1938	7 Dec	Ibrox	3	1
1954	8 Dec	Glasgow	2	4
1955	29 May	Budapest	1	3
1958	7 May	Glasgow	1	1
1960	5 June	Budapest	3	3
1980	31 May	Budapest	1	3
1987	9 Sept	Glasgow	2	0
2004	18 Aug	Glasgow	0	3
2018	27 Mar	Budapest	1	0

		v ICELAND	*S*	*I*
WC1984	17 Oct	Glasgow	3	0
WC1985	28 May	Reykjavik	1	0
EC2002	12 Oct	Reykjavik	2	0
EC2003	29 Mar	Glasgow	2	1
WC2008	10 Sept	Reykjavik	2	1
WC2009	1 Apr	Glasgow	2	1

		v IRAN	*S*	*I*
WC1978	7 June	Cordoba	1	1

		v ISRAEL	*S*	*I*
WC1981	25 Feb	Tel Aviv	1	0
WC1981	28 Apr	Glasgow	3	1
1986	28 Jan	Tel Aviv	1	0
NL2018	**11 Oct**	**Haifa**	**1**	**2**
NL2018	**20 Nov**	**Glasgow**	**3**	**2**

		v ITALY	*S*	*I*
1931	20 May	Rome	0	3
WC1965	9 Nov	Glasgow	1	0
WC1965	7 Dec	Naples	0	3
1988	22 Dec	Perugia	0	2
WC1992	18 Nov	Ibrox	0	0
WC1993	13 Oct	Rome	1	3
WC2005	26 Mar	Milan	0	2
WC2005	3 Sept	Glasgow	1	1
EC2007	28 Mar	Bari	0	2
EC2007	17 Nov	Glasgow	1	2
2016	29 May	Ta'Qali	0	1

		v JAPAN	*S*	*J*
1995	21 May	Hiroshima	0	0
2006	13 May	Saitama	0	0
2009	10 Oct	Yokohama	0	2

		v KAZAKHSTAN	*S*	*K*
EC2019	**21 Mar**	**Astana**	**0**	**3**

		v KOREA REPUBLIC	*S*	*KR*
2002	16 May	Busan	1	4

		v LATVIA	*S*	*L*
WC1996	5 Oct	Riga	2	0
WC1997	11 Oct	Celtic Park	2	0
WC2000	2 Sept	Riga	1	0
WC2001	6 Oct	Glasgow	2	1

		v LIECHTENSTEIN	*S*	*L*
EC2010	7 Sept	Glasgow	2	1
EC2011	8 Oct	Vaduz	1	0

		v LITHUANIA	*S*	*L*
EC1998	5 Sept	Vilnius	0	0
EC1999	9 Oct	Glasgow	3	0
EC2003	2 Apr	Kaunas	0	1
EC2003	11 Oct	Glasgow	1	0
EC2006	6 Sept	Kaunas	2	1
EC2007	8 Sept	Glasgow	3	1
EC2010	3 Sept	Kaunas	0	0
EC2011	6 Sept	Glasgow	1	0
WC2016	8 Oct	Hampden	1	1
WC2017	1 Sept	Vilnius	3	0

		v LUXEMBOURG	*S*	*L*
1947	24 May	Luxembourg	6	0
EC1986	12 Nov	Glasgow	3	0
EC1987	2 Dec	Esch	0	0
2012	14 Nov	Luxembourg	2	1

		v MALTA	*S*	*M*
1988	22 Mar	Valletta	1	1
1990	28 May	Valletta	2	1
WC1993	17 Feb	Ibrox	3	0
WC1993	17 Nov	Valletta	2	0
1997	1 June	Valletta	3	2
WC2016	4 Sept	Ta'Qali	5	1
WC2017	4 Sept	Glasgow	2	0

		v MEXICO	*S*	*M*
2018	3 June	Mexico City	0	1

		v MOLDOVA	*S*	*M*
WC2004	13 Oct	Chisinau	1	1
WC2005	4 June	Glasgow	2	0

		v MOROCCO	*S*	*M*
WC1998	23 June	St Etienne	0	3

		v NETHERLANDS	*S*	*N*
1929	4 June	Amsterdam	2	0
1938	21 May	Amsterdam	3	1
1959	27 May	Amsterdam	2	1
1966	11 May	Glasgow	0	3
1968	30 May	Amsterdam	0	0
1971	1 Dec	Amsterdam	1	2
WC1978	11 June	Mendoza	3	2
1982	23 Mar	Glasgow	2	1
1986	29 Apr	Eindhoven	0	0
EC1992	12 June	Gothenburg	0	1
1994	23 Mar	Glasgow	0	1
1994	27 May	Utrecht	1	3
EC1996	10 June	Villa Park	0	0
2000	26 Apr	Arnhem	0	0
EC2003	15 Nov	Glasgow	1	0
EC2003	19 Nov	Amsterdam	0	6
WC2009	28 Mar	Amsterdam	0	3
WC2009	9 Sept	Glasgow	0	1
2017	9 Nov	Aberdeen	0	1

		v NEW ZEALAND	*S*	*NZ*
WC1982	15 June	Malaga	5	2
2003	27 May	Tynecastle	1	1

		v NIGERIA	*S*	*N*
2002	17 Apr	Aberdeen	1	2
2014	28 May	Craven Cottage	2	2

		v NORTH MACEDONIA	*S*	*M*
WC2008	6 Sept	Skopje	0	1
WC2009	5 Sept	Glasgow	2	0
WC2012	11 Sept	Glasgow	1	1
WC2013	10 Sept	Skopje	2	1

		v NORWAY	*S*	*N*
1929	26 May	Oslo	7	3
1954	5 May	Glasgow	1	0
1954	19 May	Oslo	1	1
1963	4 June	Bergen	3	4
1963	7 Nov	Glasgow	6	1
1974	6 June	Oslo	2	1
EC1978	25 Oct	Glasgow	3	2
EC1979	7 June	Oslo	4	0
WC1988	14 Sept	Oslo	2	1
WC1989	15 Nov	Glasgow	1	1
1992	3 June	Oslo	0	0
WC1998	16 June	Bordeaux	1	1
2003	20 Aug	Oslo	0	0
WC2004	9 Oct	Glasgow	0	1
WC2005	7 Sept	Oslo	2	1
WC2008	11 Oct	Glasgow	0	0
WC2009	12 Aug	Oslo	0	4
2013	19 Nov	Molde	1	0

		v PARAGUAY	*S*	*P*
WC1958	11 June	Norrkoping	2	3

		v PERU	*S*	*P*
1972	26 Apr	Glasgow	2	0
WC1978	3 June	Cordoba	1	3
1979	12 Sept	Glasgow	1	1
2018	30 May	Lima	0	2

		v POLAND	*S*	*P*
1958	1 June	Warsaw	2	1
1960	4 May	Glasgow	2	3
WC1965	23 May	Chorzow	1	1
WC1965	13 Oct	Glasgow	1	2
1980	28 May	Poznan	0	1
1990	19 May	Glasgow	1	1
2001	25 Apr	Bydgoszcz	1	1
2014	5 Mar	Warsaw	1	0
EC2014	14 Oct	Warsaw	2	2
EC2015	8 Oct	Glasgow	2	2

		v PORTUGAL	*S*	*P*
1950	21 May	Lisbon	2	2
1955	4 May	Glasgow	3	0
1959	3 June	Lisbon	0	1
1966	18 June	Glasgow	0	1
EC1971	21 Apr	Lisbon	0	2
EC1971	13 Oct	Glasgow	2	1
1975	13 May	Glasgow	1	0
EC1978	29 Nov	Lisbon	0	1
EC1980	26 Mar	Glasgow	4	1
WC1980	15 Oct	Glasgow	0	0
WC1981	18 Nov	Lisbon	1	2

			S	*P*
WC1992	14 Oct	Ibrox	0	0
WC1993	28 Apr	Lisbon	0	5
2002	20 Nov	Braga	0	2
2018	**14 Oct**	**Glasgow**	**1**	**3**

v QATAR

			S	*Q*
2015	5 June	Easter Road	1	0

v REPUBLIC OF IRELAND

			S	*RI*
WC1961	3 May	Glasgow	4	1
WC1961	7 May	Dublin	3	0
1963	9 June	Dublin	0	1
1969	21 Sept	Dublin	1	1
EC1986	15 Oct	Dublin	0	0
EC1987	18 Feb	Glasgow	0	1
2000	30 May	Dublin	2	1
2003	12 Feb	Glasgow	0	2
NC2011	29 May	Dublin	0	1
EC2014	14 Nov	Hampden	1	0
EC2015	13 June	Dublin	1	1

v ROMANIA

			S	*R*
EC1975	1 June	Bucharest	1	1
EC1975	17 Dec	Glasgow	1	1
1986	26 Mar	Glasgow	3	0
EC1990	12 Sept	Glasgow	2	1
EC1991	16 Oct	Bucharest	0	1
2004	31 Mar	Glasgow	1	2

v RUSSIA

			S	*R*
EC1994	16 Nov	Glasgow	1	1
EC1995	29 Mar	Moscow	0	0

v SAN MARINO

			S	*SM*
EC1991	1 May	Serravalle	2	0
EC1991	13 Nov	Glasgow	4	0
EC1995	26 Apr	Serravalle	2	0
EC1995	15 Nov	Glasgow	5	0
WC2000	7 Oct	Serravalle	2	0
WC2001	28 Mar	Glasgow	4	0
EC2019	**24 Mar**	**Serravalle**	**2**	**0**

v SAUDI ARABIA

			S	*SA*
1988	17 Feb	Riyadh	2	2

v SERBIA

			S	*Se*
WC2012	8 Sept	Glasgow	0	0
WC2013	26 Mar	Novi Sad	0	2

v SLOVAKIA

			S	*Sl*
WC2016	11 Oct	Trnava	0	3
WC2017	5 Oct	Glasgow	1	0

v SLOVENIA

			S	*Sl*
WC2004	8 Sept	Glasgow	0	0
WC2005	12 Oct	Celje	3	0
2012	29 Feb	Koper	1	1
WC2017	26 Mar	Hampden	1	0
WC2017	8 Oct	Ljubljana	2	2

v SOUTH AFRICA

			S	*SA*
2002	20 May	Hong Kong	0	2
2007	22 Aug	Aberdeen	1	0

v SPAIN

			S	*Sp*
WC1957	8 May	Glasgow	4	2
WC1957	26 May	Madrid	1	4
1963	13 June	Madrid	6	2
1965	8 May	Glasgow	0	0
EC1974	20 Nov	Glasgow	1	2
EC1975	5 Feb	Valencia	1	1
1982	24 Feb	Valencia	0	3
WC1984	14 Nov	Glasgow	3	1
WC1985	27 Feb	Seville	0	1
1988	27 Apr	Madrid	0	0
2004	3 Sept	Valencia	1	1

Match abandoned after 60 minutes; floodlight failure.

EC2010	12 Oct	Glasgow	2	3
EC2011	11 Oct	Alicante	1	3

v SWEDEN

			S	*Sw*
1952	30 May	Stockholm	1	3
1953	6 May	Glasgow	1	2
1975	16 Apr	Gothenburg	1	1
1977	27 Apr	Glasgow	3	1
WC1980	10 Sept	Stockholm	1	0
WC1981	9 Sept	Glasgow	2	0
WC1990	16 June	Genoa	2	1
1995	11 Oct	Stockholm	0	2
WC1996	10 Nov	Ibrox	1	0
WC1997	30 Apr	Gothenburg	1	2
2004	17 Nov	Easter Road	1	4
2010	11 Aug	Stockholm	0	3

v SWITZERLAND

			S	*Sw*
1931	24 May	Geneva	3	2
1946	15 May	Glasgow	3	1
1948	17 May	Berne	1	2
1950	26 Apr	Glasgow	3	1
WC1957	19 May	Basle	2	1
WC1957	6 Nov	Glasgow	3	2
1973	22 June	Berne	0	1
1976	7 Apr	Glasgow	1	0
EC1982	17 Nov	Berne	0	2
EC1983	30 May	Glasgow	2	2
EC1990	17 Oct	Glasgow	2	1
EC1991	11 Sept	Berne	2	2
WC1992	9 Sept	Berne	1	3
WC1993	8 Sept	Aberdeen	1	1
WC1996	18 June	Villa Park	1	0
2006	1 Mar	Glasgow	1	3

v TRINIDAD & TOBAGO

			S	*TT*
2004	30 May	Easter Road	4	1

v TURKEY

			S	*T*
1960	8 June	Ankara	2	4

v UKRAINE

			S	*U*
EC2006	11 Oct	Kiev	0	2
EC2007	13 Oct	Glasgow	3	1

v URUGUAY

			S	*U*
WC1954	19 June	Basle	0	7
1962	2 May	Glasgow	2	3
1983	21 Sept	Glasgow	2	0
WC1986	13 June	Nezahualcoyotl	0	0

v USA

			S	*USA*
1952	30 Apr	Glasgow	6	0
1992	17 May	Denver	1	0
1996	26 May	New Britain	1	2
1998	30 May	Washington	0	0
2005	12 Nov	Glasgow	1	1
2012	26 May	Jacksonville	1	5
2013	15 Nov	Glasgow	0	0

v USSR

			S	*USSR*
1967	10 May	Glasgow	0	2
1971	14 June	Moscow	0	1
WC1982	22 June	Malaga	2	2
1991	6 Feb	Ibrox	0	1

v YUGOSLAVIA

			S	*Y*
1955	15 May	Belgrade	2	2
1956	21 Nov	Glasgow	2	0
WC1958	8 June	Vasteras	1	1
1972	29 June	Belo Horizonte	2	2
WC1974	22 June	Frankfurt	1	1
1984	12 Sept	Glasgow	6	1
WC1988	19 Oct	Glasgow	1	1
WC1989	6 Sept	Zagreb	1	3

v ZAIRE

			S	*Z*
WC1974	14 June	Dortmund	2	0

WALES

v ALBANIA			*W*	*A*
EC1994	7 Sept	Cardiff	2	0
EC1995	15 Nov	Tirana	1	1
2018	**20 Nov**	**Elbasan**	**0**	**1**

v ANDORRA			*W*	*A*
EC2014	9 Sept	La Vella	2	1
EC2015	13 Oct	Cardiff	2	0

v ARGENTINA			*W*	*A*
1992	3 June	Tokyo	0	1
2002	13 Feb	Cardiff	1	1

v ARMENIA			*W*	*A*
WC2001	24 Mar	Erevan	2	2
WC2001	1 Sept	Cardiff	0	0

v AUSTRALIA			*W*	*A*
2011	10 Aug	Cardiff	1	2

v AUSTRIA			*W*	*A*
1954	9 May	Vienna	0	2
1955	23 Nov	Wrexham	1	2
EC1974	4 Sept	Vienna	1	2
1975	19 Nov	Wrexham	1	0
1992	29 Apr	Vienna	1	1
EC2005	26 Mar	Cardiff	0	2
EC2005	30 Mar	Vienna	0	1
2013	6 Feb	Swansea	2	1
WC2016	6 Oct	Vienna	2	2
WC2017	2 Sept	Cardiff	1	0

v AZERBAIJAN			*W*	*A*
EC2002	20 Nov	Baku	2	0
EC2003	29 Mar	Cardiff	4	0
WC2004	4 Sept	Baku	1	1
WC2005	12 Oct	Cardiff	2	0
WC2008	6 Sept	Cardiff	1	0
WC2009	6 June	Baku	1	0

v BELARUS			*W*	*B*
EC1998	14 Oct	Cardiff	3	2
EC1999	4 Sept	Minsk	2	1
WC2000	2 Sept	Minsk	1	2
WC2001	6 Oct	Cardiff	1	0

v BELGIUM			*W*	*B*
1949	22 May	Liege	1	3
1949	23 Nov	Cardiff	5	1
EC1990	17 Oct	Cardiff	3	1
EC1991	27 Mar	Brussels	1	1
WC1992	18 Nov	Brussels	0	2
WC1993	31 Mar	Cardiff	2	0
WC1997	29 Mar	Cardiff	1	2
WC1997	11 Oct	Brussels	2	3
WC2012	7 Sept	Cardiff	0	2
WC2013	15 Oct	Brussels	1	1
EC2014	16 Nov	Brussels	0	0
EC2015	12 June	Cardiff	1	0
EC2016	1 July	Lille	3	1

v BOSNIA-HERZEGOVINA			*W*	*BH*
2003	12 Feb	Cardiff	2	2
2012	15 Aug	Llanelli	0	2
EC2014	10 Oct	Cardiff	0	0
EC2015	10 Oct	Zenica	0	2

v BRAZIL			*W*	*B*
WC1958	19 June	Gothenburg	0	1
1962	12 May	Rio de Janeiro	1	3
1962	16 May	São Paulo	1	3
1966	14 May	Rio de Janeiro	1	3
1966	18 May	Belo Horizonte	0	1
1983	12 June	Cardiff	1	1
1991	11 Sept	Cardiff	1	0
1997	12 Nov	Brasilia	0	3
2000	23 May	Cardiff	0	3
2006	5 Sept	Cardiff	0	2

v BULGARIA			*W*	*B*
EC1983	27 Apr	Wrexham	1	0
EC1983	16 Nov	Sofia	0	1
EC1994	14 Dec	Cardiff	0	3
EC1995	29 Mar	Sofia	1	3
2006	15 Aug	Swansea	0	0
2007	22 Aug	Burgas	1	0

			W	*B*
EC2010	8 Oct	Cardiff	0	1
EC2011	12 Oct	Sofia	1	0

v CANADA			*W*	*C*
1986	10 May	Toronto	0	2
1986	20 May	Vancouver	3	0
2004	30 May	Wrexham	1	0

v CHILE			*W*	*C*
1966	22 May	Santiago	0	2
2014	4 June	Valparaiso	0	2

v CHINA			*W*	*C*
2018	22 Mar	Nanning	6	0

v COSTA RICA			*W*	*CR*
1990	20 May	Cardiff	1	0
2012	29 Feb	Cardiff	0	1

v CROATIA			*W*	*C*
2002	21 Aug	Varazdin	1	1
2010	23 May	Osijek	0	2
WC2012	16 Oct	Osijek	0	2
WC2013	26 Mar	Swansea	1	2
EC2019	**8 June**	**Osijek**	**1**	**2**

v CYPRUS			*W*	*C*
WC1992	14 Oct	Limassol	1	0
WC1993	13 Oct	Cardiff	2	0
2005	16 Nov	Limassol	0	1
EC2006	11 Oct	Cardiff	3	1
EC2007	13 Oct	Nicosia	1	3
EC2014	13 Oct	Cardiff	2	1
EC2015	3 Sept	Nicosia	1	0

v CZECHOSLOVAKIA			*W*	*C*
WC1957	1 May	Cardiff	1	0
WC1957	26 May	Prague	0	2
EC1971	21 Apr	Swansea	1	3
EC1971	27 Oct	Prague	0	1
WC1977	30 Mar	Wrexham	3	0
WC1977	16 Nov	Prague	0	1
WC1980	19 Nov	Cardiff	1	0
WC1981	9 Sept	Prague	0	2
EC1987	29 Apr	Wrexham	1	1
EC1987	11 Nov	Prague	0	2
WC1993	28 Apr	Ostrava†	1	1
WC1993	8 Sept	Cardiff†	2	2

†Czechoslovakia played as RCS (Republic of Czechs and Slovaks).

v DENMARK				
WC1964	21 Oct	Copenhagen	0	1
WC1965	1 Dec	Wrexham	4	2
EC1987	9 Sept	Cardiff	1	0
EC1987	14 Oct	Copenhagen	0	1
1990	11 Sept	Copenhagen	0	1
EC1998	10 Oct	Copenhagen	2	1
EC1999	9 June	Liverpool	0	2
2008	19 Nov	Brondby	1	0
2018	**9 Sept**	**Aarhus**	**0**	**2**
NL2018	**16 Nov**	**Cardiff**	**1**	**2**

v ESTONIA			*W*	*E*
1994	23 May	Tallinn	2	1
2009	29 May	Llanelli	1	0

v FAROE ISLANDS			*W*	*F*
WC1992	9 Sept	Cardiff	6	0
WC1993	6 June	Toftir	3	0

v FINLAND			*W*	*F*
EC1971	26 May	Helsinki	1	0
EC1971	13 Oct	Swansea	3	0
EC1987	10 Sept	Helsinki	1	1
EC1987	1 Apr	Wrexham	4	0
WC1988	19 Oct	Swansea	2	2
WC1989	6 Sept	Helsinki	0	1
2000	29 Mar	Cardiff	1	2
EC2002	7 Sept	Helsinki	2	0
EC2003	10 Sept	Cardiff	1	1
WC2009	28 Mar	Cardiff	0	2
WC2009	10 Oct	Helsinki	1	2
2013	16 Nov	Cardiff	1	1

v FRANCE			*W*	*F*
1933	25 May	Paris	1	1
1939	20 May	Paris	1	2
1953	14 May	Paris	1	6
1982	2 June	Toulouse	1	0
2017	10 Nov	Paris	0	2

v GEORGIA			W	G
EC1994	16 Nov	Tbilisi	0	5
EC1995	7 June	Cardiff	0	1
2008	20 Aug	Swansea	1	2
WC2016	9 Oct	Cardiff	1	1
WC2017	6 Oct	Tbilisi	1	0

v GERMANY			W	G
EC1995	26 Apr	Dusseldorf	1	1
EC1995	11 Oct	Cardiff	1	2
2002	14 May	Cardiff	1	0
EC2007	8 Sept	Cardiff	0	2
EC2007	21 Nov	Frankfurt	0	0
WC2008	15 Oct	Moenchengladbach	0	1
WC2009	1 Apr	Cardiff	0	2

v EAST GERMANY			W	EG
WC1957	19 May	Leipzig	1	2
WC1957	25 Sept	Cardiff	4	1
WC1969	16 Apr	Dresden	1	2
WC1969	22 Oct	Cardiff	1	3

v WEST GERMANY			W	WG
1968	8 May	Cardiff	1	1
1969	26 Mar	Frankfurt	1	1
1976	6 Oct	Cardiff	0	2
1977	14 Dec	Dortmund	1	1
EC1979	2 May	Wrexham	0	2
EC1979	17 Oct	Cologne	1	5
WC1989	31 May	Cardiff	0	0
WC1989	15 Nov	Cologne	1	2
EC1991	5 June	Cardiff	1	0
EC1991	16 Oct	Nuremberg	1	4

v GREECE			W	G
WC1964	9 Dec	Athens	0	2
WC1965	17 Mar	Cardiff	4	1

v HUNGARY			W	H
WC1958	8 June	Sanviken	1	1
WC1958	17 June	Stockholm	2	1
1961	28 May	Budapest	2	3
EC1962	7 Nov	Budapest	1	3
EC1963	20 Mar	Cardiff	1	1
EC1974	30 Oct	Cardiff	2	0
EC1975	16 Apr	Budapest	2	1
1985	16 Oct	Cardiff	0	3
2004	31 Mar	Budapest	2	1
2005	9 Feb	Cardiff	2	0
EC2019	**11 June**	**Budapest**	**0**	**1**

v ICELAND			W	I
WC1980	2 June	Reykjavik	4	0
WC1981	14 Oct	Swansea	2	2
WC1984	12 Sept	Reykjavik	0	1
WC1984	14 Nov	Cardiff	2	1
1991	1 May	Cardiff	1	0
2008	28 May	Reykjavik	1	0
2014	5 Mar	Cardiff	3	1

v IRAN			W	I
1978	18 Apr	Tehran	1	0

v ISRAEL			W	I
WC1958	15 Jan	Tel Aviv	2	0
WC1958	5 Feb	Cardiff	2	0
1984	10 June	Tel Aviv	0	0
1989	8 Feb	Tel Aviv	3	3
EC2015	28 Mar	Haifa	3	0
EC2015	6 Sept	Cardiff	0	0

v ITALY			W	I
1965	1 May	Florence	1	4
WC1968	23 Oct	Cardiff	0	1
WC1969	4 Nov	Rome	1	4
1988	4 June	Brescia	1	0
1996	24 Jan	Terni	0	3
EC1998	5 Sept	Liverpool	0	2
EC1999	5 June	Bologna	0	4
EC2002	16 Oct	Cardiff	2	1
EC2003	6 Sept	Milan	0	4

v JAMAICA			W	J
1998	25 Mar	Cardiff	0	0

v JAPAN			W	J
1992	7 June	Matsuyama	1	0

v KUWAIT			W	K
1977	6 Sept	Wrexham	0	0
1977	20 Sept	Kuwait	0	0

v LATVIA			W	L
2004	18 Aug	Riga	2	0

v LIECHTENSTEIN			W	L
2006	14 Nov	Swansea	4	0
WC2008	11 Oct	Cardiff	2	0
WC2009	14 Oct	Vaduz	2	0

v LUXEMBOURG			W	L
EC1974	20 Nov	Swansea	5	0
EC1975	1 May	Luxembourg	3	1
EC1990	14 Nov	Luxembourg	1	0
EC1991	13 Nov	Cardiff	1	0
2008	26 Mar	Luxembourg	2	0
2010	11 Aug	Llanelli	5	1

v MALTA			W	M
EC1978	25 Oct	Wrexham	7	0
EC1979	2 June	Valletta	2	0
1988	1 June	Valletta	3	2
1998	3 June	Valletta	3	0

v MEXICO			W	M
WC1958	11 June	Stockholm	1	1
1962	22 May	Mexico City	1	2
2012	27 May	New Jersey	0	2
2018	29 May	Pasadena	0	0

v MOLDOVA			W	M
EC1994	12 Oct	Kishinev	2	3
EC1995	6 Sept	Cardiff	1	0
WC2016	5 Sept	Cardiff	4	0
WC2017	5 Sept	Chisinau	2	0

v MONTENEGRO			W	M
2009	12 Aug	Podgorica	1	2
EC2010	3 Sept	Podgorica	0	1
EC2011	2 Sept	Cardiff	2	1

v NETHERLANDS			W	N
WC1988	14 Sept	Amsterdam	0	1
WC1989	11 Oct	Wrexham	1	2
1992	30 May	Utrecht	0	4
WC1996	5 Oct	Cardiff	1	3
WC1996	9 Nov	Eindhoven	1	7
2008	1 June	Rotterdam	0	2
2014	4 June	Amsterdam	0	2
2015	13 Nov	Cardiff	2	3

v NEW ZEALAND			W	NZ
2007	26 May	Wrexham	2	2

v NORTH MACEDONIA			W	M
WC2013	6 Sept	Skopje	1	2
WC2013	11 Oct	Cardiff	1	0

v NORWAY			W	N
EC1982	22 Sept	Swansea	1	0
EC1983	21 Sept	Oslo	0	0
1984	6 June	Trondheim	0	1
1985	26 Feb	Wrexham	1	1
1985	5 June	Bergen	2	4
1994	9 Mar	Cardiff	1	3
WC2000	7 Oct	Cardiff	1	1
WC2001	5 Sept	Oslo	2	3
2004	27 May	Oslo	0	0
2008	6 Feb	Wrexham	3	0
2011	12 Nov	Cardiff	4	1

v PANAMA			W	P
2017	14 Nov	Cardiff	1	1

v PARAGUAY			W	P
2006	1 Mar	Cardiff	0	0

v POLAND			W	P
WC1973	28 Mar	Cardiff	2	0
WC1973	26 Sept	Katowice	0	3
1991	29 May	Radom	0	0
WC2000	11 Oct	Warsaw	0	0
WC2001	2 June	Cardiff	1	2
WC2004	13 Oct	Cardiff	2	3
WC2005	7 Sept	Warsaw	0	1
2009	11 Feb	Vila Real	0	1

v PORTUGAL

			W	P
1949	15 May	Lisbon	2	3
1951	12 May	Cardiff	2	1
2000	2 June	Chaves	0	3
EC2016	6 July	Lille	0	2

v QATAR

			W	Q
2000	23 Feb	Doha	1	0

v REPUBLIC OF IRELAND

			W	RI
1960	28 Sept	Dublin	3	2
1979	11 Sept	Swansea	2	1
1981	24 Feb	Dublin	3	1
1986	26 Mar	Dublin	1	0
1990	28 Mar	Dublin	0	1
1991	6 Feb	Wrexham	0	3
1992	19 Feb	Dublin	1	0
1993	17 Feb	Dublin	1	2
1997	11 Feb	Cardiff	0	0
EC2007	24 Mar	Dublin	0	1
EC2007	17 Nov	Cardiff	2	2
NC2011	8 Feb	Dublin	0	3
2013	14 Aug	Cardiff	0	0
WC2017	24 Mar	Dublin	0	0
WC2017	9 Oct	Cardiff	0	1
NL2018	**6 Sept**	**Cardiff**	**4**	**1**
NL2018	**16 Oct**	**Dublin**	**1**	**0**

v ROMANIA

			W	R
EC1970	11 Nov	Cardiff	0	0
EC1971	24 Nov	Bucharest	0	2
1983	12 Oct	Wrexham	5	0
WC1992	20 May	Bucharest	1	5
WC1993	17 Nov	Cardiff	1	2

v RUSSIA

			W	R
EC2003	15 Nov	Moscow	0	0
EC2003	19 Nov	Cardiff	0	1
WC2008	10 Sept	Moscow	1	2
WC2009	9 Sept	Cardiff	1	3
EC2016	20 June	Toulouse	3	0

v SAN MARINO

			W	SM
WC1996	2 June	Serravalle	5	0
WC1996	31 Aug	Cardiff	6	0
EC2007	28 Mar	Cardiff	3	0
EC2007	17 Oct	Serravalle	2	1

v SAUDI ARABIA

			W	SA
1986	25 Feb	Dahran	2	1

v SERBIA

			W	S
WC2012	11 Sept	Novi Sad	1	6
WC2013	10 Sept	Cardiff	0	3
WC2016	12 Nov	Cardiff	1	1
WC2017	11 June	Belgrade	1	1

v SERBIA-MONTENEGRO

			W	SM
EC2003	20 Aug	Belgrade	0	1
EC2003	11 Oct	Cardiff	2	3

v SLOVAKIA

			W	S
EC2006	7 Oct	Cardiff	1	5
EC2007	12 Sept	Trnava	5	2
EC2016	11 June	Bordeaux	2	1
EC2019	**24 Mar**	**Cardiff**	**1**	**0**

v SLOVENIA

			W	Sl
2005	17 Aug	Swansea	0	0

v SPAIN

			W	S
WC1961	19 Apr	Cardiff	1	2
WC1961	18 May	Madrid	1	1
1982	24 Mar	Valencia	1	1
WC1984	17 Oct	Seville	0	3
WC1985	30 Apr	Wrexham	3	0
2018	**11 Oct**	**Cardiff**	**1**	**4**

v SWEDEN

			W	S
WC1958	15 June	Stockholm	0	0
1988	27 Apr	Stockholm	1	4
1989	26 Apr	Wrexham	0	2
1990	25 Apr	Stockholm	2	4
1994	20 Apr	Wrexham	0	2
2010	3 Mar	Swansea	0	1
2016	5 June	Stockholm	0	3

v SWITZERLAND

			W	S
1949	26 May	Berne	0	4
1951	16 May	Wrexham	3	2
1996	24 Apr	Lugano	0	2
EC1999	31 Mar	Zurich	0	2
EC1999	9 Oct	Wrexham	0	2
EC2010	12 Oct	Basle	1	4
EC2011	8 Oct	Swansea	2	0

v TRINIDAD & TOBAGO

			W	TT
2006	27 May	Graz	2	1
2019	**20 Mar**	**Wrexham**	**1**	**0**

v TUNISIA

			W	T
1998	6 June	Tunis	0	4

v TURKEY

			W	T
EC1978	29 Nov	Wrexham	1	0
EC1979	21 Nov	Izmir	0	1
WC1980	15 Oct	Cardiff	4	0
WC1981	25 Mar	Ankara	1	0
WC1996	14 Dec	Cardiff	0	0
WC1997	20 Aug	Istanbul	4	6

v UKRAINE

			W	U
WC2001	28 Mar	Cardiff	1	1
WC2001	6 June	Kiev	1	1
2016	28 Mar	Kiev	0	1

v REST OF UNITED KINGDOM

1951	5 Dec	Cardiff	3	2
1969	28 July	Cardiff	0	1

v URUGUAY

			W	U
1986	21 Apr	Wrexham	0	0
2018	26 Mar	Nanning	0	1

v USA

			W	USA
2003	27 May	San Jose	0	2

v USSR

			W	USSR
WC1965	30 May	Moscow	1	2
WC1965	27 Oct	Cardiff	2	1
WC1981	30 May	Wrexham	0	0
WC1981	18 Nov	Tbilisi	0	3
1987	18 Feb	Swansea	0	0

v YUGOSLAVIA

			W	Y
1953	21 May	Belgrade	2	5
1954	22 Nov	Cardiff	1	3
EC1976	24 Apr	Zagreb	0	2
EC1976	22 May	Cardiff	1	1
EC1982	15 Dec	Titograd	4	4
EC1983	14 Dec	Cardiff	1	1
1988	23 Mar	Swansea	1	2

NORTHERN IRELAND

v ALBANIA

			NI	A
WC1965	7 May	Belfast	4	1
WC1965	24 Nov	Tirana	1	1
EC1982	15 Dec	Tirana	0	0
EC1983	27 Apr	Belfast	1	0
WC1992	9 Sept	Belfast	3	0
WC1993	17 Feb	Tirana	2	1
WC1996	14 Dec	Belfast	2	0
WC1997	10 Sept	Zurich	0	1
2010	3 Mar	Tirana	0	1

v ALGERIA

			NI	A
WC1986	3 June	Guadalajara	1	1

v ARGENTINA

			NI	A
WC1958	11 June	Halmstad	1	3

v ARMENIA

			NI	A
WC1996	5 Oct	Belfast	1	1
WC1997	30 Apr	Erevan	0	0
EC2003	29 Mar	Erevan	0	1
EC2003	10 Sept	Belfast	0	1

v AUSTRALIA

			NI	A
1980	11 June	Sydney	2	1
1980	15 June	Melbourne	1	1
1980	18 June	Adelaide	2	1

		v AUSTRIA	*NI*	*A*
WC1982	1 July	Madrid	2	2
EC1982	13 Oct	Vienna	0	2
EC1983	21 Sept	Belfast	3	1
EC1990	14 Nov	Vienna	0	0
EC1991	16 Oct	Belfast	2	1
EC1994	12 Oct	Vienna	2	1
EC1995	15 Nov	Belfast	5	3
WC2004	13 Oct	Belfast	3	3
WC2005	12 Oct	Vienna	0	2
NL2018	**12 Oct**	**Vienna**	**0**	**1**
NL2018	**18 Nov**	**Belfast**	**1**	**2**

		v AZERBAIJAN	*NI*	*A*
WC2004	9 Oct	Baku	0	0
WC2005	3 Sept	Belfast	2	0
WC2012	14 Nov	Belfast	1	1
WC2013	11 Oct	Baku	0	2
WC2016	11 Nov	Belfast	4	0
WC2017	10 June	Baku	1	0

		v BARBADOS	*NI*	*B*
2004	30 May	Waterford	1	1

		v BELARUS	*NI*	*B*
2016	27 May	Belfast	3	0
EC2019	**24 Mar**	**Belfast**	**2**	**1**
EC2019	**11 June**	**Barysaw**	**1**	**0**

		v BELGIUM	*NI*	*B*
WC1976	10 Nov	Liege	0	2
WC1977	16 Nov	Belfast	3	0
1997	11 Feb	Belfast	3	0

		v BOSNIA-HERZEGOVINA	*NI*	*B*
NL2018	**8 Sept**	**Belfast**	**1**	**2**
NL2018	**15 Oct**	**Sarajevo**	**0**	**2**

		v BRAZIL	*NI*	*B*
WC1986	12 June	Guadalajara	0	3

		v BULGARIA	*NI*	*B*
WC1972	18 Oct	Sofia	0	3
WC1973	26 Sept	Sheffield	0	0
EC1978	29 Nov	Sofia	2	0
EC1979	2 May	Belfast	2	0
WC2001	28 Mar	Sofia	3	4
WC2001	2 June	Belfast	0	1
2008	6 Feb	Belfast	0	1

		v CANADA	*NI*	*C*
1995	22 May	Edmonton	0	2
1999	27 Apr	Belfast	1	1
2005	9 Feb	Belfast	0	1

		v CHILE	*NI*	*C*
1989	26 May	Belfast	0	1
1995	25 May	Edmonton	1	2
2010	30 May	Chillan	0	1
2014	4 June	Valparaiso	0	2

		v COLOMBIA	*NI*	*C*
1994	4 June	Boston	0	2

		v COSTA RICA	*NI*	*CR*
2018	3 June	San Jose	0	3

		v CROATIA	*NI*	*C*
2016	15 Nov	Belfast	0	3

		v CYPRUS	*NI*	*C*
EC1971	3 Feb	Nicosia	3	0
EC1971	21 Apr	Belfast	5	0
WC1973	14 Feb	Nicosia	0	1
WC1973	8 May	London	3	0
2002	21 Aug	Belfast	0	0
2014	5 Mar	Nicosia	0	0

		v CZECHOSLOVAKIA	*NI*	*C*
WC1958	8 June	Halmstad	1	0
WC1958	17 June	Malmo	2	1*

**After extra time*

		v CZECH REPUBLIC	*NI*	*C*
WC2001	24 Mar	Belfast	0	1
WC2001	6 June	Teplice	1	3
WC2008	10 Sept	Belfast	0	0
WC2009	14 Oct	Prague	0	0
WC2016	4 Sept	Prague	0	0
WC2017	4 Sept	Belfast	2	0

		v DENMARK	*NI*	*D*
EC1978	25 Oct	Belfast	2	1
EC1979	6 June	Copenhagen	0	4
1986	26 Mar	Belfast	1	1
EC1990	17 Oct	Belfast	1	1
EC1991	13 Nov	Odense	1	2
WC1992	18 Nov	Belfast	0	1
WC1993	13 Oct	Copenhagen	0	1
WC2000	7 Oct	Belfast	1	1
WC2001	1 Sept	Copenhagen	1	1
EC2006	7 Oct	Copenhagen	0	0
EC2007	17 Nov	Belfast	2	1

		v ESTONIA	*NI*	*E*
2004	31 Mar	Tallinn	1	0
2006	1 Mar	Belfast	1	0
EC2011	6 Sept	Tallinn	1	4
EC2011	7 Oct	Belfast	1	2
EC2019	**21 Mar**	**Belfast**	**2**	**0**
EC2019	**8 June**	**Tallinn**	**2**	**1**

		v FAROE ISLANDS	*NI*	*F*
EC1991	1 May	Belfast	1	1
EC1991	11 Sept	Landskrona	5	0
EC2010	12 Oct	Toftir	1	1
EC2011	10 Aug	Belfast	4	0
EC2014	11 Oct	Belfast	2	0
EC2015	4 Sept	Torshavn	3	1

		v FINLAND	*NI*	*F*
WC1984	27 May	Pori	0	1
WC1984	14 Nov	Belfast	2	1
EC1998	10 Oct	Belfast	1	0
EC1998	9 Oct	Helsinki	1	4
2003	12 Feb	Belfast	0	1
2006	16 Aug	Helsinki	2	1
2012	15 Aug	Belfast	3	3
EC2015	29 Mar	Belfast	2	1
EC2015	11 Oct	Helsinki	1	1

		v FRANCE	*NI*	*F*
1928	21 Feb	Paris	0	4
1951	12 May	Belfast	2	2
1952	11 Nov	Paris	1	3
WC1958	19 June	Norrkoping	0	4
1982	24 Mar	Paris	0	4
WC1982	4 July	Madrid	1	4
1986	26 Feb	Paris	0	0
1988	27 Apr	Belfast	0	0
1999	18 Aug	Belfast	0	1

		v GEORGIA	*NI*	*G*
2008	26 Mar	Belfast	4	1

		v GERMANY	*NI*	*G*
1992	2 June	Bremen	1	1
1996	29 May	Belfast	1	1
WC1996	9 Nov	Nuremberg	1	1
WC1997	20 Aug	Belfast	1	3
EC1999	27 Mar	Belfast	0	3
EC1999	8 Sept	Dortmund	0	4
2005	4 June	Belfast	1	4
EC2016	21 June	Paris	0	1
WC2016	11 Oct	Hanover	0	2
WC2017	5 Oct	Belfast	1	3

		v WEST GERMANY	*NI*	*WG*
WC1958	15 June	Malmo	2	2
WC1960	26 Oct	Belfast	3	4
WC1961	10 May	Hamburg	1	2
1966	7 May	Belfast	0	2
1977	27 Apr	Cologne	0	5
EC1982	17 Nov	Belfast	1	0
EC1983	16 Nov	Hamburg	1	0

		v GREECE	*NI*	*G*
WC1961	3 May	Athens	1	2
WC1961	17 Oct	Belfast	2	0
1988	17 Feb	Athens	2	3
EC2003	2 Apr	Belfast	0	2
EC2003	11 Oct	Athens	0	1
EC2014	14 Oct	Piraeus	2	0
EC2015	8 Oct	Belfast	3	1

		v HONDURAS	*NI*	*H*
WC1982	21 June	Zaragoza	1	1

		v HUNGARY	*NI*	*H*
WC1988	19 Oct	Budapest	0	1
WC1989	6 Sept	Belfast	1	2
2000	26 Apr	Belfast	0	1
2008	19 Nov	Belfast	0	2
EC2014	7 Sept	Budapest	2	1
EC2015	7 Sept	Belfast	1	1

		v ICELAND	*NI*	*I*
WC1977	11 June	Reykjavik	0	1
WC1977	21 Sept	Belfast	2	0
WC2000	11 Oct	Reykjavik	0	1
WC2001	5 Sept	Belfast	3	0
EC2006	2 Sept	Belfast	0	3
EC2007	12 Sept	Reykjavik	1	2

		v ISRAEL	*NI*	*I*
1968	10 Sept	Jaffa	3	2
1976	3 Mar	Tel Aviv	1	1
WC1980	26 Mar	Tel Aviv	0	0
WC1981	18 Nov	Belfast	1	0
1984	16 Oct	Belfast	3	0
1987	18 Feb	Tel Aviv	1	1
2009	12 Aug	Belfast	1	1
WC2013	26 Mar	Belfast	0	2
WC2013	15 Oct	Tel Aviv	1	1
2018	**11 Sept**	**Belfast**	**3**	**0**

		v ITALY	*NI*	*I*
WC1957	25 Apr	Rome	0	1
1957	4 Dec	Belfast	2	2
WC1958	15 Jan	Belfast	2	1
1961	25 Apr	Bologna	2	3
1997	22 Jan	Palermo	0	2
2003	3 June	Campobasso	0	2
2009	6 June	Pisa	0	3
EC2010	8 Oct	Belfast	0	0
EC2011	11 Oct	Pescara	0	3

		v KOREA REPUBLIC	*NI*	*KR*
2018	24 Mar	Belfast	2	1

		v LATVIA	*NI*	*L*
WC1993	2 June	Riga	2	1
WC1993	8 Sept	Belfast	2	0
EC1995	26 Apr	Riga	1	0
EC1995	7 June	Belfast	1	2
EC2006	11 Oct	Belfast	1	0
EC2007	8 Sept	Riga	0	1
2015	13 Nov	Belfast	1	0

		v LIECHTENSTEIN	*NI*	*L*
EC1994	20 Apr	Belfast	4	1
EC1995	11 Oct	Eschen	4	0
2002	27 Mar	Vaduz	0	0
EC2007	24 Mar	Vaduz	4	1
EC2007	22 Aug	Belfast	3	1

		v LITHUANIA	*NI*	*L*
WC1992	28 Apr	Belfast	2	2
WC1993	25 May	Vilnius	1	0

		v LUXEMBOURG	*NI*	*L*
2000	23 Feb	Luxembourg	3	1
WC2012	11 Sept	Belfast	1	1
WC2013	10 Sept	Luxembourg	2	3

		v MALTA	*NI*	*M*
WC1988	21 May	Belfast	3	0
WC1989	26 Apr	Valletta	2	0
2000	28 Mar	Valletta	3	0
WC2000	2 Sept	Belfast	1	0
WC2001	6 Oct	Valletta	1	0
2005	17 Aug	Ta'Qali	1	1
2013	6 Feb	Ta'Qali	0	0

		v MEXICO	*NI*	*M*
1966	22 June	Belfast	4	1
1994	11 June	Miami	0	3

		v MOLDOVA	*NI*	*M*
EC1998	18 Nov	Belfast	2	2
EC1999	31 Mar	Chisinau	0	0

		v MONTENEGRO	*NI*	*M*
2010	11 Aug	Podgorica	0	2

		v MOROCCO	*NI*	*M*
1986	23 Apr	Belfast	2	1
2010	17 Nov	Belfast	1	1

		v NETHERLANDS	*NI*	*N*
1962	9 May	Rotterdam	0	4
WC1965	17 Mar	Belfast	2	1
WC1965	7 Apr	Rotterdam	0	0
WC1976	13 Oct	Rotterdam	2	2
WC1977	12 Oct	Belfast	0	1
2012	2 June	Amsterdam	0	6

		v NEW ZEALAND	*NI*	*N*
2017	2 June	Belfast	1	0

		v NORWAY	*NI*	*N*
1922	25 May	Bergen	1	2
EC1974	4 Sept	Oslo	1	2
EC1975	29 Oct	Belfast	3	0
1990	27 Mar	Belfast	2	3
1996	27 Mar	Belfast	0	2
2001	28 Feb	Belfast	0	4
2004	18 Feb	Belfast	1	4
2012	29 Feb	Belfast	0	3
WC2017	26 Mar	Belfast	2	0
WC2017	8 Oct	Oslo	0	1

		v PANAMA	*NI*	*P*
2018	30 May	Panama City	0	0

		v POLAND	*NI*	*P*
EC1962	10 Oct	Katowice	2	0
EC1962	28 Nov	Belfast	2	0
1988	23 Mar	Belfast	1	1
1991	5 Feb	Belfast	3	1
2002	13 Feb	Limassol	1	4
EC2004	4 Sept	Belfast	0	3
EC2005	30 Mar	Warsaw	0	1
WC2009	28 Mar	Belfast	3	2
WC2009	5 Sept	Chorzow	1	1
EC2016	12 June	Nice	0	1

		v PORTUGAL	*NI*	*P*
WC1957	16 Jan	Lisbon	1	1
WC1957	1 May	Belfast	3	0
WC1973	28 Mar	Coventry	1	1
WC1973	14 Nov	Lisbon	1	1
WC1980	19 Nov	Lisbon	0	1
WC1981	29 Apr	Belfast	1	0
EC1994	7 Sept	Belfast	1	2
EC1995	3 Sept	Lisbon	1	1
WC1997	29 Mar	Belfast	0	0
WC1997	11 Oct	Lisbon	0	1
2005	15 Nov	Belfast	1	1
WC2012	16 Oct	Porto	1	1
WC2013	6 Sept	Belfast	2	4

		v QATAR	*NI*	*Q*
2015	31 May	Crewe	1	1

		v REPUBLIC OF IRELAND	*NI*	*RI*
EC1978	20 Sept	Dublin	0	0
EC1979	21 Nov	Belfast	1	0
WC1988	14 Sept	Belfast	0	0
WC1989	11 Oct	Dublin	0	3
WC1993	31 Mar	Dublin	0	3
WC1993	17 Nov	Belfast	1	1
EC1994	16 Nov	Belfast	0	4
EC1995	29 Mar	Dublin	1	1
1999	29 May	Dublin	1	0
NC2011	24 May	Dublin	0	5
2018	**15 Nov**	**Dublin**	**0**	**0**

		v ROMANIA	*NI*	*R*
WC1984	12 Sept	Belfast	3	2
WC1985	16 Oct	Bucharest	1	0
1994	23 Mar	Belfast	2	0
2006	27 May	Chicago	0	2
EC2014	14 Nov	Bucharest	0	2
EC2015	13 June	Belfast	0	0

		v RUSSIA	*NI*	*R*
WC2012	7 Sept	Moscow	0	2
WC2013	14 Aug	Belfast	1	0

v SAN MARINO			*NI*	*SM*
WC2008	15 Oct	Belfast	4	0
WC2009	11 Feb	Serravalle	3	0
WC2016	8 Oct	Belfast	4	0
WC2017	1 Sept	Serravalle	3	0

v ST KITTS & NEVIS			*NI*	*SK*
2004	2 June	Basseterre	2	0

v SERBIA			*NI*	*S*
2009	14 Nov	Belfast	0	1
EC2011	25 Mar	Belgrade	1	2
EC2011	2 Sept	Belfast	0	1

v SERBIA-MONTENEGRO			*NI*	*SM*
2004	28 Apr	Belfast	1	1

v SLOVAKIA			*NI*	*S*
1998	25 Mar	Belfast	1	0
WC2008	6 Sept	Bratislava	1	2
WC2009	9 Sept	Belfast	0	2
2016	4 June	Trnava	0	0

v SLOVENIA			*NI*	*S*
WC2008	11 Oct	Maribor	0	2
WC2009	1 Apr	Belfast	1	0
EC2010	3 Sept	Maribor	1	0
EC2011	29 Mar	Belfast	0	0
2016	28 Mar	Belfast	1	0

v SOUTH AFRICA			*NI*	*SA*
1924	24 Sept	Belfast	1	2

v SPAIN			*NI*	*S*
1958	15 Oct	Madrid	2	6
1963	30 May	Bilbao	1	1
1963	30 Oct	Belfast	0	1
EC1970	11 Nov	Seville	0	3
EC1972	16 Feb	Hull	1	1
WC1982	25 June	Valencia	1	0
1985	27 Mar	Palma	0	0
WC1986	7 June	Guadalajara	1	2
WC1988	21 Dec	Seville	0	4
WC1989	8 Feb	Belfast	0	2
WC1992	14 Oct	Belfast	0	0
WC1993	28 Apr	Seville	1	3
1998	2 June	Santander	1	4
2002	17 Apr	Belfast	0	5
EC2002	12 Oct	Albacete	0	3
EC2003	11 June	Belfast	0	0
EC2006	6 Sept	Belfast	3	2
EC2007	21 Nov	Las Palmas	0	1

v SWEDEN			*NI*	*S*
EC1974	30 Oct	Solna	2	0
EC1975	3 Sept	Belfast	1	2
WC1980	15 Oct	Belfast	3	0
WC1981	3 June	Solna	0	1
1996	24 Apr	Belfast	1	2
EC2007	28 Mar	Belfast	2	1
EC2007	17 Oct	Stockholm	1	1

v SWITZERLAND			*NI*	*S*
WC1964	14 Oct	Belfast	1	0
WC1964	14 Nov	Lausanne	1	2
1998	22 Apr	Belfast	1	0
2004	18 Aug	Zurich	0	0
WC2017	9 Nov	Belfast	0	1
WC2017	12 Nov	Basel	0	0

v THAILAND			*NI*	*T*
1997	21 May	Bangkok	0	0

v TRINIDAD & TOBAGO			*NI*	*TT*
2004	6 June	Bacolet	3	0

v TURKEY			*NI*	*T*
WC1968	23 Oct	Belfast	4	1
WC1968	11 Dec	Istanbul	3	0
2013	15 Nov	Adana	0	1
EC1983	30 Mar	Belfast	2	1
EC1983	12 Oct	Ankara	0	1
WC1985	1 May	Belfast	2	0
WC1985	11 Sept	Izmir	0	0
EC1986	12 Nov	Izmir	0	0
EC1987	11 Nov	Belfast	1	0
EC1998	5 Sept	Istanbul	0	3
EC1999	4 Sept	Belfast	0	3
2010	26 May	New Britain	0	2
2013	15 Nov	Adana	0	1

v UKRAINE			*NI*	*U*
WC1996	31 Aug	Belfast	0	1
WC1997	2 Apr	Kiev	1	2
EC2002	16 Oct	Belfast	0	0
EC2003	6 Sept	Donetsk	0	0
EC2016	16 June	Lyon	2	0

v URUGUAY			*NI*	*U*
1964	29 Apr	Belfast	3	0
1990	18 May	Belfast	1	0
2006	21 May	New Jersey	0	1
2014	30 May	Montevideo	0	1

v USSR			*NI*	*USSR*
WC1969	19 Sept	Belfast	0	0
WC1969	22 Oct	Moscow	0	2
EC1971	22 Sept	Moscow	0	1
EC1971	13 Oct	Belfast	1	1

v YUGOSLAVIA			*NI*	*Y*
EC1975	16 Mar	Belfast	1	0
EC1975	19 Nov	Belgrade	0	1
WC1982	17 June	Zaragoza	0	0
EC1987	29 Apr	Belfast	1	2
EC1987	14 Oct	Sarajevo	0	3
EC1990	12 Sept	Belfast	0	2
EC1991	27 Mar	Belgrade	1	4
2000	16 Aug	Belfast	1	2

REPUBLIC OF IRELAND

v ALBANIA			*RI*	*A*
WC1992	26 May	Dublin	2	0
WC1993	26 May	Tirana	2	1
EC2003	2 Apr	Tirana	0	0
EC2003	7 June	Dublin	2	1

v ALGERIA			*RI*	*A*
1982	28 Apr	Algiers	0	2
2010	28 May	Dublin	3	0

v ANDORRA			*RI*	*A*
WC2001	28 Mar	Barcelona	3	0
WC2001	25 Apr	Dublin	3	1
EC2010	7 Sept	Dublin	3	1
EC2011	7 Oct	Andorra La Vella	2	0

v ARGENTINA			*RI*	*A*
1951	13 May	Dublin	0	1
†1979	29 May	Dublin	0	0
1980	16 May	Dublin	0	1
1998	22 Apr	Dublin	0	2
2010	11 Aug	Dublin	0	1

†*Not considered a full international.*

v ARMENIA			*RI*	*A*
EC2010	3 Sept	Erevan	1	0
EC2011	11 Oct	Dublin	2	1

v AUSTRALIA			*RI*	*A*
2003	19 Aug	Dublin	2	1
2009	12 Aug	Limerick	0	3

v AUSTRIA			*RI*	*A*
1952	7 May	Vienna	0	6
1953	25 Mar	Dublin	4	0
1958	14 Mar	Vienna	1	3
WC2013	10 Sept	Vienna	0	1
1962	8 Apr	Dublin	2	3
EC1963	25 Sept	Vienna	0	0
EC1963	13 Oct	Dublin	3	2
1966	22 May	Vienna	0	1
1968	10 Nov	Dublin	2	2
EC1971	30 May	Dublin	1	4
EC1971	10 Oct	Linz	0	6
EC1995	11 June	Dublin	1	3
EC1995	6 Sept	Vienna	1	3
WC2013	26 Mar	Dublin	2	2

			RI	A
wc2013	10 Sept	Vienna	0	1
wc2016	12 Nov	Vienna	1	0
wc2017	11 June	Dublin	1	1

v BELARUS

			RI	B
2016	31 May	Cork	1	2

v BELGIUM

			RI	B
1928	12 Feb	Liege	4	2
1929	30 Apr	Dublin	4	0
1930	11 May	Brussels	3	1
wc1934	25 Feb	Dublin	4	4
1949	24 Apr	Dublin	0	2
1950	10 May	Brussels	1	5
1965	24 Mar	Dublin	0	2
1966	25 May	Liege	3	2
wc1980	15 Oct	Dublin	1	1
wc1981	25 Mar	Brussels	0	1
EC1986	10 Sept	Brussels	2	2
EC1987	29 Apr	Dublin	0	0
wc1997	29 Oct	Dublin	1	1
wc1997	16 Nov	Brussels	1	2
EC2016	18 June	Bordeaux	0	3

v BOLIVIA

			RI	B
1994	24 May	Dublin	1	0
1996	15 June	New Jersey	3	0
2007	26 May	Boston	1	1

v BOSNIA-HERZEGOVINA

			RI	BH
2012	26 May	Dublin	1	0
EC2015	13 Nov	Zenica	1	1
EC2015	16 Nov	Dublin	2	0

v BRAZIL

			RI	B
1974	5 May	Rio de Janeiro	1	2
1982	27 May	Uberlandia	0	7
1987	23 May	Dublin	1	0
2004	18 Feb	Dublin	0	0
2008	6 Feb	Dublin	0	1
2010	2 Mar	Emirates	0	2

v BULGARIA

			RI	B
wc1977	1 June	Sofia	1	2
wc1977	12 Oct	Dublin	0	0
EC1979	19 May	Sofia	0	1
EC1979	17 Oct	Dublin	3	0
wc1987	1 Apr	Sofia	1	2
wc1987	14 Oct	Dublin	2	0
2004	18 Aug	Dublin	1	1
wc2009	28 Mar	Dublin	1	1
wc2009	6 June	Sofia	1	1

v CAMEROON

			RI	C
wc2002	1 June	Niigata	1	1

v CANADA

			RI	C
2003	18 Nov	Dublin	3	0

v CHILE

			RI	C
1960	30 Mar	Dublin	2	0
1972	21 June	Recife	1	2
1974	12 May	Santiago	2	1
1982	22 May	Santiago	0	1
1991	22 May	Dublin	1	1
2006	24 May	Dublin	0	1

v CHINA PR

			RI	CPR
1984	3 June	Sapporo	1	0
2005	29 Mar	Dublin	1	0

v COLOMBIA

			RI	C
2008	29 May	Fulham	1	0

v COSTA RICA

			RI	C
2014	6 June	Philadephia	1	1

v CROATIA

			RI	C
1996	2 June	Dublin	2	2
EC1998	5 Sept	Dublin	2	0
EC1999	4 Sept	Zagreb	0	1
2001	15 Aug	Dublin	2	2
2004	16 Nov	Dublin	1	0
2011	10 Aug	Dublin	0	0
EC2012	10 June	Poznan	1	3

v CYPRUS

			RI	C
wc1980	26 Mar	Nicosia	3	2
wc1980	19 Nov	Dublin	6	0
wc2001	24 Mar	Nicosia	4	0
wc2001	6 Oct	Dublin	4	0
wc2004	4 Sept	Dublin	3	0
wc2005	8 Oct	Nicosia	1	0
EC2006	7 Oct	Nicosia	2	5
EC2007	17 Oct	Dublin	1	1
2008	15 Oct	Dublin	1	0
wc2009	5 Sept	Nicosia	2	1

v CZECHOSLOVAKIA

			RI	C
1938	18 May	Prague	2	2
EC1959	5 Apr	Dublin	2	0
EC1959	10 May	Bratislava	0	4
wc1961	8 Oct	Dublin	1	3
wc1961	29 Oct	Prague	1	7
EC1967	21 May	Dublin	0	2
EC1967	22 Nov	Prague	2	1
wc1969	4 May	Dublin	1	2
wc1969	7 Oct	Prague	0	3
1979	26 Sept	Prague	1	4
1981	29 Apr	Dublin	3	1
1986	27 May	Reykjavik	1	0

v CZECH REPUBLIC

			RI	C
1994	5 June	Dublin	1	3
1996	24 Apr	Prague	0	2
1998	25 Mar	Olomouc	1	2
2000	23 Feb	Dublin	3	2
2004	31 Mar	Dublin	2	1
EC2006	11 Oct	Dublin	1	1
EC2007	12 Sept	Prague	0	1
2012	29 Feb	Dublin	1	1

v DENMARK

			RI	D
wc1956	3 Oct	Dublin	2	1
wc1957	2 Oct	Copenhagen	2	0
wc1968	4 Dec	Dublin	1	1
	(abandoned after 51 mins)			
wc1969	27 May	Copenhagen	0	2
wc1969	15 Oct	Dublin	1	1
EC1978	24 May	Copenhagen	3	3
EC1979	2 May	Dublin	2	0
wc1984	14 Nov	Copenhagen	0	3
wc1985	13 Nov	Dublin	1	4
wc1992	14 Oct	Copenhagen	0	0
wc1993	28 Apr	Dublin	1	1
2002	27 Mar	Dublin	3	0
2007	22 Aug	Copenhagen	4	0
wc2017	11 Nov	Copenhagen	0	0
wc2017	14 Nov	Dublin	1	5
NL2018	**13 Oct**	**Dublin**	**0**	**0**
NL2018	**19 Nov**	**Aarhus**	**0**	**0**
EC2019	**7 June**	**Copenhagen**	**1**	**1**

v ECUADOR

			RI	E
1972	19 June	Natal	3	2
2007	23 May	New Jersey	1	1

v EGYPT

			RI	E
wc1990	17 June	Palermo	0	0

v ENGLAND

			RI	E
1946	30 Sept	Dublin	0	1
1949	21 Sept	Everton	2	0
wc1957	8 May	Wembley	1	5
wc1957	19 May	Dublin	1	1
1964	24 May	Dublin	1	3
1976	8 Sept	Wembley	1	1
EC1978	25 Oct	Dublin	1	1
EC1980	6 Feb	Wembley	0	2
1985	26 Mar	Wembley	1	2
EC1988	12 June	Stuttgart	1	0
wc1990	11 June	Cagliari	1	1
EC1990	14 Nov	Dublin	1	1
EC1991	27 Mar	Wembley	1	1
1995	15 Feb	Dublin	1	0
	(abandoned after 27 mins)			
2013	29 May	Wembley	1	1
2015	7 June	Dublin	0	0

		v ESTONIA	*RI*	*E*
WC2000	11 Oct	Dublin	2	0
WC2001	6 June	Tallinn	2	0
EC2011	11 Nov	Tallinn	4	0
EC2011	15 Nov	Dublin	1	1
		v FAROE ISLANDS	*RI*	*F*
EC2004	13 Oct	Dublin	2	0
EC2005	8 June	Toftir	2	0
WC2012	16 Oct	Torshavn	4	1
WC2013	7 June	Dublin	3	0
		v FINLAND	*RI*	*F*
WC1949	8 Sept	Dublin	3	0
WC1949	9 Oct	Helsinki	1	1
1990	16 May	Dublin	1	1
2000	15 Nov	Dublin	3	0
2002	21 Aug	Helsinki	3	0
		v FRANCE	*RI*	*F*
1937	23 May	Paris	2	0
1952	16 Nov	Dublin	1	1
WC1953	4 Oct	Dublin	3	5
WC1953	25 Nov	Paris	0	1
WC1972	15 Nov	Dublin	2	1
WC1973	19 May	Paris	1	1
WC1976	17 Nov	Paris	0	2
WC1977	30 Mar	Dublin	1	0
WC1980	28 Oct	Paris	0	2
WC1981	14 Oct	Dublin	3	2
1989	7 Feb	Dublin	0	0
WC2004	9 Oct	Paris	0	0
WC2005	7 Sept	Dublin	0	1
WC2009	14 Nov	Dublin	0	1
WC2009	18 Nov	Paris	1	1
EC2016	26 June	Lyon	1	2
2018	28 May	Paris	0	2
		v GEORGIA	*RI*	*G*
EC2003	29 Mar	Tbilisi	2	1
EC2003	11 June	Dublin	2	0
WC2008	6 Sept	Mainz	2	1
WC2009	11 Feb	Dublin	2	1
2013	2 June	Dublin	3	0
EC2014	7 Sept	Tbilisi	2	1
EC2015	7 Sept	Dublin	1	0
WC2016	6 Oct	Dublin	1	0
WC2017	2 Sept	Tbilisi	1	1
EC2019	**26 Mar**	**Dublin**	**1**	**0**
		v GERMANY	*RI*	*G*
1935	8 May	Dortmund	1	3
1936	17 Oct	Dublin	5	2
1939	23 May	Bremen	1	1
1994	29 May	Hanover	2	0
WC2002	5 June	Ibaraki	1	1
EC2006	2 Sept	Stuttgart	0	1
EC2007	13 Oct	Dublin	0	0
WC2012	12 Oct	Dublin	1	6
WC2013	11 Oct	Cologne	0	3
EC2014	14 Oct	Gelsenkirchen	1	1
EC2015	8 Oct	Dublin	1	0
		v WEST GERMANY	*RI*	*WG*
1951	17 Oct	Dublin	3	2
1952	4 May	Cologne	0	3
1955	28 May	Hamburg	1	2
1956	25 Nov	Dublin	3	0
1960	11 May	Dusseldorf	1	0
1966	4 May	Dublin	0	4
1970	9 May	Berlin	1	2
1975	1 Mar	Dublin	1	0†
1979	22 May	Dublin	1	3
1981	21 May	Bremen	0	3†
1989	6 Sept	Dublin	1	1

†*v West Germany 'B'*

		v GIBRALTAR	*RI*	*G*
EC2014	11 Oct	Dublin	7	0
EC2015	4 Sept	Faro	4	0
EC2019	**23 Mar**	**Gibraltar**	**1**	**0**
EC2019	**10 June**	**Dublin**	**2**	**0**
		v GREECE	*RI*	*G*
2000	26 Apr	Dublin	0	1
2002	20 Nov	Athens	0	0
2012	14 Nov	Dublin	0	1

		v HUNGARY	*RI*	*H*
1934	15 Dec	Dublin	2	4
1936	3 May	Budapest	3	3
1936	6 Dec	Dublin	2	3
1939	19 Mar	Cork	2	2
1939	18 May	Budapest	2	2
WC1969	8 June	Dublin	1	2
WC1969	5 Nov	Budapest	0	4
WC1989	8 Mar	Budapest	0	0
WC1989	4 June	Dublin	2	0
1991	11 Sept	Gyor	2	1
2012	4 June	Budapest	0	0
		v ICELAND	*RI*	*I*
EC1962	12 Aug	Dublin	4	2
EC1962	2 Sept	Reykjavik	1	1
EC1982	13 Oct	Dublin	2	0
EC1983	21 Sept	Reykjavik	3	0
1986	25 May	Reykjavik	2	1
WC1996	10 Nov	Dublin	0	0
WC1997	6 Sept	Reykjavik	4	2
2017	28 Mar	Dublin	0	1
		v IRAN	*RI*	*I*
1972	18 June	Recife	2	1
WC2001	10 Nov	Dublin	2	0
WC2001	15 Nov	Tehran	0	1
		v ISRAEL	*RI*	*I*
1984	4 Apr	Tel Aviv	0	3
1985	27 May	Tel Aviv	0	0
1987	10 Nov	Dublin	5	0
EC2005	26 Mar	Tel Aviv	1	1
EC2005	4 June	Dublin	2	2
		v ITALY	*RI*	*I*
1926	21 Mar	Turin	0	3
1927	23 Apr	Dublin	1	2
EC1970	8 Dec	Rome	0	3
EC1971	10 May	Dublin	1	2
1985	5 Feb	Dublin	1	2
WC1990	30 June	Rome	0	1
1992	4 June	Foxboro	0	2
WC1994	18 June	New York	1	0
2005	17 Aug	Dublin	1	2
WC2009	1 Apr	Bari	1	1
WC2009	10 Oct	Dublin	2	2
2011	7 June	Liege	2	0
EC2012	18 June	Poznan	0	2
2014	31 May	Craven Cottage	0	0
EC2016	22 June	Lille	1	0
		v JAMAICA	*RI*	*J*
2004	2 June	Charlton	1	0
		v KAZAKHSTAN	*RI*	*K*
WC2012	7 Sept	Astana	2	1
WC2013	15 Oct	Dublin	3	1
		v LATVIA	*RI*	*L*
WC1992	9 Sept	Dublin	4	0
WC1993	2 June	Riga	2	1
EC1994	7 Sept	Riga	3	0
EC1995	11 Oct	Dublin	2	1
2013	15 Nov	Dublin	3	0
		v LIECHTENSTEIN	*RI*	*L*
EC1994	12 Oct	Dublin	4	0
EC1995	3 June	Eschen	0	0
WC1996	31 Aug	Eschen	5	0
WC1997	21 May	Dublin	5	0
		v LITHUANIA	*RI*	*L*
WC1993	16 June	Vilnius	1	0
WC1993	8 Sept	Dublin	2	0
WC1997	20 Aug	Dublin	0	0
WC1997	10 Sept	Vilnius	2	1
		v LUXEMBOURG	*RI*	*L*
1936	9 May	Luxembourg	5	1
WC1953	28 Oct	Dublin	4	0
WC1954	7 Mar	Luxembourg	1	0
EC1987	28 May	Luxembourg	2	0
EC1987	9 Sept	Dublin	2	1

v MALTA			*RI*	*M*
EC1983	30 Mar	Valletta	1	0
EC1983	16 Nov	Dublin	8	0
WC1989	28 May	Dublin	2	0
WC1989	15 Nov	Valletta	2	0
1990	2 June	Valletta	3	0
EC1998	14 Oct	Dublin	5	0
EC1999	8 Sept	Valletta	3	2

v MEXICO			*RI*	*M*
1984	8 Aug	Dublin	0	0
WC1994	24 June	Orlando	1	2
1996	13 June	New Jersey	2	2
1998	23 May	Dublin	0	0
2000	4 June	Chicago	2	2
2017	2 June	New Jersey	1	3

v MOLDOVA			*RI*	*M*
WC2016	9 Oct	Chisinau	3	1
WC2017	6 Oct	Dublin	2	0

v MONTENEGRO			*RI*	*M*
WC2008	10 Sept	Podgorica	0	0
WC2009	14 Oct	Dublin	0	0

v MOROCCO			*RI*	*M*
1990	12 Sept	Dublin	1	0

v NETHERLANDS			*RI*	*N*
1932	8 May	Amsterdam	2	0
1934	8 Apr	Amsterdam	2	5
1935	8 Dec	Dublin	3	5
1955	1 May	Dublin	1	0
1956	10 May	Rotterdam	4	1
WC1980	10 Sept	Dublin	2	1
WC1981	9 Sept	Rotterdam	2	2
EC1982	22 Sept	Rotterdam	1	2
EC1983	12 Oct	Dublin	2	3
EC1988	18 June	Gelsenkirchen	0	1
WC1990	21 June	Palermo	1	1
1994	20 Apr	Tilburg	1	0
WC1994	4 July	Orlando	0	2
EC1995	13 Dec	Liverpool	0	2
1996	4 June	Rotterdam	1	3
WC2000	2 Sept	Amsterdam	2	2
WC2001	1 Sept	Dublin	1	0
2004	5 June	Amsterdam	1	0
2006	16 Aug	Dublin	0	4
2016	27 May	Dublin	1	1

v NIGERIA			*RI*	*N*
2002	16 May	Dublin	1	2
2004	29 May	Charlton	0	3
2009	29 May	Fulham	1	1

v NORTHERN IRELAND			*RI*	*NI*
EC1978	20 Sept	Dublin	0	0
EC1979	21 Nov	Belfast	0	1
WC1988	14 Sept	Belfast	0	0
WC1989	11 Oct	Dublin	3	0
WC1993	31 Mar	Dublin	3	0
WC1993	17 Nov	Belfast	1	1
EC1994	16 Nov	Belfast	4	0
EC1995	29 Mar	Dublin	1	1
1999	29 May	Dublin	0	1
NC2011	24 May	Dublin	5	0
2018	**15 Nov**	**Dublin**	**0**	**0**

v NORTH MACEDONIA			*RI*	*M*
WC1996	9 Oct	Dublin	3	0
WC1997	2 Apr	Skopje	2	3
EC1999	9 June	Dublin	1	0
EC1999	9 Oct	Skopje	1	1
EC2011	26 Mar	Dublin	2	1
EC2011	4 June	Podgorica	2	0

v NORWAY			*RI*	*N*
WC1937	10 Oct	Oslo	2	3
WC1937	7 Nov	Dublin	3	3
1950	26 Nov	Dublin	2	2
1951	30 May	Oslo	3	2
1954	8 Nov	Dublin	2	1
1955	25 May	Oslo	3	1
1960	6 Nov	Dublin	3	1
1964	13 May	Oslo	4	1
1973	6 June	Oslo	1	1
1976	24 Mar	Dublin	3	0
1978	21 May	Oslo	0	0

			RI	*N*
WC1984	17 Oct	Oslo	0	1
WC1985	1 May	Dublin	0	0
1988	1 June	Oslo	0	0
WC1994	28 June	New York	0	0
2003	30 Apr	Dublin	1	0
2008	20 Aug	Oslo	1	1
2010	17 Nov	Dublin	1	2

v OMAN			*RI*	*O*
2012	11 Sept	London	4	1
2014	3 Sept	Dublin	2	0
2016	31 Aug	Dublin	4	0

v PARAGUAY			*RI*	*P*
1999	10 Feb	Dublin	2	0
2010	25 May	Dublin	2	1

v POLAND			*RI*	*P*
1938	22 May	Warsaw	0	6
1938	13 Nov	Dublin	3	2
1958	11 May	Katowice	2	2
1958	5 Oct	Dublin	2	2
1964	10 May	Kracow	1	3
1964	25 Oct	Dublin	3	2
1968	15 May	Dublin	2	2
1968	30 Oct	Katowice	0	1
1970	6 May	Dublin	1	2
1970	23 Sept	Dublin	0	2
1973	16 May	Wroclaw	0	2
1973	21 Oct	Dublin	1	0
1976	26 May	Poznan	2	0
1977	24 Apr	Dublin	0	0
1978	12 Apr	Lodz	0	3
1981	23 May	Bydgoszcz	0	3
1984	23 May	Dublin	0	0
1986	12 Nov	Warsaw	0	1
1988	22 May	Dublin	3	1
EC1991	1 May	Dublin	0	0
EC1991	16 Oct	Poznan	3	3
2004	28 Apr	Bydgoszcz	0	0
2013	19 Nov	Poznan	0	0
2008	19 Nov	Dublin	2	3
2013	6 Feb	Dublin	2	0
2013	19 Nov	Poznan	0	0
EC2015	29 Mar	Dublin	1	1
EC2015	11 Oct	Warsaw	1	2
2018	**11 Sept**	**Wroclaw**	**1**	**1**

v PORTUGAL			*RI*	*P*
1946	16 June	Lisbon	1	3
1947	4 May	Dublin	0	2
1948	23 May	Lisbon	0	2
1949	22 May	Dublin	1	0
1972	25 June	Recife	1	2
1992	7 June	Boston	2	0
EC1995	26 Apr	Dublin	1	0
EC1995	15 Nov	Lisbon	0	3
1996	29 May	Dublin	0	1
WC2000	7 Oct	Lisbon	1	1
WC2001	2 June	Dublin	1	1
2005	9 Feb	Dublin	1	0
2014	10 June	New Jersey	1	5

v ROMANIA			*RI*	*R*
1988	23 Mar	Dublin	2	0
WC1990	25 June	Genoa	0	0*
WC1997	30 Apr	Bucharest	0	1
WC1997	11 Oct	Dublin	1	1
2004	27 May	Dublin	1	0

v RUSSIA			*RI*	*R*
1994	23 Mar	Dublin	0	0
1996	27 Mar	Dublin	0	2
2002	13 Feb	Dublin	2	0
EC2002	7 Sept	Moscow	2	4
EC2003	6 Sept	Dublin	1	1
EC2010	8 Oct	Dublin	2	3
EC2011	6 Sept	Moscow	0	0

v SAN MARINO			*RI*	*SM*
EC2006	15 Nov	Dublin	5	0
EC2007	7 Feb	Serravalle	2	1

v SAUDI ARABIA			*RI*	*SA*
WC2002	11 June	Yokohama	3	0

v SCOTLAND

			RI	*S*
WC1961	3 May	Glasgow	1	4
WC1961	7 May	Dublin	0	3
1963	9 June	Dublin	1	0
1969	21 Sept	Dublin	1	1
EC1986	15 Oct	Dublin	0	0
EC1987	18 Feb	Glasgow	1	0
2000	30 May	Dublin	1	2
2003	12 Feb	Glasgow	2	0
NC2011	29 May	Dublin	1	0
EC2014	14 Nov	Hampden	0	1
EC2015	13 June	Dublin	1	1

v SERBIA

			RI	*S*
2008	24 May	Dublin	1	1
2012	15 Aug	Belgrade	0	0
2014	5 Mar	Dublin	1	2
WC2016	5 Sept	Belgrade	2	2
WC2017	5 Sept	Dublin	0	1

v SLOVAKIA

			RI	*S*
EC2007	28 Mar	Dublin	1	0
EC2007	8 Sept	Bratislava	2	2
EC2010	12 Oct	Zilina	1	1
EC2011	2 Sept	Dublin	0	0
2016	29 Mar	Dublin	2	2

v SOUTH AFRICA

			RI	*SA*
2000	11 June	New Jersey	2	1
2009	8 Sept	Limerick	1	0

v SPAIN

			RI	*S*
1931	26 Apr	Barcelona	1	1
1931	13 Dec	Dublin	0	5
1946	23 June	Madrid	1	0
1947	2 Mar	Dublin	3	2
1948	30 May	Barcelona	1	2
1949	12 June	Dublin	1	4
1952	1 June	Madrid	0	6
1955	27 Nov	Dublin	2	2
EC1964	11 Mar	Seville	1	5
EC1964	8 Apr	Dublin	0	2
WC1965	5 May	Dublin	1	0
WC1965	27 Oct	Seville	1	4
WC1965	10 Nov	Paris	0	1
EC1966	23 Oct	Dublin	0	0
EC1966	7 Dec	Valencia	0	2
1977	9 Feb	Dublin	0	1
EC1982	17 Nov	Dublin	3	3
EC1983	27 Apr	Zaragoza	0	2
1985	26 May	Cork	0	0
WC1988	16 Nov	Seville	0	2
WC1989	26 Apr	Dublin	1	0
WC1992	18 Nov	Seville	0	0
WC1993	13 Oct	Dublin	1	3
WC2002	16 June	Suwon	1	1
EC2012	14 June	Gdansk	0	4
2013	11 June	New York	0	2

v SWEDEN

			RI	*S*
WC1949	2 June	Stockholm	1	3
WC1949	13 Nov	Dublin	1	3
1959	1 Nov	Dublin	3	2
1960	18 May	Malmo	1	4
EC1970	14 Oct	Dublin	1	1
EC1970	28 Oct	Malmo	0	1
1999	28 Apr	Dublin	2	0
2006	1 Mar	Dublin	3	0
WC2013	22 Mar	Stockholm	0	0
WC2013	6 Sept	Dublin	1	2
EC2016	13 June	Paris	1	1

v SWITZERLAND

			RI	*S*
1935	5 May	Basle	0	1
1936	17 Mar	Dublin	1	0
1937	17 May	Berne	1	0
1938	18 Sept	Dublin	4	0
1948	5 Dec	Dublin	0	1
EC1975	11 May	Dublin	2	1
EC1975	21 May	Berne	0	1
1980	30 Apr	Dublin	2	0
WC1985	2 June	Dublin	3	0
WC1985	11 Sept	Berne	0	0
1992	25 Mar	Dublin	2	1
EC2002	16 Oct	Dublin	1	2
EC2003	11 Oct	Basle	0	2
WC2004	8 Sept	Basle	1	1
WC2005	12 Oct	Dublin	0	0
2016	25 Mar	Dublin	1	0

v TRINIDAD & TOBAGO

			RI	*TT*
1982	30 May	Port of Spain	1	2

v TUNISIA

			RI	*T*
1988	19 Oct	Dublin	4	0

v TURKEY

			RI	*T*
EC1966	16 Nov	Dublin	2	1
EC1967	22 Feb	Ankara	1	2
EC1974	20 Nov	Izmir	1	1
EC1975	29 Oct	Dublin	4	0
2014	25 May	Dublin	1	2
1976	13 Oct	Ankara	3	3
1978	5 Apr	Dublin	4	2
1990	26 May	Izmir	0	0
EC1990	17 Oct	Dublin	5	0
EC1991	13 Nov	Istanbul	3	1
EC2000	13 Nov	Dublin	1	1
EC2000	17 Nov	Bursa	0	0
2003	9 Sept	Dublin	2	2
2014	25 May	Dublin	1	2
2018	23 Mar	Antalya	0	1

v URUGUAY

			RI	*U*
1974	8 May	Montevideo	0	2
1986	23 Apr	Dublin	1	1
2011	29 Mar	Dublin	2	3
2017	4 June	Dublin	3	1

v USA

			RI	*USA*
1979	29 Oct	Dublin	3	2
1991	1 June	Boston	1	1
1992	29 Apr	Dublin	4	1
1992	30 May	Washington	1	3
1996	9 June	Boston	1	2
2000	6 June	Boston	1	1
2002	17 Apr	Dublin	2	1
2014	18 Nov	Dublin	4	1
2018	2 June	Dublin	2	1

v USSR

			RI	*USSR*
WC1972	18 Oct	Dublin	1	2
WC1973	13 May	Moscow	0	1
EC1974	30 Oct	Dublin	3	0
EC1975	18 May	Kiev	1	2
WC1984	12 Sept	Dublin	1	0
WC1985	16 Oct	Moscow	0	2
EC1988	15 June	Hanover	1	1
1990	25 Apr	Dublin	1	0

v WALES

			RI	*W*
1960	28 Sept	Dublin	2	3
1979	11 Sept	Swansea	1	2
1981	24 Feb	Dublin	1	3
1986	26 Mar	Dublin	0	1
1990	28 Mar	Dublin	1	0
1991	6 Feb	Wrexham	3	0
1992	19 Feb	Dublin	0	1
1993	17 Feb	Dublin	2	1
1997	11 Feb	Cardiff	0	0
EC2007	24 Mar	Dublin	1	0
EC2007	17 Nov	Cardiff	2	2
NC2011	8 Feb	Dublin	3	0
2013	14 Aug	Cardiff	0	0
WC2017	24 Mar	Dublin	0	0
WC2017	9 Oct	Cardiff	1	0
NL2018	**6 Sept**	**Cardiff**	**1**	**4**
NL2018	**16 Oct**	**Dublin**	**0**	**1**

v YUGOSLAVIA

			RI	*Y*
1955	19 Sept	Dublin	1	4
1988	27 Apr	Dublin	2	0
EC1998	18 Nov	Belgrade	0	1
EC1999	1 Sept	Dublin	2	1

OTHER BRITISH AND IRISH INTERNATIONAL MATCHES 2018–19

FRIENDLIES

▪ *Denotes player sent off.*

ENGLAND

Tuesday, 11 September 2018

England (0) 1 *(Rashford 54)*

Switzerland (0) 0 30,256

England: (3142) Butland; Walker, Tarkowski (Stones 61), Maguire; Dier; Alexander-Arnold (Trippier 78), Loftus-Cheek (Lingard 61), Delph (Henderson 68), Rose (Chilwell 78); Rashford, Welbeck (Kane 61).
Switzerland: (3511) Sommer; Schar, Djourou, Akanji (Mehmedi 46); Lichtsteiner, Zakaria (Fernandes 66), Xhaka, Freuler (Zuber 66), Rodriguez (Moubandje 46); Shaqiri (Seferovic 80); Gavranovic (Ajeti 66).
Referee: Clement Turpin.

Thursday, 15 November 2018

England (2) 3 *(Lingard 25, Alexander-Arnold 27, Wilson 77)*

USA (0) 0 68,155

England: (4231) Pickford (McCarthy 46); Alexander-Arnold, Keane, Dunk, Chilwell (Dier 57); Delph, Winks (Loftus-Cheek 69); Alli (Henderson 57), Sancho, Lingard (Rooney 57); Wilson (Rashford 78).
USA: (4231) Guzan; Yedlin, Miazga, Brooks, Villafana (Moore 88); Trapp (Acosta 70), McKennie (Lletget 76); Green (Adams 62), Pulisic, Weah (Saief 76); Wood.
Referee: Jesus Gil Manzano.

SCOTLAND

Friday, 7 September 2018

Scotland (0) 0

Belgium (1) 4 *(Lukaku 28, Hazard E 46, Batshuayi 52, 60)* 20,196

Scotland: (352) Gordon; Souttar, Mulgrew (O'Donnell 68), Tierney; Fraser, McGinn (Shinnie 73), McDonald (Snodgrass 53), Armstrong (Jack 53), Robertson; McGregor C (Russell 68), Griffiths (Naismith 46).
Belgium: (343) Courtois; Kompany (Vermaelen 46), Boyata, Vertonghen; Hazard T, Tielemans, Dembele (Verstraete 85), Castagne (Meunier 46); Mertens (Carrasco 46), Lukaku (Batshuayi 46), Hazard E (Vanaken 55).
Referee: Luca Banti.

Sunday, 14 October 2018

Scotland (0) 1 *(Naismith 90)*

Portugal (1) 3 *(Helder Costa 43, Eder 74, Bruma 84)* 20,000

Scotland: (442) Gordon; O'Donnell, Hendry, McKenna, Robertson; McGregor C, Armstrong (McDonald 77), McGinn (Shinnie 67), Forrest; Naismith, McBurnie (Mackay-Steven 76).
Portugal: (433) Beto (Claudio Ramos 86); Cedric, Neto, Dias (Pedro Mendes 56), Rodrigues; Danilo Pereira (William Carvalho 90), Sergio Oliveira (Sanches 56), Bruno Fernandes (Fernandes 68); Bruma (Rafa Silva 90), Eder, Helder Costa.
Referee: Ruddy Buquet.

WALES

Thursday, 11 October 2018

Wales (0) 1 *(Vokes 89)*

Spain (3) 4 *(Alcacer 8, 29, Sergio Ramos 19, Bartra 74)* 50,232

Wales: (352) Hennessey; Gunter, Williams A (Chester 46), Davies B (Richards 62); Roberts C, Allen (Smith 61), Ramsey, Ampadu (King 50), John (Lawrence T 62); Wilson (Brooks 46), Vokes.
Spain: (4312) de Gea (Arrizabalaga 46); Azpilicueta (Jonny 62), Albiol, Sergio Ramos (Bartra 46), Gaya; Suso (Rodrigo 81), Rodri, Saul (Koke 46); Ceballos; Morata, Alcacer (Aspas 73).
Referee: Anthony Taylor.

Tuesday, 20 November 2018

Albania (0) 1 *(Balaj 59 (pen))*

Wales (0) 0 3000

Albania: (352) Berisha; Ismajli, Mavraj, Veseli; Uzuni, Basha, Lila (Memushaj 60), Xhaka, Hysaj; Grezda (Lilaj 68), Balaj.
Wales: (433) Ward; Gunter, Lockyer, Lawrence J, Roberts C (Freeman 79); Allen (Ramsey 56), James (Woodburn 55), King; Brooks (Bale 59), Vokes (Matondo 78), Wilson.
Referee: Dejan Jakimovksi.

Wednesday, 20 March 2019

Wales (0) 1 *(Woodburn 90)*

Trinidad and Tobago (0) 0 10,326

Wales: (442) Ward (Davies A 46); Gunter, Williams (Lawrence T 61), Dummett (John 61), Taylor; Hedges, Vaulks, Evans, Thomas; Roberts T (Matondo 70), Woodburn.
Trinidad and Tobago: (442) Phillip; David, Cyrus, Bateau, Hodge; George, Hyland, Paul (Hackshaw 81), Garcia (Peltier 60); Lewis, Plaza (Cato 46).
Referee: Tim Marshall.

NORTHERN IRELAND

Tuesday, 11 September 2018

Northern Ireland (2) 3 *(Davis 13, Dallas 42, Whyte 67)*

Israel (0) 0 17,895

Northern Ireland: (433) Carson (McGovern 46); McNair, Evans J, Cathcart, Lewis; Davis, Evans C (Norwood 46), Saville (Smith 71); Dallas (Ferguson 77), Grigg (Whyte 65), Jones (Washington 65).
Israel: (442) Haimov; Dasa (Biton 65), Tawatha (Scheimann 40), Habashi (Kapiloto 46), Yeini; Tibi, Natcho, Peretz, Micha (Turgeman 58); Hemed (Saba 59), Dabbur (Glazer 75).
Referee: Bas Nijhuis.

Thursday, 15 November 2018

Republic of Ireland (0) 0

Northern Ireland (0) 0 31,241

Republic of Ireland: (541) Randolph; Coleman, Lenihan (Christie 84), Duffy, Egan, McClean (Stevens 66); O'Dowda (Curtis 46), Hendrick, Whelan (Hourihane 36), Brady; Robinson (Maguire 66 (Hogan 79)).
Northern Ireland: (433) Peacock-Farrell; Smith (Ward 74), Cathcart, Evans J, Lewis; Evans C (McNair 65), Davis, Saville; Whyte (Jones 62), Boyce (Lafferty 71), Dallas.
Referee: Slavko Vincic.

REPUBLIC OF IRELAND

Tuesday, 11 September 2018

Poland (0) 1 *(Klich 87)*

Republic of Ireland (0) 1 *(O'Brien 53)* 25,455

Poland: (4411) Szczesny; Kedziora, Glik (Bednarek 61), Kaminski, Reca (Pietrzak 73); Blaszczykowski (Frankowski 81), Krychowiak (Szymanski 72), Linetty, Kurzawa (Kadzior 46); Milik; Piatek (Klich 61).
Republic of Ireland: (3511) Randolph; Keogh, Egan, Long; Christie (Doherty 55), O'Dowda (Judge 90), Williams (Hourihane 72), Hendrick (Meyler 56), Stevens; Robinson (Burke 63); O'Brien (Horgan 81).
Referee: Boris Marhefka.

BRITISH AND IRISH INTERNATIONAL MANAGERS

England
Walter Winterbottom 1946–1962 (after period as coach); Alf Ramsey 1963–1974; Joe Mercer (caretaker) 1974; Don Revie 1974–1977; Ron Greenwood 1977–1982; Bobby Robson 1982–1990; Graham Taylor 1990–1993; Terry Venables (coach) 1994–1996; Glenn Hoddle 1996–1999; Kevin Keegan 1999–2000; Sven-Goran Eriksson 2001–2006; Steve McClaren 2006–2007; Fabio Capello 2008–2012; Roy Hodgson 2012–2016; Sam Allardyce 2016 for one match; Gareth Southgate from November 2016.

Northern Ireland
Peter Doherty 1951–1952; Bertie Peacock 1962–1967; Billy Bingham 1967–1971; Terry Neill 1971–1975; Dave Clements (player-manager) 1975–1976; Danny Blanchflower 1976–1979; Billy Bingham 1980–1994; Bryan Hamilton 1994–1998; Lawrie McMenemy 1998–1999; Sammy McIlroy 2000–2003; Lawrie Sanchez 2004–2007; Nigel Worthington 2007–2011; Michael O'Neill from December 2011.

Scotland (since 1967)
Bobby Brown 1967–1971; Tommy Docherty 1971–1972; Willie Ormond 1973–1977; Ally MacLeod 1977–1978; Jock Stein 1978–1985; Alex Ferguson (caretaker) 1985–1986 Andy Roxburgh (coach) 1986–1993; Craig Brown 1993–2001; Berti Vogts 2002–2004; Walter Smith 2004–2007; Alex McLeish 2007; George Burley 2008–2009; Craig Levein 2009–2012; Gordon Strachan 2013–2017; Alex McLeish 2018–19; Steve Clarke from May 2019.

Wales (since 1974)
Mike Smith 1974–1979; Mike England 1980–1988; David Williams (caretaker) 1988; Terry Yorath 1988–1993; John Toshack 1994 for one match; Mike Smith 1994–1995; Bobby Gould 1995–1999; Mark Hughes 1999–2004; John Toshack 2004–2010; Gary Speed 2010–2011; Chris Coleman 2012–2017; Ryan Giggs from January 2018.

Republic of Ireland
Liam Tuohy 1971–1972; Johnny Giles 1973–1980 (after period as player-manager); Eoin Hand 1980–1985; Jack Charlton 1986–1996; Mick McCarthy 1996–2002; Brian Kerr 2003–2006; Steve Staunton 2006–2007; Giovanni Trapattoni 2008–2013; Martin O'Neill 2013–2018; Mick McCarthy from November 2018.

Steve Clarke was appointed as Scotland's new Head Coach in May. (Action Images via Reuters/Lee Smith)

BRITISH AND IRISH INTERNATIONAL APPEARANCES 1872–2019

This is a list of full international appearances by Englishmen, Irishmen, Scotsmen and Welshmen in matches against the Home Countries and against foreign nations. It does not include unofficial matches against Commonwealth and Empire countries. The year indicated refers to the player's international debut season; i.e. 2019 is the 2018–19 season. **Bold** type indicates players who have made an international appearance in season 2018–19.

As at July 2019.

ENGLAND

Abbott, W. 1902 (Everton) 1
Abraham, K. O. T. (Tammy) 2018 (Chelsea) 2
A'Court, A. 1958 (Liverpool) 5
Adams, T. A. 1987 (Arsenal) 66
Adcock, H. 1929 (Leicester C) 5
Agbonlahor, G. 2009 (Aston Villa) 3
Alcock, C. W. 1875 (Wanderers) 1
Alderson, J. T. 1923 (Crystal Palace) 1
Aldridge, A. 1888 (WBA, Walsall Town Swifts) 2
Alexander-Arnold, T. J. 2018 (Liverpool) 6
Allen, A. 1888 (Aston Villa) 1
Allen, A. 1960 (Stoke C) 3
Allen, C. 1984 (QPR, Tottenham H) 5
Allen, H. 1888 (Wolverhampton W) 5
Allen, J. P. 1934 (Portsmouth) 2
Allen, R. 1952 (WBA) 5
Alli, B. J. (Dele) 2016 (Tottenham H) 37
Alsford, W. J. 1935 (Tottenham H) 1
Amos, A. 1885 (Old Carthusians) 2
Anderson, R. D. 1879 (Old Etonians) 1
Anderson, S. 1962 (Sunderland) 2
Anderson, V. A. 1979 (Nottingham F, Arsenal, Manchester U) 30
Anderton, D. R. 1994 (Tottenham H) 30
Angus, J. 1961 (Burnley) 1
Armfield, J. C. 1959 (Blackpool) 43
Armitage, G. H. 1926 (Charlton Ath) 1
Armstrong, D. 1980 (Middlesbrough, Southampton) 3
Armstrong, K. 1955 (Chelsea) 1
Arnold, J. 1933 (Fulham) 1
Arthur, J. W. H. 1885 (Blackburn R) 7
Ashcroft, J. 1906 (Woolwich Arsenal) 3
Ashmore, G. S. 1926 (WBA) 1
Ashton, C. T. 1926 (Corinthians) 1
Ashton, D. 2008 (West Ham U) 1
Ashurst, W. 1923 (Notts Co) 5
Astall, G. 1956 (Birmingham C) 2
Astle, J. 1969 (WBA) 5
Aston, J. 1949 (Manchester U) 17
Athersmith, W. C. 1892 (Aston Villa) 12
Atyeo, P. J. W. 1956 (Bristol C) 6
Austin, S. W. 1926 (Manchester C) 1

Bach, P. 1899 (Sunderland) 1
Bache, J. W. 1903 (Aston Villa) 7
Baddeley, T. 1903 (Wolverhampton W) 5
Bagshaw, J. J. 1920 (Derby Co) 1
Bailey, G. R. 1985 (Manchester U) 2
Bailey, H. P. 1908 (Leicester Fosse) 5
Bailey, M. A. 1964 (Charlton Ath) 2
Bailey, N. C. 1878 (Clapham R) 19
Baily, E. F. 1950 (Tottenham H) 9
Bain, J. 1877 (Oxford University) 1
Baines, L. J. 2010 (Everton) 30
Baker, A. 1928 (Arsenal) 1
Baker, B. H. 1921 (Everton, Chelsea) 2
Baker, J. H. 1960 (Hibernian, Arsenal) 8
Ball, A. J. 1965 (Blackpool, Everton, Arsenal) 72
Ball, J. 1928 (Bury) 1
Ball, M. J. 2001 (Everton) 1
Balmer, W. 1905 (Everton) 1
Bamber, J. 1921 (Liverpool) 1
Bambridge, A. L. 1881 (Swifts) 3
Bambridge, E. C. 1879 (Swifts) 18
Bambridge, E. H. 1876 (Swifts) 1
Banks, G. 1963 (Leicester C, Stoke C) 73
Banks, H. E. 1901 (Millwall) 1
Banks, T. 1958 (Bolton W) 6
Bannister, W. 1901 (Burnley, Bolton W) 2
Barclay, R. 1932 (Sheffield U) 3
Bardsley, D. J. 1993 (QPR) 2
Barham, M. 1983 (Norwich C) 2
Barkas, S. 1936 (Manchester C) 5
Barker, J. 1935 (Derby Co) 11
Barker, R. 1872 (Herts Rangers) 1
Barker, R. R. 1895 (Casuals) 1
Barkley, R. 2013 (Everton, Chelsea) 29
Barlow, R. J. 1955 (WBA) 1
Barmby, N. J. 1995 (Tottenham H, Middlesbrough, Everton, Liverpool) 23
Barnes, J. 1983 (Watford, Liverpool) 79
Barnes, P. S. 1978 (Manchester C, WBA, Leeds U) 22
Barnet, H. H. 1882 (Royal Engineers) 1
Barrass, M. W. 1952 (Bolton W) 3
Barrett, A. F. 1930 (Fulham) 1
Barrett, E. D. 1991 (Oldham Ath, Aston Villa) 3
Barrett, J. W. 1929 (West Ham U) 1
Barry, G. 2000 (Aston Villa, Manchester C) 53
Barry, L. 1928 (Leicester C) 5
Barson, F. 1920 (Aston Villa) 1
Barton, J. 1890 (Blackburn R) 1
Barton, J. 2007 (Manchester C) 1
Barton, P. H. 1921 (Birmingham) 7
Barton, W. D. 1995 (Wimbledon, Newcastle U) 3
Bassett, W. I. 1888 (WBA) 16
Bastard, S. R. 1880 (Upton Park) 1
Bastin, C. S. 1932 (Arsenal) 21
Batty, D. 1991 (Leeds U, Blackburn R, Newcastle U, Leeds U) 42
Baugh, R. 1886 (Stafford Road, Wolverhampton W) 2
Bayliss, A. E. J. M. 1891 (WBA) 1
Baynham, R. L. 1956 (Luton T) 3
Beardsley, P. A. 1986 (Newcastle U, Liverpool, Newcastle U) 59
Beasant, D. J. 1990 (Chelsea) 2
Beasley, A. 1939 (Huddersfield T) 1
Beats, W. E. 1901 (Wolverhampton W) 2
Beattie, J. S. 2003 (Southampton) 5
Beattie, T. K. 1975 (Ipswich T) 9
Beckham, D. R. J. 1997 (Manchester U, Real Madrid, LA Galaxy) 115
Becton, F. 1895 (Preston NE, Liverpool) 2
Bedford, H. 1923 (Blackpool) 2
Bell, C. 1968 (Manchester C) 48
Bennett, W. 1901 (Sheffield U) 2
Benson, R. W. 1913 (Sheffield U) 1
Bent, D. A. 2006 (Charlton Ath, Tottenham H, Sunderland, Aston Villa) 13
Bentley, D. M. 2008 (Blackburn R, Tottenham H) 7
Bentley, R. T. F. 1949 (Chelsea) 12
Beresford, J. 1934 (Aston Villa) 1
Berry, A. 1909 (Oxford University) 1
Berry, J. J. 1953 (Manchester U) 4
Bertrand, R. 2013 (Chelsea, Southampton) 19
Bestall, J. G. 1935 (Grimsby T) 1
Betmead, H. A. 1937 (Grimsby T) 1
Betts, M. P. 1877 (Old Harrovians) 1
Betts, W. 1889 (Sheffield W) 1
Beverley, J. 1884 (Blackburn R) 3
Birkett, R. H. 1879 (Clapham R) 1
Birkett, R. J. E. 1936 (Middlesbrough) 1
Birley, F. H. 1874 (Oxford University, Wanderers) 2
Birtles, G. 1980 (Nottingham F) 3
Bishop, S. M. 1927 (Leicester C) 4
Blackburn, F. 1901 (Blackburn R) 3
Blackburn, G. F. 1924 (Aston Villa) 1

Blenkinsop, E. 1928 (Sheffield W) 26
Bliss, H. 1921 (Tottenham H) 1
Blissett, L. L. 1983 (Watford, AC Milan) 14
Blockley, J. P. 1973 (Arsenal) 1
Bloomer, S. 1895 (Derby Co, Middlesbrough) 23
Blunstone, F. 1955 (Chelsea) 5
Bond, R. 1905 (Preston NE, Bradford C) 8
Bonetti, P. P. 1966 (Chelsea) 7
Bonsor, A. G. 1873 (Wanderers) 2
Booth, F. 1905 (Manchester C) 1
Booth, T. 1898 (Blackburn R, Everton) 2
Bothroyd, J. 2011 (Cardiff C) 1
Bould, S. A. 1994 (Arsenal) 2
Bowden, E. R. 1935 (Arsenal) 6
Bower, A. G. 1924 (Corinthians) 5
Bowers, J. W. 1934 (Derby Co) 3
Bowles, S. 1974 (QPR) 5
Bowser, S. 1920 (WBA) 1
Bowyer, L. D. 2003 (Leeds U) 1
Boyer, P. J. 1976 (Norwich C) 1
Boyes, W. 1935 (WBA, Everton) 3
Boyle, T. W. 1913 (Burnley) 1
Brabrook, P. 1958 (Chelsea) 3
Bracewell, P. W. 1985 (Everton) 3
Bradford, G. R. W. 1956 (Bristol R) 1
Bradford, J. 1924 (Birmingham) 12
Bradley, W. 1959 (Manchester U) 3
Bradshaw, F. 1908 (Sheffield W) 1
Bradshaw, T. H. 1897 (Liverpool) 1
Bradshaw, W. 1910 (Blackburn R) 4
Brann, G. 1886 (Swifts) 3
Brawn, W. F. 1904 (Aston Villa) 2
Bray, J. 1935 (Manchester C) 6
Brayshaw, E. 1887 (Sheffield W) 1
Bridge W. M. 2002 (Southampton, Chelsea, Manchester C) 36
Bridges, B. J. 1965 (Chelsea) 4
Bridgett, A. 1905 (Sunderland) 11
Brindle, T. 1880 (Darwen) 2
Brittleton, J. T. 1912 (Sheffield W) 5
Britton, C. S. 1935 (Everton) 9
Broadbent, P. F. 1958 (Wolverhampton W) 7
Broadis, I. A. 1952 (Manchester C, Newcastle U) 14
Brockbank, J. 1872 (Cambridge University) 1
Brodie, J. B. 1889 (Wolverhampton W) 3
Bromilow, T. G. 1921 (Liverpool) 5
Bromley-Davenport, W. E. 1884 (Oxford University) 2
Brook, E. F. 1930 (Manchester C) 18
Brooking, T. D. 1974 (West Ham U) 47
Brooks, J. 1957 (Tottenham H) 3
Broome, F. H. 1938 (Aston Villa) 7
Brown, A. 1882 (Aston Villa) 3
Brown, A. 1971 (WBA) 1
Brown, A. S. 1904 (Sheffield U) 2
Brown, G. 1927 (Huddersfield T, Aston Villa) 9
Brown, J. 1881 (Blackburn R) 5
Brown, J. H. 1927 (Sheffield W) 6
Brown, K. 1960 (West Ham U) 1
Brown, W. 1924 (West Ham U) 1
Brown, W. M. 1999 (Manchester U) 23
Bruton, J. 1928 (Burnley) 3
Bryant, W. I. 1925 (Clapton) 1
Buchan, C. M. 1913 (Sunderland) 6
Buchanan, W. S. 1876 (Clapham R) 1
Buckley, F. C. 1914 (Derby Co) 1
Bull, S. G. 1989 (Wolverhampton W) 13
Bullock, F. E. 1921 (Huddersfield T) 1
Bullock, N. 1923 (Bury) 3
Burgess, H. 1904 (Manchester C) 4
Burgess, H. 1931 (Sheffield W) 4
Burnup, C. J. 1896 (Cambridge University) 1
Burrows, H. 1934 (Sheffield W) 3
Burton, F. E. 1889 (Nottingham F) 1
Bury, L. 1877 (Cambridge University, Old Etonians) 2
Butcher, T. 1980 (Ipswich T, Rangers) 77
Butland, J. 2013 (Birmingham C, Stoke C) 9
Butler, J. D. 1925 (Arsenal) 1
Butler, W. 1924 (Bolton W) 1
Butt, N. 1997 (Manchester U, Newcastle U) 39
Byrne, G. 1963 (Liverpool) 2
Byrne, J. J. 1962 (Crystal Palace, West Ham U) 11
Byrne, R. W. 1954 (Manchester U) 33

Cahill, G. J. 2011 (Bolton W, Chelsea) 61
Callaghan, I. R. 1966 (Liverpool) 4
Calvey, J. 1902 (Nottingham F) 1
Campbell, A. F. 1929 (Blackburn R, Huddersfield T) 8
Campbell, F. L. 2012 (Sunderland) 1
Campbell, S. 1996 (Tottenham H, Arsenal, Portsmouth) 73
Camsell, G. H. 1929 (Middlesbrough) 9
Capes, A. J. 1903 (Stoke) 1
Carr, J. 1905 (Newcastle U) 2
Carr, J. 1920 (Middlesbrough) 2
Carr, W. H. 1875 (Owlerton, Sheffield) 1
Carragher, J. L. 1999 (Liverpool) 38
Carrick, M. 2001 (West Ham U, Tottenham H, Manchester U) 34
Carroll, A. T. 2011 (Newcastle U, Liverpool) 9
Carson, S. P. 2008 (Liverpool, WBA) 4
Carter, H. S. 1934 (Sunderland, Derby Co) 13
Carter, J. H. 1926 (WBA) 3
Catlin, A. E. 1937 (Sheffield W) 5
Caulker, S. A. 2013 (Tottenham H) 1
Chadwick, A. 1900 (Southampton) 2
Chadwick, E. 1891 (Everton) 7
Chalobah, N. N. 2019 (Watford) 1
Chamberlain, M. 1983 (Stoke C) 8
Chambers, H. 1921 (Liverpool) 8
Chambers, C. 2015 (Arsenal) 3
Channon, M. R. 1973 (Southampton, Manchester C) 46
Charles, G. A. 1991 (Nottingham F) 2
Charlton, J. 1965 (Leeds U) 35
Charlton, R. 1958 (Manchester U) 106
Charnley, R. O. 1963 (Blackpool) 1
Charsley, C. C. 1893 (Small Heath) 1
Chedgzoy, S. 1920 (Everton) 8
Chenery, C. J. 1872 (Crystal Palace) 3
Cherry, T. J. 1976 (Leeds U) 27
Chilwell, B. J. 2019 (Leicester C) 7
Chilton, A. 1951 (Manchester U) 2
Chippendale, H. 1894 (Blackburn R) 1
Chivers, M. 1971 (Tottenham H) 24
Christian, E. 1879 (Old Etonians) 1
Clamp, E. 1958 (Wolverhampton W) 4
Clapton, D. R. 1959 (Arsenal) 1
Clare, T. 1889 (Stoke) 4
Clarke, A. J. 1970 (Leeds U) 19
Clarke, H. A. 1954 (Tottenham H) 1
Clay, T. 1920 (Tottenham H) 4
Clayton, R. 1956 (Blackburn R) 35
Clegg, J. C. 1872 (Sheffield W) 1
Clegg, W. E. 1873 (Sheffield W, Sheffield Alb) 2
Clemence, R. N. 1973 (Liverpool, Tottenham H) 61
Clement, D. T. 1976 (QPR) 5
Cleverley, T. W. 2013 (Manchester U) 13
Clough, B. H. 1960 (Middlesbrough) 2
Clough, N. H. 1989 (Nottingham F) 14
Clyne, N. E. 2015 (Southampton, Liverpool) 14
Coates, R. 1970 (Burnley, Tottenham H) 4
Cobbold, W. N. 1883 (Cambridge University, Old Carthusians) 9
Cock, J. G. 1920 (Huddersfield T, Chelsea) 2
Cockburn, H. 1947 (Manchester U) 13
Cohen, G. R. 1964 (Fulham) 37
Cole, A. 2001 (Arsenal, Chelsea) 107
Cole, A. A. 1995 (Manchester U) 15
Cole, C. 2009 (West Ham U) 7
Cole, J. J. 2001 (West Ham U, Chelsea) 56
Colclough, H. 1914 (Crystal Palace) 1
Coleman, E. H. 1921 (Dulwich Hamlet) 1
Coleman, J. 1907 (Woolwich Arsenal) 1
Collymore, S. V. 1995 (Nottingham F, Aston Villa) 3
Common, A. 1904 (Sheffield U, Middlesbrough) 3
Compton, L. H. 1951 (Arsenal) 2
Conlin, J. 1906 (Bradford C) 1
Connelly, J. M. 1960 (Burnley, Manchester U) 20
Cook, L. J. 2018 (Bournemouth) 1
Cook, T. E. R. 1925 (Brighton) 1
Cooper, C. T. 1995 (Nottingham F) 2
Cooper, N. C. 1893 (Cambridge University) 1

Cooper, T. 1928 (Derby Co) 15
Cooper, T. 1969 (Leeds U) 20
Coppell, S. J. 1978 (Manchester U) 42
Copping, W. 1933 (Leeds U, Arsenal, Leeds U) 20
Corbett, B. O. 1901 (Corinthians) 1
Corbett, R. 1903 (Old Malvernians) 1
Corbett, W. S. 1908 (Birmingham) 3
Cork, J. F. P. 2018 (Burnley) 1
Corrigan, J. T. 1976 (Manchester C) 9
Cottee, A. R. 1987 (West Ham U, Everton) 7
Cotterill, G. H. 1891 (Cambridge University, Old Brightonians) 4
Cottle, J. R. 1909 (Bristol C) 1
Cowan, S. 1926 (Manchester C) 3
Cowans, G. S. 1983 (Aston Villa, Bari, Aston Villa) 10
Cowell, A. 1910 (Blackburn R) 1
Cox, J. 1901 (Liverpool) 3
Cox, J. D. 1892 (Derby Co) 1
Crabtree, J. W. 1894 (Burnley, Aston Villa) 14
Crawford, J. F. 1931 (Chelsea) 1
Crawford, R. 1962 (Ipswich T) 2
Crawshaw, T. H. 1895 (Sheffield W) 10
Crayston, W. J. 1936 (Arsenal) 8
Creek, F. N. S. 1923 (Corinthians) 1
Cresswell, A. W. 2017 (West Ham U) 3
Cresswell, W. 1921 (South Shields, Sunderland, Everton) 7
Crompton, R. 1902 (Blackburn R) 41
Crooks, S. D. 1930 (Derby Co) 26
Crouch, P. J. 2005 (Southampton, Liverpool, Portsmouth, Tottenham H) 42
Crowe, C. 1963 (Wolverhampton W) 1
Cuggy, F. 1913 (Sunderland) 2
Cullis, S. 1938 (Wolverhampton W) 12
Cunliffe, A. 1933 (Blackburn R) 2
Cunliffe, D. 1900 (Portsmouth) 1
Cunliffe, J. N. 1936 (Everton) 1
Cunningham, L. 1979 (WBA, Real Madrid) 6
Curle, K. 1992 (Manchester C) 3
Currey, E. S. 1890 (Oxford University) 2
Currie, A. W. 1972 (Sheffield U, Leeds U) 17
Cursham, A. W. 1876 (Notts Co) 6
Cursham, H. A. 1880 (Notts Co) 8

Daft, H. B. 1889 (Notts Co) 5
Daley, A. M. 1992 (Aston Villa) 7
Danks, T. 1885 (Nottingham F) 1
Davenport, P. 1985 (Nottingham F) 1
Davenport, J. K. 1885 (Bolton W) 2
Davies, K. C. 2011 (Bolton W) 1
Davis, G. 1904 (Derby Co) 2
Davis, H. 1903 (Sheffield W) 3
Davison, J. E. 1922 (Sheffield W) 1
Dawson, J. 1922 (Burnley) 2
Dawson, M. R. 2011 (Tottenham H) 4
Day, S. H. 1906 (Old Malvernians) 3
Dean, W. R. 1927 (Everton) 16
Deane, B. C. 1991 (Sheffield U) 3
Deeley, N. V. 1959 (Wolverhampton W) 2
Defoe, J. C. 2004 (Tottenham H, Portsmouth, Tottenham H, Sunderland) 57
Delph, F. 2015 (Aston Villa, Manchester C) 20
Devey, J. H. G. 1892 (Aston Villa) 2
Devonshire, A. 1980 (West Ham U) 8
Dewhurst, F. 1886 (Preston NE) 9
Dewhurst, G. P. 1895 (Liverpool Ramblers) 1
Dickinson, J. W. 1949 (Portsmouth) 48
Dier, E. J. E. 2016 (Tottenham H) 40
Dimmock, J. H. 1921 (Tottenham H) 3
Ditchburn, E. G. 1949 (Tottenham H) 6
Dix, R. W. 1939 (Derby Co) 1
Dixon, J. A. 1885 (Notts Co) 1
Dixon, K. M. 1985 (Chelsea) 8
Dixon, L. M. 1990 (Arsenal) 22
Dobson, A. T. C. 1882 (Notts Co) 4
Dobson, C. F. 1886 (Notts Co) 1
Dobson, J. M. 1974 (Burnley, Everton) 5
Doggart, A. G. 1924 (Corinthians) 1
Dorigo, A. R. 1990 (Chelsea, Leeds U) 15
Dorrell, A. R. 1925 (Aston Villa) 4
Douglas, B. 1958 (Blackburn R) 36
Downing, S. 2005 (Middlesbrough, Aston Villa, Liverpool, West Ham U) 35
Downs, R. W. 1921 (Everton) 1
Doyle, M. 1976 (Manchester C) 5
Drake, E. J. 1935 (Arsenal) 5
Drinkwater, D. N. 2016 (Leicester C) 3
Dublin, D. 1998 (Coventry C, Aston Villa) 4
Ducat, A. 1910 (Woolwich Arsenal, Aston Villa) 6
Dunn, A. T. B. 1883 (Cambridge University, Old Etonians) 4
Dunn, D. J. I. 2003 (Blackburn R) 1
Dunk, L. C. 2019 (Brighton & HA) 1
Duxbury, M. 1984 (Manchester U) 10
Dyer, K. C. 2000 (Newcastle U, West Ham U) 33

Earle, S. G. J. 1924 (Clapton, West Ham U) 2
Eastham, G. 1963 (Arsenal) 19
Eastham, G. R. 1935 (Bolton W) 1
Eckersley, W. 1950 (Blackburn R) 17
Edwards, D. 1955 (Manchester U) 18
Edwards, J. H. 1874 (Shropshire Wanderers) 1
Edwards, W. 1926 (Leeds U) 16
Ehiogu, U. 1996 (Aston Villa, Middlesbrough) 4
Ellerington, W. 1949 (Southampton) 2
Elliott, G. W. 1913 (Middlesbrough) 3
Elliott, W. H. 1952 (Burnley) 5
Evans, R. E. 1911 (Sheffield U) 4
Ewer, F. H. 1924 (Casuals) 2

Fairclough, P. 1878 (Old Foresters) 1
Fairhurst, D. 1934 (Newcastle U) 1
Fantham, J. 1962 (Sheffield W) 1
Fashanu, J. 1989 (Wimbledon) 2
Felton, W. 1925 (Sheffield W) 1
Fenton, M. 1938 (Middlesbrough) 1
Fenwick, T. W. 1984 (QPR, Tottenham H) 20
Ferdinand, L. 1993 (QPR, Newcastle U, Tottenham H) 17
Ferdinand, R. G. 1998 (West Ham U, Leeds U, Manchester U) 81
Field, E. 1876 (Clapham R) 2
Finney, T. 1947 (Preston NE) 76
Flanagan, J. P. 2014 (Liverpool) 1
Fleming, H. J. 1909 (Swindon T) 11
Fletcher, A. 1889 (Wolverhampton W) 2
Flowers, R. 1955 (Wolverhampton W) 49
Flowers, T. D. 1993 (Southampton, Blackburn R) 11
Forman, Frank 1898 (Nottingham F 9
Forman, F. R. 1899 (Nottingham F) 3
Forrest, J. H. 1884 (Blackburn R) 11
Forster, F. G. 2013 (Celtic, Southampton) 6
Fort, J. 1921 (Millwall) 1
Foster, B. 2007 (Manchester U, Birmingham C, WBA) 8
Foster, R. E. 1900 (Oxford University, Corinthians) 5
Foster, S. 1982 (Brighton & HA) 3
Foulke, W. J. 1897 (Sheffield U) 1
Foulkes, W. A. 1955 (Manchester U) 1
Fowler, R. B. 1996 (Liverpool, Leeds U) 26
Fox, F. S. 1925 (Millwall) 1
Francis, G. C. J. 1975 (QPR) 12
Francis, T. 1977 (Birmingham C, Nottingham F, Manchester C, Sampdoria) 52
Franklin, C. F. 1947 (Stoke C) 27
Freeman, B. C. 1909 (Everton, Burnley) 5
Froggatt, J. 1950 (Portsmouth) 13
Froggatt, R. 1953 (Sheffield W) 4
Fry, C. B. 1901 (Corinthians) 1
Furness, W. I. 1933 (Leeds U) 1

Galley, T. 1937 (Wolverhampton W) 2
Gardner, A. 2004 (Tottenham H) 1
Gardner, T. 1934 (Aston Villa) 2
Garfield, B. 1898 (WBA) 1
Garraty, W. 1903 (Aston Villa) 1
Garrett, T. 1952 (Blackpool) 3
Gascoigne, P. J. 1989 (Tottenham H, Lazio, Rangers, Middlesbrough) 57
Gates, E. 1981 (Ipswich T) 2
Gay, L. H. 1893 (Cambridge University, Old Brightonians) 3
Geary, F. 1890 (Everton) 2
Geaves, R. L. 1875 (Clapham R) 1

Gee, C. W. 1932 (Everton) 3
Geldard, A. 1933 (Everton) 4
George, C. 1977 (Derby Co) 1
George, W. 1902 (Aston Villa) 3
Gerrard, S. G. 2000 (Liverpool) 114
Gibbins, W. V. T. 1924 (Clapton) 2
Gibbs, K. J. R. 2011 (Arsenal) 10
Gidman, J. 1977 (Aston Villa) 1
Gillard, I. T. 1975 (QPR) 3
Gilliat, W. E. 1893 (Old Carthusians) 1
Goddard, P. 1982 (West Ham U) 1
Gomez, J. D. 2018 (Liverpool) 7
Goodall, F. R. 1926 (Huddersfield T) 25
Goodall, J. 1888 (Preston NE, Derby Co) 14
Goodhart, H. C. 1883 (Old Etonians) 3
Goodwyn, A. G. 1873 (Royal Engineers) 1
Goodyer, A. C. 1879 (Nottingham F) 1
Gosling, R. C. 1892 (Old Etonians) 5
Gosnell, A. A. 1906 (Newcastle U) 1
Gough, H. C. 1921 (Sheffield U) 1
Goulden, L. A. 1937 (West Ham U) 14
Graham, L. 1925 (Millwall) 2
Graham, T. 1931 (Nottingham F) 2
Grainger, C. 1956 (Sheffield U, Sunderland) 7
Gray, A. A. 1992 (Crystal Palace) 1
Gray, M. 1999 (Sunderland) 3
Greaves, J. 1959 (Chelsea, Tottenham H) 57
Green, F. T. 1876 (Wanderers) 1
Green, G. H. 1925 (Sheffield U) 8
Green, R. P. 2005 (Norwich C, West Ham U) 12
Greenhalgh, E. H. 1872 (Notts Co) 2
Greenhoff, B. 1976 (Manchester U, Leeds U) 18
Greenwood, D. H. 1882 (Blackburn R) 2
Gregory, J. 1983 (QPR) 6
Grimsdell, A. 1920 (Tottenham H) 6
Grosvenor, A. T. 1934 (Birmingham) 3
Gunn, W. 1884 (Notts Co) 2
Guppy, S. 2000 (Leicester C) 1
Gurney, R. 1935 (Sunderland) 1

Hacking, J. 1929 (Oldham Ath) 3
Hadley, H. 1903 (WBA) 1
Hagan, J. 1949 (Sheffield U) 1
Haines, J. T. W. 1949 (WBA) 1
Hall, A. E. 1910 (Aston Villa) 1
Hall, G. W. 1934 (Tottenham H) 10
Hall, J. 1956 (Birmingham C) 17
Halse, H. J. 1909 (Manchester U) 1
Hammond, H. E. D. 1889 (Oxford University) 1
Hampson, J. 1931 (Blackpool) 3
Hampton, H. 1913 (Aston Villa) 4
Hancocks, J. 1949 (Wolverhampton W) 3
Hapgood, E. 1933 (Arsenal) 30
Hardinge, H. T. W. 1910 (Sheffield U) 1
Hardman, H. P. 1905 (Everton) 4
Hardwick, G. F. M. 1947 (Middlesbrough) 13
Hardy, H. 1925 (Stockport Co) 1
Hardy, S. 1907 (Liverpool, Aston Villa) 21
Harford, M. G. 1988 (Luton T) 2
Hargreaves, F. W. 1880 (Blackburn R) 3
Hargreaves, J. 1881 (Blackburn R) 2
Hargreaves, O. 2002 (Bayern Munich, Manchester U) 42
Harper, E. C. 1926 (Blackburn R) 1
Harris, G. 1966 (Burnley) 1
Harris, P. P. 1950 (Portsmouth) 2
Harris, S. S. 1904 (Cambridge University, Old Westminsters) 6
Harrison, A. H. 1893 (Old Westminsters) 2
Harrison, G. 1921 (Everton) 2
Harrow, J. H. 1923 (Chelsea) 2
Hart, C. J. J. 2008 (Manchester C) 75
Hart, E. 1929 (Leeds U) 8
Hartley, F. 1923 (Oxford C) 1
Harvey, A. 1881 (Wednesbury Strollers) 1
Harvey, J. C. 1971 (Everton) 1
Hassall, H. W. 1951 (Huddersfield T, Bolton W) 5
Hateley, M. 1984 (Portsmouth, AC Milan, Monaco, Rangers) 32
Hawkes, R. M. 1907 (Luton T) 5
Haworth, G. 1887 (Accrington) 5
Hawtrey, J. P. 1881 (Old Etonians) 2
Haygarth, E. B. 1875 (Swifts) 1
Haynes, J. N. 1955 (Fulham) 56
Healless, H. 1925 (Blackburn R) 2
Heaton, T. 2016 (Burnley) 3
Hector, K. J. 1974 (Derby Co) 2
Hedley, G. A. 1901 (Sheffield U) 1
Hegan, K. E. 1923 (Corinthians) 4
Hellawell, M. S. 1963 (Birmingham C) 2
Henderson, J. B. 2011 (Sunderland, Liverpool) 51
Hendrie, L. A. 1999 (Aston Villa) 1
Henfrey, A. G. 1891 (Cambridge University, Corinthians) 5
Henry, R. P. 1963 (Tottenham H) 1
Heron, F. 1876 (Wanderers) 1
Heron, G. H. H. 1873 (Uxbridge, Wanderers) 5
Heskey, E. W. I. 1999 (Leicester C, Liverpool, Birmingham C, Wigan Ath, Aston Villa) 62
Hibbert, W. 1910 (Bury) 1
Hibbs, H. E. 1930 (Birmingham) 25
Hill, F. 1963 (Bolton W) 2
Hill, G. A. 1976 (Manchester U) 6
Hill, J. H. 1925 (Burnley, Newcastle U) 11
Hill, R. 1983 (Luton T) 3
Hill, R. H. 1926 (Millwall) 1
Hillman, J. 1899 (Burnley) 1
Hills, A. F. 1879 (Old Harrovians) 1
Hilsdon, G. R. 1907 (Chelsea) 8
Hinchcliffe, A. G. 1997 (Everton, Sheffield W) 7
Hine, E. W. 1929 (Leicester C) 6
Hinton, A. T. 1963 (Wolverhampton W, Nottingham F) 3
Hirst, D. E. 1991 (Sheffield W) 3
Hitchens, G. A. 1961 (Aston Villa, Internazionale) 7
Hobbis, H. H. F. 1936 (Charlton Ath) 2
Hoddle, G. 1980 (Tottenham H, Monaco) 53
Hodge, S. B. 1986 (Aston Villa, Tottenham H, Nottingham F) 24
Hodgetts, D. 1888 (Aston Villa) 6
Hodgkinson, A. 1957 (Sheffield U) 5
Hodgson, G. 1931 (Liverpool) 3
Hodkinson, J. 1913 (Blackburn R) 3
Hogg, W. 1902 (Sunderland) 3
Holdcroft, G. H. 1937 (Preston NE) 2
Holden, A. D. 1959 (Bolton W) 5
Holden, G. H. 1881 (Wednesbury OA) 4
Holden-White, C. 1888 (Corinthians) 2
Holford, T. 1903 (Stoke) 1
Holley, G. H. 1909 (Sunderland) 10
Holliday, E. 1960 (Middlesbrough) 3
Hollins, J. W. 1967 (Chelsea) 1
Holmes, R. 1888 (Preston NE) 7
Holt, J. 1890 (Everton, Reading) 10
Hopkinson, E. 1958 (Bolton W) 14
Hossack, A. H. 1892 (Corinthians) 2
Houghton, W. E. 1931 (Aston Villa) 7
Houlker, A. E. 1902 (Blackburn R, Portsmouth, Southampton) 5
Howarth, R. H. 1887 (Preston NE, Everton) 5
Howe, D. 1958 (WBA) 23
Howe, J. R. 1948 (Derby Co) 3
Howell, L. S. 1873 (Wanderers) 1
Howell, R. 1895 (Sheffield U, Liverpool) 2
Howey, S. N. 1995 (Newcastle U) 4
Huddlestone, T. A. 2010 (Tottenham H) 4
Hudson, A. A. 1975 (Stoke C) 2
Hudson, J. 1883 (Sheffield) 1
Hudson-Odoi C. J. 2019 (Chelsea) 2
Hudspeth, F. C. 1926 (Newcastle U) 1
Hufton, A. E. 1924 (West Ham U) 6
Hughes, E. W. 1970 (Liverpool, Wolverhampton W) 62
Hughes, L. 1950 (Liverpool) 3
Hulme, J. H. A. 1927 (Arsenal) 9
Humphreys, P. 1903 (Notts Co) 1
Hunt, G. S. 1933 (Tottenham H) 3
Hunt, Rev. K. R. G. 1911 (Leyton) 2
Hunt, R. 1962 (Liverpool) 34
Hunt, S. 1984 (WBA) 2
Hunter, J. 1878 (Sheffield Heeley) 7
Hunter, N. 1966 (Leeds U) 28
Hurst, G. C. 1966 (West Ham U) 49

Ince, P. E. C. 1993 (Manchester U, Internazionale, Liverpool, Middlesbrough) 53
Ings, D. 2016 (Liverpool) 1
Iremonger, J. 1901 (Nottingham F) 2

Jack, D. N. B. 1924 (Bolton W, Arsenal) 9
Jackson, E. 1891 (Oxford University) 1
Jagielka, P. N. 2008 (Everton) 40
James. D. B. 1997 (Liverpool, Aston Villa, West Ham U, Manchester C, Portsmouth) 53
Jarrett, B. G. 1876 (Cambridge University) 3
Jarvis, M. T. 2011 (Wolverhampton W) 1
Jefferis, F. 1912 (Everton) 2
Jeffers, F. 2003 (Arsenal) 1
Jenas, J. A. 2003 (Newcastle U, Tottenham H) 21
Jenkinson, C. D. 2013 (Arsenal) 1
Jezzard, B. A. G. 1954 (Fulham) 2
Johnson, A. 2005 (Crystal Palace, Everton) 8
Johnson, A. 2010 (Manchester C) 12
Johnson, D. E. 1975 (Ipswich T, Liverpool) 8
Johnson, E. 1880 (Saltley College, Stoke) 2
Johnson, G. M. C. 2004 (Chelsea, Portsmouth, Liverpool) 54
Johnson, J. A. 1937 (Stoke C) 5
Johnson, S. A. M. 2001 (Derby Co) 1
Johnson, T. C. F. 1926 (Manchester C, Everton) 5
Johnson, W. H. 1900 (Sheffield U) 6
Johnston, H. 1947 (Blackpool) 10
Jones, A. 1882 (Walsall Swifts, Great Lever) 3
Jones, H. 1923 (Nottingham F) 1
Jones, H. 1927 (Blackburn R) 6
Jones, M. D. 1965 (Sheffield U, Leeds U) 3
Jones, P. A. 2012 (Manchester U) 27
Jones, R. 1992 (Liverpool) 8
Jones, W. 1901 (Bristol C) 1
Jones, W. H. 1950 (Liverpool) 2
Joy, B. 1936 (Casuals) 1

Kail, E. I. L. 1929 (Dulwich Hamlet) 3
Kane, H. E. 2015 (Tottenham H) 39
Kay, A. H. 1963 (Everton) 1
Kean, F. W. 1923 (Sheffield W, Bolton W) 9
Keane, M. V. 2017 (Burnley, Everton) 7
Keegan, J. K. 1973 (Liverpool, Hamburger SV, Southampton) 63
Keen, E. R. L. 1933 (Derby Co) 4
Kelly, M. R. 2012 (Liverpool) 1
Kelly, R. 1920 (Burnley, Sunderland, Huddersfield T) 14
Kennedy, A. 1984 (Liverpool) 2
Kennedy, R. 1976 (Liverpool) 17
Kenyon-Slaney, W. S. 1873 (Wanderers) 1
Keown, M. R. 1992 (Everton, Arsenal) 43
Kevan, D. T. 1957 (WBA) 14
Kidd, B. 1970 (Manchester U) 2
King, L. B. 2002 (Tottenham H) 21
King, R. S. 1882 (Oxford University) 1
Kingsford, R. K. 1874 (Wanderers) 1
Kingsley, M. 1901 (Newcastle U) 1
Kinsey, G. 1892 (Wolverhampton W, Derby Co) 4
Kirchen, A. J. 1937 (Arsenal) 3
Kirkland, C. E. 2007 (Liverpool) 1
Kirton, W. J. 1922 (Aston Villa) 1
Knight, A. E. 1920 (Portsmouth) 1
Knight, Z. 2005 (Fulham) 2
Knowles, C. 1968 (Tottenham H) 4
Konchesky, P. M. 2003 (Charlton Ath, West Ham U) 2

Labone, B. L. 1963 (Everton) 26
Lallana, A. D. 2013 (Southampton, Liverpool) 34
Lambert, R. L. 2013 (Southampton, Liverpool) 11
Lampard, F. J. 2000 (West Ham U, Chelsea) 106
Lampard, F. R. G. 1973 (West Ham U) 2
Langley, E. J. 1958 (Fulham) 3
Langton, R. 1947 (Blackburn R, Preston NE, Bolton W) 11
Latchford, R. D. 1978 (Everton) 12
Latheron, E. G. 1913 (Blackburn R) 2
Lawler, C. 1971 (Liverpool) 4
Lawton, T. 1939 (Everton, Chelsea, Notts Co) 23
Leach, T. 1931 (Sheffield W) 2
Leake, A. 1904 (Aston Villa) 5
Lee, E. A. 1904 (Southampton) 1
Lee, F. H. 1969 (Manchester C) 27
Lee, J. 1951 (Derby Co) 1
Lee, R. M. 1995 (Newcastle U) 21
Lee, S. 1983 (Liverpool) 14
Leighton, J. E. 1886 (Nottingham F) 1
Lennon, A. J. 2006 (Tottenham H) 21
Lescott, J. P. 2008 (Everton, Manchester C) 26
Le Saux, G. P. 1994 (Blackburn R, Chelsea) 36
Le Tissier, M. P. 1994 (Southampton) 8
Lilley, H. E. 1892 (Sheffield U) 1
Linacre, H. J. 1905 (Nottingham F) 2
Lindley, T. 1886 (Cambridge University, Nottingham F) 13
Lindsay, A. 1974 (Liverpool) 4
Lindsay, W. 1877 (Wanderers) 1
Lineker, G. 1984 (Leicester C, Everton, Barcelona, Tottenham H) 80
Lingard, J. E. 2017 (Manchester U) 24
Lintott, E. H. 1908 (QPR, Bradford C) 7
Lipsham, H. B. 1902 (Sheffield U) 1
Little, B. 1975 (Aston Villa) 1
Livermore, J. C. 2013 (Tottenham H, WBA) 7
Lloyd, L. V. 1971 (Liverpool, Nottingham F) 4
Lockett, A. 1903 (Stoke) 1
Lodge, L. V. 1894 (Cambridge University, Corinthians) 5
Lofthouse, J. M. 1885 (Blackburn R, Accrington, Blackburn R) 7
Lofthouse, N. 1951 (Bolton W) 33
Loftus-Cheek, R. I. 2018 (Chelsea) 10
Longworth, E. 1920 (Liverpool) 5
Lowder, A. 1889 (Wolverhampton W) 1
Lowe, E. 1947 (Aston Villa) 3
Lucas, T. 1922 (Liverpool) 3
Luntley, E. 1880 (Nottingham F) 2
Lyttelton, Hon. A. 1877 (Cambridge University) 1
Lyttelton, Hon. E. 1878 (Cambridge University) 1

Mabbutt, G. 1983 (Tottenham H) 16
Macaulay, R. H. 1881 (Cambridge University) 1
Macrae, S. 1883 (Notts Co) 5
Maddison, F. B. 1872 (Oxford University) 1
Madeley, P. E. 1971 (Leeds U) 24
Magee, T. P. 1923 (WBA) 5
Maguire, J. H. 2018 (Leicester C) 20
Makepeace, H. 1906 (Everton) 4
Male, C. G. 1935 (Arsenal) 19
Mannion, W. J. 1947 (Middlesbrough) 26
Mariner, P. 1977 (Ipswich T, Arsenal) 35
Marsden, J. T. 1891 (Darwen) 1
Marsden, W. 1930 (Sheffield W) 3
Marsh, R. W. 1972 (QPR, Manchester C) 9
Marshall, T. 1880 (Darwen) 2
Martin, A. 1981 (West Ham U) 17
Martin, H. 1914 (Sunderland) 1
Martyn, A. N. 1992 (Crystal Palace, Leeds U) 23
Marwood, B. 1989 (Arsenal) 1
Maskrey, H. M. 1908 (Derby Co) 1
Mason, C. 1887 (Wolverhampton W) 3
Mason, R. G. 2015 (Tottenham H) 1
Matthews, R. D. 1956 (Coventry C) 5
Matthews, S. 1935 (Stoke C, Blackpool) 54
Matthews, V. 1928 (Sheffield U) 2
Maynard, W. J. 1872 (1st Surrey Rifles) 2
McCall, J. 1913 (Preston NE) 5
McCann, G. P. 2001 (Sunderland) 1
McCarthy, A. S. 2019 (Southampton) 1
McDermott, T. 1978 (Liverpool) 25
McDonald, C. A. 1958 (Burnley) 8
Macdonald, M. 1972 (Newcastle U) 14
McFarland, R. L. 1971 (Derby Co) 28
McGarry, W. H. 1954 (Huddersfield T) 4
McGuinness, W. 1959 (Manchester U) 2
McInroy, A. 1927 (Sunderland) 1
McMahon, S. 1988 (Liverpool) 17
McManaman, S. 1995 (Liverpool, Real Madrid) 37
McNab, R. 1969 (Arsenal) 4
McNeal, R. 1914 (WBA) 2
McNeil, M. 1961 (Middlesbrough) 9
Meadows, J. 1955 (Manchester C) 1
Medley, L. D. 1951 (Tottenham H) 6

Meehan, T. 1924 (Chelsea) 1
Melia, J. 1963 (Liverpool) 2
Mercer, D. W. 1923 (Sheffield U) 2
Mercer, J. 1939 (Everton) 5
Merrick, G. H. 1952 (Birmingham C) 23
Merson, P. C. 1992 (Arsenal, Middlesbrough, Aston Villa) 21
Metcalfe, V. 1951 (Huddersfield T) 2
Mew, J. W. 1921 (Manchester U) 1
Middleditch, B. 1897 (Corinthians) 1
Milburn, J. E. T. 1949 (Newcastle U) 13
Miller, B. G. 1961 (Burnley) 1
Miller, H. S. 1923 (Charlton Ath) 1
Mills, D. J. 2001 (Leeds U) 19
Mills, G. R. 1938 (Chelsea) 3
Mills, M. D. 1973 (Ipswich T) 42
Milne, G. 1963 (Liverpool) 14
Milner, J. P. 2010 (Aston Villa, Manchester C, Liverpool) 61
Milton, C. A. 1952 (Arsenal) 1
Milward, A. 1891 (Everton) 4
Mitchell, C. 1880 (Upton Park) 5
Mitchell, J. F. 1925 (Manchester C) 1
Moffat, H. 1913 (Oldham Ath) 1
Molyneux, G. 1902 (Southampton) 4
Moon, W. R. 1888 (Old Westminsters) 7
Moore, H. T. 1883 (Notts Co) 2
Moore, J. 1923 (Derby Co) 1
Moore, R. F. 1962 (West Ham U) 108
Moore, W. G. B. 1923 (West Ham U) 1
Mordue, J. 1912 (Sunderland) 2
Morice, C. J. 1872 (Barnes) 1
Morley, A. 1982 (Aston Villa) 6
Morley, H. 1910 (Notts Co) 1
Morren, T. 1898 (Sheffield U) 1
Morris, F. 1920 (WBA) 2
Morris, J. 1949 (Derby Co) 3
Morris, W. W. 1939 (Wolverhampton W) 3
Morse, H. 1879 (Notts Co) 1
Mort, T. 1924 (Aston Villa) 3
Morten, A. 1873 (Crystal Palace) 1
Mortensen, S. H. 1947 (Blackpool) 25
Morton, J. R. 1938 (West Ham U) 1
Mosforth, W. 1877 (Sheffield W, Sheffield Alb, Sheffield W) 9
Moss, F. 1922 (Aston Villa) 5
Moss, F. 1934 (Arsenal) 4
Mosscrop, E. 1914 (Burnley) 2
Mozley, B. 1950 (Derby Co) 3
Mullen, J. 1947 (Wolverhampton W) 12
Mullery, A. P. 1965 (Tottenham H) 35
Murphy, D. B. 2002 (Liverpool) 9

Neal, P. G. 1976 (Liverpool) 50
Needham, E. 1894 (Sheffield U) 16
Neville, G. A. 1995 (Manchester U) 85
Neville, P. J. 1996 (Manchester U, Everton) 59
Newton, K. R. 1966 (Blackburn R, Everton) 27
Nicholls, J. 1954 (WBA) 2
Nicholson, W. E. 1951 (Tottenham H) 1
Nish, D. J. 1973 (Derby Co) 5
Norman, M. 1962 (Tottenham H) 23
Nugent, D. J. 2007 (Preston NE) 1
Nuttall, H. 1928 (Bolton W) 3

Oakley, W. J. 1895 (Oxford University, Corinthians) 16
O'Dowd, J. P. 1932 (Chelsea) 3
O'Grady, M. 1963 (Huddersfield T, Leeds U) 2
Ogilvie, R. A. M. M. 1874 (Clapham R) 1
Oliver, L. F. 1929 (Fulham) 1
Olney, B. A. 1928 (Aston Villa) 2
Osborne, F. R. 1923 (Fulham, Tottenham H) 4
Osborne, R. 1928 (Leicester C) 1
Osgood, P. L. 1970 (Chelsea) 4
Osman, L. 2013 (Everton) 2
Osman, R. 1980 (Ipswich T) 11
Ottaway, C. J. 1872 (Oxford University) 2
Owen, J. R. B. 1874 (Sheffield) 1
Owen, M. J. 1998 (Liverpool, Real Madrid, Newcastle U) 89
Owen, S. W. 1954 (Luton T) 3
Oxlade-Chamberlain, A. M. D. 2012 (Arsenal, Liverpool) 32

Page, L. A. 1927 (Burnley) 7
Paine, T. L. 1963 (Southampton) 19
Pallister, G. A. 1988 (Middlesbrough, Manchester U) 22
Palmer, C. L. 1992 (Sheffield W) 18
Pantling, H. H. 1924 (Sheffield U) 1
Paravicini, P. J. de 1883 (Cambridge University) 3
Parker, P. A. 1989 (QPR, Manchester U) 19
Parker, S. M. 2004 (Charlton Ath, Chelsea, Newcastle U, West Ham U, Tottenham H) 18
Parker, T. R. 1925 (Southampton) 1
Parkes, P. B. 1974 (QPR) 1
Parkinson, J. 1910 (Liverpool) 2
Parlour, R. 1999 (Arsenal) 10
Parr, P. C. 1882 (Oxford University) 1
Parry, E. H. 1879 (Old Carthusians) 3
Parry, R. A. 1960 (Bolton W) 2
Patchitt, B. C. A. 1923 (Corinthians) 2
Pawson, F. W. 1883 (Cambridge University, Swifts) 2
Payne, J. 1937 (Luton T) 1
Peacock, A. 1962 (Middlesbrough, Leeds U) 6
Peacock, J. 1929 (Middlesbrough) 3
Pearce, S. 1987 (Nottingham F, West Ham U) 78
Pearson, H. F. 1932 (WBA) 1
Pearson, J. H. 1892 (Crewe Alex) 1
Pearson, J. S. 1976 (Manchester U) 15
Pearson, S. C. 1948 (Manchester U) 8
Pease, W. H. 1927 (Middlesbrough) 1
Pegg, D. 1957 (Manchester U) 1
Pejic, M. 1974 (Stoke C) 4
Pelly, F. R. 1893 (Old Foresters) 3
Pennington, J. 1907 (WBA) 25
Pentland, F. B. 1909 (Middlesbrough) 5
Perry, C. 1890 (WBA) 3
Perry, T. 1898 (WBA) 1
Perry, W. 1956 (Blackpool) 3
Perryman, S. 1982 (Tottenham H) 1
Peters, M. 1966 (West Ham U, Tottenham H) 67
Phelan, M. C. 1990 (Manchester U) 1
Phillips, K. 1999 (Sunderland) 8
Phillips, L. H. 1952 (Portsmouth) 3
Pickering, F. 1964 (Everton) 3
Pickering, J. 1933 (Sheffield U) 1
Pickering, N. 1983 (Sunderland) 1
Pickford, J. L. 2018 (Everton) 19
Pike, T. M. 1886 (Cambridge University) 1
Pilkington, B. 1955 (Burnley) 1
Plant, J. 1900 (Bury) 1
Platt, D. 1990 (Aston Villa, Bari, Juventus, Sampdoria, Arsenal) 62
Plum, S. L. 1923 (Charlton Ath) 1
Pointer, R. 1962 (Burnley) 3
Pope, N. D. 2018 (Burnley) 1
Porteous, T. S. 1891 (Sunderland) 1
Powell, C. G. 2001 (Charlton Ath) 5
Priest, A. E. 1900 (Sheffield U) 1
Prinsep, J. F. M. 1879 (Clapham R) 1
Puddefoot, S. C. 1926 (Blackburn R) 2
Pye, J. 1950 (Wolverhampton W) 1
Pym, R. H. 1925 (Bolton W) 3

Quantrill, A. 1920 (Derby Co) 4
Quixall, A. 1954 (Sheffield W) 5

Radford, J. 1969 (Arsenal) 2
Raikes, G. B. 1895 (Oxford University) 4
Ramsey, A. E. 1949 (Southampton, Tottenham H) 32
Rashford, M. 2016 (Manchester U) 32
Rawlings, A. 1921 (Preston NE) 1
Rawlings, W. E. 1922 (Southampton) 2
Rawlinson, J. F. P. 1882 (Cambridge University) 1
Rawson, H. E. 1875 (Royal Engineers) 1
Rawson, W. S. 1875 (Oxford University) 2
Read, A. 1921 (Tufnell Park) 1
Reader, J. 1894 (WBA) 1
Reaney, P. 1969 (Leeds U) 3
Redknapp, J. F. 1996 (Liverpool) 17
Redmond, N. D. J. 2017 (Southampton) 1
Reeves, K. P. 1980 (Norwich C, Manchester C) 2

Regis, C. 1982 (WBA, Coventry C) 5
Reid, P. 1985 (Everton) 13
Revie, D. G. 1955 (Manchester C) 6
Reynolds, J. 1892 (WBA, Aston Villa) 8
Rice, D. 2019 (West Ham U) 3
Richards, C. H. 1898 (Nottingham F) 1
Richards, G. H. 1909 (Derby Co) 1
Richards, J. P. 1973 (Wolverhampton W) 1
Richards, M. 2007 (Manchester C) 13
Richardson, J. R. 1933 (Newcastle U) 2
Richardson, K. 1994 (Aston Villa) 1
Richardson, K. E. 2005 (Manchester U) 8
Richardson, W. G. 1935 (WBA) 1
Rickaby, S. 1954 (WBA) 1
Ricketts, M. B. 2002 (Bolton W) 1
Rigby, A. 1927 (Blackburn R) 5
Rimmer, E. J. 1930 (Sheffield W) 4
Rimmer, J. J. 1976 (Arsenal) 1
Ripley, S. E. 1994 (Blackburn R) 2
Rix, G. 1981 (Arsenal) 17
Robb, G. 1954 (Tottenham H) 1
Roberts, C. 1905 (Manchester U) 3
Roberts, F. 1925 (Manchester C) 4
Roberts, G. 1983 (Tottenham H) 6
Roberts, H. 1931 (Arsenal) 1
Roberts, H. 1931 (Millwall) 1
Roberts, R. 1887 (WBA) 3
Roberts, W. T. 1924 (Preston NE) 2
Robinson, J. 1937 (Sheffield W) 4
Robinson, J. W. 1897 (Derby Co, New Brighton Tower, Southampton) 11
Robinson, P. W. 2003 (Leeds U, Tottenham H, Blackburn R) 41
Robson, B. 1980 (WBA, Manchester U) 90
Robson, R. 1958 (WBA) 20
Rocastle, D. 1989 (Arsenal) 14
Rodriguez, J. E. 2013 (Southampton) 1
Rodwell, J. 2012 (Everton) 3
Rooney, W. M. 2003 (Everton, Manchester U, D.C. United) 120
Rose, D. L. 2016 (Tottenham H) 27
Rose, W. C. 1884 (Swifts, Preston NE, Wolverhampton W) 5
Rostron, T. 1881 (Darwen) 2
Rowe, A. 1934 (Tottenham H) 1
Rowley, J. F. 1949 (Manchester U) 6
Rowley, W. 1889 (Stoke) 2
Royle, J. 1971 (Everton, Manchester C) 6
Ruddlesdin, H. 1904 (Sheffield W) 3
Ruddock, N. 1995 (Liverpool) 1
Ruddy, J. T. G. 2013 (Norwich C) 1
Ruffell, J. W. 1926 (West Ham U) 6
Russell, B. B. 1883 (Royal Engineers) 1
Rutherford, J. 1904 (Newcastle U) 11

Sadler, D. 1968 (Manchester U) 4
Sagar, C. 1900 (Bury) 2
Sagar, E. 1936 (Everton) 4
Salako, J. A. 1991 (Crystal Palace) 5
Sancho, J. M. 2019 (Borussia Dortmund) 6
Sandford, E. A. 1933 (WBA) 1
Sandilands, R. R. 1892 (Old Westminsters) 5
Sands, J. 1880 (Nottingham F) 1
Sansom, K. G. 1979 (Crystal Palace, Arsenal) 86
Saunders, F. E. 1888 (Swifts) 1
Savage, A. H. 1876 (Crystal Palace) 1
Sayer, J. 1887 (Stoke) 1
Scales, J. R. 1995 (Liverpool) 3
Scattergood, E. 1913 (Derby Co) 1
Schofield, J. 1892 (Stoke) 3
Scholes, P. 1997 (Manchester U) 66
Scott, L. 1947 (Arsenal) 17
Scott, W. R. 1937 (Brentford) 1
Seaman, D. A. 1989 (QPR, Arsenal) 75
Seddon, J. 1923 (Bolton W) 6
Seed, J. M. 1921 (Tottenham H) 5
Settle, J. 1899 (Bury, Everton) 6
Sewell, J. 1952 (Sheffield W) 6
Sewell, W. R. 1924 (Blackburn R) 1
Shackleton, L. F. 1949 (Sunderland) 5
Sharp, J. 1903 (Everton) 2
Sharpe, L. S. 1991 (Manchester U) 8
Shaw, G. E. 1932 (WBA) 1
Shaw, G. L. 1959 (Sheffield U) 5
Shaw, L. P. H. 2014 (Southampton, Manchester U) 8
Shawcross, R. J. 2013 (Stoke C) 1
Shea, D. 1914 (Blackburn R) 2
Shearer, A. 1992 (Southampton, Blackburn R, Newcastle U) 63
Shellito, K. J. 1963 (Chelsea) 1
Shelton A. 1889 (Notts Co) 6
Shelton, C. 1888 (Notts Rangers) 1
Shelvey, J. 2013 (Liverpool, Swansea C) 6
Shepherd, A. 1906 (Bolton W, Newcastle U) 2
Sheringham, E. P. 1993 (Tottenham H, Manchester U, Tottenham H) 51
Sherwood, T. A. 1999 (Tottenham H) 3
Shilton, P. L. 1971 (Leicester C, Stoke C, Nottingham F, Southampton, Derby Co) 125
Shimwell, E. 1949 (Blackpool) 1
Shorey, N. 2007 (Reading) 2
Shutt, G. 1886 (Stoke) 1
Silcock, J. 1921 (Manchester U) 3
Sillett, R. P. 1955 (Chelsea) 3
Simms, E. 1922 (Luton T) 1
Simpson, J. 1911 (Blackburn R) 8
Sinclair, T. 2002 (West Ham U, Manchester C) 12
Sinton, A. 1992 (QPR, Sheffield W) 12
Slater, W. J. 1955 (Wolverhampton W) 12
Smalley, T. 1937 (Wolverhampton W) 1
Smalling, C. L. 2012 (Manchester U) 31
Smart, T. 1921 (Aston Villa) 5
Smith, A. 1891 (Nottingham F) 3
Smith, A. 2001 (Leeds U, Manchester U, Newcastle U) 19
Smith, A. K. 1872 (Oxford University) 1
Smith, A. M. 1989 (Arsenal) 13
Smith, B. 1921 (Tottenham H) 2
Smith, C. E. 1876 (Crystal Palace) 1
Smith, G. O. 1893 (Oxford University, Old Carthusians, Corinthians) 20
Smith, H. 1905 (Reading) 4
Smith, J. 1920 (WBA) 2
Smith, Joe 1913 (Bolton W) 5
Smith, J. C. R. 1939 (Millwall) 2
Smith, J. W. 1932 (Portsmouth) 3
Smith, Leslie 1939 (Brentford) 1
Smith, Lionel 1951 (Arsenal) 6
Smith, R. A. 1961 (Tottenham H) 15
Smith, S. 1895 (Aston Villa) 1
Smith, S. C. 1936 (Leicester C) 1
Smith, T. 1960 (Birmingham C) 2
Smith, T. 1971 (Liverpool) 1
Smith, W. H. 1922 (Huddersfield T) 3
Solanke, D. A. 2018 (Liverpool) 1
Sorby, T. H. 1879 (Thursday Wanderers, Sheffield) 1
Southgate, G. 1996 (Aston Villa, Middlesbrough) 57
Southworth, J. 1889 (Blackburn R) 3
Sparks, F. J. 1879 (Herts Rangers, Clapham R) 3
Spence, J. W. 1926 (Manchester U) 2
Spence, R. 1936 (Chelsea) 2
Spencer, C. W. 1924 (Newcastle U) 2
Spencer, H. 1897 (Aston Villa) 6
Spiksley, F. 1893 (Sheffield W) 7
Spilsbury, B. W. 1885 (Cambridge University) 3
Spink, N. 1983 (Aston Villa) 1
Spouncer, W. A. 1900 (Nottingham F) 1
Springett, R. D. G. 1960 (Sheffield W) 33
Sproston, B. 1937 (Leeds U, Tottenham H, Manchester C) 11
Squire, R. T. 1886 (Cambridge University) 3
Stanbrough, M. H. 1895 (Old Carthusians) 1
Staniforth, R. 1954 (Huddersfield T) 8
Starling, R. W. 1933 (Sheffield W, Aston Villa) 2
Statham, D. J. 1983 (WBA) 3
Steele, F. C. 1937 (Stoke C) 6
Stein, B. 1984 (Luton T) 1
Stephenson, C. 1924 (Huddersfield T) 1
Stephenson, G. T. 1928 (Derby Co, Sheffield W) 3
Stephenson, J. E. 1938 (Leeds U) 2
Stepney, A. C. 1968 (Manchester U) 1
Sterland, M. 1989 (Sheffield W) 1
Sterling, R. S. 2013 (Liverpool, Manchester C) 51

Steven, T. M. 1985 (Everton, Rangers, Marseille) 36
Stevens, G. A. 1985 (Tottenham H) 7
Stevens, M. G. 1985 (Everton, Rangers) 46
Stewart, J. 1907 (Sheffield W, Newcastle U) 3
Stewart, P. A. 1992 (Tottenham H) 3
Stiles, N. P. 1965 (Manchester U) 28
Stoker, J. 1933 (Birmingham) 3
Stone, S. B. 1996 (Nottingham F) 9
Stones, J. 2014 (Everton, Manchester C) 38
Storer, H. 1924 (Derby Co) 2
Storey, P. E. 1971 (Arsenal) 19
Storey-Moore, I. 1970 (Nottingham F) 1
Strange, A. H. 1930 (Sheffield W) 20
Stratford, A. H. 1874 (Wanderers) 1
Streten, B. 1950 (Luton T) 1
Sturgess, A. 1911 (Sheffield U) 2
Sturridge, D. A. 2012 (Chelsea, Liverpool) 26
Summerbee, M. G. 1968 (Manchester C) 8
Sunderland, A. 1980 (Arsenal) 1
Sutcliffe, J. W. 1893 (Bolton W, Millwall) 5
Sutton, C. R. 1998 (Blackburn R) 1
Swan, P. 1960 (Sheffield W) 19
Swepstone, H. A. 1880 (Pilgrims) 6
Swift, F. V. 1947 (Manchester C) 19

Tait, G. 1881 (Birmingham Excelsior) 1
Talbot, B. 1977 (Ipswich T, Arsenal) 6
Tambling, R. V. 1963 (Chelsea) 3
Tarkowski, J. A. 2018 (Burnley) 2
Tate, J. T. 1931 (Aston Villa) 3
Taylor, E. 1954 (Blackpool) 1
Taylor, E. H. 1923 (Huddersfield T) 8
Taylor, J. G. 1951 (Fulham) 2
Taylor, P. H. 1948 (Liverpool) 3
Taylor, P. J. 1976 (Crystal Palace) 4
Taylor, T. 1953 (Manchester U) 19
Temple, D. W. 1965 (Everton) 1
Terry, J. G. 2003 (Chelsea) 78
Thickett, H. 1899 (Sheffield U) 2
Thomas, D. 1975 (QPR) 8
Thomas, D. 1983 (Coventry C) 2
Thomas, G. R. 1991 (Crystal Palace) 9
Thomas, M. L. 1989 (Arsenal) 2
Thompson, A. 2004 (Celtic) 1
Thompson, P. 1964 (Liverpool) 16
Thompson, P. B. 1976 (Liverpool) 42
Thompson T. 1952 (Aston Villa, Preston NE) 2
Thomson, R. A. 1964 (Wolverhampton W) 8
Thornewell, G. 1923 (Derby Co) 4
Thornley, I. 1907 (Manchester C) 1
Tilson, S. F. 1934 (Manchester C) 4
Titmuss, F. 1922 (Southampton) 2
Todd, C. 1972 (Derby Co) 27
Toone, G. 1892 (Notts Co) 2
Topham, A. G. 1894 (Casuals) 1
Topham, R. 1893 (Wolverhampton W, Casuals) 2
Towers, M. A. 1976 (Sunderland) 3
Townley, W. J. 1889 (Blackburn R) 2
Townrow, J. E. 1925 (Clapton Orient) 2
Townsend, A. D. 2013 (Tottenham H, Newcastle U, Crystal Palace) 13
Tremelling, D. R. 1928 (Birmingham) 1
Tresadern, J. 1923 (West Ham U) 2
Trippier, K. J. 2017 (Tottenham H) 16
Tueart, D. 1975 (Manchester C) 6
Tunstall, F. E. 1923 (Sheffield U) 7
Turnbull, R. J. 1920 (Bradford) 1
Turner, A. 1900 (Southampton) 2
Turner, H. 1931 (Huddersfield T) 2
Turner, J. A. 1893 (Bolton W, Stoke, Derby Co) 3
Tweedy, G. J. 1937 (Grimsby T) 1

Ufton, D. G. 1954 (Charlton Ath) 1
Underwood, A. 1891 (Stoke C) 2
Unsworth, D. G. 1995 (Everton) 1
Upson, M. J. 2003 (Birmingham C, West Ham U) 21
Urwin, T. 1923 (Middlesbrough, Newcastle U) 4
Utley, G. 1913 (Barnsley) 1

Vardy, J. R. 2015 (Leicester C) 26
Vassell, D. 2002 (Aston Villa) 22
Vaughton, O. H. 1882 (Aston Villa) 5
Veitch, C. C. M. 1906 (Newcastle U) 6
Veitch, J. G. 1894 (Old Westminsters) 1
Venables, T. F. 1965 (Chelsea) 2
Venison, B. 1995 (Newcastle U) 2
Vidal, R. W. S. 1873 (Oxford University) 1
Viljoen, C. 1975 (Ipswich T) 2
Viollet, D. S. 1960 (Manchester U) 2
Von Donop 1873 (Royal Engineers) 2

Wace, H. 1878 (Wanderers) 3
Waddle, C. R. 1985 (Newcastle U, Tottenham H, Marseille) 62
Wadsworth, S. J. 1922 (Huddersfield T) 9
Wainscoat, W. R. 1929 (Leeds U) 1
Waiters, A. K. 1964 (Blackpool) 5
Walcott, T. J. 2006 (Arsenal) 47
Walden, F. I. 1914 (Tottenham H) 2
Walker, D. S. 1989 (Nottingham F, Sampdoria, Sheffield W) 59
Walker, I. M. 1996 (Tottenham H, Leicester C) 4
Walker, K. A. 2012 (Tottenham H, Manchester C) 48
Walker, W. H. 1921 (Aston Villa) 18
Wall, G. 1907 (Manchester U) 7
Wallace, C. W. 1913 (Aston Villa) 3
Wallace, D. L. 1986 (Southampton) 1
Walsh, P. A. 1983 (Luton T) 5
Walters, A. M. 1885 (Cambridge University, Old Carthusians) 9
Walters, K. M. 1991 (Rangers) 1
Walters, P. M. 1885 (Oxford University, Old Carthusians) 13
Walton, N. 1890 (Blackburn R) 1
Ward, J. T. 1885 (Blackburn Olympic) 1
Ward, P. 1980 (Brighton & HA) 1
Ward, T. V. 1948 (Derby Co) 2
Ward-Prowse, J. M. E. 2017 (Southampton) 2
Waring, T. 1931 (Aston Villa) 5
Warner, C. 1878 (Upton Park) 1
Warnock, S. 2008 (Blackburn R, Aston Villa) 2
Warren, B. 1906 (Derby Co, Chelsea) 22
Waterfield, G. S. 1927 (Burnley) 1
Watson, D. 1984 (Norwich C, Everton) 12
Watson, D. V. 1974 (Sunderland, Manchester C, Werder Bremen, Southampton, Stoke C) 65
Watson, V. M. 1923 (West Ham U) 5
Watson, W. 1913 (Burnley) 3
Watson, W. 1950 (Sunderland) 4
Weaver, S. 1932 (Newcastle U) 3
Webb, G. W. 1911 (West Ham U) 2
Webb, N. J. 1988 (Nottingham F, Manchester U) 26
Webster, M. 1930 (Middlesbrough) 3
Wedlock, W. J. 1907 (Bristol C) 26
Weir, D. 1889 (Bolton W) 2
Welbeck, D. N. T. M. 2011 (Manchester U, Arsenal) 42
Welch, R. de C. 1872 (Wanderers, Harrow Chequers) 2
Weller, K. 1974 (Leicester C) 4
Welsh, D. 1938 (Charlton Ath) 3
West, G. 1969 (Everton) 3
Westwood, R. W. 1935 (Bolton W) 6
Whateley, O. 1883 (Aston Villa) 2
Wheeler, J. E. 1955 (Bolton W) 1
Wheldon, G. F. 1897 (Aston Villa) 4
White, D. 1993 (Manchester C) 1
White, T. A. 1933 (Everton) 1
Whitehead, J. 1893 (Accrington, Blackburn R) 2
Whitfeld, H. 1879 (Old Etonians) 1
Whitham, M. 1892 (Sheffield U) 1
Whitworth, S. 1975 (Leicester C) 7
Whymark, T. J. 1978 (Ipswich T) 1
Widdowson, S. W. 1880 (Nottingham F) 1
Wignall, F. 1965 (Nottingham F) 2
Wilcox, J. M. 1996 (Blackburn R, Leeds U) 3
Wilkes, A. 1901 (Aston Villa) 5
Wilkins, R. C. 1976 (Chelsea, Manchester U, AC Milan) 84
Wilkinson, B. 1904 (Sheffield U) 1
Wilkinson, L. R. 1891 (Oxford University) 1
Williams, B. F. 1949 (Wolverhampton W) 24
Williams, O. 1923 (Clapton Orient) 2
Williams, S. 1983 (Southampton) 6

Williams, W. 1897 (WBA) 6
Williamson, E. C. 1923 (Arsenal) 2
Williamson, R. G. 1905 (Middlesbrough) 7
Willingham, C. K. 1937 (Huddersfield T) 12
Willis, A. 1952 (Tottenham H) 1
Wilshaw, D. J. 1954 (Wolverhampton W) 12
Wilshere, J. A. 2011 (Arsenal) 34
Wilson, C. 2019 (Bournemouth) 3
Wilson, C. P. 1884 (Hendon) 2
Wilson, C. W. 1879 (Oxford University) 2
Wilson, G. 1921 (Sheffield W) 12
Wilson, G. P. 1900 (Corinthians) 2
Wilson, R. 1960 (Huddersfield T, Everton) 63
Wilson, T. 1928 (Huddersfield T) 1
Winks, H. B. 2018 (Tottenham H) 3
Winckworth, W. N. 1892 (Old Westminsters) 2
Windridge, J. E. 1908 (Chelsea) 8
Wingfield-Stratford, C. V. 1877 (Royal Engineers) 1
Winterburn, N. 1990 (Arsenal) 2
Wise, D. F. 1991 (Chelsea) 21
Withe, P. 1981 (Aston Villa) 11
Wollaston, C. H. R. 1874 (Wanderers) 4
Wolstenholme, S. 1904 (Everton, Blackburn R) 3
Wood, H. 1890 (Wolverhampton W) 3
Wood, R. E. 1955 (Manchester U) 3
Woodcock, A. S. 1978 (Nottingham F, Cologne, Arsenal) 42
Woodgate, J. S. 1999 (Leeds U, Newcastle U, Real Madrid, Tottenham H) 8
Woodger, G. 1911 (Oldham Ath) 1
Woodhall, G. 1888 (WBA) 2
Woodley, V. R. 1937 (Chelsea) 19
Woods, C. C. E. 1985 (Norwich C, Rangers, Sheffield W) 43
Woodward, V. J. 1903 (Tottenham H, Chelsea) 23
Woosnam, M. 1922 (Manchester C) 1
Worrall, F. 1935 (Portsmouth) 2
Worthington, F. S. 1974 (Leicester C) 8
Wreford-Brown, C. 1889 (Oxford University, Old Carthusians) 4
Wright, E. G. D. 1906 (Cambridge University) 1
Wright, I. E. 1991 (Crystal Palace, Arsenal, West Ham U) 33
Wright, J. D. 1939 (Newcastle U) 1
Wright, M. 1984 (Southampton, Derby Co, Liverpool) 45
Wright, R. I. 2000 (Ipswich T, Arsenal) 2
Wright, T. J. 1968 (Everton) 11
Wright, W. A. 1947 (Wolverhampton W) 105
Wright-Phillips, S. C. 2005 (Manchester C, Chelsea, Manchester C) 36
Wylie, J. G. 1878 (Wanderers) 1

Yates, J. 1889 (Burnley) 1
York, R. E. 1922 (Aston Villa) 2
Young, A. 1933 (Huddersfield T) 9
Young, A. S. 2008 (Aston Villa, Manchester U) 39
Young, G. M. 1965 (Sheffield W) 1
Young, L. P. 2005 (Charlton Ath) 7

Zaha, D. W. A. 2013 (Manchester U) 2
Zamora, R. L. 2011 (Fulham) 2

NORTHERN IRELAND

Addis, D. J. 1922 (Cliftonville) 1
Aherne, T. 1947 (Belfast Celtic, Luton T) 4
Alexander, T. E. 1895 (Cliftonville) 1
Allan, C. 1936 (Cliftonville) 1
Allen, J. 1887 (Limavady) 1
Anderson, J. 1925 (Distillery) 1
Anderson, T. 1973 (Manchester U, Swindon T, Peterborough U) 22
Anderson, W. 1898 (Linfield, Cliftonville) 4
Andrews, W. 1908 (Glentoran, Grimsby T) 3
Armstrong, G. J. 1977 (Tottenham H, Watford, Real Mallorca, WBA, Chesterfield) 63

Baird, C. P. 2003 (Southampton, Fulham, Reading, Burnley, WBA, Derby Co) 79
Baird, G. 1896 (Distillery) 3
Baird, H. C. 1939 (Huddersfield T) 1
Balfe, J. 1909 (Shelbourne) 2
Bambrick, J. 1929 (Linfield, Chelsea) 11
Banks, S. J. 1937 (Cliftonville) 1
Barr, H. H. 1962 (Linfield, Coventry C) 3
Barron, J. H. 1894 (Cliftonville) 7
Barry, J. 1888 (Cliftonville) 3
Barry, J. 1900 (Bohemians) 1
Barton, A. J. 2011 (Preston NE) 1
Baxter, R. A. 1887 (Distillery) 1
Baxter, S. N. 1887 (Cliftonville) 1
Bennett, L. V. 1889 (Dublin University) 1
Best, G. 1964 (Manchester U, Fulham) 37
Bingham, W. L. 1951 (Sunderland, Luton T, Everton, Port Vale) 56
Black, K. T. 1988 (Luton T, Nottingham F) 30
Black, T. 1901 (Glentoran) 1
Blair, H. 1928 (Portadown, Swansea T) 4
Blair, J. 1907 (Cliftonville) 5
Blair, R. V. 1975 (Oldham Ath) 5
Blanchflower, J. 1954 (Manchester U) 12
Blanchflower, R. D. 1950 (Barnsley, Aston Villa, Tottenham H) 56
Blayney, A. 2006 (Doncaster R, Linfield) 5
Bookman, L. J. O. 1914 (Bradford C, Luton T) 4
Bothwell, A. W. 1926 (Ards) 5
Bowler, G. C. 1950 (Hull C) 3
Boyce, L. 2011 (Werder Bremen, Ross Co, Burton Alb) 19
Boyle, P. 1901 (Sheffield U) 5
Braithwaite, R. M. 1962 (Linfield, Middlesbrough) 10
Braniff, K. R. 2010 (Portadown) 2
Breen, T. 1935 (Belfast Celtic, Manchester U) 9
Brennan, B. 1912 (Bohemians) 1
Brennan, R. A. 1949 (Luton T, Birmingham C, Fulham) 5
Briggs, W. R. 1962 (Manchester U, Swansea T) 2
Brisby, D. 1891 (Distillery) 1
Brolly, T. H. 1937 (Millwall) 4
Brookes, E. A. 1920 (Shelbourne) 1
Brotherston, N. 1980 (Blackburn R) 27
Brown, J. 1921 (Glenavon, Tranmere R) 3
Brown, J. 1935 (Wolverhampton W, Coventry C, Birmingham C) 10
Brown, N. M. 1887 (Limavady) 1
Brown, W. G. 1926 (Glenavon) 1
Browne, F. 1887 (Cliftonville) 5
Browne, R. J. 1936 (Leeds U) 6
Bruce, A. 1925 (Belfast Celtic) 1
Bruce, A. S. 2013 (Hull C) 2
Bruce, W. 1961 (Glentoran) 2
Brunt, C. 2005 (Sheffield W, WBA) 65
Bryan, M. A. 2010 (Watford) 2
Buckle, H. R. 1903 (Cliftonville, Sunderland, Bristol R) 3
Buckle, J. 1882 (Cliftonville) 1
Burnett, J. 1894 (Distillery, Glentoran) 5
Burnison, J. 1901 (Distillery) 2
Burnison, S. 1908 (Distillery, Bradford, Distillery) 8
Burns, J. 1923 (Glenavon) 1
Burns, W. 1925 (Glentoran) 1
Butler, M. P. 1939 (Blackpool) 1

Camp, L. M. J. 2011 (Nottingham F) 9
Campbell, A. C. 1963 (Crusaders) 2
Campbell, D. A. 1986 (Nottingham F, Charlton Ath) 10
Campbell, James 1897 (Cliftonville) 14
Campbell, John 1896 (Cliftonville) 1
Campbell, J. P. 1951 (Fulham) 2
Campbell, R. M. 1982 (Bradford C) 2
Campbell, W. G. 1968 (Dundee) 6
Capaldi, A. C. 2004 (Plymouth Arg, Cardiff C) 22
Carey, J. J. 1947 (Manchester U) 7
Carroll, E. 1925 (Glenavon) 1
Carroll, R. E. 1997 (Wigan Ath, Manchester U, West Ham U, Olympiacos, Notts Co, Linfield) 45
Carson, J. G. 2011 (Ipswich T) 4
Carson, S. 2009 (Coleraine) 1
Carson, T. 2018 (Motherwell) 5
Casement, C. 2009 (Ipswich T) 1

Casey, T. 1955 (Newcastle U, Portsmouth) 12
Caskey, W. 1979 (Derby Co, Tulsa Roughnecks) 8
Cassidy, T. 1971 (Newcastle U, Burnley) 24
Cathcart, C. G. 2011 (Blackpool, Watford) 45
Caughey, M. 1986 (Linfield) 2
Chambers, R. J. 1921 (Distillery, Bury, Nottingham F) 12
Chatton, H. A. 1925 (Partick Thistle) 3
Christian, J. 1889 (Linfield) 1
Clarke, C. J. 1986 (Bournemouth, Southampton, QPR, Portsmouth) 38
Clarke, R. 1901 (Belfast Celtic) 2
Cleary, J. 1982 (Glentoran) 5
Clements, D. 1965 (Coventry C, Sheffield W, Everton, New York Cosmos) 48
Clingan, S. G. 2006 (Nottingham F, Norwich C, Coventry C, Kilmarnock) 39
Clugston, J. 1888 (Cliftonville) 14
Clyde, M. G. 2005 (Wolverhampton W) 3
Coates, C. 2009 (Crusaders) 6
Cochrane, D. 1939 (Leeds U) 12
Cochrane, G. 1903 (Cliftonville) 1
Cochrane, G. T. 1976 (Coleraine, Burnley, Middlesbrough, Gillingham) 26
Cochrane, M. 1898 (Distillery, Leicester Fosse) 8
Collins, F. 1922 (Celtic) 1
Collins, R. 1922 (Cliftonville) 1
Condy, J. 1882 (Distillery) 3
Connell, T. E. 1978 (Coleraine) 1
Connor, J. 1901 (Glentoran, Belfast Celtic) 13
Connor, M. J. 1903 (Brentford, Fulham) 3
Cook, W. 1933 (Celtic, Everton) 15
Cooke, S. 1889 (Belfast YMCA, Cliftonville) 3
Coote, A. 1999 (Norwich C) 6
Coulter, J. 1934 (Belfast Celtic, Everton, Grimsby T, Chelmsford C) 11
Cowan, J. 1970 (Newcastle U) 1
Cowan, T. S. 1925 (Queen's Island) 1
Coyle, F. 1956 (Coleraine, Nottingham F) 4
Coyle, L. 1989 (Derry C) 1
Coyle, R. I. 1973 (Sheffield W) 5
Craig, A. B. 1908 (Rangers, Morton) 9
Craig, D. J. 1967 (Newcastle U) 25
Craigan, S. J. 2003 (Partick Thistle, Motherwell) 54
Crawford, A. 1889 (Distillery, Cliftonville) 7
Croft, T. 1922 (Queen's Island) 3
Crone, R. 1889 (Distillery) 4
Crone, W. 1882 (Distillery) 12
Crooks, W. J. 1922 (Manchester U) 1
Crossan, E. 1950 (Blackburn R) 3
Crossan, J. A. 1960 (Sparta-Rotterdam, Sunderland, Manchester C, Middlesbrough) 24
Crothers, C. 1907 (Distillery) 1
Cumming, L. 1929 (Huddersfield T, Oldham Ath) 3
Cunningham, W. 1892 (Ulster) 4
Cunningham, W. E. 1951 (St Mirren, Leicester C, Dunfermline Ath) 30
Curran, S. 1926 (Belfast Celtic) 4
Curran, J. J. 1922 (Glenavon, Pontypridd, Glenavon) 5
Cush, W. W. 1951 (Glenavon, Leeds U, Portadown) 26

Dallas, S. A, 2011 (Crusaders, Brentford, Leeds U) 40
Dalrymple, J. 1922 (Distillery) 1
Dalton, W. 1888 (YMCA, Linfield) 11
D'Arcy, S. D. 1952 (Chelsea, Brentford) 5
Darling, J. 1897 (Linfield) 22
Davey, H. H. 1926 (Reading, Portsmouth) 5
Davis, S. 2005 (Aston Villa, Fulham, Rangers, Southampton, Rangers) 111
Davis, T. L. 1937 (Oldham Ath) 1
Davison, A. J. 1996 (Bolton W, Bradford C, Grimsby T) 3
Davison, J. R. 1882 (Cliftonville) 8
Dennison, R. 1988 (Wolverhampton W) 18
Devine, A. O. 1886 (Limavady) 4
Devine, J. 1990 (Glentoran) 1
Dickson, D. 1970 (Coleraine) 4
Dickson, T. A. 1957 (Linfield) 1
Dickson, W. 1951 (Chelsea, Arsenal) 12
Diffin, W. J. 1931 (Belfast Celtic) 1
Dill, A. H. 1882 (Knock, Down Ath, Cliftonville) 9
Doherty, I. 1901 (Belfast Celtic) 1
Doherty, J. 1928 (Portadown) 1
Doherty, J. 1933 (Cliftonville) 2
Doherty, L. 1985 (Linfield) 2
Doherty, M. 1938 (Derry C) 1
Doherty, P. D. 1935 (Blackpool, Manchester C, Derby Co, Huddersfield T, Doncaster R) 16
Doherty, T. E. 2003 (Bristol C) 9
Donaghey, B. 1903 (Belfast Celtic) 1
Donaghy, M. M. 1980 (Luton T, Manchester U, Chelsea) 91
Donnelly, L. 1913 (Distillery) 1
Donnelly, L. F. P. 2014 (Fulham) 1
Donnelly, M. 2009 (Crusaders) 1
Doran, J. F. 1921 (Brighton) 3
Dougan, A. D. 1958 (Portsmouth, Blackburn R, Aston Villa, Leicester C, Wolverhampton W) 43
Douglas, J. P. 1947 (Belfast Celtic) 1
Dowd, H. O. 1974 (Glenavon, Sheffield W) 3
Dowie, I. 1990 (Luton T, West Ham U, Southampton, C Palace, West Ham U, QPR) 59
Duff, M. J. 2002 (Cheltenham T, Burnley) 24
Duggan, H. A. 1930 (Leeds U) 8
Dunlop, G. 1985 (Linfield) 4
Dunne, J. 1928 (Sheffield U) 7

Eames, W. L. E. 1885 (Dublin University) 3
Eglington, T. J. 1947 (Everton) 6
Elder, A. R. 1960 (Burnley, Stoke C) 40
Elleman, A. R. 1889 (Cliftonville) 2
Elliott, S. 2001 (Motherwell, Hull C) 39
Elwood, J. H. 1929 (Bradford) 2
Emerson, W. 1920 (Glentoran, Burnley) 11
English, S. 1933 (Rangers) 2
Enright, J. 1912 (Leeds C) 1
Evans, C. J. 2009 (Manchester U, Hull C, Blackburn R) 53
Evans, J. G. 2007 (Manchester U, WBA, Leicester C) 80

Falloon, E. 1931 (Aberdeen) 2
Farquharson, T. G. 1923 (Cardiff C) 7
Farrell, P. 1901 (Distillery) 2
Farrell, P. 1938 (Hibernian) 1
Farrell, P. D. 1947 (Everton) 7
Feeney, J. M. 1947 (Linfield, Swansea T) 2
Feeney, W. 1976 (Glentoran) 1
Feeney, W. J. 2002 (Bournemouth, Luton T, Cardiff C, Oldham Ath, Plymouth Arg) 46
Ferguson, G. 1999 (Linfield) 5
Ferguson, S. K. 2009 (Newcastle U, Millwall) 39
Ferguson, W. 1966 (Linfield) 2
Ferris, J. 1920 (Belfast Celtic, Chelsea, Belfast Celtic) 6
Ferris, R. O. 1950 (Birmingham C) 3
Fettis, A. W. 1992 (Hull C, Nottingham F, Blackburn R) 25
Finney, T. 1975 (Sunderland, Cambridge U) 14
Fitzpatrick, J. C. 1896 (Bohemians) 2
Flack, H. 1929 (Burnley) 1
Flanagan, T. M. 2017 (Burton Alb) 1
Fleming, J. G. 1987 (Nottingham F, Manchester C, Barnsley) 31
Forbes, G. 1888 (Limavady, Distillery) 3
Forde, J. T. 1959 (Ards) 4
Foreman, T. A. 1899 (Cliftonville) 1
Forsythe, J. 1888 (YMCA) 2
Fox, W. T. 1887 (Ulster) 2
Frame, T. 1925 (Linfield) 1
Fulton, R. P. 1928 (Larne, Belfast Celtic) 21

Gaffikin, G. 1890 (Linfield Ath) 15
Galbraith, W. 1890 (Distillery) 1
Gallagher, P. 1920 (Celtic, Falkirk) 11
Gallogly, C. 1951 (Huddersfield T) 2
Gara, A. 1902 (Preston NE) 3
Gardiner, A. 1930 (Cliftonville) 5
Garrett, J. 1925 (Distillery) 1
Garrett, R. 2009 (Linfield) 5
Gaston, R. 1969 (Oxford U) 1
Gaukrodger, G. 1895 (Linfield) 1
Gault, M. 2008 (Linfield) 1
Gaussen, A. D. 1884 (Moyola Park, Magherafelt) 6
Geary, J. 1931 (Glentoran) 2
Gibb, J. T. 1884 (Wellington Park, Cliftonville) 10
Gibb, T. J. 1936 (Cliftonville) 1
Gibson W. K. 1894 (Cliftonville) 14

Gillespie, K. R. 1995 (Manchester U, Newcastle U, Blackburn R, Leicester C, Sheffield U) 86
Gillespie, S. 1886 (Hertford) 6
Gillespie, W. 1889 (West Down) 1
Gillespie, W. 1913 (Sheffield U) 25
Goodall, A. L. 1899 (Derby Co, Glossop) 10
Goodbody, M. F. 1889 (Dublin University) 2
Gordon, H. 1895 (Linfield) 3
Gordon R. W. 1891 (Linfield) 7
Gordon, T. 1894 (Linfield) 2
Gorman, R. J. 2010 (Wolverhampton W) 9
Gorman, W. C. 1947 (Brentford) 4
Gough, J. 1925 (Queen's Island) 1
Gowdy, J. 1920 (Glentoran, Queen's Island, Falkirk) 6
Gowdy, W. A. 1932 (Hull C, Sheffield W, Linfield, Hibernian) 6
Graham, W. G. L. 1951 (Doncaster R) 14
Gray, P. 1993 (Luton T, Sunderland, Nancy, Luton T, Burnley, Oxford U) 26
Greer, W. 1909 (QPR) 3
Gregg, H. 1954 (Doncaster R, Manchester U) 25
Griffin, D. J. 1996 (St Johnstone, Dundee U, Stockport Co) 29
Grigg, W. D. 2012 (Walsall, Brentford, Milton Keynes D, Wigan Ath) 13

Hall, G. 1897 (Distillery) 1
Halligan, W. 1911 (Derby Co, Wolverhampton W) 2
Hamill, M. 1912 (Manchester U, Belfast Celtic, Manchester C) 7
Hamill, R. 1999 (Glentoran) 1
Hamilton, B. 1969 (Linfield, Ipswich T, Everton, Millwall, Swindon T) 50
Hamilton, G. 2003 (Portadown) 5
Hamilton, J. 1882 (Knock) 2
Hamilton, R. 1928 (Rangers) 5
Hamilton, W. D. 1885 (Dublin Association) 1
Hamilton, W. J. 1885 (Dublin Association) 1
Hamilton, W. J. 1908 (Distillery) 1
Hamilton, W. R. 1978 (QPR, Burnley, Oxford U) 41
Hampton, H. 1911 (Bradford C) 9
Hanna, J. 1912 (Nottingham F) 2
Hanna, J. D. 1899 (Royal Artillery, Portsmouth) 1
Hannon, D. J. 1908 (Bohemians) 6
Harkin, J. T. 1968 (Southport, Shrewsbury T) 5
Harland, A. I. 1922 (Linfield) 2
Harris, J. 1921 (Cliftonville, Glenavon) 2
Harris, V. 1906 (Shelbourne, Everton) 20
Harvey, M. 1961 (Sunderland) 34
Hastings, J. 1882 (Knock, Ulster) 7
Hatton, S. 1963 (Linfield) 2
Hayes, W. E. 1938 (Huddersfield T) 4
Hazard, C. 2018 (Celtic) 1
Healy, D. J. 2000 (Manchester U, Preston NE, Leeds U, Fulham, Sunderland, Rangers, Bury) 95
Healy, P. J. 1982 (Coleraine, Glentoran) 4
Hegan, D. 1970 (WBA, Wolverhampton W) 7
Henderson, J. 1885 (Ulster) 3
Hewison, G. 1885 (Moyola Park) 2
Hill, C. F. 1990 (Sheffield U, Leicester C, Trelleborg, Northampton T) 27
Hill, M. J. 1959 (Norwich C, Everton) 7
Hinton, E. 1947 (Fulham, Millwall) 7
Hodson, L. J. S. 2011 (Watford, Milton Keynes D, Rangers) 24
Holmes, S. P. 2002 (Wrexham) 1
Hopkins, J. 1926 (Brighton) 1
Horlock, K. 1995 (Swindon T, Manchester C) 32
Houston, J. 1912 (Linfield, Everton) 6
Houston, W. 1933 (Linfield) 1
Houston, W. J. 1885 (Moyola Park) 2
Hughes, A. W. 1998 (Newcastle U, Aston Villa, Fulham, QPR, Brighton & HA, Melbourne C, Kerala Blasters, Hearts) 112
Hughes, J. 2006 (Lincoln C) 2
Hughes, M. A. 2006 (Oldham Ath) 2
Hughes, M. E. 1992 (Manchester C, Strasbourg, West Ham U, Wimbledon, Crystal Palace) 71
Hughes, P. A. 1987 (Bury) 3
Hughes, W. 1951 (Bolton W) 1
Humphries, W. M. 1962 (Ards, Coventry C, Swansea T) 14
Hunter, A. 1905 (Distillery, Belfast Celtic) 8
Hunter, A. 1970 (Blackburn R, Ipswich T) 53
Hunter, B. V. 1995 (Wrexham, Reading) 15
Hunter, R. J. 1884 (Cliftonville) 3
Hunter, V. 1962 (Coleraine) 2

Ingham, M. G. 2005 (Sunderland, Wrexham) 3
Irvine, R. J. 1962 (Linfield, Stoke C) 8
Irvine, R. W. 1922 (Everton, Portsmouth, Connah's Quay, Derry C) 15
Irvine, W. J. 1963 (Burnley, Preston NE, Brighton & HA) 23
Irving, S. J. 1923 (Dundee, Cardiff C, Chelsea) 18

Jackson, T. A. 1969 (Everton, Nottingham F, Manchester U) 35
Jamison, J. 1976 (Glentoran) 1
Jenkins, I. 1997 (Chester C, Dundee U) 6
Jennings, P. A. 1964 (Watford, Tottenham H, Arsenal, Tottenham H) 119
Johnson, D. M. 1999 (Blackburn R, Birmingham C) 56
Johnston, H. 1927 (Portadown) 1
Johnston, R. S. 1882 (Distillery) 5
Johnston, R. S. 1905 (Distillery) 1
Johnston, S. 1890 (Linfield) 4
Johnston, W. 1885 (Oldpark) 2
Johnston, W. C. 1962 (Glenavon, Oldham Ath) 2
Jones, J. 1930 (Linfield, Hibernian, Glenavon) 23
Jones, J. 1956 (Glenavon) 3
Jones, J. L. 2018 (Kilmarnock) 9
Jones, S. 1934 (Distillery, Blackpool) 2
Jones, S. G. 2003 (Crewe Alex, Burnley) 29
Jordan, T. 1895 (Linfield) 2

Kavanagh, P. J. 1930 (Celtic) 1
Keane, T. R. 1949 (Swansea T) 1
Kearns, A. 1900 (Distillery) 6
Kee, P. V. 1990 (Oxford U, Ards) 9
Keith, R. M. 1958 (Newcastle U) 23
Kelly, H. R. 1950 (Fulham, Southampton) 4
Kelly, J. 1896 (Glentoran) 1
Kelly, J. 1932 (Derry C) 11
Kelly, P. J. 1921 (Manchester C) 1
Kelly, P. M. 1950 (Barnsley) 1
Kennedy, A. L. 1923 (Arsenal) 2
Kennedy, P. H. 1999 (Watford, Wigan Ath) 20
Kernaghan, N. 1936 (Belfast Celtic) 3
Kirk, A. R. 2000 (Hearts, Boston U, Northampton T, Dunfermline Ath) 11
Kirkwood, H. 1904 (Cliftonville) 1
Kirwan, J. 1900 (Tottenham H, Chelsea, Clyde) 17

Lacey, W. 1909 (Everton, Liverpool, New Brighton) 23
Lafferty, D. P. 2012 (Burnley) 13
Lafferty, K. 2006 (Burnley, Rangers, FC Sion, Palermo, Norwich C, Hearts, Rangers) 73
Lavery, S. F. 2018 (Everton) 1
Lawrie, J. 2009 (Port Vale) 3
Lawther, R. 1888 (Glentoran) 2
Lawther, W. I. 1960 (Sunderland, Blackburn R) 4
Leatham, J. 1939 (Belfast Celtic) 1
Ledwidge, J. J. 1906 (Shelbourne) 2
Lemon, J. 1886 (Glentoran, Belfast YMCA) 3
Lennon, N. F. 1994 (Crewe Alex, Leicester C, Celtic) 40
Leslie, W. 1887 (YMCA) 1
Lewis, J. 1899 (Glentoran, Distillery) 4
Lewis, J. P. 2018 (Norwich C) 10
Little, A. 2009 (Rangers) 9
Lockhart, H. 1884 (Rossall School) 1
Lockhart, N. H. 1947 (Linfield, Coventry C, Aston Villa) 8
Lomas, S. M. 1994 (Manchester C, West Ham U) 45
Loyal, J. 1891 (Clarence) 1
Lund, M. C. 2017 (Rochdale) 3
Lutton, R. J. 1970 (Wolverhampton W, West Ham U) 6
Lynas, R. 1925 (Cliftonville) 1
Lyner, D. R. 1920 (Glentoran, Manchester U, Kilmarnock) 6
Lytle, J. 1898 (Glentoran) 1

Madden, O. 1938 (Norwich C) 1
Magee, G. 1885 (Wellington Park) 3
Magennis, J. B. D. 2010 (Cardiff C, Aberdeen, St Mirren, Kilmarnock, Charlton Ath, Bolton W) 44
Magill, E. J. 1962 (Arsenal, Brighton & HA) 26
Magilton, J. 1991 (Oxford U, Southampton, Sheffield W, Ipswich T) 52
Maginnis, H. 1900 (Linfield) 8
Mahood, J. 1926 (Belfast Celtic, Ballymena) 9
Mannus, A. 2004 (Linfield, St Johnstone) 9
Manderson, R. 1920 (Rangers) 5
Mansfield, J. 1901 (Dublin Freebooters) 1
Martin, C. 1882 (Cliftonville) 3
Martin, C. 1925 (Bo'ness) 1
Martin, C. J. 1947 (Glentoran, Leeds U, Aston Villa) 6
Martin, D. K. 1934 (Belfast Celtic, Wolverhampton W, Nottingham F) 10
Mathieson, A. 1921 (Luton T) 2
Maxwell, J. 1902 (Linfield, Glentoran, Belfast Celtic) 7
McAdams, W. J. 1954 (Manchester C, Bolton W, Leeds U) 15
McAlery, J. M. 1882 (Cliftonville) 2
McAlinden, J. 1938 (Belfast Celtic, Portsmouth, Southend U) 4
McAllen, J. 1898 (Linfield) 9
McAlpine, S. 1901 (Cliftonville) 1
McArdle, R. A. 2010 (Rochdale, Aberdeen, Bradford C) 7
McArthur, A. 1886 (Distillery) 1
McAuley, G. 2005 (Lincoln C, Leicester C, Ipswich T, WBA, Rangers) 80
McAuley, J. L. 1911 (Huddersfield T) 6
McAuley, P. 1900 (Belfast Celtic) 1
McBride, S. D. 1991 (Glenavon) 4
McCabe, J. J. 1949 (Leeds U) 6
McCabe, W. 1891 (Ulster) 1
McCambridge, J. 1930 (Ballymena, Cardiff C) 4
McCandless, J. 1912 (Bradford) 5
McCandless, W. 1920 (Linfield, Rangers) 9
McCann, G. S. 2002 (West Ham U, Cheltenham T, Barnsley, Scunthorpe U, Peterborough U) 39
McCann, P. 1910 (Belfast Celtic, Glentoran) 7
McCartan, S. V. 2017 (Accrington S, Bradford C) 2
McCarthy, J. D. 1996 (Port Vale, Birmingham C) 18
McCartney, A. 1903 (Ulster, Linfield, Everton, Belfast Celtic, Glentoran) 15
McCartney, G. 2002 (Sunderland, West Ham U, Sunderland) 34
McCashin, J. W. 1896 (Cliftonville) 5
McCavana, W. T. 1955 (Coleraine) 3
McCaw, J. H. 1927 (Linfield) 6
McClatchey, J. 1886 (Distillery) 3
McClatchey, T. 1895 (Distillery) 1
McCleary, J. W. 1955 (Cliftonville) 1
McCleery, W. 1922 (Cliftonville, Linfield) 10
McClelland, J. 1980 (Mansfield T, Rangers, Watford, Leeds U) 53
McClelland, J. T. 1961 (Arsenal, Fulham) 6
McCluggage, A. 1922 (Cliftonville, Bradford, Burnley) 13
McClure, G. 1907 (Cliftonville, Distillery) 4
McConnell, E. 1904 (Cliftonville, Glentoran, Sunderland, Sheffield W) 12
McConnell, P. 1928 (Doncaster R, Southport) 2
McConnell, W. G. 1912 (Bohemians) 6
McConnell, W. H. 1925 (Reading) 8
McCourt, F. J. 1952 (Manchester C) 6
McCourt, P. J. 2002 (Rochdale, Celtic, Barnsley, Brighton & HA, Luton T) 18
McCoy, R. K. 1987 (Coleraine) 1
McCoy, S. 1896 (Distillery) 1
McCracken, E. 1928 (Barking) 1
McCracken, R. 1921 (Crystal Palace) 4
McCracken, R. 1922 (Linfield) 1
McCracken, W. R. 1902 (Distillery, Newcastle U, Hull C) 16
McCreery, D. 1976 (Manchester U, QPR, Tulsa Roughnecks, Newcastle U, Hearts) 67
McCrory, S. 1958 (Southend U) 1
McCullough, K. 1935 (Belfast Celtic, Manchester C) 5
McCullough, L. 2014 (Doncaster R) 6
McCullough, W. J. 1961 (Arsenal, Millwall) 10
McCurdy, C. 1980 (Linfield) 1
McDonald, A. 1986 (QPR) 52
McDonald, R. 1930 (Rangers) 2
McDonnell, J. 1911 (Bohemians) 4
McElhinney, G. M. A. 1984 (Bolton W) 6
McEvilly, L. R. 2002 (Rochdale) 1
McFaul, W. S. 1967 (Linfield, Newcastle U) 6
McGarry, J. K. 1951 (Cliftonville) 3
McGaughey, M. 1985 (Linfield) 1
McGibbon, P. C. G. 1995 (Manchester U, Wigan Ath) 7
McGinn, N. 2009 (Celtic, Aberdeen, Gwangju, Aberdeen) 56
McGivern, R. 2009 (Manchester C, Hibernian, Port Vale, Shrewsbury) 24
McGovern, M. 2010 (Ross Co, Hamilton A, Norwich C) 29
McGrath, R. C. 1974 (Tottenham H, Manchester U) 21
McGregor, S. 1921 (Glentoran) 1
McGrillen, J. 1924 (Clyde, Belfast Celtic) 2
McGuire, E. 1907 (Distillery) 1
McGuire, J. 1928 (Linfield) 1
McIlroy, H. 1906 (Cliftonville) 1
McIlroy, J. 1952 (Burnley, Stoke C) 55
McIlroy, S. B. 1972 (Manchester U, Stoke C, Manchester C) 88
McIlvenny, P. 1924 (Distillery) 1
McIlvenny, R. 1890 (Distillery, Ulster) 2
McKay, W. R. 2013 (Inverness CT, Wigan Ath) 11
McKeag, W. 1968 (Glentoran) 2
McKeague, T. 1925 (Glentoran) 1
McKee, F. W. 1906 (Cliftonville, Belfast Celtic) 5
McKelvey, H. 1901 (Glentoran) 2
McKenna, J. 1950 (Huddersfield T) 7
McKenzie, H. 1922 (Distillery) 2
McKenzie, R. 1967 (Airdrieonians) 1
McKeown, N. 1892 (Linfield) 7
McKie, H. 1895 (Cliftonville) 3
Mackie, J. A. 1923 (Arsenal, Portsmouth) 3
McKinney, D. 1921 (Hull C, Bradford C) 2
McKinney, V. J. 1966 (Falkirk) 1
McKnight, A. D. 1988 (Celtic, West Ham U) 10
McKnight, J. 1912 (Preston NE, Glentoran) 2
McLaughlin, C. G. 2012 (Preston NE, Fleetwood T, Millwall) 35
McLaughlin, J. C. 1962 (Shrewsbury T, Swansea T) 12
McLaughlin, R. 2014 (Liverpool, Oldham Ath) 5
McLean, B. S. 2006 (Rangers) 1
McLean, T. 1885 (Limavady) 1
McMahon, G. J. 1995 (Tottenham H, Stoke C) 17
McMahon, J. 1934 (Bohemians) 1
McMaster, G. 1897 (Glentoran) 3
McMichael, A. 1950 (Newcastle U) 40
McMillan, G. 1903 (Distillery) 2
McMillan, S. T. 1963 (Manchester U) 2
McMillen, W. S. 1934 (Manchester U, Chesterfield) 7
McMordie, A. S. 1969 (Middlesbrough) 21
McMorran, E. J. 1947 (Belfast Celtic, Barnsley, Doncaster R) 15
McMullan, D. 1926 (Liverpool) 3
McNair, P. J. C. 2015 (Manchester U, Sunderland, Middlesbrough) 29
McNally, B. A. 1986 (Shrewsbury T) 5
McNinch, J. 1931 (Ballymena) 3
McPake, J. 2012 (Coventry C) 1
McParland, P. J. 1954 (Aston Villa, Wolverhampton W) 34
McQuoid, J. J. B. 2011 (Millwall) 5
McShane, J. 1899 (Cliftonville) 4
McVeigh, P. M. 1999 (Tottenham H, Norwich C) 20
McVicker, J. 1888 (Linfield, Glentoran) 2
McWha, W. B. R. 1882 (Knock, Cliftonville) 7
Meek, H. L. 1925 (Glentoran) 1
Mehaffy, J. A. C. 1922 (Queen's Island) 1
Meldon, P. A. 1899 (Dublin Freebooters) 2
Mercer, H. V. A. 1908 (Linfield) 1
Mercer, J. T. 1898 (Distillery, Linfield, Distillery, Derby Co) 12
Millar, W. 1932 (Barrow) 2
Miller, J. 1929 (Middlesbrough) 3
Milligan, D. 1939 (Chesterfield) 1
Milne, R. G. 1894 (Linfield) 28
Mitchell, E. J. 1933 (Cliftonville, Glentoran) 2
Mitchell, W. 1932 (Distillery, Chelsea) 15

Molyneux, T. B. 1883 (Ligoniel, Cliftonville) 11
Montgomery, F. J. 1955 (Coleraine) 1
Moore, C. 1949 (Glentoran) 1
Moore, P. 1933 (Aberdeen) 1
Moore, R. 1891 (Linfield Ath) 3
Moore, R. L. 1887 (Ulster) 2
Moore, W. 1923 (Falkirk) 1
Moorhead, F. W. 1885 (Dublin University) 1
Moorhead, G. 1923 (Linfield) 4
Moran, J. 1912 (Leeds C) 1
Moreland, V. 1979 (Derby Co) 6
Morgan, G. F. 1922 (Linfield, Nottingham F) 8
Morgan, S. 1972 (Port Vale, Aston Villa, Brighton & HA, Sparta Rotterdam) 18
Morrison, R. 1891 (Linfield Ath) 2
Morrison, T. 1895 (Glentoran, Burnley) 7
Morrogh, D. 1896 (Bohemians) 1
Morrow, S. J. 1990 (Arsenal, QPR) 39
Morrow, W. J. 1883 (Moyola Park) 3
Muir, R. 1885 (Oldpark) 2
Mulgrew, J. 2010 (Linfield) 2
Mulholland, T. S. 1906 (Belfast Celtic) 2
Mullan, G. 1983 (Glentoran) 4
Mulligan, J. 1921 (Manchester C) 1
Mulryne, P. P. 1997 (Manchester U, Norwich C, Cardiff C) 27
Murdock, C. J. 2000 (Preston NE, Hibernian, Crewe Alex, Rotherham U) 34
Murphy, J. 1910 (Bradford C) 3
Murphy, N. 1905 (QPR) 3
Murray, J. M. 1910 (Motherwell, Sheffield W) 3

Napier, R. J. 1966 (Bolton W) 1
Neill, W. J. T. 1961 (Arsenal, Hull C) 59
Nelis, P. 1923 (Nottingham F) 1
Nelson, S. 1970 (Arsenal, Brighton & HA) 51
Nicholl, C. J. 1975 (Aston Villa, Southampton, Grimsby T) 51
Nicholl, H. 1902 (Belfast Celtic) 3
Nicholl, J. M. 1976 (Manchester U, Toronto Blizzard, Sunderland, Toronto Blizzard, Rangers, Toronto Blizzard, WBA) 73
Nicholson, J. J. 1961 (Manchester U, Huddersfield T) 41
Nixon, R. 1914 (Linfield) 1
Nolan, I. R. 1997 (Sheffield W, Bradford C, Wigan Ath) 18
Nolan-Whelan, J. V. 1901 (Dublin Freebooters) 5
Norwood, O. J. 2011 (Manchester U, Huddersfield T, Reading, Brighton & HA) 57

O'Boyle, G. 1994 (Dunfermline Ath, St Johnstone) 13
O'Brien, M. T. 1921 (QPR, Leicester C, Hull C, Derby Co) 10
O'Connell, P. 1912 (Sheffield W, Hull C) 5
O'Connor, M. J. 2008 (Crewe Alex, Scunthorpe U, Rotherham U) 11
O'Doherty, A. 1970 (Coleraine) 2
O'Driscoll, J. F. 1949 (Swansea T) 3
O'Hagan, C. 1905 (Tottenham H, Aberdeen) 11
O'Hagan, W. 1920 (St Mirren) 2
O'Hehir, J. C. 1910 (Bohemians) 1
O'Kane, W. J. 1970 (Nottingham F) 20
O'Mahoney, M. T. 1939 (Bristol R) 1
O'Neill, C. 1989 (Motherwell) 3
O'Neill, J. 1962 (Sunderland) 1
O'Neill, J. P. 1980 (Leicester C) 39
O'Neill, M. A. M. 1988 (Newcastle U, Dundee U, Hibernian, Coventry C) 31
O'Neill, M. H. M. 1972 (Distillery, Nottingham F, Norwich C, Manchester C, Norwich C, Notts Co) 64
O'Reilly, H. 1901 (Dublin Freebooters) 3
Owens, J. 2011 (Crusaders) 1

Parke, J. 1964 (Linfield, Hibernian, Sunderland) 14
Paterson, M. A. 2008 (Scunthorpe U, Burnley, Huddersfield T) 22
Paton, P. R. 2014 (Dundee U) 4
Patterson, D. J. 1994 (Crystal Palace, Luton T, Dundee U) 17
Patterson, R. 2010 (Coleraine, Plymouth Arg) 5
Peacock, R. 1952 (Celtic, Coleraine) 31
Peacock-Farrell, B. 2018 (Leeds U) 9
Peden, J. 1887 (Linfield, Distillery) 24
Penney, S. 1985 (Brighton & HA) 17
Percy, J. C. 1889 (Belfast YMCA) 1
Platt, J. A. 1976 (Middlesbrough, Ballymena U, Coleraine) 23
Pollock, W. 1928 (Belfast Celtic) 1
Ponsonby, J. 1895 (Distillery) 9
Potts, R. M. C. 1883 (Cliftonville) 2
Priestley, T. J. M. 1933 (Coleraine, Chelsea) 2
Pyper, Jas. 1897 (Cliftonville) 7
Pyper, John 1897 (Cliftonville) 9
Pyper, M. 1932 (Linfield) 1

Quinn, J. M. 1985 (Blackburn R, Swindon T, Leicester C, Bradford C, West Ham U, Bournemouth, Reading) 46
Quinn, S. J. 1996 (Blackpool, WBA, Willem II, Sheffield W, Peterborough U, Northampton T) 50

Rafferty, P. 1980 (Linfield) 1
Ramsey, P. C. 1984 (Leicester C) 14
Rankine, J. 1883 (Alexander) 2
Rattray, D. 1882 (Avoniel) 3
Rea, R. 1901 (Glentoran) 1
Reeves, B. N. 2015 (Milton Keynes D) 2
Redmond, R. 1884 (Cliftonville) 1
Reid, G. H. 1923 (Cardiff C) 1
Reid, J. 1883 (Ulster) 6
Reid, S. E. 1934 (Derby Co) 3
Reid, W. 1931 (Hearts) 1
Reilly, M. M. 1900 (Portsmouth) 2
Renneville, W. T. J. 1910 (Leyton, Aston Villa) 4
Reynolds, J. 1890 (Distillery, Ulster) 5
Reynolds, R. 1905 (Bohemians) 1
Rice, P. J. 1969 (Arsenal) 49
Roberts, F. C. 1931 (Glentoran) 1
Robinson, P. 1920 (Distillery, Blackburn R) 2
Robinson, S. 1997 (Bournemouth, Luton T) 7
Rogan, A. 1988 (Celtic, Sunderland, Millwall) 18
Rollo, D. 1912 (Linfield, Blackburn R) 16
Roper, E. O. 1886 (Dublin University) 1
Rosbotham, A. 1887 (Cliftonville) 7
Ross, W. E. 1969 (Newcastle U) 1
Rowland, K. 1994 (West Ham U, QPR) 19
Rowley, R. W. M. 1929 (Southampton, Tottenham H) 6
Rushe, F. 1925 (Distillery) 1
Russell, A. 1947 (Linfield) 1
Russell, S. R. 1930 (Bradford C, Derry C) 3
Ryan, R. A. 1950 (WBA) 1

Sanchez, L. P. 1987 (Wimbledon) 3
Saville, G. A. 2018 (Millwall, Middlesbrough) 15
Scott, E. 1920 (Liverpool, Belfast Celtic) 31
Scott, J. 1958 (Grimsby) 2
Scott, J. E. 1901 (Cliftonville) 1
Scott, L. J. 1895 (Dublin University) 2
Scott, P. W. 1975 (Everton, York C, Aldershot) 10
Scott, T. 1894 (Cliftonville) 13
Scott, W. 1903 (Linfield, Everton, Leeds C) 25
Scraggs, M. J. 1921 (Glentoran) 2
Seymour, H. C. 1914 (Bohemians) 1
Seymour, J. 1907 (Cliftonville) 2
Shanks, T. 1903 (Woolwich Arsenal, Brentford) 3
Sharkey, P. G. 1976 (Ipswich T) 1
Sheehan, Dr G. 1899 (Bohemians) 3
Sheridan, J. 1903 (Everton, Stoke C) 6
Sherrard, J. 1885 (Limavady) 3
Sherrard, W. C. 1895 (Cliftonville) 3
Sherry, J. J. 1906 (Bohemians) 2
Shields, R. J. 1957 (Southampton) 1
Shiels, D. 2006 (Hibernian, Doncaster R, Kilmarnock) 14
Silo, M. 1888 (Belfast YMCA) 1
Simpson, W. J. 1951 (Rangers) 12
Sinclair, J. 1882 (Knock) 2
Slemin, J. C. 1909 (Bohemians) 1
Sloan, A. S. 1925 (London Caledonians) 1
Sloan, D. 1969 (Oxford U) 2
Sloan, H. A. de B. 1903 (Bohemians) 8
Sloan, J. W. 1947 (Arsenal) 1
Sloan, T. 1926 (Cardiff C, Linfield) 11
Sloan, T. 1979 (Manchester U) 3
Small, J. M. 1887 (Clarence, Cliftonville) 4

Smith, A. W. 2003 (Glentoran, Preston NE) 18
Smith, E. E. 1921 (Cardiff C) 4
Smith, J. E. 1901 (Distillery) 2
Smith, M. 2016 (Peterborough U, Hearts) 6
Smyth, P. 2018 (QPR) 2
Smyth, R. H. 1886 (Dublin University) 1
Smyth, S. 1948 (Wolverhampton W, Stoke C) 9
Smyth, W. 1949 (Distillery) 4
Snape, A. 1920 (Airdrieonians) 1
Sonner, D. J. 1998 (Ipswich T, Sheffield W, Birmingham C, Nottingham F, Peterborough U) 13
Spence, D. W. 1975 (Bury, Blackpool, Southend U) 29
Spencer, S. 1890 (Distillery) 6
Spiller, E. A. 1883 (Cliftonville) 5
Sproule, I. 2006 (Hibernian, Bristol C) 11
Stanfield, O. M. 1887 (Distillery) 30
Steele, A. 1926 (Charlton Ath, Fulham) 4
Steele, J. 2013 (New York Red Bulls) 3
Stevenson, A. E. 1934 (Rangers, Everton) 17
Stewart, A. 1967 (Glentoran, Derby Co) 7
Stewart, D. C. 1978 (Hull C) 1
Stewart, I. 1982 (QPR, Newcastle U) 31
Stewart, R. K. 1890 (St Columb's Court, Cliftonville) 11
Stewart, T. C. 1961 (Linfield) 1
Swan, S. 1899 (Linfield) 1

Taggart, G. P. 1990 (Barnsley, Bolton W, Leicester C) 51
Taggart, J. 1899 (Walsall) 1
Taylor, M. S. 1999 (Fulham, Birmingham C, unattached) 88
Thompson, A. L. 2011 (Watford) 2
Thompson, F. W. 1910 (Cliftonville, Linfield, Bradford C, Clyde) 12
Thompson, J. 1897 (Distillery) 1
Thompson, J. 2018 (Rangers) 2
Thompson, P. 2006 (Linfield, Stockport Co) 8
Thompson, R. 1928 (Queen's Island) 1
Thompson, W. 1889 (Belfast Ath) 1
Thunder, P. J. 1911 (Bohemians) 1
Todd, S. J. 1966 (Burnley, Sheffield W) 11
Toner, C. 2003 (Leyton Orient) 2
Toner, J. 1922 (Arsenal, St Johnstone) 8
Torrans, R. 1893 (Linfield) 1
Torrans, S. 1889 (Linfield) 26
Trainor, D. 1967 (Crusaders) 1
Tuffey, J. 2009 (Partick Thistle, Inverness CT) 8
Tully, C. P. 1949 (Celtic) 10
Turner, A. 1896 (Cliftonville) 1
Turner, E. 1896 (Cliftonville) 1
Turner, W. 1886 (Cliftonville) 3
Twomey, J. F. 1938 (Leeds U) 2

Uprichard, W. N. M. C. 1952 (Swindon T, Portsmouth) 18

Vassell, K. T. 2019 (Rotherham U) 2
Vernon, J. 1947 (Belfast Celtic, WBA) 17

Waddell, T. M. R. 1906 (Cliftonville) 1
Walker, J. 1955 (Doncaster R) 1
Walker, T. 1911 (Bury) 1
Walsh, D. J. 1947 (WBA) 9
Walsh, W. 1948 (Manchester C) 5
Ward, J. J. 2012 (Derby Co, Nottingham F) 35
Waring, J. 1899 (Cliftonville) 1
Warren, P. 1913 (Shelbourne) 2
Washington, C. J. 2016 (QPR, Sheffield U) 20
Watson, J. 1883 (Ulster) 9
Watson, P. 1971 (Distillery) 1
Watson, T. 1926 (Cardiff C) 1
Wattie, J. 1899 (Distillery) 1
Webb, C. G. 1909 (Brighton & HA) 3
Webb, S. M. 2006 (Ross Co) 4
Weir, E. 1939 (Clyde) 1
Welsh, E. 1966 (Carlisle U) 4
Whiteside, N. 1982 (Manchester U, Everton) 38
Whiteside, T. 1891 (Distillery) 1
Whitfield, E. R. 1886 (Dublin University) 1
Whitley, Jeff 1997 (Manchester C, Sunderland, Cardiff C) 20
Whitley, Jim 1998 (Manchester C) 3
Whyte, G. 2019 (Oxford U) 5
Williams, J. R. 1886 (Ulster) 2
Williams, M. S. 1999 (Chesterfield, Watford, Wimbledon, Stoke C, Wimbledon, Milton Keynes D) 36
Williams, P. A. 1991 (WBA) 1
Williamson, J. 1890 (Cliftonville) 3
Willighan, T. 1933 (Burnley) 2
Willis, G. 1906 (Linfield) 4
Wilson, D. J. 1987 (Brighton & HA, Luton T, Sheffield W) 24
Wilson, H. 1925 (Linfield) 2
Wilson, K. J. 1987 (Ipswich T, Chelsea, Notts Co, Walsall) 42
Wilson, M. 1884 (Distillery) 3
Wilson, R. 1888 (Cliftonville) 1
Wilson, S. J. 1962 (Glenavon, Falkirk, Dundee) 12
Wilton, J. M. 1888 (St Columb's Court, Cliftonville, St Columb's Court) 7
Winchester, C. 2011 (Oldham Ath) 1
Wood, T. J. 1996 (Walsall) 1
Worthington, N. 1984 (Sheffield W, Leeds U, Stoke C) 66
Wright, J. 1906 (Cliftonville) 6
Wright, T. J. 1989 (Newcastle U, Nottingham F, Manchester C) 31

Young, S. 1907 (Linfield, Airdrieonians, Linfield) 9

SCOTLAND

Adam, C. G. 2007 (Rangers, Blackpool, Liverpool, Stoke C) 26
Adams, J. 1889 (Hearts) 3
Agnew, W. B. 1907 (Kilmarnock) 3
Aird, J. 1954 (Burnley) 4
Aitken, A. 1901 (Newcastle U, Middlesbrough, Leicester Fosse) 14
Aitken, G. G. 1949 (East Fife, Sunderland) 8
Aitken, R. 1886 (Dumbarton) 2
Aitken, R. 1980 (Celtic, Newcastle U, St Mirren) 57
Aitkenhead, W. A. C. 1912 (Blackburn R) 1
Albiston, A. 1982 (Manchester U) 14
Alexander, D. 1894 (East Stirlingshire) 2
Alexander, G. 2002 (Preston NE, Burnley) 40
Alexander, N. 2006 (Cardiff C) 3
Allan, D. S. 1885 (Queen's Park) 3
Allan, G. 1897 (Liverpool) 1
Allan, H. 1902 (Hearts) 1
Allan, J. 1887 (Queen's Park) 2
Allan, T. 1974 (Dundee) 2
Ancell, R. F. D. 1937 (Newcastle U) 2
Anderson, A. 1933 (Hearts) 23
Anderson, F. 1874 (Clydesdale) 1
Anderson, G. 1901 (Kilmarnock) 1
Anderson, H. A. 1914 (Raith R) 1
Anderson, J. 1954 (Leicester C) 1
Anderson, K. 1896 (Queen's Park) 3
Anderson, R. 2003 (Aberdeen, Sunderland) 11
Anderson, W. 1882 (Queen's Park) 6
Andrews, P. 1875 (Eastern) 1
Anya, I. 2013 (Watford, Derby Co) 29
Archer, J. G. 2018 (Millwall) 1
Archibald, A. 1921 (Rangers) 8
Archibald, S. 1980 (Aberdeen, Tottenham H, Barcelona) 27
Armstrong, M. W. 1936 (Aberdeen) 3
Armstrong, S. 2017 (Celtic, Southampton) 15
Arnott, W. 1883 (Queen's Park) 14
Auld, J. R. 1887 (Third Lanark) 3
Auld, R. 1959 (Celtic) 3

Bain, S. 2018 (Celtic) 3
Baird, A. 1892 (Queen's Park) 2
Baird, D. 1890 (Hearts) 3
Baird, H. 1956 (Airdrieonians) 1
Baird, J. C. 1876 (Vale of Leven) 3
Baird, S. 1957 (Rangers) 7
Baird, W. U. 1897 (St Bernard) 1
Bannan, B. 2011 (Aston Villa, Crystal Palace, Sheffield W) 27

Bannon, E. J. 1980 (Dundee U) 11
Barbour, A. 1885 (Renton) 1
Bardsley, P. A. 2011 (Sunderland) 13
Barker, J. B. 1893 (Rangers) 2
Barr, D. 2009 (Falkirk) 1
Barrett, F. 1894 (Dundee) 2
Bates, D. 2019 (Hamburger SV) 4
Battles, B. 1901 (Celtic) 3
Battles, B. jun. 1931 (Hearts) 1
Bauld, W. 1950 (Hearts) 3
Baxter, J. C. 1961 (Rangers, Sunderland) 34
Baxter, R. D. 1939 (Middlesbrough) 3
Beattie, A. 1937 (Preston NE) 7
Beattie, C. 2006 (Celtic, WBA) 7
Beattie, R. 1939 (Preston NE) 1
Begbie, I. 1890 (Hearts) 4
Bell, A. 1912 (Manchester U) 1
Bell, C. 2011 (Kilmarnock) 1
Bell, J. 1890 (Dumbarton, Everton, Celtic) 10
Bell, M. 1901 (Hearts) 1
Bell, W. J. 1966 (Leeds U) 2
Bennett, A. 1904 (Celtic, Rangers) 11
Bennie, R. 1925 (Airdrieonians) 3
Bernard, P. R. J. 1995 (Oldham Ath) 2
Berra, C. D. 2008 (Hearts, Wolverhampton W, Ipswich T) 41
Berry, D. 1894 (Queen's Park) 3
Berry, W. H. 1888 (Queen's Park) 4
Bett, J. 1982 (Rangers, Lokeren, Aberdeen) 25
Beveridge, W. W. 1879 (Glasgow University) 3
Black, A. 1938 (Hearts) 3
Black, D. 1889 (Hurlford) 1
Black, E. 1988 (Metz) 2
Black, I. 2013 (Rangers) 1
Black, I. H. 1948 (Southampton) 1
Blackburn, J. E. 1873 (Royal Engineers) 1
Blacklaw, A. S. 1963 (Burnley) 3
Blackley, J. 1974 (Hibernian) 7
Blair, D. 1929 (Clyde, Aston Villa) 8
Blair, J. 1920 (Sheffield W, Cardiff C) 8
Blair, J. 1934 (Motherwell) 1
Blair, J. A. 1947 (Blackpool) 1
Blair, W. 1896 (Third Lanark) 1
Blessington, J. 1894 (Celtic) 4
Blyth, J. A. 1978 (Coventry C) 2
Bone, J. 1972 (Norwich C) 2
Booth, S. 1993 (Aberdeen, Borussia Dortmund, Twente) 21
Bowie, J. 1920 (Rangers) 2
Bowie, W. 1891 (Linthouse) 1
Bowman, D. 1992 (Dundee U) 6
Bowman, G. A. 1892 (Montrose) 1
Boyd, G. I. 2013 (Peterborough U, Hull C) 2
Boyd, J. M. 1934 (Newcastle U) 1
Boyd, K. 2006 (Rangers, Middlesbrough) 18
Boyd, R. 1889 (Mossend Swifts) 2
Boyd, T. 1991 (Motherwell, Chelsea, Celtic) 72
Boyd, W. G. 1931 (Clyde) 2
Bradshaw, T. 1928 (Bury) 1
Brand, R. 1961 (Rangers) 8
Brandon, T. 1896 (Blackburn R) 1
Brazil, A. 1980 (Ipswich T, Tottenham H) 13
Breckenridge, T. 1888 (Hearts) 1
Bremner, D. 1976 (Hibernian) 1
Bremner, W. J. 1965 (Leeds U) 54
Brennan, F. 1947 (Newcastle U) 7
Breslin, B. 1897 (Hibernian) 1
Brewster, G. 1921 (Everton) 1
Bridcutt, L. 2013 (Brighton & HA, Sunderland) 2
Broadfoot, K. 2009 (Rangers) 4
Brogan, J. 1971 (Celtic) 4
Brophy, E. 2019 (Kilmarnock) 1
Brown, A. 1890 (St Mirren) 2
Brown, A. 1904 (Middlesbrough) 1
Brown, A. D. 1950 (East Fife, Blackpool) 14
Brown, G. C. P. 1931 (Rangers) 19
Brown, H. 1947 (Partick Thistle) 3
Brown, J. B. 1939 (Clyde) 1
Brown, J. G. 1975 (Sheffield U) 1
Brown, R. 1884 (Dumbarton) 2
Brown, R. 1890 (Cambuslang) 1
Brown, R. 1947 (Rangers) 3
Brown, R. jun. 1885 (Dumbarton) 1
Brown, S. 2006 (Hibernian, Celtic) 55
Brown, W. D. F. 1958 (Dundee, Tottenham H) 28
Browning, J. 1914 (Celtic) 1
Brownlie, J. 1909 (Third Lanark) 16
Brownlie, J. 1971 (Hibernian) 7
Bruce, D. 1890 (Vale of Leven) 1
Bruce, R. F. 1934 (Middlesbrough) 1
Bryson, C. 2011 (Kilmarnock, Derby Co) 3
Buchan, M. M. 1972 (Aberdeen, Manchester U) 34
Buchanan, J. 1889 (Cambuslang) 1
Buchanan, J. 1929 (Rangers) 2
Buchanan, P. S. 1938 (Chelsea) 1
Buchanan, R. 1891 (Abercorn) 1
Buckley, P. 1954 (Aberdeen) 3
Buick, A. 1902 (Hearts) 2
Burchill, M. J. 2000 (Celtic) 6
Burke, C. 2006 (Rangers, Birmingham C) 7
Burke O. J. 2016 (Nottingham F, RB Leipzig, WBA) 8
Burley, C. W. 1995 (Chelsea, Celtic, Derby Co) 46
Burley, G. E. 1979 (Ipswich T) 11
Burns, F. 1970 (Manchester U) 1
Burns, K. 1974 (Birmingham C, Nottingham F) 20
Burns, T. 1981 (Celtic) 8
Busby, M. W. 1934 (Manchester C) 1

Cadden, C. 2018 (Motherwell) 2
Caddis, P. M. 2016 (Birmingham C) 1
Cairney, T. 2017 (Fulham) 2
Cairns, T. 1920 (Rangers) 8
Calderhead, D. 1889 (Q of S Wanderers) 1
Calderwood, C. 1995 (Tottenham H) 36
Calderwood, R. 1885 (Cartvale) 3
Caldow, E. 1957 (Rangers) 40
Caldwell, G. 2002 (Newcastle U, Hibernian, Celtic, Wigan Ath) 55
Caldwell, S. 2001 (Newcastle U, Sunderland, Burnley,Wigan Ath) 12
Callaghan, P. 1900 (Hibernian) 1
Callaghan, W. 1970 (Dunfermline Ath) 2
Cameron, C. 1999 (Hearts, Wolverhampton W) 28
Cameron, J. 1886 (Rangers) 1
Cameron, J. 1896 (Queen's Park) 1
Cameron, J. 1904 (St Mirren, Chelsea) 2
Campbell, C. 1874 (Queen's Park) 13
Campbell, H. 1889 (Renton) 1
Campbell, Jas 1913 (Sheffield W) 1
Campbell, J. 1880 (South Western) 1
Campbell, J. 1891 (Kilmarnock) 2
Campbell, John 1893 (Celtic) 12
Campbell, John 1899 (Rangers) 4
Campbell, K. 1920 (Liverpool, Partick Thistle) 8
Campbell, P. 1878 (Rangers) 2
Campbell, P. 1898 (Morton) 1
Campbell, R. 1947 (Falkirk, Chelsea) 5
Campbell, W. 1947 (Morton) 5
Canero, P. 2004 (Leicester C) 1
Carabine, J. 1938 (Third Lanark) 3
Carr, W. M. 1970 (Coventry C) 6
Cassidy, J. 1921 (Celtic) 4
Chalmers, S. 1965 (Celtic) 5
Chalmers, W. 1885 (Rangers) 1
Chalmers, W. S. 1929 (Queen's Park) 1
Chambers, T. 1894 (Hearts) 1
Chaplin, G. D. 1908 (Dundee) 1
Cheyne, A. G. 1929 (Aberdeen) 5
Christie, A. J. 1898 (Queen's Park) 3
Christie, R. 2018 (Celtic) 5
Christie, R. M. 1884 (Queen's Park) 1
Clark, J. 1966 (Celtic) 4
Clark, R. B. 1968 (Aberdeen) 17
Clarke, S. 1988 (Chelsea) 6
Clarkson, D. 2008 (Motherwell) 2
Cleland, J. 1891 (Royal Albert) 1
Clements, R. 1891 (Leith Ath) 1
Clunas, W. L. 1924 (Sunderland) 2
Collier, W. 1922 (Raith R) 1
Collins, J. 1988 (Hibernian, Celtic, Monaco, Everton) 58
Collins, R. Y. 1951 (Celtic, Everton, Leeds U) 31
Collins, T. 1909 (Hearts) 1

Colman, D. 1911 (Aberdeen) 4
Colquhoun, E. P. 1972 (Sheffield U) 9
Colquhoun, J. 1988 (Hearts) 2
Combe, J. R. 1948 (Hibernian) 3
Commons, K. 2009 (Derby Co, Celtic) 12
Conn, A. 1956 (Hearts) 1
Conn, A. 1975 (Tottenham H) 2
Connachan, E. D. 1962 (Dunfermline Ath) 2
Connelly, G. 1974 (Celtic) 2
Connolly, J. 1973 (Everton) 1
Connor, J. 1886 (Airdrieonians) 1
Connor, J. 1930 (Sunderland) 4
Connor, R. 1986 (Dundee, Aberdeen) 4
Conway, C. 2010 (Dundee U, Cardiff C) 7
Cook, W. L. 1934 (Bolton W) 3
Cooke, C. 1966 (Dundee, Chelsea) 16
Cooper, D. 1980 (Rangers, Motherwell) 22
Cormack, P. B. 1966 (Hibernian, Nottingham F) 9
Cowan, J. 1896 (Aston Villa) 3
Cowan, J. 1948 (Morton) 25
Cowan, W, D. 1924 (Newcastle U) 1
Cowie, D. 1953 (Dundee) 20
Cowie, D. M. 2010 (Watford, Cardiff C) 10
Cox, C. J. 1948 (Hearts) 1
Cox, S. 1949 (Rangers) 24
Craig, A. 1929 (Motherwell) 3
Craig, J. 1977 (Celtic) 1
Craig, J. P. 1968 (Celtic) 1
Craig, T. 1927 (Rangers) 8
Craig, T. B. 1976 (Newcastle U) 1
Crainey, S. D. 2002 (Celtic, Southampton, Blackpool) 12
Crapnell, J. 1929 (Airdrieonians) 9
Crawford, D. 1894 (St Mirren, Rangers) 3
Crawford, J. 1932 (Queen's Park) 5
Crawford, S. 1995 (Raith R, Dunfermline Ath, Plymouth Arg) 25
Crerand, P. T. 1961 (Celtic, Manchester U) 16
Cringan, W. 1920 (Celtic) 5
Crosbie, J. A. 1920 (Ayr U, Birmingham) 2
Croal, J. A. 1913 (Falkirk) 3
Cropley, A. J. 1972 (Hibernian) 2
Cross, J. H. 1903 (Third Lanark) 1
Cruickshank, J. 1964 (Hearts) 6
Crum, J. 1936 (Celtic) 2
Cullen, M. J. 1956 (Luton T) 1
Cumming, D. S. 1938 (Middlesbrough) 1
Cumming, J. 1955 (Hearts) 9
Cummings, G. 1935 (Partick Thistle, Aston Villa) 9
Cummings, J. 2018 (Nottingham F) 2
Cummings, W. 2002 (Chelsea) 1
Cunningham, A. N. 1920 (Rangers) 12
Cunningham, W. C. 1954 (Preston NE) 8
Curran, H. P. 1970 (Wolverhampton W) 5

Dailly, C. 1997 (Derby Co, Blackburn R, West Ham U, Rangers) 67
Dalglish, K. 1972 (Celtic, Liverpool) 102
Davidson, C. I. 1999 (Blackburn R, Leicester C, Preston NE) 19
Davidson, D. 1878 (Queen's Park) 5
Davidson, J. A. 1954 (Partick Thistle) 8
Davidson, M. 2013 (St Johnstone) 1
Davidson, S. 1921 (Middlesbrough) 1
Dawson, A. 1980 (Rangers) 5
Dawson, J. 1935 (Rangers) 14
Deans, J. 1975 (Celtic) 2
Delaney, J. 1936 (Celtic, Manchester U) 13
Devine, A. 1910 (Falkirk) 1
Devlin, P. J. 2003 (Birmingham C) 10
Dewar, G. 1888 (Dumbarton) 2
Dewar, N. 1932 (Third Lanark) 3
Dick, J. 1959 (West Ham U) 1
Dickie, M. 1897 (Rangers) 3
Dickov, P. 2001 (Manchester C, Leicester C, Blackburn R) 10
Dickson, W. 1888 (Dundee Strathmore) 1
Dickson, W. 1970 (Kilmarnock) 5
Divers, J. 1895 (Celtic) 1
Divers, J. 1939 (Celtic) 1
Dixon, P. A. 2013 (Hudderfield T) 3
Dobie, R. S. 2002 (WBA) 6
Docherty, T. H. 1952 (Preston NE, Arsenal) 25
Dodds, D. 1984 (Dundee U) 2
Dodds, J. 1914 (Celtic) 3
Dodds, W. 1997 (Aberdeen, Dundee U, Rangers) 26
Doig, J. E. 1887 (Arbroath, Sunderland) 5
Donachie, W. 1972 (Manchester C) 35
Donaldson, A. 1914 (Bolton W) 6
Donnachie, J. 1913 (Oldham Ath) 3
Donnelly, S. 1997 (Celtic) 10
Dorrans, G. 2010 (WBA, Norwich C) 12
Dougal, J. 1939 (Preston NE) 1
Dougall, C. 1947 (Birmingham C) 1
Dougan, R. 1950 (Hearts) 1
Douglas, A. 1911 (Chelsea) 1
Douglas, B. 2018 (Wolverhampton W) 1
Douglas, J. 1880 (Renfrew) 1
Douglas, R. 2002 (Celtic, Leicester C) 19
Dowds, P. 1892 (Celtic) 1
Downie, R. 1892 (Third Lanark) 1
Doyle, D. 1892 (Celtic) 8
Doyle, J. 1976 (Ayr U) 1
Drummond, J. 1892 (Falkirk, Rangers) 14
Dunbar, M. 1886 (Cartvale) 1
Duncan, A. 1975 (Hibernian) 6
Duncan, D. 1933 (Derby Co) 14
Duncan, D. M. 1948 (East Fife) 3
Duncan, J. 1878 (Alexandra Ath) 2
Duncan, J. 1926 (Leicester C) 1
Duncanson, J. 1947 (Rangers) 1
Dunlop, J. 1890 (St Mirren) 1
Dunlop, W. 1906 (Liverpool) 1
Dunn, J. 1925 (Hibernian, Everton) 6
Durie, G. S. 1988 (Chelsea, Tottenham H, Rangers) 43
Durrant, I. 1988 (Rangers, Kilmarnock) 20
Dykes, J. 1938 (Hearts) 2

Easson, J. F. 1931 (Portsmouth) 3
Elliott, M. S. 1998 (Leicester C) 18
Ellis, J. 1892 (Mossend Swifts) 1
Evans, A. 1982 (Aston Villa) 4
Evans, R. 1949 (Celtic, Chelsea) 48
Ewart, J. 1921 (Bradford C) 1
Ewing, T. 1958 (Partick Thistle) 2

Farm, G. N. 1953 (Blackpool) 10
Ferguson, B. 1999 (Rangers, Blackburn R, Rangers) 45
Ferguson, D. 1988 (Rangers) 2
Ferguson, D. 1992 (Dundee U, Everton) 7
Ferguson, I. 1989 (Rangers) 9
Ferguson, J. 1874 (Vale of Leven) 6
Ferguson, R. 1966 (Kilmarnock) 7
Fernie, W. 1954 (Celtic) 12
Findlay, R. 1898 (Kilmarnock) 1
Fitchie, T. T. 1905 (Woolwich Arsenal, Queen's Park) 4
Flavell, R. 1947 (Airdrieonians) 2
Fleck, R. 1990 (Norwich C) 4
Fleming, C. 1954 (East Fife) 1
Fleming, J. W. 1929 (Rangers) 3
Fleming, R. 1886 (Morton) 1
Fletcher, D. B. 2004 (Manchester U, WBA, Stoke C) 80
Fletcher, S. K. 2008 (Hibernian, Burnley, Wolverhampton W, Sunderland, Sheffield W) 33
Forbes, A. R. 1947 (Sheffield U, Arsenal) 14
Forbes, J. 1884 (Vale of Leven) 5
Ford, D. 1974 (Hearts) 3
Forrest, J. 1958 (Motherwell) 1
Forrest, J. 1966 (Rangers, Aberdeen) 5
Forrest, J. 2011 (Celtic) 30
Forsyth, A. 1972 (Partick Thistle, Manchester U) 10
Forsyth, C. 2014 (Derby Co) 4
Forsyth, R. C. 1964 (Kilmarnock) 4
Forsyth, T. 1971 (Motherwell, Rangers) 22
Fox, D. J. 2010 (Burnley, Southampton) 4
Foyers, R. 1893 (St Bernards) 2
Fraser, D. M. 1968 (WBA) 2
Fraser, J. 1891 (Moffat) 1
Fraser, J. 1907 (Dundee) 1
Fraser, M. J. E. 1880 (Queen's Park) 5
Fraser, R. 2017 (Bournemouth) 9
Fraser, W. 1955 (Sunderland) 2
Freedman, D. A. 2002 (Crystal Palace) 2

Fulton, W. 1884 (Abercorn) 1
Fyfe, J. H. 1895 (Third Lanark) 1

Gabriel, J. 1961 (Everton) 2
Gallacher, H. K. 1924 (Airdrieonians, Newcastle U, Chelsea, Derby Co) 20
Gallacher, K. W. 1988 (Dundee U, Coventry C, Blackburn R, Newcastle U) 53
Gallacher, P. 1935 (Sunderland) 1
Gallacher, P. 2002 (Dundee U) 8
Gallagher, P. 2004 (Blackburn R) 1
Galloway, M. 1992 (Celtic) 1
Galt, J. H. 1908 (Rangers) 2
Gardiner, I. 1958 (Motherwell) 1
Gardner, D. R. 1897 (Third Lanark) 1
Gardner, R. 1872 (Queen's Park, Clydesdale) 5
Gemmell, T. 1955 (St Mirren) 2
Gemmell, T. 1966 (Celtic) 18
Gemmill, A. 1971 (Derby Co, Nottingham F, Birmingham C) 43
Gemmill, S. 1995 (Nottingham F, Everton) 26
Gibb, W. 1873 (Clydesdale) 1
Gibson, D. W. 1963 (Leicester C) 7
Gibson, J. D. 1926 (Partick Thistle, Aston Villa) 8
Gibson, N. 1895 (Rangers, Partick Thistle) 14
Gilchrist, J. E. 1922 (Celtic) 1
Gilhooley, M. 1922 (Hull C) 1
Gilks, M. 2013 (Blackpool) 3
Gillespie, G. 1880 (Rangers, Queen's Park) 7
Gillespie, G. T. 1988 (Liverpool) 13
Gillespie, Jas 1898 (Third Lanark) 1
Gillespie, John 1896 (Queen's Park) 1
Gillespie, R. 1927 (Queen's Park) 4
Gillick, T. 1937 (Everton) 5
Gilmour, J. 1931 (Dundee) 1
Gilzean, A. J. 1964 (Dundee, Tottenham H) 22
Glass, S. 1999 (Newcastle U) 1
Glavin, R. 1977 (Celtic) 1
Glen, A. 1956 (Aberdeen) 2
Glen, R. 1895 (Renton, Hibernian) 3
Goodwillie, D. 2011 (Dundee U, Blackburn R) 3
Goram, A. L. 1986 (Oldham Ath, Hibernian, Rangers) 43
Gordon, C. A. 2004 (Hearts, Sunderland, Celtic) 54
Gordon, J. E. 1912 (Rangers) 10
Gossland, J. 1884 (Rangers) 1
Goudle, J. 1884 (Abercorn) 1
Gough, C. R. 1983 (Dundee U, Tottenham H, Rangers) 61
Gould, J. 2000 (Celtic) 2
Gourlay, J. 1886 (Cambuslang) 2
Govan, J. 1948 (Hibernian) 6
Gow, D. R. 1888 (Rangers) 1
Gow, J. J. 1885 (Queen's Park) 1
Gow, J. R. 1888 (Rangers) 1
Graham, A. 1978 (Leeds U) 11
Graham, G. 1972 (Arsenal, Manchester U) 12
Graham, J. 1884 (Annbank) 1
Graham, J. A. 1921 (Arsenal) 1
Grant, J. 1959 (Hibernian) 2
Grant, P. 1989 (Celtic) 2
Gray, A. 1903 (Hibernian) 1
Gray, A. D. 2003 (Bradford C) 2
Gray, A. M. 1976 (Aston Villa, Wolverhampton W, Everton) 20
Gray, D. 1929 (Rangers) 10
Gray, E. 1969 (Leeds U) 12
Gray, F. T. 1976 (Leeds U, Nottingham F, Leeds U) 32
Gray, W. 1886 (Pollokshields Ath) 1
Green, A. 1971 (Blackpool, Newcastle U) 6
Greer, G. 2013 (Brighton & HA) 11
Greig, J. 1964 (Rangers) 44
Griffiths, L. 2013 (Hibernian, Celtic) 19
Groves, W. 1888 (Hibernian, Celtic) 3
Gulliland, W. 1891 (Queen's Park) 4
Gunn, B. 1990 (Norwich C) 6

Haddock, H. 1955 (Clyde) 6
Haddow, D. 1894 (Rangers) 1
Haffey, F. 1960 (Celtic) 2
Hamilton, A. 1885 (Queen's Park) 4
Hamilton, A. W. 1962 (Dundee) 24
Hamilton, G. 1906 (Port Glasgow Ath) 1
Hamilton, G. 1947 (Aberdeen) 5
Hamilton, J. 1892 (Queen's Park) 3
Hamilton, J. 1924 (St Mirren) 1
Hamilton, R. C. 1899 (Rangers, Dundee) 11
Hamilton, T. 1891 (Hurlford) 1
Hamilton, T. 1932 (Rangers) 1
Hamilton, W. M. 1965 (Hibernian) 1
Hammell, S. 2005 (Motherwell) 1
Hanley, G. C. 2011 (Blackburn R, Newcastle U, Norwich C) 29
Hannah, A. B. 1888 (Renton) 1
Hannah, J. 1889 (Third Lanark) 1
Hansen, A. D. 1979 (Liverpool) 26
Hansen, J. 1972 (Partick Thistle) 2
Harkness, J. D. 1927 (Queen's Park, Hearts) 12
Harper, J. M. 1973 (Aberdeen, Hibernian, Aberdeen) 4
Harper, W. 1923 (Hibernian, Arsenal) 11
Harris, J. 1921 (Partick Thistle) 2
Harris, N. 1924 (Newcastle U) 1
Harrower, W. 1882 (Queen's Park) 3
Hartford, R. A. 1972 (WBA, Manchester C, Everton, Manchester C) 50
Hartley, P. J. 2005 (Hearts, Celtic, Bristol C) 25
Harvey, D. 1973 (Leeds U) 16
Hastings, A. C. 1936 (Sunderland) 2
Haughney, M. 1954 (Celtic) 1
Hay, D. 1970 (Celtic) 27
Hay, J. 1905 (Celtic, Newcastle U) 11
Hegarty, P. 1979 (Dundee U) 8
Heggie, C. 1886 (Rangers) 1
Henderson, G. H. 1904 (Rangers) 1
Henderson, J. G. 1953 (Portsmouth, Arsenal) 7
Henderson, W. 1963 (Rangers) 29
Hendry, E. C. J. 1993 (Blackburn R, Rangers, Coventry C, Bolton W) 51
Hendry, J. 2018 (Celtic) 3
Hepburn, J. 1891 (Alloa Ath) 1
Hepburn, R. 1932 (Ayr U) 1
Herd, A. C. 1935 (Hearts) 1
Herd, D. G. 1959 (Arsenal) 5
Herd, G. 1958 (Clyde) 5
Herriot, J. 1969 (Birmingham C) 8
Hewie, J. D. 1956 (Charlton Ath) 19
Higgins, A. 1885 (Kilmarnock) 1
Higgins, A. 1910 (Newcastle U) 4
Highet, T. C. 1875 (Queen's Park) 4
Hill, D. 1881 (Rangers) 3
Hill, D. A. 1906 (Third Lanark) 1
Hill, F. R. 1930 (Aberdeen) 3
Hill, J. 1891 (Hearts) 2
Hogg, G. 1896 (Hearts) 2
Hogg, J. 1922 (Ayr U) 1
Hogg, R. M. 1937 (Celtic) 1
Holm, A. H. 1882 (Queen's Park) 3
Holt, D. D. 1963 (Hearts) 5
Holt, G. J. 2001 (Kilmarnock, Norwich C) 10
Holton, J. A. 1973 (Manchester U) 15
Hope, R. 1968 (WBA) 2
Hopkin, D. 1997 (Crystal Palace, Leeds U) 7
Houliston, W. 1949 (Queen of the South) 3
Houston, S. M. 1976 (Manchester U) 1
Howden, W. 1905 (Partick Thistle) 1
Howe, R. 1929 (Hamilton A) 2
Howie, H. 1949 (Hibernian) 1
Howie, J. 1905 (Newcastle U) 3
Howieson, J. 1927 (St Mirren) 1
Hughes, J. 1965 (Celtic) 8
Hughes, R. D. 2004 (Portsmouth) 5
Hughes, S. R. 2010 (Norwich C) 1
Hughes, W. 1975 (Sunderland) 1
Humphries, W. 1952 (Motherwell) 1
Hunter, A. 1972 (Kilmarnock, Celtic) 4
Hunter, J. 1909 (Dundee) 1
Hunter, J. 1874 (Third Lanark, Eastern, Third Lanark) 4
Hunter, W. 1960 (Motherwell) 3
Hunter, R. 1890 (St Mirren) 1
Husband, J. 1947 (Partick Thistle) 1
Hutchison, D. 1999 (Everton, Sunderland, West Ham U) 26
Hutchison, T. 1974 (Coventry C) 17
Hutton, A. 2007 (Rangers, Tottenham H, Aston Villa) 50
Hutton, J. 1887 (St Bernards) 1

Hutton, J. 1923 (Aberdeen, Blackburn R) 10
Hyslop, T. 1896 (Stoke, Rangers) 2

Imlach, J. J. S. 1958 (Nottingham F) 4
Imrie, W. N. 1929 (St Johnstone) 2
Inglis, J. 1883 (Rangers) 2
Inglis, J. 1884 (Kilmarnock Ath) 1
Irons, J. H. 1900 (Queen's Park) 1
Irvine, B. 1991 (Aberdeen) 9
Iwelumo, C. R. 2009 (Wolverhampton W, Burnley) 4

Jack, R. 2018 (Rangers) 2
Jackson, A. 1886 (Cambuslang) 2
Jackson, A. 1925 (Aberdeen, Huddersfield T) 17
Jackson, C. 1975 (Rangers) 8
Jackson, D. 1995 (Hibernian, Celtic) 28
Jackson, J. 1931 (Partick Thistle, Chelsea) 8
Jackson, T. A. 1904 (St Mirren) 6
James, A. W. 1926 (Preston NE, Arsenal) 8
Jardine, A. 1971 (Rangers) 38
Jarvie, A. 1971 (Airdrieonians) 3
Jenkinson, T. 1887 (Hearts) 1
Jess, E. 1993 (Aberdeen, Coventry C, Aberdeen) 18
Johnston, A. 1999 (Sunderland, Rangers, Middlesbrough) 18
Johnston, L. H. 1948 (Clyde) 2
Johnston, M. 1984 (Watford, Celtic, Nantes, Rangers) 38
Johnston, R. 1938 (Sunderland) 1
Johnston, W. 1966 (Rangers, WBA) 22
Johnstone, D. 1973 (Rangers) 14
Johnstone, J. 1888 (Abercorn) 1
Johnstone, J. 1965 (Celtic) 23
Johnstone, Jas 1894 (Kilmarnock) 1
Johnstone, J. A. 1930 (Hearts) 3
Johnstone, R. 1951 (Hibernian, Manchester C) 17
Johnstone, W. 1887 (Third Lanark) 3
Jordan, J. 1973 (Leeds U, Manchester U, AC Milan) 52

Kay, J. L. 1880 (Queen's Park) 6
Keillor, A. 1891 (Montrose, Dundee) 6
Keir, L. 1885 (Dumbarton) 5
Kelly, H. T. 1952 (Blackpool) 1
Kelly, J. 1888 (Renton, Celtic) 8
Kelly, J. C. 1949 (Barnsley) 2
Kelly, L. M. 2013 (Kilmarnock) 1
Kelso, R. 1885 (Renton, Dundee) 7
Kelso, T. 1914 (Dundee) 1
Kennaway, J. 1934 (Celtic) 1
Kennedy, A. 1875 (Eastern, Third Lanark) 6
Kennedy, J. 1897 (Hibernian) 1
Kennedy, J. 1964 (Celtic) 6
Kennedy, J. 2004 (Celtic) 1
Kennedy, S. 1905 (Partick Thistle) 1
Kennedy, S. 1975 (Rangers) 5
Kennedy, S. 1978 (Aberdeen) 8
Kenneth, G. 2011 (Dundee U) 2
Ker, G. 1880 (Queen's Park) 5
Ker, W. 1872 (Queen's Park) 2
Kerr, A. 1955 (Partick Thistle) 2
Kerr, B. 2003 (Newcastle U) 3
Kerr, P. 1924 (Hibernian) 1
Key, G. 1902 (Hearts) 1
Key, W. 1907 (Queen's Park) 1
King, A. 1896 (Hearts, Celtic) 6
King, J. 1933 (Hamilton A) 2
King, W. S. 1929 (Queen's Park) 1
Kingsley, S. 2016 (Swansea C) 1
Kinloch, J. D. 1922 (Partick Thistle) 1
Kinnaird, A. F. 1873 (Wanderers) 1
Kinnear, D. 1938 (Rangers) 1
Kyle, K. 2002 (Sunderland, Kilmarnock) 10

Lambert, P. 1995 (Motherwell, Borussia Dortmund, Celtic) 40
Lambie, J. A. 1886 (Queen's Park) 3
Lambie, W. A. 1892 (Queen's Park) 9
Lamont, W. 1885 (Pilgrims) 1
Lang, A. 1880 (Dumbarton) 1
Lang, J. J. 1876 (Clydesdale, Third Lanark) 2
Latta, A. 1888 (Dumbarton) 2
Law, D. 1959 (Huddersfield T, Manchester C, Torino, Manchester U, Manchester C) 55
Law, G. 1910 (Rangers) 3
Law, T. 1928 (Chelsea) 2
Lawrence, J. 1911 (Newcastle U) 1
Lawrence, T. 1963 (Liverpool) 3
Lawson, D. 1923 (St Mirren) 1
Leckie, R. 1872 (Queen's Park) 1
Leggat, G. 1956 (Aberdeen, Fulham) 18
Leighton, J. 1983 (Aberdeen, Manchester U, Hibernian, Aberdeen) 91
Lennie, W. 1908 (Aberdeen) 2
Lennox, R. 1967 (Celtic) 10
Leslie, L. G. 1961 (Airdrieonians) 5
Levein, C. 1990 (Hearts) 16
Liddell, W. 1947 (Liverpool) 28
Liddle, D. 1931 (East Fife) 3
Lindsay, D. 1903 (St Mirren) 1
Lindsay, J. 1880 (Dumbarton) 8
Lindsay, J. 1888 (Renton) 3
Linwood, A. B. 1950 (Clyde) 1
Little, R. J. 1953 (Rangers) 1
Livingstone, G. T. 1906 (Manchester C, Rangers) 2
Lochhead, A. 1889 (Third Lanark) 1
Logan, J. 1891 (Ayr) 1
Logan, T. 1913 (Falkirk) 1
Logie, J. T. 1953 (Arsenal) 1
Loney, W. 1910 (Celtic) 2
Long, H. 1947 (Clyde) 1
Longair, W. 1894 (Dundee) 1
Lorimer, P. 1970 (Leeds U) 21
Love, A. 1931 (Aberdeen) 3
Low, A. 1934 (Falkirk) 1
Low, J. 1891 (Cambuslang) 1
Low, T. P. 1897 (Rangers) 1
Low, W. L. 1911 (Newcastle U) 5
Lowe, J. 1887 (St Bernards) 1
Lundie, J. 1886 (Hibernian) 1
Lyall, J. 1905 (Sheffield W) 1

Macari, L. 1972 (Celtic, Manchester U) 24
Mackail-Smith, C. 2011 (Peterborough U, Brighton & HA) 7
Mackay-Steven, G. 2013 (Dundee U, Aberdeen) 2
Mackie, J. C. 2011 (QPR) 9
Madden, J. 1893 (Celtic) 2
Maguire, C. 2011 (Aberdeen) 2
Main, F. R. 1938 (Rangers) 1
Main, J. 1909 (Hibernian) 1
Maley, W. 1893 (Celtic) 2
Maloney, S. R. 2006 (Celtic, Aston Villa, Celtic, Wigan Ath, Chicago Fire, Hull C) 47
Malpas, M. 1984 (Dundee U) 55
Marshall, D. J. 2005 (Celtic, Cardiff C, Hull C) 29
Marshall, G. 1992 (Celtic) 1
Marshall, H. 1899 (Celtic) 2
Marshall, J. 1885 (Third Lanark) 4
Marshall, J. 1921 (Middlesbrough, Llanelly) 7
Marshall, J. 1932 (Rangers) 3
Marshall, R. W. 1892 (Rangers) 2
Martin, B. 1995 (Motherwell) 2
Martin, C. H. 2014 (Derby Co) 17
Martin, F. 1954 (Aberdeen) 6
Martin, N. 1965 (Hibernian, Sunderland) 3
Martin, R. K. A. 2011 (Norwich C) 29
Martis, J. 1961 (Motherwell) 1
Mason, J. 1949 (Third Lanark) 7
Massie, A. 1932 (Hearts, Aston Villa) 18
Masson, D. S. 1976 (QPR, Derby Co) 17
Mathers, D. 1954 (Partick Thistle) 1
Matteo, D. 2001 (Leeds U) 6
Maxwell, W. S. 1898 (Stoke C) 1
May, J. 1906 (Rangers) 5
May, S. 2015 (Sheffield W) 1
McAllister, J. R. 2004 (Livingston) 1
McAdam, J. 1880 (Third Lanark) 1
McAllister, B. 1997 (Wimbledon) 3
McAllister, G. 1990 (Leicester C, Leeds U, Coventry C) 57
McArthur, D. 1895 (Celtic) 3
McArthur, J. 2011 (Wigan Ath, Crystal Palace) 32
McAtee, A. 1913 (Celtic) 1

McAulay, J. 1884 (Arthurlie) 1
McAulay, J. D. 1882 (Dumbarton) 9
McAulay, R. 1932 (Rangers) 2
Macauley, A. R. 1947 (Brentford, Arsenal) 7
McAvennie, F. 1986 (West Ham U, Celtic) 5
McBain, E. 1894 (St Mirren) 1
McBain, N. 1922 (Manchester U, Everton) 3
McBride, J. 1967 (Celtic) 2
McBride, P. 1904 (Preston NE) 6
McBurnie, O. R. 2018 (Swansea C) 7
McCall, A. 1888 (Renton) 1
McCall, A. S. M. 1990 (Everton, Rangers) 40
McCall, J. 1886 (Renton) 5
McCalliog, J. 1967 (Sheffield W, Wolverhampton W) 5
McCallum, N. 1888 (Renton) 1
McCann, N. 1999 (Hearts, Rangers, Southampton) 26
McCann, R. J. 1959 (Motherwell) 5
McCartney, W. 1902 (Hibernian) 1
McClair, B. 1987 (Celtic, Manchester U) 30
McClory, A. 1927 (Motherwell) 3
McCloy, P. 1924 (Ayr U) 2
McCloy, P. 1973 (Rangers) 4
McCoist, A. 1986 (Rangers, Kilmarnock) 61
McColl, I. M. 1950 (Rangers) 14
McColl, R. S. 1896 (Queen's Park, Newcastle U, Queen's Park) 13
McColl, W. 1895 (Renton) 1
McCombie, A. 1903 (Sunderland, Newcastle U) 4
McCorkindale, J. 1891 (Partick Thistle) 1
McCormack, R. 2008 (Motherwell, Cardiff C, Leeds U, Fulham) 13
McCormick, R. 1886 (Abercorn) 1
McCrae, D. 1929 (St Mirren) 2
McCreadie, A. 1893 (Rangers) 2
McCreadie, E. G. 1965 (Chelsea) 23
McCulloch, D. 1935 (Hearts, Brentford, Derby Co) 7
McCulloch, L. 2005 (Wigan Ath, Rangers) 18
MacDonald, A. 1976 (Rangers) 1
McDonald, J. 1886 (Edinburgh University) 1
McDonald, J. 1956 (Sunderland) 2
McDonald, K. D. 2018 (Fulham) 5
MacDougall, E. J. 1975 (Norwich C) 7
McDougall, J. 1877 (Vale of Leven) 5
McDougall, J. 1926 (Airdrieonians) 1
McDougall, J. 1931 (Liverpool) 2
McEveley, J. 2008 (Derby Co) 3
McFadden, J. 2002 (Motherwell, Everton, Birmingham C) 48
McFadyen, W. 1934 (Motherwell) 2
Macfarlane, A. 1904 (Dundee) 5
Macfarlane, W. 1947 (Hearts) 1
McFarlane, R. 1896 (Greenock Morton) 1
McGarr, E. 1970 (Aberdeen) 2
McGarvey, F. P. 1979 (Liverpool, Celtic) 7
McGeoch, A. 1876 (Dumbreck) 4
McGeouch, D. 2018 (Hibernian) 2
McGhee, J. 1886 (Hibernian) 1
McGhee, M. 1983 (Aberdeen) 4
McGinlay, J. 1994 (Bolton W) 13
McGinn, J. 2016 (Hibernian, Aston Villa) 15
McGonagle, W. 1933 (Celtic) 6
McGrain, D. 1973 (Celtic) 62
McGregor, A. J. 2007 (Rangers, Besiktas, Hull C, Rangers) 42
McGregor, C. W. 2018 (Celtic) 13
McGregor, J. C. 1877 (Vale of Leven) 4
McGrory, J. 1928 (Celtic) 7
McGrory, J. E. 1965 (Kilmarnock) 3
McGuire, W. 1881 (Beith) 2
McGurk, F. 1934 (Birmingham) 1
McHardy, H. 1885 (Rangers) 1
McInally, A. 1989 (Aston Villa, Bayern Munich) 8
McInally, J. 1987 (Dundee U) 10
McInally, T. B. 1926 (Celtic) 2
McInnes, D. 2003 (WBA) 2
McInnes, T. 1889 (Cowlairs) 1
McIntosh, W. 1905 (Third Lanark) 1
McIntyre, A. 1878 (Vale of Leven) 2
McIntyre, H. 1880 (Rangers) 1
McIntyre, J. 1884 (Rangers) 1
MacKay, D. 1959 (Celtic) 14
Mackay, D. C. 1957 (Hearts, Tottenham H) 22
Mackay, G. 1988 (Hearts) 4
Mackay, M. 2004 (Norwich C) 5
McKay, B. 2016 (Rangers) 1
McKay, J. 1924 (Blackburn R) 1
McKay, R. 1928 (Newcastle U) 1
McKean, R. 1976 (Rangers) 1
McKenna, S. 2018 (Aberdeen) 12
McKenzie, D. 1938 (Brentford) 1
Mackenzie, J. A. 1954 (Partick Thistle) 9
McKeown, M. 1889 (Celtic) 2
McKie, J. 1898 (East Stirling) 1
McKillop, T. R. 1938 (Rangers) 1
McKimmie, S. 1989 (Aberdeen) 40
McKinlay, D. 1922 (Liverpool) 2
McKinlay, T. 1996 (Celtic) 22
McKinlay, W. 1994 (Dundee U, Blackburn R) 29
McKinnon, A. 1874 (Queen's Park) 1
McKinnon, R. 1966 (Rangers) 28
McKinnon, R. 1994 (Motherwell) 3
MacKinnon, W. 1883 (Dumbarton) 4
MacKinnon, W. W. 1872 (Queen's Park) 9
McLaren, A. 1929 (St Johnstone) 5
McLaren, A. 1947 (Preston NE) 4
McLaren, A. 1992 (Hearts, Rangers) 24
McLaren, A. 2001 (Kilmarnock) 1
McLaren, J. 1888 (Hibernian, Celtic) 3
McLaughlin, J. P. 2018 (Aberdeen) 1
McLean, A. 1926 (Celtic) 4
McLean, D. 1896 (St Bernards) 2
McLean, D. 1912 (Sheffield W) 1
McLean, G. 1968 (Dundee) 1
McLean, K. 2016 (Aberdeen, Norwich C) 8
McLean, T. 1969 (Kilmarnock) 6
McLeish, A. 1980 (Aberdeen) 77
McLeod, D. 1905 (Celtic) 4
McLeod, J. 1888 (Dumbarton) 5
MacLeod, J. M. 1961 (Hibernian) 4
MacLeod, M. 1985 (Celtic, Borussia Dortmund, Hibernian) 20
McLeod, W. 1886 (Cowlairs) 1
McLintock, A. 1875 (Vale of Leven) 3
McLintock, F. 1963 (Leicester C, Arsenal) 9
McLuckie, J. S. 1934 (Manchester C) 1
McMahon, A. 1892 (Celtic) 6
McManus, S. 2007 (Celtic, Middlesbrough) 26
McMenemy, J. 1905 (Celtic) 12
McMenemy, J. 1934 (Motherwell) 1
McMillan, I. L. 1952 (Airdrieonians, Rangers) 6
McMillan, J. 1897 (St Bernards) 1
McMillan, T. 1887 (Dumbarton) 1
McMullan, J. 1920 (Partick Thistle, Manchester C) 16
McNab, A. 1921 (Morton) 2
McNab, A. 1937 (Sunderland, WBA) 2
McNab, C. D. 1931 (Dundee) 6
McNab, J. S. 1923 (Liverpool) 1
McNair, A. 1906 (Celtic) 15
McNamara, J. 1997 (Celtic, Wolverhampton W) 33
McNamee, D. 2004 (Livingston) 4
McNaught, W. 1951 (Raith R) 5
McNaughton, K. 2002 (Aberdeen, Cardiff C) 4
McNeill, W. 1961 (Celtic) 29
McNiel, H. 1874 (Queen's Park) 10
McNiel, M. 1876 (Rangers) 2
McNulty, M. 2019 (Reading) 2
McPhail, J. 1950 (Celtic) 5
McPhail, R. 1927 (Airdrieonians, Rangers) 17
McPherson, D. 1892 (Kilmarnock) 1
McPherson, D. 1989 (Hearts, Rangers) 27
McPherson, J. 1875 (Clydesdale) 1
McPherson, J. 1879 (Vale of Leven) 8
McPherson, J. 1888 (Kilmarnock, Cowlairs, Rangers) 9
McPherson, J. 1891 (Hearts) 1
McPherson, R. 1882 (Arthurlie) 1
McQueen, G. 1974 (Leeds U, Manchester U) 30
McQueen, M. 1890 (Leith Ath) 2
McRorie, D. M. 1931 (Morton) 1
McSpadyen, A. 1939 (Partick Thistle) 2
McStay, P. 1984 (Celtic) 76
McStay, W. 1921 (Celtic) 13
McSwegan, G. 2000 (Hearts) 2

McTavish, J. 1910 (Falkirk) 1
McTominay, S. F. 2018 (Manchester U) 9
McWattie, G. C. 1901 (Queen's Park) 2
McWilliam, P. 1905 (Newcastle U) 8
Meechan, P. 1896 (Celtic) 1
Meiklejohn, D. D. 1922 (Rangers) 15
Menzies, A. 1906 (Hearts) 1
Mercer, R. 1912 (Hearts) 2
Middleton, R. 1930 (Cowdenbeath) 1
Millar, J. 1897 (Rangers) 3
Millar, J. 1963 (Rangers) 2
Miller, A. 1939 (Hearts) 1
Miller, C. 2001 (Dundee U) 1
Miller, J. 1931 (St Mirren) 5
Miller, K. 2001 (Rangers, Wolverhampton W, Celtic, Derby Co, Rangers, Bursaspor, Cardiff C, Vancouver Whitecaps) 69
Miller, L. 2006 (Dundee U, Aberdeen) 3
Miller, P. 1882 (Dumbarton) 3
Miller, T. 1920 (Liverpool, Manchester U) 3
Miller, W. 1876 (Third Lanark) 1
Miller, W. 1947 (Celtic) 6
Miller, W. 1975 (Aberdeen) 65
Mills, W. 1936 (Aberdeen) 3
Milne, J. V. 1938 (Middlesbrough) 2
Mitchell, D. 1890 (Rangers) 5
Mitchell, J. 1908 (Kilmarnock) 3
Mitchell, R. C. 1951 (Newcastle U) 2
Mochan, N. 1954 (Celtic) 3
Moir, W. 1950 (Bolton W) 1
Moncur, R. 1968 (Newcastle U) 16
Morgan, H. 1898 (St Mirren, Liverpool) 2
Morgan, L. 2018 (St Mirren) 2
Morgan, W. 1968 (Burnley, Manchester U) 21
Morris, D. 1923 (Raith R) 6
Morris, H. 1950 (East Fife) 1
Morrison, J. C. 2008 (WBA) 46
Morrison, T. 1927 (St Mirren) 1
Morton, A. L. 1920 (Queen's Park, Rangers) 31
Morton, H. A. 1929 (Kilmarnock) 2
Mudie, J. K. 1957 (Blackpool) 17
Muir, W. 1907 (Dundee) 1
Muirhead, T. A. 1922 (Rangers) 8
Mulgrew, C. P. 2012 (Celtic, Blackburn R) 41
Mulhall, G. 1960 (Aberdeen, Sunderland) 3
Munro, A. D. 1937 (Hearts, Blackpool) 3
Munro, F. M. 1971 (Wolverhampton W) 9
Munro, I. 1979 (St Mirren) 7
Munro, N. 1888 (Abercorn) 2
Murdoch, J. 1931 (Motherwell) 1
Murdoch, R. 1966 (Celtic) 12
Murphy, F. 1938 (Celtic) 1
Murphy, J. 2018 (Rangers) 2
Murray, I. 2003 (Hibernian, Rangers) 6
Murray, J. 1895 (Renton) 1
Murray, J. 1958 (Hearts) 5
Murray, J. W. 1890 (Vale of Leven) 1
Murray, P. 1896 (Hibernian) 2
Murray, S. 1972 (Aberdeen) 1
Murty, G. S. 2004 (Reading) 4
Mutch, G. 1938 (Preston NE) 1

Naismith, S. J. 2007 (Kilmarnock, Rangers, Everton, Norwich C) 49
Napier, C. E. 1932 (Celtic, Derby Co) 5
Narey, D. 1977 (Dundee U) 35
Naysmith, G. A. 2000 (Hearts, Everton, Sheffield U) 46
Neil, R. G. 1896 (Hibernian, Rangers) 2
Neill, R. W. 1876 (Queen's Park) 5
Neilson, R. 2007 (Hearts) 1
Nellies, P. 1913 (Hearts) 2
Nelson, J. 1925 (Cardiff C) 4
Nevin, P. K. F. 1986 (Chelsea, Everton, Tranmere R) 28
Niblo, T. D. 1904 (Aston Villa) 1
Nibloe, J. 1929 (Kilmarnock) 11
Nicholas, C. 1983 (Celtic, Arsenal, Aberdeen) 20
Nicholson, B. 2001 (Dunfermline Ath) 3
Nicol, S. 1985 (Liverpool) 27
Nisbet, J. 1929 (Ayr U) 3
Niven, J. B. 1885 (Moffat) 1

O'Connor, G. 2002 (Hibernian, Lokomotiv Moscow, Birmingham C) 16
O'Donnell, F. 1937 (Preston NE, Blackpool) 6
O'Donnell, P. 1994 (Motherwell) 1
O'Donnell, S. G. 2018 (Kilmarnock) 9
Ogilvie, D. H. 1934 (Motherwell) 1
O'Hare, J. 1970 (Derby Co) 13
O'Neil, B. 1996 (Celtic, Wolfsburg, Derby Co, Preston NE) 7
O'Neil, J. 2001 (Hibernian) 1
Ormond, W. E. 1954 (Hibernian) 6
O'Rourke, F. 1907 (Airdrieonians) 1
Orr, J. 1892 (Kilmarnock) 1
Orr, R. 1902 (Newcastle U) 2
Orr, T. 1952 (Morton) 2
Orr, W. 1900 (Celtic) 3
Orrock, R. 1913 (Falkirk) 1
Oswald, J. 1889 (Third Lanark, St Bernards, Rangers) 3

Palmer, L. J. 2019 (Sheffield W) 1
Parker, A. H. 1955 (Falkirk, Everton) 15
Parlane, D. 1973 (Rangers) 12
Parlane, R. 1878 (Vale of Leven) 3
Paterson, C. T. O. 2016 (Hearts, Cardiff C) 12
Paterson, G. D. 1939 (Celtic) 1
Paterson, J. 1920 (Leicester C) 1
Paterson, J. 1931 (Cowdenbeath) 3
Paton, A. 1952 (Motherwell) 2
Paton, D. 1896 (St Bernards) 1
Paton, M. 1883 (Dumbarton) 5
Paton, R. 1879 (Vale of Leven) 2
Patrick, J. 1897 (St Mirren) 2
Paul, H. McD. 1909 (Queen's Park) 3
Paul, W. 1888 (Partick Thistle) 3
Paul, W. 1891 (Dykebar) 1
Pearson, S. P. 2004 (Motherwell, Celtic, Derby Co) 10
Pearson, T. 1947 (Newcastle U) 2
Penman, A. 1966 (Dundee) 1
Pettigrew, W. 1976 (Motherwell) 5
Phillips, J. 1877 (Queen's Park) 3
Phillips, M. 2012 (Blackpool, QPR, WBA) 14
Plenderleith, J. B. 1961 (Manchester C) 1
Porteous, W. 1903 (Hearts) 1
Pressley, S. J. 2000 (Hearts) 32
Pringle, C. 1921 (St Mirren) 1
Provan, D. 1964 (Rangers) 5
Provan, D. 1980 (Celtic) 10
Pursell, P. 1914 (Queen's Park) 1

Quashie, N. F. 2004 (Portsmouth, Southampton, WBA) 14
Quinn, J. 1905 (Celtic) 11
Quinn, P. 1961 (Motherwell) 4

Rae, G. 2001 (Dundee, Rangers, Cardiff C) 14
Rae, J. 1889 (Third Lanark) 2
Raeside, J. S. 1906 (Third Lanark) 1
Raisbeck, A. G. 1900 (Liverpool) 8
Rankin, G. 1890 (Vale of Leven) 2
Rankin, R. 1929 (St Mirren) 3
Redpath, W. 1949 (Motherwell) 9
Reid, J. G. 1914 (Airdrieonians) 3
Reid, R. 1938 (Brentford) 2
Reid, W. 1911 (Rangers) 9
Reilly, L. 1949 (Hibernian) 38
Rennie, H. G. 1900 (Hearts, Hibernian) 13
Renny-Tailyour, H. W. 1873 (Royal Engineers) 1
Rhind, A. 1872 (Queen's Park) 1
Rhodes, J. L. 2012 (Huddersfield T, Blackburn R, Sheffield W) 14
Richmond, A. 1906 (Queen's Park) 1
Richmond, J. T. 1877 (Clydesdale, Queen's Park) 3
Ring, T. 1953 (Clyde) 12
Rioch, B. D. 1975 (Derby Co, Everton, Derby Co) 24
Riordan, D. G. 2006 (Hibernian) 3
Ritchie, A. 1891 (East Stirlingshire) 1
Ritchie, H. 1923 (Hibernian) 2
Ritchie, J. 1897 (Queen's Park) 1
Ritchie, M. T. 2015 (Bournemouth, Newcastle U) 16
Ritchie, P. S. 1999 (Hearts, Bolton W, Walsall) 7
Ritchie, W. 1962 (Rangers) 1
Robb, D. T. 1971 (Aberdeen) 5

Robb, W. 1926 (Rangers, Hibernian) 2
Robertson, A. 1955 (Clyde) 5
Robertson, A. 2014 (Dundee U, Hull C, Liverpool) 30
Robertson, D. 1992 (Rangers) 3
Robertson, G. 1910 (Motherwell, Sheffield W) 4
Robertson, G. 1938 (Kilmarnock) 1
Robertson, H. 1962 (Dundee) 1
Robertson, J. 1931 (Dundee) 2
Robertson, J. 1991 (Hearts) 16
Robertson, J. N. 1978 (Nottingham F, Derby Co) 28
Robertson, J. G. 1965 (Tottenham H) 1
Robertson, J. T. 1898 (Everton, Southampton, Rangers) 16
Robertson, P. 1903 (Dundee) 1
Robertson, S. 2009 (Dundee U) 2
Robertson, T. 1889 (Queen's Park) 4
Robertson, T. 1898 (Hearts) 1
Robertson, W. 1887 (Dumbarton) 2
Robinson, R. 1974 (Dundee) 4
Robson, B. G. G. 2008 (Dundee U, Celtic, Middlesbrough) 17
Ross, M. 2002 (Rangers) 13
Rough, A. 1976 (Partick Thistle, Hibernian) 53
Rougvie, D. 1984 (Aberdeen) 1
Rowan, A. 1880 (Caledonian, Queen's Park) 2
Russell, D. 1895 (Hearts, Celtic) 6
Russell, J. 1890 (Cambuslang) 1
Russell, J. S. S. 2015 (Derby Co, Kansas City) 12
Russell, W. F. 1924 (Airdrieonians) 2
Rutherford, E. 1948 (Rangers) 1

St John, I. 1959 (Motherwell, Liverpool) 21
Saunders, S. 2011 (Motherwell) 1
Sawers, W. 1895 (Dundee) 1
Scarff, P. 1931 (Celtic) 1
Schaedler, E. 1974 (Hibernian) 1
Scott, A. S. 1957 (Rangers, Everton) 16
Scott, J. 1966 (Hibernian) 1
Scott, J. 1971 (Dundee) 2
Scott, M. 1898 (Airdrieonians) 1
Scott, R. 1894 (Airdrieonians) 1
Scoular, J. 1951 (Portsmouth) 9
Sellar, W. 1885 (Battlefield, Queen's Park) 9
Semple, W. 1886 (Cambuslang) 1
Severin, S. D. 2002 (Hearts, Aberdeen) 15
Shankly, W. 1938 (Preston NE) 5
Sharp, G. M. 1985 (Everton) 12
Sharp, J. 1904 (Dundee, Woolwich Arsenal, Fulham) 5
Shaw, D. 1947 (Hibernian) 8
Shaw, F. W. 1884 (Pollokshields Ath) 2
Shaw, J. 1947 (Rangers) 4
Shearer, D. 1994 (Aberdeen) 7
Shearer, R. 1961 (Rangers) 4
Shinnie, A. M. 2013 (Inverness CT) 1
Shinnie, G. 2018 (Aberdeen) 6
Sillars, D. C. 1891 (Queen's Park) 5
Simpson, J. 1895 (Third Lanark) 3
Simpson, J. 1935 (Rangers) 14
Simpson, N. 1983 (Aberdeen) 5
Simpson, R. C. 1967 (Celtic) 5
Sinclair, G. L. 1910 (Hearts) 3
Sinclair, J. W. E. 1966 (Leicester C) 1
Skene, L. H. 1904 (Queen's Park) 1
Sloan, T. 1904 (Third Lanark) 1
Smellie, R. 1887 (Queen's Park) 6
Smith, A. 1898 (Rangers) 20
Smith, D. 1966 (Aberdeen, Rangers) 2
Smith, G. 1947 (Hibernian) 18
Smith, H. G. 1988 (Hearts) 3
Smith, J. 1924 (Ayr U) 1
Smith, J. 1935 (Rangers) 2
Smith, J. 1968 (Aberdeen, Newcastle U) 4
Smith, J. 2003 (Celtic) 2
Smith, J. E. 1959 (Celtic) 2
Smith, Jas 1872 (Queen's Park) 1
Smith, John 1877 (Mauchline, Edinburgh University, Queen's Park) 10
Smith, N. 1897 (Rangers) 12
Smith, R. 1872 (Queen's Park) 2
Smith, T. M. 1934 (Kilmarnock, Preston NE) 2
Snodgrass, R. 2011 (Leeds U, Norwich C, Hull C, West Ham U) 26

Somers, P. 1905 (Celtic) 4
Somers, W. S. 1879 (Third Lanark, Queen's Park) 3
Somerville, G. 1886 (Queen's Park) 1
Souness, G. J. 1975 (Middlesbrough, Liverpool, Sampdoria) 54
Souttar, J. 2019 (Hearts) 3
Speedie, D. R. 1985 (Chelsea, Coventry C) 10
Speedie, F. 1903 (Rangers) 3
Speirs, J. H. 1908 (Rangers) 1
Spencer, J. 1995 (Chelsea, QPR) 14
Stanton, P. 1966 (Hibernian) 16
Stark, J. 1909 (Rangers) 2
Steel, W. 1947 (Morton, Derby Co, Dundee) 30
Steele, D. M. 1923 (Huddersfield) 3
Stein, C. 1969 (Rangers, Coventry C) 21
Stephen, J. F. 1947 (Bradford) 2
Stevenson, G. 1928 (Motherwell) 12
Stevenson, L. 2018 (Hibernian) 1
Stewart, A. 1888 (Queen's Park) 2
Stewart, A. 1894 (Third Lanark) 1
Stewart, D. 1888 (Dumbarton) 1
Stewart, D. 1893 (Queen's Park) 3
Stewart, D. S. 1978 (Leeds U) 1
Stewart, G. 1906 (Hibernian, Manchester C) 4
Stewart, J. 1977 (Kilmarnock, Middlesbrough) 2
Stewart, M. J. 2002 (Manchester U, Hearts) 4
Stewart, R. 1981 (West Ham U) 10
Stewart, W. G. 1898 (Queen's Park) 2
Stockdale, R. K. 2002 (Middlesbrough) 5
Storrier, D. 1899 (Celtic) 3
Strachan, G. D. 1980 (Aberdeen, Manchester U, Leeds U) 50
Sturrock, P. 1981 (Dundee U) 20
Sullivan, N. 1997 (Wimbledon, Tottenham H) 28
Summers, W. 1926 (St Mirren) 1
Symon, J. S. 1939 (Rangers) 1

Tait, T. S. 1911 (Sunderland) 1
Taylor, G. J. 2019 (Kilmarnock) 1
Taylor, J. 1872 (Queen's Park) 6
Taylor, J. D. 1892 (Dumbarton, St Mirren) 4
Taylor, W. 1892 (Hearts) 1
Teale, G. 2006 (Wigan Ath, Derby Co) 13
Telfer, P. N. 2000 (Coventry C) 1
Telfer, W. 1933 (Motherwell) 2
Telfer, W. D. 1954 (St Mirren) 1
Templeton, R. 1902 (Aston Villa, Newcastle U, Woolwich Arsenal, Kilmarnock) 11
Thompson, S. 2002 (Dundee U, Rangers) 16
Thomson, A. 1886 (Arthurlie) 1
Thomson, A. 1889 (Third Lanark) 1
Thomson, A. 1909 (Airdrieonians) 1
Thomson, A. 1926 (Celtic) 3
Thomson, C. 1904 (Hearts, Sunderland) 21
Thomson, C. 1937 (Sunderland) 1
Thomson, D. 1920 (Dundee) 1
Thomson, J. 1930 (Celtic) 4
Thomson, J. J. 1872 (Queen's Park) 3
Thomson, J. R. 1933 (Everton) 1
Thomson, K. 2009 (Rangers, Middlesbrough) 3
Thomson, R. 1932 (Celtic) 1
Thomson, R. W. 1927 (Falkirk) 1
Thomson, S. 1884 (Rangers) 2
Thomson, W. 1892 (Dumbarton) 4
Thomson, W. 1896 (Dundee) 1
Thomson, W. 1980 (St Mirren) 7
Thornton, W. 1947 (Rangers) 7
Tierney, K. 2016 (Celtic) 12
Toner, W. 1959 (Kilmarnock) 2
Townsley, T. 1926 (Falkirk) 1
Troup, A. 1920 (Dundee, Everton) 5
Turnbull, E. 1948 (Hibernian) 8
Turner, T. 1884 (Arthurlie) 1
Turner, W. 1885 (Pollokshields Ath) 2

Ure, J. F. 1962 (Dundee, Arsenal) 11
Urquhart, D. 1934 (Hibernian) 1

Vallance, T. 1877 (Rangers) 7
Venters, A. 1934 (Cowdenbeath, Rangers) 3

Waddell, T. S. 1891 (Queen's Park) 6
Waddell, W. 1947 (Rangers) 17
Wales, H. M. 1933 (Motherwell) 1
Walker, A. 1988 (Celtic) 3
Walker, F. 1922 (Third Lanark) 1
Walker, G. 1930 (St Mirren) 4
Walker, J. 1895 (Hearts, Rangers) 5
Walker, J. 1911 (Swindon T) 9
Walker, J. N. 1993 (Hearts, Partick Thistle) 2
Walker, R. 1900 (Hearts) 29
Walker, T. 1935 (Hearts) 20
Walker, W. 1909 (Clyde) 2
Wallace, I. A. 1978 (Coventry C) 3
Wallace, L. 2010 (Hearts, Rangers) 10
Wallace, R. 2010 (Preston NE) 1
Wallace, W. S. B. 1965 (Hearts, Celtic) 7
Wardhaugh, J. 1955 (Hearts) 2
Wark, J. 1979 (Ipswich T, Liverpool) 28
Watson, A. 1881 (Queen's Park) 3
Watson, J. 1903 (Sunderland, Middlesbrough) 6
Watson, J. 1948 (Motherwell, Huddersfield T) 2
Watson, J. A. K. 1878 (Rangers) 1
Watson, P. R. 1934 (Blackpool) 1
Watson, R. 1971 (Motherwell) 1
Watson, W. 1898 (Falkirk) 1
Watt, A. P. 2016 (Charlton Ath) 1
Watt, F. 1889 (Kilbirnie) 4
Watt, W. W. 1887 (Queen's Park) 1
Waugh, W. 1938 (Hearts) 1
Webster, A. 2003 (Hearts, Dundee U, Hearts) 28
Weir, A. 1959 (Motherwell) 6
Weir, D. G. 1997 (Hearts, Everton, Rangers) 69
Weir, J. 1887 (Third Lanark) 1
Weir, J. B. 1872 (Queen's Park) 4
Weir, P. 1980 (St Mirren, Aberdeen) 6
White, John 1922 (Albion R, Hearts) 2
White, J. A. 1959 (Falkirk, Tottenham H) 22
White, W. 1907 (Bolton W) 2
Whitelaw, A. 1887 (Vale of Leven) 2
Whittaker, S. G. 2010 (Rangers, Norwich C) 31
Whyte, D. 1988 (Celtic, Middlesbrough, Aberdeen) 12
Wilkie, L. 2002 (Dundee) 11
Williams, G. 2002 (Nottingham F) 5
Wilson, A. 1907 (Sheffield W) 6
Wilson, A. 1954 (Portsmouth) 1
Wilson, A. N. 1920 (Dunfermline, Middlesbrough) 12
Wilson, D. 1900 (Queen's Park) 1
Wilson, D. 1913 (Oldham Ath) 1
Wilson, D. 1961 (Rangers) 22
Wilson, D. 2011 (Liverpool) 5
Wilson, G. W. 1904 (Hearts, Everton, Newcastle U) 6
Wilson, Hugh 1890 (Newmilns, Sunderland, Third Lanark) 4
Wilson, I. A. 1987 (Leicester C, Everton) 5
Wilson, J. 1888 (Vale of Leven) 4
Wilson, M. 2011 (Celtic) 1
Wilson, P. 1926 (Celtic) 4
Wilson, P. 1975 (Celtic) 1
Wilson, R. P. 1972 (Arsenal) 2
Winters, R. 1999 (Aberdeen) 1
Wiseman, W. 1927 (Queen's Park) 2
Wood, G. 1979 (Everton, Arsenal) 4
Woodburn, W. A. 1947 (Rangers) 24
Wotherspoon, D. N. 1872 (Queen's Park) 2
Wright, K. 1992 (Hibernian) 1
Wright, S. 1993 (Aberdeen) 2
Wright, T. 1953 (Sunderland) 3
Wylie, T. G. 1890 (Rangers) 1

Yeats, R. 1965 (Liverpool) 2
Yorston, B. C. 1931 (Aberdeen) 1
Yorston, H. 1955 (Aberdeen) 1
Young, A. 1905 (Everton) 2
Young, A. 1960 (Hearts, Everton) 8
Young, G. L. 1947 (Rangers) 53
Young, J. 1906 (Celtic) 1
Younger, T. 1955 (Hibernian, Liverpool) 24

WALES

Adams, H. 1882 (Berwyn R, Druids) 4
Aizlewood, M. 1986 (Charlton Ath, Leeds U, Bradford C, Bristol C, Cardiff C) 39
Allchurch, I. J. 1951 (Swansea T, Newcastle U, Cardiff C, Swansea T) 68
Allchurch, L. 1955 (Swansea T, Sheffield U) 11
Allen, B. W. 1951 (Coventry C) 2
Allen, J. M. 2009 (Swansea C, Liverpool, Stoke C) 51
Allen, M. 1986 (Watford, Norwich C, Millwall, Newcastle U) 14
Ampadu, E. K. C. R. 2018 (Chelsea) 8
Arridge, S. 1892 (Bootle, Everton, New Brighton Tower) 8
Astley, D. J. 1931 (Charlton Ath, Aston Villa, Derby Co, Blackpool) 13
Atherton, R. W. 1899 (Hibernian, Middlesbrough) 9

Bailiff, W. E. 1913 (Llanelly) 4
Baker, C. W. 1958 (Cardiff C) 7
Baker, W. G. 1948 (Cardiff C) 1
Bale, G. F. 2006 (Southampton, Tottenham H, Real Madrid) 77
Bamford, T. 1931 (Wrexham) 5
Barnard, D. S. 1998 (Barnsley, Grimsby T) 22
Barnes, W. 1948 (Arsenal) 22
Bartley, T. 1898 (Glossop NE) 1
Bastock, A. M. 1892 (Shrewsbury T) 1
Beadles, G. H. 1925 (Cardiff C) 2
Bell, W. S. 1881 (Shrewsbury Engineers, Crewe Alex) 5
Bellamy, C. D. 1998 (Norwich C, Coventry C, Newcastle U, Blackburn R, Liverpool, West Ham U, Manchester C, Liverpool, Cardiff C) 78
Bennion, S. R. 1926 (Manchester U) 10
Berry, G. F. 1979 (Wolverhampton W, Stoke C) 5
Blackmore, C. G. 1985 (Manchester U, Middlesbrough) 39
Blake, D. J. 2011 (Cardiff C, Crystal Palace) 14
Blake, N. A. 1994 (Sheffield U, Bolton W, Blackburn R, Wolverhampton W) 29
Blew, H. 1899 (Wrexham) 22
Boden, T. 1880 (Wrexham) 1
Bodin, B. P. 2018 (Preston NE) 1
Bodin, P. J. 1990 (Swindon T, Crystal Palace, Swindon T) 23
Boulter, L. M. 1939 (Brentford) 1
Bowdler, H. E. 1893 (Shrewsbury T) 1
Bowdler, J. C. H. 1890 (Shrewsbury T, Wolverhampton W, Shrewsbury T) 4
Bowen, D. L. 1955 (Arsenal) 19
Bowen, E. 1880 (Druids) 2
Bowen, J. P. 1994 (Swansea C, Birmingham C) 2
Bowen, M. R. 1986 (Tottenham H, Norwich C, West Ham U) 41
Bowsher, S. J. 1929 (Burnley) 1
Boyle, T. 1981 (Crystal Palace) 2
Bradley, M. S. 2010 (Walsall) 1
Bradshaw, T. W. C. 2016 (Walsall, Barnsley) 3
Britten, T. J. 1878 (Parkgrove, Presteigne) 2
Brooks, D. R. 2018 (Sheffield U, Bournemouth) 12
Brookes, S. J. 1900 (Llandudno) 2
Brown, A. I. 1926 (Aberdare Ath) 1
Brown, J. R. 2006 (Gillingham, Blackburn R, Aberdeen) 3
Browning, M. T. 1996 (Bristol R, Huddersfield T) 5
Bryan, T. 1886 (Oswestry) 2
Buckland, T. 1899 (Bangor) 1
Burgess, W. A. R. 1947 (Tottenham H) 32
Burke, T. 1883 (Wrexham, Newton Heath) 8
Burnett, T. B. 1877 (Ruabon) 1
Burton, A. D. 1963 (Norwich C, Newcastle U) 9
Butler, J. 1893 (Chirk) 3
Butler, W. T. 1900 (Druids) 2

Cartwright, L. 1974 (Coventry C, Wrexham) 7
Carty, T. See McCarthy (Wrexham).
Challen, J. B. 1887 (Corinthians, Wellingborough GS) 4
Chapman, T. 1894 (Newtown, Manchester C, Grimsby T) 7
Charles, J. M. 1981 (Swansea C, QPR, Oxford U) 19
Charles, M. 1955 (Swansea T, Arsenal, Cardiff C) 31

Charles, W. J. 1950 (Leeds U, Juventus, Leeds U, Cardiff C) 38
Chester, J. G. 2014 (Hull C, WBA, Aston Villa) 35
Church, S. R. 2009 (Reading, Charlton Ath) 38
Clarke, R. J. 1949 (Manchester C) 22
Coleman, C. 1992 (Crystal Palace, Blackburn R, Fulham) 32
Collier, D. J. 1921 (Grimsby T) 1
Collins, D. L. 2005 (Sunderland, Stoke C) 12
Collins, J. M. 2004 (Cardiff C, West Ham U, Aston Villa, West Ham U) 51
Collins, W. S. 1931 (Llanelly) 1
Collison, J. D. 2008 (West Ham U) 16
Conde, C. 1884 (Chirk) 3
Cook, F. C. 1925 (Newport Co, Portsmouth) 8
Cornforth, J. M. 1995 (Swansea C) 2
Cotterill, D. R. G. B. 2006 (Bristol C, Wigan Ath, Sheffield U, Swansea C, Doncaster R, Birmingham C) 24
Coyne, D. 1996 (Tranmere R, Grimsby T, Leicester C, Burnley, Tranmere R) 16
Crofts, A. L. 2016 ((Gillingham, Brighton & HA, Norwich C, Scunthorpe U) 29
Crompton, W. 1931 (Wrexham) 3
Cross, E. A. 1876 (Wrexham) 2
Crosse, K. 1879 (Druids) 3
Crossley, M. G. 1997 (Nottingham F, Middlesbrough, Fulham) 8
Crowe, V. H. 1959 (Aston Villa) 16
Cumner, R. H. 1939 (Arsenal) 3
Curtis, A. T. 1976 (Swansea C, Leeds U, Swansea C, Southampton, Cardiff C) 35
Curtis, E. R. 1928 (Cardiff C, Birmingham) 3

Daniel, R. W. 1951 (Arsenal, Sunderland) 21
Darvell, S. 1897 (Oxford University) 2
Davies, A. 1876 (Wrexham) 2
Davies, A. 1904 (Druids, Middlesbrough) 2
Davies, A. 1983 (Manchester U, Newcastle U, Swansea C, Bradford C) 13
Davies, A. 2019 (Barnsley) 1
Davies, A. O. 1885 (Barmouth, Swifts, Wrexham, Crewe Alex) 9
Davies, A. R. 2006 (Yeovil T) 1
Davies, A. T. 1891 (Shrewsbury T) 1
Davies, B. T. 2013 (Swansea C, Tottenham H) 46
Davies, C. 1972 (Charlton Ath) 1
Davies, C. M. 2006 (Oxford U, Verona, Oldham Ath, Barnsley) 7
Davies, D. 1904 (Bolton W) 3
Davies, D. C. 1899 (Brecon, Hereford) 2
Davies, D. W. 1912 (Treharris, Oldham Ath) 2
Davies, E. Lloyd 1904 (Stoke, Northampton T) 16
Davies, E. R. 1953 (Newcastle U) 6
Davies, G. 1980 (Fulham, Manchester C) 16
Davies, Rev. H. 1928 (Wrexham) 1
Davies, Idwal 1923 (Liverpool Marine) 1
Davies, J. E. 1885 (Oswestry) 1
Davies, Jas 1878 (Wrexham) 1
Davies, John 1879 (Wrexham) 1
Davies, Jos 1888 (Newton Heath, Wolverhampton W) 7
Davies, Jos 1889 (Everton, Chirk, Ardwick, Sheffield U, Manchester C, Millwall, Reading) 11
Davies, J. P. 1883 (Druids) 2
Davies, Ll. 1907 (Wrexham, Everton, Wrexham) 13
Davies, L. S. 1922 (Cardiff C) 23
Davies, O. 1890 (Wrexham) 1
Davies, R. 1883 (Wrexham) 3
Davies, R. 1885 (Druids) 1
Davies, R. O. 1892 (Wrexham) 2
Davies, R. T. 1964 (Norwich C, Southampton, Portsmouth) 29
Davies, R. W. 1964 (Bolton W, Newcastle U, Manchester C, Manchester U, Blackpool) 34
Davies, S. 2001 (Tottenham H, Everton, Fulham) 58
Davies, S. I. 1996 (Manchester U) 1
Davies, Stanley 1920 (Preston NE, Everton, WBA, Rotherham U) 18
Davies, T. 1886 (Oswestry) 1
Davies, T. 1903 (Druids) 4
Davies, W. 1884 (Wrexham) 1
Davies, W. 1924 (Swansea T, Cardiff C, Notts Co) 17
Davies, William 1903 (Wrexham, Blackburn R) 11
Davies, W. C. 1908 (Crystal Palace, WBA, Crystal Palace) 4
Davies, W. D. 1975 (Everton, Wrexham, Swansea C) 52
Davies, W. H. 1876 (Oswestry) 4
Davis, G. 1978 (Wrexham) 3
Davis, W. O. 1913 (Millwall Ath) 5
Day, A. 1934 (Tottenham H) 1
Deacy, N. 1977 (PSV Eindhoven, Beringen) 12
Dearson, D. J. 1939 (Birmingham) 3
Delaney, M. A. 2000 (Aston Villa) 36
Derrett, S. C. 1969 (Cardiff C) 4
Dewey, F. T. 1931 (Cardiff Corinthians) 2
Dibble, A. 1986 (Luton T, Manchester C) 3
Dorman, A. 2010 (St Mirren, Crystal Palace) 3
Doughty, J. 1886 (Druids, Newton Heath) 8
Doughty, R. 1888 (Newton Heath) 2
Duffy, R. M. 2006 (Portsmouth) 13
Dummett, P. 2014 (Newcastle U) 5
Durban, A. 1966 (Derby Co) 27
Dwyer, P. J. 1978 (Cardiff C) 10

Eardley, N. 2008 (Oldham Ath, Blackpool) 16
Earnshaw, R. 2002 (Cardiff C, WBA, Norwich C, Derby Co, Nottingham F, Cardiff C) 59
Easter, J. M. 2007 (Wycombe W, Plymouth Arg, Milton Keynes D, Crystal Palace, Millwall) 12
Eastwood, F. 2008 (Wolverhampton W, Coventry C) 11
Edwards, C. 1878 (Wrexham) 1
Edwards, C. N. H. 1996 (Swansea C) 1
Edwards, D. A. 2008 (Luton T, Wolverhampton W, Reading) 43
Edwards, G. 1947 (Birmingham C, Cardiff C) 12
Edwards, H. 1878 (Wrexham Civil Service, Wrexham) 8
Edwards, J. H. 1876 (Wanderers) 1
Edwards, J. H. 1895 (Oswestry) 3
Edwards, J. H. 1898 (Aberystwyth) 1
Edwards, L. T. 1957 (Charlton Ath) 2
Edwards, R. I. 1978 (Chester, Wrexham) 4
Edwards, R. O. 2003 (Aston Villa, Wolverhampton W) 15
Edwards, R. W. 1998 (Bristol C) 4
Edwards, T. 1932 (Linfield) 1
Egan, W. 1892 (Chirk) 1
Ellis, B. 1932 (Motherwell) 6
Ellis, E. 1931 (Nunhead, Oswestry) 3
Emanuel, W. J. 1973 (Bristol C) 2
England, H. M. 1962 (Blackburn R, Tottenham H) 44
Evans, B. C. 1972 (Swansea C, Hereford U) 7
Evans, C. M. 2008 (Manchester C, Sheffield U) 13
Evans, D. G. 1926 (Reading, Huddersfield T) 4
Evans, H. P. 1922 (Cardiff C) 6
Evans, I. 1976 (Crystal Palace) 13
Evans, J. 1893 (Oswestry) 3
Evans, J. 1912 (Cardiff C) 8
Evans, J. H. 1922 (Southend U) 4
Evans, L. 2018 (Wolverhampton W, Sheffield U, Wigan Ath) 4
Evans, Len 1927 (Aberdare Ath, Cardiff C, Birmingham) 4
Evans, M. 1884 (Oswestry) 1
Evans, P. S. 2002 (Brentford, Bradford C) 2
Evans, R. 1902 (Clapton) 1
Evans, R. E. 1906 (Wrexham, Aston Villa, Sheffield U) 10
Evans, R. O. 1902 (Wrexham, Blackburn R, Coventry C) 10
Evans, R. S. 1964 (Swansea T) 1
Evans, S. J. 2007 (Wrexham) 7
Evans, T. J. 1927 (Clapton Orient, Newcastle U) 4
Evans, W. 1933 (Tottenham H) 6
Evans, W. A. W. 1876 (Oxford University) 2
Evans, W. G. 1890 (Bootle, Aston Villa) 3
Evelyn, E. C. 1887 (Crusaders) 1
Eyton-Jones, J. A. 1883 (Wrexham) 4

Farmer, G. 1885 (Oswestry) 2
Felgate, D. 1984 (Lincoln C) 1
Finnigan, R. J. 1930 (Wrexham) 1
Fletcher, C. N. 2004 (Bournemouth, West Ham U, Crystal Palace) 36
Flynn, B. 1975 (Burnley, Leeds U, Burnley) 66
Fon Williams, O. 2016 (Inverness CT) 1

Ford, T. 1947 (Swansea T, Aston Villa, Sunderland, Cardiff C) 38
Foulkes, H. E. 1932 (WBA) 1
Foulkes, W. I. 1952 (Newcastle U) 11
Foulkes, W. T. 1884 (Oswestry) 2
Fowler, J. 1925 (Swansea T) 6
Freeman, K. S. 2019 (Sheffield U) 1
Freestone, R. 2000 (Swansea C) 1

Gabbidon, D. L. 2002 (Cardiff C, West Ham U, QPR, Crystal Palace) 49
Garner, G. 2006 (Leyton Orient) 1
Garner, J. 1896 (Aberystwyth) 1
Giggs, R. J. 1992 (Manchester U) 64
Giles, D. C. 1980 (Swansea C, Crystal Palace) 12
Gillam, S. G. 1889 (Wrexham, Shrewsbury, Clapton) 5
Glascodine, G. 1879 (Wrexham) 1
Glover, E. M. 1932 (Grimsby T) 7
Godding, G. 1923 (Wrexham) 2
Godfrey, B. C. 1964 (Preston NE) 3
Goodwin, U. 1881 (Ruthin) 1
Goss, J. 1991 (Norwich C) 9
Gough, R. T. 1883 (Oswestry White Star) 1
Gray, A. 1924 (Oldham Ath, Manchester C, Manchester Central, Tranmere R, Chester) 24
Green, A. W. 1901 (Aston Villa, Notts Co, Nottingham F) 8
Green, C. R. 1965 (Birmingham C) 15
Green, G. H. 1938 (Charlton Ath) 4
Green, R. M. 1998 (Wolverhampton W) 2
Grey, Dr W. 1876 (Druids) 2
Griffiths, A. T. 1971 (Wrexham) 17
Griffiths, F. J. 1900 (Blackpool) 2
Griffiths, G. 1887 (Chirk) 1
Griffiths, J. H. 1953 (Swansea T) 1
Griffiths, L. 1902 (Wrexham) 1
Griffiths, M. W. 1947 (Leicester C) 11
Griffiths, P. 1884 (Chirk) 6
Griffiths, P. H. 1932 (Everton) 1
Griffiths, T. P. 1927 (Everton, Bolton W, Middlesbrough, Aston Villa) 21
Gunter, C. R. 2007 (Cardiff C, Tottenham H, Nottingham F, Reading) 95

Hall, G. D. 1988 (Chelsea) 9
Hallam, J. 1889 (Oswestry) 1
Hanford, H. 1934 (Swansea T, Sheffield W) 7
Harrington, A. C. 1956 (Cardiff C) 11
Harris, C. S. 1976 (Leeds U) 24
Harris, W. C. 1954 (Middlesbrough) 6
Harrison, W. C. 1899 (Wrexham) 5
Hartson, J. 1995 (Arsenal, West Ham U, Wimbledon, Coventry C, Celtic) 51
Haworth, S. O. 1997 (Cardiff C, Coventry C) 5
Hayes, A. 1890 (Wrexham) 2
Hedges, R. P. 2018 (Barnsley, Aberdeen) 3
Henley, A. D. 2016 (Blackburn R) 2
Hennessey, W. R. 2007 (Wolverhampton W, Crystal Palace) 84
Hennessey, W. T. 1962 (Birmingham C, Nottingham F, Derby Co) 39
Hersee, A. M. 1886 (Bangor) 2
Hersee, R. 1886 (Llandudno) 1
Hewitt, R. 1958 (Cardiff C) 5
Hewitt, T. J. 1911 (Wrexham, Chelsea, South Liverpool) 8
Heywood, D. 1879 (Druids) 1
Hibbott, H. 1880 (Newtown Excelsior, Newtown) 3
Higham, G. G. 1878 (Oswestry) 2
Hill, M. R. 1972 (Ipswich T) 2
Hockey, T. 1972 (Sheffield U, Norwich C, Aston Villa) 9
Hoddinott, T. F. 1921 (Watford) 2
Hodges, G. 1984 (Wimbledon, Newcastle U, Watford, Sheffield U) 18
Hodgkinson, A. V. 1908 (Southampton) 1
Holden, A. 1984 (Chester C) 1
Hole, B. G. 1963 (Cardiff C, Blackburn R, Aston Villa, Swansea C) 30
Hole, W. J. 1921 (Swansea T) 9
Hollins, D. M. 1962 (Newcastle U) 11
Hopkins, I. J. 1935 (Brentford) 12
Hopkins, J. 1983 (Fulham, Crystal Palace) 16
Hopkins, M. 1956 (Tottenham H) 34
Horne, B. 1988 (Portsmouth, Southampton, Everton, Birmingham C) 59
Howell, E. G. 1888 (Builth) 3
Howells, R. G. 1954 (Cardiff C) 2
Hugh, A. R. 1930 (Newport Co) 1
Hughes, A. 1894 (Rhos) 2
Hughes, A. 1907 (Chirk) 1
Hughes, C. M. 1992 (Luton T, Wimbledon) 8
Hughes, E. 1899 (Everton, Tottenham H) 14
Hughes, E. 1906 (Wrexham, Nottingham F, Wrexham, Manchester C) 16
Hughes, F. W. 1882 (Northwich Victoria) 6
Hughes, I. 1951 (Luton T) 4
Hughes, J. 1877 (Cambridge University, Aberystwyth) 2
Hughes, J. 1905 (Liverpool) 3
Hughes, J. I. 1935 (Blackburn R) 1
Hughes, L. M. 1984 (Manchester U, Barcelona, Manchester U, Chelsea, Southampton) 72
Hughes, P. W. 1887 (Bangor) 3
Hughes, W. 1891 (Bootle) 3
Hughes, W. A. 1949 (Blackburn R) 5
Hughes, W. M. 1938 (Birmingham) 10
Humphreys, J. V. 1947 (Everton) 1
Humphreys, R. 1888 (Druids) 1
Hunter, A. H. 1887 (FA of Wales Secretary) 1
Huws, E. W. 2014 (Manchester C, Wigan Ath, Cardiff C) 11

Isgrove, L. J. 2016 (Southampton) 1

Jackett, K. 1983 (Watford) 31
Jackson, W. 1899 (St Helens Rec) 1
James, D. O. 2019 (Swansea C) 4
James, E. 1893 (Chirk) 8
James, E. G. 1966 (Blackpool) 9
James, L. 1972 (Burnley, Derby Co, QPR, Burnley, Swansea C, Sunderland) 54
James, R. M. 1979 (Swansea C, Stoke C, QPR, Leicester C, Swansea C) 47
James, W. 1931 (West Ham U) 2
Jarrett, R. H. 1889 (Ruthin) 2
Jarvis, A. L. 1967 (Hull C) 3
Jenkins, E. 1925 (Lovell's Ath) 1
Jenkins, J. 1924 (Brighton & HA) 8
Jenkins, R. W. 1902 (Rhyl) 1
Jenkins, S. R. 1996 (Swansea C, Huddersfield T) 16
Jenkyns, C. A. L. 1892 (Small Heath, Woolwich Arsenal, Newton Heath, Walsall) 8
Jennings, W. 1914 (Bolton W) 11
John, D. C. 2013 (Cardiff C, Rangers, Swansea C) 7
John, R. F. 1923 (Arsenal) 15
John, W. R. 1931 (Walsall, Stoke C, Preston NE, Sheffield U, Swansea T) 14
Johnson, A. J. 1999 (Nottingham F, WBA) 15
Johnson, M. G. 1964 (Swansea T) 1
Jones, A. 1987 (Port Vale, Charlton Ath) 6
Jones, A. F. 1877 (Oxford University) 1
Jones, A. T. 1905 (Nottingham F, Notts Co) 2
Jones, Bryn 1935 (Wolverhampton W, Arsenal) 17
Jones, B. S. 1963 (Swansea T, Plymouth Arg, Cardiff C) 15
Jones, Charlie 1926 (Nottingham F, Arsenal) 8
Jones, Cliff 1954 (Swansea T, Tottenham H, Fulham) 59
Jones, C. W. 1935 (Birmingham) 2
Jones, D. 1888 (Chirk, Bolton W, Manchester C) 14
Jones, D. E. 1976 (Norwich C) 8
Jones, D. O. 1934 (Leicester C) 7
Jones, Evan 1910 (Chelsea, Oldham Ath, Bolton W) 7
Jones, F. R. 1885 (Bangor) 3
Jones, F. W. 1893 (Small Heath) 1
Jones, G. P. 1907 (Wrexham) 2
Jones, H. 1902 (Aberaman) 1
Jones, Humphrey 1885 (Bangor, Queen's Park, East Stirlingshire, Queen's Park) 14
Jones, Ivor 1920 (Swansea T, WBA) 10
Jones, Jeffrey 1908 (Llandrindod Wells) 3
Jones, J. 1876 (Druids) 1
Jones, J. 1883 (Berwyn Rangers) 3
Jones, J. 1925 (Wrexham) 1
Jones, J. L. 1895 (Sheffield U, Tottenham H) 21
Jones, J. Love 1906 (Stoke, Middlesbrough) 2

Jones, J. O. 1901 (Bangor) 2
Jones, J. P. 1976 (Liverpool, Wrexham, Chelsea, Huddersfield T) 72
Jones, J. T. 1912 (Stoke, Crystal Palace) 15
Jones, K. 1950 (Aston Villa) 1
Jones, Leslie J. 1933 (Cardiff C, Coventry C, Arsenal 11
Jones, M. A. 2007 (Wrexham) 2
Jones, M. G. 2000 (Leeds U, Leicester C) 13
Jones, P. L. 1997 (Liverpool, Tranmere R) 2
Jones, P. S. 1997 (Stockport Co, Southampton, Wolverhampton W, QPR) 50
Jones, P. W. 1971 (Bristol R) 1
Jones, R. 1887 (Bangor, Crewe Alex) 3
Jones, R. 1898 (Leicester Fosse) 1
Jones, R. 1899 (Druids) 1
Jones, R. 1900 (Bangor) 2
Jones, R. 1906 (Millwall) 2
Jones, R. A. 1884 (Druids) 4
Jones, R. A. 1994 (Sheffield W) 1
Jones, R. S. 1894 (Everton) 1
Jones, S. 1887 (Wrexham, Chester) 2
Jones, S. 1893 (Wrexham, Burton Swifts, Druids) 6
Jones, T. 1926 (Manchester U) 4
Jones, T. D. 1908 (Aberdare) 1
Jones, T. G. 1938 (Everton) 17
Jones, T. J. 1932 (Sheffield W) 2
Jones, V. P. 1995 (Wimbledon) 9
Jones, W. E. A. 1947 (Swansea T, Tottenham H) 4
Jones, W. J. 1901 (Aberdare, West Ham U) 4
Jones, W. Lot 1905 (Manchester C, Southend U) 20
Jones, W. P. 1889 (Druids, Wynnstay) 4
Jones, W. R. 1897 (Aberystwyth) 1

Keenor, F. C. 1920 (Cardiff C, Crewe Alex) 32
Kelly, F. C. 1899 (Wrexham, Druids) 3
Kelsey, A. J. 1954 (Arsenal) 41
Kenrick, S. L. 1876 (Druids, Oswestry, Shropshire Wanderers) 5
Ketley, C. F. 1882 (Druids) 1
King, A. P. 2009 (Leicester C) 50
King, J. 1955 (Swansea T) 1
Kinsey, N. 1951 (Norwich C, Birmingham C) 7
Knill, A. R. 1989 (Swansea C) 1
Koumas, J. 2001 (Tranmere R, WBA, Wigan Ath) 34
Krzywicki, R. L. 1970 (WBA, Huddersfield T) 8

Lambert, R. 1947 (Liverpool) 5
Latham, G. 1905 (Liverpool, Southport Central, Cardiff C) 10
Law, B. J. 1990 (QPR) 1
Lawrence, E. 1930 (Clapton Orient, Notts Co) 2
Lawrence, J. A. 2019 (Anderlecht) 5
Lawrence, S. 1932 (Swansea T) 8
Lawrence, T. M. 2016 (Leicester C, Derby Co) 19
Lea, A. 1889 (Wrexham) 4
Lea, C. 1965 (Ipswich T) 2
Leary, P. 1889 (Bangor) 1
Ledley, J. C. 2006 (Cardiff C, Celtic, Crystal Palace, Derby Co) 77
Leek, K. 1961 (Leicester C, Newcastle U, Birmingham C, Northampton T) 13
Legg, A. 1996 (Birmingham C, Cardiff C) 6
Lever, A. R. 1953 (Leicester C) 1
Lewis, B. 1891 (Chester, Wrexham, Middlesbrough, Wrexham) 10
Lewis, D. 1927 (Arsenal) 3
Lewis, D. 1983 (Swansea C) 1
Lewis, D. J. 1933 (Swansea T) 2
Lewis, D. M. 1890 (Bangor) 2
Lewis, J. 1906 (Bristol R) 1
Lewis, J. 1926 (Cardiff C) 1
Lewis, T. 1881 (Wrexham) 2
Lewis, W. 1885 (Bangor, Crewe Alex, Chester, Manchester C, Chester) 27
Lewis, W. L. 1927 (Swansea T, Huddersfield T) 6
Llewellyn, C. M. 1998 (Norwich C, Wrexham) 6
Lloyd, B. W. 1976 (Wrexham) 3
Lloyd, J. W. 1879 (Wrexham, Newtown) 2
Lloyd, R. A. 1891 (Ruthin) 2
Lockley, A. 1898 (Chirk) 1
Lockyer, T. A. 2018 (Bristol R) 5
Lovell, S. 1982 (Crystal Palace, Millwall) 6
Lowndes, S. R. 1983 (Newport Co, Millwall, Barnsley) 10
Lowrie, G. 1948 (Coventry C, Newcastle U) 4
Lucas, P. M. 1962 (Leyton Orient) 4
Lucas, W. H. 1949 (Swansea T) 7
Lumberg, A. 1929 (Wrexham, Wolverhampton W) 4
Lynch, J. J. 2013 (Hudderfield T) 1

MacDonald, S. B. 2011 (Swansea C, Bournemouth) 4
Maguire, G. T. 1990 (Portsmouth) 7
Mahoney, J. F. 1968 (Stoke C, Middlesbrough, Swansea C) 51
Mardon, P. J. 1996 (WBA) 1
Margetson, M. W. 2004 (Cardiff C) 1
Marriott, A. 1996 (Wrexham) 5
Martin, T. J. 1930 (Newport Co) 1
Marustik, C. 1982 (Swansea C) 6
Mates, J. 1891 (Chirk) 3
Matonda, R. 2019 (Manchester C, Schalke 04) 3
Matthews, A. J. 2011 (Cardiff C, Celtic, Sunderland) 14
Matthews, R. W. 1921 (Liverpool, Bristol C, Bradford) 3
Matthews, W. 1905 (Chester) 2
Matthias, J. S. 1896 (Brymbo, Shrewsbury T, Wolverhampton W) 5
Matthias, T. J. 1914 (Wrexham) 12
Mays, A. W. 1929 (Wrexham) 1
McCarthy, T. P. 1889 (Wrexham) 1
McMillan, R. 1881 (Shrewsbury Engineers) 2
Medwin, T. C. 1953 (Swansea T, Tottenham H) 30
Melville, A. K. 1990 (Swansea C, Oxford U, Sunderland, Fulham, West Ham U) 65
Mepham, C. J. 2018 (Brentford, Bournemouth) 6
Meredith, S. 1900 (Chirk, Stoke, Leyton) 8
Meredith, W. H. 1895 (Manchester C, Manchester U) 48
Mielczarek, R. 1971 (Rotherham U) 1
Millership, H. 1920 (Rotherham Co) 6
Millington, A. H. 1963 (WBA, Crystal Palace, Peterborough U, Swansea C) 21
Mills, T. J. 1934 (Clapton Orient, Leicester C) 4
Mills-Roberts, R. H. 1885 (St Thomas' Hospital, Preston NE, Llanberis) 8
Moore, G. 1960 (Cardiff C, Chelsea, Manchester U, Northampton T, Charlton Ath) 21
Morgan, C. 2007 (Milton Keynes D, Peterborough U, Preston NE) 23
Morgan, J. R. 1877 (Cambridge University, Derby School Staff) 10
Morgan, J. T. 1905 (Wrexham) 1
Morgan-Owen, H. 1902 (Oxford University, Corinthians) 4
Morgan-Owen, M. M. 1897 (Oxford University, Corinthians) 13
Morison, S. W. 2011 (Millwall, Norwich C) 20
Morley, E. J. 1925 (Swansea T, Clapton Orient) 4
Morris, A. G. 1896 (Aberystwyth, Swindon T, Nottingham F) 21
Morris, C. 1900 (Chirk, Derby Co, Huddersfield T) 27
Morris, E. 1893 (Chirk) 3
Morris, H. 1894 (Sheffield U, Manchester C, Grimsby T) 3
Morris, J. 1887 (Oswestry) 1
Morris, J. 1898 (Chirk) 1
Morris, R. 1900 (Chirk, Shrewsbury T) 6
Morris, R. 1902 (Newtown, Druids, Liverpool, Leeds C, Grimsby T, Plymouth Arg) 11
Morris, S. 1937 (Birmingham) 5
Morris, W. 1947 (Burnley) 5
Moulsdale, J. R. B. 1925 (Corinthians) 1
Murphy, J. P. 1933 (WBA) 15
Myhill, G. O. 2008 (Hull C, WBA) 19

Nardiello, D. 1978 (Coventry C) 2
Nardiello, D. A. 2007 (Barnsley, QPR) 3
Neal, J. E. 1931 (Colwyn Bay) 2
Neilson, A. B. 1992 (Newcastle U, Southampton) 5
Newnes, J. 1926 (Nelson) 1
Newton, L. F. 1912 (Cardiff Corinthians) 1
Nicholas, D. S. 1923 (Stoke, Swansea T) 3
Nicholas, P. 1979 (Crystal Palace, Arsenal, Crystal Palace, Luton T, Aberdeen, Chelsea, Watford) 73
Nicholls, J. 1924 (Newport Co, Cardiff C) 4
Niedzwiecki, E. A. 1985 (Chelsea) 2

Nock, W. 1897 (Newtown) 1
Nogan, L. M. 1992 (Watford, Reading) 2
Norman, A. J. 1986 (Hull C) 5
Nurse, M. T. G. 1960 (Swansea T, Middlesbrough) 12
Nyatanga, L. J. 2006 (Derby Co, Bristol C) 34

O'Callaghan, E. 1929 (Tottenham H) 11
Oliver, A. 1905 (Bangor, Blackburn R) 2
Oster, J. M. 1998 (Everton, Sunderland) 13
O'Sullivan, P. A. 1973 (Brighton & HA) 3
Owen, D. 1879 (Oswestry) 1
Owen, E. 1884 (Ruthin Grammar School) 3
Owen, G. 1888 (Chirk, Newton Heath, Chirk) 4
Owen, J. 1892 (Newton Heath) 1
Owen, T. 1879 (Oswestry) 1
Owen, Trevor 1899 (Crewe Alex) 2
Owen, W. 1884 (Chirk) 16
Owen, W. P. 1880 (Ruthin) 12
Owens, J. 1902 (Wrexham) 1

Page, M. E. 1971 (Birmingham C) 28
Page, R. J. 1997 (Watford, Sheffield U, Cardiff C, Coventry C) 41
Palmer, D. 1957 (Swansea T) 3
Parris, J. E. 1932 (Bradford) 1
Parry, B. J. 1951 (Swansea T) 1
Parry, C. 1891 (Everton, Newtown) 13
Parry, E. 1922 (Liverpool) 5
Parry, M. 1901 (Liverpool) 16
Parry, P. I. 2004 (Cardiff C) 12
Parry, T. D. 1900 (Oswestry) 7
Parry, W. 1895 (Newtown) 1
Partridge, D. W. 2005 (Motherwell, Bristol C) 7
Pascoe, C. 1984 (Swansea C, Sunderland) 10
Paul, R. 1949 (Swansea T, Manchester C) 33
Peake, E. 1908 (Aberystwyth, Liverpool) 11
Peers, E. J. 1914 (Wolverhampton W, Port Vale) 12
Pembridge, M. A. 1992 (Luton T, Derby Co, Sheffield W, Benfica, Everton, Fulham) 54
Perry, E. 1938 (Doncaster R) 3
Perry, J. 1994 (Cardiff C) 1
Phennah, E. 1878 (Civil Service) 1
Phillips, C. 1931 (Wolverhampton W, Aston Villa) 13
Phillips, D. 1984 (Plymouth Arg, Manchester C, Coventry C, Norwich C, Nottingham F) 62
Phillips, L. 1971 (Cardiff C, Aston Villa, Swansea C, Charlton Ath) 58
Phillips, T. J. S. 1973 (Chelsea) 4
Phoenix, H. 1882 (Wrexham) 1
Pipe, D. R. 2003 (Coventry C) 1
Poland, G. 1939 (Wrexham) 2
Pontin, K. 1980 (Cardiff C) 2
Powell, A. 1947 (Leeds U, Everton, Birmingham C) 8
Powell, D. 1968 (Wrexham, Sheffield U) 11
Powell, I. V. 1947 (QPR, Aston Villa) 8
Powell, J. 1878 (Druids, Bolton W, Newton Heath) 15
Powell, Seth 1885 (Oswestry, WBA) 7
Price, H. 1907 (Aston Villa, Burton U, Wrexham) 5
Price, J. 1877 (Wrexham) 12
Price, L. P. 2006 (Ipswich T, Derby Co, Crystal Palace) 11
Price, P. 1980 (Luton T, Tottenham H) 25
Pring, K. D. 1966 (Rotherham U) 3
Pritchard, H. K. 1985 (Bristol C) 1
Pryce-Jones, A. W. 1895 (Newtown) 1
Pryce-Jones, W. E. 1887 (Cambridge University) 5
Pugh, A. 1889 (Rhostyllen) 1
Pugh, D. H. 1896 (Wrexham, Lincoln C) 7
Pugsley, J. 1930 (Charlton Ath) 1
Pullen, W. J. 1926 (Plymouth Arg) 1

Ramsey, A. J. 2009 (Arsenal) 58
Rankmore, F. E. J. 1966 (Peterborough U) 1
Ratcliffe, K. 1981 (Everton, Cardiff C) 59
Rea, J. C. 1894 (Aberystwyth) 9
Ready, K. 1997 (QPR) 5
Reece, G. I. 1966 (Sheffield U, Cardiff C) 29
Reed, W. G. 1955 (Ipswich T) 2
Rees, A. 1984 (Birmingham C) 1
Rees, J. M. 1992 (Luton T) 1
Rees, R. R. 1965 (Coventry C, WBA, Nottingham F) 39
Rees, W. 1949 (Cardiff C, Tottenham H) 4
Ribeiro, C. M. 2010 (Bristol C) 2
Richards, A. 1932 (Barnsley) 1
Richards, A. D. J. (Jazz) 2012 (Swansea C, Cardiff C) 14
Richards, D. 1931 (Wolverhampton W, Brentford, Birmingham) 21
Richards, G. 1899 (Druids, Oswestry, Shrewsbury T) 6
Richards, R. W. 1920 (Wolverhampton W, West Ham U, Mold) 9
Richards, S. V. 1947 (Cardiff C) 1
Richards, W. E. 1933 (Fulham) 1
Ricketts, S. D. 2005 (Swansea C, Hull C, Bolton W, Wolverhampton W) 52
Roach, J. 1885 (Oswestry) 1
Robbins, W. W. 1931 (Cardiff C, WBA) 11
Roberts, A. M. 1993 (QPR) 2
Roberts, C. R. J. 2018 (Swansea C) 10
Roberts, D. F. 1973 (Oxford U, Hull C) 17
Roberts, G. W. 2000 (Tranmere R) 9
Roberts, I. W. 1990 (Watford, Huddersfield T, Leicester C, Norwich C) 15
Roberts, Jas 1913 (Wrexham) 2
Roberts, J. 1879 (Corwen, Berwyn R) 7
Roberts, J. 1881 (Ruthin) 2
Roberts, J. 1906 (Bradford C) 2
Roberts, J. G. 1971 (Arsenal, Birmingham C) 22
Roberts, J. H. 1949 (Bolton W) 1
Roberts, N. W. 2000 (Wrexham, Wigan Ath) 4
Roberts, P. S. 1974 (Portsmouth) 4
Roberts, R. 1884 (Druids, Bolton W, Preston NE) 9
Roberts, R. 1886 (Wrexham) 3
Roberts, R. 1891 (Rhos, Crewe Alex) 2
Roberts, R. L. 1890 (Chester) 1
Roberts, S. W. 2005 (Wrexham) 1
Roberts, T. 2019 (Leeds U) 5
Roberts, W. 1879 (Llangollen, Berwyn R) 6
Roberts, W. 1883 (Rhyl) 1
Roberts, W. 1886 (Wrexham) 4
Roberts, W. H. 1882 (Ruthin, Rhyl) 6
Robinson, C. P. 2000 (Wolverhampton W, Portsmouth, Sunderland, Norwich C, Toronto Lynx) 52
Robinson, J. R. C. 1996 (Charlton Ath) 30
Robson-Kanu, T. H. 2010 (Reading, WBA) 44
Rodrigues, P. J. 1965 (Cardiff C, Leicester C, Sheffield W) 40
Rogers, J. P. 1896 (Wrexham) 3
Rogers, W. 1931 (Wrexham) 2
Roose, L. R. 1900 (Aberystwyth, London Welsh, Stoke, Everton, Stoke, Sunderland) 24
Rouse, R. V. 1959 (Crystal Palace) 1
Rowlands, A. C. 1914 (Tranmere R) 1
Rowley, T. 1959 (Tranmere R) 1
Rush, I. 1980 (Liverpool, Juventus, Liverpool) 73
Russell, M. R. 1912 (Merthyr T, Plymouth Arg) 23

Sabine, H. W. 1887 (Oswestry) 1
Saunders, D. 1986 (Brighton & HA, Oxford U, Derby Co, Liverpool, Aston Villa, Galatasaray, Nottingham F, Sheffield U, Benfica, Bradford C) 75
Savage, R. W. 1996 (Crewe Alex, Leicester C, Birmingham C) 39
Savin, G. 1878 (Oswestry) 1
Sayer, P. A. 1977 (Cardiff C) 7
Scrine, F. H. 1950 (Swansea T) 2
Sear, C. R. 1963 (Manchester C) 1
Shaw, E. G. 1882 (Oswestry) 3
Sherwood, A. T. 1947 (Cardiff C, Newport Co) 41
Shone, W. W. 1879 (Oswestry) 1
Shortt, W. W. 1947 (Plymouth Arg) 12
Showers, D. 1975 (Cardiff C) 2
Sidlow, C. 1947 (Liverpool) 7
Sisson, H. 1885 (Wrexham Olympic) 3
Slatter, N. 1983 (Bristol R, Oxford U) 22
Smallman, D. P. 1974 (Wrexham, Everton) 7
Smith, M. 2018 (Manchester C) 7
Southall, N. 1982 (Everton) 92
Speed, G. A. 1990 (Leeds U, Everton, Newcastle U, Bolton W) 85
Sprake, G. 1964 (Leeds U, Birmingham C) 37
Stansfield, F. 1949 (Cardiff C) 1
Stevenson, B. 1978 (Leeds U, Birmingham C) 15
Stevenson, N. 1982 (Swansea C) 4

Stitfall, R. F. 1953 (Cardiff C) 2
Stock, B. B. 2010 (Doncaster R) 3
Sullivan, D. 1953 (Cardiff C) 17
Symons, C. J. 1992 (Portsmouth, Manchester C, Fulham, Crystal Palace) 37

Tapscott, D. R. 1954 (Arsenal, Cardiff C) 14
Taylor, G. K. 1996 (Crystal Palace, Sheffield U, Burnley, Nottingham F) 15
Taylor, J. 1898 (Wrexham) 1
Taylor, J. W. T. 2015 (Reading) 1
Taylor, N. J. 2010 (Wrexham, Swansea C, Aston Villa) 42
Taylor, O. D. S. 1893 (Newtown) 4
Thatcher, B. D. 2004 (Leicester C, Manchester C) 7
Thomas, C. 1899 (Druids) 2
Thomas, D. A. 1957 (Swansea T) 2
Thomas, D. S. 1948 (Fulham) 4
Thomas, E. 1925 (Cardiff Corinthians) 1
Thomas, G. 1885 (Wrexham) 2
Thomas, G. S. 2018 (Leicester C) 3
Thomas, H. 1927 (Manchester U) 1
Thomas, Martin R. 1987 (Newcastle U) 1
Thomas, Mickey 1977 (Wrexham, Manchester U, Everton, Brighton & HA, Stoke C, Chelsea, WBA) 51
Thomas, R. J. 1967 (Swindon T, Derby Co, Cardiff C) 50
Thomas, T. 1898 (Bangor) 2
Thomas, W. R. 1931 (Newport Co) 2
Thomson, D. 1876 (Druids) 1
Thomson, G. F. 1876 (Druids) 2
Toshack, J. B. 1969 (Cardiff C, Liverpool, Swansea C) 40
Townsend, W. 1887 (Newtown) 2
Trainer, H. 1895 (Wrexham) 3
Trainer, J. 1887 (Bolton W, Preston NE) 20
Trollope, P. J. 1997 (Derby Co, Fulham, Coventry C, Northampton T) 9
Tudur-Jones, O. 2008 (Swansea C, Norwich C, Hibernian) 7
Turner, H. G. 1937 (Charlton Ath) 8
Turner, J. 1892 (Wrexham) 1
Turner, R. E. 1891 (Wrexham) 2
Turner, W. H. 1887 (Wrexham) 5

Van Den Hauwe, P. W. R. 1985 (Everton) 13
Vaughan, D. O. 2003 (Crewe Alex, Real Sociedad, Blackpool, Sunderland, Nottingham F) 42
Vaughan, Jas 1893 (Druids) 4
Vaughan, John 1879 (Oswestry, Druids, Bolton W) 11
Vaughan, J. O. 1885 (Rhyl) 4
Vaughan, N. 1983 (Newport Co, Cardiff C) 10
Vaughan, T. 1885 (Rhyl) 1
Vaulks, W. R. 2019 (Rotherham U) 3
Vearncombe, G. 1958 (Cardiff C) 2
Vernon, T. R. 1957 (Blackburn R, Everton, Stoke C) 32
Villars, A. K. 1974 (Cardiff C) 3
Vizard, E. T. 1911 (Bolton W) 22
Vokes, S. M. 2008 (Bournemouth, Wolverhampton W, Burnley, Stoke C) 62

Walley, J. T. 1971 (Watford) 1
Walsh, I. P. 1980 (Crystal Palace, Swansea C) 18
Ward, D. 1959 (Bristol R, Cardiff C) 2
Ward, D. 2000 (Notts Co, Nottingham F) 5
Ward, D. 2016 (Liverpool, Leicester C) 6
Warner, J. 1937 (Swansea T, Manchester U) 2
Warren, F. W. 1929 (Cardiff C, Middlesbrough, Hearts) 6
Watkins, A. E. 1898 (Leicester Fosse, Aston Villa, Millwall) 5
Watkins, M. J. 2018 (Norwich C) 2
Watkins, W. M. 1902 (Stoke, Aston Villa, Sunderland, Stoke) 10
Webster, C. 1957 (Manchester U) 4
Weston, R. D. 2000 (Arsenal, Cardiff C) 7
Whatley, W. J. 1939 (Tottenham H) 2
White, P. F. 1896 (London Welsh) 1
Wilcock, A. R. 1890 (Oswestry) 1
Wilding, J. 1885 (Wrexham Olympians, Bootle, Wrexham) 9
Williams, A. 1994 (Reading, Wolverhampton W, Reading) 13
Williams, A. E. 2008 (Stockport Co, Swansea C, Everton) 86
Williams, A. L. 1931 (Wrexham) 1
Williams, A. P. 1998 (Southampton) 2
Williams, B. 1930 (Bristol C) 1
Williams, B. D. 1928 (Swansea T, Everton) 10
Williams, D. G. 1988 (Derby Co, Ipswich T) 13
Williams, D. M. 1986 (Norwich C) 5
Williams, D. R. 1921 (Merthyr T, Sheffield W, Manchester U) 8
Williams, E. 1893 (Crewe Alex) 2
Williams, E. 1901 (Druids) 5
Williams, G. 1893 (Chirk) 6
Williams, G. C. 2014 (Fulham) 7
Williams, G. E. 1960 (WBA) 26
Williams, G. G. 1961 (Swansea T) 5
Williams, G. J. 2006 (West Ham U, Ipswich T) 2
Williams, G. J. J. 1951 (Cardiff C) 1
Williams, G. O. 1907 (Wrexham) 1
Williams, H. J. 1965 (Swansea T) 3
Williams, H. T. 1949 (Newport Co, Leeds U) 4
Williams, J. H. 1884 (Oswestry) 1
Williams, J. J. 1939 (Wrexham) 1
Williams, J. P. 2013 (Crystal Palace) 17
Williams, J. T. 1925 (Middlesbrough) 1
Williams, J. W. 1912 (Crystal Palace) 2
Williams, R. 1935 (Newcastle U) 2
Williams, R. P. 1886 (Caernarvon) 1
Williams, S. G. 1954 (WBA, Southampton) 43
Williams, W. 1876 (Druids, Oswestry, Druids) 11
Williams, W. 1925 (Northampton T) 1
Wilson, H. 2013 (Liverpool) 11
Wilson, J. S. 2013 (Bristol C) 1
Witcomb, D. F. 1947 (WBA, Sheffield W) 3
Woodburn, B. 2018 (Liverpool) 10
Woosnam, A. P. 1959 (Leyton Orient, West Ham U, Aston Villa) 17
Woosnam, G. 1879 (Newtown Excelsior) 1
Worthington, T. 1894 (Newtown) 1
Wynn, G. A. 1909 (Wrexham, Manchester C) 11
Wynn, W. 1903 (Chirk) 1

Yorath, T. C. 1970 (Leeds U, Coventry C, Tottenham H, Vancouver Whitecaps) 59
Young, E. 1990 (Wimbledon, Crystal Palace, Wolverhampton W) 21

REPUBLIC OF IRELAND

Aherne, T. 1946 (Belfast Celtic, Luton T) 16
Aldridge, J. W. 1986 (Oxford U, Liverpool, Real Sociedad, Tranmere R) 69
Ambrose, P. 1955 (Shamrock R) 5
Anderson, J. 1980 (Preston NE, Newcastle U) 16
Andrews, K. J. 2009 (Blackburn R, WBA) 35
Andrews, P. 1936 (Bohemians) 1
Arrigan, T. 1938 (Waterford) 1
Arter, H. N. 2015 (Bournemouth) 16

Babb, P. A. 1994 (Coventry C, Liverpool, Sunderland) 35
Bailham, E. 1964 (Shamrock R) 1
Barber, E. 1966 (Shelbourne, Birmingham C) 2
Barrett, G. 2003 (Arsenal, Coventry C) 6
Barry, P. 1928 (Fordsons) 2
Beglin, J. 1984 (Liverpool) 15
Bennett, A. J. 2007 (Reading) 2
Bermingham, J. 1929 (Bohemians) 1
Bermingham, P. 1935 (St James' Gate) 1
Best, L. J. B. 2009 (Coventry C, Newcastle U) 7
Bonner, P. 1981 (Celtic) 80
Boyle, A. 2017 (Preston NE) 1
Braddish, S. 1978 (Dundalk) 2
Bradshaw, P. 1939 (St James' Gate) 5
Brady, F. 1926 (Fordsons) 2
Brady, R. 2013 (Hull C, Norwich C, Burnley) 45
Brady, T. R. 1964 (QPR) 6
Brady, W. L. 1975 (Arsenal, Juventus, Sampdoria, Internazionale, Ascoli, West Ham U) 72
Branagan, K. G. 1997 (Bolton W) 1
Breen, G. 1996 (Birmingham C, Coventry C, West Ham U, Sunderland) 63

Breen, T. 1937 (Manchester U, Shamrock R) 5
Brennan, F. 1965 (Drumcondra) 1
Brennan, S. A. 1965 (Manchester U, Waterford) 19
Brown, J. 1937 (Coventry C) 2
Browne, A. J. 2017 (Preston NE) 3
Browne, W. 1964 (Bohemians) 3
Bruce, A. S. 2007 (Ipswich T) 2
Buckley, L. 1984 (Shamrock R, Waregem) 2
Burke, F. 1952 (Cork Ath) 1
Burke, G. D. 2018 (Shamrock R, Preston NE) 3
Burke, J. 1929 (Shamrock R) 1
Burke, J. 1934 (Cork) 1
Butler, P. J. 2000 (Sunderland) 1
Butler, T. 2003 (Sunderland) 2
Byrne, A. B. 1970 (Southampton) 14
Byrne, D. 1929 (Shelbourne, Shamrock R, Coleraine) 3
Byrne, J. 1928 (Bray Unknowns) 1
Byrne, J. 1985 (QPR, Le Havre, Brighton & HA, Sunderland, Millwall) 23
Byrne, J. 2004 (Shelbourne) 2
Byrne, P. 1931 (Dolphin, Shelbourne, Drumcondra) 3
Byrne, P. 1984 (Shamrock R) 8
Byrne, S. 1931 (Bohemians) 1

Campbell, A. 1985 (Santander) 3
Campbell, N. 1971 (St Patrick's Ath, Fortuna Cologne) 11
Cannon, H. 1926 (Bohemians) 2
Cantwell, N. 1954 (West Ham U, Manchester U) 36
Carey, B. P. 1992 (Manchester U, Leicester C) 3
Carey, J. J. 1938 (Manchester U) 29
Carolan, J. 1960 (Manchester U) 2
Carr, S. 1999 (Tottenham H, Newcastle U) 44
Carroll, B. 1949 (Shelbourne) 2
Carroll, T. R. 1968 (Ipswich T, Birmingham C) 17
Carsley, L. K. 1998 (Derby Co, Blackburn R, Coventry C, Everton) 39
Cascarino, A. G. 1986 (Gillingham, Millwall, Aston Villa, Celtic, Chelsea, Marseille, Nancy) 88
Chandler, J. 1980 (Leeds U) 2
Chatton, H. A. 1931 (Shelbourne, Dumbarton, Cork) 3
Christie, C. S. F. 2015 (Derby Co, Middlesbrough, Fulham) 23
Clark, C. 2011 (Aston Villa, Newcastle U) 32
Clarke, C. R. 2004 (Stoke C) 2
Clarke, J. 1978 (Drogheda U) 1
Clarke, K. 1948 (Drumcondra) 2
Clarke, M. 1950 (Shamrock R) 1
Clinton, T. J. 1951 (Everton) 3
Coad, P. 1947 (Shamrock R) 11
Coffey, T. 1950 (Drumcondra) 1
Coleman, S. 2011 (Everton) 53
Colfer, M. D. 1950 (Shelbourne) 2
Colgan, N. 2002 (Hibernian, Barnsley) 9
Collins, F. 1927 (Jacobs) 1
Conmy, O. M. 1965 (Peterborough U) 5
Connolly, D. J. 1996 (Watford, Feyenoord, Wolverhampton W, Excelsior, Feyenoord, Wimbledon, West Ham U, Wigan Ath) 41
Connolly, H. 1937 (Cork) 1
Connolly, J. 1926 (Fordsons) 1
Conroy, G. A. 1970 (Stoke C) 27
Conway, J. P. 1967 (Fulham, Manchester C) 20
Corr, P. J. 1949 (Everton) 4
Courtney, E. 1946 (Cork U) 1
Cox, S. R. 2011 (WBA, Nottingham F) 30
Coyle, O. C. 1994 (Bolton W) 1
Coyne, T. 1992 (Celtic, Tranmere R, Motherwell) 22
Crowe, G. 2003 (Bohemians) 2
Cummins, G. P. 1954 (Luton T) 19
Cuneen, T. 1951 (Limerick) 1
Cunningham, G. R. 2010 (Manchester C, Bristol C) 4
Cunningham, K. 1996 (Wimbledon, Birmingham C) 72
Curtis, D. P. 1957 (Shelbourne, Bristol C, Ipswich T, Exeter C) 17
Curtis, R. 2019 (Portsmouth) 2
Cusack, S. 1953 (Limerick) 1

Daish, L. S. 1992 (Cambridge U, Coventry C) 5
Daly, G. A. 1973 (Manchester U, Derby Co, Coventry C, Birmingham C, Shrewsbury T) 48
Daly, J. 1932 (Shamrock R) 2
Daly, M. 1978 (Wolverhampton W) 2
Daly, P. 1950 (Shamrock R) 1
Davis, T. L. 1937 (Oldham Ath, Tranmere R) 4
Deacy, E. 1982 (Aston Villa) 4
Delaney, D. F. 2008 (QPR, Ipswich T, Crystal Palace) 9
Delap, R. J. 1998 (Derby Co, Southampton) 11
De Mange, K. J. P. P. 1987 (Liverpool, Hull C) 2
Dempsey, J. T. 1967 (Fulham, Chelsea) 19
Dennehy, J. 1972 (Cork Hibernians, Nottingham F, Walsall) 11
Desmond, P. 1950 (Middlesbrough) 4
Devine, J. 1980 (Arsenal, Norwich C) 13
Doherty, G. M. T. 2000 (Luton T, Tottenham H, Norwich C) 34
Doherty, M. J. 2018 (Woverhampton W) 7
Donnelly, J. 1935 (Dundalk) 10
Donnelly, T. 1938 (Drumcondra, Shamrock R) 2
Donovan, D. C. 1955 (Everton) 5
Donovan, T. 1980 (Aston Villa) 2
Douglas, J. 2004 (Blackburn R, Leeds U) 8
Dowdall, C. 1928 (Fordsons, Barnsley, Cork) 3
Doyle, C. 1959 (Shelbourne) 1
Doyle, C. A. 2007 (Birmingham C, Bradford C) 4
Doyle, D. 1926 (Shamrock R) 1
Doyle, K. E. 2006 (Reading, Wolverhampton W, Colorado Rapids) 63
Doyle, L. 1932 (Dolphin) 1
Doyle, M. P. 2004 (Coventry C) 1
Duff, D. A. 1998 (Blackburn R, Chelsea, Newcastle U, Fulham) 100
Duffy, B. 1950 (Shamrock R) 1
Duffy, S. P. M. 2014 (Everton, Blackburn R, Brighton & HA) 29
Duggan, H. A. 1927 (Leeds U, Newport Co) 5
Dunne, A. P. 1962 (Manchester U, Bolton W) 33
Dunne, J. 1930 (Sheffield U, Arsenal, Southampton, Shamrock R) 15
Dunne, J. C. 1971 (Fulham) 1
Dunne, L. 1935 (Manchester C) 2
Dunne, P. A. J. 1965 (Manchester U) 5
Dunne, R. P. 2000 (Everton, Manchester C, Aston Villa, QPR) 80
Dunne, S. 1953 (Luton T) 15
Dunne, T. 1956 (St Patrick's Ath) 3
Dunning, P. 1971 (Shelbourne) 2
Dunphy, E. M. 1966 (York C, Millwall) 23
Dwyer, N. M. 1960 (West Ham U, Swansea T) 14

Eccles, P. 1986 (Shamrock R) 1
Egan, J. 2017 (Brentford, Sheffield U) 4
Egan, R. 1929 (Dundalk) 1
Eglington, T. J. 1946 (Shamrock R, Everton) 24
Elliot, R. 2014 (Newcastle U) 4
Elliott, S. W. 2005 (Sunderland) 9
Ellis, P. 1935 (Bohemians) 7
Evans, M. J. 1998 (Southampton) 1

Fagan, E. 1973 (Shamrock R) 1
Fagan, F. 1955 (Manchester C, Derby Co) 8
Fagan, J. 1926 (Shamrock R) 1
Fahey, K. D. 2010 (Birmingham C) 16
Fairclough, M. 1982 (Dundalk) 2
Fallon, S. 1951 (Celtic) 8
Fallon, W. J. 1935 (Notts Co, Sheffield W) 9
Farquharson, T. G. 1929 (Cardiff C) 4
Farrell, P. 1937 (Hibernian) 2
Farrell, P. D. 1946 (Shamrock R, Everton) 28
Farrelly, G. 1996 (Aston Villa, Everton, Bolton W) 6
Feenan, J. J. 1937 (Sunderland) 2
Finnan, S. 2000 (Fulham, Liverpool, Espanyol) 53
Finucane, A. 1967 (Limerick) 11
Fitzgerald, F. J. 1955 (Waterford) 2
Fitzgerald, P. J. 1961 (Leeds U, Chester) 5
Fitzpatrick, K. 1970 (Limerick) 1
Fitzsimons, A. G. 1950 (Middlesbrough, Lincoln C) 26
Fleming, C. 1996 (Middlesbrough) 10

Flood, J. J. 1926 (Shamrock R) 5
Fogarty, A. 1960 (Sunderland, Hartlepools U) 11
Folan, C. C. 2009 (Hull C) 7
Foley, D. J. 2000 (Watford) 6
Foley, J. 1934 (Cork, Celtic) 7
Foley, K. P. 2009 (Wolverhampton W) 8
Foley, M. 1926 (Shelbourne) 1
Foley, T. C. 1964 (Northampton T) 9
Forde, D. 2011 (Millwall) 24
Foy, T. 1938 (Shamrock R) 2
Fullam, J. 1961 (Preston NE, Shamrock R) 11
Fullam, R. 1926 (Shamrock R) 2

Gallagher, C. 1967 (Celtic) 2
Gallagher, M. 1954 (Hibernian) 1
Gallagher, P. 1932 (Falkirk) 1
Galvin, A. 1983 (Tottenham H, Sheffield W, Swindon T) 29
Gamble, J. 2007 (Cork C) 2
Gannon, E. 1949 (Notts Co, Sheffield W, Shelbourne) 14
Gannon, M. 1972 (Shelbourne) 1
Gaskins, P. 1934 (Shamrock R, St James' Gate) 7
Gavin, J. T. 1950 (Norwich C, Tottenham H, Norwich C) 7
Geoghegan, M. 1937 (St James' Gate) 2
Gibbons, A. 1952 (St Patrick's Ath) 4
Gibson, D. T. D. 2008 (Manchester U, Everton) 27
Gilbert, R. 1966 (Shamrock R) 1
Giles, C. 1951 (Doncaster R) 1
Giles, M. J. 1960 (Manchester U, Leeds U, WBA, Shamrock R) 59
Given, S. J. J. 1996 (Blackburn R, Newcastle U, Manchester C, Aston Villa, Stoke C) 134
Givens, D. J. 1969 (Manchester U, Luton T, QPR, Birmingham C, Neuchatel X) 56
Gleeson, S. M. 2007 (Wolverhampton W, Birmingham C) 4
Glen, W. 1927 (Shamrock R) 8
Glynn, D. 1952 (Drumcondra) 2
Godwin, T. F. 1949 (Shamrock R, Leicester C, Bournemouth) 13
Golding, J. 1928 (Shamrock R) 2
Goodman, J. 1997 (Wimbledon) 4
Goodwin, J. 2003 (Stockport Co) 1
Gorman, W. C. 1936 (Bury, Brentford) 13
Grace, J. 1926 (Drumcondra) 1
Grealish, A. 1976 (Orient, Luton T, Brighton & HA, WBA) 45
Green, P. J. 2010 (Derby Co, Leeds U) 20
Gregg, E. 1978 (Bohemians) 8
Griffith, R. 1935 (Walsall) 1
Grimes, A. A. 1978 (Manchester U, Coventry C, Luton T) 18

Hale, A. 1962 (Aston Villa, Doncaster R, Waterford) 14
Hamilton, T. 1959 (Shamrock R) 2
Hand, E. K. 1969 (Portsmouth) 20
Harrington, W. 1936 (Cork) 5
Harte, I. P. 1996 (Leeds U, Levante) 64
Hartnett, J. B. 1949 (Middlesbrough) 2
Haverty, J. 1956 (Arsenal, Blackburn R, Millwall, Celtic, Bristol R, Shelbourne) 32
Hayes, A. W. P. 1979 (Southampton) 1
Hayes, J. 2016 (Aberdeen) 4
Hayes, W. E. 1947 (Huddersfield T) 2
Hayes, W. J. 1949 (Limerick) 1
Healey, R. 1977 (Cardiff C) 2
Healy, C. 2002 (Celtic, Sunderland) 13
Heighway, S. D. 1971 (Liverpool, Minnesota K) 34
Henderson, B. 1948 (Drumcondra) 2
Henderson, W. C. P. 2006 (Brighton & HA, Preston NE) 6
Hendrick, J. P. 2013 (Derby Co, Burnley) 49
Hennessy, J. 1965 (Shelbourne, St Patrick's Ath) 5
Herrick, J. 1972 (Cork Hibernians, Shamrock R) 3
Higgins, J. 1951 (Birmingham C) 1
Hogan, S. A. 2018 (Aston Villa) 5
Holland, M. R. 2000 (Ipswich T, Charlton Ath) 49
Holmes, J. 1971 (Coventry C, Tottenham H, Vancouver Whitecaps) 30
Hoolahan, W. 2008 (Blackpool, Norwich C) 43
Horgan, D. J. 2017 (Preston NE, Hibernian) 6
Horlacher, A. F. 1930 (Bohemians) 7
Houghton, R. J. 1986 (Oxford U, Liverpool, Aston Villa, Crystal Palace, Reading) 73
Hourihane, C. 2017 (Aston Villa) 12
Howlett, G. 1984 (Brighton & HA) 1
Hoy, M. 1938 (Dundalk) 6
Hughton, C. 1980 (Tottenham H, West Ham U) 53
Hunt, N. 2009 (Reading) 3
Hunt, S. P. 2007 (Reading, Hull C, Wolverhampton W) 39
Hurley, C. J. 1957 (Millwall, Sunderland, Bolton W) 40
Hutchinson, F. 1935 (Drumcondra) 2

Ireland S .J. 2006 (Manchester C) 6
Irwin, D. J. 1991 (Manchester U) 56

Jordan, D. 1937 (Wolverhampton W) 2
Jordan, W. 1934 (Bohemians) 2
Judge, A. C. 2016 (Brentford, Ipswich T) 6

Kavanagh, G. A. 1998 (Stoke C, Cardiff C, Wigan Ath) 16
Kavanagh, P. J. 1931 (Celtic) 2
Keane, R. D. 1998 (Wolverhampton W, Coventry C, Internazionale, Leeds U, Tottenham H, Liverpool, Tottenham H, LA Galaxy) 146
Keane, R. M. 1991 (Nottingham F, Manchester U) 67
Keane, T. R. 1949 (Swansea T) 4
Kearin, M. 1972 (Shamrock R) 1
Kearns, F. T. 1954 (West Ham U) 1
Kearns, M. 1971 (Oxford U, Walsall, Wolverhampton W) 18
Kelly, A. T. 1993 (Sheffield U, Blackburn R) 34
Kelly, D. T. 1988 (Walsall, West Ham U, Leicester C, Newcastle U, Wolverhampton W, Sunderland, Tranmere R) 26
Kelly, G. 1994 (Leeds U) 52
Kelly, J. 1932 (Derry C) 4
Kelly, J. A. 1957 (Drumcondra, Preston NE) 47
Kelly, J. P. V. 1961 (Wolverhampton W) 5
Kelly, M. J. 1988 (Portsmouth) 4
Kelly, N. 1954 (Nottingham F) 1
Kelly, S. M. 2006 (Tottenham H, Birmingham C, Fulham, Reading) 38
Kendrick, J. 1927 (Everton, Dolphin) 4
Kenna, J. J. 1995 (Blackburn R) 27
Kennedy, M. F. 1986 (Portsmouth) 2
Kennedy, M. J. 1996 (Liverpool, Wimbledon, Manchester C, Wolverhampton W) 34
Kennedy, W. 1932 (St James' Gate) 3
Kenny, P. 2004 (Sheffield U) 7
Keogh, A. D. 2007 (Wolverhampton W, Millwall) 30
Keogh, J. 1966 (Shamrock R) 1
Keogh, R. J. 2013 (Derby Co) 25
Keogh, S. 1959 (Shamrock R) 1
Kernaghan, A. N. 1993 (Middlesbrough, Manchester C) 22
Kiely, D. L. 2000 (Charlton Ath, WBA) 11
Kiernan, F. W. 1951 (Shamrock R, Southampton) 5
Kilbane, K. D. 1998 (WBA, Sunderland, Everton, Wigan Ath, Hull C) 110
Kinnear, J. P. 1967 (Tottenham H, Brighton & HA) 26
Kinsella, J. 1928 (Shelbourne) 1
Kinsella, M. A. 1998 (Charlton Ath, Aston Villa, WBA) 48
Kinsella, O. 1932 (Shamrock R) 2
Kirkland, A. 1927 (Shamrock R) 1

Lacey, W. 1927 (Shelbourne) 3
Langan, D. 1978 (Derby Co, Birmingham C, Oxford U) 26
Lapira, J. 2007 (Notre Dame) 1
Lawler, J. F. 1953 (Fulham) 8
Lawlor, J. C. 1949 (Drumcondra, Doncaster R) 3
Lawlor, M. 1971 (Shamrock R) 5

Lawrence, L. 2009 (Stoke C, Portsmouth) 15
Lawrenson, M. 1977 (Preston NE, Brighton & HA, Liverpool) 39
Lee, A. D. 2003 (Rotherham U, Cardiff C, Ipswich T) 10
Leech, M. 1969 (Shamrock R) 8
Lenihan, D. P. 2018 (Blackburn R) 2
Lennon, C. 1935 (St James' Gate) 3
Lennox, G. 1931 (Dolphin) 2
Long, K. F. 2017 (Burnley) 11
Long, S. P. 2007 (Reading, WBA, Hull C, Southampton) 82
Lowry, D. 1962 (St Patrick's Ath) 1
Lunn, R. 1939 (Dundalk) 2
Lynch, J. 1934 (Cork Bohemians) 1

Macken, A. 1977 (Derby Co) 1
Macken J. P. 2005 (Manchester C) 1
Mackey, G. 1957 (Shamrock R) 3
Madden, O. 1936 (Cork) 1
Madden, P. 2013 (Scunthorpe U) 1
Maguire, J. 1929 (Shamrock R) 1
Maguire, S. P. 2018 (Preston NE) 6
Mahon, A. J. 2000 (Tranmere R) 2
Malone, G. 1949 (Shelbourne) 1
Mancini, T. J. 1974 (QPR, Arsenal) 5
Martin, C. 1927 (Bo'ness) 1
Martin, C. J. 1946 (Glentoran, Leeds U, Aston Villa) 30
Martin, M. P. 1972 (Bohemians, Manchester U, WBA, Newcastle U) 52
Maybury, A. 1998 (Leeds U, Hearts, Leicester C) 10
McAlinden, J. 1946 (Portsmouth) 2
McAteer, J. W. 1994 (Bolton W, Liverpool, Blackburn R, Sunderland) 52
McCann, J. 1957 (Shamrock R) 1
McCarthy, J. 1926 (Bohemians) 3
McCarthy, J. 2010 (Wigan Ath, Everton) 41
McCarthy, M. 1932 (Shamrock R) 1
McCarthy, M. 1984 (Manchester C, Celtic, Lyon, Millwall) 57
McClean, J. J. 2012 (Sunderland, Wigan Ath, WBA, Stoke C) 67
McConville, T. 1972 (Dundalk, Waterford) 6
McDonagh, Jacko 1984 (Shamrock R) 3
McDonagh, J. 1981 (Everton, Bolton W, Notts Co, Wichita Wings) 25
McEvoy, M. A. 1961 (Blackburn R) 17
McGeady, A. J. 2004 (Celtic, Spartak Moscow, Everton, Sunderland) 93
McGee, P. 1978 (QPR, Preston NE) 15
McGoldrick, D. J. 2015 (Ipswich T, Sheffield U) 10
McGoldrick, E. J. 1992 (Crystal Palace, Arsenal) 15
McGowan, D. 1949 (West Ham U) 3
McGowan, J. 1947 (Cork U) 1
McGrath, M. 1958 (Blackburn R, Bradford) 22
McGrath, P. 1985 (Manchester U, Aston Villa, Derby Co) 83
McGuire, W. 1936 (Bohemians) 1
McKenzie, G. 1938 (Southend U) 9
McLoughlin, A. F. 1990 (Swindon T, Southampton, Portsmouth) 42
McLoughlin, F. 1930 (Fordsons, Cork) 2
McMillan, W. 1946 (Belfast Celtic) 2
McNally, J. B. 1959 (Luton T) 3
McPhail, S. 2000 (Leeds U) 10
McShane, P. D. 2007 (WBA, Sunderland, Hull C, Reading) 33
Meagan, M. K. 1961 (Everton, Huddersfield T, Drogheda) 17
Meehan, P. 1934 (Drumcondra) 1
Meyler, D. J. 2013 (Sunderland, Hull C, Reading) 26
Miller, L. W. P. 2004 (Celtic, Manchester U, Sunderland, Hibernian) 21
Milligan, M. J. 1992 (Oldham Ath) 1
Monahan, P. 1935 (Sligo R) 2
Mooney, J. 1965 (Shamrock R) 2
Moore, A. 1996 (Middlesbrough) 8
Moore, P. 1931 (Shamrock R, Aberdeen, Shamrock R) 9
Moran, K. 1980 (Manchester U, Sporting Gijon, Blackburn R) 71
Moroney, T. 1948 (West Ham U, Evergreen U) 12
Morris, C. B. 1988 (Celtic, Middlesbrough) 35
Morrison, C. H. 2002 (Crystal Palace, Birmingham C, Crystal Palace) 36
Moulson, C. 1936 (Lincoln C, Notts Co) 5
Moulson, G. B. 1948 (Lincoln C) 3
Muckian, C. 1978 (Drogheda U) 1
Muldoon, T. 1927 (Aston Villa) 1
Mulligan, P. M. 1969 (Shamrock R, Chelsea, Crystal Palace, WBA, Shamrock R) 50
Munroe, L. 1954 (Shamrock R) 1
Murphy, A. 1956 (Clyde) 1
Murphy, B. 1986 (Bohemians) 1
Murphy, D. 2007 (Sunderland, Ipswich T, Newcastle U, Sheffield W) 32
Murphy, J. 1980 (Crystal Palace) 3
Murphy, J. 2004 (WBA, Scunthorpe U) 2
Murphy, P. M. 2007 (Carlisle U) 1
Murray, T. 1950 (Dundalk) 1

Newman, W. 1969 (Shelbourne) 1
Nolan. E. W. 2009 (Preston NE) 3
Nolan, R. 1957 (Shamrock R) 10

Obafemi, M. O. 2019 (Southampton) 1
O'Brien, A. 2007 (Newcastle U) 5
O'Brien, A. A. 2019 (Millwall) 5
O'Brien, A. J. 2001 (Newcastle U, Portsmouth) 26
O'Brien, F. 1980 (Philadelphia F) 3
O'Brien J. M. 2006 (Bolton W, West Ham U) 5
O'Brien, L. 1986 (Shamrock R, Manchester U, Newcastle U, Tranmere R) 16
O'Brien, M. T. 1927 (Derby Co, Walsall, Norwich C, Watford) 4
O'Brien, R. 1976 (Notts Co) 5
O'Byrne, L. B. 1949 (Shamrock R) 1
O'Callaghan, B. R. 1979 (Stoke C) 6
O'Callaghan, K. 1981 (Ipswich T, Portsmouth) 21
O'Cearuill, J. 2007 (Arsenal) 2
O'Connell, A. 1967 (Dundalk, Bohemians) 2
O'Connor, T. 1950 (Shamrock R) 4
O'Connor, T. 1968 (Fulham, Dundalk, Bohemians) 7
O'Dea, D. 2010 (Celtic, Toronto, Metalurh Donetsk) 20
O'Dowda, C. J. R. 2016 (Oxford U, Bristol C) 15
O'Driscoll, J. F. 1949 (Swansea T) 3
O'Driscoll, S. 1982 (Fulham) 3
O'Farrell, F. 1952 (West Ham U, Preston NE) 9
O'Flanagan, K. P. 1938 (Bohemians, Arsenal) 10
O'Flanagan, M. 1947 (Bohemians) 1
O'Halloran, S. E. 2007 (Aston Villa) 2
O'Hanlon, K. G. 1988 (Rotherham U) 1
O'Kane, E. C. 2016 (Bournemouth, Leeds U) 7
O'Kane, P. 1935 (Bohemians) 3
O'Keefe, E. 1981 (Everton, Port Vale) 5
O'Keefe, T. 1934 (Cork, Waterford) 3
O'Leary, D. 1977 (Arsenal) 68
O'Leary, P. 1980 (Shamrock R) 7
O'Mahoney, M. T. 1938 (Bristol R) 6
O'Neill, F. S. 1962 (Shamrock R) 20
O'Neill, J. 1952 (Everton) 17
O'Neill, J. 1961 (Preston NE) 1
O'Neill, K. P. 1996 (Norwich C, Middlesbrough) 13
O'Neill, W. 1936 (Dundalk) 11
O'Regan, K. 1984 (Brighton & HA) 4
O'Reilly, J. 1932 (Brideville, Aberdeen, Brideville, St James' Gate) 20
O'Reilly, J. 1946 (Cork U) 2
O'Shea, J. F. 2002 (Manchester U, Sunderland) 118

Pearce, A. J. 2013 (Reading, Derby Co) 9
Peyton, G. 1977 (Fulham, Bournemouth, Everton) 33
Peyton, N. 1957 (Shamrock R, Leeds U) 6
Phelan, T. 1992 (Wimbledon, Manchester C, Chelsea, Everton, Fulham) 42
Pilkington, A. N. J. 2013 (Norwich C, Cardiff C) 9
Potter, D. M. 2007 (Wolverhampton W) 5

Quinn, A. 2003 (Sheffield W, Sheffield U) 8
Quinn, B. S. 2000 (Coventry C) 4
Quinn, N. J. 1986 (Arsenal, Manchester C, Sunderland) 91
Quinn, S. 2013 (Hull C, Reading) 18

Randolph, D. E. 2013 (Motherwell, West Ham U, Middlesbrough) 38
Reid, A. M. 2004 (Nottingham F, Tottenham H, Charlton Ath, Sunderland, Nottingham F) 29
Reid, C. 1931 (Brideville) 1
Reid, S. J. 2002 (Millwall, Blackburn R) 23
Rice, D. 2018 (West Ham U) 3
Richardson, D. J. 1972 (Shamrock R, Gillingham) 3
Rigby, A. 1935 (St James' Gate) 3
Ringstead, A. 1951 (Sheffield U) 20
Robinson, C. J. 2019 (Preton NE) 8
Robinson, J. 1928 (Bohemians, Dolphin) 2
Robinson, M. 1981 (Brighton & HA, Liverpool, QPR) 24
Roche, P. J. 1972 (Shelbourne, Manchester U) 8
Rogers, E. 1968 (Blackburn R, Charlton Ath) 19
Rowlands, M. C. 2004 (QPR) 5
Ryan, G. 1978 (Derby Co, Brighton & HA) 18
Ryan, R. A. 1950 (WBA, Derby Co) 16

Sadlier, R. T. 2002 (Millwall) 1
Sammon, C. 2013 (Derby Co) 9
Savage, D. P. T. 1996 (Millwall) 5
Saward, P. 1954 (Millwall, Aston Villa, Huddersfield T) 18
Scannell, T. 1954 (Southend U) 1
Scully, P. J. 1989 (Arsenal) 1
Sheedy, K. 1984 (Everton, Newcastle U) 46
Sheridan, C. 2010 (Celtic, CSKA Sofia) 3
Sheridan, J. J. 1988 (Leeds U, Sheffield W) 34
Slaven, B. 1990 (Middlesbrough) 7
Sloan, J. W. 1946 (Arsenal) 2
Smyth, M. 1969 (Shamrock R) 1
Squires, J. 1934 (Shelbourne) 1
Stapleton, F. 1977 (Arsenal, Manchester U, Ajax, Le Havre, Blackburn R) 71
Staunton, S. 1989 (Liverpool, Aston Villa, Liverpool, Aston Villa) 102
St Ledger-Hall, S. P. 2009 (Preston NE, Leicester C) 37
Stevens, E. J. 2018 (Sheffield U) 10
Stevenson, A. E. 1932 (Dolphin, Everton) 7
Stokes, A. 2007 (Sunderland, Celtic) 9
Strahan, F. 1964 (Shelbourne) 5
Sullivan, J. 1928 (Fordsons) 1
Swan, M. M. G. 1960 (Drumcondra) 1
Synnott, N. 1978 (Shamrock R) 3

Taylor, T. 1959 (Waterford) 1
Thomas, P. 1974 (Waterford) 2
Thompson, J. 2004 (Nottingham F) 1
Townsend, A. D. 1989 (Norwich C, Chelsea, Aston Villa, Middlesbrough) 70
Traynor, T. J. 1954 (Southampton) 8
Treacy, K. 2011 (Preston NE, Burnley) 6
Treacy, R. C. P. 1966 (WBA, Charlton Ath, Swindon T, Preston NE, WBA, Shamrock R) 42
Tuohy, L. 1956 (Shamrock R, Newcastle U, Shamrock R) 8
Turner, C. J. 1936 (Southend U, West Ham U) 10
Turner, P. 1963 (Celtic) 2

Vernon, J. 1946 (Belfast Celtic) 2

Waddock, G. 1980 (QPR, Millwall) 21
Walsh, D. J. 1946 (Linfield, WBA, Aston Villa) 20
Walsh, J. 1982 (Limerick) 1
Walsh, M. 1976 (Blackpool, Everton, QPR, Porto) 21
Walsh, M. 1982 (Everton) 4
Walsh, W. 1947 (Manchester C) 9
Walters, J. R. 2011 (Stoke C, Burnley) 54
Ward, S. R. 2011 (Wolverhampton W, Burnley) 50
Waters, J. 1977 (Grimsby T) 2
Watters, F. 1926 (Shelbourne) 1
Weir, E. 1939 (Clyde) 3
Westwood, K. 2009 (Coventry C, Sunderland, Sheffield W) 21
Whelan, G. D. 2008 (Stoke C, Aston Villa) 87
Whelan, R. 1964 (St Patrick's Ath) 2
Whelan, R. 1981 (Liverpool, Southend U) 53
Whelan, W. 1956 (Manchester U) 4
White, J. J. 1928 (Bohemians) 1
Whittaker, R. 1959 (Chelsea) 1
Williams, D. S. 2018 (Blackburn R) 1
Williams, J. 1938 (Shamrock R) 1
Williams, S. 2018 (Millwall) 3
Wilson, M. D. 2011 (Stoke C, Bournemouth) 25

BRITISH AND IRISH INTERNATIONAL GOALSCORERS 1872–2019

Where two players with the same surname and initials have appeared for the same country, and one or both have scored, they have been distinguished by reference to the club which appears *first* against their name in the international appearances section.
Bold type indicates players who have scored international goals in season 2018–19.

ENGLAND

A'Court, A.	1
Adams, T. A.	5
Adcock, H.	1
Alcock, C. W.	1
Alexander-Arnold, T. J.	**1**
Allen, A.	3
Allen, R.	2
Alli, B. J. (Dele)	3
Amos, A.	1
Anderson, V.	2
Anderton, D. R.	7
Astall, G.	1
Athersmith, W. C.	3
Atyeo, P. J. W.	5
Bache, J. W.	4
Bailey, N. C.	2
Baily, E. F.	5
Baines, L. J.	1
Baker, J. H.	3
Ball, A. J.	8
Bambridge, A. L.	1
Bambridge, E. C.	11
Barclay, R.	2
Barkley, R.	**4**
Barmby, N. J.	4
Barnes, J.	11
Barnes, P. S.	4
Barry, G.	3
Barton, J.	1
Bassett, W. I.	8
Bastin, C. S.	12
Beardsley, P. A.	9
Beasley, A.	1
Beattie, T. K.	1
Beckham, D. R. J.	17
Becton, F.	2
Bedford, H.	1
Bell, C.	9
Bent, D. A.	4
Bentley, R. T. F.	9
Bertrand, R.	1
Bishop, S. M.	1
Blackburn, F.	1
Blissett, L.	3
Bloomer, S.	28
Bond, R.	2
Bonsor, A. G.	1
Bowden, E. R.	1
Bowers, J. W.	2
Bowles, S.	1
Bradford, G. R. W.	1
Bradford, J.	7
Bradley, W.	2
Bradshaw, F.	3
Brann, G.	1
Bridge, W. M.	1
Bridges, B. J.	1
Bridgett, A.	3
Brindle, T.	1
Britton, C. S.	1
Broadbent, P. F.	2
Broadis, I. A.	8
Brodie, J. B.	1
Bromley-Davenport, W.	2
Brook, E. F.	10
Brooking, T. D.	5
Brooks, J.	2
Broome, F. H.	3
Brown, A.	4
Brown, A. S.	1
Brown, G.	5
Brown, J.	3
Brown, W.	1
Brown, W. M.	1
Buchan, C. M.	4
Bull, S. G.	4
Bullock, N.	2
Burgess, H.	4
Butcher, T.	3
Byrne, J. J.	8
Cahill, G. J.	5
Campbell, S. J.	1
Camsell, G. H.	18
Carroll, A. T.	2
Carter, H. S.	7
Carter, J. H.	4
Caulker, S. A.	1
Chadwick, E.	3
Chamberlain, M.	1
Chambers, H.	5
Channon, M. R.	21
Charlton, J.	6
Charlton, R.	49
Chenery, C. J.	1
Chivers, M.	13
Clarke, A. J.	10
Cobbold, W. N.	6
Cock, J. G.	2
Cole, A.	1
Cole, J. J.	10
Common, A.	2
Connelly, J. M.	7
Coppell, S. J.	7
Cotterill, G. H.	2
Cowans, G.	2
Crawford, R.	1
Crawshaw, T. H.	1
Crayston, W. J.	1
Creek, F. N. S.	1
Crooks, S. D.	7
Crouch, P. J.	22
Currey, E. S.	2
Currie, A. W.	3
Cursham, A. W.	2
Cursham, H. A.	5
Daft, H. B.	3
Davenport, J. K.	2
Davis, G.	1
Davis, H.	1
Day, S. H.	2
Dean, W. R.	18
Defoe, J. C.	20
Devey, J. H. G.	1
Dewhurst, F.	11
Dier, E. J. E.	3
Dix, W. R.	1
Dixon, K. M.	4
Dixon, L. M.	1
Dorrell, A. R.	1
Douglas, B.	11
Drake, E. J.	6
Ducat, A.	1
Dunn, A. T. B.	2
Eastham, G.	2
Edwards, D.	5
Ehiogu, U.	1
Elliott, W. H.	3
Evans, R. E.	1
Ferdinand, L.	5
Ferdinand, R. G.	3
Finney, T.	30
Fleming, H. J.	9
Flowers, R.	10
Forman, Frank	1
Forman, Fred	3
Foster, R. E.	3
Fowler, R. B.	7
Francis, G. C. J.	3
Francis, T.	12
Freeman, B. C.	3
Froggatt, J.	2
Froggatt, R.	2
Galley, T.	1
Gascoigne, P. J.	10
Geary, F.	3
Gerrard, S. G.	21
Gibbins, W. V. T.	3
Gilliatt, W. E.	3
Goddard, P.	1
Goodall, J.	12
Goodyer, A. C.	1
Gosling, R. C.	2
Goulden, L. A.	4
Grainger, C.	3
Greaves, J.	44
Grovesnor, A. T.	2
Gunn, W.	1
Haines, J. T. W.	2
Hall, G. W.	9
Halse, H. J.	2
Hampson, J.	5
Hampton, H.	2
Hancocks, J.	2
Hardman, H. P.	1
Harris, S. S.	2
Hassall, H. W.	4
Hateley, M.	9
Haynes, J. N.	18
Hegan, K. E.	4
Henfrey, A. G.	2
Heskey, E. W.	7
Hilsdon, G. R.	14
Hine, E. W.	4
Hinton, A. T.	1
Hirst, D. E.	1
Hitchens, G. A.	5
Hobbis, H. H. F.	1
Hoddle, G.	8
Hodgetts, D.	1
Hodgson, G.	1
Holley, G. H.	8
Houghton, W. E.	5
Howell, R.	1
Hughes, E. W.	1
Hulme, J. H. A.	4
Hunt, G. S.	1
Hunt, R.	18
Hunter, N.	2
Hurst, G. C.	24
Ince, P. E. C.	2
Jack, D. N. B.	3
Jagielka, P. N.	3
Jeffers, F.	1
Jenas, J. A.	1
Johnson, A.	2
Johnson, D. E.	6
Johnson, E.	2
Johnson, G. M. C.	1
Johnson, J. A.	2
Johnson, T. C. F.	5
Johnson, W. H.	1
Kail, E. I. L.	2
Kane, H. E.	**22**
Kay, A. H.	1
Keane, M. V.	**1**
Keegan, J. K.	21
Kelly, R.	8
Kennedy, R.	3
Kenyon-Slaney, W. S.	2
Keown, M. R.	2
Kevan, D. T.	8
Kidd, B.	1
King, L. B.	2
Kingsford, R. K.	1
Kirchen, A. J.	2
Kirton, W. J.	1
Lallana, A. D.	3
Lambert, R. L.	3
Lampard, F. J.	29
Langton, R.	1
Latchford, R. D.	5
Latheron, E. G.	1
Lawler, C.	1
Lawton, T.	22
Lee, F.	10
Lee, J.	1
Lee, R. M.	2
Lee, S.	2
Lescott, J.	1
Le Saux, G. P.	1
Lindley, T.	14
Lineker, G.	48
Lingard, J. E.	**4**
Lofthouse, J. M.	3
Lofthouse, N.	30
Hon. A. Lyttelton	1
Mabbutt, G.	1
Macdonald, M.	6
Maguire, J. H.	1
Mannion, W. J.	11
Mariner, P.	13
Marsh, R. W.	1
Matthews, S.	11
Matthews, V.	1
McCall, J.	1
McDermott, T.	3
McManaman, S.	3
Medley, L. D.	1
Melia, J.	1
Mercer, D. W.	1
Merson, P. C.	3
Milburn, J. E. T.	10
Miller, H. S.	1
Mills, G. R.	3
Milner, J. P.	1
Milward, A.	3
Mitchell, C.	5
Moore, J.	1
Moore, R. F.	2
Moore, W. G. B.	2
Morren, T.	1

Morris, F.	1
Morris, J.	3
Mortensen, S. H.	23
Morton, J. R.	1
Mosforth, W.	3
Mullen, J.	6
Mullery, A. P.	1
Murphy, D. B	1
Neal, P. G.	5
Needham, E.	3
Nicholls, J.	1
Nicholson, W. E.	1
Nugent, D. J.	1
O'Grady, M.	3
Osborne, F. R.	3
Owen, M. J.	40
Own goals	33
Oxlade-Chamberlain, A. M. D.	6
Page, L. A.	1
Paine, T. L.	7
Palmer, C. L.	1
Parry, E. H.	1
Parry, R. A.	1
Pawson, F. W.	1
Payne, J.	2
Peacock, A.	3
Pearce, S.	5
Pearson, J. S.	5
Pearson, S. C.	5
Perry, W.	2
Peters, M.	20
Pickering, F.	5
Platt, D.	27
Pointer, R.	2
Quantrill, A.	1
Ramsay, A. E.	3
Rashford, M.	**7**
Revie, D. G.	4
Redknapp, J. F.	1
Reynolds, J.	3
Richards, M.	1
Richardson, K. E.	2
Richardson, J. R.	2
Rigby, A.	3
Rimmer, E. J.	2
Roberts, F.	2
Roberts, H.	1
Roberts, W. T.	2
Robinson, J.	3
Robson, B.	26
Robson, R.	4
Rooney, W. M.	53
Rowley, J. F.	6
Royle, J.	2
Rutherford, J.	3
Sagar, C.	1
Sandilands, R. R.	3
Sansom, K.	1
Schofield, J.	1
Scholes, P.	14
Seed, J. M.	1
Settle, J.	6
Sewell, J.	3
Shackleton, L. F.	1
Sharp, J.	1
Shearer, A.	30
Shelton, A.	1
Shepherd, A.	2
Sheringham, E. P.	11
Simpson, J.	1
Smalling, C. L.	1
Smith, A.	1
Smith, A. M.	2
Smith, G. O.	11
Smith, Joe	1
Smith, J. R.	2
Smith, J. W.	4
Smith, R.	13
Smith, S.	1
Sorby, T. H.	1
Southgate, G.	2
Southworth, J.	3
Sparks, F. J.	3
Spence, J. W.	1
Spiksley, F.	5
Spilsbury, B. W.	5
Steele, F. C.	8
Stephenson, G. T.	2
Sterling, R. S.	**8**
Steven, T. M.	4
Stewart, J.	2
Stiles, N. P.	1
Storer, H.	1
Stone, S. B.	2
Stones, J.	2
Sturridge, D. A.	8
Summerbee, M. G.	1
Tambling, R. V.	1
Taylor, P. J.	2
Taylor, T.	16
Terry, J. G.	6
Thompson, P. B.	1
Thornewell, G.	1
Tilson, S. F.	6
Townley, W. J.	2
Townsend, A. D.	3
Trippier, K. J.	1
Tueart, D.	2
Upson, M. J.	2
Vardy, J. R.	7
Vassell, D.	6
Vaughton, O. H.	6
Veitch, J. G.	3
Viollet, D. S.	1
Waddle, C. R.	6
Walcott, T. J.	8
Walker, W. H.	9
Wall, G.	2
Wallace, D.	1
Walsh, P.	1
Waring, T.	4
Warren, B.	2
Watson, D. V.	4
Watson, V. M.	4
Webb, G. W.	1
Webb, N.	4
Wedlock, W. J.	2
Welbeck D. N. T. M.	16
Weller, K.	1
Welsh, D.	1
Whateley, O.	2
Wheldon, G. F.	6
Whitfield, H.	1
Wignall, F.	2
Wilkes, A.	1
Wilkins, R. G.	3
Willingham, C. K.	1
Wilshaw, D. J.	10
Wilshere J. A.	2
Wilson, C.	**1**
Wilson, G. P.	1
Winckworth, W. N.	1
Windridge, J. E.	7
Wise, D. F.	1
Withe, P.	1
Wollaston, C. H. R.	1
Wood, H.	1
Woodcock, T.	16
Woodhall, G.	1
Woodward, V. J.	29
Worrall, F.	2
Worthington, F. S.	2
Wright, I. E.	9
Wright, M.	1
Wright, W. A.	3
Wright-Phillips, S. C.	6
Wylie, J. G.	1
Yates, J.	3
Young, A. S.	7

NORTHERN IRELAND

Anderson, T.	4
Armstrong, G.	12
Bambrick, J.	12
Barr, H. H.	1
Barron, H.	3
Best, G.	9
Bingham, W. L.	10
Black, K.	1
Blanchflower, D.	2
Blanchflower, J.	1
Boyce, L.	1
Brennan, B.	1
Brennan, R. A.	1
Brotherston, N.	3
Brown, J.	1
Browne, F.	2
Brunt, C.	3
Campbell, J.	1
Campbell, W. G.	1
Casey, T.	2
Caskey, W.	1
Cassidy, T.	1
Cathcart, C. G.	2
Chambers, J.	3
Clarke, C. J.	13
Clements, D.	2
Cochrane, T.	1
Condy, J.	1
Connor, M. J.	1
Coulter, J.	1
Croft, T.	1
Crone, W.	1
Crossan, E.	1
Crossan, J. A.	10
Curran, S.	2
Cush, W. W.	5
Dallas, S. A.	**3**
Dalton, W.	4
D'Arcy, S. D.	1
Darling, J.	1
Davey, H. H.	1
Davis, S.	**12**
Davis, T. L.	1
Dill, A. H.	1
Doherty, L.	1
Doherty, P. D.	3
Dougan, A. D.	8
Dowie, I.	12
Dunne, J.	4
Elder, A. R.	1
Elliott, S.	4
Emerson, W.	1
English, S.	1
Evans, C.	**2**
Evans, J. G.	**3**
Feeney, W.	1
Feeney, W. J.	5
Ferguson, S. K.	1
Ferguson, W.	1
Ferris, J.	1
Ferris, R. O.	1
Finney, T.	2
Gaffkin, J.	4
Gara, A.	3
Gaukrodger, G.	1
Gibb, J. T.	2
Gibb, T. J.	1
Gibson, W.	1
Gillespie, K. R.	2
Gillespie, W.	13
Goodall, A. L.	2
Griffin, D. J.	1
Gray, P.	6
Grigg, W. D.	**2**
Halligan, W.	1
Hamill, M.	1
Hamilton, B.	4
Hamilton, W. R.	5
Hannon, D. J.	1
Harkin, J. T.	2
Harvey, M.	3
Healy, D. J.	36
Hill, C. F.	1
Hughes, A.	1
Hughes, M. E.	5
Humphries, W.	1
Hunter, A. (Distillery)	1
Hunter, A. (Blackburn R)	1
Hunter, B. V.	1
Irvine, R. W.	3
Irvine, W. J.	8
Johnston, H.	2
Johnston, S.	2
Johnston, W. C.	1
Jones, S. (Distillery)	1
Jones, S. (Crewe Alex)	1
Jones, J.	1
Kelly, J.	4
Kernaghan, N.	2
Kirwan, J.	2
Lacey, W.	3
Lafferty, K.	20
Lemon, J.	2
Lennon, N. F.	2
Lockhart, N.	3
Lomas, S. M.	3
Magennis, J. B. D.	**6**
Magilton, J.	5
Mahood, J.	2
Martin, D. K.	3
Maxwell, J.	2
McAdams, W. J.	7
McAllen, J.	1
McAuley, G.	9
McAuley, J. L.	1
McCann, G. S.	4
McCartney, G.	1
McCandless, J.	2
McCandless, W.	1
McCaw, J. H.	1
McClelland, J.	1
McCluggage, A.	2
McCourt, P.	2
McCracken, W.	1
McCrory, S.	1
McCurdy, C.	1
McDonald, A.	3
McGarry, J. K.	1
McGrath, R. C.	4
McGinn, N.	**4**
McIlroy, J.	10
McIlroy, S. B.	5
McKenzie, H	1
McKnight, J.	2
McLaughlin, C. G.	1
McLaughlin, J. C.	6
McMahon, G. J.	2
McMordie, A. S.	3
McMorran, E. J.	4
McNair, P. J. C.	**1**
McParland, P. J.	10
McWha, W. B. R.	1
Meldon, P. A	1
Mercer, J. T.	1
Millar, W.	1
Milligan, D.	1

Milne, R. G. 2
Molyneux, T. B. 1
Moreland, V. 1
Morgan, S. 3
Morrow, S. J. 1
Morrow, W. J. 1
Mulryne, P. P. 3
Murdock, C. J. 1
Murphy, N. 1

Neill, W. J. T. 2
Nelson, S. 1
Nicholl, C. J. 3
Nicholl, J. M. 1
Nicholson, J. J. 6

O'Boyle, G. 1
O'Hagan, C. 2
O'Kane, W. J. 1
O'Neill, J. 2
O'Neill, M. A. 4
O'Neill, M. H. 8
Own goals 10

Paterson, M. A. 3
Patterson, D. J. 1
Patterson, R. 1
Peacock, R. 2
Peden, J. 7
Penney, S. 2
Pyper, James 2
Pyper, John 1

Quinn, J. M. 12
Quinn, S. J. 4

Reynolds, J. 1
Rowland, K. 1
Rowley, R. W. M. 2
Rushe, F. 1

Sheridan, J. 2
Sherrard, J. 1
Sherrard, W. C. 2
Shields, D. 1
Simpson, W. J. 5
Sloan, H. A. de B. 4
Smyth, P. 1
Smyth, S. 5

Spence, D. W. 3
Sproule, I. 1
Stanfield, O. M. 11
Stevenson, A. E. 5
Stewart, I. 2

Taggart, G. P. 7
Thompson, F. W. 2
Torrans, S. 1
Tully, C. P. 3
Turner, A. 1

Walker, J. 1
Walsh, D. J. 5
Ward, J. J. 4
Washington, C. J. 4
Welsh, E. 1
Whiteside, N. 9
Whiteside, T. 1
Whitley, Jeff 2
Whyte, G. 1
Williams, J. R. 1
Williams, M. S. 1
Williamson, J. 1
Wilson, D. J. 1
Wilson, K. J. 6
Wilson, S. J. 7
Wilton, J. M. 2
Young, S. 1

N.B. In 1914 Young goal should be credited to Gillespie W v Wales

SCOTLAND

Aitken, R. (Celtic) 1
Aitken, R. (Dumbarton) 1
Aitkenhead, W. A. C. 2
Alexander, D. 1
Allan, D. S. 4
Allan, J. 2
Anderson, F. 1
Anderson, W. 4
Andrews, P. 1
Anya, I. 3
Archibald, A. 1
Archibald, S. 4
Armstrong, S. 1

Baird, D. 2
Baird, J. C. 2
Baird, S. 2
Bannon, E. 1
Barbour, A. 1
Barker, J. B. 4
Battles, B. Jr 1
Bauld, W. 2
Baxter, J. C. 3
Beattie, C. 1
Bell, J. 5
Bennett, A. 2
Berra, C. D. 4
Berry, D. 1
Bett, J. 1
Beveridge, W. W. 1
Black, A. 3
Black, D. 1
Bone, J. 1
Booth, S. 6
Boyd, K 7
Boyd, R. 2
Boyd, T. 1
Boyd, W. G. 1
Brackenridge, T. 1
Brand, R. 8
Brazil, A. 1
Bremner, W. J. 3
Broadfoot, K. 1
Brown, A. D. 6
Brown, S. 4
Buchanan, P. S. 1
Buchanan, R. 1
Buckley, P. 1
Buick, A. 2
Burke, C. 2
Burke, O. J. 1
Burley, C. W. 3
Burns, K. 1

Cairns, T. 1
Caldwell, G. 2
Calderwood, C. 1
Calderwood, R. 2
Caldow, E. 4
Cameron, C. 2
Campbell, C. 1
Campbell, John (Celtic) 5
Campbell, John (Rangers) 4
Campbell, J. (South Western) 1
Campbell, P. 2
Campbell, R. 1
Cassidy, J. 1
Chalmers, S. 3
Chambers, T. 1
Cheyne, A. G. 4
Christie, A. J. 1
Clarkson, D. 1
Clunas, W. L. 1
Collins, J. 12
Collins, R. Y. 10
Combe, J. R. 1
Commons, K. 2
Conn, A. 1
Cooper, D. 6
Craig, J. 1
Craig, T. 1

Crawford, S. 4
Cunningham, A. N. 5
Curran, H. P. 1

Dailly, C. 6
Dalglish, K. 30
Davidson, D. 1
Davidson, J. A. 1
Delaney, J. 3
Devine, A. 1
Dewar, G. 1
Dewar, N. 4
Dickov, P. 1
Dickson, W. 4
Divers, J. 1
Dobie, R. S. 1
Docherty, T. H. 1
Dodds, D. 1
Dodds, W. 7
Donaldson, A. 1
Donnachie, J. 1
Dougall, J. 1
Drummond, J. 2
Dunbar, M. 1
Duncan, D. 7
Duncan, D. M. 1
Duncan, J. 1
Dunn, J. 2
Durie, G. S. 7

Easson, J. F. 1
Elliott, M. S. 1
Ellis, J. 1

Ferguson, B. 3
Ferguson, J. 6
Fernie, W. 1
Fitchie, T. T. 1
Flavell, R. 2
Fleming, C. 2
Fleming, J. W. 3
Fletcher, D. 5
Fletcher, S. K. 10
Forrest, J. 5
Fraser, M. J. E. 3
Fraser, R. 1
Freedman, D. A. 1

Gallacher, H. K. 23
Gallacher, K. W. 9
Gallacher, P. 1
Galt, J. H. 1
Gemmell, T. (St Mirren) 1
Gemmell, T. (Celtic) 1
Gemmill, A. 8
Gemmill, S. 1
Gibb, W. 1
Gibson, D. W. 3
Gibson, J. D. 1
Gibson, N. 1
Gillespie, Jas. 3
Gillick, T. 3
Gilzean, A. J. 12
Goodwillie, D. 1
Gossland, J. 2
Goudie, J. 1
Gough, C. R. 6
Gourlay, J. 1
Graham, A. 2
Graham, G. 3
Gray, A. 7
Gray, E. 3
Gray, F. 1
Greig, J. 3
Griffiths, L. 4
Groves, W. 4

Hamilton, G. 4
Hamilton, J. (Queen's Park) 3
Hamilton, R. C. 15
Hanley, G. C. 1
Harper, J. M. 2
Hartley, P. J. 1

Harrower, W. 5
Hartford, R. A. 4
Heggie, C. W 4
Henderson, J. G. 1
Henderson, W. 5
Hendry, E. C. J. 3
Herd, D. G. 3
Herd, G. 1
Hewie, J. D. 2
Higgins, A. (Newcastle U) 1
Higgins, A. (Kilmarnock) 4
Highet, T. C. 1
Holt, G.J. 1
Holton, J. A. 2
Hopkin, D. 2
Houliston, W. 2
Howie, H. 1
Howie, J. 2
Hughes, J. 1
Hunter, W. 1
Hutchison, D. 6
Hutchison, T. 1
Hutton, J. 1
Hyslop, T. 1

Imrie, W. N. 1

Jackson, A. 8
Jackson, C. 1
Jackson, D. 4
James, A. W. 4
Jardine, A. 1
Jenkinson, T. 1
Jess, E. 2
Johnston, A. 2
Johnston, L. H. 1
Johnston, M. 14
Johnstone, D. 2
Johnstone, J. 4
Johnstone, Jas. 1
Johnstone, R. 10
Johnstone, W. 1
Jordan, J. 11

Kay, J. L. 5
Keillor, A. 3
Kelly, J. 1
Kelso, R. 1
Ker, G. 10
King, A. 1
King, J. 1
Kinnear, D. 1
Kyle, K. 1

Lambert, P. 1
Lambie, J. 1
Lambie, W. A. 5
Lang, J. J. 2
Latta, A. 2
Law, D. 30
Leggat, G. 8
Lennie, W. 1
Lennox, R. 3
Liddell, W. 6
Lindsay, J. 6
Linwood, A. B. 1
Logan, J. 1
Lorimer, P. 4
Love, A. 1
Low, J. (Cambuslang) 1
Lowe, J. (St Bernards) 1

Macari, L. 5
MacDougall, E. J. 3
MacFarlane, A. 1
MacLeod, M. 1
Mackay, D. C. 4
Mackay, G. 1
MacKenzie, J. A. 1
Mackail-Smith, C. 1
Mackie, J. C. 2
MacKinnon, W. W. 5

Madden, J. 5
Maloney, S. R. 7
Marshall, H. 1
Marshall, J. 1
Martin, C. H. 3
Mason, J. 4
Massie, A. 1
Masson, D. S. 5
McAdam, J. 1
McAllister, G. 5
McArthur, J. 4
McAulay, J. D. 1
McAvennie, F. 1
McCall, J. 1
McCall, S. M. 1
McCalliog, J. 1
McCallum, N. 1
McCann, N. 3
McClair, B. J. 2
McCoist, A. 19
McColl, R. S. 13
McCormack, R. 2
McCulloch, D. 3
McCulloch, L. 1
McDougall, J. 4
McFadden, J.* 15
McFadyen, W. 2
McGhee, M. 2
McGinlay, J. 4
McGregor, J. 1
McGrory, J. 6
McGuire, W. 1
McInally, A. 3
McInnes, T. 2
McKie, J. 2
McKimmie, S. 1
McKinlay, W. 4
McKinnon, A. 1
McKinnon, R. 1
McLaren, A. 4
McLaren, J. 1
McLean, A. 1
McLean, K. 1
McLean, T. 1
McLintock, F. 1
McMahon, A. 6
McManus, S. 2
McMenemy, J. 5
McMillan, I. L. 2
McNeill, W. 3
McNiel, H. 5
McPhail, J. 3
McPhail, R. 7
McPherson, J. (Kilmarnock) 7
McPherson, J. (Vale of Leven) 1
McPherson, R. 1
McQueen, G. 5
McStay, P. 9
McSwegan, G. 1
Meiklejohn, D. D. 3
Millar, J. 2
Miller, K. 18
Miller, T. 2
Miller, W. 1
Mitchell, R. C. 1
Morgan, W. 1
Morris, D. 1
Morris, H. 3
Morrison, J. C. 3
Morton, A. L. 5
Mudie, J. K. 9
Mulgrew, C. P. 3
Mulhall, G. 1
Munro, A. D. 1
Munro, N. 2
Murdoch, R. 5
Murphy, F. 1
Murray, J. 1

Napier, C. E. 3
Narey, D. 1
Naismith, S. J. 9
Naysmith, G. A. 1
Neil, R. G. 2
Nevin, P. K. F. 5
Nicholas, C. 5
Nisbet, J. 2

O'Connor, G. 4
O'Donnell, F. 2
O'Hare, J. 5
Ormond, W. E. 2
O'Rourke, F. 1
Orr, R. 1
Orr, T. 1
Oswald, J. 1
Own goals 21

Parlane, D. 1
Paul, H. McD. 2
Paul, W. 5
Pettigrew, W. 2
Phillips, M. 1
Provan, D. 1

Quashie, N. F. 1
Quinn, J. 7
Quinn, P. 1

Rankin, G. 2
Rankin, R. 2
Reid, W. 4
Reilly, L. 22
Renny-Tailyour, H. W. 1
Rhodes, J. L. 3
Richmond, J. T. 1
Ring, T. 2
Rioch, B. D. 6
Ritchie, J. 1
Ritchie, M. T. 3
Ritchie, P. S. 1
Robertson, A. (Clyde) 2
Robertson, A. 3
Robertson, J. 3
Robertson, J. N. 8
Robertson, J. T. 2
Robertson, T. 1
Robertson, W. 1
Russell, D. 1
Russell, J. S. S. 1

Scott, A. S. 5
Sellar, W. 4
Sharp, G. 1
Shaw, F. W. 1
Shearer, D. 2
Simpson, J. 1
Smith, A. 5
Smith, G. 4
Smith, J. 1
Smith, John 13
Snodgrass, R. 7
Somerville, G. 1
Souness, G. J. 4
Speedie, F. 2
St John, I. 9
Steel, W. 12
Stein, C. 10
Stevenson, G. 4
Stewart, A. 1
Stewart, R. 1
Stewart, W. E. 1
Strachan, G. 5
Sturrock, P. 3

Taylor, J. D. 1
Templeton, R. 1
Thompson, S. 3
Thomson, A. 1
Thomson, C. 4
Thomson, R. 1
Thomson, W. 1
Thornton, W. 1

Waddell, T. S. 1
Waddell, W. 6
Walker, J. 2
Walker, R. 7
Walker, T. 9
Wallace, I. A. 1
Wark, J. 7
Watson, J. A. K. 1
Watt, F. 2
Watt, W. W. 1
Webster, A. 1
Weir, A. 1
Weir, D. 1
Weir, J. B. 2
White, J. A. 3
Wilkie, L. 1
Wilson, A. (Sheffield W) 2
Wilson, A. N. (Dunfermline Ath) 13
Wilson, D. (Liverpool) 1
Wilson, D. (Queen's Park) 2
Wilson, D. (Rangers) 9
Wilson, H. 1
Wylie, T. G. 1

Young, A. 5

WALES

Allchurch, I. J. 23
Allen, J. M. 2
Allen, M. 3
Astley, D. J. 12
Atherton, R. W. 2

Bale, G. F. 31
Bamford, T. 1
Barnes, W. 1
Bellamy, C. D. 19
Blackmore, C. G. 1
Blake, D. 1
Blake, N. A. 4
Bodin, P. J. 3
Boulter, L. M. 1
Bowdler, J. C. H. 3
Bowen, D. L. 1
Bowen, M. 3
Boyle, T. 1
Brooks, D. R. 1
Bryan, T. 1
Burgess, W. A. R. 1
Burke, T. 1
Butler, W. T. 1

Chapman, T. 2
Charles, J. 1
Charles, M. 6
Charles, W. J. 15
Church, S. R. 3
Clarke, R. J. 5
Coleman, C. 4
Collier, D. J. 1
Collins, J. 3
Cotterill, D. R. G. B. 2
Crosse, K. 1
Cumner, R. H. 1
Curtis, A. 6
Curtis, E. R. 3

Davies, D. W. 1
Davies, E. Lloyd 1
Davies, G. 2
Davies, L. S. 6
Davies, R. T. 9
Davies, R. W. 6
Davies, Simon 6
Davies, Stanley 5
Davies, W. 6
Davies, W. H. 1
Davies, William 5
Davis, W. O. 1
Deacy, N. 4
Doughty, J. 6
Doughty, R. 2
Durban, A. 2
Dwyer, P. 2

Earnshaw, R. 16
Eastwood, F. 4
Edwards, D. A. 3
Edwards, G. 2
Edwards, R. I. 4
England, H. M. 4
Evans, C. 2
Evans, I. 1
Evans, J. 1
Evans, R. E. 2
Evans, W. 1
Eyton-Jones, J. A. 1

Fletcher, C. 1
Flynn, B. 7
Ford, T. 23
Foulkes, W. I. 1
Fowler, J. 3

Giles, D. 2
Giggs, R. J. 12
Glover, E. M. 7
Godfrey, B. C. 2
Green, A. W. 3
Griffiths, A. T. 6
Griffiths, M. W. 2
Griffiths, T. P. 3

Harris, C. S. 1
Hartson, J. 14
Hersee, R. 1
Hewitt, R. 1
Hockey, T. 1
Hodges, G. 2
Hole, W. J. 1
Hopkins, I. J. 2
Horne, B. 2
Howell, E. G. 3
Hughes, L. M. 16
Huws, E. W. 1

James, D. O. 1
James, E. 2
James, L. 10
James, R. 7
Jarrett, R. H. 3
Jenkyns, C. A. 1
Jones, A. 1
Jones, Bryn 6
Jones, B. S. 2
Jones, Cliff 16
Jones, C. W. 1
Jones, D. E. 1
Jones, Evan 1
Jones, H. 1
Jones, I. 1
Jones, J. L. 1
Jones, J. O. 1
Jones, J. P. 1
Jones, Leslie J. 1
Jones, R. A. 2
Jones, W. L. 6

Keenor, F. C. 2
King, A. P. 2
Koumas, J. 10
Krzywicki, R. L. 1

Lawrence, T. M. 3
Ledley, J. C. 4
Leek, K. 5
Lewis, B. 4
Lewis, D. M. 2
Lewis, W. 8
Lewis, W. L. 3

** The Scottish FA officially changed Robson's goal against Iceland on 10 September 2008 to McFadden.*

Llewelyn, C. M	1
Lovell, S.	1
Lowrie, G.	2
Mahoney, J. F.	1
Mays, A. W.	1
Medwin, T. C.	6
Melville, A. K	3
Meredith, W. H.	11
Mills, T. J.	1
Moore, G.	1
Morgan, J. R.	2
Morgan-Owen, H.	1
Morgan-Owen, M. M.	2
Morison, S.	1
Morris, A. G.	9
Morris, H.	2
Morris, R.	1
Morris, S.	2
Nicholas, P.	2
O'Callaghan, E.	3
O'Sullivan, P. A.	1
Owen, G.	2
Owen, W.	4
Owen, W. P.	6
Own goals	14
Palmer, D.	3
Parry, P. I.	1
Parry, T. D.	3
Paul, R.	1
Peake, E.	1
Pembridge, M.	6
Perry, E.	1
Phillips, C.	5
Phillips, D.	2
Powell, A.	1
Powell, D.	1
Price, J.	4
Price, P.	1
Pryce-Jones, W. E.	3
Pugh, D. H.	2
Ramsey, A. J.	**14**
Reece, G. I.	2
Rees, R. R.	3
Richards, R. W.	1
Roach, J.	2
Robbins, W. W.	4
Roberts, C. R. J.	**1**
Roberts, J. (Corwen)	1
Roberts, Jas.	1
Roberts, P. S.	1
Roberts, R. (Druids)	1
Roberts, W. (Llangollen)	2
Roberts, W. (Wrexham)	1
Roberts, W. H.	1
Robinson, C. P.	1
Robinson, J. R. C.	3
Robson-Kanu, T. H.	5
Rush, I.	28
Russell, M. R.	1
Sabine, H. W.	1
Saunders, D.	22
Savage, R. W.	2
Shaw, E. G.	2
Sisson, H.	4
Slatter, N.	2
Smallman, D. P.	1
Speed, G. A.	7
Symons, C. J.	2
Tapscott, D. R.	4
Taylor, G. K.	1
Taylor, N. J.	1
Thomas, M.	4
Thomas, T.	1
Toshack, J. B.	12
Trainer, H.	2
Vaughan, D. O.	1
Vaughan, John	2
Vernon, T. R.	8
Vizard, E. T.	1
Vokes, S. M.	**11**
Walsh, I.	7
Warren, F. W.	3
Watkins, W. M.	4
Wilding, J.	4
Williams, A.	1
Williams, A. E.	2
Williams, D. R.	2
Williams, G. E.	1
Williams, G. G.	1
Williams, W.	1
Wilson, H.	**2**
Woodburn, B.	**2**
Woosnam, A. P.	3
Wynn, G. A.	1
Yorath, T. C.	2
Young, E.	1

REPUBLIC OF IRELAND

Aldridge, J.	19
Ambrose, P.	1
Anderson, J.	1
Andrews, K.	3
Barrett, G.	2
Bermingham, P.	1
Bradshaw, P.	4
Brady, L.	9
Brady, R.	**8**
Breen, G.	7
Brown, J.	1
Burke, G. D.	1
Byrne, D.	1
Byrne, J.	4
Cantwell, N.	14
Carey, J.	3
Carroll, T.	1
Cascarino, A.	19
Christie, C. S. F.	2
Clark, C.	2
Coad, P.	3
Coleman, S.	1
Connolly, D. J.	9
Conroy, T.	2
Conway, J.	3
Cox, S. R.	4
Coyne, T.	6
Cummins, G.	5
Curtis, D.	8
Daly, G.	13
Davis, T.	4
Dempsey, J.	1
Dennehy, M.	2
Doherty, G. M. T.	4
Donnelly, J.	4
Donnelly, T.	1
Doyle, K. E.	14
Duff, D. A.	8
Duffy, B.	1
Duffy, S. P. M.	**3**
Duggan, H.	1
Dunne, J.	13
Dunne, L.	1
Dunne, R. P.	8
Eglington, T.	2
Elliott, S. W.	1
Ellis, P.	1
Fagan, F.	5
Fahey, K.	3
Fallon, S.	2
Fallon, W.	2
Farrell, P.	3
Finnan, S.	2
Fitzgerald, P.	2
Fitzgerald, J.	1
Fitzsimons, A.	7
Flood, J. J.	4
Fogarty, A.	3
Foley, D.	2
Fullam, J.	1
Fullam, R.	1
Galvin, A.	1
Gavin, J.	2
Geoghegan, M.	2
Gibson, D. T. D.	1
Giles, J.	5
Givens, D.	19
Gleeson, S. M.	1
Glynn, D.	1
Grealish, T.	8
Green, P. J.	1
Grimes, A. A.	1
Hale, A.	2
Hand, E.	2
Harte, I. P.	11
Haverty, J.	3
Healy, C.	1
Hendrick, J. P.	**2**
Holland, M. R.	5
Holmes, J.	1
Hoolahan, W.	3
Horlacher, A.	2
Houghton, R.	6
Hourihane, C.	**1**
Hughton, C.	1
Hunt, S. P.	1
Hurley, C.	2
Ireland, S. J.	4
Irwin, D.	4
Jordan, D.	1
Judge, A. C.	1
Kavanagh, G. A.	1
Keane, R. D.	68
Keane, R. M.	9
Kelly, D.	9
Kelly, G.	2
Kelly, J.	2
Kennedy, M.	4
Keogh, A.	2
Keogh, R. J.	1
Kernaghan, A. N.	1
Kilbane, K. D.	8
Kinsella, M. A.	3
Lacey, W.	1
Lawrence, L.	2
Lawrenson, M.	5
Leech, M.	2
Long, S. P.	17
Mancini, T.	1
Martin, C.	6
Martin, M.	4
McAteer, J. W.	3
McCann, J.	1
McCarthy, M.	2
McClean, J. J.	10
McEvoy, A.	6
McGeady, A. G.	5
McGee, P.	4
McGrath, P.	8
McLoughlin, A. F.	2
McPhail, S. J. P.	1
Miller, L. W. P.	1
Mooney, J.	1
Moore, P.	7
Moran, K.	6
Morrison, C. H.	9
Moroney, T.	1
Mulligan, P.	1
Murphy, D.	3
O'Brien, A. A.	**1**
O'Brien, A. J.	1
O'Callaghan, K.	1
O'Connor, T.	2
O'Dea, D.	1
O'Farrell, F.	2
O'Flanagan, K.	3
O'Keefe, E.	1
O'Leary, D. A.	1
O'Neill, F.	1
O'Neill, K. P.	4
O'Reilly, J. (Brideville)	2
O'Reilly, J. (Cork)	1
O'Shea, J. F.	3
Own goals	14
Pearce, A. J.	2
Pilkington, A. N. J.	1
Quinn, N.	21
Reid, A. M.	4
Reid, S. J.	2
Ringstead, A.	7
Robinson, M.	4
Rogers, E.	5
Ryan, G.	1
Ryan, R.	3
St Ledger-Hall, S.	3
Sheedy, K.	9
Sheridan, J.	5
Slaven, B.	1
Sloan, J.	1
Squires, J.	1
Stapleton, F.	20
Staunton, S.	7
Strahan, J.	1
Sullivan, J.	1
Townsend, A. D.	7
Treacy, R.	5
Touhy, L.	4
Waddock, G.	3
Walsh, D.	5
Walsh, M.	3
Walters, J. R.	14
Ward, S. R.	3
Waters, J.	1
White, J. J.	2
Whelan, G. D.	2
Whelan, R.	3
Williams, S.	**1**
Wilson, M. D.	1

SOUTH AMERICA

COPA AMERICA 2019

▪ *Denotes player sent off.*

GROUP A

Brazil v Bolivia	3-0
Venezuela v Peru	0-0
Bolivia v Peru	1-3
Brazil v Venezuela	0-0
Peru v Brazil	0-5
Bolivia v Venezuela	1-3

Group A Table	P	W	D	L	F	A	GD	Pts
Brazil	3	2	1	0	8	0	8	7
Venezuela	3	1	2	0	3	1	2	5
Peru	3	1	1	1	3	6	–3	4
Bolivia	3	0	0	3	2	9	–7	0

GROUP B

Argentina v Colombia	0-2
Paraguay v Qatar	2-2
Colombia v Qatar	1-0
Argentina v Paraguay	1-1
Qatar v Argentina	0-2
Colombia v Paraguay	1-0

Group B Table	P	W	D	L	F	A	GD	Pts
Colombia	3	3	0	0	4	0	4	9
Argentina	3	1	1	1	3	3	0	4
Paraguay	3	0	2	1	3	4	–1	2
Qatar	3	0	1	2	2	5	–3	1

GROUP C

Uruguay v Ecuador	4-0
Japan v Chile	0-4
Uruguay v Japan	2-2
Ecuador v Chile	1-2
Chile v Uruguay	0-1
Ecuador v Japan	1-1

Group C Table	P	W	D	L	F	A	GD	Pts
Uruguay	3	2	1	0	7	2	5	7
Chile	3	2	0	1	6	2	4	6
Japan	3	0	2	1	3	7	–4	2
Ecuador	3	0	1	2	2	7	–5	1

QUARTER-FINALS

Brazil v Paraguay 0-0
Brazil won 4-3 on penalties.
Venezuela v Argentina 0-2
Colombia v Chile 0-0
Chile won 5-4 on penalties.
Uruguay v Peru 0-0
Peru won 5-4 on penalties.

SEMI-FINALS

Brazil v Argentina 2-0
Chile v Peru 0-3

THIRD PLACE PLAY-OFF

Argentina v Chile 2-1

COPA AMERICA FINAL 2019

Rio de Janeiro, Sunday 7 July 2019

Brazil (2) 3 *(Everton 15, Jesus 45, Richarlison 90 (pen))*

Peru (1) 1 *(Guerrero 44 (pen))*

Brazil: Allison; Alves, Marquinhos, Thiago Silva, Sandro, Arthur, Casemiro, Jesus▪, Countinho (Militao 77), Everton (Allan 90), Firmino (Richarlison 75).
Peru: Gallese; Advincula, Zambrano, Abram, Trauco, Tapia (Gonzales 82), Yotun (Ruidiaz 78), Flores, Cueva, Carrillo (Polo 86), Guerrero.
Referee: Roberto Tobar (Chile)

COPA SUDAMERICANA 2018

SECOND STAGE – FIRST LEG

General Diaz v Millonarios	1-1
Nacional v Botafogo	2-1
Sol de America v Nacional	0-0
Sao Paulo v Colon	0-1
Boston River v Banfield	1-0
Fluminense v Defensor Sporting	2-0
Athletico Paranaense v Penarol	2-0
Deportivo Cali v Bolivar	4-0
LDU Quito v Vasco da Gama	3-1
Caracas v Sport Huancayo	2-0
Deportivo Cuenca v Jorge Wilstermann	2-2
Defensa y Justicia v El Nacional	2-0
Lanus v Junior	1-0
San Lorenzo v Deportes Temuco	3-0
Match awarded 3-0 to San Lorenzo after Deportes Temuco fielded an ineligible player. Original match 1-2.	
Bahia v Cerro	2-0
Rampla Juniors v Santa Fe	0-0

SECOND STAGE – SECOND LEG

		(agg)
Millonarios v General Diaz	4-0	5-1
Botafogo v Nacional	2-0	3-2
Nacional v Sol de America	1-0	1-0
Colon v Sao Paulo	0-1	1-1
Colon won 5-3 on penalties.		
Banfield v Boston River	2-0	2-1
Defensor Sporting v Fluminense	0-1	0-3
Penarol v Athletico Paranaense	1-4	1-6
Bolivar v Deportivo Cali	1-2	1-6
Vasco da Gama v LDU Quito	1-0	2-3
Sport Huancayo v Caracas	3-4	3-6
Jorge Wilstermann v Deportivo Cuenca	2-2	4-4
Deportivo Cuenca won 6-5 on penalties.		
El Nacional v Defensa y Justicia	1-0	1-2
Junior v Lanus	1-0	1-1
Junior won 3-2 on penalties.		
Deportes Temuco v San Lorenzo	1-0	1-3
Cerro v Bahia	1-1	1-3
Santa Fe v Rampla Juniors	2-0	2-0

ROUND OF 16 – FIRST LEG

Santa Fe v Millonarios	0-0
Bahia v Botafogo	2-1
San Lorenzo v Nacional	3-1
Junior v Colon	1-0
Defensa y Justicia v Banfield	2-0
Deportivo Cuenca v Fluminense	0-2
Caracas v Athletico Paranaense	0-2
LDU Quito v Deportivo Cali	1-0

ROUND OF 16 – SECOND LEG

		(agg)
Millonarios v Santa Fe	0-0	0-0
Santa Fe won 5-3 on penalties.		
Botafogo v Bahia	2-1	3-3
Bahia won 5-4 on penalties.		
Nacional v San Lorenzo	2-0	3-3
Nacional won on away goals.		
Colon v Junior	1-1	1-2
Banfield v Defensa y Justicia	0-0	0-2
Fluminense v Deportivo Cuenca	2-0	4-0
Athletico Paranaense v Caracas	2-1	4-1
Deportivo Cali v LDU Quito	1-0	1-1
Deportivo Cali won 3-1 on penalties.		

QUARTER-FINALS – FIRST LEG

Santa Fe v Deportivo Cali	1-1
Bahia v Athletico Paranaense	0-1
Fluminense v Nacional	1-1
Junior v Defensa y Justicia	2-0

QUARTER-FINALS – SECOND LEG

		(agg)
Deportivo Cali v Santa Fe	1-2	2-3
Athletico Paranaense v Bahia	0-1	1-1
Athletico Paranaense won 4-1 on penalties.		
Nacional v Fluminense	0-1	1-2
Defensa y Justicia v Junior	3-1	3-3
Junior won on away goals.		

SEMI-FINALS – FIRST LEG

Santa Fe v Junior	0-2
Athletico Paranaense v Fluminense	2-0

SEMI-FINALS – SECOND LEG

		(agg)
Junior v Santa Fe	1-0	3-0
Fluminense v Athletico Paranaense	0-2	0-4

FINAL – FIRST LEG

Junior v Athletico Paranaense 1-1

FINAL – SECOND LEG

		(agg)
Athletico Paranaense v Junior	1-1	2-2
aet; Athletico Paranaense won 4-3 on penalties.		

RECOPA SUDAMERICANA 2018

FINAL – FIRST LEG
Independiente v Gremio 1-1

FINAL – SECOND LEG *(agg)*
Gremio v Independiente 0-0 1-1
aet; Gremio won 5-4 on penalties.

COPA LIBERTADORES 2018

SECOND STAGE – FIRST LEG
Deportivo Tachira v Santa Fe 2-3
Chapecoense v Nacional 0-1
Oriente Petrolero v Jorge Wilstermann 1-2
Carabobo v Guarani 1-0
Olimpia v Junior 1-0
Universidad de Concepcion v Vasco da Gama 0-4
Banfield v Independiente del Valle 1-1
Santiago Wanderers v Melgar 1-1

SECOND STAGE – SECOND LEG *(agg)*
Santa Fe v Deportivo Tachira 0-0 3-2
Nacional v Chapecoense 1-0 2-0
Jorge Wilstermann v Oriente Petrolero 2-2 4-3
Guarani v Carabobo 6-0 6-1
Junior v Olimpia 3-1 3-2
Vasco da Gama v Universidad de Concepcion 2-0 6-0
Independiente del Valle v Banfield 2-2 3-3
Banfield won on away goals.
Melgar v Santiago Wanderers 0-1 1-2

THIRD STAGE – FIRST LEG
Santiago Wanderers v Santa Fe 1-2
Banfield v Nacional 2-2
Vasco da Gama v Jorge Wilstermann 4-0
Junior v Guarani 1-1

THIRD STAGE – SECOND LEG *(agg)*
Santa Fe v Santiago Wanderers 3-0 5-1
Nacional v Banfield 1-0 3-2
Jorge Wilstermann v Vasco da Gama 4-0 4-4
Vasco da Gama won 3-2 on penalties.
Guarani v Junior 0-0 0-1

GROUP STAGE

GROUP A
Defensor Sporting v Gremio 1-1
Monagas v Cerro Porteno 0-2
Cerro Porteno v Defensor Sporting 2-1
Gremio v Monagas 4-0
Defensor Sporting v Monagas 3-1
Cerro Porteno v Gremio 0-0
Monagas v Defensor Sporting 1-0
Gremio v Cerro Porteno 5-0
Defensor Sporting v Cerro Porteno 0-1
Monagas v Gremio 1-2
Gremio v Defensor Sporting 1-0
Cerro Porteno v Monagas 3-2

Group A Table	P	W	D	L	F	A	GD	Pts
Gremio	6	4	2	0	13	2	11	14
Cerro Porteno	6	4	1	1	8	8	0	13
Defensor Sporting	6	1	1	4	5	7	–2	4
Monagas	6	1	0	5	5	14	–9	3

GROUP B
Colo-Colo v Atletico Nacional 0-1
Delfin v Bolivar 1-1
Bolivar v Colo-Colo 1-1
Atletico Nacional v Delfin 4-0
Colo-Colo v Delfin 0-2
Bolivar v Atletico Nacional 1-0
Atletico Nacional v Bolivar 4-1
Delfin v Colo-Colo 1-2
Delfin v Atletico Nacional 1-0
Colo-Colo v Bolivar 2-0
Bolivar v Delfin 2-1
Atletico Nacional v Colo-Colo 0-0

Group B Table	P	W	D	L	F	A	GD	Pts
Atletico Nacional	6	3	1	2	9	3	6	10
Colo-Colo	6	2	2	2	5	5	0	8
Bolivar	6	2	2	2	6	9	–3	8
Delfin	6	2	1	3	6	9	–3	7

GROUP C
Atletico Tucuman v Libertad 0-2
The Strongest v Penarol 1-0
Libertad v The Strongest 3-0
Penarol v Atletico Tucuman 3-1
The Strongest v Atletico Tucuman 1-2
Libertad v Penarol 2-1
Atletico Tucuman v The Strongest 3-0
Penarol v Libertad 2-0
Atletico Tucuman v Penarol 1-0
The Strongest v Libertad 1-3
Penarol v The Strongest 2-0
Libertad v Atletico Tucuman 0-0

Group C Table	P	W	D	L	F	A	GD	Pts
Libertad	6	4	1	1	10	4	6	13
Atletico Tucuman	6	3	1	2	7	6	1	10
Penarol	6	3	0	3	8	5	3	9
The Strongest	6	1	0	5	3	13	–10	3

GROUP D
Flamengo v River Plate 2-2
Santa Fe v Emelec 1-1
Emelec v Flamengo 1-2
River Plate v Santa Fe 0-0
Flamengo v Santa Fe 1-1
Emelec v River Plate 0-1
Santa Fe v Flamengo 0-0
River Plate v Emelec 2-1
Santa Fe v River Plate 0-1
Flamengo v Emelec 2-0
River Plate v Flamengo 0-0
Emelec v Santa Fe 0-3

Group D Table	P	W	D	L	F	A	GD	Pts
River Plate	6	3	3	0	6	3	3	12
Flamengo	6	2	4	0	7	4	3	10
Santa Fe	6	1	4	1	5	3	2	7
Emelec	6	0	1	5	3	11	–8	1

GROUP E
Racing v Cruzeiro 4-2
Vasco da Gama v Universidad de Chile 0-1
Universidad de Chile v Racing 1-1
Cruzeiro v Vasco da Gama 0-0
Racing v Vasco da Gama 4-0
Universidad de Chile v Cruzeiro 0-0
Cruzeiro v Universidad de Chile 7-0
Vasco da Gama v Racing 1-1
Vasco da Gama v Cruzeiro 0-4
Racing v Universidad de Chile 1-0
Cruzeiro v Racing 2-1
Universidad de Chile v Vasco da Gama 0-2

Group E Table	P	W	D	L	F	A	GD	Pts
Cruzeiro	6	3	2	1	15	5	10	11
Racing	6	3	2	1	12	6	6	11
Vasco da Gama	6	1	2	3	3	10	–7	5
Universidad de Chile	6	1	2	3	2	11	–9	5

GROUP F
Nacional v Estudiantes 0-0
Real Garcilaso v Santos 2-0
Estudiantes v Real Garcilaso 3-0
Santos v Nacional 3-1
Real Garcilaso v Nacional 0-0
Estudiantes v Santos 0-1
Santos v Estudiantes 2-0
Nacional v Real Garcilaso 4-0
Real Garcilaso v Estudiantes 0-0
Nacional v Santos 1-0
Santos v Real Garcilaso 0-0
Estudiantes v Nacional 3-1

Group F Table	P	W	D	L	F	A	GD	Pts
Santos	6	3	1	2	6	4	2	10
Estudiantes	6	2	2	2	6	4	2	8
Nacional	6	2	2	2	7	6	1	8
Real Garcilaso	6	1	3	2	2	7	–5	6

GROUP G

Millonarios v Corinthians	0-0
Deportivo Lara v Independiente	1-0
Corinthians v Deportivo Lara	2-0
Independiente v Millonarios	1-0
Millonarios v Deportivo Lara	4-0
Independiente v Corinthians	0-1
Deportivo Lara v Millonarios	2-1
Corinthians v Independiente	1-2
Deportivo Lara v Corinthians	2-7
Millonarios v Independiente	1-1
Corinthians v Millonarios	0-1
Independiente v Deportivo Lara	2-0

Group G Table	P	W	D	L	F	A	GD	Pts
Corinthians	6	3	1	2	11	5	6	10
Independiente	6	3	1	2	6	4	2	10
Millonarios	6	2	2	2	7	4	3	8
Deportivo Lara	6	2	0	4	5	16	–11	6

GROUP H

Alianza Lima v Boca Juniors	0-0
Junior v Palmeiras	0-3
Palmeiras v Alianza Lima	2-0
Boca Juniors v Junior	1-0
Palmeiras v Boca Juniors	1-1
Alianza Lima v Junior	0-2
Boca Juniors v Palmeiras	0-2
Junior v Alianza Lima	1-0
Junior v Boca Juniors	1-1
Alianza Lima v Palmeiras	1-3
Boca Juniors v Alianza Lima	5-0
Palmeiras v Junior	3-1

Group H Table	P	W	D	L	F	A	GD	Pts
Palmeiras	6	5	1	0	14	3	11	16
Boca Juniors	6	2	3	1	8	4	4	9
Junior	6	2	1	3	5	8	–3	7
Alianza Lima	6	0	1	5	1	13	–12	1

KNOCKOUT STAGE

ROUND OF 16 – FIRST LEG

Racing v River Plate	0-0
Colo-Colo v Corinthians	1-0
Flamengo v Cruzeiro	0-2
Estudiantes v Gremio	2-1
Atletico Tucuman v Atletico Nacional	2-0
Boca Juniors v Libertad	2-0
Cerro Porteno v Palmeiras	0-2
Independiente v Santos	3-0

Independiente awarded 3-0 victory after Santos fielded an ineligible player, original match 0-0.

ROUND OF 16 – SECOND LEG *(agg)*

River Plate v Racing	3-0	3-0
Corinthians v Colo-Colo	2-1	2-2
Colo-Colo won on away goals.		
Cruzeiro v Flamengo	0-1	2-1
Gremio v Estudiantes	2-1	3-3
Gremio won on 5-3 on penalties.		
Atletico Nacional v Atletico Tucuman	1-0	1-2
Libertad v Boca Juniors	2-4	2-6
Palmeiras v Cerro Porteno	0-1	2-1
Santos v Independiente	0-0	0-3

Match abandoned after 81 minutes due to crowd disturbance.

QUARTER-FINALS – FIRST LEG

Independiente v River Plate	0-0
Colo-Colo v Palmeiras	0-2
Boca Juniors v Cruzeiro	2-0
Atletico Tucuman v Gremio	0-2

QUARTER-FINALS – SECOND LEG *(agg)*

River Plate v Independiente	3-1	3-1
Palmeiras v Colo-Colo	2-0	4-0
Cruzeiro v Boca Juniors	1-1	1-3
Gremio v Atletico Tucuman	4-0	6-0

SEMI-FINALS – FIRST LEG

River Plate v Gremio	0-1
Boca Juniors v Palmeiras	2-0

SEMI-FINALS – SECOND LEG *(agg)*

Gremio v River Plate	1-2	2-2
River Plate won on away goals.		
Palmeiras v Boca Juniors	2-2	2-4

FINAL – FIRST LEG

Boca Juniors v River Plate 2-2

FINAL – SECOND LEG

River Plate v Boca Juniors 3-1

aet; River Plate won 5-3 on aggregate.
Second leg played in Madrid.

ASIA

2019 AFC ASIAN CUP

**After extra time.*

GROUP A

United Arab Emirates v Bahrain	1-1
Thailand v India	1-4
Bahrain v Thailand	0-1
India v United Arab Emirates	0-2
United Arab Emirates v Thailand	1-1
India v Bahrain	0-1

Group A Table	P	W	D	L	F	A	GD	Pts
United Arab Emirates	3	1	2	0	4	2	2	5
Thailand	3	1	1	1	3	5	–2	4
Bahrain	3	1	1	1	2	2	0	4
India	3	1	0	2	4	4	0	3

GROUP B

Australia v Jordan	0-1
Syria v Palestine	0-0
Jordan v Syria	2-0
Palestine v Australia	0-3
Australia v Syria	3-2
Palestine v Jordan	0-0

Group B Table	P	W	D	L	F	A	GD	Pts
Jordan	3	2	1	0	3	0	3	7
Australia	3	2	0	1	6	3	3	6
Palestine	3	0	2	1	0	3	–3	2
Syria	3	0	1	2	2	5	–3	1

GROUP C

China PR v Kyrgyzstan	2-1
Korea Republic v Philippines	1-0
Philippines v China PR	0-3
Kyrgyzstan v Korea Republic	0-1
Korea Republic v China PR	2-0
Kyrgyzstan v Philippines	3-1

Group C Table	P	W	D	L	F	A	GD	Pts
Korea Republic	3	3	0	0	4	0	4	9
China PR	3	2	0	1	5	3	2	6
Kyrgyzstan	3	1	0	2	4	4	0	3
Philippines	3	0	0	3	1	7	–6	0

GROUP D

Iran v Yemen	5-0
Iraq v Vietnam	3-2
Vietnam v Iran	0-2
Yemen v Iraq	0-3
Vietnam v Yemen	2-0
Iran v Iraq	0-0

Group D Table	P	W	D	L	F	A	GD	Pts
Iran	3	2	1	0	7	0	7	7
Iraq	3	2	1	0	6	2	4	7
Vietnam	3	1	0	2	4	5	–1	3
Yemen	3	0	0	3	0	10	–10	0

GROUP E
Saudi Arabia v Korea DPR 4-0
Qatar v Lebanon 2-0
Lebanon v Saudi Arabia 0-2
Korea DPR v Qatar 0-6
Saudi Arabia v Qatar 0-2
Lebanon v Korea DPR 4-1

Group E Table	P	W	D	L	F	A	GD	Pts
Qatar	3	3	0	0	10	0	10	9
Saudi Arabia	3	2	0	1	6	2	4	6
Lebanon	3	1	0	2	4	5	–1	3
Korea DPR	3	0	0	3	1	14	–13	0

GROUP F
Japan v Turkmenistan 3-2
Uzbekistan v Oman 2-1
Oman v Japan 0-1
Turkmenistan v Uzbekistan 0-4
Oman v Turkmenistan 3-1
Japan v Uzbekistan 2-1

Group F Table	P	W	D	L	F	A	GD	Pts
Japan	3	3	0	0	6	3	3	9
Uzbekistan	3	2	0	1	7	3	4	6
Oman	3	1	0	2	4	4	0	3
Turkmenistan	3	0	0	3	3	10	–7	0

ROUND OF 16
Jordan v Vietnam 1-1*
Vietnam won 4-2 on penalties.
Thailand v China PR 1-2
Iran v Oman 2-0
Japan v Saudi Arabia 1-0
Australia v Uzbekistan 0-0*
Australia won 4-2 on penalties.
United Arab Emirates v Kyrgyzstan 3-2*
Korea Republic v Bahrain 2-1*
Qatar v Iraq 1-0

QUARTER-FINALS
Vietnam v Japan 0-1
China PR v Iran 0-3
Korea Republic v Qatar 0-1
United Arab Emirates v Australia 1-0

SEMI-FINALS
Iran v Japan 0-3
Qatar v United Arab Emirates 4-0

ASIAN CUP 2019 FINAL
Abu Dhabi, Friday 1 February 2019
Japan (0) 1 *(Minamino 69)*
Qatar (2) 3 *(Ali 12, Hatem 27, Afif 83 (pen))* 36,776
Japan: Gonda; Sakai, Tomiyasu, Yoshida, Nagatomo, Haraguchi (Muto 62), Shibasaki, Shiotani (Ito 84), Doan, Osako, Minamino (Inui 89).
Qatar: Al Sheeb; Ro-Ro, Al-Rawl, Khoukhi (Al-Hajri 61), Salman, Hassan, Al-Haydos (Boudiaf 74), Hatem, Madibo, Afif, Ali (Alaaeldin 90).
Referee: Ravshan Irmatov (Uzbekistan).

NORTH AMERICA

MAJOR LEAGUE SOCCER 2018

EASTERN CONFERENCE

	P	W	D	L	F	A	GD	Pts
New York Red Bulls	34	22	5	7	62	33	29	71
Atlanta United	34	21	6	7	70	44	26	69
New York City	34	16	8	10	59	45	14	56
DC United	34	14	9	11	60	50	10	51
Columbus Crew	34	14	9	11	43	45	–2	51
Philadelphia Union	34	15	5	14	49	50	–1	50
Montreal Impact	34	14	4	16	47	53	–6	46
NE Revolution	34	10	11	13	49	55	–6	41
Toronto	34	10	6	18	59	64	–5	36
Chicago Fire	34	8	8	18	48	61	–13	32
Orlando City	34	8	4	22	43	74	–31	28

WESTERN CONFERENCE

	P	W	D	L	F	A	GD	Pts
Sporting Kansas City	34	18	8	8	65	40	25	62
Seattle Sounders	34	18	5	11	52	37	15	59
Los Angeles	34	16	9	9	68	52	16	57
FC Dallas	34	16	9	9	52	44	8	57
Portland Timbers	34	15	9	10	54	48	6	54
Real Salt Lake	34	14	7	13	55	58	–3	49
LA Galaxy	34	13	9	12	66	64	2	48
Vancouver Whitecaps	34	13	8	13	54	67	–13	47
Houston Dynamo	34	10	8	16	58	58	0	38
Minnesota United	34	11	3	20	49	71	–22	36
Colorado Rapids	34	8	7	19	36	63	–27	31
San Jose Earthquakes	34	4	9	21	49	71	–22	21

EASTERN KNOCKOUT ROUND
New York City v Philadephia Union 3-1
DC United v Columbus Crew 2-2
aet; Columbus Crew won 3-1 on penalties.

WESTERN KNOCKOUT ROUND
Los Angeles v Real Salt Lake 2-3
FC Dallas v Portland Timbers 1-2

EASTERN SEMI-FINALS – FIRST LEG
Columbus Crew v New York Red Bulls 1-0
New York City v Atlanta United 0-1

EASTERN SEMI-FINALS – SECOND LEG *(agg)*
New York Red Bulls v Columbus Crew 3-0 3-1
Atlanta United v New York City 3-1 4-1

WESTERN SEMI-FINALS – FIRST LEG
Real Salt Lake v Sporting Kansas City 1-1
Portland Timbers v Seattle Sounders 2-1

WESTERN SEMI-FINALS – SECOND LEG *(agg)*
Sporting Kansas City v Real Salt Lake 4-2 5-3
Seattle Sounders v Portland Timbers 3-2 4-4
aet; Portland Timbers won 4-2 on penalties.

EASTERN CHAMPIONSHIP – FIRST LEG
Atlanta United v New York Red Bulls 3-0

EASTERN CHAMPIONSHIP – SECOND LEG *(agg)*
New York Red Bulls v Atlanta United 1-0 1-3

WESTERN CHAMPIONSHIP – FIRST LEG
Portland Timbers v Sporting Kansas City 0-0

WESTERN CHAMPIONSHIP – SECOND LEG *(agg)*
Sporting Kansas City v Portland Timbers 2-3 2-3

MLS CUP FINAL 2018
Atlanta, Saturday 8 December 2018
Atlanta United (1) 2 *(Martinez 39, Escobar 54)*
Portland Timbers (0) 0 73,019
Atlanta United: Guzan; Escobar, Larentowicz, Parkhurst, Gonzalez Pirez, Garza (McCann 90), Nagbe, Remedi, Gressel, Martinez (Villalba 76), Almiron (Barco 90).
Portland Timbers: Attinella; Valentin, Mabiala, Ridgewell, Villafana, Chara, Guzman (Powell 82), Polo (Asprilla 68), Valeri, Blanco, Ebobisse (Melano 59).
Referee: Alan Kelly.

AFRICA

2018–19 TOTAL CAF CHAMPIONS LEAGUE

FIRST ROUND – FIRST LEG

Saint George v KCCA	0-0
Zanaco v Mbabane Swallows	1-2
Wydad Casablanca v Williamsville AC	7-2
Aduana Stars v ES Setif	1-0
Al-Ahly v CF Mounana	4-0
MFM v MC Alger	2-1
Horoya v Generation Foot	2-1
Young Africans v Township Rollers	1-2
Gor Mahia v Esperance de Tunis	0-0
Etoile du Sahel v Plateau United	4-2
AS Togo-Port v Al-Hilal	2-0
ZESCO United v ASEC Mimosas	0-1
TP Mazembe v UD Songo	4-0
Difaa El Jadidi v AS Vita Club	1-0
1° de Agosto v Bidvest Wits	1-0
Rayon Sports v Mamelodi Sundowns	0-0

FIRST ROUND – SECOND LEG

		(agg)
KCCA v Saint George	1-0	1-0
Mbabane Swallows v Zanaco	1-0	3-1
Williamsville AC v Wydad Casablanca	2-0	4-7
ES Setif v Aduana Stars	4-0	4-1
CF Mounana v Al-Ahly	1-3	1-7
MC Alger v MFM	6-0	7-2
Generation Foot v Horoya	0-2	1-4
Township Rollers v Young Africans	0-0	2-1
Esperance de Tunis v Gor Mahia	1-0	1-0
Plateau United v Etoile du Sahel	1-0	3-4
Al-Hilal v AS Togo-Port	3-1	3-3
AS Togo-Port won on away goals		
ASEC Mimosas v ZESCO United	1-2	2-2
ZESCO United won on away goals		
UD Songo v TP Mazembe	3-0	3-4
AS Vita Club v Difaa El Jadidi	2-2	2-3
Bidvest Wits v 1° de Agosto	1-0	1-1
1° de Agosto won 3-2 on penalties		
Mamelodi Sundowns v Rayon Sports	2-0	2-0

GROUP STAGE

GROUP A

Al-Ahly v Esperance de Tunis	0-0
Township Rollers v KCCA	1-0
KCCA v Al-Ahly	2-0
Esperance de Tunis v Township Rollers	4-1
Esperance de Tunis v KCCA	3-2
Al-Ahly v Township Rollers	3-0
KCCA v Esperance de Tunis	0-1
Township Rollers v Al-Ahly	0-1
Esperance de Tunis v Al-Ahly	0-1
KCCA v Township Rollers	1-0
Al-Ahly v KCCA	4-3
Township Rollers v Esperance de Tunis	0-0

Group A	P	W	D	L	F	A	GD	Pts
Al-Ahly	6	4	1	1	9	5	4	13
Esperance de Tunis	6	3	2	1	8	4	4	11
KCCA	6	2	0	4	8	9	–1	6
Township Rollers	6	1	1	4	2	9	–7	4

GROUP B

MC Alger v Difaa El Jadidi	1-1
TP Mazembe v ES Setif	4-1
Difaa El Jadidi v TP Mazembe	0-2
ES Setif v MC Alger	0-1
TP Mazembe v MC Alger	1-0
ES Setif v Difaa El Jadidi	2-1
Difaa El Jadidi v ES Setif	1-1
MC Alger v TP Mazembe	1-1
ES Setif v TP Mazembe	1-1
Difaa El Jadidi v MC Alger	2-0
TP Mazembe v Difaa El Jadidi	1-1
MC Alger v ES Setif	1-2

Group B	P	W	D	L	F	A	GD	Pts
TP Mazembe	6	3	3	0	10	4	6	12
ES Setif	6	2	2	2	7	9	–2	8
Difaa El Jadidi	6	1	3	2	6	7	–1	6
MC Alger	6	1	2	3	4	7	–3	5

GROUP C

AS Togo-Port v Horoya	1-2
Mamelodi Sundowns v Wydad Casablanca	1-1
Wydad Casablanca v AS Togo-Port	3-0
Horoya v Mamelodi Sundowns	2-2
AS Togo-Port v Mamelodi Sundowns	1-0
Horoya v Wydad Casablanca	1-1
Mamelodi Sundowns v AS Togo-Port	2-1
Wydad Casablanca v Horoya	2-0
Horoya v AS Togo-Port	2-1
Wydad Casablanca v Mamelodi Sundowns	1-0
AS Togo-Port v Wydad Casablanca	0-0
Mamelodi Sundowns v Horoya	0-0

Group C	P	W	D	L	F	A	GD	Pts
Wydad Casablanca	6	3	3	0	8	2	6	12
Horoya	6	2	3	1	7	7	0	9
Mamelodi Sundowns	6	1	3	2	5	6	–1	6
AS Togo-Port	6	1	1	4	4	9	–5	4

GROUP D

ZESCO United v Mbabane Swallows	1-1
1° de Agosto v Etoile du Sahel	1-1
Mbabane Swallows v 1° de Agosto	1-0
Etoile du Sahel v ZESCO United	2-1
Mbabane Swallows v Etoile du Sahel	0-3
ZESCO United v 1° de Agosto	0-0
1° de Agosto v ZESCO United	2-1
Etoile du Sahel v Mbabane Swallows	2-0
Mbabane Swallows v ZESCO United	0-3
Etoile du Sahel v 1° de Agosto	1-1
ZESCO United v Etoile du Sahel	1-1
1° de Agosto v Mbabane Swallows	2-1

Group D	P	W	D	L	F	A	GD	Pts
Etoile du Sahel	6	3	3	0	10	4	6	12
1° de Agosto	6	2	3	1	6	5	1	9
ZESCO United	6	1	3	2	7	6	1	6
Mbabane Swallows	6	1	1	4	3	11	–8	4

QUARTER-FINALS – FIRST LEG

1° de Agosto v TP Mazembe	0-0
Esperance de Tunis v Etoile du Sahel	2-1
ES Setif v Wydad Casablanca	1-0
Horoya v Al-Ahly	0-0

QUARTER-FINALS – SECOND LEG

		(agg)
TP Mazembe v 1° de Agosto	1-1	1-1
1° de Agosto won on away goals		
Etoile du Sahel v Esperance de Tunis	0-1	1-3
Wydad Casablanca v ES Setif	0-0	0-1
Al-Ahly v Horoya	4-0	4-0

SEMI-FINALS – FIRST LEG

Al-Ahly v ES Setif	2-0
1° de Agosto v Esperance de Tunis	1-0

SEMI-FINALS – SECOND LEG

		(agg)
ES Setif v Al-Ahly	2-1	2-3
Esperance de Tunis v 1° de Agosto	4-2	4-3

FINAL – FIRST LEG

Al-Ahly v Esperance de Tunis	3-1

FINAL – SECOND LEG

Esperance de Tunis v Al-Ahly	3-0
Esperance de Tunis won 4-3 on aggregate	

UEFA YOUTH LEAGUE 2018–19

CHAMPIONS LEAGUE PATH

GROUP A
Monaco v Atletico Madrid 0-2
Club Brugge v Borussia Dortmund 1-1
Atletico Madrid v Club Brugge 1-2
Borussia Dortmund v Monaco 0-2
Club Brugge v Monaco 2-3
Borussia Dortmund v Atletico Madrid 3-4
Monaco v Club Brugge 3-1
Atletico Madrid v Borussia Dortmund 4-0
Atletico Madrid v Monaco 3-0
Borussia Dortmund v Club Brugge 2-1
Monaco v Borussia Dortmund 1-1
Club Brugge v Atletico Madrid 3-1

Group A Table	P	W	D	L	F	A	GD	Pts
Atletico Madrid	6	4	0	2	15	8	7	12
Monaco	6	3	1	2	9	9	0	10
Club Brugge	6	2	1	3	10	11	−1	7
Borussia Dortmund	6	1	2	3	7	13	−6	5

GROUP B
Inter Milan v Tottenham H 1-1
Barcelona v PSV Eindhoven 2-1
PSV Eindhoven v Inter Milan 2-1
Tottenham H v Barcelona 1-1
PSV Eindhoven v Tottenham H 2-2
Barcelona v Inter Milan 2-1
Tottenham H v PSV Eindhoven 2-0
Inter Milan v Barcelona 0-2
Tottenham H v Inter Milan 2-4
PSV Eindhoven v Barcelona 1-1
Inter Milan v PSV Eindhoven 3-0
Barcelona v Tottenham H 0-2

Group B Table	P	W	D	L	F	A	GD	Pts
Barcelona	6	3	2	1	8	6	2	11
Tottenham H	6	2	3	1	10	8	2	9
Inter Milan	6	2	1	3	10	9	1	7
PSV Eindhoven	6	1	2	3	6	11	−5	5

GROUP C
Crvena Zvezda v Napoli 1-1
Liverpool v Paris Saint-Germain 5-2
Paris Saint-Germain v Crvena Zvezda 2-1
Napoli v Liverpool 1-1
Liverpool v Crvena Zvezda 2-1
Paris Saint-Germain v Napoli 0-0
Napoli v Paris Saint-Germain 2-5
Crvena Zvezda Zvezda v Liverpool 0-2
Napoli v Crvena Zvezda 5-3
Paris Saint-Germain v Liverpool 3-2
Liverpool v Napoli 5-0
Crvena Zvezda v Paris Saint-Germain 0-1

Group C Table	P	W	D	L	F	A	GD	Pts
Liverpool	6	4	1	1	17	7	10	13
Paris Saint-Germain	6	4	1	1	13	10	3	13
Napoli	6	1	3	2	9	15	−6	6
Crvena Zvezda	6	0	1	5	6	13	−7	1

GROUP D
Schalke 04 v Porto 0-3
Galatasaray v Lokomotiv Moscow 0-1
Lokomotiv Moscow v Schalke 04 0-0
Porto v Galatasaray 2-2
Lokomotiv Moscow v Porto 2-1
Galatasaray v Schalke 04 3-0
Porto v Lokomotiv Moscow 2-1
Schalke 04 v Galatasaray 1-2
Lokomotiv Moscow v Galatasaray 0-1
Porto v Schalke 04 3-0
Galatasaray v Porto 0-2
Schalke 04 v Lokomotiv Moscow 1-4

Group D Table	P	W	D	L	F	A	GD	Pts
Porto	6	4	1	1	13	5	8	13
Lokomotiv Moscow	6	3	1	2	8	5	3	10
Galatasaray	6	3	1	2	8	6	2	10
Schalke 04	6	0	1	5	2	15	−13	1

GROUP E
Benfica v Bayern Munich 3-0
Ajax v AEK Athens 6-0
Bayern Munich v Ajax 2-2
AEK Athens v Benfica 1-3
Ajax v Benfica 3-0
AEK Athens v Bayern Munich 0-4
Bayern Munich v AEK Athens 2-0
Benfica v Ajax 3-3
AEK Athens v Ajax 1-8
Bayern Munich v Benfica 2-2
Benfica v AEK Athens 3-0
Ajax v Bayern Munich 1-2

Group E Table	P	W	D	L	F	A	GD	Pts
Ajax	6	3	2	1	23	8	15	11
Benfica	6	3	2	1	14	9	5	11
Bayern Munich	6	3	2	1	12	8	4	11
AEK Athens	6	0	0	6	2	26	−24	0

GROUP F
Shakhtar Donetsk v Hoffenheim 1-2
Manchester C v Lyon 1-4
Hoffenheim v Manchester C 5-2
Lyon v Shakhtar Donetsk 2-0
Shakhtar Donetsk v Manchester C 1-1
Hoffenheim v Lyon 3-1
Lyon v Hoffenheim 3-3
Manchester C v Shakhtar Donetsk 4-1
Lyon v Manchester C 2-0
Hoffenheim v Shakhtar Donetsk 1-1
Shakhtar Donetsk v Lyon 1-1
Manchester C v Hoffenheim 2-1

Group F Table	P	W	D	L	F	A	GD	Pts
Hoffenheim	6	3	2	1	15	10	5	11
Lyon	6	3	2	1	13	8	5	11
Manchester C	6	2	1	3	10	14	−4	7
Shakhtar Donetsk	6	0	3	3	5	11	−6	3

GROUP G
Viktoria Plzen v CSKA Moscow 1-1
Real Madrid v Roma 3-1
CSKA Moscow v Real Madrid 1-4
Roma v Viktoria Plzen 3-4
Roma v CSKA Moscow 3-1
Real Madrid v Viktoria Plzen 3-2
CSKA Moscow v Roma 1-2
Viktoria Plzen v Real Madrid 1-2
CSKA Moscow v Viktoria Plzen 1-1
Roma v Real Madrid 1-6
Viktoria Plzen v Roma 2-4
Real Madrid v CSKA Moscow 2-1

Group G Table	P	W	D	L	F	A	GD	Pts
Real Madrid	6	6	0	0	20	7	13	18
Roma	6	3	0	3	14	17	−3	9
Viktoria Plzen	6	1	2	3	11	14	−3	5
CSKA Moscow	6	0	2	4	6	13	−7	2

GROUP H
Valencia v Juventus 0-1
Young Boys v Manchester U 1-2
Juventus v Young Boys 2-1
Manchester U v Valencia 4-0
Young Boys v Valencia 3-3
Manchester U v Juventus 4-1
Valencia v Young Boys 0-1
Juventus v Manchester U 2-2
Manchester U v Young Boys 6-2
Juventus v Valencia 3-0
Valencia v Manchester U 1-2
Young Boys v Juventus 4-2

Group H Table	P	W	D	L	F	A	GD	Pts
Manchester U	6	5	1	0	20	7	13	16
Juventus	6	3	1	2	11	11	0	10
Young Boys	6	2	1	3	12	15	−3	7
Valencia	6	0	1	5	4	14	−10	1

DOMESTIC CHAMPIONS PATH

FIRST ROUND – FIRST LEG

Altinordu v HJK Helsinki	1-1
Zilina v Montpellier	1-5
FC Basel v Hamilton Academical	2-2
Dynamo Kyiv v Septemvri Sofia	1-0
KR Reykjavik v Elfsborg	1-2
Anderlecht v Admira Wacker Modling	0-0
Midtjylland v Bohemians	2-1
Chelsea v Molde	10-1
AEL Limassol v PAOK	1-2
Sigma Olomouc v Maribor	4-1
Gabala v Sheriff Tiraspol	1-1
Hertha Berlin v Lech Poznan	2-0
Astana v Vllaznia	3-1
Anzhi Makhachkala v Maccabi Tel Aviv	3-2
Viitorul Constanta v Dinamo Zagreb	0-1
Minsk v Illes Akademia	1-0

FIRST ROUND – SECOND LEG

		(agg)
HJK Helsinki v Altinordu	1-2	2-3
Montpellier v Zilina	2-0	7-1
Hamilton Academical v FC Basel	2-2	4-4
Hamilton Academicals won 3-2 on penalties.		
Septemvri Sofia v Dynamo Kyiv	1-5	1-6
Elfsborg v KR Reykjavik	1-0	3-1
Admira Wacker Modling v Anderlecht	1-1	1-1
Anderlecht won on away goals.		
Bohemians v Midtjylland	1-2	2-4
Molde v Chelsea	0-4	1-14
PAOK v AEL Limassol	2-0	4-1
Maribor v Sigma Olomouc	2-3	3-7
Sheriff Tiraspol v Gabala	1-3	2-4
Lech Poznan v Hertha Berlin	2-3	2-5
Vllaznia v Astana	0-4	1-7
Maccabi Tel Aviv v Anzhi Makhachkala	3-0	5-3
Dinamo Zagreb v Viitorul Constanta	2-0	3-0
Illes Akademia v Minsk	3-3	3-4

SECOND ROUND – FIRST LEG

Anderlecht v Dynamo Kyiv	1-1
Midtjylland v Hamilton Academical	2-0
Altinordu v Montpellier	2-4
Elfsborg v Chelsea	0-3
PAOK v Minsk	2-1
Gabala v Hertha Berlin	1-3
Astana v Dinamo Zagreb	1-1
Sigma Olomouc v Maccabi Tel Aviv	1-1

SECOND ROUND – SECOND LEG

		(agg)
Dynamo Kyiv v Anderlecht	2-1	3-2
Hamilton Academical v Midtjylland	1-2	1-4
Montpellier v Altinordu	1-0	5-2
Chelsea v Elfsborg	6-0	9-0
Minsk v PAOK	0-1	1-3
Hertha Berlin v Gabala	1-0	4-1
Dinamo Zagreb v Astana	3-1	4-2
Maccabi Tel Aviv v Sigma Olomouc	2-2	3-3
Sigma Olomouc won on away goals.		

PLAY-OFFS

Dinamo Zagreb v Lokomotiv Moscow	1-1
Dinamo Zagreb won 5-4 on penalties.	
Hertha Berlin v Paris Saint-Germain	2-1
Chelsea v Monaco	3-1
PAOK v Tottenham H	0-1
Dynamo Kyiv v Juventus	3-0
Midtjylland v Roma	1-1
Midtylland won 4-3 on penalties.	
Sigma Olomouc v Lyon	0-2
Montpellier v Benfica	2-1

KNOCKOUT STAGE

ROUND OF 16

Atletico Madrid v Real Madrid	1-2
Dinamo Zagreb v Liverpool	1-1
Dinamo Zagreb won 4-3 on penalties.	
Hoffenheim v Dynamo Kyiv	0-0
Hoffenheim won 4-3 on penalties.	
Lyon v Ajax	2-2
Lyon won 6-5 on penalties.	
Barcelona v Hertha Berlin	3-0
Porto v Tottenham H	2-0
Midtjylland v Manchester U	3-1
Chelsea v Montpellier	2-1

QUARTER-FINALS

Porto v Midtyjlland	3-0
Barcelona v Lyon	3-2
Chelsea v Dinamo Zagreb	2-2
Chelsea won 4-2 on penalties.	
Hoffenheim v Real Madrid	4-2

SEMI-FINALS

Hoffenheim v Porto	0-3
Barcelona v Chelsea	3-3
Chelsea won 5-4 on penalties.	

UEFA YOUTH LEAGUE FINAL 2018–2019

Nyon, Monday 29 April 2019

Porto (1) 3 *(Vieira 17, Queiros 55, Sousa 75)*

Chelsea (0) 1 *(Redan 53)* 227

Porto: Costa; Esteves, Queiros, Leite, Lopes, Ndiaye, Torres, Vieira (Ferreira 71), Fabio Silva (Takang 89), Baro (Borges 89), Mario (Sousa 63).
Chelsea: Ziger; Lamptey (Brown 76), Colley, Guehi, Maatsen, McEachran, Gallagher (Anjorin 76), Gilmour, Redan, McCormick, Familio-Castillo.
Referee: Francois Letexier (France).

ENGLAND C 2018–19

Dublin, Sunday 27 May 2018

Republic of Ireland Amateurs (1) 4 *(Stritch 15, Murphy 46, Hayes 81, 86)*

England C (1) 2 *(Pennell 39, Walker 58)*

Republic of Ireland Amateurs: O'Connell (Power 73); McCormac (Albor 78), McCarthy, Horgan (Fitzgerald 59), Murray, Hyland, Buckley (Doherty 66), Walsh (Foley 59), Stritch (Clarke 66), Murphy (Hayes 59), Daly-Butz.
England C: McHale (Van der Vliet 46); Ling (Brown 56), Staunton, Horsfall, Pennell, Miley, Adams (Wheatley 76), Wright (Crawford 67), Koroma (Walker 46), Okenabirhie, Marsh-Brown.

Leyton Orient, Wednesday 10 October 2018

England C (0) 1 *(Pavey 65 (pen))*

Estonia U23 (0) 0 635

England C: Killip (Huddart 51); Tinkler, Ekpiteta, Maguire (Pennell 87), Binnom-Williams (Millish 51), Croasdale, Pavey (Willoughby 75), Walker (Taylor 72), Fonguck, Hardy, Williams.

Salford, Tuesday 19 March 2019

England C (1) 2 *(Peate 25(og), Willoughby 53)*

Wales C (1) 2 *(McLaggon 31, Roscoe 63)* 709

England C: Killip (Huddart 83); Trotman, Maguire, Mellish, Jones (Happe 53), Taylor, James (Rowley 70), Olley, Williams (White 49), Hardy, Willoughby (Goodship 81).
Wales C: Ramsay; Rees, Lewis, Peate, Hugh (Robert 90), Edwards, Venables, Green (Patten 77, Jones (Roscow 57), McLaggon (Thomas 68), Evans (Brookwell 57).

Tallin, Wednesday 5 June 2019

Estonia U23C (0) 2 *(Poom 88, Usta 90)*

England C (0) 0

England C: Kilip (Huddart 70); Trottman, Longe-King, Dickenson, Brown, Croasdale, White, Hardy (Galliford 55), Mason-Clark (Lowe 64), Willoughby, Rowley (Fonguck 59).

UEFA UNDER-19 CHAMPIONSHIP 2017–18

FINALS IN FINLAND

GROUP A
Norway v Portugal 1-3
Finland v Italy 0-1
Finland v Norway 2-3
Portugal v Italy 2-3
Portugal v Finland 3-0
Italy v Norway 1-1

Group A Table	P	W	D	L	F	A	GD	Pts
Italy	3	2	1	0	5	3	2	7
Portugal	3	2	0	1	8	4	4	6
Norway	3	1	1	1	5	6	–1	4
Finland	3	0	0	3	2	7	–5	0

Italy and Portugal qualify for 2019 World Cup.

GROUP B
Turkey v England 2-3
France v Ukraine 1-2
Ukraine v England 1-1
Turkey v France 0-5
Ukraine v Turkey 1-0
England v France 0-5

Group B Table	P	W	D	L	F	A	GD	Pts
Ukraine	3	2	1	0	4	2	2	7
France	3	2	0	1	11	2	9	6
England	3	1	1	1	4	8	–4	4
Turkey	3	0	0	3	2	9	–7	0

Ukraine and France qualify for 2019 World Cup.

SEMI-FINAL
Italy v France 2-0
Ukraine v Portugal 0-5

WORLD CUP PLAY-OFF
Norway v England 3-0
Norway qualify for 2019 World Cup.

FINAL
Italy v Portugal 3-4
aet.

UEFA UNDER-19 CHAMPIONSHIP 2018–19

QUALIFYING ROUND

GROUP 1 (GEORGIA)
Azerbaijan v Israel 1-4
Georgia v Liechtenstein 7-0
Israel v Liechtenstein 2-1
Georgia v Azerbaijan 1-2
Liechtenstein v Azerbaijan 0-3
Israel v Georgia 1-1

Group 1 Table	P	W	D	L	F	A	GD	Pts
Israel	3	2	1	0	7	3	4	7
Azerbaijan	3	2	0	1	6	5	1	6
Georgia	3	1	1	1	9	3	6	4
Liechtenstein	3	0	0	3	1	12	–11	0

GROUP 2 (ESTONIA)
Finland v Denmark 0-0
Italy v Estonia 3-0
Denmark v Estonia 3-0
Italy v Finland 3-0
Estonia v Finland 0-0
Denmark v Italy 0-1

Group 2 Table	P	W	D	L	F	A	GD	Pts
Italy	3	3	0	0	7	0	7	9
Denmark	3	1	1	1	3	1	2	4
Finland	3	0	2	1	0	3	–3	2
Estonia	3	0	1	2	0	6	–6	1

GROUP 3 (CZECH REPUBLIC)
North Macedonia v Croatia 1-1
Czech Republic v Luxembourg 2-1
Croatia v Luxembourg 2-1
Czech Republic v North Macedonia 2-1
Luxembourg v North Macedonia 0-2
Croatia v Czech Republic 2-2

Group 3 Table	P	W	D	L	F	A	GD	Pts
Czech Republic	3	2	1	0	6	4	2	7
Croatia	3	1	2	0	5	4	1	5
North Macedonia	3	1	1	1	4	3	1	4
Luxembourg	3	0	0	3	2	6	–4	0

GROUP 4 (WALES)
Sweden v San Marino 2-1
Wales v Scotland 1-2
Scotland v San Marino 5-0
Sweden v Wales 1-2
San Marino v Wales 0-2
Scotland v Sweden 2-2

Group 4 Table	P	W	D	L	F	A	GD	Pts
Scotland	3	2	1	0	9	3	6	7
Wales	3	2	0	1	5	3	2	6
Sweden	3	1	1	1	5	5	0	4
San Marino	3	0	0	3	1	9	–8	0

GROUP 5 (TURKEY)
England v Moldova 4-0
Iceland v Turkey 2-1
England v Iceland 3-1
Turkey v Moldova 3-0
Moldova v Iceland 1-1
Turkey v England 1-0

Group 5 Table	P	W	D	L	F	A	GD	Pts
Turkey	3	2	0	1	5	2	3	6
England	3	2	0	1	7	2	5	6
Iceland	3	1	1	1	4	5	–1	4
Moldova	3	0	1	2	1	8	–7	1

GROUP 6 (MALTA)
France v Malta 1-0
Lithuania v Belgium 0-5
France v Lithuania 7-0
Belgium v Malta 1-1
Belgium v France 2-2
Malta v Lithuania 2-1

Group 6 Table	P	W	D	L	F	A	GD	Pts
France	3	2	1	0	10	2	8	7
Belgium	3	1	2	0	8	3	5	5
Malta	3	1	1	1	3	3	0	4
Lithuania	3	0	0	3	1	14	–13	0

GROUP 7 (HUNGARY)
Austria v Kosovo 0-0
Slovenia v Hungary 1-2
Austria v Slovenia 2-2
Hungary v Kosovo 0-0
Kosovo v Slovenia 1-4
Hungary v Austria 2-1

Group 7 Table	P	W	D	L	F	A	GD	Pts
Hungary	3	2	1	0	4	2	2	7
Slovenia	3	1	1	1	7	5	2	4
Austria	3	0	2	1	3	4	–1	2
Kosovo	3	0	2	1	1	4	–3	2

GROUP 8 (ALBANIA)
Norway v Slovakia 1-2
Ukraine v Albania 1-0
Slovakia v Albania 3-0
Ukraine v Norway 1-2
Albania v Norway 0-1
Slovakia v Ukraine 1-4

Group 8 Table	P	W	D	L	F	A	GD	Pts
Ukraine	3	2	0	1	6	3	3	6
Norway	3	2	0	1	4	3	1	6
Slovakia	3	2	0	1	6	5	1	6
Albania	3	0	0	3	0	5	–5	0

GROUP 9 (NORTHERN IRELAND)
Serbia v Kazakhstan 2-2
Northern Ireland v Poland 0-0
Poland v Kazakhstan 4-0
Serbia v Northern Ireland 3-1
Kazakhstan v Northern Ireland 2-3
Poland v Serbia 1-4

Group 9 Table	P	W	D	L	F	A	GD	Pts
Serbia	3	2	1	0	9	4	5	7
Poland	3	1	1	1	5	4	1	4
Northern Ireland	3	1	1	1	4	5	–1	4
Kazakhstan	3	0	1	2	4	9	–5	1

GROUP 10 (REPUBLIC OF IRELAND)
Bosnia-Herzegovina v Republic of Ireland 1-3
Netherlands v Faroe Islands 5-0
Republic of Ireland v Faroe Islands 3-0
Netherlands v Bosnia-Herzegovina 6-0
Faroe Islands v Bosnia-Herzegovina 1-2
Republic of Ireland v Netherlands 2-1

Group 10 Table	P	W	D	L	F	A	GD	Pts
Republic of Ireland	3	3	0	0	8	2	6	9
Netherlands	3	2	0	1	12	2	10	6
Bosnia-Herzegovina	3	1	0	2	3	10	–7	3
Faroe Islands	3	0	0	3	1	10	–9	0

GROUP 11 (CYPRUS)
Cyprus v Montenegro 0-0
Russia v Latvia 1-1
Montenegro v Latvia 1-2
Russia v Cyprus 2-0
Latvia v Cyprus 0-1
Montenegro v Russia 0-2

Group 11 Table	P	W	D	L	F	A	GD	Pts
Russia	3	2	1	0	5	1	4	7
Cyprus	3	1	1	1	1	2	–1	4
Latvia	3	1	1	1	3	3	0	4
Montenegro	3	0	1	2	1	4	–3	1

GROUP 12 (SWITZERLAND)
Spain v Andorra 5-0
Belarus v Switzerland 0-1
Spain v Belarus 3-0
Switzerland v Andorra 2-0
Andorra v Belarus 0-2
Switzerland v Spain 1-2

Group 12 Table	P	W	D	L	F	A	GD	Pts
Spain	3	3	0	0	10	1	9	9
Switzerland	3	2	0	1	4	2	2	6
Belarus	3	1	0	2	2	4	–2	3
Andorra	3	0	0	3	0	9	–9	0

GROUP 13 (BULGARIA)
Romania v Bulgaria 1-1
Greece v Gibraltar 4-0
Bulgaria v Gibraltar 6-0
Greece v Romania 5-3
Gibraltar v Romania 0-8
Bulgaria v Greece 0-3

Group 13 Table	P	W	D	L	F	A	GD	Pts
Greece	3	3	0	0	12	3	9	9
Romania	3	1	1	1	12	6	6	4
Bulgaria	3	1	1	1	7	4	3	4
Gibraltar	3	0	0	3	0	18	–18	0

ELITE ROUND

GROUP 1 (RUSSIA)
Republic of Ireland v Romania 5-0
Azerbaijan v Russia 0-0
Republic of Ireland v Azerbaijan 3-1
Russia v Romania 0-0
Romania v Azerbaijan 4-0
Russia v Republic of Ireland 0-2

Group 1 Table	P	W	D	L	F	A	GD	Pts
Republic of Ireland	3	3	0	0	10	1	9	9
Romania	3	1	1	1	4	5	–1	4
Russia	3	0	2	1	0	2	–2	2
Azerbaijan	3	0	1	2	1	7	–6	1

GROUP 2 (ENGLAND)
England v Czech Republic 4-1
Greece v Denmark 2-2
Greece v England 2-1
Czech Republic v Denmark 3-1
Denmark v England 2-2
Czech Republic v Greece 3-1

Group 2 Table	P	W	D	L	F	A	GD	Pts
Czech Republic	3	2	0	1	7	6	1	6
Greece	3	1	1	1	5	6	–1	4
England	3	1	1	1	7	5	2	4
Denmark	3	0	2	1	5	7	–2	2

GROUP 3 (CROATIA)
Norway v Hungary 0-0
Germany v Croatia 2-1
Germany v Norway 0-1
Hungary v Croatia 0-2
Croatia v Norway 2-3
Hungary v Germany 0-3

Group 3 Table	P	W	D	L	F	A	GD	Pts
Norway	3	2	1	0	4	2	2	7
Germany	3	2	0	1	5	2	3	6
Croatia	3	1	0	2	5	5	0	3
Hungary	3	0	1	2	0	5	–5	1

GROUP 4 (NETHERLANDS)
Spain v Slovenia 1-1
Wales v Netherlands 1-2
Spain v Wales 5-1
Netherlands v Slovenia 2-0
Slovenia v Wales 3-0
Netherlands v Spain 0-1

Group 4 Table	P	W	D	L	F	A	GD	Pts
Spain	3	2	1	0	7	2	5	7
Netherlands	3	2	0	1	4	2	2	6
Slovenia	3	1	1	1	4	3	1	4
Wales	3	0	0	3	2	10	–8	0

GROUP 5 (FRANCE)
France v Poland 0-0
Switzerland v Israel 0-3
France v Switzerland 3-2
Israel v Poland 1-0
Poland v Switzerland 0-0
Israel v France 0-3

Group 5 Table	P	W	D	L	F	A	GD	Pts
France	3	2	1	0	6	2	4	7
Israel	3	2	0	1	4	3	1	6
Poland	3	0	2	1	0	1	–1	2
Switzerland	3	0	1	2	2	6	–4	1

GROUP 6 (PORTUGAL)
Turkey v Scotland 1-3
Portugal v Cyprus 3-0
Scotland v Cyprus 4-0
Portugal v Turkey 3-0
Cyprus v Turkey 2-2
Scotland v Portugal 0-4

Group 6 Table	P	W	D	L	F	A	GD	Pts
Portugal	3	3	0	0	10	0	10	9
Scotland	3	2	0	1	7	5	2	6
Turkey	3	0	1	2	3	8	–5	1
Cyprus	3	0	1	2	2	9	–7	1

GROUP 7 (ITALY)
Ukraine v Serbia 2-2
Italy v Belgium 2-2
Serbia v Belgium 0-2
Italy v Ukraine 3-1
Belgium v Ukraine 2-5
Serbia v Italy 0-2

Group 7 Table	P	W	D	L	F	A	GD	Pts
Italy	3	2	1	0	7	3	4	7
Ukraine	3	1	1	1	8	7	1	4
Belgium	3	1	1	1	6	7	–1	4
Serbia	3	0	1	2	2	6	–4	1

Final Tournament in Armenia 14–27 July 2019.

UEFA UNDER-17 CHAMPIONSHIP 2018–19

QUALIFYING ROUND

GROUP 1 (SWEDEN)
Montenegro v Sweden 0-2
Netherlands v Liechtenstein 10-1
Sweden v Liechtenstein 5-0
Netherlands v Montenegro 6-0
Liechtenstein v Montenegro 0-2
Sweden v Netherlands 4-6

Group 1 Table	P	W	D	L	F	A	GD	Pts
Netherlands	3	3	0	0	22	5	17	9
Sweden	3	2	0	1	11	6	5	6
Montenegro	3	1	0	2	2	8	–6	3
Liechtenstein	3	0	0	3	1	17	–16	0

GROUP 2 (BOSNIA-HERZEGOVINA)
Iceland v Ukraine 2-2
Bosnia-Herzegovina v Gibraltar 8-0
Ukraine v Gibraltar 11-0
Bosnia-Herzegovina v Iceland 1-1
Gibraltar v Iceland 0-8
Ukraine v Bosnia-Herzegovina 3-2

Group 2 Table	P	W	D	L	F	A	GD	Pts
Ukraine	3	2	1	0	16	4	12	7
Iceland	3	1	2	0	11	3	8	5
Bosnia-Herzegovina	3	1	1	1	11	4	7	4
Gibraltar	3	0	0	3	0	27	–27	0

GROUP 3 (SLOVENIA)
Austria v Malta 7-0
Bulgaria v Slovenia 0-1
Austria v Bulgaria 2-1
Slovenia v Malta 2-1
Malta v Bulgaria 1-3
Slovenia v Austria 1-1

Group 3 Table	P	W	D	L	F	A	GD	Pts
Austria	3	2	1	0	10	2	8	7
Slovenia	3	2	1	0	4	2	2	7
Bulgaria	3	1	0	2	4	4	0	3
Malta	3	0	0	3	2	12	–10	0

GROUP 4 (NORTH MACEDONIA)
Faroe Islands v Israel 0-6
Spain v North Macedonia 1-0
Spain v Faroe Islands 6-0
Israel v North Macedonia 4-1
North Macedonia v Faroe Islands 4-0
Israel v Spain 0-3

Group 4 Table	P	W	D	L	F	A	GD	Pts
Spain	3	3	0	0	10	0	10	9
Israel	3	2	0	1	10	4	6	6
North Macedonia	3	1	0	2	5	5	0	3
Faroe Islands	3	0	0	3	0	16	–16	0

GROUP 5 (CYPRUS)
Cyprus v Switzerland 0-3
Scotland v Kosovo 2-1
Switzerland v Kosovo 0-1
Scotland v Cyprus 1-1
Kosovo v Cyprus 1-0
Switzerland v Scotland 1-1

Group 5 Table	P	W	D	L	F	A	GD	Pts
Kosovo	3	2	0	1	3	2	1	6
Scotland	3	1	2	0	4	3	1	5
Switzerland	3	1	1	1	4	2	2	4
Cyprus	3	0	1	2	1	5	–4	1

GROUP 6 (DENMARK)
Georgia v Denmark 1-3
Russia v Estonia 6-0
Russia v Georgia 7-1
Denmark v Estonia 5-2
Estonia v Georgia 1-0
Denmark v Russia 1-0

Group 6 Table	P	W	D	L	F	A	GD	Pts
Denmark	3	3	0	0	9	3	6	9
Russia	3	2	0	1	13	2	11	6
Estonia	3	1	0	2	3	11	–8	3
Georgia	3	0	0	3	2	11	–9	0

GROUP 7 (POLAND)
Finland v Poland 1-2
France v Luxembourg 4-0
Poland v Luxembourg 7-3
France v Finland 2-1
Luxembourg v Finland 0-2
Poland v France 1-3

Group 7 Table	P	W	D	L	F	A	GD	Pts
France	3	3	0	0	9	2	7	9
Poland	3	2	0	1	10	7	3	6
Finland	3	1	0	2	4	4	0	3
Luxembourg	3	0	0	3	3	13	–10	0

GROUP 8 (ALBANIA)
Azerbaijan v Norway 1-4
Czech Republic v Albania 6-0
Czech Republic v Azerbaijan 2-0
Norway v Albania 3-1
Albania v Azerbaijan 1-0
Norway v Czech Republic 0-1

Group 8 Table	P	W	D	L	F	A	GD	Pts
Czech Republic	3	3	0	0	9	0	9	9
Norway	3	2	0	1	7	3	4	6
Albania	3	1	0	2	2	9	–7	3
Azerbaijan	3	0	0	3	1	7	–6	0

GROUP 9 (HUNGARY)
Romania v Hungary 0-0
Serbia v Lithuania 2-1
Hungary v Lithuania 3-0
Serbia v Romania 2-2
Lithuania v Romania 0-4
Hungary v Serbia 1-0

Group 9 Table	P	W	D	L	F	A	GD	Pts
Hungary	3	2	1	0	4	0	4	7
Romania	3	1	2	0	6	2	4	5
Serbia	3	1	1	1	4	4	0	4
Lithuania	3	0	0	3	1	9	–8	0

GROUP 10 (TURKEY)
Northern Ireland v Slovakia 0-1
Turkey v San Marino 6-0
Slovakia v San Marino 8-0
Turkey v Northern Ireland 1-1
San Marino v Northern Ireland 0-6
Slovakia v Turkey 3-0

Group 10 Table	P	W	D	L	F	A	GD	Pts
Slovakia	3	3	0	0	12	0	12	9
Northern Ireland	3	1	1	1	7	2	5	4
Turkey	3	1	1	1	7	4	3	4
San Marino	3	0	0	3	0	20	–20	0

GROUP 11 (PORTUGAL)
Belarus v Wales 2-2
Portugal v Kazakhstan 10-0
Wales v Kazakhstan 0-1
Portugal v Belarus 3-0
Kazakhstan v Belarus 1-2
Wales v Portugal 1-5

Group 11 Table	P	W	D	L	F	A	GD	Pts
Portugal	3	3	0	0	18	1	17	9
Belarus	3	1	1	1	4	6	–2	4
Kazakhstan	3	1	0	2	2	12	–10	3
Wales	3	0	1	2	3	8	–5	1

GROUP 12 (MOLDOVA)
Latvia v Greece 1-1
Belgium v Moldova 1-0
Greece v Moldova 1-0
Belgium v Latvia 5-0
Moldova v Latvia 2-2
Greece v Belgium 0-3

Group 12 Table	P	W	D	L	F	A	GD	Pts
Belgium	3	3	0	0	9	0	9	9
Greece	3	1	1	1	2	4	–2	4
Latvia	3	0	2	1	3	8	–5	2
Moldova	3	0	1	2	2	4	–2	1

GROUP 13 (CROATIA)
Italy v Andorra 7-0
Armenia v Croatia 0-3
Italy v Armenia 3-0
Croatia v Andorra 3-0
Andorra v Armenia 3-0
Croatia v Italy 0-3

Group 13 Table	P	W	D	L	F	A	GD	Pts
Italy	3	3	0	0	13	0	13	9
Croatia	3	2	0	1	6	3	3	6
Andorra	3	1	0	2	3	10	–7	3
Armenia	3	0	0	3	0	9	–9	0

ELITE ROUND

GROUP 1 (TURKEY)
Romania v Austria 1-5
Italy v Turkey 2-0
Italy v Romania 3-0
Austria v Turkey 0-0
Turkey v Romania 1-3
Austria v Italy 1-4

Group 1 Table	P	W	D	L	F	A	GD	Pts
Italy	3	3	0	0	9	1	8	9
Austria	3	1	1	1	6	5	1	4
Romania	3	1	0	2	4	9	–5	3
Turkey	3	0	1	2	1	5	–4	1

GROUP 2 (NETHERLANDS)
Israel v Czech Republic 0-1
Netherlands v Northern Ireland 5-0
Czech Republic v Northern Ireland 2-0
Netherlands v Israel 2-0
Northern Ireland v Israel 0-0
Czech Republic v Netherlands 2-5

Group 2 Table	P	W	D	L	F	A	GD	Pts
Netherlands	3	3	0	0	12	2	10	9
Czech Republic	3	2	0	1	5	5	0	6
Israel	3	0	1	2	0	3	–3	1
Northern Ireland	3	0	1	2	0	7	–7	1

GROUP 3 (DENMARK)
Croatia v Denmark 3-2
England v Switzerland 5-2
England v Croatia 0-0
Denmark v Switzerland 1-1
Switzerland v Croatia 1-1
Denmark v England 2-3

Group 3 Table	P	W	D	L	F	A	GD	Pts
England	3	2	1	0	8	4	4	7
Croatia	3	1	2	0	4	3	1	5
Switzerland	3	0	2	1	4	7	–3	2
Denmark	3	0	1	2	5	7	–2	1

GROUP 4 (GERMANY)
Germany v Belarus 1-1
Iceland v Slovenia 2-1
Germany v Iceland 3-3
Slovenia v Belarus 1-1
Belarus v Iceland 1-4
Slovenia v Germany 0-1

Group 4 Table	P	W	D	L	F	A	GD	Pts
Iceland	3	2	1	0	9	5	4	7
Germany	3	1	2	0	5	4	1	5
Belarus	3	0	2	1	3	6	–3	2
Slovenia	3	0	1	2	2	4	–2	1

GROUP 5 (NEUTRAL – SWITZERLAND)
Kosovo v Ukraine 0-2
Spain v Greece 2-0
Ukraine v Greece 0-1
Spain v Kosovo 1-0
Greece v Kosovo 2-0
Ukraine v Spain 0-1

Group 5 Table	P	W	D	L	F	A	GD	Pts
Spain	3	3	0	0	4	0	4	9
Greece	3	2	0	1	3	2	1	6
Ukraine	3	1	0	2	2	2	0	3
Kosovo	3	0	0	3	0	5	–5	0

GROUP 6 (SCOTLAND)
Poland v Russia 2-3
Portugal v Scotland 2-0
Portugal v Poland 2-1
Russia v Scotland 3-0
Scotland v Poland 1-1
Russia v Portugal 1-2

Group 6 Table	P	W	D	L	F	A	GD	Pts
Portugal	3	3	0	0	6	2	4	9
Russia	3	2	0	1	7	4	3	6
Poland	3	0	1	2	4	6	–2	1
Scotland	3	0	1	2	1	6	–5	1

GROUP 7 (HUNGARY)
Belgium v Bosnia-Herzegovina 1-0
Norway v Hungary 0-1
Hungary v Bosnia-Herzegovina 1-0
Belgium v Norway 3-0
Bosnia-Herzegovina v Norway 1-2
Hungary v Belgium 2-4

Group 7 Table	P	W	D	L	F	A	GD	Pts
Belgium	3	3	0	0	8	2	6	9
Hungary	3	2	0	1	4	4	0	6
Norway	3	1	0	2	2	5	–3	3
Bosnia-Herzegovina	3	0	0	3	1	4	–3	0

GROUP 8 (SERBIA)
Sweden v France 0-2
Slovakia v Serbia 1-3
Slovakia v Sweden 0-0
France v Serbia 1-0
Serbia v Sweden 1-2
France v Slovakia 3-0

Group 8 Table	P	W	D	L	F	A	GD	Pts
France	3	3	0	0	6	0	6	9
Sweden	3	1	1	1	2	3	–1	4
Serbia	3	1	0	2	4	4	0	3
Slovakia	3	0	1	2	1	6	–5	1

FINAL TOURNAMENT (REPUBLIC OF IRELAND)

GROUP A
Czech Republic v Belgium 1-1
Republic of Ireland v Greece 1-1
Belgium v Greece 3-0
Republic of Ireland v Czech Republic 1-1
Belgium v Republic of Ireland 1-1
Greece v Czech Republic 0-2

Group A Table	P	W	D	L	F	A	GD	Pts
Belgium	3	1	2	0	5	2	3	5
Czech Republic	3	1	2	0	4	2	2	5
Republic of Ireland	3	0	3	0	3	3	0	3
Greece	3	0	1	2	1	6	–5	1

GROUP B
Netherlands v Sweden 2-0
England v France 1-1
Netherlands v England 5-2
France v Sweden 4-2
France v Netherlands 2-0
Sweden v England 1-3

Group B Table	P	W	D	L	F	A	GD	Pts
France	3	2	1	0	7	3	4	7
Netherlands	3	2	0	1	7	4	3	6
England	3	1	1	1	6	7	–1	4
Sweden	3	0	0	3	3	9	–6	0

GROUP C
Iceland v Russia 3-2
Hungary v Portugal 1-0
Iceland v Hungary 1-2
Portugal v Russia 2-1
Portugal v Iceland 4-2
Russia v Hungary 2-3

Group C Table	P	W	D	L	F	A	GD	Pts
Hungary	3	3	0	0	6	3	3	9
Portugal	3	2	0	1	6	4	2	6
Iceland	3	1	0	2	6	8	–2	3
Russia	3	0	0	3	5	8	–3	0

GROUP D

Spain v Austria 3-0
Germany v Italy 1-3
Spain v Germany 1-0
Italy v Austria 2-1
Italy v Spain 4-1
Austria v Germany 1-3

Group D Table	P	W	D	L	F	A	GD	Pts
Italy	3	3	0	0	9	3	6	9
Spain	3	2	0	1	5	4	1	6
Germany	3	1	0	2	4	5	–1	3
Austria	3	0	0	3	2	8	–6	0

QUARTER-FINALS

France v Czech Republic 6-1
Belgium v Netherlands 0-3
Italy v Portugal 1-0
Hungary v Spain 1-1
Spain won 5-4 on penalties.

FIFA U17 WORLD CUP PLAY-OFF

Hungary v Belgium 1-1
Hungary won 5-4 on penalties.

SEMI-FINALS

Netherlands v Spain 1-0
France v Italy 1-2

FINAL

Tallaght Stadium, Dublin, Sunday 19 May 2019

Netherlands (3) 4 *(Hansen 20, Bannis 37, Maatsen 45, Unuvar 70)*

Italy (0) 2 *(Colombo 56, 89)*

Netherlands: Raatsie; Hoever (Allouch 90), Bogarde, Rensch, Salah-Eddine (Kasanwirjo 69), Taylor, Hansen (Unuvar 69), Maatsen 45, Brobbey, Taabouni (Proper 86), Bannis (de Schutter 90).
Italy: Molla; Lamanna, Panada (Bonfante 90), Moretti (Ruggeri 46), Pirola, Tongya (Giovane 82), Esposito, Cudrig (Colombo 46), Udogie, Brentan (Sekulov 47), Dalle Mura.
Referee: Espen Eskas (Norway).

UEFA UNDER-21 CHAMPIONSHIP 2017–19

QUALIFYING ROUND

GROUP 1

Belarus v San Marino 1-0
San Marino v Moldova 0-2
Moldova v Croatia 0-3
Belarus v Greece 0-2
Greece v Moldova 5-1
Czech Republic v Belarus 1-1
Moldova v Greece 0-2
Croatia v Belarus 2-1
Croatia v Czech Republic 5-1
Belarus v Moldova 3-1
San Marino v Greece 0-5
Croatia v San Marino 5-0
Czech Republic v San Marino 3-1
Greece v Croatia 1-1
Moldova v Czech Republic 1-3
Greece v San Marino 4-0
Czech Republic v Croatia 2-1
San Marino v Belarus 0-2
Greece v Czech Republic 3-0
Croatia v Moldova 4-0
San Marino v Czech Republic 0-2
Moldova v Belarus 2-2
Moldova v San Marino 1-0
Belarus v Croatia 0-4
Czech Republic v Greece 1-2
Belarus v Czech Republic 1-0
Croatia v Greece 2-0
Czech Republic v Moldova 1-0
San Marino v Croatia 0-4
Greece v Belarus 2-0

Group 1 Table	P	W	D	L	F	A	GD	Pts
Croatia	10	8	1	1	31	5	26	25
Greece	10	8	1	1	26	5	21	25
Czech Republic	10	5	1	4	14	15	–1	16
Belarus	10	4	2	4	11	14	–3	14
Moldova	10	2	1	7	8	23	–15	7
San Marino	10	0	0	10	1	29	–28	0

GROUP 2

Estonia v Northern Ireland 1-2
Albania v Estonia 0-0
Northern Ireland v Albania 1-0
Estonia v Slovakia 1-2
Iceland v Albania 2-3
Estonia v Spain 0-1
Slovakia v Northern Ireland 1-0
Slovakia v Iceland 0-2
Albania v Iceland 0-0
Slovakia v Spain 1-4
Northern Ireland v Estonia 4-2
Spain v Iceland 1-0
Albania v Northern Ireland 1-1
Estonia v Iceland 2-3
Spain v Slovakia 5-1
Northern Ireland v Spain 3-5
Albania v Slovakia 2-3
Northern Ireland v Iceland 0-0
Slovakia v Albania 4-1
Spain v Estonia 3-1
Iceland v Estonia 5-2
Spain v Albania 3-0
Iceland v Slovakia 2-3
Spain v Northern Ireland 1-2
Iceland v Northern Ireland 0-1
Albania v Spain 0-1
Slovakia v Estonia 2-0
Estonia v Albania 2-2
Iceland v Spain 2-7
Northern Ireland v Slovakia 1-0

Group 2 Table	P	W	D	L	F	A	GD	Pts
Spain	10	9	0	1	31	10	21	27
Northern Ireland	10	6	2	2	15	11	4	20
Slovakia	10	6	0	4	17	18	–1	18
Iceland	10	3	2	5	16	19	–3	11
Albania	10	1	4	5	9	17	–8	7
Estonia	10	0	2	8	11	24	–13	2

GROUP 3

Lithuania v Faroe Islands 3-0
Faroe Islands v Denmark 0-3
Georgia v Poland 0-3
Denmark v Lithuania 6-0
Finland v Faroe Islands 1-1
Poland v Finland 3-3
Denmark v Georgia 5-2
Finland v Denmark 0-5
Lithuania v Poland 0-2
Faroe Islands v Georgia 3-1
Georgia v Finland 2-2
Faroe Islands v Poland 2-2
Georgia v Lithuania 1-0
Poland v Denmark 3-1
Georgia v Faroe Islands 1-0
Lithuania v Finland 0-2
Georgia v Denmark 2-2
Poland v Lithuania 1-0
Faroe Islands v Finland 1-3
Lithuania v Georgia 0-0
Denmark v Finland 2-0
Poland v Faroe Islands 1-1
Finland v Poland 1-3
Lithuania v Denmark 0-2
Finland v Georgia 1-2

Denmark v Poland	1-1
Faroe Islands v Lithuania	2-2
Finland v Lithuania	0-2
Poland v Georgia	3-0
Denmark v Faroe Islands	3-0

Group 3 Table	P	W	D	L	F	A	GD	Pts
Denmark	10	7	2	1	30	8	22	23
Poland	10	6	4	0	22	9	13	22
Georgia	10	3	3	4	11	19	–8	12
Finland	10	2	3	5	13	21	–8	9
Lithuania	10	2	2	6	7	16	–9	8
Faroe Islands	10	1	4	5	10	20	–10	7

GROUP 4

Latvia v Andorra	0-0
Latvia v Ukraine	1-1
Netherlands v England	1-1
Andorra v Ukraine	0-6
Scotland v Netherlands	2-0
England v Latvia	3-0
Netherlands v Latvia	3-0
England v Scotland	3-1
Latvia v Scotland	0-2
Ukraine v Netherlands	1-1
Andorra v England	0-1
Ukraine v England	0-2
Netherlands v Andorra	8-0
Scotland v Latvia	1-1
Scotland v Ukraine	0-2
Andorra v Scotland	1-1
Andorra v Netherlands	0-1
England v Ukraine	2-1
Scotland v Andorra	3-0
England v Netherlands	0-0
Ukraine v Latvia	3-2
Latvia v England	1-2
Ukraine v Andorra	1-0
Netherlands v Scotland	1-2
England v Andorra	7-0
Ukraine v Scotland	3-1
Latvia v Netherlands	0-3
Scotland v England	0-2
Netherlands v Ukraine	3-0
Andorra v Latvia	0-0

Group 4 Table	P	W	D	L	F	A	GD	Pts
England	10	8	2	0	23	4	19	26
Netherlands	10	5	3	2	21	6	15	18
Ukraine	10	5	2	3	18	12	6	17
Scotland	10	4	2	4	13	13	0	14
Latvia	10	0	4	6	5	18	–13	4
Andorra	10	0	3	7	1	28	–27	3

GROUP 5

Republic of Ireland v Kosovo 1-0
Norway v Kosovo 0-3

Match awarded 3-0 to Kosovo. Norway fielded an ineligible player.

Israel v Azerbaijan	3-1
Kosovo v Norway	3-2
Azerbaijan v Republic of Ireland	1-3
Norway v Israel	0-0
Germany v Kosovo	1-0
Republic of Ireland v Norway	0-0
Germany v Azerbaijan	6-1
Republic of Ireland v Israel	4-0
Norway v Germany	3-1
Azerbaijan v Germany	0-7
Kosovo v Israel	0-4
Azerbaijan v Kosovo	0-0
Israel v Germany	2-5
Norway v Republic of Ireland	2-1
Germany v Israel	3-0
Kosovo v Azerbaijan	2-0
Israel v Norway	1-3
Kosovo v Germany	0-0
Republic of Ireland v Azerbaijan	1-0
Azerbaijan v Israel	1-1
Kosovo v Republic of Ireland	1-1
Azerbaijan v Norway	1-3
Republic of Ireland v Germany	0-6
Israel v Republic of Ireland	3-1
Germany v Norway	2-1
Israel v Kosovo	3-0
Norway v Azerbaijan	1-1
Germany v Republic of Ireland	2-0

Group 5 Table	P	W	D	L	F	A	GD	Pts
Germany	10	8	1	1	33	7	26	25
Norway	10	4	3	3	15	13	2	15
Republic of Ireland	10	4	2	4	12	15	–3	14
Israel	10	4	2	4	17	18	–1	14
Kosovo	10	3	3	4	9	12	–3	12
Azerbaijan	10	0	3	7	6	27	–21	3

GROUP 6

Belgium v Malta	2-1
Cyprus v Malta	2-1
Hungary v Malta	2-1
Sweden v Cyprus	4-1
Belgium v Turkey	0-0
Cyprus v Turkey	2-1
Belgium v Sweden	1-1
Cyprus v Belgium	0-2
Turkey v Hungary	0-0
Sweden v Malta	3-0
Belgium v Cyprus	3-2
Malta v Turkey	0-1
Hungary v Sweden	2-2
Cyprus v Hungary	0-2
Turkey v Belgium	1-2
Hungary v Cyprus	4-0
Turkey v Sweden	0-3
Belgium v Hungary	3-0
Cyprus v Sweden	0-1
Turkey v Malta	4-2
Malta v Sweden	0-4
Malta v Belgium	0-4
Turkey v Cyprus	4-0
Sweden v Hungary	1-0
Hungary v Belgium	0-3
Sweden v Turkey	0-1
Malta v Hungary	2-1
Malta v Cyprus	1-1
Hungary v Turkey	1-2
Sweden v Belgium	0-3

Group 6 Table	P	W	D	L	F	A	GD	Pts
Belgium	10	8	2	0	23	5	18	26
Sweden	10	6	2	2	19	8	11	20
Turkey	10	5	2	3	14	10	4	17
Hungary	10	3	2	5	12	14	–2	11
Cyprus	10	2	1	7	8	23	–15	7
Malta	10	1	1	8	8	24	–16	4

GROUP 7

Austria v Gibraltar	3-0
Gibraltar v Armenia	0-3
Russia v Armenia	0-0
Serbia v Gibraltar	4-0
Armenia v North Macedonia	0-3
Russia v Gibraltar	3-0
Armenia v Gibraltar	1-0
Russia v Austria	1-0
North Macedonia v Serbia	0-2
Armenia v Austria	0-5
Gibraltar v North Macedonia	1-0
Serbia v Russia	3-2
Armenia v Russia	1-2
Austria v Serbia	1-3
Armenia v Serbia	0-1
North Macedonia v Austria	0-4
North Macedonia v Russia	3-4
Gibraltar v Serbia	0-6
Austria v North Macedonia	2-0
Gibraltar v Russia	0-5
Austria v Armenia	2-1
Serbia v North Macedonia	2-1
North Macedonia v Armenia	3-3
Russia v Serbia	1-2
Gibraltar v Austria	0-5
Russia v North Macedonia	5-1
Serbia v Austria	0-0
North Macedonia v Gibraltar	6-1
Austria v Russia	3-2
Serbia v Armenia	0-0

Group 7 Table	P	W	D	L	F	A	GD	Pts
Serbia	10	8	2	0	23	5	18	26
Austria	10	7	1	2	25	7	18	22
Russia	10	6	1	3	25	13	12	19
Armenia	10	2	3	5	9	16	–7	9
North Macedonia	10	2	1	7	17	24	–7	7
Gibraltar	10	1	0	9	2	36	–34	3

GROUP 8

Bosnia-Herzegovina v Liechtenstein	6-0
Switzerland v Bosnia-Herzegovina	1-0
Liechtenstein v Romania	0-2
Bosnia-Herzegovina v Romania	1-3
Switzerland v Wales	0-3
Romania v Switzerland	1-1
Portugal v Wales	2-0
Liechtenstein v Wales	1-3
Switzerland v Romania	0-2
Bosnia-Herzegovina v Portugal	3-1
Liechtenstein v Switzerland	0-2
Romania v Portugal	1-1
Wales v Bosnia-Herzegovina	0-4
Portugal v Switzerland	2-1
Wales v Romania	0-0
Bosnia-Herzegovina v Wales	1-0
Portugal v Liechtenstein	7-0
Switzerland v Portugal	2-4
Liechtenstein v Bosnia-Herzegovina	0-4
Bosnia-Herzegovina v Switzerland	3-0
Wales v Liechtenstein	2-1
Portugal v Romania	1-2
Romania v Bosnia-Herzegovina	2-0
Switzerland v Liechtenstein	3-0
Wales v Portugal	0-2
Liechtenstein v Portugal	0-9
Romania v Wales	2-0
Wales v Switzerland	3-1
Portugal v Bosnia-Herzegovina	4-2
Romania v Liechtenstein	4-0

Group 8 Table	P	W	D	L	F	A	GD	Pts
Romania	10	7	3	0	19	4	15	24
Portugal	10	7	1	2	33	11	22	22
Bosnia-Herzegovina	10	6	0	4	24	11	13	18
Wales	10	4	1	5	11	14	–3	13
Switzerland	10	3	1	6	11	18	–7	10
Liechtenstein	10	0	0	10	2	42	–40	0

GROUP 9

Luxembourg v Kazakhstan 1-2
Match awarded 3-0 to Kazakhstan; Luxembourg fielded ineligible player.

Kazakhstan v Montenegro	1-1
Slovenia v Luxembourg	3-1
Bulgaria v Luxembourg	0-1
France v Kazakhstan	4-1
Luxembourg v Slovenia	1-1
France v Montenegro	2-1
Bulgaria v Kazakhstan	2-2
Montenegro v Slovenia	1-3
Luxembourg v France	2-3
Kazakhstan v Bulgaria	1-1
Slovenia v Montenegro	2-0
France v Bulgaria	3-0
Slovenia v France	1-3
Bulgaria v Montenegro	3-1
Kazakhstan v France	0-3
Luxembourg v Montenegro	1-3
Kazakhstan v Luxembourg	3-0
Bulgaria v Slovenia	3-0
Montenegro v France	0-2
Kazakhstan v Slovenia	0-0
Bulgaria v France	0-1
Slovenia v Kazakhstan	2-1
Montenegro v Bulgaria	0-0
France v Luxembourg	2-0
Montenegro v Luxembourg	3-0
Slovenia v Bulgaria	1-1
Montenegro v Kazakhstan	5-1
France v Slovenia	1-1
Luxembourg v Bulgaria	1-0

Group 9 Table	P	W	D	L	F	A	GD	Pts
France	10	9	1	0	24	6	18	28
Slovenia	10	4	4	2	14	12	2	16
Montenegro	10	3	2	5	15	15	0	11
Kazakhstan	10	2	4	4	13	18	–5	10
Bulgaria	10	2	4	4	10	11	–1	10
Luxembourg	10	2	1	7	7	21	–14	7

PLAY-OFF – FIRST LEG

Greece v Austria	0-1
Poland v Portugal	0-1

PLAY-OFF – SECOND LEG

Austria v Greece 1-0
Austria won 2-0 on aggregate.
Portugal v Poland 1-3
Poland won 3-2 on aggregate.

UEFA UNDER-21 CHAMPIONSHIP 2017–19

FINALS IN ITALY AND SAN MARINO

GROUP A

Poland v Belgium	3-2
Italy v Spain	3-1
Spain v Belgium	2-1
Italy v Poland	0-1
Belgium v Italy	1-3
Spain v Poland	5-0

Group A Table	P	W	D	L	F	A	GD	Pts
Spain	3	2	0	1	8	4	4	6
Italy	3	2	0	1	6	3	3	6
Poland	3	2	0	1	4	7	–3	6
Belgium	3	0	0	3	4	8	–4	0

GROUP B

Serbia v Austria	0-2
Germany v Denmark	3-1
Denmark v Austria	3-1
Germany v Serbia	6-1
Austria v Germany	1-1
Denmark v Serbia	2-0

Group B Table	P	W	D	L	F	A	GD	Pts
Germany	3	2	1	0	10	3	7	7
Denmark	3	2	0	1	6	4	2	6
Austria	3	1	1	1	4	4	0	4
Serbia	3	0	0	3	1	10	–9	0

GROUP C

Romania v Croatia	4-1
England v France	1-2
England v Romania	2-4
France v Croatia	1-0
Croatia v England	3-3
France v Romania	0-0

Group C Table	P	W	D	L	F	A	GD	Pts
Romania	3	2	1	0	8	3	5	7
France	3	2	1	0	3	1	2	7
England	3	0	1	2	6	9	–3	1
Croatia	3	0	1	2	4	8	–4	1

SEMI-FINALS

Germany v Romania	4-2
Spain v France	4-1

FINAL

Stadio Friuli, Udine, Sunday 30 June 2019

Spain (1) 2 *(Fabián 7, Dani Olmo 69)*

Germany (0) 1 *(Amiri 88)* 23,232

Spain: Sivera; Vallejo, Unai Nunez, Fabian Ruiz (Merino 78), Ceballos, Oyarzabal (Soler 55), Martin Aguirregabiria, Dani Olmo, Junior Firpo, Marc Roca, Fornals (Mayoral 72).
Germany: Nubel; Henrichs, Klostermann, Tah, Baumgartl, Eggestein (Nmecha 78), Oztunali (Richter 72), Dahoud, Waldschmidt, Serdar (Neuhaus 61), Amiri.
Referee: Srdan Jovanovic (Serbia).

ENGLAND UNDER-21 RESULTS 1976–2019

EC *UEFA Competition for Under-21 Teams*

Bold type indicates matches played in season 2018–19.

Year	*Date*		*Venue*		
			v ALBANIA	*Eng*	*Alb*
EC1989	Mar	7	Shkroda	2	1
EC1989	April	25	Ipswich	2	0
EC2001	Mar	27	Tirana	1	0
EC2001	Sept	4	Middlesbrough	5	0
			v ANDORRA	*Eng*	*And*
EC2017	Oct	10	Andorra la Vella	1	0
EC2018	**Oct**	**11**	**Chesterfield**	**7**	**0**
			v ANGOLA	*Eng*	*Ang*
1995	June	10	Toulon	1	0
1996	May	28	Toulon	0	2
			v ARGENTINA	*Eng*	*Arg*
1998	May	18	Toulon	0	2
2000	Feb	22	Fulham	1	0
			v AUSTRIA	*Eng*	*Aus*
1994	Oct	11	Kapfenberg	3	1
1995	Nov	14	Middlesbrough	2	1
EC2004	Sept	3	Krems	2	0
EC2005	Oct	7	Leeds	1	2
2013	June	26	Brighton	4	0
			v AZERBAIJAN	*Eng*	*Az*
EC2004	Oct	12	Baku	0	0
EC2005	Mar	29	Middlesbrough	2	0
2009	June	8	Milton Keynes	7	0
EC2011	Sept	1	Watford	6	0
EC2012	Sept	6	Baku	2	0
			v BELARUS	*Eng*	*Bel*
2015	June	11	Barnsley	1	0
			v BELGIUM	*Eng*	*Bel*
1994	June	5	Marseille	2	1
1996	May	24	Toulon	1	0
EC2011	Nov	14	Mons	1	2
EC2012	Feb	29	Middlesbrough	4	0
			v BOSNIA-HERZEGOVINA	*Eng*	*B-H*
EC2015	Nov	12	Sarajevo Canton	0	0
EC2016	Oct	11	Walsall	5	0
			v BRAZIL	*Eng*	*B*
1993	June	11	Toulon	0	0
1995	June	6	Toulon	0	2
1996	June	1	Toulon	1	2
			v BULGARIA	*Eng*	*Bul*
EC1979	June	5	Pernik	3	1
EC1979	Nov	20	Leicester	5	0
1989	June	5	Toulon	2	3
EC1998	Oct	9	West Ham	1	0
EC1999	June	8	Vratsa	1	0
EC2007	Sept	11	Sofia	2	0
EC2007	Nov	16	Milton Keynes	2	0
			v CHINA PR	*Eng*	*CPR*
2018	May	26	Toulon	2	1
			v CROATIA	*Eng*	*Cro*
1996	Apr	23	Sunderland	0	1
2003	Aug	19	West Ham	0	3
EC2014	Oct	10	Wolverhampton	2	1
EC2014	Oct	14	Vinkovci	2	1
EC2019	**June**	**24**	**Serravale**	**3**	**3**
			v CZECHOSLOVAKIA	*Eng*	*Cz*
1990	May	28	Toulon	2	1
1992	May	26	Toulon	1	2
1993	June	9	Toulon	1	1
			v CZECH REPUBLIC	*Eng*	*CzR*
1998	Nov	17	Ipswich	0	1
EC2007	June	11	Arnhem	0	0
2008	Nov	18	Bramall Lane	2	0
EC2011	June	19	Viborg	1	2
2015	Mar	27	Prague	1	0
			v DENMARK	*Eng*	*Den*
EC1978	Sept	19	Hvidovre	2	1
EC1979	Sept	11	Watford	1	0
EC1982	Sept	21	Hvidovre	4	1
EC1983	Sept	20	Norwich	4	1
EC1986	Mar	12	Copenhagen	1	0
				Eng	*Den*
EC1986	Mar	26	Manchester	1	1
1988	Sept	13	Watford	0	0
1994	Mar	8	Brentford	1	0
1999	Oct	8	Bradford	4	1
2005	Aug	16	Herning	1	0
2011	Mar	24	Viborg	4	0
2017	Mar	27	Randers	4	0
2018	**Nov**	**20**	**Esbjerg**	**5**	**1**
			v EQUADOR	*Eng*	*E*
2009	Feb	10	Malaga	2	3
			v FINLAND	*Eng*	*Fin*
EC1977	May	26	Helsinki	1	0
EC1977	Oct	12	Hull	8	1
EC1984	Oct	16	Southampton	2	0
EC1985	May	21	Mikkeli	1	3
EC2000	Oct	10	Valkeakoski	2	2
EC2001	Mar	23	Barnsley	4	0
EC2009	June	15	Halmstad	2	1
EC2013	Sept	9	Tampere	1	1
EC2013	Nov	14	Milton Keynes	3	0
			v FRANCE	*Eng*	*Fra*
EC1984	Feb	28	Sheffield	6	1
EC1984	Mar	28	Rouen	1	0
1987	June	11	Toulon	0	2
EC1988	April	13	Besancon	2	4
EC1988	April	27	Highbury	2	2
1988	June	12	Toulon	2	4
1990	May	23	Toulon	7	3
1991	June	3	Toulon	1	0
1992	May	28	Toulon	0	0
1993	June	15	Toulon	1	0
1994	May	31	Aubagne	0	3
1995	June	10	Toulon	0	2
1998	May	14	Toulon	1	1
1999	Feb	9	Derby	2	1
EC2005	Nov	11	Tottenham	1	1
EC2005	Nov	15	Nancy	1	2
2009	Mar	31	Nottingham	0	2
2014	Nov	17	Paris	2	3
2016	May	29	Toulon	2	1
2016	Nov	14	Bondoufle	2	3
EC2019	**June**	**18**	**Cesena**	**1**	**2**
			v GEORGIA	*Eng*	*Geo*
EC1996	Nov	8	Batumi	1	0
EC1997	April	29	Charlton	0	0
2000	Aug	31	Middlesbrough	6	1
			v GERMANY	*Eng*	*Ger*
1991	Sept	10	Scunthorpe	2	1
EC2000	Oct	6	Derby	1	1
EC2001	Aug	31	Frieburg	2	1
2005	Mar	25	Hull	2	2
2005	Sept	6	Mainz	1	1
EC2006	Oct	6	Coventry	1	0
EC2006	Oct	10	Leverkusen	2	0
EC2009	June	22	Halmstad	1	1
EC2009	June	29	Malmo	0	4
2010	Nov	16	Wiesbaden	0	2
2015	Mar	30	Middlesbrough	3	2
2017	Mar	24	Wiesbaden	0	1
EC2017	June	27	Tychy	2	2
2019	**Mar**	**26**	**Bournemouth**	**1**	**2**
			v EAST GERMANY	*Eng*	*EG*
EC1980	April	16	Sheffield	1	2
EC1980	April	23	Jena	0	1
			v WEST GERMANY	*Eng*	*WG*
EC1982	Sept	21	Sheffield	3	1
EC1982	Oct	12	Bremen	2	3
1987	Sept	8	Ludenscheid	0	2
			v GREECE	*Eng*	*Gre*
EC1982	Nov	16	Piraeus	0	1
EC1983	Mar	29	Portsmouth	2	1
1989	Feb	7	Patras	0	1
EC1997	Nov	13	Heraklion	0	2
EC1997	Dec	17	Norwich	4	2

				Eng	Gre
EC2001	June	5	Athens	1	3
EC2001	Oct	5	Ewood Park	2	1
EC2009	Sept	8	Tripoli	1	1
EC2010	Mar	3	Doncaster	1	2

v GUINEA

				Eng	Gui
2016	May	23	Toulon	7	1

v HUNGARY

				Eng	Hun
EC1981	June	5	Keszthely	2	1
EC1981	Nov	17	Nottingham	2	0
EC1983	April	26	Newcastle	1	0
EC1983	Oct	11	Nyiregyhaza	2	0
1990	Sept	11	Southampton	3	1
1992	May	12	Budapest	2	2
1999	April	27	Budapest	2	2

v ICELAND

				Eng	Ice
2011	Mar	28	Preston	1	2
EC2011	Oct	6	Reykjavik	3	0
EC2011	Nov	10	Colchester	5	0

v ISRAEL

				Eng	Isr
1985	Feb	27	Tel Aviv	2	1
2011	Sept	5	Barnsley	4	1
EC2013	June	11	Jerusalem	0	1

v ITALY

				Eng	Italy
EC1978	Mar	8	Manchester	2	1
EC1978	April	5	Rome	0	0
EC1984	April	18	Manchester	3	1
EC1984	May	2	Florence	0	1
EC1986	April	9	Pisa	0	2
EC1986	April	23	Swindon	1	1
EC1997	Feb	12	Bristol	1	0
EC1997	Oct	10	Rieti	1	0
EC2000	May	27	Bratislava	0	2
2000	Nov	14	Monza*	0	0
2002	Mar	26	Valley Parade	1	1
EC2002	May	20	Basle	1	2
2003	Feb	11	Pisa	0	1
2007	Mar	24	Wembley	3	3
EC2007	June	14	Arnhem	2	2
2011	Feb	8	Empoli	0	1
EC2013	June	5	Tel Aviv	0	1
EC2015	June	24	Olomouc	1	3

**Abandoned 11 mins; fog.*

2016	Nov	10	Southampton	3	2
2018	**Nov**	**15**	**Ferrara**	**2**	**1**

v JAPAN

				Eng	Jap
2016	May	27	Toulon	1	0

v KAZAKHSTAN

				Eng	Kaz
EC2015	Oct	13	Coventry	3	0
EC2016	Oct	6	Aktobe	1	0

v LATVIA

				Eng	Lat
1995	April	25	Riga	1	0
1995	June	7	Burnley	4	0
EC2017	Sept	5	Bournemouth	3	0
EC2018	**Sept**	**11**	**Jelgava**	**2**	**1**

v LITHUANIA

				Eng	Lith
EC2009	Nov	17	Vilnius	0	0
EC2010	Sept	7	Colchester	3	0
EC2013	Oct	15	Ipswich	5	0
EC2014	Sept	5	Zaliakalnis	1	0

v LUXEMBOURG

				Eng	Lux
EC1998	Oct	13	Greven Macher	5	0
EC1999	Sept	3	Reading	5	0

v MALAYSIA

				Eng	Mal
1995	June	8	Toulon	2	0

v MEXICO

				Eng	Mex
1988	June	5	Toulon	2	1
1991	May	29	Toulon	6	0
1992	May	25	Toulon	1	1
2001	May	24	Leicester	3	0
2018	May	29	Toulon	0	0
2018	June	9	Toulon	2	1

v MOLDOVA

				Eng	Mol
EC1996	Aug	31	Chisinau	2	0
EC1997	Sept	9	Wycombe	1	0
EC2006	Aug	15	Ipswich	2	2

				Eng	Mol
EC2013	Sept	5	Reading	1	0
EC2014	Sept	9	Tiraspol	3	0

v MONTENEGRO

				Eng	M
EC2007	Sept	7	Podgorica	3	0
EC2007	Oct	12	Leicester	1	0

v MOROCCO

				Eng	Mor
1987	June	7	Toulon	2	0
1988	June	9	Toulon	1	0

v NETHERLANDS

				Eng	N
EC1993	April	27	Portsmouth	3	0
EC1993	Oct	12	Utrecht	1	1
2001	Aug	14	Reading	4	0
EC2001	Nov	9	Utrecht	2	2
EC2001	Nov	13	Derby	1	0
2004	Feb	17	Hull	3	2
2005	Feb	8	Derby	1	2
2006	Nov	14	Alkmaar	1	0
EC2007	June	20	Heerenveen	1	1
2009	Aug	11	Groningen	0	0
EC2017	Sept	1	Doetinchem	1	1
EC2018	**Sept**	**6**	**Norwich**	**0**	**0**

v NORTHERN IRELAND

				Eng	NI
2012	Nov	13	Blackpool	2	0

v NORTH MACEDONIA

				Eng	M
EC2002	Oct	15	Reading	3	1
EC2003	Sept	5	Skopje	1	1
EC2009	Sept	4	Prilep	2	1
EC2009	Oct	9	Coventry	6	3

v NORWAY

				Eng	Nor
EC1977	June	1	Bergen	2	1
EC1977	Sept	6	Brighton	6	0
1980	Sept	9	Southampton	3	0
1981	Sept	8	Drammen	0	0
EC1992	Oct	13	Peterborough	0	2
EC1993	June	1	Stavanger	1	1
1995	Oct	10	Stavanger	2	2
2006	Feb	28	Reading	3	1
2009	Mar	27	Sandefjord	5	0
2011	June	5	Southampton	2	0
EC2011	Oct	10	Drammen	2	1
EC2012	Sept	10	Chesterfield	1	0
EC2013	June	8	Petah Tikva	1	3
EC2015	Sept	7	Drammen	1	0
EC2016	Sept	6	Colchester	6	1

v PARAGUAY

				Eng	Par
2016	May	25	Toulon	4	0

v POLAND

				Eng	Pol
EC1982	Mar	17	Warsaw	2	1
EC1982	April	7	West Ham	2	2
EC1989	June	2	Plymouth	2	1
EC1989	Oct	10	Jastrzebie	3	1
EC1990	Oct	16	Tottenham	0	1
EC1991	Nov	12	Pila	1	2
EC1993	May	28	Zdroj	4	1
EC1993	Sept	7	Millwall	1	2
EC1996	Oct	8	Wolverhampton	0	0
EC1997	May	30	Katowice	1	1
EC1999	Mar	26	Southampton	5	0
EC1999	Sept	7	Plock	1	3
EC2004	Sept	7	Rybnik	3	1
EC2005	Oct	11	Hillsborough	4	1
2008	Mar	25	Wolverhampton	0	0
EC2017	June	22	Kielce	3	0
2019	**Mar**	**21**	**Bristol**	**1**	**1**

v PORTUGAL

				Eng	Por
1987	June	13	Toulon	0	0
1990	May	21	Toulon	0	1
1993	June	7	Toulon	2	0
1994	June	7	Toulon	2	0
EC1994	Sept	6	Leicester	0	0
1995	Sept	2	Lisbon	0	2
1996	May	30	Toulon	1	3
2000	Apr	16	Stoke	0	1
EC2002	May	22	Zurich	1	3
EC2003	Mar	28	Rio Major	2	4
EC2003	Sept	9	Everton	1	2
EC2008	Nov	20	Agueda	1	1
2008	Sept	5	Wembley	2	0
EC2009	Nov	14	Wembley	1	0
EC2010	Sept	3	Barcelos	1	0
2014	Nov	13	Burnley	3	1
EC2015	June	18	Uherske Hradiste	0	1
2016	May	19	Toulon	1	0

v QATAR

				Eng	Q
2018	June	1	Toulon	4	0

			v REPUBLIC OF IRELAND	*Eng*	*RoI*
1981	Feb	25	Liverpool	1	0
1985	Mar	25	Portsmouth	3	2
1989	June	9	Toulon	0	0
EC1990	Nov	13	Cork	3	0
EC1991	Mar	26	Brentford	3	0
1994	Nov	15	Newcastle	1	0
1995	Mar	27	Dublin	2	0
EC2007	Oct	16	Cork	3	0
EC2008	Feb	5	Southampton	3	0

			v ROMANIA	*Eng*	*Rom*
EC1980	Oct	14	Ploesti	0	4
EC1981	April	28	Swindon	3	0
EC1985	April	30	Brasov	0	0
EC1985	Sept	10	Ipswich	3	0
2007	Aug	21	Bristol	1	1
EC2010	Oct	8	Norwich	2	1
EC2010	Oct	12	Botosani	0	0
2013	Mar	21	Wycombe	3	0
2018	Mar	24	Wolverhampton	2	1
EC2019	**June**	**21**	**Cesena**	**2**	**4**

			v RUSSIA	*Eng*	*Rus*
1994	May	30	Bandol	2	0

			v SAN MARINO	*Eng*	*SM*
EC1993	Feb	16	Luton	6	0
EC1993	Nov	17	San Marino	4	0
EC2013	Oct	10	San Marino	4	0
EC2013	Nov	19	Shrewsbury	9	0

			v SCOTLAND	*Eng*	*Sco*
1977	April	27	Sheffield	1	0
EC1980	Feb	12	Coventry	2	1
EC1980	Mar	4	Aberdeen	0	0
EC1982	April	19	Glasgow	1	0
EC1982	April	28	Manchester	1	1
EC1988	Feb	16	Aberdeen	1	0
EC1988	Mar	22	Nottingham	1	0
1993	June	13	Toulon	1	0
2013	Aug	13	Sheffield	6	0
EC2017	Oct	6	Middlesbrough	3	1
2018	June	6	Toulon	3	1
EC2018	**Oct**	**16**	**Edinburgh**	**2**	**0**

			v SENEGAL	*Eng*	*Sen*
1989	June	7	Toulon	6	1
1991	May	27	Toulon	2	1

			v SERBIA	*Eng*	*Ser*
EC2007	June	17	Nijmegen	2	0
EC2012	Oct	12	Norwich	1	0
EC2012	Oct	16	Krusevac	1	0

			v SERBIA-MONTENEGRO	*Eng*	*S-M*
2003	June	2	Hull	3	2

			v SLOVAKIA	*Eng*	*Slo*
EC2002	June	1	Bratislava	0	2
EC2002	Oct	11	Trnava	4	0
EC2003	June	10	Sunderland	2	0
2007	June	5	Norwich	5	0
EC2017	June	19	Kielce	2	1

			v SLOVENIA	*Eng*	*Slo*
2000	Feb	12	Nova Gorica	1	0
2008	Aug	19	Hull	2	1

			v SOUTH AFRICA	*Eng*	*SA*
1998	May	16	Toulon	3	1

			v SPAIN	*Eng*	*Spa*
EC1984	May	17	Seville	1	0
EC1984	May	24	Sheffield	2	0
1987	Feb	18	Burgos	2	1
1992	Sept	8	Burgos	1	0
2001	Feb	27	Birmingham	0	4
2004	Nov	16	Alcala	0	1
2007	Feb	6	Derby	2	2
EC2009	June	18	Gothenburg	2	0
EC2011	June	12	Herning	1	1

			v SWEDEN	*Eng*	*Swe*
1979	June	9	Vasteras	2	1
1986	Sept	9	Ostersund	1	1
EC1988	Oct	18	Coventry	1	1
EC1989	Sept	5	Uppsala	0	1
EC1998	Sept	4	Sundvall	2	0
EC1999	June	4	Huddersfield	3	0
2004	Mar	30	Kristiansund	2	2
EC2009	June	26	Gothenburg	3	3
2013	Feb	5	Walsall	4	0
EC2015	Jun	21	Olomouc	1	0
EC2017	June	16	Kielce	0	0

			v SWITZERLAND	*Eng*	*Swit*
EC1980	Nov	18	Ipswich	5	0
EC1981	May	31	Neuenburg	0	0
1988	May	28	Lausanne	1	1
1996	April	1	Swindon	0	0
1998	Mar	24	Brugglifeld	0	2
EC2002	May	17	Zurich	2	1
EC2006	Sept	6	Lucerne	3	2
EC2015	Nov	16	Brighton	3	1
EC2016	Mar	26	Thun	1	1

			v TURKEY	*Eng*	*Tur*
EC1984	Nov	13	Bursa	0	0
EC1985	Oct	15	Bristol	3	0
EC1987	April	28	Izmir	0	0
EC1987	Oct	13	Sheffield	1	1
EC1991	April	30	Izmir	2	2
1991	Oct	15	Reading	2	0
EC1992	Nov	17	Orient	0	1
EC1993	Mar	30	Izmir	0	0
EC2000	May	29	Bratislava	6	0
EC2003	April	1	Newcastle	1	1
EC2003	Oct	10	Istanbul	0	1

			v UKRAINE	*Eng*	*Uk*
2004	Aug	17	Middlesbrough	3	1
EC2011	June	15	Herning	0	0
EC2017	Nov	10	Kiev	2	0
EC2018	Mar	27	Sheffield	2	1

			v USA	*Eng*	*USA*
1989	June	11	Toulon	0	2
1994	June	2	Toulon	3	0
2015	Sept	3	Preston	1	0

			v USSR	*Eng*	*USSR*
1987	June	9	Toulon	0	0
1988	June	7	Toulon	1	0
1990	May	25	Toulon	2	1
1991	May	31	Toulon	2	1

			v UZBEKISTAN	*Eng*	*Uzb*
2010	Aug	10	Bristol	2	0

			v WALES	*Eng*	*Wales*
1976	Dec	15	Wolverhampton	0	0
1979	Feb	6	Swansea	1	0
1990	Dec	5	Tranmere	0	0
EC2004	Oct	8	Blackburn	2	0
EC2005	Sept	2	Wrexham	4	0
2008	May	5	Wrexham	2	0
EC2008	Oct	10	Cardiff	3	2
EC2008	Oct	14	Villa Park	2	2
EC2013	Mar	5	Derby	1	0
EC2013	May	19	Swansea	3	1

			v YUGOSLAVIA	*Eng*	*Yugo*
EC1978	April	19	Novi Sad	1	2
EC1978	May	2	Manchester	1	1
EC1986	Nov	11	Peterborough	1	1
EC1987	Nov	10	Zemun	5	1
EC2000	Mar	29	Barcelona	3	0
2002	Sept	6	Bolton	1	1

BRITISH & IRISH UNDER-21 TEAMS 2018–19

▪ *Denotes player sent off.*

ENGLAND

UEFA UNDER-21 CHAMPIONSHIPS 2017–19

Thursday, 6 September 2018

England U21 (0) 0

Netherlands U21 (0) 0 16,369

England U21: (433) Henderson; Wan Bissaka, Konsa, Fry, Chilwell; Onomah (Davies 65), Cook, Sessegnon R; Maddison (Solanke 76), Calvert-Lewin (Abraham 76), Gray.
Referee: Roi Reinshreiber.

Tuesday, 11 September 2018

Latvia U21 (1) 1 *(Jurkovskis 28)*

England U21 (1) 2 *(Abraham 40, Mount 73)* 1037

England U21: (4231) Henderson; Walker-Peters, Clarke-Salter, Tomori, Kenny; Dowell, Davies; Lookman (Sessegnon R 63), Solanke, Mount; Abraham (Calvert-Lewin 80 (Onomah 89)).
Referee: Peter Kralovic.

Thursday, 11 October 2018

England U21 (3) 7 *(Lookman 9, Konsa 28, Calvert-Lewin 45, 49 (pen), Solanke 81, Nelson 90, Garcia 90 (og))*

Andorra U21 (0) 0 7147

England U21: (433) Henderson; Kenny (Dasilva 72), Fry, Konsa, Walker-Peters; Foden, Cook, Davies; Lookman (Nelson 72), Calvert-Lewin (Solanke 72), Sessegnon R.
Referee: Urs Schnyder.

Tuesday, 16 October 2018

Scotland U21 (0) 0

England U21 (0) 2 *(Nelson 60, Dowell 90)* 4122

Scotland U21: (433) Doohan; Porteous, Bates, Taylor, Smith; Cadden, Ross McCrorie, Campbell; Shaw (Middleton 46), Morgan, Gilmour (Ferguson 61).
England U21: (4231) Henderson; Wan Bissaka, Tomori, Clarke-Salter, Dasilva; Onomah (Foden 71), Dowell; Nelson (Sessegnon R 73), Solanke, Barnes; Abraham (Calvert-Lewin 87).
Referee: Marco Di Bello.

UEFA UNDER-21 CHAMPIONSHIPS 2017–19 FINALS IN ITALY

Tuesday, 18 June 2019

England U21 (0) 1 *(Foden 54)*

France U21 (0) 2 *(Ikone 89, Wan Bissaka 90 (og))* 11,228

England U21: (433) Henderson; Wan Bissaka, Tomori, Clarke-Salter, Dasilva; Maddison, Choudhury▪, Foden; Sessegnon R (Calvert-Lewin 74), Solanke (Mount 71), Gray (Abraham 75).
Referee: Srdjan Jovanovic.

Friday, 21 June 2019

England U21 (0) 2 *(Gray 79, Abraham 87)*

Romania U21 (0) 4 *(Puscas 76 (pen), Hagi 85, Coman 88, 90)* 8440

England U21: (433) Henderson; Dasilva (Abraham 77), Clarke-Salter, Kenny, Tomori; Dowell, Barnes (Sessegnon R 46 (Foden 57)), Gray; Mount, Calvert-Lewin, Maddison.
Referee: Andreas Ekberg.

Monday, 24 June 2019

Croatia U21 (1) 3 *(Brekalo 39, 82, Vlasic 62)*

England U21 (1) 3 *(Nelson 11 (pen), Maddison 48, Kenny 70)*

England U21: (433) Henderson; Kenny, Clarke-Salter (Konsa 49), Tomori, Kelly; Foden, Dowell (Mount 56), Maddison (Gibbs-White 73); Gray, Abraham, Nelson.
Referee: Orel Grinfeld.

FRIENDLIES

Thursday, 15 November 2018

Italy U21 (1) 1 *(Kean 42)*

England U21 (1) 2 *(Solanke 8, 53)*

England U21: (4231) Henderson; Walker-Peters, Clarke-Salter (Kelly 4), Tomori, Dasilva; Cook, Davies (Dowell 69); Gray (Nelson 63), Foden, Sessegnon R (Abraham 69); Solanke (Calvert-Lewin 63).

Tuesday, 20 November 2018

Denmark U21 (1) 1 *(Ingvartsen 42)*

England U21 (2) 5 *(Gray 31, Solanke 39, 47, Calvert-Lewin 81, 87 (pen))*

England U21: (442) Henderson; Walker-Peters (Tomori 70), Dasilva (Kelly 61), Simpson, Konsa; Cook (Davies 70), Gray (Sessegnon R 73), Foden (Calvert-Lewin 61), Dowell; Solanke, Nelson.

Thursday, 21 March 2019

England U21 (1) 1 *(Calvert-Lewin 13)*

Poland U21 (1) 1 *(Szymanski 34)*

England U21: (442) Gunn; Kenny, Dasilva, Dowell (Choudhury 80), Tomori; Kelly, Lookman (Barnes 72), Maddison, Calvert-Lewin (Solanke 72); Foden (Davies 72), Nelson (Gray 72).

Tuesday, 26 March 2019

England U21 (1) 1 *(Solanke 43)*

Germany U21 (1) 2 *(Dahoud 27, Uduokhai 90)*

England U21: (433) Henderson; Walker-Peters, Fry (Konsa 68), Clarke-Salter, Sessegnon R (Dasilva 82); Foden, Davies (Calvert-Lewin 68), Dowell (Choudhury 67); Barnes (Lookman 81), Solanke (Maddison 82), Gray.

SCOTLAND

UEFA UNDER-21 CHAMPIONSHIPS 2017–19

Thursday, 6 September 2018

Scotland U21 (1) 3 *(Hornby 45 (pen), 70, 83)*

Andorra U21 (0) 0 2125

Scotland U21: (433) Fulton; Williamson, Bates, Porteous, Smith; Gilmour (Ferguson 78), Ross McCrorie, Mallan (Campbell 72); Cadden, Hornby (Shaw 85), Johnston M.
Referee: Dejan Jakimovski.

Tuesday, 11 September 2018

Holland U21 (0) 1 *(Koopmeiners 70)*

Scotland U21 (0) 2 *(Hornby 54, 89 (pen))* 6830

Scotland U21: (433) Robby McCrorie; Magennis, Cadden, Bates, Porteous; Hornby, Ross McCrorie, Smith; Johnston M (Gilmour 70), Campbell (Ferguson 39), Mallan (McIntyre 77).
Referee: Antti Munukka.

Friday, 12 October 2018

Ukraine U21 (1) 3 *(Zubkov 32, 56, Kovalenko 90)*

Scotland U21 (1) 1 *(Morgan 1)* 4367

Scotland U21: (433) Robby McCrorie; Porteous, Bates, Taylor, Smith; Campbell (Gilmour 90), Ross McCrorie, Cadden; Mallan, Brophy (Middleton 69), Morgan.
Referee: Bojan Pandzic.

Tuesday, 16 October 2018

Scotland U21 (0) 0

England U21 (0) 2 *(Nelson 60, Dowell 90)* 4122

Scotland U21: (433) Doohan; Porteous, Bates, Taylor, Smith; Cadden, Ross McCrorie, Campbell; Shaw (Middleton 46), Morgan, Gilmour (Ferguson 61).
England U21: (4231) Henderson; Wan Bissaka, Tomori, Clarke-Salter, Dasilva; Onomah (Foden 71), Dowell; Nelson (Sessegnon R 73), Solanke, Barnes; Abraham (Calvert-Lewin 87).
Referee: Marco Di Bello.

FRIENDLY

Friday, 22 March 2019

Scotland U21 (0) 0

Mexico U21 (0) 0

Scotland U21: (442) Doohan; Brandon, Harvie, Johnston G, Maguire; Ross McCrorie, Campbell, Turnbull, McAllister; Hastie, Hornby.

Monday, 25 March 2019

Sweden U21 (2) 2 *(Asoro 7, Mbunga-Kimpioka 38)*

Scotland U21 (1) 1 *(Maguire 23)*

Scotland U21: (442) Robby McCrorie; Campbell, Harvie, Holsgrove, House; Johnston G, Johnston M, Mackie, Maguire; Ross McCrorie, Wilson.

WALES

UEFA UNDER-21 CHAMPIONSHIPS 2017–19

Friday, 7 September 2018

Wales U21 (2) 2 *(Thomas 5, 18)*

Liechtenstein U21 (0) 1 *(Graber L 78)* 307

Wales U21: (442) Pilling; Harries (Broadhead 53), Poole, Coxe, Norrington-Davies; Baker, James, Morrell, Thomas; Harris M, Matondo (Babos 72).
Referee: Laurent Kopriwa.

Tuesday, 11 September 2018

Wales U21 (0) 0

Portugal U21 (1) 2 *(Andre Horta 34, Joao Felix 73)* 625

Wales U21: (433) Pilling; Coxe, Cooper, Harries, Norrington-Davies; Morrell (Lemonheigh-Evans 74), Poole, Baker (Babos 79); James, Broadhead (Matondo 56), Thomas.
Referee: Mykola Balakin.

Friday, 12 October 2018

Romania U21 (0) 2 *(Man 55, Puscas 71)*

Wales U21 (0) 0 12,588

Wales U21: (442) Evans O; Norrington-Davies, Cooper, Poole, Lewis; James, Broadhead, Baker (Christie-Davies 90), Morrell; Harris M (Lemonheigh-Evans 62), Cullen (Babos 62).
Referee: Boris Marhefka.

Tuesday, 16 October 2018

Wales U21 (2) 3 *(Morrell 36, Lemonheigh-Evans 38, 87)*

Switzerland U21 (0) 1 *(Zeqiri 76)* 242

Wales U21: (541) Evans O; Lewis, Davies, Poole, Harries, Norrington-Davies; Lemonheigh-Evans, Burton (Christie-Davies 90), Morrell, Broadhead (Babos 61); Harris M (Touray 80).
Referee: Erik Lambrechts.

FRIENDLIES

Sunday, 9 June 2019

Albania (0) 2 *(Broja 48, 60)*

Wales (0) 1 *(Pugh 80)*

Wales: Absolom: Lewis, Dasilva (Cullen 60), Poole, Norrington-Davies, Cooper, Burton (Price 60), Evans J (Clifton 46), Harris M (Touray 60), Broadhead (Pugh 60), Babos (Huggins 46).

Tuesday, 11 June 2019

Albania (2) 3 *(Bullari 9, Mala 14, Broja 65)*

Wales (1) 1 *(Lewis 90 (pen))*

Wales: Ratcliffe, Lewis, Dasilva (Cullen 46), Poole, Norrington-Davies, Cabango, Evans J (Burton 60), Clifton, Harris M (Pugh 46), Touray (Mooney 60), Broadhead (Evans K 60).

NORTHERN IRELAND

UEFA UNDER-21 CHAMPIONSHIPS 2017–19

Tuesday, 11 September 2018

Spain U21 (0) 1 *(Mir 90)*

N Ireland U21 (2) 2 *(Lavery 4, Donnelly 8 (pen))* 3400

N Ireland U21: (352) Hazard; Donnelly, Ballard, Johnson; McDonagh, Dunwoody (Gorman 74), Holden (Bird 78), Sykes, Burns; Lavery (McGonigle 61), Smyth.
Referee: Jonathan Lardot.

Thursday, 11 October 2018

Iceland U21 (0) 0

N Ireland U21 (0) 1 *(Ballard 90)* 337

N Ireland U21: (433) Hazard; McDonagh, Ballard, Donnelly, Bird; Thompson, Gorman (Sykes 74), Burns; Smyth, Lavery (Parkhouse 82), Holden (Roy 77).
Referee: Jens Maae.

Tuesday, 16 October 2018

N Ireland U21 (0) 1 *(Sykes 62)*

Slovakia U21 (0) 0 5452

N Ireland U21: (352) Hazard; Ballard, Donnelly, Johnson; McDonagh, Roy (Dummigan 79), Thompson (Gorman 89), Sykes, Burns; Lavery (Parkhouse 83), Smyth.
Referee: Eitan Shmuelevitz.

FRIENDLIES

Friday, 22 March 2019

N Ireland U21 (1) 1 *(Lavery 18)*

Bulgaria U21 (0) 0

N Ireland U21: (442) Thompson; Amos, Finlayson, Balmer, Bird; Kerr, McClean, Palmer, Kelly; Lavery, Galllagher.

Monday 25 March 2019

Mexico (1) 1 *(Lopez 18)*

Northern Ireland (0) 2 *(Parkhouse 55, Lavery 87)*

Northern Ireland: Dunne, Toal, Kerr, Balmer (Bird 65), McCalmont, Gallagher (McClean 65), Galbraith (Palmer 76), Dunwoody, Burns (Amos 88), Boyd-Munce (Lavery 76), Parkhouse (Kelly 76).

REPUBLIC OF IRELAND

UEFA UNDER-21 CHAMPIONSHIPS 2017–19

Friday, 7 September 2018

Kosovo U21 (0) 1 *(Hasani 64)*

Republic of Ireland U21 (0) 1 *(Curtis 82)* 1000

Republic of Ireland U21: (442) O'Hara; Kane (Hale 77), Whelan, Sweeney, Manning (Mulraney 77); Charsley, Kinsella, Curtis, Cullen; Shaughnessy, Grego-Cox.
Referee: Petr Ardeleanu.

Tuesday, 11 September 2018

Republic of Ireland U21 (0) 0

Germany U21 (2) 6 *(Seydel 6, Teuchert 22 (pen), 66, 73 (pen), Serdar 83 (pen), 86)* 2325

Republic of Ireland U21: (433) O'Hara; McLaughlin (Donnellan 16), Delaney, Shaughnessy, Whelan; Charsley, Cullen, Kinsella; Manning (McGrath 54), Grego-Cox, Mulraney (Quigley 88).
Referee: Alejandro Hernandez Hernandez.

Thursday, 11 October 2018

Israel U21 (1) 3 *(Kanichowsky 15, Plakushchenko 77, Cohen 90)*

Republic of Ireland U21 (0) 1 *(Hale 64)* 120

Republic of Ireland U21: (433) O'Hara; Whelan, Delaney (McGrath 86), Sweeney, Kane; Cullen, Shipley (Hale 59), Kinsella; Charsley, Grego-Cox (Mulraney 85), Curtis.
Referee: Lawrence Visser.

Tuesday, 16 October 2018

Germany U21 (2) 2 *(Serra 32, Oztunali 40)*

Republic of Ireland U21 (0) 0 3229

Republic of Ireland U21: (433) Bossin; Whelan, Delaney, Sweeney, Kane (Dunne 65); Donnellan, Cullen, Kinsella; McGrath, Hale (Grego-Cox 77), Shipley.
Referee: Karim Abed.

Sunday, 24 March 2019

Republic of Ireland U21 (2) 3 *(Idaz 34, 68, Farrugia 38)*

Luxembourg U21 (0) 0 4772

Republic of Ireland U21: (442) Kelleher; Masterson, Leahy, O'Connor L, O'Shea; Elbouzedi (O'Connor M 90), Ronan (Mandroiu 86), Molumby (Lennon 78), Coventry; Farrugia (Drinan 90), Idaz (Kavanagh 90).
Referee: Timotheos Christofi.

UEFA REGIONS' CUP 2018–19

FINALS IN BAVARIA

GROUP A

West Slovakia v Istanbul	1-3
Bavaria v Normandie	1-0
Istanbul v Normandie	2-1
Bavaria v West Slovakia	1-1
Istanbul v Bavaria	0-1
Normandie v West Slovakia	2-0

	P	W	D	L	F	A	GD	Pts
Bavaria	3	2	1	0	3	1	2	7
Istanbul	3	2	0	1	5	3	2	6
Normandie	3	1	0	2	3	3	0	3
West Slovakia	3	0	1	2	2	6	–4	1

GROUP B

Hradec Kralove Region v Castile and Leon	0-3
S Fed U – Southern Region v Dolny Slask	0-1
Hradec Kralove Region v S Fed U – Southern Region	1-0
Dolny Slask v Castile and Leon	1-1
Dolny Slask v Hradec Kralove Region	2-2
Castile and Leon v S Fed U – Southern Region	1-2

	P	W	D	L	F	A	GD	Pts
Dolny Slask	3	1	2	0	4	3	1	5
Castile and Leon	3	1	1	1	5	3	2	4
Hradec Kralove Region	3	1	1	1	3	5	–2	4
S Fed U – Southern Region	3	1	0	2	2	3	–1	3

FINAL

Bavaria v Dolny Slask 2-3

BRITISH UNDER-21 APPEARANCES 1976–2019

Bold type indicates players who made an international appearance in season 2018–19.

ENGLAND

Ablett, G. 1988 (Liverpool)	1
Abraham, K. O. T. (Tammy) 2017 (Chelsea)	**26**
Akpom, C. A. 2015 (Arsenal)	5
Adams, N. 1987 (Everton)	1
Adams, T. A. 1985 (Arsenal)	5
Addison, M. 2010 (Derby Co)	1
Afobe, B. T. 2012 (Arsenal)	2
Agbonlahor, G. 2007 (Aston Villa)	16
Albrighton, M. K. 2011 (Aston Villa)	8
Alexander-Arnold, T. J. 2018 (Liverpool)	3
Alli, B. J. (Dele) 2015 (Tottenham H)	2
Allen, B. 1992 (QPR)	8
Allen, C. 1980 (QPR, Crystal Palace)	3
Allen, C. A. 1995 (Oxford U)	2
Allen, M. 1987 (QPR)	2
Allen, P. 1985 (West Ham U, Tottenham H)	3
Allen, R. W. 1998 (Tottenham H)	3
Alnwick, B. R. 2008 (Tottenham H)	1
Ambrose, D. P. F. 2003 (Ipswich T, Newcastle U, Charlton Ath)	10
Ameobi, F. 2001 (Newcastle U)	19
Ameobi, S. 2012 (Newcastle U)	5
Amos, B. P. 2012 (Manchester U)	3
Anderson, V. A. 1978 (Nottingham F)	1
Anderton, D. R. 1993 (Tottenham H)	12
Andrews, I. 1987 (Leicester C)	1
Ardley, N. C. 1993 (Wimbledon)	10
Armstrong, A. J. 2018 (Newcastle U)	5
Ashcroft, L. 1992 (Preston NE)	1
Ashton, D. 2004 (Crewe Alex, Norwich C)	9
Atherton, P. 1992 (Coventry C)	1
Atkinson, B. 1991 (Sunderland)	6
Awford, A. T. 1993 (Portsmouth)	9
Bailey, G. R. 1979 (Manchester U)	14
Baines, L. J. 2005 (Wigan Ath)	16
Baker, G. E. 1981 (Southampton)	2
Baker, L. R. 2015 (Chelsea)	17
Baker, N. L. 2011 (Aston Villa)	3
Ball, M. J. 1999 (Everton)	7
Bamford, P. J. 2013 (Chelsea)	2
Bannister, G. 1982 (Sheffield W)	1
Barker, S. 1985 (Blackburn R)	4
Barkley, R. 2012 (Everton)	5
Barmby, N. J. 1994 (Tottenham H, Everton)	4
Barnes, H. L. 2019 (Leicester C)	**4**
Barnes, J. 1983 (Watford)	2
Barnes, P. S. 1977 (Manchester C)	9
Barrett, E. D. 1990 (Oldham Ath)	4
Barry, G. 1999 (Aston Villa)	27
Barton, J. 2004 (Manchester C)	2
Bart-Williams, C. G. 1993 (Sheffield W)	16
Batty, D. 1988 (Leeds U)	7
Bazeley, D. S. 1992 (Watford)	1
Beagrie, P. 1988 (Sheffield U)	2
Beardsmore, R. 1989 (Manchester U)	5
Beattie, J. S. 1999 (Southampton)	5
Beckham, D. R. J. 1995 (Manchester U)	9
Berahino, S. 2013 (WBA)	11
Bennett, J. 2011 (Middlesbrough)	3
Bennett, R. 2012 (Norwich C)	2
Bent, D. A. 2003 (Ipswich T, Charlton Ath)	14
Bent, M. N. 1998 (Crystal Palace)	2
Bentley, D. M. 2004 (Arsenal, Blackburn R)	8
Beeston, C 1988 (Stoke C)	1
Benjamin, T. J. 2001 (Leicester C)	1
Bertrand, R. 2009 (Chelsea)	16
Bertschin, K. E. 1977 (Birmingham C)	3
Bettinelli, M. 2015 (Fulham)	1
Birtles, G. 1980 (Nottingham F)	2
Blackett, T. N. 2014 (Manchester U)	1
Blackstock, D. A. 2008 (QPR)	2
Blackwell, D. R. 1991 (Wimbledon)	6
Blake, M. A. 1990 (Aston Villa)	8
Blissett, L. L. 1979 (Watford)	4
Bond, J. H. 2013 (Watford)	5
Booth, A. D. 1995 (Huddersfield T)	3
Bothroyd, J. 2001 (Coventry C)	1
Bowyer, L. D. 1996 (Charlton Ath, Leeds U)	13
Bracewell, P. 1983 (Stoke C)	13
Bradbury, L. M. 1997 (Portsmouth, Manchester C)	3
Bramble, T. M. 2001 (Ipswich T, Newcastle U)	10
Branch, P. M. 1997 (Everton)	1
Bradshaw, P. W. 1977 (Wolverhampton W)	4
Breacker, T. 1986 (Luton T)	2
Brennan, M. 1987 (Ipswich T)	5
Bridge, W. M. 1999 (Southampton)	8
Bridges, M. 1997 (Sunderland, Leeds U)	3
Briggs, M. 2012 (Fulham)	2
Brightwell, I. 1989 (Manchester C)	4
Briscoe, L. S. 1996 (Sheffield W)	5
Brock, K. 1984 (Oxford U)	4
Broomes, M. C. 1997 (Blackburn R)	2
Brown, M. R. 1996 (Manchester C)	4
Brown, W. M. 1999 (Manchester U)	8
Bull, S. G. 1989 (Wolverhampton W)	5
Bullock, M. J. 1998 (Barnsley)	1
Burrows, D. 1989 (WBA, Liverpool)	7
Butcher, T. I. 1979 (Ipswich T)	7
Butland, J. 2012 (Birmingham C, Stoke C)	28
Butt, N. 1995 (Manchester U)	7
Butters, G. 1989 (Tottenham H)	3
Butterworth, I. 1985 (Coventry C, Nottingham F)	8
Bywater, S. 2001 (West Ham U)	6
Cadamarteri, D. L. 1999 (Everton)	3
Caesar, G. 1987 (Arsenal)	3
Cahill, G. J. 2007 (Aston Villa)	3
Callaghan, N. 1983 (Watford)	9
Calvert-Lewin, D. N. 2018 (Everton)	**17**
Camp, L. M. J. 2005 (Derby Co)	5
Campbell, A. P. 2000 (Middlesbrough)	4
Campbell, F. L. 2008 (Manchester U)	14
Campbell, K. J. 1991 (Arsenal)	4
Campbell, S. 1994 (Tottenham)	11
Carbon, M. P. 1996 (Derby Co)	4
Carr, C. 1985 (Fulham)	1
Carr, F. 1987 (Nottingham F)	9
Carragher, J. L. 1997 (Liverpool)	27
Carroll, A. T. 2010 (Newcastle U)	5
Carroll, T. J. 2013 (Tottenham H)	17
Carlisle, C. J. 2001 (QPR)	3
Carrick, M. 2001 (West Ham U)	14
Carson, S. P. 2004 (Leeds U, Liverpool)	29
Casper, C. M. 1995 (Manchester U)	1
Caton, T. 1982 (Manchester C)	14
Cattermole, L. B. 2008 (Middlesbrough, Wigan Ath, Sunderland)	16
Caulker, S. R. 2011 (Tottenham H)	10
Chadwick, L. H. 2000 (Manchester U)	13
Challis, T. M. 1996 (QPR)	2
Chalobah, N. N. 2012 (Chelsea)	40
Chamberlain, M. 1983 (Stoke C)	4
Chambers, C. 2015 (Arsenal)	22
Chaplow, R. D. 2004 (Burnley)	1
Chapman, L. 1981 (Stoke C)	1
Charles, G. A. 1991 (Nottingham F)	4
Chettle, S. 1988 (Nottingham F)	12
Chilwell, B. J. 2016 (Leicester C)	**10**
Chopra, R. M. 2004 (Newcastle U)	1

Choudhury, H. D. 2018 (Leicester C) 7
Clark, L. R. 1992 (Newcastle U) 11
Clarke, P. M. 2003 (Everton) 8
Clarke-Salter, J. L. 2018 (Chelsea) 12
Christie, M. N. 2001 (Derby Co) 11
Clegg, M. J. 1998 (Manchester U) 2
Clemence, S. N. 1999 (Tottenham H) 1
Cleverley, T. W. 2010 (Manchester U) 16
Clough, N. H. 1986 (Nottingham F) 15
Clyne, N. E. 2012 (Crystal Palace) 8
Cole, A. 2001 (Arsenal) 4
Cole, A. A. 1992 (Arsenal, Bristol C, Newcastle U) 8
Cole, C. 2003 (Chelsea) 19
Cole, J. J. 2000 (West Ham U) 8
Coney, D. 1985 (Fulham) 4
Connolly, C. A. 2018 (Everton) 4
Connor, T. 1987 (Brighton & HA) 1
Cook, L. J. 2018 (Bournemouth) 14
Cooke, R. 1986 (Tottenham H) 1
Cooke, T. J. 1996 (Manchester U) 4
Cooper, C. T. 1988 (Middlesbrough) 8
Cork, J. F. P. 2009 (Chelsea) 13
Corrigan, J. T. 1978 (Manchester C) 3
Cort, C. E. R. 1999 (Wimbledon) 12
Cottee, A. R. 1985 (West Ham U) 8
Couzens, A. J. 1995 (Leeds U) 3
Cowans, G. S. 1979 (Aston Villa) 5
Cox, N. J. 1993 (Aston Villa) 6
Cranie, M. J. 2008 (Portsmouth) 16
Cranson, I. 1985 (Ipswich T) 5
Cresswell, R. P. W. 1999 (York C, Sheffield W) 4
Croft, G. 1995 (Grimsby T) 4
Crooks, G. 1980 (Stoke C) 4
Crossley, M. G. 1990 (Nottingham F) 3
Crouch, P. J. 2002 (Portsmouth, Aston Villa) 5
Cundy, J. V. 1991 (Chelsea) 3
Cunningham, L. 1977 (WBA) 6
Curbishley, L. C. 1981 (Birmingham C) 1
Curtis, J. C. K. 1998 (Manchester U) 16

Daniel, P. W. 1977 (Hull C) 7
Dann, S. 2008 (Coventry C) 2
Dasilva, J. R. 2018 (Chelsea) 13
Davenport, C. R. P. 2005 (Tottenham H) 8
Davies, A. J. 2004 (Middlesbrough) 1
Davies, C. E. 2006 (WBA) 3
Davies, K. C. 1998 (Southampton, Blackburn R, Southampton) 3
Davies, T. 2018 (Everton) 12
Davis, K. G. 1995 (Luton T) 3
Davis, P. 1982 (Arsenal) 11
Davis, S. 2001 (Fulham) 11
Dawson, C. 2012 (WBA) 15
Dawson, M. R. 2003 (Nottingham F, Tottenham H) 13
Day, C. N. 1996 (Tottenham H, Crystal Palace) 6
D'Avray, M. 1984 (Ipswich T) 2
Deehan, J. M. 1977 (Aston Villa) 7
Defoe, J. C. 2001 (West Ham U) 23
Delfouneso, N. 2010 (Aston Villa) 17
Delph, F. 2009 (Leeds U, Aston Villa) 4
Dennis, M. E. 1980 (Birmingham C) 3
Derbyshire, M. A. 2007 (Blackburn R) 14
Dichio, D. S. E. 1996 (QPR) 1
Dickens, A. 1985 (West Ham U) 1
Dicks, J. 1988 (West Ham U) 4
Dier, E. J. E. 2013 (Sporting Lisbon, Tottenham H) 9
Digby, F. 1987 (Swindon T) 5
Dillon, K. P. 1981 (Birmingham C) 1
Dixon, K. M. 1985 (Chelsea) 1
Dobson, A. 1989 (Coventry C) 4
Dodd, J. R. 1991 (Southampton) 8
Donowa, L. 1985 (Norwich C) 3
Dorigo, A. R. 1987 (Aston Villa) 11
Dowell, K. O. 2018 (Everton) 17
Downing, S. 2004 (Middlesbrough) 8
Dozzell, J. 1987 (Ipswich T) 9
Draper, M. A. 1991 (Notts Co) 3
Driver, A. 2009 (Hearts) 1
Duberry, M. W. 1997 (Chelsea) 5
Dunn, D. J. I. 1999 (Blackburn R) 20
Duxbury, M. 1981 (Manchester U) 7
Dyer, B. A. 1994 (Crystal Palace) 10
Dyer, K. C. 1998 (Ipswich T, Newcastle U) 11
Dyson, P. I. 1981 (Coventry C) 4

Eadie, D. M. 1994 (Norwich C) 7
Ebanks-Blake, S. 2009 (Wolverhampton W) 1
Ebbrell, J. 1989 (Everton) 14
Edghill, R. A. 1994 (Manchester C) 3
Ehiogu, U. 1992 (Aston Villa) 15
Ejaria, O. D. 2018 (Liverpool) 1
Elliott, P. 1985 (Luton T) 3
Elliott, R. J. 1996 (Newcastle U) 2
Elliott, S. W. 1998 (Derby Co) 3
Etherington, N, 2002 (Tottenham H) 3
Euell, J. J. 1998 (Wimbledon) 6
Evans, R. 2003 (Chelsea) 2

Fairclough, C. 1985 (Nottingham F, Tottenham H) 7
Fairclough, D. 1977 (Liverpool) 1
Fashanu, J. 1980 (Norwich C, Nottingham F) 11
Fear, P. 1994 (Wimbledon) 3
Fenton, G. A. 1995 (Aston Villa) 1
Fenwick, T. W. 1981 (Crystal Palace, QPR) 11
Ferdinand, A. J. 2005 (West Ham U) 17
Ferdinand, R. G. 1997 (West Ham U) 5
Fereday, W. 1985 (QPR) 5
Fielding, F. D. 2009 (Blackburn R) 12
Flanagan, J. 2012 (Liverpool) 3
Flitcroft, G. W. 1993 (Manchester C) 10
Flowers, T. D. 1987 (Southampton) 3
Foden, P. W. 2019 (Manchester C) 9
Ford, M. 1996 (Leeds U) 2
Forster, N. M. 1995 (Brentford) 4
Forsyth, M. 1988 (Derby Co) 1
Forster-Caskey, J. D. 2014 (Brighton & HA) 14
Foster, S. 1980 (Brighton & HA) 1
Fowler, R. B. 1994 (Liverpool) 8
Fox, D. J. 2008 (Coventry C) 1
Froggatt, S. J. 1993 (Aston Villa) 2
Fry, D. J. 2018 (Middlesbrough) 11
Futcher, P. 1977 (Luton T, Manchester C) 11

Gabbiadini, M. 1989 (Sunderland) 2
Gale, A. 1982 (Fulham) 1
Gallen, K. A. 1995 (QPR) 4
Galloway, B. J. 2017 (Everton) 3
Garbutt, L. S. 2014 (Everton) 11
Gardner, A. 2002 (Tottenham H) 1
Gardner, C. 2008 (Aston Villa) 14
Gardner, G. 2012 (Aston Villa) 5
Gascoigne, P. J. 1987 (Newcastle U) 13
Gayle, H. 1984 (Birmingham C) 3
Gernon, T. 1983 (Ipswich T) 1
Gerrard, P. W. 1993 (Oldham Ath) 18
Gerrard, S. G. 2000 (Liverpool) 4
Gibbs, K. J. R. 2009 (Arsenal) 15
Gibbs, N. 1987 (Watford) 5
Gibbs-White, M. A. 2019 (Wolverhampton W) 1
Gibson, B. J. 2014 (Middlesbrough) 10
Gibson, C. 1982 (Aston Villa) 1
Gilbert, W. A. 1979 (Crystal Palace) 11
Goddard, P. 1981 (West Ham U) 8
Gomez, J. D. 2015 (Liverpool) 7
Gordon, D. 1987 (Norwich C) 4
Gordon, D. D. 1994 (Crystal Palace) 13
Gosling, D. 2010 (Everton, Newcastle U) 3
Grant, A. J. 1996 (Everton) 1
Grant, L. A. 2003 (Derby Co) 4
Granville, D. P. 1997 (Chelsea) 3
Gray, A. 1988 (Aston Villa) 2
Gray, D. R. 2016 (Leicester C) 26

Grealish, J. 2016 (Aston Villa) 7
Greening, J. 1999 (Manchester U, Middlesbrough) 18
Griffin, A. 1999 (Newcastle U) 3
Grimes, M. J. 2016 (Swansea C) 4
Gunn, A. 2015 (Manchester C, Southampton) 12
Guppy, S. A. 1998 (Leicester C) 1

Haigh, P. 1977 (Hull C) 1
Hall, M. T. J. 1997 (Coventry C) 8
Hall, R. A. 1992 (Southampton) 11
Hamilton, D. V. 1997 (Newcastle U) 1
Hammill, A. 2010 (Wolverhampton W) 1
Harding, D. A. 2005 (Brighton & HA) 4
Hardyman, P. 1985 (Portsmouth) 2
Hargreaves, O. 2001 (Bayern Munich) 3
Harley, J. 2000 (Chelsea) 3
Harrison, J. D. 2018 (Manchester C) 2
Hart, C. J. J. (Joe) 2007 (Manchester C) 21
Hateley, M. 1982 (Coventry C, Portsmouth) 10
Hause, K. P. D. 2015 (Wolverhampton W) 10
Hayden, I. 2017 (Newcastle U) 3
Hayes, M. 1987 (Arsenal) 3
Hazell, R. J. 1979 (Wolverhampton W) 1
Heaney, N. A. 1992 (Arsenal) 6
Heath, A. 1981 (Stoke C, Everton) 8
Heaton, T. D. 2008 (Manchester U) 3
Henderson, D. B. 2018 (Manchester U) 11
Henderson, J. B. 2011 (Sunderland, Liverpool) 27
Hendon, I. M. 1992 (Tottenham H) 7
Hendrie, L. A. 1996 (Aston Villa) 13
Hesford, I. 1981 (Blackpool) 7
Heskey, E. W. I. 1997 (Leicester C, Liverpool) 16
Hilaire, V. 1980 (Crystal Palace) 9
Hill, D. R. L. 1995 (Tottenham H) 4
Hillier, D. 1991 (Arsenal) 1
Hinchcliffe, A. 1989 (Manchester C) 1
Hines, Z. 2010 (West Ham U) 2
Hinshelwood, P. A. 1978 (Crystal Palace) 2
Hirst, D. E. 1988 (Sheffield W) 7
Hislop, N. S. 1998 (Newcastle U) 1
Hoddle, G. 1977 (Tottenham H) 12
Hodge, S. B. 1983 (Nottingham F, Aston Villa) 8
Hodgson, D. J. 1981 (Middlesbrough) 6
Holding, R. S. 2016 (Bolton W, Arsenal) 5
Holdsworth, D. 1989 (Watford) 1
Holgate, M. 2017 (Everton) 6
Holland, C. J. 1995 (Newcastle U) 10
Holland, P. 1995 (Mansfield T) 4
Holloway, D. 1998 (Sunderland) 1
Horne, B. 1989 (Millwall) 5
Howe, E. J. F. 1998 (Bournemouth) 2
Howson, J. M. 2011 (Leeds U) 1
Hoyte, J. R. 2004 (Arsenal) 18
Hucker, P. 1984 (QPR) 2
Huckerby, D. 1997 (Coventry C) 4
Huddlestone, T. A. 2005 (Derby Co, Tottenham H) 33
Hughes, S. J. 1997 (Arsenal) 8
Hughes, W. J. 2012 (Derby Co) 22
Humphreys, R. J. 1997 (Sheffield W) 3
Hunt, N. B. 2004 (Bolton W) 10

Ibe, J. A. F. 2015 (Liverpool) 4
Impey, A. R. 1993 (QPR) 1
Ince, P. E. C. 1989 (West Ham U) 2
Ince, T. C. 2012 (Blackpool, Hull C) 18
Ings, D. W. J. 2013 (Burnley) 13
Iorfa, D. 2016 (Wolverhampton W) 13

Jackson, M. A. 1992 (Everton) 10
Jagielka, P. N. 2003 (Sheffield U) 6
James, D. B. 1991 (Watford) 10
James, J. C. 1990 (Luton T) 2
Jansen, M. B. 1999 (Crystal Palace, Blackburn R) 6
Jeffers, F. 2000 (Everton, Arsenal) 16
Jemson, N. B. 1991 (Nottingham F) 1
Jenas, J. A. 2002 (Newcastle U) 9
Jenkinson, C. D. 2013 (Arsenal) 14
Jerome, C. 2006 (Cardiff C, Birmingham C) 10
Joachim, J. K. 1994 (Leicester C) 9
Johnson, A. 2008 (Middlesbrough) 19
Johnson, G. M. C. 2003 (West Ham U, Chelsea) 14
Johnson, M. 2008 (Manchester C) 2
Johnson, S. A. M. 1999 (Crewe Alex, Derby Co, Leeds U) 15
Johnson, T. 1991 (Notts Co, Derby Co) 7
Johnston, C. P. 1981 (Middlesbrough) 2
Jones, D. R. 1977 (Everton) 1
Jones, C. H. 1978 (Tottenham H) 1
Jones, D. F. L. 2004 (Manchester U) 1
Jones, P. A. 2011 (Blackburn R) 9
Jones, R. 1993 (Liverpool) 2

Kane, H. E. 2013 (Tottenham H) 14
Keane, M. V. 2013 (Manchester U, Burnley) 16
Keane, W. D. 2012 (Manchester U) 3
Keegan, G. A. 1977 (Manchester C) 1
Kelly, L. C. 2019 (Bournemouth) 4
Kelly, M. R. 2011 (Liverpool) 8
Kenny, J. 2018 (Everton) 16
Kenny, W. 1993 (Everton) 1
Keown, M. R. 1987 (Aston Villa) 8
Kerslake, D. 1986 (QPR) 1
Kightly, M. J. 2008 (Wolverhampton W) 7
Kilcline, B. 1983 (Notts C) 2
Kilgallon, M. 2004 (Leeds U) 5
King, A. E. 1977 (Everton) 2
King, L. B. 2000 (Tottenham H) 12
Kirkland, C. E. 2001 (Coventry C, Liverpool) 8
Kitson, P. 1991 (Leicester C, Derby Co) 7
Knight, A. 1983 (Portsmouth) 2
Knight, I. 1987 (Sheffield W) 2
Knight, Z. 2002 (Fulham) 4
Konchesky, P. M. 2002 (Charlton Ath) 15
Konsa, E. 2018 (Charlton Ath, Brentford) 7
Kozluk, R. 1998 (Derby Co) 2

Lake, P. 1989 (Manchester C) 5
Lallana, A. D. 2009 (Southampton) 1
Lampard, F. J. 1998 (West Ham U) 19
Langley, T. W. 1978 (Chelsea) 1
Lansbury, H. G. 2010 (Arsenal, Nottingham F) 16
Lascellas, J. 2014 (Newcastle U) 2
Leadbitter, G. 2008 (Sunderland) 3
Lee, D. J. 1990 (Chelsea) 10
Lee, R. M. 1986 (Charlton Ath) 2
Lee, S. 1981 (Liverpool) 6
Lees, T. J. 2012 (Leeds U) 6
Lennon, A. J. 2006 (Tottenham H) 5
Le Saux, G. P. 1990 (Chelsea) 4
Lescott, J. P. 2003 (Wolverhampton W) 2
Lewis, J. P. 2008 (Peterborough U) 5
Lingard, J. E. 2013 (Manchester U) 11
Lita, L. H. 2005 (Bristol C, Reading) 9
Loach, S. J. 2009 (Watford) 14
Loftus-Cheek, R. I. 2015 (Chelsea) 17
Lookman, A. 2018 (Everton) 11
Lowe, D. 1988 (Ipswich T) 2
Lowe, J. J. 2012 (Blackburn R) 11
Lukic, J. 1981 (Leeds U) 7
Lund, G. 1985 (Grimsby T) 3

McCall, S. H. 1981 (Ipswich T) 6
McCarthy, A. S. 2011 (Reading) 3
McDonald, N. 1987 (Newcastle U) 5
McEachran, J. M. 2011 (Chelsea) 13
McEveley, J. 2003 (Blackburn R) 1
McGrath, L. 1986 (Coventry C) 1
MacKenzie, S. 1982 (WBA) 3
McLeary, A. 1988 (Millwall) 1
McLeod, I. M. 2006 (Milton Keynes D) 1
McMahon, S. 1981 (Everton, Aston Villa) 6

McManaman, S. 1991 (Liverpool) 7
McQueen, S. J. 2017 (Southampton) 1
Mabbutt, G. 1982 (Bristol R, Tottenham H) 7
Maddison, J. D. 2018 (Norwich C, Leicester C) 9
Maguire, J. H. 2012 (Sheffield U) 1
Maitland-Niles, A. C. 2018 (Arsenal) 4
Makin, C. 1994 (Oldham Ath) 5
Mancienne, M. I. 2008 (Chelsea) 30
March, S. B. 2015 (Brighton & HA) 3
Marney, D. E. 2005 (Tottenham H) 1
Marriott, A. 1992 (Nottingham F) 1
Marsh, S. T. 1998 (Oxford U) 1
Marshall, A. J. 1995 (Norwich C) 4
Marshall, B. 2012 (Leicester C) 2
Marshall, L. K. 1999 (Norwich C) 1
Martin, L. 1989 (Manchester U) 2
Martyn, A. N. 1988 (Bristol R) 11
Matteo, D. 1994 (Liverpool) 4
Mattock, J. W. 2008 (Leicester C) 5
Matthew, D. 1990 (Chelsea) 9
Mawson, A. R. J. 2017 (Swansea C) 6
May, A. 1986 (Manchester C) 1
Mee, B. 2011 (Manchester C) 2
Merson, P. C. 1989 (Arsenal) 4
Middleton, J. 1977 (Nottingham F, Derby Co) 3
Miller, A. 1988 (Arsenal) 4
Mills, D. J. 1999 (Charlton Ath, Leeds U) 14
Mills, G. R. 1981 (Nottingham F) 2
Milner, J. P. 2004 (Leeds U, Newcastle U, Aston Villa) 46
Mimms, R. 1985 (Rotherham U, Everton) 3
Minto, S. C. 1991 (Charlton Ath) 6
Mitchell, J. 2017 (Derby Co) 1
Moore, I. 1996 (Tranmere R, Nottingham F) 7
Moore, L. 2012 (Leicester C) 10
Moore, L. I. 2006 (Aston Villa) 5
Moran, S. 1982 (Southampton) 2
Morgan, S. 1987 (Leicester C) 2
Morris, J. 1997 (Chelsea) 7
Morrison, R. R. 2013 (West Ham U) 4
Mortimer, P. 1989 (Charlton Ath) 2
Moses, A. P. 1997 (Barnsley) 2
Moses, R. M. 1981 (WBA, Manchester U) 8
Moses, V. 2011 (Wigan Ath) 1
Mount, M. T. 2019 (Chelsea) 4
Mountfield, D. 1984 (Everton) 1
Muamba, F. N. 2008 (Birmingham C, Bolton W) 33
Muggleton, C. D. 1990 (Leicester C) 1
Mullins, H. I. 1999 (Crystal Palace) 3
Murphy, D. B. 1998 (Liverpool) 4
Murphy, Jacob K. 2017 (Norwich C) 6
Murray, P. 1997 (QPR) 4
Murray, M. W. 2003 (Wolverhampton W) 5
Mutch, A. 1989 (Wolverhampton W) 1
Mutch, J. J. E. S. 2011 (Birmingham C) 1
Myers. A. 1995 (Chelsea) 4

Naughton, K. 2009 (Sheffield U, Tottenham H) 9
Naylor, L. M. 2000 (Wolverhampton W) 3
Nelson, R. L. (Arsenal) 6
Nethercott, S. H. 1994 (Tottenham H) 8
Neville, P. J. 1995 (Manchester U) 7
Newell, M. 1986 (Luton T) 4
Newton, A. L. 2001 (West Ham U) 1
Newton, E. J. I. 1993 (Chelsea) 2
Newton, S. O. 1997 (Charlton Ath) 3
Nicholls, A. 1994 (Plymouth Arg) 1
Nketiah, E. K. 2018 (Arsenal) 4
Nmecha, L. 2018 (Manchester C) 3
Noble, M. J. 2007 (West Ham U) 20
Nolan, K. A. J. 2003 (Bolton W) 1
Nugent, D. J. 2006 (Preston NE) 14

Oakes, M. C. 1994 (Aston Villa) 6
Oakes, S. J. 1993 (Luton T) 1
Oakley, M. 1997 (Southampton) 4
O'Brien, A. J. 1999 (Bradford C) 1
O'Connor, J. 1996 (Everton) 3
O'Hara, J. D. 2008 (Tottenham H) 7
Ojo, O. B. (Sheyi) 2018 (Liverpool) 1
Oldfield, D. 1989 (Luton T) 1
Olney, I. A. 1990 (Aston Villa) 10
O'Neil, G. P. 2005 (Portsmouth) 9
Onomah, J. O. P. 2017 (Tottenham H) 8
Onuoha, C. 2006 (Manchester C) 21
Ord, R. J. 1991 (Sunderland) 3
Osman, R. C. 1979 (Ipswich T) 7
Owen, G. A. 1977 (Manchester C, WBA) 22
Owen, M. J. 1998 (Liverpool) 1
Oxlade-Chamberlain, A. M. D. 2011 (Southampton, Arsenal) 8

Painter, I. 1986 (Stoke C) 1
Palmer, C. L. 1989 (Sheffield W) 4
Palmer, K. R. 2016 (Chelsea) 6
Parker, G. 1986 (Hull C, Nottingham F) 6
Parker, P. A. 1985 (Fulham) 8
Parker, S. M. 2001 (Charlton Ath) 12
Parkes, P. B. F. 1979 (QPR) 1
Parkin, S. 1987 (Stoke C) 5
Parlour, R. 1992 (Arsenal) 12
Parnaby, S. 2003 (Middlesbrough) 4
Peach, D. S. 1977 (Southampton) 6
Peake, A. 1982 (Leicester C) 1
Pearce, I. A. 1995 (Blackburn R) 3
Pearce, S. 1987 (Nottingham F) 1
Pearce, T. M. 2018 (Leeds U) 2
Pennant, J. 2001 (Arsenal) 24
Pickering N. 1983 (Sunderland, Coventry C) 15
Pickford, J. L. 2015 (Sunderland) 14
Platt, D. 1988 (Aston Villa) 3
Plummer, C. S. 1996 (QPR) 5
Pollock, J. 1995 (Middlesbrough) 3
Porter, G. 1987 (Watford) 12
Potter, G. S. 1997 (Southampton) 1
Powell, N. E. 2012 (Manchester U) 2
Pressman, K. 1989 (Sheffield W) 1
Pritchard, A. D. 2014 (Tottenham H) 9
Proctor, M. 1981 (Middlesbrough, Nottingham F) 4
Prutton, D. T. 2001 (Nottingham F, Southampton) 25
Purse, D. J. 1998 (Birmingham C) 2

Quashie, N. F. 1997 (QPR) 4
Quinn, W. R. 1998 (Sheffield U) 2

Ramage, C. D. 1991 (Derby Co) 3
Ramsdale, A. C. 2018 (Bournemouth) 1
Ranson, R. 1980 (Manchester C) 10
Rashford, M. 2017 (Manchester U) 1
Redknapp, J. F. 1993 (Liverpool) 19
Redmond, N. D. J. 2013 (Birmingham C, Norwich C, Southampton) 38
Redmond, S. 1988 (Manchester C) 14
Reeves, K. P. 1978 (Norwich C, Manchester C) 10
Regis, C. 1979 (WBA) 6
Reid, N. S. 1981 (Manchester C) 6
Reid, P. 1977 (Bolton W) 6
Reo-Coker, N. S. A. 2004 (Wimbledon, West Ham U) 23
Richards, D. I. 1995 (Wolverhampton W) 4
Richards, J. P. 1977 (Wolverhampton W) 2
Richards, M. 2007 (Manchester C) 15
Richards, M. L. 2005 (Ipswich T) 1
Richardson, K. E. 2005 (Manchester U) 12
Rideout, P. 1985 (Aston Villa, Bari) 5
Ridgewell, L. M. 2004 (Aston Villa) 8
Riggott, C. M. 2001 (Derby Co) 8
Ripley, S. E. 1988 (Middlesbrough) 8
Ritchie, A. 1982 (Brighton & HA) 1
Rix, G. 1978 (Arsenal) 7
Roberts, A. J. 1995 (Millwall, Crystal Palace) 5
Roberts, B. J. 1997 (Middlesbrough) 1
Robins, M. G. 1990 (Manchester U) 6
Robinson, J. 2012 (Liverpool, QPR) 10

Robinson, P. P. 1999 (Watford) 3
Robinson, P. W. 2000 (Leeds U) 11
Robson, B. 1979 (WBA) 7
Robson, S. 1984 (Arsenal, West Ham U) 8
Rocastle, D. 1987 (Arsenal) 14
Roche, L. P. 2001 (Manchester U) 1
Rodger, G. 1987 (Coventry C) 4
Rodriguez, J. E. 2011 (Burnley) 1
Rodwell, J. 2009 (Everton) 21
Rogers, A. 1998 (Nottingham F) 3
Rosario, R. 1987 (Norwich C) 4
Rose, D. L. 2009 (Tottenham H) 29
Rose, M. 1997 (Arsenal) 2
Rosenior, L. J. 2005 (Fulham) 7
Routledge, W. 2005 (Crystal Palace, Tottenham H) 12
Rowell, G. 1977 (Sunderland) 1
Rudd, D. T. 2013 (Norwich C) 1
Ruddock, N. 1989 (Southampton) 4
Rufus, R. R. 1996 (Charlton Ath) 6
Ryan, J. 1983 (Oldham Ath) 1
Ryder, S. H. 1995 (Walsall) 3

Samuel, J. 2002 (Aston Villa) 7
Samways, V. 1988 (Tottenham H) 5
Sansom, K. G. 1979 (Crystal Palace) 8
Scimeca, R. 1996 (Aston Villa) 9
Scowcroft, J. B. 1997 (Ipswich T) 5
Seaman, D. A. 1985 (Birmingham C) 10
Sears, F. D. 2010 (West Ham U) 3
Sedgley, S. 1987 (Coventry C, Tottenham H) 11
Sellars, S. 1988 (Blackburn R) 3
Selley, I. 1994 (Arsenal) 3
Serrant, C. 1998 (Oldham Ath) 2
Sessegnon, K. R. (Ryan) 2018 (Fulham) 10
Sharpe, L. S. 1989 (Manchester U) 8
Shaw, L. P. H. 2013 (Southampton, Manchester U) 5
Shaw, G. R. 1981 (Aston Villa) 7
Shawcross, R. J. 2008 (Stoke C) 2
Shearer, A. 1991 (Southampton) 11
Shelton, G. 1985 (Sheffield W) 1
Shelvey, J. 2012 (Liverpool, Swansea C) 13
Sheringham, E. P. 1988 (Millwall) 1
Sheron, M. N. 1992 (Manchester C) 16
Sherwood, T. A. 1990 (Norwich C) 4
Shipperley, N. J. 1994 (Chelsea, Southampton) 7
Sidwell, S. J. 2003 (Reading) 5
Simonsen, S. P. A. 1998 (Tranmere R, Everton) 4
Simpson, J. B. 2019 (Bournemouth) 1
Simpson, P. 1986 (Manchester C) 5
Sims, S. 1977 (Leicester C) 10
Sinclair, S. A. 2011 (Swansea C) 7
Sinclair, T. 1994 (QPR, West Ham U) 5
Sinnott, L. 1985 (Watford) 1
Slade, S. A. 1996 (Tottenham H) 4
Slater, S. I. 1990 (West Ham U) 3
Small, B. 1993 (Aston Villa) 12
Smalling, C. L. 2010 (Fulham, Manchester U) 14
Smith, A. 2000 (Leeds U) 10
Smith, A. J. 2012 (Tottenham H) 11
Smith, D. 1988 (Coventry C) 10
Smith, M. 1981 (Sheffield W) 5
Smith, M. 1995 (Sunderland) 1
Smith, T. W. 2001 (Watford) 1
Snodin, I. 1985 (Doncaster R) 4
Soares, T. J. 2006 (Crystal Palace) 4
Solanke, D. A. 2015 (Chelsea, Liverpool, Bournemouth) 18
Sordell, M. A. 2012 (Watford, Bolton W) 14
Spence, J. 2011 (West Ham U) 1
Stanislaus, F. J. 2010 (West Ham U) 2
Statham, B. 1988 (Tottenham H) 3
Statham, D. J. 1978 (WBA) 6
Stead, J. G. 2004 (Blackburn R, Sunderland) 11
Stearman, R. J. 2009 (Wolverhampton W) 4
Steele, J. 2011 (Middlesbrough) 7
Stein, B. 1984 (Luton T) 3
Stephens, J. 2015 (Southampton) 8
Sterland, M. 1984 (Sheffield W) 7
Sterling, R. S. 2012 (Liverpool) 8
Steven, T. M. 1985 (Everton) 2
Stevens, G. A. 1983 (Brighton & HA, Tottenham H) 8
Stewart, J. 2003 (Leicester C) 1
Stewart, P. 1988 (Manchester C) 1
Stockdale, R. K. 2001 (Middlesbrough) 1
Stones, J. 2013 (Everton) 12
Stuart, G. C. 1990 (Chelsea) 5
Stuart, J. C. 1996 (Charlton Ath) 4
Sturridge, D. A. 2010 (Chelsea) 15
Suckling, P. 1986 (Coventry C, Manchester C, Crystal Palace) 10
Summerbee, N. J. 1993 (Swindon T) 3
Sunderland, A. 1977 (Wolverhampton W) 1
Surman, A. R. E. 2008 (Southampton) 4
Sutch, D. 1992 (Norwich C) 4
Sutton, C. R. 1993 (Norwich C) 13
Swift, J. D. 2015 (Chelsea, Reading) 13
Swindlehurst, D. 1977 (Crystal Palace) 1

Talbot, B. 1977 (Ipswich T) 1
Targett, M. R. 2015 (Southampton) 12
Taylor, A. D. 2007 (Middlesbrough) 13
Taylor, M. 2001 (Blackburn R) 1
Taylor, M. S. 2003 (Portsmouth) 3
Taylor, R. A. 2006 (Wigan Ath) 4
Taylor, S. J. 2002 (Arsenal) 3
Taylor, S. V. 2004 (Newcastle U) 29
Terry, J. G. 2001 (Chelsea) 9
Thatcher, B. D. 1996 (Millwall, Wimbledon) 4
Thelwell, A. A. 2001 (Tottenham H) 1
Thirlwell, P. 2001 (Sunderland) 1
Thomas, D. 1981 (Coventry C, Tottenham H) 7
Thomas, J. W. 2006 (Charlton Ath) 2
Thomas, M. 1986 (Luton T) 3
Thomas, M. L. 1988 (Arsenal) 12
Thomas, R. E. 1990 (Watford) 1
Thompson, A. 1995 (Bolton W) 2
Thompson, D. A. 1997 (Liverpool) 7
Thompson, G. L. 1981 (Coventry C) 6
Thorn, A. 1988 (Wimbledon) 5
Thornley, B. L. 1996 (Manchester U) 3
Thorpe, T. J. 2013 (Manchester U) 1
Tiler, C. 1990 (Barnsley, Nottingham F) 13
Tomkins, J. O. C. 2009 (West Ham U) 10
Tomori, O. O. (Fikayo) 2018 (Chelsea) 15
Tonge, M. W. E. 2004 (Sheffield U) 2
Townsend, A. D. 2012 (Tottenham H) 3
Trippier, K. J. 2011 (Manchester C) 2
Tuanzebe, A. 2018 (Manchester U) 1

Unsworth, D. G. 1995 (Everton) 6
Upson, M. J. 1999 (Arsenal) 11

Vassell, D. 1999 (Aston Villa) 11
Vaughan, J. O. 2007 (Everton) 4
Venison, B. 1983 (Sunderland) 10
Vernazza, P. A. P. 2001 (Arsenal, Watford) 2
Vieria, R. A. 2018 (Leeds U) 3
Vinnicombe, C. 1991 (Rangers) 12

Waddle, C. R. 1985 (Newcastle U) 1
Waghorn, M. T. 2012 (Leicester C) 5
Walcott, T. J. 2007 (Arsenal) 21
Wallace, D. L. 1983 (Southampton) 14
Wallace, Ray 1989 (Southampton) 4
Wallace, Rod 1989 (Southampton) 11
Walker, D. 1985 (Nottingham F) 7
Walker, I. M. 1991 (Tottenham H) 9
Walker, K. 2010 (Tottenham H) 7
Walker-Peters, K. L. 2018 (Tottenham H) 11
Walsh, G. 1988 (Manchester U) 2
Walsh, P. A. 1983 (Luton T) 4
Walters, K. 1984 (Aston Villa) 9

Walton, C. T. 2017 (Brighton & HA) 1
Wan Bissaka, A. 2019 (Crystal Palace) 3
Ward, P. 1978 (Brighton & HA) 2
Ward-Prowse, J. M. E. 2013 (Southampton) 31
Warhurst, P. 1991 (Oldham Ath, Sheffield W) 8
Watmore, D. I. 2015 (Sunderland) 13
Watson, B. 2007 (Crystal Palace) 1
Watson, D. 1984 (Norwich C) 7
Watson, D. N. 1994 (Barnsley) 5
Watson, G. 1991 (Sheffield W) 2
Watson, S. C. 1993 (Newcastle U) 12
Weaver, N. J. 2000 (Manchester C) 10
Webb, N. J. 1985 (Portsmouth, Nottingham F) 3
Welbeck, D. 2009 (Manchester U) 14
Welsh, J. J. 2004 (Liverpool, Hull C) 8
Wheater, D. J. 2008 (Middlesbrough) 11
Whelan, P. J. 1993 (Ipswich T) 3
Whelan, N. 1995 (Leeds U) 2
Whittingham, P. 2004 (Aston Villa, Cardiff C) 17
White, D. 1988 (Manchester C) 6
Whyte, C. 1982 (Arsenal) 4
Wickham, C. N. R. 2011 (Ipswich T, Sunderland) 17
Wicks, S. 1982 (QPR) 1
Wilkins, R. C. 1977 (Chelsea) 1
Wilkinson, P. 1985 (Grimsby T, Everton) 4
Williams, D. 1998 (Sunderland) 2
Williams, P. 1989 (Charlton Ath) 4
Williams, P. D. 1991 (Derby Co) 6
Williams, S. C. 1977 (Southampton) 14
Wilshere, J. A. 2010 (Arsenal) 7
Wilson, C. E. G. 2014 (Bournemouth) 1
Wilson, J. A. 2015 (Manchester U) 1
Wilson, M. A. 2001 (Manchester U, Middlesbrough) 6
Winks, H. 2017 (Tottenham H) 2
Winterburn, N. 1986 (Wimbledon) 1
Wisdom, A. 2012 (Liverpool) 10
Wise, D. F. 1988 (Wimbledon) 1
Woodcook, A. S. 1978 (Nottingham F) 2
Woodgate, J. S. 2000 (Leeds U) 1
Woodhouse, C. 1999 (Sheffield U) 4
Woodman, F. J. 2017 (Newcastle U) 6
Woodrow, C. 2014 (Fulham) 9
Woods, C. C. E. 1979 (Nottingham F, QPR, Norwich C) 6
Worrall, J. A. 2018 (Nottingham F) 3
Wright, A. G. 1993 (Blackburn R) 2
Wright, M. 1983 (Southampton) 4
Wright, R. I. 1997 (Ipswich T) 15
Wright, S. J. 2001 (Liverpool) 10
Wright, W. 1979 (Everton) 6
Wright-Phillips, S. C. 2002 (Manchester C) 6

Yates, D. 1989 (Notts Co) 5
Young, A. S. 2007 (Watford, Aston Villa) 10
Young, L. P. 1999 (Tottenham H, Charlton Ath) 12

Zaha, D. W. A. 2012 (Crystal Palace, Manchester U) 13
Zamora, R. L. 2002 (Brighton & HA) 6

NORTHERN IRELAND

Allen, C. 2009 (Lisburn Distillery) 1
Amos, D. 2019 (Doncaster R) 2
Armstrong, D. T. 2007 (Hearts) 1

Bagnall, L. 2011 (Sunderland) 1
Bailie, N. 1990 (Linfield) 2
Baird, C. P. 2002 (Southampton) 6
Ball, D. 2013 (Tottenham H) 2
Ball, M. 2011 (Norwich C) 5
Ballard, D. G. 2019 (Arsenal) 3
Balmer, K. 2019 (Ballymena U) 2
Beatty, S. 1990 (Chelsea, Linfield) 2
Bird, P. M. 2019 (Notts Co) 4
Black, J. 2003 (Tottenham H) 1
Black, K. T. 1990 (Luton T) 1
Black, R. Z. 2002 (Morecambe) 1
Blackledge, G. 1978 (Portadown) 1
Blake, R. G. 2011 (Brentford) 2
Blayney, A. 2003 (Southampton) 4
Boyd-Munce, C. S. 2019 (Birmingham C) 1
Boyce, L. 2010 (Cliftonville, Werder Bremen) 8
Boyle, W. S. 1998 (Leeds U) 7
Braniff, K. R. 2002 (Millwall) 11
Breeze, J. 2011 (Wigan Ath) 4
Brennan, C. 2013 (Kilmarnock) 13
Brobbel, R. 2013 (Middlesbrough) 9
Brotherston, N. 1978 (Blackburn R) 1
Browne, G. 2003 (Manchester C) 5
Brunt, C. 2005 (Sheffield W) 2
Bryan, M. A. 2010 (Watford) 4
Buchanan, D. T. H. 2006 (Bury) 15
Buchanan, W. B. 2002 (Bolton W, Lisburn Distillery) 5
Burns, A. 2014 (Linfield) 1
Burns, B. 2018 (Glenavon, Hearts) 5
Burns, L. 1998 (Port Vale) 13

Callaghan, A. 2006 (Limavady U, Ballymena U, Derry C) 15
Campbell, S. 2003 (Ballymena U) 1
Camps, C. 2015 (Rochdale) 1
Capaldi, A. C. 2002 (Birmingham C, Plymouth Arg) 14
Carlisle, W. T. 2000 (Crystal Palace) 9
Carroll, R. E. 1998 (Wigan Ath) 11
Carson, J. G. 2011 (Ipswich T, York C) 12
Carson, S. 2000 (Rangers, Dundee U) 2
Carson, T. 2007 (Sunderland) 15
Carvill, M. D. 2008 (Wrexham, Linfield) 8
Casement, C. 2007 (Ipswich T, Dundee) 18
Cathcart, C. 2007 (Manchester U) 15
Catney, R. 2007 (Lisburn Distillery) 1
Chapman, A. 2008 (Sheffield U, Oxford U) 7
Charles, D. 2017 (Fleetwood T) 3
Clarke, L. 2003 (Peterborough U) 4
Clarke, R. 2006 (Newry C) 7
Clarke, R. D. J. 1999 (Portadown) 5
Clingan, S. G. 2003 (Wolverhampton W, Nottingham F) 11
Close, B. 2002 (Middlesbrough) 10
Clucas, M. S. 2011 (Preston NE, Bristol R) 11
Clyde, M. G. 2002 (Wolverhampton W) 5
Colligan, L. 2009 (Ballymena U) 1
Conlan, L. 2013 (Burnley, Morecambe) 11
Connell, T. E. 1978 (Coleraine) 1
Cooper, J. 2015 (Glenavon) 5
Coote, A. 1998 (Norwich C) 12
Convery, J. 2000 (Celtic) 4

Dallas, S. 2012 (Crusaders, Brentford) 2
Davey, H. 2004 (UCD) 3
Davis, S. 2004 (Aston Villa) 3
Devine, D. 1994 (Omagh T) 1
Devine, D. G. 2011 (Preston NE) 2
Devine, J. 1990 (Glentoran) 1
Devlin, C. 2011 (Manchester U, unattached, Cliftonville) 11
Dickson, H. 2002 (Wigan Ath) 1
Doherty, B. 2018 (Derry C) 4
Doherty, J. E. 2014 (Watford, Leyton O, Crawley T) 6
Doherty, M. 2007 (Hearts) 2
Dolan, J. 2000 (Millwall) 6
Donaghy, M. M. 1978 (Larne) 1
Donnelly, L. F. P. 2012 (Fulham, Hartlepool U, Motherwell) 23
Donnelly, M. 2007 (Sheffield U, Crusaders) 5
Donnelly, R. 2013 (Swansea C) 1
Dowie, I. 1990 (Luton T) 1
Drummond, W. 2011 (Rangers) 2
Dudgeon, J. P. 2010 (Manchester U) 4
Duff, S. 2003 (Cheltenham T) 1

Duffy, M. 2014 (Derry C, Celtic) 9
Duffy, S. P. M. 2010 (Everton) 3
Dummigan, C. 2014 (Burnley, Oldham Ath) 18
Dunne, D. 2019 (Cliftonville) 1
Dunwoody, J. 2017 (Stoke C) 3

Elliott, S. 1999 (Glentoran) 3
Ervin, J. 2005 (Linfield) 2
Evans, C. J. 2009 (Manchester U) 10
Evans, J. 2006 (Manchester U) 3

Feeney, L. 1998 (Linfield, Rangers) 8
Feeney, W. 2002 (Bournemouth) 8
Ferguson, M. 2000 (Glentoran) 2
Ferguson, S. 2009 (Newcastle U) 11
Finlayson, D. 2019 (Rangers) 1
Fitzgerald, D. 1998 (Rangers) 4
Flanagan, T. M. 2012 (Milton Keynes D) 1
Flynn, J. J. 2009 (Blackburn R, Ross Co) 11
Fordyce, D. T. 2007 (Portsmouth, Glentoran) 12
Friars, E. C. 2005 (Notts Co) 7
Friars, S. M. 1998 (Liverpool, Ipswich T) 21

Galbraith, E. S. W. 2019 (Manchester U) 1
Gallagher, C. 2019 (Glentoran) 2
Garrett, R. 2007 (Stoke C, Linfield) 14
Gault, M. 2005 (Linfield) 2
Gibb, S. 2009 (Falkirk, Drogheda U) 2
Gilfillan, B. J. 2005 (Gretna, Peterhead) 9
Gillespie, K. R. 1994 (Manchester U) 1
Glendinning, M. 1994 (Bangor) 1
Glendinning, R. 2012 (Linfield) 3
Gordon, S. 2017 (Motherwell) 2
Gorman, D. A. 2015 (Stevenage, Leyton Orient) 13
Gorman, R. J. 2012 (Wolverhampton W, Leyton Orient) 4
Graham, G. L. 1999 (Crystal Palace) 5
Graham, R. S. 1999 (QPR) 15
Gray, J. P. 2012 (Accrington S) 11
Gray, P. 1990 (Luton T) 1
Griffin, D. J. 1998 (St Johnstone) 10
Grigg, W. D. 2011 (Walsall) 10

Hall, B. 2018 (Notts Co) 3
Hamilton, G. 2000 (Blackburn R, Portadown) 12
Hamilton, W. R. 1978 (Linfield) 1
Hanley, N. 2011 (Linfield) 1
Harkin, M. P. 2000 (Wycombe W) 9
Harney, J. J. 2014 (West Ham U) 1
Harvey, J. 1978 (Arsenal) 1
Hawe, S. 2001 (Blackburn R) 2
Hayes, T. 1978 (Luton T) 1
Hazard, C. 2019 (Celtic) 3
Hazley, M. 2007 (Stoke C) 3
Healy, D. J. 1999 (Manchester U) 8
Hegarty, C. 2011 (Rangers) 7
Herron, C. J. 2003 (QPR) 2
Higgins, R. 2006 (Derry C) 1
Hodson, L. J. S. 2010 (Watford) 10
Holden, R. 2019 (Bristol C) 2
Holmes, S. 2000 (Manchester C, Wrexham) 13
Howland, D. 2007 (Birmingham C) 4
Hughes, J. 2006 (Lincoln C) 7
Hughes, M. A. 2003 (Tottenham H, Oldham Ath) 12
Hughes, M. E. 1990 (Manchester C) 1
Hunter, M. 2002 (Glentoran) 1

Ingham, M. G. 2001 (Sunderland) 4

Jarvis, D. 2010 (Aberdeen) 2
Johns, C. 2014 (Southampton) 1
Johnson, D. M. 1998 (Blackburn R) 11
Johnson, R. A. 2015 (Stevenage) 13
Johnston, B. 1978 (Cliftonville) 1
Julian, A. A. 2005 (Brentford) 1

Kane, A. M. 2008 (Blackburn R) 5
Kane, M. 2012 (Glentoran) 1
Kee, B. R. 2010 (Leicester C, Torquay U, Burton Alb) 10
Kee, P. V. 1990 (Oxford U) 1
Kelly, D. 2000 (Derry C) 11
Kelly, J. 2019 (Maidenhead U) 2
Kelly, N. 1990 (Oldham Ath) 1
Kennedy, B. J. 2017 (Stevenage) 8
Kennedy, M. C. P. 2015 (Charlton Ath) 7
Kerr, N. 2019 (Glentoran) 2
Kirk, A. R. 1999 (Hearts) 9
Knowles, J. 2012 (Blackburn R) 2

Lafferty, D. 2009 (Celtic) 6
Lafferty, K. 2006 (Burnley) 2
Lavery, C. 2011 (Ipswich T, Sheffield W) 7
Lavery, S. 2017 (Everton) 10
Lawrie, J. 2009 (Port Vale, AFC Telford U) 9
Lennon, N. F. 1990 (Manchester C, Crewe Alex) 2
Lester, C. 2013 (Bolton W) 1
Lewis, J. 2017 (Norwich C) 1
Lindsay, K. 2006 (Larne) 1
Little, A. 2009 (Rangers) 6
Lowry, P. 2009 (Institute, Linfield) 6
Lund, M. 2011 (Stoke C) 6
Lyttle, G. 1998 (Celtic, Peterborough U) 8

McAlinden, L. J. 2012 (Wolverhampton W) 3
McAllister, M. 2007 (Dungannon Swifts) 4
McArdle, R. A. 2006 (Sheffield W, Rochdale) 19
McAreavey, P. 2000 (Swindon T) 7
McBride, J. 1994 (Glentoran) 1
McCaffrey, D. 2006 (Hibernian) 8
McCallion, E. 1998 (Coleraine) 1
McCalmont, A. 2019 (Leeds U) 1
McCann, G. S. 2000 (West Ham U) 11
McCann, P. 2003 (Portadown) 1
McCann, R. 2002 (Rangers, Linfield) 2
McCartan, S. V. 2013 (Accrington S) 9
McCartney, G. 2001 (Sunderland) 5
McCashin, S. 2011 (Jerez Industrial, unattached) 2
McChrystal, M. 2005 (Derry C) 9
McClean, J. 2010 (Derry C) 3
McClean, K. 2019 (St Johnstone) 2
McClure, M. 2012 (Wycombe W) 1
McCourt, P. J. 2002 (Rochdale, Derry C) 8
McCoy, R. K. 1990 (Coleraine) 1
McCreery, D. 1978 (Manchester U) 1
McCullough, L. 2013 (Doncaster R) 8
McDaid, R. 2015 (Leeds U) 5
McDermott, C. 2017 (Derry C) 4
McDonagh, J. D. C. 2015 (Sheffield U, Derry C) 9
McEleney, S. 2012 (Derry C) 2
McElroy, P. 2013 (Hull C) 1
McEvilly, L. R. 2003 (Rochdale) 9
McFlynn, T. M. 2000 (QPR, Woking, Margate) 19
McGeehan, C. 2013 (Norwich C) 3
McGibbon, P. C. G. 1994 (Manchester U) 1
McGivern, R. 2010 (Manchester C) 6
McGlinchey, B. 1998 (Manchester C, Port Vale, Gillingham) 14
McGonigle, J. 2017 (Coleraine) 4
McGovern, M. 2005 (Celtic) 10
McGowan, M. V. 2006 (Clyde) 2
McGurk, A. 2010 (Aston Villa) 1
McIlroy, T. 1994 (Linfield) 1
McKay, W. 2009 (Leicester C, Northampton T) 7
McKenna, K. 2007 (Tottenham H) 6
McKeown, R. 2012 (Kilmarnock) 12
McKnight, D. 2015 (Shrewsbury T, Stalybridge Celtic) 5
McKnight, P. 1998 (Rangers) 3
McLaughlin, C. G. 2010 (Preston NE, Fleetwood T) 7
McLaughlin, P. 2010 (Newcastle U, York C) 10
McLaughlin, R. 2012 (Liverpool, Oldham Ath) 6
McLean, B. S. 2006 (Rangers) 1
McLean, J. 2009 (Derry C) 4
McLellan, M. 2012 (Preston NE) 1

McMahon, G. J. 2002 (Tottenham H)	1
McMenamin, L. A. 2009 (Sheffield W)	4
McNair, P. J. C. 2014 (Manchester U)	2
McNally, P. 2013 (Celtic)	1
McQuilken, J. 2009 (Tescoma Zlin)	1
McQuoid, J. J. B. 2009 (Bournemouth)	8
McVeigh, A. 2002 (Ayr U)	1
McVeigh, P. M. 1998 (Tottenham H)	11
McVey, K. 2006 (Coleraine)	8
Magee, J. 1994 (Bangor)	1
Magee, J. 2009 (Lisburn Distillery)	1
Magennis, J. B. D. 2010 (Cardiff C, Aberdeen)	16
Magilton, J. 1990 (Liverpool)	1
Magnay, C. 2010 (Chelsea)	1
Maloney, L. 2015 (Middlesbrough)	6
Marshall, R. 2017 (Glenavon)	1
Matthews, N. P. 1990 (Blackpool)	1
Meenan, D. 2007 (Finn Harps, Monaghan U)	3
Melaugh, G. M. 2002 (Aston Villa, Glentoran)	11
Millar, K. S. 2011 (Oldham Ath, Linfield)	11
Millar, W. P. 1990 (Port Vale)	1
Miskelly, D. T. 2000 (Oldham Ath)	10
Mitchell, A. 2012 (Rangers)	3
Mitchell, C. 2017 (Burnley)	10
Moreland, V. 1978 (Glentoran)	1
Morgan, D. 2012 (Nottingham F)	4
Morgan, M. P. T. 1999 (Preston NE)	1
Morris, E. J. 2002 (WBA, Glentoran)	8
Morrison, O. 2001 (Sheffield W, Sheffield U)	7
Morrow, A. 2001 (Northampton T)	1
Morrow, S. 2005 (Hibernian)	4
Mulgrew, J. 2007 (Linfield)	10
Mulryne, P. P. 1999 (Manchester U, Norwich C)	5
Murray, W. 1978 (Linfield)	1
Murtagh, C. 2005 (Hearts)	1
Nicholl, J. M. 1978 (Manchester U)	1
Nixon, C. 2000 (Glentoran)	1
Nolan, L. J. 2014 (Crewe Alex, Southport)	4
Norwood, O. J. 2010 (Manchester U)	11
O'Connor, M. J. 2008 (Crewe Alex)	3
O'Hara, G. 1994 (Leeds U)	1
O'Kane, E. 2009 (Everton, Torquay U)	4
O'Neill, J. P. 1978 (Leicester C)	1
O'Neill, M. A. M. 1994 (Hibernian)	1
O'Neill, S. 2009 (Ballymena U)	4
Owens, C. 2018 (QPR)	2
Palmer, C. 2019 (Rangers)	**2**
Parkhouse, D. 2017 (Sheffield U)	**8**
Paterson, M. A. 2007 (Stoke C)	2
Patterson, D. J. 1994 (Crystal Palace)	1
Paul, C. D. 2017 (QPR)	3

Peacock-Farrell, B. 2018 (Leeds U)	1
Quigley, C. 2017 (Dundee)	2
Quinn, S. J. 1994 (Blackpool)	1
Ramsey, C. 2011 (Portadown)	3
Ramsey, K. 2006 (Institute)	1
Reid, J. T. 2013 (Exeter C)	2
Robinson, S. 1994 (Tottenham H)	1
Rooney, L. J. 2017 (Plymouth Arg)	1
Roy, A. 2019 (Derry C)	**2**
Scullion, D. 2006 (Dungannon Swifts)	8
Sendles-White J. 2013 (QPR, Hamilton A)	12
Sharpe, R. 2013 (Derby Co, Notts Co)	6
Shiels, D. 2005 (Hibernian)	6
Shields, S. P. 2013 (Dagenham & R)	2
Shroot, R. 2009 (Harrow B, Birmingham C)	4
Simms, G. 2001 (Hartlepool U)	14
Singleton, J. 2015 (Glenavon)	2
Skates, G. 2000 (Blackburn R)	4
Sloan, T. 1978 (Ballymena U)	1
Smylie, D. 2006 (Newcastle U, Livingston)	6
Smyth, P. 2017 (Linfield, QPR)	**12**
Stewart, J. 2015 (Swindon T)	2
Stewart, S. 2009 (Aberdeen)	1
Stewart, T. 2006 (Wolverhampton W, Linfield)	19
Sykes, M. 2017 (Glenavon)	**10**
Taylor, J. 2007 (Hearts, Glentoran)	10
Taylor, M. S. 1998 (Fulham)	1
Teggart, N. 2005 (Sunderland)	2
Tempest, G. 2013 (Notts Co)	6
Thompson, A. L. 2011 (Watford)	11
Thompson, J. 2017 (Rangers, Blackpool)	**13**
Thompson, P. 2006 (Linfield)	4
Toal, E. 2019 (Derry C)	**1**
Toner, C. 2000 (Tottenham H, Leyton Orient)	17
Tuffey, J. 2007 (Partick Thistle)	13
Turner, C. 2007 (Sligo R, Bohemians)	12
Ward, J. J. 2006 (Aston Villa, Chesterfield)	7
Ward, M. 2006 (Dungannon Swifts)	1
Ward, S. 2005 (Glentoran)	10
Waterman, D. G. 1998 (Portsmouth)	14
Waterworth, A. 2008 (Lisburn Distillery, Hamilton A)	7
Webb, S. M. 2004 (Ross Co, St Johnstone, Ross Co)	6
Weir, R. J. 2009 (Sunderland)	8
Wells, D. P. 1999 (Barry T)	1
Whitley, J. 1998 (Manchester C)	17
Whyte, G. 2015 (Crusaders)	7
Willis, P. 2006 (Liverpool)	1
Winchester, C. 2011 (Oldham Ath)	13
Winchester, J. 2013 (Kilmarnock)	1

SCOTLAND

Adam, C. G. 2006 (Rangers)	5
Adam, G. 2011 (Rangers)	6
Adams, J. 2007 (Kilmarnock)	1
Aitken, R. 1977 (Celtic)	16
Albiston, A. 1977 (Manchester U)	5
Alexander, N. 1997 (Stenhousemuir, Livingston)	10
Allan, S. 2012 (WBA)	10
Anderson, I. 1997 (Dundee, Toulouse)	15
Anderson, R. 1997 (Aberdeen)	15
Andrews, M. 2011 (East Stirlingshire)	1
Anthony, M. 1997 (Celtic)	3
Archdeacon, O. 1987 (Celtic)	1
Archer, J. G. 2012 (Tottenham H)	14
Archibald, A. 1998 (Partick Thistle)	5
Archibald, S. 1980 (Aberdeen, Tottenham H)	5
Archibald, T. V. 2018 (Brentford)	1
Arfield, S. 2008 (Falkirk, Huddersfield T)	17
Armstrong, S. 2011 (Dundee U)	20

Bagen, D. 1997 (Kilmarnock)	4
Bain, K. 1993 (Dundee)	4
Baker, M. 1993 (St Mirren)	10
Baltacha, S. S. 2000 (St Mirren)	3
Bannan, B. 2009 (Aston Villa)	10
Bannigan, S. 2013 (Partick Thistle)	3
Bannon, E. J. 1979 (Hearts, Chelsea, Dundee U)	7
Barclay, J. 2011 (Falkirk)	1
Bates, C. 2019 (Hamburger SV)	**4**
Beattie, C. 2004 (Celtic)	7
Beattie, J. 1992 (St Mirren)	4
Beaumont, D. 1985 (Dundee U)	1
Bell, D. 1981 (Aberdeen)	2
Bernard, P. R. J. 1992 (Oldham Ath)	15
Berra, C. 2005 (Hearts)	6
Bett, J. 1981 (Rangers)	7
Black, E. 1983 (Aberdeen)	8
Blair, A. 1980 (Coventry C, Aston Villa)	5
Bollan, G. 1992 (Dundee U, Rangers)	17

Bonar, P. 1997 (Raith R) 4
Booth, C. 2011 (Hibernian) 4
Booth, S. 1991 (Aberdeen) 14
Bowes, M. J. 1992 (Dunfermline Ath) 1
Bowman, D. 1985 (Hearts) 1
Boyack, S. 1997 (Rangers) 1
Boyd, K. 2003 (Kilmarnock) 8
Boyd, T. 1987 (Motherwell) 5
Brandon, J. 2019 (Hearts) 1
Brazil, A. 1978 (Hibernian) 1
Brazil, A. 1979 (Ipswich T) 8
Brebner, G. I. 1997 (Manchester U, Reading, Hibernian) 18
Brighton, T. 2005 (Rangers, Clyde) 7
Broadfoot, K. 2005 (St Mirren) 5
Brophy, E. 2017 (Hamilton A, Kilmarnock) 3
Brough, J. 1981 (Hearts) 1
Brown, A. H. 2004 (Hibernian) 1
Brown, S. 2005 (Hibernian) 10
Browne, P. 1997 (Raith R) 1
Bryson, C. 2006 (Clyde) 1
Buchan, J. 1997 (Aberdeen) 13
Burchill, M. J. 1998 (Celtic) 15
Burke, A. 1997 (Kilmarnock) 4
Burke, C. 2004 (Rangers) 3
Burke, O. J. 2018 (WBA) 9
Burley, C. W. 1992 (Chelsea) 7
Burley, G. E. 1977 (Ipswich T) 5
Burns, H. 1985 (Rangers) 2
Burns, T. 1977 (Celtic) 5
Burt, L. 2017 (Rangers) 5

Cadden, C. 2017 (Motherwell) 12
Caddis, P. 2008 (Celtic, Dundee U, Celtic, Swindon T) 13
Cairney, T. 2011 (Hull C) 6
Caldwell, G. 2000 (Newcastle U) 19
Caldwell, S. 2001 (Newcastle U) 4
Cameron, G. 2008 (Dundee U) 3
Cameron, K. M. 2017 (Newcastle U) 3
Campbell, A. 2018 (Motherwell) 15
Campbell, R. 2008 (Hibernian) 6
Campbell, S. 1989 (Dundee) 3
Campbell, S. P. 1998 (Leicester C) 15
Canero, P. 2000 (Kilmarnock) 17
Cardwell, H. 2014 (Reading) 1
Carey, L. A. 1998 (Bristol C) 1
Carrick, D. 2012 (Hearts) 1
Casey, J. 1978 (Celtic) 1
Chalmers, J. 2014 (Celtic, Motherwell) 2
Christie, M. 1992 (Dundee) 3
Christie, R. 2014 (Inverness CT, Celtic) 9
Clark, R. B. 1977 (Aberdeen) 3
Clarke, S. 1984 (St Mirren) 8
Clarkson, D. 2004 (Motherwell) 13
Cleland, A. 1990 (Dundee U) 11
Cole, D. 2011 (Rangers) 2
Collins, J. 1988 (Hibernian) 8
Collins, N. 2005 (Sunderland) 7
Connolly, P. 1991 (Dundee U) 3
Connor, R. 1981 (Ayr U) 2
Conroy, R. 2007 (Celtic) 4
Considine, A. 2007 (Aberdeen) 5
Cooper, D. 1977 (Clydebank, Rangers) 6
Cooper, N. 1982 (Aberdeen) 13
Coutts, P. A. 2009 (Peterborough U, Preston NE) 7
Crabbe, S. 1990 (Hearts) 2
Craig, M. 1998 (Aberdeen) 2
Craig, T. 1977 (Newcastle U) 1
Crainey, S. D. 2000 (Celtic) 7
Crainie, D. 1983 (Celtic) 1
Crawford, S. 1994 (Raith R) 19
Creaney, G. 1991 (Celtic) 11
Cummings, J. 2015 (Hibernian) 8
Cummings, W. 2000 (Chelsea) 8
Cuthbert, S. 2007 (Celtic, St Mirren) 13

Dailly, C. 1991 (Dundee U) 34
Dalglish, P. 1999 (Newcastle U, Norwich C) 6
Dargo, C. 1998 (Raith R) 10
Davidson, C. I. 1997 (St Johnstone) 2
Davidson, H. N. 2000 (Dundee U) 3
Davidson, M. 2011 (St Johnstone) 1
Dawson, A. 1979 (Rangers) 8
Deas, P. A. 1992 (St Johnstone) 2
Dempster, J. 2004 (Rushden & D) 1
Dennis, S. 1992 (Raith R) 1
Diamond, A. 2004 (Aberdeen) 12
Dickov, P. 1992 (Arsenal) 4
Dixon, P. 2008 (Dundee) 2
Docherty, G. 2017 (Hamilton A) 4
Dodds, D. 1978 (Dundee U) 1
Dods, D. 1997 (Hibernian) 5
Doig, C. R. 2000 (Nottingham F) 13
Donald, G. S. 1992 (Hibernian) 3
Donnelly, S. 1994 (Celtic) 11
Doohan, R. 2018 (Celtic) 5
Dorrans, G. 2007 (Livingston) 6
Dow, A. 1993 (Dundee, Chelsea) 3
Dowie, A. J. 2003 (Rangers, Partick Thistle) 14
Duff, J. 2009 (Inverness CT) 1
Duff, S. 2003 (Dundee U) 9
Duffie, K. 2011 (Falkirk) 6
Duffy, D. A. 2005 (Falkirk, Hull C) 8
Duffy, J. 1987 (Dundee) 1
Durie, G. S. 1987 (Chelsea) 4
Durrant, I. 1987 (Rangers) 4
Doyle, J. 1981 (Partick Thistle) 2

Easton, B. 2009 (Hamilton A) 3
Easton, C. 1997 (Dundee U) 21
Edwards, M. 2012 (Rochdale) 1
Elliot, B. 1998 (Celtic) 2
Elliot, C. 2006 (Hearts) 9
Esson, R. 2000 (Aberdeen) 7

Fagan, S. M. 2005 (Motherwell) 1
Ferguson, B. 1997 (Rangers) 12
Ferguson, D. 1987 (Rangers) 5
Ferguson, D. 1992 (Dundee U) 7
Ferguson, D. 1992 (Manchester U) 5
Ferguson, I. 1983 (Dundee) 4
Ferguson, I. 1987 (Clyde, St Mirren, Rangers) 6
Ferguson, L. 2019 (Aberdeen) 3
Ferguson, R. 1977 (Hamilton A) 1
Feruz, I. 2012 (Chelsea) 4
Findlay, S. 2012 (Celtic) 13
Findlay, W. 1991 (Hibernian) 5
Fitzpatrick, A. 1977 (St Mirren) 5
Fitzpatrick, M. 2007 (Motherwell) 4
Flannigan, C. 1993 (Clydebank) 1
Fleck, J. 2009 (Rangers) 4
Fleck, R. 1987 (Rangers, Norwich C) 6
Fleming, G. 2008 (Gretna) 1
Fletcher, D. B. 2003 (Manchester U) 2
Fletcher, S. 2007 (Hibernian) 7
Forrest, A. 2017 (Ayr U) 1
Forrest, J. 2011 (Celtic) 4
Foster, R. M. 2005 (Aberdeen) 5
Fotheringham, M. M. 2004 (Dundee) 3
Fowler, J. 2002 (Kilmarnock) 3
Foy, R. A. 2004 (Liverpool) 5
Fraser, M. 2012 (Celtic) 5
Fraser, R. 2013 (Aberdeen, Bournemouth) 10
Fraser, S. T. 2000 (Luton T) 4
Freedman, D. A. 1995 (Barnet, Crystal Palace) 8
Fridge, L. 1989 (St Mirren) 2
Fullarton, J. 1993 (St Mirren) 17
Fulton, J. 2014 (Swansea C) 2
Fulton, R. 2017 (Liverpool, Hamilton A) 11
Fulton, M. 1980 (St Mirren) 5
Fulton, S. 1991 (Celtic) 7
Fyvie, F. 2012 (Wigan Ath) 8

Gallacher, K. W. 1987 (Dundee U)	7
Gallacher, P. 1999 (Dundee U)	7
Gallacher, S. 2009 (Rangers)	2
Gallagher, P. 2003 (Blackburn R)	11
Galloway, M. 1989 (Hearts, Celtic)	2
Gardiner, J. 1993 (Hibernian)	1
Gauld, R. 2013 (Dundee U, Sporting Lisbon)	11
Geddes, R. 1982 (Dundee)	5
Gemmill, S. 1992 (Nottingham F)	4
Germaine, G. 1997 (WBA)	1
Gilles, R. 1997 (St Mirren)	7
Gillespie, G. T. 1979 (Coventry C)	8
Gilmour, B. C. 2019 (Arsenal)	**4**
Glass, S. 1995 (Aberdeen)	11
Glover, L. 1988 (Nottingham F)	3
Goodwillie, D. 2009 (Dundee U)	9
Goram, A. L. 1987 (Oldham Ath)	1
Gordon, C. S. 2003 (Hearts)	5
Gough, C. R. 1983 (Dundee U)	5
Graham, D. 1998 (Rangers)	8
Grant, P. 1985 (Celtic)	10
Gray, D. P. 2009 (Manchester U)	2
Gray, S. 1987 (Aberdeen)	1
Gray S. 1995 (Celtic)	7
Griffiths, L. 2010 (Dundee, Wolverhampton W)	11
Grimmer, J. 2014 (Fulham)	1
Gunn, B. 1984 (Aberdeen)	9
Hagen, D. 1992 (Rangers)	8
Hamill, J. 2008 (Kilmarnock)	11
Hamilton, B. 1989 (St Mirren)	4
Hamilton, C. 2018 (Hearts)	3
Hamilton, J. 1995 (Dundee, Hearts)	14
Hamilton, J. 2014 (Hearts)	8
Hammell, S. 2001 (Motherwell)	11
Handling, D. 2014 (Hibernian)	3
Handyside, P. 1993 (Grimsby T)	7
Hanley, G. 2011 (Blackburn R)	1
Hanlon, P. 2009 (Hibernian)	23
Hannah, D. 1993 (Dundee U)	16
Hardie, R. 2017 (Rangers)	8
Harper, K. 1995 (Hibernian)	7
Hartford, R. A. 1977 (Manchester C)	1
Hartley, P. J. 1997 (Millwall)	1
Harvie, D. 2018 (Aberdeen, Ayr U)	5
Hastie, J. 2019 (Motherwell)	**1**
Hegarty, P. 1987 (Dundee U)	6
Henderson, L. 2015 (Celtic)	9
Hendrie, S. 2014 (West Ham U)	3
Hendry, J. 1992 (Tottenham H)	1
Henly, J. 2014 (Reading)	1
Herron, J. 2012 (Celtic)	2
Hetherston, B. 1997 (St Mirren)	1
Hewitt, J. 1982 (Aberdeen)	6
Hogg, G. 1984 (Manchester U)	4
Holsgrove, J. 2019 (Reading)	**1**
Holt, J. 2012 (Hearts)	7
Hood, G. 1993 (Ayr U)	3
Horn, R. 1997 (Hearts)	6
Hornby, F. D. I. 2018 (Everton)	**8**
House, B. 2019 (Reading)	**1**
Howie, S. 1993 (Cowdenbeath)	5
Hughes, R. D. 1999 (Bournemouth)	9
Hughes, S. 2002 (Rangers)	12
Hunter, G. 1987 (Hibernian)	3
Hunter, P. 1989 (East Fife)	3
Hutton, A. 2004 (Rangers)	7
Hutton, K. 2011 (Rangers)	1
Hyam, D. J. 2014 (Reading)	5
Iacovitti, A. 2017 (Nottingham F)	4
Inman, B. 2011 (Newcastle U)	2
Irvine, G. 2006 (Celtic)	2
Jack, R. 2012 (Aberdeen)	19
James, K. F. 1997 (Falkirk)	1
Jardine, I. 1979 (Kilmarnock)	1
Jess, E. 1990 (Aberdeen)	14
Johnson, G. I. 1992 (Dundee U)	6
Johnston, A. 1994 (Hearts)	3
Johnston, F. 1993 (Falkirk)	1
Johnston, G. 2019 (Liverpool)	**2**
Johnston, M. 1984 (Partick Thistle, Watford)	3
Johnston, M. A. 2018 (Celtic)	**7**
Jones, J. C. 2017 (Crewe Alex)	4
Jordan, A. J. 2000 (Bristol C)	3
Jules, Z. K. 2017 (Reading)	3
Jupp, D. A. 1995 (Fulham)	9
Kelly, L. A. 2017 (Reading)	11
Kelly, S. 2014 (St Mirren)	1
Kennedy, J. 2003 (Celtic)	15
Kennedy, M. 2012 (Kilmarnock)	1
Kenneth, G. 2008 (Dundee U)	8
Kerr, B. 2003 (Newcastle U)	14
Kerr, F. 2012 (Birmingham C)	3
Kerr, J. 2018 (St Johnstone)	6
Kerr, M. 2001 (Kilmarnock)	1
Kerr, S. 1993 (Celtic)	10
Kettings, C. D. 2012 (Blackpool)	3
King, A. 2014 (Swansea C)	1
King, C. M. 2014 (Norwich C)	1
King, W. 2015 (Hearts)	8
Kingsley, S. 2015 (Swansea C)	6
Kinniburgh, W. D. 2004 (Motherwell)	3
Kirkwood, D. 1990 (Hearts)	1
Kyle, K. 2001 (Sunderland)	12
Lambert, P. 1991 (St Mirren)	11
Langfield, J. 2000 (Dundee)	2
Lappin, S. 2004 (St Mirren)	10
Lauchlan, J. 1998 (Kilmarnock)	11
Lavety, B. 1993 (St Mirren)	9
Lavin, G. 1993 (Watford)	7
Lawson, P. 2004 (Celtic)	10
Leighton, J. 1982 (Aberdeen)	1
Lennon, S. 2008 (Rangers)	6
Levein, C. 1985 (Hearts)	2
Leven, P. 2005 (Kilmarnock)	2
Liddell, A. M. 1994 (Barnsley)	12
Lindsey, J. 1979 (Motherwell)	1
Locke, G. 1994 (Hearts)	10
Love, D. 2015 (Manchester U)	5
Love, G. 1995 (Hibernian)	1
Loy, R. 2009 (Dunfermline Ath, Rangers)	5
Lynch, S. 2003 (Celtic, Preston NE)	13
McAllister, G. 1990 (Leicester C)	1
McAllister, K. 2019 (Derby Co)	**1**
McAllister, R. 2008 (Inverness CT)	2
McAlpine, H. 1983 (Dundee U)	5
McAnespie, K. 1998 (St Johnstone)	4
McArthur, J. 2008 (Hamilton A)	2
McAuley, S. 1993 (St Johnstone)	1
McAvennie, F. 1982 (St Mirren)	5
McBride, J. 1981 (Everton)	1
McBride, J. P. 1998 (Celtic)	2
McBurnie, O. 2015 (Swansea C)	12
McCabe, R. 2012 (Rangers, Sheffield W)	3
McCall, A. S. M. 1988 (Bradford C, Everton)	2
McCann, K. 2008 (Hibernian)	4
McCann, N. 1994 (Dundee)	9
McCart, J. 2017 (Celtic)	1
McClair, B. 1984 (Celtic)	8
McCluskey, G. 1979 (Celtic)	6
McCluskey, S. 1997 (St Johnstone)	14
McCoist, A. 1984 (Rangers)	1
McConnell, I. 1997 (Clyde)	1
McCormack, D. 2008 (Hibernian)	1
McCormack, R. 2006 (Rangers, Motherwell, Cardiff C)	13
McCracken, D. 2002 (Dundee U)	5
McCrorie, Robby 2018 (Rangers)	**6**

McCrorie, Ross 2017 (Rangers)	**11**
McCulloch, A. 1981 (Kilmarnock)	1
McCulloch, I. 1982 (Notts Co)	2
McCulloch, L. 1997 (Motherwell)	14
McCunnie, J. 2001 (Dundee U, Ross Co, Dunfermline Ath)	20
MacDonald, A. 2011 (Burnley)	6
MacDonald, C. 2017 (Derby Co)	2
MacDonald, J. 1980 (Rangers)	8
MacDonald, J. 2007 (Hearts)	11
McDonald, C. 1995 (Falkirk)	5
McDonald, K. 2008 (Dundee, Burnley)	14
McEwan, C. 1997 (Clyde, Raith R)	17
McEwan, D. 2003 (Livingston)	2
McFadden, J. 2003 (Motherwell)	7
McFadzean C. 2015 (Sheffield U)	3
McFarlane, D. 1997 (Hamilton A)	3
McGarry, S. 1997 (St Mirren)	3
McGarvey, F. P. 1977 (St Mirren, Celtic)	3
McGarvey, S. 1982 (Manchester U)	4
McGeough, D. 2012 (Celtic)	10
McGhee, J. 2013 (Hearts)	20
McGhee, M. 1981 (Aberdeen)	1
McGinn, J. 2014 (St Mirren, Hibernian)	9
McGinn, S. 2009 (St Mirren, Watford)	8
McGinnis, G. 1985 (Dundee U)	1
McGlinchey, M. R. 2007 (Celtic)	1
McGregor, A. 2003 (Rangers)	6
McGregor, C. W. 2013 (Celtic)	5
McGrillen, P. 1994 (Motherwell)	2
McGuire, D. 2002 (Aberdeen)	2
McHattie, K. 2012 (Hearts)	6
McInally, J. 1989 (Dundee U)	1
McIntyre, T. P. 2019 (Reading)	**1**
McKay, B. 2012 (Rangers)	4
McKay, B. 2013 (Hearts)	1
McKean, K. 2011 (St Mirren)	1
McKenna, S. 2018 (Aberdeen)	5
McKenzie, R. 2013 (Kilmarnock)	4
McKenzie, R. 1997 (Hearts)	2
McKimmie, S. 1985 (Aberdeen)	3
McKinlay, T. 1984 (Dundee)	6
McKinlay, W. 1989 (Dundee U)	6
McKinnon, R. 1991 (Dundee U)	6
McLaren, A, 1989 (Hearts)	11
McLaren, A. 1993 (Dundee U)	4
McLaughlin, B. 1995 (Celtic)	8
McLaughlin, J. 1981 (Morton)	10
McLean, E. 2008 (Dundee U, St Johnstone)	2
McLean, S. 2003 (Rangers)	4
McLeish, A. 1978 (Aberdeen)	6
McLean, K. 2012 (St Mirren)	11
MacLeod, A. 1979 (Hibernian)	3
McLeod, J. 1989 (Dundee U)	2
MacLeod, L. 2012 (Rangers)	8
MacLeod, M. 1979 (Dumbarton, Celtic)	5
McManus, D. J. 2014 (Aberdeen, Fleetwood T)	4
McManus, T. 2001 (Hibernian)	14
McMillan, S. 1997 (Motherwell)	4
McMullan, P. 2017 (Celtic)	1
McNab, N. 1978 (Tottenham H)	1
McNally, M. 1991 (Celtic)	2
McNamara, J. 1994 (Dunfermline Ath, Celtic)	12
McNaughton, K. 2002 (Aberdeen)	1
McNeil, A. 2007 (Hibernian)	1
McNichol, J. 1979 (Brentford)	7
McNiven, D. 1977 (Leeds U)	3
McNiven, S. A. 1996 (Oldham Ath)	1
McParland, A. 2003 (Celtic)	1
McPhee, S. 2002 (Port Vale)	1
McPherson, D. 1984 (Rangers, Hearts)	4
McQuilken, J. 1993 (Celtic)	2
McStay, P. 1983 (Celtic)	5
McWhirter, N. 1991 (St Mirren)	1
Mackay-Steven, G. 2012 (Dundee U)	3
Mackie, S. 2019 (Hibernian)	**1**
Magennis, K. 2019 (St Mirren)	**1**
Maguire, B. 2019 (Motherwell)	**2**
Maguire, C. 2009 (Aberdeen)	12
Main, A. 1988 (Dundee U)	3
Malcolm, R. 2001 (Rangers)	1
Mallan, S. 2017 (St Mirren, Barnsley, St Mirren)	**9**
Maloney, S. 2002 (Celtic)	21
Malpas, M. 1983 (Dundee U)	8
Marr, B. 2011 (Ross Co)	1
Marshall, D. J. 2004 (Celtic)	10
Marshall, S. R. 1995 (Arsenal)	5
Martin, A. 2009 (Leeds U, Ayr U)	12
Mason, G. R. 1999 (Manchester C, Dunfermline Ath)	2
Mathieson, D. 1997 (Queen of the South)	3
May, E. 1989 (Hibernian)	2
May, S. 2013 (St Johnstone, Sheffield W)	8
Meldrum, C. 1996 (Kilmarnock)	6
Melrose, J. 1977 (Partick Thistle)	8
Middleton, G. 2018 (Rangers)	**6**
Millar, M, 2009 (Celtic)	1
Miller, C. 1995 (Rangers)	8
Miller, J. 1987 (Aberdeen, Celtic)	7
Miller, K. 2000 (Hibernian, Rangers)	7
Miller, W. 1991 (Hibernian)	7
Miller, W. F. 1978 (Aberdeen)	2
Milne, K. 2000 (Hearts)	1
Milne, R. 1982 (Dundee U)	3
Mitchell, C. 2008 (Falkirk)	7
Money, I. C. 1987 (St Mirren)	3
Montgomery, N. A. 2003 (Sheffield U)	2
Morgan, L. 2017 (Celtic)	**9**
Morrison, S. A. 2004 (Aberdeen, Dunfermline Ath)	12
Muir, L. 1977 (Hibernian)	1
Mulgrew, C. P. 2006 (Celtic, Wolverhampton W, Aberdeen)	14
Murphy J. 2009 (Motherwell)	13
Murray, H. 2000 (St Mirren)	3
Murray, I. 2001 (Hibernian)	15
Murray, N. 1993 (Rangers)	16
Murray, R. 1993 (Bournemouth)	1
Murray, S. 2004 (Kilmarnock)	2
Narey, D. 1977 (Dundee U)	4
Naismith, J. 2014 (St Mirren)	1
Naismith, S. J. 2006 (Kilmarnock, Rangers)	15
Naysmith, G. A. 1997 (Hearts)	22
Neilson, R. 2000 (Hearts)	1
Nesbitt, A. 2017 (Celtic)	2
Ness, J, 2011 (Rangers)	2
Nevin, P. 1985 (Chelsea)	5
Nicholas, C. 1981 (Celtic, Arsenal)	6
Nicholson, B. 1999 (Rangers)	7
Nicholson, S. 2015 (Hearts)	8
Nicol, S. 1981 (Ayr U, Liverpool)	14
Nisbet, S. 1989 (Rangers)	5
Noble, D. J. 2003 (West Ham U)	2
Notman, A. M. 1999 (Manchester U)	10
O'Brien, B. 1999 (Blackburn R, Livingston)	6
O'Connor, G. 2003 (Hibernian)	8
O'Donnell, P. 1992 (Motherwell)	8
O'Donnell, S. 2013 (Partick Thistle)	1
O'Halloran, M. 2012 (Bolton W)	2
O'Hara, M. 2015 (Kilmarnock, Dundee)	2
O'Leary, R. 2008 (Kilmarnock)	2
O'Neil, B. 1992 (Celtic)	7
O'Neil, J. 1991 (Dundee U)	1
O'Neill, M. 1995 (Clyde)	6
Orr, N. 1978 (Morton)	7
Palmer, L. J. 2011 (Sheffield W)	8
Park, C. 2012 (Middlesbrough)	1
Parker, K. 2001 (St Johnstone)	1
Parlane, D. 1977 (Rangers)	1
Paterson, C. 1981 (Hibernian)	2
Paterson, C. 2012 (Hearts)	12

Paterson, J. 1997 (Dundee U)	9
Pawlett, P. 2012 (Aberdeen)	7
Payne, G. 1978 (Dundee U)	3
Peacock, L. A. 1997 (Carlisle U)	1
Pearce, A. J. 2008 (Reading)	2
Pearson, S. P. 2003 (Motherwell)	8
Perry, R. 2010 (Rangers, Falkirk, Rangers)	16
Polworth, L. 2016 (Inverness CT)	1
Porteous, R. 2018 (Hibernian)	**8**
Pressley, S. J. 1993 (Rangers, Coventry C, Dundee U)	26
Provan, D. 1977 (Kilmarnock)	1
Prunty, B. 2004 (Aberdeen)	6
Quinn, P. C. 2004 (Motherwell)	3
Quinn, R. 2006 (Celtic)	9
Quitongo, J. 2017 (Hamilton A)	1
Rae, A. 1991 (Millwall)	8
Rae, G. 1999 (Dundee)	6
Ralston, A. 2018 (Celtic)	5
Redford, I. 1981 (Rangers)	6
Reid, B. 1991 (Rangers)	4
Reid, C. 1993 (Hibernian)	3
Reid, M. 1982 (Celtic)	2
Reid, R. 1977 (St Mirren)	3
Reilly, A. 2004 (Wycombe W)	1
Renicks, S. 1997 (Hamilton A)	1
Reynolds, M. 2007 (Motherwell)	9
Rhodes, J. L. 2011 (Huddersfield T)	8
Rice, B. 1985 (Hibernian)	1
Richardson, L. 1980 (St Mirren)	2
Ridgers, M. 2012 (Hearts)	5
Riordan, D. G. 2004 (Hibernian)	5
Ritchie, A. 1980 (Morton)	1
Ritchie, P. S. 1996 (Hearts)	7
Robertson, A. 1991 (Rangers)	1
Robertson, A. 2013 (Dundee U, Hull C)	4
Robertson, C. 1977 (Rangers)	1
Robertson, C. 2012 (Aberdeen)	10
Robertson, D. 2007 (Dundee U)	4
Robertson, D. A. 1987 (Aberdeen)	7
Robertson, G. A. 2004 (Nottingham F, Rotherham U)	15
Robertson, H. 1994 (Aberdeen)	2
Robertson, J. 1985 (Hearts)	2
Robertson, L. 1993 (Rangers)	3
Robertson, S. 1998 (St Johnstone)	2
Roddie, A. 1992 (Aberdeen)	5
Ross, G. 2007 (Dunfermline Ath)	1
Ross, N. 2011 (Inverness CT)	2
Ross, T. W. 1977 (Arsenal)	1
Rowson, D. 1997 (Aberdeen)	5
Ruddy, J. 2017 (Wolverhampton W)	1
Russell, J. 2011 (Dundee U)	11
Russell, R. 1978 (Rangers)	3
Salton, D. B. 1992 (Luton T)	6
Sammut, R. A. M. 2017 (Chelsea)	3
Samson, C. I. 2004 (Kilmarnock)	6
Saunders, S. 2011 (Motherwell)	2
Scobbie, T. 2008 (Falkirk)	12
Scott, M. 2006 (Livingston)	1
Scott, P. 1994 (St Johnstone)	4
Scougall, S. 2012 (Livingston, Sheffield U)	2
Scrimgour, D. 1997 (St Mirren)	3
Seaton, A. 1998 (Falkirk)	1
Severin, S. D. 2000 (Hearts)	10
Shankland, L. 2015 (Aberdeen)	4
Shannon, R. 1987 (Dundee)	7
Sharp, G. M. 1982 (Everton)	1
Sharp, R. 1990 (Dunfermline Ath)	4
Shaw, O. 2019 (Hibernian)	**2**
Sheerin, P. 1996 (Southampton)	1
Sheppard, J. 2017 (Reading)	2
Shields, G. 1997 (Rangers)	2
Shinnie, A. 2009 (Dundee, Rangers)	3
Shinnie, G. 2012 (Inverness CT)	2
Simmons, S. 2003 (Hearts)	1
Simpson, N. 1982 (Aberdeen)	11
Sinclair, G. 1977 (Dumbarton)	1
Skilling, M. 1993 (Kilmarnock)	2
Slater, C. 2014 (Kilmarnock, Colchester U)	9
Smith, B. M. 1992 (Celtic)	5
Smith, C. 2008 (St Mirren)	2
Smith, C. 2015 (Aberdeen)	1
Smith, D. 2012 (Hearts)	4
Smith, D. L. 2006 (Motherwell)	2
Smith, G. 1978 (Rangers)	1
Smith, G. 2004 (Rangers)	8
Smith, H. G. 1987 (Hearts)	2
Smith, L. 2017 (Hearts, Ayr U)	**12**
Smith, S. 2007 (Rangers)	1
Sneddon, A. 1979 (Celtic)	1
Snodgrass, R. 2008 (Livingston)	2
Soutar, D. 2003 (Dundee)	11
Souttar, J. 2016 (Dundee U, Hearts)	11
Speedie, D. R. 1985 (Chelsea)	1
Spencer, J. 1991 (Rangers)	3
Stanton, P. 1977 (Hibernian)	1
Stanton, S. 2014 (Hibernian)	1
Stark, W. 1985 (Aberdeen)	1
St Clair, H. 2018 (Chelsea)	3
Stephen, R. 1983 (Dundee)	1
Stevens, G. 1977 (Motherwell)	1
Stevenson, L. 2008 (Hibernian)	8
Stewart, C. 2002 (Kilmarnock)	1
Stewart, J. 1978 (Kilmarnock, Middlesbrough)	3
Stewart, M. J. 2000 (Manchester U)	17
Stewart, R. 1979 (Dundee U, West Ham U)	12
Stillie, D. 1995 (Aberdeen)	14
Storie, C. 2017 (Aberdeen)	2
Strachan, G. D. 1998 (Coventry C)	7
Sturrock, P. 1977 (Dundee U)	9
Sweeney, P. H. 2004 (Millwall)	8
Sweeney, S. 1991 (Clydebank)	7
Tapping, C. 2013 (Hearts)	1
Tarrant, N. K. 1999 (Aston Villa)	5
Taylor, G. J. 2017 (Kilmarnock)	**14**
Teale, G. 1997 (Clydebank, Ayr U)	6
Telfer, P. N. 1993 (Luton T)	3
Templeton, D. 2011 (Hearts)	2
Thomas, D. 2017 (Motherwell)	6
Thomas, K. 1993 (Hearts)	8
Thompson, S. 1997 (Dundee U)	12
Thomson, C. 2011 (Hearts)	2
Thomson, J. A. 2017 (Celtic)	1
Thomson, K. 2005 (Hibernian)	6
Thomson, W. 1977 (Partick Thistle, St Mirren)	10
Tolmie, J. 1980 (Morton)	1
Tortolano, J. 1987 (Hibernian)	2
Toshney, L. 2012 (Celtic)	5
Turnbull, D. 2019 (Motherwell)	**1**
Turner, I. 2005 (Everton)	6
Tweed, S. 1993 (Hibernian)	3
Wales, G. 2000 (Hearts)	1
Walker, A. 1988 (Celtic)	1
Walker, J. 2013 (Hearts)	1
Wallace, I. A. 1978 (Coventry C)	1
Wallace, L. 2007 (Hearts)	10
Wallace, M. 2012 (Hudderfield T)	4
Wallace, R. 2004 (Celtic, Sunderland)	4
Walsh, C. 1984 (Nottingham F)	5
Wark, J. 1977 (Ipswich T)	8
Watson, A. 1981 (Aberdeen)	4
Watson, K. 1977 (Rangers)	2
Watt, A. 2012 (Celtic)	9
Watt, E. 2018 (Wolverhampton W)	3
Watt, M. 1991 (Aberdeen)	12
Watt. S. M. 2005 (Chelsea)	5
Webster, A. 2003 (Hearts)	2
Whiteford, A. 1997 (St Johnstone)	1

Whittaker, S. G. 2005 (Hibernian) 18
Whyte, D. 1987 (Celtic) 9
Wighton, C. R. 2017 (Dundee) 6
Wilkie, L. 2000 (Dundee) 6
Will, J. A. 1992 (Arsenal) 3
Williams, G. 2002 (Nottingham F) 9
Williamson, R. 2018 (Dunfermline) 4
Wilson, D. 2011 (Liverpool, Hearts) 13
Wilson, I. 2018 (Kilmarnock) 7
Wilson, M. 2004 (Dundee U, Celtic) 19
Wilson, S. 1999 (Rangers) 7
Wilson, T. 1983 (St Mirren) 1
Wilson, T. 1988 (Nottingham F) 4
Winnie, D. 1988 (St Mirren) 1
Woods, M. 2006 (Sunderland) 2
Wotherspoon, D. 2011 (Hibernian) 16
Wright, P. 1989 (Aberdeen, QPR) 3
Wright, Stephen 1991 (Aberdeen) 14
Wright, Scott 2018 (Aberdeen) 5
Wright, T. 1987 (Oldham Ath) 1
Wylde, G. 2011 (Rangers) 7

Young, Darren 1997 (Aberdeen) 8
Young, Derek 2000 (Aberdeen) 5

WALES

Abbruzzese, R. 2018 (Cardiff C) 3
Absolom, K. 2019 (Ostersund) 1
Adams, N. W. 2008 (Bury, Leicester C) 5
Alfei, D. M. 2010 (Swansea C) 13
Aizlewood, M. 1979 (Luton T) 2
Allen, J. M. 2008 (Swansea C) 13
Anthony, B. 2005 (Cardiff C) 8

Babos, A. 2018 (Derby Co) 7
Baddeley, L. M. 1996 (Cardiff C) 2
Baker, A. T. 2019 (Sheffield W) 3
Balcombe, S. 1982 (Leeds U) 1
Bale, G. 2006 (Southampton, Tottenham H) 4
Barnhouse, D. J. 1995 (Swansea C) 3
Basey, G. W. 2009 (Charlton Ath) 1
Bater, P. T. 1977 (Bristol R) 2
Beevers, L. J. 2005 (Boston U, Lincoln C) 7
Bellamy, C. D. 1996 (Norwich C) 8
Bender, T. J. 2011 (Colchester U) 4
Birchall, A. S. 2003 (Arsenal, Mansfield T) 12
Bird, A. 1993 (Cardiff C) 6
Blackmore, C. 1984 (Manchester U) 3
Blake, D. J. 2007 (Cardiff C) 14
Blake, N. A. 1991 (Cardiff C) 5
Blaney, S. D. 1997 (West Ham U) 3
Bloom, J. 2011 (Falkirk) 1
Bodin, B. P. 2010 (Swindon T, Torquay U) 21
Bodin, P. J. 1983 (Cardiff C) 1
Bond, J. H. 2011 (Watford) 1
Bowen, J. P. 1993 (Swansea C) 5
Bowen, M. R. 1983 (Tottenham H) 3
Boyle, T. 1982 (Crystal Palace) 1
Brace, D. P. 1995 (Wrexham) 6
Bradley, M. S. 2007 (Walsall) 17
Bradshaw, T. 2012 (Shrewsbury T) 8
Broadhead, N. 2018 (Everton) 12
Brooks, D. R. 2018 (Sheffield U) 3
Brough, M. 2003 (Notts Co) 3
Brown, J. D. 2008 (Cardiff C) 6
Brown, J. R. 2003 (Gillingham) 7
Brown, T. A. F. 2011 (Ipswich T, Rotherham U, Aldershot T) 10
Burns, W. J. 2013 (Bristol C) 18
Burton, R. 2018 (Arsenal) 4
Byrne, M. T. 2003 (Bolton W) 1

Cabango, B. 2019 (Swansea C) 1
Calliste, R. T. 2005 (Manchester U, Liverpool) 15
Carpenter, R. E. 2005 (Burnley) 1
Cassidy, J. A. 2011 (Wolverhampton W) 8
Cegielski, W. 1977 (Wrexham) 2
Chamberlain, E. C. 2010 (Leicester C) 9
Chapple, S. R. 1992 (Swansea C) 8
Charles, J. D. 2016 (Huddersfield T, Barnsley) 9
Charles, J. M. 1979 (Swansea C) 2
Christie-Davies, I. 2018 (Chelsea, Liverpool) 4
Church, S. R. 2008 (Reading) 15
Clark, J. 1978 (Manchester U, Derby Co) 2
Clifton, H. L. 2019 (Grimsby T) 2
Coates, J. S. 1996 (Swansea C) 5
Coleman, C. 1990 (Swansea C) 3
Collins, J. M. 2003 (Cardiff C) 7
Collins, M. J. 2007 (Fulham, Swansea C) 2
Collison, J. D. 2008 (West Ham U) 7
Cooper, B. 2019 (Swansea C) 3
Cornell, D. J. 2010 (Swansea C) 4
Cotterill, D. R. G. B. 2005 (Bristol C, Wigan Ath) 11
Coyne, D. 1992 (Tranmere R) 7
Coxe, C. T. 2018 (Cardiff C) 10
Craig, N. L. 2009 (Everton) 4
Critchell, K. A. R. 2005 (Southampton) 3
Crofts, A. L. 2005 (Gillingham) 10
Crowe, M. T. T. 2017 (Ipswich T) 1
Crowell, M. T. 2004 (Wrexham) 7
Cullen, L. 2018 (Swansea C) 5
Curtis, A. T. 1977 (Swansea C) 1

Dasilva, C. P. 2018 (Chelsea, Brentford) 3
Davies, A. 1982 (Manchester U) 6
Davies, A. G. 2006 (Cambridge U) 6
Davies, A. R. 2005 (Southampton, Yeovil T) 14
Davies, C. M. 2005 (Oxford U, Verona, Oldham Ath) 9
Davies, D. 1999 (Barry T) 1
Davies, G. M. 1993 (Hereford U, Crystal Palace) 7
Davies, I. C. 1978 (Norwich C) 1
Davies, K. E. 2019 (Swansea C) 1
Davies, L. 2005 (Bangor C) 1
Davies, R. J. 2006 (WBA) 4
Davies, S. 1999 (Peterborough U, Tottenham H) 10
Dawson, C. 2013 (Leeds U) 2
Day, R. 2000 (Manchester C, Mansfield T) 11
Deacy, N. 1977 (PSV Eindhoven) 1
De-Vulgt, L. S. 2002 (Swansea C) 2
Dibble, A. 1983 (Cardiff C) 3
Dibble, C. 2014 (Barnsley) 1
Doble, R. A. 2010 (Southampton) 10
Doughty, M. E. 2012 (QPR) 1
Doyle, S. C. 1979 (Preston NE, Huddersfield T) 2
Duffy, R. M. 2005 (Portsmouth) 7
Dummett, P. 2011 (Newcastle U) 3
Dwyer, P. J. 1979 (Cardiff C) 1

Eardley, N. 2007 (Oldham Ath, Blackpool) 11
Earnshaw, R. 1999 (Cardiff C) 10
Easter, D. J. 2006 (Cardiff C) 1
Ebdon, M. 1990 (Everton) 2
Edwards, C. N. H. 1996 (Swansea C) 7
Edwards, D. A. 2006 (Shrewsbury T, Luton T, Wolverhampton W) 9
Edwards, G. D. R. 2012 (Swansea C) 6
Edwards, R. I. 1977 (Chester) 2
Edwards, R. W. 1991 (Bristol C) 13
Evans, A. 1977 (Bristol R) 1
Evans, C. 2007 (Manchester C, Sheffield U) 13
Evans, J. 2018 (Swansea C) 8
Evans, J. A. J. 2014 (Fulham, Wrexham) 6
Evans, K. 1999 (Leeds U, Cardiff C) 4
Evans, K. G. 2019 (Swansea C) 1
Evans, L. 2013 (Wolverhampton W) 13
Evans, O. R. 2018 (Wigan Ath) 3
Evans, P. S. 1996 (Shrewsbury T) 1
Evans, S. J. 2001 (Crystal Palace) 2

Evans, T. 1995 (Cardiff C)	3
Fish, N. 2005 (Cardiff C)	2
Fleetwood, S. 2005 (Cardiff C)	5
Flynn, C. P. 2007 (Crewe Alex)	1
Folland, R. W. 2000 (Oxford U)	1
Foster, M. G. 1993 (Tranmere R)	1
Fowler, L. A. 2003 (Coventry C, Huddersfield T)	9
Fox, M. A. 2013 (Charlton Ath)	6
Freeman, K. 2012 (Nottingham F, Derby Co)	15
Freestone, R. 1990 (Chelsea)	1
Gabbidon, D. L. 1999 (WBA, Cardiff C)	17
Gale, D. 1983 (Swansea C)	2
Gall, K. A. 2002 (Bristol R, Yeovil T)	8
Gibson, N. D. 1999 (Tranmere R, Sheffield W)	11
Giggs, R. J. 1991 (Manchester U)	1
Gilbert, P. 2005 (Plymouth Arg)	12
Giles, D. C. 1977 (Cardiff C, Swansea C, Crystal Palace)	4
Giles, P. 1982 (Cardiff C)	3
Graham, D. 1991 (Manchester U)	1
Green, R. M. 1998 (Wolverhampton W)	16
Griffith, C. 1990 (Cardiff C)	1
Griffiths, C. 1991 (Shrewsbury T)	1
Grubb, D. 2007 (Bristol C)	1
Gunter, C. 2006 (Cardiff C, Tottenham H)	8
Haldane, L. O. 2007 (Bristol R)	1
Hall, G. D. 1990 (Chelsea)	1
Harries, C. W. T. 2018 (Swansea C)	**7**
Harris, M. T. 2018 (Cardiff C)	**13**
Harrison, E. W. 2013 (Bristol R)	14
Hartson, J. 1994 (Luton T, Arsenal)	9
Haworth, S. O. 1997 (Cardiff C, Coventry C, Wigan Ath)	12
Hedges, R. P. 2014 (Swansea C)	11
Henley, A. 2012 (Blackburn R)	3
Hennessey, W. R. 2006 (Wolverhampton W)	6
Hewitt, E. J. 2012 (Macclesfield T, Ipswich T)	10
Hillier, I. M. 2001 (Tottenham H, Luton T)	5
Hodges, G. 1983 (Wimbledon)	5
Holden, A. 1984 (Chester C)	1
Holloway, C. D. 1999 (Exeter C)	2
Hopkins, J. 1982 (Fulham)	5
Hopkins, S. A. 1999 (Wrexham)	1
Howells, J. 2012 (Luton T)	5
Huggins, D. S. 1996 (Bristol C)	1
Huggins, N. 2019 (Leeds U)	**1**
Hughes, D. 2005 (Kaiserslautern, Regensburg)	2
Hughes, D. R. 1994 (Southampton)	1
Hughes, I. 1992 (Bury)	11
Hughes, L. M. 1983 (Manchester U)	5
Hughes, R. D. 1996 (Aston Villa, Shrewsbury T)	13
Hughes, W. 1977 (WBA)	3
Huws, E. W. 2012 (Manchester C)	6
Isgrove, L. J. 2013 (Southampton)	6
Jackett, K. 1981 (Watford)	2
Jacobson, J. M. 2006 (Cardiff C, Bristol R)	15
James, D. O. 2017 (Swansea C)	**11**
James, L. R. S. 2006 (Southampton)	10
James, R. M. 1977 (Swansea C)	3
Jarman, L. 1996 (Cardiff C)	10
Jeanne, L. C. 1999 (QPR)	8
Jelleyman, G. A. 1999 (Peterborough U)	1
Jenkins, L. D. 1998 (Swansea C)	9
Jenkins, S. R. 1993 (Swansea C)	2
John, D. C. 2014 (Cardiff C)	9
Jones, C. T. 2007 (Swansea C)	1
Jones, E. P. 2000 (Blackpool)	1
Jones, F. 1981 (Wrexham)	1
Jones, G. W. 2014 (Everton)	9
Jones, J. A. 2001 (Swansea C)	3
Jones, L. 1982 (Cardiff C)	3
Jones, M. A. 2004 (Wrexham)	4
Jones, M. G. 1998 (Leeds U)	7
Jones, O. R. 2015 (Swansea C)	1
Jones, P. L. 1992 (Liverpool)	12
Jones, R. 2011 (AFC Wimbledon)	1
Jones, R. A. 1994 (Sheffield W)	3
Jones, S. J. 2005 (Swansea C)	1
Jones, V. 1979 (Bristol R)	2
Kendall, L. M. 2001 (Crystal Palace)	2
Kendall, M. 1978 (Tottenham H)	1
Kenworthy, J. R. 1994 (Tranmere R)	3
King, A. 2008 (Leicester C)	11
Knott, G. R. 1996 (Tottenham H)	1
Law, B. J. 1990 (QPR)	2
Lawless, A. 2006 (Torquay U)	1
Lawrence, T. 2013 (Manchester U)	8
Ledley, J. C. 2005 (Cardiff C)	5
Lemonheigh-Evans, C. 2019 (Bristol C)	**3**
Letheran, G. 1977 (Leeds U)	2
Letheran, K. C. 2006 (Swansea C)	1
Lewis, A. 2018 (Swansea C)	**7**
Lewis, D. 1982 (Swansea C)	9
Lewis, J. 1983 (Cardiff C)	1
Llewellyn, C. M. 1998 (Norwich C)	14
Lockyer, T. A. 2015 (Bristol R)	7
Loveridge, J. 1982 (Swansea C)	3
Low, J. D. 1999 (Bristol R, Cardiff C)	1
Lowndes, S. R. 1979 (Newport Co, Millwall)	4
Lucas, L. P. 2011 (Swansea C)	19
MacDonald, S. B. 2006 (Swansea C)	25
McCarthy, A. J. 1994 (QPR)	3
McDonald, C. 2006 (Cardiff C)	3
Mackin, L. 2006 (Wrexham)	1
Maddy, P. 1982 (Cardiff C)	2
Margetson, M. W. 1992 (Manchester C)	7
Martin, A. P. 1999 (Crystal Palace)	1
Martin, D. A. 2006 (Notts Co)	1
Marustik, C. 1982 (Swansea C)	7
Matondo, R. 2018 (Manchester C)	**8**
Matthews, A. J. 2010 (Cardiff C)	5
Maxwell, C. 2009 (Wrexham)	16
Maxwell, L. J. 1999 (Liverpool, Cardiff C)	14
Meades, J. 2012 (Cardiff C)	4
Meaker, M. J. 1994 (QPR)	2
Melville, A. K. 1990 (Swansea C, Oxford U)	2
Mepham, C. J. 2018 (Brentford)	4
Micallef, C. 1982 (Cardiff C)	3
Mooney, D. 2019 (Fleetwood T)	**1**
Morgan, A. M. 1995 (Tranmere R)	4
Morgan, C. 2004 (Wrexham, Milton Keynes D)	12
Morrell, J. J. 2018 (Bristol C)	**8**
Morris, A. J. 2009 (Cardiff C, Aldershot T)	8
Moss, D. M. 2003 (Shrewsbury T)	6
Mountain, P. D. 1997 (Cardiff C)	2
Mumford, A. O. 2003 (Swansea C)	4
Nardiello, D. 1978 (Coventry C)	1
Neilson, A. B. 1993 (Newcastle U)	7
Nicholas, P. 1978 (Crystal Palace, Arsenal)	3
Nogan, K. 1990 (Luton T)	2
Nogan, L. M. 1991 (Oxford U)	1
Norrington-Davies, R. 2018 (Sheffield U)	**10**
Nyatanga, L. J. 2005 (Derby Co)	10
Oakley, A. 2013 (Swindon T)	1
O'Brien, B. T. 2015 (Manchester C)	8
Ogleby, R. 2011 (Hearts, Wrexham)	12
Oster, J. M. 1997 (Grimsby T, Everton)	9
O'Sullivan, T. P. 2013 (Cardiff C)	15
Owen, G. 1991 (Wrexham)	8
Page, R. J. 1995 (Watford)	4
Parslow, D. 2005 (Cardiff C)	4

Partington, J. M. 2009 (Bournemouth) 8
Partridge, D. W. 1997 (West Ham U) 1
Pascoe, C. 1983 (Swansea C) 4
Pearce, S. 2006 (Bristol C) 3
Pejic, S. M. 2003 (Wrexham) 6
Pembridge, M. A. 1991 (Luton T) 1
Peniket, R. 2012 (Fulham) 1
Perry, J. 1990 (Cardiff C) 3
Peters, M. 1992 (Manchester C, Norwich C) 3
Phillips, D. 1984 (Plymouth Arg) 3
Phillips, G. R. 2001 (Swansea C) 3
Phillips, L. 1979 (Swansea C, Charlton Ath) 2
Pilling, L. 2018 (Tranmere R) 9
Pipe, D. R. 2003 (Coventry C, Notts Co) 12
Pontin, K. 1978 (Cardiff C) 1
Poole, R. L. 2017 (Manchester U) 17
Powell, L. 1991 (Southampton) 4
Powell, L. 2004 (Leicester C) 3
Powell, R. 2006 (Bolton W) 1
Price, J. J. 1998 (Swansea C) 7
Price, L. P. 2005 (Ipswich T) 10
Price, M. D. 2001 (Everton, Hull C, Scarborough) 13
Price, P. 1981 (Luton T) 1
Price, T. O. 2019 (Swansea C) 1
Pritchard, J. P. 2013 (Fulham) 3
Pritchard, M. O. 2006 (Swansea C) 4
Pugh, D. 1982 (Doncaster R) 2
Pugh, S. 1993 (Wrexham) 2
Pugh, T. 2019 (Scunthorpe U) 2
Pulis, A. J. 2006 (Stoke C) 5

Ramasut, M. W. T. 1997 (Bristol R) 4
Ramsey, A. J. 2008, (Cardiff C, Arsenal) 12
Ratcliffe, G. 2019 (Cardiff C) 1
Ratcliffe, K. 1981 (Everton) 2
Ray, G. E. 2013 (Crewe Alex) 5
Ready, K. 1992 (QPR) 5
Rees, A. 1984 (Birmingham C) 1
Rees, J. M. 1990 (Luton T) 3
Rees, M. R. 2003 (Millwall) 4
Reid, B. 2014 (Wolverhampton W) 1
Ribeiro, C. M. 2008 (Bristol C) 8
Richards, A. D. J. 2010 (Swansea C) 16
Richards, E. A. 2012 (Bristol R) 1
Roberts, A. M. 1991 (QPR) 2
Roberts, C. 2013 (Cheltenham T) 6
Roberts, C. J. 1999 (Cardiff C) 1
Roberts, C. R. J. 2016 (Swansea C) 2
Roberts, G. 1983 (Hull C) 1
Roberts, G. W. 1997 (Liverpool, Panionios, Tranmere R) 11
Roberts, J. G. 1977 (Wrexham) 1
Roberts, N. W. 1999 (Wrexham) 3
Roberts, P. 1997 (Porthmadog) 1
Roberts, S. I. 1999 (Swansea C) 13
Roberts, S. W. 2000 (Wrexham) 3
Roberts, T. W. 2018 (Leeds U) 5
Robinson, C. P. 1996 (Wolverhampton W) 6
Robinson, J. R. C. 1992 (Brighton & HA, Charlton Ath) 5
Robson-Kanu, K. H. 2010 (Reading) 4
Rodon, J. P. 2017 (Swansea C) 9
Rowlands, A. J. R. 1996 (Manchester C) 5
Rush, I. 1981 (Liverpool) 2

Savage, R. W. 1995 (Crewe Alex) 3
Saunders, C. L. 2015 (Crewe Alex) 1
Sayer, P. A. 1977 (Cardiff C) 2
Searle, D. 1991 (Cardiff C) 6
Sheehan, J. L. 2014 (Swansea C) 12
Shephard, L. 2015 (Swansea C) 2
Slatter, D. 2000 (Chelsea) 6
Slatter, N. 1983 (Bristol R) 6
Smith, D. 2014 (Shrewsbury T) 3
Smith, M. 2018 (Manchester C) 5
Somner, M. J. 2004 (Brentford) 2
Speed, G. A. 1990 (Leeds U) 3
Spender, S. 2005 (Wrexham) 6
Stephens, D. 2011 (Hibernian) 7
Stevenson, N. 1982 (Swansea C) 2
Stevenson, W. B. 1977 (Leeds U) 3
Stock, B. B. 2003 (Bournemouth) 4
Symons, C. J. 1991 (Portsmouth) 2

Tancock, S. 2013 (Swansea C) 6
Taylor, A. J. 2012 (Tranmere R) 3
Taylor, G. K. 1995 (Bristol R) 4
Taylor, J. W. T. 2010 (Reading) 12
Taylor, N. J. 2008 (Wrexham, Swansea C) 13
Taylor, R. F. 2008 (Chelsea) 5
Thomas, C. E. 2010 (Swansea C) 3
Thomas, D. G. 1977 (Leeds U) 3
Thomas, D. J. 1998 (Watford) 2
Thomas, G. S. 2018 (Leicester C) 8
Thomas, J. A. 1996 (Blackburn R) 21
Thomas, Martin R. 1979 (Bristol R) 2
Thomas, Mickey R. 1977 (Wrexham) 2
Thomas, S. 2001 (Wrexham) 5
Thompson, L. C. W. 2015 (Norwich C) 2
Tibbott, L. 1977 (Ipswich T) 2
Tipton, M. J. 1998 (Oldham Ath) 6
Tolley, J. C. 2001 (Shrewsbury T) 12
Touray, M. 2019 (Newport Co) 3
Tudur-Jones, O. 2006 (Swansea C) 3
Twiddy, C. 1995 (Plymouth Arg) 3

Valentine, R. D. 2001 (Everton, Darlington) 8
Vaughan, D. O. 2003 (Crewe Alex) 8
Vaughan, N. 1982 (Newport Co) 2
Vokes, S. M. 2007 (Bournemouth, Wolverhampton W) 14

Walsh, D. 2000 (Wrexham) 8
Walsh, I. P. 1979 (Crystal Palace, Swansea C) 2
Walsh, J. 2012 (Swansea C, Crawley T) 11
Walton, M. 1991 (Norwich C.) 1
Ward, D. 1996 (Notts Co) 2
Ward, D. 2013 (Liverpool) 6
Warlow, O. J. 2007 (Lincoln C) 2
Weeks, D. L. 2014 (Wolverhampton W) 2
Weston, R. D. 2001 (Arsenal, Cardiff C) 4
Wharton, T. J. 2014 (Cardiff C) 1
Whitfield, P. M. 2003 (Wrexham) 1
Wiggins, R. 2006 (Crystal Palace) 9
Williams, A. P. 1998 (Southampton) 9
Williams, A. S. 1996 (Blackburn R) 16
Williams, D. 1983 (Bristol R) 1
Williams, D. I. L. 1998 (Liverpool, Wrexham) 9
Williams, D. T. 2006 (Yeovil T) 1
Williams, E. 1997 (Caernarfon T) 2
Williams, G. 1983 (Bristol R) 2
Williams, G. A. 2003 (Crystal Palace) 5
Williams, G. C. 2014 (Fulham) 3
Williams, J. P. 2011 (Crystal Palace) 8
Williams, M. 2001 (Manchester U) 10
Williams, M. P. 2006 (Wrexham) 14
Williams, M. J. 2014 (Notts Co) 1
Williams, M. R. 2006 (Wrexham) 6
Williams, O. fon 2007 (Crewe Alex, Stockport Co) 11
Williams, R. 2007 (Middlesbrough) 10
Williams, S. J. 1995 (Wrexham) 4
Wilmot, R. 1982 (Arsenal) 6
Wilson, H. 2014 (Liverpool) 10
Wilson, J. S. 2009 (Bristol C) 3
Worgan, L. J. 2005 (Milton Keynes D, Rushden & D) 5
Wright, A. A. 1998 (Oxford U) 3
Wright, J. 2014 (Huddersfield T) 2

Yorwerth, J. 2014 (Cardiff C) 7
Young, S. 1996 (Cardiff C) 5

ENGLAND YOUTH GAMES 2018–19

■ *Denotes player sent off.*

ENGLAND UNDER-16

FRIENDLIES

Sunday 22 July 2018

Croatia (0) 0 England (0) 2 *(Dobbin 70, Iling-Junior 75)*

England: Chibueze; Lusala, Norris, Delap, Laing, Colwill, Dembele, Simons, Barry (Iling-Junior 41), Musiala (Dobbin 41), Bellingham.
Substitutes: Patino, John, Illing-Junior, Watt, Oluwayemi, Dobbin, Hagan, Quansah, Gordon, Ramsey, Boyce-Clarke.

Tuesday 24 July 2018

Croatia (0) 0

England (0) 0

England: Oluwayemi; Norris, Patino, Watt, Hagan, Jarel Quansah, Ramsey, John, Gordon, Dobbin, Illing-Junior.
Substitutes: Chibueze, Lusala, Laing, Colwill, Dembele, Barry, Musiala, Delap, Simons, Bellingham, Boyce-Clarke.

2018 UEFA DEVELOPMENT TOURNAMENT

Burton, Monday 20 August 2018

England (0) 1 *(Sackey)* **Scotland (0) 0**

England: Oluwayemi; Riley, Garrett, Kenneh, Davidson, Robertson, Elliott, Bellingham, Ohio, John, Hodnett.
Substitutes: Hagan, Mbete-Tabu, Boyce-Clarke, Ebiowei, Sackey, Barry, Pye.
Scotland: Ritchie; Devine, Watson, King, Morrison, Neilson, Smith, Fairley, McKinnon, Mochrie, Brooks.
Substitutes: Henderson, Fraser, Metcalfe, Hepburn, Ramsay, Hanratty, Charleston-King, Ferguson, Hutchinson, Connolly.

Burton, Friday 24 August 2018

England (0) 2 *(Ohio 62, Robertson 78)*

Turkey (1) 1 *(Elmaz 24)*

England: Oluwayemi; Sackey, Pye (Garrett 60), Vale (Bellingham 60), Hagan, Mbete-Tabu, Ebiowei (Ohio 60), Haigh (John 60), Barry, Young-Coombes (Robertson 60).

VAL-DE-MARNE TOURNAMENT

Limeil-Brevannes, Tuesday 30 October 2018

France (1) 1 *(Tramoni 17)*

England (2) 3 *(Bellingham 8, Patino 13, Barry 59)*

England: Boyce-Clarke; Egan-Riley (Watt 64), Norris, Patino (Diallo 60), Hagan, Colwill, Dembele, Bellingham, Barry (Iling-Junior 60), Musiala (Dobbin 60), John.

Plessis-Treviso, Thursday 1 November 2018

Austria (0) 2 *(Babuscu 74, 82)*

England (0) 4 *(Dobbin 51, Dembele 55, John 77, Diallo 80)*

England: Chibueze; Mbete-Tabu, Norris (Colwill 41), Kenneh (Musiala 63), Hagan (John 63), Watt, Dembele (Egan-Riley 63), Bellingham (Barry 63), Dobbin, Iling-Junior (Patino 80), Diallo.

Bonneil sur Marne, Saturday 3 November 2018

England (2) 4 *(John, Barry (2), Musiala)*

Japan (1) 1 *(Kosel)*

England: Boyce-Clarke, Egan-Riley, Mbete-Tabu, Kenneh, Patino, Colwill, John, Bellingham, Barry, Musiala, Diallo.
Substitutes: Chibueze, Norris, Hagan, Dembele, Watt, Iling-Junior, Dobbin.

AEGEAN INTERNATIONAL TOURNAMENT

Turkey, Monday 14 January 2019

England (0) 2 *(Lusala 42, Delap 72)* **Albania (0) 0**

England: Oluwayemi; Lusala, Samuels, Humphreys, Burns, Gooch, McNeill, Balagizi, Delap, Williams, Ridley.
Substitutes: Welch, Raymond, Richardson, Pye, Chibueze, Henry, Ramsey, Richards, Hamilton.

Turkey, Tuesday 15 January 2019

England (3) 5 *(Delap 3 (pen), 18, Richards 17, Richardson 43, McNeill 65)*

Moldova (1) 1 *(Covalciuc 5)*

England: Chibueze; Lusala, Pye, Welch, Burns, Gooch, Henry, Ramsey, Delap, Hamilton, Richards.
Substitutes: Oluwayemi, Samuels, Humphreys, McNeill, Balagizi, Raymond, Richardson, Williams, Ridley.

Turkey, Thursday 17 January 2019

Turkey (1) 2 *(Beyaz 30 (pen), 45)*

England (1) 1 *(Delap 2)*

England: Chibueze; Lusala, Samuels, Burns (Pye 41), Welch, McNeill (Ramsey 46), Balagizi, Henry (Richards 53), Delap, Williams (Hamilton 53), Richardson (Ridley 46).

AEGEAN INTERNATIONAL TOURNAMENT 3RD PLACE PLAY-OFF

Turkey, Saturday 19 January 2019

England (0) 1 *(Bagrintsev 79)*

Russia (0) 1 *(Richardson 47)*

England: Oluwayemi; Lusala, Pye, Humphreys, Welch, Hamilton, Balagizi, Ramsey, Ridley, McNeill, Richards.
Substitutes: Chibueze, Samuels, Burns, Delap, Raymond, Richardson, Williams, Henry, Gooch.
England won 4-2 on penalties.

2019 UEFA DEVELOPMENT TOURNAMENT

Burton, Sunday 17 February 2019

England (2) 2 *(Quansah 30, Iling-Junior 32)*

Norway (0) 1 *(Arnstad 79)*

England: Graczyk; Oyegoke (Humphreys 46), Norris (Colwill 46), Kenneh, Baptiste, Quansah, Raymond (Dembele 63), Patino, Barry (Delap 46), Diallo (Dobbin 46), Iling-Junior.

Burton, Tuesday 19 February 2019

England 4 *(John 2, Dobbin, Colwill)* **France 0**

England: Boyce-Clarke; Oyegoke (Kenneh 51), Norris (Baptiste 63), Humphreys, Colwill, Dembele, Bellingham, Musiala (Raymond 63), John, Dobbin, Iling-Junior (Diallo 63).

Burton, Thursday 21 February 2019

England 2 *(Barry 2)*

Brazil 2 *(Leonardo, Henrique)*

England: Boyce-Clarke; Baptiste, Norris, Kenneh, Patino, Colwill, Dembele, Bellingham, Barry, Musiala, Diallo.
Substitutes: Graczyk, Oyegoke, Humphreys, John, Delap, Dobbin, Raymond, Iling-Junior, Quansah.

MONTAIGU TOURNAMENT – GROUP B

Jard sur Mer, Tuesday 16 April 2019

England (1) 1 *(Barry 34)*

Argentina (1) 2 *(Sarmiento 2, Cabrera 72 (pen))*

England: Oluwayemi; Oyegoke, Humphreys, Colwill, Norris, Kenneh, Bellingham, Ohio, Musiala, Iling-Junior, Barry.
Substitutes: Boyce-Clarke, Egan-Riley, Patino, Dembele, John, Delap, Balagizi, Baptiste, Diallo.

La Copechagniere, Thursday 18 April 2019

England (3) 5 *(Diallo 5, Delap 31, John 36, Dembele 45, Patino 53)*

Ivory Coast (0) 0

England: Boyce-Clark; Egan-Riley, Kenneh, Baptiste, Iling-Junior, Patino, Balagizi, John, Dembele, Delap, Diallo.
Substitutes: Oluwayemi, Norris, Humprheys, Colwill, Bellingham, Barry, Musiala, Oyegoke, Ohio.

La Copechagniere, Saturday 20 April 2019

England (1) 3 *(Nazinho 27 (og), Bellingham 73, Musiala 76)*

Portugal (0) 1 *(Sousa 60)*

England: Oluwayemi; Baptiste, Humphreys, Colwill, Norris, Patino, Bellingham, John, Dembele, Diallo, Barry.
Substitutes: Egan-Riley, Musiala, Oyegoke, Boyce-Clarke, Ohio, Kenneh, Delap, Balagizi, Iling-Junior.

FINAL ROUND

Montaigu, Monday 22 April 2019

England (2) 4 *(Dembele 29, Delap 40, Musiala 47, Barry 68)*

Brazil (0) 0

England: Boyce-Clarke; Kenneh, Egan-Riley, Colwill, Iling-Junior, Balagizi, Bellingham, Dembele, Muslala, Delap, Ohio.
Substitutes: Oluwayemi, Baptiste, Humphreys, Norris, Oyegoke, Patino Barry, Diallo, John.

ENGLAND UNDER-17

SYRENKA CUP

Ostrowiec Swietokrzyski, Friday 7 September 2018

England (2) 6 *(Sarmiento 4, Rogers 6, Greenwood 49, Harwood Bellis 52, Gelhardt 74, 85 (pen))*

Norway (0) 0

England: Moulden; Livramento (Hodge 62), Roberts (Bondswell 62), Harwood-Bellis, Wood-Gordon, Musah (Azeez 72), Weir, Carvalho (Madueke 75), Rogers (Okoflex 72), Greenwood (Gelhardt 62), Sarmiento (Mighten 72).

Ostrowiec Swietokrzyski, Sunday 9 September 2018

Portugal (1) 1 *(Silva 28)*

England (0) 2 *(Mighten 21 (pen), Musah 90 (pen))*

England: Trafford; Livramento (Musah 60), Bondswell (Harwood-Bellis 60), Mengi (Wood-Gordon 71), Roberts, Azeez, Hodge, Madueke (Carvalho 60), Gelhart (Greenwood 71), Mighten (Sarmiento 71), Okoflex (Rogers 60).

Ostrowiec Swietokrzyski, Tuesday 11 September 2018

Belgium (1) 2 *(Baeten 9, Buhadir 73)*

England (5) 6 *(Rogers 3, 13, 44, Greenwood 16, Mighten 37, Gelhardt 74)*

England: Moulden (Trafford 46); Livramento (Mengi 46), Harwood-Bellis, Wood-Gordon, Bondswell (Roberts 46), Azeez (Hodge 46), Carvalho (Madueke (65), Musah (Weir 46), Greenwood (Gelhardt 46), Mighten (Sarmiento 46), Rogers (Okoflex 65).
England U17s win Syrenka Cup.

UNDER-17 INTERNATIONAL TOURNAMENT

Chester, Friday 12 October 2018

England (0) 3 *(Greenwood 47, Rogers 71, Gelhardt 89)*

USA (1) 1 *(Yow 16)* 1035

England: Moulden; Livramento (Elliot 62), Azeez, Harwood-Bellis, Mengi, Mighten (Hodge 70), Musah, Greenwood (Gelhardt 81), Carvalho (Knight 62), Rogers, Cirkin (Roberts 62).

Shrewsbury, Sunday 14 October 2018

England (3) 3 *(Roberts 30, Gelhardt 41, 45)*

Russia (0) 0 1472

England: Trafford; Livramento (Musah 46), Roberts, Knight (Carvalho 46), Gelhardt (Greenwood 70), Hodge, Weir, Wood-Gordon, Okoflex (Rogers 80), Cirkin (Harwood-Bellis 60), Elliott (Mighten 70).

Telford, Tuesday 16 October 2018

England (2) 3 *(Mighten 6, Greenwood 41, Rogers 50)*

Brazil (1) 1 *(Neto 12)* 3144

England: Molden; Livramento (Hodge 46), Roberts (Cirkin 46), Azeez, Harwood-Bellis, Mengi, Mighten (Elliott 46), Musah, Greenwood (Gelhardt 46), Carvalho (Knight 46), Rogers (Weir 50).

UNDER-17 FOUR NATIONS TOURNAMENT

Dublin, Thursday 8 November 2018

Republic of Ireland (1) 1 *(Ebosele 33 (pen))*

England (2) 3 *(Elliott 18, Mighten 31, Greenwood 84)*

Republic of Ireland: Corcoran; Keogh, Turner, Kelly, Furlong, Holt, Hodge, Everitt, Sobowale (Giurgi 63), Ebosele (Kennedy 90), Carty.
England: Trafford (Moulden 46); Musah, Wood-Gordon, Simeu, Cirken, Weir, Azeez, Carvalho (Roberts 46), Elliott (Knight 77), Gelhardt (Rogers 63), Mighten (Greenwood 63).

Dublin, Sunday 11 November 2018

Germany (2) 2 *(Woltemade 2, Tillman 40)*

England (1) 2 *(Musah 33, Rogers 52)* 250

England: Moulden; Musah, Simeu, Harwood-Bellis, Roberts (Wood-Gordon 16), Madueke (Elliott 74), Walcott, Bate (Azeez 46), Rogers, Greenwood (Gelhardt 84), Mighten.

Dublin, Wednesday 14 November 2018

England (0) 0 **Czech Republic (0) 0**

FRIENDLIES

Murcia, Thursday 7 February 2019

England (1) 3 *(Elliott 16, Greenwood 48, 63)*

France (2) 2 *(Bakwa 5, Soppi 32)*

England: Moulden; Matheson (Livramento 59), Cirkin (Simeu 46), Weir, Wood-Gordon, Roberts, Knight, Musah (Jenks 59), Greenwood, Carvalho, Elliott.

Murcia, Sunday 10 February 2019

England (0) 0

Hungary (0) 0

England: Broome; Livramento, Cirkin, Bate, Simeu, Wood-Gordon, Sarmiento, Musah, Gelhardt, Carvalho, Taylor-Hart.
Substitutes: Moulden, Matheson, Mnoga, Roberts, Elliott, Jenks, Mighten, Weir, Knight.

UNDER-17 EUROPEAN CHAMPIONSHIP ELITE QUALIFYING IN DENMARK – GROUP 3

Silkeborg, Thursday 21 March 2019

England (3) 5 *(Rogers 22, 80, Greenwood 30, 32 (pen), Fazlic 56 (og))*

Switzerland (0) 2 *(De Donno 52, Stergiou 68)*

England: Moulden; Livramento, Roberts, Azeez, Harwood-Bellis, Wood-Gordon, Weir, Greenwood (Gelhardt 84), Madueke (Mighten 87), Rogers, Elliott (Knight 75).

Silkeborg, Sunday 24 March 2019

England (0) 0

Croatia (0) 0

England: Moulden■; Livramento, Roberts, Azeez, Harwood-Bellis, Wood-Gordon, Weir (Bate 76), Greenwood (Gelhardt 76), Madueke (Mighten 61), Rogers, Knight (Trafford 31).

Silkeborg, Wednesday 27 March 2019

Denmark (0) 2 *(Zaar 62, Faghir 90)*

England (0) 3 *(Madueke 79, 90, Gelhardt 87)*

England: Trafford; Livramento, Roberts, Azeez, Harwood-Bellis, Wood-Gordon, Mighten (Madueke 56), Weir (Bate 56), Greenwood, Rogers (Mengi 90), Knight (Gelhardt 72).

UNDER-17 EUROPEAN CHAMPIONSHIP FINALS IN IRELAND – GROUP B

Longford, Friday 3 May 2019

England (1) 1 *(Greenwood 34 (pen))*

France (0) 1 *(Aouchiche 79)*

England: Moulden; Fagan-Walcott, Roberts, Azeez, Harwood-Bellis, Madueke (Gelhardt 89), Weir, Greenwood, Rogers, Robinson (Bondswell 54), Palmer (Bate 65).

Dublin, Monday 6 May 2019

Netherlands (3) 5 *(Brobbey, 10, 58 (pen), Bannis 35, Hansen 45, Unuvar 63)*

England (2) 2 *(Harwood-Bellis 6, Greenwood 34 (pen))*

England: Moulden; Fagan-Walcott, Roberts, Azeez, Harwood-Bellis, Weir (Jenks 81), Greenwood (Knight 71), Rogers, Gelhardt, Robinson (Bondswell 62), Palmer.

Dublin, Thursday 9 May 2019

Sweden (1) 1 *(Prica 28)*

England (1) 3 *(Greenwood 15, Jenks 76, Gelhardt 82)*

England: Trafford; Roberts, Azeez, Mengi, Madueke, Weir (Jenks 72), Greenwood (Gelhardt 65), Rogers (Sarmiento 59), Bondswell, Robinson (Bate 71), Palmer (Knight 46).

ENGLAND UNDER-18

LIMOGES FOUR NATIONS TOURNAMENT

Limoges, Wednesday 5 September 2018

Netherlands (0) 0

England (2) 3 *(Greenwood 3, Anjorin 36, Appiah 84)*

England: Ashby-Hammond; Crowe (Alese 83), Ogbeta, Laird, Saka, Garner, Appiah (Simmonds 90), Anjorin (Mumba 83), Jones (Gordon 90), Greenwood (Balogun 64), John-Jules.

Limoges, Friday 7 September 2018

Russia (0) 0

England (2) 3 *(John-Jules 14 (pen), Simmonds 38, Anjorin 49)*

England: Okonkwo (Dewhurst); Crowe, Alese, Laird, Mumba (Saka 73), Gordon (Greenwood 60), Simmonds, Jones, Mola, John-Jules (Appiah 73), Balogun.

Limoges, Sunday 9 September 2018

France (1) 1 *(Saliba 45)*

England (1) 2 *(Laird 11, Saka 75 (pen))*

England: Ashby-Hammond; Ogbeta, Alese, Laird, Sako, Garner, Simmonds, Anjorin (Gordon 68), Jones, Greenwood, Balogun (Mumba 79).

FRIENDLIES

Burton, Thursday 11 October 2018

England (2) 4 *(John-Jules 21 (pen), Anjorin 45, Appiah 50 Laird 69)*

Sweden (0) 0

England: Ashby-Hammond (Okonkwo 80); Laird (Daley-Campbell 80), Saka, Garner, Kpohomouh, Alese (Ogbeta 60), Appiah (Balogun 80), Anjorin (Gordon 59), Greenwood, Jones (Mumba 59), John-Jules (Simmonds 80).

Burton, Monday 15 October 2018

England (1) 2 *(Vicek 21 (og), John-Jules 71)*

Czech Republic (0) 2 *(Zeronik 53, Cejka 62)*

England: Dewhurst; Laird, Saka (Kpohomouh 63), Garner, Greenwood, Daley-Campbell, Ogbeta, Mumba (Appiah 74), Gordon (Anjorin 63), Simmonds (Jones 63), Balogun (John-Jules 63).
England won 5-4 on penalties.

FOUR TEAM TOURNAMENT, SPAIN

Pinatar, Thursday 15 November 2018

Netherlands (1) 2 *(Azarkan 22, Zirkzee 81 (pen))*

England (2) 2 *(John-Jules 13 (pen), Adshead 17)*

England: Ashby-Hammond■; Daley-Campbell, Thomas, Kpohomouh, Ogbeta, Appiah, Anjorin (Maghoma 73), John-Jules, Gordon (Okonkwo 7), Jones (Balogun 82), Adshead (Mumba 73).

Murcia, Saturday 17 November 2018

Republic of Ireland (0) 1 *(Idah 48)*

England (0) 3 *(John-Jules 75, 78, Balogun 90)*

Republic of Ireland: Clarke; Connell (Staunton 77), O'Sullivan (Murphy 61), McEntee, Ledwidge, Wright (Walsh 84), Coffey, Knight, Thompson (Flynn 46), Grant (Brennan 61), Ellis (Idah 46).
England: Ashby-Hammond; Daley-Campbell, Thomas, Ogbeta, Gordon (Jones 56), Balogun, Mumba (Adshead 81), Maghoma (Mola 56), Lloyd-Bennett (John-Jules 56), Binks, Whittaker (Appiah 56).

Murcia, Monday 19 November 2018

England (1) 3 *(John-Jules 18, Anjorin 51, Appiah 52)*

Belgium (0) 1 *(Ugur 66)*

England: Ashby-Hammond; Daley-Campbell (Thomas 46), Mola, Ogbeta (Kpohomouh 58), Appiah (Gordon 72), Anjorin (Lloyd-Bennett 72), John-Jules (Balogun 49), Jones (Whittaker 58), Binks, Mumba, Adshead (Maghoma 46).

SPORTS CHAIN CUP, DUBAI

Dubai, Wednesday 20 March 2019

Japan (1) 1 *(Sosuke 11)*

England (2) 4 *(Balogun 9, Doyle 17, Whittaker 69, Maghoma 84)*

England: Ashby-Hammond; Daley-Campbell, Thomas (Drameh 42), Garner, Laird, Binks, Whittaker (Maghoma 75), Doyle, Balogun (Duncan 75), Jones (Gordon 46), Ramsey (Mumba 87).

Dubai, Friday 22 March 2019

Czech Republic (0) 1 *(Szewieczek 78)*

England (0) 0

England: Wickens; Binks, Gordon (Jones 86), Crowe (Daley-Campbell 86), Ramsey (Whittaker 75), Maghoma (Doyle 85), Mumba, Mola, Williams, Duncan, Drameh.

Dubai, Sunday 24 March 2019

England (2) 3 *(Doyle 12 (pen) Balogun 28, Jones 70)*

Mexico (2) 2 *(Monreal 4, Medina 45)*

England: Griffiths; Daley-Campbell (Drameh 46), Garner, Laird (Crowe 46), Binks (Ramsey 55), Whittaker (Duncan 46), Doyle, Balogun (Maghoma 55), Jones, Mola, Williams■.

SLOVAKIA CUP

Zlate Moravce, Monday 20 May 2019

England (0) 1 *(John-Jules 25)*

Russia (0) 0

England: Okonkwo; Daley-Campbell, Ogbeta, Doyle, Alese (Binks 73), Appiah, Daly (Sibley 62), John-Jules, Ramsey, Sharif (Whittaker 62), McDonald.

Ziar nad Hronom, Tuesday 21 May 2019

Slovakia (1) 2 *(Gembicky 29, Lichy 49)*

England (1) 2 *(Mola 22, Bennett 54)* 1011

England: Dewhurst; Williams, Whittaker (Appiah 67), Cottrell (Ramsey 59), Tulloch (John-Jules 59), Binks, White (Daly 77), Mola (Ogbeta 77), Mumba (Daley-Campbell 59), Sibley (Doyle 59), Bennett.

Zlate Moravce, Thursday 23 May 2019

England (2) 2 *(Binks 8, John-Jules 33)*

Mexico (0) 0

England: Okonkwo; Daley-Campbell, Doyle, Daly (Sibley 67), John-Jules (Tulloch 67), Ramsey (Cottrell 78), Whittaker (Bennett 67), Binks, Mola (Ogbeta 78), Sharif (Appiah 67), McDonald.

SLOVAKIA CUP FINAL

Ziar nad Hronom, Friday 24 May 2019

England (0) 1 *(Dewhurst 80)*

Spain (1) 1 *(Noubi 10)*

England: Dewhurst; Daley-Campbell, Ogbeta (Mumba 58), Doyle (White 58), Williams, Appiah (Whittaker 58), John-Jules (Tulloch 58), Ramsey (Mola 51), Cottrell (Daly 51), Binks, Bennett (Sharif 58).
Spain won 4-3 on penalties.

ENGLAND UNDER-19

2018 EUROPEAN UNDER-19 CHAMPIONSHIPS, FINLAND 2018 – GROUP B

Seinajoki, Tuesday 17 July 2018

Turkey (1) 2 *(Yalcin 2, Guclu 57)*

England (2) 3 *(Tanganga 22, Brereton 45, Embleton 54)*

England: Balcombe; Sterling, Lewis, Sanders (Kirby 79), Tanganga, Chalobah, Embleton, Tavernier, Hirst, Brereton, Watts.

Seinajoki, Friday 20 July 2018

Ukraine (1) 1 *(Supriaha 39)*

England (1) 1 *(Tavernier 8)*

England: Balcombe; Sterling, Lewis, Sanders, Tanganga, Chalobah, Embleton, Tavernier, Hirst (Morrris 81), Brereton, Watts (Kirby 84).

Vaasa, Monday 23 July 2018

France (2) 5 *(Alioui 28, 56, Maolida 41, Gouiri 63, 69)*

England (0) 0

England: Balcombe; Sterling, Lewis, Tanganga, Chalobah, Embleton, Tavernier, Hirst (Brereton 63), Gallagher (Bayliss 84), Kirby, Ferguson (Sanders 46).

FIFA UNDER-20 WORLD CUP PLAY-OFF

Seinajoki, Thursday 26 July 2018

Norway (0) 3 *(Botheim 75, Markovic 86, Hauge 89)*

England (0) 0

England: Balcombe; Sterling (Kirby 82), Chalobah, Tanganga, Lewis, Embleton, Sanders, Brereton, Bayliss, Lamptey, Hirst (Ennis 80).

FRIENDLIES

Burton, Wednesday 5 September 2018

England (3) 4 *(Loader 34, 63, Foden 45, Gomes 61)*

Netherlands (1) 1 *(Aboukhlal 28 (pen)*

England: Bursik (Anderson 46); Sessegnon S, Vokins (Aarons 88), Kirby (McEachran 75), Eyoma, Panzo, Foden (Poveda-Ocampo 75), Gibbs-White, Loader (Walker 81), Gomes, Sancho (Hudson-Odoi 75).

Tubize, Monday 10 September 2018

Belgium (1) 1 *(Kargbo Jr 19)*

England (2) 2 *(Hudson-Odoi 25, Walker 41)*

England: Crellin (Anderson 46); Lamptey, McEachran (Sancho 80), Aarons, Ferguson, Panzo (Eyoma 67), Poveda-Ocampo (Vokins 89), Walker (Gomes 80), Foden, Harper, Hudson-Odoi (Loader 80).

Almada, Thursday 11 October 2018

Portugal (0) 1 *(Bras 90)*

England (0) 4 *(Smith-Rowe 60, Nmecha 63, Guehi 71, Poveda-Ocampo 89)*

England: Bursik; Aarons, Sessegnon S (Vokins 80), Gallagher (Kirby 80), Guehi, Panzo, Smith-Rowe (Poveda-Ocampo 72), Gibbs-White (Harper 72), Loader (Walker 80), Gomes (Nmecha 46), Hudson-Odoi (Lamptey 72).

Burton, Tuesday 16 October 2018

England (3) 6 *(Hudson-Odoi 16, Walker 32, 38, 77 (pen), Kirby 57, Lamptey 89)*

North Macedonia (1) 2 *(Churlinov 43, Gjorgjievski 90)*

England: Anderson; Lamptey, Vokins, Harper (Gallagher 63), Eyoma, Ferguson, Poveda-Ocampo (Sessegnon S 78), Kirby, Walker (Loader 78), Smith-Rowe (Gibbs-White 26), Hudson-Odoi.

2019 EUROPEAN UNDER-19 CHAMPIONSHIPS QUALIFYING IN TURKEY – GROUP 5

Turkey, Wednesday 14 November 2018

Moldova (0) 0

England (1) 4 *(Gallagher 24, Loader 65, Saka 85, Sessegnon S 90)*

England: Bursik; Lamptey, Sessegnon S, McEachran, Guehi (Eyoma 85), Panzo, Smith-Rowe (Poveda-Ocampo 70), Gallagher, Loader (Walker 82), Gibbs-White (Saka 82), Hudson-Odoi (Kirby 70).

Manavgat, Saturday 17 November 2018

England (1) 3 *(Sessegnon S 13, Walker 55, 77)*

Iceland (1) 1 *(Olafsson 34)*

England: Bursik; Sessegnon S (Vokins 90), Guehi, Smith-Rowe (Poveda-Ocampo 87), Gallagher (Kirby 87), Gibbs-White (Loader 78), Hudson-Odoi (Saka 90), Walker, Max, Harper, Eyoma.

Manavgat, Tuesday 20 November 2018

Turkey (0) 1 *(Takir 72)*

England (0) 0

England: Bursik; Lamptey, McEachran, Panzo, Loader (Gibbs-White 46), Walker, Kirby (Saka 63), Harper (Gallagher 71), Poveda-Ocampo (Hudson-Odoi 81), Vokins (Sessegnon S 71), Eyoma.

UNDER-19 EUROPEAN CHAMPIONSHIP ELITE QUALIFYING IN ENGLAND – GROUP 2

Burton, Wednesday 20 March 2019

England (1) 4 *(Saka 11, 56, Guehi 49, Loader 85)*

Czech Republic (1) 1 *(Selnar 10)*

England: Bursik; Aarons, Sessegnon S, Gallagher (Harper 90), Guehi, Panzo, Poveda-Ocampo (Lamptey 66), Gibbs-White (McEachran 90), Loader, Gomes (Nmecha 72), Saka (Appiah 66).

Burton, Saturday 23 March 2019

England (0) 1 *(Gibbs-White 90 (pen))*

Greece (1) 2 *(Liavas 34, Diamantis 69)*

England: Bursik; Sessegnon S, Gallagher (McEachran 64), Guehi, Panzo, Poveda-Ocampo (Aarons 65), Gibbs-White, Gomes (Nmecha 71), Walker (Loader 71), Lamptey, Appiah (Saka 46).

Burton, Tuesday 26 March 2019

Denmark (1) 2 *(Madsen 45, Jansen 71)*

England (0) 2 *(Poveda-Ocampo 63, Guehi 73)*

England: Bursik; Aarons (Poveda-Ocampo 46), Sessegnon S, Guehi, Panzo, Gibbs-White (Nmecha 46), Loader, Saka (Gallagher 74), McEachran (Walker 87), Lamptey, Harper (Gomes 74).

ENGLAND UNDER-20

EURO U20 ELITE TOURNAMENT

Burton, Thursday 6 September 2018

England (1) 2 *(Hirst 4, Embleton 60)*

Switzerland (0) 0

England: Balcombe, Edwards, Dasilva, Field, Tanganga, Kelly, Nelson (Willock C 70), Willock, Hirst, Embleton, Lewis.

Katwijk, Monday 10 September 2018

Netherlands (0) 3 *(Chong 62, Vente 74 (pen), Kadioglu 88)*

England (1) 1 *(Nketiah 7)*

England: Trott; Pearce (Dasilva 84), Vieira, Suliman, Chalobah, Willock C, Tavernier (Embleton 84), Brereton (Willock J 69), Edwards (Hirst 69), Nketiah, James.

Fylde, Thusday 11 October 2018

England (2) 2 *(Nketiah 18, Willock J 38 (pen))*

Italy (0) 1 *(Fratessi 68)*

England: Ramsdale; James, Pearce, Field, Suliman, Kelly, Eze (Edwards 84), Tavernier, Nketiah (Hurst 90), Willock J (Vieira 62), Embleton.

Budejovice, Monday 15 October 2018

Czech Republic (0) 1 *(Pfeifer 86)*

England (1) 1 *(Nketiah 39)* 2900

England: Trott; Edwards, Pearce, Field, Suliman (Wilmot 79), Kelly, Edwards, Dozzell (Tavernier 79), Hirst, Vieira, Nketiah.

Colchester, Monday 19 November 2018

England (0) 2 *(Willock J 66, Nmecha 69)*

Germany (0) 0

England: Ramsdale; James, Lewis, Field (Vieira 63), Suliman, Chalobah, Diangana (Eze 72), Willock J (Downes 89), Nketiah, Dozzell (Tavernier 63), Embleton (Nmecha 63).

Burton, Thursday 21 March 2019

England (0) 1 *(Nketiah 57)*

Poland (2) 3 *(Moder 8, Klimala 26 (pen), Kwietniewski 53)*

England: Schofield; Edwards (James 46), Pearce, Field (Hirst 87), Godfrey, Chalobah, Diangana (Eze 65), Dozzell (Vieira 65), Nketiah, Embleton (Tavernier 22), McNeil.

Penafil, Thursday 26 March 2019

Portugal (0) 1 *(Martelo 62)*

England (0) 0

England: Balcombe; James, Pearce, Vieira (Downes 65), Wilmot (Sterling 70), Godfrey, Eze, Tavernier, Hirst (McNeil 65), Willock J, Nketiah.

MAURICE REVELLO TOULON TOURNAMENT

Aubagne, Saturday 1 June 2019

England (1) 1 *(Chalobah 36)*

Japan (0) 2 *(Ominami 49, Naganuma 69)*

England: Balcombe; Pearce (Lowe 73), Field, Guehi, Chalobah, Tavernier, McNeil, Sessegnon S, Hirst (Loader 82), Edwards (Sims 73), Da Silva (Bogle 65).

Salon de Provence, Tuesday 4 June 2019

England (1) 2 *(Nketiah 8, Willock J 87)*

Portugal (3) 3 *(Paulo 21, Cardoso 39, Correia 42)*

England: Schofield (Balcombe 46); James, Chalobah, Eze, Willock J, Nketiah, McNeil (Tavernier 58), Gallagher, Lowe, Sims (Edwards 70), Shackleton (Loader 76).

Fos-sur-Mer, Friday 7 June 2019

England (1) 1 *(Willock J 45)*

Chile (0) 2 *(Jara 87, Guehi 90 (og))*

England: Balcombe; James (Field 37 (Gallagher 79)), Pearce, Guehi, Chalobah, Eze (Sims 75), Willock J, Nketiah, Tavernier, Sessegnon, Edwards (McNeil 76).

Mallemort, Tuesday 11 June 2019

England (4) 4 *(Hirst 15, 26, Nketiah 23 (pen), McNeil 29)*

Guatemala (0) 0

England: Bishop; Pearce, Gueh (Tavernier 66), Nketiah, McNeil (Edwards 66), Hirst, Bogle, Lowe, Dasilva (Gallagher 75), Loader (Sims 75), Shackleton.

SCHOOLS FOOTBALL 2018–19

BOODLES INDEPENDENT SCHOOLS FA CUP 2018–19

**After extra time.*

PRELIMINARY ROUND

Bootham v Newcastle School for Boys	4-3
Bristol GS v Sherborne	2-4
Brooke House College v Twycross House	12-0
Bournemouth Collegiate v Box Hill	5-0
Bury GS v Stockport GS	4-5
Canford v Wellington	2-0
Cheadle Hulme v Merchant Taylors, Crosby	3-2
College of the Holy Child v Lingfield College	11-1
Haberdashers' Aske's v Whitgift	1-4
KCS Wimbledon v Brighton College	3-1
King's School, Worcester v LVS Ascot	5-0
Norwich v Bedford Modern	1-2
Oswestry v Moorland	4-1
RGS Guildford v Kingston GS	2-4
Trinity v ACS Cobham	5-2

SECOND ROUND

Bede's v Berkhamsted	4-3
Bedford Modern v Trinity	2-3
Birkdale v Latymer Upper	1-5
Bolton v College of the Holy Child	3-1
Bournemouth Collegiate v City of London	0-8
Brentwood v Kingston GS	5-1
Buckswood v Repton	1-5
Cheadle Hulme v Millfield	1-4
Chigwell v University College School	0-1
Eton v Grange	6-0
Forest v King's School, Chester	3-2
Harrodian v Winchester	1-2
Harrow v Grammar School at Leeds	5-0
Highgate v Sevenoaks	1-0*
John Lyon v Bootham	3-4
KCS Wimbledon v Manchester GS	1-3
Kimbolton v Aldenham	2-1
King Edward's, Witley v St John's, Leatherhead	3-1*
King's School, Worcester v Hampton	0-4
Oldham Hulme GS v Queen Ethelburga's College	0-5
Oswestry v St Bede's College	6-0
Peterborough (withdrew) v Royal Russell (walkover)	
RGS Newcastle v Alleyn's	1-3
Sherborne v Ardingly	1-5
St Columba's Col (withdrew) v. Brooke House (walkover)	
St Edmund's, Ware v Shrewsbury	0-6
Stockport GS v Canford	3-1
Tonbridge v Lancing	5-1
Truro v Bradfield	0-8
Westminster v Dulwich College	4-4*
(Dulwich won 6-5 on penalties)	
Whitgift v Charterhouse	1-2
Wolverhampton GS v Ibstock Place	1-3

THIRD ROUND

Ardingly v Trinity	6-0
Bootham v Highgate	1-2
Bradfield v Hampton	2-3
Charterhouse v Bede's	2-0
Dulwich College v Winchester	0-3
Harrow v Alleyn's	1-1*
(Harrow won 3-0 on penalties)	
Ibstock Place v Bolton	1-2
Kimbolton v King Edward's, Witley	3-2
Millfield v Eton	4-1
Manchester GS v Brooke House College	3-5*
Oswestry v Stockport GS	4-1
Queen Ethelburga's College v Latymer Upper	6-2
Repton v Tonbridge	4-0
Royal Russell v Brentwood	6-2
Shrewsbury v Forest	3-1
University College School v City of London	4-4*
(UCS won 3-0 on penalties)	

FOURTH ROUND

Ardingly v Kimbolton	2-1
Bolton v Shrewsbury	1-3
Harrow v Hampton	1-7
Queen Ethelburga's College v Charterhouse	1-0
Millfield v Brooke House	4-3*
Oswestry v Highgate	4-0
Repton v Winchester	4-0
Royal Russell v University College School	5-0

FIFTH ROUND

Hampton v Ardingly	0-0*
(Ardingly won 5-4 on penalties)	
Repton v Queen Ethelburga's College	1-1*
(Repton won 4-1 on penalties)	
Royal Russell v Oswestry	3-1
Shrewsbury v Millfield	0-0*
(Millfield won 8-7 on penalties)	

SEMI-FINALS

Ardingly v Royal Russell	0-4
Millfield v Repton	3-0

FINAL

at Milton Keynes Dons FC, 4 March 2019

Royal Russell 2 *(Harding og, Okorogheye)*

Millfield 1 *(Harding)* 785

Royal Russell: Long S, Richardson D, Ibe A, Leeson B, Daniels N, Garvey-Williams K, John R, Newbury-Teeluck J, Okorogheye A, Taylor A, Thomas L.
Substitutes: Gallagher J, Spillane-Davis L, Atomanson I, Bello J, Mamas D.
Millfield: Scott R, Hickin J, Lamont S, Pestell C, Jones B, Harding B, LeRougetel B, Stein P, Pereira R, Gustke G, Spicer L.
Substitutes: McCallum T, Lott J, Prescott A, Clatworthy D, Ojo S.
Referee: Anthony Taylor.

INVESTEC ISFA U15 CUP FINAL

Whitgift v Alleyn's 7-2
(at Burton Albion FC)

INVESTEC ISFA U13 CUP FINAL

Aldenham v Royal Russell 2-1
(at Burton Albion FC)

UNIVERSITY FOOTBALL 2019

135th UNIVERSITY MATCH

(Sunday 10 March 2019, at The Hive, Barnet FC)

Oxford (0) 1 *(Achtelstetter 60)* **Cambridge (1) 1** *(Ringhof 45)*

(Cambridge won 4-3 on penalties)

Oxford: Langham, Ackerman, Tutton, Collins, Naylor, Thelen, Mort (Achtelstetter 54), Evans D, Barton, Cantrill, Evans M (Burton 84).

Cambridge: Ringhof, Young, Melbourne (Parker 82), Reich, Lerway, Ellis, Alexander, Rodrigues (Nwuba 55), Bull (Mortimer 67), Gallagher, Sypniewksi.

Oxford have won 55 games (2 on penalties), Cambridge 53 games (4 on penalties) and 27 games have been drawn. Oxford have scored 215 goals, Cambridge 208 goals.

NON-LEAGUE TABLES 2018–19

NATIONAL LEAGUE SYSTEM STEP 3

EVOSTIK NORTHERN PREMIER LEAGUE PREMIER DIVISION

			Home					*Away*					*Total*						
		P	*W*	*D*	*L*	*F*	*A*	*W*	*D*	*L*	*F*	*A*	*W*	*D*	*L*	*F*	*A*	*GD*	*Pts*
1	Farsley Celtic	40	13	5	2	39	20	15	1	4	43	20	28	6	6	82	40	42	90
2	South Shields	40	16	3	1	57	19	11	3	6	29	22	27	6	7	86	41	45	87
3	Warrington T¶	40	12	5	3	31	15	13	4	3	38	18	25	9	6	69	33	36	84
4	Nantwich T	40	10	6	4	34	24	9	6	5	36	35	19	12	9	70	59	11	69
5	Buxton	40	11	3	6	31	24	7	9	4	29	21	18	12	10	60	45	15	66
6	Gainsborough Trinity	40	9	4	7	30	27	10	4	6	23	14	19	8	13	53	41	12	65
7	Basford U	40	13	2	5	52	34	5	5	10	30	33	18	7	15	82	67	15	61
8	Scarborough Ath	40	9	4	7	37	27	9	3	8	33	29	18	7	15	70	56	14	61
9	Witton Alb	40	7	7	6	23	22	9	3	8	22	19	16	10	14	45	41	4	58
10	Hyde U	40	9	2	9	31	26	6	6	8	27	27	15	8	17	58	53	5	53
11	Whitby T	40	9	1	10	24	21	6	3	11	24	38	15	4	21	48	59	–11	49
12	Lancaster C	40	6	7	7	19	28	6	6	8	23	33	12	13	15	42	61	–19	49
13	Hednesford T	40	8	4	8	24	22	5	5	10	27	41	13	9	18	51	63	–12	48
14	Stafford Rangers	40	6	9	5	31	28	5	5	10	31	42	11	14	15	62	70	–8	47
15	Matlock T	40	7	5	8	32	33	5	3	12	26	46	12	8	20	58	79	–21	44
16	Bamber Bridge	40	7	5	8	39	37	3	7	10	23	30	10	12	18	62	67	–5	42
17	Stalybridge Celtic	40	7	6	7	26	27	4	3	13	20	35	11	9	20	46	62	–16	42
18	Grantham T	40	8	2	10	19	31	4	4	12	20	41	12	6	22	39	72	–33	42
19	Mickleover Sports	40	5	6	9	17	27	5	5	10	20	34	10	11	19	37	61	–24	41
20	Marine	40	4	5	11	20	31	6	5	9	19	23	10	10	20	39	54	–15	40
21	Workington	40	4	2	14	20	38	4	3	13	18	35	8	5	27	38	73	–35	29
22	North Ferriby U*																		

**North Ferriby U record expunged. ¶Warrington T won play-offs and progressed to super play-off with King's Lynn T, which they lost, so remain in Northern Premier League.*

EVOSTIK SOUTHERN LEAGUE PREMIER CENTRAL DIVISION

			Home					*Away*					*Total*						
		P	*W*	*D*	*L*	*F*	*A*	*W*	*D*	*L*	*F*	*A*	*W*	*D*	*L*	*F*	*A*	*GD*	*Pts*
1	Kettering T	42	14	1	6	51	28	16	3	2	33	13	30	4	8	84	41	43	94
2	King's Lynn T¶	42	12	7	2	40	18	11	4	6	40	23	23	11	8	80	41	39	80
3	Stourbridge	42	14	5	2	49	19	8	7	6	30	21	22	12	8	79	40	39	78
4	Alvechurch	42	12	5	4	37	25	9	5	7	29	28	21	10	11	66	53	13	73
5	Stratford T	42	13	2	6	30	22	8	7	6	25	27	21	9	12	55	49	6	72
6	Coalville T	42	9	6	6	42	28	11	1	9	36	38	20	7	15	78	66	12	67
7	Biggleswade T	42	11	5	5	29	17	7	7	7	38	37	18	12	12	67	54	13	66
8	Rushall Olympic	42	6	8	7	26	26	11	3	7	30	23	17	11	14	56	49	7	62
9	AFC Rushden & D	42	9	9	3	33	21	6	7	8	27	28	15	16	11	60	49	11	61
10	Royston T*	42	8	3	10	32	32	10	4	7	27	21	18	7	17	59	53	6	60
11	Needham Market	42	8	6	7	35	33	9	3	9	33	32	17	9	16	68	65	3	60
12	Tamworth	42	7	6	8	36	25	8	7	6	28	21	15	13	14	64	46	18	58
13	St Ives T	42	5	8	8	14	21	9	5	7	22	22	14	13	15	36	43	–7	55
14	Lowestoft T	42	9	3	9	29	26	5	6	10	26	34	14	9	19	55	60	–5	51
15	Redditch U	42	9	5	7	39	36	5	3	13	24	43	14	8	20	63	79	–16	50
16	Barwell	42	4	8	9	27	26	8	5	8	28	29	12	13	17	55	55	0	49
17	Banbury U†	42	10	6	5	34	21	3	8	10	19	34	13	14	15	53	55	–2	49
18	Hitchin T	42	10	2	9	30	24	4	4	13	20	47	14	6	22	50	71	–21	48
19	Leiston	42	7	4	10	27	33	5	7	9	27	40	12	11	19	54	73	–19	47
20	St Neots T	42	5	4	12	16	36	4	5	12	16	37	9	9	24	32	73	–41	36
21	Halesowen T	42	5	8	8	16	23	1	6	14	10	43	6	14	22	26	66	–40	32
22	Bedworth U	42	1	3	17	13	47	2	7	12	19	44	3	10	29	32	91	–59	19

**Royston T deducted 1 point for fielding an ineligible player.*
†Banbury U deducted 4 points for fielding an ineligible player.
¶King's Lynn T won play-offs and progressed to super play-off with Warrington T, which they won, so are promoted to National League North.

EVOSTIK SOUTHERN LEAGUE PREMIER SOUTH DIVISION

			Home					*Away*					*Total*						
		P	*W*	*D*	*L*	*F*	*A*	*W*	*D*	*L*	*F*	*A*	*W*	*D*	*L*	*F*	*A*	*GD*	*Pts*
1	Weymouth	42	13	6	2	49	22	12	5	4	47	29	25	11	6	96	51	45	86
2	Taunton T	42	14	6	1	56	26	12	1	8	33	30	26	7	9	89	56	33	85
3	Metropolitan Police¶	42	14	5	2	52	30	8	7	6	39	34	22	12	8	91	64	27	78
4	Salisbury	42	13	3	5	46	37	9	8	4	51	32	22	11	9	97	69	28	77
5	Poole T	42	9	6	6	41	32	11	4	6	43	27	20	10	12	84	59	25	70
6	Kings Langley	42	14	2	5	38	21	7	4	10	27	40	21	6	15	65	61	4	69
7	Harrow Bor	42	10	4	7	50	31	8	5	8	47	46	18	9	15	97	77	20	63
8	Hartley Wintney	42	10	4	7	44	33	7	8	6	38	37	17	12	13	82	70	12	63
9	Farnborough	42	12	3	6	35	27	6	5	10	37	45	18	8	16	72	72	0	62
10	Chesham U	42	7	7	7	31	31	8	7	6	23	24	15	14	13	54	55	–1	59
11	Swindon Supermarine	42	10	5	6	38	26	6	5	10	32	33	16	10	16	70	59	11	58
12	Beaconsfield T	42	9	8	4	44	33	6	5	10	21	32	15	13	14	65	65	0	58
13	Merthyr T	42	8	5	8	38	32	7	4	10	30	35	15	9	18	68	67	1	54
14	Wimborne T	42	11	5	5	42	31	4	2	15	30	44	15	7	20	72	75	–3	52
15	Dorchester T	42	5	5	11	28	40	9	5	7	39	35	14	10	18	67	75	–8	52
16	Hendon	42	8	4	9	33	33	6	6	9	31	41	14	10	18	64	74	–10	52
17	Walton Casuals	42	10	4	7	44	34	4	5	12	25	44	14	9	19	69	78	–9	51
18	Tiverton T	42	7	7	7	33	31	6	5	10	32	44	13	12	17	65	75	–10	51
19	Gosport Bor	42	10	2	9	32	35	5	3	13	31	35	15	5	22	63	70	–7	50
20	Basingstoke T	42	9	4	8	45	37	5	3	13	36	45	14	7	21	81	82	–1	49
21	Frome T	42	6	3	12	21	30	5	1	15	24	44	11	4	27	45	74	–29	37
22	Staines T	42	3	0	18	23	81	1	0	20	17	87	4	0	38	40	168	–128	12

¶Metropolitan Police won play-offs and progressed to super play-off with Tonbridge Angels, which they lost, so remain in Southern League South.

BOSTIK ISMITHIAN LEAGUE PREMIER DIVISION

			Home					*Away*					*Total*						
		P	*W*	*D*	*L*	*F*	*A*	*W*	*D*	*L*	*F*	*A*	*W*	*D*	*L*	*F*	*A*	*GD*	*Pts*
1	Dorking W	42	16	2	3	58	18	12	7	2	29	13	28	9	5	87	31	56	93
2	Carshalton Ath	42	14	3	4	41	19	7	5	9	29	30	21	8	13	70	49	21	71
3	Haringey Bor	42	13	4	4	43	27	8	4	9	30	27	21	8	13	73	54	19	71
4	Tonbridge Angels¶	42	10	3	8	27	25	11	4	6	32	21	21	7	14	59	46	13	70
5	Merstham	42	13	3	5	35	20	7	7	7	25	30	20	10	12	60	50	10	70
6	Folkestone Invicta	42	13	2	6	45	21	8	4	9	32	37	21	6	15	77	58	19	69
7	Bishop's Stortford	42	12	4	5	38	25	8	3	10	32	32	20	7	15	70	57	13	67
8	Leatherhead	42	10	4	7	27	23	9	4	8	29	19	19	8	15	56	42	14	65
9	Worthing	42	7	6	8	38	35	11	5	5	34	28	18	11	13	72	63	9	65
10	Enfield T	42	8	8	5	38	25	9	2	10	38	31	17	10	15	76	56	20	61
11	Lewes	42	8	6	7	32	26	8	6	7	29	27	16	12	14	61	53	8	60
12	Margate	42	6	6	9	20	28	10	5	6	25	20	16	11	15	45	48	–3	59
13	Brightlingsea Regent	42	9	4	8	23	23	7	7	7	26	31	16	11	15	49	54	–5	59
14	Bognor Regis T	42	7	6	8	38	32	7	9	5	33	30	14	15	13	71	62	9	57
15	AFC Hornchurch	42	7	7	7	33	25	5	7	9	24	34	12	14	16	57	59	–2	50
16	Potters Bar T	42	5	7	9	25	25	8	3	10	26	31	13	10	19	51	56	–5	49
17	Corinthian-Casuals	42	8	6	7	26	29	5	2	14	22	45	13	8	21	48	74	–26	47
18	Kingstonian	42	8	3	10	38	37	5	3	13	22	41	13	6	23	60	78	–18	45
19	Wingate & Finchley	42	6	5	10	25	34	6	2	13	32	52	12	7	23	57	86	–29	43
20	Whitehawk	42	4	7	10	25	34	6	4	11	25	38	10	11	21	50	72	–22	41
21	Burgess Hill T	42	5	4	12	19	40	4	6	11	25	51	9	10	23	44	91	–47	37
22	Harlow T	42	4	3	14	27	54	5	4	12	26	53	9	7	26	53	107	–54	34

¶Tonbridge Angels won play-offs and progressed to super play-off with Metropolitan Police, which they won, so are promoted to National League South.

NATIONAL LEAGUE SYSTEM STEP 4

EVOSTIK NORTHERN PREMIER LEAGUE DIVISION ONE WEST

			Home					*Away*					*Total*						
		P	*W*	*D*	*L*	*F*	*A*	*W*	*D*	*L*	*F*	*A*	*W*	*D*	*L*	*F*	*A*	*GD*	*Pts*
1	Atherton Collieries	38	12	1	6	53	23	14	3	2	36	11	26	4	8	89	34	55	82
2	Radcliffe¶	38	13	2	4	38	19	10	4	5	35	15	23	6	9	73	34	39	75
3	Leek T	38	10	5	4	45	18	12	3	4	33	16	22	8	8	78	34	44	74
4	Colne	38	12	1	6	35	24	10	6	3	36	20	22	7	9	71	44	27	73
5	Ramsbottom U	38	9	4	6	34	24	12	5	2	44	17	21	9	8	78	41	37	72
6	Runcorn Linnets	38	11	4	4	32	23	11	2	6	37	27	22	6	10	69	50	19	72
7	Prescot Cables	38	13	3	3	46	20	8	3	8	38	34	21	6	11	84	54	30	69
8	Mossley	38	11	4	4	27	17	8	4	7	39	34	19	8	11	66	51	15	65
9	Trafford	38	7	7	5	24	25	10	3	6	29	19	17	10	11	53	44	9	61
10	Kidsgrove Ath	38	7	6	6	28	20	8	7	4	30	20	15	13	10	58	40	18	58
11	Colwyn Bay	38	6	3	10	37	36	9	4	6	36	30	15	7	16	73	66	7	52
12	Widnes	38	6	4	9	25	28	9	2	8	35	33	15	6	17	60	61	–1	51
13	Chasetown	38	6	7	6	33	26	6	3	10	28	37	12	10	16	61	63	–2	46
14	Droylsden	38	6	3	10	31	36	6	4	9	30	36	12	7	19	61	72	–11	43
15	Newcastle T	38	7	4	8	34	34	3	6	10	18	40	10	10	18	52	74	–22	40
16	Market Drayton T	38	7	5	7	31	39	4	2	13	24	55	11	7	20	55	94	–39	40
17	Glossop North End	38	2	5	12	17	44	5	5	9	24	30	7	10	21	41	74	–33	31
18	Clitheroe	38	3	2	14	23	49	4	5	10	22	39	7	7	24	45	88	–43	28
19	Kendal T	38	2	2	15	17	48	3	2	14	15	46	5	4	29	32	94	–62	19
20	Skelmersdale U	38	1	4	14	12	48	1	3	15	12	63	2	7	29	24	111	–87	13

¶Radcliffe promoted to Northern Premier League Premier Division via play-offs.

EVOSTIK NORTHERN PREMIER LEAGUE DIVISION ONE EAST

			Home					Away					Total						
		P	W	D	L	F	A	W	D	L	F	A	W	D	L	F	A	GD	Pts
1	Morpeth T	38	16	1	2	53	19	12	3	4	37	14	28	4	6	90	33	57	88
2	Pontefract Collieries	38	14	3	2	47	17	9	4	6	44	37	23	7	8	91	54	37	76
3	Brighouse T¶	38	11	5	3	40	19	10	3	6	34	24	21	8	9	74	43	31	71
4	Sheffield FC	38	13	3	3	48	23	8	3	8	33	40	21	6	11	81	63	18	69
5	Ossett U	38	10	7	2	38	16	8	6	5	27	21	18	13	7	65	37	28	67
6	Tadcaster Alb	38	9	4	6	37	25	11	2	6	34	22	20	6	12	71	47	24	66
7	Cleethorpes T	38	9	5	5	48	32	9	5	5	42	30	18	10	10	90	62	28	64
8	Loughborough Dynamo	38	13	2	4	51	27	6	3	10	31	40	19	5	14	82	67	15	62
9	Belper T	38	7	7	5	31	31	9	4	6	35	29	16	11	11	66	60	6	59
10	Marske U	38	11	4	4	38	20	5	6	8	25	27	16	10	12	63	47	16	58
11	Stamford	38	8	6	5	26	21	5	5	9	29	36	13	11	14	55	57	–2	50
12	Frickley Ath	38	6	5	8	32	32	7	4	8	22	28	13	9	16	54	60	–6	48
13	Stocksbridge Park Steels	38	9	3	7	23	32	3	4	12	18	38	12	7	19	41	70	–29	43
14	Lincoln U	38	8	4	7	29	34	4	3	12	24	49	12	7	19	53	83	–30	43
15	AFC Mansfield	38	6	4	9	26	33	5	5	9	29	40	11	9	18	55	73	–18	42
16	Pickering T	38	2	5	12	19	41	6	6	7	26	31	8	11	19	45	72	–27	35
17	Wisbech T	38	3	7	9	25	30	3	6	10	18	40	6	13	19	43	70	–27	31
18	Spalding U	38	3	5	11	21	35	3	8	8	17	32	6	13	19	38	67	–29	31
19	Carlton T	38	2	3	14	22	40	5	3	11	24	44	7	6	25	46	84	–38	27
20	Gresley FC	38	4	2	13	17	42	3	2	14	20	49	7	4	27	37	91	–54	25

¶Brighouse T won via play-offs, but were transferred to Division One West.

EVOSTIK SOUTHERN LEAGUE DIVISION ONE CENTRAL

			Home					Away					Total						
		P	W	D	L	F	A	W	D	L	F	A	W	D	L	F	A	GD	Pts
1	Peterborough Sports	38	16	2	1	58	9	14	3	2	51	19	30	5	3	109	28	81	95
2	Bromsgrove Sporting¶	38	17	2	0	65	14	10	4	5	43	30	27	6	5	108	44	64	87
3	Corby T	38	15	0	4	57	28	9	5	5	49	32	24	5	9	106	60	46	77
4	Bedford T	38	11	2	6	36	22	10	0	9	48	30	21	2	15	84	52	32	65
5	Sutton Coldfield T	38	8	7	4	36	28	9	4	6	29	21	17	11	10	65	49	16	62
6	Berkhamsted	38	8	4	7	33	23	9	4	6	35	30	17	8	13	68	53	15	59
7	Didcot T	38	10	6	3	38	26	6	4	9	31	35	16	10	12	69	61	8	58
8	Thame U	38	10	3	6	31	24	7	3	9	29	37	17	6	15	60	61	–1	57
9	Coleshill T	38	7	4	8	28	29	9	4	6	32	29	16	8	14	60	58	2	56
10	AFC Dunstable	38	6	6	7	32	37	10	1	8	26	34	16	7	15	58	71	–13	55
11	Yaxley	38	11	0	8	46	46	4	4	11	26	46	15	4	19	72	92	–20	49
12	Cambridge C	38	7	6	6	36	27	5	5	9	22	27	12	11	15	58	54	4	47
13	Kempston R	38	3	7	9	28	39	8	3	8	30	36	11	10	17	58	75	–17	43
14	Welwyn Garden C*	38	7	3	9	23	28	4	7	8	29	36	11	10	17	52	64	–12	42
15	Aylesbury U	38	6	2	11	29	41	6	4	9	33	45	12	6	20	62	86	–24	42
16	Barton R	38	4	5	10	24	42	6	6	7	21	26	10	11	17	45	68	–23	41
17	North Leigh	38	6	4	9	37	49	3	3	13	30	57	9	7	22	67	106	–39	34
18	Kidlington	38	4	3	12	21	41	5	4	10	22	41	9	7	22	43	82	–39	34
19	Aylesbury	38	5	4	10	18	31	3	3	13	24	48	8	7	23	42	79	–37	31
20	Dunstable T	38	3	4	12	24	51	5	3	11	25	41	8	7	23	49	92	–43	31

**Welwyn Garden C deducted 1 point for fielding an ineligible player.*
¶Bromsgrove Sporting promoted to Southern League Premier Central Division via play-offs.

EVOSTIK SOUTHERN LEAGUE DIVISION ONE SOUTH

			Home					Away					Total						
		P	W	D	L	F	A	W	D	L	F	A	W	D	L	F	A	GD	Pts
1	Blackfield & Langley	38	14	2	3	43	16	12	2	5	32	18	26	4	8	75	34	41	82
2	Cirencester T	38	12	3	4	67	28	11	3	5	43	24	23	6	9	110	52	58	75
3	Yate T¶	38	12	5	2	41	23	11	1	7	33	28	23	6	9	74	51	23	75
4	Moneyfields	38	11	4	4	34	20	10	4	5	39	23	21	8	9	73	43	30	71
5	Cinderford T	38	11	4	4	36	16	10	4	5	28	23	21	8	9	64	39	25	71
6	Winchester C	38	10	4	5	48	25	11	3	5	36	21	21	7	10	84	46	38	70
7	Evesham U	38	10	4	5	36	27	9	2	8	30	26	19	6	13	66	53	13	63
8	Street	38	9	7	3	31	18	8	3	8	27	33	17	10	11	58	51	7	61
9	Bideford	38	11	3	5	29	17	7	1	11	37	51	18	4	16	66	68	–2	58
10	AFC Totton	38	11	2	6	41	24	6	3	10	31	31	17	5	16	72	55	17	56
11	Thatcham T	38	8	2	9	32	27	9	3	7	25	31	17	5	16	57	58	–1	56
12	Melksham T	38	9	2	8	30	35	8	3	8	29	35	17	5	16	59	70	–11	56
13	Larkhall Ath	38	9	1	9	25	23	7	6	6	27	28	16	7	15	52	51	1	55
14	Highworth T	38	8	4	7	34	33	5	5	9	29	38	13	9	16	63	71	–8	48
15	Bristol Manor Farm	38	9	2	8	40	36	4	5	10	25	41	13	7	18	65	77	–12	46
16	Mangotsfield U	38	6	1	12	33	35	5	3	11	31	43	11	4	23	64	78	–14	37
17	Paulton R	38	5	1	13	22	36	5	2	12	27	43	10	3	25	49	79	–30	33
18	Slimbridge	38	4	5	10	26	48	4	1	14	17	39	8	6	24	43	87	–44	30
19	Barnstaple T	38	4	1	14	23	46	2	4	13	19	54	6	5	27	42	100	–58	23
20	Fleet T	38	3	1	15	26	54	2	0	17	22	67	5	1	32	48	121	–73	16

¶Yate T promoted to Southern League Premier South Division via play-offs.

BOSTIK ISTHMIAN LEAGUE DIVISION ONE NORTH

			Home					Away					Total						
		P	W	D	L	F	A	W	D	L	F	A	W	D	L	F	A	GD	Pts
1	Bowers & Pitsea	38	15	3	1	60	13	14	2	3	36	12	29	5	4	96	25	71	92
2	Aveley	38	12	4	3	50	23	12	4	3	34	26	24	8	6	84	49	35	80
3	Maldon & Tiptree	38	11	2	6	38	23	13	5	1	48	23	24	7	7	86	46	40	79
4	Coggeshall T	38	10	4	5	35	17	12	4	3	44	26	22	8	8	79	43	36	74
5	Heybridge Swifts¶	38	13	3	3	34	19	10	2	7	36	32	23	5	10	70	51	19	74
6	Bury T	38	10	3	6	42	34	7	5	7	30	29	17	8	13	72	63	9	59
7	Grays Ath	38	7	7	5	38	33	7	4	8	27	31	14	11	13	65	64	1	53
8	AFC Sudbury	38	8	2	9	40	37	8	2	9	31	35	16	4	18	71	72	–1	52
9	Canvey Island	38	6	3	10	22	24	9	3	7	29	26	15	6	17	51	50	1	51
10	Tilbury	38	7	4	8	32	33	6	7	6	32	31	13	11	14	64	64	0	50
11	Felixstowe & Walton U	38	9	4	6	29	27	5	4	10	27	39	14	8	16	56	66	–10	50
12	Barking	38	9	1	9	31	27	4	7	8	18	36	13	8	17	49	63	–14	47
13	Brentwood T	38	8	6	5	38	28	4	3	12	33	49	12	9	17	71	77	–6	45
14	Dereham T*	38	8	2	9	39	32	6	3	10	32	50	14	5	19	71	82	–11	44
15	Great Wakering R	38	8	6	5	33	30	3	2	14	22	42	11	8	19	55	72	–17	41
16	Soham Town Rangers	38	6	2	11	25	31	6	2	11	19	33	12	4	22	44	64	–20	40
17	Basildon U	38	6	2	11	14	32	5	4	10	23	39	11	6	21	37	71	–34	39
18	Witham T	38	4	6	9	21	29	5	1	13	17	39	9	7	22	38	68	–30	34
19	Romford	38	9	2	8	35	38	1	2	16	13	44	10	4	24	48	82	–34	34
20	Mildenhall T	38	3	6	10	27	41	2	6	11	20	41	5	12	21	47	82	–35	27

**Dereham T deducted 3 points for fielding an ineligible player.*
¶Heybridge Swifts won play-offs, but were not promoted due to inferior record to other play-off winners.

BOSTIK ISTHMIAN LEAGUE DIVISION ONE SOUTH CENTRAL

			Home					Away					Total						
		P	W	D	L	F	A	W	D	L	F	A	W	D	L	F	A	GD	Pts
1	Hayes & Yeading U	38	17	1	1	69	11	12	5	2	60	25	29	6	3	129	36	93	93
2	Bracknell T	38	14	5	0	58	19	9	3	7	44	30	23	8	7	102	49	53	77
3	Cheshunt¶	38	11	7	1	44	19	11	3	5	35	24	22	10	6	79	43	36	76
4	Marlow	38	11	4	4	31	14	10	6	3	35	23	21	10	7	66	37	29	73
5	Westfield	38	12	3	4	43	26	9	4	6	34	28	21	7	10	77	54	23	70
6	Tooting & Mitcham U	38	7	8	4	31	23	11	3	5	35	29	18	11	9	66	52	14	65
7	Ware	38	8	7	4	46	33	10	2	7	44	26	18	9	11	90	59	31	63
8	Hanwell T	38	11	2	6	40	37	5	10	4	31	28	16	12	10	71	65	6	60
9	Waltham Abbey	38	9	2	8	34	36	9	0	10	29	32	18	2	18	63	68	–5	56
10	Northwood	38	6	5	8	34	32	10	1	8	31	39	16	6	16	65	71	–6	54
11	Ashford T (Middx)	38	7	4	8	25	32	8	1	10	30	38	15	5	18	55	70	–15	50
12	Bedfont Sports	38	9	5	5	46	28	4	4	11	29	48	13	9	16	75	76	–1	48
13	Chipstead	38	6	2	11	27	36	7	4	8	27	27	13	6	19	54	63	–9	45
14	Chalfont St Peter	38	6	6	7	29	30	4	7	8	23	30	10	13	15	52	60	–8	43
15	Uxbridge	38	7	3	9	24	29	4	6	9	26	42	11	9	18	50	71	–21	42
16	FC Romania	38	6	1	12	22	42	5	2	12	24	44	11	3	24	46	86	–40	36
17	South Park	38	3	2	14	18	51	6	4	9	29	41	9	6	23	47	92	–45	33
18	Hertford T	38	5	3	11	34	47	1	10	8	21	38	6	13	19	55	85	–30	31
19	Molesey	38	4	3	12	19	35	3	4	12	17	41	7	7	24	36	76	–40	28
20	Egham T	38	3	6	10	18	35	1	0	18	11	59	4	6	28	29	94	–65	18

¶Cheshunt promoted to Isthmian League Premier Division via play-offs.

BOSTIK ISTHMIAN LEAGUE DIVISION ONE SOUTH EAST

			Home					Away					Total						
		P	W	D	L	F	A	W	D	L	F	A	W	D	L	F	A	GD	Pts
1	Cray W	36	12	5	1	45	18	13	2	3	34	17	25	7	4	79	35	44	82
2	Horsham¶	36	13	3	2	41	16	10	2	6	32	22	23	5	8	73	38	35	74
3	Hastings U	36	13	3	2	46	17	8	4	6	32	28	21	7	8	78	45	33	70
4	Ashford U	36	11	2	5	41	19	10	3	5	33	17	21	5	10	74	36	38	68
5	Haywards Heath T	36	9	3	6	26	17	9	6	3	39	35	18	9	9	65	52	13	63
6	VCD Athletic	36	9	2	7	36	31	11	0	7	38	35	20	2	14	74	66	8	62
7	Hythe T	36	10	5	3	38	23	4	5	9	28	36	14	10	12	66	59	7	52
8	Whyteleafe	36	9	2	7	39	29	5	5	8	20	22	14	7	15	59	51	8	49
9	Phoenix Sports	36	7	5	6	40	35	6	5	7	25	30	13	10	13	65	65	0	49
10	Sevenoaks T	36	5	5	8	24	27	8	3	7	25	27	13	8	15	49	54	–5	47
11	Ramsgate	36	6	7	5	32	27	5	5	8	22	26	11	12	13	54	53	1	45
12	Whitstable T	36	8	6	4	21	19	3	4	11	15	36	11	10	15	36	55	–19	43
13	East Grinstead T	36	7	5	6	34	29	4	3	11	31	43	11	8	17	65	72	–7	41
14	Three Bridges	36	7	0	11	26	41	5	5	8	25	28	12	5	19	51	69	–18	41
15	Herne Bay	36	5	2	11	29	43	6	3	9	36	42	11	5	20	65	85	–20	38
16	Sittingbourne	36	5	2	11	24	36	6	2	10	25	36	11	4	21	49	72	–23	37
17	Faversham T	36	7	5	6	30	29	3	2	13	25	56	10	7	19	55	85	–30	37
18	Guernsey	36	3	3	12	24	41	4	6	8	26	36	7	9	20	50	77	–27	30
19	Greenwich Bor*	36	5	3	10	22	32	3	3	12	18	46	8	6	22	40	78	–38	27
20	Thamesmead T†																		

**Greenwich Bor deducted 3 points for fielding an ineligible player.*
†Thamesmead T record expunged.
¶Horsham promoted to Isthmian League Premier Division via play-offs.

THE BUILDBASE FA TROPHY 2018–19

**After extra time.*

EXTRA PRELIMINARY ROUND

Atherton Collieries v Runcorn Linnets	4-2
Cleethorpes T v Mossley	3-1
Sheffield v Prescot Cables	2-2, 2-6
Trafford v Colne	2-1
Glossop NE v Brighouse T	0-2
Droylsden v Widnes	2-1
Bromsgrove Sporting v Corby T	1-3
Loughborough Dynamo v Market Drayton T	5-2
Peterborough Sports v Sutton Coldfield T	2-1
Coleshill T v Kidsgrove Ath	1-2
Witham T v Coggeshall T	1-0
Uxbridge v Chalfont St Peter	1-1, 0-0*
Chalfont St Peter won 5-4 on penalties	
Felixstowe & Walton U v Grays Ath	1-3
Romford v Great Wakering R	2-3
Bedford T v Cheshunt	1-1, 2-1
Bury T v Horsham	1-2
Aveley v Tooting & Mitcham U	3-1
Didcot T v Thamesmead T	3-1
Ashford T (Middlesex) v Heybridge Swifts	4-2
Barton R v Kempston R	1-3
Whyteleafe v Bowers & Pitsea	4-1
Waltham Abbey v Hastings U	1-3
AFC Sudbury v Egham T	0-1
Ashford U v Haywards Heath T	4-4, 0-3
Blackfield & Langley v Highworth T	3-0
Evesham U v Moneyfields	1-5
Slimbridge v Winchester C	2-2, 3-3*
Slimbridge won 6-5 on penalties	

PRELIMINARY ROUND

Prescot Cables v Kendal T	5-1
Pickering T v Stocksbridge Park Steels	3-0
Marske U v Atherton Collieries	3-3, 1-0
Radcliffe v Cleethorpes T	2-3
Droylsden v Tadcaster Alb	1-1, 2-0
Trafford v Ramsbottom U	1-2
Skelmersdale U v Frickley Ath	1-3
Ossett U v Colwyn Bay	6-0
Morpeth T v Brighouse T	3-4
Clitheroe v Pontefract Collieries	3-2
Spalding U v Carlton T	1-4
Wisbech T v Kidsgrove Ath	1-2
(Tie awarded to Wisbech T – Kidsgrove Ath removed for fielding an ineligible player)	
Peterborough Sports v Cambridge C	2-4
Gresley v Newcastle T	1-2
Belper T v Stamford	0-0, 0-1
Chasetown v Lincoln U	2-1
Soham Town Rangers v AFC Mansfield	0-0, 1-2
Leek T v Loughborough Dynamo	0-0, 5-2
Corby T v Yaxley	2-3
Chipstead v Welwyn Garden C	2-1
Berkhamsted v South Park	5-1
Barking v Hayes & Yeading U	0-1
AFC Dunstable v Witham T	0-1
Hythe T v FC Romania	2-0
Grays Ath v Sevenoaks T	2-4
Aylesbury U v Mildenhall T	2-3
Didcot T v Hertford T	2-1
Greenwich Bor v Egham T	4-1
Dunstable T v Northwood	2-0
Haywards Heath T v Bracknell T	2-3
Faversham T v Sittingbourne	0-2
Phoenix Sports v Ramsgate	1-1, 0-1
Bedfont Sports v Whitstable T	1-4
Canvey Island v Cray W	2-0
Tilbury v Bedford T	1-4
Horsham v Ware	3-1
Great Wakering R v East Grinstead T	0-1
Dereham T v Kempston R	1-3
VCD Ath v Hanwell T	3-1
Aylesbury v Herne Bay	1-2
Three Bridges v Molesey	0-1
Hastings U v Whyteleafe	2-4
Ashford T (Middlesex) v Westfield	0-0, 3-2
Chalfont St Peter v Maldon & Tiptree	0-2
Brentwood T v Marlow	4-1
Aveley v Basildon U	2-1
Slimbridge v Melksham T	2-3
AFC Totton v North Leigh	1-1, 5-1
Yate T v Blackfield & Langley	1-0
Cinderford T v Moneyfields	5-0
Bideford v Street	2-3
Thatcham T v Cirencester T	2-0
Mangotsfield U v Kidlington	3-0
Larkhall Ath v Thame U	0-0, 0-1
Fleet T v Barnstaple T	2-1
Bristol Manor Farm v Paulton R	1-0

FIRST QUALIFYING ROUND

Workington v Scarborough Ath	1-0
Marine v Lancaster C	0-2
Warrington T v Prescot Cables	0-1
Pickering T v Droylsden	2-2, 3-2
Frickley Ath v Ramsbottom U	0-3
Whitby T v Witton Alb	0-1
Farsley Celtic v Brighouse T	4-1
Ossett U v Clitheroe	2-1
South Shields v North Ferriby U	4-0
Hyde U v Bamber Bridge	3-0
Cleethorpes T v Marske U	0-2
Stalybridge Celtic v Nantwich T	1-0
Gainsborough Trinity v Tamworth	0-0, 0-3
Buxton v King's Lynn T	3-3, 2-1*
(1-1 at the end of normal time)	
Kettering T v Stourbridge	2-0
AFC Rushden & Diamonds v St Ives T	2-1
Stamford v Leek T	0-0, 1-0
Cambridge C v Basford U	1-2
Carlton T v Bedworth U	1-0
Newcastle T v Chasetown	5-2
Mickleover Sports v Redditch U	1-0
St Neots T v Matlock T	1-0
Wisbech T v Yaxley	1-1, 0-2
Stafford Rangers v Rushall Olympic	2-1
AFC Mansfield v Hednesford T	1-1, 1-0
Grantham T v Halesowen T	0-4
Alvechurch v Stratford T	1-1, 0-3
Barwell v Coalville T	1-1, 3-2*
(2-2 at the end of normal time)	
Chipstead v Berkhamsted	2-1
Sittingbourne v Wingate & Finchley	1-2
Brentwood T v Whitstable T	3-1
Hythe T v Bishop's Stortford	1-2
Molesey v Walton Casuals	0-1
Kingstonian v Bedford T	1-1, 2-3
Margate v Potters Bar T	1-2
Horsham v Corinthian Casuals	3-0
Burgess Hill T v Worthing	1-1, 1-2
Dorking W v Sevenoaks T	2-1
Biggleswade T v Harrow Bor	2-1
Hitchin T v Hayes & Yeading U	0-1
Maldon & Tiptree v Royston T	0-3
Haringey Bor v Chesham U	1-1, 2-2*
Chesham U won 3-1 on penalties	
Ashford T (Middlesex) v Lewes	1-2
Lowestoft T v Enfield T	0-1
AFC Hornchurch v Ramsgate	6-0
Kempston R v Beaconsfield T	1-1, 1-3
Folkestone Invicta v Leatherhead	5-1
Merstham v East Grinstead T	2-0
Tonbridge Angels v Whyteleafe	2-1
Hendon v Staines T	2-1
VCD Ath v Leiston	1-3
Mildenhall T v Greenwich Bor	2-4*
(2-2 at the end of normal time)	
Metropolitan Police v Carshalton Ath	2-2, 1-2
Canvey Island v Brightlingsea Regent	0-1
Bracknell T v Bognor Regis T	2-2, 2-2*
Bognor Regis T won 3-2 on penalties	
Whitehawk v Harlow T	2-3
Aveley v Dunstable T	1-0
Kings Langley v Needham Market	0-2
Herne Bay v Witham T	2-1

Yate T v Dorchester T	1-1, 0-2
Gosport Bor v AFC Totton	1-2
Cinderford T v Street	2-2, 1-4
Thame U v Bristol Manor Farm	4-2
Farnborough v Merthyr T	2-3
Fleet T v Salisbury	0-3
Taunton T v Weymouth	1-3
Thatcham T v Melksham T	1-2
Poole T v Frome T	2-1
Hartley Wintney v Tiverton T	1-1, 1-5
Didcot T v Mangotsfield U	1-1, 4-2*
(2-2 at the end of normal time)	
Basingstoke T v Wimborne T	4-2
Swindon Supermarine v Banbury U	1-1, 0-3

SECOND QUALIFYING ROUND

Basford U v Stafford Rangers	4-0
Stamford v Kettering T	1-0
Stalybridge Celtic v Buxton	0-0, 2-1
Yaxley v Ramsbottom U	2-2, 1-5
AFC Mansfield v Pickering T	2-2, 0-2
St Neots T v Barwell	0-1
Lancaster C v Ossett U	1-0
Newcastle T v Workington	2-2, 0-5
Marske U v Tamworth	2-0
Halesowen T v Prescot Cables	3-2
Stratford T v Mickleover Sports	1-1, 1-0
Witton Alb v AFC Rushden & Diamonds	2-0
Farsley Celtic v Carlton T	0-0, 4-0
South Shields v Hyde U	2-1
Brightlingsea Regent v AFC Hornchurch	2-1
Lewes v Merthyr T	2-0
Chipstead v Bedford T	2-2, 0-2
Dorking W v Tonbridge Angels	1-0
Hendon v Biggleswade T	1-2
Basingstoke T v Enfield T	2-1
Royston T v Thame U	5-2
Horsham v Potters Bar T	1-0
Brentwood T v Poole T	2-2, 1-4
Herne Bay v Needham Market	0-1
Leiston v Melksham T	2-1
Salisbury v Merstham	2-0
Banbury U v Hayes & Yeading U	0-2
Carshalton Ath v Harlow T	3-1
Weymouth v Street	2-2, 1-0
Dorchester T v AFC Totton	3-1
Aveley v Beaconsfield T	1-2
Worthing v Chesham U	1-0
Walton Casuals v Bognor Regis T	2-0
Folkestone Invicta v Didcot T	3-0
Greenwich Bor v Bishop's Stortford	1-0
Tiverton T v Wingate & Finchley	2-3

THIRD QUALIFYING ROUND

Altrincham v Bradford (Park Avenue)	4-0
Blyth Spartans v Marske U	4-1
Alfreton T v Farsley Celtic	0-2
Spennymoor T v Halesowen T	8-2
Stamford v Barwell	1-1, 3-3*
Barwell won 7-6 on penalties	
Hereford v FC United of Manchester	3-1
Brackley T v Nuneaton Bor	3-0
Stratford T v South Shields	2-1
Kidderminster H v York C	1-3
Southport v Chester FC	0-0, 2-0
Leamington v Witton Alb	2-1
Darlington v AFC Telford U	0-2
Ashton U v Boston U	0-5
Pickering T v Ramsbottom U	0-0, 1-2
Basford U v Curzon Ashton	2-1
Lancaster C v Guiseley	2-2, 2-1
Stockport Co v Chorley	3-0
Stalybridge Celtic v Workington	1-2
Lewes v Hemel Hempstead T	2-2, 2-3
Bedford T v Worthing	2-1
Salisbury v East Thurrock U	2-1
Dorchester T v Hungerford T	1-0
Slough T v Western-super-Mare	2-3
Poole T v Dorking W	2-3
Weymouth v St Albans C	1-1, 2-0
Concord Rangers v Wealdstone	2-3
Truro C v Greenwich Bor	3-0
Chippenham T v Wingate & Finchley	1-1, 2-3
Beaconsfield T v Leiston	3-1
Hampton & Richmond Bor v Billericay T	0-1
Eastbourne Bor v Dartford	1-1, 3-2
Welling U v Dulwich Hamlet	1-1, 1-2
Woking v Folkestone Invicta	2-0
Basingstoke T v Torquay U	1-1*
Torquay U won 5-4 on penalties	
Carshalton Ath v Walton Casuals	2-0
Royston T v Needham Market	1-1, 0-2
Hayes & Yeading U v Brightlingsea Regent	0-0, 2-1
Gloucester C v Biggleswade T	1-3
Horsham v Bath C	1-2
Oxford C v Chelmsford C	4-0

FIRST ROUND

Southport v Solihull Moors	0-1
Lancaster C v Blyth Spartans	0-3
AFC Fylde v Stratford T	5-1
Salford C v Gateshead	3-1
Chesterfield v Basford U	5-1
Wrexham v Boston U	3-0
Barrow v FC Halifax T	1-2
Harrogate T v York C	2-1
Leamington v Hartlepool U	0-1
Workington v Ramsbottom U	0-0, 0-2
Spennymoor T v Barwell	4-0
Altrincham v Stockport Co	0-1
AFC Telford U v Farsley Celtic	4-3
Wingate & Finchley v Dulwich Hamlet	2-0
Biggleswade T v Wealdstone	2-1
Maidenhead U v Oxford C	A-A, 1-2*
First match abandoned after 75 minutes due to waterlogged pitch with Oxford C leading 0-1 (rearranged match – 1-1 at the end of normal time)	
Hereford v Billericay T	2-1
Aldershot T v Bedford T	3-3, 0-7
Carshalton Ath v Dorking W	1-0
Hemel Hempstead T v Eastleigh	2-1
Dover Ath v Havant & Waterlooville	2-2, 1-0
Woking v Maidstone U	1-1, 2-3*
(2-2 at the end of normal time)	
Ebbsfleet U v Dagenham & Redbridge	0-1
Barnet v Bath C	3-2
Bromley v Sutton U	2-1
(Tie awarded to Sutton U – Bromley removed for fielding an ineligible player)	
Truro C v Western-super-Mare	4-0
Salisbury v Braintree T	2-1
Boreham Wood v Torquay U	3-1*
(1-1 at the end of normal time)	
Leyton Orient v Beaconsfield T	4-0
Brackley T v Hayes & Yeading U	4-2
Weymouth (walkover) v Needham Market (withdrawn)	
Eastbourne Bor v Dorchester T	0-4

SECOND ROUND

Ramsbottom U v Weymouth	2-2, 3-1
Hartlepool U v AFC Telford U	1-2
Maidstone U v Oxford C	1-0
Hemel Hempstead T v Wingate & Finchley	4-2
Barnet v Dorchester T	2-1
Hereford v Brackley T	1-3
Salford C v Dagenham & Redbridge	2-0
Blyth Spartans v Boreham Wood	1-0
AFC Fylde v Biggleswade T	1-0
Spennymoor T v Sutton U	3-0
Stockport Co v Truro C	5-0
Dover Ath v Harrogate T	1-2
Chesterfield v Bedford T	1-0
Carshalton Ath v Salisbury	4-1
FC Halifax T v Solihull Moors	2-2, 0-1
Wrexham v Leyton Orient	0-1

THIRD ROUND

Ramsbottom U v AFC Fylde	5-5, 1-4
Spennymoor T v AFC Telford U	1-2
Carshalton Ath v Barnet	3-3, 1-2
Chesterfield v Brackley T	0-2
Leyton Orient v Blyth Spartans	1-0
Hemel Hempstead T v Solihull Moors	0-5
Salford C v Maidstone U	1-1, 0-3
Harrogate T v Stockport Co	2-4

QUARTER-FINALS

Brackley T v Leyton Orient	1-2
AFC Fylde v Barnet	0-0*
AFC Fylde won 4-1 on penalties	
Stockport Co v Maidstone U	1-1, 3-0
Solihull Moors v AFC Telford U	1-2

SEMI-FINALS – FIRST LEG

Leyton Orient v AFC Telford U	1-0
AFC Fylde v Stockport Co	0-0

SEMI-FINALS – SECOND LEG

AFC Telford U v Leyton Orient	1-2
Leyton Orient won 3-1 on aggregate	
Stockport Co v AFC Fylde	2-3
AFC Fylde won 3-2 on aggregate	

THE BUILDBASE FA TROPHY FINAL 2019

Wembley, Sunday 19 May 2019

AFC Fylde (0) 1 *(Rowe 60)*

Leyton Orient (0) 0 42,962 (combined with FA Vase)

AFC Fylde: Lynch; Francis-Angol, Byrne (Brewitt 12), Tunnicliffe, Bond, Croasdale, Rowe, Philliskirk, Birch (Crawford 90), Haughton (Odusina 74), Reid.
Leyton Orient: Brill; Widdowson, Coulson, McAnuff (Lee 78), Clay, Bonne, Happe (Harrold 68), Brophy, Koroma, Ekpiteta, Turley (Maguire-Drew 46).
Referee: Andrew Madley.

THE BUILDBASE FA VASE 2018–19

**After extra time.*

FIRST QUALIFYING ROUND

Alnwick T v Charnock Richard	1-2
Stokesley SC v Guisborough T	0-9
Holker Old Boys v Prestwich Heys	0-2
Goole v Barnoldswick T	1-2
Whickham v Jarrow	1-0
West Allotment Celtic v Yorkshire Amateur	3-0
Darlington Railway Ath v Bedlington Terriers	0-5
Chester-le-Street T v Sunderland Ryhope CW	1-5
Esh Winning v Whitley Bay	0-6
Bishop Auckland v Newton Aycliffe	2-2, 2-0
North Shields v Consett	1-2
Daisy Hill v Whitehaven	5-2
Harrogate Railway Ath v Silsden	3-4
Thackley v Thornaby	3-2
Dunston UTS v Heaton Stannington	2-0
Team Northumbria (removed) v Garforth T (walkover)	
Billingham T v Campion	2-0
Blyth (removed) v Crook T (walkover)	
Billingham Synthonia v Knaresborough T	3-1
Durham C v Seaham Red Star	0-5
Eccleshill U v Hebburn T	0-1
Northallerton T v Willington	2-2, 3-2
Lower Breck v West Didsbury & Chorlton	3-1
Longridge T v Vauxhall Motors	1-3
Worksop T v Grimsby Bor	2-1
Burscough v Alsager T	5-1
Wythenshawe T (withdrawn) v Rylands (withdrawn)	0-0
Winsford U v Liversedge	2-1*
(1-1 at the end of normal time)	
Maltby Main v Ashton Ath	5-1
Ashton T v St Helens T	3-1
Barton T v AFC Liverpool	3-1
AFC Blackpool v Nostell MW	3-1
Sandbach U v Athersley Recreation	5-1
Shelley v Penistone Church	2-1
AFC Emley v Litherland Remyca	3-4
Swallownest v Abbey Hey	1-0
Cammell Laird 1907 v Harworthy Colliery	2-1
Armthorpe Welfare v Worsbrough Bridge Ath	1-2
Parkgate v Chadderton	5-2*
(2-2 at the end of normal time)	
Congleton T v Bootle	1-2
Selby T v Staveley MW	0-5
Kirby Muxloe v Brocton	1-2
Nuneaton Griff v Coton Green	3-1
Littleton v Lichfield C	1-0
Coventry Sphinx v Sporting Khalsa	2-2, 0-3
FC Stratford v Bewdley T	0-1
Abbey Hulton U v Whitchurch Alport	2-3
AFC Bridgnorth v Wolverhampton Casuals	1-3
Ellesmere Rangers v Birstall U	0-4
Rugby Bor v Malvern T	3-2
Stafford T v Wednesfield	2-3
Droitwich Spa v Coventry U	2-4
Boldmere St Michaels v GNP Sports	4-1
Heather St Johns v Rocester	4-1
Rugby T (walkover) v Team Dudley (removed)	
Racing Club Warwick v Pegasus Juniors	10-0
Melton T v Ingles	2-2, 0-1
Lutterworth Ath v Cradley T	1-3
Wellington v St Martins	3-2
Dudley Sports v Shawbury U	3-1
Coventry Copsewood v Eccleshall	6-3*
(3-3 at the end of normal time)	
NKF Burbage v Lutterworth T	2-1
Gornal Ath v Stone Old Alleynians	1-2
Wellington Amateurs (walkover) v Ellistown (removed)	
Heath Hayes v Shifnal T	3-1
Dudley T (walkover) v Bardon Hill (withdrawn)	
Pershore T v Hanley T	0-4
Ashby Ivanhoe v Friar Lane & Epworth	2-0
Bolehall Swifts v Tipton T	3-0
Haughmond v Saffron Dynamo	2-4
Gedling MW v Ilkeston T	0-4
Rainworth MW v Teversal	0-3
Newark Flowserve (withdrawn) v Harrowby U (walkover)	
Leicester Road v Bottesford T	1-1, 1-2
Loughborough University v West Bridgford	6-0
Ollerton T v New Mills	1-0
Skegness T v Clay Cross T	4-1
Anstey Nomads v Eastwood Community	2-5
Borrowash Vic v Hucknall T	0-7
Clifton All Whites v Belper U	4-4, 0-3
Blidworth Welfare v Blaby & Whetstone Ath	5-3
Clipstone v Aylestone Park	1-2
South Normanton Ath v St Andrews	3-0
Oadby T v Sherwood Colliery	1-7
Dunkirk v Stapenhill	3-1*
(1-1 at the end of normal time)	
Quorn v Retford U	5-0
Holwell Sports v Pinxton	1-4
Lincoln Moorlands Railway v Kimberley MW	1-3
Radford v Selston	1-3
Framlingham T v Wisbech St Mary	3-2
Deeping Rangers v Blackstones	7-1
Woodbridge T v Eynesbury R	3-1
Gorleston v Boston T	5-1
Peterborough Northern Star v Fakenham T	2-0
Walsham Le Willows v Diss T	3-0
Newmarket T v Downham T	2-1
Bourne T v March Town U	3-4
Huntingdon T v Wroxham	0-4
Ely C v Norwich U	4-3*
(2-2 at the end of normal time)	
Stotfold v Leyton Ath	4-0
St Margaretsbury v Hadleigh U	0-3
Newbury Forest v Wivenhoe T	2-1
Wormley R v Biggleswade U	A-A, 1-2*
First match abandoned before kick-off due to an injury to a Wormley R player (rearranged match – 1-1 at the end of normal time)	
Enfield Bor v Halstead T	6-0
Clapton v Woodford T	1-1, 3-1
May & Baker Eastbrook Community v Burnham Ramblers	8-1
Stanway R v White Ensign	A-A, 4-2
First match abandoned after 83 minutes due to a serious injury to a White Ensign player with Stanway R leading 2-1	
Baldock T v Long Melford	2-1
Haverhill R v Ilford	2-1
Holland v Cornard U	4-2
Walthamstow v Takeley	1-3*
(1-1 at the end of normal time)	

Langford v Tower Hamlets 3-2
Southend Manor v Ipswich W 3-0
Stansted v Brantham Ath 1-3
London Colney v Cockfosters 2-1
Whitton U v Hatfield T 5-2
British Airways HEW v Harefield U 1-3
Rothwell Corinthians v CB Hounslow U 0-5
Spelthorne Sports v Northampton On Chenecks 5-3*
(3-3 at the end of normal time)
FC Deportivo Galicia v London Tigers 3-2
Sandhurst T v Kensington Bor 1-2
Wellingborough Whitworths v Bugbrooke St Michaels 0-2
Hanworth Villa v Bedford 5-1
Ampthill T v Edgware T 1-3
Broadfields U v Daventry T 5-0
AFC Hayes v Wembley 1-2
Rushden & Higham U v Winslow U 4-5*
(4-4 at the end of normal time)
Raunds T v Cranfield U 2-1*
(1-1 at the end of normal time)
Bicester T v AFC Spelthorne Sports Club 3-2
Southall v Reading C 3-2
Leverstock Green v Unite MK 10-0
Cricklewood W v Risborough Rangers 4-3
Burnham (walkover) v Hillingdon (removed)
St Panteleimon v Holmer Green 3-1
Shrivenham v Tytherington Rocks 9-0
Bashley v AFC Portchester 6-0
Binfield v Frimley Green 5-0
Tadley Calleva v Ascot U 3-1
Milton U v Clanfield 85 0-3
Chertsey T v Woodley U 4-2
Brimscombe & Thrupp v Ash U 5-1
Wallingford T v Abingdon U 1-4
Penn & Tylers Green v AFC Stoneham 1-3
Lydney T v Abbey Rangers 1-3
Cove v Fleet Spurs 0-2
Royal Wootton Bassett T (walkover) v Oxford C Nomads (withdrawn)
Ardley U v Holyport 1-4
Fairford T v Baffins Milton R 2-3*
(2-2 at the end of normal time)
Colliers Wood U v Stansfeld 3-1*
(0-0 at the end of normal time)
Bagshot v Sidlesham 0-5
Raynes Park Vale v Cobham 0-1
Lingfield v Epsom & Ewell 6-1
Croydon v Little Common 2-3
Sutton Ath v Cray Valley (PM) 1-2
Hassocks v K Sports 0-2
St Francis Rangers v FC Elmstead 3-1
Knaphill v AFC Varndeanians 1-4
Wick v Godalming T 2-1
Mile Oak v Selsey 2-2, 0-3
Billingshurst v Tunbridge Wells 0-3
Lordswood v Fire U Christian 2-0
Sheerwater v Lancing 2-1
Meridian v Southwick 0-1
Chessington & Hook U v Oakwood 7-0
Erith T v Arundel 5-0
Lewisham Bor (Community) v Broadbridge Heath 1-2*
(1-1 at the end of normal time)
Kent Football U v Steyning T 2-3*
(2-2 at the end of normal time)
Sporting Club Thamesmead v Midhurst & Easebourne 4-3
Westside v AC London 2-4
AFC Croydon Ath v Worthing U 4-1
AFC Uckfield T v Hollands & Blair 2-0
Glebe v Loxwood 3-0
Seaford T v Tooting Bec 1-0
Lydd T v Punjab U 1-2
Snodland T v Newhaven 2-3
Erith & Belvedere v Rushtall 1-3
Fisher v Corinthian 4-4, 2-3
East Preston v Eastbourne U 5-2
Bearsted v Bexhill U 4-1
Sheppey U v Balham 3-1
Langney W v Canterbury C 0-2
Saltdean U v Crawley Down Gatwick 2-1
Redhill v Holmesdale 2-0
Guildford C v Rochester U 4-0
Whitchurch U v Almondsbury 0-2
Devizes T v Warminster T 0-2
Calne T v Fawley 4-5
Christchurch v Folland Sports 3-0
Cowes Sports v Westbury U 3-5*
(3-3 at the end of normal time)
Chippenham Park v Bitton 0-4
Lymington T v Portland U 4-2
Oldland Abbotonians v Totton & Eling 2-3
Hamworthy U v Amesbury T 5-0
Romsey T v Bridport 4-4, 2-4
Ringwood T v Alresford T 1-2
Stockbridge v Roman Glass St George 1-3
Hallen v Fareham T 2-3
East Cowes Vic Ath v Pewsey Vale 4-3
Team Solent v Longwell Green Sports 2-3
Eversley & California v Downton 1-0
Bournemouth v Bristol Telephones 8-0
Hythe & Dibden v Bemerton Heath Harlequins 1-2*
(1-1 at the end of normal time)
Corsham T v Laverstock & Ford 1-0
Exmouth T v Callington T 4-2
Plymouth Parkway v Brislington 5-1
Tavistock v Helston Ath 3-1
Keynsham T v Sidmouth T 2-3
Bishops Lydeard v Bishop Sutton 3-0*
(0-0 at the end of normal time)
Godolphin Atlantic v Portishead T 1-0
Hengrove Ath v Newquay 1-2*
(1-1 at the end of normal time)
Wellington v Saltash U 1-3
Liskeard Ath v Bovey Tracey 1-3
Crediton U v Clevedon T 0-3
AFC St Austell v Ilfracombe T 3-1
Wincanton T v Radstock T 1-2
Witheridge (withdrawn) v Wells C (walkover)
Odd Down v Shepton Mallet 4-1
Elburton Villa v Launceston 3-1

SECOND QUALIFYING ROUND

Northallerton T v Steeton 1-2
Ashington v Crook T 6-2
Nelson v Tow Law T 5-2
Thackley v Carlisle C 5-2
Whickham v Whitley Bay 2-1*
(1-1 at the end of normal time)
Billingham T v Birtley T 3-1
Albion Sports v Silsden 0-1
Sunderland Ryhope CW v Dunston UTS 0-2
Bishop Auckland v West Allotment Celtic 3-1*
(1-1 at the end of normal time)
Brandon U v Washington 3-2*
(2-2 at the end of normal time)
Penrith v Charnock Richard 1-4
Padiham v Prestwich Heys 2-2, 2-5
Hebburn T v Billingham Synthonia 3-1
Ryton & Crawcrook Alb v Garforth T 1-2
Guisborough T v Barnoldswick T 4-2
Bedlington Terriers v Redcar Ath 2-0
Bridlington T v Consett 1-0*
(0-0 at the end of normal time)
Daisy Hill v Seaham Red Star 0-2
AFC Darwen v Garstang 1-2
Northwich Vic v Maltby Main 2-0
Swallownest v AFC Blackpool 4-1
Avro v Barnton 3-0
Irlam v Burscough 4-2
Bacup Bor v Litherland Remyca 1-4
Cammell Laird 1907 v Shelley 2-1
Glasshoughton Welfare v Parkgate 3-1
Cheadle T v Vauxhall Motors 2-2, 0-6
Bootle v Hallam 0-1
Worsbrough Bridge Ath v Squires Gate 0-2
Staveley MW v Maine Road 4-1
Wythenshawe T (withdrawn) or Rylands (withdrawn) v Hemsworth MW (walkover)
Barton T v Ashton T 4-0
Atherton LR v Sandbach U 0-4
Winsford U v Worksop T 5-0
Winterton Rangers v Rossington Main 2-0
Lower Breck v Stockport T 1-0
Chelmsley T v Tividale 3-1
Dudley Sports v Hanley T 0-4
Rugby Bor v Bustleholme 0-2
Whitchurch Alport v Shepshed Dynamo 2-3*
(2-2 at the end of normal time)
Littleton v Smethwick 0-1
Birstall U v Heather St Johns 0-4
Coventry Copsewood v Hereford Lads Club 1-2

Boldmere St Michaels v Studley	3-0
Lye T v Bolehall Swifts	2-0
Wednesfield v Bromyard T	5-2
Uttoxeter T v Walsall Wood	2-2, 4-5*
(4-4 at the end of normal time)	
Wellington Amateurs v Racing Club Warwick	6-3
NKF Burbage v Cradley T	2-1
Brocton v Nuneaton Griff	4-0
Cadbury Ath v Wem T	2-0
Coventry U v Atherstone T	2-1
Paget Rangers (walkover) v Kington T (removed)	
Saffron Dynamo v Heath Hayes	4-0
Ingles v Rugby T	0-2
Ashby Ivanhoe v Bewdley T	0-1
Black Country Rangers v Dudley T	4-0
Wolverhampton Casuals v Romulus	0-1
AFC Wulfrunians v Wellington	1-2
Stone Old Alleynians v Sporting Khalsa	3-7
Hucknall T v Harrowby U	2-0
Aylestone Park v Kimberley MW	2-1
Pinxton v Bottesford T	1-1, 0-3
Holbrook Sports v Blidworth Welfare	3-5
Belper U v Teversal	1-0
Quorn v Skegness T	4-1
Barrow T v Shirebrook T	4-1
Heanor T v Dunkirk	3-2
South Normanton Ath v Selston	1-3
Ollerton T v Long Eaton U	1-5*
(1-1 at the end of normal time)	
Arnold T v Loughborough University	0-5
Sleaford T v Sandiacre T	2-0
Eastwood Community v Sherwood Colliery	3-2
Graham St Prims v Ilkeston T	0-2
Dronfield T v Harborough T	3-1
FC Bolsover v Leicester Nirvana	1-2
Peterborough Northern Star v March Town U	1-0
Histon (walkover) v Team Bury (withdrawn)	
Walsham Le Willows v Deeping Rangers	1-4
Wroxham v Mulbarton W	3-0
Framlingham T v Swaffham T	0-0, 1-2
Woodbridge T v Pinchbeck U	2-1
Great Yarmouth T v Thetford T	3-1
Gorleston v Kirkley & Pakefield	0-2
Newmarket T v Ely C	5-2
Saffron Walden T v May & Baker Eastbrook Community	1-4
Southend Manor v Haverhill R	4-3
Hoddesdon T v FC Clacton	2-3
London Lions v Biggleswade U	0-3
Colney Heath v Langford	2-1
Brantham Ath v Takeley	3-4
Haverhill Bor v Whitton U	2-1
Little Oakley v Hadleigh U	1-0
Barkingside v Wodson Park	1-1*
Wodson Park won 4-2 on penalties	
London Colney v FC Broxbourne Bor	3-1
Coggeshall U v Sawbridgeworth T	0-4
Enfield Bor v Sporting Bengal U	3-2
Baldock T v Stanway R	1-0
Codicote v Holland	1-0
Clapton v Newbury Forest	0-2
Hadley v Enfield 1893	0-1
Stotfold v West Essex	2-4
Amersham T v Hanworth Villa	0-1
Southall v Wembley	5-0
Brackley T Saints v Crawley Green	0-1
Burton Park W v FC Deportivo Galicia	0-5
Brimsdown (walkover) v Bicester T (withdrawn)	
Leverstock Green v Raunds T	4-0
Wellingborough T v Burnham	3-2
Potton U v CB Hounslow U	2-3
St Panteleimon v Long Buckby	4-1
Cricklewood W v North Greenford U	3-6*
(3-3 at the end of normal time)	
Arlesey T v Irchester U	1-2*
(1-1 at the end of normal time)	
Kensington Bor v Northampton Sileby Rangers	4-2
Broadfields U v Edgware T	2-0
Bedfont & Feltham v Winslow U	2-0
Bugbrooke St Michaels v Spelthorne Sports	3-3, 0-2
Rayners Lane v Thrapston T	3-2
Harefield U v Oxhey Jets	4-1*
(1-1 at the end of normal time)	
Easington Sports v Brimscombe & Thrupp	1-2
Baffins Milton R v New College Swindon	14-1
Royal Wootton Bassett T v Bashley	0-4
Thame Rangers v Farnham T	1-0
Tadley Calleva v Chertsey T	0-1
Abingdon U v Alton	3-0
AFC Stoneham v Binfield	3-2
Chipping Sodbury T v Abbey Rangers	1-3
Clanfield 85 v Buckingham Ath	2-5
Shrivenham v Badshot Lea	1-4
Malmesbury Vic v Virginia Water	3-1
Cheltenham Saracens v Flackwell Heath	0-1
Longlevens v Tuffley R	0-0, 1-0
Holyport v Fleet Spurs	2-1
Redhill v Forest Hill Park	2-1*
(1-1 at the end of normal time)	
Steyning T v Punjab U	1-1*
Steyning T won 9-8 on penalties	
AFC Varndeanians v Canterbury C	0-2
Cray Valley (PM) v Hailsham T	2-0
Cobham (walkover) v Gravesham Bor (withdrawn)	
St Francis Rangers v Lordswood	0-6
Sporting Club Thamesmead v Banstead Ath	0-1
Tunbridge Wells v Bridon Ropes	1-1, 1-0
Guildford C v Rushtall	0-2
Wick v Hackney Wick	4-2
Peacehaven & Telscombe v Shoreham	3-1
AFC Uckfield T v Southwick	5-0
AC London v Erith T	2-3
Colliers Wood U v Sidlesham	0-1
Saltdean U v Littlehampton T	3-1
Selsey v Bearsted	0-2
Chatham T v Camberley T	5-1
Corinthian v Glebe	3-0
Chessington & Hook U v Sheerwater	0-5
Newhaven v Little Common	1-0
Sheppey U v Seaford T	5-3
K Sports v Deal T	1-4
East Preston v Broadbridge Heath	1-0
AFC Croydon Ath v Lingfield	5-2*
(2-2 at the end of normal time)	
Hamworthy U v Fawley	3-1
Roman Glass St George v Bemerton Heath Harlequins	3-0
Bournemouth v Christchurch	3-1
Verwood T v Alresford T	1-1, 0-1
Bridport v Warminster T	5-0
Eversley & California v Lymington T	2-1
Shortwood U v Cribbs	1-5
Swanage T & Herston v Longwell Green Sports	0-3
Fareham T v Corsham T	2-1*
(0-0 at the end of normal time)	
Bitton v Bishop's Cleeve	3-1
Petersfield T v Westbury U	1-3
New Milton T v Cadbury Heath	1-2
Totton & Eling v East Cowes Vic Ath	1-0
Sherborne T v Almondsbury	0-1
Shaftesbury v Andover New Street	5-1
United Services Portsmouth v Brockenhurst	0-2
Buckland Ath v Newquay	0-1
Odd Down v Welton R	2-1
Radstock T v Plymouth Parkway	1-3
Cullompton Rangers v Ivybridge T	0-4
Sidmouth T v Godolphin Atlantic	4-1
Saltash U v Axminster T	6-0
Bovey Tracey v Tavistock	1-2*
(1-1 at the end of normal time)	
Falmouth T v Clevedon T	2-1
Bishops Lydeard v Elburton Villa	0-4
Exmouth T v Bridgwater T	3-0
Cheddar v Newton Abbot Spurs	2-0
Camelford v Bodmin T	3-3, 0-4
Porthleven v Torpoint Ath	3-6
Wells C v AFC St Austell	2-3

FIRST ROUND

Hallam v Charnock Richard	3-1
Northwich Vic v Cammell Laird 1907	5-0
Litherland Remyca v Thackley	1-4
Prestwich Heys v Garforth T	6-2
Irlam v Handsworth Parramore	2-0
Staveley MW v Silsden	2-2, 0-2
Bedlington Terriers v Whickham	5-1
Sunderland RCA v Bridlington T	3-2*
(2-2 at the end of normal time)	
Hebburn T v City of Liverpool	4-0
Vauxhall Motors v Seaham Red Star	4-0
Squires Gate v Sandbach U	2-1
Bishop Auckland v Hemsworth MW	2-3

Swallownest v Garstang 1-1*
Garstang won 4-3 on penalties
Steeton v Avro 2-3
Runcorn T v Guisborough T 3-3, 4-2*
(2-2 at the end of normal time)
Billingham T v Dunston UTS 1-3
Winterton Rangers v Lower Breck 1-0
Nelson v Ashington 0-5
Shildon v Glasshoughton Welfare 1-0
Barton T v Brandon U 8-0
Shepshed Dynamo v Bewdley T 2-0
Cadbury Ath v Hanley T 4-0
Aylestone Park v Blidworth Welfare 0-3
Lye T v Chelmsley T 5-2
Romulus v Wellington 3-3, 3-1
Bustleholme v NKF Burbage 1-4
Coventry U v Wednesfield 5-0
Loughborough University v Heather St Johns 1-2
Wellington Amateurs v Leicester Nirvana 1-2
Belper U v Quorn 1-4
Brocton v Highgate U 3-2*
(2-2 at the end of normal time)
Heanor T v Ilkeston T 0-3
Sporting Khalsa v Winsford U 1-0
Saffron Dynamo v Bottesford T 3-3, 3-2
Barrow T v Dronfield T 0-1
Hereford Lads Club v Paget Rangers 2-0
Eastwood Community v Selston 3-0
Boldmere St Michaels v Rugby T 2-1
Hucknall T v Black Country Rangers 3-2
Worcester C v Long Eaton U 2-1
Smethwick v Walsall Wood 0-3
Baldock T v Brimsdown 3-0
Little Oakley v Enfield 1893 2-2, 0-2
Newmarket T v Deeping Rangers 0-1
Great Yarmouth T v Wroxham 3-1
Colney Heath v Histon 1-1, 0-2
FC Deportivo Galicia v Irchester U 1-2
Buckingham Ath v FC Clacton 2-2, 2-3
Newbury Forest v Newport Pagnell T 2-3
Biggleswade U v Holbeach U 2-3*
(2-2 at the end of normal time)
Haverhill Bor v Swaffham T 3-4
Enfield Bor v Kirkley & Pakefield 2-3*
(2-2 at the end of normal time)
London Colney v Wellingborough T 2-3*
(2-2 at the end of normal time)
Southend Manor v Redbridge 1-4
May & Baker Eastbrook Community v North Greenford U 4-2*
(2-2 at the end of normal time)
Thame Rangers v Crawley Green 4-2
West Essex v Godmanchester R 1-2
Takeley v Wodson Park 0-2
Codicote v Wantage T 1-7
Harefield U v Woodbridge T 0-2
Stowmarket T v Harpenden T 5-0
Sleaford T v Peterborough Northern Star 2-2, 0-2
Leverstock Green v Sawbridgeworth T 3-0
Sidlesham v Chatham T 0-2
Redhill v Peacehaven & Telscombe 2-3
Sheppey U v East Preston 4-0
Wick v Lordswood 0-3
Corinthian v Deal T 3-2
Eversley & California v Horndean 0-1
Southall v Sheerwater 6-0
Spelthorne Sports v CB Hounslow U 2-1
Rayners Lane v Abbey Rangers 2-3
Bearsted v Beckenham T 3-0
Canterbury C v Saltdean U 2-1
Broadfields U v Banstead Ath 1-7
Hanworth Villa v Pagham 2-4
Sutton Common R v Cobham 2-1
Chertsey T v Flackwell Heath 6-1
AFC Croydon Ath v Fareham T 3-0
Horsham YMCA v Kensington Bor 0-2
St Panteleimon v Cray Valley (PM) A-A, 1-3
First match abandoned after 104 minutes due to a serious injury to a St Panteleimon player with the score at 1-1 in extra time
Bedfont & Feltham v Erith T 1-2
Newhaven v Rushtall 2-1
Tunbridge Wells v AFC Uckfield T 0-2
Steyning T v Walton & Hersham 1-0
Bashley v Baffins Milton R 1-2
Saltash U v Westbury U 2-1
Brimscombe & Thrupp v Cribbs 2-3
Longwell Green Sports v Brockenhurst 1-3
Ivybridge T v Holyport 0-0, 3-0
Torpoint Ath v Sholing 0-1
Exmouth T v Elburton Villa 2-0
Cheddar v Totton & Eling 1-0*
(0-0 at the end of normal time)
Roman Glass St George v Malmesbury Vic 0-2
Andover T v Badshot Lea 1-4
Odd Down v Willand R 1-4
Alresford T v Abingdon U 1-0
Bridport v Falmouth T 0-6
Bodmin T v AFC Stoneham 2-1
Bournemouth v Newquay 6-0
Longlevens v Tavistock 1-3*
(1-1 at the end of normal time)
Cadbury Heath v Sidmouth T 5-0
AFC St Austell v Plymouth Parkway 6-1
Almondsbury v Bitton 2-1
Shaftesbury v Hamworthy U 1-2

SECOND ROUND

Hallam v Hebburn T 1-2
Vauxhall Motors v Runcorn T 1-3
Silsden v Bedlington Terriers 3-1
Newcastle Benfield v 1874 Northwich 2-0
Avro v Squires Gate 2-1
Winterton Rangers v Dunston UTS 2-1
Irlam v Hemsworth MW 3-1
Barton T v Shildon 0-2
Garstang v Sunderland RCA 2-6
Thackley v West Auckland T 0-1
Stockton T v Ashington 4-1
Prestwich Heys v Northwich Vic 0-0, 0-1
Westfields v Romulus 3-2
Shepshed Dynamo v Blidworth Welfare 3-0
Worcester C v Desborough T 0-2
Cadbury Ath v Heather St Johns 3-2
Coventry U v Boldmere St Michaels 3-0
Sporting Khalsa v Hucknall T 3-2
Quorn v Eastwood Community 1-2
Wolverhampton SC v Ilkeston T 0-2
Walsall Wood v Dronfield T 3-1
Lye T v Brocton 4-1
Stourport Swifts v NKF Burbage 0-2
Hinckley v Hereford Lads Club 3-1
Leicester Nirvana v Saffron Dynamo 3-0
Biggleswade v Norwich CBS 3-1
Cogenhoe U v Leighton T 2-0
(Tie awarded to Leighton T – Cogenhoe U removed for fielding an ineligible player)
FC Clacton v Kirkley & Pakefield 1-0
Great Yarmouth T v Godmanchester R 1-3
Enfield 1893 v Leverstock Green 1-4
Redbridge v Peterborough Northern Star 1-0
Hullbridge Sports v Irchester U 3-1
Wellingborough T v Tring Ath 0-7
May & Baker Eastbrook Community v Swaffham T 0-1
Stowmarket T v Baldock T 3-1*
(1-1 at the end of normal time)
Histon v Woodbridge T 5-4
Wantage T v Deeping Rangers 1-2
Wodson Park v Holbeach U 0-2
Newport Pagnell T v Thame Rangers 3-2
Chertsey T v Horndean 2-0
Sutton Common R v Horley T 6-1
Abbey Rangers v Lordswood 5-0
Chichester C v Windsor 0-2
Kensington Bor v Erith T 0-3
Steyning T v Banstead Ath 1-0
AFC Croydon Ath v AFC Uckfield T 1-2
Spelthorne Sports v Sheppey U 1-2
Badshot Lea v Cray Valley (PM) 0-7
Crowborough Ath v Eastbourne T 0-4
Corinthian v Canterbury C 2-4*
(2-2 at the end of normal time)
Pagham v Peacehaven & Telscombe 4-1
Bearsted v Newhaven 1-0
Southall v Chatham T 1-0*
(0-0 at the end of normal time)
Sholing v Malmesbury Vic 5-1
Exmouth T v Cadbury Heath 3-4
Almondsbury v Hamble Club 1-2
Bodmin T v Alresford T 1-0*
(0-0 at the end of normal time)
Cheddar v AFC St Austell 1-2

Newport (IW) v Cribbs 0-2
Baffins Milton R v Bournemouth 3-2
Brockenhurst v Bradford T 0-4
Willand R v Tavistock 2-1
Ivybridge T v Saltash U 1-3
Hamworthy U v Falmouth T 3-1*
(1-1 at the end of normal time)

THIRD ROUND
Shildon v Sunderland RCA 2-3
Northwich Vic v Silsden 3-0
Stockton T v Hebburn T 3-5
Avro v West Auckland T 0-2
Irlam v Winterton Rangers A-A, 2-0
First match abandoned at half time due to floodlight failure with the score 0-0
Newcastle Benfield v Runcorn T 5-4
Ilkeston T v Eastwood Community 1-2
Coventry U v Hinckley 4-0
Cadbury Ath v Desborough T 3-2
Westfields v Leicester Nirvana 0-4
Shepshed Dynamo v NKF Burbage 3-0
Lye T v Leighton T 4-0*
(0-0 at the end of normal time)
Sporting Khalsa v Walsall Wood 3-1
Histon v Leverstock Green 5-1
Godmanchester R v Holbeach U 2-0
Swaffham T v Stowmarket T 0-0, 1-2
Tring Ath v Biggleswade 1-1, 0-0*
Biggleswade won 5-3 on penalties
Hullbridge Sports v Newport Pagnell T 0-2
Deeping Rangers v FC Clacton 4-2
AFC Uckfield T v Sutton Common R 5-2
Eastbourne T v Abbey Rangers 0-1
Redbridge v Chertsey T 0-5
Bearsted v Steyning T 3-2*
(2-2 at the end of normal time)
Sheppey U v Cray Valley (PM) 0-4
Canterbury C v Southall 1-0*
(0-0 at the end of normal time)
Erith T v Windsor 1-2
Saltash U v Cribbs 2-4
Bradford T v Baffins Milton R 1-3
Willand R v Bodmin T 3-0
Cadbury Heath v AFC St Austell 4-8
Hamble Club v Hamworthy U 1-1, 1-4
Sholing v Pagham 6-2

FOURTH ROUND
Godmanchester R v Sporting Khalsa 1-0
(Tie awarded to Sporting Khalsa – Godmanchester R removed for fielding an ineligible player)
Irlam v Cadbury Ath 4-0
Hebburn T v Shepshed Dynamo 2-1
Newcastle Benfield v Northwich Vic 2-3
Sunderland RCA v West Auckland T 0-1
Coventry U v Leicester Nirvana 3-2
(Tie awarded to Leicester Nirvana – Coventry U removed for fielding an ineligible player)
Deeping Rangers v Eastwood Community 4-0
Histon v Lye T 2-1
Willand R v Hamworthy U 1-0
Canterbury C v Newport Pagnell T 3-2
AFC Uckfield T v Windsor 1-4
Cribbs v Sholing 0-2
Bearsted v Abbey Rangers 1-2*
(1-1 at the end of normal time)
Chertsey T v AFC St Austell 5-0
Biggleswade v Stowmarket T 1-0
Cray Valley (PM) v Baffins Milton R 3-1

FIFTH ROUND
Irlam v Chertsey T 0-2
Cray Valley (PM) v Abbey Rangers 3-1
Histon v Northwich Vic 1-3*
(1-1 at the end of normal time)
Sholing v Sporting Khalsa 3-1
Hebburn T v West Auckland T 0-2
Biggleswade v Windsor 6-1
Willand R v Deeping Rangers 3-2
Canterbury C v Leicester Nirvana 2-1

SIXTH ROUND
West Auckland T v Chertsey T 0-2
Canterbury C v Biggleswade 2-1
Willand R v Cray Valley (PM) 1-3
Northwich Vic v Sholing 3-1*
(1-1 at the end of normal time)

SEMI-FINALS – FIRST LEG
Northwich Vic v Chertsey T 1-1
Cray Valley (PM) v Canterbury C 1-0

SEMI-FINALS – SECOND LEG
Chertsey T v Northwich Vic 0-0*
Chertsey T won 5-3 on penalties
Canterbury C v Cray Valley (PM) 1-1
Cray Valley (PM) won 2-1 on aggregate

THE BUILDBASE FA VASE FINAL 2019
Wembley, Sunday 19 May 2019

Chertsey T (1) 3 *(Flegg 39, Baxter 105, Rowe 117)*
Cray Valley (PM) (1) 1 *(Tomlin 36)*
42,962 (combined with FA Trophy)

Chertsey T: Jupp; Welch-Turner, Maclaren (Taylor 79), Peacock, Rowe, Guentchev, Baxter (Pomroy 118), Murphy, Binns (Jackson 97), Driver (Crossley 83), Flegg.
Cray Valley (PM): Walker; Smith, Hickey, Sains (Willock 111), Tumkaya (Potter 106), Edgar, Semakula, Tomlin, Lisbie (Babalola 100), Flack (James 72), Gayle.
aet.
Referee: Ross Joyce.

THE FA YOUTH CUP 2018–19

**After extra time.*

PRELIMINARY ROUND
Chester-le-Street T v Ryton & Crawcrook Alb 0-4
Workington v Hebburn T 1-2
Stockton T v South Shields 3-4
AFC Darwen v Hyde U 0-6
FC United of Manchester v Nantwich T 2-1
Prescot Cables v Abbey Hey 4-0
Curzon Ashton v Witton Alb 10-4
Marine v Southport 2-2*
Marine won 7-6 on penalties
Stockport Co v Radcliffe 5-2
Chester FC v Sandbach U 5-1
Ashton T v Altrincham 0-5
West Didsbury & Chorlton v City of Liverpool 0-2
Litherland Remyca v Cheadle T 3-1
Ashton Ath v Mossley 4-2*
(2-2 at the end of normal time)
Bootle v Vauxhall Motors 1-0
Staveley MW v Bradford (Park Avenue) 2-4
Handsworth Parramore v York C 1-3
Steeton v Harrogate Railway Ath 2-4
Ossett U v Silsden 4-2
Farsley Celtic v Tadcaster Alb 0-8
Selby T v Frickley Ath 0-11
Rossington Main v Shelley 2-1
Pickering T (withdrawn) v Nostell MW (walkover)
Deeping Rangers v Harrowby U 7-1
Heather St Johns v Lincoln U 3-1*
(1-1 at the end of normal time)
Cleethorpes T v Eastwood Community 1-0
Dunkirk v Basford U 0-7
Grantham T v Harborough T 4-2
Bottesford T (walkover) v Sandiacre T (withdrawn)
Buxton v Blaby & Whetstone Ath 3-0
West Bridgford v Dronfield T 6-1
Alfreton T v Long Eaton U 1-3
Anstey Nomads (walkover) v Ashby Ivanhoe (withdrawn)
Mickleover Sports v Boston U 1-1*
Mickleover Sports won 4-3 on penalties
Hinckley v Aylestone Park 0-1
Spalding U v Bourne T 2-3

Newcastle T v Bedworth U 2-1*
(1-1 at the end of normal time)
Stafford Rangers v Stourbridge 0-2
Halesowen T (walkover) v Nuneaton Griff (withdrawn)
Alvechurch v Stratford T 1-4
Rushall Olympic v Leek T 4-2
Bromsgrove Sporting v Haughmond 1-3*
(1-1 at the end of normal time)
Coventry Sphinx v Coton Green 3-4
Ellesmere Rangers v Racing Club Warwick 0-4
Coleshill T v Walsall Wood 3-1
Kidderminster H v Dudley T 7-0
AFC Telford U v Evesham U 2-2*
AFC Telford won 5-3 on penalties
Leamington (walkover) v Eccleshall (withdrawn)
Lye T v Lichfield C 2-6
Nuneaton Bor v Hednesford T 6-2
Brackley T v St Ives T 4-2
Peterborough Sports v Biggleswade T 6-0
Rothwell Corinthians v Cogenhoe U 0-9
Godmanchester R (walkover) v Potton U (withdrawn)
AFC Rushden & Diamonds v Peterborough Northern Star 3-0
Huntingdon T (withdrawn) v Bugbrooke St Michaels (walkover)
Kettering T (walkover) v Desborough T (withdrawn)
Irchester U (withdrawn) v AFC Dunstable (walkover)
Kempston R v Corby T 0-6
Gorleston v March Town U 6-0
Whitton U v Ipswich W 1-5
Walsham Le Willows v Haverhill R 3-2
Mildenhall T v Histon 4-3
Dereham T v Fakenham T 6-2
Framlingham T v King's Lynn T 0-1
Wisbech St Mary v Hadleigh U 0-2
Swaffham T v Needham Market 1-5
Felixstowe & Walton U v Bury T 2-3*
(2-2 at the end of normal time)
Norwich U v Woodbridge T 5-1
Hitchin T v Barking 1-0
Cheshunt v Welwyn Garden C 0-20
Tower Hamlets v Heybridge Swifts 3-0
St Margaretsbury v Walthamstow 0-2
Redbridge v Hullbridge Sports 0-1*
(0-0 at the end of normal time)
Clapton (withdrawn) v Tring Ath (walkover)
Woodford T v Grays Ath 1-1*
Grays Ath won 3-1 on penalties
St Albans C v Ware 1-2*
(0-0 at the end of normal time)
Aveley v Potters Bar T 3-1
Royston T v Chelmsford C 1-3
Great Wakering R (walkover) v Waltham Abbey (withdrawn)
Witham T (walkover) v East Thurrock U (withdrawn)
Concord Rangers v Saffron Walden T 0-1
Hertford T v Barkingside 1-5
Romford (walkover) v Hoddesdon T (withdrawn)
Codicote v Takeley 0-1
AFC Hornchurch v Ilford 3-2
Hanwell T v Hendon 2-3
Haringey Bor v Wingate & Finchley 1-2
Colney Heath v Ashford T (Middlesex) 16-0
Staines T v Flackwell Heath 1-3
Burnham v Aylesbury 2-2*
Aylesbury won 5-3 on penalties
North Greenford U v Harefield U 0-1
Spelthorne Sports v Chalfont St Peter 0-4
Uxbridge (walkover) v Amersham T (withdrawn)
Leverstock Green v Cockfosters 3-1
Chesham U (withdrawn) v Sandhurst T (walkover)
Harrow Bor v Hayes & Yeading U 0-4
Enfield T v Wallingford T 5-1
CB Hounslow U (walkover) v Abingdon U (withdrawn)
Shrivenham v Buckingham Ath 0-4
Northwood v Brimsdown 5-0
Glebe v Dartford 2-3
Phoenix Sports v Herne Bay 6-0
Cray W v Holmesdale 4-2*
(2-2 at the end of normal time)
Sevenoaks T (withdrawn) v Tooting & Mitcham U (walkover)
Dulwich Hamlet v Fisher 3-1
Croydon v Cray Valley (PM) 3-0
Lingfield (walkover) v Lewisham Bor (Community) (withdrawn)
Welling U v Eastbourne Bor 2-4
Eastbourne U (withdrawn) v Chatham T (walkover)
Hollands & Blair (walkover) v Erith & Belvedere (withdrawn)
Ramsgate v Tonbridge Angels 1-2
Bridon Ropes v VCD Ath 3-6
Ashford U (walkover) v Erith T (withdrawn)
South Park v Abbey Rangers 4-2
Chichester C v Raynes Park Vale 1-4
Three Bridges v Steyning T 4-3
Crowborough Ath v Mile Oak 3-0
Burgess Hill T v Whitehawk 1-2
Hackney Wick v Sutton Common R 7-2
East Preston v Newhaven 0-3
Dorking W v Chertsey T 4-2
Leatherhead v Whyteleafe 2-5
Haywards Heath T v Lancing 3-0
Knaphill v Shoreham 6-1
Horley T v Loxwood 0-10
Hastings U v Metropolitan Police 1-3
Camberley T v Corinthian Casuals 13-0
Worthing U v Woking 1-1*
Woking won 3-1 on penalties
Clanfield 85 v Hungerford T 2-4
Thame U (withdrawn) v Banbury U (walkover)
Fleet Spurs v Basingstoke T 6-0
Fleet T v Thatcham T 4-1
Alton v Bracknell T 1-9
Hartley Wintney v Ascot U 4-5*
(3-3 at the end of normal time)
Windsor v Binfield 5-1
Andover T v Ardley U 1-0*
(0-0 at the end of normal time)
Christchurch v Team Solent 1-6
Sholing v Salisbury 4-0
Farnborough v Cove 3-1
Tuffley R v Bitton 6-1
Chippenham T v Yate T 2-3
Oldland Abbotonians v Cirencester T 0-2
Bishop's Cleeve v Almondsbury 1-3
Portishead T v Radstock T 4-2
Wellington v Odd Down 1-7
Torquay U v Elburton Villa 3-1
Bath C v Street 2-1
Weston-super-Mare v Helston Ath 2-5
Frome T v Wells C 0-2
Welton R v Keynsham T 1-0

FIRST QUALIFYING ROUND

Hebburn T v Carlisle C 2-1
Ryton & Crawcrook Alb v North Shields 1-7
Seaham Red Star v Consett 6-2
South Shields v Spennymoor T 3-1
Bootle v Prescot Cables 3-1*
(0-0 at the end of normal time)
Stockport T v Litherland Remyca 2-8
Stalybridge Celtic v Irlam 3-4
Curzon Ashton v Hyde U 1-1*
Hyde U won 3-1 on penalties
Chorley v Stockport Co 4-0
Daisy Hill v Ashton Ath 4-3
Marine v Chester FC 0-6
City of Liverpool v FC United of Manchester 4-1
Lancaster C (withdrawn) v Altrincham (walkover)
St Helens T (walkover) v Runcorn T (withdrawn)
Bradford (Park Avenue) v Harworthy Colliery 2-4
Garforth T v Harrogate Railway Ath 4-0
AFC Emley v Sheffield 1-6
Ossett U v Frickley Ath 3-1
Nostell MW v Stocksbridge Park Steels 2-5
Guiseley v Rossington Main 11-0
Tadcaster Alb v York C 3-1
West Bridgford v Leicester Road 5-1
Cleethorpes T v Aylestone Park 1-4
Leicester Nirvana v Long Eaton U 1-3
Heather St Johns v Anstey Nomads 2-3
Deeping Rangers v Basford U 1-2
Stamford v Matlock T 1-6
Bottesford T v Lutterworth Ath 5-1
Buxton v Mickleover Sports 1-2
Grantham T v Bourne T 3-1
Hereford v Tipton T 11-3
Lichfield C v Stourbridge 1-2
Worcester C v Malvern T 0-2
Coleshill T v Tamworth 2-0
Romulus v Kidderminster H 0-2

Newcastle T v Halesowen T	3-5*
(3-3 at the end of normal time)	
Sutton Coldfield T v Pegasus Juniors	8-0
Rushall Olympic v Racing Club Warwick	3-0
Boldmere St Michaels v AFC Telford U	0-3
Bustleholme v Nuneaton Bor	0-2
Rugby T v Leamington	11-2
Rugby Bor v Coton Green	2-1
Stratford T v Haughmond	4-1
Wellingborough T (walkover) v Biggleswade U (withdrawn)	
St Neots T v Peterborough Sports	1-4
AFC Dunstable v AFC Rushden & Diamonds	1-2
Kettering T v Bugbrooke St Michaels	1-0
Brackley T v Godmanchester R	8-1
Corby T v Cogenhoe U	2-4
Ely C v Walsham Le Willows	1-2*
(1-1 at the end of normal time)	
AFC Sudbury v Norwich U	3-1
Wroxham v Stowmarket T	4-1
Mildenhall T v Gorleston	5-2
Brantham Ath v King's Lynn T	1-5
Cornard U v Cambridge C	0-1
Dereham T v Hadleigh U	3-1
Bury T v Ipswich W	5-0
Leiston v Needham Market	2-1
Newmarket T v Great Yarmouth T	3-1*
(1-1 at the end of normal time)	
Great Wakering R v FC Broxbourne Bor	2-1*
(1-1 at the end of normal time)	
Walthamstow v Saffron Walden T	0-1*
(0-0 at the end of normal time)	
Takeley v Brentwood T	3-7
Hitchin T v Grays Ath	0-1*
(0-0 at the end of normal time)	
Tilbury v AFC Hornchurch	0-3
Sawbridgeworth T v Brightlingsea Regent	5-5*
Sawbridgeworth T won 5-4 on penalties	
Hullbridge Sports v Chelmsford C	4-1
Bishop's Stortford v Barkingside	4-3
Tower Hamlets v Romford	0-1
Welwyn Garden C v Ware	4-2
Tring Ath (walkover) v Hadley (withdrawn)	
Aveley v Witham T	1-0
Hayes & Yeading U v Bedfont Sports	3-2
Flackwell Heath v CB Hounslow U	9-0
Didcot T v Winslow U	4-1
Hendon v Chalfont St Peter	4-2
(Tie awarded to Chalfont St Peter – Hendon removed for fielding an ineligible player)	
Kings Langley v Newport Pagnell T	4-1
Wealdstone v Hemel Hempstead T	0-1
Aylesbury v Sandhurst T	5-1
London Tigers v Buckingham Ath	0-3
Colney Heath v Northwood	2-1*
(1-1 at the end of normal time)	
Wingate & Finchley v Uxbridge	2-0
Harefield U (walkover) v Edgware T (withdrawn)	
Leverstock Green v Enfield T	3-0
VCD Ath v Cray W	0-6
Folkestone Invicta v Hollands & Blair	3-0
Corinthian v East Grinstead T	6-0
Tooting & Mitcham U v Dartford	0-3
AFC Croydon Ath v Croydon	0-5
Thamesmead T v Tonbridge Angels	0-1
Dulwich Hamlet (walkover) v Lingfield (withdrawn)	
Chatham T v Phoenix Sports	1-4
Carshalton Ath v Eastbourne Bor	3-1
Chipstead v Ashford U	3-4*
(3-3 at the end of normal time)	
Lewes v Hackney Wick	6-2
Hampton & Richmond Bor v Knaphill	5-1
Three Bridges v Worthing	0-4
Crowborough Ath v Whitehawk	2-8
Sidlesham (withdrawn) v Arundel (walkover)	
Loxwood v Kingstonian	1-2
Haywards Heath T v Bognor Regis T	2-3*
(2-2 at the end of normal time)	
Redhill v Guildford C	1-2
Chessington & Hook U v Dorking W	3-3*
Dorking W won 7-5 on penalties	
Woking v South Park	2-3
Raynes Park Vale v Walton & Hersham	3-2
Balham v Whyteleafe	1-1*
Whyteleafe won 4-1 on penalties	
Camberley T (walkover) v Westfield (withdrawn)	
Newhaven v Metropolitan Police	1-3
Oxford C v Holmer Green	2-2*
Oxford C won 3-2 on penalties	
Kidlington v Banbury U	3-0
Andover T v Bracknell T	4-0
Windsor v Ascot U	1-2
Hungerford T v Fleet T	2-1
Reading C v Fleet Spurs	4-3*
(3-3 at the end of normal time)	
Winchester C v Moneyfields	0-4
Totton & Eling v Sholing	5-3
AFC Totton v Wimborne T	4-2*
(2-2 at the end of normal time)	
AFC Stoneham v AFC Portchester	1-0
Team Solent v Poole T	5-4*
(2-2 at the end of normal time)	
Brockenhurst v Farnborough	8-2
Longwell Green Sports v Cirencester T	1-7
Pewsey Vale v Malmesbury Vic	1-9
Tuffley R v Slimbridge	1-4
New College Swindon v Almondsbury	0-3
Yate T v Bristol Manor Farm	4-0
Wells C v Torquay U	0-6
Paulton R v Bridgwater T	2-4
Portishead T v Welton R	5-3
Clevedon T v Bath C	1-0
Odd Down v Helston Ath	2-1

SECOND QUALIFYING ROUND

North Shields v Seaham Red Star	3-1
Hartlepool U v Hebburn T	5-1
South Shields v Gateshead	3-1
Litherland Remyca v Irlam	4-0
City of Liverpool v Hyde U	1-3
St Helens T v Chorley	0-7
Chester FC v Wrexham	3-2
Salford C v Bootle	3-0*
(0-0 at the end of normal time)	
Daisy Hill v Altrincham	3-4
Barrow v AFC Fylde	0-5
Harrogate T v Guiseley	1-5
Garforth T v FC Halifax T	0-1
Ossett U v Harworthy Colliery	5-3*
(3-3 at the end of normal time)	
Tadcaster Alb v Stocksbridge Park Steels	5-2*
(2-2 at the end of normal time)	
Long Eaton U v Basford U	4-1
West Bridgford v Aylestone Park	0-2
Matlock T v Mickleover Sports	2-1
Grantham T v Bottesford T	2-1
Sheffield v Chesterfield	1-6
Coleshill T v Kidderminster H	0-3
Nuneaton Bor v Halesowen T	8-9
Stratford T v Sutton Coldfield T	2-5
AFC Telford U v Stourbridge	3-1
Hereford v Malvern T	4-0
Rushall Olympic v Rugby Bor	1-5
Anstey Nomads v Solihull Moors	2-3
Brackley T v Cogenhoe U	2-4
AFC Rushden & Diamonds v Kettering T	2-1
Rugby T v Wellingborough T	2-1
Mildenhall T v Wroxham	1-4
AFC Sudbury v Leiston	10-0
King's Lynn T v Cambridge C	2-0*
(0-0 at the end of normal time)	
Walsham Le Willows v Newmarket T	3-1*
(1-1 at the end of normal time)	
Sawbridgeworth T v Peterborough Sports	0-2
Bury T v Dereham T	1-2
Saffron Walden T v Great Wakering R	2-0
Leyton Orient v Romford	2-1
Brentwood T v Grays Ath	1-1*
Brentwood T won 4-3 on penalties	
Dagenham & Redbridge v Aveley	0-2
Bishop's Stortford v Braintree T	5-1
Hullbridge Sports v AFC Hornchurch	7-2
Chalfont St Peter v Kings Langley	1-2
Harefield U v Hemel Hempstead T	0-3
Welwyn Garden C v Buckingham Ath	9-0
Wingate & Finchley v Hayes & Yeading U	5-1
Tring Ath v Flackwell Heath	2-1*
(1-1 at the end of normal time)	
Colney Heath v Leverstock Green	2-5
Barnet v Boreham Wood	2-0
Folkestone Invicta v Cray W	1-4
Maidstone U v Phoenix Sports	1-2

Corinthian v Dartford	1-2
Dover Ath v Lewes	0-4
Metropolitan Police v Bromley	3-2*
(2-2 at the end of normal time)	
Dulwich Hamlet v Tonbridge Angels	2-1
Dorking W v Carshalton Ath	1-6
Bognor Regis T v Guildford C	3-1
Croydon v Camberley T	2-2*
Croydon won 4-3 on penalties	
Raynes Park Vale v Arundel	5-1
Kingstonian v Whitehawk	1-2
Ashford U v Hampton & Richmond Bor	1-5
South Park v Worthing	0-5
Sutton U v Whyteleafe	3-1
Ascot U v Hungerford T	2-1
Kidlington v Andover T	0-4
Reading C v Aylesbury	4-1
Malmesbury Vic v Didcot T	1-3
Oxford C v Maidenhead U	0-5
Totton & Eling v AFC Totton	3-1
Havant & Waterlooville v Moneyfields	1-3
AFC Stoneham v Brockenhurst	A-A, 1-4
(First match abandoned)	
Almondsbury v Team Solent	0-1
Eastleigh v Aldershot T	1-3
Torquay U v Slimbridge	1-0
Portishead T v Yate T	3-4
Clevedon T v Bridgwater T	3-0
Cirencester T v Odd Down	1-0

THIRD QUALIFYING ROUND

South Shields v Chorley	3-2
Guiseley v Ossett U	13-0
Tadcaster Alb v Altrincham	2-4
FC Halifax T v Litherland Remyca	5-0
Hartlepool U v Chester FC	2-4
Hyde U v Salford C	0-1
North Shields v AFC Fylde	2-1
Matlock T v Sutton Coldfield T	1-2
Long Eaton U v Hereford	3-1
Kidderminster H v Chesterfield	1-0
AFC Telford U v Rugby T	2-1
Rugby Bor v Solihull Moors	3-1*
(1-1 at the end of normal time)	
Cogenhoe U v Aylestone Park	1-0
Grantham T v Halesowen T	4-2
AFC Sudbury v Wroxham	11-1
Hullbridge Sports v Aveley	3-2
Barnet v Bishop's Stortford	3-1
Brentwood T v Saffron Walden T	2-1
King's Lynn T v Dereham T	2-0
Peterborough Sports v Walsham Le Willows	3-2
AFC Rushden & Diamonds v Leyton Orient	2-3
Leverstock Green v Maidenhead U	0-8
Ascot U v Wingate & Finchley	1-2
Kings Langley v Tring Ath	A-A, 9-1
(First match abandoned)	
Reading C v Hemel Hempstead T	0-4
Welwyn Garden C v Andover T	1-3*
(1-1 at the end of normal time)	
Phoenix Sports v Hampton & Richmond Bor	3-2
Croydon v Lewes	2-3
Metropolitan Police v Whitehawk	2-3
Dartford v Dulwich Hamlet	0-3
Cray W v Raynes Park Vale	3-0
Bognor Regis T v Sutton U	2-3*
(1-1 at the end of normal time)	
Carshalton Ath v Worthing	1-5
Team Solent v Moneyfields	0-1
Torquay U v Yate T	7-2
Cirencester T v Aldershot T	1-4*
(1-1 at the end of normal time)	
Clevedon T v Brockenhurst	8-1
Didcot T v Totton & Eling	1-3

FIRST ROUND

North Shields v Bury	0-7
Doncaster R v Rochdale	0-3
Fleetwood T v Carlisle U	2-1
Morecambe v Crewe Alex	0-2
Blackpool v Guiseley	4-0
Tranmere R v Accrington S	0-3
FC Halifax T v Sunderland	0-1
Salford C v Bradford C	3-1
Chester FC v Barnsley	2-1
Altrincham v Oldham Ath	1-6
South Shields v Macclesfield T	6-2
Scunthorpe U v AFC Telford U	6-1
Rugby Bor v Sutton Coldfield T	2-6
Shrewsbury T v Lincoln C	0-1
Cogenhoe U v Grantham T	2-1
Grimsby T v Mansfield T	2-3
Long Eaton U v Milton Keynes D	1-2
Port Vale v Kidderminster H	6-1
Walsall v Notts Co	1-2
Burton Alb v Coventry C	1-2
Stevenage v Colchester U	3-2
Peterborough Sports v Barnet	0-1
Cambridge U v AFC Sudbury	2-1
Leyton Orient v Southend U	3-4*
(3-3 at the end of normal time)	
Luton T v Brentwood T	4-1
Hullbridge Sports v Peterborough U	0-2
Northampton T v King's Lynn T	4-0
Worthing v Cray W	1-2
Wingate & Finchley v Kings Langley	5-3
Phoenix Sports v Andover T	1-4
Lewes v Sutton U	2-3
Charlton Ath v Whitehawk	6-0
Hemel Hempstead T v Oxford U	0-3
AFC Wimbledon v Gillingham	1-3
Maidenhead U v Dulwich Hamlet	5-0
Exeter C v Plymouth Arg	3-2
Newport Co v Yeovil T	1-2
Portsmouth v Bristol R	5-2
Forest Green R v Cheltenham T	1-3
Aldershot T v Clevedon T	1-4
Torquay U v Totton & Eling	4-1
Swindon T v Moneyfields	7-0

SECOND ROUND

Lincoln C v South Shields	4-2
Bury v Fleetwood T	3-2
Scunthorpe U v Blackpool	1-2*
(1-1 at the end of normal time)	
Mansfield T v Chester FC	2-0
Sunderland v Oldham Ath	4-1
Accrington Stanley v Notts Co	2-1
Rochdale v Milton Keynes D	2-0
Port Vale v Sutton Coldfield T	3-1
Salford C v Crewe Alex	1-2
Cogenhoe U v Coventry C	3-2
Yeovil T v Cambridge U	1-4
Charlton Ath v Southend U	2-0
Clevedon T v Sutton U	1-2
(Tie awarded to Clevedon T – Sutton U removed for fielding an ineligible player)	
Peterborough U v Luton T	3-0
Oxford U v Barnet	1-0
Stevenage v Exeter C	4-0
Northampton T v Swindon T	2-0
Maidenhead U v Torquay U	3-1
Cray W v Portsmouth	0-4
Cheltenham T v Gillingham	0-4
Wingate & Finchley v Andover T	2-2*
Andover T won 8-7 on penalties	

THIRD ROUND

Sheffield W v Stoke C	2-3
Blackburn R v Gillingham	1-2
Everton v Sunderland	4-1
Burnley v Oxford U	1-1*
Oxford U won 3-2 on penalties	
Huddersfield T v Peterborough U	0-2
Watford v Birmingham C	1-0
Preston NE v Charlton Ath	2-2*
Preston NE won 3-1 on penalties	
Leicester C v Fulham	2-1*
(1-1 at the end of normal time)	
Arsenal v Northampton T	2-0
Accrington S v Leeds U	4-2*
(2-2 at the end of normal time)	
Wolverhampton W v Wigan Ath	1-2
Hull C v Cardiff C	2-1
Maidenhead U v Nottingham F	1-5
Middlesbrough v Sheffield U	0-1
Bristol C v Crewe Alex	1-2
WBA v Lincoln C	5-1
Liverpool v Portsmouth	3-2
Manchester U v Chelsea	4-3
West Ham U v Brighton & HA	1-1*
Brighton & HA won 5-4 on penalties	

Southampton v Rotherham U	2-0
Aston Villa v Swansea C	4-2
Blackpool v Derby Co	1-2
Ipswich T v Andover T	4-0
Bolton W v Newcastle U	2-1
Bournemouth v Mansfield T	2-1
Stevenage v Bury	2-4*
(2-2 at the end of normal time)	
Cogenhoe U v Crystal Palace	1-2
Millwall v Tottenham H	1-2*
(1-1 at the end of normal time)	
Port Vale v Norwich C	2-3
Clevedon T v Manchester C	0-4
QPR v Rochdale	3-2*
(1-1 at the end of normal time)	
Cambridge U v Reading	1-3

FOURTH ROUND

Stoke C v Everton	2-2*
Everton won 3-1 on penalties	
Gillingham v Ipswich T	1-2
Derby Co v Sheffield U	3-0
Hull C v Wigan Ath	2-6
Oxford U v Bournemouth	0-3
Leicester C v Crewe Alex	4-0
Arsenal v Tottenham H	5-2*
(2-2 at the end of normal time)	
Crystal Palace v Bolton W	2-4
WBA v QPR	5-1
Manchester U v Brighton & HA	1-3
Preston NE v Norwich C	3-0
Liverpool v Accrington S	4-0
Aston Villa v Reading	4-1
Peterborough U v Bury	0-1
Watford v Southampton	2-1
Manchester C v Nottingham F	4-1

FIFTH ROUND

Preston NE v Bury	0-2
Bournemouth v Aston Villa	2-0
Arsenal v WBA	1-2
Everton v Brighton & HA	2-0
Bolton W v Leicester C	0-3
Liverpool v Wigan Ath	2-0
Derby Co v Manchester C	1-2
Watford v Ipswich T	4-1

SIXTH ROUND

Leicester C v Watford	1-2*
(1-1 at the end of normal time)	
WBA v Everton	4-3
Bournemouth v Manchester C	1-4
Bury v Liverpool	1-5

SEMI-FINALS

Liverpool v Watford	2-1
Manchester C v WBA	4-2

FA YOUTH CUP FINAL 2019

Academy Stadium, Manchester, Thursday 25 April 2019

Manchester C (1) 1 *(Touaizi 45)*

Liverpool (0) 1 *(Duncan 86)* 3878

Manchester C: Moulden; Diounkou, Garcia (Dele-Bashiru 59), Harwood-Bellis (Ogunby 116), Frimpong, McDonald, Knight (Ogbeta 90), Doyle, Touaizi, Nmecha, Bernabe (Palmer 107).
Liverpool: Jaros; Williams N, Larouci, Williams R, Boyes, Clarkson (Longstaff 78), Sharif, Cain (Bearne 101), Glatzel, Duncan, Dixon-Bonner.
Referee: Darren England.
aet; Liverpool won 5-3 on penalties.

THE FA COUNTY YOUTH CUP 2018–19

**After extra time.*

FIRST ROUND

Essex v Hertfordshire	3-0
Bedfordshire v Cornwall	0-5

SECOND ROUND

Cheshire v Sheffield & Hallamshire	7-2
Northumberland v Nottinghamshire	0-3
Lancashire v Staffordshire	4-0
Shropshire v Isle of Man	1-2
Cumberland v Westmorland	4-2
Durham v Manchester	1-4
West Riding v Liverpool	2-6
Birmingham v North Riding	6-1
Guernsey v Essex	0-5
Cornwall v Norfolk	3-4*
(3-3 at the end of normal time)	
Amateur Football Alliance v London	1-0
Kent v Gloucestershire	2-6
Middlesex v Wiltshire	14-0
Northamptonshire v Devon	4-2
Sussex (walkover) v Herefordshire (withdrawn)	
Berks & Bucks v Somerset	3-2*
(2-2 at the end of normal time)	

THIRD ROUND

Berks & Bucks v Cumberland	7-2
Lancashire v Cheshire	1-2
Manchester v Essex	4-1
Sussex v Northamptonshire	5-0
Nottinghamshire v Amateur Football Alliance	1-3
Norfolk v Isle of Man	3-1
Liverpool v Middlesex	2-1
Gloucestershire v Birmingham	3-2

FOURTH ROUND

Liverpool v Amateur Football Alliance	2-1
Gloucestershire v Cheshire	2-2*
Cheshire won 4-2 on penalties	
Sussex v Norfolk	0-1
Manchester v Berks & Bucks	4-2

SEMI-FINALS

Cheshire v Norfolk	1-3
Manchester v Liverpool	5-0

FA COUNTY YOUTH CUP FINAL 2019

Rochdale, Saturday 13 April 2019

Manchester (2) 3 *(Chukwu 1, Dyson 23, 88)*

Norfolk (0) 0 402

Manchester: Neave; Wright, Rhodes, Lockett, Hall, Adetiloye, Burrows, Doyle, Ognrinde, Chukwu, Dyson.
Substitutes: Foulds, Voss, Moncrieffe, Ditchfield, Shepherd.
Norfolk: Milligan; Tinkler, Philpott, Johnson, Ford, Rich, Wing, Cottingham, Bemrose, Forbes, Watts.
Substitutes: Lane, Upston, Lane, Gilding-Hewitt, Wengrzik.
Referee: David Rock.

THE FA SUNDAY CUP 2018–19

**After extra time.*

FIRST ROUND

Newton Aycliffe Iron Horse v Dawdon Colliery Welfare	1-3
Amble Tavern v Peterlee Catholic Club	0-2
Thornton U (withdrawn) v Queens Park (walkover)	
Dock v Campfield	0-3
Main Line Social v Melling Vic	1-3
Clay Brow v Mayfair	0-4
Lobster v Bleak House	2-1
Custys v FC Walkers Hounds	3-1
Linthwaite v Leeds City R	0-1
Oakenshaw v Canada	5-3
Mottram v Kirkdale	1-0
BRNESC (walkover) v Garston (withdrawn)	
Eastwood v Callow End	2-0
Birstall Stamford v Sporting Dynamo	8-2
AFC Jacks v Austin Ex Apprentices	6-4
Asianos v Borussia Martlesham	4-1*
(1-1 at the end of normal time)	
Global (Sunday) v Priory Sports	3-3*
Global won 5-4 on penalties	
Larkspur R v St Josephs (Luton)	0-2
AC Sportsman v Club Lewsey	1-4
Magpies 91 v Old Southall	1-7
AFC 2015 v Lambeth All Stars	2-5
Rudgwick Panthers SX v Broadwater	3-5
Watersedge Park v Lebeqs Tavern Courage	1-5

SECOND ROUND

Burradon & New Fordley v Mottram	5-1
Joker v Pineapple	4-1
Peterlee Catholic Club v Greenside	2-3
Crossflatts Village v Dengo U	2-0
Kensington Fields v Campfield	4-0
Home Bargains v Sunderland Southwick	0-1*
(0-0 at the end of normal time)	
AFC Blackburn Leisure (withdrawn) v Melling Vic (walkover)	
FC Dovecot v LIV Supplies	1-3
Custys v Oyster Martyrs	1-3
Allerton v Hope Inn Whites	4-2
Queens Park v Oakenshaw	7-0
Dawdon Colliery Welfare v Lobster	2-4
Leeds City R v BRNESC	4-1
Western Avenue v Mayfair	0-2
Blucher Blue Star v Huyton Cons	0-1
Billingham The Merlin v Rock Ferry Social	
(Tie awarded to Billingham The Merlin – Rock Ferry Social removed)	
Eastwood v OJM	0-6
Rolls Royce v Oadby Ath	0-4
Attenborough Cavaliers v Falcons	3-3*
Attenborough Cavaliers won 4-2 on penalties	
Hampton Sunday v Leighton Madrid	2-3
AFC Jacks v FC Topps	6-1
Black Horse (Redditch) v RHP Sports & Social	4-0
Newark T (Sunday) v Birstall Stamford	3-5*
(3-3 at the end of normal time)	
Real Milan v Club Lewsey	3-7
St Josephs (Luton) v Global (Sunday)	5-3
Flaunden v Old Southall	1-5
Aylesbury Flooring v NLO	4-2
Asianos v Gym U	1-4
East Christchurch SSC v Navy Inn	3-2*
(2-2 at the end of normal time)	
Barnes v Lambeth All Stars	0-5
Broadwater (walkover) v Poplar (withdrawn)	
Portland v Lebeqs Tavern Courage	4-1

THIRD ROUND

Greenside v Crossflatts Village	3-0
Queens Park v Mayfair	0-2
Leeds City R v Sunderland Southwick	0-3
Lobster v Allerton	5-3
Melling Vic v Kensington Fields	2-3
Billingham The Merlin v Joker	0-2
Oyster Martyrs v Huyton Cons	4-2
Burradon & New Fordley v LIV Supplies	6-2
AFC Jacks v OJM	4-1
Birstall Stamford v Oadby Ath	4-1
Attenborough Cavaliers v Black Horse (Redditch)	1-2
Old Southall v Club Lewsey	3-1
Leighton Madrid v Aylesbury Flooring	0-7
Gym U v St Josephs (Luton)	0-2
East Christchurch SSC v Portland	4-2
Broadwater v Lambeth All Stars	1-2
(Tie awarded to Broadwater – Lambeth All Stars removed)	

FOURTH ROUND

Burradon & New Fordley v Kensington Fields	4-0
Sunderland Southwick v Greenside	3-0
Mayfair v Lobster	2-2*
Mayfair won 9-8 on penalties	
Joker v Oyster Martyrs	1-0*
(0-0 at the end of normal time)	
Birstall Stamford v Old Southall	5-1
Black Horse (Redditch) v St Josephs (Luton)	2-2*
Black Horse (Redditch) won 3-2 on penalties	
Broadwater v East Christchurch SSC	0-3
AFC Jacks v Aylesbury Flooring	3-4*
(2-2 at the end of normal time)	

QUARTER-FINALS

Mayfair v Joker	2-2*
Joker won 5-3 on penalties	
Burradon & New Fordley v Sunderland Southwick	2-3
East Christchurch SSC v Birstall Stamford	0-2
Black Horse (Redditch) v Aylesbury Flooring	3-5

SEMI-FINALS

Sunderland Southwick v Aylesbury Flooring	0-2
Birstall Stamford v Joker	3-0

FA SUNDAY CUP FINAL 2019

Peterborough, Sunday 28 April 2019

Aylesbury Flooring (0) 3 *(Deacon 77, Freshwater 87 (pen), Goss 90)*

Birstall Stamford (1) 1 *(Seal 29)*

Aylesbury Flooring: Smith; Page, Freshwater, Jenkins (Roberts 13), Collins M, Parsons (Collins T 90), Kedzierski, Hogg, Goss, Deacon, Brown (Seaton 48).
Birstall Stamford: Shiliam; Lane, Dodd, Sibson, Armstrong, Morris (Jelly 83), Parry (Bibby 65), Barrett (Dodd 52), Young, Seal, Pallett.
Referee: Michael Salisbury.

PREMIER LEAGUE 2 2018–19

**After extra time.*

PREMIER LEAGUE 2 – LEAGUE 1

DIVISION ONE	P	W	D	L	F	A	GD	Pts
1 Everton	22	12	5	5	31	14	17	41
2 Arsenal	22	10	7	5	48	36	12	37
3 Brighton & HA	22	9	8	5	37	27	10	35
4 Liverpool	22	9	7	6	38	27	11	34
5 Blackburn R	22	9	4	9	38	37	1	31
6 Chelsea	22	9	4	9	34	33	1	31
7 Derby Co	22	9	3	10	29	34	–5	30
8 Manchester C	22	9	3	10	38	48	–10	30
9 Tottenham H	22	7	7	8	26	38	–12	28
10 Leicester C	22	8	3	11	24	33	–9	27
11 West Ham U	22	8	2	12	41	43	–2	26
12 Swansea C	22	3	7	12	28	42	–14	16

DIVISION TWO	P	W	D	L	F	A	GD	Pts
1 Wolverhampton W	22	13	4	5	45	22	23	43
2 Southampton	22	13	4	5	37	21	16	43
3 Reading	22	12	4	6	45	33	12	40
4 Newcastle U	22	13	1	8	46	37	9	40
5 Aston Villa	22	11	4	7	35	30	5	37
6 Manchester U	22	8	6	8	33	31	2	30
7 Stoke C	22	7	7	8	42	37	5	28
8 Middlesbrough	22	6	8	8	32	36	–4	26
9 WBA	22	5	9	8	33	38	–5	24
10 Fulham	22	5	7	10	26	34	–8	22
11 Norwich C	22	5	4	13	30	52	–22	19
12 Sunderland	22	2	6	14	14	47	–33	12

PROMOTION PLAY-OFFS – SEMI-FINALS

Southampton v Aston Villa 2-0
Reading v Newcastle U 2-2
Newcastle U won 3-2 on penalties

PROMOTION PLAY-OFFS – FINAL

Southampton v Newcastle U 2-1

PREMIER LEAGUE 2 – LEAGUE 2

NORTH DIVISION	P	W	D	L	F	A	GD	Pts
1 Leeds U	28	17	6	5	59	31	28	57
2 Birmingham C	28	14	6	8	47	25	22	48
3 Crewe Alex	28	13	8	7	46	37	9	47
4 Burnley	28	14	3	11	61	48	13	45
5 Nottingham F	28	12	7	9	53	42	11	43
6 Bolton W	28	13	4	11	39	42	–3	43
7 Barnsley	28	10	9	9	36	44	–8	39
8 Sheffield W	28	11	5	12	35	46	–11	38
9 Sheffield U	28	9	9	10	35	41	–6	36
10 Hull C	28	5	6	17	30	57	–27	21

SOUTH DIVISION	P	W	D	L	F	A	GD	Pts
1 Ipswich T	28	15	7	6	67	38	29	52
2 Coventry C	28	13	6	9	49	38	11	45
3 Crystal Palace	28	12	6	10	55	49	6	42
4 Charlton Ath	28	11	7	10	44	41	3	40
5 Bristol C	28	11	5	12	45	49	–4	38
6 Millwall	28	10	7	11	32	31	1	37
7 Cardiff C	28	8	8	12	41	43	–2	32
8 QPR	28	8	7	13	54	61	–7	31
9 Watford	28	6	6	16	32	50	–18	24
10 Colchester U	28	6	2	20	30	77	–47	20

Teams play each team in their own division twice, and each team in the other division once.

KNOCKOUT STAGE – SEMI-FINALS

Leeds U v Coventry C 3-2*
Ipswich T v Birmingham C 0-3

FINAL

Leeds U v Birmingham C 0-0*
Leeds U won 4-2 on penalties

FA PREMIER LEAGUE 2 – LEAGUE CUP

**After extra time.*

GROUP STAGE

Group A Table	P	W	D	L	F	A	GD	Pts
1 Stoke C	6	4	1	1	17	8	9	13
2 Sunderland	6	4	0	2	18	13	5	12
3 Peterborough U	6	2	0	4	11	18	–7	6
4 Charlton Ath	6	1	1	4	6	13	–7	4

Group B Table	P	W	D	L	F	A	GD	Pts
1 Everton	6	4	2	0	11	5	6	14
2 Blackburn R	6	3	1	2	14	6	8	10
3 Sheffield U	6	3	0	3	9	9	0	9
4 Doncaster R	6	0	1	5	6	20	–14	1

Group C Table	P	W	D	L	F	A	GD	Pts
1 Burnley	6	2	3	1	9	12	–3	9
2 Bournemouth	6	2	2	2	13	10	3	8
3 Liverpool	6	1	4	1	5	4	1	7
4 WBA	6	1	3	2	6	7	–1	6

Group D Table	P	W	D	L	F	A	GD	Pts
1 Nottingham F	6	5	1	0	17	6	11	16
2 Leicester C	6	1	3	2	8	8	0	6
3 Exeter C	6	1	3	2	7	11	–4	6
4 Norwich C	6	0	3	3	5	12	–7	3

Group E Table	P	W	D	L	F	A	GD	Pts
1 Swansea C	6	3	2	1	9	5	4	11
2 Wolverhampton W	6	3	2	1	7	5	2	11
3 Oxford U	6	2	1	3	6	7	–1	7
4 Hull C	6	1	1	4	6	11	–5	4

Group F Table	P	W	D	L	F	A	GD	Pts
1 Derby Co	6	4	1	1	18	4	14	13
2 Aston Villa	6	4	0	2	15	6	9	12
3 Plymouth Arg	6	1	3	2	6	8	–2	6
4 Bristol C	6	0	2	4	4	25	–21	2

Group G Table	P	W	D	L	F	A	GD	Pts
1 Reading	6	4	1	1	15	7	8	13
2 Fulham	6	4	0	2	16	5	11	12
3 Birmingham C	6	3	1	2	11	9	2	10
4 Colchester U	6	0	0	6	3	24	–21	0

Group H Table	P	W	D	L	F	A	GD	Pts
1 Leeds U	6	4	0	2	14	8	6	12
2 Newcastle U	6	3	2	1	11	7	4	11
3 Southampton	6	3	1	2	18	10	8	10
4 Notts Co	6	0	1	5	6	24	–18	1

ROUND OF 16

Leeds U v Fulham 2-2*
Leeds U won 5-4 on penalties
Nottingham F v Bournemouth 2-1
Reading v Newcastle U 1-2
Burnley v Leicester C 1-0
Stoke C v Blackburn R 1-4
Swansea C v Aston Villa 2-0
Derby Co v Wolverhampton W 2-1
Everton v Sunderland 2-1

QUARTER-FINALS

Burnley v Leeds U 1-3
Nottingham F v Swansea C 0-0*
Swansea C won 3-0 on penalties
Newcastle U v Derby Co 3-2*
Everton v Blackburn R 2-1

SEMI-FINALS

Leeds U v Newcastle U 0-3
Swansea C v Everton 0-2

FINAL

Everton v Newcastle U 1-0

PREMIER LEAGUE INTERNATIONAL CUP 2018–19

**After extra time.*

GROUP STAGE

GROUP A

Southampton v Dinamo Zagreb	1-0
Southampton v Porto	1-1
West Ham U v Porto	2-1
West Ham U v Dinamo Zagreb	0-2
Porto v Dinamo Zagreb	1-4
Southampton v West Ham U	3-0

Group A Table	P	W	D	L	F	A	D	Pts
Southampton	3	2	1	0	5	1	4	7
Dinamo Zagreb	3	2	0	1	6	2	4	6
West Ham U	3	1	0	2	2	6	–4	3
Porto	3	0	1	2	3	7	–4	1

GROUP B

Leicester C v Reading	0-2
Reading v Sparta Prague	2-2
Sparta Prague v Feyenoord	0-8
Leicester C v Sparta Prague	1-0
Reading v Feyenoord	2-0
Leicester C v Feyenoord	3-1

Group B Table	P	W	D	L	F	A	D	Pts
Reading	3	2	1	0	6	2	4	7
Leicester C	3	2	0	1	4	3	1	6
Feyenoord	3	1	0	2	9	5	4	3
Sparta Prague	3	0	1	2	2	11	–9	1

GROUP C

Athletic Bilbao v Wolfsburg	0-4
Norwich C v Athletic Bilbao	0-3
Tottenham H v Wolfsburg	2-1
Norwich C v Wolfsburg	2-2
Norwich C v Tottenham H	2-2
Tottenham H v Athletic Bilbao	5-4

Group C Table	P	W	D	L	F	A	D	Pts
Tottenham H	3	2	1	0	9	7	2	7
Wolfsburg	3	1	1	1	7	4	3	4
Athletic Bilbao	3	1	0	2	7	9	–2	3
Norwich C	3	0	2	1	4	7	–3	2

GROUP D

Brighton & HA v Everton	2-2
Everton v Benfica	2-0
Brighton & HA v Benfica	2-0
Everton v Bayern Munich	1-4
Bayern Munich v Benfica	0-1
Brighton & HA v Bayern Munich	0-2

Group D Table	P	W	D	L	F	A	D	Pts
Bayern Munich	3	2	0	1	6	2	4	6
Brighton & HA	3	1	1	1	4	4	0	4
Everton	3	1	1	1	5	6	–1	4
Benfica	3	1	0	2	1	4	–3	3

GROUP E

Swansea C v Villarreal	1-1
Hertha Berlin v Villarreal	0-1
Liverpool v Villarreal	0-7
Liverpool v Hertha Berlin	3-1
Swansea C v Hertha Berlin	1-4
Liverpool v Swansea C	2-0

Group E Table	P	W	D	L	F	A	D	Pts
Villarreal	3	2	1	0	9	1	8	7
Liverpool	3	2	0	1	5	8	–3	6
Hertha Berlin	3	1	0	2	5	5	0	3
Swansea C	3	0	1	2	2	7	–5	1

GROUP F

Derby Co v Paris Saint-Germain	1-1
Derby Co v PSV Eindhoven	3-1
Paris Saint-Germain v PSV Eindhoven	2-4
Derby Co v Manchester U	1-1
Manchester U v PSV Eindhoven	0-0
Manchester U v Paris Saint-Germain	3-0

Group F Table	P	W	D	L	F	A	D	Pts
Manchester U	3	1	2	0	4	1	3	5
Derby Co	3	1	2	0	5	3	2	5
PSV Eindhoven	3	1	1	1	5	5	0	4
Paris Saint-Germain	3	0	1	2	3	8	–5	1

QUARTER-FINALS

Manchester U v Reading	1-3
Tottenham H v Dinamo Zagreb	0-1
Southampton v Villareal	2-1
Leicester C v Bayern Munich	1-1*

Bayern Munich won 5-4 on penalties.

SEMI-FINALS

Reading v Bayern Munich	1-3
Southampton v Dinamo Zagreb	1-3

PREMIER LEAGUE INTERNATIONAL CUP FINAL 2019

Millwall, Thursday 2 May 2019

Bayern Munich (0) 2 *(Wriedt 46, Shabani 90)*

Dinamo Zagreb (0) 0

Bayern Munich: Wagner; Feldhahn, Mayer, Turkkalesi, Awouda, Mai, Shabani, Franzke (Kohn 90), Woo-Yeong (Rochelt 68), Wriedt, Zirkzee (Nollenberger 88).
Dinamo Zagreb: Horkas; Barisic (Baturina 84), Gjira, Gogic, Sutalo, Moro, Tolic (Gvardiol 72), Cuze, Franjic, Marin (Jovicevic 75), Sipos.
Referee: David Rock (England).

UNDER-18 PROFESSIONAL DEVELOPMENT LEAGUE 2018–19

PREMIER LEAGUE UNDER-18 DEVELOPMENT LEAGUE 1

NORTH DIVISION

	P	W	D	L	F	A	GD	Pts
1 Derby Co	22	16	3	3	63	27	36	51
2 Liverpool	22	16	3	3	59	32	27	51
3 Everton	22	14	2	6	65	34	31	44
4 Manchester U	22	12	7	3	60	39	21	43
5 Middlesbrough	22	11	2	9	52	48	4	35
6 Stoke C	22	10	2	10	42	39	3	32
7 Blackburn R	22	9	3	10	48	49	–1	30
8 Manchester C	22	7	8	7	46	34	12	29
9 WBA	22	4	6	12	44	62	–18	18
10 Wolverhampton W	22	4	2	16	22	47	–25	14
11 Newcastle U	22	3	5	14	17	62	–45	14
12 Sunderland	22	1	7	14	20	65	–45	10

SOUTH DIVISION

	P	W	D	L	F	A	GD	Pts
1 Arsenal	22	20	0	2	86	23	63	60
2 Tottenham H	22	18	2	2	81	26	55	56
3 Chelsea	22	13	5	4	42	24	18	44
4 Southampton	22	11	2	9	48	41	7	35
5 Brighton & HA	22	11	1	10	40	37	3	34
6 Aston Villa	22	9	2	11	44	47	–3	29
7 Leicester C	22	9	2	11	37	46	–9	29
8 West Ham U	22	9	2	11	38	52	–14	29
9 Fulham	22	6	6	10	36	45	–9	24
10 Reading	22	6	1	15	22	53	–31	19
11 Swansea C	22	3	3	16	19	53	–34	12
12 Norwich C	22	3	2	17	24	70	–46	11

FINAL
Derby Co v Arsenal 5-2

PREMIER LEAGUE UNDER-18 DEVELOPMENT LEAGUE 2

NORTH DIVISION

	P	W	D	L	F	A	GD	Pts
1 Sheffield W	28	17	8	3	69	22	47	59
2 Leeds U	28	19	2	7	66	37	29	59
3 Nottingham F	28	15	5	8	59	33	26	50
4 Sheffield U	28	14	8	6	48	38	10	50
5 Burnley	28	15	4	9	64	54	10	49
6 Barnsley	28	12	5	11	47	45	2	41
7 Birmingham C	28	12	3	13	55	57	–2	39
8 Hull C	28	8	5	15	44	51	–7	29
9 Bolton W	28	7	5	16	49	72	–23	26
10 Crewe Alex	28	7	5	16	43	77	–34	26

SOUTH DIVISION

	P	W	D	L	F	A	GD	Pts
1 Cardiff C	28	17	3	8	61	31	30	54
2 Ipswich T	28	17	2	9	68	52	16	53
3 Millwall	28	13	6	9	62	40	22	45
4 QPR	28	13	3	12	53	51	2	42
5 Crystal Palace	28	11	5	12	51	54	–3	38
6 Charlton Ath	28	10	5	13	46	46	0	35
7 Bristol C	28	11	2	15	42	50	–8	35
8 Watford	28	8	7	13	50	63	–13	31
9 Coventry C	28	6	6	16	33	69	–36	24
10 Colchester U	28	1	5	22	34	102	–68	8

Teams play each team in their own division twice, and each team in the other division once.

KNOCKOUT STAGE – SEMI-FINALS
Caridff C v Leeds U 2-1
Sheffield W v Ipswich T 1-0

FINAL
Sheffield W v Cardiff C 3-2

U18 PROFESSIONAL DEVELOPMENT LEAGUE CUP

**After extra time.*

Group A Table	P	W	D	L	F	A	GD	Pts
1 Middlesbrough	3	2	1	0	12	3	9	7
2 Tottenham H	3	2	1	0	7	4	3	7
3 Wolverhampton W	3	0	1	2	1	6	–5	1
4 Swansea C	3	0	1	2	2	9	–7	1

Group B Table	P	W	D	L	F	A	GD	Pts
1 Liverpool	3	3	0	0	13	2	11	9
2 Stoke C	3	2	0	1	11	7	4	6
3 Southampton	3	1	0	2	4	7	–3	3
4 Reading	3	0	0	3	2	14	–12	0

Group C Table	P	W	D	L	F	A	GD	Pts
1 Derby Co	3	3	0	0	12	3	9	9
2 Aston Villa	3	1	1	1	5	6	–1	4
3 Sunderland	3	0	2	1	4	8	–4	2
4 Brighton & HA	3	0	1	2	5	9	–4	1

Group D Table	P	W	D	L	F	A	GD	Pts
1 Everton	3	3	0	0	14	2	12	9
2 Arsenal	3	1	1	1	5	2	3	4
3 WBA	3	1	1	1	2	11	–9	4
4 Fulham	3	0	0	3	2	8	–6	0

Group E Table	P	W	D	L	F	A	GD	Pts
1 Blackburn R	3	2	0	1	8	4	4	6
2 Manchester C	3	2	0	1	8	4	4	6
3 Leicester C	3	1	0	2	5	8	–3	3
4 West Ham U	3	1	0	2	4	9	–5	3

Group F Table	P	W	D	L	F	A	GD	Pts
1 Manchester U	3	3	0	0	7	0	7	9
2 Chelsea	3	2	0	1	8	4	4	6
3 Newcastle U	3	1	0	2	2	5	–3	3
4 Norwich C	3	0	0	3	2	10	–8	0

QUARTER-FINALS
Derby Co v Tottenham H 2-0
Liverpool v Manchester U 2-3*
Stoke C v Manchester C 2-4
Middlesbrough v Everton 4-0

SEMI-FINALS
Manchester C v Manchester U 3-0
Middlesbrough v Derby Co 1-0

FINAL
Middlesbrough v Manchester C 0-1

CENTRAL LEAGUE 2018–19

NORTH	P	W	D	L	F	A	GD	Pts
1 Wigan Ath	14	9	3	2	45	17	28	30
2 Rotherham U	14	8	2	4	31	30	1	26
3 Port Vale	14	7	2	5	28	24	4	23
4 Doncaster R	14	7	2	5	23	26	–3	23
5 Notts Co	14	6	3	5	29	28	1	21
6 Morecambe	14	5	2	7	20	24	–4	17
7 Mansfield T	14	5	1	8	21	26	–5	16
8 Grimsby T	14	0	3	11	15	37	–22	3

SOUTH	P	W	D	L	F	A	GD	Pts
1 Milton Keynes D	13	9	1	3	37	21	16	28
2 Exeter C	13	7	2	4	34	15	19	23
3 AFC Wimbledon	13	7	1	5	30	17	13	22
4 Plymouth Arg	13	6	4	3	27	17	10	22
5 Bristol R	13	6	4	3	22	22	0	22
6 Southend U	13	5	3	5	27	37	–10	18
7 Peterborough U	13	4	4	5	33	37	–4	16
8 Forest Green R	13	4	0	9	23	39	–16	12
9 Cheltenham T	13	3	1	9	24	37	–13	10
10 Luton T	13	1	6	6	10	25	–15	9

CENTRAL LEAGUE CUP

NORTH	P	W	D	L	F	A	GD	Pts
1 Fleetwood T	3	2	0	1	9	4	5	6
2 Macclesfield T	3	2	0	1	7	8	–1	6
3 Huddersfield T	3	1	0	2	7	7	0	3
4 Morecambe	3	1	0	2	3	7	–4	3

NORTH CENTRAL	P	W	D	L	F	A	GD	Pts
1 Notts Co	4	4	0	0	15	5	10	12
2 Mansfield T	4	3	0	1	14	9	5	9
3 Rotherham U	4	1	0	3	6	10	–4	3
4 Doncaster R	4	1	0	3	7	12	–5	3
5 Peterborough U	4	1	0	3	7	13	–6	3

SOUTH	P	W	D	L	F	A	GD	Pts
1 Bournemouth	3	2	1	0	7	2	5	7
2 AFC Wimbledon	3	1	2	0	7	3	4	5
3 Southend U	3	1	1	1	7	6	1	4
4 Portsmouth	3	0	0	3	3	13	–10	0

SOUTH CENTRAL	P	W	D	L	F	A	GD	Pts
1 Shrewsbury T	3	3	0	0	10	3	7	9
2 Bristol R	3	2	0	1	6	5	1	6
3 Walsall	3	1	0	2	4	8	–4	3
4 Burton Alb	3	0	0	3	4	8	–4	0

SEMI-FINALS

Shrewsbury T v Bournemouth 1-2
Fleetwood T v Notts Co 0-3

FINAL

Notts Co v Bournemouth 0-2

EFL YOUTH ALLIANCE 2018–19

NORTH EAST	P	W	D	L	F	A	GD	Pts
1 Grimsby T	24	13	7	4	43	23	20	46
2 Doncaster R	24	13	5	6	54	33	21	44
3 Bradford C	24	12	7	5	39	29	10	43
4 Mansfield T	24	12	4	8	58	36	22	40
5 Hartlepool U	24	12	4	8	40	32	8	40
6 Burton Alb	24	11	4	9	42	34	8	37
7 Lincoln C	24	9	6	9	36	41	–5	33
8 Oldham Ath	24	9	4	11	47	46	1	31
9 Notts Co	24	8	6	10	36	37	–1	30
10 Chesterfield	24	9	3	12	39	44	–5	30
11 Rotherham U	24	8	4	12	42	55	–13	28
12 Scunthorpe U	24	7	2	15	29	55	–26	23
13 Huddersfield T	24	4	2	18	26	66	–40	14

NORTH WEST	P	W	D	L	F	A	GD	Pts
1 Wigan Ath	26	19	5	2	79	20	59	62
2 Rochdale	26	16	3	7	71	44	27	51
3 Preston NE	26	13	6	7	53	42	11	45
4 Bury	26	13	4	9	52	43	9	43
5 Blackpool	26	11	7	8	60	56	4	40
6 Fleetwood T	26	10	7	9	39	31	8	37
7 Tranmere R	26	9	8	9	33	34	–1	35
8 Wrexham	26	8	9	9	35	43	–8	33
9 Shrewsbury T	26	8	8	10	45	54	–9	32
10 Morecambe	26	7	6	13	31	50	–19	27
11 Carlisle U	26	7	5	14	35	51	–16	26
12 Walsall	26	6	7	13	27	41	–14	25
13 Accrington S	26	7	4	15	40	56	–16	25
14 Port Vale	26	8	1	17	40	75	–35	25

SOUTH EAST	P	W	D	L	F	A	GD	Pts
1 Northampton T	20	16	2	2	46	19	27	50
2 Peterborough U	20	11	4	5	46	30	16	37
3 Southend U	20	10	4	6	65	39	26	34
4 Stevenage	20	9	6	5	35	31	4	33
5 Luton T	20	9	4	7	35	35	0	31
6 AFC Wimbledon	20	8	4	8	36	40	–4	28
7 Cambridge U	20	7	3	10	31	32	–1	24
8 Gillingham	20	6	5	9	36	37	–1	23
9 Barnet	20	7	2	11	40	51	–11	23
10 Milton Keynes D	20	5	3	12	30	47	–17	18
11 Leyton Orient	20	2	3	15	22	61	–39	9

SOUTH WEST	P	W	D	L	F	A	GD	Pts
1 Oxford U	20	14	5	1	55	23	32	47
2 Bournemouth	20	11	7	2	52	28	24	40
3 Exeter C	20	11	1	8	39	31	8	34
4 Yeovil T	20	9	3	8	35	28	7	30
5 Swindon T	20	9	3	8	42	45	–3	30
6 Portsmouth	20	8	5	7	46	44	2	29
7 Cheltenham T	20	9	2	9	36	43	–7	29
8 Bristol R	20	7	4	9	40	42	–2	25
9 Forest Green R	20	6	5	9	35	44	–9	23
10 Plymouth Arg	20	3	4	13	21	40	–19	13
11 Newport Co	20	2	3	15	29	62	–33	9

Top six teams in South East and South West divisions qualify for Merit League 1; the remainder contest Merit League 2.

MERIT LEAGUE 1	P	W	D	L	F	A	GD	Pts
1 Southend U	11	7	2	2	24	17	7	23
2 AFC Wimbledon	11	5	5	1	25	16	9	20
3 Swindon T	11	6	2	3	23	18	5	20
4 Oxford U	11	6	2	3	21	16	5	20
5 Peterborough U	11	4	3	4	23	26	–3	15
6 Northampton T	11	4	2	5	23	26	–3	14
7 Portsmouth	11	3	4	4	18	17	1	13
8 Yeovil T	11	3	4	4	13	15	–2	13
9 Bournemouth	11	2	5	4	17	22	–5	11
10 Stevenage	11	2	4	5	15	18	–3	10
11 Exeter C	11	2	4	5	18	22	–4	10
12 Luton T	11	1	5	5	15	22	–7	8

MERIT LEAGUE 2	P	W	D	L	F	A	GD	Pts
1 Forest Green R	9	6	2	1	24	10	14	20
2 Plymouth Arg	9	6	2	1	24	10	14	20
3 Bristol R	9	5	2	2	15	11	4	17
4 Milton Keynes D	9	5	1	3	23	13	10	16
5 Cheltenham T	9	4	1	4	14	16	–2	13
6 Barnet	9	3	2	4	12	18	–6	11
7 Cambridge U	9	2	3	4	18	15	3	9
8 Gillingham	9	2	3	4	9	16	–7	9
9 Newport Co	9	2	2	5	11	23	–12	8
10 Leyton Orient	9	1	0	8	11	29	–18	3

YOUTH ALLIANCE CUP – SECTIONAL SEMI-FINALS

Grimsby T v Bury 1-2
Scunthorpe U v Wigan Ath 1-2
Exeter C v Northampton T 2-1
Southend U v Cambridge U 3-0

SECTIONAL FINALS

Bury v Wigan Ath 0-2
Southend U v Exeter C 1-2

FINAL

Exeter C v Wigan Ath 0-2

IMPORTANT ADDRESSES

The Football Association: Wembley Stadium, PO Box 1966, London SW1P 9EQ. *0800 169 1863*

Scotland: Hampden Park, Glasgow G42 9AY. *0141 616 6000*

Northern Ireland (Irish FA): Chief Executive, Donegall Avenue, Belfast, Northern Ireland BT12 6LU. *028 9066 9458*

Wales: 11/12 Neptune Court, Vanguard Way, Cardiff CF24 5PJ. *029 2043 5830*

Republic of Ireland: National Sports Campus, Abbotstown, Dublin 15. *00 353 1 8999 500*

International Federation (FIFA): Strasse 20, P.O. Box 8044, Zurich, Switzerland. *00 41 43 222 7777. Fax: 00 41 43 222 7878*

Union of European Football Associations: Secretary, Route de Geneve 46, P.O. Box 1260, Nyon 2, Switzerland. *Fax: 00 41 848 00 2727*

THE LEAGUES

The Premier League: 30 Gloucester Place, London W1U 8PL. *0207 864 9000*

The Football League: Shaun Harvey, EFL House, 10–12 West Cuff, Preston PR1 8HU. *01772 325 800. Fax 01772 325 801*

The National League: M. Tattersall, 4th Floor, Wellington House, 20 Waterloo Street, Birmingham B2 5TB. *0121 643 3143*

FA Women's Super League: Wembley Stadium, PO Box 1966, London SW1P 9EQ. *+44 844 980 8200*

Scottish Premier League: Letherby Drive, Glasgow G42 9DE. *0141 620 4140*

The Scottish League: Hampden Park, Glasgow G42 9EB. *0141 620 4160*

Welsh Premier League: 11/12 Neptune Court, Vanguard Way, Cardiff CF24 5PJ. *029 2043 5830*

Northern Ireland Football League: Mervyn Brown Suite, National Stadium at Windsor Park, Donegall Avenue, Belfast BT12 6LW. *028 9560 7150*

Football League of Ireland: D. Crowther, National Sports Campus, Abbotstown, Dublin 15. *00 353 1 8999 500*

Southern League: J. Mills, Suite 3B, Eastgate House, 121–131 Eastgate Street, Gloucester GL1 1PX. *07768 750 590*

Northern Premier League: Ms A. Firth, 23 High Lane, Norton Tower, Halifax, W. Yorkshire HX2 0NW. *01422 410 691*

Isthmian League: Kellie Discipline, PO Box 393, Dartford DA1 9JK. *01322 314 999*

Eastern Counties League: N. Spurling, 16 Thanet Road, Ipswich, Suffolk IP4 5LB. *01473 720 893*

Essex Senior League: Secretary: Ms. M. Darling, 39 Milwards, Harlow, Essex CM19 4SG. *07939 850627*

Hellenic League: John Ostinell, 2 Wynn Grove, Hazlemere HP15 7LY. *07900 081 814*

Midland League: N. Wood, 30 Glaisdale Road, Hall Green, Birmingham B28 8PX. *07967 440 007*

North West Counties League: J. Deal, 24 The Pastures, Crossens, Southport PR9 8RH. *01704 211 955*

Northern Counties East: Matt Jones, 346 Heneage Road, Grimsby DN32 9NJ. *07415 068 996*

Northern League: K. Hewitt, 21 Cherrytree Drive, Langley Park, Durham DH7 9FX. *07897 611640*

Spartan South Midlands League: M. Appleby, 15 Aintree Close, Bletchley, Milton Keynes MK3 5LP.

Southern Combination League: T. Dawes, 32 Reynolds Lane, Langney, Eastbourne BN23 7NW. *01323 764 218*

United Counties League: Ms W. Newey, Nene Valley Community Centre, Candy Street, Peterborough PE2 9RE. *07890 5184577*

Wessex League: A. Hodder, leaguesecretary.wessexleague @gmail.com. *07780 496312*

Western League: A. Radford, 19 Longney Place, Patchway, Bristol BS34 5LQ. *07872 818 868*

Combined Counties League: A. Constable, 3 Craigwell Close, Staines, Middlesex TW18 3NP. *01784 440 613*

Southern Counties East League: D. Peck, secretary@scefl.com *07710 143 944*

OTHER USEFUL ADDRESSES

Amateur Football Alliance: Jason Kilby, Unit 3, 7 Wenlock Road, London N1 7SL. *0208 733 2613*

Association of Football Badge Collectors: K. Wilkinson, 18 Hinton St, Fairfield, Liverpool L6 3AR. *0151 260 0554*

British Olympic Association: 60 Charlotte Street, London W1T 2NU. *0207 842 5700*

British Blind Sport (including football): Plato Close, Tachbrook Park, Leamington Spa, Warwickshire CV34 6WE. *01926 424 247*

British Universities and Colleges Sports Association: Vince Mayne, Chief Executive: BUCSA, 20–24 King's Bench Street, London SE1 0QX. *0207 633 5080*

England Supporters Club: Wembley Stadium, PO Box 1966, London SW1P 9EQ. *0800 389 1966*

English Schools FA: 4 Parker Court, Staffordshire Technology Park, Stafford ST18 0WP. *01785 785 970*

Fields In Trust: Woodstock Studios, 36 Woodstock Grove, London W12 8LE. *0207 427 2110*

Football Foundation: Niall Malone, Communications Manager: Whittinghton House, 19–30 Alfred Place, London WC1E 7EA. *0345 345 4555*

Football Postcard Collectors Club: PRO: John Farrelly, 163 Collingwood Road, Hillingdon, Middlesex UB8 3EW. Web: www.hobbyist.co.uk/pfcc

Football Safety Officers Association: Peter Houghton, Blackburn Rovers Enterprise Centre, Nuttall Street, Blackburn BB2 4JF. *01254 841 771.*

Institute of Groundsmanship: 28 Stratford Office Village, Walker Avenue, Wolverton, Milton Keynes MK12 5TW. *01908 312 511*

League Managers Association: St George's Park, Newborough Road, Needwood, Burton on Trent DE13 9PD. *0128 357 6350*

National Football Museum: Urbis Building, Cathedral Gardens, Todd Street, Manchester M4 3BG. *0161 605 8200*

Professional Footballers' Association: G. Taylor, 20 Oxford Court, Bishopsgate, Off Lower Moseley Street, Manchester M2 3WQ. *0161 236 0575*

Programme Monthly & Football Collectable Magazine: R. P. Matz, 11 Tannington Terrace, London N5 1LE. *020 7359 8687*

Programme Promotions: 21 Roughwood Close, Watford WD17 3HN. *01923 861 468*
Web: www.footballprogrammes.com

Referees' Association: 1C Bagshaw Close, Ryton-on-Dunsmore, Coventry CV8 3EX. *024 7642 0360*

Scottish Football Museum: Hampden Park, Glasgow G42 9BA. *0141 616 6139*

Sir Norman Chester Centre for Football Research: Department of Sociology, University of Leicester, University Road LE1 7RH. *0116 252 2741/5*

Sport England: 21 Bloomsbury Street, London WC1B 3HF.

Sports Grounds Safety Authority: East Wing, 3rd Floor, Fleetbank House, 2–6 Salisbury Square, London EC4Y 8JX. *0207 930 6693*

Sports Turf Research Institute: St Ives Estate, Harden, Bingley, West Yorkshire BD16 1AU. *01274 565 131*

The Football Supporters' Federation: 1 Ashmore Terrace, Stockton Road, Sunderland, Tyne and Wear SR2 7DE. *0330 440 0044*

The Ninety-Two Club: Mr M. Kimberley, The Ninety-Two Club, 153 Hayes Lane, Kenley, Surrey CR8 5HP.

Walking Football Association: Kemp House, 160 City Road, London EC1V 2NX. *07517 033248*

Wheelchair Football Association: c/o Nottinghamshire FA, Unit 6b, Chetwynd Business Park, Chilwell, Nottingham NG9 6RZ.

FOOTBALL CLUB CHAPLAINCY

Brian was already in his thirties when he was ordained, but there weren't many – or even any! – other clergymen who had played in a major cup final.

During an afternoon visiting the local hospital, Brian met a colleague who had been a football chaplain for many years prior to moving to his current appointment. The pair soon became firm friends and it was at the latter's suggestion that Brian applied to a nearby club that was among the minority of league clubs which had never benefited from a chaplain's ministry.

The club secretary, a sidesman at his local church, encouraged his Chairman to consider the matter, and after several meetings, the directors appointed Brian to serve as chaplain of their club.

Naturally, many of the playing staff were intrigued by Brian's pedigree and, occasionally, by invitation, he would take part in a morning's training and travel with the team when it was convenient. Of course, the highlight for Brian was the occasion when 'his' new club met his former one – but wild horses would never goad Brian to reveal which team he supported that afternoon!

THE REV

OFFICIAL CHAPLAINS TO FA PREMIERSHIP AND FOOTBALL LEAGUE CLUBS

Aston Villa – Phillip Nott
Barnsley – Peter Amos
Birmingham C – Kirk McAtear
Birmingham C Academy – Tim Atkins
Blackburn R – Ken Howles
Blackpool – Michael Ward
Bolton W – Phillip Mason
Bournemouth – Adam Parrett
Bradford C – Oliver Evans
Brentford – Stuart Cashman
Bristol C – Derek Cleave
Bristol R – David Jeal
Burnley – Barry Hunter
Burton Alb – Phil Pusey
Bury – David Ottley
Cardiff C Academy – Bryon Castle
Carlisle U – Alun Jones
Charlton Ath – Matt Baker
Charlton Ath Academy – Gareth Morgan
Chelsea – Martin Swan
Cheltenham T – Malcolm Allen
Coventry C – Simon Betteridge
Crawley T – Steve Alliston
Crewe Alex – Phil Howell
Crystal Palace – Chris Roe
Derby Co – Tony Luke
Doncaster R – Barry Miller
Everton – Harry Ross
Everton Training Ground – Henry Corbett
Fleetwood T – George Ayoma
Fulham – Gary Piper
Gillingham – Chris Gill
Huddersfield T – Dudley Martin
Ipswich T – Kevan McCormack
Leeds U – Dave Niblock
Leicester C – Andrew Hulley
Lincoln C – Canon Andrew Vaughan
Liverpool – Bill Bygroves
Luton T – David Kesterton
Macclesfield T – Chris Whiteley
Manchester C – Pete Horlock
Mansfield T – Kevin Charles
Millwall – Canon Owen Beament
Newport Co – Keith Beardmore
Northampton T – Haydon Spenceley
Norwich C – Jon Norman
Norwich C Academy – Lewis Blois
Notts Co – Liam O'Boyle
Oldham Ath – John Simmons
Peterborough U – Richard Longfoot
Peterborough U Academy – Sid Bridges
Plymouth Arg – Arthur Goode
Port Vale – John Hibberts
Portsmouth – Jonathan Jeffery and Mick Mellows
Preston NE – Chris Nelson
QPR – Joshua Baines
Reading – Steven Prince
Rochdale – Richard Bradley
Rotherham U – Baz Gascoyne
Scunthorpe U – Alan Wright
Scunthorpe U Academy – David Eames
Sheffield U – Delroy Hall
Sheffield W – Baz Gascoyne
Sheffield W Wise Old Owls – David Jeans
Shrewsbury T – Phil Cansdale
Southampton – Andy Bowerman
Southend U – Stuart Alleway and Mike Lodge
Stevenage – Jon Woodrow
Sunderland – Father Marc Lyden-Smith
Swansea C – Kevin Johns
Swansea C Academy – Eirian Wyn
Swindon T – Simon Stevenette
Tranmere R – Buddy Owen
Tranmere R (Stadium) – Matt Graham
Walsall – Peter Hart
Watford – Clive Ross
WBA – Steven Harper
West Ham U – Alan Bolding
West Ham U Academy – Philip Wright
Wolverhampton W – David Wright
Wolverhampton W Academy – Steve Davies
Wycombe W – Benedict Mwendwa Musola
Yeovil T – Jim Pearce

OTHER CHAPLAINS

EFL Offices London – Cameron Collington
EFL Offices Preston – Chris Nelson

The chaplains hope that those who read this page will see the value and benefit of chaplaincy work in football and will take appropriate steps to spread the word where this is possible. They would also like to thank the editors of the Football Yearbook for their continued support for this specialist and growing area of work.

For further information, please contact: Sports Chaplaincy UK, The Avenue Methodist Church, Wincham Road, Sale, Cheshire M33 4PL. Telephone: 0800 181 4051 or email: admin@sportschaplaincy.org.uk. Website: www.sportschaplaincy.org.uk

OBITUARIES

Ian Allen (Born: Johnstone, Renfrewshire, 27 January 1932. Died: 11 November 2018.) Ian Allen was a winger who developed in Ayrshire Junior football with Beith. He attracted attention from senior clubs and shortly after trialling with Aberdeen A he signed for Queens Park Rangers in September 1952. He made just one first-team appearance during a two-year stay at Loftus Road but fared better after moving on to Bournemouth. He played 60 first-team games for the Cherries, scoring 12 goals, before switching to non-league football with Salisbury City.

Stan Anderson (Born: Horden, Co. Durham, 27 February 1934. Died: Doncaster, 10 June 2018.) Stan Anderson was a former England Schools international who went on to sign amateur forms for Sunderland in June 1949, turning professional on reaching the age of 17. He established himself in the side at right-half during the 1953–54 season and went on to make over 400 first-team appearances for the Black Cats. He won representative honours for England U23 and B teams and two full caps, both in April 1962. Later he had a short spell with Newcastle United, assisting them to win promotion to the top flight in 1964–65 before concluding his career as player-coach of Middlesbrough where he was appointed manager in April 1966. He went on to manage AEK Athens, Doncaster Rovers and Bolton Wanderers.

Tommy Anderson (Born: Haddington, East Lothian, 4 September 1934. Died: New South Wales, Australia, 1 July 2018.) Tommy Anderson was a pacy winger who was playing first-team football for Berwick Rangers in Scotland's C Division at the age of 17. His early career was interrupted by National Service in the RAF and although he rejoined the club on demobilisation he was released in the summer of 1955. He subsequently signed for Queen of the South, embarking on a lengthy and peripatetic career in British football which continued until 1967 and saw him make senior appearances for a total of 14 different clubs, rarely staying more than 12 months anywhere. His most successful spell was with Stockport County (June 1960 to November 1961) where he scored 21 goals in 69 appearances.

Dave Andrews (Born: 14 January 1939. Died: 2 November 2018.) Dave Andrews was a prominent amateur player throughout the 1960s, winning the FA Amateur Cup with Walthamstow Avenue (1961) and Leytonstone (1968) and gaining caps for England Amateurs and the Great Britain Olympic team. He later became manager and then chairman of Leytonstone and led them through a series of mergers which resulted in the formation of Dagenham and Redbridge in 1992. He became joint chairman on the club's formation and continued as chairman through to November 2013 when he stepped down and was appointed Life President, a position he held at the time of his death.

Phil Aston (Born: Measham, 13 May 1924. Died: November 2018.) After wartime service in the RAF Phil Aston turned out for Measham Imperial in the Leicestershire Senior League. His performances at right-half soon drew wider attention and in January 1950 he made an appearance for Leicester City in a friendly against Luton Town. The following season he gained three caps for England Amateurs, then after a brief spell with Rugby Town he signed for Walsall. He made 10 Football League appearances for the Saddlers then returned to non-league football with Rugby, Bedworth and Burton Albion.

Kevin Austin (Born: Hackney, 12 February 1973. Died: 23 November 2018.) Kevin Austin was a powerful defender who had a good sense of position and read the game well. After joining Leyton Orient from Saffron Walden Town in August 1993 he went on to make more than 500 senior appearances in a career that spanned the period to 2010 and saw him also play for Lincoln City, Barnsley, Cambridge United, Bristol Rovers, Swansea City and Chesterfield. He was an ever-present for the Imps team that won promotion from Division Three in 1997–98 and won two promotions with Swansea (2004–05 and 2007–08). He was also capped for Trinidad & Tobago. When his playing career was over he went into coaching, most recently with Scunthorpe United. His early death was as a result of pancreatic cancer.

Bobby Ayre (Born: Berwick-on-Tweed, 26 March 1932. Died: 31 July 2018.) As a youngster Bobby Ayre was 'capped' by the England Army Cadet Force team and was on the books of Newcastle United as an amateur before signing professional terms for Charlton Athletic in the summer of 1950. He scored in his second appearance for the Addicks and found the net regularly during a six-year stay at The Valley, when he won England U23 honours and toured South Africa with an FA squad in the 1956 close season. He later spent two seasons at Reading, taking his record in senior football to an impressive 80 goals from 178 appearances.

Allan Ball (Born: Hetton-le-Hole, Co. Durham, 26 February 1943. Died: Dumfries, 21 July 2018.) Goalkeeper Allan Ball was a product of County Durham schools football and went on to sign for Queen of the South during the 1963–64 season. He went straight into the line-up and never looked back, staying until the end of the 1981–82 season. His totals of 725 League and Cup appearances and 507 consecutive first-team appearances are both club records. A genuine legend in the club's history, he enjoyed two testimonial matches for Queens and later played briefly for Gretna and Dalbeattie Star before retiring from the game.

Mike Balson (Born: Bridport, Dorset, 9 September 1947. Died: Florida, USA, 30 May 2019.) Mike Balson joined Exeter City as a forward but was quickly converted to defence, initially at left-back and then at left-half. He had six seasons as a regular at St James Park and in total made 305 first-team appearances before moving to South Africa to play for Highlands Park in 1974. After returning to the UK he emigrated to the USA in 1979 where he played in the NASL for Atlanta Chiefs and for a number of indoor teams. He later became a referee and administrator of the game.

Gordon Banks OBE (Born: Sheffield, 30 December 1937. Died: 12 February 2019.) Gordon Banks is justifiably the greatest goalkeeper English football has produced. A World Cup winner in 1966, his tremendous save from Pele in the 1970 World Cup finals is widely regarded as the greatest save in football history. He began his professional career with Chesterfield, where he featured in the team defeated by Manchester United in the 1956 FA Youth Cup final. Soon after establishing himself in the Spireites' first team he was sold to Leicester City. He appeared in two losing FA Cup finals and was a Football League Cup winner in 1963–64 during his time at Filbert Street before being surprisingly sold to Stoke City in April 1967. Manager Tony Waddington assembled a squad of great experience and Gordon went on to be part of the team that won the League Cup in 1972, the club's first-ever major trophy. The following October he lost an eye in a road traffic accident and this effectively ended his career in top-class football. He was, however, best known for his exploits in international rather than club football, winning 73 caps between 1963 and 1972. In addition he won a host of personal awards including FIFA Goalkeeper of the Year six times in a row (1966 to 1971) and the Football Writers' Association Footballer of the Year (1972).

Colin Barlow (Born: Manchester, 14 November 1935. Died: December 2018.) Colin Barlow was a pacy outside-right who established himself in the Manchester City team during the 1956–57 campaign after scoring on his debut in a 3-2 win at Chelsea. He stayed at Maine Road until the end of the 1962–63 season, bringing his tally to 80 goals from 189 League and Cup appearances. He later spent time on the books of Oldham Athletic and Doncaster Rovers before becoming a successful businessman and eventually being appointed Manchester City's first chief executive, holding the position between 1994 and 1997.

Mike Barnard (Born: Portsmouth, 18 July 1933. Died: 18 December 2018.) Mike Barnard was a local lad who signed amateur forms for Portsmouth in May 1951. Seven months later he turned professional but it was not until the 1953–54 season that he played regular first-team football for Pompey. An inside-forward, he went on to make over 100 League appearances for the club, all in the top flight, before injury led to a switch in focus to his cricket career. A middle order batsman, he made 285 appearances for Hampshire between 1952 and 1966 and was a member of their team which won the County Championship in 1961.

Ernie Bateman (Born: Hemel Hempstead, 5 April 1929. Died: 10 September 2018.) Ernie Bateman was a tall centre-half who joined Watford from Hemel Hempstead Town in March 1952. He spent five years at Vicarage Road, but it was only in the 1954–55 season that he featured regularly in the side. In only his second appearance he played the whole of the second half in goal after regular 'keeper Ted Bennett broke a finger and went out to play on the wing. Ernie later played for Sittingbourne, captaining their team which won the Kent League in both 1957–58 and 1958–59. His brother Colin also played for Watford in the 1950s.

Kevin Beattie (Born: Carlisle, 18 December 1953. Died: Ipswich, 16 September 2018.) Kevin Beattie was big, powerful central defender who joined Ipswich Town as an apprentice and progressed to a professional contract in the summer of 1971. He won a regular place in Bobby Robson's side in 1972–73 and enjoyed considerable success in a decade at Portman Road. He gained an FA Cup winners' medal in 1978 and was a member of the team that defeated Norwich City to win the Texaco Cup in 1973. In total he played over 300 League and Cup games for Ipswich before injuries effectively ended his career, although there were brief come backs with Colchester United and Middlesbrough. He was the PFA Young Player of the Year in 1973–74 and was capped for England at both U23 and full international levels.

Ted Bennett (Born: Kilburn, 22 August 1925. Died: 23 August 2018.) Goalkeeper Ted Bennett enjoyed a successful amateur career with Southall, winning nine England Amateur caps and also featuring for Great Britain in the 1952 Olympic Games. During this period he also made two appearances for Queens Park Rangers in 1948–49. After helping Southall reach the FA Amateur Cup semi-final in 1952–53 he signed professional forms for Watford in December 1953. He went straight into the Hornets' first team and enjoyed a successful run, missing just one game before being sidelined by a broken finger in September 1955. The following summer he moved on to sign for Gravesend & Northfleet.

Carl Bertelsen (Born: Haderslev, Denmark, 15 November 1937. Died: 11 June 2019.) Carl Bertelsen was a clever forward who developed in Denmark with his hometown club Haderslev BK, winning international honours for his country and featuring in the team that finished in fourth place in the 1964 European Championships. Shortly afterwards he became the latest Scandinavian to sign for Hal Stewart's Morton, helping them reach the League Cup semi-finals in 1964–65. He moved on for spells at Dundee and Kilmarnock where he featured in the team that reached the semi-final of the Inter Cities Fairs Cup in 1966–67. He subsequently returned to Denmark to play for OB Odense.

Tommy Best (Born: Milford Haven, 23 December 1920. Died: Hereford, 16 September 2018.) Tommy Best was stationed in Belfast when serving with the Royal Navy in the Second World War during which time he turned out for Belfast Celtic and Cliftonville, thus becoming the first black player to appear in senior football in Ireland. When peacetime football resumed he signed for Chester at the age of 26 and after impressing during his time at Sealand Road he went on to play for Cardiff City and Queens Park Rangers in Division Two. Generally featuring as a centre- or inside-forward, he eventually moved on to play for Southern League club Hereford United.

Barrie Betts (Born: Barnsley, 18 September 1932. Died: Lytham St Anne's, 10 November 2018.) Barrie Betts was a full-back who developed in local junior football before signing for Barnsley in November 1950. After waiting two years for his senior debut he appeared to be establishing himself when a persistent back injury led to his retirement from the game early in 1957. However, he went on to make a full recovery and signed for Stockport County the following November. His performances for the Hatters earned him a move to Manchester City in the summer of 1960 and he went on to captain the team, making over 100 top-flight appearances before retiring for a second time after a brief spell with Scunthorpe United.

Gordon Black (Born: Linlithgow, West Lothian, 8 July 1931. Died: Livingston, 29 November 2018.) Wing-half Gordon Black was still a teenager when he joined Hibernian from Armadale Thistle in March 1949, but although he spent five seasons at Easter Road he was unable to break into the first team. After moving on to Falkirk in October 1953 he went on to make just under 250 League and Cup appearances during a career which also saw him play for Dundee, St Johnstone and Dumbarton.

Lyall Bolton (Born: Gateshead, 11 July 1932. Died: 8 August 2018.) Lyall Bolton was a tall half-back who signed for Sunderland as a teenager from local team Close House. He went on to make three Football League appearances for the Black Cats in the mid-1950s then moved to Southern League club Chelmsford City where he was a near ever-present in his first two seasons.

Peter Brackley (Born: Brighton, 1951. Died: 14 October 2018.) Peter Brackley was a match commentator and broadcaster who began his career at BBC Radio Brighton before moving to BBC Radio Sport. He subsequently worked for ITV, Channel Four's *Football Italia* and Sky before returning to ITV in 1992. He was a lifelong Brighton & Hove Albion supporter.

Harold Bratt (Born: Salford, 8 October 1939. Died: 8 October 2018.) Harold Bratt was an England Schools international who went on to sign for Manchester United and was a member of the team that won the FA Youth Cup in 1956–57. His only first-team game for United came in a surprise League Cup defeat by Bradford City in November 1960. He went on to play two seasons as a regular at left-half for Doncaster Rovers before switching to non-league football with Altrincham.

Matt Brazier (Born: Leytonstone, 2 July 1976. Died: February 2019.) Matt Brazier was a trainee with Queens Park Rangers before progressing to the professional ranks in July 1994. Initially a left-sided midfield player he dropped back to play at full-back in the latter stages of his career. He featured for the R's in the Premier League and went on to play for Fulham, Cardiff City and Leyton Orient before retiring in 2004 having made over 200 senior appearances. His early death was due to cancer.

Tony Brimacombe (Born: Plymouth, 6 August 1939. Died: August 2018.) Tony Brimacombe came to prominence with the Loughborough Colleges side that reached the quarter-finals of the FA Amateur Cup in 1960–61 and also won representative honours for the British Universities team. After appearing for Tooting & Mitcham, Kettering Town and Barnet he signed for Plymouth Argyle in December 1965 and he went on to make 16 Football League appearances for the club over the next three seasons.

Ivor Broadis (Born: Poplar, 18 December 1922. Died: 12 April 2019.) Ivor Broadis was a creative, intelligent inside-forward who developed in wartime football, principally with Millwall and Tottenham Hotspur, before being appointed player-manager of Carlisle United in August 1946 at the age of 23. He enjoyed an excellent scoring record during his time at Brunton Park and then transferred himself to Sunderland for a substantial fee during the 1948–49 campaign. For the next eight seasons he played top-flight football with considerable success, also winning 14 England caps and appearing for his country in the 1954 World Cup finals. He returned to Carlisle as player-coach in July 1955 then went on to play for Queen of the South where he remained until April 1962. After his playing career ended he worked as a journalist for the *Newcastle Journal* and later for the *Carlisle Evening News*. He was the oldest surviving England international player at the time of his death.

Jim Brogan (Born: Glasgow, 5 June 1944. Died: Glasgow, 24 September 2018.) Jim Brogan was a left-sided defender who was a member of the successful Celtic team of the late 1960s and early 1970s. He won seven consecutive League championships (1967–68 to 1973–74), four Scottish Cups and three Scottish League Cups during his time at Parkhead as well as playing in the 1970 European Cup final. In total he made almost 350 League and Cup appearances for the club and won four full Scotland caps as well as playing for the Scottish League representative side. He was released on a free transfer in the summer of 1975 and moved south to play for Coventry City where he was initially a regular in the line-up before losing his place in the side. He concluded his career with a brief spell at Ayr United.

Tommy Brownlee (Born: Carnwath, Lanarkshire, 21 May 1935. Died: 16 December 2018.) Centre-forward Tommy Brownlee was a prolific scorer in Junior football with Broxburn Athletic and while undertaking his National Service he signed for Walsall. He scored regularly for the Saddlers' reserve team but after a brief spell at York City he moved on to Workington in the summer of 1959, where he again found the net at almost a goal a game for the club's reserves. A spell at Lancashire Combination club Netherfield saw him become their record all-time goalscorer, earning him a brief return to senior football with Bradford City, for whom he finished as top scorer in the 1964–65 season.

Cyril Bunclark (Born: Rotherham, 27 March 1931. Died: 7 July 2018.) Cyril Bunclark was a winger who joined Rotherham United from local football, signing professional forms in November 1953. He was mostly a reserve during his time at Millmoor, making two first-team appearances, scoring within 15 minutes of his debut at Hull. He moved on to Wisbech Town in the summer of 1956.

Goran Bunjevcevic (Born: Karlovac, Yugoslavia, 17 February 1973. Died: Belgrade, Serbia, 28 June 2018.) Goran Bunjevcevic was a central defender and occasional central midfield player who came to prominence playing with Red Star Belgrade. He joined Tottenham Hotspur for a substantial fee in May 2001 but his first season was marred by injury and although he was a regular in 2002–03 he then struggled to break into the team before moving on to ADO Den Haag in the summer of 2006. He won 16 caps for FR Yugoslavia and continued to work in the game, most recently as sporting director of the FA of Serbia.

Ted Burgin (Born: Stannington, Sheffield, 29 April 1927. Died: 26 March 2019.) Goalkeeper Ted Burgin joined Sheffield United from Lincolnshire League club Alford Town in March 1949 and within six months had established himself as the Blades' first-choice 'keeper. He went on to make over 300 League and Cup appearances during his time at Bramall Lane, where he was an ever-present in the team that won the Division Two title in 1952–53. He came to close to winning full England honours, touring twice with an FA squad (Australia in 1951 and South Africa in 1956), winning two England B caps and being a member of the squad for the 1954 World Cup finals. Later he spent the best part of three years at Leeds United before concluding his senior career at Rochdale, where he added a further 200 appearances and was a member of the team defeated by Norwich City in the 1961–62 League Cup final.

Albert Burnett (Born: Glasgow, 10 October 1955. Died: 21 September 2018.) Albert Burnett played at left-half for Benburb Juniors against Baillieston in the 1980 Scottish Junior Cup final at Hampden, scoring in the drawn first game, with Benburb losing out in the replay. Stepping up to the seniors, he made a single first-team appearance for Airdrieonians at the end of the 1980–81 campaign, then played a further 50 games for Dumbarton before concluding with a season at Falkirk. He later returned to the Juniors with Port Glasgow.

Terry Bush (Born: Ingoldisthorpe, Norfolk, 29 January 1943. Died: 30 July 2018.) Terry Bush was a powerful centre-forward who was on the books of Bristol City as a youngster before signing professional terms in February 1960. He scored twice on his Football League debut for City against Torquay in March 1961 but it was not until the 1964–65 season that he became established in the team. He netted 16 goals that season to help City win promotion from the old Third Division and went on to make a total of 181 first-team appearances (45 goals) before injury led to his retirement.

Eric Caldow (Born: Cumnock, 14 May 1934. Died: 4 March 2019.) Eric Caldow was a neat and efficient full-back capable of playing equally well on either flank. He was just 19 when he made his first-team debut for Rangers and spent 14 years on the club's books, making over 400 first-team appearances. He captained both club and country but suffered a broken leg playing for Scotland against England in 1963 and was never quite the same player afterwards. In his time at Ibrox he won five Scottish League titles, the Scottish Cup on two occasions and the League Cup three times. He captained the team defeated by Fiorentina in the 1960–61 European Cup Winners' Cup final. He later had a season with Stirling Albion before leaving senior football. He was also a member of the Ibrox Hall of Fame.

Bobby Campbell (Born: 13 August 1941. Died: 7 March 2019.) Bobby Campbell progressed from Ayrshire Junior football with Ardeer Recreation to St Mirren in August 1959, beginning a decade of senior football. Initially an inside-forward, he was a member of the successful Morton team of 1963–64 which won the Second Division title and also reached the League Cup final. However, at the end of the following season he followed manager Bobby Howitt to Motherwell where he was to spend six years. He bagged all five goals in a win over St Mirren in September 1966 and after dropping back to play in a more defensive role he was an ever-present in the team that won Division Two in 1968–69. Later he concluded his career with a season at Stranraer.

Len Campbell (Born: Old Kilpatrick, Dunbartonshire, 23 December 1946. Died: November 2018.) Len Campbell was a wing-half who developed in Junior football with Yoker Athletic before stepping up to the seniors with Dumbarton in November 1968. He became a regular in the line-up through to the end of the 1969–70 season before eventually reverting to Junior status and rejoining Yoker.

Tom Cargill (Born: 15 December 1944. Died: Dundee, 10 May 2019.) Half-back Tom Cargill joined Dundee from Arbroath Lads Club as a 17-year-old but failed to make the first team at Dens Park. After a successful spell on loan he made a permanent move to Arbroath in the summer of 1966 and over the next 15 years became a mainstay in the side, establishing a club record of 445 Scottish League appearances. He was inducted into the Arbroath FC Hall of Fame in 2015.

Joe Carolan (Born: Dublin, 8 September 1937. Died: September 2018.) Joe Carolan signed for Manchester United as a wing-half from Home Farm in February 1956 and later that season was a member of the United team that went on to defeat Chesterfield to win the FA Youth Cup. By November 1958, when he made his senior debut, he had switched to left-back and he went on to enjoy an 18-month run in the United line-up, also gaining two caps for the Republic of Ireland. In December 1960 he moved on to Brighton & Hove Albion then went on to a lengthy career in Southern League football, notably with Tonbridge.

Terry Casey (Born: Llanrwst, Denbighshire, 1937. Died: 19 February 2018.) Terry Casey was a half-back who captained Barnet to successive Athenian League titles in 1963–64 and 1964–65. He went on to win 10 amateur international caps for Wales. He later worked for the Football Association, the FA of Wales (director of coaching & development) and FIFA (technical director).

Steve Chalmers (Born: Glasgow, 26 December 1935. Died: 29 April 2019.) Steve Chalmers achieved immortal fame when he scored Celtic's decisive goal five minutes from time in the 1967 European Cup final win over Inter Milan, the first time a British club had won the trophy. A product of Junior football (he had been capped for the Juniors against Ireland in 1959), he enjoyed a fine career as a member of Celtic's all-conquering team of the late 1960s, winning four Scottish League titles, three Scottish Cups and the League Cup on four occasions. A fractured ankle suffered against St Johnstone in the League Cup final in October 1969 effectively ended his career at Parkhead although he later had spells with Morton (as player-coach) and Partick Thistle before leaving senior football. He won five caps for Scotland and also won representative honours for the Scottish League.

Stan Clements OBE (Born: Portsmouth, 25 June 1923. Died: 8 November 2018.) Stan Clements was a powerful centre-half who played wartime football for both Portsmouth and Southampton. He signed up for Saints in July 1944 but was mostly on the fringes of the first team until the 1951–52 season when he began to feature more regularly and had a spell as captain of the side. He moved on to Basingstoke in the summer of 1955 and later worked as a civil engineer, mostly in Africa, at one point coaching the Kenya national side. He was Southampton's oldest surviving Football League player at the time of his death aged 95.

Jimmy Coates (Born: 16 October 1929. Died: 26 April 2019.) Jimmy Coates was a forward who enjoyed a lengthy career in amateur football and won representative honours for the Royal Navy and England Amateurs, as well as being a member of the Great Britain squad for the 1956 Olympic Games. He was best known in club football for his time at Kingstonian for whom he was a member of the team that was defeated by Hendon in the 1960 FA Amateur Cup final. He later coached the Combined Services team.

Colin Collindridge (Born: Barugh Green, Barnsley, 15 November 1920. Died: April 2019.) Collin Collindridge was a tricky winger who had been on the books of Rotherham United as an amateur before the war. He signed for Sheffield United in January 1939 and went on to make over 70 wartime appearances for the Blades as well as guesting for a number of other clubs, notably Notts County. He was a regular in the line-up at Bramall Lane in the first four post-war seasons and on moving to Nottingham Forest in August 1950 he was an ever-present as the club won the Division Three South title in his first season with them. He ended his senior career with two seasons at Coventry City, finishing with career totals of 111 goals from 343 peacetime appearances.

Jimmy Collins (Born: Sorn, Ayrshire, 21 December 1937. Died: July 2018.) Jimmy Collins was something of a star in Scottish Junior football as a teenager, gaining two Junior caps and featuring for Lugar Boswell Thistle when they lost out in the 1956 Junior Cup final. He signed for Tottenham Hotspur shortly afterwards but in a six-year stay at White Hart Lane he made just two appearances before moving on to Brighton & Hove Albion in October 1962. He was a regular for the Seagulls for five seasons, making over 200 appearances and playing a key role in the team that won the Fourth Division title in 1964–65. Later he enjoyed a lengthy spell with Southern League club Wimbledon.

Jimmy Copeland (Born: Kirkconnel, Dumfries & Galloway, 23 August 1941. Died: 22 July 2018.) Forward Jimmy Copeland made his senior debut for Kilmarnock at the age of 17. However, his early career was restricted by a broken leg and although he went on to play for Dumbarton, Montrose and Clyde he was unable to gain regular first-team football. He subsequently spent two years in South Africa with Highlands Park then a further 15 years in Bermuda. He played for a Bermuda representative side against a number of touring teams including Coventry City, Tottenham Hotspur and Celtic.

Charlie Crickmore (Born: Hull, 11 February 1942. Died: Hessle, East Riding, 13 October 2018.) Charlie Crickmore was a traditional-style outside-left, quick and with the ability to cross the ball from the flanks into the penalty area. In a career spanning the period from 1959 to 1972 he scored 64 goals from 357 Football League appearances. Starting out with his hometown club Hull City, he played in turn for Bournemouth, Gillingham, Rotherham United (briefly under manager Tommy Docherty), Rotherham United, Norwich City and Notts County. The high point of his career came in his penultimate season of senior football when he was an ever-present in the Notts County team that won the Division Four title in 1970–71.

Bob Crookes (Born: Retford, 29 February 1924. Died: 20 June 2018.) Bob Crookes had a trial for Lincoln City reserves in May 1949, featuring in a Midland League game against Notts County, but then signed forms for the Magpies. He spent seven years as a part-time professional at Meadow Lane, making 185 first-team appearances and finishing the 1951–52 season as the club's top scorer. He later played in the Midland League for Worksop Town and Grantham.

Allan Crowshaw (Born: Bloxwich, 12 December 1932. Died: 3 November 2018.) Allan Crowshaw was a tall, direct winger who signed for West Bromwich Albion at the age of 17. After completing his National Service he progressed through the Albion junior and reserve teams to make his first-team debut during the 1954–55 season. Unable to win a regular place for the Baggies, he spent two seasons at Derby County, where he contributed to the 1956–57 promotion campaign and a further two at Millwall. However, it was only during the 1958–59 season that he played regular first-team football. He later played for Sittingbourne and Dartford, becoming a Vice-President of Sittingbourne, and from 2006 until his death he was club President.

John Curran (Born: 21 May 1940. Died: 24 June 2018.) John Curran was a tall defender who developed with Drumchapel Amateurs and, briefly, Duntocher Hibs prior to signing for Celtic in November 1958. Although principally a reserve in four seasons at Parkhead, he made four first-team appearances during his stay. After spending the 1962–63 campaign with Irish League club Derry City, he was reinstated as a Junior and signed for Maryhill Harp.

Tom Darling (Born: Newbattle, Midlothian, 29 April 1927. Died: Edinburgh, 31 July 2018.) Tom Darling was a solid full-back who won two Junior caps for Scotland in May 1948 while with Dalkeith Thistle. He moved into the seniors with Heart of Midlothian soon afterwards and made his first-team debut at Motherwell in September 1948. However, he managed just three more appearances during his spell at Tynecastle and in the summer of 1952 moved on to Cowdenbeath. In two seasons at Central Park he made a total of 50 first-team appearances before eventually returning to the Juniors with Newtongrange Star.

George Darwin (Born: Chester-le-Street, 16 May 1932. Died: 2019.) Inside-forward George Darwin joined Huddersfield Town from Kimblesworth Juniors at the age of 18, but in three seasons at Leeds Road he was unable to break into the first team. In November 1953 he signed for Mansfield Town and quickly earned a reputation as a tricky forward with an excellent scoring record, gaining representative honours for Division Three North and against their Southern counterparts and scoring 63 goals from 126 League outings. In the summer of 1957 he was sold to Second Division Derby County where he continued in similar vein before concluding his career with spells at Rotherham United and Barrow.

Dennis Davidson (Born: Aberdeen, 18 May 1937. Died: 26 January 2019.) A product of Aberdeen Juvenile club Torry Rangers, wing-half Dennis Davidson joined the groundstaff at Portsmouth early in 1954, signing professional forms when he reached the age of 17. Dennis spent seven seasons at Fratton Park, mostly playing in the reserve and junior teams. His single Football League appearance came in a 6-1 defeat at Charlton Athletic in the final game of the 1959–60 when he was one of three Pompey players making their senior debut.

Ray Davies (Born: Wallasey, 3 October 1931. Died: March 2019.) Ray Davies joined Tranmere Rovers in October 1949 from local junior football. Initially a centre-forward, he had switched to playing on the right wing by the time he made his first-team debut in September 1951. He enjoyed two good seasons at Prenton Park but then began a period of National Service when he was stationed with the Army in Germany. It was not until August 1955 that he was demobbed and by this time Rovers had a new manager and he became a fringe player before moving on to New Brighton in the summer of 1958.

Harold Davis (Born: Cupar, Fife, 10 May 1933. Died: 26 June 2018.) Harold Davis attracted plenty of attention from senior clubs as centre-forward with Newburgh Juniors but chose to sign professional forms for East Fife in January 1952. Shortly afterwards he was called up for National Service and was posted to Korea where he was badly wounded. He required intensive rehabilitation over two years but recovered full fitness and in October 1956 he signed for Rangers, linking up again with former Bayview manager Scott Symon. Now converted to a role at half-back, he showed great strength and pace in his new role and enjoyed considerable success during his time at Ibrox, winning four Scottish League titles, the Scottish Cup twice and the League Cup once as well as appearing in both legs of the 1960–61 European Cup Winners' Cup final when Rangers lost out to Fiorentina. He was later coach of Queen's Park (August 1965 to November 1969) and manager of Queen of the South (June to December 1970). He was also a member of the Ibrox Hall of Fame.

Joe Davis (Born: Bristol, 24 August 1938. Died: Bristol, 26 November 2018.) Joe Davis signed professional forms for Bristol Rovers as a 17-year-old but had to wait almost five years before he was called up for first-team duties. He went on to make over 200 League and Cup appearances for the Pirates, initially playing at centre-half before switching to left-back. He was Rovers' Player of the Year in 1964–65 and was the first substitute used by the club when he came on against Walsall in October 1965. He finished off with a brief spell at Swansea Town before injury ended his career.

John Dempsey (Born: Birkenhead, 2 April 1951. Died: 2018.) John Dempsey enjoyed a fine start to his career, featuring for Tranmere Rovers reserves at the age of 16 and making his Football League debut at 17, having already trialled for the England Youth team. A left-back, he signed professional forms on reaching his 18th birthday but although he went on to make a total of 65 senior appearances for Rovers he was rarely a regular in the line-up. In the summer of 1972 he signed for Northern Premier League club Ellesmere Port Town.

Peter Dolby (Born: Derby, 18 May 1940. Died: 28 February 2019.) Peter Dolby was a centre-half who played his early football with Derby Corinthians and Heanor Town. In February 1960 he was sold to Shrewsbury Town and his early appearances for the Shrews were made at inside-forward with some success; in his third senior appearance he scored two goals to knock Everton out of the League Cup. He later returned to playing in the centre of defence but lost his place in the side in the 1969–70 season. In July 1971 he had the briefest of loan periods at Crewe Alexandra, where he appeared in Watney Cup action, before returning to Gay Meadow to conclude a career which saw his final total of appearances for the Shrews reach 371.

Fred Donaldson (Born: Stoke-on-Trent, 7 April 1937. Died: Stoke-on-Trent, 24 July 2018.) Fred Donaldson was a versatile player who featured at full-back, inside-forward and wing-half during his career. A product of Potteries' junior football, he made his debut for Port Vale at the end of the 1954–55 season but then had to wait over two years for his next appearance. He spent six years on the books at Vale Park and also played for Exeter City and Chester, making a total of over 100 senior appearances before switching to non-league football with Macclesfield Town.

Vic Dougherty (Born: Glasgow, 17 January 1955. Died: March 2019.) Vic Dougherty was a product of Glasgow schools football who moved south to join Bury as an apprentice. A defender, he made 10 first-team appearances for the Shakers, all before his 18th birthday. After leaving Gigg Lane he stayed in the North West and played for a number of clubs including Mossley, Horwich RMI and Radcliffe Borough.

Bobby Doyle (Born: Dumbarton, 27 December 1953. Died: 26 February 2019.) Bobby Doyle was a creative midfield player who signed for Barnsley in December 1972 shortly after leaving school. He went on to enjoy a successful career in the lower divisions of the Football League, initially playing on the flanks before moving to a more central role. He was highly regarded at all his clubs, winning a place in the PFA Divisional Team of the Year with both Barnsley (Division Four, 1974–75) and Portsmouth (Division Three, 1982–83) and being chosen by *The People* as the Third Division Player of the Season in 1976–77 while with Peterborough United. He was a near ever-present in the Pompey team that won the Third Division title in 1982–83. He also played for Blackpool and Hull City where his career was effectively ended after he suffered a bad injury in a pre-season friendly in August 1986.

Ray Dyer (Born: Stockport, 12 May 1938. Died: 9 December 2018.) Ray Dyer was a winger who made a solitary Football League appearance for Stockport County against Gateshead in October 1956. A former England Schools triallist he had been on the books of Bolton Wanderers as an amateur before signing for Stockport. His senior career was interrupted by National Service and he went on to mostly play in local football in the Stockport area.

Brian Edgley (Born: Shrewsbury, 26 August 1937. Died: Australia, February 2019.) Brian Edgley was a local lad who was on amateur forms with Shrewsbury Town before turning professional in February 1956, shortly after making his first-team debut. Although initially a winger he went on to become a versatile forward, making over 100 first-team appearances for the Shrews and helping them win promotion from the Fourth Division in 1958–59. He later had a spell in the top flight with Cardiff City before winding down his Football League career at Brentford and Barnsley. After doing the rounds of non-league football and a spell in South Africa he emigrated to Australia where he became a successful coach, being named as Victoria State Coach of the Year in 1975 and winning the Victoria State League with Preston Makedonia in 1980.

Justin Edinburgh (Born: Basildon, 18 December 1969. Died: 8 June 2019.) Justin Edinburgh was a determined left-back who was a trainee with Southend United, establishing himself in the side during the 1989–90 promotion campaign. His performances earned him a transfer to Tottenham Hotspur in the summer of 1990 and he quickly became a first-team regular, gaining an FA Cup winners' medal in his first season at White Hart Lane. He went on to make over 200 top-flight appearances for Spurs and added a League Cup winners' medal in 1999. He moved on to Portsmouth in March 2000 but injuries began to take their toll and in 2002 he retired as a player on medical advice. He subsequently moved into management and after spells with a number of non-league clubs he enjoyed success with Newport County, taking them to the FA Trophy final in 2012 and a place in the Football League via the play-offs the following year. He then managed Gillingham (February 2015 to January 2017), Northampton Town (January 2017 to August 2017) and Leyton Orient (from November 2017). His tragic death following a cardiac arrest came just weeks after he had led Orient to the National League title and a place back in the Football League.

Bob Edwards (Born: Guildford, 22 May 1931. Died: 29 May 2019.) Inside-forward Bob Edwards made his debut for Chelsea in the 1952–53 season but, unable to establish himself in the line-up, moved to Swindon Town in the 1955 close season. He did well at the County Ground, leading the scoring charts in 1956–57 and scoring 70 goals from 185 League and Cup appearances. However, future moves to Norwich City and Northampton Town were less successful and he subsequently switched to Southern League football with King's Lynn.

Walter Edwards (Born: Mansfield Woodhouse, 26 June 1924. Died: Mansfield, 5 November 2018.) Walter Edwards was a winger who signed amateur forms for Mansfield Town in the summer of 1947, turning professional the following November after being demobbed from Army service. He made 26 appearances for the Stags before being sold to Leeds United in March 1949. However, he made just two appearances during a very brief stay at Elland Road then spent the 1949–50 season with Leicester City without breaking into the first team before leaving senior football. He was Mansfield Town's oldest surviving player at the time of his death.

Bryn Elliott (Born: Beeston, 3 May 1925. Died: 15 February 2019.) Bryn Elliott was a half-back who signed for Nottingham Forest in October 1942 and made a number of first-team appearances while on leave from military service. He was eventually demobbed in September 1947 but struggled to make an impact at the City Ground. After a brief spell in Midland League football with Boston United his career was resurrected by Southampton. He joined the Saints in October 1949, staying for a decade and making over 250 first-team appearances before eventually moving on to Poole Town.

Des Farrow (Born: Peterborough, 11 February 1926. Died: 2019.) Des Farrow was a wing-half or inside-forward who joined Queens Park Rangers in November 1944. He was a regular in the line-up in 1945–46 but was then posted with the RAF to India and it was not until the 1948–49 season that he was able to play regularly again. He made over 100 first-team appearances during his stay at Loftus Road before moving on for an unsuccessful spell with Stoke City then switching to Midland League football with Peterborough United.

Joe Fascione (Born: Coatbridge, Lanarkshire, 5 February 1945. Died: 2019.) Joe Fascione was a small but skilful winger who joined Chelsea from Kirkintilloch Rob Roy in October 1962. He was still a teenager when he made his debut for the Blues but in seven years at Stamford Bridge he was mostly a reserve, making a total of 34 senior appearances. He later spent two years with Durban City and on his return he played for Romford and Barking.

Ken Finney (Born: St Helens, 10 March 1929. Died: Warrington, 7 July 2018.) Ken Finney was a winger and occasional centre-forward who joined Stockport County from St Helens Town in December 1947 but although he made sporadic appearances it was not until the 1954–55 season that he featured regularly in the line-up. In March 1958 he moved on to Tranmere Rovers where he enjoyed a further four seasons of regular first-team football and took his total of senior appearances to just short of 400. He subsequently joined non-league Altrincham.

Tony Flower (Born: Carlton, Nottingham, 2 January 1945. Died: January 2019.) Tony Flower was a winger who joined the groundstaff at Notts County as a 15-year-old in February 1960, signing a professional contract at the age of 17. He left County for Halifax Town in the summer of 1967 where he contributed to the club's promotion campaign of 1968–69 before leaving senior football at the end of the following season. He played a total of 232 League and Cup appearances during his career, scoring 31 goals.

Andy Fraser (Born: Newtongrange, Midlothian, 29 August 1940. Died: 18 September 2018.) Andy Fraser was a tall half-back who progressed from Newtongrange Star to sign for Heart of Midlothian in June 1957. Competition for places at Tynecastle was fierce and he was restricted to just four first-team appearances during his stay. After being released at the end of the 1960–61 season he spent the summer playing in the Eastern Canada Professional League with Toronto City then signed for Hartlepools United. He went on to make 85 appearances for Pools and was a near ever-present in 1963–64 before moving back to play for Newtongrange Star.

Stewart Fraser (Born: Aberdeen, 25 September 1936. Died: December 2018.) Left half Stewart Fraser came to prominence as a member of the Banks O' Dee team that won the Scottish Junior Cup in 1957. In October that year he signed for Dundee United who were to be his only senior club. He stayed at Tannadice for a decade, contributing to the 1959–60 promotion campaign and winning representative honours for the Scottish League. However, he suffered a broken leg during the 1964–65 campaign and although he made a full return to fitness he was never able to win back a regular place in the line-up. He retired in April 1967 having made 248 League and Cup appearances and later had a spell with Brora Rangers in the Highland League. He was inducted into the Dundee United Hall of Fame in 2010.

Alan Gilzean (Born: Coupar Angus, 22 October 1938. Died: Weston-super-Mare, 8 July 2018.) Alan Gilzean was an exceptional striker who enjoyed fine careers both in Scotland and England. Signed by Dundee during the 1956–57 season, he was required to undergo a period of National Service early on, playing a few games for Aldershot Reserves during this time. He went on to head the Dundee scoring charts four seasons in a row (1960–61 to 1963–64) and he finished with the exceptional figures of 165 goals from 185 appearances. His scoring feats significantly helped the Dark Blues win the Scottish League title in 1961–62 and reach the semi-final of the European Cup the following season. In December 1964 he signed for Tottenham Hotspur where he forged a productive partnership with Jimmy Greaves which helped win the FA Cup in 1967. Later he partnered Martin Chivers up front as Spurs won the League Cup in 1970–71 and 1972–73 and the UEFA Cup in 1971–72. He subsequently spent time with Johannesburg club Highlands Park and was briefly manager of Stevenage Athletic before leaving the game. He won 22 caps for Scotland and also won representative honours for Scotland U23s and the Scottish League.

Jon Gittens (Born: Moseley, Birmingham, 22 January 1964. Died: 10 May 2019.) Jon Gittens was a quick and powerful defender who was plucked from Midlands non-league football by Southampton in October 1985. He never quite settled at The Dell and was sold to Swindon Town in the summer of 1987 where he became a first-team regular over the next four seasons. Saints bought him back for a reported £400,000 fee (10 times what they had sold him for) but again he struggled to get in the team. Moves to Middlesbrough and Portsmouth followed before he concluded his career in the lower divisions with Torquay United and Exeter City. After retiring from playing he became involved in coaching and went on to become an FA coach educator, teaching other coaches.

Freddie Glidden (Born: Newmains, Lanarkshire, 7 September 1927. Died: Armadale, West Lothian, 1 January 2019.) Freddie Glidden developed with juvenile club Murrayfield Rovers during the war and was a member of their team that won the Lord Weir Cup in 1944–45. He was then 'farmed out' to Newtongrange Star where he won Junior international honours. After making his senior debut for Heart of Midlothian in November 1951 he became a solid figure in the centre of defence. He went on to make over 200 first-team appearances, captaining the team when they won the Scottish Cup in 1956 and also played in the club's Scottish League Cup winning teams of 1954 and 1956. He subsequently ended his career with a three-year spell at Dumbarton.

Derek Grace (Born: Chiswick, 29 December 1944. Died: 8 January 2019.) Derek Grace was a wing-half or inside-forward who served an apprenticeship with Queens Park Rangers before joining Exeter City in May 1962. He spent three years at St James Park, although his only season of regular first-team football was 1963–64 when the Grecians won promotion from the old Fourth Division. He subsequently had a brief spell at Gillingham then moved into non-league football with Margate.

Johnny Graham (Born: 8 January 1945. Died: 31 October 2018.) Johnny Graham was an inside-forward with Strathclyde Juniors when he signed for Third Lanark in April 1962 but he was converted into an outside-right, where he played both for Thirds and Dundee United. He was transferred to Falkirk in January 1965 where a switch back to inside-forward revitalised his career and he went on to top the scoring charts for the Bairns four seasons in a row. He later spent two seasons with Hibernian before moving on to Ayr United where he was appointed captain and was a key figure in ensuring the club were founder members of the new Premier Division in 1975–76. He wound down his career playing in midfield back at Falkirk.

Rodney Green (Born: Halifax, 24 June 1939. Died: 21 November 2018.) Rodney Green was a big powerful centre-forward who joined Halifax Town from local football in August 1960. Over the next decade he went on to enjoy a somewhat peripatetic career, turning out for eight different clubs and concluding with a respectable tally of 106 goals from 269 appearances. He rarely stayed more than 12 months in any one place but his most productive time was at Bradford City where he topped the scoring charts in both 1962–63 and 1963–64. Towards the end of his career he played cameo roles in the promotion campaigns of both Luton Town and Watford before moving to South Africa to play for Durban United.

Johnny Haasz (Born: Budapest, Hungary, 7 July 1937. Died: 2 June 2018.) Johnny Haasz had played in Hungary with the Air Force team before leaving the country in the aftermath of the 1956 Hungarian Uprising and making his way to the UK. He was initially only allowed to play as an amateur but after scoring regularly for Midland League club Gainsborough Trinity he signed for Swansea Town. Although he was leading scorer for the Swans' reserves he made just one appearance in the first team before moving on to Workington in the summer of 1961. He played over 50 games during his stay at Borough Park and had the misfortune to score all four in a 4-0 win at Accrington Stanley which was later deleted from the official records when that club resigned from the League. He subsequently played in the Southern League for Cambridge United.

George Haigh (Born: Reddish, Stockport, 29 June 1915. Died: Middleton Cheney, Northants, 23 April 2019.) George Haigh was a centre-half who was on the books of Manchester City as an amateur before signing as a professional for Stockport County in November 1936 and making two appearances in Division Three North matches in 1938–39. He also made 60 appearances for Rochdale during the war as well as playing for RAF Morecambe. When peacetime returned he had a brief association with Wigan Athletic and also played for Lancaster City and Rossendale United. At the time of his death he was the oldest surviving former Stockport County player.

Dave Hargreaves (Born: Accrington, 27 August 1954. Died: August 2018.) Dave Hargreaves is the modern Accrington Stanley club's record scorer, netting 309 goals in 322 appearances in two spells between 1974 and 1985. His total of 56 goals in 44 appearances in 1975–76, when the club played in the Lancashire Combination, is a club record for a season. In between he spent time on the books of Blackburn Rovers, making two Second Division appearances during his stay.

David Harney (Born: Jarrow, 2 March 1947. Died: April 2019.) David Harney was a centre- or inside-forward who was on the books of Grimsby Town as a teenager but did not progress beyond the reserve team. In the summer of 1967 he moved to local rivals Scunthorpe United and began the 1967–68 season as a regular in the line-up until injury struck in November 1967, which effectively marked the end of his senior career. He played a few more games for the Iron and made one appearance during a trial at Brentford at the start of the 1969–70 season before signing for Southern League club Wimbledon.

Hugh Harra (Born: Cadder, Lanarkshire, 29 March 1936. Died: 2018.) A former Junior with Rutherglen Glencairn, Hugh Harra developed into an uncompromising wing-half or inside-forward in spells with Falkirk and Dumbarton. His best seasons were spent with Dumbarton (1962 to 1967) for whom he made over 150 first-team appearances and captained the side.

Eric Harrison MBE (Born: Mytholmroyd, Yorkshire, 5 February 1938. Died: 13 February 2019.) Eric Harrison was a hard-tackling centre half who forged a 15-year career in the lower divisions of the Football League, making over 500 League and Cup appearances. After joining Halifax Town from local football he made his first-team debut as a teenager and went on to play for Hartlepools United, Barrow and Southport. He was a member of the Barrow team that won promotion from the Fourth Division in 1966–67. He later became a highly respected youth coach firstly with Everton then with Manchester United from 1981 to 2008 during which time he developed the renowned 'Class of 92'.

Mike Harrison (Born: Ilford, 18 April 1940. Died: Spain, 27 January 2019.) Winger Mike Harrison was only 16 when he made his First Division debut for Chelsea and was a member of the team that reached the final of the FA Youth Cup in 1957–58. However, in six seasons at Stamford Bridge he was only really a regular in 1961–62 when the club were relegated from the top flight. In September 1962 he was transferred to Blackburn Rovers where he enjoyed the best years of his career, scoring 40 goals from 160 Football League appearances, most of which were in the top flight. He wound down with spells at Plymouth Argyle and Luton Town. He was capped for both England Schools and England U23s.

Johnny Hart (Born: Golborne, Lancashire, 8 June 1928. Died: 26 November 2018.) Johnny Hart was an inside-forward who was an office boy with Manchester City during the war, signing professional forms on reaching his 17th birthday. Although his career was affected by injuries he went on to score 73 goals from 178 first-team appearances, although he missed out on both the 1955 and 1956 FA Cup finals. He was leading scorer for City on three occasions and on retirement as a player in 1963 he joined the backroom staff at Maine Road, eventually having a short period as manager of the club (March to October 1973). He was inducted into the Manchester City Hall of Fame in 2006.

Keith Harvey (Born: Crediton, Devon, 25 December 1934. Died: October 2018.) Keith Harvey signed for Exeter City as a teenager in the summer of 1952 and went on to spend 17 years with the Grecians, making over 500 senior appearances, the second highest in the club's history. An effective centre-half, he established himself in the side in the second half of the 1954–55 season and apart from injury was a first choice in the line-up until he was appointed trainer for the 1966–67 campaign. He made just a handful of appearances that season before returning to the side for two further seasons as a regular. He was an ever-present in the promotion winning team of 1963–64 and was the club's Player of the Year in 1965–66.

Wally Hazelden (Born: Ashton-in-Makerfield, Lancashire, 13 February 1941. Died: February 2019.) Inside-forward Wally Hazelden was an early product of the Aston Villa youth set-up and became the club's youngest-ever first-team player when he made his debut aged 16 years and 279 days in November 1957. Although capped by England at Youth international level he was never able to establish a regular place in the side at Villa Park and in the summer of 1960 he moved on to Wigan Athletic, then members of the Lancashire Combination. He scored at almost a goal a game during his only season at Springfield Park before returning to the Midlands to sign for Southern League club Rugby Town.

Don Hazledine (Born: Arnold, Nottinghamshire, 10 July 1929. Died: 2018.) Don Hazledine was an inside-forward who joined Derby County from local football in Nottingham but in three years at the Baseball Ground he never really established himself in the side. In the summer of 1954 he moved to Northampton Town in part exchange for Frank Upton but he lasted only a season with the Cobblers before switching to Boston United, then members of the Midland League. In December 1955 he captained Boston to a sensational 6-1 FA Cup victory away to Derby with a side that included six former Rams players.

John Hellawell (Born: Keighley, 20 December 1943. Died: Leeds, 14 February 2019.) John Hellawell was an inside-forward who joined Bradford City from amateur club Salts and went on to make over 50 appearances during his time at Valley Parade. He later had spells with Rotherham United, Darlington and Bradford Park Avenue but he made little impact at all three clubs before moving on to Bromsgrove Rovers.

Alan Hercher (Born: Dingwall, 11 August 1965. Died: August 2018.) Alan Hercher was a powerful midfield player who played for Ross County and Inverness Caledonian in the Highland League before moving over to the newly formed Inverness Caledonian Thistle for the 1994–95 season. He was the club's first captain and scored a hat-trick against Arbroath in their first-ever Scottish League fixture. He spent three seasons with Thistle where he was a member of the team that won the Division Three title in 1996–97. He later returned to Highland League football with Clachnacuddin and Brora Rangers.

Ally Hill (Born: Glasgow, 25 April 1934. Died: Blairgowrie, 18 December 2018.) Ally Hill won two caps for Scotland Juniors as a teenager with Jeanfield Swifts prior to signing professional forms with Clyde at the age of 18. He stayed six years at Shawfield, where he was a member of the team that defeated Celtic to win the Scottish Cup final in 1955. After a brief spell with Dundee he moved south to Bristol City, where he had an unsuccessful time, before returning to Scotland to play for Stirling Albion and Falkirk.

Wally Hinshelwood (Born: Battersea, 27 October 1929. Died: 26 November 2018.) Wally Hinshelwood was a winger who worked as an office boy at Fulham until reaching the age of 17 when he signed professional forms. Like many players of his generation his early career was disrupted by National Service, during which he served with the Army in Hong Kong. Although unable to fully establish himself at Craven Cottage, or in a brief association with Chelsea, he went on to enjoy a useful career Reading and then Bristol City, making over 100 first-team appearances with both clubs. He concluded with spells at Millwall, Toronto Italia and Newport County.

Barrie Hole (Born: Swansea, 16 September 1942. Died: 25 March 2019.) Barrie Hole was a wing-half who joined Cardiff City as a youngster and was just 17 years old when he made his first-team debut. He spent five seasons as a first-team regular with the Bluebirds, making over 200 first-team appearances and gaining Welsh Cup winners' medals in 1964 and 1965. He later played for Blackburn Rovers, Aston Villa and Swansea City taking his total of senior appearances beyond the 450-mark. He also won representative honours for Wales at Schools and U23 levels and won 30 full caps between 1963 and 1971.

Reg Holland (Born: Sutton-in-Ashfield, 23 January 1940. Died: 3 January 2019.) Reg Holland was an England Schools international who joined Manchester United as a youngster. He enjoyed a fine career in youth football, winning England Youth caps and being a member of the United teams that won the FA Youth Cup in 1955–56 and 1956–57. Unable to break into the first team at Old Trafford, he moved on to Wrexham towards the end of the 1959–60 season. He went on to make over 100 appearances, mostly at full-back, during a six-year stay at the Racecourse Ground then spent a season with Chester before moving into non-league football with Altrincham.

Harry Hood (Born: Glasgow, 3 October 1944. Died: 26 May 2019.) Harry Hood was a skilful forward who made his name with Clyde, heading the club's scoring charts 1963–64 as the club won promotion back to the top flight. The following November he was sold to Sunderland. However, he never really settled at Roker Park and spent much of his time on the transfer list before returning to Shawfield in October 1966. His goalscoring touch returned and in March 1969 he was sold again, this time to Celtic. He enjoyed an excellent career at Parkhead where he won six Scottish League championships, four Scottish Cups and two League Cups. He later had a spell in the NASL with San Antonio Thunder and returned to play for Motherwell and Queen of the South before leaving senior football. He won representative honours for Scotland U23s and the Scottish League and toured with a Scottish FA XI in 1967. He later briefly managed Albion Rovers (February to April 1981) and Queen of the South (February to April 1982).

Tony Hopper (Born: Carlisle, 31 May 1976. Died: Carlisle, 9 October 2018.) Tony Hopper was a midfield player who made his first-team debut for Carlisle United at the age of 16. He went on to make over 100 appearances during two separate spells at Brunton Park, contributing to the club's 1996–97 promotion campaign. In between he spent six months with League of Ireland club Bohemians (where he featured in UEFA Cup action) and Workington. After leaving senior football he played for a number of clubs in the North West including Barrow, Workington and Celtic Nation. His early death was as a result of motor neurone disease.

Harry Hough (Born: Chapeltown, Sheffield, 26 September 1924. Died: 2019.) Goalkeeper Harry Hough signed for Barnsley from Thorncliffe Welfare in September 1947 and although he made his first-team debut shortly afterwards it was not until the 1951–52 season that he became first-choice at Oakwell. He went on to make over 350 appearances for the club and was an ever-present in the team that won the Division Three North title in 1954–55. Later he had two seasons at Bradford Park Avenue before joining Denaby United.

Roger Hoy (Born: Poplar, 6 December 1946. Died: New South Wales, Australia, 9 November 2018.) Roger Hoy had been on the books of West Ham United as an inside-forward but was released and signed for Tottenham Hotspur who successfully converted him to a role in defence. He provided back-up to Mike England at White Hart Lane but on moving to Crystal Palace he won a regular place in the side, contributing to their 1968–69 promotion campaign. He spent the 1970–71 season with Luton where he played as a midfielder before moving on to Cardiff City where a serious knee injury effectively ended his career.

Johnny Hubbard MBE (Born: Pretoria, South Africa, 16 December 1930. Died: Prestwick, Ayrshire, 21 June 2018.) Winger Johnny Hubbard was one of many South African stars who moved to British football in the years after the Second World War when he signed for Rangers in July 1949. He spent a successful decade at Ibrox, with the highlight coming on New Year's Day 1955 when he scored a hat-trick in the Old Firm match. He gained a Scottish Cup winners' medal in 1953 and was a member of three Scottish League winning teams (1952–53, 1955–56 and 1956–57). He also had a phenomenal record as a penalty taker, scoring more than 50 times with spot kicks. He later had a spell with Bury where he was a near ever-present in the team that won the Division Three title in 1960–61 before concluding his senior career with Ayr United.

Brian Hughes (Born: Swansea, 22 November 1937. Died: Victoria, British Columbia, Canada, 7 October 2018.) Brian Hughes was a local lad who won Schools and Youth international honours for Wales before signing professional forms for Swansea Town in July 1956. He soon progressed to the first team at the Vetch Field and made over 250 first-team appearances during his stay, a highlight coming when he lined up at left-back for the FA Cup semi-final against Preston in March 1964. He also featured for the Atlanta Chiefs team that won the NASL Championship in 1968.

Mike Hughes (Born: Llanidloes, 3 September 1940. Died: December 2018.) Mike Hughes was a hard-tackling wing-half who was playing in Cardiff City's reserve team at the age of 16. However, competition for places at Ninian Park was fierce and he managed just a solitary first-team outing during his stay. He made further progress in two seasons with Exeter City but his best football was played in a six-year spell with Chesterfield (1963 to 1969). He made over 200 appearances during his stay at Saltergate before becoming player-manager of Yeovil Town where he led the team to the Southern League championship and a place in the FA Cup third round in 1970–71. He later had a spell as coach of Torquay United.

Dennis Hunt (Born: Portsmouth, 8 September 1937. Died: Seabrook, Kent, 29 January 2019.) Dennis Hunt was a robust and uncompromising left-back who signed for Gillingham in September 1958 and went on to spend a decade with the club, making over 350 first-team appearances. A highlight came in the 1963–64 season when he was a near ever-present in the team that won the Division Four title, conceding just 30 goals. He concluded his senior career at Brentford and then became player-manager of Folkestone Town.

Ernie Hunt (Born: Swindon, 17 March 1943. Died: Gloucestershire, 20 June 2018.) Ernie Hunt became Swindon Town's youngest-ever player when he made his first-team debut in September 1959. He went on to finish as the team's leading scorer four seasons in a row and played an important role in assisting the club to promotion from Division Three in 1962–63. An attacking player with great flair, he helped Wolverhampton Wanderers win promotion to the First Division in 1966–67 and after a very brief spell at Everton he signed for Coventry City where he enjoyed some of the best years of his career. In 1970–71 he won the BBC *Match of the Day* Goal of the Season award as a result of his 'donkey-kick' goal against Everton. He concluded his career back in the West Country at Bristol City.

Ron Hunt (Born: Paddington, 19 December 1945. Died: 23 August 2018.) Centre-half Ron Hunt developed with the Pathfinders Boys Club in Slough before signing for Queens Park Rangers at the age of 17. He was still a teenager when given his first-team debut and was a key figure in the Hoops' success in 1966–67, winning both the Football League Cup and the Division Three title. Injury then restricted his appearances and he eventually retired in 1973, having played over 250 games for the club.

Cliff Huxford (Born: Stroud, 8 June 1937. Died: 3 August 2018.) Cliff Huxford was a powerful wing half who joined Chelsea as an amateur at the age of 15, progressing to professional status shortly before his 18th birthday. His career at Stamford Bridge was disrupted by National Service and in the summer of 1959 he was allowed to leave for Southampton. He went straight into the Saints line-up and was an ever-present in his first season when they lifted the Division Three title. He remained at The Dell until May 1967 by which time he had made over 300 first-team appearances and assisted the club to promotion to the First Division in 1965–66. He concluded his senior career with a season at Exeter and later played and coached with a number of non-league clubs.

Jim Iley (Born: South Kirkby, Yorkshire, 15 December 1935. Died: 18 November 2018.) Jim Iley was a solid and effective wing-half who signed for Sheffield United as a teenager. He made over 100 appearances for the Blades before moving on to Tottenham Hotspur where his performances earned him representative honours for England U23s and the Football League. A move to Nottingham Forest followed but his best years were probably spent with Newcastle United (1962 to 1969) where he made over 200 appearances and was a key figure in the team which won the Second Division title in 1964–65. He subsequently became player-manager of Peterborough United and then went on to manage Barnsley, Blackburn Rovers, Bury and Exeter City.

Gerry Irving (Born: Allerby, near Maryport, 19 September 1937. Died: 2018.) Gerry Irving joined Workington as a winger and made a single appearance for them, lining up at Oldham Athletic in October 1956. After a spell with Aspatria he signed for Queen of the South in August 1959 with whom he went on to make over 150 senior appearances before eventually moving on to Morecambe, initially as a player before switching to coaching.

Lennart Johansson (Born: Bromma, Stockholm, 5 November 1929. Died: Stockholm, 4 June 2019.) Lennart Johansson was the longest serving president of UEFA, holding the position between 1990 and 2007. During that time he oversaw the introduction of the Champions League in place of the European Cup and the complete transformation of UEFA. He was president of the Swedish Football Association (SvFF) between 1984 and 1991 and was elected to the top position in UEFA in 1990. He unsuccessfully stood for president of FIFA in 1998 when he lost out to Sepp Blatter. In 2001 the Allsvenskan [Swedish League] championship trophy was named the Lennart Johansson Pokal in his honour.

Tommy Johnson (Born: Stockton, 5 March 1926. Died: 9 December 2018.) Tommy Johnson was a wing-half or inside-forward who made a number of wartime appearances for Middlesbrough before joining Darlington where he featured in the 1947–48 season. He later played in non-league football for Stockton and Horden CW before briefly returning to senior football with Bradford Park Avenue where he was principally a reserve, making just a single first-team appearance. He went on to join the back-room staff at Hartlepools United staying 25 years, before spending a further decade as physio at Middlesbrough.

Brian Jordan (Born: Bentley, South Yorks, 31 January 1932. Died: December 2018.) Half-back Brian Jordan signed for Derby County as a part-time professional in October 1951 but failed to make a breakthrough at the Baseball Ground and after dropping down to the Midland League with Denaby United he was given a second chance by Rotherham United. He spent five years on the books at Millmoor and also had spells with Middlesbrough and York City, making a total of 51 appearances before leaving senior football.

Tom Kay (Died: 24 July 2018.) Wing-half Tom Kay progressed from Juvenile club Cowdenbeath Royals to sign for Cowdenbeath in February 1960 but after just a handful of games at Central Park he was sidelined by a broken leg. He later spent two seasons in the Southern League with Bedford Town before he returned to Scotland and became involved in coaching, notably with Hill of Beath Swifts.

Charlie Kelsall (Born: Buckley, Flintshire, 15 April 1921. Died: Hawarden, Deeside, 20 April 2019.) A product of West Cheshire League club Buckley Town, Charlie Kelsall signed for Wrexham in August 1939, shortly before war broke out. He went on to play 23 wartime games for the Robins and one for New Brighton (for which they were fined by the Football League) before spending most of the remainder of the war serving with the Army in India. He returned to the Racecourse Ground and remained until the end of the 1951–52 season, although he was mostly a reserve during this time, making a further 41 appearances.

Mick Kennedy (Born: Salford, 9 April 1961. Died: 9 February 2019.) Mick Kennedy was a combative central midfield player who spent most of his career in the lower divisions of the Football League. Starting out at Halifax Town in the Fourth Division, he moved up the leagues with Huddersfield Town (Third Division) and Middlesbrough (Second Division). He played his best football with Portsmouth (1984–1988) where he was club captain and led the team to promotion to the First Division in 1986–87. He continued to play through to the end of the 1993–94 season, his final games being with Wigan Athletic. He won two full caps for the Republic of Ireland and was inducted into the Pompey Hall of Fame in 2018.

Ian Larnach (Born: Ferryhill, Co. Durham, 10 July 1951. Died: April 2019.) Ian Larnach was a centre-forward who made two appearances for Darlington as a teenager, scoring in his only start against Notts County in March 1970. He later played for South Shields and Spennymoor before returning to Feethams to work with the reserve and youth teams.

Pat Laverty (Born: Gorseinon, near Swansea, 24 May 1934. Died: March 2019.) Pat Laverty was an inside-forward who had a trial for the Wales Amateur team before joining Sheffield United from Cheshire League club Wellington Town in May 1956. However, he was mostly a reserve during four seasons at Bramall Lane, making only seven first-team appearances. He featured fairly regularly for Southend United in 1960–61 before rejoining Wellington Town.

Jimmy Lawton (Born: Middlesbrough, 6 July 1942. Died: 17 January 2019.) Jimmy Lawton was a centre- or inside-forward who was a regular for Darlington in the early 1960s and led the club's scoring charts with 25 goals in the 1964–65 season. He was sold to Swindon Town in September 1965 the day after his goal knocked them out of the League Cup, and later played under his former colleague Ken Furphy at Watford although he was unable to repeat the goalscoring form he had shown with the Quakers. He eventually returned to Darlington but a knee injury ended his career at the age of 27.

Fred Leeder (Born: New Hartley, Seaton, 15 September 1936. Died: August 2018.) Full-back Fred Leeder made a single top-flight appearance for Everton against Chelsea in January 1958, deputising for the injured Jimmy Tansey. He moved on to Darlington where he featured more regularly and then to Southport where he was mostly a first choice at right-back. He later played in non-league football with Runcorn and New Brighton.

Geoff Lees (Born: Rotherham, 1 October 1933. Died: 6 June 2019.) Geoff Lees was a wing-half who was on the books of Barnsley as a youngster without making the first team. He completed his National Service with the 5th Regiment Royal Horse Artillery who had a renowned soccer team and later spent two years with Bradford City, making three first-team appearances towards the end of the 1955–56 season. After a career in teaching he returned to Oakwell as one of the club's youth team coaches.

Lawrie Leslie (Born: Edinburgh, 17 March 1935. Died: Wilmington, Kent, 4 June 2019.) Goalkeeper Lawrie Leslie joined Hibernian after completing his National Service and was a member of the team defeated by Clyde in the Scottish Cup final of 1958. He moved on to Airdrieonians, where his performances won him representative honours for both Scotland and the Scottish League and earned him a move to West Ham United. He was chosen as Hammer of the Year in his first season with the club but after suffering a broken leg he lost his place and moved on to spells with Stoke City (where he was a League Cup runner-up), Millwall and Southend United.

Derek Lewin (Born: Manchester, 18 May 1930. Died: March 2019.) Derek Lewin was an amateur inside-forward who made 10 first-team appearances for Oldham Athletic, all bar one in the 1953–54 season. In December 1954 he signed for Bishop Auckland and he played and scored in each of the club's consecutive FA Amateur Cup final wins of 1955, 1956 and 1957. He also won five England Amateur caps and was a member of the Great Britain squad for the 1956 Melbourne Olympic Games. In addition for his experience with Oldham he made a solitary Football league appearance for Accrington Stanley and was one of three Bishop Auckland players who assisted Manchester United in the aftermath of the Munich Disaster, although he did not play in the first team. He was later a director of Blackpool FC and served as a member of the Lancashire FA Council and the FA Council.

Ronnie Lewis (Born: Belfast, 10 February 1932. Died: 2018.) Inside-forward Ronnie Lewis was capped for Northern Ireland Schools and Youth teams, featuring alongside both Jimmy McIlroy and Billy Bingham in the youth set-up. He joined Burnley from Cliftonville Olympic in the summer of 1949 but failed to make a breakthrough at Turf Moor. After spending a season with Southern League club Weymouth he returned to senior football with Barrow for whom he made five appearances in the 1954–55 season. He was later active in non-league football in Lancashire for many years.

Jimmy Linton (Born: Glasgow, 2 December 1930. Died: Milton Keynes, 7 November 2018.) Goalkeeper Jimmy Linton was a member of the Kirkintilloch Rob Roy Juveniles team that reached the Secondary Juvenile Cup final in 1951 and within a matter of weeks he had signed professional forms for Notts County. He had to wait until completing his National Service with the Army before eventually making his debut at Huddersfield Town in November 1952. He went on to make over 100 Football League appearances for the Terriers and then moved to Watford, for whom he was a near ever-present in the team that won promotion from Division Four in 1959–60. After taking his total of senior appearances beyond the 200-mark he moved into non-league football with Poole Town.

Jim Lynn (Born: 7 November 1947. Died: 9 September 2018.) Jim Lynn was a winger who scored the goal that won the Scottish Junior Cup final for Blantyre Victoria against Penicuik Athletic at Hampden in 1970. He went on to make 81 senior appearances, turning out for Albion Rovers and Stenhousemuir before returning to Junior football with Carluke Rovers for the 1973–74 season.

Bobby McCool (Born: Edinburgh, 11 August 1942. Died: 22 March 2019.) Bobby McCool started out as a winger, making four first-team appearances for Third Lanark while still a teenager. In the summer of 1962 he played for Hamilton Steelers in the Eastern Canada Professional League and on his return he signed for Cheltenham Town. He went on to forge a lengthy career in the Southern League firstly with the Robins and then with Gloucester City.

Terry McDonald (Born: Belfast, 5 February 1947. Died: Eccleston, near Chorley, 6 August 2018.) Terry McDonald won Schools and Youth international honours for Northern Ireland and as a youngster spent 18 months on the books of Middlesbrough where he featured in the reserve team. He was still a teenager when he signed for Southport in July 1965 and he went on to contribute to the club's run to the FA Cup fifth round in 1965–66 and to the following season's promotion campaign. He subsequently spent two seasons with Barrow before an ankle injury effectively ended his senior career.

Roy McDowell (Born: Jedburgh, 11 June 1947. Died: March 2019.) Central defender Roy McDowell enjoyed two spells with Berwick Rangers between 1971 and 1981, making over 350 appearances in total and helping them with the Second Division title in 1978–79. In between he spent six months with League of Ireland club Drogheda United. He later spent time as manager of Jeanfield Swifts before becoming a director and then chairman of Berwick Rangers in the early 1990s.

Jimmy McGowan (Born: Glasgow, 31 July 1939. Died: Sutton-in-Ashfield, 6 January 2019.) Jimmy McGowan was an inside-forward who developed with Kirkintilloch Rob Roy. He moved into the seniors with St Johnstone in January 1960 but made just a single first team appearance during his stay in Perth. He moved south, making three appearances for Mansfield Town in 1961–62 then playing in the Southern League for Margate and Burton Albion.

Hugh McIlvanney OBE (Born: Kilmarnock, 2 February 1934. Died: 24 January 2019.) Hugh McIlvanney was a journalist who began his career at the *Kilmarnock Standard* and went on to become the leading sports journalist of his era, spending 30 years at the *Observer* and 25 years at the *Sunday Times* before retiring in 2016. He was awarded the OBE in 1996 and was Sports Journalist of the Year on seven occasions.

Jimmy McIlroy MBE (Born: Lambeg, Co. Antrim, 25 October 1931. Died: Nelson, Lancs, 20 August 2018.) Jimmy McIlroy was one of the most skilful inside-forwards of his era, a player who could unlock a defence with the most subtle of touches. He was a regular with Irish League club Glentoran when Burnley signed him in March 1950. A regular for the Clarets from October 1950 until his departure in March 1963, he made almost 500 appearances during his stay at Turf Moor. He played a significant role for Burnley in 1959–60 when they won the Football League title, despite carrying an injury for most of that season. He was a member of the Clarets team that reached the quarter finals of the European Cup in 1960–61 before finishing second in the League and beaten finalists in the FA Cup the following season. He was surprisingly allowed to leave for Stoke City where he helped the Potters secure the Division Two title in 1962–63 while the following season he was a member of their team that lost out to Leicester City in the League Cup final. In January 1966 he became player-manager of Oldham Athletic, a post he held until August 1968. Jimmy was capped for Northern Ireland on 55 occasions and was a member of the team that reached the quarter-finals of the 1958 World Cup tournament.

Ian MacKenzie (Born: Rotherham, 27 September 1950. Died: Harby, Notts, August 2018.) Ian MacKenzie was a centre-half or defensive midfield player who developed in the youth set-up at Sheffield United and went on to spend seven years with the club as a professional. He was mostly a reserve at Bramall Lane although he made 53 first-team appearances during his stay. In the summer of 1975 he signed for Mansfield Town and went on to make a useful contribution for the Stags in 1976–77 when they won the Division Three title. He retired from the game in 1978 due to a persistent knee injury.

Billy McNeill MBE (Born: Bellshill, Lanarkshire, 2 March 1940. Died: Glasgow, 22 April 2019.) Billy McNeill was one of the greatest players in the history of Celtic. A towering and immense centre-half from 1957 to 1975 he established a club record total of appearances and as captain lifted a total of 23 trophies. Most important of all he led the Lisbon Lions to victory over Inter Milan in 1967 to become the first British club to win the European Cup. Celtic won every cup available to them that season and to this he was able to add nine consecutive Scottish League titles (1965–66 to 1973–74), seven Scottish Cups and six League Cups. After retiring as a player he turned to management, briefly with Clyde and then Aberdeen before returning to Parkhead. He had two spells as manager of Celtic, adding a further four league titles and four domestic cups to his tally. In between he spent time in England with both Manchester City (where he gained a promotion in 1984–85) and Aston Villa. He won 29 caps for Scotland between 1961 and 1972.

Davie McParland (Born: Larkhall, Lanarkshire, 5 May 1935. Died: 14 July 2018.) David McParland joined Partick Thistle as a teenager during the 1953–54 season and went on to stay with the club for more than 20 years. He was a versatile player featuring both on the wing and at wing-half and made over 500 first-team appearances for the Jags. He gained a League Cup runners-up prize in 1958–59 and also won representative honours for Scotland U23s and the Scottish League. In September 1968 he was appointed assistant manager of the club and two years later he took over as manager. Thistle won promotion from the Second Division in his first campaign in charge and the following season sensationally defeated Celtic 4-1 to win the League Cup. He remained in charge at Firhill until May 1974 and also had spells as manager of both Queen's Park (July 1974 to May 1976) and Hamilton Academical (June 1978 to October 1982).

Billy McPheat (Born: Caldercruix, Lanarkshire, 4 September 1942. Died: Glasgow, 6 April 2019.) Billy McPheat was a robust, tall inside-forward who did well enough in Airdrie schools football to earn a deal with Sunderland. He made a goalscoring debut against Leeds United at the age of 18 and his career was progressing well until he suffered a broken leg in August 1962. It was some time before he was able to return to action and after a brief spell with Hartlepools United he returned to Scotland in the summer of 1966, signing for Airdrieonians. He made over 100 appearances during a five-year stay at Broomfield before leaving the senior game.

Paul Madeley (Born: Beeston, Leeds, 20 September 1944. Died: Leeds, 23 July 2018.) Paul Madeley joined Leeds United from Farsley Celtic in the summer of 1962 and went on to become one of the cornerstones of Don Revie's successful team of the 1960s and '70s. A genuinely versatile player who excelled in a variety of roles, he enjoyed a 19-year career at Elland Road, making over 700 first-team appearances. He was a member of two Football League winning teams (1968–69 and 1973–74), played in three FA Cup finals in four years (gaining a winners' medal in 1972) and also won both the Football League Cup (1967–68) and the Inter Cities Fairs Cup (1970–71). He gained 24 full caps for England between 1971 and 1977 and also won representative honours for the Football League.

Barrie Martin (Born: Birmingham, 29 September 1935. Died: Blackpool, 27 February 2019.) Full-back Barrie Martin signed professional forms for Blackpool at the age of 18 but had to wait four years for his senior debut. He was a regular in the line-up from the 1959–60 season and went on to make over 200 appearances for the Seasiders before moving on to Oldham in the summer of 1964. He concluded his career with three seasons at Tranmere Rovers, contributing to their 1966–67 promotion campaign.

Phil Masinga (Born: Klerksdorp, North West Province, South Africa, 28 June 1969. Died: Johannesburg, 13 January 2019.) Phil Masinga was a striker who arrived at Leeds United along with his colleague in the South Africa national team, Lucas Radebe, in August 1994. He featured fairly regularly in the side over the next two seasons, although often being used as a substitute and moved on to play in Switzerland with St Gallen. Later he spent time in Italy with Salernitana. He had played in South Africa's first international match of the modern era and in total won 58 caps, featuring in the side that won the Africa Cup of Nations in 1996 and in the 1998 World Cup finals. His early death was as a result of cancer.

David Meek (Born: York, 1930. Died: 30 October 2018.) David Meek was a reporter who briefly covered York City for the *Yorkshire Post* before switching to work for the *Manchester Evening News*. He took over coverage of Manchester United after Tom Jackson lost his life in the Munich Air Disaster and reported on the club until his retirement in 1996. He was also a long-standing contributor to the United programme over many years.

Mickey Metcalf (Born: Liverpool, 24 May 1939. Died: 26 December 2018.) Mickey Metcalf was a skilful forward who signed for Wrexham in May 1957 but it was not until the 1960–61 campaign that he gained a regular place in the side. In December 1963 he moved on to sign for Chester where he enjoyed the best seasons of his career, notably in 1964–65 when he was a member of the team that scored 119 goals, and he finished as leading scorer with 37 League and Cup goals. He eventually left senior football at the end of the 1968–69 season with a very creditable record of 157 goals from 384 appearances. He continued to play non-league football with the likes of Altrincham and Bangor City for several seasons.

Graeme Morrison (Born: Falkirk, 29 October 1976. Died: 25 September 2018.) Graeme Morrison was a central defender who spent five years on the books of Celtic in the 1990s, where he captained the reserve team and also gained experience in a loan spell with League of Ireland club Dundalk. He spent the summer of 1999 in Finland playing for TPV Tampere then returned to Scotland to play for Morton and Stirling Albion. He later became involved in coaching including a spell with Sauchie Juniors. His early death was due to pancreatic cancer.

Gordon Morritt (Born: Rotherham, 8 February 1942. Died: York, November 2018.) Gordon Morritt was a goalkeeper who joined Rotherham United from local football in the summer of 1961 but although he made his first-team debut within weeks of signing he was rarely a first choice. He was also a useful centre-forward and in October 1964 made an outfield appearance in a League Cup tie at Swansea Town; he also played (and scored) regularly as a forward with the club's reserve team. After a spell in South Africa with Durban City he returned to continue his career with spells at Doncaster Rovers, Northampton Town, York City, Rochdale and Darlington, taking his total of senior appearances to exactly 300.

Cliff Myers (Born: Southwark, 23 September 1946. Died: 8 February 2019.) Cliff Myers was a versatile forward who was on the books of both Charlton Athletic and Brentford as a youngster without establishing himself as a first-team regular. In January 1968 he signed for Southern League club Yeovil Town where he became a key player in the team that won the league title in 1970–71. In November 1972 he had the satisfaction of scoring the goal that knocked Brentford out of the FA Cup and the following summer he returned to the Football League, signing for Torquay United. He went on to make 94 League and Cup appearances before eventually returning to non-league football.

Kit Napier (Born: Dunblane, 26 September 1943. Died: Durban, South Africa, 31 March 2019.) Kit Napier was a tall, slim striker best known for the six years he spent with Brighton & Hove Albion (1966–1972) when his goals helped the team win promotion to Division Two in 1971–72. His final tally of 99 goals for the Seagulls is the third highest in the club's history. His career had begun with spells at Blackpool and Preston North End with little success. It was only when he dropped down the divisions to play for Workington that he began to blossom. He moved on to Newcastle United, but had few chances at St James' Park, and then Brighton before concluding his career at Blackburn Rovers. He later emigrated to South Africa where he played for Durban United.

Gordon Neate (Born: Reading, 14 March 1941. Died: Reading, 9 May 2019.) Gordon Neate joined Reading on amateur forms as a 15-year-old, stepping up to the professional ranks at the age of 17. A full-back, although never a regular first-team player, he went on to make over 100 first-team appearances for the Royals before injuries brought on his retirement. He was subsequently appointed groundsman and he stayed in post until retiring in 2009, having given the club 53 years' service.

Billy Neville (Born: Cork, 15 May 1935. Died: 29 September 2018.) Centre-forward Billy Neville signed for West Ham United from Limerick junior club Wembley Rovers in November 1956, and after progressing through the club's junior and reserve teams he went on to make three first-team appearances, all in September 1957. The following month he was capped for the Republic of Ireland B team, scoring in the 1-1 draw with Romania at Dalymount Park. He was retained for the 1958–59 season but then contracted tuberculosis which ended his playing career at the age of 22.

Ron Newman (Born: Fareham, 19 January 1934. Died: Tampa, Florida, USA, 27 August 2018.) Ron Newman enjoyed two distinct careers in the game, firstly as a player in the Football League and then as a player and coach in the United States. A winger with Portsmouth in the 1950s, he had to wait until the 1959–60 season to establish himself in the side and then spent three seasons as a first-team regular. Unsuccessful spells with Leyton Orient and Crystal Palace followed before he signed for Gillingham where he was a member of the team that won the Division Three title in 1963–64. In the United States he played for Atlanta Chiefs and Dallas Tornado then successfully turned to coaching, notably with Dallas Tornado (NASL champions in 1971) and San Diego Sockers with whom he won eight Major Indoor Soccer League titles between 1982 and 1992. He was inducted into the US National Soccer Hall of Fame in 1992.

Graham Newton (Born: Bilston, 22 December 1942. Died: February 2019.) Graham Newton was a wing-half or inside-forward who was on the books of both Wolverhampton Wanderers and Blackpool as a youngster without making a senior appearance. In February 1962 he signed for Walsall where he played in 34 League and Cup games, later gaining further experience with both Coventry City and Bournemouth. He did well, playing for Atlanta Chiefs over a four-year period (1967–1970) and was a member of their team that won the NASL championship in 1968. His Football League career ended with a brief spell at Port Vale.

Reece Nicholson (Born: Bircotes, Nottinghamshire, 4 April 1936. Died: 22 March 2019.) Reece Nicholson was a skilful inside-forward who joined Doncaster Rovers from Harworth Colliery Institute at the start of the 1953–54 season. Although mostly a reserve during five years at Belle Vue, he made 30 first team appearances during his stay. He subsequently spent a season with Cambridge City before enjoying a lengthy career in Midland League football.

Flemming Nielsen (Born: Copenhagen, 24 February 1934. Died: 16 November 2018.) Flemming Nielsen was a tall, skilful midfield player who developed in domestic football in Denmark with B93 and AB, also gaining international honours and a silver medal at the 1960 Olympic Games. In 1961 he moved to play in Serie A with Atalanta where he played for the Italian League representative team before eventually joining the 'Scandinavian Invasion' at Morton in January 1965. He stayed 18 months at Cappielow, making 36 appearances, before returning to Denmark to play for B93.

Dusan Nikolic (Born: Belgrade, 23 January 1953. Died: Belgrade, 15 December2018.) Dusan Nikolic was a hard-tackling midfield player who made his name with Red Star Belgrade, with whom he also won international honours for Yugoslavia. In October 1980 he signed for Bolton Wanderers and he was a regular in his first season with the club but added just one more appearance the following season and in January 1982 he returned to Yugoslavia, signing for Teteks Tetevo.

George O'Hara (Born: 1933. Died: Glasgow, 7 September 2018.) George O'Hara was an inside-left who joined Dundee from Shettleston Juniors in August 1955. He went on to make over 70 appearances during his stay but lost his place in the side and chose to move south, signing for Southend United. The move was not a success and within a month he was back in Scotland with Queen of the South where he made a number of appearances before leaving the senior game in the summer of 1960.

Ian Oliver (Died: 7 February 2019.) Ian Oliver made his senior debut for Berwick Rangers as a 17-year-old and went on to serve the club for over 50 years as player, coach, physio, groundsman and caretaker manager. A centre-forward, he played in the Chirnside United team that lost out to Third Lanark in the first round of the Scottish Cup in January 1958 and soon afterwards he was signed by Berwick. However, his stay at Shielfield was a brief one and he made just five appearances before returning to Chirnside for the start of the 1958–59 campaign.

Lindsay Parsons (Born: Bristol, 20 March 1946. Died: 12 April 2019.) Defender Lindsay Parsons joined Bristol Rovers as an apprentice on leaving school, graduating to a professional contract in April 1964. It was not until the 1970–71 season that he fully established himself in the line-up and between September 1970 and March 1974 he went on a run of 199 consecutive League and Cup appearances. He was a member of the team that won the Watney Cup in 1972–73 and the following season he was a near ever-present as Rovers clinched promotion from Division Three. He ended his career at Torquay United before continuing in non-league football for several seasons. He was later manager of Cheltenham Town (May 1992 to 1995).

Ron Peplow (Born: Willesden, 4 May 1935. Died: 15 March 2019.) Ron Peplow was a versatile player who developed with Rugby Juniors BC of North Kensington and then with Southall as an amateur before stepping up to the senior ranks with Brentford in August 1955. He spent six years as a professional at Griffin Park and although never a first choice in the side he made 66 first-team appearances. Later he played for Folkestone Town and Ashford Town.

Gordon Phillips (Born: Uxbridge, 17 November 1946. Died: 3 September 2018.) Goalkeeper Gordon Phillips played in Hayes' first team as a 16-year-old and two weeks after signing for Brentford he made his first-team debut in an FA Cup tie against Margate the day before his 17th birthday. He went on to make over 200 first-team appearances for the Bees and although not always a regular in the side, he was ever-present in the 1971–72 season when they won promotion from the old Fourth Division.

Justin Phillips (Born: Derby, 17 December 1971. Died: Duffield, Derbyshire, 12 June 2018.) Justin Phillips was a tall central defender who represented England at Schools and Youth international levels. He joined Derby County as a trainee before becoming a professional in July 1990 but spent much of his four years at the Baseball Ground sidelined by injury. He made three first-team appearances, all towards the end of the 1990–91 season, and later spent time on loan with Cork City during 1993–94.

Fred Pickering (Born: Blackburn, 19 January 1941. Died: 9 February 2019.) Fred Pickering joined Blackburn Rovers from school as a full-back and went on to captain the Rovers team that won the FA Youth Cup in 1959–60. It was not until early in 1961 that he switched to playing as a centre-forward and he was a revelation in his new role, scoring two in his first appearance against Manchester City. His performances at Ewood Park drew admirers from rival clubs and in March 1964 he was sold to Everton for a substantial fee. He scored a hat-trick on his debut for the Toffees and two months later scored a hat-trick on his England debut against the USA (the last England player to achieve this feat). He won a further two caps, scoring two more goals, for the national side. He led the Everton scoring charts in both 1964–65 and 1965–66 but was injured in the closing stages of the latter campaign, causing him to miss out on a place in the Cup final team. He later enjoyed some success with both Birmingham City (a place in the FA Cup semi-final in 1967–68) and Blackpool (promotion to the top flight in 1969–70) before ending his career back at Ewood Park.

John Pickup (Born: Stoke-on-Trent, 6 September 1929. Died: Endon, Staffordshire, 19 July 2018.) Inside left John Pickup was on Stoke City's books from September 1946 before undertaking his National Service with the RAF. In five years on the club's books he featured regularly for the reserve and junior teams, but only made one first-team appearance, in the home game with Huddersfield Town in November 1949. He later moved on to play for Stafford Rangers.

Darren Pitcher (Born: Stepney, 12 October 1969. Died: November 2018.) Darren Pitcher won England Youth international honours and was a member of the Charlton Athletic team that lost out to Coventry in the final of the 1986–87 FA Youth Cup. He signed a professional contract with the Addicks in January 1988 and between 1990 and 1994 he was firmly established in the side as a defensive midfield player, making over 200 appearances for the club. In July 1994 he moved on to Crystal Palace where his career continued to progress before he suffered a serious knee injury in August 1996.

Ralph Prouton (Born: Southampton, 1 March 1926. Died: Bath, 12 September 2018.) Although better known as a wicketkeeper batsman who made 52 appearances for Hampshire, Ralph Prouton also enjoyed a brief career as a soccer player. He had three years at Arsenal without breaking into the first team then spent the 1952–53 season with Swindon Town, for whom he made 16 appearances at left-half. Later he had spells with Tonbridge and Bath City.

Kevin Randall (Born: Ashton-under-Lyne, 20 August 1945. Died: 28 March 2019.) Kevin Randall was one of the best lower division strikers in the 1960s and '70s. He had been a professional at Bury in 1965–66 but received few opportunities there and it was only after he moved on to Chesterfield in the summer of 1966 that his career began to blossom. He recorded a double-figure goals tally in each of six seasons at Saltergate and he was a member of the team that won the Division Four title in 1969–70. His total of 96 League goals has been bettered by only two other players in the club's history. He moved on to Notts County and then Mansfield Town, assisting both to promotion, but by the time he had joined York City in October 1978 injuries had begun to catch up on him and he became less prolific. After retirement he continued to work in the game including a spell as Chesterfield manager (June 1987 to October 1988). At the time of his death he was a member of Burnley's scouting staff.

Hugh Reid (Died: Dundee, 25 September 2018.) Hugh Reid was a right-back who spent his early career with Lochee United Juveniles and Carnoustie Panmure. He was signed by Dundee in October 1955 and in a 12-year spell at Dens Park made a total of 146 appearances, scoring a solitary goal. Later he had a spell with Highland League club Keith.

John Reid (Born Edinburgh, 23 July 1935. Died: 2019.) John Reid was an outside-right who signed for Airdrieonians from Tranent Juniors in August 1954. In his first season at Broomfield he helped the club win the Scottish B Division title and reach the semi finals of both the League Cup and the Scottish Cup. However, National Service then intervened to disrupt his career. Stationed at RAF Uxbridge he was allowed to play for Watford by his parent club and in his only appearance, on Christmas Day 1956, he scored in a 2-1 win over Ipswich Town. He returned briefly to Scotland then spent an unproductive season at Norwich City before concluding his career in senior football at Barrow.

Jose Antonio Reyes (Born: Utrera, Spain, 1 September 1983. Died: Utrera, Spain, 1 June 2019.) Jose Antonio Reyes was a pacy and skilful left-sided attacking player who developed with Sevilla before joining Arsenal in the January 2004 transfer window. In his first term at Highbury he contributed to the club's unbeaten Premier League-winning season and the following season he was a member of the side that won the FA Cup. In 2005–06 he was a substitute in the team that lost to Barcelona in the Champions League final. He spent 2006–07 on a season-long loan deal with Real Madrid and then continued to play with a number of teams in La Liga including Atletico Madrid and Sevilla. Most recently he was playing for Extremadura in the Segunda Division. He won 21 full caps for Spain. His death was as a result of a road traffic accident.

John Richmond (Born: Derby, 17 September 1938. Died: August 2018.) Half-back John Richmond captained the Derby Boys team and progressed from local club Derby Corinthians to sign for Derby County in January 1956. He made his senior debut against Huddersfield Town in April 1958, marking a young Denis Law, but in just over seven seasons at the Baseball Ground he mostly featured in the Central League team. In recent years he was treasurer of Derby County Former Players Association.

Gordon Riddick (Born: Langleybury, Hertfordshire, 6 November 1943. Died: 24 August 2018.) Gordon Riddick was a versatile player who made over 400 senior appearances in a career that spanned the period 1961 to 1977. He played more than 100 games for each of Luton Town, Gillingham and Brentford and also spent time with Charlton Athletic, Orient and Northampton. He scored Orient's 3,000th Football League goal at Middlesbrough in March 1971 while in the closing stages of his career he captained Brentford.

Jim Riddle (Born: Arbroath, 27 March 1946. Died: Dundee, 8 May 2019.) Defender Jim Riddle was a product of the Arbroath Lads' Club and Carnoustie Panmure before stepping up to the seniors with Arbroath in the summer of 1963. He captained the Arbroath side that won the Combined Reserve League Autumn Series title in 1963–64 and after spending part of the 1966–67 season on loan to Brechin City he returned to Gayfield, going on to make 72 first-team appearances.

John Ritchie (Born: Auchterderran, Fife, 12 June 1947. Died: 1 June 2018.) Goalkeeper John Ritchie joined Cowdenbeath in June 1964 and made over 100 appearances in the following three seasons. However, he is best known for his association with Brechin City for whom he played almost 350 first-team games in two separate spells, also serving as manager from January 1987 to May 1993, leading them to the Second Division championship in 1989–90 and a further promotion from the Second Division in 1992–93. In between his two spells as a player at Glebe Park he spent time with Bradford City and Dundee United. At the time of his death he was goalkeeping coach at Arbroath.

Dennis Roach (Born: April, 1940. Died: Mudeford, Dorset, 16 May 2019.) Dennis Roach played Southern League football in the 1960s and '70s for Barnet, Bedford Town and Hillingdon Borough but later became much better known as one of the most powerful football agents in the game. He represented players such as Johan Cruyff, Paul Gascoigne, Glenn Hoddle and Trevor Francis through his company PRO International and was at one time president of the FIFA-recognised International Association of Football Agents.

Johnny Robinson (Born: Chorley, 18 April 1936. Died: June 2019.) Johnny Robinson was an apprentice electrician at Leyland Motors where he was playing for the works team when he signed for Bury in September 1954. A winger, he went on to make 126 first-team appearances for the Shakers, mostly in the old Second Division. He later had a brief trial with Oldham Athletic (July to September 1961) before leaving senior football.

Ian Ross (Born: Glasgow, 26 January 1947. Died: February 2019.) Ian Ross was a versatile defender who spent over six years with Liverpool after signing as a 17-year-old but was mostly a mainstay of the club's reserve team. In February 1972 he was sold to Aston Villa, and after helping them win promotion from the Third Division in his first season he went on to captain the team that won the Football League Cup and returned to the top flight in 1974–75. After leaving Villa Park he had two-and-a-half seasons of regular first-team football with Peterborough United before moving into coaching. He was manager of Valur, KR Reykjavik and Keflavik in Iceland as well as Huddersfield Town (March 1992 to July 1993) and Berwick Rangers (from March 1996).

Ray Russell (Born: Walsall, 9 March 1930. Died: 2018.) Ray Russell was an inside-left who was on the books of West Bromwich Albion as a youngster before making his name as a goalscorer in Birmingham League football with Kidderminster Harriers and Burton Albion. He signed for Shrewsbury Town in May 1954 and scored on his debut at Brentford soon afterwards. He went on to net 61 goals from 177 appearances for the Shrews, enjoying his best season in 1958–59 when he hit 27 as the team won promotion from Division Four.

Nigel Saddington (Born: Sunderland, 9 December 1965. Died: 24 January 2019.) Nigel Saddington was a central defender who developed in non-league football in the North East before signing for Doncaster Rovers shortly after the start of the 1984–85 season. He made a number of first-team appearances during his time at Belle Vue, then returned to the North East where he signed for Sunderland after a trial period. He enjoyed the best seasons of his career in a three-year spell at Carlisle United where he was club captain and made over 100 first-team appearances. His senior career ended after he was diagnosed with ME at the age of 25 although he later turned out for Gateshead and Nissan of the Wearside League.

Emiliano Sala (Born: Cululu, Santa Fe, Argentina, 31 October 1990. Died: English Channel, 21 January 2019.) Emiliano Sala developed in youth football in Argentina prior to moving to France to sign for Bordeaux. After maturing in a series of loan spells he joined Nantes in July 2015 where his goalscoring exploits earned him a move to Cardiff City in the January 2019 transfer window. Tragically he was killed in an air accident before he was able to make his debut for the Bluebirds.

Frank Sandeman (Born: Dundee, 28 August 1936. Died: Newport-on-Tay, 23 November 2018.) Frank Sandeman was a wing-half who developed in Junior football with Dundee St Joseph's before signing for Montrose in December 1956. After making over 200 appearances he moved on to East Stirlingshire, where he was a member of the team that won promotion to the top flight in 1962–63. After brief spells with Heart of Midlothian and Arbroath he concluded his career at Brechin City, signing as a player in October 1966 before becoming player-manager (March 1969 to January 1971).

Geoff Scott (Born: Birmingham, 31 October 1956. Died: October 2018.) Geoff Scott was on the books of Aston Villa as a youngster but drifted into non-league football before his career was revived by a move to Stoke City in April 1977. He was a near ever-present in the Potters' team that won promotion to the top flight in 1977–78 and subsequently moved on to play for Leicester City, Charlton Athletic, Middlesbrough, Northampton Town and Cambridge United before a serious knee injury ended his career. He was later secretary of the Stoke City Old Boys Association.

Walter Selway (Born: Dundee, 1927. Died: Alford, Aberdeenshire, 14 July 2018.) Centre-forward Walter Selway developed in Junior football with Dundee Osborne and Alyth United before joining the senior ranks with Brechin City towards the end of the 1953–54 season. He enjoyed an excellent scoring record in three seasons at Glebe Park and a further two at Montrose finishing with a career tally of 75 goals from 161 League and Cup appearances before leaving senior football.

Jimmy Shanks (Died: 13 March 2019.) Jimmy Shanks was a defender who was playing reserve-team football for Airdrieonians while still at school. He went on to make over 250 appearances for the club and was a member of the team that won the Scottish League Division B and reached the semi-finals of both the Scottish Cup and Scottish League Cup in 1954–55. In September 1963 he transferred to Stranraer where he added a further century of appearances before leaving senior football. Jim worked as a school teacher and served as Scottish Schools FA President from 1988 to 1990.

Ronnie Sheed (Born: Provan, Glasgow, 8 May 1947. Died: 16 June 2018.) Ronnie Sheed was a busy midfield player who signed for Kilmarnock from East Kilbride Thistle in November 1969. His early career was hampered after he suffered a broken leg playing against Motherwell in the opening weeks of the 1970–71 season but he fought his way back to fitness and went on to play more than 150 games for Killie before leaving in the summer of 1977. He later had a spell with Partick Thistle before switching to amateur football.

John Shepherd (Born: Kensington, 29 May 1932. Died: 11 June 2018.) John Shepherd was playing in the Kensington & District Sunday League for Kensal House when he signed amateur forms for Millwall in April 1951. He contracted polio shortly afterwards but made a full recovery and went on to make a sensational start to his Football League career. He scored four goals on his debut against Leyton Orient in October 1952 and netted hat-tricks on four occasions in his first 12 appearances. His Millwall tally was 78 goals from 166 games and he later went on to assist Brighton & Hove Albion and Gillingham before switching to Southern League football with Ashford Town.

Peter Skipper (Born: Hull, 11 April 1958. Died: 23 April 2019.) Peter Skipper was a powerful central defender best known for his two spells with Hull City. A local boy who made a few appearances as a youngster for the Tigers he moved to Darlington for two seasons before returning to Boothferry Park in the summer of 1982. Ever-present in League matches in his first three seasons back, he helped the club to promotions in both 1982–83 and 1984–85. When the Tigers' regular 'keeper was injured en route to the Full Members Cup match at Southampton in November 1986 he played the whole match in goal. Further spells with Oldham Athletic and Walsall followed before he wound down his career on non-contract terms with Wrexham and Wigan Athletic.

Alan Skirton (Born: Bath, 23 January 1939. Died: May 2019.) Alan Skirton was a winger who excelled with Southern League club Bath City as a teenager, earning him a move to Arsenal. He missed the whole of the 1959–60 season through injury but once fit again he began to establish himself in the first team at Highbury. In seven seasons with the Gunners he made over 150 first-team appearances before moving on to Blackpool, where he was leading scorer in the 1967–68 season. After concluding his senior career with spells at Bristol City and Torquay United he spent 10 years as commercial manager at Bath City and a further 21 years in a similar role at Yeovil Town.

Bill Slater OBE, CBE (Born: Clitheroe, 29 April 1927. Died: 18 December 2018.) Bill Slater played as an amateur for both Blackpool and Brentford in the years after the war, turning out for Blackpool in the 1951 FA Cup final, the last amateur to appear in a Cup final. He won 20 caps for England Amateurs and also appeared for the Great Britain Olympic team before becoming a part-time professional with Wolverhampton Wanderers. He went on to make over 300 appearances at Molineux where he played in three Football League championship-winning teams and was an FA Cup winner in 1960. He won 20 full caps for England and was the Football Writers Association's Footballer of the Year in 1960 (the only part-time player to win the award).

Alan Smith (Born: Newcastle, 15 October 1921. Died: 27 May 2019.) Alan Smith was a winger who signed for Arsenal in May 1946 after being demobbed from the Army. He made three appearances for the Gunners in a six-month spell, moving on to Brentford, then also members of the First Division, at the end of 1946. He stayed in senior football until the end of the 1949–50 season but was principally a reserve both at Griffin Park and with Leyton Orient before moving into the Southern League with Tonbridge.

Billy Smith (Born: Arbroath, 1936. Died: 4 November 2018.) Centre-half Billy Smith signed for Rangers shortly after the start of the 1953–54 season but his only first-team experience at Ibrox came with a couple of appearances at the end of the 1957–58 season. He fared better in a three-year spell with Dundee but it was only when he dropped down to play for Forfar Athletic that he played regular first-team football, making 86 appearances during his time at Station Park.

Ken Smith (Born: Consett, Co. Durham, 7 December 1927. Died: 6 December 2018.) Ken Smith was an inside-forward who featured in Scottish Junior football for Montrose Roselea while stationed at RAF Montrose on National Service, helping them to win the Angus Junior League in 1947–48. On demobilisation he played briefly for Annfield Plain before signing for Blackpool in April 1949. However, the nearest he came to first-team football for the Seasiders was being selected as a travelling reserve and in August 1952 he moved on to Gateshead. He enjoyed seven seasons of regular first-team football at Redheugh Park, scoring 78 goals from 278 League and Cup appearances before dropping into non-league football with Ashington.

Tommy Smith MBE (Born: Liverpool, 5 April 1945. Died: Waterloo, Crosby, 12 April 2019.) Tommy Smith joined the groundstaff at Liverpool on leaving school, signing a professional contract on reaching the age of 17. He developed into a fearsome central defender who was a consistent performer throughout his career. He made over 600 appearances for the Reds in a career that spanned the period from 1962 to 1978. One of the stars of Bill Shankly's team, he was a member of four Football League title-winning sides and was twice an FA Cup winner. He also gained UEFA Cup winners' medals in 1973 and 1976 and a European Cup winners' medal in 1977. After 16 years at Anfield he concluded his career with a season at Swansea City, helping the team win promotion from Division Three in 1978–79. He won a solitary cap for England, playing against Wales in May 1971.

John Smout (Born: Newtown, 30 October 1941. Died: Newtown, 18 February 2019.) Goalkeeper John Smout was playing for his local team Newtown in the Mid Wales League when signed by Crystal Palace in August 1965. He was mostly third choice in his season at Crystal Palace and on the only occasion he featured in the first team he was carried off with an injury. He then spent two seasons with Exeter City, where he was an ever-present in 1967–68 before returning to play for Newtown again.

Vichai Srivaddhanaprabha (Born: Bangkok, 5 June 1958. Died: Leicester, 27 October 2018.) Vichai Srivaddhanaprabha was a Thai businessman who became a billionaire through his King Power company. He was the lead figure in the Asia Football Investments consortium which bought the then Championship club Leicester City in August 2010. Under his ownership the club won promotion to the top flight and in 2015–16 became Premier League champions. He also owned the VR Polo Club in Bangkok and Belgian second division football team OH Leuven. His death was as a result of a helicopter crash which occurred as he was leaving the King Power Stadium following Leicester's home game against West Ham United.

John Steeples (Born: Doncaster, 28 April 1959. Died: March 2019.) John Steeples was a wide attacking player who spent three seasons with Grimsby Town in the early 1980s. He was mostly a reserve during his time at Blundell Park, although he was a member of the team that defeated Wimbledon 3-2 to win the first ever Football League Group Cup final in April 1982. He later played for Scarborough and Grantham.

Dave Stewart (Born: Glasgow, 11 March 1947. Died: 13 November 2018.) Goalkeeper David Stewart was a Scottish Junior Cup winner with Kilsyth Rangers in 1967 and signed for Ayr United shortly afterwards. A near ever-present in the team that won promotion from the Second Division in 1968–69 he made over 250 appearances for Ayr before being sold to Leeds United in October 1973. He spent the next six seasons at Elland Road providing back-up to David Harvey although he played in the 1975 European Cup final when Leeds lost to Bayern Munich in Paris. Later he had 18 months as a reserve at West Bromwich Albion and ended his senior career with Swansea City where he played every game of the 1981–82 season as the Swans clinched promotion to the First Division. He won a single cap for Scotland, appearing against East Germany in September 1977.

Roger Sugden (Born: Stanningley, West Yorkshire, 15 October 1945. Died: Edinburgh, 6 July 2018.) Roger Sugden played his early football with Musselburgh Windsor and Haddington Athletic before signing for Cowdenbeath in August 1963. A pacy winger, he went on to make over 200 senior appearances during his time at Central Park and was a member of the team that won promotion from the Second Division in 1969–70. Shortly afterwards injury effectively ended his senior career and he returned to the Juniors with Dalkeith Thistle.

John Sutherland (Born: Cork, 10 February 1932. Died: Nantwich, 6 February 2019.) Full-back John Sutherland won an FA of Ireland Minor Cup winners' medal with Cork junior club Evergreen in 1948 and had a trial with Southampton before signing up for Everton in May 1950. He had to wait six years for his first-team debut at Goodison and after making half-a-dozen appearances he joined Chesterfield in the 1957 close season. He fared much better in lower division football and was an ever-present at Saltergate in 1957–58 before spending two seasons with Crewe Alexandra where he took his total of senior appearances beyond the 100-mark before a serious knee injury led to his retirement.

Alan Swan (Born: 2 June 1950. Died: Johannesburg, South Africa, 24 January 2019.) Alan Swan was a left-back who joined Clyde from Shettleston Juniors in December 1969 and went on to make over 150 first-team appearances during his stay at Shawfield. A highlight came in the 1972–73 season when he was a member of the team that won the Second Division title. At the end of the 1974–75 season he emigrated to South Africa where he played for the Johannesburg-based club Highlands Park for several seasons.

Alex Tait (Born: West Sleekburn, Northumberland, 28 November 1933. Died: Tutbury, Staffordshire, 22 January 2019.) Alex Tait was a lively striker with an eye for goal who played with Newcastle United's nursery team while still at school. On leaving education he signed a professional contract for the club but never really established himself in the side during an eight-year spell at St James' Park, best remembered for his hat-trick in a 6-2 win over Sunderland in December 1956. He moved on to Bristol City in the summer of 1960 where he enjoyed a good scoring record (133 appearances, 44 goals). After a season at Doncaster Rovers he became player-manager of Burton Albion in the 1965 close season.

Mike Thalassitis (Born: Edmonton, 19 January 1993. Died: Essex, 15 March 2019.) Michael Thalassitis was a striker who developed in the youth set-up at Stevenage and went on to make a total of seven appearances, all from the substitutes' bench, scoring in the 4-1 League Cup defeat to Southampton in August 2012. He subsequently played for a number of teams, mostly at Conference South level, before leaving the game. He represented Cyprus at U19 and U21 levels. He was better known as a reality television star who appeared in such programmes as *Love Island* and *Celebs Go Dating*.

Peter Thompson (Born: Carlisle, 27 November 1942. Died: Ashford, Kent, 30 December 2018.) Peter Thompson signed for Preston North End at the age of 17 and initially featured in the first team at centre-forward before switching to playing on the left wing where his skills were better used. His career really took off when he moved to Liverpool in the summer of 1963 and he went on to become one of the key players in Bill Shankly's legendary side of that era. A member of the team that won the Football League title in 1963–64 and 1965–66, he was an FA Cup winner in 1965 and the following year gained a European Cup Winners' Cup runners-up medal. In total he made over 400 League and Cup appearances for the Anfield club before injuries took their toll and he moved on to conclude his career with Bolton Wanderers. He won 16 full caps for England between 1964 and 1970 and also gained representative honours for England U23s and the Football League.

Alan Thomson (Born: Clarkston, Glasgow, 6 September 1946. Died: Birmingham, 22 July 2018.) Alan Thomson was a Scotland Schools international who was on the books of Rangers as a youngster without making the first team. After moving on to Hamilton Academical in August 1966 he established himself as a regular at centre-forward and finished as leading scorer in two of his three seasons with the club. He spent the 1969–70 season with Albion Rovers before work sent him to live abroad.

Dennis Thrower (Born: Ipswich, 1 August 1938. Died: Ipswich, 5 August 2018.) Dennis Thrower was a wing-half who was just 18 when he made his senior debut for Ipswich Town, but after another appearance shortly afterwards it was another six years before he returned to the first-team line-up. In total he made 31 appearances for the team before moving on to sign for Bury Town in 1965.

Arthur Turner (Born: Poplar, 22 January 1921. Died: Sevenoaks, 25 January 2019.) Arthur Turner signed for Charlton Athletic on amateur forms during the Second World War and made over 50 appearances for them, finishing as top scorer in both 1944–45 and 1945–46. He became the first amateur player to appear in an FA Cup final at Wembley when he lined up for the Addicks in the 1946 final. He later signed for Colchester United, scoring 74 goals in 94 Southern League appearances and then played for them in Division Three South, scoring their first-ever Football League goal in a 1-1 draw at Swindon Town in August 1950.

Johnny Valentine (Born: 13 March 1930. Died: Forres, Moray, 17 February 2019.) Centre-half Johnny Valentine developed with Buckie Thistle and had trials with Hibernian and Aberdeen before signing for Queen's Park in February 1953. He enjoyed a useful amateur career, making over 100 appearances for the Hampden club and winning 10 caps for Scotland Amateurs before moving on to Rangers where he was mostly a reserve. Later he concluded his career with two seasons at St Johnstone, contributing to their success in winning the Second Division title in 1959–60.

Peter Vine (Born: Abingdon, 11 December 1940. Died: 30 April 2018.) Peter Vine was an inside-forward who signed amateur forms for Southampton in April 1956, turning professional in December 1957. A member of the Saints team that reached the semi-final of the FA Youth Cup in 1956–57 and an England Youth international, he made a solitary senior appearance, featuring at inside-right at Bury in March 1959.

Harry Walden (Born: Walgrave, Northamptonshire, 22 December 1940. Died: 23 September 2018.) Harry Walden was a pacy winger whose goals helped Kettering Town to reach the FA Cup second round in 1960–61, earning him a move to Luton Town in January 1961. He went straight into the Hatters' line-up but then suffered an injury and it was not until the 1961–62 season that he featured regularly in the side. In June 1964 he moved on to Northampton Town, helping the Cobblers win promotion to the top flight in his first season. He stayed until the club descended into the Third Division then returned to Kettering where he continued to play until 1973.

Jim Walker (Died: 2019.) Jim Walker developed with Bonnybridge Wellstood Juveniles and Clydebank Juniors before signing for Rangers in February 1954. Although restricted by National Service he played occasional friendly games during his time at Ibrox and two Scottish League games in December 1956. He was only a reserve in a brief spell with Southend United and returned to Scotland to establish himself firstly with St Johnstone from November 1958 and then East Fife (1962–1967). He made over 200 appearances during his time at Bayview before ending his senior career with Forfar Athletic.

Johnny Walker (Born: Glasgow, 17 December 1928. Died: Reading, 23 January 2019.) Inside-forward Johnny Walker was one of the stars of the Campsie Black Watch team that reached the final of the Scottish Secondary Juvenile Cup in 1947 and he signed professional forms for Wolves immediately after the game. He never quite managed to establish himself in the side at Molineux but later enjoyed a very successful career out of the top flight with both Southampton (1952–1957) and Reading (1957–1965). His final total of 542 senior appearances is testament to his reliability while during his time at Elm Park he captained the side.

Don Wallace (Born: 22 November 1932. Died: 4 December 2018.) Goalkeeper Don Wallace excelled in Junior football with Bonnybridge Juniors before stepping up to the seniors with Alloa Athletic early in 1957. In a short senior career he made 13 first-team appearances before moving on.

Duncan Welbourne (Born: Scunthorpe, 28 July 1940. Died: 14 January 2019.) Duncan Welbourne was a robust defender who developed in a six-year spell with Grimsby Town (1957–1963), making over 100 first-team appearances for the Mariners. However, he is best known for his performances for Watford where he was a model of consistency, playing over 450 games including a consecutive run of 280 Football League games. Highlights of his time at Vicarage Road included being ever-present in the team that won Division Three in 1968–69 and also assisting the team to a place in the FA Cup semi-final the following season. He moved on to Southport in July 1974 where he became player-coach.

Chris Weller (Born: Reading, 25 December 1939. Died: Wimborne, 4 June 2018.) Inside-forward Chris Weller had been an amateur with Reading before joining Bournemouth on a professional contract in September 1959. After waiting 12 months for his senior debut he burst on the scene with seven goals in his first 13 appearances. With the exception of a six-month spell at Bristol Rovers, he remained at Dean Court until the end of the 1966–67 season, playing over 100 first-team games. He later had a lengthy spell with Southern League club Yeovil Town, helping them win the title and reach the FA Cup third round in 1970–71.

Bob Whitehead (Born: Ashington, 22 September 1936. Died: March 2019.) Right-back Bob Whitehead signed for Newcastle United as a 17-year-old, but in seven seasons at St James' Park he mostly provided back-up to Dick Keith, making a total of 20 first-team appearances. He spent the 1961–62 campaign with Southern League club Cambridge City before returning to senior football once more with Darlington where he was a regular in the line-up for 18 months.

Danny Williams (Born: Maltby, near Rotherham, 20 November 1924. Died: Newmarket, 3 February 2019.) Danny Williams was one of the all-time great figures in the history of Rotherham United. He joined the club as a left-half during the Second World War, making 95 appearances in the emergency competitions before continuing as a part-time professional when peacetime football returned. He was a regular in the Millers' line-up for the best part of 14 seasons and rarely missed a game during the 1950–51 campaign when the Division Three North title was won. He amassed a club record total of 500 first-team appearances and on retirement joined the backroom staff at Millmoor before serving as manager from July 1962 to May 1965. He later had two spells in charge of Swindon Town as well as managing both Sheffield Wednesday and Mansfield Town. His greatest feat as a manager was in the 1968–69 season when he won promotion from the Third Division with Swindon Town as well as the League Cup, defeating Arsenal in extra time in the final.

Gareth Williams (Born: Hendon, 30 October 1941. Died: Las Palmas, Gran Canaria, Spain, 4 June 2018.) Gareth Williams was a powerful wing-half who joined Cardiff City from local football in the closing stages of the 1958–59 season, but it was not until April 1963 that he established himself as a first-team regular at Ninian Park. He went on to become a key member of the side and club captain, featuring in the teams which reached the quarter-final of the European Cup Winners' Cup (1964–65) and semi-final of the League Cup (1965–66). He was surprisingly allowed to leave for Bolton Wanderers in October 1967 and later concluded his senior career with a couple of seasons at Bury.

Graham Williams (Born: Wrexham, 31 December 1936. Died: 25 November 2018.) Graham Williams was an outside-left who was briefly with Bradford City before being sold to Everton in March 1956. He spent three full seasons at Goodison but was mostly a back-up player during his stay. He did better when dropping down to the Second Division with Swansea Town, making 100 appearances and also winning five full caps for Wales. Later he had spells with Wrexham, Wellington Town, Tranmere Rovers (where he was a promotion winner in 1966–67) and Port Vale before leaving senior football.

Joe Williams (Died: Bangor, North Wales, 8 March 2018.) Joe Williams enjoyed his best seasons with Holyhead Town (1960–1970) for whom he was a member of the team that won the Welsh League North title in 1963–64 and the North Wales Coast Challenge Cup in 1966–67. He won three caps for Wales Amateurs and also featured for the North Wales Coast FA in their fixtures against the Scottish Junior FA.

Ernest Womersley (Born: Liversedge, 28 August 1932. Died: Cleckheaton, 15 September 2018.) Ernest Womersley was a winger or inside-forward who signed for Huddersfield Town in September 1949. He mostly featured in the club's Central League and Yorkshire League teams, making two first-team appearances, both in the 1950–51 season. He stayed at Leeds Road until the summer of 1957 and then had a season with Bradford City without breaking into the side before joining Stocksbridge Works.

Roy Woolcott (Born: Leyton, 29 July 1946. Died: Waltham Abbey, 16 December 2019.) Roy Woolcott was a tall centre-forward who progressed from amateur football with Eton Manor to a professional contract with Tottenham Hotspur during the 1967–68 season. However, during a five-year stay at White Hart Lane he made just a single appearance for Spurs, lining up at Ipswich Town in December 1969. He had a successful loan spell with Gillingham in 1971–72, scoring five goals from 13 appearances, before switching to non-league football with Chelmsford City. He helped the Essex club reach the FA Cup third round in 1972–73 but then a back injury restricted his appearances.

Brian Wright (Died: Derry, 15 March 2019.) Brian Wright developed in Irish football firstly with Derry City and Distillery before moving south to play for Sligo Rovers. He was the youngest player to appear in an Irish Cup final when he turned out for Derry City against Glenavon in the 1957 final at the age of 15. He spent most of the 1962–63 season with Port Vale, scoring two goals in 15 first-team outings. He subsequently returned to Ireland and later went on to score Finn Harps' first-ever League of Ireland goal in a 10-2 defeat to Shamrock Rovers in August 1969.

George Yardley (Born: Kirkcaldy, 8 October 1942. Died: Dalgety Bay, Fife, 14 November 2018.) George Yardley initially signed for East Fife as a second-choice goalkeeper but he was also a capable outfield player. He was capped for Scotland Amateurs against Wales in May 1960 as a 'keeper but made most of his appearances at Bayview as a centre-forward with just occasional outings between the sticks. He later played for Forfar Athletic and Montrose and spent time in Australia before returning to look for a club. A one-match trial with Luton Town was followed by a longer spell with Tranmere Rovers where his goalscoring feats helped fire the club to promotion in 1966–67. A serious kidney injury suffered in March 1968 led to a lengthy stay in hospital and it was some time before he was able to play again. He returned to Prenton Park to bring his record for Rovers to 81 goals from 149 appearances.

Jake Young (Died: 8 May 2019.) Jake Young was a defender who signed for Dundee from Junior outfit Carnoustie Panmure shortly after the start of the 1954–55 season. He made little progress at Dens Park but went on to enjoy a useful career as an effective centre-half with both Arbroath and East Fife. During his time at Gayfield he was a near ever-present in the team that won promotion from the Second Division and reached the League Cup quarter-finals in 1958–59. After further spells with St Mirren and Keith he was appointed player-manager of Forfar Athletic in August 1967, successfully turning round the fortunes of the club.

Ian Nannestad, Soccer History Magazine
www.soccer-history.co.uk

THE FOOTBALL RECORDS

BRITISH FOOTBALL RECORDS

ALL-TIME PREMIER LEAGUE CHAMPIONSHIP SEASONS ON POINTS AVERAGE

	Team	*Season*	*P*	*W*	*D*	*L*	*F*	*A*	*Pts*	*Pts Av*
1	Manchester C	2017–18	38	32	4	2	106	27	100	2.63
2	Manchester C	2018–19	38	32	2	4	95	23	98	2.58
3	Chelsea	2004–05	38	29	8	1	72	15	95	2.50
4	Chelsea	2016–17	38	30	3	5	85	33	93	2.45
5	Manchester U	1999–2000	38	28	7	3	97	45	91	2.39
6	Chelsea	2005–06	38	29	4	5	72	22	91	2.39
7	Arsenal	2003–04	38	26	12	0	73	26	90	2.36
	Manchester U	2008–09	38	28	6	4	68	24	90	2.36
9	Manchester C	2011–12	38	28	5	5	93	29	89	2.34
	Manchester U	2006–07	38	28	5	5	83	27	89	2.34
	Manchester U	2012–13	38	28	5	5	86	43	89	2.34
12	Arsenal	2001–02	38	26	9	3	79	36	87	2.28
	Manchester U	2007–08	38	27	6	5	80	22	87	2.28
	Chelsea	2014–15	38	26	9	3	73	32	87	2.28
15	Chelsea	2009–10	38	27	5	6	103	32	86	2.26
	Manchester C	2013–14	38	27	5	6	102	37	86	2.26
17	Manchester U	1993–94	42	27	11	4	80	38	92	2.19
18	Manchester U	2002–03	38	25	8	5	74	34	83	2.18
19	Manchester U	1995–96	38	25	7	6	73	35	82	2.15
20	Leicester C	2015–16	38	23	12	3	68	36	81	2.13
21	Blackburn R	1994–95	42	27	8	7	80	39	89	2.11
22	Manchester U	2000–01	38	24	8	6	79	31	80	2.10
	Manchester U	2010–11	38	23	11	4	78	37	80	2.10
24	Manchester U	1998–99	38	22	13	3	80	37	79	2.07
25	Arsenal	1997–98	38	23	9	6	68	33	78	2.05
26	Manchester U	1992–93	42	24	12	6	67	31	84	2.00
27	Manchester U	1996–97	38	21	12	5	76	44	75	1.97

PREMIER LEAGUE EVER-PRESENT CLUBS

	P	*W*	*D*	*L*	*F*	*A*	*Pts*
Manchester U	1038	648	224	166	1989	930	2168
Arsenal	1038	565	260	213	1845	1014	1955
Chelsea	1038	558	257	223	1770	1004	1931
Liverpool	1038	529	262	247	1774	1046	1849
Tottenham H	1038	446	257	335	1547	1306	1595
Everton	1038	377	296	365	1357	1311	1427

TOP TEN PREMIER LEAGUE APPEARANCES

1	Barry, Gareth	653	**6=**	Heskey, Emile	516
2	Giggs, Ryan	632	**6=**	Milner, James	516
3	Lampard, Frank	609	**8**	Schwarzer, Mark	514
4	James, David	572	**9**	Carragher, Jamie	508
5	Speed, Gary	535	**10**	Neville, Phil	505

TOP TEN PREMIER LEAGUE GOALSCORERS

1	Shearer, Alan	260	**6**	Aguero, Sergio	164
2	Rooney, Wayne	208	**7**	Fowler, Robbie	163
3	Cole, Andrew	187	**8**	Defoe, Jermain	162
4	Lampard, Frank	177	**9**	Owen, Michael	150
5	Henry, Thierry	175	**10**	Ferdinand, Les	149

SCOTTISH PREMIER LEAGUE SINCE 1998–99

	P	W	D	L	F	A	Pts
Celtic	789	580	120	89	1833	593	1860
Rangers	637	423	119	95	1328	536	1378
Aberdeen	789	316	180	293	1005	1013	1128
Hearts	751	296	186	269	969	907	1059
Motherwell	789	278	168	343	983	1190	1002
Kilmarnock	789	261	203	325	946	1131	986
Hibernian	639	223	168	248	854	892	837
Dundee U	680	214	184	282	842	1021	823

Rangers deducted 10 pts in 2011–12; Hearts deducted 15 pts in 2013–14; Dundee U deducted 3 pts in 2015–16.

DOMESTIC LANDMARKS 2018–19

AUGUST 2018

6 Blackpool manager Gary Bowyer resigned after just one game of the season. He became the first managerial casualty of the new season.

14 Nathan Wood became the youngest player to play in a competitive match for Middlesbrough at 16 years and 75 days. His debut came in the Carabao Cup tie with Notts Co when he appeared as a 62nd-minute substitute. The tie ended 3-3 with Middlesbrough eventually winning 4-3 on penalties. Wood also became the first player born in 2002 to play in a competitive match in any of England's professional leagues or domestic cups.

SEPTEMBER 2018

5 Luke Matheson became Rochdale's youngest debutant in the EFL Trophy tie against Bury at the age of 15 years and 336 days. Matheson appeared as a 13th minute substitute and went on to win the man-of-the-match award.

25 Fifteen-year-old Harvey Elliott became the youngest player to play in a competitive match for Fulham. He appeared as an 81st-minute substitute in Fulham's 3-1 victory at Millwall in the Carabao Cup 3rd round. At 15 years and 174 days old, he became the first 15-year-old to appear for Fulham.

OCTOBER 2018

27 Tragedy struck Leicester City as chairman Vichai Srivaddhanaprabha was killed in a helicopter crash in a car park outside the King Power Stadium.

NOVEMBER 2018

4 Sergio Aguero scored his 150th Premier League goal in Manchester City's 6-1 victory over Southampton at the Etihad Stadium.

DECEMBER 2018

8 Liverpool's James Milner made his 500th Premier League appearance in his side's 4-0 victory over Bournemouth at Dean Court. A Mohamed Salah hat-trick and a Steve Cook own goal sealed the victory for Liverpool.

21 Jordan Henderson of Liverpool made his 300th Premier League appearance in the 2-0 victory against Wolverhampton W at Molineux.

29 Ethan Walker became Preston North End's youngest ever league player with his appearance as substitute in the 1-1 home draw with Aston Villa.

JANUARY 2019

3 Liverpool lost for the first time this season in the 2-1 defeat by Manchester City at the Etihad Stadium.

21 Emiliano Sala, Cardiff City's record signing, was lost on board a plane that disappeared near the Channel Islands.

FEBRUARY 2019

22 FIFA impose a transfer embargo on Chelsea for breaching rules in relation to youth players. The embargo is to last two transfer windows.

APRIL 2019

2 Mike Dean became to first Premier League referee to issue 100 red cards in his career. The landmark was reached with his dismissal of Ashley Young of Manchester United in their 2-1 defeat at Wolves.

6 Luton Town's unbeaten run of 28 games became a new club record. It began with a 2-0 home win over Walsall on 20 October 2018 and ended with a 1-3 defeat at Charlton on 13 April 2019.

13 Lincoln City's unbeaten run of 19 games became a new club record. It began with a 2-1 home win over Cambridge on 29 December 2018 and ended with a 0-1 defeat to Carlisle United on 19 April.

22 Aston Villa's tenth successive league win 1-0 at home to Millwall became a new club record.

23 Shane Long scored the fastest goal in Premier League history in Southampton's 1-1 draw at Watford. Long scored after 7.69 seconds to take the record from Tottenham's Ledley King who scored after 9.82 seconds against Bradford City in December 2000.

MAY 2019

4 Harvey Elliott became the youngest ever Premier League player at 16 years, 30 days with his appearance for Fulham against Wolverhampton Wanderers at Molineux. Elliott was a 88th minute substitute in his team's 0-1 defeat.

12 Liverpool finish second in the Premier League with a record number of points for finishing runners-up. A final day victory over Wolverhampton Wanderers at Anfield was not enough as Manchester City defeated Brighton 4-1 to secure the title.

19 Manchester City became the first team to complete the English Domestic treble. Their 6-0 defeat of Watord in the FA Cup Final followed on from their EFL League Cup defeat of Chelsea on penalties and pipping Liverpool to the Premier League title.

EUROPEAN CUP AND CHAMPIONS LEAGUE RECORDS

MOST WINS BY CLUB

Real Madrid	13	1956, 1957, 1958, 1959, 1960, 1966, 1998, 2000, 2002, 2014, 2016, 2017, 2018.
AC Milan	7	1963, 1969, 1989, 1990, 1994, 2003, 2007.
Liverpool	6	1977, 1978, 1981, 1984, 2005, 2019.
Bayern Munich	5	1974, 1975, 1976, 2001, 2013.
Barcelona	5	1992, 2006, 2009, 2011, 2015.

MOST APPEARANCES IN FINAL
Real Madrid 15; AC Milan 11; Bayern Munich 10

MOST FINAL APPEARANCES PER COUNTRY
Spain 29 (18 wins, 11 defeats)
Italy 28 (12 wins, 16 defeats)
England 22 (13 wins, 9 defeats)
Germany 17 (7 wins, 10 defeats)

MOST CHAMPIONS LEAGUE/EUROPEAN CUP APPEARANCES
181 Iker Casillas (Real Madrid, Porto)
166 Cristiano Ronaldo (Manchester U, Real Madrid, Juventus)
157 Xavi (Barcelona)
151 Ryan Giggs (Manchester U)
144 Raul (Real Madrid, Schalke)
139 Paolo Maldini (AC Milan)
135 Lionel Messi (Barcelona):
132 Andreas Iniesta (Barcelona)
131 Clarence Seedorf (Ajax, Real Madrid, Internazionale, AC Milan)
130 Paul Scholes (Manchester U)
130 Gianluigi Buffon (Parma, Juventus, Paris Saint-Germain)
128 Roberto Carlos (Internazionale, Real Madrid, Fenerbahce)
127 Xabi Alonso (Real Sociedad, Liverpool, Real Madrid, Bayern Munich)

MOST WINS WITH DIFFERENT CLUBS
Clarence Seedorf (Ajax) 1995; (Real Madrid) 1998; (AC Milan) 2003, 2007.

MOST WINNERS MEDALS
6 Francisco Gento (Real Madrid) 1956, 1957, 1958, 1959, 1960, 1966.
5 Alfredo Di Stefano (Real Madrid) 1956, 1957, 1958, 1959, 1960.
5 Jose Maria Zarraga (Real Madrid) 1956, 1957, 1958, 1959, 1960.
5 Paolo Maldini (AC Milan) 1989, 1990, 1994, 2003, 2007.
5 Cristiano Ronaldo (Manchester U, Real Madrid) 2008, 2014, 2016, 2017, 2018.

CHAMPIONS LEAGUE BIGGEST WINS
HJK Helsinki 10, Bangor C 0 19.7.2011
Liverpool 8 Besiktas 0 6.11.2007
Real Madrid 8 Malmo 0 8.12.2015

MOST SUCCESSIVE CHAMPIONS LEAGUE APPEARANCES
Real Madrid (Spain) 21 1997–98 to 2017–18.
Manchester U (England) 18: 1996–97 to 2013–14.

MOST SUCCESSIVE EUROPEAN CUP APPEARANCES
Real Madrid (Spain) 15: 1955–56 to 1969–70.

MOST SUCCESSIVE WINS IN THE CHAMPIONS LEAGUE
Barcelona (Spain) 11: 2002–03.

LONGEST UNBEATEN RUN IN THE CHAMPIONS LEAGUE
Manchester U (England) 25: 2007–08 to 2009 (Final).

MOST GOALS OVERALL
127 Cristiano Ronaldo (Manchester U, Real Madrid, Juventus).
112 Lionel Messi (Barcelona).
71 Raul (Real Madrid, Schalke).
60 Ruud van Nistelrooy (PSV Eindhoven, Manchester U, Real Madrid).
60 Karim Benzema (Lyon, Real Madrid).
58 Andriy Shevchenko (Dynamo Kyiv, AC Milan, Chelsea, Dynamo Kyiv).
53 Robert Lewandowski (Borussia Dortmund, Bayern Munich).
51 Thierry Henry (Monaco, Arsenal, Barcelona).
50 Filippo Inzaghi (Juventus, AC Milan).
49 Alfredo Di Stefano (Real Madrid).
49 Zlatan Ibrahimovic (Ajax, Juventus, Internazionale, Barcelona, AC Milan, Paris Saint-Germain).
47 Eusebio (Benfica).

MOST GOALS IN CHAMPIONS LEAGUE MATCH
5 Lionel Messi, Barcelona v Bayer Leverkusen (25, 42, 49, 58, 84 mins) (7-1), 7.3.2012.
5 Luiz Adriano, Shaktar Donetsk v BATE (28, 36, 40, 44, 82 (0-7), 21.10.2014.

MOST GOALS IN ONE SEASON
17 Cristiano Ronaldo 2013–14
16 Cristiano Ronaldo 2015–16
15 Cristiano Ronaldo 2017–18
14 Jose Altafini 1962–63
14 Ruud van Nistelrooy 2002–03
14 Lionel Messi 2011–12

MOST GOALS SCORED IN FINALS
7 Alfredo Di Stefano (Real Madrid), 1956 (1), 1957 (1 pen), 1958 (1), 1959 (1), 1960 (3).
7 Ferenc Puskas (Real Madrid), 1960 (4), 1962 (3).

HIGHEST SCORE IN A EUROPEAN CUP MATCH
European Cup
14 KR Reykjavik (Iceland) 2 Feyenoord (Netherlands) 12 *(First Round First Leg 1969–70)*
Champions League
12 Borussia Dortmund 8, Legia Warsaw 4 22.11.2016

HIGHEST AGGREGATE IN A EUROPEAN CUP MATCH
Benfica (Portugal) 18, Dudelange (Luxembourg) 0
8-0 (h), 10-0 (a) *(Preliminary Round 1965–66)*

FASTEST GOALS SCORED IN CHAMPIONS LEAGUE

10.12 sec	Roy Makaay for Bayern Munich v Real Madrid, 7.3.2007.
10.96 sec	Jonas for Valencia v Bayer Leverkusen, 1.11.2011.
20.07 sec	Gilberto Silva for Arsenal at PSV Eindhoven, 25.9.2002.
20.12 sec	Alessandro Del Piero for Juventus at Manchester U, 1.10.1997.

YOUNGEST CHAMPIONS LEAGUE GOALSCORER
Peter Ofori-Quaye for Olympiacos v Rosenborg at 17 years 195 days in 1997–98.

FASTEST HAT-TRICK SCORED IN CHAMPIONS LEAGUE
Bafetimbi Gomis, 8 mins for Lyon in Dinamo Zagreb v Lyon (1-7) 7.12.2011

MOST GOALS BY A GOALKEEPER
Hans-Jorg Butt (for three different clubs)
Hamburg 13.9.2000, Bayer Leverkusen 12.5.2002, Bayern Munich 8.12.2009 – all achieved against Juventus.

LANDMARK GOALS CHAMPIONS LEAGUE
1st Daniel Amokachi, Club Brugge v CSKA Moscow 17 minutes 25.11.1992
1,000th Dmitri Khokhlov, PSV Eindhoven v Benfica 41 minutes 9.12.1998
5,000th Luisao, Benfica v Hapoel Tel Aviv 21 minutes 14.9.2010

HIGHEST SCORING DRAW
Hamburg 4, Juventus 4 13.9.2000
Chelsea 4, Liverpool 4 14.4.2009
Bayer Leverkusen 4, Roma 4 20.10.2015

MOST CLEAN SHEETS
10: Arsenal 2005–06 (995 minutes with two goalkeepers Manuel Almunia 347 minutes and Jens Lehmann 648 minutes).

EUROPEAN CUP AND CHAMPIONS LEAGUE RECORDS – continued

CHAMPIONS LEAGUE ATTENDANCES AND GOALS FROM GROUP STAGES ONWARDS

Season	*Attendances*	*Average*	*Goals*	*Games*
1992–93	873,251	34,930	56	25
1993–94	1,202,289	44,529	71	27
1994–95	2,328,515	38,172	140	61
1995–96	1,874,316	30,726	159	61
1996–97	2,093,228	34,315	161	61
1997–98	2,868,271	33,744	239	85
1998–99	3,608,331	42,451	238	85
1999–2000	5,490,709	34,973	442	157
2000–01	5,773,486	36,774	449	157
2001–02	5,417,716	34,508	393	157
2002–03	6,461,112	41,154	431	157
2003–04	4,611,214	36,890	309	125
2004–05	4,946,820	39,575	331	125
2005–06	5,291,187	42,330	285	125
2006–07	5,591,463	44,732	309	125
2007–08	5,454,718	43,638	330	125
2008–09	5,003,754	40,030	329	125
2009–10	5,295,708	42,366	320	125
2010–11	5,474,654	43,797	355	125
2011–12	5,225,363	41,803	345	125
2012–13	5,773,366	46,187	368	125
2013–14	5,713,049	45,704	362	125
2014–15	5,207,592	42,685	361	125
2015–16	5,116,690	40,934	347	125
2016–17	5,398,851	43,191	380	125
2017–18	5,744,918	45,959	401	125
2018–19	5,746,629	45,973	366	125

HIGHEST AVERAGE ATTENDANCE IN ONE EUROPEAN CUP SEASON

1959–60 50,545 from a total attendance of 2,780,000.

GREATEST COMEBACKS

Werder Bremen beat Anderlecht 5-3 after being three goals down in 33 minutes on 8.12.1993. They scored five goals in 23 second-half minutes.

Deportivo La Coruna beat Paris Saint-Germain 4-3 after being three goals down in 55 minutes on 7.3.2001. They scored four goals in 27 second-half minutes.

Liverpool after being three goals down to AC Milan in the first half on 25.5.2005 in the Champions League Final. They scored three goals in five second-half minutes and won the penalty shoot-out after extra time 3-2.

Liverpool three goals down to FC Basel in 29 minutes on 12.11.2002. They scored three second half goals in 24 minutes to draw 3-3.

MOST SUCCESSFUL MANAGER

Bob Paisley 3 wins, 1977, 1978, 1981 (Liverpool).

Carlo Ancelotti 3 wins, 2002–03, 2006–07 (AC Milan), 2013–14 (Real Madrid).

Zinedine Zidane 3 wins, 2015–16, 2016–17, 2017–18 (Real Madrid).

REINSTATED WINNERS EXCLUDED FROM NEXT COMPETITION

1993 Marseille originally stripped of title. This was rescinded but they were not allowed to compete the following season.

INTERNATIONAL LANDMARKS 2018–19

AUGUST 2018

13 Manchester City and Spain's David Silva announced his retirement from international football. His international debut came in 2006 in a home friendly with Romania which ended in a 1-0 victory for the Romanians. He went on to make 125 appearances for Spain, scoring 35 times and was in the World Cup winning side of 2010. He helped Spain to win the 2008 and 2012 European Championships.

SEPTEMBER 2018

6 Pepe made his 100th international appearance for Portugal in the 1-1 home friendly draw with Croatia. Pepe scored the Portugal equaliser in the 32nd minute. Ivan Perisic had put Croatia 1-0 ahead in the 18th minute.

11 Ivan Rakitic made his 100th international appearance for Croatia in the Nations League Group A4 6-0 defeat by Spain in Elche.

OCTOBER 2018

11 Robert Lewandowski made his 100th international appearance for Poland in the 2-3 defeat by Portugal in the Nations League Group A3 in Chorzow.

13 Martin Skrtel made his 100th international appearance for Slovakia in the Nations League Group B1 1-2 defeat by Czech Republic in Trnava.

20 Cristiano Ronaldo became the first player to score 400 league goals in Europe's top five leagues. His fifth goal for Juventus in the 1-1 home draw with Genoa added to his 84 Premier League goals for Manchester U and his 311 La Liga goals for Real Madrid.

NOVEMBER 2018

15 Axel Witsel made his 100th international appearance for Belgium in the 2-0 Nations League Group A2 victory over Iceland at Heysel Stadium.

17 Giorgio Chiellini made his 100th international appearance for Italy in the Nations League Group A3 0-0 draw with Portugal in Milan.

17 Roderick Briffa made his 100th international appearance for Malta in the 0-5 home defeat by Kosovo in the Nations League Group D3.

18 Vasilis Torosidis made his 100th international appearance for Greece in the 0-1 defeat to Estonia at the OAKA Stadium in Athens in the Nations League Group C2.

19 Thomas Muller made his 100th international appearance for Germany. Muller was a 66th minute substitute in the 2-2 draw with Netherlands in Group A1 of the Nations League. Netherlands scored twice in the final five minutes after being 2-0 down to secure a place in the Nations League finals.

MARCH 2019

24 Eden Hazard made his 100th international appearance for Belgium in the 2-0 away win against Cyprus in the Euro 2020 qualifying Group I match. Hazard opened the scoring after 10 minutes – his 30th international goal – and Chelsea teammate Michy Batshuayi doubled the lead after 18 minutes.

24 Edin Dzeko made his 100th international appearance for Bosnia-Herzegovina in the Euro 2020 qualifying Group J match against Armenia. Bosnia-Herzegovina ran out 2-1 winners with goals from Rade Krunic and Deni Milosevic. Henrikh Mikhitaryan hit an injury time consolation goal for Armenia.

JUNE 2019

9 West Bromwich Albion striker Salomon Rondon became Venezuela's all-time leading goalscorer with two goals in the 3-0 victory against USA in Cincinnati. His brace took him to 24 goals beating the previous record holder Juan Arango's total of 23.

11 USA Women record the highest Women's World Cup win with their 13-0 defeat of Thailand. Alex Morgan top scored with 5 goals, 4 in the second half.

13 Brazil women's striker Marta scored the opening goal against Australia in Group C to become the first player to score at five World Cups.

TOP TEN PREMIER LEAGUE AVERAGE ATTENDANCES 2018–19

1	Manchester U	74,498
2	Arsenal	59,899
3	West Ham U	58,336
4	Tottenham H	54,216
5	Manchester C	54,130
6	Liverpool	52,983
7	Newcastle U	51,121
8	Chelsea	40,437
9	Everton	38,780
10	Leicester C	31,851

TOP TEN FOOTBALL LEAGUE AVERAGE ATTENDANCES 2018–19

1	Aston Villa	36,029
2	Leeds U	34,033
3	Sunderland	32,157
4	Nottingham F	28,144
5	Derby Co	26,850
6	Sheffield U	26,175
7	Norwich C	26,014
8	Stoke C	25,200
9	Sheffield W	24,429
10	West Brom A	24,148

TOP TEN AVERAGE ATTENDANCES

1	Manchester U	2006–07	75,826
2	Manchester U	2007–08	75,691
3	Manchester U	2012–13	75,530
4	Manchester U	2011–12	75,387
5	Manchester U	2014–15	75,335
6	Manchester U	2008–09	75,308
7	Manchester U	2016–17	75,290
8	Manchester U	2015–16	75,279
9	Manchester U	2013–14	75,207
10	Manchester U	2010–11	75,109

TOP TEN AVERAGE WORLD CUP FINALS CROWDS

1	In USA	1994	68,991
2	In Brazil	2014	52,621
3	In Germany	2006	52,491
4	In Mexico	1970	50,124
5	In South Africa	2010	49,669
6	In West Germany	1974	49,098
7	In England	1966	48,847
8	In Italy	1990	48,388
9	In Brazil	1950	47,511
10	In Russia	2018	47,371

TOP TEN ALL-TIME ENGLAND CAPS

1	Peter Shilton	125
2	Wayne Rooney	120
3	David Beckham	115
4	Steven Gerrard	114
5	Bobby Moore	108
6	Ashley Cole	107
7	Bobby Charlton	106
	Frank Lampard	106
9	Billy Wright	105
10	Bryan Robson	90

TOP TEN ALL-TIME ENGLAND GOALSCORERS

1	Wayne Rooney	53
2	Bobby Charlton	49
3	Gary Lineker	48
4	Jimmy Greaves	44
5	Michael Owen	40
	Tom Finney	30
6	Nat Lofthouse	30
	Alan Shearer	30
9	Vivian Woodward	29
	Frank Lampard	29

GOALKEEPING RECORDS

(without conceding a goal)

FA PREMIER LEAGUE
Edwin van der Sar (Manchester U) in 1,311 minutes during the 2008–09 season.

FOOTBALL LEAGUE
Steve Death (Reading) 1,103 minutes from 24 March to 18 August 1979.

SCOTTISH PREMIER LEAGUE
Fraser Forster (Celtic) in 1,215 minutes from 6 December 2013 to 25 February 2014.

MOST CLEAN SHEETS IN A SEASON

Petr Cech (Chelsea) 24 2004–05

MOST CLEAN SHEETS OVERALL IN PREMIER LEAGUE

Petr Cech (Chelsea and Arsenal) 201 games.

MOST GOALS FOR IN A SEASON

		Goals	Games
FA PREMIER LEAGUE			
2017–18	Manchester C	106	38
FOOTBALL LEAGUE			
Division 4			
1960–61	Peterborough U	134	46
SCOTTISH PREMIER LEAGUE			
2016–17	Celtic	106	38
SCOTTISH LEAGUE			
Division 2			
1937–38	Raith R	142	34

MOST GOALS AGAINST IN A SEASON

		Goals	Games
FA PREMIER LEAGUE			
1993–94	Swindon T	100	42
FOOTBALL LEAGUE			
Division 2			
1898–99	Darwen	141	34
SCOTTISH PREMIER LEAGUE			
1999–2000	Aberdeen	83	36
2007–08	Gretna	83	38
SCOTTISH LEAGUE			
Division 2			
1931–32	Edinburgh C	146	38

MOST LEAGUE GOALS IN A SEASON

		Goals	Games
FA PREMIER LEAGUE			
1993–94	Andy Cole (Newcastle U)	34	40
1994–95	Alan Shearer (Blackburn R)	34	42
2017–18	Mohamed Salah (Liverpool)	32	38
FOOTBALL LEAGUE			
Division 1			
1927–28	Dixie Dean (Everton)	60	39
Division 2			
1926–27	George Camsell (Middlesbrough)	59	37
Division 3(S)			
1936–37	Joe Payne (Luton T)	55	39
Division 3(N)			
1936–37	Ted Harston (Mansfield T)	55	41
Division 3			
1959–60	Derek Reeves (Southampton)	39	46
Division 4			
1960–61	Terry Bly (Peterborough U)	52	46
FA CUP			
1887–88	Jimmy Ross (Preston NE)	20	8
LEAGUE CUP			
1986–87	Clive Allen (Tottenham H)	12	9
SCOTTISH PREMIER LEAGUE			
2000–01	Henrik Larsson (Celtic)	35	37
SCOTTISH LEAGUE			
Division 1			
1931–32	William McFadyen (Motherwell)	52	34
Division 2			
1927–28	Jim Smith (Ayr U)	66	38

MOST FA CUP FINAL GOALS

Ian Rush (Liverpool) 5: 1986(2), 1989(2), 1992(1)

SCORED IN EVERY PREMIERSHIP GAME

Arsenal 2001–02: 38 matches

FEWEST GOALS FOR IN A SEASON

		Goals	Games
FA PREMIER LEAGUE			
2007–08	Derby Co	20	38
FOOTBALL LEAGUE			
Division 2			
1899–1900	Loughborough T	18	34
SCOTTISH PREMIER LEAGUE			
2010–11	St Johnstone	23	38
SCOTTISH LEAGUE			
New Division 1			
1980–81	Stirling Alb	18	39

FEWEST GOALS AGAINST IN A SEASON

		Goals	Games
FA PREMIER LEAGUE			
2004–05	Chelsea	15	38
FOOTBALL LEAGUE			
Division 1			
1978–79	Liverpool	16	42
SCOTTISH PREMIER LEAGUE			
2001–02	Celtic	18	38
SCOTTISH LEAGUE			
Division 1			
1913–14	Celtic	14	38

MOST LEAGUE GOALS IN A CAREER

	Goals	Games	Season
FOOTBALL LEAGUE			
Arthur Rowley			
WBA	4	24	1946–48
Fulham	27	56	1948–50
Leicester C	251	303	1950–58
Shrewsbury T	152	236	1958–65
	434	619	
SCOTTISH LEAGUE			
Jimmy McGrory			
Celtic	1	3	1922–23
Clydebank	13	30	1923–24
Celtic	396	375	1924–38
	410	408	

MOST HAT-TRICKS

Career
37: Dixie Dean (Tranmere R, Everton, Notts Co, England)

Division 1 (one season post-war)
6: Jimmy Greaves (Chelsea), 1960–61

Three for one team in one match
West, Spouncer, Hooper, Nottingham F v Leicester Fosse, Division 1, 21 April 1909
Loasby, Smith, Wells, Northampton T v Walsall, Division 3S, 5 Nov 1927
Bowater, Hoyland, Readman, Mansfield T v Rotherham U, Division 3N, 27 Dec 1932
Barnes, Ambler, Davies, Wrexham v Hartlepools U, Division 4, 3 March 1962
Adcock, Stewart, White, Manchester C v Huddersfield T, Division 2, 7 Nov 1987

MOST CUP GOALS IN A CAREER

FA CUP (pre-Second World War)
Henry Cursham 48 (Notts Co)

FA CUP (post-war)
Ian Rush 43 (Chester, Liverpool)

LEAGUE CUP
Geoff Hurst 49 (West Ham U, Stoke C)
Ian Rush 49 (Chester, Liverpool, Newcastle U)

GOALS PER GAME (Football League to 1991–92)

Goals per game	Division 1		Division 2		Division 3		Division 4		Division 3(S)		Division 3(N)	
	Games	Goals	Games	Goals	Games	Goals	Games	Goals	Games	Goals	Games	Goals
0	2465	0	2665	0	1446	0	1438	0	997	0	803	0
1	5606	5606	5836	5836	3225	3225	3106	3106	2073	2073	1914	1914
2	8275	16550	8609	17218	4569	9138	4441	8882	3314	6628	2939	5878
3	7731	23193	7842	23526	3784	11352	4041	12123	2996	8988	2922	8766
4	6229	24920	5897	23588	2837	11348	2784	11136	2445	9780	2410	9640
5	3752	18755	3634	18170	1566	7830	1506	7530	1554	7770	1599	7995
6	2137	12822	2007	12042	769	4614	786	4716	870	5220	930	5580
7	1092	7644	1001	7007	357	2499	336	2352	451	3157	461	3227
8	542	4336	376	3008	135	1080	143	1144	209	1672	221	1768
9	197	1773	164	1476	64	576	35	315	76	684	102	918
10	83	830	68	680	13	130	8	80	33	330	45	450
11	37	407	19	209	2	22	7	77	15	165	15	165
12	12	144	17	204	1	12	0	0	7	84	8	96
13	4	52	4	52	0	0	0	0	2	26	4	52
14	2	28	1	14	0	0	0	0	0	0	0	0
17	0	0	0	0	0	0	0	0	0	0	1	17
	38164	**117060**	**38140**	**113030**	**18768**	**51826**	**18631**	**51461**	**15042**	**46577**	**14374**	**46466**

Extensive research by statisticians has unearthed seven results from the early years of the Football League which differ from the original scores. These are 26 January 1889 Wolverhampton W 5 Everton 0 (not 4-0), 16 March 1889 Notts Co 3 Derby Co 5 (not 2-5), 4 January 1896 Arsenal 5 Loughborough 0 (not 6-0), 28 November 1896 Leicester Fosse 4 Walsall 2 (not 4-1), 21 April 1900 Burslem Port Vale 2 Lincoln C 1 (not 2-0), 25 December 1902 Glossop NE 3 Stockport Co 0 (not 3-1), 26 April 1913 Hull C 2 Leicester C 0 (not 2-1).

GOALS PER GAME (from 1992–93)

Goals per game	Premier		Championship/Div 1		League One/Div 2		League Two/Div 3	
	Games	Goals	Games	Goals	Games	Goals	Games	Goals
0	882	0	1219	0	1161	0	1182	0
1	1904	1904	2778	2778	2776	2776	2848	2848
2	2537	5074	3778	7556	3779	7558	3714	7428
3	2221	6663	3226	9678	3287	9861	3197	9591
4	1567	6268	2068	8272	2074	8296	1969	7876
5	782	3910	1105	5525	1112	5560	1041	5205
6	372	2232	492	2952	462	2772	427	2562
7	151	1057	170	1190	177	1239	175	1225
8	66	528	50	400	52	416	53	424
9	18	162	9	81	19	171	19	171
10	5	50	7	70	5	50	6	60
11	1	11	2	22	0	0	3	33
	10506	**27859**	**14904**	**38524**	**14904**	**38699**	**14634**	**37423**

New Overall Totals (since 1992)		Totals (up to 1991–92)		Complete Overall Totals (since 1888–89)	
Games	54948	Games	143119	Games	198067
Goals	142505	Goals	426420	Goals	568925
Goals per game	2.59		2.98		2.87

A CENTURY OF LEAGUE AND CUP GOALS IN CONSECUTIVE SEASONS

	League	Cup	Season
George Camsell			
Middlesbrough	59	5	1926–27
(101 goals)	33	4	1927–28

(Camsell's cup goals were all scored in the FA Cup.)

Steve Bull			
Wolverhampton W	34	18	1987–88
(102 goals)	37	13	1988–89

(Bull had 12 in the Sherpa Van Trophy, 3 Littlewoods Cup, 3 FA Cup in 1987–88; 11 Sherpa Van Trophy, 2 Littlewoods Cup in 1988–89.)

PENALTIES

Most in a season (individual)

Division 1 — *Goals* / *Season*

Francis Lee (Manchester C) 13 1971–72

Also scored 1 in League Cup and 2 in FA Cup.

Most awarded in one game

Five Crystal Palace (1 scored, 3 missed) v Brighton & HA (1 scored), Div 2 1988–89

Most saved in a season

Division 1

Paul Cooper (Ipswich T) 8 (of 10) 1979–80

MOST GOALS IN A GAME

FA PREMIER LEAGUE

4 Mar 1995	Andy Cole (Manchester U) 5 goals v Ipswich T
19 Sept 1999	Alan Shearer (Newcastle U) 5 goals v Sheffield W
22 Nov 2009	Jermain Defoe (Tottenham H) 5 goals v Wigan Ath
27 Nov 2010	Dimitar Berbatov (Manchester U) 5 goals v Blackburn R
3 Oct 2015	Sergio Aguero (Manchester C) 5 goals v Newcastle U

FOOTBALL LEAGUE

Division 1

14 Dec 1935	Ted Drake (Arsenal) 7 goals v Aston Villa

Division 2

5 Feb 1955	Tommy Briggs (Blackburn R) 7 goals v Bristol R
23 Feb 1957	Neville Coleman (Stoke C) 7 goals v Lincoln C

Division 3(S)

13 Apr 1936	Joe Payne (Luton T) 10 goals v Bristol R

Division 3(N)

26 Dec 1935	Bunny Bell (Tranmere R) 9 goals v Oldham Ath

Division 3

24 Apr 1965	Barrie Thomas (Scunthorpe U) 5 goals v Luton T
20 Nov 1965	Keith East (Swindon T) 5 goals v Mansfield T
16 Sept 1969	Steve Earle (Fulham) 5 goals v Halifax T
2 Oct 1971	Alf Wood (Shrewsbury T) 5 goals v Blackburn R
10 Sept 1983	Tony Caldwell (Bolton W) 5 goals v Walsall
4 May 1987	Andy Jones (Port Vale) 5 goals v Newport Co
3 Apr 1990	Steve Wilkinson (Mansfield T) 5 goals v Birmingham C
5 Sept 1998	Giuliano Grazioli (Peterborough U) 5 goals v Barnet
6 Apr 2002	Lee Jones (Wrexham) 5 goals v Cambridge U

Division 4

26 Dec 1962	Bert Lister (Oldham Ath) 6 goals v Southport

FA CUP

20 Nov 1971	Ted MacDougall (Bournemouth) 9 goals v Margate (*1st Round*)

LEAGUE CUP

25 Oct 1989	Frankie Bunn (Oldham Ath) 6 goals v Scarborough

SCOTTISH LEAGUE

Premier Division

17 Nov 1984	Paul Sturrock (Dundee U) 5 goals v Morton

Premier League

23 Aug 1996	Marco Negri (Rangers) 5 goals v Dundee U
4 Nov 2000	Kenny Miller (Rangers) 5 goals v St Mirren
25 Sept 2004	Kris Boyd (Kilmarnock) 5 goals v Dundee U
30 Dec 2009	Kris Boyd (Rangers) 5 goals v Dundee U
13 May 2012	Gary Hooper (Celtic) 5 goals v Hearts

Division 1

14 Sept 1928	Jimmy McGrory (Celtic) 8 goals v Dunfermline Ath

Division 2

1 Oct 1927	Owen McNally (Arthurlie) 8 goals v Armadale
2 Jan 1930	Jim Dyet (King's Park) 8 goals v Forfar Ath
18 Apr 1936	John Calder (Morton) 8 goals v Raith R
20 Aug 1937	Norman Hayward (Raith R) 8 goals v Brechin C

SCOTTISH CUP

12 Sept 1885	John Petrie (Arbroath) 13 goals v Bon Accord (*1st Round*)

LONGEST SEQUENCE OF CONSECUTIVE DEFEATS

FOOTBALL LEAGUE Division 2	*Team*	*Games*
1898–99	Darwen	18

LONGEST UNBEATEN SEQUENCE

FA PREMIER LEAGUE	*Team*	*Games*
May 2003–Oct 2004	Arsenal	49
FOOTBALL LEAGUE – League 1		
Jan 2011–Nov 2011	Huddersfield T	43

LONGEST UNBEATEN CUP SEQUENCE

Liverpool	25 rounds	League/Milk Cup	1980–84

LONGEST UNBEATEN SEQUENCE IN A SEASON

FA PREMIER LEAGUE	*Team*	*Games*
2003–04	Arsenal	38
FOOTBALL LEAGUE – Division 1		
1920–21	Burnley	30
SCOTTISH PREMIERSHIP		
2016–17	Celtic	38

LONGEST UNBEATEN START TO A SEASON

FA PREMIER LEAGUE	*Team*	*Games*
2003–04	Arsenal	38
FOOTBALL LEAGUE – Division 1		
1973–74	Leeds U	29
1987–88	Liverpool	29

LONGEST SEQUENCE WITHOUT A WIN IN A SEASON

FA PREMIER LEAGUE	*Team*	*Games*
2007–08	Derby Co	32
FOOTBALL LEAGUE Division 2	*Team*	*Games*
1983–84	Cambridge U	31

LONGEST SEQUENCE WITHOUT A WIN FROM SEASON'S START

FOOTBALL LEAGUE Division 4	*Team*	*Games*
1970–71	Newport Co	25

LONGEST SEQUENCE OF CONSECUTIVE SCORING (individual)

FA PREMIER LEAGUE		
Jamie Vardy (Leicester C)	13 in 11 games	2015–16
FOOTBALL LEAGUE RECORD		
Tom Phillipson (Wolverhampton W)	23 in 13 games	1926–27

LONGEST WINNING SEQUENCE

FA PREMIER LEAGUE	*Team*	*Games*
2017-18	Manchester C	18
FOOTBALL LEAGUE – Division 2		
1904–05	Manchester U	14
1905–06	Bristol C	14
1950–51	Preston NE	14
FROM SEASON'S START – Division 3		
1985–86	Reading	13
SCOTTISH PREMIER LEAGUE		
2003–04	Celtic	25

HIGHEST WINS

Highest win in a First-Class Match
(Scottish Cup 1st Round)

Arbroath	36 Bon Accord	0	12 Sept 1885

Highest win in an International Match

England	13 Ireland	0	18 Feb 1882

Highest win in an FA Cup Match

Preston NE *(1st Round)*	26 Hyde U	0	15 Oct 1887

Highest win in a League Cup Match

West Ham U *(2nd Round, 2nd Leg)*	10 Bury	0	25 Oct 1983
Liverpool *(2nd Round, 1st Leg)*	10 Fulham	0	23 Sept 1986

Highest win in an FA Premier League Match

Manchester U	9 Ipswich T	0	4 Mar 1995
Tottenham H	9 Wigan Ath	1	22 Nov 2009

Highest win in a Football League Match
Division 2 – highest home win

Newcastle U	13 Newport Co	0	5 Oct 1946

Division 3(N) – highest home win

Stockport Co	13 Halifax T	0	6 Jan 1934

Division 2 – highest away win

Burslem Port Vale 0	Sheffield U	10	10 Dec 1892

Highest wins in a Scottish League Match
Scottish Premier League – highest home win

Celtic	9 Aberdeen	0	6 Nov 2010

Scottish Division 2 – highest home win

Airdrieonians	15 Dundee Wanderers	1	1 Dec 1894

Scottish Premier League – highest away win

Hamilton A	0 Celtic	8	5 Nov 1988

MOST HOME WINS IN A SEASON

Brentford won all 21 games in Division 3(S), 1929–30

RECORD AWAY WINS IN A SEASON

Doncaster R won 18 of 21 games in Division 3(N), 1946–47

CONSECUTIVE AWAY WINS

FA PREMIER LEAGUE
Chelsea 11 games (2007–08 (3), 2008–09 (8)).
Manchester C 11 games (2016–17 (1), 2017–18 (10))

FOOTBALL LEAGUE
Division 1
Tottenham H 10 games (1959–60 (2), 1960–61 (8))

HIGHEST AGGREGATE SCORES

FA PREMIER LEAGUE

Portsmouth	7 Reading	4	29 Sept 2007

Highest Aggregate Score England
Division 3(N)

Tranmere R	13 Oldham Ath	4	26 Dec 1935

Highest Aggregate Score Scotland
Division 2

Airdrieonians	15 Dundee Wanderers	1	1 Dec 1894

MOST WINS IN A SEASON

		Wins	*Games*
FA PREMIER LEAGUE			
2017–18 & 2018–19	Manchester C	32	38
FOOTBALL LEAGUE Division 3(N)			
1946–47	Doncaster R	33	42
SCOTTISH PREMIERSHIP			
2016–17	Celtic	34	38
SCOTTISH LEAGUE Division 1			
1920–21	Rangers	35	42

FEWEST WINS IN A SEASON

		Wins	*Games*
FA PREMIER LEAGUE			
2007–08	Derby Co	1	38
FOOTBALL LEAGUE Division 2			
1899–1900	Loughborough T	1	34
SCOTTISH PREMIER LEAGUE			
1998–99	Dunfermline Ath	4	36
SCOTTISH LEAGUE Division 1			
1891–92	Vale of Leven	0	22

UNDEFEATED AT HOME OVERALL

Liverpool 85 games (63 League, 9 League Cup, 7 European, 6 FA Cup), Jan 1978–Jan 1981

UNDEFEATED AT HOME LEAGUE

Chelsea 86 games, March 2004–October 2008

UNDEFEATED AWAY

Arsenal 19 games, FA Premier League 2001–02 and 2003–04 (only Preston NE with 11 in 1888–89 had previously remained unbeaten away) in the top flight.

MOST POINTS IN A SEASON

(three points for a win)

		Points	*Games*
FA PREMIER LEAGUE			
2017–18	Manchester C	100	38
FOOTBALL LEAGUE Championship			
2005–06	Reading	106	46
SCOTTISH PREMIER LEAGUE			
2001–02	Celtic	103	38
SCOTTISH LEAGUE League One			
2013–14	Rangers	102	36

MOST POINTS IN A SEASON

(under old system of two points for a win)

		Points	*Games*
FOOTBALL LEAGUE Division 4			
1975–76	Lincoln C	74	46
SCOTTISH LEAGUE Division 1			
1920–21	Rangers	76	42

FEWEST POINTS IN A SEASON

		Points	*Games*
FA PREMIER LEAGUE			
2007–08	Derby Co	11	38
FOOTBALL LEAGUE Division 2			
1904–05	Doncaster R	8	34
1899–1900	Loughborough T	8	34
SCOTTISH PREMIER LEAGUE			
2007–08	Gretna	13	38
SCOTTISH LEAGUE Division 1			
1954–55	Stirling Alb	6	30

NO DEFEATS IN A SEASON

FA PREMIER LEAGUE

2003–04	Arsenal	won 26, drew 12

FOOTBALL LEAGUE

Division 1

1888–89	Preston NE	won 18, drew 4

Division 2

1893–94	Liverpool	won 22, drew 6

SCOTTISH LEAGUE

Premiership

2016–17	Celtic	won 34, drew 4

Division 1

1898–99	Rangers	won 18

League One

2013–14	Rangers	won 33, drew 3

ONE DEFEAT IN A SEASON

FA PREMIER LEAGUE		Defeats	Games
2004–05	Chelsea	1	38
2018–19	Liverpool	1	38
FOOTBALL LEAGUE			
Division 1			
1990–91	Arsenal	1	38
SCOTTISH PREMIER LEAGUE			
2001–02	Celtic	1	38
2013–14	Celtic	1	38
SCOTTISH LEAGUE			
Division 1			
1920–21	Rangers	1	42
Division 2			
1956–57	Clyde	1	36
1962–63	Morton	1	36
1967–68	St Mirren	1	36
New Division 1			
2011–12	Ross Co	1	36
New Division 2			
1975–76	Raith R	1	26

MOST DEFEATS IN A SEASON

FA PREMIER LEAGUE		Defeats	Games
1994–95	Ipswich T	29	42
2005–06	Sunderland	29	38
2007–08	Derby Co	29	38
FOOTBALL LEAGUE			
Division 3			
1997–98	Doncaster R	34	46
SCOTTISH PREMIER LEAGUE			
2005–06	Livingston	28	38
SCOTTISH LEAGUE			
New Division 1			
1992–93	Cowdenbeath	34	44

MOST DRAWN GAMES IN A SEASON

FA PREMIER LEAGUE		Draws	Games
1993–94	Manchester C	18	42
1993–94	Sheffield U	18	42
1994–95	Southampton	18	42
FOOTBALL LEAGUE			
Division 1			
1978–79	Norwich C	23	42
Division 3			
1997–98	Cardiff C	23	46
1997–98	Hartlepool U	23	46
Division 4			
1986–87	Exeter C	23	46
SCOTTISH PREMIER LEAGUE			
1998–99	Dunfermline Ath	16	38
SCOTTISH LEAGUE			
Premier Division			
1993–94	Aberdeen	21	44
New Division 1			
1986–87	East Fife	21	44

SENDINGS-OFF

SEASON

451 (League alone) 2003–04

(Before rescinded cards taken into account)

DAY

19 (League) 13 Dec 2003

FA CUP FINAL

Kevin Moran, Manchester U v Everton	1985
Jose Antonio Reyes, Arsenal v Manchester U	2005
Pablo Zabaleta, Manchester C v Wigan Ath	2013
Chris Smalling, Manchester U v Crystal Palace	2016
Victor Moses, Chelsea v Arsenal	2017

QUICKEST

FA Premier League

Andreas Johansson, Wigan Ath v Arsenal (7 May 2006) and Keith Gillespie, Sheffield U v Reading (20 January 2007) both in 10 seconds

Football League

Walter Boyd, Swansea C v Darlington, Div 3 as substitute in zero seconds 23 Nov 1999

MOST IN ONE GAME

Five: Chesterfield (2) v Plymouth Arg (3)	22 Feb 1997
Five: Wigan Ath (1) v Bristol R (4)	2 Dec 1997
Five: Exeter C (3) v Cambridge U (2)	23 Nov 2002
Five: Bradford C (3) v Crawley T (2)*	27 Mar 2012

**All five sent off after final whistle for fighting*

MOST IN ONE TEAM

Wigan Ath (1) v Bristol R (4)	2 Dec 1997
Hereford U (4) v Northampton T (0)	6 Sept 1992

MOST SUCCESSFUL MANAGERS

Sir Alex Ferguson CBE
Manchester U

1986–2013, 25 major trophies:
13 Premier League, 5 FA Cup, 4 League Cup, 2 Champions League, 1 Cup-Winners' Cup.

Aberdeen

1976–86, 9 major trophies:
3 League, 4 Scottish Cup, 1 League Cup, 1 Cup-Winners' Cup.

Bob Paisley – Liverpool

1974–83, 13 major trophies:
6 League, 3 European Cup, 3 League Cup, 1 UEFA Cup.

Bill Struth – Rangers

1920–54, 30 major trophies:
18 League, 10 Scottish Cup, 2 League Cup.

LEAGUE CHAMPIONSHIP HAT-TRICKS

Huddersfield T	1923–24 to 1925–26
Arsenal	1932–33 to 1934–35
Liverpool	1981–82 to 1983–84
Manchester U	1998–99 to 2000–01
Manchester U	2006–07 to 2008–09

MOST FA CUP MEDALS

Ashley Cole 7 (Arsenal 2002, 2003, 2005; Chelsea 2007, 2009, 2010, 2012).

MOST LEAGUE MEDALS

Ryan Giggs (Manchester U) 13: 1993, 1994, 1996, 1997, 1999, 2000, 2001, 2003, 2007, 2008, 2009, 2011 and 2013.

MOST SENIOR MATCHES

1,390 Peter Shilton (1,005 League, 86 FA Cup, 102 League Cup, 125 Internationals, 13 Under-23, 4 Football League XI, 20 European Cup, 7 Texaco Cup, 5 Simod Cup, 4 European Super Cup, 4 UEFA Cup, 3 Screen Sport Super Cup, 3 Zenith Data Systems Cup, 2 Autoglass Trophy, 2 Charity Shield, 2 Full Members Cup, 1 Anglo-Italian Cup, 1 Football League play-offs, 1 World Club Championship)

MOST LEAGUE APPEARANCES (750+ matches)

1,005 Peter Shilton (286 Leicester C, 110 Stoke C, 202 Nottingham F, 188 Southampton, 175 Derby Co, 34 Plymouth Arg, 1 Bolton W, 9 Leyton Orient) 1966–97
931 Tony Ford (355 Grimsby T, 9 Sunderland (loan), 112 Stoke C, 114 WBA, 68 Grimsby T, 5 Bradford C (loan), 76 Scunthorpe U, 103 Mansfield T, 89 Rochdale) 1975–2002
909 Graeme Armstrong (204 Stirling A, 83 Berwick R, 353 Meadowbank Thistle, 268 Stenhousemuir, 1 Alloa Ath) 1975–2001
863 Tommy Hutchison (165 Blackpool, 314 Coventry C, 46 Manchester C, 92 Burnley, 178 Swansea C, 68 Alloa Ath) 1965–91
833 Graham Alexander (159 Scunthorpe U, 150 Luton T, 370 Preston NE, 154 Burnley) 1990–2012
824 Terry Paine (713 Southampton, 111 Hereford U) 1957–77
790 Neil Redfearn (35 Bolton W, 10 Lincoln C (loan), 90 Lincoln C, 46 Doncaster R, 57 Crystal Palace, 24 Watford, 62 Oldham Ath, 292 Barnsley, 30 Charlton Ath, 17 Bradford C, 22 Wigan Ath, 42 Halifax T, 54 Boston U, 9 Rochdale) 1982–2004
788 David James (89 Watford, 214 Liverpool, 67 Aston Villa, 91 West Ham U, 93 Manchester C, 134 Portsmouth, 81 Bristol C, 19 Bournemouth) 1988–2013
782 Robbie James (484 Swansea C, 48 Stoke C, 87 QPR, 23 Leicester C, 89 Bradford C, 51 Cardiff C) 1973–94
777 Alan Oakes (565 Manchester C, 211 Chester C, 1 Port Vale) 1959–84
774 Dave Beasant (340 Wimbledon, 20 Newcastle U, 133 Chelsea, 6 Grimsby T (loan), 4 Wolverhampton W (loan), 88 Southampton, 139 Nottingham F, 27 Portsmouth, 1 Tottenham H (loan), 16 Brighton & HA) 1979–2003
771 John Burridge (27 Workington, 134 Blackpool, 65 Aston Villa, 6 Southend U (loan), 88 Crystal Palace, 39 QPR, 74 Wolverhampton W, 6 Derby Co (loan), 109 Sheffield U, 62 Southampton, 67 Newcastle U, 65 Hibernian, 3 Scarborough, 4 Lincoln C, 3 Aberdeen, 3 Dumbarton, 3 Falkirk, 4 Manchester C, 3 Darlington, 6 Queen of the S) 1968–96
770 John Trollope (all for Swindon T) 1960–80†
764 Jimmy Dickinson (all for Portsmouth) 1946–65
763 Stuart McCall (395 Bradford C, 103 Everton, 194 Rangers, 71 Sheffield U) 1982–2004
761 Roy Sproson (all for Port Vale) 1950–72
760 Mick Tait (64 Oxford U, 106 Carlisle U, 33 Hull C, 240 Portsmouth, 99 Reading, 79 Darlington, 139 Hartlepool U) 1975–97
758 Ray Clemence (48 Scunthorpe U, 470 Liverpool, 240 Tottenham H) 1966–87
758 Billy Bonds (95 Charlton Ath, 663 West Ham U) 1964–88
757 Pat Jennings (48 Watford, 472 Tottenham H, 237 Arsenal) 1963–86
757 Frank Worthington (171 Huddersfield T, 210 Leicester C, 84 Bolton W, 75 Birmingham C, 32 Leeds U, 19 Sunderland, 34 Southampton, 31 Brighton & HA, 59 Tranmere R, 23 Preston NE, 19 Stockport Co) 1966–88
755 Jamie Cureton (98 Norwich C, 5 Bournemouth (loan), 174 Bristol R, 108 Reading, 43 QPR, 30 Swindon T, 52 Colchester U, 8 Barnsley (loan), 12 Shrewsbury (loan), 88 Exeter C, 19 Leyton Orient, 35 Cheltenham T, 83 Dagenham & R) 1992–2016
753 Andy Millen (71 St.Johnstone, 111 Alloa Ath, 119 Hamilton A, 57 Kilmarnock, 51, Hibernian, 18 Raith Rovers, 60 Ayr U, 44 G.Morton, 89 Clyde, 114 St.Mirren, 19 Queen's Park) 1986–2012

† *record for one club*

CONSECUTIVE
401 Harold Bell (401 Tranmere R; 459 in all games) 1946–55

YOUNGEST PLAYERS

FA Premier League appearance
Harvey Elliott, 16 years 30 days, Wolves v Fulham, 4.5.2019

FA Premier League scorer
James Vaughan, 16 years 271 days, Everton v Crystal Palace 10.4.2005

Football League appearance
Reuben Noble-Lazarus, 15 years 45 days, Barnsley v Ipswich T, FL Championship 30.9.2008

Football League scorer
Ronnie Dix, 15 years 180 days, Bristol Rovers v Norwich C, Division 3S, 3.3.1928

FA Cup appearance (any round)
Andy Awford, 15 years 88 days as substitute Worcester City v Boreham Wood, 3rd Qual. rd, 10.10.1987

FA Cup goalscorer
George Williams, 16 years 66 days, Milton Keynes D v Nantwich T, 12.11.2011

FA Cup appearance (competition rounds)
Luke Freeman, 15 years 233 days, Gillingham v Barnet 10.11.2007

FA Cup Final appearance
Curtis Weston, 17 years 119 days, Millwall v Manchester U, 22.5.2004

FA Cup Final scorer
Norman Whiteside, 18 years 18 days, Manchester United v Brighton & HA, 1983

FA Cup Final captain
David Nish, 21 years 212 days, Leicester C v Manchester C, 1969

League Cup appearance
Connor Wickham, 16 years 133 days, Ipswich T v Shrewsbury T, 11.8.2009

League Cup goalscorer
Connor Wickham, 16 years 133 days, Ipswich T v Shrewsbury T, 11.8.2009

League Cup Final scorer
Norman Whiteside, 17 years 324 days, Manchester U v Liverpool, 1983

League Cup Final captain
Barry Venison, 20 years 7 months 8 days, Sunderland v Norwich C, 1985

Scottish Premier League appearance
Scott Robinson, 16 years 45 days, Hearts v Inverness CT, 26.4.2008

Scottish Football League appearance
Jordan Allan, 14 years 189 days, Airdrie U v Livingston, 26.4.2013

Scottish Premier League scorer
Fraser Fyvie, 16 years 306 days, Aberdeen v Hearts, 27.1.2010

OLDEST PLAYERS

FA Premier League appearance
John Burridge, 43 years 162 days, Manchester C v QPR, 14.5.95

Football League appearance
Neil McBain, 52 years 4 months, New Brighton v Hartlepools U, Div 3N, 15.3.47 (McBain was New Brighton's manager and had to play in an emergency)

Division 1 appearance
Stanley Matthews, 50 years 5 days, Stoke C v Fulham, 6.2.65

INTERNATIONAL RECORDS

MOST GOALS IN AN INTERNATIONAL

Record/World Cup	Archie Thompson (Australia) 13 goals v American Samoa	11.4.2001
England	Howard Vaughton (Aston Villa) 5 goals v Ireland, at Belfast	18.2.1882
	Steve Bloomer (Derby Co) 5 goals v Wales, at Cardiff	16.3.1896
	Willie Hall (Tottenham H) 5 goals v N. Ireland, at Old Trafford	16.11.1938
	Malcolm Macdonald (Newcastle U) 5 goals v Cyprus, at Wembley	16.4.1975
Northern Ireland	Joe Bambrick (Linfield) 6 goals v Wales, at Belfast	1.2.1930
Wales	John Price (Wrexham) 4 goals v Ireland, at Wrexham	25.2.1882
	John Doughty (Newton Heath) 4 goals v Ireland, at Wrexham	3.3.1888
	Mel Charles (Cardiff C) 4 goals v N. Ireland, at Cardiff	11.4.1962
	Ian Edwards (Chester) 4 goals v Malta, at Wrexham	25.10.1978
Scotland	Alexander Higgins (Kilmarnock) 4 goals v Ireland, at Hampden Park	14.3.1885
	Charles Heggie (Rangers) 4 goals v Ireland, at Belfast	20.3.1886
	William Dickson (Dundee Strathmore) 4 goals v Ireland, at Belfast	24.3.1888
	William Paul (Partick Thistle) 4 goals v Wales, at Paisley	22.3.1890
	Jake Madden (Celtic) 4 goals v Wales, at Wrexham	18.3.1893
	Duke McMahon (Celtic) 4 goals v Ireland, at Celtic Park	23.2.1901
	Bob Hamilton (Rangers) 4 goals v Ireland, at Celtic Park	23.2.1901
	Jimmy Quinn (Celtic) 4 goals v Ireland, at Dublin	14.3.1908
	Hughie Gallacher (Newcastle U) 4 goals v N. Ireland, at Belfast	23.2.1929
	Billy Steel (Dundee) 4 goals v N. Ireland, at Hampden Park	1.11.1950
	Denis Law (Manchester U) 4 goals v N. Ireland, at Hampden Park	7.11.1962
	Denis Law (Manchester U) 4 goals v Norway, at Hampden Park	7.11.1963
	Colin Stein (Rangers) 4 goals v Cyprus, at Hampden Park	17.5.1969

MOST GOALS IN AN INTERNATIONAL CAREER

		Goals	*Games*
England	Wayne Rooney (Everton, Manchester U)	53	120
Scotland	Denis Law (Huddersfield T, Manchester C, Torino, Manchester U)	30	55
	Kenny Dalglish (Celtic, Liverpool)	30	102
Northern Ireland	David Healy (Manchester U, Preston NE, Leeds U, Fulham, Sunderland, Rangers, Bury)	36	95
Wales	Gareth Bale (Southampton, Tottenham H, Real Madrid)	31	77
Republic of Ireland	Robbie Keane (Wolverhampton W, Coventry C, Internazionale, Leeds U, Tottenham H, Liverpool, Tottenham H, LA Galaxy)	68	146

HIGHEST SCORES

World Cup Match	Australia	31	American Samoa	0	2001
European Championship	San Marino	0	Germany	13	2006
Olympic Games	Denmark	17	France	1	1908
	Germany	16	USSR	0	1912
Olympic Qualifying Tournament	Vanuatu	46	Micronesia	0	2015
Other International Match	Libya	21	Oman	0	1966
	Abandoned after 80 minutes as Oman refused to play on.				
European Cup	KR Reykjavik	2	Feyenoord	12	1969
European Cup-Winners' Cup	Sporting Lisbon	16	Apoel Nicosia	1	1963
Fairs & UEFA Cups	Ajax	14	Red Boys Differdange	0	1984

GOALSCORING RECORDS

World Cup Final	Geoff Hurst (England) 3 goals v West Germany	1966
World Cup Final tournament	Just Fontaine (France) 13 goals	1958
World Cup career	Miroslav Klose (Germany) 16 goals	2002, 2006, 2010, 2014
Career	Artur Friedenreich (Brazil) 1,329 goals	1910–30
	Pele (Brazil) 1,281 goals	*1956–78
	Franz 'Bimbo' Binder (Austria, Germany) 1,006 goals	1930–50
World Cup Finals fastest	Hakan Sukur (Turkey) 10.8 secs v South Korea	2002

**Pele subsequently scored two goals in Testimonial matches making his total 1,283.*

MOST CAPPED INTERNATIONALS IN THE BRITISH ISLES

England	Peter Shilton	125 appearances	1970–90
Northern Ireland	Pat Jennings	119 appearances	1964–86
Scotland	Kenny Dalglish	102 appearances	1971–86
Wales	Chris Gunter	95 appearances	2007–2019
Republic of Ireland	Robbie Keane	146 appearances	1998–2016

THE PREMIER LEAGUE AND FOOTBALL LEAGUE FIXTURES 2019–20

All fixtures subject to change.

Community Shield

Sunday, 4 August 2019
Manchester C v Liverpool

Premier League

Friday, 9 August 2019
Liverpool v Norwich C

Saturday, 10 August 2019
Bournemouth v Sheffield U
Burnley v Southampton
Crystal Palace v Everton
Leicester C v Wolverhampton W
Tottenham H v Aston Villa
Watford v Brighton & HA
West Ham U v Manchester C

Sunday, 11 August 2019
Manchester U v Chelsea
Newcastle U v Arsenal

Saturday, 17 August 2019
Arsenal v Burnley
Aston Villa v Bournemouth
Brighton & HA v West Ham U
Chelsea v Leicester C
Everton v Watford
Manchester C v Tottenham H
Norwich C v Newcastle U
Sheffield U v Crystal Palace
Southampton v Liverpool
Wolverhampton W v Manchester U

Saturday, 24 August 2019
Aston Villa v Everton
Bournemouth v Manchester C
Brighton & HA v Southampton
Liverpool v Arsenal
Manchester U v Crystal Palace
Norwich C v Chelsea
Sheffield U v Leicester C
Tottenham H v Newcastle U
Watford v West Ham U
Wolverhampton W v Burnley

Saturday, 31 August 2019
Arsenal v Tottenham H
Burnley v Liverpool
Chelsea v Sheffield U
Crystal Palace v Aston Villa
Everton v Wolverhampton W
Leicester C v Bournemouth
Manchester C v Brighton & HA
Newcastle U v Watford
Southampton v Manchester U
West Ham U v Norwich C

Saturday, 14 September 2019
Aston Villa v West Ham U
Bournemouth v Everton
Brighton & HA v Burnley
Liverpool v Newcastle U
Manchester U v Leicester C
Norwich C v Manchester C
Sheffield U v Southampton
Tottenham H v Crystal Palace
Watford v Arsenal
Wolverhampton W v Chelsea

Saturday, 21 September 2019
Arsenal v Aston Villa
Burnley v Norwich C
Chelsea v Liverpool
Crystal Palace v Wolverhampton W
Everton v Sheffield U
Leicester C v Tottenham H
Manchester C v Watford
Newcastle U v Brighton & HA
Southampton v Bournemouth
West Ham U v Manchester U

Saturday, 28 September 2019
Aston Villa v Burnley
Bournemouth v West Ham U
Chelsea v Brighton & HA
Crystal Palace v Norwich C
Everton v Manchester C
Leicester C v Newcastle U
Manchester U v Arsenal
Sheffield U v Liverpool
Tottenham H v Southampton
Wolverhampton W v Watford

Saturday, 5 October 2019
Arsenal v Bournemouth
Brighton & HA v Tottenham H
Burnley v Everton
Liverpool v Leicester C
Manchester C v Wolverhampton W
Newcastle U v Manchester U
Norwich C v Aston Villa
Southampton v Chelsea
Watford v Sheffield U
West Ham U v Crystal Palace

Saturday, 19 October 2019
Aston Villa v Brighton & HA
Bournemouth v Norwich C
Chelsea v Newcastle U
Crystal Palace v Manchester C
Everton v West Ham U
Leicester C v Burnley
Manchester U v Liverpool
Sheffield U v Arsenal
Tottenham H v Watford
Wolverhampton W v Southampton

Saturday, 26 October 2019
Arsenal v Crystal Palace
Brighton & HA v Everton
Burnley v Chelsea
Liverpool v Tottenham H
Manchester C v Aston Villa
Newcastle U v Wolverhampton W
Norwich C v Manchester U
Southampton v Leicester C
Watford v Bournemouth
West Ham U v Sheffield U

Saturday, 2 November 2019
Arsenal v Wolverhampton W
Aston Villa v Liverpool
Bournemouth v Manchester U
Brighton & HA v Norwich C
Crystal Palace v Leicester C
Everton v Tottenham H
Manchester C v Southampton
Sheffield U v Burnley
Watford v Chelsea
West Ham U v Newcastle U

Saturday, 9 November 2019
Burnley v West Ham U
Chelsea v Crystal Palace
Leicester C v Arsenal
Liverpool v Manchester C
Manchester U v Brighton & HA
Newcastle U v Bournemouth
Norwich C v Watford
Southampton v Everton
Tottenham H v Sheffield U
Wolverhampton W v Aston Villa

Saturday, 23 November 2019
Arsenal v Southampton
Aston Villa v Newcastle U
Bournemouth v Wolverhampton W
Brighton & HA v Leicester C
Crystal Palace v Liverpool
Everton v Norwich C
Manchester C v Chelsea
Sheffield U v Manchester U
Watford v Burnley
West Ham U v Tottenham H

Saturday, 30 November 2019
Burnley v Crystal Palace
Chelsea v West Ham U
Leicester C v Everton
Liverpool v Brighton & HA
Manchester U v Aston Villa
Newcastle U v Manchester C
Norwich C v Arsenal
Southampton v Watford
Tottenham H v Bournemouth
Wolverhampton W v Sheffield U

Tuesday, 3 December 2019
Arsenal v Brighton & HA
Burnley v Manchester C
Leicester C v Watford
Sheffield U v Newcastle U
Wolverhampton W v West Ham U
Manchester U v Tottenham H

Wednesday, 4 December 2019
Chelsea v Aston Villa
Southampton v Norwich C
Crystal Palace v Bournemouth
Liverpool v Everton

Saturday, 7 December 2019
Aston Villa v Leicester C
Bournemouth v Liverpool
Brighton & HA v Wolverhampton W
Everton v Chelsea
Manchester C v Manchester U
Newcastle U v Southampton
Norwich C v Sheffield U
Tottenham H v Burnley
Watford v Crystal Palace
West Ham U v Arsenal

Saturday, 14 December 2019
Arsenal v Manchester C
Burnley v Newcastle U
Chelsea v Bournemouth
Crystal Palace v Brighton & HA
Leicester C v Norwich C
Liverpool v Watford
Manchester U v Everton
Sheffield U v Aston Villa

Southampton v West Ham U
Wolverhampton W v Tottenham H

Saturday, 21 December 2019
Aston Villa v Southampton
Bournemouth v Burnley
Brighton & HA v Sheffield U
Everton v Arsenal
Manchester C v Leicester C
Newcastle U v Crystal Palace
Norwich C v Wolverhampton W
Tottenham H v Chelsea
Watford v Manchester U
West Ham U v Liverpool

Thursday, 26 December 2019
Aston Villa v Norwich C
Bournemouth v Arsenal
Chelsea v Southampton
Crystal Palace v West Ham U
Everton v Burnley
Leicester C v Liverpool
Manchester U v Newcastle U
Sheffield U v Watford
Tottenham H v Brighton & HA
Wolverhampton W v Manchester C

Saturday, 28 December 2019
Arsenal v Chelsea
Brighton & HA v Bournemouth
Burnley v Manchester U
Liverpool v Wolverhampton W
Manchester C v Sheffield U
Newcastle U v Everton
Norwich C v Tottenham H
Southampton v Crystal Palace
Watford v Aston Villa
West Ham U v Leicester C

Wednesday, 1 January 2020
Arsenal v Manchester U
Brighton & HA v Chelsea
Burnley v Aston Villa
Liverpool v Sheffield U
Manchester C v Everton
Newcastle U v Leicester C
Norwich C v Crystal Palace
Southampton v Tottenham H
Watford v Wolverhampton W
West Ham U v Bournemouth

Saturday, 11 January 2020
Aston Villa v Manchester C
Bournemouth v Watford
Chelsea v Burnley
Crystal Palace v Arsenal
Everton v Brighton & HA
Leicester C v Southampton
Manchester U v Norwich C
Sheffield U v West Ham U
Tottenham H v Liverpool
Wolverhampton W v Newcastle U

Saturday, 18 January 2020
Arsenal v Sheffield U
Brighton & HA v Aston Villa
Burnley v Leicester C
Liverpool v Manchester U
Manchester C v Crystal Palace
Newcastle U v Chelsea
Norwich C v Bournemouth
Southampton v Wolverhampton W
Watford v Tottenham H
West Ham U v Everton

Tuesday, 21 January 2020
Aston Villa v Watford
Bournemouth v Brighton & HA
Everton v Newcastle U
Leicester C v West Ham U
Manchester U v Burnley
Sheffield U v Manchester C
Wolverhampton W v Liverpool

Wednesday, 22 January 2020
Chelsea v Arsenal
Crystal Palace v Southampton
Tottenham H v Norwich C

Saturday, 1 February 2020
Bournemouth v Aston Villa
Burnley v Arsenal
Crystal Palace v Sheffield U
Leicester C v Chelsea
Liverpool v Southampton
Manchester U v Wolverhampton W
Newcastle U v Norwich C
Tottenham H v Manchester C
Watford v Everton
West Ham U v Brighton & HA

Saturday, 8/15 February 2020*
Arsenal v Newcastle U
Aston Villa v Tottenham H
Brighton & HA v Watford
Chelsea v Manchester U
Everton v Crystal Palace
Manchester C v West Ham U
Norwich C v Liverpool
Sheffield U v Bournemouth
Southampton v Burnley
Wolverhampton W v Leicester C
**Fixtures to be decided as part of winter break. Five fixtures will take place on each of 8 and 15 February.*

Saturday, 22 February 2020
Arsenal v Everton
Burnley v Bournemouth
Chelsea v Tottenham H
Crystal Palace v Newcastle U
Leicester C v Manchester C
Liverpool v West Ham U
Manchester U v Watford
Sheffield U v Brighton & HA
Southampton v Aston Villa
Wolverhampton W v Norwich C

Saturday, 29 February 2020
Aston Villa v Sheffield U
Bournemouth v Chelsea
Brighton & HA v Crystal Palace
Everton v Manchester U
Manchester C v Arsenal
Newcastle U v Burnley
Norwich C v Leicester C
Tottenham H v Wolverhampton W
Watford v Liverpool
West Ham U v Southampton

Saturday, 7 March 2020
Arsenal v West Ham U
Burnley v Tottenham H
Chelsea v Everton
Crystal Palace v Watford
Leicester C v Aston Villa
Liverpool v Bournemouth
Manchester U v Manchester C
Sheffield U v Norwich C
Southampton v Newcastle U
Wolverhampton W v Brighton & HA

Saturday, 14 March 2020
Aston Villa v Chelsea
Bournemouth v Crystal Palace
Brighton & HA v Arsenal
Everton v Liverpool
Manchester C v Burnley
Newcastle U v Sheffield U
Norwich C v Southampton
Tottenham H v Manchester U
Watford v Leicester C
West Ham U v Wolverhampton W

Saturday, 21 March 2020
Burnley v Watford
Chelsea v Manchester C
Leicester C v Brighton & HA
Liverpool v Crystal Palace
Manchester U v Sheffield U
Newcastle U v Aston Villa
Norwich C v Everton
Southampton v Arsenal
Tottenham H v West Ham U
Wolverhampton W v Bournemouth

Saturday, 4 April 2020
Arsenal v Norwich C
Aston Villa v Wolverhampton W
Bournemouth v Newcastle U
Brighton & HA v Manchester U
Crystal Palace v Burnley
Everton v Leicester C
Manchester C v Liverpool
Sheffield U v Tottenham H
Watford v Southampton
West Ham U v Chelsea

Saturday, 11 April 2020
Burnley v Sheffield U
Chelsea v Watford
Leicester C v Crystal Palace
Liverpool v Aston Villa
Manchester U v Bournemouth
Newcastle U v West Ham U
Norwich C v Brighton & HA
Southampton v Manchester City
Tottenham H v Everton
Wolverhampton W v Arsenal

Saturday, 18 April 2020
Arsenal v Leicester C
Aston Villa v Manchester U
Bournemouth v Tottenham H
Brighton & HA v Liverpool
Crystal Palace v Chelsea
Everton v Southampton
Manchester C v Newcastle U
Sheffield U v Wolverhampton W
Watford v Norwich C
West Ham U v Burnley

Saturday, 25 April 2020
Aston Villa v Crystal Palace
Bournemouth v Leicester C
Brighton & HA v Manchester C
Liverpool v Burnley
Manchester U v Southampton
Norwich C v West Ham U
Sheffield U v Chelsea
Tottenham H v Arsenal
Watford v Newcastle U
Wolverhampton W v Everton

Saturday, 2 May 2020
Arsenal v Liverpool
Burnley v Wolverhampton W
Chelsea v Norwich C
Crystal Palace v Manchester U
Everton v Aston Villa
Leicester C v Sheffield U
Manchester C v Bournemouth
Newcastle U v Tottenham H
Southampton v Brighton & HA
West Ham U v Watford

Saturday, 9 May 2020
Aston Villa v Arsenal
Bournemouth v Southampton
Brighton & HA v Newcastle U
Liverpool v Chelsea
Manchester U v West Ham U
Norwich C v Burnley
Sheffield U v Everton
Tottenham H v Leicester C
Watford v Manchester C
Wolverhampton W v Crystal Palace

Sunday, 17 May 2020
Arsenal v Watford
Burnley v Brighton & HA
Chelsea v Wolverhampton W

Crystal Palace v Tottenham H
Everton v Bournemouth
Leicester C v Manchester U
Manchester C v Norwich C
Newcastle U v Liverpool
Southampton v Sheffield U
West Ham U v Aston Villa

EFL Championship

Friday, 2 August 2019
Luton T v Middlesbrough

Saturday, 3 August 2019
Barnsley v Fulham
Blackburn R v Charlton Ath
Brentford v Birmingham C
Millwall v Preston NE
Nottingham F v WBA
Reading v Sheffield W
Stoke C v QPR
Swansea C v Hull C
Wigan Ath v Cardiff C

Sunday, 4 August 2019
Bristol C v Leeds U

Monday, 5 August 2019
Huddersfield T v Derby Co

Saturday, 10 August 2019
Birmingham C v Bristol C
Cardiff C v Luton T
Charlton Ath v Stoke C
Derby Co v Swansea C
Fulham v Blackburn R
Hull C v Reading
Leeds U v Nottingham F
Middlesbrough v Brentford
Preston NE v Wigan Ath
QPR v Huddersfield T
Sheffield W v Barnsley
WBA v Millwall

Saturday, 17 August 2019
Barnsley v Charlton Ath
Blackburn R v Middlesbrough
Brentford v Hull C
Bristol C v QPR
Huddersfield T v Fulham
Luton T v WBA
Millwall v Sheffield W
Nottingham F v Birmingham C
Reading v Cardiff C
Stoke C v Derby Co
Swansea C v Preston NE
Wigan Ath v Leeds U

Tuesday, 20 August 2019
Birmingham C v Barnsley
Derby Co v Bristol C
Hull C v Blackburn R
Middlesbrough v Wigan Ath
Sheffield W v Luton T

Wednesday, 21 August 2019
Cardiff C v Huddersfield T
Charlton Ath v Nottingham F
Fulham v Millwall
Leeds U v Brentford
Preston NE v Stoke C
QPR v Swansea C
WBA v Reading

Saturday, 24 August 2019
Barnsley v Luton T
Blackburn R v Cardiff C
Charlton Ath v Brentford
Derby Co v WBA
Fulham v Nottingham F
Huddersfield T v Reading
Hull C v Bristol C
Middlesbrough v Millwall
Preston NE v Sheffield W
QPR v Wigan Ath
Stoke C v Leeds U
Swansea C v Birmingham C

Saturday, 31 August 2019
Birmingham C v Stoke C
Brentford v Derby Co
Bristol C v Middlesbrough
Cardiff C v Fulham
Leeds U v Swansea C
Luton T v Huddersfield T
Millwall v Hull C
Nottingham F v Preston NE
Reading v Charlton Ath
Sheffield W v QPR
WBA v Blackburn R
Wigan Ath v Barnsley

Saturday, 14 September 2019
Barnsley v Leeds U
Blackburn R v Millwall
Charlton Ath v Birmingham C
Derby Co v Cardiff C
Fulham v WBA
Huddersfield T v Sheffield W
Hull C v Wigan Ath
Middlesbrough v Reading
Preston NE v Brentford
QPR v Luton T
Stoke C v Bristol C
Swansea C v Nottingham F

Saturday, 21 September 2019
Birmingham C v Preston NE
Brentford v Stoke C
Bristol C v Swansea C
Cardiff C v Middlesbrough
Leeds U v Derby Co
Luton T v Hull C
Millwall v QPR
Nottingham F v Barnsley
Reading v Blackburn R
Sheffield W v Fulham
WBA v Huddersfield T
Wigan Ath v Charlton Ath

Saturday, 28 September 2019
Barnsley v Brentford
Blackburn R v Luton T
Charlton Ath v Leeds U
Derby Co v Birmingham C
Fulham v Wigan Ath
Huddersfield T v Millwall
Hull C v Cardiff C
Middlesbrough v Sheffield W
Preston NE v Bristol C
QPR v WBA
Stoke C v Nottingham F
Swansea C v Reading

Tuesday, 1 October 2019
Blackburn R v Nottingham F
Hull C v Sheffield W
Leeds U v WBA
Middlesbrough v Preston NE
Reading v Fulham
Stoke C v Huddersfield T
Wigan Ath v Birmingham C

Wednesday, 2 October 2019
Barnsley v Derby Co
Brentford v Bristol C
Cardiff C v QPR
Charlton Ath v Swansea C
Luton T v Millwall

Saturday, 5 October 2019
Birmingham C v Middlesbrough
Bristol C v Reading
Derby Co v Luton T
Fulham v Charlton Ath
Huddersfield T v Hull C
Millwall v Leeds U
Nottingham F v Brentford
Preston NE v Barnsley
QPR v Blackburn R
Sheffield W v Wigan Ath
Swansea C v Stoke C
WBA v Cardiff C

Saturday, 19 October 2019
Barnsley v Swansea C
Blackburn R v Huddersfield T
Brentford v Millwall
Cardiff C v Sheffield W
Charlton Ath v Derby Co
Hull C v QPR
Leeds U v Birmingham C
Luton T v Bristol C
Middlesbrough v WBA
Reading v Preston NE
Stoke C v Fulham
Wigan Ath v Nottingham F

Tuesday, 22 October 2019
Birmingham C v Blackburn R
Millwall v Cardiff C
QPR v Reading
Sheffield W v Stoke C
Swansea C v Brentford
WBA v Barnsley

Wednesday, 23 October 2019
Bristol C v Charlton Ath
Derby Co v Wigan Ath
Fulham v Luton T
Huddersfield T v Middlesbrough
Nottingham F v Hull C
Preston NE v Leeds U

Saturday, 26 October 2019
Birmingham C v Luton T
Bristol C v Wigan Ath
Huddersfield T v Barnsley
Hull C v Derby Co
Middlesbrough v Fulham
Millwall v Stoke C
Nottingham F v Reading
Preston NE v Blackburn R
QPR v Brentford
Sheffield W v Leeds U
Swansea C v Cardiff C
WBA v Charlton Ath

Saturday, 2 November 2019
Barnsley v Bristol C
Blackburn R v Sheffield W
Brentford v Huddersfield T
Cardiff C v Birmingham C
Charlton Ath v Preston NE
Derby Co v Middlesbrough
Fulham v Hull C
Leeds U v QPR
Luton T v Nottingham F
Reading v Millwall
Stoke C v WBA
Wigan Ath v Swansea C

Saturday, 9 November 2019
Barnsley v Stoke C
Birmingham C v Fulham
Cardiff C v Bristol C
Hull C v WBA
Leeds U v Blackburn R
Millwall v Charlton Ath
Nottingham F v Derby Co
Preston NE v Huddersfield T
QPR v Middlesbrough
Reading v Luton T
Sheffield W v Swansea C
Wigan Ath v Brentford

Saturday, 23 November 2019
Blackburn R v Barnsley
Brentford v Reading
Bristol C v Nottingham F
Charlton Ath v Cardiff C
Derby Co v Preston NE

Fulham v QPR
Huddersfield T v Birmingham C
Luton T v Leeds U
Middlesbrough v Hull C
Stoke C v Wigan Ath
Swansea C v Millwall
WBA v Sheffield W

Tuesday, 26 November 2019
Cardiff C v Stoke C
Fulham v Derby Co
Huddersfield T v Swansea C
Luton T v Charlton Ath
Millwall v Wigan Ath
Reading v Leeds U

Wednesday, 27 November 2019
Blackburn R v Brentford
Hull C v Preston NE
Middlesbrough v Barnsley
QPR v Nottingham F
Sheffield W v Birmingham C
WBA v Bristol C

Saturday, 30 November 2019
Barnsley v Hull C
Birmingham C v Millwall
Brentford v Luton T
Bristol C v Huddersfield T
Charlton Ath v Sheffield W
Derby Co v QPR
Leeds U v Middlesbrough
Nottingham F v Cardiff C
Preston NE v WBA
Stoke C v Blackburn R
Swansea C v Fulham
Wigan Ath v Reading

Saturday, 7 December 2019
Blackburn R v Derby Co
Cardiff C v Barnsley
Fulham v Bristol C
Huddersfield T v Leeds U
Hull C v Stoke C
Luton T v Wigan Ath
Middlesbrough v Charlton Ath
Millwall v Nottingham F
QPR v Preston NE
Reading v Birmingham C
Sheffield W v Brentford
WBA v Swansea C

Tuesday, 10 December 2019
Bristol C v Millwall
Charlton Ath v Huddersfield T
Leeds U v Hull C
Nottingham F v Middlesbrough
Preston NE v Fulham
Stoke C v Luton T

Wednesday, 11 December 2019
Barnsley v Reading
Birmingham C v QPR
Brentford v Cardiff C
Derby Co v Sheffield W
Swansea C v Blackburn R
Wigan Ath v WBA

Saturday, 14 December 2019
Barnsley v QPR
Birmingham C v WBA
Brentford v Fulham
Bristol C v Blackburn R
Charlton Ath v Hull C
Derby Co v Millwall
Leeds U v Cardiff C
Nottingham F v Sheffield W
Preston NE v Luton T
Stoke C v Reading
Swansea C v Middlesbrough
Wigan Ath v Huddersfield T

Saturday, 21 December 2019
Blackburn R v Wigan Ath
Cardiff C v Preston NE
Fulham v Leeds U
Huddersfield T v Nottingham F
Hull C v Birmingham C
Luton T v Swansea C
Middlesbrough v Stoke C
Millwall v Barnsley
QPR v Charlton Ath
Reading v Derby Co
Sheffield W v Bristol C
WBA v Brentford

Thursday, 26 December 2019
Barnsley v WBA
Blackburn R v Birmingham C
Brentford v Swansea C
Cardiff C v Millwall
Charlton Ath v Bristol C
Hull C v Nottingham F
Leeds U v Preston NE
Luton T v Fulham
Middlesbrough v Huddersfield T
Reading v QPR
Stoke C v Sheffield W
Wigan Ath v Derby Co

Sunday, 29 December 2019
Birmingham C v Leeds U
Bristol C v Luton T
Derby Co v Charlton Ath
Fulham v Stoke C
Huddersfield T v Blackburn R
Millwall v Brentford
Nottingham F v Wigan Ath
Preston NE v Reading
QPR v Hull C
Sheffield W v Cardiff C
Swansea C v Barnsley
WBA v Middlesbrough

Wednesday, 1 January 2020
Birmingham C v Wigan Ath
Bristol C v Brentford
Derby Co v Barnsley
Fulham v Reading
Huddersfield T v Stoke C
Millwall v Luton T
Nottingham F v Blackburn R
Preston NE v Middlesbrough
QPR v Cardiff C
Sheffield W v Hull C
Swansea C v Charlton Ath
WBA v Leeds U

Saturday, 11 January 2020
Barnsley v Huddersfield T
Blackburn R v Preston NE
Brentford v QPR
Cardiff C v Swansea C
Charlton Ath v WBA
Hull C v Fulham
Leeds U v Sheffield W
Luton T v Birmingham C
Middlesbrough v Derby Co
Reading v Nottingham F
Stoke C v Millwall
Wigan Ath v Bristol C

Saturday, 18 January 2020
Birmingham C v Cardiff C
Bristol C v Barnsley
Derby Co v Hull C
Fulham v Middlesbrough
Huddersfield T v Brentford
Millwall v Reading
Nottingham F v Luton T
Preston NE v Charlton Ath
QPR v Leeds U
Sheffield W v Blackburn R
Swansea C v Wigan Ath
WBA v Stoke C

Saturday, 25 January 2020
Barnsley v Preston NE
Blackburn R v QPR
Brentford v Nottingham F
Cardiff C v WBA
Charlton Ath v Fulham
Hull C v Huddersfield T
Leeds U v Millwall
Luton T v Derby Co
Middlesbrough v Birmingham C
Reading v Bristol C
Stoke C v Swansea C
Wigan Ath v Sheffield W

Saturday, 1 February 2020
Birmingham C v Nottingham F
Cardiff C v Reading
Charlton Ath v Barnsley
Derby Co v Stoke C
Fulham v Huddersfield T
Hull C v Brentford
Leeds U v Wigan Ath
Middlesbrough v Blackburn R
Preston NE v Swansea C
QPR v Bristol C
Sheffield W v Millwall
WBA v Luton T

Saturday, 8 February 2020
Barnsley v Sheffield W
Blackburn R v Fulham
Brentford v Middlesbrough
Bristol C v Birmingham C
Huddersfield T v QPR
Luton T v Cardiff C
Millwall v WBA
Nottingham F v Leeds U
Reading v Hull C
Stoke C v Charlton Ath
Swansea C v Derby Co
Wigan Ath v Preston NE

Tuesday, 11 February 2020
Barnsley v Birmingham C
Blackburn R v Hull C
Brentford v Leeds U
Nottingham F v Charlton Ath
Swansea C v QPR
Wigan Ath v Middlesbrough

Wednesday, 12 February 2020
Bristol C v Derby Co
Huddersfield T v Cardiff C
Luton T v Sheffield W
Millwall v Fulham
Reading v WBA
Stoke C v Preston NE

Saturday, 15 February 2020
Birmingham C v Brentford
Cardiff C v Wigan Ath
Charlton Ath v Blackburn R
Derby Co v Huddersfield T
Fulham v Barnsley
Hull C v Swansea C
Leeds U v Bristol C
Middlesbrough v Luton T
Preston NE v Millwall
QPR v Stoke C
Sheffield W v Reading
WBA v Nottingham F

Saturday, 22 February 2020
Barnsley v Middlesbrough
Birmingham C v Sheffield W
Brentford v Blackburn R
Bristol C v WBA
Charlton Ath v Luton T
Derby Co v Fulham
Leeds U v Reading
Nottingham F v QPR
Preston NE v Hull C
Stoke C v Cardiff C

Swansea C v Huddersfield T
Wigan Ath v Millwall

Tuesday, 25 February 2020
Cardiff C v Nottingham F
Fulham v Swansea C
Huddersfield T v Bristol C
Luton T v Brentford
QPR v Derby Co
WBA v Preston NE

Wednesday, 26 February 2020
Blackburn R v Stoke C
Hull C v Barnsley
Middlesbrough v Leeds U
Millwall v Birmingham C
Sheffield W v Charlton Ath
Reading v Wigan Ath

Saturday, 29 February 2020
Blackburn R v Swansea C
Cardiff C v Brentford
Fulham v Preston NE
Huddersfield T v Charlton Ath
Hull C v Leeds U
Luton T v Stoke C
Middlesbrough v Nottingham F
Millwall v Bristol C
QPR v Birmingham C
Reading v Barnsley
Sheffield W v Derby Co
WBA v Wigan Ath

Saturday, 7 March 2020
Barnsley v Cardiff C
Birmingham C v Reading
Brentford v Sheffield W
Bristol C v Fulham
Charlton Ath v Middlesbrough
Derby Co v Blackburn R
Leeds U v Huddersfield T
Nottingham F v Millwall
Preston NE v QPR
Stoke C v Hull C
Swansea C v WBA
Wigan Ath v Luton T

Saturday, 14 March 2020
Blackburn R v Bristol C
Cardiff C v Leeds U
Fulham v Brentford
Huddersfield T v Wigan Ath
Hull C v Charlton Ath
Luton T v Preston NE
Middlesbrough v Swansea C
Millwall v Derby Co
QPR v Barnsley
Reading v Stoke C
Sheffield W v Nottingham F
WBA v Birmingham C

Tuesday, 17 March 2020
Barnsley v Millwall
Brentford v WBA
Bristol C v Sheffield W
Charlton Ath v QPR
Derby Co v Reading
Preston NE v Cardiff C

Wednesday, 18 March 2020
Birmingham C v Hull C
Leeds U v Fulham
Nottingham F v Huddersfield T
Stoke C v Middlesbrough
Swansea C v Luton T
Wigan Ath v Blackburn R

Saturday, 21 March 2020
Barnsley v Blackburn R
Birmingham C v Huddersfield T
Cardiff C v Charlton Ath
Hull C v Middlesbrough
Leeds U v Luton T
Millwall v Swansea C
Nottingham F v Bristol C
Preston NE v Derby Co
QPR v Fulham
Reading v Brentford
Sheffield W v WBA
Wigan Ath v Stoke C

Saturday, 4 April 2020
Blackburn R v Leeds U
Brentford v Wigan Ath
Bristol C v Cardiff C
Charlton Ath v Millwall
Derby Co v Nottingham F
Fulham v Birmingham C
Huddersfield T v Preston NE
Luton T v Reading
Middlesbrough v QPR
Stoke C v Barnsley
Swansea C v Sheffield W
WBA v Hull C

Friday, 10 April 2020
Birmingham C v Swansea C
Brentford v Charlton Ath
Bristol C v Hull C
Cardiff C v Blackburn R
Leeds U v Stoke C
Luton T v Barnsley
Millwall v Middlesbrough
Nottingham F v Fulham
Reading v Huddersfield T
Sheffield W v Preston NE
WBA v Derby Co
Wigan Ath v QPR

Monday, 13 April 2020
Barnsley v Wigan Ath
Blackburn R v WBA
Charlton Ath v Reading
Derby Co v Brentford
Fulham v Cardiff C
Huddersfield T v Luton T
Hull C v Millwall
Middlesbrough v Bristol C
Preston NE v Nottingham F
QPR v Sheffield W
Stoke C v Birmingham C
Swansea C v Leeds U

Saturday, 18 April 2020
Birmingham C v Charlton Ath
Brentford v Preston NE
Bristol C v Stoke C
Cardiff C v Derby Co
Leeds U v Barnsley
Luton T v QPR
Millwall v Blackburn R
Nottingham F v Swansea C
Reading v Middlesbrough
Sheffield W v Huddersfield T
WBA v Fulham
Wigan Ath v Hull C

Saturday, 25 April 2020
Barnsley v Nottingham F
Blackburn R v Reading
Charlton Ath v Wigan Ath
Derby Co v Leeds U
Fulham v Sheffield W
Huddersfield T v WBA
Hull C v Luton T
Middlesbrough v Cardiff C
Preston NE v Birmingham C
QPR v Millwall
Stoke C v Brentford
Swansea C v Bristol C

Saturday, 2 May 2020
Birmingham C v Derby Co
Brentford v Barnsley
Bristol C v Preston NE
Cardiff C v Hull C
Leeds U v Charlton Ath
Luton T v Blackburn R
Millwall v Huddersfield T
Nottingham F v Stoke C
Reading v Swansea C
Sheffield W v Middlesbrough
WBA v QPR
Wigan Ath v Fulham

EFL League One

Saturday, 3 August 2019
AFC Wimbledon v Rotherham U
Blackpool v Bristol R
Burton Alb v Ipswich T
Bury v Milton Keynes D
Coventry C v Southend U
Doncaster R v Gillingham
Lincoln C v Accrington S
Peterborough U v Fleetwood T
Shrewsbury T v Portsmouth
Sunderland v Oxford U
Tranmere R v Rochdale
Wycombe W v Bolton W

Saturday, 10 August 2019
Accrington S v Bury
Bolton W v Coventry C
Bristol R v Wycombe W
Fleetwood T v AFC Wimbledon
Gillingham v Burton Alb
Ipswich T v Sunderland
Milton Keynes D v Shrewsbury T
Oxford U v Peterborough U
Portsmouth v Tranmere R
Rochdale v Doncaster R
Rotherham U v Lincoln C
Southend U v Blackpool

Saturday, 17 August 2019
AFC Wimbledon v Accrington S
Blackpool v Oxford U
Burton Alb v Rotherham U
Bury v Gillingham
Coventry C v Bristol R
Doncaster R v Fleetwood T
Lincoln C v Southend U
Peterborough U v Ipswich T
Shrewsbury T v Rochdale
Sunderland v Portsmouth
Tranmere R v Bolton W
Wycombe W v Milton Keynes D

Tuesday, 20 August 2019
Accrington S v Shrewsbury T
Bolton W v Doncaster R
Bristol R v Tranmere R
Fleetwood T v Wycombe W
Gillingham v Blackpool
Ipswich T v AFC Wimbledon
Milton Keynes D v Lincoln C
Oxford U v Burton Alb
Portsmouth v Coventry C
Rochdale v Sunderland
Rotherham U v Bury
Southend U v Peterborough U

Saturday, 24 August 2019
Bolton W v Ipswich T
Bristol R v Oxford U
Coventry C v Gillingham
Doncaster R v Lincoln C
Fleetwood T v Accrington S
Milton Keynes D v Peterborough U
Portsmouth v Rotherham U
Rochdale v Blackpool
Shrewsbury T v Burton Alb
Sunderland v AFC Wimbledon
Tranmere R v Bury
Wycombe W v Southend U

Saturday, 31 August 2019
AFC Wimbledon v Wycombe W
Accrington S v Milton Keynes D
Blackpool v Portsmouth
Burton Alb v Bristol R
Bury v Doncaster R
Gillingham v Bolton W
Ipswich T v Shrewsbury T
Lincoln C v Fleetwood T
Oxford U v Coventry C
Peterborough U v Sunderland
Rotherham U v Tranmere R
Southend U v Rochdale

Saturday, 7 September 2019
Bolton W v Bury
Bristol R v Accrington S
Coventry C v Blackpool
Doncaster R v Rotherham U
Fleetwood T v Oxford U
Milton Keynes D v AFC Wimbledon
Portsmouth v Southend U
Rochdale v Ipswich T
Shrewsbury T v Peterborough U
Sunderland v Burton Alb
Tranmere R v Gillingham
Wycombe W v Lincoln C

Saturday, 14 September 2019
AFC Wimbledon v Shrewsbury T
Accrington S v Sunderland
Blackpool v Milton Keynes D
Burton Alb v Coventry C
Bury v Portsmouth
Gillingham v Wycombe W
Ipswich T v Doncaster R
Lincoln C v Bristol R
Oxford U v Tranmere R
Peterborough U v Rochdale
Rotherham U v Bolton W
Southend U v Fleetwood T

Tuesday, 17 September 2019
Bolton W v Oxford U
Bristol R v Gillingham
Coventry C v AFC Wimbledon
Doncaster R v Blackpool
Fleetwood T v Bury
Milton Keynes D v Ipswich T
Portsmouth v Burton Alb
Rochdale v Lincoln C
Shrewsbury T v Southend U
Sunderland v Rotherham U
Tranmere R v Peterborough U
Wycombe W v Accrington S

Saturday, 21 September 2019
AFC Wimbledon v Bristol R
Accrington S v Blackpool
Bolton W v Sunderland
Bury v Coventry C
Doncaster R v Peterborough U
Fleetwood T v Rochdale
Gillingham v Ipswich T
Lincoln C v Oxford U
Milton Keynes D v Southend U
Rotherham U v Shrewsbury T
Tranmere R v Burton Alb
Wycombe W v Portsmouth

Saturday, 28 September 2019
Blackpool v Lincoln C
Bristol R v Rotherham U
Burton Alb v Bury
Coventry C v Doncaster R
Ipswich T v Tranmere R
Oxford U v Gillingham
Peterborough U v AFC Wimbledon
Portsmouth v Bolton W
Rochdale v Wycombe W
Shrewsbury T v Fleetwood T
Southend U v Accrington S
Sunderland v Milton Keynes D

Saturday, 5 October 2019
AFC Wimbledon v Rochdale
Accrington S v Oxford U
Bolton W v Blackpool
Bury v Bristol R
Doncaster R v Portsmouth
Fleetwood T v Ipswich T
Gillingham v Southend U
Lincoln C v Sunderland
Milton Keynes D v Burton Alb
Rotherham U v Coventry C
Tranmere R v Shrewsbury T
Wycombe W v Peterborough U

Saturday, 12 October 2019
Blackpool v Rotherham U
Bristol R v Milton Keynes D
Burton Alb v Bolton W
Coventry C v Tranmere R
Ipswich T v Wycombe W
Oxford U v Doncaster R
Peterborough U v Lincoln C
Portsmouth v Gillingham
Rochdale v Accrington S
Shrewsbury T v Bury
Southend U v AFC Wimbledon
Sunderland v Fleetwood T

Saturday, 19 October 2019
AFC Wimbledon v Portsmouth
Accrington S v Ipswich T
Bolton W v Rochdale
Bury v Blackpool
Doncaster R v Bristol R
Fleetwood T v Burton Alb
Gillingham v Peterborough U
Lincoln C v Shrewsbury T
Milton Keynes D v Coventry C
Rotherham U v Oxford U
Tranmere R v Southend U
Wycombe W v Sunderland

Tuesday, 22 October 2019
Blackpool v Wycombe W
Bristol R v Bolton W
Burton Alb v AFC Wimbledon
Ipswich T v Rotherham U
Oxford U v Bury
Peterborough U v Accrington S
Portsmouth v Lincoln C
Rochdale v Milton Keynes D
Shrewsbury T v Gillingham
Southend U v Doncaster R
Sunderland v Tranmere R

Wednesday, 23 October 2019
Coventry C v Fleetwood T

Saturday, 26 October 2019
Accrington S v Gillingham
Bristol R v Portsmouth
Burton Alb v Blackpool
Bury v AFC Wimbledon
Fleetwood T v Milton Keynes D
Lincoln C v Bolton W
Oxford U v Rochdale
Peterborough U v Coventry C
Rotherham U v Wycombe W
Shrewsbury T v Sunderland
Southend U v Ipswich T
Tranmere R v Doncaster R

Saturday, 2 November 2019
AFC Wimbledon v Lincoln C
Blackpool v Peterborough U
Bolton W v Fleetwood T
Coventry C v Accrington S
Doncaster R v Burton Alb
Gillingham v Rotherham U
Ipswich T v Bury
Milton Keynes D v Tranmere R
Portsmouth v Oxford U
Rochdale v Bristol R
Sunderland v Southend U
Wycombe W v Shrewsbury T

Saturday, 16 November 2019
Blackpool v AFC Wimbledon
Bolton W v Milton Keynes D
Bristol R v Sunderland
Burton Alb v Southend U
Bury v Peterborough U
Coventry C v Rochdale
Doncaster R v Shrewsbury T
Gillingham v Lincoln C
Oxford U v Ipswich T
Portsmouth v Fleetwood T
Rotherham U v Accrington S
Tranmere R v Wycombe W

Saturday, 23 November 2019
AFC Wimbledon v Gillingham
Accrington S v Bolton W
Fleetwood T v Tranmere R
Ipswich T v Blackpool
Lincoln C v Bury
Milton Keynes D v Rotherham U
Peterborough U v Burton Alb
Rochdale v Portsmouth
Shrewsbury T v Bristol R
Southend U v Oxford U
Sunderland v Coventry C
Wycombe W v Doncaster R

Saturday, 7 December 2019
Blackpool v Fleetwood T
Bolton W v AFC Wimbledon
Bristol R v Southend U
Burton Alb v Lincoln C
Bury v Wycombe W
Coventry C v Ipswich T
Doncaster R v Milton Keynes D
Gillingham v Sunderland
Oxford U v Shrewsbury T
Portsmouth v Peterborough U
Rotherham U v Rochdale
Tranmere R v Accrington S

Saturday, 14 December 2019
AFC Wimbledon v Doncaster R
Accrington S v Portsmouth
Fleetwood T v Gillingham
Ipswich T v Bristol R
Lincoln C v Tranmere R
Milton Keynes D v Oxford U
Peterborough U v Bolton W
Rochdale v Bury
Shrewsbury T v Coventry C
Southend U v Rotherham U
Sunderland v Blackpool
Wycombe W v Burton Alb

Saturday, 21 December 2019
Blackpool v Shrewsbury T
Bolton W v Southend U
Bristol R v Peterborough U
Burton Alb v Rochdale
Bury v Sunderland
Coventry C v Lincoln C
Doncaster R v Accrington S
Gillingham v Milton Keynes D
Oxford U v Wycombe W
Portsmouth v Ipswich T
Rotherham U v Fleetwood T
Tranmere R v AFC Wimbledon

Thursday, 26 December 2019
Blackpool v Accrington S
Bristol R v AFC Wimbledon
Burton Alb v Tranmere R
Coventry C v Bury
Ipswich T v Gillingham
Oxford U v Lincoln C
Peterborough U v Doncaster R
Portsmouth v Wycombe W
Rochdale v Fleetwood T

Shrewsbury T v Rotherham U
Southend U v Milton Keynes D
Sunderland v Bolton W

Sunday, 29 December 2019
AFC Wimbledon v Oxford U
Accrington S v Burton Alb
Bolton W v Shrewsbury T
Bury v Southend U
Doncaster R v Sunderland
Fleetwood T v Bristol R
Gillingham v Rochdale
Lincoln C v Ipswich T
Milton Keynes D v Portsmouth
Rotherham U v Peterborough U
Tranmere R v Blackpool
Wycombe W v Coventry C

Wednesday, 1 January 2020
AFC Wimbledon v Southend U
Accrington S v Rochdale
Bolton W v Burton Alb
Bury v Shrewsbury T
Doncaster R v Oxford U
Fleetwood T v Sunderland
Gillingham v Portsmouth
Lincoln C v Peterborough U
Milton Keynes D v Bristol R
Rotherham U v Blackpool
Tranmere R v Coventry C
Wycombe W v Ipswich T

Saturday, 4 January 2020
Blackpool v Bolton W
Bristol R v Bury
Burton Alb v Milton Keynes D
Coventry C v Rotherham U
Ipswich T v Fleetwood T
Oxford U v Accrington S
Peterborough U v Wycombe W
Portsmouth v Doncaster R
Rochdale v AFC Wimbledon
Shrewsbury T v Tranmere R
Southend U v Gillingham
Sunderland v Lincoln C

Saturday, 11 January 2020
Blackpool v Bury
Bristol R v Doncaster R
Burton Alb v Fleetwood T
Coventry C v Milton Keynes D
Ipswich T v Accrington S
Oxford U v Rotherham U
Peterborough U v Gillingham
Portsmouth v AFC Wimbledon
Rochdale v Bolton W
Shrewsbury T v Lincoln C
Southend U v Tranmere R
Sunderland v Wycombe W

Saturday, 18 January 2020
AFC Wimbledon v Peterborough U
Accrington S v Southend U
Bolton W v Portsmouth
Bury v Burton Alb
Doncaster R v Coventry C
Fleetwood T v Shrewsbury T
Gillingham v Oxford U
Lincoln C v Blackpool
Milton Keynes D v Sunderland
Rotherham U v Bristol R
Tranmere R v Ipswich T
Wycombe W v Rochdale

Saturday, 25 January 2020
Blackpool v Tranmere R
Bristol R v Fleetwood T
Burton Alb v Accrington S
Coventry C v Wycombe W
Ipswich T v Lincoln C
Oxford U v AFC Wimbledon
Peterborough U v Rotherham U
Portsmouth v Milton Keynes D
Rochdale v Gillingham
Shrewsbury T v Bolton W
Southend U v Bury
Sunderland v Doncaster R

Tuesday, 28 January 2020
Accrington S v Peterborough U
AFC Wimbledon v Burton Alb
Bolton W v Bristol R
Bury v Oxford U
Doncaster R v Southend U
Fleetwood T v Coventry C
Gillingham v Shrewsbury T
Lincoln C v Portsmouth
Milton Keynes D v Rochdale
Rotherham U v Ipswich T
Tranmere R v Sunderland
Wycombe W v Blackpool

Saturday, 1 February 2020
Accrington S v AFC Wimbledon
Bolton W v Tranmere R
Bristol R v Coventry C
Fleetwood T v Doncaster R
Gillingham v Bury
Ipswich T v Peterborough U
Milton Keynes D v Wycombe W
Oxford U v Blackpool
Portsmouth v Sunderland
Rochdale v Shrewsbury T
Rotherham U v Burton Alb
Southend U v Lincoln C

Saturday, 8 February 2020
AFC Wimbledon v Fleetwood T
Blackpool v Southend U
Burton Alb v Gillingham
Bury v Accrington S
Coventry C v Bolton W
Doncaster R v Rochdale
Lincoln C v Rotherham U
Peterborough U v Oxford U
Shrewsbury T v Milton Keynes D
Sunderland v Ipswich T
Tranmere R v Portsmouth
Wycombe W v Bristol R

Tuesday, 11 February 2020
AFC Wimbledon v Ipswich T
Blackpool v Gillingham
Burton Alb v Oxford U
Bury v Rotherham U
Coventry C v Portsmouth
Doncaster R v Bolton W
Lincoln C v Milton Keynes D
Peterborough U v Southend U
Shrewsbury T v Accrington S
Sunderland v Rochdale
Tranmere R v Bristol R
Wycombe W v Fleetwood T

Saturday, 15 February 2020
Accrington S v Lincoln C
Bolton W v Wycombe W
Bristol R v Blackpool
Fleetwood T v Peterborough U
Gillingham v Doncaster R
Ipswich T v Burton Alb
Milton Keynes D v Bury
Oxford U v Sunderland
Portsmouth v Shrewsbury T
Rochdale v Tranmere R
Rotherham U v AFC Wimbledon
Southend U v Coventry C

Saturday, 22 February 2020
AFC Wimbledon v Blackpool
Accrington S v Rotherham U
Fleetwood T v Portsmouth
Ipswich T v Oxford U
Lincoln C v Gillingham
Milton Keynes D v Bolton W
Peterborough U v Bury
Rochdale v Coventry C
Shrewsbury T v Doncaster R
Southend U v Burton Alb
Sunderland v Bristol R
Wycombe W v Tranmere R

Saturday, 29 February 2020
Blackpool v Ipswich T
Bolton W v Accrington S
Bristol R v Shrewsbury T
Burton Alb v Peterborough U
Bury v Lincoln C
Coventry C v Sunderland
Doncaster R v Wycombe W
Gillingham v AFC Wimbledon
Oxford U v Southend U
Portsmouth v Rochdale
Rotherham U v Milton Keynes D
Tranmere R v Fleetwood T

Saturday, 7 March 2020
AFC Wimbledon v Bolton W
Accrington S v Tranmere R
Fleetwood T v Blackpool
Ipswich T v Coventry C
Lincoln C v Burton Alb
Milton Keynes D v Doncaster R
Peterborough U v Portsmouth
Rochdale v Rotherham U
Shrewsbury T v Oxford U
Southend U v Bristol R
Sunderland v Gillingham
Wycombe W v Bury

Saturday, 14 March 2020
Blackpool v Sunderland
Bolton W v Peterborough U
Bristol R v Ipswich T
Burton Alb v Wycombe W
Bury v Rochdale
Coventry C v Shrewsbury T
Doncaster R v AFC Wimbledon
Gillingham v Fleetwood T
Oxford U v Milton Keynes D
Portsmouth v Accrington S
Rotherham U v Southend U
Tranmere R v Lincoln C

Saturday, 21 March 2020
AFC Wimbledon v Tranmere R
Accrington S v Doncaster R
Fleetwood T v Rotherham U
Ipswich T v Portsmouth
Lincoln C v Coventry C
Milton Keynes D v Gillingham
Peterborough U v Bristol R
Rochdale v Burton Alb
Shrewsbury T v Blackpool
Southend U v Bolton W
Sunderland v Bury
Wycombe W v Oxford U

Saturday, 28 March 2020
Accrington S v Coventry C
Bristol R v Rochdale
Burton Alb v Doncaster R
Bury v Ipswich T
Fleetwood T v Bolton W
Lincoln C v AFC Wimbledon
Oxford U v Portsmouth
Peterborough U v Blackpool
Rotherham U v Gillingham
Shrewsbury T v Wycombe W
Southend U v Sunderland
Tranmere R v Milton Keynes D

Saturday, 4 April 2020
AFC Wimbledon v Bury
Blackpool v Burton Alb
Bolton W v Lincoln C
Coventry C v Peterborough U

Doncaster R v Tranmere R
Gillingham v Accrington S
Ipswich T v Southend U
Milton Keynes D v Fleetwood T
Portsmouth v Bristol R
Rochdale v Oxford U
Sunderland v Shrewsbury T
Wycombe W v Rotherham U

Friday, 10 April 2020
AFC Wimbledon v Sunderland
Accrington S v Fleetwood T
Blackpool v Rochdale
Burton Alb v Shrewsbury T
Bury v Tranmere R
Gillingham v Coventry C
Ipswich T v Bolton W
Lincoln C v Doncaster R
Oxford U v Bristol R
Peterborough U v Milton Keynes D
Rotherham U v Portsmouth
Southend U v Wycombe W

Monday, 13 April 2020
Bolton W v Gillingham
Bristol R v Burton Alb
Coventry C v Oxford U
Doncaster R v Bury
Fleetwood T v Lincoln C
Milton Keynes D v Accrington S
Portsmouth v Blackpool
Rochdale v Southend U
Shrewsbury T v Ipswich T
Sunderland v Peterborough U
Tranmere R v Rotherham U
Wycombe W v AFC Wimbledon

Saturday, 18 April 2020
AFC Wimbledon v Milton Keynes D
Accrington S v Bristol R
Blackpool v Coventry C
Burton Alb v Sunderland
Bury v Bolton W
Gillingham v Tranmere R
Ipswich T v Rochdale
Lincoln C v Wycombe W
Oxford U v Fleetwood T
Peterborough U v Shrewsbury T
Rotherham U v Doncaster R
Southend U v Portsmouth

Saturday, 25 April 2020
Bolton W v Rotherham U
Bristol R v Lincoln C
Coventry C v Burton Alb
Doncaster R v Ipswich T
Fleetwood T v Southend U
Milton Keynes D v Blackpool
Portsmouth v Bury
Rochdale v Peterborough U
Shrewsbury T v AFC Wimbledon
Sunderland v Accrington S
Tranmere R v Oxford U
Wycombe W v Gillingham

Sunday, 3 May 2020
AFC Wimbledon v Coventry C
Accrington S v Wycombe W
Blackpool v Doncaster R
Burton Alb v Portsmouth
Bury v Fleetwood T
Gillingham v Bristol R
Ipswich T v Milton Keynes D
Lincoln C v Rochdale
Oxford U v Bolton W
Peterborough U v Tranmere R
Rotherham U v Sunderland
Southend U v Shrewsbury T

EFL League Two

Saturday, 3 August 2019
Bradford C v Cambridge U
Carlisle U v Crawley T
Colchester U v Port Vale
Crewe Alex v Plymouth Arg
Exeter C v Macclesfield T
Forest Green R v Oldham Ath
Leyton Orient v Cheltenham T
Morecambe v Grimsby T
Newport Co v Mansfield T
Northampton T v Walsall
Salford C v Stevenage
Scunthorpe U v Swindon T

Saturday, 10 August 2019
Cambridge U v Newport Co
Cheltenham T v Scunthorpe U
Crawley T v Salford C
Grimsby T v Bradford C
Macclesfield T v Leyton Orient
Mansfield T v Morecambe
Oldham Ath v Crewe Alex
Plymouth Arg v Colchester U
Port Vale v Northampton T
Stevenage v Exeter C
Swindon T v Carlisle U
Walsall v Forest Green R

Saturday, 17 August 2019
Bradford C v Oldham Ath
Carlisle U v Mansfield T
Colchester U v Cambridge U
Crewe Alex v Walsall
Exeter C v Swindon T
Forest Green R v Grimsby T
Leyton Orient v Stevenage
Morecambe v Cheltenham T
Newport Co v Plymouth Arg
Northampton T v Macclesfield T
Salford C v Port Vale
Scunthorpe U v Crawley T

Tuesday, 20 August 2019
Cambridge U v Scunthorpe U
Cheltenham T v Carlisle U
Crawley T v Crewe Alex
Grimsby T v Colchester U
Macclesfield T v Morecambe
Mansfield T v Leyton Orient
Oldham Ath v Exeter C
Plymouth Arg v Salford C
Port Vale v Forest Green R
Stevenage v Bradford C
Swindon T v Northampton T
Walsall v Newport Co

Saturday, 24 August 2019
Bradford C v Forest Green R
Cambridge U v Oldham Ath
Carlisle U v Salford C
Cheltenham T v Swindon T
Colchester U v Northampton T
Grimsby T v Port Vale
Leyton Orient v Crawley T
Macclesfield T v Scunthorpe U
Mansfield T v Stevenage
Morecambe v Exeter C
Newport Co v Crewe Alex
Plymouth Arg v Walsall

Saturday, 31 August 2019
Crawley T v Cheltenham T
Crewe Alex v Bradford C
Exeter C v Mansfield T
Forest Green R v Newport Co
Northampton T v Plymouth Arg
Oldham Ath v Colchester U
Port Vale v Cambridge U
Salford C v Leyton Orient
Scunthorpe U v Carlisle U
Stevenage v Macclesfield T
Swindon T v Morecambe
Walsall v Grimsby T

Saturday, 7 September 2019
Bradford C v Northampton T
Cambridge U v Forest Green R
Carlisle U v Exeter C
Cheltenham T v Stevenage
Colchester U v Walsall
Grimsby T v Crewe Alex
Leyton Orient v Swindon T
Macclesfield T v Crawley T
Mansfield T v Scunthorpe U
Morecambe v Salford C
Newport Co v Port Vale
Plymouth Arg v Oldham Ath

Saturday, 14 September 2019
Crawley T v Mansfield T
Crewe Alex v Cambridge U
Exeter C v Leyton Orient
Forest Green R v Colchester U
Northampton T v Newport Co
Oldham Ath v Grimsby T
Port Vale v Plymouth Arg
Salford C v Cheltenham T
Scunthorpe U v Morecambe
Stevenage v Carlisle U
Swindon T v Macclesfield T
Walsall v Bradford C

Tuesday, 17 September 2019
Carlisle U v Forest Green R
Cheltenham T v Bradford C
Crawley T v Plymouth Arg
Exeter C v Port Vale
Leyton Orient v Crewe Alex
Macclesfield T v Newport Co
Mansfield T v Cambridge U
Morecambe v Walsall
Salford C v Grimsby T
Scunthorpe U v Oldham Ath
Stevenage v Northampton T
Swindon T v Colchester U

Saturday, 21 September 2019
Bradford C v Carlisle U
Cambridge U v Swindon T
Colchester U v Leyton Orient
Crewe Alex v Salford C
Forest Green R v Stevenage
Grimsby T v Macclesfield T
Newport Co v Exeter C
Northampton T v Crawley T
Oldham Ath v Morecambe
Plymouth Arg v Cheltenham T
Port Vale v Mansfield T
Walsall v Scunthorpe U

Saturday, 28 September 2019
Carlisle U v Oldham Ath
Cheltenham T v Crewe Alex
Crawley T v Walsall
Exeter C v Grimsby T
Leyton Orient v Port Vale
Macclesfield T v Colchester U
Mansfield T v Plymouth Arg
Morecambe v Northampton T
Salford C v Forest Green R
Scunthorpe U v Bradford C
Stevenage v Cambridge U
Swindon T v Newport Co

Saturday, 5 October 2019
Bradford C v Swindon T
Cambridge U v Macclesfield T
Colchester U v Stevenage
Crewe Alex v Exeter C
Forest Green R v Crawley T
Grimsby T v Mansfield T
Newport Co v Carlisle U
Northampton T v Leyton Orient

Oldham Ath v Cheltenham T
Plymouth Arg v Scunthorpe U
Port Vale v Morecambe
Walsall v Salford C

Saturday, 12 October 2019
Carlisle U v Crewe Alex
Cheltenham T v Newport Co
Crawley T v Colchester U
Exeter C v Forest Green R
Leyton Orient v Walsall
Macclesfield T v Port Vale
Mansfield T v Oldham Ath
Morecambe v Bradford C
Salford C v Cambridge U
Scunthorpe U v Northampton T
Stevenage v Grimsby T
Swindon T v Plymouth Arg

Saturday, 19 October 2019
Bradford C v Crawley T
Cambridge U v Exeter C
Colchester U v Morecambe
Crewe Alex v Swindon T
Forest Green R v Mansfield T
Grimsby T v Leyton Orient
Newport Co v Scunthorpe U
Northampton T v Salford C
Oldham Ath v Macclesfield T
Plymouth Arg v Carlisle U
Port Vale v Stevenage
Walsall v Cheltenham T

Tuesday, 22 October 2019
Bradford C v Port Vale
Cambridge U v Grimsby T
Carlisle U v Northampton T
Cheltenham T v Macclesfield T
Crewe Alex v Colchester U
Mansfield T v Salford C
Morecambe v Forest Green R
Newport Co v Crawley T
Oldham Ath v Walsall
Plymouth Arg v Leyton Orient
Scunthorpe U v Exeter C
Swindon T v Stevenage

Saturday, 26 October 2019
Colchester U v Newport Co
Crawley T v Swindon T
Exeter C v Plymouth Arg
Forest Green R v Crewe Alex
Grimsby T v Cheltenham T
Leyton Orient v Carlisle U
Macclesfield T v Bradford C
Northampton T v Cambridge U
Port Vale v Oldham Ath
Salford C v Scunthorpe U
Stevenage v Morecambe
Walsall v Mansfield T

Saturday, 2 November 2019
Bradford C v Exeter C
Cambridge U v Crawley T
Carlisle U v Macclesfield T
Cheltenham T v Forest Green R
Crewe Alex v Port Vale
Mansfield T v Colchester U
Morecambe v Leyton Orient
Newport Co v Salford C
Oldham Ath v Northampton T
Plymouth Arg v Grimsby T
Scunthorpe U v Stevenage
Swindon T v Walsall

Saturday, 16 November 2019
Colchester U v Bradford C
Crawley T v Morecambe
Exeter C v Cheltenham T
Forest Green R v Plymouth Arg
Grimsby T v Newport Co
Leyton Orient v Scunthorpe U
Macclesfield T v Mansfield T
Northampton T v Crewe Alex
Port Vale v Carlisle U
Salford C v Swindon T
Stevenage v Oldham Ath
Walsall v Cambridge U

Saturday, 23 November 2019
Carlisle U v Cambridge U
Cheltenham T v Colchester U
Crawley T v Exeter C
Crewe Alex v Morecambe
Leyton Orient v Forest Green R
Newport Co v Oldham Ath
Northampton T v Grimsby T
Plymouth Arg v Bradford C
Salford C v Macclesfield T
Scunthorpe U v Port Vale
Swindon T v Mansfield T
Walsall v Stevenage

Saturday, 7 December 2019
Bradford C v Newport Co
Cambridge U v Plymouth Arg
Colchester U v Salford C
Exeter C v Northampton T
Forest Green R v Scunthorpe U
Grimsby T v Swindon T
Macclesfield T v Crewe Alex
Mansfield T v Cheltenham T
Morecambe v Carlisle U
Oldham Ath v Leyton Orient
Port Vale v Walsall
Stevenage v Crawley T

Saturday, 14 December 2019
Carlisle U v Grimsby T
Cheltenham T v Cambridge U
Crawley T v Port Vale
Crewe Alex v Mansfield T
Leyton Orient v Bradford C
Newport Co v Stevenage
Northampton T v Forest Green R
Plymouth Arg v Morecambe
Salford C v Exeter C
Scunthorpe U v Colchester U
Swindon T v Oldham Ath
Walsall v Macclesfield T

Saturday, 21st December 2019
Bradford C v Salford C
Cambridge U v Leyton Orient
Colchester U v Carlisle U
Exeter C v Walsall
Forest Green R v Swindon T
Grimsby T v Scunthorpe U
Macclesfield T v Plymouth Arg
Mansfield T v Northampton T
Morecambe v Newport Co
Oldham Ath v Crawley T
Port Vale v Cheltenham T
Stevenage v Crewe Alex

Thursday, 26 December 2019
Carlisle U v Bradford C
Cheltenham T v Plymouth Arg
Crawley T v Northampton T
Exeter C v Newport Co
Leyton Orient v Colchester U
Macclesfield T v Grimsby T
Mansfield T v Port Vale
Morecambe v Oldham Ath
Salford C v Crewe Alex
Scunthorpe U v Walsall
Stevenage v Forest Green R
Swindon T v Cambridge U

Sunday, 29 December 2019
Bradford C v Mansfield T
Cambridge U v Morecambe
Colchester U v Exeter C
Crewe Alex v Scunthorpe U
Forest Green R v Macclesfield T
Grimsby T v Crawley T
Newport Co v Leyton Orient
Northampton T v Cheltenham T
Oldham Ath v Salford C
Plymouth Arg v Stevenage
Port Vale v Swindon T
Walsall v Carlisle U

Wednesday, 1 January 2020
Bradford C v Morecambe
Cambridge U v Mansfield T
Colchester U v Crawley T
Crewe Alex v Carlisle U
Forest Green R v Exeter C
Grimsby T v Salford C
Newport Co v Cheltenham T
Northampton T v Stevenage
Oldham Ath v Scunthorpe U
Plymouth Arg v Swindon T
Port Vale v Macclesfield T
Walsall v Leyton Orient

Saturday, 4 January 2020
Carlisle U v Newport Co
Cheltenham T v Oldham Ath
Crawley T v Forest Green R
Exeter C v Crewe Alex
Leyton Orient v Northampton T
Macclesfield T v Cambridge U
Mansfield T v Grimsby T
Morecambe v Port Vale
Salford C v Walsall
Scunthorpe U v Plymouth Arg
Stevenage v Colchester U
Swindon T v Bradford C

Saturday, 11 January 2020
Carlisle U v Plymouth Arg
Cheltenham T v Walsall
Crawley T v Bradford C
Exeter C v Cambridge U
Leyton Orient v Grimsby T
Macclesfield T v Oldham Ath
Mansfield T v Forest Green R
Morecambe v Colchester U
Salford C v Northampton T
Scunthorpe U v Newport Co
Stevenage v Port Vale
Swindon T v Crewe Alex

Saturday, 18 January 2020
Bradford C v Scunthorpe U
Cambridge U v Stevenage
Colchester U v Macclesfield T
Crewe Alex v Cheltenham T
Forest Green R v Salford C
Grimsby T v Exeter C
Newport Co v Swindon T
Northampton T v Morecambe
Oldham Ath v Carlisle U
Plymouth Arg v Mansfield T
Port Vale v Leyton Orient
Walsall v Crawley T

Saturday, 25 January 2020
Carlisle U v Walsall
Cheltenham T v Northampton T
Crawley T v Grimsby T
Exeter C v Colchester U
Leyton Orient v Newport Co
Macclesfield T v Forest Green R
Mansfield T v Bradford C
Morecambe v Cambridge U
Salford C v Oldham Ath
Scunthorpe U v Crewe Alex
Stevenage v Plymouth Arg
Swindon T v Port Vale

Tuesday, 28 January 2020
Bradford C v Cheltenham T
Cambridge U v Salford C
Colchester U v Swindon T
Crewe Alex v Leyton Orient
Forest Green R v Carlisle U

Grimsby T v Stevenage
Newport Co v Macclesfield T
Northampton T v Scunthorpe U
Oldham Ath v Mansfield T
Plymouth Arg v Crawley T
Port Vale v Exeter C
Walsall v Morecambe

Saturday, 1 February 2020
Cambridge U v Colchester U
Cheltenham T v Morecambe
Crawley T v Scunthorpe U
Grimsby T v Forest Green R
Macclesfield T v Northampton T
Mansfield T v Carlisle U
Oldham Ath v Bradford C
Plymouth Arg v Newport Co
Port Vale v Salford C
Stevenage v Leyton Orient
Swindon T v Exeter C
Walsall v Crewe Alex

Saturday, 8 February 2020
Bradford C v Grimsby T
Carlisle U v Swindon T
Colchester U v Plymouth Arg
Crewe Alex v Oldham Ath
Exeter C v Stevenage
Forest Green R v Walsall
Leyton Orient v Macclesfield T
Morecambe v Mansfield T
Newport Co v Cambridge U
Northampton T v Port Vale
Salford C v Crawley T
Scunthorpe U v Cheltenham T

Tuesday, 11 February 2020
Bradford C v Stevenage
Carlisle U v Cheltenham T
Colchester U v Grimsby T
Crewe Alex v Crawley T
Exeter C v Oldham Ath
Forest Green R v Port Vale
Leyton Orient v Mansfield T
Morecambe v Macclesfield T
Newport Co v Walsall
Northampton T v Swindon T
Salford C v Plymouth Arg
Scunthorpe U v Cambridge U

Saturday, 15 February 2020
Cambridge U v Bradford C
Cheltenham T v Leyton Orient
Crawley T v Carlisle U
Grimsby T v Morecambe
Macclesfield T v Exeter C
Mansfield T v Newport Co
Oldham Ath v Forest Green R
Plymouth Arg v Crewe Alex
Port Vale v Colchester U
Stevenage v Salford C
Swindon T v Scunthorpe U
Walsall v Northampton T

Saturday, 22 February 2020
Carlisle U v Morecambe
Cheltenham T v Mansfield T
Crawley T v Stevenage
Crewe Alex v Macclesfield T
Leyton Orient v Oldham Ath
Newport Co v Bradford C
Northampton T v Exeter C
Plymouth Arg v Cambridge U
Salford C v Colchester U
Scunthorpe U v Forest Green R
Swindon T v Grimsby T
Walsall v Port Vale

Saturday, 29 February 2020
Bradford C v Plymouth Arg
Cambridge U v Carlisle U
Colchester U v Cheltenham T
Exeter C v Crawley T
Forest Green R v Leyton Orient
Grimsby T v Northampton T
Macclesfield T v Salford C
Mansfield T v Swindon T
Morecambe v Crewe Alex
Oldham Ath v Newport Co
Port Vale v Scunthorpe U
Stevenage v Walsall

Saturday, 7 March 2020
Carlisle U v Colchester U
Cheltenham T v Port Vale
Crawley T v Oldham Ath
Crewe Alex v Stevenage
Leyton Orient v Cambridge U
Newport Co v Morecambe
Northampton T v Mansfield T
Plymouth Arg v Macclesfield T
Salford C v Bradford C
Scunthorpe U v Grimsby T
Swindon T v Forest Green R
Walsall v Exeter C

Saturday, 14 March 2020
Bradford C v Leyton Orient
Cambridge U v Cheltenham T
Colchester U v Scunthorpe U
Exeter C v Salford C
Forest Green R v Northampton T
Grimsby T v Carlisle U
Macclesfield T v Walsall
Mansfield T v Crewe Alex
Morecambe v Plymouth Arg
Oldham Ath v Swindon T
Port Vale v Crawley T
Stevenage v Newport Co

Tuesday, 17 March 2020
Colchester U v Crewe Alex
Crawley T v Newport Co
Exeter C v Scunthorpe U
Forest Green R v Morecambe
Grimsby T v Cambridge U
Leyton Orient v Plymouth Arg
Macclesfield T v Cheltenham T
Northampton T v Carlisle U
Port Vale v Bradford C
Salford C v Mansfield T
Stevenage v Swindon T
Walsall v Oldham Ath

Saturday, 21 March 2020
Bradford C v Macclesfield T
Cambridge U v Northampton T
Carlisle U v Leyton Orient
Cheltenham T v Grimsby T
Crewe Alex v Forest Green R
Mansfield T v Walsall
Morecambe v Stevenage
Newport Co v Colchester U
Oldham Ath v Port Vale
Plymouth Arg v Exeter C
Scunthorpe U v Salford C
Swindon T v Crawley T

Saturday, 28 March 2020
Colchester U v Mansfield T
Crawley T v Cambridge U
Exeter C v Bradford C
Forest Green R v Cheltenham T
Grimsby T v Plymouth Arg
Leyton Orient v Morecambe
Macclesfield T v Carlisle U
Northampton T v Oldham Ath
Port Vale v Crewe Alex
Salford C v Newport Co
Stevenage v Scunthorpe U
Walsall v Swindon T

Saturday, 4 April 2020
Bradford C v Colchester U
Cambridge U v Walsall
Carlisle U v Port Vale
Cheltenham T v Exeter C
Crewe Alex v Northampton T
Mansfield T v Macclesfield T
Morecambe v Crawley T
Newport Co v Grimsby T
Oldham Ath v Stevenage
Plymouth Arg v Forest Green R
Scunthorpe U v Leyton Orient
Swindon T v Salford C

Friday, 10 April 2020
Crawley T v Leyton Orient
Crewe Alex v Newport Co
Exeter C v Morecambe
Forest Green R v Bradford C
Northampton T v Colchester U
Oldham Ath v Cambridge U
Port Vale v Grimsby T
Salford C v Carlisle U
Scunthorpe U v Macclesfield T
Stevenage v Mansfield T
Swindon T v Cheltenham T
Walsall v Plymouth Arg

Monday, 13 April 2020
Bradford C v Crewe Alex
Cambridge U v Port Vale
Carlisle U v Scunthorpe U
Cheltenham T v Crawley T
Colchester U v Oldham Ath
Grimsby T v Walsall
Leyton Orient v Salford C
Macclesfield T v Stevenage
Mansfield T v Exeter C
Morecambe v Swindon T
Newport Co v Forest Green R
Plymouth Arg v Northampton T

Saturday, 18 April 2020
Crawley T v Macclesfield T
Crewe Alex v Grimsby T
Exeter C v Carlisle U
Forest Green R v Cambridge U
Northampton T v Bradford C
Oldham Ath v Plymouth Arg
Port Vale v Newport Co
Salford C v Morecambe
Scunthorpe U v Mansfield T
Stevenage v Cheltenham T
Swindon T v Leyton Orient
Walsall v Colchester U

Saturday, 25 April 2020
Bradford C v Walsall
Cambridge U v Crewe Alex
Carlisle U v Stevenage
Cheltenham T v Salford C
Colchester U v Forest Green R
Grimsby T v Oldham Ath
Leyton Orient v Exeter C
Macclesfield T v Swindon T
Mansfield T v Crawley T
Morecambe v Scunthorpe U
Newport Co v Northampton T
Plymouth Arg v Port Vale

NATIONAL LEAGUE FIXTURES 2019–20

All fixtures subject to change.

Saturday, 3 August 2019
Aldershot T v AFC Fylde
Barnet v Yeovil T
Chesterfield v Dover Ath
Chorley v Bromley
Dagenham & R v Woking
Eastleigh v Notts Co
Ebbsfleet U v FC Halifax T
Harrogate T v Solihull Moors
Hartlepool U v Sutton U
Stockport Co v Maidenhead U
Torquay U v Boreham Wood
Wrexham v Barrow

Tuesday, 6 August 2019
AFC Fylde v Chorley
Barrow v Harrogate T
Boreham Wood v Wrexham
Bromley v Ebbsfleet U
Dover Ath v Dagenham & R
FC Halifax T v Hartlepool U
Maidenhead U v Chesterfield
Notts Co v Stockport Co
Solihull Moors v Torquay U
Sutton U v Barnet
Woking v Aldershot T
Yeovil T v Eastleigh

Saturday, 10 August 2019
AFC Fylde v Ebbsfleet U
Barrow v Eastleigh
Boreham Wood v Chesterfield
Bromley v Torquay U
Dover Ath v Wrexham
FC Halifax T v Dagenham & R
Maidenhead U v Hartlepool U
Notts Co v Barnet
Solihull Moors v Aldershot T
Sutton U v Chorley
Woking v Harrogate T
Yeovil T v Stockport Co

Tuesday, 13 August 2019
Aldershot T v Bromley
Barnet v Dover Ath
Chesterfield v Woking
Chorley v Solihull Moors
Dagenham & R v Boreham Wood
Eastleigh v Sutton U
Ebbsfleet U v Yeovil T
Harrogate T v Notts Co
Hartlepool U v AFC Fylde
Stockport Co v Barrow
Torquay U v Maidenhead U
Wrexham v FC Halifax T

Saturday, 17 August 2019
AFC Fylde v Woking
Aldershot T v FC Halifax T
Barnet v Chesterfield
Barrow v Yeovil T
Boreham Wood v Sutton U
Dagenham & R v Harrogate T
Dover Ath v Torquay U
Hartlepool U v Bromley
Maidenhead U v Chorley
Notts Co v Wrexham
Solihull Moors v Ebbsfleet U
Stockport Co v Eastleigh

Saturday, 24 August 2019
Bromley v Boreham Wood
Chesterfield v Barrow
Chorley v Hartlepool U
Eastleigh v Dagenham & R
Ebbsfleet U v Notts Co
FC Halifax T v AFC Fylde
Harrogate T v Stockport Co
Sutton U v Dover Ath
Torquay U v Aldershot T
Woking v Solihull Moors
Wrexham v Barnet
Yeovil T v Maidenhead U

Monday, 26 August 2019
AFC Fylde v Harrogate T
Aldershot T v Sutton U
Barnet v Torquay U
Barrow v FC Halifax T
Boreham Wood v Ebbsfleet U
Dagenham & R v Yeovil T
Dover Ath v Woking
Hartlepool U v Wrexham
Maidenhead U v Bromley
Notts Co v Chorley
Solihull Moors v Eastleigh
Stockport Co v Chesterfield

Saturday, 31 August 2019
Bromley v AFC Fylde
Chesterfield v Dagenham & R
Chorley v Boreham Wood
Eastleigh v Barnet
Ebbsfleet U v Aldershot T
FC Halifax T v Solihull Moors
Harrogate T v Dover Ath
Sutton U v Maidenhead U
Torquay U v Hartlepool U
Woking v Barrow
Wrexham v Stockport Co
Yeovil T v Notts Co

Tuesday, 3 September 2019
Barnet v Aldershot T
Barrow v Hartlepool U
Chesterfield v FC Halifax T
Dagenham & R v Bromley
Dover Ath v Ebbsfleet U
Eastleigh v Boreham Wood
Harrogate T v Chorley
Notts Co v Solihull Moors
Stockport Co v AFC Fylde
Woking v Torquay U
Wrexham v Maidenhead U
Yeovil T v Sutton U

Saturday, 7 September 2019
AFC Fylde v Barnet
Aldershot T v Barrow
Boreham Wood v Dover Ath
Bromley v Chesterfield
Chorley v Stockport Co
Ebbsfleet U v Eastleigh
FC Halifax T v Yeovil T
Hartlepool U v Woking
Maidenhead U v Dagenham & R
Solihull Moors v Wrexham
Sutton U v Notts Co
Torquay U v Harrogate T

Saturday, 14 September 2019
Barnet v Maidenhead U
Barrow v Solihull Moors
Chesterfield v Torquay U
Dagenham & R v Hartlepool U
Dover Ath v Chorley
Eastleigh v Bromley
Harrogate T v Boreham Wood
Notts Co v FC Halifax T
Stockport Co v Aldershot T
Woking v Ebbsfleet U
Wrexham v Sutton U
Yeovil T v AFC Fylde

Saturday, 21 September 2019
AFC Fylde v Eastleigh
Aldershot T v Wrexham
Boreham Wood v Stockport Co
Bromley v Notts Co
Chorley v Woking
Ebbsfleet U v Barrow
FC Halifax T v Barnet
Hartlepool U v Dover Ath
Maidenhead U v Harrogate T
Solihull Moors v Yeovil T
Sutton U v Chesterfield
Torquay U v Dagenham & R

Tuesday, 24 September 2019
AFC Fylde v Wrexham
Aldershot T v Yeovil T
Boreham Wood v Notts Co
Bromley v Woking
Chorley v Barrow
Ebbsfleet U v Barnet
FC Halifax T v Harrogate T
Hartlepool U v Chesterfield
Maidenhead U v Dover Ath
Solihull Moors v Stockport Co
Sutton U v Dagenham & R
Torquay U v Eastleigh

Saturday, 28 September 2019
Barnet v Solihull Moors
Barrow v Maidenhead U
Chesterfield v Aldershot T
Dagenham & R v Chorley
Dover Ath v FC Halifax T
Eastleigh v Hartlepool U
Harrogate T v Sutton U
Notts Co v AFC Fylde
Stockport Co v Torquay U
Woking v Boreham Wood
Wrexham v Ebbsfleet U
Yeovil T v Bromley

Saturday, 5 October 2019
Boreham Wood v Solihull Moors
Bromley v Barrow
Chesterfield v Eastleigh
Chorley v Aldershot T
Dagenham & R v Barnet
Dover Ath v Notts Co
Harrogate T v Ebbsfleet U
Hartlepool U v Yeovil T
Maidenhead U v FC Halifax T
Sutton U v Stockport Co
Torquay U v AFC Fylde
Woking v Wrexham

Tuesday, 8 October 2019
AFC Fylde v Chesterfield
Aldershot T v Dover Ath
Barnet v Bromley
Barrow v Boreham Wood
Eastleigh v Maidenhead U
Ebbsfleet U v Torquay U
FC Halifax T v Chorley
Notts Co v Dagenham & R
Solihull Moors v Sutton U
Stockport Co v Hartlepool U
Wrexham v Harrogate T
Yeovil T v Woking

Saturday, 12 October 2019
AFC Fylde v Sutton U
Aldershot T v Hartlepool U
Barnet v Woking
Barrow v Dover Ath
Eastleigh v Chorley
Ebbsfleet U v Maidenhead U
FC Halifax T v Boreham Wood
Notts Co v Torquay U
Solihull Moors v Bromley
Stockport Co v Dagenham & R
Wrexham v Chesterfield
Yeovil T v Harrogate T

Saturday, 26 October 2019
Boreham Wood v AFC Fylde
Bromley v FC Halifax T
Chesterfield v Notts Co
Chorley v Yeovil T
Dagenham & R v Wrexham
Dover Ath v Stockport Co
Harrogate T v Aldershot T
Hartlepool U v Barnet
Maidenhead U v Solihull Moors
Sutton U v Ebbsfleet U
Torquay U v Barrow
Woking v Eastleigh

Tuesday, 29 October 2019
Boreham Wood v Aldershot T
Bromley v Stockport Co
Chesterfield v Yeovil T
Chorley v Ebbsfleet U
Dagenham & R v Barrow
Dover Ath v Eastleigh
Harrogate T v Barnet
Hartlepool U v Solihull Moors
Maidenhead U v AFC Fylde
Sutton U v FC Halifax T
Torquay U v Wrexham
Woking v Notts Co

Saturday, 2 November 2019
AFC Fylde v Dover Ath
Aldershot T v Maidenhead U
Barnet v Chorley
Barrow v Sutton U
Eastleigh v Harrogate T
Ebbsfleet U v Chesterfield
FC Halifax T v Torquay U
Notts Co v Hartlepool U
Solihull Moors v Dagenham & R
Stockport Co v Woking
Wrexham v Bromley
Yeovil T v Boreham Wood

Saturday, 16 November 2019
Barnet v Stockport Co
Boreham Wood v Maidenhead U
Bromley v Harrogate T
Chesterfield v Chorley
Dagenham & R v Aldershot T
Eastleigh v Wrexham
Ebbsfleet U v Hartlepool U
Notts Co v Barrow
Solihull Moors v AFC Fylde
Torquay U v Sutton U
Woking v FC Halifax T
Yeovil T v Dover Ath

Saturday, 23 November 2019
AFC Fylde v Dagenham & R
Aldershot T v Notts Co
Barrow v Barnet
Chorley v Torquay U
Dover Ath v Solihull Moors
FC Halifax T v Eastleigh
Harrogate T v Chesterfield
Hartlepool U v Boreham Wood
Maidenhead U v Woking
Stockport Co v Ebbsfleet U
Sutton U v Bromley
Wrexham v Yeovil T

Tuesday, 26 November 2019
Barnet v Ebbsfleet U
Barrow v Chorley
Chesterfield v Hartlepool U
Dagenham & R v Sutton U
Dover Ath v Maidenhead U
Eastleigh v Torquay U
Harrogate T v FC Halifax T
Notts Co v Boreham Wood
Stockport Co v Solihull Moors
Woking v Bromley
Wrexham v AFC Fylde
Yeovil T v Aldershot T

Saturday, 30 November 2019
AFC Fylde v Notts Co
Aldershot T v Chesterfield
Boreham Wood v Woking
Bromley v Yeovil T
Chorley v Dagenham & R
Ebbsfleet U v Wrexham
FC Halifax T v Dover Ath
Hartlepool U v Eastleigh
Maidenhead U v Barrow
Solihull Moors v Barnet
Sutton U v Harrogate T
Torquay U v Stockport Co

Saturday, 7 December 2019
Barnet v AFC Fylde
Barrow v Aldershot T
Chesterfield v Bromley
Dagenham & R v Maidenhead U
Dover Ath v Boreham Wood
Eastleigh v Ebbsfleet U
Harrogate T v Torquay U
Notts Co v Sutton U
Stockport Co v Chorley
Woking v Hartlepool U
Wrexham v Solihull Moors
Yeovil T v FC Halifax T

Saturday, 21 December 2019
AFC Fylde v Yeovil T
Aldershot T v Stockport Co
Boreham Wood v Harrogate T
Bromley v Eastleigh
Chorley v Dover Ath
Ebbsfleet U v Woking
FC Halifax T v Notts Co
Hartlepool U v Dagenham & R
Maidenhead U v Barnet
Solihull Moors v Barrow
Sutton U v Wrexham
Torquay U v Chesterfield

Thursday, 26 December 2019
Barnet v Boreham Wood
Barrow v AFC Fylde
Chesterfield v Solihull Moors
Dagenham & R v Ebbsfleet U
Dover Ath v Bromley
Eastleigh v Aldershot T
Harrogate T v Hartlepool U
Notts Co v Maidenhead U
Stockport Co v FC Halifax T
Woking v Sutton U
Wrexham v Chorley
Yeovil T v Torquay U

Saturday, 28 December 2019
AFC Fylde v Stockport Co
Aldershot T v Barnet
Boreham Wood v Eastleigh
Bromley v Dagenham & R
Chorley v Harrogate T
Ebbsfleet U v Dover Ath
FC Halifax T v Chesterfield
Hartlepool U v Barrow
Maidenhead U v Wrexham
Solihull Moors v Notts Co
Sutton U v Yeovil T
Torquay U v Woking

Wednesday, 1 January 2020
AFC Fylde v Barrow
Aldershot T v Eastleigh
Boreham Wood v Barnet
Bromley v Dover Ath
Chorley v Wrexham
Ebbsfleet U v Dagenham & R
FC Halifax T v Stockport Co
Hartlepool U v Harrogate T
Maidenhead U v Notts Co
Solihull Moors v Chesterfield
Sutton U v Woking
Torquay U v Yeovil T

Saturday, 4 January 2020
Barnet v FC Halifax T
Barrow v Ebbsfleet U
Chesterfield v Sutton U
Dagenham & R v Torquay U
Dover Ath v Hartlepool U
Eastleigh v AFC Fylde
Harrogate T v Maidenhead U
Notts Co v Bromley
Stockport Co v Boreham Wood
Woking v Chorley
Wrexham v Aldershot T
Yeovil T v Solihull Moors

Saturday, 18 January 2020
AFC Fylde v Torquay U
Aldershot T v Chorley
Barnet v Dagenham & R
Barrow v Bromley
Eastleigh v Chesterfield
Ebbsfleet U v Harrogate T
FC Halifax T v Maidenhead U
Notts Co v Dover Ath
Solihull Moors v Boreham Wood
Stockport Co v Sutton U
Wrexham v Woking
Yeovil T v Hartlepool U

Saturday, 25 January 2020
Boreham Wood v Barrow
Bromley v Barnet
Chesterfield v AFC Fylde
Chorley v FC Halifax T
Dagenham & R v Notts Co
Dover Ath v Aldershot T

Harrogate T v Wrexham
Hartlepool U v Stockport Co
Maidenhead U v Eastleigh
Sutton U v Solihull Moors
Torquay U v Ebbsfleet U
Woking v Yeovil T

Saturday, 1 February 2020
AFC Fylde v Boreham Wood
Aldershot T v Harrogate T
Barnet v Hartlepool U
Barrow v Torquay U
Eastleigh v Woking
Ebbsfleet U v Sutton U
FC Halifax T v Bromley
Notts Co v Chesterfield
Solihull Moors v Maidenhead U
Stockport Co v Dover Ath
Wrexham v Dagenham & R
Yeovil T v Chorley

Saturday, 8 February 2020
Boreham Wood v FC Halifax T
Bromley v Solihull Moors
Chesterfield v Wrexham
Chorley v Eastleigh
Dagenham & R v Stockport Co
Dover Ath v Barrow
Harrogate T v Yeovil T
Hartlepool U v Aldershot T
Maidenhead U v Ebbsfleet U
Sutton U v AFC Fylde
Torquay U v Notts Co
Woking v Barnet

Saturday, 15 February 2020
AFC Fylde v Maidenhead U
Aldershot T v Boreham Wood
Barnet v Harrogate T
Barrow v Dagenham & R
Eastleigh v Dover Ath
Ebbsfleet U v Chorley
FC Halifax T v Sutton U
Notts Co v Woking
Solihull Moors v Hartlepool U
Stockport Co v Bromley
Wrexham v Torquay U
Yeovil T v Chesterfield

Saturday, 22 February 2020
Boreham Wood v Yeovil T
Bromley v Wrexham
Chesterfield v Ebbsfleet U
Chorley v Barnet
Dagenham & R v Solihull Moors
Dover Ath v AFC Fylde
Harrogate T v Eastleigh
Hartlepool U v Notts Co
Maidenhead U v Aldershot T
Sutton U v Barrow
Torquay U v FC Halifax T
Woking v Stockport Co

Saturday, 29 February 2020
Barnet v Barrow
Boreham Wood v Hartlepool U
Bromley v Sutton U
Chesterfield v Harrogate T
Dagenham & R v AFC Fylde
Eastleigh v FC Halifax T
Ebbsfleet U v Stockport Co
Notts Co v Aldershot T
Solihull Moors v Dover Ath
Torquay U v Chorley
Woking v Maidenhead U
Yeovil T v Wrexham

Saturday, 7 March 2020
AFC Fylde v Solihull Moors
Aldershot T v Dagenham & R
Barrow v Notts Co
Chorley v Chesterfield
Dover Ath v Yeovil T
FC Halifax T v Woking
Harrogate T v Bromley
Hartlepool U v Ebbsfleet U
Maidenhead U v Boreham Wood
Stockport Co v Barnet
Sutton U v Torquay U
Wrexham v Eastleigh

Saturday, 14 March 2020
AFC Fylde v Aldershot T
Barrow v Wrexham
Boreham Wood v Torquay U
Bromley v Chorley
Dover Ath v Chesterfield
FC Halifax T v Ebbsfleet U
Maidenhead U v Stockport Co
Notts Co v Eastleigh
Solihull Moors v Harrogate T
Sutton U v Hartlepool U
Woking v Dagenham & R
Yeovil T v Barnet

Saturday, 21 March 2020
Aldershot T v Woking
Barnet v Sutton U
Chesterfield v Maidenhead U
Chorley v AFC Fylde
Dagenham & R v Dover Ath
Eastleigh v Yeovil T
Ebbsfleet U v Bromley
Harrogate T v Barrow
Hartlepool U v FC Halifax T
Stockport Co v Notts Co
Torquay U v Solihull Moors
Wrexham v Boreham Wood

Saturday, 28 March 2020
AFC Fylde v Hartlepool U
Barrow v Stockport Co
Boreham Wood v Dagenham & R
Bromley v Aldershot T
Dover Ath v Barnet
FC Halifax T v Wrexham
Maidenhead U v Torquay U
Notts Co v Harrogate T
Solihull Moors v Chorley
Sutton U v Eastleigh
Woking v Chesterfield
Yeovil T v Ebbsfleet U

Saturday, 4 April 2020
Aldershot T v Solihull Moors
Barnet v Notts Co
Chesterfield v Boreham Wood
Chorley v Sutton U
Dagenham & R v FC Halifax T
Eastleigh v Barrow
Ebbsfleet U v AFC Fylde
Harrogate T v Woking
Hartlepool U v Maidenhead U
Stockport Co v Yeovil T
Torquay U v Bromley
Wrexham v Dover Ath

Friday, 10 April 2020
Bromley v Maidenhead U
Chesterfield v Stockport Co
Chorley v Notts Co
Eastleigh v Solihull Moors
Ebbsfleet U v Boreham Wood
FC Halifax T v Barrow
Harrogate T v AFC Fylde
Sutton U v Aldershot T
Torquay U v Barnet
Woking v Dover Ath
Wrexham v Hartlepool U
Yeovil T v Dagenham & R

Monday, 13 April 2020
AFC Fylde v FC Halifax T
Aldershot T v Torquay U
Barnet v Wrexham
Barrow v Chesterfield
Boreham Wood v Bromley
Dagenham & R v Eastleigh
Dover Ath v Sutton U
Hartlepool U v Chorley
Maidenhead U v Yeovil T
Notts Co v Ebbsfleet U
Solihull Moors v Woking
Stockport Co v Harrogate T

Saturday, 18 April 2020
Bromley v Hartlepool U
Chesterfield v Barnet
Chorley v Maidenhead U
Eastleigh v Stockport Co
Ebbsfleet U v Solihull Moors
FC Halifax T v Aldershot T
Harrogate T v Dagenham & R
Sutton U v Boreham Wood
Torquay U v Dover Ath
Woking v AFC Fylde
Wrexham v Notts Co
Yeovil T v Barrow

Saturday, 25 April 2020
AFC Fylde v Bromley
Aldershot T v Ebbsfleet U
Barnet v Eastleigh
Barrow v Woking
Boreham Wood v Chorley
Dagenham & R v Chesterfield
Dover Ath v Harrogate T
Hartlepool U v Torquay U
Maidenhead U v Sutton U
Notts Co v Yeovil T
Solihull Moors v FC Halifax T
Stockport Co v Wrexham

THE SCOTTISH PREMIER LEAGUE AND SCOTTISH LEAGUE FIXTURES 2019–20

All fixtures subject to change.

SPFL Premiership

Saturday, 3 August 2019
Aberdeen v Hearts
Celtic v St Johnstone
Hibernian v St Mirren
Livingston v Motherwell
Ross Co v Hamilton A

Sunday, 4 August 2019
Kilmarnock v Rangers

Saturday, 10 August 2019
Hamilton A v Kilmarnock
Hearts v Ross Co
Motherwell v Celtic
Rangers v Hibernian
St Johnstone v Livingston
St Mirren v Aberdeen

Saturday, 24 August 2019
Celtic v Hearts
Hamilton A v Motherwell
Hibernian v St Johnstone
Kilmarnock v Aberdeen
Ross Co v Livingston
St Mirren v Rangers

Saturday, 31 August 2019
Aberdeen v Ross Co
Hearts v Hamilton A
Livingston v St Mirren
Motherwell v Hibernian
Rangers v Celtic
St Johnstone v Kilmarnock

Saturday, 14 September 2019
Aberdeen v St Johnstone
Hamilton A v Celtic
Hearts v Motherwell
Kilmarnock v Hibernian
Rangers v Livingston
Ross Co v St Mirren

Saturday, 21 September 2019
Celtic v Kilmarnock
Hibernian v Hearts
Livingston v Aberdeen
Motherwell v Ross Co
St Johnstone v Rangers
St Mirren v Hamilton A

Saturday, 28 September 2019
Hamilton A v Livingston
Hibernian v Celtic
Kilmarnock v Ross Co
Rangers v Aberdeen
St Johnstone v Motherwell
St Mirren v Hearts

Saturday, 5 October 2019
Aberdeen v Hibernian
Hearts v Kilmarnock
Livingston v Celtic
Motherwell v St Mirren
Rangers v Hamilton A
Ross Co v St Johnstone

Saturday, 19 October 2019
Celtic v Ross Co
Hamilton A v Hibernian
Hearts v Rangers
Kilmarnock v Livingston
Motherwell v Aberdeen
St Mirren v St Johnstone

Saturday, 26 October 2019
Aberdeen v Celtic
Hibernian v Ross Co
Kilmarnock v St Mirren
Livingston v Hearts
Rangers v Motherwell
St Johnstone v Hamilton A

Wednesday, 30 October 2019
Celtic v St Mirren
Hamilton A v Aberdeen
Hibernian v Livingston
Motherwell v Kilmarnock
Ross Co v Rangers
St Johnstone v Hearts

Saturday, 2 November 2019
Aberdeen v Kilmarnock
Hamilton A v Ross Co
Hearts v Celtic
Motherwell v Livingston
Rangers v St Johnstone
St Mirren v Hibernian

Saturday, 9 November 2019
Celtic v Motherwell
Hearts v St Mirren
Kilmarnock v Hamilton A
Livingston v Rangers
Ross Co v Aberdeen
St Johnstone v Hibernian

Saturday, 23 November 2019
Celtic v Livingston
Hamilton A v Rangers
Hibernian v Motherwell
Kilmarnock v Hearts
St Johnstone v Aberdeen
St Mirren v Ross Co

Saturday, 30 November 2019
Aberdeen v St Mirren
Hibernian v Kilmarnock
Livingston v Hamilton A
Motherwell v St Johnstone
Rangers v Hearts
Ross Co v Celtic

Wednesday, 4 December 2019
Aberdeen v Rangers
Celtic v Hamilton A
Hearts v Livingston
Kilmarnock v St Johnstone
Ross Co v Hibernian
St Mirren v Motherwell

Saturday, 7 December 2019
Hamilton A v St Mirren
Hibernian v Aberdeen
Livingston v Kilmarnock
Motherwell v Hearts
Rangers v Ross Co
St Johnstone v Celtic

Saturday, 14 December 2019
Aberdeen v Hamilton A
Celtic v Hibernian
Hearts v St Johnstone
Motherwell v Rangers
Ross Co v Kilmarnock
St Mirren v Livingston

Saturday, 21 December 2019
Celtic v Aberdeen
Hamilton A v Hearts
Hibernian v Rangers
Kilmarnock v Motherwell
Livingston v Ross Co
St Johnstone v St Mirren

Thursday, 26 December 2019
Aberdeen v Livingston
Hamilton A v St Johnstone
Hearts v Hibernian
Rangers v Kilmarnock
Ross Co v Motherwell
St Mirren v Celtic

Sunday, 29 December 2019
Celtic v Rangers
Hearts v Aberdeen
Livingston v Hibernian
Motherwell v Hamilton A
St Johnstone v Ross Co
St Mirren v Kilmarnock

Wednesday, 22 January 2020
Aberdeen v Motherwell
Hibernian v Hamilton A
Kilmarnock v Celtic
Livingston v St Johnstone
Rangers v St Mirren
Ross Co v Hearts

Saturday, 25 January 2020
Celtic v Ross Co
Hamilton A v Livingston
Hearts v Rangers
Motherwell v Hibernian
St Johnstone v Kilmarnock
St Mirren v Aberdeen

Saturday, 1 February 2020
Hamilton A v Celtic
Hibernian v St Mirren
Kilmarnock v Ross Co
Livingston v Motherwell
Rangers v Aberdeen
St Johnstone v Hearts

Wednesday, 5 February 2020
Aberdeen v St Johnstone

Hearts v Kilmarnock
Motherwell v Celtic
Rangers v Hibernian
Ross Co v Livingston
St Mirren v Hamilton A

Wednesday, 12 February 2020
Celtic v Hearts
Hamilton A v Aberdeen
Hibernian v Ross Co
Kilmarnock v Rangers
Livingston v St Mirren
St Johnstone v Motherwell

Saturday, 15 February 2020
Aberdeen v Celtic
Hearts v Hamilton A
Kilmarnock v Hibernian
Motherwell v St Mirren
Rangers v Livingston
Ross Co v St Johnstone

Saturday, 22 February 2020
Aberdeen v Ross Co
Celtic v Kilmarnock
Hamilton A v Motherwell
Hibernian v Livingston
St Johnstone v Rangers
St Mirren v Hearts

Wednesday, 4 March 2020
Hibernian v Hearts
Kilmarnock v Aberdeen
Livingston v Celtic
Motherwell v Ross Co
Rangers v Hamilton A
St Mirren v St Johnstone

Saturday, 7 March 2020
Aberdeen v Hibernian
Celtic v St Mirren
Hamilton A v Kilmarnock
Hearts v Motherwell
Ross Co v Rangers
St Johnstone v Livingston

Saturday, 14 March 2020
Hibernian v St Johnstone
Kilmarnock v St Mirren
Livingston v Hearts
Motherwell v Aberdeen
Rangers v Celtic
Ross Co v Hamilton A

Saturday, 21 March 2020
Celtic v St Johnstone
Hamilton A v Hibernian
Hearts v Ross Co
Livingston v Aberdeen
Motherwell v Kilmarnock
St Mirren v Rangers

Saturday, 4 April 2020
Aberdeen v Hearts
Hibernian v Celtic
Kilmarnock v Livingston
Rangers v Motherwell
Ross Co v St Mirren
St Johnstone v Hamilton A

SPFL Championship

Saturday, 3 August 2019
Alloa Ath v Partick Thistle
Arbroath v Queen of the South
Ayr U v Greenock Morton
Dundee U v Inverness CT
Dunfermline v Dundee

Saturday, 10 August 2019
Dundee v Ayr U
Inverness CT v Arbroath
Greenock Morton v Alloa Ath
Partick Thistle v Dundee U
Queen of the South v Dunfermline

Saturday, 24 August 2019
Alloa Ath v Arbroath
Ayr U v Queen of the South
Dundee v Inverness CT
Dunfermline v Dundee U
Greenock Morton v Partick Thistle

Saturday, 31 August 2019
Arbroath v Dunfermline
Dundee U v Dundee
Inverness CT v Greenock Morton
Partick Thistle v Ayr U
Queen of the South v Alloa Ath

Saturday, 14 September 2019
Arbroath v Partick Thistle
Ayr U v Dundee U
Dundee v Alloa Ath
Dunfermline v Inverness CT
Queen of the South v Greenock Morton

Saturday, 21 September 2019
Alloa Ath v Ayr U
Dundee U v Arbroath
Inverness CT v Queen of the South
Greenock Morton v Dundee
Partick Thistle v Dunfermline

Saturday, 28 September 2019
Arbroath v Ayr U
Dundee U v Greenock Morton
Dunfermline v Alloa Ath
Inverness CT v Partick Thistle
Queen of the South v Dundee

Saturday, 5 October 2019
Alloa Ath v Dundee U
Ayr U v Inverness CT
Dundee v Arbroath
Greenock Morton v Dunfermline
Partick Thistle v Queen of the South

Saturday, 19 October 2019
Arbroath v Greenock Morton
Dundee v Partick Thistle
Dunfermline v Ayr U
Inverness CT v Alloa Ath
Queen of the South v Dundee U

Saturday, 26 October 2019
Alloa Ath v Queen of the South
Ayr U v Dundee
Dundee U v Dunfermline
Greenock Morton v Inverness CT
Partick Thistle v Arbroath

Tuesday, 29 October 2019
Alloa Ath v Dundee
Dundee U v Partick Thistle
Dunfermline v Arbroath
Greenock Morton v Ayr U
Queen of the South v Inverness CT

Saturday, 2 November 2019
Arbroath v Alloa Ath
Ayr U v Partick Thistle
Dundee v Greenock Morton
Dunfermline v Queen of the South
Inverness CT v Dundee U

Saturday, 9 November 2019
Alloa Ath v Dunfermline
Arbroath v Inverness CT
Dundee v Dundee U
Partick Thistle v Greenock Morton
Queen of the South v Ayr U

Saturday, 16 November 2019
Ayr U v Dunfermline
Dundee U v Queen of the South
Inverness CT v Dundee
Greenock Morton v Arbroath
Partick Thistle v Alloa Ath

Saturday, 30 November 2019
Alloa Ath v Inverness CT
Ayr U v Arbroath
Dundee v Queen of the South
Dunfermline v Partick Thistle
Greenock Morton v Dundee U

Saturday, 7 December 2019
Arbroath v Dundee
Dundee U v Alloa Ath
Dunfermline v Greenock Morton
Inverness CT v Ayr U
Queen of the South v Partick Thistle

Saturday, 14 December 2019
Arbroath v Dundee U
Ayr U v Alloa Ath
Dundee v Dunfermline
Greenock Morton v Queen of the South
Partick Thistle v Inverness CT

Saturday, 21 December 2019
Alloa Ath v Greenock Morton
Dundee U v Ayr U
Inverness CT v Dunfermline
Partick Thistle v Dundee
Queen of the South v Arbroath

Saturday, 28 December 2019
Ayr U v Queen of the South
Dundee U v Dundee
Dunfermline v Alloa Ath
Inverness CT v Arbroath
Greenock Morton v Partick Thistle

Saturday, 4 January 2020
Alloa Ath v Partick Thistle
Arbroath v Greenock Morton
Dundee v Inverness CT
Dunfermline v Ayr U
Queen of the South v Dundee U

Saturday, 11 January 2020
Alloa Ath v Arbroath
Dundee v Ayr U

Inverness CT v Queen of the South
Greenock Morton v Dunfermline
Partick Thistle v Dundee U

Saturday, 25 January 2020
Arbroath v Partick Thistle
Ayr U v Inverness CT
Dundee U v Greenock Morton
Dunfermline v Dundee
Queen of the South v Alloa Ath

Saturday, 1 February 2020
Dundee U v Arbroath
Inverness CT v Alloa Ath
Greenock Morton v Dundee
Partick Thistle v Ayr U
Queen of the South v Dunfermline

Saturday, 15 February 2020
Alloa Ath v Dundee U
Arbroath v Queen of the South
Ayr U v Greenock Morton
Dundee v Partick Thistle
Dunfermline v Inverness CT

Saturday, 22 February 2020
Arbroath v Ayr U
Dundee U v Inverness CT
Greenock Morton v Alloa Ath
Partick Thistle v Dunfermline
Queen of the South v Dundee

Saturday, 29 February 2020
Alloa Ath v Ayr U
Dundee v Arbroath
Dunfermline v Dundee U
Inverness CT v Partick Thistle
Queen of the South v Greenock Morton

Tuesday, 3 March 2020
Ayr U v Dundee U
Dundee v Alloa Ath
Inverness CT v Greenock Morton
Partick Thistle v Queen of the South

Wednesday, 4 March 2020
Arbroath v Dunfermline

Saturday, 7 March 2020
Alloa Ath v Inverness CT
Ayr U v Dundee
Dundee U v Partick Thistle
Dunfermline v Queen of the South
Greenock Morton v Arbroath

Saturday, 14 March 2020
Arbroath v Inverness CT
Dundee v Dunfermline
Greenock Morton v Dundee U
Partick Thistle v Alloa Ath
Queen of the South v Ayr U

Saturday, 21 March 2020
Ayr U v Partick Thistle
Dundee U v Alloa Ath
Dunfermline v Greenock Morton
Inverness CT v Dundee
Queen of the South v Arbroath

Saturday, 28 March 2020
Alloa Ath v Dunfermline
Arbroath v Dundee U
Dundee v Queen of the South
Inverness CT v Ayr U
Partick Thistle v Greenock Morton

Saturday, 4 April 2020
Alloa Ath v Dundee
Ayr U v Dunfermline
Dundee U v Queen of the South
Greenock Morton v Inverness CT
Partick Thistle v Arbroath

Saturday, 11 April 2020
Ayr U v Alloa Ath
Dundee v Greenock Morton
Dunfermline v Arbroath
Inverness CT v Dundee U
Queen of the South v Partick Thistle

Saturday, 18 April 2020
Alloa Ath v Queen of the South
Arbroath v Dundee
Dundee U v Dunfermline
Greenock Morton v Ayr U
Partick Thistle v Inverness CT

Saturday, 25 April 2020
Alloa Ath v Greenock Morton
Ayr U v Arbroath
Dundee v Dundee U
Dunfermline v Partick Thistle
Queen of the South v Inverness CT

Saturday, 2 May 2020
Arbroath v Alloa Ath
Dundee U v Ayr U
Inverness CT v Dunfermline
Greenock Morton v Queen of the South
Partick Thistle v Dundee

SPFL League One

Saturday, 3 August 2019
Airdrieonians v Forfar Ath
Clyde v East Fife
Dumbarton v Raith R
Peterhead v Falkirk
Stranraer v Montrose

Saturday, 10 August 2019
East Fife v Peterhead
Falkirk v Dumbarton
Forfar Ath v Stranraer
Montrose v Airdrieonians
Raith R v Clyde

Saturday, 17 August 2019
Airdrieonians v Clyde
Falkirk v Montrose
Forfar Ath v East Fife
Peterhead v Dumbarton
Stranraer v Raith R

Saturday, 24 August 2019
Clyde v Falkirk
Dumbarton v Stranraer
East Fife v Airdrieonians
Peterhead v Forfar Ath
Raith R v Montrose

Saturday, 31 August 2019
Airdrieonians v Falkirk
East Fife v Raith R
Forfar Ath v Clyde
Montrose v Dumbarton
Stranraer v Peterhead

Saturday, 14 September 2019
Clyde v Stranraer
Dumbarton v Airdrieonians
Falkirk v Forfar Ath
Montrose v East Fife
Raith R v Peterhead

Saturday, 21 September 2019
Airdrieonians v Raith R
East Fife v Dumbarton
Forfar Ath v Montrose
Peterhead v Clyde
Stranraer v Falkirk

Saturday, 28 September 2019
Airdrieonians v Stranraer
Dumbarton v Clyde
Falkirk v East Fife
Forfar Ath v Raith R
Montrose v Peterhead

Saturday, 5 October 2019
Clyde v Montrose
Dumbarton v Forfar Ath
East Fife v Stranraer
Peterhead v Airdrieonians
Raith R v Falkirk

Saturday, 19 October 2019
Airdrieonians v Montrose
Clyde v Raith R
East Fife v Forfar Ath
Falkirk v Peterhead
Stranraer v Dumbarton

Saturday, 26 October 2019
Dumbarton v Peterhead
Falkirk v Clyde
Forfar Ath v Airdrieonians
Montrose v Stranraer
Raith R v East Fife

Saturday, 2 November 2019
Airdrieonians v Dumbarton
East Fife v Montrose
Forfar Ath v Falkirk
Peterhead v Raith R
Stranraer v Clyde

Saturday, 9 November 2019
Clyde v Peterhead
Dumbarton v East Fife
Falkirk v Airdrieonians
Montrose v Forfar Ath
Raith R v Stranraer

Saturday, 16 November 2019
Dumbarton v Falkirk
East Fife v Clyde
Peterhead v Montrose
Raith R v Forfar Ath
Stranraer v Airdrieonians

Saturday, 30 November 2019
Airdrieonians v East Fife
Clyde v Dumbarton
Falkirk v Stranraer
Forfar Ath v Peterhead
Montrose v Raith R

Saturday, 7 December 2019
Clyde v Forfar Ath
Dumbarton v Montrose
East Fife v Falkirk

Peterhead v Stranraer
Raith R v Airdrieonians

Saturday, 14 December 2019
Airdrieonians v Peterhead
Falkirk v Raith R
Forfar Ath v Dumbarton
Montrose v Clyde
Stranraer v East Fife

Saturday, 21 December 2019
Clyde v Airdrieonians
Montrose v Falkirk
Peterhead v East Fife
Raith R v Dumbarton
Stranraer v Forfar Ath

Saturday, 28 December 2019
Airdrieonians v Falkirk
Dumbarton v Stranraer
East Fife v Raith R
Forfar Ath v Montrose
Peterhead v Clyde

Saturday, 4 January 2020
Airdrieonians v Forfar Ath
Clyde v Stranraer
Falkirk v Dumbarton
Montrose v East Fife
Raith R v Peterhead

Saturday, 11 January 2020
Dumbarton v Clyde
East Fife v Airdrieonians
Forfar Ath v Raith R
Peterhead v Falkirk
Stranraer v Montrose

Saturday, 25 January 2020
Airdrieonians v Stranraer
Clyde v East Fife
Falkirk v Forfar Ath
Peterhead v Dumbarton
Raith R v Montrose

Saturday, 1 February 2020
Airdrieonians v Raith R
East Fife v Dumbarton
Forfar Ath v Clyde
Montrose v Peterhead
Stranraer v Falkirk

Saturday, 8 February 2020
Clyde v Montrose
Dumbarton v Airdrieonians
Falkirk v East Fife
Peterhead v Forfar Ath
Stranraer v Raith R

Saturday, 15 February 2020
Airdrieonians v Clyde
East Fife v Peterhead
Forfar Ath v Stranraer
Montrose v Dumbarton
Raith R v Falkirk

Saturday, 22 February 2020
Dumbarton v Forfar Ath
East Fife v Stranraer
Falkirk v Montrose
Peterhead v Airdrieonians
Raith R v Clyde

Saturday, 29 February 2020
Clyde v Falkirk
Dumbarton v Raith R
Forfar Ath v East Fife
Montrose v Airdrieonians
Stranraer v Peterhead

Saturday, 7 March 2020
Airdrieonians v East Fife
Clyde v Dumbarton
Falkirk v Peterhead
Montrose v Stranraer
Raith R v Forfar Ath

Saturday, 14 March 2020
Dumbarton v Falkirk
East Fife v Montrose
Forfar Ath v Airdrieonians
Peterhead v Raith R
Stranraer v Clyde

Saturday, 21 March 2020
Airdrieonians v Dumbarton
Clyde v Peterhead
Falkirk v Stranraer
Montrose v Forfar Ath
Raith R v East Fife

Saturday, 28 March 2020
East Fife v Clyde
Forfar Ath v Falkirk
Peterhead v Montrose
Raith R v Airdrieonians
Stranraer v Dumbarton

Saturday, 4 April 2020
Clyde v Forfar Ath
Dumbarton v Peterhead
Falkirk v Airdrieonians
Montrose v Raith R
Stranraer v East Fife

Saturday, 11 April 2020
Airdrieonians v Montrose
East Fife v Forfar Ath
Falkirk v Clyde
Peterhead v Stranraer
Raith R v Dumbarton

Saturday, 18 April 2020
Clyde v Raith R
Dumbarton v East Fife
Forfar Ath v Peterhead
Montrose v Falkirk
Stranraer v Airdrieonians

Saturday, 25 April 2020
Airdrieonians v Peterhead
East Fife v Falkirk
Forfar Ath v Dumbarton
Montrose v Clyde
Raith R v Stranraer

Saturday, 2 May 2020
Clyde v Airdrieonians
Dumbarton v Montrose
Falkirk v Raith R
Peterhead v East Fife
Stranraer v Forfar Ath

SPFL League Two

Saturday, 3 August 2019
Brechin C v Annan Ath
Cove Rangers v Edinburgh C
Elgin C v Cowdenbeath
Stenhousemuir v Albion R
Stirling Alb v Queen's Park

Saturday, 10 August 2019
Albion R v Cove Rangers
Annan Ath v Elgin C
Cowdenbeath v Stirling Alb
Edinburgh C v Brechin C
Queen's Park v Stenhousemuir

Saturday, 17 August 2019
Annan Ath v Albion R
Brechin C v Queen's Park
Cove Rangers v Cowdenbeath
Edinburgh C v Stirling Alb
Elgin C v Stenhousemuir

Saturday, 24 August 2019
Albion R v Brechin C
Cowdenbeath v Annan Ath
Queen's Park v Elgin C
Stenhousemuir v Edinburgh C
Stirling Alb v Cove Rangers

Saturday, 31 August 2019
Albion R v Stirling Alb
Annan Ath v Stenhousemuir
Cove Rangers v Queen's Park
Cowdenbeath v Brechin C
Elgin C v Edinburgh C

Saturday, 14 September 2019
Brechin C v Cove Rangers
Edinburgh C v Annan Ath
Queen's Park v Albion R
Stenhousemuir v Cowdenbeath
Stirling Alb v Elgin C

Saturday, 21 September 2019
Albion R v Edinburgh C
Annan Ath v Stirling Alb
Elgin C v Cove Rangers
Queen's Park v Cowdenbeath
Stenhousemuir v Brechin C

Saturday, 28 September 2019
Brechin C v Elgin C
Cove Rangers v Annan Ath
Cowdenbeath v Albion R
Edinburgh C v Queen's Park
Stirling Alb v Stenhousemuir

Saturday, 5 October 2019
Albion R v Elgin C
Brechin C v Stirling Alb
Cowdenbeath v Edinburgh C
Queen's Park v Annan Ath
Stenhousemuir v Cove Rangers

Saturday, 26 October 2019
Annan Ath v Brechin C
Cove Rangers v Albion R
Edinburgh C v Stenhousemuir
Elgin C v Queen's Park
Stirling Alb v Cowdenbeath

Saturday, 2 November 2019
Brechin C v Edinburgh C
Cowdenbeath v Cove Rangers
Elgin C v Annan Ath
Stenhousemuir v Queen's Park
Stirling Alb v Albion R

Saturday, 9 November 2019
Albion R v Stenhousemuir
Annan Ath v Cowdenbeath
Cove Rangers v Stirling Alb
Edinburgh C v Elgin C
Queen's Park v Brechin C

Saturday, 16 November 2019
Cove Rangers v Brechin C
Cowdenbeath v Queen's Park
Edinburgh C v Albion R
Stenhousemuir v Elgin C
Stirling Alb v Annan Ath

Saturday, 30 November 2019
Albion R v Cowdenbeath
Annan Ath v Cove Rangers
Brechin C v Stenhousemuir
Elgin C v Stirling Alb
Queen's Park v Edinburgh C

Saturday, 7 December 2019
Albion R v Queen's Park
Cowdenbeath v Elgin C
Edinburgh C v Cove Rangers
Stenhousemuir v Annan Ath
Stirling Alb v Brechin C

Saturday, 14 December 2019
Annan Ath v Edinburgh C
Brechin C v Cowdenbeath
Cove Rangers v Stenhousemuir
Elgin C v Albion R
Queen's Park v Stirling Alb

Saturday, 21 December 2019
Albion R v Annan Ath
Cowdenbeath v Stenhousemuir
Elgin C v Brechin C
Queen's Park v Cove Rangers
Stirling Alb v Edinburgh C

Saturday, 28 December 2019
Annan Ath v Queen's Park
Brechin C v Albion R
Cove Rangers v Elgin C
Edinburgh C v Cowdenbeath
Stenhousemuir v Stirling Alb

Saturday, 4 January 2020
Albion R v Stirling Alb
Brechin C v Cove Rangers
Cowdenbeath v Annan Ath
Elgin C v Edinburgh C
Queen's Park v Stenhousemuir

Saturday, 11 January 2020
Annan Ath v Elgin C
Cowdenbeath v Albion R
Edinburgh C v Queen's Park
Stenhousemuir v Brechin C
Stirling Alb v Cove Rangers

Saturday, 18 January 2020
Albion R v Edinburgh C
Annan Ath v Stirling Alb
Brechin C v Queen's Park
Cove Rangers v Cowdenbeath
Elgin C v Stenhousemuir

Saturday, 25 January 2020
Cove Rangers v Annan Ath
Cowdenbeath v Brechin C
Queen's Park v Albion R
Stenhousemuir v Edinburgh C
Stirling Alb v Elgin C

Saturday, 1 February 2020
Albion R v Cove Rangers
Annan Ath v Stenhousemuir
Brechin C v Elgin C
Edinburgh C v Stirling Alb
Queen's Park v Cowdenbeath

Saturday, 8 February 2020
Albion R v Brechin C
Edinburgh C v Annan Ath
Elgin C v Cove Rangers
Stenhousemuir v Cowdenbeath
Stirling Alb v Queen's Park

Saturday, 15 February 2020
Brechin C v Annan Ath
Cove Rangers v Edinburgh C
Cowdenbeath v Stirling Alb
Queen's Park v Elgin C
Stenhousemuir v Albion R

Saturday, 22 February 2020
Annan Ath v Albion R
Cove Rangers v Queen's Park
Edinburgh C v Brechin C
Elgin C v Cowdenbeath
Stirling Alb v Stenhousemuir

Saturday, 29 February 2020
Albion R v Elgin C
Brechin C v Stirling Alb
Cowdenbeath v Edinburgh C
Queen's Park v Annan Ath
Stenhousemuir v Cove Rangers

Saturday, 7 March 2020
Annan Ath v Cowdenbeath
Cove Rangers v Brechin C
Edinburgh C v Albion R
Elgin C v Stirling Alb
Stenhousemuir v Queen's Park

Saturday, 14 March 2020
Albion R v Queen's Park
Cowdenbeath v Cove Rangers
Edinburgh C v Stenhousemuir
Elgin C v Brechin C
Stirling Alb v Annan Ath

Saturday, 21 March 2020
Annan Ath v Edinburgh C
Brechin C v Cowdenbeath
Cove Rangers v Albion R
Queen's Park v Stirling Alb
Stenhousemuir v Elgin C

Saturday, 28 March 2020
Annan Ath v Brechin C
Cowdenbeath v Stenhousemuir
Edinburgh C v Cove Rangers
Elgin C v Queen's Park
Stirling Alb v Albion R

Saturday, 4 April 2020
Albion R v Annan Ath
Brechin C v Stenhousemuir
Cove Rangers v Elgin C
Queen's Park v Edinburgh C
Stirling Alb v Cowdenbeath

Saturday, 11 April 2020
Annan Ath v Cove Rangers
Brechin C v Albion R
Cowdenbeath v Queen's Park
Edinburgh C v Elgin C
Stenhousemuir v Stirling Alb

Saturday, 18 April 2020
Albion R v Cowdenbeath
Cove Rangers v Stenhousemuir
Elgin C v Annan Ath
Queen's Park v Brechin C
Stirling Alb v Edinburgh C

Saturday, 25 April 2020
Edinburgh C v Cowdenbeath
Elgin C v Albion R
Queen's Park v Cove Rangers
Stenhousemuir v Annan Ath
Stirling Alb v Brechin C

Saturday, 2 May 2020
Albion R v Stenhousemuir
Annan Ath v Queen's Park
Brechin C v Edinburgh C
Cove Rangers v Stirling Alb
Cowdenbeath v Elgin C

FOOTBALL FIXTURES 2019–20

JULY 2019

9 Tuesday	UEFA Champions League 1Q(1)
10 Wednesday	UEFA Champions League 1Q(1)
16 Tuesday	UEFA Champions League 1Q(2)
17 Wednesday	UEFA Champions League 1Q(2)
23 Tuesday	UEFA Champions League 2Q(1)
24 Wednesday	UEFA Champions League 2Q(1)
30 Tuesday	UEFA Champions League 2Q(2)
31 Wednesday	UEFA Champions League 2Q(2)

AUGUST 2019

3 Saturday	EFL commences National League commences
6 Tuesday	UEFA Champions League 3Q(1)
7 Wednesday	UEFA Champions League 3Q(1)
8 Thursday	UEFA Europa League 3Q(1)
10 Saturday	Premier League commences The Emirates FA Cup EP
12 Monday	Carabao Cup 1+
13 Tuesday	UEFA Champions League 3Q(2)
15 Thursday	UEFA Europa League 3Q(2)
18 Sunday	The Women's FA Cup PR
20 Tuesday	UEFA Champions League Play-Off (1)
21 Wednesday	UEFA Champions League Play-Off (1)
22 Thursday	UEFA Europa League Play-Off (1)
24 Saturday	The Emirates FA Cup P
26 Monday	Carabao Cup 2+
27 Tuesday	UEFA Champions League Play-Off (2)
28 Wednesday	UEFA Champions League Play-Off (2)
29 Thursday	UEFA Europa League Play-Off (2)
31 Saturday	The FA Vase 1Q

SEPTEMBER 2019

1 Sunday	The Women's FA Cup 1Q
2 Monday	EFL Trophy Group MD1+ The FA Youth Cup P+
7 Saturday	England v Bulgaria – Euro 2020 Qualifying Group A The Emirates FA Cup 1Q
10 Tuesday	England v Kosovo – Euro 2020 Qualifying Group A
14 Saturday	The FA Vase 2Q
16 Monday	The FA Youth Cup 1Q+
17 Tuesday	UEFA Champions League MD1
18 Wednesday	UEFA Champions League MD1
19 Thursday	UEFA Europa League MD1
21 Saturday	The Emirates FA Cup 2Q
22 Sunday	The Women's FA Cup 2Q
23 Monday	Carabao Cup 3+
28 Saturday	The FA Trophy EP
30 Monday	The FA Youth Cup 2Q+

OCTOBER 2019

1 Tuesday	UEFA Champions League MD2
2 Wednesday	UEFA Champions League MD2
3 Thursday	UEFA Europa League MD2
5 Saturday	The Emirates FA Cup 3Q
6 Sunday	The Women's FA Cup 3Q
7 Monday	EFL Trophy Group MD2+
11 Friday	Czech Republic v England – Euro 2020 Qualifying Group A
12 Saturday	The FA Trophy P The FA Vase 1
14 Monday	Bulgaria v England – Euro 2020 Qualifying Group A The FA Youth Cup 3Q+
19 Saturday	The Emirates FA Cup 4Q
22 Tuesday	UEFA Champions League MD3
23 Wednesday	UEFA Champions League MD3
24 Thursday	UEFA Europa League MD3
26 Saturday	The FA Trophy 1Q
28 Monday	Carabao Cup 4+

NOVEMBER 2019

2 Saturday	The FA Vase 2 The FA Youth Cup 1*
5 Tuesday	UEFA Champions League MD4
6 Wednesday	UEFA Champions League MD4
7 Thursday	UEFA Europa League MD4
9 Saturday	The Emirates FA Cup 1 The FA Trophy 2Q
10 Sunday	The Women's FA Cup 1
11 Monday	EFL Trophy Group MD3+
14 Thursday	England v Montenegro – Euro 2020 Qualifying Group A
16 Saturday	The FA Youth Cup 2*
17 Sunday	Kosovo v England – Euro 2020 Qualifying Group A
23 Saturday	The FA Trophy 3Q
26 Tuesday	UEFA Champions League MD5
27 Wednesday	UEFA Champions League MD5
28 Thursday	UEFA Europa League MD5
30 Saturday	The Emirates FA Cup 2 The FA Vase 3

DECEMBER 2019

1 Sunday	The Women's FA Cup 2
2 Monday	EFL Trophy 2+
10 Tuesday	UEFA Champions League MD6
11 Wednesday	UEFA Champions League MD6
12 Thursday	UEFA Europa League MD6

14 Saturday The FA Trophy 1
The FA Youth Cup 3*
16 Monday Carabao Cup QF+

JANUARY 2020
4 Saturday The Emirates FA Cup 3
5 Sunday The Women's FA Cup 3
6 Monday Carabao Cup SF1+
EFL Trophy 3+
11 Saturday The FA Trophy 2
The FA Vase 4
18 Saturday The FA Youth Cup 4*
20 Monday EFL Trophy QF+
25 Saturday The Emirates FA Cup 4
26 Sunday The Women's FA Cup 4
27 Monday Carabao Cup SF2+

FEBRUARY 2020
8 Saturday The FA Trophy 3
The FA Vase 5
The FA Youth Cup 5*
16 Sunday The Women's FA Cup 5
17 Monday EFL Trophy SF+
18 Tuesday UEFA Champions League 16(1)
19 Wednesday UEFA Champions League 16(1)
20 Thursday UEFA Europa League 32(1)
25 Tuesday UEFA Champions League 16(1)
26 Wednesday UEFA Champions League 16(1)
27 Thursday UEFA Europa League 32(2)
29 Saturday The FA Trophy 4
The FA Vase QF
The FA Youth Cup QF*

MARCH 2020
1 Sunday Carabao Cup Final
4 Wednesday The Emirates FA Cup 5
10 Tuesday UEFA Champions League 16(2)
11 Wednesday UEFA Champions League 16(2)
12 Thursday UEFA Europa League 16(1)
15 Sunday The Women's FA Cup QF
17 Tuesday UEFA Champions League 16(2)
18 Wednesday UEFA Champions League 16(2)
19 Thursday UEFA Europa League 16(2)
21 Saturday The Emirates FA Cup QF
The FA Trophy Semi Final 1
The FA Vase Semi Final 1
The FA Youth Cup SF*
28 Saturday The FA Trophy Semi Final 2
The FA Vase Semi Final 2

APRIL 2020
5 Sunday EFL Trophy Final
7 Tuesday UEFA Champions League QF(1)
8 Wednesday UEFA Champions League QF(1)
9 Thursday UEFA Europa League QF(1)
14 Tuesday UEFA Champions League QF(2)
15 Wednesday UEFA Champions League QF(2)
16 Thursday UEFA Europa League QF(2)
18 Saturday The Emirates FA Cup SF
19 Sunday The Emirates FA Cup SF
The Women's FA Cup SF
25 Saturday EFL League Two Ends
National League Ends
The FA Youth Cup Final
28 Tuesday UEFA Champions League SF(1)
29 Wednesday UEFA Champions League SF(1)
30 Thursday UEFA Europa League SF(1)

MAY 2020
2 Saturday EFL Championship Ends
3 Sunday EFL League One Ends
5 Tuesday UEFA Champions League SF(2)
6 Wednesday UEFA Champions League SF(2)
7 Thursday UEFA Europa League SF(2)
9 Saturday The Women's FA Cup Final
16 Saturday EFL League 2 Play-Off Final
17 Sunday Premier League Ends
The FA Trophy Final
The FA Vase Final
23 Saturday The Emirates FA Cup Final
24 Sunday EFL League 1 Play-Off Final
25 Monday EFL Championship Play-Off Final
27 Wednesday UEFA Europa League Final
30 Saturday UEFA Champions League Final

JUNE 2020
12–24 EURO 2020 Group Stage
27–30 EURO 2020 R16

JULY 2020
3–4 EURO 2020 QF
7–8 EURO 2020 SF (Wembley)
12 EURO 2020 Final (Wembley)

**closing date of round*
+week commencing

STOP PRESS

England Women reach semi-final of the FIFA Women's World Cup but are defeated 2-1 by a strong USA team … USA win Women's World Cup defeating Netherlands 2-0 in the final in Lyon … Rafa leaves Newcastle and ends up in China … Hazard gets his wish and arrives at Real Madrid … Frank Lampard returns to the Bridge to replace Sarri … Pogba will he stay or will he go? … and Lukaku? … Steve Bruce replaces Rafa at Newcastle … Barcelona sign Griezmann from Atletico Madrid for €120m … Hammers smash record for Haller.

SUMMER TRANSFER DIARY 2019

Reported fees only, otherwise Free or Undisclosed.

1 June: **Mo Eisa** Bristol C to Peterborough U; **Lamine Kone** Sunderland to Strasbourg.

3 June: **Edimilson Fernandes** West Ham U to Mainz; **Kieran Kennedy** Wrexham to Port Vale; **Shaun MacDonald** Wigan Ath to Rotherham U; **David Martin** Millwall to West Ham U; **Lucas Perez** West Ham U to Alaves; **Tyler Reid** Swansea C to Swindon T; **Ryan Watson** Milton Keynes D to Northampton T.

4 June: **Jack Bonham** Brentford to Gillingham; **Ryan Hedges** Barnsley to Aberdeen; **Mark Little** Bolton W to Bristol R; **Joe Mason** Wolverhampton W to Milton Keynes D; **Callum McManaman** Wigan Ath to Luton T; **Blair Spittal** Partick Thistle to Ross Co; **Ash Taylor** Northampton T to Aberdeen.

5 June: **Nicky Adams** Bury to Northampton T; **Steve Arnold** Shrewsbury T to Northampton T; **Fankaty Dabo** Chelsea to Coventry C; **Gary Gardner** Aston Villa to Birmingham C; **Joe Ironside** Kidderminster H to Macclesfield T; **Jota** Birmingham C to Aston Villa; **Kyle Knoyle** Swindon T to Cambridge U; **Alan McCormack** Luton T to Northampton T; **Jak McCourt** Swindon T to Macclesfield T.

7 June: **James Bolton** Shrewsbury T to Portsmouth; **Eden Hazard** Chelsea to Real Madrid – £89m; **Tom King** Millwall to Newport Co; **Daniel Powell** Northampton T to Crewe Alex.

8 June: **Lee Hodson** Rangers to Gillingham.

9 June: **Joe Newell** Rotherham U to Hibernian.

10 June: **Anwar El Ghazi** Lille to Aston Villa; **Brandon Goodship** Weymouth to Southend U; **Matt Green** Salford C to Grimsby T; **Christopher Long** Blackpool to Motherwell; **James Norwood** Tranmere R to Ipswich T.

11 June: **Ola Aina** Chelsea to Torino; **Jordan Bowery** Crewe Alex to Milton Keynes D; **Graham Carey** Plymouth Arg to CSKA Sofia; **Tom Davies** Coventry C to Bristol R; **Kyle Howkins** WBA to Newport Co; **Zeli Ismail** Walsall to Bradford C; **Harry McKirdy** Aston Villa to Carlisle; **Stuart O'Keefe** Cardiff C to Gillingham.

12 June: **Josh Hare** Eastleigh to Bristol; **Daniel James** Swansea C to Manchester U – £15m.

13 June: **Tom Brewitt** AFC Fylde to Morecambe; **Moussa Djenepo** Standard Liege to Southampton; **Jackson Longridge** Dunfermline Ath to Bradford C; **Greg Stewart** Birmingham C to Rangers; **Luke Thomas** Derby Co to Barnsley; **Jordi van Stappershoef** FC Volendam to Bristol R; **Wesley** Club Brugge to Aston Villa; **Matty Willock** Manchester U to Gillingham.

14 June: **Tahvon Campbell** Forest Green R to Cheltenham T; **Clayton Donaldson** Bolton W to Bradford C; **Ryan Edwards** Plymouth Arg to Blackpool; **Nathan Ferguson** Dulwich Hamlet to Crawley T; **Pablo Fornals** Villarreal to West Ham U – £24m; **Adam Henley** Real Salt Lake to Bradford C; **Wesley Jobello** Ajaccio to Coventry C; **Liam Kelly** Livingston to QPR; **Regan Poole** Manchester U to Milton Keynes D; **Lazar Stojsavljevic** Millwall to Newport Co; **Lee Wallace** Rangers to QPR; **Josh Wright** Bradford C to Leyton Orient.

15 June: **Tommy Elphick** Aston Villa to Huddersfield T.

17 June: **Danny Andrew** Doncaster R to Fleetwood T; **Macauley Bonne** Leyton Orient to Charlton Ath; **Zeki Fryers** Barnsley to Swindon T; **Reece Hall-Johnson** Grimsby T to Northampton T; **Kortney Hause** Wolves to Aston Villa – £3m; **Josh Pask** West Ham U to Coventry C; **Conor Wilkinson** Dagenham & R to Leyton Orient.

18 June: **Ebou Adams** Ebbsfleet to Forest Green R; **Daniel Adshead** Rochdale to Norwich C; **Yoann Barbet** Brentford to QPR; **Mathieu Baudry** Milton Keynes D to Swindon T; **Aaron Collins** Morecambe to Forest Green R; **James Hanson** AFC Wimbledon to Grimsby T; **Paudie O'Connor** Leeds to Bradford C; **Hillal Soudani** Nottingham Forest to Olympiakos.

19 June: **Patrick Bauer** Charlton Ath to Preston NE; **Craig Bryson** Derby Co to Aberdeen; **Brad Collins** Chelsea to Barnsley; **Reece James** Sunderland to Doncaster R; **Josh Morris** Scunthorpe U to Fleetwood T.

20 June: **Jack Bridge** Northampton T to Carlisle U; **Reece Brown** Forest Green R to Huddersfield T; **Jamie Devitt** Carlisle U to Blackpool; **Gervane Kastaneer** NAC Breda to Coventry C; **Daniel Leadbitter** Bristol R to Newport Co; **Adam Roscrow** Cardiff Met to AFC Wimbledon.

21 June: **Mads Juel Andersen** AC Horsens to Barnsley; **Richie Bennett** Carlisle U to Port Vale; **Matt Clarke** Portsmouth to Brighton & HA; **Andy Cook** Walsall to Mansfield T; **Paul Downing** Blackburn R to Portsmouth; **Stewart Downing** Middlesbrough to BlackburnR; **George Edmundson** Oldham Ath to Rangers; **Ellis Harrison** Ipswich T to Portsmouth; **Josh Koroma** Leyton Orient to Huddersfield T; **Beryly Lubala** Birmingham C to CrawleyT; **Zak Mills** Morecambe to Oldham Ath; **Ben Tollitt** Tranmere R to Blackpool; **Lewis Ward** Reading to Exeter C.

22 June: **Frankie Kent** Colchester U to Peterborough U.

24 June: **Sammy Ameobi** Bolton W to Nottingham F; **Ousseynou Cisse** Milton Keynes D to Gillingham; **Josip Drmic** Borussia Monchengladbach to Norwich C; **James Hardy** AFC Fylde to Walsall; **Rob Hunt** Oldham Ath to Swindon T; **Ruben Lameiras** Plymouth Arg to FC Famalicao; **Aaron Pierre** Northampton T to Shrewsbury T; **George Ray** Crewe Alex to Tranmere T; **Reuben Reid** Forest Green R to Cheltenham T; **Apostolos Vellios** Nottingham F to Atromitos; **Byron Webster** Scunthorpe U to Carlisle U.

25 June: **Elijah Adebayo** Fulham to Walsall; **Tom Aldred** Bury to Brisbane Roar; **Aaron Amadi-Holloway** Shrewsbury T to Brisbane Roar; **Jordan Cousins** QPR to Stoke C; **Adam Davies** Barnsley to Stoke C; **Christian Doidge** Forest Green R to Hibernian; **Alex Fisher** Yeovil T to Exeter C; **Macaulay Gillesphey** Carlisle U to Brisbane Roar; **Andre Gomes** Barcelona to Everton – £22m; **Lee Gregory** Millwall to Stoke C; **Matt Ingram** QPR to Hull C; **Freddie Ladapo** Plymouth Arg to Rotherham U – £500,000; **Liam Lindsay** Barnsley to Stoke C – £2m; **Nick Powell** Wigan Ath to Stoke C; **Adam Smith** Bristol R to Forest Green R; **Moses Ugbu** Al-Ain to Grimsby T; **James Vaughan** Wigan Ath to Bradford C; **Gary Woods** Hamilton A to Oldham Ath.

26 June: **Corey Blackett-Taylor** Aston Villa to Tranmere R; **Mark Cullen** Blackpool to Port Vale; **Jay Dasilva** Chelsea to Bristol C; **Luke Gambin** Luton T to Colchester U; **Elliott Hewitt** Notts Co to Grimsby R; **Tom James** Yeovil T to Hibernian; **Ryan Lloyd** Macclesfield T to Port Vale; **Kieron Morris** Walsall to Tranmere R; **Sid Nelson** Millwall to Tranmere R; **Samuel Radlinger** Hannover 96 to Barnsley; **Leandro Trossard** Genk to Brighton & HA; **Stephen Ward** Burnley to Stoke C; **Ryan Williams** Rotherham U to Portsmouth; **Calum Woods** Bradford C to Tranmere R.

27 June: **Rafael Camacho** Liverpool to Sporting Lisbon – £5m; **Joe Day** Newport Co to Cardiff C; **Joe Edwards** Walsall to Plymouth Arg; **Frank Fielding** Bristol C to Millwall; **Curtis Nelson** Oxford U to Cardiff C; **Sepp van den Berg** PEC Zwolle to Liverpool – £1.3m; **Will Vaulks** Rotherham U to Cardiff C – £2.1m; **Connor Washington** Sheffield U to Hearts.

28 June: **Jamie Allen** Burton Alb to Coventry C; **Chuks Aneke** Milton Keynes D to Charlton Ath; **Ryan Babel** Fulham to Galatasaray; **Daniel Bentley** Brentford to Bristol C; **Martin Cranie** Sheffield U to Luton T; **James Justin** Luton T to Leicester C; **Tom Lockyer** Bristol R to Charlton Ath; **Jonny Maxted** Accrington S to Exeter C; **Jay O'Shea** Bury to Brisbane Roar; **Stefan Payne** Bristol R to Tranmere R; **Darren Potter** Rotherham U to Tranmere R; **Sammie Szmodics** Colchester U to Bristol C; **Antonio Valencia** Manchester U to LDU Quito; **Jamie Walker** Wigan Ath to Hearts; **Aaron Wan-Bissaka** Crystal Palace to Manchester U – £50m; **Gary Warren** Yeovil T to Exeter C.

29 June: **Luca Connell** Bolton W to Celtic; **Emmanuel Osadebe** Cambridge U to Macclesfield T.

1 July: **Che Adams** Birmingham C to Southampton; **Lee Angol** Shrewsbury T to Leyton Orient; **Jacob Blyth** Barrow to Macclesfield T; **Kevin Dawson** Cheltenham T to Forest Green R; **Craig Dawson** WBA to Watford; **Michael Fernandes** Farnborough T to Colchester U; **Tariqe Fosu** Charlton Ath to Oxford U; **Rene Gilmartin** Colchester U to Bristol C; **Johnny Hunt** Stevenage to Hamilton A; **Danny Ings** Liverpool to Southampton – £20m; **Anssi Jaakkola** Reading to Bristol R; **Tomas Kalas** Chelsea to Bristol C; **Jack Kiersey** Everton to Walsall; **Mateo Kovacic** Real Madrid to Chelsea – £40m; **Danny Mayor** Bury to Plymouth Arg; **Liam McCarron** Carlisle to Leeds U; **Conor McLaughlin** Millwall to Sunderland; **John Mikel Obi** Middlesbrough to Trabzonspor; **Mark Milligan** Hibernian to Southend U; **Tommy Rowe** Doncaster R to Bristol C; **Matt Smith** QPR to Millwall; **Omar Sowunmi** Yeovil T to Colchester U; **Matt Targett** Southampton to Aston Villa; **Ryan Tunnicliffe** Millwall to Luton T; **Laurie Walker** Hemel Hempstead to Milton Keynes D.

2 July: **Will Aimson** Bury to Plymouth Arg; **Dominic Ball** Rotherham U to QPR; **Jake Bidwell** QPR to Swansea C; **Charlie Carter** Chesterfield to Stevenage; **Jack Clarke** Leeds U to Tottenham H; **Paul Digby** Forest Green R to Stevenage; **Shay Facey** Northampton T to Walsall; **Gabriel Martinelli** Ituano to Arsenal; **Nicky Maynard** Bury to Mansfield T; **Tanguy Ndombele** Lyon to Tottenham H – £53.8m; **John O'Sullivan** Blackpool to Morecambe; **Ethan Pinnock** Barnsley to Brentford; **Ben Purrington** Rotherham U to Charlton Ath; **Toby Sibbick** AFC Wimbledon to Barnsley; **Chris Stokes** Bury to Stevenage; **Matthew Weaire** Brighton & HA to Colchester U.

3 July: **Nicky Ajose** Charlton Ath to Exeter C; **Lee Burge** Coventry C to Sunderland; **Paul Coutts** Sheffield U to Fleetwood T; **Luke Freeman** QPR to Sheffield U; **Brendan Galloway** Everton to Luton T; **Charlie Goode** Scunthorpe U to Northampton T; **Aapo Halme** Leeds U to Barnsley; **Sullay Kaikai** NAC Breda to Blackpool; **Conor Masterson** Liverpool to QPR; **Vadaine Oliver** Morecambe to Northampton T; **Jack Payne** Huddersfield T to Lincoln V.

4 July: **Tony Andreu** Coventry C to St Mirren; **Dan Bowry** Charlton Ath to Cheltenham T; **Jevani Brown** Cambridge U to Colchester U; **Paris Cowan-Hall** Wycombe W to Colchester U; **Ander Herrera** Manchester U to Paris Saint-Germain; **Phil Jagielka** Everton to Sheffield U; **Nathaniel Knight-Percival** Bradford C to Carlisle U; **Tomas Mejias** Omonia Nicosia to Middlesbrough; **Joe Murphy** Bury to Shrewsbury T; **Kgosi Ntlhe** Rochdale to Scunthorpe U; **Luke O'Neill** Gillingham to AFC Wimbledon; **Ayoze Perez** Newcastle U to Leicester C – £30m; **Rodri** Atletico Madrid to Manchester C – £68.2m; **James Wilson** Manchester U to Aberdeen.

5 July: **Bambo Diaby** KSC Lokeren to Barnsley; **Aidan Fitzpatrick** Partick Thistle to Norwich C – £350,000; **Jorge Grant** Nottingham F to Lincoln C; **Bradley Johnson** Derby Co to Blackburn R; **Luciano Narsingh** Swansea C to Feyenoord; **Samir Nasri** West Ham U to Anderlecht; **Matthew Olosunde** Manchester U to Rotherham U; **Jack Powell** Maidstone U to Crawley T; **Tiago Silva** Feirense to Nottingham F; **Mallik Wilks** Leeds U to Barnsley.

6 July: **Marcin Bulka** Chelsea to Paris Saint-Germain; **Stephen Henderson** Nottingham F to Crystal Palace; **David Raya** Blackburn R to Brentford.

8 July: **David Amoo** Cambridge U to Port Vale; **Herbert Bockhorn** Borussia Dortmund to Huddersfield T; **Pontus Jansson** Leeds U to Brentford; **Liam Kelly** Reading to Feyenoord; **Liam Kitching** Leeds U to Forest Green R; **David Marshall** Hull C to Wigan Ath; **Tyrone Mings** Bournemouth to Aston Villa £20m; **Erik Pieters** Stoke C to Burnley; **Yuri Ribeiro** Benfica to Nottingham F; **Sherwin Seedorf** Wolverhampton W to Motherwell; **Jack Stacey** Luton T to Bournemouth £4m; **Youri Tielemans** Monaco to Leicester C.

9 July: **Dion Donohue** Portsmouth to Mansfield T; **Alex Gilliead** Shrewsbury T to Scunthorpe U; **Luke Leahy** Walsall to Bristol R; **Connor Mahoney** Bournemouth to Millwall; **Isaac Mbenza** Montpellier to Huddersfield T; **Alberto Moreno** Liverpool to Villarreal; **Alex Pattison** Middlesbrough to Wycombe W; **Nathan Ralph** Dundee to Southend U; **Jay Rodriguez** WBA to Burnley; **Noah Smerdon** Gloucester to Exeter C; **Tom White** Gateshead to Blackburn R.

10 July: **Albert Adomah** Aston Villa to Nottingham F; **Julian Borner** Arminia Bielefeld to Sheffield W; **Tom Eaves** Gillingham to Hull; **Mathias Jensen** Celta Vigo to Brentford.

11 July: **Tyler Denton** Leeds U to Stevenage; **Danny Guthrie** Mitra Kukar to Walsall; **Ezri Konsa** Brentford to Aston Villa £12m; **Wes McDonald** Birmingham C to Walsall; **Moses Odubajo** Brentford to Sheffield W; **Mat Sadler** Shrewsbury T to Walsall; **Dom Telford** Bury to Plymouth Arg; **Jordan Tunnicliffe** AFC Fylde to Crawley T.

12 July: **Karim Ansarifard** Nottingham F to Al-Sailiya; **Jon Dadi Bodvarsson** Reading to Millwall; **Mary Earps** Wolfsburg to Manchester U; **Ryan Haynes** Shrewsbury T to Newport Co; **Donald Love** Sunderland to Shrewsbury T; **Lewis Macleod** Brentford to Wigan Ath; **Jasmine Matthews** Liverpool to Bristol C; **Callum Robinson** Preston NE to Sheffield U; **Laura Vetterlein** SC Sand to West Ham U.

13 July: **Colby Bishop** Leamington to Accrington S; **Zaine Francis-Angol** AFC Fylde to Accrington S; **Sam Gallagher** Southampton to Blackburn R; **Dean Gerken** Ipswich T to Colchester U; **Kadeem Harris** Cardiff C to Sheffield W; **Jordan Willis** Coventry C to Sunderland.

14 July: **Funso Ojo** Scunthorpe U to Aberdeen £125,000; **Yann Songo'o** Plymouth Arg to Scunthorpe U.

15 July: **Ben Amos** Bolton W to Charlton Ath; **George Boyd** Sheffield W to Peterborough U; **Fabian Delph** Manchester C to Everton; **Joe Maguire** Fleetwood T to Accrington S; **Callum McFadzean** Bury to Plymouth Arg; **Dean Parrett** Gillingham to Stevenage; **Antonee Robinson** Everton to Wigan Ath; **Lamine Kaba Sherif** Leicester C to Accrington S; **Tommy Smith** Huddersfield T to Stoke C.

Compiler's pick: Harry Bell – Leam Rangers most assists 2018–19; Hedworth FC manager's player of the season 2018–19.
Compiler's player for the future: Riley Davison – Wrekenton Nou Camp and Montagu Yellows.